D1476784

A
SANSKRIT - ENGLISH DICTIONARY

ETYMOLOGICALLY AND PHILOLOGICALLY ARRANGED

with special reference to

COGNATE INDO-EUROPEAN LANGUAGES

SIR MONIER MONIER-WILLIAMS, M.A., K.C.I.E.
Boden Professor of Sanskrit
Hon. D.C.L. Oxon, Hon. LL.D. Calcutta, Hon. Ph.D. Göttingen
Hon. Fellow of University College and Sometime Fellow of Balliol College, Oxford

NEW EDITION, GREATLY ENLARGED AND IMPROVED

with the collaboration of

PROFESSOR E. LEUMANN, Ph. D.
of the University of Strassburg

PROFESSOR C. CAPPELLER, Ph. D.
of the University of Jena

And Other Scholars

MOTILAL BANARSIDASS PUBLISHERS
PRIVATE LIMITED • DELHI

First Edition Published by Oxford University Press, 1899
Reprint: Delhi, 1963, 1964, 1970, 1974, 1976, 1979,
1981, 1984, 1986, 1990, 1993, 1995, 1997

© MOTILAL BANARSIDASS PUBLISHERS PRIVATE LIMITED
All Rights Reserved

ISBN: 81-208-0069-9 (Deluxe Ed.)
ISBN: 81-208-0065-6 (Ordinary Ed.)

Also available at:
MOTILAL BANARSIDASS
41 U.A. Bungalow Road, Jawahar Nagar, Delhi 110 007
8 Mahalaxmi Chamber, Warden Road, Mumbai 400 026
120 Royapettah High Road, Mylapore, Madras 600 004
Sanas Plaza, Subhash Nagar, Pune 411 002
16 St. Mark's Road, Bangalore 560 001
8 Camac Street, Calcutta 700 017
Ashok Rajpath, Patna 800 004
Chowk, Varanasi 221 001

PRINTED IN INDIA
BY JAINENDRA PRAKASH JAIN AT SHRI JAINENDRA PRESS,
A-45 NARAINA, PHASE I, NEW DELHI 110 028
AND PUBLISHED BY NARENDRA PRAKASH JAIN FOR
MOTILAL BANARSIDASS PUBLISHERS PRIVATE LIMITED,
BUNGALOW ROAD, DELHI 110 007

PREFACE TO THE NEW EDITION.

THE first edition of this Dictionary had the advantage of being published by the Delegates of the Oxford University Press, with the support of the Secretary of State for India in Council. The present greatly enlarged and improved work enjoys the same privileges. The first edition appeared in the summer of 1872. The extent of its indebtedness to the great seven-volumed Sanskṛit-German Thesaurus compiled by the two eminent German Sanskṛitists, Otto Böhtlingk and Rudolf Roth, with the assistance of many distinguished scholars, such as Professor A. Weber of Berlin—then only completed as far as the beginning of the letter व *v*—was fully acknowledged by me in the Preface.

Having regard, however, to the entire originality of the *plan* of my own work, I did not venture to describe it as based on the great Sanskṛit-German Wörterbuch. For that plan I claimed to be alone responsible. Every particle of its detail was thought out in my own mind, and the whole work was brought to completion by me, with the co-operation of five successive assistants—whose names were duly recorded—in about twelve years from the date of my election to the Boden Professorship in the University of Oxford.

The words and the meanings of the words of a Dictionary can scarcely be proved by its compilers to belong exclusively to themselves. It is not the mere aggregation of words and meanings, but the method of dealing with them and arranging them, which gives a Dictionary the best right to be called an original production.

In saying this I am not claiming any superiority for my own method over that of the two great German Sanskṛit scholars—which, of course, has advantages of its own. Nor am I detracting one whit from the tribute of admiration which I and other lexicographers are always desirous of rendering to the colossal monument of industry and scholarship represented by their work. I am merely repeating my claim to the production of a Sanskṛit-English Dictionary on a wholly unique plan—a plan the utility of which has been now proved by experience.

It was not thought desirable to print off more than a thousand copies of the first edition of my book. These—notwithstanding the necessarily high publishing price—were sold off in a few years. It then became a question as to how the continuous demand for the Dictionary was to be met, and the Delegates decided to provide for it by a supplementary facsimile edition, produced by a photo-lithographic process. Copies printed by that process have been procurable ever since. Of course I was well satisfied with the factual evidence thus afforded of the practical utility of my Dictionary, and the more so as, along with many eulogistic reviews and notices, it met with some adverse criticism, especially at the hands of German Sanskṛitists.

Not that such criticisms discouraged me. On the contrary, as soon as I became aware of the likelihood of my volume becoming out of print, I set about preparations for a new edition on the very same general plan, although with an earnest determination to improve the original work by the light of such critical animadversions as seemed to me to be pertinent. And I must at once acknowledge that in these efforts I received valuable suggestions from Professor Ernst Leumann of the University of Strassburg, who was my first collaborator at an early stage of the new undertaking (see p. xxxi). It ought, however, to be put on record that, even before Professor Leumann's co-operation, I had made the discovery that the great increase in the number of printed Sanskṛit texts and works bearing on Sanskṛit scholarship, since the issue of my first edition, would entirely preclude the idea of my producing a mere 'réchauffé' of my former volume, with additions, however numerous, introduced from my own interleaved copy and the contributions of fellow-Sanskṛitists. It would necessitate the re-writing of the whole from beginning to end—a formidable task, tantamount to the production of an entirely new Dictionary. This task I began to put in hand alone at least twenty years ago, and it is only due to the authorities at the India Office, under whose auspices this work was inaugurated, and with whose assistance it has been printed, that I should explain the causes which have led to the unexpected delay in its publication.

In real truth I am bound to confess that I entered upon my third lexicographical career with a little too magnificent audacity, and a little too airy hopefulness, at a time when my energies were severely tried, not only by my ordinary duties of lecturing in Sanskṛit, but by other collateral activities.

Amongst the latter it may be mentioned that I had devoted myself to researches into Indian religions and philosophies, for a series of public lectures before the University, which I felt bound to give in my capacity of Boden Professor. And I certainly could not have ventured to carry on these researches —much less to have printed them in various books as trustworthy[1]—if I had not gained a 'first-hand' knowledge of my subject by placing my own mind in direct touch with the mind of the learned natives of India in their own country.

It was for this and other cognate reasons[2] that—with the consent and approbation of two successive Vice-Chancellors, and at my own expense—I undertook voyages to India on three several occasions (in 1875-6, 1876-7, 1883-4), and extended my travels from Bombay to Calcutta and the confines of Tibet—from Cashmere to Madras and the extreme South, including the chief homes of Buddhism in the island of Ceylon.

[1] Some of these books are referred to in the present Dictionary; for example, that on 'Hindūism' (published by the S. P. C. K., 13th edition); that on 'Brāhmanism' &c. (also called 'Religious Thought and Life in India;' published by Mr. J. Murray, Albemarle Street, 4th ed., referred to as RTL.); that on 'Indian Wisdom' (published by Messrs. Luzac of Great Russell Street, 4th ed., referred to as IW.); that on 'Buddhism' (also published by Mr. Murray, 2nd ed., referred to as MWB.).

[2] One of these was the founding of an Indian Institute for the promotion of Indian studies in my own University of Oxford. Another was to induce the Government of India to found six Government scholarships for enabling deserving Indians to finish their education at our University.

On each occasion I was cordially assisted by the Governor-General and local Governments of the day[1]. On each occasion, too, I found scattered throughout vast areas old fellow-students and pupils of my own administering immense provinces, and eager to help me in my investigations; and on each occasion I met to my surprise with learned and thoughtful natives—not only in the cities and towns, but even in remote villages—able and willing to converse with me in Sanskṛit, as well as in their own vernaculars, and to explain difficult points in their languages, literatures, religions, and philosophies.

It may well be believed that these Indian journeys were of great value in extending the horizon of my own knowledge, and increasing my power of improving the Dictionary, but it must be confessed that they interrupted its continuous prosecution.

And, in very deed, the intermittent character of my latest lexicographical career would have made its completion during my life-time almost hopeless, had I not been ably aided by successive assistants and fellow-workers, whose co-operation is gratefully acknowledged by me subsequently (p. xxxi); that of Professor C. Cappeller having extended over far the larger portion of the work.

And this is not all that I have to urge in extenuation of my apparent dilatoriness. A still more unavoidable cause of delay has been the unlooked-for amount of labour involved. This is fully explained in the Introduction (see p. xvi), but I may briefly mention here that it has consisted in adding about 60,000 Sanskṛit words to about 120,000—the probable amount of the first edition; in fitting the new matter into the old according to the same etymological plan; in the verification of meanings, old and new; in their justification by the insertion of references to the literature and to authorities; in the accentuation of nearly every Sanskṛit word to which accents are usually applied; in the revision and re-revision of printed proofs; until at length, after the lapse of more than a quarter of a century since the publication of the original volume, a virtually new Dictionary is sent forth.

It would, of course, be unreasonable to look for perfection in the result of our combined efforts. The law of human liability to error is especially applicable to the development of a new method of any kind. Nor are the imperfections of this volume ever likely to become better known to the most keen-sighted critics than they are to the compilers themselves.

It is said of the author of a well-known Dictionary that the number of mistakes which his critics discovered in it, were to him a source of satisfaction rather than annoyance. The larger a work, he affirmed, the more likely it was to include errors; and a hypercritical condemnation of these was often symptomatic of a narrow-mindedness which could not take in the merit of any great performance as a whole.

Without having recourse to this convenient way of discomfiting critics of the *Chidrânveshin* type, and without abating one iota of justifiable confidence in the

[1] The three Viceroys were Lord Northbrook, the late Lord Lytton, and Lord Ripon. I owe a deep debt of gratitude to Lord Ripon for receiving me as his guest at Government House, Calcutta, in 1883–4; and to Sir Richard Temple for receiving me at Government House, Belvedere, during the Prince of Wales' visit in 1875–6; and to Sir James Fergusson for receiving me at Government House, Bombay, in 1884.

general trustworthiness of the present Dictionary, its compilers can yet be keenly alive to its thoroughly human character.

Speaking for myself I may say that blended with my thankfulness for the longevity that has enabled me to see a protracted undertaking brought to a completion, is a deep consciousness that I am not young enough to consider myself infallible. Indeed it is at once the joy and sorrow of every true scholar that the older he grows the more he has to confess himself a learner rather than a teacher, and the more morbidly conscious he becomes of his own liability to a learner's mistakes.

From all true scholars I do not fear, but court, criticism. Such critics will understand how a sense of responsibility may increase with advancing age, putting an author out of conceit with his own performances, and filling him with progressively intensified cravings after an impossible perfection. They will make due allowance for the difficulties besetting the production of so many densely printed pages, often comprising column after column of unbroken serried type, and abounding with countless dots and diacritical marks. Nor will they be surprised at occasional inequalities of execution in a work representing efforts spread over numerous years. Nor will they need to be reminded that occasional distractions, trials of health and weariness of spirit are unavoidably incident, not only to the responsible head of a prolonged undertaking, but to his several assistants. Indeed it is no disparagement to those who have contributed to the detail of this work to admit that a compilation, which is the result of the collaboration of so many different personalities, must in some degree reflect the idiosyncrasies and infirmities peculiar to each.

Yet notwithstanding my desire that due weight should be given to such considerations, I may be pardoned if I express my confident expectation that the volume now offered to students of both Sanskrit and comparative philology, will supply them with the most complete and useful one-volumed Sanskrit-English Dictionary ever yet produced — a Dictionary, too, which in its gradual progress has, I trust, kept pace with the advancing knowledge and scholarship of the day.

At all events I feel sure that I may affirm for my collaborators, as well as for myself, that we have earnestly striven to secure for this new volume, even more than for the old, the possession of four principal characteristics, namely:— 1. Scholarly accuracy; 2. Practical utility; 3. Lucidity of arrangement, designed to set forth, as clearly as possible, the etymological structure of the language, and its bearing on that of the cognate languages of Europe; 4. Completeness and comprehensiveness, at least to the fullest extent attainable in the latest state of Sanskrit research, and to the utmost limit compatible with compactness and compression into a single volume.

And here it is my duty to notify, in justice as much to my assistants as to myself, that I must be held primarily responsible, not only for the plan, but for the general character of the whole Dictionary. This will be understood when I state that I have from the first exercised a strict superintendence over the details of both editions—not only in carefully supervising the manuscript, but in adding new words, in modifying or amplifying meanings, in subjoining explanations from my own literary notes—made during my sojourning at the chief seats of learning in India—in examining and re-examining every proof-sheet.

I ought to state, however, that during occasional attacks of illness I have been compelled to trust more to my collaborators than at other times[1]; and I must also make an exception in regard to the Additions, the abundance of which is justifiable by the circumstance that many of them are taken from texts and books published quite recently. For although a manuscript list of all the words and meanings in the supplementary pages was submitted for my approval, and although many words in the list have been eliminated by me, while others have been added from my own notes, yet the necessity for passing the worst winter months in a Southern climate has made it impossible for me to have at hand every new book needed for the verification of every addition which I have allowed to be retained.

With regard to a strictly personal criticism in which I have for many years been content to acquiesce without comment, I may perhaps advantageously—now that I have nearly arrived at the end of my career—make a brief explanation. Some of my critics and a few candid friends have expressed surprise that I should have devoted so much of my long tenure of the Boden Professorship to the dry, dreary and thankless drudgery of writing Dictionaries and Grammars, and to practical researches carried on among the Pandits of India in their own country, rather than to the duty of proving the profundity of my learning and my fitness to occupy a high Professorial position by editing or translating obscure Sanskṛit texts which have never been edited or translated before[2].

In explanation I must draw attention to the fact that I am only the second occupant of the Boden Chair, and that its Founder, Colonel Boden, stated most explicitly in his will (dated August 15, 1811) that the special object of his munificent bequest was to promote the translation of the Scriptures into Sanskṛit, so as 'to enable his countrymen to proceed in the conversion of the natives of India to the Christian Religion[3].'

It was on this account that, when my distinguished predecessor and teacher, Professor H. H. Wilson, was a candidate for the Chair in 1832, his lexicographical labours were put forward as his principal claim to election.

Surely then it need not be thought surprising, if following in the footsteps of my venerated master, I have made it the chief aim of my professorial life to provide facilities for the translation of our sacred Scriptures into Sanskṛit[4], and for

[1] I cannot allow myself to think that the Dictionary has suffered much from this cause, except perhaps during the collaboration of the late Dr. Schönberg, the rapid impairment of whose powers did not at first strike me so as to make me aware of the necessity for increased vigilance on my part (see p. xxxi).

[2] I believe it is held that for an Alpine climber to establish a reputation for mountaineering he must ascend some peak, however comparatively insignificant, that has never been ascended before. But the application of such a principle as a sole proof of scholarship in the present day, can no more hold good in Sanskṛit than in Greek and Latin. At all events let any one who claims a reputation for superior scholarship on that sole ground associate with Indian Pandits in their own country and he will find out that far severer proofs of his knowledge and acquirements will be required of him there.

[3] Lieutenant-Colonel Boden, of the Bombay Native Infantry, returned to England in 1807 and died at Lisbon, Nov. 21, 1811. His daughter died Aug. 24, 1827, whereupon his bequest passed to the University of Oxford, but the first election to the Chair, for some reason unknown to me, did not take place till 1832.

[4] In his address proposing himself for election to the Boden Electors, Professor H. H. Wilson laid stress on what he had done for 'the rendering of Scripture Terms into the Sanskṛit language.' It was doubtless on this account that after he was elected he urged me to compile an English-Sanskṛit Dictionary—a work never before attempted. I laboured at this for about seven years, and although the result (published in a thick volume by the Directors of the East India Company in 1851) cannot, I fear, be said to meet the needs of the present day, yet it should be borne in mind that it was *pioneering work*. Nor can it be said to have been useless, seeing that seven years after its publication the following testimony to its utility was voluntarily tendered by the Rev. J. Wenger, translator of the Bible into Sanskṛit and Editor of Dr. Yates' Sanskṛit Dic-

the promotion of a better knowledge of the religions and customs of India, as the best key to a knowledge of the religious needs of our great Eastern Dependency. My very first public lecture delivered after my election in 1860 was on 'The Study of Sanskrit in Relation to Missionary Work in India' (published in 1861).

For the rest, I have already alluded to the advantage which this Dictionary has derived from the support of the Governments of India, and I ought here to acknowledge with gratitude that, without the subsidy granted by successive Secretaries of State in Council, the present volume could not have been sold to the public at the price at which it is now offered. In regard to the Oxford University Press it will be sufficient to say that this volume adds to the countless evidences of its efficiency and of the wealth of its resources. But I may be permitted to congratulate its Delegates and Controller on their good fortune in possessing an unrivalled Oriental Press-reader in Mr. Pembrey. For more than forty years he has read the final proofs of all my books; and I can from my own experience, and without exaggeration, affirm, that I doubt whether any one can surpass him in the perfection to which he has brought the art of detecting errors due to the inadvertence of both authors and printers.

It is only necessary for me to add that having been alone responsible for the singularity of the plan of the original Dictionary, I thought it desirable to prefix to the first edition several sections of introductory explanations. In the same way my supremacy in the production of the present new work necessitates my undertaking the responsibility of writing a new series of explanations, in which I have deemed it desirable to pursue the main lines of my previous method, and not to discard any portion of the old matter which could be advantageously retained.

Indian Institute, Oxford, 1899. MONIER MONIER-WILLIAMS.

POSTSCRIPT.

This Dictionary, to which my father devoted so many years of labour, was completed by him a few days before his death, which took place at Cannes, in the south of France, on April 11, 1899. It had been his hope to see this work published shortly after his return to England. Although this desire was not granted, it was a satisfaction to him to know that the last revise had received his final corrections, and that the book would be issued from the University Press within a few weeks of his death.

May 4, 1899. M. F. Monier-Williams.

tionary:—'I received a copy of Professor Monier Williams' English and Sanskṛit Dictionary at a time when I was about to commence a translation into Sanskṛit of portions of the Old Testament. I have used it daily for the last seven years, and the more I have consulted it the more excellent I have found it. I feel bound to say that he appears to have succeeded, not only beyond my previous ideas of what was likely, but also of what was feasible, to be accomplished at the present time. The Pundits whom I employ have likewise expressed their unqualified admiration of the labour and erudition which his volume displays. The Rev. J. Parsons of Benares, who has been engaged for some years past in preparing a new Hindee version of the New Testament, has likewise derived material assistance from Professor M. W.'s work. Indian missionaries generally owe him a large debt of gratitude.'

Let me add that I hope the present Sanskṛit-English Dictionary will furnish some young scholar with materials for the compilation of a far more satisfactory English-Sanskṛit Dictionary than that which I began to compile more than half a century ago.

INTRODUCTION.

SECTION I.

Statement of the circumstances which led to the peculiar System of Sanskrit Lexicography introduced for the first time in the Monier-Williams Sanskrit-English Dictionary of 1872.

To enable me to give a clear account of the gradual development of the plan of the present work, I must go back to its earliest origin, and must reiterate what I stated in the Preface to the first edition, that my predecessor in the Boden Chair, Professor H. H. Wilson, once intended to compile a Sanskrit Dictionary in which all the words in the language were to be scientifically arranged under about 2,000 roots, and that he actually made some progress in carrying out that project. Such a scientific arrangement of the language would, no doubt, have been appreciated to the full by the highest class of scholars. Eventually, however, he found himself debarred from its execution, and commended it to me as a fitting object for the occupation of my spare time during the tenure of my office as Professor of Sanskṛit at the old East India College, Haileybury. Furthermore, he generously made over to me both the beginnings of his new Lexicon and a large MS. volume, containing a copious selection of examples and quotations (made by Pandits at Calcutta under his direction[1]) with which he had intended to enrich his own volume. It was on this account that, as soon as I had completed the English-Sanskrit part of a Dictionary of my own (published in 1851), I readily addressed myself to the work thus committed to me, and actually carried it on for some time between the intervals of other undertakings, until the abolition of the old Haileybury College on January 1, 1858.

One consideration which led my predecessor to pass on to me his project of a root-arranged Lexicon was that, on being elected to the Boden Chair, he felt that the elaboration of such a work would be incompatible with the practical objects for which the Boden Professorship was founded[2].

Accordingly he preferred, and I think wisely preferred, to turn his attention to the expansion of the second edition of his first Dictionary[3]—a task the prosecution of which he eventually intrusted to a well-known Sanskṛit scholar, the late Professor Goldstücker. Unhappily, that eminent Orientalist was singularly unpractical in some of his ideas, and instead of expanding Wilson's Dictionary, began to convert it into a vast cyclopædia of Sanskṛit learning, including essays and controversial discussions of all kinds. He finished the printing of 480 pages of his own work, which only brought him to the word *Arim-dama* (p. 87 of the present volume), when an untimely death cut short his lexicographical labours.

As to my own course, the same consideration which actuated my predecessor operated in my case, when I was elected to fill the Boden Chair in his room in 1860.

I also felt constrained to abandon the theoretically perfect ideal of a wholly root-arranged Dictionary in favour of a more practical performance, compressible within reasonable limits—and more especially as I had long become aware that the great Sanskṛit-German Wörterbuch of Böhtlingk and Roth was expanding into dimensions which would make it inaccessible to ordinary English students of Sanskṛit.

Nevertheless I could not quite renounce an idea which my classical training at Oxford had forcibly impressed upon my mind—viz. that the primary object of a Sanskṛit Dictionary should be to exhibit, by a lucid etymological arrangement, the structure of a language which, as most people know, is not only the elder sister of Greek, but the best guide to the structure of Greek, as well as of every other member of the Āryan or Indo-European family—a language, in short, which is the very key-stone of the science of comparative philology. This was in truth the chief factor in determining the plan which, as I now proceed to show, I ultimately carried into execution.

[1] This will be found in the library presented by me to the Indian Institute, Oxford.

[2] The main object was really a missionary one, as I have shown in the Preface to this volume (p. ix), and in my Life of H. H. Wilson appended to my Reminiscences of Old Haileybury College (published by A. Constable & Co.).

[3] His first Dictionary was published in 1819, and his second in 1832, while he was a candidate for the Boden Professorship.

And it will conduce to the making of what I have to say in this connexion clearer, if I draw attention at the very threshold to the fact that the Hindūs are perhaps the only nation, except the Greeks, who have investigated, independently and in a truly scientific manner, the general laws which govern the evolution of language.

The synthetical process which comes into operation in the working of those laws may be well called *saṃskaraṇa*, 'putting together,' by which I mean that every single word in the highest type of language (called Saṃskṛita[1]) is first evolved out of a primary *Dhātu*—a Sanskrit term usually translated by 'Root,' but applicable to any primordial constituent substance, whether of words, or rocks, or living organisms—and then, being so evolved, goes through a process of 'putting together' by the combination of other elementary constituents.

Furthermore, the process of 'putting together' implies, of course, the possibility of a converse process of *vyākaraṇa*, by which I mean 'undoing' or 'decomposition;' that is to say, the resolution of every root-evolved word into its component elements. So that in endeavouring to exhibit these processes of synthesis and analysis, we appear to be engaged, like a chemist, in combining elementary substances into solid forms, and again in resolving these forms into their constituent ingredients.

It seemed to me, therefore, that in deciding upon the system of lexicography best calculated to elucidate the laws of root-evolution, with all the resulting processes of verbal synthesis and analysis, which constitute so marked an idiosyncrasy of the Sanskṛit language, it was important to keep prominently in view the peculiar character of a Sanskṛit root—a peculiarity traceable through the whole family of so-called Āryan languages connected with Sanskṛit, and separating them by a sharp line of demarcation from the other great speech-family usually called Semitic[2].

And here, if I am asked a question as to what languages are to be included under the name Āryan—a question which ought certainly to be answered *in limine*, inasmuch as this Dictionary, when first published in 1872, was the first work of the kind, put forth by any English scholar, which attempted to introduce comparisons between the principal members of the Āryan family—I reply that the Āryan languages (of which Sanskṛit is the eldest sister[3], and English one of the youngest) proceeded from a common but nameless and unknown parent, whose very home somewhere in Central Asia cannot be fixed with absolute certainty, though the locality may conjecturally be placed somewhere in the region of Bactria (Balkh) and Sogdiana, or not far from Bokhara and the first course of the river Oxus[4]. From this centre radiated, as it were, eight principal lines of speech—each taking its own course and expanding in its own way—namely **the two Asiatic lines:** (A) the Indian—comprising Sanskṛit, the various ancient Prākṛits, including the Prākṛit of the Inscriptions, the Pāli[5] of the Buddhist sacred Canon, the Ardha-Māgadhī of the Jains, and the modern Prākṛits or vernacular languages of the Hindūs, such as Hindī, Marāṭhī, Gujarātī, Bengālī, Oriya &c. (B) the Iranian — comprising the Avesta language commonly called Zand or Zend[6], old Persian or Akhæmenian, Pahlavī, modern Persian, and, in connexion with these, Armenian and Pushtu; and then **the six European lines:** (A) Keltic, (B) Hellenic, (C) Italic, (D) Teutonic, (E) Slavonic, (F) Lithuanian, each branching into various sub-lines as exhibited in the present languages of Europe. It is this Asiatic and European ramification of the Āryan languages which has led to their being called Indo-European.

Now if I am asked a second question, as to what most striking feature distinguishes all these languages from the Semitic, my answer is, that the main distinction lies in the character of their roots

[1] Sanskṛit is now too Anglicized a word to admit of its being written as it ought to be written according to the system of transliteration adopted in the present Dictionary—Saṃskṛit.

[2] The name Semitic or Shemitic is applied to Assyrian, Hebrew, Aramaic (or Aramæan), Arabic, and Himyaritic, because in the tenth chapter of Genesis, Shem is represented as father of the principal nations speaking these languages—e.g. Assur (Assyria), Aram (Syria), and of Arphaxad, grandfather of Eber, from whom came the Hebrews—or Trans-Euphratian race, the name Hebrew coming from عبر, and really meaning 'one who lives beyond (a river)'—and Joktan, the father of many of the tribes inhabiting South Arabia. It is usual, too, to reckon among Semitic races the people of Abyssinia, whose sacred and literary language is the Ethiopic or Ge'ez, while their spoken dialects are Tigré for the north and north-east, and Amharic for the centre and south, all presenting affinities with the ancient Himyaritic Arabic of South Arabia (Yaman). Hence, speaking generally, we may classify Semitic languages under the two heads of:—1. 'North Semitic,' comprising Assyrian, Hebrew, and Aramaic; 2. 'South Semitic,' comprising Arabic, Himyaritic, and Ethiopic.

[3] Though the younger sisters sometimes preserve older forms.

[4] According to some German Theorists the cradle-land of the Āryans was in the steppes of Southern Russia. Others have fantastically placed it in Northern Europe. Most scholars hold to the old idea of 'somewhere in Central Asia,' and probably in the region of Bactria (Balkh) and Sogdiana, although there might have been a second centre of migration. I myself firmly believe that Balkh was once a chief ancient home of Āryan civilization. Its ruins are said to extend for twenty miles.

[5] See note 3, p. xxv, on Pāli and on the Prākṛit of the inscriptions.

[6] As to the Avesta, commonly called Zend (more correctly Zand), this is that ancient language of Eastern Īrān in which are written the sacred books of the Zoroastrians, commonly called Zend-Avesta—books which constitute the bible and prayer-book of the Pārsīs—those fugitives from Persia who are scattered everywhere throughout India, and are now among the most energetic and loyal of our Indian fellow-subjects.

or radical sounds; for although both Āryan and Semitic forms of speech are called 'inflective[1],' it should be well understood that the inflectiveness of the root in the two cases implies two very different processes.

For example, an Arabic root is generally a kind of hard tri-consonantal framework consisting of three consonants which resemble three sliding but unchangeable upright limbs, moveable backwards and forwards to admit on either side certain equally unchangeable ancillary letters used in forming a long chain of derivative words. These intervenient and subservient letters are of the utmost importance for the diverse colouring of the radical idea, and the perfect precision of their operation is noteworthy, but their presence within and without the rigid frame of the root is, so to speak, almost overpowered by the ever prominent and changeless consonantal skeleton. In illustration of this we may take the Arabic tri-consonantal root **KTB,** 'to write,' using capitals for the three radical consonants to indicate their unchangeableness; the third pers. sing. past tense is **KaTaBa**, 'he wrote,' and from the same three consonants, by means of certain servile letters, are evolved with fixed and rigid regularity a long line of derivative forms, of which the following are specimens:—**KaTB,** and **KiTāBat**, the act of writing; **KāTiB,** a writer; **maKTūB,** written; **taKTīB,** a teaching to write; **muKāTaBat**, and **taKāTuB,** the act of writing to one another; **mutaKāTiB,** one engaged in mutual correspondence; **iKTāB,** the act of dictating; **maKTaB,** the place of writing, a writing-school; **KiTāB,** a book; **KiTBat**, the act of transcribing.

In contradistinction to this, a Sanskṛit root is generally a single monosyllable[2], consisting of one or more consonants combined with a vowel, or sometimes of a single vowel only. This monosyllabic radical has not the same cast-iron rigidity of character as the Arabic tri-consonantal root before described. True, it has usually one fixed and unchangeable initial letter, but in its general character it may rather be compared to a malleable substance, capable of being beaten out or moulded into countless ever-variable forms, and often in such a way as to entail the loss of one or other of the original radical letters; new forms being, as it were, beaten out of the primitive monosyllabic ore, and these forms again expanded by affixes and suffixes, and these again by other affixes and suffixes[3], while every so expanded form may be again augmented by prepositions and again by compositions with other words and again by compounds of compounds till an almost interminable chain of derivatives is evolved. And this peculiar expansibility arises partly from the circumstance that the vowel is recognized as an independent constituent of every Sanskṛit radical, constituting a part of its very essence or even sometimes standing alone as itself the only root.

Take, for example, such a root as **Bhū,** 'to be' or 'to exist.' From this is, so to speak, beaten out an immense chain of derivatives of which the following are a few examples:—**Bhava** or **Bhavana,** being; **Bhāva,** existence; **Bhāvana,** causing to be; **Bhāvin,** existing; **Bhuvana,** the world; **Bhū** or **Bhūmi,** the earth; **Bhū-dhara,** earth-supporter, a mountain; **Bhū-dhara-ja,** mountain-born, a tree; **Bhū-pa,** an earth-protector, king; **Bhūpa-putra,** a king's son, prince, &c. &c.; **Ud-bhū,** to rise up; **Praty-ā-bhū,** to be near at hand; **Prôdbhūta,** come forth, &c.[4]

Sanskṛit, then, the faithful guardian of old Indo-European forms, exhibits these remarkable properties better than any other member of the Āryan line of speech, and the crucial question to be decided was, how to arrange the plan of my Dictionary in such a way as to make them most easily apprehensible.

On the one hand I had to bear in mind that, supposing the whole Sanskṛit language to be referable to about 2,000 roots or parent-stems[5], the plan of taking root by root and writing, as it were, the biographies of two thousand parents with sub-biographies of their numerous descendants in the order of their growth and evolution, would be to give reality to a beautiful philological dream—a dream, however, which could not receive practical shape without raising the Lexicon to a level of scientific perfection unsuited to the needs of ordinary students.

On the other hand I had to reflect that to compile a Sanskṛit Dictionary according to the usual plan

[1] As distinguished from unchangeably 'monosyllabic' like the Chinese, and 'agglutinative' like the Drāviḍian of Southern India, and like the Turkish and other members of an immense class of languages, in which there are no so-called 'inflections,' but merely affixes or suffixes 'glued' as it were to the root or body of a word, and easily separable from it, and not blending intimately with it, and so, as it were, inflecting it.

[2] Of course it is well understood that there are in Sanskṛit a certain number of dissyllabic roots, but I am here merely contrasting Semitic and Āryan roots *generally*.

[3] The *vikaraṇa* of a root may be called an 'affix,' and the verbal termination &c. a 'suffix.'

[4] For other illustrations of this see 1. *kṛi*, p. 300; 1. *śru*, p. 1100; 1. *sthā*, p. 1262 of this volume.

[5] The number of distinct Dhātus or radical forms given in some collections is 1,750, but as many forms having the same sound have different meanings, and are conjugated differently, they are held to be distinct roots and the number is thereby swelled to 2,490. It should be noted, too, that a great many of these Dhātus are modifications or developments of simpler elements, and this Dictionary does not always decide as to which of two, three or more roots is the simplest, although when roots are allied their connexion is indicated. Probably the real number of elementary radicals in Sanskṛit might be reduced to a comparatively small catalogue—even, as some think, to a list of not more than about 120 primitive roots. Many Sanskṛit roots have alternative Prākṛit forms or vice versâ, and both forms are allowed to co-exist, as *bhan* and *bhaṇ*, *dhan* and *dhaṇ*, *nṛit* and *naṭ*; others whose initials are aspirated consonants have passed into other aspirated consonants or have retained only the aspirate, as in *bhṛi*, *dhṛi*, *dhvṛi*, *hvṛi*, *hṛi* &c. Again, such a root as *svad* is probably nothing but a compound of *su* and root *ad*, and such roots as *stubh*, *stumbh*, *stambh* are plainly mere modifications of each other.

of treating each word as a separate and independent entity, requiring separate and independent explanation, would certainly fail to give a satisfactory conception of the structure of such a language as Sanskṛit, and of its characteristic processes of synthesis and analysis, and of its importance in throwing light on the structure of the whole Indo-European family of which it is the oldest surviving member.

I therefore came to the conclusion that the best solution of the difficulty lay in some middle course—some compromise by virtue of which the two lexicographical methods might be, as it were, interwoven.

It remains for me to explain the exact nature of this compromise, and I feel confident that the plan of the present work will be easily understood by any one who, before using the Dictionary, prepares the way by devoting a little time to a preliminary study of the explanations which I now proceed to give.

SECTION II.

Explanation of the Plan and Arrangement of the Work, and of the Improvements introduced into the Present Edition.

Be it notified, at the very threshold, that there are four mutually correlated lines of Sanskṛit words in this Dictionary:—(1) a main line in Nāgarī type, with equivalents in Indo-Italic type[1]; (2) a subordinate line (under the Nāgarī) in *thick* Indo-Romanic type[1]; (3) a branch line, also in thick Indo-Romanic type, branching off from either the first or the second lines with the object of grouping compound words under one head; (4) a branch line in Indo-Italic type, branching off from leading compounds with the object of grouping together the compounds of those compounds. Of course all four lines follow the usual Sanskṛit Dictionary order of the alphabet (see p. xxxvi).

The first or main line, or, as it may be called, the 'Nāgarī line,' constitutes the principal series of Sanskṛit words to which the eye must first turn on consulting the Dictionary. It comprises all the roots of the language, both genuine and artificial (the genuine being in *large* Nāgarī type), as well as many leading words in small Nāgarī, and many isolated words (also in small Nāgarī), some of which have their etymologies given in parentheses, while others have their derivation indicated by hyphens.

The second or subordinate line in thick Indo-Romanic type is used for two purposes:—(*a*) for exhibiting clearly to the eye in regular sequence under every root the continuous series of derivative words which grow out of each root; (*b*) for exhibiting those series of cognate words which, to promote facility of reference, are placed under certain *leading* words (in small Nāgarī) rather than under the roots themselves.

The third or branch line in thick Indo-Romanic type is used for grouping together under a leading word all the words compounded with that leading word.

The fourth or branch Indo-Italic line is used for grouping under a leading compound all the words compounded with that compound.

The first requires no illustration; the second is illustrated by the series of words under कृ 1. *kṛi* (p. 300) beginning with 1. **Kṛit,** p. 301, col. 3, and under कर 1. *kará* (p. 253) beginning with 1. **Karaka** (p. 254, col. 1); the third by the series of compounds under कर 1. *kará* (p. 253, col. 1), and **Káraṇa** (p. 254, col. 1); the fourth by the series of compounds under **-vīra** (p. 253, col. 3).

And this fourfold arrangement is not likely to be found embarrassing; because any one using the Dictionary will soon perceive that the four lines or series of Sanskṛit words, although following their own alphabetical order, are made to fit into each other without confusion by frequent backward and forward cross-references. In fact, it will be seen at a glance that the ruling aim of the whole arrangement is to exhibit, in the clearest manner, first the evolution of words from roots, and then the interconnexion of groups of words so evolved, as members of one family descended from a common source. Hence all the genuine roots of the language are brought prominently before the eye by large Nāgarī type; while the evolution of words from these roots, as from parent-stocks, is indicated by their being printed in thick Romanic type, and placed in regular succession either under the roots, or under some leading word connected with the same family by the tie of a common origin. It will be seen, too, that in the case of such leading words (which are always in Nāgarī type), their etymology—given in a parenthesis—applies to the whole family of cognate words placed under them, until a new series of words is introduced by a new root or new leading-word *in Nāgarī type.* In this way all repetition of etymologies is avoided, and the Nāgarī type is made to serve a very useful purpose.

It will also be seen that words which are different in meaning, but appear identical in form, are distinguished

[1] I use the expression 'Indo-Romanic' and 'Indo-Italic' to denote the expanded Roman and Italic alphabets adapted by the use of diacritical points and marks to the expression of Sanskṛit and other Indian languages. The thick Indo-Romanic type employed in this volume is a product of the Oxford Clarendon Press, and therefore named Clarendon type.

from each other by the figures 1, 2, 3, &c., placed before the Indo-Romanic or Indo-Italic transliterated forms:—see, for example, अशीत 1. *a-śīta,* अशीत 2. *aśita* (p. 113)[1]; 1. **Ā́pya,** आप्य 2. *āpya,* आप्य 3. *āpya* (pp. 142, 144); बृह् 1. *bṛih,* बृह् 2. *bṛih,* बृह् 3. *bṛih* (p. 735).

In regard to the roots of the language, it will be observed that they are treated of in the present work—both in respect of the meanings and of the exhibition of tenses, participles, and verbal forms evolved from them—more thoroughly and exhaustively than has hitherto been attempted in a Dictionary[2].

Furthermore, all the verbs formed from the roots with prepositions (as, for example, अनुकृ *anu-√kṛi,* p. 31, समभिव्याहृ *sam-abhi-vy-ā-√hṛi,* p. 1156) are arranged according to the method followed in Greek and Latin Lexicons; that is to say, such verbs are to be looked for in their own alphabetical order, and not under the roots *kṛi* and *hṛi.* The practical convenience resulting from this method, and the great advantage of exhibiting the connexion of every verb and its meanings with its derivatives, constitute in my opinion an invaluable gain, especially to the student who studies Sanskṛit as he would Greek and Latin, and makes it a guide to the study of the other members of the Indo-European family. At all events it forms one of the unique features of the present work, stamping it with an individuality of its own, and differentiating it from all other Sanskṛit Dictionaries. The labour entailed in the process—necessarily a wholly *pioneering process*—of thus rearranging the verbs in a language so rich in prepositions, can only be understood by those who have undergone it.

As to the separation of meanings it must be noted that mere amplifications of preceding meanings are separated by a comma, whereas those which do not clearly run into each other are divided by semicolons. A comma, therefore, must always be taken as marking *separate shades of meaning,* except it occurs in parenthetical observations.

Let it be observed, however, that all the meanings of a word belonging to a group are not always given in full, if they may be manifestly gathered from the other members of the group. This applies especially to participles and participial formations.

Observe too that all remarks upon meanings and all descriptive and explanatory statements are given between ( ), all remarks within remarks and comparisons with other languages between [ ].

I was told by a friendly critic, soon after the appearance of the first edition, that meanings and synonyms had been needlessly multiplied, but when the book had been fairly tested by repeated and extended application to various branches of the literature, it was found that apparently superfluous synonyms often gave the precise meanings required to suit particular passages. In the present edition—to save space—some synonyms which seemed mere surplusage have been rejected; and I fear I may have occasionally gone too far in sanctioning some of these rejections. For experience proves that the practical utility of a Dictionary is less impaired by a redundancy than by a paucity of meanings.

Again, a glance at the following pages will show that the arrangement of compound words under a leading word, as introduced in the edition of 1872, and continued with modifications in the present edition, is entirely novel.

It may perhaps be objected that there are too many of these compounds; but once more it may be urged that a Sanskṛit Dictionary must not be tried by ordinary laws in this respect, for Sanskṛit has developed more than Greek and German and any other Aryan language the faculty of forming compounds. The love of composition is indeed one of its most characteristic features. To exclude compounds from a Sanskṛit Lexicon would be, so to speak, to 'unsanskṛitize' it. Not only are there certain compounds quite peculiar to Sanskṛit, but, in the grammar, composition almost takes the place of Syntax, and the various kinds of compound words are classified and defined with greater subtlety and minuteness than in any other known language of the world. When a student is in doubt whether to translate compounds like **Indra-śatru** as Bahuvrīhis or Tatpurushas, the Dictionary is surely bound to aid in clearing up his perplexity. Even as it is, many useful compounds have, I fear, been sacrificed to the exigencies of space. The meanings of these, however, can be easily inferred from the meaning of their component members. Take, for example, such a word as **saṃyuktâkshara,** 'a compound or conjunct letter.'

Another distinctive peculiarity of this Dictionary consists in the articles on mythology, literature, religion, and philosophy, scattered everywhere throughout its pages. My own collection of notes from various sources, especially those made during my three Indian journeys and published in the books named in the Preface to this volume (see p. vi, with note), have enabled me to furnish students with much useful information on many subjects not hitherto treated of in Sanskṛit Dictionaries. It will, I feel

[1] In this first case the hyphen used in the transliterated form is no doubt sufficient to distinguish the two forms from each other. Hence, to economize space, the figures have occasionally towards the end of the work been omitted (see *samānā́, Sa-māna,* p. 1160).

[2] I must, however, here repeat the acknowledgment of my original indebtedness to 'Westergaard's Radices;' nor must I omit to mention Whitney's valuable Index of Roots, Verb-forms and Primary Derivatives.

sure, be admitted that the knowledge gained by me from personal contact with Indian Pandits and educated men in their own Universities, and with all sorts and conditions of Hindūs in their own towns and villages, has been a distinct advantage to this Dictionary. It has enabled me to give much useful information not found in other works, and to avoid many mistakes made by Sanskṛitists who have only a book-knowledge of India.

A further peculiar feature is the introduction of a large number of names of persons and places. This may be objected to as a needless extension of the scope and limits of a Dictionary. In extenuation I contend that greater liberty ought to be allowed to a Sanskṛit Dictionary in this respect than to Greek and Latin Lexicons, because Oriental alphabets have no capital letters enabling such names to be distinguished from ordinary nouns.

Then again, in regard to the names of works, which are also multiplied to an unusual extent, Sanskṛit literature is so vast that, although—as I hold—very little worthy of attention remains to be edited, yet it may often be of great importance to have attention drawn to unknown treatises, or to commentaries on well-known works ascertained to exist in manuscript in the libraries of Europe or India.

As to plants and trees, the adjective qualifying the name of a plant, as well as the name of the plant itself, ought occasionally to be marked, according to the rules of botanical science, with an initial capital letter. But it is often difficult for a non-botanist to decide as to the correct usage. It was therefore thought better to use capital letters for both substantive and adjective, especially as in the new edition, to save space, the word 'plant' is omitted. Hence the second capital letter, though often inappropriate, serves as a symbol for denoting that the epithet is that of a plant.

I need scarcely draw attention to the comparisons from cognate languages which manifestly constitute a special feature of this volume. Many doubtful comparisons have been eliminated from the present edition. A few questionable ones have, I fear, been retained or rashly inserted, but they will be easily detected (e.g. under **Ayā́sya,** p. 85).

In regard to what may be thought a needless multiplication of indecent words and meanings, offensive to European notions of delicacy, I am sorry to say that they had to be inserted, because in very truth Sanskṛit, like all Oriental languages, abounds with words of that character, and to such an extent, that to have omitted them, would have been to cut out a large percentage of the language. A story is told of a prudish lady who complimented Dr. Johnson on having omitted all bad words from his English Dictionary; whereupon he replied: 'Madam, it is true that I have done so, but I find that you have been looking for them.' In point of fact students of Sanskṛit literature cannot sometimes avoid looking for such words. Nor have I, except in rare instances, veiled their meaning under a Latin translation which only draws attention to what might otherwise escape notice.

In extenuation it may fairly be urged that in India the relationship between the sexes is regarded as a sacred mystery, and is never held to be suggestive of improper or indecent ideas.

After the foregoing explanation of the general plan of the work it remains to describe some of the more noteworthy changes and improvements introduced into the present edition.

And let me at once say that, as it was intended to give explanations of even more Sanskṛit words than are treated of in the great Wörterbuch of Böhtlingk and Roth, and in the later Wörterbuch of the former, and, as it was decided that to prevent its expansion beyond the limits of one compact volume, the number of pages in the new edition should not be augmented by much more than a hundred and fifty, it became a difficult problem to devise a method of making room for the ever-increasing number of words which, as the work grew under our hands, continually pressed more and more for admission into its purview.

Let any critic, then, who may feel inclined to pass a severe judgment on the contrivances for abbreviation in the present edition of the Dictionary, think for a moment of the difficulties in which its compilers found themselves involved. It was only gradually that the actual fact revealed itself—the very startling fact that we had to provide for the treatment of about one half more Sanskṛit words, simple and compound, than in the first edition. That is to say, calculating as I had done that the number of Sanskṛit words—simple and compound—in the first edition amounted to about 120,000, it became evident to us, as the work proceeded, that the number to be provided for in the new edition could not be reckoned at less than 180,000. It was as if a builder employed in repairing one of his own buildings had been told that he had to provide for the crowding of 1,800 human beings into a room, originally constructed by him to hold only twelve hundred.

Or perhaps the difficulty may be better illustrated thus:—A traveller, after having made a voyage round the world, starts some time afterwards for a second similar journey. The rules of the ship in which he embarks only permit of his taking a limited amount of baggage into his cabin, and naturally his first idea is to take the same box which accompanied him on the first occasion. Into this he begins by packing his possessions, with perhaps a little more compression than before. He soon finds, however, that the lapse of time has added to his acquisitions, and that no close packing will enable him to make room for them. What then is he to do? He is permitted to make his one box a little longer and deeper; but even then he has not room enough. His only resource is to make his one receptacle hold more by filling up every crevice, and fitting one article into the other by various ingenious devices.

This is an illustration of the difficulties encountered in the process of compressing the immense mass of new matter which had to be brought within the compass of the new edition. It has been possible to lengthen the pages of the new volume by about an inch, so that each column now contains about eight or nine lines more than in the first edition, and the volume has been increased in thickness by more than one hundred pages (and with the Addenda by 147 pages). These enlargements have given considerable additional space, but not nearly as much as was needed. All sorts of contrivances for contracting, abridging, and abbreviating had, therefore, to be adopted, so as to secure the greatest economy of space without impairing the completeness of the work—considerations which will, I hope, be a valid excuse for the occasional violations of uniformity which forced themselves upon us, as the need for greater comprehensiveness, within a limited circumference, became more and more imperative.

Perhaps the necessity for such measures will be better understood if I here enumerate some of the sources whence the additional matter in the present volume has been derived.

Imprimis, all the latter portion of the great seven-volumed Wörterbuch of the two great German lexicographers beginning with the letter व *v*. Next, all the additions in Geheimrath von Böhtlingk's later compilation, and especially his Nachträge. Then all my own manuscript Addenda in the interleaved copy of my first edition[1]; and lastly all the words from many important pure Sanskṛit and Buddhistic Sanskṛit works printed and published in recent years, most of which will be named in the sequel.

Doubtless, therefore, in describing the improvements which mark this new Dictionary, the first place should be given to the vast mass of new matter introduced into it. This I venture to assert, after a somewhat rough calculation, amounts to very little short of 60,000 additional Sanskṛit words with their meanings.

And a still further increase has resulted from the introduction of references to authorities, and to those portions of the literature in which the words and meanings recorded in the Dictionary occur. The reason given by me for abstaining from more than a few such references in the first edition, was that abundant quotations were to be found in the great seven-volumed Thesaurus—so often named before—which all who used my Dictionary could easily find means of consulting. In real fact, however, not a few words and meanings in the earlier portion of the first edition of my book were entered on the authority of Professor H. H. Wilson, while many more in the middle and towards the end were inserted from sources investigated independently by myself, and were not supported by any of the quotations given in the Thesaurus. It followed as a matter of course that, very soon after the publication of my first edition in 1872, the almost entire absence of independent references of my own was animadverted upon regretfully by even friendly critics.

Naturally, therefore, I determined to remedy an evident defect by introducing a large number of references and quotations into the new edition. Nor is it surprising that this determination grew and strengthened in the course of execution, so much so, indeed, that after the printing of page 60 I decided, with Professor Leumann's co-operation, to give no words and no series of meanings without quoting some authority for their use, or referring to the particular book or portion of literature in which they occur.

And further, it became a question whether we were not bound to indicate by a reference in every case not merely the particular books, but the chapter and line in which each word was to be found, and sometimes even to quote entire passages. This, in fact, as will be seen, has been occasionally done, but it soon became evident, that the immense copiousness of Sanskṛit literature—a copiousness far exceeding that of Greek and Latin—would preclude the carrying out of so desirable an object in full, or even to a somewhat less extent than in the great St. Petersburg Thesaurus—unless indeed my new Dictionary was to be enlarged to a point beyond the limits of a single compact volume. Nay, it soon became clear that the exigencies of space would make the mere enumeration of all the works in which a word occurs impossible. In the end it was found that the use of the symbol &c., would answer all the purpose of a full enumeration.

[1] Unfortunately in noting down words for insertion I omitted to quote the sources whence they were taken, as I did not at the time contemplate improving my new edition by the addition of references.

Hence it must be understood that RV.[1] &c. &c. denotes that a word occurs in the whole literature—both Vedic and Post-Vedic—beginning with the Ṛig-veda, while Mn. &c. signifies that the use of a word is restricted to the later literature beginning with Manu.

And again, when a word had not yet been met with in any published literary work, but only in native lexicons, it was decided to denote this by the letter L.

As to the words and meanings given on my authority and marked MW., many of them have been taken by me from commentaries or from the notes which I made after conversations with learned Pandits in their own country. For it seems to me that Sanskṛit Dictionaries ought sometimes to give important modern words and meanings as used by modern educated Sanskṛit scholars in India—such, for example, as the meaning of *prâṇa-pratishṭhā*[2] (see Additions under **Prâṇa**, p. 1330).

Then a third improvement in the present edition, as every true scholar will admit, is the accentuation of words occurring in accentuated texts, although it will be found, I fear, that occasional accidental omissions occur, and in cross-references the accent has often been designedly dropped. Many accents, too, which are only known from Pāṇini and the Phiṭ-sūtras have been intentionally omitted.

It is admitted that accentuation is *marked* only in the oldest Vedic texts, and that in later times it must have undergone great changes—so far at least as the *spoken* accent was concerned. And this led me to decide that in preparing a practical Dictionary which employed so many complicated diacritical marks, it would be better not to increase the complication by adding the marks of accentuation. All accentuation was, therefore, designedly omitted in the first edition. But the careful study of Pāṇini's grammar, which my higher lectures, during the period of my active occupancy of the Boden Chair (1860–1888), obliged me to carry on, forced upon me the conviction that, inasmuch as at the time when the great Indian Grammarian—the chief authority for both Vedic and classical grammar—elaborated his wonderful system, every word in Sanskṛit, as much in the ordinary language as in the Vedic, had its accent[3], a knowledge of accents must be often indispensable to a right knowledge of the meaning of words in Sanskṛit.

And in real truth the whole of Pāṇini's grammar is interpenetrated throughout by the ruling idea of the importance of accentuation to a correct knowledge of words and their meanings.

For example, we learn from Pāṇ. vi, 1, 201, that the word **ksháya** means 'abode,' but **kshayá** with the accent on the last syllable means 'destruction.' And again, from Pāṇ. vi, 1, 205, that **datta,** 'given,' which as a p. participle has the accent on the second syllable (*dattá*) is accentuated on the first syllable (i.e. is pronounced *dátta*) when it is used as a proper name. On the other hand, by Pāṇ. vi, 1, 206, **dhṛishṭa** has the accent on the first syllable, whether as a participle, or as a name (not *dhṛishṭá* at p. 519).

Further, by Pāṇ. vi, 1, 223 and vi, 2, 1 all compounds have different meanings according to the position of the accent. Hence **Indra-śatru** means either 'an enemy of Indra' or 'having Indra as an enemy,' according as the accent is on the last or first member of the compound (*Indra-śatrú* or *Índra-śatru;* see Additions, p. 1321). These examples may suffice to show the importance of accentuation in affecting meanings.

That this holds good in all languages is shown by the careful way in which accentuation is marked in modern English Dictionaries. How, indeed, could it be otherwise when the transference of an accent from one syllable to another often makes such important alteration in the sense as may be noted in the words 'gállant' and 'gallánt,' 'récord' and 'recórd,' 'présent' and 'presént,' 'aúgust' and 'augúst,' 'désert' and 'desért.' The bearing, too, of Sanskṛit accentuation on comparative philology will be evident to any one who has noted the coincidences between the accentuation of Greek and Sanskṛit words.

Manifestly then it would have been inexcusable had we omitted all accentuation in the present enlarged and improved work[4]. It must be admitted, however, that incidence of accent has not been treated with exact uniformity in every page of this volume.

In Pāṇini's system, as is well known, the position of the accent is generally denoted by some indicatory letter, attached to the technical names given by him to his affixes and suffixes, including the terminations

[1] Rig-Veda has now become an Anglicized word, and the dot under the R has been omitted in the Dictionary for simplicity.

[2] I am sorry to have to confess that imbued as I once was with false notions as to the deadness of Sanskṛit, I have sometimes omitted to give the meanings of important modern words like *prâṇa-pratishṭhā* in the body of the Dictionary.

[3] The absence of accent was only permitted in calling out to a person in the distance, Pāṇ. i, 2, 33.

[4] The importance of correct accentuation and intonation in a language, the very sound of which is held by the Hindūs to be divine, and the bearing of Sanskṛit accentuation on that of Greek, had become so impressed on me, that when I was sent as a Delegate to the Berlin International Congress of Orientalists by the Government of India in 1881, I requested Pandit Śyāmajī Kṛishṇa-varmā (who was also a Government Delegate) to illustrate my paper on Vedic hymns by repeating them with the right accentuation. The Pandit's illustrations were not only much appreciated, but received with grateful acknowledgments at the time by the eminent Chairman, Prof. A. Weber, and other Sanskṛit scholars present, but were misconstrued by one of my auditors—the well-known and most energetic Hon. Secretary of the Royal Asiatic Society. That gentleman made the Pandit's illustrative additions the subject of an extraordinary criticism in a paper on 'Oriental Congresses,' written by him and published in the Calcutta Review, No. CLXI (1885), and quite recently reprinted. A letter lately received by me from Professor A. Weber, and printed last year in the Asiatic Quarterly Review, expresses the astonishment which we both felt at the statements in that paper.

of verbs and of verbal derivatives (called *pratyaya*). Thus, by Pāṇ. vi, 1, 163 the letter *c* added to a suffix (as in *ghurac*, Pāṇ. iii, 2, 161), indicates that the derivative **bhaṅgura** formed by that suffix is accented on the *last* syllable (e.g. **bhaṅgurá**).

In Vedic texts printed in Nāgarī character the accents are denoted by certain short lines placed above and below the letters, but in the present Dictionary we have not thought it necessary to mark the accent of words printed in Nāgarī, but only of their equivalents in Romanic and Italic type, the common Udātta or acute accent being marked by ´, and the rarer Svarita by `.

And in this connexion it should be mentioned that the employment of the long prosodial mark (¯) to denote long vowels (e. g. **ā**) has manifestly one advantage. It enables the position of an accent to be indicated with greater clearness in cases where it falls on such vowels (e. g. **ā́**).

Next to the three principal improvements thus explained ought certainly to be reckoned the increased mechanical aids provided for the eye, to facilitate the search for words in pages overcrowded with complicated and closely printed type. And most conspicuous among these aids is the employment of thick 'Clarendon' type (see p. xiv, note 1) in place of the Italics of the previous edition, both for the derivatives under roots and under leading words and for the compounds under such words; thus allowing the Italic type to be reserved for compounds of compounds.

Then another improvement of the same kind has been effected by the distribution of the compounds belonging to leading words under two, three, or even more separate heads, according to the euphonic changes in the finals of these words. Thus in the first edition all the compounds belonging to the leading word **Bahis** were arranged under the one word *Bahis* (= *Vahis*); but in the present edition these compounds are far more readily found by their segregation under the five heads of **Bahis, Bahiḥ, Bahir, Bahiś,** and **Bahish** (see pp. 726, 727).

Furthermore, among useful changes must be reckoned the substitution of the short thick line (not necessarily expressive of a hyphen[1]) for the leading word in all groups of compounds whose first member is formed with that leading word. Take, for example, such an article as that which has the leading word **Agni**, at pp. 5, 6. It is easy to see that the constant repetition of **Agni** in the compounds formed with that word was unnecessary. Hence **—kaṇa, —karman** &c. are now substituted for **Agni-kaṇa, Agni-karman** &c. By referring to such an article as **Mahā**, at pp. 794–802, an idea may be formed of the space economized by this simple expedient.

And here I must admit that a few changes may possibly be held to be doubtful improvements, the real fact being that they have been forced upon us by the necessity for finding room for those 60,000 additional Sanskṛit words with their meanings, the accession of which to the pages of the Dictionary—as already mentioned—became a paramount duty.

For instance, towards the end of the work, the exigencies of space have compelled us to use Italics with hyphens, not only in the case of sub-compounds (as, for example, *-maṇi-maya* under **candra-kānta** at p. 386, col. 3, is for **candrakānta-maṇi-maya**), but also in the case of compounds falling under words combined with prepositions (as, for example, under such words as 2. **Vi-budha, Vi-bhāga,** at p. 977).

The same exigencies of space compelled us to group together all words compounded with 3. **vi** (see p. 949) and with 7. *sa* (see under **sa-kaṅkata,** p. 1123 &c.).

The same considerations, too, have obliged us to make a new departure in extending the use of the little circle ° to English words. Its ordinary use, of course, is to denote that either the first or last part of a Sanskrit word has to be supplied. For instance, such a word as *keśa-v°*, coming after 1. **Vapanīya** at p. 919 stands for *keśa-vapanīya*, while *°da*, *°data*, *°dasva* after *codati*, at p. 400, are for *coda*, *codata*, *codasva;* and similarly **°dyotana** under **Pra-dyota** at p. 680 is for **Pra-dyotana.**

The application of this expedient to English words has enabled us to effect a great saving. It must be understood that this method of abbreviation is only applied to the leading meaning which runs through a long article, or to English words in *close juxtaposition*. For example, the leading signification of **ratha** under the article 1. *rátha* (p. 865) being 'chariot,' this is shortened to 'ch°' in the remainder of the article; and 'clarified butter' in one line is shortened to 'cl° b°' in the next. By referring to such an article as **sahasra,** at p. 1195, it will be seen what a gain in space has thus been effected.

In cases like **—°ṉsa** under *kalā́* (p. 261) the ° denotes that **—°ṉsa** is not a complete word without the prefixing of **a,** which is not given because it has become blended with the final *ā* of the leading word *kalā*.

Much space, too, has been gained by the application of the symbols ^ ^ ^ ^ (adopted at Professor Leumann's suggestion) to denote the blending of short and long vowels. Thus ^ denotes the blending of two short vowels (as of *a*+*a* into *â*); ^ denotes the blending of a short with a long vowel (as of *a*+*ā* into *â*); ^ denotes the blending of a long with a short (as of *ā*+*a* into *â*); ^ denotes the blending of two long vowels (as of *ā*+*ā* into *â*), and so with the other vowels, e.g. *ê* for *a*+*i*, *ô* for *a*+*u*, *ô* for *a*+*ū* &c. (see for example **kṛitâgni** for *kṛita*+*agni*, **kṛitôdaka** for *kṛita*+*udaka*, at p. 303).

[1] Some compound words which are formed by Taddhita affixes supposed to be added to the *whole word* ought not strictly to have a hyphen.

A further economy has been effected by employing the symbol √ for root.

In this new edition, too, the letters 'mfn.' placed after the crude stems of words, have been generally substituted for the forms of the nominative cases of all adjectives, participles, and substantives (at least after the first 100 pages), such nominative forms being easily inferred from the gender. But it must be borne in mind that nearly all feminine stems in *ā* and *ī* are also nominative forms. In cases where adjectives make their feminines in *ī* this has been generally indicated, as in the previous edition. Occasionally, too, the neuter nominative form (*am*) is given as an aid to the eye in marking the change from one gender to another.

Other contrivances for abbreviation scarcely need explanation; for instance, 'N.' standing for 'name' is applicable to epithets as well as names, and when it applies to more than one person or object in a series, is omitted in all except the first; e.g. 'N. of an author, RV.; of a king, MBh.' &c.

Also, the figures 1, 2, 3 &c. have been in some cases dropped (see note 1, p. xv), and the mention of cl. 8 is often omitted after the common root *kṛi*.

Finally, I have thought it wise to shorten some of the articles on mythology, and to omit some of the more doubtful comparisons with the cognate languages of Europe.

SECTION III.

Extent of Sanskṛit Literature comprehended in the Present Edition.

I stated in the Preface to the first edition of this work—written in 1872—that I had sometimes been asked by men learned in all the classical lore of Europe, whether Sanskṛit had any literature. Happily, since then, a great advance in the prosecution of Indian studies and in the diffusion of a knowledge of India has been effected. The efforts and researches of able Orientalists in almost every country have contributed to this result, and I venture to claim for the Oxford Indian Institute and its staff of Professors and Tutors a large share in bringing this about.

Nevertheless much ignorance still prevails, even among educated English-speakers, in respect of the exact position occupied by Sanskṛit literature in India—its relationship to that of the spoken vernaculars of the country and the immensity of its range in comparison with that of the literature of Europe. I may be permitted therefore to recapitulate what I have already said in regard to the term 'Sanskṛit,' before explaining what I conceive ought to be included under the term 'Sanskṛit literature.'

By Sanskṛit, then, is meant the learned language of India—the language of its cultured inhabitants—the language of its religion, its literature, and science—not by any means a dead language, but one still spoken and written by educated men in all parts of the country, from Cashmere to Cape Comorin, from Bombay to Calcutta and Madras[1]. Sanskṛit, in short, represents, I conceive, the learned form of the language brought by the Indian branch of the great Āryan race into India. For, in point of fact, the course of the development of language in India resembles the course of Āryan languages in other countries, the circumstances of whose history have been similar.

The language of the immigrant Āryan race has prevailed over that of the aborigines, but in doing so has separated into two lines, the one taken by the educated and learned classes, the other by the unlearned—the latter again separating into various provincial sub-lines[2]. Doubtless in India, from the greater exclusiveness of the educated few, and the desire of a proud priesthood to keep the key of knowledge in their own possession, the language of the learned classes became so highly elaborated that it received the name **Saṃskṛita,** or 'perfectly constructed speech' (see p. xii), both to denote its superiority to the common dialects (called in contradistinction **Prākṛita**) and its more exclusive dedication to religious and literary purposes. Not that the Indian vernaculars are exclusively spoken languages, without any literature of their own; for some of them (as, for example, Hindī, Hindūstānī, and Tamil, the last belonging to the Drāviḍian and not Āryan family) have produced valuable literary works, although their subject-matter is often borrowed from the Sanskṛit.

Next, as to the various branches of Sanskṛit literature which ought to be embraced by a Dictionary aiming, like the present, at as much completeness as possible—these are fully treated of in my book 'Indian Wisdom' (a recent edition of which has been published by Messrs. Luzac & Co.). It will be

[1] A paper written by Pandit Śyāmajī Kṛishṇa-varmā on 'Sanskṛit as a living language in India,' was read by him at the Berlin Oriental Congress of 1881, and excited much interest. He argues very forcibly that 'Sanskṛit as settled in the *Ashṭādhyāyī* of Pāṇini was a spoken vernacular at the time when that great grammarian flourished.' In the same paper he maintains that Sanskṛit was the source of the Prākṛits, and quotes Vararuci's Prākṛita-prakāsa xii, 2 (Prakṛitiḥ saṃskṛitam, 'Sanskṛit is the source'). Of course the provincialized Prākṛits—though not, as I believe, derived directly from the learned language, but developed independently—borrowed largely from the Sanskṛit after it was thus elaborated.

[2] It has been recently stated in print that Russian furnishes an exception to the usual ramification into dialects, but Mr. Morfill informs me that it has all the characteristics of Āryan languages, separating first into Great and Little Russian and then into other dialects.

sufficient therefore to state here that Sanskṛit literature comprises two distinct periods, Vedic and Post-Vedic, the former comprising works written in an ancient form of Sanskṛit which is to the later form what the language of Chaucer is to later English.

Vedic literature begins with the Ṛig-veda (probably dating from about 1200 or 1300 B.C.), and extending through the other three Vedas (viz. the Yajur, Sāma, and Atharva-veda), with their Brāhmaṇas, Upanishads, and Sūtras, is most valuable to philologists as presenting the nearest approach to the original Āryan language. Post-Vedic literature begins with the Code of Manu (probably dating *in its earliest form* from about 500 B.C.), with its train of subsequent law-books, and extending through the six systems of philosophy, the vast grammatical literature, the immense Epics[1], the lyric, erotic, and didactic poems, the Nīti-śāstras with their moral tales and apothegms, the dramas, the various treatises on mathematics, rhetoric, prosody, music, medicine, &c., brings us at last to the eighteen Purāṇas with their succeeding Upa-purāṇas, and the more recent Tantras, many of which are worthy of study as repositories of the modern mythologies and popular creeds of India. No one person, indeed, with limited powers of mind and body, can hope to master more than one or two departments of so vast a range, in which scarcely a subject can be named, with the single exception of Historiography, not furnishing a greater number of texts and commentaries or commentaries on commentaries, than any other language of the ancient world. To convince one's self of this one need only glance at the pages of the present Dictionary, and note the numerous works named there, which, if the catalogue were complete, would probably amount to a total number not far short of the 10,000 which the Pandits of India are said to be able to enumerate.

Nor is it their mere number that astonishes us. We are appalled by the length of some of India's literary productions as compared with those of European countries. For instance, Virgil's Æneid is said to consist of 9,000 lines, Homer's Iliad of 12,000 lines, and the Odyssey of 15,000, whereas the Sanskṛit Epic poem called Mahā-bhārata contains at least 200,000 lines, without reckoning the supplement called Hari-vaṉśa[2]. In some subjects too, especially in poetical descriptions of nature and domestic affection, Indian works do not suffer by a comparison with the best specimens of Greece and Rome, while in the wisdom, depth, and shrewdness of their moral apothegms they are unrivalled.

More than this, the Hindūs had made considerable advances in astronomy, algebra, arithmetic, botany, and medicine, not to mention their superiority in grammar, long before some of these sciences were cultivated by the most ancient nations of Europe. Hence it has happened that I have been painfully reminded during the progress of this Dictionary that a Sanskṛit lexicographer ought to aim at a kind of quasi omniscience. Nor will any previous University education, such at least as was usual in my youth, enable him to explain correctly the scientific expressions which—although occasionally borrowed from the Greeks—require special explanation.

In answer then to the question: What extent of Sanskṛit literature is comprehended in this Dictionary? I reply that it aims at including every department, or at least such portions of each department as have been edited up to the present date.

And here I must plainly record my conviction that, notwithstanding the enormous extent of Sanskṛit literature, nearly all the most important portions of it—Vedic or Post-Vedic—worthy of being edited or translated have been already printed and made accessible in the principal public libraries of the world[3].

No doubt the vast area of India's philosophical literature has not yet been exhaustively explored; but its most important treatises have been published either in India or in Europe. In England we may appeal with satisfaction to the works of our celebrated scholar Colebrooke, of the late Dr. Ballantyne, and more recently of such writers as E. B. Cowell, A. E. Gough, and Colonel Jacob, all of whom have contributed to the elucidation of this most difficult, but most interesting branch of study, while among Continental scholars the names of Deussen, Garbe, and Thibaut are most distinguished.

[1] See the chapters on the Epic poems in 'Indian Wisdom,' and my edition of the 'Story of Nala,' published at the Clarendon Press, and my little work on 'Indian Epic Poetry' (now scarce).

[2] The late Professor Bühler has shown that the inscriptions of about 500 A.D. quote the Mahā-bhārata and describe it as containing 100,000 *verses*.

[3] I do not mean this remark to apply to Buddhistic literature, which is very extensive, and is partly in Sanskṛit, and has much still unedited and untranslated. The *Divyâvadāna*, edited by Professor E. B. Cowell and Mr. Neil, is an example. It is written in Sanskṛit or rather in a kind of Sanskṛitized Pāli, or Pāli disguised in Sanskṛit garb. Other Buddhist Texts, written in Sanskṛit, are now being ably edited by the well-known Tibetan traveller, Rai Śarat Candra Dās, Bahādur, C.I.E., to whom I was greatly indebted for help in my researches at Darjeeling and its neighbourhood. Much Jaina philosophical literature, too, is still unedited, although well worthy of attention, and although only occasionally referred to in this Dictionary. It is written in Sanskṛit as well as in Ardha-Māgadhī Prākṛit, for the elucidation of which Professor Leumann has done such excellent work. In fact, the Sanskṛit form of Jaina philosophical literature (now being ably expounded by Mr. Vīrcand Ghāndhi at Chicago) still offers an almost wholly unexplored field of investigation. Furthermore, it must be admitted that in some cases better editions of pure Sanskṛit works are needed. For example, a better critical edition of the Mahā-bhārata than those of Calcutta and Bombay is a desideratum. The Southern Recension of that immense work is I believe engaging the attention of Dr. Lüders, Librarian of the Indian Institute.

There is also much still to be done in what may be called Epigraphic or Inscription literature, in which Dr. Fleet, Dr. E. Hultzsch, and Professor F. Kielhorn are labouring so effectively. And I am happy to say that we have occasionally availed ourselves of their labours in the following pages.

The Tantras, too, present a field of research almost wholly untrodden by European scholars, and these books at one time attracted much curiosity as likely to present a hopeful mine for exploitation. I therefore, during my Indian journeys, searched everywhere for good MSS. of the most popular Tantras, with a view to making the best procurable example of them better known in Europe by a good printed edition and translation. Everywhere I was told that the Rudra-yāmala Tantra was held in most esteem[1]. But after a careful examination of its contents I decided that it was neither worth editing nor translating (see my 'Brāhmanism and Hindūism,' pp. 205–208).

As to translations, the long array of 'Sacred Books of the East' might well be supposed to have exhausted the whole reservoir of Sanskṛit works worthy of being translated; even admitting that the entire range of Sanskṛit literature is held to be more or less sacred. Yet the series is still incomplete[2].

Assuming then my opinion on this point to be correct, I think I may fairly claim for the present Dictionary as great an amount of comprehensiveness as existing circumstances make either possible or desirable. Of course the earlier part of the work must perforce be less complete than the later. Nor can it be said to deal with every branch of literature with equal thoroughness, but its defects are, I hope, fairly remedied by the ample Additions at the end of the volume.

SECTION IV.

Reasons for applying the Roman Alphabet to the expression of Sanskṛit, with an account of the Method of Transliteration employed in the Present Dictionary.

As I cherish the hope that this Dictionary may win its way to acceptance with the learned natives of India, I must ask European scholars to pardon my diffuseness if I state with some amplitude of detail my reasons for having applied the Roman or Latin alphabet to the expression of Sanskṛit more freely than any other Sanskṛit lexicographer.

For indeed I know full well that all who belong to the straitest sect of Hindū scholars will at once flatly deny that their divine Sanskṛit can with any propriety be exhibited to the eye clothed in any other alphabetical dress than their own 'divine Nāgarī.' *Na hi pūtaṃ syād go-kshīraṃ śva-dṛitau dhṛitam*, 'let not cow's milk be polluted by being put into a dog's skin.' How can it possibly be, they will exclaim, that the wonderful structure of our divine language and the subtle distinctions of its sacred sounds can be properly represented by such a thoroughly human and wholly un-Oriental graphic system as a modern European alphabet?

Let me, then, in the first place point out that our so-called European alphabet, as adopted by the Greeks, Romans, and modern nations of Europe, is really Asiatic, and not European in its origin. And secondly, let me try to show that it has certain features which connect it with the so-called divine Nāgarī alphabet of the Brāhmans. Nay more, that it is well suited to the expression of their venerated Sanskṛit; while its numerous accessory appliances, its types of various kinds and sizes, its capital and small letters, hyphens, brackets, stops &c., make it better suited than any other graphic system to meet the linguistic requirements of the coming century—a century which will witness such vast physical, moral, and intellectual changes, that a new order of things, and almost a new world and a new race of beings, will come into existence. In that new world some of the most inveterate prejudices and peculiarities now separating nation from nation will be obliterated, and all nationalities—brought into fraternal relationship—will recognize their kinship and solidarity.

Even during the present century the great gulf dividing the West from the East has been partially bridged over. Steam and electricity have almost destroyed the meaning of differences of latitude and longitude; and nations which were once believed to be actually and figuratively the antipodes of each other have been brought to feel that mere considerations of distance are no obstacles to the reciprocal interchange of personal intercourse, and no bar to the adoption of all that is best in each other's customs and habits of thought.

And a still more remarkable event has happened. Europe has learnt to perceive that in imparting

[1] A section of it has been printed in Calcutta.

[2] The use made of some of the series is thankfully acknowledged at p. xxxii; but it is surprising that the long line of 49 thick octavo volumes includes no complete translation of India's most sacred book—the Ṛig-veda. Only about 180 out of 1017 hymns are translated in vols. xxxii and xlvi, when a continuous English version of all the hymns might have been given in one volume. It is regrettable, too, that vol. xlii only gives about a third of the Atharva-veda hymns, and that the Bhāgavata-purāṇa, which is a bible of modern Hindūism, has no place in the list, while some volumes give translations of far less important works, and some give re-translations of works previously translated by good scholars.

some of the benefits of her modern civilization to Eastern races, she is only making a just return for the lessons imparted to her by Asiatic wisdom in past ages.

For did she not receive her Bible and her religion from an Eastern people? Did not her system of counting by twelves and sixties come to her from Babylonia, and her invaluable numerical symbols and decimal notation from India through the Arabs? Did not even her languages have their origin in a common Eastern parent? It cannot, therefore, be thought surprising if her method of expressing these languages by graphic symbols also came to her from an Eastern source.

We cannot, indeed, localize with absolute certainty the precise spot whence issued the springs of that grand flow of speech which spread in successive waves—commencing with the Sanskṛit in Asia and the Keltic in Europe—over a large proportion of those two continents. Nor can we fix, beyond all liability to question, the local source of the first known purely phonographic alphabet. But we stand on sure ground when we assert that such an alphabet is to be found inscribed on Phœnician monuments of a date quite as early as the cognate Moabite inscription on the stone of King Mesha, known to belong to the middle of the ninth century B.C.[1]

It was of course *a priori* to be expected that Phœnicia—one of the chief centres of trade, and the principal channel of communication between the Eastern and Western worlds in ancient times—should have been compelled to make use of graphic symbols of some kind to enable her to carry on her commercial dealings with other nations; and it may fairly be conjectured that a mere system of ideograms would have been quite unsuited to her needs. But this does not prove that the phonographic signs on Phœnician inscriptions were invented all at once, without any link of connexion with previously current ideographic prototypes. And it is certainly noteworthy that the discovery at Tel-el-Amarna in Egypt of letters from an ancient king of Jerusalem written on tablets in the early Babylonian cuneiform script[2] proves that a Babylonian form of ideographic writing existed in Palestine and the neighbourhood of Phœnicia as early as the fifteenth century B.C.

Those, however, who have conjectured that the Phœnician phonograms were developed out of the Babylonian cuneiform symbols, cannot be said to support their hypothesis by any satisfactory proof, literary or epigraphic.

Nor does the theory which makes the South Semitic or Himyaritic scripts[3] the precursors and prototypes of the Phœnician seem to rest on sufficiently clear evidence.

On the other hand it is certain that if we investigate the development of the Egyptian hieroglyphic ideograms, we shall find that they passed into a so-called 'hieratic' writing in which a certain number of phonograms were gradually introduced. And it is highly probable that Phœnicia in her commercial intercourse with a country so close to her shores as Egypt, or perhaps through a colony actually established there, became acquainted in very early times with this Egyptian hieratic script.

Furthermore, a careful comparison of the elaborate tables printed in the latest edition of the Encyclopædia Britannica, and in the Oxford 'Helps to the Study of the Bible'—giving the Egyptian and Phœnician symbols side by side—tends no doubt to show a certain resemblance of form between five or six of the Phœnician and corresponding Egyptian letters.

Nevertheless, the comparison by no means makes it clear that *all* the Phœnician letters were derived from Egyptian models[4], nor does it invalidate the fact that existing epigraphic evidence is in favour of regarding Phœnicia as practically the inventor of that most important factor in the world's progress—a purely phonographic alphabet.

Here, however, I seem to hear some learned native of India remark:—It may be true that the Phœnician inscriptions are prior in date to those hitherto discovered in India; but do you really mean to imply that India's admirably perfect Deva-nāgarī alphabet, which we hold to be a divine gift[5], was borrowed from the imperfect alphabet of a nation of mere money-making traders, like the Phœnicians? Is it not the case that the earliest elements of civilization and enlightenment have always originated in the East, and spread from the East to the West—not from the West to the East? And if, as is generally admitted, the symbols for numbers, which were as essential to the world's progress as letters, originated in India and passed through

[1] The Phœnician inscriptions have been deciphered by assuming that the Phœnician language must have been akin to Hebrew. Although their age cannot be ascertained with absolute certainty, yet there is good reason to believe that some of them are of greater antiquity than the cognate Moabite inscription of King Mesha which was found at Dibon, a little N.E. of Jerusalem and south of Heshbon.

[2] Some of these tablets show that diplomatic correspondence passed between Babylonia and Egypt through Palestine. In fact, 'Babylonian' was in those days the language of diplomacy, as French once was in Europe. Other tablets in Babylonian cuneiform character have proved to be letters written by the king of Jerusalem to the Egyptian monarch to whose suzerainty he appears to have been subject.

[3] There are two kinds of Himyaritic inscriptions, viz. Sabæan and Minæan.

[4] Notwithstanding the elaborate proofs given by the Abbé Van Drival in his ingenious and interesting treatise on '*l'origine de l'écriture*.'

[5] See note 2, p. xxvi.

Semitic countries into Europe, why should not alphabets have had the same origin and the same course? Did not the Hindūs invent for themselves their own grammar, their own science of language, their own systems of philosophy, logic, algebra, and music? Have they not an immense literature on these and other subjects, much of which must have been written down at least 600 years B.C.? And are there not references in this literature to the existence of writing in India in very ancient times? for instance, in the Vāsishṭha Dharma-sūtra of the later Vedic period, in the Laws of Manu[1], in Pāṇini, who lived about 400 B.C.[2], in the Pāli Canon of the Buddhists which refers to writing schools and writing materials[3]. And again, do not the actual inscriptions of King Aśoka of the third century B.C. exhibit a remarkably perfect system of alphabetical signs, and many varying forms in different districts of India, postulating several centuries of antecedent development[4]? And if no Indian epigraphs of an earlier date than the reign of Aśoka have yet been discovered, is not that due to the circumstance that the art of incising letters on stone and metal only came into use when great Hindū kings arose, whose empire was sufficiently extensive to make it necessary to issue edicts and grants to their subjects? Bearing all this in mind, may it not be contended that if there has been any plagiarism in the matter of alphabets, the borrowing may have been *from* the Hindūs rather than *by* them?

Such questions as these have often been addressed to me by learned Pandits, and it must be confessed that they are by no means to be brushed aside as unworthy of consideration. Quite the reverse. They contain many statements to which no exception can be taken. But my present object is not to furnish incontestable proof of the derivation of Indian alphabets from a Phœnician source. It is rather to point out to Indian scholars that even admitting (with some eminent authorities) that there is good ground for claiming an indigenous origin for Hindū alphabets, many of the letters composing them offer points of contact and affinity with those of Phœnicia, and therefore with those of Greece and Rome and modern Europe.

And at the outset it must be frankly acknowledged that the first phonographic alphabet brought to light on ancient Phœnician monuments constituted by no means a perfect alphabetic system. It had, no doubt, advanced beyond the ideographic stage, and even to some extent beyond the syllabic, but its phonograms were only twenty-two in number, and mainly represented consonants. It had not attained to the level of an alphabet in which vowel symbols are promoted to an equality of representation with consonantal, and treated as compeers, not as mere secondary appendages. And even to this day, the Semitic alphabets connected with the Phœnician—viz. the Hebrew, Aramæan, and Arabian—are nearly as imperfect, and very little better than, so to speak, consonantal skeletons, wanting the life-blood which vowels only can impart.

Indeed, the imperfection of the Phœnician script is well shown by the fact that the Greeks who, as every one admits, were indebted to the Phœnicians for their rudimentary consonantal method of writing, had no sooner received it (probably quite as early as 800 B.C.) than they began to remedy its defects, and gradually developed out of it a true alphabetic method of their own, which was ultimately made to flow from left to right in opposition to the Semitic method.

Similarly, too, the Romans when they had accepted the Phœnician graphic signs from the Greeks, found it necessary to improve upon them, and ultimately developed out of them an even more practical alphabetic system.

But surely these two facts may be appealed to as making it not improbable that if the Greeks and Romans, two highly intellectual races, sprung from the same Āryan stock as the Brāhmans, condescended to accept certain rudimentary phonograms from the Phœnicians, and to expand them into alphabets suited to the expression of their own languages, the Brāhmans also might have deigned, if not to accept a foreign alphabet, at least to improve their own graphic system by modifications introduced through contact with Semitic races.

Nor should it be forgotten that in later times the Hindūs did actually borrow a Semitic alphabet from Arabia for the expression of their vernacular Hindī[5].

No doubt it must be admitted that, had any overmastering conviction of the necessity for the general use of written signs taken hold of the Hindū mind in early times, India would not have consented to be beholden to other countries for even improvements in her own forms of writing.

But the most patriotic of India's patriots must acknowledge that the Hindūs have always preferred oral to written communications. Indeed, although a vast literature exists in Sanskṛit, no word exists exactly corresponding to our English word 'literature[6];' and even if such a word were available, true

[1] In Book viii, 168 written legal documents are mentioned.

[2] He gives the words *lipi* and *libi* in one of his rules (iii, 2, 21).

[3] The bark of the Bhoj (or Birch) tree and the leaf of the palm seem to have constituted the chief material used by the Hindūs till the introduction of paper by the Muhammadans. No such durable materials as Egyptian papyrus or European parchment—the latter being prohibited on account of its impurity—seem to have been employed.

[4] See note 3, p. xxv.

[5] Hindī when so transliterated is called Hindūstānī or Urdū.

[6] *Litera*, 'a letter,' is derived from *lino*, 'to smear,' just as Sanskṛit *lipi* from *lip*. If a corresponding word were to be used in Sanskṛit it would be *lipi-śāstra*. The word *akshara*, which is the Sanskṛit for a letter, properly means 'indelible,' and this meaning seems to point to the use of letters in early times for inscriptions on stones and metal. Similarly the first meaning of *lekha* is 'scratching with a sharp point.'

Indian Pandits would prefer to designate the immense series of their sacred books by such words as **Veda,** or **Vidyā** (from *vid*, 'to know'), **Śruti** (from *śru*, 'to hear'), **Śāstra** (from *śās*, 'to teach'), **Smṛiti** (from *smṛi*, 'to remember'); the reason being that, like Papias, Bishop of Hierapolis (whose date, according to Dean Farrar, is 140 A.D.), they consider 'that the things from books are not so advantageous as things from the living and abiding voice.' Nor must we forget that the climate of India was unfavourable to the preservation of such writing material as existed in ancient times.

And besides this may it not be conjectured that the invention and general diffusion of alphabetic writing was to Indian learned men, gifted with prodigious powers of memory, and equipped with laboriously acquired stores of knowledge, very much what the invention and general use of machinery was to European handicraftsmen? It seemed to deprive them of the advantage and privilege of exercising their craft. It had to be acquiesced in, and was no doubt prevalent for centuries before the Christian era, but it was not really much encouraged. And even to this day in India the man whose learning is treasured up in his own memory is more honoured than the man of far larger acquirements, whose knowledge is either wholly or partially derived from books, and dependent on their aid for its communication to others[1].

It seems, therefore, not unreasonable to assume that, when the idea of the necessity for inventing alphabetic signs began to impress itself on the minds of Semitic races, it had not taken such deep root among the inhabitants of India as to lead to the invention or general adoption of any one fixed system of writing of their own. It seems, indeed, more probable that learned men in that country viewed the art of writing too apathetically to make a stand against the introduction of alphabetical ideas from foreign sources.

At all events there can be no antecedent improbability in the theory propounded by German Sanskṛitists that an early passage of phonographic symbols took place from a Phœnician centre eastward towards Mesopotamia and India, at about the same period as their passage westward towards Europe, namely, about 800 B.C.

It is not asserted that the exact channel by which they were transmitted has been satisfactorily demonstrated. Some think—and, as it seems to me, with much plausibility—that they may have been introduced through contact with the Greeks[2]. Perhaps a more likely conjecture is that Hindū traders, passing up the Persian Gulf, had commercial dealings with Aramæan traders in Mesopotamia, and, becoming acquainted with their graphic methods, imported the knowledge and use of some of their phonetic signs into India.

This view was first propounded in the writings of the learned Professor A. Weber of Berlin, and has recently been ably argued in a work on 'Indische Palæographie,' by the late Professor Bühler of Vienna (published in 1896). If Indian Pandits will consult that most interesting standard work, they will there find a table exhibiting the most ancient of known Phœnician letters side by side with the kindred symbols used in the Moabite inscriptions of King Mesha—which, as before intimated, is known to be as old as about 850 B.C.—while in parallel columns, and in a series of other excellent tables, are given the corresponding phonographic symbols from the numerous inscriptions of King Aśoka scattered everywhere throughout Central and Northern India[3].

These inscription-alphabets are of two principal kinds:—

The first kind is now called Kharoshṭhī (or 'Ass's lip' form of writing, *lipi* being understood)[4]. This belongs to the North-west corner of the Panjāb and Eastern Afghānistān. It was used by King Aśoka for a few of his rock and stone inscriptions, and is a kind of writing the prototype of which was probably introduced into Persia about 500 B.C., and brought by Persian rulers into Northern India in the fourth

[1] Pandit Śyāmajī in his second paper, read at the Leyden Congress, said: 'We in India believe even at the present day that oral instruction is far superior to book-learning in maturing the mind and developing its powers.'

[2] Certainly, as I think, the change of direction in the writing may have been due to Greek influence. Pāṇini, who probably lived about 400 B.C., gives as an example of feminine nouns the word *Yavanānī*, which Kātyāyana interprets to mean 'the Greek alphabet;' and we know that Greek coins and imitations of Greek coins, unearthed in North-western India, prove the existence of that alphabet there before Alexander the Great's time. Hindū receptivity of Greek influences is illustrated by the number of astronomical words derived directly from the Greeks to be found scattered throughout the pages of the present Dictionary.

[3] Aśoka, who called himself Priya-darśin, and was the grandson of Candra-gupta, did for Buddhism what Constantine did for Christianity, by adopting it as his own creed. Buddhism then became the religion of the whole kingdom of Magadha, and therefore of a great portion of India; and Aśoka's edicts, inscribed on rocks and pillars (about the middle of the third century B.C.), furnish the first authentic records of Indian history. Yet the language of these inscriptions cannot be said to be exactly identical with so-called Māgadhī Prākṛit, nor with the Pāli of the Buddhist sacred scriptures, although those forms of Prākṛit may be loosely called either Māgadhī or Pāli. Nor was the name Pāli originally applied to the *language* of the Buddhist Canon, but rather to the *line or series of passages* constituting a text (cf. the use of *tantra*). According to Professor Oldenberg the Vinaya portion of the texts existed in its present form as early as 400 B.C. The later Buddhist texts were written down not long after, and commentaries have since been compiled in Pāli and the languages of Ceylon, Siam, and Burma; the Pāli of Ceylon being affected by intercourse with Kalinga (Orissa).

[4] See this Kharoshṭhī fully described in Professor Bühler's book. The first names given to it were Ariano-Pāli, Bactro-Pāli, Indo-Bactrian, North Aśoka &c. Sir A. Cunningham called it Gāndhārian. Pandit Gaurī-Śaṃkar, in his interesting work Prācīna-lipi-mālā written in Hindī, calls it *Gāndhāra-lipi*. Some think that Kharoshṭhī is derived from the name of the inventor.

century B.C. At all events, it is well known that the Persian monarchs of the Akhæmenian period employed Aramæan scribes, and that the Kharoshṭhī writing, even if originally Indian (according to Sir A. Cunningham and others), has assumed under their hands a manifestly Aramaic character, flowing like all Semitic writing from right to left. Possibly, however, as it seems to me, Grecian influences (which penetrated into India before the time of Alexander) may have partially operated in assimilating this early North-western Indian script to a Phœnician type. It may be excluded from our present inquiry, because it never became generally current in India, and never developed into a form suitable for printing.

The second kind of ancient Indian script is called Brāhma (or Brāhmī lipi). This is without doubt the oldest of the two principal forms[1]. Its claim to greater antiquity is proved by its name Brāhma—given to it by the Brāhmans, because, as they assert, it was invented by their god Brahmā[2]—an assertion which may be taken as indicating that, whatever its origin, it was moulded into its present form by the Brāhmans.

And undeniably it is this Brāhma writing (Brāhmī lipi) which has the best right to be called the true Indian Brahmanical script. It must have been the first kind of writing used when Sanskṛit literature began to be written down (perhaps six centuries B.C.), and it is the script of the Aśoka inscriptions of Central and Northern India—and even of North-western India, where it is found concurrently with the Kharoshṭhī. It was employed to express the Prākṛit dialect[3] of the Buddhist kings, and flowed, like its later development called Nāgarī, from left to right. Its first appearance on actually existing inscriptions—so far as at present discovered—cannot be placed earlier than the date of these kings in the third century B.C.

But it is important to note that the existence of the Brāhmī lipi in India must be put back to a period sufficiently early to allow for its having once flowed from right to left like the Kharoshṭhī, probably as early as the sixth century B.C. This is made clear by the direction of the letters on an ancient coin discovered by Sir A. Cunningham at Eraṇ[4]—a place in the central provinces remarkable for its monumental remains. One can scarcely accept seriously the suggestion that the position of the short ि *i* in the present Nāgarī is a survival of the original direction of the writing[5].

If then any unprejudiced Hindū scholar will examine attentively the tables in Professor Bühler's book, he will, I think, be constrained to admit that the Indian Brāhma letters have certain features which connect them with the ancient Phœnician script, and therefore with the Greek and Roman.

It should not, however, be forgotten that an interval of nearly seven centuries separates the Phœnician from the Brāhma inscription-letters, and that to make the affinity between the two alphabets clearer the side-lights afforded by collateral and intermediate Semitic scripts ought to be taken into account[6]. Nor should it be forgotten that when the Hindūs, like the Greeks, changed the direction of their writing, some of the symbols were turned round or their forms inverted, or closed up or opened out in various ways.

The further development of the Brāhma symbols into the modern Deva-nāgarī and its co-ordinate scripts[7] is easily traceable. It must, however, be borne in mind that the later Pandits tried to improve the ancient graphic signs by setting them up as upright as possible and by drawing a horizontal stroke to serve as a line from which the letters might hang down, and so secure a system of straight writing—often conspicuously absent in Hindūstānī and Persian caligraphy[8].

I here append a table consisting of seven columns, in which I have so arranged the letters as to illustrate the view that the Phœnician alphabet spread about 800 B.C. first westward towards Greece and Italy, and secondly eastward towards India.

The column marked 1 gives ten Phœnician letters. That marked 2, to the left of 1, gives the ten corresponding Greek letters; that marked 3 the corresponding Roman; and that marked 4 the corresponding English letters. Then the column marked 2, to the right of 1, gives the ten corresponding Brāhma letters; that marked 3 shows the gradual developments of the Brāhma symbols as exhibited on various inscriptions; and that marked 4 gives the corresponding letters in modern Nāgarī[9].

[1] A variation of it called Bhaṭṭiprolu is described by Bühler.

[2] In the same way the great Arabian Teacher Muhammad declared in the first Sura of the Kurān (according to Rodwell, p. 2, and Sale, p. 450 with note) that 'God taught the use of the pen.' Even some Christians may not be indisposed to agree with Hindūs and Muhammadans in holding that the faculty of writing, as an instrument for the expression of thought—although dormant through all the early ages of the world's history—is as much a divine gift as language. Muhammad's view, however, of the divine origin of writing consisted in declaring that the Kurān descended ready written from heaven.

[3] For the language of the inscriptions, see p. xxv, note 3.

[4] These letters are shown in Professor Bühler's tables.

[5] Our invaluable decimal notation certainly came from India, and may be said to conform to Semitic methods in the direction of the notation, inasmuch as units are placed on the right, while tens and hundreds are on the left.

[6] Professor Bühler's first table in his work on Indian Palæography would have been more convincing had he given examples of collateral and intermediate Semitic forms.

[7] Such as the Bengālī, the Marāṭhī, Gujarātī &c., some of which may be usefully studied as presenting forms more closely resembling the ancient Brāhma letters.

[8] A similar line is often drawn in English copybooks and on writing paper as an aid to straight writing, but always *below*, not above the letters.

[9] Dr. Lüders, of the Indian Institute, has kindly assisted me in the right formation of some of the inscription letters. The roughness of some is due to their being photographs from original impressions.

Let any one study this Table and he must, I think, admit that it indicates an original connexion or family likeness between the Phœnician and earliest Indian or Brāhma letters, whilst it also illustrates the fact that the plastic hand of the Brāhmans has greatly modified and expanded the original germs, without, however, obliterating the evident indications of their connexion with the Phœnician.

4	3	2	1	2	3			4
CORRESPONDING ENGLISH	ARCHAIC ROMAN	ARCHAIC GREEK	PHŒNICIAN	BRĀHMA	DEVELOPMENTS OF BRĀHMA			MODERN NĀGARĪ
A	A	A						अ
K	K	K						क
G	C	Γ						ग
T	T	T						त
TH*	⊗	⊗						थ
D§	D	Δ						द
P	P	Γ						प
B	B	B						ब
Y	Y							य
V	V	Y						व

* This is for the Greek *theta*, which is represented in this Dictionary, according to present usage, by *th*, although *ŧ* or *t'* would be a more scientific symbol.

§ According to Professor Bühler, the Brāhma D became Nāgarī ध *dh*, from which द *d* was evolved.

And indeed the modest equipment of twenty-two letters which satisfied the Phœnicians, Greeks, and Romans, to whom the invention of writing was a mere human contrivance for the attainment of purely human ends, could not possibly have satisfied the devout Hindū, who regarded his language as of divine origin, and therefore not to be expressed by anything short of a perfect system of equally divine symbols. Even the popular Prākṛit of King Aśoka's edicts seems to have required nearly forty symbols[1], and the

[1] Some of the inscriptions had not the full complement of vowel-signs. As a matter of fact I find that in some inscriptions a list of only thirty-five letters in all is given, while in others there are thirty-six, and in others again thirty-nine. Professor Bühler says (p. 82 of his latest work published in 1898) that the ordinary Brāhma alphabet has forty-four letters traceable in the oldest inscriptions (including the Bhaṭṭiprolu) which with *au* (derived from *o*) would make forty-five, and with the mark for Visarga which 'first occurs in the Kushana inscriptions' forty-six. The common reckoning for the vowels, as taught in indigenous schools, makes them only twelve.

amount needed for the full Brāhmī lipi, as used for the Sanskṛit of that period, could not have been less than fifty (if the symbols for *ai*, *au*, *ṛi*, *ṛī*, *ḷri*, *ḷrī*, and *ḷa* be included).

Then, if we turn to the Brāhma alphabet in its final development, called Nāgarī, we see at a glance that it is based on the scientific phonetic principle of 'one sound one symbol'—that is, every consonantal sound is represented by one invariable symbol, and every shade of vowel-sound—short, long, or prolated—has one unvarying sign (not as in English where the sound of *e* in *be* may be represented in sixteen different ways). Hence, for the expression of the perfectly constructed Sanskṛit language there are sixteen vowel-signs (including *aṃ* and *aḥ* and excluding the prolated vowel forms), and thirty-five simple consonants, as exhibited on p. xxxvi of this volume.

Of course a system of writing so highly elaborated was only perfected by degrees[1], and no doubt it is admirably adapted to the purposes it is intended to serve. Yet it is remarkable that even in its latest development, as employed in the present Dictionary, it has characteristics indicative of its probable original connexion with Semitic methods of writing, which from their exclusively consonantal character are admittedly imperfect.

For the Pandits, unlike the Greeks and Romans, cannot in my opinion be said to have adopted to the full the true alphabetic theory which assigns a separate independent position to all vowel-signs. And my reason for so thinking is that they make the commonest of all their vowels—namely short *a*[2]—inherent in every isolated consonant, and give a subordinate position above or below consonants to some of their vowel-signs. And this partially syllabic character of their consonantal symbols has compelled them to construct an immense series of intricate conjunct consonants, some of them very complicated, the necessity for which may be exemplified by supposing that the letters of the English word 'strength' were Nāgarī letters, and written **सतरेनगथ.** This would have to be pronounced *satarenagatha*, unless a conjunction of consonantal signs were employed, to express *str* and *ngth*, and unless the mark called Virāma, 'stop,' were added to the last consonant. So that with only thirty-three simple consonants and an almost indefinite number of complex conjunct consonants the number of distinct types necessary to equip a perfect Sanskṛit fount for printing purposes amounts to more than 500.

Surely, then, no one will maintain that, in these days of every kind of appliance for increased facilities of inter-communication, any language is justified in shutting itself up behind such a complex array of graphic signs, however admirable when once acquired. At all events such a system ought not to have the monopoly for the expression of a language belonging to the same family as our own and in a country forming an integral part of the British Empire. The Sanskṛit language, indeed, is a master-key to a knowledge of all the Hindū vernaculars, and should moreover be studied as a kind of linguistic bond of sympathy and fellow-feeling between the inhabitants of the United Kingdom and their Indian fellow-subjects. But to this end every facility ought to be afforded for its acquirement.

And if, as we have tried to show, the Brāhmī lipi, the Nāgarī, and the Greek and Romanic alphabets are all four related to each other—at least, in so far as they are either derived from or connected with the same rudimentary stock—it surely cannot be opposed to the fitness of things, that both the Nāgarī and Romanic alphabets should be equally applied to the expression of Sanskṛit, and both of them made to co-operate in facilitating its acquisition.

Nor let it be forgotten that in the present day the use of the English language is spreading everywhere throughout India, and that it already co-exists with Sanskṛit as a kind of *lingua franca* or medium of communication among educated persons, just as Latin once co-existed with Greek. So much so indeed, that, contemporaneously with the diffusion of the English language, the Roman graphic system, adopted by all the English-speaking inhabitants of the British Empire, has already forced itself on the acceptance of the Pandits, whether they like it or not, as one vehicle for the expression of their languages; just as centuries ago the Arabic and Persian written characters were forced upon them by their Muhammadan conquerors for the expression of Hindī.

It is on this account that I feel justified in designating the European method of transliteration employed in this Dictionary by the term 'Indo-Romanic alphabet.'

And be it understood that such an acceptance of the Romanic alphabet involves no unscientific

[1] The oldest known inscription in Sanskṛit is on a rock at Junā-garh in Kāthiāwār. It is called the Rudra-dāman inscription, and dates from the second century A.D. It is not in Nāgarī, but in old inscription letters. The Bower MS. of about 400 A.D. shows a great advance towards the Nāgarī, while Danti-durga's inscription of about 750 A.D. exhibits a complete set of symbols very similar to the Nāgarī now in use. It is noteworthy, however, that the first *manuscript* in really modern Nāgarī is not older than the eleventh century A.D.

[2] This *ă* is the *a* of our words 'vocal organ' (pronounced *vocul orgun*). Sanskṛit does not possess the sound of *a* in our 'man,' nor that of *o* in our 'on.' As a consonant cannot be pronounced without a vowel, the Brāhmans chose the commonest of their vowels for the important duty of enabling every consonant to be pronounced. Hence every consonant is named by pronouncing it with *a* (e.g. *ka*, *kha*, *ga* &c.). It is, I suppose, for a similar reason that we have used the common vowel symbol *e* for naming many of our English letters.

adaptation of it to the expression of Sanskṛit like our chaotic adaptation of it to the expression of English; or like the inaccurate use of it by native writers themselves in transliterating their own Indian words[1]. Quite the reverse. The Roman alphabet adapts itself so readily to expansion by the employment of diacritical points and marks, that it may be regarded as a thoroughly scientific instrument for the accurate expression of every Indian sound, and probably of nearly every sound in every language of the world. And it may, I think, be confidently predicted that before the twentieth century has closed, man's vision, overtasked by a constantly increasing output of literary matter, will peremptorily demand that the reading of the world's best books be facilitated by the adoption of that graphic system which is most universally applicable and most easily apprehensible. Whether, however, the Roman symbols will be ultimately chosen in preference to other competing systems as the best basis for the construction of a world's future universal alphabet no one can, of course, foretell with the same confidence.

One thing, I contend, is certain. Any ordinary scholar who consults the present work will be ready to admit that it derives much of its typographical clearness from certain apparently trifling, but really important, contrivances, possible in Romanic type, impossible in Nāgarī. One of these, of course, is the power of leaving spaces between the words of the Sanskrit examples. Surely such a sentence as *sādhu-mitrāṇy akuśalād vārayanti* is clearer than *sādhumitrāṇyakuśalādvārayanti*. Again, who will deny the gain in clearness resulting from the ability to make a distinction between such words as 'smith' and 'Smith,' 'brown' and 'Brown,' 'bath' and 'Bath?' not to speak of the power of using italics and other forms of European type. And, without doubt, the use of the hyphen for separating long compounds in a language where compounds prevail more than simple words[2], will be appreciated by all. I can only say that, without that most useful little mark, the present volume must have lost much in clearness, and still more in compactness; for, besides the obvious advantage of being able to indicate the difference between such compounds as **su-tapa** and **suta-pa** which would have been impossible in Nāgarī type, it is manifest that even the simplest compounds, like **sad-asad-viveka, sv-alpa-keśin,** would have required, without its use, an extra line to explain their analysis[3].

Fairness, however, demands that a few of the obvious defects of the Indo-Romanic system of transliteration adopted in this volume should be acknowledged. In certain cases it confessedly offends against scientific exactness; nor does it always consistently observe the rule that every simple vowel-sound should be represented by a single symbol. For instance, the Sanskṛit vowels ऋ ṛ and ॠ ṝ are not represented in this Dictionary by the symbols *ṛ* and *ṝ*, according to the practice of some German scholars—a practice adopted by the Geneva Transliteration Committee—but by *ṛi* and *ṛī*. And my reason is that, inasmuch as in English Grammar *r* is not regarded as a semi-vowel, *ṛ* and *ṝ* are unsuitable representatives of vowel-sounds. Moreover, they are open to this objection, that when the dot under the *r* is accidentally dropped or broken off, as often happens in printing, especially in India, the result is worse than if the *r* were followed by *i*. For example, *Krshṇa* is surely worse than *Krishṇa*.

So again in the case of aspirated consonants, the aspiration ought not to be represented by a second letter attached to them. Indeed, in the case of *ch* employed by Sir W. Jones for the palatal च, and *chh* for छ, the inconvenience has been so great that in the present edition I have adopted (in common with many other Sanskṛitists) the simple *c* for च, the pronunciation being the same as *c* in the Italian *dolce* or as *ch* in 'church,' the latter of which would, if a Sanskṛit word, be written 'curc.' Similarly *ch* has been adopted for छ[4].

As to the transliteration of the palatal sibilant श, I have preferred *ś* to the *ṡ* employed in the first edition, and I much prefer it to the German and French method of using *ç*. Experience proves that the cedilla is often either broken off in printing or carelessly dropped, and as a consequence important words such as Aśoka are now often wrongly printed and pronounced Acoka.

So also I should have preferred the symbol *ṣ* for the cerebral sibilant, but have felt it desirable to retain *sh* in the present edition. There is the same objection to *ṣ* as to the *ṛ* mentioned above. This

[1] Take, for example, the following transliterated words in a recent pamphlet by a native:—*Devi, puja, Durga, Purana, ashtami, Krshna, Savitri, Acoka, Civa* &c. I have even seen *crab* written for the Hindūstānī *ḳharāb*, 'bad.'

[2] Forster gives an example of one compound word consisting of 152 syllables. This might be matched by even longer specimens from what is called Campū composition.

[3] We may, at least, entertain a hope that the hyphen will not be denied to Sanskṛit for the better understanding of the more complex words, such, for example, as *vaidikamanvādipraṇīta-smṛititvāt, karmaphalarūpaśarīradhārijīvanirmitatvābhāvamā-treṇa*, taken at haphazard from Dr. Muir's Texts. We may even express a hope that German scholars and other Europeans, who speak forms of Āryan speech, all of them equally delighting in composition, may more frequently condescend to employ the hyphen for some of their own Sesquipedalia Verba, thereby imitating the practical Englishman in his Parliamentary compounds, such, for example, as *Habeas-corpus-suspension-act-continuance-Ireland-bill*.

[4] In the paper on transliteration, which I read at the Berlin International Congress, I proposed a kind of mark of accentuation to represent aspirated consonants, as, for example, *k'*, *p'*. To say (as at p. xxxvi) that aspirated *k* or *p* is like *kh* in *inkhorn* or *ph* in *uphill* is to a certain extent misleading. It is simply *k* or *p* pronounced as in Ireland with a forcible emission of the breath.

will be clear if we write the important word **Ṛishi** in the way German scholars write it, namely **Ṛṣi,** and then omit the dots thus, **Rsi.**

In regard to the nasals I have in the present edition adopted *ṅ* for ङ and *ñ* for ञ. In these changes I am glad to find myself in accord with the Geneva Transliteration Committee.

As to the method of using italic *k, kh* for च, छ and italic *g, gh* for ज, झ—adopted in the 'Sacred Books of the East'—the philological advantage thought to be gained by thus exhibiting the phonetic truth of the interchange of gutturals and palatals, appears to me to be completely outweighed by the disadvantage of representing by similar symbols sounds differing so greatly in actual pronunciation. For instance, to represent such common words as 'chinna' by '*k*hinna' and 'jaina' by '*g*aina' seems to me as objectionable as to write '*K*hina' for 'China' and '*G*apan' for 'Japan.' The plan of using italics is no safeguard, seeing that in printing popular books and papers the practice of mixing up Roman and Italic letters in the same word is never adhered to, so that it is now common to find the important Indian sect of Jains printed and pronounced 'Gains[1].'

Having felt obliged by the form in which this Dictionary is printed to dwell at full length on a matter of the utmost importance both in its bearing on the more general cultivation of Sanskrit and on the diffusion of knowledge in our Eastern Empire, I must now repeat my sense of the great assistance the cause of the transliteration of Indian languages into Romanized letters formerly received at the hands of the late Sir Charles Trevelyan. He was the first (in his able minute, dated Calcutta, January, 1834[2]) to clear away the confusion of ideas with which the subject was perplexed. He also was the first to awaken an interest in the question throughout England about forty-two years ago. His arguments induced me to take part in the movement, and our letters on the subject were published by the 'Times,' and supported by its advocacy. Since then, many Oriental books printed on a plan substantially agreeing with Sir W. Jones' Indo-Romanic system, have been published[3]. Moreover, on more than one occasion I directed the attention of the Royal Asiatic Society[4], and of the Church Missionary Society[5], and Bible Society, to this important subject, and at the Congress of Orientalists held at Berlin in September, 1881, I read a paper, and submitted a proposal for concerted international action with a view to the fixing of a common scheme of transliteration. The discussion that followed led to the appointment of the first Commission for settling a common international system of transcription, and it may, I think, be fairly assumed that the agitation thus set in motion, and carried on for so many years, was one of the principal factors in bringing about the proposed international scheme issued by the Transliteration Committee of the Geneva Oriental Congress in September, 1894.

SECTION V.

Acknowledgment of Assistance Received.

In the Preface to the first edition I made special mention of the name of an eminent scholar who was a member of the Oxford University Press Delegacy when the publication of that edition was undertaken—Dr. Robert Scott, sometime Master of Balliol, afterwards Dean of Rochester, and co-author with Dr. Liddell of the well-known Greek Lexicon. He had been one of my kindest friends, and wisest counsellors, ever since the day I went to him for advice during my first undergraduate days at Balliol, on my receiving an appointment in the Indian Civil Service, and I need scarcely repeat my sense of what this Dictionary, in its inception, owed to his support and encouragement.

Nor need I repeat the expression of my sense of obligation to my predecessor in the Boden Chair, Professor H. H. Wilson, who first led me to the study of Sanskrit about sixty years ago (in 1839), and furnished me with my first materials for an entirely new system of Sanskṛit lexicography (see p. xi). All the words and meanings marked W. in the following pages in the present work rest on his authority.

[1] Surely we ought to think of our Indian fellow-subjects who in their eagerness to learn the correct pronunciation of English would be greatly confused if told that such good old English words as *pinch, catch, chin, much, jump, jest,* ought to be written pin*k*, ca*k*, *k*in, mu*k*, *g*ump, *g*est.

[2] This will be found at p. 3 of the 'Original Papers illustrating the History of the Application of the Roman Alphabet to the Languages of India,' edited by me in 1859.

[3] Among other numberless publications a most accurate edition of the Ṛig-veda itself, edited by Professor Aufrecht, was printed in the Roman character, and published in two of the volumes of Professor Weber's Indische Studien.

[4] See especially my paper read before the R.A.S., April 21, 1890.

[5] In 1858 I wrote strong letters to the Rev. Henry Venn, deprecating the system of transliteration then adopted by the C.M.S. It has been recently remodelled on the lines of the Geneva Congress report.

Nevertheless, sincerity obliges me to confess that, during my long literary career, my mind has had to pass through a kind of painful discipline involving a gradual weakening of faith in the trustworthiness of my fellow men, not excepting that of my first venerated teacher. I began my studies, indeed, with much confidence in the thought that one man existed on whom I could lean as an almost infallible guide; but as I grew a little wiser, and my sensitiveness to error sharpened, I discovered to my surprise that I was compelled to reject much of his teaching as doubtful. Nay, I am constrained to confess that as I advanced further on the path of knowledge, my trustfulness in others, besides my old master, experienced by degrees a series of disagreeable and unexpected shocks; till now, that I have arrived at nearly the end of my journey, I find myself left with my faith in the accuracy of human beings generally—and certainly not excepting myself—somewhat distressingly disturbed. Such painful feelings result, I fear, in my own case from a gradual and inevitable growth of the critical faculty during a long lifetime, and are quite consistent with a sense of gratitude for the effective aid received from my collaborators, without which, indeed, I could not have brought this work to a conclusion.

In my original Preface I expressed my thanks to each and all of the scholars who aided me in the compilation of the first edition, and whose names in the chronological order of their services were as follow:—

The late Rev. J. Wenger, of the Baptist Mission, Calcutta; Dr. Franz Kielhorn, afterwards Superintendent of Sanskṛit Studies in Deccan College, Poona, and now Professor of Sanskṛit in the University of Göttingen; Dr. Hermann Brunnhofer; Mr. A. E. Gough, M.A., of Lincoln College, Oxford, sometime Professor in the Government Colleges of Benares, Allāhābād, and Calcutta; and lastly, Mr. E. L. Hogarth, M.A., of Brasenose College, sometime Head Master of the Government Provincial School at Calicut.

It is now my duty to express my grateful obligations to the able and painstaking Assistants who have co-operated with me in producing the present greatly enlarged and improved work.

No one but those who have taken part in similar labours can at all realize the amount of tedious toil—I might almost say dreary drudgery—involved in the daily routine of small lexicographical details, such as verifying references and meanings, making indices and lists of words, sorting and sifting an ever-increasing store of materials, revising old work, arranging and re-arranging new, writing and re-writing and interlineating 'copy,' correcting and re-correcting proofs—printed, be it remembered, in five kinds of intricate type, bristling with countless accents and diacritical points, and putting the eyesight, patience, and temper of author, collaborators, compositors, and press-readers to severe trial. I mention these matters not to magnify my own labours, but to show that I could not have prosecuted them without the able co-operation of others.

The names of my new Assistants in chronological order are as follow:—

First, Dr. Ernst Leumann (a native of Switzerland), who worked with me in Oxford from October 3, 1882, until April 15, 1884, when he accepted a teachership in the Kantonschule of Frauenfeld in Switzerland. I have already acknowledged my obligations to him.

He was succeeded by the late Dr. Schönberg (a pupil of the late Professor Bühler), who came to me in a condition of great physical weakness, and whose assistance only extended from May 20, 1884, to July 19, 1885, when he left me to die. He was a good scholar, and a good worker, but impatient of supervision, and, despite my vigilance, I found it impossible to guard against a few errors of omission and commission due to the rapid impairment of his powers.

Then followed an interval during which my sources of aid were too fitful to be recorded.

In September, 1886, Dr. Leumann, who had meanwhile been appointed Professor of Sanskṛit in the University of Strassburg, renewed his co-operation, but only in an intermittent manner, and while still resident in Germany. Unhappily the pressure of other duties obliged him in September, 1890, to withdraw from all work outside that of his Professorship. He laboured with me in a scholarly way as far as p. 474; but his collaboration did not extend beyond 355 pages, because he took no part in pp. 137–256, which represent the period of Dr. Schönberg's collaboration.

It was not till December, 1890, that Dr. Carl Cappeller, Professor of Sanskṛit in the University of Jena, began his painstaking co-operation, which, starting from the word Dāda (p. 474), he has prosecuted perseveringly to the completion of the Dictionary. And it should be put on record that, although his collaboration had to be carried on contemporaneously with the discharge of his duties at Jena—involving the necessity for a constant interchange of communications by post—yet it resulted in the production of 834 finished pages between March, 1891, and July, 1898. It should also be recorded that, from the beginning of the letter प *p*, he had a careful assistant in Dr. Blau of Berlin, who also occasionally read the proof-sheets and contributed a certain number of words for the Addenda.

Furthermore, I must express my gratitude to Herr Geheimrath Franz Kielhorn, C. I. E., Ph.D., Professor of Sanskṛit in the University of Göttingen, who was my assistant soon after the inception of the first edition, for his free and generous supervision of the grammatical portions of the present edition from about the year 1886; and his readiness to place at my disposal the experience which he gained during his labours for many years as Superintendent of Sanskṛit Studies at the Government College, Poona.

I have finally to record my grateful appreciation of the value of the principal works used or consulted by my collaborators and myself in compiling this Dictionary. Some of these, and a few important grammatical works—such as the Mahā-bhāshya (in the excellent edition of Professor Kielhorn), the Siddhânta-kaumudī &c.—besides many other texts, such as that of Manu, the Bṛihat-saṃhitā &c., did not exist in good critical editions when the great Thesaurus of the two German Lexicographers was being compiled.

Professor Ernst Leumann informs me that during the period of his collaboration he was much aided by Grassmann's Ṛig-veda, Whitney's Index Verborum to the published text of the Atharva-veda; Stenzler's Indices to the Gṛihya-sūtras of Āśvalāyana, of Pāraskara, Śāṅkhāyana, Gobhila, and the Dharma-śāstra of Gautama; the vocabularies to Aufrecht's edition of the Aitareya Brāhmaṇa; Bühler's Āpastamba Dharma-sūtra; Garbe's Vaitāna-sūtra; Hillebrandt's Śāṅkhāyana Śrauta-sūtra &c. He states that in his portion of the work his aim was rather to verify and revise the words and meanings given in the Petersburg Dictionaries than to add new and unverifiable matter. In regard to quotations he refers the reader to the Journal of the German Oriental Society, vol. xlii, pp. 161–198.

Professor C. Cappeller states that in addition to the books enumerated above he wishes to name in the first place Böhtlingk's Upanishads, his Pāṇini (2nd ed.) and Kāvyâdarśa as well as the valuable critical remarks of that honoured Nestor of Sanskṛitists on numerous texts, published in various journals; further the Jaiminīya Upanishad Brāhmaṇa edited by H. Oertel, and various Sūtra works with their indices by F. Knauer, M. Winternitz, J. Kirste, and W. Caland. For some additions contributed from the Drāhyāyaṇa Śrauta-sūtra he is indebted to Dr. J. N. Reuter of Helsingfors. He also made use of the Vaijayantī of Yādava-prakāśa (edited by G. Oppert, London, 1893); the Uṇādigaṇa-sūtra of Hemacandra (edited by J. Kirste, Vienna, 1895); the Dictionaries of Apte (Poona, 1890), of A. A. Macdonell (London, 1893), of C. Cappeller (Strassburg, 1891); Whitney's Roots, Verb-forms, and Primary Derivatives of the Sanskṛit Language (Leipzig, 1885); Lanman's Noun-inflection in the Veda (New Haven, 1880); Jacob Wackernagel's Altindische Grammatik (Göttingen, 1896); Delbrück's Altindische Syntax (Halle, 1888); Regnaud's Rhétorique Sanskrite (Paris, 1884); Lévi's Théatre Indien (Paris, 1890); Macdonell's Vedic Mythology (Strassburg, 1897), &c.

For Vedic interpretation Roth and Grassmann have been the chief authorities, but it will be seen that neither Sāyaṇa nor such modern interpreters as Pischel and Geldner in Vedische Studien (Stuttgart, 1889–1897), and Bloomfield for the Atharva-veda (in S. B. E., vol. xlii) have been neglected.

The Buddhistic portion of the Dictionary has chiefly been enriched by the following:—Aśvaghosha's Buddha-carita (edited and translated by Professor E. B. Cowell of Cambridge); Divyâvadāna (edited by Cowell and Neil, Cambridge, 1886); Jātaka-mālā (edited by H. Kern, Boston, 1891); the two Sukhāvatī-vyūhas (S. B. E., vol. xlix) and the Dharma-saṃgraha (Anecdota Oxoniensia, 1885). It is evident, that until new and complete Pāli and Prākṛit Dictionaries are published, the idiomatic Sanskṛit used by Buddhists and Jains and the authors of certain inscriptions cannot be dealt with satisfactorily.

Of course many portions of the Indische Studien (edited by Professor A. Weber of Berlin) have been consulted, and valuable aid has been received from some of the translations contained in the 'Sacred Books of the East,' as well as from many other works, the names of which will be found in the List of Works and Authors at p. xxxiii.

As to the books used by myself, many of them, of course, are identical with those named above. Others are named in the first edition, and need not be referred to again here. I ought, however, to repeat that some of the words marked MW. in the present edition rest on the authority of the Śabda-kalpa-druma of Rādhā-kānta-deva (published in eight volumes at Calcutta in the Bengālī character). I am also, of course, responsible for some words and meanings taken from my own books, such as 'Brāhmanism and Hindūism,' 'Buddhism,' 'Indian Wisdom' (see note 1 to p. vi of Preface), my Sanskṛit Grammar and Nalôpâkhyānam (with vocabulary, published by the Delegates of the Oxford University Press), text of the Śakuntalā (with index and notes, published by the same), as well as from the notes appended to my English translation of the Śakuntalā (published by Messrs. Harmsworth among Sir John Lubbock's hundred best books of the world), &c.

MONIER MONIER-WILLIAMS.

INDIAN INSTITUTE, OXFORD.

LIST OF WORKS AND AUTHORS.

[*The order is that of the English Alphabet. The letters outside the parentheses represent the abbreviated forms used in the references.*]

Abhinav(a-gupta).
Ācāranirṇ(aya).
Adbh(uta)Br(āhmaṇa).
Ādi-p(arvan of the Mahābhārata).
Ag(astya)Saṃh(itā).
Ag(ni)P(urāṇa).
Ait(areya)Ār(aṇyaka).
Ait(areya)Br(āhmaṇa).
Ait(areya)Up(anishad).
Alaṃkārak(austubha).
Alaṃkāras[1](arvasva, by Ruyyaka).
Alaṃkāras[2](arvasva, by Maṅkhaka).
Alaṃkāraś(ekhara, by Keśava-miśra).
Alaṃkārat(ilaka).
Alaṃkārav(imarśinī, by Jayaratha).
Amar(u-śataka).
Amṛitab(indu)Up(anishad).
Ānand(a-laharī).
Anaṅgar(aṅga).
An(anta)Saṃ(hitā).
Anarghar(āghava).
Anukr(amaṇikās).
Anup(ada-sūtra).
Āp(astamba's Dharma-sūtra).
Āp(astamba's)Śr(auta-sūtra).
Ap(astamba's) Y(ajña-paribhāshā-sūtra).
A(pte's Dic ionary).
Ārsh(eya)Br(āhmaṇa).
Āruṇ(eya)Up(anishad).
Āryabh(aṭa).
Āryav(idyā-sudhākara).
Ashṭāṅg(a-hṛidaya).
Ashṭāv(akra)S(aṃhitā).
Āśv(alāyana-gṛihya)P(ariśishṭa).
Āśv(alāyana)Gṛ(ihya-sūtra).
Āśv(alāyana-śākhôktā) MantraS(aṃhitā).
Āśv(alāyana)Śr(auta-sūtra).
Atharvaś(ikhā)Up(anishad).
A(tharva)V(eda).
A(tharva)V(eda). Paipp(alāda-śākhā).
A(tharva)V(eda).Pariś(ishṭa).
A(tharva-Veda)Pr(ātiśākhya).
A(tharva)V(eda).Prây(aścitta).
Ātm(a)Up(anishad), iii Kh.
Ātr(eya)Anukr(amaṇikā).
Avadānaś(ataka).
Bādar(āyaṇa's Brahma-sūtra).
Bādar(āyaṇa). Gov(indânanda's gloss).
Bādar(āyaṇa)., Sch.(i. e. Śaṃkara's Comm.).
Bālar(āmāyaṇa).
Baudh(āyana's Dharma-śāstra).
Baudh(āyana's)P(itṛimedha-sūtra).
Bhadrab(āhu-carita).
Bhag(avad-gītā).
Bh(āgavata)P(urāṇa).
Bhagavatīg(ī.ā).
Bhaktâm(ara-stotra).
Bhām(inī-vilāsa).
Bharaṭ(aka-dvātriṇśikā).
Bhar(ata's Nāṭya-śāstra).
Bh(āratītīrtha's)pañcad(aśī).
Bhartṛ(ihari).
Bhāshāp(ariccheda).
Bhāshik(a-sūtra).
Bhaṭṭ(i-kāvya).
Bh(āva)pr(akāśa).
Bhav(ishya)P(urāṇa), ii Kh. (Bhavishya- & °yôttaraP.).
Bhoj(a).
Bhojapr(abandha).
Bījag(aṇita).
B(öhtlingk &) R(oth's) D(ictionary).
Brahmab(indu)Up(anishad).
Br(āhmaṇas).
BrahmâṇḍaP(urāṇa).
BrahmaP(urāṇa).
Brahmas(iddhânta).
Brahm(a)Up(anishad).
Brahmav(aivarta)P(urāṇa).
Brahmav(idyā)Up(anishad).
Brahmôtt(ara)Kh(aṇḍa, from the SkandaP.).
Bṛ(ihad)Ār(aṇyaka)Up(anishad).
Bṛih(ad-devatā).
Bṛ(ihan)Nār(adīya)P(urāṇa), xxxviii Adhy.
B(uddha-)car(ita).
Buddh(ist literature).
Campak(a-śreshṭhi-kathānaka).
Cāṇ(akya).
Caṇḍ(a-kauśika).
Car(aka).
Caraṇ(a-vyūha).
Caurap(añcāśikā).
Chandaḥs(ūtra).
Ch(āndogya)Up(anishad).
Chandom(añjarī).
Col(ebrooke).
Cūl(ikā)Up(anishad).
Daiv(ata)Br(āhmaṇa).
Damayantī-kathā, see Nalac.
Daś(akumāra-carita).
Daśar(ūpa).
Dāṭhādh(ātu-vaṇsa).
Dāyabh(āga).
Dāyat(attva).
Devatâdhyāya = DaivBr.
Devībh(āgavata)P(urāṇa).
Devīm(āhātmya).
Dhanaṃj(aya-vijaya).
Dhanv(antari).
Dharmas(aṃgraha).
Dharmaśarm(âbhyudaya).
Dharmav(iveka).
Dhātup(āṭha).
Dhūrtan(artaka).
Dhūrtas(amāgama).
Dhyānab(indu)Up(anishad).
Dīp(ikā).
Divyâv(adāna).
Drāhy(āyaṇa).
Durgāv(ilāsa).
Dūtāṅg(ada).
Gal(anos' Dictionary).
Gaṇar(atna-mahôdadhi).
Gaṇ(êśa)P(urāṇa).
Gaṇit(âdhyāya).
Garbh(a)Up(anishad).
GārgīS(aṃhitā).
GāruḍaP(urāṇa).
Gar(uḍa)Up(anishad).
Gāthāsaṃgr(aha).
Gauragaṇ(ôddeśa).
Gaut(ama's Dharma-śāstra).
GayāMāh(ātmya).
Ghaṭ(akarpara).
Gīt(a-govinda).
Gobh(ila's)Śrāddh(a-kalpa).
Gol(âdhyāya).
Gop(atha)Br(āhmaṇa).
Goraksh(a-śataka).
Grahay(ajña-tattva).
G(rass)m(an)n.
Gṛ(ihya and) Śr(auta-Sūtra).
Gṛihyās(aṃgraha).
Gṛ(ihya)S(ūtra).
Hāl(a).
Haṇs(a)Up(anishad).
Harav(ijaya).
Hār(ita).
Hariv(aṇśa).
H(arsha)car(ita).
Hāsy(ârṇava).
Hāyan(a-ratna, by Balabhadra).
Hemac(andra).
H(emacandra's)Pariś(ishṭa-parvan).
H(emacandra's)Yog(a-śāstra).
H(emâdri's) cat(urvarga-cintāmaṇi).
Hir(aṇyakeśin's) Gṛ(ihya-sūtra).
Hir(aṇyakeśin's)P(itṛimedha-sūtra).
Hit(ôpadeśa).
Horāś(āstra).
I(ndian)W(isdom, by Sir M. Monier-Williams).
Īś(a)Up(anishad).
Jābāl(a)Up(anishad).
Jaim(ini).
Jaim(ini)Bh(ārata, āśvamedhika parvan).
Jaim(inīya)Br(āhmaṇa).
Jaim(inīya)Up(anishad).
Jain(a literature).
Jātakam(ālā).
Jyot(isha).
Kād(ambarī).
Kaiv(alya)Up(anishad).
Kaiy(aṭa or Kaiyyaṭa).
Kālac(akra).
Kālakâc(ārya-kathānaka).
Kālanirṇ(aya).
Kālid(āsa).
Kāl(ikā)P(urāṇa).
KalkiP(urāṇa).
Kalpas(ūtra).
Kalpat(aru).
Kalyāṇam(andira-stotra).
Kām(andakīya-nītisāra).
Kaṇ(âda's Vaiśeshika-sūtra).
Kaṇṭh(aśruti)Up(anishad).
Kap(ila)Saṃh(itā, from the SkandaP.).
Kap(ila's)S(āṃkhya-pravacana).
Kapishṭh(ala-Saṃhitā).
Kāraṇḍ(a-vyūha).
Kāraṇḍ.[2] (metrical recension of the text).
Karmapr(adīpa).
Kāś(ikā Vṛitti).
KāśīKh(aṇḍa, from the SkandaP.).
Kāt(antra).
Kāṭh(aka).
Kāṭh(aka)Gṛ(ihya-sūtra).
Kathârṇ(ava).
Kathās(aritsāgara).
Kaṭh(a)Up(anishad).
Kāty(āyana).
Kāty(āyana)Śr(auta-sūtra).
Kaush(ītaki)Ār(aṇyaka).
Kaush(ītaki)Up(anishad).
Kauś(ika-sūtra).
Kautukar(atnākara).
Kautukas(arvasva).
Kavik(alpa-latā).
Kavikalpat(aru).
Kāvyac(andrikā).
Kāvyâd(arśa).
Kāvyak(alpa latā).
Kāv(ya literature).
K(āvya)pr(akāśa).
Kayy(aṭa).
Ked(āra's vṛitti-ratnākara).
Ken(a)Up(anishad).
Khaṇḍapr(aśasti).
Kir(ātārjunīya).
Koshṭhipr(adīpa).
Kramadīp(ikā).
Kṛishis(aṃgraha).
Kṛishṇakarṇ(âmṛita).
Kriyāy(oga-sāra in the Padma Purāṇa).
Kshem(êndra).
Kshitīś(a-vaṇśâvalī-carita).
Kshur(ikā)Up(anishad).
Kulad(ipikā).
Kulârṇ(ava-tantra).
Kull(ūka's commentary on Manu).
Kum(āra-sambhava).
KūrmaP(urāṇa).
Kuṭṭanim(ata).
Kuval(ayânanda).
Laghuj(ātaka, by Varāha-mihira).
Laghuk(aumudī).
Lalit(a-vistara).
Laṅkāvat(āra-sūtra).
Lāṭy(āyana).
L(exicographers, esp. such as Amarasiṇha, Halâyudha, Hemacandra, &c.).
Līl(āvatī of Bhāskara).
LiṅgaP(urāṇa).
M(acdonel)l('s Dictionary, &c.).
Madanav(inoda).
Madhus(ūdana).
MāghaMāh(ātmya in the Padma Purāṇa).
M(ahā)Bh(ārata).
MahānārāyaṇaUp. (see Nār° Up°).
Mahān(āṭaka).
M(ahāvīra-)car(itra).
Mahīdh(ara).
Maitr(āyaṇī)S(aṃhitā).
Maitr(y)Up(anishad).
Malamāsat(attva).
Mālatīm(ādhava).
Mālav(ikâgnimitra).
Mallapr(akāśa).
Mall(inātha).
Mān(ava)Gṛ(ihya-sūtra).
Mān(ava)Śr(auta-sūtra).
Mān(avīya)S(amhitā of the SauraP.).
Māṇḍ(ūki)Ś(ikshā).
Māṇḍ(ūkya)Up(anishad), 12 Mantras.
Māṇḍ(ūkya)Up(anishad Gauḍ(apāda's Kārikā).
MantraBr(āhmaṇa).
Mantram(ahôdadhi).
M(a)n(u's Law-book).
Mārk(aṇḍeya)P(urāṇa).
Maś(aka).
Math(urā)Māh(ātmya).
MatsyaP(urāṇa).
Matsyas(ūkta), Śabdak.
Megh(adūta).
Megh.* (15 additional verses).
M(onier)W(illiams, 1st edition of Dictionary, with marginal notes).
M(onier) W(illiams) B(uddhism).
Mṛicch(akaṭikā).
Mudr(ārākshasa).
Mukt(ikā)Up(anishad).
Muṇḍ(aka)Up(anishad).
Nādab(indu)Up(anishad).
Nāḍīpr(akāśa), Śabdak.
Nāg(ânanda).
Naigh(aṇṭuka, commented on by Yāska).
Naish(adha-carita).
Nalac(ampū or Damayantī-kathā).
Nalôd(aya).
Nal(ôpâkhyāna).
NandiP(urāṇa).
Nār(ada)S(aṃhitā).
Nār(ada's Law-book).
Nār(adīya)P(urāṇa).
Naras(iṇha)P(urāṇa).
Nār(āyaṇa)Up(anishad).
Nāṭyaś(āstra).
N(ew) B(öhtlingk's) D(ictionary).
Nid(āna by Mādhava).
Nid(āna), Sch. (i.e. Vācaspati's Comm.).
Nidānas(ūtra).
N(ighaṇṭu)pr(akāśa).
Nīlak(aṇṭha).
Nīl(amata)P(urāṇa).
Nīlar(udra)Up(anishad).
Nirṇayas(indhu).
Nir(ukta, by Yāska).
Nītis., see Kām(andakīya-nītisāra).
Nṛis(iṇha-tāpanīya)Up(anishad).
Nyāyad(arśana).
Nyāyak(ośa).
Nyāyam(ālā-vistara).

Padap(āṭha).
PadmaP(urāṇa).
Padyas(aṃgraha).
Pañcad(aṇḍacchattra-prabandha).
Pañcad.² (metrical recension).
Pañcadaśī, see Bh(āratītīrtha's) pañcad(aśī).
Pañcar(ātra).
Pañcat(antra).
Pāṇ(ini).
Pāṇ(inīya)Ś(ikshā).
Pāpabuddhidharm(abuddhi-kathānaka).
Param(ārtha-sāra).
Parāś(ara-smṛiti).
Pār(askara's)Gṛ(ihya-sūtra).
Paraśur(āma-prakāśa).
Paribh(āshêndu-śekhara).
Pārśvan(ātha-caritra).
Pārvat(ī-pariṇaya).
Pat(añjali).
Phetk(āriṇī-tantra).
PhiṭS(ūtra).
Piṇḍ(a)Up(anishad).
Piṅg(ala)Sch(oliast, i.e. Halâyudha).
Prab(odha-candrôdaya).
Pracaṇḍ(a-pāṇḍava).
Pradyumn(a-vijaya).
Prah(asana Nāṭaka).
Prajāp(ati's Dharma-sūtra).
Prāṇ(âgnihotra)Up(anishad).
Prasaṅg(âbharaṇa).
Prasannar(āghava).
Praśn(a)Up(anishad).
Pratāp(arudrīya).
PratijñāS(ūtra).
Prāt(iśākhya).
Pravar(a texts).
Prâyaśc(itta-tattva).
Prayog(âmṛita).
Prayogar(atna).
Priy(adarśikā).
Pur(āṇas).
P(urāṇa)Sarv(asva).
Purushôtt(ama-tattva).
Pushpas(ūtra).

Rāghav(apāṇḍavīya).
Ragh(uvaṇśa).
Rājat(araṃgiṇī).
Rāmag(ītā).
Rāmapūjāś(araṇī).
Rāmat(āpanīya)Up(anishad).
Rām(a)Up(anishad).
R(āmāyaṇa).
Rāsal(ilā).
Rasar(atnâkara).
Rasat(araṃgiṇī).
Rasêndrac(intāmaṇi).
Rasik(aramaṇa).
Ratir(ahasya).
Ratnā(vali).
R(eligious) T(hought and) L(ife in India, also called 'Brāhmanism and Hindūism,' by Sir M. Monier-Williams).
RevāKh(aṇḍa).
R(ig-)V(eda, referred to as RV.).
Ṛitus(aṃhāra).
Romakas(iddhânta).
Rudray(āmala).
R(V.)Anukr(amaṇikā).
R(V.)Prāt(iśākhya).
Śabdak(alpa-druma).
Saddh(arma)P(uṇḍarīka).
Sadukt(i-karṇâmṛita).
Sāh(itya-darpaṇa).
Sahy(âdri)Kh(aṇḍa, from the SkandaP.).
Śākaṭ(āyana).
Śāktān(anda-taraṃgiṇī).
Śāktir(atnâkara).
Śak(untalā).
S(āma)V(eda).
S(āma)V(eda)Ār(aṇyaka).
Sāmav(idhāna)Br(āhmaṇa).
Śambh(alagrāma)Māh(ātmya).
Saṃgīt(a-sārasaṃgraha).
Saṃh(itā)Up(anishad-brāhmaṇa).
Śaṃkar(a-vijaya).
Sāṃkhyak(ārikā).

Sāṃkhyapr(avacana).
S(aṃkshepa)Śaṃkar(a-vijaya).
Saṃskārak(austubha).
Śāṅkh(āyana)Br(āhmaṇa).
Śāṅkh(āyana)Gṛ(ihya-sūtra).
Śāṅkh(āyana)Śr(auta-sūtra).
Śāntik(alpa).
Śāntiś(ataka).
Śārad(ā-tilaka).
Sarasv(atī-kaṇṭhâbharaṇa, by Bhoja).
Sarasv.² (by Kshemêndra).
Śārṅg(adhara)P(addhati).
Śārṅg(adhara)S(aṃhitā).
Sarvad(arśana-saṃgraha).
Sarv(a)Up(anishat-sāra).
Ś(atapatha)Br(āhmaṇa).
Śatar(udriya)Up(anishad).
Śatr(uṃjaya-māhātmya).
SauraP(urāṇa).
Sāy(aṇa).
Setub(andha).
Shaḍguruś(ishya).
Shaḍv(iṇśa)Br(āhmaṇa).
Siddh(ânta-kaumudī).
Siddhântaś(iromaṇi).
Śiksh(ā).
Śikshāp(attrī).
Śil(âṅka).
Siṇhâs(ana-dvātriṇśikā or Vikramâditya-caritra, Jaina recension).
Siṇhâs.² (metrical recension of the Ind.Off., E.I.H. 2897).
Siṇhâs.³ (recension of E.I.H. 2523).
ŚiraUp(anishad).
Śiś(upāla-vadha).
Śivag(ītā, ascribed to the PadmaP.).
ŚivaP(urāṇa).
SkandaP(urāṇa).
Smṛitik(aumudī).
Smṛitit(attva; the numbers xxix & xxx mark the additional texts Graha-yajña & Tīrtha-yātrā).

Śrāddhak(alpa-bhāshya).
Śr(auta)Sūtra.
Śrīkaṇṭh(a-carita).
Śrīm(āla)Māh(ātmya).
Śṛiṅgār(a-tilaka).
Śrutab(odha).
Subh(āshitâvali).
Śukas(aptati).
Sukh(āvatī-vyūha).
Śulbas(ūtra).
Suparṇ(âdhyāya).
Sūryad(eva-yajvan).
Sūryapr(ajñapti).
Sūryas(iddhânta).
Suśr(uta).
Suvarṇapr(abhāsa).
Svapnac(intāmaṇi).
Śvet(âśvatara)Up(anishad).
T(aittirīya)Ār(aṇyaka).
T(aittirīya)Br(āhmaṇa).
T(aittirīya)Prāt(iśākhya).
T(aittirīya)S(aṃhitā).
T(aittirīya)Up(anishad).
Tāj(aka).
TāṇḍyaBr(āhmaṇa).
Tantras(āra).
T(ārānātha Tarkavācaspati's Dictionary).
Tarkas(aṃgraha).
Tattvas(amāsa).
Tejob(indu)Up(anishad).
Tīrtha-yātrā(see Smṛititattva).
Tithyād(itya).
Toḍar(ânanda).
Uṇ(ādi)k(alpa).
Uṇ(ādi),Sch.(i.e.Ujjvaladatta).
Uṇ(ādi-sūtra).
Uṇ(ādi)vṛ(itti).
Up(anishad).
Upap(urāṇa).
UtkalaKh(aṇḍa).
Uttamac(aritra-kathānaka, prose version).
Uttamac²(aritra in about 700 verses).
Uttarar(āma-caritra).
Vāgbh(aṭâlaṃkāra).
VahniP(urāṇa).

Vait(āna-sūtra).
V(ājasaneyi)S(aṃhitā).
V(ājasaneyi-Saṃhitā) Prāt(iśākhya).
Vajracch(edikā).
Vajras(ūci).
Vām(ana)P(urāṇa).
Vām(ana's Kāvyâlaṃkāra-vṛitti).
V(aṇśa)Br(āhmaṇa).
Var(āha-mihira's)Bṛ(ihajjātaka).
Var(āha-mihira's)Bṛ(ihat) S(aṃhitā).
Var(āha-mihira's)Yogay(ātrā).
Var(āha)P(urāṇa).
Vārāhīt(antra).
Vasantar(āja's Śākuna).
Vāsant(ikā).
Vās(avadattā).
Vas(ishṭha).
Vāstuv(idyā).
Vātsyāy(ana).
VāyuP(urāṇa).
Vedântap(aribhāshā).
Vedântas(āra).
Vet(āla-pañcaviṇśatikā).
Viddh(aśālabhañjikā).
V(ikramâṅkadeva)car(ita, by Bilhaṇa).
Vikr(amôrvaśī).
Vīrac(arita).
V(ishṇu)P(urāṇa).
Vishṇ(u's Institutes).
Viśvan(ātha, astronomer).
Vop(adeva).
Vṛishabhān(ujā-nāṭikā, by Mathurā-dāsa).
Vyavahārat(attva).
W(ilson).
Yājñ(avalkya).
Yājñ., Sch. (i.e. Mitâksharā).
Yogaś(ikhā)Up(anishad).
Yogas(ūtra).
Yogat(attva)Up(anishad).
Yogavās(ishṭha-sāra).

SYMBOLS.

= denotes 'equivalent to,' 'equal,' 'the same as,' 'explained by,' &c.

( ) Between these parentheses stand all remarks upon meanings, and all descriptive and explanatory statements.

[ ] Between these brackets stand all remarks within remarks, and comparisons with other languages.

▬ denotes that the leading word in a group of compounds is to be repeated. It is generally, but not always, equivalent to a hyphen. A shortened line occurs in cases like **▬sūd**, followed by **-sūda** and **-sūdana**, which are for **Havya-sūd, havya-sūda, havya-sūdana.**

° denotes that the rest of a word is to be supplied, e. g. *°ri-in°* after *karīndra* is for *kari-indra.*

√ denotes a root.

¯ denotes that a vowel or syllable is long.

˘ denotes that a vowel or syllable is to be specially noted as short.

≚ denotes that a vowel or syllable is either long or short.

\+ is for plus.

&c. is for et cetera.

^ denotes the blending of two short vowels (as of a + a into â).

^ denotes the blending of a short with a long vowel (as of a + ā into â).

^ denotes the blending of a long with a short vowel (as of ā + a into â).

^ denotes the blending of two long vowels (as of ā + ā into â).

ABBREVIATIONS.

[In the progress of a work extending over many years it has been found almost impossible to preserve absolute uniformity in the use of abbreviations and symbols, but it is hoped that most of the inconsistencies are noticed in the following table.]

Ā. = Ātmane-pada.
abl. = ablative case.
above = a reference to some preceding word (not necessarily in the same page).
acc. = accusative case.
accord. or acc. = according.
add. = Additions.
Ādi-p. = Ādi-parvan of the Mahā-bhārata.
adj. = adjective (cf. mfn.).
adv. = adverb.
Æol. = Æolic.
alg. = algebra.
anat. = anatomy.
Angl.Sax. = Anglo-Saxon.
anom. = anomalous.
Aor. or aor. = Aorist.
Arab. = Arabic.
arithm. = arithmetic.
Arm. or Armor. = Armorican or the language of Brittany.
Armen. = Armenian.
astrol. = astrology.
astron. = astronomy.
B. = Bombay edition.
Boh. or Bohem. = Bohemian.
Br. = Brāhmaṇa.
Bret. = Breton.
C. = Calcutta edition.
c. = case.
Cat. = catalogue or catalogues.
Caus. = Causal.
cf. = confer, compare.
ch. = chapter.
cl. = class.
Class. = Classical.
col., cols. = column, columns.
Comm. = commentator or commentary.
comp. = compound.
compar. = comparative degree.
concl. = conclusion.
Cond. = Conditional.
conj. = conjectural.
cons. = consonant.
dat. = dative case.
defect. = defective.
Desid. = Desiderative.
dimin. = diminutive.
dram. = dramatic language.
du. = dual number.
ed. = edition.
e. g. = exempli gratiâ, 'for example.'
Eng. = English.
Ep. or ep. = Epic.
esp. = especially.
etym. = etymology.
f. = feminine.
fig. = figuratively.
fr. = from.
Fut. or fut. = future.
fut. p. p. = future passive participle.
g. = gaṇa.
Gaël. = Gaëlic.
gen. = genitive case.
gend. = gender.
geom. = geometry.
Germ. = German.
Gk. = Greek.
Goth. = Gothic.
Gr. = Grammar.
Hib. = Hibernian or Irish.
Hind. = Hindī.
ib. = ibidem or 'in the same place or book or text' as the preceding.
ibc. = in the beginning of a compound.
Icel. = Icelandic.
id. = idem or 'the same meaning as that of a preceding word.'
i. e. = id est.
ifc. = in fine compositi or 'at the end of a compound.'
impers. = impersonal or used impersonally.
impf. = imperfect tense.
Impv. = imperative.
ind. = indeclinable.
inf. = infinitive mood.
Inscr. = Inscriptions.
instr. = instrumental case.
Intens. = Intensive.
interpol. = interpolation.
Introd. = Introduction.
Ion. = Ionic.
irr. = irregular.
L. = lexicographers (i. e. a word or meaning which although given in native lexicons, has not yet been met with in any published text).
Lat. = Latin.
lat. = latitude.
Lett. = Lettish.
lit. = literally.
Lith. = Lithuanian.
loc. = locative case.
log. = logic.
long. = longitude.
m. = masculine gender.
math. = mathematics.
m. c. = metri causâ.
medic. = medicine.
metron. = metronymic.
mfn. = masculine, feminine, and neuter or = adjective.
Mod. = modern.
MS., MSS. = manuscript, manuscripts.
myth. = mythology.
N. = Name (also = title or epithet).
n. = neuter gender.
neg. = negative.
Nom. = Nominal verb.
nom. = nominative case.
obs. = obsolete.
onomat. = onomatopoetic (i.e. formed from imitation of sounds).
opp. to = opposed to.
opt. = optative.
orig. = originally.
Osset. = Ossetic.
others = according to others.
P. = Parasmai-pada.
p. = page and participle (cf. p. p.).
parox. = paroxytone.
part. = participle.
partic. = particular.
Pass. = Passive voice.
patr. = patronymic.
perh. = perhaps.
Pers. = Persian.
pers. = person.
pf. = perfect tense.
phil. = philosophy.
pl. = plural number.
poet. = poetry or poetic.
Pot. = Potential.
p. p. = past participle.
Pr. = proper.
Prāk. or Prākr. = Prākṛit.
Prec. = precative.
prec. = preceding.
prep. and prepos. = preposition.
pres. = present tense.
priv. = privative.
prob. = probably.
pron. = pronoun.
pronom. = pronominal.
propar. = proparoxytone.
Pruss. = Prussian.
q. v. = quod vide.
redupl. = reduplicated.
Reflex. = Reflexive or used reflexively.
rhet. = rhetoric.
rt., rts. = root, roots.
Russ. = Russian.
RV. = Ṛig-veda.
Sax. = Saxon.
sc. and scil. = scilicet.
Sch. and Schol. = Scholiast or Commentator.
Scot. = Scotch or Highland-Scotch.
seq. = sequens.
sev. = several.
sing. = singular.
Slav. = Slavonic or Slavonian.
Subj. = subjunctive.
subst. = substantive.
suff. = suffix.
superl. = superlative degree.
surg. = surgery.
s. v. = sub voce, i. e. the word in the Sanskṛit order.
Vārt. and Vārtt. = Vārttika.
vb. = verb.
Ved. = Vedic or Veda.
v. l. = varia lectio.
voc. = vocative case.
vow. = vowel.
wk. = work.
w. r. = wrong reading.
Zd. = Zend.

THE DICTIONARY ORDER OF THE NĀGARĪ LETTERS

WITH THEIR INDO-ROMANIC EQUIVALENTS AND THEIR PRONUNCIATION EXEMPLIFIED BY ENGLISH WORDS.

Vowels.

Initial.	Medial.	Equivalents and Pronunciation.	
अ	—	a	*in* mica, rural.
आ	ा	ā	„ tar, father (tār, fāther).
इ	ि	i	„ fill, lily.
ई	ी	ī	„ police (polīce).
उ	ु	u	„ full, bush.
ऊ	ू	ū	„ rude (rūde).
ऋ	ृ	ṛi	„ merrily (merṛily).
ॠ	ॄ	ṝi	„ marine (maṝine).
ऌ	ॢ	lṛi	„ revelry (revelṛi).
ॡ	ॣ	lṝi	„ the above prolonged.
ए	े	e	„ prey, there.
ऐ	ै	ai	„ aisle.
ओ	ो	o	„ go, stone.
औ	ौ	au	„ Haus (as in German).
ं		n̲ or ṃ	either true Anusvāra n̲ or the symbol of any nasal.
ः		ḥ	symbol called Visarga.

Consonants.

	Equivalents and Pronunciation.			Equivalents and Pronunciation.	
क्	k	*in* kill, seek.	द्	d	*in* dice (more like *th* in *this*).
ख्	kh	„ in*kh*orn.	ध्	dh	„ a*dh*ere (but more dental).
ग्	g	„ gun, get, dog.	न्	n	„ not, nut, in.
घ्	gh	„ lo*gh*ut.	प्	p	„ put, sip.
ङ्	ṅ	„ sing, king, sink (siṅk).	फ्	ph	„ u*ph*ill.
च्	c	„ dolce (in music).	ब्	b	„ bear, rub.
छ्	ch	„ chur*chh*ill (cur*ch*ill).	भ्	bh	„ a*bh*or.
ज्	j	„ jet, jump.	म्	m	„ map, jam.
झ्*	jh	„ he*dgeh*og (he*jh*og).	य्	y	„ yet, loyal.
ञ्	ñ	„ singe (siñj).	र्	r	„ red, year.
ट्	ṭ	„ true (ṭrue).	ल्	l	„ lull, lead.
ठ्	ṭh	„ an*th*ill (an*ṭh*ill).	ळ्	ḻ	„ (sometimes for ड् *ḍ* in Veda).
ड्	ḍ	„ drum (ḍrum).	ळ्ह्	ḻh	„ (sometimes for ढ् *ḍh* in Veda).
ढ्	ḍh	„ re*dh*aired (re*ḍh*aired).	व्	v	„ ivy (but like *w* after cons.).
ण्	ṇ	„ none (ṇone).	श्	ś	„ sure (śure).
त्	t	„ water (as in Ireland).	ष्	sh	„ shun, bush.
थ्	th	„ nut*h*ook (more dental).	स्	s	„ saint, sin, hiss.
			ह्	h	„ hear, hit.

* Sometimes printed in the form झ्, see p. 174, col. 3.

The conjunct consonants are too numerous to be exhibited above, but the most common will be found at the end of 'A Practical Sanskṛit Grammar by Monier-Williams,' published by the Delegates of the Clarendon Press, fourth edition.

For the correct pronunciation of the aspirated consonants, *kh, ch, ṭh, th, ph,* &c., see p. xxix, note 4 of the foregoing Introduction.

Observe that n̲ represents the true Anusvāra in the body of a word before the sibilants and *h*, as in *an̲śa, an̲sa, an̲hati:* *ṃ* as the symbol of any nasal will often be found at the end of a word, as in *dānaṃ ca;* but may also represent Anusvāra, when final *m* is followed by initial semivowels, sibilants and *h*, and in words formed with preposition *sam*, like *saṃ-veśa, saṃ-śaya, saṃ-hata:* the word Sanskṛit is now too Anglicized to be written Saṃskṛit. Visarga, as a substitute for final *s*, is a distinctly audible aspirate, so that the *ḥ* at the end of such a word as *devaḥ* must be clearly heard.

THE DICTIONARY ORDER OF THE INDO-ROMANIC LETTERS

WITHOUT THEIR NĀGARĪ EQUIVALENTS.

a, ā; i, ī; u, ū; ṛi, ṝi; lṛi, lṝi; e, ai; o, au;—n̲ or ṃ, ḥ;—k, kh; g, gh; ṅ;—c, ch; j, jh; ñ; ṭ, ṭh; ḍ, ḍh; ṇ;—t, th; d, dh; n;—p, ph; b, bh; m;—y, r, l, ḻ, ḻh, v;—ś, sh, s;—h.

अ A.

अ 1. *a*, the first letter of the alphabet; the first short vowel inherent in consonants. **-kāra**, m. the letter or sound *a*.

अ 2. *a* (pragṛihya, q. v.), a vocative particle [*a Ananta*, O Vishṇu], T.; interjection of pity, Ah!

अ 3. *a* (before a vowel *an*, exc. *a-ṛiṇin*), a prefix corresponding to Gk. ἀ, ἀν, Lat. *in*, Goth. and Germ. *un*, Eng. *in* or *un*, and having a negative or privative or contrary sense (*an-eka* not one; *an-anta* endless; *a-sat* not good; *a-paśyat* not seeing); rarely prefixed to Inf. (*a-svaptum* not to sleep, TāṇḍyaBr.) and even to forms of the finite verb (*a-spṛihayanti* they do not desire, BhP.; Śiś.) and to pronouns (*a-saḥ* not he, Śiś.; *a-tad* not that, BhP.); occasionally denoting comparison (*a-brāhmaṇa* like a Brahman, T.); sometimes disparagement (*a-yajña* a miserable sacrifice); sometimes diminutiveness (cf. *á-karṇa, an-udarā*); rarely an expletive (cf. *a-kupya, a-pūpa*). According to Pāṇ. vi, 2, 161, the accent may be optionally either on the first or last syllable in certain compounds formed with *a* (as *á-tīkshṇa* or *a-tīkshṇá, á-śuci* or *a-śucí, án-anna* or *an-anná*); the same applies to stems ending in *tṛi* accentuated on the first syllable before *a* is prefixed; cf. also *á-tūrta* and *a-tū́rta, á-bhinna* and *a-bhinná*, &c.

अ 4. *a*, the base of some pronouns and pronom. forms, in *asya, atra*, &c.

अ 5. *a*, the augment prefixed to the root in the formation of the imperfect, aorist, and conditional tenses (in the Veda often wanting, as in Homer, the fact being that originally the augment was only prefixed in principal sentences where it was accentuated, whilst it was dropped in subordinate sentences where the root-vowel took the accent).

अ 6. *a, as*, m., N. of Vishṇu, L. (especially as the first of the three sounds in the sacred syllable *om*).

अऋणिन् *a-ṛiṇin*, mfn. free from debt, L.

अंश् *anś*, cl. 10. P. *anśayati*, to divide, distribute, L.; also occasionally Ā. *anśayate*, L.; also *anśāpayati*, L.

अंश *áṇśa, as*, m. (probably fr. √1. *aś*, perf. *ān-áṇśa*, and not from the above √*anś* fictitiously formed to serve as rt.), a share, portion, part, party; partition, inheritance; a share of booty; earnest money; stake (in betting), RV. v, 86, 5; TāṇḍyaBr.; a lot (cf. 2. *prāś*); the denominator of a fraction; a degree of lat. or long.; a day, L.; N. of an Āditya. **-karaṇa**, n. act of dividing. **-kalpanā**, f. or **-prakalpanā**, f. or **-pradāna**, n. allotment of a portion. **-bhāgin** or **-bhāj**, mfn. one who has a share, an heir, co-heir. **-bhū**, m. partner, associate, TS. **-bhūta**, mfn. forming part of. **-vat** (for *anśumat*?), m. a species of Soma plant, Suśr. **-savarṇana**, n. reduction of fractions. **-svara**, m. key-note or chief note in music. **-hara** or **-hārin**, mfn. taking a share, a sharer. **Anśâṅśa**, m. part of a portion (of a deity), secondary incarnation. **Anśânśi**, ind. share by share. **Anśâvataraṇa**, n. descent of part of a deity; partial incarnation; title of sections 64–67 of the first book of the MBh. **Anśi-√1. kṛi**, to share.

1. **Anśaka**, mf(*ikā*)n. (ifc.) forming part.

2. **Anśaka**, *as*, m. a share; degree of lat. or long.; a co-heir, L.; (*am*), n. a day, L.

Anśala. See *anśalā* next col.

Anśin, mfn. having a share, Yājñ. **Anśi-tā**, f. the state of a sharer or co-heir, heirship.

अंशु *anśú, us*, m. a filament (especially of the Soma plant); a kind of Soma libation, ŚBr.; thread; end of a thread, a minute particle; a point, end; array, sunbeam; cloth, L.; N. of a Ṛishi, RV. viii, 5, 26; of an ancient Vedic teacher, son of a Dhanaṃjaya, VBr.; of a prince. **-jāla**, n. a collection of rays, blaze of light. **-dhara**, m. 'bearer of rays,' the sun, L. **-dhāna**, n., N. of a village, R. **-dhāraya**, m. a lamp, MaitrUp. **-nadī**, f., N. of a river. **-paṭṭa**, n. a kind of cloth. **-pati** or **-bhartṛi**, m. 'lord of rays,' the sun, L. **-mát**, mfn. fibrous, rich in filaments; rich in Soma plants or Soma juice; radiant, luminous; pointed; (*ān*), m. the sun, the moon; N. of various persons, especially of a prince of the solar race, son of A-samañjas, grandson of Sagara; (*mátī*), f., N. of a river (Yamunā?), RV. viii, 96, 13–15; Hedysarum Gangeticum, Suśr. **-matphalā**, f. Musa Paradisiaca. **-mālā**, f. a garland of light, halo. **-mālin**, m. the sun. **-vāṇa**, m. 'having rays for arrows,' the sun. **-vimarda**, m. ray-obscuration. **-hasta**, m. 'having rays for hands,' the sun, L. **Anśûdaka**, n. water which has been exposed to the rays of the sun or the moon, Bhpr. **Anśv-ādi**, a gaṇa of Pāṇ. (vi, 2, 193).

Anśuka, *am*, n. cloth; fine or white cloth, muslin [see *cīnânśuka*], L.; garment, upper garment; tie (for binding a churning-stick).

Anśula, *as*, m. radiant, T.; N. of the sage Cāṇakya, L.

अंस् *ans* (cf. √*anś*), L. See **वंस्**.

Áṅsa, *as*, m. the shoulder, shoulder-blade; corner of a quadrangle; N. of a king; (*au*), m. du. the two shoulders or angles of an altar; a share (for *anśa*); [cf. Goth. *amsa*; Gk. ὦμος, ἄσιλλα; Lat. *humerus, ansa*.] **-kūṭa**, m. the shoulder; a bull's hump, the protuberance between an ox's shoulders. **-tra** (*áṅsa-*), n. armour to protect the shoulder, RV.; a bow, Nir.; *áṅsatra-kośa*, mfn. having a cask for its tunic (probably = a Soma filter, Gmn.), RV. x, 101, 7. **-daghná**, mf(*ā́*)n. up to the shoulder, ŚBr. **-dhrī́**, f. a cooking vessel, AV. **-pṛishṭha**, n. back of the shoulder. **-phalaká**, n. shoulder-blade, ŚBr.; Suśr. **-bhāra** or **anse-bhāra**, m. a burden on the shoulder, (gaṇa *bhastrâdi*, q. v.) **-bhārika**, mf(*ī*)n. or **anse-bhārika**, mf(*ī*)n. bearing a burden on the shoulder, ib. **-mūla**, n. the acromion, L.

Ansalá, mfn. lusty, strong, ŚBr. &c.

Áṅsya (3), mfn. belonging to the shoulder, RV. i, 191, 7.

अंह् 1. *anh* (cf. √*aṅgh*), cl. 1. Ā. *anhate*, to go, set out, commence, L.; to approach, L.; cl. 10. P. *anhayati*, to send, Bhaṭṭ.; to speak, Bhaṭṭ.; to shine, L.

Anhri, *is*, m. a foot, Hpar.; root of a tree, L.; [cf. *aṅghri*.] **-pa**, m. 'root-drinker,' a tree, L. **-skandha**, m. or **-śiras**, n. a part of the foot between the ancle and the heel, L.

(**अंह्**) 2. *anh*, to press together, to strangle (conjecturable from Gk. ἄχος, ἐγγύς; Lat. *angustus, anxius*, &c.), L.

Anhatí, *is*, f. anxiety, distress, trouble, RV.; illness, L.; [cf. Lat. *ango*]; a gift (also *anhatī*, f.), L.

Áṅhas, n. anxiety, trouble, RV. &c.; sin, L.; [cf. *aghá, āgas*; Gk. ἄχνυμαι, ἄχος, ἄγος.] **-pati** or **anhasas-pátí** [VS.], m. lord of perplexity, i. e. an intercalary month; cf. *ā́nhaspatya*. **-patyá**, n. power over calamity, TS.; ĀpŚr. **Anho-múc**, mfn. delivering from distress, RV. x, 63, 9; VS.

Anhiti, *is*, f. a gift, donation, L. See *anhatī*.

Anhu, mfn. (only in compar. *anhīyas*) narrow, AitBr., see *parâ'nhu*; (*u*), n. (only in Abl. *anhós*) anxiety, distress, RV.; [cf. Gk. ἐγγύς; Goth. *aggvus*; Lat. *angustus, anxius*, &c.] **-bhédī**, f. having a narrow slit (pudendum muliebre), VS.

Anhurá, mfn. straitened, distressed, RV. x, 5, 6.

Anhūraṇá, mf(*ā*)n. distressing, RV. vi, 47, 20; (*ám*), n. distress, RV. i, 105, 17; AV.

Anhoyú, mfn. troublesome, RV. v, 15, 3.

अक् *ak*, cl. 1. P. *akati*, to move tortuously (like a snake), L. Cf. √*ag* and √*añc*.

अक 1. *aka*, the suffix *aka* (*akac*).

अक 2. *á-ka, am*, n. unhappiness, pain, trouble, TS.; sin, L.

अकच *a-kaca*, mfn. hairless, bald; cf. *ut-, ūrdhva-, vi-*; (*as*), m., N. of Ketu, the dragon's tail or descending node (having a headless trunk), L.

अकटुक *a-kaṭuka*, mfn. not acrid, not impetuous; unwearied, indefatigable.

A-kaṭu-phala, *as*, m. a kind of plant.

अकठोर *a-kaṭhora*, mfn. not hard, weak.

अकडम *akaḍama, am*, n. a kind of Tāntrik diagram. **-cakra**, n. id.

अकण्टक *a-kaṇṭaka*, mfn. thornless, free from troubles or difficulties or enemies.

अकण्ठ *a-kaṇṭha*, mfn. having no neck; having no voice, hoarse.

अकत्थन *a-katthana*, mfn. unboastful.

अकथह *akathaha, am*, n. a kind of diagram.

अकथ्य *a-kathya*, mfn. unspeakable; unutterable, unmentionable.

अकनिष्ठ *á-kanishṭha, ās*, m. pl. of whom none is the youngest (i. e. younger than the others), RV.; a class of Buddhist deities. **-ga**, m. a Buddha, L. **-pa**, m. a Buddhist king, T.

अकन्या *a-kanyā*, f. not a virgin, Mn.

अकपीवत् *akapīvat, ān*, m., N. of a Ṛishi.

अकम्पन *akampana, as*, m., N. of a prince; of a Rākshasa.

अकम्पित *a-kampita*, mfn. unshaken, firm; (*as*), m., N. of one of the 11 chief pupils (*gaṇa-dhara* or *gaṇâdhipa*) of Mahāvīra (the last Tīrtha-kara).

A-kampya, mfn. not to be shaken.

अकर *a-kara*, mfn. handless, maimed; exempt from tax or duty, privileged; not acting; (*ā*), f. Emblic Myrobalan, Phyllanthus Emblica.

अकरण *a-karaṇa, am*, n. absence of action.

A-karaṇi, *is*, f. non-accomplishment, failure, disappointment (used in imprecations, e. g. *tasyâkaraṇir evâstu* bad luck to him!), L.

A-karaṇīya, mfn. not to be done.

अकरुण *a-karuṇa*, mfn. merciless, relentless. **-tva**, n. harshness, cruelty.

अकर्कश *a-karkaśa*, mfn. not hard, tender.

अकर्ण *á-karṇa*, mf(*ā*)n. having diminutive ears, TS.; ŚBr.; without ears, deaf; without helm or rudder; without Karṇa.

A-karṇáka, mfn. without ears, TS., &c.

A-karṇya, mfn. not fit for the ears, Pāṇ. Sch.

अकर्णधार *a-karṇadhāra*, mfn. without a helmsman, destitute of a pilot.

अकर्तन *a-kartana, as*, m. a dwarf, L.

अकर्तृ *a-kartṛi, tā*, m. not an agent, N. applied to the *purusha* (in Sāṅkhya phil.); not active (in Gr.) **-tva**, n. state of non-agency.

अकर्मन् *a-karmán*, mfn. not working; not performing good works, wicked, RV. x, 22, 8; inefficient; (in Gr.) intransitive; (*a*), n. absence of work; observances; improper work, crime. **Akarma-bhoga,** m. enjoyment of freedom from action. **A-karmânvita,** mfn. unoccupied; disqualified.

A-karmaka, mfn. (in Gr.) intransitive.

A-karmaṇya, mfn. improper to be done; unfit for work; inefficient.

अकल *a-kala*, mfn. not in parts, entire; not skilled in the arts (*kalās*).

अकलङ्क *a-kalaṅka*, mfn. without stains or spots; N. of a Jaina.

अकल्क *a-kalka*, mfn. free from impurity; (*ā*), f. moonlight, L. **—tā,** f. honesty, Yājñ.

अकल्कन *a-kalkana* or *a-kalkala*, mfn. not deceitful, honourable, (T.) Bhag.

अकल्प *a-kalpá*, mf(*ā*)n. not subject to rules, uncontrolled; not admitting (any comparison *prati-mā́nam*), RV. i, 102, 6; unable to (loc. or Inf. or in comp.)

A-kalpita, mfn. not manufactured, not artificial, not pretended; natural, genuine.

अकल्मष *a-kalmasha*, mf(*ā*)n. spotless.

अकल्माष *a-kalmāsha*, *as*, m., N. of a son of the fourth Manu, Hariv.

अकल्य *a-kalya*, mf(*ā*)n. ill, sick; true (?), L.

Á-kalyāṇa, mfn. not handsome, AV.; inauspicious; (*am*), n. adversity.

अकव *á-kava*, mfn. (fr. 1. *ku*, q.v.), not contemptible, not stingy, RV.

Á-kavāri, mf(*ī*)n. not selfish, not stingy, RV. iii, 47, 5, & vii, 96, 3 [Sāy. explains by *a-kava-ari*, 'not contemptible as an enemy, or to his enemies; not having weak enemies'].

अकवच *a-kavacá*, mfn. having no coat of mail, AV. xi, 10, 22.

अकवि *á-kavi*, mfn. unwise, RV. vii, 4, 4.

अकस्मात् *a-kasmāt*, ind. without a why or a wherefore, accidentally, suddenly.

अकाण *á-kāṇa*, mf(*ā*)n. not one-eyed, not monoculous, TS. & ŚBr.

अकाण्ड *a-kāṇḍa*, mfn. without a trunk, T.; causeless, unexpected; (*e*), ind. causelessly, unexpectedly. **—pāta-jāta,** mfn. dying as soon as born. **—śūla,** n. sudden, acute pain.

अकातर *a-kātara*, mfn. not dejected.

अकाम *a-kāmá*, mf(*ā*)n. without desire or wish; unintentional, reluctant; (in Gr.) the Sandhi which causes the dropping of a final *r* before a succeeding *r*. **—karśana** (*á-kāma-*), mfn. not disappointing desires, RV. i, 53, 2. **—tas,** ind. unintentionally, unwillingly. **—tā,** f. freedom from desire, &c. **—hata** (*á-kāma-*), mfn. unaffected with desire, calm, ŚBr. xiv.

A-kāmin, mfn. = *a-kāmá*.

अकाय *a-kāyá*, mfn. bodiless, incorporeal, VS.

अकारण *a-kāraṇa*, mfn. causeless; (*am*), n. absence of a cause; (*am, ena, e, āt*), ind. causelessly. **A-kāraṇôtpanna,** mfn. produced spontaneously.

A-kārin, mfn. inactive, not performing, (gaṇa *gra-hâdi*, q. v.)

अकार्णवेष्टकिक *a-kārṇaveshṭakika*, mf(*ī*)n. not fit for ear-rings, not looking well with ear-rings, Pāṇ. Sch. See *karṇa-veshṭaka*.

अकार्य *a-kārya*, mfn. not to be done, improper; (*am*), n. a criminal action. **—kārin,** mfn. an evil-doer; neglecting duty.

अकार्ष्ण्य *a-kārshṇya*, *am*, n. absence of blackness.

अकाल *a-kāla*, *as*, m. a wrong or bad time; (mfn.), unseasonable; (*e*) or *-tas*, ind. unseasonably. **—kushmāṇḍa,** m. a pumpkin produced out of season; a useless birth. **—kusuma,** n. a flower blossoming out of season. **—ja** or **-jāta** or **akālôt-panna,** mfn. born at a wrong time, unseasonable. **—jaladôdaya** or **-meghôdaya,** m. unseasonable rising of clouds or mist. **—velā,** f. wrong or unseasonable time. **—saha,** mfn. unable to bide one's time. **—hīnam,** ind. without losing time, immediately.

A-kālikam, ind. immediately, MBh.

A-kālya, mfn. unseasonable.

अकासार *a-kāsāra*, *as*, m., N. of a teacher, BhP.

अकिञ्चन *a-kiñcana*, mfn. without anything, utterly destitute; disinterested; (*am*), n. that which is worth nothing. **—tā,** f. or **-tva,** n. voluntary poverty (as practised by Jaina ascetics).

A-kiñcaniman, *ā*, m. utter destitution, (gaṇa *pṛithv-ādi*, q. v.)

अकितव *á-kitava*, *as*, m. no gambler, VS.

अकिल्विष *a-kilvishá*, mfn. sinless, ŚBr.

अकीर्ति *a-kīrti*, *is*, f. ill-fame, disgrace. **—kara,** mfn. causing disgrace, disparaging, insulting.

अकुण्ठ *a-kuṇṭha*, mfn. not blunted, not worn out; vigorous, fixed; ever fresh, eternal. **—dhi-shṇya,** n. an eternal abode, heaven.

A-kuṇṭhita, mfn. = *a-kuṇṭha*.

अकुतस् *a-kutas*, ind. (usually in comp.), not from any quarter or cause. **Akutaś-cala,** m. not movable from any cause; N. of Śiva. **A-kuto-bhaya** or **a-kutaścid-bhaya** or **a-kutraca-bha-ya,** mfn. having no fear from any quarter, secure.

A-kutra or (Ved.) **a-kútrā,** ind. nowhere, astray, RV. i, 120, 8.

अकुत्सित *a-kutsita*, mfn. unreproached.

अकुध्र्यच् *a-kudhryáñc*, *àṅ*, *dhrīcī*, *àk* (*ku-dhri* for *kudha* for *kuha* = *kutra*), 'going nowhere' (*àk*, 4), ind. objectless, aimless, RV. x, 22, 12.

अकुप्य *a-kupya*, *am*, n. not base metal, gold or silver, Kir.; any base metal (= *kupya*, see 3. *a*). **Akupyaka,** *am*, n. gold or silver, L.

अकुमार *á-kumāra*, *as*, m. not a boy (said of Indra), RV. i, 155, 6.

अकुल *a-kula*, mfn. not of good family, low; (*as*), m., N. of Śiva, L.; (*ā*), f., N. of Pārvatī, L. **—tā,** f. lowness of family.

A-kulīna, mfn. not of good family, Mn.

अकुशल *a-kuśala*, mf(*ā*)n. inauspicious, evil; not clever; (*am*), n. evil, an evil word, Mn.

अकुसीद *a-kusīda* or *akuśīda*, mfn. taking no interest or usury, without gain.

अकुसुम *a-kusuma*, mfn. flowerless.

अकुह *a-kuha*, *as*, m. no deceiver, L.

A-kuhaka, *as*, m. id., Suśr.

अकूट *á-kūṭa*, mf(*ā*)n. having no prominence on the forehead, TS.; not deceitful, unerring (said of arms), Yājñ.; not false (said of coins), Yājñ.

अकूपार *á-kūpāra*, mfn. unbounded, RV. v, 39, 2 & x, 109, 1; (*as*), m. the sea, VS. &c.; tortoise, BhP. &c., the mythical tortoise that upholds the world; N. of a man, PBr.; N. of an Āditya, L.; (*ā*), f., N. of an Aṅgirasī, PBr.

A-kūvāra = a-kūpāra above.

अकूर्च *a-kūrca*, *as*, m. 'the guileless one,' a Buddha, L.

अकृच्छ्र *a-kṛicchra*, *as*, *am*, m. n. absence of difficulty; freedom from trouble.

A-kṛicchrin, mfn. free from difficulty or trouble.

अकृत *á-kṛita*, mf(*ā*)n. undone, not committed; not made, uncreated; unprepared, incomplete; one who has done no works; (*am*), n. an act never before committed, AitBr.; (*ā*), f. a daughter who has not been made *putrikā*, or a sharer in the privileges of a son, Pāṇ. **—kāram,** ind. in a way not done before, Pāṇ. **—jña,** mfn. not acknowledging benefits, ungrateful. **—jña-tā,** f. ingratitude. **—bud-dhi,** mfn. having an unformed mind. **—buddhi-tva,** n. ignorance. **—vraṇa,** m., N. of a commentator on the Purāṇas, VP.; of a companion of Rāma Jāmadagnya, MBh.; of a teacher. **Akṛitât-man,** mfn. having an unformed mind; not yet identified with the supreme Spirit. **Akṛitârtha,** mfn. having one's object unaccomplished, unsuccessful. **Akṛitâstra,** mfn. unpractised in arms, MBh.

A-kṛitin, mfn. unfit for work, not clever. **Akṛi-ti-tva,** n. unfitness for work.

A-kṛitya, mfn. not to be done, criminal; (*am*), n. crime. **—kārin,** mfn. evil-doer, MBh.

अकृत्त *a-kṛitta*, mfn. uncut, unimpaired. **—ruc,** mfn. possessing unimpaired splendour, RV. x, 84, 4.

अकृत्रिम *a-kṛitrima*, mf(*ā*)n. inartificial.

अकृत्स्न *á-kṛitsna*, mf(*ā*)n. incomplete.

अकृप *a-kṛipa*, mfn. merciless, unkind.

अकृपण *a-kṛipaṇa*, mfn. not miserly.

अकृश *á-kṛiśa*, mfn. not emaciated, TS.; unimpaired. **—lakshmī,** mfn. enjoying full prosperity. **A-kṛiśâśva,** mfn., N. of a king of Ayodhyā, Hariv.

अकृषीवल *á-kṛishīvala*, mf(*ā*)n. not agricultural, RV. x, 146, 6.

अकृष्ट *á-kṛishṭa*, mfn. unploughed, untilled; not drawn; (*am*), n. unploughed land, ŚBr.; (*ās*), m. plur., N. of a kind of Ṛishis, MBh.; Hariv. **—pacyá,** mfn. ripening in unploughed land, growing wild, AV.; VS.; TS.; (said of the earth) giving fruits without having been ploughed, VP.

अकृष्णकर्मन् *a-kṛishṇa-karman*, mfn. free from black deeds, guiltless, L.

अकेतन *a-ketana*, mfn. houseless.

अकेतु *a-ketú*, mfn. shapeless, unrecognisable, RV. i, 6, 3; ('unconscious,' Sāy.)

अकेश *a-keśa*, mf(*ā*, Pāṇ.; *ī*, R.) n. hairless.

अकोट *a-koṭa*, *as*, m. 'without a bend,' the Areca or Betel-nut palm, L.

अकोप *a-kopa*, *as*, m., N. of a minister of king Daśaratha, R. &c.

अकोपन *a-kopana*, mfn. not irascible.

अकोविद *a-kovida*, mfn. unwise, ignorant.

अकौशल *a-kauśala*, *am*, n. unskilfulness, Pāṇ.; cf. *ākauśala*.

अक्का *akkā*, f. (Voc. *akka*, Pāṇ.) a mother (used contemptuously); N. of a woman; [supposed to be a term of foreign origin; cf. Lat. *Acca*.]

अक्त 1. *akta*, mfn. (√*aj*), driven.

अक्त 2. *aktá*, mfn. (√*añj*), smeared over; diffused; bedaubed, tinged, characterized. Often ifc. (cf. *raktâkta*); (*am*), n. oil, ointment.

Aktā́, f. night, RV. i, 62, 8.

Aktú, *us*, m. tinge, ray, light, RV.; dark tinge, darkness, night, RV.; (*ós*, *úbhis*), ind. at night, RV.

अक्नोपन *a-knopana*, mfn. not moistening, drying, Nir.

अक्र 1. *á-kra*, mfn. (√*kṛi*), inactive, RV. i, 120, 2.

अक्र 2. *akrá*, *as*, m. a banner, RV.; a wall, fence (*prākāra*), according to Durga on Nir. vi, 17.

अक्रतु *a-kratú*, mfn. destitute of energy or power ['of sacrifices,' Sāy.], RV. x, 83, 5; AV.; foolish, RV. vii, 6, 3; free from desire, Up.

अक्रम *a-krama*, mfn. not happening successively, happening at once, Yogas.; (*as*), m. want of order, confusion.

अक्रविहस्त *á-kravi-hasta*, mfn. not having bloody hands ['not having niggardly hands, not close-fisted,' Sāy.], RV. v, 62, 6.

अक्रव्याद् *a-kravyád*, mfn. not consuming flesh (N. of an Agni), AV.; not carnivorous, Yājñ.

A-kravyâda, mfn. not carnivorous, Mn.

अक्रान्त *a-krānta*, mfn. unpassed, unsurpassed, unconquered; not doubled, RV. Prāt.; (*ā*), f. the Egg plant.

अक्रिय *a-kriya*, mfn. without works; inactive; abstaining from religious rites; impious; (*ā*), f. inactivity; neglect of duty.

अक्रीडत् *á-krīḍat*, mfn. not playing, RV. x, 79, 6.

अक्रूर *a-krūra*, mfn. not cruel, gentle; (*as*), m., N. of Kṛishṇa's paternal uncle, MBh.

अक्रोध *a-krodha*, *as*, m. suppression of anger; (mfn.), free from anger. **-máya**, mfn. free from anger, ŚBr. xiv.

A-krodhana, mfn. free from anger, Mn.; (*as*), m., N. of a prince, son of Ayutāyu, VP.

अक्लम *a-klama*, *as*, m. freedom from fatigue.

अक्लिका *aklikā*, f. the Indigo plant, L.

अक्लिन्नवर्त्मन् *a-klinna-vartman*, *a*, n., N. of a disease of the eyes, Suśr.

A-kledya, mfn. not to be wetted.

अक्लिष्ट *a-klishṭa*, mfn. untroubled; undisturbed; unwearied. **-karman** or **-kārin**, mfn. unwearied in action. **-vrata**, mfn. unwearied in keeping religious vows.

A-kleśa, *aś*, m. freedom from trouble, Mn.

अक्ष् *aksh* (perhaps a kind of old Desid. of √1. *aś*), cl. 1. 5. *akshati*, *akshṇoti* (Pāṇ. III, 1, 75; fut. *akshishyati* or *akshyati*, L.; aor. *ākshīt*, 3. du. *ākshishṭām* or *āshṭām*, L.; perf. *ānaksha* [Pāṇ. vii, 4, 60, Comm.], but Ā. p. [with the Vedic weak stem *āksh*, cf. perf. *āś-uḥ* 3. pl. &c. fr. √1. *aś*] *ākshāṇá*), to reach, RV. x, 22, 11; to pass through, penetrate, pervade, embrace, L.; to accumulate (to form the cube?), L.: Caus. *akshayati*, *ācikshat*, to cause to pervade, L.: Desid. *acikshishati* or *acikshati*, L.

1. **Áksha**, *as*, m. an axle, axis (in this sense also *am*, n., L.); a wheel, car, cart; the beam of a balance or string which holds the pivot of the beam; a snake, L.; terrestrial latitude (cf. *-karṇa*, *-bhā*, *-bhāga*); the collar-bone, ŚBr.; the temporal bone, Yājñ.; N. of a measure (= 104 aṅgula); [cf. Lat. *axis*; Gk. ἄξων; Old Germ. *ahsa*; Mod. Germ. *Achse*; Lith. *assis*.] **-karṇa**, m. the hypotenuse, especially of the triangle formed with the gnomon of a dial and its shadow; (in astron.) argument of the latitude. **-ja**, m. a diamond; a thunderbolt; N. of Vishṇu. **-dṛik-karman**, n. operation or calculation for latitude. **-dvāra**, n. the cavity in the axle of a car, Sāy. on RV. v, 30, 1. **-dhur**, f. the pin at the end of an axle, pole attached to an axle. **-dhūrtila**, m. a draft-ox, L. **-pīḍa**, m. Chrysopogon Acicularis, Suśr.; (*ā*), f., N. of a plant. **-bhā**, f. shadow of latitude. **-bhāga**, m. degree of latitude. **-bhāra**, m. a cart-load. **-saṅgám**, ind. so that the axle is caught or hooked by contact with some obstruction, MaitrS. **Akshâṅsa**, m. a degree of latitude. **Akshâgra**, n. end of an axle, or of the pole of a car; an axle. **Akshâgra-kīla** or **-kīlaka**, m. a linch-pin; the pin fastening the yoke to the pole. **Akshā-náh** (the vowel lengthened as in *upā-náh*, &c.), mfn. tied to the axle of a car, RV. x, 53, 7; (horse, Sāy.; trace attached to the horse's collar, Gmn.)

2. **Akshá**, *as*, m. (√1. *aś*, Uṇ.) a die for gambling; a cube; a seed of which rosaries are made (cf. *indrâksha*, *rudrâksha*); the Eleocarpus Ganitrus, producing that seed; a weight called *karsha*, equal to 16 māshas; Beleric Myrobalan (Terminalia Belerica), the seed of which is used as a die; a N. of the number 5; (*am*). n. sochal salt; blue vitriol (from its cube-like crystals), L. **-kāma** (*akshá-*), mfn. fond of dice, AV. **-kitava**, m. a gambler, MBh. **-kuśala**, mfn. skilled in dice. **-kshapaṇa**, m., N. of a gambler, Kathās. **-glaha**, m. gambling, playing at dice, MBh. **-ja**, m. a thunderbolt; N. of Vishṇu, L. **-tattva**, n. science of dice; *-vid*, mfn. skilled in it. **-dāya**, m. handing over the dice in gambling, Naish. [moving a piece on a board, BR.] **-devana**, n. gambling, dice-playing. **-devin** or **-dyū**, m. a gambler, a dice-player. **-dyūta**, n. gambling; cf. *ākshadyūtika*. **-dyūtâdi**, a gaṇa of Pāṇ. (iv, 4, 19). **-drugdha** (*akshá-*), mfn. hated by (unlucky at) dice, or injuring with dice (a sharper), AV. **-dhara**, mfn. holding dice; (*as*), m. Trophis Aspera (see *śākhoṭa*). **-dhūrta**, m. 'dice-rogue,' gambler, L. **-naipuṇa** or **-naipuṇya**, n. skill in gambling. **-parâjayá**, m. defeat in gambling, AV. **-pari**, ind. with exception of a single die, Pāṇ. **-pāta**, m. throw or cast of dice. **-pātana**, n. act of casting dice. **-priya**, mfn. fond of dice, or (perhaps) favoured by dice. **-bhūmi**, f. gambling-place. **-mada**, m. passion for dice. **-mātra**, n. anything as big as dice; the twinkling of an eye, a moment (cf. 4. *aksha*), L. **-mālā**, f. a string or rosary of beads, especially of Eleocarpus seeds; N. of Arundhatī, wife of Vasishṭha (from her wearing a rosary), Mn. ix, 23; N. of the mother of Vatsa. **-mālin**, mfn. wearing a rosary of seeds; N. of Śiva, MBh. **-rājá**, m. 'king of dice,' the die called Kali, VS. **-vat**, mfn. having dice; (*tī*), f. a game of dice, L. **-vāpa** = *akshâvāpá* below, Kāṭh. **-vāma**, m. an unfair gambler. **-vid**, mfn. skilful in gambling. **-vṛitta**, mfn. anything that happens in gambling. **-śauṇḍa**, mfn. fond of gambling. **-sūkta**, n. dice-hymn, N. of RV. x, 34. **-sūtra**, n. a string or rosary of Eleocarpus seeds. **-stusha**, m. Beleric Myrobalan. **-hṛidaya**, n. innermost nature of dice, perfect skill in gambling. **-hṛidaya-jña**, mfn. perfectly skilled in gambling. **Akshâtivāpa**, m. = *akshâvāpá* below, MBh. **Akshâvápana**, n. a dice-board, ŚBr. **Akshâvalī**, f. a rosary. **Akshâvāpá**, m. [ŚBr.] (cf. *aksha-vāpa* & *akshâtivāpa*), the keeper or superintendent of a gambling-table [Comm. = *dyūta-pati*, *dyūtâdhyaksha*, *aksha-goptṛi*].

3. **Aksha**, *am*, n. an organ of sense; sensual perception, L.; (*as*), m. the soul, L.; knowledge, religious knowledge, L.; a lawsuit, L.; a person born blind, L.; N. of Garuḍa, L.; of a son of Rāvaṇa; of a son of Nara, &c. **-darśaka** or **-dṛiś**, m. a judge, i. e. one who sees lawsuits. **-paṭala**, n. court of law; depository of legal document, Rājat. **-pāṭa**, m. an arena, a wrestling ground, place of contest, L. **-pāṭaka** or **-pāṭika**, m. a judge, i. e. arranger of a lawsuit, L. **-vāṭa**, L. = *-pāṭa*. **-vid**, mfn. versed in law, L.

4. **Aksha**, **aksha-caraṇa**, &c. See col. 3.

Akshaka, *as*, m. Dalbergia Oujeinensis; (*as*, *am*), m. n. the collar-bone, Suśr.; (*ī*), f., N. of a creeping plant.

अक्षण *a-kshaṇa*, mfn. inopportune.

अक्षण्वत् 1. *a-kshaṇvat*, mfn. (√*kshaṇ*), not injuring, ĀśvGṛ.

अक्षत *á-kshata*, mfn. not crushed; uninjured, unbroken, whole; (*as*), m. Śiva, L.; (*as*, *am*), m. n. a eunuch, L.; (*ā*), f. a virgin, Yājñ.; N. of a plant, Karkaṭaśṛiṅgī or Kaṅkaḍaśṛiṅgī; (*am*), n. and (*ās*), m. pl. unhusked barley-corns; N. of the descendants of Surabhi, Hariv. **-yoni**, f. a virgin, an unblemished maiden.

अक्षत्र *a-kshatra*, mfn. destitute of the Kshatriya caste, apart from the Kshatriya caste.

अक्षन् *akshan*. See *akshi*.

अक्षम *a-kshama*, mf(*ā*)n. unable to endure, impatient; incompetent (with Loc., Inf. or ifc.), envious; (*ā*), f. or *-tā*, f. impatience, envy; incompetence, inability (with Inf.)

अक्षय *a-kshaya*, mf(*ā*)n. exempt from decay, undecaying; (*as*), m., N. of the twentieth year in the cycle of Jupiter; N. of a mountain, Hariv.; (*ā*), f. the seventh day of a lunar month, if it fall on Sunday or Monday; the fourth, if it fall on Wednesday. **-guṇa**, mfn. possessing imperishable qualities; (*as*), m. Śiva. **-tā**, f. or **-tva**, n. imperishableness. **-tṛitīyā**, f., N. of a festival (the third day of the bright half of Vaiśākha, which is the first day of the Satya-yuga, and secures permanency to actions then performed). **-nīvī**, f. a permanent endowment, Buddhist Inscr. **-puruhūta**, m. Śiva. **-mati**, m., N. of a Buddhist. **-loka**, m. the undecaying world, heaven.

A-kshayin, mfn. undecaying; (*iṇī*), f., N. of Śiva's wife (?), Rājat.

A-kshayyá, mfn. undecaying; (*am*), n. or ind. 'may thy prosperity be undecaying!' (a form of blessing addressed to a Vaiśya), MBh. **-navamī**, f. the ninth day of the bright half of Āśvina. **Akshayyôdaka**, n. inexhaustible water, Yājñ. &c.

अक्षर *a-kshára*, mfn. imperishable; unalterable; (*as*), m. a sword, L.; Śiva, L.; Vishṇu, L.; (*ā*), f., see *ákshar*ā below; (*am*), n. a syllable; the syllable *om*, Mn.; a letter [(*as*), m., RāmatUp.]; a vowel; a sound; a word; N. of Brahma; final beatitude; religious austerity, sacrifice, L.; water, RV. i, 34, 4 & i, 164, 42; Achyranthes Aspera. **-kara**, m. a kind of religious meditation, Kāraṇḍ. **-cañcu** or **-cuñcu** or **-caṇa** or **-cana**, m. 'clever in writing,' a scribe, L. **-cyutaka**, n. 'supplying dropped (*cyuta*) syllables,' a kind of game, Kād. **-chandas**, n. metre regulated by the number and quality of syllables. **-jananī**, f. 'letter producer,' a reed or pen. **-jīvaka** or **-jīvika** or **-jīvin**, m. 'one who lives by writing,' a scribe. **-tūlikā**, f. a reed or pen. **-nyāsa**, m. array of syllables or letters; the alphabet. **-paṅkti**, mfn. containing five syllables; (*akshára-paṅkti*), f., N. of a metre of four lines, each containing one dactyl and one spondee, VS.; also called *paṅkti* or *haṅsa*. **-bhāj**, mfn. entitled to a share in the syllables (of a prayer), AitBr. **-mukha**, m. having the mouth full of syllables, a student, scholar, L. **-mushṭikā**, f. the art of communicating syllables or ideas by the fingers (one of the 64 Kalās), Vātsyāy. **-vinyāsa** = *-nyāsa*, Vikr. **-śás**, ind. syllable by syllable, MaitrS.; AitBr. **-śūnya**, mfn. inarticulate. **-saṃsthāna**, n. scripture, writing, L. **-samāmnāya**, m. alphabet, Pat.; BhP. **Aksharâkshara**, m. a kind of religious meditation (*samādhi*), Karaṇḍ. **Aksharâṅga**, n. part of a syllable (said of the anusvāra), RV. Prāt. **Akshare-sthā**, mfn. consisting of syllables, TāṇḍyaBr.

Aksharaka, *am*, n. a vowel.

Áksharā, f. (cf. *a-kshára*, n. above), word, speech, RV.

Aksharya, mf(*ā*)n. corresponding to the number of syllables or letters, RV. Prāt.; (*aksharyam revat*), n., N. of a Sāman, ĀrshBr.

अक्षान्ति *a-kshānti*, *is*, f. impatience, jealousy, intolerance.

अक्षार *a-kshāra*, mfn. free from alkali or factitious salt. **-lavaṇa**, n. not factitious (i. e. natural) salt; (mfn.) not composed of artificial salt, [Kullūka on] Mn. iii, 257; v, 73; xi, 109; or, according to Goldst. and NBD., better '(food) not containing acrid substances nor salt;' therefore also *akshārâlavaṇa* in the same sense, cf. *kshāra-lavaṇa*. **-lavaṇâśin**, mfn. eating *akshāra-lavaṇa*.

A-kshāra-madya-māṅsâda, mfn. not eating acrid substances nor (drinking) spirituous liquors nor eating meat, VarYogay.

अक्षि *ákshi*, n. (√1. *aś*, Uṇ.) [instr. *akshṇā*, dat. *akshṇe*, &c., fr. *akshan*, substituted for *akshi* in the weakest cases. Vedic forms are: abl. gen. *akshṇás*; loc. *akshán* (once *akshiṇi*!); du. nom, acc. *akshī́*, RV., *ákshiṇī*, *ákshyau*, and *akshyàu*, AV.; ŚBr. & AitBr.; instr. *akshī́bhyām*; gen. *akshyós*, VS., *akshyós* and *akshós* (!), AV.; plur. nom. acc. *ákshīṇi*, AV., *akshāṇi*, RV.; ifc. *aksha* is substituted, see 4. *aksha*], the eye; the number two; (*ī́*), n. du. the sun and moon, RV. i, 72, 10; [cf. Gk. ὄσσε, ὄκταλλος; Lat. *oculos*; A. S. *aegh*; Goth. *augo*; Germ. *Auge*; Russ. *oko*; Lith. *aki-s*.] **-kūṭa** or **-kūṭaka**, n. the prominent part of the forehead above the eye, Yājñ. &c. **-gata**, mfn. presented to the eye, visible, seen; hated, MBh. &c. **-gola**, m. the eyeball. **-jāha**, n. the root of the eye. **-tārā**, f. the pupil of the eye. **-nikāṇam**, ind. with half-closed eyes, Pāṇ. iii, 4, 54 Sch.; also *nikāṇam-akshi*, id. **-nimesha**, m. twinkling of an eye, a moment, Suśr. **-pakshman**, n. the eyelash. **-paṭala**, n. coat of the eye, L. **-pát**, ind. as much as could fall into the eyes, a little, RV. vi, 16, 18 & x, 119, 6. **-pāka**, m. inflammation of the eyes, Suśr. **-bhū́**, mfn. visible, perceptible, manifest, AV. xx, 136, 4; VS. **-bheshaja**, n. medicament for the eyes, collyrium, &c.; (*as*), m. a tree, Red Lodh. **-bhruva**, n. the eyes and eyebrows together. **-mat**, mfn. possessing eyes. **-loman**, n. the eyelash. **-vikūṇita**, n. a glance with the eyelids partially closed. **-saṃtarjana** (probably n.), N. of a mythic weapon, MBh. **Akshy-āmayá**, m. disease of the eye, ŚBr.; KātyŚr. **Akshy-āmayin**, mfn. having a disease of the eye, PBr.

4. **Aksha**, *am*, n. [only ifc. (f. *ī*) for *akshi*], the eye. **-caraṇa** or **-pad** or **-pāda**, m. (probably) 'having his eyes fixed in abstraction on his feet,' N. of the philosopher Gautama; cf. *ākshapāda*.

Akshan, n. substituted for *akshi*, 'the eye,' in the weakest cases, Gram. 122 [cf. Goth. *augan*]; an organ of sense, BhP. **-2. -váṭ**, mfn. having eyes, RV.; (for 1. see col. 2.)

Akshika or **akshīka,** *as,* m. the tree Dalbergia Oujeinensis, L.; see *akshaka.*

अक्षिणी *akshiṇī,* f. one of the eight conditions or privileges attached to landed property, L.

अक्षित् *a-kshít,* mfn. imperishable, not lost, MaitrS.

Á-kshita, mfn. undecayed, uninjured, undecaying; (*am*), n. water, L.; the number 100,000 millions, PBr. **Ákshitā-vasu,** m. 'possessed of undecaying wealth,' N. of Indra, RV. viii, 49, 6. **Ákshitôti,** m. 'granting permanent help,' N. of Indra, RV.

Á-kshiti, *is,* f. imperishableness, AV. &c.; (mfn.), imperishable, RV.

अक्षिब *akshiba, as,* m., L.; see *akshība.*

अक्षियत् *á-kshiyat,* mfn. not inhabiting, destitute of a dwelling, unsettled ('not decreasing in riches,' Sāy.), RV. iv, 17, 13.

अक्षीक *akshīka, as,* m., L.; see *akshika.*

अक्षीण *á-kshīṇa,* mfn. not perishing or failing, ŚBr.; not waning (the moon), ŚBr.; not diminishing in weight, Yājñ.; N. of a son of Viśvāmitra, MBh.

अक्षीब *akshība* and *akshiba,* mfn. not intoxicated, sober, L.; (*as*), m. Guilandina or Hyperanthera Moringa, L.; (*am*), n. sea salt, L.

अक्षु *ákshu, us,* m. a kind of net, RV. i, 180, 5; AV. The NBD. suggests 'axle of a car,' making *ákshu* = *áksha.*

अक्षुण्ण *a-kshuṇṇa,* mfn. unbroken, uncurtailed; not trite, new, Mālatīm.; permanent; unconquered; inexperienced, inexpert. **-tā,** f. uncurtailed condition; inexperience.

अक्षुद्र *a-kshudra,* mfn. not small; not low or vulgar, MBh.

अक्षुध् *á-kshudh,* f. satiety, VS.

A-kshudhyá, mfn. not liable to hunger, AV.

Á-kshodhuka, mfn. not hungry, MaitrS.

अक्षेत्र *á-kshetra,* mfn. destitute of fields, uncultivated, ŚBr.; (*am*), n. a bad field, Mn. x, 71; a bad geometrical figure. **-jña** [Pāṇ. vii, 3, 30] or **-vid** [*áksh°*, RV. v, 40, 5 & x, 32, 7], not finding out the way; destitute of spiritual knowledge.

A-kshetrin, mfn. having no fields, Mn. ix, 49 & 51.

A-kshaitrajñya, *am,* n. spiritual ignorance, Pāṇ. vii, 3, 30; see *āksh°.*

अक्षोट *akshoṭa, as,* m. a walnut (Pistacio nut?), Ragh.; the tree Pīlu; the tree Aleurites Triloba. Also spelt *akshoḍa* (Suśr.), *akshoḍaka, ākshoṭa, ākshoḍaka, ākhoṭa.*

अक्षोभ *a-kshobha,* mfn. unagitated, unmoved; (*as*), m. the post to which an elephant is tied, freedom from agitation, imperturbability.

A-kshobhya, mfn. immovable, imperturbable; (*as*), m., N. of a Buddha; of an author; an immense number, said by Buddhists to be 100 vivaras.

अक्षौहिणी *akshauhiṇī,* f. an army consisting of ten anīkinīs, or 21,870 elephants, 21,870 chariots, 65,610 horse, and 109,350 foot. (Since an anīkinī consists of 27 vāhinīs, and 27 is the cube of 3, *akshauhiṇī* may be a compound of 2. *aksha* and *vāhinī*; or it may possibly be connected with 1. *aksha,* axle, car.)

अक्ष्ण *akshṇa, am,* n. = *a-khaṇḍa,* Uṇ. Sch. **-yā́van,** mfn. going across, RV. viii, 7, 35.

Akshṇayā́, instr. ind. transversely, ŚBr. (Sch. circuitously, like a wheel!); wrongly, ŚBr. xiv; diagonally, Śulbas. **-kṛita** (*akshṇayā́-*), mfn. done wrongly, ŚBr. **-deśá,** m. an intermediate region, ŚBr. **-drúh,** mfn. injuring wrongly or in a bad way, RV. i, 122, 9. **-rajju,** f. diagonal line, Śulbas. **-stomī́ya,** f., N. of an Ishṭakā, TS.; ŚBr.

अखट्ट *akhaṭṭa,* m. Buchanania Latifolia.

अखट्टि *akhaṭṭi,* m. childish whim, L.

अखण्ड *a-khaṇḍa,* mfn. not fragmentary, entire, whole; (*am*), n. time, L.; (*a-khaṇḍā dvādaśī*), the twelfth day of the first half of the month Mārgaśīrsha.

A-khaṇḍana, *am,* n. not breaking, leaving entire, L.; non-refutation, admission, L.; (*as*), m. time, L.

A-khaṇḍita, mfn. unbroken, undivided, unimpaired; unrefuted. **-ṛtu** (*ṛitu*), mfn. 'not breaking the season,' bearing seasonable fruits.

अखनत् *á-khanat,* mfn. not digging, RV. x, 101, 11.

अखर्व *á-kharva,* mfn. not shortened or mutilated, RV. vii, 32, 13; not small, important; also *a-kharvan,* Hcat.; (*ā*), f., N. of a plant, L.

अखात *á-khāta,* mfn. unburied, AV.; (*as, am*), m.n. a natural pond or lake, a pool before a temple, L.

अखाद्य *a-khādya,* mfn. uneatable.

अखिद्र *á-khidra,* mf(*ā*)n. not weak, TS. &c. **-yāman** (*ákhidra-*), mfn. unwearied in course, RV. i, 38, 11.

अखिल *a-khila,* mf(*ā*)n. without a gap, complete, whole; (*ena*), ind. completely. **Akhilâtman,** m. the universal Spirit, Brahma. **Akhilī-√1. kṛi,** *-kṛitya,* ind. p. not having annihilated or rendered powerless, Śiś. ii, 34.

अखेटिक *akheṭika* or *ākheṭika, as,* m. a dog trained to the chase.

अखेदिन् *a-khedin,* mfn. not wearisome, unwearied. **Akhedi-tva,** n. continuous flow (of speech), one of the *vāg-guṇas* of Mahāvīra, Jain.

अख्खल *akhkhala,* ind. an exclamation of joy, Sāy. on RV. vii, 103, 3. **Akhkhalī-kṛítyā,** Ved. ind. p. (√1. *kṛi*), uttering the exclamation akhkhala, RV. vii, 103, 3.

अख्यात *a-khyāta,* mfn. not famous, unknown.

A-khyāti, *is,* f. infamy, bad repute, disgrace. **-kara,** mfn. causing infamy, disgraceful.

अग् *ag,* cl. 1. P. *agati,* to move tortuously, wind, L.: Caus. *agayati,* L.; cf. √*aṅg.*

1. **aga,** *as,* m. a snake [in this sense perhaps rather *a-ga*], L.; the sun, L.; a water-jar, L.

अग 2. *a-ga,* mfn. (√*gam*), unable to walk, Pāṇ. vi, 3, 77 Sch.; (*as*), m. a mountain; a tree; the number seven. **-ja,** mfn. produced on a mountain, or from a tree; (*ā*), f., N. of Pārvatī, daughter of Himālaya; (*am*), n. bitumen. **Agâtma-jā,** f. = *aga-jā,* Kir. **Agâvaha,** m., N. of a son of Vasudeva, and of others, Hariv. **Agâukas,** m. 'mountain-dweller,' a lion; 'tree-dweller,' a bird; the Śarabha, q. v.

A-gaccha, mfn. not going, L.; (*as*), m. a tree, L.

अगणित *a-gaṇita,* mfn. uncounted; inconsiderable, VP. **-pratiyāta,** mfn. returned without (or because of not) having been noticed, Śiś. **-lajja,** mfn. disregarding shame.

अगत *á-gata,* mfn. not gone; (*am*), n. not yet frequented, the dominion of death, AV.

A-gati, mfn. not going, halting; without resource, helpless; (*is*), f. stoppage, R.; want of resort or resource; unsuccessfulness, Vikr.; not cohabiting with a woman.

A-gatika, mf(*ā*)n. without resort or resources, Kathās. **-gati,** f. the resort of one who has no resort, a last resource, Yājñ. i, 345.

A-gatīka, mf(*ā*)n. not to be walked on (as an evil path), MBh.

अगद *a-gadá,* mfn. free from disease, healthy, RV. &c.; free from affliction; (*as*), m. freedom from disease, Mn.; a medicine, drug, (especially) antidote, Mn. **Agadam-kāra,** m. a physician, Naish. **Agada-veda,** m. medical science, Car.

Agadya, Nom. P. *agadyati,* to have good health, (gaṇa *kaṇḍv-ādi,* q. v.); to heal, ib.

अगदित *a-gadita,* mfn. untold.

अगन्ध *a-gandhá,* mfn. without smell.

अगम *a-gama,* mfn. not going, unable to go; (*as*), m. a mountain, L.; a tree [cf. 2. *a-ga*].

A-gamya, mfn. unfit to be walked in, or to be approached; not to be approached (sexually); inaccessible; unattainable; unintelligible; unsuitable. **-gā,** f. a woman who has illicit intercourse with a man, VarBṛ. **-rūpa,** mfn. of unsurpassed form.

A-gamyā, f. a woman with whom cohabitation is forbidden. **-gamana,** n. illicit intercourse with a woman. **-gamanīya,** mfn. relating to it, Mn. xi, 169. **-gāmin,** mfn. practising it, Gaut.

अगरी *a-garī,* f. a kind of grass (Deotar, Andropogon Serratus), L.; [cf. *garī.*]

अगरु *agaru, us, u,* m. n. Agallochum, Amyris Agallocha; cf. *aguru.*

अगर्तमित् *á-garta-mit* (cf. *garta-mít*), mfn. not buried in a hole, ŚBr.

A-garta-skandya, mfn. 'not having holes to be lept over,' not offering hindrances, ŚāṅkhBr.

अगर्व *a-garva,* mfn. free from pride.

अगर्हित *a-garhita,* mfn. undespised, unreproached, blameless.

अगव्यूति *a-gavyūtí,* mfn. without good pasturage for cattle, barren, RV. vi, 47, 20.

अगस्ति *agásti, is,* m. (according to Uṇ. iv, 179 fr. 2. *a-ga,* a mountain, and *asti,* thrower, √2. *as*), N. of a Ṛishi (author of several Vedic hymns; said to have been the son of both Mitra and Varuṇa by Urvaśī; to have been born in a water-jar; to have been of short stature; to have swallowed the ocean, and compelled the Vindhya mountains to prostrate themselves before him; to have conquered and civilized the South; to have written on medicine, &c.); the star Canopus (of which Agastya is the regent, said to be the 'cleanser of water,' because of turbid waters becoming clean at its rising, Ragh. xiii, 36); Agasti Grandiflora, Suśr. [also *-dru,* f., L.]; (*ayas*), m. pl. the descendants of Agastya; (*ī*), f. a female descendant of Agastya, Pāṇ. vi, 4, 149, Sch.

Agastīya, mfn. relating to Agasti, Pāṇ. vi, 4, 149, Comm.

Agástya (3, 4), *as,* m. = *agásti;* N. of Śiva, L. **-gītā,** *ās,* f. pl. Agastya's hymns, forming part of the Ādi-vārāha-Purāṇa. **-cāra,** m. the path of Canopus. **-mārga,** m. the path of Agastya (Canopus), i. e. the South. **-saṃhitā,** f., N. of an old compendium of the Tantra literature. **Agastyôdaya,** m. the rising of Canopus; the seventh day of the second half of Bhādra.

अगा *a-gā, ās,* m.f. (Ved.) not going, Pāṇ. iii, 2, 67 Sch.

अगातृ *a-gātṛi, tā,* m. a bad singer, TāṇḍyaBr.

अगाध *a-gādha,* mf(*ā*)n. not shallow, deep, unfathomable; (*as*), m. a hole, chasm, L.; N. of one of the five fires at the Svadhākāra, Hariv. **-jala,** mfn. having deep water; (*am*), n. deep water. **-rudhira,** n. a vast quantity of blood, Daś.

A-gādhi-tva, *am,* n. depth, Comm. on Śiś. i, 55.

अगार *agāra* (rarely *as,* m.), *am,* n. house, apartment [cf. *āgāra*]. **-dāhin,** m. 'house-burner,' an incendiary, Gaut.

Agārin, mfn. possessing a house; (*ī*), m. a householder, layman (cf. *an-agārin*), Jain.

अगिर *agira, as,* m. (√*ag*), the sun, L.; fire, L.; a Rākshasa, L.

अगिरौकस् *á-girâukas,* mfn. (*girā,* instr. of *gir,* and *okas*), not to be kept back by hymns, N. of the Maruts, RV. i, 135, 9.

अगु *á-gu,* mfn. (fr. *go* with *a*), destitute of cows, poor, RV. viii, 2, 14; (*us*), m. 'destitute of rays,' N. of Rāhu the ascending node.

A-go, f. not a cow, PārGṛ. **-tā** (*a-gó-*), f. want of cows, RV.; AV.

अगुण *a-guṇa,* mfn. destitute of qualities or attributes (said of the supreme Being, cf. *nirguṇa*); destitute of good qualities; (*as*), m. a fault. **-tā,** f. or **-tva,** n. absence of qualities or of good qualities. **-vat,** mfn. destitute of qualities; without good qualities. **-vādin,** mfn. fault-finding, censorious. **-śīla,** mfn. of a worthless character.

अगुप्त *a-gupta,* mfn. unhidden, unconcealed; unprotected; not keeping a secret.

अगुरु *a-guru,* mfn. not heavy, light; (in prosody) short as a short vowel alone or before a single consonant; (*us, u*), m.n. the fragrant Aloe wood and tree, Aquilaria Agallocha.

अगूढ *a-gūḍha*, mfn. unconcealed, manifest. **–gandha**, n. Asa Foetida. **–bhāva**, mfn. having a transparent disposition.

अगृभीत *á-gribhīta*, mfn. not seized or taken, unsubdued, RV. viii, 79, 1; TBr. **–śocis** (*ágri-bhīta-*), mfn. 'having unsubdued splendour,' N. of Agni and the Maruts, RV. v, 54, 5 & 12; viii, 23, 1; ('having inconceivable splendour,' BR.)

अगृह *a-griha*, mfn. houseless. **–tā**, f. houselessness, TāṇḍyaBr.

अगोचर *a-gocara*, mfn. not within range, unattainable, inaccessible (cf. *drishty-agocara*), imperceptible by the senses; (*am*), n. anything that is beyond the cognizance of the senses; Brahma; the not being seen, absence; (*eṇa*), instr. ind. out of the sight of any one (gen.), behind one's back, Hit.

अगोपा *á-gopā*, mfn. without a cowherd, not tended by one, RV.

अगोरुध *á-go-rudha*, mfn. not driving away the cow, RV. viii, 24, 20; ('not repelling or disdaining praise,' Sāy.)

अगोह्य *á-gohya* (4), mfn. not to be concealed or covered, bright, RV.

अगौकस् *agaukas*. See 2. *a-ga*.

अग्धाद् *agdhád*, mfn. (fr. *a* + *gdha*, p.p.p. fr. √*ghas* + *ad*), eating food which is not yet eaten, TS.; (Comm. = *dagdhád*.)

अग्ना *agnā* (for *agni* in the following comp.) **–marutau**, m. du. Agni and Marut, Pāṇ. vi, 3, 28, Sch. **–vishṇū**, voc. m. du. Agni and Vishṇu, AV.

Agnáyī, f. the wife of Agni, one of the *deva-patnyaḥ*, RV. i, 22, 12 & v, 46, 8; the Tretā-yuga, L.

अग्नि *agní*, *is*, m. (√*ag*, Uṇ.) fire; sacrificial fire (of three kinds, Gārhapatya, Āhavanīya, and Dakshiṇa); the number three, Sūryas.; the god of fire; the fire of the stomach, digestive faculty, gastric fluid; bile, L.; gold, L.; N. of various plants, Semicarpus Anacardium, Suśr., Plumbago Zeylanica and Rosea, Citrus Acida; mystical substitute for the letter *r*; in the Kātantra grammar N. of noun-stems ending in *i* and *u* [cf. Lat. *igni-s*; Lith. *ugni-s*; Slav. *ognj*]. **–kaṇa**, m. 'fire-particle,' a spark. **–karmán**, n. 'fire-act,' piling up the wood &c., ŚBr.; action of Agni, Nir.; cauterization, Suśr. **–kalpa** (*agní-*), mfn. having the nature of fire, ŚBr. **–kārikā** [L.], f. and **-kārya** [Mn. &c.], n. kindling or feeding the sacrificial fire with clarified butter &c.; the prayers said while doing so, Kathās.; cauterization. **–kāshṭha**, n. Agallochum, L. **–kukkuṭa**, m. a lighted wisp of straw, firebrand, L. **–kuṇḍa**, n. a pan with live coals, R.; a hole or enclosed space for the consecrated fire, Kathās. **–kumāra**, m. a particular preparation of various drugs; N. of a class of Bhavanavāsin deities, Jain. **–kṛita**, mfn. made by fire. **–ketu** (*agní-*), mfn. having fire as an emblem or characteristic mark (Ushas), TS.; (*us*), m., N. of a Rakshas, R. **–koṇa**, m. the south-east quarter, ruled over by Agni, L. **–krīḍā**, f. 'fire-sport,' fire-works, illuminations, &c. **–khaḍā**, f. an infernal pan or stove, Kāraṇḍ. **–garbha**, mf(*ā*)n. pregnant with fire, BṛĀrUp.; (*as*), m. a gem supposed to contain and give out solar heat (= *sūrya-kānta*), L.; N. of a frothy substance on the sea, engendered by the submarine fire, L.; N. of a man; (*ā*), f. the plant Mahājyotishmatī. **–gṛiha**, n. house or place for keeping the sacred fire, MBh.; a room fitted with hot-baths, Car. **–grantha**, m., N. of a work. **–ghaṭa**, m., N. of a hell, Kāraṇḍ. **–caya** [Śulb.], m. or **-cayana**, n. or **-citi**, f. or **-cityā́** [ŚBr.], f. arranging or preparing the sacred or sacrificial fire-place; *agni-caya*, a heap or mass of fire, R. **–cit**, mfn. arranging the sacrificial fire, or one who has arranged it, ŚBr. &c.; *án-* (neg.), ŚBr. **–cit-vat**, mfn. possessing householders that have prepared a sacred fire-place, Pāṇ. viii, 2, 10, Sch. **–já**, mfn. 'fire-born,' produced by or in fire, AV.; MaitrS.; (*as*), m., N. of Vishṇu, Hariv.; of a frothy substance on the sea (cf. *-garbha*), L. **–janman**, m. 'fire-born,' Skanda, god of war. **–jāra** or **-jāla**, m., N. of a frothy substance on the sea (cf. *-garbha* and *-já*), L. **–jihvá**, mfn. 'having Agni for tongue,' consuming the sacrifice through Agni, RV.; (*ā́*), f. tongue or flame of fire, AV.; MuṇḍUp.; the plant Methonica Superba (Lāṅgalī). **–jvalita-tejana**, mfn. having a point hardened in fire, Mn. vii, 90. **–jvāla**, m., N. of Śiva; (*ā*), f. flame of fire; a plant with red blossoms, used by dyers, Grislea Tomentosa; Jalapippalī. **–táp**, mfn. enjoying the warmth of fire, RV. v, 61, 4. **–tápas**, mfn. hot as fire, glowing, RV. x, 68, 6. **–taptá**, mfn. fire-heated, glowing, RV. vii, 104, 5. **–tā** (*agní-*), f. the state of fire, ŚBr. **–tejas** (*agní-*), mfn. having the energy of fire or of Agni, AV.; (*ās*), m. one of the seven Ṛishis of the eleventh Manvantara, Hariv. **–traya**, n. or **-tretā** [Mn.; MBh.], f. the three sacred fires, called respectively Gārhapatya, Āhavanīya, and Dakshiṇa. **–trā**, mfn., see *án-agnitrā*. **–da**, m. 'fire-giver,' incendiary, Mn.; Yājñ.; stomachic. **–1.-dagdha** (*agní-*), mfn. burnt with fire, RV. x, 103, additional verses; ŚBr.; cauterized, Suśr.; (*am*), n. a cautery. **–2.-dagdhá**, mfn. burnt on a funeral pile, RV. x, 15, 14; TBr.; (*ās*), m. pl. a class of Pitṛis who, when on earth, maintained a sacred fire, Mn. iii, 199. **–datta**, m., N. of a prince; of a Brahman, Kathās. **–damanī**, f. a narcotic plant, Solanum Jacquini. **–dāyaka**, m. = *-da*, q.v. **–dāha**, m. a particular disease; a fiery glow (in the sky), Hariv. **–diś**, f. Agni's quarter, the south-east. **–dīpana**, mf(*ī*)n. stomachic, Suśr. **–dīpta**, mfn. blazing, glowing; (*ā*), f. the plant Mahājyotishmatī. **–dīpti**, f. active state of digestion, Suśr. **–dūta** (*agní-*), mfn. having Agni for a messenger, brought by Agni, RV. x, 14, 13; AV. **–dūshita**, mfn. 'fire-marked,' branded. **–deva**, m. Agni; (*ā*), f. = *-nakshatrá*, q.v., L. **–devata** (*agní-*), mfn. having Agni for deity, ŚBr. **–daivata**, n. = *-nakshatrá*, q.v., VarBṛS. **–dh** (*agní-dh*, *dh* for *idh*; cf. *agnī́dh*), m. the priest who kindles the sacred fire, RV. ii, 1, 2; x, 41, 3; 91, 10. **–dhā́na**, n. receptacle for the sacred fire, RV. x, 165, 3; AV. **–nakshatrá**, n. the third lunar mansion, the Pleiades (Kṛittikā), ŚBr. **–nayana**, n. the act of bringing out the sacrificial fire. **–niryāsa**, m. = *-jāra*. **–nunna** (*agní-*), mfn. struck by fire or lightning, SV. **–netra** (*agní-*), mfn. having Agni for a guide, VS. **–pakva**, mfn. cooked on the fire, Mn. **–pada**, m. 'whose foot has stepped on the sacrificial fire-place,' N. of a horse, Lāṭy.; Vait. **–parikriyā**, f. care of the sacred fire, Mn. ii, 67. **–paricchada**, m. the whole apparatus of a fire-sacrifice, Mn. vi, 4. **–paridhāna**, n. enclosing the sacrificial fire with a kind of screen. **–parīkshā**, f. ordeal by fire. **–parvata**, m. 'fire-mountain,' a volcano, R. **–puccha**, n. tail or extreme point of a sacrificial fire (arranged in the shape of a bird), ĀśvŚr. **–purā́**, f. the castle of Agni, ŚBr. **–purāṇa**, n., N. of a Purāṇa. **–purogama**, mfn. having Agni for a leader. **–praṇayana**, n. = *-nayana*, q.v. **–praṇayanīya**, mfn. referring to the *-praṇayana*. **–pratishṭhā**, f. consecration of fire, especially of the nuptial fire. **–prabhā**, f. a venomous insect, Suśr. **–praveśa**, m. or **-praveśana**, n. entering the fire; self-immolation of a widow on her husband's funeral pile. **–prastara**, m. a fire-producing stone; flint; L. **–prāyaścitta**, n. or **-prāyaścitti** [ŚBr.], f. an expiatory act during the preparation of the sacrificial fire. **–bāhu**, m. smoke [cf. *-vāha*], L.; N. of a son of the first Manu, Hariv.; of a son of Priyavrata and Kāmyā, VP. **–bīja**, n. gold, L.; N. of the letter *r*, RāmatUp. **–bha**, n. 'shining like fire,' gold, L. **–bhu**, n. 'fire-produced,' water, L. **–bhū**, m. Skanda, L.; N. of a Vedic teacher, with the patron. Kāśyapa, VBr.; (in arithm.) six. **–bhūti**, m., N. of one of the eleven chief pupils (gaṇadharas) of the last Tīrthakara. **–bhrājas** (*agní-*), mfn. possessing fiery splendour, RV. v, 54, 11. **–maṇi**, m. the sun-stone (= *sūrya-kānta*). **–mát**, mfn. being near the fire, AV. (RV. has *-vát*); having or maintaining a sacrificial fire, Mn. &c.; having a good digestion, Suśr. **–mantha**, mfn. producing fire by friction; (*as*), m. Premna Spinosa, Suśr. **–manthana**, n. production of fire by friction, ĀśvŚr. **–manthanīya**, mfn. relating to such friction, ib. **–máya**, mf(*ī*)n. fiery, ŚBr.; AitBr. **–māṭhara**, m., N. of an expounder of the Ṛig-veda, VP. **–māndya**, n. slowness of digestion, dyspepsia. **–māruti**, m., N. of Agastya, L.; cf. *āgnimāruta*. **–mitra**, m., N. of a prince of the Suṅga dynasty, son of Pushyamitra, VP. **–m-indhá** (*agnim-indhá*), m. the priest who kindles the fire, RV. i, 162, 5. **–mukha** (*agní-*), mfn. having Agni for the mouth, ŚBr.; (*as*), m. a deity, a Brāhmaṇa, a tonic medicine, L.; Semicarpus Anacardium; Plumbago Zeylanica, L.; N. of a bug, Pañcat.; (*ī*), f. Semicarpus Anacardium; Gloriosa (or Methonica) Superba. **–mūḍha** (*agní-*), mfn. made insane by Agni, RV. x, 103, additional verses; AV. **–yuta**, m., N. of the author of the hymn x, 116 in the Ṛig-veda. **–yojana**, n. the act of stirring the sacrificial fire (to make it blaze up). **–rakshaṇa**, n. maintenance of the sacred domestic fire. **–raja** or **-rajas**, m. a scarlet insect, L. **–rahasya**, n. 'mystery of Agni,' title of the tenth book of the Śatapatha-Brāhmaṇa. **–rājan**, mfn., pl. 'having Agni as king,' N. of the Vasus, ŚāṅkhŚr. **–rā́śi**, m. a heap or mass of fire, a burning pile. **–ruhā**, f. the plant Māṃsarohiṇī. **–rūpa** (*agní-*), mfn. fire-shaped, RV. x, 84, 1; (*agni-rū́pa*), n. a shape of fire, ŚBr. **–retasá**, mfn. sprung from Agni's seed, ŚBr. **–rohiṇī**, f. a hard inflammatory swelling in the arm-pit, Suśr. **–loka**, m. the world of Agni, KaushUp. **–vát**, mfn. being near the fire, RV. vii, 104, 2 (= *-mát*, q.v.); 'joined to (another) fire,' N. of Agni, TS. **–varcas**, m., N. of a teacher of the Purāṇas, VP. **–varṇa**, mf(*ā*)n. having the colour of fire; hot, fiery (said of liquors), Mn. xi, 90 & 91; (*as*), m., N. of a prince, son of Sudarśana. **–vardhaka** or **-vardhana**, mfn. promoting digestion, stomachic. **–vallabha**, m. the tree Shorea Robusta; its resinous juice. **–vāṇa**, m. a fiery arrow. **–vādin**, m. 'fire-asserter,' worshipper of fire. **–vārtta**, mfn. gaining a livelihood by fire [as a blacksmith &c.], VarBṛS. **–vāsas** (*agní-*), mfn. wearing a fiery or red garment, AV. **–vāha**, m. the vehicle of fire, i.e. smoke, L. **–vidhā́**, f. manner or fashion of fire, ŚBr. **–vimocana**, n. the act of lowering the sacrificial fire (by spreading it out). **–visarpa**, m. spread of inflammation (in a tumour). **–viharaṇa**, n. removing the sacrificial fire from the Āgnīdhra to the Sadas Maṇḍapa. **–vīrya**, n. gold, L. **–vṛiddhi**, f. improvement of digestion. **–vetāla**, m., N. of a Vetāla (connected with the story of king Vikramāditya). **–velā**, f. the time at which the fire is kindled, afternoon, ĀśvGṛ. **–veśa**, m., N. of an ancient medical authority; also of other persons. **–veśman**, m. the fourteenth day of the Karma-māsa, Sūryapr. **–veśya**, m., N. of a teacher, MBh.; N. of the 22nd muhūrta, Sūryapr. **–śaraṇa** or **-śā́la** [AV.], n. or **-śālā**, f. house or place for keeping the sacrificial fire. **–śarman**, m., N. of a man. **–śikha**, mfn. having a point like fire (an arrow), R.; (*as*), m. an arrow; a lamp; a safflower plant, L.; saffron, L.; N. of Vararuci's father, Kathās.; of a Vetāla, Kathās.; (*am*), n. saffron, L.; gold, L. **–śikhā́**, f. a flame, ŚBr. &c.; the plants Gloriosa Superba and Menispermum Cordifolium. **–śuśrūshā**, f. attention to the sacrificial fire, Mn. ii, 248. **–śekhara**, n. saffron. **–śesha**, m. appendix to the chapter on Agni in the Taittirīya-Saṃhitā. **–śrí**, m(nom. pl. *-śrí-yas*)fn. having the brightness of Agni, RV. iii, 26, 5 ['approaching the fire (of lightning),' Sāy.] **–śroṇi**, f. leg of the sacrificial altar, KātyŚr. **–shṭút**, m. 'laudatory of Agni,' the first day of the Agnishṭoma sacrifice, one day of the Sattra Pañcadaśarātra, ŚBr. &c.; N. of a son of the sixth Manu, Cākshusha (by Naḍvalā), VP.; Hariv. [v.l. *-shṭubh*]. **–shṭomá**, m. 'praise of Agni,' N. of a protracted ceremony or sacrifice (forming one of the chief modifications [*saṃsthās*] of the Jyotishṭoma offered by one who is desirous of obtaining heaven; the performer is a Brahman who maintains the sacred fire, the offering is the Soma, the deities to whom the offering is made are Indra &c., the number of priests required is 16, the ceremonies continue for five days); a mantra or kalpa connected with the Agnishṭoma, L.; (*agni-shṭoma*)-*yājin*, mfn. one who has performed the A.; *-sád*, mfn. performing the A.; *-sádya*, n. the performance of A., ŚBr.; *-sāmá*, m. and *-sāmán*, n. the passage of the Sāma-veda chanted at the A.; *-hotra*, n. title of a Vedic text. **–shṭhá**, mfn. placed in, or over, or near the fire; (*as*), m. a pan, fire-pan, R. [cf. *-shṭhikā*]; a vehicle carrying the fire, ĀpŚr.; (in the Aśvamedha sacrifice) the eleventh Yūpa or sacrificial post which (of all the twenty-one) is nearest the fire, ŚBr.; (*ā́*), f. that corner of the sacrificial post which (of all the eight) is nearest the fire, ŚBr. **–shṭhikā**, f. a fire-pan [cf. *-shṭha*]. **–shvāttá** [in Epic and later texts *-svātta*], *ās*, m. plur. 'tasted by the funeral fire,' the Manes, RV. x, 15, 11; VS.; ŚBr.; in later texts N. of a class of Manes (who on earth neglected the sacrificial fire),

MBh. &c. **-saṃskāra,** m. the consecration of fire; performance of any rite in which the application of fire is essential, as the burning of a dead body, Mn.; Ragh. **-sakha,** m. 'friend of fire,' the wind, L. **-saṃkāśa** (*agni-*), mfn. resplendent like fire, ŚBr. **-sajjā,** f.? indigestion, Suśr. **-saṃcaya,** m. preparing the sacrificial fire-place; see *-cayana*. **-sambhava,** mfn. produced from fire; (*as*), m. wild safflower, L; = *-jāra*; 'the result of digestion,' chyme or chyle, L. **-saras,** n., N. of a Tīrtha, VārP. **-savá,** m. consecration of the fire, TS.; ŚBr. **-sahāya,** m. 'friend of fire,' the wind; a wild pigeon; L. **-sākshika,** mfn. taking Agni or the domestic or nuptial fire for a witness, R. &c. **-sākshika-maryāda,** mfn. one who taking Agni for a witness gives a solemn promise of conjugal fidelity. **-sāda,** m. weakness of digestion, Suśr. **-sāra,** n. a medicine for the eyes, a collyrium, L. **-sāvarṇi,** m., N. of a Manu, L. **-siṇha,** m., N. of the father of the seventh black Vāsudeva, Jain. **-sūtra,** n. thread of fire; a girdle of sacrificial grass put upon a young Brāhman at his investiture; L. **-stambha,** m. or **-stambhana,** n. the (magical) quenching of fire. **-stoka,** m. a particle of fire, spark. **-svātta,** see *-shvāttá*. **-havana,** n. a sacrificial libation, Gaut. **-hút** [VS.] or **-huta,** mfn. sacrificed by fire. **-hotṛi** (*agní-*), m. having Agni for a priest, RV. x, 66, 8. **-1. -hotra** (*agní-*), mfn. sacrificing to Agni, AV. vi, 97, 1; (*ī*), f. the cow destined for the Agnihotra, ŚBr.; AitBr.; (*agni-hotrī*)*-vatsá*, m. her calf, ŚBr. **-2. -hotrá,** n. AV. &c. oblation to Agni (chiefly of milk, oil, and sour gruel; there are two kinds of Agnihotra, one is *nitya*, i. e. of constant obligation, the other *kāmya*, i. e. optional); the sacred fire, Mn.; Yājñ. &c.; (*ag-nihotra*)*-devatā*, f. the deity of the Agnihotra; *-tvá*, n. the state of the A., MaitrS.; *-sthālī*, f. a pot used at the A., ŚBr.; *-hávanī*, f. a spoon used at the A., ŚBr.; ĀśvGṛ.; *-hút*, offering the A., AV.; *-homa*, m. a libation at the A., KātyŚr.; *agnihotrāyaṇin*, mfn. one who offers only the A., KātyŚr.; *agnihotrâvṛit*, f. (see *āvṛit*) the mere A. without recitation of Vedic formulas, KātyŚr.; *agnihotrâhuti* [ŚBr., cf. *āhuti*] and *agnihotrêshṭi* [KātyŚr., cf. *ishṭi*], f. a libation or offering at the A.; *agnihotrôcchishṭá* [ŚBr.] and *agnihotrôcche-shaṇá* [TS.], n. the remains of the A. **-hotrín,** mfn. practising the Agnihotra, maintaining the sacrificial fire, ŚBr. &c. **-homa,** m. oblation put into the fire, KātyŚr. **-hvará,** mfn. ? making a mistake in the fire-ceremonial, MaitrS. **Agnídh,** m. the priest who kindles the fire, VS.; ŚBr.; AitBr. [cf. *agnídh*]. **Agnidhra,** m. (= *agni-bāhu*), N. of two men. **Agnîndrau,** m. du. Agni and Indra, VS. **Agnîndhana,** n. kindling or feeding the fire, Mn. &c. **Agnī-parjanyau,** Voc. m. du. Agni and Parjanya, RV. vi, 52, 16. **Agnī́-váruṇau,** m. du. Agni and Varuṇa, ŚBr. **Agnī́-shómā** or **°mau,** m. du. Agni and Soma, RV.; AV.; VS.; (*agnīshoma*)*-praṇaya-na*, n. bringing out the fire and the Soma, a ceremony in the Jyotishṭomá sacrifice. **Agnīshomīya,** mfn. related or sacred to Agni and Soma, AV. &c.; (*ag-nīshomīya*)*-nirvāpa*, m. making libations with the cake sacred to Agni and Soma, a ceremony in the Darśapūrṇamāsa sacrifice; *-paśu*, m. a victim, generally a sheep or goat, sacred to Agni and Soma; *-paśv-anushṭhāna*, n. the rite connected with that victim at the Jyotishṭoma sacrifice; *-puroḍāśa*, m. cake sacred to Agni and Soma (baked in eleven bowls); *-yāga*, m. one of the three sacrifices of the Pūrṇamāsa; *agnīshomīyâikādaśa-kapāla*, m. cake sacred to Agni and Soma, see above. **Agny-agārá** [ŚBr. &c.] or **-āgāra,** m. house or place for keeping the sacred fire. **Agny-abhāva,** m. absence or want of the sacred fire; loss of appetite. **Agny-arcis,** f. or n. flame, ŚBr. **Agny-āgāra,** see *agny-agārá*. **Agny-ātmaka,** mf(*ikā*)n. having Agni's nature. **Agny-ādhāna** [KaushBr.] or **-ādhéya** [AV.; Mn. &c.], n. placing the fire on the sacrificial fire-place; the ceremony of preparing the three sacred fires Āhavanīya &c.; (*agnyādheya*)*-devatā*, f. the deity of the Agnyādheya ceremony, PārGṛ.; *-rūpá*, n. form or shape of the A., ŚBr.; *-śarkará, ās*, f. plur. (figuratively) bad performance of the A., ŚBr.; *-havís*, n. an oblation at the A., ŚBr. **Agny-ālaya,** m. = *agny-agārá*. **Agny-āhita,** m. one who has performed the Agnyādhāna, R. &c. **Agny-utpāta,** m. a fiery portent, Car.; a conflagration, PārGṛ. **Agny-utsādin,** mfn. one who lets the sacred fire go out. **Agny-uddharaṇa,** n. taking the sacred fire from its usual place (previous to a sacrifice). **Agny-upasthāná,** n. worship of Agni at the conclusion of the Agnihotra &c., ŚBr. **Agny-edhá,** m. one who kindles the fire, VS.

Agnika, *as*, m. a plant, probably Semecarpus Anacardium; a kind of serpent, Suśr.; an insect of scarlet colour, Coccinella; (*am*), n. the Acayou-nut, Suśr.

Agnisāt, ind. to the state of fire (used in comp. with √1. *kṛi* and √*bhū*, e. g. *agnisāt kṛi*, to reduce to fire, to consume by fire), cf. *bhasmasāt*.

अग्मन् *agman, a*, n. conflict, battle, L.; (connected with *ajman*, q. v.)

अग्र *ágra*, mfn. (fr. √*aṅg*, Uṇ.), foremost, anterior, first, prominent, projecting, chief, best, L.; supernumerary, L.; (*ā*), f. [scil. *rekhā*] measure of amplitude (i. e. the distance from the extremity of the gnomon-shadow to the line of the equinoctial shadow), Sūryas.; (*am*), n. foremost point or part; tip; front; uppermost part, top, summit, surface; point; and hence, figuratively, sharpness; the nearest end, the beginning; the climax or best part; goal, aim; multitude, L.; a weight, equal to a pala, L.; a measure of food given as alms, L.; (in astron.) the sun's amplitude; (*am*), ind. in front, before, ahead of; (*ágreṇa*), ind. in front, before (without or with acc.), ŚBr.; (*ágre*), ind. in front, ahead of, in the beginning, first; further on, subsequently, below (in a book); from—up to (*ā*), ŚBr.; before (in time), AitUp. &c. [cf. Gk. ἄκρον]. **-kara,** m. the fore part of the hand, finger; first ray; Śiś. **-kāya,** m. the fore part of the body. **-ga,** m. a leader. **-gaṇya,** mfn. to be counted or regarded as the foremost, principal. **-gāmin,** mfn. preceding, taking the lead. **-grāsikā,** f. the claim or right to the first morsel, Pāṇ. iii, 3, 111, Kāś. **-ja** (cf. *-já*), mfn. born first or earlier; (*as*), m. the first-born, an elder brother, Mn. &c.; a Brahman, VarBṛS. &c.; (*ā*), f. an elder sister. **-jaṅghā,** f. the fore part of the leg, the shin-bone, L. **-janman,** m. the first-born, an elder brother; a Brahman, Mn.; Yājñ. &c.; a member of one of the three highest castes, L.; Brahmā. **-já,** mfn. first-born, RV. ix, 5, 9. **-jātaka** or **-jāti,** m. a Brahman, L. **-jihvá,** n. tip of the tongue, VS. **-jyā,** f. sine of the amplitude, Sūryas. **-ṇī,** mfn. taking the lead, foremost; N. of an Agni, MBh. **-ṇīti** (*ágra-*), f. the first offering, RV. ii, 11, 14. **-tás,** ind.; see col. 3. **-tīrtha,** m., N. of a prince, MBh. **-dātṛi,** mfn. offering the best bits (to the gods), MBh. **-dānin,** m. a degraded Brāhman who receives presents from Śūdras, or takes things previously offered to the dead, BrahmavP. **-didhishú,** m. = *agre-didhishu*, TBr. **-nakha,** m. tip of a nail, R.; cf. *nakhâgra*. **-nāsikā,** f. tip of the nose, R.; cf. *nāsikâgra*. **-nirūpaṇa,** n. determining beforehand, prophecy. **-parṇī,** f. cowage, Carpopogon Pruriens. **-pā,** mfn. drinking first, MBh. **-pāṇi,** m. fore part of the hand; the right hand, L. **-pāda,** m. fore part of the foot, Śiś. **-pūjā,** f. highest act of reverence, R. **-peya,** n. precedence in drinking, AitBr. **-pradāyin,** mfn. offering first, MBh. **-praśīrṇá,** mfn. broken at the top, ŚBr. **-bīja,** mfn. (said of plants) propagated by cuttings; (*as*), m. a viviparous plant. **-bhāga** (or *agrâṇśa*), m. fore part; (in astron.) degree of amplitude, L. **-bhuj,** mfn. having the precedence in eating, TĀr.; N. of the sun, MBh. **-bhū,** mfn. being at the top, at the head of. **-bhūmi,** f. a goal, L.; the top-floor (of a house), Megh. **-mahishī,** f. the principal queen, R.; Jain. **-māṇsa,** n. the heart, L.; morbid protuberance of the liver. **-yāna,** n. stepping in front to defy the enemy. **-yāyin,** mfn. going before, taking the lead; (*ī*), m. a leader, Śāk. **-yāvan,** mfn. going before, RV. x, 70, 2. **-yodhin,** m. the foremost man or leader in a fight; a champion. **-lohitā,** f. a kind of vegetable, similar to the spinage. **-vaktra,** n., N. of a surgical instrument, Suśr. **-vat** (*ágra-*), mfn. being at the top, TS. **-śás,** ind. from the beginning, AV. **-saṃdhānī,** f. the register of human actions (kept by Yama), L. **-sandhyā,** f. early down. **-sara,** mf(*ī*)n. going in front, taking the lead. **-sānu,** m. the front part of a table-land, L. **-sārā,** f. a short method of counting immense numbers. **-sūci,** f. point of a needle, Naish. **-sena,** m., N. of Janamejaya's son. **-hasta,** m. = *-pāṇi*; the tip of an elephant's trunk, Vikr.; finger, R. **-hāyaṇa,** m. 'commencement of the year,' N. of a Hindū month (*Mārga-śīrsha*, beginning about the 12th of November). **-hāra,** m. royal donation of land to Brāhmans; land or village thus given, MBh. **Agrâṇśa** = *agra-bhāga*. **Agrâṇśu,** m. the end of a ray of light, the focal point. **Agrâkshan,** n. a side-look, R. **Agrâṅguli,** m. the finger-tip. **Agrâdvan,** mfn. having precedence in eating, RV. vi, 69, 6. **Agrânika,** n. the front of an army, vanguard, Mn. &c. **Agrâyaṇīya,** n. title of the second of the fourteen oldest (but lost) Jaina books, called Pūrvas. **Agrâśana,** mfn. eating before another (abl.), MārkP. **Agrâsana,** n. seat of honour. **Agre-gá,** &c.; see *ágre* below. **Agrêtvan,** mf(*arī*)n. going in front, AV. **Agrôpaharaṇīya,** mfn. that which has to be first or principally supplied, Suśr.

Agratás, ind. in front, before; in the beginning, first, RV. x, 90, 7; VS.; (with gen.) before, in presence of. **Agrataḥ-√1. kṛi,** to place in front or at the head, to consider most important. **Agrataḥ-sara,** mf(*ī*)n. going in front, taking the lead.

Agrimá, mfn. being in front, preceding, prior, furthest advanced; occurring further on or below (in a book, cf. *ágre*); the foremost, RV. v, 44, 9; eldest, principal, L.; (*ā*), f. the fruit Annona Reticulata.

Agriyá, mfn. foremost, principal, RV.; oldest, first-born, RV. i, 13, 10; (*as*), m. elder brother, L.; (*ám*), n. the first-fruits, the best part, RV. iv, 37, 4 and probably ix, 71, 4. **-vat,** mfn.; f. *vatī* (scil. *ṛic*), N. of the hymn Ṛig-veda ix, 62, 25, quoted in Lāṭy.

Agrīya, mfn. best, L.; (*as*), m. elder brother, L.

Ágre, ind. (loc.), see *ágra*. **-gá** [RV. ix, 86, 45] or **-gā́** [TBr. &c.], mfn. going in front or before. **-gū,** mfn. (said of the waters) moving forwards, VS.; ŚBr. **-ṇī́,** m. a leader, VS. **-tana,** mfn. occurring further on, subsequently (in a book). **-dadhús** [MaitrS.] or **-dadhishu** [KapS.] or **-didhishu** [MBh.; Gaut.], m. a man who at his first marriage takes a wife that was married before; (*agre-didhishu* or *-didhishū*), f. a married woman whose elder sister is still unmarried. **-pā́** [RV. iv, 34, 7 & 10] or **-pū́** [VS.; ŚBr.], mfn. having the precedence in drinking. **-bhrū** (√*bhram*), m. wandering in front, Pāṇ. vi, 4, 40, Comm. **-vaṇa,** n. the border of a forest, (gaṇa *rājadantâdi*, q.v.) **-vadhá,** m. hitting or killing whatever is in front, VS. **-sara,** mf(*ī*)n. going in front, preceding; best, L. **-sarika,** m. a leader, L.

Agryá, mf(*ā*)n. foremost, topmost, principal, best; proficient, well versed in (with loc.); intent, closely attentive; (*as*), m. an elder or eldest brother, L.; (*ā*), f. = *tri-phalā*, q. v.; (*am*), n. a roof, L. **-tapas,** m., N. of a Muni, Kathās.

अग्रभण *a-grabhaṇá*, mfn. (√*grabh* = √*grah*), having nothing which can be grasped, RV. i, 116, 5.

A-graha, mfn. = *mukhya* (Comm.), MBh. iii, 14189; BR. propose to read *agra-ha*, destroying the best part; (*as*), m. non-acceptance; a houseless man, i. e. a Vānaprastha, a Brāhman of the third class, L.

A-grāhin, mfn. not taking; not holding (said of a leech and of tools), Suśr.

A-grāhya, mfn. not to be conceived or perceived or obtained or admitted or trusted; to be rejected.

A-grāhyaka, mfn. not to be perceived, impalpable, MBh.

अग्राम्य *a-grāmya*, mfn. not rustic, town-made; not tame, wild.

अग्रि *agrí*, m. a word invented for the explanation of *agní*, ŚBr.

अग्रु *ágru, us*, m. unmarried, RV. v, 44, 7 & vii, 96, 4; AV.; (*ū*), f. a virgin, RV.; AV.; nom. pl. *agrúvas*, poetical N. of the ten fingers, RV.; and also of the seven rivers, RV. i, 191, 14 & iv, 19, 7; cf. Zend *aghru*.

अघ् *agh*, cl. 10. P. *aghayati*, to go wrong, sin, L.

Aghá, mfn. bad, dangerous, RV.; sinful, impure, BhP.; (*as*), m., N. of an Asura, BhP.; (*ám*), n. evil, mishap, RV.; AV.; sin, impurity, Mn. &c.; pain, suffering, L.; (*ā́s*), f. pl. the constellation usually called Maghā, RV. x, 85, 13. **-kṛit,** mfn. doing evil or harm, an evil-doer, AV. **-ghna** or **-nāśaka,** mfn. sin-destroying, expiatory; (*as*), m. 'an expiator,' N. of Vishṇu. **-deva,** m., N. of a man, Rājat. **-marshaṇa,** mfn. 'sin-effacing,' N. of a particular Vedic hymn [RV. x, 190] still used by Brāhmans as a daily prayer, Mn.; Yājñ.; Gaut.;

(*as*), m., N. of the author of that prayer, son of Madhucchandas; (plur.) his descendants, Hariv.; ĀśvŚr. **–mārá**, mfn. fearfully destructive, AV. **–rúd**, mfn. 'howling fearfully,' N. of certain female demons, AV. **–vat**, mfn. sinful; [voc. *aghavan* or *aghos*, q.v.] **–visha** (*aghá-*), mf(*ā*)n. fearfully venomous, AV. **–śaṇsa** (*aghá-*), mfn. wishing evil, wicked, RV.; TBr. **–śaṇsa-hán**, m. slaying the wicked, RV. **–śaṇsin**, mfn. confessing sin, R.; Daś. **–haraṇa**, n. removal of guilt, L. **–hārá**, m. an outrageous robber, SV.; AV. **Aghâśva**, mfn. having a bad or vicious horse, RV. i, 116, 6; (*ás*) [according to NBD. fr. *agha* + √*śvas*], m., N. of a snake, AV. **Aghâsura**, m. Agha, Kaṇsa's general, BhP. **Aghâhan**, n. inauspicious day, ŚāṅkhŚr. **Aghâugha-marshaṇa**, mfn. destroying a whole mass of sins.

Aghalá, mf(*ā*)n. fearful, AV.; ŚBr.; ŚāṅkhBr.

Aghāya, Nom. P. *aghāyáti* (part. °*yát*), to intend to injure, to threaten, RV.; AV.

Aghāyú, mfn. intending to injure, malicious, RV. &c.

अघटमान *a-ghaṭamāna*, mfn. incongruous, incoherent.

अघन *a-ghana*, mfn. not dense or solid.

अघर्म *a-gharma*, mfn. not hot, cool. **–dhāman**, m. 'having cool splendour,' the moon.

अघात *á-ghāta*, m. no injury, no damage, TBr.

A-ghātin, mfn. not fatal, not injurious, harmless.

Á-ghātuka, mfn. not injurious, MaitrS.

अघारिन् *a-ghārín*, mfn. not anointing, AV.

अघासक *a-ghāsaka*, mfn. without food or provisions.

अघृण *a-ghṛiṇa*, mfn. incompassionate.

A-ghṛiṇin, mfn. not contemptuous, not disdainful.

अघोर *á-ghora*, mfn. not terrific; (*as*), m. a euphemistic title of Śiva; a worshipper of Śiva and Durgā; (*ā*), f. the fourteenth day of the dark half of Bhādra, which is sacred to Śiva. **–ghoratará**, mfn. having a form both not terrific and terrific, MaitrS. **–ghora-rūpa**, m. 'having a form or nature both not terrific and terrific,' N. of Śiva, MBh. **–cakshus** (*ághora-*), mfn. not having an evil eye, RV. x, 85, 44. **–pathin** or **-mārga**, m. a particular sect of Śaivas who eat loathsome food and are addicted to disgusting practices. **–pramāṇa**, n. a terrific oath, L.

अघोष *a-ghosha*, *as*, m. (in Gr.) 'non-sonance, absence of all sound or soft murmur,' hard articulation or effort as applied to the hard consonants and Visarga; (mfn.), soundless, hard (as the hard consonants).

अघोस् *aghos*, ind., voc. of *agha-vat*, O sinner! Pāṇ. viii, 3, 1, Sch.; see also Pāṇ. viii, 3, 17 seqq.

अघ्नत् *á-ghnat*, mf(*atī*) n. (√*han*), not killing, not injurious, RV.

Á-ghnya (2, 3) or **a-ghnyá** (2, 3), m. 'not to be killed,' a bull, and (*ā*, *ā́*), f. a cow, RV.; AV.; (*ághnyā*), said of a cloud, RV. x, 46, 3.

अघ्रेय *a-ghreya*, mfn. (√*ghrā*), improper to be smelled at, Mn.

अङ्क् *aṅk*, cl. 1. (connected with √*añc*) Ā. *aṅkate*, *ānaṅke*, *aṅkishyate*, *aṅkitum*, to move in a curve, L.; cl. 10. P. *aṅkayati*, to move in a curve, L.; to mark, stamp, brand.

Aṅká, *as*, m. a hook, RV. i, 162, 13, &c.; part of a chariot (used in the dual), TS.; TBr.; a curve; the curve in the human, especially the female, figure above the hip (where infants sitting astride are carried by mothers, hence often = 'breast' or 'lap'); the side or flank; the body; proximity, place; the bend in the arm; any hook or crooked instrument; a curved line; a numerical figure, cipher; a figure or mark branded on an animal, &c.; any mark, line, stroke, ornament, stigma; a number; the numbers one and nine; a co-efficient; an act of a drama; a drama; a military show or sham-fight; a misdeed, a sin, L. [cf. Gk. ἀγκάς, ἀγκάλη, ἀγκών, ὄγκος, and Lat. *uncus*]. **–karaṇa**, n. the act of marking or stamping. **–kāra**, m. a champion chosen by each side to decide a battle, Bālar.; *aṅkakārī*-√1. *kri*, to choose such a champion, Bālar. **–tantra**, n., N. of a book treating of magical marks or figures. **–dhāraṇā**, f. manner of holding the body, figure, ĀśvŚr. **–parivartana**, n. turning the body, turning on the other side. **–pāda-vrata**, n., N. of a chapter in the Bhavishyottara-Purāṇa. **–pāli**, f. or **-pālikā**, f. embracing, an embrace, L. **–pālī**, f. an embrace; a nurse, L.; the plant (Piring) Medicago Esculenta. **–pāśa**, m. a peculiar concatenation of numerals or numbers. **–pāśa-vyavahāra**, m. the use of that concatenation. **–pāśâdhyāya**, m. the study of that concatenation. **–bandha**, m. branding with a mark (that resembles a headless body), Yājñ. **–bhāj**, mfn. (an infant) carried on the hip; (forced fruit) nearly ripe, early ripe, Kir.; near one's side, in one's possession, close at hand, easy of attainment. **–mukha**, n. introductory act of a drama giving a clue to the whole plot. **–loḍya**, m. ginger, Ciñcoḍa or Ciñcoṭaka. **–vidyā**, f. science of numbers, arithmetic. **Aṅkâṅká**, n. water, VS. **Aṅkâvatāra**, m. the close of a dramatic act (preparing the audience for the following one).

Aṅkati, *is*, m. wind, L.; fire, L.; Brahmā, L.; a Brāhman who maintains the sacred fire, L.; N. of a teacher of the Sāma-veda.

Aṅkana, *am*, n. the act of marking, stamping, branding, ciphering, writing; (mfn.), marking.

A'ṅkas, *as*, n. a curve or bend, RV. iv, 40, 4; cf. Gk. ἄγκος.

Aṅkasá, *am*, n. the flanks or the trappings of a horse, RV. iv, 40, 3.

Aṅkita, mfn. marked, branded; numbered, counted, calculated.

Aṅkín, mfn. possessing a hook, RV. iii, 45, 4; AV. &c.; (*ī*), m. a small drum, L.; (*inī*), f. a number of marks, (gaṇa *khalâdi*, q. v.)

Aṅkī, f. a small drum, L.

Aṅkuṭa and **aṅkuḍaka**, *as*, m. a key, L.

Aṅkupá, *am*, n. water, VS.

Aṅkura, *as*, m. a sprout, shoot, blade; a swelling, a tumour, Suśr.; a hair, L.; blood, L.; water, L.

Aṅkuraka, *as*, m. a nest, L.

Aṅkurita, mfn. sprouted.

Aṅkuśá, *as*, *am*, m. n. a hook, especially an elephant-driver's hook; (*ā*) or (*ī*), f. one of the twenty-four Jaina goddesses, L. [cf. Gk. ἄγκιστρον; Germ. *Angel*]. **–graha**, m. an elephant-driver. **–durdhara**, m. a restive elephant.

Aṅkuśita, mfn. urged on by the hook.

Aṅkuśín, mfn. having a hook, laying hold of with a hook, RV. x, 34, 7.

Aṅkūyát, mfn. (fr. a Nom. *aṅkūya*, related to *aṅka*), moving tortuously (to escape), RV. vi, 15, 17.

Aṅkūra, *as*, m. a sprout, L. See *aṅkura*.

Aṅkūsha, *as*, *am*, m. n. an ichneumon, Uṇ. Comm.; cf. *aṅgūsha*.

Aṅkya, mfn. fit or proper to be marked or counted; (*as*), m. a small drum [cf. *aṅkī*], L.

अङ्कार *aṅkāra*, *as*, m.? diminution in music, L.

अङ्कोट *aṅkoṭa*, *aṅkoṭha*, *aṅkola*, *aṅkolla*, *aṅkolaka*, *as*, m. the plant Alangium Hexapetalum. **Aṅkolla-sāra**, m. 'essence of Aṅkolla,' a poison prepared from the plant Aṅkolla, &c.

अङ्कोलिका *aṅkolikā*, f. (a corruption of *aṅka-pālikā*, q. v.), an embrace, L.

अङ्क्त्वा *aṅktvā*, ind. p. (√*añj*), having besmeared, Pāṇ. vii, 2, 62, Sch.

अङ्ख् *aṅkh*, cl. 10. P. (p. *aṅkhayát*), to stir up, mix, ŚBr.

अङ्ग् *aṅg*, cl. 1. P. *aṅgati*, *ānaṅga*, *aṅgitum*, to go (cf. √*ag*); cl. 10. P. *aṅgayati*, to mark (cf. √*aṅk*), L.

Aṅgana, *am*, n. walking, L.; 'place to walk in,' yard; see s. v.

अङ्ग 1. *aṅgá*, ind. a particle implying attention, assent or desire, and sometimes impatience; it may be rendered by well; indeed, true; please; rather; quick; *kim aṅga*, how much rather!

Aṅgī (for *aṅga* in comp. with √1. *kri* and its derivatives). **–karaṇa**, n. act of taking the side of, assenting, agreeing, promising. **–kāra**, m. agreement, promise. **–**√**1. kṛi**, to take the side of; to agree to, assent, promise, confess. **–kṛita**, mfn. agreed to, promised. **–kṛiti**, f. agreement, promise.

अङ्ग 2. *áṅga*, *am*, n. (√*am*, Uṇ.), a limb of the body; a limb, member; the body; a subordinate division or department, especially of a science, as the six Vedâṅgas; hence the number six; N. of the chief sacred texts of the Jainas; a limb or subdivision of Mantra or counsel (said to be five, viz. 1. *karmaṇām ārambhôpāyaḥ*, means of commencing operations; 2. *purusha-dravya-sampad*, providing men and materials; 3. *deśa-kāla-vibhāga*, distribution of place and time; 4. *vipatti-pratīkāra*, counteraction of disaster; 5. *kārya-siddhi*, successful accomplishment; whence *mantra* is said to be *pañcâṅga*); any subdivision, a supplement; (in Gr.) the base of a word, but in the strong cases only, Pāṇ. i, 4, 13 seqq.; anything inferior or secondary, anything immaterial or unessential, see *aṅga-tā*; (in rhetoric) an illustration; (in the drama) the whole of the subordinate characters; an expedient; a mental organ, the mind, L.; (*as*), m. sg. or (*ās*), m. pl., N. of Bengal proper or its inhabitants; (sg.), N. of a king of Aṅga; (mfn.), having members or divisions, L.; contiguous, L. **–kartana**, n. cutting off a limb. **–karman**, n. or **-kriyā**, f. a supplementary sacrificial act. **–kashāyá**, m. the essence of the body (said of the semen virile), ŚBr. **–graha**, m. 'limb-seizure,' spasm, Suśr. **–ja**, mfn. produced from or on the body; ornamental, L.; produced by a supplementary ceremony; (*as*), m. a son, L.; hair of the head, L.; the god of love, L.; intoxicating passion, L.; drunkenness, L.; a disease, L.; (*ā*), f. a daughter; (*am*), n. blood. **–janus**, m. a son. **–jāta**, mfn. produced from or on the body; ornamental; produced by a supplementary ceremony. **–jvará**, mfn. causing fever, AV. **–tā**, f. or **-tva**, n. a state of subordination or dependance; the being of secondary importance, the being unessential. **–da**, m., N. of a brother of Rāma; of a son of Gada; of an ape, son of Bālin; (*ā*), f. the female elephant of the south; (*am*), n. a bracelet worn on the upper arm. **–dvīpa**, m. one of the six minor Dvīpas. **–nyāsa**, m. ceremony of touching certain parts of the body. **–pāli**, f. an embrace, L.; see *aṅka-pāli*. **–prāyaścitta**, n. expiation of bodily impurity, especially that arising from death in a family. **–bhū**, m. son, Śiś. **–bhedá**, mfn. causing rheumatism, AV. **–marda** or **-mardaka** or **-mardin**, m. a servant who shampoos his master's body; *aṅgamarda* also rheumatism, Car. **–marsha**, m. pain in the limbs, rheumatism. **–marsha-praśamana**, n. alleviation of rheumatism. **–m-ejayatva** (*aṅgam-ej*°), n. the trembling of the body, Yogas. **–yashṭi**, f. a slender form, fairy-figure. **–yāga**, m. a subordinate sacrificial act. **–rakta**, m. the plant Guṇḍārocanī. **–rakshaṇī** or **-rakshiṇī**, f. 'body-protector,' a coat of mail, L. **–rāga**, m. application of unguents or cosmetics to the body (especially after bathing); scented cosmetic. **–rāj** or **-rāja**, m., N. of Karṇa, king of Aṅga. **–rājya**, n. kingdom of Aṅga. **–ruha**, mfn. 'growing on the body,' hair, wool, down, &c. **–lipi**, f. written character of Aṅga. **–loka**, m. the country Aṅga. **–loḍya**, m. a sort of grass; ginger, or its root. **–vāk-pāṇi-mat**, mfn. possessing mind(?), speech, and hands. **–vikṛiti**, f. change of bodily appearance, collapse; fainting, apoplexy. **–vikshepa**, m. gesticulation; movement of the limbs and arms; a kind of dance. **–vidyā**, f. knowledge of lucky or unlucky marks on the body, Chiromantia, Mn. vi, 50, &c. **–vaikṛita**, n. a wink, nod, sign. **–śás**, ind. into parts, ŚBr. **–saṃskāra**, m. or **-saṃskriyā**, f. embellishment of person, bathing, perfuming and adorning the body. **–saṃhati**, f. compactness of limb, symmetry of body. **–saṃhitā**, f. the Saṃhitā or phonetic relation between consonants and vowels in the body of a word, TS. Prāt. **–saṅga**, m. 'bodily contact,' coition, L. **–skandha**, m. a subdivision of a science. **–sparśa**, m. bodily contact. **–hāra** [Kathās.] or **-hāri** [L.], m. gesticulation. **–hīna**, mfn. limbless, mutilated; incorporeal; (*as*), m. Kāmadeva. **Aṅgâṅgi**, ind. jointly or reciprocally, related as one limb to another or to the body. **Aṅgâṅgi-tā**, f. mutual relation or correlation as between the limbs, or a limb and the body, or between subordinate and the principal, or principal and accessory. **Aṅgâṅgi-bhāva**, m. correlation between the limbs of a body; the mutual relation or correlation of the different limbs or members of anything, as in a simile or comparison between the principal parts or features of any object and those of the thing compared to it. **Aṅgâdhipa,** m. Karṇa, the king of Aṅga. **Aṅgânukūla,** mfn. agreeable to the body, Megh. **Aṅgânulepana,** n. anointing the body. **Aṅgâpūrva,** n. effect of a secondary sacrificial act, L. **Aṅgêśvara,** m. the king of Aṅga. **Aṅge-shṭhā,** mfn. situated in a member or in the body, AV. **Aṅgôñcha,** m. or **aṅgôñchana,** n. a towel, L.

Aṅgaka, *am,* n. a limb, member, body; (*ikā*), f. a bodice, a jacket, L.

Aṅgin, mfn. having limbs, corporeal, having subordinate parts, principal; having expedients.

Aṅgīya, mfn. relating to the Aṅga country, (gaṇa *gahâdi,* q. v.)

Áṅgya (3), mfn. belonging to the limbs, RV. i, 191, 7.

अङ्गण *aṅgaṇa, am,* n. See *aṅgana.*

अङ्गति *aṅgati, is,* m. (√*ag*), fire, L.; a Brāhman who maintains a sacred fire, L.; Brahmā, L.; Vishṇu, L.; cf. *aṅkati.*

अङ्गन *aṅgana, am,* n. (√*aṅg,* q.v.), the act of walking, L.; place to walk in, yard, court, area; (*ā*), f. 'a woman with well-rounded limbs,' any woman or female; (in astron.) Virgo; the female elephant of the north. **Aṅganā-gaṇa,** m. a number of women. **Aṅganā-jana,** m. a female person. **Aṅganā-priya,** m. 'dear to women,' N. of the tree Jonesia Asoca.

Aṅgaṇa, *am,* n. a yard, court, area.

अङ्गभ *aṅgabha,* m. a kind of rice, L.

अङ्गव *aṅgava, as,* m. dried fruit, L.

अङ्गस् *aṅgas, as,* n. (√*aṅj,* Uṇ.), a bird, L.

अङ्गार *áṅgāra, as,* m., (rarely) *am,* n. (√*ag* or *aṅg,* Uṇ., cf. *agni*), charcoal, either heated or not heated; (*as*), m. the planet Mars; N. of a prince of the Maruts, Hariv.; the plant Hitāvalī; (*ās*), m. pl., N. of a people and country, VP. [cf. Lith. *angli-s;* Russ. *ŭgolj;* also Germ. *Kohle;* Old Germ. *col* and *colo;* Eng. *coal*]. **-kārin** and **-krit** [Hpar.], m. charcoal-burner. **-kushṭhaka,** m. the plant Hitāvalī. **-dhānī** or **-dhānikā,** f. a portable fire-place. **-paripācita,** n. roasted food. **-parṇa,** m., N. of Citraratha, chief of the Gandharvas, MBh.; (*ī*), f. Clerodendron Siphonanthus. **-pātrī,** f. a portable fire-place. **-pushpa,** m. the plant Iṅgudī (Vulg. Ingua). **-mañjarī** or **-mañjī,** f. the shrub Cesalpinia Banducella. **-vallarī** or **-vallī,** f. (various plants), Galedupa Arborea; Ovieda Verticallata; Bhārgī; Guñjā. **-śakaṭī,** f. a portable fire-place on wheels. **-setu,** m., N. of a prince, father of Gāndhāra. **Aṅgārâvakshayaṇa,** n. an instrument for extinguishing coals, ŚBr. xiv.

Aṅgāraka, *as,* m. charcoal; heated charcoal; the planet Mars; Tuesday; N. of a prince of Sauvīra; of a Rudra; of an Asura, Kathās.; N. of two plants, Eclipta (or Verbesina) Prostrata, and white or yellow Amaranth; (*am*), n. a medicated oil in which turmeric and other vegetable substances have been boiled. **-dina,** m. n. a festival of Mars on the fourteenth of the latter half of Caitra. **-maṇi,** m. coral (amber). **-vāra,** m. Tuesday.

Aṅgārakita, mfn. charred, roasted, burnt, (gaṇa *tārakâdi,* q. v.)

Aṅgāri, *is,* f. a portable fire-place, L.

Aṅgārikā, f. the stalk of the sugar-cane; the bud of the Kiṅśuka or Butea Frondosa.

Aṅgārita, mfn. charred, roasted, (gaṇa *tārakâdi,* q. v.); 'burnt,' a kind of food not to be accepted by Jaina ascetics, Jain.; (*ā*), f. a portable fire-place, L.; a bud, L.; N. of a creeper, L.; of a river, L.; (*am*), n. the early blossom of the Kiṅśuka.

Aṅgārin, mfn. heated by the sun, though no longer exposed to its rays, VarBṛS. [generally f. (*iṇī*), scil. *diś,* the region just left by the sun]; N. of a creeper.

Aṅgārīya, mfn. fit for making charcoal, Pāṇ. v, 1, 12, Sch.

Aṅgāryā, f. a heap of charcoal, (gaṇa *pāśâdi,* q.v.)

अङ्गिका *aṅgikā.* See *aṅgaka.*

अङ्गिर् *aṅgir, ir,* m. (√*aṅg,* Uṇ.), N. of a Ṛishi, who received the Brahmavidyā from Atharvan, and imparted it to Satyavāha, the teacher of Aṅgiras, MuṇḍUp.

Aṅgira, *as,* m. = *áṅgiras,* RV. i, 83, 4 & iv, 51, 4; MBh.; Yājñ.; (cf. Gk. ἄγγελος and ἄγγαρος.)

Áṅgiras, *ās,* m., N. of a Ṛishi, author of the hymns of RV. ix, of a code of laws, and of a treatise on astronomy (he is said by some to have been born from Brahmā's mouth, and to have been the husband of Smṛiti, of Śraddhā, of two daughters of Maitreya, of several daughters of Daksha, &c.; he is considered as one of the seven Ṛishis of the first Manvantara, as a Prajāpati, as a teacher of the Brahmavidyā, which he had learnt from Satyavāha, a descendant of Bharadvāja, &c. Among his sons, the chief is Agni, others are Saṃvarta, Utathya, and Bṛihaspati; among his daughters are mentioned Sinīvālī, Kuhū, Rākā, Anumati, and Akūpārā; but the Ṛicas or Vedic hymns, the manes of Havishmat, and mankind itself are styled his offspring. In astronomy he is the planet Jupiter, and a star in Ursa Major); N. of Agni, MBh.; (*asas*), m. pl. descendants of Aṅgiras or of Agni (mostly personifications of luminous objects); the hymns of the Atharva-veda, TS.; priests who by using the magical formulas of those hymns protect the sacrifice against the effects of inauspicious accidents. **-tama** (*áṅgiras-*), mfn. having the luminous quality of the Aṅgirasas in the highest degree, said of Agni and of Ushas, RV. **-vát,** ind. like Aṅgiras, RV.; VS.; (*áṅgiras-vat*), mfn. connected with or accompanied by the Aṅgirasas, RV.; VS.

Aṅgirasa, *as,* m. an enemy of Vishṇu in his incarnation of Paraśurāma.

Aṅgirasām-ayana, *am,* n. a Sattra sacrifice.

अङ्गी *aṅgī.* See 1. *aṅga.*

अङ्गुरि *aṅgúri, is,* or *aṅgurī* [L.], f. (for *aṅguli,* q. v.), a finger, AV.; a toe; (cf. *an-aṅgurí, pañcâṅguri, sv-aṅguri.*)

Aṅgurīya or °**yaka,** *as, am,* m. n. a finger-ring.

अङ्गुल *aṅgula, as,* m. (√*ag* or *aṅg*), a finger; the thumb; a finger's breadth, a measure equal to eight barley-corns, twelve aṅgulas making a vitasti or span, and twenty-four a hasta or cubit; (in astron.) a digit, or twelfth part; N. of the sage Cāṇakya, L. **-pramāṇa** or **-māna,** n. the measure or length of an aṅgula; (mfn.), having the length of an aṅgula.

Aṅgulaka, ifc. = *aṅgula,* i. e. so many aṅgulas or fingers long.

Aṅgúli, *is,* (or *aṅgulī*), f. a finger; a toe; the thumb; the great toe; the finger-like tip of an elephant's trunk; the measure aṅgula. **-toraṇa,** n. a sectarial mark on the forehead consisting of three fingers or lines shaped like an arch or doorway (*toraṇa*), drawn with sandal or the ashes of cow-dung. **-tra,** n. a finger-protector, a contrivance like a thimble (used by archers to protect the thumb or finger from being injured by the bowstring), R. &c.; *-vat,* mfn. provided with it. **-trāṇa,** n. = *-tra,* R. **-mukha** or **aṅguli-mukha,** n. the tip of the finger, Śiś. **-mudrā** or **-mudrikā,** f. a seal-ring. **-moṭana,** n. snapping or cracking the fingers. **-veshṭaka,** m. or **-veshṭana,** n. a glove (?). **-shaṅga,** m. contact of the fingers; act of fingering; (mfn.), sticking to the fingers. **-saṃdeśa,** m. snapping or cracking the fingers as a sign. **-sphoṭana,** n. snapping or cracking the fingers. **Aṅguli-pañcaka,** n. the five fingers. **Aṅguli-parvan,** n. a finger-joint. **Aṅguli-sambhūta,** m. 'produced on the finger,' a finger nail. **Aṅguly-agrá,** n. the tip of the finger, ŚBr. **Aṅguly-ādi** (*aṅgulī-*), a gaṇa of Pāṇ. (v, 3, 108).

Aṅgulīya or **aṅgulīyaka,** *am,* n. a finger-ring; also *aṅgulīka,* L.

Aṅgúshṭha, *as,* m. the thumb; the great toe; a thumb's breadth, usually regarded as equal to an *aṅgula.* **-mātra,** mf(*ī*)n. or **-mātraka,** mf(*ikā*)n. having the length or size of a thumb.

Aṅgushṭhikā, f., N. of a shrub.

Aṅgushṭhya, *as,* m. belonging to the thumb (the thumb nail).

अङ्गूष *aṅgūsha, as,* m. (√*aṅg* or *ag*), 'moving rapidly,' an ichneumon; an arrow.

अङ्गोषिन् *aṅgoshín,* mfn. 'resonant (?), praiseworthy (?),' N. of the Soma, SV.

अङ्ग्य *áṅgya.* See col. 1.

अङ्घ् *aṅgh,* cl. 1. Ā. *aṅghate, ānaṅghe,* to go, set out, set about, commence, L.; to hasten, L.; to speak hastily, blame, L.

Aṅgha (not in use, but equivalent to *aghá*), evil, sin, L. **Aṅghâri,** m. 'an enemy to sin or evil,' N. of a celestial guard of the Soma, VS. [blazing, T.]

Aṅghas, n. sin, Hariv.

Áṅghri, *is,* m. a foot; foot of a seat; the root of a tree [cf. *aṅhri*]. **-nāmaka,** m. or **-nāman,** n. a synonym of *aṅghri,* means always foot as well as root. **-pa,** m. (drinking with the foot or root), a tree. **-parṇī** or **-valli** or **-vallikā,** f. the plant Hedysarum Lagopodioides. **-pāna,** mfn. sucking the foot or toes (as an infant), L. **-skandha,** m. the ancle.

अच् 1. *ac* (connected with √*añc,* q. v.), cl. 1. P. Ā. *ácati, áñcati,* °*te, ānañca,* °*ce,* to go, move, tend; to honour; to make round or curved; to request, ask, L.; to speak indistinctly, L. See 2. *acita, ácishṭu.*

अच् 2. *ac,* a technical term for all the vowels, Pāṇ. **Aj-anta,** mfn. ending in a vowel.

अचक्र *a-cakrá,* mfn. having no wheels; not wanting wheels, i. e. moving by itself, RV.

अचक्षुस् *a-cakshus, us,* n. a bad eye, no eye; (mfn.), blind. **A-cakshur-vishaya,** mfn. not or no longer within reach of the eyes, invisible. **Acakshush-ṭva,** n. blindness.

A-cakshúshka, mfn. destitute of eyes, ŚBr. xiv; blind.

अचण्ड *a-caṇḍa,* mfn. not of a hot temper, gentle, tractable; (*ī*), f. a tractable cow.

अचतुर *a-catura,* mfn. destitute of four, having less than four; not cunning, not dexterous.

अचन्द्र *a-candra,* mfn. moonless.

अचपल *a-capala,* mfn. not oscillating, not wavering, not fickle; unmovable, steady.

A-cāpalya, *am,* n. freedom from unsteadiness.

अचर *a-cara* or *á-carat* [RV.], mfn. immovable.

अचरम *á-carama,* mfn. not last, not least; said of the Maruts, RV. v, 58, 5.

अचर्मक *a-carmáka,* mfn. having no skin, TS.

अचल *a-cala,* mf(*ā*)n. not moving, immovable; (*as*), m. a mountain, rock; a bolt or pin; the number seven; N. of Śiva and of the first of the nine deified persons, called 'white Balas' among the Jainas; of a Devarshi, VP.; (*ā*), f. the earth; one of the ten degrees which are to be ascended by a Bodhisattva before becoming a Buddha. **-kīlā,** f. the earth. **-tvish,** m. the Kokila or Indian cuckoo. **-dhṛiti,** f. a metre of four lines, of sixteen short syllables each, also called Gītyāryā. **-pura,** n., N. of a town, Jain. **-bhrātṛi,** m., N. of a Brāhman from Oude, who became one of the eleven heads of Gaṇas among the Jainas. **-mati,** m., N. of a Māraputra. **-śreshṭha,** m. chief of mountains. **Acalâdhipa,** m. 'king of mountains,' the Himālaya. **Acalā-saptamī,** f., N. of a book in the Bhavishyottara-Purāṇa.

अचारु *a-cāru,* mfn. not pretty, Pāṇ.

अचित् *a-cít,* mfn. without understanding, RV.; irreligious, bad, RV.; (the NBD. suggests to take *a-cit* as a f. 'not-knowledge;' Sāy. sometimes explains by √*ci,* 'neglecting the Agnicayana, irreligious;') *a-cit,* f. not-spirit, matter, Sarvad.

Á-cikitvas, *ān, ushī, at,* not knowing, ignorant of, RV. i, 164, 6.

A-cítta, mfn. unnoticed, unexpected; not an object of thought; inconceivable, RV.; destitute of intellect or sense. **-pājas** and **-manas** (*ácitta-*), m., N. of two Ṛishis, MaitrS.; Kāṭh.

Á-citti, *is,* f. want of sense, infatuation, RV.; AV.; (figuratively said of) an infatuated man, RV. iv, 2, 11; VS.

अचित 1. *á-cita,* mfn. not heaped up.

अचित 2. *acita,* mfn. (√*ac*), gone, L.

Ácishṭu, mfn. moving, VS.

अचित्र *a-citrá,* mfn. not variegated, undistinguishable; (*ám*), n. undistinguishableness, darkness, RV. iv, 51, 3 & vi, 49, 11.

अचिन्ता *a-cintā,* f. thoughtlessness.

A-cintita, mfn. not thought of, unexpected, disregarded.

A-cintya, mfn. inconceivable, surpassing thought, MaitrS. &c.; (*as*), m., N. of Śiva. **-karman**, mfn. performing inconceivable actions. **-rūpa**, mfn. having an inconceivable form.

अचिर *a-cira*, mfn. not of long duration, brief; instantaneous, recent; (*am, āt, eṇa*), ind. not long, not for long; not long ago; soon, speedily; (*ā*), f. the mother of the Jaina saint Śānti. **-dyuti** or **-prabhā**, f. lightning. **-prasūtā**, f. 'having recently brought forth,' a cow that has recently calved. **-bhās**, f. lightning, Śak. **-mṛita**, mfn. recently deceased. **-rocis**, f. or **acirâṅśu**, m. or **acirâbhā**, f. lightning.

अचिष्ट *ácishṭu*. See 2. *acita*.

अचेतन *a-cetana*, mfn. without consciousness, inanimate; unconscious, insensible, senseless, fainting, &c.

A-cetás, mfn. imprudent, RV.; unconscious, insensible.

A-cetāna, mfn. thoughtless, infatuated, RV. vii, 4, 7.

A-caitanya, *am*, n. unconsciousness; insensibility; senselessness, want of spirituality; that which is destitute of consciousness, matter.

अचेष्ट *a-ceshṭa*, mfn. effortless, motionless. **-tā**, f. loss of motion from fainting, &c.

अचोदत् *a-codát*, mfn. (√*cud*), not driving or impelling, RV. v, 44, 2.

A-codás, mfn. free from compulsion or external stimulus, spontaneous, RV. ix, 79, 1.

अच्छ 1. *a-ccha*, mfn. (fr. *a*+*cha* for *chad* or *chāyā*, √*chad*), 'not shaded,' 'not dark,' pellucid, transparent, clear; (*as*), m. a crystal, L. **Acchôda**, mfn. having clear water; (*ā*), f., N. of a river; (*am*), n., N. of a lake in the Himālaya formed by the river Acchodā.

A-cchāyá, mfn. without shadow, casting no shadow, RV. x, 27, 14; ŚBr. xiv.

अच्छ 2. *accha*, *as*, m. (corruption of *ṛiksha*), a bear. **-bhalla**, m. a bear, Bālar. (cf. *bhalla*).

अच्छ 3. *áccha* (so at the end of a pāda), or usually *ácchā*, ind., Ved. to, towards (governing acc. and rarely the locative). It is a kind of separable preposition or prefix to verbs and verbal derivatives, as in the following.

A'cchā-√i or **ácchā-√gam** or **ácchā-√car**, to attain, go towards, RV. &c.

A'cchā-√2. dru, to run near, RV. iii, 14, 3.

A'cchā-√dhanv, to run towards, RV. iii, 53, 4.

A'cchā-√naksh, to go towards, approach, RV. vi, 22, 5.

A'cchā-√1. naś, to come near, RV.

A'cchā-√nī, to lead towards or to, RV.

A'cchā-√4. nu, to call out to, to cheer, RV.

A'cchā-√pat [ŚBr.] and Caus. P. *-patayati* [RV. v, 45, 9], to fly towards.

Acchā-√brū, to invite to come near, PBr.

A'cchā-√yā or **áccha-√yā**, to approach, RV.; TS.

A'cchā-√vac, to invite, RV.

Acchā-vāká, m. 'the inviter,' title of a particular priest or Ṛitvij, one of the sixteen required to perform the great sacrifices with the Soma juice.

Acchāvākīya, mfn. referring to the acchāvāka; containing the word acchāvāka, Pāṇ. v, 2, 59, Sch.; (*am*), n. the state or work of the acchāvāka, Pāṇ. v, 1, 135, Sch.

A'cchā-√vañc, Pass. *-vacyáte*, to extend itself towards, to go towards, RV. i, 142, 4.

A'cchā-√vad, to salute, RV. &c.

A'cchā-√vṛit (Opt. Ā. 1. sg. *-vavṛitīya*), to cause to come near, RV. i, 186, 10.

A'cchā-√sṛi, to flow near, RV. ix, 92, 2.

A'cchā-√syand, Caus. to flow near (aor. *-ásishyadat*), RV. ix, 81, 2: Intens. to cause to flow near (part. nom. sg. m. *-sánishyadat*), RV. ix, 110, 4.

A'cchêta, mfn. approached, attained, VS.

Acchêtya, mfn. to be approached, ĀpŚr.

A'cchôkti, *is*, f. invitation, RV.

अच्छिद्र *á-cchidra*, mfn. free from clefts or flaws, unbroken, uninterrupted, uninjured; (*am*), n. unbroken or uninjured condition, an action free from defect or flaw; (*eṇa*), ind. uninterruptedly, without break from first to last. **-kāṇḍa**, n., N. of a chapter of the Taittirīya-Brāhmaṇa. **Acchidrôti**, mfn. affording perfect protection, RV. i, 145, 3. **A'cchidrôdhnī**, f. (a cow) having a faultless udder, RV. x, 133, 7.

A'-cchidyamāna, mfn. uncut, uncurtailed, AV.; not fragile (a needle), RV. ii, 32, 4.

A'-cchinna, mfn. uncut, uncurtailed, uninjured; undivided, inseparable. **-pattra** (*ácchinna-*), mf(*ā*)n. (said of goddesses, of a bird, of an altar shaped like a bird), having the wings uncurtailed, uninjured, RV. i, 22, 11; VS.; having uninjured leaves, VS. **-parṇá**, mfn. having uninjured leaves, AV.

A-cchedika, mfn. not fit or needing to be cut, Pāṇ. vi, 2, 155, Sch.

A-cchedya, mfn. improper or impossible to be cut, indivisible.

अच्छुप्ता *a-cchuptā*, f., N. of one of the sixteen Vidyādevīs of the Jainas.

अच्छुरिका *acchurikā* or *acchurī*, f. discus, wheel, BhP.

अच्युत *á-cyuta* or *a-cyutá*, mfn. not fallen; firm, solid; imperishable, permanent; not leaking or dripping; (*as*), m., N. of Vishṇu; of Kṛishṇa; of a physician; the plant Morinda Tinctoria; N. of a gift to Agni, ŚBr. **-kshít**, m. 'having solid ground,' N. of Soma, VS. **-cyút**, mfn. shaking firm objects (said of the thunderer Indra), RV.; (said of a drum), AV. **-ja**, *ās*, m. pl. a class of Jaina deities. **-jallakin**, m., N. of a commentator of the Amara-Kosha. **-danta** or **acyutanta**, m., N. of the ancestor of a warrior tribe called Ācyutadanti or Ācyutanti (though possibly these refer to two distinct tribes). **-pājas** and **-manas** (*ácyuta-*), m., N. of two Maharshis, TĀr. **-mūrti**, m., N. of Vishṇu. **-rush**, f. inveterate hatred. **-vāsa**, m. the sacred fig-tree, Ficus Religiosa; *acyutâvāsa*, id., T. **-sthala**, n., N. of a place in the Pañjāb, MBh. **Acyutâgraja**, m. (Vishṇu's elder brother), Balarāma; Indra. **A'cyutôpādhyāya**, m. = *acyuta-jallakin*, q. v.

अज *aj*, cl. 1. P. (defect., supplemented fr. √*vī*), *ájati, ājīt, ajitum*, to drive, propel, throw, cast: Desid. *ajijishati*, to be desirous of driving [cf. Gk. ἄγω; Lat. *ago*].

1. **Ajá**, *as*, m. a drove, troop (of Maruts), AV.; a driver, mover, instigator, leader; N. of Indra, of Rudra, of one of the Maruts [*ajá ékapād*, RV., and *ajá éka-pāda*, AV.], of Agni, of the sun, of Brahmā, of Vishṇu, of Śiva, of Kāma (cf. 2. *a-ja*); the leader of a flock; a he-goat, ram [cf. Gk. αἴξ, αἰγός; Lith. *ożys*]; the sign Aries; the vehicle of Agni; beam of the sun (Pūshan); N. of a descendant of Viśvāmitra, and of Daśaratha's or Dīrghabāhu's father; N. of a mineral substance; of a kind of rice; of the moon; (*ās*), m. pl., N. of a people, RV. vii, 18, 19; of a class of Ṛishis, MBh.; (*ā*), f., N. of Prakṛiti, of Māyā or Illusion, see *a-jā* (s. v. 2. *a-já*); a she-goat; N. of a plant whose bulbs resemble the udder of a goat, Suśr. **-karṇa**, m. a goat's ear; the tree Terminalia Alata Tomentosa. **-karṇaka**, m. the Śāl-tree, Shorea Robusta. **-kūlā**, f., N. of a town of the Bodhis. **-kshīrá**, n. goat's milk, MaitrS.; cf. Pāṇ. vi, 3, 63, Sch. **-gandhā** or **-gandhikā**, f. 'smelling like a he-goat,' shrubby basil, Ocymum Gratissimum. **-gandhinī**, f. a plant, = *aja-śṛiṅgī*, q. v. **-gará**, m. ('goat-swallower'), a huge serpent, boa constrictor, AV. &c.; N. of an Asura; (*ī*), f., N. of a plant. **-gallikā**, f. 'goat's cheek,' an infantile disease. **-jīvana** or **-jīvika**, m. 'who lives by goats,' a goat-herd. **-tā**, f. a multitude of goats; the being a goat. **-tvá** [TS.; cf. Pāṇ. vi, 3, 64, Sch.] or **ajā-tva**, n. the being a goat. **-daṇḍī**, f. a plant, = *brahmadaṇḍī*. **-devatā**, *ās*, f. pl. the 25th lunar mansion. **-nāmaka**, m. 'named Aja or Vishṇu,' a mineral substance. **-pa**, m. a goat-herd. **-patha**, m. 'goat's road,' probably = *aja-vīthī*, q. v. **-pada** or **-pāda**, mfn. goat-footed. **-pād**, m., N. of the divinity called *Aja ekapād*. **-pārśva**, m. 'having black sides like a goat,' N. of Śvetakarṇa's son Rājīvalocana. **-pālá**, m. a goat-herd, VS.; N. of Daśaratha's father. **-babhru** (*ajá-*), m. said to be the father or origin of a medical plant, AV. v, 5, 8. **-bhaksha**, m. 'goat's food,' the plant Varvūra. **-māyu** (*ajá-*), m. bleating like a goat (a frog), RV. vii, 103, 6 & 10. **-māra**, m., N. of a tribe or prince, (gaṇa *kurv-ādi*, q. v.) **-mīḍha** or **-mīlha**, m., N. of a son of Suhotra (author of some Vedic hymns, RV. iv, 43 & 44); of a grandson of Suhotra; of Yudhishṭhira. **-mukha**, mfn. goat-faced; (*ī*), f., N. of a Rākshasī. **-meru**, N. of a place, Ajmīr(?). **-moda**, m. or **-modā** or **-modikā**, f. 'goat's delight,' N. of various plants, common Carroway, the species called Ajwaen (Ligusticum Ajwaen), a species of Parsley, Apium Involucratum. **-rshabhá** (*ṛish*), m. a he-goat, ŚBr. **-lambana**, n. antimony. **-loman**, m. or **-lomī**, f. Cowage, Carpopogon Pruriens; (*á*), n. goat's hair, ŚBr. &c. **-vasti**, m., N. of a tribe, (gaṇa *gṛishty-ādi* and *śubhrâdi*, q. v.); (*ayas*), m. pl. the members of that tribe, (gaṇa *yaskâdi*, q. v.) **-vāha**, m., N. of a district. **-vīthī**, f. 'goat's road,' N. of one of the three divisions of the southern path, or one of the three paths in which the sun, moon, and planets move, comprehending the asterisms *mūla, pūrvâshāḍha*, and *uttarâshāḍha*. **-śṛiṅgī**, f. 'goat's horn,' the shrub Odina Wodier, used as a charm and as a remedy for sore eyes, AV. (its fruit resembles a goat's horn). **-stunda**, n., N. of a town, Pāṇ. vi, 1, 155. **-hā**, f. = *a-jaḍā*, q. v.; the plant Ālkuśī, T. **Ajā-kṛipāṇīya**, mfn. like the goat and shears in the fable, Pāṇ. v, 3, 106, Sch. **Ajā-kshīrá**, n. goat's milk, ŚBr. &c.; cf. *aja-kshīrá*. **Ajā-gala**, m. goat's neck. **Ajāgala-stana**, m. nipple or fleshy protuberance on the neck of goats, an emblem of any useless or worthless object or person. **Ajā-jīva**, m. 'who lives by goats,' a goat-herd. **Ajā-taulvali**, m., N. of a Muni who lived on the milk of goats (an example of compounds in which the middle term is left out, gaṇa *Śākapārthivâdi*, q. v.) **Ajâda**, m. 'goat-eater,' the ancestor of a warrior tribe, Pāṇ. iv, 1, 171. **Ajâdanī**, f. a species of prickly night-shade. **Ajâdi**, a gaṇa of Pāṇ. (iv, 1, 4). **Ajântrī**, f. the pot-herb Convolvulus Argenteus. **Ajā-payas**, n. goat's milk. **Ajā-pālaka**, mfn. tending goats; (*as*), m. a goat-herd, L. **Ajâvi**, m. pl. (*ajâváyas*, ŚBr.) or **ajâviká**, n. sg. goats and sheep, small cattle. **Ajâśva**, n. goats and horses, Yājñ.; (*as*), m. Pūshan or the Sun (having goats for horses), RV. **Ajâikapād**, m., N. of Vishṇu; of one of the eleven Rudras; cf. 1. *ajá*. **Ajâiḍaka**, n. goats and rams, (gaṇa *gavâśvâdi*, q. v.)

Ajaka, *as*, m., N. of a descendant of Purūravas; of a king of Magadha; (*akā* or *ikā*), f. a young she-goat; a disease of the pupil of the eye (small reddish tumours compared to kids, protruding through the transparent cornea and discharging pus). **Ajakā-jāta**, n. the above disease.

Ajana, ájani, ájma, &c. See s. v.

अज 2. *a-já*, mfn. not born, existing from all eternity; (*ás*), m., N. of the first uncreated being, RV.; AV.; Brahmā, Vishṇu, Śiva, Kāma; (*ā*), f., N. of Prakṛiti, Māyā or Illusion (see also 1. *ajá* and 1. *ajana*).

अजकव *ajakava*, *as*, m. Śiva's bow, L.

Ajakāvá, mfn., N. of a sacrificial vessel dedicated to Mitra and Varuṇa and (according to the Comm.) having an ornament similar to the fleshy protuberance called *ajā-gala-stana*, q. v., ŚBr.; (*ás* or *ám*), m. or n. a species of venomous vermin, centipede or scorpion, RV. vii, 50, 1; (*as, am*), m. n. Śiva's bow, L.

Ajagava, *as*, m. Śiva's bow, L.; the southern portion of the path of the sun, moon, and planets; (*as*), m., N. of a snake priest, PBr.

Ajagāva, m., N. of a snake demon, TāṇḍyaBr.; cf. *ājagāva*; (*am*), n. Śiva's bow, L.; N. of the sacrificial vessel also called *ajakāvá* (q. v.), ĀpŚr.

अजघन्य *a-jaghanya*, mfn. not last; not least.

अजघ्निवस् *á-jaghnivas*, mf(*á-jaghnushī*)n. (√*han*), not having killed, RV. viii, 56, 15.

अजटा *a-jaṭā*, f. Flacourtia Cataphracta, = *ajaḍā* and *ajjhaṭā*.

अजड *a-jaḍa*, mfn. not inanimate, not torpid, not stupid; (*ā*), f. the plants Ajaṭā and Kapikacchu (Carpopogon Pruriens). **-dhī**, mfn. of a vigorous mind, energetic.

अजथ्या *ajathyā*, f. yellow jasmin.

अजन 1. *ajana*, *as*, m. (√*aj*), 'the instigator,' Brahmā; (*am*), n. act of instigating or moving. **-yoni-ja**, m. 'born from Ajana,' N. of Daksha.

Ajani, *is*, f. a path, road, Nir.

अजन 2. *a-janá*, mfn. destitute of men; desert; (*as*), m. an insignificant person.

A-janani, *is*, f. (generally used in cursing), non-birth, cessation of existence; *ajananir astu tasya*, 'may he cease to exist!' Pañcat.; cf. Pāṇ. iii, 3, 112.

A-janya, mfn. improper to be produced or born; unfit for mankind; (*am*), n. any portent unfavourable to mankind, as an earthquake.

अजन्त *aj-anta*, mfn. See **2.** *ac*.

अजप 1. *a-japa*, *as*, m. (√*jap*), one who does not repeat prayers; a reciter of heterodox works, L.; (*ā*), f. the mantra or formula called haṅsa (which consists only of a number of inhalations and exhalations).

अजप 2. *aja-pa*, m. See **1.** *ajá*.

अजम्भ *a-jambha*, *as*, m. 'toothless,' a frog.

अजय *a-jaya*, *as*, m. non-victory, defeat; (mfn.), unconquered, unsurpassed, invincible; (*as*), m., N. of Vishṇu; of a lexicographer; of a river; (*ā*), f. hemp; N. of a friend of Durgā; Māyā or Illusion.

A-jayya, mfn. invincible; improper to be won at play.

अजर *a-jára*, mfn. (√*jṛī*), not subject to old age, undecaying, ever young; (*ā*), f. the plants Aloe Perfoliata and Jīrṇapañjhī; the river Sarasvatī.

Ajarâmara, mfn. undecaying and immortal, MBh.

A-jaraka, *as*, *am*, m.n. indigestion.

A-járat, mfn. not decaying, VS.

A-jarayú, mfn. not subject to old age, RV. i, 116, 20.

A-jaras, another form for *a-jara*, used only in some cases, L.

A-jaryá, mfn. not subject to old age or decay, ŚBr.; not friable, not digestible; (*am*), n. friendship.

अजवस् *a-javás*, mfn. not quick, inactive, RV. ii, 15, 6.

अजस्र *á-jasra*, mfn. (√*jas*), not to be obstructed, perpetual, RV. &c.; (*am* [gaṇa *svar-ādi*, &c.] or *ena* [RV. vi, 16, 45]), ind. perpetually, for ever, ever.

अजहत् *a-jahat*, mfn. (pr. p. √**3.** *hā*), not dropping or losing (in comp.) **-svārthā**, f. a rhetorical figure (using a word which involves the meaning of another word previously used, as 'white ones' for 'white horses,' 'lances' for 'men with lances'). **Ajahal-liṅga**, m. (in Gr.) a noun which does not drop its original gender, when used as an adjective.

अजा *ajā*, f. a she-goat. See **1.** *ajá*.

अजागर *a-jāgara*, mfn. not awake, not wakeful, L.; (*as*), m. the plant Eclipta or Verbesina Prostrata.

अजाजि *ajāji*, *is*, or *ajājī*, f. Cuminum Cyminum; Ficus Oppositifolia; Nigella Indica.

अजात *á-jāta*, mfn. unborn, not yet born, not yet developed. **-kakud**, m. a young bull whose hump is yet undeveloped, Pāṇ. v, 4, 146, Sch. **-paksha**, mfn. having undeveloped wings. **-loman**, mf(*mnī*)n. or **-vyañjana**, mfn. whose signs of puberty are not yet developed. **-vyavahāra**, m. having no experience of business, a minor, a youth under fifteen. **-śatru** (*ájāta-*), mfn. having no enemy; having no adversary or equal (Indra), RV.; (*us*), m., N. of Śiva, of Yudhishṭhira, of a king of Kāśī, of a son of Śamīka, of a son of Vidmisāra or Bimbisāra (contemporary of Śākyamuni). **Ajātânuśaya**, mfn. having no regret. **Ajātâri**, m. having no enemy, Yudhishṭhira, Śiś.

अजानत् *a-jānat*, mfn. (pr. p. √*jñā*), not knowing, unaware.

अजानि *a-jāni*, *is* [AV.], or *a-jānika* [L.], *as*, m. having no wife.

अजामि *á-jāmi*, mfn. not of kin, not related, RV.; (in Gr.) not corresponding, Nir.; (*i*), n. '(cohabitation) not allowed between relations,' incest, RV. **-tā** (*ájāmi-*) [ŚBr.], f. or **-tva** [TBr.], n. not uniformity, variation.

अजायमान *á-jāyamāna*, mfn. (√*jan*), not being born, not subject to birth, VS.

अजिका *ajikā*, f. See *ajaka*.

अजित *a-jita*, mfn. not conquered, unsubdued, unsurpassed, invincible, irresistible; (*as*), m. a particular antidote; a kind of venomous rat; N. of Vishṇu; Śiva; one of the Saptarshis of the fourteenth Manvantara; Maitreya or a future Buddha; the second of the Arhats or saints of the present (Jaina) Avasarpiṇī, a descendant of Ikshvāku; the attendant of Suvidhi (who is the ninth of those Arhats); (*ās*), m. pl. a class of deified beings in the first Manvantara. **-keśa-kambala**, m., N. of one of the six chief heretical teachers (mentioned in Buddhist texts as contemporaries of Buddha). **-balā**, f., N. of a Jaina deity who acts under the direction of the Arhat Ajita. **-vikrama**, *as*, m. 'having invincible power,' N. of king Candragupta the second. **Ajitâtman**, mfn. having an unsubdued self or spirit. **Ajitâpīḍa**, m. having an unsurpassed crown; N. of a king, Rājat. **Ajitêndriya**, mfn. having unsubdued passions.

अजिन *ajína*, *am*, n. (probably at first the skin of a goat, *aja*); the hairy skin of an antelope, especially a black antelope (which serves the religious student for a couch, seat, covering, &c.); the hairy skin of a tiger, &c.; (*as*), m., N. of a descendant of Pṛithu, VP. **-pattrā** or **-pattrī** or **-pattrikā**, f. a bat. **-phalā**, f., N. of a plant, (gaṇa *ajâdi*, q.v.) **-yoni**, m. 'origin of skin,' an antelope, deer. **-vāsin**, mfn. clad in a skin, ŚBr. **-sandhá**, m. one who prepares skins, a furrier, VS.

अजिर *ajirá*, mfn. (√*aj*), agile, quick, rapid; (*ám*), ind. quickly; RV.; AV.; VS.; (*as*), m., N. of a Nāga priest, PBr.; (*ā*), f., N. of Durgā; of a river; (*am*), n. place to run or fight in, area, court, R. &c.; the body; any object of sense, air, wind; a frog; L. **-vatī**, f., N. of the river on which the town Śrāvasti was situated, Pāṇ. vi, 3, 119 & vi, 1, 220, Sch. **-śocis** (*ajirá-*), m. having a quick light, glittering, N. of Agni, of Soma, RV. **Ajirâdi**, a gaṇa of Pāṇ. (vi, 3, 119). **Ajirâdhirājá**, m. 'an agile emperor,' death, AV.

Ajirāya, Nom. Ā. *ajirāyate*, to be agile or quick, RV. viii, 14, 10.

Ajiriya, mfn. connected with a court &c., (gaṇa *utkarâdi*, q.v.)

अजिह्म *a-jihma*, mfn. not crooked, straight; honest, upright, Mn. &c.; (*as*), m. a frog (perhaps for *a-jihva*), L.; a fish, L. **-ga**, mfn. going straight; (*as*), m. an arrow. **Ajihmâgra**, mfn. having a straight point.

अजिह्व *a-jihva*, mfn. tongueless; (*as*), m. a frog, L.

अजीकव *ajikava*, *am*, n. Śiva's bow, L. See *ajakava*.

अजीगर्त *a-jīgarta*, *as*, m. 'that has nothing to swallow,' N. of a Ṛishi, Śunaḥśepha's father.

अजीत *á-jita*, mfn. (√*jyā*, usually *jīna*), not faded, not faint, AV.; TS., &c. **-punarvaṇya**, n. 'asking the restitution of an object which has in fact not been lost,' N. of a twofold rite to be performed by Kshatriyas, AitBr.

Á-jiti, *is*, f. the state of being uninjured, RV.; TS. &c.; cf. *á-jyāni*.

अजीर्ण *a-jīrṇa*, mfn. (√*jṛī*), not decomposed; unimpaired; undigested; (*am*), n. indigestion.

A-jīrṇi, *is*, f. indigestion, L.

A-jīrṇin, mfn. suffering from indigestion.

A-jīrti, *is*, f. indigestibleness.

अजीव *a-jīva*, mfn. lifeless.

A-jīvat, mfn. not living, destitute of a livelihood, Mn.

Á-jīvana, mfn. destitute of a livelihood, AV.

A-jīvani, *is*, f. non-existence, death; *ajīvanis tasya bhūyāt*, 'may death befall him!' Pāṇ. iii, 3, 112, Sch.

A-jīvita, *am*, n. non-existence, death.

अजुगुप्सित *a-jugupsita*, mfn. not disliked.

अजुर् *a-júr*, mfn. (√*jur*), not subject to old age or decay, RV. viii, 1, 2.

A-juryá (3; once 4, RV. vi, 17, 13), id., RV.

Á-jūryat, mfn. not subject to old age, RV. iii, 46, 1 & v, 42, 6.

अजुष्ट *á-jushṭa*, mfn. not enjoyed, unsatisfactory, RV.

A-jushṭi, *is*, f. non-enjoyment, feeling of disappointment, RV.

अजेतव्य *a-jetavya*, mfn. invincible.

A-jeya, mfn. invincible; N. of a prince, MBh.; (*am*), n., N. of a kind of antidote.

अजोष *á-josha*, mf(*ā*)n. not gratified, insatiable, RV. i, 9, 4.

Á-joshya (4), mfn. not liked, not welcome, RV. i, 38, 5.

अज्जुका *ajjukā*, f. (in the drama) a courtezan.

अज्झटा *ajjhaṭā*, f. the plant Flacourtia Cataphracta (= *ajaṭā* and *ajaḍā*).

अज्झल *ajjhala*, *as*, m. a burning coal.

अज्ञ *a-jña*, mfn. (√*jñā*), not knowing; ignorant, inexperienced; unconscious; unwise, stupid. **-tā**, f. or **-tva**, n. ignorance.

Ajñakā or **ajñikā**, f. an ignorant woman, Pāṇ. vii, 3, 47.

Á-jñāta, mfn. unknown; unexpected; unaware; (*am*), ind. without the knowledge of, MBh. **-kulaśīla**, mfn. whose lineage and character are unknown. **-keta** (*ájñāta-*), mfn. having unknown or secret designs, RV. v, 3, 11. **-bhukta**, mfn. eaten unawares, Mn. **-yakshmá**, m. an unknown or hidden disease, RV. x, 161, 1; AV. **-vāsa**, mfn. whose dwelling is unknown. **-śīla**, mfn. whose character is unknown.

Ajñātaka, mfn. unknown, (gaṇa *yāvâdi*, q.v.)

A-jñāti, *is*, m. not a kinsman, not related, Mn.

A-jñātvā, ind. not having known or ascertained.

A-jñāna, *am*, n. non-cognizance; ignorance, (in philosophy) spiritual ignorance (or a power which, consisting of the three Guṇas *sattva*, *rajas*, and *tamas*, and preventing the soul from realizing its identity with Brahma, causes self to appear a distinct personality, and matter to appear a reality); Prakṛiti, Māyā, Illusion; (mfn.), ignorant, unwise; (*āt*), ind. unawares, ignorantly. **-kṛita**, mfn. done inadvertently. **-tas**, ind. unawares, inadvertently. **-tā**, f. or **-tva**, n. ignorance. **-bandhana**, n. the bond of ignorance.

A-jñānin, mfn. ignorant, unwise.

A-jñās, mfn. having no kindred, RV. x, 39, 6.

A-jñeya, mfn. unknowable, unfit to be known.

अज्म *ájma*, *as*, m. (√*aj*), career, march, RV. [cf. Gk. ὄγμος].

Ájman, *a*, n. career, passage, battle, RV.; AV. [Lat. *agmen*].

Ájra, *as*, m. a field, a plain, RV. [Lat. *ager*; Gk. ἀγρός: cf. *ajira*].

Ajryá (3), mfn. being in or connected with a field or plain, RV. x, 69, 6.

Ajvin, mfn. (√*aj*), active, agile, used in a sacrificial formula, ĀśvŚr.

अज्यानि *á-jyāni*, *is*, f. the state of being uninjured, AV. (cf. *á-jīti*); (*ajyānayas*), nom. pl., N. of certain offerings, TBr., ĀpŚr.

A-jyeyá-tā, f. state of anything which is not to be hurt or overpowered, ŚBr.

अज्येष्ठ *a-jyeshṭhá*, mfn. not the oldest or best; (*ās*), nom. pl. of which none is the eldest (the Maruts), RV. v, 59, 6 & 60, 5; cf. *á-kanishṭha*. **-vṛitti**, mfn. not behaving as the eldest brother [Mn. ix, 110], or (*ajyeshṭha-vṛitti*) behaving like one who has no elder brother.

अञ्च 1. *añc* (connected with √*ac*, q.v.), cl. 1. P. Ā. *áñcati*, °*te*, *ānañca*, °*ce*, *añcishyati*, °*te*, *añcitum*, to bend, curve, incline, curl; to reverence (with inclined body), to honour; to tend, move, go, wander about; to request, L.: cl. 10. or Caus. *añcayati*, to unfold, make clear, produce: Desid. P. Ā. *añcicishati*, °*te*, to be desirous of bending: Pass. *añcyate* or *acyate*, to be bent.

2. Añc, only ifc., turned to, going or directed towards; see *akudhryáñc*, *áváñc*, *udáñc*, *devadryáñc*, &c.

Añca, 'curling' (of the hairs of the body, thrill of rapture), only at the end of *româñca*, q.v.

Añcati, *is,* m. or **añcatī,** f. wind, L.; fire, L.

Añcana, *am,* n. act of bending or curving.

Añcala, *as,* m. (perhaps also *am*), n. the border or end of a garment, especially of a woman's garment, of a veil, shawl. (In Bengālī, a strip of country, district.)

Añcita, mfn. bent, curved, curled, arched, handsome; gone, walked in; reverenced, honoured; distinguished. **–pattra,** m. a kind of lotus with curved leaves. **–pattrâksha,** mfn. having lotus eyes. **–bhrū,** f. a woman with arched or handsome eyebrows. **–lāṅgūla,** mfn. having a curved tail (as a monkey).

अञ्ज् *añj,* cl. 7. P. Ā. *anákti, aṅkté, ā-nañja, añjishyati* or *aṅkshyati, āñjīt, añjitum* or *aṅktum,* to apply an ointment or pigment, smear with, anoint; to decorate, prepare; to honour, celebrate; to cause to appear, make clear, RV. i, 92, 1; to be beautiful, L.; to go, L.: Caus. *añjayati, āñjijat,* to smear with; to speak; to shine; to cause to go, L. [cf. Lat. *ungo*].

Añjaka, *as,* m., N. of a son of Vipracitti, VP.

Añjana, *as,* m. a kind of domestic lizard, L.; N. of a fabulous serpent; of a tree, Pañcat.; of a mountain; of a king of Mithilā; of the elephant of the west or south-west quarter; (*ā*), f., N. of Hanumat's mother; of Pravarasena's mother; (*am*), n. act of applying an ointment or pigment, embellishing, &c.; black pigment or collyrium applied to the eyelashes or the inner coat of the eyelids; a special kind of this pigment, as lamp-black, Antimony, extract of Ammonium, Xanthorrhiza, &c.; paint, especially as a cosmetic; magic ointment; ink, L.; night, L.; fire, L. (In rhetoric) making clear the meaning of an equivocal expression, double entendre or pun, &c. **–keśa,** mf(*ī*)n. whose hair (or mane) is as black as pigment; (*ī*), f., N. of a vegetable perfume. **–nāmikā,** f. a swelling of the eyelid, stye. **–vat,** ind. like collyrium. **Añjanā-giri,** m., N. of a mountain. **Añjanâdhikā,** f. a species of lizard, L. **Añjanâmbhas,** n. eye-water. **Añjanā-vatī,** f. the female elephant of the north-east (or the west?) quarter.

Añjanaka, *as,* m. portion of a text containing the word *añjana,* (gaṇa *goshad-ādi,* q. v.); (*ī*), f., N. of a medicinal plant.

Añjanikā, f. a species of lizard, L.; a small mouse, L.; cf. *añjalikā.*

Añjanī, f. a woman (fit for the application of ointments, pigments, sandal, &c.), L.; N. of two medicinal plants.

Añjala, añjali. See s. v. below.

Añjas, *as,* n. ointment, a mixture, RV. i, 132, 2; N. of a Sāman, ĀrshBr.; (*as*), ind. quickly, instantly, RV.; BhP.; see *áñjasā.* **Añjaḥ-savá,** m. rapid preparation (of Soma), ŚBr.; AitBr. **Añjas-pā́,** mfn. drinking instantly, RV. x, 92, 2 & 94, 13.

Añjasa, mfn. straight, straightforward, honest, L.; (*ī*), f., N. of a heavenly river, RV. i, 104, 4.

Áñjasā, ind. straight on, right, truly, justly; quickly, soon, instantly. **Añjasâyana,** mf(*ī*)n. having a straight course, going straight on, TS.; AitBr.

Añjasína, mfn. going straight on, straightforward, RV. x, 32, 7.

Añjí, mfn. applying an ointment or pigment, RV.; ointment, brilliancy, RV.; unctuous, smooth, sleek (membrum virile), VS.; (*is*), m. a sender, commander, Uṇ. **–mát,** mfn. coloured, bright, adorned, RV. v, 57, 5. **–sakthá,** mfn. having coloured thighs (a victim), VS.; cf. Pāṇ. vi, 2, 199, Sch.

Añjy-etá, mfn. black and white coloured, TS.

Añjivá, mfn. slippery, smooth, AV.

Añjishṭha, *as,* or **añjishṇu,** *us,* m. 'highly brilliant,' the sun, L.

अञ्जल *añjala* only ifc. for *añjali,* q. v.

अञ्जलि *añjalí, is,* m. (√*añj*), the open hands placed side by side and slightly hollowed (as if by a beggar to receive food; hence when raised to the forehead, a mark of supplication), reverence, salutation, benediction; a libation to the Manes (two hands full of water, *udakâñjali*), VP. &c.; a measure of corn, sufficient to fill both hands when placed side by side, equal to a kuḍava. **–karman,** n. making the above respectful salutation. **–kārikā,** f. an earthen figure (with the hands joined for salutation); the plant Mimosa Natans. **–puṭa,** m. n. cavity produced in making the *añjali* salutation. **–bandhana,** n. salutation with the *añjali* raised to the forehead. **Añjalī-kṛita,** mfn. placed together to form the *añjali* salutation.

Añjalika, *as, am,* m. n., N. of one of Arjuna's arrows, MBh.; (*ā*), f. a young mouse, L.

अञ्जिक *añjika, as,* m., N. of a son of Yadu. See *añjaka.*

अञ्जिहिषा *añjihishā,* f. (fr. Desid. of √1. *aṇh*), desire of going, [°*shām cakre* (√1. *kṛi*)], Bhaṭṭ.

अञ्जी *añjī,* f. a blessing (?), T.

अञ्जीर *añjīra, am,* n. (a Persian word), a species of fig-tree (Ficus Oppositifolia); a fig. (In Bengālī) a guava.

अट् *aṭ,* cl. 1. P. Ā. *aṭati,* °*te, āṭa, aṭishyati, āṭīt, aṭitum,* to roam, wander about (sometimes with acc.; frequently used of religious mendicants): Intens. *aṭāṭyate,* to roam or wander about zealously or habitually, especially as a religious mendicant: Desid. *aṭiṭishati,* to be desirous of roaming.

Aṭaka, mfn. roaming, L.

Aṭana, mfn. roaming about, VarBṛ.; (*am*), n. act or habit of wandering about.

Aṭani, *is,* f. or **aṭanī,** f. the notched extremity of a bow.

Aṭamāna, *as,* m., N. of a prince, BhP.

Aṭavi, *is,* or usually **aṭavī,** f. 'place to roam in,' a forest. **Aṭavī-śikhara,** *ās,* m. pl., N. of a people, MBh.

Aṭavika, better **āṭavika,** *as,* m. a woodman, forester.

Aṭā, f. the act or habit of roaming or wandering about (especially as a religious mendicant).

Aṭāṭā, f. (habit of) roaming or wandering about, L.

Aṭāṭyamāna, mfn. roaming excessively.

Aṭāṭyā, f. (habit of) roaming, L.

Aṭāya, Nom. Ā. *aṭāyate,* to enter upon a roaming life, to become a religious mendicant, L.

Aṭyā, f. roaming about, one of the ten faults resulting from an excessive fondness for pleasure, Mn. vii, 47.

अटनि *aṭani.* See √*aṭ.*

अटरूष *aṭarusha* or *aṭarūsha* or *aṭarūshaka, as,* m. the shrub Justicia Adhatoda.

अटल *a-ṭala,* mfn. not shaky, firm, L.

अट्ट् *aṭṭ,* cl. 1. Ā. *aṭṭate, ānaṭṭe, aṭṭitum,* to exceed, L.; to kill, L.: cl. 10. P. *aṭṭayati,* to contemn, L.; to lessen, diminish, L.

Aṭṭa, ind. high, lofty, L.; loud, L.; (*as*), m. a watch-tower; a market, a market-place (corruption of *haṭṭa*); N. of a Yaksha, Rājat.; over-measure, L.; (*ā*), f. overbearing conduct (?), Pāṇ. iii, 1, 17, Comm.; (*am*), n. boiled rice, food, L.; (mfn.), dried, dry, L. **–pati-bhāgâkhya-gṛiha-kṛitya,** n. business of the house called the market-master's department (an office in Kashmīr), Rājat. **–sthalī,** f. site of an *aṭṭa* (?), (gaṇa *dhūmâdi,* q. v.) **–hasita,** n. loud laughter, a horse-laugh. **–hāsa,** m. id.; a name of Śiva; of a Yaksha, Kathās.; of a mountain. **–hāsaka,** m. the shrub Jasminum Multiflorum or Hirsutum. **–hāsin,** m., N. of Śiva. **–hāsya,** n. loud laughter; a horse-laugh. **Aṭ-ṭâṭṭa-hāsa,** m. very loud laughter.

Aṭṭaka, *as,* m. an apartment on the roof; tower.

Aṭṭaṭṭa, ind. very high, L.; very loud, L.

Aṭṭana, *am,* n. a weapon shaped like a discus, L.

Aṭṭāya (Nom. fr. *aṭṭā*), Ā. *aṭṭāyate,* to be overbearing (?), Pāṇ. iii, 1, 17, Comm.

अट्टाल *aṭṭāla, as,* or *aṭṭālaka, as,* m. a watch-tower; (*ikā*), f. a palace, L.; N. of a country, Rājat.

Aṭṭālikā-kāra, *as,* m. a bricklayer (son of a painter and a lascivious Śūdra woman), BrahmavP.

Aṭṭālikā-bandham, ind. (in the way that aṭṭālikās are formed), Pāṇ. iii, 4, 42, Sch.

अट्टिलिका *aṭṭilikā,* f., N. of a town, Rājat.

अड्णार *aṭṇārá, as,* m. a king of Kosala, ŚBr.

अट्या *aṭyā,* f. See √*aṭ.*

अठ् *aṭh,* cl. 1. P. Ā. *aṭhati,* °*te,* to go, L.

अठिद *aṭhida, ās,* m. pl., N. of a people, MBh.

अठिल्ला *aṭhillā,* f., N. of a Prākṛit metre.

अड् 1. *aḍ,* cl. 1. P. *aḍati,* to endeavour, L.

अडकवती *aḍakavatī,* N. of a fabulous palace on Meru; also of a city.

अड्ड् *aḍḍ,* cl. 1. P. *aḍḍati, ānaḍḍa, aḍḍitum,* to join, L.; to infer, argue, L.; to meditate, discern, L.; to attack, L.

Aḍḍana, *am,* n. a shield, L.

अण् *aṇ,* cl. 1. P. *aṇati, āṇa, aṇitum,* to sound, L.: cl. 4. Ā. *aṇyate,* to breathe, (another form of √*an,* q. v.; in this sense regarded in the Dhātu-pāṭha as a distinct rt.), L.

Aṇaka, mfn. insignificant, small, contemptible, (gaṇa *utkarâdi,* q. v.)

Aṇakīya, mfn. connected with what is insignificant, &c., ib.

Aṇavya, *am,* n. a field of (*aṇu*) Panicum Miliaceum, Pāṇ. v, 2, 4; see *aṇu.*

Aṇi, *is,* m. or **aṇī,** f. the point of a needle or of a sharp stake, L.; linch-pin, L.; the pin or bolt at the end of the pole of a carriage, L.; the corner or part of a house, L.; a boundary, L. **Aṇī-māṇḍavya,** m., N. of a Brāhman ascetic (said to have been impaled on an *aṇi* or point of a stake), MBh.

Aṇimán, *ā,* m. (fr. *aṇu,* q. v.), minuteness, fineness, thinness, ŚBr. &c.; meagreness; atomic nature; the superhuman power of becoming as small as an atom; (*áṇiman*), n. the smallest particle, ŚBr.

Aṇishṭha, mfn. (fr. *aṇu,* q. v.), most minute.

Áṇiyas, *ān, asī, as* (fr. *aṇu,* q. v.), or **aṇīyaská** [AV.], mfn. more minute than usual.

Áṇu, mf(*vī*)n. fine, minute, atomic; (*us*), m. an atom of matter; 'an atom of time,' the 54,675,000th part of a muhūrta (of 48 minutes); Panicum Miliaceum, VS.; ŚBr. xiv; MuṇḍUp.; N. of Śiva; (*áṇvī*), f. 'the subtle one,' N. of the fingers preparing the Soma juice, RV.; (*u*), n. (in prosody) the fourth part of a mātrā; (*aṇú*), ind. minutely, ŚBr. **–tara,** mfn. very fine or minute, gentle. **–taila,** n., N. of a medical oil. **–tva,** n. or **-tā,** f. minuteness, atomic nature. **–bhā,** f. lightning. **–madhya-bīja,** n., N. of a hymn. **–mātra,** mfn. having the size of an atom. **–mātrika,** mfn. having the size of an atom; containing the atomic elements (*mātrā*) of the body, Mn. i, 56. **–reṇu,** m. f. atomic dust (as seen in sun-beams). **–reṇu-jāla,** n. an aggregate of such atomic dust. **–revatī,** f. the plant Croton Polyandrum. **–vādin,** mfn. one who believes in and teaches atomism. **–vedānta,** m. title of a book. **–vrata,** *āni,* n. pl., N. of the twelve small duties or vows of the laymen adhering to the Jaina faith. **–vrīhi,** m. a fine sort of rice, L. **–śas,** ind. into or in minute particles. **Aṇū** (with √*bhū,* &c.), see s. v. **Áṇv-anta,** m. a hair-splitting question, ŚBr.

Aṇuka, mfn. fine, minute, atomic; clever, (gaṇa *yāvâdi,* q. v.); (*am*), n. an atom.

Aṇū (for *aṇu* in comp. with √*bhū* and its derivatives). **–bhāva,** m. the becoming an atom, Nir. **–√bhū,** to become minute or atomic.

Áṇva, *am,* n. fine interstice or hole in the strainer used for the Soma juice, RV.

अणुह *aṇuha, as,* m., N. of a son of Vibhrāja, MBh.

अण्ठ् *aṇṭh* or *aṭh,* cl. 1. Ā. *aṇṭhate, ānaṇṭhe, aṇṭhitum,* to go, move, tend, L.

Aṇṭhita, mfn. pained (?), Suśr.

अण्ड *aṇḍa, am,* n. (also *as,* m., L.) [√*am,* Uṇ.], an egg, a testicle; the scrotum; the musk bag; semen virile, L.; N. of Śiva (from his being identified with the Brahmâṇḍa or mundane egg). **–kaṭāha,** m. the shell of the mundane egg, VP. **–koṭara-pushpī,** f. the plant Convolvulus Argenteus (?). **–kośa** or **-kosha** or **-koshaka,** m. the scrotum; the mundane egg. **–ja,** mfn. egg-born; (*as*), m. a bird, L.; a fish, L.; a snake, L.; a lizard, L.; (*ā*), f. musk. **–jêśvara,** m. 'king of birds,' Garuḍa. **–dala,** n. egg-shell. **–dhara,** m., N. of Śiva. **–vardhana,** n. or **-vṛiddhi,** f. swelling of the scrotum, hydrocele. **–sū,** f. oviparous. **Aṇḍâkarshaṇa,** n. castration. **Aṇḍâkāra,** mfn. egg-shaped, oval, elliptical; (*as*), m. an ellipsis. **Aṇḍâkṛiti,** mfn. egg-shaped, oval, elliptical; (*is*), f. an ellipsis.

Aṇḍaka, *as,* m. the scrotum; (*am*), n. an egg.

Aṇḍara, mf(*ī*, gaṇa *gaurâdi*, q.v.)n., N. of a tribe, (gaṇa *bhṛiśâdi*, q.v.)

Aṇḍarāya, Nom. Ā. *aṇḍarāyate*, to behave like an Aṇḍara, (gaṇa *bhṛiśâdi*, q. v.)

Aṇḍālu, *us*, m. 'full of eggs,' a fish, L.

Aṇḍikā, f., N. of a weight (= 4 yava), Car.

Aṇḍīra, *as*, m. a full male, a man, L.; strong, L.

अत् 1. *at*, ind. a prefix said to imply 'surprise,' probably a contraction of *ati*, meaning 'extraordinary,' (gaṇa *ūry-ādi*, q. v.) **Ád-bhuta,** mfn. extraordinary; see s. v.

अत् 2. *at*, cl. 1. P. Ā. *átati* (Naigh.; p. *átat* or *átamāna*), to go constantly, walk, run, RV.; to obtain, L.

Atana, *as*, m. a passer on, Nir.; (*am*), n. act of passing on, Nir. **– vat,** m. one who wanders, Nir.

Atasí, átka. See s. v.

अतज्ज्ञ *a-taj-jña* (for *a-tad-jña*), mfn. not knowing that, i. e. Brahma and the soul's identity.

अतट *a-taṭa*, mfn. having no beach or shore, precipitous, Śák.; (*as*), m. a precipice; the third hell; cf. *atala*.

अतत्त्वविद् *a-tattva-vid*, mfn. not knowing the truth, i. e. the soul's identity with Brahma.

A-tattvârtha-vat, mfn. not conformable with the nature of truth.

अतथा *á-tathā*, mfn. not saying *tathā* (yes), giving a negative answer, RV. i, 82, 1. **A-tathôcita,** mfn. not deserving of such (a fate); not used to this (with gen.)

A-tathya, mfn. untrue, unreal, not really so.

अतद् *a-tad*, not that, BhP. (cf. *a-sa*). **– arha,** mfn. not deserving that; (*am*), ind. undeservedly, unjustly. **– guṇa,** m. (in rhetoric) the use of predicates not descriptive of the essential nature of the object.

अतनु 1. *a-tanu*, mfn. not thin, not small.

2. **A-tanu,** *us*, m. = *an-aṅga*, N. of Kāma.

अतन्त्र *a-tantra*, mfn. having no cords; having no (musical) strings; unrestrained; (*am*), n. not the object of a rule or of the rule under consideration.

अतन्द्र *á-tandra*, mfn. free from lassitude, alert, unwearied, RV.; AV.

A-tandrita or **a-tandrin,** mfn. id., Mn. &c.

अतप *a-tapa* (√*tap*), *ās*, m. pl. a class of deities among the Buddhists.

A-tapas or **a-tapaska** or **a-tapasya,** mfn. one who neglects *tapas* or the practice of ascetic austerities; an irreligious character.

A-tapta, mfn. not heated, cool. **– tanū** (*átapta-*), mfn. whose body or mass is not prepared in fire, raw, RV. ix, 83, 1. **– tapas,** m. whose ascetic austerity has not been (fully) endured.

Á-tapyamāna, mfn. not suffering, RV. i, 185, 4.

अतमस् *a-tamás*, mfn. without darkness, ŚBr. xiv. **A-tamâvishṭa** (irregular contraction of *a-tama-āvishṭa*), mfn. not enveloped in darkness, MaitrUp.

A-tamisra, mfn. not dark, not benighted.

अतमेरु *á-tameru*, mfn. not languid, VS.

अतर्क *a-tarka*, *as*, m. an illogical reasoner; bad logic.

A-tarkita, mfn. unconsidered, unthought of; unexpected; (*am*), ind. unexpectedly.

A-tarkya, mfn. incomprehensible, surpassing thought or reasoning. **– sahasra-śakti,** m. endowed with a thousand incomprehensible powers.

अतल *a-tala*, *am*, n. bottomless; N. of a hell beneath the earth; (*as*), m., N. of Śiva. **– sparśa** or **-spṛiś,** mfn. whose bottom cannot be reached, bottomless.

अतव्यस् *á-tavyas*, *ān*, *asī*, *as*, not stronger, not very strong, RV. v, 33, 1 & vii, 100, 5.

अतस् *átas*, ind. (ablative of the pronom. base *a*, equivalent to *asmát*), from this, than this; hence; henceforth, from that time; from this or that cause or reason. **Ata-ūrdhvam,** ind. henceforth, afterwards. **Ata-eva,** ind. for this very reason; therefore. **Ataḥ-param,** ind. henceforth, further on. **Ato-nimittam,** ind. on this ground, for this reason. **Ato-'nya,** mfn. differing from this. **Ato-'rtham,** ind. for this object.

अतस *atasa*, *as*, m. (√*at*), wind, air, L.; the soul, L.; a (missile) weapon, L.; a garment made of the fibre of (*atasī*) flax, L.; (*ám*), n. shrubs, RV.; (*ī*), f. common flax, Linum Usitatissimum; Śaṇa, Bengal sun used as hemp, Crotolaria Juncea.

अतसि *atasí*, *is*, m. (√*at*), a wandering mendicant, RV. viii, 3, 13.

Atasáyya (5), mfn. to be got by begging, RV. i, 63, 6 & ii, 19, 4.

अतस्थान *á-tasthāna* (√*sthā*), mfn. not suiting or fitting, ŚBr.

अतापस *á-tāpasa*, mfn. not an ascetic, ŚBr.

अति *áti*, ind. [probably neut. of an obsolete adj. *atin*, passing, going, beyond; see √*at*, and cf. Old Germ. *anti, unti, inti, unde, indi*, &c.; Eng. *and*; Germ. *und*; Gk. ἔτι, ἀντί; Lat. *ante*; Lith. *ant*; Arm. *ti*; Zend *aiti*]. As a prefix to verbs and their derivatives, expresses beyond, over, and, if not standing by itself, leaves the accent on the verb or its derivative; as, *ati-kram* (√*kram*), to overstep, Ved. Inf. *ati-krāme*, (fit) to be walked on, to be passed, RV. i, 105, 16; *ati-krámaṇa*, n., see s. v.

When prefixed to nouns, not derived from verbs, it expresses beyond, surpassing; as, *ati-kaśa*, past the whip; *ati-mānusha*, superhuman, &c.; see s. v.

As a separable adverb or preposition (with acc.), Ved. beyond; (with gen.) over, at the top of, RV.; AV.

Ati is often prefixed to nouns and adjectives, and rarely to verbs, in the sense excessive, extraordinary, intense; excessively, too; exceedingly, very; in such compounds the accent is generally on *áti*. **– kaṭhora,** mfn. very hard, too hard. **– katha,** mfn. exaggerated; (*ā*), f. an exaggerated tale; see also s. v. **– karshaṇa** (for *-karśana*?), n. excessive exertion. **– kalyam,** ind. very early, too early. **– kānta,** mfn. excessively beloved. **– kāya,** mfn. of extraordinary body or size, gigantic; (*as*), m., N. of a Rākshasa, R. **– kiriṭa** (*áti-*) or **-kirīṭa** [Comm.], mfn. having too small teeth, TBr. **– kutsita,** mfn. greatly despised. **– kulva** (*áti-*), mfn. too bald, VS. **– kṛicchra,** m. extraordinary pain or penance lasting twelve days, Mn.; Yājñ. **– kṛita,** mfn. overdone, exaggerated. **– kṛiśa** (*áti-*), mfn. very thin, emaciated. **– kṛishṇa** (*áti-*), mfn. very or too dark, very or too deep blue. **– kruddha,** mfn. excessively angry. **– krudh,** f. excessive anger, Kathās. **– krushṭa** (*áti-*), n. extraordinary cry or wailing, VS. **– khara,** mfn. very pungent or piercing. **– gaṇḍa,** mfn. having large cheeks or temples; (*as*), m., N. of the *yoga* (or index), star of the 6th lunar mansion. **– gandha,** mfn. having an overpowering smell; (*as*), m. sulphur; lemon-grass (Andropogon Schænunthes); the Champac flower (Michelia Champaca); a kind of jasmin. **– gandhālu,** m., N. of the creeper Putradātrī. **– garīyas,** n. (compar. of *ati-guru*), a higher or too high price; *ati-garīyasā* (instr.) √*krī*, to buy too dear, Daś. **– garvita,** mfn. very conceited. **– gahana,** mfn. very deep; very impenetrable. **– gāḍha,** mfn. very important; very intensive; (*am*), ind. exceedingly; excessively. **– guṇa,** mfn. having extraordinary qualities. **– gupta,** mfn. closely concealed, very mysterious. **– guru,** mfn. very heavy. **– go,** f. an excellent cow, Pāṇ. v, 4, 69, Sch. **– caṇḍa,** mfn. very violent. **– caraṇa,** n. excessive practice. **– cāpalya,** n. extraordinary mobility or unsteadiness. **– cira,** mfn. very long; (*am*), ind. a very long time; (*asya*), ind. for a very long time; (*āt*), ind. at last. **– chattra** or **-chattraka,** m. a mushroom; (*ā*), f. Anise (Anisum or Anethum Sowa); the plant Barleria Longifolia. **– jara** or **-jaras,** mfn. very aged, Pāṇ. vii, 2, 101, Sch. **– jala,** mfn. well watered. **– java,** m. extraordinary speed; (mfn.), very fleet. **– jāgara,** mfn. very wakeful; (*as*), m. the black curlew. **– jīrṇa,** mfn. very aged. **– jīrṇatā,** f. extreme old age. **– jīvá,** mfn. quite alive, very lively, AV. **– ḍīna,** n. extraordinary flight (of birds), MBh. **– tapasvin,** mfn. very ascetic. **– tīkshṇa,** mfn. very sharp. **– tīvra,** mfn. very sharp, pungent or acid; (*ā*), f. dūb grass. **– tṛiṇṇa,** mfn. seriously hurt. **– tṛipti,** f. too great satiety. **– tṛishṇa,** mfn. excessively thirsty, rapacious; (*ā*), f. excessive thirst. **– trasnu,** mfn. over timid. **– dagdha,** mfn. badly burnt; (*am*), n., N. of a bad kind of burn. **– dantura** (*áti-*), mfn. whose teeth are too prominent, TBr. **– darpa,** m. excessive conceit; N. of a snake; (mfn.), excessively conceited. **– darśin,** mfn. very far-sighted. **– dātṛi,** m. a very or too liberal man. **– dāna,** n. munificence; excessive munificence. **– dāruṇa,** mfn. very terrible. **– dāhá,** m. great heat; violent inflammation, TS. &c. **– dīrgha** (*áti-*), mfn. very long, too long. **– duḥkhita** (or *-dushkhita*), mfn. greatly afflicted, very sad. **– duḥsaha,** mfn. very hard to bear, quite unbearable. **– durgata,** mfn. very badly off. **– durdharsha,** mfn. very hard to approach, very haughty. **– durlambha,** mfn. very hard to attain. **– dushkara,** mfn. very difficult. **– dūra,** mfn. very distant; (*am*), n. a great distance. **– dosha,** m. a great fault. **– dhavala,** mfn. very white. **– dhenu,** mfn. distinguished for his cows, Pāṇ. i, 4, 3, Comm. **– nidra,** mfn. given to excessive sleep; (*ā*), f. excessive sleep; (*am*), ind., see s. v. (p. 14, col. 2). **– nipuṇa,** mfn. very skilful. **– nīca,** mfn. excessively low. **– pathin** (nom. *-panthās*), m. a better road than common, L. **– pada,** mfn. (in prosody) too long by one *pada* or foot. **– paroksha,** mfn. far out of sight, no longer discernible. **– paroksha-vṛitti,** mfn. (in Gr.) having a nature that is no longer discernible, i. e. obsolete. **– pātaka,** n. a very heinous sin. **– purusha** or **-pūrusha** (*áti-*) [ŚBr.], m. a first-rate man, hero. **– pūta,** mfn. quite purified, over-refined. **– peśala,** mfn. very dexterous. **– prakāśa,** mfn. very notorious. **– prage,** ind. very early, Mn. **– praṇaya,** m. excessive kindness, partiality. **– praṇudya,** ind. having pushed far forward. **– prabandha,** m. complete continuity. **– pravaraṇa,** n. excess in choosing. **– pravṛitti,** f. issuing abundantly. **– pravṛiddha,** mfn. enlarged to excess, overbearing, Mn. **– praśna,** m. an extravagant question, a question regarding transcendental objects. **– praśnya,** mfn. to be asked such a question, BṛĀrUp. **– prasakti,** f. or **-prasaṅga,** m. excessive attachment; unwarrantable stretch of a rule. **– prasiddha,** mfn. very notorious. **– prauḍha,** mfn. full-grown. **– prauḍha-yauvana,** mfn. being in the full enjoyment of youth. **– bala,** mfn. very strong or powerful; (*as*), m. an active soldier; N. of a king; (*ā*), f. a medicinal plant (Sidonia Cordifolia and Rhombifolia, or Annona Squamosa); N. of a powerful charm; of one of Daksha's daughters. **– bahu** (*áti-*), mfn. very much; too much, MaitrS. **– bālaka,** m. an infant; (mfn.), infantine. **– bāhu,** m. 'having extraordinary arms,' N. of a Ṛishi of the fourteenth Manvantara, Hariv.; N. of a Gandharva, MBh. **– bībhatsa,** mfn. excessively disagreeable. **– brahmacarya,** n. excessive abstinence or continence. **– bhāra,** m. an excessive burden; excessive obscurity (of a sentence); N. of a king. **– bhāraga,** m. 'heavy-burden-bearer,' a mule. **– bhī,** m. 'very terrific,' lightning, L. **– bhīshaṇa,** mfn. very terrific. **– bhṛita,** mfn. well filled. **– bhojana,** n. eating too much; morbid voracity. **– bhrū,** mfn. having extraordinary eyebrows. **– maṅgalya,** mfn. very auspicious; (*as*), m, Ægle or Cratæva Marmelos. **– mati** (*áti-*), f. haughtiness, RV. i, 129, 5; (mfn.), exceedingly wise, MBh. **– madhyandina,** n. high noon. **– marśa,** m. close contact. **– māná,** m. great haughtiness. **– mānin,** mfn. very haughty. **– māni-tā,** f. great haughtiness. **– māruta,** mfn. very windy; (*as*), m. a hurricane, Yājñ. **– mirmira** (*áti-*), mfn. twinkling exceedingly, TBr. **– mukta,** mfn. entirely liberated; quite free from sensual or worldly desire; seedless, barren; (*as*), m. the tree Dalbergia Oujeinensis; Gærtnera Racemosa. **– muktaka,** m. = the preceding; mountain ebony; the tree Harimantha. **– mukti** (*áti-*), f. final liberation (from death), TS.; ŚBr. xiv. **– mūrti,** f. 'highest shape,' N. of a ceremony. **– memisha** (*áti-*), mfn. (√1. *mish*), opening the eyes too much, staring, TBr. **– maithuna,** n. excess of sexual intercourse. **– mokshá,** m.; see *ati-√muc*. **– modā,** f. extraordinary fragrance; the tree Jasminum Arboreum. **– yava,** m. a sort of barley. **– yaśa** [MBh.] or **-yaśas,** mfn. very illustrious. **– yājá,** m. 'great sacrificer,' very pious, RV. vi, 52, 1. **– yuvan,** mfn. very youthful, L. **– yoga,** m. excessive union, excess. **– raṇhas,** mfn. extremely rapid, Śák. **– rakta,** mfn. very red; (*ā*), f. one of Agni's seven tongues. **– ratha,** m. a great warrior (fighting from a car), R. **– rabhasa,** m. extraordinary speed. **– rasā,** f. 'very succulent,' N. of various plants (Mūrvā, Rāsnā, Klitanaka). **– rājan,** m. an extraordinary king, Pāṇ. v, 4, 69, Sch.; one who surpasses a king [cf.

also s.v.] **-rucira**, mfn. very lovely; (*ā*), f., N. of two metres (a variety of the *Atijagatī*; another called *Cuḍikā* or *Culikā*). **-rush**, mfn. very angry. **-rūpa**, mfn. very beautiful; (*am*), n. extraordinary beauty. **-roga**, m. consumption, L. **-romaśa**, mfn. very hairy, too hairy; (*as*), m. a wild goat, a kind of monkey. **-lakshmī**, mfn. very prosperous; (*īs*), f. extraordinary prosperity. **-laṅghana**, n. excessive fasting, Suśr. **-lamba**, mfn. very extensive. **-lubdha** or **ati-lobha**, mfn. very greedy or covetous. **-lulita**, mfn. closely attached or adhering. **-lobha**, m. or **-lobha-tā**, f. excessive greediness or covetousness. **-loma** or **-lomaśa** (*áti-*) [VS.], mfn. very hairy, too hairy. **-lomaśā**, f. Convolvulus Argenteus. **-lohita**, mfn. very red. **-laulya**, n. excessive eagerness or desire. **-vaktṛi**, mfn. very loquacious. **-vakra**, mfn. very crooked or curved; (*ā*), f. one of the eight descriptions of planetary motion. **-vartula**, mfn. very round; (*as*), m. a kind of grain or pot-herb. **-vāta**, m. high wind, a storm. **-vāda**, m. abusive language; reproof; N. of a Vedic verse, AitBr. **-vādin**, mfn. very talkative. **-vālaka**, see *-bālaka* above. **-vāhana**, n. excessive toiling. **-vikaṭa**, mfn. very fierce; (*as*), m. a vicious elephant. **-vipina**, mfn. having many forests, very impenetrable, Kir. v, 18. **-vilambin**, mfn. very dilatory. **-viśrabdha-navôḍhā**, f. a fond but pert young wife. **-visha**, mfn. exceedingly poisonous; counteracting poison; (*ā*), f. the plant Aconitum Ferox. **-vṛiddhi**, f. extraordinary growth. **-vṛishṭi**, f. excessive rain. **-vṛishṭi-hata**, mfn. injured by heavy rain. **-vepathu**, m. excessive tremor; (mfn.), or *ativepathu-mat*, mfn. trembling excessively. **-vaicakshaṇya**, n. great proficiency. **-vaiśasa**, mfn. very adverse or destructive. **-vyathana**, n. infliction of (or giving) excessive pain, Pāṇ. v, 4, 61. **-vyathā**, f. excessive pain. **-vyaya**, m. lavish expenditure. **-vyāpta**, mfn. stretched too far (as a rule or principle). **-vyāpti**, f. unwarrantable stretch (of a rule or principle), Pāṇ. vi, 3, 35, Sch. **-śakta** or **-śakti**, mfn. very powerful; (*is*), f. or *atiśakti-tā*, f. great power or valour. **-śakti-bhāj**, mfn. possessing great power. **-śaṅkā**, f. excessive timidity. **-śarvará**, n. the dead of night, AV. **-śasta**, mfn. very excellent. **-śukra** (*áti-*), mfn. too bright. **-śukla**, mfn. very white, too white. **-śobhana**, mfn. very handsome. **-śrī**, mfn. very prosperous, Pāṇ. i, 2, 48, Sch. **-ślakshṇa** (*áti-*), mfn. too tender, TBr. **-saṃskṛita**, mfn. highly finished. **-sakti**, f. excessive attachment. **-sakti-mat**, mfn. excessively attached. **-saṃcaya**, m. excessive accumulation. **-saṃtapta**, mfn. greatly afflicted. **-saṃdheya**, mfn. easy to be settled or conciliated. **-samartha**, mfn. very competent. **-samīpa**, mfn. very near. **-samparka**, m. excessive (sexual) intercourse. **-sarva**, mfn. too complete, AitBr.; superior to all, see s. v. **-sādhvasa**, n. excessive fear. **-sāntapana**, n. a kind of severe penance (inflicted especially for eating unclean animal food). **-sāyam**, ind. very late in the evening. **-siddhi**, f. great perfection. **-sujana**, mfn. very moral, very friendly. **-sundara**, mfn. very handsome; (*as*, *ā*), m. f. a metre belonging to the class *Ashṭi* (also called *Citra* or *Cañcalā*). **-sulabha**, mfn. very easily obtainable. **-suhita**, mfn. excessively kind, over-kind. **-sṛishṭi** (*áti-*), f. an extraordinary or excellent creation, ŚBr. xiv. **-sevā**, f. excessive addiction (to a habit). **-saurabha**, mfn. very fragrant; (*am*), n. extraordinary fragrance. **-sauhitya**, n. excessive satiety, e.g. being spoiled, stuffed with food, &c., Mn. iv, 62. **-stuti**, f. excessive praise, Nir. **-sthira**, mfn. very stable. **-sthūla** (*áti-*), mfn. excessively big or clumsy, VS. &c.; excessively stupid. **-snigdha**, mfn. very smooth, very nice, very affectionate. **-sparśa**, m. too marked contact (of the tongue and palate) in pronunciation. **-sphira**, mfn. very tremulous. **-svapna**, m. excessive sleep; (*am*), n. excessive tendency to dreaming. **-svastha**, mfn. enjoying excellent health. **-hasita**, n. or **-hāsa**, m. excessive laughter. **-hrasva** (*áti-*), mfn. excessively short, VS. &c. **Aty-agni**, m. morbidly rapid digestion. **Áty-aṇu**, mfn. very thin, MaitrS. **Aty-adbhuta**, mfn. very wonderful; (*as*), m., N. of the Indra in the ninth Manvantara, VP.; (*am*), n. a great wonder. **Aty-adhvan**, m. a long way or journey, excessive travelling. **Aty-amarshaṇa** or **-amarshin**, mfn. quite out of temper. **Aty-amla**, mfn. very acid; (*as*), m. the tree Spondias Mangifera; (*ā*), f. a species of citron. **Atyamla-parṇī**, f. 'having very acid leaves,' N. of a medicinal plant. **Aty-alpa**, mfn. very little. **Aty-aśana**, n. immoderate eating. **Aty-aśnat**, mfn. eating too much. **Aty-asama**, mfn. very uneven, very rough. **Aty-ādara**, m. excessive deference. **Aty-ādāna**, n. taking away too much. **Áty-ānanda**, m. excessive wantonness, ŚBr.; (mfn.), excessively wanton, Suśr. **Áty-āpti**, f. complete attainment, AV. xi, 7, 22. **Aty-ārūḍhi**, f. or **-āroha**, m. mounting too high, insolence, arrogance. **Aty-āśā**, f. extravagant hope. **Áty-āśita**, mfn. (√2. *aś*), too satiate, MaitrS. **Aty-āsārin**, mfn. excessively flowing towards, TS. **Aty-āhāra**, m. excess in eating. **Aty-āhārin**, mfn. eating immoderately, gluttonous. **Aty-āhita**, n. great calamity; great danger; facing great danger; a daring action. **Aty-ukti**, f. excessive talking; exaggeration; hyperbole. **Aty-ugra**, mfn. very fierce; very pungent; (*am*), n. Asa Fœtida. **Aty-uccais**, ind. very loudly. **Atyuccair-dhvani**, m. a very loud sound; a very high note. **Aty-utkaṭa**, mfn. very imposing or immense. **Aty-utsāha**, m. excessive vigour. **Aty-udāra**, mfn. very liberal. **Aty-ulbaṇa** or **-ulvaṇa**, mfn. very conspicuous, excessive. **Aty-ushṇa**, mfn. very hot. **Aty-ūdhnī**, f. having an exceedingly large udder, Pāṇ. Sch.

अतिकथ *ati-katha*, mfn. transgressing tradition or law, deviating from the rules of caste; (see also s. v. *ati*.)

अतिकन्दक *ati-kandaka*, *as*, m. the plant Hastikanda.

अतिकल्याण *áti-kalyāṇa*, mf(*ī*)n. 'past or beyond beauty,' not beautiful, ŚBr.

अतिकश *ati-kaśa*, mfn. beyond the whip, unmanageable, Pāṇ. vi, 2, 191, Sch.

अतिकुप् *ati-√kup*, to become very angry.

अतिकूर्द् *ati-√kūrd*, to jump about.

अतिकृति *ati-kṛiti* or better *abhi-kṛiti*, q. v.

अतिकृष् *ati-√kṛish*, to drag over or beyond.

अतिकेशर *ati-keśara*, *as*, m. the plant Trapa Bispinosa.

अतिक्रम् *ati-√kram*, to step or go beyond or over or across, (Ved. Inf. *ati-krā́me*, to be walked on, RV. i, 105, 16); to pass, cross; to pass time; to surpass, excel, overcome; to pass by, neglect; to overstep, transgress, violate; to pass on or away; to step out; to part from, lose: Caus. *-krāmayati* or *-kramayati*, to allow to pass (as time); to leave unnoticed.

Ati-krama, *as*, m. passing over, overstepping; lapse (of time); overcoming, surpassing, conquering; excess, imposition, transgression, violation; neglect; determined onset.

Ati-krámaṇa, *am*, n. the act of passing over, ŚBr., surpassing, overstepping; excess; passing, spending (time).

Ati-kramaṇīya, mfn. to be passed beyond or over; generally negative *an-atikramaṇīya*, q. v.

Ati-kramin, mfn. (ifc.) exceeding, violating, &c.

Ati-kramya, ind. having passed beyond or over.

Ati-krānta, mfn. having passed or transgressed; exceeded, surpassed, overcome. **-nishedha**, mfn. one who has neglected a prohibition.

Ati-krānti, *is*, f. transgression, Kir.

Ati-krāmaka, mfn. exceeding, transgressing, L.

अतिक्षर् *ati-√kshar*, to overflow or flow through, RV. &c. (3. sg. aor. *ákshār áti*, RV. ix, 43, 5).

अतिक्षिप् *ati-√kship*, to throw beyond.

Ati-kshipta, mfn. thrown beyond; (*am*), n. (in med.) sprain or dislocation of a particular kind, Suśr.

अतिखट्व *ati-khaṭva*, mfn. beyond the bedstead, able to do without a bedstead, Pāṇ. Sch.

अतिख्या *ati-√khyā*, to survey, overlook (3. sg. impf. *áty-akhyat*), AV.; to neglect, pass over, abandon (2. sg. Conj. *áti-khyas*, 2. du. Conj. *áti-khyatam*), RV.

अतिगम् *ati-√gam* or *ati-√1. gā*, to pass by or over; to surpass, overcome; to escape; neglect; to pass away, die.

Ati-ga, mfn. (ifc.) exceeding, overcoming, surpassing (cf. *śokâtiga*); transgressing, violating.

Ati-gata, mfn. having passed; being past.

अतिगर्ज् *ati-√garj*, to speak loudly or provokingly or in a threatening voice, MBh.

अतिगव *ati-gava*, mfn. (a bull) covering the cow, L.

अतिगाह् *ati-√gāh*, 'to emerge over,' to rise upon, RV.

Ati-gāḍha, mfn. See p. 12, col. 2.

अतिगुर् *ati-√gur*, (Pot. *áti juguryā́t*), to cry out, give a shriek, RV. i, 173, 2.

अतिगुहा *ati-guhā*, f. the plant Hemionites Cordifolia.

अतिग्रह् *ati-√grah*, to take beyond or over the usual measure, ŚBr.; TBr.; ŚāṅkhŚr.; to surpass, Pāṇ. v, 4, 46, Sch.

Ati-grahá, *as*, m. act of taking over or beyond, surpassing; one who takes or seizes to an extraordinary extent; (in phil.) = *atigrāha*.

Ati-grāha, *as*, m. the object of a *graha* (q.v.) or organ of apprehension (these are eight, and their corresponding *ati-grāhas* or objects are *apāna*, 'fragrant substance;' *nāman*, 'name;' *rasa*, 'flavour;' *rūpa*, 'form;' *śabda*, 'sound;' *kāma*, 'desire;' *karman*, 'action;' *sparśa*, 'touch'), ŚBr. xiv.

Ati-grāhyà, *as*, m., N. of three successive libations made (or cups filled) at the Jyotishṭoma sacrifice, TS.; ŚBr. &c.

अतिघ *ati-gha*, *as*, m. (√*han*), 'very destructive,' a weapon, bludgeon; wrath.

Ati-ghnī́, f. utter oblivion or profound sleep (obliterating all that is disagreeable in the past, and regarded as the highest condition of bliss), ŚBr. xiv.

Ati-ghnyà (4), mfn. one who is in the condition *ati-ghnī́*, AV.

अतिचमू *ati-camū*, mfn. (victorious) over armies, L.

अतिचर् *ati-√car*, to pass by; to overtake, surpass; to transgress, offend, be unfaithful to.

Ati-cara, mfn. transient, changeable; (*ā*), f. the shrub Hibiscus Mutabilis.

Ati-caraṇa. See p. 12, col. 2.

Ati-cāra, *as*, m. passing by, overtaking, surpassing; accelerated motion, especially of planets; transgression.

Ati-cārin, mfn. surpassing, transgressing.

अतिचृत् *ati-√cṛit*, to stick on, fasten, AV.

अतिचेष्ट् *ati-√cesht*, to make extraordinary or excessive efforts.

अतिच्छन्दस् *áti-cchandas*, mfn. past worldly desires, free from them, ŚBr. xiv; (*ās*, *as*), f. n., N. of two large classes of metres; (*as*), n., N. of a particular brick in the sacrificial fire-place.

अतिजगती *ati-jagatī*, f., N. of a class of metres (belonging to those called *Aticchandas*, and consisting of four lines, each containing thirteen syllables).

अतिजन *ati-jana*, mfn. 'beyond men,' uninhabited.

अतिजात *ati-jāta*, mfn. superior to parentage.

अतिजि *ati-√ji* (aor. *áty-ajaishīt*), to conquer, AV.

अतिजीव् *ati-√jīv*, to survive; to surpass in the mode of living.

अतितत *ati-tata*, mfn. (√*tan*), stretching far, making one's self big, conceited, Śiś.

अतितप् *ati-√tap*, to be very hot, AV. xviii, 2, 36, &c.; to heat, AV. xiii, 2, 40; BhP.; to affect greatly: Caus. *-tāpayati*, to heat much.

अतितराम् *ati-tarā́m*, ind. (compar. of *áti*), above in rank (with acc.), KenaUp.; better, higher, more (with abl.), ŚBr. &c.; very much, exceedingly, excessively.

अतितृद् *ati-√trid*, to cleave, split, VS.; to pierce through, penetrate, AV.

अतितृप् *ati-√trip*, to be satiated.

अतितॄ *ati-√trī*, to pass through or by or over, cross, overcome, escape: Desid. *-titīrshati*, to be desirous of crossing or overcoming, BhP.
Ati-tārin, mfn. crossing, AitBr.
Ati-tāryà, mf(*ā*)n. to be crossed or passed over or overcome, AV.

अतित्यद् *ati-tyad*, surpassing that, Pāṇ. vii, 2, 102, Sch.

अतित्वम् *ati-tvam*, surpassing thee, Pāṇ. vii, 2, 97, Sch.; *atitvām, atitvān*, acc. sing. and pl. him that surpasses thee, them that surpass thee; (fictitious forms coined by grammarians.)

अतित्वर् *ati-√tvar*, to hasten overmuch.

अतिथि *átithi, is*, m. (*√at*, or said to be from *a-tithi*, 'one who has no fixed day for coming'), a guest, a person entitled to hospitality; N. of Agni; of an attendant on Soma; N. of Suhotra (king of Ayodhyā, and grandson of Rāma). **–kriyā**, f. hospitality. **–gvá**, m. 'to whom guests should go,' N. of Divodāsa and of another mythical hero, RV. **–tva**, n. state of a guest, hospitality. **–deva**, mfn. one to whom a guest is as a divinity, TUp. **–dvesha**, m. hatred of guests, inhospitality. **–dharma**, m. rights of hospitality, Mn. iii, 111, &c. **–dharmin**, mfn. entitled to hospitality, Mn. iii, 112. **–pati** (*átithi-*), m. a host, entertainer of a guest, AV. **–pūjana**, n. or **-pūjā**, f. showing honour to a guest. **–vat**, ind. like a guest. **–satkāra**, m. honourable treatment of a guest. **–sevā**, f. attention to a guest.
Atithin, mfn. (*√at*), travelling, RV. x, 68, 3; (*ī*), m., N. of a king (also Suhotra and Atithi, q. v.)

अतिदघ् *ati-√dagh*, to go beyond, to pass (3. sg. *áti-dhak*, 2. du. *áti-dhaktam*), RV.

अतिदत्त *ati-datta, as*, m., N. of a brother of Datta and son of Rājādhideva, Hariv.

अतिदह् *ati-√dah*, to burn or blaze across, ŚBr.; to burn or distress greatly.

अतिदा *ati-√1. dā*, to surpass in giving, RV. viii, 1, 38; to pass over in giving, KātyŚr.

अतिदान्त *ati-dānta, as*, m., N. of a prince.

अतिदाश् *ati-√dāś*, to favour with a gift, present, RV.

अतिदिव् *ati-√2. div* (ind. p. *dívyā* [=°*vya*]), to play higher, RV. x, 42, 9; to risk (in playing), MBh. ii, 2041.

अतिदिश् *ati-√diś*, to make over, transfer, assign: Pass. *-diśyate*, (in Gr.) to be overruled or attracted or assimilated.
Ati-dishṭa, mfn. overruled, attracted, influenced, inferred, substituted.
Ati-deśa, *as*, m. transfer, extended application, inference, analogy, overruling influence, assimilation; a rule providing for more than the usual rule; putting one thing instead of another, substitution; *rūpâti-deśa*, such a rule as affecting the form of a word; (mfn.), overruling, previously stated.

अतिदीप्य *ati-dīpya, as*, m. 'very brilliant,' the plant Plumbago Rosea.

अतिदृप् *ati-√drip*, to be excessively conceited.

अतिदेव *ati-deva, as*, m. a superior god; surpassing the gods.

अतिद्रु *ati-√2. dru*, to run by, pass hastily, RV.; AV.; to pass over, ŚBr.

अतिधन्वन् *ati-dhanvan, ā*, m., N. of a Vedic teacher, a descendant of Śunaka, VBr.

अतिधा *ati-√dhā*, to put away.
Ati-hita, mfn. put away or aside, AV.

अतिधाव् *ati-√1. dhāv*, to run or rush over.

अतिधृति *ati-dhriti, is*, f., N. of a class of metres (belonging to those called *Aticchandas*, and consisting of four lines, each containing nineteen syllables); (in arithm.) nineteen.

अतिध्यै *ati-√dhyai*, to meditate deeply, VP.

अतिध्वंस् *ati-√dhvans*, to raise the dust in running through or over (3. pl. Conj. aor. *ati-dhvasán*), RV. viii, 55, 5.

अतिनम् *ati-√nam*, to bend aside, keep on one side.

अतिनामन् *ati-nāman, ā*, m., N. of a Saptarshi of the sixth Manvantara.

अतिनाष्ट्र *ati-nāshṭrá*, mfn. beyond danger, out of danger, ŚBr.

अतिनिःश्वस् *ati-niḥ-√śvas*, to breathe or sigh violently.

अतिनिचृत् *ati-nicrit* (or wrongly written *ati-nivrit*), f., N. of a Vedic metre of three pādas (containing respectively seven, six and seven syllables), RV. Prāt. &c.

अतिनिद्रम् *ati-nidram*, ind. beyond sleeping time, Pāṇ. ii, 1, 6, Sch. See also *ati-nidra* s. v. *ati*.

अतिनिष्टन् *ati-nish-ṭan* (*√tan*), (perf. Pot. 3. pl. *áti nísh-ṭatanyuḥ*), to penetrate (with rays), RV. i, 141, 13.

अतिनिह्नुत्य *ati-ni-hnutya*, ind. p. (*√hnu*), denying obstinately.

अतिनी *ati-√nī*, to lead over or beyond, to help a person over anything, RV. &c.; to allow to pass away: Intens. Ā. *-neniyáte*, to bring forward, RV. vi, 47, 16.

अतिनु *ati-√3. nu*, Caus. to turn away, TS.

अतिनुद् *ati-√nud*, to drive by, AV.

अतिनेद् *ati-√ned*, to stream or flow over, foam over, TS. &c.

अतिनौ *ati-nau*, mfn. disembarked, Pāṇ. Sch.

अतिपञ्चा *ati-pañcā*, f. a girl who is past five.

अतिपटीक्षेप *ati-paṭikshepa*, v. l. for *a-paṭīkshepa, as*, m. omitting to remove or non-removal of the theatrical curtain.

अतिपठ् *ati-√paṭh*, Pass. *-paṭhyate*, to be greatly proclaimed or celebrated, MBh.

अतिपत् *ati-√2. pat*, to fall or fly by or past or beyond or over; to neglect, miss: Caus. *-pātayati*, to cause to fly by; to drag away; to make effectless.
Ati-patana, *am*, n. act of falling or flying beyond, passing, missing, transgressing.
Ati-patita, mfn. passed beyond, transgressed, missed.
Ati-pāta, *as*, m. passing away, lapse; neglect, transgression; ill-usage, opposition, contrariety.
Ati-pātita, mfn. completely displaced or broken; (*am*), n. (in med.) complete fracture of a bone.
Ati-pātin, mfn. overtaking, excelling in speed; (in med.) running a rapid course, acute; neglecting.
Ati-pātya, mfn. to be passed over, to be neglected.

अतिपत्त्र *ati-pattra, as*, m. the Teak tree; the tree Hastikanda.

अतिपद् *ati-√pad*, to go beyond (acc.), jump over; to neglect, transgress: Caus. *-pādayati*, to allow to pass by.
Ati-patti, *is*, f. going beyond, passing, lapse; *kriyâtipatti*, the passing by of an action unaccomplished, Pāṇ. iii, 3, 139.
Ati-panna, mfn. gone beyond, transgressed, missed; past.

अतिपर *ati-para*, mfn. one who has overcome his enemies; (*as*), m. a great enemy.

अतिपरी *ati-parī* (*pari-√i*), to pass round, ĀpŚr.

अतिपश् *ati-√paś*, to look beyond, look through, RV. i, 94, 7; AV.

अतिपा *ati-√1. pā*, Caus. P. *-pāyayati*, to give to drink in great quantity, Kathās.

अतिपादनिचृत् *ati-pāda-nicrit*, f., N. of a Vedic metre of three pādas (containing respectively six, eight and seven syllables).

अतिपितृ *áti-pitri, tā*, m. surpassing his own father, ŚBr. xiv.
Ati-pitāmaha, *as*, m. surpassing his own paternal grandfather, ŚBr. xiv.

अतिपू *ati-√pū*, P. to clarify or purify through (3. pl. aor. *áti apāvishuḥ*), RV. ix, 60, 2: Ā. *-pavate*, to purify or purge by flowing through (especially used of the Soma juice, which is considered to be a purgative), ŚBr. &c.

अतिपृ *ati-√1. pri*, to convey across, to help over, RV.; to cross, pass over, RV. i, 174, 9 & vi, 20, 12; to keep (a promise): Caus. *-pārayati*, to lead or convey over, RV. &c.

अतिपॄ *ati-√prī*, cl. 4. P. *-pūryati*, to become full or overflowing, MBh.

अतिप्रचित् *ati-pra-√cit, -cekite* (=*-cikite*, BR.; =Intens. *-cekitte*, Gmn.), to be clearly distinct or distinguishable, RV. i, 55, 3.

अतिप्रच्यु *ati-pra-√cyu*, to pass by, TBr.: Caus. *-cyāvayati*, to cause to pass by, ŚBr.

अतिप्रछ् *ati-√prach*, to go on asking, ŚBr. &c.

अतिप्रज्वल् *ati-pra-√jval*, to flame or blaze exceedingly, MBh.

अतिप्रणश् *ati-pra-ṇaś* (*√2. naś*), to be entirely deprived of (acc.), ŚBr.

अतिप्रणी *ati-pra-ṇī* (*√nī*), to lead by or beyond, Lāṭy., ĀśvŚr.

अतिप्रणुद् *ati-pra-ṇud* (*√nud*), to press or incite very strongly.

अतिप्रपद् *ati-pra-√pad*, Caus. *-pādayati*, to help to pass into the other world (Comm.), MBh. iv, 1717.

अतिप्रमाण *ati-pramāṇa*, mfn. beyond measure, immense.

अतिप्रयम् *ati-pra-√yam*, to give or hand over, TS.; TBr.

अतिप्रयुज् *ati-pra-√yuj*, to separate from (with instr.), TS.

अतिप्रवह् *ati-pra-√vah*, to extend or carry beyond.

अतिप्रवा *ati-pra-√2. vā*, cl. 4. P. *-vāyati*, to blow violently, MBh.

अतिप्रविद्ध *ati-pra-viddha*, mfn. (*√vyadh*), frightened away, scared, R.

अतिप्रवृत् *ati-pra-√vrit*, to issue violently (as blood from a wound), Suśr.; to have an intense effect (as venom), Suśr.

अतिप्रवे *ati-pra-√ve*, to add in weaving, weave on an additional piece, ŚāṅkhBr.

अतिप्रशंस् *ati-pra-√śans*, to praise highly.

अतिप्रश्रु *ati-pra-√śru*, cl. 5. Ā. *-śriṇve* (Ved. 3. sg.), to become known or famous more than others, RV. x, 11, 7.

अतिप्रसद् *ati-pra-√sad*, P. *-sīdati*, to become completely cheerful.

अतिप्रसृ *ati-pra-√sri*, Intens. *-sarsrite*, to outstrip, surpass, RV. ii, 25, 1.
Ati-pra-sṛita, mfn. issued violently.

अतिप्रस्था *ati-pra-√sthā*, to have an advantage over, RV. i, 64, 13 & viii, 60, 16.

अतिप्रहा *ati-pra-√2. hā*, cl. 3. Ā. *-jihīte*, to give or hand over, ŚBr.

अतिप्राणम् *ati-prāṇam*, ind. exceeding life.
Ati-prāṇa-priya, mfn. dearer than life.

अतिप्रु *ati-√pru*, to jump over, to escape, TS.

अतिप्रेषित *ati-preshita, am*, n. the time following the Praisha ceremony, KātyŚr.

अतिबाध् *ati-√bādh*, to molest or annoy exceedingly.

अतिबृह् *ati-√1. bṛih*, to push out intensely (scil. *retas*; used only for the etym. of *vṛishabha*), Nir.

अतिब्रह्मन् *ati-brahman*, *ā*, m., N. of a king.

अतिब्रू *ati-√brū* or *abhi-√brū*, to insult, abuse, MBh. iii, 15640.

अतिभा *ati-√bhā*, *-bhā́ti*, to blaze or be very bright, AV. x, 3, 17; R.

अतिभू *ati-√bhū* (perf. *-babhūva*), to originate or take rise in an excessive way, MBh. viii, 4541; P. (once Ā., TĀr.), to excel, surpass, PBr.; MBh. &c.: Desid. to intend to surpass, ĀśvŚr.

Ati-bhāva, m. superiority, overcoming.

अतिभूमि *ati-bhūmi*, *is*, f. extensive land; culmination, eminence, superiority; excess.

अतिभूष् *ati-√2. bhūsh*, to adorn one's self before (another); to adorn richly.

अतिभृ *ati-√bhṛi*, Ā. to pass or extend over (perf. 2. sg. *-jabhrishe*), RV. ix, 86, 29 & 100, 9.

Ati-bhāra, *as*, m. See s.v. *ati*.

अतिमन् *ati-√man*, *-manyate* (1. pl. *-manāmahé 'ti*), to disdain, despise, RV. &c.; to value less than one's self, ŚBr.; to pride one's self, ŚBr.

Ati-mānita, mfn. honoured highly; cf. *ati-mānā́* s.v. *ati*.

अतिमनुष्यबुद्धि *ati-manushya-buddhi*, mfn. having a superhuman intellect.

अतिमर्त्य *ati-martya*, mfn. superhuman.

अतिमर्याद *ati-maryāda*, mfn. exceeding the proper limit; (*am*), ind. beyond bounds.

अतिमर्शम् *ati-marśam*, ind. (*√mṛiś*), so as to encroach, AitBr.

अतिमात्र *ati-mātrá*, mfn. exceeding the proper measure, AV. &c.; (*ám*), ind. or *-śas*, ind. beyond measure.

अतिमानुष *ati-mānusha*, mfn. superhuman, divine, MBh. &c.

अतिमाम् *ati-mām* (acc. of *aty-aham*, q.v.), surpassing me, Pāṇ. vii, 2, 97, Sch.

अतिमाय *ati-māya*, mfn. emancipated from Māyā or Illusion; finally liberated.

अतिमार *ati-māra* or *ati-bhāra*, *as*, m., N. of a prince.

अतिमित 1. *ati-mita*, mfn. over measured, beyond measure, exceeding.

अतिमित 2. *a-timita*, mfn. not moistened.

अतिमुच् *ati-√muc*, Pass. *-mucyate*, to avoid, escape, ŚBr. &c.

Ati-mukta or **ati-muktaka**, *as*, m. 'surpassing pearls in whiteness,' N. of certain shrubs.

Ati-mukti, *is*, f. final liberation. See *ati*.

Ati-mucya, ind. p. having dismissed or given up.

Ati-mokshá, *as*, m. final liberation, ŚBr. xiv.

Ati-mokshin, mfn. escaping, TS.; Kāṭh.

अतिमृत्यु *ati-mṛityu*, mfn. overcoming death, ChUp.

अतियज् *ati-√yaj*, to neglect or pass in offering a sacrifice, TS.

अतिया *ati-√yā*, to pass over or before; to surpass, RV. &c.; to pass by, RV. i, 135, 7; to transgress, BhP.

अतियूयम् *ati-yūyam* (nom. pl. of *ati-tvam*, q.v.), surpassing thee.

अतिराज् *ati-√rāj*, to shine over (aor. Subj. 3. sg. *áti rāṭ*), RV. vi, 12, 5.

Ati-rājan, *ā*, m. a supreme king; superior to a king, Pāṇ. iv, 1, 12, Sch.; (*-rājñī*), f. (a woman) superior to a king, ib. **Ati-rājakumārī**, mfn. superior to a princess, Pāṇ. i, 2, 48, Sch.

Atirājaya, Nom. P. *atirājayati*, to surpass a king, Pāṇ. vii, 4, 2, Sch.

अतिरात्र *ati-rātrá*, mfn. prepared or performed over-night, RV. vii, 103, 7; (*ás*), m. an optional part of the Jyotishṭoma sacrifice; commencement and conclusion of certain sacrificial acts; the concluding Vedic verse chanted on such occasions, AV. &c.; N. of a son of Cākshusha the sixth Manu. **–savanīya-paśu**, m. the victim sacrificed at the Atirātra.

अतिरि *ati-ri*, neut. of *ati-rai*, q.v.

अतिरिच् *ati-√ric*, Pass. *-ricyate*, to be left with a surplus, to surpass (in a good or bad sense with abl. or acc.); to be superior, predominate, prevail: Caus. *-recayati*, to do superfluously, to do too much, ŚBr. &c.

Áti-rikta, mfn. left with or as a surplus, left apart; redundant, unequalled; different from (with abl.) **–tā**, f. redundancy, &c. **Atiriktâṅga**, mfn. having a redundant limb or finger or toe; (*am*), n. a redundant limb or finger or toe.

Ati-reka or **atī-reká** [only once, ŚBr.], *as*, m. surplus, excess; redundancy; difference.

Ati-rekin, mfn. surpassing.

अतिरुच् 1. *ati-√ruc*, to shine over or along, RV. &c.; to surpass in shining.

2. **Ati-rúc**, m. a horse's fetlock or knee, VS.

अतिरुह् *ati-√ruh*, to climb or ascend over, RV. ix, 17, 5; to grow higher, RV. x, 90, 2.

अतिरै *ati-rai*, *ās*, *ās*, *i*, exceeding one's income, extravagant, Pāṇ. Sch.

अतिलङ्घ् *ati-√laṅgh*, Caus. *-laṅghayati*, to transgress, Kathās.

अतिलिहा *atilihā* or *aṭhillā*, f., N. of a Prākṛit metre (of four lines, each containing sixteen Mātras).

अतिवच् *ati-√vac*, to blame; to speak too loudly either in blaming or praising.

अतिवद् *ati-√vad*, to speak louder or better; to surpass or overpower in disputing, TBr. &c.; to ask for too much, AV.

अतिवयम् *ati-vayam* (nom. pl. of *aty-aham*, q.v.), surpassing me.

अतिवह् *ati-√vah*, to carry over or across; to pass by; to pass (time), Daś.: Caus. *-vāhayati*, to let pass, get over or through, endure; to let time pass, spend.

Ati-vāhana, *am*, n. excessive toiling or enduring.

Ati-vāhika, mfn. 'swifter than the wind,' N. of the liṅga-śarīra (but see *ātivāhika*); (*as*), m. an inhabitant of the lower world.

Ati-vāhya, mfn. to be passed (as time, &c.); (*am*), n. the passing of time.

Ati-voḍhṛi, *ḍhā*, m. one who carries over or across, ŚBr.

अतिवा *ati-√2. vā*, cl. 2. P. *-vāti*, to blow beyond, AV.: cl. 4. P. *-vāyati*, to blow violently; (*ati-vāyati*), pr.p.loc.ind. the wind blowing strongly, MBh.

अतिवास *ati-vāsa*, *as*, m. a fast on the day before performing the Śrāddha.

अतिविधा *ati-vi-√dhā*, cl. 3. Ā. *-dhatte*, to distribute too much, ŚBr.

अतिविराज् *ati-vi-√rāj*, to shine or be brilliant exceedingly, MBh. &c.

अतिविलङ्घ् *ati-vi-√laṅgh*, Caus. *-laṅghayati*, to pass by without taking notice of, BhP.

अतिविलुड् *ati-vi-√luḍ*, Caus. *-loḍayati*, to disturb, destroy, MBh.

अतिविवृत् *ati-vi-√vṛit*, Caus. *-vartayati*, to separate too far, to make too great distinction between, RV. Prāt.

अतिविश्रम्भ् *ati-vi-√śrambh*, Caus. *-śrambhayati*, to make too familiar or too intimate, Car.

Ati-vi-śrabdha, mfn. entirely trusting or confiding in; (*am*), ind. quite confidently.

अतिविश्व *ati-viśva*, *as*, m. 'superior to all or to the universe,' N. of a Muni, Hariv.

अतिविश्वस् *ati-vi-√śvas*, to confide or trust too much (generally with *na*, neg.)

अतिवी *ati-√vī*, to outstrip, RV. v, 44, 7.

अतिवृंहित *ati-vṛiṇhita*, mfn. (*√vṛiṇh*), strengthened, MBh. v, 499.

अतिवृत् *ati-√vṛit*, to pass beyond, surpass, cross; to get over, overcome; to transgress, violate, offend, especially by unfaithfulness; to pass away; to delay.

Ati-vartana, *am*, n. a pardonable offence or misdemeanour.

Ati-vartin, mfn. passing beyond, crossing, passing by, surpassing; guilty of a pardonable offence.

Ati-vṛitti, *is*, f. surpassing; hyperbolical meaning; (in med.) excessive action.

अतिवृध् *ati-√vṛidh*, to surpass in growing, grow beyond, ŚBr.

Ati-vṛiddha, mfn. very large; very old.

अतिवृष् *ati-√vṛish*, to rain violently.

अतिवेल *ati-vela*, mfn. passing the proper boundary, excessive; (*am*), ind. excessively.

अतिव्यध् *ati-√vyadh* (Ved. Inf. *ati-vídhe*, RV. v, 62, 9), to pierce through, RV.; AV.

Ati-viddha, mfn. pierced through, wounded.

Ati-vyādhin, mfn. piercing through, wounding, VS.; ŚBr. xiv.

Ati-vyādhya, mfn. vulnerable.

अतिव्रज् *ati-√vraj*, to pass by; to fly over, RV. i, 116, 4; to pass or wander through.

अतिशंस् *ati-√śaṇs*, to recite beyond measure, to continue reciting; to omit in reciting, AitBr.

अतिशक्करी *ati-śakkarī* or *ati-śakvarī*, f. a class of metres of four lines, each containing fifteen syllables. It has eighteen varieties.

अतिशक्र *ati-śakra*, mfn. superior to Indra.

अतिशङ्क् *ati-√śaṅk*, to suspect strongly, Lāṭy.; to suspect falsely; to be concerned about.

अतिशय *ati-śaya*, &c. See 1. *ati-√1. śī*.

अतिशस्त्र *ati-śastra*, mfn. superior to weapons.

अतिशाक्कर *atiśākvara*, mfn. written in or connected with the Ati-śakvarī metre.

अतिशि *ati-√śi*, cl. 3. Ā. *-śíśite*, to sharpen up (a weapon) for attacking, RV. i, 36, 16.

अतिशिष् *ati-√2. śish*, to leave remaining: Pass. *-śishyate*, to remain.

Ati-śishṭa, mfn. remaining, TS. &c.

Ati-śesha, *as*, m. remainder, remnant (especially of time), ChUp.

अतिशी 1. *ati-√1. śī*, *-śete*, to precede in lying down, MBh.; to surpass, excel; to act as an incubus, annoy, L.: Pass. *-śayyate*, to be excelled or surpassed.

Ati-śaya, *as*, m. pre-eminence, eminence; superiority in quality or quantity or numbers; advantageous result; one of the superhuman qualities attributed to Jaina Arhats; (mfn.), pre-eminent, superior, abundant, ŚāṅkhBr. &c.; (*am* or *ena*), ind. eminently, very. **Atiśayôkti**, f. hyperbolical language; extreme assertion; verbosity.

Ati-śayana, mf(*ī*)n. eminent, abundant; (*am*), ind. excessively; (*ī*), f., N. of a metre of four lines, also called *Citralekhā*.

Ati-śayita, mfn. surpassing, superior.

Ati-śayin, mfn. excelling, abounding.

Ati-śāyana, *am*, n. excelling; excessiveness.

Ati-śāyin, mfn. excelling, abounding; excessive.

अतिशी 2. *ati-√3. śī*, to fall or drop beyond, Kāṭh.; to get out from (acc.), leave, ChUp.

अतिशीतम् *ati-śītam*, ind. past or beyond the cold, after the winter.

अतिशीलय *ati-śīlaya*, Nom. P. °*yati*, to practise or use excessively.

अतिशुभ् *ati-√śubh*, to be brilliant; to please: Caus. *-śobhayati*, to make brilliant, adorn.

अतिश्रेष्ठ *ati-śreshṭha*, mfn. superior to the best, best of all. **–tva**, n. pre-eminence.

Ati-śreyasi, *is*, m. a man superior to the most excellent woman.

अतिश्लिष् *ati-√ślish*, to fasten or tie over.

अतिश्व *ati-śva*, mf(*ī*)n. superior to, or worse

than, a dog, Pāṇ. v, 4, 96; (*ā*), m., N. of a tribe (?), (gaṇa *pakshâdi*, q. v.)

अतिषक्त *áti-shakta* or (in later texts) *ati-sakta*, mfn. (√*sañj*), connected with, AV. &c.

अतिषित *áti-shita*, mfn. tied or bound round (so as to prevent the flow of any liquid), RV. x, 73, 9.

अतिष्कन्द् *ati-shkand* (√*skand*), to cover (said of a bull), RV. v, 52, 3; to leap or jump over, Ved. Inf. (dat.) *ati-shkáde*, RV. viii, 67, 19; Ved. Inf. (abl.) *-shkádas*, RV. x, 108, 2; to omit, *án-ati-skandat*, mfn. not omitting anything, uniform, TBr.

Ati-shkádvan, mf(*arī*)n. jumping over, transgressing.

अतिष्ठिघम् *ati-shṭígham* (√*stigh*), ind. so as to overwhelm, MaitrS.

अतिष्टु *ati-shṭu* (√*stu*), to go on too far in reciting hymns of praise, PBr.; Lāṭy.

अतिष्ठत् *á-tishṭhat*, mfn. not standing, unstable, RV.

अतिष्ठा 1. *ati-shṭhā* (√*sthā*), to be at the head of, govern, RV.; AV.; to jut over or out, TBr.

2. Ati-shṭhā, f. precedence, superiority, ŚBr. &c.; (*ās*), m. f. or *ati-shṭhâvan*, m. or *atishṭhā-vat* [AV.], mfn. superior in standing, surpassing.

अतिसंधा *ati-sam-√dhā*, to overreach, deceive, Śāk.; to wrong or injure, VarBṛS.

Ati-sandhám, ind. so as to violate an agreement or any fixed order, ŚBr.

Ati-sam-dhāna, *am*, n. overreaching, cheating.

Ati-sandhita, mfn. overreached, cheated.

Ati-sam-dheya, mfn. easy to be conciliated, easy to be settled.

अतिसर्व *ati-sarva*, mfn. superior to all, Pāṇ. Sch.; (*as*), m. the Supreme.

अतिसांवत्सर *ati-sāṃvatsara*, mfn. extending over more than a year, Mn.

अतिसाम्या *ati-sāmyā*, f. the sweet juice of the Bengal Madder, Rubia Manjith.

अतिसृ *ati-√sṛi*, Caus. to cause to pass through: Pass. *-sāryate*, to be purged, Suśr.

Ati-sará, *as*, m. effort, exertion, AV.

Ati-sāra or **atī-sāra**, *as*, m. purging, dysentery.

Ati-sārakin or **atī-sārakin** or **ati-sārin** or **atī-sārin**, mfn. afflicted with purging or dysentery.

अतिसृज् *ati-√sṛij*, to glide over or along, RV.; to send away, dismiss, abandon; to leave as a remnant; to remit, forgive; to give away, present; to create in a higher degree, ŚBr. xiv.

Ati-sargá, *as*, m. act of parting with, dismissal, giving away; granting permission, leave; *atisargáṃ √1. dā*, to bid any one farewell, MaitrS.

Ati-sarjana, *am*, n. the act of giving away, granting; liberality; a gift; sending out of the world, killing.

Ati-sṛijya, mfn. to be dismissed, ŚBr.

Á'ti-sṛishṭi, *is*, f. a higher creation, ŚBr. xiv.

अतिसृप् *ati-√sṛip*, to glide or creep over, get over, RV. &c.

अतिसेन *ati-sena*, *as*, m., N. of a prince.

अतिसेव् *ati-√sev*, to use or enjoy immoderately, to practise excessively; cf. *ati-sevā* s.v. *ati*.

अतिसौपर्ण *ati-sauparṇa*, mfn. superior to (the powers of) Suparṇa or Garuḍa.

अतिस्त्रि *ati-stri*, mf(*is* or *ī*)n. surpassing a woman, L.; see Gram. 123. *b*.

अतिस्रंस् *ati-√sraṇs*, to drop or turn away from, to escape, RV. vi, 11, 6.

अतिस्रु *ati-√sru*, to flow over or flow excessively.

Ati-srāvita, mfn. caused to flow excessively (as a wound), Suśr.

Ati-sruta, mfn. that which has been flowing over (N. of Soma), VS.

अतिस्वृ *ati-√svṛi*, to hold or sustain a note, PBr.; ChUp.

Ati-svārya, mfn. the last of the seven notes, TS. Prāt.

अतिहन् *ati-√han*, Desid. *-jighāṇsati* (for *-jighāsati* fr. √2. *hā*?), to try to escape, AitBr.

Ati-hata, mfn. firmly fixed, ŚBr.; utterly destroyed, Car.

अतिहस्तय *ati-hastaya*, Nom. (fr. *ati-hasta*), P. *atihastayati*, to stretch out the hands; (fr. *ati-hastin*), to overtake on an elephant.

अतिहा *ati-√2. hā*, to jump over, RV. &c.; to pass jumping from one place to another.

अतिहिमम् *ati-himam*, ind. after the frost; past the cold.

अतिहृ *ati-√hṛi*, to hold over; to reach over; to cause to jut over; to add.

अतिह्वे *ati-√hve* (1. sg. Ā. *-hvaye*), to call over to one's side, TBr.

अती *ati* (√*i*), cl. 2. P. *aty-eti*, *-etum*, to pass by, elapse, pass over, overflow; to pass on; to get over; (Ved. Inf. *áty-etavai*), to pass through, RV. v, 83, 10; to defer; to enter; to overcome, overtake, outdo; to pass by, neglect; to overstep, violate; to be redundant; to die; Intens. *atîyate*, to overcome.

Atita, mfn. gone by, past, passed away, dead; one who has gone through or got over or beyond, one who has passed by or neglected; negligent; passed, left behind; excessive; (*as*), m., N. of a particular Śaiva sect; (*am*), n. the past. **—kāla**, m. the past time or tense. **—nauka**, mfn. passed out of a ship, landed.

Atītvarī, f. a female transgressor, bad woman, VS.

Aty-aya, aty-āya, see s. v.

अतीक्ष्ण *á-tīkshṇa*, mfn. not sharp, blunt; not severe or rigid.

अतीन्द्रिय *atîndriya*, mfn. beyond the (cognizance of the) senses; (*as*), m. (in Sāṅkhya phil.) the soul; (*am*), n., N. of Pradhāna; the mind.

अतीरेक *atī-reká*. See *ati-√ric*.

अतीव *atîva*, ind. exceedingly, very; excessively, too; quite; surpassing (with acc.): Compar. *atîva-tarām*, ind. exceedingly, excessively, Śiś. iv. 25.

अतीव्र *a-tīvra*, mfn. not sharp, blunt; not pungent.

अतीष् *atîsh* (√*ish*), to pass by (acc.), MaitrS.

अतीसार *atī-sāra*. See *ati-√sṛi*.

अतुङ्ग *a-tuṅga*, mfn. not tall, short, dwarfish.

अतुन्द *a-tunda*, mfn. not stout, thin.

अतुर *á-tura*, mfn. not liberal, not rich, AV.

अतुल *a-tula*, mfn. unequalled; (*as*), m. (destitute of weight), the Sesamum seed and plant.

A-tulya, mfn. unequalled.

अतुष *a-tushá*, mfn. without husks, ŚBr.

अतुषारकर *a-tushāra-kara*, *as*, m. 'having not cold rays,' the sun.

अतुष्टि *a-tushṭi*, *is*, f. displeasure, discontent.

अतुहिन *a-tuhina*, not cold. **—dhāman** or **-raśmi** or **-ruci**, m. 'having not cold light,' the sun, VarBṛS.

अतूतुजि *á-tūtuji*, mfn. not quick, slow, RV. vii, 28, 3.

अतूर्त *á-tūrta* [RV. viii, 99, 7] or *a-tū́rta* [RV.], mfn. not outrun, not outdone, not obstructed, unhurt; (*a-tū́rtam*), n. illimited space, RV. x, 149, 1. **—daksha**, m. 'having designs that cannot be obstructed,' N. of the Aśvins, RV. viii, 26, 1. **—pathin** (*átūrta-*), m(nom. *-panthās*)fn. having a path that cannot be obstructed, RV.

अतृणाद *á-tṛiṇâda*, *as*, m. 'not an eater of grass,' a newly-born calf, ŚBr. xiv.

A-tṛiṇyā, f. a small quantity or short supply of grass, Pāṇ. vi, 2, 156, Sch.

अतृदिल *á-tṛidila*, mfn. 'having no interstices,' solid, RV. x, 94, 11.

अतृप *a-tṛipá*, mfn. not satisfied, RV. iv, 5, 14.

Á'tṛipṇuvat, mfn. insatiable, RV. iv, 19, 3.

A-tṛipta, mfn. unsatisfied, insatiable, eager. **—dṛiś**, mfn. looking with eagerness.

A-tṛipti, *is*, f. unsatisfied condition, insatiability.

अतृषित *á-tṛishita*, mfn. not thirsty, not greedy, RV. x, 94, 11.

Á'-tṛishṇaj, mfn. not thirsty, RV. x, 94, 11.

A-tṛishyá, mfn. beyond the reach of thirst, AV.

Á'-tṛishyat, mfn. not thirsting after, not greedy, not eager, RV. i, 71, 3.

अतेजस् *a-tejas*, *as*, n. absence of brightness or vigour; dimness, shade, shadow; feebleness, dulness, insignificance; (*a-tejás*), mfn. [AV.] or *a-tejáska* [ŚBr. xiv] or *a-tejasvin*, mfn. not bright, dim, not vigorous. **A-tejo-máya**, mfn. not consisting of light or brightness, ŚBr. xiv.

अतोषणीय *a-toshaṇīya*, mfn. not to be pleased or appeased.

अत्क *átka*, *as*, (√*at*), m. a traveller, L.; a limb or member, L.; armour, mail, garment, RV.; N. of an Asura, RV.

अत्कील *atkīla*, *as*, m., N. of an ancient Ṛishi (*utkīla*, q.v.), ĀśvŚr.

अत्तलि *attali*, *is*, m., N. of a man.

अत्तव्य *attavya*, mfn. (√*ad*), fit or proper to be eaten, Mn.

A'tti, *is*, m. an eater, ŚBr. xiv.

Attṛi, *tā*, m. an eater, AV. &c.; f. *attrī́*, TS.

अत्ता *attā*, f. (probably a colloquialism borrowed from the Deccan, said to occur chiefly in dramas), a mother, L.; mother's sister, L.; elder sister, L.; (in Prākṛit) a mother-in-law, L. See *akkā*.

Atti, *is*, or **attikā**, f. elder sister, L.

अत्त्र *attra*. See 3. & 4. *atra*, p. 17, col. 2.

अत्त्रि *attri*. See *átri*, p. 17, col. 2.

अत्न *atna*, *as*, or *atnu*, *us*, m. (√*at*), the sun, L.

A'tya (2, 3), *as*, m. a courser, steed, RV.

अत्यंहस् *áty-aṇhas*, mfn. beyond the reach of evil or distress, VS.

Aty-aṇhá, *as*, m., N. of a man, TBr.

अत्यग्नि *aty-agni*, *is*, m. too rapid digestion; (mfn.), surpassing fire. **—somârka**, mfn. brighter than fire or the moon or the sun.

अत्यग्निष्टोम *aty-agnishṭoma*, *as*, m., N. of the second of the seven modifications of the Jyotishṭoma sacrifice; the Vedic verse chanted at the close of that ceremony.

अत्यग्र *áty-agra*, mfn. whose point is jutting over, TS.

अत्यङ्कुश *aty-aṅkuśa*, mfn. past or beyond the (elephant-driver's) hook, unmanageable.

अत्यङ्गुल *aty-aṅgula*, mfn. exceeding an aṅgula (finger's breadth).

अत्यतिक्रम् *aty-ati-√kram*, to approach for sexual intercourse, MBh.

अत्यतिरिच् *aty-ati-√ric*, Pass. *-ricyate*, to surpass exceedingly.

अत्यनिल *aty-anila*, mfn. surpassing the wind.

अत्यनुसृ *aty-anu-√sṛi*, Caus. *-sārayati*, to pursue excessively, MBh.

अत्यन्त *aty-anta*, mfn. beyond the proper end or limit; excessive, very great, very strong; endless, unbroken, perpetual; absolute, perfect; (*am*), ind. excessively, exceedingly; in perpetuity; absolutely, completely; to the end; (*āya*), dat. ind. for ever, perpetually, Pat.; quite, Pat. **—kopana**, mfn. very passionate. **—ga**, mfn. going very much or very fast, Pāṇ. iii, 2, 48. **—gata**, mfn. completely pertinent; always applicable, Nir.; gone for ever, Ragh. **—gati**, f. complete accomplishment; (in Gr.) the sense of 'completely.' **—gāmin**, mfn. = *-ga* above. **—guṇin**, mfn. having extraordinary qualities. **—tiraskṛita-vācya-dhvani**, f. (in rhetoric) a metaphoric or hyperbolical use of depreciatory language. **—pīḍana**, n. act of giving excessive pain. **—vāsin**, m. a student who perpetually resides with his teacher.

—saṃyoga, m. (in Gr.) immediate proximity. **—samparka,** m. excessive sexual intercourse. **—sukumāra,** mfn. very tender; (*as*), m. a kind of grain, Panicum Italicum. **Atyantâbhāva,** m. absolute non-existence.

Aty-antika, mfn. too close; (*am*), n. too great nearness, ŚBr.

Atyantīna, mfn. going far, Pāṇ. v, 2, 11.

अत्यभिसृत *aty-abhi-sṛita,* mfn. (√*sṛi*), having approached too much, having come too close, MBh. i, 3854.

अत्यय *aty-aya, as,* m. (fr. √*i* with *ati,* see *ati*), passing, lapse, passage; passing away, perishing, death; danger, risk, evil, suffering; transgression, guilt, vice; getting at, attacking, Yājñ. ii, 12; overcoming, mastering (mentally); a class, ChUp.

Atyayika. See *ātyayika.*

Atyayin, mfn. passing, Pāṇ. iii, 2, 157.

अत्यराति *aty-arāti, is,* m., N. of a son of Janantapa, AitBr.

अत्यर्थ *aty-artha,* mfn. 'beyond the proper worth,' exorbitant, excessive; (*am*), ind. excessively, exceedingly.

अत्यर्द् *aty-√ard,* to press hard, distress greatly, Bhaṭṭ.

अत्यर्ह् *aty-√arh* (Subj. *-arhāt*), to excel in worth, RV. ii, 23, 15.

अत्यवसृज् *aty-ava-√sṛij,* to let loose, let go.

अत्यवि *áty-avi, is,* m. passing over or through the strainer (consisting of sheep's wool or a sheep's tail; said of the Soma), RV.

अत्यश् *aty-√2. aś,* to precede in eating, ŚBr.; MBh.; to eat too much, Bhag.

अत्यष्टि *aty-ashṭi, is,* f. a metre (of four lines, each containing seventeen syllables); the number seventeen. **—sāmagrī,** f., N. of a work.

अत्यस् 1. *aty-√1. as* (Imper. *-astu*) to excel, surpass, RV. vii, 1, 14; AV.

अत्यस् 2. *aty-√2. as,* to shoot beyond, overwhelm, overpower (as with arrows).

Aty-asta, mfn. one who has shot or cast beyond, Pāṇ. ii, 1, 24.

Aty-āsam, ind. ifc. after the lapse of (e.g. *dvyahâtyāsam,* after the lapse of two days), Pāṇ. iii, 4, 57, Sch.

अत्यहम् *aty-aham,* surpassing me; surpassing self-consciousness, NṛisUp.; cf. Pāṇ. vii, 2, 97, Sch.

अत्यह्न *aty-ahna,* mfn. exceeding a day in duration, Pāṇ. v. 4, 88, Sch.

अत्याकार *aty-ā-kāra, as,* m. (√1. *kṛi*), contempt, blame, Pāṇ. v, 1, 134.

अत्याक्रम् *aty-ā-√kram* (ind. p. *-krámya*) to walk past, TS.; ŚBr.

अत्याचार *aty-ācāra, as,* m. performance of works of supererogation; (mfn.), negligent of or departing from the established customs.

अत्यादित्य *aty-āditya,* mfn. surpassing the sun.

अत्यादृ *aty-ā-√dṛi,* to take great care of, be anxious about.

अत्याधम् *aty-ā-√dham, -dhamati,* to breathe violently, Suśr.

अत्याधा *aty-ā-√dhā,* to place in a higher rank, ŚBr.

Aty-ā-dhāna, *am,* n. act of imposing or placing upon, Pāṇ.; imposition, deception, L.

Aty-ā-hita, mfn. disagreeable, Mbh. &c.; (*am*), n. disagreeableness, Śāk. &c. (Prākṛit *accāhida*).

अत्याय *aty-āya, as,* m. (√*i*), the act of going beyond, transgression, excess, Pāṇ. iii, 1, 141; (*am,* 4), ind. going beyond, RV. viii, 101, 14.

अत्यायत् *aty-ā-√yat,* Ā. to make extraordinary efforts for (loc.), Daś.

अत्याया *aty-ā-√yā,* to pass by, RV.

अत्यायु *atyāyu,* n., N. of a sacrificial vessel, PBr.

अत्याल *aty-āla, as,* m. Plumbago Rosea.

अत्याश्रमिन् *aty-āśramin, ī,* m. 'superior to the (four) Āśramas,' an ascetic of the highest degree.

अत्यासद् *aty-ā-√sad,* Caus. ind. p. *-sādya,* passing through.

Aty-ā-sanna, mfn. being too close.

अत्यासृ *aty-ā-√sṛi,* to run near, Kauś.

Aty-ā-sārin, mfn. flowing near violently, TS.

अत्युक्था *aty-uktā* or *-ukthā,* f., N. of a class of metres (of four lines, each containing two syllables).

अत्युक्ष् *aty-√2. uksh* (perf. 2. sg. *-vavakshitha*) to surpass, RV.

अत्युत्क्रम् *aty-ut-√kram,* to surpass, excel.

अत्युद्धा *aty-ud-dhā* (√2. *hā*), to surpass, ŚBr. xiv.

अत्युपध *aty-upadha,* mfn. superior to any test, tried, trustworthy, L.

अत्युपयज् *aty-upa-√yaj,* to continue offering sacrifices, ŚBr.

अत्युह् *aty-√uh.* See *aty-√1. ūh.*

अत्यूमशा *aty-ūmaśā,* ind. a particle of abuse (used in comp. with √1. *as, bhū,* 1. *kṛi;* gaṇa *ūry-ādi,* q.v.)

अत्यूर्मि *áty-ūrmi,* mfn. overflowing, bubbling over, RV. ix, 17, 3.

अत्यूह् 1. *aty-√1. ūh,* to convey across. Spelt *aty-uh* in some forms, possibly belonging to √*vah.*

अत्यूह् 2. *aty-√2. ūh, -ohate,* to contemn, RV. viii, 69, 14.

Aty-ūha, *as,* m. excessive deliberation; a gallinule, a peacock, Car.; (*ā*), f. the plant Jasminum Villosum or Nyctanthes Tristis.

अत्यृज् *aty-√ṛij,* to convey across (towards an object), admit to, AitBr.

अत्येष् *aty-√esh* (Subj. 2. sg. *-eshas*) to glide over, AV. ix, 5, 9.

अत्र 1. *á-tra* (or Ved. *á-trā*), ind. (fr. pronominal base *a;* often used in sense of loc. case *asmin*), in this matter, in this respect; in this place, here; at this time; there; then. **—daghná,** mf(*ā*)n. reaching so far up, having this (or that) stature, ŚBr. **—bhavat,** mfn. his Honour, your Honour, &c. (used honorifically in dramatic language). **Atrâiva,** ind. on this very spot.

Atratya, mfn. connected with this place, produced or found here, L.

अत्र 2. *a-tra,* mfn. (√*trai*), (only for the etym. of *kshattra*), 'not enjoying or affording protection,' BṛĀrUp.

अत्र 3. *atrá, as,* m. (for *at-tra,* fr. √*ad*), a devourer, demon, RV.; AV.; a Rākshasa.

4. **Átra,** *am,* n. (for *at-tra*), food, RV. x, 79, 2.

Átri, *is,* m. (for *at-tri,* fr. √*ad*), a devourer, RV. ii, 8, 5; N. of a great Ṛishi, author of a number of Vedic hymns; (in astron.) one of the seven stars of the Great Bear; (*atrayas*), pl. m. the descendants of Atri. **—caturaha,** m. 'the four days of Atri,' N. of a sacrifice. **—jāta,** m. 'produced by Atri,' the moon. **—dṛig-ja** or **-netra-ja** or **-netra-prasūta** or **-netra-prabhava** or **-netra-sūta** or **-netra-bhū,** m. 'produced by Atri's look,' the moon; (in arithm.) the number one. **—bhāradvājikā,** f. marriage of descendants of Atri with those of Bhāradvāja. **—vát,** ind. like Atri, RV. **—saṃhitā** or **-smṛiti,** f. the code ascribed to Atri.

Atrín, *ī,* m. a devourer, demon, RV.; a Rākshasa.

अत्रप *a-trapa,* mfn. destitute of shame.

अत्रपु *a-trapú* or *a-trapús,* mfn. not tinned, MaitrS.; Kāṭh.; KapS.

अत्रस्नु *á-trasnu* [ŚBr.; Ragh. xiv, 47] or *a-trāsa,* mfn. fearless.

अत्रिजात *a-tri-jāta,* mfn. 'not born thrice' (but twice), a man belonging to one of the first three classes; [for *atri-jāta,* see under *atri.*]

अत्वक्क *a-tvák-ka* [TS.] or *a-tvác* [ŚBr.], mfn. skinless.

अत्वरा *a-tvarā,* f. freedom from haste.

अथ *átha* (or Ved. *áthā*), ind. (probably fr. pronom. base *a*), an auspicious and inceptive particle (not easily expressed in English), now; then; moreover; rather; certainly; but; else; what? how else? &c. **—kim,** ind. how else? what else? certainly, assuredly, sure enough. **—kimu,** ind. how much more; so much the more. **—ca,** ind. moreover, and likewise. **—tu,** ind. but, on the contrary. **—vā,** ind. or; (when repeated) either or; or rather; or perhaps; what? is it not so? &c. **—vâpi,** ind. or, rather. **Athâtas,** ind. now. **Athânantaram,** ind. now. **Athâpi,** ind. so much the more; moreover; therefore; thus.

Áthô, ind. (= *atha* above), now; likewise; next; therefore. **—vā,** ind. = *atha-vā,* Mn. iii, 202.

अथरि *athari, is,* or *atharī,* f. (said to be fr. √*at,* to go, or fr. an obsolete √*ath*), flame [Gmn.; 'the point of an arrow or of a lance,' NBD.; 'finger,' Naigh.], RV. iv, 6, 8.

1. **Atharya** [VS.] and **atharyú** [RV. vii, 1, 1], mfn. flickering, lambent.

2. **Atharya,** Nom. P. *atharyati,* to move tremulously, flicker, Naigh.

अथर्वन् *átharvan, ā,* m. (said to be fr. an obsolete word *athar,* fire), a priest who has to do with fire and Soma; N. of the priest who is said to have been the first to institute the worship of fire and offer Soma and prayers (he is represented as a Prajāpati, as Brahmā's eldest son, as the first learner and earliest teacher of the Brahma-vidyā, as the author of the Atharva-veda, as identical with Aṅgiras, as the father of Agni, &c.); N. of Śiva, Vasishṭha [Kir. x, 10], Soma, Prāṇa; (*ā, a*), m. n. the fourth or Atharva-veda (said to have been composed by Atharvan, and consisting chiefly of formulas and spells intended to counteract diseases and calamities); (*átharvāṇas*), pl. m. descendants of Atharvan, often coupled with those of Aṅgiras and Bhṛigu; the hymns of the Atharva-veda.

1. **Atharva** (in comp. for *atharvan*). **—bhūta,** *ās,* m. pl. 'who have become Atharvans,' N. of the twelve Maharshis. **—vát,** ind. like Atharvan or his descendants, RV. **—vid,** m. one versed in the Atharva-veda (a qualification essential to the special class of priests called Brahmans). **—veda,** m., N. of the fourth Veda (see above). **—śikhā,** f., N. of an Upanishad. **—śiras,** n. id.; N. of a kind of brick, TBr.; (*ās*), m., N. of Mahāpurusha. **—hṛidaya,** n., N. of a Pariśishṭa. **Atharvâṅgirás,** m. a member of the sacerdotal race or class called *Atharvâṅgirasas,* m. pl., i. e. the descendants of Atharvan and of Aṅgiras; the hymns of the Atharva-veda. **Atharvâṅgirasa,** mfn. connected with the sacerdotal class called Atharvâṅgiras; (*am*), n. the work or office of the Atharvâṅgiras; (*ās*), m. pl. the hymns of the Atharva-veda.

2. **Atharva,** *as,* m., N. of Brahmā's eldest son (to whom he revealed the Brahma-vidyā), MuṇḍUp.

Atharvaṇa, *as,* m., N. of Śiva.

Atharvaṇi, *is,* better **ātharvaṇi,** m. a Brahman versed in the Atharva-veda, L.; a family priest, L.

Atharvāṇa, *am,* n. the Atharva-veda or the ritual of it, MBh. **—vid,** m. one versed in that ritual.

Atharví, f. ['female priest,' Gmn.; BR.] pierced by the point (of an arrow or of a lance), RV. i, 112, 10; cf. *atharí.*

अद् 1. *ad,* cl. 2. P. *átti, āda, atsyati, attum,* to eat, consume, devour; Ved. Inf. *áttave,* RV.: Caus. *ādáyati* &°*te* (once *adayate* [ĀpŚr.]), to feed [cf. Lith. *edmi;* Slav. *jamj* for *jadmj;* Gk. ἔδω; Lat. *edo;* Goth. rt. *AT,* pres. *ita;* Germ. *essen;* Eng. *to eat;* Arm. *utem*]. **Ad-ādi,** mfn. belonging to the second class of roots called *ad,* &c., cf. Pāṇ. ii, 4, 72.

Attavya, átti, attṛí, 4. **átra** &c., see s. v.

2. **Ad,** mfn., ifc. 'eating,' as *matsyâd,* eating fish.

Ada or **adaka,** mfn., chiefly ifc., eating.

1. **Adát,** mfn. eating, RV. x, 4, 4, &c.

Ádana, *am,* n. act of eating; food, RV. vi, 59, 3.

Adanīya, mfn. to be eaten, what may be eaten.

Ádman, adya, advan, see s. v.

अदक्ष *a-daksha,* mfn. not dexterous, unskilful, awkward.

A-dakshiṇá, mfn. not dexterous, not handy; not right, left; inexperienced, simple-minded; not giving or bringing in a dakshiṇā or present to the priest, RV. x, 61, 10, &c. **-tva**, n. awkwardness; not bringing in a dakshiṇā.

Adakshiṇīyá, mfn. not entitled to a dakshiṇā, ŚBr.

Adakshiṇyá, mfn. not fit to be used as a dakshiṇā, TS.

अदग्ध *a-dagdha*, mfn. not burnt.

अदण्ड *a-daṇḍa*, mfn. exempt from punishment; (*am*), n. impunity.

A-daṇḍanīya, mfn. = *a-daṇḍyá*.

A-daṇḍyá, mfn. not deserving punishment, PBr.; Mn. &c.; exempt from it, ŚBr.; Mn. viii, 335.

अदत् 2. *a-dát* [RV.] or *adatka* [ChUp.], mfn. toothless. (For 1. *adát*, see above.)

अदत्त *á-datta*, mfn. not given; given unjustly; not given in marriage; one who has given nothing, AV.; (*ā*), f. an unmarried girl; (*am*), n. a donation which is null and void, Comm. on Yājñ.

Á-dattvā, ind. not having given, AV. xii, 4, 19, &c.

A-datrayā́, ind. not through a present, RV. v, 49, 3.

अदद्र्यञ्च् *adadry-añc*, *aṅ*, *īcī*, *ak* (fr. *adas* + *añc*), inclining or going to that, L.

अदन *ádana*, *adanīya*. See √*ad*.

अदन्त 1. *a-danta*, mfn. toothless; (*as*), m. a leech, L.

A-dantáka [TS.] or **a-dántaka** [ŚBr.], mfn. toothless.

A-dantya, mfn. not suitable for the teeth; not dental; (*am*), n. toothlessness.

अदन्त 2. *ad-anta*, mfn. (in Gr.) ending in *at*, i. e. in the short inherent vowel *a*.

अदब्ध *á-dabdha*, mfn. (√*dambh* or *dabh*), not deceived or tampered with, unimpaired, unbroken, pure, RV. **-dhīti** (*ádabdha-*), mfn. whose works are unimpaired, RV. vi, 51, 3. **-vrata-pramati** (*ádabdha-*), mfn. of unbroken observances and superior mind (or 'of superior mind from having unbroken observances'), RV. ii, 9, 1. **Adabdhā́yu**, m. having unimpaired vigour (or 'leaving uninjured the man who sacrifices'), VS. **Ádabdhāsu**, mfn. having a pure life, AV. v, 1, 1.

A-dábha, mfn. not injuring, benevolent, RV. v, 86, 5.

A-dabhra, mfn. not scanty, plentiful, RV. viii, 47, 6; strong.

A-dambha, mfn. free from deceit, straightforward; (*as*), m., N. of Śiva; absence of deceit; straightforwardness.

A-dambhi-tva, *am*, n. sincerity.

अदमुद्र्यञ्च् *adamudry-añc*, *aṅ*, *īcī*, *ak*, going to that, L.

Adamuy-añc or **adamūy-añc**, id., L.

अदम्य *a-damya*, mfn. untamable.

अदय *a-dayá*, mfn. (√*day*), merciless, unkind, RV. x, 103, 7; (*am*), ind. ardently.

A-dayālu, mfn. unkind.

अदर *a-dara*, mfn. not little, much.

Adaraka, *as*, m., N. of a man.

अदर्श 1. *a-darśa* (for *ā-darśa*), *as*, m. a mirror.

अदर्श 2. *a-darśa*, *as*, m. day of new moon.

A-darśana, *am*, n. non-vision, not seeing; disregard, neglect; non-appearance, latent condition, disappearance; (mfn.), invisible, latent. **-patha**, n. a path beyond the reach of vision.

A-darśanīya, mfn. invisible; (*am*), n. invisible condition.

अदल *a-dala*, mfn. leafless; (*as*), m. the plant Eugenia (or Barringtonia) Acutangula; (*ā*), f. Socotorine Aloe (Perfoliata or Indica).

अदशन् *á-daśan*, *a*, not ten, ŚBr. **Á-daśa-māsya**, mfn. not ten months old, ŚBr.

अदस् *adás*, nom. m. f. *asaú* (voc. *ásau*, MaitrS.), n. *adás*, (opposed to *idám*, q. v.), that; a certain; (*adas*), ind. thus, so; there. **Adaḥ-kṛitya**, having done that. **Ado-bhavati**, he becomes that. **Ado-máya**, mfn. made of that, containing that, ŚBr. xiv. **Ado-mūla**, mfn. rooted in that.

Adayíya, mf(*ī*)n. belonging to that or those, Naish.

Adasya, Nom. P. *adasyati*, to become that.

अदाक्षिण्य *a-dākshiṇya*, *am*, n. incivility.

अदातृ *a-dātṛi*, mfn. not giving; not liberal, miserly; not giving (a daughter) in marriage; not paying, not liable to payment.

अदान *á-dāna*, *am*, n. (√1. *dā*), not giving, act of withholding, AV. &c.; (mfn.), not giving.

A-dānyá, mfn. not giving, miserly, AV.

A-dāmán, mfn. not liberal, miserly, RV.

A-dāyin, mfn. not giving, Nir.

Á-dāśu [RV. i, 174, 6] or **á-dāśuri** [RV. viii, 45, 15] or **á-dāśvas** [RV.; Compar. *ádāśūshṭara*, RV. viii, 81, 7], mfn. not worshipping the deities, impious.

1. **Á-diti**, *is*, f. having nothing to give, destitution, RV.; for 2. *aditi*, 3. *á-diti*, see below.

अदान्त *a-dānta*, mfn. unsubdued.

अदाभ्य *á-dābhya* (3, 4), mfn. free from deceit, trusty; not to be trifled with, RV.; (*as*), m., N. of a libation (*graha*) in the Jyotishṭoma sacrifice.

अदायाद *a-dāyādá*, mf(*ī́*, in later texts *ā*)n. not entitled to be an heir; destitute of heirs.

A-dāyika, mfn. unclaimed from want of persons entitled to inherit; not relating to inheritance.

अदार *a-dāra*, *as*, m. having no wife.

अदारसृत् *á-dāra-sṛit*, mfn. not falling into a crack or rent, AV.; N. of a Sāman, PBr.

अदास *a-dāsa*, *as*, m. not a slave, a freeman.

अदाहुक *á-dāhuka*, mfn. not consuming by fire, MaitrS.

A-dāhya, mfn. incombustible.

अदिक्क *a-dikka*, mfn. having no share in the horizon, banished from beneath the sky, ŚBr.

अदिति 2. *aditi*, *is*, m. (√*ad*), devourer, i. e. death, BṛĀrUp.

अदिति 3. *á-diti*, mfn. (√4. *dā* or *do*, *dyati*; for 1. *á-diti*, see above), not tied, free, RV. vii, 52, 1; boundless; unbroken, entire, unimpaired, happy, RV.; VS.; (*is*), f. freedom, security, safety; boundlessness, immensity; inexhaustible abundance; unimpaired condition, perfection; creative power; N. of one of the most ancient of the Indian goddesses ('Infinity' or the 'Eternal and Infinite Expanse,' often mentioned in RV., daughter of Daksha and wife of Kaśyapa, mother of the Ādityas and of the gods); a cow, milk, RV.; the earth, Naigh.; speech, Naigh. (cf. RV. viii, 101, 15); (*ī*), f. du. heaven and earth, Naigh. **-ja**, m. a son of Aditi, an Āditya, a divine being. **-tvá**, n. the condition of Aditi, or of freedom, unbrokenness, RV. vii, 51, 1; the state of the goddess Aditi, BṛĀrUp. **-nandana**, m. = *-ja*, q. v.

अदित्सत् *á-ditsat* [RV. vi, 53, 3, &c.] or *a-ditsu*, mfn. (Desid. fr. √1. *dā*), not inclined to give.

अदिप्रभृति *adi-prabhṛiti* = *ad-ādi*. See √*ad*.

अदीक्षित *á-dīkshita*, mfn. one who has not performed the initiatory ceremony (*dīkshā*) connected with the Soma sacrifice; one who is not concerned in that ceremony; one who has not received Brāhmanical consecration.

अदीन *á-dīna*, mfn. not depressed; noble-minded; (*as*), m., N. of a prince (also called Ahīna). **-sattva**, mfn. possessing unimpaired goodness. **Adīnātman**, mfn. undepressed in spirit.

अदीपित *a-dīpita*, mfn. unilluminated.

अदीर्घ *á-dīrgha*, mfn. not long. **-sūtra**, mfn. not tedious, prompt, L.

अदुःख *a-duḥkha*, mfn. free from evil or trouble, propitious. **-navamī**, f. the propitious ninth day in the first fortnight of Bhādrapada (when women worship Devī to avert evil for the ensuing year).

अदुग्ध *á-dugdha*, mfn. not milked out, RV. vii, 32, 22; not sucked out, Suśr.

अदुच्छुन *a-ducchuná*, mfn. free from evil, propitious, RV. ix, 61, 17.

अदुर्ग *a-durga*, mfn. not difficult of access; destitute of a strong hold or fort. **-vishaya**, m. an unfortified country.

अदुर्मख *á-durmakha*, mfn. not reluctant, unremitting, cheerful, RV. viii, 75, 14.

अदुर्मङ्गल *á-durmaṅgala*, mf(nom. *īḥ*)n. not inauspicious, RV. x, 85, 43.

अदुर्वृत्त *a-durvṛitta*, mfn. not of a bad character or disposition.

अदुष्कृत् *á-dush-kṛit*, mfn. not doing evil, RV. iii, 33, 13.

अदुष्ट *a-dushṭa*, mfn. not vitiated, not bad, not guilty, Mn. viii, 388; innocent. **-tva**, n. the being not vitiated; innocence.

अदू *á-dū*, mfn. dilatory, without zeal, not worshipping, RV. vii, 4, 6.

अदून *á-dūna*, mfn. (√2. *du*), uninjured.

अदूर *a-dūra*, mfn. not distant, near; (*am*), n. vicinity; (*e*), (*āt*), (*atas*), ind. (with abl. or gen.) not far, near; soon. **-bhava**, mfn. situated at no great distance.

अदूषित *a-dūshita*, mfn. unvitiated; unspotted, irreproachable. **-dhī**, mfn. possessing an uncorrupted mind.

अदृढ *a-dṛiḍha*, mfn. not firm; not decided.

अदृपित *á-dṛipita*, mfn. not infatuated, not vain, RV.

Á-dṛipta, mfn. id., RV. **-kratu** (*ádṛipta-*), mfn. sober-minded, RV.

Ádṛipyat, mfn. not being infatuated, RV. i, 151, 8.

अदृश् *a-dṛiś*, mfn. (√*dṛiś*), blind, L.

A-dṛiśya, mfn. invisible, latent; not fit to be seen; (cf. *a-dreśya*.) **-karaṇa**, n. act of rendering invisible; N. of a part of a treatise on magic.

A-dṛiśyat, mfn. invisible, L.; (*atī*), f., N. of Vasishṭha's daughter-in-law.

A-dṛishṭa or **á-dṛishṭa** [ŚBr.], mfn. unseen, unforeseen; invisible; not experienced; unobserved, unknown; unsanctioned; (*as*), m., N. of a particular venomous substance or of a species of vermin, AV.; (*am*), n. unforeseen danger or calamity; that which is beyond the reach of observation or consciousness (especially the merit or demerit attaching to a man's conduct in one state of existence and the corresponding reward or punishment with which he is visited in another); destiny, fate: luck, bad luck. **-karman**, mfn. one who has not seen practice. **-kāma**, m. passionate attachment to an object that has never been seen. **-ja**, mfn. produced or resulting from fate. **-nara** or **-purusha**, m. a treaty concluded by the parties personally (in which no third mediator is seen). **-para-sāmarthya**, m. one who has not experienced the power of an enemy. **-pūrva**, mfn. never seen before. **-phala**, mfn. having consequences that are not yet visible; (*am*), n. a result or consequence which is not yet visible or hidden in the future. **-rūpa**, mfn. having an invisible shape. **-vat**, mfn. connected with or arising from destiny; lucky or unlucky; fortunate. **-hán**, m. destroyer of venomous vermin, RV. i, 191, 8 & 9. **Adṛishṭārtha**, mfn. having an object not evident to the senses (as a science), transcendental. **Adṛishṭāśrutapūrvatva**, n. the state of never having been seen or heard before.

A-dṛishṭi, *is*, or **a-dṛishṭikā**, f. a displeased or malicious look, an evil eye, L.

अदेय *a-deya*, mfn. improper or unfit to be given; (*am*) or **-dāna**, n. an illegal gift.

अदेव *á-deva*, mfn. not divine, not of divine origin, not referring to any deity, RV.; godless, impious, RV.; (*as*), m. one who is not a god, ŚBr. xiv; Mn. **-mātṛika**, mfn. 'not having the gods or clouds as mothers, not suckled by any deity,' not rained upon.

A-dévaka, mf(*ā*)n. not referring to or intended for any deity, ŚBr.

A-devatā, f. one who is not a deity, Nir.

Á-devatra, mfn. not devoted to the gods, RV. v, 61, 6.

Á-devayat [RV. ii, 26, 1] or **ádevayu** [RV.], mfn. indifferent to the gods, irreligious.

A-daiva, mfn. not referring to or connected with the gods or with their action; not predetermined by them or by fate.

अदेवृघ्नी *á-devṛi-ghnī*, f. not killing her brother-in-law, AV. xiv, 2, 18.

अदेश *a-deśa*, *as*, m. a wrong place, an improper place. **-kāla**, n. wrong place and time. **-ja**, mfn. produced in a wrong place. **-stha**, mfn. out of place, in the wrong place; one absent from his country, an absentee.

A-deśya, mfn. not on the spot, not present on the occasion referred to, Mn. viii, 53 (v.l. *a-deśa*); not to be ordered or advised.

अदोमद *a-doma-dá* or *a-doma-dhá*, mfn. not occasioning inconvenience, AV.

अदोमय *ado-máya*, &c. See *adás*.

अदोह *a-doha*, *as*, m. (√*duh*), the season when milking is impracticable, KātyŚr.

A-dogdhṛi, mfn. not milking; not exacting; not caring for, BhP.

अद्ग *ádga*, *as*, m. (√*ad*), a sacrificial cake (*puroḍāśa*) made of rice, Uṇ.; a cane(?), AV. i, 27, 3.

अद्धा *ad-dhā́*, ind. (fr. *ad* or *a*, this), Ved. in this way; manifestly; certainly, truly. **-tama**, mfn. quite manifest, AitĀr.; (*ā́m*), ind. most certainly, ŚBr. **-purusha**, m., see *an-addhāpurushá*. **-bodheya**, *ās*, m. pl. adherents of a particular Śākhā or recension of the white Yajur-veda.

Addhātí, *is*, m. a sage, RV. x, 85, 16; AV.

अद्धालोहकर्ण *addhyā-loha-kárṇa*, mfn. having ears quite red, VS.; cf. *adhirūḍhā-kárṇa*.

अद्भुत *ádbhuta* [once *adbhutá*, RV. i, 120, 4], mfn. (see 1. *at*), supernatural, wonderful, marvellous; (*as*), m. the marvellous (in style); surprise; N. of the Indra of the ninth Manvantara; (*am*), n. a marvel, a wonder, a prodigy. **-karman**, mfn. performing wonderful works; exhibiting wonderful workmanship. **-kratu** (*ádbhuta-*), mfn. possessing wonderful intelligence, RV. **-gandha**, mfn. having a wonderful smell. **-tama**, n. an extraordinary wonder. **-tva**, n. wonderfulness. **-darśana**, mfn. having a wonderful aspect. **-dharma**, m. 'a system or series of marvels or prodigies,' N. of one of the nine aṅgas of the Buddhists. **-brāhmaṇa**, n., N. of a portion of a Brāhmaṇa belonging to the Sāma-veda. **-bhīma-karman**, mfn. performing wonderful and fearful works. **-rasa**, m. the marvellous style (of poetry). **-rāmāyaṇa**, n., N. of a work ascribed to Vālmīki. **-rūpa**, mfn. having a wonderful shape. **-śānti**, m. or f., N. of the sixty-seventh Pariśishṭa of the Atharva-veda. **-saṃkāśa**, mfn. resembling a wonder. **-sāra**, m. 'wonderful resin' of the Khadira tree (Mimosa Catechu); N. of a book on the essence of prodigies. **-svana**, m. 'having a wonderful voice,' N. of Śiva. **Ádbhutainas**, mfn. one in whom no fault is visible, RV. **Adbhutôttarakāṇḍa**, n., N. of a work, an appendix to or imitation of the Rāmāyaṇa. **Adbhutôpama**, mfn. resembling a wonder.

अद्मन् *ádman*, *a*, n. (√*ad*), eating, a meal, RV. i, 58, 2.

Adma (in comp. for *adman*). **-sád**, m. seated (with others) at a meal, companion at table, RV. **-sádya**, n. commensality, RV. viii, 43, 19. **-sádvan**, mfn. companion at a meal, RV. vi, 4, 4.

Admani, *is*, m. fire, Uṇ.

Admara, mfn. gluttonous, Pāṇ. iii, 2, 160.

1. **Adya**, mfn. fit or proper to be eaten; (*am*), ifc. (cf. *annâdya*, *havir-adya*), n. food.

अद्य 2. *a-dyá* (Ved. *adyā́*), ind. (fr. pronom. base *a*, this, with *dya* for *dyu*, q.v., Lat. *ho-die*), to-day; now-a-days; now. **-dina** or **-divasa**, m. n. the present day. **-pūrvam**, ind. before now. **-prabhṛiti**, ind. from and after to-day. **-śva**, mfn. comprising the present and the following day, PBr. **-śvīna**, mfn. likely to happen to-day or (*śvas*) to-morrow, Pāṇ. v, 2, 13; (*ā*), f. a female near delivery, ib. **-sutyā́**, f. preparation and consecration of the Soma on the same day, ŚBr. &c. **Adyâpi**, ind. even now, just now; to this day; down to the present time; henceforth. **Adyâvadhi**, mfn. beginning or ending to-day; from or till to-day. **Adyā-śvá**, n. the present and the following day, TS. **Adyâiva**, ind. this very day.

Adyatana, mf(*ī*)n. extending over or referring to to-day; now-a-days, modern; (*as*), m. the period of a current day, either from midnight to midnight, or from dawn to dark; (*ī*), f. (in Gr.) the aorist tense (from its relating what has occurred on the same day). **-bhūta**, m. the aorist.

Adyatanīya, mfn. extending over or referring to to-day; current now-a-days.

अद्यु *á-dyu*, mfn. not burning or not sharp, RV. vii, 34, 12.

A-dyút, mfn. destitute of brightness, RV. vi, 39, 3.

अद्यूत्य *a-dyūtyà* (4), *am*, n. unlucky gambling, RV. i, 112, 24; (mfn.), not derived from gambling, honestly obtained.

अद्रव *a-drava*, mfn. not liquid.

अद्रव्य *a-dravya*, *am*, n. a nothing, a worthless thing; (mfn.), having no possessions.

अद्रि *ádri*, *is*, m. (√*ad*, Uṇ.), a stone, a rock, a mountain; a stone for pounding Soma with or grinding it on; a stone for a sling, a thunderbolt; a mountain-shaped mass of clouds; a cloud (the mountains are the clouds personified, and regarded as the enemies of Indra); a tree, L.; the sun, L.; N. of a measure; the number seven; N. of a grandson of Pṛithu. **-karṇī**, f. the plant Clitoria Ternatea Lin. **-kīlā**, f. the earth, L. **-kṛita-sthalī**, f., N. of an Apsaras. **-ja**, mfn. produced from or found among rocks or mountains; (*ā*), f. the plant Saiṇhalī; N. of Pārvatī or Durgā; (*am*), n. red chalk. **-já**, mfn. produced from (the friction of) stones, RV. iv, 40, 5; N. of the soul, KaṭhUp. **-jūta** (*ádri-*), mfn. excited by (the friction of) stones, RV. iii, 58, 8. **-tanayā**, f. 'mountain-daughter,' N. of Pārvatī; N. of a metre (of four lines, each containing twenty-three syllables). **-dugdha** (*ádri-*), mfn. not pressed out or extracted with stones, RV. **-dvish**, m. the enemy of mountains or clouds, i. e. Indra, L. **-nandinī**, f., N. of Pārvatī. **-pati**, m. 'lord of mountains,' the Himālaya. **-barhas** (*ádri-*), mfn. fast as a rock, RV. x, 63, 3; TBr. **-budhna** (*ádri-*), mfn. rooted in or produced on a rock or mountain, RV. x, 108, 7; VS. **-bhíd**, mfn. splitting mountains or clouds, RV. vi, 73, 1; (*t*), m., N. of Indra, L. **-bhū**, mfn. mountain-born, found or living among mountains; (*ūs*), f. the plant Salvinia Cucullata. **-mātṛi** (*ádri-*), mfn. having a rock or mountain for a mother, RV. ix, 86, 3. **-mūrdhan**, m. the head or summit of a mountain. **-rāj** or **-rāja**, m. 'king of mountains,' the Himālaya. **-vat** (voc. *vas*), m. armed with stones or thunderbolts, RV. **-vahni**, m. fire on or in a mountain or rock. **-śayya**, m. 'having the mountain for a couch,' Śiva, L. **-śṛiṅga**, n. a mountain-peak. **-shuta** (*ádri-*), mfn. prepared with stones, RV. **-saṃhata** (*ádri-*), mfn. expressed with stones, RV. ix, 98, 6. **-sānu**, mfn. lingering on the mountains, RV. vi, 65, 5. **-sāra**, m. 'essence of stones,' iron. **-sāra-maya**, mfn. made of iron. **Adrindra** or **adrîśa**, m. 'lord of mountains,' the Himālaya.

Adrikā, f., N. of an Apsaras.

अद्रुह् *a-drúh* (nom. *a-dhrúk*), mfn. free from malice or treachery, RV.

A-druhāṇa [RV. v, 70, 2] or **a-druhvan** [SV.], mfn. id.

A-droghá, mfn. free from falsehood, true, RV.; (*á-drogham*), ind. without falsehood, RV. viii, 60, 4. **-vāc** (*ádrogha-*), mfn. free from malice or treachery in speech, RV.; AV. **Ádroghâvita**, mfn. loving freedom from malice or treachery, AV.

A-droha, *as*, m. freedom from malice or treachery. **-vṛitti**, f. conduct free from malice or treachery.

A-drohin, mfn. free from malice or treachery.

अद्रेश्य *a-dreśya*, mfn. invisible, MuṇḍUp.

अद्वन् *advan*, mfn. (√*ad*), ifc. (e.g. *agrâdvan*), eating.

अद्वय *a-dvaya*, mfn. not two, without a second, only, unique; (*as*), m., N. of a Buddha; (*am*), n. non-duality, unity; identity (especially the identity of Brahma with the human soul or with the universe, or of spirit and matter); the ultimate truth. **-vādin**, m. one who teaches *advaya* or identity, a Buddha; a Jaina; (cf. *advaita-vādin*.) **Advayânanda**, m., N. of an author, and of a founder of the Vaishṇava sect in Bengal (who lived at the close of the fifteenth century).

Á-dvayat [RV. iii, 29, 5] or **á-dvayas** [RV. i, 187, 3 & viii, 18, 6], mfn. free from duplicity.

Á-dvayāvin [RV.] or **á-dvayu** [RV. viii, 18, 15], mfn. free from double-dealing or duplicity.

अद्वार् *á-dvār*, f. not a door, ŚBr.; MBh.

Á-dvāra, *am*, n. a place without a door; an entrance which is not the proper door, ŚBr. xiv, &c.

अद्विज *a-dvija*, mfn. destitute of Brāhmans, Mn. viii, 22.

अद्वितीय *a-dvitīya*, mfn. without a second, sole, unique; matchless.

अद्विषेण्य *a-dvishenyá* (5), mfn. (√*dvish*), not malevolent, RV.

A-dveshá, mfn. not malevolent (nom. du. f. °*é*), RV. viii, 68, 10 & x, 45, 12. **-rāgin**, mfn. free from malevolence and passionate desire.

Adveshás, ind. without malevolence, RV.

Adveshin, mfn. free from malevolence.

Adveshṭṛi, *ṭā*, m. not an enemy, a friend.

अद्वैत *á-dvaita*, mfn. destitute of duality, having no duplicate, ŚBr. xiv, &c.; peerless; sole, unique; epithet of Vishṇu; (*am*), n. non-duality; identity of Brahmă or of the Paramātman or supreme soul with the Jīvātman or human soul; identity of spirit and matter; the ultimate truth; title of an Upanishad; (*ena*), ind. solely. **-vādin**, *ī*, m. one who asserts the doctrine of non-duality. **Advaitânanda**, m. = *advayânanda*, q. v. **Advaitôpanishad**, f., N. of an Upanishad.

A-dvaidha, mfn. not divided into two parts, not shared; not disunited; free from malice, straightforward.

अध *ádha* or *ádhā*, ind., Ved. (=*átha*; used chiefly as an inceptive particle), now; then, therefore; moreover, so much the more; and, partly. **Ádha—ádha**, as well as, partly partly. **Adhapriya**, mfn. (you who are) now pleased (voc. du. °*yā*), RV. viii, 8, 4.

अधः *adhaḥ*, &c. See अधस्.

अधन *a-dhana*, mfn. destitute of wealth.

A-dhanya, mfn. not richly supplied with corn or other produce; not prosperous; unhappy.

अधम *adhamá*, mfn. (see *ádhara*), lowest, vilest, worst; very low or vile or bad (often ifc., as in *narâdhama*, the vilest or worst of men); (*as*), m. an unblushing paramour; (*ā*), f. a low or bad mistress [cf. Lat. *infimus*]. **-bhṛita** or **-bhṛitaka**, m. a servant of the lowest class, a porter. **-ṛṇa** (*ṛi*) or **-ṛṇika** (*ṛi*), m. one reduced to inferiority by debt, a debtor. **-śākha** (?), N. of a region, (*gaṇa gahâdi*, q. v.) **Adhamâṅga**, n. 'the lowest member,' the foot. **Adhamâcāra**, mfn. guilty of vile conduct. **Adhamārdha**, n. the lower half, the lower part. **Adhamârdhya**, mfn. connected with or referring to the lower part, Pāṇ. iv, 3, 5.

अधमर्ण *adhama-ṛṇa*, &c. See *adhamá*.

अधर *ádhara*, mfn. (connected with *adhás*), lower, inferior; tending downwards; low, vile; worsted, silenced; (*as*), m. the lower lip, the lip; (*ā́t*), abl. ind., see s. v. below; (*asmāt*), abl. ind. below, L.; (*ā*), f. the lower region, nadir; (*am*), n. the lower part; a reply; Pudendum Muliebre, L. [Lat. *inferus*]. **-kaṇṭhá**, m. n. the lower neck, lower part of the throat, VS. **-kāya**, m. the lower part of the body. **-tas**, ind. below, Pāṇ. v, 3, 35, Sch. **-pāna**, n. 'drinking the lip,' kissing. **-madhu**, n. the moisture of the lips. **-sapatna** (*ádhara-*), mfn. whose enemies are worsted or silenced, MaitrS. **-svastika**, n. the nadir. **-hanú**, f. the lower jaw-bone, AV. **Adharâmṛita**, n. the nectar of the lips. **Adharâraṇí**, f. the lower of the two pieces of wood used in producing fire by friction, ŚBr. &c. **Adharâvalopa**, m. biting the lip. **Adharī-kṛita**, mfn. worsted, eclipsed, excelled, Śāk. (v. l.) **Adharī-bhūta**, mfn. worsted (as in a process), Yājñ. ii, 17. **Adharedyus**, ind. the day before yesterday, Pāṇ. v, 3, 22. **Adharôttara**, mfn. lower and higher; worse and better; question and answer; nearer and further; sooner and later; upside down, topsy-turvy. **Adhar'oshṭha** or **adharâushṭha**, m. the lower lip; (*am*), n. the lower and upper lip.

Adharaya, Nom. P. *adharayati*, to make inferior, put under; eclipse, excel.

Adharastāt, ind. below, L.

Adharāk, ind. beneath, in the lower region, i. e. in the south, VS.

Adharācīna [RV. ii, 17, 5] or **adharācyà** [(5); AV.], mfn. or **adharā́ñc**, *ā́n*, *ā́cī*, *ā́k*, Ved. tending downwards, to the nadir or the lower region, tending towards the south.

Adharā́t, ind. below, beneath, RV. & AV.; in the south, AV. **-tāt** (*adharā́t-*), ind. below, beneath, RV. x, 36, 14.

Adharīṇa, mfn. vilified, L.

अधर्म *á-dharma, as*, m. unrighteousness, injustice, irreligion, wickedness; demerit, guilt; N. of a Prajāpati (son of Brahmā, husband of Hiṇsā or Mṛishā); N. of an attendant of the sun; (*ā*), f. unrighteousness (personified and represented as the bride of death). **-cārin**, mfn. practising wickedness. **-tas**, ind. unrighteously, unjustly. **-daṇḍana**, n. unjust punishment, Mn. viii, 127. **-máya**, mfn. made up of wickedness, ŚBr. xiv. **Adharmâtman**, mfn. having a wicked spirit or disposition. **Adharmâstikāya**, m. the category (*astikāya*) of *adharma* (one of the five categories of the Jaina ontology).

Adharmin, mfn. unrighteous, wicked, impious.

Adharmishṭha, mfn. most wicked, impious.

Adharmya, mfn. unlawful, contrary to law or religion, wicked.

अधवा *a-dhavā*, f. one who has no husband, a widow (usually *vi-dhavā*, q. v.), L.

अधस् *adhás*, ind. (see *ádhara*), below, down; in the lower region; beneath, under; from under (with acc., gen., and abl.); also applied to the lower region and to the Pudendum Muliebre [cf. Lat. *infra*]. **Adha-upâsana**, n. sexual intercourse, Comm. on BṛĀrUp. **Adhaḥ-kara**, m. the lower part of the hand. **Adhaḥ-kāya**, m. the lower part of the body. **Adhaḥ-kṛita**, mfn. cast down. **Adhaḥ-kṛishṇâjinam**, ind. under the black skin, KātyŚr. **Adhaḥ-kriyā**, f. (= *apamāna*), disgrace, humiliation. **Adhaḥ-khanana**, n. undermining. **Adhaḥ-padma**, n. (in architecture) a part of a cupola. **Adhaḥ-pāta**, m. a downfall. **Adhaḥ-pushpī**, f. 'having flowers looking downwards,' two plants, Pimpinella Anisum and Elephantopus Scaber (or Hieracium?). **Adhaḥ-pravāha**, m. a downward current. **Adhaḥ-prastara**, m. seat or bed of turf or grass (for persons in a state of impurity). **Adhaḥ-prāk-śāyin**, mfn. sleeping on the ground towards the east. **Adhaḥ-śayá**, mfn. sleeping on the ground, ŚBr. **Adhaḥ-śayya**, mfn. having a peculiar couch on the ground; (*a*), f. act of sleeping on the ground and on a peculiar couch. **Adhaḥ-śiras**, mfn. holding the head downward; head foremost; (*ās*), m., N. of a hell, VP. **Adhaḥ-stha**, mfn. placed low or below; inferior. **Adhaḥ-sthita**, mfn. standing below; situated below. **Adhaḥ-svastika**, n. the nadir. **Adhaś-cara**, m. 'creeping on the ground,' a thief. **Adhas-tarā́m**, ind. very far down, ŚBr. **Adhas-tala**, n. the room below anything. **Adhas-padá**, mfn., Ved. placed under the feet, under foot; (*ám*), n. the place under the feet; (*ám*) (ind.) under foot. **Adho-akshá**, mfn. being below (or not coming up to) the axle, RV. iii, 33, 9. **Adho-'ksham** [KātyŚr.] or **adho-'kshena** [ĀśvŚr.], ind. under the axle. **Adho-'ksha-ja**, m., N. of Vishṇu or Kṛishṇa; the sign Śravaṇā. **Adho-gata**, mfn. gone down, descended. **Adho-gati**, f. or **-gama**, m. or **-gamana**, n. descent, downward movement, degradation. **Adho-gati** and **-gāmin**, mfn. going downwards, descending. **Adho-ghaṇṭā**, f. the plant Achyranthes Aspera. **Adho-'ṅga**, n. the anus; Pudendum Muliebre. **Adho-jānú**, ind. below the knee, ŚBr. **Adho-jihvikā**, f. the uvula. **Adho-dāru**, n. the under timber. **Adho-diś**, f. the lower region, the nadir. **Adho-drishṭi**, f. a downcast look; (mfn.), having a downcast look. **Adho-deśa**, m. the lower or lowest part (especially of the body). **Adho-dvāra**, n. the anus; Pudendum Muliebre. **Adho-nābham** or **-nābhi** [MaitrS.], ind. below the navel. **Adho-nilaya**, m. 'lower abode,' the lower regions, hell. **Adho-'para**, n. the anus. **Adhôpahāsa** (*adhás-up*), m. sexual intercourse, ŚBr. xiv. **Adho-bandhana**, n. an under girth. **Adho-bhakta**, n. a dose of medicine to be taken after eating. **Adho-bhava**, mfn. lower. **Adho-bhāga**, m. the lower or lowest part, especially of the body. **Adho-bhāga-dosha-hara**, mfn. curing or strengthening the lower part of the body. **Adho-bhuvana**, n. the lower world. **Adho-bhūmi**, f. lower ground; land at the foot of a hill. **Adho-marman**, n. the anus. **Adho-mukha**, mf(*ā* [Śiś.] or *ī*)n. having the face downwards; headlong; upside down; (*as*), m. Vishṇu; a division of hell, VP.; (*ā*), f. the plant Premna Esculenta. **Adho-yantra**, n. the lower part of an apparatus; a still. **Adho-rakta-pitta**, n. discharge of blood from the anus and the urethra. **Adhó-rāma**, m. (a goat) having peculiar white or black marks on the lower part (of the body), VS.; ŚBr. **Adho-lamba**, m. a plummet; the perpendicular. **Adho-loka**, m. the lower world. **Adho-vadana**, mfn. = *adho-mukha*. **Adhó-varcas**, mfn. tumbling downwards, AV. v, 11, 6. **Adho-vaśa**, m. Pudendum Muliebre. **Adho-vāyu**, m. vital air passing downwards; breaking wind. **Adho-'vêkshin**, mfn. looking down. **Adho-'śvam**, ind. under the horse, KātyŚr. **Adho-'sra-pitta**, n. = *adho-rakta-pitta*, q. v.

Adhastana, mfn. lower, being underneath; preceding (in a book).

Adhástāt, ind. = *adhás*, q. v. **Adhastād-diś**, f. the lower region, the nadir. **Adhástāl-lakshman**, mfn. having a mark at the lower part (of the body), MaitrS.

अधा *ádhā*, Ved. See *ádha*.

अधमार्गव *adhāmārgava, as*, m. the plant Achyranthes Aspera.

अधारणक *a-dhāraṇaka*, mfn. unable to support, unremunerative.

अधार्मिक *a-dhārmika*, mfn. unjust, unrighteous, wicked.

अधार्य *a-dhārya*, mfn. unfit or improper to be held or carried or kept up.

अधि 1. *adhi, is*, m. (better *ādhi*, q. v.), anxiety; (*is*), f. a woman in her courses (= *avi*, q. v.), L.

अधि 2. *ádhi*, ind., as a prefix to verbs and nouns, expresses above, over and above, besides.

As a separable adverb or preposition; (with abl.) Ved. over; from above; from; from the presence of; after, AitUp.; for; instead of, RV. i, 140, 11; (with loc.) Ved. over; on; at; in comparison with; (with acc.) over, upon, concerning. **Adhy-adhi**, ind. on high, just above, KātyŚr.

Adhika, mfn. additional; subsequent, later; surpassing (in number or quantity or quality), superior, more numerous; abundant; excellent; supernumerary, redundant; secondary, inferior; intercalated; (*am*), n. surplus; abundance; redundancy; hyperbole; ind. exceedingly; too much; more. **-kshaya-kārin**, mfn. causing excessive waste. **-tā**, f. addition, excess, redundancy, preponderance. **-tithi**, m. f. an intercalary lunar day. **-tva**, n. = *-tā*, q. v. **-danta**, m. a redundant tooth which grows over another, Suśr.; (cf. *adhi-danta*.) **-dina**, n. a redundant, i. e. an intercalated day; (cf. *adhi-dina*.) **-māṇsârman**, n. proud flesh in the eye; (cf. *adhimāṇsa*.) **-māsa**, m. an intercalated month. **-rddhi** (*ṛid*), mfn. abundantly prosperous. **-vākyôkti**, f. exaggeration, hyperbole. **-shāshṭika**, mfn. (containing or costing) more than sixty. **-saṃvatsara**, m. an intercalated month. **-sāptatika**, mfn. (containing or costing) more than seventy. **Adhikâṅga**, mf(*ī*)n. having some redundant member or members, Mn. iii, 8; (*am*), n. belt worn over the coat of mail, L. **Adhikâdhika**, mfn. outdoing one another. **Adhikârtha**, mfn. exaggerated. **Adhikârtha-vacana**, n. exaggeration, hyperbole, Pāṇ. ii, 1, 33.

अधिकन्धरम् *adhi-kandharam*, ind. upon or as far as the neck, Śiś.

अधिकर्ण *adhi-karṇa, as*, m., N. of a snake demon, Hariv.

अधिकर्मकर *adhi-karmakara, as*, m. and *adhi-karmakṛit, t*, m. See *adhi-√1. kṛi* below.

अधिकल्पिन् *adhi-kalpin, ī*, m. a sharp gambler, VS.

अधिकार्म *adhi-kārma, am*, n., N. of some place unknown, Pāṇ. vi, 2, 91.

अधिकृ *adhi-√1. kṛi*, to place at the head, appoint; to aim at, regard; to refer or allude to; to superintend, be at the head of (loc.), MBh. iv, 241: Ā. *-kurute*, to be or become entitled to (acc.), MBh. iii, 1345; to be or become superior to, overcome, Pāṇ. i, 3, 33.

Adhi-karaṇa, *am*, n. the act of placing at the head or of subordinating government, supremacy, magistracy, court of justice; a receptacle, support; a claim; a topic, subject; (in philosophy) a substratum; a subject (e. g. *ātman* is the *adhi-karaṇa* of knowledge); a category; a relation; (in Gr.) government; location, the sense of the locative case; relationship of words in a sentence (which agree together, either as adjective and substantive, or as subject and predicate, or as two substantives in apposition); (in rhetoric) a topic; a paragraph or minor section; (mfn.), having to superintend. **-bhojaka**, m. a judge. **-maṇḍapa**, m. n. the hall of justice. **-mālā**, f. a compendium of the topics of the Vedānta by Bhāratī-tīrtha. **-siddhānta**, m. a syllogism or conclusion which involves others, Nyāyad. &c. **Adhikaraṇâitāvattva**, n. fixed quantity of a substratum.

Adhikaraṇika or better **ādhikaraṇika**, *as*, m. a government official; a judge or magistrate.

Adhi-karaṇya, *am*, n. authority, power.

Adhi-karman, *a*, n. superintendence. **Adhi-karmakara** or **-karmakṛit**, m. an overseer, superintendent. **Adhi-karma-kṛita**, m. person appointed to superintend an establishment.

Adhikarmika, *as*, m. overseer of a market, L.

Adhi-kāra, *as*, m. authority; government, rule, administration, jurisdiction; royalty, prerogative; title; rank; office; claim, right, especially to perform sacrifices with benefit; privilege; ownership; property; reference, relation; a topic, subject; a paragraph or minor section; (in Gr.) government; a governing-rule (the influence of which over any number of succeeding rules is called anu-vṛitti, q. v.) **-stha**, mfn. established in an office. **Adhikārâḍhya**, mfn. invested with rights or privileges.

Adhi-kārin, mfn. possessing authority; entitled to; fit for; (*ī*), m. a superintendent, governor; an official; a rightful claimant; a man, L. **Adhi-kāri-tā**, f. or **-tva**, n. authority; rightful claim; ownership, &c.

Adhi-kṛita, mfn. placed at the head of; appointed; ruled, administered; claimed; (*as*), m. a superintendent (especially a comptroller of public accounts). **-tva**, n. the being engaged in or occupied with.

Adhi-kṛiti, *is*, f. a right, privilege; possession.

Adhi-kṛitya, ind. p. having placed at the head, having made the chief subject; regarding; concerning; with reference to.

अधिक्रम् *adhi-√kram*, to ascend, mount up to.

Adhi-krama, *as*, m. an invasion, attack, L.

Adhi-kramaṇa, *am*, n. act of invading, L.

अधिक्रीड् *adhi-√krīḍ*, to play or dance over (acc.), MaitrS.; TBr.

अधिक्षि *adhi-√1. kshi* (3. du. *-kshitáḥ*; 3. pl. *-kshiyánti*) to be settled in or over, be extended over or along (acc. or loc.), RV.; MBh. i, 722 & 730; to rest upon, ŚBr.

अधिक्षित् *adhi-kshít, t*, m. (√2. *kshi*), a lord, ruler, RV. x, 92, 14.

अधिक्षिप् *adhi-√kship*, to throw upon; to bespatter; to insult, scold; to superinduce (disease).

Adhikshipad-abja-netra, mfn. having eyes which eclipse the lotus.

Adhi-kshipta, mfn. insulted; scolded; thrown down; placed, fixed; despatched.

Adhi-kshepa, *as*, m. abuse, contempt; dismissal.

अधिगण् *adhi-√gaṇ*, to enumerate; to value highly, BhP.

अधिगम् *adhi-√gam*, to go up to, approach, overtake; to approach for sexual intercourse; to fall in with; to meet, find, discover, obtain; to accomplish; to study, read: Desid. P. *adhi-jigamishati*, to seek; Ā. *adhi-jigāṇsate*, to be desirous of studying or reading.

Adhi-gata, mfn. found, obtained, acquired; gone over, studied, learnt.

Adhi-gantavya, mfn. attainable, to be studied.

Adhi-gantṛi, *tā*, m. one who attains or acquires.

Adhi-gama, *as*, m. the act of attaining, acquisition; acquirement, mastery, study, knowledge; mercantile return, profit, &c.

Adhi-gamana, *am*, n. acquisition; finding; acquirement, reading, study; marriage, copulation.

Adhi-gamanīya or **-gamya**, mfn. attainable; practicable to be learnt.

अधिगर्त्य *ádhi-gartya* (5), mfn. being on the driver's seat, RV. v, 62, 7.

अधिगव *adhi-gavá*, mfn. being on or in a cow, derived from a cow, AV. ix, 6, 39.

अधिगा *adhi-√1. gā*, P. to obtain; P. (aor. Subj. 2. pl. *-gāta* or *-gātana*) to remember, notice, RV. & AV.; P. or generally Ā. (*-jage, -agīshṭa, -agīshyata*, Pāṇ.) to go over, learn, read, study; to attempt, resolve: Caus. P. *-gāpayati*, to cause to go over or teach: Desid. Caus. *-jigāpayishati*, to be desirous of teaching, Pāṇ. ii, 4, 51.

अधिगुण *adhi-guṇa*, mfn. possessing superior qualities, Megh.

अधिगुप्त *adhi-gupta*, mfn. protected.

अधिगृहम् *adhi-gṛiham*, ind. in the house, in the houses, Śiś. iii, 45.

अधिग्रीवम् *adhi-grīvam*, ind. upon the neck, up to the neck.

अधिचङ्क्रम *adhi-caṅkramá*, mfn. (*√kram*), walking or creeping over, AV. xi, 9, 16.

अधिचर् *adhi-√car*, to walk or move on or over, RV. vii, 88, 3, &c.; to be superior to (acc.), AitĀr.

Adhi-caraṇa, *am*, n. the act of walking or moving or being on or over.

अधिचि *adhi-√1. ci*, to pile upon, AV.; ŚBr.

अधिजन् *adhi-√jan*, to be born.

Adhi-ja, mfn. born, superior by birth, Pāṇ. iii, 2, 101, Sch.

Adhi-janana, *am*, n. birth, Mn. ii, 169.

अधिजानु *adhi-jānu*, ind. on the knees, Śiś.

अधिजि *adhi-√ji* (Subj. 2. sg. *-jayāsi*) to win in addition, RV. vi, 35, 2.

अधिजिह्व *adhi-jihva*, *as*, m. or *-jihvikā*, f. a peculiar swelling of the tongue or epiglottis, Suśr.

अधिज्य *ádhi-jya*, mfn. having the bowstring (*jyā*) up or stretched, strung, ŚBr. &c.

अधिज्योतिषम् *adhi-jyotisham*, ind. on the luminaries (treated of in the Upanishads), TUp.

अधितिष्ठति *adhi-tishṭhati*. See *adhi-shṭhā*.

अधित्यका *adhityakā*, f. (fr. *adhi-tya*, a derivation of *adhi*; cf. Pāṇ. v, 2, 34), land on the upper part of a mountain, table land, Śiś.; Ragh. &c.

अधिदण्डनेतृ *adhi-daṇḍa-netṛi*, *tā*, m. 'presiding over punishment,' N. of Yama, BhP.

अधिदन्त *adhi-danta*, *as*, m. a redundant tooth, Pāṇ. vi, 2, 188, Sch.; Suśr.

अधिदार्व *adhi-dārva*, mfn. (fr. *dāru*), wooden.

अधिदिन *adhi-dina*, *am*, n. an intercalated day.

अधिदिश् *adhi-√diś* (aor. Subj. Ā. 3. sg. *-didishṭa*) to bestow, RV. x, 93, 15.

अधिदीधिति *adhi-dīdhiti*, mfn. having excessive lustre, Śiś. i, 24.

अधिदेव *adhi-deva*, *as*, m. or *-devatā*, f. a presiding or tutelary deity. **Adhi-devam** or **-devatám** [ŚBr.], ind. concerning the gods or the deity.

अधिदेवन *adhi-dévana*, *am*, n. a table or board for gambling, AV.; ŚBr.

अधिदैव *adhi-daiva* or *-daivata*, *am*, n. a presiding or tutelary deity; the supreme deity; the divine agent operating in material objects; (*am*), ind. on the subject of the deity or the divine agent.

Adhi-daivika, mfn. spiritual.

अधिद्रु *adhi-√2. dru*, to cover (said of a bull), ŚBr.: Caus. *-drāvayati*, to cause to cover, ŚBr.

अधिधा *adhi-√dhā* (Pass. 3. sg. *-dhāyi*, RV.) Ved. to place upon; to give, share between (dat. or loc.), RV.; Ā. (aor. *-adhita*; perf. *-dadhe*, p. *-dádhāna*) to acquire additionally, RV.

अधिधृ *adhi-√dhṛi*, Caus. P. *-dhārayati*, Ved. to carry over or across.

अधिनम् *adhi-√nam*, Intens. Ā. *-námnate*, to incline over, RV. i, 140, 6.

अधिनाथ *adhi-nātha*, *as*, m. a supreme lord, chieftain; N. of the author of the Kālayogaśāstra.

अधिनिधा *adhi-ni-√dhā*, Ved. to place upon; to impart, grant.

अधिनिर्णिज् *ádhi-nirṇij*, mfn. covered over, veiled, RV. viii, 41, 10.

अधिनिर्मुच् *adhi-nir-√muc*, Pass. *-mucyate*, to escape from, PBr.

अधिनिर्हन् *adhi-nir-√han* (perf. 2. sg. *-jaghantha*) to destroy, root out from, RV. i, 80, 4.

अधिनिवस् *adhi-ni-√5. vas*, to dwell in.

अधिनिव्यध् *adhi-ni-√vyadh* (Imper. 3. du. *-vidhyatām*) to pierce through, AV. viii, 6, 24.

अधिनिषद् *adhi-ni-shad* (*√sad*), (perf. 3. pl. *-sheduḥ*) to settle in a place, RV. i, 164, 39.

अधिनी *adhi-√nī* (aor. 2. pl. *-naishṭa*) to lead away from (abl.), RV. viii, 30, 3; to raise above the ordinary measure, enhance, RV. x, 89, 6.

अधिनृत् *adhi-√nṛit* (Imper. *-nṛityatu*) to dance upon (acc.), AV.

अधिन्यस् *adhi-ny-√2. as*, to throw upon, KapS.

अधिप *adhi-pa*, *as*, m. a ruler, commander, regent, king.

Ádhi-pati, *is*, m. = *adhi-pa*; (in med.) a particular part of the head (where a wound proves instantly fatal). **-vatī** (*ádhipati-*), f. containing the lord in herself, MaitrUp.

Ádhi-patnī, f. a female sovereign or ruler.

Adhi-pā́, *ās*, m., Ved. a ruler, king, sovereign.

अधिपथम् *adhi-pathám*, ind. over or across a road, ŚBr.

अधिपांशुल *adhi-pāṅsula* or *-pansula*, mfn. being dusty above; dusty.

अधिपुरन्ध्रि *adhi-purandhri*, ind. towards a wife, Śiś. vi, 32.

अधिपुरुष *adhi-purusha* or *-pūrusha* [VP.], *as*, m. the Supreme Spirit.

अधिपूतभृतम् *adhi-pūta-bhṛitam*, ind. over the (vessel) full of purified Soma, KātyŚr.

अधिपेषण *adhi-péshaṇa*, mfn. serving to pound or grind upon, ŚBr.

अधिप्रजम् *adhi-prajam*, ind. on procreation as a means of preserving the world (treated of in the Upanishads), TUp.

अधिप्रधाव् *adhi-pra-√1. dhāv*, to approach hastily from, TBr.

अधिप्रष्टियुग *ádhi-prashṭi-yuga*, *am*, n. yoke for attaching a fourth horse laid upon the *prashṭi* or foremost of three horses (used on sacrificial occasions), ŚBr.

अधिप्रसू *adhi-pra-√1. sū*, to send away from, Kāṭh.

अधिबाध् *adhi-√bādh*, to vex, annoy.

अधिब्रू *adhi-√brū*, Ved. to speak in favour of (dat.) or favourably to (dat.), intercede for.

अधिभुज् *adhi-√3. bhuj*, to enjoy.

Ádhi-bhojana, *am*, n. an additional gift, RV. vi, 47, 23.

अधिभू *adhi-bhū*, *ūs*, m. (*√bhū*), a master, a superior, L.

Adhi-bhūta, *am*, n. the spiritual or fine substratum of material or gross objects; the all-penetrating influence of the Supreme Spirit; the Supreme Spirit itself; nature; (*ám*), ind. on material objects (treated of in the Upanishads), ŚBr. xiv; TUp.

अधिमन् *adhi-√man*, to esteem highly.

अधिमन्थ *adhi-mantha* or *adhī-mantha*, *as*, m. 'great irritation of the eyes,' severe ophthalmia.

Adhi-mánthana, *am*, n. friction for producing fire, RV. iii, 29, 1; (mfn.), suitable for such friction (as wood), ŚBr.

Adhi-manthita, mfn. suffering from ophthalmia.

अधिमांस *adhi-māṅsa* or *-māṅsaka*, *as*, m. proud flesh or cancer (especially in the eyes or the back part of the gums). **Adhimāṅsârman**, n. ophthalmic disease produced by proud flesh or cancer.

अधिमात्र *adhi-mātra*, mfn. above measure, excessive; (*am*), ind. on the subject of prosody. **-kāruṇika**, m. 'exceedingly merciful,' N. of a Mahā-brāhmaṇa, Buddh.

अधिमास *adhi-māsa*, *as*, m. an additional or intercalary month.

अधिमुक्त *adhi-mukta*, mfn. (*√muc*), inclined, propense, Buddh.; confident, ib.

Adhi-mukti, *is*, f. propensity; confidence.

Adhi-muktika, *as*, m., N. of Mahā-kāla, Buddh.

अधिमुह्य *adhi-muhya*, *as*, m., N. of Śākyamuni in one of his thirty-four former births.

अधियज्ञ *adhi-yajña*, *as*, m. the chief or principal sacrifice, Bhag.; influence or agency affecting a sacrifice; (mfn.), relating to a sacrifice, Mn.; (*ám*), ind. on the subject of sacrifice, ŚBr.; Nir.

अधियत् *adhi-√yat*, to fasten, RV. i, 64, 4: Caus. Ā. *-yātáyate*, to reach, join, RV. vi, 6, 4.

अधियम् *adhi-√yam* (Imper. 2. pl. *-yacchata*) to erect or stretch out over, RV. i, 85, 11; Ā. (aor. 3. pl. *-ayaṅsata*) to strive up to (loc.), RV. x, 64, 2.

अधिया *adhi-√yā*, to escape, Bhaṭṭ.

अधियुज् *adhi-√yuj*, to put on, load.

अधिरज्जु *ádhi-rajju*, mfn. carrying a rope, fastening, fettering, AV.

अधिरथ *ádhi-ratha*, mfn. being upon or over a car; (*as*), m. a charioteer; N. of a charioteer who was a prince of Aṅga and Karṇa's foster-father; (*am*), n. a cart-load, RV.

Adhi-rathyam, ind. on the high road.

अधिराज् *adhi-rāj*, *ṭ*, m. a supreme king.

Adhi-rājá, *as*, or **-rājan**, *ā*, m. an emperor.

Adhi-rājya, *am*, n. supremacy, imperial dignity; an empire; N. of a country. **-bhāj**, m. possessor of imperial dignity.

Adhi-rāshṭra, *am*, n. = *adhi-rājya*.

अधिरुक्म *ádhi-rukma*, mfn. wearing gold, RV. viii, 46, 33.

अधिरुह् *adhi-√ruh*, cl. 1. P. or poet. Ā. to rise above, ascend, mount: Caus. *-ropayati*, to raise, place above.

Adhi-rūḍha, mfn. ascended, mounted. **-samādhi-yoga**, mfn. engaged in profound meditation.

Adhirūḍhā-kárṇa, mfn. = *addhyā-loha-kárṇa*, q. v., MaitrS.; cf. *adhīloha-kárṇa*.

Adhi-ropaṇa, *am*, n. the act of raising or causing to mount.

Adhi-ropita, mfn. raised, placed above.

Adhi-roha, *as*, m. ascent, mounting, overtopping; (mfn.), riding, mounted, Śiś.

Adhi-róhaṇa, *am*, n. act of ascending or mounting or rising above; (*ī*), f. a ladder, flight of steps, L.

Adhi-rohin, mfn. rising above, ascending, &c.; (*iṇī*), f. a ladder, flight of steps.

अधिलोकम् *adhi-lokám*, ind. on the universe (treated of in the Upanishads), ŚBr.; TUp.

Adhi-loka-nātha, m. lord of the universe.

अधिवच् *adhi-√vac* (aor. Imper. 2. sg. *-vocā*, 2. du. *-vocatam*, 2. pl. *-vocata*) to speak in favour of, advocate, RV.; VS.

Adhi-vaktṛí, *tā*, m. an advocate, protector, comforter, RV.; VS.

Adhi-vacana, *am*, n. an appellation, epithet.

Adhi-vāká, *as*, m. advocacy, protection, RV. viii, 16, 5; AV.

अधिवद् *adhi-√vad*, to speak, pronounce over or at, ŚBr.; TBr.

Adhi-vādá, *as*, m. offensive words, MaitrS.

अधिवप् *adhi-√2. vap*, Ā. -*vapate*, to put on, fasten, RV. i, 92, 4; to scatter, TS.

अधिवस् 1. *adhi-√4. vas*, Ā. -*vaste*, to put on or over (as clothes, &c.), RV. x, 75, 8.

Adhi-vastra, mfn. clothed, RV. viii, 26, 13.

1. **Adhi-vāsá** [ŚBr.] or **adhī-vāsá** [RV.; ŚBr. &c.], *as*, m. or 1. **adhī-vāsas** [Vait.], *as*, n. an upper garment, mantle.

अधिवस् 2. *adhi-√5. vas*, to inhabit; to settle or perch upon.

2. **Adhi-vāsa**, *as*, m. an inhabitant; a neighbour; one who dwells above; a habitation, abode, settlement, site; sitting before a person's house without taking food till he ceases to oppose or refuse a demand (commonly called 'sitting in dharṇā'); pertinacity. **—bhūmi**, f. a dwelling-place, settlement.

1. **Adhi-vāsana**, *am*, n. causing a divinity to dwell in an image; sitting in dharṇā (see above).

Adhi-vāsin, mfn. inhabiting, settled in. **Adhivāsi-tā**, f. settled residence.

Adhy-ushita, see s. v.

अधिवाज्यकुलाद्य *adhivājya-kulâdya*, m., N. of a country, MBh.

अधिवास् *adhi-√vās*, to scent, perfume.

3. **Adhi-vāsa**, *as*, m. perfume, fragrance; application of perfumes or fragrant cosmetics.

2. **Adhi-vāsana**, *am*, n. application of perfumes, &c.; the ceremony of touching a vessel containing fragrant objects (that have been presented to an idol); preliminary purification of an image.

Adhi-vāsita, mfn. scented, perfumed.

अधिवाहन *adhi-vāhana*, *as*, m., N. of a man (said to be a son of Aṅga).

अधिविकर्तन *adhi-vi-kártana*, *am*, n. the act of cutting off or cutting asunder, RV. x, 85, 35.

अधिविक्रम् *adhi-vi-√kram*, Ā. to come forth on behalf of (dat.), KātyŚr.

अधिविज्ञान *adhi-vijñāna*, *am*, n. the highest knowledge.

अधिविद् *adhi-√3. vid*, cl. 6. P. -*vindati*, to obtain; to marry in addition to.

Adhi-vinnā, f. a wife whose husband has married again; a neglected or superseded wife.

Adhi-vettavyā, f. a wife in addition to whom it is proper to marry another.

Adhi-vettṛi, *tā*, m. a husband who marries an additional wife.

Adhi-vedana, *am*, n. marrying an additional wife.

Adhi-vedanīyā or **-vedyā**, f. = -*vettavyā*.

अधिविद्यम् *adhi-vidyam*, ind. on the subject of science (treated of in the Upanishads), TUp.

अधिविधा *adhi-vi-√dhā*, to distribute or scatter over, ŚBr. &c.

अधिवियत् *adhi-vi-√yat*, Caus. -*yātayati*, to subjoin, annex, Kaṭh.

अधिविराज् *adhi-vi-√rāj*, to surpass in brightness, RV.

अधिविश् *adhi-√viś*, Caus. -*veśayati*, to cause to sit down; to place upon.

अधिवृज् *adhi-√vṛij*, cl. 7. P. -*vṛinákti*, to place near or over (the fire), ŚBr.

अधिवृत् *adhi-√vṛit* (Pot. 3. pl. -*vavṛityuḥ*) to move or pass along or over (loc.), RV. x, 27, 6: Caus. id., TBr.

अधिवृध् *adhi-√vṛidh*, P. (Subj. -*vardhat*) to refresh, gladden, RV. vi, 38, 3; Ā. -*várdhate*, to prosper through or by (loc.), RV. ix, 75, 1.

अधिवेदम् *adhi-vedám*, ind. concerning the Veda, ŚBr. xiv.

अधिवेलम् *adhi-velam*, ind. on the shore, Śiś. iii, 71.

अधिव्ये *adhi-√vye*, to envelop.

Adhi-vīta, mfn. wrapped up, enveloped in.

अधिशस्त *adhi-śasta*, mfn. (√*śaṅs*), (=*abhi-śasta*), notorious, MBh. xiii, 3139.

अधिशी *adhi-√śī*, to lie down upon, to lie upon, to sleep upon (loc., but generally acc.)

Adhi-śaya, *as*, m. addition, anything added or given extra, Laṭy.

Adhi-śayana, mfn. lying on, sleeping on.

Adhi-śayita, mfn. recumbent upon; used for lying or sleeping upon.

अधिश्रि *adhi-√śri* (Ved. Inf. *ádhi-śrayi-tavai*, ŚBr.) to put in the fire; to spread over, AV.

Adhi-śraya, *as*, m. a receptacle.

Adhi-śrayaṇa, *am*, n. the act or ceremony of putting on the fire; (*ī*), f. a fire-place, oven.

Adhi-śrayaṇīya, mfn. relating to or connected with the Adhi-śrayaṇa.

Adhi-śrita, mfn. put on the fire (as a pot); resided in, dwelt in; occupied by.

अधिषु *adhi-shu* (√*3. su*), to extract or prepare the Soma juice, RV. ix, 91, 2.

Adhi-shávaṇa, *am*, n. (generally used in the dual), hand-press for extracting and straining the Soma juice; (mfn.), used for extracting and straining the Soma juice.

Adhi-shavaṇyà (6), m. du. the two parts of the hand-press for extracting and straining the Soma juice, RV. i, 28, 2.

अधिष्कन्द् *adhi-shkand* (√*skand*), (aor. 3. sg. -*shkán*) to cover in copulation, RV. x, 61, 7; AV.

Adhi-shkannā, f. (a cow) covered (by the bull), TS.

अधिष्ठा *adhi-shṭhā* (√*sthā*), to stand upon, depend upon; to inhabit, abide; to stand over; to superintend, govern; to step over or across; to overcome; to ascend, mount; to attain, arrive at.

Adhi-shṭhātṛi, mfn. superintending, presiding, governing, tutelary; (*ā*), m. a ruler; the Supreme Ruler (or Providence personified and identified with one or other of the Hindū gods); a chief; a protector.

Adhi-shṭhána, *am*, n. standing by, being at hand, approach; standing or resting upon; a basis, base; the standing-place of the warrior upon the car, SāmavBr.; a position, site, residence, abode, seat; a settlement, town; standing over; government, authority, power; a precedent, rule; a benediction, Buddh. **—deha** or **-śarīra**, n. the intermediate body which serves to clothe and support the departed spirit during its several residences in the Pitṛi-loka or world of spirits (also called the Preta-śarīra).

Adhi-shṭhāyaka, mfn. governing, superintending, guarding.

Adhi-shṭhita, mfn. settled; inhabited; superintended; regulated; appointed; superintending.

Adhi-shṭheya, mfn. to be superintended or governed.

अधिष्वन् *adhi-shvan* (√*svan*), to roar along or over (3. sg. aor. Pass. in the sense of P. *adhi-shvāṇi*), RV. ix, 66, 9.

अधिसंवस् *adhi-saṃ-√5. vas* (3. pl. -*vásante*) to dwell or reside together, TS. (quoted in TBr.)

अधिसंवृत् *adhi-saṃ-√vṛit* (impf. *sám-avar-tatâdhi*) to originate from, RV. x, 129, 4.

अधिसंधा *adhi-saṃ-√dhā* (perf. 3. pl. -*da-dhúḥ*) to put or join together, RV. iii, 3, 3.

अधिसृप् *adhi-√sṛip*, to glide along, ŚāṅkhŚr.

अधिस्त्रि *adhi-stri*, ind. concerning a woman or a wife, Pāṇ. ii, 1, 6, Sch.

Adhi-strī, f. a superior woman, Hariv.

अधिस्पर्ध् *adhi-√spardh* (3. pl. p. -*spár-dhante* & perf. -*paspṛidhre*) to compete for an aim, strive at (loc.), RV.

अधिस्पृश् *adhi-√spṛiś*, to touch lightly or slightly, ŚBr.: Caus. (Pot. -*sparśáyet*) to cause to reach to, to extend to, TS.

अधिस्रु *adhi-√sru*, to trickle or drop off, ŚBr.

अधिहरि *adhi-hari*, ind. concerning Hari, Pāṇ. ii, 1, 6, Sch.

अधिहस्ति *adhi-hasti*, ind. on an elephant, Ragh.

अधिहु *adhi-√hu* (impf. 3. pl. -*ájuhavta*) to make an oblation upon or over, RV. i, 51, 5.

अधिहृ *adhi-√hṛi*, to procure, furnish.

अधी *adhī* (√*i*), *adhy-éti* or *ádhy-eti* (exceptionally *adhīyati*, RV. x, 32, 3), to turn the mind towards, observe, understand, RV. & AV.; chiefly Ved. (with gen. [cf. Pāṇ. ii, 3, 72] or acc.) to mind, remember, care for, long for, RV. &c.; to know, know by heart, TS.; ŚBr.; Up. &c.; to go over, study, MBh. iii, 13689; to learn from (a teacher's mouth, abl.), MBh. iii, 10713; to declare, teach, ŚBr. x; Up.: Ā. *adhīté* or (more rarely) *adhīyate* (Mn. iv, 125; Pot. 3. pl. *adhīyīran*, Kauś.; Mn. x, 1) to study, learn by heart, read, recite: Caus. *adhy-āpa-yati* (aor. -*āpipat*, Pāṇ. ii, 4, 51) to cause to read or study, teach, instruct: Caus. Desid. *adhy-āpipa-yishati*, to be desirous of teaching Pāṇ. ii, 4, 51: Desid. *adhīshishati*, to be desirous of studying, Pāṇ. viii, 3, 61, Sch.

Adhīta, mfn. attained; studied, read; well read, learned. **—véda**, m. one who has studied the Vedas or whose studies are finished, ŚBr. xiv.

Adhīti, *is*, f. perusal, study, TĀr.; desire, recollection, RV. ii, 4, 8; AV.

Adhītin, mfn. well read, proficient, (gaṇa *ishṭâdi*, q.v.) &c.; occupied with the study of the Vedas, Kum.

Adhītya, ind. p. having gone over, having studied.

Adhīyat, mfn. remembering, proficient.

Adhīyāná, mfn. reading, studying; (*as*), m. a student; one who goes over the Veda either as a student or a teacher.

Adhy-ayana, *am*, n. reading, studying, especially the Vedas (one of the six duties of a Brāhman). **—tapasī**, n. du. study and penance. **—puṇya**, n. religious merit acquired by studying.

Adhy-ayanīya, mfn. fit to be read or studied.

Adhy-āpaka, mfn. a teacher (especially of sacred knowledge). **Adhyāpakôdita**, m. styled a teacher.

Adhy-āpana, *am*, n. instruction, lecturing.

Adhy-āpayitṛi, *tā*, m. a teacher, RPrāt.

Adhy-āpita, mfn. instructed, Mn.; Kum. iii, 6.

Adhy-āpya, mfn. fit or proper to be instructed.

Adhy-āya, *as*, m. a lesson, lecture, chapter; reading; proper time for reading or for a lesson; ifc. a reader (see *vedâdhyāya*), Pāṇ. iii, 2, 1, Sch. **—śata-pāṭha**, m. 'Index of One Hundred Chapters,' N. of a work.

Adhy-āyin, mfn. engaged in reading, a student.

Adhy-etavya or **-eya**, mfn. to be read.

Adhy-etṛi, *tā*, m. a student, reader.

Adhy-eshyamāṇa, mf(*ā*)n. (fut. p.) intending to study, about to read, Mn.

अधीकार *adhī-kāra* (= *adhi-kāra*), *as*, m. superintendence over (loc.), Mn. xi, 63; authorization, capability, MBh.

अधीक्ष् *adhīksh* (√*īksh*), to expect.

अधीन *adhīna*, mfn. (fr. *adhi*), ifc. resting on or in, situated; depending on, subject to, subservient to. **—tā**, f. or **-tva**, n. subjection, dependence.

अधीमन्थ *adhī-mantha* = *adhi-mantha*, q.v.

अधीर *á-dhīra*, mfn. imprudent, RV. i, 179, 4; AV.; not fixed, movable; confused; deficient in calm self-command; excitable; capricious; querulous; weak-minded, foolish; (*ā*), f. lightning; a capricious or bellicose mistress. **—tā**, f. want of confidence.

अधीलोहकर्ण *adhīloha-kárṇa*, mfn. = *ad-dhyāloha-karṇa*, q.v., TS.

अधीवास *adhī-vāsá* = 1. *adhi-vāsá*, q.v.

2. **Adhī-vāsas**, ind. over the garment, KātyŚr.

अधीश *adhīśa*, *as*, m. a lord or master over (others).

Adhīśvara, *as*, m. a supreme lord or king, an emperor; an Arhat, Jain.

अधीष्ट *adhīshṭa*, mfn. (√*3. ish*), solicited, asked for instruction (as a teacher), Pāṇ.; (*as*? or *am*), m. n. instruction given by a teacher solicited for it, Pāṇ. Sch.

Adhy-eshaṇa, *am*, *ā*, m. f. solicitation, asking for instruction.

अधुना *adhunā*, ind. at this time, now.

Adhunātána, mf(*ī*)n. belonging to or extending over the present time, ŚBr.

अधुर *a-dhura,* mfn. not laden.

अधूमक *a-dhūmaka,* mfn. smokeless.

अधृत *á-dhṛita,* mfn. not held, unrestrained, uncontrolled; unquiet, restless, TS.; (*as*), m., N. of Vishṇu.

Á-dhṛiti, *is,* f. want of firmness or fortitude; laxity, absence of control or restraint; incontinence; (mfn.), unsteady.

अधृष्ट *á-dhṛishṭa,* mfn. (√*dhṛish*), not bold, modest; not overcome, invincible, irresistible.

A-dhṛishya, mfn. unassailable, invincible; unapproachable; proud; (*ā*), f., N. of a river.

अधेनु *á-dhenu,* mfn. yielding no milk, RV. i, 117, 20; AV.; not nourishing, RV. x, 71, 5.

अधैर्य *a-dhairya, am,* n. want of self-command; excitement; excitability; (mfn.), without self-command; excitable.

अध्यंस *adhy-aṅsa,* mfn. being on the shoulder, ĀśvGṛ.

अध्यक्त *adhy-akta,* mfn. (√*añj*), equipped, prepared.

अध्यक्ष *ádhy-aksha,* mf(*ā*)n. perceptible to the senses, observable; exercising supervision; (*as*), m. an eye-witness; an inspector, superintendent; the plant Mimusops Kauki (*Kshīrikā*).

अध्यक्षरम् *adhy-aksharam,* ind. on the subject of syllables; above all syllables (as the mystic *om*).

अध्यग्नि *adhy-agni,* ind. over or by the nuptial fire (property given to the bride). **Adhyagni-kṛita,** n. property given to the wife at the wedding. **Adhyagny-upāgata,** n. property received by a wife at the wedding.

अध्यञ्च् *adhy-añc, aṅ, īcī, ak,* tending upwards, eminent, superior, Pāṇ. vi, 2, 53.

अध्यण्डा *adhy-aṇḍā,* f. the plants Carpopogon Pruriens (cowage) and Flacourtia Cataphracta.

अध्यधिक्षेप *adhy-adhikshepa, as,* m. excessive censure, Yājñ. iii, 228; gross abuse.

अध्यधीन *adhy-adhīna,* mfn. completely subject to or dependent on (as a slave), Mn.

अध्यन्तेन *adhy-anténa,* ind. close to, ŚBr.

अध्यपविच् *adhy-apa-√vic, -vinákti,* to put into by singling out from, ŚBr.

अध्ययन *adhy-ayana,* &c. See *adhí.*

अध्यर्ध *ádhy-ardha,* mf(*ā*)n. 'having an additional half,' one and a half. **-kaṅsa,** m. n. one and a half kaṅsa; (mf(*ī*)n.), amounting to or worth one and a half kaṅsa. **-kākiṇika,** mfn. amounting to or worth one and a half kākiṇī. **-kārshāpaṇa** or **-kārshāpaṇika,** mfn. amounting to or worth one and a half kārshāpaṇa. **-khārika,** mfn. amounting to or worth one and a half khārī. **-paṇya,** mfn. amounting to or worth one and a half paṇa. **-pādya,** mfn. amounting to one foot and a half. **-pratika,** mfn. amounting to one and a half kārshāpaṇa. **-māshya,** mfn. amounting to or worth one and a half māsha. **-viṅśatikīna,** mfn. amounting to or worth one and a half score or thirty. **-śata** or **-śatya,** mfn. amounting to or bought with one hundred and fifty. **-śatamāna** or **-śātamāna,** mfn. amounting to or worth one and a half śatamāna. **-śāṇa** or **-śāṇya,** mfn. amounting to or worth one and a half śāṇa. **-śūrpa,** mfn. amounting to or worth one and a half śūrpa. **-sahasra** or **-sāhasra,** mfn. amounting to or worth one thousand five hundred. **-suvarṇa** or **-sauvarṇika,** mfn. amounting to or worth one and a half suvarṇa.

Adhy-ardhaka, mfn. amounting to or worth one and a half.

अध्यर्बुद *adhy-arbuda* or *-arvuda, am,* n. a congenital tumour, goitre.

अध्यवरुह् *adhy-ava-√ruh,* to step downwards upon, TBr.

अध्यवसो *adhy-ava-√so,* cl. 4. P. *-syati,* to undertake, attempt, accomplish; to determine, consider, ascertain.

Adhy-ava-sāna, *am,* n. attempt, effort, exertion; energy, perseverance; determining; (in rhetoric) concise and forcible language.

Adhy-ava-sāya, *as,* m. id.; (in phil.) mental effort, apprehension. **-yukta,** mfn. resolute.

Adhy-ava-sāyita, mfn. attempted.

Adhy-ava-sāyin, mfn. resolute.

Adhy-ava-sita, mfn. ascertained, determined, apprehended.

Adhy-ava-siti, *is,* f. exertion, effort.

अध्यवहन् *adhy-ava-√han,* to thrash upon, TBr.

Adhy-avahánana, mfn. serving as an implement on which anything is thrashed, ŚBr.

अध्यशन *adhy-aśana, am,* n. eating too soon after a meal (before the last meal is digested).

अध्यस् *adhy-√2. as,* to throw or place over or upon; (in phil.) to attribute or impute wrongly.

Adhy-asta, mfn. placed over; disguised; supposed.

Adhy-āsa, *as,* m. See s. v.

अध्यस्थ *adhy-asthá, am,* n. the upper part of a bone, TS.

Adhy-asthi, *i,* n. a bone growing over another, Suśr.

अध्यह् *adhy-√ah,* perf. *-āha,* to speak on behalf of (dat.), AV. i, 16, 2.

अध्याक्रम् *adhy-ā-√kram,* to attack; to choose, Śāk.

अध्यागम् *adhy-ā-√gam,* to meet with.

अध्याचर् *adhy-ā-√car,* to use, Mn. &c.

अध्याण्डा *ádhy-āṇḍā,* f. = *adhy-aṇḍā,* ŚBr.

अध्यात्म *adhy-ātma, am,* n. the Supreme Spirit; (mfn.), own, belonging to self; (*ám*), ind. concerning self or individual personality. **-cetas,** m. one who meditates on the Supreme Spirit. **-jñāna,** n. knowledge of the Supreme Spirit or of *ātman.* **-dṛiś,** mfn. knowing the Supreme Spirit. **-rati,** m. a man delighting in the contemplation of the Supreme Spirit. **-rāmāyaṇa,** n. a Rāmāyaṇa, in which Rāma is identified with the universal spirit (it forms part of the Brahmāṇḍa-Purāṇa). **-vid,** mfn. = *-dṛiś.* **-vidyā,** f. = *-jñāna.* **-śāstra,** n., N. of a work. **Adhyātmôttara-kāṇḍa,** n. the last book of the Adhyātma-rāmāyaṇa.

Adhy-ātmika or better **ādhyātmika,** mf(*ī*)n. relating to the soul or the Supreme Spirit.

अध्याधा *adhy-ā-√dhā,* to place upon.

अध्यापक *adhy-āpaka,* &c. See *adhí.*

अध्याभृ *adhy-ā-√bhṛi* (impf. *ádhy-ā́bharat*) to bring near from, VS.

अध्यारुह् *adhy-ā-√ruh,* to ascend up on high, mount: Caus. *-ropayati,* to cause to mount.

Adhy-ārūḍha, mfn. mounted up, ascended; above, superior to (instr.); below, inferior to (abl.)

Adhy-āropa, *as,* m. (in Vedānta phil.) wrong attribution, erroneous transferring of a statement from one thing to another.

Adhy-āropaṇa, *am, ā,* n. f. id.

Adhy-āropita, mfn. (in Vedānta phil.) erroneously transferred from one thing to another.

अध्यावप् *adhy-ā-√2. vap, -ā́-vapati,* to scatter upon, ŚBr.

Adhy-ā-vāpa, *as,* m. the act of sowing or scattering upon, KātyŚr.

अध्यावस् *adhy-ā-√5. vas,* to inhabit, dwell in (acc. or loc.)

अध्यावाहनिक *adhy-ā-vāhanika, am,* n. that part of a wife's property which she receives when led in procession from her father's to her husband's house.

अध्यास् *adhy-√ās,* to sit down or lie down upon, to settle upon; to occupy as one's seat or habitation; to get into, enter upon; to be directed to or upon; to affect, concern; to preside over, influence, rule; to cohabit with: Caus. P. *adhy-āsayati,* to cause to sit down, Bhaṭṭ.: Desid. (p. *adhy-āsisishamāṇa*) to be about to rise up to (acc.), Bhaṭṭ.

Adhy-āsana, *am,* n. act of sitting down upon, L.; presiding over, L.; a seat, settlement, BhP.

Adhy-āsita, mfn. seated down upon; seated in a presidential chair; settled, inhabited; (*am*), n. sitting upon, Ragh. ii, 52.

Adhy-āsin, mfn. sitting down or seated upon.

Adhy-āsīna, mfn. seated upon.

अध्यास *adhy-āsa, as,* m. (√*2. as*), imposing (as of a foot), Yājñ.; (in phil.) = *adhy-āropa;* an appendage, RPrāt.

अध्यासञ्ज् *adhy-ā-√sañj* (1. sg. *-sajāmi*) to hang up, suspend, AV. xiv, 2, 48.

अध्यासद् *adhy-ā-√sad,* to sit upon (acc.), Kauś.: Caus. (1. sg. *ádhy-ā́-sādayāmi*) to set upon (loc.), TBr.

अध्याहरण *adhy-ā-haraṇa, am,* n. (√*hṛi*), act of supplying (elliptical language); supplement; act of inferring, inference.

Adhy-āharaṇīya or **-āhartavya,** mfn. to be supplied; to be inferred.

Adhy-āhāra, *as,* m. act of supplying (elliptical language), Pāṇ. vi, 1, 139, &c.

Adhy-āhṛita, mfn. supplied, argued.

अध्युत्था *adhy-ut-thā* (√*sthā*), to turn away from, PBr.

अध्युद्धि *adhy-ud-dhi,* f. See *ádhy-ūdhnī.*

अध्युद्धृ *adhy-ud-dhṛi* (√*hṛi*), (Imper. 2. sg. *ádhy-úd-dhara*) to draw (water) from, AV. xii, 3, 36.

अध्युद्भृ *adhy-ud-√bhṛi,* to take or carry away from, AV.

अध्युषित *adhy-ushita,* mfn. 1. (√*2. vas*), (°*te*), loc. ind. at daybreak, MBh.; 2. (√*5. vas*) inhabited; occupied.

अध्युष्ट *adhy-ushṭa,* mfn. (invented as the Sanskrit representative of the Prākrit *addhuṭṭha,* which is derived from *ardha-caturtha*), three and a half. **-valaya,** m. forming a ring coiled up three and a half times (as a snake).

अध्युष्ट्र *adhy-ushṭra, as,* m. a conveyance drawn by camels.

अध्यूढ *adhy-ūḍha,* mfn. (√*vah*), raised, exalted; affluent; abundant; (*as*), m. the son of a woman pregnant before marriage [cf. 1. *sahôḍha*]; Śiva; (*ā*), f. a wife whose husband has married an additional wife. **-ja,** m. the son of a woman pregnant before marriage.

अध्यूध्नी *ádhy-ūdhnī,* f. (fr. *ūdhan*) [MaitrS.; KātyŚr.] or *adhy-ud-dhi,* f. (√*dhā*) [ĀpŚr.], a tubular vessel above the udder, or above the scrotum.

अध्यूषिवस् *adhy-ūshivas, ān, ushī, at* (perf. p. √*5. vas*), one who has dwelt in, Pāṇ. iii, 2, 108, Sch.

अध्यूह् *adhy-√1. ūh,* to lay on, overlay; to place upon; to raise above.

Adhy-ūhana, *am,* n. putting on a layer (of ashes).

अध्यृध् *adhy-√ṛidh,* to expand, ŚBr. xiv.

अध्येतव्य *adhy-etavya,* &c. See *adhí.*

अध्येध् *adhy-√edh,* to increase, prosper.

अध्येषण *adhy-eshaṇa.* See *adhíshṭa.*

अध्रि *á-dhri,* mfn. (√*dhṛi*), unrestrained, irresistible, AV. v, 20, 10. **-gu** (*ádhri°*), mfn. (m. pl. *āvas*), irresistible, RV.; (*us*), m., N. of a heavenly killer of victims, RV.; N. of a formula concluding with an invocation of Agni, ŚBr. &c. **-ja** (*ádhri-*), mfn. irresistible, RV. v, 7, 10. **-pushpalikā,** f. a species of the Pān plant, Piper Betel.

A-dhriyamāṇa, mfn. (pr. Pass. p. √*dhṛi*), not held; not to be got hold of, not forthcoming, not surviving or existing, dead, (gaṇa *cārv-ādi,* q.v.)

अध्रुव *á-dhruva,* mf(*ā*)n. not fixed, not permanent; uncertain, doubtful; separable.

अध्रुष *adhrusha, as,* m. (etymology doubtful), quinsy, sore throat, Suśr.

अध्वन् *ádhvan, ā,* m. a road, way, orbit; a journey, course; distance; time, Buddh. & Jain.; means, method, resource; the zodiac (?), sky, air, L.; a place; a recension of the Vedas and the school upholding it; assault (?); ifc. *adhva, as.*

Adhva (in comp. for *adhvan*). **-gá**, mf(*ā*)n. road-going, travelling; (*as*), m. a traveller; a camel, a mule; (*ā*), f. the river Ganges. **-gát**, m. a traveller, AV. xiii, 1, 36. **-gaty-anta** or **-gantavya**, m. measure of length applicable to roads. **-ga-bhogya**, m. 'traveller's delight,' the tree Spondias Mangifera. **-gamana**, n. act of travelling. **-gāmin**, mfn. wayfaring. **-jā**, f. the plant Svarṇulī. **-pati**, m. lord of the roads, VS. **-ratha**, m. a travelling car. **-śalya**, m. the plant Achyranthes Aspera. **Adhvâdhipa** or **adhvêśa** m. an officer in charge of the public roads, police-officer, Rājat.

Adhvanīna, *as*, m. a traveller, Pāṇ.; Yājñ. i, 111.

Adhvanya, *as*, m. id., Pāṇ. v, 2, 16.

अध्वर *a-dhvará*, mfn. (√*dhvṛi*), not injuring, AV.; TS.; (*ás*), m. a sacrifice (especially the Soma sacrifice); N. of a Vasu; of the chief of a family; (*am*), n. sky or air, L. **-karmán**, n. performance of the Adhvara or any act connected with it, ŚBr. **-kalpā**, f., N. of an optional sacrifice (Kāmyeshṭi). **-kāṇḍa**, n., N. of the book in the Śatapatha-Brāhmaṇa which refers to Adhvaras. **-kṛit**, m. performing an Adhvara, VS. **-ga**, mfn. intended for an Adhvara. **-dīkshaṇīyā**, f. consecration connected with the Adhvara. **-dhishṇyá**, m. a second altar at the Soma sacrifice, ŚBr. **-prāyaścittí**, f. expiation connected with the Adhvara. **-vat** (*ádhvará-*), mfn. containing the word Adhvara, ŚBr. **-śrí**, mfn. embellishing the Adhvara, RV. **-samishṭa-yajus**, n., N. of an aggregate of nine libations connected with the Adhvara. **-stha** or **adhvare-shṭhá** [RV. x, 77, 7], mfn. standing at or engaged in an Adhvara.

Adhvarīya, Nom. P. (2. sg. °*rīyási*; p. °*rīyát*) to perform an Adhvara, RV.

Adhvarya, Nom. P. (p. °*ryát*) to be engaged in an Adhvara, RV. i, 181, 1.

Adhvaryú, *us*, m. one who institutes an Adhvara; any officiating priest; a priest of a particular class (as distinguished from the *Hotṛi*, the *Udgātṛi*, and the *Brahman* classes. The Adhvaryu priests 'had to measure the ground, to build the altar, to prepare the sacrificial vessels, to fetch wood and water, to light the fire, to bring the animal and immolate it;' whilst engaged in these duties, they had to repeat the hymns of the Yajur-veda; hence that Veda itself is also called Adhvaryu); (*adhvaryavas*), pl. the adherents of the Yajur-veda; (*us*), f. the wife of an Adhvaryu priest, Pāṇ. iv, 1, 66, Sch. **-kāṇḍa**, n., N. of a book of mantras or prayers intended for Adhvaryu priests. **-kratu**, m. sacrificial act performed by the Adhvaryu, Pāṇ. ii, 4, 4. **-veda**, m. the Yajur-veda.

अध्वस्मन् *a-dhvasmán*, mfn. unveiled, RV.

अध्वान्त *a-dhvānta*, *am*, n. (not positive darkness), twilight, gloom, shade. **-śātrava**, m. 'an enemy to shade,' the plant Cassia Fistula or Bignonia Indica.

अन् 1. *an-*, occasionally अन *ana-*, (before a vowel) the substitute for 3. *a*, or *a* privative.

अन् 2. *an*, cl. 2. P. *ániti* or *ánati*, *āna*, *anishyati*, *ānīt* [RV. x, 129, 2], to breathe, respire, gasp; to live, L.; to move, go, L. [cf. Gk. ἄνεμος; Lat. *animus*]: Caus. *ānayati*: Desid. *aninishati*.

Aná, *as*, m. breath, respiration, ŚBr.; ChUp. **-vat-tva**, n. the state of being endowed with breath or life, Nir.

Anana, *am*, n. breathing, living, Nir.

अनंश *an-aṅsa* or *an-aṅsin*, mfn. portionless; not entitled to a share in an inheritance.

अनंशुमत्फला *an-aṅsumat-phalā*, f. the plantain (= *aṅsumat-phalā*).

अनकदुन्दुभ *anaka-dundubha*, *as*, m., N. of Kṛishṇa's grandfather.

Anaka-dundubhi or better **ānakadundubhi**, *is*, m., N. of Kṛishṇa's father (Vasudeva; said to be derived from the beating of drums at his birth).

अनकस्मात् *an-akasmāt*, ind. not without a cause or an object; not accidentally, not suddenly.

अनकाममार *an-akāma-māra*, mfn. not killing undesiredly, AitĀr.

अनक्ष् *an-áksh* (nom. *an-ák*), mfn. blind, RV. ii, 15, 7.

An-akshá, mf(*ā*)n. id., RV. ix, 73, 6 & x, 27, 11.

An-akshi, n. a bad eye, L.

An-akshika, mfn. eyeless, TS.

अनक्षर *an-akshara*, mfn. unfit to be uttered; unable to articulate a syllable.

अनक्षसङ्गम् *án-aksha-saṅgam* [MaitrS.] or *án-aksha-stambham* [ŚBr.], ind. so as not to interfere with the axle-tree.

अनगार *an-agāra*, *as*, m. 'houseless,' a vagrant ascetic, L.

An-agārikā, f. the houseless life of such an ascetic, Buddh.

अनग्न *á-nagna*, mf(*ā*)n. not naked. **-tā** (*a-nagná-*), f. the not being naked, ŚBr.

अनग्नि *an-agní* (*án-agni*, Nir.), *is*, m. non-fire; substance differing from fire; absence of fire; (mfn.), requiring no fire or fire-place; not maintaining a sacred fire, irreligious; unmarried; dispensing with fire; 'having no fire in the stomach;' dyspeptic. **-trā** (*án-agni-*), mfn. not maintaining the sacred fire, RV. i, 189, 3. **-dagdha** (*án-agni-*), mfn. not burnt with fire; not burnt on the funeral pile (but buried), RV. x, 15, 14; (*ās*), m. pl., N. of a class of manes, Mn. iii, 199. **-shvātta**, *ās*, m. pl. id., L. (see *agni-dagdhá*, *agni-shvāttá*).

अनघ *an-agha*, mf(*ā*)n. sinless; faultless; uninjured; handsome, L.; (*as*), m. white mustard, L.; N. of Śiva and others. **Anaghâshṭamī**, f., N. of an eighth day (spoken of in the fifty-fifth Adhyāya of the Bhavishyottara-Purāṇa).

अनङ्कुश *an-aṅkuśa*, mfn. unrestrained.

अनङ्ग *an-aṅgá*, mf(*ā*)n. bodiless, incorporeal; (*as*), m., N. of Kāma (god of love, so called because he was made bodiless by a flash from the eye of Śiva, for having attempted to disturb his life of austerity by filling him with love for Pārvatī); (*am*), n. the ether, air, sky, L.; the mind, L.; that which is not the *aṅga*. **-krīḍā**, f. amorous play; N. of a metre (of two verses, the first containing sixteen long syllables, the second thirty-two short ones). **-devī**, f., N. of a queen of Kashmīr. **-pāla**, m., N. of a king's chamberlain at Kashmīr. **-m-ejaya** (*an-aṅgam-*), mfn. not shaking the body (?), (gaṇa *cārv-ādi*, q.v.) **-raṅga**, m., N. of an erotic work. **-lekhā**, f. a love letter; N. of a queen of Kashmīr. **-śekhara**, m., N. of a metre (of four verses, each containing fifteen iambi). **-senā**, f., N. of a dramatic personage. **Anaṅgâpīḍa**, m., N. of a king of Kashmīr. **Anaṅgâsuhṛid**, m. 'Kāma's enemy,' Śiva.

An-aṅgaka, *as*, m. the mind, L.

अनङ्गुरि *an-aṅgurí*, mfn. destitute of fingers, AV.

अनच्छ *an-accha*, mfn. unclear, turbid.

अनजका *an-ajakā* or *an-ajikā*, f. a miserable little goat, Pāṇ. vii, 3, 47.

अनञ्जन *an-añjana*, mfn. free from collyrium or pigment or paint; (*am*), n. the sky, atmosphere, L.

अनडुह् *anaḍ-úh*, *ḍvā́n*, m. (fr. *ánas*, a cart, and √*vah*, to drag), an ox, bull; the sign Taurus. **Anaḍuj-jihvā**, f. the plant Gojihvā, Elephantopus Scaber. **Anaḍud-da**, *as*, m. donor of a bull or ox.

Anaḍutka, mfn. ifc. for *anaḍuh*, (gaṇa *ura-ādi* and gaṇa *ṛiśyādi*, q.v.)

Anaḍuha, *as*, m. ifc. for *anaḍuh*; N. of the chief of a certain Gotra (?), (gaṇa *śarad-ādi*, q.v.)

Anaḍuhī [ŚBr.] or **anaḍvāhī** [Pāṇ.], f. a cow.

अनणु *án-aṇu*, mfn. not minute or fine, coarse, ŚBr.; (*us*), m. coarse grain, peas, &c.

An-aṇīyas, mfn. not at all minute; vast, mighty, Śiś. iii, 4.

अनत *a-nata*, mfn. not bent, not bowed down; not changed into a lingual consonant, RPrāt.; erect; stiff; haughty.

अनति- *an-ati-*, not very-, not too-, not past-. (Words commencing with *an-ati* are so easily analysed by referring to *ati*, &c., that few need be enumerated.) **Án-atikrama**, m. not transgressing, ŚBr.; moderation, propriety. **An-atikramaṇīya**, mfn. not to be avoided, not to be transgressed, inviolable. **An-atidṛiśyá**, mfn. not transparent, opaque, ŚBr.; (or = *aty-adṛiśya*), quite indiscernible. **Án-atidbhuta**, mfn. unsurpassed, RV. viii, 90, 3. **Án-atineda**, m. not foaming over, MaitrS. **Án-atirikta**, mfn. not abundant, ŚBr. **Án-atireca**, n. not abundance, MaitrS. **An-ativṛitti**, f. congruity. **An-ativyādhyá**, mfn. invulnerable, AV. ix, 2, 16. **An-atyanta-gati**, f. the sense of 'not exceedingly,' sense of diminutive words. **Án-atyaya**, m. the not going across, ŚBr.; (mfn.), unperishable, unbroken. **An-atyudyá**, mfn. (= *aty-an-udya*), quite unfit to be mentioned, far above any expression, AV. x, 7, 28.

अनदत् *án-adat*, mfn. not eating, not consuming, RV. iii, 1, 6; AV. &c.

अनद्धा *án-addhā* or (with particle *u*) *án-addhô*, ind. not truly, not really, not definitely, not clearly, ŚBr. **-purushá**, m. one who is not a true man, one who is of no use either to gods or men or the manes, ŚBr.; AitBr.; KātyŚr.

अनद्यतन *an-adyatana*, *as*, m. a tense (either past or future) not applicable to the current day, Pāṇ.

अनधस् *án-adhas*, ind. not below, TBr.

अनधिक *an-adhika*, mfn. having no superior, not to be enlarged or excelled; boundless; perfect.

अनधिकार *an-adhikāra*, *as*, m. absence of authority or right or claim. **-carcā**, f. unjustifiable interference, intermeddling, officiousness.

An-adhikārin, mfn. not entitled to.

An-adhikṛita, mfn. not placed at the head of, not appointed.

अनधिगत *an-adhigata*, mfn. not obtained, not acquired; not studied. **-manoratha**, mfn. one who has not obtained his wish, disappointed. **-śāstra**, mfn. unacquainted with the Śāstras.

An-adhigamya or **an-adhigamanīya**, mfn. unattainable.

अनधिष्ठान *an-adhishṭhāna*, *am*, n. want of superintendence.

An-adhishṭhita, mfn. not placed over, not appointed; not present.

अनधीन *an-adhīna* or *an-adhīnaka*, mfn. not subject to, independent; (*as*), m. an independent carpenter who works on his own account (see *kauṭataksha*).

अनध्यक्ष *an-adhyaksha*, mfn. not perceptible by the senses, not observable; without a superintendent.

अनध्ययन *an-adhyayana*, *am*, n. not reading or studying; intermission of study, Mn. &c.

An-adhyāya, *as*, m. id.; a time when there is intermission of study, Mn. **-divasa**, m. a vacation day, holiday.

अननङ्गमेजय *an-anaṅgamejaya*, mfn. not leaving the body unshaken (?); cf. *an-aṅgamejaya*.

अननुख्याति *án-anukhyāti*, *is*, f. not perceiving, MaitrS.

अननुज्ञात *an-anujñāta*, mfn. not agreed to, not permitted; denied.

अननुध्यायिन् *án-anudhyāyin*, mfn. not missing, not missing anything, AitBr.; not insidious, TBr.

अननुभावक *an-anubhāvaka*, mfn. unable to comprehend. **-tā**, f. non-comprehension; unintelligibility.

अननुभाषण *an-anubhāshaṇa*, *am*, n. 'not repeating (for the sake of challenging) a proposition,' tacit assent.

अननुभूत *an-anubhūta*, mfn. not perceived, not experienced, unknown.

अननुमत *an-anumata*, mfn. not approved or honoured, not liked, disagreeable, unfit.

अननुयाज *an-anuyājá* or *an-anūyājá* [TS.], mfn. without a subsequent or final sacrifice.

अननुषङ्गिन् *an-anushaṅgin*, mfn. not attached to, indifferent to.

अननुष्ठान *an-anushṭhāna*, *am*, n. non-observance, neglect; impropriety.

अननूक्त *án-anûkta* [ŚBr. xiv] or *an-anûkti* [KātyŚr.], mfn. not recited or studied; not responded to.

अननृत *an-anṛita*, mf(ā)n. not false, true, Śiś. vi, 39.

अनन्त *an-antá*, mf(ā)n. endless, boundless, eternal, infinite; (*as*), m., N. of Vishṇu; of Śesha (the snake-god); of Śesha's brother Vāsuki; of Kṛishṇa; of his brother Baladeva; of Śiva; of Rudra; of one of the Viśva-devas; of the 14th Arhat, &c.; the plant Sinduvāra, Vitex Trifolia; Talc; the 23rd lunar asterism, Śravaṇa; a silken cord (tied round the right arm at a particular festival); the letter *ā*; a periodic decimal fraction? (*ā*), f. the earth; the number one; N. of Pārvatī and of various females, the plant Śārivā; Periploca Indica or Asclepias Pseudosarsa or Asthmatica (the root of which supplies a valuable medicine); (*am*), n. the sky, atmosphere; Talc. **-kara**, mfn. rendering endless, magnifying indefinitely, Pāṇ. iii, 2, 21; R. v, 20, 26. **-ga**, mfn. going or moving for ever or indefinitely, Pāṇ. iii, 2, 48. **-guṇa**, mfn. having boundless excellencies. **-caturdaśī**, f. the fourteenth lunar day (or full moon) of Bhādra, when Ananta is worshipped. **-cāritra**, m., N. of a Bodhisattva. **-jit**, m., N. of the fourteenth Jaina Arhat of the present Avasarpiṇī. **-tā** (*anantá-*), f. eternity, infinity, ŚBr. xiv. **-tāna**, mfn. extensive. **-tīrtha**, m., N. of an author. **-tīrtha-kṛit**, m. = Anantajit. **-tṛitīyā**, f. the third day of Bhādra (said to be sacred to Vishṇu). **-tṛitīyā-vrata**, N. of the twenty-fourth Adhyāya of the Bhavishyottara-Purāṇa. **-tva**, n. = *-tā*, q. v. **-dṛishṭi**, m., N. of Śiva. **-deva**, m., N. of various persons, especially of a king of Kashmīr. **-nemi**, m., N. of a king of Mālava, a contemporary of Śākyamuni. **-pāra**, mfn. of boundless width. **-pāla**, m., N. of a warrior chief in Kashmīr. **-bhaṭṭa**, m., N. of a man. **-mati**, m., N. of a Bodhisattva. **-māyin**, mfn. endlessly illusory or delusive or deceitful. **-mūla**, m. the medicinal plant Śārivā. **-rāma**, m., N. of a man. **-rāśi**, m. (in arithm.) an infinite quantity; a periodic decimal fraction (?). **-rūpa**, mfn. having innumerable forms or shapes. **-vat**, mfn. eternal, infinite; (*ān*), m. (in the Upanishads) one of Brahmā's four feet (earth, intermediate space, heaven, and ocean). **-varman**, m., N. of a king. **-vāta**, m. a disease of the head (like tetanus). **-vikramin**, m., N. of a Bodhisattva. **-vijaya**, m., N. of Yudhishṭhira's conch-shell. **-vīrya**, m., N. of the twenty-third Jaina Arhat of a future age. **-vrata**, n. ceremony or festival in honour of Ananta or Vishṇu (on the day of the full moon in Bhādra); N. of the 102nd Adhyāya of the Bhavishyottara-Purāṇa. **-śakti**, mfn. omnipotent; (*is*), m., N. of a king. **-śayana**, n. Travancore. **-śīrshā**, f., N. of the snake king Vāsuki's wife. **-śushma** (*anantá-*), mfn. possessing boundless strength or endlessly roaring (?), RV. i, 64, 10. **Anantâtman**, m. the infinite spirit. **Anantâśrama**, **anantêśvara**, &c., names of persons unknown.

Anantaka, mfn. endless, boundless, eternal, infinite; (*am*), n. the infinite (i.e. infinite space).

Anantya, mfn. infinite, eternal; (*am*), n. infinity, eternity.

अनन्तर *an-antará*, mf(ā)n. having no interior; having no interstice or interval or pause; uninterrupted, unbroken; continuous; immediately adjoining, contiguous; next of kin, &c.; compact, close; (*as*), m. a neighbouring rival, a rival neighbour; (*am*), n. contiguousness; Brahma or the supreme soul (as being of one entire essence); (*am*), ind. immediately after; after; afterwards. **-ja**, m. 'next-born,' the son of a Kshatriyā or Vaiśyā mother by a father belonging to the caste immediately above the mother's, Mn. x, 41. **-jāta**, m. id., Mn. x, 6; also the son of a Śūdrā mother by a Vaiśya father.

Án-antaraya, *as*, m. non-interruption, ŚBr. & PBr.; (cf. *antaraya*.)

Án-antarāyam, ind. without a break, ŚBr. & AitBr.

Án-antarita, mfn. not separated by any interstice; unbroken.

Án-antariti, *is*, f. not excluding or passing over, TS.; AitBr.

Anantarīya, mfn. concerning or belonging to the next of kin, &c., (gaṇa *gahâdi*, q. v.)

अनन्तर्हित *án-antar-hita*, mfn. (√*dhā*), not concealed, manifest; not separated by a break.

अनन्द *a-nanda*, mfn. joyless, cheerless; (*ās*), m. pl., N. of a purgatory, Up.

अनन्ध *án-andha*, mfn. not blind, TBr. &c.

अनन्न *án-anna*, *am*, n. rice or food undeserving of its name, ŚBr. xiv.

अनन्य *an-anyá*, mf(ā)n. no other, not another, not different, identical; self; not having a second, unique; not more than one, sole; having no other (object), undistracted; not attached or devoted to any one else, TS. **-gati**, f. sole resort or resource. **-gati** or **-gatika**, mfn. having only one (or no other) resort or resource left. **-gāmin**, mfn. going to no other. **-guru**, m. 'having no other as a Guru,' N. of Kṛishṇa, Śiś. i, 35. **-citta**, mf(ā)n. or **-cetas**, mfn. giving one's undivided thought to (with loc.) **-codita**, mfn. self-impelled. **-ja**, m., N. of Kāma or Love. **-tā**, f. or **-tva**, n. identity. **-dṛishṭi**, mfn. gazing intently. **-deva**, mfn. having no other god. **-nishpādya**, mfn. to be accomplished by no other. **-pūrvā**, f. a female who never belonged to another, a virgin, Ragh. **-pratikriya**, mfn. having no other means of resistance or redress. **-bhava**, mfn. originating in or with no other. **-bhāva**, mfn. thinking of the only one, i. e. of the Supreme Spirit. **-manas** or **-manaska** or **-mānasa**, mfn. exercising undivided attention. **-yoga**, m. not suitable to any others; (*am*), ind. not in consequence of any other (word), RPrāt. **-vishaya**, mfn. exclusively applicable. **-vishayâtman**, mfn. having the mind fixed upon one (or the sole) object. **-vṛitti**, mfn. closely attentive. **-sādhāraṇa**, mfn. not common to any one else, not belonging to any other. **-hṛita**, mfn. not carried off by another, safe. **Ananyânubhava**, m., N. of the teacher of Prakāśātman. **Ananyârtha**, mfn. not subservient to another object; principal. **Ananyâśrita**, mfn. not having resorted to another; independent; (*am*), n. (in law) unencumbered property.

An-anyādṛiśa, mf(ī)n. not like others, Kathās.

अनन्वय *an-anvaya*, *as*, m. want of connexion; (in rhetoric) comparison of an object with its own ideal, (as, 'a lady-like lady.')

An-anvita, mfn. unconnected, inconsecutive, desultory, incoherent, irrelevant, irregular; not attended with, destitute of.

अनन्ववचार *án-anvavacāra* [ŚBr.] or *án-anvavâya* [MaitrS.], *as*, m. or *án-anvavâyana* [ŚBr.], *am*, n. (√*car* and √*i* with *anu* and *ava*), not following or going after any one (in a sneaking manner).

अनन्वाभक्त *án-anvābhakta*, mfn. (√*bhaj*), not receiving a share, not interested in (loc.), ŚBr.

अनप *an-apa*, mfn destitute of water, L.

अनपकरण *an-apakaraṇa*, *am*, n. (in law) non-payment, non-delivery.

An-apakarman, *a*, n. id., Mn. viii, 4.

An-apakāra, *as*, m. harmlessness.

An-apakārin, mfn. not harming, innocuous.

An-apakṛita, mfn. unharmed; (*am*), n. no offence, MBh.

An-apakriyā, f. = *an-apakaraṇa*, Mn.

अनपकर्ष *an-apakarsha*, *as*, m. (√*kṛish*), m. non-degradation, superiority.

अनपक्रम *án-apakrama*, *as*, m. not going away.

Án-apakramin, mfn. not departing from; devoted, attached to.

An-apakrāma, *as*, m. not retreating or withdrawing from, AitBr.

An-apakrāmuká, mf(*á*)n. not running away, MaitrS.; PBr.

अनपग *án-apaga* [TS.] or *an-apagá* [ŚBr.], mf(ā)n. not departing from (abl. or in comp.)

अनपच्युत *án-apacyuta*, mfn. not falling off, holding fast (a yoke), RV. x, 93, 12; never dropping off, keeping to or faithful for ever, RV.

अनपजय्यम् *an-apajayyám*, ind. (√*ji*), so that its victorious character cannot be reversed, ŚBr.

अनपत्य *an-apatyá*, mf(ā)n. childless; (*ám*), n. childlessness, RV. iii, 54, 18. **-tā**, f. childlessness, Śāk. &c. **-vat** (*ánapatya-*), mfn. childless, AV.

Anapatyaka, mfn. childless.

अनपत्रप *an-apatrapa*, mfn. shameless.

अनपदेश *an-apadeśa*, *as*, m. an invalid argument.

अनपधृष्य *an-apadhṛishya*, ind. p. not having overpowered, AitBr.

अनपनिहितम् *an-apanihitám*, ind. without leaving out anything, ŚBr.

अनपयति *an-apayati*, ind. (loc. pr. p. √*i* with *apa*?), 'before the sun makes a start,' very early, L.

अनपर *an-apará*, mfn. without another; having no follower; single, sole (as N. of Brahma), ŚBr. xiv.

अनपराद्ध *án-aparāddha*, mfn. one who has not injured anybody, MBh.; faultless, ŚBr.; (*ám*), ind. without injury, ŚBr. xiv.

An-aparādha, *as*, m. innocence, innocuousness; (mfn.), innocent, faultless; free from defects. **-tva**, n. freedom from fault.

Anaparâdhin, mfn. innocent.

अनपलाशुक *an-apalāshuka*, mfn. not thirsty, Pāṇ. vi, 2, 160, Sch.

अनपवाचन *an-apavācana*, mfn. impossible to be talked away or wished away, AV. viii, 8, 9.

अनपवृज्य *an-apavṛijyá*, mfn. not to be finished (as a way; 'free from objects that should be shunned as impure,' Sāy.), RV. i, 146, 3.

अनपव्ययत् *án-apavyayat* (*apa-vy-ayat*), mfn. unremitting, RV. vi, 75, 7.

अनपसर *an-apasara*, mfn. 'having no hole to creep out of,' inexcusable, unjustifiable; (*as*), m. a usurper, Mn. viii, 198.

An-apasaraṇá, *am*, n. not leaving a place or withdrawing from it, ŚBr.

अनपस्पृश् *án-apaspṛiś*, mfn. not refusing, not obstinate, AV.

अनपस्फुर् *án-apasphur* [RV. viii, 69, 10] or *án-apasphura* [RV. vi, 48, 11], mf(ā)n. or *án-apasphurat* [RV. iv, 42, 10; AV.], mfn. 'not withdrawing,' not refusing to be milked (said of a cow).

अनपहतपाप्मन् *án-apahata-pāpman*, mfn. (said of the Pitṛis to distinguish them from the Devas) not freed from evil, ŚBr.

An-apahanana, *am*, n. not repelling from, PBr.

अनपाकरण *an-apâkaraṇa*, *am*, n. (in law) non-payment, non-delivery.

An-apâkarman, *a*, n. id.

अनपाय *an-apâya*, mfn. without obstacles, prosperous; (*as*), m. freedom from mischief; (in phil.) the state of not being abridged or deprived of (abl.); N. of Śiva.

Ánapâyin, mfn. not going or passing away; constant in the same state; invariable.

अनपावृत् *án-apâvṛit*, ind. without turning away, unremittingly, RV. vi, 32, 5 & x, 89, 3.

अनपाश्रय *an-apâśraya*, mfn. not dependent.

अनपुंसक *a-napuṇsaka*, *am*, n. (in Gr.) not a neuter.

अनपूपीय *an-apūpīya* or *an-apūpya*, mfn. unfit for cakes. See *apūpa*.

अनपेक्ष *an-apêksha*, mfn. regardless, careless; indifferent; impartial; irrespective of; irrelevant; (*ā*), f. disregard, carelessness; (*án-apêksham*), ind. irrespectively, carelessly, ŚBr. **-tva**, n. disregard; irrelevance; irrespectiveness; (*āt*), ind. from having no reference to, since (it) has no reference to.

An-apêkshita, mfn. disregarded; unheeded; unexpected.

An-apêkshin, mfn. regardless of; indifferent to.

An-apêkshya, ind. p. disregarding, irrespective of.

अनपेत *án-apêta*, mfn. not gone off, not past; not separated, faithful to, possessed of.

अनपोद्धार्य *an-apôddhāryá*, mfn. of which nothing is to be taken off, ŚBr.

अनप्त *án-apta*, mfn. not watery, RV. ix, 16, 3.

अनप्नस् *an-apnás*, mfn. destitute of means, RV. ii, 23, 9, [cf. Lat. *inops*.]

अनप्सरस् an-apsaras, ās, f. unlike an Apsaras, unworthy of an Apsaras.

अनफा anaphā, f. a particular configuration of the planets. [Gk. ἀναφή.]

अनभिज्ञ an-abhijña, mfn. unacquainted with, ignorant, Comm. on Mn. ii, 125.

अनभिद्रुह् án-abhidruh, mfn. not malicious, RV. ii, 41, 5.

अनभिप्रेत an-abhiprêta, am, n. an occurrence different from what was intended.

अनभिभूत an-abhibhūta, mfn. not overcome, unsurpassed; not beset, unobstructed.

अनभिमत an-abhimata, mfn. not to one's mind, disliked, Hit.

अनभिमानुक án-abhimānuka, mfn. not having evil intentions against (acc.), MaitrS.; AitBr.

अनभिम्लात an-abhi-mlāta, mfn. unfaded. **-varṇa** (ánabhimlāta-), mfn. of unfaded colour or brightness, RV. ii, 35, 13.

An-abhimlāna, as, m. 'non-fading,' N. of the chief of a Gotra, (gaṇa śivâdi, q.v.)

अनभिरूप an-abhirūpa, mfn. not corresponding; not handsome, not pleasing.

अनभिलक्षित an-abhilakshita, as, m. 'destitute of (right) marks or symbols,' an impostor.

अनभिलाष an-abhilāsha, as, m. non-relish; want of appetite; want of desire.

An-abhilāshin, mfn. not desirous.

अनभिवादुक an-abhivāduka, mfn. not greeting, GopBr.; Vait.

An-abhivādya, mfn. not to be greeted.

अनभिव्यक्त an-abhivyakta, mfn. indistinct.

अनभिशस्त án-abhiśasta [RV. ix, 88, 7] or án-abhiśasti [VS.] or an-abhiśastenyá [VS.] or án-abhiśastya [Naigh.], mfn. blameless, faultless.

अनभिषङ्ग an-abhishaṅga or an-abhishvaṅga, as, m. absence of connection or attachment.

अनभिसन्धान an-abhisandhāna, am, n. absence of design; disinterestedness.

An-abhisandhi, is, m. id. **-kṛita**, mfn. done undesignedly.

अनभिसम्बन्ध an-abhisambandha, mfn. unconnected; (as), m. no connection.

अनभिस्नेह an-abhisneha, mfn. without affection, cold, unimpassioned, Bhag.

अनभिहित án-abhihita, mfn. not named; not fastened, ŚBr.; (as), m., N. of the chief of a Gotra, (gaṇa upakâdi, q.v.)

अनभीशु an-abhīśú, mfn. without bridles, having no bridles, RV.

अनभ्यनुज्ञा an-abhyanujñā, f. non-permission.

अनभ्यवचारुक án-abhyavacāruka, mf(ā)n. not attacking, MaitrS.

अनभ्यारूढ án-abhyārūḍha, mfn. not ascended, not mounted, AV.; not attained, ŚBr.

Án-abhyāroha, as, m. not ascending, ŚBr.

An-abhyārohyá, mfn. not to be ascended, ŚBr.

अनभ्याश an-abhyāśa or an-abhyāsa, mfn. not near, distant. **An-abhyāśam-itya**, mfn. improper to be approached, Pāṇ. vi, 3, 70, Comm.

अनभ्यास an-abhyāsa, as, m. want of practice or skill.

अनभ्र an-abhra, mf(ā)n. cloudless. **-vṛishṭi**, f. 'cloudless rain,' any unexpected acquisition or advantage, Kir. iii, 5.

An-abhraka, ās, m. pl. 'cloudless,' N. of a class of divinities, Buddh.

अनभ्रि an-abhrí, mfn. not dug out with a spade (said of rain-water), AV.

अनम a-nama, as, m. 'one who makes no salutation to others,' a Brāhman, L.

Á-namasyu, mfn. not bowing, RV. x, 48, 6.

अनमितम्पच an-amitam-paca, mfn. 'not cooking what has not first been measured,' niggardly, miserly (= mitam-paca, q.v.)

अनमित्र an-amitrá, mfn. having no enemies, AV.; (ám), n. the having no enemies, AV.; VS.; (as), m., N. of various persons, particularly a king of Ayodhyā.

अनमीव an-amīvá, mf(ā́)n., Ved. free from disease, well, comfortable; salubrious, salutary; (ám), n. good health, happy state, RV. x, 14, 11.

अनम्बर an-ambara, mfn. wearing no clothing, naked; (as), m. a Jaina mendicant; cf. dig-ambara.

अनय 1. a-naya, as, m. bad management; bad conduct (gambling, &c.)

अनय 2. an-aya, as, m. evil course, ill luck; misfortune, adversity; (cf. ayânaya s.v. aya.) **Anayam-gata**, mfn. fallen into misfortune.

अनरण्य an-araṇya, as, m., N. of a king of Ayodhyā, said by some to have been Pṛithu's father.

अनरुस् án-arus, mfn. not sore or wounded, ŚBr.

अनर्गल an-argala, mfn. without bars or checks, free, licentious.

अनर्घ an-argha, mfn. priceless, invaluable; (as), m. wrong value. **-rāghava**, n., N. of a drama (by Murāri, treating of Rāma).

An-arghya, mfn. priceless, invaluable, Kum. i, 59, &c.; not valuable, L. **-tva**, n. pricelessness, Hit.

अनर्जुन an-arjuna, mfn. without Arjuna, MBh.

अनर्थ an-artha, as, m. non-value; a worthless or useless object; disappointing occurrence, reverse, evil; nonsense; (mfn.), worthless, useless, bad; unfortunate; having no meaning; having not that (but another) meaning; nonsensical. **-kara**, mfn. doing what is useless or worthless; unprofitable; producing evil or misfortune. **-tva**, n. uselessness, &c. **-darśin**, mfn. minding useless or worthless things. **-nāśin**, m. 'Evil-destroyer,' Śiva. **-buddhi**, mfn. having a worthless intellect. **-bhāva**, mfn. having a bad nature, malicious. **-lupta**, mfn. freed from all that is worthless. **-saṃśaya**, m. non-risk of money or wealth.

An-arthaka, mfn. useless, vain, worthless; meaningless, nonsensical.

An-arthyá, mfn. worthless, useless, ŚBr.

अनर्पण án-arpaṇa, am, n. non-surrendering, not giving up, AV. xii, 4, 33.

अनर्मन् anarmán, mfn. = an-arván, q.v., AV. vii, 7, 1.

अनर्व an-arvá, mf(ā́)n. or an-arván, mfn. not to be limited, not to be obstructed, irresistible, RV.

An-arváṇa, mfn. id., RV. viii, 31, 12; (as), m., N. of the god Pūshan, RV. v, 51, 11 & x, 92, 14.

अनर्विश् ánar-viś, ṭ, m. seated on the car (ánas), a driver, RV. i, 121, 7.

अनर्शनि án-arśani, is, m., N. of a demon slain by Indra, RV. viii, 32, 2.

अनर्शराति án-arśa-rāti, mfn. giving uninjurious things, one whose gifts do not hurt, RV. viii, 99, 4.

अनर्ह an-arha, mf(ā)n. or an-arhat, mfn. undeserving of punishment or of reward; unworthy; inadequate, unsuitable.

Anarhya-tā, f. the not being properly estimated; unworthiness; inadequacy, unsuitableness.

अनल anala, as, m. (√an), fire; the god of fire; digestive power, gastric juice; bile, L.; wind, L.; N. of Vasudeva; of a Muni; of one of the eight Vasus; of a monkey; of various plants (Plumbago Zeylanica and Rosea; Semicarpus Anacardium); the letter r; the number three; (in astron.) the fiftieth year of Bṛihaspati's cycle; the third lunar mansion or Kṛittikā (?). **-da** (fr. 3. da), mfn. quenching fire (said of water), Kir. v, 25. **-dīpana**, mfn. exciting the digestion, stomachic. **-prabhā**, f. the plant Halicacabum Cardiospermum. **-priyā**, f. Agni's wife. **-vāṭa**, m., N. of ancient Pattana. **-sāda**, m. dyspepsia. **Analânanda**, m., N. of a Vedāntic writer, author of the Vedānta-kalpataru.

अनलंकरिष्णु an-alaṃkarishṇu, mfn. not given to the use of ornaments; unornamented.

अनलम् an-alam, ind. not enough; insufficiently.

अनलस an-alasa, mfn. not lazy, active.

अनलि anali, is, m. the tree Sesbana Grandiflora.

अनल्प an-alpa, mfn. not a little, much, numerous. **-ghosha**, mfn. very clamorous, very noisy. **-manyu**, mfn. greatly enraged.

अनवकाश an-avakāśa, mf(ā)n. having no opportunity or occasion; uncalled for, inapplicable, Pāṇ. i, 4, 1, Sch.

अनवक्रामम् an-avakrāmam, ind. not stepping upon, ĀpŚr.

अनवगाहिन् an-avagāhin, mfn. (√gāh), not dipping into, not studying.

An-avagāhya, mfn. unfathomable.

अनवगीत an-avagīta, mfn. not made an object of contemptuous song, uncensured.

अनवग्रह an-avagraha, mfn. resistless; not to be intercepted.

अनवग्लायत् án-avaglāyat, mfn. not growing remiss, AV. iv, 4, 7.

अनवच्छिन्न an-avacchinna, mfn. not intersected, uninterrupted; not marked off, unbounded, immoderate; undiscriminated. **-hāsa**, m. continuous or immoderate laughter.

अनवतप्त an-avatapta, as, m., N. of a serpent king, Buddh.; of a lake (= Rāvaṇa-hrada), ib.

अनवत्त्व anavat-tva. See √an.

अनवद्य an-avadyá, mf(ā́)n. irreproachable, faultless; unobjectionable; (ā), f., N. of an Apsaras. **-tā**, f. or **-tva**, n. faultlessness. **-rūpa** (anavadyá-), mf(ā)n. of faultless form or beauty, RV. x, 68, 3, &c. **Anavadyâṅga**, mf(ī)n. having faultless body or limbs.

अनवद्राण an-avadrāṇá, mfn. (√drā), not going to sleep, not sleepy, AV. viii, 1, 13.

अनवधर्ष्य an-avadharshyà (6), mfn. not to be defied, AV. viii, 2, 10.

अनवधान an-avadhāna, am, n. inattention, inadvertence; (mfn.), inattentive, careless. **-tā**, f. inadvertency.

अनवधि an-avadhi, mfn. unlimited.

अनवधृष्य an-avadhṛishya, mfn. impossible to be put down or injured, ŚBr.

अनवन an-avana, mf(ī, Śiś. vi, 37)n. 'affording no help or protection,' causing distress; (am), n. non-protection, Pāṇ. i, 3, 66.

अनवनामितवैजयन्त an-avanāmita-vaijayanta, as, m. 'having victorious banners unlowered,' 'ever glorious,' a future universe, Buddh.

अनवपृग्ण án-avapṛigṇa, mfn. (√pṛic), not closely united, but spreading all around, RV. i, 152, 4.

अनवबुध्यमान an-avabudhyamāna, mfn. deranged, L.

अनवब्रव an-avabravá, mfn. (√brū), irreproachable, RV. x, 84, 5.

अनवभ्रराधस् an-avabhrá-rādhas, mfn. (√bhṛi), having or giving undiminished (or durable) wealth, RV.

अनवम an-avama, mf(ā)n. not low; exalted.

अनवमर्शम् án-avamarśam, ind. without touching, ŚBr.

An-avamṛiśyá, mfn. not fit to be touched, ŚBr.

अनवर an-avara, mfn. not inferior; excellent.

अनवरत *an-avarata*, mfn. incessant; (*am*), ind. incessantly.

अनवरथ *an-avaratha*, *as*, m., N. of a son of Madhu and father of Kuruvatsa, VP.

अनवरार्ध्य *an-avarârdhya*, mfn. chief, principal, L.

अनवलम्ब *an-avalamba*, mfn. having no support, not propped up.

An-avalambana, *am*, n. independence.

An-avalambita, mfn. not supported or propped up, not dependent.

अनवलेप *an-avalepa*, mfn. free from veneer, unvarnished, plain, unassuming.

अनवलोभन *an-avalobhana*, *am*, n. (for °*lopana*, 'cutting off,' Comm.), N. of a ceremony observed by a pregnant woman to prevent miscarriage (treated of in an Upanishad), ĀśvGṛ.

अनवस *an-avasá*, mfn. (probably fr. √*so* with *ava*), not making to halt, not stopping, RV. vi, 66, 7.

अनवसर *an-avasara*, mfn. having no interval of leisure, busy; coming when there is no such interval, inopportune; (*as*), m. absence of leisure; unseasonableness.

अनवसाद्य *an-avasādya*, ind. p. (Caus. of *ava*-√*sad*), not discouraging, not annoying.

अनवसान *an-avasāna*, mfn. (√*so*), having no termination, free from death; endless.

An-avasita, mfn. not set, not terminated; (*ā*), f., N. of a species of the Trishṭubh metre (consisting of four lines with eleven feet in each).

Án-avasyat, mfn. unceasing, RV. iv, 13, 3.

अनवस्कर *an-avaskara*, mfn. free from dirt, clean, cleansed.

अनवस्थ *an-avastha*, mfn. unsettled, unstable; (*ā*), f. unsettled condition or character; instability, unsteady or loose conduct; (in phil.) non-finality (of a proposition), endless series of statements.

An-avasthāna, mfn. unstable, fickle, BhP.; (*as*), m. wind; (*am*), n. instability; unsteadiness or looseness of conduct.

An-avasthāyin, mfn. transient.

An-avasthita, mfn. unsettled, unsteady, loose in conduct. **–citta**, mfn. unsteady-minded. **–citta-tva**, n. unsteadiness of mind. **–tva**, n. unsteadiness, instability.

An-avasthiti, *is*, f. instability; unsteadiness; looseness of character.

अनवस्यत् *án-ava-syat*. See *an-avasāna*.

अनवहित *an-avahita*, mfn. heedless, inattentive.

अनवह्वर *án-avahvara*, mfn. not crooked, straightforward, RV. ii, 41, 6.

अनवाच् *an-avāc*, mfn. not speechless.

अनवाञ्च् *an-avāñc*, *ān*, *ācī*, *āk*, not inclining downwards, looking up or straightforward.

अनवानत् *án-avânat*, mfn. (√*an*), not taking breath, not respiring, ŚBr.

An-avânam, ind. without breathing between, in one breath, without interruption, *uno tenore*, AitBr. **Anavâna-tā**, f. uninterruptedness, contiguity.

अनवाप्त *an-avâpta*, mfn. not obtained.

An-avâpti, *is*, f. non-attainment.

अनवाय *an-avâyá*, mfn. uninterrupted, unyielding, RV. vii, 104, 2.

अनविथ्य *an-avithya*, mfn. (fr. *avi*, q. v.), not suited to sheep.

अनवेक्ष *an-avêksha*, mfn. regardless; (*am*), ind. irrespectively; without regard to; (*ā*), f. or **an-avêkshaṇa**, n. regardlessness.

अनव्रत *an-avrata*, mfn. not destitute of ascetic exercises; (*as*), m. a Jaina devotee of that description.

अनशन *án-aśana*, *am*, n. abstinence from food, fasting (especially as a form of suicide adopted from vindictive motives); (mfn.), fasting. **–tā** (*anaśaná-*), f. not eating, ŚBr.

An-aśanāyá, mfn. not hungry, ŚBr.

Án-aśita, *am*, n. condition of not having eaten, fasting.

Án-aśnat, mfn. not eating, RV. i, 164, 20, &c.

Án-aśnan-t-sāṅgamaná, m. the sacrificial fire in the Sabhā (which is approached before breakfast), ŚBr.

An-aśnāna, mf(*ā*)n. not eating.

अनश्रु *an-aśrú*, mfn. tearless, RV. x, 18, 7; VS.

अनश्व *an-aśvá*, mfn. having no horse or horses, RV. [cf. ἄνιππος]; (*as*), m. something that is not a horse, Pañcat. **–dā** (*án-aśva-*), mfn. one who does not give horses, RV. v, 54, 5.

अनश्वन् *an-aśvan*, *ā*, m., N. of Parīkshit's father, MBh. i, 3793 seqq.

अनश्वर *a-naśvara*, mfn. imperishable.

A-nashṭa, mfn. undestroyed, unimpaired. **–paśu** (*ánashṭa-*), mfn. having one's cattle unimpaired, RV. x, 17, 3. **–vedas** (*ánashṭa-*), mfn. having one's property unimpaired, RV. vi, 54, 8.

अनस् *ánas*, *as*, n. (√*an*, Uṇ.), a cart, RV. &c.; a mother, L.; birth, L.; offspring, living creature, L.; boiled rice, L. **–vat** (*ánas-*), mfn. yoked to a cart, RV.; AV.

Anaḍ-úh, ánar-viś, ano-ratha, &c. See s.v.

अनसूय *an-asūya*, mfn. not spiteful, not envious; (*ā*), f. freedom from spite; absence of ill-will or envy; N. of a daughter of Daksha; of one of Śakuntalā's friends.

An-asūyaka or **an-asūyu**, mfn. not spiteful or envious.

अनसूरि *an-a-sūri*, *is*, m. not unwise, intelligent, ChUp.

अनस्तमित *án-astam-ita*, mfn. not gone down; not subject to setting or declining.

अनस्थ *an-asthá* [RV. viii, 1, 34; AV.] or *an-ásthaka* [MaitrS.] or *an-asthán* [RV. i, 164, 4; Mn.] or *an-asthi* [KātyŚr.] or *anasthika* [TS.] or *an-ásthika* [ŚBr.; Yājñ.] or *anasthi-mat*, mfn. boneless.

अनहंकार *an-ahaṃkāra*, *as*, m. non-egotism, absence of self-conceit or of the tendency to regard self as something distinct from the Supreme Spirit; freedom from pride; (mfn.), free from self-conceit.

An-ahaṃkṛita, mfn. free from self-conceit.

An-ahaṃkṛiti, *is*, f. = *an-ahaṃkāra*; (mfn.), free from self-conceit or pride.

An-aham-vādin, mfn. = *an-ahaṃkṛita*.

अनहन् *an-ahan*, *as*, n. a non-day, no day, an evil or unlucky day, L.

अना *anā́*, ind. (fr. pronom. base *a*), hereby, thus, indeed, RV.

अनाकार *an-ākāra*, mfn. shapeless.

अनाकारित *an-ākārita*, mfn. not claimed, not exacted.

अनाकाल *án-ākāla*, *as*, m. unseasonable time, ŚBr.; (in law-books) famine. **–bhṛita**, m. a slave who became so voluntarily to avoid starvation in a time of scarcity (also spelt *annākāla-bhṛita*).

अनाकाश *an-ākāśá*, mfn. having no ether or transparent atmosphere, differing from ether, ŚBr, xiv; opaque, dark; (*am*), n. non-ether.

अनाकुल *an-ākula*, mf(*ā*)n. not beset; not confused; unperplexed, calm, consistent, regular.

अनाकृत *án-ākṛita*, mfn. unreclaimed, unreclaimable, RV. i, 141, 7; not taken care of, PBr.

अनाक्रान्त *an-ākrānta*, mfn. unassailed, unassailable; (*ā*), f. the Prickly Nightshade (Solanum Jacquini).

अनाक्षारित *an-ākshārita*, mfn. unreproached.

अनाक्षित् *án-ākshit*, mfn. not residing or resting, ŚBr.

अनाग *án-āga*, mf(*ā*)n. See *án-āgas*.

अनागत *án-āgata*, mfn. (√*gam*), not come, not arrived; future; not attained, not learnt; unknown; (*am*), n. the future. **–vat**, mfn. connected with or relating to the future. **–vidhātṛi**, m. 'disposer of the future,' provident; N. of a fish, Pañcat. **Anāgatâbādha**, m. future trouble. **Anāgatârtavā**, f. a girl who has not yet attained to puberty. **Anāgatâvekshaṇa**, n. act of looking at that which is not yet come or the future.

An-āgati, *is*, f. non-arrival; non-attainment; non-accession.

An-āgama, *as*, m. non-arrival; non-attainment; (mfn.), not come, not present; (in law) not constituting an accession to previous property, but possessed from time immemorial, and therefore without documentary proof. **Anāgamôpabhoga**, m. enjoyment of such property.

Án-āgamishyat, mfn. one who will not approach, AV.

An-āgamya, mfn. unapproachable, unattainable.

An-āgāmin, mfn. not coming, not arriving; not future, not subject to returning; (*ī*), m., N. of the third among the four Buddhist orders

An-āgāmuka, mfn. not in the habit of coming, not likely to come, Pāṇ. vi, 2, 160, Sch.

अनागस् *án-āgas*, mfn. sinless, blameless, RV. &c.; (*an-āgás*), mfn. not injuring, RV. x, 165, 2. **Anāgās-tvá**, n. sinlessness, RV. **Anāgo-hatyā́**, f. murder of an innocent person, AV. x, 1, 29.

Án-āga, mf(*ā*)n. sinless, RV.; (*ā*), f., N. of a river.

अनागूर्तिन् *án-āgūrtin*, mfn. one who has not recited the Āgur, ŚBr.

अनाचरण *an-ācaraṇa*, *am*, n. non-performance of what is right or customary, improper behaviour; misconduct.

An-ācāra, *as*, m. id.; (mfn.), improper in behaviour; regardless of custom or propriety or law; unprincipled; uncommon, curious, Kauś.

Anācārin, mfn. not acting properly.

अनाचार्यभोगीन *an-ācārya-bhogīna*, mfn. unfit or improper for a spiritual teacher to eat or enjoy.

अनाछृण्ण *án-āchṛiṇṇa*, mfn. not poured upon, TS.

अनाजानत् *án-ājānat*, mfn. (√*jñā*), not learning or perceiving, AV.

An-ājñapta, mfn. not commanded. **–kārin**, mfn. doing what has not been commanded.

An-ājñāta, mfn. unknown, surpassing all that has ever been known; (*án-ājñātam*), ind. in an unknown, i. e. inexplicable way or manner, TS.

अनाढ्य *án-āḍhya*, mfn. not wealthy, poor, ŚBr. &c. **An-āḍhyam-bhavishṇu**, mfn. not becoming wealthy, becoming poor (?), Pāṇ. vi, 2, 160, Sch.

अनातत *án-ātata*, mfn. not stretched or strung, VS.

अनातप *an-ātapa*, *as*, m. freedom from the blaze of the sun; shade; (mfn.), shady.

अनातुर *an-āturá* [once *án-ātura*, AV. xii, 2, 49], mfn. free from suffering or weariness, RV. &c.; well.

अनात्मन् *an-ātman*, *ā*, m. not self, another; something different from spirit or soul; (*an-ātmán*), mfn. not spiritual, corporeal; destitute of spirit or mind, ŚBr.

An-ātma (in comp. for *an-ātman*). **–jña**, mfn. destitute of spiritual knowledge or true wisdom. **–pratyavêkshā**, f. reflection that there is no spirit or self, Buddh. **–vat**, mfn. not self-possessed; (*vat*), ind. unlike one's self.

An-ātmaka, mfn. unreal, Buddh.

An-ātmanīna, mfn. not adapted to self; disinterested.

An-ātmya, mfn. impersonal, TUp.; (*am*), n. want of affection for one's own family, BhP.

अनात्यन्तिक *an-ātyantika*, mfn. not perpetual, not final; intermittent, recurrent.

अनाथ *a-nātha*, mf(*ā*)n. having no master or protector; widowed; fatherless; helpless, poor; (*ám*), n. want of a protector, helplessness, RV. x, 10, 11. **–piṇḍa-da** or **-piṇḍika**, m. 'giver of cakes or food to the poor,' N. of a merchant (in whose garden Śākyamuni used to instruct his disciples). **–sabhā**, f. a poor-house.

अनाद *a-nāda, as*, m. absence of sound (in pronouncing aspirated letters), RPrāt.

A-nādin, mfn. not sounding.

अनाददान *an-ādadāna*, mfn. not accepting.

अनादर *an-ādara, as*, m. disrespect, contemptuous neglect; (*an-ādará*), mfn. indifferent, ŚBr.; ChUp.

An-ādaraṇa, *am*, n. disrespectful behaviour, neglect.

An-ādarin, mfn. disrespectful, irreverent.

An-ādṛita, mfn. not respected, disrespected.

An-ādṛitya, ind. p. without respecting, regardless.

अनादि *an-ādi*, mfn. having no beginning, existing from eternity. **-tva**, n. state of having no beginning. **-nidhana**, mfn. having neither beginning nor end, eternal. **-mat**, mfn. having no beginning. **-madhyânta**, mfn. having no beginning, middle or end. **Anādy-ananta**, mfn. without beginning and without end, Up. **An-ādyanta**, mfn. without beginning and end; (*as*), m., N. of Śiva.

अनादिष्ट *án-ādishṭa*, mfn. not indicated; not commanded or instructed; not allowed.

अनादीनव *an-ādīnava*, mfn. faultless, Śiś.

अनादृत *an-ādṛita*. See *an-ādara*.

अनादेय *an-ādeya*, mfn. unfit or improper to be received, unacceptable, inadmissible.

अनादेशकर *anādeśa-kara*, mfn. doing what is not commanded or not allowed, BhP.

अनाद्य 1. *an-ādya*, mfn. = *an-ādi*, q. v.

अनाद्य 2. *an-ādyá*, mf(*ā́*)n. (= *an-adya*), not eatable, AV.; ŚBr.; Mn.

अनाधृष् *án-ādhṛish*, mfn. (√*dhṛish*), not checking, AV. vi, 21, 3.

Á́n-ādṛishṭa, mfn. unchecked, unimpaired, invincible, perfect, RV.; VS.

An-ādhṛishṭi, *is*, m. 'superior to any check,' N. of a son of Śūra; of a son of Ugrasena (general of the Yādavas).

An-ādhṛishyá, mfn. invincible, not to be meddled with, RV. &c.

अनानत *án-ānata*, mfn. unbent, not humbled, RV.; (*as*), m., N. of a Ṛishi of the SV.

अनानुकृत्य *an-ānukṛityá*, mfn. (*ānu* for *anu*), inimitable, unparalleled, RV. x, 68, 10 & 112, 5.

अनानुजा *an-ānujā*, f. (being) no younger sister, TS.

अनानुद *an-ānudá*, mfn. (√1. *dā* with *ānu* for *anu*), not giving way, obstinate, RV.

अनानुदिष्ट *án-ānudishṭa*, mfn. (√*diś* with *ānu* for *anu*), unsolicited, RV. x, 160, 4.

अनानुपूर्व्य *an-ānupūrvya, am*, n. separation of the different parts of a compound word by the intervention of others; the not coming in regular order, tmesis, RPrāt. **-saṃhitā**, f. the manner of constructing a sentence with the above tmesis.

अनानुभूति *án-ānubhūti, is*, f. 'inattention, neglect' (*tayas*), pl. neglectful or irreligious people, RV. vi, 47, 17.

अनापद् *an-āpad, t*, f. absence of misfortune or calamity, Mn.

An-āpanna, mfn. not realized, unattained; not fallen into distress.

अनापान *an-āpāna, as*, m., N. of a prince (son of Aṅga).

अनापि *án-āpi*, mf(nom. *iḥ*)n. having no friends, RV. x, 39, 6; (Indra), RV. viii, 21, 13.

अनापूयित *án-āpūyita*, mfn. not stinking, ŚBr.

अनाप्त *án-āpta*, mfn. unattained, unobtained, RV. i, 100, 2, &c.; unsuccessful in the effort to attain or obtain; not apt, unfit, Mn. viii, 294; (*as*), m. a stranger.

An-āpti, *is*, f. non-attainment.

An-āpyá (4), mfn. unattainable, RV. vii, 66, 11; AitBr.

अनाप्लुत *an-āpluta*, mfn. unbathed, unwashed. **An-āplutâṅga**, mfn. having an unwashed body, MBh.

अनाबयु *anābayu*, m., N. of a plant, AV.

अनाबाध *an-ābādha*, mfn. free from obstacles or troubles.

अनाभयिन् *an-ābhayin*, mfn. fearless (N. of Indra), RV. viii, 2, 1.

अनाभू *án-ābhū*, mfn. neglectful, disobliging, RV. i, 51, 9; MaitrS.

अनाभ्युदयिक *an-ābhyudayika*, mfn. inauspicious, ill-omened, unlucky.

अनामन् *á-nāman*, mfn. nameless, ŚBr. xiv; infamous; (*ā*), m. the ring-finger, Hcat. **Anāmatva**, n. namelessness.

A-nāmaka, mfn. nameless, infamous; (*as*), m. the intercalary month; (*am*), n. piles, hæmorrhoids.

Á-nāmikā, f. the ring-finger, ŚBr. xiv, &c.

अनामन *anāmaná, as* or *am*, m. or n., N. of a disease, AV.

अनामय *an-āmayá*, mf(*ā́*)n. not pernicious, AV.; free from disease, healthy, salubrious; (*as*), m. Śiva; (*am*), n. health.

Á́n-āmayat, mfn. 'not causing pain' (°*yatā*), instr ind. in good health, VS.

An-āmayitnú, mfn. salubrious, curative, RV. x, 137, 7.

अनामिन् *á-nāmin*, mfn. unbending, RV.

A-nāmya, mfn. impossible to be bent.

अनामिष *an-āmisha*, mfn. without flesh; bootless, profitless.

अनामृण *an-āmṛiṇá*, mfn. having no enemy that can injure, RV. i, 33, 1.

अनामृत *án-āmṛita*, mfn. not struck by death, TS.

अनाम्नात *an-āmnāta*, mfn. not handed down in sacred texts.

अनायक *a-nāyaka*, mf(*ā*)n. having no leader or ruler, disorderly.

अनायत *án-āyata*, mfn. not tied or fastened, RV. iv, 13, 5 & 14, 5; close, continuous, unseparated; unextended, having no length.

अनायतन *án-āyatana* or *an-āyataná, am*, n. that which is not really a resting-place or an altar, ŚBr.; (*an-āyataná*), mfn. having no resting-place or altar, AV. **-vat**, mfn. = the last, AitBr.

अनायत्त *an-āyatta*, mfn. independent, uncontrolled. **-vṛitti**, mfn. having an independent livelihood. **-vṛitti-tā**, f. independence.

अनायसाग्र *an-āyasâgra*, mfn. having no iron point.

अनायास *an-āyāsa, as*, m. absence of exertion, facility, ease, idleness, neglect; (mfn.), easy, ready; (*ena*), ind. easily. **-kṛita**, mfn. done readily or easily; (*am*), n. (in med.) an infusion prepared extemporaneously.

अनायुध *an-āyudhá*, mfn. weaponless; having no implements (for sacrifice), RV. iv, 5, 14 & viii, 96, 9.

अनायुषा *an-āyushā*, f. or *an-āyus*, f., N. of the mother of Bala and Vṛitra.

An-āyushya, mfn. not imparting long life, fatal to long life.

अनारत *an-ārata*, mfn. without interruption, continual; (*am*), ind. continually.

अनारभ्य 1. *an-ārabhya*, mfn. improper or impracticable to be commenced or undertaken. **-tva**, n. impossibility of being commenced.

2. **An-ārabhya**, ind. p. without commencing (used in comp. in the sense 'detached'). **-vāda**, m. a detached remark (upon sacrifices, &c.) **Anārabhyâdhīta**, mfn. taught or studied or read as a detached subject (not as part of a regular or authoritative treatise).

An-ārambha, *as*, m. absence of beginning, non-commencement, not attempting or undertaking; (mfn.), having no commencement.

अनारम्बण *an-ārambaṇá*, mfn. (for *anālambana*), having no support, ŚBr. xiv; ChUp.

अनारम्भण *an-ārambhaṇá*, mfn. intangible, giving no support, RV.; ŚBr.; BṛĀrUp.

अनारुह्य *an-āruhya*, ind. p. not having surmounted.

अनारोग्य *an-ārogya, am*, n. sickness; (mfn.), unhealthy. **-kara**, mfn. unwholesome, unhealthy, causing sickness.

अनार्जव *an-ārjava, am*, n. crookedness, moral or physical; disease, L.

अनार्त *án-ārta*, mfn. not sick, well.

Á́n-ārti, *is*, f. painlessness.

अनार्तव *an-ārtava*, mfn. unseasonable.

अनार्त्विजीन *an-ārtvijīna*, mfn. unfit or unsuitable for a priest.

अनार्य *an-ārya*, mfn. not honourable or respectable, vulgar, inferior; destitute of Āryas; (*as*), m. not an Ārya. **-karmin**, m. doing work unbecoming an Ārya or becoming only a non-Ārya. **-ja**, mfn. of vile or unworthy origin; (*am*), n. Agallochum, being a produce of the country of Mlecchas or barbarians. **-jushṭa**, mfn. practised, observed, or possessed by non-Āryas. **-tā**, f. vileness, unworthiness, Mn. x, 58. **-tikta**, m. the medicinal plant Gentiana Cherayta. **-tva**, n. = *-tā*, q. v.

An-āryaka, *am*, n. Agallochum or Aloe wood (Aquila Agallocha).

अनार्ष *an-ārsha*, mfn. not belonging to a Ṛishi or to a Vedic hymn; not belonging to the Saṃhitā text (e.g. the word *iti*, added for grammatical purposes in the Pada-pāṭha to certain words, RPrāt.); not applied to a Ṛishi, not added to his name (as an affix), Pāṇ. iv, 1, 78.

Á́n-ārsheya, mfn. not connected with the Ṛishis, AV.

अनालम्ब *an-ālamba*, mfn. unsupported, without stay or support; (*as*), m. want of support; despondency; (*ī*), f. Śiva's lute.

An-ālambana, mfn. unsupported; desponding.

An-ālambukā [Kāṭh.] or better **an-ālambhuká** [TBr.; KapS.], f. 'intangible,' a woman during menstruation.

अनालाप *an-ālāpa*, mfn. not talkative, reserved, taciturn; (*as*), m. reserve, taciturnity.

अनालोचित *an-ālocita*, mfn. unseen, unbeheld; unweighed, unconsidered, rash, imprudent.

An-ālocya, ind. p. not having considered.

अनावयस् *án-āvayas*, mfn. (cf. *āvayá* & *á-pravīta*), not having the power of causing conception, AV. vii, 90, 3.

अनावरणिन् *an-āvaraṇin, inas*, m. pl. 'without cover or clothes,' N. of a religious sect, (? = *an-ambara*, q. v.).

अनाविद्ध *án-āviddha*, mfn. not wounded, unhurt, RV. vi, 75, 1, &c.

अनाविल *an-āvila*, mfn. not turbid, clear, pure, not marshy.

अनावृत् *án-āvṛit*, mfn. not returning, RV. x, 95, 14.

Á́n-avṛitta, mfn. not turned about or round; not retreating; not frequented or approached, AV.; not chosen.

An-āvṛitti, *is*, f. non-return to a body, final emancipation.

अनावृत *án-āvṛita*, mfn. uncovered, ŚBr. xiv, undressed; uninclosed, open.

अनावृष्टि *an-āvṛishṭi, is*, f. want of rain, drought.

अनावेदित *an-āvedita*, mfn. not notified, not made known.

अनाव्याध *an-āvyādhá*, mfn. impossible to be broken or forced open, AV. xiv, 1, 64.

अनाव्रस्क *án-āvraska, as*, m. (√*vraśc*), not falling or dropping off, TS.; uninjured condition, KaushBr.; (*an-āvraská*), mfn. not falling or dropping off, AV. xii, 4, 47.

अनाश 1. an-āśa, mfn. (fr. āśā), hopeless, despairing.

अनाश 2. a-nāśa, mfn. (√2. naś), undestroyed, living.

1. **A-nāśin**, mfn. imperishable.

A-nāśya, mfn. indestructible.

अनाशक án-āśaka, am, n. fasting, abstaining from food even to death. **-nivṛitta**, m. one who has abandoned the practice of fasting. **Anāśakâyana**, n. a course of fasting (as a penance), ChUp.

2. **An-āśin**, mfn. not eating.

Án-āśvas, *vān, ushī, vat*, not having eaten, fasting, TS.; TBr. (without *an* the form would be *āśivas*, see Pāṇ. iii, 2, 109).

अनाशस्त an-āśastá, mfn. not praised [Gmn.; 'not to be trusted,' NBD.], RV. i, 29, 1.

अनाशिस् an-āśis, mfn. not desirable, not agreeable, Rājat. **Án-āśīr-dā**, mfn. not giving a blessing, RV. x, 27, 1.

An-āśīr-ka, mfn. not containing a prayer or blessing, TS.

अनाशु an-āśú, mfn. not quick, slow, RV.; superl. *an-āśishṭa*, mfn., AitBr.; not having quick horses, RV. i, 135, 9 (Sāy. derives the word in the last sense from √2. *naś* or √1. *aś*: *a-nāśú* or *an-āśú*).

अनाश्चर्य an-āścarya, mfn. not wonderful.

अनाश्रमिन् an-āśramin, ī, m. one who does not belong to or follow any of the four Āśramas or religious orders to which Brāhmans at different periods of life are bound to attach themselves.

An-āśrama-vāsa or **an-āśrame-vāsa**, *as*, m. one who does not belong to the Āśramas; non-residence in a religious retreat.

अनाश्रय an-āśraya, as, m. non-support, absence of any person or thing to depend upon; defencelessness, self-dependence, isolation; (mfn.), defenceless; unprotected; isolated.

An-āśrita, mfn. not supported, detached; disengaged, independent; non-inherent.

अनाष्ट्र a-nāshṭrá, mfn. free from dangers or dangerous opponents, ŚBr.; (cf. *ati-nāshṭrá*.)

अनास् an-ás, mfn. having no mouth or face (N. of demons), RV. v, 29, 10.

अनास a-nāsa, mfn. noseless.

A-nāsiká, mfn. noseless, TS.

अनासादित an-āsādita, mfn. not met with, not found or obtained, not encountered or attacked; not occurred; not having happened; non-existent. **-vigraha**, mfn. unused to war.

An-āsādya, mfn. not attainable.

अनास्था an-āsthā, f. unfixedness, want of confidence; disrespect; want of consideration; want of faith or devotedness; unconcern, indifference.

An-āsthāná, mfn. having or yielding no basis or fulcrum (as the sea), RV. i, 116, 5.

अनास्माक an-āsmāká, mfn. not belonging to us, AV. xix, 57, 5.

अनास्राव an-āsrāvá, mfn. not causing pain, AV. ii, 3, 2.

अनास्वाद an-āsvāda, as, m. want of taste, insipidity; (mfn.), without taste, insipid.

An-āsvādita, mfn. untasted.

अनाहत an-āhata, mfn. unbeaten, unwounded, intact; new and unbleached (as cloth); produced otherwise than by beating; not multiplied; (*am*), n. the fourth of the mystical *cakras* or circles of the body. **-nāda**, m. a sound produced otherwise than by beating; the sound *om*.

अनाहवनीय án-āhavanīya, as, m. no Āhavanīya fire, ŚBr.

अनाहार an-āhāra, as, m. not taking food, abstinence; non-seizure; non-production; (mfn.), one who abstains from food.

An-āhārin, mfn. not taking (food); fasting.

An-āhārya, mfn. not to be seized or taken, not producible, Mn. viii, 202; not to be bribed, Vishṇus.; not to be eaten.

अनाहिताग्नि án-āhitâgni, is, m. one who has not performed the Agnyādhāna.

अनाहुति án-āhuti, is, f. non-sacrificing, RV. x, 37, 4 & 63, 12; a sacrifice unworthy of its name, ŚBr.

अनाहूत an-āhūta, mfn. uncalled, uninvited. **Anāhūtôpajalpin**, m. an uncalled-for boaster. **Anāhūtôpavishṭa**, mfn. seated as an uninvited guest.

अनाह्लाद an-āhlāda, as, m. absence of joy; (mfn.), gloomy, not cheerful.

An-āhlādita, mfn. not exhilarated.

अनिःशस्त a-niḥśasta, mfn. blameless [Gmn.; 'not repelled or refused,' NBD.], RV. iv, 34, 11.

अनिकामतस् a-nikāmatas [BhP.] or *a-nikāmam* [ŚBr.], ind. involuntarily, unintentionally.

अनिकेत a-niketa or *a-niketana*, mfn. houseless.

अनिक्षिप्तधूर a-nikshipta-dhūra, as, m., N. of a Bodhisattva or deified Buddhist saint.

अनिक्षु an-ikshu us, m. (see 3. *a*), 'not (true) sugar-cane,' a sort of long grass or reed, Saccharum Spontaneum.

अनिगीर्ण a-nigīrṇa, mfn. not swallowed, not suppressed (as an ellipsis), Sāh.

अनिग्रह a-nigraha, mfn. unrestrained; (*as*), m. non-restraint; non-refutation; not owning one's self refuted. **-sthāna**, n. (in phil.) occasion of non-refutation.

अनिघातेषु a-nighātêshu, us, m. 'having arrows that strike no one,' N. of a man.

अनिङ्ग an-iṅga [APrāt.] or *an-iṅgya* [RPrāt.], mfn. not divisible (said of words).

An-iṅgayat, mfn. not dividing, RPrāt.

अनिच्छ an-iccha or *an-icchaka* or *an-icchat*, mfn. undesirous, averse, unwilling; not intending.

An-icchā, f. absence of wish or design, indifference.

An-icchu, mfn. = *an-iccha*, Vishṇus.

अनिजक a-nijaka, mfn. not one's own, belonging to another.

अनित an-ita, mfn. not gone to, not having obtained, Ragh. ix, 37; destitute of; (*am*), n. not deviating from (abl.), KaushBr. **-bhā** (*án-ita-*), f., N. of a river, RV. v, 53, 9.

अनित्य a-nitya, mfn. not everlasting, transient; occasional, incidental; irregular, unusual; unstable; uncertain; (*am*), ind. occasionally. **-karman**, n. or **-kriyā**, f. an occasional act of worship, sacrifice for a special purpose. **-tā**, f. or **-tva**, n. transient or limited existence. **-datta** or **-dattaka** or **-datrima**, m. a son surrendered by his parents to another for temporary or preliminary adoption. **-pratyavêkshā**, f. consciousness that all is passing away, Buddh. **-bhāva**, m. transitoriness. **-sama**, m. sophism, consisting in generalizing what is exceptional (as perishableness). **-sama-prakaraṇa**, n. a section in the Nyāya discussing that sophism. **-samāsa**, m. a compound, the sense of which may be equally expressed by resolving it into its constituent parts.

अनिदान a-nidāna, mfn. causeless, groundless.

अनिद्र a-nidra, mf(*ā*)n. sleepless, awake; (*ā*), f. sleeplessness.

A-nidrita, mfn. not asleep, awake.

अनिधृष्ट a-nidhṛishṭa, mfn. unchecked, unsubdued, L.

अनिध्म an-idhmá, mfn. having or requiring no fuel, RV. ii, 35, 4 & x, 30, 4.

अनिन an-iná, mfn. strengthless, feeble, RV. i, 150, 2.

अनिन्दा á-nindā, f. no reproach, AV. xi, 8, 22.

A-nindanīya, mfn. unblamable, faultless.

A-nindita, mfn. irreproachable, virtuous.

A-nindyá (3, 4), mfn. id., RV.; ŚBr. &c.

अनिन्द्र an-indrá, mf(*á*)n. dispensing with or disregarding Indra, RV.

अनिन्द्रिय an-indriya, am, n. that which is not the senses, the soul, the reason, L.

अनिपद्यमान á-nipadyamāna [*a-nipádyamāna*, AV.], mfn. not falling down (to sleep), untiring, RV. i, 164, 31 & x, 177, 3.

अनिपात a-nipāta, as, m. (not a fall), continuance of life.

अनिपुण a-nipuṇa, mf(*ā*)n. unskilled, not clever or conversant.

अनिबद्ध á-nibaddha, mfn. not tied down, not bound, RV. iv, 13, 5; unattached, incoherent, unconnected. **-pralāpin**, mfn. chattering incoherently, talking at random, Yājñ.

अनिबाध a-nibādha, mfn. unobstructed, unlimited; (*ás*), m. liberty, RV.

अनिभृत a-nibhṛita, mfn. not private, not reserved, immodest, bold, public.

अनिभृष्ट á-nibhṛishṭa, mfn. unabated, undefeated, RV. x, 116, 6. **-tavishi** (*ánibhṛishṭa-*), mfn. having unabated power, RV.

अनिभ्य an-ibhya, mfn. not wealthy.

अनिमन् animan = *aṇiman*, q.v., L.

अनिमन्त्रित a-nimantrita, mfn. uninvited. **-bhojin**, mfn. eating without being invited.

अनिमान a-nimāná, mfn. unbounded, RV.

अनिमित्त a-nimitta, mf(*ā*)n. having no adequate occasion, causeless, groundless; (*am*), n. absence of an adequate cause or occasion, groundlessness. **-tas**, ind. groundlessly, Mn. iv, 144. **-nirākṛita**, mfn. groundlessly rejected, Śak. **-liṅga-nāśa**, m. 'unaccountable loss of distinct vision,' N. of an ophthalmic disease ending in total blindness (perhaps amaurosis).

अनिमिष् a-nimish, m. 'without winking,' N. of a god, BhP.; (*ánimisham* or *ánimishā*), acc. or instr. ind. without winking, i. e. vigilantly or incessantly, RV.

A-nimishá, mfn. not winking, looking steadily, vigilant, RV. &c.; open (as eyes or flowers); (*as*), m. not winking; a god, BhP.; a fish, L.; (*ám*), ind. vigilantly, RV. i, 24, 6. **Animishâksha**, mf(*ī*)n. one whose eyes are fixed. **Animishâcārya**, m., N. of Bṛihaspati.

Á-nimishat, mfn. not winking, vigilant, RV.

A-nimesha, mfn. = *animishá*; (*ánimesham*), ind. vigilantly, RV. i, 31, 12 & 164, 21.

अनियत a-niyata, mfn. not regulated, uncontrolled, not fixed, uncertain, unrestricted, irregular, casual; not unaccentuated, RPrāt. **-puṃskā**, f. 'having no fixed husband,' a woman unchaste in conduct. **-vṛitti**, mfn. having no fixed or regular employment or income. **Aniyatâṅka**, m. (in arithm.) an indeterminate digit. **A-niyatâtman**, m. one whose self or spirit is not regulated or under proper control.

A-niyama, *as*, m. absence of control or rule or fixed order or obligation, unsettledness; indecorous or improper conduct; uncertainty, doubt; (mfn.), having no rule, irregular.

A-niyamita, mfn. having no rule; irregular.

अनियुक्त a-niyukta, mfn. not appointed, not authoritative; (*as*), m. an assessor at a court who has not been formally appointed and is not entitled to vote.

A-niyoga, *as*, m. non-application, Lāṭy.; an unfitting employment or commission.

A-niyogin, mfn. not attached or clinging to.

अनिर an-irá, mfn. destitute of vigour, RV. iv, 5, 14; (*án-irā*), f. want of vigour, languor, RV.; VS.

अनिराकरिष्णु a-nirākarishṇu, mfn. not obstructive, not censorious, Pāṇ. vi, 2, 160, Sch.

A-nirākṛita, mfn. unobstructed.

अनिराहित á-nirāhita, mfn. not to be kept off from (abl.), AV. xii, 2, 35.

अनिरुक्त á-nirukta, mfn. unuttered, not articulated; not explained (because of being clear by itself); unspeakable, TUp. **-gāna**, n. indistinct singing; humming (of hymns), a particular mode of chanting the Sāma-veda.

अनिरुद्ध *a-niruddha*, mfn. unobstructed, ungovernable, self-willed; *(as)*, m. a spy, a secret emissary (?); the son of Pradyumna (a form of Kāma, and husband of Ushā); Śiva; N. of an Arhat (contemporary of Śākyamuni); of a descendant of Vṛishṇi; *(am)*, n. the rope for fastening cattle, L. **-patha**, n. 'an unobstructed path,' the atmosphere, ether, L. **-bhāvinī**, f. Aniruddha's wife.

अनिरुप्त *a-nirupta*, mfn. (√2. *vap*), not distributed, not shared.

अनिरूपित *a-nirūpita*, mfn. not determined, undefined.

अनिर्घात *á-nirghāta*, *as*, m. not wresting or tearing from, TS.; TBr.

अनिर्जित *a-nirjita*, mfn. unconquered.

अनिर्णय *a-nirṇaya*, *as*, m. uncertainty, want of decision.

A-nirṇīta, mfn. unascertained, undetermined.
A-nirṇeya, mfn. not to be decided.

अनिर्दश *a-nirdaśa* or *a-nir-daśāha*, mf(*ā*)n. within the ten days of impurity after childbirth or a death, Mn. &c.; *(am)*, ind. id. (used adverbially).

अनिर्दिष्ट *a-nirdishṭa*, mfn. (√*diś*), unexplained, undefined.

A-nirdiśya, mfn. undefinable, inexplicable.
A-nirdeśa, *as*, m. absence of rule or direction.
A-nirdeśya, mfn. undefinable, inexplicable, incomparable.

अनिर्धारित *a-nirdhārita*, mfn. undetermined, unascertained, undefined.

A-nirdhārya, mfn. undeterminable, not to be agreed upon.

अनिर्भर *a-nirbhara*, mfn. not excessive, little, slight, light.

अनिर्भेद *a-nirbheda*, *as*, m. not blurting out,' not revealing.

अनिर्मल *a-nirmala*, mfn. dirty, foul, turbid.

A-nirmālyā, f. the plant Mendicago Esculenta.

अनिर्लोचित *a-nirlocita*, mfn. not carefully looked at, not considered.

अनिर्लोडित *a-nirloḍita*, mfn. not examined thoroughly, Śiś. ii, 27.

अनिर्वचनीय *a-nirvacanīya*, mfn. unutterable, indescribable; not to be mentioned.

Anirvācya, mfn. id.

अनिर्वर्त्यमान *a-nirvartyamāna*, mfn. not being brought to a close.

अनिर्वाण *a-nirvāṇa*, mfn. unextinguished.

अनिर्वाह *a-nirvāha*, *as*, m. non-accomplishment, non-completion; inconclusiveness; insufficiency of income.

A-nirvāhya, mfn. difficult to be managed.

अनिर्विण्ण *a-nirviṇṇa*, mfn. not downcast.

A-nirvid, mfn. free from causes of depression, undesponding, unwearied.

A-nirveda, *as*, m. non-depression, self-reliance.

अनिर्वृत *a-nirvṛita*, mfn. discontented; unhappy; discomposed.

A-nirvṛiti, *is*, f. discontent.

अनिर्वृत्त *a-nirvṛitta*, mfn. unaccomplished, unfulfilled.

A-nirvṛitti, *is*, f. incompleteness.

अनिर्वेश *a-nirveśa* (= *akṛita-nirveśa*), mfn. not having expiated one's sins, BhP.

अनिल *ánila*, *as*, m. (√*an*, cf. Irish *anal*), air or wind; the god of wind; one of the forty-nine Anilas or winds; one of the eight demi-gods, called Vasus; wind as one of the humors or *rasas* of the body; rheumatism, paralysis, or any affection referred to disorder of the wind; N. of a Ṛishi and other persons; the letter *y*; the number forty-nine. **-kumāra**, *ās*, m pl. 'wind-princes,' a class of deities, Jain. **-ghna**, mfn. curing disorders arising from wind. **-ghnaka**, m. the large tree Terminalia Belerica. **-paryaya** or **-paryāya**, m. pain and swelling of the eyelids and outer parts of the eye. **-prakṛiti**, mfn. 'having an airy or windy nature,' N. of the planet Saturn. **-vyādhi**, m. derangement of the (internal) wind. **-sakha** or **-sārathi** [MBh.], m. 'the friend of wind,' N. of fire. **-han** or **-hṛit**, mfn. = *-ghna*. **Anilâtmaja**, m. the son of the wind, Hanumat or Bhīma. **Anilântaka**, m. 'wind-destroying,' the plant Iṅgudī or Aṅgāra-pushpa. **Anilâpaha**, mfn. = *anila-ghna*. **Anilâmaya**, m. morbid affection of the wind, flatulence, rheumatism. **Anilâyana**, n. way or course of the wind, Suśr. **Anilâśin**, mfn. 'feeding on the wind,' fasting; *(ī)*, m. a snake, L., cf. *vāyu-bhaksha*.

अनिलम्भसमाधि *a-nilambha-samādhi*, *is*, m. 'unsupported meditation,' N. of a peculiar kind of meditation, Buddh.

अनिलय *a-nilaya*, mf(*ā*)n. having no resting-place, restless, AitBr.; ĀśvŚr.

A-nilayana, *am*, n. no home or refuge, TUp.

अनिवर्तन *a-nivartana*, mfn. not turning back or away, steadfast; improper to be abandoned, right.

A-nivartin, mfn. not turning back, brave, not returning. **Anivarti-tva**, n. not turning back, brave resistance.

A-nivṛitta, mfn. not turning back, brave.

अनिवारित *a-nivārita*, mfn. unhindered, unimpeded, unopposed, unforbidden, unchecked.

A-nivārya, mfn. not to be warded off, inevertible, unavoidable, irresistible.

अनिविशमान *á-niviśamāna*, mf(*ā*)n. not retiring to rest, restless, RV. vii, 49, 1.

अनिवृत *á-nivṛita*, mfn. (√1. *vṛi*), unchecked, not impeded, RV. iii, 29, 6.

अनिवेदित *a-nivedita*, mfn. untold, unmentioned. **-vijñāta**, mfn. known without being told.

A-nivedya, ind. p. not having announced.

अनिवेशन *a-niveśaná*, mf(*ā́*)n. affording no place of rest, RV. i, 32, 10.

अनिश *a-niśa*, mfn. 'nightless,' sleepless; uninterrupted, incessant (only in comp.); *(am)*, ind. incessantly, continually.

Á-niśita, mfn. incessant, VS.; ŚBr.; *(am)*, ind. incessantly, RV. ii, 38, 8 & ix, 96, 2. **-sarga** (*áni-śita-*), mfn. having an incessant flow, RV. x, 89, 4.

अनिश्चित *a-niścita*, mfn. unascertained, not certain.

A-niścitya, ind. p. not having ascertained.

अनिश्चिन्त्य *a-niścintya*, mfn. not to be thought of, inconceivable, incomprehensible.

अनिषङ्ग *a-nishaṅgá*, mfn. having no quiver, unarmed, RV. i, 31, 13.

अनिषव्य *an-ishavyá*, mf(*ā́*)n. not to be wounded or killed with arrows, RV. x, 108, 6.

अनिषिद्ध *a-nishiddha*, mfn. unprohibited, unforbidden.

A-nisheddhṛá, mf(*ā́*)n. unimpeded, ŚBr.

अनिषु *an-ishu*, mfn. having no arrows, having bad arrows. **-dhanvá**, mfn. without arrows and a bow, TĀr.

अनिष्कासित *a-nishkāsita* or *a-nishkāsin*, mfn. without remains of food, ĀpŚr.

अनिष्कृत *á-nishkṛita* or *án-ishkṛita*, mfn. not done with, unfinished, not settled, RV. **Anish-kṛitâinas**, mfn. having one's guilt not settled, i. e. unexpiated, L.

अनिष्ट 1. *an-ishṭa*, mfn. (√3. *ish*), unwished, undesirable, disadvantageous, unfavourable; bad, wrong, evil, ominous; *(ā)*, f. the plant Sida Alba; *(am)*, n. evil, disadvantage. **-graha**, m. an evil planet. **-dushṭa-dhī**, mfn. having an evil and corrupt mind. **-prasaṅga**, m. connection with a wrong object or a wrong argument or a wrong rule. **-phala**, n. evil result. **-śaṅkā**, f. foreboding or fear of evil or misfortune. **-sūcaka**, mfn. foreboding evil, ominous. **-hetu**, m. an evil omen. **An-ishṭâpādana**, n. not obtaining what is desired or (fr. *anishṭa* and *āpādana*) obtaining what is not desired. **An-ishṭâpti**, f. id. **An-ishṭâśaṅsin**, mfn. indicating or boding evil. **Anishṭôtprekshaṇa**, n. expectation of evil.

अनिष्ट 2. *án-ishṭa*, mfn. (√*yaj*), not offered in sacrifice; not honoured with a sacrifice.

An-ishṭin, *ī*, m. one who does not sacrifice or has not sacrificed, KātyŚr.

अनिष्टृत *á-nishṭṛita*, mfn. unhurt, unchecked, RV. viii, 33, 9; VS.

अनिष्ठा *a-nishṭhā*, f. unsteadfastness, unsteadiness.

अनिष्ठुर *a-nishṭhura*, mfn. not harsh.

अनिष्ण *a-nishṇa* or *a-nishṇāta*, mfn. unskilled.

अनिष्पत्ति *a-nishpatti*, *is*, f. non-accomplishment, incompletion.

A-nishpanna, mfn. imperfect, incomplete.

अनिष्पत्त्रम् *a-nish-pattram*, ind. so that the arrow does not come out (on the other side), i. e. not with excessive force, KātyŚr.

अनिसर्ग *a-nisarga*, mfn. unnatural, unnaturally affected.

अनिस्तब्ध *a-nistabdha*, mfn. not rendered immovable or stiff; not paralysed; not fixed.

अनिस्तीर्ण *a-nistīrṇa*, mfn. not crossed over; not set aside; not rid of; unanswered, unrefuted. **Anistīrṇâbhiyoga**, m. (a defendant) who has not yet (by refutation) got rid of a charge.

अनीक *ánīka*, *as*, *am*, m. n. (√*an*), face; appearance, splendour; edge, point; front, row, array, march; army, forces; war, combat. **-vat** (*ánīka-*), mfn. having a face, or constituting the face, or occupying the front or foremost rank (N. of Agni), VS. &c. **-vidāraṇa**, m. 'shatterer of armies,' N. of a man. **-śás**, ind. in rows or marching columns, AV. **-stha**, m. a warrior or combatant; an armed or royal guard, a sentinel, L.; the trainer of an elephant, an elephant-driver, L.; a mark, a sign, signal, L.; a military drum, L.

Anīkinī, f. an army, a host, forces; a certain force; three Camūs or one-tenth of an Akshauhiṇī (or of a complete army; 2187 elephants and as many cars, 6561 horses, and 10935 foot); a lotus.

अनीक्षण *an-īkshaṇa*, *am*, n. not seeing or looking at.

अनीच *a-nīca*, mf(*ā*)n. not low, decent, respectable; not pronounced with the Anudātta accent. **-darśin**, m., N. of a Buddha. **A-nīcânuvartin**, mfn. not keeping low company; *(ī)*, m. a faithful lover or husband.

A-nīcais, ind. not in a low voice, loudly.

अनीड *á-nīḍa*, mfn. having no nest, RV. x, 55, 6; having no settled abode, i. e. incorporeal, Up.; *(as)*, m., N. of Agni or fire, L.

अनीति 1. *a-nīti*, *is*, f. impropriety, immorality, injustice; impolicy, foolish conduct, indiscretion. **-jña** or **-vid**, mfn. clever in immoral conduct or (fr. *a* and *nītijña*) ignorant of morality or policy, not politic or discreet.

अनीति 2. *an-īti*, *is*, f. freedom from a calamitous season.

अनीदृश *an-īdṛiśa*, mfn. unlike, dissimilar.

अनीप्सित *an-īpsita*, mfn. undesired.

अनीरशन *a-nīraśana* (*a-nir-raśana*), mfn. not destitute of a waistband, having zones or girdles.

अनीलवाजिन् *anīla-vājin*, mfn. 'white-horsed,' Arjuna, Kir. xiv, 26.

अनीश *an-īśa*, mfn. one who has not a lord or superior, paramount; powerless, unable; *(as)*, m. Vishṇu; *(ā)*, f. powerlessness, helplessness, Up. **-tva**, n. powerlessness.

Án-īśvara, mf(*ā*)n. without a superior, AV.; unchecked, paramount; without power, unable; not belonging to the Deity; atheistical. **-tā**, f. or **-tva**, n. absence of a supreme ruler. **-vādin**, m.

'one who denies a supreme ruler of the universe,' an atheist.

अनीह *an-īha*, mfn. listless, indifferent; (*as*), m., N. of a king of Ayodhyā; (*ā*), f. indifference, apathy, disinclination.

An-īhita, mfn. disagreeable, displeasing, unwished; (*am*), n. disinclination, apathy.

अनीळ *á-nīla* [RV. x, 55, 6] = *á-nīḍa*, q.v.

अनु 1. *anu*, mfn. = *aṇu*, q. v., L.

अनु 2. *ánu*, *us*, m. a non-Āryan man, RV.; N. of a king (one of Yayāti's sons); of a non-Āryan tribe, MBh. &c.

अनु 3. *ánu*, ind. (as a prefix to verbs and nouns, expresses) after, along, alongside, lengthwise, near to, under, subordinate to, with.

(When prefixed to nouns, especially in adverbial compounds), according to, severally, each by each, orderly, methodically, one after another, repeatedly.

(As a separable preposition, with accusative) after, along, over, near to, through, to, towards, at, according to, in order, agreeably to, in regard to, inferior to, Pāṇ. i, 4, 86.

(As a separable adverb) after, afterwards, thereupon, again, further, then, next.

Ánu-ka, mf(*ā*)n. subordinate, dependent, TS.; ŚBr.; 'being after,' lustful, Pāṇ. v, 2, 74.

Anu-tamám, (superl.) ind. most, ŚBr.

अनुकथ् *anu-√kath*, to relate after (some one or something else); to repeat (what has been heard).

Anu-kathana, *am*, n. orderly narration, discourse, conversation.

Anu-kathita, mfn. related after (something else), Pāṇ. vi, 2, 190, Sch.; repeated.

अनुकनीयस् *anu-kanīyas*, *ān*, *asī*, *as*, the next youngest, Pāṇ. vi, 2, 189.

अनुकपोलम् *anu-kapolam*, ind. along the cheek, Śiś. v, 35.

अनुकम् *anu-√kam*, Caus. (impf. *-akāmayata*) to desire (with Inf.), AitBr.

Anu-kāmá, *as*, m. desire, VS.; (mfn.), according to one's desire, agreeable, RV.; (*ám*), ind. as desired, at pleasure, RV. **–kṛit**, mfn. fulfilling one's desire, RV. ix, 11, 7.

Anukāmin, mfn. desirous, TS.

Anukāmīna, mfn. one who acts as he pleases, Pāṇ. v, 2, 11.

अनुकम्प् *anu-√kamp*, to sympathize with, compassionate: Caus. P. (impf. *-akampayat*) id., Kum.

Anu-kampaka, *as*, m. 'sympathizer,' N. of a king; (mfn.), ifc. sympathizing with, compassionating.

Anu-kampana, *am*, n. sympathy, compassion.

Anu-kampanīya, mfn. pitiable.

Anu-kampā, f. id.

Anu-kampāyin, mfn. condoling.

Anu-kampita, mfn. compassionated. **Anukampitâtman**, mfn. having a compassionate spirit.

Anu-kampin, mfn. sympathizing with.

Anu-kampya, mfn. pitiable, worthy of sympathy; (*as*), m. an ascetic, L.; expeditious (explained by *tarasvin*, perhaps for *tapasvin*), L.

अनुकर्ष *anu-karsha*. See *anu-√kṛish*.

अनुकल्प *anu-kalpa*. See *anu-√klṛip*.

अनुकाङ्क्ष् *anu-√kāṅksh*, to long for, desire.

Anu-kāṅkshā, f. desire after.

Anu-kāṅkshin, mfn. longing for.

अनुकाल *anu-kāla*, mfn. opportune, occasional; (*am*), ind. opportunely, occasionally.

अनुकीर्त् *anu-√kīrt*, to relate after or in order; to narrate.

Anu-kīrtana, *am*, n. the act of narrating or proclaiming or publishing.

अनुकुञ्चित *anu-kuñcita*, mfn. bent, made crooked.

अनुकुष् *anu-√kush*, to drag along, Pāṇ. iii, 1, 25, Sch.

अनुकूज् *anu-√kūj*, to follow in cooing or singing or groaning.

अनुकूल *anu-kūla*, mf(*ā*)n. following the bank (*kūla*) or slope or declivity; according to the current, AV.; favourable, agreeable; conformable to; friendly, kind, well-disposed; (*as*), m. a faithful or kind and obliging husband; (*ā*), f. Croton Polyandrum; N. of a metre; (*am*), n. (in poetry) narrative of calamity leading finally to happiness. **–tā**, f. concord, good-will, favour, conformity, consent; prosperity. **–nāyaka**, m. a kind husband or lover. **–vāyu**, m. a favourable wind.

Anukūlaya, Nom. P. *anukūlayati*, to act in a friendly way towards, favour.

अनुकृ *anu-√kṛi*, to do afterwards, to follow in doing; to imitate, copy; to equal; to requite; to adopt: Caus. *-kārayati*, to cause to imitate.

Anu-kará, mfn. imitating, ŚBr.; (*ás*), m. an assistant, AV. xii, 2, 2.

Anu-karaṇa, *am*, n. the act of imitation or of following an example; resemblance, similarity.

Anu-kartṛi, mfn. an imitator, imitating; (*tā*), m. a mimic, actor, performer.

Anu-karman, *a*, n. imitation; a subsequent rite or ceremony; (*ā*), m., N. of one of the Viśvedevās, MBh.

Anu-kāra, *as*, m. imitation, resemblance.

Anu-kārin, mfn. imitating, acting, mimicking.

Anu-kārya, mfn. to be imitated or copied, to be acted (dramatically); (*am*), n. subsequent business, R.

Anu-kṛita, mfn. imitated, made like.

Anu-kṛiti, *is*, f. imitation, a copy, compliance.

Anu-kṛitya, mfn. fit to be imitated, Pañcat.

Anu-kriyā, f. imitation, doing anything in like manner or subsequently; a subsequent rite.

अनुकृत् *anu-√2. kṛit* (p. *-kṛintat*) to go on destroying, MBh. xiii, 2906.

अनुकृप् *anu-√kṛip*, *-kṛipate*, to mourn for, long for, RV. i, 113, 10; Nom. Ā. *-kṛipāyate*, to compassionate, condole with, MBh.

अनुकृश् *anu-√kṛiś*, Caus. *-karśayati*, to emaciate.

अनुकृष् *anu-√kṛish*, to drag or draw after, attract: Caus. *-karshayati*, to cause to drag after, draw, attract; to subject.

Anu-karsha, *as*, m. attraction, drawing; invoking, summoning by incantation; the bottom or the axle-tree of a carriage; grammatical attraction (including a subsequent in a preceding rule); lagging behind in a ceremony; delayed performance of a duty.

Anu-karshaṇa, *am*, n. = *anu-karsha*.

Anu-karshan, *ā*, m. the bottom of a carriage, L.

Anu-kṛishṭa, mfn. drawn after, attracted; included or implied in a subsequent rule.

अनुकॄ *anu-√1. kṝī* (1. sg. *-kirāmi*) to scatter along, AV.; to strew, fill with, crowd: Pass. *-kīryate*, to become crowded or filled.

Anu-kīrṇa, mfn. crowded, crammed full.

अनुकॢप् *anu-√klṛip*, to follow in order, TS.: Caus. *-kalpayati*, to cause to follow or imitate in order.

Anu-kalpa, *as*, m. permission to adopt an alternative or substitute (e. g. instead of Kuśa grass you may use Dūrbā), Mn. &c.

Anu-kalpita, mfn. followed by (instr.), MBh.

Anu-klṛipti, *is*, f. (in Vaiśeshika phil.) agreement.

अनुक्त *an-ukta*, mfn. (*√vac*), unuttered, unsaid, unheard of, extraordinary. **–nimitta**, n. a reason which is uttered or unheard of or extraordinary; (mfn.), having such a reason.

An-ukti, *is*, f. the not speaking, improper speech.

An-ukthá, mfn. hymnless, not singing hymns, RV. v, 2, 3; not followed by an uktha, AitBr.

अनुक्रकच *anu-krakaca*, mfn. dentated like a saw, serrated.

अनुक्रन्द् *anu-√krand* (perf. Ā. *-cakrade*) to shout or cry after one, RV. viii, 3, 10.

अनुक्रम् *anu-√kram*, to go on, go after, follow; to go through in order, enumerate, supply with an abstract or index.

Anu-krama, *as*, m. succession, arrangement, order, method; an index showing the successive contents of a book; (*am*) or (*eṇa*) or (*āt*), ind. in due order.

Anu-kramaṇa, *am*, n. proceeding methodically or in order; following.

Anu-kramaṇikā or **anu-kramaṇī**, f. a table or chapter of contents, index to a collection of Vedic hymns (giving the first word of each hymn, the number of verses, name and family of poets, names of deities and metres).

Anu-krānta, mfn. gone over, read, or done in due order; enumerated, mentioned in the Anukramaṇī.

अनुक्री *anu-krī*, mfn. (*√krī*), bought subsequently (i. e. not early on the first day), PBr.; Lāṭy. &c.; (cf. *pari-krī*, *śata-krī*.)

अनुक्रीड् *anu-√krīḍ*, to play, Pāṇ. i, 3, 21.

अनुक्रुश् *anu-√kruś*, to shout at, RV. iv, 38, 5: Caus. (ind. p. *-krośya*) to join in lamenting, show sympathy for, MBh. xiii, 285.

Anu-krośa, *as*, m. tenderness, compassion.

अनुक्षणम् *anu-kshaṇam*, ind. momentarily, perpetually, every instant.

अनुक्षत्तृ *anu-kshattṛi*, *tā*, m. a door-keeper's or charioteer's mate or attendant, VS.

अनुक्षपम् *anu-kshapam*, ind. night after night, Kir.

अनुक्षर् *anu-√kshar* (3. pl. *-ksharanti*; Imper. 2. sg. *-kshara*) to flow into or upon, RV.

अनुक्षि 1. *anu-√2. kshi*, *-kshiyati* (Imper. 2. sg. *-kshiya*) to settle along, AV.

अनुक्षि 2. *anu-√4. kshi*, Pass. (p. *-kshīyamāṇa*) to decay or vanish gradually, BhP.

अनुक्षेत्र *anu-kshetra*, *am*, n. stipend given to temple-servants in Orissa (in commutation probably of the proceeds of an endowment).

अनुखञ्ज *anu-khañja*, *as*, m., N. of a country.

अनुख्या *anu-√khyā* (perf. 2. du. *-cakhyathuḥ*) to descry, RV. vii, 70, 4, &c.

Ánu-khyāti, *is*, f. act of descrying or revealing, TS.; AitBr.

Anu-khyātṛi, *tā*, m. a discoverer, revealer, AitBr.

अनुगङ्गम् *anu-gaṅgam*, ind. along the Ganges, Pat.

अनुगण् *anu-√gaṇ*, to count over.

Anu-gaṇita, mfn. counted over.

Anu-gaṇitin, mfn. one who has counted over, (gaṇa *ishṭâdi*, q. v.)

अनुगम् *anu-√gam*, cl. 1. P. *-gacchati*, *-gantum*, to go after, follow, seek, approach, visit, arrive; to practise, observe, obey, imitate; to enter into; to die out, be extinguished: Caus. *-gamayati*, to imitate, cause to die out.

Anu-gá, mf(*ā*)n. going after, following, corresponding with, adapted to; a companion; a follower, a servant; (ifc.) followed by; (*ā*), f., N. of an Apsaras.

Anu-gata, mfn. followed by; having anything (as a skin) hanging behind; following; a follower; acquired; extinguished; tallying with; (*am*), n. moderate time (in music). **Anugatârtha**, mfn. having a corresponding meaning.

Anu-gati, *is*, f. following, imitation, dying out.

Anu-gatika, *as*, m. a follower, an imitator.

Anu-gantavya, mfn. to be followed (as a husband by a wife in death); worthy of being imitated; to be looked for or discovered, Pāṇ. vi, 1, 7, Sch.

Anu-gama, *as*, m. or **anu-gamana**, *am*, n. following, going after in life or death; postcremation of a widow; imitating, approaching.

Anu-gamya, mfn. to be followed or imitated.

Anu-gāmin, mfn. following, a companion.

Anu-gāmuka, mfn. habitually or constantly following or attending.

अनुगर्ज् *anu-√garj*, to shout or roar after.

Anu-garjita, *am*, n. roaring after, echo, Kum.

अनुगवम् *anu-gavam*, ind. so as to suit (or follow) the cows, Pāṇ. v, 4, 83.

अनुगवीन *anu-gavīna*, *as*, m. a cowherd, Pāṇ. v, 2, 15.

अनुगा *anu-√1. gā*, to go after, follow; to act in conformity to, or according to the wishes of, RV.

अनुगादिन् *anu-gādin*, mfn. repeating another's words, Pāṇ. v, 4, 13.

अनुगायस् *ánu-gāyas*, mfn. (√*gai*), followed by shouts or hymns, RV. viii, 5, 34; ('to be praised in hymns,' Sāy.)

अनुगाह् *anu-√gāh*, to plunge after, be immersed in.

Anu-gāḍha, mfn. plunged or immersed in.

अनुगिरम् *anu-giram*, ind. on the mountain, Ragh.

अनुगु *anu-gu*, ind. behind the cows, Pāṇ. v, 2, 15.

अनुगुण *anu-guṇa*, mf(*ā*)n. having similar qualities, congenial to; according or suitable to; (*am*), ind. according to one's merits, Kathās.; (*as*), m. natural peculiarity.

Anu-guṇaya, Nom. P. *-guṇayati*, to favour, Kir.

अनुगुप्त *anu-gupta*, mfn. protected, sheltered, concealed.

अनुगृध् *anu-√gṛidh* (pr. p. *-gṛidhyat*) to be greedy after (loc.), MBh. xii, 372.

अनुगॄ *anu-√1. gṝi*, *-gṛiṇāti*, to join in praising, RV. i, 147, 2; to rejoin, answer, ŚāṅkhŚr.; to repeat, BhP.

अनुगै *anu-√gai*, to sing after or to (a person or tune); to celebrate in song: Caus. *-gāpayati*, to make one sing after or to.

Anu-gītā, f. 'an after-song,' N. of part of the fourteenth book of the Mahābhārata (chaps. 16-92).

Anu-gīti, *is*, f., N. of a metre (of two verses, the first containing twenty-seven, the second thirty-two mātrās).

अनुगोदम् *anu-godam*, ind. near the Godāvarī.

अनुग्र *án-ugra*, or *an-ugrá*, mf(*ā*)n. not harsh or violent, mild, gentle, RV. &c.

अनुग्रह् *anu-√grah*, to follow in taking or plundering, MBh. iv, 996; to support; to uphold; to receive, welcome; to treat with kindness, favour, oblige; to foster.

Anu-gṛihīta, mfn. favoured, obliged.

Anu-graha, *as*, m. favour, kindness, showing favour, conferring benefits, promoting or furthering a good object; assistance; facilitating by incantations; rear-guard; N. of the eighth or fifth creation, VP. **–kātara**, mfn. anxious to please or for favour. **–sarga**, m. (in Sāṅkhya phil.) creation of the feelings or mental conditions.

Anu-grahaṇa, *am*, n. = *anu-graha*.

Anu-grahita, mfn. occupied, engaged, R. i, 7, 15.

Anu-grahin, *ī*, m. proficient in magic skill.

Anu-grāhaka, mf(*ikā*)n. favouring, furthering, facilitating; favourable, kind, gracious.

Anu-grāhin, mfn. gracious, favourable.

Anu-grāhya, mfn. to be favoured or furthered.

Anu-jighṛikshā, f. desire to show favour or kindness; intention to include, Nyāyam.

अनुग्रामम् *anu-grāmam*, ind. village after village, Pāṇ. iv, 3, 61; into a village, Lāṭy.

अनुग्रासक *anu-grāsaka*, *as*, m. a mouthful (of boiled rice, &c.); the equivalent of a mouthful.

अनुघट्ट् *anu-√ghaṭṭ*, to stroke, rub lengthwise.

अनुघुष् *anu-√ghush* (Ved. ind. p. *-ghúshyā*) to name aloud, RV. i, 162, 18.

अनुघ्रा *anu-√ghrā*, 'to smell at,' kiss, Kathās.

Anu-jighrá, mfn. snuffling at, AV. viii, 8, 8.

अनुचक्ष् *anu-√caksh* (perf. *-cacáksha*; impf. Ā. *-acashṭa*) to look at or up to, RV.

अनुचर् *anu-√car*, to walk or move after or along; to follow, pursue, seek after; to follow out, adhere to, attend; to behave: Caus. *-cārayati*, to let or cause to traverse: Intens. p. *-carcūryámāṇa*, continuing following, RV. x, 124, 9.

Anu-cará, mf(*ī*)n. following, attending; (*ás*), m. companion, follower, servant; (*ī*, rarely *ā*), f. a female attendant.

Anu-cāraka, *as*, m. a follower, attendant, (gaṇa *mahishy-ādi*, q. v.); (*ikā*), f. a female follower or attendant.

Anu-cārin, mfn. following, attending.

अनुचर्चि *anu-carci*, mfn. reciting or repeating (in a chorus), ĀśvŚr.

अनुचि *anu-√2. ci* (Imper. Ā. *-cikitām*) to remember, AV. vi, 53, 1.

अनुचित 1. *anu-cita*, mfn. (√1. *ci*), set or placed along or lengthwise or in rows, AitBr.

अनुचित 2. *an-ucita*, mfn. improper, wrong, unusual, strange. **Anucitârtha**, m. an unusual meaning.

अनुचिन्त् *anu-√cint*, to meditate, consider, recal to mind: Caus. to make to consider.

Anu-cintana, *am*, n. or **anu-cintā**, f. thinking of, meditating upon, recalling, recollecting; anxiety.

Anu-cintita, mfn. recollected, recalled, thought of.

अनुच्च *an-ucca*, mfn. not high, low, humble; (= *an-udātta*), accentless, APrāt.

An-uccais, ind. not aloud, in a low voice.

अनुच्चार *an-uccāra*, *as*, m. or *an-uccāraṇa*, *am*, n. non-pronunciation, skipping words (in reciting hymns). See *uc-√car*.

अनुच्छाद *anu-cchādá*, *as*, m. (√*chad*), a garment which hangs down (probably that part of the lower garment which hangs down in front from the waist to the feet), ŚBr.

अनुच्छित्ति *an-uc-chitti*, *is*, f. (√*chid*), not cutting off, non-extirpation, non-destruction, indestructibility. **–dharman** (*ánucchitti-*), mfn. possessing the virtue (or faculty) of being indestructible, ŚBr. xiv.

1. **An-uc-chindat**, mfn. not destroying.

An-uc-chinna, mfn. not cut off, unextirpated.

An-uc-cheda, *as*, m. = *an-uc-chitti*.

An-uc-chedya, mfn. indestructible, not severable.

अनुच्छिद् *anu-cchid* (√*chid*), to cut along or lengthwise.

2. **Anu-cchindat**, mfn. cutting lengthwise.

अनुच्छिष्ट *an-ucchishṭa*, mfn. (√*śish* with *ud*), without remains or leavings of food, pure; not mere remains, Ragh.

अनुच्छो *anu-ccho* (√*cho*), cl. 4. P. (Imper. 2. sg. *-chya*) to cut open or cut up, AV. ix, 5, 4.

अनुजन् *anu-√jan*, cl. 4. Ā. *-jāyate*, to follow in being born or produced or arising; to take after (one's parents), Ragh.

Anu-ja, mfn. born after, later, younger; (*as*), m. a younger brother, a cadet; the plant Trāyamāṇa; (*am*), n. the plant Prapauṇḍarīka; (*ā*), f. a younger sister, TS.

Anu-janman, *ā*, m. a younger brother, younger.

Anu-jāta, mfn. after-born, later, younger; taking after (one's parents), Pañcat.; born again, regenerated by the sacred cord; (*as*), m. a younger brother; (*ā*), f. a younger sister.

अनुजनम् *anu-janam*, ind. according to people, popularly.

अनुजप् *anu-√jap*, to follow or imitate in muttering.

अनुजल्प् *anu-√jalp*, to follow in talking; Ā. *-jalpate*, to entertain by conversation.

अनुजागृ *anu-√jāgṛi*, to watch as an attendant.

अनुजि *anu-√ji*, to subdue: Desid. *-jigīshate*, to be desirous of subduing.

अनुजिघृक्षा *anu-jighṛikshā*. See *anu-√grah*.

अनुजिघ्र *anu-jighrá*. See *anu-√ghrā*.

अनुजीर्ण *anu-jīrṇa*, mfn. grown old or decayed after or in consequence of, Pāṇ. iii, 4, 72, Sch.

अनुजीव् *anu-√jīv*, to follow or imitate in living; to live for any one; to live by or upon something; to live submissively under, be dependent on: Caus. *-jīvayati*, to restore to life, Daś.

Anu-jīvin, mfn. living by or upon; dependent; (*ī*), m. a dependent, follower; N. of a crow, Pañcat.

Anujīvisāt-kṛita, mfn. made wholly subservient, Kir.

Anu-jīvya, mfn. to be followed in living.

अनुजुष् *anu-√1. jush*, to seek, ŚāṅkhGṛ.; to devote one's self to, indulge in, BhP.

अनुज्झत् *an-ujjhat*, mfn. not quitting.

An-ujjhita, mfn. undiminished, unimpaired, not left or lost.

अनुज्ञा 1. *anu-√jñā*, to permit, grant, allow, consent; to excuse, forgive; to authorize; to allow one to depart, dismiss, bid farewell to; to entreat; to behave kindly: Caus. *-jñāpayati*, to request, ask permission, ask for leave to depart, to take leave: Desid. *-jijñāsati* or *-te*, to wish to allow or permit, Pāṇ. i, 3, 58.

Anu-jñapti, *is*, f. authorization, permission.

2. **Anu-jñā**, f. assent, assenting, permission; leave to depart; allowance made for faults; an order or command. **–prārthanā** or **anujñâishaṇā**, f. asking permission, taking leave.

Anu-jñāta, mfn. assented to, permitted, allowed; ordered, directed, instructed; accepted; authorized, honoured; allowed to depart, dismissed.

Anu-jñāna, *am*, n. = 2. *anu-jñā*.

Anu-jñāpaka, *as*, m. one who commands or enjoins.

Anu-jñāpana, *am*, n. = *anu-jñapti*.

अनुज्येष्ठ *anu-jyeshṭha*, mfn. next eldest, Pāṇ. vi, 2, 189, Sch.; (*ám*), ind. after the eldest, according to seniority, MaitrS.; MBh.

अनुतक्ष् *anu-√taksh* (impf. 2. pl. *-átakshata*) to create or procure for the help of (dat.), RV. i, 86, 3; TS.

अनुतटम् *anu-taṭam*, ind. along the shore, Megh.

अनुतन् *anu-√tan*, to extend along, to carry on, continue, develop.

अनुतप् *anu-√tap*, to heat, Suśr.; to vex, annoy, AV. xix, 49, 7: Pass. *-tapyáte* (rarely *-tapyati* [MBh. i, 5055]), to suffer afterwards, repent; to desiderate, miss: Caus. *-tāpayati*, to distress.

Anu-tapta, mfn. heated; filled with regret; (*ā*), f., N. of a river, VP.

Anu-tāpa, *as*, m. repentance, heat.

Anu-tāpana, mfn. occasioning remorse, repentance or sorrow.

Anu-tāpin, mfn. penitent, regretting.

अनुतर *anu-tara*. See *anu-√tṝi* below.

अनुतर्क् *anu-√tark*, to follow in thought, to regard as or take for.

अनुतर्ष *anu-tarsha*, *as*, m. thirst, wish, desire, L.; a drinking vessel (used for drinking spirituous liquors), L.

Anu-tarshaṇa, *am*, n. a vessel from which spirituous liquor is drunk, L.; distributing liquor, L.

Anu-tarshula, mfn. causing desire, MBh.

अनुतिलम् *anu-tilam*, ind. grain after grain (of Sesamum), by grains, very minutely, (gaṇa *parimukhâdi*, q. v.)

अनुतिष्ठमान *anu-tishṭhamāna*. See 1. *anu-shṭhā*.

अनुतुन्न *anu-tunna*, mfn. (√*tud*), depressed or repressed (in sound), muffled, PBr.

अनुतूलय *anu-tūlaya*, Nom. P. *-tūlayati*, to rub lengthwise (with a brush or cotton).

अनुतृद् *anu-√tṛid* (Imper. 2. sg. *-tṛindhi*; impf. 2. du. *-atṛintam*; perf. *-tatarda*) to split open, RV.

अनुतृप् *anu-√tṛip*, to take one's fill (or refreshment) after or later than another.

अनुतॄ *anu-√tṛī* (3. pl. *-taranti*) to follow across or to the end, AV. vi, 122, 2.

Anu-tara, *am,* n. fare, freight, L.

अनुत्क *an-utka,* mfn. free from regret, not regretting, self-complacent, not repenting of.

अनुत्कर्ष *an-utkarsha, as,* m. non-elevation, inferiority.

अनुत्त *á-nutta,* mfn. not cast down, invincible, RV. **-manyu** (*á-nutta-*), m. 'of invincible wrath,' Indra, RV. vii, 31, 12; viii, 6, 35 & 96, 19.

अनुत्तम *an-uttama,* mf(*ā*)n. unsurpassed, incomparably the best or chief, excellent; excessive; not the best; (in Gr.) not used in the *uttama* or first person. **An-uttamâmbhas,** n. (in Sāṅkhya phil.) indifference to and consequent abstinence from sensual enjoyment (as fatiguing). **An-uttamâmbhasika,** n. indifference to and abstinence from sensual enjoyment (as involving injury to external objects).

अनुत्तर *an-uttara,* mfn. chief, principal; best, excellent; without a reply, unable to answer, silent; fixed, firm; low, inferior, base; south, southern; (*am*), n. a reply which is coherent or evasive and therefore held to be no answer; (*ās*), m. pl. a class of gods among the Jainas. **-yoga-tantra,** n. title of the last of the four Bauddhatantras. **Anuttarôpapātika,** *ās,* m. pl. a class of gods, Jain. **Anuttarôpapātika-daśā,** *ās,* f. pl. title of the ninth aṅga of the Jainas treating of those gods.

अनुत्तान *an-uttāna,* mfn. lying with the face towards the ground; not supine; not flat, Suśr.

अनुत्थान *an-utthāna, am,* n. (*√sthā*), the not rising, want of exertion or of energy, Rājat.

An-utthita, mfn. not risen, not grown up (as grain).

अनुत्पत्ति *an-utpatti, is,* f. failure, non-production; (mfn.), not (yet) produced, Buddh. **-sama,** *as, ā,* m. f. (in Nyāya phil.) arguing against a thing by trying to show that nothing exists from which it could spring.

Anutpattika-dharma-kshānti, *is,* f. acquiescence in the state which is still future, preparation for a future state, Buddh.

An-utpanna, mfn. unborn, unproduced; uneffected, unaccomplished.

An-utpāda, *as,* m. non-production, not coming into existence; not taking effect. **-kshānti,** f. acquiescence in not having to undergo another birth.

An-utpādana, *am,* n. not producing, non-production.

An-utpādya, mfn. not to be created, eternal.

अनुत्सन्न *án-utsanna,* mfn. not lost, ŚBr. vii.

अनुत्साह *an-utsāha, as,* m. non-exertion, want of effort; want of energy or determination; listlessness; (mfn.), deficient in determination. **-tā,** f. want of determination, Sāh.

अनुत्सुक *an-utsuka,* mfn. not eager, calm, retiring; moderate. **-tā,** f. moderateness, Vikr.

अनुत्सूत्र *an-utsūtra,* mfn. not anomalous.

अनुत्सेक *an-utseka, as,* m. absence of arrogance or highmindedness.

An-utsekin, mfn. not arrogant or puffed up, Śak.

अनुदक *an-udaká,* mf(*ā́*)n. waterless, RV. vii, 50, 4, &c.; (*am*), ind. without touching water, KātyŚr.; without adding water, ib.

अनुदग्र *an-udagra,* mfn. not lofty, low; not projecting.

अनुदण्डि *anu-daṇḍi, is,* f. back-bone, MBh.

अनुदय *an-udaya, as,* m. non-rising, the not rising (of a luminary).

1. **Án-udita,** mfn. not risen, not appeared.

अनुदर *an-udara,* mf(*ā*)n. (see 3. *a*) thin, lank, Pat.

अनुदह् *anu-√dah,* to burn up, RV. &c.; to take fire (aor. Subj. 2. sg. *-dakshi*[!for *dhakshi*]), RV. ii, 1, 10; to be consumed by fire subsequently after (acc.), MBh. xii, 8107.

अनुदा *anu-√1. dā* (Pass. *-dāyi*) to permit, restore, RV.; to give way, yield, RV.; AV.; to remit, AV.; to pay one out (?), MBh. vii, 9499.

Anu-da. See *anānudá.*

Anu-datta, mfn. granted, remitted, given back, Pāṇ. vii, 4, 47, Comm.

Anu-déya, *am,* n. a present, RV. vi, 20, 11; (*anu-déyī*), f. a bride's maid (Gmn. & Sāy.), RV. x, 85, 6; 135, 5 & 6; ['gift,' NBD.]

अनुदात्त *an-udātta,* mfn. not raised, not elevated, not pronounced with the Udātta accent, grave; accentless, having the neutral general tone neither high nor low (i. e. both the grave or non-elevated accent explained by Pāṇini as *sannatara,* q. v.—which immediately precedes the Udātta, and also the general accentless, neutral tone, neither high nor low, explained as *eka-śruti*); having the one monotonous ordinary intonation which belongs to the generality of syllables in a sentence; (*as*), m. one of the three accents to be observed in reading the Vedas, the grave accent. **-tara,** m. 'more than Anudātta, still lower in sound than Anudātta,' i. e. the *very* Anudātta accent (or a syllable having this accent which immediately precedes a syllable having the Udātta or Svarita accent, and is therefore more depressed than the ordinary Anudātta, Pāṇ. i, 2, 31, Sch.), Pāṇ. i, 2, 40, Sch. **Anudāttâdi,** n. (in Gr.) a nominal base of which the first syllable is Anudātta. **Anudāttêt,** m. a verbal root having for its Anubandha the Anudātta accent to indicate that it takes the Ātmane-pada terminations only; also *anudāttôpadeśa.* **Anudāttôdaya,** n. a syllable immediately preceding the Anudātta accent.

अनुदार 1. *an-udāra,* mfn. niggardly, mean.

अनुदार 2. *anu-dāra,* mfn. adhered to or followed by a wife.

अनुदिग्ध *anu-digdha,* mfn. (*√dih*), covered (ifc.), Car.

अनुदित 2. *án-udita,* mfn. unsaid, unuttered; unutterable, blamable (cf. *a-vadyá*), RV. x, 95, 1; AV. v, 1, 2 (see 1. *án-udita* s. v. *an-udaya*).

अनुदिनम् *anu-dinam,* ind. every day.

अनुदिवसम् *anu-divasam,* ind. id.

अनुदिश् *anu-√diś,* to point out for, assign.

Anu-diśam, ind. in every quarter.

Anu-deśa, *as,* m. a rule or injunction pointing back to a previous rule; reference to something prior.

Anu-deśin, mfn. pointing back, referring back; being the object of an Anudeśa; residing at the same place, ĀśvGṛ.

अनुदुष् *anu-√dush,* to become demoralized as a result of, MBh. v, 4543.

अनुदृभ् *anu-√dṛibh,* to make into bundles or chains, KaushBr.

अनुदृश् *anu-√dṛiś* (ind. p. *-dṛíśya,* RV. x, 130, 7) to survey, behold; to keep in view or in mind, to foresee: Caus. P. *-darśayati,* to show, tell, teach: Pass. *-dṛiśyate* (also perf. Ā. *-dadṛiśe,* RV. viii, 1, 34), to become or be visible.

Anu-darśana, *am,* n. consideration, regard.

Anu-darśin, mfn. considering, foreseeing.

Anu-dṛishṭi, *is,* f., N. of the ancestress of Ānudṛishṭineya, (gaṇa *śubhrâdi* and *kalyāṇy-ādi.*)

Anu-drashṭavya, mfn. to be observed, visible.

अनुदॄ *anu-√dṝī,* Pass. *-dīryate,* to break through after (another); to be scattered or confused in consequence of the confusion of others.

अनुदेहम् *anu-deham,* ind. behind the body, Śiś. ix, 73.

अनुदैर्घ्य *anu-dairghya,* mfn. longitudinal.

अनुद्गीर्ण *an-udgīrṇa,* mfn. not vomited forth, not disdained; not spurned.

अनुद्धत *án-uddhata,* mfn. (*√han*), not lifted up, humble; unsurpassed; unopposed; (*as*), m. not a high place, TBr.

अनुद्धरण *an-uddharaṇa, am,* n. (*√hṛi*), non-removal; not offering, not establishing or proving.

An-uddhāra, *as,* m. non-partition, not taking a share; non-removal.

Án-uddhṛita, mfn. non-removed, not taken away; uninjured, undestroyed; unoffered; undivided, unpartitioned; unestablished, unproved. **An-uddhṛitâbhyastamaya,** m. sunset (*abhy-astamaya*) taking place whilst the Āhavanīya fire continues unremoved from the Gārhapatya, KātyŚr.

अनुद्भट *an-udbhaṭa,* mfn. not exalted, unassuming.

अनुद्य *an-udya,* mfn. unutterable, Pāṇ. iii, 1, 101, Sch.

Án-udyamāna, mfn. not being spoken, ŚBr.

अनुद्यत *an-udyata,* mfn. (*√yam*), inactive, idle, destitute of perseverance.

अनुद्यूत *anu-dyūta, am,* n. continuation of the play at dice, N. of the chapters 70-79 in the second book of the MBh.

अनुद्योग *an-udyoga, as,* m. absence of exertion or effort, inactivity, laziness.

An-udyogin, mfn. inactive, lazy, indifferent.

अनुद्र *an-udrá,* mfn. waterless, RV. x, 115, 6.

अनुद्रु *anu-√2. dru,* to run after, follow; to accompany; to pursue; to run over in reciting, AitBr.

Anu-druta, mfn. followed, pursued; having followed or pursued; accompanied; (*am*), n. a measure of time in music (half a Druta, or one-fourth of a Mātrā or of the time taken to articulate a short vowel).

अनुद्वाह *an-udvāha, as,* m. non-marriage, celibacy.

अनुद्विग्न *an-udvigna,* mfn. free from apprehension or perplexity, easy in mind, Mṛicch. &c.

An-udvega, mfn. free from anxiety; (*as*), m. freedom from uneasiness. **-kara,** mfn. not causing apprehension, not overawing.

अनुद्विष् *anu-√dvish,* to wreak one's anger upon, BhP.

अनुधन्व् *anu-√dhanv* (perf. Ā. 3. sg. *-dadhanvé*) to run near, RV. ii, 5, 3.

अनुधम् *anu-√dham* (3. pl. *dhámanty ánu*) to sprinkle over, RV. viii, 7, 16.

अनुधा *anu-√dhā,* to add in placing upon, Lāṭy.; to stimulate to, RV. vi, 36, 2; to concede, allow, (Pass. aor. *-dhāyi*) RV. vi, 20, 2.

अनुधाव् 1. *anu-√1. dhāv,* to run after, run up to; to follow; to pursue.

1. **Anu-dhāvana,** *am,* n. chasing, pursuing, running after; close pursuit of any object, going after a mistress.

Anu-dhāvita, mfn. pursued, run after (literally or figuratively).

अनुधाव् 2. *anu-√2. dhāv,* to cleanse.

2. **Anu-dhāvana,** *am,* n. cleansing, purification

अनुधी *anu-√dhī* (p. Ā. *-dídhyāna;* impf. P. 3. pl. *-dīdhiyuḥ*) to think of, RV. iii, 4, 7 & x, 40, 10; AV.

अनुधूपित *ánu-dhūpita,* mfn. (*√dhūp*), puffed up, proud, RV. ii, 30, 10.

अनुधे *anu-√dhe,* Caus. *-dhāpayati,* to cause to suck, to put to the breast, ŚBr. xiv.

अनुध्यै *anu-√dhyai,* to consider attentively, think of, muse; to miss, Kāṭh.; to bear a grudge, TS.

Anu-dhyā́, f. sorrow, AV. vii, 114, 2.

Anu-dhyāna, *am,* n. meditation, religious contemplation, solicitude.

Anu-dhyāyin, mfn. contemplating, meditating; missing, MaitrS.

अनुध्वंस् *anu-√dhvaṇs,* Ā. (perf. *-dadhvasé*) to fall or drop upon, TS.

अनुनद् *anu-√nad,* to sound towards (acc.): Caus. P. *-nādayati,* to make resonant or musical.

Anu-nāda, *as,* m. sound, vibration, Śiś.; reverberation, echo.

Anu-nādita, mfn. made to resound.

Anu-nādin, mfn. resounding, echoing, resonant.

अनुनन्द् *anu-√nand,* to enjoy.

अनुनम् *anu-√nam*, Ā. to incline to, RV. v, 32, 10: Caus. P. *-nāmayati*, to cause to bow, BhP.

अनुनय *anu-naya*, &c. See *anu-√nī*.

अनुनासिक *anu-nāsika*, mfn. nasal, uttered through the nose (as one of the five nasal consonants, or a vowel, or the three semivowels *y, v, l*, under certain circumstances; in the case of vowels and semivowels, the mark ँ is used to denote this nasalization); the nasal mark ँ; (*am*), n. a nasal twang; speaking through the nose (a fault in pronunciation). **-tva**, n. nasality. **-lopa**, m. dropping of a nasal sound or letter. **Anunāsikâdi**, m. a compound letter commencing with a nasal. **Anunāsikânta**, m. a radical ending in a nasal. **Anunāsikôpadha**, mfn. having a nasal penultimate; succeeding a syllable with a nasal sound.

अनुनिक्रम् *anu-ni-√kram, -krāmati* (Subj. *-krāmāt*) to follow in the steps, TS.; ŚBr.

अनुनिक्ष् *anu-√niksh*, to pierce along, AV.

अनुनितुद् *anu-ni-√tud* (impf. 3. pl. *-atudan*) to wound with a stab, goad, PBr.

अनुनिपद् *anu-ni-√pad, -padyate*, to lie down by the side of, ŚBr.; Kauś.

अनुनियुज् *anu-ni-√yuj*, to attach to, place under the authority of, AitBr.; PBr.; Kāṭh.

अनुनिर्जिहान *anu-nir-jihāna*, mfn. (pr. p. Ā. √2. *hā*), proceeding out of, BhP.

अनुनिर्दह् *anu-nir-√dah* (Imper. 2. sg. *-daha*) to burn down in succession, AV. ix, 2, 9.

अनुनिर्देश *anu-nirdeśa, as*, m. description or relation following a previous model.

अनुनिर्वप् *anu-nir-√2. vap*, to take out from for scattering or sharing subsequently, TS.; ŚBr. &c.

Anu-nirvāpyà, mfn. to be taken out and shared subsequently, TS.; (*ā*), f., N. of a ceremony, KaushBr.

अनुनिर्वा *anu-nir-√2. vā, -vāti*, to become extinct, go out after.

अनुनिवृज् *anu-ni-√vṛij* (impf. 3. sg. *-vriṇak*) to plunge into (loc.), RV. vii, 18, 12.

अनुनिवृत् *anu-ni-√vṛit*, Caus. *-vartayati*, to bring back, AitBr.

अनुनिशम् 1. *anu-ni-√śam* (ind. p. *-śamya*) to hear, perceive, BhP.; to consider, MBh. xii, 6680.

अनुनिशम् 2. *anu-niśam*, ind. every night, Kathās. &c.

अनुनिशीथम् *anu-niśītham*, ind. at midnight, Kir.

अनुनी *anu-√nī* (Subj. 2. sg. *-nayas*; aor. Subj. 2. sg. *-neshi*, 2 pl. *-neshathā*) to bring near, lead to, RV.; to induce, win over, conciliate, pacify, supplicate.

Anu-naya, *as*, m. conciliation, salutation, courtesy, civility, showing respect or adoration to a guest or a deity; humble entreaty or supplication, reverential deportment; regulation of conduct, discipline, tuition; (mfn.), conciliatory, kind; (*am*), ind. fitly, becomingly. **-pratigha-prahāṇa**, n. abandoning the obstacles to conciliatory behaviour, Buddh. **Anunayâmantraṇa**, n. conciliatory address.

Anu-nayamāna, mfn. conciliating, honouring.

Anu-nayin, mfn. courteous, supplicating.

Anu-nāyaka, mf(*ikā*)n. submissive, humble.

Anu-nāyikā, f. a female character subordinate to a *nāyikā* or leading female character in a drama.

Anu-ninīshu, mfn. desirous of conciliating.

Anu-nīta, mfn. disciplined, taught; obtained; respected; pleased, pacified; humbly entreated.

Anu-nīti, *is*, f. conciliation, courtesy, supplication.

Anu-neya, mfn. to be conciliated, Mṛicch.

अनुनु *anu-√4. nu*, Intens. (impf. 3 pl. *-nonavur*; pr. p. nom. pl. m. *-nônuvatas*) to follow with acclamations of praise, RV. i, 80, 9 & viii, 92, 33.

अनुनृत् *anu-√nṛit*, to dance after (acc.), R.; Kathās.; to dance before (acc.), MBh.

अनुन्नत *an-unnata*, mfn. not elevated, not lifted up. **-gātra**, mfn. having limbs that are not too stout, prominent or protuberant, Buddh. **An-unnatânata**, mfn. not raised nor lowered, level.

अनुन्मत्त *an-unmatta*, mfn. not mad, sane, sober, not wild.

Án-unmadita, mfn. id., AV. vi, 111, 1-4.

Án-unmāda, *as*, m. not being mad, soberness, MaitrS.; (mfn.) = *an-unmatta*.

अनुपकारिन् *an-upakārin*, mfn. not assisting, disobliging, ungrateful, not making a return for benefits received; unserviceable, useless.

An-upakṛita, mfn. unassisted.

अनुपक्षित *án-upakshita*, mfn. uninjured, undecaying, RV. iii, 13, 7 & x, 101, 5; AV. vi, 78, 2.

अनुपगीतम् *án-upagītam*, ind. so that no other person accompanies in singing, ŚBr.

अनुपघाताર्जित *an-upaghātârjita*, mfn. acquired without detriment (to the paternal estate).

An-upaghnat, mfn. not detrimental, Mn.; not touching, Lāṭy.

अनुपच् *anu-√pac*, to make ripe by degrees, BhP.: Pass. to become ripe by degrees, MBh. xiv, 497.

अनुपजीवनीय *an-upajīvanīyá*, mfn. yielding no livelihood, (Compar. *-tara*, 'yielding no livelihood at all') ŚBr. vi; having no livelihood, ŚBr. vi.

अनुपठ् *anu-√paṭh*, to say after, read through, repeat, BhP.; Suśr.

Anu-paṭhita, mfn. read through (aloud), recited.

Anu-paṭhitin, *ī*, m. (one who has read through or recited), proficient, (gaṇa *ishṭâdi*, q. v.)

अनुपत् *anu-√pat*, to pass by (acc.) flying, ĀśvGṛ.; to fly after, run after, go after, follow: Caus. (Imper. 2. sg. *-pātaya*) to fly along, AV. vi, 134, 3; to throw (a person) down together with oneself, R.

Anu-patana, *am*, n. falling on or upon; following; (in mathem.) proportion.

Anu-patita, mfn. fallen, descended; followed.

Anu-pāta. See s. v.

अनुपति *anu-pati*, ind. after the husband, KātyŚr.

अनुपथ *ánu-patha*, mfn. following the road, RV. v, 52, 10; (*as*), m. a road followed after another, BhP.; a servant, BhP.; (*am*), ind. along the road.

अनुपद् 1. *anu-√pad*, to follow, attend, be fond of; to enter; to enter upon; to notice, understand; to handle.

2. **Anu-pád**, mfn. coming to pass, VS. xv, 8.

Anu-pada, mfn. following closely, L.; (*as*), m., N. of a man or tribe, (gaṇa *upakâdi*, q. v.); (*am*), n. a chorus, refrain, burden of a song or words sung again after regular intervals; N. of an Upāṅga belonging to the Sāma-veda; (*am*), ind. step by step; word for word; on the heels of, close behind or after. **-sūtra**, n. a commentary explaining the text (of a Brāhmaṇa) word for word.

Anu-padavī, f. a road followed after another, BhP.

Anu-padin, *ī*, m. a searcher, an inquirer, one who follows or seeks for, Pāṇ. v, 2, 90.

Anupadīnā, f. a boot, buskin, Pāṇ. v, 2, 9.

अनुपदस्त *an-upadasta* [Kauś.] or *an-upadasya* [ŚāṅkhŚr.] or *án-upadasyat* [TS.] or *án-upadasvat* [AV.] or *án-upadāsuka* [TS.], mfn. not drying up, not decaying.

अनुपदिष्ट *an-upadishṭa*, mfn. untaught, uninstructed.

An-upadeshṭṛi, *ṭā*, m. one who does not teach.

अनुपध *an-upadha, as*, m. 'having no penultimate,' a letter or syllable (as a sibilant or *h*) not preceded by another.

अनुपधिशेष *an-upadhi-śesha*, mfn. in whom there is no longer a condition of individuality, Buddh.

अनुपनाह *an-upanāha, as*, m. want of close attachment or adherence (?), Buddh.

अनुपन्यस्त *an-upanyasta*, mfn. not laid down clearly, not established, Yājñ.

An-upanyāsa, *as*, m. failure of proof or determination, uncertainty, doubt.

अनुपपत्ति *an-upapatti, is*, f. non-accomplishment; failure of proof; inconclusive argumentation; irrelevancy, inapplicability; insufficiency of means, adversity.

An-upapanna, mfn. not done, unaccomplished, uneffected; unproved; irrelevant, inconclusive, inapplicable; impossible; inadequately supported.

An-upapādaka, *ās*, m. pl. 'having no material parent,' N. of a class of Buddhas, called Dhyāni-buddhas.

अनुपप्लव *an-upaplava*, mfn. free from disaster or overwhelming calamity.

An-upapluta, mfn. not overwhelmed (with calamity).

अनुपबाध *an-upabādhá*, mf(*ā*)n. unobstructed, ŚBr.

अनुपभुक्त *an-upabhukta*, mfn. unenjoyed, unpossessed.

An-upabhujyamāna, mfn. not being enjoyed.

अनुपम *an-upama*, mf(*ā*)n. incomparable, matchless; excellent, best; (*ā*), f. the female elephant of the south-east or of the north-east. **-mati**, m., N. of a contemporary of Śākya-muni.

An-upamita, mfn. uncompared, matchless.

An-upameya, mfn. incomparable.

अनुपमर्दन *an-upamardana, am*, n. non-demolition or refutation of a charge.

अनुपयुक्त *an-upayukta*, mfn. unsuited, unsuitable, improper; useless, unserviceable.

An-upayoga, *as*, m. unserviceableness, uselessness.

An-upayogin, mfn. unsuitable, useless.

अनुपरत *án-uparata*, mfn. uninterrupted, not stopped.

अनुपरागम् *anu-parā-√gam*, to follow one who is escaping, MaitrS.

अनुपरापत् *anu-parā-√pat*, to fly or hasten by the side of another, AitBr.

अनुपराभू *anu-parā-√bhū*, to spoil or destroy after another, TS.; AitBr.: Caus. *-bhāvayati*, id., TS.

अनुपरामृश् *anu-parā-√mṛiś*, to seize, ŚBr.

अनुपरास्रु *anu-parā-√sru*, (said of a leaky vessel) to flow with water subsequently, Kāṭh.

अनुपरिकॄ *anu-pari-√1. kṝ*, to scatter alongside, to bestrew, Kauś.

अनुपरिक्रम् *anu-pari-√kram*, to walk round in order, to make the circuit of, visit in a regular round.

Anu-parikramaṇa, *am*, n. walking round in order, AitĀr.

Anu-parikrā́mam, ind. while walking round in order, TS.; ŚBr.; PārGṛ.

अनुपरिगा *anu-pari-√1. gā*, to make the round of, traverse, MBh.

अनुपरिचारम् *anu-paricāram*, ind. = *anu-parikrā́mam*, KapS.

अनुपरिणी *anu-pari-ṇī* (√*nī*), to lead or carry about, Kauś.

अनुपरिधि *anu-paridhi*, ind. along or at the three Paridhis of the sacrificial fire, KātyŚr.

अनुपरिपाटिक्रम *anu-paripāṭi-krama, as*, m. regular order, VarBṛS.

अनुपरिया *anu-pari-√yā*, to pass through in order, ĀśvGṛ.

अनुपरिवृत् *anu-pari-√vṛit*, to return, be repeated, ŚBr. xiv.

अनुपरिश्रित् *anu-pariśrit*, ind. along or at the surrounding fence, KātyŚr.

अनुपरिस्रु *anu-pari-√sru*, to run after, BhP.

अनुपरिहारम् *anu-pari-hāram*, ind. surrounding, TS.

अनुपरी *anu-parí* (√*i*), *-pary-eti* (3. pl. *-pári-yanti*, AV. xv, 17, 8, irreg. *-paryanti*, Kauś.), to follow in going round, to make the round of.

अनुपरे *anu-parê (-parā-√i)*, (Imper. 2. sg. *-párehi*; impf. *-páraît*) to follow in walking off, RV. x, 18, 1; TS.

अनुपर्यागा *anu-pary-ā-√1. gā* (aor. 3. pl. *-āgur*) to revolve, return to, AitBr.

अनुपर्याधा *anu-pary-ā-√dhā* (Pot. *-dadhyāt*) to place round in order, AitBr.

अनुपर्यावृत् *anu-pary-ā-√vṛit*, to follow in going off, to follow, TS.; ŚBr.; AitBr.

अनुपर्युक्ष् *anu-pary-√1. uksh*, to sprinkle round, Gobh.; Gaut.

अनुपर्ये *anu-pary-ê (-ā-√i), -pary-áiti*, to make the whole round of, ŚBr. &c.

अनुपलक्षित *an-upalakshita*, mfn. untraced, unperceived, unmarked, indiscriminated.

An-upalakshya, mfn. not to be traced, imperceptible. **–vartman**, mfn. having ways that cannot be traced.

अनुपलब्ध *an-upalabdha*, mfn. unobtained, unperceived, unascertained.

An-upalabdhi, *is*, f. non-perception, non-recognition. **–sama**, *as, ā*, m. f. trying to establish a fact (e. g. the reality and eternity of sound) from the impossibility of perceiving the non-perception of it, sophistical argument, Nyāyad.

An-upalabhyamāna, mfn. not being perceived, Pāṇ. vi, 3, 80, Sch.

An-upalambha, *as*, m. non-perception.

An-upalambhana, *am*, n. want of apprehension or knowledge.

Án-upalābha, *as*, m. not catching, TS.

अनुपलाल *anupalāla*, *as*, m., N. of a demon dangerous to children, AV. viii, 6, 2.

अनुपवीतिन् *an-upavitin, ī*, m. one uninvested with the sacred thread.

अनुपश् *anu-√paś*, P. Ā. *-paśyati*, °*te*, to look at, perceive, notice, discover, RV. &c.; to consider, reflect upon (acc.), MBh. &c.; to look upon as, take as, ib.; (perf. Ā. p. *-paspaśānd*) to show (as the path), RV. x, 14, 1; AV. vi, 28, 3; (Nir. x, 20.)

Anu-paśya, mfn. perceiving, seeing, Yogas.

Ánu-spashṭa, mfn. noticed, RV. x, 160, 4.

अनुपशय *an-upaśaya*, *as*, m. any aggravating circumstance (in a disease).

अनुपशान्त *an-upaśānta*, mfn. not calm; (*as*), m., N. of a Buddhist mendicant.

अनुपसर्ग *an-upasarga*, *as*, m. a word that is not an Upasarga, q. v., or destitute of one; that which needs no additions (as a divine being).

अनुपसेचन *an-upasecanā*, mfn. having nothing that moistens (e. g. no sauce), AV. xi, 3, 24.

अनुपस्कृत *an-upaskṛita*, mfn. unfinished, unpolished; not cooked; genuine; blameless; unrequited.

अनुपस्थान *an-upasthāna*, *am*, n. not coming near, Lāṭy.; not being at hand, absence.

An-upasthāpana, *am*, n. not placing near, not producing, not offering; not having ready or at hand.

An-upasthāpayat, mfn. not presenting, not having at hand.

An-upasthāpita, mfn. not placed near, not ready, not at hand, not offered or produced.

An-upasthāyin, mfn. absent, distant.

Án-upasthita, mfn. not come near, not present, not at hand; not complete, ŚBr.; (*am*), n. a word not *upasthita*, q. v.

Án-upasthiti, *is*, f. absence, not being at hand; incompleteness, ŚBr.

अनुपहत *an-upahata*, mfn. unimpaired, unvitiated; not rendered impure. **–krushṭa**, mfn. whose organs of hearing are unimpaired, Buddh.

अनुपहूत *án-upahūta*, mfn. not called upon or invited, ŚBr.; not accompanied with invitations, ib.

Án-upahūyamāna, mfn. not being invited, MaitrS.

अनुपा 1. *anu-√1. pā*, to drink after or thereupon, follow in drinking, drink at: Caus. (Pot. *-pāyáyet*) to cause to drink afterwards, ŚBr.

Anu-pāna, *am*, n. a fluid vehicle in medicine; drink taken with or after medicine; drink after eating; drink to be had near at hand, (Comm. on) ChUp. i, 10, 3.

Anu-pānīya, *am*, n. drink to be had near at hand, Comm. on ChUp. i, 10, 3; (mfn.), fit to be drunk after; serving as a liquid vehicle of medicine.

अनुपा 2. *anu-√2. pā*, Caus. P. Ā. *-pālayati*, °*te*, to preserve, keep, cherish; to wait for, expect.

Anu-pālana, *am*, n. preserving, keeping up.

Anu-pālayat, mfn. keeping, maintaining.

Anu-pālin, mfn. preserving, keeping up.

Anu-pālu, n., N. of a plant, wild Calladium (?).

अनुपाकृत *an-upâkṛita*, mfn. not rendered fit for sacrificial purposes, Mn. v, 7; Yājñ. **–māṉsa**, n. flesh of an animal not prepared for sacrifice.

अनुपाख्य *an-upâkhya*, mfn. not clearly discernible, Pāṇ. vi, 3, 80.

अनुपात *anu-pāta*, *as*, m. falling subsequently upon, alighting or descending upon in succession; following; going, proceeding in order, or as a consequence; a degree of latitude opposite to one given, the Antæci (?); proportion (in arithm.); arithmetical progression, rule of three.

Anu-pātaka, *am*, n. a crime similar to a *mahāpātaka*, q. v. (falsehood, fraud, theft, adultery, &c.)

Anu-pātam, ind. in regular succession.

Anu-pātin, mfn. following as a consequence or result.

अनुपान *anu-pāna*. See 1. *anu-√1. pā*.

अनुपानत्क *an-upānatka*, mfn. shoeless, KātyŚr.

अनुपायिन् *an-upâyin*, mfn. not using means or expedients.

अनुपार्श्व *anu-pārśva*, mfn. along or by the side; lateral.

अनुपाल् *anu-√pāl*. See 2. *anu-√2. pā*.

अनुपावृत्त *an-upâvṛitta*, *ās*, m. pl., N. of a people, MBh.

अनुपासन *an-upâsana*, *am*, n. want of attention to.

An-upâsita, mfn. not attended to, neglected.

अनुपिश् *anu-√piś* (perf. *-pipeśa*) to fasten along, AV.

अनुपिष् *anu-√pish* (ind. p. *-pishya*) to strike against, to touch, KātyŚr.

अनुपुरुष *anu-purusha*, *as*, m. the before-mentioned man, Pāṇ. vi, 2, 190; a follower, ib. Sch.

अनुपुष् *anu-√push*, to go on prospering, VS.; to prosper after another (acc.), ShaḍvBr.

Anu-pushpa, *as*, m. a kind of reed (Saccharum Sara Roxb.)

अनुपू *anu-√pū*, Ā. (*ánu-pavate*) to purify in passing along, ŚBr.

अनुपूर्व *anu-pūrva*, mf(*ā*)n. regular, orderly, in successive order from the preceding; (*ám*), ind. in regular order, from the first, RV. &c.; (*eṇa*), ind. in regular order or succession, from the first, from the beginning, from above downwards. **–keśa, -gātra, -daṇshṭra, -nābhi, -pāṇi-lekha**, mfn. having regular hair, regularly shaped limbs, regular teeth, a regularly shaped navel, regular lines in the hands (all these are epithets given to Buddha, some of them also to Mahāvīra), Buddh. & Jain. **–ja**, mfn. descended in a regular line, KātyŚr. **–vatsā** (*anupūrvá-*), f. a cow which calves regularly, AV. ix, 5, 29. **–śas**, ind. = *anu-pūrvám*.

Anupūrvya, mfn. regular, orderly, KātyŚr.

अनुपृक्त *anu-pṛikta*, mfn. mixed with, MBh.

अनुपृष्ठ्य *anu-prishṭhya*, mf(*ā*)n. (held or extended) lengthwise, KātyŚr.

अनुपॄ *anu-√pṛī*, Caus. (Imper. *-pūrayatu*) to fill, Gīt.

अनुपेत *án-upêta* [ŚBr.] or *anupêta-pūrva* [ĀśvGṛ.], mfn. not yet entered at a teacher's (for instruction).

अनुपोषण *an-upôshaṇa*, *am*, n. not fasting.

अनुप्त *an-upta*, mfn. (√2. *vap*), unsown (as seed). **–sasya**, mfn. fallow, meadow (ground, &c.), L.

An-uptrima, mfn. grown without being sown, L.

अनुप्रकम्प् *anu-pra-√kamp*, Caus. (Pot. *-kampayet*, 3. pl. °*yeyur*) to follow in shaking or agitating, AitBr.; ĀpŚr.

अनुप्रछ् *anu-√prach* (with acc. of the person and thing), to ask, to inquire after.

Anupraśna. See s. v.

अनुप्रजन् *anu-pra-√jan*, to be born after; (with *prajām*) to propagate again and again, BhP.: Caus. *-janayati*, to cause to be born subsequently.

अनुप्रज्ञा *anu-pra-√jñā* (pr. p. *-jānát*) to track, trace, discover, RV. iii, 26, 8, &c.

Anu-prajñāna, *am*, n. tracking, tracing.

अनुप्रणुद् *anu-pra-ṇud* (√*nud*), to push away from one's self; to frighten away, put to flight.

अनुप्रतिक्रामम् *anu-prati-krāmam*, ind. (√*kram*), returning, TS. v.

अनुप्रतिधा *anu-prati-√dhā*, to offer after another (acc.), AitBr. (Pass. *-dhīyate*).

अनुप्रतिष्ठा *anu-prati-shṭhā* (√*sthā*), to follow in getting a firm footing or in prospering, TS.; ChUp.: Desid. *-tishṭhāsati*, to wish to get a firm footing after, Gobh.

अनुप्रथ् *anu-√prath*, Ā. *-prathate*, to extend or spread along (acc.), TS.; to praise, (Comm. on) VS. viii, 30.

अनुप्रदा *anu-pra-√1. dā*, to surrender, make over, Buddh.; to add.

Anu-pradāna, *am*, n. a gift, donation, Buddh.; addition, increase, Prāt.

अनुप्रधाव् *anu-pra-√1. dhāv*, to rush after, RV. x, 145, 6, &c.: Caus. (perf. *-dhāvayām cakāra*) to drive after, ŚBr.

Anu-pradhāvita, mfn. hurried, eager, Daś.

अनुप्रपत् *anu-pra-√pat* (aor. 3. pl. *-paptan*) to fly towards, RV. vi, 63, 6.

Anu-prapātam, ind. going in succession, Pāṇ. iv, 3, 56, Sch.

अनुप्रपद् *anu-pra-√pad*, to enter or approach or arrive after; to follow, act in conformance to.

Anu-prapanna, mfn. following after, conformed to.

Anu-prapādam, ind. going in succession, Pāṇ. iv, 3, 56, Sch.

अनुप्रपा *anu-pra-√1. pā*, P. (3. pl. *-pibanti*) to drink one after the other, AitBr.; Ā. (3. pl. *-pipate* [sic] & *-pibate*) to drink after another (acc.), TS.; Kāṭh.

अनुप्रभा *anu-pra-√bhā*, to shine upon, TBr.

अनुप्रभूत *anu-pra-bhūta*, mfn. passing through, penetrating, (*ánu prá-bhūta*) RV. viii, 58, 2; penetrated, ChUp.

अनुप्रभूष् *anu-pra-√bhūsh* (p. *-bhūshat*) to serve, attend, offer, RV. ix, 29, 1.

अनुप्रमाण *anu-pramāṇa*, mfn. having a suitable size or length.

अनुप्रमुच् *anu-pra-√muc*, to let loose or go successively, RV. iv, 22, 7.

अनुप्रमुद् *anu-pra-√mud*, Caus. *-modayati*, to consent, MārkP.

अनुप्रयम् *anu-pra-√yam*, to offer, TS.

अनुप्रया *anu-pra-√yā*, to follow after, TBr.; to start after, accompany.

अनुप्रयुज् *anu-pra-√yuj*, to employ after, add after (abl.), Pāṇ.; to join, follow, AV. &c.

Anu-prayujyamāna, mfn. being employed in addition or after or afterwards.

Anu-prayoktavya, mfn. to be joined or employed in addition or after.

Anu-prayoga, *as*, m. additional use.

अनुप्ररुह् *anu-pra-√ruh*, to grow in accordance with, ŚBr.

Anu-praroha, mfn. coming up or growing in accordance with.

अनुप्रवचन *anu-pra-vacana, am,* n. study of the Veda with a teacher. **Anupravacanâdi,** a gaṇa of Pāṇ. (v. 1, 111).

Anupravacanīya, mfn. belonging to, or necessary for *anupravacana,* ĀśvGṛ.; Gobh.

अनुप्रवद् *anu-pra-√vad,* to repeat another's words, TS.; AitBr.; to speak of, Nir.: Caus. *-vādayati,* to cause to resound, to play (an instrument), ŚāṅkhŚr.

अनुप्रवह् *anu-pra-√vah,* to drag (or carry) about; to go or get forward, RV. x, 2, 3.

अनुप्रविश् *anu-pra-√viś,* to follow in entering, enter; to attack.

Anu-praviśya, ind. p. having entered into.

Anu-praveśa, *as,* m. or **anu-praveśana** [gaṇa *anupravacanâdi,* q. v.], *am,* n. entrance into; imitation, L.

Anu-praveśanīya, mfn. connected with entering, (gaṇa *anupravacanâdi,* q. v.)

अनुप्रवृज् *anu-pra-√vṛij, -prá-vṛiṇakti,* to send or throw after, ŚBr.

अनुप्रवृत् *anu-pra-√vṛit* (impf. *-prâvartata;* perf. *-vāvṛite*) to proceed along or after, RV.

Anu-pravṛitta, mfn. following after (acc.), BhP.

अनुप्रव्रज् *anu-pra-√vraj,* to follow into exile, R. v, 36, 61.

अनुप्रशुच् *anu-pra-√1. śuc, -śocate,* to regret or mourn deeply, MBh.

अनुप्रश्न *anu-praśna, as,* m. a subsequent question (having reference to what has been previously said by the teacher).

अनुप्रसञ्ज् *anu-pra-√sañj,* to adhere to, fasten, ŚBr.

Anu-prasakta, mfn. strongly attached, Śiś.

Anu-prasakti, *is,* f. close connection with.

अनुप्रसद् *anu-pra-√sad,* to be content or satisfied with (acc.)

अनुप्रसूत *anu-prasūta,* mfn. (√4. *su*), created afterwards, MBh. xiii, 7361.

अनुप्रसृ *anu-pra-√sṛi,* Caus. (impf. 3. pl. *-prâsārayanta*) to extend over, RV. x, 56, 5: Intens. part. *-sársrāṇa,* moving along (acc.), RV. v, 44, 3.

अनुप्रसृप् *anu-pra-√sṛip,* to creep towards or after, TS.; ŚBr.: Caus. (Opt. 3. pl. *-sarpayeyuḥ*) to cause to pass round (acc.), ĀśvŚr.

अनुप्रस्तृ *anu-pra-√stṛi,* to scatter along or upon, Kauś.

अनुप्रस्था *anu-pra-√sthā,* to start after another: Caus. *-sthāpayati,* to cause to follow, BhP.

Anu-prastha, mfn. latitudinal; according to width, following the breadth or latitude.

अनुप्रहित *anu-pra-hita,* mfn. (√*hi*), sent after, Uttarar.

अनुप्रहृ *anu-pra-√hṛi,* to throw into the fire, TS.; ŚBr. &c.

Anu-praháraṇa, *am,* n. throwing into the fire, ŚBr. &c.

अनुप्राण् *anu-prâṇ* (√*an*), cl. 2. P. *-prâṇiti,* to breathe after, TUp.

अनुप्राप् *anu-prâp* (√*āp*), to come or go up to, reach, attain; to arrive; to get; to get back; to get by imitating.

Anu-prâpta, mfn. arrived, returned; obtained; having reached, having got.

अनुप्रास् *anu-prâs* (√*2. as*), *-prâsyati,* to throw after, ŚBr., KātyŚr.

Anu-prâsa, *as,* m. alliteration, repetition of similar letters, syllables, and words, Kpr. &c.

अनुप्रे *anu-prê* (√*i*), cl. 2. P. *-praiti,* to follow, RV. &c.; to follow in death, ŚBr.; to seek after, AV.; AitBr.

अनुप्रेक्ष् *anu-prêksh* (√*īksh*), to follow with the eyes.

अनुप्रेष् *anu-prêsh* (√*ish*), Caus. P. *-prêshayati,* to send forth after.

Anu-praishá, *as,* m. a subsequent invitation, ŚBr.

अनुप्रोह् *anu-prôh* (√1. *ūh*), to insert, ĀpŚr.

अनुप्लु *anu-√plu,* to float (as clouds) after; to follow.

Anu-plava, *as,* m. a companion or follower, Ragh.

अनुबन्ध् *anu-√bandh,* to attach, tie; to bind (by an obligation); to stick, adhere, follow, endure; to be followed by, BhP.

Anu-baddha, mfn. bound to, obliged to, connected with, related to, belonging to; followed by.

Anu-badhnat, mfn. following, seeking, Kir.

Anu-bandha, *as,* m. binding, connection, attachment; encumbrance; clog; uninterrupted succession; sequence, consequence, result; intention, design; motive, cause; obstacle; inseparable adjunct or sign of anything, secondary or symptomatic affection (supervening on the principal disease); an indicatory letter or syllable attached to roots, &c. (marking some peculiarity in their inflection; e. g. an *i* attached to roots, denotes the insertion of a nasal before their final consonant); a child or pupil who imitates an example set by a parent or preceptor; commencement, beginning; anything small or little, a part, a small part; (in arithm.) the junction of fractions; (in phil.) an indispensable element of the Vedânta; (*ī*), f hickup, L.; thirst, L.

Anu-bandhaka, mf(*ikā*)n. connected, allied; related.

Anu-bandhana, *am,* n. binding, connection, succession, unbroken series.

Anu-bandhin, mfn. connected with, attached; having in its train or as a consequence, resulting; continuous, lasting, permanent. **Anubandhi-tva,** n. the state of being accompanied or attended or followed.

Anu-bandhya, mfn. principal, primary, liable to receive an adjunct (as a root, a disease); (cf. *anū-bándhya.*)

अनुबल *anu-bala, am,* n. rear-guard, an auxiliary army following another.

अनुबाध् *anu-√bādh,* Pass. (p *-bādhyamāna*) to be oppressed or tormented, Rājat.; Kathās.

अनुबुध् *anu-√budh,* to awake; to recollect; to learn (by information): Caus. *-bodhayati,* to communicate; to remind, Śāk.

Anu-bodha, *as,* m. recollection; an after-thought, L.; reviving the scent of a faded perfume, replacing perfumes.

Anu-bodhana, *am,* n. recollecting, reminding.

Anu-bodhita, mfn. reminded; convinced by recollection.

अनुब्राह्मण *anu-brāhmaṇa, am,* n. a work resembling a Brāhmaṇa, Pāṇ. iv, 2, 62; (*am*), ind. according to the Brāhmaṇa, Lāṭy.

Anu-brāhmaṇika [Comm. on Lāṭy.], *as,* or **anu-brāhmaṇin** [ĀśvŚr.; Vait.], *ī,* m. a knower of an *anu-brāhmaṇa.*

अनुब्रू *anu-√brū,* cl. 2. P. *-braviti,* to pronounce, recite; to utter; to address, invite (with dat.), ŚBr. &c.; to repeat another's words, learn by heart (by repeating another's words), RV. v, 44, 13; ŚBr.

अनुभज् *anu-√bhaj,* to worship, BhP

अनुभा *anu-√bhā,* to shine after another (acc.), RV. iii, 6, 7; Up.

अनुभाष् *anu-√bhāsh,* to speak to, address; to confess.

Anu-bhāshaṇa, *am.* See *an-anubhāshaṇa.*

Anu-bhāshitṛi, mfn. speaking to, saying, Ragh.

अनुभास *anu-bhāsa, as,* m. a kind of crow.

अनुभिद् *anu-√bhid,* to split or break along, ŚBr.

Anu-bhitti, ind. along a mat, KātyŚr.

अनुभुज् *anu-√bhuj,* to suffer the consequence of one's actions; to enjoy successively, Kum.; to enjoy, participate; to pass (an asterism), BhP.

Anu-bhoga, *as,* m. (in law) enjoyment, a grant of hereditary land in return for service.

अनुभू *anu-√bhū,* to enclose, embrace, ChUp.; to be after, attain, equal, RV. &c.; to be useful, to help; ŚBr.; ŚāṅkhŚr.; to turn or incline to, RV. x, 147, 1; to notice, perceive, understand; to experience, to attempt.

Anu-bhava, *as,* m. perception, apprehension, fruition; understanding; impression on the mind not derived from memory; experience, knowledge derived from personal observation or experiment; result, consequence. **–siddha,** mfn. established by experience or perception. **Anubhavârūḍha,** mfn. subjected to trial or experiment.

Anu-bhāva, *as,* m. sign or indication of a feeling (*bhāva*) by look or gesture, Kpr. &c.; dignity, authority, consequence; firm opinion, ascertainment, good resolution, belief.

Anu-bhāvaka, mf(*ikā*)n. causing to apprehend, making to understand. **–tā,** f. understanding.

Anu-bhāvana, *am,* n. the act of indicating feelings by sign or gesture, Sāh.

Anu-bhāvin, mfn. perceiving, knowing; being an eye-witness, Mn. viii, 69; Āp.; showing signs of feeling.

Anu-bhū, mfn. perceiving, understanding (ifc.)

Anu-bhūta, mfn. perceived, understood, apprehended; resulted, followed as a consequence; that has experienced, tasted, tried or enjoyed.

Anu-bhūti, *is,* f. perception; knowledge from any source but memory; (in phil.) knowledge gained by means of the four Pramāṇas (perception by the senses, inference, comparison, and verbal authority); dignity, consequence. **–prakāśa,** m., N. of a metrical paraphrase of the twelve principal Upanishads by Vidyāraṇya-muni. **–svarūpâcārya,** m., N. of the author of the grammar Sārasvatī-prakriyā.

Anu-bhūya, ind. having experienced.

Anu-bhūyamāna, mfn. being under trial; being experienced or enjoyed.

अनुभृ *anu-√bhṛi,* to support, Kāṭh.; to insert, enter, RV. x, 61, 5; AV.

Anu-bhartṛi, mf(*trī*)n. supporting, strengthening (Gmn.), penetrating (NBD.), RV. i, 88, 6.

अनुभ्राज् *anu-√bhrāj,* to illuminate.

अनुभ्रातृ *anu-bhrātṛi, tā,* m. a younger brother.

अनुमद् *anu-√mad,* to rejoice over, to gladden, to praise, RV. &c.

Anu-mádya (4, 5), mfn. to be praised in succession, to be granted with acclamation or praise, RV.; AV.

अनुमध्यम *anu-madhyama,* mfn. next oldest to the middle, Pāṇ. vi, 2, 189, Sch.

अनुमन् *anu-√man,* to approve, assent to, permit, grant: Caus. P. *-mānayati,* to ask for permission or leave, ask for (acc.), Yājñ.; to honour.

Anu-mata, mfn. approved, assented to, permitted, allowed; agreeable, pleasant; loved, beloved; concurred with, being of one opinion; (*am*), n. consent, permission, approbation; (*e*), loc. ind. with consent of. **–karma-kārin,** mfn. doing what is allowed, acting according to an agreement.

Ánu-mati, *is,* f. assent, permission, approbation; personified as a goddess, RV.; AV. &c.; the fifteenth day of the moon's age (on which it rises one digit less than full, when the gods or manes receive oblations with favour); also personified as a goddess, VP.; oblation made to this goddess. **–pattra,** n. (in law) a deed expressing assent.

Anu-manana, *am,* n. assenting, Nir.

Anu-mantṛi, mfn. consenting to, permitting, TBr. &c.

Anu-manyamāna, mfn. minding, assenting.

1. **Anu-māná,** *as,* m. permission, consent, TBr.; Kāṭh.

अनुमन्त्र् *anu-√mantr,* to accompany with or consecrate by magic formulas; to dismiss with a blessing.

Anu-mantraṇa, *am,* n. consecration by hymns and prayers. **–mantra,** m. a hymn used in consecrating.

Anu-mantrita, mfn. so consecrated.

अनुमरण *anu-maraṇa.* See *anu-√mṛi.*

अनुमरु *anu-maru, us,* m. (used in the pl.) a country next to a desert, R. iv, 43, 19.

अनुमा 1. *anu-√2. mā,* Intens. (impf. *amīmed ánu*) to roar or bleat towards, RV. i, 164, 28.

अनुमा 2. *anu-√3. mā,* to be behind in

measure, to be unable to equal, RV.; to infer, conclude, guess, conjecture: Pass. *-mīyate*, to be inferred or supposed.

3. **Anu-mā**, f. inference, a conclusion from given premises.

2. **Anu-māna**, *am*, n. the act of inferring or drawing a conclusion from given premises; inference, consideration, reflection; guess, conjecture; one of the means of obtaining true knowledge (see *pramāṇa*). **-khaṇḍa**, n. or **-cintāmaṇi**, m. or **-prakāśa**, m. works on *anumāna*. **-maṇi-dīdhiti**, f. a similar work written by Raghunātha. **Anumānôkti**, f. inferential argument, reasoning.

Anu-māpaka, mf(*ikā*)n. causing an inference (as an effect).

Anu-mita, mfn. inferred, conjectured.

Anu-miti, *is*, f. conclusion from given premises.

Anu-mimāna, mfn. p. Ā. concluding, inferring.

Anu-mīyamāna, mfn. Pass. p. being inferred.

Anu-méya, mfn. to be measured, AV. vi, 137, 2; inferable, to be inferred, proved or conjectured.

अनुमाद्य *anu-mādya*. See *anu-√mad*.

अनुमाषम् *anu-māsham*, ind. like a kidney bean, (gaṇa *parimukhâdi*, q. v.)

अनुमिद् *anu-√2. mid, -medyati*, to become fat after another, TBr.

अनुमुद् *anu-√mud*, to join in rejoicing, RV. viii, 1, 14, &c.; to sympathize with, to rejoice; to allow with pleasure, express approval, applaud, permit: Caus. *-modayati*, to express approval, permit.

Anu-moda, *as*, m. a subsequent pleasure, the feeling of pleasure from sympathy.

Anu-modaka, mf(*ikā*)n. assenting, showing sympathetic joy.

Anu-modana, *am*, n. pleasing, causing pleasure, applauding; assent, acceptance; sympathetic joy.

Anu-modita, mfn. pleased, delighted, applauded; agreeable, acceptable.

अनुमुह् *anu-√muh*, to feel distressed at, to be troubled about or after another, MBh. i, 143.

अनुमृ *anu-√mṛi*, to follow in death, TBr. &c.

Anu-maraṇa, *am*, n. following in death; post-cremation or concremation of a widow; the burning of a widow with (her husband's corpse or with part of his dress when his body is not on the spot; cf. *saha-maraṇa*).

Anu-marishyat, mfn. about to follow in death.

Anu-mṛitā, f. the woman who burns with a part of her husband's dress.

अनुमृग्य *anumṛigya*, mfn. (*√mṛig*), to be sought after, BhP. **-dāśu**, mfn. granting all that is sought.

अनुमृज् *anu-√mṛij*, to rub lengthways for polishing or cleaning, AV.; ŚBr. &c.: Intens. part. *-mármṛijāna*, stretching (the arms) repeatedly towards, RV. x, 142, 5.

अनुमृश् *anu-√mṛiś*, to grasp, seize, RV. &c.; to consider, think of, reflect: Caus. *-marśayati*, to touch or take hold of for the sake of examining, Kāṭh.

Anu-márśam, ind. so as to seize or take hold of, ŚBr.; KātyŚr.

अनुम्लुच् *anu-√mluc* (only used for the etymol. of *anu-mlócantī* below), to rise from the resting-place (?), ŚBr.

Anu-mlócantī [VS.] or **anu-mlocā** [Hariv.], f., N. of an Apsaras.

अनुयजुस् *anu-yajus*, ind. according to the Yajus-formula, KātyŚr.

Anu-yāga, *as*, m. a subsequent or after-sacrifice, Pāṇ. vii, 3, 62, Sch.

Anu-yājá, *as*, m. a secondary or final sacrifice, RV. x, 51, 8 & 9 and 182, 2; ŚBr. &c. **-prasava**, m. permission to perform an Anuyāja, KātyŚr. **-praisha**, *ās*, m. pl. the formulas belonging to the Anuyāja, KātyŚr. **-vat** (*anuyājá-*), mfn. having secondary sacrifices, MaitrS.; AitBr. **Anuyājânumantraṇa**, n. reciting those formulas, KātyŚr. **Anuyājârtha**, mfn. belonging to or used at an Anuyāja, KātyŚr.

अनुयत् *anu-√yat*, Ā. *-yatate*, to strive to attain to or to reach, RV. ix, 92, 3.

अनुयम् *anu-√yam* (3. pl. *-yacchanti*; Imper. *-yacchatu*; p. fem. *-yácchamānā*) to direct, guide, give a direction to, RV. i, 123, 13; iv, 57, 7 & vi, 75, 6; (perf. 3. pl. *-yemuḥ*, Ā. 3. du. *-yemáte*) to follow, RV.

Á́nu-yata, mfn. followed (in hostile manner), RV. v, 41, 13.

अनुयवम् *anu-yavam*, ind. like barley, (gaṇa *parimukhâdi*, q. v.)

अनुया 1. *anu-√yā*, to go towards or after, follow; to imitate, equal.

2. **Anu-yā́**, mfn. following, VS. xv, 6.

Anu-yāta, mfn. following; followed; practised.

Anu-yātavya, mfn. to be followed.

Anu-yātṛi, m. a follower, companion.

Anu-yātra, *am, ā*, n. f. retinue, attendance; that which is required for a journey.

Anu-yātrika, mfn. following, attendant, Śāk.

Anu-yāna, *am*, n. going after, following.

Anu-yāyin, mfn. going after; a follower, a dependant, attendant; following, consequent upon.

Anuyāyi-tā, f. or **-tva**, n. succession.

अनुयुज् *anu-√yuj*, to join again, ŚBr.; AitBr.; to question, examine; to order; to enjoin: Caus. *-yojayati*, to place upon; to add, Kauś.: Desid. *-yuyukshati*, to intend to question, MBh.

Anu-yukta, mfn. ordered, enjoined; asked, inquired; examined, questioned; reprehended.

Anu-yuktin, *ī*, m. one who has enjoined, examined, (gaṇa *ishṭâdi*, q. v.)

Anu-yugam, ind. according to the Yugas or four ages, Mn. i, 84.

Anu-yoktṛi, *tā*, m. an examiner, inquirer, teacher.

Anu-yoga, *as*, m. a question, examination; censure, reproof, Nyāyad.; religious meditation, spiritual union. **-kṛit**, m. an Ācārya or spiritual teacher.

Anu-yogin, mfn. ifc. combining, uniting; connected with; questioning.

Anu-yojana, *am*, n. question, questioning.

Anu-yojya, mfn. to be examined or questioned, Mn.; to be enjoined or ordered; censurable; a servant, agent, delegate, Śāk.

अनुयू *anu-yū*, mfn. (*√2. yu*), depending, dependent, ŚBr. xi.

अनुयूपम् *anu-yūpam*, ind. along the Yūpa or sacrificial post, (gaṇa *parimukhâdi*, q. v.)

अनुरक्ष् *anu-√1. raksh*, to guard while following, ŚāṅkhŚr.; to guard, take care of.

Anu-rakshaṇa, *am*, n. the act of guarding.

अनुरज्जु *anu-rajju*, ind. along the rope, KātyŚr.

अनुरञ्ज् *anu-√rañj*, to become red in imitation of; to be attached or devoted: Caus. P. *-rañjayati*, to win, conciliate, gratify.

Anu-rakta, mfn. fond of, attached, pleased; beloved. **-praja**, mfn. beloved by his subjects. **-loka**, m. a person to whom every one is attached.

Anu-rakti, *is*, f. affection, love, devotion.

Anu-rañjaka, mf(*ikā*)n. attaching, conciliating.

Anu-rañjana, *am*, n. the act of attaching or conciliating affection, love; pleasing.

Anu-rañjita, mfn. conciliated, delighted.

Anu-rāga, *as*, m. attachment, affection, love, passion; red colour, Śiś. ix, 8, &c. **-vat**, mfn. affectionate, attached, in love with; red, Śiś. ix, 10, &c.

Anurāgêṅgita, n. gesture expressive of passion.

Anu-rāgin, mfn. impassioned, attached; causing love; (*iṇī*), f. personification of a musical note.

Anuragi-tā, f. the state of being in love with.

अनुरणन *anu-raṇana*, *am*, n. sounding conformably to, echoing, Sāh.

अनुरथ *anu-ratha*, *as*, m., N. of a son of Kuruvatsa and father of Puruhotra, VP.; (*am*), ind. behind the carriage, Pāṇ. ii, 1, 6, Sch.

Anu-rathyā, f. a path along the margin of a road, side road, R. ii, 6, 17.

अनुरम् *anu-√ram*, P. *-ramati*, to cease to go or continue, stop, ŚāṅkhŚr.: Ā. to be fond of.

Anu-rata, mfn. fond of, attached to.

Anu-rati, *is*, f. love, affection; attachment.

अनुरस् *anu-√1. ras*, to answer to a cry or to a sound.

Anu-rasita, *am*, n. echo, Mālatim.; Uttarar.

अनुरस *anu-rasa*, *as*, m. (in poetry) a subordinate feeling or passion; a secondary flavour (as a little sweetness in a sour fruit, &c.), Suśr. &c.

अनुरहसम् *anu-rahasam*, ind. in secret, apart, Pāṇ. v, 4, 81.

अनुराज् *anu-√rāj*, to be brilliant or shine in accordance with (said of corresponding metres), RV.

अनुरात्रम् *anu-rātram*, ind. in the night, AitBr.

अनुराध् *anu-√rādh*, to carry to an end; to finish with (gen.), TBr.

Anu-rāddha, mfn. effected, accomplished; obtained, BhP.

Anu-rādha, mfn., see *anūrâdhā*; born under the asterism Anurādhā, Pāṇ. iv, 3, 34; (*as*), m., N. of a Buddhist; (*ās*), m. pl. and (*ā*) [AV. &c.], f. the seventeenth of the twenty-eight Nakshatras or lunar mansions (a constellation described as a line of oblations). **-grāma**, m. or **-pura**, n. the ancient capital of Ceylon founded by the above-named Anurādha.

अनुरिच् *anu-√ric*, Pass. *-ricyate*, to be emptied after, TS.

अनुरिष् *anu-√rish*, cl. 4. P. *-rishyati*, to be injured after (acc.), ChUp.

अनुरी *anu-√rī*, cl. 4. Ā. *-rīyate*, to flow after, RV. i, 85, 3; (p. *-rī́yamāṇa*) VS. x, 19.

अनुरु 1. *anu-√ru*, to imitate the cry or answer to the cry of (acc.)

Anu-ruta, mfn. resounding with, VarBṛS.

अनुरु 2. *an-uru*, mf(*us* or *vī*)n. not great.

अनुरुच् *anu-√ruc*, Caus. P. *-rocayati*, to choose, prefer, MBh.

अनुरुद् *anu-√rud*, to lament, bewail.

अनुरुध् 1. *anu-√rudh*, to bar (as a way), MBh. xiii, 1649; to surround, confine, overcome, BhP. &c.; cl. 4. Ā. *-rudhyate* or ep. P. *-rudhyati* (2. sg. *-rudhyase*, RV. viii, 43, 9, &c.), to adhere to, be fond of, love; to coax, soothe, entreat.

Anu-ruddha, mfn. checked, opposed; soothed, pacified; (*as*), m., N. of a cousin of Śākyamuni.

2. **Anu-rúdh**, mfn. adhering to, loving, VS. xxx, 9; (cf. *anū-rúdh*.)

Anu-rodha, *as*, m. obliging or fulfilling the wishes (of any one); obligingness, compliance; consideration, respect; reference or bearing of a rule.

Anu-ródhana, *am*, n. obliging or fulfilling the wishes of; means for winning the affection of, AV.

Anu-rodhin, mfn. complying with, compliant, obliging, having respect or regard to. **Anurodhi-tā**, f. the state of being so, Kathās.

अनुरुह् *anu-√ruh*, P. to ascend, mount, RV. x, 13, 3: Ā. to grow, RV.

Anu-ruhā, f. a grass (Cyperus Pertenius).

Anu-rohá, *as*, m. mounting or growing up to, MaitrS.; PBr.

अनुरूप *ánu-rūpa*, mfn. following the form, conformable, corresponding, like, fit, suitable; adapted to, according to; (*as*), m. the Antistrophe which has the same metre as the Stotriya or Strophe; the second of three verses recited together; (*am*), n. conformity, suitability; (*am, eṇa*), ind. ifc. conformably, according. **-ceshṭa**, mfn. endeavouring to act becomingly. **-tas**, ind. conformably.

अनुरेवती *anu-revatī*, f., N. of a plant.

अनुलक्ष्य *anu-lakshya*, ind. p. conforming to.

अनुलग्न *anu-lagna*, mfn. attached to; followed; intent on, pursuing after.

अनुलभ् *anu-√labh*, to grasp or take hold of (from behind), ŚBr.; KātyŚr.: Desid. *-lipsate*, to intend to grasp, ib.

अनुला *anulā*, f., N. of a female Arhat or Buddhist saint; also of a queen of Ceylon.

अनुलाप *anu-lāpa, as,* m. (√*lap*), repetition of what has been said, tautology.

अनुलास *anu-lāsa* or *-lāsya, as,* m. a peacock.

अनुलिप् *anu-√lip,* P. to anoint, besmear; Ā. to anoint one's self after (bathing): Caus. *-lepayati,* to cause to be anointed.

Anu-lipta, mfn. smeared, anointed. **Anuliptâṅga,** mfn. having the limbs anointed.

Anu-lepa, *as,* m. unction, anointing, bedaubing.

Anu-lepaka, mfn. anointing the body with unguents, L.; (*ikā*), f. (gaṇa *mahishy-ādi,* q.v.)

Anu-lepana, *am,* n. anointing the body; unguent so used; oily or emollient application.

अनुली *anu-√lī,* to disappear after, BhP.

अनुलुभ् *anu-√lubh,* Caus. *-lobhayati,* to long for, desire, R.

अनुलोम *anu-loma,* mf(*ā*)n. 'with the hair or grain' (opposed to *prati-loma,* q.v.), in a natural direction, in order, regular, successive; conformable; (*ā*), f. a woman of a lower caste than that of the man's with whom she is connected, Yājñ.; (*ās*), m. 'descendants of an anulomā,' mixed castes, (gaṇa *upakâdi,* q.v.); (*ám*), ind. in regular order, ŚBr. &c. **–kalpa,** m. the thirty-fourth of the Atharva-pariśishṭas. **–kṛishṭa,** mfn. ploughed in the regular direction (with the grain). **–ja,** mfn. offspring of a mother inferior in caste to the father [Mn.; Yājñ.], (as the Mūrdhāvasikta of a Brāhman father and Kshatriyā mother, and so on with the Ambashṭha Nishāda or Pāraśava, Māhishya, Ugra, Karaṇa.) **–pariṇītā,** f. married in regular gradation. **Anulomaya,** mfn. having fortune favourable. **Anulomârtha,** mfn. one who holds favourable views on any question.

Anu-lomana, *am,* n. due regulation, sending or putting in the right direction, Suśr.; carrying off by the right channels, purging, Suśr.

Anu-lomaya, Nom. P. *anu-lomayati,* to stroke or rub with the hair, Pāṇ. iii, 1, 25, Sch.; to send in the right direction or so as to carry off by the right channels, Suśr.

अनुल्बण *an-ulbaṇá,* mf(*ā*)n. not excessive, not prominent, keeping the regular measure, RV. &c.

अनुवंश *anu-vaṅśa, as,* m. a genealogical list or table; collateral branch of a family, Hariv.; (*am*), ind. according to race or family; (mf(*ā*)n.), of a corresponding family, of equal birth.

Anuvaṅśya, mfn. relating to a genealogical list.

अनुवक्र *anu-vakra,* mfn. somewhat crooked or oblique. **–ga,** mfn. having a somewhat oblique course (as a planet, &c.), Suśr.

अनुवच् *anu-√vac,* to recite the formulas inviting to the sacrificial ceremony; to repeat, reiterate, recite; to communicate; to study: Caus. *-vācayati,* to cause to recite the inviting formulas, to cause to invite for some sacrificial act, KātyŚr.

Anu-vaktávya, mfn. to be repeated, ŚBr.

Anu-vaktṛi, mfn. speaking after; replying.

Anu-vácana, *am,* n. speaking after, repetition, reciting, reading; lecture; a chapter, a section; recitation of certain texts in conformity with injunctions (*praîsha*) spoken by other priests.

Anu-vacanīya, mfn. referring to the *anuvacana,* (gaṇa *anupravacanâdi,* q.v.)

Anu-vāká, *as,* m. saying after, reciting, repeating, reading; a chapter of the Vedas, a subdivision or section. **–saṅkhyā,** f. the fourth of the eighteen Pariśishṭas of the Yajur-veda. **Anuvākânukramaṇī,** f. a work referring to the Ṛig-veda, attributed to Śaunaka.

Anu-vākyà, mfn. to be recited, TBr.; to be repeated, reiterated, Gobh.; (*ā*), f. the verse to be recited by the Hotṛi or Maitrāvaruṇa priest, in which the god is invoked to partake of the offering intended for him, ŚBr. **Anuvākyà-vat** [ŚBr.] or **anuvākyā-vat** [ĀśvŚr.], mfn. furnished or accompanied with an Anuvākyā.

Anu-vác, *k,* f. = *anu-vākyà,* ŚBr.; AitBr.

Anu-vācana, *am,* n. the act of causing the Hotṛi to recite the passages of the Ṛig-veda in obedience to the injunction (*praîsha*) of the Adhvaryu priest, KātyŚr. **–praisha,** m. an injunction to recite as above, KātyŚr.

Anûkta, &c. See s.v., p. 42.

अनुवत्सर *anu-vatsará, as,* m. the fourth year in the Vedic cycle of five years, TBr. &c.; a year, L.; (*am*), ind. every year, yearly.

Anuvatsarīṇa [TBr. &c.] or **anuvatsarīya** [MānŚr.], mfn. referring to the *anuvatsará.*

अनुवद् *anu-√vad,* P. (with acc.) to repeat the words of; to imitate (in speaking); to resound; to repeat, insist upon; (according to Pāṇ. i, 3, 49, also Ā. if without object or followed by a Gen.) Pass. (*anûdyate*) to be expressed correspondingly; cf. *anûdita* s. v.

Anu-vāda, *as,* m. saying after or again, repeating by way of explanation, explanatory repetition or reiteration with corroboration or illustration, explanatory reference to anything already said; translation; a passage of the Brāhmaṇas which explains or illustrates a rule (*vidhi*) previously propounded (such a passage is sometimes called *anuvāda-vacana*); confirmation, Nir.; slander, reviling, L.

Anu-vādaka or **anu-vādin,** mfn. repeating with comment and explanation, corroborative, concurrent, conformable, in harmony with; (the masculine of the last is also the name of any one of the three notes of the gamut.)

Anu-vādita, mfn. translated.

Anu-vādya, mfn. to be explained by an anuvāda, to be made the subject of one; (*am*), n. the subject of a predicate. **–tva,** n. the state of requiring to be explained by an anuvāda.

Anûdita. See s. v.

अनुवनम् *anu-vanam,* ind. along side of a wood, Kir.; (cf. Pāṇ. ii, 1, 15.)

अनुवप् *anu-√2. vap,* P. to scatter over, Nir.; Ā. to scatter as dust, AV.: Pass. *ánu upyáte,* to be scattered as dust, RV. i, 176, 2.

अनुवर्ण् *anu-√varṇ,* to mention, describe, recount; to praise.

अनुवर्तन *anu-vartana,* &c. See *anu-√vṛit.*

अनुवश *anu-vaśa, as,* m. obedience to the will of; (mfn.), obedient to the will of.

अनुवषट्कृ *anu-vashaṭ-kṛi* (√*1. kṛi*), *-karoti* (Pot. *-kuryāt*) to make a secondary exclamation of *vashaṭ,* ŚBr.; AitBr.; KaushBr.; ŚāṅkhŚr.

Anu-vashaṭkāra, *as,* m. or **-váshaṭkṛita,** *am,* n. a secondary exclamation of *vashaṭ.*

अनुवस् 1. *anu-√4. vas,* to clothe, cover, RV. vi, 75, 18; AV. &c.

Anu-vasita, mfn. dressed up, wrapped.

अनुवस् 2. *anu-√5. vas,* to settle after another (acc.); to dwell near to; to inhabit along with: Caus. *-vāsayati,* to leave (the calf) with (the cow), TBr.

Anu-vāsin, mfn. residing, resident.

अनुवह् *anu-√vah,* to convey or carry along; to take after, Comm. on Mn. iii, 7.

Anu-vaha, *as,* m. 'bearing after,' one of the seven tongues of fire.

अनुवा 1. *anu-√vā,* cl. 2. P. *-vāti,* to blow upon, blow along or after, RV. &c.

2. Anu-vā́, f. blowing after, TS.; (cf. *anvā.*)

Anu-vāte, ind. with the wind blowing in the same direction, to windward, Mn. ii, 203.

अनुवाक *anu-vāká.* See *anu-√vac.*

अनुवारम् *anu-vāram,* ind. time after time.

अनुवाश् *anu-√vāś,* to roar in reply to (acc.), VarBṛS.

अनुवास् *anu-√vās,* to perfume.

Anu-vāsa, *as,* m. perfuming (especially the clothes); an oily enema; administering oily enemata.

Anu-vāsana, *am,* n. id.

Anu-vāsita, mfn scented, perfumed, fumigated; prepared or administered as an enema.

Anu-vāsya or **-vāsanīya,** mfn. to be scented or fumigated; requiring an enema.

अनुविकस् *anu-vi-√kas,* to blow, expand, as a flower.

अनुविकाश् *anu-vi-√kāś,* Intens. *-cākaśīti,* to penetrate with one's vision, AV.

अनुविकृ *anu-vi-√1. kṛi,* to shape after, ŚBr.

अनुविकॄ *anu-vi-√1. kṝi,* to bestrew, ŚBr.; to scatter separately, ĀpŚr.

अनुविक्रम् *anu-vi-√kram,* Ā. to step or walk after, follow, AV. &c.

अनुविचर् *anu-vi-√car,* to walk or pass through, RV. vi, 28, 4; to walk up to, RV. viii, 32, 19.

अनुविचल् *anu-vi-√cal,* to follow in changing place, AV.

अनुविचिन्त् *anu-vi-√cint,* to recal to mind, Buddh.; to meditate upon, ib.

अनुवितन् *anu-vi-√tan,* to extend all along or all over, ŚBr.

अनुविद् 1. *anu-√1. vid,* cl. 2. P., Ved. *-vetti,* to know thoroughly, RV. &c.

अनुविद् 2. *anu-√3. vid,* cl. 6. P. Ā. *-vindati,* °*te,* to find, obtain, discover, RV. &c.; to marry, MBh.; to deem, Gīt.

Ánu-vitta, mfn. found, obtained, at hand, ŚBr. xiv, &c.

Ánu-vitti, *is,* f. finding, ŚBr.

Anu-vidvás, mfn. perf. p. having found, AV.

अनुविधा *anu-vi-√dhā,* to assign to in order; to regulate, lay down a rule: Pass. *-dhīyate,* to be trained to follow rules; to yield or conform to (gen.)

Anu-vidhātavya, mfn. to be performed according to an order.

Anu-vidhāna, *am,* n. acting conformably to order, obedience.

Anu-vidhāyin, mfn. conforming to, compliant; imitating, Śiś. vi, 23.

अनुविधाव् *anu-vi-√1. dhāv,* to flow or run along (acc. or loc.), Kāṭh.; KaṭhUp.; to flow through, RV. viii, 17, 5.

अनुविनद् *anu-vi-√nad,* Caus. P. *-nādayati,* to make resonant or musical.

अनुविनर्द् *anu-vi-√nard,* to answer with roars, Hariv.

अनुविनश् *anu-vi-√2. naś,* to disappear, perish, vanish after or with another (acc.), AV. &c.

Anu-vi-nāśa, *as,* m. perishing after.

अनुविनिःसृ *anu-vi-niḥ-√sṛi,* to go or come out in order, MārkP.

अनुविन्द *anu-vinda, as,* m., N. of a king of Oujein.

अनुविपश् *anu-vi-√paś, -ví-paśyati,* to look at, view, ŚBr.; PBr.

अनुविभू *anu-vi-√bhū,* to equal, correspond to, ŚBr.

अनुविमृश् *anu-vi-√mṛiś,* to consider, Daś.

अनुविराज् *anu-vi-√rāj,* to be bright after or along, RV. v, 81, 2.

अनुविली *anu-vi-√lī,* to dissolve (as salt in water), ŚBr. xiv.

अनुविवा *anu-vi-√vā,* to blow while passing through, TBr.

अनुविविश् *anu-vi-√viś,* to settle along separately, TS.

अनुविवृत् *anu-vi-√vṛit,* to run along, RV. viii, 103, 2: Caus. Ā. *-vartayate,* to follow hastily, AV.

अनुविश् *anu-√viś,* to enter after; to enter; to follow.

Anu-veśa, *as,* m. or **-veśana,** *am,* n. entering after, following.

अनुविश्व *anu-viśva, ās,* m. pl., N. of a people in the north-east, VarBṛS.

अनुविषण्ण *anu-vi-shaṇṇa,* mfn. (√*sad*), fixed upon, ChUp.

अनुविषिच् *anu-vi-shic* (√*sic*), to pour in addition to (acc.), AV.

अनुविष्टम्भ anu-vishṭambha, as, m. the being impeded in consequence of, Nir.

अनुविष्ठा anu-vi-shṭhā (√sthā), to extend over, RV. &c.

अनुविष्णु anu-vishṇu, ind. after Vishṇu.

अनुविष्यन्द् anu-vi-shyand (√syand), to flow over or along or upon, ŚBr.

अनुविसृ anu-vi-√sṛi, to extend or stream over, TBr.

अनुविसृज् anu-vi-√sṛij, to shoot at or towards; to send along (acc.), RV. v, 53, 6.

अनुविस्तृत anu-vistṛita, mfn. (√stṛi), 'extended, spread out,' large, roomy, R.

अनुविस्मित anu-vismita, mfn. one who is astonished after another, R.

अनुविस्रंस् anu-vi-√sraṇs, Caus. -sraṇsayati, to separate, loose, ŚBr.

अनुविहन् anu-vi-√han, to interrupt, derange, MBh.

अनुवी anu-vī (√i), cl. 2. P. -vyeti, to follow or join in going off or separating, VS.; ŚBr.; to extend along, TBr.

अनुवीक्ष् anu-vīksh (√īksh), to survey, examine.

अनुवीज् anu-√vīj, to fan.

अनुवृ anu-√vṛi, to cover, KaushBr. &c.; to surround: Caus. Ā. -vārayate, to hinder, prevent.

अनुवृत् anu-√vṛit, Ā. to go after; to follow, pursue; to follow from a previous rule, be supplied from a previous sentence; to attend; to obey, respect, imitate; to resemble; to assent; to expect: Caus. P. -vartayati, to roll after or forward; to follow up, carry out; to supply.

Anu-vartana, am, n. obliging, serving or gratifying another; compliance, obedience; following, attending; concurring; consequence, result; continuance; supplying from a previous rule.

Anu-vartanīya, mfn. to be followed; to be supplied from a previous rule.

Anu-vartin, mfn. following, compliant, obedient, resembling. **Anuvarti-tva,** n. the state of being so.

Ánu-vartman, mfn. following attending, AV. &c.; (a), n. a path previously walked by another, BhP.

Anu-vṛit, mfn. walking after, following, MaitrS.; PBr.

Anu-vṛitta, mfn. following, obeying, complying; rounded off; (am), n. obedience, conformity, compliance.

Anu-vṛitti, is, f. following, acting suitably to, having regard or respect to, complying with, the act of continuance; (in Pāṇini's Gr.) continued course or influence of a preceding rule on what follows; reverting to; imitating, doing or acting in like manner.

अनुवृध् anu-√vṛidh, to grow, increase.

अनुवृष् anu-√vṛish, to rain upon or along, AV.; TS.

अनुवेदि anu-vedi, ind. along the ground prepared for sacrifice, KātyŚr. **Anu-vedy-antám,** ind. along the edge of the sacrificial ground, ŚBr.

अनुवेन् anu-√ven, to allure, entice, RV.

अनुवेलम् anu-velam, ind. now and then.

अनुवेल्लित anu-vellita, am, n. (√vell), bandaging, securing with bandages (in surgery); a kind of bandage applied to the extremities, Suśr.; (mfn.), bent in conformity with, bent under.

अनुवेष्ट् anu-√vesht, to be fixed to, cling to, Kāṭh.: Caus. P. -veshṭayati, to wind round, cover.

अनुवैनेय anuvaineya, N. of a country.

अनुव्यञ्जन anu-vyañjana, am, n. a secondary mark or token, Buddh.

अनुव्यध् anu-√vyadh, cl. 4. P. -vidhyati, to strike afterwards, Mn.; to penetrate, pierce through, wound.

Anu-viddha, mfn. pierced, penetrated; intermixed, full of, abounding in; set (as a jewel).

Anu-vedha or **anu-vyādha,** as, m. piercing; obstructing; blending, intermixture.

अनुव्यम् anu-vyàm, ind. (√vī), behind, after, inferior to, ŚBr.; PBr.

अनुव्यवगा anu-vy-ava-√1. gā, cl. 3. P. -jigāti, to come between in succession to another, ŚBr.

अनुव्यवसो anu-vy-ava-√so, to perceive.

अनुव्यवे anu-vy-avê (√i), cl. 2. P. -avaiti, to follow in intervening or coming between, ŚBr.

अनुव्यश् anu-vy-√1. aś, to overtake, reach, ŚBr.

अनुव्याख्या anu-vy-ā-√khyā, to explain further, ShaḍvBr.; ChUp.

Anu-vyākhyāna, am, n. that portion of a Brāhmaṇa which explains or illustrates difficult Sūtras, texts or obscure statements occurring in another portion, ŚBr. xiv.

अनुव्यास्था anu-vy-ā-√sthā, Caus. -sthāpayati, to send away in different directions, TBr.

अनुव्याहृ anu-vy-ā-√hṛi, to utter in order or repeatedly, MaitrUp.; to curse, ŚBr. &c.

Anu-vyāharaṇa, am, n. repeated utterance, R.

Anu-vyāhāra, as, m. cursing, execration, KātyŚr.

Anu-vyāhārin, mfn. execrating, cursing, ŚBr.

अनुव्युच्चर् anu-vy-uc-√car, to follow in going forth, ŚBr.

अनुव्यूह् anu-vy-√1. ūh, to move apart after, PBr.; to distribute, ŚBr.

अनुव्रज् anu-√vraj, to go along, ĀśvŚr.; to follow (especially a departing guest, as a mark of respect); to visit seriatim; to obey, do homage.

Anu-vrajana, am, n. following as above, Hcat.

Anu-vrajya, mfn. to be followed (as by the relatives of a dead person to the cemetery), Yājñ. iii, 1.

Anu-vrajyā, f. = anu-vrajana, Mn. &c.

अनुव्रत ánu-vrata, mfn. devoted to, faithful to, ardently attached to (with gen. or acc.)

अनुशंस् anu-√śaṇs, to recite or praise after another, TS. &c.; (Ved. Inf. (dat.) anu-śáse) to join in praising, RV. v, 50, 2.

अनुशक् anu-√śak, to be able to imitate or come up with, RV. x, 43, 5: Desid. Caus. P. -śikshayati, to teach, instruct.

Anu-śikshin, mfn. exercising one's self in, practising, Daś. &c.

अनुशतिक anu-śatika, mfn. accompanied with or bought for a hundred. **Anuśatikādi,** a gaṇa of Pāṇ. (vii, 3, 20) containing the compounds the derivatives of which have Vṛiddhi in both parts, as ānuśātika, &c.

अनुशप् anu-√śap, to curse, MBh.

अनुशब्दित anu-śabdita, mfn. verbally communicated; spoken of.

Anu-śabdya, ind. p. having communicated, Hariv.

अनुशम् anu-√śam, to become calm after or in consequence of, BhP.

अनुशय anu-śaya, &c. See anu-√1. śī.

अनुशर anu-śara, as, m. (√śṛī), N. of a Rākshasa.

अनुशस्त्र anu-śastra, am, n. any subsidiary weapon or instrument, anything used in place of a regular surgical instrument (as a finger-nail), Suśr.

अनुशास् anu-√śās, to rule, govern; to order; to teach, direct, advise, address; to punish, chastise, correct.

Anu-śāsaka, mfn. one who governs, instructs, directs or punishes.

Anu-śāsat, mfn. showing (the way), RV. i, 139, 4.

Anu-śāsana, am, n. instruction, direction, command, precept, RV. x, 32, 7, &c. **— para,** mfn. obedient.

Anu-śāsanīya or **-śāsya,** mfn. to be instructed.

Anu-śāsita, mfn. directed; defined by rule.

Anu-śāsitṛi, mfn. governing, instructing, Bhag.

Anu-śāsin, mfn. punishing, Vikr.

Anu-śishṭa, mfn. taught, revealed; adjudged, done conformably to law.

Anu-śishṭi, is, f. instruction, teaching, ordering.

Anu-śishya, ind. part. having ruled or ordered.

अनुशिक्ष् anu-śiksh, &c. See anu-√śak.

अनुशिख anu-śikha, as, m., N. of a Nāga or snake priest, PBr.

अनुशिवम् anu-śivam, ind. after Śiva.

अनुशिशु ánu-śiśu, us, f. followed by its young (as by a foal, &c.), ŚBr.; KātyŚr.

अनुशी anu-√1. śī, cl. 2. Ā. -śete, to sleep with, lie along or close, adhere closely to.

Anu-śaya, as, m. close connection as with a consequence, close attachment to any object; (in phil.) the consequence or result of an act (which clings to it and causes the soul after enjoying the temporary freedom from transmigration to enter other bodies); repentance, regret; hatred; ancient or intense enmity; (ī), f. a disease of the feet, a boil or abscess on the upper part; a boil on the head. **— vat,** mfn. = anu-śayin.

Anu-śayāna, mfn. repenting, regretting; (ā), f. a heroine or female character who regrets the loss of her lover (in dramas).

Anu-śayitavya, mfn. to be regretted.

Anu-śayin, mfn. having the consequence of an act, connected as with a consequence; devotedly attached to, faithful; repentant, penitent, regretful, sorry for; hating deeply.

Anu-śāyin, mfn. lying or extending along, Nir.

अनुशीलय anu-śīlaya, Nom. P. -śīlayati, to practise in imitation of, BhP.

Anu-śīlana, am, n. constant practice or study (of a science, &c.), repeated and devoted service.

Anu-śīlita, mfn. studied carefully, attended to.

अनुशुच् anu-√1. śuc, to mourn over, regret, bewail: Caus. P. -śocayati, to mourn over.

Anu-śoka, as, m. sorrow, repentance, regret, L.

Anu-śocaka, mfn. grieving, one who repents; occasioning repentance.

Anu-śocana, am, n. sorrow, repentance.

Anu-śocita, mfn. regretted, repented of.

Anu-śocin, mfn. regretful, sorrowful.

अनुशुष् anu-√śush, to dry up gradually, ŚBr. xiv, &c.; to become emaciated by gradual practice of religious austerity, Kauś.; to languish after another.

अनुशोभिन् anu-śobhin, mfn. shining.

अनुश्रथ् anu-√śrath, cl. 6. P. -śrinthati, to untie, TS.: Caus. P. (aor. Subj. 2. sg. -śiśrathaḥ) to frighten [BR.; 'to abolish,' Sāy.], RV. iv, 32, 22: Ā. -śrathayate, to annihilate or soften the effect of, RV. v, 59, 1.

अनुश्रु anu-√śru, cl. 5. P. -śṛinoti, to hear repeatedly (especially what is handed down in the Veda): Desid. Ā. -śuśrūshate, to obey.

Anu-śrava, as, m., Vedic tradition (acquired by repeated hearing), L.

Anu-śruta, mfn. handed down by Vedic tradition.

अनुश्वस् anu-√śvas, to breathe continually.

अनुषच् anu-shac (√sac), to adhere to, keep at the side of, RV. &c.

अनुषञ्ज् anu-shañj (√sañj), cl. 1. Ā. or Pass. -shajjate, -shajyate, to cling to, adhere, be attached to.

Anu-shak or **anu-shaṭ,** ind. in continuous order, one after the other, (gaṇa svar-ādi, q. v.); cf. ānushák.

Anu-shakta, mfn. closely connected with, supplied from something preceding.

Anu-shaṅga, as, m. close adherence, connection, association, conjunction, coalition, commixture; connection of word with word, or effect with cause;

necessary consequence, the connection of a subsequent with a previous act; (in the Dhātupāṭha) the nasals connected with certain roots ending in consonants (as in *trimph*); tenderness, compassion, L.

Anu-shaṅgika, mfn. consequent, following as a necessary result; connected with, adhering to, inherent, concomitant.

Anu-shaṅgin, mfn. addicted or attached to, connected with, or 'common, prevailing,' Mn. vii, 52.

Anu-shañjana, *am,* n. connection with what follows, concord; grammatical relation.

Anu-shañjanīya, mfn. to be connected, supplied.

अनुषण्ड *anushaṇḍa, as* or *am,* m. or n., N. of a place or country, (gaṇa *kacchâdi,* q. v.)

अनुषत्य *anu-shatyá,* mfn. being conformable to truth (*satya*), RV. iii, 26, 1.

अनुषिच् *anu-shic* (√*sic*), Ved. to pour upon or into; to drip upon.

Anu-shiktá, mfn. dripped upon, TS.

Anu-sheka, *as,* m. or **-shecana,** *am,* n. rewatering or sprinkling over again, L.

अनुषिध् *anu-shidh* (√*sidh*), Intens. (p. *-séshidhat*) to bring back along the path, RV. i, 23, 15.

अनुष्टब्ध *anu-shṭabdha,* mfn. (√*stambh*), (used for an etymology) raised, KaushBr.

अनुष्टु *anu-shṭu* (√*stu*), to praise, RV.

Ánu-shṭuti, *is,* f. praise, RV.

अनुष्टुभ् 1. *anu-shṭubh* (√*stubh*), to praise after, to follow in praising, Nir.

2. **Anu-shṭúbh,** *p* (nom. °*shṭúk,* TS.), f. following in praise or invocation; a kind of metre consisting of four Pādas or quarter-verses of eight syllables each (according to the DaivBr., quoted in Nir. vii, 12, so called because it *anushṭobhati,* i. e. follows with its praise the Gāyatrī, which consists of three Pādas), RV. x, 130, 4, &c.; (in later metrical systems, the Anushṭubh constitutes a whole class of metres, consisting of four times eight syllables); hence the number eight; speech, Sarasvatī, L.; (mfn.), praising, RV. x, 124, 9. **Anushṭúp-karmíṇa,** mfn. being performed with an *anushṭubh* verse, ŚBr. **Anushṭúp-chandas,** mfn. having *anushṭubh* for metre, MaitrS. **Anushṭup-śiras** or **-śīrshan** [AitBr.], mfn. having an *anushṭubh* verse at the head. **Anushṭub-garbhā,** f. a metre (like that in RV. i, 187, 1) of the class Ushṇih, RPrāt.

Anu-shṭobhana, *am,* n. praising after, DaivBr.

अनुष्ट्र *an-ushṭra, as,* m. no camel, i.e. a bad camel.

अनुष्ठा *anu-shṭhā* (√*sthā*), to stand near or by; to follow out; to carry out, attend to; to perform, do, practise; to govern, rule, superintend; to appoint: Pass. *-shṭhīyate,* to be done; to be followed out: Desid. *-tishṭhāsati,* to be desirous of doing, &c.

Anu-tishṭhamāna, mfn. following out, carrying out, performing, attending to.

Anu-shṭhá, mfn. standing after, i.e. in succession, RV. i, 54, 10.

Anu-shṭhātavya, mfn. to be accomplished.

Anu-shṭhātṛí, *tā,* m. the undertaker of any work, AV. &c.

Anu-shṭhāna, *am,* n. carrying out, undertaking; doing, performance; religious practice; acting in conformity to; (*ī*), f. performance, action, Kauś. **-krama,** m. the order of performing religious ceremonies. **-śarīra,** n. (in Sāṅkhya phil.) the body which is intermediate between the *liṅga-* or *sūkshma-* and the *sthūla-śarīra* (generally called the *adhishṭhāna-śarīra,* q. v.) **-smāraka,** mf(*ikā*)n. reminding of religious ceremonies.

Anu-shṭhāpaka, mf(*ikā*)n. causing to perform.

Anu-shṭhāpana, *am,* n. the causing to perform an act.

Anu-shṭhāyin, mfn. doing, performing an act.

Anu-shṭhi, *is,* f. 'being near, present, at hand,' only inst. *anu-shṭhyā,* ind. immediately, ŚBr. &c.

Anu-shṭhita, mfn. done, practised; effected, executed, accomplished; followed, observed; done conformably.

Anu-shṭhú or **-shṭhuyá,** presently, immediately.

Anu-shṭheya, mfn. to be effected, done or accomplished; to be observed; to be proved or established.

Anu-shṭhyā. See *anu-shṭhi.*

अनुष्ण *an-ushṇa,* mf(*ā*)n. not hot, cold; apathetic; lazy, L.; (*am*), n. the blue lotus, Nymphæa Cærulea; (*ā*), f., N. of a river. **-gu,** m. 'having cold rays,' the moon. **-vallikā,** f. the plant Nila-dūrbā. **Anushṇâśīta,** mfn. neither hot nor cold.

An-ushṇaka, mfn. not hot, cold; chilly, &c.

अनुष्यन्द् *anu-shyand* (√*syand*), Ved. Inf. *-shyáde* [RV. ii, 13, 2] and Caus. *-syandayádhyai* [RV. iv, 22, 7], to run along: *-syandate* & *-shyandate* with a differentiation in meaning like that in *abhi-shyand,* q. v., Pāṇ. viii, 3, 72.

Anu-shyandá, *as,* m. a hind-wheel, ŚBr.

अनुष्वधम् *anu-shvadhám* (fr. *sva-dhā*), ind. according to one's will, voluntary, RV.

अनुष्वापम् *anu-shvâpam,* ind. (√*svap*), continuing to sleep, RV. viii, 97, 3.

अनुसंया *anu-saṃ-√yā,* to go up and down (as guards); to go to or towards.

अनुसंरक्त *anu-saṃrakta,* mfn. attached or devoted to.

अनुसंरभ् *anu-saṃ-√rabh,* Ā. to catch hold of, RV. x, 103, 6; to catch hold of mutually, AV.

अनुसंवत्सरम् *anu-saṃvatsaram,* ind. year after year.

अनुसंवह् *anu-saṃ-√vah,* to draw or run by the side of, AV.; to convey along, TBr.

अनुसंवा *anu-saṃ-√2. vā,* to blow towards in order, TBr.

अनुसंविचर् *anu-saṃ-vi-√car,* to visit successively, make the round of, MBh.

अनुसंविद् *anu-saṃ-√1. vid,* to know together with, or in consequence of (something else), AV. x, 7, 17 & 26.

अनुसंविश् *anu-saṃ-√viś,* to retire for sleep after, AV.; TBr. &c.

अनुसंवीत *anu-saṃ-vīta,* mfn. (√*vye*), wrapped up, covered, MBh.

अनुसंव्रज् *anu-saṃ-√vraj,* to go after, follow, ĀśvŚr. &c.

अनुसंसृ *anu-saṃ-√sṛi,* Caus. P. *-sārayati,* to cause to follow, to pass or go on before, MBh.

अनुसंसृप् *anu-saṃ-√sṛip,* to creep or crawl after, ŚBr.; TBr.

Anu-saṃ-sarpam, ind. creeping after, KātyŚr.

अनुसंसृष्ट *anu-saṃ-sṛishṭa,* mfn. joined to (instr.), BhP.

अनुसंस्था *anu-saṃ-√sthā,* P. to follow (a road), BhP.: Ā. to become finished after, ŚBr.; AitBr.: Caus. P. *-sthāpayati,* to encourage, R.

Anu-saṃ-sthita, mfn. following; dead or deceased after (another), Ragh.

अनुसंस्पृश् *anu-saṃ-√spṛiś,* Caus to cause to touch after, ŚBr.

अनुसंस्मृ *anu-saṃ-√smṛi,* to remember, to long for (the dead or absent).

अनुसंस्यन्द् *anu-saṃ-√syand,* Intens. (p. nom. m. *ánu saṃ-sánishyadat*) to run after, VS. ix, 14; (cf. Pāṇ. vii, 4, 65.)

अनुसंहितम् *anu-saṃhitam,* ind. according to the Saṃhitā text, RPrāt.

अनुसंहृ *anu-saṃ-√hṛi,* to drag (the foot), Kauś.; to compress, reduce a subject, Lāṭy.

अनुसंकल् *anu-saṃ-√2. kal,* to drive or convey along or after, ĀśvGṛ.

अनुसंक्रम् *anu-saṃ-√kram,* to walk or go up to, to reach, AV.

अनुसंख्या *anu-saṃ-√khyā,* Caus. P. *-khyāpayati,* to cause to observe, show, ŚBr.

अनुसंग्रह् *anu-saṃ-√grah,* to oblige, favour; to salute by laying hold of the feet.

अनुसंचर् *anu-saṃ-√car,* to walk along side, to follow, join; to visit; to pursue, seek after; to penetrate, traverse, cross; to become assimilated: Caus. P. *-cārayati,* to join, become identified or assimilated with.

Anu-saṃ-cará, mfn. following or accompanying (with acc.), TBr.

अनुसंचिन्त् *anu-saṃ-√cint,* to meditate.

अनुसंज्वर् *anu-saṃ-√jvar,* to feel distressed after (another), BṛĀrUp. (*anu-saṃ-car,* ŚBr. xiv); to be troubled, become envious.

अनुसंतन् *anu-saṃ-√tan,* to overspread, diffuse, extend everywhere; to join on, continue.

Anu-sáṃ-tati, *is,* f. continuation, MaitrS.

अनुसंतॄ *anu-saṃ-√tṝi,* to carry to the end, go on (in spinning), AV. vi, 122, 1; ĀśvŚr.

अनुसंदह् *anu-saṃ-√dah,* to burn up along the whole length, AV.

अनुसंदिश् *anu-saṃ-√diś,* to assign, to make over.

अनुसंदृश् *anu-saṃ-√dṛiś* (ind. p. *-dṛiśya*) to consider successively, MBh. xii, 12024.

अनुसंधा *anu-saṃ-√dhā,* to explore, ascertain, inspect, plan, arrange; to calm, compose, set in order; to aim at.

Anu-saṃdhātavya, mfn. to be explored, to be investigated, to be looked after, &c.

Anu-saṃdhāna, *am,* n. investigation, inquiry, searching into, close inspection, setting in order, arranging, planning; aiming at; plan, scheme, congruous or suitable connection; (in the Vaiśeshika phil.) the fourth step in a syllogism (i. e. the application).

Anu-saṃdhānin, mfn. investigating, searching, skilful at concerting or carrying out schemes.

Anu-saṃdhāyin, mfn. id.

Anu-saṃdheya, mfn. to be investigated, worthy of inquiry or scrutiny, &c.

अनुसन्ध्यम् *anu-sandhyam,* ind. evening after evening, every twilight.

अनुसमय *anu-samaya.* See *anu-sam-√i.*

अनुसमश् *anu-sam-√1. aś,* to overtake, reach, ŚBr.

अनुसमस् *anu-sam-√2. as, -sám-asyati,* to add further, ŚBr.

अनुसमाचर् *anu-sam-ā-√car,* to carry out, accomplish, BhP.

अनुसमाधा *anu-sam-ā-√dhā,* to calm, compose.

अनुसमाप् *anu-sam-√āp,* Caus. P. to complete or accomplish further or subsequently, KātyŚr.

Anu-samāpana, *am,* n. regular completion, KātyŚr.

अनुसमारभ् *anu-sam-ā-√rabh,* Ā. to place one's self in order after, cling to (acc.), TS.; TBr.: Caus. Ā. (impf. *-ârambhayata*) to cause to cling to one's self (loc.), TS.

अनुसमारुह् *anu-sam-ā-√ruh,* to rise after, TBr.

अनुसमाहृ *anu-sam-ā-√hṛi,* to join or bring in order again, ChUp.

अनुसमि *anu-sam-√i,* cl. 2. P. *-eti,* to visit conjointly or successively; to join in following or being guided by; to join, become assimilated with.

Anu-samaya, *as,* m. regular connection (as of words), Nyāyad. &c.

अनुसमीक्ष् *anu-sam-√īksh,* to keep in view, have in view, ŚBr.

अनुसमुद्रम् *anu-samudram,* ind. along the sea, Pāṇ. iv, 3, 10.

अनुसम्प्रया *anu-sam-pra-√yā,* to go towards, AV. xi, 1, 36.

अनुसम्प्राप् *anu-sam-prâp* (√*āp*), to arrive, reach, get.

Anu-samprâpta, mfn. arrived, come.

अनुसम्बद्ध **anu-sambaddha**, mfn. (√*bandh*), connected with, accompanied by.

अनुसम्भिद् *anu-sam-√bhid*, to bring into contact, combine, Kāṭh.

अनुसम्भू *anu-sam-√bhū*, to be produced after, proceed after, ŚBr.

अनुसम्मन् *anu-sam-√man*, to approve, MBh.

अनुसवनम् *anu-savanám*, ind. at every sacrifice, TBr. &c.; constantly, BhP.

अनुसातम् *anu-sātam*, ind. according to delight.

अनुसानु *anu-sānu*, ind. along a table-land or summit, from ridge to ridge.

अनुसाम *anu-sāma*, mfn. at every Sāman-verse (?), Pāṇ. v, 4, 75.

अनुसायम् *anu-sāyam*, ind. evening after evening, every evening, (gaṇa *parimukhâdi*, q.v.)

अनुसार *anu-sāra*, *anu-sārin*, &c. See under *anu-√sṛi* below.

अनुसिच् *anu-√sic*. See *anu-√shic*.

अनुसिद्ध *anu-siddha*, mfn. (√3. *sidh*), gradually effected or realized, BhP.

अनुसीतम् *anu-sītám*, ind. along the furrow, TS.; (gaṇa *parimukhâdi*, q.v.)

अनुसीरम् *anu-sīram*, ind. along the plough, (gaṇa *parimukhâdi*, q.v.)

अनुसू *anu-sū*, *ūs*, m., N. of a work, Pāṇ Comm.

अनुसूचक *anu-sūcaka*, mf(*ikā*)n. (√*sūc*), indicative of, pointing out.

Anu-sūcana, *am*, n. pointing out, indication.

अनुसूपम् *anu-sūpam*, ind. in every condiment.

अनुसृ *anu-√sṛi*, to go after: Caus. P. *-sārayati*, to pursue.

Anu-sara, mf(*ī*)n. following, a companion.

Anu-saraṇa, *am*, n. following, going after; tracking, conformity to, consequence of; custom, habit, usage.

Anu-sāra, *as*, m. going after, following; custom, usage; nature, natural state or condition of anything; prevalence, currency; received or established authority, especially of codes of law; accordance, conformity to usage; consequence, result; (*eṇa*), or **-tas**, ind. conformably to.

Anu-sāraka or **anu-sārin**, mfn. following, attendant on, according or conformable to; penetrating, scrutinizing, investigating.

Anu-sāryaka, *am*, n. a fragrant substance.

Anu-sṛita, mfn. followed, conformed to.

Anu-sṛiti, *is*, f. going after, following, conforming to; N. of a woman, (gaṇa *kalyāṇy-ādi*, q.v.)

अनुसृज् *anu-√sṛij*, to dismiss, let go, RV. x, 66, 8, &c.: P. Ā. *-sṛijati*, °*te*, to create successively, ŚBr. &c.: Pass. to be created in succession to, TS.

Anu-sṛishṭa, mfn. created in succession, VS.

अनुसृप् *anu-√sṛip*, to glide after or towards, to approach.

Anu-sarpa, *as*, m. a serpent-like being, AV.

अनुसेव् *anu-√sev*, to practise, observe.

Anu-sevin, mfn. practising, observing, habitually addicted to.

अनुसैन्य *anu-sainya*, *am*, n. the rear of an army, L.

अनुसोमम् *anu-somam*, ind. according to the (practice with the) Soma, as with the Soma, KātyŚr.

अनुस्कन्दम् *anu-skandam*, ind. having gone into in succession, Pāṇ. iii, 4, 56, Sch.

अनुस्तरण *anu-staraṇa*, *as*, m. (√*stṛi*), an animal which is fit to be chosen as a secondary victim; *anu-stáraṇī*, f. the cow sacrificed at the funeral ceremony, TS. &c.

अनुस्तोत्र *anu-stotra*, *am*, n. 'praising after,' N. of a treatise relating to the Sāma-veda.

अनुस्नेहम् *anu-sneham*, ind. after (adding) oil, Suśr.

अनुस्पष्ट *ánu-spashṭa*. See *anu-√paś*.

अनुस्पृश् *anu-√spṛiś*, to touch, extend to, RV. iv, 4, 2.

अनुस्फुर् *anu-√sphur*, to whizz towards, RV. vi, 67, 11.

Anu-sphurá, mfn. whizzing (as an arrow), AV.

अनुस्मृ *anu-√smṛi*, to remember, recollect: Caus. P. *-smārayati* or *-smarayati*, to remind (with acc.), Kir. v, 14.

Anu-smaraṇa, *am*, n. remembering, repeated recollection.

Anu-smṛita, mfn. remembered.

Anu-smṛiti, *is*, f. cherished recollection, recalling some idea to the exclusion of all others.

अनुस्यूत *anu-syūta*, mfn. (√*siv*), sewed consecutively, strung together or connected regularly and uninterruptedly.

अनुस्रयामन् *án-usra-yāman*, *ā*, m. not going out during daylight, RV. iv, 32, 24.

अनुस्वान *anu-svāna*, *as*, m. sounding conformably, Sāh.

अनुस्वार *anu-svāra*, *as*, m. (√*svṛi*), after-sound, the nasal sound which is marked by a dot above the line, and which always belongs to a preceding vowel. **-vat**, mfn. having the Anusvāra. **-vyavâya**, m. separation between two sounds caused by an Anusvāra. **Anusvārâgama**, m. an augment consisting in the addition of an Anusvāra.

अनुह *anuha*, *as*, m., N. of a son of Vibhrātra and father of Brahma-datta, VS.

अनुहव *anu-havá*. See *anu-√hve*.

अनुहा *anu-√2. hā*, cl. 3. Ā. *-jihite*, to run after, catch, AV. &c.; to follow, join, RV.

अनुहुंकृ *anu-huṃ-√kṛi*, to roar in imitation of.

अनुहुर्छ् *anu-√hurch*, to fall down after another, Kāṭh.

अनुहृ *anu-√hṛi*, to imitate; to resemble: Ā. *-harate*, to take after (one's parents).

Anu-haraṇa, *am*, n. or **-hāra**, *as*, m. imitation; resemblance.

Anu-harat, mfn. imitating; (*an*), m., N. of a man, (gaṇa *anuśatikâdi*, q.v.)

Anu-haramāṇa, mfn. imitating.

Anu-hāraka, mf(*ikā*)n. imitating.

Anu-hārya, mfn. to be imitated; (*as*), m. = *anv-ā-hārya*, L.

अनुहोड *anu-hoḍa*, *as*, m. a cart(?), (gaṇa *anuśatikâdi*, q.v.)

अनुह्राद *anu-hrāda* or *-hlāda*, *as*, m., N. of a son of Hiraṇya-kaśipu, Hariv.

अनुह्वे *anu-√hve*, to call again, call after, call back, RV.; AV.: Intens. *-johavīti*, to call repeatedly, AV.

Anu-havá, *as*, m. inviting, stirring up, AV.

अनूक *ánūka*, *as*, *am*, m. n. (√*añc* with *anu*), the backbone, spine; the back part of the altar; a former state of existence; (*am*), n. race, family, L.; peculiarity of race, disposition, character, VarBṛS. &c.; (*ā*), f., N. of an Apsaras, Hariv.

Anūkyà (3, 4), mfn. belonging to the backbone, ŚBr.; backbone, RV. x, 163, 2; AV.

अनूकाश *anū-kāśá*, *as*, m. (√*kāś*), reflection (of light), clearness, VS.; TS. &c.; regard, reference, AitBr.

अनूक्ष् *anûksh* (√1. *uksh*), (p. Ā. *ánu ... ukshámāṇa*; perf. *ánu ... vavâksha*) to sprinkle, bedew, RV. iii, 7, 6 & vi, 66, 4.

अनूचीन *anūcīná*, mfn. (fr. *anv-añc*), coming after, successive, RV. iv, 54, 2; Śulb. **-garbhá**, mfn. born in successive order, ŚBr. **Anūcīnâhám**, ind. on successive days, ŚBr.

1. **Anûcyà**, *am*, n. elbow-piece of a seat, AV. &c.

अनूच्यते *anûcyate*, Pass. of *anu-√vac*, q.v., p. 38, col. 1.

Anûkta, mfn. spoken after, recited after; occurring in the (sacred) text; studied; (*am*), n. study.

Anûkti, *is*, f. mentioning after, repeated mention, repetition by way of explanation; study of the Veda. **-tva**, n. state of requiring repetition or explanation.

Anûcāná, mfn. one so well versed in the Vedas and Vedâṅgas as to be able to repeat them; one who repeats his lesson after his master; devoted to learning; well-behaved (√*uc*).

2. **Anûcya**, mfn. to be repeated or learnt; (cf. *araṇye-'nûcya*.)

अनूज्जि *anûj-ji* (*anu-ud-√ji*), (aor. Subj. 1. sg. *ánûj-jesham*) to be victorious after, VS. ii, 15; KātyŚr.

अनूढ *an-ūḍha*, mfn. (√*vah*), not borne, not carried; (*ā*), f. an unmarried woman. **-māna**, mfn. bashful. **Anūḍhā-gamana**, n. 'going after an unmarried woman,' fornication. **Anūḍhā-bhrātṛi**, m. the brother of an unmarried woman; the brother of the concubine of a king.

अनूति *án-ūti*, *is*, f. no help, RV. vi, 29, 6.

अनूत्क्रम् *anût-√kram*, to go up or out after, ŚBr.

अनूत्था *anûtthā* (√*sthā*), *anûttishṭhati*, to rise after, VS. &c.

अनूत्पत् *anût-√pat*, to fly up after another (acc.), raise one's self into the air, jump up afterwards.

अनूत्पा 1. *anût-√1. pā*, *-pibati*, to drink up or empty by drinking after another, ŚBr.

अनूत्पा 2. *anût-√5. pā* (3. pl. *-pipate*) to rise along, TBr.; (cf. *ut-√5. pā*.)

अनूत्सारम् *anût-sāram*, ind. while leaving a place or retiring successively, AitBr.

अनूत्सृज् *anût-√sṛij*, to dismiss towards, TS.

अनूद् *anûd* (√*ud*), (impf. 3. pl. *anv-aundan*) to wet along, Kāṭh.

अनूदक *an-ūdaka*, *am*, n. (metri causa for *an-udaka*), want of water, aridity, R. i, 20, 16.

अनूदस् *anûd-√2. as*, *-asyati*, to toss up behind or after, ŚBr.

अनूदि *anûd-√i*, to go up or out after (another), AV. &c.

अनूदित *anûdita*, mfn. (√*vad*), spoken after, spoken according to. See also *anu-√vad*.

1. **Anûdya**, mfn. to be spoken to afterwards.

2. **Anûdya**, ind. having said afterwards or in reply.

Anûdyamāna, mfn. spoken in reply to or according to.

अनूदे *anûd-ê* (*-ā-√i*), cl. 2. P. *anûd-aiti*, to rise or come up after, ŚBr. &c.

अनूदृंह् *anûd-√dṛiṇh* (Pot. 3. pl. *anûd-dṛiṇheyuḥ*) 'to fix or fasten during,' keep waiting until (*ā*), ŚBr.

अनूद्देश *anûddeśa*, *as*, m. (√*diś*), describing, mentioning according to or conformably with, Sāh.

अनूद्रु *anûd-√2. dru*, to run after (acc.), Kāṭh.

अनूद्धा *anûd-dhā* (√*2. hā*), to set off or start after, TBr.

अनूद्धृ *anûd-dhṛi* (√*hṛi*), to take out from subsequently, TS.

अनूद्वा *anûd-√2. vā*, *-vāti*, to disperse or dissipate by following (the wind *vāyum*), ŚBr.

अनूधस् *an-ūdhás*, *ās*, f. udderless, RV. x, 115, 1.

अनून *án-ūna*, mf(*ā*)n. or *an-ūnaka* [L.], mfn. not less, not inferior to (abl.), Ragh.; whole, entire; having full power; (*ā*), f., N. of an Apsaras, Hariv. **-guru**, mfn. of undiminished weight, very heavy. **-varcas** (*ánūna-*), mfn. having full splendour, RV. x, 140, 2.

अनूनी *anūn-√nī*, cl. 1. P. *-nayati*, to take out and fill after another, TBr.; ŚBr.

अनूप *anūpá*, mfn. (fr. 2. *áp*, q.v., with *anu*), situated near the water, watery, L.; (*ás*), m. a watery country, Mn. &c.; pond, RV.; bank of a river; a buffalo (cf. *ānūpa*), L.; N. of a Ṛishi, teacher of the Sāma-veda. **-ja**, n. growing near the water, VarBṛS.; ginger. **-deśa**, m. a marshy country. **-prāya**, mfn. marshy. **-vilāsa**, m., N. of a work.

Anūpyà (4), mfn. being in ponds or bogs (as water), AV.

अनूपदस् *anūpa-√das*, to fail (or become extinct) after (acc.), PBr.

अनूपधा *anūpa-√dhā* (generally P.), to place upon, pile up after or in addition to, TS.; ŚBr.

अनूपधृ *anūpa-√dhṛi*, Caus. *-dhārayati*, to hold towards in addition to, Lāṭy.

अनूपविश् *anūpa-√viś*, to sit down in order, ĀśvŚr.; Lāṭy.; to lie down or incline the body (said of a parturient animal), ŚBr.

अनूपसदम् *anūpasadam*, ind. at every Upasad (q.v.), KātyŚr.

अनूपस्था *anūpa-√sthā*, Ā. to approach in order, ŚBr.; AitBr.

अनूबन्ध्य *anū-bándhya*, mfn. to be fastened (as a sacrificial animal) for slaughtering, ŚBr. &c.

अनूयाज *anū-yājá* = *anu-yājá*, q.v., TS.

अनूराध *anū-rādhá*, mfn. causing welfare, happiness, AV.; (*ás*), m. f. plur. = *anu-rādhās*, q.v., TS.; TBr.; Kāṭh.

अनूरु *an-ūru*, mfn. thighless; (*us*), m. the charioteer of the sun, the dawn, Rājat. &c. **-sārathi**, m. whose charioteer is Anūru, i.e. the sun, Śiś.

अनूरुध् *anū-rúdh*, mfn. = *anu-rudh*, q.v., RV. iii, 55, 5.

अनूर्जित *an-ūrjita*, mfn. not strong, weak; not proud.

अनूर्ध्व *an-ūrdhva*, mfn. not high, low. **-bhās** (*án-ūrdhva-*), mfn. one whose splendour does not rise, who lights no sacred fires, RV. v, 77, 4.

A'n-ūrdhvam-bhāvuka, n. not rising upwards, not reaching the heaven, TS.

अनूर्मि *án-ūrmi*, mfn. 'not waving or fluctuating,' inviolable, RV. viii, 24, 22.

अनूला *anūlā*, f., N. of a river in Kaśmīra.

अनूवृज् *anū-vṛíj*, only du. *-vṛíjau*, m. f. a part of the body near the ribs, AV. ix, 4, 12.

अनूषर *an-ūshara*, mf(*ā*)n. not salted, not saline, ĀśvGṛ.; Hcat.

अनूषित *anūshita*, mfn. (√5. *vas* with *anu*), living near another, Pāṇ. iii, 4, 72, Sch.

अनूष्मपर *an-ūshma-para*, mfn. (in Gr.) not followed by a sibilant.

अनूह *an-ūha*, mfn. thoughtless, careless.

An-ūhya, mfn. inconceivable, MaitrUp.

अनृक्क *an-ṛik-ka*. See *an-ṛíc* below.

अनृक्षर *an-ṛiksharā́*, mfn. thornless (as a path or a couch), RV.

अनृच् *an-ṛíc* [RV. x, 105, 8, &c.] or *an-ṛica* [Mn.], mfn. not containing a verse from the Ṛig-veda, hymnless, not conversant with the Ṛig-veda; (*an-ṛicám*), ind. not in conformity with the Ṛic, MaitrS.

An-ṛik-ka (or **an-ṛic-ka**), mfn. containing no Ṛic, Pāṇ. v, 4, 74, Kāś.

अनृजु *án-ṛiju*, mfn. not straight, crooked, perverse, wicked, RV. iv, 3, 13, &c.

अनृण *an-ṛiṇá*, mf(*ā*)n. free from debt. **-tā**, f. or **-tva**, n. freedom from debt.

An-ṛiṇin, mfn. unindebted, free from debt.

An-ṛiṇya-tā, f. freedom from debt, R.

अनृत *án-ṛita*, mf(*ā*)n. not true, false; (*am*), n. falsehood, lying, cheating; agriculture, L. **-deva** (*ánṛita-*), m. one whose gods are not true, RV. vii, 104, 14. **-dvish**, mfn. persecuting untruth, RV. vii, 66, 13. **-maya**, mfn. full of untruth, false. **-vadana**, n. speaking falsehood, lying. **-vāc** [AV. &c.], **-vādin**, mfn. speaking untruth. **-vrata**, mfn. false to vows or engagements. **Anṛitâkhyāna**, n. telling a falsehood. **Anṛitâbhisandha**, mfn. id., ChUp.

Anṛitin, mfn. telling untruths, lying, a liar.

अनृतु *an-ṛitu*, *us*, m. unfit season; (*ú*), ind. unseasonably, MaitrS. **-kanyā**, f. a girl before menstruation. **-pā** (*án-ṛitu-*), mfn. not drinking in time, RV. iii, 53, 8.

अनृशंस *a-nṛiśaṇsa*, mf(*ā*)n. not cruel, mild. **-tā**, f. mildness, kindness.

अनेक *an-eka*, mfn. not one, many, much; separated. **-kāma** (*áneka-*), mfn. having many wishes, ŚBr. **-kālam**, ind. a long time, for a long time. **-kālâvadhi**, ind. long since. **-kṛit**, m. 'doing much,' N. of Śiva. **-gotra**, m. having more families than one, i.e. two, belonging to two families (or to one as an adopted son). **-cara**, mfn. gregarious. **-citta-mantra**, m. one whose counsels are many-minded. **-ja**, mfn. born more than once; (*as*), m. a bird, L. **-tā**, f. or **-tva**, n. muchness, manifold condition. **-tra**, ind. in many places. **-dharma-kathā**, f. different exposition of the law. **-dhā**, ind. in various ways, often. **-dhā-prayoga**, m. using repeatedly. **-pa**, mfn. 'drinking oftener than once,' an elephant (because he drinks with his trunk and with his mouth), Ragh. **-bhārya**, mfn. having more wives than one. **-mukha**, mfn. having several faces, having different ways. **-yuddha-vijayin**, m. victorious in many battles. **-randhra**, mfn. having many holes or weaknesses or troubles. **-rūpa**, mf(*ā*)n. multiform; of various kinds or sorts; fickle, of variable mind. **-locana**, m. 'having several (three) eyes,' N. of Śiva. **-vacana**, n. the plural number. **-varṇa**, (in algebra compounded with various words to denote) many unknown quantities (colours representing *x*, *y*, *z*, &c., e.g. *aneka-varṇa-guṇana*, multiplication of many unknown quantities). **-vāram**, ind. many times, repeatedly. **-vidha**, mfn. of many kinds, in different ways, various. **-śapha**, mfn. cloven-hoofed, Pāṇ. i, 2, 73, Comm. **-śabda**, mfn. expressed by several words, synonymous. **-śas**, ind. in great numbers, several times, repeatedly. **Anekâkāra**, mfn. multiform. **Anekâkshara**, mfn. polysyllabic, having more than one syllable. **Anekâgra**, mfn. engaged in various pursuits. **Anekâc**, mfn. having more than one vowel or syllable (*ac* in Gr. being the technical term for vowel). **Anekârtha**, mfn. having more than one meaning (as a word). **Anekârtha-dhvani-mañjarī**, f. and **anekârtha-saṃgraha**, m., N. of two works on words. **Anekâl**, mfn. consisting of more than one letter (*al* being the technical term for letter). **Anekâśraya** or **anekâśrita**, mfn. (in Vaiśeshika phil.) dwelling or abiding in more than one.

A'n-ekākin, mfn. not alone, accompanied by, ŚBr.

An-ekānta, mfn. not alone and excluding every other, uncertain. **-tva**, n. uncertainty. **-vāda**, m. scepticism. **-vādin**, m. a sceptic; a Jaina, an Arhat of the Jainas.

Anekī-karaṇa, *am*, n. making manifold.

Anekī-bhavat, mfn. being manifold, i.e. divided in two.

Anekīya, mfn. having several, (gaṇa *utkarâdi*, q.v.)

अनेजत् *an-ejat*, mfn. (√*ej*), not moving, immovable.

अनेड *an-eḍa*, *as*, m. (*an* being an expletive or denoting comparison), stupid, foolish, L.

An-eḍa-mūka, mfn. deaf and dumb, L.; blind, L.; wicked, fraudulent, L.

अनेद्य *á-nedya* (4), mfn. (√*nid*), not to be blamed, RV.

अनेन 1. *an-enā́*, mfn. without stags, RV. vi, 66, 7; (cf. *enī́*.)

अनेनस् *an-enás*, mfn. blameless, sinless, not liable to error, RV. &c.; N. of various personages.

An-enasyá, *am*, n. freedom from fault, sin, ŚBr.

अनेमन् *á-neman*, mfn. = *praśasya* (to be praised), Naigh.

अनेव *án-eva*, ind. otherwise, AV. xvi, 7, 4.

अनेहस् *an-ehás*, mfn. (√*īh*), without a rival, incomparable, unattainable; unmenaced, unobstructed; RV.; (*ā*), m. time, Bālar.; BhP.

अनैकान्त *an-aikānta*, mfn. (fr. *ekānta*), variable, unsteady; (in logic) occasional, as a cause not invariably attended by the same effects.

An-aikāntika, mfn. unsteady, variable, having many objects or purposes; (*am*), n. (in Vaiśeshika phil.) the fallacy of undistributed middle. **-tva**, n. unsteadiness, uncertainty, Nyāyad.

An-aikya, *am*, n. (*eka*), want of oneness, plurality, the existence of many; want of union, anarchy.

अनैपुण *a-naipuṇa* or *a-naipuṇya*, *am*, n. unskilfulness, Pāṇ. vii, 3, 30; (see *ānaipuṇa*.)

अनैश्वर्य *an-aiśvarya*, *am*, n. 'non-power,' weakness, Pāṇ. vii, 3, 30; (see *ānaiśvarya*.)

अनो *ano*, ind. no, not, L.

अनोकशायिन् *an-oka-śāyin*, *ī*, m. not sleeping in a house (as a beggar), L.

An-oka-ha, *as*, m. 'not quitting his home or his place,' a tree, Ragh. &c.

अनोंकृत *an-oṃ-kṛita*, mfn. not accompanied by the holy syllable *om*, Mn. ii, 74.

अनोरथ *ano-ratha*, *ās*, m. pl. waggon (*anas*) and chariot, AitBr.

Ano-vāhá, mfn. driving a waggon or carriage, TS.; ŚBr.

Ano-vāhyà, mfn. to be driven on a carriage, TS.; (*am*), ind. in waggon-loads, KātyŚr.

अनौचित्य *an-aucitya*, *am*, n. unfitness, Sāh.

अनौजस्य *an-aujasya*, *am*, n. want of vigour, Sāh.

अनौद्धत्य *an-auddhatya*, *am*, n. freedom from haughtiness, Sāh.; not standing high (said of the water of a river), Kir.

अनौपम्य *an-aupamya*, mfn. unparalleled.

अनौरस *an-aurasa*, *as*, m. not one's own son, adopted.

अन्त् *ant*, cl. 1. P. *antati*, to bind, L.; (cf. √*and*, *īnt*.)

अन्त *ánta*, *as*, m. end, limit, boundary, term; end of a texture; end, conclusion; end of life, death, destruction (in these latter senses sometimes neut.); a final syllable, termination; last word of a compound; pause, settlement, definite ascertainment, certainty; whole amount; border, outskirt (e.g. *grāmânte*, in the outskirts of the village); nearness, proximity, presence; inner part, inside; condition, nature; (*e*), loc. c. in the end, at last; in the inside; (*am*), ind. as far as (ifc., e.g. *udakântam*, as far as the water); (mfn.), near, handsome, agreeable, L. [cf. Goth. *andeis*, Theme *andja*; Germ. *Ende*; Eng. *end*: with *anta* are also compared the Gk. ἄντα, ἀντί; Lat. *ante*; the Goth. *anda* in *anda-vaurd*, &c.; and the Germ. *ent*, e.g. in *entsagen*]. **-kara**, **-karaṇa**, **-kārin**, mfn. causing death, mortal, destructive. **-kāla**, m. time of death, death. **-kṛit**, mfn. making an end; (*t*), m. death. **-kṛid-daśā**, *ās*, f. pl., N. of the eighth of the twelve sacred Aṅga texts of the Jainas (containing ten chapters). **-ga**, mfn. going to the end, thoroughly conversant with. **-gata** (*ánta-*), mfn. gone to the end; being at the end of; thoroughly penetrating, TS. **-gati** (*ánta-*) [ŚBr.] or **-gāmin**, mfn. going to the end, perishing. **-gamana**, n. the act of going to the end, finishing; going to the end of life, dying. **-cara**, mfn. going to the frontiers, walking about the frontiers, R. **-ja**, mfn. last born. **-jāti**, see *antya-jāti*. **-tás**, ind. from the end, from the term; lastly, finally; in the lowest way; in part; within. **-dīpaka**, n. a figure in rhetoric. **-pāla**, m. a frontier-guard. **-bhava**, mfn. being at the end, last. **-bhāj**, mfn. standing at the end (of a word), RPrāt. **-rata**, mfn. delighting in destruction. **-līna**, mfn. hidden, concealed. **-lopa**, m. (in

Gr.) the dropping of the final of a word. **-vat** (*ánta-*), mfn. having an end or term, limited, perishable, AV. &c.; containing a word which has the meaning of *anta*, AitBr.; (*-vat*), ind. like the end; like the final of a word, Pat. **-vahni**, m. the fire of the end (by which the world is to be burnt). **Anta-vāsin** = *ante-vāsin*, q.v., L. **Anta-velā**, f. hour of death, ChUp. **-śayyā**, f. a bed or mat on the ground; death; the place for burial or burning; bier; L. **-satkriyā**, f. the funeral ceremonies, Rājat. **-sad**, m. a pupil (who dwells near his teacher). **-stha**, mfn. standing at the end; see also *antaḥ-sthá*. **-svarita**, m. the Svarita accent on the last syllable of a word; (*am*), n. a word thus accentuated. **Antâdi**, *ī*, du. m. end and beginning, (gaṇa *rājadantâdi*, q. v.) **Antâvasāyin** (or **antâvaśāyin**), m. a barber, L.; a Cāṇḍāla, MārkP. &c., cf. *ante-'vasāyin*; N. of a Muni, L. **Ante-'vasāyin**, m. a man living at the end of a town or village, a man belonging to the lowest caste, MBh. &c. **Ante-vāsa**, m. a neighbour, companion, AitBr. **Ante-vāsín**, mfn. dwelling near the boundaries, dwelling close by, L.; (*ī*), m. a pupil who dwells near or in the house of his teacher, ŚBr. &c.; = *ante-'vasāyin*, q.v., L.; (*i*), ind. in statu pupillari, (gaṇa *dvidaṇḍy-ādi*, q. v.) **Antôdātta**, m. the acute accent on the last syllable; (mfn.), having the acute accent on the last syllable.

1. **Antaká**, *as*, m. border, boundary, ŚBr.

2. **Ántaka**, mfn. making an end, causing death; (*as*), m. death; Yama, king or lord of death, AV. &c.; N. of a man favoured by the Aśvins, RV. i, 112, 6; N. of a king. **-drúh**, Nom. *-dhrúk*, f. demon of death, RV. x, 132, 4.

1. **Ántama** [once *antamá*, RV. i, 165, 5], mfn. next, nearest, RV.; intimate (as a friend), RV.

2. **Antamá**, mfn. the last, TS.; ŚBr. &c.

Antaya, Nom. P. *antayati*, to make an end of, L.

Antika, antima, antya, &c. See *antika*, p. 45.

अन्तः *antáḥ* (for *antár*, see col. 2). **-karaṇa**, n. the internal organ, the seat of thought and feeling, the mind, the thinking faculty, the heart, the conscience, the soul. **-kalpa**, m. a certain number of years, Buddh. **-kuṭila**, mfn. internally crooked; fraudulent; (*as*), m. a couch, L. **-kṛimi**, m. a disease caused by worms in the body. **-koṭara-pushpī** = *aṇḍa-koṭara-pushpī*, q.v., Car. **-koṇa**, m. the inner corner. **-kopa**, m. inward wrath. **-kośá**, n. the interior of a store-room, AV. **-paṭa**, m. n. a cloth held between two persons who are to be united (as bride and bridegroom, or pupil and teacher) until the right moment of union is arrived. **-padam** or **-pade**, ind. in the middle of an inflected word, Prāt. **-paridhāna**, n. the innermost garment. **-paridhi**, ind. in the inside of the pieces of wood forming the paridhi, KātyŚr. **-parśavyá**, n. flesh between the ribs, VS. **-pavitrá**, the Soma when in the straining-vessel, ŚBr. **-paśu**, ind. from evening till morning (while the cattle are in the stables), KātyŚr. **-pātá** [ŚBr.] or **-pātya** [KātyŚr.], *as*, m. a post fixed in the middle of the place of sacrifice; (in Gr.) insertion of a letter, RPrāt. **-pātita** or **-pātin**, mfn. inserted, included in. **-pātrá**, n. the interior of a vessel, AV. **-pādam**, ind. within the Pāda of a verse, RPrāt.; Pāṇ. **-pārśvyá**, n. flesh between or at both sides, VS. **-pāla**, m. one who watches the inner apartments of a palace, R. **-pura**, n. the king's palace, the female apartments, gynæceum; those who live in the female apartments; a queen. **-pura-cara**, m. guardian of the women's apartments. **-pura-jana**, m. the women of the palace. **-pura-pracāra**, m. the gossip of the women's apartments. **-pura-rakshaka** or **-pura-vartin** or **-purâdhyaksha**, m. superintendent of the women's apartments, chamberlain. **-pura-sahāya**, *as*, m. belonging to the women's apartments (as a eunuch, &c.) **-purika**, m. superintendent of the gynæceum or harem; (*ā*), f. a woman in the harem. **-pūya**, mfn. ulcerous. **-péya**, n. supping up, drinking, RV. x, 107, 9. **-prakṛiti**, f. the heart, the soul, the internal nature or constitution of a man. **-prajña**, mfn. internally wise, knowing one's self. **-pratishṭhāna**, n. residence in the interior. **-pratishṭhita**, mfn. residing inside. **-śará**, m. interior reed or cane, TS.; an internal arrow or disease. **-śarīra**, n. the internal and spiritual part of man. **-śalya** (*antáḥ-*), mfn. having a pin or extraneous body sticking inside, ŚBr. **-śilā**, f. = *antra-śilā*. **-śleshá** [MaitrS.; VS.], m. or **-śléshaṇa** [ŚBr.; AitBr.], n. internal support. **-saṃjña**, mfn. internally conscious, Mn. i, 49, &c. **-sattvā**, f. a pregnant woman; the marking nut (Semecarpus Anacardium). **-sadasám**, ind. in the middle of the assembly, ŚBr. **-sāra**, mfn. having internal essence; (*as*), m. internal treasure, inner store or contents. **-sukha**, mfn. internally happy. **-senam**, ind. into the midst of the armies. **-sthá** (generally written *antasthá*), mfn. being in the midst or between, ŚBr. &c.; (*as, ā*), m. f. a term applied to the semivowels, as standing between the consonants and vowels, Prāt. &c.; (*ā*), f. interim, meantime, PBr. **-stha-mudgara**, m. (in anatomy) the malleus of the ear. **-sthā-chandas**, n., N. of a class of metres. **-sveda**, m. 'sweating internally,' an elephant, L.

Antáḥ-√khyā, to deprive of, conceal from, RV.

Antáḥ-√paś, to look between, look into, RV.

Antáḥ-√sthā, to stand in the way of, stop, RV.

अन्तम *ántama* and *antamá*. See s.v. *ánta*.

अन्तर् *antár*, ind. within, between, amongst, in the middle or interior.

(As a prep. with loc.) in the middle, in, between, into; (with acc.) between; (with gen.) in, in the middle.

(Ifc.) in, into, in the middle of, between, out of the midst of [cf. Zend *antarĕ*; Lat. *inter*; Goth. *undar*].

Antar is sometimes compounded with a following word like an adjective, meaning interior, internal, intermediate. **-agni**, m. the interior fire, digestive force, Suśr.; (mfn.), being in the fire, Kauś. **-aṅga**, mfn. interior, proximate, related, being essential to, or having reference to the essential part of the *aṅga* or base of a word; (*am*), n. any interior part of the body, VarBṛS. **-aṅga-tva**, n. the state or condition of an Antaraṅga. **-avayava**, m. an inner limb or part. **-ākāśa**, m. intermediate place, KaushBr.; the sacred ether or Brahma in the interior part or soul of man. **-ākūta**, n. hidden intention. **-āgama**, m. (in Gr.) an additional augment between two letters. **-āgāra**, m. the interior of a house, Yājñ. **-âtmaka**, mf(*ī*)n. interior, MaitrUp. **-ātmán**, m. the soul; the internal feelings, the heart or mind, MaitrS. &c. **-âtmêshṭakam**, ind. in the space between one's self and the (sacrificial) bricks, KātyŚr. **-ādhāna** (*antár-*), mfn. 'having a bit inside,' bridled, TBr. **-āpaṇa**, m. a market inside (a town), R. **-āya**, see *antar-√i*. **-ārāma**, mfn. rejoicing in one's self (not in the exterior world), Bhag. **-āla** or **-ālaka** [L.], n. intermediate space; (*e*), loc. ind. in the midst, in midway (*āla* is probably for *ālaya*). **-indriya**, n. (in Vedânta phil.) an internal organ (of which there are four, viz. *manas*, *buddhi*, *ahaṃkāra*, and *citta*). **-īpa**, n. (fr. 2. *ap*), an island, Pāṇ. vi, 3, 97. **-ushya**, m. (√5. *vas*), an intermediate resting-place, KaushBr.; cf. *daśântarushyá*. **-gaṅgā**, f. the under-ground Ganges (as supposed to communicate under-ground with a sacred spring in Mysore). **-gaḍu**, mfn. 'having worms within,' unprofitable, useless. **-gata**, &c., see *antar-√gam*. **-garbha**, mfn. inclosing young, pregnant, KātyŚr. **-giri**, m. 'situated among the mountains,' N. of a country, MBh. **-guda-valaya**, m. (in anat.) the sphincter muscle. **-gūḍha-visha**, mfn. having hidden poison within. **-gṛiha** or **-geha**, n. interior of the house, inner apartment; (*am*), ind. in the interior of a house. **-goshṭha** (*antár-*), mfn. being inside of the stable, MaitrS.; (*as*), m. inside of a stable, MānGṛ. **-ghaṇa** or **-ghana** or **-ghāta**, m. a place between the entrance-door and the house; N. of a village, Pāṇ. iii, 3, 78, Sch. **-ja**, mfn. bred in the interior (of the body, as a worm). **-jaṭhara**, n. the stomach, L. **-janman**, n. inward birth. **-jambhá**, m. the inner part of the jaws, ŚBr. **-jala-cara**, mfn. going in the water. **-jāta**, mfn. inborn, inbred, innate. **-jānu**, ind. between the knees; holding the hands between the knees, Hcat.; (mfn.), holding the hands between the knees. **-jñāna**, n. inward knowledge. **-jyotis** (*antár-*), mfn. having the soul enlightened, illuminated, ŚBr. xiv; Bhag. **-jvalana**, n. internal heat, inflammation. **-dagdhá**, mfn. burnt inwardly. **-dadhana**, n. the distillation of spirituous liquor (or a substance used to cause fermentation), L. **-dadhāna**, mfn. vanishing, disappearing, hiding one's self; (cf. *antar-√dhā*.) **-daśā**, f. (in astrol.) intermediate period. **-daśâha**, n. an interval of ten days; (*āt*), ind. before the end of ten days, Mn. **-dāvá**, m. the middle of a fire, AV. **-dāha**, m. internal heat, or fever. **-diś**, f. = *-deśá* below, MānGṛ. **-duḥkha**, mfn. afflicted in mind, sad. **-dushṭa**, mfn. internally bad, wicked, vile. **-dṛishṭi**, mfn. looking into one's own soul. **-deśá**, m. an intermediate region of the compass, AV. **-dvāra**, n. a private or secret door within the house, L. **-dhā**, &c., see s. v. *antar-√dhā*, p. 44. **-dhyāna**, n. profound inward meditation. **-nagara**, n. the palace of a king, R. **-nivishṭa**, mfn. gone within, being within. **-nishṭha**, mfn. engaged in internal reflection. **-bāshpa**, m. suppressed tears; (mfn.), containing tears. **-bhavana**, n. the interior of a house. **-bhāva**, &c., see *antár-√bhū*, p. 44, col. 2. **-bhāvanā**, f. inward meditation or anxiety; (in arithm.) rectification of numbers by the differences of the products. **-bhūmi**, f. the inner part of the earth. **-bhauma**, mfn. being in the interior of the earth, subterranean, R. **-manas**, mfn. sad, perplexed, L. **-mukha**, mfn. going into the mouth; (*am*), n. a kind of scissors used in surgery, Suśr. **-mudra**, m. 'sealed inside,' N. of a form of devotion. **-mṛita**, mfn. still-born, Suśr. **-yāmá**, m. a Soma libation performed with suppression of the breath and voice, VS.; ŚBr. &c. **-yāma-graha**, m. id. **-yāmin**, m. 'checking or regulating the internal feelings,' the soul, ŚBr. xiv; MuṇḍUp. **-yoga**, m. deep thought, abstraction. **-lamba**, mfn. acute-angular; (*as*), m. a triangle in which the perpendicular falls within, an acute-angled triangle. **-līna**, mfn. inherent. **-loma** (*antár-*), mfn. (said of anything) the hairy side of which is turned inwards, MaitrS.; covered with hair on the inner side. **-vaṇśa**, m. = *antaḥ-pura*. **-vaṇśika**, m. superintendent of the women's apartments. **-vaṇa**, mfn. situated in a forest, Pāṇ.; (*am*), ind. within a forest, Pāṇ. Sch. **-vat** (*antár-*), mf(*vatī* [RV.] or *vatnī*)n. pregnant, RV. &c. **-vami**, m. flatulence, indigestion. **-vartá**, m. the act of filling up gaps with grass, TS. **-vartin** or **-vasat**, mfn. internal, included, dwelling in. **-vasu**, m., N. of a Soma sacrifice, KātyŚr. **-vastra**, n. an under garment, Kathās. **-vāṇi**, mfn. skilled in sacred sciences. **-vâvat**, ind. inwardly, RV. **-vāsas**, n. an inner or under garment, Kathās. **-vigāhana**, n. entering within, L. **-vidvás**, mfn. (perf. p. √1. *vid*), knowing exactly, RV. i, 72, 7. **-vega**, m. internal uneasiness or anxiety; inward fever. **-vedí**, ind. within the sacrificial ground, ŚBr. &c.; (*ī*), f. the Doab or district between the Gaṅgā and Yamunā rivers; (*ayas*), m. pl., N. of the people living there, R. **-veśman**, n. the inner apartments, the interior of a building. **-veśmika**, m. superintendent of the women's apartments. **-hanana**, n. abolishing, Pāṇ. viii, 4, 24, Sch. **-hanana**, m., N. of a village, Pāṇ. viii, 4, 24, Sch. **-hastám**, ind. in the hand, within reach of the hand, AV. **-hastīna**, mfn. being in the hand or within reach, AitBr. **-hāsa**, m. laughing inwardly; suppressed laughter; (*am*), ind. with suppressed laugh. **-hita**, &c., see *antar-√dhā*, p. 44. **-hṛidaya**, mfn. turned inwards in mind, MaitrUp.

अन्तर *ántara*, mf(*ā*)n. being in the interior, interior; near, proximate, related, intimate; lying adjacent to; distant; different from; exterior; (*am*), n. the interior; a hole, opening; the interior part of a thing, the contents; soul, heart, supreme soul; interval, intermediate space or time; period; term; opportunity, occasion; place; distance, absence; difference, remainder; property, peculiarity; weakness, weak side; representation; surety, guaranty; respect, regard; (ifc.), different, other, another, e.g. *deśântaram*, another country; (*am*), or *-tás*, ind. in the interior, within [cf. Goth. *anthar*, Theme *anthara*; Lith. *antra-s*, 'the second;' Lat. *alter*]. **-cakra**, n. the whole of the thirty-two intermediate regions of the compass, VarBṛS.; a technical term in augury. **-jña**, mfn. knowing the interior, prudent, provident, foreseeing. **-tama**, mfn. nearest; immediate, intimate, internal; like, analogous; (*as*), m. a congenial letter, one of the same class. **-tara** (*ántara-*), mfn. nearer; very intimate, TS.; ŚBr. **-da**, mfn. (√3. *dā*), cutting or hurting the interior or heart. **-diśá** [VS.], f. an intermediate region or quarter of the compass; (cf. *antarā-diś* and *antar-deśá*.) **-pūrusha**, m. the internal man, the soul, Mn. viii, 85. **-prabhava,** mfn. of mixed origin or caste, Mn. i, 2. **-praśna,** m. an inner question; a question which is contained in and arises from what has been previously stated. **-stha, -sthāyin, -sthita,** mfn. interposed, internal, situated inside, inward; separate, apart. **Antarâpatyā,** f. a pregnant woman, L. **Antarā-bharā́,** see *antarā́*.

Antarā́, ind. in the middle, inside, within, among, between; on the way, by the way; near, nearly, almost; in the meantime, now and then; for some time; (with acc. and loc.) between, during, without. **Antarā́ṅsa,** m. the part of the body between the shoulders, the breast, ŚBr. **Antarā-diś,** f. = *antar-diśā́*, q.v. **Antarā-bharā́,** mfn. bringing close to, procuring, RV. viii, 32, 12. **Antarā-bhava-deha,** m. or **-bhava-sattva,** n. the soul in its middle existence between death and regeneration. **Antarā-vedī,** f. a veranda resting on columns, L. **Antarā-śṛiṅgam,** ind. between the horns, KātyŚr.

Antarīya, *am*, n. an under or lower garment, L.

Antare, ind. amidst, among, between; with regard to, for the sake of, on account of.

A̍ntareṇa, ind. amidst, between; (with acc.) within, between, amidst, during; except, without, with regard to, with reference to, on account of.

Antarya, mfn. interior, (gaṇa *dig-ādi*, q. v.)

अन्तरञ्ज् *antar-√añj*, to assume, take up into one's self, VS.

अन्तरय *antar-aya*, &c. See *antar-√i*.

अन्तराधा *antar-ā-√dhā*, Ā. *-dhatte*, to receive into one's self, contain, RV. ix, 73, 8; ŚBr.

अन्तराय *antarāya*. See *antar-√i*.

अन्तराल *antar-āla*. See s. v. *antar*.

अन्तरास् *antar-√ās*, to sit down into (acc.), RV. ix, 78, 3.

अन्तरि *antar-√i*, *-ayati*, to come between, Mṛicch.; (perf. *-ayāṃ cakāra*) to conceal, cause to disappear, Śiś. iii, 24; *-eti*, to stand in any one's way, separate; to exclude from (abl., rarely gen.); to pass over, omit; to disappear: Intens. *-īyate*, to walk to and fro between (as a mediator), RV.

1. **Antar-aya,** *as*, m. impediment, hindrance, ĀpŚr.; (cf. *án-antaraya*.)

2. **Antar-aya,** Nom. P. *-ayati*, see *antar-√i*.

Antar-ayaṇa, *am*, n. going under, disappearing, Pāṇ. viii, 4, 25.

Antar-ayana, *as*, m., N. of a country, Pāṇ. viii, 4, 25.

Antar-āya, *as*, m. intervention, obstacle.

Antár-ita, mfn. gone within, interior, hidden, concealed, screened, shielded; departed, retired, withdrawn, disappeared, perished; separated, excluded; impeded; (*am*), n. (?) remainder (in arithmetic); a technical term in architecture.

Antár-iti, *is*, f. exclusion, MaitrS.

अन्तरिक्ष *antáriksha*, *am*, n. the intermediate space between heaven and earth; (in the Veda) the middle of the three spheres or regions of life; the atmosphere or sky; the air; talc. **-kshit,** mfn. dwelling in the atmosphere, ChUp. **-ga** or **-cara,** mfn. passing through the atmosphere; (*as*), m. a bird. **-prā́,** mfn. (√1. *prī*), travelling through the atmosphere, RV. **-prút,** mfn. (√*pru*), floating over the atmosphere, RV. i, 116, 3. **-yānī,** f., N. of a brick, TS. **-loká,** m. the intermediate region or sky as a peculiar world, ŚBr. **-saṃśita** (*antáriksha-*), mfn. sharpened in the atmosphere, AV. **-sád,** mfn. dwelling in the atmosphere, RV. iv, 40, 5, &c. **-sádya,** n. residence in the atmosphere, ŚBr. **Antárikshâyatana,** mfn. having its abode in the atmosphere, ŚBr. **Antarikshôdara,** mfn. having an interior as comprehensive as the atmosphere.

Antárikshya (5), mfn. atmospheric, RV.

Antarīksha, *am*, n. = *antáriksha*.

अन्तरिष् *antár-√3. ish* (3. pl. *-icchanti*) to wish, long for, RV. viii, 72, 3.

अन्तरुपाती *antar-upâtī* (√*i*), *-upâtyeti*, to enter over a threshold or boundary, Kauś.

अन्तर्गम् *antár-√gam*, to go between (so as to exclude from [abl.]), ŚBr.

Antar-gata or **-gāmin,** mfn. gone between or into, being in, included in; being in the interior, internal, hidden, secret; disappeared, perished; slipped out of the memory, forgotten. **-manas,** mfn. whose mind is turned inwards, engaged in deep thought, sad, perplexed. **Antargatôpamā,** f. a concealed simile (the particle of comparison being omitted).

अन्तर्गा *antár-√1. gā*, to go between, RV.; to separate, exclude from (with abl.), ŚBr.

अन्तर्धा 1. *antar-√dhā*, Ā. *-dhatte*, to place within, deposit; to receive within; to hide, conceal, obscure; to hide one's self: Pass. *-dhīyate*, to be received within, to be absorbed; to be rendered invisible; to disappear, vanish; to cease: Caus. *-dhāpayati*, to render invisible, to cause to disappear.

2. **Antar-dhā,** f. concealment, covering, Pāṇ. Sch.

Antar-dhāna, *am*, n. disappearance, invisibility; *antardhānam √i* or *√gam*, to disappear; (*as*), m., N. of a son of Pṛithu. **-gata,** mfn. disappeared. **-cara,** mfn. going invisibly.

Antar-dhāpita, mfn. rendered invisible.

Antar-dhāyaka, mf(*ikā*)n. rendering invisible.

Antar-dhí, *is*, m. concealment, covering, AV.; disappearance; interim, meantime, ShaḍvBr.

Antar-hita, mfn. placed between, separated; covered, concealed, hidden, made invisible, vanished, invisible; hidden from (with abl.) **Antarhitât-man,** m. 'of concealed mind,' N. of Śiva.

अन्तर्भू *antár-√bhū*, to be (contained or inherent or implied) in, RV. vii, 86, 2, &c.

Antar-bhava, mfn. being within, inward, internal, generated internally.

Antar-bhavana. See s. v. *antár*.

Antar-bhāva, *as*, m. the being included by (loc.), internal or inherent nature or disposition.

Antar-bhāvanā. See s. v. *antár*.

Antar-bhāvita, mfn. included, involved.

Antar-bhūta, mfn. being within, internal, inner. **-tva,** n.; see *antar-bhāva*.

Antar-bhūmi. See s. v. *antár*.

अन्तर्यम् *antár-√yam* (Imper. 2. sg. *-yaccha*) to hinder, stop, RV. x, 102, 3; VS.; TS.; (Imper. *-yacchatu*) to keep inside, ĀśvGṛ.

अन्तर्वस् *antar-√5. vas*, to dwell inside, abide in the interior, Śiś.; to stop in the midst of, MBh.; (cf. *antar-ushya* s. v. *antár*.)

अन्तर्हन् *antar-√han*, forms the ind. p. *-hatya*, Pāṇ. i, 4, 65, Sch., and the Pass. *-hanyate*, Pāṇ. viii, 4, 24, Sch.

अन्तश्चर् *antáś-√car*, to move between, to move within, RV. &c.

अन्तश्छिद् *antáś-√chid*, to cut off, intercept, ŚBr.

अन्तस् *antas* for *antár*, see p. 43, col. 2. **-tapta,** mfn. internally heated or harassed. **-tāpa,** m. inward heat, Śāk.; Mālatīm. **-tushāra,** mfn. having dew in the interior. **-toya,** mfn. containing water inside, Megh. **-patha** (*ántas-*), mfn. being on the way, RV. v, 52, 10.

Antastya, *am*, n. intestines, AitBr.

अन्ति 1. *ánti*, ind. before, in the presence of, near, RV.; AV.; (with gen.) within the proximity of, to [cf. Lat. *ante*; Gk. ἀντί]. **-gṛiha** (*ánti-*), m. neighbour, RV. x, 95, 4. **-tama,** mfn. very near, Pāṇ. Comm. **-tas** (*ánti-*), ind. from near, RV. **-deva** (*ánti-*), mfn. being in the presence of the gods, near the gods, RV. i, 180, 7. **-mitra** (*ánti-*), mfn. having friends near one's self, VS. **-vāma** (*ánti-*), mf(*ā*)n. at hand with wealth or loveliness, RV. vii, 77, 4. **-shad,** mfn. sitting near, Pat. **-sumna** (*ánti-*), mfn. at hand with kindness, AV. **A̍nty-ūti** (4), mfn. at hand with help, RV. i, 138, 1.

1. **Antika,** mfn. (with gen. or abl.) near, proximate, L. (compar. *nedīyas*, superl. *nedishṭha*); (*am*), n. vicinity, proximity, near, e.g. *antika-stha*, remaining near; (*ám*), ind. (with gen. or ifc.) until, near to, into the presence of; (*ā́t*), ind. from the proximity; near, close by; within the presence of; (*é*), ind. (with gen. or ifc.) near, close by, in the proximity or presence of; (*ena*), ind. (with gen.) near. **-gati,** f. going near. **-tā,** f. nearness, vicinity, contiguity. **Antikâśraya,** m. contiguous support (as that given by a tree to a creeper), L.

1. **Antima,** mfn. ifc. immediately following (e.g. *daśântima*, 'the eleventh'); very near, L.

अन्ति 2. *anti*, *is*, f. an elder sister (in theatrical language), L. For 1. *ánti*, see col. 2.

Antikā, f. an elder sister (in theatrical language; perhaps a corruption of *attikā*), L.; a fire-place, L.; the plant Echites Scholaris.

Antī, f. an oven, L.

अन्तिक 2. *antika*, mfn. (fr. *anta*), only ifc. reaching to the end of, reaching to (e.g. *nāsântika*, reaching to the nose), lasting till, until.

2. **Antima,** mfn. final, ultimate, last. **Anti-mâṅka,** m. the last unit, nine.

Antya, mfn. last in place, in time, or in order; ifc. immediately following, e.g. *ashṭamântya*, the ninth; lowest in place or condition, undermost, inferior, belonging to the lowest caste; (*as*), m. the plant Cyperus Hexastachyus Communis; (*am*), n. the number 1000 billions; the twelfth sign of the zodiac; the last member of a mathematical series. **-karman,** n. or **-kriyā,** f. funeral rites. **-ja,** mfn. of the lowest caste; (*as*), m. a Śūdra; a man of one of seven inferior tribes (a washerman, currier, mimic, Varuḍa, fisherman, Meda or attendant on women, and mountaineer or forester). **-ja-gamana,** n. intercourse (between a woman of the higher caste) with a man of the lowest caste. **-janman** or **-jāti** or **-jātīya,** mfn. of the lowest caste. **-jā-gamana,** n. intercourse (between a man of the higher caste) with a woman of the lowest caste. **-dhana,** n. last member of an arithmetical series. **-pada** or **-mūla,** n. (in arithm.) the last or greatest root (in the square). **-bha,** n. the last Nakshatra (Revatī); the last sign of the zodiac, the sign Pisces. **-yuga,** m. the last or Kali age. **-yoni,** f. the lowest origin, Mn. viii, 68; (mfn.), of the lowest origin. **-varṇa,** *as*, *ā*, m. f. a man or woman of the last tribe, a Śūdra. **-vipulā,** f., N. of a metre. **Antyâva-sāyin,** *ī*, *inī*, m. f. a man or woman of low caste (the son of a Cāṇḍāla by a Nishādī, especially a Cāṇḍāla, Śvapaca, Kshattṛi, Sūta, Vaidehaka, Māgadha, and Āyogava), Mn. &c. **Antyâhuti,** f. funeral oblation or sacrifice. **Antyêshṭi,** f. funeral sacrifice. **Antyêshṭi-kriyā,** f. funeral ceremonies.

Antyaka, *as*, m. a man of the lowest tribe, L.

अन्तेवासिन् *ante-vāsín*. See p. 43, col. 1.

अन्त्र *antra*, *am*, n. (contr. of *antara*; Gk. ἔντερον), entrail, intestine (cf. *āntrá*); (*ī*), f. the plant Convolvulus Argenteus or Ipomœa Pes Capræ Roth. **-kūja,** m. or **-kūjana,** n. or **-vikūjana,** n. rumbling of the bowels. **-m-dhami** (*antram-*), f. indigestion, inflation of the bowels from wind. **-pācaka,** m. the plant Æschynomene Grandiflora. **-maya,** mfn. consisting of entrails. **-vardhman,** n. or **-vṛiddhi,** f. inguinal hernia, rupture. **-śilā,** f., N. of a river. **-sraj,** f. a kind of garland worn by Nara-siṃha. **Antrâda,** m. worms in the intestines.

अन्द् *and*, cl. 1. P. *andati*, to bind, L.

Andu, *us*, or **andū,** *ūs*, f. the chain for an elephant's feet; a ring or chain worn on the ancle.

Anduka or **andūka,** *as*, m. id., L.

अन्दिका *andikā*, f. (for *antikā*, q.v.), fire-place.

अन्दोलय *andolaya*, Nom. P. *andolayati*, to agitate, to swing.

Andolana, *am*, n. swinging, oscillating.

Andolita, mfn. agitated, swung.

अन्द्रक *andraka*=*ārdraka*, q. v.

अन्ध् *andh*, cl. 10. P. *andhayati*, to make blind, Śiś.

Andhá, mf(*ā*)n. blind; dark; (*am*), n. darkness; turbid water, water; (*ās*), m. pl., N. of a people. **-kāra,** m. n. darkness. **-kāra-maya,** mfn. dark. **-kāra-saṃcaya,** m. intensity of darkness. **-kārita,** mfn. made dark, dark, Kād.; (cf. gaṇa *tārakâdi*.) **-kūpa,** m. a well of which the mouth is hidden; a well over-grown with plants, &c.; a particular hell. **-m-karaṇa** (*andham-*), mf(*ī*)n. making blind. **-tamasa,** n. great, thick, or intense darkness, Pāṇ. v, 4, 79; Ragh. **-tā,** f. or **-tva,** n. blindness. **-tāmasa,** n. = *-tamasa*, L. **-tā-**

misra, m. complete darkness of the soul; (*am*), n. the second or eighteenth of the twenty-one hells, Mn. &c.; doctrine of annihilation after death. **–dhī**, mfn. mentally blind. **–pūtanā**, f. a female demon causing diseases in children, Suśr. **–mūshā**, f. a small covered crucible with a hole in the side. **–mūshikā**, f. the grass Lepocercis Serrata. **–m-bhavishṇu** (*andham-*), mfn. becoming blind, Pāṇ. iii, 2, 57. **–m-bhāvuka** (*andham-*), mfn. id., ib.; Kauś. **–rātrī**, f. dark night (?), AV. **Andhâlajī**, f. a blind boil, one that does not suppurate, Suśr. **Andhâhi** (or *andhâhika*), m. a 'blind,' i.e. not poisonous snake; (*is, is*), m. f. the fish called kucikā. **Andhī-√1. kṛi**, to make blind, to blind. **Andhīkṛita**, mfn. made blind. **Andhīkṛitâtman**, mfn. blinded in mind. **Andhī-gu**, *us*, m., N. of a Ṛishi, PBr. **Andhī-√bhū**, to become blind. **Andhībhūta**, mfn. become blind.

Andhaka, mfn. blind; (*as*), m., N. of an Asura (son of Kaśyapa and Diti); of a descendant of Yadu and ancestor of Kṛishṇa and his descendants; N. of a Muni. **–ghātin** or **–ripu**, m. 'the slayer or enemy of the Asura Andhaka,' N. of Śiva. **–varta**, m., N. of a mountain, Pāṇ. iv, 3, 91, Sch. **–vṛishṇi**, *ayas*, m. pl. descendants of Andhaka and Vṛishṇi. **Andhakâri** or **andhakâsuhṛid**, m. 'enemy of the Asura Andhaka,' N. of Śiva.

1. **Á́ndhas**, *as*, n. darkness, obscurity, RV.

Andhikā, f. night, L.; a kind of game (blindman's buff), L.; a woman of a particular character (one of the classes of women), L.; a disease of the eye, L.; another disease, L.; =*sarshapī*, L.

अन्धस् 2. *ándhas*, *as*, n. (Gk. ἄνθος), a herb; the Soma plant; Soma juice, RV.; VS.; juice, ŚBr.; grassy ground, RV. vii, 96, 2; food, MBh. iii, 13244; BhP.

अन्धु *andhu*, *us*, m. a well, Rājat.

अन्धुल *andhula*, *as*, m. the tree Acacia Sirissa.

अन्ध्र *andhra*, *as*, m., N. of a people (probably modern Telingana); of a dynasty; a man of a low caste (the offspring of a Vaideha father and Kārāvara mother, who lives by killing game), Mn. x, 36. **–jāti**, f. the Andhra tribe. **–jātīya**, mfn. belonging to the Andhra tribe. **–bhṛitya**, *ās*, m. pl. a dynasty of the Andhras.

अन्न *anna*, mfn. (√*ad*), eaten, L.; (*ánnam*), n. food or victuals, especially boiled rice; bread corn; food in a mystical sense (or the lowest form in which the supreme soul is manifested, the coarsest envelope of the Supreme Spirit); water, Naigh.; Vishṇu; earth, L. **–kāma** (*ánna-*), mfn. desirous of food, RV. x, 117, 3. **–kāla**, m. meal-time, proper hour for eating; time at which a convalescent patient begins to take food, Bhpr. **–koshṭhaka**, m. cupboard, granary; Vishṇu, the sun, L. **–gati**, f. the œsophagus, gullet. **–gandhi**, m. dysentery, diarrhœa. **–ja** or **–jāta**, mfn. springing from or occasioned by food as the primitive substance. **–jala**, n. food and water, bare subsistence. **–jit**, mfn. obtaining food by conquest (explanation of *vāja-jít*), ŚBr. **–jīvana** (*ánna-*), mfn. living by food, ŚBr. **–tejas** (*ánna-*), mfn. having the vigour of food, AV. **–da** or **–dātṛi**, mfn. giving food; N. of Śiva and Durgā, L. **–dāna**, n. the giving of food. **–dāyin**, mfn. = *-da* above. **–devatā**, f. the divinity supposed to preside over articles of food. **–dosha**, m. a fault committed by eating prohibited food, Mn. v, 4. **–dvesha**, *as*, m. want of appetite, dislike of food. **–pati** (*ánna-*), m. the lord of food, N. of Savitṛi, Agni, Śiva. **–patnī**, f. a goddess presiding over food, AitBr.; ĀśvŚr. **–patya** (*ánna-*), n. the lordship over food, MaitrS. **–pū́**, mfn. (explanation of *keta-pū́*), purifying food, ŚBr. **–pūrṇa**, mfn. filled with or possessed of food; (*ā*), f., N. of a goddess, a form of Durgā. **–péya**, n. explains the word *vāja-péya*, q. v., ŚBr. **–pradá**, mfn. = *-da* above, ŚBr. **–pralaya**, mfn. being resolved into food or the primitive substance after death, L. **–prâśa**, m. or **–prâśana**, n. putting rice into a child's mouth for the first time (one of the Saṃskāras; see *saṃskāra*), Mn. ii, 34; Yājñ. i, 12. **–bubhukshu**, mfn. desirous of eating food. **–brahman**, n. Brahma as represented by food. **–bhaksha**, m. or **–bhakshaṇa**, n. eating of food. **–bhāgá**, m. a share of food, AV. iii, 30, 6. **–bhuj**, mfn. eating food; (*k*), m. a N. of Śiva, MBh. xii, 10382. **–maya**, mf(*ī*)n. made from food, composed of food or of boiled rice. **–maya-kośa**, m. the gross material body (which is sustained by food = *sthūla-śarīra*). **–mala**, n. excrement; spirituous liquor, cf. Mn. xi, 93. **–rakshā**, f. caution in eating food. **–rasa**, m. essence of food, chyle; meat and drink, nutriment, taste in distinguishing food. **–lipsā**, f. desire for food, appetite. **–vat** (*ánna-*), mfn. Ved. possessed of food, RV. x, 117, 2, &c. **–vastra**, n. food and clothing, the necessaries of life. **–vāhi-srotas**, n. the œsophagus, gullet. **–vikāra**, m. transformation of food; disorder of the stomach from indigestion; the seminal secretion. **–víd**, mfn. (√2. *vid*), acquiring food, AV. vi, 116, 1; (√1. *vid*), knowing food. **–śesha**, m. leavings, offal. **–saṃskāra**, m. consecrating of food. **–hartṛi**, mfn. taking away food. **–homá**, m. a sacrifice connected with the Aśvamedha, ŚBr. **Annâkāla**, see *anākāla*. **Annâcchādana**, n. food and clothing. **Annâttṛi** or **annâdin** [Mn. ii, 188], mfn. eating food. **Annâdá**, mf(*ī*, *ā*)n. eating food; Superl. of the fem. *annâdī-tamā*, 'eating the most,' N. of the fore-finger, ŚBr. **Annâdana**, n. eating of food. **Annâdya**, n. food in general, proper food. **Annâdya-kāma**, mfn. desirous of food. **Annâyu**, m. (coined for the etymology of *vāyu*), 'living by food, desirous of food,' AitUp. **Annârthin**, mfn. asking for food. **Annā-vṛidh** (final *a* lengthened), mfn. prospering by food, RV. x, 1, 4. **Annâhārin**, mfn. eating food.

Á́nniyat, mfn. being desirous of food, RV. iv, 2, 7.

अन्नम्भट्ट *annambhaṭṭa*, *as*, m., N. of the author of the Tarka-saṃgraha, q. v.

अन्य 1. *ánya* (3), *am*, n. inexhaustibleness (as of the milk of cows), AV. xii, 1, 4; (cf. *ánya*.)

अन्य 2. *anyá*, *as, ā, at*, other, different; other than, different from, opposed to (abl. or in comp.); another; another person; one of a number; *anya anya* or *eka anya*, the one, the other; *anyac ca*, and another, besides, moreover [cf. Zend *anya*; Armen. *ail*; Lat. *alius*; Goth. *aljis*, Theme *alja*; Gk. ἄλλος for ἄλjo-s; cf. also ἔνιοι]. **–kāma**, mfn. loving another. **–kārukā**, f. a worm bred in excrement, L. **–kṛita** (*anyá-*), mfn. done by another, RV. **–kshetrá**, n. another territory or sphere, AV. **–ga** or **–gāmin**, mfn. going to another, adulterous. **–gotra**, mfn. of a different family. **–citta**, mf(*ā*)n. whose mind is fixed on some one or something else. **–codita**, mfn. moved by another. **–ja** or **–jāta** (*anyá-*) [RV.], mfn. born of another (family, &c.), of a different origin. **–janman**, n. another birth, being born again. **–tas**, see s. v. **–tā**, f. difference. **–durvaha**, mfn. difficult to be borne by another. **–devata** or **–devatya** [MaitrS.; ŚBr.] or **–daivata**, mfn. having another divinity, i. e. addressed to another divinity. **–dharma**, m. different characteristic; characteristic of another; (mfn.), having different characteristics. **–dhī**, mfn. one whose mind is alienated, L. **–nābhi** (*anyá-*), mfn. of another family, AV. i, 29, 1. **–para**, mfn. devoted to something else, zealous in something else. **–pushṭa**, *as*, m. or *ā*, f. [Kum. i, 46] 'reared by another,' the kokila or Indian cuckoo (supposed to be reared by the crow). **–pūrvā**, f. a woman previously betrothed to one and married to another. **–bīja-ja** or **–bīja-samudbhava** or **–bījôtpanna**, m. 'born from the seed of another,' an adopted son. **–bhṛit**, m. 'nourishing another,' a crow (supposed to sit upon the eggs of the kokila). **–bhṛita**, *as*, m. or *ā*, f. [Ragh. viii, 58] = *-pushṭā* above. **–manas** or **–manaska**, mfn. whose mind is fixed on something else, absent, versatile; having another mind in one's self, possessed by a demon. **–mātṛi-ja**, m. a half-brother (who has the same father but another mother), Yājñ. **–rājan**, mfn. having another for king, subject to another, ChUp. **–rāshṭrīya**, mfn. from another kingdom, belonging to another kingdom, ŚBr. **–rūpa**, n. another form; (*eṇa*), in another form, disguised; (*anyá-rūpa*), mf(*ā*)n. having another form, changed, altered, RV. &c. **–rūpin**, mfn. having another shape. **–liṅga** or **–liṅgaka**, mfn. having the gender of another (word, viz. of the substantive), an adjective. **–varṇa** (*anyá-*), mf(*ā*)n. having another colour. **–vāpá**, m. 'sowing for others,' i. e. 'leaving his eggs in the nests of other birds,' the kokila or Indian cuckoo, VS. **–vrata** (*anyá-*), m. devoted to others, infidel, RV.; VS. **–śākhaka**, m. a Brāhman who has left his school, L.; an apostate, L. **–saṃgama**, m. intercourse with another, adulterous intercourse. **–sādhāraṇa**, mfn. common to others. **–strī-ga**, m. going to another's wife, an adulterer, Mn. **Anyā-dṛiksha** [L.] or **anyā-dṛiś** [VS. &c.], mfn. or **anyā-dṛiśa**, mf(*ī*)n. of another kind, like another. **Anyâdhīna**, mfn. subject to others, dependent. **Anyâśrayaṇa**, n. going to another (as an inheritance). **Anyâśrita**, mfn. gone to another. **Anyâsakta**, mfn. intent on something else. **Anyâsādhāraṇa**, mfn. not common to another, peculiar. **Anyôḍhā**, f. married to another, another's wife, Sāh. **Anyôtpanna**, mfn. begotten by another. **Anyôdarya**, mfn. born from another womb, RV. vii, 4, 8; (*as*), m. a stepmother's son, Yājñ.

Anyaká, mfn. another, other, RV.

Anya-tama, mfn. any one of many, either, any.

Anya-tará, *as, ā, at*, either of two, other, different; *anyatara anyatara*, the one, the other; *anyatarasyām*, loc. f. either way, Pāṇ. **–tas** (*anyatará-*), ind. on one of two sides, ŚBr.; KātySr.; either way (= *anyatarasyām*), VPrāt. **Anyataráto-danta**, mf(*ā*)n. having teeth on one side (only), ŚBr. **Anyatare-dyus**, ind. on either of two days, Pāṇ. v, 3, 22.

Anyá-tas, ind. from another; from another motive; on one side (*anyataḥ anyataḥ*, on the one, on the other side); elsewhere; on the other side, on the contrary, in one direction; towards some other place. **Anyáta-eta**, mf(*-enī*)n. variegated on one side, VS. xxx, 19. **Anyataḥ-kshṇút**, mfn. sharp on one side, ŚBr. **Anyátaḥ-plakshā**, f., N. of a lotus pond in Kurukshetra, ŚBr. **Anyatoghātín**, mfn. striking in one direction, ŚBr. **Anyáto-dat**, mfn. = *anyataráto-danta*, q. v., TS. **Anyáto-'raṇya**, n. a land which is woody only on one side, VS. xxx, 19. **Anyato-vāta**, m. a disease of the eye, Suśr.

Anyatastya, *as*, m. 'opponent, adversary,' in comp. with **-jāyín**, mfn. overwhelming adversaries, ŚBr. xiv.

Anyat-kāraka, mfn. making mistakes, Pāṇ. vi, 3, 99 (the neut. form appears to be used in comp. when error of any kind is implied; other examples besides the following are given). **Anyat-√1. kṛi**, to make a mistake, Pat. **Anyad-āśā** or **-āśis**, f. a bad desire or hope (?), Pāṇ. vi, 3, 99.

Anyá-tra, ind. (= *anyasmin*, loc. of 2. *anyá*), elsewhere, in another place (with abl.); on another occasion; (ifc.) at another time than; otherwise, in another manner; to another place; except, without, MānGṛ.; Jain. [cf. Goth. *aljathrō*]. **–manas** (*anyátra-*), mfn. having the mind directed to something else, inattentive, ŚBr. xiv.

Anyathaya, P. *anyathayati*, to alter, Sāh.

Anyá-thā, ind. otherwise, in a different manner (with *atas, itas*, or *tatas* = in a manner different from this; *anyathā anyathā*, in one way, in another way); inaccurately, untruly, falsely, erroneously; from another motive; in the contrary case, otherwise [cf. Lat. *aliuta*]. **–kāra**, m. doing otherwise, changing; (*am*), ind. otherwise, in a different manner, Pāṇ. iii, 4, 27. **–√1. kṛi**, to act otherwise, alter, violate (a law), destroy (a hope), &c. **–kṛita**, mfn. changed. **–khyāti**, f. (in Sāṅkhya phil.) the assertion that something is not really what it appears to be according to sensual perception; N. of a philosophical work. **–tva**, n. an opposite state of the case, difference. **–bhāva**, m. alteration, difference. **–bhūta**, mfn. changed. **–vādin** (or *anya-vādin*), mfn. speaking differently; (*ī*), m. speaking inconsistently; (in law) prevaricating or a prevaricator. **–vṛitti**, mfn. altered, disturbed by strong emotion. **–siddha**, mfn. wrongly defined, wrongly proved or established; effected otherwise, unessential. **–siddha-tva**, n. or **–siddhi**, f. wrong arguing, wrong demonstration; that demonstration in which arguments are referred to untrue causes. **–stotra**, n. irony, Yājñ. ii, 204.

Anya-dā, ind. at another time; sometimes; one day, once; in another case [cf. Old Slav. *inogda*, *inŭda*].

Anyad-āśā, **-āśis**, &c. See *anyat-kāraka*.

Anyadīya, mfn. (Pāṇ. vi, 3, 99) belonging to another, Daś.

Anyarhi, ind. at another time, L.

Anyedyuka [Car.] or **anyedyushka** [Suśr.], mfn. occurring on another day; (*as*), m. a chronic fever.

Anye-dyús, ind. on the other day, on the following day, AV. &c.; the other day, once, Pañcat.

Anyonya or **anyo-'nya** (said to be fr. *anyas*, nom. sing. m., and *anya*; cf. *paraspara*; in most cases the first *anya* may be regarded as the subject of the sentence, while the latter assumes the acc., inst., gen., or loc. cases as required by the verb; but there are many instances in which the first *anya*, originally a nominative, is equivalent to an oblique case); one another, mutual; (*am*), or *-tas*, ind. mutually. **-kalaha**, m. mutual quarrel. **-ghāta**, m. mutual conflict, killing one another. **-paksha-nayana**, n. transposing (of numbers) from one side to another. **-bheda**, m. mutual division or enmity. **-mithuna**, n. mutual union; (*as*), m. united mutually. **-vibhāga**, m. mutual partition (of an inheritance). **-vṛitti**, m. mutual effect of one upon another. **-vyatikara**, m. reciprocal action, relation or influence. **-saṃśraya**, m. reciprocal relation (of cause and effect). **-sâpeksha**, mfn. mutually relating. **-hārâbhihata**, mfn. (two quantities) mutually multiplied by their denominators. **Anyonyâpahṛita**, mfn. taken or secreted from one another, taken secretly. **Anyonyâbhāva**, m. mutual non-existence, mutual negation, relative difference. **Anyonyâśraya**, m. mutual or reciprocal support or connection or dependance; mutually depending. **Anyonyâśrita**, mfn. mutually supported or depending. **Anyonyôkti**, f. conversation.

अन्यङ्ग *a-nyaṅga*, mfn. 'spotless,' in comp. with **-śveta**, mfn. white and without spot (as a sacrificial animal), AitBr.

अन्यतस् *anyá-tas*, &c. See s.v. 2. *anyá*.

Anyá-thā, anya-dā, &c. See ib.

अन्या *ányā* (3), f. inexhaustible (as the milk of a cow), RV. viii, 1, 10 & 27, 11; SV.

अन्याय *a-nyāya*, *as*, m. unjust or unlawful action; impropriety, indecorum; irregularity, disorder. **-vartin** or **-vṛitta**, mfn. acting unjustly; following evil courses.

A-nyāyin or **a-nyāyya**, mfn. unjust, improper, indecorous, unbecoming.

अन्यून *á-nyūna*, mf(*ā*)n. not defective, not less than (with abl.); entire, complete. **A-nyū-nâtt ikta** [ŚBr.] or **a-nyūnâdhika**, mfn. not too little and not too much; neither deficient nor excessive.

अन्योकस् *á-ny-okas*, mfn. not remaining in one's habitation (*okas*), AV.

अन्वक्ष *anv-aksha*, mfn. (fr. 4. *aksha*), following, L.; (*am*), ind. afterwards, immediately after, R. &c., cf. gaṇa *śarad-ādi*.

अन्वक्षरसन्धि *anv-akshara-sandhi*, *is*, m. a kind of Sandhi in the Vedas, RPrāt.

अन्वङ्गम् *anv-aṅgám*, ind. after every member or part, ŚBr.

अन्वञ्च् *anváñc*, *aṅ*, *ūcī* and *ūcī*, *ak* (√*añc*), following the direction of another, going after, following; lying lengthwise; (*anūci*), loc. ind. in the rear, behind; (*ak*), ind. afterwards; behind (with acc.) **Anvag-bhāvam**, ind. afterwards, L.; friendly disposed, Pāṇ. iii, 4, 64. **Anvag-bhūya**, ind. becoming friendly disposed, ib.

अन्वञ्ज् *anv-√añj*, to anoint, ŚBr.; Kauś.

अन्वतिषिच् *anv-ati-√sic*, to pour out over or along, TBr.

अन्वती *anv-ati* (√*i*), cl. 2. P. *-atyeti*, to pass over to, follow, ŚBr.

अन्वधिरुह् *anv-adhi-√ruh*, to ascend after another, Lāṭy.

अन्वध्यस् *anv-adhy-√2. as*, to throw upon after another, MānŚr.

अन्वध्यायम् *anv-adhyāyam*, ind. according to the chapters (of the Veda), according to the sacred texts, Nir.

अन्वपक्रम् *anv-apa-√kram*, to run away after another, TBr.

अन्वभिषिच् *anv-abhi-shic* (√*sic*), Ā. *-siñcate*, to have one's self anointed by another (with acc.), MBh. xii, 2803 (both editions).

अन्वय *anv-aya*, *as*, m. (√*i*, see *anv-√i*), following, succession; connection, association, being linked to or concerned with; the natural order or connection of words in a sentence, syntax, construing; logical connection of words; logical connection of cause and effect, or proposition and conclusion; drift, tenor, purport; descendants, race, lineage, family. **-jña**, m. a genealogist. **-vat**, mfn. having a connection (as a consequence), following, agreeing with; belonging to race or family; (*vat*), ind. in connection with, in the sight of, Mn. viii, 332. **-vyatireka**, n. agreement and contrariety; a positive and negative proposition; species and difference; rule and exception; logical connection and disconnection. **-vyatirekin**, mfn. (in phil.) affirmative and negative. **-vyāpti**, f. an affirmative argument.

Anvayin, mfn. connected (as a consequence); belonging to the same family, Rājat. **Anvayi-tva**, n. the state of being a necessary consequence.

अन्वर्च् *anv-√arc*, to honour with shouts or songs of jubilee, RV. v, 29, 2.

अन्वर्ज् *anv-√arj*, to let go, ŚBr.

अन्वर्त् *anvart* (according to NBD.) shortened for *anu-vart* (√*vṛit*), to go after, demand (a girl in marriage), AV. xiv, 1, 56. For the abbreviation, cf. *anvā*, *apvà*, *a-bhva*.

Anvartitṛi for **anu-vartitṛi**, *tā*, m. a wooer, RV. x, 109, 2.

अन्वर्थ *anv-artha*, mf(*ā*)n. conformable to the meaning, agreeing with the true meaning, Ragh. iv, 12; having the meaning obvious, intelligible, clear. **-grahaṇa**, n. the literal acceptation of the meaning of a word (as opposed to the conventional). **-samjñā**, f. a term whose meaning is intelligible in itself (opposed to such technical terms as *bha*, *ghu*, &c.)

अन्वव् *anv-√av*, to encourage, RV. viii, 7, 24.

अन्ववकृ *anv-ava-√1. kri*, to despise, refuse, MaitrS.

अन्ववकॄ *anv-ava-√1. kṝi*, to scatter or strew about (with instr.), Yājñ.

Anv-avakiraṇa, *am*, n. scattering about successively, L.

अन्ववक्रम् *anv-ava-√kram*, to descend or enter in succession, ŚBr. xiv.

अन्ववगा *anv-ava-√1. gā*, to go and join another, ŚBr.

अन्ववचर् *anv-ava-√car*, to insinuate one's self into, enter stealthily, TS. &c.

Anv-avacāra, *as*, m. See *án-anvavacāra*.

अन्ववधा *anv-ava-√dhā*, to place into successively, ĀpŚr.

अन्ववपा *anv-ava-√1. pā*, Ved. Inf. *-pātoh*, to drink after others, ŚāṅkhBr.

अन्ववप्लु *anv-ava-√plu*, *-plavate*, to dive after, TBr.

अन्ववमृश् *anv-ava-√mṛiś*, to touch or come in contact with or along, Gobh.

अन्ववरुह् *anv-ava-√ruh*, to ascend or enter upon after another, MBh.

अन्ववलुप् *anv-ava-√lup*, Pass. *-lupyate*, to drop off after another, PBr.

अन्ववसृज् *anv-ava-√sṛij*, to let go along or towards, TS.; TBr.

Anv-avasarga, *as*, m. letting down, slackening, TPrāt.; Pat.; permission to do as one likes, Pāṇ. i, 4, 96.

अन्ववसो *anv-ava-√so*, *-syati*, to adhere to, cling to, TBr. &c.; to long for, desire, ŚBr. &c.

Anv-ava-sāyín, mfn. adhering to, depending on (gen.), TS.; ŚBr.

Anv-ava-sita, mfn. seized by, ŚāṅkhBr.

अन्ववस्था *anv-ava-√sthā*, to descend after another, ŚBr.

अन्ववस्रु *anv-ava-√sru*, Caus. *-srāvayati*, to cause to flow down upon or along, TS.; TBr.; ŚBr.

अन्ववहन् *anv-ava-√han*, to throw down by striking, ŚBr.

अन्ववहृ *anv-ava-√hṛi*, to lower (the shoulder), ŚāṅkhGṛ.

अन्ववार्ज् *anv-avârj* (√*arj*), to cause to go after or in a particular direction, ŚBr.; to afflict with (instr.), AitUp.

अन्ववास् *anv-avâs* (√*2. as*), to place upon (dat.), TS.

अन्ववे *anv-avê* (√*i*), cl. 2. P. *-avaiti*, to follow, walk up to or get into.

Anv-avāya, *as*, m. race, lineage, MBh.

Anv-avāyana, *am*, n. See *án-anvavāyana*.

अन्ववेक्ष् *anv-avêksh* (√*iksh*), to look at, inspect.

Anv-avekshā, f. regard, consideration.

अन्वश् *anv-√1. aś*, cl. 5. P. Ā. *-aśnoti*, *-nute*, to reach, come up to, equal, RV.; AV.

अन्वष्टका *anv-ashṭakā*, f. the ninth day in the latter half of the three (or four) months following the full moon in Āgrahāyaṇa, Pausha, Māgha (& Phālguna), Mn. iv, 150.

Anvashṭakya, *am*, n. a Śrāddha or funeral ceremony performed on the Anvashṭakās.

अन्वस् *anv-√1. as*, to be near, Lāṭy.; to be at hand, RV.; AitBr.; to reach, RV.

अन्वस्त *ánv-asta*, mfn. (√*2. as*), shot along, shot; interwoven (as in silk), chequered, ŚBr.

अन्वह् *anv-√ah*, perf. *-āha*, to pronounce (especially a ceremonial formula, ŚBr. &c.)

अन्वहम् *anv-ahám*, ind. day after day, every day.

अन्वा *anvā* (for 2. *anu-vā*, q.v.), blowing after, TāṇḍyaBr.; GopBr.

अन्वाकृ *anv-ā-√1. kri*, to give to any one to take with him, to give a portion to a daughter, ŚāṅkhBr.

Anv-ā-kṛiti, *is*, f. shaping after, imitation, ŚāṅkhGṛ.

अन्वाक्रम् *anv-ā-√kram*, Ā. to ascend towards or to, TS.: P. to visit in succession, BhP.

अन्वाक्शायम् *anv-ā-kśâyam*, ind. (*kśā* for *khyā*), reciting successively, MaitrS.

अन्वाख्या *anv-ā-√khyā*, to enumerate, Lāṭy.

Anv-ākhyāna, *am*, n. an explanation keeping close to the text, ŚBr.; a minute account or statement, Pat.

अन्वागम् *anv-ā-√gam*, to follow, come after, VS.; ŚBr. &c.: Desid. *-jigāṅsati*, to wish or intend to follow, ŚBr.

अन्वागा *anv-ā-√1. gā*, to follow, RV. i, 126, 3.

अन्वाचक्ष् *anv-ā-√caksh*, to name after, ŚBr.

अन्वाचम् *anv-ā-√cam*, to follow in rinsing the mouth, ĀśvGṛ.

अन्वाचय *anv-ācaya*, *as*, m. (√*ci*), laying down a rule of secondary importance (after that which is *pradhāna* or primary); connecting of a secondary action with the main action (e.g. the conjunction *ca* is sometimes used *anvācaye*). **-śish-ṭa**, mfn. propounded as a rule or matter of secondary importance.

Anv-ācita, mfn. secondary, inferior.

अन्वाचर् *anv-ā-√car*, to follow or imitate in doing, BhP.

अन्वाजे *anvāje* (√*aj*?), only used in connection with √*1. kri*, e.g. *anvāje kri*, to support, aid, assist, Pāṇ. i, 4, 73.

अन्वातन् *anv-ā-√tan*, to extend, spread, RV. viii, 48, 13, &c.; to overspread, extend over, VS.

अन्वादा *anv-ā-√1. dā*, Ā. to resume, ŚBr.

अन्वादिश् *anv-ā-√diś*, to name or mention afresh, Pāṇ.

Anv-ādishṭa, mfn. mentioned again, referring to a previous rule, Pāṇ. vi, 2, 190.

Anv-ādeśa, *as,* m. mentioning after, a repeated mention, referring to what has been stated previously, re-employment of the same word in a subsequent part of a sentence, the employment again of the same thing to perform a subsequent operation.

Anv-ādeśaka, mfn. referring to a previous statement, TPrāt.

अन्वाधा *anv-ā-√dhā*, to add in placing upon, place upon: Ā. & P. to add fuel (to the fire), AitBr. &c.; to deliver over to a third person (in law).

Anv-ādhāna, *am,* n. adding or putting fuel (on the three sacred fires); depositing.

1\. **Anv-ādhi,** *is,* m. a bail or deposit given to any one for being delivered to a third person, Gaut.

Anv-ādheya or **-ādheyaka,** *am,* n. property presented after marriage to the wife by her husband's family, Mn. &c.

Anv-āhita, mfn. deposited with a person to be delivered ultimately to the right owner.

अन्वाधाव् *anv-ā-√1.dhāv*, to run after, Kāṭh.

अन्वाधी *anv-ā-√dhī*, to recollect, remember, think of, AV.; TĀr.

2\. **Anv-ādhi,** *is,* m. repentance, remorse, L.

Anv-ādhyá, *ās,* m. pl. a kind of divinity, ŚBr.

अन्वानी *anv-ā-√nī*, to lead to or along.

अन्वानु *anv-ā-√nu*, Intens. *-nónavīti*, to sound through, RV. x, 68, 12.

अन्वान्त्र्य *ánv-āntrya*, mfn. being in the entrails, AV.

अन्वाप् *anv-√āp*, to attain, reach, AitBr.: Desid. *anv-īpsati*, to harmonize in opinion, agree, VP.

अन्वाभज् *anv-ā-√bhaj*, P. and Ā. to cause to take a share after or with another, ŚBr. &c.

Anv-ā-bhakta, mfn. entitled to take a share after or with another.

अन्वाभू *anv-ā-√bhū*, to imitate, equal, TS. &c.

अन्वायत् *anv-ā-√yat*, Caus. *-yātayati*, to dispose or add in regular sequence, bring into connection with (loc. or abl.), ŚBr. &c.

Anv-ā-yatta, mfn. (with loc. or acc.) connected with, being in accordance with, being entitled to, TS. &c.

Anv-āyātya, mfn. to be brought in connection with, to be added, to be supplied, ĀśvŚr.

अन्वायतन *anv-āyatana*, mfn. latitudinal.

अन्वारभ् *anv-ā-√rabh*, to catch or seize or touch from behind; to place one's self behind or at the side of, keep at the side of, AV. &c.: Caus. *-rambhayati*, to place behind another (with loc.), TS.

Anv-ārábhya, mfn. to be touched from behind, ŚBr.

Anv-ārambhá, *as,* m. touching from behind, TBr.; KātyŚr.

Anv-ārambhaṇa, *am,* n. id., KātyŚr.

Anv-ārambhaṇīyā, f. an initiatory ceremony, KātyŚr.

अन्वारुह् *anv-ā-√ruh*, to follow or join by ascending; to ascend: Caus. *-rohayati*, to place upon.

Anv-ārohá, *ās,* m. pl., N. of certain Japas uttered at the Soma-libations, TS.

Anv-ārohaṇa, *am,* n. (a widow's) ascending the funeral pile after or with the body of a husband, (gaṇa *anupravacanādi*, q. v.)

Anv-ārohaṇīya, mfn. belonging to the Anvārohaṇa, or rite of cremation, ibid.

अन्वालभ् *anv-ā-√labh*, to lay hold of, grasp, handle, take in the hand or with the hand, RV. x, 130, 7, &c.

Anv-ālabhana or **anv-ālambhana,** *am,* n. a handle (?), MBh. iii, 17156.

अन्वालोच् *anv-ā-√loc*, Caus. *-locayati*, to consider attentively.

अन्वावप् *anv-ā-√2. vap*, 'to scatter in addition,' to add, Kauś.

अन्वावह् *anv-ā-√vah*, to convey to or in the proximity of, RV. x, 29, 2.

अन्वाविश् *anv-ā-√viś*, to enter, occupy, possess; to follow, act according to, ChUp. &c.

अन्वावृत् *anv-ā-√vṛit*, to roll near or along, RV. v, 62, 2; to revolve or move after, follow, VS. &c.: Intens. *-varīvartti* (impf. 3. pl. *ánv āvarīvuḥ* for °*vṛituḥ*), to drive or move after or along, RV. x, 51, 6; TS.

अन्वाशी *anv-ā-√śī*, to lie along, be extended over, AV.

अन्वाश्रित *anv-ā-śrita*, mfn. (√*śri*), one who has gone along; placed or situated along.

अन्वास् *anv-√ās*, to take a seat subsequently; to be seated at or near or round (with acc.); to live in the proximity of (with gen.), Hcat.; to be engaged in (especially in a religious act).

Anv-āsana, *am,* n. sitting down after (another); service; regret, affliction, L.; a place where work is done, manufactory, house of industry, L.; an unctuous or cooling enema, L.

Anv-āsīna, mfn. sitting down after, seated alongside of.

Anv-āsyamāna, mfn. being accompanied by, attended by.

अन्वास्था *anv-ā-√sthā*, to go towards, to meet, attain, VS. &c.

अन्वाहित *anv-ā-hita.* See *anv-ā-√dhā*.

अन्वाहृ *anv-ā-√hṛi*, to make up, supply, ŚBr. &c.

Anv-ā-haraṇa, *am,* n. making up, supplying, Comm. on Lāṭy.

Anv-ā-hāra, *as,* m. id., Lāṭy.

Anv-āhāryà, *as,* m. a gift, consisting of food prepared with rice, presented to the Ṛitvij priest at the Darśapūrṇamāsa ceremonies, TS. &c.; (*am* or *akam*), n. the monthly Śrāddha (q. v.) held on the day of new moon (according to Mn. iii, 123 it should be of meat eaten after the presentation of a Piṇḍa or ball of rice). **—pácana,** m. the southern sacrificial fire, used in the Anvāhārya sacrifice, ŚBr. &c.

अन्वाह्वे *anv-ā-√hve*, to call to one's side in order or after another, Kauś.

अन्वि *anv-√i*, to go after or alongside, to follow; to seek; to be guided by; to fall to one's share, RV. iv, 4, 11; Ved. Inf. *ánv-etave*, to reach or join [BR.], to imitate [Gmn.], RV. vii, 33, 8; *ánv-etavaí*, to go along (with acc.), RV. i, 24, 8; vii, 44, 5.

Anv-aya. See p. 46, col. 1.

Anv-ita, mfn. gone along with; joined, attended, accompanied by, connected with, linked to; having as an essential or inherent part, endowed with, possessed of, possessing; acquired; reached by the mind, understood; following; connected as in grammar or construction. **Anvitârtha,** mfn. having a clear meaning understood from the context, perspicuous.

Ánv-iti, *is,* f. following after, VS.

Anv-īyamāna, mfn. being followed.

अन्विध् *anv-√idh* or *anv-√indh*, to kindle, AV.

अन्विष् *anv-√3. ish*, cl. 1. P. *-icchati*, to desire, seek, seek after, search, aim at, AV. &c.: cl. 4. P. *-ishyati*, id., R. &c., Caus. *-eshayati*, id., Mṛicch. &c.

Anv-ishṭa or **anv-ishyamāṇa,** mfn. sought, required.

Anv-esha, *as,* m. [Śāk.] or **anv-eshaṇa,** *am, ā,* n. f. seeking for, searching, investigating.

Anv-eshaka, mf(*ikā*)n. or **anv-eshin** or **anv-eshṭṛi** [Pāṇ. v, 2, 90, &c.], mfn. searching, inquiring.

Anv-eshṭavya or **anv-eshya,** mfn. to be searched, to be investigated.

अन्वीक्ष् *anv-√īksh*, to follow with one's looks, to keep looking or gazing, AV. &c.; to keep in view, ŚBr.

Anv-īkshaṇa, *am,* n. or **anv-īkshā,** f. examining, inquiry, Comm. on Nyāyad.; meditation, BhP.

Anv-īkshitávya, mfn. to be kept in view or in mind, ŚBr.

अन्वीत *anv-ita* = *anv-ita*, q.v., Bālar.; Kir.

अन्वीपम् *anv-īpám*, ind. (fr. 2. *ap*), along the water, along the river, MaitrS.; cf. Pāṇ. vi, 3, 98, Sch.

अन्वृ *anv-√ṛi* (cl. 3. P. *-iyarti*), aor. Ā. *-arta*, to follow in rising, RV. v, 52, 6.

अन्वृचम् *anv-ṛicám*, ind. verse after verse, ŚBr.

अन्वृजु *ánv-ṛiju*, mfn. moving straightforwards or in the right way (N. of Indra), MaitrS.

अन्वृध् *anv-√ṛidh*, cl. 6. P. *-ṛidháti*, to carry out, accomplish, RV. vii, 87, 7.

अन्वे *anv-ê* (*ā-√i*), cl. 2. P. *-aiti*, to come after, to follow as an adherent or attendant, RV. i, 161, 3, &c.

अन्वेतवे *ánv-etave*, &c. See *anv-√i*.

अप् 1. *áp*, n. (gen. *apás*), work (according to NBD.), RV. i, 151, 4.

अप् 2. *áp* (in Ved. used in sing. and plur., but in the classical language only in plur., *ā́pas*), f. water; air, the intermediate region, Naigh.; the star δ Virginis; the Waters considered as divinities. Ifc. *ap* may become *apa* or *īpa*, *ūpa* after *i*- and *u*-stems respectively. [Cf. Lat. *aqua*; Goth. *ahva*, 'a river;' Old Germ. *aha*, and *affa* at the end of compounds; Lith. *uppė*, 'a river;' perhaps Lat. *amnis*, 'a river,' for *apnis*; cf. also ἀφρός.] **Ápa-vat,** mfn. watery, AV. xviii, 4, 24. **Apaḥ-saṃvarta,** m. destruction (of the world) by water, Buddh. **Apāṃ-vatsa,** m. 'calf of the waters,' N. of a star. **Apā́ṃ-nápāt** [RV.; VS.] or **apāṃ-naptṛi** [Pāṇ. iv, 2, 27] or **apāṃ-garbha** [VS.] or **apo-naptṛi** [Pāṇ. iv, 2, 27], m. 'grandson of the waters,' N. of Agni or fire as sprung from water. **Apāṃ-naptriya** [Pāṇ. iv, 2, 27] or **apāṃ-naptrīya** [Kāṭh.] or **apo-naptriya** [PBr.] or **apo-naptrīya** [MaitrS.; TS.; AitBr. &c.], mfn. relating to Agni. **Apāṃ-nātha,** m. the ocean, L. **Apāṃ-nidhi,** m. the ocean, L.; N. of a Sāman. **Apām-pati** or **ap-pati** [Mn.], m. the ocean; N. of Varuṇa. **Apām-pitta** or **ap-pitta,** n. fire; a plant; L. **Ap-kṛitsna,** n. deep meditation performed by means of water, Buddh. **Ap-cara,** m. an aquatic animal, Mn. vii, 72. **Ap-saras,** see s. v.

Aptyá (3), mfn. watery, RV. i, 124, 5.

Ápya (2, 3), mf(*ā́pyā*; once *ā́pī*, RV. vi, 67, 9)n. being in water, coming from water, connected with water, RV. (cf. 3. *ā́pya*).

Apsavá, apsavyà, apsā́. See s. v.

Apsu, for words beginning thus, see s. v. *apsu*.

Ab-, for words beginning thus, see s. v. *ab-indhana*, *ab-ja*, &c.

अप *ápa*, ind. (as a prefix to nouns and verbs, expresses) away, off, back (opposed to *úpa*, *ánu*, *sam*, *pra*); down (opposed to *ud*). **—tarám,** ind. farther off, MaitrS.

When prefixed to nouns, it may sometimes = the neg. particle *a*, e. g. *apa-bhī*, fearless; or may express deterioration, inferiority, &c. (cf. *apa-pāṭha*). (As a separable particle or adverb in Ved., with abl.) away from, on the outside of, without, with the exception of [cf. Gk. ἀπό; Lat. *ab*; Goth. *af*; Eng. *of*].

अपकरुण *apa-karuṇa*, mfn. cruel.

अपकलङ्क *apa-kalaṅka*, *as,* m. a deep stain or mark of disgrace, L.

अपकल्मष *apa-kalmasha*, mf(*ā*)n. stainless, sinless.

अपकष् *apa-√kash*, to scrape off, AV.

अपकषाय *apa-kashāya*, mfn. sinless, MarkP.

अपकाम *apa-kāmá*, *as,* m. aversion, abhorrence, RV. vi, 75, 2: AV.; abominableness, AV.; (*ám*), ind. against one's liking, unwillingly, AV.

अपकीर्ति *apa-kīrti, is,* f. infamy, disgrace.

अपकुक्षि *apa-kukshi, is,* m. a bad or ill-shaped belly (?), Pāṇ. vi, 2, 187; (also used as a *Bahu-vrīhi* and *Avyayī-bhāva.*)

अपकुञ्ज *apa-kuñja, as,* m., N. of a younger brother of the serpent-king Śesha, Hariv.

अपकृ *apa-√1. kṛi,* to carry away, remove, drag away; (with gen. or acc.) to hurt, wrong, injure: Caus. *-kārayati,* to hurt, wrong.

Apa-karaṇa, *am,* n. acting improperly; doing wrong, L.; ill-treating, offending, injuring, L.

Apa-kartṛi, mfn. injurious, offensive.

Apa-karman, *a,* n. discharge (of a debt), Mn. viii, 4; evil doing, L.; violence, L.; any impure or degrading act, L.

Apa-kāra, *as,* m. wrong, offence, injury, hurt; despise, disdain. **-gir** [L.], f. or **-śabda** [Pāṇ. viii, 1, 8, Sch.], m. an offending or menacing speech. **-tā,** f. wrong, offence. **Apakārârthin,** mfn. malicious, malevolent.

Apa-kāraka or **apa-kārin,** mfn. acting wrong, doing ill to (with gen.); offending, injuring.

Apa-kṛita, mfn. done wrongly or maliciously, offensively or wickedly committed; practised as a degrading or impure act (e.g. menial work, funeral rites, &c.); (*am*), n. injury, offence.

Apa-kṛiti, *is,* f. oppression, wrong, injury.

Apa-kṛitya, *am,* n. damage, hurt, Pañcat.

Apa-kriyā, f. a wrong or improper act; delivery, clearing off (debts), Yājñ. iii, 234; offence.

अपकृत् *apa-√2. kṛit,* cl. 6. P. *-kṛintati,* to cut off, Kauś.

अपकृष् *apa-√kṛish,* cl. 1. P. *-karshati,* to draw off or aside, drag down, carry away, take away, remove; to omit, diminish; to put away; to anticipate a word &c. which occurs later (in a sentence); to bend (a bow); to detract, debase, dishonour: Caus. *-karshayati,* to remove, diminish, detract.

Apa-karsha, *as,* m. drawing or dragging off or down, detraction, diminution, decay; lowering, depression; decline, inferiority, infamy; anticipation, Nyāyam.; (in poetry) anticipation of a word occurring later. **-sama,** *as, ā,* m. f. a sophism in the Nyāya (e.g. 'sound has not the quality of shape as a jar has, therefore sound and a jar have no qualities in common').

Apa-karshaka, mf(*ikā*)n. drawing down, detracting (with gen.), Sāh.

Apa-karshaṇa, mfn. taking away, forcing away, removing, diminishing; (*am*), n. taking away, depriving of; drawing down; abolishing, denying; anticipation, Nyāyam.

Apa-kṛishṭa, mfn. drawn away, taken away, removed, lost; dragged down, brought down, depressed; low, vile, inferior; (*as*), m. a crow, L. **-cetana,** mfn. mentally debased. **-jāti,** mfn. of a low tribe. **-tā,** f. or **-tva,** n. inferiority, vileness.

अपकॄ *apa-√1. kṝi,* Ā. *apa-s-kirate* (Pāṇ. vi, 1, 142) to scrape with the feet, Uttarar.; (cf. *ava-√s-kṝi*): P. *apa-kirati,* to spout out, spurt, scatter, Pāṇ. i, 3, 21, Comm.; to throw down, L.

अपक्ति *a-pakti, is,* f. (√*pac*), immaturity; indigestion.

A-pakva, mf(*ā*)n. unripe, immature; undigested. **-tā,** f. immaturity; incompleteness. **-buddhi,** mfn. of immature understanding. **Apakvâśin,** mfn. eating raw, uncooked food.

अपक्रम् *apa-√kram,* to go away, retreat, retire from, RV. x, 164, 1, &c.; to glide away; to measure off by steps, Kauś.: Caus. *-kramayati,* to cause to run away, PBr.: Desid. *-cikramishati,* to intend to run away or escape (with abl.), ŚBr.

Apa-kramá, *as,* m. going away, ŚBr. &c.; flight, retreat, L.; (mfn.), not being in the regular order (a fault in poetry).

Apa-krámaṇa, *am,* n. or **apa-krāma,** *as,* m. passing off or away, retiring.

Apa-kramin, mfn. going away, retiring.

Apa-krānta, mfn. gone away; (*am*), n. (= *atītam*) that which is past, Bālar.

Ápa-krānti, *is,* f. = *apa-krámaṇa,* MaitrS.

Apa-krāmuka, mfn. = *apa-kramin,* TS.; PBr.

अपक्री *apa-√krī,* to buy, AV.; ŚBr. (see *ava-√krī*).

अपक्रुश् *apa-√kruś,* to revile.

Apa-krośa, *as,* m. reviling, abusing, L.

अपक्ष *a-pakshá,* mfn. without wings, AV. &c.; without followers or partisans, MBh.; not on the same side or party; adverse, opposed to. **-tā,** f. opposition, hostility. **-pāta,** m. impartiality. **-pucchá,** mfn. without wings and tail, ŚBr. &c.

अपक्षि *apa-√4. kshi,* Pass. *-kshīyate,* to decline, wane (as the moon), TS.; ŚBr.

Apa-kshaya, *as,* m. decline, decay, wane, VP.

Apa-kshita, mfn. waned, BhP.

Apa-kshīṇa, mfn. declined, decayed, L.

अपक्षिप् *apa-√kship,* to throw away or down, take away, remove.

Apa-kshipta, mfn. thrown down or away.

Apa-kshepaṇa, *am,* n. throwing down, &c.

अपगम् *apa-√gam,* to go away, depart; to give way, vanish.

Apa-ga, mf(*ā*)n. going away, turning away from (abl.), AV. i, 34, 5; (cf. *án-apaga*); (*ā*), f. = *āpa-gā,* L.

Apa-gata, mfn. gone, departed, remote, gone off; dead, diseased. **-vyādhi,** mfn. one who has recovered from a disease.

Apa-gama, *as,* m. going away; giving way; departure, death.

Apa-gamana, *am,* n. id.

अपगर *apa-gara, as,* m. (√*1. gṝi*), reviler (special function of a priest at a sacrifice), PBr.; Lāṭy. &c.; (cf. *abhigará.*)

अपगर्जित *apa-garjita,* mfn. thunderless (as a cloud), Kathās.

अपगल्भ *apa-galbhá,* mfn. wanting in boldness, embarrassed, perplexed, VS.; TS.

अपगा *apa-√1. gā,* to go away, vanish, retire (with abl.), VS. &c.

अपगुर् *apa-√gur,* to reject, disapprove, threaten, RV. v, 32, 6, &c.; to inveigh against any one: Intens. part. *apa-járgurāṇa* (see s. v. *apa-√2. gṝi*).

Apa-gāram or **apa-goram,** ind. disapproving, threatening (?), Pāṇ. vi, 1, 53.

Apa-goraṇa, *am,* n. threatening, Comm. on TS.

अपगुह् *apa-√guh* (Subj. 2. sg. P. *-gūhas,* Ā. *-gūhathās*; impf. 3. pl. *ápāgūhan*; aor. *-aghukshat*) to conceal, hide, RV.; AV.

Ápa-gūḍha, mfn. hidden, concealed, RV.

Apa-gū́hamāna, mfn. hiding, AV. xix, 56, 2; (*ápa gū́h°*) RV. vii, 104, 17.

Apa-gohá, *as,* m. hiding place, secret, RV. ii, 15, 7.

अपगॄ *apa-√2. gṝi,* Intens. part. *-járgurāṇa,* mfn. (Gmn. & NBD.) devouring, RV. v, 29, 4.

अपगोपुर *apa-gopura,* mfn. without gates (as a town).

अपगै *apa-√gai,* to break off singing, cease to sing, GopBr.; Vait.

अपग्रह् *apa-√grah,* to take away, disjoin, tear off.

अपघट् *apa-√ghaṭ,* Caus. *-ghāṭayati,* to shut up.

अपघन 1. *apa-ghana, as,* m. (√*han*), (Pāṇ. iii, 3, 81) a limb or member (as a hand or foot), Naish.

Apa-ghā́ta, *as,* m. striking off, warding off, ŚBr.; (cf. Pāṇ. iii, 3, 81, Sch.)

Apa-ghātaka, mf(*ikā*)n. (ifc.) warding off.

Apa-ghātin, mfn. id. See *apa-√han.*

अपघन 2. *apa-ghana,* mfn. cloudless.

अपच *a-paca,* mfn. not able to cook, a bad cook, Pāṇ. vi, 2, 157 seq., Sch.

अपचर् *apa-√car,* to depart; to act wrongly.

Apa-carita, mfn. gone away, departed, dead; (*am*), n. fault, offence, Śāk.

Apa-cāra, *as,* m. want, absence; defect; fault, improper conduct, offence; unwholesome or improper regimen.

Apa-cārin, mfn. departing from, disbelieving in, infidel, Mn.; doing wrong, wicked.

अपचाय् *apa-cāy,* to fear, TBr.; to respect, honour, ŚBr.; TBr.

Apa-cāyita, mfn. honoured, respected, Pāṇ. vii, 2, 30, Sch.

Apa-cāyin, mfn. not rendering due respect, showing want of respect, MBh.; *vṛiddhâpacāyi-tva,* n. the not rendering due respect to old men, MBh. xiii, 6705.

अपचि 1. *apa-√2. ci* (Imper. 2. sg. *-cikīhi*) to pay attention to, to respect, AV. i, 10, 4.

1. **Ápa-cita,** mfn. (Pāṇ. vii, 2, 30) honoured, respected, ŚBr. &c.; respectfully invited, BhP.; (*am*), n. honouring, esteeming.

1. **Apa-citi,** *is,* f. honouring, reverence, Śiś. **-mat** (*ápaciti-*), mfn. honoured, TS.; ŚBr.; KātyŚr.

अपचि 2. *apa-√1. ci, -cinoti,* to gather, collect: Pass. *-cīyate,* to be injured in health or prosperity; to grow less; to wane; (with abl.) to lose anything, MBh.

Apa-caya, *as,* m. diminution, decay, decrease, decline; N. of several planetary mansions.

2. **Apa-cita,** mfn. diminished, expended, wasted; emaciated, thin, Śāk. &c.

2. **Apa-citi,** *is,* f. loss, L.; expense, L.; N. of a daughter of Marīci, VP.; (for 3. *ápa-citi,* see below.)

Apa-cī, f. a disease consisting in an enlargement of the glands of the neck, Suśr.

Apa-cetṛi, *tā,* m. a spendthrift, L.

अपचिकीर्षा *apa-cikīrshā,* f. (√*1. kṛi* Desid.), desire of hurting any one.

अपचित् 1. *apa-√cit,* Caus. Ā. (Subj. *-cetáyātai*) to abandon, turn off from (abl.), VS. ii, 17: Desid. *-cikitsati,* to wish to leave or to abandon any one (abl.), AV. xiii, 2, 15.

2. **Apa-cít,** *t,* f. a noxious flying insect, AV.

Apa-cetas, mfn. not favourable to (with abl.), TBr.

अपचिति 3. *ápa-citi, is,* f. (= ἀπότισις, √*3. ci*), compensation, either recompense [TS. &c.] or retaliation, revenge, punishing, RV. iv, 28, 4, &c.

अपच्छद् *apa-cchad* (√*chad*), Caus. *-cchādayati,* to take off a cover, ĀpŚr.

Apa-cchattra, mfn. not having a parasol, Kathās.

अपच्छाय *apa-cchāya,* mfn. shadowless, having no shadow (as a deity or celestial being); having a bad or unlucky shadow; (*ā*), f. an unlucky shadow, a phantom, apparition.

अपच्छिद् 1. *apa-cchid* (√*chid*), to cut off or away, ŚBr. &c.

2. **Apa-cchíd,** *t,* f. a cutting, shred, chip, ŚBr.; PBr.

Apa-ccheda, *as, am,* m. n. cuttting off or away; separation.

Apa-cchedana, *am,* n. id.

अपच्यु *apa-√cyu* (aor. Ā. 2. sg. *-cyoshṭhāḥ*) to fall off, go off, desert, RV. x, 173, 2: Caus. (aor. *-cucyavat*) to expel, RV. ii, 41, 10.

Apa-cyavá, *as,* m. pushing away, RV. i, 28, 3.

अपजात *apa-jāta, as,* m. a bad son who has turned out ill, Pañcat.

अपजि *apa-√ji,* to ward off, keep off or out, ŚBr.; Kāṭh.; PBr.

Apa-jaya, *as,* m. defeat, discomfiture, L.

Apa-jayya, mfn. See *an-apajayyám.*

अपजिघांसु *apa-jighāṅsu,* mfn. (√*han* Desid.), desirous of keeping off, wishing to avert, AitBr.

अपजिहीर्षु *apa-jihīrshu,* mfn. (√*hṛi* Desid.), wishing to carry off or take away, Rājat.

अपज्ञा *apa-√jñā, -jānīte,* to dissemble, conceal, Pāṇ. i, 3, 44.

Apa-jñāna, *am,* n. denying, concealing, L.

अपज्य *apa-jya,* mfn. without a bowstring, MBh.

अपञ्चीकृत *a-pañcī-kṛita, am,* n. (in Vedānta phil.) 'not compounded of the five gross elements,' the five subtle elements.

अपटान्तर *a-paṭântara*, mfn. 'not separated by a curtain,' adjoining (v. l. *a-padântara*, q.v.), L.

अपटी *apaṭī*, f. a screen or wall of cloth (especially surrounding a tent), L. **-kshepa**, m. 'tossing aside the curtain;' (*eṇa*), ind. with a toss of the curtain, precipitate entrance on the stage (indicating hurry and agitation); (cf. *paṭīkshepa*.)

अपटु *a-paṭu*, mfn. not clever, awkward, uncouth; ineloquent; sick, diseased, L. **-tā**, f. or **-tva**, n. awkwardness.

अपठ *a-paṭha*, *as*, m. unable to read, Pāṇ. vi, 2, 157 seq., Sch.

अपण्डित *a-paṇḍita*, mfn. unlearned, illiterate.

अपण्य *a-paṇya*, mfn. unfit for sale; (*am*), n. an unsaleable article, Gaut.

अपतक्ष् *apa-√taksh* (3. pl. *-takshṇuvanti* & impf. *apâtakshan*) to chip off, AV. x, 7, 20; ŚBr.

अपतन्त्र *apa-tantra*, *as*, m. spasmodic contraction (of the body or stomach), emprosthotonos, Hcat.

Apa-tantraka, *as*, m. id., Suśr.

Apa-tānaka, *as*, m. id., Suśr.

Apa-tānakin, mfn. affected with spasmodic contraction, Suśr.

अपति *á-pati*, *is*, m. not a husband or master, AV. viii, 6, 16; (*is*), f. 'without a husband or master,' either an unmarried person or a widow. **-ghnī** (*á-pati-*), f. not killing a husband, RV. x, 85, 44; AV. **-tā**, f. state of being without a husband. **-putrā**, f. without a husband and children. **-vratā**, f. an unfaithful or unchaste wife.

A-patikā = *a-pati*, f., Nir.

अपतीर्थ *apa-tīrtha*, *as*, *am*, m. n. a bad or improper Tīrtha, q. v.

अपतूल *ápa-tūla*, mf(*ā*)n. without a tuft, without a panicle, TS.

अपतृप् *apa-√tṛip*, Caus. *-tarpayati*, to starve, cause to fast, Car.; Suśr.

Apa-tarpaṇa, *am*, n. fasting (in sickness), Suśr.

अपत्त्र *a-pattra*, mfn. leafless; (*ā*), f., N. of a plant.

अपत्नीक *a-patnīka*, mfn. not having a wife, AitBr.; KātyŚr.; where the wife is not present, KātyŚr.

अपत्य *ápatya*, *am*, n. (fr. *ápa*), offspring, child, descendant; a patronymical affix, Sāh. **-kāma**, mfn. desirous of offspring. **-jīva**, m., N. of a plant. **-tā**, f. state of childhood, Mn. iii, 16. **-da**, mfn. giving offspring; (*ā*), f., N. of various plants. **-patha**, m. 'path of offspring,' the vulva, Suśr. **-pratyaya**, m. a patronymical affix, Sāh. **-vat** (*ápatya-*), mfn. possessed of offspring, AV. xii, 4, 1. **-vikrayin**, m. 'seller of his offspring,' a father who receives a gratuity from his son-in-law. **-śatru**, m. 'having his descendants for enemies,' a crab (said to perish in producing young). **-sáć**, m(acc. sg. *-sáćam*)fn. accompanied with offspring, RV. **-Apatyârtha-śabda**, m. a patronymic.

अपत्रप् *apa-√trap*, to be ashamed or bashful, turn away the face.

Apa-trapaṇa, *am*, n. or **-trapā**, f. bashfulness; embarrassment.

Apa-trapishṇu, mfn. bashful, Pāṇ. iii, 2, 136.

अपत्रस् *apa-√tras* (impf. 3. pl. *-atrasan*) to flee from in terror, RV. x, 95, 8, MBh.

Apa-trasta, mfn. (ifc. or with abl.) afraid of, fleeing or retiring from in terror, Pāṇ. ii, 1, 38.

अपथ *á-patha*, *am*, n. not a way, absence of a road, pathless state, AV. &c.; wrong way, deviation; heresy, heterodoxy, L.; (mf(*ā*)n.), pathless, roadless, Pāṇ. ii, 4, 30, Sch.; (*ā*), f., N. of various plants. **-gāmin**, mfn. going by a wrong road, pursuing bad practices, heretical. **-prapanna**, mfn. out of place, in the wrong place, misapplied.

A-pathin, °*nthās*, m. absence of road, Pāṇ. v, 4, 72.

A-pathya, mfn. unfit; unsuitable; inconsistent; (in med.) unwholesome as food or drink in particular complaints. **-nimitta**, mfn. caused by unfit food or drink. **-bhuj**, mfn. eating what is forbidden.

अपद् *a-pád* or *á-pad* [only ŚBr. xiv], mfn. nom. m. *a-pắd*, f. *a-pắd* [RV. i, 152, 3 & vi, 59, 6] or *a-pádī* [RV. x, 22, 14], footless, RV.; AV.; ŚBr.

Á-pada, *am*, n. no place, no abode, AV.; the wrong place or time, Kathās. &c.; (mfn.), footless, Pañcat. **-ruhā** or **-rohiṇī**, f. the parasitical plant Epidendron Tesselloides. **-stha**, mfn. not being in its place; out of office. **A-padântara**, mfn. 'not separated by a foot,' adjoining, contiguous (v. l. *a-paṭântara*, q.v.), L.; (*am*), ind. without delay, immediately, MBh.

अपदक्षिणम् *apa-dakshiṇam*, ind. away from the right, to the left side, KātyŚr.

अपदम *apa-dama*, mfn. without self-restraint; of wavering fortune.

अपदव *apa-dava*, mfn. free from forest-fire.

Apa-davâpad, mfn. free from the calamity of fire.

अपदश *apa-daśa*, mfn. (fr. *daśan*), (any number) off or beyond ten, L.; (fr. *daśā*), without a fringe (as a garment), MBh.

अपदस् *apa-√das* (3. pl. *-dasyanti*) to fail, i. e. become dry, RV. i, 135, 8.

अपदह् *apa-√dah*, to burn up, to burn out so as to drive out, RV. vii, 1, 7, &c.

अपदान *apa-dāna*, *am*, n. (√*dai*?), a great or noble work, R. ii, 65, 4; Śāk. (v. l.); (in Pāli for *ava-dāna*, q. v.) a legend treating of former and future births of men and exhibiting the consequences of their good and evil actions.

अपदार्थ *a-padārtha*, *as*, m. nonentity.

अपदिश् *apa-√diś* (ind. p. *-diśya*) to assign, KātyŚr.; to point out, indicate; to betray, pretend, hold out as a pretext or disguise, Ragh. &c.

Apa-diśam, ind. in an intermediate region (of the compass), half a point, L.

Apa-dishṭa, mfn. assigned as a reason or pretext.

Apa-deśa, *as*, m. assigning, pointing out, KātyŚr.; pretence, feint, pretext, disguise, contrivance; the second step in a syllogism (i. e. statement of the reason); a butt or mark, L.; place, quarter, L.

Apa-deśin, mfn. assuming the appearance or semblance of; pretending, feigning, Daś.

Apa-deśya, mfn. to be indicated, to be stated, Mn. viii, 54; Daś.

अपदुष्पद् *ápa-dushpad*, 'not a failing step,' a firm or safe step, RV. x, 99, 3.

अपदॄ *apa-√dṝī*, Intens. p. *apa-dárdrat*, mfn. tearing open, RV. vi, 17, 5.

अपदेवता *apa-devatā*, f. an evil demon.

अपदोष *apa-dosha*, mfn. faultless.

अपद्रव्य *apa-dravya*, *am*, n. a bad thing.

अपद्रा *apa-√drā* (Imper. 3. pl. *-drāntu*, 2. sg. *-drāhi*) to run away, RV. x, 85, 32; AV.

अपद्रु *apa-√2. dru*, id., ŚBr. &c.

अपद्वार *apa-dvāra*, *am*, n. a side-entrance (not the regular door), Suśr.

अपधम् *apa-√dham* (3. pl. *-dhamanti*, impf. *ápâdhamat*, 2. sg. *-adhamas*) to blow away or off, RV.

अपधा 1. *apa-√dhā* (Imper. *-dadhātu*; aor. Pass. *-dhāyi*) to take off, place aside, RV. iv, 28, 2; vi, 20, 5 & x, 164, 3.

2. **Apa-dhā́**, f. hiding, shutting up, RV. ii, 12, 3.

अपधाव् *apa-√dhāv*, to run away, AV.; ŚBr.; to depart (from a previous statement), prevaricate, Mn. viii, 54.

अपधुरम् *apa-dhurám*, away from the yoke, TBr.

अपधू *apa-√dhū* (1. sg. *-dhūnomi*) to shake off, ŚāṅkhGṛ.

Apa-dhūma, mfn. free from smoke, Ragh.

अपधृष् *apa-√dhṛish*, *-dhṛis ṇoti*, to overcome, subdue, KaushBr.; (cf. *an-apadhṛishya*.)

अपध्यै *apa-√dhyai*, to have a bad opinion of, curse mentally, MBh. &c.

Apa-dhyāna, *am*, n. envy, jealousy, MBh. &c.; meditation upon things which are not to be thought of, Jain.

अपध्वंस् *apa-√dhvaṇs*, *-dhvaṇsati*, to scold, revile, [Comm. on] MBh. i, 5596 ('to drive or turn away,' NBD.); to fall away, be degraded (NBD.), Hariv. 720.

Apa-dhvaṇsá, *as*, m. concealment, AV.; 'falling away, degradation,' in comp. with **-ja**, mfn. 'born from it,' a child of a mixed or impure caste (whose father belongs to a lower [Mn. x, 41, 46] or higher [MBh. xiii, 2617] caste than its mother's).

Apa-dhvaṇsin, mfn. causing to fall, destroying, abolishing.

Apa-dhvasta, mfn. degraded; reviled; abandoned, destroyed; (*as*), m. a vile wretch lost to all sense of right, L.

अपध्वान्त *apa-dhvānta*, mfn. (√*dhvan*), sounding wrong, ChUp.

अपनम् *apa-√nam*, (with abl.) bend away from, give way to [NBD.], to bow down before [Gmn.], RV. vi, 17, 9.

Á́pa-nata, mfn. bent outwards, bulging out, ŚBr.; KaushBr.

Apa-nāma, *as*, m. curve, flexion, Śulb.

अपनश् *apa-√2. naś*, 'to disappear,' Imper. *-naśya*, be off, KaushBr.

अपनस *apa-nasa*, mfn. without a nose, L.

अपनह् *apa-√nah*, to bind back, AV.; (ind. p. *-nahya*) to loosen, MBh. iii, 13309.

अपनाभि *ápa-nābhi*, mfn. 'without a navel,' without a focal centre (as the Vedi), TS.

अपनामन् *apa-nāman*, *a*, n. a bad name, Pāṇ. vi, 2, 187; (mfn.), having a bad name, ib.

अपनिद्र 1. *apa-nidra*, mfn. sleepless.

अपनिद्र 2. *apa-ni-dra*, mfn. (√*drā*), opening (as a flower), Śiś.; Kir.

Apa-ni-drat, mfn. id., Naish.

अपनिधा *apa-ni-√dhā*, to place aside, hide, conceal, TBr. &c.; to take off, AV.

अपनिर्वाण *apa-nirvāṇa*, mfn. not yet extinct, Śāk.

अपनिली *apa-ni-√lī*, Ā. (Imper. 3. pl. *-layantām*) to hide one's self, disappear, RV. x, 84, 7; ŚBr.

अपनिह्नु *apa-ni-√hnu*, to deny, conceal, ChUp. &c.

अपनी *apa-√nī*, to lead away or off; to rob, steal, take or drag away; to remove, frighten away; to put off or away (as garments, ornaments, or fetters); to extract, take from; to deny, Comm. on Mn. viii, 53. 59; to except, exclude from a rule, Comm. on RPrāt.: Desid *-ninīshati*, to wish to remove, Comm. on Mn. i, 27.

Apa-naya, *as*, m. leading away, taking away; bad policy, bad or wicked conduct.

Apa-nayana, *am*, n. taking away, withdrawing; destroying, healing; acquittance of a debt.

Apa-nīta, mfn. led away from; taken away, removed; paid, discharged; contradictory; badly executed, spoiled; (*am*), n. imprudent or bad behaviour.

Apa-nīti, *is*, f. taking away from (abl.), Nyāyam.

Apa-netṛi, *tā*, m. a remover, taking away.

अपनु *apa-√3. nu*, to put aside, ŚāṅkhGṛ.

अपनुद् *apa-√nud*, to remove, RV. &c.

Apa-nutti, *is*, f. removing, taking or sending away; expiation, Mn. & Yājñ.

Apa-nuda, mfn. (ifc. e. g. *śokâpanuda*, q.v.) removing, driving away.

Apa-nunutsu, mfn. desirous of removing, expiating (with acc.), Mn. xi, 101.

Apa-noda, *as*, m. = *apa-nutti*.

Apa-nodana, mfn. removing, driving away, Mn.; (*am*), n. removing, driving away, Kauś.; Mn.

Apa-nodya, mfn. to be removed.

अपन्नगृह *á-panna-gṛiha*, mfn. whose house has not fallen in, VS. vi, 24.

A-panna-da, mfn. = *á-panna-dat*, q. v., Gaut.

Á́-panna-dat, mf(*atī*)n. whose teeth have not fallen out, TS.; TBr.

अपपद् *apa-√pad*, to escape, run away.

अपपरे *apa-parê* (√*i*), (perf. 1. sg. *ápa párêto asmi; ápa asmi* may also be taken by itself as fr. 1. *apâs*) to go off, RV. x, 83, 5.

अपपर्यावृत् *apa-pary-ā-√vṛit*, to turn (the face) away from, Gobh.

अपपाठ *apa-pāṭha, as*, m. a mistake in reading, Pāṇ. iv, 4, 64, Sch.; a wrong reading (in a text), VPrāt.

अपपात्र *apa-pātra*, mfn. 'not allowed to use vessels (for food),' people of low caste, Mn. x, 51; Āp.
Apa-pātrita, mfn. id.

अपपादत्र *apa-pādatra*, mfn. having no protection for the feet, shoeless, Rājat.

अपपान *apa-pāna, am*, n. a bad or improper drink.

अपपित्व *apa-pitvá, am*, n. (probably for *-pittvá* fr. √2. *pat*; cf. *abhi-pitvá, ā-pitvá, pra-pitvá*; but cf. also *api-tvá*, s. v. *ápi*), turning away, separation, RV. iii, 53, 24.

अपपिवस् *á-papivas*, m(gen. *á-pupushas*)fn. (perf. p.), who has not drunk, AV. vi, 139, 4.

अपपूत *apa-pūta, au*, m. du. badly formed buttocks, Pāṇ. vi, 2, 187; (mfn.), having badly formed buttocks, ib.

अपपृ *apa-√1. pṛi* (aor. Subj. 2. sg. *parshi*) to drive or scare away from (abl.), RV. i, 129, 5.

अपप्रगा *apa-pra-√1. gā* (aor. *-prāgāt*) to go away from, yield to, RV. i, 113, 16.

अपप्रजाता *apa-prajātā*, f. a female that has had a miscarriage, Suśr.

अपप्रदान *apa-pradāna, am*, n. a bribe.

अपप्रु *apa-√pru, ápa-pravate*, Ved. to leap or jump down, ŚBr. &c.

अपप्रुथ् *apa-√pruth* (Imper. 2. sg. *-protha*; p. *-próthat*) to blow off, RV. vi, 47, 30 & ix, 98, 11.

अपप्रे *apa-prê* (√*i*), (3. pl. *-pra-yánti* or *-prá-yanti*; Opt. *-prêyāt*) to go away, withdraw, RV. x, 117, 4; ŚBr.

अपप्रोषित *apa-prôshita, am*, n. (√5. *vas*), the having departed, a wrong departure or evil caused thereby, (neg. *án-*) ŚBr.

अपप्लु *apa-√plu*, to spring down, MBh.: Caus. *-plāvayati*, to wash off, TS. &c.

अपबर्हिस् *ápa-barhis*, mfn. not having the portion constituting the Barhis, ŚBr.; KātyŚr.

अपबाध् *apa-√bādh*, Ā. to drive away, repel, remove, RV. &c.: Caus. P. id., AV. xii, 1, 49: Desid. Ā. *-bībhatsate*, to abhor from (abl.), AitBr.

अपबाहुक *apa-bāhuka, as*, m. a bad arm, stiffness in the arm, L.

अपब्रू *apa-√brū* (impf. *-brávat*) to speak some mysterious or evil words upon, AV. vi, 57, 1.

अपभज् *apa-√bhaj*, P. (Subj. 1. pl. *-bhajāma*) to cede or transfer a share to, RV. x, 108, 9; ŚBr.; to satisfy the claims of (acc.), KātyŚr.; to divide into parts, PBr.; ŚāṅkhŚr.

अपभय *apa-bhaya*, mf(ā)n. fearless, undaunted.
Apa-bhī, mfn. id.

अपभरणी *apa-bháraṇī*, f. pl. (√*bhṛi*), the last lunar mansion, TS.; TBr.
Apa-bhartavai, Inf. to take away, RV. x, 14, 2.
Apa-bhartṛi, mfn. taking away, RV. ii, 33, 7; destroying.

अपभाष् *apa-√bhāsh*, to revile, Kum. v, 83.
Apa-bhāshaṇa, *am*, n. abuse, bad words, L.

अपभिद् *apa-√bhid* (Imper. 2. sg. *-bhindhí* for *-bhinddhi*) to drive away, RV. viii, 45, 40.

अपभू *apa-√bhū* (Imper. *-bhavatu* & *-bhūtu* [RV. i, 131, 7]; aor. Subj. 2. sg. *-bhūs*, 2. pl. *-bhūtana*) to be absent, be deficient, RV.; AV.; TS.
Ápa-bhūti, *is*, f. defect, damage, AV. v, 8, 5.

अपभ्रंश *apa-bhranśá* (or *apa-bhransa*), *as*, m. falling down, a fall, TS. &c.; a corrupted form of a word, corruption; ungrammatical language; the most corrupt of the Prākṛit dialects.
Apa-bhrashṭa, mfn. corrupted (as a Prākṛit dialect), Kathās.

अपम *apamá*, mfn. (fr. *ápa*), the most distant, the last, RV. x, 39, 3; AV. x, 4, 1; (*as*), m. (in astron.) the declination of a planet. **-kshetra**, see *krānti-kshetra*. **-jyā**, f. the sine of the declination. **-maṇḍala** (or *apa-maṇḍala*) or **-vṛitta**, n. the ecliptic.

अपमन्यु *apa-manyu*, mfn. free from grief.

अपमर्द *apa-marda, as*, m. (√*mṛid*), what is swept away, dirt.

अपमर्श *apa-marśa, as*, m. (√*mṛiś*), touching, grazing, Śak. (v. l. for *abhi-marśa*).

अपमा *apa-√3. mā* (ind. p. *-máya*; cf. Pāṇ. vi, 4, 69) to measure off, measure, AV. xix, 57, 6.

अपमान *apa-māna, as*, m. (or *am*, n.), (√*man*), disrespect, contempt, disgrace.
Apa-mānita, mfn. dishonoured, disgraced, ŚāṅkhGṛ. &c.
Apa-mānin, mfn. dishonouring, despising.
Apa-mānya, mfn. disreputable, dishonourable.

अपमार्ग 1. *apa-mārga, as*, m. a by-way, Pañcat.

अपमित्य *apa-mitya*. See *apa-√me*.

अपमुख *apa-mukha*, mfn. having the face averted, Pāṇ. vi, 2, 186; having an ill-formed face or mouth, ib.; (*am*), ind. except the face, &c., ib.

अपमूर्धन् *apa-mūrdhan*, mfn. headless.

अपमृज् *apa-√mṛij*, cl. 2. P. Ā. *-mārshṭi* (1. pl. *-mṛijmahe*; Imper. 2. du. *-mṛijcthām*) to wipe off, remove, AV.; ŚBr. &c.
2. **Apa-mārga**, *as*, m. wiping off, cleansing, Śiś.
Apa-mārjana, *am*, n. cleansing; a cleansing remedy, detergent, Suśr.; (mfn.) wiping off, moving away, destroying, BhP.
Ápa-mṛishṭa, mfn. wiped off, cleansed, VS. &c.

अपमृत्यु *apa-mṛityu, us*, m. sudden or accidental death; a great danger or illness (from which a person recovers).

अपमृषित *apa-mṛishita*, unintelligible (as a speech), Pāṇ. i, 2, 20, Sch.

अपमे *apa-√me*, cl. 1. Ā. *-mayate* (ind. p. *-mitya* or *-māya*) to be in debt to, owe, Pāṇ. iii, 4, 19, Sch.
Apa-mitya, *am*, n. debt, AV. vi, 117, 1; ĀśvŚr.

अपम्यक्ष् *apa-√myaksh* (Imper. 2. sg. *-myaksha*) to keep off from (abl.), RV. ii, 28, 6.

अपम्लुक्त *ápa-mlukta*, mfn. (√*mluc*), retired, hidden, RV. x, 52, 4.

अपयज् *apa-√yaj* (1. pl. *-yajāmasi*) to drive off by means of a sacrifice, Kauś.

अपयशस् *apa-yaśas, as*, n. disgrace, infamy. **-kara**, mfn. occasioning infamy, disgraceful.

अपया *apa-√yā*, to go away, depart, retire from (abl.); to fall off: Caus. *-yāpayati*, to carry away by violence, BhP.
Apa-yāta, mfn. gone away, having retired.
Apa-yātavya, *am*, n. impers. to be gone away, Kathās.
Apa-yāna, *am*, n. retreat, flight; (in astron.) declination.

अपयु *apa-√1. yu, -yuyoti* (Imper. 2. sg. *-yuyodhi*, 2. pl. *-yuyotana*) to repel, disjoin, RV.

अपयुज् *apa-√yuj*, Ā. *-yuṅkte*, to loose one's self or be loosened from (abl.), ŚBr.

अपर 1. *a-para*, mfn. having nothing beyond or after, having no rival or superior. **-vát**, mfn. having nothing following, ŚBr. **-1. -s-para**, mfn. 'not reciprocal, not one (by the other,' only in comp. with *-sambhūta*, mfn. not produced one by the other, Bhag. **Á-parâdhīna**, mfn. not dependent on another, ŚBr. **A-parârdhya**, mfn. without a maximum, unlimited in number, ĀśvŚr.

अपर 2. *ápara*, mf(ā)n. (fr. *ápa*), posterior, later, latter (opposed to *pūrva*; often in comp.); following; western; inferior, lower (opposed to *pára*); other, another (opposed to *svá*); different (with abl.); being in the west of; distant, opposite. Sometimes *apara* is used as a conjunction to connect words or sentences, e. g. *aparaṃ-ca*, moreover; (*as*), m. the hind foot of an elephant, Śiś.; (*ā*), f. the west, L.; the hind quarter of an elephant, L.; the womb, L.; (*ī*), f. (used in the pl.) or (*ám*) [RV. vi, 33, 5], n. the future, RV.; ŚBr.; (*áparam* [AV.] or *aparám* [RV.]), ind. in future, for the future; (*aparam*), ind. again, moreover, PārGṛ.; Pañcat.; in the west of (abl.), KātyŚr.; (*eṇa*), ind. (with acc.) behind, west, to the west of, KātyŚr. [cf. Goth. and Old Germ. *afar*, and the Mod. Germ. *aber*, in such words as *Aber-mal, Aber-witz*]. **-kānyakubja**, m., N. of a village in the western part of Kānyakubja, Pāṇ. vii, 3, 14, Sch. **-kāya**, m. the hind part of the body. **-kāla**, m. a later period, KātyŚr. **-godāna**, n. (in Buddhist cosmogony) a country west of the Mahā-meru. **-já**, mfn. born later, VS. **-jana**, sg. or pl. m. inhabitants of the west, GopBr.; KātyŚr. **-tā**, f. distance; posteriority (in place or time); opposition, contrariety, relativeness; nearness. **-tra**, ind. in another place; (*ekatra, aparatra*, in one place, in the other place, Pāṇ. vi, 1, 194, Sch.) **-tva**, n. = *-tā*, q. v. **-dakshiṇam**, ind. south-west, (gaṇa *tishṭhadgv-ādi*, q. v.) **-nidāgha**, m. the latter part of the summer. **-pakshá**, m. the latter half of the month, ŚBr.; the other or opposing side, the defendant. **-pakshīya**, mfn. belonging to the latter half of the month, (gaṇa *gakâdi*, q. v.) **-pañcāla**, m. pl. the western Pañcālas, Pāṇ. vi, 2, 103, Sch. **-para**, m(*ās* or *e*)fn. pl. one and the other, various, Pāṇ. vi, 1, 144, Sch. **-purushá**, m. a descendant, ŚBr. x. **-praṇeya**, mfn. easily led by others, tractable. **-bhāva**, m. after-existence, succession, continuation, Nir. **-rātrá**, m. the latter half of the night, the end of the night, the last watch. **-loka**, m. another world, paradise. **-vaktrā**, f. a kind of metre of four lines (having every two lines the same). **-vat**, see 1. *a-para*. **-varshā**, *ās*, f. pl. the latter part of the rains. **-śarad**, f. the latter part of the autumn. **-śvas**, ind. the day after to-morrow, Gobh. **-sakthá**, n. the hind thigh, ŚBr. **-sad**, mfn. being seated behind, PBr. **-2. -s-para**, mfn. pl. one after the other, Pāṇ. vi, 1, 144. **-svastika**, n. the western point in the horizon. **-hemanta**, m. n. the latter part of winter. **-haimana**, mfn. belonging to the latter half of the winter season, Pāṇ. vii, 3, 11, Sch. **Aparâgni**, *ī*, m. du. the southern and the western fire (of a sacrifice), KātyŚr. **Aparânta**, mfn. living at the western border; (*as*), m. the western extremity, the country or the inhabitants of the western border; the extreme end or term; 'the latter end,' death. **Aparântaka**, mf(*ikā*)n. living at the western border, VarBṛS. &c.; (*ikā*), f. a metre consisting of four times sixteen mātrās; (*am*), n., N. of a song, Yājñ. **Aparânta-jñāna**, n. prescience of one's latter end. **Aparâpara**, m(*ās* or *e*)fn. pl. another and another, various, L. **Aparârka**, m. the oldest known commentator of Yājñavalkya's law-book. **Aparârka-candrikā**, f. the name of his comment. **Aparârdha**, m. the latter, the second half. **Aparâhṇá**, m. afternoon, the last watch of the day. **Aparâhṇaka**, mfn. 'born in the afternoon,' a proper name, Pāṇ. iv, 3, 28. **Aparâhṇa-tana** [L.] or **aparâhṇe-tana** [Pāṇ. iv, 3, 24], mfn. belonging to or produced at the close of the day. **Aparêtarā**, f. opposite to or other than the west, the east, L. **Aparedyús**, ind. on the following day, MaitrS. &c.

अपरञ्ज् *apa-√rañj, -rajyate*, to become unfavourable to, MBh.; Kir. ii, 49.
Apa-rakta, mfn. having a changed colour, grown pale, Śak.; unfavourable, VarBṛS.
Apa-rāga, *as*, m. aversion, antipathy, Mn. vii, 154.

अपरत *apa-rata*, mfn. (√*ram*), turned off from, unfavourable to (abl.), Nir.; resting, BhP.

अपरव *apa-rava, as*, m. contest, dispute; discord. **Aparavôjjhita**, mfn. free from dispute, undisputed.

अपरस्पर 1. *a-paraspara*. See 1. *a-para*.
2. **Aparas-para**. See 2. *ápara*.

अपराङ्मुख ***a-parāṅ-mukha,*** mfn. with unaverted face, not turned away from (gen.), Ragh.

अपराजयिन् ***á-parājayin,*** mfn. never losing (at play), TBr.

Á-parājita, mf(*ā*)n. unconquered, unsurpassed, RV. &c.; (*as*), m. a poisonous insect, Suśr.; Vishṇu; Śiva; one of the eleven Rudras, Hariv.; a class of divinities (constituting one portion of the so-called Anuttara divinities of the Jainas); N. of a serpent-demon, MBh.; of a son of Kṛishṇa, BhP.; of a mythical sword, Kathās.; (*ā*), f. (with *diś*) the north-east quarter, AitBr. &c.; Durgā; several plants, Clitoria Ternatea, Marsilea Quadrifolia, Sesbania Ægyptiaca; a species of the Śarkarī metre (of four lines, each containing fourteen syllables).

Á-parājishṇu, mfn. unconquerable, invincible, ŚBr. xiv.

अपराध् ***apa-√rādh, -rādhyati*** or ***-rādhnoti,*** to miss (one's aim, &c.), AV. &c.; to wrong, offend against (gen. or loc.); to offend, sin.

Apa-rāddha, mfn. having missed; having offended, sinned; criminal, guilty; erring. **-pṛishatka** or **aparāddhêshu,** m. an archer whose arrows miss the mark, L.

Ápa-rāddhi, *is,* f. wrong, mistake, ŚBr.

Apa-rāddhṛi, mfn. offending, an offender.

Apa-rādha, *as,* m. offence, transgression, fault; mistake; *aparādhaṃ √1. kṛi,* to offend any one (gen.) **-bhañjana,** m. 'sin-destroyer,' N. of Śiva. **-bhañjana-stotra,** n. a poem of Śaṅkarācārya (in praise of Śiva).

Apa-rādhin, mfn. offending; criminal; guilty.

Aparādhi-tā, f. or **-tva,** n. criminality, guilt.

अपरापरण ***a-parāparaṇá,*** *as,* m. not having descendants or offspring, AV. xii, 5, 45.

अपराभाव ***á-parābhāva,*** *as,* m. the state of not succumbing or not breaking down, TBr.

Á-parābhūta, mfn. not succumbing, not breaking down, ŚBr.

अपरामृष्ट ***a-parāmṛishṭa,*** mfn. untouched.

अपरासिक्त ***á-parāsikta,*** mfn. not poured on one's side, not spilled (as the semen virile), ŚBr.

अपराहत ***á-parāhata,*** mfn. not driven off, AV. xviii, 4, 38.

अपरिकलित ***a-parikalita,*** mfn. unknown, unseen.

अपरिक्रम ***a-parikrama,*** mfn. not walking about, unable to walk round, R. ii, 63, 42.

A-parikrāmam, ind. without going about, standing still, KātyŚr.

अपरिक्लिन्न ***a-pariklinna,*** mfn. not moist, not liquid, dry.

अपरिगण्य ***a-pariganya,*** mfn. incalculable.

अपरिगत ***a-parigata,*** mfn. unobtained, unknown, Kād.

अपरिग्रह ***a-parigraha,*** *as,* m. not including, Comm. on TPrāt.; non-acceptance, renouncing (of any possession besides the necessary utensils of ascetics), Jain.; deprivation, destitution, poverty; (mfn.), destitute of possession; destitute of attendants or of a wife, Kum. i, 54.

A-parigrāhya, mfn. unfit or improper to be accepted, not to be taken.

अपरिचयिन् ***a-paricayin,*** mfn. (*√2. ci*), having no acquaintances, misanthropic.

A-paricita, mfn. unacquainted with, unknown to.

A-pariceya, mfn. unsociable.

अपरिच्छद ***a-paricchada,*** mfn. (*√chad*), without retinue, unprovided with necessaries, Mn. viii, 405.

A-paricchanna, mfn. uncovered, unclothed.

A-paricchādita, mfn. id.

अपरिच्छिन्न ***a-paricchinna,*** mfn. without interval or division, uninterrupted, continuous; connected; unlimited; undistinguished.

A-pariccheda, *as,* m. want of distinction or division; want of discrimination, Śāk.; want of judgment; continuance.

अपरिज्यानि ***a-parijyāni,*** *is,* f. 'not falling into decay,' *ishṭāpūrtasyâparijyāni,* f., N. of a sacrificial ceremony, AitBr.

अपरिणयन ***a-pariṇayana,*** *am,* n. (*√nī*), non-marriage, celibacy.

A-pariṇītā, f. an unmarried woman.

अपरिणाम ***a-pariṇāma,*** *as,* m. (*√nam*), unchangeableness. **-darśin,** mfn. not providing for a change, improvident.

A-pariṇāmin, mfn. unchanging.

अपरितोष ***a-paritosha,*** mfn. unsatisfied, discontented, Śāk.

अपरिपक्व ***a-paripakva,*** mfn. not quite ripe (as fruits, or a tumour [Suśr.]); not quite mature.

अपरिपर ***á-paripara,*** mfn. not going by a tortuous course, AV. xviii, 2, 46; MaitrS.

अपरिभिन्न ***á-paribhinna,*** mfn. not broken into small pieces, not crumbled, ŚBr.

अपरिमाण ***á-parimāṇa,*** mfn. without measure, immeasurable, immense; (*am*), n. immeasurableness.

Á-parimita, mfn. unmeasured, either indefinite or unlimited, AV.; ŚBr. &c. **-guṇa-gaṇa,** mfn. of unbounded excellences. **-dhā,** ind. into an unlimited number of pieces or parts, MaitrUp. **-vidha** (*áparimita-*), mfn. indefinitely multiplied, ŚBr. **Áparimitâlikhita,** mfn. having an indefinite number of lines, ŚBr.; KātyŚr.

A-parimeya, mfn. immeasurable, illimitable.

अपरिमोष ***á-parimosha,*** *as,* m. not stealing, TS.

अपरिम्लान ***a-parimlāna,*** *as,* m. 'not withering, not decaying,' the plant Gomphrena Globosa.

अपरियाणि ***a-pariyāṇi,*** *is,* f. inability to walk about (used in execrations), Pāṇ. viii, 4, 29, Kāś.

अपरिलोप ***a-parilopa,*** *as,* m. non-loss; non-damage, RPrāt.

अपरिवर्गम् ***á-parivargam,*** ind. without leaving out, uninterruptedly, completely, TS.; TBr.; ĀpŚr.

अपरिवर्तनीय ***a-parivartanīya,*** mfn. not to be exchanged.

अपरिवाद्य ***a-parivādya,*** mfn. (*√vad*), not to be reprimanded, Gaut.

अपरिविष्ट ***á-parivishṭa,*** mfn. not enclosed, unbounded, RV. ii, 13, 8.

अपरिवीत ***á-parivīta,*** mfn. (*√vye*), not covered, ŚBr.

अपरिवृत ***a-parivṛita,*** mfn. not hedged in or fenced, Mn. & Gaut.; (cf. *á-parīvṛita.*)

अपरिशेष ***a-pariśesha,*** mfn. not leaving a remainder, all-surrounding, all-enclosing, Sāṅkhyak.

अपरिश्लथम् ***a-pariślatham,*** ind. not loosely, very firmly, Uttarar.

अपरिष्कार ***a-parishkāra,*** *as,* m. want of polish or finish; coarseness, rudeness.

A-parishkṛita, mfn. unpolished, unadorned, coarse.

अपरिसमाप्तिक ***a-parisamāptika,*** mfn. not ending, endless, Comm. on BṛĀrUp.

अपरिसर ***a-parisara,*** mfn. non-contiguous, distant.

अपरिस्कन्दम् ***a-pariskandam,*** ind. so as not to jump or leap about, Bhaṭṭ.

अपरिहरणीय ***a-pariharaṇīya,*** mfn. not to be avoided, inevitable; not to be abandoned or lost; not to be degraded.

A-parihārya, mfn. id., Gaut. &c.

अपरिहाण ***a-parihāṇa*** or ***a-parhāṇa,*** *am,* n. the state of not being deprived of anything, KaushBr.

अपरिह्वृत ***á-parihvṛita,*** mfn. unafflicted, not endangered, RV.; (cf. Pāṇ. vii, 2, 32.)

अपरीक्षित ***a-parīkshita,*** mfn. untried, unproved; not considered, inconsiderate.

अपरीत ***á-parīta,*** mfn. unobstructed, irresistible, RV.; (*as*), m., N. of a people (v. l.)

अपरीवृत ***á-parīvṛita,*** mfn. (*√1. vṛi*), unsurrounded, RV. ii, 10, 3; (cf. *a-parivṛita.*)

अपरुध् ***apa-√2. rudh,*** to expel, drive out (from possession or dominion), RV. x, 34, 2 & 3; AV. &c.: Desid. Pass. p. *apa-rurutsyamāna,* wished or intended to be expelled, Kāṭh.

Apa-roddhṛi, *ā,* m. one who keeps another off, a repeller, TS.

Apa-rodha, *as,* m. exclusion, prohibition (*an-*, neg.), KātyŚr.

Apa-ródhuka, mfn. detaining, hindering, MaitrS.

अपरुष ***a-parusha,*** mf(*ā*)n. not harsh.

अपरूप ***ápa-rūpa,*** *am,* n. monstrosity, deformity, AV. xii, 4, 9; (mfn.), deformed, ill-looking, odd-shaped, L.

अपरेद्युस् ***apare-dyús.*** See 2. *ápara.*

अपरोक्ष ***a-paroksha,*** mfn. not invisible; perceptible; (*am*), ind. (with gen.) in the sight of; (*áparokshāt*), ind. perceptibly, manifestly, ŚBr. xiv.

Aparokshaya, Nom. P. °*yati,* to make perceptible, L.; to take a view of (acc.), MBh.

अपर्ण ***a-parṇá,*** mfn. leafless, TS.; (*ā*), f., 'not having even leaves (for food during her religious austerities),' N. of Durgā or Pārvatī, Kum. v, 28.

अपर्तु ***apa-rtú*** (*ṛitu*), mfn. untimely, unseasonable, AV. iii, 28, 1; not corresponding to the season (as rain), BhP.; (*us*), m. not the right time, not the season, Gaut.; Āp.; (*u*), ind. not in correspondence with the season, Gaut.

अपर्यन्त ***a-paryantá,*** mfn. unbounded, unlimited, ŚBr. x, xiv, &c.

अपर्याप्त ***a-paryāpta,*** mfn. (*√āp*), incomplete; unable, incompetent, insufficient; not enough; unlimited, unbounded, L. **-vat,** mfn. not competent to (Inf.), Ragh. xvi, 28.

अपर्याय ***a-paryāya,*** *as,* m. want of order or method.

अपर्यासित ***a-paryāsita,*** mfn. (Caus. perf. Pass. p. *√2. as*), not thrown down or annihilated, Kir. i, 41.

अपर्वन् ***a-parván,*** *a,* n. not a point of junction, RV. iv, 19, 3; a day which is not a *parvan* (a day in the lunar month, as the full and change of the moon, and the eighth and fourteenth of each half month); (mfn.), without a joint. **Aparva-daṇḍa,** m. a kind of sugar-cane. **A-parva-bhaṅga-nipuṇa,** mfn. skilled in breaking a passage where there is no joint (i. e. where there is no possibility of bending), Kām.

A-párvaka, mfn. jointless, ŚBr.

अपर्हाण ***a-parhāṇa*** = ***a-parihāṇa,*** q. v.

अपल ***1. apala,*** *am,* n. a pin or bolt, L.

अपल ***2. a-pala,*** mfn. fleshless.

अपलप् ***apa-√lap,*** to explain away, to deny, conceal: Caus. Ā. *-lāpayate,* to outwit, Bhaṭṭ.

Apa-lapana, *am,* n. denial or concealment of knowledge, evasion, turning off the truth, detraction; concealing, hiding; affection, regard, L.; the part between the shoulder and the ribs, Suśr.

Apa-lapita, mfn. denied, concealed; suppressed, embezzled, Comm. on Mn. viii, 400.

Apa-lāpa, *as,* m. = *apa-lapana.* **-daṇḍa,** m. a fine imposed on one who denies or evades (in law).

Apa-lāpin, mfn. one who denies, evades or conceals (with gen.)

अपलाल ***a-palāla,*** *as,* m., N. of a Rakshas.

अपलाश ***a-palāśá,*** mfn. leafless, RV. x, 27, 14.

अपलाषिका ***apa-lāshikā*** (or ***apa-lāsikā***), f. thirst, L.

Apa-lāshin, mfn. free from desire, Pāṇ. iii, 2, 144.

Apa-lāshuka, mfn. free from desire, Pāṇ. vi, 2, 160, Sch.

अपलिख् *apa-√likh* (Subj. *-likhāt*) to scrape off, AV. xiv, 2, 68.

अपलित *á-palita,* mfn. not grey, AV.

अपलुपम् *apa-lupam,* ind. (according to Pāṇ. iii, 4, 12, Sch.) Ved. Inf. of *apa-√lup,* to cut off.

अपल्पूलनकृत *á-palpūlana-kṛita,* mfn. not soaked or macerated, ŚBr.

अपवक्तृ *apa-vaktṛí, tā,* m. 'speaking away,' warning off, averting, RV. i, 24, 8; AV. v, 15, 1.

Apa-vācana, *am,* n. See *an-apavācaná.*

अपवत् *ápa-vat.* See s.v. 2. *áp.*

अपवद् *apa-√vad,* P. to revile, abuse, TBr. &c.; to distract, divert, console by tales, PārGṛ.; Yājñ.; (in Gr.) to except, RPrāt.; (Ā. only) to disown, deny, contradict, Pāṇ. i, 3, 77, Sch.: Caus. *-vādayati,* to oppose as unadvisable; to revile; (in Gr.) to except, RPrāt.

Apa-vadamāna, mfn. reviling, speaking ill of (dat.), Bhaṭṭ.

Apa-vāda, *as,* m. evil speaking, reviling, blaming, speaking ill of (gen.); denial, refutation, contradiction; a special rule setting aside a general one, exception (opposed to *utsarga,* Pāṇ. iii, 1, 94, Sch.), RPrāt.; Pāṇ. Sch.; order, command, Kir.; a peculiar noise made by hunters to entice deer, Śiś. vi, 9. **–pratyaya,** m. an exceptional affix, Pāṇ. iii, 1, 94, Sch. **–sthala,** n. case for a special rule or exception, Pāṇ. Sch.

Apa-vādaka, mfn. reviling, blaming, defaming; opposing, objecting to; excepting, excluding, Comm. on TPrāt.

Apa-vādita, mfn. blamed; opposed, objected to.

Apa-vādin, mfn. blaming, Śak.

Apa-vādya, mfn. to be censured; to be excepted, Comm. on TPrāt.

अपवध् *apa-√vadh* (aor. *-avadhīt*) to cut off, split, RV. x, 146, 4; to repel, avert, VS.; ŚBr.

अपवन 1. *a-pavana,* mfn. without air, sheltered from wind.

अपवन 2. *apa-vana, am,* n. a grove, L.

अपवप् *apa-√2. vap* (Subj. 2. sg. *-vapas* [Padap. *-vapa*]; impf. 2. sg. *-ávapas,* 3. sg. *-ávapat*) to disperse, drive off, destroy, RV.; AV.; TS.

अपवरक *apa-varaka,* &c. See *apa-√1. vṛi.*

अपवर्ग *apa-varga,* &c. See *apa-√vṛij.*

अपवर्त *apa-varta,* &c. See *apa-√vṛit.*

अपवस् *apa-√2. vas* (Subj. *-ucchat,* Imper. *-ucchatu*) to drive off by excessive brightness, RV.; AV.; to become extinct, AV. iii, 7, 7.

Apa-vāsá, *as,* m. extinction, disappearance, AV. iii, 7, 7; N. of a plant, L.

अपवह् *apa-√vah,* to carry off; to deduct; to give up: Caus. *-vāhayati,* to have (something) carried off or taken away; to drive away, Daś.; Pañcat.

Apa-vāhá, *as,* m. 'carrying off (water),' a channel, TS.; 'carrying off,' see *Vasishṭhâpavāha;* deduction, subtraction; N. of a metre; of a people.

Apa-vāhaka, *as,* m. deduction, subtraction.

Apa-vāhana, *am,* n. carrying off, Hit.; Daś.; subtraction.

Apa-vāhya, mfn. to be carried away, R.

Apôḍha. See s.v., p. 56, col. 3.

अपवा *apa-√vā, -vắti,* to exhale, perspire, RV. i, 162, 10; (Imper. *-vātu*) to blow off, RV. viii, 18, 10.

अपवाद *apa-vāda,* &c. See *apa-√vad.*

अपविक्षत *apa-vikshata,* mfn. unwounded, Śak. (v. l.)

अपविघ्न *apa-vighna,* mfn. unobstructed, unimpeded; *(am),* n. freedom from obstruction, MBh. i, 6875.

अपविच् *apa-√vic,* cl. 7. *-vinakti* (impf. *ápâvinak*) to single out from, select, AV.; ŚBr.; cl. 3. *-vevekti,* id., Kauś.

अपवित्र *a-pavitra,* mf(*ā*)n. impure.

अपविद्ध *apa-viddha.* See *apa-√vyadh.*

अपविश् *apa-√viś,* Caus. (Imper. 2. sg. *-veśayā*) to send away, AV. ix, 2, 25.

अपविषा *apa-vishā,* f. 'free from poison,' the grass Kyllingia Monocephala.

अपविष्णु *apa-vishṇu,* ind. except or without Vishṇu.

अपवी *apa-√vī, -veti,* to turn away from, be unfavourable to, RV. v, 61, 18 & x, 43, 2.

अपवीण *apa-vīṇa,* mfn. having a bad or no lute, Pāṇ. vi, 2, 187; *(ā),* f. a bad lute, ib.; *(am),* ind. without a lute, ib.

अपवीरवत् *á-pavīra-vat,* mfn. not armed with a lance, RV. x, 60, 3.

अपवृ *apa-√1. vṛi* (impf. 2. sg. *ápâvṛiṇos,* 3. sg. *ápâvṛiṇot;* Subj. *-varat;* aor. 2. & 3. sg. *-āvar* [Padap. *-avar*], 3. sg. Ā. *-avṛita;* aor. Subj. 1. sg. *-vam* [for *varm,* RV. x, 28, 7], 3. sg. *-var,* 3. pl. *-vran,* Imper. 2. sg. [in RV.] once *ápa vṛidhi* and five times *ápā vṛidhi* [cf. *apā-√1. vṛi* and ib. *ápā-vṛita*]; perf. 2. sg. *-vavártha,* 3. sg. *-vavāra*) to open, uncover, exhibit, RV.; (ind. p. *-vṛítya*) ŚBr. xiv; (cf. *apā-√1. vṛi*): Caus. *-vārayati,* 'to hide, conceal,' see *apa-vārita.*

Apa-varaka, *as,* m. an inner apartment, lying-in chamber, Kathās.

Apa-varaṇa, *am,* n. covering, L.; garment, L.

Apa-vartṛi, *tā,* m. one who opens, RV. iv, 20, 8.

Apa-vāraṇa, *am,* n. covering, concealment, L.

Apa-vārita, mfn. covered, concealed, Mṛicch. &c.; *(am),* ind. (in theatrical language) secretly, apart, aside (speaking so that only the addressed person may hear, opposed to *prakāśam*), Sāh.

Apa-vāritakena, ind. = *apa-vāritam.*

Apa-vārya, ind. p. = *apa-vāritam.*

अपवृज् *apa-√vṛij,* Ā. *-vṛiṅkte* (Imper. 2. sg. *-vṛiṅkshva;* Subj. 1. sg. *-vṛiṇḍjai;* aor. P. 3. sg. *ápâvṛik*) to turn off, drive off, AV.; ŚBr.; to tear off, AV.; (with *ádhvānam*) carpere viam [BR.], RV. x, 117, 7; to leave off, determine, fulfil, ŚBr. &c.: Caus. *-varjayati,* to quit, get rid of; to sever, turn off from; to transmit, bestow, grant, MBh. &c.

Apa-varga, *as,* m. completion, end (e. g. *pañcâpavarga,* coming to an end in five days), KātyŚr. &c.; the emancipation of the soul from bodily existence, exemption from further transmigration; final beatitude; BhP. &c.; gift, donation, ĀśvŚr.; restriction (of a rule), Suśr.; Śulb. **–da,** mf(*ā*)n. conferring final beatitude.

Apa-varjana, *am,* n. completion, discharging a debt or obligation, Hariv.; transmitting, giving in marriage (a daughter), MBh.; final emancipation or beatitude, L.; abandoning, L.

Apa-varjanīya, mfn. to be avoided.

Apa-varjita, mfn. abandoned, quitted, got rid of, given or cast away; made good (as a promise), discharged (as a debt).

Apa-varjya, ind. p. excepting, except.

Apa-vṛikta, mfn. finished, completed.

Apa-vṛikti, *is,* f. fulfilment, completion.

अपवृत् *apa-√vṛit,* to turn away, depart; to move out from, get out of the way, slip off: Caus. P. (Ved. Imper. 2. sg. *-vartayā*) to turn or drive away from, RV. ii, 23, 7 &c.; (in arithm.) to divide; to reduce to a common measure.

Apa-varta, *as,* m. (in arithm. or alg.) reduction to a common measure; the divisor (which is applied to both or either of the quantities of an equation).

Apa-vartaka, *as,* m. a common measure, L.

Apa-vartana, *am,* n. taking away, removal, Suśr.; ademption, Mn. ix, 79; reduction of a fraction to its lowest terms; division without remainder; divisor.

Apa-vartita, mfn. taken away; removed; divided by a common measure without remainder.

Apa-vṛitta, mfn. reversed, inverted, overturned; finished, carried to the end (perhaps for *apa-vṛikta*), ŚāṅkhŚr.; KātyŚr. &c.; *(am),* n. (in astron.) ecliptic.

Apa-vṛitti, *is,* f. slipping off; end, L.

अपवे *apa-√ve* (Imper. 2. sg. *-vaya*) to unweave what has been woven, RV. x, 130, 1.

अपवेन् *apa-√ven* (Subj. 2. sg. *-venas*) to turn away from, be unfavourable to, AV. iv, 8, 2.

अपवेष्ट् *apa-√vesht,* Caus. *-veshṭayati,* to strip off, PBr.

अपव्यध् *apa-√vyadh* (Subj. 3. du. *-vidhyatām*) to drive away, throw away, RV. vii, 75, 4, &c.; to pierce (with arrows), MBh.; to reject, neglect.

Apa-viddha, mfn. pierced; thrown away, rejected, dismissed, removed. **–putra,** m. a son rejected by his natural parents and adopted by a stranger, Mn.; Yājñ.; one of the twelve objects of filiation in law. **–loka,** mfn. 'who has given up the world,' dead, BhP.

Apa-vedha, *as,* m. piercing anything in the wrong direction or manner (spoiling a jewel by so piercing it), Mn. xi, 286.

अपव्यय *apa-vyaya, as,* m. (√*i*), prodigality, L.

Apa-vyayamāna, mfn. See *apa-√vye.*

अपव्यादा *apa-vy-ā-√1. dā* (see *vy-ā-√1. dā*), to open (the lips), ŚBr.

अपव्याहृ *apa-vy-ā-√hṛi* (Pot. *-haret*) to speak wrongly or unsuitably, ŚBr.; KātyŚr.

अपव्ये *apa-√vye,* P. Ā. *-vyayati* (1. sg. *-vyaye*) to uncover, RV. vii, 81, 1; AV.: Ā. (pr. p. *-vyayamāna*) to extricate one's self, deny, Mn.

अपव्रज् *apa-√vraj,* to go away, ĀśvŚr.

अपव्रत *ápa-vrata,* mfn. disobedient, unfaithful, RV.; perverse, RV. v, 40, 6; (x, 103, additional verse, =) AV. iii, 2, 6 = VS. xvii, 47.

अपशकुन *apa-śakuna, am,* n. a bad omen.

अपशङ्क *apa-śaṅka,* mfn. fearless, having no fear or hesitation; *(am),* ind. fearlessly, Śiś.

अपशब्द *apa-śabda, as,* m. bad or vulgar speech; any form of language not Sanskrit; ungrammatical language; (*apa-bhraṇśa.*)

अपशम *apa-śama, as,* m. cessation, L.

अपशव्य *a-paśavyá.* See *a-paśu.*

अपशातय *apa-śātaya* (cf. √*śad*), Nom. P. (Imper. 2. sg. *-śātaya*) to throw or shoot off (an arrow), AV.

अपशिरस् *ápa-śiras* [ŚBr. xiv] or *apa-śirsha* or *ápa-śīrshan* [ŚBr. xiv], mfn. headless.

अपशिष् *apa-√śish,* to leave out, ŚBr.

अपशु 1. *á-paśu, us,* m. not cattle, i. e. cattle not fit to be sacrificed, TS.; ŚBr. **–han** (*á-paśu-*), mf(*ghnī*)n. not killing cattle, AV. xiv, 1, 62.

2. **A-paśú,** mfn. deprived of cattle, poor, TS.; ŚBr.; having no victim, ĀśvGṛ. **–tā** (*apaśú-*), f. want of cattle, MaitrS.

A-paśavyá, mfn. not fit or useful for cattle, TBr.; ŚBr.; ŚāṅkhGṛ.

अपशुच् 1. *apa-śuc, k,* m. (√1. *śuc*), 'without sorrow,' the soul, L.

Apa-śoka, mfn. sorrowless, Ragh.; *(as),* m. the tree Jonesia Asoka.

अपशुच् 2. *apa-√2. śuc,* Intens. p. *-śóśucat,* mfn. driving off by flames, RV. i, 97, 1.

अपश्चादघ्वन् *á-paścā-daghvan* [SV.; AV. xix, 55, 5] or better *á-paścād-daghvan* [RV. vi, 42, 1; MaitrS.], mfn. not staying behind, not coming short of, not being a loser.

अपश्चिम *a-paścima,* mfn. not having another in the rear, last; not the last.

अपश्नथ् *apa-√śnath* (aor. Imper. 2. pl. *-śnathishṭana*) to push away, repel, RV. ix, 101, 1.

अपश्य *a-paśyá,* mfn. not seeing, RV. i, 148, 5.

A-paśyat, mfn. id., RV. x, 135, 3; (in astron.) not being in view of, VarBṛ.; not noticing; not considering, not caring for, Yājñ. ii, 3.

A-paśyanā, f. not seeing, Buddh.

अपश्रि *apa-√śri,* to retire from, Lāṭy.

Apa-śrayá, *as,* m. a bolster, AV. xv, 3, 8.

Apa-śrita, mfn. retired from, retreated, absconded, RV.; AV.; ŚBr.

अपश्री *apa-śrī,* mfn. deprived of beauty, Śiś.

अपश्वस् *apa-√śvas* cl. 2. P. *-śvasiti,* used to explain *apâniti* (cf. *apân*), Comm. on ChUp.

Apa-śvāsa, *as*, m. one of the five vital airs (see *apâna*), L.

अपष्ठ *apa-shṭha*, *as*, *am*, m. n. (√*sthā*), the end or point of the hook for driving an elephant, Pāṇ. viii, 3, 97; (cf. *apāshṭhá*.)

Apa-shṭhu, mfn. contrary, opposite, L.; perverse, L.; left, L.; (*u*), ind. perversely, badly, Śiś. xv, 17 (v. l. *um*); properly, L.; handsomely, L.; (*us*), m. time, L.

Apa-shṭhura or **-shṭhula**, mfn. opposite, contrary, L.

अपस् 1. *ápas*, *as*, n. (fr. 1. *áp*), work, action, especially sacred act, sacrificial act, RV. [Lat. *opus*.]

2. **Apás**, mfn. active, skilful in any art, RV.; (*ásas*), f. pl., N. of the hands and fingers (when employed in kindling the sacred fire and in performing the sacrifices), RV.; of the three goddesses of sacred speech, RV.; VS.; of the active or running waters, RV.; AV. **-tama** (*apás-*), mfn. (superl.), most active, RV.; most rapid, RV. x, 75, 7. **-pati**, m., N. of a son of Uttānapāda, VP.

1. **Apasya**, Nom. P. (Subj. °*syát*) to be active, RV. i, 121, 7.

1. **Apasyā́**, f. activity, RV. v, 44, 8; vii, 45, 2; (cf. *sv-apasyā́*; for 2. *apasyā̀*, see 2. *apasyà* below.)

Apasyú, mfn. active, RV.

अपस् 3. *apás*, mfn. (fr. 2. *áp*), watery. (So some passages of the Ṛig-veda [i, 95, 4, &c.] may (according to NBD. and others) be translated where the word is applied to the running waters, see 2. *apás* at end & *apás-tama*.)

2. **Apasyà**, mf(*sī́*)n. watery, melting, dispersing, RV. x, 89, 2; VS. x, 7; (2. *apasyā̀*), f. a kind of brick (twenty are used in building the sacrificial altar), ŚBr.; KātyŚr.

अपसच् *apa-√sac* (perf. Ā. 3. pl. *-saścire*, 1. pl. P. *-saścima*) to escape, evade (with acc.), RV. v, 20, 2; VS. xxxviii, 20.

अपसद *apa-sada*, *as*, m. the children of six degrading marriages (of a Brāhman with the women of the three lower classes, of a Kshatriya with women of the two lower, and of a Vaiśya with one of the Śūdra, Mn. x, 10 seqq., but cf. MBh. xiii, 2620 seqq. and *apadhvaṇsa-ja*); an outcast (often ifc.; see *brāhmaṇâpasada*).

अपसमम् *apa-samam*, ind. last year (? gaṇa *tishṭhadgv-ādi*, q. v.)

अपसर्जन *apa-sarjana*, *am*, n. (√*sṛij*), abandonment, L.; gift or donation, L.; final emancipation of the soul, L.; (cf. *apa-√vṛij*.)

अपसलवि *apa-salavi*, ind. to the left (opposed to *pra-salavi*; cf. *ava-salavi*), ŚBr.; the space between the thumb and the forefinger (sacred to the Manes).

Apa-salaiḥ, ind. to the left, ĀśvGṛ.

अपसव्य *apa-savya*, mfn. not on the left side, right, Mn. iii, 214; (with auguries) from the right to the left, moving to the left, MBh.; VarBṛS. &c.; (*am*, *ena*), ind. to the left, from the right to the left, KātyŚr. &c. **Apasavyam √1. kṛi** = *pradakshiṇam kṛi*, to circumambulate a person keeping the right side towards him, Kauś. &c.; to put the sacred thread over the right shoulder, Yājñ. i, 232. **Apasavya-vat**, mfn. having the sacred thread over the right shoulder, Yājñ. i, 250.

अपसिद्धान्त *apa-siddhānta*, *as*, m. an assertion or statement opposed to orthodox teaching or to settled dogma, Nyāyad. &c.

अपसिध् *apa-√2. sidh* (Imper. 2. sg. *-sédha* or *-sedha*, 3. sg. *-sedhatu*, 3. pl. *-sedhantu*; pr. p. *-sédhat*) to ward off, remove, drive away, RV. &c.

अपसू *apa-√1. sū* (1. sg. *-suvāmi*; Imper. 2. sg. *-suva*; aor. Subj. *-sāvishat*) to drive off, RV. x, 37, 4 & 100, 8; AV.; VS.

अपसृ *apa-√sṛi* (impf. *-sarat*) to slip off from (abl.), RV. iv, 30, 10; to go away, retreat; Caus. *-sārayati*, to make or let go away, remove.

Apa-sara, *as*, m. (in geom.) distance; see *an-apasara*.

Apa-saraṇa, *am*, n. going away, retreating.

Apa-sāra, *as*, m. a way for going out, escape, Mṛicch.; Pañcat.

Apa-sāraṇa, *am*, n. removing to a distance; dismissing; banishment, Mcar.

Apa-sārita, mfn. removed, put away.

Apa-sṛiti, *is*, f. = *apa-sara*.

अपसृप् *apa-√sṛip*, to glide or move off; to retreat.

Apa-sarpa, *as*, m. a secret emissary or agent, spy, Bālar.

Apa-sarpaṇa, *am*, n. going back, retreating.

Apa-sṛipti, *is*, f. going away from (abl.)

अपस्कम्भ *apa-skambhá*, *as*, m. fastening, making firm, AV. iv, 6, 4.

अपस्कृ *apa-√skṛī*. See *apa-√3. kṛī*.

Apa-skara, *as*, m. any part of a carriage, a wheel, &c., Pāṇ. vi, 1, 149; fæces (cf. *avaskara*), Vet.; anus, L.; vulva, L.

Apa-skāra, *as*, m. under part of the knee, L.

अपस्खल *apa-skhalá*, *as*, m. slipping [‘outside of a threshing-floor,’ Sāy.], ŚBr.

अपस्तम *apás-tama*. See 2. *apás*.

अपस्तम्ब *apa-stamba*, *as*, m. a vessel inside or on one side of the chest containing vital air, Bhpr.

Apa-stambha, *as*, m. id., Suśr.

Apa-stambhinī, f., N. of a plant.

अपस्नात *apa-snāta*, mfn. bathing during mourning or upon the death of a relation, R. ii, 42, 22.

Apa-snāna, *am*, n. funeral bathing (upon the death of a relative, &c.), L.; impure water in which a person has previously washed, Mn. iv, 132.

अपस्पति *apas-pati*. See 2. *apás*.

अपस्पृ *apa-√spṛi*, Ā. (impf. 3. pl. *-spriṇvata*) to extricate from, deliver from, KaushBr.; (3. pl. *-spṛinvate*) to refresh [Gmn.; ‘to alienate,’ BR.], RV. viii, 2, 5.

अपस्पृश् *apa-spṛiś*. See *án-apaspṛiś*.

अपस्फिग *apa-sphiga*, mfn. one who has badly formed buttocks, Pāṇ. vi, 2, 187; (*am*), ind. except the buttocks, ib.

अपस्फुर् 1. *apa-√sphur* (aor. Subj. 2. sg. *-spharīs*) to move suddenly aside or to lash out (as a cow during milking), RV. vi, 61, 14.

2. **Apa-sphúr**, mfn. bounding or bursting forth, (or figuratively) splashing out (said of the Soma), RV. viii, 69, 10; (cf. *án-apasphur*, &c.)

अपस्मार *apa-smāra*, *as*, m. epilepsy, falling sickness, Suśr. &c.

Apa-smārin, mfn. epileptic, convulsed, Mn. &c.

Apa-smṛiti, mfn. forgetful, BhP.; absent in mind, confused, ib.

अपस्य *apasya*, *apasyú*. See अपस्.

अपस्वर *apa-svara*, *as*, m. an unmusical note or sound, L.

अपस्वान *apa-svāna*, *as*, m. a hurricane, Āp.

अपहन् *apa-√han* (Subj. 3. sg. *-han*; Imper. 2. sg. *-jahi*, 2. du. *-hatam*; 2. pl. *-hatá* or *-hata*; perf. *-jaghāna*; pr. p. *-ghnát*; Intens. p. nom. m. *-jáṅghanat*) to beat off, ward off, repel, destroy, RV. &c.

Apa-ghā́ta, **apa-jighāṇsu**. See s. v.

Apa-ha, mfn. ifc. keeping back, repelling, removing, destroying (e. g. *śokâpaha*, q. v.)

Ápa-hata, mfn. destroyed, warded off, killed. **-pāpman** (*ápahata-*), mfn. having the evil warded off, free from evil, ŚBr.

Apa-hati, *is*, f. removing, destroying, AitBr. &c.

Apa-hanana, *am*, n. warding off; (cf. *apa-ghā́ta*, s. v.)

Apa-hantṛí, mf(*trī*, Ragh.)n. beating off, destroying, ŚBr. &c.

अपहर *apa-hara*, &c. See *apa-√hṛi*.

अपहल *apa-hala*, mfn. having a bad plough, Pāṇ. vi, 2, 187, Sch.

अपहस् *apa-√has*, to deride: Caus. *-hāsayati*, to deride, ridicule.

Apa-hasita, *am*, n. silly or causeless laughter, Sāh.

Apa-hāsa, *as*, m. id., L.; a mocking laugh, R.

Apa-hāsya, mfn. to be laughed at, R.

अपहस्त *apa-hasta*, *am*, n. striking or throwing away or off, MBh. iii, 545 [‘the back of the hand,’ Comm.]

Apa-hastaya, Nom. P. °*yati*, to throw away, push aside, repel, (generally used in the perf. Pass. p.)

Apa-hastita, mfn. thrown away, repelled, Mālatīm. &c.

अपहा 1. *apa-√2. hā*, Ā. *-jihīte* (aor. 3. pl. *-ahāsata*, Subj. 1. pl. *-hāsmahi*), to run away from (abl.) or off, RV.

अपहा 2. *apa-√3. hā*, Ā. (aor. Subj. 2. sg. *-hāsthāḥ*) to remain behind, fall short, not reach the desired end, AV. xviii, 3, 73: Pass. *-hīyate*, to grow less, decrease (in strength, *balam*), Suśr.

Apa-hāni, *is*, f. diminishing, vanishing, Up.

Apa-hāya, ind. p. quitting, MBh. &c.; leaving, avoiding, Hariv.; leaving out of view, Śāk. &c.; excepting, except, Ragh.

अपहि *apa-√hi*, to throw off, disengage or deliver one's self from (acc.), BhP.

अपहिंकार *ápa-him-kāra*, mfn. without the syllable *him* (which is pronounced in singing the Sāma verses), ŚBr.

अपहृ *apa-√hṛi*, to snatch away, carry off, plunder; to remove, throw away: Caus. *-hārayati*, see *apa-hārita* below.

Apa-hara, mfn. (ifc.) carrying off, Bhām.

Apa-haraṇa, *am*, n. taking away, carrying off; stealing, Mn.

Apa-haraṇīya, mfn. to be taken away, carried off, stolen, &c.

Apa-haras, mfn. not pernicious, PBr.

Apa-hartṛi, *tā*, m. (with gen. [Mn. viii, 190, 192] or acc. [Pāṇ. iii, 2, 135, Sch.] or ifc.) taking away, carrying off, stealing, Mn. &c.; removing (faults), expiating, Mn. xi, 161.

Apa-hāra, *as*, m. taking away, stealing; spending another person's property; secreting, concealment, e. g. *ātmâpahāram* √1. *kṛi*, to conceal one's real character, Śāk.

Apa-hāraka, mfn. one who takes away, seizes, steals, &c.; a plunderer, a thief; (cf. *ātmâpahāraka*, *vāg-apahāraka*.)

Apa-hāraṇa, *am*, n. causing to take away.

Apa-hārita, mfn. carried off, R.; Ragh. iii, 50.

Apa-hārin, mfn. = *apa-hāraka*.

Apa-hṛita, mfn. taken away, carried off, stolen, &c. **-vijñāna**, mfn. bereft of sense.

Apa-hṛiti, *is*, f. carrying off.

अपहेला *apa-helā*, f. contempt, L.

अपह्नु *apa-√hnu*, Ā. (1. sg. *-hnuvé*) to refuse, RV. i, 138, 4; to conceal, disguise, deny, Kāṭh. &c.; to excuse one's self, give satisfaction to, ŚBr.; TBr.

Apa-hnavá, *as*, m. concealment, denial of or turning off of the truth; dissimulation; appeasing, satisfying, ŚBr.; affection, love, R.; = *apa-hnuti*, Sāh.

Apa-hnuta, mfn. concealed, denied.

Apa-hnuti, *is*, f. ‘denial, concealment of truth,’ using a simile in other than its true or obvious application, Kpr.; Sāh.

Apa-hnuvāna, mfn. pr. p. Ā. concealing, denying (any one, dat.), Naish.

Apa-hnotṛi, mfn. one who conceals or denies or disowns, Comm. on Mn. viii, 190.

अपह्रास *apa-hrāsa*, *as*, m. diminishing, reducing, Suśr.

अपाक् *ápāk* & 1. *ápāka*. See *ápāñc*.

अपाक 2. *a-pāka*, mfn. (√*pac*), immature, raw, unripe (said of fruits and of sores); (*as*), m. immaturity; indigestion, Suśr. **-ja**, mfn. not produced by cooking or ripening; original; natural. **-śāka**, n. ginger.

A-pākin, mfn. unripe; undigested.

अपाकृ *apâ-√1. kṛi*, to remove, drive away, (Ved. Inf. *apâkartoḥ*) MaitrS.; to cast off, reject, desist from, MBh. &c.; to select for a present, PBr.; KātyŚr.; to reject (an opinion).

Apâ-karaṇa, *am*, n. driving away, removal, KātyŚr.; payment, liquidation.

Apâ-karishṇu, mfn. (with acc.) 'outdoing,' surpassing.

Apâ-karman, *a*, n. payment, liquidation,

Apâ-kṛita, mfn. taken away, removed, destroyed, void of; paid.

Apâ-kṛiti, *is*, f. taking away, removal, RV. viii, 47, 2; evil conduct, rebelling (Comm. = *vikāra*), Kir. i, 27.

अपाकृष् *apâ-√kṛish* (Inf. *-krashṭum*) to turn off or away, avert, remove, R. &c.

अपाकॄ *apâ-√1. kṛī*, to throw any one off; to abandon, to contemn.

अपाक्ष *apâksha*, mfn. = *adhy-aksha* or *praty-aksha*, L.

अपाङ्क्तेय *a-pāṅkteya*, mfn. 'not in a line or row,' not in the same class, inadmissible into society, ejected from caste, Mn. &c.

A-pāṅktya, mfn. id., Mn.; Gaut. **Apāṅktyôpahata**, mfn. defiled or contaminated by the presence of impure or improper persons, Mn. iii, 183.

अपाङ्ग *apâṅga*, mfn. without limbs or without a body, L.; (*as*), m. (ifc. f. *ā* or *ī*) the outer corner of the eye, Śak. &c.; a sectarial mark or circlet on the forehead, R.; N. of Kāma (the god of love), L.; = *apâmārgá*, L. **-darśana**, n. or **-drishṭi**, f. a side glance, a leer. **-deśa**, m. the place round the outer corner of the eye. **-netra**, mf(*ā*)n. casting side glances, Vikr.

Apâṅgaka, *as*, m. = *apâmārgá*.

अपाच् *apâc* (√*ac*), (Imper. *-aca*) to drive away, RV. ix, 97, 54.

अपाज् *apâj* (√*aj*), (impf. *-ājat*; p. *apâjat*; Imper. 2. sg. *-aja*) to drive away, RV.; AitBr.

अपाञ्च् *ápāñc*, *āṅ*, *ācī*, *āk* (fr. 2. *añc*), going or situated backwards, behind, RV. & AV.; western (opposed to *prāñc*), ib.; southern, L.

Ápāk, ind. westward, RV.; VS. **-tás** [AV. viii, 4, 19; cf. RV. vii, 104, 19] or **-tāt** (*ápāk-*) [RV. vii, 104, 19], ind. from behind.

1. **Ápāka**, mfn. coming from a distant place, distant, RV.; VS.; (*āt*), ind. from a distant place, RV. viii, 2, 35. **-cakshas** (*ápāka-*), mfn. shining far, RV. viii, 75, 7. For 2. *a-pāka*, see p. 53, col. 3.

Apākā́ (an old instr. case of 1. *ápāñc*), ind. far, RV. i, 129, 1.

Apācī, f. the south, L. **Apācitarā**, f. 'other than the south,' the north, L.

Apācīna, mfn. situated backwards, behind, western, RV. vii, 6, 4 & 78, 3; AV. vi, 91, 1; turned back, L.; southern, L.

Apācyá (4), mfn. western, RV. viii, 28, 3; AitBr.; southern, L.

अपाञ्जस् *apâñjas* (?), Pāṇ. vi, 2, 187.

अपाटव *a-pāṭava*, *am*, n. awkwardness, inelegance, L.; sickness, disease, L.

अपाठ्य *a-pāṭhya*, mfn. illegible.

अपाणिग्रहण *a-pāṇigrahaṇa*, *am*, n. celibacy.

A-pāṇi-pāda, mfn. without hands and feet, Up.

अपाती *apâti* (√*i*), to escape (with acc.), GopBr.

अपात्र *a-pātra*, *am*, n. a worthless or common utensil; an undeserving or worthless object, unfit recipient, unworthy to receive gifts, Bhag.; Kathās. **-kṛityā**, f. acting unbecomingly, doing degrading offices (as for a Brāhman to receive wealth improperly acquired, to trade, to serve a Śūdra, and to utter an untruth), Mn. xi, 125. **-dāyin**, mfn. giving to the undeserving. **-bhṛit**, mfn. supporting the unworthy, cherishing the undeserving.

A-pātrī-karaṇa, *am*, n. = *a-pātra-kṛityā*, Mn. xi, 69.

अपाद् *a-pád*. See *a-pád*, p. 49, col. 2.

A-pāda, mfn. not divided into Pādas, not metrical. **A-pādâdi**, m. not the beginning of a Pāda, VPrāt. **A-pādâdi-bhāj**, mfn. not standing at the beginning of a Pāda, RPrāt. **A-pādântīya**, mfn. not standing at the end of a Pāda.

A-pādáka, mfn. footless, TS.

Á-pādya, mf(*ā*)n. (or *ápādya*?), N. of certain Ishṭis (performed with the *cavana vaiśvasṛija*), TBr.

अपादा *apâ-√1. dā*, Ā. to take off or away, ŚBr.; Kauś.

Apâ-dātṛí, *tā*, m. one who takes off, TBr.

Apâ-dāna, *am*, n. taking away, removal, ablation; a thing from which another thing is removed; hence the sense of the fifth or ablative case, Pāṇ.

अपाधा *apâ-√dhā* (Subj. 1. sg. *-dadhāni*) to take off, loosen from, KaushBr.

अपाध्वन् *apâdhvan*, *ā*, m. a bad road, Pāṇ. vi, 2, 187.

अपान् *apân* (√*an*), *apâniti* or *apânati* [AV. xi, 4, 14], to breathe out, expire, ŚBr. xiv; ChUp.; pr. p. *apânát*, mf(*tī*)n. breathing out, RV. x, 189, 2; AV.

Apāná, *as*, m. (opposed to *prāṇá*), that of the five vital airs which goes downwards and out at the anus; the anus, MBh. (in this sense also (*am*), n., L.); N. of a Sāman, PBr.; ventris crepitus, L. **-dā́**, mfn. giving the vital air Apāna, VS. xvii, 15. **-dṛíh**, m(nom. *-dhṛík*)fn. strengthening the vital air Apāna, TS. **-dvāra**, n. the anus. **-pavana**, m. the vital air Apāna, L. **-pā́**, mfn. protecting the Apāna, VS. **-bhṛít**, f. 'cherishing the vital air,' a sacrificial brick, ŚBr. **-vāyu**, m. the air Apāna, L.; ventris crepitus, L. **Apānôdgāra**, m. ventris crepitus.

अपानुद् *apā-√nud* (the *ā* of *apā* always in the antepenultimate of a śloka, therefore *apā* metrically for *apa*; see *apa-√nud*), to remove, repel, repudiate, MBh.; Mn.

अपानृत *apânṛita*, mfn. free from falsehood, true, R. ii, 34, 38.

अपान्तरतमस् *apântara-tamas*, *ās*, m., N. of an ancient sage (who is identified with Kṛishṇa Dvaipāyana), MBh.; Hariv.

अपांनपात् *apâṃ-nápāt*, &c. See 2. *áp*.

अपाप *a-pāpa*, mf(*ā*)n. sinless, virtuous, pure. **-kāśin** (*á-pāpa-*), mfn. not ill-looking, VS. **-kṛit** (*á-pāpa-*), mfn. not committing sin, ŚBr. **-purī**, f., N. of a town; also written *pāpa-purī*, q. v. **-vasyasa** (*á-pāpa-*), n. not a wrong order, no disorder, ŚBr.; (cf. *pāpa-vasyasá*.) **-viddha** (*á-pāpa-*), mfn. not afflicted with evil, VS. xl, 8.

अपामंभविष्णु *á-pāmam-bhavishṇu*, mfn. not becoming diseased with herpes, MaitrS.; (cf. *pāmam-bhavishṇú*.)

अपामार्ग *apâ-mārgá*, *as*, m. (√*mṛij*), the plant Achyranthes Aspera (employed very often in incantations, in medicine, in washing linen, and in sacrifices), AV.; VS. &c.

Apâ-mārjana, *am*, n. cleansing, keeping back, removing (of diseases and other evils). **-stotra**, n. 'removing of diseases,' N. of a hymn.

अपामित्य *apâ-mítya*, n. (cf. *apa-mítya*), equivalent, MaitrS.

अपामृत्यु *apā-mṛityu* = *apa-mṛityu*, L.

अपाय *apâya*. See *apê*.

अपार् *apâr* (*apa-√ṛi*), to open by removing anything, RV. v, 45, 6 (Subj. Ā. 3. sg. *ápa ṛinutá*); ix, 10, 6 (3. pl. *ápa ṛinvanti*) & 102, 8 (impf. 2. sg. *ṛiṇór ápa*).

अपार *a-pārá*, mfn. not having an opposite shore, TS.; not having a shore, unbounded, boundless (applied to the earth, or to heaven and earth [*ródasī*], &c.), RV. &c.; (*as*), m. 'not the opposite bank,' the bank on this side (of a river), MBh. viii, 2381; (*am*), n. (in Sāṅkhya phil.) 'a bad shore,' 'the reverse of *pāra*,' a kind of mental indifference or acquiescence; the reverse of mental acquiescence, L.; the boundless sea. **-pāra**, mfn. carrying over the boundless sea (of life), VP.; (*am*), n. non-acquiescence, L.

A-pāraṇīya, mfn. not to be got over, not to be carried to the end or triumphed over, MBh.; BhP. &c.

A-pārayat, mfn. incompetent, impotent (with Inf. or loc.); not able to resist, MBh.

अपारमार्थिक *a-pāramārthika*, mf(*ī*)n. not concerned about the highest truth.

अपार्छ् *apârch* (*apa-√ṛich*), to retire, L.

अपार्जित *apârjita*, mfn. (√*ṛij* with *apa*), flung away, L.

अपार्ण *apârṇa*, mfn. (fr. *apâr* above, BR. see *abhy-arṇa*), distant, far from (abl.), Nir.

अपार्थ *apârtha*, mfn. without any object, useless; unmeaning, BhP. &c.; (*am*), n. incoherent argument. **-karaṇa**, n. a false plea in a lawsuit.

Apârthaka, mfn. useless, Mn. viii, 78, &c.

अपार्थिव *a-pārthiva*, mfn. not earthly, Ragh.

अपाल *a-pāla*, mf(*ā*)n. unguarded, unprotected, undefended; (*ā́*), f., N. of a daughter of Atri, RV. viii, 91, 7, &c.

अपालङ्क *apālaṅka*, *as*, m. the plant Cassia Fistula; (see *pālaṅka*.)

अपालम्ब *apâ-lambá*, *as*, m. a kind of break let down from a carriage to stop it, ŚBr.; KātyŚr.

अपालि 1. *a-pāli*, mfn. having no tip of the ear, Suśr.

अपालि 2. *apâli*, mfn. free from bees, &c., L. (see *ali*).

अपावृ *apā-√1. vṛi* (*apā* = *apa*, cf. *apa-√1. vṛi*), *-vṛiṇoti*, to open, uncover, reveal, Lāṭy.; Up. &c.

Apā-vṛit, mfn. unrestrained, BhP.; (cf. *an-apāvṛit*.)

Ápā-vṛita, mfn. open, laid open, RV. i, 57, 1, &c.; covered, L.; unrestrained, self-willed, L.

Ápā-vṛiti, *is*, f. a place of concealment, hiding-place, RV. viii, 66, 3.

अपावृक्त *apâ-vṛikta* (√*vṛij*), removed, avoided, RV. viii, 80, 8.

अपावृत् *apâ-√vṛit* (aor. Ā. 3. pl. *apa āvṛitsata* [v. l. *av°*]) to turn or move away, ŚāṅkhŚr.

Apâ-vartana, *am*, n. turning away or from, retreat, L.; repulse, L.

Apâ-vṛitta, mfn. (for *apă-*, the vowel being metrically lengthened in the antepenultimate of a śloka), (with abl.) turned away from, R.; abstaining from, rejecting, MBh.; (*am*), n. the rolling on the ground (of a horse), L.

Apâ-vṛitti, *is*, f. = *ud-vartana*, L.

Apâ-vṛitya, ind. p. turning away from (with abl.), AV. xii, 2, 34.

अपाव्य *ápāvya*, mfn., N. of particular gods & Mantras, TS. (Comm. = *apa-āvya*); TBr. (Comm. = *apa-avya*, fr. √*av*).

अपाश्या *a-pāśyā*, f. no great number of nooses or fetters, Pāṇ. vi, 2, 156, Sch.

अपाश्रय 1. *apâśraya*, mfn. helpless, destitute.

अपाश्रि *apâ-√śri*, P. Ā. *-śrayati*, *°te*, to resort to; to use, practise.

2. **Apâ-śraya**, *as*, m. the upper portion of a bed or couch on which the head rests, Daś.; refuge, recourse, the person or thing to which recourse is had for refuge; an awning spread over a court or yard, R. v, 11, 19.

Apâ-śrita, mfn. resting on; resorting to.

अपाष्टि *apâshṭi*. See *áyo-'pāshṭi*.

Apâshṭhá, *as*, m. (fr. √*sthā* with *apa*, APrāt.; cf. *apashṭha*), the barb of an arrow, AV. iv, 6, 5; (cf. *śatâpāshṭha*.) **-vat** (*apâshṭhá-*), mfn. having barbs, RV. x, 85, 34.

Apâshṭhi = *apâshṭi* in comp. with **-há** or **-hán**, mfn. killing with the claws, ŚBr.

अपास् 1. *apâs* (√1. *as*), 'to be absent from, not to participate in,' see *apa-parê*.

अपास् 2. *apâs* (√2. *as*), to fling away, throw away or off, discard; to scare, drive away; to leave behind; to take no notice of, disregard.

Apâsana, *am*, n. throwing away, placing aside, KātyŚr.; killing, slaughter, L.

Apâsita, mfn. thrown down, injured, destroyed, L.

Apâsta, mfn. thrown off, set aside; driven away; carried off or away, abandoned, discarded; disregarded; contemned.

Apâsya, ind. p. having thrown away or discarded; having left, having disregarded; having excepted.

Apâsyat, mfn. discarding, throwing off, &c.

अपासङ्ग *apā-saṅga, as*, m. (√*sañj*)?, Kāṭh.; =*upāsaṅga*, L.

अपासि *apâsi*, mfn. having a bad or no sword.

अपासु *apâsu*, mfn. lifeless, Naish.

अपासृ *apâ-√sṛi* (*apa-ā-*; or *apā* for *apa*, the *ā* standing in the antepenultimate of a śloka), to turn off from, avoid (with abl.), Yājñ. ii, 262.

Apâ-saraṇa, *am*, n. departing, L.

Apâ-sṛita, mfn. gone, departed, gone away, L.

अपास्था *apâ-√sthā*, to go off towards, AitBr.; ŚāṅkhŚr. (v. l. *upâ-√sthā*, q. v.)

अपाहन् *apâ-√han*, to throw off or back, ShaḍvBr.

अपाहाय *apā-hāya*, ind. p. (fr. √3. *hā* with *apa*, the *a* being metrically lengthened), quitting, MBh.; disregarding, ib.; excepting, except, ib.

अपाहृ *apâ-√hṛi*, Ā. to take off, ŚBr.

अपि *ápi*, or sometimes *pi* (see *pi-dṛibh*, *pi-dhā*, *pi-nah*), expresses placing near or over, uniting to, annexing, reaching to, proximity, &c. [cf. Gk. ἐπί; Zend *api*; Germ. and Eng. prefix *be*]; in later Sanskṛit its place seems frequently supplied by *abhi*. (As a separable adv.) and, also, moreover, besides, assuredly, surely; *api api* or *api-ca*, as well as; *na vâpi* or *na apivā* or *na nacâpi*, neither, nor; *câpi*, (and at the beginning of a sentence) *api-ca*, moreover.

Api is often used to express emphasis, in the sense of even, also, very; e. g. *anyad api*, also another, something more; *adyâpi*, this very day, even now; *tathâpi*, even thus, notwithstanding; *yady api*, even if, although; *yadyapi tathâpi*, although, nevertheless; *na kadâcid api*, never at any time: sometimes in the sense of but, only, at least, e. g. *muhūrtam api*, only a moment.

Api may be affixed to an interrogative to make it indefinite, e. g. *ko 'pi*, any one; *kutrâpi*, anywhere.

Api imparts to numerals the notion of totality, e. g. *caturṇām api varṇānām*, of all the four castes.

Api may be interrogative at the beginning of a sentence.

Api may strengthen the original force of the Potential, or may soften the Imperative, like the English 'be pleased to;' sometimes it is a mere expletive.

Api tu, but, but yet.

Api-tvá, *am*, n. having part, share, AV.; ŚBr.; (cf. *apa-pitvá*.) **Api-tvin**, mfn. having part, sharing, ŚBr.

Api-nāma (in the beginning of a phrase), perhaps, in all probability, I wish that, Mṛicch.; Śāk. &c.

Ápi-vat, mf(*vatī*)n. See *api-√vat*.

अपिकक्ष *api-kakshá, as*, m. the region of the arm-pits and shoulder-blades (especially in animals), RV. iv, 40, 4; x, 134, 7; Lāṭy.; N. of a man & (*ās*), m. pl. his descendants.

Api-kakshya (5), mfn. connected with the region of the arm-pits, RV. i, 117, 22.

अपिकर्ण *api-karṇá, am*, n. the region of the ears, RV. vi, 48, 16.

अपिकृ *api-√1. kṛi*, to bring into order, arrange, prepare, TS.; TBr.; PBr.

अपिकृत् *api-√2. kṛit* (1. sg. *-kṛintāmi*, fut. 1. sg. *-kartsyāmi*) to cut off, VS.; AV.; TS.; ŚBr.

अपिक्षै *api-√kshai*, Caus. *-kshāpayati*, to consume by fire, AV. xii, 5, 44 & 51.

अपिगम् *api-√gam*, Ved. to go into, enter, approach, join, [aor. Subj. 3. pl. *ápi gman*, RV. v, 33, 10] RV. &c.; to approach a woman, RV. i, 179, 1.

अपिगा *api-√1. gā*, Ved. to enter, get into, mingle with, RV. vii, 21, 5, &c.

अपिगीर्ण *api-gīrṇa*, mfn. praised, L.

अपिगुण *api-guṇa*, mfn. excellent, MBh. xii, 2677.

अपिग्रह *api-√grah* (with or without *mukham, nāsike*, &c.), to close (the mouth, nose, &c.), ŚBr.; AitBr.; ChUp.

1. **Api-gṛihya**, ind. p. closing the mouth, TS.

2. **Api-gṛihya** [Ved., Pāṇ. iii, 1, 118] or **api-grāhya** [ib., Comm.], *am*, n. impers. (with abl.) the mouth to be closed before (a bad smell, &c.)

अपिघस् *api-√ghas*, to eat off or away (perf. 3. pl. *-jakshuḥ*), ŚBr.; (aor. Ā. 3. sg. *-gdha* [fr. *gh-s-ta*], which by Sāy. is derived fr. √*han*), RV. i, 158, 5.

अपिच्छिल *a-picchila*, mfn. clear, free from sediment or soil.

अपिज *api-já, as*, m. born after or in addition to (N. of Prajāpati and other divinities), VS.

अपिण्ड *a-piṇḍa*, mfn. without funeral balls.

अपित् 1. *a-pít*, mfn. (√*pi*), not swelling, dry, RV. vii, 82, 3.

अपित् 2. *a-pit*, mfn. (in Gr.) not having the *it* or Anu-bandha *p*, Pāṇ.

अपितृ *á-pitṛi, tā*, m. not a father, ŚBr. xiv. **-devatya** (*á-pitṛi-*), mfn. not having the Manes as deities, ŚBr.

A-pitṛika, mfn. not ancestral or paternal, uninherited; fatherless, Āp.

A-pitrya, mfn. not inherited, not ancestral or paternal, Mn. ix, 205.

अपिदह् *api-√dah, -dahati* (impf. *-adahat*) to touch with fire, to singe, TS.; Kāṭh.

अपिदो *api-√do* (1. sg. *-dyāmi*) to cut off, AV. iv, 37, 3.

अपिधम् *api-√dham*, to blow upon, Kauś.

अपिधा *api-√dhā*, Ved. to place upon or into, put to, give; chiefly Ved. to shut, close, cover, conceal (in later texts more usually *pi-√dhā*, q. v.)

Api-dhāna, *am*, n. placing upon, covering, KātyŚr.; a cover, a cloth for covering, RV. &c.; a lid, BhP.; a bar, Kum.; (*ī*), f. a cover, Āp.; (cf. *pi-dhāna*.) **-vat** (*apidhāna-*), mfn. 'having a cover,' concealed, RV. v, 29, 12.

Api-dhí, *is*, m. 'that which is placed upon the fire,' a gift to Agni, RV. i, 127, 7.

Ápi-hita, mfn. put to, placed into, RV.; shut, covered, concealed, RV. &c.; (cf. *pi-hita*)

Ápi-hiti, *is*, f. a bar, MaitrS.; PBr.

अपिधाव् *api-√dhāv*, to run into, Vait.

अपिनह् *api-√nah*, to tie on, fasten (usually *pi-√nah*, q. v.); to tie up, close, stop up (Ved.; later on *pi-√nah*, q. v.)

Ápi-naddha, mfn. closed, concealed, RV. x, 68, 8; ŚBr.; (cf. *pi-naddha*.)

अपिनी *api-√nī*, to lead towards or to, bring to a state or condition, TS.; ŚBr.; AitBr.

Api-netṛi, *tā*, m. one who leads towards (gen.), ŚBr.

अपिपक्ष *api-pakshá, as*, m. the region or direction to the side, TS.

अपिपथ् *api-√path*, Caus. *-pāthayati*, to lead upon a path (acc.), KaushBr.; ŚāṅkhŚr.

अपिपद् *api-√pad*, to go in, enter, ŚBr.

अपिपास *a-pipāsá*, mfn. free from thirst or desire, ŚBr. xiv; ChUp.

अपिपृच् *api-√pṛic* (aor. 3. sg. *aprāg ápi*) to mix with (loc.), AV. x, 4, 26; (*-pṛiñcanti*, AV. v, 2, 3, according to BR. a mistake for *-vṛiñjanti*.)

अपिप्राण *api-prāṇa*, mf(*ī*)n. uttered or produced with every breath, RV. i, 186, 11.

अपिबन्ध् *api-√bandh*, Ā. to fasten upon, put on (a wreath), ĀśvGṛ.

Api-baddha, mfn. fastened, R. iii, 68, 42.

अपिभाग *ápi-bhāga*, mfn. having part in, sharing in, ŚBr.

अपिभू *api-√bhū*, to be in, AV.; to have part in, RV.; AitBr.

अपिमन्त्र *api-mantra*, mfn. giving an explanation or an account of, Kāṭh.

अपिमृष् *api-√mṛish*, Ā. *-mṛishyate* (1. sg. *-mṛishye*; aor. Subj. 2. sg. *-mṛishṭhās*) to forget, neglect, RV.

अपियाच् *api-√yāc*, Caus. *-yācáyate*, to despise, refuse (?), AV. xii, 4, 38.

अपिरिप्त *ápi-ripta*, mfn. (√*rip*), 'smeared over,' i. e. grown blind, RV. i, 118, 7; viii, 5, 23.

अपिरुह् *api-√ruh*, *ápi-rohati*, to grow together, grow whole again, TS.

अपिवत् *api-√vat* (Opt. 1. pl. *-vatema*; pr. p. *-vátat*) to understand, comprehend, RV. vii, 3, 10; 60, 6; Caus. (Imper. 2. sg. *-vātaya*; pr. p. *-vātáyat*; aor. 3. pl. *avīvatan*, RV. x, 13, 5) to cause to understand, make intelligible to (with or without dat.), RV.; (1. pl. *-vātayāmasi*) to excite, awaken, RV. i, 128, 2.

Ápi-vatī (scil. *vāc*), f. of a conjecturable adj. *ápivatya*, intelligible, TBr. ['containing the word *api* or what is meant by *api*,' Comm. & BR.]

अपिवप् *api-√2. vap* (1. sg. *-vapāmi*) to scatter upon, AV.; ŚBr.; TBr.

Api-vāpá, *as*, m. 'scattering upon,' N. of particular Puroḍāśa, TBr.

अपिवान्यवत्सा *apivānya-vatsā*=*abhivānyā*, q. v., Kauś.

अपिवृ *api-√1. vṛi* (perf. Ā. *-vavre*) to conceal, RV. iii, 38, 8.

Ápi-vṛita, mfn. concealed, covered, RV.

अपिवृज् *api-√vṛij* (3. pl. *-vṛiñjanti*; aor. 3. pl. *avṛijann ápi*, RV. x, 48, 3) 'to turn to,' procure to, bestow upon (dat. or loc.), RV.

अपिवृत् *api-√vṛit*, Caus. (impf. 2. sg. *-avartayas*) to throw into (acc.), RV. i, 121, 13.

अपिव्ये *api-√vye* (1. pl. P. *-vyayāmasi*) to cover, AV. i, 27, 1.

अपिव्रत *ápi-vrata*, mfn. sharing in the same religious acts, related by blood, ŚBr.; KātyŚr.

अपिव्रश्च् *api-√vraśc* (perf. Imper. 2. du. *-vavṛiktam*, RV. vi, 62, 10) to strike off, cut off, RV.; AV.

अपिशर्वर *api-śarvara*, mfn. 'contiguous to the night,' being at the beginning or end of the night, AitBr.; (*ám*), n. the time early in the morning, RV.

अपिशल *apiśala, as*, m., N. of a man; (*ās*), m. pl. the descendants of Apiśala. See *āpiśali*.

अपिशस् *api-śás*, f. (only used in abl. *-śásas*) slitting, ripping up, MaitrS.; AitBr.

अपिशुन *a-piśuna*, mfn. unmalicious, upright, honest.

अपिशॄ *api-√śṝ*, P. to break off, AV.; Ā. id., ŚBr.: Pass. *-śīryate*, to break, PBr.

Ápi-śīrṇa, mfn. broken, AV. iv, 3, 6.

अपिष्टुत *api-shṭuta*, mfn. (√*stu*), praised, L.

अपिष्ठा *api-shṭhā* (√*sthā*), to stand (too) near, stand in any one's way, AV. iii, 13, 4 & v, 13, 5.

Api-shṭhitá, mfn. approached, RV. i, 145, 4.

अपिसंगृभाय *api-saṃ-gṛibhāya*, Nom. P. (Imper. 2. sg. *-gṛibhāya*) to assume, RV. x, 44, 4.

अपिसिच् *api-√sic*, to sprinkle with, L.

अपिसृ *api-√sṛi*, to flow upon, ŚBr.; TBr.

अपिसृज् *api-√sṛij*, P. to place to or upon, TS.; ŚBr.: P. & Ā. to add to, mingle to, Lāṭy.

अपिहन् *api-√han* (3. pl. *ghnanti*) to remove or suppress (pregnancy, *sūtum*), TS.

अपिहित *ápi-hita*, &c. See *api-√dhā*.

अपिह्नु *api-√hnu* (3. du. *ápi hnutaḥ*) to refuse, RV. viii, 31, 7.

अपिह्वे *api-hve* (1. sg. Ā. *-huve*) to call in addition to (or besides), RV. x, 19, 4.

अपी 1. *ápī*. See *ápya*.

अपी 2. *apī* (√*i*), (Ved.) *ápy-eti*, to go in or near; to enter into or upon; to come near, approach (also in copulation, RV. ii, 43, 2, ind. p. *apītyā*); to partake, have a share in; to join; to pour out (as a river).

Api-yát, mfn. entering the other world, dying, RV. i, 162, 20; dissolving, disappearing, BhP.

1. **Ápīta**, mfn. gone into, entered, ŚBr. x (used for the etym. of *svapiti*), ChUp.; (cf. *svâpyayá*.)

Ápīti, *is*, f. entering into, RV. i, 121, 10; dissolving, dissolution, ŚBr.; Up.

Apy-aya, *as*, m. joint, juncture, Kauś.; Śulb.; pouring out (of a river), PBr.; entering into, vanishing (the contrary of *prabhava* or *utpatti*), Up. &c.; (cf. *svâpyayá*.) **-dīkshita**, m., N. of a Drāviḍa saint and writer (of the sixteenth century, author of various works, celebrated as a Śaiva, and thought to be an incarnation of Śiva; also *apyāya°* or *apyai°*, &c.)

Apy-ayana, *am*, n. union, copulating, L.

अपीच्य *apīcyà* (3, 4), mfn. (fr. *api-añc*), secret, hidden, RV.; very handsome (v. l. *apīvya*), BhP.

अपीजू *api-jū́*, m(du. *-jū́vā*)fn. impelling, RV. ii, 31, 5.

अपीडन *a-pīḍana*, *am*, n. not giving pain, gentleness, kindness.

A-pīḍayat, mfn. not paining.

A-pīḍā, f. id.; (*ayā*), ind. not unwillingly.

अपीत 2. *a-pīta*, mfn. not drunk; not having drunk, MBh. ii, 1902.

A-pītvā, ind. p. not having drunk, without drinking.

अपीनस *apī-nasa*, *as*, m. (*apī* for *api*; cf. *pī-nasa*), dryness of the nose, want of the pituitary secretion and loss of smell, cold, Suśr.

अपीवृत *ápī-vṛita*. See *api-√1. vṛi*.

अपीव्य *apīvya*, mfn. See *apīcyà*.

अपुंस् *a-puṇs* (nom. *-pumān*), m. not a man, a eunuch, Mn. iii, 49, &c. **-tva**, n. the state of a eunuch.

A-puṇskā, f. without a husband, Bhaṭṭ.

अपुच्छ *a-puccha*, mfn. tailless; (*ā*), f. the tree Dalbergia Śiśu.

अपुण्य *a-puṇya*, mfn. impure, wicked. **-kṛit**, mfn. acting wickedly, wicked.

अपुत्र *á-putra*, *as*, m. not a son, ŚBr. xiv; (*a-pútra*), mf(*ā*)n. sonless, ŚBr. &c. **-tā** (*aputrá-*), f. sonlessness, ŚBr.

A-putraka, mf(*ikā*)n. sonless, Kathās.; Daś.

A-putrika, *as*, m. the father of a daughter not fit to be adopted as a son because of her not having any male offspring.

A-putriya, mfn. sonless, childless, ŚāṅkhGṛ. &c.

अपुनर् *a-punár*, ind. not again, only once, RV. x, 68, 10. **-anvaya**, mfn. not returning, dead. **-āvartana**, n. or **-āvṛitti**, f. final exemption from life or transmigration, Jain.; Up. **-ukta**, n. or **-ukti**, f. no (superfluous) repetition. **-dīyamāna** (*á-punar-*), mfn. not being given back, AV. xii, 5, 44. **-bhava**, m. not occurring again, Car.; exemption from further transmigration, final beatitude, BhP. **-bhāva**, m. id. **-√bhū**, not to recover consciousness, ŚBr. **A-punaḥ-prâpya**, mfn. irrecoverable.

अपुराण *a-purāṇa* or *a-purātana*, mfn. not old, modern, new.

अपुरुष *a-purusha*, mfn. unmanly. **A-purushârtha**, m. a rite which is not for the benefit of the sacrificer; not the chief object of the soul.

अपुरोगव *á-purogava*, mfn. without a leader, AV. xx, 135, 7; AitBr.

A-puro-'nuvâkyâka, mfn. without a Puronuvākyā, ŚBr.

A-puroruk̂ka, mfn. without a Puroruc, ŚBr.

Á-purohita, *as*, m. not a Purohita, ŚBr.; (mfn.), without a Purohita, AitBr.

अपुष्कल *a-pushkala*, mfn. 'not eminent,' mean, low, Veṇis.; Hcar.

अपुष्ट *a-pushṭa*, mfn. unnourished, lean; soft, L.; invalid, unimportant, Kpr.

अपुष्प *a-pushpá*, mf(*ā́*)n. not flowering, RV. &c.; (*as*), m. the glomerous fig tree. **-phala** or **-phala-da**, m. 'bearing fruits without flowering,' 'having neither flowers nor fruits,' the jack tree, Artocarpus Integrifolia, the glomerous fig tree.

अपुस् *apus*, *us*, n., v. l. for *vápus*, Naigh.

अपूजक *a-pūjaka*, mfn. irreverent.

A-pūjā, f. irreverence, disrespect.

A-pūjita, mfn. not reverenced or worshipped.

A-pūjya, mfn. not to be worshipped or revered.

अपूत *á-pūta*, mfn. impure, ŚBr.; KātyŚr.; not purified (by purificatory rites), Mn.; Gaut.

अपूप *apūpá*, *as*, m. (cf. *pūpa*), cake of flour, meal, &c., RV. &c.; a kind of fine bread; honeycomb, ChUp.; wheat, L. **-nābhi** (*apūpá-*), m. having a navel consisting of a cake, AV. x, 9, 5. **-maya**, mfn. consisting of cake, Pāṇ. v, 4, 21, Sch. **-vat** (*apūpá-*), mfn. accompanied with cake, RV.; AV. **Apūpâdi**, a gaṇa of Pāṇ. (v, 1, 4). **Apūpâpihita**, mfn. covered with cake, AV. xviii, 3, 68.

1. **Apūpīya**, mfn. fit for cakes, Pāṇ. v, 1, 4.

2. **Apūpīya**, Nom. P. °*yati*, to have a desire for cakes, KātyŚr.

Apūpya, mfn. = 1. *apūpīya*, Pāṇ. v, 1, 4; *as*, m. flour, meal, L.

अपूरणी *apūraṇī*, f. the silk cotton tree (Bombax Heptaphyllum).

अपूरुष *a-pūrushá*, mfn. lifeless, inanimate, RV. x, 155, 3. **-ghna** (*á-pūrusha-*), mfn. not killing men, RV. i, 133, 6.

अपूर्ण *a-pūrṇa*, mfn. not full or entire, incomplete, deficient; (*am*), n. an incomplete number, a fraction. **-kāla**, mfn. premature; (*as*), m. incomplete time. **-kāla-ja**, mfn. born before the proper time, abortive. **-tā**, f. incompleteness.

A-pūrti, *is*, f. non-accomplishment (of wishes), MBh.

A-pūryamāṇa, mfn. not getting full, KātyŚr.

अपूर्व *a-pūrvá*, mf(*ā*)n. unpreceded, unprecedented, ŚBr. xiv, &c.; not having existed before, quite new; unparalleled, incomparable, extraordinary; not first; preceded by *a*, Pāṇ. viii, 3, 17; (*as*), m., N. of a sacrifice (offered to Prajāpati), PBr.; Vait.; (*am*), n. the remote or unforeseen consequence of an act (as heaven of religious rites), Nyāyam.; a consequence not immediately preceded by its cause; (*éṇa*), ind. never before, AV. x, 8, 33. **-karman**, n. a religious rite or sacrifice (the power of which on the future is not before seen). **-tā**, f. or **-tva**, n. the being unpreceded, the not having existed before, incomparableness, &c. **-pati**, f. one who has had no husband before, Pat. **-vat**, ind. singularly, unlike anything else.

A-pūrvīya, mfn. referring to the remote or unforeseen consequence of an act, L.

Á-pūrvya (4), mf(*ā*)n. unpreceded, first, RV.; incomparable, RV.

अपृक्त *a-pṛikta*, mfn. unmixed, uncombined (said of a word [as *ā* and *u*, Prāt.] or an affix [Pāṇ.] consisting of a single letter, i. e. of one not combined with another).

अपृणत् *á-pṛiṇat*, mfn. 'not filling, not propitiating by gifts,' stingy, RV.

अपृथक् *a-pṛithak*, ind. not separately, with, together with, collectively. **-śruti**, mfn. not audible separately, RPrāt. **Apṛithag-dharmaśīla**, mfn. of the same religion.

अपृष्ट *a-pṛishṭa*, mfn. unasked, Gaut. &c.

अपे *apé* (*√i*), P. Ā. *apâiti*, *ápâyati* (impf. Ā. *ápâyata*, RV. x, 72, 6) to go away, withdraw, retire, run away, escape; to vanish, disappear.

Apâya, *as*, m. going away, departure; destruction, death, annihilation; injury, loss; misfortune, evil, calamity.

Apâyin, mfn. going away, departing, vanishing, perishable.

Apêta, mfn. escaped, departed, gone; having retired from, free from (abl. or in comp.) **-bhī**, mfn. one whose fear is gone, Mn. vii, 197. **-rākshasī**, f. the plant Ocimum Sanctum (also *aprêta-r°*).

Apêhi (Imper. 2. sg. in comp.) means 'excluding, expelling.' **-praghasā** (scil. *kriyā*), f. a ceremony from which gluttons are excluded, (gaṇa *mayūravyaṇsakâdi*.) **-vāṇijā** (scil. *kriyā*), f. a ceremony from which merchants are excluded, ib. **-vātā** (scil. *latā*), f. 'useful in expelling wind,' the plant Poederia Foetida, Suśr.

अपेक्ष् *apêksh* (*√īksh*), to look away, to look round, AV.; ŚBr.; to have some design; to have regard to, to respect; to look for, wait for; to expect, hope; to require, have an eye to, Sāh.; with *na*, not to like, Kathās.

Apêkshaṇa, *am*, n. = *apêkshā*, L.

Apêkshaṇīya, mfn. to be considered or regarded; to be looked for or expected; to be wished or required; desirable.

Apêkshā, f. looking round or about, consideration of, reference, regard to (in comp.; rarely loc.); dependence on, connection of cause with effect or of individual with species; looking for, expectation, hope, need, requirement; (*ayā*), ind. with regard to (in comp.) **-buddhi**, f. (in Vaiśeshika phil.) a mental process, the faculty of arranging and methodizing, clearness of understanding.

Apêkshita, mfn. considered; referred to; looked for, expected; wished, required.

Apêkshitavya = *apêkshaṇīya*, q. v.

Apêkshin, mfn. considering, respecting, regardful of, looking to (in comp.; rarely gen.); looking for, expecting, requiring; depending on. **Apêkshitā**, f. expectation, Kum. iii, 1.

1. **Apêkshya** = *apêkshaṇīya*.

2. **Apêkshya**, ind. p. with regard or reference to.

अपेज् *apêj* (*√ij*), *ápêjate*, to drive away, RV. v, 48, 2 & vi, 64, 3.

अपेन्द्र *ápêndra*, mfn. without Indra, ŚBr.

अपेय *a-peya*, mf(*ā*)n. unfit for drinking, not to be drunk, Mn. &c.

अपेशल *a-peśala*, mfn. unclever.

A-peśás, mfn. shapeless, RV. i, 6, 3.

अपेष् 1. *apêsh* (*√ish*), (aor. 3. sg. *ápa aíyeḥ*) to withdraw from (abl.), RV. v, 2, 8.

अपेहिप्रघसा *apêhi-praghasā*, &c. See *apê*.

अपैशुन *a-paiśuna*, *am*, n. non-calumny, Bhag.

अपोगण्ड *a-pogaṇḍa*, mfn. not under sixteen years of age, Mn. viii, 148; a child or infant, L.; timid, L.; flaccid, L.; having a limb too many or too few, L.

अपोच्छद् *apôcchad* (*ud-√chad*), (ind. p. *-chādya*) to uncover, ĀśvŚr.

अपोढ *apôḍha*, mfn. (*√vah*), carried off, removed, taken away.

अपोत्कृष् *apôt-kṛish* (*√kṛish*), (ind. p. *-kṛishya*) to disjoin, Kauś.

अपोदक *ápôdaka*, mf(*ā*)n. waterless, watertight, RV. i, 116, 3; not watery, not fluid, AV.; (*ikā*), f. the pot-herb Basella Rubra or Lucida, L.

अपोदि *apôd-i* (*√i*), to go away altogether, withdraw from (abl.), AV.; ŚBr.; AitBr.

Apôd-itya, (mfn.) n. impers. to be completely gone away from (abl.), ŚBr.

अपोदूह् *apôd-√1. ūh*, to strip off, TBr.

अपोद्धार्य *apôd-dhārya*. See *an-apôddhāryá*.

अपोनप्तृ *apó-naptṛi*, &c. See 2. *áp*.

अपोभ् *apôbh* (*√ubh*), (Imper. 2. pl. *ápômbhata*) to bind, fetter, AV. viii, 8, 11.

Apôbdha, mfn. bound, TS.

Apómbhana, *am*, n. a fetter, TS.

अपोर्णु *apôrṇu* (*√ūrṇu*), *ápa ūrṇoti*, *ápôrṇute*, once *apôrṇauti* [KātyŚr.], to uncover, unveil, open, RV.; AV.; ŚBr.: Ā. to uncover one's self, TS.; ŚBr.

Apôrṇavana, *am*, n. untying, Comm. on ĀpŚr.

अपोष् *apósh* (*√ush*) = *apa-√2. vas*, q. v.

अपोह् *apôh* (*√1. ūh*), *-ūhati* (impf. *ápâúhat*) to strip off, push away, frighten away, RV. &c.; to remove or heal (diseases), Suśr.; Ā. to keep away from one's self, avoid, Mn.; to give up, Ragh.; (in disputation) to object, deny, Sāh.

Apôha, *as*, m. pushing away, removing; (in disputation) reasoning, arguing, denying.

Apôhana, *am*, n. id.

Apôhanīya, mfn. to be taken away, or removed, or expiated.

Apôhita, mfn. removed; (in disputation) denied (the opposite of *sthāpita*).

Apôhya, mfn. = *apôhanīya*.

अपौरुष *a-paurusha*, *am*, n. unmanliness; superhuman power; (mfn.), unmanly; superhuman.

A-paurusheya, mfn. not coming from men, ShaḍvBr.

अपौल्कस *á-paulkasa*, *as*, m. not a Paulkasa, ŚBr.

अपौष्कल्य *a-paushkalya*, *am*, n. immaturity.

अप्त *apta*. See *án-apta*.

अप्तस् *aptas*, *as*, n. a sacrificial act, Uṇ.

Aptúr (only acc. sg. & pl. *úram* & *úras*), m. (fr. 1. *áp* + √*tvar*), active, busy (said of the Aśvins, of Soma, of Agni, of Indra), RV.

Aptúrya (4), *am*, n. zeal, activity, RV. iii, 12, 8 & 51, 9.

Apna-rā́j, mfn. (*apna* = *ápnas* below), presiding over property, RV. x, 132, 7.

Ápnas, *as*, n. possession, property, RV. [cf. Lat. *ops*]; work, sacrificial act, Naigh.; Uṇ.; progeny, Naigh.; shape, ib. **-vat** (*ápnas-*), mfn. giving property, profitable, RV. **Apnaḥ-sthá**, m. possessor, RV. vi, 67, 3.

अप्तु *aptú*, mfn. small, tender [Comm.; but perhaps connected with *aptúr* above, because also applied to the Soma], MaitrS.; TS.; ŚBr.; body, Uṇ. **-mát**, mfn. containing the word *aptú*, MaitrS.

Aptor-yāmá, *as* [ŚBr. &c] or **-yāman**, *ā* [PBr.; Lāṭy.], m. a particular way of offering the Soma sacrifice.

अप्त्य *aptyá*. See 2. *áp*.

अप्नवान *ápnavāna*, *as*, m., N. of a Ṛishi (appointed with the Bhṛigus), RV. iv, 7, 1; the arm, Naigh. **-vát**, ind. like Apnavāna, RV. viii, 102, 4.

अप्पति *ap-pati*, *is*, m. See 2. *áp*.

अप्पदीक्षित *appadīkshita* or *apyadīkshita*, *as*, m., N. of an author = *apyaya-dīkshita*, q. v.

अप्पित्त *ap-pitta*, *am*, n. See 2. *áp*.

अप्य *ápya*. See 2. *áp*.

अप्यत्यर्ज् *apy-aty-√arj* (3. pl. *-arjanti*) to add over and above, AitBr.

अप्यद् *apy-√ad*, to eat off, ŚBr. xiv: Caus. *-ādayati*, to give more (food) to eat, AitBr.

अप्यय *apy-aya*. See 2. *apí*.

अप्यर्धम् *ápy-ardham*, ind. within proximity, near to (gen.), ŚBr.; (cf. *abhy-ardhás*.)

अप्यस् *apy-√1. as*, *-asti* (1. pl. *-shmasi*; Imper. *-astu*; Opt. *-shyāt*), Ved. (with loc. or local adv.) to be in, be closely connected with, RV &c.; to belong to (as a share), RV.; ŚBr.

अप्यस् *apy-√2. as* (Subj. Ā. 2. sg. *-asyāthāḥ*) to insert, AitBr.

अप्याहृ *apy-ā-√hṛi* (Pot. *ápy ā́ haret*) to take or assume in addition, TS.

अप्युत *apy-uta* = *api*+*uta*, q. v.

अप्रकट *a-prakaṭa*, mf(*ā*)n. unmanifested, unapparent; (*am*), ind. without having been perceived, Kathās.

अप्रकम्प *a-prakampa*, mfn. unshaken; firm, steady; unanswered, unrefuted. **-tā**, f. firmness, stability, unanswerableness.

A-prakampin, mfn. not shaking, steady, AitĀr.

अप्रकर *a-prakara*, mfn. not acting excellently, L.

A-prakaraṇa, *am*, n. not the principal topic, not relevant to the main subject.

A-prakṛita, mfn. not principal, not relevant to the main topic under discussion, not chief; occasional or incidental; not natural.

A-prakṛiti, *is*, f. not an inherent or inseparable property, accidental property or nature.

अप्रकर्षित *a-prakarshita*, mfn. not exceeded; unsurpassed.

A-prakṛishṭa, *as*, m. a crow, L.; (cf. *apakṛishṭa*.)

अप्रकल्पक *a-prakalpaka*, mf(*ikā*)n. not prescribing as obligatory.

A-praklṛipta, mfn. not explicitly enjoined. **-tā**, f. the state of not being explicitly enjoined, KātyŚr.

अप्रकाण्ड *a-prakāṇḍa*, mfn. stemless, L.; (*as*), m. a bush, a shrub, L.

अप्रकाश *a-prakāśa*, mf(*ā*)n. not shining, dark; not visible, hidden, secret, Mn.; not manifest or evident; (*am*), ind. in secret, Mn. viii, 351; (*as*), m. indistinctness, darkness, Ragh. i, 68.

A-prakāśaka, mf(*ikā*)n. not rendering bright, making dark.

A-prakāśamāna, mfn. not manifested, unrevealed.

A-prakāśita, mfn. id.

A-prakāśya, mfn. not to be manifested.

अप्रकेत *a-praketá*, mfn. indiscriminate, unrecognizable, RV. x, 129, 3.

अप्रक्षित *á-prakshita*, mfn. undiminished, inexhaustible, RV, i, 55, 8.

अप्रखर *a-prakhara*, mfn. dull, obtuse, L.; bland, mild, L.

अप्रख्यता *a-prakhya-tā*, f. want of a striking or dignified appearance, MBh. xii, 5881.

अप्रगम *a-pragama*, mfn. (in speech or discussion) going too fast for others to follow, not to be surpassed.

अप्रगल्भ *a-pragalbha*, mf(*ā*)n. not arrogant, modest; timid.

अप्रगुण *a-praguṇa*, mfn. perplexed, L.

अप्रग्रह *a-pragraha* [TPrāt.] or *a-pragṛihya* [RPrāt.], *as*, m. not a vowel called *pragṛihya* (q. v.)

A-pragrāha, mfn. unrestrained, L.

अप्रचङ्कश *á-pracaṅkaśa*, mf(*ā*)n. without power of seeing, AV. viii, 6, 16.

अप्रचुर *a-pracura*, mfn. little, few.

अप्रचेतस् *á-pracetas*, mfn. deficient in understanding, foolish, RV.; AV. xx, 128, 2.

A-pracetita, mfn. not having been perceived, Bhaṭṭ.

अप्रचोदित *a-pracodita*, mfn. undesired, not bidden or commanded, unasked, Mn. iv, 248.

अप्रच्छिन्न *a-pracchinna*, mfn. not split, ĀśvGṛ.

A-pracchedya, mfn. inscrutable, L.

अप्रच्याव *a-pracyāva*, *as*, m. not falling in, PBr.

A-pracyāvuka, mf(*ā*)n. not decaying, KaushBr.

Á-pracyuta, mfn. unmoved, RV. ii, 28, 8; (with abl.) not fallen or deviating from, observing, following, Mn. xii, 116.

Á-pracyuti, *is*, f. not decaying, ŚBr.; ŚāṅkhŚr.

अप्रज *á-praja*, mf(*ā*)n. (√*jan*), without progeny, childless, RV. i, 21, 5; Mn. &c.; (*ā*), f. not bearing, unprolific, MBh. i, 4491.

1. **Á-prajajñi**, mfn. not generative, having no power of begetting, ŚBr.

Á-prajanishṇu, mfn. id., MaitrS.

Á-prajas [AV.] or **a-prajás** [ŚBr. &c.; cf. Pāṇ. v, 4, 122], mfn. without progeny, childless. **-tā** (*aprajás-*), f. or **aprajās-tvá**, n. childlessness, AV.

A-prajasyá, *am*, n. childlessness, TS.

A-prajātā, f. not having brought forth (cf. *a-prajā* above), MBh. v, 3047.

अप्रजज्ञि 2. *á-prajajñi*, mfn. (√*jñā*), inexperienced, inexpert, RV. x, 71, 9.

A-prajña, mfn. not knowing, RāmatUp.

A-prajñāta, mfn. not known, TS.; Mn. i, 5.

A-prajñātrá, mfn. (fr. *pra-jñātṛi*), not knowing, erring, being wrong, TS.

अप्रणाश *á-praṇāśa*, *as*, m not perishing, ŚBr.; PBr.

अप्रणीत *a-praṇīta*, mfn. (√*nī*), unconsecrated, profane, Mn. ix, 317; (*am*), n. the act of frying clarified butter without consecrated water, ĀśvŚr.

अप्रणोद्य *a-praṇodya*, mfn. (√*nud*), not to be turned away (as a guest), Mn. iii, 105; Gaut.

अप्रतर्क्य *a-pratarkya*, mfn. not to be discussed, L.; incomprehensible by reason, undefinable, Mn. i, 5 & xii, 29; BhP. &c.

अप्रता *a-pratā́* (Ved. loc. fr. *pratí*), ind. without recompense, for nothing, RV. viii, 32, 16.

अप्रताप *a-pratāpa*, *as*, m. want of brilliancy, dullness; meanness, want of dignity.

अप्रति *a-pratí*, mfn. without opponents, irresistible, RV.; BhP.; (*í*), n. irresistibly, RV. vii, 83, 4 & 99, 5; AV.; (*á*), ind., see s. v. above. **-1. -rūpa**, mf(*ā*)n. of unequalled form, incomparable, R. &c. [cf. 2. *a-pratirūpa*, p. 58]. **-rūpa-kathā**, f. incomparable or unanswerable discourse, L. **-vīrya**, mfn. of irresistible power, R. iv, 35, 4 & 38, 13.

अप्रतिकर *a-pratikara*, mfn. trusted, confidential, L.; (*eṇa*), ind. without recompense, Rājat.; (cf. *a-pratā́*.)

A-pratikarman, mfn. of unparalleled deeds, R.

A-pratikāra [Veṇis.] or **a-pratīkāra** [Mn. xii, 80; Kād.], mfn. not admitting of any relief or remedy.

A-pratikārin, mfn. (said of patients) not using a remedy, not permitting the employment of a remedy, Suśr.

अप्रतिकूल *a-pratikūla*, mf(*ā*)n. not resisting, not obstinate.

अप्रतिख्यात *á-pratikhyāta*, mfn. not seen, TBr.

अप्रतिगृह्य *a-pratigṛihyá*, mfn. one from whom one must not accept anything, ŚBr. xiv.

A-pratigrahaṇa, *am*, n. not accepting (a girl into marriage), not marrying, R.

Á-pratigrāhaka, mf(*ikā*)n. not accepting, ŚBr.; ĀśvŚr.

A-pratigrāhya, mfn. unacceptable.

अप्रतिघ *a-pratigha*, mfn. (√*han*), not to be kept off, not to be vanquished, Mn. xii, 28, &c.

अप्रतिद्वन्द्व *a-pratidvandva*, mfn. 'not having an adversary in battle,' not to be vanquished, irresistible, R. &c. **-tā**, f. unrivalledness.

अप्रतिधुर *a-pratidhurá*, mfn. without a match in going at the pole of a carriage (as a horse), ŚBr.

अप्रतिधृष्ट *á-pratidhṛishṭa*, mfn. 'irresistible,' in comp. with **-śavas**, mfn. of irresistible power, RV. i, 84, 2.

A-pratidhṛishyá, mfn. irresistible, VS. &c.

अप्रतिनोद *á-pratinoda*, *as*, m. not repelling, MaitrS.; PBr.

अप्रतिपक्ष *a-pratipaksha*, mfn. without a rival or opponent.

अप्रतिपण्य *a-pratipaṇya*, mfn. not to be bartered or exchanged.

अप्रतिपत्ति *a-pratipatti*, *is*, f. non-ascertainment; not understanding, Nyāyad.; the state of being undecided or confused, Sāh. &c.; non-performance, failure.

Á-pratipad, mfn. confused (*vikala*), VS. xxx, 8.

A-pratipadyamāna, mfn. not consenting to (acc.), Śak.

A-pratipanna, mfn. unascertained; unaccomplished.

अप्रतिबन्ध *a-pratibandha*, *as*, m. absence of obstruction; (mfn.) unimpeded, undisputed, direct (inheritance), not collateral or presumptive.

अप्रतिबल *a-pratibala*, mfn. of unequalled power, R.

अप्रतिबोध *a-pratibodha*, mfn. without consciousness, Ragh. viii, 57. **-vat**, mfn. id., MārkP.

अप्रतिब्रुवत् *á-pratibruvat*, mfn. not contradicting, AV. iii, 8, 3.

अप्रतिभ *a-pratibha*, mfn. modest, bashful, L.; (*ā*), f. shyness, timidity, Nyāyad.

अप्रतिम *a-pratima*, mf(*ā*)n. unequalled, incomparable, without a match.

A-pratimāná, mfn. incomparable, RV. viii, 96, 17.

A-pratimeya, mfn. id., Hariv.

अप्रतिमन्यूयमान *á-pratimanyūyamāna*, mfn. being unable to show resentment or to retaliate anger for anger, AV. xiii, 1, 31.

अप्रतियत्नपूर्व *a-pratiyatna-pūrva*, mf(*ā*)n. not produced ('by force' =) artificially, natural, Śiś.

अप्रतियोगिन् *a-pratiyogin*, mfn. not opposed to, not incompatible with; not correlative to.

अप्रतियोधिन् *a-pratiyodhin*, mfn. 'not having an adversary,' irresistible, MBh.; (cf. gaṇa *gamy-ādi.*)

अप्रतिरथ *á-pratiratha*, mfn. id., ŚBr., Śāk.; (*as*), m., N. of a Ṛishi (son of Indra and composer of the hymn RV. x, 103); N. of a son of Rantināra, VP.; (*am*), n., N. of the above-named hymn (composed by Apratiratha), MaitrS.; ŚBr. &c.

अप्रतिरव *a-pratirava*, mfn. uncontested, undisputed.

अप्रतिरूप 2. *á-pratirūpa*, mf(*ā*)n. not corresponding with, unfit, ŚBr. xiv; odious, disagreeable, R. &c. (For 1. see *a-prati.*)

अप्रतिलब्धकाम *a-pratilabdha-kāma*, mfn. never satiated in one's desires.

अप्रतिवादिन् *á-prativādin*, mfn. not contradicting, TS. &c.

अप्रतिशंसत् *á-pratiśaṃsat*, mfn. not reciting or shouting towards, ŚBr.

Á-pratiśasta, mfn. not shouted towards, id.

अप्रतिशासन *a-pratiśāsana*, mfn. not subject to the orders of another, not giving a counter or rival order, completely under subjection.

अप्रतिषिक्त *á-pratishikta*, mfn. not poured upon, not moistened, MaitrS.

A-pratishekyá, mfn. (a ceremony) at which there is no pouring upon, MaitrS.; ĀpŚr.

अप्रतिषिद्ध *a-pratishiddha*, mfn. (√2. *sidh*), unprohibited, unforbidden, Suśr.

A-pratishedha, *as*, m. 'non-prohibition,' non-negation, an invalid objection, Nyāyad.

अप्रतिष्कुत *á-pratishkuta*, mfn. not to be kept off, unrestrainable, RV.

अप्रतिष्कृत *a-pratishkṛita*, mfn. to whom nothing has been opposed, Nir.

अप्रतिष्टब्ध *a-pratishṭabdha*, mfn. not supported by (instr.), Āp.; (cf. *a-pratistabdha* below.)

अप्रतिष्ठ *a-pratishṭha*, mfn. having no solid ground, no value, fluctuating, unsafe, MBh.; Mn. iii, 180, &c.; (*as*), m., N. of a hell, VP.

Á-pratishṭhā, f. instability, TBr.

A-pratishṭhāná, mfn. having no solid ground, AV. xi, 3, 49.

Á-pratishṭhāyuka, mfn. id., MaitrS.

Á-pratishṭhita, mfn. id., ŚBr.; AitBr.; TBr.; unlimited, BhP.; Jain.

अप्रतिसंक्रम *a-pratisaṃkrama*, mfn. having no intermixture.

अप्रतिसंख्या *a-pratisaṃkhyā*, f. 'not observing,' in comp. with **-nirodha**, m. the unobserved annihilation of an object, Buddh.

अप्रतिस्तब्ध *a-pratistabdha*, mfn. unrestrained, Bhaṭṭ.; (cf. *a-pratishṭabdha* above.)

अप्रतिहत *a-pratihata*, mfn. uninterrupted, unobstructed, irresistible; unaffected, unimpaired, indestructible, uninjured; not passed away, PārGṛ. **-netra**, m. 'whose eyes are unimpeded,' N. of a deity, Buddh.

अप्रतिहार *a-pratihāra*, *as*, m. not stopping, PBr.; (mfn.), without the syllables contained in the *pratihāra* (q.v.), Lāṭy.

A-pratihārya, mfn. not to be repelled, irresistible, R.

अप्रतीकार *a-pratīkāra*. See *a-pratikāra.*

अप्रतीक्ष *a-pratīksha*, mfn. not looking backward, ĀpŚr.; (*á-pratīksham*), ind. without looking backward, ŚBr.

अप्रतीघातिता *a-pratīghātitā*, f. the state of not having (or meeting with) obstacles, of not being restrainable, MBh. xii, 9138.

अप्रतीत *á-pratīta*, mfn. unapproached, unattackable, RV.; AV. vii, 25, 1; not understood, uncommon (as an expression), Sāh. &c.; not merry, sad, R.

A-pratīti, *is*, f. the state of not being understood; mistrust, want of confidence.

अप्रतीत्त *á-pratītta*, mfn. not given back, AV. vi, 117, 1.

अप्रतीप *a-pratīpa*, mfn. not contradictory, not obstinate; (*as*), m., N. of a king of Magadha, VP.

अप्रतुल *a-pratula*, *as*, m. want of weight, want, L.

अप्रत्त *a-pratta*, mfn. (for *a-pradatta*), not given back, PBr.; (*ā*), f. 'not given away (in marriage),' a girl, Nir.; Gaut.

अप्रत्यक्ष *a-pratyaksha*, mfn. not present to the sight, invisible, imperceptible. **-tā**, f. imperceptibility. **-śishṭa**, mfn. not distinctly taught.

अप्रत्यय *a-pratyaya*, *as*, m. distrust, disbelief, doubt; not an affix, Pāṇ. i, 1, 69; (mfn.), distrustful (with loc.), Śāk.; causing distrust; having no affix. **-stha**, mfn. (in Gr.) not pertaining to an affix.

अप्रत्याख्यात *a-pratyākhyāta*, mfn. uncontradicted, unrefuted, assented to.

A-pratyākhyāna, *am*, n. non-refutation.

A-pratyākhyeya, mfn. not to be contradicted, undeniable.

अप्रत्याम्नाय *a-pratyāmnāya*, *as*, m. not a contradictory statement, RPrāt.

अप्रत्यालभमान *á-pratyālabhamāna*, mfn. not offering resistance, ŚBr.

अप्रत्यृत *a-pratyṛita*, mfn. (=*an-arvá*), not encountering any resistance in (loc.), Nir.

अप्रथित *a-prathita*, mfn. not spread, Nir.

अप्रदग्ध *á-pradagdha*, mfn. not burnt, ŚBr.

अप्रददि *á-pradadi*, mfn. not liberal, AV. xx, 128, 8.

A-pradānavat, mfn. id., R.

अप्रदाह *á-pradāha*, *as*, m. not consuming by fire, ŚBr.; TBr.

अप्रदीप्ताग्नि *a-pradīptâgni*, mfn. dyspeptic.

अप्रदुग्ध *á-pradugdha*, mfn. not milked to the end, RV. iii, 55, 16.

अप्रदृपित *á-pradṛipita*, mfn. not thoughtless, not careless, RV. i, 145, 2.

अप्रधान *a-pradhāna*, mfn. not principal, subordinate, secondary, Pāṇ. ii, 3, 19, &c. **-tā**, f. or **-tva**, n. inferiority.

अप्रधृष्य *a-pradhṛishya*, mfn. not to be vanquished, invincible, MBh.; Pañcat.

अप्रपदन *á-prapadana*, *am*, n. a bad place of refuge, ŚBr.

Á-prapāda, *as*, m. non-abortiveness, TS.; TBr.

Á-prapāduka, mfn. not abortive, MaitrS.

अप्रपाणा *a-prapāṇá*, mfn. not containing drinkable water, AV. xx, 128, 8.

अप्रबल *a-prabala*, mfn. inefficacious, weak.

अप्रभ *a-prabha*, mfn. obscure; dull, L.

अप्रभु *á-prabhu*, mfn. wanting power, unable, incompetent (with loc.), RV. ix, 73, 9; AitBr. &c. **-tva**, n. want of power, insufficiency, MBh. &c.

A-prabhūta, mfn. insufficient, inadequate.

Á-prabhūti, *is*, f. (Ved. instr. °*tī*), little effort, RV. x, 124, 7.

अप्रभ्रंश *á-prabhraṇśa*, *as*, m. not getting deprived of, not losing (with abl.), ŚBr.

अप्रमत्त *á-pramatta*, mfn. not careless, careful, attentive, vigilant, ŚBr. &c. **-vat**, mfn. id., MBh. xii, 8889.

A-pramāda, *as*, m. care, vigilance, MBh. &c.; (mfn.), 'careful, cautious,' see *-tā* below; (*á-pramādam*), ind. attentively, carefully, AV.; VS.; without interruption, AV. **-tā**, f. the being cautious, Yājñ. iii, 314.

A-pramādin, mfn. careful, Mn. ii, 115, &c.

अप्रमद *a-pramada*, *as*, m. not pleasure, joylessness, MBh. xii, 10414.

अप्रमय *a-prámaya*, mfn. imperishable, ŚBr. xiv; (cf. *a-prāmi-satya.*)

Á-pramāyuka, mfn. not dying suddenly, AV. xix, 44, 3; TBr.

A-pramīya, mfn. (that) which ought not to perish, ShaḍvBr.

अप्रमा *a-pramā*, f. a rule which is no authority (see *a-pramāṇa*); incorrect knowledge.

A-pramāṇa, *am*, n. a rule which is no standard of action, MBh.; Śāk. &c.; (in discussion) a statement of no importance or authority. **-vid**, mfn. incapable of weighing evidence, BhP. **-śubha**, *ās*, m. pl. 'of immeasurable virtue,' N. of a class of divinities, Buddh. **Apramāṇâbha**, *ās*, m. pl. 'of unlimited splendour,' N. of a class of divinities, Buddh.

A-pramita, mfn. unbounded, unmeasured; not proved, not established by authority.

A-prameya, mfn. immeasurable, unlimited, unfathomable, Mn. i, 3 & xii, 94, &c.; not to be proved. **Aprameyâtman**, m. 'of inscrutable spirit,' N. of Śiva. **Aprameyânubhāva**, mfn. of unlimited might.

अप्रमायुक *á-pramāyuka*. See *a-prámaya.*

A-pramīya. See ib.

अप्रमुदिता *a-pramuditā*, f. 'joylessness,' (in Sāṅkhya phil.) N. of one of the eight Asiddhis.

A-pramoda, *as*, m. joylessness, Mn. iii, 61 = MBh. xiii, 2487.

A-pramodamānā, f., N. of another of the above Asiddhis.

अप्रमूर *á-pramūra*, mfn. not foolish, prudent, RV. i, 90, 2.

अप्रमृष्य *a-pramṛishyá*, mfn. not to be destroyed, indestructible, RV.

अप्रयत *a-prayata*, mfn. not intent (on devotion), not prepared (in mind) for any important action or performance, Mn.; Āp.; (once said of food) Āp.

A-prāyatya, *am*, n. the state of being *a-prayata*, BhP.; Āp.

अप्रयत्न *a-prayatna*, *as*, m. absence of effort, indifference; (mfn.), indifferent, apathetic in (loc.), Mn. vi, 26.

अप्रयाज *a-prayājá*, mfn. without a Prayāja, TS.

अप्रयाणक *a-prayāṇaka*, *am*, n. halt (on a journey), Pañcat.

A-prayāṇi, *is*, f. not going, not moving (used in execrations), Pāṇ. viii, 4, 29, Kāś.

A-prayāpaṇi, *is*, f. not allowing to go (used in execrations), Pāṇ. viii, 4, 30, Sch.

अप्रयावम् *á-prayāvam* [VS. xi, 75; AV. xix, 55, 1] or *á-prayāvan* [AV. iii, 5, 1], ind. (√1. *yu*), not carelessly, attentively; (cf. *á-prāyu.*)

Á-prayucchat, mfn. attentive, RV.; AV.

Á-prayuta, mfn. id., RV. vii, 100, 2.

Á-prayutvan, mfn. id., RV. vi, 48, 10.

अप्रयास *a-prayāsa*, *as*, m. absence of toil; (*ena*), ind. easily, Yājñ. iii, 115.

अप्रयुक्त *á-prayukta*, mfn. not used or applied, MaitrS.; (of words) not in use, Pat.; unsuitable, Pañcat. **-tā**, f. or **-tva**, n. unusualness (of expressions), Sāh.

A-prayoga, *as*, m. non-application; the not being in use (of words), Pat.

A-prayojaka, mf(*ikā*)n. not causing or effecting; aimless.

अप्रलम्बम् *a-pralambam*, ind. without delay, L.

अप्रवदत् *a-pravadat*, mf(*atī*)n. not roaring, ĀśvGṛ.

अप्रवर्ग्य *á-pravargya*, mfn. without the Pravargya ceremony, ŚBr.; KātyŚr.

अप्रवर्तक *a-pravartaka*, mf(*ikā*)n. abstaining from action, inert; not exciting to action.

A-pravartana, *am*, n. the act of refraining from, not engaging in; not exciting to any action.

A-pravṛitta, mfn. not acting, not engaged in; not commenced, not instigated.

A-pravṛitti, *is*, f. not proceeding; no further effect or applicability of a precept, KātyŚr.; abstaining from action, inertion; non-excitement; (in med.) suppression of the natural evacuations, constipation, ischury, &c.

अप्रवीण *a-pravīṇa*, mfn. unskilful.

अप्रवीता *á-pravītā*, f. (see *pra-√vī*), not impregnated, RV. iii, 55, 5; iv, 7, 9; ŚBr.; KātyŚr.

अप्रवृद्ध *a-pravṛiddha*, mfn. not excessively grown, (gaṇa *pravṛiddhâdi*, q. v.)

अप्रवेद *á-praveda*, mf(*ā*)n. (said of heaven and earth, together with *á-trasnu*), not insidious, ŚBr.

अप्रव्लय *a-pravlaya*, *as*, m. not sinking down, AitBr.

अप्रशस्त 1. *a-praśastá*, mfn. not praised, fameless, RV. ii, 41, 16 & iv, 28, 4; not good, inferior, worthless; (*am*), n. dirt, natural excretion, Mn. xi, 255.

2. **Á-praśasta**, mfn. not praised, blamable, RV. i, 167, 8.

A-praśasya, mfn. not praiseworthy.

अप्रसक्त *a-prasakta*, mfn. not addicted, not attached to.

A-prasakti, *is*, f. non-addiction, non-attachment to (loc.), Mn. i, 89.

A-prasaṅga, *as*, m. (in Nyāya phil.) want of connection with; non-applicability, KātyŚr.

अप्रसन्न *a-prasanna*, mfn. not quiet, not clear; turbid, muddy; displeased, unfavourable.

A-prasāda, *as*, m. disfavour, disapprobation.

A-prasādya, mfn. not to be propitiated; unappeasable, implacable.

अप्रसव 1. *a-prasava*, *as*, m. (√3. *su*), not preparing the Soma juice, KātyŚr.

अप्रसव 2. *a-prasava*, mfn. (√4. *su*), not being prolific; (*as*), m. non-propagation. **—dharmin**, mfn. (in Sāṅkhya phil.) not having the property of producing (one of the characteristics of Purusha).

A-prasūtā, f. 'not giving birth to,' a barren woman.

अप्रसह्य *a-prasahya*, mfn. intolerable, MBh.; irresistible, ib.

A-prasahishṇu, mfn. quite unable (to), Śiś. i, 54.

A-prasāha, mfn. not subjected to any force, ChUp.

अप्रसिद्ध *a-prasiddha*, mfn. not settled, unestablished; unknown, uncelebrated; unusual, uncommon, of no real existence, not current, not generally known. **—pada**, n. an obsolete word.

अप्रसूत *á-prasūta*, mfn. (√1. *sū*), not allowed, ŚāṅkhŚr. (of persons); ŚBr. (of things).

अप्रस्तुत *a-prastuta*, mfn. unconnected with, irrelevant, unsuitable to the time or subject; not principal, not being the chief subject-matter; indirect, accidental or extraneous; not laudable, R. **—praśaṇsā** or **-stuti**, f. 'conveying the subject-matter by that which is not the subject-matter,' (in rhetoric) implied or indirect expression.

A-prastāvika, mf(*ī*)n. irrelevant to the subject-matter, Mālatīm.

अप्रस्रंस *á-prasraṇsa*, *as*, m. not falling down, TBr.; Kāṭh.; AitBr.

अप्रहत *a-prahata*, mfn. unhurt, intact; untilled, waste, L.

Á-prahan, m(acc. °*haṇam*)fn. not hurting, RV. vi, 44, 4.

अप्रहावन् *á-prahāvan*, mf(*varī*)n. not diminishing, not vanishing, MaitrS.

अप्रहित *á-prahita*, mfn. not stirred up, RV. viii, 99, 7; not sent out, AV. vi, 29, 2.

अप्रहृत *á-prahṛita*, mfn. (a stick) not advanced for striking, ŚBr.

अप्राकरणिक *a-prākaraṇika*, mfn. not connected with the subject-matter, Comm. on Mn. iii, 285.

A-prākṛita, mfn. not principal; not original; special, particular; not vulgar, extraordinary, Mcar.

अप्राग्र्य *a-prâgrya*, mfn. secondary, L.

अप्राचीन *a-prācīna*, mfn. not eastern, western; not old, modern, recent.

अप्राज्ञ *a-prājña*, mfn. unlearned, ignorant. **—tā**, f. ignorance, Mn. iv, 167.

अप्राण 1. *á-prâṇa*, *as*, m. no breath, MaitrUp.

2. **A-prāṇá**, mfn. inanimate, lifeless, AV.; ŚBr.

Á-prāṇat, mfn. id., AV. x, 8, 11; Lāṭy.

अप्रातिलोम्य *a-prātilomya*, *am*, n. the not being hostile to, Rājat.

अप्रादेशिक *a-prādeśika*, mfn. not pointing to or suggestive of (the etymol. of a word), Nir. i, 13.

अप्राधान्य *a-prādhānya*, *am*, n. non-superiority, inferiority, subordination.

अप्राप्त *á-prâpta*, mfn. unobtained; unarrived; not accomplished, Yājñ. ii, 243; not yet full-grown, Mn. ix, 88; not resulting (from any rule), Pāṇ. viii, 2, 33, Sch. **—kāla**, mfn. out of season, inopportune, ill-timed; under age; (*am*), n. an irregular debate, Nyāyad. **—yauvana**, mfn. not arrived at puberty. **—vikalpa** [Pāṇ. i, 4, 53, Comm.], m. or **-vibhāshā** [Pāṇ. i, 3, 43, Sch.], f. the optional permission of an operation which without such permission would not take place at all. **—vyavahāra**, mfn. a minor in law; under age, not of years to engage in law or public business. **Aprāptâvasara**, mfn. unseasonable, inopportune, Hit.

A-prâpti, *is*, f. non-attainment, non-acquisition.

1. **A-prâpya**, mfn. unobtainable, MBh. &c.; superl. *-tama*, Mṛicch.

2. **A-prâpya**, ind. p. not having obtained; not reaching. **—kārin**, mfn. acting on any object without direct contact with it, Comm. on Nyāyad. **—grahaṇa**, n. perception of an object though the senses are not in any direct connection with it, Nyāyad.

अप्रामाणिक *a-prāmāṇika*, mfn. unauthentic; unauthoritative.

A-prāmāṇya, *am*, n. absence or insufficiency of proof or authority.

अप्रामिसत्य *a-prāmi-satya* (√*mī* with *prā* = *pra*, cf. *a-prámaya*), 'of imperishable truthfulness,' unalterably true, RV. viii, 61, 4.

अप्रायत्य *a-prāyatya*. See *a-prayata*.

अप्रायु *á-prāyu*, mfn. (√1. *yu* with *prā* = *pra* [cf. *á-prayāvam*]; Padap. *á-prâyu* fr. *āyú* or *âyus*), not careless, assiduous, RV. i, 89, 1 & viii, 24, 18; (*u*), ind. assiduously, RV. v, 80, 3.

Á-prāyus, mfn. (Padap. *á-prâyus* fr. *âyus*) id., RV. i, 127, 5.

अप्रार्थक *a-prârthaka*, mfn. not demanding in marriage, Comm. on Mn. iii, 27.

अप्रावृत *á-prāvṛita*, mfn. not covered, ŚBr. &c.

अप्राशन *a-prâśana*, *am*, n. not eating, MBh.

A-prâśitṛi, mfn. not eating, MBh.

A-prâśitriyá, mfn. not fit for food called *prâśitrá* (q. v.), TS.

अप्रिय *á-priya*, mfn. disagreeable, disliked; unkind, unfriendly; (*as*), m. a foe, an enemy, Mn.; N. of a Yaksha, Buddh.; (*ā*), f. a sort of skeat fish, Silurus Pungentissimus. **—m-vada**, see *apriya-vādin*. **—kara**, mfn. 'not giving pleasure,' disagreeable, Mn. vii, 204. **—bhāgin**, mfn. unfortunate. **—vādin** [Mn. ix, 81], mfn. or **apriyam-vada** [Yājñ. i, 73], mf(*ā*)n. speaking unkindly or harshly.

A-prīti, *is*, f. dislike, aversion, enmity, Mṛicch.; pain. **—kara**, mfn. unkind, adverse; disagreeable, Mn. xii, 28. **Aprīty-ātmaka**, mf(*ikā*)n. consisting of pain.

A-preman, *a*, n. dislike, aversion, L.; (mfn.), unfriendly, L.

अप्रेत *á-prêta*, mfn. not gone away, ŚBr. **—rākshasī**, f. a plant (also called *prêta-rākshasī* or *apêta-rākshasī*, q. v.)

अप्रैष *a-praisha*, mfn. not invoked with a *praísha* (q. v.) mantra, Comm. on ĀśvŚr.

अप्रोक्षित *á-prókshita*, mfn. not sprinkled, not consecrated, ŚBr. &c.

अप्रोदित *á-prôdita*, mfn. not uttered, TS.

अप्रोषित *a-prôshita*, mfn. not departed, not absent.

Á-prôshivas, m(nom. *vān*)fn. not gone away, staying, RV. viii, 60, 19.

अप्रौढ *a-prauḍha*, mf(*ā*)n. not arrogant, timid, gentle; not capable of (Inf.), Rājat.; (*ā*), f. an unmarried girl; one very recently married and not come to womanhood.

अप्लव *á-plava*, mf(*ā*)n. without a ship, AV. xix, 50, 31, &c.; not swimming. **—vat**, mfn. without a ship, MBh. **A-plavêsa**, mfn. unable to swim.

अप्वा *apvā́* (3; *ápvā*, Naigh.), f., N. of a disease (got in danger), RV. x, 103, 12 (voc. *apve*); AV. ix, 8, 9 (acc. *apvām*).

Apuvāya, Nom. Ā. °*yáte*, to get ill, become spoiled, TS.; (cf. *anvart*.)

अप्सरस् *ap-sarás*, *ās* [RV.; AV. &c.], or *apsarā́* [AV. &c.], f. (fr. 2. *áp* + √*sṛi*), 'going in the waters or between the waters of the clouds,' a class of female divinities (sometimes called 'nymphs;' they inhabit the sky, but often visit the earth; they are the wives of the Gandharvas (q.v.) and have the faculty of changing their shapes at will; they are fond of the water; one of their number, Rambhā, is said to have been produced at the churning of the ocean). **Apsaraḥ-pati**, m. 'lord of the Apsarasas,' Indra, L. **Apsaras-tīrtha**, n. a pool in which the Apsarasas bathe, Śāk. **Apsarā-patí**, m. 'lord of the Apsarasas,' N. of the Gandharva Śikhaṇḍin, AV. iv, 37, 7.

Apsarāya, Nom. Ā. *apsarāyate*, to behave like an Apsaras, Pāṇ. iii, 1, 11, Comm.

Apsarāyita, mfn. made or grown an Apsaras, Naish.

Ap-savá, mfn. giving water, RV. x, 65, 3.

Apsavyà, mfn. (fr. 2. *apsú*, q.v.), being in the water (Varuṇa), MaitrS.; Kāṭh.; cf. Pāṇ. vi, 3, 1, Comm.

Ap-sá, mfn. (√*san*), giving water, RV.

अप्सस् *ápsas*, *as*, n. 'the hidden part of the body,' the secret charms (of a wife), RV.; AV.; SV. ['breast or κόλπος,' Gmn.; 'cheek,' BR.; 'forehead, face,' NBD.]; hidden fault, sin, MaitrS.; Kāṭh.; (*apsvas*) KapS.

अप्सु 1. *á-psu*, mfn. without food, RV. vii, 4, 6.

अप्सु 2. *apsú* (loc. pl. of 2. *áp*, q. v.), in the water or waters. **—kshít**, mfn. dwelling within the clouds, in the region between heaven and earth, RV. i, 139, 11. **—cara**, mfn. (Ved.) going in the waters, Pāṇ. vi, 3, 1, Comm. **—já** [TS.] or **-já** [RV. viii, 43, 28, &c.], mfn. born in the waters. **—jit**, mfn. vanquishing among the waters or in the region of the clouds (N. of Indra), RV. **—dīkshā**, f. consecration in water. **—mát**, mfn. possessed of or shining in the waters (e. g. the lightning which does not lose its brilliant nature in the clouds), MaitrS. &c.; containing the word *apsú*, ŚBr.; N. of an Agni, ĀpŚr. **—yogá**, m. the connecting power in water, AV. x, 5, 5. **—yoni** (*apsú-*), mfn. born from the waters, TS.; ŚBr. **—váh**, m(nom. pl. *-vā́has*)fn. driving in water, SV. **—shád**, mfn. dwelling in the waters, RV. iii, 3, 5; AV.; VS. **—shádas**, n. dwelling in the waters, MaitrS. **—shomá**, m. 'Soma in water,' a cup filled with water, ŚBr.; KātyŚr. **—saṃśita** (*apsú-*), mfn. raised or excited in the waters, AV. x, 5, 33. **—homya**, m., N. of a man, MBh. ii, 107.

अफल *a-phalá*, mf(*ā́*)n. unfruitful, barren, RV. x, 97, 15, &c.; vain, unproductive, RV. x, 71, 5, &c.; deprived of virility, R. i, 49, 1 & 11; (*as*), m. Tamarix Indica; (*ā*), f. the Aloe (Aloes Perfoliata); Flacourtia Cataphracta. **—kāṅkshin**, mfn. disinterested, not looking to beneficial consequences. **—tā**, f. or **-tva**, n. barrenness, unprofitableness. **—prêpsu**, mfn. one who desires no recompense, Bhag. **A-phalâkāṅkshin**, mfn. = *a-phala-kāṅkshin*, q.v., Bhag.

अफल्गु *a-phalgu*, mfn. not vain, productive, profitable, Śiś. iii, 76.

अफुल्ल *a-phulla*, mf(*ā*)n. unblown (a rose), L.

अफेन *a-phena*, mf(*ā*)n. frothless; (*am*), n. opium, L.

अबण्ड *á-baṇḍa*, mf(*ā*)n. not crippled, ŚBr.

अबद्ध *á-baddha*, mfn. unbound, unrestrained, at liberty, TS. &c.; unmeaning, nonsensical, N. **—mukha**, mfn. foul-mouthed, scurrilous, L. **—mūla**, mfn. whose root does not hold fast, is not firm. **—vat**, mfn. unmeaning, ungrammatical, BhP.

A-baddhaka, mfn. unmeaning, nonsensical, L. **Á-badhira,** mfn. not deaf, RV. viii, 45, 17.

1. **A-badhya,** mfn. unmeaning, nonsensical, L.

A-banddhrá (or defectively written *a-bandhrá*), mfn. without bonds or ligatures, AV. iv, 16, 7.

A-bandhaka, mfn. not binding; *(as)*, m., N. of a man, & *(ās)*, m. pl. his descendants, (gaṇa *upakâdi.*)

A-bandhaná, mfn. without fetters, free, RV. iii, 55, 6.

1. **A-bandhya,** mfn. not to be fettered or bound.

A-bandhrá. See *a-banddhrá.*

अबध *a-badha.* See *a-vadha.*

2. **A-badhya.** See *a-vadhya.*

अबधा *abadhā*, f. segment of the basis of a triangle; (cf. *ăbādhā* and *avabadhā.* In Jaina Prākṛit *ăbāhā* or *ăvăhā.*)

अबन्धु *a-bandhú*, mfn. without kindred, without companions, friendless, RV. i, 53, 9 & viii, 21, 4; AV. vi, 122, 2. **-kṛit** *(á-bandhu-)*, mfn. causing want of companions, AV. iv, 19, 1.

A-bāndhava, mfn. having no relation or kindred, lone, Mn. x, 55. **-kṛita,** mfn. not caused by relation or kindred, Śāk.

अबन्ध्य 2. *a-bandhya*, mf(*ā*)n. not barren, not unfruitful, fruitful, productive; (cf. *a-vandhya*, which is perhaps the better spelling.)

अबल *a-balá*, mf(*ā́*)n. weak, feeble, RV. v, 30, 9, &c.; *(as)*, m. the plant Tapia Cratæva; a king of Magadha, VP.; *(ā)*, f. a woman, Śāk. &c.; N. of a woman, Kathās.; (= *acalā*) one of the ten Buddhist earths; *(am)*, n. want of strength, weakness. **-dhanvan** *(abalá-)*, mfn. possessing a weak bow, AV. iii, 19, 7. **-vat,** mfn. strengthless, Veṇis. **A-balâbala,** mfn. 'neither powerful nor powerless,' N. of Śiva.

Á-balīyas, mfn. (compar.) weaker, ŚBr.; superl. *abalishṭha*, mfn. weakest, PBr.

A-balyà [ŚBr.] or **á-balya** [ŚBr. xiv], *am*, n. weakness, sickness.

अबलास *a-balāsá*, mfn. not causing consumption, AV. viii, 2, 18.

अबहिर् *a-bahir*, ind. 'not outside,' in the interior, in one's heart, BhP. **-dhā** *(á-bahir-)*, ind. not outside, ŚBr. **-vāsas,** mfn. without an upper garment, BhP.

अबहु *a-bahu*, mfn. not many, few. **Abahv-akshara,** mfn. having not many (i. e. not more than two) syllables, RPrāt. **Abahv-ac,** mfn. id., Pāṇ. Sch.

अबाध *a-bādha*, mfn. unobstructed, unrestrained; free from pain; *(ā)*, f. freedom from pain, MārkP.; = *a-badhā*, q. v.

A-bādhaka, mf(*ā*)n. unimpeded, Kathās.

Á-bādhita, mfn. unimpeded, unobstructed, RV. x, 92, 8, &c.; unrefuted; not forbidden, Comm. on Mn. iv, 5.

A-bādhya, mfn. not to be opposed or pained.

अबान्धव *a-bāndhava.* See *a-bandhú.*

अबालिश *a-bāliśa*, mfn. not childish, Nir. ix, 10; R.

अबालेन्दु *a-bālêndu, us*, m. 'not the infantine moon,' full moon, Ragh. vi, 53.

अबाह्य *a-bāhyá*, mfn. not exterior, internal, Ragh. xiv, 50; without an exterior, ŚBr. xiv.

अबिन्धन *ab-indhana, as*, m. 'having water (*ap*) for fuel,' submarine fire, Ragh. xiii, 14.

अबिभीवस् *á-bibhīvas*, m (instr. °*bhyushā*; nom. pl. °*bhyushas*) fn. (perf. p.) fearless, confident, RV. i, 6, 7; 11, 5 & ix, 53, 2; AV. iii, 14, 3.

Á-bibhyat, mfn. (pr. p.) id., RV. vi, 23, 2.

अबीज *a-bīja*, mfn. seedless; impotent, Mn. ix, 79.

A-bījaka, mfn. unsown, Mn. x, 71.

अबीभत्सा *á-bībhatsā*, f. non-disgust, TBr.

अबुद्ध *a-buddha*, mfn. unwise, foolish; not seen or noticed, KaushBr.; R. **-tva,** n. foolishness.

A-buddhi, *is*, f. want of understanding; ignorance; stupidity; (mfn.), ignorant, stupid; *(a-buddhyā)*, ind. unintentionally. **-pūrva** or **-pūrvaka,** mfn. not preceded by intelligence; beginning with non-intelligence; *(am)*, ind. ignorantly. **-mat,** mfn. unwise, foolish. **-stha,** mfn. not being in the conscience of, Comm. on Mn. iii, 266.

A-budh [BṛĀrUp.] or **a-budhá** [ŚBr. xiv], mfn. stupid, foolish; *(a-budha)*, *as*, m. a fool, Hit.

A-budhyá, mfn. not to be awakened, RV. iv, 19, 3.

Á-budhyamāna, mfn. not being awake, RV.

A-bodha, *as*, m. non-perception; ignorance, stupidity; (mfn.), ignorant, stupid; puzzled, perplexed. **-gamya,** mfn. incomprehensible.

A-bodhanīya, mfn. unintelligible; not to be awakened or aroused.

अबुध्न *a-budhná*, mfn. bottomless, RV. i, 24, 7 & viii, 77, 5.

अब्ज *ab-ja*, mfn. (fr. 2. *áp* and √*jan*), born in water; *(as)*, m. the conch; the moon; the tree Barringtonia Acutangula; N. of Dhanvantari (physician of the gods, produced at the churning of the ocean); a son of Viśāla; *(am)*, n. a lotus; a milliard (cf. *padma*). **-ja,** m. 'sprung (at the creation) from the lotus (which arose from the navel of Vishṇu),' N. of Brahmā. **-dṛiś** or **-nayana,** mfn. lotus-eyed, having large fine eyes. **-nābha,** m. 'whose navel is a lotus,' N. of Vishṇu. **-netra,** mfn. = *-dṛiś.* **-bāndhava,** m. 'friend of the lotus,' the sun. **-bhava** [BhP.] or **-bhū** [Daś.], m. Brahmā. **-bhoga,** m. the root of a lotus, L. **-yoni,** m. (= *-ja* above) N. of Brahmā, Hcat. **-vāhana,** m. 'carrying the moon (on his forehead),' N. of Śiva. **-hasta,** m. the sun (represented as holding a lotus in one hand), L. **Abjâda,** m. 'eating lotus-leaves,' a swan, VarBṛS.

Ab-já, mfn. born in water, RV. iv, 40, 5 & vii, 34, 16.

Ab-jit, mfn. conquering waters, RV.

Abjinī, f. a multitude of lotus flowers, (gaṇa *pushkarâdi.*) **-pati,** m. the sun, Kathās.

Áb-da, mfn. giving water, L.; *(as)*, m. a year; a cloud, Bhaṭṭ.; the grass Cyperus Rotundus; N. of a mountain, L.; *(ā́)*, f., see *abdayā́* below. **-tantra,** n., N. of an astronomical work. **-vāhana,** m. (for *abja-vāhana*, q. v.), N. of Śiva, L. **-śata,** n. a century. **-sahasra,** n. a thousand years. **-sāra,** m. a kind of camphor. **Abdârdha,** n. a half year.

Abdayā́ (instr. of *ab-dā́*), ind. out of desire of giving water, RV. v, 54, 3.

Abdi-mát, mfn. possessed of clouds (*abdi* = *abda*), RV. v, 42, 14.

Ab-durga, *am*, n. a fortress surrounded by a moat or lake.

Ab-daivata, mfn. having the waters as divinities, praising the waters (said of certain hymns; see *ab-liṅga* below), Mn. viii, 106 & xi, 132.

Ab-dhi, *is*, m. (√*dhā*), a pond, lake, L.; the ocean, Hit. &c.; (hence) the numeral 4. **-kapha,** m. cuttle fish bone, being considered as the froth of the sea. **-ja,** mfn. born in the ocean; *(au)*, m. du. the Aśvins, L.; *(ā)*, f. spirituous liquor, L. **-jīvin,** m. a fisherman, Kathās. **-jhasha,** m. a sea-fish. **-tanaya,** *au*, m. du. the Aśvins, Kathās. **-dvīpā,** f. earth, L. **-nagarī,** f., N. of Dvārakā, the capital of Kṛishṇa. **-navanītaka,** m. the moon. **-phena,** m. cuttle fish bone. **-maṇḍūkī,** f. the pearl oyster. **-śayana,** m. 'sleeping on the ocean (at the periods of the destruction and renovation of the world),' N. of Vishṇu. **-sāra,** m. a gem. **Abdhy-agni,** m. submarine fire.

Ab-bindu, *us*, m. a tear, BhP.

Ab-bhaksha, mfn. living upon water, Yājñ. iii, 286; Gaut.; *(as)*, m. a snake, L.

Ab-bhakshaṇa, *am*, n. living upon water (a kind of fasting), BhP.

Ab-liṅga, *āni*, n. pl. [Yājñ. iii, 30] or **ab-liṅgā,** *ās*, f. pl. [Gaut.], N. of some Vedic verses [RV. x, 9, 1-3] addressed to the waters; (cf. *ab-daivata* above.)

अब्रह्मचर्य *a-brahmacarya*, mfn. not keeping a vow of continence, unchaste, Nir.

A-brahmacaryaka, *am*, n. incontinence, L.

अब्रह्मण्य *a-brahmaṇya*, mfn. not favourable to Brāhmans, MBh.; BhP.; *(am)*, n. an unbrahmanical or sacrilegious act, used as an exclamation, meaning 'help!' 'a disgraceful deed is perpetrated!' Pañcat.; Kathās.; (Prākṛit *abbamhaṇṇaṃ*), Śāk.

Á-brahman, mfn. not a *brahmán*, ŚBr.; without devotion (*bráhman*), RV.; without Brāhmans, Mn. ix, 322; *(á)*, n. not the *bráhman*, TBr. **Abrahmá-tā,** f. want of devotion, RV. v, 33, 3; VS. **A-brahma-bandhūka,** mfn. without *brahmabandhū* (q. v.), Pāṇ. vi, 2, 173, Kāś. **A-brahma-vid,** mfn. not knowing Brahma or the Supreme Spirit.

1. **Á-brāhmaṇa,** *as*, m. not a Brāhman, AV. &c.; *(ī)*, f. not a Brāhmaṇī; *(a-brāhmaṇá)*, mfn. without Brāhmans, ŚBr.

A-brāhmaṇya, *am*, n. violation of the duty of a Brāhman, ĀśvŚr.

अब्रुवत् *a-bruvat*, mfn. (pr. p.), not speaking, silent, Yājñ. ii, 76.

अभक्त *á-bhakta*, mfn. not received as a share, RV. i, 129, 5 & iii, 30, 7; not attached to, detached, unconnected with; not eaten. **-cchanda,** m. or **-ruci,** f. want of appetite.

A-bhakti, *is*, f. want of devotion to, want of faith. **-mat,** mfn. undevoted to, unbelieving.

अभक्ष *a-bhaksha, as*, m. or *a-bhakshaṇa, am*, n. not eating anything, fasting.

Á-bhakshita, mfn. not eaten.

A-bhakshya, mfn. not to be eaten by (instr. or gen., Mn.) **-bhakshaṇa,** n. eating of prohibited food, RāmatUp. **-bhakshin,** mfn. eating forbidden food.

अभग *a-bhagá*, mfn. without enjoyment, unfortunate, AV. v, 31, 11.

अभग्न *a-bhagna*, mfn. unbroken, entire; uninterrupted. **-kāma,** mf(*ā*)n. whose desire or wishes are not disturbed, Ragh.

A-bhaṅgura, mf(*ā*)n. not fragile; unchangeable, invariable, firm; (not curved), flat, plain, Suśr.

A-bhajyamāna, mfn. (Pass.) not being detached; not being vanquished, &c.

अभद्र *a-bhadra*, mfn. inauspicious, mischievous; *(am)*, n. mischief.

अभय *á-bhaya*, mf(*ā*)n. unfearful, not dangerous, secure; *(a-bháya)*, mfn. fearless, undaunted, ŚBr. xiv; *(as)*, m., N. of Śiva; of a natural son of Bimbisāra; of a son of Idhmajihva, BhP.; of a river in Krauñcadvīpa, BhP.; *(ā)*, f. the plant Terminalia Chebula; *(á-bhayam)*, n. (ifc. f. *ā*) absence or removal of fear, peace, safety, security, RV. &c. (cf. *ábhaya-tama* below); 'safety,' (applied as proper name to) a child of Dharma and his reign in Plakshadvīpa, BhP.; a kind of symbol procuring security, Hcat.; a sacrificial hymn recited to obtain personal security, Kauś.; the root of a fragrant grass, Andropogon Muricatum. **-giri-vāsin,** m. pl. 'dwelling on the mountain of safety,' N. of a division of Kātyāyana's pupils, Buddh. **-giri-vihāra,** m. Buddhist monastery on the Abhayagiri. **-m-kará** [RV. x, 152, 2; AV. &c.] or **-m-kṛit** [ŚBr.], mfn. causing safety. **-jāta,** m., N. of a man, (gaṇa *gargâdi*, q. v.) **-ḍiṇḍima,** m. a war-drum, L. **-tama** *(ábhaya-)*, n. greatest safety, RV. x, 17, 5. **-da,** mfn. giving fearlessness or safety; *(as)*, m. an Arhat of the Jainas; N. of a king (the son of Manasyu and father of Sudhanvan), Hariv.; VP. **-dakshiṇā,** f. promise or present of protection from danger, Mn. iv, 247, &c. **-dāna,** n. giving assurance of safety. **-m-dada,** m., N. of Avalokiteśvara, Buddh. **-pattra,** n. (a modern term), a written document or paper granting assurance of safety, a safe conduct. **-prada,** mfn. giving safety, Mn. iv, 232, &c. **-pradāna,** n. = *-dāna*, Pañcat. **-yācanā,** f. asking for safety, Ragh. xi, 78. **-vacana,** n. [Pañcat.] or **-vāc,** f. [Hit.] assurance of safety. **-sáni,** mfn. giving safety, VS. xix, 48. **Abhayânanda,** m., N. of a man.

अभर्तृका *a-bhartṛikā*, f. an unmarried woman; a widow.

अभव *a-bhava, as*, m. non-existence; destruction, end of the world.

A-bhavanīya, mfn. what is not to be, what will not be.

A-bhavan-mata-yoga or **a-bhavan-mata-sambandha,** *as*, m. want of fitness between words and the ideas expressed by them (a defect in composition).

A-bhavya, mfn. not to be, not predestined; what ought not to be, improper. **-haṃsa,** m. a swan as it ought not to be (i. e. with black wings), L.

A-bhāva, *as*, m. non-existence, nullity, absence; non-entity, negation (the seventh category in Kaṇāda's system); proof from non-existence (one of the six pramāṇas in Vedānta phil. ['since there are no mice, therefore there must be cats here'], see *pramāṇa*); annihilation, death.

A-bhāvanā, *am,* f. n. absence of judgment or right perception.

A-bhāvanīya, mfn. not to be inferred or contemplated.

A-bhāvayitṛi, mfn. not perceiving, not inferring, not comprehending.

A-bhāvin, mfn. what is not to be or will not be, not destined to be.

A-bhāvya, mfn. id.

अभवदीय *a-bhavadīya,* mfn. not belonging to your Honour, Daś.

अभस्त्र *a-bhastra,* mfn. without bellows.

A-bhastrakā or **a-bhastrikā,** f. a badly made or inferior pair of bellows (i. e. small), said to mean also (a woman) who has no bellows, Pāṇ. vii, 3, 47.

अभाग *a-bhāgá,* mf(*ā*)n. having no share, RV. x, 83, 5, &c.

A-bhāgin, mfn. having no share; not participating in, excluded from (gen.)

A-bhāgya, mfn. unfortunate, wretched.

अभाषण *a-bhāshuṇa, am,* n. not speaking, silence.

अभि *abhí,* ind. (a prefix to verbs and nouns, expressing) to, towards, into, over, upon.

(As a prefix to verbs of motion) it expresses the notion of moving or going towards, approaching, &c.

(As a prefix to nouns not derived from verbs) it expresses superiority, intensity, &c.; e. g. *abhi-tāmra, abhi-nava,* q. v.

(As a separate adverb or preposition) it expresses (with acc.) to, towards, in the direction of, against; into, ŚBr. & KātyŚr.; for, for the sake of; on account of; on, upon, with regard to; by, before, in front of; over. It may even express one after the other, severally, Pāṇ. i, 4, 91, e. g. *vṛiksham vṛiksham abhi,* tree after tree [cf. Gk. ἀμφί; Lat. *ob;* Zend *aibi, aiwi;* Goth. *bi;* Old High Germ. *bī*].

Abhika, mfn. (Pāṇ. v, 2, 74) lustful, libidinous, Ragh. xix, 4; (cf. 1. *abhīka* and *anuka*); (*as*), m. a lover, Naish.

Abhi-tarám [MaitrS.] or **abhi-tarám** [ŚBr.; AitBr. (see 2. *abhí*)], ind. nearer.

Abhí-tas, ind. near to, towards, MBh. &c.; near, in the proximity or presence of (gen.), Bhag. &c.; (with acc.) on both sides, ŚBr. &c.; (with acc.) before and after, ĀśvŚr.; KātyŚr.; Gaut.; (with acc.) on all sides, everywhere, about, round; entirely, MBh.; quickly, L. **Abhitaḥ-sara,** mfn. running on both sides, Up. **Abhitaś-cara,** *ās,* m. pl. the attendants, retinue, MBh. &c.

Abhito (in Sandhi for *abhitas*). **-deva-yajana-mātra-deśa,** mfn. whose space on all sides suffices for a sacrificial ground, KātyŚr. **-bhāvin,** mfn. being on both sides, Pāṇ. vi, 2, 182. **-rātrám,** ind. near (i. e. either just at the beginning or end of) the night, ŚBr. **-'sthi** (*abhitó-*), mfn. surrounded by bones (as the eyes), ŚBr.

अभिकम् *abhi-√kam* (fut. *-kamishyate*) to desire, love, TBr.: Caus. *-kāmayate,* id., MBh.; BhP.

Abhi-kāma, *as,* m. (ifc. f. *ā*) affection, desire, N.; BhP.; (mf(*ā*)n.), affectionate, loving, desirous (with acc. or ifc.); (*am*), ind. with desire, L.; (cf. *ābhikāmika.*)

अभिकम्प् *abhi-√kamp, -kampate,* to tremble vehemently, MBh. iii, 15721: Caus. *-kampayati,* to stir, allure, KātyŚr.

अभिकाङ्क्ष् *abhi-√kāṅksh, -kāṅkshati,* °*te,* rarely Caus. *-ayate,* to long for, desire; to strive.

Abhi-kāṅkshā, f. longing for, desire (with acc. or ifc.)

Abhi-kāṅkshita, mfn. longed for, wished, desired.

Abhi-kāṅkshin, mfn. longing for, desiring (with acc. [BhP.] or ifc. [Mn. iv, 91, &c.]).

अभिकाल *abhi-kāla, as,* m., N. of a village, R. ii, 68, 17.

अभिकाश् *abhi-√kāś,* Intens. *-cākaśīti* (1. sg. °*śīmi;* Imper. 2. sg. °*śīhi;* impf. 1. sg. *-acākaśam*) to illuminate, irradiate, VS.; to look on, to perceive, RV.; ŚBr. xiv.

अभिकुत्स् *abhi-√kuts,* to revile, inveigh against, R. ii, 75, 2.

अभिकुष् *abhi-√kush, -kushṇāti,* to tear, pull at, pinch, Suśr.

अभिकूज् *abhi-√kūj,* to twitter, warble, R.

अभिकृ *abhi-√1. kṛi,* to do with reference to or in behalf of, ŚBr.; (perf. 2. pl. *-cakrá*) to procure, effect, AV. iii, 9, 1; (with *niveśam*) to settle.

Abhi-karaṇa. See *svapnâbhikáraṇa.*

Abhi-kṛiti, *is,* f., N. of a metre (containing one hundred syllables), RPrāt. &c.

Abhi-kṛitvarī, f. 'producing (diseases),' a female demon, AV. ii, 8, 2.

अभिकृष् *abhi-√kṛish, -karshati,* to overpower, MBh. iii, 15064.

अभिकॄ *abhi-√1. kṝi, -kirati,* to pour over, throw over, cover.

अभिक्लृप् *abhi-√klṛip,* Ā. (p. *-kálpamāna*) to be adequate to, be in accordance with (acc.), VS. xiii, 25: Caus. *-kalpayati,* to put in order, R.

Abhí-klṛipta, mfn. being adequate to, in accordance with, ŚBr.; Up.

अभिक्नूयम् *abhi-knúyam,* ind. (√*knūy*), so as to bemoisten, ŚBr. xiv.

अभिक्रतु *abhí-kratu,* mfn. insolent, haughty, RV. iii, 34, 10.

अभिक्रन्द् *abhi-√krand* (aor. 2. sg. *-kran*) to shout at, roar at, neigh or whinny at, RV.; AV.; Lāṭy.: Caus. (aor. *-acikradat*), id., RV. ix, 68, 2 & 82, 1: Intens. (p. *-kánikradat*), id., RV.

Abhi-kranda, *as,* m. a shout, MBh.; *indrasyâbhikranda,* m., N. of a Sāman.

अभिक्रम् *abhi-√kram* (aor. *-akramīt;* ind. p. *-krámya*) to step or go near to, approach, RV. &c.; to attack, overpower, RV. vi, 49, 15 & ix, 40, 1; to step upon; to undertake, begin, RPrāt.; (with *gamanāya*) to get on one's way, R. i, 77, 18: Caus. *-kramayati,* to bring near, TS.

Abhi-krama, *as,* m. stepping near, approaching; assault, attack, L.; overpowering, PBr.; Gaut.; ascending; undertaking, attempt, beginning. **-nāśa,** m. unsuccessful effort, Bhag.

Abhi-kramaṇa, *am,* n. stepping near, approaching, Gaut. &c.

Abhi-krānta, mfn. approached; attacked; begun; (*am*), n. = *abhí-krānti,* PBr.

Abhí-krānti, *is,* f., Ved. overpowering, bringing into one's possession, TS.; AitBr. &c.

Abhi-krāntin, mfn. one who has undertaken (the study of), i. e. conversant with (loc.), Lāṭy.

Abhi-krāmam, ind. so as to step near, KātyŚr.

अभिक्री *abhi-√krī,* to buy for a special purpose, ŚBr.

अभिक्रुध् *abhi-√krudh,* to be angry with (acc.), Pāṇ. i, 4, 38, Sch.; Vikr.

Abhi-kruddha, mfn. being angry, MBh.; BhP.

अभिक्रुश् *abhi-√kruś,* to cry out at, call out to, to call to (in a scolding manner), AV. &c.; to lament with tears, bemoan, R. iv, 24, 22.

Abhi-krośaka, *as,* m. a reviler (*nindaka*), VS.

अभिक्षत्तृ *abhi-kshattṛí, tā,* m. (√*kshad*), 'one who carves and distributes (food),' an host, RV. ii, 29, 2 & vii, 21, 8; ['a destroyer,' Sāy.]

अभिक्षदा *a-bhiksha-dá* [Padap. *abhi-kshadá*], mfn. giving without being asked, RV. vi, 50, 1; [according to the Padap. (cf. *abhi-kshattṛí*) 'destroying, a destroyer,' Sāy.]

Á-bhikshita, mfn. not asked for alms, ŚBr.

अभिक्षम् *abhi-√ksham* (Opt. *-kshameta;* Imper. 2. pl. *-kshámadhvam*) to be gracious, propitious to (dat. or loc.), RV.; to pardon (perf. Opt. 2. sg. *-cakshamithāḥ*), RV. ii, 33, 7.

अभिक्षर् *abhi-√kshar* (aor. 3. sg. *-akshāḥ,* RV. ix, 97, 45) to flow near or round, RV.; ŚBr.; to pour on, AV.

अभिक्षिप् *abhi-√kship* (only P., Pāṇ. i, 3, 80; pr. p. *-kshipát*) to fling at (as the lash of a whip at a horse), RV. v, 83, 3; to excel, Bhaṭṭ.

अभिखन् *abhi-√khan,* to dig up, turn up (the soil), ŚBr. &c.

अभिख्या 1. *abhi-√khyā* (Subj. 1. 2. 3. sg. *-khyam, -khyas* & *-khyás, -khyát;* impf. 3. sg. *abhy ákhyat;* ind. p. *-khyáya*) to see, view, perceive, RV.; to cast a kind or gracious look upon any one, to be gracious, RV.; (impf. 3. pl. *abhí ákhyan*) TS.: Caus. *-khyāpayati,* to make known, Mn. &c.

2. **Abhi-khyá,** f. a gracious look, RV. x, 112, 10; splendour, RV. i, 148, 5 & viii, 23, 5; beauty, Ragh. &c.; fame, glory, Kathās.; telling, L.; 'calling, addressing,' a name, appellation.

Abhi-khyāta, mfn. become known, manifested, MBh.; (neg. *an-*) Yājñ. iii, 301.

Abhi-khyātṛí, *tá,* m. a supervisor (N. of Indra), RV. iv, 17, 17.

Abhi-khyāna, *am,* n. fame, glory, L.

अभिगम् *abhi-√gam, -gacchati,* to go near to, approach (with acc.); to follow, Kaṭh.; R.; to meet with, find; to cohabit (said of men and women), Yājñ. ii, 205, &c.; to undertake; to get, gain, obtain, AV.; ŚBr. &c.; (with *mánasā* or *medháyā* or *hṛidayena*) to understand, RV. iii, 60, 1; TS.; ŚBr.: Caus. *-gamayati,* to study, MBh. i, 1295.

Abhi-gacchat, mfn. approaching, &c.

Abhi-gata, mfn. approached, &c.

Abhi-gantṛi, *tā,* m. one who understands, ŚBr.; 'one who pursues,' insidious, Kaṭh.; one who has intercourse with a woman.

Abhi-gama, *as,* m. (gaṇa *anuśatikâdi,* q. v.), approaching; visiting, Megh.; Ragh. v, 11; sexual intercourse, Yājñ. ii, 291.

Abhi-gamana, *am,* n. = *abhi-gama;* the act of cleansing and smearing with cowdung the way leading to the image of the deity (one of the five parts of the *upâsana* with the Rāmānujas), Sarvad.

1. **Abhi-gamya,** mfn. to be visited, Kum. vi, 56, &c.; accessible, tempting (for a visit), Ragh. i, 16.

2. **Abhi-gamya,** ind. p. having approached.

Abhi-gāmin, mfn. having sexual intercourse with (in comp.), Mn. iii, 45; Yājñ. ii, 282, &c.

अभिगर *abhi-gará.* See *abhi-√1. gṝi* below.

अभिगर्ज् *abhi-√garj,* to roar at, bawl at, raise savage or ferocious cries, MBh. &c.

Abhi-garjana, *am,* n. ferocious roaring, uproar, R.

Abhi-garjita, *am,* n. a savage cry, uproar, R.

अभिगा *abhi-√1. gā, -jígāti* (impf. *-ajigāt;* aor. Subj. *-gāt*) to go near to, to approach, arrive at, RV. &c.; to get, gain.

अभिगाह् *abhi-√gāh,* Ā. (p. *-gāhamāna*) to penetrate into (acc.), RV. x, 103, 7.

अभिगुप्त *abhi-gupta,* mfn. guarded, protected.

Abhi-gupti, *is,* f. guarding, protecting, ŚBr. &c.

Abhi-goptṛi, mfn. guarding, protecting, ŚBr.

अभिगुम्फित *abhi-gumphita,* mfn. strung together, interwoven, Śiś.

अभिगुर् *abhi-√gur* (Subj. *-jugurat;* Opt. 2. sg. *-juguryās*) to assent, agree, approve of, RV.

Abhí-gūrta, mfn. approved of, RV. i, 162, 15; TS.

Abhí-gūrti, *is,* f. song of praise, RV. i, 162, 6 & 12.

Abhi-gūrya, (Ved.) ind. p. having approved of, RV. ii, 37, 3.

अभिगृध्न *abhi-gṛidhna,* mfn. See *mithyâbhigṛidhna.*

अभिगॄ *abhi-√1. gṝi, -gṛiṇāti,* to call to or address with approbation; to join in (acc.); to welcome, praise; to approve of, accept propitiously, allow.

Abhi-gará, *as,* m. a calling out in approbation (part of the sacrificial ceremony), VS.; KātyŚr.; the priest who calls out approvingly (to the other priests), MaitrS.; Lāṭy.; (cf. *apagara.*)

अभिगै *abhi-√gai* (Imper. 2. sg. *-gáya* or *-gāya;* 2. pl. *-gāyata*) to call or sing to (acc.), RV.; to enchant, AitBr.; to sing (a hymn, &c.), ŚBr. &c.; to fill with song, R.; to celebrate in song, R.

Abhi-gīta, mfn. addressed or praised in song, RV. ix, 96, 23.

Abhi-geshṇa, mfn. calling to, AitBr.

अभिग्रस्त *abhi-grasta,* mfn. = *abhi-panna* (overcome), L.

अभिग्रह् *abhi-√grah, -gṛihṇāti,* to take hold of, take up (from the soil), TS. &c.; to accept, receive, MBh.; to set (as a blossom), BhP.; to lay together, to fold (the hands), see *abhigṛihīta-pāṇi* below;

Caus. *-grāhayati*, to catch, surprise, e.g. *rūpâbhi-grāhita*, taken in the very act, Daś.

Abhi-gṛihīta, mfn. taken hold of, &c. **-pāṇi**, mfn. having the hands joined, BhP.

Abhi-graha, *as*, m. seizing, taking hold of; attack, onset, L.; defiance, challenge, L.; robbing, plundering, L.; authority, L.; a vow, Jain.

Abhi-grahaṇa, *am*, n. robbing, L.

Abhi-grahītṛí, mfn. one who seizes, MaitrS.

अभिघर्षण *abhi-gharshaṇa*, *am*, n. (√*ghṛish*), rubbing, friction, L.; possession by an evil spirit, L.

अभिघात *abhi-ghāta*, *as*, m. (√*han*), striking, attack; infliction of injury, damage, Mn. xii, 77, &c.; striking back, driving away, warding off; abrupt or vehement articulation (of Vedic text), VPrāt.; (*am*), n. an irregular combination of consonants, i.e. the combination of the fourth letter of gutturals, cerebrals, &c. with the first or third letter, of the second with the first letter, and of the third with the second letter of those classes of consonants.

Abhi-ghātaka, mf(*ikā*)n. counteracting, removing.

Abhi-ghātita, mfn. struck, wounded (ifc. as *śarâbhighātita*, wounded by arrows).

Abhi-ghātin, mfn. (generally ifc.) striking, attacking, hurting; inflicting injury; (*ī*), m. an assailant, enemy, Hit.

अभिघृ *abhi-√ghṛi* (perf. Pass. p. *abhí-ghṛita*, see below): Caus. *-ghārayati*, to cause to trickle down, TS. &c.; to sprinkle with, ŚBr. &c.

Abhi-ghāra, *as*, m. sprinkling over, ŚāṅkhGṛ.; scattering over, mingling with, Gobh.; ghee or clarified butter, L.

Abhi-ghāraṇa, *am*, n. the act of sprinkling ghee, besprinkling, Kauś.; KātyŚr.

Abhí-ghārita, mfn. sprinkled with, AV. &c.

Abhi-ghārya, mfn. to be sprinkled.

Abhí-ghṛita, mfn. sprinkled (as ghee), dropped upon, TS.; sprinkled with, BhP.

अभिघ्रा *abhi-√ghrā*, *-jighrati* (ind. p. *-jighrya*, Gobh.) to snuffle, smell at; to bring the nose close to another's forehead in caressing, or as a token of affection, TS. &c.; to smell, scent, Kād.

Abhi-ghrāṇa, *am*, n. smelling at, caressing, Comm. on Gobh.

Abhi-jighraṇa, *am*, n. id., Gobh.

Abhi-jíghrat, mf(du. *antī*)n. caressing, RV. i, 185, 5.

अभिचक्ष् *abhi-√caksh*, *-cashṭe* (2. sg. *-cakshase*, RV. v, 3, 9; Ved. Inf. *-cákshe*, RV.) to look at, view, perceive, RV.; BhP.; to cast a kind or gracious look upon any one, RV.; to address, BhP.; to assail with harsh language, RV. vii, 104, 8; to call, BhP.

Abhi-cákshaṇa, *am*, n. conjuring, incantation, AV. vi, 127, 2; (*ā*), f. (in augury or astron.) observation (of the sky), AV. ix, 2, 21.

Abhi-cákshya, mfn. manifest, RV. viii, 4, 7.

अभिचर् *abhi-√car* (Ved. Inf. *abhí-caritavai*, TBr., & *abhi-caritos*, Kāṭh.; cf. Pāṇ. iii, 4, 13, Sch.) to act wrongly towards any one; to be faithless (as a wife); to charm, enchant, bewitch, RV. x, 34, 14 (Subj. 2. pl. *-caratâbhí*); AV. &c.; *pūrvâbhicaritā* (f. perf. Pass. p.) = *pūrva-dig-gāminī*, R. i, 34, 10.

Abhi-cara, *as*, m. a servant, L.

Abhi-caraṇíya, mfn. fit for enchanting or exorcising, ŚBr. &c.; (neg. *an-*), Comm. on Mn. xi, 197.

Abhi-cārá, *as*, m. exorcising, incantation, employment of spells for a malevolent purpose, AV. &c.; magic (one of the Upapātakas or minor crimes). **-kalpa**, m., N. of a work on incantations (belonging to the Atharva-veda). **-jvara**, m. a fever caused by magical spells. **-mantra**, m. a formula or prayer for working a charm, an incantation. **-yajña** or **-homa**, m. a sacrifice for the same purpose.

Abhi-cāraka, mf(*ikā*)n. enchanting, exorcising, conjuring, VarBṛS. &c.; a conjurer, a magician.

Abhi-cāraṇíya, mfn. to be enchanted, L.

Abhi-cārita, mfn. enchanted, charmed.

Abhi-cārin, mfn. enchanting, AV. x, 1, 9.

Abhi-cārya, mfn. = *abhi-cāraṇíya*, L.

Abhí-cāra, *as*, m. exorcising, incantation, Āp.

अभिचाकश् *abhi-cākaś*. See *abhi-√kāś*.

अभिचिन्त् *abhi-√cint* (impf. *-acintayat*) to reflect on, MBh. xiii, 4341.

अभिचिह्नय *abhi-cihnaya*, Nom. P. (perf. Pass. p. *-cihnita*) to mark, characterize, R. iv, 42, 12.

अभिचुद् *abhi-√cud*, Caus. *-codayati*, to impel, drive; to inflame, animate, embolden; to invite; to fix, settle; to announce, inquire for (acc.), MBh. i, 2913.

अभिचैद्यम् *abhi-caidyam*, ind. against the prince of the Cedis (i.e. Śiśupāla), Śiś. ii, 1.

अभिच्छद् *abhi-cchad* (√*chad*), *abhí-cchādayati*, to cover over, ŚBr.; Kauś.

अभिच्छायम् *abhi-cchāyám*, ind. in darkness, AV. xiii, 1, 57.

अभिजन् *abhi-√jan*, cl. 4. Ā. *-jāyate* (Ved. Inf. *abhí-janitos*, ŚBr.) to be born for or to, RV. i, 168, 2, &c.; to claim as one's birthright; to be born or produced; to be reproduced or born again, Bhag. &c.; to become: Caus. *-janayati* (with *abhijñānam*) to reanimate, revivify, Sarvad.

Abhi-ja, mfn. ifc. produced all around, L.

Abhi-jana, *as*, m. family, race; descendants; ancestors; noble descent; the head or ornament of a family, L.; native country, Pāṇ. iv, 3, 90; fame, notoriety, Rājat. &c. **-vat**, mfn. of noble descent, Śāk. &c.

Abhi-jāta, mfn. born in consequence of; born, produced; noble, well-born; obtained by birth, inbred; fit, proper, L.; wise, learned, L.; handsome, R.; Kum. i, 46; (*am*), n. nativity, BhP.; high birth, nobility. **-tā**, f. high birth, nobility.

Abhi-jāti, *is*, f. descent, birth, Comm. on Nir. ix, 4; ifc. °*tīya* (f. *ā*), R. vi, 10, 24.

अभिजप् *abhi-√jap*, to mutter over or whisper to, R.

अभिजभ् *abhi-√jabh*, Intens. (p. *-jáñjabhāna*) to try to swallow, open the mouth to do so, AV. v, 20, 6; Kauś.

अभिजल्प् *abhi-√jalp*, to address; to accompany with remarks; to advocate; to settle by conversation, MBh. iv, 711.

अभिजि *abhi-√ji*, *-jayati*, to conquer completely, acquire by conquest, AV.; TS. &c.: Desid. *-jigīshati*, to try to win, attack, Suśr.

Abhi-jaya, *as*, m. conquest, complete victory.

Abhi-jít, mfn. victorious, VS. xv, 7; born under the constellation Abhijit, Pāṇ. iv, 3, 36, (cf. *ābhijita*); (*t*), m., N. of a Soma sacrifice (part of the great sacrifice Gavām-ayana), AV.; ŚBr. &c.; N. of a son [Hariv.] or of the father [VP.] of Punarvasu; of Vishṇu, L.; N. of a star (α Lyræ), L.; of the 20th (or 22nd) Nakshatra, AV. &c.; the eighth Muhūrta of the day (about midday), Kauś. &c. **Abhijid-viśvajitau**, f. du. the two Soma sacrifices called Abhijit and Viśvajit, ŚBr. **Abhijin-muhūrta**, m. the eighth Muhūrta (the period comprising twenty-four minutes before and twenty-four after midday).

Abhi-jita, *as*, m., N. of a Nakshatra (see *abhijit*), MBh.; of the eighth Muhūrta (see *abhi-jit*), MBh.; Hariv.

Abhí-jiti, *is*, f. victory, conquest, ŚBr.; AitBr.

अभिजिघ्रण *abhi-jighraṇa*. See *abhi-√ghrā*.

अभिजुष् *abhi-√jush* (Subj. *-jújoshat*; pr. p. *-jushāṇá*) to be pleased with, like, RV. iv, 23, 1 & 4.

Abhi-jushṭa, mfn. visited, frequented, surrounded by, possessed of, MBh. &c.

अभिजृम्भ् *abhi-√jṛimbh*, to open the mouth wide (for swallowing), R. vi, 2, 18.

अभिज्ञा *abhi-√jñā*, *-jānāti*, °*nīte*, to recognize, perceive, know, be or become aware of; to acknowledge, agree to, own; to remember (either with the fut. p. or with *yad* and impf.), Pāṇ. iii, 2, 112 seqq.; Bhaṭṭ.

Abhi-jña, mf(*ā*)n. knowing, skilful, clever; understanding, conversant with (gen. or ifc.); (*ā*), f. remembrance, recollection, Pāṇ. iii, 2, 112; supernatural science or faculty of a Buddha (of which five are enumerated, viz. 1. taking any form at will; 2. hearing to any distance; 3. seeing to any distance; 4. penetrating men's thoughts; 5. knowing their state and antecedents). **-tā**, f. [Ragh. vii, 61] or **-tva**, n. the knowledge of.

Abhi-jñāna, *am*, n. remembrance, recollection; knowledge, L.; ascertainment; a sign or token of remembrance; any sign or token serving as a proof for (loc. or *prati*), R.; = *abhijñāna-śakuntala*, q.v., Sāh. **-pattra**, n. certificate. **-śakuntala**, n. title of a play of Kālidāsa, i.e. (the *nāṭaka* or play) on the subject of 'token-(recognized)-Śakuntalā,' Śāk.

Abhi-jñāpaka, mfn. making known, BhP.

Abhi-jñāyam. See *yathâbhijñāyam*.

अभिज्ञु *abhi-√jñú*, ind. on the knees, RV.; up to the knees, RV. i, 37, 10 & viii, 92, 3.

अभिज्वल् *abhi-√jval*, to blaze forth, MBh.; Caus. *-jvālayati*, to enlighten, illuminate, Vait.: Intens. *-jājvalīti*, to blaze up, rise suddenly (as anger, &c.)

अभिडीन *abhi-ḍīna*, *am*, n. (√*ḍī*), act of flying towards, MBh.

अभितंस् *abhi-√taṇs* (perf. 3. pl. *-tatasré*), to shake out of, rob, RV. iv, 50, 2 & x, 89, 15.

अभितड् *abhi-√taḍ*, *-tāḍayati*, to thump, hit, beat, wound, bruise; (in astron.) to eclipse the greater part of a disk, VarBṛS.

Abhi-tāḍita, mfn. knocked, struck.

अभितन् *abhi-√tan*, to stretch or spread across or over, be prominent, (aor. 1. pl. *-tatánāma*) RV. i, 160, 5 & v, 54, 15; to extend or enlarge in front of, (perf. Ā. 2. sg. *-tatnishe*) RV. viii, 6, 25 & ix, 108, 6.

अभितप् *abhi-√tap*, to irradiate with heat, to heat, AV. &c.; to pain, distress: Pass. *-tapyate*, to suffer intensely: Caus. *-tāpayati*, to distress.

Abhi-tapta, mfn. scorched, burnt; afflicted about (acc.), R.

Abhi-tāpa, *as*, m. extreme heat, Śiś. &c.; agitation, affliction, emotion; great pain.

अभितरम् *abhi-tarám*, &c. See *abhí*.

अभितर्ज् *abhi-√tarj*, *-tarjayati*, to scold, abuse.

अभितस् *abhí-tas*, ind. See *abhí*.

अभिताम्र *abhi-tāmra*, mf(*ā*)n. very red, dark-red, murry-coloured, MBh.; Ragh. xv, 49, &c.

अभितिग्मरश्मि *abhi-tigmaraśmi*, ind. towards the sun, Śiś. ix, 11.

अभितुष् *abhi-√tush*, *-tushyati*, to be glad or pleased, Kathās.

अभितृद् *abhi-√tṛid*, *-tṛiṇatti* (Imper. 2. sg. *-tṛindhi* [for *tṛind-dhi*]; aor. Subj. 2. sg. *-tárdas*, RV. vi, 17, 1) to burst open, open, procure (waters) by bursting (the clouds) or by boring (i.e. digging a well), RV. &c.; to procure (*vā́jam*, *vā́jān*, *gā́ḥ*, *gandharvā́m*), RV.; *annâdyam*, &c., ŚBr. &c.: Desid. (Subj. 3. pl. *-títṛitsān*) to try to open, RV. x, 74, 4.

Abhi-tṛitti, *is*, f. the act of procuring or gaining, Kāṭh.

अभितृप् *abhi-√tṛip*, Caus. *-tarpayati* (pr. p. f. pl. *-tarpáyantīḥ*, AV.) to satiate, refresh.

Abhi-tṛipta, mfn. satiated, refreshed.

अभितॄ *abhi-√tṛī*, to come near, approach (Ā. 3. du. *-tarete*), RV. i, 140, 3; to overtake, get up to, MBh. vii, 280.

अभित्ति *á-bhitti*, *is*, f. not bursting, VS. xi, 64; no wall, Kathās.; (mfn.), having no walls, i.e. no solid foundation, Śiś. iv, 53.

अभित्यज् *abhi-√tyaj*, to abandon, R. ii, 47, 5 (ed. Bomb.)

अभित्रास *abhi-trāsa*, *as*, m. putting in fear, intimidating, Āp.

अभित्रिपिष्टप *abhi-tripishṭapa*, mfn. being over the three worlds, Hariv.

अभित्वर् *abhi-√tvar*, to be in haste.

अभित्सर् *abhi-√tsar* (3. pl. *-tsáranti*) to catch, entrap, RV. viii, 2, 6.

Abhi-tsāra, *as*, m. catching, entrapping, Kāṭh.

अभिदक्षिणम् *abhi-dakshiṇam*, ind. to or towards the right, Kauś.; KātyŚr.; Lāṭy.

अभिददि *abhi-dadí*. See *abhi-√1. dā*.

अभिदधत् *abhi-dadhat*, mfn. pr. p. of 1. *abhi-√dhā*, q. v.

अभिदर्शन *abhi-darśana*. See *abhi-√dṛiś*.

अभिदष्ट *abhi-√dashṭa*, mfn. (√*daṇś*), bitten.

अभिदह् *abhi-√dah*, to singe, burn, RV. ii, 4, 7 (aor. p. *abhí-dákshat* [Padap. -*dhákshat*]), ŚBr. &c.

अभिदा *abhi-√1. dā*, -*dadāti*, to give, bestow (for a purpose), MBh. iii, 13309.

Abhi-dadí, *is*, m. an oblation of boiled rice (*caru*) upon which ghee has been sprinkled, TS.

Abhi-dāpana, *am*, n. the being trampled on by elephants as a punishment (?).

अभिदास् *abhi-√dās*, Ved. -*dāsati* (Subj. 3. sg. -*dāsat* [RV. vi, 5, 4] or -*dā́sāt*, AV. v, 6, 10) to consider and treat as an enemy.

अभिदिप्सु *abhi-dipsú*, mfn. (*dips*, Desid. of √*dambh*), 'wishing to deceive,' inimical, cunning, RV. ii. 23, 10 & 13.

अभिदिश् *abhi-√diś*, to point out, PBr.

अभिदिह् *abhi-√dih*, to wrap up, envelop in, ĀpŚr.

Abhí-digdha, mfn. polished, glazed (in the fire, *tápasā*), i. e. sharp, AV. v, 18, 8.

अभिदी *abhi-√2. dī* (Imper. 2. sg. -*didīhi*) to radiate, beam forth or towards, RV. ix, 108, 9.

अभिदीक्ष् *abhi-√dīksh*, to consecrate one's self (for a purpose, acc.), PBr.

अभिदीप् *abhi-√dīp*, to blaze towards, Hariv.: Caus. *dīpayati*, to cause to shine, make brilliant, Car.; to blaze or shine all round, AV. iv, 19, 3.

अभिदु *abhi-√2. du* (pr. p. m. nom. -*dunván*) to burn or pain by burning, AV. v, 22, 2.

अभिदुष् *abhi-√dush*, -*dūshayati*, to contaminate; to wound.

Abhi-dushṭa, mfn. contaminated, MBh.

Abhi-dūshita, mfn. wounded, injured, Suśr.

अभिदुह् *abhi-√duh*, to milk in addition to, TBr.; Caus. P. to cause to milk in addition to, ĀpŚr.

Abhi-dohana, *am*, n. milking upon, ĀpŚr.

Abhi-dohya, *am*, n. (impers.) to be milked upon, ĀpŚr.

अभिदूति *abhi-dūti*, ind. to or towards a female messenger, Śiś, ix, 56 (quoted in Sāh.)

अभिदृश् *abhi-√dṛiś* (Inf. -*drashṭum*) to look at: Caus. -*darśayati*, to show; to point out, denounce any one (acc.), MBh. i, 7740: Pass. -*dṛiśyate*, to be visible, be in view, appear, Mn. ix, 308, &c.

Abhi-darśana, *am*, n. becoming visible, appearance, Mn. ix, 274.

अभिदेवन *abhi-devana*, *am*, n. a board for playing at dice, MBh. ix, 760.

अभिद्यु *abhí-dyu*, mfn. directed to heaven, tending or going to heaven, RV.; heavenly, bright, RV.; ŚBr.

अभिद्रा *abhi-√2. drā* (aor. Subj. -*drāsat*) to overtake, RV. viii, 47, 7.

अभिद्रु *abhi-√2. dru*, to run up to or near, RV. x, 75, 2, &c.; to attack, overrun, infest.

Abhi-druta, mfn. run towards, attacked.

Abhi-drutya, ind. p. having attacked.

अभिद्रुह् 1. *abhi-√druh*, -*drúhyati* (aor. Subj. 3. pl. -*druhan*; perf. 1. p. -*dudróha*) to hate, seek to injure or maliciously assail, RV. &c.: Desid. (p. -*dudrukshat*) id., Kāṭh.

Abhi-drugdha, mfn. injured, oppressed, BhP.; injuring, oppressing, MBh. v, 2160; PārGr.

2. **Abhi-drúh**, mfn. seeking to injure, inimical, RV. i, 122, 9 (nom. -*dhrúk*) & ii, 27, 16; (cf. *an-abhidruh*.)

Abhi-druhyamāṇa, mfn. being injured.

Abhi-drohá, *as*, m. injuring, RV.; Mn. &c.

अभिधन्व् *abhi-√dhanv* (aor. 3. pl. -*ádhanvishuḥ* & perf. Ā. -*dadhanviré*) to come up in haste, RV. iv, 31, 6; ix, 13, 7 & 24, 2.

अभिधम् *abhi-√dham* (p. m. du. -*dhámantā*) to blow towards or against, RV. i, 117, 21.

Abhi-dhmāta, mfn. blown on (as an instrument), Kathās.

अभिधर्म *abhi-dharma*, *as*, m. the dogmas of Buddhist philosophy or metaphysics. — **kośa**, m., N. of a work on the preceding. — **piṭaka**, m. 'basket of metaphysics,' N. of the third section of Buddhist writings.

अभिधर्षण *abhi-dharshaṇa*, *am*, n. (√*dhṛish*), possession by demoniac spirits, L.

अभिधा 1. *abhi-√dhā*, -*dadhāti*, to surrender any one to (dat.; aor. Subj. 2. du. -*dhātam*), RV. i, 120, 8; to bring upon (dat.), RV. ii, 23, 6: Ā. (rarely P.) to put on or round, put on the furniture of a horse (cf. *abhí-hita* below), RV. &c.; to cover (a country) with an army, MBh. ii, 1090; to cover, protect, RV. viii, 67, 5 (aor. Pot. 2. pl. -*dhetana*), &c.; (in classical Sanskṛit generally) to set forth, explain, tell, speak to, address, say, name (cf. *abhí-hita* below): Pass. -*dhīyate*, to be named or called: Caus. -*dhāpayate*, to cause to name, ĀśvGṛ.: Desid. Ā. -*dhítsate*, to intend to cover one's self, RV. x, 85, 30.

2. **Abhi-dhā**, f. name, appellation; the literal power or sense of a word, Sāh.; a word, sound, L.; (*ā́s*), m. f. surrounding, VS. xxii, 3. — **dhvaṇsin**, mfn. losing one's name. — **mūla**, mfn. founded on the literal meaning of a word.

Abhi-dhātavya, mfn. to be told or named; to be manifested.

Abhi-dhātṛi, mfn. saying, telling, Śiś.

Abhi-dhāna, *am*, n. telling, naming, speaking, speech, manifesting; a name, title, appellation, expression, word; a vocabulary, dictionary; putting together, bringing in close connection, VPrāt.; (compar. -*tara*) KaushBr.; (*ī*), f., see s.v. — **cintāmaṇi**, m. 'the jewel that gives every word,' N. of Hemacandra's vocabulary of synonyms. — **tva**, n. the state of being used as a name. — **mālā**, f. a dictionary. — **ratnamālā**, f., N. of Halāyudha's vocabulary.

Abhi-dhānaka, *am*, n. a sound, noise, L.

Abhi-dhā́nī, f. a halter, AV.; ŚBr.; AitBr.

Abhi-dhānīya, mfn. to be named, L.

Abhi-dhāya, ind. p. having said, having called.

Abhi-dhāyaka, mfn. naming, expressing, expressive of, denominating, RPrāt. &c.; telling, speaking. — **tva**, n. the state of being expressive.

Abhi-dhāyam, ind. ifc. See *gotrâbhidhāyam*.

Abhi-dhāyin, mfn. = *abhi-dhāyaka*; (cf. *pṛishṭâbhidhāyin*.)

Abhi-dhitsā, f. desire of expressing or naming, Kpr.

Abhi-dheya, mfn. to be named or mentioned; to be expressed, to be spoken of, Pāṇ. iii, 3, 51, Sch. &c.; being spoken of, being expressed, Sāh.; (*am*), n. signification, meaning; 'that which is expressed or referred to,' the substantive. — **tā**, f. signification, meaning. — **rahita**, mfn. having no sense or meaning, unmeaning, nonsensical.

Abhí-hita, abhí-hiti. See s. v.

अभिधाव् *abhi-√dhāv*, -*dhāvati*, to run up towards, to rush upon, attack, RV. &c.

Abhi-dhāvaka, mfn. running up, hastening towards, Yājñ. ii, 234; assailing, an assailant.

Abhi-dhāvana, *am*, n. running up, attack.

अभिधि *abhi-√3. dhi* (impf. 3. pl. *abhy-adhinvan*) to satisfy, Kāṭh.; PBr.

अभिधी *abhi-√dhī* (perf. 1. sg. -*dīdhayā*; p. Ā. -*dī́dhyāna*, RV. iv, 33, 9) to reflect upon, consider, RV. iii, 38, 1 & x, 32, 4.

अभिधू *abhi-√dhū* (p. -*dhūnvat*) to shake, TĀr.

अभिधृ *abhi-√dhṛi*, Caus. -*dhārayati*, to uphold, maintain, MBh.

अभिधृष् *abhi-√dhṛish*, to overpower, (impf. 3. pl. -*adhṛishṇuvan*) Kāṭh.; (perf. 3. pl. -*dādhṛishuḥ*) AV. i, 27, 3: Caus. -*dharshayati*, id., MBh.

Abhi-dhṛishṇú, mfn. powerful over (acc.), ŚBr.

अभिध्मात *abhi-dhmāta*. See *abhi-√dham*.

अभिध्यै *abhi-√dhyai*, -*dhyāyati*, to direct one's intention to, set one's heart upon, intend, desire, TS.; ŚBr. &c.; to meditate, Mn. i, 8, &c.

Abhi-dhyā, f. wish, longing for, desire.

Abhi-dhyāna, *am*, n. desiring, longing for (loc.), Mn. xii, 5, &c.; meditation, Up.

Abhi-dhyāyin, mfn. (ifc.) giving one's attention to, MārkP.

Abhi-dhyeya, mfn. deserving attention, BhP.; (neg. *an-*) MBh.

अभिध्वंस् *abhi-√dhvaṇs*, Caus. -*dhvaṇsayati*, to sprinkle with dust, dust, Kāṭh.

Abhi-dhvasta, mfn. afflicted by (instr.), MBh. v, 3230.

अभिध्वन् *abhi-√dhvan*, to resound, whiz (as arrows), Śiś. xx, 13.

अभिनक्ष् *abhi-√naksh*, -*nákshati* (perf. 3. pl. -*nanakshúḥ*; p. P. -*nákshat*, Ā. -*nákshamāṇa*) to approach, come to, arrive at, RV.; AV.

अभिनद् *abhi-√nad*, to sound towards (acc.), BhP.; to sound, raise a noise, Hariv.: Caus. -*nādayati* (perf. Pass. p. -*nādita* or for the sake of the metre -*nadita* [R.]), to cause to sound, fill with noise.

अभिनद्ध *abhi-naddha*, mfn. (√*nah*), 'tied round,' *abhi-naddhâksha*, mfn. blindfold, ChUp.

Abhi-nahana, *am*, n. a bandage (over the eyes), ChUp.

अभिनन्द् *abhi-√nand*, to please, AV. ix, 2, 2; to rejoice at, salute, welcome, greet, hail; to praise, applaud, approve (often with *na* neg. 'to refuse'); to acknowledge: Caus. -*nandayati*, to gladden, R.

Abhi-nánda, *as*, m. the delight, pleasure (of sensuality), ŚBr. xiv; ChUp.; wish, desire for (ifc.), Suśr.; N. of the first month; N. of a commentator on the Amara-kosha; N. of the author of the Yoga-vāsishṭhasāra; (*ā*), f. delight, L.; wish, L.

Abhi-nandana, *am*, n. delighting, L.; praising, applauding, L.; wish, desire, L.; (*as*), m., N. of the fourth Jaina Arhat of the present Avasarpiṇī.

Abhi-nandanīya, mfn. to be acknowledged or applauded, Śāk.

Abhi-nandita, mfn. delighted, made happy, saluted, applauded, &c.

Abhi-nanditṛi, mfn. gladdening, MBh.

Abhi-nandin, mfn. rejoicing at, wishing, desiring (ifc.)

1. **Abhi-nandya**, mfn. = *abhi-nandanīya*, Śāk.; Ragh. v, 31.

2. **Abhi-nandya**, ind. p. having rejoiced at; having gladdened.

अभिनभस् *abhi-nabhas*, ind. towards the sky.

Abhi-nabhyám, ind. near the clouds or the sky, RV. x, 119, 12.

अभिनम् *abhi-√nam* (aor. 3. sg. -*anamat* or -*anān* [Kāṭh.]) to bow or bend or turn towards.

Abhi-nata, mfn. bent, inclined, KaushBr. &c.

Abhi-namra, mf(*ā*)n. deeply bowed or curved, Ragh. xiii, 32.

Abhi-nāmin, *ī*, m., N. of a Ṛishi in the sixth Manvantara, VP.

अभिनय *abhi-naya*. See 1. *abhi-√nī*.

अभिनर्द् *abhi-√nard*, P. (ep. also Ā.) to roar towards, MBh.; to roar, R.

अभिनव *abhi-nava*, mf(*ā*)n. quite new or young, very young, fresh; modern (cf. -*kālidāsa* & -*śākaṭāyana* below); N. of two men, Rājat.; not having experience, L. — **kālidāsa**, m. the modern Kālidāsa, i. e. Mādhavācārya. — **gupta**, m., N. of a well-known author. — **candrârgha-vidhi**, m. 'a ceremony performed at the time of the new moon,' N. of the 114th chapter in the BhavP. ii. — **yauvana**, mf(*ā*)n. youthful, Hit. — **vaiyākaraṇa**, m. a modern grammarian. — **śākaṭāyana**, m. the modern Śākaṭāyana. **Abhinavī-√bhū**, to become new, Comm. on Bhaṭṭ. **Abhinavôdbhid**, m. a new bud.

अभिनश् *abhi-√1. naś* (aor. Subj. 3. sg. -*naṭ*, RV. vii, 104, 23) to attain, reach, RV.

अभिनहन *abhi-nahana*. See *abhi-naddha*.

अभिनासिकाविवरम् *abhi-nāsikāvivaram*, ind to the opening of the nose, Śiś. ix, 52.

अभिनिःसृ *abhi-niḥ-√sṛi*, to stream forth, issue, Suśr.

Abhi-niḥ-sṛita, mfn. issued or issuing from (abl.), ChUp. (= KaṭhUp.); Yājñ. &c.

अभिनिःसृज् *abhi-niḥ-√sṛij*, to pour out towards, ŚBr.

अभिनिःसृप् *abhi-niḥ-√srip*, to move towards, ĀśvŚr.

अभिनिःस्तन् *abhi-niḥ-√stan*, to sound heavily (as a drum), Pāṇ. viii. 3, 86, Sch.

Abhi-nishṭāna, *as,* m. 'a sound which dies away,' the Visarga, APrāt.; ĀśvGṛ. &c.

Abhi-nistāna, *as,* m. = *abhi-niśhṭāna*, Pāṇ. viii, 3, 86.

अभिनिक्रम् *abhi-ni-√kram* (aor. 2. sg. *-akramīs*) to tread down (with acc.), RV. x, 60, 6.

अभिनिगद् *abhi-ni-√gad*, to speak to, Kauś.

अभिनिधन *abhi-nidhana*, *am,* n., N. of different verses of the Sāma-veda, KātyŚr. &c.

अभिनिधा *abhi-ni-√dhā*, P. to place upon or into (loc.), ŚBr.; Ā. to place upon one's self (as a burden), AitBr.; to touch slightly with (instr.), ŚBr.; KātyŚr. &c.: Pass. *-dhīyate*, 'to be touched by each other,' be in close contact (as the letters *e*, *o* & *a* in the Sandhi called *abhinihita*, q. v.), Prāt.

Abhi-ni-dhāna, *am,* n. placing upon, KātyŚr.; (*as*), m. [APrāt. & TPrāt.] or (*am*), n. [RPrāt.] 'touching' or close contact (of letters in pronunciation, especially in the cases where initial *a* is suppressed after *e* & *o*).

Abhi-ní-hita, mfn. touched with (instr.; also *án-* neg.), ŚBr.; (*as*), m. 'close contact,' N. of a special Sandhi (by which final *e* & *o* are brought into close contact with the initial *a* of the following word, which in the old language probably was not entirely suppressed), Prāt.

अभिनिध्यै *abhi-ni-√dhyai*, to give attention to, R.

अभिनिनर्तम् *abhi-ni-nartam*, ind. (√*nṛit*), so as to accomplish step by step, i. e. repeating separately, KaushBr.; (cf. *abhy-ā-gāram*.)

अभिनिनी *abhi-ni-√nī*, to pour out (water &c.) upon, Comm. on KātyŚr.; (cf. *ni-√nī*.)

अभिनिपत् *abhi-ni-√pat*, Caus. *-pātayati*, to throw down, MBh.

Abhi-ni-pāta, *as,* m. = *abhini-dhāna* (m. or n.) above, Comm. on APrāt.

अभिनिपीड् *abhi-ni-√pīḍ*, to press, squeeze, trouble, MBh. &c.

Abhi-nipīḍita, mfn. pained, tormented.

अभिनिमन्त् *abhi-ni-√mantr*, to summon, invite, Hariv.

अभिनिम्रुच् *abhi-ni-√mruc*, *-mrócati* (said of the sun) to set upon anybody who is sleeping or has not finished his work, TS.; TBr.; Kāṭh.

Abhi-ni-mrukta, mfn. upon whom while not doing any work or while sleeping the sun has set, TBr.; (wrongly written *abhi-nir-mukta*) Mn. ii, 221 & BhP.

अभिनिम्लुच् *abhi-ni-√mluc* = *-√mruc* before, Mn. ii, 219; (cf. *ni-√mruc* & *ni-√mluc*.)

अभिनिम्लुप्त *abhi-ni-mlupta* = *abhi-ni-mrukta* above, Gobh.

अभिनियुक्त *abhi-niyukta*, mfn. (√*yuj*), occupied in.

अभिनिरस् *abhi-nir-√2. as*, to throw towards, Kauś.

अभिनिर्गम् *abhi-nir-√gam*, to go out or away from (abl.), R.

अभिनिर्जित *abhi-nirjita*, mfn. (√*ji*), conquered, MBh. xiv, 2220.

अभिनिर्णुद् *abhi-nir-ṇud* (√*nud*), (Pot. *-ṇudet*) to drive out, frighten away, MBh. xii, 10728.

अभिनिर्दिश् *abhi-nir-√diś*, to point out, indicate, TS. &c.; to appoint, characterize, Mn. x, 20; to settle, fix, MBh.; VarBṛS.

अभिनिर्भर्त्स् *abhi-nir-√bharts* (ind. p. *-bhartsya*) to scold thoroughly, R. ii, 78, 19.

अभिनिर्मित *abhi-nirmita*, mfn. (√*3. mā*), made, created, R. iii, 76, 30; Kir. v, 3.

अभिनिर्मुक्त *abhi-nir-mukta* for *abhi-ni-mrukta*, q. v.

अभिनिर्या *abhi-nir-√yā*, to march out, go out towards (dat.) or from (abl.), MBh. &c.

Abhi-niryāṇa, *am,* n. march of an assailant, L.

अभिनिर्वद् *abhi-nir-√vad*, to declare with regard to (acc.), PBr.

अभिनिर्वप् *abhi-nir-√2. vap*, to share out or add anything to another thing (either acc. & loc. [TS.] or instr. & acc. [AitBr.]).

अभिनिर्वृत् *abhi-nir-√vrit*, to result from, proceed, MBh.: Caus. *-vartayati*, to produce, accomplish, Hariv. &c.

Abhi-nirvṛitta, mfn. resulting from, MBh. &c.

Abhi-nirvṛitti, *is,* f. resulting, proceeding, accomplishment.

अभिनिलीयमानक *abhi-ni-līyamānaka*, mfn. (√*lī*), (a bird) lying down in its nest in the presence of (a spectator), VarBṛS.

अभिनिवर्तम् *abhi-ni-vártam*, ind. (√*vṛit*), so as to turn back towards (acc.), TS.; ŚBr.; Kāṭh.

अभिनिविश् *abhi-ni-√viś*, *-viśate*, to enter (with acc.), Pāṇ. i, 4, 47, Sch.; to disembogue (as a river) into (acc.), BhP.; to devote one's self entirely to (acc.), Daś. &c.: Caus. *-veśayati*, to cause to enter, lead into (acc.), BhP.; to cause to sit down upon (loc.), Śiś.; to cause any one to devote himself entirely to, MBh. &c.; (with *manas* or *ātmānam*) to devote one's attention to (loc.), BhP.

Abhi-nivishṭa, mfn. entered or plunged into; intent on (loc. or in comp.); endowed with, Ragh. ii, 75; determined, persevering. **–tā,** f. state of being persevering, Sāh.

Abhi-niveśa, *as,* m. application, intentness, study, affection, devotion (with loc. or ifc.); determination (to effect a purpose or attain an object), tenacity, adherence to (loc.), Kum. v, 7, &c.

Abhi-niveśita, mfn. made to enter into, plunged into.

Abhi-niveśin, mfn. intent upon, devoted to, Yājñ. iii, 134; determined.

अभिनिशम् *abhi-ni-√śam* (ind. p. *-śāmya*) to perceive, notice, Daś.

अभिनिश्चित *abhi-niścita*, mfn. (√*2. ci*), quite convinced of, MBh. xii, 10635; settled or fixed with regard to (acc.), MBh. iii, 1085.

अभिनिश्रि *abhi-ni-√śri*, to pass (from one thing) to another (acc.), Āp.

अभिनिषद् *abhi-ni-shad* (√*sad*), to sit down or settle round (perf. 3. sg. *-shasāda*), RV. vii, 15, 2; (Opt. 1. pl. *-shīdema*) AV. xii, 1, 29.

अभिनिष्कारिन् *abhi-nish-kārín*, mfn. intending anything evil against, injuring, AV. x, 1, 31; (cf. *abhi-kṛitvarī*.)

Abhi-nish-kṛita, mfn. directed against (as an evil action), AV. x, 1, 12.

अभिनिष्क्रम् *abhi-nish-√kram*, to go out towards; to lead towards (as a door), Pāṇ. iv, 3, 86; to leave the house in order to become an anchorite, Buddh. & Jain.

Abhi-nishkramaṇa, *am,* n. going forth; leaving the house in order to become an anchorite, Buddh. & Jain.

Abhi-nishkrānta, mfn. gone out towards; descended from (abl.), R.; having left the house (abl.) in order to become an anchorite, Mn. vi, 41; Buddh. & Jain. **–gṛihâvāsa,** mfn. having left his house (for becoming an anchorite), Buddh.

अभिनिष्टान *abhi-nishṭāna*. See *abhi-niḥ-√stan*.

अभिनिष्ठिव् *abhi-ni-√shṭhiv*, to spit upon, ŚBr.; Kauś.

अभिनिष्पत् *abhi-nish-√pat*, to fly out towards (acc.), AV. vii, 64, 1; to spring forth, shoot forth.

Abhi-nishpatana, *am,* n. springing forth, issuing.

अभिनिष्पद् *abhi-nish-√pad*, to come to (acc.), ŚBr.; to enter into, become (with acc.), ŚBr. xiv; ChUp.; to appear, ChUp.: Caus. *-pādayati*, to bring to (acc.), ŚBr.

Abhi-nishpatti, *is,* f. appearance, Comm. on ChUp.

अभिनिस्यन्द् *abhi-ni-√syand* (or *-shyand*), to trickle upon, MBh. xii, 3881.

Abhi-ni-shyanda, *as,* m. trickling, R.

अभिनिहन् *abhi-ni-√han* (p. *-ghnat*) to beat, strike, MBh. &c.

Abhi-ni-hata, mfn. put on (as on a spit), (*abhí níhata*) RV. i, 162, 11; for *abhi-ní-hita*, q. v., APrāt.

अभिनिहित *abhi-ní-hita*. See *abhi-ni-√dhā*.

अभिनिह्नव *abhi-nihnava*, *as,* m. (√*hnu*), denial, L.; N. of a Sāman.

अभिनी 1. *abhi-√nī* (perf. Opt. *-ninīyāt*, RV. vii, 88, 2; aor. Subj. 2. sg. *-neshi*, RV. vi, 61, 14) to conduct towards, bring near, RV. &c.; to represent dramatically, act; to adduce, quote, L.

Abhi-naya, *as,* m. (indication of a passion or purpose by look, gesture, &c.) acting, dramatic action (expressive of sentiment).

Abhi-nīta, mfn. brought near; performed, L.; highly finished or ornamented, L.; fit, proper, MBh. &c.; = *marshin* or *amarshin* (? patient or impatient), L.

Abhi-nīti, *is,* f. gesture, expressive gesticulation, L.; friendship, civility, L.

Abhi-netavya, mfn. to be represented dramatically.

Abhi-netṛi, *tā́*, m. one who brings near, RV. iv, 20, 8; ŚBr.

Abhi-neya, mfn. = *abhi-netavya*.

अभिनी 2. *abhi-nī* (*-ni-√i*), (Imper. *-nyè̀tu*) to enter into (as in approaching a woman), RV. x, 149, 4.

अभिनील *abhi-nīla*, mfn. very black or dark.

अभिनु 1. *abhi-√3. nu*, Ā. (3. pl. *abhí navante*) to turn one's self towards (acc.), RV. ix, 100, 1.

अभिनु 2. *abhi-√4. nu*, P. Ā. (pr. 1. pl. *-navāmahe*, 3. pl. *-navante*; impf. P. 3. pl. *-anāvan*; aor. 1. sg. *-anūshi*, 3. du. *-anūshātām*, 3. pl. *-anūshata* [very frequently] or *-nūshata*, RV. ix, 103, 3) to shout towards (acc.), RV.: Intens. (1. pl. *-nonumas*), id., RV.

अभिनुद् *abhi-√nud*, to push, press: Caus. *-nodayati*, to excite, spur or urge on.

अभिनृत् *abhi-√nṛit*, *-nṛityati*, to dance towards (acc.) or in imitation of (acc.), BhP.

अभिनृम्ण *abhi-nṛimṇa*, mf(*ā*)n. exceedingly propitious, BhP.

अभिन्न *á-bhinna*, mfn. (√*bhid*), uncut, unbroken, ŚBr. &c.; uninterrupted, RV. vi, 28, 2; (*a-bhinná*) AV.; (in arithm.) 'undivided,' integer, whole (as numbers); unchanged, unaltered, not different from (abl. or in comp.) **–gati,** mfn. not changing its course, Śāk. **–taraka,** mfn. (compar.) not at all different, Pat. **–tā,** f. or **-tva,** n. [R.] 'non-difference,' identity; (with numbers) wholeness. **–parikarmâshṭaka,** n. the eight processes in working whole numbers. **–sthiti,** mfn. not breaking its rules, Śāk. **Abhinnâtman,** mfn. 'of undaunted spirit,' firm.

अभिन्यस् *abhi-ny-√2. as*, *-asyati*, to depress (as fire), KātyŚr.

Abhi-nyāsa, *as,* m. a kind of fever, Bhpr.

अभिन्युब्ज् *abhi-ny-√ubj*, to press down, hold down, AV. viii, 8, 6; Kauś.

अभिपच् *abhi-√pac*, to boil up (as milk), Suśr.

अभिपठित *abhi-paṭhita*, mfn. denominated, named, Suśr.

अभिपत् 1. *abhi-√1. pat*, *-patyate*, to be lord over (acc.), RV. viii, 102, 9; pr. p. *-pātyamāna*, possessing, RV. x, 132, 3.

अभिपत् 2. *abhi-√2. pat*, to fly near, hasten near; to rush towards, assail; to fall down upon (acc.), AV. vi, 124, 1 & 2 (aor. *abhy-àpapta* & *abhy-àpaptat*), &c.; to fall or come into (acc.); to fly through or over, MBh. v, 3051; to overtake in flying, MBh. viii, 1910: Caus. *-pātayati*, to throw after with (instr.), TBr.; to throw upon (dat. or loc.); to throw down; to pass (time).

Abhi-patana, *am*, n. flying towards.

Abhi-pāta, *as*, m. hastening near, Kād.

Abhi-pātin, mfn. hastening near; running to the help of (in comp.), MBh. iii, 284.

Abhi-pitvá, *am*, n. (cf. *apa-pitvá*), approaching, visiting, putting up (for the night at an inn), RV.; (with or without the gen. pl. *áhnām*) close or departure of the day, evening, RV.

अभिपद् *abhi-√pad*, to come near or towards, approach; to approach (a deity) for imploring her help, Śiś. ix, 27; to come up (as an auxiliary), assist; to seize, catch, overpower, master, RV. x, 71, 9; ŚBr. &c.; to take possession of, Mn. i, 30, &c.; to accept, R.; to undertake, devote one's self to (acc.)

Abhí-patti, *is*, f. seizing, ŚBr.

Abhí-panna, mfn. approaching for imploring the help of, L.; assisted, MBh. &c.; seized, overpowered, ŚBr. &c.; undertaking, taking in hand; undertaken, taken in hand; one who has acted wrongly towards (in comp.), MBh. xii, 68, 50 & 58; distant, L.; dead, L.

अभिपद्म *abhi-padma*, mfn. (said of elephants) having red spots on the skin, MBh. i, 7013.

अभिपरावद् *abhi-parā-√vad*, to speak to, address, ŚBr.; KaushBr.

अभिपरिग्रह् *abhi-pari-√grah*, to clasp, embrace, MānGṛ.

अभिपरिग्लान *abhi-pari-glāna*, mfn. (√*glai*), tired, exhausted, MBh. i, 4489.

अभिपरिप्लुत *abhi-paripluta*, mfn. overflowed with (as *medasā, rajasā* [said of a wife during menstruation, MBh. iii, 523; cf. *abhi-pluta* below], &c.); attacked, afflicted by (instr.; as by anger, sorrow, compassion, &c.), MBh. &c.

अभिपरिष्वञ्ज् *abhi-pari-shvañj* (√*svañj*), (p. *-shvajat*) to embrace, R.

अभिपरिहन् *abhi-pari-√han*, to overpower entirely, ŚBr.

अभिपरिहृ *abhi-pari-√hṛi*, P. to move round (in a circle), ŚBr.: P. with *ātmānam* [Kauś.] or Caus. Ā. (Opt. 3. pl. *-hārayeran*) [ĀśvŚr.] to move round one's self.

Abhi-pari-hāra, *as*, m. moving round, (*an-*, neg.), ĀśvŚr.

अभिपरीत *abhi-parīta*, mfn. (√*i*), filled or taken with, seized by (instr., in comp.), MBh. &c.

अभिपरीवृत *abhi-parī-vṛita*, mfn. (√*vṛi*), filled or taken with (instr.; as with anger), R.

अभिपरे *abhi-parê* (√*i*), (Imper. 2. sg. *-párêhi*) to go away towards (acc.), AV. xiv, 2, 34 & 35.

अभिपर्याधा *abhi-pary-ā-√dhā* (= *pary-ā-√dhā*, q. v.), to surround (as a pan with fire), ŚBr.

अभिपर्यावृत् *abhi-pary-ā-√vṛit*, Ā. to turn one's self towards (acc.), AV.; TS. &c.; to turn one's self round (acc.), AitBr.

अभिपर्यासिच् *abhi-pary-ā-√sic*, to pour out round, AitBr.

अभिपर्यूह् *abhi-pary-√1. ūh*, *abhí páry ūhate*, to carry or bring towards (acc.), TS.

अभिपर्ये *abhi-pary-ê* (√*i*), (said of the time) 'to pass round' (acc.), i. e. to pass away or elapse, ŚBr.

अभिपले *abhi-palê* (√*i*), to follow after any one running away (acc.), PBr.; (cf. *palê*.)

अभिपश् *abhi-√paś*, *-paśyati*, to look upon or at, view, RV. &c.; to perceive, notice, MBh. i, 5002, &c.; (with gen.), BhP.; to know, ChUp.

अभिपा 1. *abhi-√1. pā*, to drink of, Gobh.

Abhi-pīta, mfn. watered (as the earth by rain), MBh. xii, 12844.

अभिपा 2. *abhi-√2. pā*, *-pā́ti*, to guard, RV.; VS.; to behold with attention, RV. viii, 59, 3: Caus. P. *-pālayati*, to protect, assist, MBh. &c.

Abhi-pāla, *as*, m. protector, MBh.

Abhi-pālana, *am*, n. protecting, R.

अभिपिङ्गल *abhi-piṅgala*, mfn. 'very red,' reddish-brown, Hariv.

अभिपित्व *abhi-pitvá*. See *apa-√2. pat*.

अभिपिश् *abhi-√piś* (impf. *-apiṇśat*, perf. Ā. 3. pl. *-pipiśre*) to adorn with (instr.), RV. v, 60, 4; x, 68, 11; TBr.

अभिपीड् *abhi-√pīḍ*, to oppress, torment.

Abhi-pīḍita, mfn. pressed (as the soil by the foot or by an army), ShaḍvBr. &c.; oppressed, tormented, afflicted, MBh. &c.

अभिपुथ् *abhi-√puth*, Caus. *-pothayati*, to throw with violence upon (loc.), Hariv.

अभिपुष्प *abhi-pushpa*, mfn. covered with flowers, R.; (*am*), n. an excellent flower, L.

अभिपू *abhi-√pū*, *-pavate*, to flow purified towards or for (acc. or dat.), RV.; to blow towards, TS.; TBr.; to make bright, glorify, AV.; TS.

अभिपूज् *abhi-√pūj*, to honour, reverence greatly; to approve of.

Abhi-pūjita, mfn. honoured; approved, assented to, Mn. vi, 58, &c.

अभिपूर्व *abhi-pūrva*, mfn. following in regular order, PBr.; (*ám* [AV.; ŚBr.] or *eṇa* [PBr.]), ind. in regular order, successively.

अभिपृष्ठे *abhi-pṛishṭhe*, ind. at the back of, behind, Kum.

अभिपॄ *abhi-√pṝī* (Imper. 2. sg. *-pṛiṇīhi*) to fill up, PārGṛ.; *-pūryate*, to become full or abundant, PārGṛ.; MBh.: Caus. *-pūrayati*, to make full, fill, ŚBr. &c.; to load with, Kathās.; to cover with (as with arrows), MBh. vi, 1721; to present with (instr.), Hariv.; Kathās.; (said of sorrows, &c.) to fill the heart of any one, overwhelm; to accomplish, R. vii, 35, 14.

Abhi-pūraṇa, *am*, n. filling, KātyŚr.

Abhi-pūrṇa, mfn. full of (instr. or gen.)

Abhi-pūrta, *am*, n. that which has been fulfilled, AV. ix, 5, 13.

Abhi-pūrya, mfn. to be filled, MaitrS.

अभिप्यै *abhi-√pyai* (perf. Ā. p. *-pipyā́na*) to swell, abound with (instr.), RV. vii, 36, 6.

अभिप्रकम्प् *abhi-pra-√kamp*, Caus. *-kampayati*, to stir, allure, ŚBr.

अभिप्रकाश् *abhi-pra-√kāś*, *-kāśate*, to become visible, MBh. (*cakshushā*, 'to the eye'); R.

अभिप्रक्रम् *abhi-pra-√kram*, P. *-krāmati*, to go up to (acc.), ŚBr.; Kauś.

Abhi-pra-kramya, mfn. to be stepped upon or walked on, PBr.

अभिप्रक्षर् *abhi-pra-√kshar*, to stream towards (acc.), ŚBr.

Abhi-pra-ksharita, mfn. poured out, ŚBr.

अभिप्रक्षल् *abhi-pra-√kshal*, *-kshālayati*, to clean thoroughly, polish up (as a jewel), Vikr.

अभिप्रगाह् *abhi-pra-√gāh*, *-gā́hate*, to dip or plunge into, penetrate, RV. ix, 99, 2 & 110, 2: Caus. (ind. p. *-gāhya*) to immerse, dip, ŚaṅkhŚr.

अभिप्रगै *abhi-pra-√gai* (Imper. 2. pl. *-gāyata*) to begin to praise, RV.

अभिप्रचक्ष् *abhi-pra-√caksh* (Ved. Inf. *-cákshe*) to see, RV. i, 113, 6.

अभिप्रचुद् *abhi-pra-√cud*, Caus. *-codayati*, to impel, induce, persuade, MBh.; R.

अभिप्रच्यु *abhi-pra-√cyu* (Imper. 2. sg. Ā. *-cyavasva*) to move towards, arrive at (acc.), VS.; TS.

अभिप्रछ् *abhi-√prach*, to ask or inquire after, MBh. &c.

Abhi-pṛishṭa, mfn. inquired after, BhP.

Abhi-praśnin, mfn. inclined to ask, inquisitive, VS.

अभिप्रजन् *abhi-pra-√jan* (3. pl. Ā. *-jāyante*) to bring forth, bear, RV. v, 19, 1: Caus. *-janayati*, to generate for the sake of (acc.), ŚBr.

अभिप्रज्वल् *abhi-pra-√jval* (perf. *-jajvāla*) to flare up, MBh.

अभिप्रणक्ष् *abhi-pra-ṇaksh* (√*naksh*), (perf. Ā. *-nanakshé*) to overpower, RV. viii, 51, 8.

अभिप्रणद् *abhi-pra-ṇad* (√*nad*), (perf. 3. pl. *-neduḥ*) to begin to roar or sound, Bhaṭṭ.

अभिप्रणम् *abhi-pra-ṇam* (√*nam*), to bow before (dat. or acc.), MBh. &c.

Abhi-praṇata, mfn. bent, bowing before.

अभिप्रणी *abhi-pra-ṇī* (√*nī*), (aor. Subj. 2. sg. *-ṇeshi*) to bring towards (acc.), RV. i, 31, 18.

Abhi-praṇaya, *as*, m. affection, L.; (cf. *praṇaya*.)

Abhi-praṇīta, mfn. brought to (as fire to the altar), Bhaṭṭ.; (cf. *pra-ṇī*.)

अभिप्रणु *abhi-pra-ṇu* (√4. *nu*), (aor. Ā. 3. pl. *-ánūshata*) to shout towards, praise highly, RV. iv, 32, 9: Intens. (1. pl. *-ṇonumas* [frequently]; perf. 3. pl. *-ṇonuvuḥ*) id., RV.

अभिप्रतन् *abhi-pra-√tan*, to spread over (acc.), KaushUp.

अभिप्रतप्त *abhi-pratapta*, mfn. 'intensely heated,' dried up, Suśr.; exhausted with pain or fever, R.

अभिप्रतारिन् *abhi-pratārin*, *ī*, m., N. of a descendant of Kaksha-sena, ChUp.

अभिप्रतिगॄ *abhi-prati-√1. gṝī*, 'to call out to (acc.) alternately,' answer in singing, TS.; (cf. *prati-√1. gṝī*.)

अभिप्रतिपद् *abhi-prati-√pad*, P. (fut. *-patsyati*) to begin with or at (acc.), AitBr.

अभिप्रतिपिष् *abhi-prati-√pish* (perf. *-pipesha*) to dash or crush out, ŚBr.

अभिप्रत्यवरुह् *abhi-praty-ava-√ruh*, to step down upon (acc.), AitBr.

अभिप्रत्यवे *abhi-praty-avê* (√*i*), to move down towards, ŚBr.

अभिप्रत्ये *abhi-praty-ê* (√*i*), to come back towards (acc.), ŚBr.

अभिप्रथ् *abhi-√prath* (perf. Ā. *-paprathe*) to spread, extend itself towards (acc.), RV. ix, 80, 3: Caus. *-prathayati*, to spread or scatter over (acc.), TS.; to spread (as one's fame), MBh.

Abhi-prathana, *am*, n. spreading over, L.

अभिप्रदक्षिणम् *abhi-pra-dakshiṇam*, ind. to the right (e.g. with √1. *kṛi*, to circumambulate keeping the object on the right), R.

अभिप्रदर्शन *abhi-pra-darśana*, *am*, n. pointing out, indicating, Sāh.

अभिप्रदिश् *abhi-pra-√diś*, Caus. *-deśayati*, to urge on, R.

अभिप्रदॄ *abhi-pra-√dṝī* (perf. 3. pl. *-dadrur* = *abhi-jagmuḥ*, Sāy. fr. *-√2. drā*, 'to run towards') to put forth by bursting or opening, RV. iv, 19, 5: Pass. *-dīryate*, to be scattered or divided asunder, MBh. viii, 3976.

अभिप्रद्रा *abhi-pra-√2. drā*. See *-√dṝī*.

अभिप्रद्रु *abhi-pra-√2. dru* (perf. Ā. *-dudruve*) to rush towards (acc.), assail, MBh.

अभिप्रधर्षण *abhi-pra-dharshaṇa*, *am*, n. oppressing, injuring, MBh. iii, 14937.

अभिप्रपच् *abhi-pra-√pac*, Pass. *-pacyate*, 'to get ripe,' develop itself, Suśr.

अभिप्रपद् *abhi-pra-√pad*, to come towards, reach at, enter into (acc.), ŚBr. &c.; to resort to (acc.), MBh. &c.; to undertake, MBh.

Abhi-prapanna, mfn. approached, attained.

अभिप्रपश् *abhi-pra-√paś* (impf. *-prāpaśyat*) to look out after (acc.), RV. x, 113, 4.

अभिप्रपीड् *abhi-pra-√pīḍ*, Caus. *-pīḍayati*, to cause pain, torture, MBh. &c.

अभिप्रपॄ *abhi-pra-√pṝī*, *-pūryate*, to be filled, fill one's self completely, MBh. xv, 678.

अभिप्रभङ्गिन् *abhi-pra-bhaṅgin*, mfn. (√*bhañj*), breaking completely, RV. viii, 45, 35.

अभिप्रभू *abhi-pra-√bhū* (Ved. Inf. aor. *abhí pra-bhūshánī*) to assist, RV. x, 132, 1.

अभिप्रभृ *abhi-pra-√bhṛi* (1. pl. *-bharāmahe*) to offer to (dat.), RV. iv, 56, 5; (Imper. 2. sg. *-bhara*) to throw, dart, RV. viii, 89, 4.

अभिप्रमथ् *abhi-pra-√math*, Caus. *-manthayati*, to churn thoroughly, Suśr.

अभिप्रमन् *abhi-pra-√man*, Ā. (3. pl. *-manvate*) to take any one for, look upon him as, AV. vi, 84, 1.

अभिप्रमन्द् *abhi-pra-√1. mand* (1. & 2. sg. Ā. *-mande, -mandase*; perf. P. 3. pl. *-mandiḥ*) to gladden, RV.; P. (Imper. 2. sg. *-manda*) to confuse, infatuate, RV. vi, 18, 9.

अभिप्रमुर् *abhi-pra-múr*, mfn. (√*mṛi*), bruising, crushing, RV. x, 115, 2.

अभिप्रमृश् *abhi-pra-√mṛiś* (Imper. 2. sg. *-mṛiśa*; aor. Subj. 2. sg. *-mṛikshas* & 2. pl. *-mṛikshata*) to seize, grasp: Intens. (p. nom. m. *-marmṛiśat*) id., RV. i, 140, 5.

अभिप्रया *abhi-pra-√yā* (Imper. 2. pl. *-yāthána*) to come towards, approach, RV. viii, 27, 6; to set out, march off, go to battle, MBh. &c.

Abhi-pra-yāyam, ind. so as to approach, KātyŚr.

Abhi-pra-yāyín, mfn. approaching, TS.

अभिप्रयुज् *abhi-pra-√yuj*, *-prá-yuṅkte*, to seize, grasp, bring in one's possession, TS.; TBr.; KaushBr.

अभिप्ररुह् *abhi-pra-√ruh*, to put forth or produce shoots, Suśr.

अभिप्रवह् *abhi-pra-√vah*, to carry or bring towards, AitBr.

अभिप्रविप् *abhi-pra-√vip* (Opt. 3. pl. *-véperan*) to move against (acc.), threaten, TS.

अभिप्रविश् *abhi-pra-√viś*, to disembogue into (acc.), BhP.

Abhi-pra-vishṭa, mfn. fallen or come into (acc.), R.

Abhi-pra-veśa, *as*, m. entering into, MBh. i, 2871.

अभिप्रवृत् *abhi-pra-√vṛit*, Ā. to advance up to (acc.), AitBr.; KaushUp.; to disembogue into (acc.), R.; to go forth, advance, ĀśvGṛ.; (see also *abhi-pra-vṛitta*): Caus. *-vartayati*, to cause to advance against, throw against (acc.), TS.; (dat.), SV.

Abhi-pravartana, *am*, n. coming or flowing forth (said of the sweat), Suśr.

Abhi-pravṛitta, mfn. being performed, advancing, proceeding, MBh. viii, 3464; occupied or engaged in, Bhag.

अभिप्रवृध् *abhi-pra-vṛidh*, Caus. *-vardhayati* (generally used in the perf. Pass. p. *-vardhita*) to enlarge, Suśr.; render prosperous, MBh.

अभिप्रवृष् *abhi-pra-√vṛish*, to pour down rain, MBh. &c.

अभिप्रव्रज् *abhi-pra-√vraj*, to step or advance towards, ChUp.; KaushUp.

अभिप्रशंस् *abhi-pra-√śaṉs*, to praise highly, MBh.

अभिप्रशुध् *abhi-pra-√śudh*, Caus. *-śodhayati*, to clean thoroughly, Suśr.

अभिप्रश्निन् *abhi-praśnín*. See *abhi-√prach*.

अभिप्रश्वस् *abhi-pra-√śvas*, to blow towards (acc.), AitBr.

अभिप्रसद् *abhi-pra-√sad* (p. *-sīdat*; perf. 3. pl. *-seduḥ*) to sit down or settle along (acc.), RV. iv, 1, 13 & x, 32, 1: Caus. *-sādayati*, to cause to be well-disposed or gracious, pray for grace or favour, MBh. &c.

अभिप्रसह् *abhi-pra-√sah*, to be able to (Inf.), Kir. xii, 18.

अभिप्रसुप्त *abhi-pra-supta*, mfn. (√*svap*), fallen asleep, MBh.

अभिप्रसू *abhi-pra-√1. sū* (3. pl. *-suvanti*) to drive towards (acc.), Nir.

1. **Abhi-pra-sūta**, mfn. engaged, induced, ordered, Nir.

अभिप्रसूत 2. *abhi-pra-sūta*, mfn. (√*4. su*), generated, born, MBh. v, 964.

अभिप्रसृ *abhi-pra-√sṛi*, Caus. (ind. p. *-sāryá*) to stretch one's self out towards (acc.), ŚBr.; Ā. (Pot. *-sārayīta*) to stretch out (as a foot) towards or upon (loc.), Āp.

Abhi-pra-sāraṇa, *am*, n. stretching out the feet towards (gen.), Āp.

Abhi-pra-sṛita, mfn. devoted to, R.; (cf. *pra-sṛita*.)

अभिप्रसृप् *abhi-pra-√sṛip* (p. *-sárpat*) to creep near, AV. viii, 6, 22.

अभिप्रस्कन्द् *abhi-pra-√skand*, to jump into (acc.), ŚāṅkhBr.

अभिप्रस्तु *abhi-pra-√stu*, to praise with a *stoma* (q. v.), TS.

अभिप्रस्तृ *abhi-pra-√stṛi*, to scatter, ŚBr.

अभिप्रस्था *abhi-pra-√sthā* (aor. Subj. 2. pl. *-sthāta*; perf. 3. pl. *-tasthuḥ*) to start or advance towards, reach, RV.; AV. &c.; to surpass, have the precedence of (with or without acc.), RV. i, 74, 8 & x, 65, 15; (cf. *ati-pra-√sthā*): Caus. to drive (as the cattle to pasture), ChUp.

Abhi-pra-sthita, mfn. one who has set out, started, MBh. &c.

अभिप्रहन् *abhi-pra√-han* (3. pl. *-ghnánti*) to overpower, RV. vi, 46, 10; ŚBr.

Abhi-pra-hata, mfn. struck at, hurt, Suśr.

अभिप्रहा *abhi-pra-√2. hā*, *-jihite*, to jump or fly upwards in the direction of (acc.), ŚāṅkhŚr.

अभिप्रहित *abhi-prá-hita*, mfn. (√*hi*), sent hither, AV. x, 1, 15.

अभिप्राण् *abhi-prâṇ* (√*an*), *-prâṇiti*, to exhale, breathe forth towards (acc.), ŚBr.; to exhale, breathe forth, AitBr.; TBr. &c.

Abhi-prâṇana, *am*, n. exhaling (opposed to *apânana*, q. v.), L.

अभिप्रातर् *abhi-prâtár*, ind. towards morning, early, ŚBr. xiv; (according to some Comm. 'on the fourth day early in the morning').

अभिप्राप् *abhi-prâp* (√*āp*), to reach, obtain, ŚBr.; ChUp.

Abhi-prâpaṇa. See *arthâbhiprāpaṇa*.

Abhi-prâpta, mfn. reached, obtained.

Abhi-prâpti, *is*, f. arrival, Nir.

Abhi-prêpsu, mfn. desirous of gaining, Mn. &c.

अभिप्राय *abhi-prâya*. See *abhi-prê*.

अभिप्रार्च् *abhi-prârc* (√*arc*), to celebrate in song, RV. viii, 49, 1 & 69, 4.

अभिप्रार्थ् *abhi-prârth* (√*arth*), to long for, wish, R.

अभिप्राश् *abhi-prâś* (√*2. aś*), to eat in addition to (acc.) another thing (in order to get rid of the taste of it), ChUp.

अभिप्रास् *abhi-prâs* (√*2. as*), to throw upon (acc.), ŚBr.; KātyŚr.

अभिप्री 1. *abhi-√prī*, Caus. to gladden, refresh, Car.

2. **Abhi-prí**, mfn. gladdening, RV. i, 162, 3 & ix, 31, 3.

Abhi-prīta, mfn. pleased, (*an-*, neg.) AitBr.

Abhi-prīti, *is*, f. pleasing, pleasure, PBr.

अभिप्रु *abhi-√pru*, to hasten near or towards, RV. iv, 58, 8; to jump into, ŚBr.

Abhi-prava, *as*, m. = *abhi-plavá* below, Kāṭh.

अभिप्रुष् *abhi-√prush*, *-prushṇute*, *-prushāyati* [RV. x, 26, 3], to sprinkle with, RV.

अभिप्रे *abhi-prê* (√*i*), *-praîti* (Imper. 2. sg. *-prêhi*, 2. pl. *prêta*, RV.; AV.) to go near to, approach; to approach with one's mind, to think of, Pāṇ. i, 4, 32, &c.; to aim at, intend.

Abhi-prâya, *as*, m. aim, Pāṇ. i, 3, 72; purpose, intention, wish, R. &c.; opinion, Mn. vii, 57, &c.; meaning, sense (as of a word or of a passage).

Abhi-prêta, mfn. meant, intended, R. &c.; accepted, approved, Nir. &c.; to whom one's heart is devoted, dear, MBh.; Śāk. &c.

Abhi-prêtya, ind. intending, meaning by, Nir.

अभिप्रेक्ष् *abhi-prêksh* (√*īksh*), (generally ind. p. *-prêkshya*) to look at, to see, view, MBh. &c.

अभिप्रेप्सु *abhi-prêpsu*. See *abhi-prâp*.

अभिप्रेर् *abhi-prêr* (√*īr*), Caus. *-prêrayati*, to drive forwards, push on, Suśr.

Abhi-prêraṇa, *am*, n. pushing, setting in motion (as a see-saw).

अभिप्रेष् *abhi-prêsh* (√*1. ish*), (1. sg. *-prêshyāmi*) to summon, command, AV.

Abhi-prêshita, mfn. that which has been commanded or ordered, (*án-*, neg.) ŚBr.

अभिप्रोक्षण *abhi-prôkshaṇa*, *am*, n. (√*uksh*), sprinkling upon, affusion.

अभिप्लु *abhi-√plu*, to swim or navigate towards, approach, ŚBr. &c.; to overflow, &c. (see *abhi-pluta*); to jump near to, Hariv. &c.: Caus. (said of the sea) to wash, Kauś.

Abhi-plavá, *as*, m., N. of a religious ceremony (lasting six days and performed five times during the sacrifice Gavām-ayana), ŚBr. &c.

Abhi-pluta, mfn. overflowed, overrun; overwhelmed, affected by, labouring under (instr.), MBh. &c.; (*rajasā*, said of a wife during menstruation; cf. *abhi-pari-pluta* above), Mn. iv, 41.

अभिबल *abhi-bala*, *am*, n. (in dramatic language) overreaching or deceiving anybody by disguise, Sāh.

अभिबाध् *abhi-√bādh*, *-bādhate*, to check, stop, RV. viii, 5, 34; to attack (in battle), MBh. xii, 3731; to cause pain, afflict, R.

Abhi-bādhitṛi, mfn. causing pain, Hariv.; (v. l. *adhi-bādhitṛi*.)

अभिबुद्धि *abhi-buddhi*, *is*, f. (in Sāṅkhya phil.) N. of a function of the intellect (comprising *adhyavasāya*, *abhimāna*, *icchā*, *kartavyatā*, and *kriyā*).

अभिभज् *abhi-√bhaj*, to turn or flee towards (acc.), Hariv.

अभिभञ्ज् *abhi-√2. bhañj* (p. gen. pl. f. *-bhañjatīnấm*) to break down, destroy, RV. x, 103, 8.

Abhi-bhaṅgá, mfn. breaking down, destroying, RV. ii, 21, 3.

अभिभर्तृ *abhi-bhartṛi*, ind. towards the husband, Śiś. ix, 35; before (i. e. in presence of) the husband, Śiś. ix, 77.

अभिभर्त्स् *abhi-√bharts* (ind. p. *-bhartsya*) to scold, threaten so as to terrify, R.; to deride, ridicule, MBh. iii, 10921.

अभिभव *abhi-bhavá*. See 1. *abhi-√bhū* below.

अभिभा 1. *abhi-√bhā*, to glitter (around), be bright, appear, MBh. &c.

2. **Abhi-bhā́**, f. 'apparition, phenomenon,' inauspicious omen, RV. ii, 42, 1; AV.; (with Buddh.) act of overpowering, superiority, L. **Abhibhâyatana**, n. 'abode of superiority,' N. of the eight sources of superiority with Buddhists, L.

अभिभार *abhí-bhāra*. See *abhi-√bhṛi*.

अभिभाष् *abhi-√bhāsh*, to address, speak to (acc.), MBh. &c.; converse with (instr.), Mn. &c.; to utter, say (*abhibhāshante*, 'people use to say,' Nir.); to confess, Mn. xi, 103.

Abhi-bhāshaṇa, *am*, n. the act of addressing or speaking to, ĀśvŚr. &c.

Abhi-bhāshita, mfn. addressed, spoken to.

Abhi-bhāshin, mfn. addressing, speaking to.

Abhi-bhāshya, mfn. to be addressed.

Abhi-bhāshyamāṇa, mfn. being addressed.

अभिभुज् *abhi-√3. bhuj*, P. to be useful to (acc.), ŚāṅkhŚr.

अभिभू 1. *abhi-√bhū*, to overcome, overpower, predominate, conquer, surpass, overspread; to attack, defeat, humiliate; to approach, come near to (acc.), RV. iv, 31, 3; AV.; to be victorious or prospering in (loc.), RV. v, 37, 5.

Abhi-bhavá, mfn. overpowering, powerful, AV.

i, 29, 4; (*as*), m. prevailing, overpowering, predominance, Bhag. &c.; defeat, subjugation under (instr. or abl., or in comp.); disregard, disrespect; humiliation, mortification.

Abhi-bhavana, *am*, n. overpowering, Lalit.; the state of being overpowered, Mn. vi, 62.

Abhi-bhavanīya, mfn. to be overcome.

Abhi-bhāvaka, mfn. overpowering, surpassing, Comm. on Nyāyad.

Abhi-bhāvana, *am*, n. causing to overcome, making victorious, L.

Abhi-bhāvin, mfn. (ifc.) overpowering, Ragh. i, 14, &c.

Abhi-bhāvuka, mfn. = *abhi-bhāvaka*, L.

Abhi-bhú or 2. **abhi-bhū́,** mfn. one who surpasses, a superior (with or without acc.), RV.; AV.; VS.; (Compar. *abhibhū́tara*, RV. viii, 97, 10); (*us*), m., N. of a month, Kāṭh.; (*ū́s*), m., N. of a die, TS.; Kāṭh.; of a prince of the Nāgas, PārGṛ.

Abhi-bhūta, mfn. surpassed, defeated, subdued, humbled; overcome, aggrieved, injured.

Abhí-bhūti, *is*, f. superior power, overpowering, RV. iv, 38, 9; ŚBr.; KātyŚr.; disrespect, humiliation, L.; (mfn.), overpowering, superior, RV.; AV.

Abhibhūty-ójas (6), mfn. having superior power, RV.

Abhi-bhū́ya, *am*, n. superiority, AV. xix, 37, 3.

Abhi-bhū́van, mf(*varī*)n. superior, victorious over, RV. x, 159, 5 & 6.

अभिभृ *abhi-√bhṛi* (Subj. *-bhárāti*) to lay or throw upon (as a fault or blame), RV. v, 3, 7.

Abhí-bhāra, mfn. very heavy, ŚBr.

अभिमद् *abhi-√mad* (p. *-mā́dyat*) to be inebriated, ŚBr.; (cf. *abhi-√1. mand* below.)

Abhi-māda, *as*, m. intoxication, inebriety, L.

Abhi-mādyat-ká, mfn. partially intoxicated, half-drunk, ŚBr.

अभिमन् *abhi-√man, -manyate* (Subj. *-manyāte*, RV. x, 27, 11) to think of, long for, desire, RV. &c.; (aor. Subj. 2. sg. *-mansthāḥ*, 3. sg. *-mansta*; Ved. Inf. *abhi-mantoḥ*, ŚBr.) to intend to injure, be insidious, threaten, injure, VS.; AV. &c.; to kill, AitBr. (aor. *-amansta*); KātyŚr.; to allow, agree, MBh. ii, 1374, &c.; to think of self, be proud of; to think, suppose, imagine, take for (acc.)

Abhi-mata, mfn. longed for, wished, desired; loved, dear; allowed, ĀśvGṛ.; supposed, imagined; (*am*), n. desire, wish. **-tā,** f. agreeableness, desirableness; desire, love.

Abhi-mati, *is*, f. self-reference, referring all objects to self (as the act of Ahaṃkāra or personality), BhP.

Abhi-manas, mfn. 'having the mind directed towards,' desirous of, longing for (acc.), R. &c.

Abhi-manasya, Nom. Ā. (Opt. *-manasyéta*) 'to have the mind directed towards,' be pleased with, like, AV. xi, 3, 25.

Abhi-manāya, Nom. Ā. (Opt. *-manāyeta*) to long for, desire, Bhaṭṭ.; (cf. gaṇa *bhṛiśâdi*): Desid. *-mimānayishate*, Pat.

Abhi-mantavya, mfn. to be considered, Pañcat.; to be desired.

Abhi-mantṛi, *tā*, m. one who refers all objects to self (N. of Iśvara, together with *ahaṃkāra*; cf. *abhi-mati* above), Mn. i, 14; one who injures or threatens, GopBr.

Abhí-mantos, Ved. Inf. See s. v. *abhi-√man.*

Abhi-manyu, *us*, m., N. of a son of Manu Cākshusha; of a son of Arjuna (by Subhadrā); of two kings of Kaśmīra, Rājat. **-pura,** n., N. of a town, Rājat. **-svāmin,** m., N. of a temple, Rājat.

Abhí-māti, mfn. insidious, RV. v, 23, 4 & x, 18, 9; (*is*), f. striving to injure, RV.; an enemy, foe, RV.; AV.; ŚBr. **-jit,** mfn. subduing the enemies, VS. **-shā́h** [RV.] or **-shāhá** [RV.; AV.], mfn. conquering enemies. **-shā́hya** (7), n. conquering enemies, RV. iii, 37, 3. **-hán,** mfn. striking or destroying one's enemies, RV.; VS.

Abhi-mātin, mfn. insidious, RV. i, 85, 3.

Abhi-māna, *as*, m. intention to injure, insidiousness, KātyŚr.; high opinion of one's self, self-conceit, pride, haughtiness; (in Sāṅkhya phil.) = *abhi-mati* above; conception (especially an erroneous one regarding one's self), Sāh. &c.; affection, desire; N. of a Ṛishi in the sixth Manvantara, VP. **-tā,** f. pride, arrogance. **-vat,** mfn. conceiving or having ideas about self; proud, arrogant. **-śālin,** mfn. proud, arrogant, Kir. ii, 48. **-śūnya,** mfn. void of conceit, humble.

Abhi-mānita, *am*, n. copulation, sexual intercourse, L.

Abhi-mānin, mfn. thinking of one's self, proud, self-conceited; (ifc.) imagining one's self to be or to possess, laying claim to, arrogating to one's self; (*ī*), m., N. of an Agni, VP.; BhP. **Abhimāni-tā,** f. or **-tva,** n. the state of self-conceitedness.

Abhi-mānuka, mfn. insidious (with acc.), ŚBr.; (cf. *án-abhimānuka.*)

Abhī-māna. See *nir-abhīmāna.*

Abhī-mānin, *ī*, m., N. of an Agni, MārkP.

अभिमन्त्र् *abhi-√mantr*, Ā. to address or consecrate with a Mantra (acc. & instr.; or rarely dat. & acc. [RV. x, 191, 3]); to address with any formula (as when inviting a guest [R.], &c.)

Abhi-mantraṇa, *am*, n. making anything sacred by a special formula (called *abhi-mantraṇa-mantra*), consecrating; addressing, Kauś.

Abhi-mantrita, mfn. consecrated by a certain formula.

अभिमन्थ् *abhi-√manth*, to churn or rub (for eliciting fire), ŚBr. xiv.

Abhi-mantha, *as*, m. (ophthalmia) = *adhi-mantha*, q. v.

Abhi-manthana, *am*, n. the upper piece of wood (*araṇi*) which is churned in the lower one (for kindling the fire), Kauś.

अभिमन्द् *abhi-√1. mand*, P. (3. pl. aor. *-á-mandishuḥ*) to gladden, RV. viii, 50, 3; Ā. (2. sg. *-mandase*) to be pleased with, enjoy (with loc.), RV. x, 50, 2; (cf. *abhi-√mad* above.)

अभिमर *abhi-mara.* See *abhi-√mṛi.*

अभिमर्द *abhi-marda.* See *abhi-√mṛid.*

अभिमर्शन *abhi-marśana.* See *abhi-√mṛiś.*

अभिमा 1. *abhi-√3. mā*, to measure upon, ŚBr.; KātyŚr.

2. **Abhi-mā́,** f. measure (with regard to the breadth), MaitrS.

अभिमाति *abhí-māti.* See *abhi-√man.*

अभिमाद *abhi-māda.* See *abhi-√mad.*

अभिमान *abhi-māna.* See *abhi-√man.*

अभिमाय *abhi-māya*, mfn. (fr. *māyā*), perplexed, confused, L.

अभिमारुतम् *abhi-mārutam*, ind. against the wind.

अभिमिथ् *abhi-√mith*, to address with insulting speech, insult, ŚBr.; ĀśvŚr.; ŚāṅkhŚr.

Abhi-methana, *am*, n. insulting or injurious speech, Vait.

Abhi-méthikā, f. id., ŚBr.

अभिमिह् *abhi-√mih* (pr. p. gen. sg. m. *-mehatas*) to wet (by urining upon), Yājñ. ii, 293.

Abhi-mihya, mfn. to be wetted (by urining upon), ŚBr.

अभिमुख *abhi-mukha*, mf(*ī*, rarely *ā*)n. with the face directed towards, turned towards, facing (with acc., dat., gen.; or ifc.); (ifc.) going near, approaching (as *yauvanâbhimukhī*, 'approaching puberty, marriageable,' Pañcat.); (ifc.) disposed to, intending to, ready for; taking one's part, friendly disposed (with gen. or instr.), R.; (*am*), ind. towards (often used in a hostile manner, Kir. vi, 14, &c.), in the direction of, in front or presence of, near to (acc., gen.; or ifc.); (*e*), ind. in front or presence of (gen.; or ifc.), R.; (*ī*), f. one of the ten Bhūmis to be passed by a Bodhisattva before becoming a Buddha. **-tā,** f. presence, proximity.

Abhimukhaya, Nom. P. °*yati*, to face, Kir. xii, 19.

Abhimukhī (for *abhimukha* in comp. with √1. *kṛi* and √*bhū*). **-karaṇa,** n. turning the face towards, addressing, Pāṇ. ii, 3, 47, Sch. **-√1. kṛi,** to turn the face towards, address; to cause to turn the face forward, push forward, Daś. **-bhūta,** mfn. being in presence of or facing; (said of the fate) being favourable to.

अभिमुच् *abhi-√muc*, P. *-muñcati*, to let go, let loose, MBh. xii, 10949: Ā. to throw or shoot (as arrows), MBh. vii, 3967.

अभिमुह् *abhi-√muh*, to lose consciousness, faint away, Suśr.

अभिमूर्छित *abhi-mūrchita*, mfn. augmented, intensified, Suśr.; excited, stirred up (as by passions), MBh. i, 7794.

अभिमृ *abhi-√mṛi*, Ā. (impf. *-amriyata*) to touch or defile while dying, TS.

Abhi-mara, *as*, m. killing, slaughter, L.; combat, L.; treachery, mutiny, L.; binding in fetters, L.

Abhi-mṛita, mfn. afflicted or rendered impure by the death of (instr.), defiled, Kāṭh.; ĀśvGṛ.

अभिमृक्ष् *abhi-√mṛiksh* (impf. Ā. 3. sg. *-amṛikshata*) to smear, anoint, MBh. xiii, 1486: Caus. (impf. 1. sg. *-amṛikshayam*), id., MBh. xiii, 7426.

अभिमृज् *abhi-√mṛij* (ind. p. *-mṛijya*) to wipe, cleanse, Suśr.: Caus. (impf. *-amārjayat*), id., R. iv, 6, 16.

अभिमृड् *abhi-√mṛiḍ* (Ved. Imper. 2. sg. *-mṛiḍā*) to protect graciously from (abl.), RV. x, 25, 3.

अभिमृद् *abhi-√mṛid*, to oppress, to devastate, destroy, MBh. &c.; (in astron.) to be in opposition to, VarBṛS.

Abhi-marda, *as*, m. devastation (of a country &c. by an enemy), MBh.; battle, L.; spirituous liquor, L.

Abhi-mardana, mfn. (ifc.) oppressing; (*am*), n. oppression.

Abhi-mardin, mfn. (ifc.) oppressing, R.; one who devastates.

अभिमृश् *abhi-√mṛiś*, P. (1. pl. *-mṛiśāmasi*; Ved. Inf. *-mṛíśe*, RV. ii, 10, 5) to touch, come in contact with, RV. &c.: Ā. *-mṛiśate*, id., RV. i, 145, 4, &c.: Caus. to cause to touch, ŚāṅkhŚr.: Intens. (p. *-marmṛiśat*) 'to intend to bring in contact with one's self,' to long for (acc.), RV. iii, 38, 1; (AitBr.)

Abhi-marśa (or less correctly **abhi-marsha,** Mn. viii, 352, &c.), *as*, m. touching, contact, Kum. &c.; (ifc. f. *ā*), Śak.; grasping, seizing (as by the hair), BhP.

Abhi-marśaka (or less correctly **abhi-marshaka,** R.), mfn. touching, coming in contact with.

Abhi-marśana (or less correctly **abhi-marshaṇa,** R.), *am*, n. touching, contact, KātyŚr.; Yājñ. &c.; (mfn.), (ifc.) = *abhi-marśaka*, R.; BhP.

Abhi-mṛishṭa, mfn. touched; struck (as by a weapon), BhP. **-ja,** mfn. 'born from (women) touched (by others),' illegitimate (?), MBh. ii, 2422; summoned, invited, BhP.

अभिम्रक्ष् *abhi-√mraksh.* See *abhi-√mṛiksh.*

अभिम्लात *abhi-mlāta.* See *an-abhimlāta.*

अभियज् *abhi-√yaj*, to honour with sacrifices, Gobh. &c.; to offer (a sacrifice), MBh.; to honour (aor. Ā. 3. sg. *-ayashṭa*), RV. vi, 47, 25.

Abhi-yashṭavya, mfn. to be honoured with sacrifices, Gobh.

Abhijya, mfn. id., L.; (*as*), m. a god, L.

अभिया 1. *abhi-√yā*, to go up to in a hostile manner, attack, assail, RV. i, 174, 5 (aor. Subj. *-yāsishat*); AV. &c.; to go up to, approach, obtain, MBh. &c.; to devote one's self to, take up (as *pāshaṇḍam*, 'heterodoxies'), BhP.: Caus. to cause to approach, send towards, BhP.

2. **Abhi-yā,** mfn. going up to, approaching, L.; assailing, L.; (said of a prince) 'going all round,' i. e. vigilant, careful, MBh.

Abhi-yāta, mfn. approached; attacked.

Abhi-yāti, *is*, or **-yātin,** *ī*, m. an assailant, enemy, L.

Abhi-yātṛi, *tā*, m. id., R. ii, 2, 21.

Abhi-yāna, *am*, n. coming near, approaching, L.; attacking, MBh.

Abhi-yāyin, mfn. going towards, approaching (with acc. or ifc.); (ifc.) attacking, Ragh. xii, 43.

अभियाच् *abhi-√yāc*, to ask for, solicit, request.

Abhi-yācana, *am*, n. asking for, entreaty, request; (cf. *satyâbhiyācana.*)

Abhi-yācita, mfn. asked for, requested.

Abhi-yāćñā, f. id., L.

अभियुज् 1. *abhi-√yuj*, Ā. *-yuṅkte*, to put to (as horses to a carriage) for a special purpose (acc.), ŚBr.: P. to put to (as horses) subsequently, ŚBr.: Ā. to summon, invite to (dat.), R. vii, 61, 9: P. to order, charge with (loc.), MBh. xiv, 2637: Ā. (rarely P.) to encounter, attack, assail; to accuse of (acc.), Mn. viii, 183, &c.: P. Ā. to undertake, apply to, make one's self ready to (acc. or Inf.): Caus. to furnish with, make anybody share in (instr.), MBh. &c.

Abhi-yukta, mfn. applied, intent on (loc.); diligent, versed in (loc.); appointed; attacked (by an enemy), assailed; blamed, rebuked, L.; (in law) accused, charged, prosecuted, a defendant, Yājñ. &c.

Abhi-yúgvan, mfn. attacking, RV. vi, 45, 15; VS.

2. **Abhi-yúj**, *k*, f. an assailant, enemy, RV.

Abhi-yujyamāna, mfn. (in law) being persecuted (as a defendant).

Abhi-yoktavya, mfn. (in law) to be accused or prosecuted, Mn. viii, 50.

Abhi-yoktṛi, mfn. assailing, attacking; (*tā*), m. an enemy, Hit.; (in law) a plaintiff, claimant, pretender, accuser, Mn. viii, 52 & 58, &c.

Abhi-yoga, *as*, m. application; energetic effort, exertion, perseverance in, constant practice (with loc. or inf.); attack, assault, Kum. vii, 50, &c.; (in law) a plaint, a charge, accusation, Yājñ. &c. **-pattra**, n. a petition or writing of complaint.

Abhi-yogin, mfn. intent upon, absorbed in attacking; (in law) accusing, Yājñ. ii, 11; (*ī*), m. a plaintiff, prosecutor.

Abhi-yogya, mfn. assailable, L.

Abhi-yojana, *am*, n. putting to (as horses) subsequently, Sāy. on ŚBr. (cf. *abhi-√yuj*).

Abhi-yojya, mfn. assailable.

अभियुत *abhi-yuta*, mfn. inclosed in (acc.), Nir. ii, 19.

अभियुध् *abhi-√yudh* (pr. Subj. 2. sg. *-yúdhyās*; aor. 2. sg. *-yodhīs*, 3. sg. *-áyodhīt*, 2. du. *-yodhishṭam*, p. *-yodhānā*) to fight against (acc.), RV.; to acquire by fighting, RV.; to fight, Hariv.; BhP.

अभिरक्ष् *abhi-√raksh*, P. Ā. *-rákshati*, °*te* (p. *-rákshamāṇa*, RV. x, 157, 4) to guard, protect, preserve, RV. &c.; 'to govern or command' (cf. *abhi-rakshita*).

Abhi-rakshaṇa, *am*, n. guarding, protection, MBh. &c.

Abhi-rakshā, f. protection, VarBṛS.

Abhi-rakshita, mfn. protected, preserved, guarded; governed, commanded, Bhag. &c.

Abhi-rakshitṛi, mfn. one who preserves, a protector of (gen.), Mn. vii, 35.

Abhi-rakshya, mfn. to be protected, VarBṛS.

अभिरञ्ज् *abhi-rañj*, *-rajyate*, to be pleased with (instr.): Caus. P. 'to colour' (cf. *abhi-rañjita*).

Abhi-rakta, mfn. devoted to, MBh. &c.

Abhi-rañjita, mfn. tinted, coloured, R.

अभिरभ् *abhi-√rabh*, Ā. (perf. 3. pl. *-rebhire*) to embrace, BhP.: Caus. perf. Pass. p. *-rambhita*, see below.

Abhi-rambhita, mfn. embraced, BhP.; seized by (acc.!), BhP.

अभिरम् *abhi-√ram*, *-ramate*, to dwell, ĀśvGṛ.; to repose, ŚāṅkhGṛ.; Mn. iii, 251; Yājñ. i, 251; to delight in, be delighted, MBh. &c.: Caus. *-rāmayati*, to gladden, MBh. &c.; to delight in, to be delighted.

Abhi-rata, mfn. reposing, Yājñ. i, 251; pleased or contented with (loc.), satisfied; engaged in, attentive to (loc.), performing, practising.

Abhi-rati, *is*, f. pleasure, delighting in (loc. or in comp.), Ragh. ix, 7, &c.; N. of a world, Buddh.

Abhi-ramaṇa, *am*, n. delighting in, delighting.

Abhi-ramaṇīya, mfn. delightful.

Abhi-rāma, mf(*ā*)n. pleasing, delightful, agreeable, beautiful; (*as*), m., N. of Śiva; 1. (*am*), ind. so as to be agreeable to (in comp.), Śāk.; (for 2. *abhi-rāmam*, see s. v. below.) **-tā**, f. loveliness, beauty, Śiś. i, 16, &c.; the state of being agreeable to (in comp.), Mcar. **-tva**, n. = *-tā*. **-pasupati**, m., N. of a poet. **-maṇi**, n., N. of a drama of Sundaramiśra; (cf. Wilson, Hindu Theatre, ii, 395.)

अभिरस् *abhi-√1. ras*, to neigh towards (acc.), KātyŚr.

अभिराज् 1. *abhi-√rāj*, *-rājate*, to shine, be brilliant, MBh. iii, 10960.

2. **Abhi-rāj**, mfn. reigning everywhere, Kauś.

Abhi-rāja, *as*, m., N. of a Burmese king.

Abhí-rāshṭra, mfn. overpowering or conquering dominions, RV. x, 174, 5.

अभिराध् *abhi-√rādh*, Caus. *-rādhayati*, to propitiate, conciliate, ŚBr. &c.: Caus. Pass. *-rādhyate*, to be rendered propitious, R.: Caus. Desid. *-rirādhayishati*, to intend to render propitious, ŚBr.

Abhi-rāddha, mfn. rendered propitious, propitiated, conciliated, Śiś. i, 71.

अभिरामम् 2. *abhi-rāmam*, ind. referring to Rāma.

अभिरिभ् *abhi-√ribh*, *-rebhati*, to howl towards (acc.), BhP. (v. l. for *abhi-√1. ru*, q. v.)

अभिरिष् *abhi-√rish* (Subj. *-réshāt*) to fail, miscarry, AV. iv, 35, 1.

अभिरु *abhi-√1. ru*, *-rauti* (v. l. *-rebhati*) to roar or howl towards (acc.), BhP.; (Imper. 2. sg. *-ruva*) AV. v, 20, 3.

Abhi-ruta, mfn. filled with roaring or any noise, resounding with (in comp.), MBh. &c.; (*am*), n. cries, R.; singing (as of birds), R.

अभिरुच् *abhi-√ruc*, Ā. to be bright, shine, R.; MārkP.; to please any one (dat.), Vikr.: Caus. P. to delight, amuse, MBh. xiii, 476 (v. l. *abhi-√ram*, Caus.): P. Ā. to be pleased with, approve of, be inclined to, like, MBh. &c.

Abhi-ruci, *is*, f. delighting in, being pleased with (loc. or in comp.), BhP. &c.

Abhi-rucita, mfn. pleasing, agreeable to; pleased with, delighting in (loc. or in comp.); (cf. *yathābhirucita*); (*as*), m., N. of a prince of the Vidyādharas, Kathās.

Abhi-rucira, mfn. very bright, R. iii, 39, 5.

अभिरुदित *abhi-rudita*, mfn. cried, uttered in a lamenting manner, R.

Abhi-rorudá, mfn. causing tears (indicative of strong passion), AV. vii, 38, 1.

अभिरुध् *abhi-√rudh*, to keep off, MBh. viii, 4308.

Abhi-roddhṛi, mfn. one who wards off, MaitrS.

अभिरुषित *abhi-rushita*, mfn. very angry, MBh. viii, 1747.

अभिरुह् *abhi-ruh* (perf. 3. pl. *-ruruhuḥ*) to ascend, mount, RV. v, 7, 5, &c.

Abhi-ruhya, ind. p. having ascended.

अभिरूप *abhi-rūpa*, mf(*ā*)n. corresponding with (dat.), conformable to, ŚBr.; AitBr.; pleasing, handsome, beautiful, AV. viii, 9, 9; Mn. &c.; wise, learned, Mn. iii, 144; Śāk.; (*as*), m. the moon, L.; Śiva, L.; Vishṇu, L.; Kāmadeva, L. **-tā**, f. the state of being learned or well educated, Kād. **-pati**, m. 'having an agreeable master,' (a rite) to secure such a master in the next world, L. **-vat**, mfn. handsome, beautiful, MBh. iii, 10070.

Abhi-rūpaka, mfn. = *abhi-rūpa*, Pāṇ. viii, 1, 8, Sch.; (gaṇa *śreṇy-ādi* and *śramaṇādi*, q. v.)

अभिरै *abhi-√rai*, to back towards (acc.), TĀr.

अभिरोरुद *abhi-rorudá*. See *abhi-rudita*.

अभिलक्ष् *abhi-√laksh*, Pass. *-lakshyate*, to appear, MBh. viii, 1045.

Abhi-lakshaṇa, *am*, n. the act of marking (with signs), Hcat.

Abhi-lakshita, mfn. fixed or indicated by (as by special signs); determined for, selected as, MBh. xii, 13223; indicated, pointed out, R. ii, 57, 2; appearing, visible, Hariv.; (*an-* or *na*, neg.) unseen, unperceived, MBh. i, 5822; Yājñ. iii, 59.

Abhi-lakshya, mfn. to be fixed or indicated by, distinguishable through (in comp.); (*am*), ind. towards a mark or aim, R. ii, 63, 23. **Abhilakshyī-kṛitya**, ind. p. (√1. *kṛi*), aiming at a mark, directing towards.

अभिलङ्घ् *abhi-√laṅgh*, Caus. to jump across or over; to transgress, violate; to injure, MBh. xii, 3565.

Abhi-laṅghana, *am*, n. jumping over (gen.), R.; violating, acting contrary to (in comp.), MBh. xiii, 2194.

Abhi-laṅghin, mfn. violating, acting contrary to (in comp.), MBh. xiii, 4964.

अभिलप् *abhi-√lap*, to talk or speak about, AitBr.; KaushBr.

Abhi-lapya, mfn. See *nir-abhilapya*.

Abhi-lāpa, *as*, m. expression, word, Sāh. &c.; declaration (as of the object of a vow), Kād.; (cf. *abhīlāpalāp*.)

अभिलभ् *abhi-labh*, Ā. to take or lay hold of, BhP.; to reach, obtain, gain, MBh. &c.: Desid. (p. P. *-lipsat*) to intend to catch or obtain, MBh. i, 2940.

Abhi-lipsā, f. desire of obtaining.

अभिलष् *abhi-√lash*, *-lashati*, to desire or wish for (acc.), covet, crave.

Abhi-lashaṇa, *am*, n. craving after, desiring.

Abhi-lashaṇīya, mfn. desirable, to be coveted.

Abhi-lashita, mfn. desired, wished; (*am*), n. desire, wish, will.

Abhi-lāsha (or less correctly **abhi-lāsa**), *as*, m. (ifc. f. *ā*), desire, wish, covetousness, affection (with loc. or ifc.)

Abhi-lāshaka, mfn. wishing, desiring (with acc.), R.

Abhi-lāshin, mfn. id. (with loc. or ifc.), Śāk. &c.; (less correctly *abhi-lāsin*, Megh. &c.)

Abhi-lāshuka, mf(*ā*)n. id. (with acc. [Kir.] or ifc. [Kathās.])

अभिलाव *abhi-lāva*, *as*, m. (√*lū*), cutting, reaping, mowing, Pāṇ. iii, 3, 28.

अभिलिख् *abhi-√likh*, to engrave, write upon, draw, paint: Caus. to cause to paint, have anything painted, Kathās.; to cause to write down, Yājñ. i, 318.

Abhi-lekhana, *am*, n. writing upon, inscribing.

Abhi-lekhita, *am*, n. a written document, Yājñ. ii, 149.

अभिलिप् *abhi-√lip*, to smear with, TS.; Kauś.: Caus. id., MBh. xiii, 7427.

अभिली *abhi-√lī*, *-līyate*, to adhere to, cling to (acc.), MBh.; Daś.

Abhi-līna, mfn. adhering to, clinging to (acc.), Megh. &c.; 'adhered to,' chosen (as a seat by birds or bees), Hariv.; Ragh. iii, 8.

अभिलुप् *abhi-√lup* (p. *-lumpat*) to rob, plunder, BhP.

Abhi-lupta, mfn. disturbed, injured.

अभिलुभ् *abhi-√lubh*, Caus. *-lobhayati*, to entice, allure.

अभिलुलित *abhi-lulita*, mfn. touched or grazed by (anything); shaken about, agitated, Śāk.

अभिलूता *abhi-lūtā*, f. a kind of spider, Suśr.

अभिलोक् *abhi-√lok*, Caus. (p. *-lokayat*) to view, look at (from a height), R. vi, 2, 7.

अभिवच् *abhi-√vac* (= *abhy-anu-√vac*), 'to declare or utter a verse with reference to,' only perf. Pass. p. *abhy-ukta*, q. v.; to say to (acc.), tell, MBh. &c.

अभिवञ्चित *abhi-vañcita*, mfn. cheated, deceived, MBh. v, 7506.

अभिवत् *abhi-vát*, mfn. containing the word *abhí*, ŚBr.

अभिवद् *abhi-√vad*, P. (rarely Ā., e.g. MBh. v, 923) to address or salute with reverence, ŚBr. &c.; to declare with reference to, express by, name, call, ŚBr. &c.; to say, speak, BhP.; Up.: Caus. *-vādayati*, °*te*, to address or salute reverently; to present one's self to (dat.), ŚāṅkhGṛ.: Ā. to salute through another person (acc. or instr.), Pāṇ. i, 4, 53, Comm.: P. to cause to recite, BhP.; 'to cause to sound,' play (on an instrument), MBh. iii, 14386.

Abhi-vadana, *am*, n. salutation, MBh. iii, 1835; addressing, Comm. on Kum. vi, 2.

Abhi-vāda, *as*, m. reverential salutation, Mn. ii, 120 seqq.; Gaut.; (v. l. *ati-vāda*) opprobrious or unfriendly speech, abuse, MBh. xii, 9972.

Abhi-vādaka, mfn. a saluter, saluting, Comm.

on Mn. ii, 125; having the intention to salute, N.; (cf. *abhi-vandaka*); civil, polite, L.

Abhi-vādana, *am*, n. respectful salutation (including sometimes the name or title of the person so addressed and followed by the mention of the person's own name); salutation (of a superior or elder by a junior or inferior, and especially of a teacher by his disciple; in general it is merely lifting the joined hands to the forehead and saying *aham abhivādaye*, I salute). **-śīla**, mfn. one who habitually salutes, respectful.

Abhi-vādanīya, mfn. deserving respectful salutation, MBh. iii, 10035; (said of the name) used for the salutation, ĀśvGṛ.; Gobh.

Abhi-vādayitṛi, mfn. saluting respectfully, Comm. on Mn. ii, 123.

Abhi-vādita, mfn. saluted respectfully.

Abhi-vādin, mfn. telling, enunciating, describing, Nir.; (*ī*), m. an explainer, interpreter, MaitrUp.

Abhi-vādya, mfn. to be respectfully saluted, MBh. &c.

अभिवध् *abhi-√vadh* (aor. *-avadhīt*) to strike, MBh.; R.

अभिवन् *abhi-√van* (impf. 3. pl. *-avanvan*) to long for, desire, RV. i, 51, 2.

Abhi-vānyā̀ [TBr.] or **abhivānya-vatsā** [AitBr.] (or **apivānya-vatsā** [Kauś.]), f. a cow who suckles an adopted calf; (cf. also *ni-vānyā̀*, &c.)

अभिवन्द् *abhi-√vand*, Ā. (rarely P.) to salute respectfully, MBh. &c.

Abhi-vandaka, mfn. having the intention to salute, Jain.

Abhi-vandana, *am*, n. saluting respectfully, MBh. &c.

अभिवप् *abhi-√2. vap* (impf. 3. pl. *-vapánta*; Ved. ind. p. *-úpyā*) to scatter over, cover with (instr.), RV. ii, 15, 9 & vii, 56, 3.

अभिवम् *abhi-√vam*, to spit upon, TS.; ŚBr.

अभिवयस् *abhí-vayas*, mfn. very youthful, fresh, RV. x, 160, 1.

अभिवर्णन *abhi-varṇana*, *am*, n. description, Kathās.

Abhi-varṇita, mfn. described, MBh.; Suśr.

अभिवल्ग् *abhi-√valg*, to jump towards, MBh. vi, 3265; (said of boiling water) to bubble up, AV. xii, 3, 29.

अभिवश् *abhi-√vaś*, *-vashṭi* (perf. Ā. *-vāvaśe*, p. 1. *-vāvaśānā́*, RV. i, 164, 28; for 2. *-vāvaśānā́* see *abhi-√vāś*), P. to rule or be master over (acc.), RV. ii, 25, 3: P. Ā. to long for, desire, RV.

अभिवस् 1. *abhi-√4. vas*, *-vaste*, to wrap one's self up in (acc.), Kauś.: Caus. (impf. *-ávāsayat*) to clothe, cover, RV.; TS. &c.

Abhi-vāsa, *as*, m. covering, Nyāyam.

Abhi-vāsana, *am*, n. id., Comm. on TS. & on Nyāyam.

Abhi-vā́sas, ind. over the garment, ŚBr.; (*as*), n. (scil. *aṅgirasām*) 'the cover of the Aṅgiras,' N. of a Sāman.

Abhi-vā́sya, mfn. to be covered, TBr.

अभिवस् 2. *abhi-√5. vas*. See *abhy-ushita*.

अभिवह् *abhi-√vah* (3. pl. *-váhanti*; Pot. 3. pl. *-vaheyuḥ*; aor. Subj. 2. sg. *-vakshi*, 3. du. *-voḷhā́m* [RV. viii, 32, 29 & 93, 24]) to convey or carry near to or towards, RV.; ŚBr.; AitBr.: Caus. *-vāhayati* (incorrectly for *ati-v°*), to pass (time), Rājat.

Abhi-vahana, *am*, n. carrying near to, Nir.

Abhivāha-tás, ind. in consequence of the flowing towards, TS.

Abhi-vāhya, *am*, n. conveyance, transmission, Mn. i, 94.

Abhi-voḍhri, *ḍhā*, m. one who conveys towards, Car.

Abhy-ū̆ḍhi, *is*, f. conveying towards, TBr.

अभिवा *abhi-√2. vā* (perf. *-vavau*, ŚBr.) to blow upon or towards, RV. vii, 35, 4 & x, 169, 1; ŚBr. &c.

Abhi-vātám, ind. windwards, ŚBr.

अभिवाञ्छ् *abhi-√vāñch*, to long for, desire, MBh. &c.: Caus. id., MBh. xii, 2907.

Abhi-vāñchā, f. longing for, desire (ifc.), Kathās.

Abhi-vāñchita, *am*, n. wish, desire, R. &c.

अभिवात *abhi-vāta*, mf(*ā*)n. (√*vai*), ill, sick, Lāṭy.

अभिवान्या *abhi-vānyā̀*. See *abhi-√van*.

अभिवाश् *abhi-√vāś* (aor. 3. pl. *-avāvaśanta*; perf. 3. pl. *-vavāśire* or *-vāvaśre*, p. 2. *-vāvaśānā́* [RV. x, 123, 3; cf. *abhi-√vaś*]) to low (as a cow) or roar towards, RV.; Nir.

Abhi-vāśat, mfn. lowing (as a cow) or roaring towards, MBh.; VarBṛS.

Abhi-vāsin. See *bastâbhivāsin*.

अभिविक्रम *abhi-vikrama*, mfn endowed with great courage, R.

अभिविक्षिप् *abhi-vi-√kship*, to flap one's wings over, ĀpŚr.

Abhi-vi-kshepa, *as*, m. flapping one's wings over, Comm. on ĀpŚr.

अभिविख्या *abhi-vi-√khyā*, to look at, view, VS.; Gobh.

Abhi-vikhyāta, mfn. universally known, renowned, known as, called, MBh. &c.

अभिविचक्ष् *abhi-vi-√caksh*, *-cashṭe*, to look towards, RV. iii, 55, 9; AV. ii, 10, 4.

अभिविचर् *abhi-vi-√car*, Ā. (Subj. 3. pl. *-caranta*) to go near to (acc.), RV. iii, 4, 5: Caus. *-cārayati*, to consider, reflect upon, Nir.

अभिविज् *abhi-√vij* (aor. Subj. Ā. *-vikta*) to tip over (a vessel), RV. i, 162, 15.

Abhi-vegá, *as*, m. tottering, vacillation, RV. x, 27, 1.

अभिविजंह् *abhi-vi-√jaṇh*, Intens. *-jáṅgahe* (Ved. 3. sg.) to struggle, move in convulsions, AV. v, 19, 4.

अभिविज्ञा *abhi-vi-√jñā* (impf. 1. pl. *-ajanīmas!*) to be aware of, perceive, AitBr.

Abhi-vijñapta, mfn. notified, made known.

Abhi-vi-jñāya, ind. p. being aware of, perceiving, MBh. &c.

अभिविज्वल् *abhi-vi-√jval*, to flame or blaze against or opposite to, Bhag.

अभिवितन् *abhi-vi-√tan* (Imper. 2. sg. *-tanu*) to stretch (the string) over or across (the bow), AV. i, 1, 3: P. Ā. (3. pl. *-tanvanti*, *-tanvate*) to stretch over, cover, ŚBr.; ŚāṅkhŚr.

अभिविद् 1. *abhi-√1. vid*, Caus. *-vedayati*, to report, relate, R. (v. l.)

अभिविद् 2. *abhi-√3. vid*, to find, obtain, ŚBr.: Ā. (3. pl. *-vindate*) to know, MBh. iii, 13698.

अभिविदीपित *abhi-vi-dīpita*, mfn. entirely inflamed, MBh. xiv, 2033.

अभिविदृश् *abhi-vi-√dṛiś*, Caus. *-darśayati*, to show to (gen.), ĀpŚr.

अभिविद्युत् *abhi-vi-√1. dyut* (aor. *-dyaut*) to break open, open by force, RV. iv, 4, 6.

अभिविद्रुत *abhi-vi-druta*, mfn. (√*2. dru*), run towards, MBh. vi, 1776; run away, fled, MBh. vi, 4614.

अभिविधा *abhi-vi-√dhā*, to bring near to or in contact with (acc.), ŚBr.

Abhi-vidhi, *is*, m. complete comprehension or inclusion, Pāṇ. ii, 1, 13; (*au*), loc. ind. inclusively, Pāṇ. iii, 3, 44 & v, 4, 53.

Abhi-vi-hita, mfn. covered entirely, Lāṭy.

अभिविधाव् *abhi-vi-√1. dhāv*, to run near to, RV. x, 29, 3.

अभिविनद् *abhi-vi-√nad*, to raise a loud noise, R.

अभिविनीत *abhi-vinīta*, mfn. well disciplined, well educated, versed in (loc.), R. &c.

अभिविनुद् *abhi-vi-√nud*, Caus. *-nodayati*, to gladden, cause to rejoice, MBh. xii, 898.

अभिविपण्यु *abhi-vi-paṇyu*, mfn. (= *aihikâmushmika-karma-rahita*) absolutely indifferent, BhP.

अभिविपश् *abhi-vi-√paś*, *-páśyati*, to look at, view, RV.; ŚBr.; Nir.; to look hither, RV. iii, 23, 2.

अभिविबुध् *abhi-vi-√budh*, *-budhyate*, to notice, learn from.

अभिविभज् *abhi-vi-√bhaj*, Ā. to distribute, Suśr.

अभिविभा *abhi-vi-√bhā*, *-bhāti*, to illuminate, RV. vii, 5, 2; AV. xiii, 2, 42.

अभिविमन्थ् *abhi-vi-√manth* (Opt. *-mathnīyāt*) to grind, triturate, ŚBr.

अभिविमान *abhi-vimāna*, mfn. endowed with the faculty called *abhimāna* ('self-reference'), ChUp.

अभिविमृज् *abhi-vi-√mṛij* (ind. p. *-mṛijya*) to rub in, rub with, Kauś.

अभिविया *abhi-vi-√yā*, *-yāti*, to approach, visit, RV. i, 48, 7.

अभिविराज् *abhi-vi-√rāj* (= *vi-√rāj*, 'to govern'), Nir.; to shine, be radiant, MBh. &c.

Abhi-virājita, mfn. quite bright or brilliant, MBh.

अभिविरुच् *abhi-vi-√ruc*, Ā. (impf. *-arocata*) to shine or be brilliant over, MBh. vi, 1669 (v. l. *ati-vi-√ruc*).

अभिविली *abhi-vi-√lī*, Caus. (ind. p. *-lāpya*) to cause to melt, Suśr.

अभिविवस् *abhi-vi-√2. vas* (Pot. *-ucchet*) to shine forth during or at the time of (acc.), ĀśvŚr.; PBr.; (Ā. *-uccheta*) ŚāṅkhŚr.

अभिविवृद्धि *abhi-vi-vṛiddhi*, *is*, f. increased prosperity, VarBṛS.

अभिविश् *abhi-√viś*, Caus., perf. Pass. p. *-veśita*, 'caused to enter upon,' directed towards, BhP.

Abhi-vishṭa, mfn. 'entered by,' seized by, being in the power of (in comp.), R.

अभिविशंस् *abhi-vi-√śaṇs*, *-śáṇsati*, to divide (verses) in reciting, TS.; (cf. *vi-√śaṇs*.)

अभिविशङ्किन् *abhi-vi-śaṅkin*, mfn. afraid of (abl.)

अभिविशॄ *abhi-vi-√śṝ*, Pass. (impf. *-aśīryata*) to be torn to pieces, MBh. vii, 4378.

अभिविश्रुत *abhi-viśruta*, mfn. widely celebrated, MBh. &c.

अभिविश्वस् *abhi-vi-√śvas*, Caus. *-śvāsayati*, to render confident, MBh. iii, 10021; Suśr.

अभिविषञ्ज् *abhi-vi-shañj* (√*sañj*), Pass. *-shajjate*, to be entirely devoted to, have one's heart set upon (loc.), BhP.

अभिविष्ठा *abhi-vi-shṭhā* (√*sthā*), Ā. (2. sg. *-tishṭhase*, perf. 3. sg. *-tasthe*) to extend one's self towards or over, RV. v, 8, 7 & vi, 21, 7.

अभिविष्यन्द् *abhi-vi-shyand* (√*syand*), Caus. to pour water upon, moisten, Kauś.

अभिविसृज् *abhi-vi-√sṛij*, Ā. (impf. 3. pl. *-asṛijanta*) to throw or shout towards (acc.), Kāṭh.; to assume from (abl.), KaushUp.

अभिविहृ *abhi-vi-√hṛi* (Pot. 3. pl. *-hareyuḥ*) to divide, ĀśvŚr.

अभिवी *abhi-ví* (√*i*), (3. pl. *abhí ví yanti*) to come towards from different parts, RV. vi, 9, 5.

अभिवीक्ष् *abhi-vīksh* (√*īksh*), Ā. *-vīkshate* (rarely P., e. g. impf. *-vyaikshat*, AitUp.) to look at, view, perceive, MBh.; Mn. &c.; to examine, Suśr.; to look upon as (nom.), behave as (nom.) with regard to (acc.), MBh. xv, 379; to be affected towards.

Abhi-vīkshita, mfn. seen, perceived.

Abhi-vīkshya, ind. p. having seen or observed.

अभिवीज् *abhi-√vīj*, Caus. to fan, MBh. xii, 6347, &c.

अभिवीत *abhí-vīta*, mf(*ā*)n. (√*1. vī*), desired, RV. vii, 27, 4; driven, impelled by (in comp.), ŚBr.

अभिवीर *abhí-vīra*, mfn. surrounded by heroes, RV. x, 103, 5.

अभिवृ 1. *abhi-√1. vṛi*, Caus. *-vārayati*, to keep off, fend off, MBh.

1. **Abhi-vṛita**, mfn. surrounded by, R. vi, 92, 83.

Abhí-vṛita, mfn. surrounded by, bordered by, RV.; (said of a cow) covered by (the bull), RV. i, 164, 29.

अभिवृ 2. *abhi-√2. vṛi*, *-vṛiṇīte*, to choose, prefer, Kāṭh.; (perf. 3. pl. *-vavrire*) to select, MBh. xii, 4861.

2. **Abhi-vṛita**, mfn. chosen, selected, MBh. v, 5971.

अभिवृत् *abhi-√vṛit*, to go towards, approach, ŚBr. &c.; to attack, RV. v, 31, 5; (ind. p. *-vṛitya*) x, 174, 2, &c.; to be victorious (perf. *-vāvṛité*), RV. x, 174, 1; to turn up, arise, R. &c.; to take place, happen, exist, MBh. &c.: Caus. P. (aor. *-avīvṛitat*) to conquer, RV. x, 174, 3; AV.; 'to render victorious in,' place over (dat.), RV. x, 174, 1; to drive over (with a cart), RV. ii, 34, 9.

Abhi-vartá, *as*, m. (= *abhī-v°*) N. of a Sāman, TS.

Abhi-vartin, mfn. coming towards, approaching, Hariv.; going towards (in comp.), R.

Abhí-vṛitti, *is*, f. coming towards, TBr.

Abhī-vartá, mfn. rendering victorious, RV. x, 174, 1 & 3; (*ás*), m. victorious attack, victory, VS.; N. of different Sāmans (especially of the hymn RV. x, 174) supposed to render victorious, ĀśvGṛ.; Lāṭy.

Abhī-vṛit, mfn. 'approaching' (Sāy.), RV. i, 35, 4; the form (acc. m. *abhī́-vṛitam*) is however better derived fr. *abhī́-vṛita* by BR. & Gmn.

अभिवृध् *abhi-√vṛidh*, to grow higher than (acc.), surpass, RV.; AV. (i, 29, 1, perf. *-vāvṛidhé* for *-vāvṛité*, cf. RV. i, 174, 1), &c.; to grow up, grow or increase more and more, MBh. &c.; to prosper, Mn. &c.: Caus. P. (aor. *-avīvṛidhat*) to increase, strengthen, render prosperous, AV. i, 29, 1 & 3 (for *abhi-√vṛit*, cf. RV. x, 174, 1 & 3); MBh. &c.

Abhi-vṛiddha, mfn. increased, augmented.

Abhi-vṛiddhi, *is*, f. growth, increase, VarBṛS.; Suśr.; increase, prosperity, MBh.; Mn. vii, 109.

अभिवृष् *abhi-√vṛish*, P. (aor. *-ávarshīt*) to rain upon, RV. vii, 103, 3; AV. &c.: P. (sometimes Ā.) to bedew, cover with (instr.) a shower (as of arrows or blossoms, &c.), MBh. &c.; (said of gods) to cause to rain, VarBṛS. &c.

Abhi-varsha, *as*, m. rain, BhP.

Abhi-varshaṇa, *am*, n. raining upon, Kauś.; ĀśvŚr.; raining, R.; (cf. *kāmâbhivarshaṇa*.)

Abhi-varshin, mfn. raining, R.; BhP.

Abhí-vṛishṭa, mfn. rained upon, RV. vii, 103, 4, &c.; covered with (instr.); (said of clouds) having rained, MBh. vii, 8104; also (*am*), n. impers. it has been raining, VarBṛS.; (cf. *yathâbhivṛishṭam*.)

अभिवृह् *abhi-√vṛih*, Caus. (Imper. 2. sg. *-vṛiṅhaya*) to strengthen, encourage, MBh. vii, 2136.

अभिवेग *abhi-vegá*. See *abhi-√vij*.

अभिवेधिन् *abhi-vedhin*. See *abhi-√vyadh*.

अभिवेष्ट् *abhi-√vesht*, Caus. to cover with (instr.), Kathās. &c.

अभिव्यञ्ज् *abhi-vy-√añj*, Pass. *-vyajyate*, to be manifested, become manifest.

Abhi-vyakta, mfn. manifest, evident, distinct, Śāk.; Ragh. &c.; (*am*), ind. manifestly, Yājñ.; N.

Abhi-vyakti, *is*, f. manifestation, distinction, Pāṇ. viii, 1, 15; Sāh. &c.

Abhi-vyañjaka, mfn. revealing, manifesting, BhP.; Sāh.; indicative, showing.

Abhi-vyañjana, *am*, n. making manifest, L.

अभिव्यध् *abhi-√vyadh*, P. (rarely Ā., e.g. MBh. viii, 4591) to wound, TS. &c.

Abhi-viddha, mfn. wounded, MBh. iv, 1691.

Abhi-vedhin, mfn. (in geom.) cutting (as one line another).

Abhi-vyādhin, mfn. wounding, AV. i, 19, 1.

अभिव्यन् *abhi-vy-√an*, *-aniti*, to breathe through, to fill with breath, ŚBr.; (aor. *-ānīt*) to breathe upon, ŚBr.; Kāṭh.

अभिव्यादा *abhi-vy-ā-√1. dā* (impf. *-vyâdadāt*) to open one's mouth for swallowing (with acc.), ŚBr.; Kāṭh.

Abhi-vyādāna, *am*, n. 'swallowing,' i. e. suppressing (a vowel), RPrāt.

अभिव्याप् *abhi-vy-√āp* (ind. p. *-vyāpya*), (said of a rule) to extend to (acc.), have value unto (acc.), Pāṇ. ii, 1, 134, Sch.

Abhi-vyāpaka, mfn. (in Gr.) extending to (acc.; as a rule), including, comprehending.

Abhi-vyāpin, mfn. id.

Abhi-vyāpta, mfn. included, comprehended.

Abhi-vyāpti, *is*, f. inclusion, comprehension (= *abhi-vi-dhi*, q. v.), Pāṇ. vi, 4, 53, Sch.

1. **Abhi-vyāpya**, ind. p. up to a certain point, inclusive.

2. **Abhi-vyāpya**, mfn. to be included, Suśr.

अभिव्याहृ *abhi-vy-ā-√hṛi*, to utter, pronounce, TS. &c.; to speak or converse about (acc.), TS. &c.: Caus. to cause to pronounce, Kauś.; to pronounce, Mn. ii, 172.

Abhi-vyāharaṇa, *am*, n. = *abhi-vyāhāra*, Comm. on Nir.

Abhi-vyāhāra, *as*, m. pronunciation. utterance, ChUp. &c.; an articulate significant word or phrase, Nir.

Abhi-vyāhārin, mfn. (ifc. e. g. *kokilâbhivyāhārin*) speaking like (a cuckoo), Pāṇ. vi, 2, 80, Sch.

Abhi-vyāhṛita, mfn. pronounced, spoken; addressed, ŚBr.; (*am*), n. what has been said, AitUp.; what is being said, Pāṇ. iii, 2, 188, Comm.

Abhi-vyāhṛitya, mfn. to be said, AitBr.

अभिव्युक्ष् *abhi-vy-√1. uksh* (Opt. *-ukshet*) to sprinkle towards (acc.), ŚBr.

अभिव्युदस् *abhi-vy-ud-√2. as*, to give up or abandon entirely, BhP.

अभिव्ये *abhi-√vye* (Imper. 2. sg. Ā. *-vyayasva*) to wrap one's self into (acc.), RV. iii, 53, 19.

अभिव्रज् *abhi-√vraj* (p. *-vrájat*) to go up to (acc.), RV.; (ind. p. *-vrajya*) to pass through, Kauś.; to go to (acc.), BhP.

अभिव्लङ्ग *abhi-vlaṅgá*, *as*, m. turning off, shaking off, RV. i, 133, 4.

अभिव्ली *abhi-√vlī* (impf. *-avlīyata*) to sink down, fall down, PBr.

अभिशंस् *abhi-√śaṇs*, to accuse, blame, calumniate, TS. &c.; (2. sg. *-śaṇsasi*; ind. p. *-śasya*) to praise, R. ii, 11, 16 & 23, 8.

Abhi-śaṇsaka, mfn. accusing, L.; insulting, L.

Abhi-śaṇsana, *am*, n. accusation; insult (with gen.), Mn. viii, 268; 'accusation,' ifc. e. g. *anṛitâbhiśaṇsana* [Gaut.] or *mithyâbhiśaṇsana* [Yājñ. ii, 289] a false accusation.

Abhi-śaṇsin. See *mithyâbhiśaṇsin*.

Abhi-śás (only instr. *-śásā*), f. accusation, imprecation, RV. x, 164, 3.

Abhi-śasta, mfn. accused, blamed, calumniated; defamed, infamous, MBh. &c.; threatened, Mn. xi, 112; see also s. v.

Abhi-śastaka, mfn. accused, defamed, Yājñ.; caused by imprecation (as a disease), Suśr.

Abhí-śasti, *is*, f. curse, imprecation, damnation, RV.; AV.; effect of imprecation, misfortune, evil, RV.; VS.; one who curses or injures, RV.; AV.; blame, ŚBr.; 'accusation' (ifc.; see *mithyâbhiśasti*); calumny, defamation, L.; asking, begging, L. **-kṛit**, mfn. accusing, ĀpŚr. **-cā́tana**, mfn. keeping off imprecation, RV. iii, 3, 6. **-pā́**, mfn. defending from imprecations, RV.; VS.; AV. **-pā́van**, mfn. id., RV.; VS.

Abhi-śastenya, &c. See *án-abhiśasta*.

अभिशङ्क् *abhi-√śaṅk*, Ā. (rarely P., e.g. aor. Subj. 2. sg. *-śaṅkīḥ*, MBh. v, 5000: but Ā. *-śaṅkithāḥ*, MBh. iii, 1166) to doubt, suspect (with acc.; rarely with gen., e.g. Mn. viii, 96), have doubts about (acc.; rarely gen., e.g. MBh. v, 6078).

Abhi-śaṅkā, f. suspicion (with gen.), R.; apprehension, fear, Kathās.

Abhi-śaṅkita, mfn. having doubts; suspecting; being alarmed, being in solicitude (v. l. *ati-śaṅkita*), Hariv.; Bhaṭṭ.; (*am*), ind. (*an-*, neg.) without fear or shyness, MarkP.

Abhi-śaṅkin, mfn. doubting, suspecting, MBh.

Abhi-śaṅkya, mfn. suspicious, MBh. iii, 1167; (*an-*, neg.) MBh. ii, 190.

अभिशप् *abhi-√śap*, P. to curse, MBh. &c.: Caus. (ind. p. *-śāpya*) to conjure, implore with solemnity, Yājñ. ii, 108.

Abhi-śapana, *am*, n. false accusation, calumny, L.

Abhi-śapta, mfn. cursed, accursed, calumniated, reviled, defamed, MBh.; Hariv. &c. [often v. l. *abhi-śasta*]; (cf. *mithyâbhiśapta*.)

Abhi-śāpa, *as*, m. curse, Nir. &c.; charge, accusation, Yājñ. ii, 12 & 99 (cf. *abhī-śāpa* & *mithyâbhiśāpa*); false accusation, calumny, L. **-jvara**, m. fever caused by a curse; (cf. *abhi-śastaka* at end.)

Abhi-śāpana, *am*, n. pronouncing a curse, L.

Abhī-śāpa, *as*, m. charge, accusation, Yājñ. ii, 110.

अभिशब्दय *abhi-śabdaya*, Nom. P. (pr. p. *°yat*) to name, call, ĀśvŚr.: Pass. *-śabdyate*, to be called, MārkP.

Abhi-śabdita, mfn. announced, mentioned, Mn. vi, 82; named, MBh.; Suśr.

अभिशम् *abhi-√śam*, *-śāmyati*, to be calmed, cease, MBh. xii, 6020.

अभिशस्त *abhi-śasta*, mfn. perf. Pass. p. fr. *abhi-√śaṇs*, q. v., but sometimes (e. g. Comm. on MBh. v, 1277 & on Mn. xii, 112) derived fr. *abhi-√śas*, which does not occur.

अभिशास् *abhi-√śās*, *-śā́sati*, to assign, allot, RV. vi, 54, 2; to rule, govern, MBh. xiii, 4582.

Abhi-śāstṛi, mfn. one who assigns, allots, TBr.

अभिशिक्ष् *abhi-√śiksh*, Caus. to teach (with acc.), MBh. i, 8033; (with double acc.) Hariv. 4910.

अभिशी 1. *abhi-√1. śī*, to lie upon (acc.), ŚBr.

अभिशी 2. *abhi-√3. śī* (Imper. 3. sg. Ā. *-śīyatām*) to fall down upon, TBr.

अभिशीत *abhi-śīta* or *abhi-śyāta*, mfn. (√*śyai*), cold, chilly, Pāṇ. vi, 1, 26, Kāś.

Abhi-śīna or **abhi-śyāna**, mfn. coagulated, congealed, Pāṇ. vi, 1, 26.

अभिशुच् 1. *abhi-√1. śuc*, to mourn, MBh. xii, 11242.

अभिशुच् 2. *abhi-√2. śuc* (Imper. *-śocatu*; Subj. 2. sg. *-śocas*) to flame towards, burn, consume, RV.; VS.; KātyŚr.; to burn, torment, AV.; VS.; KātyŚr.: Caus. (aor. Subj. 3. pl. *-śūśucan*) to burn, consume (by fire), VS.; TS.: Intens. (p. *-śóśucāna*), id., RV. x, 87, 9 & 14.

Abhi-śoká, *as*, m. ardour, AV. i, 25, 3.

Abhi-śocá, mfn. shining, glowing with heat, AV. iv, 37, 10.

Abhi-śócana, *am*, n. a tormenting spirit or demon, AV. ii, 4, 2 & iv, 9, 5.

Abhi-śocayishṇú, mfn. causing heat or torments, AV. vi, 20, 3.

अभिशुन *abhí-śuna*, mfn. successful, having an advantage over (as one wrestler over another), TBr.

अभिशुभ् *abhi-√śubh*, Ā. (part. f. *-śúmbhamānā*) to adorn one's self with (acc.), RV. i, 92, 10; (3. pl. *-śobhante*) to be bright, Hariv.

Abhi-śobhita, mfn. adorned, looking bright or smart, Hariv.; Kathās.

अभिशौरि *abhi-śauri*, ind. towards Sauri (or Kṛishṇa).

अभिश्चुत् *abhi-√ścut*, Caus. P. (aor. *-acuścutat*) to sprinkle with, KātyŚr.; Kauś.: Ā. to scatter over one's self, cover one's self with (instr.), Kauś.

अभिश्नथ् *abhi-√śnath*, to pierce through, (Ved. Inf. [abl.] *-śnáthaḥ* [with *abibhet*, he was afraid] of being pierced through), RV. x, 138, 5; (Gmn., combining *abhi-śnáthaḥ* with *vájrāt*, takes *abhiśnáth* as an adj. 'piercing through, killing').

अभिश्यात *abhi-śyāta* and *-śyāna*. See *abhi-śīta* and *-śīna*.

अभिश्रि *abhi-√śri* (aor. *-aśrait*) to spread, extend (as brightness), AV. xiii, 2, 9; (perf. 3. pl. *-śiśriyuḥ*) to resort to, MBh. i, 8274.

1. **Abhi-śrī́**, mfn. (Ved. du. *-śriyā*) attached to each other, RV. i, 144, 6; AV. viii, 2, 14; arranging, putting in order (with acc.), TBr.; (*ī́s*), m. (or f., RV. x, 130, 5) one who arranges, puts or keeps in order, RV.

अभिश्रिष् *abhi-śrísh* (abl. *-śríshas*), f. a ligature, RV. viii, 1, 12.

अभिश्री 2. *abhi-√śri* (3. pl. *-śriṇanti*, p. *-śriṇát;* plusq. 3. pl. *-aśiśrayuḥ*) to mix, mingle, RV.; *-śriṇāti*, 'to prepare or dress,' produce, cause, TBr.; (by BR. placed under *abhi-√śri*.)

3. **Abhi-śrí**, nom. pl. *-śriyas*, f. anything added by mingling, RV. ix, 79, 5 & 86, 27.

अभिश्रु *abhi-√śru* (p. *-śriṇvat*) to hear, learn, Hariv. 4583; BhP.

Abhi-śravaṇa, *am*, n. repeating Vedic texts (while sitting down to a Śrāddha), L.

Abhi-śrāvá, *as*, m. hearing (a prayer), granting an answer, RV. i, 185, 10 & x, 12, 1.

Abhi-śrutá, mf(*ā*)n. renowned, AV. vi, 138, 1.

Abhi-śrutya, ind. p. hearing of, learning, MBh. i, 4427.

अभिश्वस् *abhi-√śvas* (p. *-śvasát;* Ved. Inf. (abl.) *-śvásas*) to blow towards or hither, RV. i, 140, 5 & 92, 8; (p. *-śvasat*) to whistle, R.; to groan, R.

Abhi-śvāsa, *as*, m. blowing (into a flame), KātyŚr.

अभिषच् 1. *abhi-shac* (√*sac*), Ā. *-sacate*, to turn to, be favourable to (acc.), RV.: P. *-sishakti*, to approach for revering, RV. vii, 67, 3.

2. **Abhi-shác**, m(acc. *-ācam*; n. pl. *-ācas*)fn. following, accompanying, RV. vi, 63, 9; AV. xviii, 4, 44; paying attention to, devoted to, favourable, RV.

अभिषञ्ज् *abhi-shañj* (√*sañj*), *-shajati* (Pāṇ. viii, 3, 65, Sch.) 'to be in close contact with,' have a claim to or lay claim to, MBh. iv, 95 (v. l. *abhi-√2. pat*); to put a slur upon (acc.), revile, curse.

Abhi-shakta, mfn. possessed by evil spirits, L.; humiliated, defeated, L.; reviled, cursed.

Abhi-shaṅga, *as*, m. (ifc. f. *ā*, Ragh. xiv, 77) propensity or inclination to, BhP.; the state of being possessed by evil spirits (cf. *bhūtâbhishaṅga*) or disturbed in mind, MBh.; humiliation, defeat, MBh.; Ragh.; Kum.; curse or imprecation, MBh.; false accusation, calumny, L. (cf. *mithyâbhishaṅga*); oath, L.; embracing, L. **-jvara**, m. a fever supposed to be caused by evil spirits.

Abhi-shaṅgin, mfn. humiliating, defeating, MBh. iv, 2108.

Abhī-shaṅga, *as*, m. curse or imprecation, L.

अभिषद् *abhi-shad* (√*sad*), *-sīdati*, to besiege, RV. ix, 7, 5; Ved. (impf.) *-ashīdat* or *-asīdat*, &c., Pāṇ. viii, 3, 119, in classical Sanskrit only forms with *sh* are allowed, Pāṇ. viii, 3, 63 & 118.

Abhí-shaṇṇa, mfn. besieged, oppressed, TS.; Kāṭh.

अभिषव *abhi-shava*, &c. See *abhi-shu*.

अभिषह् *abhi-shah* (√*sah*), (perf. Subj. *-sāsahat*, Prec. 2. sg. *-sāsahīshṭhās*, p. P. *-sāhvás* & Ā. *-sehāná*) to overpower, conquer, RV.; (aor. Ā. 1. sg. *-asākshi*) to gain, win, RV. x, 159, 1; Kauś.; Nir.; to tolerate, allow, pardon, (Pass. *-sahyate*) Sāh.

Abhi-shaha, *as*, m. = *nigraha* (q. v.), L.

Abhi-shahya, ind. p. with √1. *kṛi*, 'to treat by force,' commit a rape, violate (a female), Mn. viii, 367.

Abhī-sháh, m(nom. *-shāṭ*)fn. overpowering, RV. vii, 4, 8; AV.; Nir.; (*-shāhā*), instr. ind. by force, ŚBr.

Abhī-shāha, *ās*, m. pl., N. of a people, MBh. viii, 127.

अभिषात *abhí-shāta*, mfn. gained, RV. v, 41, 14.

अभिषिच् *abhi-shic* (√*sic*), P., rarely Ā. (e. g. MBh. vii, 4593; Bhaṭṭ.) to sprinkle, water, wet, RV. i, 121, 6 (pr. p. *-siñcát*), &c.; to consecrate, anoint, appoint by consecration, AV. &c.: Ā. (Imper. 2. sg. *-shiñcasva*, sometimes v. l. Pass. *-shicyasva*) to consecrate one's self or have one's self consecrated, MBh.; Hariv.; R.: Ā. or Pass. to bathe, MBh. xii, 8894 & xiii, 1702: Caus. P. to water, wet: P. (rarely Ā.) to consecrate, anoint: Ā. (with or without [Nir.] *ātmānam*) to have one's self consecrated: Desid. *-shishikshati* & Intens. *-sesicyate*, Pāṇ., Sch. & Comm.

Abhi-shikta, mfn. sprinkled; anointed, installed, enthroned; (cf. *mūrdhâbhishikta*.)

Abhi-sheká, *as*, m. anointing, inaugurating or consecrating (by sprinkling water), inauguration of a king, royal unction; the water or liquid used at an inauguration, ŚBr. &c.; religious bathing, ablution, MBh. &c.; bathing of the divinity to whom worship is offered, L.; (cf. *mahâbhisheka* & *mūrdhâbhisheka*.) **-śālā**, f. the hall of coronation.

Abhishekârdra-śiras, mfn. wet on the head with the royal unction. **Abhishekâha**, m. day of inauguration.

Abhi-shektavya, mfn. to be consecrated or anointed, Kathās.

Abhi-shektṛi, *tā*, m. one who consecrates (by sprinkling), VS.; ŚBr.

Abhishekya, mfn. worthy of inauguration (*abhisheka*), Kauś.; KātyŚr.; (said of the elephant) used for the inauguration, Jain. (Prākrit *abhisekka*).

Abhi-shecana, *am*, n. sprinkling, MBh.; BhP.; initiation, inauguration, R. &c.

Abhi-shecanīya, mfn. worthy of inauguration, ŚBr.; belonging to inauguration (as vessels, &c.), ŚBr. &c.; (*as*), m., N. of a sacrificial ceremony performed at the inauguration of a king, ŚBr.; AitBr. &c.

Abhi-shecita, mfn. caused to be sprinkled, watered, wetted, Hariv.; inaugurated.

Abhi-shecya, mfn. to be anointed, R.

अभिषिध् *abhi-shidh*, *-shedhati*, Pāṇ. viii, 3, 65, Sch.: Caus. Desid. *-shishedhayishati*, ib., 64, Sch.

Abhi-shiddha, mf(*ā*)n. driven hither, AitBr.

अभिषिव् *abhi-shiv* (√*siv*), to sew round, ŚāṅkhŚr.

अभिषिषेणयिषु *abhi-shisheṇayishu*. See *abhi-sheṇá*.

अभिषु *abhi-shu* (√3. *su*), (3. pl. *-shuṇvánti;* ind. p. *-shútya*) to press out (with stones) the Soma juice (or any other juice), ŚBr. &c.; to press out with the help of any liquid, Mn. vi, 10 (Pass. 3. pl. *-shūyante*); Suśr.; (fut. p. *-soshyat*, cf. Pāṇ. viii, 3, 117) to moisten, Bhaṭṭ.: Caus. *-shāvayati*, Pāṇ. viii, 3, 65, Comm.

Abhi-shava, *as*, m. pressing out (the juice of the Soma plant), ĀśvŚr.; KātyŚr.; distillation, L.; religious bathing, ablution (preparatory to religious rites), L.; drinking Soma juice, sacrifice, L.; ferment, yeast, any substance producing vinous fermentation, L.; (*am*), n. sour gruel, VP.

Abhi-shavaṇa, *am*, n. pressing out (the juice of the Soma plant), Nir.; (*abhi-shávanīs*), Ved. nom. pl. f. the utensils used for pressing out (the Soma juice), AV. ix, 6, 1, 16; (cf. *adhi-shávana*.)

Abhi-shavaṇīya, mfn. to be expressed (as Soma juice).

Abhi-shāvaka, *as*, m. the priest (or any one) who expresses the Soma juice, L.

Abhí-shuta, mfn. expressed (as Soma juice), ŚBr. &c.; (*am*), n. (= *abhi-shava*, n.) sour gruel, L.

Abhi-shotṛi, *tā*, m. = *abhi-shāvaka*, ŚBr.; KātyŚr.

Abhi-sāvakīya, Nom. P. °*yati*, to long for a *sāvaka* (q. v.), Pāṇ. viii, 3, 65, Comm.

Abhi-susūsh, mfn. desirous of expressing Soma juice, Pāṇ. viii, 3, 117, Sch.

अभिषुक *abhi-shuka*, *as*, m., N. of a plant, Suśr.

अभिषू *abhi-shū* (√1. *sū*), *-shuvati*, to endow with (instr.), Kāṭh.; to consecrate for a purpose (acc.), ŚBr.; impf. *-ashuvat*, Pāṇ. viii, 3, 63: Desid. *-susūshati*, ib., 64, Comm.

अभिषूद् *abhi-shūd* (√*sūd*), Caus. to kill, destroy, R. i, 27, 19.

अभिषेण *abhi-sheṇá*, *as*, m. directing arrows against, RV. vi, 44, 17.

Abhi-shisheṇayishu, mfn. (fr. Desid.) desirous of marching against, Śiś. vi, 64.

Abhi-sheṇana, *am*, n. marching against (in comp.) with an army, Rājat.

Abhi-sheṇaya, Nom. P. *-sheṇayati* (impf. *-asheṇayat*, Pāṇ. viii, 3, 63), to assail with an army, to march with an army against (acc.), Veṇīs. &c.: Desid. *-shisheṇayishati*, Pāṇ. viii, 3, 64, Sch.

अभिषो *abhi-sho* (√*so*), (1. sg. *-shyāmi*) to fetter, chain, AV. iv, 16, 9; (pr. p. *-shyat*) to put an end to, destroy, Bhaṭṭ.; impf. *-ashyat*, Pāṇ. viii, 3, 63.

अभिष्टन् *abhi-shṭan* (√*stan*), (Imper. 2. sg. *-shṭana*) to thunder, AV. vi, 126, 2: Caus. id., TS.: Intens. (Imper. 2. sg. *-taṅstanīhi*) to roar, AV. v, 20, 1.

Abhi-shṭaná, *as*, m. roaring, hollow noise, RV. i, 80, 14.

अभिष्टम्भ् *abhi-shṭambh* (√*stambh*), *-shṭabhnoti* or *-shṭabhnāti*, impf. *-ashṭabhnāt*, perf. *-tashṭambha*, Pāṇ. viii, 3, 63 seqq.

अभिष्टव *abhi-shṭava*. See *abhi-shṭu*.

अभिष्टि *abhi-shṭí*, *is*, m. (*s-ti*, fr. √1. *as*, cf. 1. pl. *s-más*, &c.) an assistant, protector ['one who is superior or victorious,' NBD.], (generally said of Indra), RV.; VS.; (*abhi-shṭis*), f. assistance, protection, help, RV.; AV.; VS.; (cf. *sv-abhishṭi*.) **-kṛit**, mfn. procuring help, assisting, RV. **-dyumna** (*abhishṭí-*), mf(*ā*)n. 'whose glory is protecting or superior,' being of benevolent majesty, RV. iv, 51, 7. **-pā́**, m(nom. *-pā́*)fn. protecting with assistance, RV. ii, 20, 2; (the nom. *-pā́* being irregular for *-pā́ḥ*, Gmn. proposes the emendation [adopted by the NBD.] *abhishṭi* (Ved. instr.) *pāsi jánān* instead of *abhishṭipā́si jánān*). **-mát**, mfn. rendering assistance, RV. i, 116, 11. **-śavas** (*abhíshṭi-*), mfn. rendering powerful assistance, RV. iii, 59, 8.

अभिष्टु *abhi-shṭu* (√*stu*), *-shṭauti* (impf. *-ashṭaut*, Pāṇ. viii, 3, 63, or also *-astaut*, Pāṇ. viii, 3, 119, Kāś.; Subj. 1. pl. *-shṭavāma*, RV. viii, 100, 3; Imper. 2. sg. *-shṭuhi*, RV. i, 54, 2) to praise, extol, RV. &c.: Ā. (3. sg.) *-shṭuvate*, id., MBh. xii, 7715.

Abhi-shṭava, *as*, m. praise, eulogy, BhP.

Abhí-shṭuta, mfn. praised, RV.; AV. &c.; praised or addressed (with *oṇkāras*), consecrated, Yājñ. iii, 307.

Abhi-shṭuvat, mfn. pr. p. P. praising, Hariv.

Abhi-shṭuvāna, mfn. pr. p. Ā. praising, BhP.

Abhi-shṭūya, irreg. ind. p. praising, BhP. &c.

अभिष्टुभ् *abhi-shṭubh* (√*stubh*), *-shṭobhati* (impf. *-ashṭobhat*, Pāṇ. viii, 3, 63) to sing or recite in addition to, Lāṭy.

अभिष्ठा *abhi-shṭhā* (√*sthā*), *-tishṭhati* (aor. *-asthāt*, RV., *-ashṭhāt*, Pāṇ. viii, 3, 63; perf. p. *-tashṭhivás*, RV. iv, 4, 9) to tread or step upon (acc.), RV.; AV.; TS.; ŚBr.; to overpower, defeat, RV.; AV.; VS.; to extend or rise over (acc.), RV. i, 149, 4 & iii, 14, 4; to step or advance towards (acc.), PBr.; Kauś.; to stay, live, MBh. xii, 3316; to stop, ib., 4475.

Abhí-shṭhita, mfn. trampled upon, defeated, RV. x, 166, 2; AV.; stepped upon, serving as basis, ŚBr.

अभिष्ठिव् *abhi-√shṭhiv* (perf. *-tishṭheva*, perf. Pass. p. *-shṭhyūta*) to spit upon, ŚBr.

अभिष्णात *abhi-shṇāta*, *ās*, m. pl. (√*snā*), N. of a family, Hariv. 1466 (v. l. *abhi-glāna* and *ati-glāna*).

अभिष्यत् *abhi-shyat*, mfn. pr. p. fr. *abhi-sho*, q. v.; (*an*) or (*abhishyantas*, n. sg.), m., N. of a son of Kuru, MBh. i, 3740.

अभिष्यन्द् *abhi-shyand* (√*syand*), *-syandate* (or also *-shyandate*, if said intransitively of lifeless objects, Pāṇ. viii, 3, 72) to run towards or along (generally said of liquids), AV. v, 5, 9 (perf. *-sishyade*, said of a plant growing or running along the stem and branches of a tree), &c.

Abhi-shyanda or **-syanda**, *as*, m. oozing or flowing, L.; running at the eyes, Suśr.; great increase or enlargement, Ragh.; Kum. (Cf. *pittâbhishyanda*, *raktâbh*°, *vātâbh*°, *śleshmâbh*°.)

Abhi-shyandamāna, mfn. (said of a cloud) raining, Uttarar.

Abhi-shyandin or **-syandin**, mfn. oozing, trickling, Suśr.; laxative, Suśr.; causing defluxions or serious effusions, Suśr. **Abhishyandi-** or **abhisyandi-ramaṇa**, n. a smaller city appended to a larger one, suburb, L.

अभिष्वञ्ज् *abhi-shvañj* (√*svañj*), *-shvajate* (impf. *-ashvajata*, Pāṇ. viii, 3, 63; perf. *-shasvaje* or *-shasvañje*, ib., 118, Kāś.) to embrace, MBh. viii, 1652: (exceptionally) P. (Opt. *-shvajet*), id., MBh. xii, 8796.

Abhi-shvaṅga, *as*, m. intense attachment or affection to (loc. [MBh. &c.], rarely instr. [Kathās.]).

Abhi-shvaṅgin, mfn. intensely attached to or mad for, MaitrUp.

अभिसंयत्त *abhi-saṃ-yatta*, mfn. (√*yat*), being taken care of or governed by (v. l. *abhi-sampanna*), MBh. vii, 5173.

अभिसंया *abhi-saṃ-√yā*, *-yāti*, to visit, approach to (acc.), RV. ix, 86, 15; Kāṭh.; to approach in hostile manner, assail, MBh. viii, 1826.

अभिसंयुज् *abhi-saṃ-√yuj*, Caus. to bring in close contact with (instr.), Hariv.

Abhi-saṃyukta, mfn. furnished or endowed with, R.

Abhi-saṃyoga, *as*, m. (in Mīmāṅsā phil.) close contact or relation to.

अभिसंरक्त *abhi-saṃ-rakta*, mfn. (√*rañj*), intensely attached to (in comp.), R.

अभिसंरभ् *abhi-saṃ-√rabh*, Ā. (3. pl. *-rabhante*; Opt. 1. pl. *-rabhemahi*) to take hold of (for support), RV.

Abhi-saṃrabdha, mfn. excited, furious, MBh. &c.

Abhi-saṃrambha, *as*, m. fury, rage, MBh. xiv, 874.

अभिसंराधन *abhi-saṃ-rādhana*, *am*, n. pacifying, conciliating, BhP.

अभिसंवस् 1. *abhi-saṃ-√4. vas*, Ā. (pr. p. 1. *-vásāna*) to wrap one's self into (acc.), AV. xii, 3, 52.

अभिसंवस् 2. *abhi-saṃ-√5. vas*, Ā. (pr. p. 2. *-vásāna*) to settle round (acc.) together, TBr.; Lāṭy.

अभिसंवाञ्छ् *abhi-saṃ-√vāñch*, to long for, KenaUp.

अभिसंविद् 1. *abhi-saṃ-√1. vid* (perf. 3. pl. *-vidús*) to know thoroughly, AV. iii, 21, 5.

अभिसंविद् 2. *abhi-saṃ-√3. vid*, Ā. (pr. p. *-vidānā*) to meet each other [BR.], VS. xxix, 6 ('to relate, explain,' Comm.)

अभिसंविश् *abhi-saṃ-√viś*, P. Ā. (Imper. 2. pl. *-sáṃ-viśadhvam*) to meet round or near, surround, AV. &c.; to enter into, dissolve in, TUp.; NṛisUp.

अभिसंवीक्ष् *abhi-saṃ-vīksh* (√*īksh*), to look at in astonishment, gaze at, Kād.

अभिसंवृ *abhi-saṃ-√1. vṛi* (impf. *-vṛiṇot*) to cover, conceal, MBh. v, 7239.

Abhi-saṃvṛita, mfn. covered, concealed, MBh. &c.; surrounded by, accompanied by, ib.; filled with, furnished with, ib.

अभिसंवृत् *abhi-saṃ-√vṛit*, Ā. (Imper. *-vartatām*) to turn one's self towards, AV. vi, 102, 1.

Abhi-saṃvṛitta, mfn. undertaking, beginning to (Inf.), R.

अभिसंवृद्ध *abhi-saṃvṛiddha*, mfn. (said of a tree) 'having grown a very long time,' very old, MBh. xii, 5805.

अभिसंशीन *abhi-saṃśīna* or °*śyāna*, mfn. (√*śyai*), coagulated, congealed, Pāṇ. vi, 1, 26, Kāś.

अभिसंश्रि *abhi-saṃ-√śri*, P. to resort to (for refuge), have recourse to (acc.), ŚBr. &c.; to give way to, devote one's self to (acc.), MBh. xii, 518; to attain, (Pass. *-śrīyate*) MBh. xii, 10977.

Abhi-saṃśraya, *as*, m. refuge, R.; connection, MBh. i, 2398.

Abhi-saṃśrita, mfn. who has resorted to any one (for refuge), MBh. xii, 2766; (for a visit), MBh.

अभिसंश्रु *abhi-saṃ-√śru* (ind. p. *-śrutya*) to hear, learn, R.

अभिसंश्लिष् *abhi-saṃ-√ślish* (ind. p. *-ślishya*) to cling to each other, MBh. vi, 3127.

अभिसंसु *abhi-saṃ-√3. su* (3. du. *-sáṃ-sunutas*) to press out (Soma juice) together for the sake of (acc.), TBr.

अभिसंसृ *abhi-saṃ-√sṛi* (ind. p. *-sṛitya*) to run against or assail each other, BhP.

Abhi-saṃ-sāram, ind. running near in crowds, ŚBr.

Abhi-saṃ-sṛita, mfn. one who has come near, MBh. viii, 4417.

अभिसंस्कृ *abhi-saṃ-s-√1. kṛi*, *-s-karoti*, to shape, form, ŚBr.: Ā. (Subj. 1. sg. *-s-karávai*) to render or make one's self (*ātmānam*) anything (wished to be, acc.), ŚBr.

Abhi-saṃskāra, *as*, m. 'the being formed,' development (as of seeds), Car.; preparation, ib.; conception, idea, Buddh.

Abhi-saṃskṛita, mfn. consecrated, MBh.

अभिसंस्तम्भ् *abhi-saṃ-√stambh* (ind. p. *-stabhya*) to support, render firm, Kauś.; R.

अभिसंस्तीर्ण *abhi-saṃ-stīrṇa*, mfn. (√*stṛī*), entirely covered with, MBh. xii, 7613.

अभिसंस्तु *abhi-saṃ-√stu* (pr. p. *-stuvat*) to praise highly, MBh. xiii, 3695.

Abhi-saṃstava, *as*, m. praise, L.

Abhi-saṃstuta, mfn. highly praised, MBh.; BhP.

अभिसंस्था *abhi-saṃ-√sthā*, *-tishṭhate*, to stop at, finish at (acc.), ŚāṅkhŚr.: Caus. to cause to stop or finish at (acc.), ChUp.

Abhi-saṃstham, ind. in regular order, GopBr.

Abhi-saṃsthita, mfn. stopping or standing or watching at some place, MBh.; reflecting upon (loc.), MBh. iv, 553.

अभिसंस्पृश् *abhi-saṃ-√spṛiś*, to wash one's self, MBh. iii, 8080; to seize, ib. xii, 2140.

अभिसंस्मृ *abhi-saṃ-√smṛi*, to recollect (with acc.), MBh. iii, 15758.

अभिसंस्रु *abhi-saṃ-√sru*, to unite in flowing into (acc.), ŚBr.

अभिसंस्वञ्ज् *abhi-saṃ-√svañj*, Ā. (Imper. 2 sg. *-svajasva*) to embrace, AV. xii, 3, 12.

अभिसंस्वृ *abhi-saṃ-√svṛi* (impf. 3. pl. *-asvaran* [four times] or *-ásvaran* [once]) to praise or call or invite unanimously, RV.

अभिसंहन् *abhi-saṃ-√han* (ind. p. *-hatya*) to combine, confederate, MBh.

Abhi-saṃ-hata, mfn. attacked, assailed, BhP.

अभिसंहित *abhi-saṃ-hita*. See *-saṃ-√dhā*.

अभिसंक्रुध् *abhi-saṃ-√krudh* (pr. p. *-krudhyat*) to be angry with (acc.), Bhaṭṭ.

Abhi-saṃkruddha, mfn. angry with (acc.), MBh. iv, 1572; (gen.), ib. iii, 682.

अभिसंक्रुश् *abhi-saṃ-√kruś* (ind. p. *-kruśya*) to call out to, R.

अभिसंक्षिप् *abhi-saṃ-√kship* (ind. p. *-kshipya*) to compress, render quite small (the body by magical power), MBh. v, 283.

Abhi-saṃkshipta, mfn. one who has compressed his body so as to render it small, MBh. i, 5368.

Abhi-saṃkshepa, *as*, m. compressing, L.

अभिसंख्या 1. *abhi-saṃ-√khyā* (perf. Pass. p. *-khyāta*) to enumerate, R.

Abhi-saṃkhya, mfn. inferable, clearly ascertainable, Jaim.; 2. (*ā*), f. number, MBh. i, 617.

Abhi-saṃkhyeya, mfn. to be enumerated, R.

अभिसंगम् *abhi-saṃ-√gam* (ind. p. *-gátya*, AV. xi, 1, 16, or *-gamya*, R.; BhP.) to approach together, RV. ix, 14, 7 (aor. Ā. 3. pl. *-agmata*), &c.; to join in welcoming, BhP.; to meet with, R.

Abhi-saṃ-gata, mfn. together with (in comp.), BhP.

अभिसंगुप्त *abhi-saṃgupta*, mfn. guarded, protected, MBh. iii, 274.

अभिसंगृ *abhi-saṃ-√1. gṛi*, to promise, Kauś.

अभिसंग्रह् *abhi-saṃ-√grah*, to grasp at once with several fingers, Gobh.

अभिसच् *abhi-√sac*. See *abhi-shac*.

अभिसंचर् *abhi-saṃ-√car* (3. pl. *-cáranti*, pr. p. f. du. *-cárantī*) to go up to, seek for, RV.

Abhi-saṃcārin, mfn. 'moving in every direction,' inconstant, changeable, Nir.

अभिसंचि *abhi-saṃ-√1. ci*, Ā. *-cinute* (Opt. 1. sg. *-cinvīya*) to pile up (the sacrificial fire) for the benefit of (one's self, *ātmānam*), ŚBr.

अभिसंचिन्त् *abhi-saṃ-√cint* (ind. p. *-cintya*) to remember, MBh. vii, 5551.

अभिसंजात *abhi-saṃjāta*, mfn. (√*jan*), produced (as joy, *harsha*), Hariv.

अभिसंज्ञा *abhi-saṃ-√jñā* (3. pl. *-jānate*, Subj. *-jānāntai*, impf. *-ajānata*) to agree, allow, concede anything (dat.) to (acc.), MaitrS.; TS.; ŚBr.

Abhi-saṃjñita, mfn. (fr. 2. *saṃjñā*, cf. *saṃjñita*), called, named, MBh. &c.

अभिसंज्वर् *abhi-saṃ-√jvar*, to envy, regard with spite, MBh. v, 1615.

अभिसत्कृ *abhi-satkṛi* (√1. *kṛi*), (ind. p. *-kṛitya*) to honour, receive (a guest) with reverence, MBh. ii, 2549.

Abhi-satkṛita, mfn. honoured, received with reverence, MBh. &c.

अभिसत्वन् *abhí-satvan*, *ā*, m. surrounded by heroes, RV. x, 103, 5; (cf. *abhí-vīra*.)

अभिसंतन् *abhi-saṃ-√tan* (3. pl. *-tanvanti*) to use for bridging over or stretching across, TBr.; PBr.

Abhi-saṃtata, mfn. spread over, covered with (in comp.), Hariv. (v. l. *abhi-saṃ-vṛita*).

अभिसंतप् *abhi-saṃ-√tap* (Subj. *-tapāti*) to press hard on all sides, AV. ii, 12, 6.

Abhi-saṃtapta, mfn. tormented, MBh. &c.

अभिसंतॄ *abhi-saṃ-√tṛī*, to cross over towards (acc.), AitBr.

अभिसंत्यज् *abhi-saṃ-√tyaj* (ind. p. *-tyajya*) to abandon, give up, desist from (acc.), MBh.

अभिसंत्रस्त *abhi-saṃtrasta*, mfn. (√*tras*), terrified, much alarmed, R.

अभिसंदष्ट *abhi-saṃdashṭa* (*abhí sáṃdashṭa*), mfn. (√*daṃś*), compressed or tightened together, TS.

अभिसंदेह *abhi-saṃdeha*, *am*, n. organ of generation, (du. acc. °*he*) MBh. v, 7494 (v. l. *abhi-saṃdoha*).

अभिसंधम् *abhi-saṃ-√dham* (1. sg. *-dhamāmi*) to blow at, AV. viii, 2, 4.

अभिसंधा 1. *abhi-saṃ-√dhā* (3. du. *-dhattas*; Imper. 2. sg. *-dhehi*; aor. *-adhāt*) to snap at (acc.) for devouring, RV. x, 87, 3; AV.; ŚBr.; Kāṭh.; to take aim at (dat. or acc.), MBh. &c.; to aim at, have in view (with acc.; rarely dat.), ib.; to acknowledge unanimously, (perf. 3. pl. *-dadhuḥ*) RV. i, 101, 6; to overcome, master, Mn. &c.; to win (as by presents), R. iv, 54, 5; to ally, associate with (instr.)

Abhi-saṃ-hita, mfn. aimed at; agreed upon, R. v, 82, 5; acknowledged by (in comp.), MBh. xii, 4793; overcome; (ifc.) connected with, attached to, MBh. &c.

Abhi-sandhaka, mfn. ifc. deceiving ['calumniating,' Comm.], Mn. iv, 195.

2. **Abhi-saṃdhā**, f. 'speech, declaration' (only ifc., cf. *anṛitābhisandha* & *satyābhisandha*).

Abhi-saṃdhāna, *am*, n. the being allied or connected, connection between (in comp.), MBh. i, 3639; 'speech, deliberate declaration' (only ifc., cf. *satyābh*°); attachment or interest in any object; special agreement; overcoming, deceiving, Ragh. xvii, 76; making peace or alliance, L.

Abhi-saṃdhāya, ind. p. aiming at, having in view; coming to an agreement regarding (acc.), Mn. ix, 52; overcoming, Mālatīm. &c.; bringing in contact with (as an arrow with a bow), place upon (instr.), R. v, 36, 42.

Abhi-saṃdhi, *is*, m. speaking or declaring deliberately, purpose, intention, object, meaning; special agreement, Sāh.; cheating, deceiving; making peace or alliance, L.; joint, junction, L. **–kṛita**, mfn. done intentionally. **–pūrva**, mfn. that which has been intended, aimed at, Gaut. **–pūrvakam**, ind. with some intention, purposely, VP.

अभिसंनम् *abhi-saṃ-√nam* (Opt. *-namet*) to alter, modify, ĀśvŚr.; ŚāṅkhŚr.

अभिसंनह् *abhi-saṃ-√nah* (3. pl. *-nahyanti*) to bind or string together, Kauś.: Ā. (impf.

3. du. *-anahyetām*) to arm one's self against (acc.), TS.

Abhi-saṃ-naddha, mfn. armed, MBh. iii, 14883.

अभिसंनिविष्ट *abhi-saṃ-ni-vishṭa*, mfn. (√*viś*), being united or combined in, Comm. on BṛĀrUp.

अभिसंनी *abhi-saṃ-√nī*, to lead to or upon (loc.), MBh. xii, 6566.

अभिसंनु *abhi-saṃ-√4. nu*, Ā. (3. pl. *-navante*; aor. 3. pl. *-anūshata*) to rejoice or cheer together at or towards (acc.), RV.

अभिसप् *abhi-√sap* (3. pl. Ā. *-sápante*) to carry on, manage, RV. vii, 38, 5.

अभिसमय *abhi-samaya*. See *abhi-sam-√i*.

अभिसमवाय *abhi-samavāya*, *as*, m. (√*i*), union, association, L.

अभिसमस् *abhi-sam-√2. as*, to put together, group, collect, Car.

अभिसमागम् *abhi-sam-ā-√gam*, to approach together, Nir.; to come to (acc.), MBh. xi, 445.

अभिसमापद् *abhi-sam-ā-√pad*, Ā. (perf. *-pede*) to enter upon (acc.), R. ii, 12, 1.

अभिसमायम् *abhi-sam-ā-√yam*, *-yácchati*, to fasten to (acc.), TBr.

अभिसमाया *abhi-sam-ā-√yā*, to approach together, MBh. v, 1974.

अभिसमायुक्त *abhi-sam-ā-yukta*, mfn. connected or endowed with (instr.), MBh. xii, 3478.

अभिसमारुह् *abhi-sam-ā-√ruh* (impf. 3. pl. *-árohan*) to enter upon (the sacrificial fire-place) for a purpose (acc.), TBr.

अभिसमावृत् *abhi-sam-ā-√vṛit*, Ved. (3. pl. *-āvartante* & impf. *-āvartanta*; fut. p. *-vartsyamāna*) to return home, TBr. &c.

अभिसमासिच् *abhi-sam-ā-√sic*, to pour together, Kauś.

अभिसमाहित *abhi-sam-ā-hita*, mfn. (√*dhā*), fastened to, connected with (instr.), R.

अभिसमाहृ *abhi-sam-ā-√hṛi*, to scrape up or together, Kauś.

अभिसमि *abhi-sam-√i*, *-eti* (3. pl. *-yanti*, Imper. *-yantu*), Ved. to approach together, come together or meet at (acc.), RV. i, 125, 7; AV. &c.; (Opt. 3. pl. *-īyuḥ*) to invade, TS.

Abhi-samaya, *as*, m. agreement, Car.; clear understanding, Buddh.

अभिसमिन्ध् *abhi-sam-√indh*, to set on fire, kindle, PBr.

अभिसमीक्ष्य *abhi-sam-īkshya*, ind. p. (√*īksh*), seeing, viewing, R.; noticing, perceiving, learning from, RPrāt.; Suśr.; considering, with reference to, Suśr.; Car.

अभिसमीर् *abhi-sam-√īr*, Caus. (perf. Pass. p. *-īrita*) to put in motion, MBh. x, 579.

अभिसमुब्ज् *abhi-sam-√ubj*, to spread a covering upon (acc.), PBr.

अभिसमूह् *abhi-sam-√1. ūh*, *-ūhati*, to heap up, PBr.; to heap up and cover with (as with ashes, instr.), TS.; ŚBr.

अभिसमृ *abhi-sam-√ṛi*, Ā. (aor. Opt. *-arīta*) to reach, seize, RV. ix, 79, 3.

अभिसमे *abhi-sam-ê* (*-ā-√i*), Ved. (Imper. *abhí . . . . sam-âitu* [AV. vi, 102, 1] or *á . . . . abhí sám-etu* [RV. vi, 19, 9]) to join in coming near (acc.), approach together.

Abhi-sam-êta, mfn. assembled, ŚBr. xiv.

अभिसम्पच् *abhi-sam-√pac*, Pass. (3. pl. *-pacyante*) to become ripe up to a certain time (acc.), PBr.

अभिसम्पत् *abhi-sam-√pat* (p. *-patat*; perf. 3. pl. *-petuḥ*) to fly to, hasten to (acc.), MBh. vii, 7295, &c.

Abhi-sampāta, *as*, m. concourse, war, battle, L.

अभिसम्पद् 1. *abhi-sam-√pad*, Ved. *-padyate*, to become; to become similar to, be changed to (acc.), ŚBr. &c.; to come to, arrive at, obtain, ŚBr. xiv; Up.: Caus. *-pādayati*, to make equal to, change into (acc.), ŚBr.; AitBr.

Abhi-sampatti, *is*, f. becoming anything, becoming similar or equal to, KātyŚr.

2. **Abhi-sampád,** *t*, f. id., ŚBr.

Abhi-sámpanna, mfn. becoming similar to, being changed to (acc.), ŚBr.; RPrāt.; being in accordance with, agreeing with (instr.), Uttarar.

अभिसम्पराय *abhi-samparâya*, *as*, m. (√*i*), futurity, Lalit.

अभिसम्पू *abhi-sam-√pū*, *-pavate*, to blow along over or towards (acc.), TBr.

अभिसम्पूज् *abhi-sam-√pūj* (generally ind. p. *-pūjya*) to honour, revere greatly, MBh.; MārkP.

अभिसम्प्रपद् *abha-sam-pra-√pad*, *-padyate* (= *abhi-sam-√pad*) to be changed to, assume or obtain the shape of (acc.), Up.

अभिसम्प्रया *abhi-sam-pra-√yā* (ind. p. *-yāya*) to go towards, MBh. vi, 3762 (v. l. *abhi-vārayitvā*).

अभिसम्प्रवृत् *abhi-sam-pra-√vṛit*, Caus. to change (? as a battle-field, *raṇâjiràm*), MBh. i, 1184.

Abhi-sam-pravṛitta, mfn. having begun, VarBṛS.

अभिसम्प्राप् *abhi-sam-prâp* (√*āp*), to reach, come to, arrive at, obtain, L.

अभिसम्प्रेक्ष् *abhi-sam-prêksh* (√*īksh*), (ind. p. *-prêkshya*) to look at, perceive, MBh.; R.

अभिसम्प्लु *abhi-sam-√plu* (ind. p. *-plutya*) to bathe, MBh. xii, 365 (*an-* neg.)

Abhi-sam-pluta, mfn. poured upon, overflowed with, MBh. ix, 3279; deeply engaged in (in comp.), R.

अभिसम्बन्ध् *abhi-sam-√bandh*, *-badhnāti*, to refer to (acc.), mean by, Comm. on BṛĀrUp.: Pass. *-badhyate*, 'to be referred to,' belong to, require to be connected with (instr. [Pat.] or acc. [Pāṇ. ii, 1, 6 & 2, 11, Sch. &c.]).

Abhi-sambaddha, mfn. connected, (*an-* neg.) Suśr.

Abhi-sambandha, *as*, m. connection with, relation to (instr.), Jaim.; being connected with, belonging to, Sāh.; Pāṇ., Sch.; sexual connection, MBh. xiii, 2924; Mn. v, 63.

अभिसम्बाध *abhi-sambādha*, mfn. pressed together, crowded, R.

अभिसम्बुद्ध *abhi-sam-buddha*, mfn. deeply versed in, MBh. iii, 12515; having attained the Bodhi, Buddh.

Abhi-sam-bodhana, *am*, n. attaining the Bodhi, Buddh.

अभिसम्भग्न *abhi-sam-bhagna*, mfn. broken, crashed, MBh. viii, 2801.

अभिसम्भू *abhi-sam-√bhū*, Ved. (perf. 2. sg. *-babhūtha*) to reach, come to, arrive at, RV. x, 18, 8, &c.; to obtain the shape of (acc.), be changed into, ŚBr.: Caus. to salute, BhP.

अभिसम्भृत *abhi-sam-bhṛita*, mfn. endowed with (in comp.), MBh. xii, 12959 (v. l. *abhi-samvṛita*).

अभिसम्मत *abhi-sam-mata*, mfn. honoured, esteemed, MārkP. &c.

अभिसम्मुख *abhi-sam-mukhá*, mf(*ā*)n. looking respectfully towards (acc.), ŚBr.

अभिसम्मूढ *abhi-sam-mūḍha*, mfn. entirely confused, MBh. iii, 12219.

अभिसम्मूर्छ् *abhi-sam-√mūrch* (p. *-mūrchat*) to assume a solid form with regard to or in connection with (acc.), ŚBr.

अभिसर *abhi-sara*, &c. See *abhi-√sṛi*.

अभिसर्ग *abhi-sarga*, &c. See *abhi-√sṛij*.

अभिसर्पण *abhi-sarpaṇa*. See *abhi-√sṛip*.

अभिसान्त्व् *abhi-√sāntv* (p. *-sāntvayat*; ind. p. *-sāntvya*) to conciliate, pacify, comfort, MBh. iv, 383; R. ii, 32, 39; MārkP.

Abhi-sāntva, *as*, m. consolation, conciliation, R. v, 56, 44.

Abhi-sāntvita, mfn. conciliated, pacified, Kām.

अभिसायम् *abhi-sāyam*, ind. about evening, at sunset, ChUp.; (cf. *abhi-prātár*.)

अभिसार *abhi-sāra*, &c. See *abhi-√sṛi*.

अभिसावक *abhi-sāvaka*, &c. See *abhi-shu*.

अभिसिध् 1. *abhi-√1. sidh*, *-sedhati*, Pāṇ. viii, 3, 113, Sch.

अभिसिध् 2. *abhi-√3. sidh*, *-sidhyati*, to be accomplished, MBh. xii, 7427; to obtain, win (with acc.), ChUp.

Abhi-siddhi, *is*, f. the state of being effected or realized, AgP.

अभिसुसूष् *abhi-susūsh*. See *abhi-shu*.

अभिसूचित *abhi-sūcita*, mfn. pointed out, MBh. iii, 2939.

अभिसृ *abhi-√sṛi* (3. pl. impf. *-asaran*, perf. *-sasrur*) to flow towards (acc.), RV. i, 52, 5 & ix, 82, 3; to approach, go towards, advance in order to meet, attack, MBh. &c.; to go to a rendezvous (said of lovers), Sāh.: Caus. to lead towards, Kathās.; to cause to attack, lead to battle, MBh. iii, 665 (v. l.); to invite to a rendezvous, Sāh.; to approach, visit, MBh. i, 1221; Mṛicch.

Abhi-sara, *as*, m. (ifc. f. *ā*) a companion, Daś.

Abhi-saraṇa, *am*, n. meeting, rendezvous (of lovers), Sāh. &c.

Abhi-sartṛi, mfn. attacking, assailant, VS. xxx, 14.

Abhi-sāra, *as*, m. attack, assault, R.; meeting, rendezvous (of lovers), Sāh.; Gīt. &c.; 'pay for coming,' messenger's pay, Buddh.; companion, L.; a purificatory rite, L.; (*eṇa*), instr. (with *sarveṇa*) = *sarvâbhisāreṇa*, q. v., MBh. iii, 639; (cf. *lohâbhisāra* & *abhīsāra*); (*ās*), m. pl., N. of a people, MBh. &c.; (*ī*), f., N. of a town, MBh. ii, 1027. **–sthāna,** n. a place of rendezvous (of lovers), Sāh.

Abhi-sārikā, f. a woman who goes to meet her lover or keeps an assignation, Kum. vi, 43; Ragh. xvi, 12, &c.

Abhi-sārin, mfn. going to meet, Vikr.; (*iṇī*), f. = *abhi-sārikā*, L.; N. of a species of the Trishṭubh metre (as that in RV. x, 23, 5, in which two Pādas contain twelve instead of eleven syllables, and which therefore is said to *approach* another metre called Jagatī), RPrāt.

Abhi-sisārayishu, mfn. intending to go to a rendezvous or to visit (a lover), Śiś. x, 20.

Abhi-sṛita, mfn. gone near (acc.), MBh. vii, 4449; Gīt.; one who has approached (for attacking), MBh.; directed towards (in comp.), VarBṛS.; visited by (instr.), Kathās.

Abhi-sṛitya, ind. p. having gone near (acc.)

Abhi-sāra, *as*, m. assault, MBh. vii, 8785.

अभिसृज् *abhi-√sṛij* (impf. *-asṛijat*; aor. Pass. *-ásarji* [RV. ix, 106, 12] & 3. pl. *-asṛigran* [RV. ix, 88, 6] or *-asṛikshata* [RV. i, 135, 6 & ix, 63, 25]) to pour into or upon (acc.), pour out for a purpose (acc.) or for the sake of (acc.), RV.; AV.; AitBr.; to let loose in a special direction, ŚBr.; AitBr.; (aor. Subj. 2. sg. *-srās* for *-srāksh-s*) to throw upon, AV. xi, 2, 19; to surrender, give, grant, allow, permit, R. &c.; to assail, attack, ŚBr. xiv.

Abhi-sarga, *as*, m. creation, MBh. xii, 13801.

Abhi-sarjana, *am*, n. for *ati-s°* (q. v.), L.

Abhi-sṛishṭa, mfn. 'let loose in a special direction,' running towards (acc. or loc.), RV.; allowed to, R.; uttered, Hariv.; surrendered, given, granted, R. &c.

अभिसृप् *abhi-sṛip* (Imper. 2. sg. *-sarpa*) to approach silently or softly, AV.; Kāṭh.; Nir.

Abhi-sarpaṇa, *am*, n. approaching; the ascent (of sap in the trees).

अभिसेवन *abhi-sevana*, *am*, n. practising, cultivating, Suśr.

अभिस्कन्द् *abhi-√skand* (perf. *-caskanda*) to ascend, AV vii, 115, 2.

Abhi-skándam, ind. running near, AV. v, 14, 11.

अभिस्कम्भ् *abhi-√skambh,* Caus. (p. *-skabhāyat*), Pāṇ. iii, 1, 84, Comm.

अभिस्तृ *abhi-√stṛi,* to scatter over, cover, TBr.; Suśr.

अभिस्थिरम् *abhi-sthirám,* ind. very firmly, intensely, ŚBr.

अभिस्निग्ध *abhi-snigdha.* See *an-abhisn°.*

Abhi-sneha, *as,* m. affection, desire, BhP.

अभिस्पृश् *abhi-spṛiś* (Opt. *-spṛiśet*) to touch, MBh. i, 2931; to influence, affect, Suśr.

अभिस्फुरित *abhi-sphurita,* mfn. expanded to the full (as a blossom).

अभिस्फूर्ज् *abhi-√sphūrj, -sphūrjati,* to sound towards, AV. xii, 5, 20.

अभिस्मि *abhi-√smi* (p. *-smayat*) to smile upon, MBh. iii, 8732.

अभिस्यन्द् *abhi-√syand.* See *abhi-shyand.*

अभिस्रंस् *abhi-√sraṇs;* aor. Subj. 2. sg. *-srās,* which is better derived fr. *abhi-√srij,* q. v.

अभिस्रु *abhi-√sru* (Imper. 3. pl. *-sravantu*) to cause to flow near, RV. x, 9, 4; (p. *-sravanta* for *-sravat*) MBh. xiii, 901.

अभिस्वयमातृण्णम् *abhi-svayamātṛiṇṇám,* ind. on the brick (used in sacrifices and called) *svayam-ātṛiṇṇā* (q. v.), ŚBr.

अभिस्वृ *abhi-√svṛi* (Imper. 2. sg. *-svara,* 3. pl. *-svarantu*) to join in praising or invoking, RV.; to keep a note (in singing) up to (acc.), PBr.

Abhi-svár (instr. *-svárā*), f. invocation, RV. ii, 21, 5 & viii, 97, 12; (*-svaré*), dat. ind. 'for calling into one's presence,' just behind (with gen.), RV. iii, 45, 2 & x, 117, 8; VS.

Abhi-svartṛi, *tā,* m. an invoker, RV. x, 78, 4.

अभिहन् *abhi-√han* (2. sg. Imper. *-jahi,* impf. *-hán* [RV. v, 29, 2] & perf. *-jaghantha*) to thump at, strike, kill, RV. &c.; to beat (as a drum, &c.), MBh. vi, 1535; Bhag. &c.; to afflict, visit with (instr.), MBh. xiii, 4375; MārkP.: Desid. *-jighāṇsati,* to intend to strike down, RV. vii, 59, 8.

Abhi-ghāta, abhi-ghātita. See s. v.

Abhí-hata, mfn. struck, smitten, killed, AV. xi, 10, 22, &c.; attacked, R.; beaten (as a drum, &c.), R.; VarBṛS.; afflicted, visited with, MBh. &c.; (in arithm.) multiplied.

Abhi-hati, *is,* f. striking (as of an arrow), Kād.; (in arithm.) multiplication; the product of multiplied numbers.

Abhi-hatya, ind. p. striking, killing, Mn. xi, 206, &c.

अभिहर *abhi-hara,* &c. See *abhi-√hṛi.*

अभिहर्य *abhi-√hary* (3. pl. *-háryanti;* Subj. Ā. *-haryata* [AV. iii, 30, 1]) to wish anything to be near, call it near, TS.; to like, love, RV. x, 112, 6; AV.; (*-haryati*) ŚBr. xiv (cf. *abhi-√hṛi,* Caus. Pass.)

अभिहव *abhi-hava.* See *abhi-√hu* & *√hve.*

अभिहस्य *abhi-hásya,* mfn. ridiculous, AV vi, 30, 2.

Abhi-hāsa, *as,* m. jest, joke, ĀśvŚr.

अभिहा *abhi-√2. hā* (ind. p. *-hāya*) to rush upon, seize hastily, Kāṭh.; AitBr.

अभिहिङ्कृ *abhi-hiṅkṛi* (√1. *kṛi*), Ved. (3. pl. *-hiṅ-kurvanti*) to make a sound towards, low or roar or neigh towards, Kāṭh.; PBr. &c.

Abhi-hiṅkāra, *as,* m. the sound *hiṅ* (used) in addition to (a certain *japa* formula), ĀśvŚr.

अभिहित *abhí-hita,* mfn. (√*dhā*), harnessed or put to (as a horse), RV.; AV.; ŚBr.; named, called, Mn. iii, 141, &c.; held forth, said, declared, spoken, MBh.; Mn. &c.; spoken to, Kum. &c.; (*as*), m., N. of a chief, L.; (*am*), n. a name, expression, word. **–tā,** f. [Sarvad.] or **-tva,** n. the having been said or stated or named; a holding forth, declaration, L.; authority, test, L.

Abhi-hiti, *is,* f. telling, manifesting, title, L.

अभिहु *abhi-√hu,* to make an oblation upon (acc.) or for the sake of (acc.), shed or pour over (acc.), ŚBr. &c.

1. **Abhi-hava,** *as,* m. pouring the oblation upon.

Abhi-havana, *am,* n. id., ĀśvŚr.

Abhí-huta, mfn. poured upon with an oblation, shed or poured over, AV. vi, 133, 2; AitBr.; ŚBr. &c.

Abhí-hotavai, Ved. Inf. to pour upon (an oblation), MaitrS.

Abhi-homa, *as,* m. = 1. *abhi-hava,* Vait.

अभिहूति *abhi-hūti.* See *abhi-√hve.*

अभिहृ *abhi-√hṛi,* to bring, offer, ŚBr. &c.; to pull off, tear off, MBh. iii, 14610: Caus. *-hārayati,* to have brought to by, send by, Hariv.; to bring, offer, MBh. iv, 2364; to put on (as a cuirass), ib. iv, 1011 seqq.; to assail, attack, MBh.: Pass. *-hāryate* incorrectly for *-haryati* (see *abhi-√hary*), BṛĀrUp.

Abhi-hara, mfn. (ifc.) carrying off, removing, L.

Abhi-haraṇa, *am,* n. bringing or conveying near, MBh.; Ragh.

Abhi-haraṇīya, mfn. to be brought near.

Abhi-hartavya, mfn. id.

Abhi-hartṛi, *tā,* m. one who carries off, takes by violence (ifc.), MBh. iii, 15761.

Abhi-hāra, *as,* m. bringing near, Pat. (cf. *ābhi-hārika*); robbing, seizing anything (in the owner's presence), MBh. xiii, 3047; brisk attack, L.; effort, L.; arming, taking up arms, L.; mingling together, Car. &c.

Abhi-hārya, mfn. = *abhi-haraṇīya.*

अभिहृष् *abhi-√hṛish,* Caus. (p. *-harshayat*) to gladden, MBh. vi, 1833; xii, 1894.

अभिहेष् *abhi-√hesh* (p. dat. m. *-heshate*) to neigh towards, AitBr.; MBh. viii, 4471.

अभिह्रुत् *abhi-hrút,* mfn. (√*hvṛi*), causing a fall or damage, injurious, RV. i, 189, 6; AV. vi, 4, 2; f. (abl. *-hrútas*) fall, damage, injury, RV. i, 128, 5 & x, 63, 11.

Abhí-hruti, *is,* f. fall, damage, injury, RV. i, 166, 8; AV. vi, 3, 3.

Abhi-hvārá, *as,* m. a crooked or damaging way or place, AV. vi, 76, 3.

अभिह्वे *abhi-√hve,* to call near, ŚBr.

2. **Abhi-hava,** *as,* m. calling near, Pāṇ. iii, 3, 72.

Abhi-hūti, *is,* f. calling near (as the gods to the sacrifice), Nir.

अभी 1. *a-bhī,* mfn. fearless, R.; Ragh. **–pada** (v. l. *-pāda*), m. 'whose foot or step is without fear,' N. of a Ṛishi, VBr.

1. **A-bhīka,** mfn. fearless, L.

A-bhīta, mf(*ā*)n. id., R. **–vat,** ind. fearlessly, MBh. xii, 3730; R. &c.

1. **A-bhīti,** *is,* f. fearlessness, L.

Á-bhīru, m(acc. °*rvam,* 4; nom. pl. °*ravas*)fn. fearless, RV.; Mn. vii, 190; not terrific (nom. pl. f. °*ravas*), RV. viii, 46, 7; (*us*), m., N. of a prince, MBh. i, 2689; N. of Bhairava or Śiva; (*us*) [L.] or (*ū*) [Suśr.], f. the plant Asparagus Racemosus. **–pattrī,** f. the above plant Asp. Rac.

A-bhīruka, mfn. fearless, MBh. vii, 2522.

A-bhīruṇa [AV. vii, 89, 3] or *a-bhīrūṇa* [VS.], mfn. not terrific.

अभी 2. *abhí* (√*i*), *abhy-èti* (Imper. 2. sg. *abhīhi;* impf. 3. pl. *-āyan,* 3. sg. Ā. *-āyata;* ind. p. *abhītya*) to come near, approach, go up to or towards (acc.), RV. &c.; (with *sakāśam* or *samīpam* or *pārśve*) id., Pañcat.; to go along or after (acc.), RV. &c.; to enter, join, go over to, Mn.; Bhaṭṭ.; (with a pr. p.) to begin to, (perf. 3. pl. *abhīyuḥ*) ŚBr.; to reach, obtain, RV. &c.; to get or fall into (acc.), MBh. &c.; to come to, fall to one's share (with acc.), Bhaṭṭ.; (said of the sun) to rise (as if he came nearer; also with *abhitarām* [q. v.] instead of *abhi*), AitBr., (with *astam*) to set, MBh. i, 1797 (cf. *abhy-aya*): Pass. *abhīyate,* to be perceived, known, BhP.: Intens. (1. pl. *-īmahe*) to ask, request, RV. i, 24, 3.

2. **Abhī́ti,** *is,* f. assault, RV. ii, 33, 3 & vii, 21, 9.

Abhī́tvan, mf(*varī*)n. attacking, VS.; AitBr.

Abhy-aya, *as,* m. approaching (as of darkness), KātyŚr.; setting (of the sun), ib.

Abhy-āyuka, mfn. coming up to (acc.), KapS.

अभीक 2. *abhīka,* mfn. (= *abhika,* q. v.), longing after, lustful, libidinous, Pāṇ. v, 2, 74; (*as*), m. a lover; a master, L.; a poet, L.

अभीक 3. *abhī́ka, am,* n. (fr. *abhi-añc;* cf. *ánūka*), meeting together, collision, RV. ix, 92, 5; (*e*), loc. ind. in the presence of (gen.), near, towards, RV.; (with √*muc* or √1. *as* with *āré*) away from, out of (abl.), RV.; (with verbs expressing defending from, as √3. *pā* & √*urushya*) from (with abl.), RV.; before (as before midday; with abl.), RV. iv, 28, 3.

अभीक्ष् *abhī́ksh* (√*īksh*), Ā. (impf. 3. du. *-aikshetām*) to look towards (acc.), RV. x, 121, 6.

अभीक्ष्ण *abhīkshṇa,* mfn. (contr. of *abhi-kshaṇa,* cf. Nir. ii, 25), constant, perpetual, L.; in comp. for *abhīkshṇam,* q. v.; (*am*), ind. repeatedly, again and again, perpetually, constantly; presently, at once; very, exceedingly (in comp. *abhīkshṇa-*), Rājat. **–śas,** ind. constantly, R.; Suśr.

अभीचार *abhī-cāra.* See *abhi-√car.*

अभीज्य *abhījya.* See *abhi-√yaj.*

अभीत *a-bhīta,* &c. See 1. *a-bhī.*

अभीन्ध् *abhī́ndh* (√*indh*), *abhī́ndhe* (for °*nddhe*) to surround with flames, inflame, AV. xi, 3, 18; ŚBr.

Abhī́ddha, mfn. inflamed, RV. i, 164, 26 & x, 190, 1; VS.

अभीप *abhī́pa,* m. or n. (fr. 2. *áp* with *abhi;* cf. *anūpá*), only in comp. with **-tás,** ind. from the waters or clouds [Gmn.], 'at the right time' [NBD. (fr. √*āp* with *abhi*)], RV. i, 164, 52.

अभीपद *abhī-pāda.* See 1. *a-bhī.*

अभीप्स् *abhīps* (Desid.), &c. See *abhy-√āp.*

अभीम *a-bhīma,* mfn. unterrific, causing no fear; (*as*), m., N. of Vishnu.

अभीमान *abhi-māna.* See *nir-abhimāna.*

Abhī-mānin. See *abhi-√man.*

अभीमोदमुद् *abhīmoda-múd* (or *abhī-moda-múd,* fr. irreg. Intens.), mfn. (√*mud*), excessively joyful, AV. xi, 7, 26 & 8, 24; (cf. *abhīlāpa-láp.*)

अभीर् *abhī́r* (√*īr*), Caus. (p. *-īrāyat*) to bring near, TBr.

Abhī́raṇī, f. a kind of serpent, L.

अभीर *abhīra* (incorrectly) for *ābhīra,* q. v.

अभीराजी *abhīrājī,* f., N. of a poisonous insect, Suśr.

अभीरु *á-bhīru,* &c. See 1. *a-bhī.*

अभीलापलप् *abhīlāpa-láp* (or *abhi-lāpaláp,* fr. irreg. Intens.), mfn. (√*lap*), excessively whimpering, AV. xi, 8, 25; (cf. *abhīmoda-múd.*)

अभीवर्ग *abhī-vargá, as,* m. (√*vṛij*), circuit, compass, AV. iii, 5, 2; vi, 54, 2 & xi, 2, 4.

अभीवर्त *abhī-vartá.* See *abhi-√vṛit.*

अभीवृत *abhī́-vṛita.* See 1. *abhi-√1. vṛi.*

अभीशाप *abhī-śāpa.* See *abhi-√śap.*

अभीशु *abhī́śu, us,* m. (fr. √1. *aś* with *abhi,* Nir. iii, 9), chiefly Ved. rein, bridle, RV. &c.; ray of light, Naigh.; (through incorrect interpretation of *dáśābhīśu,* q. v.) arm, finger, Naigh.; N. of a Ṛishi, VBr.

Abhīshu, *us,* m. (incorrectly for *abhīśu*) rein, bridle, MBh. vii, 8180; ray of light, Śiś. i, 22. **–mat,** mfn. 'having rays of light,' radiant, bright, Śiś. xvi, 50; (*ān*), m. the sun, Śiś. vi, 63.

अभीष् *abhī́sh* (√3. *ish*), *abhī́cchati* (Subj. *abhī́cchāt*) to seek for, long for (acc.), AV.; AitBr.; to intend to (Inf.), Kathās.

Abhī́shṭa, mfn. wished, desired, dear, TS. &c.; (*as*), m. a lover, Pañcat.; Sāh. (cf. *-tama* below); (*ā*), f. a mistress; betel, L.; (*am*), n. wish. **–tama,** mfn. (superl.) dearest, Pañcat.; (*as*), m. a dearest lover, Sāh. **–tā,** f. state of being desired. **–devatā,** f. beloved goddess, favourite deity (invoked in the last prayer before death), Pañcat. **–lābha,** m. or **-siddhi,** f. the gaining a desired object.

Abhishṭi, *is*, f. wish, PBr.

Abhy-eshaṇa, *am*, n. (only for the explan. of *abhishṭi*) approaching (either in a friendly or hostile manner), Sāy. on RV. vii, 19, 8 & i, 9, 1; desiring, wishing for, Sāy. on RV. i, 116, 11 & iv, 11, 4.

Abhy-eshaṇīya, mfn. (only for the explan. of *abhishṭi*) to be desired, Sāy. on RV. i, 119, 8.

अभीषङ्ग *abhī-shaṅga.* See *abhi-shañj.*

अभीषह् *abhī-sháh.* See *abhi-shah.*

अभीष्मद्रोण *a-bhīshma-droṇa*, mfn. without Bhīshma and Droṇa, Veṇis.

अभीसार *abhī-sāra.* See *abhi-√sṛi.*

अभुक्त *a-bhukta*, mfn. uneaten; unenjoyed, unused, unexpended; one who has not eaten, enjoyed or expended. **-pūrva**, mfn. what has not been enjoyed before, MBh. xii, 180, 32. **-vat**, mfn. one who has not eaten, MBh.; Suśr.

A-bhúj, mfn. one who has not experienced or enjoyed, RV. x, 95, 11.

A-bhujishya, *as, ā*, m. f. not liberal, stingy, ŚāṅkhŚr.; not a servant. **Abhujishyā-tva**, n. the state of a woman who lives independently, Mṛicch.; (cf. *a-bhaújishya.*)

A-bhuñjat, mfn. not being useful to, not liberal, stingy, RV. i, 120, 12 & viii, 1, 6; not eating.

A-bhuñjāna, mfn. not eating, fasting, R.; Gaut.

अभुग्न *a-bhugna*, mfn. not bent, straight; free from disease, well.

अभुज *a-bhuja*, mfn. armless, maimed.

अभुव *a-bhuva*, *am*, n. (√*bhū*), 'no real or common being,' a monster, MaitrS.; (cf. *a-bhva.*)

A-bhū, *ūs*, m. 'unborn,' N. of Vishṇu, L.

A-bhūta, mfn. whatever has not been or happened. **-tadbhāva**, m. the becoming or changing into anything which one has not been before, Pāṇ. iii, 1, 12, Comm. **-tva**, n. 'the state of not having existed or happened any time,' impossibility, Comm. on Kāvyād. **-dosha**, mfn. faultless. **-pūrva**, mfn. unprecedented, R. &c. **-prādurbhāva**, m. the becoming manifest of what has not been before. **-rajas**, *asas*, m. pl., N. of a class of deities (supposed to have existed in the fifth Manvantara), VP. **-śatru**, mfn. having no enemy. **Abhūtârtha**, *as*, m. anything unheard of or impossible, Sāh. (v. l.) **Abhūtâharaṇa**, *am*, n. relating anything which in fact has not happened, a wrong account (given for deceiving or puzzling anybody), Sāh.; Daśar. &c.

A-bhūti, *is*, f. non-existence, ŚBr. xiv; 'want of power,' wretchedness, AV.; VS.; mischief, calamity, MBh.

अभूमि *a-bhūmi*, *is*, f. non-earth, anything but earth, KātyŚr.; no proper place or receptacle or object for (gen.), Śāk. &c. **-ja**, mfn. produced in unfit or unsuitable ground, Suśr. **-sâhvaya**, m. 'named *a-bhūmi* (*bhūmi*=*dharā*, earth), i. e. *a-dhara*,' lip, Kāvyād.

अभूयःसंनिवृत्ति *a-bhūyaḥ-saṃnivṛitti*, *is*, f. no return any more, Ragh. x, 28.

A-bhūyishṭha, mfn. few, scanty.

A-bhūri, mfn. few, some.

अभूष *a-bhūsha*, mfn. unadorned, Bhaṭṭ.

A-bhūshita, mfn. id.

अभृत *a-bhṛita*, mfn. not receiving hire, not paid, Mn. viii, 231.

A-bhṛitaka, mfn. id., MBh. vii, 4463.

A-bhṛityâtman, mfn. 'not behaving as a servant,' disobedient towards (loc.), Kād.

अभृश *a-bhṛiśa*, mfn. not much, little, few.

अभेद *a-bheda*, *as*, m. non-fracture, compactness, closeness of array, RPrāt. &c.; absence of difference or distinction, identity; (mfn.) not different, identical, VP.

A-bhedaka, mfn. not dividing, not causing any distinction, Pat.

A-bhedin, mfn. not different, Sarvad.

A-bhedya, mfn. not to be divided or broken or pierced; indivisible; not to be betrayed (as a secret formula), BhP.; (*am*), n. a diamond, L. **-tā**, f. or **-tva**, n. [R.] indivisibility, impenetrability.

अभोक्तृ *a-bhoktṛi*, mfn. not enjoying, not using, abstemious.

A-bhoktavya, mfn. not to be enjoyed or used.

A-bhoga, *as*, m. non-enjoyment, Megh. &c.

Abhog-ghán, m(nom. pl. *-ghánas*)fn. (fr. *a-bhoj*=*á-bhuñjat*), killing the stingy, RV. i, 64, 3.

A-bhogya, mfn. not to be enjoyed, Megh. (v. l. for *a-bhoga*, q. v.); not to be enjoyed sexually, MBh. xiii, 4529.

A-bhojana, *am*, n. not eating, fasting, KātyŚr.; Mn. &c.; (*āni*), n. pl. id., Kathās.

A-bhojita, mfn. not fed, not feasted.

A-bhojin, mfn. not eating, fasting.

A-bhojya, mfn. uneatable, Hariv.; not to be eaten, prohibited as food, Gaut. &c.; one whose food is not allowed to be eaten, Mn. xi, 152. **A-bhojyânna**, mfn. one whose food is not allowed to be eaten, Mn. iv, 221.

A-bhaújishya, *am*, n. 'not the state of a servant,' independence, Suparṇ.; (cf. *a-bhujishya* s. v. *a-bhukta.*)

अभौतिक *a-bhautika*, mfn. not relating to or produced by the gross elements, not material, Comm. on Nyāyad. &c.

अभ्यग्नि *abhy-agni*, *is*, m., N. of a son of Etaśa or Aitaśa, AitBr.; KaushBr.; (*i*), ind. towards the fire, Pāṇ. ii, 1, 14, Sch.

अभ्यग्र *abhy-agra*, mf(*ā*)n. having the point turned or directed towards (acc.), ĀpŚr.; quick, KaushBr.; ŚāṅkhŚr.; constant, perpetual, Āp.; fresh (as blood), Bhaṭṭ.; near, L.; (*am*), n. proximity, L.

अभ्यघाय *abhy-aghāya*, Nom. P. *-aghāyáti*, to intend to injure, AV. vii, 70, 3.

अभ्यङ्क *abhy-aṅka*, mf(*ā*)n. recently marked (as cattle), Pāṇ. ii, 1, 14, Kāś.

अभ्यज् *abhy-aj* (√*aj*), (Imper. or Subj. 1. du. *-ájāva*) to combine, unite, RV. i, 179, 3.

अभ्यञ्ज् *abhy-√añj*, P. to smear, anoint, TS.; AitBr. &c.: Ā. to anoint one's self: Ā. (3. pl. *abhy áñjate*) to decorate, RV. ix, 86, 43: Ā. *-aṅkté*, to decorate one's self, TS. (quoted in Pāṇ. ii, 3, 62, Kāś.); (in Pass. sense; p. *-añjānd*) to be decorated, RV. ii, 8, 4.

Abhy-àkta, mfn. oiled, anointed, ŚBr.; Mn. iv, 44, &c.; decorated, AV. x, 1, 25.

Abhy-aṅga, *as*, m. rubbing with unctuous substances, inunction, Mn. ii, 178, &c.; unguent, Suśr. &c.

Abhy-añjaka, mfn. (ifc.) rubbing (the feet) with unctuous substances, Kathās.

Abhy-áñjana, *am*, n. rubbing with unctuous substances, inunction (especially of the feet, once [BhP.] said of the hairs), KātyŚr.; Mn. &c.; unguent (used for rubbing the feet; cf. *áñjana*), ŚBr. &c.; (5) ornament, embellishment, RV.

Abhy-añjanyà, mfn. whose feet are to be rubbed with unguents, TBr.

Abhy-añjya, mfn. to be rubbed with unguents (as a foot), Kathās.

अभ्यतिक्रम् *abhy-ati-√kram* (ind. p. *-kramya*; Inf. *-krāntum*) to step over, walk through, R.; to overpower, MBh. xiv, 1551; to transgress, violate, MBh. i, 199.

अभ्यतिक्षर् *abhy-ati-√kshar* (impf. *-aksharat*) to flow over to (acc.), TBr.; AitBr.

अभ्यतित *abhy-atita*, mfn. (√*at*), one who has walked towards (acc.), one who visits (used for the etym. of *atithi*), Nir.

अभ्यतिनी *abhy-ati-√nī*, to bring or place upon (loc.), Kauś.

अभ्यतिरिच् *abhy-ati-√ric*, Pass. *-áti-ricyate* or *-ati-ricyáte* (Subj. *abhy-áti-ricyātai*; Pot. *-áti-ricyeta*) Ved. to remain for the sake of (acc.), TS.; ŚBr. &c.

अभ्यतिवद् *abhy-ati-√vad*, P. (=*ati-√vad*, q. v.) 'to speak louder or better,' surpass in disputing, PBr.

अभ्यतिवृत् *abhy-ati-√vṛit*, *-vartate*, to drive past, MBh. vii, 1391 (v. l.)

अभ्यतिसृज् *abhy-ati-√sṛij* (1. pl. *-áti-sṛijāmas*) to let pass, AV. x, 5, 15=xvi, 1, 5.

अभ्यती *abhy-atí* (√*i*), (ind. p. *-atītya*) to pass over (acc.), R.; to get through towards (acc.), ŚBr.

Abhy-atīta, mfn. passed away (as time), MBh. iii, 12547; dead, Mn. iv, 252; MBh. vii, 1061.

अभ्यत्यृज् *abhy-aty-√ṛij*, to carry over or transfer upon (acc.), AitBr.

अभ्यधिक *abhy-adhika*, mf(*ā*)n. surpassing (in number, power, kind), R.; exceeding the common measure, pre-eminent, extraordinary, MBh. &c.; superior to, more excellent than, having more authority or power than, more than (abl. or instr. or in comp.), MBh. &c.; augmented by (abl. [VarBṛS.] or instr. or in comp.); (*am*), ind. exceedingly, MBh. xiii, 580, &c.

अभ्यध्वम् *abhy-adhvam*, ind. upon the way, KātyŚr.; (*é*), loc. ind. on the way, AV. iv, 28, 2.

अभ्यनुज्ञा 1. *abhy-anu-√jñā*, to assent to, approve, allow, permit, concede, MBh. &c.; to authorize, direct, MBh. ii, 1225; to allow one to depart, dismiss, MBh. &c.; (ind. p. *-jñāya*; Inf. *-jñātum*) to take leave, ask for leave to depart, MBh. xiv, 146; R.: Caus. (ind. p. *-jñāpya*; fut. p. *-jñāpayishyat*) to ask for leave to depart, MBh.

2. **Abhy-anujñā**, f. (ifc. f. *ā*) assent, approval, Ragh. ii, 69; Nyāyad.; authorization, permission, RPrāt.; ĀśvGṛ.; granting leave of absence, dismissing, R. &c.

Abhy-anujñāta, mfn. assented to, approved, Mn. ii, 1; authorized, allowed to, MBh. &c.; (*an-*, neg.) Mn. ii, 229; favoured by (instr.), R. iii, 36, 19; allowed to depart, dismissed, MBh. &c.

Abhy-anujñāna, *am*, n. assenting to, approval, Comm. on Nyāyad.; authorization, permission, R. i, 3, 14.

Abhy-anujñāpana, *am*, n. causing to assent to.

अभ्यनुप्रछ् *abhy-anu-√prach*, to inquire after, ask for, MBh. xii, 1933 & xiii, 2169.

अभ्यनुमुद् *abhy-anu-√mud*, Caus. (perf. Pass. p. *-modita*; p. necess. *-modanīya*) to assent to, approve of, MBh. i, 4447; Inscr.

अभ्यनुयुज् *abhy-anu-√yuj* (ind. p. *-yujya*) to apply to, ask, MBh. xii, 5667.

अभ्यनुवच् *abhy-anu-√vac* (perf. *-anûvāca*) to declare or state or utter with reference to (acc.), AitBr.: Pass. (3. pl. *-anûcyante*) to be referred to by some statement or verse, ŚBr.

Abhy-anûkta, mfn. stated or uttered with reference to (acc.), ŚBr.; AitBr.; ChUp.; (cf. *abhy-ukta.*)

अभ्यनुवद् *abhy-anu-√vad*, P. (=*abhy-anu-√vac*) to utter with reference to (acc.), ŚBr.

अभ्यनुशास् *abhy-anu-√śās* (Imper. 1. p. *-śāsāni*) to indicate, denote, ChUp.

अभ्यनुसृ *abhy-anu-√sṛi* (ind. p. *-sṛitya*, v. l. *-sṛijya*) to learn by investigating, Hariv. 1440.

अभ्यनुसृज् *abhy-anu-√sṛij* (ind. p. *-sṛijya*) id., ib.

अभ्यन्तर *abhy-antara*, mf(*ā*)n. interior, being inside of, included in (loc.; gen. or in comp. [cf. *gaṇâbhyantara*]), MBh. ii, 2282, &c.; initiated in, conversant with (loc.), R.; Megh.; next, nearly related, intimate, Pañcat.; (*am*), n. inner part, interior, inside, middle, Śāk. &c.; (generally loc.; ifc.) interval, space of time, Mṛicch.; Pañcat.; Hit.; (*am*), ind. (ifc.) into, Kathās. &c. **-kalā**, *ās*, f. pl. the secret arts or the arts of coquetry, Daś. **-tas**, ind. in the interior, inwards, Suśr. **-dosha-kṛit**, mfn. 'doing a wrong to one's own land,' raising a sedition or mutiny, VarBṛS. **Abhyantarâyāma**, m. curvature of the spine by spasm, emprosthonos, Suśr.; (cf. *bāhyâyāma.*)

Abhy-antaraka, *as*, m. an intimate friend, L.

Abhyantarī (for *abhyantara* in comp. with √1. *kṛi* and its derivatives). **-karaṇa**, n. initiating in (loc.), Daś. **-√1. kṛi**, to put between, insert, Pat. **-kṛita**, mfn. initiated in (loc.), R.; made intimate, Pañcat.

अभ्यपक्रम् *abhy-apa-√kram*, *-krāmati*, to go away towards (acc.), ŚBr.; (aor. Subj. 2. sg. *-ápakramīs*) to come up to, AV. xii, 2, 18.

अभ्यपश्रि *abhy-apa-√śri*, Ā. to retire towards (acc.), ShaḍvBr.

अभ्यपान् *abhy-apán* (√*an*), to breathe towards (acc.), AitBr.

अभ्यम् *abhy-√am, abhy-ámīti* (VS. [quoted in Pāṇ. vii, 2, 34, Sch.; cf. also ib. 3, 95, Sch.]; 2. sg. *-ámīshi*; 3. pl. Subj. *-amánti* & impf. Ā. *-ámanta*) to advance violently against, pain, hurt, RV. i, 189, 3; vii, 25, 2 & x, 86, 8; VS.

Abhy-amana, *am*, n. paining, oppression, Nir. **-vat**, mfn. paining, hurting, ib.

Abhy-amita or **abhy-ānta**, mfn. (perf. Pass. p.) diseased, sick, L.

Abhy-amitrīṇa [Bhaṭṭ.] or °*trīya* or °*trya* [Bhaṭṭ.], mfn. [apparently derivatives fr. *abhy-amitram* (see below s. v.), but probably originally derived from the rt., which is also indicated by the parallel form *abhy-amin* (see below)] advancing against or attacking (the enemy), Pāṇ. v, 2, 17.

Abhy-amitrīṇa-tā, f. a good opportunity to attack the enemy, Rājat.

Abhy-amin, mfn. attacking, Pāṇ. iii, 2, 157.

अभ्यमित्र *abhy-amitra* (basis of *abhy-amitram* & its derivatives °*trīṇa*, &c.), Pāṇ. v, 2, 17; (*am*), ind. against the enemy, Veṇīs.

Abhy-amitrīṇa, &c. See *abhy-√am*.

अभ्यय *abhy-aya*. See 2. *abhí*.

अभ्ययोध्यम् *abhy-ayodhyam*, ind. towards or against Ayodhyā, Bhaṭṭ.

अभ्यरि *abhy-ari*, ind. towards or against the enemy, L.

अभ्यर्कबिम्बम् *abhy-arkabimbam*, ind. towards the disk of the sun, Śāk.

अभ्यर्च् *abhy-√arc* (3. pl. *-arcanti* & impf. *-arcan* [RV. iv, 1, 14]; Imper. 2. sg. *-arca*, 2. pl. *-arcata*; Ā. 1. sg. *-arce* & aor. *-arcase* [RV. x, 64, 3]) to praise, celebrate in song (instr.), RV.; AV.; VS.; (ind. p. *-arcya*) to worship, reverence, MBh.; Mn. &c.

Abhy-arcana, *am*, n. worship, reverence, Mn. ii, 176, &c.

Abhy-arcanīya, mfn. = *abhy-arcya*.

Abhy-arcā, f. = *abhy-arcana* above, L.

Abhy-arcita, mfn. reverenced, MBh. ii, 1390, &c.; incorrectly for *abhy-arthita*, MBh. v, 1532.

Abhy-arcya, mfn. to be reverenced, VarBṛS. &c.

अभ्यर्ण *abhy-arṇa*, mfn. (fr. √*ṛi* or according to Pāṇ. vii, 2, 25 fr. √*ard*, in which case it should be written *abhy-arṇṇa*) near, proximate, Ragh. ii, 32, &c.; (*am*), n. proximity, Mālatīm. &c. **-tā**, f. proximity, Kād.

अभ्यर्त् *abhy-√art* (aor. Ā. 2. pl. *-artiḍhvam*) [NBD.] incorrectly for *abhy-√arth*, PBr.; cf. *anvart* (*anv-art*?).

अभ्यर्थ् *abhy-√arth*, Ā. (Opt. 2. sg. *-arthayethās*; rarely P., e.g. fut. *-arthayishyati*, Kathās.) to request, ask for (acc. or dat. or loc. or in comp. with *artham*), MBh. iii, 16990, &c.; (see also *abhy-√art*.)

Abhy-arthana, *am*, n. asking, requesting; generally (*ā*), f., id., Kum. i, 53, &c.

Abhy-arthanīya, mfn. to be requested or asked.

Abhy-arthita, mfn. asked, invited, Mn. ii, 189, &c.; (*am*), n. request, Yājñ. ii, 88; (cf. *yathābhyarthitam*.)

Abhy-arthin, mfn. (ifc.) asking, Kathās.

1. **Abhy-arthya**, mfn. = *abhy-arthanīya*.

2. **Abhy-arthya**, ind. p. asking, requesting, Kathās.

अभ्यर्द् *abhy-√ard*, to oppress, afflict, pain, R.: Caus. id., BhP.

Abhy-arṇṇa, mfn. (as *ni-shaṇṇa* fr. *ni-shad*). See *abhy-arṇa*.

Abhy-ardita, mfn. (fr. Caus.) distressed, oppressed, MBh. i, 4116; Pāṇ. vii, 2, 25, Sch.

अभ्यर्ध *abhy-ardhá*, *as*, m. only (*é*) loc. ind. opposite to, in the face of (abl.), ŚBr. **-yájvan** (6), mfn. (said of Pūshan) receiving sacrifices apart or separate ones, RV. vi, 50, 5.

Abhy-ardhás, ind. apart, separate from (abl.), MaitrS.; TS.

अभ्यर्ष् *abhy-√arsh* (Imper. 2. sg. *-arshā* (most frequently in RV.); p. *-árshat*) to flow or run near (acc.), RV.; to cause to flow near, afford, RV.; (aor. or plusq. *-ānarshat*) TĀr.

अभ्यर्हण *abhy-arhaṇa*, *am*, n. reverencing, honouring, BhP.

Abhy-arhaṇīya, mfn. to be greatly honoured, venerable. **-tā**, f. honourableness, Mn. ix, 23.

Abhy-arhita, mfn. greatly honoured, venerable, Kād.; (cf. Pāṇ. ii, 2, 34, Comm.); more honoured, Kād.; more important than (abl.); fit, proper, becoming, L.

अभ्यलंकृत *abhy-alaṃkṛita*, mfn. decorated, R. iii, 53, 36.

Abhy-alaṃkāra, *as*, m. (ifc. f. *ā*), decoration, MBh. iii, 16166.

अभ्यल्प *abhy-alpa*, mfn. very small, AitBr.

अभ्यव् *abhy-√av* (aor. *-āvīt*) to refresh, RV. ix, 97, 35.

अभ्यवकर्षण *abhy-avakarshaṇa*, *am*, n. (√*kṛish*), extraction, drawing out, L.

अभ्यवकाश *abhy-avakāśa*, *as*, m. (√*kāś*), an open space, Kauś.

अभ्यवकॄ *abhy-ava-√kṝi* (Pass. 3. pl. *-kīryante*) to throw or cast on, pour on, cover, R.; Lalit.

Abhy-ava-kīrṇa, mfn. covered, R.

अभ्यवक्रन्द् *abhy-ava-√krand*, to call out towards (acc.), Kāṭh.

अभ्यवगाह् *abhy-ava-√gāh*, Caus. to ride or walk (horses) into the ford, Comm. on TBr.

अभ्यवचर् *abhy-ava-√car* (Subj. 3. pl. *-cárān*) to approach, assail, ŚBr.: Caus. (Opt. *-cārayet*) to send away, MBh. xii, 3779.

अभ्यवज्वल् *abhy-ava-√jval*, Caus. *-jvālayate*, to enlighten, illumine, GopBr.

अभ्यवतन् *abhy-ava-√tan, -tanoti*, to send out or spread (as rays, instr.) towards (acc.), ŚBr.: Pass. (3. pl. *-tāyante*) to be sent out or spread (as rays) towards (acc.), ŚBr.

अभ्यवदा 1. *abhy-ava-√1. dā*, to place into (loc.), Car.

अभ्यवदा 2. *abhy-ava-√3. dā*, to cut off in addition to, ŚBr.

Abhy-ava-dānyà (or *-dā́nya*), mfn. depriving of (gen.), ŚBr. xiv.

अभ्यवदुग्ध *abhy-ava-dugdha*, mfn. that upon which milk has been milked, Kauś.

अभ्यवधा *abhy-ava-√dhā* (perf. Pass. p. *-hita*) to allay, lay (as dust), R. ii, 40, 33.

अभ्यवनम् *abhy-ava-√nam*, Caus. (ind. p. *-nāmya*) to bow, incline, MBh. iii, 10062.

अभ्यवनिज् *abhy-ava-√nij*, P. *-nenekti*, to wipe or wash, clean, Kauś.; (aor. Ā. 1. sg. *-nikshi*) AV. x, 5, 15: Caus. to cause to wash, Kauś.

अभ्यवनी *abhy-ava-√nī*, to lead down (into water), ŚBr.; AitBr.; (perf. *-ninā́ya*) to pour into or upon (acc.), AitBr.; PBr.

अभ्यवपत् *abhy-ava-√pat*, to fly near, AitBr.

अभ्यवमन् *abhy-ava-√man, -manyate*, to despise, reject, Mn. iv, 249.

अभ्यवरुह् *abhy-ava-√ruh*, to step down upon, ŚBr.; (perf. p. *-rūḍhavat*) R. v, 52, 15.

अभ्यववृत् *abhy-ava-√vṛit*, Ā. (Opt. 3. pl *-várteran*) to turn one's self away from (abl.), TBr.: Caus. P. to turn towards or to this side, ŚBr.

अभ्यवसृ *abhy-ava-√sṛi* (ind. p. *-sṛitya*) to retire from (abl.) towards (acc.), MBh. vii, 8479.

अभ्यवसृज् *abhy-ava-√sṛij* (1. p. *-sṛijāmi*) to dismiss towards (acc.), AV. xvi, 1, 6; to dismiss (as rays), MBh. xii, 3295; to throw, shoot (as arrows), MBh.; R.

अभ्यवस्कन्द् *abhy-ava-√skand* (ind. p. *-skandya*) to jump down or into, MBh.; to meet, encounter, MBh. iv, 1549.

Abhy-avaskanda, *as*, m. or °**dana**, *am*, n. impetuous assault, L.

अभ्यवस्थित *abhy-ava-sthita*, mfn. resisting (with acc.), BhP.

अभ्यवस्यन्द् *abhy-ava-√syand*, to drive (on a carriage) towards, ŚBr.

अभ्यवहृ *abhy-ava-√hṛi*, to throw down into water (acc.; *apáḥ* or *samudrám* or *hradám*), VS.; ŚBr.; ĀśvŚr.; (cf. *abhy-ava-√nī*); to bring near, ŚBr.; to take food, eat, Suśr.; Car. &c.: Caus. to cause to throw down (into water), Lāṭy.; to attack (as an enemy), MBh. iii, 16369; to take food, eat, MBh. iii, 15905; to cause to eat, Daś.

Abhy-avahárana, *am*, n. throwing away or down, ŚBr.; KātyŚr.; taking food, eating, Vishṇus.; Comm. on Yājñ.

Abhy-avahāra, *as*, m. taking food, Mn. vi, 59, &c.

Abhy-avahārin. See *satṛiṇābh°*.

Abhy-avahārya, mfn. eatable, R.; Pāṇ. Sch. & Comm.; (*am*), n. [Vikr.] or (*āṇi*), n. pl. [MBh.] food, eating.

अभ्यवास् *abhy-avā́s* (√2. *as*), (Opt. *-avā́syet*) to throw upon (acc.), Kauś.

अभ्यवे *abhy-avê* (√*i*), *-avaìti*, to go down, descend (into water, as in bathing), AitBr.; ŚBr.; KātyŚr.; (fut. 3. pl. *-avàishyanti*) to condescend, ŚBr.; (impf. 3. pl. *-avā̀yan*) to perceive, TS.

Abhy-avā̀yana, *am*, n. going down, ŚBr.

अभ्यवेक्ष् *abhy-avêksh* (√*īksh*), *-avêkshate*, to look at or upon, ŚBr.; MBh. ii, 2686.

अभ्यश् *abhy-√1. aś, -aśnoti* (frequently Opt. or Prec. 1. sg. *-aśyām*, 3. sg. *-aśyās* [RV. iv, 5, 7], 1. pl. *-aśyāma*; aor. P. *-ānaṭ* and Ā. *-āshṭa*; perf. 1. pl. *-ānaśma*, 3. pl. *-ānaśuḥ*) to pervade, reach to, gain, RV.; (Subj. 1. du. *-aśnávāva*, 1. pl. *-aśnávāma*) to overpower, RV.

Abhy-aśana, *am*, n. reaching to, gaining, Nir.

Abhy-āśa, *as*, m. (also written 1. **abhy-āsa**), reaching to, pervading, Yājñ. iii, 114; (with *yad* and Pot.) prospect, any expected result or consequence, ChUp.; proximity (with gen. or abl.), R. &c.; (mfn.) near, Kum. vi, 2; (*am*), ind. near, at hand, AitBr.; PBr.; (*e*), loc. ind. near (with gen. or abl.), R. &c.; (*āt*), abl. in comp. with (a perf. Pass. p., as) *āgata*, &c., arrived from near at hand, &c., Pāṇ. ii, 1, 39, Sch. & vi, 3, 2, Sch. **Abhyāśī-√bhū**, to come near to, Pat.

अभ्यस् 1. *abhy-√1. as, -ásti* (1. pl. *abhí shmas*, but 3. pl. *abhí sánti* and pr. p. *abhí sát* [according to Pāṇ. viii, 3, 87 *abhismas*, but *abhishanti* and *abhishat*]; Subj. *-asat*, 1. pl. *-ásāma*, 3. pl. *-ásan*; Pot. sg. *-shyām, -shyās, -shyāt*, 1. and 3. pl. *-shyāma, -shyuḥ* or *-shyuḥ*; perf. 1. sg. *-āsa*) to be over, reign over, excel, surpass, overpower, RV.; AV.; to fall to one's share, Pāṇ. i, 4, 91.

Abhi-shṭí. See s. v.

अभ्यस् 2. *abhy-√2. as* (ind. p. *-asya*) to throw towards or upon, ŚBr.; AitBr.; (p. gen. sg. *-asyatas*) to throw (as arrows), MBh. i, 5479; to add, Śulb.: P. (rarely Ā.) *-asyati* (but also Pot. *-aset*, Mn.; p. *-asat*, MBh. iii, 1450; R.; Yājñ. iii, 204: Ā. *-asate*, Mn. iv, 149) to concentrate one's attention upon (acc.), practise, exercise, study, MBh. &c.; to repeat, double; to multiply, Sūryas. &c.: Caus. to cause to practise or study, teach, Comm. on Śiś. ix, 79.

Abhy-asana, *am*, n. practice, exercise, R. &c.

Abhy-asanīya, mfn. to be practised, Kathās.; to be studied; to be repeated; (in Gr.) to be reduplicated.

Abhy-asitavya, mfn. to be practised, Comm. on Nyāyam.

Abhy-asta, mfn. accumulated by repeated practice (as food), Suśr.; practised, exercised, Mṛicch. &c.; learnt by heart, repeated, studied, Ragh. i, 8, &c.; multiplied, Nir.; Sūryas.; (in Gr.) reduplicated (as roots), Nir.; (*am*), n. the reduplicated base of a root, Pāṇ.

2. **Abhy-āsa**, *as*, m. the act of adding anything, Śulb.; (in Gr.) 'what is prefixed,' the first syllable of a reduplicated radical, Pāṇ.; reduplication, Nir.; repetition, Mn. xii, 74, &c.; (in poetry) repetition of the last verse of a stanza [Nir.] or of the last word of a chapter [Comm. on AitBr.]; (in arithm.) multiplication; repeated or permanent exercise, disci-

pline, use, habit, custom; repeated reading, study; military practice, L.; (in later Vedânta phil.) inculcation of a truth conveyed in sacred writings by means of repeating the same word or the same passage; (in Yoga phil.) the effort of the mind to remain in its unmodified condition of purity (sattva). **–tā**, f. constant practice, use, habit. **–nimitta**, n. the cause of the reduplication-syllable, Pāṇ. Comm. **–parivartin** (for *abhyāśa-*), mfn. wandering about or near, N. **–yoga**, m. the practice of frequent and repeated meditation on any deity or on abstract spirit, repeated recollection. **–vat**, m. (in Yoga phil.) 'being in the condition called *abhyāsa*,' i. e. a Yogin of the first degree. **–vyavâya**, m. interval caused by the reduplication-syllable, Pāṇ. Comm. **Abhyāsâkūpâra**, n. 'the sea of meditation,' N. of a verse of the SV.

Abhyāsin, mfn. (ifc.) practising, repeating, Gaut.; = *abhyāsa-vat*, q. v., Sarvad.

अभ्यसूय *abhy-asūya*, Nom. P. Ā. *-asūyati*, °*te*, to show indignation, be indignant at, MBh. &c.

Abhy-asūyaka, mfn. indignant, Bhag.

Abhy-asūyā, f. indignation, anger, Megh.; envy, jealousy, Kum. iii, 4; Ragh.

अभ्यस्तम् *abhy-ástam*, with √*i* [Pot. *-iyāt*, ŚBr.; AitBr.] or √1. *gā* [aor. *-agāt*, ŚBr.], (said of the sun) to set upon anybody (acc.) who is not working or while anything (acc.) is not done or performed; (cf. *abhi-ni-√mruc*.)

Abhy-astam-aya, *as*, m. See *anuddhṛitâbh*°.

Abhy-astam-ita, mfn. one on whom while not (working or) being asleep the sun has set, Gaut.

अभ्याकर्ष *abhy-ākarsha*, *as*, m. (√*kṛish*), a striking of the flat of the hand upon the breast in defiance (a practice common to wrestlers and pugilists), MBh. i, 7109.

अभ्याकाङ्क्षित *abhy-ākāṅkshita*, *am*, n. a groundless complaint, false accusation, L.

अभ्याकारम् *abhy-ā-kāram*, ind. (√1. *kṛi*), by or in drawing near to one's self, AitBr.; ŚBr. (Kāṇva Rec.)

अभ्याक्रामम् *abhy-ā-krā́mam*, ind. (√*kram*), by or in stepping towards repeatedly, AV. x, 7, 42.

अभ्याक्रुश् *abhy-ā-√kruś* (impf. 3. pl. *-âkrośan*) to assail with harsh language, revile, ŚāṅkhŚr.

अभ्याख्या *abhy-ā-√khyā* (Inf. *-khyātum* = *mithyâbhiyoktum*) to accuse falsely, Comm. on Kir. xiii, 58.

Abhy-ākhyāta, mfn. accused falsely, calumniated, Kauś.; TUp.

Abhy-ākhyāna, *am*, n. a false or groundless accusation, calumny, Buddh.; Jain.

अभ्यागम *abhy-ā-√gam* (fut. p. neg. *án-abhyāgamishyat*, ŚBr.) to come near to, approach, visit, ŚBr. &c.; (with *cintām*) to happen to think, R. iii, 4, 20.

Abhy-āgata, mfn. come, arrived, MBh. &c.; (with *kramāt*) inherited, Yājñ. ii, 119; (*as*), m. (opposed to *atithi*) an uninvited guest, BhP.; a guest in general, Hit. &c.

Abhy-āgama, *as*, m. approaching, arrival, visit, visitation, Ragh. &c.; arriving at or enjoying a result, Nyāyad.; neighbourhood, L.; rising (to receive a guest), L.; war, battle, L.; encountering, striking, killing, L.; enmity, L.

Abhy-ā-gamana, mfn. arrival, visit, R. i, 8, 24; Kir.; (cf. *kālâbh*°.)

अभ्यागा *abhy-ā-√1. gā* (aor. *abhy-ágāt*) to approach, come to (acc.), RV. i, 164, 27; MBh.; (gen.), BhP.; (said of evil) to visit, MBh. iii, 1120; to begin to (Inf.), Mn. x, 108.

अभ्यागारम् *abhy-ā-gāram*, ind. (√1. *gṛī*), so as to call or shout to each other (at the different steps of a dance), i. e. repeating separately, KaushBr. (see also *abhi-ni-nartam*); cf. *apa-gāram*.

अभ्यागारे *abhy-āgāre*, loc. ind. in the house, ĀśvGṛ.; v. l. *abhy-ācāre* [PārGṛ.] and *abhy-ācare* [MānGṛ.], 'in the reach or compass.'

Abhy-āgārika, mfn. diligent in supporting a family, L.

अभ्याघात *abhy-āghāta*, *as*, m. (√*han*), assault, attack, Mn. ix, 272; interruption, Comm. on PBr.

Abhy-āghātin, mfn. attacking, Pāṇ. iii, 2, 142.

Abhy-āghātya, mfn. recited with interruption, PBr.

अभ्याघारम् *abhy-ā-ghāram*. See *punar-abh*°.

अभ्याचक्ष् *abhy-ā-√caksh* (impf. *-âcashṭa*) to look at (acc.), BhP.; to speak, BhP.

अभ्याचर् *abhy-ā-√car* (pr. p. acc. pl. f. *abhy-ā-cárantīs*) to approach (with acc.), RV. viii, 96, 15; to undertake, practise, MBh. xii, 9719.

Abhy-ācare, loc. ind. See *abhy-āgāre*.

Abhy-ācārá, *as*, m. approaching (as an enemy), assault, AV. x, 3, 2; mishap, an accident, KaushBr.; (*e*), loc. ind. See *abhy-āgāre*.

अभ्याज् *abhy-áj* (√*aj*), (Imper. 2. sg. *-âja*) to drive near, Pāṇ. viii, 1, 8, Sch.

अभ्याज्ञाय *abhy-ā-jñāyá*, *as*, m. order, command, ŚBr.

अभ्यातन् *abhy-ā-√tan*, Ā. (impf. 3. pl. *-âtanvata*) to take aim at, shoot, TS.

Abhy-ātāná, *ā́s*, m. pl. 'aiming at,' N. of certain war-songs, TS.; Kauś. **–tvá**, n. the state of those war-songs, TS.

अभ्यातप् *abhy-ā-√tap* (3. pl. *-tapanti*) to torment, pain, RV. vii, 83, 5.

अभ्यातॄ *abhy-ā-√tṛī* (Imper. 2. sg. *-tara*) to come up to (acc.), RV. viii, 75, 15.

अभ्यात्मम् *abhy-ātmám*, ind., Ved. towards one's self, ŚBr. &c.

Abhyātma (in comp. for *abhyātmám*). **–taram**, ind. more towards one's self, ĀśvŚr. **Abhyātmâgra**, mfn. having the points turned towards one's self, ĀśvGṛ.

अभ्यादा *abhy-ā-√1. dā*, Ā. (rarely P., Hariv.) to seize, snatch away, (Pot. *-dadīta*) MBh. i, 3558 = xii, 10999 = xiii, 4985: Ā. to put on (as a wreath), Hariv.; (with *vākyam*) to take up the word, commence to speak, MBh. v, 3384.

Abhy-ā-tta, mfn. encompassing, ChUp.

Abhy-ādāna, *am*, n. beginning, Pāṇ. viii, 2, 87.

अभ्यादाव्य *abhy-ā-dāvyà*, *as*, m. (√2. *du*), N. of the non-sacrificial fire which in coming close to the sacrificial one blazes up together with it, MaitrS.

अभ्यादिश् *abhy-ā-√diś* (Intens. p. *-dédiśāna*) to aim at (in hostile manner), RV. vi, 44, 17.

अभ्याद्रु *abhy-ā-√2. dru* (perf. *-dudrāva*) to run towards (acc.), ŚBr.

अभ्याधा *abhy-ā-√dhā*, chiefly Ved. to lay on (fuel, &c.), VS., &c.; to place the fire upon, SBr. &c.

Abhy-ādhāna, *am*, n. laying on (fuel), ŚBr.; Kauś.

Abhy-ā́hita, mfn. laid on (as fuel), ŚBr.; ChUp. **–paśu**, m. a present or duty (usual in some districts of India), Pāṇ. vi, 3, 10, Sch.; (v. l. *abhyarhita-paśu*.)

अभ्यानन *abhy-ānana*, mfn. having the face turned towards, BhP.

अभ्यानी *abhy-ā-√nī* (ind. p. *-nīya*) to pour into, mix with, AitBr.

अभ्यानृत् *abhy-ā-√nṛit* (pr. p. *-nṛ́tyat*) to dance towards, hasten near, TBr.

अभ्यान्त *abhy-ānta* = *abhy-amita*, q. v.

अभ्याप् *abhy-√āp*, *-āpnóti*, to reach to, get, obtain, ŚBr.: Caus. *-āpáyati*, to bring to an end, ŚBr.: Desid. P. *abhîpsati* (rarely Ā., MBh. v, 17), to strive to reach, ask for, desire, MBh. &c.

Abhîpsat, mf(*atī*, MBh. i, 6469; R.; *antī*, Mn. v, 156)n. (pr. p.) longing for, desiring.

Abhîpsita, mfn. desired, acceptable, dear.

Abhîpsin, mfn. (ifc.) = *abhîpsat*, KaṭhUp.

Abhîpsu, mfn. id. (with acc., N. &c.; with Inf., Śiś. i, 14).

Abhy-āpti, *is*, f. obtaining, AitĀr.

अभ्यापत *abhy-ā-√pat*, to jump on, hasten near to, rush towards (acc. without or with *prati*), MBh.; Kathās.: Caus. to extend (a string) towards (acc.), Śulb.

Abhy-āpāta, *as*, m. calamity, misfortune, L.

अभ्यापद् *abhy-ā-√pad* (Pot. *-padyeta*) to enter into, come to (acc.), ĀśvGṛ.

Abhy-ā-pādam, ind. so as to enter into or pass through (acc.), Nir. vii, 26.

अभ्याभू *abhy-ā-√bhū* (Pot. *-bhávet*) to happen to, occur to (acc.), ŚBr.; AitBr.

अभ्यामर्द *abhy-āmarda*, *as*, m. war, battle, L.

अभ्यायम् *abhy-ā-√yam*, P. (3. pl. *-yacchanti*) to lengthen (as a syllable in speaking), AitBr.; to draw or pull (as the udder in sucking), Kāṭh.; Ā. (Imper. 2. sg. *-yacchasva*) to assume ('to grant,' Comm.), VS. iii, 38: P. (Subj. 3. pl. *-yaman*; ind. p. *-yátya*) to aim at, RV. viii, 92, 31; ŚBr.; AitBr.; for *abhy-ā-√gam*, KaushBr.

Abhy-ā-yaṉsénya, mfn. (said of the Aśvins) one who allows himself to be drawn near (for accepting the sacrificial oblation), RV. i, 34, 1.

अभ्याया *abhy-ā-√yā*, to come up to, approach, MBh. &c.

अभ्यायु *abhy-ā-√2. yu*, Ā. (3. pl. *-yuvate*) to strive towards (acc.), AitBr.

अभ्यायुक *abhy-āyuka*. See 2. *abhí*.

अभ्यारभ् *abhy-ā-√rabh*, Ā. to lay hold of (acc.), ŚBr.; AitBr.: P. (impf. *-ārabhat*) to commence, MBh. iii, 10724.

Abhy-ārambhá, *as*, m. beginning, ŚBr.; re-beginning, repetition, PBr.

अभ्यारम् *abhy-ā́ram*, ind. (cf. *ārá*) near, at hand, RV. viii, 72, 11.

अभ्यारुह् *abhy-ā-√ruh*, *-ā́-rohati*, to ascend, mount, step upon, AV.; TS.; ŚBr.: Caus. (Subj. 1. sg. *-roháyāṇi*) to cause to ascend, ŚBr.

Abhy-ā́rūḍha, mfn. ascended, TS.; (cf. *án*-neg.)

Abhy-ārohá, *as*, m. ascending, ŚBr. (cf. *án*-neg.); increase, growth (as of days), ŚBr.; 'ascending in devotion,' praying, ŚBr. xiv.

Abhy-ārohaṇīya, *as*, m., N. of a sacrificial ceremony, ĀśvŚr.; Lāṭy.

Abhy-āróhuka, mfn. ascending, MaitrS.

Abhy-ārohya. See *an*- neg.

अभ्यावध् *abhy-ā-√vadh* (aor. *-âvadhīt*) to strike, R. i, 45, 17 (v. l.)

अभ्यावह् *abhy-ā-√vah* (3. pl. Imper. *-vahantu* and impf. *-avahan*) to convey, bring towards (acc.), RV. i, 51, 10; 134, 1 & vi, 63, 7.

अभ्याविश् *abhy-ā-√viś* (impf. *-âviśat*) to rush into (acc.), MBh. vii, 5812: P. Ā. to enter into, penetrate, MBh.

अभ्यावृत् *abhy-ā-√vṛit*, *-vártate* (Imper. 2. sg. *-vavṛitsva*; P. impf. 3. sg. *-âvart* [RV. vii, 59, 4]) to roll (as a cart) towards, come up to or towards (acc.), approach, RV.; AV.; VS.: Caus. (Ved.) *-vavartati*, id., RV. x, 64, 1; *-vartayati*, to repeat, ŚāṅkhGṛ.

Abhy-ā-vártam, ind. so as to repeat, repeatedly, ŚBr.; PBr.

Abhy-āvartin, mfn. coming near, coming repeatedly, VS. (voc.); Kauś.; returning (as days), AitBr. (*an*- neg.); (*ī*), m., N. of a king (son of Cayamāna and descendant of Pṛithu), RV. vi, 27, 5 & 8.

Abhy-ā́vṛitta, mfn. come near, approached, VS. viii, 58; (with acc.) ŚBr.; turned towards, KātyŚr.

Abhy-āvṛitti, *is*, f. repetition, Pāṇ.; Jaim.

Abhy-ā-vṛitya, ind. p. turning one's self towards (acc.), MBh. v, 4128.

अभ्याश *abhy-āśa*, *as*, m. See *abhy-√1. aś*.

अभ्यास *abhy-āsa*. See (*abhy-√1. as* and) 2. *abhy-√2. as*.

अभ्यासक्त *abhy-ā-sakta*, mfn. (√*sañj*), closely linked together (as days by beginning a day with the same ceremony which has been performed at the end of the preceding day), ĀśvŚr.; Comm. on PBr.

Abhy-āsaṅgya, mfn. to be closely linked together (as days; see before), PBr.; Vait.; (*as*), m., N. of a Pañcāha, PBr.; ĀpŚr.

अभ्यासद् *abhy-ā-√sad* (Ved. Inf. *-sádam*) to sit down into (acc.), RV. ix, 3, 1 & 30, 4; to attain, obtain, Kir. v, 52.

Abhy-āsādana, *am*, n. attacking an enemy, L.

Abhy-āsādayitavya, mfn. to be allowed to approach, MBh. iii, 17101.

अभ्यासिच् *abhy-ā-√sic*, to pour on, Gobh.; Suśr.

अभ्याहन् *abhy-ā-√han* (Imper. 2. sg. *-jahí*; perf. Ā. *-jaghne*) to strike, wound, RV. ix, 85, 2; MBh.; ChUp.; to impede (Inf. *-hanitum*), Hariv.

Abhy-āhata, mfn. struck, wounded, MBh. &c.; seized by, afflicted with, MBh. &c.; impeded, Bhaṭṭ., (*an-*, neg.) ĀśvŚr.; MārkP.

Abhy-āhanana, *am*, n. impeding, interruption, Comm. on PBr.

अभ्याहित *abhy-ā́hita*. See *abhy-ā-√dhā*.

अभ्याहृ *abhy-ā-√hṛi*, to bring near, hand over, MBh.; R.; to carry off, R. ed. Bomb. i, 61, 7.

Abhy-āhāra, *as*, m. bringing near, ŚBr.; carrying off, robbery, L.

अभ्याह्वे *abhy-ā-√hve*, *-hváyate*, to address (with the *āhāva* formula), TS.; ŚBr.; AitBr.; (pr. p. *-hvayat*) to shout at, challenge, attack, PBr.

अभ्युक्त *abhy-ukta*, mfn. declared or uttered (as a verse) with reference to (acc.), ŚBr.; Up.

अभ्युक्ष् *abhy-√1. uksh*, P. *-uksháti* (ind. p. *-ukshya*) to sprinkle over, besprinkle, ŚBr. &c.: Ā. (perf. *-vavakshe*) to cover with sparks, RV. i, 146, 2.

Abhy-ukshaṇa, *am*, n. sprinkling over, wetting, KātyŚr.; Lāṭy; Ragh. xvi, 57.

Abhy-ukshita, mfn. besprinkled, R.; Mṛicch.

अभ्युच् *abhy-√uc*, *-ucyati*, to like, take pleasure in visiting, TS.

Abhy-ucita, mfn. usual, customary, R.

अभ्युच्चर् *abhy-uc-√car* (Imper. 2. sg. *-carā*) to rise over (acc.), RV. viii, 25, 21.

अभ्युच्चि *abhy-uc-√1. ci*, to bring together in one place, Comm. on Bād.; to treat (a subject) in connection with (another), ib.

Abhy-uccaya, *as*, m. increase, Nir.; Bhaṭṭ.

Abhy-uccita, mfn. increased, Comm. on Nir.

अभ्युच्छ्रय *abhy-ucchraya*, *as*, m. (*√śri*), 'elevation,' in comp. with **-vat**, mfn. having a great elevation, being higher than (abl.), MBh. iii, 11699.

Abhy-úcchrita, mfn. raised aloft, elevated, ŚBr. &c.; prominent, VarBṛS.; Ragh. ix, 62; excellent through (instr.), Ragh. xvi, 2. **-kara**, mfn. with uplifted proboscis, MBh. iii, 15735.

अभ्युज्जि *abhy-uj-√ji*, to obtain by conquering, GopBr.

अभ्युज्जीव् *abhy-uj-√jīv*, *-jīvati*, to preserve life, MBh. v, 4538.

अभ्युत्क्रम् *abhy-ut-√kram*, to go up to, ascend, Vait.: P. (fut. 1. pl. *-kramishyāmas*, ŚBr.) and Caus. P. *-kramayati* [ŚBr.] or *-krāmayati* [ĀśvGṛ.] to cause to go or step towards (loc.)

अभ्युत्क्रुश् *abhy-ut-√kruś* (Subj. 1. pl. *-krośāma*) to raise loud acclamations towards (acc.), AitBr.

Abhy-utkrushṭa, mfn. applauded with loud acclamations, AitBr. (*an-* neg.)

Abhy-utkrośana, *am*, n. loud acclamation, Sāy. on AitBr. **-mantra**, m. a hymn of applause (with which Indra is addressed), ib.

अभ्युत्तॄ *abhy-ut-√tṝ* (3. pl. *-út-taranti*) to cross, ŚBr.; (1. pl. *-tarema*) to cross over towards, penetrate to (acc.), RV. x, 53, 8.

अभ्युत्था *abhy-ut-thā* (*√sthā*), (impf. *-úd-atishṭhat*; perf. *-út-tasthau*) to rise for going towards (acc.), AV. xv, 8, 5; ŚBr. &c.; to rise from a seat to do any one (acc.) honour, Śāk. &c.; (with *ātithya-karma*) id., MBh. viii, 634; to rise in rebellion, MārkP.; to leave off, desist from (abl.), Comm. on ChUp.

Abhy-utthāna, *am*, n. rising from a seat through politeness, Pañcat.; rising, setting out, R.; rebellion, Hariv.; elevation, gaining a high position, gaining authority, respectability, Bhag.; Ragh.; (said of destiny) gaining efficacy, power, MBh. xiii, 343; rise, origin, birth, MBh. xii.

Abhy-utthāyin, mfn. rising from a seat to do any one honour, Comm. on KātyŚr. (*an-* neg.)

Abhy-utthita, mfn. risen, R. &c.; risen from the seat to do any one (acc.) honour, Hariv.; BhP.; appeared, visible, Ragh. i, 53, &c.; risen for doing anything, making one's self ready for (acc.), Nir.; (Inf.), MBh. xii, 4130; ready, Hariv.; BhP.

Abhy-uttheya, mfn. to be greeted reverentially (i. e. by rising from one's seat), Comm. on KātyŚr.

अभ्युत्पत् *abhy-ut-√pat* (p. *-patat*; perf. *-papāta*) to fly or jump or rush up to (acc.), Hariv.; Kathās.: Caus. *-út-pātayati*, to cause to fly up to (acc.), ŚBr.

Abhy-utpatana, *am*, n. springing or leaping against any one, Ragh. ii, 27.

अभ्युत्सद् *abhy-ut-√sad*, Caus. (Ved. aor. *-sādayām akaḥ* [*akar*, *√1. kṛi*]) to cause to set out towards (acc.; for obtaining), MaitrS. (quoted by Pāṇ. iii, 1, 42).

अभ्युत्सर्ज् *abhy-ut-√sarj* (Pot. *-út-sarjet*) to rattle towards (acc.), TS.

अभ्युत्सह् *abhy-ut-√sah*, to be able to resist (with acc.), MBh. vi, 2351; to feel competent, venture (with Inf.), MBh. iii, 13206; Ragh. v, 22.

अभ्युत्सिच् *abhy-ut-√sic* (ind. p. *-sícya*) to fill up by pouring, ŚBr.; to sprinkle with (instr., *adbhis*), ŚāṅkhGṛ.

अभ्युत्सृज् *abhy-ut-√sṛij*, to throw (as an arrow) towards (dat.), MBh. vii, 8852: Desid. (p. *-sisṛikshat*) to be about to give up (as one's life), MBh. xii, 833.

अभ्युत्स्मि *abhy-ut-√smi* (only p. *-smayat*) to smile on (acc.), smile, MBh.; Hariv.

अभ्युद् *abhy-√ud* (p. *-undát*; Imper. 2. pl. *-undátta* [for *unttá*, see Whitney's Gr. § 690]) to wet, flow over, RV.; ŚBr.; AitBr.

अभ्युदन् *abhy-ud-√an*, *-ániti*, to breathe towards or upon (acc.), ŚBr.

अभ्युदवसो *abhy-ud-ava-√so*, *-syati*, to set out or go towards (acc.), AitBr.

अभ्युदानी *abhy-ud-ā-√nī*, to lead up (out of water), MānŚr.; MānGṛ.; Gobh. (cf. *ud-ā√nī*); to fetch out from, MānŚr.

अभ्युदाहृ *abhy-ud-ā-√hṛi*, to give an example in addition, Āp.

Abhy-udāharaṇa, *am*, n. an example or illustration of a thing by its reverse, L.

अभ्युदि *abhy-ud-√i* (2. sg. *-eshi*; Imper. 2. sg. *-úd-ihi*; Pot. *-iyāt* [ŚBr.], *-īyāt* [MBh. iii, 2010 & 10272]; fut. *-ud-ayishyati*, MBh. iv, 688), (said of the sun) to rise over (acc.), rise, RV. viii, 93, 1; AV. &c.; to engage in combat with (acc.), MBh. (Pot. *-īyāt*, see before), to finish off at (acc.), PBr.

Abhy-udaya, *as*, m. sunrise or rise of luminaries (during or with reference to some other occurrence), KātyŚr.; Jaim.; beginning, commencing (as of darkness, &c.), R.; elevation, increase, prosperity, happiness, good result, Mn. iii, 254; R. &c.; a religious celebration, festival, Mn. ix, 84. **Abhyudayêshṭi**, f., N. of an expiatory sacrifice, Jaim.; (cf. *abhyudi-têshṭi*.)

Abhy-udayin, mfn. rising, Rājat.

1. **Abhy-udita**, mfn. risen (as the sun or luminaries), MBh.; R.; Mn. iv, 104; one over whom (while sleeping) the sun has risen, Mn. ii, 221; Comm. on TS.; engaged in combat, MBh. iii, 15362; arisen, happened; elevated, prosperous; (*abhyúdita*), *am*, n. (said of the sun or the moon) rising (during some other occurrence), ŚBr.; KātyŚr.; (*ā*), f., N. of the ceremony (to be performed at the *abhyúdita*), KaushBr. **-śāyi-tā**, f. the state of lying asleep while the sun has risen, MBh. xiii, 5093. **Abhy-uditêshṭi**, f. = *abhyudayêshṭi*, KaushBr.; ŚāṅkhŚr.

अभ्युदित 2. *abhy-udita*, mfn. (*√vad*), expressed (in words), KenaUp. (*an-* neg.); see *abhi-√vad*.

अभ्युदीक्ष् *abhy-ud-√īksh*, Ā. (impf. *-aikshata*) to look towards (acc.), R.

अभ्युदीर् *abhy-ud-√īr*, Caus. (p. *-īrayat*) to raise (one's voice), MBh. i, 2170: Pass. *-īryate*, to be stirred up, be intensified, Suśr.

Abhy-udīrita, mfn. 'raised (as the voice), said,' (*e*), loc. ind. after it had been said by (instr.), Kathās.

अभ्युदूह् *abhy-ud-√1. ūh* (impf. *auhat*) to move or push farther out, AitBr.

अभ्युदे *abhy-udê* (*√i*), (ind. p. *-ētya*) to go out in order to meet any one (acc.), AV. xv, 11, 2 & 12, 2.

अभ्युद्ग *abhy-udga*, mfn. fr. *√ubj*, Pat. on Pāṇ. Śivasūtra 5 & viii, 3, 38.

अभ्युद्गत *abhy-ud-gata*, mfn. risen (as the moon); one who has gone out in order to meet any one (acc.), MBh. i, 3572; extended (as fame), R.; Lalit. **-rāja**, m., N. of a Kalpa, Buddh.

Abhy-udgama, *as*, m. rising from a seat to honour any one, Kathās.

Abhy-udgamana, *am*, n. id., L.

अभ्युद्गा *abhy-ud-√1. gā* (aor. 2. sg. *-úgās*; 3. sg. *-úd-agāt*) to rise over or during (acc.), RV. viii, 93, 4; ŚBr.

अभ्युद्दिश् *abhy-ud-√diś*, to point at anything above with reference to, MānGṛ.

अभ्युद्दृष्ट *abhy-ud-drishṭa*, mfn. having become visible (as the moon) during anything, KātyŚr.; *án-* (neg.), one during the sacrifice of whom the moon has not become visible, ŚBr.; KātyŚr.; (*abhy-uddrishṭā*), f., N. of a ceremony, KaushBr. **Abhy-uddṛishṭêshṭi**, f., N. of a ceremony (beginning only after the moon has become visible), KaushBr.; ŚāṅkhŚr.

अभ्युद्द्रु *abhy-ud-√2. dru*, *-drávati*, to run up to (acc.), TBr.

अभ्युद्धा *abhy-ud-dhā* (*√2. hā*), Ā. (3. pl. *-uj-jihate*) to rise together with, ChUp.

अभ्युद्धृ *abhy-ud-dhṛi* (*√hṛi*), Ved. to take out (especially one fire in order to add it to another), TS.; ŚBr. &c.; to take or draw out, draw (as water), MBh. &c.; to take up, lift up, ŚāṅkhŚr.; MBh. xii, 12322; to re-obtain, Yājñ. ii, 119; to elevate, render prosperous, MBh.; Sāh. &c.: Caus. (ind. p. *-ud-dhārya*) to raise, lift up, MBh. iii, 13326.

Abhy-uddhṛita, mfn. taken up, &c.; drawn (as water), Yājñ. i, 17; collected (for a purpose), Mṛicch.

अभ्युद्यत *abhy-ud-yata*, mfn. (*√yam*), raised, lifted up, MBh. &c.; offered, Mn. iv, 247 seq.; prepared for, engaged in, ready for (Inf. [Hariv. &c.] or dat. [VarBṛS.] or loc. [Mn. ix, 302] or in comp. [Megh.]); (for *abhy-udgata*), received kindly, welcomed, BhP.

अभ्युन्नत *abhy-unnata*, mfn. (*√nam*), raised, elevated, VarBṛS.; Śāk. &c.

अभ्युन्नी *abhy-un-√nī*, to pour upon, scoop towards, ŚBr.; PBr.; Lāṭy.

अभ्युपगम् *abhy-upa-√gam*, to go near to, approach, arrive at (acc.), MBh. &c.; to obtain; to assent, agree to, Daś. &c.: Caus. (ind. p. *-gamayya*) to prevail on any one to assent, Daś. (see also *abhy-upagamita*).

Abhy-upagata, mfn. gone near to, approached, arrived at; agreed, assented to, admitted, MBh.; Śāk. &c.

Abhy-upagantavya, mfn. to be gone to or set out for (dat.), MBh. xiv, 327; to be assented to or agreed upon, Pāṇ. i, 2, 55, Kāś.; to be admitted, Comm. on Bād. and on Nyāyam.

Abhy-upagantṛi, mfn. one who assents or admits, Comm. on ChUp.

Abhy-upagama, *as*, m. going near to, approaching, arriving at, L.; an agreement, contract, Mn. ix, 53; assenting to, admitting, Sāh. &c.; (as a statement) Comm. on Bād. **-siddhānta**, m. an admitted axiom, Nyāyad.

Abhy-upagamita, mfn. 'made to consent,' obtained by assent or free consent (as a slave for a fixed term), Comm. on Yājñ.

अभ्युपधा *abhy-upa-√dhā*, *-úpa-dadhāti*, to place upon, TS.; to cover with (instr.), ŚBr.: P. Ā. (3. pl. *-úpa-dadhati*, Subj. 1. pl. *-dádhāmahai*) to place upon (the fire) in addition or together with, ŚBr.

अभ्युपनिवृत् *abhy-upa-ni-√vṛit*, to return, be repeated, KaushBr.

अभ्युपपद् *abhy-upa-√pad*, Ā. *-padyate*, to approach in order to help, MBh. &c.; to ask for help, R. iii, 14, 7; to furnish with, MBh. ii, 187.

Abhy-upapatti, *is*, f. approaching in order to assist, protection, defence (ifc. [Mn.; Daś.] or with gen. [MBh. i, 112]); favour, the conferring of a benefit or kindness; agreement, assent, Comm. on Nyāyad.; impregnation of a woman (especially of a brother's widow, as an act of duty), L.

Abhy-upapanna, mfn. protected, rescued; asking for protection or help, Mṛicch.; agreed to, admitted; agreeing to.

अभ्युपमन्त्र् *abhy-upa-√mantr* (impf. *-mantrayat*) to address with a formula, MBh. viii, 4720.

अभ्युपया *abhy-upa-√yā*, to approach, go towards (acc. or dat.), MBh. vii, 1967; R.; (with *śamam*) to enter the state of rest, MarkP.

अभ्युपयुक्त *abhy-upayukta*, mfn. (√*yuj*), employed, used, Comm. on Pat.

अभ्युपलक्ष् *abhy-upa-√laksh* (perf. Pass. p. *-lakshita*) to perceive, notice, R. v, 28, 11.

अभ्युपविश् *abhy-upa-√viś*, to sit down upon (acc.), MBh. v, 3244; Gobh. (v. l. *adhy-upa-√viś*); to sit down, Rājat.

अभ्युपशान्त *abhy-upa-śānta*, mfn. (√*śam*), allayed, calmed.

अभ्युपसद् *abhy-upa-√sad*, Caus. (ind. p. *-sādya*) to reach (as a town).

अभ्युपसृ *abhy-upa-√sṛi*, to come near, R.

अभ्युपसेव् *abhy-upa-√sev*, *-sevate*, to observe religiously, MBh. iii, 13432.

अभ्युपस्था *abhy-upa-√sthā*, to honour, BhP.: Caus. to cause to bring near, R. iv, 38, 28.

Abhy-upa-sthita, mfn. come, arrived, Kathās.; attended or accompanied by (instr.), MBh. iii, 16132.

अभ्युपाकृ *abhy-upâ-√1. kṛi*, to prepare or make preparations (for a sacred action, see *upâ-√1. kṛi*) with reference to (acc.) or in connection with (acc.), MaitrS.; ŚāṅkhŚr.; KātyŚr.

अभ्युपाकृष् *abhy-upâ-√kṛish*, to draw towards one's self, BhP.

अभ्युपागत *abhy-upâ-gata*, mfn. come near, approached, Lalit.; (with *vyasanāya*, said of a sad fate), R.

अभ्युपादा *abhy-upâ-√1. dā* (ind. p. *-dāya*) to pick up (as fruits from the ground), MBh. xii, 672.

अभ्युपाया *abhy-upâ-√yā*, to come up to, approach, Kathās.

अभ्युपावहृ *abhy-upâva-√hṛi*, *-upâva-harati*, to bring or set down upon (acc.), ŚBr.; to lower (as one's arms, *bāhū*), VS. x, 25; ŚBr.

अभ्युपावृत् *abhy-upâ-√vṛit*, *-upâ-vartate* (also P., aor. Subj. 1. & 3. sg. *-upâ-vṛitam*, *-upâ-vṛitat*) to turn one's self or go towards (acc.), TS.; ŚBr.; AitBr.

Abhy-upâ-vṛitta, mfn. turned or gone towards (acc.), ŚBr.; returned, R.

अभ्युपाहृ *abhy-upâ-√hṛi* (impf. *-upâharat*, which might also be *-upâharat* fr. *abhy-upa-√hṛi*) to bring near, offer, MBh. xv, 11.

अभ्युपे 1. *abhy-upê* (√*i*), *-upâiti* (3. pl. *-úpayanti*) to go near, approach, arrive at, enter, RV. vi, 28, 4; ŚBr. &c.; (with *apaḥ*) to bathe, KātyŚr.; Mn. xi, 259; Yājñ.; to approach (in copulation), Hit.; to go to meet any one (acc.), BhP.; to enter a state or condition, obtain, share, AitBr. (Ved. Inf. *-upâitos*); MBh. &c.; to admit as an argument or a position, RPrāt. (perf. p. gen. pl. *-upêyushām*); Comm. on Nyāyam. and on Bād.; to select as (acc.), MBh. i, 811; to agree with, approve of, Daś. (see *abhy-upêta*): Pass. *-upêyate*, to be approved of, admitted, Sarvad.

Abhy-upâya, *as*, m. an agreement, promise, engagement, Āp.; a means, an expedient, MBh.; Mn. xi, 210, &c.

Abhy-upâyana, *am*, n. a complimentary gift, an inducement, BhP.

Abhy-upêta, mfn. approached, arrived at (acc.), MBh. i, 3592; Ragh. v, 14; (with *gṛiham*) staying in a house, VarBṛS.; furnished with (in comp. [VarBṛS.] or instr.); agreed upon, assented to, Daś.; promised, Megh.

Abhy-upêtavya, mfn. to be admitted or assented to, Comm. on Nyāyam.

Abhy-upêtya, ind. p. having arrived at (acc.); having entered, Nir.; having assented or agreed to. **Abhyupetyâśuśrūshā**, f. breach of a contracted service, a title of law treating of disputes between the master and a servant who has broken his agreement, Comm. on Yājñ. ii, 182 seqq.

Abhy-upêyivas, mf(*yushī*)n. (perf. p.) having approached, arrived at (acc.), R.; Bhaṭṭ.; having admitted, RPrāt. (see 1. *abhy-upê*).

अभ्युपे 2. *abhy-upê* (*-upâ-√i*), (Imper. 2. sg. *-upaihi*) to approach (for refuge, *śaraṇam*), R. vi, 9, 39.

अभ्युपेक्ष् *abhy-upêksh* (√*īksh*), (perf. p. *-upêkshitavat*) to overlook, allow, MBh. xvi, 160.

अभ्युल्लसत् *abhy-ullasat*, mfn. (√*las*), gleaming, flashing, Śiś. v, 2.

अभ्युष् *abhy-√ush* (impf. 3. pl. *-ushṇán*; Ved. Inf. *-ushas*) to burn, consume by fire, RV. ix, 97, 39; Kāṭh.

Abhy-usha or **abhy-ūsha** or **abhy-osha**, *as*, m. a kind of cake of grain &c. (half dressed, slightly scorched, or parched so as to be eaten from the hand), (gaṇa *apūpâdi*, q. v.)

Abhyushīya or **abhyūshīya** or **abhyushya** or **abhyūshya** or **abhy-oshīya** or **abhy-oshya**, mfn. consisting of, or belonging to, or fit for the above cake or preparation of parched grain, (gaṇa *apūpâdi*, q. v.)

Abhy-ushṭa-miśrá, mfn. partly burnt, ŚBr.

अभ्युषित *abhy-ushita*, mfn. (√5. *vas*), having dwelt, having passed the night with, R. iii, 17, 2.

अभ्यूढि *abhy-ūḍhi*. See *abhi-√vah*.

अभ्यूर्णु *abhy-√ūrṇu*, *abhy-ūrṇoti* (Imper. 2. sg. *-ūrṇuhi*) to cover, conceal, RV. viii, 79, 2 & x, 18, 11; AV.: Ā. *-ūrṇuté* (p. f. *-ūrṇvānā*) to cover or conceal one's self, AV. xiv, 1, 27; RV. v, 41, 19.

अभ्यूष *abhy-ūsha*. See *abhy-usha*. **-khādikā**, f. 'eating of *abhyūsha*-grains,' N. of a play, Vātsyāy.

अभ्यूह् 1. *abhy-√1. ūh*, to cover with (instr.), TS.; ŚBr.; KātyŚr.

अभ्यूह् 2. *abhy-√2. ūh*, Ā. (aor. *-auhishṭa*, p. *-ohasāna*) to watch for, lie in ambush for (acc.), RV. vi, 17, 8 & 9: P. *-ūhati*, to infer, guess, Nir.

Abhy-ūḍha, mfn. concluded, inferred, Nir.

Abhy-ūha, *as*, m. reasoning, deduction, inference, conjecture, Nir.; Mālatim.

Abhy-ūhitavya, mfn. to be inferred, Nir.

1. **Abhy-ūhya**, mfn. id., L.

2. **Abhy-ūhya**, ind. p. having deduced by reasoning, having inferred, Suśr.; Pāṇ. vii, 4, 23, Kāś. &c.

अभ्यृ *abhy-√ṛi*, *-ṛiṇoti* (perf. 3. pl. *abhy-āruh*) to run towards, reach, RV. i, 35, 9 & iii, 1, 4.

Abhy-arṇa. See s.v., p. 76, col. 1.

अभ्यृच्छ् *abhy-√ṛich*, *-archati*, to come to, visit or afflict with, MBh. iii, 11875; (impf. *-ârchat*) to strive against (acc.), strive to overpower, MBh. iii, 11726.

अभ्यृञ्ज् *abhy-√ṛiñj*, Ā. *-ṛijyate* (P. pr. p. *-ṛijyat*) to stretch out the hand for, hasten towards (acc.), RV. i, 140, 2 & vi, 37, 3.

अभ्यृष् *abhy-√ṛish*. See *abhy-√arsh*.

अभ्ये *abhy-ê* (√*i*), *-âyati* [RV. viii, 55, 1] or *-âiti* [VS.], to go near, come to, approach, RV. &c.

Abhy-êtya, ind. p. having approached, N.; Pañcat. &c.

अभ्येषण *abhy-eshaṇa*. See *abhīsh*.

अभ्र् *abhr*, cl. 1. P. *abhrati* (perf. *ānabhra*) to err or wander about, Bhaṭṭ.

अभ्र *abhrá* (sometimes spelt *abbhra*, according to the derivation *ab-bhra*, 'water-bearer;' cf. Comm. on ChUp. ii, 15, 1), *am*, n. (rarely *as*, m., AV. ix, 6, 47 & TS.) cloud, thunder-cloud, rainy weather, RV. &c.; sky, atmosphere, Śiś. ix, 3; (in arithmetic) a cypher; [NBD.] dust, AV. xi, 3, 6; (in med.) talc, mica; gold, L.; camphor, L.; the ratan (Calamus Rotang), L.; Cyperus Rotundus, L.; [cf. Gk. ὄμβρος & Lat. *imber*.] **-m-liha** (*abhram-l°*), mfn. [Pāṇ. iii, 2, 32] 'cloud-licking,' what touches the clouds, high, lofty, Ragh. xiv, 29, &c.; (*as*), m. wind, Pāṇ. iii, 2, 32, Sch.; Sāh. **-gaṅgā**, f. the celestial Gaṅgā, Kād. **-ghana**, mfn. thickly covered with clouds, Ragh. **-m-kasha** (*abhram-k°*), mfn. [Pāṇ. iii, 2, 42] 'grazing (hurting) the clouds,' very high, Kād.; (*as*), m. wind, Pāṇ. iii, 2, 42, Sch. **-jā**, mfn. 'born from clouds,' caused by rainy weather, AV. i, 12, 3. **-taru**, m., N. of a certain phenomenon, VarBṛS. **-nāga**, *ās*, m. pl., N. of the eight elephants supporting the globe, L. **-patha**, m. sky, atmosphere, L. **-piśāca** or **-piśācaka**, m. 'sky-demon,' N. of Rāhu (the descending node personified), L. **-pushpa**, m. the cane Calamus Rotang, L.; (*am*), n. 'a flower in the clouds,' castle in the air, anything impossible, Naish.; (cf. *ambara-pushpa*.) **-prúsh**, f. the sprinkling of the clouds, rain, RV. x, 77, 1. **-maṇsī**, f. the plant Valeriana Jaṭāmāṇsī, L. **-mātaṅga**, m. Airāvata, Indra's elephant, L. **-mālā**, f. a line or succession of clouds, L. **-roha**, n. lapis lazuli, L. **-lipta**, mf(*ī*)n. partly overspread with clouds, Pāṇ. iv, 1, 51, Sch. **-varsha** (*abhrá-*), mfn. dripping or raining from the clouds, RV. ix, 88, 6. **-vāṭika** for *āmra-vāṭika*, q. v. **-vilipta**, mf(*ī*)n. = *-lipta*, q. v., Pāṇ. iv, 1, 51, Kāś. **-vṛiksha**, m. = *-taru*, q. v., VarBṛS. **-śiras**, n. a head formed of the sky, Śiś. **-sáni**, mfn. procuring clouds, TS. **Abhrânadhyāya**, m. pause in the study on account of rainy weather, Gobh. **Abhrâvakāśika** [Mn. vi, 23, &c.] or **°kāśin** [R. iii, 10, 4], mfn. having the clouds for shelter, open to the sky (as an ascetic). **Abhrôttha**, mfn. 'cloud-born,' Indra's thunderbolt, L.

Abhraka, *am*, n. talc, mica, Bhpr. &c. **-bhasman**, n. calx of talc, L. **-sattva**, n. steel, L.

Abhrayanti, f. (pr. p. fr. *abhraya*, Nom. P.) 'forming clouds, bringing rainy weather,' N. of one of the seven Kṛittikās, TS.; TBr.

Abhrāya, Nom. Ā. *°yate*, to create clouds, Pāṇ. iii, 1, 17.

Abhrāyita, mfn. 'shaped like a cloud,' similar to a cloud, Bhām.

Abhrita, mf(*ā*)n. covered with clouds, (gaṇa *tārakâdi*, q. v.), Ragh. iii, 12.

Abhriya (once **abhriyá**, RV. x, 68, 12), mfn. belonging to or produced from clouds, RV.; AV.; (*as, am*), m. n. thunder-cloud, RV.

Abhrīya, mfn. belonging to or produced from talc.

Abhrya, *as*, m. 'clothed only by the air' or 'having the clouds for shelter' (cf. *abhrâvakāśika*), a naked ascetic, (gaṇa *śâkhâdi*, q. v.)

अभ्रम *a-bhrama*, mfn. not blundering; steady, clear; (*as*), m. not erring, steadiness, composure, BhP.

A-bhramu, *us*, f. the female elephant of the east (the mate of Airāvata). **-priya** [Vcar.] or **-vallabha** [L.], m. the male elephant of the east or Airāvata.

अभ्रातृ *a-bhrātṛí*, mfn. brotherless, RV. i, 124, 7 (nom. sg. f. *tā́*); iv, 5, 5 (nom. pl. f. *târas*); AV. i, 17, 1 (nom. pl. f. *abhrātaras*); Nir. iii, 5 (acc. sg. f. *°trīm*). **-ghnī** (*ábhrātṛi-*), f. (√*han*), not killing a brother, AV. xiv, 1, 62. **-matī**, f. brotherless, Nir. &c.

A-bhrātṛika, mf(*ā*)n. brotherless, Nir. &c.

अभ्रातृव्य *a-bhrātṛivyá*, mf(*ā*)n. having no rival, RV. viii, 21, 13; ŚBr. &c.; (*am*), n., N. of a verse of the SV.

अभ्रान्त *a-bhrānta*, mfn. unperplexed, not mistaken, not in error; clear, composed.

A-bhrānti, *is*, f. absence of perplexity or error.

अभ्रि *ábhri*, f. a wooden scraper or shovel, a spatula, spade, VS.; AV.; ŚBr. &c. **-khāta** (*ábhri-*), mfn. dug up with a spatula, AV. iv, 7, 5 & 6.

अभ्रेष *a-bhresha*, *as*, m. non-deviation, fitness, propriety, Pāṇ. iii, 3, 37; Vait.

अभ्व *á-bhva* [RV.] or *a-bhvà* [AV.] or *a-bhvá* [ŚBr.], mfn. (cf. *a-bhuva*) monstrous, immense, terrible, RV. i, 39, 8 & 63, 1; (*am*), n. immense power, monstrosity, horror, RV.; ŚBr.; a monster, RV. vi, 71, 5; AV.; ŚBr.

अम् 1. *am*, ind. quickly, a little, (gaṇa *cādi*, q. v.)

अम् 2. *am*, the termination *am* in the comparative and other forms used as ind., e. g. *pratarám*, &c., (gaṇa *svar-ādi*, q. v.)

अम् 3. *am*, *amati*, to go, L.; to go to or towards, L.; to serve or honour, L.; to sound, L.; (Imper. Ā. 2. sg. *amīshva*; aor. *āmīt*; cf. *abhy-√am*) to fix, render firm, TS.; (perf. p. acc. sg. *emushám* for *emivāṅsam*) to be pernicious or dangerous, RV. viii, 77, 10: Caus. *āmáyati* (impf. *ámayat*; aor. Subj. *āmamat*) to be afflicted or sick, RV.; AV.; VS. (cf. *án-āmayat*).

1. **Áma**, *as*, m. impetuosity, violence, strength, power, RV.; VS.; AV.; depriving of sensation, fright, terror, RV.; disease, L. **-vat** (*áma-*), mfn. impetuous, violent, strong, RV.; (*vat*), ind. impetuously, RV. v, 58, 1.

1. **Amata**, *as*, m. sickness, disease, Uṇ.; death, L.; time, L.; dust, Comm. on Uṇ.

1. **Ámati**, *is*, f. want, indigence, RV.; VS.; AV.; (*is*), mfn. poor, indigent, RV. x, 39, 6. **Amatīván**, mfn. poor, indigent, RV. viii, 19, 26.

Ámatra, mfn. violent, strong, firm, RV. i, 61, 9 & iv, 23, 6; (*am*), n. a large drinking vessel, RV.; Pāṇ. iv, 2, 14; (*as*), m. id., RV. iii, 36, 4.

Amatraka, *am*, n. a drinking vessel, vessel, BhP.

Amatrín, mfn. having the large drinking vessel called *ámatra*, RV. vi, 24, 9.

Amani, *is*, f. road, way, Uṇ.

1. **Amita** or **ānta**, mfn. perf. Pass. p. *√am*, Pāṇ. vii, 2, 28.

Aminá, mfn. impetuous, RV. vi, 19, 1 & x, 116, 4.

अम 2. *áma*, mfn. (pron.; cf. *amu*) this, AV. xiv, 2, 71 (quoted in ŚBr. xiv & ĀśvGṛ.) [The word is also explained by *prāṇa*, 'soul,' cf. Comm. on ChUp. v, 2, 6.]

Amá, amát. See ss. vv.

अमङ्गल *a-maṅgala*, mfn. inauspicious, unlucky, evil, Ragh. xii, 43, &c.; (*as*), m. the castor oil tree, Ricinus Communis, L.; (*am*), n. inauspiciousness, ill-luck, Kum.; Veṇīs.

A-maṅgalya, mfn. inauspicious, unlucky, L.; (*am*), n. inauspiciousness, ill-luck, BhP.

अमज्जक *a-majjáka*, mfn. having no marrow, TS.

अमणिव *a-maṇiva*, mfn. [NBD.] having no jewels, ŚāṅkhŚr.

अमण्ड *amaṇḍa*, *as*, m. the castor oil tree, Ricinus Communis (cf. *āmaṇḍa* & *maṇḍa*).

अमण्डित *a-maṇḍita*, mfn. unadorned.

अमत 2. *á-mata* mfn. (*√man*), not felt, not perceptible by the mind, ŚBr. xiv; not approved of, unacceptable. **-padârtha**, mfn. having an unacceptable second sense, Kpr.; Sāh.

2. **A-mati**, *is*, f. 'unconsciousness,' generally (*tyā*), instr. ind. unconsciously, Mn. iv, 222 & v, 20; Gaut. **-pūrva** or **-pūrvaka**, mfn. unconscious, unintentional.

अमति 3. *amáti*, *is*, f. form, shape, splendour, lustre, RV.; VS.; time, Uṇ.; moon, L.

अमत्र *ámatra*. See *√am*.

अमत्सर *a-matsara*, mfn. unenvious, disinterested, Mn. iii, 231, &c.; (*am*), n. disinterestedness, Hcat.

A-matsarin, mfn. disinterested, Hcat.; not sticking to, not having one's heart set upon (loc.), R.

A-mātsarya, *am*, n. disinterestedness, MBh. v, 1640. **-tā**, f. id., Lalit.

अमद *a-mada*, mfn. cheerless, Bhaṭṭ.

A-madana, *as*, m., N. of Śiva, BhP.

A-madya-pa, mfn. not drinking intoxicating liquors, Suśr. **-madyat**, mfn. being (inebriated or) joyful without (having drunk) any intoxicating liquor, Kām.

अमधु *a-mádhu*, *u*, n. no sweetness, ŚBr.

A-madhavya, mfn. not worthy of the sweetness (of the Soma), AitBr.

अमध्यम *á-madhyama*, *-āsas*, (Ved.) m. pl. of whom none is the middle one, RV. v, 59, 6; (cf. *á-kanishtha*.)

A-madhyastha, mfn. not indifferent.

अमनस् *á-manas*, *as*, n. non-perception, want of perception, ŚBr. xiv; (*a-manás*), mfn. without perception or intellect, ŚBr. xiv; silly, ChUp.

A-manaska, mfn. without perception or intellect, Sarvad.; silly, KaṭhUp.; not well-disposed, low-spirited, Kād.

A-manī (for *a-manás* in comp. with *√bhū* and its derivatives). **-bhāva**, m. the state of not having perception or intellect, MaitrUp.

A-mano (in comp. for *a-manas*). **-jña**, mfn. disagreeable, KātyŚr.; (Prākṛit *a-maṇuṇṇa*) Jain. **-rama-tā**, f. unpleasantness, Śiś.

A-mantú, mfn. silly, ignorant, RV. x, 22, 8 & 125, 4.

A-mantṛi, mfn. not thinking, MaitrUp.

अमनाक् *a-manāk*, ind. not little, greatly.

अमनि *amani*. See *√am*.

अमनुष्य *a-manushya*, *as*, m. no man, any other being but a man, KātyŚr.; R. ii, 93, 21 (*nâmanushye*, 'only with men'); a demon, Pāṇ. ii, 4, 23. **-tā**, f. unmanliness. **-nishevita**, mfn. not inhabited by men.

A-mānava, mfn. 'not human, superhuman,' and 'not being a descendant of Manu,' Śiś. i, 67.

Á-mānusha, mf(*ī*)n. not human, anything but a man, RV. x, 95, 8; superhuman, divine, celestial, R. &c.; inhuman, brutal, RV.; (mf(*ā*)n.), without men, not inhabited by men, Kathās.; (*as*), m. not a man, ŚBr.; AitBr.; Mn. ix, 284; (*ī*), f. a female animal, Gaut. **-loka**, m. 'the celestial world,' heaven, Kād.

A-mānushya, mfn. not human, MBh. xiv, 266.

अमनोज्ञ *a-mano-jña*, &c. See *á-manas*.

अमन्तृ *a-mantṛí*, &c. See *á-manas*.

अमन्त्र *a-mantra*, *as*, m. not a Vedic verse or text or any formula; (mf(*ā*)n.), unaccompanied by Vedic verses or texts, Mn. iii, 121; unentitled to or not knowing Vedic texts (as a Śūdra, a female, &c.), Mn. ix, 18 & xii, 114; not using or applying Mantra formulas, Bhām. **-jña**, mfn. not knowing Vedic texts, Mn. iii, 129. **-vat**, mfn. unaccompanied by Vedic verses, Up. **-vid**, mfn. not knowing the formulas or texts of the Veda, Mn. iii, 133; (*t*), m., N. of a prince.

A-mantraka, mf(*ikā*)n. unaccompanied by Vedic verses, Mn. ii, 66; (*am*), n. no Vedic verse or formula, VarBṛS.

अमन्द *á-manda*, mfn. not slow, active, merry, RV. i, 126, 1; not dull, bright; not little, much, important, Rājat. &c.; (*am*), ind. (in comp. *amanda-*) intensily, Bhaṭṭ.; (*as*), m. a tree, L.

अमन्यमान *á-manyamāna*, mfn. not understanding, RV. i, 33, 9; not being aware of, RV. ii, 12, 10.

अमन्युत *á-manyuta*, mf(*ā*)n. not affected with secret anger, AV. xii, 3, 31.

अमम *a-mama*, mfn. without egotism, devoid of all selfish or worldly attachment or desire, Buddh.; Jain.; indifferent, not caring for (loc.), Mn. vi, 26; (*as*), m. the twelfth Jaina saint of a future Utsarpiṇī. **-tā**, f. or **-tva**, n. disinterestedness; indifference.

अमम्रि *á-mamri*, mfn. (*√mṛi*), immortal, undying, AV. viii, 2, 26.

A-mára, mf(*ā*, Mn. ii, 148; *ī*, R. i, 34, 16)n. undying, immortal, imperishable, ŚBr. xiv, &c.; (*as*), m. a god, a deity, MBh. &c.; hence (in arithm.) the number 33; N. of a Marut, Hariv.; the plant Euphorbia Tirocalli, Suśr.; the plant Tiaridium Indicum, L.; a species of pine, L.; quicksilver, L.; N. of Amarasiṅha; of a mountain (see *-parvata*); mystical signification of the letter *u*; (*ā*), f. the residence of Indra, L.; the umbilical cord, L.; after-birth, L.; a house-post, L.; N. of several plants, Panicum Dactylon, Cocculus Cordifolius, &c., L.; (*ī*), f. the plant Sanseviera Roxburghiana, L. **-kaṇṭaka**, n. 'peak of the immortals,' N. of part of the Vindhya range (near the source of the Soṇā and Narmadā). **-koṭa**, m. 'fortress of immortals,' N. of the capital of a Rājput state. **-kosha**, m., N. of the Sanskṛit dictionary of Amara or Amara-siṅha. **-kosha-kaumudī**, f. title of a commentary on Amara-siṅha's dictionary. **-gaṇa**, m. the assemblage of immortals, L. **-guru**, m. 'teacher of the gods,' Bṛihaspati, the planet Jupiter, VarBṛS.; Kād. **-candra**, m., N. of the author of the Bāla-bhārata. **-ja**, m., N. of a plant, L. **-m-jaya** (*amaram-j°*), mfn. conquering the gods, BhP. **-taṭinī**, f. 'river of the gods,' N. of the Ganges. **-tā** [Sāh.], f. or **-tva** [MBh. &c.], n. the condition of the gods (i. e. immortality). **-datta**, m., N. of a lexicographer; of a prince, Kathās. **-dāru**, m. the tree Pinus Deodaru Roxb. **-deva**, m. a N. of Amarasiṅha. **-dvija**, m. a Brāhman who lives by attending a temple or idol, by superintending a temple, L. **-dvish**, m. 'foe of the gods,' N. of an Asura, Kathās. **-pa**, m. 'lord of the gods,' N. of Indra, VarBṛS. **-pati**, m. id. **-parvata**, m., N. of a mountain, MBh. ii, 1193. **-pura**, n. 'the residence of the immortals,' paradise, Bhaṭṭ.; N. of various towns. **-purī**, f., N. of a town, Pañcat. **-pushpa** or **-pushpaka** m. the plants Saccharum Spontaneum, Pandanus Odoratissimus & Magnifera Indica. **-pushpikā**, f. a kind of anise (Anethum Sowa Roxb.), L. **-prakhya** or **-prabha**, mfn. like an immortal. **-prabhu**, m. 'lord of the immortals,' one of the thousand names of Vishṇu, MBh. **-bhartṛi**, m. 'supporter of the gods,' N. of Indra, L. **-mālā**, f. title of a dictionary (said to be by the same author as the Amara-kosha). **-ratna**, n. 'jewel of the gods,' crystal (also *amala-ratna*), L. **-rāj** [VarBṛS.] or **-rāja** [R.], m. 'king of the gods,' N. of Indra. **-rāja-mantrin**, m. = *amara-guru*, q. v., VarBṛS. **-rāja-śatru**, m. 'enemy of *amara-rāja* (q. v.),' N. of Rāvaṇa, R. vi, 35, 1. **-loka-tā**, f. 'state of the abode of the gods,' the bliss of heaven, Mn. ii, 5. **-vat**, ind. like an immortal. **-vallarī**, f. the plant Cassyta Filiformis Lin., L. **-śakti**, m., N. of a king, Pañcat. **-sadas**, n. the assemblage of the gods, VarBṛS. **-sarit**, f. 'river of the gods,' N. of the Ganges. **-siṅha**, m. 'god-lion,' N. of a renowned lexicographer (probably of the sixth century A. D.; he was a Buddhist, and is said to have adorned the court of Vikramāditya, being included among the nine gems). **-strī**, f. 'wife of the gods,' an Apsaras or nymph of heaven, L. **Amarâṅganā**, f. id., Kathās. **Amarâcārya**, m. (= *amara-guru*, q. v.), N. of Bṛihaspati, BhP. **Amarâdri**, m. = *amara-parvata*, q. v., BhP.; N. of Sumeru or Meru, L. **Amarâdhipa**, m. = *amara-pa*, q. v., R. ii, 74, 19; N. of Śiva. **Amarâpagā**, f. = *amara-taṭinī* & *-sarit*, q. v., Kād. **Amarâri**, m. an enemy of the gods, R.; an Asura, hence (*amarâri*)-*pūjya*, m. (= *asurâcārya*, q. v.), N. of Śukra, the planet Venus, VarBṛS. **Amarā-vatī**, f. (cf. Pāṇ. vi, 3, 119) 'the abode of the immortals,' Indra's residence, MBh.; Hariv. &c.; N. of a town in Berar. **Amarī-√bhū**, to become immortal (said of brave warriors dying in battle), Bālar. **Amarêjya**, m. = *amara-guru*, q. v., VarBṛS.; Sūryas. **Amarêśa**, m. = *amara-pa*, q. v., VarBṛS.; Sāh.; N. of Śiva or Rudra, R. **Amarêśvara**, m. = *amara-pa*, q. v., Śak.; Ragh. xix, 15; N. of Vishṇu, R. i, 77, 29; N. of a Liṅga. **Amarêśvara-tīrtha**, m., N. of a Tīrtha, ŚivaP. **Amarôpama**, mfn. like an immortal, MBh.

A-maraṇa, *am*, n. the not dying, immortality, L.

A-maraṇīya, mfn. immortal, L. **-tā**, f. immortality, L.

Á-marishṇu, mfn. immortal (v. l. for *á-mavishṇu*, q. v.)

Á-marta, mfn. immortal, RV. v, 33, 6.

Á-martya (4), mfn. immortal, RV.; AV.; VS.; imperishable, divine, RV.; (*as*), m. a god, L. **-tā** [MBh.], f. or **-tva** [L.], n. immortality. **-bhāva**, m. the condition of immortals, immortality, Ragh. vii, 50. **-bhuvana**, n. 'world of the immortals,' the heaven, L.

अमरु *amaru*, *us*, m., N. of a king, the author of the *Amaru-śataka*, q. v. **-śataka**, n. the hundred verses of Amaru.

अमर्दित *a-mardita*, mfn. (√*mṛid*), unthreshed; unsubdued; not trodden down.

अमर्धत् *á-mardhat*, mfn. not getting tired or inactive, RV. iii, 25, 4; v, 43, 1 & vii, 76, 5; not making tired, RV. vii, 76, 2.

Á-mṛidhra, mf(*ā*)n. not getting tired, unremitting, indefatigable, RV.; unceasing, RV.

अमर्मन् *a-marmán*, mfn. having no vital part, invulnerable, RV. iii, 32, 4; v, 32, 5 & vi, 26, 3; (*a*), n. not a vital part of the body, Suśr.

A-marma (in comp. for *a-marman*). **-jāta**, mfn. not originating in a vital part of the body (as a disease), Suśr. **-vedhi-tā**, f. the state of not inflicting severe injury on others, absence of acrimony (one of the thirty-five Vāg-guṇas of a Tīrthaṃkara), Jain.

अमर्याद *a-maryāda*, mfn. having no limits, transgressing every bound, R.

अमर्ष *a-marsha*, *as*, m. (√*mṛish*), non-endurance, Pāṇ. iii, 3, 145; impatience, indignation, anger, passion, MBh.; R. &c.; (*as*), m., N. of a prince, VP. **-ja**, mfn. springing from impatience or indignation, MBh. **-vat**, mfn. not bearing, intolerant, passionate, wrathful, angry, L. **-hāsa**, m. an angry laugh, a sarcastic sneer, MBh.

A-marshaṇa, mfn. = *amarsha-vat*, MBh. &c.; impatient (cf. *raṇâmarshaṇa*); (*as*), m. (= *amarsha*), N. of a prince, BhP.; (*am*), n. impatience of (gen.), MBh. xiii, 2159.

A-marshita, mfn. = *amarsha-vat*, q. v., MBh. &c.

A-marshin, mfn. id., MBh. &c.

अमल *a-mala*, mf(*ā*)n. spotless, stainless, clean, pure, shining; (*as*), m. crystal (cf. *amara-ratna*), BhP.; N. of a poet; of Nārāyaṇa, L.; (*ā*), f., N. of the goddess Lakshmī, L.; (= *amarā*, q. v.) the umbilical cord, L.; the tree Emblica Officinalis Gærtn., L.; the plant Saptalā, L.; (*am*), n. talc, L. **-garbha**, m., N. of a Bodhi-sattva, L. **-patatrin**, m. the wild goose, L. **-maṇi**, m. or **-ratna**, n. (cf. *amara-ratna*) crystal, L. **-saṃyuta**, mfn. 'not defiled by any spot,' endowed with purity, MBh. **Amalâtman**, mfn. of undefiled mind. **Amalī-√1. kṛi**, to purify, VarBṛS. **Amalôdarī**, f., N. of a female poet.

Amalaya, Nom. P. °*yati*, to make spotless, whiten, make brilliant, Kir. v, 44.

A-malina, mfn. stainless, free from dirt, clean. **-dhī**, mfn. of a pure mind.

À-malīmasa, mfn. not impure, Rājat.

अमलातक *a-malātaka* or *a-malānaka*, *am*, n. (= *a-mlāna*, q. v.) globe-amaranth (Gomphræna Globosa), (cf. *amilātaka*.)

अमवत् *áma-vat*. See 1. *áma*.

अमविष्णु *a-mavishṇu*, mfn. (√*mū* = √1. *mīv*, NBD.), immovable, RV. x, 94, 11.

अमस *amasa*, *as*, m. disease, Uṇ.; a fool, L.; time, L.; (cf. 1. *amata* & 3. *amáti*.)

अमसृण *a-masṛiṇa*, mfn. not soft, harsh, L.

अमस्तक *a-mastaka*, mfn. headless.

अमस्तु *a-mastu*, mfn. without thickened milk or sour cream, Kauś.

अमस्वन् *ámas-van*, mf(*varī*)n. for *támas-van*, q. v., MaitrS.

अमहीयमान *á-mahīyamāna*, mf(*ā*)n. 'not high-spirited,' down-cast, sad, RV. iv, 18, 13; PBr.

A-mahīyu, *us*, m., N. of a Ṛishi (composer of the hymn RV. ix, 61); (cf. *āmahīyava*.)

अमा 1. *amā́*, ind. (Ved. instr. fr. 2. *áma*, q.v.) (chiefly Ved.) at home, in the house, in the house of (gen.), with, RV. &c.; together, Pāṇ. iii, 1, 122; (*ā*), f. = *amā-vāsyā*, q. v., Comm. on Ragh. xiv, 80 (in a verse quoted from Vyāsa); Comm. on Sūryas; also *amânta*, m. the end of the *amā(-vāsyā)* night, ib. **-√1. kṛi** (gaṇa *sākshād-ādi*, q. v.), Ved. to have or take with one's self, AV.; ŚBr. &c. **-júr**, *ūr*, f. living at home, growing old at home (as a maiden), RV. ii, 17, 7; viii, 21, 15 & x, 39, 3. **-vasī**, f. = *-vāsyā*, q. v., L. **-vasu**, m., N. of a prince (a descendant of Purūravas), MBh.; Hariv.; VP. **-vasyā**, f. = *-vāsyā*, q. v., Kāṭh.; Pāṇ. iii, 1, 122. **-vāsī**, f. = *-vāsyā*, q. v., MBh. i, 4644 & R. vi, 72, 66 (only loc. °*syām*, which might be a metrical abbreviation for °*syāyām*). **-vāsyā**, n. [NBD.] neighbourhood, AV. iv, 36, 3 [perhaps for *-vāśya*, 'lowing (of cows) at home,' as the word is used together with *ā-gara* & *prati-krośa*]; mfn. born in an *amā-vāsyā* night, Pāṇ. iv, 3, 30 (cf. *āmāvāsyá*); N. of a Vedic teacher, VBr.; (*-vāsyā*), f. (scil. *rātri*; fr. √5. *vas*, 'to dwell,' with *amā́*, 'together') the night of new moon (when the sun and moon 'dwell together'), the first day of the first quarter on which the moon is invisible, AV.; ŚBr. &c.; a sacrifice offered at that time; N. of the Acchodā river, MatsyaP. **-vāsyaka**, mfn. (= *-vāsya*) born in an *amā-vāsyā* night, Pāṇ. iv, 3, 30. **-haṭha**, m., N. of a snake demon, MBh. i, 2157. **Amêshṭá**, mfn. sacrificed at home, VS. **Amôtá**, &c., see s. v.

1. **Amā́t**, ind. (abl.) from near at hand, RV. v, 53, 8 & ix, 97, 8.

Amā́tya (4), *as*, m. (fr. 1. *amā́*, cf. Pāṇ. iv, 2, 104, Sch.) inmate of the same house, belonging to the same house or family, RV. vii, 15, 3; VS.; ĀśvGṛ.; KātyŚr.; 'a companion (of a king),' minister, MBh.; Mn. &c.

अमा 2. *a-mā* (√3. *mā*), f. (= *a-pramāṇa*) not an authority, not a standard of action, Nyāyam. **-tva**, n. the not being an authority, ib.

2. **A-māt**, m(nom. sg. *ān*)fn. (pr. p. √3. *mā*), not measuring, not affording room or space, boundless (in qualities), Śiś. xiii, 2; Nalod.

A-mātrá, mfn. without measure, boundless (as Indra), RV. i, 102, 7; (as Brahman), BṛĀrUp.; not metrical or prosodical, MāṇḍUp.; having the measure or quantity of the letter *a*, VPrāt.; (*ayā*), ind. (instr. f.) in a boundless manner, Kathās.

A-māna, *am*, n. = 2. *a-mā*, Nyāyam. **-tā**, f. = *amā-tva* (s. v. 2. *a-mā*), ib.

A-miti, *is*, f. = 2. *a-mā*, ib.; boundlessness, Naish.

अमांस *a-māṇsa*, *am*, n. not flesh, anything but flesh, KātyŚr.; (mfn.), without flesh, PārGṛ.; feeble, thin, L. **-bhaksha**, mfn. not eating flesh, Kathās. **A-māṇsâśana**, mfn. id., Vishṇus. **Á-māṇsâśin**, mfn. id., ŚBr. xiv; KātyŚr.; PārGṛ.

A-māṇsáka, mfn. without flesh, TS.

अमातृ *á-mātṛi*, *tā*, f. not a mother, ŚBr. xiv. **A-mātā-putra**, mfn. (gaṇa *kāshṭhâdi*, q. v.) 'having neither mother nor son,' only in comp., e. g. *amātāputrâdhyāpaka*, m. a teacher who cares for neither mother nor son (on account of being entirely absorbed in his work), Pāṇ. viii, 1, 67, Kāś.

A-mātṛika, mfn. motherless, Āp.

अमात्य *a-mā́tya*. See 1. *amā́*.

अमात्र *a-mātrá*. See 2. *a-mā*.

अमात्सर्य *a-mātsarya*. See *a-matsara*.

अमानन *a-mānana*, *am*, n. disrespect, Hit.

अमानव *a-mānava*. See *a-manushya*.

अमानस्य *a-mānasya* = *āmanasya*, q. v., L.

अमानिन् *a-mānin*, mfn. (√*man*), not proud, modest, MBh. **Amāni-tā**, f. or **-tva** [Bhag. &c.], n. modesty, humility.

अमानुष *a-mānusha*, &c. See *a-manushya*.

अमामसी *amā-mắsī*, v. l. for *-vắsī*, q. v., L.

अमाय *a-māyá*, mfn. not cunning, not sagacious, ŚBr.; AitBr.; free from deceit, guileless, Bhaṭṭ.; (*ā*), f. absence of delusion or deceit or guile, (*ayā*), instr. ind. guilelessly, sincerely, Mn. ii, 51; BhP.; Hit.

A-māyika, mfn. without illusion or deceit, void of trick or guile, Comm. on Kir.; not illusory, real, Kap.

A-māyin, mfn. void of trick or guile, MBh. iii, 1357; BhP.; (Prākṛit *a-māī*) Jain.

अमार *a-māra*, *as*, m. non-destruction, Rājat.

A-māraka, mfn. not killing, Sāy. on RV. i, 84, 4.

अमार्ग *a-mārga*, *as*, m. a bad road, (also figuratively) an evil path, Rājat.; Kathās.; (*eṇa*), instr. ind. in a dishonourable manner, MBh. ii, 2035; (mfn.), pathless, L. **-prasṛit**, mfn. (√*sṛi*), one who is out of the right way, Car.

अमार्जित *a-mārjita*, mfn. uncleansed, unwashed, MBh. iii, 2577.

अमावसी *amā-vasī*, &c. See 1. *amā́*.

Amā-vāsyā. See ib.

अमाष *a-māsha*, mfn. not producing kidney-beans, Pat.; without or except kidney-beans, Hcat.; (*ās*), m. pl. no beans, ĀpŚr.

अमाहठ *amā-haṭha*. See 1. *amā́*.

अमित 1. *amita*. See √*am*.

अमित 2. *á-mita*, mfn. (√3. *mā*), unmeasured, boundless, infinite, RV. &c.; without a certain measure, ŚBr.; Suśr. &c.; (*á-mitam*), ind. immensely, RV. iv, 16, 5. **-kratu** (*ámita-*), mfn. of unbounded energy, RV. i, 102, 6. **-gati**, m., N. of a Vidyādhara, Kathās.; N. of a Jaina author. **-tejas**, mfn. of boundless glory, MBh. **-tva**, n. boundlessness, Hariv. **-dyuti**, mfn. of infinite splendour. **-dhvaja**, m., N. of a son of Dharmadhvaja, VP. **-ruci**, m., N. of a deity, Buddh. **-vikrama**, m. 'of unbounded valour,' a N. of Vishṇu. **-vīrya**, mfn. of immense strength, AV. xix, 34, 8. **Amitâkshara**, mfn. not containing a fixed number of syllables, Nir.; RPrāt. **Amitâtman**, mfn. of an immense mind, MBh. iii, 11924. **Amitâbha**, *ās*, m. pl. 'of unmeasured splendour,' N. of certain deities in the eighth Manvantara, VP.; (*as*), m. sg. = *amitâyus*. **Amitâyus**, m., N. of a Dhyāni-buddha, Buddh. **Ámitâujas**, mfn. of unbounded energy, almighty, RV. i, 11, 4; Mn. i, 4. 16 & 36; N. of Brahman's *paryaṅka*, KaushUp.; N. of a man, (gaṇa *bāhv-ādi*, q. v.)

A-miti. See 2. *a-mā*.

अमित्र *amítra*, *as*, *ā*, m. f. (fr. √*am* [Uṇ. iv, 173] or perhaps *a-mitra*, 'not a friend' [Pāṇ. vi, 2, 116, 'not having a friend'], but see *abhy-amitrīṇa*, &c.) an enemy, adversary, foe, RV. &c.; (mfn.), not having a friend. **-khādá**, mfn. 'devouring his enemies,' N. of Indra, RV. x, 152, 1. **-ghāta**, mfn. (Ved.) killing enemies, Pāṇ. iii, 2, 88, Sch.; (*as*), m. (= Ἀμιτροχάτης) N. of Bindusāra (the son of Candragupta). **-ghātin** or **-ghna**, mfn. killing enemies, MBh.; R. **-jit**, mfn. 'conquering enemies,' N. of a son of Suvarṇa, VP. **-tapana**, mfn. tormenting enemies, AitBr. **-tā**, f. enmity, Mṛicch.; Pañcat. **-dámbhana**, mfn. hurting enemies, RV. ii, 23, 3 & iv, 15, 4. **-varman**, m., N. of a man, Daś. **-saha**, v. l. for *mitra-saha*, q. v. **-sāhá**, mfn. (for *-khādá* in RV.) enduring or overcoming enemies (N. of Indra), AV. i, 20, 4. **-senā́**, f. hostile army, SV. (= AV. iii, 1, 3); AV. v, 20, 6. **-hán**, mfn. killing enemies, RV.; VS. **-hū**, mfn. calling or inviting evil-doers, Saṃhitop. p. 7. **Amitrā-yúdh** (for °*tra-*), mfn. fighting with enemies, RV. iii, 29, 15.

Amitraya, Nom. P. (p. °*yát*) to have hostile intentions, RV.

Amitrayú, mfn. hostile, AV. xx, 127, 13.

Amitrāya, Nom. P. p. °*yát* = *amitrayát* above, AV. vii, 84, 2 (cf. RV. x, 180, 3): Ā. °*yate*, to have hostile intentions, Pañcat.

Amitrín, mfn. hostile, RV. i, 120, 8.

Amitríya, mfn. id., RV. vi, 17, 1; viii, 31, 3 & ix, 61, 20.

अमिथित *á-mithita*, mfn. not reviled; unprovoked, RV. viii, 45, 37.

A-mithyā, ind. not falsely, truthfully, Ragh.

अमिन् *amin*, mfn. (fr. 1. *ama*), sick, L.

अमिन *aminá*. See √*am*.

अमिनत् *á-minat*, mfn. (√1. *mī*), not violating or transgressing, not altering, RV.; (Ved. du. f. °*atī*) unalterable, RV. iv, 56, 2.

Á-mīta-varṇa, mf(*ā*)n. of unaltered colour, RV. iv, 51, 9.

अमिलातक *a-milātaka* = *a-malātaka*, q. v.

अमिश्र *á-miśra*, mfn. 'unmixed,' exclusive (i.e. without participation of others), ŚBr.

A-miśraṇa, *am*, n. = *a-yāvana*, q. v., Comm. on RPrāt.

A-miśraṇīya, mfn. immiscible, L.

A-miśrita, mfn. unmixed, unblended.

अमिष *amisha*=*āmisha*, q. v., Uṇ.

अमीतवर्ण *á-mīta-varṇa.* See *á-minat.*

अमीमांसा *a-mīmāṅsā*, f. (√*man*), absence of reasoning or investigation, L.

A-mīmāṅsya, mfn. not to be reasoned about or discussed, Mn. ii, 10.

अमीव *amīva*, n. (√*am*), pain, grief, R.; BhP.; (*ámīvā*), f. distress, terror, fright, RV.; AV.; VS.; tormenting spirit, demon, RV.; AV.; affliction, disease, RV. **-cátana,** mf(*ī*)n. driving away pains, diseases, or tormenting spirits, RV.; AV. **-hán,** mfn. destroying pains, killing evil spirits, RV.; BhP.

अमु *amu*, a pronom. base, used in the declension of the pronom. *adás*, that (e. g. acc. *amúm*, *amū́m*; instr. *amunā*, *amuyā*; dat. *amúshmai*, *amushyai*, &c.) **-vat,** ind. like such person or thing (referred to without name), KātyŚr. **Amū-dṛiksha** or **-dṛiś** or **-dṛiśa,** mfn. like such a one, L.

Amuka, mf(*ā*)n. such and such a person or thing, a thing or person referred to without name, Yājñ.

Amútas, ind. from there, there, RV.; AV.; from above, from the other world, from heaven, ŚBr.; Nir.; hereupon, upon this; (=abl. *amushmāt*) from that one, Daś.

Amútra, ind. there, AV.; ŚBr. &c.; there above, i. e. in the other world, in the life to come, VS.; ŚBr. &c.; there, i. e. in what precedes or has been said, ŚBr.; here, Kathās. **-bhūya,** n. being or going there (in the other world), dying, AV. vii, 53, 1 (= VS. xxvii, 29). **Amutrârtham,** ind. for the sake of (existence in the) other world, Mn. vii, 95.

Amúthā, ind. thus, in that manner, like that, Nir.; with √1. *as*, 'to be thus' (a euphemistic expression used in the sense of) to fare very ill, ŚBr.

Amuyā́, ind. (instr. f.) in that manner, thus or thus, RV.; AV.; with √1. *as* or √*bhū*, to be gone, be lost, ŚBr.

Amúrhi, ind. at that time, then, ŚBr.; BṛĀrUp.

Amushmin (loc. sg. of *adás*), ind. in the other world, L.; (forms the base of *āmushmika*, q. v.)

Amúshya (gen. sg. of *adás*), of such a one. **-kula,** mfn. belonging to the family of such a one, (gaṇas *pratijanâdi* & *manojñâdi*, q. v.) **-putra,** m. the son of such a one (i. e. of a good family, of known origin), (gaṇa *manojñâdi*, q. v.)

Amū-dṛiksha, &c. See *amu.*

अमुक्त *a-mukta*, mfn. not loosed, not let go; not liberated from birth and death; not liberated from Rāhu, still eclipsed, Vishṇus.; (*am*), n. a weapon that is always grasped and not thrown (as a knife, a sword, &c.) **-hasta,** mf(*ā*)n. 'one whose hand is not open (to give),' sparing, economical, Mn. v, 150. **-hasta-tā,** f. economy, frugality, Vishṇus.

A-mukti, *is*, f. non-liberation, L.

A-múc, *k*, f. not setting at liberty, ŚBr.

Á-mucī, f. 'not setting at liberty,' N. of an evil spirit, AV. xvi, 6, 10.

अमुख *a-mukhá* [TS.] or *á-mukha* [ŚBr. xiv], mfn. having no mouth.

A-mukhya, mfn. not chief, inferior, Jaim. &c.

अमुग्ध *á-mugdha*, mfn. not foolish, not perverse, ŚBr.

A-mūḍha, mfn. not infatuated, not perplexed; (*āni*), n. pl. (in Sāṅkhya phil.) 'not gross,' N. of the five subtle elements (*tan-mātra*, q. v.)

अमूर *á-mūra*, mf(*ā*)n. not ignorant, wise, intelligent, sharp-sighted, RV.; (v. l. *a-mura*) AV. v, 1, 9 & 11, 5.

अमूर्त *á-mūrta*, mfn. formless, shapeless, unembodied, ŚBr. xiv; Up. &c.; not forming one body, consisting of different parts, Sūryas.; (*as*), m., N. of Śiva. **-rajas** or **-rajasa** or **-rayasa,** m. a son of Kuśa (by Vaidarbhī), MBh.; R. (ed. Bomb. *asūrti-rajasa*, q. v.); VP.

A-mūrti, *is*, f. shapelessness, absence of shape or form; (mfn.), formless; (*is*), m., N. of Vishṇu, MBh. xiii; (*ayas*), m. pl. a class of Manes (who have no definite form), Hariv. **-mat,** m. = *amūrta-rajas*, q. v., VP.

अमूल *a-mūlá*, mf(*ā*, cf. Pāṇ. iv, 1, 64, Comm.)n. rootless, baseless, ŚBr. &c.; without authority, not resting on authority, Comm. on Yājñ.; (*ā*), f. 'without root,' a bulbous plant [NBD.], AV. v, 31, 4; the plant Methonica Superba, L.

A-mūlya, mfn. invaluable, priceless.

अमृक्त *á-mṛikta*, mfn. unhurt, RV.

अमृडय *a-mṛiḍayá*, mfn. pitiless, TS.

अमृणाल *a-mṛiṇāla*, *am*, n. the root of a fragrant grass (used for tatties or screens, &c., commonly called Kaskas, Andropogon Muricatus).

अमृत *a-mṛíta* (cf. Pāṇ. vi, 2, 116), mfn. not dead, MBh.; immortal, RV. &c.; imperishable, RV.; VS.; beautiful, beloved, L.; (*as*), m. an immortal, a god, RV. &c.; N. of Śiva; of Vishṇu, MBh. xiii; of Dhanvantari, L.; the plant Phaseolus Trilobus Ait.; the root of a plant, L.; (*ā*), f. a goddess, RV. &c.; spirituous liquor, L.; Emblica Officinalis, Terminalia Citrina Roxb., Cocculus Cordifolius, Piper Longum, Ocymum Sanctum; N. of the mother of Parikshit, MBh. i, 3794; of Dākshāyaṇī, MatsyaP.; of a sister of Amṛitodana, Buddh.; of a river, Hcat.; of the first *kalā* of the moon, BrahmaP.; (*am*), n. collective body of immortals, RV.; world of immortality, heaven, eternity, RV.; VS.; AV.; (also *āni*, n. pl., RV. i, 72, 1 & iii, 38, 4); immortality, RV.; final emancipation, L.; the nectar (conferring immortality, produced at the churning of the ocean), ambrosia, RV. (or the voice compared to it, N.; Ragh.); nectar-like food; antidote against poison, Suśr.; N. of a medicament, Śiś. ix, 36; medicament in general, Buddh.; the residue of a sacrifice (cf. *amṛita-bhuj*); unsolicited alms, Mn. iv, 4 & 5; water, Naigh.; milk, L.; clarified butter, L. (cf. *pañcâmṛita*); boiled rice, L.; anything sweet, a sweetmeat, R. vii, 7, 3; a pear, L.; food, L.; property, L.; gold, L.; quicksilver, L.; poison, L.; a particular poison, L.; a ray of light, Ragh. x, 59; N. of a metre, RPrāt.; of a sacred place (in the north), Hariv. 14095; of various conjunctions of planets (supposed to confer long life), L.; the number 'four,' L. **-kara** or **-kiraṇa,** m. 'nectar-rayed,' the moon, Kād. **-kuṇḍa,** n. the vessel containing the Amṛita or nectar. **-keśava,** m., N. of a temple (built by Amṛita-prabhā), Rājat. **-kshāra,** n. sal ammoniac, L. **-gati,** f., N. of a metre (consisting of four times ten syllables). **-garbhá,** m. child of immortality (said of sleep), AV. vi, 46, 1. **-cit,** mfn. piled up (as sacrificial bricks) for the sake of immortality, MaitrS. **-citi,** f. the piling up (of sacrificial bricks) conferring immortality, ŚBr. **-jaṭā,** f. the plant Valeriana Jaṭāmāṅsī. **-jā,** f. 'produced by the Amṛita,' the plant Yellow Myrobalan. **-taraṅgiṇī,** f. 'having nectar-waves,' moonlight, L. **-tā,** f. immortality, L. **-tejas,** m., N. of a Vidyādhara prince, Kathās. **-tvá,** n. = *-tā*, RV.; AV.; VS. &c. **-dīdhiti** [Kād.] or **-dyuti** [Naish.], m. 'nectar-rayed,' the moon. **-drava,** mfn. shedding ambrosia (said of the rays of the moon), Śiś. ix, 36. **-dhārā,** f. 'stream of Amṛita,' N. of a metre. **-nādôpanishad,** f. 'the sound of immortality,' N. of an Upanishad. **-pa,** mfn. drinking nectar; (*as*), m., N. of a Dānava, MBh. i, 2537; N. of Vishṇu, MBh. xiii. **-pakshá,** m. the immortal wing (of sacrificial fire), ŚBr.; (*amṛíta-paksha*), mfn. (= *hiraṇya-paksha*, q. v.) having golden wings, ŚBr. **-prabha,** m., N. of a Vidyādhara, Kathās.; (*ā*), f., N. of several women, Rājat. **-prâśana** or **-prâśin,** m. 'living on Amṛita,' a god, R. **-phala,** m. a pear tree, L.; the plant Trichosanthes Diœca Roxb.; (*am*), n. a pear, L.; the fruit of Trichosanthes D. Roxb.; (*ā*), f. the vine, L.; the plant Emblica Officinalis Gærtn. **-bandhu** (*amṛíta-*), m. friend or keeper of immortality, RV. x, 72, 5; 'friend of Nectar,' a horse (so called because produced from the ocean along with the Nectar), L. **-bindûpanishad,** f. 'drop of nectar,' N. of an Upanishad of the Atharva-veda. **-bhavana,** n., N. of a monastery (built by Amṛita-prabhā), Rājat. **-bhuj,** m. = *-prâśana*, q. v., Mcar.; one who eats the residue of a sacrifice, Bhag. **-bhojana,** mfn. one who eats the residue of a sacrifice, Mn. iii, 285. **-mati,** f. (= *-gati*, q. v.) N. of a metre. **-manthana,** n. 'the churning for the Amṛita,' N. of the chapters 17–19 of MBh. i. **-máya,** mf(*ī*)n. immortal, ŚBr. xiv; consisting of or full of Amṛita, Pañcat. &c. **-mālinī,** f. 'having an everlasting garland,' N. of Durgā. **-yajña,** m. a sacrifice for obtaining immortality, Kāṭh. **-yoga,** m. (in astrol.) a certain Yoga. **-yoní,** m. the home of the immortals, ŚBr. **-raśmi,** m. = *-kara*, q. v., Kathās.; Bhaṭṭ. **-rasa,** m. nectar, Hit. &c.; (*ā*), f. dark-coloured grapes, L. **-latā** or **-latikā,** f. a creeping plant that gives nectar, Pañcat. **-loka,** m. the world of the immortals, AitBr. **-vapus,** m. 'of immortal form,' N. of Vishṇu, MBh. xiii; of Śiva. **-vardhana,** m., N. of a poet (quoted in Śārṅgadhara's anthology). **-varshin,** mfn. giving a shower of nectar, Śak. (v. l.) **-vallarī** or **-vallī** [Suśr.], f. the creeping plant Cocculus Cordifolius. **-vākā,** f., N. of a bird, ŚBr. x. **-vindûpanishad,** see *-bind°*. **-śāstra,** n., N. of a work, Buddh. **-sambhava,** mfn. produced from nectar, MBh. xiii, 7200; (*ā*), f. = *-vallarī*, q. v. **-sahôdara,** m. 'brother of Nectar,' a horse (cf. *-bandhu*), L. **-sāra-ja,** m. 'produced from the essence of ambrosia,' raw sugar, L. **-sū,** m. (√3. *su*), 'distilling nectar,' the moon, L. **-sôdara,** m. = *-sahôdara*. **-sravā,** f., N. of a plant, L. **-srāva,** m. a flow or current of water, Sūryas. **-srut,** mfn. (= *-drava*, q. v.), Kum. i, 46; Śiś. ix, 68. **-harītakī,** f., N. of a medicament. **-hrada,** m. a lake of nectar, Śak. **Amṛitâṅśu,** m. the moon, Kathās. **Amṛitâkara,** m. 'a mine of nectar,' N. of a man, Rājat. **Amṛitâkshara,** n. anything imperishable, Up. **Amṛitânanda,** m., N. of a man, Buddh. **Amṛitândhas,** m. 'whose food is ambrosia,' a god, L. **Amṛitâpidhānā,** n. water sipped after eating nectar-like food so as to overlay it like a cover, TĀr.; ĀśvGṛ.; MānGṛ. (cf. *amṛitôpastáraṇa*). **Amṛitā-phala,** n. (= *amṛita-phala*, n., q. v.) the fruit of Trichosanthes, L. **Amṛitâbhishikta,** mfn. anointed with nectar, ŚBr. **Amṛitâśa,** m. = *amṛita-prâśana*, q. v., MBh. xii; N. of Vishṇu, MBh. xiii. **Amṛitâśana,** m. = *amṛita-prâśana*, q. v., L. **Amṛitâśma,** m.?, Pāṇ. v, 4, 94, Sch. **Amṛitâshṭamī-tapas,** n., N. of a work. **Amṛitâsaṅga,** n. blue vitriol, Car. **Amṛitâsu,** mfn. whose soul is immortal, AV. v, 1, 1 & 7. **Amṛitâharaṇa,** m. 'nectar-stealer,' N. of Garuḍa; (*am*), n., N. of a Pariśishṭa work of the SV. **Amṛitâhuti,** f., N. of an oblation (offered to the gods), AitBr. **Amṛitâhva,** n. a pear, L. **Amṛitī-karaṇa,** n. changing into nectar. **Amṛitêśa,** m. 'lord of the immortals,' N. of Śiva, PadmaP. **Amṛite-śaya,** m. 'lying on Amṛita,' N. of Vishṇu, Hariv. **Amṛitêśvara,** m. = *amṛitêśa*, q. v., Rājat.; N. of a medicament, Bhpr. **Amṛitêshṭakā,** f. a burnt or baked (and therefore imperishable) brick (used for the sacrificial altar), ŚBr. **Amṛitôtpatti,** f. the production of the Amṛita (N. of a chapter of the first book of the Rāmāyaṇa, relating how the Amṛita was obtained by the gods). **Amṛitôtpanna,** n. impure carbonate of zinc, L.; (*ā*), f. a fly, L. **Amṛitôdana,** m., N. of a son of Siṅhahanu, and uncle of Śākyamuni. **Amṛitôdbhava** or **amṛitôpama,** n. = *amṛitôtpanna*, n., q. v., L. **Amṛitôpastáraṇa,** n. water sipped as a substratum for the nectar-like food, ĀśvGṛ. & MānGṛ.; an imperishable substratum, TĀr. (cf. *amṛitâpidhānā*).

Amṛitaka, *am*, n. the nectar of immortality.

Amṛitāya, Nom. Ā. °*yate*, to turn into nectar, Kād.; (p. °*yamāna*) to be like nectar, Ragh. ii, 61.

Amṛitāyana, mfn. nectar-like, BhP.

अमृत्पात्रप *á-mṛit-pātra-pa*, mfn. not drinking from a clay vessel, MaitrS.

A-mṛin-maya, mfn. not made of clay, TBr.; Śulb.; KātyŚr. **-pa** [PBr.] or **-pāyin** (*á-mṛin-maya-*) [ŚBr. xiv & PārGṛ.], mfn. = *á-mṛit-pātra-pa*.

अमृत्यु *á-mṛityu*, *us*, m. non-death, immortality, ŚBr. xiii; KaushUp.; (mfn.), immortal, RV.

अमृध्र *á-mṛidhra.* See *á-mardhat.*

अमृषा *a-mṛishā́*, ind. not falsely, certainly, surely, ŚBr. xiv; BhP. **-bhāshi-tva,** n. speaking truthfully (one of the qualities of a good spy), Comm. on Kir. **Amṛishôdya,** n. true speech, Bhaṭṭ. vi, 57.

अमृष्ट *a-mṛishṭa*, mfn. (√*mṛij*), not rubbed or washed, unclean, R. (v. l.) **-bhuj** or **-bhojin,** mfn. not eating delicate food or dainties (cf. 1. *mṛishṭa*), R. i, 6, 8 (i, 6, 11 ed. Bomb.) **-mṛija,** mfn. of unimpaired purity, Bhaṭṭ.

अमृष्यमाण *á-mṛishyamāṇa*, mfn. (√*mṛish*), not bearing, not tolerating, ŚBr. xii, &c.

अमेक्षण *a-mekshaṇa*, mfn. having no *mekshaṇa* or mixing instrument.

अमेदस्क *a-medáska*, mfn. without fat, lean, TS.; Suśr.

अमेधस् *a-medhas*, mfn. unintelligent, foolish, an idiot, Pāṇ. v, 4, 122.

अमेध्य *a-medhyá*, mfn. not able or not allowed to sacrifice, not fit for sacrifice, impure, unholy, nefarious, foul, ŚBr.; Mn. &c.; (*am*), n. fæces, excrement, KātyŚr.; Mn. ix, 282; Yājñ. &c. **—kuṇapâśin**, mfn. feeding on carrion. **—tā**, f. or **-tva**, n. impurity, foulness, filthiness. **—yukta**, mfn. filthy, foul. **—lipta**, mfn. smeared with ordure, Mn. iv, 56; BhP. **—lepa**, m. smearing with ordure. **Amedhyâkta**, mfn. soiled with ordure, Mn.

अमेन *a-mená*, *as*, m. having no wife, a widower, RV. v, 31, 2.

अमेनि *a-mení*, mfn. not casting or throwing, not able to throw, AV. v, 6, 9 & 10; VS.; TBr.

अमेय *a-meya*, mfn. immeasurable, MBh. viii, 1975; Kathās. **Ameyâtman**, mfn. possessing immense powers of mind, magnanimous, MBh.; Ragh. x, 18; (*ā*), m., N. of Vishṇu, MBh. xiii.

अमेष्ट *améshṭá*. See 1. *amá*.

अमेह *á-meha*, *as*, m. retention of urine, TS.; Kāṭh.; PBr.

अमोक्य *a-mokyá*, mfn. (√*muc*), that cannot be unloosed, AV. iii, 6, 5.

A-mocana, *am*, n. not loosening or letting go, L.

A-mocanīya, mfn. not to be liberated.

A-mocita, mfn. not liberated, confined.

A-mocya, mfn. = °*canīya*, q. v., Ragh. iii, 65.

अमोक्ष *a-moksha*, mfn. (√*moksh*), unliberated, unloosed, L.; (*as*), m. want of freedom, bondage, confinement; non-liberation (from mundane existence).

A-mokshayat, mfn. not liberating, Yājñ. ii, 300.

अमोचन *a-mocana*, &c. See *a-mokyá*.

अमोघ *a-mogha*, mf(*ā*)n. unerring, unfailing, not vain, efficacious, succeeding, hitting the mark; productive, fruitful; (*á-mogha*), *as*, m. the not erring, the not failing, ŚBr.; N. of Śiva; of Vishṇu, MBh. xiii; of Skanda, MBh. iii, 14632; of a minister of an Asura king at war with Kārttikeya, SkandaP.; of a river, L.; (*ā*), f. trumpet flower, Bignonia Suaveolens, Roxb.; a plant of which the seed is used as a vermifuge, Erycibe Paniculata Roxb.; Terminalia Citrina Roxb.; N. of a spear, MBh. iii, 16990 & R. i, 29, 12; (with or without *rātri*) 'the unfailing one,' a poetical N. of the night, MBh.; a mystical N. of the letter *ksh* (being the last one of the alphabet); N. of Durgā, L.; of the wife of Śāntanu; of one of the mothers in Skanda's suite, MBh. ix, 2639. **—kiraṇa**, *āni*, n. pl. 'the unerring rays,' N. of the rays immediately after sunrise and before sunset, VarBṛS. **—daṇḍa**, m. 'unerring in punishment,' N. of Śiva. **—darśana**, m. 'of an unfailing eye,' N. of a Nāga, Buddh. **—darśin**, m., N. of a Bodhisattva. **—dṛiś**, mfn. of an unfailing look or eye, BhP. **—nandinī**, f., N. of a Śikshā-text. **—patana**, mfn. 'not falling in vain,' reaching the aim, Rājat. **—pāśa**, m., N. of a Lokeśvara, Buddh. **—bala**, mfn. of never-failing strength (said of the horse Uccaiḥśravas). **—bhūti**, m., N. of a king of the Pañjāb. **—rāja**, m., N. of a Bhikshu, Lalit. **—varsha**, m., N. of a Caulukya prince. **—vāc**, mfn. whose words are not vain, BhP. **—vāñchita**, mfn. never disappointed, L. **—vikrama**, m. 'of unerring valour,' N. of Śiva. **—siddhi**, m., N. of the fifth Dhyānibuddha. **Amoghâkshī**, f., N. of Dākshāyaṇī, MatsyaP. **Amoghâcārya**, m., N. of an author.

अमोत *amôtá*, mfn. woven at home, AV.; Kauś. **—pútraka**, m. a child protected at home ['a weaver's boy,' NBD.], AV. xx, 127, 5.

Amótaka, *as*, m. protected at home (as a child) ['a weaver,' NBD.], AV. xx, 127, 5.

अमौत्रधौत *a-mautra-dhauta*, mfn. not washed (by a washerman) with alkaline lye, KātyŚr.

अमौन *a-mauná*, *am*, n. the state of not being a Muni or not keeping the vows of a Muni, ŚBr. xiv.

अम्नस् *amnás*, mfn. unawares, AV. viii, 6, 19; Kāṭh.; APrāt. [according to Pāṇ. viii, 2, 70 the word is liable to become *amnar* in Sandhi].

अम्ब् *amb*, cl. 1. P. *ambati*, to go, L.: cl. 1. Ā. *ambate*, to sound, L.

अम्ब *ámba*. See *ambá*.

अम्बक *ambaka*, *am*, n. Śiva's eye, Bālar. (cf. *try-ambaka*); an eye, L.; copper, L.

अम्बया *ambayā*. See *ambá*.

अम्बर *ámbara*, *am*, n. circumference, compass, neighbourhood, RV. viii, 8, 14; (ifc. f. *ā*) clothes, apparel, garment, MBh. &c.; cotton, L.; sky, atmosphere, ether, Naigh.; MBh. &c.; (hence) a cipher, Sūryas.; N. of the tenth astrological mansion, VarBṛ.; the lip; saffron, L.; a perfume (Ambra), L.; N. of a country, MatsyaP.; (*ās*), m. pl., N. of a people, VarBṛS. **—ga**, mfn. sky-going, Suśr. **—cara**, mfn. id., Kathās.; a bird, Pañcat.; a Vidyādhara, Kathās. **—cārin**, m. a planet. **—da**, n. 'giving clothes,' cotton. **—nagarī**, f., N. of a town. **—pushpa**, n. 'a flower in the sky,' anything impossible; (cf. *abhra-pushpa*.) **—prabhā**, f., N. of a princess, Kathās. **—maṇi**, m. 'sky-jewel,' the sun, Sāh.; Bālar. **—yuga**, n. 'pair of vestments,' the two principal female garments (upper and lower). **—śaila**, m. a high mountain (touching the sky). **—sthalī**, f. the earth, L. **Ambarâdhikārin**, m. superintendent over the robes (an office at court), Rājat. **Ambarânta**, m. the end of a garment; the horizon. **Ambarâukas**, m. 'sky-dweller,' a god, Kum. v, 79.

अम्बरीष *ambarísha*, *as*, *am*, m. n. a frying-pan, TS. v; KātyŚr.; (*as*), m., N. of a hell, Jain.; remorse, L.; war, battle, L.; a young animal, colt, L.; the sun, R. v, 3, 5; sky, atmosphere, Comm. on Uṇ.; the hog-plum plant (Spondias Magnifera), L.; N. of a Rājarshi (son of the king Vṛishāgir, and composer of the hymns RV. i, 100 & ix, 98), RV. i, 100, 17; of a descendant of Manu Vaivasvata and son of Nābhāga (celebrated for his devotion to Vishṇu), MBh. &c.; N. of a Rājarshi (descendant of Sagara and ancestor of Daśaratha), R.; N. of a son of the patriarch Pulaha, VāyuP. &c.; N. of Śiva, L.; of Vishṇu, L.; of Gaṇeśa, Kathās. **—putra**, m. son of Ambarīsha, whence the N. of a country, (gaṇa *rājanyâdi*.)

अम्बर्य *ambarya*, Nom. P. °*ryati*, to bring together, collect, (gaṇa *kaṇḍv-ādi*.)

अम्बष्ठ *amba-shṭha*, *as*, m. (fr. *amba* and *stha?*, Pāṇ. viii, 3, 97), N. of a country and of its inhabitants, MBh.; VarBṛS. &c.; of the king of that country, MBh. vii, 3399 seqq.; the offspring of a man of the Brāhman and a woman of the Vaiśya caste (a man of the medical caste, Mn. x, 47; an elephant-driver, BhP.), Mn. x; Yājñ. &c.; (*ā*), f. Jasminum Auriculatum, L.; Clypea Hernandifolia, Suśr.; Oxalis Corniculata, Suśr.; (*ā*), f. an Ambashṭha woman [Comm. on Mn. x, 15]; (*ī*), f. [Mn. x, 19], id.

Ambashṭhakī, f. Clypea Hernandifolia, L.

Ambashṭhikā, f. Clerodendrum Siphonanthus.

अम्बा *ambá*, f. (Ved. voc. *ámbe* [VS.] or *amba* [RV.], in later Sanskrit *amba* only, sometimes a mere interjection, ĀśvŚr.), a mother, good woman (as a title of respect); N. of a plant; N. of Durgā (the wife of Śiva); N. of an Apsaras, L.; N. of a daughter of a king of Kāśi, MBh.; N. of one of the seven Kṛittikās, TS.; Kāṭh.; TBr.; a term in astrol. (to denote the fourth condition which results from the conjunction of planets?). In the South-Indian languages, *ambā* is corrupted into *ammā*, and is often affixed to the names of goddesses, and females in general [Germ. *Amme*, 'a nurse;' Old Germ. *amma*, Them. *ammôn*, *ammûn*]. **—gaṅgā**, f. a river in Ceylon. **—janman**, n., N. of a Tīrtha, MBh. iii, 6051.

Ambayā, f. mother (a N. of rivers), KaushUp.

Ambāḍā or **ambālā**, f. mother, Pāṇ. vii, 3, 107, Comm. (voc. °*ḍe* & °*le*) & Kāś. (in Veda voc. optionally °*ḍa* & °*la*).

Ambālikā, f. (voc. *ámbālike*), mother, VS.; N. of a plant; N. of a daughter of a king of Kāśi (wife of Vicitravīrya, and mother of Pāṇḍu), MBh.

Ambālī, f. mother, TS. vii (voc. *ámbāli* for *ambāle* as mentioned by Pāṇ. vi, 1, 118).

Ambí, *is*, f. mother, RV. i, 23, 16; Superl. voc. *ámbitame*, 'O dearest mother!' RV. ii, 41, 16; (cf. *ambí*.)

Ambikā, f. (voc. *ámbike*), mother, good woman (as a term of respect), VS. & TS. (cf. Pāṇ. vi, 1, 118); Pāṇ. vii, 3, 107, Comm. (voc. °*ke*) & Kāś. (in Veda voc. optionally °*ka* & °*ke*); a N. applied to the harvest (as the most productive season), Kāṭh.; a sister of Rudra, VS.; ŚBr.; N. of Pārvatī (the wife of Śiva), Hariv.; Yājñ. &c.; of the wife of Rudra Ugraretas, BhP.; of one of the mothers in Skanda's retinue, MBh. ix, 2630; of a daughter of the king of Kāśi (wife of Vicitravīrya, and mother of Dhṛitarāshṭra), MBh. &c. (cf. *ambālikā*); one of the female domestic deities of the Jainas, L.; N. of a place in Bengal, L.; N. of two rivers, Hcat.; the plant Wrightia Antidysenterica. **—pati**, m., N. of Śiva; N. of Rudra or Śiva, TĀr.; Kād. &c. **—putra** or **-suta**, m., N. of Dhṛitarāshṭra.

Ambikeya, *as*, m. (for *āmbikeya*, q. v.) N. of Dhṛitarāshṭra, MBh. iii, 219 & 250; of Gaṇeśa, L.; of Kārttikeya, L.

Ambí, f. = *ambí*, q. v., RV. viii, 72, 5 (acc. *ambyàm*) & Kāṭh.

अम्बु *ámbu*, n. water, Naigh.; MBh. &c.; a kind of Andropogon, VarBṛS.; Bhpr.; N. of a metre (consisting of ninety syllables), RPrāt.; the number 'four,' VarBṛ. **—kaṇa**, m. 'a drop of water,' a shower, L. **—kaṇṭaka** or **-kirāta**, m. the short-nosed alligator, L. **—kīśa** or **-kūrma**, m. a porpoise (especially the Gangetic, Delphinus Gangeticus), L. **—keśara**, m. lemon tree, L. **—kriyā**, f. a funeral rite (= *jala-kriyā*), Bhaṭṭ. **—ga**, mfn. 'water-goer,' living in water. **—ghana**, m. hail, frozen rain, L. **—cara**, mfn. moving in the water, aquatic. **—cāmara**, n. 'water-chowrī,' the aquatic plant Valisneria. **—cārin**, mfn. moving in water (as a fish, &c.), Mn. xii, 57 (cf. *ap-cara* s. v. 2. *áp*). **—ja**, mfn. produced in water, water-born, aquatic; (*as*), m. the plant Barringtonia Acutangula Gærtn.; a lotus (Nymphæa Nelumbo); a muscle-shell, R. vii, 7, 10; the thunderbolt of Indra ('cloud-born'), L. **—janman**, n. a lotus (Nymphæa Nelumbo), Naish. **—ja-bhū**, m. 'being in a lotus,' the god Brahmā. **—ja-stha**, mfn. sitting on a lotus. **—jâksha**, mf(*ī*)n. lotus-eyed. **—jānanā**, f. 'having a lotus face,' N. of the tutelary deity of the Ojishṭha family, BrahmaP. **—taskara**, m. 'water-thief,' the sun, L. **—tāla**, m. (= *-cāmara*) the plant Valisneria. **—da**, m. 'giving water,' a cloud; the plant Cyperus Hexastychius Communis; *ambudâranya*, n., N. of a forest. **—deva** or **-daiva**, n. 'having the waters as deity,' N. of the astrological mansion Pūrvāshāḍhā, VarBṛS. **—dhara**, m. 'water-holder,' a cloud. **—dhi**, m. 'receptacle of waters,' the ocean; the number 'four;' (*ambudhi*)-*kāminī*, f. a river, Bhām.; *-sravā*, f. the plant Aloes Perfoliata. **—nātha**, m. 'lord of the waters,' the ocean, Hariv. **—nidhi**, m. 'treasury of waters,' the ocean. **—nivaha**, m. 'water-bearer,' a cloud, VarBṛS. **—1. -pa**, m. 'drinking water,' the plant Cassia Tora or Alata, L. **—2. -pa**, m. 'lord of the waters,' Varuṇa, R. vii, 3, 18. **—pakshin**, m. aquatic bird, Kathās. **—pati**, m. = 2. *-pa*, VarBṛS.; the ocean. **—pattrā**, f. (= *-da*), the plant Cyperus Hex. C. **—paddhati**, f. or **-pāta**, m. current, stream, flow of water, L. **—prasāda**, m. or **-prasādana**, n. the clearing nut tree, Strychnos Potatorum (the nuts of this plant are generally used in India for purifying water [cf. Mn. vi, 67]; they are rubbed upon the inner surface of a vessel, and so precipitate the impurities of the fluid it contains). **—bhṛit**, m. a cloud, L.; talc, L.; the grass Cyperus Pertenuis, L. **—mat**, mfn. watery, having or containing water; (*tī*), f., N. of a river, MBh. iii, 6026. **—mātra-ja**, mfn. produced only in water. **—muc**, m. a cloud, Kir. v, 12, Śiś. **—yantra**, n. clepsydra, VarBṛS. **—raya**, m. a current, R. ii, 63, 43. **—rāja**, m. = *-nātha*, Nalod.; = 2. *-pa*, Hariv. **—rāśi**, m. 'heap of waters,' the ocean, Kum.; Ragh. &c. **—ruha**, n. (ifc. f. *ā*) 'water-growing,' the day-lotus, R. &c.; (*ā*), f. Hibiscus Mutabilis. **—ruhiṇī**, f. the lotus, Kathās. **—rohiṇī**, f. id., L. **—vācī**, f. four days in Āshāḍha (the tenth to the thirteenth of the dark half of the month, when the earth is supposed to be unclean, and agriculture is prohibited), BrahmavP. ii, 77; (*ambuvācī*)-*tyāga*, m. the thirteenth of the same; *-prada*, n. the tenth in the second half of the month Āshāḍha. **—vāsinī** or **-vāsī**, f. the trumpet flower (Bignonia Suaveolens). L. **—vāha**, m. a cloud, Kum.; Megh. &c.; the grass Cyperus Pertenuis; a water-carrier, L.; talc, L.; the number 'seventeen,' L. **—vāhin**, mfn. carrying or conveying water; (*inī*), f. a wooden baling vessel, L.; N. of a river (v. l. *madhu-vāhinī*), MBh. vi, 334; VP. **—vetasa**, m. a kind of cane or reed growing in water. **—śi-**

rīshikā, f., N. of a plant, Bhpr. **—śītā**, f., N. of a river, R. iv, 41, 16. **—sarpiṇī**, f. 'water-glider,' a leech, L. **—secanī**, f. (= *-vāhinī*) a wooden baling vessel, L.

अम्बूकृत *ambū-kṛita*, mfn. (*ambū* used onomatopoetically to denote by trying to utter *mb* the effect caused by shutting the lips on pronouncing a vowel), pronounced indistinctly (so that the words remain too much in the mouth); [in later writers derived fr. *ambu*, water] sputtered, accompanied with saliva, Pat.; Lāṭy. (*an-*, neg.); (*am*), n. a peculiar indistinct pronunciation of the vowels, RPrāt.; Pat.; roaring (of beasts) accompanied with emission of saliva, Uttarar.; Mālatim.

अम्ब्य *ambyà*, *as*, m. 'a chanter' (an error of Sāy.'s on RV. viii, 72, 5; cf. *ambí*).

अम्भ् *ambh*, *ambhate*, to sound, L.

Ambhaṇa, *am*, n. 'sounding,' the body of the Vīṇā lute, AitĀr.

अम्भस् *ámbhas*, n. (cf. *abhrá*, *ámbu*), water, RV. &c.; the celestial waters, AitUp.; power, fruitfulness, VS. & AV.; (*āṅsi*), n. pl. collective N. for gods, men, Manes, and Asuras, TBr. &VP.; (hence) (*as*), sg. the number 'four;' mystical N. of the letter *v*; N. of a metre (consisting of 82 syllables), RPrāt.; (*asā*), instr. in comp. for *ambhas* (e. g. *ambhasā-kṛita*, 'done by water'), Pāṇ. vi, 3, 3; (*asī*), n. du. heaven and earth, Naigh. [ὄμβρος, *imber*].

Ambhaḥ (in comp. for *ambhas*). **—pati**, m. 'the lord of the waters,' Varuṇa. **—śyāmāka**, m. water hair-grass, Car. **—sāra**, m. a pearl, L. **—sū**, m. smoke, L. **—stha**, mfn. standing in water, Hit.

Ambho (in comp. for *ambhas*). **—ja**, n. (ifc. f. *ā*) 'water-born,' the day-lotus; (*as*), m. the plant Calamus Rotang, L.; the Sārasa or Indian crane, L. **—ja-khaṇḍa**, n. a group of lotus flowers, Pāṇ. iv, 2, 51, Kāś. **—ja-janman**, m., N. of Brahmā (born in a lotus). **—janma-jani**, m. (= *ja-janman*) Brahmā, BhP. **—janman**, n. (= *-ja*) 'water-born,' the lotus, BhP. **—ja-yoni**, m. id. **—jinī**, f. the lotus plant, Kathās. &c.; an assemblage of lotus flowers or a place where they abound, (gaṇa *pushkarâdi*, q. v.) **—da**, m. a cloud, MBh. &c.; the plant Cyperus Hexastychius Communis Nees. **—dhara**, m. a cloud, Mṛicch. &c. **—dhi**, m. 'receptacle of waters,' the ocean; (*ambudhi*)*-pallava* or *-vallabha*, m. coral, L. **—nidhi**, m. the ocean. **—muc**, m. 'water-shedder,' a cloud, Kād. **—rāśi**, m. (= *-nidhi*) the ocean. **—ruh**, n. 'water-growing,' the lotus. **—ruha**, n. (ifc. f. *ā*) id., Kum. &c.; (*as*), m. (= *-ja*, m.) the Indian crane; N. of a son of Viśvāmitra, MBh. xiii, 258.

अम्भिणी *ambhiṇí* (for °*bhṛiṇí*), f., N. of a preceptress (who transmitted the white Yajur-veda to Vāc, speech), ŚBr. xiv; (cf. *āmbhṛiṇī*.)

Ambhṛiṇá, mfn. (cf. *ámbhas*, ὄβριμος, ὄμβριμος), powerful, great [Naigh.], RV. i, 133, 5 ['roaring terribly,' Sāy.]; (*ás*), m. a vessel (used in preparing the Soma juice), VS. & ŚBr.; N. of a Ṛishi (father of Vāc), RAnukr.; (cf. *āmbhṛiṇī*.)

अम्मय *am-maya*, mf(*ī*)n. (for *ap-maya*; Pāṇ. iv, 3, 144, Siddh.), formed from or consisting of water, watery, Ragh. x, 59; BhP.

अम्यक् *ámyak*, ind. 'towards, here' (Nir. & Sāy. on RV. i, 169, 3); but see √*myaksh*.

अम्र *amra*, *as*, m. = *āmra*, q. v., L.

Amrāta, *as*, m. = *āmrāta*, q. v., L.

Amrātaka, *as*, m. = *āmrāt*°, q. v., VarBṛS.

अम्ल *amla*, mfn. sour, acid, Mn. v, 114, &c.; (*as*), m. (with or without *rasa*) acidity, vinegar, Suśr.; wood sorrel (Oxalis Corniculata), Suśr.; (*ī*), f. Oxalis Corniculata, L.; (*am*), n. sour curds, Suśr. **—kāṇḍa**, n., N. of a plant. **—keśara**, m. citron tree. **—cukrikā**, f. or **-cūḍa**, m. a kind of sorrel. **—jambīra**, m. lime tree. **—tā**, f. sourness, Suśr. **—drava**, m. the acid juice (of fruits), Bhpr. **—nāyaka**, m. sorrel. **—nimbūka**, m. the lime. **—niśā**, f. the plant Curcuma Zerumbet Roxb. **—pañcaka** or **-pañca-phala**, n. a collection of five kinds of sour vegetables and fruits. **—pattra**, m. the plant Oxalis and other plants. **—panasa**, m. the tree Artocarpus Lacucha Roxb. **—pitta**, n. acidity of stomach. **—phala**, m. the tamarind tree, Magnifera Indica; (*am*), n. the fruit of this tree, Suśr. **—bhedana**, m. sorrel, L. **—meha**, m. acid urine (a disease), Suśr. **—rasa**, mfn. having a sour taste; (*as*), m. sourness, acidity. **—ruhā**, f. a kind of betel. **—loṇikā** or **-loṇī** or **-lolikā**, f. wood sorrel (Oxalis Corniculata). **—varga**, m. a class of plants with acid leaves or fruits (as the lime, orange, pomegranate, tamarind, sorrel, and others), Suśr. **—vallī**, f. the plant Pythonium Bulbiferum Schott. **—vāṭaka**, m. hog-plum (Spondias Magnifera). **—vāṭikā**, f. a kind of betel. **—vāstūka**, n. sorrel. **—vṛiksha**, m. the tamarind tree. **—vetasa**, m. a kind of dock or sorrel, Rumex Vesicarius, MBh. iii, 11568; Suśr.; (*am*), n. vinegar (obtained from fruit), L. **—śāka**, m. a sort of sorrel (commonly used as a pot-herb). **—sāra**, m. the lime; a kind of sorrel; (*am*), n. rice water after fermentation. **—haridrā**, f. the plant Curcuma Zerumbet Roxb. **Amlâṅkuśa**, m. a kind of sorrel. **Amlâdhyushita**, n. a disease of the eyes (caused by eating acid food), Suśr. **Amlībhūta**, mfn. become sour, Suśr. **Amlôdgāra**, m. sour eructation, L.

Amlaka, *as*, m. the plant Artocarpus Lakuca; (*ikā*), f. a sour taste in the mouth, acidity of stomach, Suśr.; the tamarind tree; wood sorrel (Oxalis Corniculata). **—vaṭaka**, m. a sort of cake, Bhpr.

Amliman, *ā*, m. sourness, L.

Amlīkā, f. (= *amlikā*, q.v.) acidity of stomach, Suśr.; wood sorrel, L.

अम्लान *a-mlāna*, mfn. (√*mlai*), unwithered, clean, clear; bright, unclouded (as the mind or the face), MBh. &c.; (*as*), m. globe-amaranth (Gomphræna Globosa L.), Hcat.

A-mlāni, *is*, f. vigour, freshness, L.

A-mlānin, mfn. clean, clear, L.; (*inī*), f. an assemblage of globe-amaranths, L.

A-mlāyin, mfn. unfading, Kathās.

अय् *ay* = √*i*, only supposed to be a separate rt. on account of such forms of √*i*, as *ayate* [RV. i, 127, 3], &c. See √*i*.

Áya, *as*, m. going (only ifc., cf. *abhyastam-aya*); (with *gavām*) 'the going or the turn of the cows,' N. of a periodical sacrifice, MBh.; a move towards the right at chess, Pat. (cf. *ayấnaya*); Ved. a die, RV. x, 116, 9; AV. &c.; the number 'four;' good luck, favourable fortune, Nalod. **—vat**, mfn. happy, Kir. v, 20. **—śobhin**, mfn. bright with good fortune, Śiś. **Ayânaya**, see s. v. **Ayânvita**, mfn. fortunate, lucky, Ragh. iv, 26; (*as*), m., N. of Śaṅkarācārya, L.

Ayátha, *am*, n. a foot, RV. x, 28, 10 & 11; (mfn.) prosperous, PārGṛ.

Áyana, mfn. going, VS. xxii, 7; Nir.; (*am*), n. walking, a road, a path, RV. iii, 33, 7, &c. (often ifc., cf. *naimishâyana*, *purushâyana*, *praśamâyana*, *samudrâyana*, *svedâyana*); (in astron.) advancing, precession, Sūryas.; (with gen. [e. g. *áṅgirasām*, *ādityā́nām*, *gavām*, &c.] or ifc.) 'course, circulation,' N. of various periodical sacrificial rites, AV.; ŚBr. &c.; the sun's road north and south of the equator, the half year, Mn. &c.; the equinoctial and solstitial points, VarBṛS. &c.; way, progress, manner, ŚBr.; place of refuge, Mn. i, 10; a treatise (*śāstra*, cf. *jyotishām-ayana*), L. **—kalā**, *ās*, f. pl. the correction (in minutes) for ecliptic deviation, Sūryas. **—graha**, m. a planet's longitude as corrected for ecliptic deviation, ib. **—dṛik-karman**, n. calculation for ecliptic deviation, ib. **—bhāga**, m. (in astron.) the amount of precession, ib. **—vṛitta**, n. the ecliptic. **Ayanâṅśa**, m. = *ayana-bhāga*, Sūryas. **Ayanânta**, m. solstice, ib.

अयक्ष्म *a-yakshmá*, mf(*ā́*)n. not consumptive, not sick, healthy, VS.; AV.; causing health, salubrious, RV. ix, 49, 1; VS.; AV.; (*ám*), n. health, VS. **—m-káraṇa**, mf(*ī*)n. producing health, AV. xix, 2, 5. **—tāti** (*ayakshmá-*), f. health, AV. iv, 25, 5. **—tvá**, n. id., ŚBr.

अयक्ष्यमाण *a-yakshyamāṇa*, mfn. not wishing or not about to institute a sacrifice, Jaim.

A-yajamāna, mfn. not instituting a sacrifice, VS. &c.

A-yajúshka, mfn. without a Yajus-formula, ŚBr.; (*am*), ind. id., TBr.

A-yajús, n. 'not a Yajus-formula,' (*úshā*), instr. without a Yajus-formula, MaitrS. **Á-yajush-kṛita**, mfn. not consecrated with a Yajus-formula, ŚBr.; Lāṭy.

Á-yajña, *as*, m. not a real sacrifice, ŚBr. & TBr.; non-performance of a sacrifice, Mn. iii, 120; Lāṭy.; Gaut.; (*a-yajñá*), mfn. not offering a sacrifice, RV. vii, 6, 3 & x, 138, 6. **—sac** (*á-yajña-*), m (nom. pl. *ācas*) fn. not performing a sacrifice, RV. vi, 67, 9.

A-yajñiyá, mfn. not fit for sacrifice, ŚBr. (once *á-yajñiya*); profane, unworthy, RV. x, 124, 3 & AV. xii, 2, 37.

A-yajñīya, mfn. not fit for sacrifice, KapS.

Á-yajyu, mfn. not sacrificing, impious, RV.

Á-yajvan, mfn. id., RV. &c.; Mn. xi, 14 & 20.

अयज्ञदत्त *a-yajñadatta*, *as*, m. not Yajñadatta, i. e. the vile Yajñadatta, Pāṇ. vi, 2, 159, Kāś.

अयत् *a-yat*, mfn. (√*yam*), not making efforts, Bhaṭṭ.

Á-yata, mfn. unrestrained, uncontrolled.

A-yati, *is*, m. no ascetic, Bhag.; N. of one of the six sons of Nahusha, MBh. i, 3155.

अयतत् *á-yatat*, mfn. (√*yat*), not going side by side, RV. ii, 24, 5 ['not making efforts,' Gmn.]

A-yatna, *as*, m. absence of effort or exertion; (*ena* [Mn. v, 47, &c.], *āt*, or in comp. *ayatna-*), ind. without effort or exertion. **—kārin**, mfn. making no exertion, idle. **—kṛita** or **-ja**, mfn. easily or readily produced, spontaneous, L. **—tas**, ind. without effort or exertion. **—bālavyajanī-√bhū** (perf. 3. pl. *-babhūvuḥ*) to become or be changed into a fan without effort, Ragh. xvi, 33. **—vat**, mfn. inactive, idle.

अयथ *ayátha*. See col. 2.

अयथा *a-yathā*, ind. not as it should be, unfitly, BhP. **—kṛita**, mfn. done unfitly, VarBṛS. **—jātīyaka**, mfn. contrary to what should be the case, Pat. on Pāṇ. ii, 1, 10. **—tatham**, ind. not so as it should be, Pāṇ. vii, 3, 31; Mn. iii, 240. **—tathā**, ind. given by Pat. on Pāṇ. vii, 3, 31 as the base of *āyathātathya* (whereas Pāṇ. derives it from *-tatham*, q. v.) **—devatam** (*á-yathā-*), ind. not consonant or suitable to a deity, TBr. **—dyotana**, n. intimation of something that should not be, Pāṇ. ii, 1, 10, Comm. **—puram**, ind. not as formerly, Pāṇ. vii, 3, 31. **—pūrva**, mfn. not being so as before, Ragh. xii, 88; BhP.; (*á-yathāpūrvam*), ind. not in regular order, TBr. **—balam**, ind. not according to one's strength, Śiś. **Ayathâbhipreta**, mfn. not desired, not agreeable, Pāṇ. iii, 4, 59. **A-yathā-mātram**, ind. not according to measure or quantity (a defect in the pronunciation of vowels), RPrāt. **A-yathâmukhīna**, mfn. having the face turned away, Bhaṭṭ. **Á-yathâyatham**, ind. not as it ought to be, unsuitably, ŚBr. **A-yathârtha**, mf(*ā*)n. incorrect, incongruous, Śāk. &c.; (*am*), ind. incorrectly, Jaim. **A-yathā-vat**, ind. incorrectly, Bhag. **A-yathā-śāstra-kārin**, mfn. not acting in accordance with the scripture. **Ayathā-sthita**, mfn. not being in order, deranged, Kād. **A-yathêshṭa**, mfn. not according to wish, not intended, Pāṇ. viii, 2, 1 & 116, Comm. **A-yathôktam**, ind. not in accordance with what has been stated, RPrāt. **A-yathôcita**, mfn. unsuitable, Pañcat.

अयदीक्षित *aya-dīkshita*, *as*, m., N. of an author (nephew of Apyaya-dikshita, q. v.)

अयन *áyana*. See √*ay*, col. 2.

अयन्त्र *a-yantrá*, *am*, n. non-restraint, not a means of restraining, RV. x, 46, 6; (cf. *paśv-ayantra*.)

A-yantraṇā, f. not putting on a bandage, not dressing, Suśr.

A-yantrita, mfn. unhindered, unrestrained, self-willed, Mn. ii, 118, &c.

अयभ्या *á-yabhyā*, f. (a woman) with whom one ought not to cohabit, AV. xx, 128, 8.

अयम् *ayám*, this one. See *idám*.

अयमित *a-yamita*, mfn. 'unchecked.' **—nakha**, mfn. with untrimmed nails, Megh.

अयव 1. *á-yava*, *as*, m. the dark half of the month, VS.; ŚBr.

Á-yavan, *ā*, m. [ŚBr.] or **á-yavas**, n. [VS.], id. 1. **Á-yāva**, *as*, or **á-yāvan**, *ā*, m., id., TS.

अयव 2. *a-yava*, mfn. producing bad or no barley, Pāṇ. vi, 2, 108, Pat. & 172, Kāś.; (*as*), m., N. of one of the seven species of worms in the intestines, Suśr.

A-yavaka, mfn. producing bad or no barley, Pāṇ. vi, 2, 117, Pat. & 174, Kāś.

2. **A-yāva**, mfn. not made of barley, KātyŚr.

अयवत् *aya-vat.* See *áya.*

अयशस् *a-yaśas*, n. infamy, R.; Mn. viii, 128, &c.; (*ás*), mfn. devoid of fame, disgraced, ŚBr. xiv; KātyŚr. **–kara**, mf(*ī*)n. causing dishonour, disgraceful, MBh. &c.

Ayaśasya, mfn. = *ayaśas-kara*, q. v., R.; BhP.; Suśr.

अयस् *áyas*, n. iron, metal, RV. &c.; an iron weapon (as an axe, &c.), RV. vi, 3, 5 & 47, 10; gold, Naigh.; steel, L.; [cf. Lat. *æs, ær-is* for *æs-is*; Goth. *ais*, Thema *aisa*; Old Germ. *êr*, 'iron;' Goth. *eisarn*; Mod. Germ. *Eisen.*] **–kaṇsa**, m. an iron goblet, Pāṇ. viii, 3, 46, Sch. **–karṇī**, f.? (cf. *adhīloha-kárṇa* and *adhirūḍhā-k°*), ib. **–kāṇḍa**, m. n. 'a quantity of iron' or 'excellent iron,' (gaṇa *kaskâdi*, q. v.) **–kānta**, m. (gaṇa *kaskâdi*) 'iron-lover,' the loadstone (cf. *kāntâyasa*), Ragh. xvii, 63, &c. **–kānta-maṇi**, m. id., Mālatīm. **–kāma**, m. a blacksmith, Pāṇ. viii, 3, 46, Sch. **–kāra**, m. id., Pāṇ. ii, 4, 10, Sch. & viii, 3, 46, Sch. **–kuṇḍa**, m. an iron pitcher, L. **–kumbha**, m. or **-kumbhī**, f. an iron pot or boiler, Pāṇ. viii, 3, 46, Sch. **–kuśā**, f. a rope partly consisting of iron, ib. **–kṛiti**, f. a medical preparation of iron, Suśr. **–tāpá**, mfn. one who heats iron, VS. **–tuṇḍa**, mfn. having an iron point, Hariv. **–pātrá**, m. an iron vessel, AV. viii, 10, 22; Suśr. (v. l.); (*am* or *ī*), n. f. id., Pāṇ. viii, 3, 46, Sch. **–máya**, mf(*ī*)n. Ved. made of iron or of metal, RV. v, 30, 15, &c.; BhP.; (*as*), m., N. of a son of Manu Svārocisha, Hariv.; (*ī*), f., N. of one of the three residences of the Asuras, AitBr.; *ayasmayâdi*, a gaṇa of Pāṇ. (i, 4, 20).

Ayaḥ (in comp. for *ayas*). **–kaṇapa**, m. a certain iron weapon, MBh. i, 8257. **–kāya**, m. 'of an iron body,' N. of a Daitya, Kathās. **–kiṭṭa**, n. rust of iron, L. **–pāna**, n. 'iron-drink,' N. of a hell, BhP. **–piṇḍa**, m. a ball or lump of iron, Suśr. **–pratimā**, f. iron image, L. **–śaṅku**, m. an iron bolt, Ragh. xii, 95; Rājat.; (*us*), m., N. of an Asura, Hariv. & MārkP. **–śaphá**, mfn. having iron hoofs, TĀr. **–śayá**, mf(*ā*)n. lying in iron (said of fire), VS.; KātyŚr.; (cf. *ayā-śayá.*) **–śipra** (*áyaḥ-*), mfn. (said of the Ṛibhus) having iron cheeks (on the helmet), RV. iv, 37, 4. **–śiras**, m., N. of an Asura, Hariv. **–śīrshan** (*áyaḥ-*), mfn. having an iron head, RV. viii, 101, 3. **–śūla**, n. 'an iron dart,' a painful or violent act, Pāṇ. v, 2, 76. **–śṛiṅga** (*áyaḥ-*), mfn. having iron horns, MaitrS. **–sthūṇa** (*áyaḥ-*), mfn. having iron pillars, RV. v, 62, 8; (*as*), m., N. of a Ṛishi, ŚBr. xi; (gaṇa *śivâdi*, q. v.); (*ās*), m. pl. his descendants, (gaṇa *yaskâdi*, q. v.); (*ī*), f., (gaṇa *gaurâdi*, q. v.)

Ayaś (in comp. for *ayas*). **–cūrṇa**, n. a powder prepared from iron (used for curing worms), Suśr.

Ayo (in comp. for *ayas*). **–agra** (*áyo-*), mf(*ā*)n. iron pointed, RV. x, 99, 6. **–gava** and **-gū**, see s. v. **–guḍa**, m. an iron ball, Mn. iii, 133; Car. **–'gra** or **-'graka**, n. a pestle, L. **–ghana**, m. an iron hammer, Pāṇ. iii, 3, 82; Ragh. xiv, 33, &c. **–jāla** (*áyo-*), mfn. having or carrying iron snares (as demons), AV. xix, 66; (*am*), n. iron net-work, R. **–daṇshṭra** (*áyo-*), mfn. iron-toothed, RV. i, 88, 5 & x, 87, 2. **–datī**, f. 'having teeth like iron,' a proper name, Pāṇ. v, 4, 143, Kāś. **–darvi**, f. an iron spoon, Bhpr. **–dāha**, m. the burning property of iron (used as an instance of metaphorical speech, for iron does not possess the property of burning, but the fire by which the iron is heated). **–'pāshṭi** (*áyo-*), mfn. having iron claws, RV. x, 99, 8; (cf. *apāshṭhá.*) **–bāhu**, m. 'iron-armed,' N. of a son of Dhṛitarāshṭra, MBh. i, 2733. **–maya**, mf(*ī*)n. made of iron, R.; Mn. &c. (Ved. *ayas-máya*, q. v.) **–mala**, n. rust of iron, L. **–mukha** (*áyo-*), mfn. having an iron mouth, AV. xi, 10, 3; having an iron beak, MBh. xii, 12072; iron-pointed (as a plough [Mn. x, 84] or a stake for impaling criminals [R. iii, 53, 53]); (*as*), m. an arrow, Ragh. v, 55; N. of a Dānava, Hariv. & VP.; of a mountain, Hariv. & R. **–rajas**, n. = *-mala*, q. v., L. **–rasá**, m. id., ŚBr.; KātyŚr. **–vikāra**, m. iron-work, any iron fabric, Pāṇ. iv, 1, 42. **–'śana**, mfn. eating or living on rust of iron, Hariv. **–hata** (*áyo-*), mfn. embossed in iron-work, RV. ix, 1, 2 & 80, 2. **–hanu** (*áyo-*), mfn. iron-jawed, RV. vi, 71, 4. **–hṛidaya**, mfn. iron-hearted, stern, Ragh. ix, 9.

Ayasa, *am*, n. (only ifc.) = *ayas*, e. g. *kṛishṇâyasa, lohâyasa*, q. v.

अयसे *áyase*, Ved. Inf. fr. √*i*, q. v.

अया *ayā́*, ind. (fr. pronom. base *a* = *aná-yā*), in this manner, thus, RV.

अयाचक *a-yācaka*, mfn. (√*yāc*), 'one who does not ask or solicit' [a misspelling for *a-pācaka*, NBD.], MBh. xii, 342.

A-yācat, mfn. id., MBh. xiii, 3053.

A-yācamāna, mfn. id., KaushUp.

Á-yācita, mfn. not asked for, unsolicited, TĀr.; Mn. &c.; (*as*), m., N. of the Ṛishi Upavarsha, L. **–vrata**, n. the obligation of eating such food only as has been obtained without solicitation; (mfn.), keeping the above obligation, Āp. (quoted by Kullūka on Mn.)

Ayācitâhṛita, mfn. offered without having been solicited, Yājñ. i, 215. **Ayācitôpanīta**, mfn. id., Comm. on Mn. iv, 247.

A-yācin, mfn. not soliciting, (gaṇa *grahâdi.*)

अयाज्य *a-yājyá*, mfn. (√*yaj*), a person for whom one must not offer sacrifices, outcast, degraded, ŚBr. xiv; KātyŚr.; Mn. &c.; not to be offered in a sacrifice. **–tva**, *am*, n. the state of not being fit for a sacrificial offering, Jaim. **–yājana** [Mn. iii, 65] or **-saṃyājya** [Mn. xi, 59], n. sacrificing for an outcast (one of the sins called Upapātaka).

अयाट्कार *ayāṭ-kārá*, *as*, m. pronouncing the word *áyāṭ* (aor. fr. √*yaj*, quoted fr. VS. xxi, 47), ŚBr. i.

अयात *á-yāta*, mfn. not gone, AV. x, 8, 8.

A-yātayāma, mfn. not worn out by use, not weak, fresh, ŚBr.; MBh. iii, 11005 & BhP.; (*āni*), n. pl., N. of certain texts of the Yajur-veda (revealed to Yājñavalkya), VP. & BhP. **–tā** (*ayātayāmá-*), f. unweakened strength, freshness, ŚBr. & AitBr. **–tva** (*áyātayāma-*), n. id., TS. ii.

Á-yātayāman, mf(*mnī*)n. not weak, fresh, ŚBr. & AitBr.

अयातु *á-yātu*, *us*, m. not a demon, RV. vii, 34, 8 & 104, 16.

अयात्रा *a-yātrā*, f. the state of not being passable (as the sea), R. iv, 27, 16.

अयाथातथ्य *a-yāthātathya*, *am*, n. (= *ā-yathātathya*), the state of being *a-yathātatham*, q. v., Pāṇ. vii, 3, 31; Bhaṭṭ.

अयाथापुर्य *a-yāthāpurya*, *am*, n. (= *āyathā-purya*), the state of being *a-yathāpuram*, q. v., Pāṇ. vii, 3, 31.

अयाथार्थिक *a-yāthârthika*, mfn. not suitable = *a-yathârtha*, q. v., L.

A-yāthârthya, *am*, n. the being *a-yathârtha* (q. v.), incongruousness, L.

अयान *a-yāna*, *am*, n. not moving, halting, stopping, L.; (= *sva-bhāva*), 'natural disposition or temperament,' L.

अयानय *ayânaya*, *am*, n. good and bad luck, L.; (*as*), m. a particular movement of the pieces on a chess or backgammon board, Pāṇ. v, 2, 9 (cf. *aya*).

Ayânayīna, *as*, m. a piece at chess or backgammon so moved, Pāṇ. v, 2, 9.

अयाम *á-yāma*, *as*, m. not a path, TS.; not a night-watch,' any time during daylight.

Á-yāman, *a*, n. (Ved. loc. °*man*) no march or expedition, RV. i, 181, 7 & viii, 52, 5.

अयाव 1. & 2. *a-yāva.* See 1. & 2. *a-yava.*

Á-yāvan. See 1. *á-yava.*

अयावन *a-yāvana*, *am*, n. not causing to mix or to unite, RPrāt.

अयाशय *ayā-śayá*, mfn. = *ayaḥ-śaya*, q. v., MaitrS.; (cf. *avā-śriṅgá.*)

अयाशु *a-yāśú*, mfn. unfit for copulation, AV. viii, 6, 15.

अयास् *ayā́s* (2, twice 3 [i. e. *aïā́s*] RV. i, 167, 4 & vi, 66, 5), mfn. (fr. *a* + √*yas*?; see *ayā́sya*), agile, dexterous, nimble, RV.; (*ās*), n. (ind.) fire, Uṇ.

Ayā́sya (4), mfn. (= ἀΐζηος, Windisch; cf. *ayā́s* & *aïā́s* before), agile, dexterous, valiant, RV.; (*as*), m., N. of an Aṅgiras (composer of the hymns RV. ix, 44-66 & x, 67 & 68), RV. x, 67, 1 & 108, 8; ŚBr. xiv.

अयासोमीय *ayāsomīya*, *am*, n., N. of some verses of the SV. (so called from their beginning with the words *ayā́ sóma*).

अयि *ayi*, ind. a vocative particle (especially used in dramas); a particle of encouragement or introducing a kind inquiry.

अयिन् *ayin*, mfn. only ifc., e. g. *aty-ayin*, *anv-ayin*, &c.

अयुक्छद *a-yuk-chada*, &c. See *a-yúj.*

Á-yukta, mfn. (√*yuj*), not yoked, RV. x, 27, 9; ŚBr.; KātyŚr.; not harnessed, RV. ix, 97, 20; ShaḍvBr.; not connected, not united (as vowels); not added, not joined; not applied or made use of (see *-cāra* below); to be supplied (see *-padârtha* below); not attentive, not devout, RV. v, 33, 3; ŚBr. &c.; not suited, unfit, unsuitable, MBh. &c.; not dexterous, silly, R.; BhP.; (*á-yuktam*), ind. not being yoked, ŚBr. xii. **–kṛit**, mfn. committing wrong acts. **–cāra**, m. (a king &c.) who does not appoint spies, R. iii, 37, 7 & 10. **–tā**, f. or **-tva**, n. the not being used, the not being suitable. **–padârtha**, m. the sense of a word not given but to be supplied. **–rūpa**, mfn. unfit, unsuitable, Kum.

A-yukti, *is*, f. unsuitableness, unreasonableness, want of conformity (to correct principles or to analogy), Sarvad. **–yukta**, mfn. applied in an unsuitable way, Bhpr.; inexpert (as a surgeon), Suśr.

A-yuga, *am*, n. 'not a pair,' one, VarBṛS.; (mfn.) odd, L. **Ayugârcis**, m. 'having odd (i. e. seven) flames,' fire, Śiś.

A-yugapad, ind. not at once, not simultaneously, Nyāyad. **–grahaṇa**, n. apprehending gradually and not simultaneously, ib. **–bhāva**, m. non-simultaneousness, successiveness, ib.

A-yugū, *ūs*, f. 'without a companion,' the only daughter (of a mother), Gobh.

A-yugma, mf(*ā*)n. odd, ĀśvŚr. &c.; Mn. iii, 48. **–cchada**, m. = *a-yuk-chada*, q. v., Kir. i, 16. **–netra**, m. 'having an odd number of eyes' (i. e. three), N. of Śiva, Kum. iii, 51 & 69. **–pattra** or **-parṇa**, m. = *-cchada*, q. v., L. **–pādayamaka**, n. (a species of alliteration) the repetition of the odd (i. e. the first and third) Pādas of a stanza (in such a manner that the sense of the sounds repeated is different in the first and third Pāda), Comm. on Bhaṭṭ. x, 10. **–locana**, m. (= *-netra*), Śiva, Kād. **–śara**, m. 'having an odd number of arrows (i. e. five),' N. of the god of love, Daś.

A-yuṅga, mfn. = *a-yugma*, ŚBr. iii, xiii.

A-yúj, mfn. id., ŚBr. &c., Mn. iii, 277. **Ayuk-chada**, m. 'having odd (i. e. seven, cf. *sapta-parṇa*) leaves,' the plant Alstonia Scholaris, Śiś. vi, 50. **Ayuk-palāśa**, m. id., L. **Ayuk-pāda-yamaka**, n. = *ayugma-p°*, q. v., Comm. on Bhaṭṭ. x, 10. **Ayuk-śakti**, m. 'having an odd number of (i. e. nine) powers,' Śiva, L. **Ayug-aksha**, m. = *ayugma-netra*, q. v., L. **Ayug-ishu**, m. = *ayugma-śara*, q. v., L. **Ayug-dhātu**, mfn. having an odd number of elements or component parts, KātyŚr. **Ayug-bāṇa**, m. = *ayugma-śara*, q. v., L. **Ayuṅ-netra**, m. = *ayugma-netra*, q. v., L.

A-yujá, mfn. 'without a companion,' not having an equal, RV. viii, 62, 2; = *a-yugma*, q. v., ĀśvŚr. & ĀśvGṛ.

A-yujin, mfn. = *a-yugma*, q. v., PBr.

1. **A-yoga**, *as*, m. separation, disjunction; separation from a lover, Daśar.; unfitness, unsuitableness, nonconformity, Kāvyād.; impossibility, Comm. on Kum. iii, 14; inefficacy of a remedy, Suśr.; medical treatment counter to the symptoms, non-application or mis-application of remedies, Suśr.; vigorous effort, exertion, L.; inauspicious conjunction of planets, L.; N. of a certain conjunction of planets. **–kshema** (*á-yoga-*), m. no secure possession of what has been acquired, no prosperity, ŚBr. & AitBr. **–vāha**, m. '(sounds) which occur (in the actual language) without being given (by grammarians) together with (the other letters of the alphabet),' a term for Anusvāra, Visarjanīya, Upadhmānīya, Jihvāmūlīya, and the Yamas, Pat. on Śivasūtra 5 and on Pāṇ. viii, 3, 5.

A-yogya, mfn. unfit, unsuitable, useless, KātyŚr.

&c.; incapable, not qualified for, Yājñ. ii, 235; Bhaṭṭ.; not adequate to, not a match for (loc.), Veṇis.; (in Sāṅkhya phil.) not ascertainable &c. by the senses, immaterial. **–tā**, f. or **-tva**, n. unfitness, unsuitableness.

A-yauktika, mfn. incongruous, Kap.

A-yaugapadya, *am*, n. non-contemporaneous existence, unsimultaneousness, Nyāyad.

A-yaugika, mfn. having no regular derivation.

अयुत 1. *á-yuta*, mfn. (√1. *yu*), unimpeded, AV. xix, 51, 1; N. of a son of Rādhika, BhP. **–siddha**, mfn. (in phil.) proved to be not separated (by the intervention of space), proved to be essentially united (as organic bodies, &c.) **–siddhi**, f. establishing by proof that certain objects or ideas are essentially united and logically inseparable.

अयुत 2. *a-yúta*, *am*, n. [*as*, m. only MBh. iii, 801], 'unjoined, unbounded,' ten thousand, a myriad, RV.; AV. &c.; in comp. a term of praise (see *ayutâdhyāpaka*), (gaṇa *kāshṭhâdi*, q. v.) **–jit**, m., v. l. for *ayutā-jit* below. **–nāyin**, m., N. of a king, MBh. i, 3773. **–śas**, ind. by myriads, MBh. iii, 1763. **–homa**, m., N. of a sacrifice, BhavP. **Ayutā-jit**, m., N. of a king (son of Sindhudvīpa and father of Ṛituparṇa), BrahmaP.; of another king (son of Bhajamāna), VP. **Ayutâdhyāpaka**, m. an excellent teacher, Pāṇ. viii, 1, 67, Kāś. **Ayutâyu**, m., N. of a son of Jayasena Ārāvin, VP.; of a son of Śrutavat, VP. **Ayutâśva**, m. (= *ayutā-jit* above) N. of a son of Sindhudvīpa, VP.

अयुद्ध *á-yuddha*, mfn. (√*yudh*), unconquered, irresistible, RV. viii, 45, 3 & x, 27, 10; (*am*), n. not war, absence of war, peace, MBh. &c. **–sena** (*á-yuddha-*), mfn. whose arrows or armies are unconquered, irresistible, RV. x, 138, 5.

Á-yuddhvī, Ved. ind. without fighting, RV. x, 108, 5.

A-yudha, *as*, m. a non-fighter, Pāṇ. v, 1, 121.

A-yudhyá, mfn. unconquerable, RV. x, 103, 7.

A-yoddhṛí, m(nom. °*ddhā́*)fn. id., RV. i, 32, 6; not fighting.

A-yodhyá (3, 4), mf(*ā́*)n. not to be warred against, irresistible, AV.; R.; (*ā*), f. the capital of Rāma (the modern Oude, on the river Sarayu, described in R. i, 5). **Ayodhyā-kāṇḍa**, n., N. of R. ii. **Ayodhyâdhipati**, m. the sovereign of Ayodhyā. **Ayodhyā-vāsin**, mfn. inhabiting Ayodhyā.

A-yaudhika, *as*, m. not a warrior, (gaṇa *cārv-âdi*, q. v.)

अयुपित *á-yupita*, mfn. not confused or troubled, MaitrS.

अयुवमारिन् *a-yuva-mārin*, mfn. [NBD.] where no young people die, AitBr.

अयूप *a-yūpa*, *as*, m. not a sacrificial post, Jaim.; without sacrificial posts, MānGṛ.

अये *aye*, ind. a vocative particle, an interjection (of surprise, recollection, fatigue, fear, passion, especially used in dramas; cf. *ayi*).

अयोग 2. *ayoga*, *as*, m. [NBD.] = *ayogava*, MBh. xii.

Ayogava, *as*, m. the offspring of a Śūdra man and Vaiśya woman (whose business is carpentry), Mn. x, 32; (since the word occurs only in the loc. *ayogave* and is by both commentaries said to imply the female of this mixed tribe, the original reading is probably, as suggested by BR, *ayoguvi*, loc. fr. *ayogū*, q. v.)

Ayogū́, *ūs*, m. id., VS. xxx, 5; cf. *áyogava*; (*ūs*), f. id.? see *ayogava*.

अयोद्धृ *a-yoddhṛí*, &c. See *á-yuddha*.

अयोनि *á-yoni*, *is*, m. f. any place other than the pudendum muliebre, ŚBr.; Mn. xi, 173; Gaut.; (*a-yoni*), mfn. = *a-yoni-ja* below, MaitrS.; without origin or beginning (said of Brahma), Kum. ii, 9; (= *antya-yoni*) of an unworthy or unimportant origin, MBh. xiii, 1885; (in rhetoric) 'having no source that can be traced,' original; (*is*), m., N. of Brahma (see before); of Śiva, PadmaP. **–ja**, mf(*ā*)n. not born from the womb, not produced in the ordinary course of generation, generated equivocally, MBh. &c. **–ja-tīrtha**, n., N. of a Tīrtha, VāyuP. **–ja-tva**, n. the state of not being born from a womb, Rājat. **–jêśa**, m., N. of Śiva. **–jêśvara-tīrtha**, n. = *-ja-tīrtha*, q. v., VāyuP. **–sambhava**, mfn. = *a-yoni-ja*, q. v., L.

A-yonika, mfn. without the verse containing the word *yoni* (i. e. VS. xxiii, 2), KātyŚr.

अयौधिक *a-yaudhika*. See *á-yuddha*.

अर *ara*, mfn. (√*ṛi*), swift, speedy, L.; little (only for the etym. of *udara*), Comm. on TUp.; ifc. 'going,' cf. *samará*; (*ás*), m. the spoke or radius of a wheel, RV. &c.; the spoke of an altar formed like a wheel, Śulb.; a spoke of the time-wheel, viz. a Jaina division of time (the sixth of an Avasarpiṇī or Utsarpiṇī); the eighteenth Jaina saint of the present Avasarpiṇī; N. of an ocean in Brahmā's world (only for a mystical interpretation of *araṇya*), ChUp.; (*am*), n. the spoke of a wheel, L.; (*áram*), ind., see s. v. **–ghaṭṭa**, m. a wheel or machine for raising water from a well (Hind. ارهٹ), Pañcat.; a well, Rājat. **–ghaṭṭaka**, m. = *-ghaṭṭa*, q. v., L. **–nemi**, m., N. of Brahmadatta (king of Kośala), Buddh. **–manas** (*ará-*) & **-mati** (*ará-*), see s. v. *áram*. **Arântara**, *āṇi*, n. pl. the intervals of the spokes.

Araka, *as*, m. the spoke of a wheel, Suśr.; the Jaina division of time called *ara*, L.; the plant Blyxa Octandra; another plant, Gardenia Enneandra.

Ari, *is*, m., v. l. for *arin* below.

Arin, *i*, n. 'having spokes,' a wheel, discus, BhP.; RāmatUp.

अरक्षत् *a-rakshat*, mfn. (√1. *raksh*), not guarding, Mn. viii, 304 & 307.

A-rakshita, mfn. not guarded, MBh.; Mn. &c.

A-rakshitṛi, mfn. one who does not guard, R.

अरक्षस् *a-rakshás*, mfn. (√3. *raksh*), harmless, honest, RV.

A-rakshasyá, mfn. free from evil spirits, MaitrS.

अरगराट *aragárāṭa*, *as*, m. (? a valley), AV. vi, 69, 1.

अरंकृ *aram-*√1. *kṛi*, &c. See *áram*.

Aram-√gam, &c. See *áram*.

Aram-gará and **-ghushá**. See *áram*.

अरङ्गिन् *a-raṅgin*, mfn. passionless, L.

Araṅgi-sattva, *ās*, m. pl. a class of deities, Buddh.

A-raja, mfn. (for *a-rajás* below), dustless, R. vi; (*ā*), f., N. of a daughter of Uśanas, R. vii, 80, 8 seqq.

A-rajás, mfn. dustless, ŚBr. xiv; N.; free from passion or desire, MBh. xiv, 1283; (*ās*), f. 'not having the monthly courses,' a young girl.

A-rajas-ka, mfn. dustless; without the quality called *rajas*, NṛisUp.

Arajāya, Nom. Ā. °*yate*, 'to become dustless' or 'to lose the monthly courses,' (gaṇa *bhṛiśâdi*, q. v.)

अरज्जु *a-rajjú*, mfn. not having or consisting of cords ['not a cord or rope,' NBD.], RV. ii, 13, 9 & vii, 84, 2.

अरटु *araṭu*, *us*, m. the tree Colosanthes Indica Bl.; (cf. *aralu*.)

Araṭvá, mfn. made of the wood of the above tree; (*as*), m., N. of a man, RV. viii, 46, 27.

Araḍu, *us*, m. = *araṭu* above, AV. xx, 131, 18.

Araḍuka, mfn. made of the wood of the above tree, (gaṇa *ṛiśyâdi*, q. v.)

अरडा *araḍā*, f., N. of a goddess, Gobh.

अरण 1. *áraṇa*, mf(*ī*)n. (√*ṛi*), foreign, distant, RV.; AV.; ŚBr.; (*am*), n. (only for the etym. of *aráṇi*) the being fitted (as a piece of wood), Nir.; a refuge, BhP.

1. **Aráṇi**, *is*, f. 'being fitted into' or 'turning round,' the piece of wood (taken from the Ficus Religiosa or Premna Spinosa) used for kindling fire by attrition, RV. &c. (generally distinction is made between the lower one and the upper one, *adharâraṇi* & *uttarâraṇi*, the former may also be meant by *araṇi* alone without *adhara*); (figuratively) a mother, Hariv. (cf. *pāṇḍavâraṇi* & *surâraṇi*); (*is*), m. the plant Premna Spinosa, L.; the sun, L.; (*ī*), du. f. the two Araṇis (used for kindling the fire), RV. &c. **–mat**, mfn. being contained in the Araṇis (as fire), ĀśvŚr.

Araṇikā, f. the plant Premna Spinosa, L.

Aráṇī, f. = 1. *aráṇi*, RV. v, 9, 3, &c. **–ketu**, m. the plant Premna Spinosa, L.

अरण 2. *a-raṇa*, mfn. without fighting (as death, i. e. natural death), Bhaṭṭ.

अरणि 2. *á-raṇi*, *is*, f. discomfort, pain, AV. i, 18, 2.

अरण्य *áraṇya*, *am*, n. (fr. 1. *áraṇa*; fr. √*ṛi*, Uṇ.), a foreign or distant land, RV. i, 163, 11 & vi, 24, 10; a wilderness, desert, forest, AV.; VS. &c.; (*as*), m. the tree also called Kaṭphala, L.; N. of a son of the Manu Raivata, Hariv. 434; of a Sādhya, ib. 11536; of a teacher (disciple of Pṛithvidhara). **–kaṇā**, f. wild cumin seed, L. **–kadalī**, f. the wood or wild plantain, L. **–karpāsī**, f. = *-kārpāsī* below. **–kāka**, m. the wood-crow, L. **–kāṇḍa**, n., N. of R. iii (describing Rāma's life in the wilderness). **–kārpāsī**, f. the wild cotton-shrub, L. **–kulathikā**, f. the plant Glycine Labialis Lin., L. **–kusumbha**, m. the plant Carthamus Tinctorius, L. **–ketu**, m., N. of a plant, L. (cf. *araṇī-ketu*.) **–gaja**, m. a wild elephant, Pañcat. **–gata**, mfn. gone into a forest, Pat. on Pāṇ. ii, 1, 24, Comm. **–gholī**, f., N. of a vegetable, L. **–caṭaka**, m. a wood-sparrow, L. **–cara**, mfn. living in forests, wild, Pañcat. **–ja**, mfn. produced or born in a forest, L.; *araṇyajârdrakā*, f. wild ginger, L. **–jīra**, m. wild cumin, L. **–jīva**, mfn. = *-cara*, L. **–tulasī**, f. the plant Ocimum Adscendens. **–dvādaśī**, f. the twelfth day of the month Mārgaśīrsha; with or without *-vrata*, n., N. of a ceremony performed on this day, BhavP. **–dharma**, m. forest usage, wild or savage state, Pañcat. **–dhānya**, n. wild rice, L. **–nṛipati**, m. 'king of the forest,' the tiger, N. **–parvan**, n., N. of the first section of MBh. iii. **–bhava**, mfn. growing in a forest, wild, Pañcat. **–bhāga** (*áraṇya-*), mfn. forming part of the forest, ŚBr. xiii. **–makshikā**, f. the gad-fly, L. **–mārjāra**, m. wild cat, Pañcat. **–mudga**, m. a kind of bean, L. **–yāna**, n. going into a forest, Bhaṭṭ.; (cf. *-gata* above.) **–rakshaka**, m. forest-keeper, superintendent of a forest district, L. **–rajanī**, f. the plant Curcuma Aromatica, L. **–rāj**, m. = *-nṛipati*, N.; a lion, ib. **–rājya**, n. the sovereignty of the forest, Hit. **–rudita**, n. 'weeping in a forest,' i. e. weeping in vain, with no one to hear, Pañcat. **–vat**, ind. like a wilderness, Hit. **–vāyasa**, m. a raven, L. **–vāsa**, m. living in a forest, R. **–vāsin**, mfn. living in a forest, MBh. iii, 15632; (*ī*), m. a forest beast, Hit.; 'forest-dweller,' a hermit, MBh. iii, &c.; (*inī*), f., N. of a plant. **–vāstuka** or **-vāstūka**, m., N. of a plant. **–śāli**, m. wild rice. **–śūraṇa**, m., N. of a plant. **–śvan**, m. a wolf, L.; a jackal, L. **–shashṭhikā** or **-shashṭhī**, f., N. of a festival celebrated by females on the sixth day of the light half of the month Jyaishṭha. **–haladī**, f. the plant Curcuma Aromatica, Bhpr. **Araṇyâdhīti**, f. or **araṇyâdhyayana**, n. reading or study in a forest, Sāy. on TĀr. **Araṇyâyana**, n. going into a forest, becoming a hermit, ChUp. **Araṇye-geya**, &c., see s. v. *araṇye*. **Araṇyâukas**, m. 'whose abode is the forest,' a Brāhman who has left his family and become an anchorite, Śāk.

Araṇyaka, *am*, n. a forest, Yājñ. iii, 192; the plant Melia Sempervirens, L.

Araṇyānī or °**nī́**, f. a wilderness, desert, large forest, RV. x, 146, 4; AV. &c.; the goddess of the wilderness and desert, RV. x, 146, 1-6.

Araṇyīya, mfn. 'containing a forest' or 'near to a forest,' (gaṇa *utkarâdi*, q. v.)

Araṇye (in comp. for *araṇya* chiefly used for figurative expressions or as names, Pāṇ. ii, 1, 44 & vi, 3, 9). **–geya**, mfn. to be sung in the forest, Lāṭy.; Up. **–tilaka**, *ās*, m. pl. 'wild sesamum growing in a forest and containing no oil,' anything which disappoints expectation, Pāṇ. ii, 1, 44, Sch. & vi, 3, 9, Sch. **–'nuvākyà**, mfn. to be recited in the forest, TBr. **–'nūcya**, m. 'to be recited in the forest,' N. of an oblation (so called because of its being offered with a verse which is to be recited in a forest), ŚBr.; KātyŚr.

अरत *a-rata*, mfn. (√*ram*), dull, languid, apathetic, L.; disgusted, displeased with, Nalod.; (*am*), n. non-copulation, L. **–trapa**, m. 'not ashamed of copulation,' a dog, L.

1. **A-rati**, *is*, f. dissatisfaction, discontent, dulness, languor, Buddh.; Jain. &c.; anxiety, distress, regret, MBh.; BhP. &c.; anger, passion, L.; a bilious disease, L.; (mfn.), discontented, L. **–jña**, mfn. 'not knowing pleasure,' dull, spiritless, BhP.

A-ratika, mfn. without Rati (the wife of Kāma), Kathās.

1. **A-ratní**, mfn. 'disgusted, discontented' [NBD.], RV. viii, 80, 8.
A-rantos, Ved. Inf. not to like, AitBr.
A-ramaṇīya-tā, f. unpleasantness, Pāṇ. v, 1, 121, Kāś.
1. **A-rámati**, mfn. without relaxation or repose, RV. ii, 38, 4 & viii, 31, 12.
Á-ramamāṇa, mfn. id. RV. ix, 72, 3.

अरति 2. *aratí, is,* m. (√ṛi, cf. *ara, áram*), 'moving quickly,' a servant, assistant, manager, administrator, RV. (for RV. v, 2, 1, see 2. *aratní.*)

अरत्नि 2. *aratní, is,* m. the elbow, RV. v, 2, 1 (according to the emendation of BR.); ŚBr.; ĀśvŚr.; a corner, RV. x, 160, 4; a cubit of the middle length, from the elbow to the tip of the little finger, a fist, RV. viii, 80, 8 (cf. 1. *a-ratnī*); AV.; ŚBr. &c.; ifc. with numbers (e.g. *pañcâratnyas,* 'five fists'), Pāṇ. i, 1, 58, Comm. & vi, 2, 29 & 30, Sch.; (*is*), f. the elbow, BhP.; (cf. *ratni.*) **-mātrá**, mf(*ī*)n. one ell in length, ŚBr. &c.; (*ám*), n. a distance of only an ell, ŚBr.
Aratnika, *as,* m. the elbow, Yājñ. iii, 86.

अरत्निन् *á-ratnin,* mfn. not possessing wealth or precious things, TBr.

अरथ *a-rathá,* mfn. having no car, RV.; VS.; AV.
A-rathin, *ī,* m. a warrior who does not fight in a car, or owns no car, MBh.
Á-rathī, *īs,* m. not a charioteer, RV. vi, 66, 7.

अरध्र *á-radhra,* mfn. not pliant or obedient, RV. vi, 18, 4 & 62, 3.

अरन्तुक *arantuka, as,* m., N. of a Tīrtha, MBh. iii, 7078.

अरन्तोस् *a-rantos.* See *a-rata.*

अरप *a-rapá,* mfn. unhurt, VS. viii, 5.
A-rapás, mfn. unhurt, safe, RV.; AV.; not hurting, beneficial, RV. viii, 18, 9.

अरपचन *arapacana, as,* m. a mystical collective N. of the five Buddhas (each being represented by a letter).

अरम् *áram,* ind. (√ṛi; see *ara*), readily, fitly, suitably, so as to answer a purpose (with dat.), RV.; (with *purú* or *prithú*) enough, sufficiently, RV. i, 142, 10 & v, 66, 5; with dat. (e.g. *bhaktáya*), id., Pāṇ. viii, 2, 18, Kāś. [cf. *álam* & Gk. ἄρα]. **-ish** (*áram-*), mfn. hastening near (to help), RV. viii, 46, 17.
Ará (in comp. = *áram*). **-maṇas** (*ará-*), mfn. ready to serve, obedient, RV. vi, 17, 10. 2. **Arámati**, f. 'readiness to serve, obedience, devotion,' (generally personified as) a goddess protecting the worshippers of the gods and pious works in general, RV.; (mfn.), patient [NBD.], RV. x, 92, 4 & 5.
Áram (in comp. for *áram*). **-√1. kṛi** (Subj. *-kárat* or *-karat,* 1. pl. *-kriṇavāma;* Imper. 1. sg. *-karāṇi;* aor. 3. pl. *-ákran*) to prepare, make ready, RV.; to serve (with or without dat.), RV. **-kṛít**, mfn. preparing (a sacrifice), serving (as a worshipper), RV. **-kṛita** (*áram-*), mfn. prepared, ready, RV. & AV. **-kṛiti** (*áram-*), f. service, RV. vii, 29, 3. **-kṛityā**, Ved. ind. p. having prepared, being ready, RV. x, 51, 5. **-√gam** (Imper. 2. du. *-gantam;* Opt. 2. sg. *-gamyās,* 1. pl. *-gamema*) to come near (in order to help), assist, attend (with dat.), RV. & SV. **-gamá**, mfn. coming near (in order to help), ready to help, RV. vi, 42, 1 & viii, 46, 17; AV. **-gará**, m. (√1. *gṛi*), 'one who bestows praise, who hymns the gods?' AV. xx, 135, 13. **-ghushá**, mfn. sounding aloud, AV. x, 4, 4.

अरममाण *á-ramamāṇa,* &c. See *a-rata.*

अरमुडि *aramuḍi, is,* m. a king of Nepāl, Rājat.

अरर *arará, am,* n. a covering, a sheath, L.; (*as, ī*), m. f. the leaf of a door, a door, L.; (*am*), n. id., Mcar.; (*as*), m. an awl, L.; a part of a sacrifice, L.; fighting, war, L.
Arari, *is,* m. a door-leaf, Rājat.; (cf. *dvārârari.*)

अररका *ararākā,* f., N. of the ancestress of a celebrated Hindū family, (gaṇa *gargâdi,* q.v.); (*ās*), m. pl. the descendants of Ararākā, Pat.; (cf. *ārarākya.*)

अररिन्द *ararínda, am,* n. a vessel or a utensil used in preparing the Soma juice, RV. i, 139, 10; water, Naigh.

अररिवस् *á-rarivas,* m(nom. °*vān;* gen. abl. *á-rarushas*)fn. (√*rā*), 'not liberal,' envious, hard, cruel, unfriendly (N. of evil spirits, who strive to disturb the happiness of man), RV.
A-ráru, mfn. id., RV. i, 129, 3; (*us*), m., Ved. N. of a demon or Asura, RV. x, 99, 10; VS. &c.; a weapon, Uṇ.

अररे *arare,* ind. a vocative particle (expressing haste), L.

अरर्य *ararya,* Nom. P. °*ryati,* to work with an awl (*ārā,* q. v.; cf. *arā* below), (gaṇa *kaṇḍv-ādi,* q. v.)

अरलु *aralu* = *araṭu,* q. v., Kauś.; Suśr.
Araluka, *as,* m. id., Suśr.

अरव *a-rava,* mfn. noiseless.

अरविन्द *aravinda, am,* n. (fr. *ara* & *vinda,* Pāṇ. iii, 1, 138, Kāś.), a lotus, Nelumbium Speciosum or Nymphæa Nelumbo, Śāk. &c.; (*as*), m. the Indian crane, L.; copper, L. **-dala-prabha**, n. copper, L. **-nābha**, m. Vishṇu (from whose navel sprung the lotus that bore Brahmā at the creation), BhP. **-sad**, m. 'sitting on a lotus,' N. of Brahmā, Bhaṭṭ.
Aravindinī, f. (gaṇa *pushkarâdi,* q. v.) an assemblage of lotus flowers, Kād. &c.

अरश्मन् *a-raśmán,* m(nom. pl. *ānas*)fn. having no ropes or reins, RV. ix, 97, 20.
A-raśmika, mfn. without reins, ĀśvGṛ.

अरस *a-rasá,* mf(*ā*)n. sapless, tasteless, NṛisUp.; not having the faculty of tasting, ŚBr. xiv; weak, effectless, having no strength, RV. i, 191, 16; AV.; (*as*), m. absence of sap or juice, L. **-jña**, mfn. having no taste for, not taking interest in, MBh. xii, 6719. **Arasâśa**, m. the eating of sapless or dry food, Kauś. **Arasâśin**, mfn. eating sapless or dry food, Kauś.
A-rasayitṛi, mfn. one who does not taste, MaitrUp.
A-rasika, mfn. devoid of taste, unfeeling, dull.

अरसीठक्कुर *arasī-ṭhakkura, as,* m., N. of a poet (mentioned in Śārṅgadhara's anthology).

अरहस् *a-rahas, as,* n. absence of secrecy, Pāṇ. iii, 1, 12, Kāś. (v. l.)
Arahāya, Nom. Ā. °*yate,* to become public, ib. (v. l.)
A-rahita, mfn. not deprived of, possessed of.

अरा *arā,* f. (= *ārā*), an awl, Comm. on MBh. xv, 19.

अराग *a-rāga,* mfn. unimpassioned, cool, Veṇis.
A-rāgin, mfn. id.; not coloured, Suśr. **A-rāgitā**, f. indifference with regard to (loc.), Sāh.

अराजन् *á-rājan, ā,* m. not a king, ŚBr. & AitBr. **Arāja-tā**, f. the want of a king, AitBr. **A-rājânvayin**, mfn. not belonging to the family of a king, Rājat.
A-rājáka, mfn. having no king, TBr. &c.; (*am*), n. want of a king, anarchy, BhP.
A-rājanyá, mfn. without the Rājanya- or Kshatriya-caste, ŚBr.
A-rājin, mfn. without splendour, RV. viii, 7, 23.

अराटकी *arāṭakí,* f., N. of a plant, AV. iv, 37, 6.

अराड *arāḍa,* mf(*ī*)n. (= *ucchrita-śṛiṅga*) having high horns, MaitrS.; (compar. of fem. °*ḍítarā*) ŚBr. iv.
Arāḍyà, mfn. id., TS.

अराण *arāṇá,* aor. p. √ṛi, q.v.

अराणि *arāṇi* or *arāli, is,* m., N. of a son of Viśvāmitra, MBh. xiii, 257.

अराति *á-rāti, is,* f. 'non-liberality,' enviousness, malignity, RV.; failure, adversity, RV.; AV.; ŚBr.; TBr.; particular evil spirits (who frustrate the good intentions and disturb the happiness of man), ib.; (*is*), m. an enemy, Ragh. xii, 89; (in arithm.) the number six (there being six sins or internal enemies, cf. *shaḍ-varga*). **-dūshaṇa**, mfn. destroying adversity, AV. xix, 34, 4. **-dūshi**, mfn. id., AV. ii, 4, 6. **-nud**, mfn. expelling enemies, MBh. iii, 1702. **-bhaṅga**, m. defeat of a foe, L. **-há**, mfn. = *-dūshaṇa,* q. v., AV. xix, 35, 2. **Arāti-ván**, mfn. hostile, inimical, RV.
Arātiya, Nom. P. (Subj. °*tiyāt*) to be malevolent, have hostile intentions against (dat.), AV. iv, 36, 1.
Arātīya, Nom. P. °*tīyáti* (p. °*tīyát* [RV. i, 99, 1, &c.]; Subj. °*tīyāt*), Ved. id.
Arātiyú, mfn. hostile, AV. x, 6, 1.

अराद्धि *á-rāddhi, is,* f. ill-success, mischance, VS. xxx, 9.
A-rādhás, mfn. not liberal, hard, stingy, selfish, RV. & AV.

अराय *á-rāya,* mfn. id., RV. viii, 61, 11 (Nir. vi, 25); (*a-rāya*), *as,* m. an evil spirit, AV.; (*ī*), f. id., RV. x, 155, 1 & 2; AV. **-kshâyaṇa**, n. anything that serves to destroy evil spirits, AV. ii, 18, 3. **-câtana**, n. id., ib.

अराल *arāla,* mfn. (cf. *ará,* fr. √ṛi; Intens. for *arāra?*), crooked, curved, Uttarar. (*an-,* neg. 'straight'), &c.; crisped or curled (as hair), Ragh. &c.; (gaṇa *śārṅgaravâdi,* q. v.) 'Crispus,' N. of a Vedic teacher, VBr.; (*as*), m. a bent or crooked arm or hand, L.; the resin of the plant Shorea Robusta, L.; an elephant in rut, L.; (*ā, ī*), f. (gaṇa *bahv-ādi,* q. v.) a disloyal or unchaste woman, L.; a modest woman, L. **-pakshma-nayana**, mfn. whose eyelashes are curved, N. xi, 33.

अरालि *arāli,* v. l. for *arāṇi,* q. v.

अरावन् 1. *a-rāvan,* mfn. 'not liberal,' envious, hostile, RV.

अरावन् 2. *árāvan, ā,* m. = *arvan,* a steed, horse [NBD.; = *ara-vat,* 'having spokes or wheels,' 'a cart,' Ludwig; = *gamana-vat,* 'moving,' Sāy.], RV. vii, 68, 7.

अराष्ट्र *á-rāshṭra, am,* n. not a kingdom, ŚBr.

अरि 1. *arí,* mfn. (√ṛi), attached to, faithful, RV.; (*is*), m. a faithful or devoted or pious man, RV. **-gūrtá**, mfn. praised by devoted men, RV. i, 186, 3. **-dhâyas** (*arí-*), mf(acc. pl. °*yasas*)n. willingly yielding milk (as a cow), RV. i, 126, 5. **-shṭutá**, mfn. (√*stu*), praised with zeal (Indra), RV. viii, 1, 22.

अरि 2. *a-rí,* mfn. (√*rā;* = 1. *arí,* 'assiduous,' &c., Gmn.), 'not liberal,' envious, hostile, RV.; (*is*), m. an enemy, RV.; MBh. &c.; (*áris*), m. id., AV. vii, 88, 1 & xiii, 1, 29; (in astron.) a hostile planet, VarBṛS.; N. of the sixth astrological mansion, ib.; (in arithm.) the number six (cf. *arāti*); a species of Khadira or Mimosa, L. **-karshaṇa**, m. harasser of enemies, N. **-ghna**, m. a destroyer of enemies, R. v. **-cintana**, n. or **-cintā**, f. plotting against an enemy, administration of foreign affairs, L. **-jana**, n. a number of enemies, Kathās. **-jit**, m. 'conquering enemies,' N. of a son of Kṛishṇa (and of Bhadrā), BhP. **-tā**, f. or **-tva**, n. enmity. **-dānta**, m. 'enemy-subdued,' N. of a prince, Hariv. 6628 (v. l. *ati-dānta,* q. v.) **-nandana**, mfn. gratifying or affording triumph to an enemy, Hit. **-nipāta**, m. invasion or incursion of enemies, Hit. **-nuta**, mfn. praised even by enemies, Bhaṭṭ. **-m-dama**, mfn. (Pāṇ. iii, 2, 46, Sch.) foe-conquering, victorious, N. &c.; (*as*), m. N. of Śiva; of the father of Sanaśruta, AitBr.; of a Muni, Kathās. **-pura**, n. an enemy's town. **-marda**, m. the plant Cassia Sophora. **-mardana**, mfn. foe-trampling, enemy-destroying, MBh. &c.; (*as*), m., N. of a son of Śvaphalka, Hariv.; of a king of owls, Pañcat. **-mitra**, m. an ally or friend of an enemy. **-m-ejaya**, m. 'shaking enemies,' N. of a Nāga priest, PBr.; of a son of Śvaphalka, Hariv.; of Kuru, ib. **-meda**, m. a fetid Mimosa, Vachellia Farnesiana, L.; (*ās*), m. pl., N. of a people, VarBṛS. **-medaka**, m., N. of an insect, Suśr. **-rāshṭra**, n. an enemy's country. **-loka**, m. a hostile tribe or an enemy's country, L. **-siṅha**, m., N. of an author. **-sūdana**, m. destroyer of foes. **-soma**, m. a kind of Soma plant, MBh. xiv, 247. **-ha**, m. 'killing enemies,' N. of a prince (son of Avacīna), MBh. i, 3771; of another prince (son of Devātithi), ib., 3776. **-han**, mfn. killing or destroying enemies, N.; Ragh. ix, 23.

अरिक्त *a-rikta*, mfn. not empty, KātyŚr.; BhP.; not with empty hands, ŚāṅkhGṛ.; abundant, BhP. iv, 22, 11.

A-riktha-bhāj, mfn. not entitled to a share of property, not an heir, (in a verse quoted by the) Comm. on Yājñ.

A-rikthīya, mfn. id., Mn. ix, 147.

अरित्र *aritrí, tā́*, m. (√*ṛi*), a rower, RV. ii, 42, 1 & ix, 95, 2; [cf. Gk. ἐρέτης, ἐρετμόν, &c.; Lat. *ratis, remex*, &c.]

Arítra, mfn. (Pāṇ. iii, 2, 184) propelling, driving, RV. x, 46, 7; (*arítra*), *as*, m. an oar, ŚBr. iv; (*arítra* [RV. i, 46, 8] or *áritra* [AV. v, 4, 5]), *am*, n. (ifc. f. *ā*) an oar; (cf. *dáśâritra, nityâr°, śátâr°, sv-aritrá*); [Lat. *aratrum*.] **-gādha**, mfn. oar-deep, shallow, Pāṇ. vi, 2, 4, Kāś. **-pára̱ṇa**, mf(*ī*)n. crossing over by means of oars, RV. x, 101, 2.

अरिन् *arin, i*, n. See *ara*.

अरिप्र *a-riprá*, mf(*ā́*)n. spotless, clear, RV. & AV.; faultless, blameless, RV.

अरिफित *a-riphita*, mfn. (said of the Visarga) not changed into *r*, Prāt.

A-repha, mfn. without the letter *r*. **-jāta**, mfn. id., Up. **-vat**, mfn. id., RPrāt.

A-rephin, mfn. = *a-riphita*, RPrāt.

अरिषण्य *á-rishaṇya*, mfn. not failing, certain, to be depended upon, RV. ii, 39, 4.

A'-rishaṇyat, mfn. id., RV.

A'-rishṭa, mf(*ā*)n. unhurt, RV. &c.; proof against injury or damage, RV.; secure, safe, RV.; boding misfortune (as birds of ill-omen, &c.), AdbhBr.; Hariv.; fatal, disastrous (as a house), R. ii, 42, 22; (*as*), m. a heron, L.; a crow, L.; the soap-berry tree, Sapindus Detergens Roxb. (the fruits of which are used in washing, Yājñ. i, 186); cf. *arishṭaka;* Azadirachta Indica, R. ii, 94, 9; garlic, L.; a distilled mixture, a kind of liquor, Suśr.; N. of an Asura (with the shape of an ox, son of Bali, slain by Kṛishṇa or Vishṇu), Hariv.; BhP.; of a son of Manu Vaivasvata, VP. (v. l. for *dishṭa*); ill-luck, misfortune (see *arishṭa*, n.), MBh. xii, 6573; (*ā*), f. a bandage, Suśr.; a medical plant, L.; N. of Durgā, SkandaP.; N. of a daughter of Daksha and one of the wives of Kaśyapa, Hariv.; (*am*), n. bad or ill-luck, misfortune; a natural phenomenon boding misfortune, VarBṛS.; BhP. &c.; sign or symptom of approaching death; good fortune, happiness, MBh. iv, 2126; buttermilk, L.; vinous spirit, L.; a woman's apartment, the lying-in chamber (cf. *arishṭa-gṛiha* & *-śayyā* below), L. **-karman**, m., N. of a prince, VP. **-gātu** (*árishṭa-*), mfn. having a secure residence, RV. v, 44, 3. **-gu** (*árishṭa-*), mfn. whose cattle are unhurt, AV. x, 3, 10. **-gṛiha**, n. a lying-in chamber, L. **-grāma** (*árishṭa-*), mfn. (said of the Maruts) whose troop is unbroken, i. e. complete in number, RV. i, 166, 6. **-tāti** (*arishṭá-*), f. safeness, security, RV. x & AV.; (mfn.) = *arishṭasya kara*, making fortunate, auspicious, Pāṇ. iv, 4, 143. **-dushṭa-dhī**, mfn. (= *vivaśa*) apprehensive of death, alarmed at its approach, L. **-nemi** (*árishṭa-*), mfn. the felly of whose wheel is unhurt (N. of Tārkshya), RV.; (*is*), m., N. of a man (named together with Tārkshya), VS. xv, 18; (said to be the author of the hymn RV. x, 178) RAnukr.; N. of various princes, MBh.; VP.; of a Gandharva, BhP.; of the twenty-second of the twenty-four Jaina Tīrthaṃkaras of the present Avasarpiṇī. **-nemin**, m., N. of a brother of Garuḍa (= Aruṇa, Comm.), R. v, 2, 10; of a Muni, R. vii, 90, 5; of the twenty-second Tīrthaṃkara (see *-nemi*), L. **-pura**, n., N. of a town, Pāṇ. vi, 2, 100. **-bharman**, mfn. yielding security, RV. viii, 18, 4 (voc.) **-mathana**, m. 'killer of the Asura Arishṭa,' N. of Śiva (i. e. Vishṇu). **-ratha** (*árishṭa-*), mfn. whose carriage is unhurt, RV. x, 6, 3. **-vīra** (*árishṭa-*), mfn. whose heroes are unhurt, RV. i, 114, 3 & AV. iii, 12, 1. **-śayyā**, f. a lying-in couch, Ragh. iii, 15. **-sūdana** or **-han**, m. (= *-mathana*, q.v.) N. of Vishṇu, L. **Arishṭâśrita-pura**, n., N. of a town, Pāṇ. vi, 2, 100, Sch. **A'-rishṭâsu**, mfn. whose vital power is unhurt, AV. xiv, 2, 72.

A-rishṭaka, *as*, m. (= *á-rishṭa*, m.) the soap-berry tree (the fruits of which are used in washing, Mn. v, 120), Suśr.; (*akā* or *ikā*), f., N. of a plant, VarBṛS.

A'-rishṭi, *is*, f. Ved. safeness, security, RV. &c.

A'-rishyat, mfn. not being hurt, RV. & AV.

अरीळ्ह *á-rīḷha*, mfn. (for *á-rīḍha*, √*rih* = *lih*), not licked, RV. iv, 18, 10.

अरीति *a-rīti*, f. (in rhetoric) deficiency of style, a defect in the choice of expressions.

A-rītika, *am*, n. id., L.

अरीहण *arīhaṇa, as*, m. the first N. of the following gaṇa. **Arīhaṇâdi**, a gaṇa of Pāṇ. (iv, 2, 80).

अरु *aru, us*, m. the sun, L.; the red-blossomed Khadira tree, L.; for *arus*, n. only in comp. with **-ṃ-tuda**, mf(*ā*)n. (Pāṇ. iii, 2, 35 & vi, 3, 67) 'beating or hurting a wound,' causing torments, painful, Mn. ii, 161, &c. **Arū-√1. kṛi**, to wound, L.

Aruṇshikā, f. (fr. *arūṇshi*, pl. of *arus*, n.), scab on the head, Suśr.

अरुग्ण *á-rugṇa*, mfn. unbroken, RV. vi, 39, 2.

A-ruj, mfn. painless (as a tumour), Suśr.; free from disease, sound, healthy.

A-ruja, mf(*ā*)n. painless (as a tumour, &c.), Suśr.; free from disease, sound, Suśr. &c.; brisk, gay, R. vii, 84, 16; (*as*), m. the plant Cassia Fistula; N. of a Dānava, Hariv. 14286.

अरुच् *a-rúc*, mfn. lightless, RV. vi, 39, 4.

A-ruci, *is*, f. want of appetite, disgust, Suśr.; aversion, dislike, Sāh.; Kād. (with *upari*).

A'-rucita, mfn. not agreeable or suitable to, ŚBr. xiv.

A-rucira, mfn. disagreeable, disgusting.

A-rucya, mfn. id., L.

अरुज् *a-ruj* & *a-ruja*. See *á-rugṇa*.

अरुण *aruṇá*, mf(*ā́* [RV. v, 63, 6, &c.] or *ī́* [RV. x, 61, 4, & (nom. pl. *aruṇā́yas*) 95, 6])n. (√*ṛi*, Uṇ.), reddish-brown, tawny, red, ruddy (the colour of the morning opposed to the darkness of night), RV. &c.; perplexed, L.; dumb, L.; (*as*), m. red colour, BhP.; the dawn (personified as the charioteer of the sun), Mn. x, 33, &c.; the sun, Śak.; a kind of leprosy (with red [cf. AV. v, 22, 3 & vi, 20, 3] spots and insensibility of the skin), L.; a little poisonous animal, Suśr.; the plant Rottleria Tinctoria, L.; molasses, L.; N. of a teacher, TS.; ŚBr.; TBr.; of the composer of the hymn RV. x, 91 (with the patron. Vaitahavya), RAnukr.; of the Nāga priest Āṭa, PBr.; of a son of Kṛishṇa, BhP.; of the Daitya Mura, ib.; of an Asura, MBh. xvi, 119 (v. l. *varuṇa*); of the father of the fabulous bird Jaṭāyu, MBh. iii, 16045; (*áruṇa*), *as*, m., N. of a pupil of Upaveśi (cf. *aruṇá*, m. above), ŚBr. xiv; (*ās*), m. pl., N. of a class of Ketus (seventy-seven in number), VarBṛS.; (named as the composers of certain Mantras) Kāṭh.; (*ā*), f. the plants Betula, madder (Rubia Manjith), Téori, a black kind of the same, Colocynth or bitter apple, the plant that yields the red and black berry used for the jewellers' weight (called Retti), L.; N. of a river, MBh. iii, 7022 & ix, 2429 seq.; (*ī́s*), f. red cow (in the Vedic myths), RV. & SV.; the dawn, RV.; (*ám*), n. red colour, RV. x, 168, 1; gold, AV. xiii, 4, 51; a ruby, BhP. **-kamala**, n. the red lotus. **-kara**, m. 'having red rays,' the sun, Kād. **-kiraṇa**, m. id., VarBṛS. **-ketu-brāhmaṇa**, n. the Brāhmaṇa of the Aruṇāḥ Ketavaḥ (see *aruṇās* above), AitrAnukr. **-cūḍa**, m. 'red-combed,' a cock, L. **-jyotis**, m., N. of Śiva. **-tā**, f. red colour, Śiś. ix, 14; Suśr. **-tva**, n. id., Hcat. **-datta**, m., N. of an author, Comm. on Uṇ. iii, 159; iv, 117 & 184. **-dūrvā́**, f. reddish fennel, ŚBr; KātyŚr. **-netra**, m. 'red-eyed,' a pigeon, L. **-piśaṅgá**, mfn. reddish-brown, TS. **-pushpa** (*aruṇá-*), mfn. having red flowers, ŚBr.; the blossom of a certain grass, KātyŚr.; (*ī*), f. the plant Pentapetes Phœnicea, L. **-priyā**, f., N. of an Apsaras, Hariv. 12470. **-psu** (*aruṇá-*), mfn. of a red appearance, RV. **-babhru** (*aruṇá-*), mfn. reddish-yellow, VS. xxiv, 2. **-yúj**, mfn. furnished with red (rays of light), RV. vi, 65, 2. **-locana**, mfn. red-eyed (as in anger), MārkP.; (*as*), m. = *-netra*, q. v., L. **-sārathi**, m. 'whose charioteer is Aruṇa,' the sun, L. **-smṛiti**, f., N. of a work. **Aruṇâgraja**, m. 'the first-born of Aruṇa,' Garuḍa (the bird of Vishṇu), L.; (cf. *aruṇânuja* below.) **Aruṇâtmaja**, m. 'son of Aruṇa,' Jaṭāyu (see *aruṇa*, m. above), L. **Aruṇâditya**, m. one of the twelve shapes of the sun, SkandaP. **Aruṇânuja**, m. 'the younger brother of Aruṇa,' Garuḍa, Kād. (cf. *aruṇâgraja* above & *aruṇâvaraja* below). **Aruṇâmnāya-vidhi**, m., N. of part of the Kāṭh. (cf. *aruṇīya-vidhi*). **Aruṇârcis**, m. the rising sun, Daś. **Aruṇâvaraja**, m. = *aruṇânuja* above, L. **Aruṇâśva**, mfn. driving with red horses (N. of the Maruts), RV. v, 57, 4. **Aruṇī-kṛita**, mfn. reddened, turned or become red, Kād.; Sāh. **Aruṇaitá**, mfn. yellow-dappled, TS. **Aruṇôda**, n., N. of a lake, VP.; of one of the seas surrounding the world, Jain. **Aruṇôdaya**, m. break of day, dawn, Mn. x, 33; *-saptamī*, f. the seventh day in the bright half of Māgha, L. **Aruṇôpala**, m. a ruby, L.

Aruṇaya, Nom. P. °*yati*, to redden, Kād.; (perf. Pass. p. *aruṇita*) reddened, Śiś. vi, 32; Kum. v, 11.

Aruṇi, *is*, m., N. of a Muni, BhP. (cf. *āruṇi*).

Aruṇiman, *ā*, m. redness, ruddiness, Sāh.; Bālar.

Aruṇīya-vidhi, *is*, m. = *aruṇâmnāya-vidhi* above, Sāy. on TĀr.

अरुतहनु *á-ruta-hanu*, mfn. one whose cheeks or jaws are not broken, RV. x, 105, 7.

अरुद्ध *a-ruddha*, mfn. not hindered.

अरुंतुद *aruṃ-tuda*. See *aru*.

अरुन्धती *a-rundhatī*, f. a medicinal climbing plant, AV.; the wife of Vasishṭha, R. &c.; the wife of Dharma, Hariv.; the little and scarcely visible star Alcor (belonging to the Great Bear, and personified as the wife of one of its seven chief stars, Vasishṭha, or of all the seven, the so-called seven Ṛishis; at marriage ceremonies Arundhatī is invoked as a pattern of conjugal excellence by the bridegroom), ĀśvGṛ. &c.; N. of a kind of supernatural faculty (also called *kuṇḍalinī*). **-jāni** or **-nātha**, m. 'husband of Arundhatī,' Vasishṭha (one of the seven Ṛishis or saints, and stars in the Great Bear), L. **-vaṭa**, m., N. of a Tīrtha, MBh. iii, 8019. **-sahacara**, m. 'companion of Arundhatī,' Vasishṭha.

अरुन्मुख *arun-mukha, ās*, m. pl. (an irregular form developed fr. *arur-magha* below), N. of certain Yatis, KaushUp.

Arur-magha, *ās*, m. pl. (cf. *púnar-magha*), N. of certain miserly evil spirits (as the Paṇis, &c.), AitBr.

अरुश *aruśa, am*, n., N. of a Tantra. **-hán**, m. (*aruśa* = *arushá*?) striking the red (clouds), N. of Indra ['killing enemies,' Sāy.], RV. x, 116, 4.

अरुष 1. *a-rush*, mfn. not angry, good-tempered, Pañcat.

अरुष 1. *arushá*, mf(*árushī*, RV. i, 92, 1 & 2; x, 5, 5)n. red, reddish (the colour of Agni and his horses; of cows; of the team of Ushas, the Aśvins, &c.), RV. & VS.; (*ás*), m. the sun, the day, RV. vi, 49, 3 & vii, 71, 1 (cf. *arūsha*); (*ā́s, ásas*), m. pl. the red horses of Agni, RV.; AV.; (*árushī*), f. the dawn, RV.; a red mare (a N. applied to the team of Agni and Ushas, and to Agni's flames), RV.; (*ám*), n. shape, Naigh. **-stūpa** (*arushá-*), mfn. having a fiery tuft (as Agni), RV. iii, 29, 3.

2. **Arusha**, Nom. P. *árushati*, to go, Naigh.

Arushya, Nom. P. *arushyati*, v. l. for *árushati*.

अरुस् *árus*, mfn. wounded, sore, ŚBr.; (*us*), n. a sore or wound, AV. v, 5, 4; ŚBr. &c.; the sun, Uṇ.; ind. a joint, L. **-srāṇa**, n. (defectively written *aru-sr°*) a kind of medical preparation for wounds, AV. ii, 3, 3 & 5.

Aru (& **arū-√1. kṛi**). See s. v.

Arush (in comp. for *árus*). **-kara**, mfn. causing wounds, wounding, Suśr.; (*as*), m. the tree Semecarpus Anacardium; (*am*), n. the nut of that tree, Suśr. **-kṛita** (*árush-*), mfn. wounded, ŚBr.

Arushka, ifc. for *árus*, Car.; (*as*), m. (= *arush-kara* above) Semecarpus Anacardium, L.

अरुहा *a-ruhā*, f., N. of a plant, L.

अरूक्ष *á-rūksha*, mfn. soft, MaitrS. **-tā** (*a-rūkshá-*), f. softness, ŚBr.

A'-rūkshita, mfn. soft, supple, RV. iv, 11, 1.

A'-rūkshṇa, mfn. soft, tender, AV. viii, 2, 16.

अरूप *a-rūpa*, mf(*ā*)n. formless, shapeless,

PBr.; ŚvetUp.; NṛisUp.; ugly, ill-formed, R. **—jña** (*á-rūpa-*), mfn. not distinguishing the shape or colour, ŚBr. xiv. **—tā**, f. ugliness. **—tva**, n. id., Kathās.; want of any characteristic quality, Jaim. **—vat**, mfn. ugly.

A-rūpaka, mfn. shapeless, immaterial, MBh. iii, 12984; (in rhetoric) without figure or metaphor, literal.

A-rūpaṇa, *am*, n. not a figurative expression, Kāvyād.

A-rūpin, mfn. shapeless, R. i, 23, 15.

अरूष *arūsha*, *as*, m. (for *arusha*, m., q. v.) the sun, Uṇ.; a kind of snake, L.

अरे *are*, ind. interjection of calling, VS.; ŚBr. &c. (cf. *arare*, *arere*, and *re*).

अरेणु *a-reṇú*, mfn. not dusty (said of the gods and their cars and roads), RV.; not earthly, celestial, RV. i, 56, 3; (*ávas*), m. pl. the gods, RV. x, 143, 2.

अरेतस् *a-retás*, mfn. not receiving seed, ŚBr. xiv.

A-retás-ka, mfn. seedless, ŚBr.

अरेपस् *a-repás*, mfn. spotless, RV.; VS.; AV.

अरेफ *a-repha.* See *a-riphita.*

अरेरे *arere*, ind. (probably *are 're*, repetition of *are*, q. v.), interjection of calling to inferiors or of calling angrily, L.

अरोक *a-roka*, mfn. (√*ruc*), not bright, darkened, L. **—dat** or **-danta**, mfn. having black or discoloured teeth, Pāṇ. v, 4, 144.

A-rocaka, mfn. not shining, Kauś.; causing want of appetite or disgust, Suśr.; (*as*), m. want or loss of appetite, disgust, indigestion, Suśr. &c.

A-rocakin, mfn. suffering from want of appetite or indigestion, Suśr.; Hcat.; (in rhetoric) having a fastidious or cultivated taste.

A-rocamāna, mfn. not shining, Mn. iii, 62; not pleasing; (*as*), m. (gaṇa *cārv-ādi*, q. v.)

A-rocishṇu, mfn. dark, L.; disagreeable, L.

A-rocuká, mfn. not pleasing, MaitrS.

अरोग *a-roga*, mf(*ā*)n. free from disease, healthy, well, Mn. &c.; (*as*), m. health, Hit.; (*ā*), f., N. of Dākshāyaṇī in Vaidyanātha, MatsyaP. **—tā**, f. health, Bhpr. **—tva**, n. id., R. vii, 36, 16.

Á-rogaṇa, mfn. freeing from disease, AV. ii, 3, 2.

A-rogin, mfn. healthy, L. **Arogi-tā**, f. healthiness, health, Hit.; Vet.

A-rogya, mfn. healthy, L. **—tā**, f. health, R. ii, 70, 7.

अरोदन *a-rodana*, *am*, n. not weeping.

अरोध्य *a-rodhya*, mfn. (√2. *rudh*), not to be hindered or obstructed, unobstructed.

अरोपण *a-ropaṇu*, *um*, n. (√*ruh*), not planting or fixing.

अरोम *a-roma*, mf(*ā*)n. hairless, MBh. i, 8010.

A-romaśa, mfn. id., VarBṛS.

अरोष *a-rosha*, *as*, m. freedom from anger, gentleness, MBh, x, 712.

A-roshaṇa, mfn. not inclined to anger, MBh.

अरोहिणीक *a-rohiṇī-ka*, mfn. without Rohiṇī, Kathās.

अरौद्र *a-raudra*, mfn. not formidable.

अर्क् *ark.* See *arkaya*, col. 2.

अर्क *arká*, *as*, m. (√*arc*), Ved. a ray, flash of lightning, RV. &c.; the sun, RV. &c.; (hence) the number 'twelve,' Sūryas.; Sunday; fire, RV. ix, 50, 4; ŚBr.; BṛĀrUp.; crystal, R. ii, 94, 6; membrum virile, AV. vi, 72, 1; copper, L.; the plant Calotropis Gigantea (the larger leaves are used for sacrificial ceremonies; cf. *arka-kośī*, *-parṇá*, *-palāśá*, &c. below); *arka*, &c.; a religious ceremony, ŚBr.; BṛĀrUp.; (cf. *arkâśvamedha* below); praise, hymn, song (also said of the roaring of the Maruts and of Indra's thunder), RV. & AV.; one who praises, a singer, RV.; N. of Indra, L.; a learned man (cf. RV. viii, 63, 6), L.; an elder brother, L.; N. of a physician, BrahmavP. (cf. *arka-cikitsā* below); (*as*, *am*), m. n. (with *agneḥ*, *indrasya*, *gautamasaḥ*, &c.) N. of different Sāmans; food, Naigh. & Nir. (cf. RV. vii, 9, 2). **—kara**, m. sunbeam, Naish. **—kāntā**, f. the plant Polanisia Icosandra, W. **—kāshṭha**, n. wood from the Arka plant, KātyŚr. **—kuṇḍa-tīrtha**, n., N. of a Tīrtha, SkandaP. **—kośī**, f. a bud of the Arka plant, ŚBr. x. **—kshīra**, n. the milky juice of the Arka plant, Suśr. **—kshetra**, n. 'the field of the sun,' N. of a sacred place in Orissa. **—graha**, m. eclipse of the sun, VarBṛS. **—grīva**, m., N. of a Sāman. **—candana**, n. red sanders, L. **—cikitsā**, f. Arka's (see *arka*, m. at end) 'medical art,' i. e. work on medicine. **—ja**, mfn. 'sun-born,' coming from the sun; (*as*), m. the planet Saturn, VarBṛS. &c.; (*au*), m. du., N. of the Aśvins, L. **—tanaya**, m. (= *-ja*), the planet Saturn, VarBṛ.; N. of Karṇa, L.; of Manu Vaivasvata and Manu Sāvarṇi, MBh.; (*ā*), f., N. of the rivers Yamunā and Tapatī, MBh. **—tvá**, n. brightness, ŚBr. x. **—tvish**, f. the light of the sun. **—dina**, n. a solar day. **—dhānā́**, *ā́s*, f. pl. seeds of the Arka plant, ŚBr. x. **—nandana**, m. (= *-ja*, q. v.) N. of the planet Saturn, VarBṛS.; N. of Karṇa, L. **—nayana**, n., N. of an Asura, Hariv. **—pattra**, n. the leaf of the Arka plant, MBh. i, 715; (*as*), m. the Arka plant; (*ā*), f. a kind of birth-wort (Aristolochia Indica), L. **—parṇá**, n. the leaf of the Arka plant, ŚBr.; KātyŚr.; (*as*), m. the Arka plant; N. of a snake demon, MBh. i, 2551. **—pādapa**, m. the tree Melia Azadirachta Lin., L. **—putra**, m. (= *-ja*, q. v.) the planet Saturn, VarBṛS. & VarBṛ.; N. of Karṇa, L.; of Yama, L. **—pushpâdya**, m., N. of a Sāman. **—pushpikā**, f. the plant Gynandropsis Pentaphylla, L. **—pushpī**, f. the plant Hibiscus Hirtus, Suśr. **—pushpôttara**, n., N. of a Sāman. **—prakāśa**, mf(*ā*)n. bright like the sun, MBh. ii, 313; (*as*), m., N. of a medical work (cf. *-cikitsā* above); of a work on jurisprudence. **—prabhā-jāla**, n. (a multitude of) sun-beams, MBh. iii, 12541. **—priyā**, f. the plant Hibiscus Rosa Sinensis, L. **—bandhu** or **-bāndhava**, m. a N. of Buddha Śākya-muni, L. **—bhaktā**, f. = *-kāntā*, q. v. **—maṇḍala**, n. the disc of the sun. **—maya**, mfn. composed of the Arka plant, ĀpŚr. **—mūlá**, n. the root of the Arka plant, ŚBr. x; (*ā*), f. (= *-pattrā*, q. v.) Aristolochia Indica, L. **—ripu**, m. 'enemy of the sun,' Rāhu, Kād. **—reto-ja**, m. 'son of Sūrya,' Revanta, L. **—lavaṇa**, n. saltpetre, L. **—lūsha**, m., N. of a man, (gaṇa *karṇâdi* & *vid-ādi*, q. v.) **—vat** (*arká-*), mfn. possessing or holding the thunderbolt, TS.; containing the word *arká*, PBr.; receiving the oblation in the Arka ceremony, MaitrS. **—varsha**, m. a solar year. **—vallabha**, m. the plant Pentapetes Phœnicea, L. **—vidha** (*arká-*), mfn. Arka-like, ŚBr. x. **—vedha**, m., N. of a plant, L. **—vrata**, n. the rule or law of the sun (i. e. levying taxes, subjecting the people to imposts, or drawing their wealth as imperceptibly as the sun evaporates water), Mn. ix, 305. **—śaśi-śatru**, m. 'enemy of sun and moon,' Rāhu, VarBṛS. (cf. *-ripu* above). **—śiras**, n., N. of a Sāman. **—śoká**, m. the heat of rays, RV. vi, 4, 7. **—samudgá**, m. the tip of an Arka-bud (see *kośī*), ŚBr. x. **—sāti** (*arká-*), f. invention of hymns, poetical inspiration, RV. i, 174, 7; vi, 20, 4 & 26, 3. **—suta**, m. (= *-tanaya*, q. v.) N. of Karṇa, L.; (*ā*), f., N. of the river Yamunā, L. **—sūnu**, m. (= *-ja*, q. v.) the planet Saturn; N. of Yama, L. **—sôdara**, m. Indra's elephant Airāvata. **—stubh**, mfn. singing hymns, ŚāṅkhŚr. **—hitā**, f. = *-kāntā*, q. v. **Arkâṅśa**, m. a digit or the twelfth part of the sun's disc, L. **Arkâgrā**, f. the sun's measure of amplitude, Sūryas. **Arkâśman**, m. heliotrope, girasol, crystal, L. **Arkâśvamedha**, n. [Pāṇ. ii, 4, 4, Kāś.] or °**dhaú**, m. du. [AV. xi, 7, 7, & ŚBr.], the Arka ceremony and the Aśvamedha sacrifice; °*dhá-vat*, mfn. containing the two, TS.; °*dhin*, mfn. performing the two, TS. **Arkâshṭhīlā́**, f. a grain of the fruit of the Arka plant, ŚBr. x. **Arkâhuti**, *ayas*, f. pl., N. of five sacrificial offerings, ĀpŚr. **Arkâhva**, m. 'named (after) Arka,' the stone Sūryakānta, L.; the plant Pinus Webbiana, L. **Arkêndu-saṃgama**, m. the instant of conjunction of the sun and moon. **Arkôpala**, m. (= *arkâhva* above) Sūryakānta, Naish.

Arkaya, Nom. P. °*yati*, to heat, L.; to praise, L.

Arkín, mfn. radiant with light, RV. viii, 101, 13; praising, RV. i, 7, 1; 10, 1 & 38, 15.

Arkīya, mfn. belonging to Arka, (gaṇa *utkarâdi*, q. v.)

Arkyà, *am*, n., N. of a Śastra and of a Sāman, TS.; ŚBr.; PBr.

अर्ग *arga*, *as*, m., N. of a Ṛishi of the SV. (with the patron. Aurava).

अर्गट *argaṭa*, *as*, m., N. of a poet, Śārṅg.; the plant Barleria Cærulea.

अर्गड *argaḍa* (in the word *sārgaḍa*, q. v.) v. l. for *argala*, ŚBr. xiv.

अर्गल *argala*, mfn. a wooden bolt or pin for fastening a door or the cover of a vessel, Ragh. &c.; a bar, check, impediment, ib.; a wave, L.; (*as* or *am*), m. or n., N. of a hell, PadmaP. v. **Argalā-nirgama**, m., N. of an astrological treatise. **Argalā-stuti**, f. or **-stotra**, n. a hymn introductory to the Devīmāhātmya.

Argalikā, f. a small door pin, L.

Argalita, mfn. fastened by a bolt, Kād.; Kathās.

Argalīya or **argalya**, mfn. belonging to a bolt, (gaṇa *apūpâdi*, q. v.)

अर्घ् *argh*, cl. 1. P. *arghati*, to be worth, be of value, Pañcat.; (cf. √*arh.*)

अर्घ *argha*, *as*, m. (√*arh*), worth, value, price, Mn.; Yājñ.; (often ifc., cf. *dhanârghá*, *mahârgha*, *śatârghá*, *sahasrârghá*); (*ás*), m. respectful reception of a guest (by the offering of rice, dūrva-grass, flowers, or often only of water), ŚBr. xiv, &c. (often confounded with *arghya*, q. v.); a collection of twenty pearls (having the weight of a Dharaṇa), VarBṛS. **—dāna**, n. presentation of a respectful offering. **—pātra**, n. (for *arghya-pātra*) the small vessel in which water is offered to the guest on his arrival, Kathās. **—balâbala**, n. rate of price, proper price, the cheapness or dearness of commodities, Mn. ix, 329 (cf. *arghasya hrāsaṃ vṛiddhiṃ vā*, Yājñ. ii, 249). **—saṃsthāpana**, n. fixing the price of commodities, appraising, assize (it is the act of a king or ruler, in concert with the traders, and should be done once a week or once a fortnight), Mn. viii, 402. **Arghâpacaya**, m. 'diminution of price,' (*ena*), instr. ind. cheaper, Gaut. **Arghârha**, mfn. worthy of or requiring a respectful offering, a superior. **Arghêśvara**, m., N. of Śiva; (cf. *arghīśa.*)

Arghīśa, *as*, m. ('*arghin*' for *argha*) = *arghêśvara*, q. v., L.

Arghya, mfn. 'valuable,' see *an-arghya*; (gaṇa *daṇḍâdi*, q. v., '*argham arhati*') deserving a respectful reception (as a guest), PārGṛ.; Yājñ. &c.; belonging to or used at the respectful reception of a guest, Gobh.; Yājñ. &c.; (*am*), n. (Pāṇ. v, 4, 25) water offered at the respectful reception of a guest, ĀśvGṛ. &c.; (probably for *ārghya*, q. v.) a kind of honey, L. **—pātra**, n., see *argha-p°*. **Arghyârha**, m. the plant Pterospermum Suberifolium, L.

अर्घट *arghaṭa*, *am*, n. (= *pārghaṭa*, q. v.) ashes, L.

अर्च् 1. *arc*, cl. 1. P. *árcati* (Subj. *árcāt*; impf. *ārcat*; aor. *ārcīt*, Bhaṭṭ.; perf. *ānarca*, 3. pl. *ānarcuḥ* [MBh. iii, 988, &c.], but Ved. *ānṛicúḥ* [RV.]; perf. Ā. (Pass.) *ānarce* [Bhaṭṭ], but Ved. *sám ānṛice* [RV. i, 160, 4]; fut. p. *arcishyat* [Mn. iv, 251]; ind. p. *arcya* [Mn. &c.; cf. Pāṇ. vii, 1, 38, Sch.] or *arcitvā* [R. iii, 77, 15]; Ved. Inf. *ṛicáse* [RV. vi, 39, 5 & vii, 61, 6]) to shine, be brilliant, RV.; to praise, sing (also used of the roaring of the Maruts and of a bull [RV. iv, 16, 3]), RV.; AV; ŚBr.; to praise anything to another (dat.), recommend, RV.; to honour or treat with respect, MBh. &c.; to adorn, VarBṛS.: exceptionally Ā. (1. pl. *arcāmahe*) to honour, MBh. ii, 1383: Caus. (2. sg. *arcayas*) to cause to shine, RV. iii, 44, 2: P. Ā. to honour or treat with respect, Mn.; MBh. &c.: Desid. *arcicishati*, to wish to honour, Pāṇ. vi, 1, 3, Sch.: Ved. Pass. *ṛicyáte* (p. *ṛicyámāna*) to be praised, RV.

2. **Árc**, m(instr. *arcā́*)fn. shining, brilliant [Gmn.], RV. vi, 34, 4.

Arcaka, mfn. honouring, worshipping, Mn. xi, 224; (*as*), m. a worshipper, BhP.

Árcat, mfn. (pr. p.) shining, RV.; praising, RV.; (*an*), m., N. of a Ṛishi (son of Hiraṇyastūpa), Nir. x, 32 (commenting on RV. x, 149, 5). **Arcáddhūma**, mfn. whose smoke is shining, RV. x, 46, 7.

Arcátri, mfn. (said of the Maruts) roaring, RV. vi, 66, 10.
Arcatryà (4), mfn. (fr. *arcatra*, 'praise') to be raised, RV. vi, 24, 1.
Arcana, mf(*ī*)n. ifc. honouring, praising, Nir.; (*am, ā*), n. f. homage paid to deities and to superiors, MBh. &c. (cf. *vibudhârcana* and *surârcana*).
Arcanānas, m. 'who has a rattling carriage,' N. of a Ṛishi, RV. v, 64, 7 & AV. xviii, 3, 15.
Arca-nas, mfn. (fr. *arcā* below), 'one whose nose is like that of an idol,' Kāś. & Pat. on Pāṇ. v, 4, 118. [The rule perhaps originally meant to explain the above N. *arcanānas*, taking it for *arcanā-nas*, 'whose nose shows submission or devotion.']
Arcanīya, mfn. to be worshipped, venerable.
Arcā́, f. (Pāṇ. ii, 3, 43 & v, 2, 101) worship, adoration, ŚBr. xi; Mn. &c.; an image or idol (destined to be worshipped), VarBṛS. &c.; body, Jain. **-vat**, mfn. (= 1. *ārca*, q. v.) worshipped, Pāṇ. v, 2, 101, Sch. **-vidhi**, m. rules for worship or adoration, RāmatUp.
Arcí, *is*, m. (chiefly Ved.) ray, flame, RV. &c.; (*is*), m. (for *aṅśa*) N. of one of the twelve Ādityas, Comm. on KaushBr. **-netrâdhipati**, m., N. of a Yaksha, L. **-mát**, m(du. *-mántā*)fn. shining, blazing, RV. x, 61, 15; MuṇḍUp. **-vát**, mfn. id., RV. vii, 81, 2 & ix, 67, 24.
Arcita, mfn. honoured, worshipped, respected, saluted, MBh.; Mn. &c.; offered with reverence, Mn. iv, 213 (*an-*, neg.) & 235; Yājñ. i, 167.
Arcitin, mfn. honouring (with loc.), (gaṇa *ishṭâdi*, q. v.)
Arcitṛi, *tā*, m. a worshipper, R. v, 32, 7.
Arcín, mfn. (said of Varuṇa's foot) shining, RV. viii, 41, 8; = *arcátri*, q. v., RV. ii, 34, 1 & v, 45, 1; N. of a man.
Arcís, n. ray of light, flame, light, lustre, RV. (once pl. *arciṅshi*, RV. vii, 62, 1); AV.; ŚBr. &c.; (*is*), f. id., ŚBr. ii; Up. &c.; (*is*), f., N. of the wife of Kṛiśāśva and mother of Dhūmaketu, BhP. **-Arcish-mat**, mfn. brilliant, resplendent, R. &c.; (*ān*), m. fire, the god of fire, Hariv.; a flame, VarBṛS.; (*atī*), f. one of the ten stages (through which a Bodhisattva must rise before becoming a Buddha), Buddh.
1. **Arcya**, mfn. to be honoured or worshipped.
2. **Arcya**, ind. p. See √*arc*.

अर्ज् 1. *arj*, cl. 1. P. *arjati* (perf. 3. pl. *ānarjuḥ*) to procure, acquire, Naish. & Bhaṭṭ.: Ā. *arjate*, to go, L.; to stand firm, L.; to procure, L.; to be of good health, L.: Caus. *arjayati*, °*te*, (aor. *ārjijat*, Bhaṭṭ.) to procure, acquire, obtain, MBh.; Mn. &c.
Arjaka, mfn. procuring, acquiring, L.; (*as*), m. the plant Ocimum Gratissimum, L.
Arjana, *am*, n. (Pāṇ. iii, 1, 20, Comm.) procuring, acquiring, gaining, earning, Mn. xii, 79, &c.
Arjanīya, mfn. to be acquired or procured, Kathās.
Arjita, mfn. acquired, gained, earned; (cf. *svârjita* and *svayam-arjita*.)

अर्जुन *árjuna*, mfn. (cf. *ṛijrá* and √*raj*) white, clear (the colour of the day, RV. vi, 9, 1; of the dawn, RV. i, 49, 3; of the lightning; of the milk; of silver, &c.); made of silver, AV. iv, 37, 4; (*as*), m. the white colour, L.; a peacock, L.; cutaneous disease, Sāy. on RV. i, 122, 5; the tree Terminalia Árjuna W. and A.; N. of a man, RV. i, 122, 5; of Indra, VS.; ŚBr.; of the third of the Pāṇḍava princes (who was a son of Indra and Kuntī), MBh. &c.; of a son of Kṛitavīrya (who was slain by Paraśurāma), ib.; of a Śākya (known as a mathematician); of different other persons; the only son of his mother, L.; (*ī*), f. a cow, MBh. xiii, 3596; a kind of serpent, (voc. *árjuni*) AV. ii, 24, 7; a procuress, bawd, L.; N. of Ushā (wife of Aniruddha), L.; of the river Bāhudā or Karatoyā, L.; (°*nyau* or °*nyas*), f. du. or pl., N. of the constellation Phalgunī, RV. x, 85, 13; ŚBr.; (*am*), n. silver, AV. v, 28, 5 & 9; gold, L.; slight inflammation of the conjunctiva or white of the eye, Suśr.; a particular grass (used as a substitute for the Soma plant), PBr. &c.; (= *rūpa*) shape, Naigh.; (*ās*), m. pl. the descendants of Arjuna, Pāṇ. ii, 4, 66, Sch. **-kāṇḍa** (*árjuna-*), mfn. having a white appendage, AV. ii, 8, 3. **-cchavi**, mfn. having a white colour, white. **-tas**, ind. on the side of Arjuna. **-dhvaja**, m. 'having a white banner,' N. of Hanumat, L. **-pākī**, f., N. of a plant and its fruits, (gaṇa *harītaky-ādi*, q.v.) **-pāla**, m., N. of a prince (the son of Śamīka), BhP. **-pura**, n., N. of a town, BrahmāṇḍaP. ii. **-purusha**, n. the plants Arjuna (i. e. Terminalia Arjuna) and Purusha (i. e. Rottleria Tinctoria), (gaṇa *gavâśvâdi*, q. v.) **-miśra**, n., N. of a commentator on MBh. vi. **-śirīsha**, n. the plants Terminalia Arjuna and Śirīsha (q. v.), (gaṇa *gavâśvâdi*, q. v.) **-sakhi**, m. 'having Arjuna for his friend,' N. of Kṛishṇa, L. **-siṅha**, m., N. of a prince, Inscr. **Arjunâbhra**, n., N. of a medicament. **Arjunârishṭa-saṃchanna**, mfn. covered with Arjuna and Nimb trees. **Arjunârcana-kalpalatā**, f. or **arjunârcā-pārijāta**, m., N. of two works. **Arjunâhva**, m. 'named Arjuna,' N. of a tree, L. **Arjunêśvara-tīrtha**, n., N. of a Tīrtha, ŚivaP. Rev. **Arjunôpama**, m. 'similar to the Arjuna tree,' the teak tree (Tectona Grandis), L.
Arjunaka, *as*, m., N. of a hunter, MBh. xiii, 18; a worshipper of Arjuna, Pāṇ. iv, 3, 98; vi, 1, 197, Sch.
Arjunasa, mfn. overgrown with Arjuna plants, (gaṇa *tṛiṇâdi*, q. v.)
Arjunāva, *as*, m., N. of a man, (gaṇa *dhūmâdi*, q. v.); (cf. *ārjunāda*.)
Arjunīyā-damana, *am*, n. 'the taming of Arjunīyā,' N. of the 104th chapter of PadmaP. iv.

अर्ण *árṇa*, *as, am*, m. n. a wave, flood, stream, RV.; BhP.; (figuratively applied to the) tumult of battle, RV. v, 50, 4; (*as*), m. a letter, syllable, RāmatUp.; N. of a metre (comprising ten feet, and belonging to the class called Daṇḍaka); the teak tree (see *arjunôpama* above), L.; N. of a man (see *árṇā-citrárathā* below); (*ā*), f. a river, L.; (*ās*), m. pl., N. of a people, BhP. **-sāti** (*árṇa-*), f. (only loc. °*tau*) conquering or obtaining streams [NBD.; 'tumult of battle,' BR. & Gmn.], RV. i, 63, 6; ii, 20, 8 & iv, 24, 4. **Árṇā-citrárathā**, m. du. Arṇa and Citraratha, RV. iv, 30, 18. **Arṇôdara**, m., N. of a teacher (v. l. *ūrṇôdara*, q. v.), VāmP.
Arṇavá, mfn. agitated, foaming, restless, RV.; VS.; AV.; (*ás*), m. a wave, flood, RV.; the foaming sea, RV.; VS.; the ocean of air (sometimes personified as a demon with the epithet *mahā́n* or *tanayitnús*), RV.; AV.; (*as*, rarely *am* [MBh. xiii, 7362]), m. n. the sea; (hence) the number 'four,' Sūryas.; N. of two metres (cf. *árṇa*, m.); N. of a work on jurisprudence. **-ja**, m. 'sea-born,' cuttle-fish, L. **-nemi**, f. 'having the sea as a felly round itself,' the earth, Daś. **-pati**, m. 'lord of the seas,' the ocean, Bālar. **-pota**, m. a boat or ship. **-bhava**, m. 'existing in the sea,' a muscle, L. **-mandira**, m. 'whose abode is the sea,' Varuṇa, L. **-mala**, n. = *-ja* above. **-yāna**, n. = *-pota* above. **-varṇana**, n. 'description of the sea,' N. of a work. **-sarid-āśrita**, mfn. living on the bank of the sea and of rivers, VarBṛS. **Arṇavânta**, m. the extremity of the ocean. **Arṇavôdbhava**, m. = *agni-jāra*, q. v.
Árṇas, n. a wave, flood, stream, RV.; the foaming sea, RV.; the ocean of air, RV.; river, Naigh.; water (ifc. *arṇas-ka*), Bālar.; N. of different metres, RPrāt. &c. **-vat**, mfn. containing many waves, Nir. x, 9.
Arṇasá, mfn. (fr. *árṇas*) agitated, foaming, RV. v, 54, 6; (fr. *árṇa*) full of waves, (gaṇa *tṛiṇâdi*, q.v.)
Arṇo (in Sandhi for *árṇas*). **-da**, 'yielding water,' a cloud, L.; the plant Cyperus Rotundus. **-nidhi**, m. 'receptacle of the waves,' the ocean, Bālar.; (cf. *arṇava-pati*.) **-bhava**, m. = *arṇava-bhava* above, L. **-vṛit**, mfn. (√1. *vṛi*) including the waters, RV. ii, 19, 2.

अर्तगल *arta-gala*, *as*, m. = *ārta-gala*, q.v., L.

अर्तन *artaná*, mfn. (√*ṛit*), reviling [BR.; = *duḥkhin*, Comm.], VS. xxx, 19; (*am*), n. censure, blame, L.
Ártuka, mfn. provoking, quarrelsome, ŚBr.

अर्ति *arti*, *is*, f. = *ārti*, pain, Suśr.; Kathās.; = *ārtnī*, the end of a bow, L.

अर्तिका *artikā*, f. an elder sister (in theatrical language), L.; (cf. *atti, attikā*, and *antikā*.)

अर्थ् *arth*, cl. 10. Ā. *arthayate* (2. du. *arthayethe*, RV. x, 106, 7; Subj. 2. sg. *arthayāse*, RV. i, 82, 1); rarely cl. 1. Ā. (1. pl. *arthāmahe*, MBh. iii, 8613) to strive to obtain, desire, wish, request, ask for (acc.; rarely Inf. [Bhaṭṭ. *yoddhum*]); to supplicate or entreat any one (acc., rarely abl. [Kathās.]); to point out the sense of, comment upon, Comm. on Mṛicch.

अर्थ *ártha*, *as, am*, m. n. [in RV. i–ix only n.; in RV. x six times n. and thrice m.; in later Sanskrit only m.] aim, purpose (very often *artham, arthena, arthāya*, and *arthe* ifc. or with gen. 'for the sake of, on account of, in behalf of, for'); cause, motive, reason, Mn. ii, 213, &c.; advantage, use, utility (generally named with *kāma* and *dharma*, see *tri-varga*; used in wishing well to another, dat. or gen., Pāṇ. ii, 3, 73); thing, object (said of the membrum virile, ŚBr. xiv); object of the senses, VarBṛS.; (hence) the number 'five,' Sūryas.; substance, wealth, property, opulence, money; (hence in astron.) N. of the second mansion, the mansion of wealth (cf. *dhana*), VarBṛS.; personified as the son of Dharma and Buddhi, BhP.; affair, concern (Ved. often acc. *ártham* with √*i* or *gam*, to go to one's business, take up one's work, RV. &c.); (in law) lawsuit, action; having to do with (instr.), wanting, needing anything (instr.), ŚBr. &c.; sense, meaning, notion (cf. *artha-śabdau* and *arthāt* s. v. below and *vedatattvârtha-vid*); manner, kind, L.; prohibition, prevention, L.; price (for *argha*, q. v.), L.; (*āt*), abl. ind., see s. v. below; (*e*), loc. ind. with √1. *kṛi*, (gaṇa *sākshād-ādi*, q. v.) **-kara**, mf(*ī*)n. (Pāṇ. iii, 2, 20, Sch.) producing advantage, useful, Hit. **-karman**, n. an action on purpose (opposed to *guṇa-karman*, q. v.) **-kāma**, *am*, n. [R. ii, 86, 6, v. l.] or *au*, m. du. [R. ii, 86, 6; Mn. iv, 176] or *ās*, m. pl. [Mn. ii, 13] utility and desire, wealth and pleasure; (mfn.) desirous of wealth, N.; MBh. xii, 220; desiring to be useful. **-kāraka**, m., N. of a son of Dyutimat, MārkP. (v. l. *andha-k*°, VP.) **-kāraṇāt**, ind. ifc. for the sake or on account of, R.; Hcat. **-kārśya**, n. poverty, Ragh. v, 21. **-kāsin**, mfn. only apparently (i. e. not really) of use or utility, BhP. **-kilbishin**, mfn. dishonest in money matters, Mn. viii, 141. **-kṛiccha**, n. sg. [R. iv, 7, 9] or pl. [N.] a difficult matter. **-kṛit**, mfn. causing profit, useful. **-kṛita**, mfn. made for a special purpose, Jaim.; made only with regard to utility, interested (as friendship), BhP.; caused by the sense of a word (opposed to *śabda-k*° and *deśa-k*°), Comm. on VPrāt. **-kṛitya**, n. [R.] or **-kṛityā**, f. [Megh.] settling a matter or affair. **-kovida**, mfn. expert in any matter, experienced, R. vi, 4, 8. **-kriyā**, f. an action performed with a special purpose, Sarvad.; the being useful (to others), Lalit. **-gata**, mfn. = *gatârtha*, (gaṇa *āhitâgny-ādi*, q.v.) **-gati**, f. understanding the sense, Pat. **-garīyas**, mfn. (compar.) highly significant. **-guṇa**, m. preference or advantage in regard to the sense, Kpr. **-gṛiha**, n. a treasury, Hariv. **-grahaṇa**, n. abstraction of money; (in Gr.) apprehension of meaning; signification. **-grāhin**, mfn. choosing advantage, Āp. **-ghna**, mfn. destroying wealth, wasteful, extravagant, Mn. ix, 80 & Yājñ. i, 73; destroying advantage, causing loss or damage, Vātsy. **-citta**, mfn. thinking on or desirous of wealth. **-citra**, n. 'variety in sense,' a pun, Kpr. **-cintaka**, mfn. knowing or considering what is useful, Vātsy.; (cf. *sarvârtha-c*°.) **-cintana**, n. or **-cintā**, f. attention or consideration of affairs, Sāh. **-jāta**, n. sg. & pl. collection of goods, money, Mṛicch.; things, objects, Śāk.; Daś. **-jña**, mfn. = *-kovida* above, R. iii, 71, 1; understanding the sense (of a word), Nir. &c. **-tattva**, n. the real object or nature or cause of anything (in comp.), Mn. xii, 102; R. i, 1, 16; the true state of a case, fact of the matter. **-tantra**, n. the doctrine of utility, BhP.; (mfn.) subject to, i. e. acting according to one's interest, BhP. **-tas**, ind. towards a particular object, Sāṅkhyak.; Mcar.; (ifc.) for the sake of, Pañcat.; in fact, really, truly, R. &c.; for the profit of; with respect to the sense, VarBṛS. (opposed to *grantha-tas* and *sūtra-tas*, Jain.) **-tṛish**, mfn. greedy after money, BhP. **-tṛishṇā**, f. desire for wealth or money, VP.; BhP. **-da**, mfn. conferring advantage, profitable, Kathās.; munificent, Mn. ii, 109. **-datta**, m., N. of wealthy merchants, Kathās.; Vet. **-darśaka**, m. 'seeing lawsuits,' a judge, L.; (cf. *aksha-d*°.) **-darśana**, n. consideration of a case, Mālav. **-dāna**, n. donation of money, present, MBh.; a present given with a (selfish) purpose, Hcat. **-dūshaṇa**, n. spoiling of (another's or one's own) property, either 'unjust seizure of property' or 'prodigality,' Mn. vii, 48 & 51, &c. **-dṛiś**. f. an eye on (i.e. consideration of) the truth, BhP **-drishṭi**, f. seeing profit, BhP. **-dosha**, m. a mistake with regard to the meaning, Sāh.; Kpr. **-dravya-virodha**, m. opposition between the purpose and the thing, KātyŚr.; Jaim. **-nāśa**, m. loss of money. **-nibandhana**, mfn. having its cause in wealth, contingent on affluence and respectability, MBh. i, 5141. **-nirvṛitti,** f. fulfilling of a purpose, KātyŚr.; R. **-niścaya,** m. decision of a matter, R. iv, 31, 32; determinate view of a matter, L. **-nyūna,** mfn. 'deficient in wealth,' poor, MBh. **-pati,** m. 'lord of wealth,' a rich man, VarBṛS. &c.; a king, Ragh. &c.; N. of Kubera, L.; of the grandfather of the poet Bāṇa, Kād.; (cf. *ārtha-patya.*) **-pada,** n., N. of the Vārttikas on Pāṇ., R. vii, 36, 45. **-para,** mfn. intent on gaining wealth, niggardly, R. **-parigraha,** m. possession of wealth, R. v, 43, 6; (mfn.) dependent on money, MBh. iii, 1292. **-pāla,** m., N. of a man, Daś. **-prakṛiti,** f. 'the principal thing required for a special aim,' N. of the five constituent elements of a drama, Sāh.; Daśar. **-prayoga,** m. application of wealth to usury. **-prasaṃkhyā,** f. considering the aim, KātyŚr. **-prâpti,** f. acquisition of wealth; 'attainment of meaning,' i. e. the state of being clear by itself, Car. **-bandha,** m. 'binding the sense together,' a word or sentence, Śāk.; Vikr. **-bhāj,** mfn. entitled to a share in the division of property. **-bhṛita,** mfn. having high wages (as a servant). **-bheda,** m. distinction or difference of meaning. **-bhraṇśa,** m. loss of fortune, ruin, VarBṛS.; failing of an aim or of an intention. **-matta,** mfn. proud of money, Daś. **-manas,** mfn. having an aim in view, Gobh. **-maya,** mfn. useful, Bhām. **-mātra,** *ā, am,* f. n. property, money, Pañcat.; Kathās.; (mfn.) being only the matter itself, Yogas. **-yukta,** mfn. significant, Kum. i, 13. **-yukti,** f. gain, profit. **-rāśi,** m. great wealth, Daś. **-ruci,** mfn. = *-citta,* Mudr. **-lābha,** m. acquisition of wealth. **-lubdha,** mfn. greedy of wealth, covetous, niggardly, Daś. **-leśa,** m. a little wealth. **-lopa,** m. failing or non-existence of an aim, Jaim.; KātyŚr. **-lobha,** m. desire of wealth, avarice. **-vat,** mfn. wealthy; full of sense, significant, Pāṇ. i, 2, 45, &c.; suitable to the object, fitting, RPrāt.; KātyŚr.; full of reality, real; (*ān*), m. a man, L.; (*artha-vat*), ind. according to a purpose, Mn. v, 134; Yājñ. iii, 2. **-vat-tā,** f. or **-vat-tva,** n. significance, importance. **-vargīya,** *ās* or *āṇi,* m. or n. pl. 'treating of the category of objects,' N. of certain Buddhist texts. **-varjita,** mfn. unimportant, Kathās. **-varman,** m., N. of a rich merchant, Kathās. **-vāda,** m. explanation of the meaning (of any precept), KātyŚr.; Nyāyad. &c.; praise, eulogium, Uttarar. **-vādin,** mfn. relating facts, Pañcat. **-vijñāna,** n. comprehension of meaning (one of the six or eight exercises of the understanding), L. **-vid,** mfn. knowing the sense, Ragh. iii, 21. **-vidyā,** f. knowledge of practical life, MBh. vii, 169. **-vināśa,** m. loss of one's fortune, VarBṛS. **-vināśana,** mfn. causing a loss or disadvantage, MBh. **-viniścaya,** m. 'a disquisition treating of the objects,' N. of a Buddhist text. **-vipatti,** f. failing of an aim, R. ii, 19, 40. **-vṛiddhi,** f. accumulation of wealth. **-vaikalya,** n. incongruity in the facts, deviation from truth, Mn. viii, 95. **-vyakti,** f. clearness of the sense, Sāh.; Kpr. &c. **-vyaya,** m. expenditure; *-saha,* mfn. 'allowing expenditure,' prodigal, L. **-śabdau,** m. du. = *śabdârthau,* word and sense, (*gaṇa rājadantâdi.*) **-śālin,** mfn. wealthy; (*ī*), m. a wealthy man. **-śāstra,** n. a book treating of practical life (cf. *-vidyā* above) and political government (cf. *-cintana* above), MBh. &c. **-śāstraka,** n. id., AgP. **-śauca,** n. purity, honesty in money matters (cf. *-prayoga* above), Mn. v, 106; Kām. **-śrī,** f. great wealth, Kathās. **-saṃśaya,** m. danger in regard to one's fortune, MBh. **-saṃsthāna,** n. accumulation of wealth; treasury, L. **-saṃgraha,** m. accumulation of wealth, Ragh. xvii, 60; treasury, L.; 'compendium of objects (treated of),' N. of one of the Pūrva-mīmāṅsā texts. **-saṃgrahin,** mfn. accumulating wealth, MBh. ii, 2569. **-saṃcaya,** m. sg. & pl. collection of wealth, property, MBh. **-saṃnyāsin,** mfn. renouncing an advantage. **-saṃpādana,** n. carrying out of an affair, Mn. vii, 168. **-sambandha,** m. possession of wealth, Mudr.; connection of the sense with the word or sentence (cf. *-bandha* above), L. **-sambandhin,** mfn. concerned or interested in an affair, Mn. viii, 64; Yājñ. ii, 71. **-sādhaka,** mf(*ikā*)n. promoting an aim, useful, profitable, MBh. i, 4785, &c.; (cf. *svârtha-sādhaka*); (*as*), m. the plant Putramjīva Roxburghii, N.; N. of a minister of king Daśaratha, R. i, 7, 3. **-sāra,** m. n. a considerable property, Pañcat.; (Hit.) **-siddha,** mfn. clear in itself, self-evident; (*as*), m., N. of the tenth day of the Karma-māsa, Sūryapr.; N. of Śākyamuni in one of his previous births (as a Bodhisattva). **-siddhaka,** m. the plant Vitex Negundo, L. **-siddhi,** f. acquisition of wealth, Car.; success, Ragh. ii, 21; N. of a particular magical faculty; (*is*), m., N. of a son of Pushya, Hariv. **-hara,** mfn. inheriting wealth, Vishṇus. **-hāni,** f. loss of wealth, MBh.; VarBṛS. **-hāraka,** mf(*ikā*)n. stealing money; (*ikā*), f., N. of a female demon, MārkP. **-hārin,** mfn. stealing money, Kathās. **-hīna,** mfn. 'deprived of sense,' unmeaning, nonsensical; deprived of wealth, poor, L. **Arthâgama,** m. sg. [Vātsy.] or pl. [MBh. iii, 88] receipt or collection of property, income, acquisition of wealth. **Arthâdhikāra,** m. office of treasurer, Hit. **Arthâdhikārin,** mfn. a treasurer. **Arthântara,** n. another matter, a different or new circumstance, a similar case (often with *ny-√2. as,* to introduce some other matter as an illustration, see *arthântara-nyāsa* below); a different meaning, Nyāyad.; opposite or antithetical meaning, difference of meaning or purport, L. **Arthântara-nyāsa,** m. introduction of some other matter (an illustration of a particular case by a general truth or of a general truth by a particular case), Sāh.; Kāvyād. &c. **Arthântarâkshepa,** m. 'throwing in another fact,' i. e. establishing any disagreement with a statement by introducing a similar case (showing the impossibility of that statement), Kāvyād. **Arthânvita,** mfn. possessed of wealth, rich; possessed of sense, significant. **Arthâpatti,** f. inference from circumstances, a disjunctive hypothetical syllogism. **Arthâpatti-sama,** *ā, am,* f. n. an inference by which the quality of any object is attributed to another object because of their sharing some other quality in common, Nyāyad.; Sarvad. **Arthâbhāva,** m. absence or want of an aim, KātyŚr. &c. **Arthâbhinirvṛitti,** f. accomplishment or successful issue of any matter, MBh. v, 4548. **Arthâbhiprâpaṇa,** n. obtaining or pointing out the sense. **Arthârjana,** n. acquisition of property, Hit. **Arthârtha,** mfn. effective for the accomplishment of the aim in view, Gobh.; (*am*), ind. on account of money, Kathās. **Arthârtha-tattva-jña,** mfn. 'knowing the essence of the very aim of anything,' knowing thoroughly, R. **Arthârthin,** mfn. desirous of gaining wealth, MBh. iii, 1288; desirous of making a profit, selfish; °*thi-tā,* f. desire of wealth. **Arthâlaṃkāra,** m. embellishment of the sense by poetical figures, &c. (opposed to *śabdâlaṃkāra,* embellishment of the sound by rhymes, &c.); N. of a work. **Arthâvamarda,** m. 'wasting of wealth,' prodigality. **Arthâvṛitti,** f. (in rhetoric) re-occurrence of words of the same sense, Kāvyād. **Arthêt,** mfn. (√*i*), active, hasty (said of running waters), VS. x, 3. **Arthêpsu-tā,** f. desire of wealth, MBh. i, 6126. **Arthêhā,** f. id. **Arthâika-tva,** n. congruity or harmony of the purpose (with the thing), Jaim. **Arthâikya,** n. id., Comm. on Nyāyam. **Arthôtpāda,** m. (in rhetoric) 'production of a (different) sense,' putting words in an artificial order so that they give a different sense. **Arthôtsarga,** m. expenditure of money, Mudrar. **Arthôpakshepaka,** mfn. 'indicating or suggesting a matter (so as to facilitate the understanding of the plot),' a N. applied to the parts of a drama called *vishkambha, cūlikā, aṅkâsya, aṅkâvatāra,* and *praveśaka,* qq.vv., Sāh.; Daśar. **Arthôpakshepaṇa,** n. suggesting or indicating a matter, Sāh. **Arthôpama,** n. a simile which merely states the object of comparison (without adding the tertium comparationis or any particle of comparison, e. g. 'he is a lion,' said in praise), Nir. **Arthôpârjana,** n. = *arthârjana* above. **Arthôshman,** m. glow or pride of wealth, condition of being wealthy, L. **Arthâugha,** m. a heap of effects or property, MBh. iii, 15307; a treasure, L.

Arthanā, f. request, entreaty, Kathās.; Naish.

Arthanīya, mfn. to be requested, asked for.

Artham, acc. ind. See s. v. *ártha.*

Arthāt, abl. ind. according to the state of the case, according to the circumstance, as a matter of fact; according to the sense, that is to say, Sāh. &c.

Arthāpaya, Nom. P. *arthāpayati* (Pāṇ. iii, 1, 25, Comm.) to treat as money, i.e. to hide cautiously, Naish.

Arthika, mfn. wanting anything, MBh. i, 5619; (cf. *kanyârthika*); (*as*), m. a prince's watchman (announcing by song or music the hours of the day, especially those of rising and going to rest), L.

Arthita, mfn. asked, desired, requested; (*am*), n. wish, desire, L.

Arthitavya, mfn. = *arthanīya,* q. v., MBh. iii, 3038.

Arthín, mfn. active, industrious, RV.; (cf *arthêt* above); one who wants or desires anything (instr. or in comp.; cf. *putrârthin, balârthin*); supplicating or entreating any one (gen.); longing for, libidinous, R. i, 48, 18; (*ī*), m. one who asks for a girl in marriage, a wooer, Yājñ. i, 60; Kathās.; a beggar, petitioner, suitor, Mn. xi, 1, &c.; one who supplicates with prayers, VarBṛS.; a plaintiff, prosecutor, Mn. viii, 62 & 79; Yājñ. ii, 6; a servant, L.; a follower, companion, L.

Arthi (in comp. for *arthín*). **-tā,** f. the condition of a suppliant, Kād.; wish, desire for (instr., Mn. ix, 203), asking, request, MBh. &c. **-tva,** n. condition of a suppliant, Megh.; request, Mālav.; Kathās. **-bhāva,** m. condition of a beggar, VarYogay. **-sāt,** ind. with √*1. kṛi,* to grant anything (acc.) to one who asks for it, Kathās.

Arthīya, mfn. ifc. destined for, Mn. xii, 16; relating to (cf. *evam-arthīya* and *tad-arthīya*).

Arthya, mf(*ā,* Pāṇ. iv, 4, 92)n. = *arthanīya,* q. v., L.; proper, fit, R.; Ragh.; Kum.; rich, Pañcat.; Kathās.; intelligent, wise, L.; = *dhruva,* L.; (*am*), n. red chalk, L.

अर्द् *ard,* Ved. cl. 6. P. (Imper. 3. pl. *ṛidantu;* impf. 3. pl. *ā́rdan*) to move, be moved, be scattered (as dust), RV. iv, 17, 2 & vii, 104, 24: cl. 1. P. *ardati* (*árdati,* 'to go, move,' Naigh.) to dissolve, AV. xii, 4, 3; (aor. *ārdīt,* Bhaṭṭ., perf. *ānarda,* Pāṇ. vii, 4, 71, Sch.) to torment, hurt, kill, L.; to ask, beg for (acc.), Ragh. v, 17: cl. 7. *ṛiṇatti,* to kill, Naigh.: Caus. *ardayati* (Subj. *ardayāti*; Imper. 2. sg. *ardaya*; impf. *ā́rdayat,* 2. sg. *ardáyas*; aor. *ārdidat* or [after *mā*] *ardayīt,* Pāṇ. iii, 1, 51) to make agitated, stir up, shake vehemently, AV. iv, 15, 6 & 11; vi, 49, 2; to do harm, torment, distress, MBh. &c. (generally used in perf. Pass. p. *ardita,* q. v.); to strike, hurt, kill, destroy, RV.; AV. &c.: Desid. *ardidishati*; [Lat. *ardeo.*]

Ardana, mfn. moving restlessly, Nir. vi, 33; ifc. (cf. *janârdana*) disturbing, distressing, tormenting, R.; BhP. &c.; annihilating, destroying, BhP.; (cf. *mahishârdana*); (*as*), m. a N. of Śiva, MBh. xiii, 1147; (*ā*), f. request, L.; (*am*), n. pain, trouble, excitement, Suśr.

Ardani, *is,* m. sickness, disease, L.; asking, request, L.; fire, L.

Ardita, mfn. asked, requested, begged, L.; injured, pained, afflicted, tormented, wounded, MBh. &c.; killed, destroyed, ib.; (*am*), n., N. of a disease (spasm of the jaw-bones, trismus, tetanus; or hemiplegia, i. e. paralysis of the muscles on one side of the face and neck), Suśr.

Arditin, mfn. having spasms of the jaw-bones, Suśr.

Ardyamāna, mfn. (Pass. p. fr. Caus.) being distressed or afflicted or troubled.

अर्दिधिषु *ardidhishu,* mfn. (√*ṛidh,* Desid.), desirous of increasing or making anything (acc.) prosperous, Bhaṭṭ.

अर्ध 1. *árdha, as,* m., Ved. side, part; place, region, country; (cf. *ápy-ardham, abhy-ardhá, parârdhá*); [Lat. *ordo;* Germ. *ort.*]

2. **Ardhá,** mfn. (m. pl. *ardhe* or *ardhās,* Pāṇ. i, 1, 33) half, halved, forming a half [cf. Osset. *ardag*]; *ardhá . . . ardhá* (or *néma . . . ardhá,* RV. x, 27, 18), one part, the other part; (*ás, ám*), m. n. (ifc. f. *ā*) the half, RV. vi, 30, 1, &c.; (*ám*), n. 'one part of two,' with √*1. kṛi,* to give or leave to anybody (acc.) an equal share of (gen.), RV. ii, 30, 5 & vi, 44, 18; a part, party, RV. iv, 32, 1 & vii, 18, 16; (*e*), loc. ind. in the middle, Śāk. (*Ardha* in comp. with a subst. means 'the half part of anything' [cf. Pāṇ. ii, 2, 2], with an adj. or past Pass. p. [cf. Pāṇ. v, 4, 5] 'half;' also with an adj. indicating measure [cf. Pāṇ. vii, 3, 26 & 27]; a peculiar kind of compound is formed with ordinals [cf. Pāṇ. i, 1, 23, Comm.], e. g. *ardha-tṛitīya,* containing a half for its third, i. e. two and a half; *ardha-caturtha,* having a half for its fourth, three and a half.) **-ṛicá,** m. = *ardhá-rcá* below, VS. xix. 25. **-kaṅsika,** mfn = *ārdhak°,* q.v., measuring half a *kaṅsa,* Pāṇ. vii, 3, 27, Sch. **-kathana,** n. relating only half (not to the end of a story), Veṇis. (v. l. *-ka-*

thita, 'half-related'). **-karṇa**, m. 'half the diameter,' radius. **-kārshika**, mfn. having the weight of half a *karsha*, Suśr. **-kāla**, m. a N. of Śiva, L. **-kīla**, n., N. of a Tīrtha, MBh. iii, 7024. **-kūṭa**, m. a N. of Śiva, L. **-kṛita**, mfn. half done, half performed. **-kṛishṭa**, mfn. half drawn out from (in comp.), Śāk. **-ketu**, m., N. of a Rudra, VāyuP. **-kaiśika**, mf(*ī*)n. having half the breadth of a hair, Suśr. **-koṭī**, f. half a *koṭī*, i. e. five millions, Hit. **-kosha**, m. a moiety of one's treasure. **-kauḍavika**, mfn. = *ārdhak°*, q. v., measuring half a *kuḍava*, Pāṇ. vii, 3, 27, Sch. **-krośa**, m. half a league. **-kshetra**, *āṇi*, n. pl., N. of particular lunar mansions, Sūryapr. **-khāra**, n. or **-khārī**, f. half a *khārī*, Pāṇ. v, 4, 101. **-gaṅgā**, f. 'half the Gaṅgā,' N. of the river Kāverī, L. (cf. *ardha-jāhnavī* below). **-garbhá**, m. half a descendant (?), RV. i, 164, 36. **-guccha**, m. a necklace of sixteen (or twenty-four) strings, VarBṛS. **-gola**, m. a hemisphere. **-cakravartin** or **-cakrin**, m. 'half a *cakravartin*,' N. of the nine black Vāsudevas (of the Jainas), L. **-caturtha**, mfn. pl. (see above, 2. *ardhá* at end) three and a half, Suśr. &c.; (Jaina Prākṛit *addhuttha*, see s. v. *adhyushṭa*.) **-candana-lipta**, mfn. half rubbed with sandal, MBh. xiii, 888. **-candra**, m. half-moon; the semicircular marks on a peacock's tail, L.; the semicircular scratch of the finger nail, L.; an arrow, the head of which is like a half-moon, MBh.; R.; Kathās.; (cf. *ardhacandra-mukha* and *ardhacandrôpama* below); the hand bent into a semicircle or the shape of a claw (as for the purpose of seizing anybody by the neck; generally acc. °*am* with √ 1. *dā*, to seize any one by his neck), Kathās.; Pañcat.; Vet.; N. of the Anusvāra (from its being written in the older MSS. in a semilunar form), RāmatUp.; N. of a constellation, VarBṛS.; (*ā*), f. the plant Convolvulus Torpethum; (mfn.) crescent-shaped, of a semilunar form, Hcat.; (*ardhacandra*)-*kuṇḍa*, n., N. of a mystical figure of semilunar form; -*bhāgin*, mfn. seized by the neck; -*mukha*, mfn. (an arrow) the head of which is like a half-moon, Ragh. xii, 96; *ardhacandrâkāra* or *ardhacandrâ-kṛita*, mfn. half-moon-shaped, crescent-shaped; *ardhacandrôpama*, mfn. 'like a half-moon,' of semilunar form (said of an arrow, the head of which is like a half-moon), R. **-candraka**, m. (= *ardha-candra*) the hand bent into a semicircle for grasping any one's throat, ifc. *dattârdhacandraka*, mfn. 'seized at the throat,' Kathās.; (*am*), n. the semilunar point of an arrow, Śārṅg.; (*ikā*), f., N. of a climbing plant (Gynandropsis Pentaphylla or Convolvulus Torpethum; see *ardhacandrā* above). **-colaka**, m. a short bodice, L. **-jaratīya**, n. (fr. pr. p. *jarat*, √ *jṛi*), (according to the rule of half an aged woman) incompatibility in argument, Pat. on Pāṇ. iv, 1, 78; Sarvad. **-jāhnavī**, f. = -*gaṅgā*. **-jīvakā** or **-jyā**, f. = *jyârdha*, the sine of an arc. **-tanu**, f. half a body. **-tikta**, mfn. 'half-bitter,' the plant Gentiana Chirata. **-tūra**, m. a particular kind of musical instrument, L. **-tṛitīya**, mf(*ā*)n. pl. (see above, 2. *ardhá* at end) two and a half, ĀśvŚr.; AitĀr. **-trayodaśa**, mf(*ā*)n. pl. twelve and a half, AitĀr.; Yājñ. ii, 165 & 204. **-dagdha**, mfn. half-burnt. **-divasa**, m. 'half a day,' midday, R.; (cf. *ardha-rātra* below.) **-devá**, m. demi-god, RV. iv, 42, 8 & 9. **-drauṇika**, mfn. = *ārdhadr°*, q. v., measuring half a *droṇa*, Pāṇ. vii, 3, 26, Sch. **-dhāra**, n. 'half-edged, i. e. single-edged,' a knife or lancet with a single edge (the blade two inches long, the handle six, used by surgeons), Suśr. **-nārāca**, m. a particular kind of arrow, MBh. ii, 1855. **-nārī-nara-vapus**, mfn. having a body half man and half woman (said of Rudra), VāyuP. ii. **-nārī-naṭêśvara**, m. Śiva. **-nārīśa** or **-nārīśvara**, m. 'the lord who is half female (and half male),' a form of Śiva. **-nāva**, n. half a boat, Pāṇ. v, 4, 100. **-niśā**, f. midnight. **-pakva**, mfn. half ripe, Bhpr. **-pañcadaśa**, mfn. pl. fourteen and a half, ŚāṅkhŚr. **-pañcan**, mfn. pl. four and a half, VarBṛS. **-pañcama**, mfn. pl. id., Mn. iv, 95; Āp.; Gaut. **-pañcamaka**, mfn. bought for four and a half, Pat. **-pañcāśat**, f. twenty-five, Mn. viii, 268. **-paṇa**, m. a measure containing half a *paṇa*, Mn. viii, 404. **-patha**, m. 'half-way,' (*e*), loc. ind. midway, Yājñ. ii, 198. **-pada**, n. half a Pāda (or the fourth part of a verse), Lāṭy. **-padyā**, f. a brick measuring half a foot, KātyŚr. **-paryaṅka**, m. sitting half (i. e. partly) upon the hams (a particular posture practised in meditation; cf. *paryaṅka*), Lalit. **-pāñcālaka**, mfn. belonging to half the Pañcālas (as a country), Pat. **-pāda**, m. half the fourth part; (*ā*), f. the plant Phyllanthus Niruri, L. **-pādika**, mfn. having only half a foot, Mn. viii, 325. **-pārāvata**, m. a kind of pigeon, L.; partridge, L. **-pīta**, mfn. half-drunk, Śāk. **-purusha**, m. half the length of a man, KātyŚr. **-purushīya**, mfn. having half the length of a man, KātyŚr. **-pulāyita**, n. a half-gallop, canter. **-pushpā**, f. the plant Sida Rhomboidea, L. **-pūrṇa**, mfn. half-full. **-prasthika**, mfn. = *ārdhapr°*, q. v., measuring half a *prastha*, Pāṇ. vii, 3, 27, Sch. **-prahara**, m. half a watch (one hour and a half). **-praharikā**, f. id. (?), PSarv. **-bṛigalá**, n. half a portion, ŚBr. **-bṛihatī**, f. 'having half the usual breadth,' a kind of sacrificial brick, KātyŚr. &c. **-bhāga**, m. a half, Kum. v, 50. **-bhāgika** or **-bhāgin**, mfn. receiving half a share, Yājñ. ii, 134. **-bhāj**, mfn. containing the half of (gen.), PBr.; taking or sharing half, Mn. viii, 39; (-*bhā́j*), m. a sharer, companion, AV. vi, 86, 3. **-bhāskara**, m. midday, R. **-bhūmi**, f. half the land, MBh. i, 7444. **-bheda**, m. hemiplegia (cf. *ardita*, n.), Suśr.; (cf. *ava-bhedaka*.) **-māgadhaka**, mfn. belonging to half the Magadhas (as a country), Pat. **-māgadhī**, f. a variety of the Māgadhī dialect (being the language of the sacred literature of the Jains). **-māṇava** [L.] or **-māṇavaka** [VarBṛS.], m. a necklace of twelve strings. **-mātra**, n. the half, middle, VPrāt. &c.; (*ā*), f. half a short syllable; (mfn.) having the quantity of half a short syllable, TPrāt.; hence (*as*), m. a N. of the peculiar sound called *yama* (q. v.), RāmatUp. **-mātrika**, mfn. (= -*mātra*, mfn.) having the quantity of half a short syllable, Comm. on VPrāt.; (*ā*), f. half a short syllable, RPrāt. **-mārge**, loc. ind. half-way, midway, Kathās. **-māsá**, m. half a month, VS.; AV. &c.; (*ardhamāsa*)-*tama*, mfn. done or happening every half month or fortnight, Pāṇ. v, 2, 57; -*śás*, ind. every half month, ŚBr.; -*sahasrá*, n. a thousand of half months, ŚBr. **-māsika**, mfn. lasting half a month, Yājñ. ii, 177. **-mushṭi**, m. a half-clenched hand, L. **-yāma**, m. (= -*prahara* above) half a watch, Bhpr. **-ratha**, m. a warrior who fights on a car along with another, MBh. v, 5816 & 5820. **-rāja**, m., N. of a Prākṛit poet. **-rātra**, m. midnight, Mn. &c.; *ardharātrârdhadivasa*, m. 'the time when day and night are half and half, i. e. equal,' the equinox, R. **-rūḍha**, mfn. half grown or developed, Megh. **-rcá** (*ṛic*; cf. -*ṛicá* above), m. half a verse, AV. ix, 10, 19; ŚBr. &c.; (*ardharca*)-*śás*, ind. by hemistichs, AV. xx, 135, 5; ŚBr. &c.; -*śasya*, mfn. to be recited in hemistichs, Vait.; *ardharcâdi*, a gaṇa of Pāṇ. (ii, 4, 31); *ardharcântara*, n. another hemistich, KātyŚr. **-rcya** (*ṛi*), mf(*ā*)n. = *ardharca-śasya* above, AitĀr. **-lakshmī-hari**, m. 'half Lakshmī and half Hari,' one of the forms of Vishṇu, L. (cf. *ardha-nārī-naṭêśvara* above). **-likhita**, mfn. half painted, Śāk. **-vartman**, n. = -*patha* above, Naish. **-vaśā́**, f. half a cow, MaitrS. **-vastra-saṃvīta**, mfn. clothed or enveloped in half-garments. **-vidhu**, m. the half-moon, Bālar. **-visarga**, m. the sound Visarga before k, kh, p, ph (so called because its sign [⌣⌢] is the half of that of the Visarga [꞉]). **-vīkshaṇa**, n. a side-look, glance, leer, L. **-vṛiddha**, mf(*ā*)n. middle-aged, L. **-vṛiddhi**, f. the half of the interest or rent, Mn. viii, 150. **-vaināśika**, m. 'arguing half-perishableness,' N. of the followers of Kaṇāda. **-vyāma**, m. half a fathom (see *vyāma*), KātyŚr. **-vyāsa**, m. 'half the diameter,' radius. **-vratá**, n. the half portion of milk, ŚBr.; KātyŚr. **-śata**, n. fifty, Mn. viii, 311; one hundred and fifty, ib. 267. **-śaphara**, m. a kind of fish, L. **-śabda**, mfn. having a low voice. **-śas**, ind. by halves, KātyŚr. **-śiras**, n. the half head, ĀpŚr. **-śesha**, mfn. half left, R. (cf. *ardhâva-śesha* below). **-śyāma**, mfn. half dark or clouded, Śāk. **-śruta**, mfn. half heard, Veṇis. **-śloka**, m. half a Śloka. **-shashṭha**, mfn. pl. five and a half, PārGṛ. **-saṃjāta-sasya**, mf(*ā*)n. having its crops half grown, MBh. iii, 3007. **-saptadaśa**, mfn. pl. sixteen and a half, KātyŚr. **-saptama**, mfn. pl. six and a half, PārGṛ. **-sapta-śata**, mf(*ā*)n. pl. or *āni*, n. pl. three hundred and fifty, R. **-sama**, mfn. 'half equal,' N. of metres, in which the first and third and the second and fourth Pādas are equal; -*muktāvalī*, f., N. of a work. **-samasyā**, f. supplying an idea which is only half expressed, Naish. **-sīrin**, mfn. a cultivator (who takes half the crop for his labour), Yājñ. i, 166. **-soma**, m. half the Soma, KātyŚr. **-hāra**, m. a necklace of sixty-four (or of forty) strings, VarBṛS. **-hrasva**, n. the quantity of half a short vowel, Pāṇ. i, 2, 32. **Ardhâṅśa**, m. a half, the half. **Ardhâṅśin**, mfn. sharing a half. **Ardhâkāra**, m. 'half the letter *a*,' a N. of the *avagraha*, q. v. **Ardhâkshi**, n. = *ardha-vīkshaṇa* above, Mṛicch. **Ardhâṅga**, n. half the body. **Ardhâcita**, mfn. (said of a girdle, &c.) half-set (as with gems), Ragh. vii, 10; Kum. vii, 61. **Ardhânumātrā**, f. 'half a small *mātrā*,' i. e. the eighth part of the quantity of a short syllable, VPrāt. **Ardhâdhve**, loc. ind. = *ardha-mārge* above, ĀpŚr. **Ardhântarâikapadatā**, f. (in rhetoric) placing a single word (which belongs grammatically to one hemistich) into the other half or hemistich of the verse, Sāh. **Ardhâmbu**, mfn. consisting half of water, L. **Ardhârdha**, mfn. 'half of the half of,' the fourth part of, Pañcat.; -*bhāga*, m. a quarter, Ragh. x, 57; -*hāni*, f. deduction of a half in every case, Yājñ. ii, 207. **Ardhâvabheda** and °**daka**, m. = *ardha-bheda* above, Car.; (mfn.) dividing into halves. **Ardhâvalīḍha**, mfn. half-chewed, Śāk. **Ardhâvaśesha**, mfn. = *ardha-śesha* above, R. **Ardhâśana**, n. half a meal, L. **Ardhâsana**, n. half a seat (it is considered a mark of high respect to make room for a guest on one's own seat), Śāk.; Ragh. vi, 73, &c.; greeting kindly, L. **Ardhâstamaya**, m. half (i. e. partial) setting of the sun or the moon, VarBṛS. **Ardhī-kṛita**, mfn. divided into halves. **Ardhêḍā**, f. 'half the *iḍā*,' the syllable *up* inserted in some Sāman verses, PBr. **Ardhêndu**, m. (= *ardha-candra* above) a half-moon or crescent, Naish.; the semicircular impression of a finger nail, L.; an arrow with a crescent-shaped head, L.; the hand expanded in a semicircular form like a claw, L.; the constellation also called *ardhacandra* (q. v.), VarBṛS.; (*ardhêndu*)-*mauli*, m. 'whose diadem is a half-moon,' Śiva, Megh.; Bālar. **Ardhêndra**, mfn. that of which a half belongs to Indra, TS.; ŚBr. **Ardhôkta**, mfn. half-uttered, said imperfectly or indistinctly. **Ardhôkti**, f. 'half-speech,' speaking incompletely, broken or interrupted speech. **Ardhôdaya**, m. half (i. e. partial) rising of the sun or the moon. **Ardhôdita**, mfn. (fr. 1. *ud-ita*) half-risen, Pañcat.; (fr. 2. *udita*) half-uttered. **Ardhôna**, mf(*ā*)n. diminished by half a short syllable, RPrāt. **Ardhôruka**, mfn. reaching to the middle of the thighs; (*am*), n. a short petticoat, Daś.; Rājat.

Ardhaka, mfn. forming a half, Bhpr.; (*am*), n. the half, Hcat.; N. of a wrong pronunciation of the vowels, Pat.; (*as*), m. water-snake, L. **-ghātin**, mfn. 'killing the water-snake (?),' N. of Rudra, AV. xi, 2, 7 (*adhvaga-gh°*, AV. Paipp.)

Ardhika, mf(*ī*, Pāṇ. v, 1, 48)n. measuring a half, Yājñ. ii, 296; (ifc., cf. Pāṇ. iv, 3, 4, Comm.) forming the half of, Mn. iii, 1, &c.; (= *ardha-sīrin* above) receiving half the crop for his labour, Vishṇus. (cf. *ārdhika*).

Ardhin, mfn. forming a half, TS.; giving half (the *dakshiṇā*), Lāṭy.; receiving half (the *dakshiṇā*), Mn. viii, 210.

1. **Ardhya**, mfn. forming the half of (gen.), Śulb.

अर्धुक *ardhuka*, mfn. (√*ṛidh*), prospering, ŚBr.

2. **Ardhya** (3), mfn. to be accomplished, RV. i, 156, 1; to be obtained, RV. v, 44, 10.

अर्पय *arpaya*, Caus. of √*ṛi*, q. v.

Arpaṇa, mf(*ī*)n. procuring, MBh. xiii, 1007; consigning, entrusting; (*árpaṇa*), n. inserting, fixing, R.; piercing, AV. xii, 3, 22; placing in or upon, Ragh. ii, 35; offering, delivering, consigning, entrusting of (gen. or in comp.); giving back, Hit.

Arpaṇīya, mfn. to be delivered or entrusted, Kathās.

Árpita [eight times in RV.; cf. Pāṇ. vi, 1, 209 seq.] or **arpitá** [RV. i, 164, 48, &c.], mfn. inserted, fixed, RV.; VS. &c.; fixed upon (as the eyes or the mind); thrown, cast into (loc.; said of an arrow), Ragh. viii, 87; placed in or upon, Ragh. ix, 78, &c.; (said of a document or of a sketch) transferred to (a plate or portrait, i. e. 'engraved' or 'painted'), Ragh. xvii, 79; Śāk.; Kum. iii, 42; offered, delivered, entrusted, Yājñ. ii, 164, &c.; given back, Ragh. xix, 10, &c. **-kara**, mfn. 'having given one's hand,' married, L. **Arpitôpta**, mfn. (gaṇa *rāja-dantâdi*, q. v.)

1. **Arpya**, ind. p. See *prârpyā*.

2. **Arpya**, mfn. to be delivered, consignable.

अर्पिस *arpisa*, m. the heart, Uṇ.

अर्ब् *arb*, cl. 1. P. *arbati* (perf. *ānarba*, L.) to go, L.; to hurt, L.

अर्बुक *arbuka*, *ās*, m. pl., N. of a people, MBh. ii, 1119.

अर्बुद *árbuda*, *as*, m., Ved. a serpent-like demon (conquered by Indra, a descendant of Kadrū, therefore called Kādraveya, ŚBr.; AitBr.; said to be the author of RV. x, 94, RAnukr.), RV. &c.; (*ás*), m. id., RV. i, 51, 6 & x, 67, 12; (*am*), n., N. of the above-named hymn, RV. x, 94, ĀśvŚr.; (*as*, *am*), m. n. a long round mass (said especially of the shape of the fœtus in the second half of the first month [Nir. xiv, 6] or in the second month [Yājñ. iii, 75 & 89]); a swelling, tumour, polypus, Suśr. &c.; (*árbudu*), n. (also m., L.) ten millions, VS. xvii, 2, &c.; (*as*), m., N. of a mountain in the west of India (commonly called Abū, a place of pilgrimage of the Jainas, and celebrated for its Jaina temples); (*ās*), m. pl., N. of a people, VarBṛS.; BhP. &c. **-parvata**, m. the mountain Arbuda. **-śikhara**, m. id., Hit. **Arbudâkāra**, m. 'shaped like a tumour,' the plant Cordia Myxa, L. **Arbudâraṇya**, n., N. of a forest, NarasP.

Árbudi, *is*, m. a serpent-like demon (probably = *árbuda* and *arbudá*, m. above, but called *índra-medhin*, q. v.), AV. xi, 9 & 10 (in almost every verse); (cf. *ny-àrbudi*.)

Arbudin, mfn. afflicted with a swelling or tumour, Suśr.

Arbudha, *as*, m. = *árbuda*, m. above, Kāṭh. Anukr.

अर्भ *árbha*, mf(*ā*)n. little, small, unimportant, RV.; (*arbhá*), mfn. id., AV. vii, 56, 3; (*as*), m. child, boy, BhP. [Lat. *orbus*; Gk. ὀρφανός].

Arbhaká, mfn. small, minute, RV.; AV.; VS.; weak, RV. vii, 33, 6; AV.; (used together with *kumāraká*) young, childish, RV. viii, 30, 1 & 69, 15; emaciated, L.; similar, L.; (*as*), m. a boy, child, Ragh. &c.; the young of any animal, Śāk. (v. l.), Kād.; a fool, idiot, L.

Árbhaga, mfn. youthful, RV. i, 116, 1.

अर्म *árma*, *ās*, m. pl. ruins, rubbish, VS. xxx, 11; TS. &c.; often ifc. in names of old villages half or entirely gone to ruin (e. g. *guptârma*, *kukkuṭârma*, *bṛihad-arma*, &c., qq. vv.), Pāṇ. vi, 2, 90 seq. & viii, 2, 2, Sch.; (*as*), m. = *arman*, q. v., Uṇ.

Armaká, *am*, n. rubbish, ruins, RV. i, 133, 3.

Armaṇa, *as*, *am*, m. n. a measure of one droṇa, Suśr.

Arman, *a*, n. a disease of the eyes, Suśr.

अर्य 1. *aryá* (2, once 3, RV. iv, 1, 7), mfn. (√*ṛi*), kind, favourable, RV.; attached to, true, devoted, dear, RV.; excellent, L.; (*ás*), m. a master, lord, Naigh.; Pāṇ. iii, 1, 103; (cf. 3. *árya*.) **-pati** (*aryá-*), mf(*patnī*)n. (said of the dawns and of the waters) having kind or favourable lords(?), RV. vii, 6, 5 & x, 43, 8.

2. **Aryà**, mf(*à*)n. (= 1. *aryá*) kind, favourable, RV. i, 123, 1.

3. **Árya**, *as*, m. (= 1. *aryá*) 'master, lord,' a Vaiśya, VS. &c.; Pāṇ. iii, 1, 103; (*ā*), f. a woman of the third caste, the wife of a Vaiśya, VS. &c., Pāṇ. iv, 1, 49, Comm.; (*ī*), f. the wife of any particular Vaiśya, Pāṇ. iv, 1, 49, Siddh.; (cf. *aryāṇī*.) **-jārā** (*árya-*), f. the mistress of a Vaiśya, VS. xxiii, 30. **-patnī**, see *-pati* s. v. 1. *aryá*. **-varya**, m. a Vaiśya of rank, Daś. **-śveta**, m. (v. l. *ārya-śv°*), N. of a man, (gaṇa *śivâdi*, q. v.)

Aryamán, *ā*, m. a bosom friend, play-fellow, companion, (especially) a friend who asks a woman in marriage for another, RV.; AV.; ŚBr.; TBr.; N. of an Āditya (who is commonly invoked together with Varuṇa and Mitra, also with Bhaga, Bṛihaspati, and others; he is supposed to be the chief of the Manes, Bhag. &c.; the milky way is called his path [*aryamṇáḥ pánthāḥ*, TBr.]; he presides over the Nakshatra Uttaraphalgunī, VarBṛS.; his name is used to form different male names, Pāṇ. v, 3, 84), RV. &c.; the sun, Śiś. ii, 39; the Asclepias plant, L.

Aryama (in comp. for *aryamán*). **-gṛiha-pati** (*aryamá-*), mfn. having Aryaman as *gṛiha-pati* (i. e. as keeper of the precedence in a grand sacrifice), MaitrS. **-datta**, m., N. of a man, Pāṇ. v, 3, 84, Sch. **-devā**, f. or **-daivata**, n. 'having Aryaman for its deity,' N. of the mansion Uttaraphalgunī, L. **-bhūti** and **-rādha**, m., N. of two Vedic teachers, VBr. **Aryamâkhya**, n. the mansion Uttaraphalgunī, VarYogay.

Aryamika, *as*, m. a shortened name for *Aryama-datta*, Pāṇ. v, 3, 84.

Aryamiya or **aryamila**, *as*, m. id., ib.

Aryamyà (4), mfn. intimate, very friendly, RV. v, 85, 7.

Aryāṇī, f. a mistress, Pāṇ. iv, 1, 49, Siddh.; a woman of the third or Vaiśya caste, Pāṇ. iv, 1, 49, Comm.

अर्व् *arv*, cl. 1. P. *arvati* (perf. *ānarva*, L.) to hurt, kill, L.

अर्व *arva* and *arvaṇa*. See *an-arvá*.

Árvat, mfn. running, hasting, RV. v, 54, 14 & AV. iv, 9, 2; low, inferior, vile, Uṇ.; (*ān*), m. a courser, horse, RV.; VS.; AV.; BhP.; the driver of a horse, RV. x, 40, 5 & 74, 1; N. of a part of the sacrificial action, RV. ii, 33, 1 & viii, 71, 12; (*árvatī*), f. a mare, RV.; AV.; a bawd, procuress, L.

Árvan, mfn. running, quick (said of Agni and Indra), RV.; low, inferior, vile, Uṇ.; (*ā*), m. a courser, horse, RV.; AV.; ŚBr.; N. of Indra (see before), L.; one of the ten horses of the moon, L.; a short span, L.; (cf. *ārāvan*.)

Árvaśa or **arvaśá**, mfn. running, quick (said of Indra and of the gods), RV. x, 92, 6.

अर्वाच् *arvā́c*, *vā́n̄*, *vā́cī*, *vā́k*, Ved. (fr. *añc* with *arva*, 'near' or 'hither') coming hitherward, coming to meet any one, turned towards, RV. &c.; being on this side (of a river), L.; being below or turned downwards, AV.; ŚBr.; ChUp.; (acc. *arvā́ñcam*) with √*nud*, to push down, RV. viii, 14, 8; (*ā́k*), ind., see ss. vv. *arvā́k* and *arvā́g*.

Arvā́k, ind. (gaṇa *svar-ādi*, q. v.) hither (opposite to *párāk*, *parás*, *parástāt*), RV.; AV.; ŚBr.; (with abl., ŚBr. &c.; with instr., RV. x, 129, 6; AV.) on this side, from a certain point, before, after; on the lower side, ChUp.; (with loc.) within, near, Śāk. (v. l.) **-kālika-tā**, f. the belonging to a proximate time, the state of being more modern (than anything else), Mn. xii, 96. **-kūla**, n. the near bank of a river. **-catvāriṅśá**, mfn. pl. under forty, ŚBr. **-tana**, mf(*ā*)n. being on this side of, not reaching up to, BhP. **-pañcāśá**, mfn. pl. under fifty, ŚBr. **-śatá**, mfn. pl. under a hundred, ib. **-shashṭhá**, mfn. pl. under sixty, ib. **-sāman** (*arvā́k-*), m. pl., N. of the three days during which a Soma sacrifice is performed, ŚBr. **-srotas**, mfn. (said of a creation of beings) in which the current of nutriment tends downwards, VP.

Arvāké, loc. ind. (opposed to *parāké*, q. v.) in the proximity, near, RV. viii, 9, 15.

Arvā́g (in comp. for *arvā́k*). **-aśītá**, mfn. pl. under eighty, ŚBr. **-bila** (*arvā́g-*), mfn. having the mouth downwards, ŚBr. xiv. **-vasu** (*arvā́g-*), mfn. offering riches, VS. xv, 19; ŚBr.; (*us*), m. (for *arvā-vasu*, q. v.), N. of a Hotṛi of the gods, GopBr. **-viṅśá**, mfn. pl. under twenty, ŚBr.

Arvācin, mfn. turned towards, KaushĀr.

Arvā́cīna or **arvācīná**, mf(*ā*)n. turned towards, favouring, RV.; turned towards (in a hostile manner), RV. vi, 25, 3; (with abl.) being on this side or below, ŚBr.; belonging to a proximate time, posterior, recent; (for *avācīna*) reverse, contrary, L.; (*arvācīnam*) ind. (with abl.) 'on this side of,' thenceforward, thence onward, ŚBr.; less than (abl.), ib.

अर्वावत् *arvā-vát*, *t*, f. proximity, RV.; (in all passages opposed to *parā-vát*, q. v.)

अर्वावसु *arvā-vásu*, *us*, m., N. of a Hotṛi or Brahman of the gods, ŚBr.; KaushUp.; of a son of Raibhya, MBh. &c.

अर्वुक *arvuka*, v. l. for *arbuka*, q. v.

अर्श *arśa*, *as*, m. (√*ṛiś*), 'damage,' see *án-arśa-rāti*; (for *arśas*) hemorrhoids, piles, L.

Árśas, n. piles, hemorrhoids, VS. xii, 97, &c. **Arśa-ādi**, a gaṇa of Pāṇ. (v, 2, 127).

Arśasa, mfn. (Pāṇ. v, 2, 127) afflicted with hemorrhoids, Mn. iii, 7; Suśr.

Arśasāná, mfn. striving to hurt, malicious, RV.; (*as*), m. (= *ardani*, q. v.) fire, Uṇ.

Árśasin, mfn. = *arśasa*, Hcat.

Arśin, mfn. id., L.

Arśo (in comp. for *árśas*). **-ghora**, mfn. destroying hemorrhoids, Suśr.; (*as*), m. the plant Amorphophallus Campanulatus, L.; one part of buttermilk with three parts of water, L.; (*ī*), f. the plant Curculigo Archioides Lin., L. **-yuj**, mfn. afflicted with hemorrhoids, L. **-roga**, m. hemorrhoids. **-roga-yuta** or **-rogin**, mfn. afflicted with hemorrhoids. **-vartman**, n. a tumour in the corner of the eye, Suśr. **-hita**, m. the marking nut plant (Semecarpus Anacardium), L.

अर्षण *arshaṇa* or *arshaṇin*, mfn. (√1. *ṛish*), flowing, movable, Nir.

अर्षणी *arshaṇí*, f. (√2. *ṛish*), a pricking or piercing pain, AV. ix, 8, 13, 16 & 21.

अर्ष्टृ *arshṭṛí*, mfn. (√*ṛij* or 2. *ṛish*?) = *ārtam gacchat* (Comm.), falling into misery, TS.; TBr.; (only in an obscure formula together with *ish-tárga*, q. v.)

अर्ह् *arh*, cl. 1. P. *árhati*, rarely Ā. *arhate* [MBh. iii, 1580; R.], (p. *árhat* [see below]; Ved. Inf. *arháse* [RV. x, 77, 1]; perf. 3. pl. *ānarhuḥ*, Pāṇ. vi, 1, 39, Sch., but Ved. *ānṛihuḥ* [cf. *ānṛicúḥ*, √*arc*], Pāṇ. vi, 1, 36) to deserve, merit, be worthy of; to have a claim to, be entitled to (acc.); to be allowed to do anything (Inf.); to be obliged or required to do anything (acc.); to be worth, counterbalance; to be able; (*arhasi*, 2. sg. with an Inf. is often used as a softened form of Imper.; e. g. *dātum arhasi*, 'be pleased to give;' *śrotum arhasi*, 'deign to listen,' for *śṛiṇu*): Caus. (Opt. *arhayet*, Mn. iii, 3 & 119; aor. *ārjihat*, Bhaṭṭ.) to honour: Desid. *arjihishati* [cf. Gk. ἄρχω].

Arha, mf(*ā*)n. meriting, deserving (praise or blame, cf. *pūjârha*, *nindârha*), worthy of, having a claim or being entitled to (acc. or Inf. or in comp.); being required, obliged, allowed (with Inf.); becoming, proper, fit (with gen. or ifc.), Pañcat.; worth (in money), costing, R.; (cf. *śatârha*, *sahasrârha*); (*as*), m. a N. of Indra, L.; (*ā*), f. or (*āṇi*), n. pl. worship, ChUp.

Arhaṇa, mfn. having a claim to, being entitled to (in comp.), BhP.; (*am*), n. deserving, meriting, Pāṇ. iii, 3, 111; worship, honour, treating any one (gen.) with respect, Mn. iii, 54, BhP.; a present of honour, MBh. i, 130; BhP.; (*ā*), f. worship, honour, N.; Ragh. &c.; (*arháṇā*), Ved. instr. ind. according to what is due, RV. i, 127, 6; x, 63, 4 & 92, 7.

Árhat, mfn. deserving, entitled to (acc.), RV.; used in a respectful address for *arhasi*, Pāṇ. iii, 2, 133; able, allowed to (acc.), RV.; worthy, venerable, respectable, ŚBr.; AitBr. &c. (see *arhat-tama* below); praised, celebrated, L.; (*an*), m. a Buddha who is still a candidate for Nirvāṇa; (= *kshapanaka*) a Jaina; an Arhat or superior divinity with the Jainas; the highest rank in the Buddhist hierarchy, L. **-tama**, mfn. (superl.) most worthy, most venerable, Mn. iii, 128; BhP. **-tva**, n. the dignity of an Arhat, Kathās.

Arhanta, mfn. worthy, L.; (*as*), m. a Buddha, L.; a Buddhist mendicant, L.; a N. of Śiva, L.

Arhantikā, f., N. of a Buddhist nun, Daś.

Arhita, mfn. honoured, worshipped, L.

Arhya, mfn. worthy ('of praise,' *stotum*), L.

अर्हरिष्वणि *arharishvaṇi*, mfn. (said of Indra) exultant [formed by irregular redupl. of √*hṛish*, BR.; *arhari-shvaṇi*, 'making enemies cry aloud,' Sāy.], RV. i, 56, 4.

अल् *al*, cl. 1. P. *alati*, to adorn, L.; to be competent or able, L.; to prevent, L. [The rt. is evidently invented for the derivation of *alam*, q. v.]

अल *ala*, *am*, n. the sting in the tail of a scorpion (or a bee), L.; (cf. *ali* and *alin*); (= *āla*, q. v.) yellow orpiment, L. **-gardá**, m. a water-serpent (the black variety of the Cobra de Capello, Coluber Nāga), Suparṇ.; Suśr.; (*ā*), f. a large poisonous leech, Suśr.; (cf. *alī-garda*.) **-gardha**, m. (= *-gardá*), a water-serpent, L. **Alâyudha**, m. 'whose weapon is the sting from the tail of a scorpion,' N. of a Rākshasa, MBh. vii, 8004.

अलक *alaka, as, am,* m. n. (ifc. f. *ā*) a curl, lock, Ragh. &c.; (*as*), m. (= *alarka*, q. v.) a mad dog, L.; (*ās*), m. pl., N. of a people, VarBṛS.; of the inhabitants of Kubera's residence Alakā, MBh. iii, 11813; (*ā*), f. (gaṇa *kshipakâdi*, q. v.) a girl from eight to ten years of age, L.; N. of the capital of Kubera (situated on a peak of the Himālaya inhabited also by Śiva), Kum. vi, 37, &c.; N. of a town in Nishadha, Kathās. **–nandā**, f. a young girl from eight to ten years old, L.; N. of a river that runs from the Himālaya mountains and falls into the Gaṅgā, MBh. i, 6456; VP. **–prabhā**, f. the capital of Kubera, L. **–priya**, m. the plant Terminalia Tomentosa, L. **–saṃhati**, f. rows of curls. **Alakâdhipa** or **alakâdhipati** [Suśr.], m. 'lord of Alakā,' a N. of Kubera. **Alakânta**, m. the end of a curl, a ringlet. **Alakêśvara**, m. 'lord of Alakā,' a N. of Kubera, Ragh. xix, 15.

अलकम् *álakam*, ind. in vain, for nothing, RV. x, 71, 6 & 108, 7.

अलक्त *alakta, as,* m. (said to be for *a-rakta*), red juice or lac (obtained from the red resin of certain trees and from the cochineal's red sap), L. **–rasa**, m. the Alakta juice, R. ii, 60, 18; Bhpr.

Alaktaka, *as,* m. rarely *am,* n., id., Kum. &c.

अलक्षण *a-lakshaṇa, am,* n. (√*laksh*), a bad, inauspicious sign, Mn. iv, 156; (*a-lakshaṇá*), mf(*ā*)n. having no signs or marks, without characteristic, ŚBr.; KātyŚr.; Mn. i, 5; having no good marks, inauspicious, unfortunate, Ragh. xiv, 5.

A-lakshita, mfn. unseen, unperceived, unobserved, MBh.; uncharacterized, having no particular mark, ŚBr.; KātyŚr. **Alakshitântaka**, mfn. suddenly dead, L. **Alakshitôpasthita**, mfn. one who has approached unobserved.

A-lakshya, mfn. invisible, unobserved, MBh. &c.; unmarked, not indicated, Sāh.; having no particular marks, insignificant in appearance (see *-janma-tā* below); (*as*), m., N. of a Mantra spoken to exorcise a weapon, R. i, 30, 5. **–gati**, mfn. moving invisibly. **–janma-tā**, f. being of insignificant birth or origin, Kum. v, 72. **–liṅga**, mfn. disguised, incognito.

अलक्ष्मी *a-lakshmī, is,* f. evil fortune, bad luck; distress, poverty; (mfn.) causing misfortune, ŚāṅkhGṛ.

अलखान *alakhāna, as,* m., N. of a king of Gurjara, Rājat.

अलगर्द *ala-gardá* and °*rdha*. See *ala*.

अलग्न *a-lagna*, mfn. (√*lag*), not joined or connected.

A-láglam, ind. unconnectedly, in a stammering manner, ŚBr. iii.

अलघु *a-laghu*, mfn. not light, heavy; not short, long (as a syllable in prosody); not quick, slow, Mṛicch.; weighty, significant, Daś.; serious, solemn; intense, violent. **–pratijña**, mfn. solemnly pledged or promised. **Alaghûpala**, m. 'heavy stone,' a rock, L. **Alaghûshman**, m. intense heat.

A-laghīyas, mfn. (compar.) not insignificant, mighty, Śiś. ii, 58.

अलंकरण *alam-karaṇa,-kārá*, &c. See *álam*.

अलङ्घन *a-laṅghana, am,* n. not surmounting, not transgressing, not passing over or beyond.

A-laṅghanīya, mfn. insurmountable, impassable, not to be crossed; not to be reached or caught (by hastening), Śak.; not to be transgressed, inviolable. **–tā**, f. impassableness, insurmountableness, inaccessibility; inviolability.

A-laṅghayat, mfn. not transgressing, Ragh. ix, 9.

A-laṅghya, mfn. impassable (as a river); inviolable (as a command or prohibition), BhP.

अलज *alajá, as,* m. a kind of bird, VS. xxiv, 34. **–cit** [TS.; Kāṭh.] or **-cita** [Śulb.], mfn. piled up (as the sacrificial altar) in the shape of the bird Alaja.

अलजि *alají, is,* f. inflammation of the eye (at the edge of the cornea), AV. ix, 8, 20.

Alajī, f. id., Suśr.

अलज्ज *a-lajja*, mf(*ā*, Naish.)n. shameless.

अलञ्जर *alañjara* = *aliñjara*, q. v., L.

अलंजुष *alám-jusha*. See *álam*.

अलति *alati, is,* m. a kind of song, L.

अलंतम *alam-tama, -tarām*. See *álam*.

अलपत् *á-lapat*, mfn. not chattering, not speaking nonsense, AV. viii, 2, 3.

अलब्ध *a-labdha*, mfn. unobtained. **–nātha**, mfn. without a patron. **–nidra**, mfn. not obtaining sleep, unable to fall asleep, BhP. **–bhūmika-tva**, n. the state of not obtaining any degree (*bhūmi*) of deep meditation, Yogas. **Alabdhâbhîpsita**, mfn. disappointed in one's desire.

A-labhamāna, mfn. not gaining, &c.

A-labhya, mfn. unobtainable, Kum. v, 43, &c.

अलम् *álam*, ind. (later form of *áram*, q. v.), enough, sufficient, adequate, equal to, competent, able. (*Alam* may govern a dat. [*jīvitavai* (Ved. Inf. dat.) *álam*, AV. vi, 109, 1, or *alaṃ jīvanāya*, Mn. xi, 76, &c., sufficient for living] or Inf. [Pāṇ. iii, 4, 66; *alaṃ vijñātum*, able to conceive, Nir. ii, 3] or instr. [Pāṇ. ii, 3, 27, Siddh.; *alaṃ śaṅkayā*, enough, i. e. away with fear!] or gen. [*alaṃ prajāyāḥ*, capable of obtaining progeny, PBr.] or may be used with the fut. [*alaṃ hanishyati*, he will be able to kill, Pāṇ. iii, 3, 154, Sch.] or with an ind. [Pāṇ. iii. 4, 18; *alaṃ bhuktvā*, enough of eating, i. e. do not eat more; *alaṃ vicārya*, enough of consideration].) **–artha-tā**, f. or **-artha-tva**, n. having the sense of *alam*, Pat. **–ātardana**, mfn. easy to perforate, Nir. vi, 2. **–paśu**, &c. (i. e. *alaṃ-paśu*, &c.), see s. v. *alaṃ* below.

Alaṃ (in comp. for *álam*). **–karaṇa**, n. making ready, preparation, Kauś.; (ifc. f. *ā*, Kathās.) decoration, ornament, KātyŚr. &c. **–karaṇin**, mfn. possessed of an ornament, Kathās. **–karishṇu**, mfn. (Pāṇ. iii, 2, 136) fond of ornament, Nir.; (with acc.) decorating, Pāṇ. ii, 3, 69, Sch.; (*an-*, neg., see also s. v.) Pāṇ. vi, 2, 160, Sch.; (*us*), m., N. of Śiva. **–kartṛi**, mfn. one who decorates, L. **–karmiṇa**, mfn. competent for any act or work, Pāṇ. v, 4, 7. **–kārá**, m. the act of decorating, R. ii, 40, 13; (ifc. f. *ā*, R. v, 18, 6) ornament, decoration, ŚBr.; TBr. &c.; (in rhetoric) an ornament of the sense or the sound (cf. *arthâl°* and *śabdâl°*); (*alaṃkāra*)-*kārikā*, f., *-kaustubha*, m., *-candrikā*, f., *-cūḍāmaṇi*, m., *-mañjarī*, *-mālā*, *-muktâvalī*, f. different works on rhetoric; *-vatī*, f. 'the decorated one,' N. of the ninth Lambaka in the Kathāsaritsāgara; *-śāstra*, n. a manual or text-book of rhetoric; *-śīla*, m., N. of a prince of the Vidyādharas, Kathās.; *-suvarṇa*, n. gold used for ornaments, L.; *-sūra*, m., N. of a kind of meditation, Buddh.; *-hīna*, mfn. unadorned. **–kāraka**, m. ornament, Mn. vii, 220. **–kārya**, mfn. to be adorned or decorated, Sāh. **–kāla**, m. for *-kāra*, ornament, Nalod. **–kumāri**, mfn. fit for marrying a young girl, Pat. **–√1. kṛi** (cf. *áraṃ-√1. kṛi* s. v. *áram*), to make ready, prepare, ŚBr., (ind. p. *-kṛitvā*, q.v.); to decorate, ornament, R. &c., (ind. p. *-kṛitya*, q. v.); to impede, check, violate (with gen.), Mn. viii, 16. **–kṛita** (*álaṃ-*), mfn. adorned, decorated, ŚBr. &c.; (cf. *áraṃ-kṛita* s. v. *áram*.) **–kṛiti**, f. ornament, Kathās.; rhetorical ornament (cf. *-kāra* above), Sāh.; Kāvyād. **–kṛitya**, ind. p. having decorated, TBr.; Mn. iii, 28 & v, 68. **–kṛitvā**, ind. p. having made ready, having prepared, Pāṇ. i, 4, 64, Sch. **–kriyā**, f. decorating, L.; rhetorical ornament. **–gāmin**, mfn. (= *anugavīna*) going after or watching (as cows) in a proper manner, Pāṇ. v, 2, 15, Sch. **–jīvika**, mfn. sufficient for livelihood, Pat. **–jusha** (*aláṃ-*), mfn. sufficient, ŚBr. iii. **–tama**, mfn. very well able to (Inf.), BhP. **–tarām**, ind. (compar. of *alaṃ*) exceedingly, Kum. xiv, 16 & xv, 28; very much better or easier to (Inf.), Śiś. ii, 106. **–dhana**, mfn. possessing sufficient wealth, Mn. viii, 162. **–dhūma**, m. 'smoke enough,' thick smoke, L. **–paśu**, mfn. able to keep cattle, KātyŚr. **–purushīṇa**, mfn. sufficient for a man, Pāṇ. v, 4, 7. **–pūrva**, mfn. being preceded by the word *alam*, Pat. **–prajanana**, mfn. (cf. *alaṃ prajāyāḥ* above s. v. *álam*) able to beget or generate, ĀśvŚr. **–bala**, mfn. 'equal to any power,' N. of Śiva. **–bhūshṇu**, mfn. able, competent, L. **–manas**, mfn. satisfied in mind, BhP.; (cf. *arámanas* s. v. *áram*.)

अलम्पट *a-lampaṭa*, mfn. not libidinous, chaste, BhP.

अलम्बुष *alambusha, as,* m. the palm of the hand with the fingers extended, L.; N. of a plant, L.; of a Rākshasa, MBh. vii, 4065 & 4072; (*ā*), f. a barrier, a line or anything not to be crossed, L.; a sort of sensitive plant, Bhpr.; N. of an Apsaras, MBh. ix, 2931 seqq.; Kathās.

अलम्म *alamma, as,* m., N. of a Ṛishi, PBr.

अलय *a-laya, as,* m. (√*lī*), non-dissolution, permanence, R. iii, 71, 10 (v. l. *an-aya*); (mfn.) restless, Śiś. iv, 57.

अलयस् *alayas*. See 2. *ali*.

अलर्क *alarka, as,* m. a mad dog or one rendered furious, Suśr.; a fabulous animal, like a hog with eight legs, MBh.; R.; MārkP.; the plant Calatropis Gigantea Alba, Suśr.; (cf. *dīrghâlarka*); N. of a king, Hariv. &c.

अलर्ति *alarti* (3. sg.) and *alarshi* (2. sg.), Intens. fr. √*ṛi*, q. v.

Álarshi-rāti, mfn. eager to bestow, SV. (v. l. *án-arśa-rāti*, q. v., RV.)

अललाभवत् *alalā-bhávat*, mfn. (said of the waters) sounding cheerfully, RV. iv, 18, 6.

अलले *alale*, ind. (cf. *arare*), a word of no import occurring in the dialect or gibberish of the Piśācas (a class of goblins introduced in plays, &c.), L.

अलवण *a-lavaṇa*, mfn. not salty, Pāṇ. v, 1, 121.

अलवस् *alávas*. See 2. *ali*.

अलवाल *alavāla* or °*laka, as,* m. = *ālavāla*, q. v., L.

अलस् *a-las*, mfn. (√*las*), not shining, L.

अलस *a-lasá*, mf(*ā*)n. inactive, without energy, lazy, idle, indolent, tired, faint, ŚBr.; AitBr. &c.; (*as*), m. a sore or ulcer between the toes, Suśr.; (= *a-lasaka* below) tympanitis, Bhpr.; N. of a small poisonous animal, Suśr.; N. of a plant, L.; (*ā*), f. the climbing plant Vitis Pedata Wall, L. **–gamana**, mf(*ā*)n. going lazily, Megh. **–tā**, f. or **-tva**, n. idleness. **Alasī-√bhū**, to become tired, Bhpr. **Alasêkshaṇa**, mf(*ā*)n. having languishing or tired looks, Rājat.

A-lasaka, *as,* m. tympanitis, flatulence (intumescence of the abdomen, with constipation and wind), Car.; Suśr.

A-lāsya, mfn. (said of peacocks) not dancing, idle, Ragh. xvi, 14.

अलसाला *alasâlā*, f.?, AV. vi, 16, 4.

अलाक *alāka, as,* m. (= *alarka*) the plant Calotropis Gigantea, Car.

अलाञ्छन *a-lāñchana*, mfn. spotless, Bālar.

अलाण्डु *alâṇḍu, us,* m., N. of a noxious animal, AV. ii, 31, 2 & 3.

अलात *alāta, am,* n. a fire-brand, coal, MBh. &c. **–śānti**, f., N. of the fourth chapter of Gauḍapāda's commentary on the MāṇḍUp. **Alātākshī**, f. 'having fiery eyes,' N. of one of the mothers in Skanda's retinue, MBh. ix, 2626.

अलातृण *a-lātṛiṇá*, mfn. (√*lā* = √*rā*?, BR.) not granting anything, miserly, RV. i, 166, 7 & iii, 30, 10; (Nir. vi, 2.)

अलाबु *alâbu, us,* f. the bottle-gourd (Lagenaria Vulgaris Ser), Suśr. &c.; (*us, u*), m. n. a vessel made of the bottle-gourd, AV. &c.; (used by Brāhmanical ascetics) Mn. vi, 54; Jain.; (*u*), n. the fruit of the bottle-gourd, MBh. ii, 2196, &c. **–gandhi**, mfn. smelling of the bottle-gourd, AV. Paipp. **–pātrá**, n. a jar made of the bottle-gourd, AV. viii, 10, 29. **–maya**, mfn. made of a bottle-gourd, Yājñ. iii, 60. **–vīṇā**, f. a lute of the shape of a bottle-gourd, Lāṭy. **–suhṛid**, m. 'friend of the bottle-gourd,' sorrel, L.

Alâbuka, *am,* n. the fruit of the bottle-gourd, AV. xx, 132, 1 & 2; (*ā*), f. the bottle-gourd, L. **Alābukêśvara**, n., N. of a Tīrtha, SkandaP.

Alābū, *ūs,* f. (= *alâbu* above) the bottle-gourd, Pāṇ. iv, 1, 66, Comm.; Uṇ. **–kaṭa**, n. the down of the bottle-gourd, Pāṇ. v, 2, 29, Comm.

अलाभ *a-lābha, as,* m. non-acquirement, Mn. vi, 57; want, deficiency, ĀśvGṛ. &c.; loss (in selling goods), Mn. ix, 331; loss (of life, *prâṇa*), Mn. xi, 80.

अलायुध *alâyudha.* See *ala.*

अलाय्य *alāyya* (4), mfn. a N. of Indra [BR.; 'an assailant,' fr. √*ṛi,* Sāy.], RV. ix, 67, 30.

अलार *alāra, as,* m. a kind of Aloe plant, L.; *(am),* n. a door, L.

अलास *alāsa, as,* m. inflammation and abscess at the root of the tongue, Suśr.

अलास्य *alāsya,* mfn. See *a-lasá* above.

अलि 1. *ali, is,* m. (for *alin,* fr. *ala,* q. v.) 'possessed of a sting,' a (large black) bee, Ragh. &c.; a scorpion, L.; a crow, L.; the Indian cuckoo, L.; spirituous liquor, L. **–kula,** n. a swarm of bees, VarBṛS.; *(alikula)-priyā* or *-saṃkulā,* f. 'fond of or full of swarms of bees,' the plant Rosa Glandulifera, L. **–garda** or **-gardha,** m. = *ala-garda,* q.v., L. **–jihvā** or **-jihvikā,** f. the uvula or soft palate, L. **–dūrvā,** f., N. of a plant, L. **–pattrikā,** f., N. of a shrub, L. **–parṇī,** f. the plant Tragia Involucrata Lin., L. **–priya,** n. the red lotus, Nymphæa Rubra, L.; *(ā),* f. the trumpet flower (Bignonia Suaveolens), L. **–mālā,** f. a line or swarm of bees, Mālatīm. **–modā,** f. the plant Premna Spinosa, L. **–mohinī,** f., N. of a plant, L. **–vallabhā,** f. = *-priyā,* q. v., L. **–virāva,** m. or **-viruta,** n. song or hum of the bee, L.

Alin, *ī,* m. 'possessed of a sting (*ala,* q. v.),' a (large black) bee, BhP. &c.; a scorpion, L.; the Scorpion (in the zodiac), VarBṛS.; *(inī),* f. a female bee, Śiś. vi, 72; a swarm of bees, BhP.

अलि 2. *ali* (in the Apabhraṇśa dialect) for *ari,* enemy (pl. *alayas* for *arayas*), Pat.; also *alávas* is mentioned as a corrupt pronunciation for *aráyas,* ŚBr.

अलिंश *alíṅśa, as,* m. a kind of demon, AV. viii, 6, 1.

अलिक *alika, as,* m. = *alīka,* the forehead, Bālar.; N. of a Prākṛit poet. **–lekhā,** f. an impression or mark upon the forehead, Kād.

अलिक्लव *alíklava, as,* m. a kind of carrion bird, AV. xi, 2, 2 & 9, 9.

अलिगर्द *ali-garda* and *-gardha.* See 1. *ali.*

अलिगु *a-ligu, us,* m., N. of a man; (gaṇa *gargâdi,* q. v.)

अलिङ्ग *a-liṅga, am,* n. absence of marks, Comm. on Nyāyad.; (mfn.) having no marks, Nir.; MuṇḍUp. &c.; (in Gr.) having no gender.

A-liṅgin, mfn. 'not wearing the usual frontal marks, skin, staff, &c.,' a pretended ascetic or student, L.; (cf. *sa-liṅgin.*)

अलिञ्जर *aliñjara, as,* m. a small earthen water-jar, MBh. iii, 12756; (cf. *alañjara.*)

अलिन *álina, ās,* m. pl., N. of a tribe, RV. vii, 18, 7.

अलिन्द *alinda, as,* m. (ifc. f. *ī,* gaṇa *gaurâdi,* q. v.) a terrace before a house-door, Śāk. &c.; *(ās),* m. pl., N. of a people, MBh. vi, 371; VP.

Alindaka, *as,* m. a terrace before a house-door, L.

अलिपक *alipaka, as,* m. (= 1. *ali* above) a bee, L.; the Indian cuckoo, L.; a dog, L.

Alimaka, *as,* m. a bee, L.; the Indian cuckoo, L.; a frog, L.; the plant Bassia Latifolia, L.; the filaments of the lotus, L.

Alimpaka or **alimbaka,** *as,* m. = *alimaka.*

अलिप्सा *a-lipsā,* f. freedom from desire.

अलीक *álīka,* mf(*ā,* Naish.)n. unpleasing, disagreeable (as a serpent), AV. v, 13, 5; untrue, false, pretended, MBh. &c.; little, L.; *(am),* n. anything displeasing, ĀśvŚr.; R. ii, 52, 25; falsehood, untruth, Mn. xi, 55, &c.; the forehead (cf. *alika*); heaven, L. **–tā,** f. falsehood, vanity. **–matsya,** m. a kind of dish tasting like fish ('mock-fish,' made of the flour of a sort of bean fried with Sesamum oil), Bhpr. **–supta** or **-suptaka,** n. pretended sleep, Kathās.

Alīkayu, *us,* m., N. of a Brāhman (with the patron. Vācaspatya), KaushBr.

Alīkāya, Nom. Ā. °*yate,* to be deceived, (gaṇa *sukhâdi,* q. v.)

Alīkin, mfn. 'possessed of *alīka,*' (gaṇa *sukhâdi,* q. v.); disagreeable, L.; false, deceiving, L.

Alīkya, mfn. 'like *alīka,*' (gaṇa *dig-ādi* and *vargyâdi,* q. v.); belonging to falsehood, false, L.

अलीगर्द *alīgarda* = *ali-garda,* q. v., L.

अलु *alu, us,* f. (= *ālu,* q. v.) a small water-pot, L.

अलुप्त *a-lupta,* mfn. not cut off, undiminished. **–mahiman,** mfn. of undiminished glory.

अलुब्ध *a-lubdha,* mfn. not covetous, not avaricious, Gaut. **–tva,** n. freedom from covetousness.

A-lubhyat, mfn. not becoming disordered, not disturbed, AV. iii, 10, 11.

A-lobha, *as,* m. 'non-confusion,' steadiness, AitBr.; absence of cupidity, moderation, Hit.

A-lobhin, mfn. not desiring.

अलूक्ष *a-lūksha,* mfn. (= *á-rūksha,* q. v.) not harsh, soft, greasy, TUp. &c. **Alūkshânta-tva,** n. the having greasy substances (like butter) near at hand (for oblations), TBr. i, 1, 6, 6.

अलून *a-lūna,* mfn. uncut, unshorn.

अले *ale* or *alele,* ind. (cf. *are* and *arere*), unmeaning words in the dialect of the demons or Piśācas (introduced in plays, &c.), L.

अलेपक *a-lepaka,* mfn. stainless.

अलेश *a-leśa,* mfn. not little, much, large; *(am),* ind. 'not a bit,' not at all, L. **A-leśâiṅga,** mfn. 'not moving a bit,' firm, steady, L.

अलोक *a-loka, as,* m. 'not the world,' the end of the world, R. i, 37, 12; the immaterial or spiritual world, Jain.; (*á-lokās*), m. pl. not the people, ŚBr. xiv; (*a-loká*), mfn. not having space, finding no place, ŚBr. **–sāmānya,** mfn. not common among ordinary people, Mālatīm.

A-lokanīya, mfn. invisible, imperceptible, L.

A-lokita, mfn. unseen, L.

A-lokyá, mf(*â*)n. unusual, unallowed, ŚBr.; Mn. ii, 161. **–tā** (*alokyá-*), f. loss of the other world, ŚBr. xiv.

A-locana, mf(*ā*)n. without eyes; without windows (to look through), Car.

A-laukika, mf(*ī*)n. not current in the world, uncommon, unusual (especially said of words); not relating to this world, supernatural. **–tva,** n. rare occurrence (of a word), Sāh.

अलोप *a-lopa, as,* m. not dropping (as a letter or syllable), Lāṭy.; TPrāt.; dropping of the letter *a,* VPrāt. **Alopâṅga,** mfn. not defective in a single limb, AitBr.

अलोमक *a-lomáka* [TS.] or *a lómaka* [ŚBr.], mf(Ved. °*makā,* class. °*mikā* [Mn. iii, 8; but also AitBr.], Pāṇ. vii, 3, 45, Comm.)n. hairless.

A-loman, mfn. id., Gaut. **A-lomaharshaṇa,** mfn. not causing erection of the hair of the body (from joy).

अलोल *a-lola,* mfn. unagitated, firm, steady; *(ā),* f. (also *lolā,* q. v.), N. of a metre (containing four lines, each of fourteen syllables).

Alolu-tva = *alolup-tva* below, Bhag.

A-lolupa, mfn. = *a-lola,* MBh. iii, 153; free from desire, Āp.; *(as),* m., N. of a son of Dhṛitarāshṭra, MBh. i, 2738. **–tva** [ŚvetUp.] or **aloluptva** [Bhag. xvi, 2, v.l.], n. freedom from any desire.

A-lolupyamāna, mfn. not greedy, Gaut.

अलोह *aloha,* mfn. not made of iron, MBh. i, 5755; *(as),* m., N. of a man, (gaṇa 1. *naḍâdi,* q. v.)

अलोहित *a-lohitá* [TS.] or *a-lóhita* [ŚBr. xiv], mfn. bloodless; *(am),* n. Nymphæa Rubra, L.

अलौकिक *a-laukika.* See *a-loka.*

अल्ग *algá, au,* m. du. the groin, VS. xxv, 6.

अल्प *álpa,* mf(*ā*)n. (m. pl. *e* or *ās,* Pāṇ. i, 1, 33) small, minute, trifling, little, AV. &c.; *(am),* ind. (opposed to *bahu*) little, Mn. ii, 149 & x, 60; *(ena),* instr. ind. (with a perf. Pass. p., Pāṇ. ii, 3, 33) 'for little,' cheap, Daś.; easily, R. iv, 32, 7; *(āt),* abl. ind. (with a perf. Pass. p.) without much trouble, easily, Pāṇ. ii, 3, 33; (in comp. with a past Pass. p.) ii, 1, 39 & vi, 3, 2. **–kārya,** n. small matter. **–keśī,** f., N. of a plant (or perhaps the root of sweet flag), L. **–krīta,** mfn. bought for little money, cheap. **–gandha,** n. the red lotus, L. **–ceshṭita,** mfn. 'making little effort,' inert. **–cchada,** mfn. scantily clad. **–jña,** mfn. knowing little, ignorant. **–tanu,** mfn. small-bodied, L. **–tara,** mfn. (compar., cf. *alpīyas*), smaller, RPrāt.; KātyŚr. &c. **–tā,** f. or **-tva,** n. smallness, minuteness; insignificance. **–dakshiṇa,** mfn. defective in presents (as a ceremony), Mn. xi, 39 & 40. **–darśana** [MBh. i, 5919] or **-dṛishṭi,** mfn. of confined views, narrow-minded. **–dhana,** mfn. of little wealth, not affluent, Mn. iii, 66 & xi, 40. **–dhī,** mfn. weak-minded, having little sense, foolish, Hit. **–nishpatti,** mfn. of little or rare occurrence (as a word), Nir. ii, 2. **–pattra,** m. 'having little leaves,' N. of a plant (a species of the Tulasi), L.; *(ī),* f. the plants Curculigo Orchioides and Anethum Sowa, L. **–padma,** n. the red lotus, L. **–parīvāra,** mfn. having a small retinue. **–paśu** (*álpa-*), mfn. having a small number of cattle, AV. xii, 4, 25. **–pāyin,** mfn. sucking little or not sufficiently (as a leech), Suśr. **–puṇya,** mf(*ā*)n. whose religious merit is small, MBh. iii, 2650; R. vi, 95, 20. **–prajas,** mfn. having few descendants or few subjects. **–prabhāva,** mfn. of little weight or consequence, insignificant; *(alpaprabhāva)-tā,* f. or *-tva,* n. insignificance. **–pramāṇa,** mfn. of little weight or measure; of little authority, resting on little evidence. **–pramāṇaka,** m. common cucumber (Cucumis Sativus), L. **–prayoga,** mfn. of rare application or use, Nir. **–prâṇa,** m. (in Gr.) slight breathing or weak aspiration (the effort in uttering the vowels, the semivowels *y, r, l, v,* the consonants *k, c, ṭ, t, p, g, j, ḍ, d, b,* and the nasals, is said to be accompanied with slight aspiration, but practically *alpaprâṇa* is here equivalent to unaspirated, as opposed to *mahā-prâṇa,* q. v.), Pāṇ. i, 1, 9, Sch.; (mfn.) 'having short breath,' not persevering, soon tired, Suśr.; pronounced with slight breathing, Kāvyād. **–bala,** mfn. of little strength, feeble. **–balaprâṇa,** mfn. of little strength and little breath, i. e. weak and without any power of endurance, N. **–bahu-tva,** n. the being little or much. **–bādha,** mfn. causing little annoyance or inconvenience, Yājñ. ii, 156; having little pain or trouble, MBh. **–buddhi,** mfn. weak-minded, unwise, silly, Mn. xii, 74. **–bhāgya,** mf(*ā*)n. 'having little fortune,' unfortunate, MBh.; R. &c. **–bhāshin,** mfn. speaking little, taciturn. **–mati,** mfn. = *-buddhi* above, Suśr. **–madhyama,** mfn. thin-waisted. **–mātra,** n. a little, a little merely; a short time, a few moments, L. **–mārisha,** m. Amaranthus Polygamus, L. **–mūrti,** mfn. 'small-bodied,' diminutive (as a star), Sūryas.; *(is),* f. a small figure or object. **–mūlya,** mfn. of small value. **–medhas,** mfn. (Pāṇ. v, 4, 122, Sch.) of little understanding, ignorant, silly, KaṭhUp. &c. **–m-paca,** mfn. (= *mitam-paca,* q. v.) cooking little, stingy, L. **–ruj** or **-ruja,** mfn. 'of little pain,' not painful, Bhpr. **–vayas,** mfn. young in age (as a horse), L. **–vādin,** mfn. speaking little, taciturn. **–vid,** mfn. knowing little, ChUp. **–vidya,** mfn. ignorant, uneducated, Mn. xi, 36. **–vishaya,** mfn. of limited range or capacity, Ragh. i, 2. **–vyāhārin,** mfn. = *-bhāshin* above, Lāṭy. **–śakti,** mfn. of little strength, weak, feeble, Hit. **–śayu** (*álpa-*), m. a species of troublesome insect, AV. iv, 36, 9. **–śarīra,** mfn. having a small body, R. v, 35, 31. **–śas,** ind. in a low degree, a little, ŚBr.; (Pāṇ. ii, 1, 38) seldom, now and then (opposed to *prāya-śas*), Mn. xii, 20 & 21; *(alpaśaḥ)-paṅkti,* f., N. of a metre. **–śesha,** mfn. 'at which little is left,' nearly finished, R.; Kād. **–sattva,** mfn. having little strength or courage, Kathās. **–saṃnicaya,** mfn. having only small provisions, poor, R. i, 6, 7. **–sambhāra,** mfn. id., superl. *-tama,* very poor, Gobh. **–saras,** n. a small pond (one which is shallow or dry in the hot season), L. **–sāra,** mfn. of little value, Mn. xi, 164; *(as),* m. 'a little valuable object,' a jewel, trinket, Jain. **–snāyu,** mfn. having few sinews. **–sva,** mfn. having little property, GopBr.; Vait. **Alpâkāṅkshin,** mfn. desiring little, satisfied with little. **Alpâjya,** mfn. with little ghee, ŚBr. **Alpâñji,** mfn. covered with minute spots, VS. xxiv, 4. **Alpâtyaya,**

mfn. causing little pain, Suśr. **Alpâmbu-tîrtha**, n., N. of a Tīrtha, SkandaP. **Alpâyus**, mfn. short-lived, Mn. iv, 157; 'of few years,' a goat, L. **Alpârambha**, m. a gradual beginning; (mfn.) having little or moderate zeal in worldly affairs, Jain. **Alpâlpa**, mfn. very little, Mn. vii, 129; Megh. **Alpâsthi**, n. 'having a little kernel,' the fruit of Grewia Asiatica, L. **Alpâhâra**, mfn. taking little food, moderate, abstinent, Buddh.; Jain. **Alpâhârin**, mfn. id., L. **Alpī-√1. kṛi**, to make small, L. **Alpī-√bhū**, (p. *-bhavat*) to become smaller, Kathās. **Alpêccha**, mfn. having little or moderate wishes, Jain. **Alpêcchu**, mfn. id. **Alpêtara**, mfn. 'other than small,' large; (*alpêtara*)-*tva*, n. largeness, Ragh. v, 22. **Alpêśâkhya**, mfn. 'named after an insignificant chief or master,' of low origin, Buddh. **Alpôna**, mfn. slightly defective, not quite complete or not finished. **Alpôpâya**, m. small means.

Alpaka, mf(*ikā*)n. small, minute, trifling, Mn. &c.; (*ám*), ind. little, Naigh.; ŚBr.; (*ât*), abl. ind. shortly after, ŚBr.; (*as*), m. the plants Hedysarum Alhagi and Premna Herbacea, L.

Alpaya, Nom. P. °*yati*, to lessen, reduce, diminish, Bālar.; Naish. xxii, 54; perf. Pass. p. *alpita*, mfn. lessened in value or influence, Naish. i, 15.

Alpishṭha, mfn. least, smallest, Pāṇ. v, 3, 64. **-kīrti**, mfn. of very little reputation, L.

Alpīyas, mfn. (Pāṇ. v, 3, 64; cf. *alpa-tara* above) smaller, less, KātyŚr.; Mn. &c.; very small. **Alpīyah-khā**, f. having a very small vulva, Suśr.

अल्ला *allā*, f. (voc. *alla*), a mother, Pāṇ. vii, 3, 107, Sch.

अव् *av*, cl. 1. P. *ávati* (Imper. 2. sg. *avatāt*, RV. viii, 2, 3; p. *ávat*; impf. *ávat*, 2. sg. 1. *ávaḥ* [for 2. *ávaḥ* see √*vṛi*]; perf. 3. sg. *āva*, 2. pl. *āvá*, RV. viii, 7, 18; 2. sg. *āvitha*; aor. *āvīt*, 2. sg. *āvīs*, *avīs*, and *avishas*, Imper. *avishṭu*, 2. sg. *aviḍḍhí* [once, RV. ii, 17, 8] or *aviḍḍhi* [six times in RV.], 2. du. *avishṭam*, 3. du. *avishṭām*, 2. pl. *avishṭanā*, RV. vii, 18, 25; Prec. 3. sg. *avyās*; Inf. *ávitave*, RV. vii, 33, 1; Ved. ind. p. *āvyā*, RV. i, 166, 13) to drive, impel, animate (as a car or horse), RV.; Ved. to promote, favour; (chiefly Ved.) to satisfy, refresh; to offer (as a hymn to the gods), RV. iv, 44, 6; to lead or bring to (dat.: *ūtáye*, *vāja-sātaye*, *kshatrāya*, *svastáye*), RV.; (said of the gods) to be pleased with, like, accept favourably (as sacrifices, prayers or hymns), RV.; (chiefly said of kings or princes) to guard, defend, protect, govern, BhP.; Ragh. ix, 1; VarBṛS. &c.: Caus. (only impf. *āvayat*, 2. sg. *āvayas*) to consume, devour, RV.; AV.; VS.; ŚBr. [cf. Gk. ἀΐω; Lat. *aveo*?].

1. **Áva**, *as*, m. favour, RV. i, 128, 5; (cf. *niravá*.)

Ávat, mfn. pr. p., see √*av*. **-taram** (*ávat-*), ind. (compar.) 'more favourably' or 'with greater pleasure,' v. l. of TS. instead of *áva-tara* in VS. xvii, 6.

Avana, *am*, n. favour, preservation, protection, Nir.; BhP. &c.; (cf. *an-avana*); (= *tarpaṇa*) satisfaction, L.; joy, pleasure, L.; (for the explan. of 2. *ēva*) desire, wish, Nir.; speed, L.; 1. (*ī*), f. the plant Ficus Heterophylla, L.; N. of a river, Hariv.; (for 2. *avanī* see *avánī*.)

अव 2. *áva*, ind. (as a prefix to verbs and verbal nouns expresses) off, away, down, RV. &c.; (exceptionally as a preposition with abl.) down from, AV. vii, 55, 1; (for another use of this preposition, see *ava-kokila*.) **-tarám**, ind. (compar.) farther away, RV. i, 129, 6.

अव 3. *ava* (only gen. du. *avór* with *vām*, 'of you both,' corresponding to *sá tvám*, 'thou,' &c.), this, RV. vi, 67, 11; vii, 67, 4 & (*vā* for *vām*) x, 132, 5 [Zd. pron. *ava*; Slav. *ovo*; cf. also the syllable αὐ in αὐ-τός, αὖ, αὖθι, &c.; Lat. *au-t*, *au-tem*, &c.]

अवऋति *áva-ṛiti* for *áva-rti*, q. v., VS. xxx, 12.

अवंश *a-vaṅśa*, *as*, m. a low or despised family; (*ám*), n. 'that which has no pillars or support,' the ether, RV. ii, 15, 2; iv, 56, 3 & vii, 78, 1.

A-vaṅśya, mfn. not belonging to the family, Pat.

अवक *ávaka*, *as*, m. a grassy plant growing in marshy land (Blyxa Octandra Rich., otherwise called Śaivāla), MaitrS.; (*ā*), f. (gaṇa *kshipakâdi*, q. v.), id., VS.; TS.; ŚBr. &c. **Avakâdá**, mfn. eating the above plant, AV. iv, 37, 8–10. **Avákôlba**, mf(*ā*)n. covered or surrounded with Avakā plants, AV. viii, 7, 9.

Avakin, mfn. filled with Avakā plants, Comm. on KātyŚr.

अवकट *ava-kaṭa*, mfn. (formed like *ut-kaṭa*, *pra-kaṭa*, *vi-kaṭa*, *saṃ-kaṭa*), Pāṇ. v, 2, 30.

Ava-kaṭikā, f. dissimulation, L.

अवकर *ava-kara*. See *ava-*√1. *kṛī*.

अवकर्णय *ava-karṇaya*, Nom. P. °*yati*, not to listen or attend to, Kād.

अवकर्त *ava-karta*, &c. See *ava-*√2. *kṛit*.

अवकलित *ava-kalita*, mfn. (√2. *kal*), seen, observed, L.

अवकल्कन *ava-kalkana*, *am*, n. mingling, mixing together, L.

अवकल्पित *ava-kalpita*. See *ava-*√*klṛip*.

अवकाङ्क्ष् *ava-*√*kāṅksh*, to desire, long for, Car.; p. neg. *an-avakāṅkshamāṇa*, not wishing impatiently (said of ascetics who, having renounced all food, expect death without impatience), Jain.

अवकाश् *ava-*√*kāś*, *-kāśate*, to be visible, be manifest, ŚBr.: Caus. P. *-kāśayati* (fut. p. *-kāśayishyat*) to cause to look at, ŚBr.; KātyŚr.: Intens. p. *-cākaśat*, shining, AV. xiii, 4, 1; seeing, RV.; AV. xiii, 2, 12 (& vi, 80, 1).

Ava-kāśá, *as*, m. (ifc. f. *ā*) place, space; room, occasion, opportunity, (*avakāśam* √1. *kṛi* or *dā*, to make room, give way, admit, ŚBr. &c.; *avakāśam* √*labh* or *āp*, to get a footing, obtain a favourable opportunity, Śāk. &c.; to find scope, happen, take place; *avakāśam* √*rudh*, not to give way, hinder, Megh.); interval, aperture, Suśr. (°*śena*, instr. ind. between, PBr.); intermediate time, ŚBr.; 'a glance cast on anything,' N. of certain verses, during the recitation of which the eyes must be fixed on particular objects (which therefore are called *avakāśya*, q. v.), ŚBr.; KātyŚr. **-da**, mfn. giving opportunity, granting the use of (in comp.), Mn. ix, 271 & 278; Yājñ. ii, 276. **-vat** (*avakāśá-*), mfn. spacious, ŚBr.

Ava-kāśya, mfn. 'to be looked at,' admitted in the recitation of the Avakāśa verses, KātyŚr.

अवकिरण *ava-kiraṇa*. See *ava-*√1. *kṛī*.

Áva-kīrṇa, &c. See ib.

अवकीलक *ava-kīlaka*, *as*, m. a peg or plug, MBh. xiv, 1236.

अवकुञ्चन *ava-kuñcana*, *am*, n. curving, flexure, contraction, Suśr.

अवकुट् *ava-*√*kuṭ* (ind. p. *-kuṭya*) to break or cut into pieces, Suśr.

अवकुटार *ava-kuṭāra*, mfn. (cf. *ava-kaṭa*), Pāṇ. v, 2, 30.

Ava-kuṭārikā, f. = *ava-kaṭikā*, q. v., L.

अवकुण्ठन *ava-kuṇṭhana*, *am*, n. (= *ava-guṇṭhana*, q. v.) investing, surrounding, covering, Hcar.

Ava-kuṇṭhita, mfn. invested, surrounded, L.

अवकुत्स् *ava-*√*kuts*, to blame, revile, L.

Ava-kutsita, *am*, n. blame, censure, Nir. i, 4.

अवकुष् *ava-*√*kush*, to rub downwards, L.

अवकूज् *ava-*√*kūj* (Opt. *-kūjet*) to make a sound, utter (with *na*, neg. not to make any allusion to, be silent), MBh. xii, 4037.

अवकूल् *ava-*√*kūl*, to singe, burn, Suśr.

अवकृ *ava-*√1. *kṛi* (ind. p. *-kṛitvā* [*mukhāny*] *ava*) to direct downwards (as the face), BhP.

Ava-kṛita, mfn. directed downwards (as a root), Kathās.

Ava-kriyā, f. non-performance of prescribed acts, L.

अवकृत् *ava-*√2. *kṛit* (ind. p. *-kṛitya*) to cut off, ŚBr.; KātyŚr.; (p. *-kṛintat*) to destroy, MBh. i, 6810: Caus. (Opt. *-kartayet*) to cause to cut off, Mn. viii, 281.

Ava-karta, *as*, m. a part cut off, strip, N.

Ava-kartana, *am*, n. cutting off, N.

Ava-kartin. See *carmâvak°*.

Ava-karttṛi. See *carmâvak°*.

Ava-kṛitta, mfn. cut off, KātyŚr.; Suśr.

अवकृश् *ava-*√*kṛiś*, Caus. (3. pl. *-karśáyanti*) to emaciate, make lean or mean-looking, RV. vi, 24, 7.

अवकृष् *ava-*√*kṛish*, *-karshati* (ind. p. *-kṛishya*; once [MBh. xiii, 5007] Pass. Opt. *-kṛishyeta* in the sense of P. or Ā.) to draw off or away, take off (as a garment or wreath, &c.), MBh. &c.; to turn off, remove, KātyŚr.; to drag down (see *ava-kṛishṭa* below); to entice, allure, Kād.

Ava-karshaṇa, *am*, n. taking off, &c., L.

Ava-kṛishṭa, mfn. dragged down, being underneath anything (in comp.), Suśr.; 'removed,' being at some distance, KātyŚr.; (also compar. *avakṛishṭa-tara*, mfn. 'farther off from' [abl.], Comm. on APrāt.); inferior, low, outcast, Mn. vii, 126 & viii, 177; Yājñ. iii, 262, &c.

अवकॄ *ava-*√1. *kṝi*, *-kirati* (impf. *avâkirat*; ind. p. *-kīrya*) to pour out or down, spread, scatter, ĀśvGṛ. &c.; (Pot. *-kiret*) to spill one's semen virile, TĀr. (cf. *áva-kīrṇa* and °*ṛṇin* below); to shake off, throw off, leave, TBr.; MBh.; to bestrew, pour upon, cover with, fill, MBh. &c.: Pass. *-kīryate* (perf. *-cakre*, MBh. iii, 12306; according to Pāṇ. iii, 1, 87, Comm. also Ā. *-kirate*, aor. *avâkīrshṭa*) to extend in different directions, disperse, pass away, MBh. &c.: Ā. (aor. 3. pl. *avâkīrshata*) to fall off, become faithless, PBr.; (cf. *ava-*√*s-kṛī*.)

Ava-kara, *as*, m. dust or sweepings, Gaut. &c. **-kūṭa**, m. heap of sweepings, Kād.

Ava-kiraṇa, *am*, n. sweepings, Car.

Áva-kīrṇa, mfn. who has spilt his semen virile, i. e. violated his vow of chastity, TĀr.; poured upon, covered with, filled, MBh. i, 7840, &c.; (cf. *sapta-dvārâvakīrṇa*.) **-jaṭā-bhāra**, mfn. whose tresses of hair are scattered or have become loose, Daś.

Ava-kīrṇin, mfn. (= *áva-kīrṇa*) who has violated his vow of chastity, ĀśvŚr. &c.

अवकॢप् *ava-*√*klṛip*, *-kalpate*, to correspond to, answer, be right, TS. &c.; to be fit for, serve to (dat.), BhP.; Sarvad.: Caus. *-kalpayati*, to put in order, prepare, make ready, ŚBr. &c.; to employ becomingly, ŚBr.; to consider as possible, Pāṇ. iii, 3, 147, Sch.: Desid. of Caus. (impf. 3. pl. *avâcikalpayishan*) to wish to prepare or to make ready, AitBr.

Ava-kalpita, mfn. (gaṇa *śreṇy-ādi*, q. v.)

Ava-klṛipta, mfn. corresponding with, right, fit, ŚBr.; (*án-*, neg.), TS.; ŚBr.

Ava-klṛipti, *is*, f. considering as possible, Pāṇ. iii, 3, 145 (*an-*, neg.)

अवकेश *ava-keśa*, mfn. having the hair hanging down, AV. vi, 30, 2.

Ava-keśin, mfn. 'having its filaments (*keśa* = *kesara*, q. v.) turned downwards (so that they remain uncopulated),' unfruitful, barren (as a plant), L.

अवकोकिल *ava-kokila*, mfn. (= *avakrushṭaḥ kokilayā*) called down to by the koïl (singing in a tree above?), Pāṇ. ii, 2, 18, Comm.

अवकोल्ब *avâkôlba*. See *ávaka*.

अवक्तव्य *a-vaktavya*, mfn. not to be said, indescribable, NṛisUp. &c.

A-vaktṛi, mfn. who does not speak, MaitrUp.

A-vaktra, mf(*ā*)n. having no mouth (as a vessel), Suśr.

अवक्र *a-vakra*, mfn. not crooked, straight, ĀśvŚr. &c.; upright, honest.

अवक्रक्षिन् *ava-krakshin*, mfn. (cf. *krákshamāṇa*) rushing down, RV. viii, 1, 2.

अवक्रन्द् *ava-*√*krand* (Imper. *-krandatu*, 2. sg. *-kranda*; aor. 3. sg. *-cakradat*, 2. sg. *-cakradas*) to cry out, roar, RV.: Caus. (aor. *-acikradat*) to rush down upon (acc.) with a loud cry, RV. ix, 75, 3.

Ava-krandá, *as*, m. roaring, neighing, VS. xxii, 7 & xxv, 1.

Ava-krandana, *am*, n. crying, weeping aloud, L.

अवक्रम् *ava-*√*kram* (Opt. *-krāmet*) to step down upon (acc.), TĀr.; (aor. 3. pl. *-kramuḥ* [cf. Pāṇ. vi, 1, 116]; pr. p. *-krāmat*) to tread down, overcome, RV. vi, 75, 7 & vii, 32, 27; VS.; AV.; ŚBr.; to descend (into a womb), Buddh.; Jain.: Caus. (p. *-kramayat*) to cause to go down, KātyŚr.

Ava-kramaṇa, *am,* n. descending (into a womb), conception, Buddh.; Jain.
Ava-krānti, *is,* f. id., ib.
Ava-krāmin, mfn. running away, AV. v, 14, 10.

अवक्रिया *ava-kriyā.* See *ava-√1. kṛi.*

अवक्री *ava-√krī,* only Ā. *-krīṇīte* (Pāṇ. i, 3, 18; but also P. Pot. *-krīṇīyāt,* BṛĀrUp. [*apa-krīṇīyāt,* ŚBr. xiv]; ind. p. *-krīya,* ŚāṅkhŚr.) to purchase for one's self, hire, bribe.
Ava-kraya, *as,* m. letting out to hire, Yājñ. ii, 238; rent, revenue, Pāṇ. iv, 4, 50.

अवक्रीड् *ava-√krīḍ,* Ā. to play (?), L.

अवक्रुष्ट *ava-krushṭa,* mfn. 'called down to,' see *ava-kokila.*
Ava-krośa, *as,* m. a discordant noise, L.; an imprecation, L.; abuse, L.

अवक्लिन्नपक्व *avaklinna-pakva,* mfn. trickling because of being over-ripe, (gaṇa *rājadantâdi,* q. v.)
Ava-kloda, *as,* m. or **-kledana,** *am,* n. trickling, descent of moisture, L.; fetid discharge, L.

अवक्वण *ava-kvaṇa, as,* m. a discordant or false note, L.

अवक्वाथ *ava-kvātha, as,* m. imperfect digestion or decoction, L.

अवक्षर् *ava-√kshar,* Caus. (ind. p. *-kshārayitvā*) to cause to flow down upon (acc.), ĀśvGṛ.

अवक्षालन *ava-kshālana, am,* n. (√2. *kshal*) washing by immersion or dipping in.

अवक्षि *ava-√4. kshi* (Pot. *-kshiṇuyāt*) to remove, Lāṭy.; Kauś.: Pass. *-kshīyate,* to waste away, L.
Ava-kshaya, *as,* m. destruction, waste, loss, L.
Ava-kshayaṇa. See *aṅgārâvakshayaṇa.*
Ava-kshīṇa, mfn. wasted, emaciated, L.

अवक्षिप् *ava-√kship, -kshipati* (Subj. *-kshipát,* RV. iv, 27, 3; p. *-kshipát,* mfn., RV. x, 68, 4) to throw down, cause to fly down or away, hurl, RV. &c.; to revile, MBh. ii, 1337 (v. l. *apa* for *ava*); to grant, yield, MBh. xiii, 3030: Caus. (aor. Subj. 3. pl. *-cikshipan*) to cause to fall down, AV. xviii, 4, 12 & 13.
Ava-kshipta, mfn. thrown down; said sarcastically, imputed, insinuated, L.; blamed, reviled, L.
Ava-kshepa, *as,* m. blaming, reviling, scolding, Pāṇ. vi, 3, 73, Comm.
Ava-kshepaṇa, *am,* n. throwing down, overcoming, Pāṇ. i, 3, 32, &c.; reviling, blame, despising, Pāṇ. v, 3, 95 & vi, 2, 195; (*ī*), f. bridle, L.

अवक्षुत *ava-kshuta,* mfn. sneezed upon, Mn. iv, 213 & v, 125; MBh. xiii, 4367.

अवक्षुद् *ava-√kshud* (ind. p. *-kshudya*) to stamp or pound or rub to pieces, Suśr.

अवक्षै *ava-√kshai,* only p. p.
Ava-kshāṇa, mfn. burnt down, MaitrS.; TS.
Áva-kshāma, mfn. (cf. Pāṇ. viii, 2, 53) meagre, lean, AV. vi, 37, 3.
Ava-kshāyam, ind. so as to give a blow, ĀpŚr.

अवक्ष्णु *ava-√kshṇu* (1. sg. *-kshṇaumi*) to rub off, efface, RV. x, 23, 2.

अवखण्ड् *ava-√khaṇḍ, -khaṇḍayati,* to break into pieces, BhP.; Kād.; to annihilate, destroy, Comm. on BṛĀrUp.
Ava-khaṇḍana, *am,* n. breaking into pieces, Kād.; destroying, Comm. on BṛĀrUp.

अवखाद *ava-khādá, as,* m. 'a devourer, destroyer' [Gmn.], or mfn. 'devouring, destroying' [NBD.], RV. i, 41, 4.

अवख्या *ava-√khyā* (Imper. 2. pl. *-khyáta;* impf. *avâkhyat*) to look down, RV. viii, 47, 11; (with acc.) to see, perceive, RV. i, 161, 4 & x, 27, 3; TS.: Caus. *-khyāpayati,* to cause to look at, ŚBr.

अवगण् *ava-√gaṇ* (ind. p. *-gaṇayya*) to disregard, disrespect, Pañcat.
Ava-gaṇana, *am,* n. disregard, contempt, L.
Ava-gaṇita, mfn. disregarded, Pañcat.; despised, L.

अवगण *ava-gaṇa,* mfn. separated from one's companions, isolated, MBh. iii, 4057; (v. l. *ava-guṇa,* MBh. xiii, 5207.)

अवगण्ड *ava-gaṇḍa, as,* m. (= *yuva-gaṇḍa,* q. v.) a boil or pimple upon the face, L.

अवगथ *ava-gatha.* See *ava-√1. gā.*

अवगदित *ava-gadita,* mfn. unsaid, L.

अवगध *avagadha, ās,* m. pl., N. of a people, AitĀr.

अवगम् *ava-√gam, -gacchati* (Subj. *-gácchāt;* ind. p. *-gátya,* RV. vi, 75, 5; Ved. Inf. *áva-gantos,* TS.) to go down, descend to (acc. or loc.), RV.; AV.; (with acc.) to come to, visit, approach, RV.; AV.; ŚBr.; to reach, obtain, TS.; AitBr.; to get power or influence, TS.; to go near, undertake, MBh. v, 740; to hit upon, think of, conceive, learn, know, understand, anticipate, assure one's self, be convinced: to recognize, consider, believe any one (acc.) to be (acc.), MBh. iii, 2483, &c.: Caus. P. (3. pl. *-gamayanti;* Imper. 2. sg. *-gamaya*) to bring near, procure, AV. iii, 3, 6; TS.; to cause to know, teach, Mālav. &c.
Ava-gata, mfn. conceived, known, learnt, understood, comprehended; assented to, promised, L.
Ava-gati, *is,* f. conceiving, guessing, anticipating, Sāh.
Ava-gantavya, mfn. to be known or understood; intended to be understood, meant.
Áva-gantos. See s. v. *ava-√gam.*
Ava-gama, *as,* m. understanding, comprehension, intelligence, Bhag. ix, 2, &c.
Ava-gamaka, mfn. making known, conveying a sense, expressive of.
Ava-gamana, *am,* n. the making known, proclamation, L.
Ava-gamayitṛi, mfn. (fr. Caus.) one who procures, TS.
Ava-gamin, mfn. ifc. conceiving, understanding, BhP.
Ava-gamya, mfn. intelligible.

अवगर्हित *ava-garhita,* mfn. despised, R. ii, 21, 19 (v. l. *garhita*).

अवगल् *ava-√gal* (impf. *avâgalat*) to fall down, slip down, Śiś. viii, 34; Rājat.
Ava-galita, mfn. fallen down, BhP.

अवगल्भ् *ava-√galbh, -galbhate* or *-galbhāyate,* to be brave, valiant, Pāṇ. iii, 1, 11, Kāś.

अवगा *ava-√1. gā* (aor. Subj. *-gāt*) to pass away, be wanting, AV. xii, 3, 46; (aor. 2. sg. *-gās,* 3. sg. *avâgāt*) to go to, join with (instr.), RV. i, 174, 4; (acc.) KātyŚr.
Ava-gatha, mfn. bathed early in the morning, Uṇ.

अवगाण *avagāṇa, ās,* m. pl., N. of a people (the modern Afghāns), VarBṛS.

अवगाह् *ava-√gāh, -gāhate* (ind. p. *-gāhya,* Kum. i, 1, &c.; pr. p. P. *-gāhat,* R.; Ved. Inf. *-gāhe,* Pāṇ. iii, 4, 14, Kāś.) to plunge into, bathe in (loc.); to go deep into, be absorbed in (loc. or acc.)
Ava-gāḍha, mfn. immersed, bathed, plunged into (acc. [R.; Śak.]; loc. [Āp.; MBh. i, 5300]; rarely gen. [R. iv, 43, 32]); often in comp. [Śak.; Mṛicch.]); that in which one bathes, MBh. iii, 8236; deepened, low, Śak.; Suśr.; curdling (as blood), Suśr.; having disappeared, vanished, MBh. iv, 2238. **-vat,** mfn. bathing, plunging, diving.
Ava-gāha, *as,* m. plunging, bathing; a bucket, L.
Ava-gāhana, *am,* n. immersion, bathing.
Ava-gāhita, mfn. that in which one bathes (as a river), MBh. iii, 8230 & xiii, 1821.

अवगीत *ava-gīta,* mfn. (√*gai*), sung depreciatingly; sung of frequently, well known, trite, Rājat.; censured, blamable, despicable, vile, Hariv.; Kir. ii, 7; (*am*), n. satire in song, blame, censure, L.

अवगुण *ava-guṇa,* mfn. deficient in good qualities (see *ava-gaṇa*).

अवगुण्ठ् *ava-√guṇṭh, -guṇṭhayati* (ind. p. *-guṇṭhya*) to cover with, conceal, ŚāṅkhGṛ. &c.
Ava-guṇṭhana, *am,* n. hiding, veiling, Mṛicch.; Kād.; (often *kṛitâvaguṇṭhana,* 'enveloped in'); a veil, Sāh. &c.; a peculiar intertwining of the fingers in certain religious ceremonies, L.; sweeping, L. **-vat,** mfn. covered with a veil, Mālav.; Śak.
Ava-guṇṭhikā, f. a veil, L.
Ava-guṇṭhita, mfn. covered, concealed, veiled, screened, MBh.; Mn. iv, 49, &c. **-mukha,** mfn. having the face veiled.

अवगुण्डित *ava-guṇḍita,* mfn. pounded, ground, pulverulent, L.

अवगुर् *ava-√gur* (Pot. *-guret,* Mn. iv, 169; impf. *avâgurat,* BhP.; ind. p. *-gūrya,* Mn. iv, 165; xi, 206 & 208) to assail any one (loc. or dat.) with threats.
Ava-gūraṇa, *am,* n. rustling, roaring, Uttarar.
Ava-gūrṇa, mfn. assailed with threats, Pāṇ. viii, 2, 77, Sch.
Ava-gorana, *am,* n. menacing, Gaut. &c.
Ava-gorya, mfn. to be menaced, Pat.

अवगुह् *ava-√guh, -gūhati* [AV. xx, 133, 4; ŚBr.], °*te* [KātyŚr. &c.], to cover, hide, conceal, put into or inside; to embrace, VarBṛS.; Pañcat.
Ava-gūhana, *am,* n. hiding, concealing, KātyŚr.; embracing.

अवगॄ *ava-√gṛī,* only Ā. (Pāṇ. i, 3, 51 [p. *-giramāṇa,* Bhaṭṭ.; aor. *avâgīrshṭa,* Pāṇ. iii, 1, 87, Sch.], but P. Subj. *-garat,* AV. xvi, 7, 4) to swallow down: Intens. (Subj. 2. sg. *-jalgulas*), id., RV. i, 28, 1.
Ava-gīrṇa, mfn. swallowed down, Pat.

अवगै *ava-√gai.* See *ava-gīta.*

अवग्रह् *ava-√grah, -gṛihṇāti* (Pot. *-gṛihṇīyāt*) to let loose, let go, Lāṭy.; to keep back from (abl.), impede, stop, PBr.; Car.; Kād.; to divide, Suśr.; (in Gr.) to separate (as words or parts of a word), ŚāṅkhŚr. &c. (cf. *ava-grāham* below); to perceive (with one's senses), distinguish, Bhp.; Suśr.: Caus. (ind. p. *-grāhya*) to separate (into pieces).
1. **Ava-gṛihya,** mfn. (in Gr.) separable, Prāt. &c.
2. **Ava-gṛihya,** ind. p. having separated, laying hold with the feet (*pādābhyām*), Suśr.; forcibly, by force, Śiś. v, 49.
Ava-graha, *as,* m. separation of the component parts of a compound, or of the stem and certain suffixes and terminations (occurring in the Pada-text of the Vedas), Prāt. &c.; the mark or the interval of such a separation, Prāt.; the syllable or letter after which the separation occurs, VPrāt.; Pāṇ. viii, 4, 26; the chief member of a word so separated, Prāt.; obstacle, impediment, restraint, PBr. &c.; (= *varsha-pratibandha,* Pāṇ. iii, 3, 51) drought, Ragh.; Kathās.; nature, original temperament, L.; 'perception with the senses,' a form of knowledge, Jain.; an imprecation or term of abuse, L.; an elephant's forehead, L.; a herd of elephants, L.; an iron hook with which elephants are driven, L. **Avagrahântara,** n. (= *ava-graha*) the interval of the separation called Avagraha, RPrāt.
Ava-grahaṇa, *am,* n. the act of impeding or restraining, L.; disrespect, L.; (*ī*), f. = *gṛihâvagrahaṇī,* q. v., L.
Ava-grāha, *as,* m. obstacle, impediment (used in imprecations), Pāṇ. iii, 3, 45; (Pāṇ. iii, 3, 51; cf. also *ava-graha*) drought, Rājat.; (v. l. for *ava-gāha,* q. v.) a bucket, L.; (*am*), ind. so as to separate (the words), AitBr., (cf. *padâvagrāham*); the forehead of an elephant, L.

अवघटरिका *ava-ghaṭarikā,* f., N. of a musical instrument, ŚāṅkhŚr.; (cf. *ghāṭari.*)

अवघट्ट् *ava-√ghaṭṭ,* Caus. (p. *-ghaṭṭayat*) to push away, push open, R. v, 15, 10 (Gorresio); to push together, rub, Suśr.; to stir up, Car.; Suśr.
Ava-ghaṭṭa, *as,* m. a cave, cavern, L.
Ava-ghaṭṭana, *am,* n. pushing together, rubbing, Suśr.; coming into contact with each other, MBh. iv, 354.
Ava-ghaṭṭita, mfn. rubbed or pushed together, Hariv. 4720.

अवघात *ava-ghāta,* &c. See *ava-√han.*

अवघुष् *ava-√ghush* (Pass. impf. *-ghushyata*) to proclaim aloud, Hariv. 3522.
Ava-ghushita, mfn. approved of, Pāṇ. vii, 2, 23, Kāś.
Ava-ghushṭa, mfn. 'proclaimed aloud,' offered publicly (as food), MBh. xiii, 1576; (cf. *ghushṭânna* and *saṃghushṭa*); sent for, summoned, MBh. i, 5321; addressed aloud (to attract attention),

Hariv. 4696; filled with cries or noise, MBh. xiii, 522.

Ava-ghosha, *as*, m. See *jayâvaghosha*.

Ava-ghoshaṇa, *am*, n. proclaiming, L.

अवघूर्ण् *ava-√ghūrṇ* (p. *-ghūrṇamāna*) to move to and fro, be agitated, Daś.

Ava-ghūrṇa, mfn. shaking, agitated, BhP.

Ava-ghūrṇita, mfn. id., MBh. ix, 3239.

अवघृष् *ava-√ghṛish* (ind. p. *-ghṛishya*; 3. pl. *-ghṛishyanti* for Pass. °*shyante*) to rub off, rub to pieces, Suśr.; Pañcat.: Caus. (p. *-gharshayat*) to rub or scratch off, Suśr.; to rub with, ib.

Ava-gharshaṇa, *am*, n. rubbing off, scrubbing, Suśr.; Yājñ. iii, 60.

अवघोटित *ava-ghoṭita*, mfn. (√*ghuṭ*), (said of a palanquin) 'covered' or 'cushioned (?),' MBh. iii, 13155.

अवघ्रा *ava-√ghrā* (Imper. 2. pl. *-jighrata*; Pot. *-jighret* [TS.; Mn. iii, 218] or *-ghrāyāt* [ĀśvŚr.]; ind. p. *-ghrāya*) to smell at, VS. &c.; to touch with the mouth, kiss, PārGṛ. &c.: Caus. *-ghrāpayati*, to cause to smell at, TS.; ŚBr.; TBr.

Ava-ghra, mfn. 'kissing,' being in immediate contact with, ĀpŚr.; (*as*), m. (= *ava-ghrāṇa*) smelling at, ib.

Ava-ghrāṇa, *am*, n. smelling at, KātyŚr.; smelling, BhP.

Ava-ghrāta, mfn. kissed, R. ii, 20, 21.

Ava-ghrāpaṇa, *am*, n. causing to smell at, ĀpŚr.

Ava-ghrāyam, ind. so as to smell at, KātyŚr.

Ava-ghréya, mfn. to be smelt at, TBr.

अवच *avaca*, 'lower,' in *uccâvaca*, q. v.

अवचक्ष् *ava-√caksh*, Ā. *-cáshṭe* (impf. *-cakshata*; aor. 1. sg. *-acacaksham*, 2. sg. *-cakshi*; Ved. Inf. *-cákshe*) to look down upon, RV.; to perceive, RV. iv, 58, 5 (Inf. in Pass. sense: 'to be seen by') & v, 30, 2.

Ava-cakshaṇam, ind. (gaṇa *gotrâdi*, q. v.)

अवचत्नुक *avacatnuka* (*as*, m.?), N. of a country, AitBr.

अवचन *a-vacana*, *am*, n. absence of a special assertion, KātyŚr. &c.; (mfn.) not expressing anything, Jaim.; not speaking, silent, Śak. **-kara**, mfn. not doing what one is bid or advised.

A-vacanīya, mfn. not to be spoken, improper, Mn. viii, 269. **-tā**, f. or **-tva**, n. impropriety of speech.

A-vacas-kara, mfn. silent, not speaking.

अवचन्द्रमस *ava-candramasá*, *am*, n. disappearance of the moon, ŚBr.

अवचर् *ava-√car* (3. pl. *-caranti*) to come down from (abl.), RV. x, 59, 9: Caus. (Pot. *-cārayet*; ind. p. *-cārya*) to apply (in med.), Suśr.

Ava-cara, *as*, m. the dominion or sphere or department of (in comp., see *kāmâvacara*, *dhyānâv*°, &c.), Buddh.; (cf. *tālâvacara* & *yajñâvacará*.)

Ava-carantikā́, f. (dimin. of pr. p. f. °*ntī*) stepping down from (abl.), AV. v, 13, 9; (cf. *pravartamānaká*.)

Ava-cāraṇa, *am*, n. (in med.) application, Suśr.

Ava-cārita, mfn. (in med.) applied, Suśr.

अवचि 1. *ava-√*1. *ci* (p. *-cinvat*, MBh. iii, 13151; ind. p. *-citya*; Inf. *-cetum*, Kathās.) to gather, collect (as fruits from a tree, *vrikshaṃ phalāni* [double acc.], Pāṇ. i, 4, 51, Kāś.); (p. f. *-cinvatī*) to draw back or open one's garment, RV. iii, 61, 4.

Ava-caya, *as*, m. gathering (as flowers, fruits, &c.), Śak. &c.

Ava-cāyin, mfn. gathering, Kathās.

Ava-cicīshā, f. (Desid.) a desire to gather, Śiś. vi, 10.

Ava-cita, mfn. gathered.

अवचि 2. *ava-√*2. *ci* (3. pl. *-cinvanti*) to examine, MBh. iii, 10676 seq.

अवचूड *ava-cūḍa*, *as*, m. the pendent crest or streamer of a standard, Śiś. v, 13; (*ā*), f. a pendent tuft or garland (an ornament of peacock-feathers hanging down), Śiś. iii, 5.

Ava-cūla, *as*, m. = *ava-cūḍa*, m., Kād.

Ava-cūlaka, *am*, n. a chowrī or brush (formed of a cow's tail, peacock's feathers, &c., for warding off flies), L.

अवचूरि *ava-cūri*, *is*, or *-cūrikā*, f. a gloss, short commentary.

अवचूर्ण् *ava-√cūrṇ*, *-cūrṇayati* (ind. p. *-cūrṇya*) to sprinkle or cover with meal, dust, &c., Hariv.; Suśr.; (cf. Pāṇ. iii, 1, 25, Sch.)

Ava-cūrṇana, *am*, n. sprinkling with, Suśr.

Ava-cūrṇita, mfn. sprinkled with powder, &c., MBh. &c.; (with flowers) MBh. ii, 813.

अवचूल *ava-cūla*. See *ava-cūḍa*, col. 1.

अवचृत् *ava-√cṛit* (Pot. *-critét*) to let loose, TS.

अवच्छद् *ava-cchad* (√*chad*), *-cchādayati* (ind. p. *-cchādya*) to cover over, overspread, KātyŚr. &c.; to cover, conceal, Kād.; Kathās.; to obscure, leave in darkness, BhP.

Ava-cchada, *as*, m. a cover, R. iii, 56, 48.

Ava-cchanna, mfn. covered over, overspread, covered with (instr.), BhP.; Kād. &c.; filled (as with anger), MBh. xii, 5835.

अवच्छिद् *ava-cchid* (√*chid*), to refuse any one, Kād.: Pass. *áva-cchidyate*, to be separated from (abl.), TS.

Ava-cchinna, mfn. separated, detached, Lāṭy. &c.; (in logic) predicated (i. e. separated from everything else by the properties predicated), distinguished, particularised, Sarvad. &c.

Ava-ccheda, *as*, m. anything cut off (as from clothes), ĀśvŚr.; part, portion (as of a recitation), ib.; separation, discrimination; (in logic) distinction, particularising, determining; a predicate (the property of a thing by which it is distinguished from everything else). **Avacchedâvaccheda**, m. removing distinctions, generalising, L.

Ava-cchedaka, mfn. distinguishing, particularising, determining; (*as*), m. 'that which distinguishes,' a predicate, characteristic, property, L.

Ava-cchedana, n. cutting off, L.; dividing, L.; discriminating, distinguishing, L.

Ava-cchedya, mfn. to be separated.

अवच्छुरित *ava-cchurita* or °*taka*, *am*, n. a horse-laugh, L.

अवच्छो *ava-ccho* (√*cho*), (ind. p. *-cchāya*) to cut off; to skin, ŚBr.

Ava-cchāta, mfn. skinned, L.; reaped, KātyŚr.; emaciated (as by abstinence), Gaut.

Ava-cchita, mfn. skinned, L.; reaped, ŚBr.

अवजि *ava-√ji* (impf. *avâjayat*; ind. p. *-jitya*) to spoil (i. e. deprive of by conquest), win, MBh.; Mn. xi, 80, &c.; to ward off, MBh. xiii, 124; to conquer, MBh.: Desid. (p. *-jigīshat*) to wish to win or recover, ŚāṅkhŚr.

Ava-jaya, *as*, m. overcoming, winning by conquest, Ragh. vi, 62, &c.

Ava-jita, mfn. won by conquest, R. iii, 54, 6; contemned, L.

Ava-jiti, *is*, f. conquest, victory, Kir. vi, 43.

अवजृम्भ् *ava-√jṛimbh*, Ā. to yawn, Car.

अवज्ञा 1. *ava-√jñā*, *-jānāti* (ind. p. *-jñāya*; perf. Pass. *-jajñe*, Bhaṭṭ.) to disesteem, have a low opinion of, despise, treat with contempt, MBh. &c.; to excel, Kāvyād.

2. **Ava-jñā**, f. contempt, disesteem, disrespect (with loc. or gen.); (*ayā*), instr. ind. with disregard, indifferently, Kathās.; (cf. *sâvajñam*.) **Avajñôpahata**, mfn. treated with contempt, humiliated.

Ava-jñāta, mfn. despised, disrespected; given (as alms) with contempt, Bhag. xvii, 22.

Ava-jñāna, *am*, n. (Pāṇ. iii, 3, 55) = 2. *ava-jñā*, Ragh. i, 79; Hit.

Ava-jñeya, mfn. to be contemned, disesteemed, MBh. &c.; Yājñ. i, 153.

अवज्युत् *ava-√jyut*, Caus. *-jyotayati*, to light up or cause a light to shine upon, illumine, ŚBr.

Ava-jyotana, *am*, n. causing a light to shine upon, illumining, KātyŚr.

Ava-jyótya, ind. p. having lighted (a lamp), ŚBr.; KātyŚr.; ŚāṅkhŚr.

अवज्वल् *ava-√jval*, Caus. *-jvalayati* [ĀśvŚr.] or *-jvāl*° [Kauś.], to set on fire.

अवट *avaṭá*, *as*, m. a hole, vacuity in the ground, SV.; VS. &c.; a hole in a tooth, VarBṛS.; any depressed part of the body, a sinus, Yājñ. iii, 98; a juggler, L.; N. of a man, (gaṇa *gargâdi*, q. v.) **-kacchapa**, m. a tortoise in a hole (said of an inexperienced man who has seen nothing of the world), (gaṇa *pātresamitâdi*, q. v.) **-virodhana**, m. a particular hell, BhP. **Avaṭôdā**, f., N. of a river, BhP.

Avaṭi, *is*, m. a hole in the ground, L.

Avaṭu, *us*, m. f. the back or nape of the neck, Suśr.; a hole in the ground, L.; a well, L.; N. of a tree, L.; (*u*), n. a hole, rent, L. **-ja**, m. a hind curl, the hair on the back of the head.

Avaṭyà, mfn. being in a hole, VS. xvi, 38.

Avatá, *as*, m. a well, cistern, RV.; (cf. *avatká*.)

अवटङ्क *avaṭaṅka*, *as*, m., N. of a Prākrit poet.

अवटीट *ava-ṭīṭa*, mf(*ā*)n. flat-nosed, Pāṇ. v, 2, 31; (*am*), n. the condition of having a flat nose, ib., Sch.; (cf. *ava-nāṭa* & *ava-bhraṭa*.)

अवडङ्ग *avaḍaṅga* or *avadraṅga*, *as*, m. a market, mart, L.

अवडीन *ava-ḍīna*, *am*, n. (√*ḍī*), the flight of a bird, flying downwards, MBh. viii, 1899 & 1901.

अवत *avatá*. See above, s. v. *avaṭá*.

अवतंस *ava-taṇsa*, *as*, *am*, m. n. (ifc. f. *ā*), (√*taṇs*), a garland, ring-shaped ornament, ear-ornament, ear-ring, crest, R. &c. **Avataṇsī-√**1. **kṛi**, to employ as a garland, Kād.

Ava-taṇsaka, *as*, *am*, m. n. (ifc. f. *ā*), id., R. &c.; N. of a Buddhist text.

Ava-taṇsana, *am*, n. a garland, L.; pushing on a carriage, Car.

Ava-taṇsita, mfn. having a garland, L.; (cf. *śūlâvat*°.)

अवतक्षण *ava-takshaṇa*, *am*, n. (√*taksh*), anything cut in pieces (as chopped straw), Kauś.

अवतड् *ava-√taḍ*, Caus. *-tāḍayati*, to strike downwards, Nir. iii, 11.

अवतन् *ava-√tan*, *-tanoti* (ind. p. *-tatya*) to stretch or extend downwards, Kauś.; to overspread, cover, VarBṛS.; (Imper. 2. sg. P. *-tanu* [AV. vii, 90, 3] or *-tanuhi* [four times in RV.; cf. Pāṇ. vi, 4, 106, Comm.], Ā. *-tanushva*, RV. ii, 33, 14) to loosen, undo (especially a bowstring), RV.; AV.; ŚBr.

Áva-tata, mfn. extended downwards, AV. ii, 7, 3; Hariv.; overspread, canopied, covered, MBh. &c. **-dhanvan** (*ávatata-*), mfn. whose bow is unbent, VS. iii, 61.

Ava-tati, *is*, f. stretching, extending, L.

Ava-tāná, *as*, m. 'unbending of a bow,' N. of the verses VS. xiv, 54–63, ŚBr.; a cover (spread over climbing plants), MBh. ii, 355; R. v, 16, 28; N. of a man, Pāṇ. ii, 4, 67, Kāś.

अवतप् *ava-√tap*, *-tapati*, to radiate heat (or light) downwards, AV. xii, 4, 39: Caus. (ind. p. *-tāpya*) to heat or illuminate from above, MBh. v, 7162.

Ava-tapta, mfn. heated, L. **Avatapte-nakula-sthita**, n. an ichneumon's standing on hot ground (metaphorically said of a person's inconstancy), Pāṇ. ii, 1, 47, Sch.

Ava-tāpin, mfn. heated from above (by the sun), ŚBr.; KātyŚr.

अवतमस *ava-tamasa*, *am*, n. (Pāṇ. v, 4, 79) slight darkness, obscurity, Śiś. xi, 57.

अवतरम् *ava-tarám*. See 2. *áva*.

अवतर्पण *ava-tarpaṇa*, *am*, n. (√*tṛip*), a soothing remedy, Suśr.

अवतान्त *áva-tānta*, mfn. (√*tam*), fainting away, TS.

अवतुन्न *ava-tunna*, mfn. (√*tud*), pushed off, Car.

अवतूलय *ava-tūlaya*, Nom. P. °*yati* = *tūlair avakushṇāti*, L.

अवतृद् *ava-√tṛid*, *-tṛiṇatti*, to split, make holes through, Kāṭh.; to silence (as a drum), ŚāṅkhŚr.

Ava-tarda, *as*, m. splitting, perforation, KaushĀr.

Ava-tṛiṇṇa, mfn. split, having holes (*án-* neg. holeless, entire, uninjured, ŚBr.)

अवतृ *ava-√tṛī*, cl. 1. P. *-tarati* (perf. *-tatāra*, 3. pl. *-teruḥ*; Inf. *-taritum* [e.g. Hariv. 3511] or *-tartum* [e.g. MBh. i, 2509; R. vii, 30, 12]; ind. p. *-tīrya*) to descend into (loc. or acc.), alight from, alight (abl.), VS.; to descend (as a deity) in becoming incarnate, MBh.; to betake one's self to (acc.), arrive at, MBh.; to make one's appearance, arrive, Sarvad.; to be in the right place, to fit, TPrāt.; to undertake: Ved. cl. 6. P. (Imper. 2. sg. *-tira*; impf. *-átirat*, 2. sg. *-átiras*, 2. du. *-atiratam*; aor. 2. sg. *-tārīs*) to overcome, overpower, RV.; AV.: Ved. cl. 4. (p. fem. *-tīryatī*) to sink, AV. xix, 9, 8: Caus. *-tārayati* (ind. p. *-tārya*) to make or let one descend, bring or fetch down (acc. or loc.) from (abl.), MBh. &c.; to take down, take off, remove, turn away from (abl., Ragh. vi, 30), ib.; 'to set a-going, render current,' see *ava-tārita* below; to descend (?), AV. vii, 107, 1.

Ava-tara, *as*, m. descent, entrance, Śiś. i, 43; opportunity, Naish.

Ava-taraṇa, *am*, n. descending, alighting, R.; Śak.; 'rushing away, sudden disappearance,' or for *ava-tāraṇa*, see *bhārâvat°*; (cf. *stanyâvataraṇa*); translating, L. **-maṅgala**, n. 'auspicious act performed at the appearance (of a guest),' solemn reception.

Ava-taraṇikā, f. the introductory words of a work (e.g. *gaṇeśāya namaḥ*), Sāh.

Ava-taritavya, n. impers. to be alighted, Mṛicch.

Ava-tāra, *as*, m. (Pāṇ. iii, 3, 120) descent (especially of a deity from heaven), appearance of any deity upon earth (but more particularly the incarnations of Vishṇu in ten principal forms, viz. the fish, tortoise, boar, man-lion, dwarf, the two Rāmas, Kṛishṇa, Buddha, and Kalki, MBh. xii, 12941 seqq.); any new and unexpected appearance, Ragh. iii, 36 & v, 24, &c.; (any distinguished person in the language of respect is called an Avatāra or incarnation of a deity); opportunity of catching any one, Buddh.; a Tīrtha or sacred place, L.; translation, L. **-kathā**, f. 'account of an Avatāra,' N. of a chapter in Anantānandagiri's Śaṅkaravijaya. **-dvādaśa-kīrtana**, n. 'giving an account of the twelve Avatāras,' N. of a chapter of the work Ūrdhvāmnāya-saṃhitā. **-mantra**, m. a formula by which descent to the earth is effected, Kathās. **-vādâvalī**, f., N. of a controversial work by Purushottama.

Ava-tāraka, mfn. 'making one's appearance,' see *raṅgâvat°*.

Ava-tāraṇa, *am*, n. causing to descend, R. &c.; taking or putting off, Kād.; 'removing' (as a burden), see *bhārâvat°*; descent, appearance (= *ava-taraṇa*), MBh. i, 312 & 368; translation, L.; worship, L.; possession by an evil spirit, L.; the border of a garment, L.

Ava-tārita, mfn. caused to descend, fetched down from (abl.); taken down, laid down or aside, removed; set a-going, rendered current, accomplished, Rājat.

Ava-tārin, mfn. 'making one's appearance,' see *raṅgâvat°*; making a descent in the incarnation of (in comp.), RāmatUp.; ifc. appearing, Mālatīm.

Ava-titīrshu, mfn. intending to descend, Kathās.

Ava-tīrṇa, mfn. alighted, descended; got over (a disease), Kathās.; translated, L. **Avatīrṇarṇa** (*a-ṛi*), mfn. freed from debt, L.

अवतोका *áva-tokā*, f. a woman (or a cow, L.) miscarrying from accident, AV. viii, 6, 9 & VS. xxx, 15.

अवत्क *avatká*, *am*, n. (? fr. *avatá*, q. v.), a little hole (? 'a remedy,' NBD.), AV. ii, 3, 1.

अवत्त *áva-tta* & *ava-ttin*. See *ava-√do*.

अवत्तरम् *ávat-taram*. See *√av*.

अवत्रस्त *ava-trasta*, mfn. (*√tras*), terrified, Hariv. 2520 (v. l. *apa-dhvasta*).

अवत्विष् *ava-√tvish*, to glitter, shine, L.; to give, L.; to dwell, L.

अवत्सर् *ava-√tsar* (impf. *áva tsarat*) to fly away, RV. i, 71, 5.

Ava-tsārá, *as*, m., N. of a man (descendant of Kaśyapa [RAnukr.; ĀśvŚr.] and son of Prasravaṇa [KaushBr.]), RV. v, 44, 10.

अवत्सीय *a-vatsīya*, mfn. not suitable for a calf, Pāṇ. vi, 2, 155, Sch.

अवदंश *ava-daṅśa*, *as*, m. any pungent food (which excites thirst), stimulant, Hariv.; Suśr.

अवदत् *á-vadat*, mfn. not speaking, RV. x, 117, 7.

A-vadanta, *as*, m. 'not speaking,' a baby, L.

अवदत्त *ava-datta*, mfn. (*√1. dā*), Pāṇ. vii, 4, 47, Siddh.

अवदय् *ava-√day*, *-dayate* (1. sg. *-daye*) to give or pay a sum of money (for the purpose of silencing or keeping one off), AV. xvi, 17, 11; ŚBr.; PBr.

अवदल् *ava-√dal*, *-dalati*, to burst, crack asunder, Suśr.

Ava-dalita, mfn. burst, cracked, L.

अवदह् *ava-√dah* (impf. 2. sg. *ávâdahas*) 'to burn down from,' expel from (abl.) with heat or fire, RV. i, 33, 7; (ind. p. *-dahya*) to burn down, consume, Suśr.

Ava-dagdha, mfn. burnt down, Kauś.

Ava-dāgha, *as*, m. (gaṇa *nyaṅkv-ādi*, q. v.)

Ava-dāha, *as*, m. 'burning down,' the root of the fragrant grass Andropogon Muricatus, L. **Avadāhêshṭa**, n. id., L.

अवदात *ava-dāta*, mfn. (*√dai*), cleansed, clean, clear, Pāṇ. Sch.; Bhaṭṭ.; pure, blameless, excellent, MBh. &c.; of white splendour, dazzling white, ib.; clear, intelligible, Sāh.; (*as*), m. white colour, L.

1. **Ava-dāna**, *am*, n. a great or glorious act, achievement (object of a legend, Buddh.), Śak.; Ragh. xi, 21; Kum. vii, 48. (For 2. *ava-dāna* see *ava-√do*.)

अवदावद *a-vadāvada*, mfn. undisputed, uncontested, AitBr.

अवदिश् *ava-√diś* (Imper. 2. pl. *-didishṭana*) to show or practise (kindness &c.), RV. x, 132, 6: Caus. (aor. Subj. 1. sg. *-dediśam*) to inform, RV. viii, 74, 15.

अवदिह् *ava-√dih*, cl. 2. P. *-degdhi*, to besmear, Kauś.

अवदीप् *ava-√dīp* (p. *-dīpyamāna*) to burst out in a flame, ĀśvŚr.: Caus. to kindle, Kauś.; MānGṛ.

अवदुह् *ava-√duh* (aor. Subj. Ā. 3. sg. *-dhukshata*) to give milk to (dat.), RV. vi, 48, 13: Caus. *-dohayati*, to pour over with milk, Car.

Ava-doha, *as*, m. milk, L.

अवदृश् *ava-√dṛiś*, Pass. *-dṛiśyate*, to be inferred or inferrible, BhP.

अवदॄ *ava-√dṝī* (aor. Subj. *-darshat*, RV. ix, 74, 7; Pot. *-dṛiṇīyāt*, ŚBr.; ind. p. *-dīrya*, Suśr.) to split or force open, to rend or tear asunder: Caus. (Pot. *-dārayet*; p. *-dārayat*) to cause to burst, rend or split, R. vi, 4, 22; Ragh. xiii, 3: Pass. *-dīryate*, to be split, burst, ŚBr. &c.

Ava-daraṇa, *am*, n. breaking (as a boil &c.), bursting, separating, Suśr.

Ava-dāra, *as*, m. 'breaking through,' acc. *°ram* with *√i*, to break or burst through, VarBṛS.

Ava-dāraka, mfn. splitting open, i. e. digging (the earth), L.

Ava-dāraṇa, mfn. breaking, shattering in pieces, MBh. i, 1179; (*am*), n. breaking, shattering, Sāh.; breaking open, bursting open, R. ii, 77, 16; Suśr.; 'opening (the ground),' a spade or hoe, L.

Ava-dārita, mfn. rent or burst open, MBh. &c.

Ava-dīrṇa, mfn. torn, rent, MBh. &c.; melted, liquefied, L.; 'bewildered,' see *bhayâvadīrṇa*.

अवदो *ava-√do*, *-dyati* (ind. p. *-dāya*, ĀśvGṛ.; BhP.) Ved. to cut off, divide (especially the sacrificial cake and other objects offered in a sacrifice), ŚBr. &c.; to cut into pieces, BhP.; (aor. Pot. Ā. 1. sg. *-dishīya* [derived fr. *ava-√1. dā*, 'to present,' by Gmn.]; perhaps fr. *ava-√day* above) to appease, satisfy with (instr.), RV. ii, 33, 5.

Áva-tta, mfn. cut off, divided, VS. xxi, 43, &c.; (cf. *catur-avattá*, *pañcâvatta*, & *yathâvattam*.)

Avattin, mfn. (after a cardinal num.) 'dividing into so many parts,' see *catur-av°* & *pañcâv°*.

2. **Ava-dāna**, *am*, n. cutting or dividing into pieces, ŚBr. &c.; a part, portion, ŚBr.; KātyŚr.; = *ava-dāha* (see s.v. *ava-√dah*), L.

Avadānīyá, *am*, n. particle or portion (of meat), Kāṭh.; TBr.

Avadānya, mfn. (cf. *abhy-avad°*) 'niggardly,' (gaṇa *cārv-ādi*, q. v.)

Ava-deya, mfn. to be divided, Comm. on Nyāyam.

Ava-dyat, mfn. (pr. p.) breaking off, Kir. xv, 48.

अवदोह *ava-doha*. See *ava-√duh*.

अवद्य *a-vadyá*, mfn. (Pāṇ. iii, 1, 101) 'not to be praised,' blamable, low, inferior, RV. iv, 18, 5 & vi, 15, 12; BhP.; disagreeable, L.; (*ám*), n. anything blamable, want, imperfection, vice, RV. &c.; blame, censure, ib.; shame, disgrace, RV.; AV. **-gohana**, mfn. concealing imperfection, RV. i, 34, 3. **-pa**, see *mithó-avadya-pa*. **-bhí**, f. fear of vices or sin, RV. x, 107, 3. **-vat** (*avadyá-*), mfn. disgraceful, lamentable, AV. vii, 103, 1.

अवद्युत् *ava-√dyut*, Caus. *-dyotayati*, to illustrate, show, indicate, Comm. on BṛĀrUp.

Ava-dyotaka, mfn. illustrating, making clear, Comm. on Nyāyad.

Ava-dyótana, *am*, n. illustrating, ib.

Ava-dyotin, mfn. = *-dyotaka*.

अवद्रङ्ग *avadraṅga*. See *avadaṅga*.

अवद्रै *ava-√drai* (fut. p. *-drāsyát*) to fall asleep, ŚBr.; (cf. *an-avadrāṇá*.)

अवध *a-vadhá*, mfn. (*√vadh*), not hurting, innoxious, beneficent [Gmn.; 'indestructible,' NBD.], RV. i, 185, 3; (*as*), m. the not striking or hurting, Gaut.; absence of murder, Mn. v, 39. **A-vadhârha**, mfn. not worthy of death, L.

A-vadhyá, mfn. not to be killed, inviolable, VS. viii, 46; Mn. ix, 249, &c. **-tā** (*avadhyá-*), f. inviolability, ŚBr. &c. **-tva**, n. id., R.; Ragh. x, 44.

A-vadhrá, mfn. innoxious, beneficent, RV. vii, 82, 10.

अवधम् *ava-√dham*, *-dhamati*, (said of spirituous liquor) to stir up (as the parts of the body), Car.: Pass. to shake, tremble, shudder, Bhpr.

अवधर्ष्य *ava-dharshya*. See *an-avadh°*.

अवधा *ava-√dhā*, P. (aor. 3. pl. *-ádhuḥ*, RV.; Imper. 2. sg. *-dhehi* & perf. 3. pl. *-dadhuḥ*, AV.; ind. p. *-dhāya*; rarely Ā., e.g. perf. *-dadhe*, MBh. i, 4503) to place down, plunge into (loc.), deposit, RV. i, 158, 5 & ix, 13, 4, &c.; to place or turn aside, ŚBr.: Pass. (Imper. *-dhīyatām*) to be applied or directed (as the mind), Hit.: Caus. (Pot. *-dhāpayet*) to cause to put into (loc.), ĀśvGṛ.

Ava-dhātavya, *am*, n. impers. to be attended to.

Ava-dhāna, *am*, n. attention, attentiveness, intentness, Kum. iv, 2; Śiś. ix, 11, &c.; (cf. *sâvadhāna*.) **-tā**, f. [Pañcat.] or **-tva**, n. [L.] attentiveness.

Avadhānin, mfn. 'attentive,' (gaṇa *ishṭâdi*, q. v.)

Ava-dhí, *is*, m. attention, L.; a term, limit, ŚBr. &c.; conclusion, termination, Kum. iv, 43; Kathās. &c.; surrounding district, environs, neighbourhood, Pāṇ. iv, 2, 124; a hole, pit, L.; period, time, L.; (*i*), ind. until, up to (in comp.), Kathās.; (*es*), abl. ind. until, up to, as far as, as long as (gen. [Megh.], or in comp.) **-jñāna**, n. 'perception extending as far as the furthest limits of the world,' i. e. the faculty of perceiving even what is not within the reach of the senses, N. of the third degree of knowledge, Jain. **-jñānin**, mfn. having the above knowledge, Jain. **-mat**, mfn. limited, bounded, Pāṇ. v, 3, 35, Sch.

Ava-dhīyámāna, mfn. (Pass. p.) being confined within (acc., ? AV. xii, 5, 30; or loc., R. v, 11, 13).

Ava-dheya, *am*, n. = *-dhātavya*, q. v., Hcat.

Áva-hita, mfn. plunged into (loc.); fallen into (as into water or into a hole of the ground), RV. i, 105, 17 & x, 137, 1, &c.; placed into, confined within, ŚBr. &c.; (gaṇa *pravṛiddhâdi*, q. v.) attentive, R. &c. **-tā**, f. application, attention, L. **Avahitâñjali**, mfn. with joined hands, L.

अवधाव् *ava-√1. dhāv*, *-dhāvati*, to run down, drop down from (abl.), RV. i, 162, 11 & AV. ii, 3, 1.

अवधी *ava-√dhī* (impf. *-didhet*) to watch or lie in wait for (dat.), RV. x, 144, 3.

अवधीर् *ava-√dhīr* (ind. p. *-dhīrya*) to disregard, disrespect, repudiate, Śiś. ix, 59; Kathās.; Hit.

Ava-dhīraṇa, *am*, n. or °**nā**, f. treating with disrespect, repudiating, Śak.; Ragh. viii, 47.

Ava-dhīrita, mfn. disrespected, disregarded, Śak. &c.; surpassed, excelled, Sāh.

Ava-dhīrin, mfn. despising, L.; excelling, Daś.

अवधू *ava-√dhū*, Ved: P. (Imper. 2. sg. *-dhūnuhi*, 2. pl. *-dhūnutā*) to shake off or out or down, RV. x, 66, 14 & 134, 3; KātyŚr. &c.: Ā. (2. sg. *-dhūnushé*; impf. 2. sg. *-dhūnuthās*; aor. *-adhūshata*; perf. Pot. *-dudhuvīta*; p. *-dhūnvānā*) to shake off (as enemies or evil spirits or anything disagreeable), frighten away, RV.; AV.; ŚBr.: Caus. (Pot. *-dhūnayet*) to shake, Mn. iii, 229.

Áva-dhūta, mfn. shaken off (as evil spirits), VS. i, 14; removed, shaken away, BhP. &c.; discarded, expelled, excluded, MBh. &c.; disregarded, neglected, rejected, Daś. &c.; touched, R. vi, 82, 62; shaken, agitated (especially as plants or the dust by the wind), fanned, MBh. &c.; that upon which anything unclean has been shaken out or off (cf. *ava-kshuta*), Mn. v, 125; MBh. xiii, 1577; unclean, BhP.; one who has shaken off from himself worldly feeling and obligation, a philosopher (*brahma-vid*), BhP.; Rājat.; (*as*), m., N. of a Śaiva philosopher; (*am*), n. rejecting, repudiating, MBh. iv, 352 (= Hariv. 4717). **-praṇipāta**, mf(*ā*)n. rejecting an act of homage, Vikr. **-vesha**, mfn. 'wearing unclean clothes' or 'wearing the clothes of one who is rejected,' or 'having discarded clothes,' BhP.

Ava-dhūnana, *am*, n. shaking, causing to shake, MBh. viii, 4380; Mn. iii, 230, &c.; agitation, shaking (of the earth), Car.

Ava-dhūya, ind. p. shaking off, rejecting, discarding, MBh. &c.; disregarding, Comm. on Śiś. v, 5.

अवधूक *a-vadhū-ka*, mfn. having no wife, L.

अवधूपित *ava-dhūpita*, mfn. perfumed with incense, R. ii, 83, 16 (v. l.)

अवधूलन *ava-dhūlana*, *am*, n. (cf. *dhūli*) scattering over, strewing, Bhpr.

Ava-dhūlita, mfn. scattered over, covered, Śārṅg.

अवधृ *ava-√dhṛi*, Caus. *-dhārayati* (ind. p. *dhārya*; Pass. *-dhāryate*) to consider, ascertain, determine accurately, limit, restrict, MBh. &c.; to hear, learn, ib.; to conceive, understand, make out, become acquainted with, ib.; to reflect upon, think of (acc. or a phrase with *iti*), Śak. (Prākṛit ind. p. *odhāria*), Pañcat. &c.; to communicate, Kathās.: Pass. *-dhriyate*, to be ascertained, be certain, Comm. on BṛĀrUp.

Ava-dhāra, *as*, m. accurate determination, limitation, Suśr.

Ava-dhāraka, mfn. determining; bearing upon, meaning; restricting, TPrāt.

Ava-dhāraṇa, *am*, n. ascertainment, affirmation, emphasis; stating or holding with positiveness or assurance; accurate determination, limitation (of the sense of words), restriction to a certain instance or instances with exclusion of any other, VPrāt.; Pāṇ. ii, 1, 8; viii, 1, 62, &c.; (mfn.) restrictive, L.

Ava-dhāraṇīya, mfn. to be ascertained, determined or known, (*an-*, neg.) Ragh. xiii, 5; to be considered as ascertained or determined, Hariv. 6252; to be restricted to (instr.)

Ava-dhārita, mfn. ascertained, known, certain; heard, learnt, Mālav. &c.; (ifc. with *śreṇy-ādi*) 'known as,' (gaṇa *kṛitâdi*, q. v.)

Avadhāritin, mfn. (gaṇa *ishṭâdi*, q. v.)

Ava-dhārya, mfn. to be ascertained or known; 'to be made out or understood,' see *dur-avadh°*.

Ava-dhṛita, mfn. ascertained, determined, certain, KaushBr. &c.; heard, learnt, MBh. xiii, 3544; understood, made out, Comm. on Mn. iii, 135; (*āni*), n. pl. (in Sāṅkhya phil.) the organs of senses.

अवधृष्य *ava-dhṛishya*. See *an-avadh°*.

अवध्य *a-vadhyá*. See *a-vadhá*.

अवध्यै *ava-√dhyai* (perf. *-dadhyau*) to think ill of (acc.), disregard, BhP.

Ava-dhyāta, mfn. disregarded, R. i, 25, 12; BhP.; Car.

Ava-dhyāna, *am*, n. disregard, BhP.

Ava-dhyāyin, mfn. disregarding (ifc.), BhP.

Ava-dhyeya, mfn. to be disregarded, BhP.

अवध्र *a-vadhrá*. See *a-vadhá*.

अवध्वंस् *ava-√dhvaṅs*, Ā. (perf. *-dadhvase*) to be scattered or dispersed, RV. x, 113, 7; *-dhvaṅsate*, to sprinkle, strew with (instr.), Pāṇ. iii, 1, 25, Siddh.: Caus. *-dhvaṅsayati*, id., Pāṇ. iii, 1, 25, Sch.

Ava-dhvaṅsá, *as*, m. sprinkling, L.; meal, dust, AV. v, 22, 3; abandoning, L.; despising, disrespect, L.

Ava-dhvasta, mfn. sprinkled, Kauś.; spotted, stippled, ĀśvŚr.; abandoned, L.; despised, L.; (cf. *apa-dhvasta*.)

अवन *avana*. See *√av*.

अवनक्ष् *ava-√naksh* (2. du. *-nakshathas*) to overtake any one (gen.), RV. i, 180, 2.

अवनक्षत्र *ava-nakshatra*, *am*, n. disappearance of the luminaries, Kauś.

अवनम् *ava-√nam* (p. *-namat*; ind. p. *-namya*) to bow, make a bow to, BhP.; Śiś. ix, 74; Kathās.; (perf. Ā. 3. pl. *-nanāmire*) to bow down (as the head), MBh. i, 5336: Caus. (ind. p. *-nāmya*) to bend down, MBh. iii, 10043; Hariv. 3685; to bend (a bow), MBh. viii, 4606.

Ava-nata, mfn. bowed, bent down, MBh. &c.; bending, stooping; deepened, not projecting, R. vi, 23, 12, &c. **-kāya**, mfn. bending the body, crouching down. **-mukha**, mfn. with downcast countenance. **-śīrshan**, mfn. bowing the head. **Avanatânana**, mfn. = *avanata-mukha* above, MBh. i, 6121. **Avanatôttarakāya**, mfn. bowing the upper part of the body, Ragh. ix, 60.

Ava-nati, *is*, f. setting (of luminaries), Śiś. ix, 8; bowing down, stooping, L.; parallax, VarBṛS.; Sūryas.

Ava-namra, mf(*ā*)n. bowed, bent, Kum. iii, 54; Kathās.

Ava-nāma, *as*, m. bending, bowing, L.

Ava-nāmaka, mfn. what depresses or causes to bow or bend, L.

Ava-nāmita, mfn. bent down, MBh. i, 7586, &c.; (cf. *an-avanāmita-vaij°*.)

Ava-nāmin, mfn. being bent down (as the branches of a tree), MBh. i, 2855 & iii, 11059; Hariv. 4947.

अवनर्द् *ava-√nard* (Pot. *-nardet*) to slur or trill (a term applicable to chanting in the Hindū ritual), PBr.; (cf. *ni-√nard*.)

अवनश् *ava-√2. naś* (perf. 3. pl. *-neśuḥ*) to disappear, perish, MBh. iv, 1728.

अवनह् *ava-√nah* (ind. p. *-nahya*) to cover with (instr.), KātyŚr.

Áva-naddha, mfn. bound on, tied, covered with (instr. or in comp.), AV. &c.; (cf. *carmâvanaddha*); (*am*), n. a drum, L.

Ava-nāha, *as*, m. binding or putting on, L.

अवनाट *ava-nāṭa*, mf(*ā*)n. = *ava-ṭīṭa*, q. v., Pāṇ. v, 2, 31. **-nāsika**, mfn. flat-nosed, Hcar.

अवनि *aváni*, *is*, f. course, bed of a river, RV.; stream, river, RV.; the earth, Naigh.; R.; Pañcat. &c.; the soil, ground, Megh.; any place on the ground, Sūryas.; (*ayas*), f. pl. the fingers, Naigh. **-m-gata**, mfn. prostrate on the ground. **-cara**, mfn. roving over the earth, vagabond. **-ja**, m. 'son of the earth,' the planet Mars, VarBṛ. **-pa**, m. 'lord of the earth,' a king, VarBṛS. **-pati**, m. id., Ragh. x, 87; Pañcat. **-pāla**, m. 'protector of the earth,' a king, Bhag.; Ragh. xi, 93. **-pālaka**, m. id. **-bhṛit**, m. 'earth-supporter,' a mountain, a king, Naish. **-maṇḍala**, n. globe of the earth. **-ruh** [L.] or **-ruha** [Daś.], m. 'grown from the earth,' a tree. **-suta**, m. = *-ja* above, VarBṛS. **Avanīśa** or **avanīśvara**, m. 'lord of the earth,' a king, VarBṛS.

1. **Avanī**, f. the earth, R.; Pañcat. **-dhara**, m. 'earth-upholder,' a mountain. **-dhra**, m. id., MBh. xiii, 1847 seq. **-pati**, m. = *avani-p°* above, Kathās. **-pāla**, m. = *avani-p°* above, BhP. **-bhṛit**, m. (= *avani-bh°* above) a king, Naish.

अवनिज् *ava-√nij* (ind. p. *-nijya*; perf. Ā. *-nije* for *-ninije*) to wash (especially the feet), BhP.: Ā. *-nenikte* (1. sg. *-nenije*) to wash one's self, ŚBr.; AitBr.; ŚāṅkhGṛ.: Caus. *-nejayati*, to cause to wash, ŚBr.; KātyŚr.; PārGṛ.

Ava-nikta, mfn. washed, BhP.

Ava-nektṛi. See *pādâvan°*.

Ava-nega. See *prātar-avanegá*.

Ava-négya, mfn. serving for washing, ŚBr.

Ava-neja. See *pādâvan°*.

Ava-néjana, mf(*ī*)n. washing, serving for washing (the feet), BhP.; (*am*), n. ablution (of hands [ŚBr.] or feet [Mn. ii, 209; BhP.]); water for washing (hands [AV. xi, 3, 13] or feet, cf. *pādâvan°*).

Ava-nejya. See *pādâvan°*.

अवनिनी *ava-ni-√nī* (ind. p. *-nīya*) to put or bring into (water), ŚāṅkhŚr.; ŚāṅkhGṛ.; to pour down, ŚāṅkhGṛ.

अवनिश्चय *ava-niścaya*, *as*, m. inference, deduction, ascertainment, L.

अवनिष्ठिव् *ava-ni-√shṭhiv* (p. *-shṭhīvat*) to spit upon, Mn. viii, 282.

Ava-nishṭhīvana, *am*, n. spitting upon, L.

अवनी 2. *ava-√nī* (fut. 2. sg. *-neshyasi*) to lead or bring down into (water), ŚBr.; to put into (loc.), Gobh.; *-nayati*, Ved. to pour down or over, AV.; VS. &c.

Ava-naya, *as*, m. = *ava-nāya*, L.

Ava-nayana, *am*, n. = *ava-nāya*, L.; pouring down, ĀśvŚr.; KātyŚr.

Ava-nāya, *as*, m. (Pāṇ. iii, 3, 26) placing down, L.

Áva-nīta, mfn. led or pushed down into (loc.), RV. i, 116, 8 & 118, 7.

Ava-nīya, mfn. to be poured out or down, TS.

Ava-nīyamāna, mfn. (Pass. p.) being led down into water (as a horse), KātyŚr.

Ava-neya, mfn. to be led away, R. vii, 46, 9.

अवनु *ava-√3. nu*, Ā. (3. pl. *-navante*) to move towards (acc.), RV. ix, 86, 27.

अवन्तक *avantaka*, *ās*, m. pl., N. of a people, VarBṛS.; N. of a Buddhist school.

Avanti, *ayas*, m. pl., N. of a country and its inhabitants, MBh. vi, 350; VarBṛS. &c.; (*is*), m., N. of a river. **-khaṇḍa**, n. a portion of the Skanda-purāṇa. **-deva**, m. (= *-varman*, q. v.) N. of a king, Rājat. **-nagarī**, f. the city of the Avantis, Oujein, Kād. **-pura**, n. id., Hariv. 4906; N. of a town in Kāśmīra, built by Avantivarman, Rājat.; (*ī*), f. Oujein, Mṛicch. **-brahma**, m. a Brāhman living in the country of the Avantis, Pāṇ. v, 4, 104, Kāś. **-bhūpāla**, m. the king of Avanti, i. e. Bhoja. **-vatī**, f., N. of the wife of Pālaka, Kathās. **-vardhana**, m., N. of a son of Pālaka, ib. **-varman**, m., N. of a king, Rājat.; of a poet, Śārṅg. **-sundarī**, f., N. of a woman, Daś. **-sena**, m., N. of a man, Kād. **-soma**, m. sour gruel (prepared from the fermentation of rice-water), L. **-svāmin**, m., N. of a sanctuary built by Avantivarman, Rājat. **Avantīśvara**, m. id., ib. **Avanty-aśmaka**, n. sg. or *ās*, m. pl. the Avantis and the Aśmakas, (gaṇa *rājadantâdi* and *kārtakaujapâdi*, q. v.)

Avantikā, f. the modern Oujein (one of the seven sacred cities of the Hindūs, to die at which secures eternal happiness); the language of the Avantis, Sāh.

Avantī, f. (Pāṇ. iv, 1, 65, Sch.) Oujein, N. &c.; the queen of Oujein, Pāṇ. iv, 1, 176, Sch.; (cf. *āvantya*); (= *avanti*) N. of a river. **-deśa**, m. the region of Avanti. **-nagara**, n. the city Avanti, Kād. **-saras**, n., N. of a Tīrtha, SkandaP.

अवन्ध्य *a-vandhya*, mf(*ā*)n. = 2. *a-bandhya*, q. v.; (*as* or *am* and *ā*), m. or n. and f., N. of a place.

अवपट् *ava-√paṭ* (ind. p. *-pāṭya*) to split, tear into pieces, Suśr.; Kād.: Pass. *-pāṭyate*, to crack, flaw, split, Suśr.

Ava-pāṭikā, f. laceration of the prepuce, Suśr.

अवपत् *ava-√pat* (p. *-pátat*, RV. x, 97, 17; ind. p. *-patya*, see *ava-pāta*; impf. *avâpatat*, MBh. &c.) to fly down, jump down, fall down: Caus. (p. *-pātayat*) to throw down, Kathās.

Ava-patana, *am*, n. falling down; (cf. *avarâvap°*.) Jaina Prākṛit *ovaḍaṇa*, see *śastrâvapāta*.

Ava-patita, mfn. fallen down from (in comp.), R. ii, 28, 12; that upon which anything (in comp.) has fallen down (see *keśa-kīṭâvap°*); (said of the voice) unclear, (*an-*, neg.) Car.

Ava-pāta, *as*, m. falling down, Mṛicch.; (*an-*, neg.) AitBr.; (cf. *śastrâvap°*); descent, descending upon; flying down, Hit.; a hole or pit for catching game in, Ragh. xvi, 78; (*am*), ind. with *ava-patya* (ind. p.), falling or flying down like (in comp.)

Ava-pātana, *am*, n. felling, knocking or throwing down, Mn. xi, 64; Yājñ. ii, 223; BhP.; (in dramatical language) a scene during which a person enters the stage in terror but leaves it at the end in good humour, Sāh.

अवपद् *ava-√pad, -padyate* (Subj. P. *-padāti*, RV. ix, 73, 9; Prec. Ā. 3. sg. *-padīshṭa*, RV. vii, 104, 17; aor. Subj. Ā. 3. sg. *-pādi*, RV. i, 105, 3; Ved. Inf. (abl.) *-pádas*, RV. ii, 29, 6) Ved. to fall down, glide down into (acc.), RV. &c.; (Imper. Ā. 3. pl. *-padyantām*; Subj. P. 2. sg. *-patsi*; Pot. P. 1. sg. *-padyeyam*) to drop from (abl.), be deprived of (abl.), AV.; AitBr.; PBr.; (Subj. Ā. 1. sg. *-padyai*) to fall, meet with an accident, AitBr.; (fut. 3. pl. *-patsyanti*) to throw down, Kāṭh.: Caus. (Imper. 2. sg. *-pādaya*; ind. p. *-pādya*) to cause to glide or go down, AV.; Suśr.

Ava-panna, mfn. fallen down, that upon which anything has fallen down, MārkP.; see *keśa-kīṭāvap°* and *kīṭâvap°*; 'fallen down,' see *svayam-avapanná*.

Ava-pādá, *as*, m. falling, TBr.; Kāṭh.

अवपश् *ava-√paś*, P. *-paśyati* (2. pl. *-paśyata*; p. *-páśyat*) to look down upon (acc.), RV.; AV. xviii, 4, 37: Ā. *-paśyate*, to look upon, AV. ix, 4, 19.

अवपाक *a-vapā-ka*, mfn. having no omentum (cf. *vapā́*), ŚBr.; KātyŚr.

अवपात्रित *ava-pātrita*, mfn. a person not allowed by his kindred to eat or drink from the same vessel; (cf. *apa-pātrita*.)

अवपान *ava-pā́na*, *am*, n. drinking, RV. i, 136, 4 & x, 43, 2; a pond or pool for watering, RV. vii, 98, 1; viii, 4, 10 & x, 106, 2.

अवपाशित *ava-pāśita*, mfn. having a snare laid upon, snared, R. iii, 59, 18 & vii, 6, 59.

अवपिण्डित *ava-piṇḍita*, mfn. (said of dew-drops) fallen down in the shape of little globules (*piṇḍa*, q.v.), Kathās.

अवपिष् *ava-√pish* (ind. p. *-pishya*) to crush or grind into pieces, grind, Suśr.

अवपीड् *ava-√pīḍ* (ind. p. *-pīḍya*) to press down, compress, MBh. i, 6292; (Pot. *-pīḍayet*) to press out (as a wound), Suśr.

Ava-pīḍa, *as*, m. pressing down, Suśr.; one of the five sternutatories or drugs producing sneezing, Suśr.; Bhpr.

Ava-pīḍaka, *as*, m. (= *-pīḍa*) a sternutatory, Car.

Ava-pīḍana, *am*, n. the act of pressing down, Suśr.; pressing down (the eye-lids), Comm. on Nyāyad.; a sternutatory, Suśr.; (*ā*), f. damage, violation, Mn. viii, 287.

Ava-pīḍita, mfn. pressed down, thrown down, MBh. xiv, 1944; pressed, oppressed; pressed out (as a wound), Suśr.

अवपुञ्जित *ava-puñjita*, mfn. collected into small heaps (as sweepings).

अवपुथ् *ava-√puth*, Caus. (p. *-pothayat*; Pot. *-pothayet*) to throw or knock down, Hariv.

Ava-pothikā, f. anything used for knocking down, as stones &c. thrown from the walls of a city on the besiegers, MBh. iii, 641.

Ava-pothita, mfn. thrown or knocked down, MBh. vi, 5505; Hariv.

अवपूर्ण *ava-pūrṇa*, mfn. filled with (in comp.), Hariv. 11993; VarBṛS.

अवप्रज्जन *ava-prajjana*, *am*, n. (√*prij*), the end of the warp of a web (opposed to 2. *pra-vayaṇa*, q.v.), AitBr.

अवप्रस्नुत *ava-pra-snuta* or *-sruta*, mfn. wetted by the fluid excretion (of a bird), KātyŚr.

अवप्लु *ava-√plu*, Ā. (perf. *-pupluve*) to jump down (as from a cart), MBh. vii, 5196 & 6887.

Ava-pluta, mfn. plunged into, ĀśvGṛ.; jumped down from, MBh. &c.; gone away from, departed from, MBh. ii, 1452; Hariv. 4760; (*am*), n. jumping down, MBh. ix, 3193.

Ava-plutya, ind. p. jumping down, MBh. &c.; jumping away from (abl.), MBh. vii, 568; hastening away or off, Hariv. 15340.

अवबधा *ava-badhā*, f. = *abadhā*, q.v.

अवबन्ध् *ava-√bandh*, Ā. (ind. p. *-badhya*) to tie or fix on, put on, Kauś.; PārGṛ.; MBh. vii, 80.

Ava-baddha, mfn. put on (as a helmet), MBh. ix, 3096; fastened on, fixed, sticking (as an arrow or a nail, &c.), MBh. vi, 1787; Suśr. &c.; captivated, attached to, MBh. xii, 1438; Kathās.

Ava-bandha, *as*, m. 'palsy,' see *vartmâvab°*.

अवबाढ *áva-bāḍha*, mfn. (√*baṇh*), digged out, discovered (said of the *valagá*, q.v.), TS.; ĀpŚr.

अवबाध् *ava-√bādh*, Ā. (1. pl. *-bādhāmahe*; perf. 3. sg. *-babādhé*) Ved. to keep off, RV. ii, 14, 4 & x, 128, 9; AV. &c.

अवबाहुक *ava-bāhuka*, *as*, m. spasm in the arm, Suśr.

अवबुध् *ava-√budh, -budhyate* (fut. 3. pl. *-bhotsyante*, MBh. iii, 1363; rarely P., e.g. *-budhyati*, Hariv. 10385; 2. sg. *-budhyasi*, MBh. vi, 2921) to become sensible or aware of, perceive, know: Caus. (impf. *-bodhayat*) to make one aware of, remind of, MBh. i, 5811, &c.; to cause to know, inform, explain, Bālar. &c.: Pass. *-budhyate*, to be learnt by (instr.), BhP.

Ava-buddha, mfn. learnt (as skilfulness, *kauśala*), MBh. iv, 69.

Ava-boddhavya, mfn. to be kept in mind, MBh. ii, 2435.

Ava-bodha, *as*, m. waking, being awake, Bhag. vi, 17; Kum. ii, 8; perception, knowledge, Ragh. vii, 38, &c.; faculty of being resolute in judgment or action [Comm.], BhP.; teaching, L.

Ava-bodhaka, mfn. awakening (as faculties), teaching, BhP.

Ava-bodhana, *am*, n. informing, teaching, instruction, Daś.; Pañcat.

Ava-bodhanīya, mfn. to be reminded, admonished, censured, Kād.

Ava-bodhita, mfn. awakened, MBh. iii, 16812; Ragh. xii, 23.

अवब्रव *ava-brava*. See *an-avabravá*.

अवभञ्ज् *ava-√bhañj* (ind. p. *-bhajya*) to break off, smash, MBh.; Kum. iii, 74.

Ava-bhagna, mfn. broken off, MBh.; R.; broken, injured (as honour), R. iv, 22, 14.

Ava-bhaṅga, *as*, m. breaking off (as of the shaft of a bow), Sāh.; hollowing or sinking (of the nose), Suśr.

Ava-bhañjana, *am*, n. breaking or tearing off, Suśr.

अवभर्जन *ava-bharjana*, *am*, n. (√*bhṛij*), 'frying,' destroying (as seeds), BhP.

Ava-bharjita, mfn. 'fried,' destroyed (as seeds), BhP.

अवभर्त्स् *ava-√bharts* (p. *-bhartsayat*) to deter by threatening, MBh. iii, 15096; to deter by scolding, scold, MBh. v, 641 & 7115; R.

अवभा *ava-√bhā, -bhāti*, to shine downwards, RV. i, 154, 6 (v. l. *-bhāri*, fr. *ava-√bhṛi*, VS. vi, 3); to shine, be brilliant, Hariv. 13100; to appear, become manifest, MBh. iii, 10094; BhP.; Rājat.

अवभाषण *ava-bhāshaṇa*, *am*, n. speaking against, speaking, Sāh.

Ava-bhāshita, mfn. spoken against, reviled, Kām.; (see *ava-√bhās*.)

अवभास् *ava-√bhās, -bhāsate*, to shine forth, be brilliant, MBh.; BhP.; to become manifest, appear as (instr.): Caus. P. (p. *-bhāsayat*, wrongly written *-bhāshayat*, MBh. xii, 8345) to illuminate, MBh. &c.; to make manifest, Suśr.

Ava-bhāsa, *as*, m. splendour, lustre, light; appearance (especially ifc. with words expressing a colour), Jain.; Suśr.; (in Vedānta phil.) manifestation; reach, compass, see *śravaṇâvabh°*. **-kara,** m., N. of a Devaputra, Lalit. **-prabha,** *ās*, m. pl., N. of a class of deities, Buddh. **-prâpta,** m., N. of a world, Buddh.

Ava-bhāsaka, mfn. (in Vedānta phil.) illuminating, making manifest.

Ava-bhāsana, *am*, n. shining, Bhpr.; becoming manifest, Sāh.; (in Ved. phil.) illuminating. **-śikhin,** m., N. of a Nāga demon, Buddh.

Ava-bhāsita, mfn. shining, bright, MBh. xii, 13221; illumined, lighted, MBh. (wrongly written *ava-bhāshita*, vii, 6672), &c.

Ava-bhāsin, mfn. shining, bright, VarBṛS.; Suśr. (said of the outer skin of a snake); making manifest, Nyāyam

अवभिद् *ava-√bhid* (impf. 2. sg. *-bhinat* or *-ábhinat* or *-abhinat*; 3. sg. *-abhinat*; aor. 3. sg. *-bhet*) to split, pierce, RV.; AV.; TS.; ŚBr.

Ava-bhinna, mfn. pierced, MBh. vi, 1774; broken, injured, ŚBr.

Ava-bhedaka, mfn. 'piercing (the head),' aching (as hemiplegia); (cf. *ardha-bheda*.)

Ava-bhedin, mfn. splitting, dividing, VS.

अवभुज् *ava-√1. bhuj*, to incurve, Kauś.

Ava-bhugna, mfn. bent down, MBh. i, 5891.

अवभृ *ava-√bhṛi*, P. (impf. *ávābharat* or *-bharat*, 2. sg. *-bharas*; Ved. Imper. 2. sg. *-bharā*) to throw or push or press down or into, RV.; to throw or cut off, RV. ii, 20, 6 & x, 171, 2: Ā. *-bharate*, to sink down or disappear (as foam), RV. i, 104, 3; to lower, RV. viii, 19, 23: Pass. (Subj. *-bhriyāte*; aor. *-bhāri*) to be pressed upon or in (acc.), RV. v, 31, 12; VS. vi, 3 (see *ava-√bhā*).

Ava-bhṛiti, *is*, f., N. of a town (residence of the Āvabhṛitya kings), Comm. on BhP.

Ava-bhṛithá (once *-bhṛ́itha*, AV. ix, 6, 63), *as*, m. 'carrying off, removing,' purification or ablution of the sacrificer and sacrificial vessels after a sacrifice, RV. viii, 73, 23, &c.; a supplementary sacrifice (see below); cf. *jīvitâvabh°*. **-yájūṃshi,** n. pl. the Yajus-formulas used for the Ava-bhṛitha, TS. **-sāman,** n., N. of a Sāman, Lāṭy. **-snapana,** n. bathing or ablution after a sacrificial ceremony, BhP. **-snāna,** n. id. **Avabhṛithêshṭi,** f. a supplementary sacrifice to atone for defects in a principal and preceding one, Lāṭy.; KātyŚr.

Ava-bhra. See *an-avabhrá-rādhas*.

अवभ्रट *ava-bhraṭa*, mf(*ā*)n. = *ava-ṭīṭa*, q.v., Pāṇ. v, 2, 31.

अवम *avamá*, mf(*ā*)n. undermost, inferior, lowest, base, RV. &c.; next, intimate, RV.; last, youngest, RV. vi, 21, 5; (ifc. with numerals) less by, RPrāt.; (*am*), n. (scil. *dina*) or (*āni*), n. pl. the difference (expressed in days of twenty-four hours) existing between the lunar months and the corresponding solar ones, VarBṛS. &c.

अवमज्ज् *ava-√majj* (p. f. *-majjantī*) to immerse, R. ii, 95, 14.

अवमथ् *ava-√math* (ind. p. *-mathya*) to cleanse (as a wound) by pricking or stirring (with an instrument), Suśr.

Ava-mantha or **°nthaka,** *as*, m. swellings caused by boils or contusions, Suśr.

अवमन् *ava-√man*, Ā. (Pot. *-manyeta*, aor. Subj. 2. sg. *-maṃsthāḥ*, 2. pl. *-madhvam*, Bhaṭṭ.; ep. also P. *-manyati*, fut. *-maṃsyati*, MBh. iv, 444) to despise, treat contemptuously, MBh. &c.; to repudiate, refuse, ib.: Pass. *-manyate*, to be treated contemptuously: Caus. (Pot. *-mānayet*) to despise, treat contemptuously, Mn. ii, 50.

Ava-mata, mfn. despised, disregarded, contemned, Mn. vii, 150, &c. **Avamatâṅkuśa,** mfn. 'disdaining the hook,' a restive elephant, L.

Ava-mati, *is*, f. aversion, dislike, L.; disregard, contempt, L.; (*is*), m. a master, owner, L.

Ava-matya, ind. p. despising, Kum. v, 53; BhP.

Ava-mantavya, mfn. to be treated with disrespect, contemptible, MBh.; Mn. ii, 226 & vii, 8, &c.

Ava-mantṛi, mfn. despising, disrespectful towards (gen. [MBh. i, 1705] or acc. [Bālar.] or in comp. [BhP.])

Ava-manya, ind. p. = *-matya*, MBh. v, 7533; xvi, 73 & 75.

Ava-manyaka, mfn. = *-mantṛi*, MBh. iii, 1176 (with gen.); VP. (ifc.)

Ava-māna, *as*, m. (ifc. f. *ā*, Kathās.) disrespect contempt, Mn. ii, 162, &c.; dishonour, ignominy, MBh. iii, 226, &c. **-tā,** f. dishonourableness.

Ava-mānana, *am*, *ā*, n. f. disrespect, Sāh.; Daśar.; Kathās.; abuse, insult, Bālar.

Ava-mānanīya, mfn. = *-mantavya*, L.
Ava-mānita, mfn. disrespected, despised, MBh. &c.; neglected, not taken notice of, Suśr.
Ava-mānin, mfn. contemning, despising (ifc.), R. v, 81, 6; Śak. **Avamāni-tā**, f. or **-tva**, n. disrespectfulness.
Ava-mānya, mfn. = *-mantavya*, MBh. i, 1467; Mn. ix, 82.

अवमर्द *ava-marda*, &c. See *ava-√mṛid*.

अवमर्श *ava-marśa*, &c. See *ava-√mṛiś*.

अवमा *ava-√3. mā* (ind. p. *-máya*) to measure off, TS.

अवमान *ava-māna*, &c. See *ava-√man*.

अवमार्जन *ava-mārjana*. See *ava-√mṛij*.

अवमिह् *ava-√mih*, *-mehati*, to urine towards or upon (acc.), ŚBr.; MārkP.; to urine, BhP.; to pour out (as Soma), RV. ix, 74, 4.
Ava-mehana, *am*, n. urining upon, BhP.
Ava-mehanīya, mfn. to be urined upon, (*an-* neg.) Gobh.

अवमुच् *ava-√muc*, P. (p. *-muñcát*) to loosen, AV. viii, 2, 2; to let go, VarBṛS.; (ind. p. *-mucya*) to unharness, MBh. iii, 2870; (generally ind. p. *-mucya*) to take off (as a garment &c.), MBh. &c.: Ā. (p. *-muñcámāna*) to liberate one's self from, strip off, AV. viii, 1, 4.
Ava-mocana, *am*, n. loosening; setting at liberty, L.; 'where horses are unharnessed,' stage, a place for resting or settling, BhP.

अवमुष् *ava-√mush*, to take away, Kāṭh.

अवमूत्र् *ava-√mūtr* (p. *-mūtrayat*) to urine upon, Mn. viii, 282; VarBṛS.
Ava-mūtraṇa, *am*, n. urining upon, Car.
Ava-mūtrita, mfn. urined upon; wetted by the fluid excretion (of an insect), Suśr.

अवमूर्छ् *ava-√mūrch* (Pot. *-mūrchet*) to be appeased or allayed (as a quarrel), MBh. v, 811.

अवमूर्धशय *ava-mūrdha-śaya*, mfn. lying with the head hanging down, (gaṇa *pārśvādi*, q. v.)

अवमृज् *ava-√mṛij*, *-mārshṭi* (ind p. *-mṛijya*) to wipe or rub off, Comm. on TBr.; to wipe or rub, clean by wiping, ŚBr. &c.: Pass. (Pot. *-mṛijyeta* with the sense of Ā.) to rub one's (limbs, *gātrāṇi*), MBh. xiii, 5006.
Ava-mārjana, *am*, n. an instrument (or 'water,' Sāy.) for rubbing down (a horse), a curry-comb [Gmn. Transl.], RV. i, 163, 5 ['that which is rubbed off,' NBD.]; wipings, MBh. iii, 13373.

अवमृद् *ava-√mṛid* (impf. *avâmṛidnāt*; p. *-mṛidnat*) 'to grind down,' crush, tread down, MBh.; Hariv.; R.; to rub, MBh. iv, 468.
Ava-marda, *as*, m. oppression, giving pain, MBh. xii, 2183; R.; a kind of eclipse, VarBṛS.; N. of an owl, Kathās.
Ava-mardana, mfn. crushing, oppressing, giving pain, R. iii, 35, 114; (*am*), n. rubbing (as of hands and feet), Pañcat.; oppression, giving pain, MBh. iii, 12313; R.
Ava-mardita, mfn. crushed, destroyed, MBh. iii, 874; R.

अवमृश् *ava-√mṛiś* (Pot. *-mṛiśét*; Subj. 3. pl. *-mṛiśān*; aor. *avâmṛikshat*; ind. p. 1. *-mṛiśya*) Ved. to touch, AV. vii, 64, 2; TS. &c.; to reflect upon, BhP.: Caus. to cause to touch, ŚBr.
Ava-marśa, *as*, m. (ifc. f. *ā*) touch, contact, Śak. (v. l.); reflecting upon, Daśar.
Ava-márśam, ind. so as to touch, ŚBr.; (cf. *án-avam°*.)
Ava-marśita, mfn. touched, i. e. disturbed (as a sacrifice), BhP.
2. **Ava-mṛiśya**. See *an-avamṛiśyá*.

अवय *avaya*. See *śatâvaya*.

अवयज् 1. *ava-√yaj*, P.Ā. *-yájati* (Imper. 2. sg. P. *-yaja* & Ā. *-yakshva*; Pot. *-yajeta*) Ved. to offer a sacrifice for satisfying the claims of, to get rid of or remove by means of a sacrifice, RV. &c.
2. **Ava-yáj**, Nom. *-yâṭ* (cf. Pāṇ. iii, 2, 72 & viii, 2, 67), f. share of the sacrificial oblation, RV. i, 173, 12; AV. ii, 35, 1.

Ava-yájana, *am*, n. 'removing by means of a sacrifice,' expiation, VS.; means for expiation, PBr.
Ava-yáj. See 2. *ava-yáj*.

अवयव *ava-yava*, &c. See *ava-√1. yu*.

अवया *ava-√yā* (perf. 3. pl. *-yayuḥ*; p. gen. pl. *-yātâm*) to go or come down, RV. i, 94, 12 & 168, 4; (Ved. Inf. *ava-yaí*) to go away (opposed to *upa-yaí*, 'to come up'), RV. viii, 47, 12; (aor. Subj. *-yāsat*; Prec. 2. sg. *-yāsisīshṭhāḥ* [cf. Pāṇ. iii, 1, 34, Comm.]; aor. 1. sg. *-ayāsisham*) to avert, appease, RV. iv, 1, 4; vi, 66, 5; VS. iii, 48.
Ava-yāta, *am*, n., N. of a Tīrtha, (gaṇa *dhūmâdi*, q. v.) **-heḷas** (*ávayāta-*), mfn. whose anger is appeased, RV. i, 171, 6.
Ava-yātṛí, mfn. one who averts or appeases, RV. i, 129, 11 & viii, 48, 2 (= AV. ii, 2, 2).
Ava-yâna, *am*, n. going down, AV. viii, 1, 6; retreat, Lalit.; appeasing, RV. i, 185, 8.

अवयास *ava-yāsá*, *as*, m. (√*yas*), N. of an evil spirit in Yama's world, TS.

अवयु *ava-√1. yu* (p. fem. *-yuvatī*) to separate from (abl.), Nir. iv, 11: Caus. *-yāvayati*, to keep off, Nir. ix, 42.
Ava-yava, *as*, m. (ifc. f. *ā*) a limb, member, part, portion, Pāṇ. &c.; a member or component part of a logical argument or syllogism, Nyāyad. &c. **-dharma**, m. the property or quality of a part, Pāṇ. ii, 3, 20, Kāś. **-rūpaka**, n. a simile by which two things are only compared with regard to their parts, Kāvyād. **-śas**, ind. part by part, BhP. **Avayavârtha**, m. the meaning of the component parts of a word.
Avayavin, mfn. having portions or subdivisions, a whole, BhP. &c.; (*ī*), m. a syllogism, Nyāyad. &c. **Avayavi-rūpaka**, n. a simile by which two things are only compared as wholes, Kāvyād.
Ava-yuti, *is*, f. 'separation,' (°*tyā*), instr. ind. separately, Comm. on ĀpŚr.

अवयुन *a-vayuná*, mfn. undistinguishable, indistinct, dark, RV. vi, 21, 3.

अवर *ávara*, mf(*ā*)n. (fr. 2. *áva*), below, inferior, RV.; AV.; VS.; low, mean, unimportant, of small value, ŚBr.; Up.; Mn. &c.; posterior, hinder, later, last, younger, RV. &c.; nearer, RV.; AV.; western, ŚBr.; preceding (with abl., opposed to *pára*), ŚBr.; RPrāt.; (*ā*), f. 'after-birth,' see *avarâvapatana* below; (= *aparā*, q. v.) the hind quarter of an elephant, L.; N. of Durgā, L.; (*am*), n. ifc. (f. *ā*) the least, the lowest degree, lowest sum (cf. *kārshāpaṇâvara*, *trirātrâvara*, *try-avara*, *daśâvara*, *saṃvatsarâvara*); the hind thigh of an elephant, L.; (*eṇa*), instr. ind. below (with acc.), ŚBr. **-ja**, mf(*ā*)n. of low birth, inferior; younger, junior, R. iii, 75, 10; BhP.; (*as*), m. a Śūdra, Mn. ii, 223; a younger brother, R.; Rājat.; (with abl.) MBh. iv, 1012; (*ā*), f. a younger sister, Ragh.; BhP. **-tara** (*ávara-*), mfn. (compar.) farther down, ŚBr. **-tas**, ind. (Pāṇ. v, 3, 29) below &c., L.; at least, Pat. **-para**, mf(*ā*)n. preceding and following, AitĀr.; (*ám*), ind. one upon the other, AV. xi, 3, 20; successively, TBr. (cf. *avaras-pará* below). **-purusha**, m. a descendant, ChUp. **-vayas**, mfn. younger, Āp. **-varṇa**, m. 'a low or despised caste,' see *-varṇa-ja*; 'belonging to a low caste,' a Śūdra, L. **-varṇa-ja**, m. 'born in a low caste,' a Śūdra, Mn. iii, 241 & ix, 248. **-vrata**, m. the sun, L. **-śaila**, *ās*, m. pl. 'living or originated on the western mountain (in the monastery called *avara-śaila-saṅghârāma*),' N. of a Buddhist school. **-stāt**, ind. below &c., Pāṇ. v, 3, 29 & 41. **-s-pará**, mfn. [Padap. *avara-para*] having the last first or the hindermost foremost, inverted, VS. xxx, 19. **Avarârdha**, m. ifc. the least part, the minimum, Pāṇ. v, 4, 57; (*am*), ind. at least, Kauś. **Avarârdha-tás**, ind. from below, ŚBr. **Avarârdhya**, mfn. being on the lower or nearer side, ŚBr.; beginning from below, ib.; (*am*), n. ifc. (f. *ā*) the least part, the minimum, KaushBr.; Lāṭy.; mfn. being the minimum, Lāṭy.; (cf. *an-avarârdhya*.) **Avarâvapatana**, n. dropping of or discharge of the secundines, miscarriage, PārGṛ. **Avarâvara**, mfn. lowest, most inferior of all, R. v, 53, 24; 69, 21. **Avarôkta**, mfn. named last, KātyŚr.
Avarīṇa, mfn. (= *adharīṇa*, q. v.) vilified, censured, L.

Avarya, Nom. P. °*ryati*, to become lower, (gaṇa *kaṇḍv-ādi*, q. v.)

अवरङ्गसाह *avaraṅga-sāha* = Aurungzeb (a Muhammedan king of the 17th century; *sāha* = the Persian شاه).

अवरत *ava-rata*. See *an-avarata*.
Ava-rati, *is*, f. stopping, ceasing, L.

अवरम्ब् *ava-√ramb* (p. *-rámbamāṇa*) to hang down, RV. viii, 1, 34, = *ava-√lamb*, q. v.

अवराध् *ava-√rādh* (aor. 2. sg. *-arātsīs*) to commit a fault, AV. v, 6, 6; *-rādhnoti*, to turn out ill, fail, AitBr.

अवरिफ् *ava-√riph* (p. *-riphat*) to utter a murmuring guttural sound, Kāṭh.

अवरीण *avarīṇa*. See *ávara*.

अवरीयस् *a-varīyas*, *ān*, m., N. of a son of the Manu Sāvarṇa, Hariv. 465.

अवरुच् *ava-√ruc*, *-rócate*, to shine down, AV. iii, 7, 3.
Ava-rokin, mfn. shining, brilliant, VS. xxiv, 6.
Ava-rocaka, *as*, m. want of appetite, Suśr.

अवरुज् *ava-√ruj* (ind. p. *-rujya*) to break off (as shrubs), MBh. i, 5884.
Ava-rugṇa, mfn. broken, torn, Hariv. 3565.

अवरुणम् *a-varuṇám*, ind. without falling into the power of Varuṇa, MaitrS.
A-varuṇyá, mfn. not belonging to or fallen into the power of Varuṇa, ŚBr.

अवरुदित *ava-rudita*, mfn. (√*rud*), that upon which tears have fallen, MBh. xiii, 4367.

अवरुध् *ava-√2. rudh*, P. (aor. *-rudhat*) to obstruct, enclose, contain, RV. x, 105, 1; (Inf. *-roddhum*) to check, keep back, restrain, R. iii, 1, 33; to expel, Kauś.; ŚāṅkhŚr.; R. ii, 30, 9; *-ruṇaddhi*, to seclude, put aside, remove, ŚBr.; KaushBr.; ShaḍvBr.; to shut in, (aor. Ā. *avâruddha* and Pass. *avârodhi*) Pāṇ. iii, 1, 64, Sch.; to keep anything (acc., as one's grief) locked up (in one's bosom, acc.), Bhaṭṭ.; (ind. p. *-rudhya*) to keep one's self (*ātmānam*) wrapped up in one's self (*ātmani*), BhP.; (impf. *avâruṇat*) to confine within, besiege, Daś.: Ā. *-rundhe* (for °*nddhe*, AV.; impf. *avârundha*, TS.; ind. p. *-rudhya*, ib.; Ved. Inf. *-rúdham*, ib. and *-rúndham*, MaitrS.) chiefly Ved. to reach, obtain, gain: P. (p. f. *-rundhatī*; cf. *anu-√rudh*) to be attached to, like, BhP.: Desid. Ā. *-rurutsate*, Ved. to wish to obtain or gain, TS. &c.: Intens. P. (Subj. 2. sg. *-rorudhas*) to expel from (the dominion), R. ii, 58, 20.
Ava-ruddha, mfn. hindered, checked, stopped, kept back, Śak.; Sāh.; shut in, enclosed, Mn. viii, 236, &c.; imprisoned, secluded (as in the inner apartments), Yājñ. ii, 290, &c.; expelled, MBh. iv, 2011, &c.; wrapped up, covered, VarBṛS.; disguised, Daś.; Ved. obtained, gained, ŚBr. &c. **-deha**, mfn. having the person imprisoned, incarcerated, BhP.
Áva-ruddhi, f. only dat. °*ddhyai*, for the obtainment of (gen.), AitBr.; ŚBr.
Ava-ruddhikā, f. a woman secluded in the inner apartments, Rājat.
Ava-rúdham, Ved. Inf., see *ava-√rudh*.
Ava-rudhyamāna, mfn. being enclosed or surrounded, BhP.
Ava-rúndham, Ved. Inf., see *ava-√rudh*.
1. **Ava-rodha**, *as*, m. hindrance, obstruction, injury, harm, Suśr. &c.; seclusion, imprisonment, Āp.; Comm. on Yājñ.; an enclosure, confinement, besieging, Hit.; a covering, lid, L.; a fence, pen, L.; the inner apartments of a palace, the queen's or women's apartments, MBh. i, 1812; R. &c.; a palace, L.; (*ās*), (or in comp. *avarodha-*) m. pl. 'the women's apartments,' the wives of a king, Śak.; Ragh. &c. **Avarodhâyana**, n. a seraglio, L.
Ava-rodhaka, mfn. hindering, L.; being about to besiege (with acc.), R. i, 71, 16; (*as*), m. a guard, L.; (*ikā*), f. a female of the inner apartments, L.; (cf. *ava-ruddhikā*); (*am*), n. a barrier, fence, L.
1. **Ava-ródhana**, mf(*ī*)n. procuring, KaushUp.; (*am*), n. siege, blockade, R. i, 3, 33; secluding, imprisonment, Āp.; a closed or private place, the innermost part of anything, RV. ix, 113, 8; obtaining,

KaushUp.; the inner or women's apartments (in a royal palace); (*āni*), n. pl. = *ava-rodhās*, m. pl.

Ava-rodhika, *as*, m. a guard of the queen's apartments, L.

Ava-rodhin, mfn. (ifc.) obstructing, hindering, Naish.; wrapping up, covering, Kād.

अवरुह् *ava-√ruh*, P. (p. *-róhat*; ind. p. *-ruhya*; also Ā., e. g. MBh. ix, 3470; R. ii, 7, 11 & iv, 49, 25) to descend, alight, dismount, RV. v, 78, 4, &c.; 'to descend from,' i. e. to be deprived of (one's dominion, *aiśvaryāt*), BhP.: Caus. (impf. *avâropayat* [v. l. °*rohayat*], Ragh. i, 54; Imper. 2. sg. *-ropaya*, MBh. iv, 1318 & ix, 3468, 2. pl. Ā. *-rohayadhvam*, MBh. iii, 15609) to cause to descend, take down from (abl.): Pass. *-ropyate*, to be lowered or lessened, MBh. xii, 8501.

Ava-rūḍha, mfn. come near, approached, AV. vi, 140, 1; descended, dismounted, alighted.

2. **Ava-rodha,** *as*, m. (√1. *rudh* = √*ruh*), 'moving down,' see 1. *rodha*; (= *ava-roha* below) a shoot or root sent down by a branch (of the Indian fig-tree), AitBr.

2. **Ava-rodhana,** *am*, n. descending motion (opposed to *ud-rodhana*, q. v.), AitBr.

Ava-ropaṇa, *am*, n. planting, MBh. xiii, 2991; causing to descend, L.; depriving, diminishing, L.

Ava-ropita, mfn. caused to descend; taken down from (abl.); deprived of (as of one's dominion, *rājyāt* &c.), MBh. iv, 2101; R.; MārkP.; lowered, lessened, Mn. i, 82; curtailed, lost (as dominions, *rāshṭrāṇi*), BhP.; silenced (in dispute), BhP.

Ava-ropya, ind. p. having made or making to descend, Gobh.; Hariv. 9721; planting, MBh. i, 7063.

Ava-roha, *as*, m. descent, L.; (in music) descending from a higher tone to a lower one, Comm. on Mṛicch.; mounting, L.; a shoot or root sent down by a branch (especially of the Indian fig-tree; cf. 2. *ava-rodha*), Kauś.; PārGṛ.; R. ii, 52, 96; (= *latôdgama*) a creeping plant climbing up to the top of a tree, L.; heaven, L. **-vat,** mfn. possessed of *avaroha*-shoots (as the Indian fig-tree), (gaṇa *balâdi*, q. v.), Pat. **-śākhin,** m. 'having branches with *avaroha*-shoots,' the Indian fig-tree, L.

Ava-rohaka, *as*, m., see *aśvâv*°; (*ikā*), f. the plant Physalis Flexuosa, L.

Ava-rohaṇa, mf(*ī*)n. alighting, descending, MārkP.; (*am*), n. descending, alighting from (abl. [MBh. i, 462], or in comp. [Kathās.]); (in music = *ava-roha*) descending from a higher tone to a lower one, Comm. on Mṛicch.; the place of descending BhP.

Ava-rohita and °**tīya,** mfn. (gaṇa *utkarâdi*, q. v.)

Ava-rohin, mfn. descending, VarBṛS.; = *avaroha-vat*, q. v. (gaṇa *balâdi*, q. v.); (*ī*), m. the Indian fig-tree, L.

अवरूप *ava-rūpa*, mf(*ā*)n. mis-shapen, deformed, degenerated, Kauś. 136.

अवरोकिन् *ava-rokín*, &c. See *ava-√ruc.*

अवर्चस् *a-varcás*, mfn. having no vigour or energy, AV. iv, 22, 3; ŚBr. v.

अवर्जनीय *a-varjanīya*, mfn. inevitable. **-tā,** f. or **-tva,** n. inevitableness, Jaim.; Comm. on Nyāyad.

A-varjushī, f., AV. vii, 50, 2, v. l. for *vavarjúshī*, perf. p. f. fr. √*vṛij*, q. v.

अवर्ण 1. *a-varṇa*, mfn. having no outward appearance, ŚvetUp.; colourless (Comm.; said of Nara and Nārāyaṇa), MBh. iii, 8384; (*as*), m. 'no praise,' blame, speaking ill of, Ragh. xiv, 38 & 57; Rājat. **-kāraka,** mfn. 'not praising,' speaking ill of, Buddh.; Jain. **-vāda,** m. censure, blame, L. **-saṃyoga,** m. no connection with any caste, Āp.

A-varṇya, mfn. indescribable, Up.; not to be predicated, Comm. on Nyāyad. **-sama,** m. a sophism in which the argument still to be proved is confounded with the admitted one, Nyāyad.; Sāh.

अवर्ण 2. *a-varṇa*, *as*, m. the vowel *a* or *ā*, APrāt.

अवर्तमान *a-vartamāna*, mfn. 'not belonging to the present time,' (gaṇa *cārv-ādi*, q. v.)

अवर्ति *áva-rti*, *is*, f. (*ṛiti* fr. √*ṛi*), bad fortune, poverty, distress, RV.; AV.; (cf. *áva-ṛiti*.)

अवर्त्र *a-vartrá*, mfn. 'having nothing that restrains,' unimpeded, RV. vi, 12, 3.

A-varmán, mfn. having no armour, AV. xi, 10, 23.

अवर्धमान *a-vardhamāna*, mfn. 'not growing,' (gaṇa *cārv-ādi*, q. v.)

अवर्ष *a-varsha*, *am*, n. want of rain, drought, MBh. xii, 1208; R.; (*ā*), f. id., MBh. xiii, 4579.

A-varshaṇa, *am*, n. id., Vet.

A-varshin, mfn. not raining, Hcat.

A-varshuka, mfn. id., TS.; ŚBr.

A-varshṭos, Ved. Inf. not to rain, AitBr.

A-varshyá, mf(*ā*)n. being active in rainless bright weather, VS. xvi, 38; MaitrS.; not coming from rain (as water), TS. vii.

अवलक्ष *a-valaksha*, mfn. = *baláksha*, q. v., L.

अवलग् *ava-√lag*, Caus. *-lagayati*, to fasten to, Comm. on KātyŚr.

Ava-lagita, *am*, n. an addition made in the prologue of a drama and not having any particular reference to the latter, Sāh.

Ava-lagna, mfn. hanging down from (in comp.), Ragh. xvi, 68, &c.; (*as, am*), m. n. the waist, Śiś. ix, 49, &c.

अवलङ्घ् *ava-√laṅgh*, (ind. p. *-laṅghya*) to pass or spend (time).

Ava-laṅghita, mfn. passed (as time), Kathās.

अवलम्ब् *ava-√lamb*, *-lambate* (ind. p. *-lambya*; exceptionally P., e. g. Pot. *-lambet*, MBh. i, 8443, ed. Bomb.) to hang down, glide or slip down, descend, TUp. &c.; (pr. p. P. *-lambat*) to set (as the sun), MBh. iv, 1040; to catch hold of, cling to, hang to, hold on or support one's self by, rest upon as a support, depend upon (generally acc.; but also loc. [MBh. i, 8443] or instr. [Megh. 108]); to hold up anything (to prevent its falling down), Śak.; Ragh. vii, 9, &c.; to enter a state or condition (as *māyām, mānushyatvam, dhairyam*, &c.); to devote one's self to (acc.), Kum. ii, 15; 'to incline towards,' choose as a direction, Kathās.: Caus. (ind. p. *-lambya*) to hang up, Pañcat.; Kathās.; to grasp (for support), Mālav.

Ava-lamba, mf(*ā*)n. hanging down from (loc., R.) or to (in comp., MBh. xiii, 982); (*as*), m. hanging on or from, Megh.; depending, resting upon, L.; dependance, support, a prop, a stay, Ragh. xix, 50, &c. (cf. *nir-aval*°); a perpendicular, L.; (cf. *prishṭhyâval*°.)

Ava-lambaka, mfn. hanging down, Hcat.; (*as*), m. (in geom.) a perpendicular; (*am*), n., N. of a metre.

Ava-lambana, mf(*ī*)n. hanging on, clinging to, Bhpr.; leaning against (loc.), BhP.; (*am*), n. hanging down, L.; depending upon, dependance, support, Śak. &c.; making a halt, stopping at (loc. adv.), Hit.

Ava-lambita, mfn. hanging down, hanging on, suspended from, clinging to, Śak. &c.; crouching or settling down, Hit.; depending upon, resting upon as a support, Ragh. ix, 69; Vikr. &c.; placed upon, Suśr.; supported or protected by; (in Pass. sense) clung to, caught hold of, Śiś. vi, 10; (fr. Caus.) having been made to hang down, let down (as a basket by a string), Kathās.

Ava-lambitavya, mfn. to be caught hold of or grasped, to be clung to.

Ava-lambin, mfn. hanging down so as to rest upon, hanging on or from, depending on; clinging to, reclining, resting upon.

अवलिख् *ava-√likh* (Pot. *-likhet*; ind. p. *-likhya*) to scratch, graze, Suśr.

Ava-lekha, *as*, m. anything scraped off, Suśr.; (*ā*), f. drawing, painting, BhP.

Ava-lekhana, *am*, n. brushing, combing, ĀśvŚr.; Āp.; Gaut.; (*ī*), f. brush, comb, Kauś.

अवलिप् *ava-√lip*, P. (ind. *-lipya*) to smear, KaushBr.; ŚāṅkhŚr.; Suśr.: Ā. (p. *-limpamāna*) to smear one's self, BhP.

Ava-liptá, mfn. smeared, MBh. i, 6391; viii, 2059; Suśr.; Vet.; furred (as the tongue), Suśr.; (= *ápi-ripta*, q. v.) blind (?), VS. xxiv, 3; Kauś.; proud, arrogant, Mn. iv, 79; MBh. &c. **-tā,** f. or **-tva,** n. [R.] pride, arrogance.

Ava-lepa, *as*, m. glutinousness (as of the mouth), Suśr.: ointment, L.; ornament, L.; pride, haughtiness, BhP.; Ragh. &c.; (cf. *an-* neg.)

Ava-lepana, *am*, n. ointment; proud behaviour, R. i, 44, 9 & 36.

अवलिह् *ava-√lih*, P. *-leḍhi* (impf. *avâleṭ*; Pot. *-lihet* [MBh. xiii, 2286; VarBṛS.] or *-lihyāt*; ind. p. *-lihya*; rarely Ā. 1. sg. *-lihe*, MBh. i, 667) to lick, lap, AitBr.; Kāṭh. &c.: Intens. (p. *-lelihat*) to flicker (as a flame), MBh. i, 1181.

Ava-līḍha, mfn. licked, lapped, MBh. &c.; touched (by a flickering object), R. iii, 43, 3; touched (as by a finger-nail), Hariv. 7050; (cf. *ardhâval*°); (*ā*), f. disregard, L.

Ava-leha, *as*, m. licking, lapping, VarBṛS.; an extract, electuary, Suśr.

Ava-lehaka, mfn. licking, MBh. xiii, 2173; (*ikā*), f. (= *-leha* before) an extract, electuary, Suśr.

Ava-lehana, *am*, n. licking; = *-lehikā*, Bhpr.

Ava-lehin, mfn. lickerish, fond of dainties [BR.; '*sṛikkiṇī lelihāna*, i. e. *sadā kruddha*,' Comm.], MBh. xiii, 519.

अवली *ava-√lī*, Ā. (p. *-līyamāna*; impf. 3. pl. *avâlīyanta*) to stick to (loc.), Suśr.; to bow, stoop, MBh. viii, 939; to hide one's self in (loc.), R. vi, 99, 43 (pr. p. P. *-līyat*).

Ava-līna, mfn. sitting down (as a bird), VarBṛS.; cowering down in, hiding one's self in (loc.), R. v, 25, 13; 'engaged in' (in comp.), beginning to, Nalod. ii, 46.

अवलीला *ava-līlā*, f. 'play, sport,' (*ayā*), instr. ind. quite easily.

अवलुञ्च् *ava-√luñc* (ind. p. *-luñcya*) to tear out (as hairs), MBh. iii, 10760 seqq.; MārkP.

Ava-luñcana, *am*, n. tearing out (of hairs), R. vi, 98, 25; opening or unstitching (of a seam), Suśr.

अवलुण्ठन *ava-luṇṭhana*, *am*, n. (√*luṇṭh*), robbing, Kathās.; wallowing on the ground, L.

Ava-luṇṭhita, mfn. robbed, L.; rolled or wallowed on the ground, L.

अवलुप् *ava-√lup*, P. Ā. (3. pl. *-lumpanti*) to cut or take off, TS.; TĀr.; ShaḍvBr.; to take away by force, wrest, MBh. vi, 381; to suppress, extinguish; to rush or dash upon (as a wolf on his prey); (cf. *vṛikâvalupta*.)

Ava-lupti, *is*, f. falling off, PBr.

Ava-lumpana, *am*, n. rushing upon (as of a wolf), MBh. i, 5586.

Ava-lopa, *as*, m. interruption, BhP.

Ava-lopya, mfn. to be torn off, Bhaṭṭ.

अवलून *ava-lūna*, mfn. (√*lū*), cut off, L.

अवलेख *ava-lekha*, &c. See *ava-√likh.*

अवलेप *ava-lepa*, &c. See *ava-√lip.*

अवलेह *ava-leha*, &c. See *ava-√lih.*

अवलोक् *ava-√lok*, cl. 1. Ā. *-lokate*, to look, Sāh.; Hit.: cl. 10. P. *-lokayati* (p. *-lokayat*; ind. p. *-lokya*) to look upon or at, view, behold, see, notice, observe, MBh. &c.

Ava-loka, *as*, m. looking upon or at, viewing, Vikr.; Śiś. ix, 71; Sāh.; look, glance, BhP.; (*eshu*), loc. pl. ind. before the (looks or) eyes of (gen.), MBh. i, 7902.

Ava-lokaka, mfn. wishing to view (as a spy), R. vi, 101, 13.

Ava-lokana, *am*, n. seeing, beholding, viewing, observing, Ragh. xi, 60, &c.; a look, glance, Ragh. x, 14, &c.; 'looking like,' appearance of (in comp.), BhP.; (*ā*), f. the aspect (of planets), VarBṛS.

Ava-lokanīya, mfn. worthy to be looked at, Lalit.

Ava-lokayitavya, mfn. to be observed, VarBṛS.

Ava-lokayitṛi, mfn. one who views.

Ava-lokita, mfn. seen, viewed, observed; viewed by, i. e. being in sight of a planet, VarBṛS.; MārkP.; (*as*), m. = *avalokitêśvara* below; (*ā*), f., N. of a woman, Mālatim.; (*am*), n. looking at, beholding, L. **-vrata,** m., N. of a Buddhist. **Avalokitêśvara,** m., N. of a Bodhi-sattva, worshipped by the northern Buddhists.

Ava-lokin, mfn. looking, Kum. v, 49; looking at, beholding (ifc.), Kathās.

Ava-lokya, mfn. to be looked at, MBh. xiii, 5001; PSarv.

अवलोप *ava-lopa*, &c. See *ava-√lup.*

अवलोभन *ava-lobhana.* See *an-aval°.*

अवलोम *ava-loma*, mfn., Pāṇ. v, 4, 75.

अवल्गुज *a-valgu-ja, as*, m. the plant Vernonia Anthelminthica, Suśr.

अवल्गुली *avalgulī*, f., N. of a poisonous insect, Suśr.

अववद् *ava-√vad* (aor. Subj. 1. pl. *-vādishma*) to speak ill of or against (gen.), AitBr.; (cf. *dur-avavada.*)

Ava-vadana, *am*, n. speaking ill of, Sāy. on AitBr.

Ava-vadita, mfn. instructed, taught, Buddh.

Ava-vaditṛi, *tā*, m. one who speaks finally, who gives the definitive opinion, AitBr.

Ava-vāda, *as*, m. speaking ill of, evil report, L.; a command, order, L.; trust, confidence, L.; instruction, teaching, Buddh.

अववर्ति *avavarti*, aor. Ā. fr. *√vṛit*, q. v.

अववर्षण *ava-varshaṇa.* See *ava-√vṛish.*

अववा *ava-√vā, -vāti*, to blow down, RV. x, 60, 11; (said of fire compared to a bull) to snort (i. e. to crackle) towards, RV. i, 58, 5.

अवविद्ध *ava-viddha.* See *ava-√vyadh.*

अववी *ava-√vī, -veti*, to eat, enjoy, RV. x, 23, 4.

अववृज् *ava-√vṛij*, to disjoin, separate, Kāṭh.: Caus. (Pot. 3. pl. *-varjáyeyuḥ*) to remove, TBr.

अववृष् *ava-√vṛish* (p. *-várshat*) Ved. to rain upon, VS. xxii, 26, &c.

Ava-varshaṇa, *am*, n. raining upon, KātyŚr.

A'va-vṛishṭa, mfn. rained upon, TBr.

अवव्यध् *ava-√vyadh, -vidhyati*, to throw down into (loc.), RV. ix, 73, 8; (opposed to *abhy-ā-róhati*; Comm. = *pramādyati*) to fall or sink down, TS.; (Pot. *-vidhyet*) 'to throw down from,' deprive of (loc.), TBr.

A'va-viddha, mfn. thrown down into (loc.), RV. i, 182, 6 & vii, 69, 7.

अवव्ये *ava-√vye* (p. *-vyáyat*) to pull off (as clothes), RV. ', 13, 4.

अवव्रश्च् *ava-√vraśc* (Imper. 2. sg. *-vriścā*; impf. *-avṛiścat*) to splinter, cut off, RV. i, 51, 7 & vii, 18, 17.

Ava-vráśca, *as*, m. splinter, chip, ŚBr. xii.

अवश *a-vaśá*, mf(*ā*)n. unsubmissive to another's will, independent, unrestrained, free, AV. vi, 42, 3 & 43, 3, &c.; not having one's own free will, doing something against one's desire or unwillingly, Mn. v, 33; Bhag. &c. **–ga,** mfn. not being in any one's (gen.) power. **–m-gama,** n. 'not submissive to each other,' N. of a special Sandhi (in which the two sounds meeting each other remain unchanged), RPrāt. **A-vaśī-bhūta,** mfn. unrestrained, independent, L.; uninfluenced by magic, L. **Avaśêndriya-citta,** mfn. whose mind and senses are not held in subjection, Hit.

A-vaśin, mfn. not having one's own free will; not exercising one's own will, not independent, Āp.

Avaśi-tva, n. not being master of one's self, MBh. xiv, 1001.

A-vaśya-, in comp. with a fut. p. p. (and with some other words) for *a-vaśyam*, Pāṇ. vi, 1, 144, Comm.; (*avaśyam*), ind. necessarily, inevitably, certainly, at all events, by all means; *avaśyam eva*, most surely; (cf. *āvaśyaka.*) **–karman,** n. any necessary action or performance, AitĀr. **–kārya,** mfn. (gaṇa *mayūravyaṇsakâdi*, q. v.) to be necessarily done, R. ii, 96, 8; (*āṇi*), n. pl. necessary performances, MBh. i, 7899; viii, 10. **–pācya,** mfn. to be necessarily cooked, Pāṇ. vii, 3, 65, Sch. **–m-bhāvin,** mfn. necessarily being, MBh. i, 6144; Hit. **–m-bhāvi-tā,** f. [Comm. on Mṛicch.] or **-tva,** n. [Bhpr.] the being necessarily.

अवशप्त *ava-śapta*, mfn. cursed, MBh. xiii, 7221.

अवशस् *ava-śas* (only instr. *-śásā*), f. (*√śaṇs*), wrong desire, AV. vi, 45, 2.

अवशा *á-vaśā*, f. not a cow, a bad cow, AV. xii, 4, 17 & 42.

अवशातन *ava-śātana, am*, n. (*√śad*, Caus.), withering, drying up, Suśr.

अवशि *ava-√śi* (Imper. 2. sg. *-śiśīhi*) to deliver from, remove, RV. x, 105, 8.

अवशिरस् *ava-śiras*, mfn. having the head turned down, Kauś.

Ava-śīrshaka, mfn. id., Suśr.

अवशिष् *ava-√śish*, Pass. *-śíshyate*, to be left as a remnant, remain, TBr.; ŚBr.; MBh. &c.: Caus. (Pot. *-śeshayet*) to leave as a remnant, MBh. v, 2638; R. v, 26, 38.

Ava-śishṭa, mfn. left, remaining.

Ava-śishṭaka, *am*, n. remainder, Yājñ. ii, 47.

Ava-śesha, *am*, n. leavings, remainder, Mn. viii, 159, &c.; often ifc., e. g. *ardhâv°, kathâv°, pītâv°*, q. v.; (*am*), ind. ifc. so as to leave as a remnant, Daś.; (cf. *nir-av°.*) **–tā,** f. the being left as a remainder, BhP.

Ava-śeshita, mfn. left as a remnant, remaining, MBh. i, 5129, &c.; (cf. *kathā-mātrâv°* and *nāma-mātrâv°.*)

Ava-śeshya, mfn. to be left or kept remaining.

अवशी *ava-√3. śī*, Ā. (3. pl. *-śīyante*; Imper. *-śīyatām*) to fall or drop off, AV. xviii, 3, 60; TS.; Kāṭh.; ŚBr.; PBr.

अवशीत *ava-śīta* and *-śīna.* See *ava-śyā.*

अवशुष् *ava-√śush, -śushyati*, to become dry, VāyuP. ii; (*-śushyate*) MārkP.

अवशॄ *ava-√śṝī* (impf. *avâśṛiṇāt*) to break (as any one's anger), PBr.: Pass. (impf. *-śīryata*) to be dispersed, fly in every direction, R. i, 37, 13, ed. Bomb.

Ava-śīrṇa, mfn. broken, shattered, Kauś.; MBh. xiii, 1503.

अवशेष *ava-śesha*, &c. See *ava-√śish.*

अवश्चुत् *ava-√ścut* (perf. *-cuścota*) to trickle down, TBr.

अवश्या *ava-śyā*, f. (*√śyai*), hoar-frost, dew, L.

Ava-śīta or **-śyāta,** mfn. cooled, cool, Pāṇ. vi, 1, 26, Kāś.

Ava-śīna or **-śyāna,** mfn. coagulated, Pāṇ. vi, 1, 26.

Ava-śyāya, *as*, m. (Pāṇ. iii, 1, 141) hoar-frost, dew, Nir.; MBh. xii, 5334; R.; pride, L. **–paṭa,** m. a kind of cloth, L.

अवश्रथ् *ava-√śrath*, Caus. (Imper. 2. sg. *-śrathāya*, Padap. *°thaya*) to loosen, RV. i, 24, 15.

अवश्रयण *ava-śrayaṇa, am*, n. (*√śri*), taking (anything) from off the fire (opposed to *adhi-śr°*, q. v.), Sāh.

अवश्वसम् *ava-śvasám*, Ved. Inf. fr. *√śvas*, to blow away, AV. iv, 37, 3.

अवश्वित् *ava-√śvit* (aor. *-aśvait*) to shine down, RV. i, 124, 11.

अवषट्कार *a-vashaṭkāra*, mfn. without the exclamation *vashaṭ*, KātyŚr.

A'-vashaṭkṛita, mfn. id., ŚBr. iv.

अवष्टम्भ् *ava-shṭambh* (*√stambh*), *-shṭabhnoti* (&c., Pāṇ. viii, 3, 63 seqq.; generally ind. p. *-shṭabhya*, ĀśvŚr. &c.) to lean or rest upon, Pāṇ. viii, 3, 68, &c.; to bar, barricade, R. iii, 56, 7; *-shṭabhnāti* (Kathās.; Inf. *-shṭabdhum*, ib.; Pass. aor. *avâshṭambhi*, Rājat.) to seize, arrest, R. v, 25, 52, &c.

Ava-shṭabdha, mfn. standing firm, R. iii, 74, 24; supported by (acc.), resting on, R. v, 31, 50; grasped, seized, arrested, VarBṛS.; Kathās.; standing near, Pāṇ. viii, 3, 68; R. v, 56, 129; (said of time) being near, approaching, Pāṇ. v, 2, 13; VāyuP.; (cf. *ava-stabdha* below.)

1. **Ava-shṭabhya,** ind. p. See *ava-shṭambh.*

2. **Ava-shṭabhya,** mfn. to be seized or stopped, Kathās.

Ava-shṭambha, *as*, m. leaning or resting upon, Suśr. &c.; having recourse to anything, applying, Pañcat.; Sāh.; self-confidence, resoluteness, Suśr.; Pañcat. (cf. *sâvashṭ°*); beginning, L.; obstruction, impediment, L.; a post or pillar, L.; gold, L. **–maya,** mfn. (said of an arrow) shot with resoluteness (?), Ragh. iii, 53.

Ava-shṭambhana, *am*, n. having recourse to (in comp.), Pañcat.

Ava-stabdha, mfn. stiff (with cold &c.), Pāṇ. viii, 3, 68, Sch.

अवष्ठ्यूत *ava-shṭhyūta*, mfn. spit upon, ŚBr.

अवष्वन् *ava-shvan* (*√svan*), *-shvaṇati* (impf. *avâshvaṇat*; perf. p. Ā. *-shashvāṇa*) to smack (one's lips) or otherwise make a noise in eating, Pāṇ. viii, 3, 63 seqq.; (cf. *ava-√svan.*)

Ava-shvāṇa, *as*, m. noisy eating, smacking, L.

अवस् 1. *ávas*, n. (*√av*), favour, furtherance, protection, assistance, RV.; AV.; VS.; refreshing, RV.; enjoyment, pleasure, RV.; wish, desire (as of men for the gods &c., RV., or of the waters for the sea, RV. viii, 16, 2); (cf. *sv-ávas.*)

A'vas-vat, mfn. desirous, AV. iii, 26, 6; TS. v.

A'vasvad-vat, mfn. united with the desirous one [NBD.], MaitrS.

Avasá, *am*, n. Ved. refreshment, food, provisions, viaticum, RV. i, 93, 4; 119, 6; vi, 61, 1, &c.; (with *pad-vát*) 'food that has feet,' i. e. cattle, RV. x, 169, 1; (*as*), m. a king, Uṇ.

Avasya, Nom. P. (p. dat. sg. m. *avasyaté*) to seek favour or assistance, RV. i, 116, 23.

Avasyú, mfn. desiring favour or assistance, RV.; VS. (v, 32 & xviii, 45, nom. sg. m. *°syúḥ*); (said of Indra) desirous of helping or assisting, RV. iv, 16, 11 & v, 31, 10; (cf. Pāṇ. vi, 1, 116); (*us*), m., N. of a Ṛishi (with the patron. Ātreya, composer of the hymn RV. v, 31).

अवस् 2. *avás* (once, before *m*, *avár*, RV. i, 133, 6; cf. Pāṇ. viii, 2, 70), ind. (fr. 2. *áva*) downwards, RV.; (as a prep.) down from (abl. or instr.), RV.; below (with instr.), RV. i, 164, 17 & 18; x, 67, 4. **–tāt** (*avás-*), ind. (Pāṇ. v, 3, 40) below, RV.; VS.; ŚBr.; before (in time), TBr.; (as a prep. with gen.) below, ŚBr.; (*avástāt*)*-prapadana*, mfn. (anything) attained from below (as heaven), ŚBr.

Avā-śṛiṅgá, mfn. (fr. *avaḥ-*, cf. *ayā-śayá*) whose horns are turned downwards, TS. ii.

अवसक्थिका *ava-sakthikā*, f. (= *paryaṅka*, q. v.) sitting on the hams (or also 'the cloth tied round the legs and knees of a person sitting on his hams,' L.), Mn. iv, 112; Gaut.

अवसंचक्ष्य *ava-saṃ-cakshya*, mfn. to be shunned or avoided, Pāṇ. ii, 4, 54, Pat.

अवसञ्ज् *ava-√sañj* (ind. p. *-sajya*; Imper. 3. pl. Pass. *-sajyantām*) to suspend, attach to, append, MBh. xv, 436, Hariv.; R.; (cf. *ava-√sṛij* at end); to charge with (a business; acc.), R. iv, 42, 7: Ā. *-sajjate*, to adhere or cleave to, not leave undisturbed, MBh. xiii, 2198.

Ava-sakta, mfn. suspended from, attached to (as to the shoulder or to the branch of a tree &c.), bound round, MBh. &c.; being in contact with, Pañcat.; belonging to, BhP.; (in Pass. sense) hung with (as with wreaths), Hariv. 10049; charged with (a business), R. iv, 42, 8.

Ava-sañjana, *am*, n. (= *nivīta*, q. v.) the Brāhmanical thread hanging over the shoulder, Comm. on KātyŚr.

अवसंडीन *ava-sam-ḍīna, am*, n. (*√ḍī*), the united downward flight of birds, MBh. viii, 1901 (v. l.)

अवसथ *avasatha, as*, m. (for *ā-vasatha*, q. v.) habitation, Hcat.; a village, L.; a college, school, L.; (*am*), n. a house, dwelling, L.

Avasathin, mfn. having a habitation, Hcat.

Avasathya, mfn. (for *āvas°*, q. v.) belonging to a house, domestic, L.; (*as*), m. a college, school, L.

अवसद् *ava-√sad*, P. *-sīdati* (rarely Ā., e. g. Pot. *-sīdeta*, MBh. i, 5184; impf. *-sīdata*, R. iv, 58, 6) to sink (as into water), Suśr.; BhP.; to sink down, faint, grow lean [TS.; PBr.], become exhausted or disheartened, slacken, come to an end, perish: Caus. (p. *-sādayat*; ind. p. *-sādya*) to cause to sink (as into water), Suśr.; to render downhearted, dispirit, ruin, ChUp.; MBh. &c.; to frustrate, MBh. xii, 2634; R. v, 51, 2.

Ava-sanna, mfn. sunk down, pressed down (as

by a burden, BhP.; R. ii, 52, 22); sunken (as eyes), Suśr.; (opposed to *ut-sanna*) deep (as a wound), Suśr.; languid, dispirited, distressed, unhappy, KātyŚr.; MBh. iv, 198, &c.; ended, terminated, Hit.; (as the eyesight; said of a blind person) Ragh. ix, 77; (in law) beaten in a cause.

Ava-sāda, *as*, m. sinking (as of a chair), Suśr.; the growing faint (as of a sound), ib.; failing, exhaustion, fatigue, lassitude, ib.; defeat, Mālav.; want of energy or spirit (especially as proceeding from doubtful or unsuccessful love), L.; (in law) badness of a cause, L.; end, termination, L.; (cf. *nir-av°*.)

Ava-sādaka, mfn. causing to sink, frustrating, R. iv, 26, 19; exhausting, tiresome, wearisome, L.; ending, finishing, L.

Ava-sādana, *am*, n. oppressing, disheartening; the state of being disheartened, Car.; an escharotic, removing proud flesh by escharotic applications, Suśr.

Ava-sādita, mfn. made to sink, exhausted, dispirited; frustrated, R. v, 51, 2.

अवसभ *áva-sabha*, only in f. (*ā*), excluded from a (husband's) company [Sāy]; fallen into wrong (i. e. into men's) company [NBD.], ŚBr. i, 3, 1, 21.

अवसर *ava-sara*. See *ava-√sṛi*.

अवसर्ग *ava-sarga*. See *ava-√sṛij*.

Ava-sárjana. See ib.

अवसर्प *ava-sarpa*, &c. See *ava-√sṛip*.

अवसलवि *ava-salavi*, ind. = *apa-s°*, q. v., Gobh.

Ava-savi, ind. to the left, ŚāṅkhŚr.

Ava-savya, mfn. not left, right, L.

अवसा *áva-sā* and *-sātṛí*. See *ava-√so*.

अवसाद *ava-sāda*, &c. See *ava-√sad*.

अवसान 1. *á-vasāna*, mfn. (√4. *vas*), not dressed, RV. iii, 1, 6.

अवसान 2. *ava-sāna*, &c. See *ava-√so*.

अवसाम *ava-sāma*, mfn., Pāṇ. v, 4, 75.

अवसाय *ava-sāya*, &c. See *ava-√so*.

अवसिच् *ava-√sic* (p. *-siñcat*; ind. p. *-sicya*) to sprinkle, pour upon (acc. or loc.), KātyŚr.; ĀśvGṛ.; Kauś.; Gobh.; to pour out, Gobh.: Caus. (Pot. *-secayet*) to sprinkle, bedew, MBh. xiii, 5056; VarBṛS.

Ava-sikta, mfn. sprinkled, MBh.; Hariv.; R.

Ava-siñcita, mfn. id., MBh. vii, 7319.

Ava-seka, *as*, m. sprinkling, irrigating (as the ground), Mṛicch.; syringing, administering a clyster, Suśr.; bleeding (with leeches), Suśr.

Ava-sekima, *as*, m. a kind of cake (pulse ground and fried with oil or butter), L.

Ava-secana, *am*, n. sprinkling, KātyŚr.; Suśr.; water used for irrigating (trees), Mn. iv, 151; bathing, MBh. iii, 8231; bleeding, Suśr.

Ava-secita, mfn. = *-sikta*, MBh. vi, 4434.

अवसिध् *ava-√2. sidh* (impf. *avâsedhat*, v. l. *apâs°*) to keep back or off from (abl.), MBh. vii, 7397.

अवसुप्त *ava-supta*, mfn. (√*svap*), asleep, R. ii, 56, 1.

अवसृ *ava-√sṛi*, Caus. to move anything aside or away, Kauś.

Ava-sara, *as*, m. 'descent (of water),' rain, L.; occasion, moment, favourable opportunity, Śak. &c.; seasonableness, appropriate place for anything (gen.), Kathās.; any one's (gen.) turn, Pañcat.; leisure, advantageous situation, L.; (= *mantra*) consultation in private (?), L.; a year, L.; (*e*), loc. ind. at the right moment, Kathās. **-kāle** or **-velāyām** [Pañcat.], loc. ind. on a favourable opportunity.

Ava-sāraṇa, *am*, n. moving away, L.

अवसृज् *ava-√sṛij* (Subj. *-sṛijāt* [RV. x, 108, 5] or *-sṛiját* [RV. i, 174, 4] or *-sṛijat* [RV. i, 55, 6 & x, 113, 4]; Imper. 2. sg. *-sṛijā* or *-sṛijă*; impf. *-ásṛijat*; perf. Pot. *-sasṛijyāt*, RV. i, 24, 13; p. *-sṛiját*, RV. ii, 3, 10) to fling, throw (as arrows or the thunderbolt), RV. iv, 27, 3; AV. iv, 6, 7; TS. &c.; to throw or put into (loc.), Mn. i, 8; MBh. iii, 12769; Ved. to let off, let loose, let go, send, dismiss, abandon, surrender (as to misfortune, *aghâya*, RV. i, 189, 5), RV.; AV. &c.; to give up (as one's anger &c.), MBh. v, 1822 & vi, 5848, (or one's life, *prāṇān*) xii, 88; to pardon, RV. vii, 86, 5; (any one's life, *prāṇān*) MBh. iii, 3052; to deliver (a woman), RV. x, 138, 2; to be delivered, bring forth, AV. i, 11, 3; to produce, form, shape, Hariv. 7057; BhP.: Ā. (impf. 3. pl. *ávâsṛijanta*) to relax, lose energy and power, RV. iv, 19, 2; (impf. *avâsṛijat* for *°sajat*, fr. *-√sañj*, BR.) to attach to (loc.), MBh. i, 1973.

Ava-sarga, *as*, m. (gaṇa *nyaṅkv-ādi*, q. v.) letting loose, letting go (*an-* neg.) Jaim.; relaxation, laxity, L.; following one's own inclinations, independence, L.

Ava-sárjana, *am*, n. liberation, VS. xii, 64.

Ava-sarjita, mfn. (= *visṛishṭavat*, Comm.) who has abandoned, R. vii, 56, 23.

Áva-sṛishṭa, mfn. let loose, RV. x, 4, 3; thrown (as arrows or the thunderbolt), RV. vi, 75, 16 & vii, 46, 3; AV. i, 3, 9 (cf. *rudrâv°*); (*ava-sṛishṭá*), mfn. made over, dismissed, sent, RV. x, 28, 11 & 91, 14; brought forth (from the womb), BhP.; fallen down from or upon (in comp.), BhP.

अवसृप् *ava-√sṛip*, *-sárpati*, (said of the sun) to set, VS. xvi, 7; (p. loc. m. *-sarpati*) Lāṭy.; to flow back (as the sea in low tide), MBh. xiii, 7257 (v. l. *ava-sarpita*, mfn. 'caused to flow back'); to creep to or approach unawares, TS.; AV. viii, 6, 3; to flow over gradually, AV. xi, 1, 17.

Ava-sarpa, *as*, m. 'one who approaches unawares,' a spy, L.; (cf. *apa-sarpa*.)

Ava-sarpaṇa, *am*, n. 'descent,' the place from which Manu descended after he had left his ark, ŚBr. i; going down to, MārkP.; (cf. *rathyâvas°*.)

Ava-sarpiṇī, f. 'going or gliding down gradually,' a descending period of a long duration and alternating with the 'ascending one' (*ut-sarpiṇī*, q. v.; both the ascending [*ut-s°*] and descending [*ava-s°*] cycle are divided into six stages each: good-good, good, good-bad, bad-good, bad, bad-bad), Jain.; Āryabh.

Ava-sarpita, mfn., see s. v. *ava-√sṛip*.

अवसो *ava-√so*, *-syati* (Imper. 2. du. *-syatam*; aor. Subj. *-sāt*) to loosen, deliver from, RV. vi, 74, 3 & vii, 28, 4; TS.; ŚBr.; (Imper. 2. sg. *-sya*; aor. *ávâsāt*, TBr. &c.; aor. 3. pl. *ávâsur*, RV. i, 179, 2; ind. p. *-sāya*, RV. i, 104, 1; Ved. Inf. *-sai*, RV. iii, 53, 20) Ved. to unharness (horses), put up at any one's house, settle, rest, RV. &c.; to take one's abode or standing-place in or upon (loc), AV. ix, 2, 14; TBr.; to finish, terminate (one's work), ŚāṅkhŚr.; RPrāt. &c.; to be finished, be at an end, be exhausted, Kir. xvi, 17; to choose or appoint (as a place for dwelling or for a sacrifice); TS.; ŚBr.; (Pot. 2. sg. *-seyās*; cf. Pāṇ. vi, 4, 67) to decide, Bhaṭṭ.; to obtain, BhP.: Caus. *-sāyayati* (ind. p. *-sâyya*) to cause to take up one's abode in or upon (loc.), TS.; AitBr.; ŚBr.; (ind. p. *-sāyya*) to complete, Ragh. v, 76; (Inf. [in Pass. sense] *-sāyayitum*) to ascertain, clearly distinguish, Kir. ii, 29: Pass. *-sīyate* (cf. Pāṇ. vi, 4, 66) to be obtained, BhP.; to be insisted upon, MBh. xii, 554 (ed. Bomb. in active sense 'to insist upon'); to be ascertained, BhP.; Sarvad.

Áva-sā, f. liberation, deliverance, RV. iv, 23, 3; 'halt, rest,' see *an-avasá*.

Ava-sātṛí, *tā*, m. a liberator, RV. x, 27, 9.

2. **Ava-sāna**, *am*, n. (cf. *ava-mocana*) 'where the horses are unharnessed,' stopping, resting-place, residence, RV. x, 14, 9; AV.; ŚBr.; MBh.; a place chosen or selected for being built upon, MānGṛ.; (ifc. f. *ā*, Ragh. i, 95) conclusion, termination, cessation, Mn. ii, 71; Śak. &c.; death, Śak.; Pañcat.; boundary, limit, L.; end of a word, last part of a compound or period, end of a phrase, Prāt.; Pāṇ.; the end of the line of a verse or the line of a verse itself, AAnukr.; VPrāt.; KātyŚr.; N. of a place, (gaṇa *takshaśilâdi*, q. v.) **-darśá**, mfn. looking at one's place of destination or residence, AV. vii, 41, 1; seeing the end of (gen.), PBr. **-bhūmi**, f. 'place of limit,' the highest limit, Kād.

Avasānaka, mf(*ikā*)n. attaining an end by (in comp.)

Avasānika, mfn. forming the end of (in comp.), R. ii, 56, 25.

Avasānyà, mfn. belonging to the line of a verse, VS. xvi, 33.

1. **Ava-sāya**, ind. p. (Pāṇ. vi, 4, 69), see *-√so*.

2. **Ava-sāya**, *as*, m. (Pāṇ. iii, 1, 141) 'taking up one's abode,' see *yatra-kāmâvasāya*; termination, conclusion, end, L.; remainder, L.; determination, ascertainment, L.

Ava-sāyaka, mfn. (said of an arrow, *sāyaka*) 'bringing to a close,' destructive, Kir. xv, 37.

Ava-sāyin, mfn. 'taking up one's abode, settling,' see *antâv°* and *ante-'v°*, *yatra-kāmâv°*

Ava-sāyya, ind. p. (fr. Caus.), see *ava-√so*.

Áva-sita, mfn. one who has put up at any place, who dwells, rests, resides, RV. i, 32, 15 & iv, 25, 8; ŚBr.; KātyŚr.; brought to his abode (as Agni), TS.; ended, terminated, finished, completed, MBh. i, 4678, &c.; one who has given up anything (abl., MBh. xii, 7888; or in comp., Yājñ. ii, 183); determined, fixed, BhP.; ascertained, BhP.; known, understood; one who is determined to (loc.), BhP.; being at end of the line of a verse (see *ava-sāna*), RPrāt.; VPrāt.; stored (as grain &c.), L.; gone, L.; (*am*), n. 'a dwelling-place,' see *navâvasitá*.

Ava-seya, mfn. to be ascertained, be understood, be made out, be learnt from, Jain. Comm. &c.; 'to be brought to a close,' be destroyed, L.

Ava-sai, Ved. Inf., see *ava-√so* above.

अवस्कन्द् *ava-√skand* (ind. p. *-skandya*) to jump down from (abl.), BhP.; to approach hastening from (abl.), ShaḍvBr.; to storm, assault (as a city &c.), R.; Mālav. &c.

Ava-skanda, *as*, m. assault, attack, storm, Pañcat.; Hit.; Kathās.

Ava-skandana, *am*, n. id., L.; descending, L.; bathing, L.; (in law) accusation.

Ava-skandita, mfn. attacked, L.; gone down, L.; bathed, bathing, L.; (in law) accused, refuted (?), L.

Ava-skandin, mfn. 'covering (a cow),' see *gaurâv°*; ifc. attacking, Mcar.

Ava-skanna, mfn. spilt (as semen virile), Hariv. 1786; 'attacked,' overpowered (as by love), R. vi, 95, 41.

अवस्कर *ava-s-kara*. See *ava-√s-kṛī*.

अवस्कव *ava-skavá*, *as*, m. (√*sku*), a kind of worm, AV. ii, 31, 4.

अवस्कृ *ava-√s-kṛi* (√3. *kṛi*), Ā. (perf. 3. pl. *ava-caskarire*) to scrape with the feet, Śiś. v, 63; (cf. *apa-√s-kṛī* s. v. *apa-√kṛī*.)

Ava-s-kara, *as*, m. ordure, fæces, Pāṇ. vi, 1, 148; the privities, L.; a place for fæces &c., privy, closet, MBh. iii, 14676; Rājat.; a place for sweepings &c., Comm. on Yājñ.; (cf. *ava-kara*.) **-mandira**, n. water-closet, Rājat.

Ava-s-karaka, *as*, m., N. of an insect (originating from fæces), Pāṇ. iv, 3, 28.

अवस्तात् *avás-tāt*. See 2. *avás*.

अवस्तु *a-vastu*, n. a worthless thing, Kum. v, 66; insubstantiality, the unreality of matter, Kap.; Vedântas. **-tā**, f. or **-tva**, n. [Kap.] insubstantiality, unreality.

अवस्तृ *ava-√stṛī*, P. *-striṇāti* (1. sg. *-striṇāmi*; ind. p. *-stírya*) to strew, scatter, VS. v, 25; TS.; ŚBr.; (perf. *-tastāra*) to scatter over, cover with (instr.), MBh. vii, 1568: Ā. (perf. *-tastare*) to penetrate (as a sound), Kir. xiv, 29.

Ava-staraṇa, *am*, n. strewing, KātyŚr.; a cover for a bed, blanket, Āp.

Ava-stāra, *as*, m. (Pāṇ. iii, 3, 120) 'a litter, bed,' (cf. *nir-av°*.)

Ava-stīrṇa, mfn. strewed, covered with (instr.), Kauś.; Suśr.

अवस्त्र *a-vastra*, mfn. without clothes, naked. **-tā**, f. nakedness, N.

अवस्था *ava-√sthā*, P. *-tishṭhati* (impf. *-atishṭhat*; aor. Subj. *-sthāt*; perf. Ā. 3. sg. *-tasthe*; perf. p. P. *-tasthivás*) to go down into (acc.), reach down to (acc.), RV.; ŚBr.; (aor. Subj. 2. pl. *-sthāta*) to go away from (abl.), RV. v, 53, 8; (aor. Subj. 1. sg. *-sthām*) to be separated from or deprived of (abl.), RV. ii, 27, 17: Ā. (Pāṇ. i, 3, 22; rarely P., e. g. Bhag. xiv, 23; BhP. &c.) to take one's stand, remain standing, ĀśvGṛ. &c.; to stay, abide, stop at any place (loc.), MBh. &c.; to abide in a state or condition (instr.), MBh. i, 5080; BhP. &c.; (with ind. p.) to remain or continue (doing anything), MBh. i, 5770; iii, 187 (ed. Bomb.), &c.; to be found, exist, be present, MBh.; Yājñ. i, 272, &c.; (perf. 1. sg. *-tasthe*) to fall to, fall into the possession of (dat.), RV. x, 48, 5; to enter, be absorbed in (loc.),

Mn. vi, 81; to penetrate (as sound or as fame), MBh. xiii, 1845: Pass. *-sthīyate*, to be settled or fixed or chosen, Śak.: Caus. (generally ind. p. *-sthāpya*) to cause to stand or stop (as a carriage or an army &c.), let behind, MBh. &c.; to place upon (loc.), fix, set, array, ĀśvGṛ. &c.; to cause to enter or be absorbed in (loc.), MBh. iii, 12502; to render solid or firm, R. v, 35, 36; to establish (by arguments), Comm. on Nyāyad.: Pass. Caus. *-sthāpyate*, to be kept firm ['to be separated,' BR.], BhP.

Ava-sthá, *as*, m. membrum virile, AV. vii, 90, 3 (cf. *upá-stha*); (*ā*), f. appearance (in a court of justice), Mn. viii, 60; 'stability, consistence,' cf. *an-avastha*; state, condition, situation (five are distinguished in dramas, Sāh.), circumstance of age [Pāṇ. v, 4, 146; vi, 2, 115, &c.] or position, stage, degree; (*ās*), f. pl. the female organs of generation, RV, v, 19, 1. **Avasthā-catushṭaya**, n. the four periods or states of human life (viz. childhood, youth, manhood, and old age). **Avasthā-traya**, n. the three states (viz. waking, dreaming, and sound sleep), RāmatUp.; BhP. **Avasthā-dvaya**, n. the two states of life (viz. happiness and misery). **Avasthā́-van**, mfn. possessed of stability, TS.

Ava-sthāna, *am*, n. standing, taking up one's place, R. v, 5, 18; situation, condition, Pañcat.; Hit.; residing, abiding, dwelling, Vedāntas.; Sāh.; stability, Rājat.; (cf. *an-av°*.)

Ava-sthāpana, *am*, n. exposing (goods for sale), Daś.

Ava-sthāyin, mfn. staying, residing in, Kād.; placed (behind, *paścāt*; as an army); abiding in a particular condition, Comm. on Bād.

Ava-sthita, mfn. standing near (sometimes with acc., e.g. Hariv. 14728; R. v, 73, 26), placed, having its place or abode, ĀśvŚr.; MaitrUp.; MBh. &c.; (with a pr. p.) continuing to do anything, R. iii, 30, 19; engaged in, prosecuting, following, practising (with loc. [MBh. ii, 1228; Mn. &c.] or in comp. [Bhag. iv, 23; Hit.]); obeying or following (the words or commands of; loc.), BhP.; Bhaṭṭ.; giving one's self up to (e.g. to compassion or pride), MBh. xiii, 272; R. v, 58, 13; contained in (loc.), Mn. xii, 119; Bhag. ix, 4 & xv, 11; being incumbent upon (loc.), Kum. ii, 28; ready for (dat.), Pañcat.; firm, fixed, determined, KaṭhUp.; R. &c.; steady, trusty, to be relied on, Mn. vii, 60, &c.; (cf. *an-av°*.)

Ava-sthiti, *is*, f. residence, BhP.; Kathās.; abiding, stability, see *an-av°*; following, practising, L.

अवस्ना *ava-√snā*, Caus. *-snāpayati*, to wash, Kauś.

Ava-snāta, mfn. (water) in which any one has bathed, MBh. xiii, 5014.

अवस्पृ *ava-√spṛi* (aor. Subj. *-spárat*, 2. sg. *-spar*; Imper. 2. sg. *-spṛidhi* & 2. du. *-spṛitam*) to defend, preserve from (abl.), RV.

Ava-spartṛi (only Voc. *°rtar*), m. a preserver, saviour, RV. ii, 23, 8.

अवस्फुर् *ava-√sphur* (fut. *-sphurishyati*) to cast away, Nir. v, 17.

अवस्फूर्ज् *ava-√sphūrj* (p. *-sphū́rjat*) Ved. to thunder, make a noise like a thunder-clap, VS.; TS.; ŚBr. &c.; to snort, MBh. vi, 774 (ed. Bomb.); Suśr.; to fill with noise, MBh. vii, 321; Hariv. 13279.

Ava-sphūrja, *as*, m. the rolling of thunder, PārGṛ.

अवस्मि *ava-√smi*, Ā. (impf. 3. pl. *-smayanta*) to flash down (said of lightning), RV. i, 168, 8.

अवस्य *avasya*, Nom. P. See 1. *ávas*.

अवस्यन्द् *ava-√syand*, Ā. (p. *-syandamāna*) to flow or trickle down, BhP.

Ava-syandana, *am*, n. (gaṇa *gahâdi*, q. v.)

Ava-syandita, *am*, n. (in rhetoric) attributing to one's own words a sense not originally meant, Sāh.; Daśar. &c.

अवस्यु *avasyú*. See 1. *ávas*.

अवस्रंस् *ava-√sraṇs*, Ā. (p. *-sraṇsamāna*) falling down, Suśr.

Ava-srásas, Ved. Inf. (abl.) from falling down, RV. ii, 17, 5.

Ava-srasta, mfn. fallen down, Suśr.

अवस्रु *ava-√sru*, Caus. (p. *-srāvayat*) to cause to flow down, KātyŚr.

Ava-sruta, mfn. run or dropped down, ĀśvGṛ.

अवस्वत् *ávas-vat*. See 1. *ávas*.

अवस्वन् *ava-√svan* (aor. *-ásvanīt*) to fly down with noise, RV. iv, 27, 3; (cf. *ava-shvan*.)

Ava-svanya, mfn. roaring, MaitrS.; VS. xvi, 31.

अवस्वृ *ava-√svṛi* (Subj. *-svarāti*) to sound (as an instrument), RV. viii, 69, 9; (Pot. *-svaret*) to sustain with gradually lowered voice, Lāṭy.

अवहन् *ava-√han* (Subj. 2. sg. *-han*, RV. v, 32, 1 & vi, 26, 5; Imper. 2. pl. *-hantanā*, RV. ii, 34, 9; Imper. 2. sg. *-jahi*; impf. 2. & 3. sg. *-ahan* or *ahan*; perf. 2. sg. *-jaghantha*) to throw down, strike, hit, RV.; AV.; MBh. ii, 915; Ved. to drive away, expel, keep off, fend off, RV.; AV. &c.; chiefly Ved. to thresh, RV. i, 191, 2 (p. fem. *-ghnatī*); TS. &c.: Ā. *-jighnate*, to throw down, RV. i, 80, 5: Caus. (Pot. *-ghātayet*) to cause to thresh, ŚBr. xiv: Intens. (Imper. 2. sg. *-jaṅghanīhi*) to drive away, fend off, AV. v, 20, 8.

Ava-ghāta, *as*, m. a blow, Sāh. &c.; threshing corn by bruising it with a wooden pestle in a mortar of the same material, Jaim.; Kathās. &c.; (for *ava-ghaṭṭa*, q.v.) a hole in the ground, L.

Ava-ghātin, mfn. ifc. threshing, BhP.; striking, L.

Ava-jaghnat, mfn. (irreg. p. in Pass. sense; = *-hanyamāna*, Comm.) being beaten or struck by (instr.), MBh. iv, 1424.

Ava-hata, mfn. threshed, winnowed, KātyŚr.

Ava-hanana, *am*, n. threshing, winnowing, KātyŚr.; BhP.; (cf. *adhy-avah°*); the left lung, Yājñ. iii, 94; Comm. on Vishṇus.

Ava-hantṛi, *tā́*, m. one who throws off or wards off, RV. iv, 25, 6.

अवहर्षित *ava-harshita*, mfn. (√*hṛish*), caused to shiver, MBh. ix, 2786.

अवहस् *ava-√has*, to laugh at, deride, MBh. &c.

Ava-hasana, *am*, n. deriding, MBh. i, 144.

Ava-hāsa, *as*, m. jest, joke, Bhag. xi, 42; BrahmaP.; derision, MBh.; R.; Kathās.

Ava-hāsya, mfn. to be derided, exposed to ridicule, ridiculous, MBh. i, 7039. **-tā**, f. ridiculousness, MBh. iii, 17193; Kathās.

अवहस्त *ava-hasta*, *as*, m. the back of the hand, L.

अवहा *ava-√3. hā* (aor. 3. sg. *ávāhāḥ* [for *°hās-t*]; perf. 3. sg. *-jahā́*; ind. p. *-hāya*) to leave, quit, RV. i, 116, 3 & viii, 45, 37; TS.; MBh. xiii, 6208: Pass. *-hīyate* (fut. *-hāsyate*, Kāṭh.) to be left remaining, remain behind, MBh. iii, 11558; 'to remain behind,' i.e. to be excelled, R. v, 2, 11; (1. sg. *-hīye*) to be abandoned, RV. x, 34, 5: Caus. (aor. Subj. 2. sg. *-jīhipas*) to cause to remain behind on or to deviate from (a path; abl.), RV. iii, 53, 19.

अवहालिका *ava-hālikā*, f. (√*hal*), a wall, hedge, L.; (cf. *nir-av°*.)

अवहित *áva-hita*. See *ava-√dhā*.

अवहित्थ *avahittha*, *am*, n. (corrupted fr. *a-bahiḥ-stha*?) dissimulation; (*ā*), f. id., Daśar.; Sāh. &c.

अवहु *ava-√hu* (3. pl. *-juhvati*) to shed (as drops of sweat), RV. v, 7, 5.

अवहृ *ava-√hṛi*, Ā. *-harate* (generally ind. p. *-hṛitya*) to move down (as the arms), take down, put down or aside, KātyŚr.; Lāṭy.; (P. Imper. 2. sg. *-hara* MBh. iv, 1304: P. *-harati*, to bring together, amass (?), Pāṇ. v, 1, 52: Caus. to cause to pay taxes, Āp.: Caus. Pass. (3. pl. *-hāryante*) to be caused to pay taxes, MBh. ii, 249.

Ava-haraṇa, *am*, n. putting aside, throwing away, KātyŚr.

Ava-hāra, *as*, m. truce, suspension of arms, MBh.; cessation of playing &c., Kathās.; summoning, inviting, L.; a thief, L.; a marine monster, L.; (= *dharmântara*) apostacy, abandoning a sect or cast (?), L.; (= *apanetavya-dravya* or *upan°*) a tax, duty (?), L.

Ava-hāraka, mfn. one who stops fighting &c.; (*as*), m. a marine monster, L.; (cf. *yuddhâvahārika*.)

Ava-hārya, mfn. to be caused to pay (as a person), Mn. viii, 198; to be caused to be paid (as a sum), Mn. viii, 145.

Ava-hṛita, mfn. for *apa-h°*, taken off, MBh. vii, 1787; MārkP.

अवहेल *ava-hela*, *am*, *ā*, n.f. (√*hel* for *heḍ*), disrespect, L.; (*ayā*), instr. ind. without any trouble, quite easily, Kathās.; (cf. *sâvahelam*.)

Ava-helana, *am*, n. disrespect, L.

Ava-helita, mfn. disrespected, L.; (*am*), n. disrespect, L.

अवह्वर *ava-hvara*. See *án-av°*.

अवह्वे *ava-√hve*, Ā. (1. sg. *-hvaye*) to call down from, RV. v, 56, 1.

अवाक् *avāk*. See 1. *a-vā́c* and *ávāñc*.

अवाकिन् *a-vākin*, mfn. (√*vac*), not speaking, ChUp.

1. **A-vāk-ká**, mfn. speechless, ŚBr. x.

1. **A-vā́c**, mfn. id., ŚBr. xiv; VarBṛS. **A-vāk-śruti**, mfn. deaf and dumb, L.

A-vācaka, mfn. not expressive of, Kpr.; Sāh.

A-vācanīya, mfn. not to be read, Bālar.

1. **A-vācya**, mfn. not to be addressed, Mn. ii, 128; improper to be uttered, R.; Kathās.; (*a-vācyaṃ karma* = *maithunam*) Comm. on ŚBr.; 'not distinctly expressed,' see *-tva*. **-tā**, f. reproach, calumny, Kir. xi, 53; BhP. **-tva**, n. the not being distinctly expressed, Sāh. **-deśa**, m. 'unmentionable region,' the vulva, Comm. on ŚBr.

अवाकृ *avâ-√1. kṛi* (Imper. 2. sg. *-kṛidhi*) to ward off, remove, RV. viii, 53, 4.

अवागम् *avâ-√gam* (aor. 1. pl. *áva âgan-ma*) to undertake, begin, RV. iii, 31, 14.

अवाग्र *avâgra*, mfn. having the point turned aside, ĀpŚr.; (cf. *avāg-agra*.)

अवाचि *avâ-√1. ci*, *-cinoti* (= *bhogena vyayī-karoti*, Comm.) to dissipate what is accumulated, use up, MBh. xii, 5952.

अवाच्छिद् *avâ-√chid* (ind. p. *-chidya*) to tear away or out from (abl.), Vikr.

अवाज् *avâj* (√*oj*), *ávâjati*, to drive down, RV. i, 161, 10.

अवाजिन् *á-vājin*, *ī*, m. a bad horse, RV. iii, 53, 23.

अवाञ्च् *ávāñc*, *āṅ*, *āci*, *āk* (fr. 2. *añc*), turned downwards, being or situated below, lower than (abl.), RV. iv, 25, 6; AV. x, 2, 11; ŚBr. xiv; (*avāñcam*), ind. downwards, Śulb.; (*ávācī*), f. (with *diś*) the direction downwards (i.e. towards the ground), VS. xxii, 24; ŚBr. xiv; Up.; (without *diś*) the southern quarter, L.; (*avāk*), ind., see s. v.

Avāk, ind. downwards, headlong, ĀśvGṛ.; Kauś.; Mn. viii, 75. **-pushpī**, f. 'having its flowers turned downwards,' the plant Anethum Sowa Roxb., L. **-śākha**, mfn. having shoots turned downwards (as the Ficus Indica), KaṭhUp. **-siras**, mfn. having the head downwards, headlong, Mn.; MBh. &c.; having its upper end turned downwards, VarBṛS. **-śīrsha**, mfn. having the head turned downwards, MBh. xiii, 2929. **-śṛiṅga**, mfn. (said of the moon) whose crescent is turned downwards, VarBṛS.

2. **Avāk-ka**, mf(*ā*)n. (only for the etym. of *ávakā*) turned downwards, ŚBr. ix.

Avāg (in Sandhi for *avāk*). **-agra**, mfn. having the point turned downwards, Āp. (wrongly written *avāṅ-agra*). **-gati**, f. the way downwards (to the hell), MBh. xiv, 490. **-gamana-vat**, mfn. (said of the Apāna) taking its course downwards, Vedāntas. **-bhāga**, m. the part below, ground, L. **-vadana**, mfn. having the face turned downwards, BhP.

Avāṅ (in Sandhi for *avāk*). **-agra**, see *avāg-agra*. **-nābhi**, ind. below the navel. **-niraya**, m. the hell below (the earth), MBh. xiv, 1008; (cf. *tiryaṅ-nir°*.) **-mukha**, mf(*ī*)n. having the face turned downwards, looking down, MBh. &c.; turned downwards; (*as*), m., N. of a Mantra spoken over a weapon, R. i, 30, 4.

Avācīna, mf(*ā*)n. directed downwards, being or

situated below (abl.), AV. x, 4, 25; xiii, 1, 30; ŚBr.; (*as*), m., N. of a king, MBh. i, 3770 seqq. **-śīrshán**, mf(*°rshṇī*)n. having the head turned downwards, headlong, ŚBr. iv. **-hasta**, mfn. having the hand turned downwards, Kauś. **Avācīnâgra**, mfn. = *avāg-agra*, q. v., AitBr.

2. **Avācya**, mfn. southern, southerly, L.

Avâñcita, mfn. (perf. Pass. p. √*añc*) turned downwards (as the face), Sāh.

अवात 1. *a-vātá*, mf(*ā́*)n. (√*vai*), not dried up, fresh, RV. i, 52, 4; 62, 10 & viii, 79, 7.

A-vāna, mfn. id., MBh. ii, 704 (v. l. *a-vāta*); wet, Kād.; dry, L.

अवात 2. *a-vātá*, mf(*ā́*)n. windless, RV. i, 38, 7; (*ám*), n. the windless atmosphere, RV. vi, 64, 4 & x, 129, 2.

A-vātala, mfn. not flatulent, Suśr.

अवात 3. *á-vāta*, mf(*ā*)n. (√*van*), unattacked, untroubled, RV.

अवातित *avâtita*, mfn. (√*at*), (only for the etym. of *avatá*) gone down, Nir. x, 13.

अवाद् *avâd* (√*ad*), (Pot. 1. pl. *-adimahi*) to cause to eat food, VS. iii, 58.

अवादिन् *a-vādin*, mfn. (gaṇa *grāhy-ādi*, q. v.) not speaking, not disputing, peaceable, L.

अवान् *avân* (√*an*), *avâniti*, to breathe or inhale, ŚBr. iv; (cf. *án-avânat*.)

अवान *a-vāna*. See 1. *a-vātá*.

अवान्तर *avântará*, mfn. intermediate, TS.; ŚBr.; respectively different, respective (generally said with regard to two things only), Vedāntas.; Sāh. &c.; (*ám*), ind. differently from (abl.), MaitrS.; (*ám*), ind. between, ŚBr. **-díś**, f. an intermediate region of the compass, ŚBr.; BṛĀrUp.; Nir.; Śulb.; (*avântara-dik*)*-srakti*, mfn. (said of the Vedi) having its corners turned towards intermediate regions of the compass, KātyŚr. **-diśā́**, f. = *-diś*, q. v., MaitrS.; VS. xxiv, 26. **-dīkshá**, mfn. performing an intermediate consecration, ŚBr. iii. **-dīkshā́**, f. an intermediate consecration, ĀpŚr.; MānŚr.; *avântara-dīkshâdi*, a gaṇa, Comm. on Pāṇ. v, 1, 94. **-dīkshin**, mfn. = *-dīkshá*, q. v., Pāṇ. v, 1, 94, Comm. **-deśá**, m. a place situated in an intermediate region, ŚBr.; KātyŚr. **-bheda**, m. subdivision, Kap. **Avântarêḍā**, f. an Iḍā subdivided into five parts, AitBr.; KātyŚr.; ĀśvŚr.

अवाप् *avâp* (√*āp*), *-āpnoti* (Imper. 2. sg. *-āpnuhi*) to reach, attain, obtain, gain, get, Up.; Mn.; MBh. &c.; to get by division (as a quotient), Sūryas.; to suffer (e. g. blame or unpleasantness or pain), Mn.; Ragh. xviii, 34; Pañcat.: Caus. to cause to obtain anything (acc.), Naish. viii, 89.

Avâpa, mfn. See *dur-avâpa*.

Avâpta, mfn. one who has attained or reached, KaṭhUp.; obtained, got; (*am*), n. 'got by division,' a quotient, Comm. on VarBṛ. **-vat**, mfn. reaching, obtaining; entertaining (as a belief), L.

Avâptavya, mfn. to be obtained, Bhag.; Ragh.

Avâpti, *is*, f. obtaining, getting, R.; Kum. v, 64, &c.; (in arithm.) a quotient.

1. **Avâpya**, ind. p. having obtained, Ragh. iii, 33, &c.

2. **Avâpya**, mfn. to be obtained, Mn. xi, 185; Pañcat.

अवापित *a-vāpita*, mfn. (√*vap*), not sown (as grain, *dhānya*) but planted, L.

अवापोह् *avâpôh* (√1. *ūh*), (ind. p. *°pôhya*) to remove, Suśr.

अवाय *avâya*, *as*, m. (√*i*), going down (into water, in comp.), KātyŚr.; 'yielding,' see *an-avâyá*.

अवायु *a-vāyú*, mfn. without wind, ŚBr. xiv.

अवार *avārá*, *as*, *am*, m. n. (fr. 2. *áva*, but formed after *a-pāra*, q. v.) Ved. this side, the near bank of a river, VS. xxx, 16; TS. &c. **-tas** (*avārá-*), ind. to this side, RV. x, 65, 6. **-pāra**, m. (Pāṇ. iv, 2, 93 & v, 2, 11) the ocean, L.; (cf. *pārâvāra*.) **-pārīṇa**, mfn. deriv. fr. *avāra-pāra*, Pāṇ. iv, 2, 93 & v, 2, 11.

Avārīṇa, mfn. deriv. fr. *avāra*, Pāṇ. iv, 2, 93, Comm.; v, 2, 11, Siddh.

1. **Avāryà**, mfn. being on the near side of a river, VS. xvi, 42 & xxv, 1.

अवारणीय *a-vāraṇīya*, mfn. (√1. *vṛi*), not to be stopped or kept back, not to be warded off, unrestrainable, (as water) MBh. i, 693; (as a weapon) MBh. iv, 2112 & v, 1888; Kathās.; 'not to be remedied, incurable,' i. e. treating of incurable sicknesses, Suśr.

Avārikā, f. the plant Coriandrum Sativum.

A-vārita, mfn. unimpeded, unobstructed; (*am*), ind. without obstacles, at pleasure, MBh. xiii, 3294; xiv, 2686; Mudr.; Kathās. **-dvāra**, mfn. having open doors, Naish. iii, 41.

A-vāritavya, mfn. not to be impeded or hindered, not to be kept off.

2. **A-vārya**, mfn. not to be kept back or warded off, unrestrainable, irresistible, Hariv. 10805 & 15067; R.; (*vārya* with *na* neg.) MBh. v, 7375; 'incurable,' see *-tā*. **-kratu** (*avāryá-*), (6) mfn. of irresistible power, RV. viii, 92, 8. **-tā**, f. incurableness, Suśr.

अवारुह् *avâ-√ruh*, Caus. (fut. sg. *-rohayitā*) to bring down from (abl.)

अवार्छ् *avârch* (√*ṛich*), *avârchati* (sic; Pot. *avârchet*) to fall down, become damaged, TS.; ŚBr.

अवार्ज् *avârj* (√*ṛij*), (3. pl. *avârjanti*) to dismiss, ŚBr. iv.

अवालोच् *avâ-√loc*, Ā. (perf. *-luloce*) to consider, Bhaṭṭ.

अवावट *avāvaṭa*, *as*, m. the son of a woman by any other man than her first husband, Comm. on Mn. x, 5.

अवावन् *avāvan*, mf(*vari*)n. (√*oṇ*, Pāṇ. iv, 1, 7, Comm.), one who carries off, a thief, L.

अवाशृङ्ग *avā-śriṅgá*. See 2. *avás*.

अवास् *avâs* (√2. *as*), (Ved. ind. p. *avâsyā*) to put down, RV. i, 140, 10.

अवासस् *a-vāsas*, mfn. unclothed, L.

अवासिच् *avâ-√sic*, to pour into (loc.), Gobh.

अवासिन् *a-vāsin*, mfn. (gaṇa *grāhy-ādi*, q. v.)

अवास्तव *a-vāstava*, mfn. unsubstantial, unreal, fictitious; unfounded, irrational (as an argument).

A-vāstú, mfn. having no home, AV. xii, 5, 45.

अवाहन *a-vāhaná*, mfn. having no vehicle or carriage, not driving in a carriage, ŚBr. iv.

अवि *ávi*, mfn. (√*av*), favourable, kindly disposed, AV. v, 1, 9; (*is*), m. f. a sheep, RV. (mentioned with reference to its wool being used for the Soma strainer); AV. &c.; the woollen Soma strainer, RV.; (*ís*), m. a protector, lord, L.; the sun, L.; air, wind, L.; a mountain, L.; a wall or enclosure, L.; a cover made of the skin of mice, L.; (*is*), f. an ewe, AV. x, 8, 31; (= *a-vī*, q. v.; cf. also *adhi*) a woman in her courses, L. [cf. Lith. *awi-s*; Slav. *ovjza*; Lat. *ovi-s*; Gk. ὄϊ-ς; Goth. *avistr*]. **-kaṭa**, m. a flock of sheep, Pāṇ. v, 2, 29, Comm.; *avikaṭôraṇa*, m. tribute or tax consisting of a ram to be paid (to the king) by the owner of a flock of sheep, Pāṇ. vi, 3, 10, Pat. **-gandhikā**, f. the plant Ocimum Villosum; (cf. *aja-gandhā*.) **-dugdha**, n. the milk of an ewe, L. **-dūsa**, n. id., Pāṇ. iv, 2, 36, Comm. **-paṭa**, m. = *avīnāṃ vistāra*, Pāṇ. v, 2, 29, Comm. **-pālá**, m. a shepherd, VS. xxx, 11; ŚBr. iv; MBh. iii, 14700. **-priya**, m. 'liked by sheep,' the grass Panicum Frumentaceum, L.; (*ā*), f., N. of another plant, L. **-bhuj**, m. 'enjoying (i. e. devouring) sheep,' a wolf, L. **-mat** (*ávi-*), mfn. possessing sheep, RV. iv, 2, 5; AV. vi, 37, 1. **-marīsa**, n. = *-dugdha* above, Pāṇ. iv, 2, 36, Comm. **-sodha**, n. id., ib. **-sthala**, n. 'sheep-place,' N. of a town, MBh. v, 934 (ed. Bomb.) & 2595.

Avika, *as*, m. a sheep, Pāṇ. v, 4, 28; (*ā*), f. an ewe, RV. i, 126, 7; AV. xx, 129, 17 (*avikā*); Mn.; Kathās.; (*am*), n. a diamond, L.

Avita, avitṛi, avithya. See ss. vv.

अविकच *a-vikaca*, mfn. closed, shut (as a flower).

A-vikacita, mfn. unblown.

अविकत्थन *a-vikatthana*, mfn. not boasting, MBh.; Ragh. xiv, 73, &c.

अविकथयत् *a-vikathayat*, mfn. not talking vainly or idly, Āp.

अविकर्ष *a-vikarsha*, *as*, m. absence of separation, RPrāt.

A-vikṛishṭa, mfn. not separated, RPrāt.; not robbed or plundered, AitBr.

अविकल *a-vikala*, mfn. unimpaired, entire, MaitrUp.; MBh. xii, 11943, &c.; regular, orderly, Śiś. xi, 10.

अविकल्प *a-vikalpa*, *as*, m. absence of alternative, positive precept; (mfn.) not distinguished or particularized, BhP. &c.; not deliberating long or hesitating, Kathās.; Pañcat.; (*am*), ind. without hesitation, Kād.; Pañcat.; Kathās.

A-vikalpita, mfn. undoubted, Sarvad.

अविकार *a-vikāra*, *as*, m. non-change of form or nature, non-alteration, VPrāt.; Gaut.; Jaim.; (mfn.) unchangeable, immutable, VPrāt.; (gaṇa *cārv-ādi*, q. v.) **-vat**, mfn. not exhibiting any alteration, Kām. **-sadṛiśa**, mfn. (gaṇa *cārv-ādi*, q. v.)

A-vikārin, mfn. unchangeable, invariable (as truth), MBh. xii, 5979 & (superl. *°ri-tama*) 5986, &c.; unchangeable (in character), faithful, Mn. vii, 190; without change, without being changed, Suśr.; not exhibiting any alteration (in one's features), Kathās.

A-vikārya, mfn. invariable, Bhag. ii, 25.

A-vikṛita, mfn. unchanged, TPrāt.; not prepared, not changed by artificial means, being in its natural condition, Āp.; Gaut.; (said of cloth) not dyed, Gaut.; not developed (in its shape), ŚBr. iii; not deformed, not monstrous, Gaut. **A'vikṛitâṅga**, mfn. having undeveloped limbs (as an embryo), ŚBr. iv.

A-vikṛiti, *is*, f. unchangeableness, Sāy. on RV. i, 164, 36.

A-vikriya, mf(*ā*)n. unchangeable, invariable, Ragh. x, 17; BhP.; not showing any alteration (in one's features), Kathās.; not exhibiting any difference, quite similar, Rājat.; (*ā*), f. 'unchangeableness,' see *avikriyâtmaka* below. **-tva**, n. unchangeableness, Sāy. on RV. i, 164, 36; Kull. on Mn. vi, 92. **Avikriyâtmaka**, mfn. whose nature is unchangeableness, Vedāntas.

अविक्रम *a-vikrama*, mfn. without heroism, Kir. ii, 15; (*as*), m. non-prohibition of the change of a Visarga into an Ūshman, RPrāt.

A-vikrānta, mfn. unsurpassed, L.; not valiant, feeble, L.

अविक्रय *a-vikraya*, *as*, m. non-sale.

A'-vikrīta, mfn. who has not sold, RV. iv, 24, 9.

A-vikreya, mfn. not to be sold, unsaleable, MBh. v, 1402; R. i, 61, 17 (ed. Bomb.)

अविक्लव *a-viklava*, mf(*ā*)n. not confused or bewildered, not unsteady, MBh. i, 2070; BhP.

अविक्लिन्नाक्ष *a-viklinnâksha*, mfn. whose eyes do not water, ĀpŚr.

अविक्षत *a-vikshata*, mfn. unhurt, MBh. xii, 3604.

अविक्षित् *a-vikshit*, *t*, m., N. of a king, MBh. i, 231; (son of Kuru) 3740 seqq.; xiv, 82.

A'-vikshita, mfn. undiminished, RV. vii, 1, 24 & viii, 32, 8.

A'-vikshiṇa, mfn. id., ŚBr. i.

अविक्षिप *a-vikshipa*, mfn. unable to distribute or dispense, &c., Pāṇ. vi, 2, 157 seq., Sch.; (*as*), m., N. of a son of Śvaphalka, Hariv. 1917; (cf. *giri-kshipa*.)

A-vikshipta, mfn. not frustrated, MBh. xii, 8683.

अविक्षुब्ध *á-vikshubdha*, mfn. undisturbed (as a sacrifice), ŚBr.

A'-vikshobha, *as*, m. the not being disturbed, MaitrS.; TBr.

अविखण्डित *a-vikhaṇḍita*, mfn. undisturbed, MārkP.

अविगर्हित *a-vigarhita*, mfn. unreproached.

अविगलित *a-vigalita*, mfn. inexhaustible, BhP.

अविगान a-vigāna, mf(*ā*)n. without discord, concordant, unanimous, Rājat.

A-vigīta, mfn. not being out of harmony with each other, Comm. on Bād.

अविगुण a-viguṇa, mfn. not incomplete, not in a bad state, normal, Bhpr.

अविग्न a-vigna, *as*, m. the plant Carissa Carandas, L.; (cf. *a-vighnā*, *ā-vigna*, & *vighna*.)

अविग्रह a-vigraha, *as*, m. (said of a word) the not occurring in a separate form (but only in a compound), RPrāt.; bodiless; indisputable (as the Dharma), Rājat.

अविघात a-vighāta, *as*, m. no hindrance or obstacle, APrāt.; Sāṅkhyak. &c.; (mfn.) unimpeded, BhP.

A-vighna, mfn. without obstacle, unimpeded, uninterrupted, R.; Śak.; (*ā*), f. = *a-vigna*, q. v.; (*am*), n. want of obstacle, undisturbedness, Ragh. i, 91; (*ena*), instr. ind. without obstacle, R. **-karaṇa-vrata**, n., N. of a particular rite on the fourth day of Phālguna, VārP. **-tas**, ind. without obstacle, Rājat. **-vrata**, n. = *-karaṇa-vrata* above.

A-vighnita, mfn. undisturbed, R. i, 62, 12.

अविचक्षण a-vicakshaṇa, mfn. not discerning, not clever, ignorant, Mn. iii, 115 & viii, 150.

अविचर्त्य a-vicartyá. See *a-vicṛityá.*

अविचल a-vicala, mfn. immovable, steady, firm, MBh.; MārkP. **Avicalêndriya**, mfn. whose senses do not waver, i. e. are under control, BhP.

A-vicalat, mfn. not moving, Naish. iv, 93.

A-vicalita, mfn. not deviating, steadily fixed (as the mind), Mālatīm.; not deviating from (abl.), Comm. on TPrāt.

Á-vicācala, mfn. not staggering, standing firmly, AV. x, 8, 4.

Á-vicācalat, mfn. id., AV. vi, 87, 1 & 2.

Á-vicācali, mfn. id., RV. x, 173, 1 & 2; (cf. Pāṇ. iii, 2, 171, Comm.)

A-vicālita, mfn. unmoved, unshaken.

A-vicālin, mfn. not falling off from (abl.), Kathās.; invariable, Pat.

A-vicālya, mfn. not to be moved from its place, MBh. xv, 213.

अविचार a-vicāra, *as*, m. want of discrimination, error, folly, Rājat.; Vet.; (mfn.) undiscriminating, unwise, Kathās.; (*am*), ind. [MBh. ix, 2376; VarBṛS.] or in comp. *avicāra-* [Daś.], unhesitatingly. **-jña**, mfn. not knowing or clever at discrimination, Kathās.

A-vicāraṇa, *am*, n. non-deliberation, non-hesitation; (*āt*), abl. ind. unhesitatingly, R. iii, 28, 27.

A-vicāraṇīya, mfn. not needing deliberation, Ragh. xiv, 46, &c.

A-vicārayat, mfn. not deliberating or hesitating, Mn.; R.

A-vicārita, mfn. unconsidered, not deliberated, Hit. xii, 16; not requiring deliberation, certain, clear, Mn. viii, 295; MBh. xiv, 1344; (*am*), ind. unhesitatingly, Hariv. 3853; R. &c.

1\. **A-vicārya**, ind. p. without considering, unreflectingly.

2\. **A-vicārya**, mfn. not requiring deliberation, Kathās.

अविचालित a-vicālita, &c. See *a-vicala.*

अविचिकित्सत् á-vicikitsat, mfn. not having doubts, ŚBr. iv.

A-vicikitsā, f. absence of uncertainty, Āp.

अविचिन्तन a-vicintana, *am*, n. not thinking of, MBh. iii, 69.

A-vicintitṛi, *tā*, m. one who does not think of (gen.), MBh. v, 2446.

A-vicintya, mfn. not to be comprehended or conceived, MBh. iii, 12980.

अविचृत्य a-vicṛityá [VS. xii, 65] or *a-vicartyá* [TS. iv], mfn. not to be loosened.

अविचेतन a-vicetaná, mfn. unintelligible, RV. viii, 100, 10; AV. xx, 135, 7.

Á-vicetas, mfn. unwise, RV. ix, 64, 21.

अविच्छन्दत् a-vicchindat, mfn. not separating from each other, ĀśvGṛ.

A-vicchinna, mfn. uninterrupted, continual, ĀśvGṛ.; ŚāṅkhGṛ.; Hariv. &c. **-pāta**, m. continually falling (on one's knees), Daś.

Á-viccheda, *as*, m. uninterruptedness, continuity, AV. ix, 6, 38; ŚBr.; Sarvad. &c.; (*āt*), abl. ind. [Kād.] or (*ena*), instr. ind. [Comm. on Nyāyad.] or in comp. *aviccheda-* [MBh. viii, 2514], uninterruptedly.

अविच्युत a-vicyuta, mfn. not lost, inamissible, Yājñ. i, 212; without deviation or mistake, Yājñ. iii, 112.

अविजाता á-vijātā, f. (a woman) who has not brought forth, VS. xxx, 15.

A-vijātīya, mfn. of the same species, L.

अविजानत् á-vijānat, mfn. not understanding or knowing, ignorant, RV. i, 164, 5; KenaUp.; Mn. iii, 97; Yājñ. ii, 258.

A-vijña, mfn. ignorant. **-tā**, f. ignorance.

Á-vijñāta, mfn. unknown, ŚBr. xiv; KenaUp.; Mn.; indistinct, doubtful, VS.; ŚBr. &c.; not noticed, passed unawares (as the time), BhP.; (*as*), m., N. of a son of Anala, Hariv. 156 (ed. Bomb.) **-gati**, mfn. whose course is unknown, BhP.; (*is*), m., N. of a son of Anila, Hariv. 156. **-gada** (*ávijñāta-*), mf(*ā*)n. speaking unintelligibly, AV. xii, 4, 16.

A-vijñātṛi, mfn. not perceiving, ChUp.; ignorant, Nir. ii, 3; (*tā*), m. a N. of Vishṇu, MBh. xiii, 7000.

A-vijñāna, mfn. not having any information, Kathās.; (*am*), n. 'no knowledge,' (*āt*), abl. ind. without knowing, unawares, Mn. ii, 220; MBh. v, 5443; Hariv.; R. **-tva**, n. undiscernibleness, NṛisUp. **-vat**, mfn. not possessing knowledge, KaṭhUp.

A-vijñeya, mfn. undistinguishable, undiscernible, Mn. i, 5 & xii, 29; Bhag. xiii, 15; Jaim.

अविजितिन् a-vijitin, mfn. not victorious, AitBr.

A-vijitya, ind. p. not having conquered, MBh. v, 1150 = 4337.

अविडीन a-viḍīna, *am*, n. 'not flying apart,' a direct flight, MBh.

अवित avita, mfn. (√*av*), protected, L.; (cf. *ádroghâvita*.)

Avitṛi, mfn. a favourer, protector, RV.; BhP.; (f. *avitrī*) MBh. xii, 9449.

अवितत्करण a-vitat-karaṇa (& *a-vitad-bhāshaṇa*), *am*, n. (with the Pāśupatas) doing (and speaking) what in general is held to be unsuitable or nonsensical (*vi-tad*) but is admitted by the Pāśupatas from their own view.

अवितथ a-vitatha, mfn. not untrue, true, MBh. &c.; not vain or futile, see below; (*am*), ind. not falsely, according to truth, Mn. ii, 144; MBh. iii, 11946, &c.; (*ena*), ind. id., Up.; MBh. v, 1692; (*ājñām*) *avitathām* √1. *kṛi* or *avitathī*-√1. *kṛi*, 'to make true or effective,' fulfil (an order); (*am*), n. a species of the Atyashṭi metre. **-kriya**, mfn. whose work is not vain or ineffectual, R. ii, 47, 5. **Avitathâbhisandhi**, mfn. whose intentions are not futile, i. e. successive, BhP. **Avitathī-√1. kṛi**, see above. **Avitathêhita**, mfn. whose wishes are not frustrated, BhP.

अवितद्भाषण a-vitad-bhāshaṇa. See *a-vitat-karaṇa.*

अवितर्क a-vitarka, *as*, m., N. of a man, Buddh.

A-vitarkita, mfn. unforeseen, R. ii, 69, 21.

अवितवे ávitave, Ved. Inf. √*av*, q. v.

अवितारिन् á-vitārin, mfn. not passing away, permanent, RV. viii, 5, 6.

अवितृ avitṛi. See *avita.*

अवितृप्त a-vitṛipta, mfn. unsatisfied, (as in one's wishes, *kāmānām*) R. iv, 35, 9; BhP. **-kāma**, mfn. having the desires unsatisfied, BhP. **-tā**, f. the being unsatisfied, Kir. ii, 29. **-dṛiś**, mfn. having one's eyes unsatisfied, BhP.

अवित्ति á-vitti, *is*, f. (√3. *vid*), the not finding, ŚBr. xiii; the not possessing, poverty, AV. xvi, 6, 10.

अवित्यज a-vityaja, *as*, *am*, m. n. quicksilver, L.

अविथुर á-vithura, mfn. not staggering, firm, RV. i, 87, 1; ĀśvŚr.

अविथ्य avithya, mfn. (fr. *ávi*), fit or suited for sheep, Pāṇ. v, 1, 8; (*ā*), f. (probably) N. of a plant (like *ajathyā*, q. v.), ib., Sch.

अविदग्ध a-vidagdha, mfn. not burnt, Kauś.; Nir.; not digested, Suśr.; not ripe (as a tumour, *śotha* or *śopha*), Suśr.; Bhpr.; not turned sour, Suśr.; inexperienced, stupid, Pañcat.

A-vidāhin, mfn. not producing heartburn (on account of being imperfectly digested), Car.; Suśr.

अविदस्य a-vidasyá, mfn. not ceasing, permanent, inexhaustible, RV. vii, 39, 6.

A-vidāsin, mfn. not drying up (as a pond), perennial, ĀśvGṛ.; Gobh.; BhP.

अविदान्त a-vidānta, *as*, m. 'unsubdued,' N. of a son of Śatadhanvan, Hariv. 2037 (v. l. *ati-datta*).

अविदित á-vidita, mfn. unknown, ŚBr. x, xi, xiv; KenaUp.; R.; without the knowledge of (gen.), Kathās.; (*e*), loc. ind. [MBh. v, 5971] or (*am*), acc. ind. [Kathās.] without the knowledge of (gen.); (*am*), ind. so that nobody knows, Mṛicch.

अविदीधयु á-vidīdhayu, mfn. (√*dhyai*), not deliberating or hesitating, RV. iv, 31, 7.

अविदुष्टर á-vidushṭara. See *a-vidya.*

अविदूर a-vidūra, mfn. not very distant, near, R.; Kum. vii, 41; (*am*), n. proximity, (*am*) ind. near to, R. ii, 45, 33; (*e*), loc. ind. not far off (with abl.), near, MBh. iii, 16093; R.; BhP.; (*āt*), abl. ind. id., R. **-tas**, ind. near, R.

अविदोष a-vidosha, mfn. faultless, Lāṭy.

अविदोह á-vidoha, *as*, m. not a bad milking, MaitrS.

अविद्ध a-viddha, mfn. unpierced, not perforated (as pearls), Kum. vii, 10; 'unimpaired,' see below. **-karṇā** or **-karṇī**, f. the plant Cissampelos Hexandra; (cf. *viddha-karṇā*.) **-dṛiś**, mfn. of unimpaired sight, all-seeing, BhP. **-nas**, mfn. (said of a bull) having the nose not bored (by a nose-ring), BhP. **-varcas**, mfn. of unimpaired glory, BhP.

अविद्य a-vidya, mfn. unlearned, unwise, Mn. ix, 205, &c.; (*ávidyā*), f. ignorance, spiritual ignorance, AV. xi, 8, 23; VS. xl, 12-14; ŚBr. xiv; (in Vedānta phil.) illusion (personified as Māyā); ignorance together with non-existence, Buddh. **Avidyā-maya**, mfn. consisting of ignorance.

Á-vidvas, mfn. (perf. p.) not knowing, ignorant, RV.; AV. &c.; comp. *á-vidush-ṭara*, mfn. quite ignorant, RV. x, 2, 4.

अविद्यमान a-vidyamāna, mfn. (√3. *vid*; pr. Pass. p.), not present or existent, absent, KātyŚr.; Lāṭy.; Mn. &c. **-tā**, f. the not being present, Comm. on Nyāyad. **-tva**, n. id., Comm. on BṛĀrUp. **-vat**, ind. as if not being present, Pāṇ. iii, 1, 3, Comm.; viii, 1, 72.

अविद्रिय a-vidriyá, mfn. (√*dṛī*), not to be split or dispersed, indestructible, RV. i, 46, 15.

अविद्वस् á-vidvas. See *a-vidya.*

अविद्विष् a-vidvish, mfn. not an enemy, L.; not having enemies; (*she*), dat., see s. v.

A-vidvishāṇa, mfn. not inimical, KātyŚr.; Lāṭy.

Á-vidvishe, Ved. Inf. for preventing enmity, AV. i, 34, 5.

Á-vidvesha, *as*, m. non-enmity, AV. iii, 30, 1.

अविधवा a-vidhavā́, f. not a widow, RV. x, 18, 7; ŚāṅkhGṛ. &c.

अविधा avidhā, ind. an interjection (said to correspond to the Prākrit *avihā* or *aviha*, used in calling for help), Comm. on Śak.

अविधान a-vidhāna, *am*, n. absence of fixed rule, the not being prescribed, KātyŚr. **-tas**, ind. not according to what is prescribed, irregularly, Mn. ix, 144 & xii, 7.

A-vidhi, *is*, m. '= *a-vidhāna*,' (*inā*), instr. ind. = *avidhāna-tas*, q. v., MuṇḍUp.; Mn. v, 33; Āp. &c. **-pūrvakam**, ind. not according to rule, Bhag. ix, 23 & xvi, 17.

अविन *avina, as*, m. (√*av*), an officiating priest at a sacrifice, Uṇ.

अविनय *a-vinaya, as*, m. want of good manners or modesty, bad or rude behaviour, Mn. vii, 40 & 41; Śak. &c.; (mf(*ā*)n.) misbehaving, Comm. on Kap.

A-vināyin, mfn. (gaṇa *grāhy-ādi*, q.v.)

A-vinīta, mfn. badly trained or brought up, ill-mannered, misbehaving, Mn. iv, 67; Yājñ. iii, 155; R. &c.; (*ā*), f. an immodest or unchaste woman.

अविनाभाव *a-vinābhāva, as*, m. necessary connection of one thing with another, inherent and essential character, Sāh.; Sarvad. &c.

A-vinābhāvin, mfn. necessarily connected with, inherent, Comm. on Nyāyad. **Avinābhāvi-tva**, n. the being necessarily connected with, Comm. on Kap.

अविनाश *a-vināśa, as*, m. non-destruction, non-putrefaction (of a body), Kād.

A-vināśin, mfn. imperishable, ŚBr. xiv; Bhag. ii, 17, &c.; not decaying or putrefying, Kād. **Avināśi-tva**, n. imperishableness, ŚBr. xiv.

A-vināśya, mfn. indestructible, MBh. xv, 926.

अविनिगम *a-vinigama, as*, m. an illogical conclusion, L.

अविनिपात *a-vinipāta, as*, m. not doing wrong or erring, ŚāṅkhGṛ.

A-vinipātita, mfn. erred, done wrong, MBh. xii, 3348.

A-vinipātin, mfn. not erring (in one's duties, *dharmeshu*), Āp.

अविनिर्णय *a-vinirṇaya, as*, m. indecision, irresolution (in one's actions, *karmaṇām*), MBh. xiv, 998.

अविनिवर्तिन् *a-vinivartin*, mfn. not turning back, not fugitive (in battle).

अविनीत *a-vinīta*. See *a-vinaya*.

अविनोद *a-vinoda, as*, m. non-diversion, tediousness, Vikr.

अविन्ध्य *a-vindhya, as*, m., N. of a minister of Rāvaṇa, R.; (*ā*), f., N. of a river, Hariv. 7603.

अविपक्व *a-vipakva*, mfn. undigested, Bhpr.; immature. **–karaṇa**, mfn. having immature or insufficiently developed organs (of mind), Yājñ. iii, 141. **–kashāya**, mfn. whose passions or sins have not yet ripened, i. e. are not yet quite extinguished, BhP. **–buddhi**, mfn. having an immature or inexperienced mind, BhP.

A-vipāka, *as*, m. indigestion, Suśr. **–tā**, f. suffering from indigestion, ib.

अविपक्ष *a-vipaksha*, mfn. having no adversary, unopposed.

अविपद् *a-vipad, t*, f. no calamity, ease.

A-vipadyat, mfn. not decaying or dying, BhP.

अविपरिहृत *a-viparihṛita*, mfn. = *samāna* (?), AitĀr.

अविपर्यय *a-viparyaya, as*, m. non-inversion, absence of inverted order, Nir.; (*āt*), abl. ind. 'without mistake or misapprehension,' without any doubt, Sāṅkhyak.

अविपर्यासम् *á-viparyāsam*, ind. so that there is no interchange, ŚBr. iii.

अविपश्चित् *a-vipaścit*, mfn. unwise, ignorant, Kauś.; Bhag. ii, 42.

अविपाक *a-vipāka*. See *a-vipakva*.

अविपुल *a-vipula*, mfn. insignificant, small, slender.

अविप्र *a-viprá*, mfn. not spiritually excited, not inspired, RV. vi, 45, 2 & viii, 61, 9.

अविप्रकृष्ट *a-viprakṛishṭa*, mfn. not remote, near (as time), Pāṇ. v, 4, 20; near (in rank), Pāṇ. ii, 4, 5.

अविप्रक्रमण *a-viprakramaṇa, am*, n. not quitting or retiring, Āp.

अविप्रणाश *a-vipraṇāśa, as*, m. (said of the actions) the not perishing, continuing through their fruits, MBh. xv, 923.

अविप्रयुक्त *a-viprayukta*, mfn. not separated, Gaut.

अविप्रलब्ध *a-vipralabdha*, mfn. not deceitful, BhP.

A-vipralambhaka, mfn. not deceiving.

अविप्रवास *a-vipravāsa, as*, m. not staying in a foreign country, ŚāṅkhGṛ.

अविप्रहत *a-viprahata*, mfn. untrodden (as a forest or path), R. i, 26, 12 & iii, 74, 4.

अविप्रिय *avi-priya*. See *ávi*.

अविप्लुत *a-vipluta*, mfn. unviolated, observed without deviation, Mn. iii, 2; Yājñ. i, 52; BhP. &c.; undeviating, steadily observing (the vow of chastity), Mn. ii, 249; MBh. xii, 12033. **–mati**, mfn. whose mind is not deviating, Yājñ. iii, 161. **–mano-buddhi**, mfn. id., Kathās.

अविफल *a-viphala*, mfn. not fruitless or vain.

अविबुध *a-vibudha*, mfn. not wise, ignorant; (*as*), m. not a god.

अविब्रुवत् *a-vibruvat*, mfn. not saying or addressing, MBh. i, 3449 & xv, 281; not explaining, MBh. vii, 9226 (ed. Bomb.?, BR.)

अविभक्त *a-vibhakta*, mfn. undivided, Lāṭy.; Bhag. xiii, 16; Rājat.; 'not shared,' see *-tva*; unseparated, joint (as co-heirs who have not divided their inheritance), Mn. ix, 215; BhP. **–tva**, n. the not being shared, Jaim.; the not being distinguished (from each other), ib.

A-vibhaktin, mfn. unseparated (as co-heirs who have not divided their inheritance), Kauś.

A-vibhajya, ind. p. not dividing (the inheritance), Kum. iv, 27.

A-vibhāga, *as*, m. no separation, no distinction between (gen.), Pāṇ. i, 2, 33, Kāś.; Suśr. &c.; no division, Gaut.; undivided inheritance, L.; (*ena*), instr. ind. without distinction, in the same way, Pāṇ. i, 2, 33, Sch. **–vid**, mfn. not knowing the distinction between or the classification of (gen.), MBh. viii, 3455.

A-vibhāgin, mfn. not dividing or sharing, L.

A-vibhāgya, mfn. not to be divided, Lāṭy.

A-vibhājya, mfn. id., L. **–tā**, f. or **-tva**, n. indivisibility, unfitness for partition, L.

अविभावन *a-vibhāvana*, n. or °*nā*, f. non-perception, non-discrimination, L.

A-vibhāvanīya, mfn. imperceptible, L.

A-vibhāvita, mfn. unperceived (as indistinct voice or speech), Bālar.

A-vibhāvya, mfn. undistinguishable, imperceptible (as indistinct speech), MBh. xii, 3491 & Ragh. vii, 35; (as stars) Śiś. ix, 12.

A-vibhāvyamāna, mfn. (Pass. p.) not being perceived, Kād.

अविभिन्न *a-vibhinna*, mfn. not separated from (abl.), Kathās.; unchanged, ib.

अविभुज् *avi-bhuj*. See *ávi*.

अविभ्रंशिन् *á-vibhraṅśin*, mfn. not crumbling to pieces, ŚBr. iii; KātyŚr.; Gobh.

A-vibhrashṭa, mfn. uninjured, Comm. on Bṛ-ArUp.

अविभ्रम *a-vibhrama, as*, m. non-confusion (of mind), prudence, MBh. iv, 1887; mfn. (said of anger) not capricious or not pretended, Śak. (v.l.)

A-vibhrānta, mfn. not distorted, firm (as the eye-brows), Daś.

अविमत्त *a-vimatta, ās*, m. pl., N. of a family, (gaṇa *kārtakaujapādi*, q.v.)

अविमनस् *a-vimanas*, mfn. not absent in mind, Āp.

A-vimāna, *as*, m. non-disrespect, veneration, Hariv. 12039.

अविमित *a-vimita*, mfn. unmeasured, immense (as strength, *vikrama*), BhP.

अविमुक्त *á-vimukta*, mfn. not loosened, not unharnessed, ŚBr.; (*as*), m., N. of a Tīrtha near Benares, MBh. iii, 8057; Hariv. 1578 seqq. &c. **Avimuktâpīḍa**, m., N. of a king, Rājat. **Avimuktêśa**, m. a particular form of Śiva; (*avimuktêśa*)-*māhātmya*, n., N. of a work. **Avimuktêśvara**, m. = *avimuktêśa*, Daś.; (*avimuktêśvara*)-*liṅga*, n., N. of a Liṅga, ŚivaP.; SkandaP.

A-vimucyamāna, mfn. (Pass. p.) not being extended, AitBr.

A-vimokyá, mfn. not to be loosened, AV. vi, 63, 1.

A-vimoksha, *as*, m. no final liberation, Bād.

A-vimocana, *am*, n. not liberating, not running to any one's help, Gaut.

अविमूढ *a-vimūḍha, ās*, m. pl. a particular class of Ṛishis, MBh. i, 7683.

अवियुक्त *a-viyukta*, mfn. undivided, conjoined, Ragh. xiii, 31; Veṇis.; Kām.; not separated from (instr.), Vikr.

A-viyoga, *as*, m. no separation from, not being deprived of (instr.), Daś. **–tṛitīyā**, f., N. of a certain festival; (*aviyogatṛitīyā*)-*vrata*, n., N. of the eighteenth chapter of BhavP. ii.

A-viyogin, mfn. not liable to separation, MBh. xii, 8816.

अविरक्त *a-virakta*, mfn. not indifferent, attached to, Jain. (Prākrit °*ratta*) &c.

अविरण *á-viraṇa, as*, m. no recovery (from defeat), RV. i, 174, 8.

अविरत *a-virata*, mfn. not desisting from (abl.), KaṭhUp.; KātyŚr.; uninterrupted, Megh.; (*am*), ind. uninterruptedly, continually, BhP.; Mṛicch. &c.

A-virati, *is*, f. incontinence, intemperance, Yogas.

A-viramat, mfn. not desisting from (abl.), Kathās.

A-virāmam, ind. uninterruptedly, Gīt.

अविरल *a-virala*, mf(*ā*)n. contiguous, close, dense, compact, MBh. &c.; incessant, numerous, Ratnāv.; vehement, Kād.; (*am*), ind. contiguously, closely, Śak.; Mālatīm.; Uttarar. **–dhārâsāra**, m. incessant down-pour of heavy rain, Vikr.

अविरविकन्याय *avir-avika-nyāya, as*, m. = *avy-avika-nyāya*, q. v., Pat.

अविरहित *a-virahita*, mfn. unseparated, Vikr.; not separated from, not being without (instr.), Kir. v, 52; Kād.

अविराग *a-virāga, as*, m., N. of a Prākṛit poet.

अविराधयत् *á-virādhayat*, mfn. not opposing one's self to, not being at variance with (instr.), AV. ii, 36, 4.

अविरुद्ध *a-viruddha*, mfn. unobstructed, unimpeded, Vikr.; not incompatible with, consistent with (instr. or in comp.), KātyŚr.; Gaut. &c.

A-virodha, *as*, m. non-opposition to, living or being in agreement with (in comp. or instr.), MBh. xiii, 1935; Hariv. 8752; R.; non-incompatibility, consistency, harmony, Yājñ. ii, 186, &c.

A-virodhita, mfn. not refused, Śiś. x, 69.

A-virodhin, mfn. not being out of harmony with, not being obstructive to (gen. or in comp.), Gaut. &c.

अविरेचन *a-virecana, am*, n. anything which constipates or stops the passage of the food.

A-virecanīya, mfn. not to be purged, Suśr.

A-virecya, mfn., id.

अविलक्षित *a-vilakshita*, mfn. not perceived, not perceivable, BhP.

अविलग्नम् *a-vilagnam*, ind. so as not to cling or stick to, VarBṛS.

अविलङ्घन *a-vilaṅghana, am*, n. non-transgression, not trespassing.

A-vilaṅghanīya, mfn. not to be exceeded or transgressed, prescribed, fixed.

A-vilaṅghya, mfn. not to be surpassed, Kathās.

अविलम्ब *a-vilamba, as*, m. non-delay, following immediately, Comm. on Ragh. x, 6 & Kum. iii, 58; (mfn.) not delaying, prompt, expeditious, L.; (*am*), ind. without delay, Hariv. 16160; Vikr.; Śak. (v. l. °*lambitam*); (*ena*), ind. id.

A-vilambana, *am*, n. non-delay, MBh. i, 5227; (mfn.) not delaying, prompt, L.

A-vilambita, mfn. not delaying, expeditious, Kathās.; not pronounced slowly, KātyŚr.; Lāṭy.; TPrāt.; (*am*), ind. without delay, Śak.; Kathās.

अविला *avilā*, f. an ewe, L.; (cf. *ávi.*)

अविलिख *a-vilikha*, mfn. unable to write or paint, writing or painting badly, Pāṇ. vi, 2, 157 seq., Sch.

अविलुप्त *a-vilupta*, mfn. undamaged, unhurt, BhP.; Rājat.; Kathās.

A-vilopa, *as*, m. non-injury, not harming (with gen.), MBh. v, 3232; absence of break or interruption (in the Saṃhitā), RPrāt.

अविवक्षत् *a-vivakshat*, mfn. not intending to speak, Sarvad.

A-vivakshā, f. not declaring especially, i.e. considering to be unessential, Pat.

A-vivakshita, mfn. not intended to be stated or expressed, Pāṇ. Sch. &c. **–tva**, n. the not being intended to be expressed, Pat.

A-vivākyá, mfn. indisputable; N. of the tenth day of a certain Soma sacrifice, TS. vii; AitBr.; ĀśvŚr.; KātyŚr.

अविवदिष्णु *a-vivadishṇu*, mfn. not causing dispute, ĀśvGṛ.

A-vivāda, *as*, m. non-dispute, agreement; (mfn.) not disputed, agreed upon, Comm. on Nyāyad.

Á-vivādin, mfn. not quarrelling with (*abhí*), ŚBr. iii.

अविवाहिन् *a-vivāhin*, mfn. interdicted as to marriage, not to be married, Mn. ix, 238.

A-vivāhya, mfn. not to be married (as a girl), PSarv.; one to whom one ought not to ally one's self by marriage, Lāṭy.; MBh. i, 3376.

अविविक्त *a-vivikta*, mfn. unseparated, Vedāntas.; undiscriminated, uninvestigated, L.; indiscriminate, confounded, L.; not separated from the public, not retired or secluded, L.

A-viveka, *as*, m. absence of judgment or discrimination, Pañcat.; Kathās.; non-separation, non-distinction, Kap.; (*am*), ind., see *a-vivecam*. **–tā**, f. want of judgment, inconsiderateness, Pañcat.; Hit.

A-vivekin, mfn. not separated, undistinguished, uniform, Sāṅkhyak. &c.; undiscriminating, ignorant, Comm. on BṛĀrUp. &c.; (said of a country) destitute of men that can discriminate, Kathās.

A-vivecaka, mfn. undiscriminating, Sāṅkhyak.

A-vivecanā, f. want of judgment, L.

A-vivecam, ind. so as not to part or separate, ĀśvŚr.; (*a-vivekam* in the same sense) ĀpŚr.

अविवेनत् *á-vivenat*, mfn. not disaffected, favourable, RV. iv, 24, 6.

Á-vivenam, ind. favourably, RV. iv, 25, 3.

अविशङ्क *a-viśaṅka*, mfn. having no doubts, not hesitating, MBh. iii, 2171 & xiii, 2747; (*ā*), f. 'no hesitation,' (*ayā*), instr. ind. undoubtingly, without hesitation, MBh.; Hariv. &c.

A-viśaṅkita, mfn. unapprehensive, not having doubts, not hesitating, MBh. v, 490; BhP. &c.; (*am*), ind. without hesitation, R. v, 90, 13; Suśr.

अविशस्तृ *a-viśastṛí*, *tā́*, m. an unskilful cutter up or killer (of animals), RV. i, 162, 20.

अविशुद्ध *a-viśuddha*, mfn. not clear or pure, BhP.; not examined with regard to cleanness or purity, Kām.

अविशेष *a-viśesha*, *as*, m. non-distinction, non-difference, uniformity, Kap.; (mfn.) without difference, uniform, BhP.; Kap. &c.; (*āṇi*), n. pl. (in Sāṅkhya phil.) N. of the (five) elementary substances, (cf. *tan-mātra*); (*āt*), ind. or in comp. *aviśesha-* [e.g. *aviśesha-śruteḥ*, *aviśeshôpadeśāt*, KātyŚr.] without a special distinction or difference, KātyŚr.; Jaim.; Gaut.; Śulb.; not differently, equally, Comm. on Nyāyad.; (*eṇa*), ind. without a special distinction or difference, Āp.; Comm. on Yājñ. &c. **–jña-tā**, f. want of discrimination or judgment, Kathās. **–tas**, ind. without difference, Mn. ix, 125; R.; Kathās. **–vat**, mfn. not making a difference between (loc.), Yājñ. iii, 154. **–sama**, m. a kind of sophism, Nyāyad.; Sarvad.

अविश्रम्भ *a-viśrambha*, *as*, m. want of confidence, diffidence, MBh. &c. **–tā**, f. id., Kād.

A-viśrambhin, mfn. diffident, Bhaṭṭ.

अविश्रान्त *a-viśrānta*, mfn. unwearied; incessant, Śak.

A-viśrāmam, ind. so as not to rest.

अविश्व *a-viśva*, *am*, n. not the universe, BhP. **–m-inva** (*á-viśvam-inva*), mf(*ā*)n. not all-embracing, not pervading everything, RV. i, 164, 10 & ii, 40, 3. **–vinna** (*á-viśva-*), mf(*ā*)n. (v. l. of *á-viśvam-inva*) not perceived everywhere, AV. ix, 9, 10.

अविश्वसत् *a-viśvasat*, mfn. not confiding, Rājat.; Kathās.

A-viśvasanīya, mfn. not to be trusted. **–tva**, n. the not deserving confidence, Mālav.

A-viśvasta, mfn. not trusted, suspected, doubted, L.; = *a-viśvasat*, R. iii, 1, 25, &c.

A-viśvāsa, *as*, m. mistrust, suspicion, MBh. xii, 5160; R. &c.; (mfn.) not inspiring with confidence, mistrusted, L.; (*ā*), f. a cow calving after long intervals, L.

A-viśvāsin, mfn. mistrustful, Megh. &c.

अविष 1. *a-vishá*, mf(*ā*)n. not poisonous, RV.; AV.; VS.; Suśr.; (*ā*), f. the plant Curcuma Zedoaria.

अविष 2. *avisha*, *as*, m. (√*av*), the ocean, Uṇ.; (cf. *tavisha*); (*ī*), f. a river, Uṇ.; the earth, L.

अविषक्त *a-vishakta*, mfn. not clinging or sticking to; unrestrained, unchecked, Kir. xiii, 24.

अविषम *a-vishama*, mfn. not different, equal, BhP.; (*am*), ind. not unfavourably, BhP.

अविषय *a-vishaya*, *as*, m. anything out of reach, anything impossible or improper, MBh. xiii, 2207; Śak.; Kathās.; not a proper object for (gen.), Mālatīm.; Veṇīs.; (mfn.) not having an object, NṛisUp. **–manas**, mfn. one whose mind is not turned to the objects of sense, Mālav. **A-vishayī-karaṇa**, n. the not making anything (gen.) an object, Vedāntas.

अविषह्य *a-vishahya*, mfn. not bearable, not wearable, MBh.; BhP.; intolerable, insupportable, BhP.; R.; Ragh.; Kum. iv, 30; irresistible, MBh. &c.; unfeasible, impracticable, MBh.; R. (ii, 20, 33, superl. *-tama*); inaccessible (to the eyes, *cakshu-shām*), MBh. xiv, 611; indeterminable (as a boundary), Mn. viii, 265.

अविषाण *a-vishāṇá*, mfn. not having horns, ŚBr. v.

अविषाद *a-vishāda*, *as*, m. non-depression, cheerfulness, courage, MBh. i, 7100.

A-vishādin, mfn. intrepid, MBh. iii, 14078.

अविष्ठ *ávishṭha*, mfn. (superl. of √*av*) gladly accepting, RV. vii, 28, 5.

Avishyát, mfn. helping readily, RV. x, 115, 6; desirous of (acc. [RV. i, 58, 2] or loc. [RV. vii, 3, 2] or Inf. [RV. viii, 51, 3]).

Avishyā́, f. desire, ardour, RV. ii, 38, 3.

Avishyú, mfn. desirous, vehement, RV.; AV.

अविसंवाद *a-visaṃvāda*, *as*, m. non-contradiction, Sarvad.; non-violation of one's promise, MBh. xii, 9240.

A-visaṃvādin, mfn. not contradictory, coinciding, agreeing, MārkP.; Rājat.; Daś. **A-visaṃvādi-tā**, f. not violating (i.e. keeping) a promise, Kām.

अविसर्गिन् *a-visargin*, mfn. unintermittent (as a fever), Bhpr.

अविसर्पिन् *a-visarpin*, *ī*, m., N. of a hell, TĀr.

अविसोढ *avi-soḍha*. See *ávi*.

अविस्तीर्ण *a-vistīrṇa*, mfn. not extended, of small extent or circuit, Kād.

A-vistṛita, mfn. not spread or expanded, BhP.

अविस्पन्दित *a-vispandita*, mfn. not quivering, Kum. iii, 47.

अविस्पष्ट *a-vispashṭa*, mf(*ā*)n. not clear or plain, indistinct, obscure, Nir. &c.; (*am*) n. indistinct speech, Mn. iv, 99; anything indistinct, MBh. iii, 16446.

अविस्मित *a-vismita*, mfn. not proud, BhP.

अविस्मृत *a-vismṛita*, mfn. not forgotten, Mudr.

A-vismṛiti, *is*, f. not forgetting, remembering, L.

अविस्यन्दित *a-visyandita*. See *a-vispand°*.

अविस्रंस *a-visraṇsa*, *as*, m. not falling asunder, AitBr.; PBr.

अविस्राव्य *a-visrāvya*, mfn. (water) that cannot be caused to flow off, MBh. xii, 2634; not to be bled, Suśr.

अविस्वरम् *a-visvaram*, ind. without dissonance, MārkP.

अविहत *a-vihata*, mfn. not refused or sent away, BhP.; unobstructed, unimpeded, BhP.; Megh.

अविहर्यतक्रतु *a-viharyata-kratu*, mfn. one whose will cannot be averted, RV. i, 63, 2 ['doer of acts undesired (by his foes),' Sāy.]

अविहस्त *a-vihasta*, mfn. not unclever, experienced in (loc.), R. v, 81, 31.

अविहिंसक *a-vihiṇsaka*, mfn. not injuring anybody, MBh. (sometimes with the gen. *bhūtānām*).

A-vihiṇsana, *am*, n. not injuring, BhP.

A-vihiṇsā, f. id., MBh. xii, 9421.

A-vihiṇsra, mfn. not injurious, BhP.

अविहित *a-vihita*, mfn. unprescribed, forbidden, Āp.; undone, uneffected, L.

अविह्रुत *á-vihruta*, mfn. unbent, unbroken, RV. v, 66, 2 & x, 170, 1; AV. vi, 26, 1.

Á-vihvarat, mfn. undeviating, RV. iv, 36, 2.

अविह्वल *a-vihvala*, mf(*ā*)n. not disquieted, merry, MBh. v, 7164; not hesitating, having courage, Kathās.

अवी *a-vī*, *īs*, f. (√*vī*), a woman in her courses, L.

अवीक्षण *a-vîkshaṇa*, *am*, n. not looking at, not regarding, L.

A-vîkshita, mfn. not seen before, Naish.

A-vîkshin, mfn. ifc. not seeing, Naish. i, 28.

अवीङ्गित *á-vīṅgita*, mfn. unmoved, TBr.

अवीचि *a-vīci*, mfn. waveless, L.; (*is*), m. a particular hell, Yājñ. iii, 224; Buddh. &c. **–mat**, m. (sc. *naraka*), id., BhP. **–saṃśoshaṇa**, m. a particular Samādhi, Kāraṇḍ.

अवीज *a-vīja*, &c. See *a-bīja*.

अवीत *á-vīta*, mf(*ā*)n. (√*vī*), not enjoyed (as the sacrificial oblation), RV. iv, 48, 1.

अवीर *a-vīra*, mfn. unmanly, weak, RV. vii, 61, 4 & x, 95, 3; having no sons, RV. vii, 4, 6; without heroes, Bālar.; (*ā*), f. (a woman) who has no husband, a widow, RV. x, 86, 9; BhP.; one who has neither husband nor son, Mn. iv, 213; Yājñ. i, 163; (*ám*), n. a country destitute of heroes or men, ŚBr. **–jushṭa**, mfn. not liked by men, Mṛicch. **–tā** (*a-vīra-*), f. want of sons, RV. iii, 16, 5 (dat. °*tāyai*); vii, 1, 11 (instr. °*tā*) & 19 (dat. °*te*). **–purusha**, m. a weak man, Kathās. **–han**, mf(*-ghnī*)n. not killing men, not pernicious to men, RV. i, 91, 19; VS.; AV.

A-vīryá, mf(*ā*)n. weak, ineffective, ŚBr. **–vat** (*á-vīrya-*), mfn. weak, powerless, MaitrS.

अवृक *a-vṛiká*, mfn. not hurting, inoffensive, RV.; unendangered, safe, RV.; (*ám*), n. safety, RV.

अवृक्ष *a-vṛiksha*, mfn. treeless, destitute of trees, Lāṭy.; R. iv, 43, 28 (ed. Bomb.)

A-vṛikshaka, mfn. id., R. iv, 44, 35 (= iv, 43, 28, ed. Bomb.)

अवृजिन *á-vṛijina*, mfn. not intriguing straightforward, RV. ii, 27, 2; ŚBr. xiv.

अवृत 1. *á-vṛita*, mfn. unchecked, RV.

अवृत 2. *a-vṛita*, mfn. uninvited, Gaut.

अवृत्त *a-vṛitta*, mfn. not happened, Kathās.; not dead, still living, R. vi, 8, 10.

A-vṛitti, *is*, f. inadequate support, absence of subsistence or livelihood, Mn.; Āp.; Gaut.; (mfn.) not happening or occurring.

A-vṛitti-ka, mfn. not having to live upon, Kathās.; not yielding livelihood (as a country).

अवृथा *a-vṛithā*, ind. not in vain, profitably, L. **A-vṛithârtha-tā**, f. successfulness in gaining one's object or 'correctness of meaning,' Śiś. vi, 47.

अवृद्धिक *a-vṛiddhi-ka*, mfn. not bearing interest, Yājñ. ii, 63.

A-vṛidhá, mfn. not rendering prosperous or refreshing (the gods with sacrifices), RV. vii, 6, 3.

अवृष्टि *á-vṛishṭi, is,* f. want of rain, drought (famine), ŚBr. xi; Kauś.; VarBṛS. **-kāma**, mfn. not wishing rain, ĀpŚr.

अवृह *a-vṛiha, ās,* m. pl. a class of Buddhist divinities, Lalit.

अवे *avé* (√*i*), *-eti* (impf. *-ayat*; Pot. 1. sg. *-iyām*; pr. p. f. *avā-yatī́*, RV. viii, 91, 1) to go down, go down to (acc.), go to, RV.; (Imper. 3. pl. Ā. *ávâyantām*) to rush down, AV. xi, 10, 8 (cf. *ávê*); (Imper. *ávâitu*) to go away, RV. v, 49, 5; AV. i, 11, 4; to look upon, consider, Śak.; Vikr.; Bhaṭṭ.; to perceive, conceive, understand, learn, know, MBh. &c.; (with Inf.) Kathās.: Intens. (1. pl. *-īmahe*) to beg pardon for, conciliate, RV. i, 24, 14 & vii, 58, 5.

Avêta, mfn. elapsed, passed, (*án-*, neg.) TS.; one who has gained, obtained (with acc.), Pāṇ. v, 1, 134.

अवेक्ष् *avêksh* (√*īksh*), *avêkshate*, to look towards, look at, behold, TS.; ŚBr. &c.; (1. sg. *īkshe*) to perceive, observe, experience, RV. viii, 79, 9; R.; Bhag. &c.: Ā. (rarely P., e.g. 2. sg. *avêkshasi*, MBh. ii, 2158) to have in view, have regard to, take into consideration, Mn.; MBh. &c.: Caus. *avêkshayati*, to cause to look at, KātyŚr.

Avêkshaṇa, *am*, n. looking towards or at, Gaut.; Sāh.; (said of planets) the being in sight, VarBṛS.; the act of considering, attention, observation, Ragh. xiv, 85, &c.

Avêkshaṇīya, mfn. to be respected, Ragh. xiv, 67.

Avêkshā, f. observation, care, attention to (loc.), Mn. vii, 101; R.; BhP.

Avêkshitavya, mfn. to be observed attentively, Suśr.

Avêkshin, mfn. looking towards or at, Pañcat.; attentive to (acc.), MBh. v, 1423.

Avêkshya, mfn. to be attended to, MBh. ii, 2591; Yājñ. iii, 63; R.

अवेणि *a-veṇi*, mfn. having no braid of hair, L.; not commingled (as the waters of rivers), L.; single, being by itself, Buddh.; (cf. *āveṇika*.)

अवेद *á-veda, ās,* m. pl. not the Vedas, ŚBr. xiv. **-vid**, mfn. not knowing the Vedas, GopBr.; Mn. iv, 192. **-vidvas**, m (dat. *-vidushe*) fn. id., MBh. xii, 8967. **-vihita**, mfn. not prescribed in the Vedas, Mn. v, 43. **A-vedôkta**, mfn. id., MBh. xiii, 4397.

1. **A-vedana**, *am*, n. not knowing, Mn. v, 60.

A-vedayāna, mfn. (pr. p. Ā.) not knowing, not ascertaining, Mn. viii, 32.

1. **A-vedi**, *is*, f. ignorance, BṛĀrUp.

Á-vedin, mfn. having no knowledge, ŚBr. xiv; BhP.; MārkP.

1. **A-vedya**, mfn. not to be known, unascertainable, MBh. xii, 11765; (*ā*), f. (in Sāṅkhya phil.) non-admission of the Ahaṃkāra.

अवेदन 2. *a-vedana*, mfn. painless, Suśr.

अवेदि 2. *a-vedi*, mfn. without a Vedi or sacrificial altar, KātyŚr.

अवेद्य *a-vedya*, mf(*ā*)n. (√3. *vid*), not to be married, Mn. x, 24; (*as*), m. a calf, L.

अवेध्य *a-vedhya*, mfn. unpierceable, not to be pierced, Kathās.

अवेनत् *á-venat*, mfn. not having any wish or desire, RV. x, 27, 16.

अवेन्व् *avênv* (√*inv*), (Imper. 2. du. *-invatam*) to send down (as rain), RV. vii, 64, 2.

अवेल *a-vela, as,* m. (?), denial or concealment of knowledge, L.; (*ā*), f. wrong time, Lāṭy.; chewed betel, L.; (*am*), ind. untimely, Kathās.

अवेष्टि *ávêshṭi, is,* f. (√*yaj*), appeasing or expiation by sacrifices, ŚBr.; TBr.

अवैदिक *a-vaidika*, mfn. non-Vedic.

A-vaidya, mfn. unlearned, Gaut.; Jaim.

अवैध *a-vaidha*, mfn. not conformable to rule, unprescribed, Comm. on Mn. v, 50 & 55; vi, 31.

अवैधव्य *a-vaidhavya, am,* n. non-widowhood, MBh. iii, 16725 & 16873; v, 362.

अवैभीदक *á-vaibhīdaka*, mfn. not having its origin on a Vibhīdaka tree, MaitrS.

अवैरहत्य *a-vairahatyá, am,* n. the non-destruction of men, AV. vi, 29, 3; (*a-vīrahatya*) ĀpŚr.

अवोक्षण *avôkshaṇa, am,* n. besprinkling, bedewing with (in comp.), Sāy. on ŚBr.: bedewing one's self, Gaut.

अवोद *avôda*, mfn. (Pāṇ. vi, 4, 29), dripping, wet, L.

अवोदेव *avó-deva.* See 2. *avás.*

अवोष *avôsha, as,* m., N. of a king of ants.

Avôshīya or **avôshya**, mfn. relating to *avôsha*, (gaṇa *apūpâdi*, q. v.)

अवोह् *avôh* (√1. *ūh*), (Pot. *ávôhet*) to push down, TS. vi.

अव्य *ávya*, mfn. (said of the woollen Soma strainer) coming from sheep (*ávi*, q.v.), RV.; (*as, am*), m. n. the woollen Soma strainer, RV.

अव्यक्त *a-vyakta*, mfn. undeveloped, not manifest, unapparent, indistinct, invisible, imperceptible, Up.; Pāṇ.; Mn. &c.; (in alg.) unknown as quantity or number; speaking indistinctly; (*as*), m. (= *paramâtman*) the universal Spirit, Mn. ix, 50; N. of Vishṇu, L.; of Śiva, L.; of Kāma, L.; a fool, L.; N. of an Upanishad; (*am*), n. (in Sāṅkhya phil.) 'the unevolved (Evolver of all things),' the primary germ of nature, primordial element or productive principle whence all the phenomena of the material world are developed, KaṭhaUp.; Sāṅkhyak. &c.; (*am*), ind. indistinctly. **-kriyā**, f. algebraic calculation, L. **-gaṇita**, n. id. **-gati**, mfn. going imperceptibly. **-pada**, mfn. inarticulate. **-rāga**, m. dark-red (the colour of the dawn), L. **-rāśi**, m. (in alg.) an unknown number or indistinct quantity. **-lakshaṇa**, mfn. 'whose marks are imperceptible,' N. of Śiva. **-vyakta**, mfn. id. **-sāmya**, n. equation of unknown quantities. **Avyaktânukaraṇa**, n. the imitating of inarticulated sound, Pāṇ. v, 4, 57 & vi, 1, 98.

A-vyañjana, mf(*ā*)n. without the marks of puberty; without consonants, Up.; (*as*), m. an animal without horns (though of age to have them), L.

अव्यग्र *a-vyagra*, mf(*ā*)n. unconfused, steady, cool, deliberate, MaitrUp.; MBh. &c.; unoccupied, Uttarar.; not in danger, undisturbed, safe, MBh.; R.; (*am*), ind. coolly, deliberately, Hariv. 9034; R. &c.

अव्यङ्ग 1. *a-vyaṅga*, mf(*ā*, AgP.)n. not mutilated, perfect, KātyŚr.; BhP. &c.; (*ā*), f. (for *adhyaṇḍā*, q.v.) the plant Carpopogon Pruriens Roxb., L. **-tā**, f. the not being mutilated, MBh. xiii, 5599 seqq.

Avyaṅgâṅga, mf(*ī*)n. perfect, entire, Mn. iii, 10.

अव्यङ्ग 2. *avyaṅga, as* or *am,* m. n. the girdle of the Maga priests, BhavP. i; (*viyaṅga* or *viyāṅga*) VarBṛS. [cf. Zend *aiwyāoṅhana*].

अव्यचस् *á-vyacas*, mfn. not spacious, AV. xix, 68, 1.

अव्यण्डा *avy-aṇḍā* = *adhy-a°*, q. v., L.

अव्यत् *á-vyat*, mfn. (√*vī*; cf. *a-vī*), only f. °*tī*, not longing for copulation, RV. x, 95, 5.

अव्यतिक्रम *a-vyatikrama, as,* m. non-transgression, Āp.

अव्यतिकीर्ण *a-vyatikīrṇa*, mfn. unmixed, unblended, distinct, separate, L.

अव्यतिचार *a-vyaticāra, as,* m. the absence of mutual permutation, ĀśvŚr.

अव्यतिमोह *á-vyatimoha, as,* m. the not confounding by error, ŚBr. xiii.

अव्यतिरेक *a-vyatireka, as,* m. non-exclusion, non-exception, Jaim.; Nyāyad.; (mfn.), (= *a-vyabhicārin*) unerring, L.

A-vyatirekin, mfn. unerring.

अव्यतिषक्त *á-vyatishakta*, mfn. not intermingled, ŚBr. xii.

A-vyatishaṅgam, ind. without exchanging one for another, ĀpŚr.

अव्यथ *a-vyatha*, mfn. untroubled; intrepid, Daś.; painless, L.; (*as*), m. a snake, L.; (*á-vyathā*), f. absence of tremor, firmness, VS.; TBr.; the plant Terminalia Citrina Roxb., L.; the plant Hibiscus Mutabilis, L. **-tva**, n. painlessness, Bhpr.

A-vyathamāna, mfn. not trembling, VS.; TS.

A-vyathí, mfn. not tremulous, not unsteady, sure-footed, safe, RV.; unfailing (as help), RV. i, 112, 6; (*is*), f. sure-footedness, RV.

A-vyathin, mfn., Pāṇ. iii, 2, 157.

A-vyathisha, *as,* m. the sun, Uṇ.; the ocean, Uṇ.; (*ī*), f. the earth, Uṇ.; night, Uṇ.

A-vyathishyai, Ved. Inf. (Pāṇ. iii, 4, 10), for not trembling, for rendering sure-footed, KapS.; (*a-vyáthishe!*) MaitrS.

A-vyathyá, mfn. (Pāṇ. iii, 1, 114), unshakable, RV. ii, 35, 5; AitBr.

अव्यनत् *á-vyanat* (4), mfn. not breathing, RV. x, 120, 2.

अव्यन्त *a-vyanta*, mfn. not very distant, growing near (abl.), ĀpŚr.

अव्यपदेश *a-vyapadeśa, as,* m. no designation or pointing to, Āp. **-rūpin**, mfn. whose shape admits of no name or appellation, BhP.

A-vyapadeśya, mfn. not to be defined, MāṇḍUp.; RāmatUp.

अव्यपेत *a-vyapêta*, mfn. not separated, contiguous, Kāvyâd.

अव्यपोह्य *a-vyapôhya*, mfn. undeniable, incontestable, Rājat.

अव्यभिचार *a-vyabhicāra, as,* m. non-failure, absolute necessity, Kap. &c.; 'non-deviation,' conjugal fidelity, Mn. ix, 101; non-transgression, Mn. viii, 122; (mfn.) constant, Bhag. xiv, 26; (*āt, eṇa*) ind. with absolute necessity, Pāṇ. Kāś. & Sch. **-vat** mfn. absolutely determined, inevitable, MBh. ii, 871

A-vyabhicārin, mfn. not going astray, unfailing, Śak.; Rājat. &c.; steady, permanent, MBh. xiv, 1111; Bhag. xiii, 10, &c.; faithful, Kathās. &c.

अव्यय 1. *avyáya* or rarely *ávyaya* [only RV. viii, 97, 2 & ix, 86, 34], mfn. (*ávi*) made of sheep's skin (as the woollen Soma strainer), RV.; belonging to or consisting of sheep, RV. viii, 97, 2.

अव्यय 2. *a-vyaya*, mf(*ā*)n. not liable to change, imperishable, undecaying, Up.; Mn. &c.; 'not spending,' parsimonious; (*as*), m., N. of Vishṇu or Śiva, L.; of a son of Manu Raivata, Hariv. 433; of a Nāga demon, MBh. i, 2157 (ed. Bomb.); the non-spending, parsimony; (*am*), n. [or (*as*), m., L.] an indeclinable word, particle, Pāṇ.; APrāt. &c.; (in Vedânta) a member or corporeal part of an organized body, L. **-tva**, n. imperishableness, Hit. (v. l.); the state of an indeclinable word, Pat. **-vat**, mfn. consisting of an indeclinable word, Pat. **Avyayâtman**, mfn. imperishable, VP. **Avyayī-bhāva**, m. 'unchangeable state,' an indeclinable compound, Pāṇ.; (*avyayībhāva*)*-samāsa*, m. id., Pāṇ. i, 1, 41, Sch.

अव्यर्ण *a-vyarṇa*, mfn. (√*ard*; cf. Pāṇ. vii, 2, 24) unoppressed, Bhaṭṭ.

अव्यर्थ *a-vyartha*, mfn. not useless, profitable, fruitful; effectual, efficacious.

अव्यर्धुक *á-vyardhuka*, mfn. not losing anything (instr.), TS.; TBr.

Á-vyṛiddha, mfn. undiminished, ŚBr. xii.

Á-vyṛiddhi, *is*, f. no ill-success, AV. x, 2, 10.

अव्यलीक *a-vyalīka*, mfn. having no uneasiness or unpleasantness; well off, MBh. v, 698; not false, true, veracious, BhP.; Daśar.; (*am*), ind. truly, BhP.

अव्यवच्छिन्न *á-vyavacchinna*, mfn. uninterrupted, ŚBr. & AitBr. (together with *sáṃtata*); Hariv. 3580; (*am*), ind. or in comp. *avyavacchinna-* [MBh. vii, 4746] uninterruptedly.

Á-vyavaccheda, *as,* m. uninterruptedness, ŚBr.; AitBr.

अव्यवधान *a-vyavadhāna, am,* n. non-interruption, contiguity, Pāṇ. Kāś. &c.; non-separation, BhP.; Comm. on Mn. xi, 201; (mfn.) uninterrupted, BhP.; without a cover (as the ground), Kād.

A-vyavahita, mfn. not separated, adjoining,

contiguous, Pāṇ. Sch. &c.; uninterrupted (as worship), BhP.; separated by the letter *a*, VPrāt.

अव्यवलम्बिन् *a-vyavalambin*, mfn. unsupported, not sure-footed, KaushBr.

अव्यवसायिन् *a-vyavasāyin*, mfn. inactive, negligent, remiss, Bhag. ii, 41.

A-vyavasita, mfn. id., R. iv, 26, 13.

अव्यवस्त *a-vyavasta*, mfn. (*sta* for *sita*?, √*si*), not tied or fastened, ĀśvŚr.

अव्यवस्थ *a-vyavastha*, mfn. irregular, without rule; (*ā*), f. irregularity.

A-vyavasthita, mfn. not conformable to law or practice; not in due order, unmethodical.

अव्यवस्रंस *a-vyavasraṇsa*, *as*, m. not falling asunder, PBr.

अव्यवहार्य *a-vyavahārya*, mfn. not to be practised, MāṇḍUp.; RāmatUp.; not to be discussed in law, unactionable, L.

अव्यवहित *a-vyavahita*. See *a-vyavadhāna*.

अव्यवानम् *á-vyavānam*, ind. (√*an*), without breathing between, MaitrS.

अव्यवाय *a-vyavāya*, *as*, m. not entering between, non-separation, KātyŚr.; Lāṭy.; uninterrupted contiguity, Jaim.; Nyāyam.

अव्यविकन्याय *avy-avika-nyāya*, *as*, m. (only instr. °*ena*) after the fashion of *avi* and *avika* (i. e. though *avi* and *avika* both mean 'a goat,' a derivation in the sense of 'goat's flesh' can be formed only from *avika* [*āvikam*], not from *avi* [*aver mānsam*]), Pat.

अव्यसन *a-vyasana*, mfn. free from evil practices, MBh. xii, 3910; Yājñ. i, 309.

A-vyasanin, mfn. id., Mn. vii, 53; Suśr. &c.

अव्यस्त *a-vyasta*, mfn. undecomposed, undispersed, not separated, Lāṭy.

अव्याकृत *á-vyākṛita*, mfn. undeveloped, unexpounded, ŚBr. xiv; BhP.; (*am*), n. elementary substance from which all things were created, considered as one with the substance of Brahma, L.

अव्याक्षेप *a-vyākshepa*, *as*, m. the not being confused or unsteady-minded, resolution, Ragh. x, 6.

अव्याख्येय *a-vyākhyeya*, mfn. inexplicable, unintelligible; inexpressible, Bhām.

अव्याज *a-vyāja*, *as*, m. 'absence of fraud, simplicity,' (only in comp.) without fraud or artifice, Śak.; Mālav.; (mfn.) not pretended or artificial, Mālatīm.; Rājat. &c.

अव्यापक *a-vyāpaka*, mfn. not spread over or pervading the whole, not an invariable concomitant, special, peculiar. **-tā**, f. or **-tva**, n. non-comprehensiveness or generalization, speciality.

A-vyāpin, mfn. not pervading, not comprehensive, Kap. &c.

A-vyāpta, mfn. not pervaded with, Mn. v, 128.

A-vyāpti, *is*, f. 'non-comprehensiveness,' inadequate pervasion or extent (of a definition; e.g. 'man is a cooking animal,' which does not extend to savages who eat raw food), Sāh.; Comm. on Kap.

A-vyāpya, ind. p. not pervading generally, not extending to the whole circumstances, L. **-vṛitti**, mfn. being of limited application, of partial inherence (with reference to place and time, as pain, pleasure, love, hatred, virtue, vice, &c.)

अव्यापन्न *a-vyāpanna*, mfn. not dead, Megh.

अव्यापार *a-vyāpāra*, *as*, m. cessation from work, L.; not one's own business, Pañcat. (& Hit.)

अव्यायाम *a-vyāyāma*, *as*, m. non-exertion, want of bodily exercise, Suśr.; Kām.

अव्यावर्तनीय *a-vyāvartanīya*, mfn. not to be taken back, Comm. on Yājñ.

Á-vyāvṛitta, mfn. undivided, Comm. on Nyāyad.; simultaneous, TS. vi; TBr.

A-vyāvṛitti, *is*, f. not turning away from (abl.), not neglecting, ĀśvŚr.; Lāṭy.

अव्याहत *a-vyāhata*, mfn. unresisted, unimpeded, MBh.; R. &c.; not disappointed, not contradictory, L.

अव्याहारिन् *a-vyāhārin*, mfn. not speaking, (gaṇa *grāhy-ādi*, q. v.)

A-vyāhṛita, *am*, n. not speaking, MBh. v, 1271 (= xii, 11029).

अव्युच्छिन्न *a-vyucchinna*, mfn. uninterrupted, MBh. iii, 355; Hariv. 2355, &c.

A-vyucchettṛi, *tā*, m. one who does not injure (with gen.), MBh. xii, 2901.

अव्युत्पन्न *a-vyutpanna*, mfn. not ensuing or following, Veṇīs.; underived (as a word), having no etymology, Pāṇ. vii, 2, 8, Pat.; unaccomplished, inexperienced, BhP. &c.

अव्युष्ट *á-vyushṭa*, mfn. not yet shining (as the dawn), RV. ii, 28, 9.

Á-vyushṭi, *is*, f. the not becoming light, TS. i.

अव्यूढ *á-vyūḍha*, mfn. not moved asunder or separated, ŚBr. v.

A-vyūha, *as*, m. indivisibility, Nyāyad.; non-separation, non-resolution (of semivowels and compound vowels), RPrāt.

अव्यृद्ध *á-vyṛiddha*, &c. See *á-vyardhuka*.

अव्येष्यत् *á-vyeshyat*, mfn. (√*i*, fut. p.) not disappearing, AV. xii, 4, 9.

अव्रण *a-vraṇá*, mf(*ā*)n. unhurt, unscarred, sound, VS. xl, 8; BhP.; (generally said of bows, swords, sticks &c.) without rents or splinters or notches, entire, KātyŚr.; Mn.; MBh. &c.

अव्रत *a-vratá*, mf(*ā*)n. lawless, disobedient, wicked, RV.; AV.; SV.; not observing religious rites or obligations, Gobh.; Mn.; MBh. &c. **-vat**, mfn. not observing religious rites, MBh. xii, 2305.

A-vratika, mfn. = *avrata-vat*, q. v., MBh. xii, 1336.

A-vratin, mfn. id., MBh. xiii, 1601; R.

A-vratyá, *am*, n. anything out of harmony with, or violating, a religious obligation, ŚBr.; AitBr.; AitĀr.; (mfn.) with *karman*, id., Gobh. **Avratyôpacāra**, m. practising anything that offends one's religious obligations, ĀśvŚr.; ĀśvGṛ.

Á-vrātya, *as*, m. not a Vrātya, AV. xv, 13, 6; (*am*), n. = *a-vratyá*, n., q. v., Vishṇus.

अव्राजिन् *a-vrājin*, mfn. 'not wandering,' (gaṇa *grāhy-ādi*, q. v.)

अश् 1. *aś* (in classical Sanskṛit only) Ā. *aśnute* (aor. 3. pl. *āśishata*, Bhaṭṭ.; perf. *ānaśe*, Pāṇ. vii, 4, 72. Vedic forms are: *aśnoti*, &c.; Subj. *aśnavat*, &c.; aor. P. *ānaṭ* (2. & 3. sg., frequently in RV.) & Ā. *ashṭa* or *áshṭa*, 3. pl. *āśata* (frequently in RV.) or *ákshishur* [RV. i, 163, 10], Subj. *ákshat* [RV. x, 11, 7], Pot. 1. pl. *aśema*, Prec. *aśyās* (2. & 3. sg.) &c., Pot. Ā. 1. sg. *aśīya* & pl. *aśīmahi*, Imper. *ashṭu* [VS.]; perf. *ānaṇśa* (thrice in RV.) or *ānāśa* [RV. vi, 16, 26] or *āśa* [RV. viii, 47, 6], 2. pl. *ānaśá*, 3. pl. *ānaśúḥ* (frequently in RV.) or *āśuḥ* [RV. iv, 33, 4], Ā. *ānaśé*, Subj. 1. pl. *anaśāmahai* [RV. viii, 27, 22], Pot. 1. sg. *ānaśyām*, p. *ānaśāná* [AV.]; Inf. *ashṭave*, RV. iv, 30, 19) to reach, come to, arrive at, get, gain, obtain, RV. &c.; (said of an evil, *aṇhati*, *áṇhas*, *gráhi*) to visit, RV.; AV. vi, 113, 1; to master, become master of, RV.; to offer, RV.; to enjoy, MBh. xii, 12136; to pervade, penetrate, fill, Naigh.; Bhaṭṭ. ii, 30; to accumulate, L.: Desid. *aśiśishate*, Pāṇ. vii, 2, 74: Intens. *aśāśyate*, Pāṇ. iii, 1, 22, Pat.

1. **Aśana**, mfn. reaching, reaching across, Nir.

Aśāya, Nom. Ā. (impf. *aśāyata*) to reach, RV. x, 92, 1.

Aśin, mfn. reaching far, lasting long, Nir.

अश् 2. *aś*, *aśnāti* (Pot. *aśnīyāt*; p. *aśnát* (see s. v. 1. *aśna*); aor. Subj. *aśīt*, RV. x, 87, 17; fut. p. *aśishyát*, ŚBr., perf. *āśa*, RV. i, 162, 9 & iii, 36, 8; perf. p. *āśivas*, see *án-āśvas* s. v. *án-āśaka*; Pass. p. *aśyámāna*, AV. xii, 5, 38) to eat, consume (with acc. [this only in classical Sanskṛit] or gen.), RV. &c.; to enjoy, Bhag. ix, 20, &c.; Caus. *āśayati* (Pāṇ. i, 3, 87, Sch.; aor. *āśiśat*, ib. i, 1, 59, Sch.) to cause to eat, feed, Mn.; (with double acc.; cf. Pāṇ. i, 4, 52, Kāś.) BhP.; (cf. *āśita*): Desid. *aśiśishati* (Pāṇ. vi, 1, 2, Sch.) to wish to eat, ŚBr.; ChUp.: Intens. *aśāśyate*, Pāṇ. iii, 1, 22, Pat.

2. **Áśana**, *am*, n. eating, ŚBr. &c.; food, ŚBr. &c. [often ifc., e.g. *mūla-phalâśana*, mf(*ā*)n. having roots and fruit for food, Mn. &c.]; (*ā*), f. = *aśanāyā́*, q. v., ŚBr. xi; ChUp. **-kṛit**, mfn. preparing food, AV. ix, 6, 13. **-pati**, m. (voc.) lord of food, ŚBr. vi. **-vat**, mfn. possessed of food, Nir. x, 12 & 13. **Aśanânaśaná**, n. eating and fasting, AV. xix, 6, 2; ŚBr. i.

Aśanāya, Nom. P. °*yati* (Pāṇ. vii, 4, 34) to desire food, be hungry, ŚBr.; ChUp.

Aśanāyā́ or °**nāyā**, f. desire of eating or consuming, hunger, ŚBr.; AitBr. &c. **-pipāse** (*aśanāyā́-*), f. nom. du. hunger and thirst, ŚBr. xiv. **-vat**, mfn. hungry, Vedāntas.

Aśanāyita, mfn. hungry, L.

Aśanāyuka, mfn. id., ŚBr. vii, xi, xii.

Aśanīya, Nom. P. °*yati*, to be greedy for food (without being hungry), Pāṇ. vii, 4, 34, Sch.

Aśitá, mf(*ā*)n. eaten, AV. xii, 5, 37 & 38; ŚBr. i; (*am*), n. the place where anybody has eaten, Pāṇ. ii, 3, 68, Kāś. **-m-gavīna**, mfn. for *āśit°*, q. v., L. **Aśitá-vat**, mfn. (Padap. °*ta-vat*) one who has eaten, AV. ix, 6, 38.

Aśitavyà, mfn. (impers.) to be eaten, MaitrS.; ŚBr. i.

Aśitá-vat. See *aśitá*.

Aśitṛi, *tā*, m. an eater, ŚBr. ii.

Aśitra, *am*, n. food, Kāṭh.; (cf. *prâśitrá*.)

Aśiśishu, mfn. (fr. Desid.), hungry, Kauś.

1. **Áśishṭha**, mfn. (superl.) 'eating most' (as an equivalent for *aśitama*), ŚBr.

Aśitama, mfn. (superl.) 'eating most,' VS. ii, 20 (voc.); (cf. *aśita-tanu*.)

अशकुन *a-śakuna*, *am*, n. (ifc. f. *ā*) an inauspicious omen, Śiś. ix, 83; Kathās. **Aśakuni-√bhū**, to turn into an inauspicious omen, Naish. iii, 9.

अशकुम्भी *aśa-kumbhī*, f. the aquatic plant Pistia Stratiotes, L.

अशक्त *a-śakta*, mfn. unable, incompetent (with Inf. or loc. or dat.), Mn.; MBh. &c.

A-śakti, *is*, f. inability, incapability.

A-śaknuvat, mfn. (p. P.) unable to (Inf.), Mṛicch.

A-śaknuvāna, mfn. (p. Ā.) id., Bhaṭṭ.

A-śakya, mfn. impossible, impracticable, KātyŚr.; MBh. &c.; impossible to be composed (as a book, Mn. xii, 94) or to be executed (as an order, Kathās.), not to be overcome, invincible, R. vi, 17, 8; Pañcat. **-tā**, f. or **-tva**, n. impossibility (with Inf.), Sarvad.

Aśakyârtha, mfn. unavailing, L.

अशङ्क *a-śaṅka*, mfn. fearless, Hit.; secure, certain, to be relied on, MBh. xii, 4169; (*am*), ind. without fear, Daś.; Kathās.; (*ayā*), instr. f. ind., id., R. ii, 49, 17.

A-śaṅkita, mfn. fearless, confident, MBh.; Rājat.; undoubted, certain, Mn. xii, 108; (*am*), ind. without fear, Kād.; Kathās.; Rājat.; unexpectedly, suddenly, Kathās.

A-śaṅkya, mfn. not to be mistrusted, secure, MBh.; not to be expected, Rājat.

अशठ *a-śaṭha*, mf(*ā*)n. not false, sincere, honest, Mn. iii, 246; MBh. xii, 12550, &c.

अशत *á-śata*, *am*, n. not a full hundred, ŚBr. iv. **-dakshiṇa** (*á-śata-*), mfn. where the Dakshiṇā is less than a hundred, ib.

अशत्रु *a-śatrú*, mfn. one who has no adversary or whom no enemy defies (especially said of Indra), RV.; without opposition from enemies, RV. v, 2, 12; (*us*), m. the moon, L.; (*ú*), n. condition of having no enemy, AV. vi, 40, 2.

अशन् *áśan*, m. (connected with √1. *aś*) [only *áśnā* (instr.) and *áśnas*, perhaps better derived from *áśman*, q. v., cf. Whitney's Gr. § 425 e], stone, rock, RV. x, 68, 8; a stone for slinging, missile stone, RV. ii, 30, 4 & iv, 28, 5; (NBD.) the firmament, RV. i, 164, 1; 173, 2; x, 27, 15; [in the first two of these three passages the form *áśnas* has before been taken as nom. sg. m. fr. 1. *aśna*, q. v.]

Aśáni, *is*, f. (rarely m., R.; Pāṇ. Sch.) the thunderbolt, a flash of lightning, RV. &c.; the tip of a missile, RV. x, 87, 4; (in astronomy) a subdivision of the phenomena called Ulkās, VarBṛS.; (*is*), m. one of the nine names of Rudra, PārGṛ.; N. of Śiva, MBh. xiii; (*ayas*), m. pl., N. of a warrior tribe, (gaṇa *parśv-ādi*, q. v.) **-prabha**, m., N. of a Rākshasa, R. vi, 69, 11. **-mat** (*aśáni-*), mfn. possessing the thunderbolt, RV. iv, 17, 13. **-hata**, mfn. struck by lightning, Kāṭh.

Aśanika, mfn. = *aśanau kuśala*, (gaṇa *ākarshâdi*, q. v.)

Aśanin, mfn. = *aśáni-mat*, q.v., MBh. xiii, 1157.

Aśanī, f. = *aśáni*, the thunderbolt, ŚBr. xi (voc.); R. iii, 35, 40.

अशन 1. & 2. *aśana*. See √1. & 2. *aś*.

अशन 3. *aśana* for 2. *asana*, q. v.

अशनाय *aśanāya*, &c. See √2. *aś*.

अशनीय *aśanīya*. See √2. *aś*.

अशपत् *á-śapat*, mfn. not cursing, AV. vi, 37, 3 & vii, 59, 1.

अशब्द *á-śabda*, mfn. soundless, ŚBr. xiv; Āp.; TPrāt.; not Vedic, Jaim.

अशम् *á-śam*, ind. 'non-welfare,' harm, AV ii, 25, 1; ŚBr. ii.

अशम *a-śama*, *as*, m. disquietude, uneasiness, L.; 'not resting,' in comp. with **-rathambhāvuka** (*áśama-*), mfn. being changed into a never-resting carriage, TBr.

अशरण *a-śaraṇa*, mf(*ā*)n. destitute of refuge, defenceless, R.; Megh.; Śak. &c. **Aśaraṇīkṛita**, mfn. deprived of refuge, VarBṛS.; (Pañcat.)

A-śaraṇya, mfn. not yielding refuge, MBh.; R.; destitute of refuge, wanting refuge, R. iii, 55, 65; Daś.

अशरमय *á-śaramaya*, mfn. not made of reeds, MaitrS.

A-śaravyá, mf(*ā́*)n. not to be reached by arrows, ŚBr. v.

अशरीर *a-śarīra*, mf(*ā*)n. bodiless, incorporeal, AitBr.; ŚBr. xiv, &c.; not coming from a visible body (as a voice), R. iv, 63, 6; Kathās.; (*as*), m., N. of Kāma, Śiś. ix, 61; (*am*), n. (in rhetoric) absence of the verb in a sentence.

A-śarīrin, mfn. incorporeal, RāmatUp.; not coming from a visible body (as a voice), R.; Uttarar. &c.

अशर्मन् *a-śarman*, *a*, n. unhappiness, Kir.

अशवाग्नि *á-śavágni*, *is*, m. 'not a corpse-fire' or fire kindled to burn a corpse, ŚBr. xii.

अशस् *a-śás*, mfn. (√*śaṇs*), not blessing or wishing well, cursing, hating, RV. ii, 34, 9 & iv, 4, 15.

Á-śasta, mfn. 'ineffable' or 'unwished,' AV. vi, 45, 1. **-vāra** (*áśasta-*), mfn. having indescribable treasures, RV. x, 99, 5 ['who is not asked for wealth, i. e. who grants it of his own accord,' Sāy.]

Á-śasti, *is*, f. not wishing well, curse, RV. vi, 68, 6; (generally personified) a curser, hater, RV.; AV.; VS. **-hán**, mfn. averting curses or cursers, RV.

1. **A-śastra**, mf(*ā*)n. having no invocation, MārkP.

अशस्त्र 2. *a-śastra*, mfn. (√1. *śas*), weaponless, unarmed, MBh. &c. **-pāṇi**, mfn. not having a sword in one's hand, Veṇīs.

अशाखा *a-śākhā*, f., N. of a grass, L.

अशान्त *á-śānta*, mfn. unappeased, indomitable, violent, wild, MaitrS.; ŚBr.; BhP.; restless, unresigned, L.; unconsecrated, not sacred, ŚBr. **-tā**, f. want of tranquillity, passionateness, Kathās.

A-śānti, *is*, f. restlessness, anxiety, L.; non-cessation, Suśr. **-kara**, mfn. causing mischief, BhP.

A-śāmya, mfn. unappeasable, Hariv. 4207.

अशाय *aśāya*, Nom. Ā. See √1. *aś*.

अशाश्वत *a-śāśvata*, mf(*ī*)n. not permanent or eternal, transient, MaitrUp.; MBh. &c.

अशासत् *a-śāsat*, mfn. not punishing, Mn. ix, 254.

A-śāsana, *am*, n. want of government, anarchy, L.

A-śāstra, mf(*ā*)n. not prescribed in the Śāstras, unscriptural, Jaim. **-vihita** or **-siddha**, mfn. not enjoined or established by the Śāstras.

A-śāstrīya, mfn. = *a-śāstra*, q. v.

A-śāsyá (4), mfn. unblamable, RV. viii, 33, 17; not to be punished, MBh. v, 3542.

अशिक *aśika*, v.l. for *asika*, q. v.

अशिक्षित *a-śikshita*, mfn. not learnt (as manners &c.), Kām.; untaught (with acc. [Śak.; Kathās.] or loc. or Inf.)

अशित *aśitá*, *aśitavyà*, &c. See √2. *aś*.

अशिथिर *á-śithira*, mfn. not loose, tight, firm, MaitrS.

Á-śithila, mf(*ā*)n. id., ŚBr. **-m-bhāva** (*áśithilam-bh°*), m. the becoming tight or firm, TS. vii; TBr.

अशिन् *aśin*. See √1. *aś*.

अशिपद *a-śipadá*, mf(*á*)n. not causing, i.e. averting the sickness called Śipada, RV. vii, 50, 4.

अशिमिद *a-śimidá*, mf(*ā*)n. not destructive like a Śimidā, RV. vii, 50, 4; VS. xxxviii, 7.

अशिमिविद्विष् *a-śimi-vidvísh*, mfn. (*śimi* = *karman*, Comm.), not unfavourable to or counteracting the labours of men (N. of the seven Parjanyas or rain-clouds), TĀr. (quoted by Sāy. on RV. ii, 12, 12).

अशिर *aśira*, *as*, m. (√2. *aś*), 'consumer,' fire, L.; the sun, L.; N. of a Rākshasa and (*ā*), f. of his wife, L.; (*am*), n. a diamond, L.

अशिरस् *a-śiras*, mfn. headless, Mn. ix, 237. **A-śiraḥ-snāna**, n. bathing the whole body except the head, L.

A-śiraska, mfn. headless, MBh. iii, 15745.

अशिव *á-śiva*, mf(*ā*)n. unkind, envious, pernicious, dangerous, RV.; AV.; MBh. &c.; (*as*), m., N. of a demon causing disease, Hariv. 9560; (*am*), n. ill-luck, RV. i, 116, 24; x, 23, 5; MBh. &c.

अशिशिर *a-śiśira*, mf(*ā*)n. not cool, hot, Śak. **-kara**, m. 'having hot rays,' the sun, Kād. **-kiraṇa**, m. id., ib. **-tā**, f. heat, Megh. **-raśmi**, m. = *-kara*, q. v., Kir. v, 31.

अशिशिषु *aśiśishu*. See √2. *aś*.

अशिश्वी *á-śiśu*, mf(*á-śiśvī*, but according to Pāṇ. iv, 1, 62, also Ved. *a-śiśu*)n. childless, without young ones, RV. i, 120, 8 & iii, 55, 6.

Aśiśvikā, f. a childless woman, L.

अशिष्ट 1. *a-śishṭa*, mfn. (√*śās*), untrained, badly trained, ill-behaved, rude, Āp.; MBh. &c. **-tā**, f. or **-tva**, n. rudeness.

A-śishya, mfn. not to be taught (as a person), not deserving to, or not capable of being instructed, MBh. v, 1009; Pañcat.; (a thing) that need not be taught or which it is unnecessary to teach, Pāṇ. i, 2, 53.

अशिष्ट 2. *á-śishṭa*, mfn. (√*śish*), not left, AV. ii, 31, 3.

अशिष्ठ *aśishṭha*. See √2. *aś*.

अशीत 1. *a-śīta*, mfn. not cold, warm, hot. **-kara**, m. = *aśiśira-kara*, q. v. **-tanu**, mfn. (only voc.) having a hot body, TS. & TBr. (v. l. for *aśītama* of VS.) **-ruc**, m. = *-kara*, Śiś. ix, 5.

A-śītala, mf(*ā*)n. hot, Śiś. ix, 86.

अशीत 2. *aśīta*, mfn. ifc. 'the eightieth,' see *arvāg-aśītá*.

Aśīti, *is*, f. eighty, RV. ii, 18, 6; AV. &c. **-tama**, mfn. the eightieth, MBh. &c. (in the numeration of the chapters). **-bhāga**, m. the eightieth part, Mn. viii, 140. **Aśītishṭaka**, mfn. having eighty Ishṭakās, ŚBr. x.

Aśītika, mfn. measuring eighty, R.; an octogenarian, VarBṛS. **Aśītikâvara**, mfn. being at least eighty years of age, Gaut.

अशीर्ण *a-śīrṇa*, mfn. unimpaired, L.

Á-śīrya, mfn. indestructible, ŚBr. xiv.

अशीर्षक *a-śīrshaka*, mfn. headless, TS.

A-śīrshán, mfn. id., RV. iv, 1, 11; AV.

A-śīrshika, mfn. id., (gaṇa *vrīhy-ādi*, q. v.)

A-śīrshin, mfn. id., Pāṇ. v, 2, 116, Kāś.

अशील *a-śīla*, mf(*ā*)n. ill-behaved, vulgar, MBh. xii, 4619; R. &c.; (*am*), n. bad manners, depravity, Kathās.

अशुक्ल *á-śukla*, mf(*ā*)n. not white, ŚBr. vii. **-vat** (*á-śukla-*), mfn. not containing the word *śukla*, ŚBr. vi.

अशुचि *a-śuci*, mfn. (Pāṇ. vi, 2, 161) impure, foul, Mn. &c. **-kara**, mfn. making dirty, soiling, Āp. **-tā**, f. or **-tva**, n. impurity. **-bhāva**, m. id., MBh. i, 782. **-lipta**, mfn. soiled, Ap.

A-śauca, *am*, n. (= *āśauca*, q. v., Pāṇ. vii, 3, 30) impurity, contamination, defilement (contracted by the death of a relation, or by the commission of prohibited acts, &c.), Mn. xi, 183; uncleanness, Pañcat.; Vet.

अशुद्ध *á-śuddha*, mfn. impure, ŚBr.; Mn.; inaccurate, wrong (especially said of mistakes of copyists and of errata in printing); unknown, unascertained, L. **-vāsaka**, m. 'having impure abodes,' a vagrant, suspicious character.

A-śuddhi, *is*, f. impurity, Yogas.

A-śodhita, mfn. uncleansed, unclean; uncorrected, unrevised, inaccurate.

अशुन *á-śuna*, *am*, n. (AV. xiv, 2, 16) for *śūna* (RV. iii, 33, 13), q. v.

अशुभ *a-śubha*, mfn. not beautiful or agreeable, disagreeable; inauspicious, Vet.; bad, vicious (as thought or speech), MBh. i, 3077 seq. &c.; (*as*), m., N. of a lexicographer; (*á-śubha*), *am*, n. a shameful deed, sin, ŚBr. ii; Bhag. &c.; misfortune, harm, mischief, Suśr.; VarBṛS. &c. **-darśana**, mfn. ugly, R. iii, 1, 21.

अशुश्रूषा *a-śuśrūshā*, f. non-desire of hearing, disobedience, neglect of service or respect, MBh. v, 1535.

A-śuśrūshu, mfn. not desirous of hearing or learning, GopBr.; Bhag.; Hariv.; disobedient towards (gen.), MBh. xii, 8405.

अशुष *aśúsha*, mfn. (√2. *aś*), consuming, voracious, RV. ['not causing to dry up, not extinguished,' Sāy., as if fr. √*śush*].

अशुष्क *a-śushka*, mf(*ā*)n. not dry, moist, fresh, ŚāṅkhŚr.; Gobh.; Mn. xi, 64. **A-śushkâgra**, mf(*ā*)n. not having a dry point, KātyŚr.

A-śoshya, mfn. not to be dried up, not drying up, permanent (as a pond), Bhag. ii, 24; VarBṛS.

अशूद्र *á-śūdra*, *as*, m. not a Śūdra, VS. xxx, 22; KātyŚr. **Á-śūdrôcchishṭin**, mfn. not coming into contact with Śūdras or with leavings, ŚBr. xiv.

अशून्य *a-śūnya*, mf(*ā*)n. not empty, KātyŚr. &c.; not vain or useless, Rājat. **-tā** (*aśūnyá-*), f. non-emptiness, Ragh. xix, 13; completion (as of seasons), ŚBr. x. **-śayana**, n. the day on which Viśvakarman rests, VāmP.; (*aśūnyaśayana*)-*dvitīyā*, f. and *-vrata*, n., N. of ceremonies on that occasion, MatsyaP.; BhavP. ii. **Aśūnyôpasthā**, f. (a woman) whose womb is not empty, married, MantraBr.; PārGṛ.

अशूला *a-śūlā*, f. the tree Vitex Alata, L.

अशृङ्ग *a-śṛiṅga*, mf(*ī*)n. without horns, PBr.; Rājat.; having no top, L.

अशृण्वत् *á-śṛiṇvat*, mfn. not hearing or liking to hear, TS. vii; Pañcat.

अशृत *a-śṛita*, mfn. uncooked, ŚBr.

अशृथित *á-śṛithita*, mfn. (√*śrath*), not loosened, not becoming loose, RV. x, 94, 11.

अशेव *á-śeva*, mf(*ā*)n. not causing pleasure, pernicious, RV. vii, 34, 13; x, 53, 8.

अशेष *a-śesha*, mf(*ā*)n. without remainder, entire, perfect, all; (*as*), m. non-remainder, KātyŚr.; (*am*), ind. entirely, wholly, Kum. v, 82; (*eṇa*), ind. id., MBh. &c. **-tas**, ind. id., Mn.; MBh. &c. **-tā**, f. totality, Pāṇ. ii, 1, 6, Sch. **-tva**, n. id., Jaim. **-sāmrājya**, m. 'possessed of complete sovereignty,' N. of Śiva, L.

Aśeshaya, Nom. P. (ind. p. °*shayitvā*) to finish entirely, Kum. vii, 29.

A-śéshas, mfn. without descendants, RV. vii, 1, 11.

Aśeshita, mfn. completely annihilated, Veṇīs.

अशैक्ष *a-śaiksha*, *as*, m. 'no longer a pupil,' an Arhat, Buddh.

अशोक 1. *a-śoka*, mf(*ā*)n. (√1. *śuc*), not causing sorrow, N.; Lalit.; not feeling sorrow, Nalod.; (*as*), m. the tree Jonesia Asoka Roxb. (a tree of moderate size belonging to the leguminous class with magnificent red flowers), MBh. &c.; N. of a minister of king Daśaratha, R. i, 7, 3; of a well-known king (in Pāṭaliputra), MBh.; Buddh. &c.; (*ā*), f., N. of a medicinal plant, L.; a female name, (gaṇa *śubhrâdi*, q. v.); N. of one of the female deities of the Jainas, L.; (*am*), n. the blossom of the Aśoka plant, Vikr., (cf. Pāṇ. iv, 3, 166, Siddh.); quicksilver, L. **-kara**, m. 'rendering sorrowless,' N. of a Vidyā-dhara, Kathās.; (ī), f. a female name, Kathās. **-taru**, m. the Aśoka tree, N. **-tīrtha**, n., N. of a Tīrtha, MBh. iii, 8338; SkandaP. **-trirātra**, m., N. of a feast which lasts three nights, BhavP. ii. **-datta**, m., N. of a man, Kathās. **-dvādaśī** and **-pūrṇimā**, f., N. of certain holidays, MatsyaP.; BhavP. ii. **-mañjarī**, f., N. of a metre. **-mālā**, f. a female name, Kathās. **-rohiṇī**, f., N. of a medicinal plant, Suśr. **-vanikā**, f. a grove of Aśoka trees, R. **-vardhana**, m., N. of a king, BhP.; VP. **-vega**, m. = *-datta*, q.v., Kathās. **-vrata**, n., N. of a certain ceremony, BhavP. ii. **-shashṭhī**, f. the sixth day in the first half of the month Caitra, BhavP. ii. **Aśokâri**, m. 'enemy of the Aśoka tree,' the plant Nauclea Kadamba Roxb. **Aśokâshṭamī**, f. the eighth day in the first half of the month Caitra. **Aśokêśvara-tīrtha**, n., N. of a Tīrtha, ŚivaP. Rev.

A-śoca, mfn.? = *an-ahaṃkriti*, L.

A-śocanīya, mfn. not to be lamented, Kād.

A-śocya, mfn. id., MBh. &c.; (*am*), n. impers. id., Hariv. 6062. **-tā**, f. the state of being not to be lamented, Ragh. viii, 27. **-tva**, n. id., MBh. iv, 523.

अशोक 2. *á-śoka*, mfn. (√3. *śuc*), without heat, ŚBr. xiv.

अशोभमान *a-śobhamāna*, *as*, m. (gaṇa *cārvādi*, q. v.)

अशोष्य *a-śoshya*. See *a-śushka*.

अशौच *a-śauca*. See *a-śuci*.

अशौटीर्य *a-śauṭīrya*, *am*, n. want of self-confidence, unmanliness, MBh. xii, 3605, ed. Bomb.

A-śauṇḍīrya, *am*, n. id., MBh. xii, 3605, ed. Calc.; Mṛicch.

अशौर्य *a-śaurya*, *am*, n. want of heroism.

अश्न 1. *áśna*, mfn. (√2. *aś*), 'voracious' [RV. i, 164, 1 & 173, 2], see *áśan* at end; (*as*), m., N. of a demon, RV. ii, 14, 5; 20, 5; vi, 4, 3.

Aśnát, mfn. eating, consuming, RV. vii, 67, 7 & viii, 5, 31, &c.; (cf. *án-aśnat*.)

Aśni, mfn. 'eating,' only in the comp. **Áśnyushṇi**, mfn. 'burning him who eats' [Comm.] or 'consuming and burning' (N. of an Agni), TĀr.

Aśnīta-pibatā, f. invitation to eat and to drink, (gaṇa *mayūravyaṅsakâdi*, q. v.)

Aśnītapibatīya, Nom. P. °*yati*, to have the intention of inviting to eat and drink, Bhaṭṭ. v, 92.

1. **Aśman**, *ā*, m. an eater, AV. xviii, 4, 54.

अश्न 2. *aśna*, *as*, m. (cf. *áśan*), a stone, RV. viii, 2, 2; a cloud, Naigh.

1. **Aśma**, ifc. for 2. *áśman*, a stone, Pāṇ. v, 4, 94.

Aśmaka, *as*, m. (gaṇa *ṛiśyâdi*, q. v.) N. of a son of Vasishṭha and Madayantī, MBh.; VP.; (*ās*), m. pl., N. of a warrior tribe, Pāṇ. iv, 1, 173; R. &c.; (cf. *avanty-aśmakās*); (*ī*), f., N. of several women, Hariv. &c. **-sumantu**, m., N. of a Ṛishi, MBh. xii, 1592.

2. **Áśman**, *ā*, m. (once *aśmán*, ŚBr. iii), a stone, rock, RV. &c.; a precious stone, RV. v, 47, 3; ŚBr. vi; any instrument made of stone (as a hammer &c.), RV. &c.; thunderbolt, RV. &c.; a cloud, Naigh.; the firmament, RV. v, 30, 8; 56, 4; vii, 88, 2 [cf. Zd. *asman*; Pers. *aṣmān*; Lith. *akmů*; Slav. *kamy*]. **-máya**, mf(*ī*)n. made of stone, RV. iv, 30, 20; x, 67, 3; 101, 10; (cf. *aśma-máya*.) **-vat** (*áśman-*), mfn. stony, RV. x, 53, 8; AV. xii, 2, [26 &] 27; (cf. *aśma-vat*.)

2. **Aśma** (in comp. for 2. *áśman*). **-kadalī**, f., N. of a plant, L. **-kuṭṭa**, mfn. breaking or bruising with a stone (as grain), Mn. vi, 17; R. **-kuṭṭaka**, mfn. id., Yājñ. iii, 49. **-ketu**, m., N. of a plant, L. **-gandhā** (*áśma-*), f., N. of a plant, ŚBr. xiii; KātyŚr.; (cf. *aśva-gandhā*.) **-garbha** or **-garbha-ja**, n. an emerald. L. **-ghna**, m., N. of a plant, L. **-cakra** (*áśma-*), mfn. furnished with a disk of stone, RV. x, 101, 7. **-cita**, mfn. covered with stones, PBr. **-ja**, n. 'rock-born,' bitumen, L.; iron, L.; (cf. Mn. ix, 321.) **-jatu**, n. bitumen, Car. **-tā**, f. the state (hardness) of a stone, Kathās. **-dāraṇa**, m. an instrument for breaking stones, L. **-didyu** (*áśma-*), mfn. whose missile weapons are stones or thunderbolts, RV. v, 54, 3. **-nagara**, n., N. of the town in which Kālakeya resided, R. vii. **-purá**, f. a castle built on a rock, ŚBr. iii. **-pushpa**, n. benzoin (styrax), L. **-bhāla**, n. a stone mortar, L. **-bhid**, m. the plant Coleus Scutellarioides (supposed to dissolve stone in the bladder), Suśr. **-bheda** [L.] or **-bhedaka** [Suśr.], m. id. **-máya**, mf(*ī*)n. (= *aśman-máya*, q. v.) made of stone, ŚBr.; KātyŚr.; Mn. **-mūrdhan**, mfn. having a head of stone, AitBr. **-yoni**, m. = *-garbha*, q. v., L. **-vat**, mfn. (= *áśman-vat*, q. v.) stony, Suśr. **-varmán**, n. a wall or shield of stone, AV. v, 10, 1-7. **-varsha**, n. a shower of stones, MBh. **-vrishṭi**, f. id., R. iii, 38, 8. **-vraja** (*áśma-*), mfn. whose stall or pen is a rock, RV. iv, 1, 13; x, 139, 6. **-sāra**, m. n. iron, Suśr.; (*as*), m. sapphire, L.; (*aśmasāra*)*-maya*, mfn. made of iron, MBh. ii, 1836; R. iv, 22, 15. **-sārin**, m., N. of a man. **-hanman** (*áśma-*), n. a stroke of the thunderbolt, RV. vii, 104, 5. **Aśmâdi**, a gaṇa of Pāṇ. (iv, 2, 80). **Aśmâpidhāna**, mfn. covered by a stone, PBr. **Aśmârma**, n. a heap of ruins, stones of a ruin, Pāṇ. vi, 2, 91. **Áśmâsya** (4), mfn. 'having a stone-mouth or a stone-source,' flowing from a rock, RV. ii, 24, 4. **Aśmôttha**, n. (= *aśma-ja*, q. v.) 'rock-produced,' bitumen, L.

1. **Aśmanta**, *am*, n. a fire-place, L.; a field, L.; (*as*), m., N. of a Marutvat, Hariv. 11546; [? cf. Gk. *κάμινος*; Lat. *caminus*], (v. l. *aśvanta*.)

1. **Aśmantaka**, *am*, n. a fire-place, L.; a shade for a lamp, Daś.; (*as*), m. (= *aśmāntaka*, q. v.) N. of a plant, PārGr.; Suśr. &c.

Aśmarī, f. (Pāṇ. iv, 2, 80), (in comp. sometimes *aśmari*, Suśr.) strangury, stone or gravel (the disease), Suśr. &c. **-ghna**, m. the tree Cratæva Roxburghii (used as a lithontriptic), L. **-bhedana**, n. a lithontriptic, Suśr. **-hara**, m. the tree Pentaptera Arjuna or another plant (used as a lithontriptic), L.

Aśmāntaka, *as*, m., N. of a plant (from the fibres of which a Brāhman's girdle may be made), Mn. ii, 43.

अश्मन्त 2. *a-śmanta*, mfn. (? √*śam*), inauspicious, L.; unbounded, L.; (*am*), n. death, L.; (v. l. *aśvanta* and this perhaps for *asv-anta*, 'end of life'?)

अश्र 1. *aśra* ifc. for *áśri* (q. v.), e. g. *catur-aśra*, *try-aśra*, qq. vv.

अश्र 2. *aśra* for *asra* (a tear, blood), q. v.

अश्रद्दधान *á-śraddadhāna*, mfn. (p. Ā. *śrad-√dhā*) not trusting in (gen., Bhag. ix, 3), unbelieving, ŚBr. xii; MBh. &c.

A-śraddhá, mfn. (fr. *śraddhā́*), id., RV. vii, 6, 3; AV. xii, 2, 51; (*á-śraddhā*), f. want of trust, unbelief, VS.; AV.; ŚBr.; Mn.

A-śraddhita, mfn. unbelieving, BhP.

A-śraddheya, mfn. incredible, R. &c.

A-śrāddha, mfn. not performing funeral rites, L.; (*am*), n. food which has no relation to funeral rites, Āp. **-bhojin**, mfn. one who has taken a vow not to eat during the performance of the Śrāddha ceremonies, Pāṇ. iii, 2, 80, Sch.

A-śrāddhin, mfn. not performing funeral rites, Mn. iv, 223.

A-śrāddheya, mfn. not fit for funeral rites, MBh. xiii, 4363.

अश्रम *a-śramá*, mfn. indefatigable, RV. vii, 69, 7; (*á-śrama*), mfn. id., RV. vi, 21, 12; (*ena*), instr. ind. without fatigue, Ragh. ii, 67.

A-śramaṇá, mfn. indefatigable, RV. x, 94, 11; (*á-śramaṇa*), *as*, m. not an ascetic, ŚBr. xiv.

Á-śramishṭha, mfn. (superl.) quite indefatigable, RV. iv, 4, 12.

Á-śrānta, mfn. unwearied, RV. x, 62, 11; AV. xix, 25, 1; Kathās.; (*am*), n. unweariedly, Uttarar.

अश्रवण *a-śravaṇa*, *am*, n. not hearing, Vedāntas.; (*āt*), abl. ind. on account of not hearing, i. e. not seeing anything declared in the sacred texts, Lāṭy.

A-śravaṇīya, mfn. inaudible, ChUp.

A-śrāvya, mfn. unfit to be heard, Sāh.

अश्रात *á-śrāta*, mfn. uncooked, RV. x, 179, 1.

अश्राद्ध *a-śrāddha*, &c. See *á-śraddadhāna*.

अश्राव्य *a-śrāvya*. See *a-śravaṇa*.

अश्रि *áśri*, *is*, f. the sharp side of anything, corner, angle (of a room or house), edge (of a sword), ŚBr.; KātyŚr.; often ifc., e. g. *ashṭâśri*, *trir-áśri*, *cátur-aśri*, *śatâśri*, q. v.; (cf. *aśra*); [cf. Lat. *acies*, *acer*; Lith. *assmů*]. **-mat**, mfn. cornered, Nir. vi, 23.

1. **Aśrī**, f. = *áśri*, ShaḍvBr.

अश्रित *á-śrita*, mfn.? RV. iv, 7, 6.

अश्री 2. *a-śrī*, f. ill-luck (personified as a goddess), Kathās. **-mat**, mfn. inglorious, unpleasant, R. i, 6, 16 (ed. Bomb.)

A-śrīka, mfn. unlucky, MBh. iii, 12261.

A-śrīrá, mf(*ā́*)n. unpleasant, ugly, RV.

A-ślika, mfn. unpropitious, Mn. iv, 206.

A-ślīlá, mfn. = *a-śrīrá*, q. v., AV.; ŚBr.; AitBr.; (especially said of speech) coarse, vulgar, Kāṭh.; PBr.; MBh. &c.; (*am*), n. rustic language, low abuse, Daś.; Sāh. &c. **-tā**, f. or **-tva**, n. rustic language, Sāh. &c. **-dṛiḍha-rūpā**, f. (a woman) of an unpleasant but strong figure, Pāṇ. vi, 2, 42. **-parivāda**, m. ill-report, Yājñ. i, 33.

अश्रीवी *aśrivī* = *asrivī*, q. v., MaitrS.

अश्रु *áśru*, n. (*us*, m. only once ŚBr. vi and once R.) a tear, RV. x, 95, 12 & 13; AV. &c. with √*muc* or √*kṛi* [MBh. xii, 12491] or √*vṛit*, Caus. [R.] to shed tears [supposed to stand for *daśru* fr. √*daṅś*: cf. Gk. *δάκρυ*; Lat. *lacryma* for *dacryma*; Goth. *tagrs*; Eng. *tear*; Mod. Germ. *Zähre*]. **-karman**, n. shedding tears, MBh. xii, 12491. **-nāli**, f. Fistula Lacrymalis. **-nipāta**, m. flow of tears, MBh. iii, 327, &c. **-paripluta**, mfn. bathed in tears. **-pāta**, m. = *-nipāta*, q. v., MBh. xiv, 1638; Sāh.; N. of a particular part of a horse's head, VarBṛS. **-pūrṇa**, mfn. filled with tears. **-pravāha**, m. = *-nipāta*, q. v., Pañcat. **-plāvita**, n. a flood of tears, Kād. **-mukhá**, mf(*ī*)n. having tears on the face, AV. xi, 9, 7; R.; Vikr.; (*ās*), m. pl. a collective name for father, grandfather, and great-grandfather, BrahmaP. **-locana**, mfn. having tears in the eyes, MBh. iv, 485. **-vilocana**, mfn. id., VarBṛS. **Aśrûpahata**, mfn. affected by tears, Vikr.

अश्रुत *á-śruta*, mfn. unheard, ŚBr. xiv, &c.; not heard from the teacher, not taught, Jaim.; (hence) contrary to the Vedas, L.; untaught, not learned, MBh. v, 1000 & 1369; (*as*), m., N. of a son of Kṛishṇa, Hariv. 6190; of a son of Dyutimat, VP.; (*ā*), f., N. of the wife of Aṅgiras, Kathās. **-vat**, ind. as if it were not heard, Rājat. **-vraṇa**, m., N. of a son of Dyutimat, VP.

Á-śruti, *is*, f. oblivion, ŚBr. xiii; R.; not a Vedic text, KātyŚr. **-tva**, n. 'inaudibleness,' indistinctness, RPrāt. **-dhara**, mfn. not striking the hearing, VPrāt.; not knowing the Veda, L.

अश्रेयस् *a-śreyas*, mfn. (compar.) not the better, inferior, Mn. x, 64; MBh.; (*as*), n. mischief, MBh. iii, 1195; v, 7079; Kathās.

A-śreyaska, mfn. fatal, noxious, MBh. iii, 75.

A-śreshṭha, mfn. not the best, inferior, L.

अश्रेष्मन् *a-śreshmán*, mfn. (√2. *śrish*), without bands, AV. iii, 9, 2.

अश्रोतृ *a-śrotṛí*, mfn. one who does not hear, ChUp.; MaitrUp.

A-śrotrá, mfn. without ears, ŚBr. xiv.

Á-śrotriya, mfn. not versed in the Veda, Kāṭh.; ŚBr. &c.; performed by Brāhmans who are not versed in the Veda, Pañcat.

अश्लाघा *a-ślāghā*, f. modesty, Nir. iv, 10.

A-ślāghya, mfn. not to be praised, base, Mṛicch.

अश्लिक *a-ślika*. See 2. *a-śrī*.

A-ślīlá. See ib.

अश्लेषा *a-śleshā*, f. sg. or *ās*, f. pl. (= *ā-śleshā́*, q. v.) N. of the seventh (in later times the ninth) lunar mansion (containing five stars), MBh. xiii, 3262; Jyot.; VarBṛS. **-bhava** or **-bhū**, m. the Ketu (or descending node), L.

अश्लोण *á-śloṇa*, mf(ā)n. not lame, AV.

अश्व 1. *áśva* (2. rarely 3, RV.), *as*, m. (√1. *aś*, Uṇ.), ifc. f. *ā*, a horse, stallion, RV. &c.; the horse (in the game of chess); the number 'seven' (that being the number of the horses of the sun); the archer (in the Zodiac), VarBṛ.; a particular kind of lover (horse-like in strength), L.; N. of a teacher (with the patron. Sāmudri), ŚBr. xiii; of a son of Citraka, Hariv. 1921; of a Dānava, MBh. i, 2532; (*ā*), f. (gaṇa *ajâdi*, q. v.) a mare, RV. &c. [Zd. *aspa*; Lat. *equus*; Gk. *ἵππος*, &c.] **-kandikā**, f. = *-gandhā*, q. v., L. **-karṇa**, m. the ear of a horse, KātyŚr.; (mfn.) 'resembling the ear of a horse,' said of a particular fracture of the bones, Suśr.; (*as*); m. the tree Vatica Robusta (so called from the shape of its leaves), R.; Suśr.; N. of a mountain, Buddh. **–karṇaka**, mfn. (= *-karṇa*, mfn.) said of a particular fracture of the bones, Suśr.; (*as*), m. the tree Vatica Robusta, Suśr. **–kaśā**, f. a whip for a horse, Nir. ix, 19. **–kuṭī**, f. a stable for horses, Pañcat. **–kuṇapá**, n. the carcass of a horse, TS. vii. **–keśa**, *ās*, m. pl., N. of a people, MārkP. **–kovida**, mfn. skilled in horses, N. **–kranda** (*áśva-*), m., N. of a mythical being, Suparṇ.; MBh. i, 1488 ('N. of Yaksha,' Comm.) **–krīta**, mf(*ī*, Pāṇ. iv, 1, 50) n. bought (in exchange) for a horse, Pāṇ. vi, 2, 151, Sch. **–kshabhá**, mf(*ā́*)n.? AV. xix, 49, 1. **–khura**, m. a horse's hoof, Suśr.; Pañcat.; a perfume (apparently a dried shell-fish), L.; (*ī*), f. the plant Clitoria Ternatea, L. **–gati**, f. 'the pace of a horse,' N. of a metre (containing four verses of eighteen [or sixteen?] syllables each). **–gandhā**, f. the plant Physalis Flexuosa, Suśr.; Comm. on KātyŚr. **–gupta**, m., N. of a teacher, Buddh. **–goyuga**, n. a pair of horses; (cf. Pāṇ. v, 2, 29, Comm.) **–goshṭha**, n. a stable for horses, Pāṇ. v, 2, 29, Comm. **–grīva**, m. 'horse-neck,' N. of an Asura, MBh.; R.; of a son of Citraka, Hariv. 1920. **–ghāma**, m., N. of a place, Rājat. **–ghāsa**, m. (Pāṇ. ii, 1, 36, Comm.) fodder for horses, Kathās. **–ghosha**, m., N. of a Buddhist patriarch. **–ghna**, m. 'horse-bane,' a kind of Oleander (Nerium Odorum), L. **–cakra**, m., N. of a man, MBh. iii, 10272. **–calana-śālā**, f. a riding-house, Pañcat. **–cikitsā**, f. 'veterinary art,' a work of Jayadatta. **–jaghana**, mfn. having the lower limbs like those of a horse, VarBṛ. **–jit**, mfn. gaining horses by conquest, RV. ii, 21, 1; ix, 59, 1; AV.; (*t*), m., N. of a Buddhist Bhikshu. **–tará**, see below s.v. **–tīrtha**, n., N. of a place of pilgrimage near Kānyakubja on the Gaṅgā, MBh. iii, 11052; xiii, 216. **–ttha, -tthāma, -tthāman**, see ss. vv. below. **–trirātra**, m. (gaṇa *yuktârohyādi*, q.v.) N. of a ceremony, ŚāṅkhŚr.; Lāṭy. **–tvá**, n. the state of a horse, ŚBr. xiii. **–da**, mfn. giving horses, Mn. iv, 231. **–danshṭrā**, f. (= *śva-danshṭrā*, q.v.) the plant Tribulus Lanuginosus, L. **–dā́**, mfn. = *-da*, q.v., RV.; (cf. *án-aśva-dā*.) **–dāvan**, mfn. id., RV. v, 18, 3 (voc.) **–dūta**, m. a messenger on horseback, Lalit. **–nadī**, f., N. of a river, MBh. iii, 17132. **–naya**, m. a horse-herd, one who has the charge of a drove of grazing horses, ChUp. **–nāśaka**, m. = *-ghna*, L. **–nibandhika**, m. 'a horse-fastener,' groom, Inscr. **–nirṇij** (*áśva-*), mfn. decorated with horses, RV. x, 76, 3. **–pá**, m. a groom, VS. xxx, 11. **–pati** (*áśva-*), m. lord of horses, RV. viii, 21, 3 (voc.; said of Indra); VS. xvi, 24; N. of a Kaikeya, ŚBr. x; of a brother-in-law of Daśaratha, R. ii, 1, 2; of an Asura, MBh.; Hariv.; of a king of Madras and father of Sāvitrī, MBh.; (*aśvapaty*)-*ādi*, a gaṇa of Pāṇ. (iv, 1, 84). **–parṇa** (*áśva-*), mfn. having horses for wings, RV. i, 88, 1; vi, 47, 31; (*ī*), f., N. of a river, ŚivaP. Rev. **–pastya** (*áśva-*, 5), mfn. having horses in the stable, filling the stable with horses, RV. ix, 86, 41. **–pāda**, mfn. horse-footed, (gaṇa *hasty-ādi*, q.v.); (*as*), m., N. of a Siddha, Rājat. **–pāla**, m. (f. *ī*, gaṇa *revaty-ādi*, q.v.) a groom, Ratnāv.; one who has to guard the sacrificial horse, ŚāṅkhŚr. **–pucchaka**, m., N. of a plant, L.; (*ikā*), f. the plant Glycine Debilis, L. **–pṛishṭha** (*áśva-*), mfn. carried on horseback, RV. viii, 26, 24; (*am*), n. horseback. **–peja** or **-peya**, m., N. of a man, Pāṇ. iv, 3, 106, Kāś. **–peśas** (*áśva-*), mfn. decorated with horses, RV. ii, 1, 16. **–praṇīta** (*áśva-*), mfn. carried near by a horse, ŚBr. vii. **–prapatana**, n., Pāṇ. v, 1, 111, Comm.; °*tanīya*, mfn. referring to it, ib. **–bandha**, m. = *-nibandhika*, q.v., MBh. iv, 62; R. **–bandhaka**, m. id., R. **–bandhana**, n. fastening of horses; (mf(*ī*)n.) used for fastening horses. **–balā**, f. the vegetable Trigonella Fœnum Græcum, Suśr. **–bāhu**, m., N. of a son of Citraka, Hariv. 1920 & 2088. **–budhna** (*áśva-*), mf(*ā*)n. 'based on horses,' carried by horses, RV. x, 8, 3. **–budhya** (*áśva-*), mfn. based on horses, consisting of horses (as wealth), RV. i, 92, 7 & 8; 121, 14. **–bhāra**, m. the load of a horse, (gaṇa *vanśâdi*, q.v.) **–mandurā**, f. = *-goshṭha*, q.v., Kād. **–mahishikā**, f. the natural enmity of a horse and a buffalo, L. **–māra** or **-māraka**, m. = *-ghna*, q.v., Suśr. **–māla**, m. a kind of serpent, L. **–mitra**, m., N. of a teacher of the Gobhila family, VBr. **–m-ishṭi** (*áśvam-ishṭi*), mfn. wishing for horses, RV. viii, 61, 7; procuring horses, RV. ii, 6, 2. **–mukha**, mf(*ī*)n. having the head of a horse, VarBṛS.; (*ás*), m., N. of a mythical being, Suparṇ.; a Kiṃnara, Kād.; (*ī*), f. a Kiṃnarī, R.; Kum. i, 11; (*ās*), m. pl., N. of a people, VarBṛS. (v.l. *śva-mukha*). **–1. -medhá**, m. the horse-sacrifice (a celebrated ceremony, the antiquity of which reaches back to the Vedic period; the hymns i, 162 & 163 of the RV. [= VS. xxii seqq.], referring to it, are however of comparatively late origin; in later times its efficacy was so exaggerated, that a hundred such sacrifices entitled the sacrificer to displace Indra from the dominion of Svarga; kings who engaged in it spent enormous sums in gifts to the Brāhmans; it is said that the horse was sometimes not immolated, but kept bound during the ceremony), VS. xviii, 22; TS.; Ragh. &c., (cf. *arkâśvamedhá*); (*aśvamedha*)-*kāṇḍa*, n., N. of ŚBr. xiii (treating of the Aśvamedha); *-ja*, m., N. of a king, BhP.; *-tvá*, n. the state of an Aśv., ŚBr. x; *-datta*, m., N. of a king, MBh. i, 3838; VP.; *-yājín*, m. engaged in an Aśv., ŚBr. xiii, xiv; (*aśvamedhá*)-*vat*, mfn. receiving an Aśv.; ind. as with the Aśv., KātyŚr.; *aśvamedhêśvara*, m., N. of a king, MBh. ii, 1066. **–2. -medha** (*áśva-*), m., N. of a descendant of Bharata, RV. v, 27, 4–6. **–medhaka**, m. (= *aśvamedha-ja* above) N. of a king, BhP. **–medhika**, mfn. relating to the Aśvamedha, MBh. i, 354 & 605; (cf. *āśvamedhika*); (*as*), m. a horse fit for the Aśv., L. **–medhin**, mfn. engaged in an Aśv., PBr. **–medhīya**, m. = *-medhika* (q.v.), m., L. **–mohaka**, m. = *-ghna*, q.v., L. **–yajña**, m. a sacrifice offered for the benefit of one's horses, Gobh. **–yúj**, mfn. harnessing horses, RV. v, 54, 2; having horses put to (as a carriage), R. v, 27, 14; born under the constellation Aśvayuj, Pāṇ. iv, 3, 36 (cf. *āśvayuja*); (*k*), f. sg., N. of a constellation (the head of Aries), Pāṇ. iv, 3, 36; VarBṛS. &c.; (*-yújau*), f. du. id., AV. xix, 7, 5; TBr.; (*k*), m. the month Āśvina (Sept.–Oct.), VarBṛS. **–yuja**, m. the month Āśvina, Kauś.; VarBṛS. **–yūpá**, m. the post to which the sacrificial horse is bound, RV. i, 162, 6. **–yoga** (*áśva-*), mf(*ā*)n. 'having horses put to,' reaching quickly, RV. i, 186, 7. **–raksha**, m. a groom, L. **–rathá**, m. a carriage drawn by horses, ŚBr. v; KātyŚr.; (mfn.) driving in such a carriage, PBr.; (*ā*), f., N. of a river, MBh. iii, 11681. **–rāja**, m. 'king of horses,' N. of the horse Uccaiḥśravas (q.v.), MBh. i, 1097; N. of Śākyamuni, Lalit. **–rādhas** (*áśva-*), mfn. equipping or furnishing horses, RV. v, 10, 4; x, 21, 2. **–ripu**, m. 'enemy of horses,' a buffalo, Bhpr. **–rodhaka**, m. = *-ghna*, q.v., L. **–lalita**, n. a species of the Vikṛiti metre. **–lālā**, f. a kind of snake, L. **–loman**, m. horse-hair, L. **–vaktra**, m. (= *-mukha*, q.v.) a Kiṃnara, L. **–vaḍava**, *am*, n. sg. or *au*, m. du. a horse and a mare, Pāṇ. ii, 4, 12; (*ās*), m. pl. horses and mares, Pāṇ. ii, 4, 27, Kāś. **–vat** (*áśva-*), mfn. rich in horses, AV. vi, 68, 3; (*t*), n. 'consisting of horses,' possession of horses, RV. viii, 46, 5; ix, 105, 4; AV. xviii, 3, 61; (cf. *áśvā-vat*); (mfn.) containing the word *aśva*, PBr.; (*tī*), f., N. of a river, MBh. xiii, 7651; of an Apsaras, VP. **–vadana**, *ās*, m. pl., N. of a people, VarBṛS. **–vaha**, m. a horseman, L. **–1. -vāra**, m. (= *-vālá*, q.v.) Saccharum Spontaneum, Pāṇ. viii, 2, 18, Comm.; (cf. *āśvavāra*.) **–2. -vāra**, m. a horseman, R.; Śiś. iii, 66, &c.; a groom, L. **–vāraka**, m. a groom, L. **–vāraṇa**, m. = *-ripu*, q.v., L. **–vālá**, m. hair from the tail of a horse, KātyŚr.; the reed Saccharum Spontaneum, ŚBr. iii. **–vāha**, m. a horseman, L. **–vikrayin**, m. a horse-dealer, L. **–1. -vid**, m. (√1. *vid*), 'skilled in training horses,' a N. of Nala, L. **–2. -vid**, mfn. (√3. *vid*), procuring horses, RV. ix, 55, 3; 61, 3. **–vṛishá**, m. a stallion, ŚBr. xiv. **–vaidya**, m. a veterinary surgeon. **–vrata**, n., N. of a Sāman. **–śaká**, n. excrements of a horse, ŚBr. vi. **–śakṛit**, n. id., KātyŚr.; f., N. of a river, Hariv. 6445. **–śaṅku**, m., N. of a Dānava, MBh. i, 2531. **–śatru**, m. = *-ripu*, q.v., L. **–śaphá**, m. a horse's hoof, ŚBr. xiii; KātyŚr.; (*aśvaśapha*)-*budhna*, mfn. having ground shaped like a horse's hoof, ĀpŚr.; *-mātrá*, having the measure of a horse-hoof, ŚBr. i. **–śākhoṭa**, m., N. of a plant. **–śālā**, f. a stable for horses, MBh. **–śāva**, m. a foal. **–śāstra**, n. a text-book of veterinary science; N. of a work of Nakula. **–śiras**, n. a horse's head, MBh.; (mfn.) having the head of a horse (N. of Nārāyaṇa), MBh. xii, 13100 seqq.; (*ās*), m., N. of a Dānava, MBh.; Hariv.; of a king (named in connection with Nārāyaṇa), VārP. **–śīrsha**, m. 'having the head of a horse,' a form of Vishṇu, AgP. **–ścandra** (*áśva-*), brilliant with horses, RV. vi, 35, 4. **–shaḍgava**, n. a set or team of six horses, Pāṇ. v, 2, 29, Comm. **–shā**, mfn. (Ved.) = *-sā*, q.v., Pāṇ. viii, 3, 110, Pat. **–sáni**, mfn. gaining or procuring horses, VS. viii, 12; (cf. gaṇa *savanâdi*, q.v.) **–sā́**, mfn. id., RV. **–sādá**, m. a horseman, VS. xxx, 13. **–sādin**, m. id., Ragh. vii, 44. **–sārathya**, n. management of horses and cars, horsemanship and driving, Mn. x, 47. **–sukta**, n., N. of a Sāman. **–sūktin**, m., N. of the author of the hymns RV. viii, 14 & 15. **–sūtra**, n. a text-book on the management of horses, MBh. ii, 255. **–sūnṛita**, mf(*ā*)n. pleased with horses, RV. v, 79, 1–10 (voc.) **–sṛigālikā**, f. the natural enmity between the horse and the jackal, L. **–sena**, m., N. of a Nāga, MBh. i, 803, 8237; of a son of Kṛishṇa, BhP.; of the father of the twenty-third Arhat of the present Avasarpiṇī, L. **–stomīya**, n. 'relating to the praise of the sacrificial horse,' N. of the hymn RV. i, 162, ŚBr. xiii; (*as*), m. (sc. *homa*), N. of an oblation, ĀpŚr. **–sthāna**, n. a stable for horses, Yājñ. i, 278; (mfn.) born in a stable, Pāṇ. iv, 3, 35, Sch. **–hana**, m. = *-ghna*, q.v., Car. **–hanu**, m., N. of a man, Hariv. 1943. **–hantṛi**, m. = *-ghna*, q.v., Suśr. **–hayá**, mfn. driving horses, RV. ix, 96, 2; x, 26, 5. **–havis**, n., N. of a sacrificial ceremony, MaitrS. **–hāraka**, m. a horse-stealer, Mn. xi, 51. **–hṛidaya**, n. horsemanship, L.; (*ā*), f. a N. of the Apsaras Rambhā, Kād. **Aśvâksha**, m., N. of a plant, L. **Aśvâjanī**, f. a whip, RV. v, 62, 7; vi, 75, 13. **Aśvâdi**, two gaṇas of Pāṇ. (iv, 1, 110 & v, 1, 39). **Aśvâdhika**, mfn. superior in horses, strong in cavalry. **Aśvâdhyaksha**, m. a guardian of horses, N.; Pañcat. **Aśvânīka**, n. cavalry, Mālav. **Aśvântaka**, m. = *aśva-ghna*, q.v., L. **Aśvâbhidhānī**, f. a halter, AV.; ŚBr.; *aśvâbhidhānī-krita*, mfn. having the halter put on, ŚBr. vi. **Aśvā-magha**, mfn. rich in horses, RV. vii, 71, 1. **Aśvâyurveda**, m. veterinary science. **Aśvâyus**, m., N. of a king, MatsyaP. **Aśvâri**, m. = *aśva-ripu*, q.v., L. **Aśvârudha**, mfn. mounted, sitting on horseback, Kathās. **Aśvâroha**, m. a horseman, Kathās.; (*ā*), f. = *aśva-gandhā*, q.v., L. **Áśvā-vat**, mfn. (Pāṇ. vi, 3, 131) furnished with horses, together with a horse or horses, RV.; consisting of horses, RV.; (*t*), n. (= *áśva-vat*, q.v.) possession of horses, RV.; (*tī*), f., N. of a river, ŚivaP. Rev. **Aśvâvatāna**, m., N. of a man, (gaṇa *gopavanâdi* and *vidâdi*, q.v.) **Aśvâvarohaka**, m. or °**hikā**, f. = *aśva-gandhā*, q.v. **Áśvêshita**, mfn. driven by horses, RV. viii, 46, 28. **Aśvôrasa**, n. a principal horse, Pāṇ. v, 4, 93, Sch.

2. **Aśva**, Nom. P. *aśvati*, to behave like a horse, Pāṇ. iii, 1, 11, Sch.

Aśvaká, *as*, m. a small or bad horse, VS. xxiii, 18; a sparrow, L.; (*ās*), m. pl., N. of a people, MBh. vi, 351, &c. (cf. *aśmaka*); (*ikā*), f. a little mare, Pāṇ. vii, 3, 46.

Aśvakinī, f. the Nakshatra Aśvinī, L.

Aśvatará, *as*, m. (Pāṇ. v, 3, 91) a mule, AV. iv, 4, 8; ŚBr. &c.; (compar. of *aśva*) a better horse, Pat.; a male calf, L.; one of the chiefs of the Nāgas, MBh.; Hariv. &c.; N. of a Gandharva, L.; (*ā*), f. a better mare, Pat.; (*ī́*), f. a she-mule, AV. viii, 8, 22; MBh. &c. **Aśvatarâśva**, m., N. of a man, Comm. on ChUp.; (cf. *āśvatarâśvi*.) **Aśvatarī-ratha**, m. a car drawn by a she-mule, AitBr.; ChUp.; KātyŚr.

Aśvatthá, *as*, m. (*ttha* = *stha*, 'under which horses stand') the holy fig tree, Ficus Religiosa, AV.; ŚBr. &c.; a vessel made of its wood, RV. i, 135, 8; x, 97, 5; the upper (or male) *araṇi* made of its wood, AV. vi, 11, 1; ŚBr. xi; KātyŚr.; the plant Thespesia Populneoides, L.; N. of a Nakshatra (also called Śroṇā), Pāṇ. iv, 2, 5 & 22; a N. of the sun, MBh. iii, 151; (*ās*), m. pl., N. of a people, VarBṛS.; (*ā*), f. day of full moon in the month Āśvina (in which month the fruit of the Ficus Religiosa generally becomes ripe); (*ī*), f. the small Pippala tree, L.; (mfn.) 'relating to the Nakshatra Aśvattha,' (with *muhūrta*) the moment in which the moon enters that Nakshatra, Pāṇ. iv, 2, 5, Sch. **–kuṇa**, m. the fruit season of the holy fig tree, (gaṇa *pilv-ādi*, q.v.) **–bheda**, m. the tree Ficus Benjamina.

Aśvatthaka, mfn. to be done (as paying debts) when the Aśvattha tree bears, Pāṇ. iv, 3, 48; (*ikā*), f. = *āśvatthī*, q.v., L.

Aśvatthāma, mfn. (for *aśva-sth°*) having the strength of a horse, Pat.

Aśvatthāman, mfn. id., Pāṇ. iv, 1, 85, Siddh.; (*ā*), m., N. of a son of Droṇa, MBh.; of one of the seven Ṛishis of the period of Manu Sāvarṇi, Hariv. 453.

Aśvatthika, mf(*ī*)n., °**tthila**, °**tthīya**, mfn. (gaṇas *parpâdi*, *kumudâdi*, *kāśâdi*, and *utkarâdi*, qq. vv.)

Aśvathá, *as*, m., N. of a man, RV. vi, 47, 24.

Aśvaya, Nom. Ā. °*yate* = *aśvataram ācashṭe*, L.

Aśvayā́, f. desire to get horses, RV. viii, 46, 10; ix, 64, 4.

Aśvayú, mfn. desiring horses, RV.

Aśvalá, *as*, m., N. of the Hotṛi-priest of Janaka king of Vaideha, ŚBr. xiv; (cf. *āśvalāyana*.)

Aśvasya, Nom. P. °*syati*, to wish for the stallion, Pāṇ. vii, 1, 51.

Aśvāya, Nom. P. (p. °*yát*) to wish for horses, RV.; (cf. Pāṇ. vii, 4, 37.)

Aśvika, mf(*ī*)n. (gaṇas *parpâdi* and *kumudâdi*, qq. vv.)

Aśvin, mfn. possessed of horses, consisting of horses, RV.; mounted on horseback, MārkP.; (*ī*), m. a cavalier; horse-tamer, RV.; (*inā* or *inau*), m. du. 'the two charioteers,' N. of two divinities (who appear in the sky before the dawn in a golden carriage drawn by horses or birds; they bring treasures to men and avert misfortune and sickness; they are considered as the physicians of heaven), RV. &c.; a N. of the Nakshatra presided over by the Aśvins, VarBṛS.; the number 'two,' ib.; Sūryas.; (for *aśvi-sutau*) the two sons of the Aśvins, viz. Nakula and Sahadeva, MBh. v, 1816; (*inī*), f., N. of the wife of the two Aśvins (who in later times was considered as their mother; cf. *aśvinī-putrau* below), RV. v, 46, 8; the head of Aries or the first of the 28 Nakshatras, Jyot.; VarBṛS.; (*aśvini*, shortened for the sake of metre) Sūryas.; (*i*), n. (= *aśva-vat*, n., q. v.) richness in horses, RV. i, 53, 4. **Aśvi-devatāka**, mfn. whose divinities are the Aśvins, L. **Aśvina-kṛita**, mfn. (irreg. for *aśvi-k*°) done by the Aśvins, VS. xx, 35. **Aśvinī-kumāra**, m. the son of Aśvinī (said to be the father of the first physician), BrahmavP. i. **Aśvinī-putrau** or **-sutau**, m. du. the twin sons of Aśvinī, L. **Aśvi-mat**, mfn. (any Mantra) containing the word Aśvin, Pāṇ. iv, 4, 126.

Aśviyá, *ā́*, Ved. n. pl. troops of horses, RV. iv, 17, 11.

1. **Aśvīya**, Nom. P. °*yati*, to desire horses, Pāṇ. vii, 1, 51, Sch.: Desid. *aśvīyiyishati* or *aśiśvīyishati*, Pāṇ. vi, 1, 3, Comm.

2. **Aśvīya**, mfn. (gaṇa *apûpâdi*, q. v.) conducive to horses, L.; (Pāṇ. iv, 2, 48) a number of horses or horsemen with horses, Kād.; Kathās.

1. **Áśvya** (3, rarely 2), mfn. (gaṇa *apûpâdi*, q.v.) belonging to or coming from horses, RV.; ŚBr. xiv; consisting of horses, RV.; (*am*), n. a number of horses, possession of horses, RV.

2. **Aśvyá** (3), *as*, m. 'son of Aśva,' N. of Vaśa, RV. i, 112, 10; viii, 46, 21 & 33; N. of another man, RV. viii, 24, 14.

अश्वन्त *aśvanta*, v. l. for *aśmanta*, q. v.

अश्वस्तन *a-śvastana*, mf(*ī*)n. not for to-morrow, not provided for to-morrow, PBr.; Yājñ. i, 128; MBh. — **vid**, mfn. ignorant of the future, BhP. — **vidhātṛi**, mfn. not providing for the future, MBh. xii, 8920. — **vidhāna**, n. non-provision for the future, Mn. xi, 16 (= MBh. xii, 6050).

A-śvastanika, mfn. = *a-śvastana*, Mn. iv, 7.

अष *ash*, cl. 1. P. Ā. *ashati*, °*te*, to go, move, L.; to shine, L.; to take or receive, L.; (cf. √3. *as*.)

अषडक्षीण *a-shaḍakshīṇa*, mfn. (fr. *shash*, *akshi*), not seen by six eyes, i. e. known by two persons only, secret, Pāṇ. v, 4, 7.

अषतर *áshatara*, mfn. (compar. fr. '*asha*' fr. √1. *aś*?) more acceptable, RV. i, 173, 4.

अषाढ *á-shāḍha* (or in RV. *á-shālha*), mfn. not to be overcome, invincible, RV.; VS.; born under the Nakshatra Ashāḍhā, Pāṇ. iv, 3, 34; (*as*), m. the month (generally called) Āshāḍha, L.; a staff made of Palāśa wood (carried by the student during the performance of certain vows), L.; N. of a teacher, Kāṭh.; ŚBr. i; (cf. *āshāḍhi*); (*ā*), f., N. of a brick (used for the sacrificial altar), ŚBr.; (*ā́* or *ā́s*), f. sg. or pl., N. of two lunar mansions (distinguished as *pûrvā* and *uttarā*, 'the former' and 'the latter,' and reckoned either as the eighteenth and nineteenth [TBr.] or as the twentieth and twenty-first [VP. &c.]), AV. xix, 7, 4, &c.

Ashāḍhaka, *as*, m. the month Āshāḍha, L.

Ashāḍhin, mfn. wearing the staff (of Palāśa wood) called Ashāḍha, Kād.

अष्ट 1. *ashṭa*, mfn. (√*aksh*; cf. *nir*-√*aksh*) 'marked, branded,' only in comp. with 1. **-karṇa**, mfn. branded on the ear, Pāṇ. vi, 3, 115; (*ī*), f. a cow branded on the ear, RV. x, 62, 7.

अष्ट 2. *ashṭa*, fr. √1. *aś*. See *á-samashṭa-k*°.

अष्टन् (*ashṭan*), *ashṭaú* [RV.; AV. &c.] or *ashṭā́* [RV. viii, 2, 41] or *ashṭá* [RV. x, 27, 15; AV. &c.], pl. eight (other forms are: gen. *ashṭānām*, Mn. &c.; instr. *ashṭabhís*, RV. ii, 18, 4; ŚBr. &c.; loc. *ashṭāsú*, ŚBr. &c.); [Lat. *octo*; Gk. ὀκτώ; Goth. *ahtau*; Mod. Germ. *acht*; Engl. *eight*; Lith. *asztûni*; Slav. *osmj*.]

3. **Ashṭa** (in comp. for *ashṭan*). — **kapāla**, mfn. = *ashṭā́-kap*°, q. v., Pāṇ. vi, 3, 46, Comm. — 2. **-karṇa**, m. 'eight-eared,' N. of Brahman (who is supposed to have four heads), L. — **kṛítvas**, ind. eight times, AV. xi, 2, 9; KātyŚr.; (cf. *ashṭaú kṛítvas*, id., ŚB.) — **koṇa**, m. an octogon, L. — **khaṇḍa**, m., N. of a collection of different passages of the RV. — **gava**, n. a flock of eight cows, Pāṇ. vi, 3, 46, Comm., (cf. *ashṭā-gava*); (mfn.) drawn by eight oxen, MBh. viii, 799. — **guṇa**, mfn. eightfold, Mn. viii, 400; (*am*), n. 'eight qualities,' in comp., e. g. *ashṭaguṇâśraya*, mfn. endowed with the eight qualities (as a king), L. — **gṛihīta**, mfn. = *ashṭā-gṛih*°, q. v., KātyŚr. — **catvāriṇśa**, mfn. the forty-eighth. — **catvāriṇśat**, f. = *ashṭā́-catv*°, q. v., Pāṇ. vi, 3, 49. — **taya**, n. (in later language for *ashṭā-taya*, q. v.) a collection of eight different things. — **triṇśa**, mfn. the thirty-eighth, MBh. — **triṇśat**, f. = *ashṭā-tr*°, q. v., MBh. — **tva**, n. condition of eight, Pāṇ. vii, 2, 84, Sch. — **daṇshṭra**, m. (= *ashṭā-d*°, q. v.) N. of a Dānava, Hariv. 12935. — **dala**, mfn. having a flower of eight leaves, Sāh.; (*am*), n. a lotus flower with eight leaves. — **diś**, °*śas*, f. pl. the eight cardinal points of the compass collectively, L.; (*ashṭa-dik*)-*pāla*, *ās*, m. pl. the eight regents of the cardinal points, as Indra of the East, &c.; (see *dik-pati* and *-pāla*.) — **dhā́**, ind. (Pāṇ. v, 3, 42 seq.) eightfold, in eight parts or sections, AV. xiii, 3, 19; VS. &c.; (*ashṭadhā*)-*vihitá*, mfn. divided into eight parts, ŚBr. vi. — **dhātu**, m. pl. the eight metals collectively (as gold, silver, copper, tin, lead, brass, iron, and steel). — **navata**, mfn. the ninety-eighth. — **navati**, f. = *ashṭā́-n*°, q. v. — **navatitama**, mfn. = *-navata*, q. v. — **pañcāśa**, mfn. the fifty-eighth. — **pañcāśat**, f. = *ashṭā́-p*°, q.v. — **pañcāśattama**, mfn. = *-pañcāśa*, q.v. — **pati** (*ashṭá-*), mf(*-patnī*)n (*-pat*), having eight husbands, TĀr. — **pattra**, mfn. and (*am*), n. = *-dala*, q. v. — **pad**, m. (nom. *-pād*) 'having eight legs,' a spider, L.; the fabulous animal generally called Śarabha, L. — **pada**, mf(*ā*)n. having eight Padas (as a metre), RPrāt. — **padikā**, f. the plant Vallaris Dichotomus Wall., MBh. xiii, 2831, ed. Bomb.; v. l. *-pādikā*, ed. Calc. — **pāda**, mfn. having eight legs, MBh. iii, 10665; (*as*), m. a kind of spider, L.; the fabulous animal Śarabha, L. — **pādikā**, see *-padikā* above. — **putra** (*ashṭá-*), mf(*ā*)n. having eight sons, AV. viii, 9, 21; TĀr. — **purusha** (*ashṭá-*), mfn. consisting of eight persons, TĀr. — **pushpikā**, f. a wreath made with eight different kinds of flowers, Kād. — **maṅgala**, n. a collection of eight lucky things (for certain great occasions, such as a coronation &c.), e. g. a lion, a bull, an elephant, a water-jar, a fan, a flag, a trumpet, and a lamp; (or, according to others, a Brāhman, a cow, fire, gold, ghee, the sun, water, and a king); (*as*), m. a horse with a white face, tail, mane, breast, and hoofs, L. — **māna**, n. a measure (one *kuḍava*, q. v.), Śārṅg. — **mūrti**, m. 'eight-formed,' a N. of Śiva (as identified with the five elements, mind, egotism, and Prakṛiti [matter]; or, according to the opening of the Śakuntalā, with the five elements, the sun and moon and the sacrificing priest), MBh. iii, 1939; Ragh. &c. — **mūrti-dhara**, m. 'possessing eight forms,' a N. of Śiva. — **mūlī**, f. a collection of eight roots from different plants, VarBṛS. — **yoni** (*ashṭá-*), mf(*ī*)n. having eight places of origin, AV. viii, 9, 21; TĀr. — **ratna**, n. 'the eight jewels,' N. of a collection of eight Ślokas on ethics. — **rasâśraya**, mfn. endowed with the eight rasas (or sentiments of poetry). — **rcá**, m. (fr. *ṛic*), m. a hymn consisting of eight verses, ŚBr. ix. — **loha**, n. = *-dhātu*, q. v., Hcat. — **varga**, mfn. being in rows of eight each, KātyŚr.; (*as*), m. a class of eight principal medicaments (viz. Ṛishabha, Jīvaka, Medā, Mahāmedā, Ṛiddhi, Vṛiddhi, Kākolī, and Kshīrakākolī), L. — **varsha**, mf(*ā*)n. eight years old, Mn. ix, 94. — **vikalpa**, mfn. of eight kinds, Sāṅkhyak. — **vidha**, mfn. eightfold, of eight kinds, Mn. vii, 154, &c. — **vṛishá**, mfn. having eight bulls (?), AV. v, 16, 8. — **śata**, n. a hundred and eight, VarBṛS.; Jain.; eight hundred, Yājñ. i, 302; (*ī*), f. id., Sūryas.; (*ashṭaśata*)-*sāhasra*, mfn. consisting of eight hundred thousand, MBh. iv, 288. — **śataka**, n. a hundred and eight, MBh. iii, 158. — **śravaṇa** or **-śravas**, m. (= *-karṇa*, q. v.) 'eight-eared,' N. of Brahman, L. — **shashṭa**, mfn. the sixty-eighth. — **shashṭi**, f. sixty-eight, Kathās. — **shashṭitama**, mfn. = *-shashṭa*, q. v. — **saptati**, f. seventy-eight. — **saptatitama**, mfn. the seventy-eighth. — **sāhasraka**, mf(*ikā*)n. consisting of eight thousand (i. e. ślokas, as one of the Buddhist Prajñāpāramitās). — **stanā** [MaitrS.] or **ashṭá-stanā** [ŚBr.], f. (a cow) whose udder has eight teats; (cf. *ashṭā-stanā*.)

Ashṭā (in comp. for *ashṭan*). — **kapāla** (*ashṭā́-*), mfn. (an oblation) prepared or offered in eight pans, VS.; AitBr.; ŚBr. — **gava**, mfn. (a car) drawn by eight oxen, Pāṇ. vi, 3, 46, Comm. — **gṛihītá**, mfn. (said of ghee) drawn eight times, ŚBr. vi. — **cakra** (*ashṭā́-*), mf(*ā*)n. having eight wheels, AV. — **catvāriṇśá**, mfn. the forty-eighth, VS.; ŚBr.; consisting of forty-eight verses, N. of a Stoma. — **catvāriṇśaka**, mfn. lasting forty-eight years, PārGṛ.; = *-catvāriṇśin*, q. v., Pāṇ. v, 1, 94, Comm. — **catvāriṇśat** (*ashṭā́-*), f. forty-eight, ŚBr.; (*ashṭā́-catvāriṇśad*)-*akshara*, mf(*ā*)n. consisting of forty-eight syllables, ŚBr.; (*ashṭācatvāriṇśad*)-*ishṭaka*, mfn. consisting of forty-eight Ishṭakās, ŚBr. — **catvāriṇśin**, mfn. performing a vow that lasts forty-eight years, Pāṇ. v, 1, 94, Comm. — **taya**, *āni*, n. pl. eight different things, AitBr. — **triṇśá**, mfn. 'the thirty-eighth,' with *śatá*, a hundred augmented by thirty-eight, ŚBr. x. — **triṇśat**, f. thirty-eight, KātyŚr. — **daṇshṭra**, mfn. having eight tusks, APrāt.; N. of a son of Virūpa, author of the hymn RV. x, 111, RAnukr.; ĀśvŚr. — **daśá**, mfn. the eighteenth, VS.; ŚBr.; connected with an eighteen-fold Stoma, PBr. — **daśan** (*ashṭā́-*), mfn. eighteen, ŚBr. &c.; (*ashṭādaśa*)-*dhā*, ind. in eighteen parts, Sāṅkhyak.; **-bhujā**, f. 'having eighteen arms,' a N. of Durgā, L.; **-rcá**, n. (*ṛic*), a hymn consisting of eighteen verses or lines, AV. xix, 23, 15. — **daśama**, mfn. the eighteenth. — **diś**, f. pl. = *ashṭa-diś*, q. v., Hcat. — **navati** (*ashṭā́-*), f. ninety-eight, ŚBr. x; Rājat. — **paksha** (*ashṭā́-*), mf(*ā*)n. having eight side-pillars, AV. ix, 3, 21. — **pañcāśat** (*ashṭā́-*), f. fifty-eight, ŚBr. vi. — **pad** (*ashṭā́-*), mfn., only f. *-padī* (a verse) having eight lines, eightfold (as speech or verses), RV.; AV.; (in ritual language) a pregnant animal, VS.; ŚBr.; KātyŚr. (also neg. *án-ashṭāpadī*, 'not a pregnant animal,' ŚBr.); a wild sort of jasmin, L. — **pada**, m. 'having eight legs,' a spider, L.; a worm, L.; the fabulous animal Śarabha, L.; a wild sort of jasmin, L.; a pin or bolt, L.; the mountain Kailāsa, L.; (*as* or *am*), m. n. (gaṇa *ardharcâdi*, q. v.) a kind of chequered cloth or board for drafts, dice, &c., Hariv.; R. &c.; (= *-prush*, q. v.) gold, MBh. xii, 10983; Kum. vii, 10; (*ā*), f. (i. e. *ṛic*) a verse consisting of eight Padas, APrāt. — **parṇa**, mfn. having eight leaves, APrāt. — **pādya**, mfn. eightfold, Mn. viii, 337; Gaut. — **prush** (*ashṭā́-*), mfn. (nom. n. *-prúṭ!*) having (i. e. marked by a sign similar to) eight drops (as a golden coin, cf. *ashṭā-pada*), TS. — **yogá**, m. a carriage and eight, AV. vi, 91, 1. — **ratha**, m., N. of a son of Bhīmaratha, Hariv. 1744. — **vakra**, m., N. of a Brāhman (a son of Kahoḍa), MBh. iii, 10599 seqq. &c.; of another man, Kathās. — **vandhura** (*ashṭā́-*), mfn. having eight seats (as a cart), RV. x, 53, 7. — **viṇśá**, mfn. the twenty-eighth, AV. xix, 8, 2; consisting of twenty-eight, VarBṛS.; consisting of twenty-eight verses (as a certain Stoma). — **viṇśati** (*ashṭā́-*), f. twenty-eight, VS.; ŚBr. &c.; (*ashṭāviṇśati*)-*dhā*, ind. twenty-eightfold, Kap.; *-śata*, n. a hundred and twenty-eight, PBr. — **śata** (*ashṭā́-*), n. a hundred and eight, ŚBr. x. — **śapha** (*ashṭā́-*), mfn. having eight hoofs or claws, ŚBr. vi. — **shashṭi**, f. sixty-eight, RPrāt. — **saptati** (*ashṭā́-*), f. seventy-eight, ŚBr. xiii. — **stanā** (*ashṭā́-*), f. = *ashṭa-stanā*, q. v. TS.

Ashṭa or **ashṭā** with the final *ă* blended in comp. **Ashṭâkshara,** mf(*ā*)n. containing eight syllables, VS.; AitBr.; ŚBr.; (*as*), m., N. of an author. **Ashṭâṅga,** mf(*ā*)n. consisting of eight parts or members (as medical science [MBh. ii, 224 & 442] or a kingdom [MBh. xv, 177] &c.); (in comp.) the eight parts (as of an army [MBh. ii, 197]; or of a court, viz. the law, the judge, assessors, scribe, and astrologer, gold, fire, and water, L.); (*ashṭâṅga*)-*naya* or -*pāta* [see *sâshṭâṅga-pātam*] or -*praṇāma*, m. prostration of the eight parts of the body (in performing very profound obeisance; the eight parts are the hands, breast, forehead, eyes, throat, and middle of the back; or the first four, with the knees and feet; or these six, with the speech and mind), L.; -*hṛidaya*, n., N. of a medical work of Vāgbhaṭa; *ashṭâṅgârghya*, n. an offering of eight articles (water, milk, Kuśa grass, curds, ghee, rice, barley, and mustard; or honey, red oleander flowers, and sandal are substituted for the last three). **Ashṭâdhyāyī,** f. 'a collection of eight books or chapters,' N. of ŚBr. xi; also of Pāṇini's grammar. **Ashṭâra,** mfn. having eight spokes, NṛisUp.; (*ashṭâra*)-*cakra-vat*, mfn. 'having a wheel with eight spokes,' a N. of Mañjuśrī, Buddh. **Ashṭâśîti,** f. eighty-eight; (*ashṭâśîti*)-*śata*, *āni*, n. pl. a hundred and eighty-eight, BhP. **Ashṭâśri,** mfn. having eight corners, ŚBr. **Ashṭâsri,** mfn. id., MBh. iii, 10665. **Ashṭâha,** mfn. lasting eight days (as a certain Soma sacrifice), KātyŚr.

Áshṭaka, mf(*ā* or *ikā*, Śulb.; cf. Pāṇ. vii, 3, 45, Comm.)n. consisting of eight parts, ŚBr.; RPrāt. &c.; one who is acquainted with the eight books of Pāṇini's grammar, Pāṇ. iv, 2, 65, Sch.; (*as*), m., N. of a son of Viśvāmitra (author of the hymn RV. x, 104), AitBr.; ĀśvŚr.; MBh. &c.; (*ā*), f. the eighth day after full moon (especially that in the months Hemanta and Śiśira, on which the progenitors or manes are worshipped, ĀśvGṛ.; Mn. &c.; *ashṭakā* is therefore also a N. of the worship itself or the oblations offered on those days, Kauś. &c.), AV. xv, 16, 2; ŚBr. &c.; (*ā*), f. a N. of the Acchodā river, Matsya-P.; (*am*), n. a whole consisting of eight parts (as each of the eight Ashṭakas of the RV., or as TS. i, or as Pāṇini's grammar &c.) **Ashṭakâṅga,** n. a kind of dice-board having eight divisions, L.

Ashṭakin, mfn. one who performs an Ashṭakā, (gaṇa *vrīhy-ādi*, q. v.)

Ashṭakya, mfn. relating to an Ashṭakā, (gaṇa *gav-ādi*, q. v.)

Ashṭamá, mf(*í*)n. the eighth, RV. ii, 5, 2; x, 114, 9; AV. &c.; (*as*), m. (Pāṇ. v, 3, 51 seq.) the eighth part, Mn. x, 120; (mfn.) forming the eighth part of (gen.), Gaut.; Śulb.; (*ī*), f. (i. e. *rātri*) the eighth day (night) in a half-month, ĀśvGṛ.; Mn. iv, 128, &c. **-kālika,** mfn. one who omitting seven meals partakes only of the eighth, Mn. vi, 19.

Ashṭamaka, mfn. the eighth, Yājñ. ii, 244; (*ikā*), f. a śukti or weight of four tolas.

1. **Ashṭi,** f., N. of a metre consisting of sixty-four syllables (like that in RV. ii, 22, 1, RPrāt.); the number 'sixteen,' Sūryas.

Ashṭin, mfn. consisting of eight members or syllables, RPrāt.

अष्टि 2. *ashṭi*, *is*, f. (√1. *aś*), reaching, AV. vi, 54, 1; (cf. *jarád-ashṭi*, *vyàshṭi*, *sámashṭi*.)

अष्टि 3. *ashṭi*, *is*, f. (= *asthi*, q. v.) the kernel or stone of a fruit, BhP.

Ashṭhi, *is*, f. id., L. **Ashṭhī-vát,** -*vántau*, m. du. (Pāṇ. viii, 2, 12) 'bony,' the knees, RV.; AV.; ŚBr.; (cf. *ūrv-ashṭhīvá*); (*ashṭhīvad*)-*daghná*, mfn. reaching up to the knee, ŚBr. xiii.

Ashṭhīlā, f. id., MBh. iii, 10629; v, 2758; a round pebble or stone, Suśr.; a ball, globe, MBh. i, 4494 seqq., (cf. *arkâshṭhīlā*); (= *vātâshṭhīlā*, q. v.) a globular swelling below the navel, produced by wind, Suśr.; (*ashṭhīla*, m. or n.) Hcat.

Ashṭhīlikā, f. a kind of abscess, Suśr.

Ashṭhī-vát. See *ashṭhi*.

अष्ट्रा *áshṭrā*, f. a prick or goad for driving cattle (regarded as the badge of the agriculturist, Kauś.), RV.; [Zd. *astrā*; Lith. *akstinas*.] **-vín,** mfn. obeying the goad (as a bull), RV. x, 102, 8.

अस् 1. *as*, cl. 2. P. *ásti* (2. sg. *ási*, 1. sg. *ásmi*; pl. *smási* or *smás*, *sthá*, *sánti*; (rarely Ā., e. g. 1. pl. *smahe*, MBh. xiii, 13); Subj. *ásat*; Imper. *astu*, 2. sg. *edhi* (fr. *as-dhi*, cf. Pāṇ. vi, 4, 119); Pot. *syāt*; impf. *āsīt*, rarely *ās* [only in RV. x; cf. Pāṇ. vii, 3, 97]; perf. 1. & 3. sg. *ā́sa*, 2. sg. *ā́sitha*, 3. pl. *āsúḥ*; p. m. *sát*, f. *satī́*) to be, live, exist, be present; to take place, happen; to abide, dwell, stay; to belong to (gen. or dat.); to fall to the share of, happen to any one (gen.); to be equal to (dat.), ŚBr. xiv; Mn. xi, 85; to turn out, tend towards any result, prove (with dat.); to become, BṛĀrUp. &c., (cf. Pāṇ. v, 4, 51–55); to be (i. e. used as copula, but not only with adj., but also with adv. [e. g. *túshṇīm āsīt*, MBh. iii, 4041], and often with part., [e. g. perf. Pass. p. *prasthitāḥ sma*, N.; fut. p. p. *hantavyo 'smi*, N.; fut. p. especially with Pot., and only in ŚBr., as *yádi dāsyán-t-syāt*, 'if he should intend to give']; the pf. *āsa* helps to form the periphrastic perf., and *asmi* &c. the fut.); [cf. Gk. ἐσ-τί; Lat. *es-t*; Goth. *is-t*; Lith. *es-ti*.]

अस् 2. *as*, cl. 4. P. *ásyati* (p. *ásyat*; impf. *ā́syat*, AV. [cf. *parâs* and *vy-as*]; fut. p. *asishyát*; aor. *ā́sthat* [Nir. ii, 2; Pāṇ. vii, 4, 17; cf. *vy-as*]; perf. P. *ā́sa* [cf. *parâs*], Ā. *āse* [cf. *vy-as*]; Ved. Inf. *ástave*, VS.) to throw, cast, shoot at (loc., dat., or gen.), RV. &c.; to drive or frighten away, Nalod. iv, 36; see also 1. *astá* s. v.

1. **Ásana,** *am*, n. (√2. *as*), throwing, sending, a shot, RV. i, 112, 21; 130, 4; AV.; (mfn.) one who throws or discharges, L.; (*ā*), f. a missile, an arrow, RV.

अस् 3. *as*, *asati*, °*te* = √*ash*, q. v.

अस *a-sa*, *as*, (Pāṇ. vi, 1, 132) not he, Śiś. i, 69; (cf. *a-tad*.)

असंयत् *á-saṃyat*, mfn. (√*i*), 'not entering (into),' i. e. not pleasing (to one's mind), AV. xviii, 1, 14.

असंयत *á-saṃyata*, mfn. not kept together, TS. v; not shut (as a door), R. ii, 71, 34; unbridled, MBh. xiii, 2261; recited inattentively, Up. **Asaṃyatâtman,** mfn. having the soul uncontrolled.

A-saṃyama, *as*, m. non-restraint (as of one's senses), Hit.

असंयत्त *á-saṃyatta*, mfn. unopposed, RV. i, 83, 3.

असंयाज्य *a-saṃyājya*, mfn. one with whom nobody is allowed to sacrifice, Mn. ix, 248.

असंयुक्त *a-saṃyukta*, mfn. unconnected, Jaim.; uncombined (as vowels in hiatus), RPrāt.

A-saṃyoga, *as*, m. absence of union or connection, Jaim.; for *a-saṃtyāga*, q. v., MBh. xii, 2797; not a conjunct consonant, Pāṇ. i, 2, 5; iv, 1, 54; (mfn.) one with whom intercourse is forbidden, Āp.

असंयुत *a-saṃyuta*, mfn. not combined, unmixed, BhP.; not put together (as the hands), PSarv.; (*as*), m. a N. of Vishṇu, L.

असंरोध *a-saṃrodha*, *as*, m. non-injury, (*ena*), instr. ind. without injury to (with gen.), MBh. xiv, 1282.

असंरोह *á-saṃroha*, *as*, m. non-junction (as of roads), TS. ii.

असंलक्ष्य *a-saṃlakshya*, mfn. not perceptible, Sāh.

असंवत्सर *a-saṃvatsara*, *as*, m. 'not one year, not a whole year,' in comp. with **-bhṛita** (*ás*°), mfn. not maintained a whole year (as a sacred fire), ŚBr.; KātyŚr. **-bhṛitin,** mfn. one who does not maintain (a fire) a whole year, KātyŚr. **-vāsin,** mfn. not staying a whole year (with the teacher), AitĀr.

असंवर *a-saṃvara*, mfn. not to be concealed, Naish. i, 53.

A-saṃvārya, mfn. not to be warded off, MBh.

Á-saṃvṛita, mfn. uncovered, unconcealed, ŚBr. xiv; bare (as the ground), R.; (*am*), n., N. of a hell, Mn. iv, 81.

असंविज्ञात *a-saṃvijñāta*, mfn. not agreeing with, Gaut.

A-saṃvijñāna, *am*, n. unintelligible, Mcar.

असंविद *a-saṃvidá*, mfn. unconscious, ŚBr.

Á-saṃvidāna, mfn. not agreeing together, ŚBr. x (ChUp.)

असंवृत *á-saṃvṛita*. See *a-saṃvara*.

असंवृत्ति *a-saṃvṛitti*, *is*, f. non-completion.

असंव्यवहार्य *a-saṃvyavahārya*, mfn. with whom intercourse is forbidden, Kām.

असंव्यवहितम् *a-saṃvyavahitam*, ind. without interval, immediately, BhP.

असंव्याथ *a-saṃvyātha*, *as*, m. absence of disarrangement or irregular order, PBr.

असंव्याहारिन् *a-saṃvyāhārin*, mfn. (gaṇa *grāhy-ādi*, q. v.)

असंव्लय *a-saṃvlaya*, *as*, m. the not sinking down, TBr.

असंशब्द्य *a-saṃśabdya*, mfn. not worth mentioning, MBh. iii, 10695.

असंशय *a-saṃśaya*, *as*, m. absence of doubt, certainty, R. v, 23, 25; (*am*), ind. without doubt, Mn.; N. &c.

असंश्रव *a-saṃśrava*, *as*, m. the being out of hearing, (*e*), loc. out of the hearing of (gen.), Mn. ii, 203.

A-saṃśravaṇe, ind. = *a-saṃśrave*, ĀśvŚr.

A-saṃśrāvam, ind. id. (with gen.), VPrāt. (v. l. °*vyam*).

असंश्लिष्ट *a-saṃślishṭa*, mfn. not in close contact, PBr.; (*as*), m. a N. of Śiva.

A-saṃślesha, *as*, m. non-contact, Comm. on BṛĀrUp.

असंसक्त *a-saṃsakta*, mfn. unconnected, incoherent, Bhpr.; (said of the eyebrows) not joining, VarBṛS.; not attached to, indifferent to (loc.), R. vii, 3, 2; Hariv.; (*am*), ind. unconnectedly, separately, MānŚr.; MānGṛ.

असंसूक्तगिल *a-saṃsūkta-gilá*, mfn. swallowing without chewing (as Rudra's dogs), AV. xi, 2, 30.

असंसृति *a-saṃsṛiti*, *is*, f. not passing through a new course of existence.

असंसृष्ट *a-saṃsṛishṭa*, mfn. having no connection with, unacquainted, MBh. xii, 3841; not mixed with (instr.), KātyŚr.; ĀśvŚr.; unadulterated, undefiled (as food, Jain.; or as the mind by bad qualities, VP.)

Á-saṃsṛishṭi, *is*, f. non-mixture, MaitrS.

असंस्कार *a-saṃskāra*, *as*, m. non-consecration, PārGṛ.; want of embellishment or care, natural state, Śak.; Kād.

A-saṃskṛita, mfn. not prepared, ŚāṅkhGṛ.; not consecrated, Mn.; Yājñ.; unadorned, Pañcat.; unpolished, rude (as speech). **Asaṃskṛitâlakin,** mfn. having unadorned curls, Kād.

असंस्तव *a-saṃstava*, mfn. unknown, unacquainted, not on terms of friendship, Śak. (v. l.)

A-saṃstuta, mfn. id., Vātsy.; Śak.; Kir.; Kād.

असंस्थान *a-saṃsthāna*, mfn. disfigured, R.

Á-saṃsthita, mfn. not being fixed, moving continually, AitBr.; ŚBr.; not arrayed in one place, not collected, scattered, Kām.; Hit.; unaccomplished, AV. vi, 50, 2; ŚBr.; AitBr.

असंस्वादम् *a-saṃsvādam*, ind. without tasting, Gobh.

असंहत *a-saṃhata*, mfn. not coagulated (as blood), Suśr.; not formed into a ball (as fæces), Bhpr.; unconnected, BhP.; having no acquaintances or relations, not living in common MBh. xiii, 5207; disagreeing, disunited, Pañcat.; (*as*), m. a form of array (loose or open order of troops), Kām.

असंहार्य *a-saṃhārya*, mfn. irresistible, insuperable, MBh.; Hariv.; R.; not to be diverted (from an opinion or purpose), not to be misled, unbribable, MBh.; R.

असंहित *a-saṃhita*, mfn. unconnected, Prāt.

असकल *a-sakala*, mfn. not all, not entire, Kauś.; Megh.; VarBṛS.

असकृत् *a-sakṛit*, ind. not (only) once, often, repeatedly, ChUp.; Mn.; MBh. &c.; with *saṃvatsarasya*, oftener than once a year, PārGṛ. **-samâdhi,** m. repeated meditation, Buddh. **Asakṛid-garbhavāsa,** m. repeated birth. **Asakṛid-bhava,** m. 'produced more than once,' a tooth, VarBṛS.

असकौ *asakaú*, m. f. = *asaú* (see s. v. *adás*),

only used in connection with *yakáḥ* and *yakā́* (for *yáḥ* and *yā́*), VS. xxiii, 22 & 23; (cf. Pāṇ. vii, 2, 107.)

असक्त *a-sakta*, mfn. not stopped or intercepted by or at (loc.; said of arrows and of a sword), MBh. iii, 1602; xiv, 2189; (in the same sense *a-saṅga*, Ragh. iii, 63); free from ties, independent, Sāṅkhyak.; detached from worldly feelings or passions, unattached or indifferent to (loc.), Mn. ii, 13; Ragh. &c.; (*am*), ind. without obstacle or resistance, Hariv. 9741; R. iii, 75, 6; uninterruptedly, Kir. iv, 31; Kām.; immediately, at once, Daś.

A-sakti, *is*, f. the being detached from worldly feelings or passions, Bhag. xiii, 9.

असक्थ *a-saktha* or *a-sakthi*, mfn. without thighs, Pāṇ. v, 4, 121.

असक्र *á-sakra*, mfn. (√*saśc*), not ceasing to flow or drying up, RV. vi, 63, 8; (Nir. vi, 29.)

असखि *a-sakhi*, *ā*, m. an untrustworthy friend, Comm. on Uṇ.

असगोत्र *a-sagotra*, mf(*ā*)n. not belonging to the same family with (gen.), Gobh.; Mn. iii, 5; MBh.

असंकर *a-saṃkara*, *as*, m. non-mixture of caste, Gaut.; (mfn.) with *dharma*, id., MBh. xiv, 2777; (*as*), m. absence of confusion, Nyāyad.

असंकल्प *a-saṃkalpa*, *as*, m. absence of desire, BhP.; (*am*), n. id., R. i, 67, 15.

A-saṃkalpanīya, mfn. not to be desired, ChUp.

A-saṃkalpayat, mfn. having no desire, Kauś.

A-saṃkalpita, mfn. not determined, R. ii, 22, 24.

असंकसुक *a-saṃkasuka*, mfn. not undetermined, firm, steady, Mn. vi, 43.

असंकीर्ण *a-saṃkīrṇa*, mfn. unmixed; not unclean, Suśr.

असंकुल *a-saṃkula*, mfn. not crowded; (*as*), m. a broad road, L.

असंकेतित *a-saṃketita*, mfn. one with whom nothing has been concerted, Daś. — **tva**, n. the not being settled by agreement, Sāh.

असंक्रान्त *a-saṃkrānta*, *as*, m. an intercalary month, Hcat.

Asaṃkrānti-māsa, *as*, m. id.

असंख्य *a-saṃkhya*, mf(*ā*)n. innumerable, exceedingly numerous, Mn.; Suśr. &c.

A-saṃkhyaka, mfn. id., AgP.

Á-saṃkhyāta, mfn. uncounted, innumerable, AV. xii, 3, 28; VS.; ŚBr.; Kauś.

A-saṃkhyeya, mfn. innumerable, MBh.; BhP. &c.; (*ás*), m. a N. of Śiva, L.; (*ám*), n. an innumerable multitude, AV. x, 8, 24; an exceedingly large number, Buddh. — **guṇa**, mfn. innumerably multiplied, unnumbered. — **tā**, f. innumerableness, Suśr.

असङ्ग *á-saṅga* or *a-saṅgá*, mfn. free from ties, independent, ŚBr. xiv (BṛĀrUp.); NṛisUp.; moving without obstacle (as a cart, a vessel, a flag, &c.), MBh. ii, 944; Hariv. &c.; having no attachment or inclination for or interest in; (see also s. v. *a-sakta*); (*as*), m. non-attachment, non-inclination, Mn. vi, 75; Bh.; N. of a son of Yuyudhāna, Hariv. 9207; VP.; a N. of Vasubandhu, Buddh.; 'non-impediment,' generally (*ena*), instr. ind. without obstacle, Hariv. 10187; R.; (*āt*), abl. ind. unobstructedly, at pleasure, Bālar. — **cārin**, mfn. moving without obstacle, R. v, 42, 4. — **vat**, mfn. 'not attached to' (loc.), R. iii, 37, 23 [according to NBD. a mistake for *saṅga-vat*].

A-saṅgin, mfn. not attached to the world, BhP.; free from worldly desire, MārkP. **Asaṅgi-tva**, n. non-attachment to the world, MBh. xii. — **sattva**, *ās*, m. pl., N. of certain deities, Buddh.

A-sajjamāna, mfn. not hesitating, MBh. v, 1532.

Asajjitātman, mfn. having a soul free from attachments, BhP.

असंगत *a-saṃgata*, mfn. (Pāṇ. v, 1, 121) ununited, unassociated with, BhP.; uneven, unequal, Pañcat. (Hit.); unpreferred, disesteemed, L.; unbecoming, unpolished, rude, L.

A-saṃgati, *is*, f. 'incongruity, improbability,' N. of a rhetorical figure, Sāh.; Kpr. &c.; non-association with, MBh. xii.

A-saṃgama, *as*, m. not associating with; (for *a-saṅga*, m., q. v.) = *vairāgya*, no attachment to (loc.), BhP.

असंघट्ट *a-saṃghaṭṭa*, *as*, m. non-collision, Ragh. xiv, 86.

असचद्विष् *a-saca-dvish*, mfn. hating or persecuting the non-worshippers [BR.; Gmn.] or not persecuting worshippers [NBD.], RV. viii, 20, 24 (voc.)

असच्छाखा *asac-chākhā* and *-chāstra*. See *á-sat*.

असजात *á-sajāta*, mfn. not related by blood, VS. v, 23.

A-sajātyá, mf(*ā́*)n. without consanguinity, RV. x, 39, 6.

असज्जन *asaj-jana*. See *á-sat*.

असंचय *a-saṃcaya*, mfn. having no provisions, MBh. xiii, 2018. — **vat**, mfn. id., TĀr.

A-saṃcayika, mfn. id., Mn. vi, 43 (v. l.)

Á-saṃcita, mfn. not piled, not completely arranged (as the sacrificial altar), ŚBr. ii.

असंचर *a-saṃcara*, *as*, m. not a passage which is frequented or accessible, KātyŚr.

Á-saṃcarat, mfn. (pr. p.) not moving about (said of a Prāṇa), ŚBr. xiv.

A-saṃcāra, *as*, m. no disarrangement (as of verses), Lāṭy.

A-saṃcārya, mfn. inaccessible to (instr.), Hariv. 3637.

असंछन्न *a-saṃchanna*, mfn. not covered, ŚBr.

असंज्ञ *a-saṃjña*, mfn. senseless, Bhpr.; not having full consciousness, R.; (*á-saṃjñā*), f. disunion, discord, AV. xii, 5, 34; ŚBr.; not a name, Pāṇ. iv, 3, 149. — **tva**, n. the not having full consciousness, MBh. xiv, 1001 (ed. Bomb.)

Á-saṃjñapta, mfn. not suffocated (as a victim), ŚBr. xiii.

Á-saṃjñāna, *am*, n. discord with (instr.), TS. v.

Asaṃjñi-sattva, *ās*, m. pl. = *asaṅgi-s.*, q. v.

असंज्वर *a-saṃjvara*, mfn. feeling no (heat of) anger or grief, Mn. iv, 185.

असत् *á-sat*, mf(*á-satī*)n. [in RV. seven times *ásat* and five times *ā́sat* with lengthening of the accentuated vowel] not being, not existing, unreal, RV. vii, 134, 8; AV.; Up.; Kum. iv, 12; untrue, wrong, RV.; bad, ŚBr.; Mn. &c.; (*n*), m. Indra, L.; (*tī*), f., see s. v. below; (*t*), n. non-existence, nonentity, RV.; AV. &c.; untruth, falsehood, RV. vii, 104, 8; evil, Ragh. i, 10; (*ntas*), m. pl. bad or contemptible men, MBh. &c. — **kara-tva**, n. incapability of effecting anything, Kap. — **kalpanā**, f. a wrong supposition, Śak. — **kāra**, m. doing injury, offence, MBh. i, 6355. — **kārya**, n. bad or illicit occupation, Mn. xii, 32; (*asatkārya*)-*vādin*, m. one who (like a Naiyāyika) holds that an effect is non-existent in its cause before production. — **kṛita**, mfn. badly treated, MBh. iii, 2755 & 2918; (*am*), n. offence, ib. 2981. — 1. **-kṛitya**, ind. p. not taking notice of (acc.), MBh. xiii, 2766. — 2. **-kṛitya**, mfn. one who does evil actions, L. — **tā**, f. non-existence, L. — 1. **-tva**, n. id., NṛisUp.; non-presence, absence, Nyāyam. — **patha**, m. a bad road, L.; (mfn.) not being on the right path, BhP. — **parigraha**, mfn. receiving unfit presents, or from improper persons, Mn. xi, 194; xii, 32. — **putra**, mfn. having no son, Mn. ix, 154. — **pramudita**, n. (in Sāṅkhya phil.) one of the eight Asiddhis. — **saṃsarga**, m. evil company. — **saṅga**, m. 'attached to evil,' N. of a doorkeeper (in the Prabodhacandrodaya).

Asac (in comp. for *asat*). — **chākhā**, f. an unreal branch (?), AV. x, 7, 21. — **chāstra**, n. heretical doctrine, Mn. xi, 65.

Asaj (in comp. for *asat*). — **jana**, m. a bad or wicked man, R.; Ragh. xii, 46, &c.; a malignous man, Kād. — **jāti-miśra**, m., N. of a person (in the Dhūrtasaṃgraha).

Asati, f. an unfaithful or unchaste wife, MBh.; R. &c. — **suta**, m. the son of an unchaste wife, L.

2. **A-sattva**, mfn. strengthless, without energy, R.

A-satyá, mfn. untrue, false, lying, RV. iv, 5, 5; MBh. &c.; (*am*), n. untruth, falsehood, Mn. &c. — **tā**, f. untruth, Sāh. — **vāda**, m. a lie, Daś. — **vādin**, mfn. speaking falsely, a liar. — **śīla**, mf(*ā*)n. having an inclination to falsehood, R. — **sandha**, mfn. treacherous, base, R. iii, 57, 20; Hit. — **sannibha**, mfn. improbable, unlikely, L.

Asad (in comp. for *asat*). — **adhyetṛi**, m. a Brāhman who reads heterodox works, L. — **āgraha**, mfn. = *-graha*, mfn., BhP. — **ācāra**, mfn. following evil practices, wicked; (*as*), m. evil practice. — **ācārin**, mfn. = *-ācāra*, mfn. — **graha**, mfn. performing mischievous or malignous tricks, BhP.; (*as*), m. caprice, idle or childish desire, BhP.; VP. &c. — **grāha**, mfn. = *-graha*, mfn., Hariv. 15479; R.; BhP.; (*as*), m. = *-graha*, m., ib. — **grāhin**, mfn. = *-graha*, mfn., R. ii, 1, 18 (v. l. *-grahin*). — **dṛiś**, mfn. evil-eyed, L. — **dharma**, m. evil practice or custom, MBh. xiii, 2215. — **buddhi**, mfn. foolish, BhP. — **bhāva**, m. non-existence, absence, Vedāntas. &c.; an evil temperament or disposition, L. — **vāc**, mfn. whose speech is untrue, a liar, BhP. — **vāda**, m. heterodoxy, BhP. — **vṛitti**, f. low or degrading occupation or profession; (mfn.) following evil practices, BhP. — **vyavahāra**, mfn. and (*as*), m. = *-ācāra*, mfn. and m. — **vyavahārin**, mfn. = *-ācārin*.

1. **Asan** (in comp. for *asat*). — **mati**, f. a wrong opinion, BhP.; 'no intention,' acc. °*tim* with √1. *kṛi*, not to care for (loc.), BhP. — **mantrá**, m. untrue speech, AV. iv, 9, 6. — **māna**, m. for *a-sammāna*, q. v.

असदृश *a-sadṛiśa*, mf(*ī*)n. (gaṇa *cārv-ādi*, q. v.) unlike, dissimilar; improper, MBh. iii, 16061; Mṛicch.; (*as*), m., N. of a Prākṛit poet. — **tva**, n. dissimilarity, VarBṛS. — **vyavahārin**, mfn. behaving improperly. **Asadṛiśôpama**, n. (in rhetoric) a dissimilar simile.

असद्यस् *a-sadyas*, ind. not on the same day, not immediately, KātyŚr.

असन् (2. *asán*), n. Ved. the base of some cases (viz. instr. *asnā́*, gen. abl. *asnás*, gen. pl. *asnā́m*) of *ásṛij*, q. v., AV.; VS.; MaitrS. &c.

असन 2. *asana*, *as*, m. the tree Terminalia Tomentosa, Jain.; Suśr.; (cf. 3. *āsana*.) — **parṇī**, f. the plant Marsilea Quadrifolia, L. (For 1. *asana* see √2. *as*.)

असनाभि *a-sanābhi* = *á-sajāta*, q. v., KapS.

असनि *asani* and *asanika*, mfn.? (gaṇa *ṛiśyādi*, q. v.)

असंतत *á-saṃtata*, mfn. interrupted, ŚBr.

असंताप *a-saṃtāpá*, mf(*ā*)n. not suffering pain or sorrow, AV. xvi, 3, 6; Comm. on Mn. iv, 185; not causing pain or sorrow, AV. iv, 26, 3; viii, 2, 14.

असंतुष्ट *a-saṃtushṭa*, mfn. discontented, displeased, Hit.

A-saṃtosha, *as*, m. displeasure, Śak.; Mālatim. — **vat**, mfn. discontented, Pañcat.

असंत्याग *a-saṃtyāga*, *as*, m. not giving up or renouncing (intercourse with; gen.), MBh. v, 1164.

A-saṃtyāgin, mfn. not giving up or abandoning, R.

A-saṃtyājya, mfn. not to be abandoned, MBh. i, 8349; not to be avoided, MBh. xii, 9950; not to be neglected or forgotten, MBh. iii, 1055.

असंदिग्ध *a-saṃdigdha*, mfn. not indistinct, MBh. xii; undoubted, unsuspected, certain, Jain. (Prākṛit °*diddha*); Pat.; (*am*), ind. without any doubt, certainly, Pañcat.; MārkP.

असंदित *á-saṃdita*, mfn. unbound, unrestrained, RV. iv, 4, 2; Mn. viii, 342.

Á-saṃdina, mfn. id., RV. viii, 104, 14.

असंदृश्य *a-saṃdṛiśya*, mfn. invisible to (gen.), Uttarar.

असंधान *a-saṃdhāna*, *am*, n. want of aim or object; disjunction.

A-saṃdhi, *is*, m. want of union or connection.

A-saṃdhita, mfn. for *a-saṃdita*, q. v. [NBD.]

A-saṃdheya, mfn. not to be made peace with, MBh. xii, 6268; Hit.; for which no amends can be made, not to be redressed, AitBr. — **tā**, f. the state of one with whom no peace is to be made, Veṇis.

असन्न *á-sanna*, mfn. restless, ŚBr.

असंनद्ध *a-saṃnaddha*, mfn. not put on (as a mail-coat), MBh. xii, 3541; not yet appertaining to (as a quality), Kāvyād.; pretending to knowledge, conceited (as a Paṇḍit or teacher), L.; proud, L.

असंनिकर्ष *a-saṃnikarsha, as,* m. want of nearness or proximity, remoteness of objects (so as to render them imperceptible), L.

A-saṃnikṛishṭa, mfn. not near, remote.

असंनिधान *a-saṃnidhāna, am,* n. non-proximity, absence, Kāvyād.; Kathās. &c.; wanting, (*āt*), abl. instr. through want of (gen.), Rājat.

A-saṃnidhi, *is,* m. (generally loc. °*dhau*) absence, Mn.; Gaut. &c.; wanting, Jaim.

असन्मति *asan-mati* & *-mantrá.* See *á-sat.*

असपत्न *á-sapatna, as,* m. not a rival, AV. i, 19, 4; (*a-sapatná*), mf(*ā́*)n. (chiefly Ved.) without a rival or adversary, undisturbed, RV. x, 159, 4 & 5; 174, 4 & 5; AV. &c.; (*ā́*), f., N. of a certain sacrificial brick, ŚBr.; KātyŚr.; (*ám*), n. undisturbed condition, peace, AV.

असपिण्ड *a-sapiṇḍa,* mfn. related more distantly than a *sa-piṇḍa,* q.v., Mn.; Yājñ. &c.

असप्तशफ *á-saptaśapha,* mf(*ā*)n. not having seven hoofs (or claws), TS. vi; ŚBr.

असबन्धु *á-sabandhu,* mfn. not related, VS. v, 23; AV.

असभ *a-sabhá,* mfn. without company, TS.

A-sabhya, mfn. unfit for an assembly, vulgar, low, Nir.; BhP. &c.

असम *a-sama,* mfn. uneven, unequal (either by birth or in surface or number), Mn. x, 73; Kir. v, 7, &c.; odd; (*á-sama*), mf(*ā*)n. unequalled, without a fellow or equal, RV.; AV. &c. **–tā,** f. the being unequalled, Naish. **–tva,** n. unfair or ungracious behaviour, MaitrUp. **–bāṇa,** m. 'having an odd number of (i. e. five) arrows,' Kāma, Gīt. **–ratha** (*ásama-*), mfn. possessed of an unequalled chariot, VS. xv, 17. **–śara,** m. = *-bāṇa,* q.v., Naish. **–sama,** mfn. unequalled, Lalit. **–sāyaka,** m. = *-bāṇa,* q. v., Kathās. **Asamâśuga,** m. id., Naish. **Asamêshu,** m. id., L. **Asamâñjas,** m., N. of a man, Hariv. 2038 seq.

A-samaná, mf(*ā́*)n. not remaining united, going in different directions, RV. i, 140, 4; vii, 5, 3; uneven (as a path), RV. vi, 46, 13.

Á-samāti, mfn. having no equal, unparalleled, RV. x, 60, 2 & 5 (AV. vi, 79, 1 for *á-samarti*?, NBD.); (*is*), m., N. of a king (with the patron. Rāthaproshṭha), RAnukr. **Ásamāty-ojas** (6), mfn. of unequalled strength, RV. vi, 29, 6.

Á-samāna, mf(*ā*)n. unequal (by birth or in qualities), different, VS. v, 23, &c.; incomparable, Daś.; (*am*), n. not a similar or corresponding condition, Mṛicch. **–kāraṇa,** mfn. not having the same cause, RPrāt. **–grāma,** mfn. not belonging to or being born in the same village, Gaut.

असमक्षम् *a-samaksham,* ind. not visibly, behind one's back, BhP.

असमग्र *a-samagra,* mfn. incomplete, unentire, partial, MBh. &c.; (*am*), [Ragh. iii, 64] or in comp. *asamagra-* [Mālav.], ind. incompletely.

असमञ्ज *a-samañja, as,* or °*ñjas, ās,* m., N. of a descendant of Ikshvāku (a son of Sagara by Keśinī and father of Aṅśumat), MBh.; Hariv. &c.

A-samañjasa, mfn. unfit, unbecoming, MBh. &c.; (*as*), m. a good-for-nothing fellow, BhP.; (*am*), n. unconformity, impropriety, unbecomingness, BhP.; Pañcat. &c.; (*am*), ind. unbecomingly, Kathās. &c.

असमद् *á-samad, t,* f. non-conflict, concord, ŚBr.

असमन *a-samaná.* See *a-sama.*

असमय *a-samaya, as,* m. non-obligation, absence of contract or agreement, Āp.; unseasonableness; unfit or unfavourable time, Kathās.; Veṇīs.

असमर्थ *a-samartha,* mf(*ā*)n. unable to (Inf., dat., loc., or in comp.); not having the intended meaning, Kpr. **–tva,** n. incapability of (in comp.), Rājat.

असमर्पण *a-samarpaṇa, am,* n. not committing or not intrusting; non-delivery, Hcat.

A-samarpita, mfn. unconsigned, not intrusted; undelivered.

असमवहितम् *á-samavahitam,* ind. so as not to touch each other, ŚBr. ix.

असमवायिन् *a-samavāyin,* mfn. not inherent, not inseparably connected with, accidental, Tarkas.

A-samavêta, mfn. id. ib.; (pl.) not all assembled, Gaut.

असमष्टकाव्य *á-samashṭa-kāvya* (7), mfn. (√ 1. *aś*), of unattainable wisdom, RV. ii, 21, 4; ix, 76, 4.

असमस्त *a-samasta,* mfn. uncompounded, Kāvyād. &c.; uncollected, L.; incomplete, L.

असमाति *á-samāti.* See *a-sama.*

Á-samāna. See ib.

असमाप्त *a-samāpta,* mfn. unfinished, unaccomplished, incomplete.

A-samāpti, *is,* f. non-completion, KātyŚr.

असमायुत *a-samāyuta,* mfn. unconnected, TĀr.

असमावर्तक *a-samāvartaka, as,* m. a religious student who has not yet completed the period of his residence with his teacher and who therefore has not yet returned home, Mn. xi, 157.

A-samāvṛittaka and °**ttika,** *as,* m. id., ib. (v. l.)

असमिध्य *a-samidhya,* ind. p. not having kindled, Mn. ii, 187.

असमीक्षित *a-samīkshita,* mfn. not perceived or ascertained, R. v, 81, 8.

A-samīkshya, ind. p. not having considered. **–kārin,** mfn. acting inconsiderately, Hit.

असमीचीन *a-samīcīna,* mfn. incorrect.

असमृद्ध *á-samṛiddha,* mfn. not successful or prosperous, AV. i, 27, 2 & 3; not fulfilled (as wishes &c.), unaccomplished, failing, ŚBr.; R. ii, 92, 16.

Á-samṛiddhi, *is,* f. (often *ayas,* f. pl.) non-accomplishment, ill-success, failure, AV.; Mn. iv, 137, &c.

असमेत *a-samêta,* mfn. 'not arrived, absent,' missing, Ragh. ix, 70.

असंपत्ति *a-saṃpatti, is,* f. ill-luck, want of success, failure, Mn. xii, 36; the not being sufficient, Hcat.

A-sampanna, mfn. unaccomplished, KaushBr.; BhP.

असंपर्क *a-saṃparka,* mfn. destitute of contact, without connection or relation.

असंपाठ्य *a-saṃpāṭhya,* mfn. not to be studied with, one with whom it is forbidden to read or study, Mn. ix, 238.

असंपात *a-saṃpāta,* mf(*ā*)n. not present or at hand, Kauś.

असंपूर्ण *a-saṃpūrṇa,* mfn. incomplete.

असंपृञ्चान *á-saṃpriñcāna,* mfn. (pr. p. Ā.) not being in contact, ŚBr. iii; KātyŚr.

असंप्रति *á-saṃprati,* ind. (gaṇa *tishṭhadgv-ādi,* q. v.; Pāṇ. ii, 1, 6) not according to the moment or to present circumstances, ŚBr. ix.

असंप्रत्त *á-saṃpratta,* mfn. not delivered or handed over, TS. ii.

A-sampradatta, mfn. not willingly given (as a girl into marriage), Hariv. 10106.

असंप्रमाद *a-saṃpramāda, as,* m. absence of carelessness, BhP.

असंप्रमोष *a-saṃpramosha, as,* m. 'the not allowing to be carried off,' not letting drop (as from memory), Yogas.

असंप्राप्त *a-saṃprâpta,* mfn. not arrived at, not having reached the aim, MBh. xiv, 2188; not reached or attained (as an object or anything desired), MBh.; Pāṇ. ii, 3, 12, Comm.

A-samprâpya, ind. p. without reaching.

असंबद्ध *a-saṃbaddha,* mfn. unconnected, separate, R. iii, 31, 20; not closely associated, distant, not related, Mn. viii, 163; Śak.; incoherent (as words or speech), unmeaning, absurd, Veṇīs. &c.; (also said of an action) Kād.; speaking unmeaningly, Mṛicch.

A-sambandha, mfn. not related, Mn. ii, 129; Kād.; (*as*), m. non-connection, Jaim.

असंबाध *a-saṃbādha,* mf(*ā*)n. unconfined, spacious, wide, large, AV. xii, 1, 2; ChUp.; MBh. &c.; unobstructed, unimpeded, L.; 'not crowded,' scarcely frequented, Kād.; (*ā*), f., N. of a metre; (*ám*), n. non-confinement, open space, AV. xviii, 2, 20.

असंबोध *a-saṃbodha, as,* m. non-knowledge, ignorance, MBh. xii, 11289.

असंभव *á-saṃbhava, as,* m. 'non-existence,' destruction, VS. xl, 10; non-happening, cessation, interruption, Mn. xi, 27; absence of, want, Mn.; MBh. &c.; impropriety, inconsistence, impossibility, KātyŚr.; Mn. &c.; (mfn.) 'non-happening,' inconsistent, impossible.

A-sambhavyám, ind. so as to prevent any restoration, AV. v, 18, 12 & 19, 11.

A-sambhāvanā, f. not regarding possible, Kād.; impossibility of comprehending, L.; want of respect, Bālar.

A-sambhāvanīya, mfn. inconceivable, incomprehensible, impossible, Mṛicch.

A-sambhāvita, mfn. id., Kād.; unworthy of (gen.), ib. **Asambhāvitôpamā,** f. a simile that implies an impossibility, Kāvyād.

A-sambhāvya, mfn. = °*bhāvanīya,* q. v., MBh. xiii, 272, &c.; (*am*), ind. = *a-saṃbhavyám,* q. v., AitBr.

Á-sambhūti, *is,* f. 'non-existence,' destruction, VS. xl, 9; ŚBr. xiv.

असंभाषा *a-saṃbhāshā,* f. absence of conversation with (instr.), PārGṛ.

A-sambhāshya, mfn. one with whom one ought not to converse, MBh.; BhP.; unfit (as a place) for conversation, Mn. viii, 55.

असंभिन्दत् *á-saṃbhindat,* mfn. not damaging, PBr.; not bringing into contact, not mingling, TBr.

Á-sambhinna, mfn. not broken or passed (as barriers or bounds), MBh.; not being in contact, separated, separate, ŚBr.

Á-sambheda, *as,* m. non-contact, the being separate, ŚBr.

A-sambhedya, mfn. not to be brought into contact, Hariv. 4504.

असंभोग *a-saṃbhoga, as,* m. non-enjoyment, Hit.; absence of sexual union, MBh. v, 1524.

A-sambhojya, mfn. one with whom one ought not to eat, Mn. ix, 238; MBh. xii, 4046.

असंभ्रम *a-saṃbhrama,* mfn. free from flurry, composed, cool, MBh. &c.; (*am*), ind. coolly, ib.

A-sambhrāntam, ind. = *a-saṃbhramam,* q.v., Mṛicch.

असंमत *a-saṃmata,* mfn. not respected, despised, Kum. iii, 5; Rājat.; unauthorized, without the consent of (in comp.), Mn. viii, 197. **A-sammatâdāyin,** mfn. taking without the consent (of the owner), MBh. xii, 5969.

A-sammati, *is,* f. dishonour, Pāṇ. iii, 1, 128.

A-sammāna, *as,* m. id., Pañcat. (v. l. *a-sanm°*).

असंमित *á-saṃmita,* mfn. not measured, immeasurable, ŚBr.

असंमुख *a-saṃmukha,* mf(*ī*)n. having the face turned away from, Kathās.

असंमुग्ध *a-saṃmugdha,* mfn. one who has lost his way, KaushBr.

A-sammūḍha, mfn. not confused, deliberate, MBh.

A-sammoha, *as,* m. calmness, composure, deliberateness, R.; Suśr.

असंमृष्ट *á-saṃmṛishṭa,* mfn. uncleansed, RV. v, 11, 3; Kāvyād.; (*am*), n. incomplete cleansing (of the sacrificial fire), ŚBr. ii; KātyŚr.

असंमोष *a-saṃmosha, as,* m. = ? *a-saṃpramosha,* q. v., Buddh.

असम्यक् *a-samyak,* ind. incorrectly, wrongly, MārkP. **–kārin,** mfn. acting improperly, Mn. ix, 259. **–krita-kārin,** mfn. not doing one's work or duty well, MBh. i, 5551 = xii, 5307. **–prayoga,** m. incorrect application, Car.

असरण *a-saraṇa, am,* n. not proceeding, not going, KātyŚr.

असरु *asaru*, *us*, m. the medicinal plant Bhumea Lacera, L.

असरूप *a-sarūpa*, mfn. not having the same form, Pāṇ. iii, 1, 94.

असर्व *á-sarva*, mfn. not complete, ŚBr.; AitBr. **-kratu** (*á-sarva-*), m. not a general sacrifice, not an optional sacrifice, ŚBr. xi. **-jña**, mfn. not knowing everything. **-vibhakti**, mfn. not taking every case-termination, defective (e.g. *yataḥ*, *yatra*, and *yadā*, considered as abl., loc., and instr. respectively), Pāṇ. i, 1, 38. **-vīra** (*á-sarva-*), mfn. not surrounded by all (his) men, AV. ix, 2, 14. **-śas**, ind. not generally, not as a rule, RPrāt.

असवर्ण *a-savarṇa*, mf(*ā*)n. of a different caste, Śak.; not homogeneous (as sounds), TPrāt.

असव्य *a-savya*, mfn. not left, VarBṛS.; (*e*), ind. on the right, L.; (cf. *apa-savya*.)

असश्चत् *a-saścát*, mf(°*ścát*, eight times as adj.; or *á-saścantī*, thrice)n. not sticking; not ceasing; not drying up, RV.; (*a-saścátas*), f. pl. (i.e. *dhārās*) inexhaustible streams, RV.; (*a-saścátā*), instr. f. ind. in an inexhaustible manner, RV. x, 69, 8.

Á-saścivas, mf(°*ścushī*)n. not ceasing, RV. ix, 86, 18.

अससत् *á-sasat*, mfn. not sleeping, RV. i, 143, 3.

असह *a-saha*, mfn. incapable of bearing (or producing young ones), PārGṛ.; not bearing or enduring (ifc. or with gen.), Mudr.; Kathās.; not able to, not capable of (Inf. or in comp.), Kathās.; intolerant, impatient, ib.; (*am*), n. the middle of the breast, L. **-tva**, n. inability to endure, Sarvad.; not tolerating, Sāh.; not being at hand, Bhpr.

A-sahana, mf(*ā*)n. not able to endure, unenduring (ifc.), Kathās.; envious, jealous, Megh.; Vikr. &c.; (*as*), m. an enemy, L.; (*am*), n. not tolerating, Sāh. **-tā**, f. weakness, Kād.

A-sahamāna, mfn. not tolerating, Mudr.

A-sahishṇu, mfn. unable to endure (with acc., loc. or ifc.), Suśr.; Rājat. &c.; impatient, unenduring, envious, quarrelsome, Kathās. &c. **-tā**, f. or **-tva**, n. inability to endure, Suśr. &c.; impatience, envy, Kathās. &c.

A-sahyá, mf(*ā*)n. unbearable, insufferable, insuperable, SV.; MBh.; impracticable, impossible, MBh. iii, 12255 seq.; with *drashṭum*, 'impossible to be seen,' i.e. invisible, Up. **-pīḍa**, mfn. causing intolerable pain, Ragh. i, 71.

असहाय *a-sahāya*, mfn. without companions, friendless, Mn. vii, 30 & 55; Śārṅg.; solitary (as a house), Pāṇ. Sch. **-tā**, f. loneliness, solitude, the life of a hermit, Mn. vi, 44. **-vat**, mfn. without companions, Mn. vi, 42.

असाक्षात् *a-sākshāt*, ind. not before the eyes, invisible; not present.

A-sākshika, mfn. unattested, unwitnessed, Mn. viii, 109. **-hata**, mfn. beaten (in law) without witnesses, Yājñ. ii, 212.

A-sākshin, mfn. incompetent as a witness, not an eye-witness, Yājñ. ii, 71; Vishṇus. **A-sākshi-tva**, n. the not being an eye-witness, Kap.

A-sākshya, *am*, n. want of evidence.

असात्म्य *a-sâtmya*, mfn. unwholesome, disagreeing (as food), Car.; Suśr.

असाद *a-sādá*, mfn. not mounted on horseback, AV. xi, 10, 24; not becoming tired, unwearied, Rājat.

असाधन *a-sādhana*, mfn. without means, destitute of resources or materials or instruments or implements, MBh. &c.; (*am*), n. not a means, anything not effective of an object, Kap.

A-sādhú, mfn. (Pāṇ. vi, 2, 160) not good, wicked, bad, ŚBr.; MBh. &c.; wrong, Comm. on TPrāt.; (*ús*), m. not an honest man, a wicked man, ŚBr.; Mn. &c.; (*ú*), n. anything bad, evil, ŚBr. (*sādhv-asādhúnī*, 'good and evil'); MBh. &c.; disfavour, disgrace, only °*únā*, instr. ind. disfavourably, ŚBr. ii; ChUp. (cf. 3. *a-sāman*); (*u*), ind. (used as an interjection of disapproval) bad! shame! Rājat. &c. **-tva**, n. wickedness, Kām. &c.; the not being approvable, VarBṛS. **-vāda**, m. disapproval, BhP. **-vṛitta**, mf(*ā*)n. having bad manners, Mn. ix, 80.

A-sādhya, mfn. not to be effected or completed, not proper or able to be accomplished, Yājñ. ii, 196; Hariv. &c.; incurable, irremediable, MBh. iv, 395; Suśr. &c.; not to be overpowered or mastered, Pañcat.; Kām.; not susceptible of proof, Comm. on Yājñ. ii, 6. **-tā**, f. incurableness, Suśr.; the state of one not to be mastered, Pañcat. **-tva**, n. incurableness, Suśr.

असाधारण *a-sādhāraṇa*, mf(*ī*)n. not common, special, specifical, Tarkas.; quite uncommon, extraordinary, Daś.; Kathās. &c.; (*am*), n. special property, L.

असानाथ्य *a-sānāthya*, n. want of help or assistance, Kathās.

असांतापिक *a-sāṃtāpika*, mfn., Pāṇ. vi, 2, 155, Sch.

असांनिध्य *a-sāṃnidhya*, *am*, n. 'non-nearness,' absence, MBh. iii, 610; R.; Śak.

असामञ्जस्य *a-sāmañjasya*, *am*, n. incorrectness, Comm. on Vedāntas.; impropriety, unbecomingness, Bād.

असामन् 1. *a-sāman*, *a*, n. (fr. 1. *sắman*), want, deficiency, ChUp.

असामन् 2. *a-sāmán*, mfn. (fr. 2. *sắman*), without a song or Sāman, ŚBr. i; not acquainted with the Sāma-veda, MBh. xii, 2312.

असामन् 3. *a-sāman*, *a*, n. only °*mnā*, instr. ind. (= *a-sādhúnā* s. v. *a-sādhú*, q. v.) in an unfriendly way, unfavourably, ChUp.

A-sāmanya, mfn. unfavourable, AitBr.

असामयिक *a-sāmayika*, mfn. unseasonable, Kir. ii, 40.

असामर्थ्य *a-sāmarthya*, *am*, n. weakness, Pañcat.; Sarvad.; (mfn.) weak, decaying (as a tree), MBh. xiii, 281.

असामान्य *a-sāmānya*, mfn. not common, special, Sāṅkhyak.; uncommon, peculiar, MBh. i, 5308; Kathās. &c.; special property, L.

असामि *á-sāmi*, mfn. not half, entire, complete, RV.; (*i*), ind. completely, RV. **-śavas** (*ásāmi-*), mfn. having complete strength, RV. v, 52, 5.

असांप्रत *a-sāmprata*, mfn. not becoming, improper, MBh. i, 6371, &c.; unseasonable, Daś.; not belonging to the present time (as Brahman), MārkP.; (*am*), ind. unfitly, improperly, MBh. v, 3255, &c.

A-sāmpratika-tā, f. improper behaviour, Bālar.

असांप्रदायिक *a-sāmpradāyika*, mfn. not traditional, not sanctioned by tradition, Uttarar.; Comm. on Mn. iii, 127, &c.

असाम्य *a-sāmya*, *am*, n. (fr. *a-sama*), difference, dissimilarity, MBh. ii, 679; BhP.

असार *a-sāra*, mfn. sapless, without strength or value, without vigour, spoiled, unfit, unprofitable, Mn. viii, 203; Suśr. &c.; (*as*), m. 'worthlessness,' see *sārâsāra*; Ricinus Communis (castor-oil tree), L.; (*ā*), f. the plant Musa Paradisiaca, L.; (*am*), n. Aloe wood, L. **-tā**, f. saplessness, unfitness, worthlessness, fragility, Yājñ. ii, 60; Ragh. viii, 50.

असावधान *a-sāvadhāna*, mfn. careless, inadvertent. **-tā**, f. carelessness.

असाहस *a-sāhasa*, *am*, n. absence of violence; absence of boldness or inconsiderate hastiness.

A-sāhasika, mf(*ī*)n. not acting boldly or inconsiderately, Śiś. ix, 59.

असाहाय्य *a-sāhāyya*, *am*, n. want of assistance or co-operation.

असि *así*, *is*, m. (√2. *as*), a sword, cimeter, knife (used for killing animals), RV.; AV. &c.; (*is*), f., N. of a river (near Benares), VāmP. (cf. *asī*); [Lat. *ensi-s*.] **-gaṇḍa**, m. = *kshudrôpadhāna* (for *kshurôp*°?), L. **-caryā**, f. exercise or practice of arms, MBh. i, 5239. **-daṇshṭra** or **-daṇshṭraka**, m. 'having swords for fangs,' the marine monster Makara (painted on the banner of Kāmadeva), L. **-dhara**, m., N. of a man, Rājat. **-dhārā**, f. the blade of a sword, Ragh. &c.; (*asidhārā*)-*patha*, m. = *asi-pathá*, q. v., Śārṅg.; -*vrata*, n. an exceedingly difficult task, Pañcat. &c. **-dhāva** or **-dhāvaka**, m. a sword- or tool-cleaner, armourer, L. **-dhenu**, f. a (small) knife, Daś.; Kathās. **-dhenukā**, f. id., Kathās. **-pattra**, n. the blade of a sword, L.; (*as*), m. 'having sword-shaped leaves,' the sugar-cane (Scirpus Kysoor Roxb.), L.; 'paved with swords,' N. of a hell, L.; (*asipattra*)-*vana*, n., N. of a hell, Mn.; Yājñ.; MBh. &c.; -*vriksha*, m. a kind of tree in the lower world [Comm.], Ragh. xiv, 48; -*vrata*, n. = *asidhārā-vrata*, q. v. **-pattraka**, m. the sugar-cane, L. **-pathá**, m. the course of the sword or knife that kills, ŚBr. xiii. **-pāṇi**, mfn. having a sword in one's hand, MBh. xii, 3737. **-pucchaka**, m. the Gangetic porpoise (Delphinus Gangeticus). **-putrikā** or **-putrī**, f. 'daughter of a sword,' a (small) knife, Hcat. **-mát**, mfn. furnished with knives or daggers, VS. xvi, 21. **-meda**, m. the fetid Mimosa (Vachellia Farnesiana), L.; (cf. *ahi-māra*, &c.) **-yashṭi**, f. = -*latā*, q. v., VarBṛS.; (Prākrit *asi-laṭṭhi*) Jain. **-latā**, f. the blade of a sword, Śiś. vi, 51. **-loman**, m., N. of a Dānava, MBh. i, 2531; Hariv. **-śimbī**, f., N. of a vegetable, L. **-hatya**, n. fighting with swords (or knives), (gaṇa *anuśatikâdi*, q. v.) **-heti**, m. a swordsman or soldier armed with a sword, L. **Asy-asi**, ind. sword against sword, L. **Asy-udyata**, mfn. (for *udyatâsi*) having the sword raised, Pāṇ. ii, 2, 36, Comm.

असिक *a-sika*, *am*, n. the part of the face between the underlip and the chin, L.; (*ās*), m. pl., N. of a people, VarBṛS. (v. l. *aśika*).

असिक्नी *ásiknī*, Ved. f. of 2. *ásita*, q. v.

असित 1. *á-sita*, mfn. unbound, TS. vii; ŚBr. xiv.

असित 2. *ásita*, mf(*ā*; Ved. *ásiknī*)n. (*sita*, 'white,' appears to have been formed from this word, which is probably original, and not a compound of *a* and *sita*; cf. *asura* and *sura*), dark-coloured, black, RV. &c.; (*as*), m. the planet Saturn, VarBṛS.; a poisonous animal (said to be a kind of mouse), L.; N. of the lord of darkness and magic, AV.; ŚBr.; ĀśvŚr.; of a descendant of Kaśyapa (composer of RV. ix, 5–24), named also Devala [RAnukr.] or Asita Devala [MBh.; Hariv.]; N. of a man (with the patron. Vārshagaṇa), ŚBr. xiv; of a son of Bharata, R.; of a Ṛishi, Buddh.; of a mountain, MBh. iii, 8364; Kathās.; (*ás*), m. a black snake, AV.; a Mantra (saving from snakes), MBh. i, 2188; (*ā*), f. a girl attending in the women's apartments (whose hair is not whitened by age), L.; the indigo plant, L.; N. of an Apsaras, MBh. i, 4819; Hariv. 12472; (*ásiknī*), f. 'the dark one,' the night, RV. iv, 17, 15; x, 3, 1; a girl attending in the women's apartments, L.; N. of a wife of Daksha, Hariv.; N. of the river Akesines (afterwards called Candra-bhāgā) in the Pañjāb, RV. viii, 20, 25 & (*asiknī́*) x, 75, 5. **-keśânta**, mfn. having black locks, N. **-grīva** (*ásita-*), mfn. having a black neck, VS. xxiii, 13; (ŚBr. xiii); (*as*), m. a peacock, MBh. xii, 4363. **-jānu**, mfn. having black knees, ĀpŚr. **-jñú**, mf(nom. -*jñū́s*)n. id., AV. xii, 1, 21. **-druma**, m. the tree Xanthochymus Pictorius, L. **-nayana**, mfn. black-eyed. **-pucchaka**, m. 'having a black tail,' N. of an animal, Car.; (cf. *kāla-pucchaka*.) **-bhrū**, mfn. having black eyelids. **-mushkaka**, m. the plant Schrebera Swietenioides, Suśr. **-mṛiga**, m., N. of a Ṛishi of the SV., ShaḍvBr.; (*ās*), m. pl. his descendants, AitBr. **-varṇa** (*ásita-*), mfn. dark-coloured, TS. **-vartman**, m. 'having a black path (of smoke),' Agni, Hcar. **Asitâksha**, mf(*ī*)n. = *asita-nayana*, q. v., Vishṇus. **Asitâṅga**, m. a form of Śiva (especially mentioned in Tantras), BrahmavP. &c. **Asitâbhra-śekhara**, m., N. of a Buddha, L. **Asitâmburuha**, m. the black lotus, L. **Asitârcis**, m. fire, L. **Asitâlu**, m., N. of a plant, L. **Asitâśman**, m. the lapis lazuli, Kir. v, 48. **Asitôtpala**, m. the blue lotus, Pañcat. **Asitôda**, n. (i.e. *saras*) N. of a mythical lake, VP. **Asitôpala**, m. = *asitâśman*, q. v., L.

Asiknikā, f. (= *asiknī*, q. v.) a girl attending in the women's apartments, Pāṇ. iv, 1, 39, Kāś.

असिद्ध *a-siddha*, mfn. imperfect, incomplete, NṛisUp.; unaccomplished, uneffected; unproved; (regarded as) not existing or (as) not having taken effect (as a rule or operation taught in grammar), Pāṇ.; not possessed of magic power. **A-siddhânta**, m. not an incontestable dogma, Suśr. **A-siddhârtha**, mfn. who has not effected his aim, R. iii, 55, 20; BhP.

Á-siddhi, *is*, f. imperfect accomplishment, failure,

TBr.; Gaut.; (in logic) want of proof, conclusion not warranted by the premises; (in Sāṅkhya phil.) incompleteness (eight forms of it are enumerated) — **da,** mfn. not giving success, BrahmavP.

असिन्व *a-sinvá,* mf(*ā́*)n. insatiable, RV. v, 32, 8; x, 89, 12.

Á-sinvat, mfn. id., RV.

असिर *ásira, as,* m. (√2. *as*), 'an arrow,' a beam, ray, RV. ix, 76, 4.

Ásishṭha, mfn. (superl.) most skilful in shooting (arrows, &c.), AV. iv, 28, 2.

असी *asī,* f. (=*asi,* f., q. v.) N. of a river (near Benares), MBh. vi, 338.

असीमन् *a-sīman,* mfn. unlimited, Bālar. **Asīma-kṛishṇa,** m., N. of a prince, BhP.

असु *ásu, us,* m. (√1. *as*), Ved. breath, life, RV.; AV. &c.; life of the spiritual world or departed spirits, RV. x, 15, 1; (in astron.) 'respiration,' = four seconds of sidereal time or one minute of arc, Sūryas.; =*prajñā,* Naigh.; (in later language only *ásavas*), m. pl. the vital breaths or airs of the body, animal life, AV.; Mn. iii, 217, &c.; (*asu*), n. grief, L.; (=*citta*) the spirit, L. — **tṛip,** mfn. enjoying or profiting by (another's) life, bringing it into one's possession, RV., (cf. *paśu-tṛip*); enjoying one's life, devoted to worldly pleasures, BhP. (once *asu-tṛipa* in the same sense). — **tṛipa,** mfn., see before. — **tyāga,** m. giving up one's life, BhP. — **dhāraṇa,** n. life, L. — **nīta** (*ásu-*), n. 'the world of spirits,' or m. 'the lord of spirits (i. e. Yama),' AV. xviii, 2, 56. — **nīti** (*ásu-*), f. the world of spirits, RV. x, 12, 4; 15, 14; 16, 2; personified as a female deity (invoked for the preservation of life, RV. x, 59, 5 & 6), or as Yama (lord of the dead, AV. xviii, 3, 59; Naigh.) — **bhaṅga,** m. breaking of life, L.; fear about life, danger of life, L. — **bhṛit,** m. a living being, a creature, man, BhP. — **mat** (*ásu-*), mfn. living, TBr.; (*ān*), m. life, the principle of vitality, the portion of the spirit connected with the attributes of existence, L. — **m-bhara,** mf(*ā*)n. only (supporting, i. e.) caring for one's life, BhP. — **vilāsa,** m., N. of a metre (of four times eleven syllables). — **sama,** m. 'dear as life,' a husband, lover, L. — **sū,** mfn. 'exciting life (as Kāma's arrows),' an arrow, Kir. xv, 5. — **sthirâdara,** mfn. continually solicitous about one's life, Rājat. **Asv-anta,** see *aśvanta.*

Ásura, mfn. (√2. *as,* Uṇ.), spiritual, incorporeal, divine, RV.; AV.; VS.; (*as*), m. a spirit, good spirit, supreme spirit (said of Varuṇa), RV.; VS.; the chief of the evil spirits, RV. ii, 30, 4 & vii, 99, 5; an evil spirit, demon, ghost, opponent of the gods, RV. viii, 96, 9; x; AV. &c. [these Asuras are often regarded as the children of Diti by Kaśyapa, see *daitya;* as such they are demons of the first order in perpetual hostility with the gods, and must not be confounded with the Rākshasas or imps who animate dead bodies and disturb sacrifices]; a N. of Rāhu, VarBṛS. &c.; the sun, L.; a cloud, Naigh. (cf. RV. v, 83, 6); (*ās*), m. pl., N. of a warrior-tribe, (gaṇa *parśv-ādi,* q. v.); of a Vedic school; (*ā*), f. night, L.; a zodiacal sign, L.; (*ī*), f. a female demon, the wife of an Asura, KaushBr.; (cf. *āsurī* and *mahâsurī*); the plant Sinapis Ramosa Roxb., L. [In later Sanskṛit *sura* has been formed from *asura,* as *sita* from *asita,* q. v.] — **kumāra,** *ās,* m. pl. the first of the ten classes of Bhavanavāsin deities, Jain. — **kshâyaṇa,** mfn. destroying the Asuras, AV. x, 10, 10; 12 & 13. — **kshiti** (*ásura-*), mfn. id., AV. x, 6, 22 & 28. — **guru,** m. 'teacher of the Asuras,' the planet Venus (or Śukra), Kād.; (cf. *amarâri-pūjya.*) — **tamasá,** n. the darkness of the (world of the) demons, ŚBr. iv. — **tvá,** n. spirituality, divine dignity, RV. iii, 55, 1; x, 55, 4 & 99, 2; the being an Asura or opponent of the gods, MaitrS.; Kathās. — **druh,** m. 'enemy of the Asuras,' a god, Śiś. ii, 35. — **dvish,** m. 'enemy of the Asuras,' a N. of Vishṇu, L. — **brahmá,** m. a priest of the Asuras, ŚBr. i. — **māyā́,** f. demoniacal magic, AV. iii, 9, 4; ŚBr.; KaushBr.; PBr. — **yoní,** m. or f. the womb of Asuras, TS. — **rakshasá,** n. a demoniacal being having the qualities of an Asura as well as of a Rakshas, ŚBr.; (*āni*), n. pl. Asuras and Rākshasas, ŚBr. — **rāj,** m. king of the Asuras (N. of the Asura Baka), MBh. i, 6208. — **ripu,** m. = *-dvish,* q. v., L. — **loka,** m. the world of the demons, Kāṭh. — **sūdana,** m. = *-dvish,* q. v., L. — **hán,** mf(*-ghnī*)n. destroying the Asuras, RV.; ŚBr. **Asurâcārya,** m. = *asura-guru,* q. v., L. **Asurâdhipa,** m. (= *asura-rāj*) a N. of Bali Vairocani, R. i, 31, 6; of Māyādhara, Kathās. **Asurârī,** m. = *asura-dvish,* q. v., Kād. **Asurâhva,** n. 'named after an Asura (i. e. after Kaṇsa, cf. *kāṇsya*),' bell-metal, L. **Asurêjya,** m. = *asura-guru,* q. v., VarBṛ. **Asurêndra,** m. lord of the Asuras, VP.

1. **Asuryà** (4), mfn. incorporeal, spiritual, divine, RV.; (Pāṇ. iv, 4, 123) demoniacal, belonging or relating to the Asuras, AitBr.; ŚBr.; (*às*), m. (= *ásura,* m., q. v.) the supreme spirit, RV. ii, 35, 2.

2. **Asuryà** (3), *am,* n. spirituality, divine nature, RV.; the incorporeal, the collective body of spiritual beings, RV. [Gmn. accentuates *asuryá* in accordance with similar cases, as 2. *samaryá* (3), n. compared with 1. *samaryà* (4), mfn.]

असुकर *a-sukara,* mfn. not easy to be done, difficult, arduous, MBh. viii, 99, &c.

असुकस् *asukas,* nom. sg. = *asakaú,* q. v., Pāṇ. vii, 2, 107, Comm.; (cf. *amuka.*)

असुख *a-sukha,* mf(*ā*)n. unhappy, sorrowful, MBh. &c.; painful, N.; not easy to (Inf.), Kir. v, 49; (*am*), n. sorrow, pain, affliction, Mn.; MBh. &c. — **pīḍita,** mfn. pained with grief, N. — **saṃcāra,** mf(*ā*)n. (a place) on which it is not easy or safe to dwell, Kām. **Asukhâvaha,** mf(*ā*)n. producing unhappiness, MBh. i, 4732. **Asukhâvishṭa,** mfn. afflicted with grief or pain. **Asukhôdaya,** mfn. causing or ending in unhappiness, Mn. iv, 70. **Asukhôdarka,** mfn. id., Mn.

A-sukhin, mfn. unhappy, sorrowful, R. &c.

असुगन्ध *a-sugandha, as,* m. a bad smell, BhP.; (mfn.) not fragrant, R.

असुगम *a-sugama,* mfn. not easily passable (as a way), BhP.; difficult to be understood, Comm.

असुत *á-suta,* mfn. (√3. *su*), not pressed out, not ready (as the Soma juice), RV.; VS.

A-sunvá, mf(*ā́*)n. 'not pressing out the Soma juice,' not worshipping the gods, RV. viii, 14, 15.

Á-sunvat, mfn. id., RV.

Á-sushvi, mfn. id., RV. iv, 24, 5; 25, 6; vi, 44, 11.

असुतर *a-sutara,* mfn. (√*tṛi*), not to be easily passed, Kir. v, 18.

असुतृप् *asu-tṛip* and *asu-tṛipa.* See *ásu.*

असुन्दर *a-sundara,* mfn. not good or right, improper, Comm. on Mn. iv, 222.

असुप्त *á-supta,* mfn. not asleep, ŚBr. xiv. — **dṛiś,** mfn. never closing the eyes in sleep, ever-seeing, L.

असुम्न *á-sumna,* mfn. contrary, adverse, VS. xxxv, 1.

असुर *ásura.* See *ásu.*

असुरक्ष *a-suraksha,* mf(*ā*)n. difficult to guard or preserve, perishable, Kir. ii, 39.

असुरसा *a-surasā,* f. the plant Basilicum Pilosum Benth., L.

असुलभ *a-sulabha,* mf(*ā*)n. difficult of attainment, rare, Śak.; Vikr. &c.

असुवर्ग्य *á-suvargya,* mfn. for *a-svargyá,* q. v., TS. v.

असुषिर *a-sushira,* mfn. not hollow, ĀpŚr. — **tva** (*ás°*), n. the not being hollow, MaitrS.

असुषुप्त *a-sushupta,* mfn. not fast asleep, NṛisUp.

असुष्वि *á-sushvi.* See *á-suta.*

असुसमाप्त *a-susamāpta,* mfn. imperfect, Nir. vi, 9 & 28.

असुसू *asu-sū.* See *ásu.*

असुस्थ *a-sustha,* mfn. unwell, indisposed, uncomfortable, Śak. — **tā,** f. indisposition, sickness.

असुहृद् *a-suhrid, t,* m. not a friend, N.; an enemy, R. v, 76, 5; (mfn.) having no friend, MBh. xii, 6485.

असू *a-sū́,* mfn. (√3. *sū*), not bringing forth, barren, RV. & AV. (acc. f. *a-svàm*); VS. (acc. f. *a-sū́m*).

A-sūta-jaratī, f. (a woman) who grows old without having brought forth a child, Pāṇ. vi, 2, 42.

A-sūti, *is,* f. non-production, obstruction, removal, Kir. ii, 56.

A-sū́tikā, f. barren (as a woman), AV. vi, 83, 3.

A-sūsū́, mfn. = *a-sū́,* q. v., AV. x, 10, 23.

असूक्ष्म *a-sūkshma,* mfn. not fine or minute, thick, gross.

असूय 1. *asūya,* Nom. P. °*yati,* rarely Ā. °*yate* (pr. p. °*yát,* RV. x, 135, 2; ŚBr.; aor. *āsūyīt,* ŚBr. iii; 3. pl. *asūyishuḥ,* Rājat.) to murmur at, be displeased or discontented with (dat. [ŚBr.; Pāṇ. i, 4, 37, &c.] or acc. [MBh.; R. &c.]): Caus. (ind. p. *asūyayitvā*) to cause to be displeased, irritate, MBh. iii, 2624 (N.)

2. **Asūya,** mfn. grumbling at, displeased with (loc.), MBh. xiii, 513; (*ā*), f. displeasure, indignation (especially at the merits or the happiness of another), envy, jealousy, Nir.; Āp.; Mn. &c.

Asūyaka, mfn. (Pāṇ. iii, 2, 146) discontented, displeased, envious, calumnious, Nir.; Mn. &c.

Asūyitṛi, mfn. displeased, envious, MBh. ii, 2515; (*an-* neg.) i, 5611.

Asūyu, mfn. id.; (see *an-asuyu.*)

असूर *a-sūrá, am,* n. 'absence of sunlight,' only (*é*), loc. ind. in the night, RV. viii, 10, 4.

असूर्क्षण *asūrkshaṇa, am,* n. disrespect, L.

असूर्त *a-sū́rta,* mfn. (said of *rájas*) 'unilluminated, enveloped in darkness' [Gmn.] or 'unvisited, unknown, remote' [Nir.; Pāṇ.; BR.], RV. x, 82, 4; AV. x, 3, 9; (cf. *sūrta* and *a-sūryá.*) — **rajasa,** m., v. l. for *amūrta-r°,* q. v.

असूर्य *a-sūryá,* mfn. (said of *támas*) sunless, RV. v, 32, 6 [(v. l. for 1. *asuryà* in ŚBr. xiv) 'demoniacal,' ĪśaUp.; 'inaccessible, unknown,' (fr. √*sṛi,* cf. *a-sū́rta*) NBD.]; (*am*), ind. at night, ShaḍvBr. — **m-paśyā,** f. the wife of a king (who being shut up in the inner apartments never sees the sun), Pāṇ. iii, 2, 36.

असृज् *ásṛij, k* (once *d,* TS. vii), n. (m. or f. only Hariv. 9296) blood, RV. i, 164, 4; AV. &c. [for the weak cases, see *asán;* besides, in later language, forms like instr. *asṛijā* (R. iii, 8, 4) and gen. *asṛijas* (Suśr.) are found]; saffron, L.; (*k*), m. the planet Mars; a kind of religious abstraction, L.

Asṛik (in comp. for *ásṛij*). — **kara,** m. 'forming blood,' lymph, chyle, L. — **tvá,** n. the state of blood, MaitrS. — **pa,** m. 'drinking blood,' a Rākshasa, L. — **pāta,** m. the falling of blood, Yājñ. iii, 293; (*ās*), m. pl. drops of blood (as from a wound), Mn. viii, 44; (cf. *asṛi-pāta.*) — **pāvan,** mfn. drinking blood, AV. ii, 25, 30. — **srāva,** mfn. bleeding, letting blood, L. — **srāvin,** mfn. bleeding, taking away blood, L.

Asṛig (in comp. for *ásṛij*). — **graha,** m. 'the blood-planet,' Mars, VarBṛS. — **dara,** m. irregular or excessive menstruation, mœnorrhagia, Suśr. — **doha,** mfn. shedding blood, bleeding, L. — **dharā,** f. the skin, L. — **dhārā,** f. a stream of blood, Kathās.; = *-dharā,* q. v., L. — **vahā,** f. a blood-vessel, L. — **vimokshaṇa,** n. blood-letting, bleeding, L.

Asṛiṅ (in comp. for *ásṛij*). — **maya,** mf(*ī*)n. consisting of blood, Śiś. xviii, 71. — **miśra,** mfn. mixed or covered with blood, L. — **mukha** (*ásṛiṅ-*), mfn. whose face is bloody, AV. xi, 9, 17.

असृणि *a-sṛiṇi,* mfn. unrestrained, BhP.

असृपात *asṛi-pāta, as,* m. (corrupt form) for *asṛik-pāta,* q. v., L.; (*ī*), f. id., L.

असृष्ट *a-sṛishṭa,* mfn. uncreated; undistributed; continued. **Asṛishṭânna,** mfn. who does not distribute food.

असेचन *a-secana,* mfn. (also *ā-sec°,* q. v.) charming, lovely, L.

A-secanaka [L.] or **a-secanīya** [Lalit.], mfn. id.

असेन्य *a-senyá* (4), mfn. not striking or wounding, not hurting (as words), RV. x, 108, 6.

असेवा *a-sevā,* f. not following or practising, Mn. ii, 96; disregard, inattention.

A-sevita, mfn. neglected, unattended to; abstained from. **Asevitêsvara-dvāra,** mfn. not waiting at the doors of the great, Hit.

A-sevya, mfn. not to be served or attended to,

Pañcat.; Kathās.; not to be visited by (gen.), Pañcat.; not to be used or practised, not to be eaten, drunk, &c.

असोढ a-soḍha, mfn. not to be endured or mastered, Pāṇ. i, 4, 26; (cf. á-shāḍha.)

असोम a-soma, as, m. not Soma juice, Kāty-Śr.; not a Soma sacrifice, ib.; (mfn.) without Soma juice, MBh. xiii, 1793. — **pa**, mfn. one who does not drink or is not admitted to drink the Soma juice, AitBr. &c.; Mn. xi, 12. — **pītha**, mfn. id., ŚāṅkhŚr. — **pīthin**, mfn. id., KātyŚr. — **yājin** (á-soma-), mfn. one who has not offered a Soma sacrifice, ŚBr. i.

असौ asaú (nom.) and ásau (voc.); see adás and amu. — √1. **kṛi**, to do such and such a thing, (gaṇa sākshād-ādi, q. v.) — **nāman**, mfn. having such and such a name, ŚBr. xiv (BṛĀrUp.) — **yaja**, m., N. of a Praisha (with the address amuka yaja), ŚāṅkhŚr.

असौन्दर्य a-saundarya, am, n. ugliness.

असौम्य a-saumya, mfn. unlovely, disagreeable, displeasing, VP.; unpropitious, R. i, 74, 10.

असौवर्ण a-sauvarṇa, mfn. not consisting of gold, Mṛicch.

असौष्ठव a-saushṭhava, am, n. want of lightness or suppleness (of body), Sāh.

असौहृद a-sauhṛida, am, n. enmity, MBh. xv, 895.

अस्कन्द á-skanda, as, m. the non-spilling (as of the semen virile), TS.; ŚBr. — **tva** (á-skanda-), n. id., MaitrS.

A-skandayat, mfn. not spilling, Āp.; not neglecting, Mn. vi, 9.

A-skandita, mfn. not neglected or forgotten (as time or a vow), MBh. xii, 7002; BhP.

A-skandin, mfn. not coagulating, Suśr.

Á-skanna, mfn. not spilt (as an oblation), VS. ii, 8; ŚBr.; MBh. xii, 2318; not covered (as a cow), AitBr. — **tva** (á-skanna-), n. the not being spilt, MaitrS.

अस्कम्भन a-skambhaná, am, n. no pillar or support ['having no pillar or support,' the ether, Gmn.], RV. x, 149, 1.

अस्कृधोयु á-skṛidhoyu, mfn. (cf. kṛidhú), not deficient, abundant, RV. vi, 22, 3; 67, 11 & vii, 53, 3.

अस्खल a-skhala, as, m. 'not shaking or slipping,' N. of an Agni, PārGṛ.

A-skhalita, mfn. unshaken, unyielding, firm; not stumbling or slipping, undeviating; uninterrupted, unimpeded, undisturbed, Ragh. v, 20; xviii, 14; BhP. &c. — **prayāṇa**, mfn. not stumbling in progress, with unfaltering step, Hit.

अस्त 1. asta, mfn. (perf. Pass. p. √2. as), thrown, cast, Ragh. xii, 91; (án-, neg.) ŚBr. iii; (only in comp.) thrown off, left off, set aside, given up (as grief, anger, a vow, &c.), VP.; Kathās. &c.; (ā), f. a missile, an arrow, AV. — **kopa**, mfn. one whose anger is laid aside, Comm. on Megh. — **tandri**, mfn. who has laid aside sloth, Kir. i, 9. — **dhī**, mfn. 'out of one's mind,' foolish. — **vyasta**, mfn. scattered hither and thither, confused, disordered, Sūryapr. 18. — **saṃkhya**, mfn. innumerable, L.

Ástṛi, mfn. (fut. p.) one who is about or intends to throw, RV. i, 61, 7; x, 133, 3; (tā), m. a thrower, shooter, RV.; AV.; (with a-pád) ŚBr.

अस्त 2. ásta, am, n. home, RV.; AV.; ŚBr.; (as), m. setting (as of the sun or of luminaries), VarBṛS.; Sūryas.; 'end, death,' see asta-samaya below; the western mountain (behind which the sun is supposed to set), MBh.; R. &c.; (in astron.) the seventh lunar mansion, VarBṛ.; (ástam), ind. at home, home, RV. &c., especially used with verbs, e. g. ástam-√i [ástam éti; pr. p. astam-yát, AV.; ŚBr.; fut. p. astam-eshyát, AV.; perf. p. ástam-ita, see below s. v.] or ástaṃ-√gam [ástam gácchati, AV. &c.; perf. p. astam-gata, MBh. &c., once in reversed order gata astaṃ, R. i, 33, 21] or astaṃ-√yā [pr. p. -yāt, Mn. iv, 37] to go down, set, RV.; AV. &c.; astam-√i, astaṃ-√gam (also Caus., see astaṃ-gamita below), or -√prāp [Kathās.], to go to one's eternal home, cease, vanish, perish, die, ŚBr. xiv; MBh. &c.; astam-√nī [-nayati], to lead to setting, cause to set, MBh. iii, 17330; (ástā), ind. v. l. for ástam, SV. — **m-yát** and **-m-yāt**, see ástam before s. v. ásta. — **kshitibhṛit**, m. 'the mountain Asta,' the western mountain (behind which the sun is supposed to set), Ratnāv. — **gamana**, n. setting (of the sun), MBh. i, 6058. — **giri**, m. = -kshitibhṛit, q. v., Śiś. ix, 1. — **m-gamita**, mfn. (Caus. perf. Pass. p.) brought to an end, destroyed, Megh. — **tāti** (ásta-), f. home, RV. v, 7, 6. — **nimagna**, mfn. set (as the sun), Ragh. xvi, 11. — **bhavana**, n. the seventh lunar mansion, VarBṛ. — **m-ayá**, m. setting (of the sun), ŚBr.; Ch-Up. &c.; disappearance, vanishing, perishing, Kaṭh-Up. (said of the senses); Ragh. — **m-áyana**, n. setting of the sun, ŚBr. xiii. — **mastaka**, m. n. (the head, i. e.) the top of the mountain Asta, Ratnāv. — **m-ita** (ást°), set (as the sun), AV. &c.; come to an end, ceased, dead, R.; Ragh. &c.; (e), loc. ind. after sunset, ĀśvGṛ. — **m-iké**, loc. ind. (fr. 2. añc, cf. samīká, &c.) at home, RV. i, 129, 9. — **mūrdhan**, m. = -mastaka, q. v., R. iii, 67, 24. — **m-eshyát**, see ástam before s. v. ásta. — **rāśi**, m. = -bhavana, q. v., VarBṛ. — **śikhara**, m. = -mastaka, q. v., Śak.; Kathās. — **samaya**, m. 'the moment of sunset' and 'the moment of end or death,' Śiś. ix, 5. **Astâcala**, m. = asta-kshitibhṛit, q. v., Hit. **Astâdri**, m. id. **Astâvalambin**, mfn. reclining on the western mountain, about to set.

Ástaka, am, n. home, AV. ii, 26, 5 (cf. sv-astaká); (as), m. going to one's eternal home, L.

Astamana, am, n. (a corruption of astam-áyana, q. v.), setting, MBh.; R. &c.

Astya, am, n. (v. l. for ásta) a house, Naigh.

अस्तब्ध a-stabdha, mfn. 'not fixed,' moving, agile (as a bird), R. iii, 79, 22; not arrogant or obstinate, unassuming, modest, MBh. v, 1360; xii, 2709. — **tā**, f. unassumingness, Kām. — **tva**, n. id., Hit.

A-stambha, mf(ā)n. without pillars, Ragh. i, 41; unassuming, Rājat.

अस्ताघ a-stāgha, mfn. 'not shallow,' very deep, Jain. (only in Prākṛit atthāha).

अस्ति 1. asti, ind. (3. sg. pr. √1. as; gaṇa cādi and svar-ādi, q. v.) sometimes used as a mere particle at the beginning of fables, Pañcat.; Kathās.; existent, present, L. — **kāya**, m. an ontological category (of which five are distinguished, viz. jīvâstikāya, ajīvâst°, dharmâst°, adharmâst°, pudgalâst°), Jain. — **kshīrā**, f. having milk (as a cow), Pāṇ. ii, 2, 24, Comm. — **tā**, f. existence, reality, Comm. on Bād.; Sarvad. — **tva**, n. id., ib. — **nâsti**, ind. partly true and partly not, doubtful, L. — **pravāda**, m., N. of the fourth of the fourteen Pūrvas or older writings of the Jainas. — **mat**, mfn. possessed of property, opulent, L.

2. **Asti**, is, f. (as-ti = s-ti, q. v.), N. of a sister of Prāpti (daughter of Jarāsandhas and wife of Kaṇsa), MBh. ii, 595; Hariv. 4955; BhP.

Astu (3. sg. Imper.), let it be, be it so; there must be or should be (implying an order). — **m-kāra**, mfn. 'one who says astu,' 'conceding, assenting unwillingly,' or 'ordering,' Pāṇ. vi, 3, 70, Comm. — **vid**, mfn. knowing that anything must be done, Rājat.

अस्तुत á-stuta, mfn. not praised (by a hymn), AitBr.; not recited (as a hymn), ib.; not liked, not popular, RV. v, 61, 8; 67, 5.

A-stuti, mfn. not praising anybody, MBh. xii.

A-stutya, mfn. not to be praised, Pañcat.

A-stotṛi, mfn. = a-stuti, q. v., MBh. i, 3314; Kum. vi, 83.

अस्तृ ástṛi. See 1. asta.

अस्तृत á-stṛita, mfn. not overcome, invincible, indestructible, RV.; AV. xix, 46; (said of the gold) KaushUp. & ĀśvGṛ. [v. l. a-srutá, ŚBr. xiv & PārGṛ.]; (a-stṛitá), mfn. id., AV. i, 20, 4 & v, 9, 7. — **yajvan** (ástṛita-), mfn. sacrificing indefatigably or invincibly, RV. viii, 43, 1.

A-stṛiti, is, f. invincibleness, PBr. (ed. a-stiti).

अस्तेन á-stena, as, m. not a thief, ŚBr. xiv. — **mānin**, mfn. not believing one's self to be a thief, Mn. viii, 197.

A-steya, am, n. not stealing, Mn.; Yājñ. &c.

अस्तोक a-stoka, mfn. not slight or little, Mālatim.

अस्तोतृ a-stotṛi. See á-stuta.

अस्तोभ a-stobha, mfn. without stoppage or pause, Lalit.; without the interjection of the sound called stobha (in the Sāman), Lāṭy.

अस्त्य astya. See 2. ásta.

अस्त्यान a-styāna, am, n. disregard, L.

अस्त्र astrá, am, n. (exceptionally as, m., Hariv. 10703, &c.), (√2. as), a missile weapon, bolt, arrow, AV. xi, 10, 16; MuṇḍUp. &c.; a weapon in general, L.; a sword, L.; a bow, L.; N. of a Mantra (pronounced, for instance, before reading a book or while kindling a fire &c.), BhavP. &c.; N. of the mystical syllable phaṭ, RāmatUp. [cf. Gk. ἄστρον and ἀστήρ, 'that which throws out or emits rays of light'(?)]. — **kaṇṭaka**, m. an arrow, L. — **kāra** or **-kāraka**, m. a maker of weapons, armourer, L. — **kārin**, m. id., L. — **kshepaka**, mfn. shooting arrows, L. — **grāma**, m. a heap or collection of different missile weapons, Veṇīs. — **cikitsaka**, m. a surgeon, L. — **cikitsā**, f. surgery, L. — **jit**, n., N. of a plant, L. — **jīva**, m. 'living on arms,' a soldier, L. — **dhāraṇa**, n. the bearing of arms, L. — **dhārin**, mfn. 'bearing arms,' a soldier, L. — **nivāraṇa**, n. warding off a blow. — **bandha**, m. an uninterrupted series of arrows, R. — **bhṛit**, m. a shooter, R. v, 43, 2. — **mantra**, m. a Mantra used to charm arrows, Ragh. v, 59. — **mārja**, m. a sword-polisher or tool-cleaner, armourer, L. — **vid**, mfn. skilled in shooting, a good marksman, Ragh. v, 59. — **vidyā**, f. the military science, L. — **vṛishṭi**, f. a shower of arrows, Ragh. iii, 58. — **śastra**, āṇi, n. pl. all sorts of arms (as arrows and swords), R. i, 23, 14. — **śikshā**, f. military exercise, L. — **sāyaka**, m. an iron arrow, L. — **hīna**, mfn. unarmed, defenceless. **Astrâgāra**, n. an arsenal, armoury, Veṇīs. (quoted in Sāh.); MatsyaP. **Astrâghāta**, n. a wound, cut. **Astrâhata**, mfn. wounded, killed. **Astrôpanishad**, f. science of arms, Mcar.

Astrāya, Nom. Ā. °yate (perf. p. °yita, mfn.) to become or turn into a weapon, Bālar.

Astrin, ī, m. an archer, BhP.; Śiś. xviii, 71.

अस्त्री a-strī, f. not a woman, MBh. ii, 1694; (with lexicographers) 'not feminine,' i. e. the masculine and neuter genders. — **jita**, mfn. not wife-subdued, Rājat. — **sambhogin**, mfn. not enjoying women (by sexual intercourse), Comm. on Mn. vi, 26. **A-stry-upâyin**, mfn. id., KātyŚr.

A-straiṇa, mfn. without wives, AV. viii, 6, 16.

अस्थ astha, only ifc. for ásthi, q. v., e. g. an-asthá, ūrv-asthá, purushâsthá, q. v.

Asthán, the base of the weak cases of ásthi, q. v., e. g. instr. asthnā, &c. (Ved. also instr. pl. asthábhis, RV. i, 84, 13; and n. pl. asthāni, Pāṇ. vii, 1, 76). — **vát**, mfn. having bones, bony, RV. i, 164, 4; ŚBr. vi; vertebrated (as an animal), Gaut.

अस्था asthá, ind.(?) at once, RV. x, 48, 10.

अस्थाघ a-sthāgha, mfn. = a-stāgha, q. v., L.

अस्थान a-sthāna, am, n. non-permanency, inconstancy (as of a sound), Jaim.; not a (fit) place for (gen.), Kād.; (e), loc. ind. [PBr.; R. &c.] or in comp. asthāna- [Megh.; Daś.], in a wrong place; in wrong time, unseasonably, unsuitably, (a-sthāne) R.; MārkP. &c.; (a-sthāna-) R. iv, 32, 6; Sāh. — **yukta**, mfn. applied in the wrong place, Sāh. — **stha-pada**, mfn. having a word in the wrong place, Kpr. — **stha-samāsa**, mfn. having a compound in the wrong place, ib.

A-sthānin, mfn. not being in one's proper place or order, ĀśvŚr.

A-sthāyin, mfn. not permanent, transient, Rājat.; Śārṅg. &c. **Asthāyi-tva**, n. non-permanency, inconstancy, Suśr.

A-sthāvara, mfn. not fixed, moving, movable; (in law, said of) movable (property, viz. money, cattle &c., as opposed to land), L.

A-sthāsnu, mfn. impatient, Kathās.

A-sthita, mfn. not lasting, RPrāt.

A-sthiti, is, f. want of order, Kād.

अस्थि ásthi, i, n. (see asthán), a bone, AV.; VS. &c.; the kernel of a fruit, Suśr. (cf. 3. ashṭi); [Lat. os, ossis assimilated fr. ostis; Gk. ὀστέον.] — **kuṇḍa**, n. a hole filled with bones (part of the hell), BrahmavP. — **kṛit**, n. marrow, L. — **ketu**, m., N. of a Ketu, VarBṛS. — **cchallita**, n. a particular fracture of the bones, Suśr. — **já**, mfn. produced in the bones, AV. i, 23, 4; (as), m. marrow, L.; (= -sambhava below) the thunderbolt, L. (cf. aksha-

ja). **-tuṇḍa,** m. 'whose mouth or beak consists of bone,' a bird, L. **-tejas,** n. marrow, L. **-toda,** m. pain in the bones, L. **-tvac,** f. the periosteum, L. **-danta-maya,** mfn. made of bones or ivory, Mn. v, 121. **-dhanvan,** m. a N. of Śiva, L. **-pañjara,** m. 'cage of bones,' a skeleton, L. **-bandhana,** n. a sinew, R. v, 42, 20. **-bhaksha,** m. 'eating bones,' a dog, L. **-bhaṅga,** m. fracture of the bones; the plant Vitis Quadrangularis, L. **-bhuj,** m. = *-bhaksha,* q. v., L. **-bhūyas** (*ásthi-*), mfn. consisting chiefly of bones, dried up, AV. v, 18, 13. **-bheda,** m. fracturing or wounding a bone; a sort of bone. **-mat,** mfn. having bones, vertebrated, Mn.; Yājñ. iii, 269. **-maya,** mf(*ī*)n. bony, consisting of bones, full of bones, Rājat. &c. **-mālā,** f. 'necklace of bones,' N. of a work. **-mālin,** m. 'having a necklace of bones, i. e. of skulls,' Śiva. **-yajña,** m. bone-sacrifice (part of a funeral ceremony), KātyŚr. **-yuj,** m. the plant Vitis Quadrangularis, L. **-vilaya,** m. the dissolving of bones (in a sacred stream). **-śṛiṅkhalā,** f. id., L. **-saṃhāra,** m. or °**rī,** f. id., L. **-saṃhāraka,** m. id., Bhpr.; 'bone-seizer,' the adjutant bird, L. **-saṃcaya,** m. or **-saṃcayana,** n. the ceremony of collecting the bones (after burning a corpse), Comm. on KātyŚr. **-sandhi,** m. a joint, Car. **-samarpaṇa,** n. throwing the bones of a dead body into the Ganges, L. **-sambhava,** mfn. consisting of bones (said of the Vajra or thunderbolt), MBh. i, 1514; 'produced in the bones,' marrow, L. **-sāra,** m. marrow, L. **-sthūṇa,** mfn. having the bones for its pillars (as the body), Mn. vi, 76. **-sneha** or **-snehaka,** m. marrow, L. **-sraṅsá,** mfn. causing the bones to fall asunder, AV. vi, 14, 1.

Asthika, *am,* n. (gaṇa *yāvâdi,* q. v.) a bone [generally only ifc. f. *ā,* e. g. R.; Yājñ. iii, 89; cf. *an-asthika* s. v. *an-asthá*].

अस्थिर *á-sthira,* mfn. unsteady, trembling, shaking, ŚBr. &c.; not permanent, transient, R.; uncertain, unascertained, doubtful, Mn. viii, 71; MBh. ii, 1965; not steady (in character), changeable, not deserving confidence, R. ii, 21, 19; Pañcat. **-tva,** n. the not being hard, Suśr.; unsteadiness, fickleness, MBh.; inconstancy, MaitrUp.; Mn. viii, 77. **A-sthirī-√bhū,** to become weak, decrease, Suśr.

A-sthūrí or **á-sthūri** [only TS. vii], mfn. not single-horsed, RV. vi, 15, 19; VS. &c.

Á-sthūla, mf(*ā*)n. not gross or bulky, delicate, ŚBr. xiv; Pañcat. &c.

Á-stheyas, mfn. (compar.) not firmer, TS. v; not firm, RV. x, 159, 5.

A-sthairya, *am,* n. instability, unsteadiness, Rājat.; Sarvad. &c.

अस्नात *a-snāta,* mfn. not bathed, BhP.

A-snātṛí, mfn. not fond of bathing, fearing the water, not a swimmer, RV. ii, 15, 5; iv, 30, 17; x, 4, 5.

A-snāna, *am,* n. not bathing, (= *naishṭhika-brahmacarya,* Comm.) MBh. xiv, 1353.

A-snāyin, mfn. one who has not bathed, Hcat.

अस्नावक *a-snāvaka,* mfn. without sinews, TS. vii.

A-snāvirá, mfn. id., VS. xl, 8.

अस्निग्ध *a-snigdha,* mfn. not smooth, harsh, hard. **-dāruka,** m. a kind of pine tree, L.

A-snehá, mfn. without unctuousness, ŚBr. xiv; Yājñ.; Ragh. iv, 75; without affection, unkind, L.; (*as*), m. want of affection, L. **-vat,** mfn. without affection, Pañcat. (v. l.)

A-snehana, *as,* m. 'without affection,' a N. of Śiva, MBh. xiii, 1203.

A-snehya, mfn. not to be made unctuous, Suśr.

अस्पन्द *a-spanda,* mfn. not quivering or moving, fixed, Uttarar.; Rājat.; unvariable (as love), BhP. **Aspandâsu,** mfn. having motionless or suppressed breath, BhP.

A-spandana, mfn. not quivering or moving, Suśr.; (cf. *garbhâspandana.*)

Á-spandamāna, mfn. id., v. l. for *á-syand°,* q. v.

A-spandayat, mfn. not causing to move, ĀśvŚr.

अस्पर्श *a-sparśa,* mfn. not having the faculty of perception by touch, ŚBr. xiv; intangible, Āp.; NṛisUp.; (*as*), m. non-contact with (instr.), MBh. iii, 11087. **-para,** mfn. not followed by a letter called *sparśa,* q. v., VPrāt.

A-sparśana, *am,* n. non-contact, avoiding the contact of anything (especially of one who is impure).

A-spṛiśat, mfn. not touching, Śārṅg.

A-spṛiśya, mfn. not to be touched, Hariv.; BhP. &c.; not tangible, MBh. xiv, 610; (*am*), n. intangibleness, BhP. **-tva,** n. intangibleness, imperceptibleness, Comm. on Jaim.; intangibility, Comm. on Mn. v, 62.

A-spṛishṭa, mfn. untouched, not brought into contact, BhP.; Kāvyād.; not touched or referred to (as by a word), Kum. vi, 75; not touched by the organs of articulation (as the vowels, the Anusvāra, and the sibilants), RPrāt.; VPrāt. **-maithunā,** f. a virgin, MānGṛ. **-rajas-tamaska,** mfn. perfectly pure, BhP.

A-spṛishṭi, *is,* f. not touching, avoiding contact.

A-sprashṭṛi, mfn. one who does not touch, MaitrUp.

अस्पष्ट *a-spashṭa,* mfn. indistinct, BhP.; Suśr. &c. **-kīrti,** mfn. not famous, unknown, BhP.

अस्पृत *á-spṛita,* mfn. not forcibly carried off (as the Soma), RV. viii, 82, 9 & ix, 3, 8.

अस्पृशत् *a-spṛiśat,* &c. See *a-sparśa.*

अस्पृह *a-spṛiha,* mfn. undesirous, Mn. vi, 96; (*ā*), f. no desire, Gaut.; BhavP. i. **-tva,** n. id., Hcat.

A-spṛihaṇīya, mfn. undesirable.

अस्फुट *a-sphuṭa,* mf(*ā*)n. indistinct, BhP.; Kathās. &c.; not quite correct, approximate (as a number), Sūryas.; (*am*), n. (in rhetoric) indistinct speech. **-phala,** n. approximate result (as the gross area of a triangle &c.) **Asphuṭâlaṃkāra,** m. an indistinct embellishment of speech, Sāh.

अस्म *asma* (fr. *a-sma*), a pronom. base from which some forms (dat. *ásmai* or *asmai,* abl. *asmā́t,* loc. *asmín*) of *idám* (q. v.) are formed; also the base of the first person plur., acc. *asmā́n* [= ἡμᾶς], instr. *asmā́bhis,* dat. *asmā́bhyam,* abl. *asmát,* in later language also *asmat-tas* [MBh. &c.], gen. *asmā́kam* [exceptionally *asmā́ka,* RV. i, 173, 10; AV.], loc. *asmā́su;* dat. loc. *asmé* (only RV.; AV.; VS.) **-trā́,** ind. (for *asmat-trā́* by defective spelling), to us, with us, among us, RV.; *asmatrā́ñc,* mfn. turned towards us, RV. vi, 44, 19. **-drúh** (nom. *-dhrúk*), mfn. (for *asmad-drúh* by defective spelling), forming a plot against us, inimical to us, RV. i, 36, 16; 176, 3; viii, 60, 7. **Asmé-hiti,** f. errand or message for us, RV. x, 108, 1.

Asmat (in comp. for *asmad* below). **-prêshita** (*asmát-*), mfn. sent or driven towards us, ŚBr. vi. **-sakhi** (*asmát-*), m(nom. °*khā*)fn. having us as friends, RV. vi, 47, 26.

Asmad, base of the first person plur., as used in comp.; also by native grammarians considered to be the base of the cases *asmā́n* &c. (see above). **-devatya,** mfn. having us as deities, PBr. **-rāta** (*asmád-*), mfn. given by us, VS. vii, 46. **-vat,** ind. like us, Kathās. **-vidha,** mfn. one similar to or like us, one of us, MBh.; R. &c.

Asmadīya, mfn. (Pāṇ. iv, 3, 1) our, ours, MBh. &c.

Asmadryáñc (4), mfn. turned towards us, RV. vii, 19, 10; (°*dryàk*), ind. towards us, RV.

Asmaya, Nom. P. °*yati,* to desire us, Pat.

Asmayú, mfn. endeavouring to attain us, desiring us, liking us, RV.

Asmāka, mfn. (fr. *asma* + *añc*?, cf. *ápāka* &c.) our, ours, RV.; (cf. *āsmāká.*)

अस्मरण *a-smaraṇa, am,* n. not remembering (with gen.), MBh. iii, 10811, &c.

A-smarat, mfn. not remembering, Lāṭy.

A-smartavya, mfn. not to be recollected.

A-smārta, mfn. not traditional, illegal.

A-smṛita, mfn. forgotten, L.; not mentioned in authoritative texts, not traditional, Comm. on KātyŚr. **-dhru** (*á-smṛita-*), m(nom. du. *-dhrū*)fn. (for *-druh,* NBD.) not thinking of or caring for enemies, RV. x, 61, 4.

A-smṛiti, *is,* f. non-remembrance, forgetting, KātyŚr.; MBh.; want of memory, forgetfulness, MBh. xiv, 999; the not being part of the institutes of law, L.; (*á-smṛiti*), ind. inattentively, AV. vii, 106, 1.

अस्मि *asmi,* 'I am,' √1. *as,* q. v. **-tā,** f. egoism, Yogas.; Comm. on Śiś. iv, 55, &c. **-māna,** m. self-conceit, L.

अस्मेर *á-smera,* mf(*ā*)n. not bashful or confused, confiding, RV. ii, 35, 4; not smiling, not merry, Bālar.

अस्मेहिति *asmé-hiti.* See *asma.*

अस्यन्दमान *á-syandamāna* (or *a-spand°*), mfn. not gliding away, RV. iv, 3, 10.

अस्यवामीय *asyavāmīya, am,* n. the hymn beginning with the words *asyá vāmásya* (RV. i, 164), Mn. xi, 250; Pāṇ. v, 2, 59, Sch.

अस्यहत्य *asya-hatyá* (or *-ha-tya*), gaṇa *anuśatikâdi,* q. v.; (see *āsyahātya.*)

Asya-heti, ib.; (see *āsyahaitika.*)

अस्र 1. *asrá,* mfn. (√2. *as*), throwing, TBr.; (*am*), n. a tear, Mn.; R. &c. (often spelt *aśra*).

अस्र 2. *asra, am,* n. blood, Ragh. xvi, 15; (cf. *ásṛij.*) **-khadira,** m. a red Mimosa, L. **-ja** or **-janman,** n. 'formed by blood,' flesh, L. **-pa,** m. (= *asṛik-pa,* q. v.) a Rākshasa, Mcar.; (*ā*), f. a leech, L.; a Ḍākinī or female imp, L. **-pattraka,** m. the plant Abelmoschus Esculentus, L. **-pitta,** n. = *rakta-pitta,* q. v., L. **-phalā,** f. the plant Boswellia Thurifera Roxb., L. **-bindu-cchadā,** f., N. of a tuberous plant. **-mātṛi** or **-mātṛikā,** f. (= *asṛik-kara,* q. v.) chyle, L. **-rodhinī,** f. the plant Mimosa Pudica, L. **Asrârjaka,** m. the white Tulasī plant, L.

Asrāya, Nom. Ā. °*yate,* to shed tears, (gaṇa *sukhâdi,* q. v.)

Asrāyamāṇaka, mfn. shedding tears, MBh. iii, 16834.

Asrin, mfn. id. (gaṇa *sukhâdi,* q. v.)

अस्र 3. *asra, as,* m. hair of the head, L.

अस्रवत् *á-sravat,* mfn. 'not flowing,' not leaky (as a ship), RV. x, 63, 10; VS. xxi, 7.

A-srutá, mfn. 'inexhaustible,' v. l. for *á-stṛita,* q. v.

A-sruva, *am,* n. granulation (of a running sore), L.

अस्राम *á-srāma,* mf(*ā*)n. not lame, AV. i, 31, 3; not withered, Gobh.

अस्रिध् *a-srídh,* mfn. not failing, not erring, RV.

Á-sridhāna, mfn. (aor. p. Ā.) id., RV. vii, 69, 7.

Á-sredhat, mfn. (pr. p. P.) id., RV.

अस्रीवयस् *asrī-váyas,* n. (fr. 1. *váyas*?), VS. xiv, 18; ŚBr. viii.

Asrī-vi, *is,* m. (cf. *rāja-vi*)?, TS. iv.

Asrī-vī́, *īs,* m. (cf. *vī* = 2. *vi*), MaitrS.

अस्रेमन् *a-sremán,* mfn. (said of Agni) faultless, perfect, RV. iii, 29, 13 & x, 8, 2.

अस्व *a-sva,* mfn. having no property, MBh. **-ga** (*á-sva-*), mfn. not going to one's own home, homeless, AV. xii, 5, 45; (*asvagā́*)*-tā,* f. homelessness, AV. ix, 2, 3; xii, 5, 40. **-cchanda,** mfn. not self-willed, dependant, L.; docile, L. **-jāti,** mfn. of a different caste, Mn. ix, 86. **-tantra,** mf(*ā*)n. not self-willed, dependant, subject, Mn. ix, 2; Gaut.; BhP.; (*asvatantra*)*-tā,* f. the not being master of one's feelings or passions, Kād. **-tā,** f. the having no property, L. **-tva,** n. id., Kathās. **-dṛiś,** mfn. not seeing one's self or soul, BhP. **-dharma,** m. neglect of one's duty, Daś. **-bhāva,** m. unnatural or unusual character or temperament; (mfn.) of a different nature, L. **-rūpa,** mfn. essentially different, L.; shapeless (opposed to *rūpa-vat*), BhP. **-veśa** (*á-sva-*), mfn. having no home of one's own, RV. vii, 37, 7. **-stha,** mf(*ā*)n. not in good health, sick, feeling uneasy, Mn. vii, 226; MBh. &c.; not being firm in itself, MBh. xii, 276 (Hit.); (*asvastha*)*-tā,* f. illness, Ratnāv. (Prākrit *assatthadā*); *-śarīra,* mfn. ill, Kād. **A-svâṅga-pūrva-pada,** mfn. (a compound) the first part of which is not (a word denoting) part of the body, Pāṇ. iv, 1, 53. **A-svâdhīna,** mfn. = *a-svatantra* above, R. iii, 33, 5 (ed. Bomb.); not independent, not doing one's own will, R. ii, 30, 33. **A-svâdhyāya,** mfn. (a Brāhman) who has not performed his repetition of the Veda, who has not repeated or does not repeat the Vedas, L.; (*as*), m. interruption or interval of repetition (prohibited on certain days of the moon, at eclipses, &c.), L.; (*a-svâdhyāya*)*-para,* mfn. not devoted to the repetition of the Vedas, MBh. xiii, 4563. **A-svârtha,** mfn. not fit for a proper object, useless, BhP.; unselfish, disinterested, L. **A-svīkāra,** m. non-acquiescence, dissent, L. **A-svīkṛita,** mfn. refused, L.

A-svaka, mf(*akā* or *ikā*, Pāṇ. vii, 3, 47)n. = *a-sva*, q. v., L.
A-svātantrya, *am*, n. dependence, MaitrUp.
A-svāsthya, *am*, n. indisposition, sickness, discomfort, BhP.; Kathās.

अस्वदित *á-svadita*, mfn. not made agreeable to the taste or sweet, ŚBr. i.
A-svādu, mfn. tasteless, AitBr.; MBh.

अस्वन *a-svana*, mfn. not having a clear sound, VarBṛS.

अस्वन्त *a-svanta*, mfn. (*sv-anta*), ending ill, having an unfavourable issue; (see also *asv-anta* s. v. *aśvanta*.)

अस्वपत् *á-svapat*, mfn. not sleeping, Suparṇ.
Á-svapna, *as*, m. sleeplessness, ŚBr. iii; ShaḍvBr. (*am*, n.); VarBṛS.; (*a-svapná*), mfn. (= ἄϋπνος) not sleeping, watchful, AV.; not dreaming, NṛisUp.; (*as*), m. 'sleepless,' a god, L.
Á-svapnaj, mfn. not sleepy, sleepless, RV. ii, 27, 9; iv, 4, 12; VS.

अस्वर *a-svara*, mfn. not loud (as the voice), indistinct, R. ii, 42, 26; having no vowel, Up.; having no accent, APrāt. Sch.; having a bad or croaking voice, L.; (*ám*), ind. in low tone, indistinctly, ŚBr. xi. **A-svarâdi**, mfn. not beginning with a vowel.
A-svaraka, mfn. unaccentuated, Pat.
A-svarita, mfn. not having the accent called Svarita, Pāṇ. Sch.

अस्वर्ग्य *a-svargyá*, mfn. not leading to heaven, ŚBr. x; Mn.; Bhag. &c.

अस्वस्थ *a-svastha*. See *a-sva*.

अस्वादु *a-svādu*. See *á-svadita*.

अस्वाधीन *a-svâdhīna*. See *a-sva*.

अस्वामिक *a-svāmika*, mf(*ā*, Kāraṇḍ.)n. having no possessor, unowned, MBh. xiii, 2633; Gaut. &c.
A-svāmin, *ī*, m. not an owner, not the owner, Mn. viii, 4.

अस्वार्थ *a-svârtha*, *a-svāsthya*. See *a-sva*.

अस्वाहाकृत *á-svāhākṛita*, mfn. not dedicated to the gods by the exclamation Svāhā, ŚBr.

अस्विन्न *a-svinna*, mfn. not thoroughly boiled, MārkP.; (*am*), n. non-application of sudorifics, Suśr.
A-sveda, mfn. not perspiring, L.; (*as*), m. suppressed perspiration, L.
A-svedana, mfn. not perspiring (as feet), VarBṛS.
A-svedya, mfn. where the application of sudorifics is prohibited, Car.

अह् 1. *ah* (defect. verb, only perf. 3. sg. *āha* & 3. pl. *āhúḥ*, RV.; AV. &c.; 2. sg. *āttha*, ŚBr. xiv (BṛĀrUp.); N.; Ragh. iii, 48; 3. du. *āhatuḥ*, Pāṇ. viii, 2, 35) to say, speak, RV. &c.; (with lexicographers) to express, signify; to call (by name, *nāmnā*), MBh. iii, 16065; to call, hold, consider, regard as (with two acc., for one of which may be substituted a phrase with *iti*), RV. &c.; to state or declare with reference to (acc.), BṛĀrUp.; Śak.; Megh.; to acknowledge, accept, state, AitBr.; Mn. &c.; to adjudge anything (acc.) to any one (gen.), Mn. ix, 44. [Cf. Hib. *ag-all*, 'speech;' *eigh-im*, 'I call;' Goth. *af-aika*, 'I deny;' Lat. *nego* for *n'-ego*, 'to say no;' *ad-ag-ium*, *ajo*, &c.]

अह् 2. *ah*, cl. 5. P. *ahnoti*, to pervade or occupy, L.

अह 1. *áha*, ind. (as a particle implying ascertainment, affirmation, certainty, &c.) surely, certainly, RV.; AV.; ŚBr.; (as explaining, defining) namely, ŚBr.; (as admitting, limiting, &c.) it is true, I grant, granted, indeed, at least, ŚBr. [For the rules of accentuation necessitated in a phrase by the particle *áha*, cf. Pāṇ. viii, 1, 24 seqq.]

अह 2. *áha*, *am*, n. (only Ved.; nom. pl. *áhā*, RV.; AV.; gen. pl. *áhānām*, RV. viii, 22, 13) = *áhar*, q. v., a day; often ifc. *ahá*, m. (e. g. *dvādaśāhá*, *try-ahá*, *shaḍ-ahá*, &c.) or n. (e. g. *puṇyâhá*, *bhadrâhá*, and *sudinâha*); see also *ahna* s. v.

अहंयाति *aham-yāti*, *-yú*, &c. See *ahám*.

अहःपति *ahaḥ-pati*, &c. See s. v. *áhar*.

अहकम् *ahakam*. See *ahám*.

अहंकरण *aham-karaṇa*, &c. See *ahám*.

अहत *á-hata*, mfn. unhurt, uninjured, AV. xii, 1, 11; VS.; not beaten (as a drum), AdbhBr.; unbeaten (as clothes in washing), unwashed, new, ŚBr. &c.; unblemished, unsoiled, BhP.; (*am*), n. unwashed or new clothes. **-tā**, f. uninjured condition, GopBr. **-vāsas** (*áhata-*), mfn. wearing new clothes, ŚBr. xiv; KātyŚr.
Á-hati, *is*, f. = *ahata-tā*, q. v., RV. ix, 96, 4.
Á-hanti, *is*, f. id., VS. xvi, 18 [vv. ll. *á-hantya*, mfn. 'indestructible,' TS. iv, and *á-hantva*, mfn. id., MaitrS.; Kāṭh.]
Á-hantya, **á-hantva**. See the preceding.
A-hanyamāna, mfn. (Pass. p.) not being struck, Āp.; BhP.

अहन् *áhan*, the base of the weak and some other cases of *áhar*, q. v., e. g. instr. *áhnā* [once *ahanā́*, RV. i, 123, 4]; dat. *áhne*; loc. *áhan* (Ved.) or *áhani* or *ahni*, &c.; nom. du. *áhanī* (see also s. v. *áhar*) and pl. *áhāni*; only Ved. are the middle cases of the pl. *áhabhyas* [RV.], *áhabhis* [RV., nine times], and *áhasu* [RV. i, 124, 9], while the later language forms them fr. the base *áhas*, q. v. **Ahni-ja**, mfn. originating or appearing during the day, VarBṛS.
Ahanā́, instr. with an earlier form of accentuation for *áhnā*. See before.
Ahanyà (4), mfn. daily, RV. i, 168, 5; 190, 3; v, 48, 3.
1. **Ahīna**, **ahna**. See ss. vv.

अहभून *ahabhū́na*, *as*, m., N. of a Ṛishi, TS. iv.

अहम् *ahám*, nom. sg. 'I,' RV. &c.; = *aham-karaṇa*, q. v., (hence declinable, gen. *ahamas*, &c.) BhP. [Zd. *azem*; Gk. ἐγώ; Goth. *ik*; Mod. Germ. *ich*; Lith. *asz*; Slav. *az*]. **-agrikā**, f. = *aham-śreshṭhikā* below, L. **-ahamikā**, f. (gaṇa *mayūravyaṅsakâdi*, q. v.) assertion or conceit of superiority, Pañcat. **-uttará**, n. id., AV. iv, 22, 1 & xii, 4, 50; (*aham-uttara*)*-tvá*, n. id., AV. iii, 8, 3. **-pūrvá**, mfn. desirous of being first, RV. i, 181, 3; R. ii, 12, 92. **-pūrvikā**, f. emulation, desire of being first, Kir. xiv, 32. **-prathamikā**, f. id., Kathās. **-buddhi**, f. = *aham-karaṇa* below, BhP.; pride, haughtiness, (*an-*, neg., mfn. 'free from pride') MBh. xiii, 5354. **-bhadrá**, n. = *aham-śreyas* below, ŚBr. i. **-bhāva**, m. = *-buddhi* before, BhP. **-mati**, f. id., ib. **-mama-tā**, f. id., ib. **-mamâbhimāna**, m. id., Comm. on ŚBr. xiv. **-māna**, m. id., ib.; egotism, VP.; (mfn.) having the conceit of individuality, VP.; MārkP.
Ahaṃ (in comp. for *ahám*). **-yāti**, m., N. of a son of Saṃyāti, MBh. i, 3767 seq.; VP. **-yú**, mfn. (Pāṇ. v, 2, 140) proud, haughty, RV. i, 167, 7. **-vādin**, mfn. 'speaking of one's self, presumptuous,' see *an-ahamv°*. **-śreyas**, n. claiming superiority for one's self, ChUp.; ŚāṅkhŚr. **-śréyasa**, n. id., ŚBr. xiv (BṛĀrUp.); KaushUp. **-śreshṭhikā**, f. id., L. **-sana**, mfn. obtaining or claiming for one's self, RV. (v, 72, 2 voc. du. incorrectly written in two words *ahám sánā*) & viii, 61, 9 (voc. sg.) **-karaṇa**, n. conceit or conception of individuality, BhP. **-kartavya**, mfn. 'to be done by self,' being the object of Ahaṃkāra, PraśnaUp. **-kāra**, m. conception of one's individuality, self-consciousness, ChUp. &c.; the making of self, thinking of self, egotism, MBh. &c.; pride, haughtiness, R. &c.; (in Sāṅkhya phil.) the third of the eight producers or sources of creation, viz. the conceit or conception of individuality, individualization; (*ahaṃkāra*)*-vat*, mfn. selfish, proud, L. **-kārin**, mfn. proud, Kathās.; Daśar. **-kārya**, mfn. = *-kartavya*, q. v., Vedāntas.; (*am*), n. 'that which is to be done by one's self,' any personal object or business, MBh. iii, 11206. **-√1. kṛi**, (Pot. *-kuryāt*) to have the conceit of individuality, BhP. **-kṛita**, mfn. conscious of one's individuality, Yājñ. iii, 151; egotistic, Bhag. xviii, 17; VP. &c.; proud, haughty, MBh. i, 8252, &c. **-kṛiti**, f. = *-karaṇa*, q. v., Bh. (*an-*, neg., adj. 'free from the conceit of individuality'). **-kriyā**, see *nir-ahaṃkriya*. **-candrasūri**, m., N. of an author, Sarvad. **-jush**, mfn. thinking only of one's self, Kum. xv, 51. **-tā**, f. self-consciousness, Comm. on BhP. **-tva**, n. the being a self or an individuality, NṛisUp. **-dhī**, f. = *-karaṇa*, q. v., BhP. **-nāman**, mfn. named 'self,' ŚBr. xiv. **-pūrvá**, &c., see s. v. *ahám*.

Ahakam, dimin. for *ahám*, 'I,' Pāṇ. i, 1, 29, Pat.

अहर् *áhar*, n. (the weak cases come fr. *áhan*, q. v., the middle ones fr. *áhas* [see below] or in RV. also fr. *áhan*, q. v.) a day, RV. &c.; a sacrificial or festival day, portion of a sacrifice appointed for one day's performance, AitBr. &c. (often ifc., as *dvādaśâhá*, &c., see s. v. 2. *áha*); day personified as one of the eight Vasus, MBh. i, 2582 seqq.; N. of an Āṅgirasa, KāṭhAnukr.; of a Tīrtha, MBh. iii, 6070; (*áhanī*), nom. du. day and night, RV.; AV. xiii, 2, 3; (cf. *áhaś ca kṛishṇám áhar árjunam ca*, 'the black and the white day,' i. e. night and day, RV. vi, 9, 1); *tád áhar*, acc. ind. on that very day, ŚBr.; *yád áhar*, acc. ind. on which day, ŚBr. **-ahar** (*áhar-*), ind. day by day, daily, RV. &c.; (*aharahaḥ*)*-karmán*, n. daily work, ŚBr. ix. **-āgama**, m. the approach of the day, Bhag. viii, 18 seq. **-ādi**, a gaṇa, Comm. on Pāṇ. viii, 2, 70. **-gaṇa**, m. a series of sacrificial days, KātyŚr. &c.; a series of days, BhP.; Jaim.; any calculated term, L.; a month, L. **-jaram**, ind. 'so that the days become old,' by and by, MantraBr.; TUp. **-jāta** (*áhar-*), mfn. born in the day or from day, not belonging to night or to the spirits of darkness, AV. **-dala**, n. midday, Sūryas. **-divá** (*áhar-*), mfn. (Pāṇ. v, 4, 77) daily, VS. xxxviii, 12; (*am*), ind. day by day, Śiś. i, 51; Pāṇ. v, 4, 77, Sch. **-divi** (*áhar-*), ind. day by day, RV. ix, 86, 41; AV. v, 21, 6. **-dṛiś**, mfn. beholding the day, living, RV. viii, 66, 10 (Nir. vi, 26). **-niśa**, n. day and night, a whole day, Mn. i, 74; iv, 97; (*am*), ind. day and night, continually, Mn. iv, 126; Pañcat. &c. **-páti**, m. (Pāṇ. viii, 2, 70, Comm.) lord of the day, VS.; MaitrS.; the sun, Ragh. x, 55; a N. of Śiva, L. **-bāndhava**, m. the sun, L. **-bhāj**, mfn. (said of a sacrificial brick) partaking of the day, ŚBr. x. **-maṇi**, m. 'the jewel of the day,' the sun, L. **-mukha**, n. commencement of the day, dawn, L. **-lokā** (*áhar-*), f., N. of a sacrificial brick, ŚBr. x; (cf. *-bhā́j* before.) **-víd**, mfn. knowing the (right) days or the fit season, RV. **-vyatyāsam**, ind. so that the order of the days is reversed, KātyŚr.
Ahaḥ (in comp. for *áhar*). **-pati**, m. = *ahar-páti*, q. v., Pāṇ. viii, 2, 70, Comm. **-śesha**, m. the remaining part of the day, Mn. xi, 204. **-saṃsthā́**, f. completion of the day, TBr. iii; Lāṭy. **-sahasrá**, n. a thousand days, ŚBr. x. **-sāmán**, n. a liturgy that is to be sung during the day, ŚBr. xi.
Ahaś (in comp. for *áhar*). **-cara**, mfn. wandering during the day, ŚāṅkhGṛ. **-śas**, ind. day by day, AitBr.
Áhas, the base of the middle cases of *áhar*, instr. pl. *áhobhis* [RV. (twice); VS.; ŚBr. &c.], dat. abl. *áhobhyas* [VS. &c.], loc. *áhassu* [ŚBr. x; AitBr. &c.] **-kara**, m. (Pāṇ. iii, 2, 21; gaṇa *kaskâdi*, q. v.) 'producing the day,' the sun, Rājat.; Bālar. **-triyāma**, n. day and night, Ragh. vii, 21.
1. **Aho** (instead of *ahā* [= *áhar*] in comp. before the letter *r*). **-ratna**, n. = *ahar-maṇi* above, Pāṇ. viii, 2, 68, Kāś. **-rathantara**, n., Pāṇ. viii, 2, 68, Comm. **-rātrá**, m. [pl., VS.; du., AV. & PBr.; sg. or pl., MBh. &c.] or n. [pl., RV. x, 190, 2; VS. &c.; du., AV.; VS. &c.; sg. or du. or pl., Mn.; MBh. &c.] = *ahar-niśa* (q. v.), a day and night, νυχθήμερον, (having twenty-four hours or thirty Muhūrtas); (*am*), ind. day and night, continually, L. **-rūpa**, n., Pāṇ. viii, 2, 68, Comm.

अहर *a-hara*, *as*, m., N. of an Asura, MBh. i, 2660 (v. l. *su-hara*); Hariv.; of a son of Manu, Hariv. 484 (v. l. *a-dūra*).
A-haraṇīya, mfn. not to be taken away.
A-hārayat, mfn. (Caus. p.) not losing (in play), Kathās.
A-hārin, mfn., gaṇa *grāhy-ādi*, q. v.
A-hārya, mfn. not to be stolen, not to be removed, Mn. ix, 189; unalterable (as a resolution or the mind &c.), MBh. v, 953; Kum. v, 8; Daś. &c.; not to be bribed, Mn. vii, 217; MBh.; (*as*), m. a mountain, L.; N. of a king, VP. **-tva**, n. the state of not being liable to be taken away, Hit.

अहरित *á-harita*, mfn. not yellow, AV.
A-harīta, *am*, n., N. of a Sāman.

अहर्ष *a-harsha*, mfn. unhappy, gloomy, sorrowful. **-máya**, mfn. not consisting of joy, ŚBr. xiv.

अहल *a-hala*, mfn. unploughed, unfurrowed?, Pāṇ. v, 4, 121; (cf. AV. xx, 131, 9.)
A-hali, mfn. id., ib.

A-halyā, f., N. of the wife of Gautama or Śaradvat, ŚBr. iii, &c.; N. of an Apsaras, L.; of a lake (cf. MBh. iii, 8087), L. — **jāra**, m. 'lover of Ahalyā (cf. R. i, 48, 15 seqq.),' Indra, Bālar. — **pati**, m. id., ib. — **hrada**, m., N. of a lake, SkandaP.; (cf. MBh. iii, 8087.) **Ahalyêśvara-tīrtha**, n., N. of a Tīrtha, ŚivaP. Rev.

अहल्लिक *ahallika, as*, m. a talker(?), ŚBr. xiv.

अहविस् *á-havis*, mfn. not offering oblations, RV. i, 182, 3. **A-havir-yājin**, mfn. offering a sacrifice without oblations, Āp.

A-havishya, *as* or *am*, m. or n. objects that are not fit to be offered as an oblation, Āp.

Á-havya-vah, m(nom. *-vāṭ*)fn. not offering a sacrifice, ŚBr. i.

अहश्चर *ahaś-cara* & *ahaś-śas*. See *áhar*.

Ahas, ahas-kara, & ahas-triyāma. See ib.

अहस्त *a-hastá*, mf(*ā*)n. handless, RV.; Mn.

अहह *ahaha*, ind. an interjection, as Ah! Aha! &c. (implying surprise, fatigue, pain, sorrow, pleasure, calling), Vikr.; Hit. &c. **Ahahâre**, ind. id., ChUp.

Ahahā, ind. id., L.

अहारयत् *a-hārayat*, &c. See *a-hara*.

अहावस् *ahā́vas*, ind. an interjection said to sound like a flourish at the end of a Sāman verse, ŚBr. iv.

अहि *áhi, is*, m. (√*aṅh*), a snake, RV. &c.; the serpent of the sky, the demon Vṛitra, RV.; (see also *áhirbudhnyà* below); a cloud, Naigh.; water, ib.; the sun, L.; a N. of Rāhu, L.; a traveller L.; the navel, L.; lead, L.; (in arithm.) the number eight; N. of a Ṛishi (with the patron. *auśanasa*) and of another (with the patron. *paidva*). [Zd. *aži*; Lat. *angui-s*; Gk. ἔχι-s, ἔχιδνα, ἔγχελυs, and ὄφιs; Lith. *ungury-s*; Russ. *ûgorj*; Armen. *ôz*; Germ. *unc.*] — **kānta**, m. 'liked by snakes (which are supposed to feed upon air),' wind, air, L. — **kośa**, m. the slough or cast-off skin of a snake, L. — **kshatra**, m. (= *-cchattra*, q.v.) N. of a country, MBh. iii, 15244. — **gopā** (*áhi-*), mfn. guarded by a serpent, RV. i, 32, 11. — **ghna** (*áhi-*), n. the slaying of the serpent or demon Vṛitra, RV. vi, 18, 14 (loc. *-ghne*); (see *-hán* below.) — **cakra**, n. a certain Tāntric diagram. — **cumbaka**, m., N. of a man, and *ahicumbakāyani, is*, m. a descendant of his, Pat. — **cchattra**, m. a kind of vegetable poison, L.; the plant Odina Pennata, L.; N. of a country, MBh. i, 5515; Hariv. &c.; (*ā*), f. sugar, L.; the city of Ahicchattra, MBh. i, 5516; Kathās. — **cchattraka**, n. a mushroom, Nir. v, 16. — **jit**, m. 'conquering the serpent,' N. of Kṛishṇa, L.; of Indra, L. — **tuṇḍika**, m. (= *āhituṇḍika*, q.v.) a snake-catcher, snake-exhibitor, L. — **dat** or **-danta**, mfn. having the teeth of a serpent, Pāṇ. v, 4, 145, Sch. — **deva** or **-daivata**, n. 'having serpents as deities,' N. of the Nakshatra Aśleshā, VarBṛS. — **dvish**, m. 'enemy of serpents,' an ichneumon, L.; a peacock, L.; 'enemy of Vṛitra,' Garuḍa, L.; Indra, L. (cf. *-jit* above). — **nakulikā**, f. the natural enmity between a snake and an ichneumon, Pat. — **nas**, mfn. having a nose like a snake, Pāṇ. v, 4, 118, Comm. — **nāman** (*áhi-*), n. any animal named snake, RV. ix, 88, 4; (*ahināma*)-*bhṛit*, m. 'bearing the name snake,' N. of Baladeva (as identified with Śesha), L. — **nirvlayanī**, f. the cast-off skin of a snake, ŚBr. xiv (BṛĀrUp.) — **patāka**, m. a kind of snake (not venomous), Suśr. — **pati**, m. 'sovereign of the snakes,' N. of Śesha, Vāsuki, and others, L. — **putraka**, m. a kind of boat, L. — **pushpa**, m. the plant Mesua Roxburghii, L. — **pūtana**, m. or °**nā**, f. sores on the hinder part of the body (of children), Suśr. — **phena**, n. (= *a-phena*, q.v.) 'the saliva or venom of a snake,' opium, L. — **bradhna**, m. (corrupted for *ahir-budhnya*, see below) N. of Śiva, L.; one of the Rudras, L. — **bhaya**, n. 'fear of a lurking snake,' a king's apprehension of treachery, L.; (*ahibhaya*)-*dā*, f. the plant Flacourtia Cataphracta Roxb., L. — **bhānu**, mfn. shining like serpents (N. of the Maruts), RV. i, 172, 1 (voc.) — **bhuj**, m. 'eating snakes,' a peacock, L.; the ichneumon plant, L.; a N. of Garuḍa, L. — **bhṛit**, m. 'carrying serpents,' Śiva, L. — **mat**, mfn. 'possessed of snakes,' the base of *āhimata*, q.v. — **manyu** (*áhi-*), mfn. enraged like serpents (N. of the Maruts), RV. i, 64, 8 & 9. — **mardanī**, f. 'killing snakes,' the ichneumon plant, L. — **māya** (*áhi-*), mfn. multiform or versatile like a snake, showing the same variety of colour and shape, RV. — **māra** or **-māraka**, m. (= *asi-meda*, q.v.) the plant Vachellia Farnesiana, L. — **meda** or **-medaka**, m. id., L. — **ripu**, m. (= *-avish*, q.v.) a peacock, L. — **latā**, f. = *-mardanī*, L.; the plant Betel, L. — **locana**, m., N. of a servant of Śiva, L. — **lolikā**, f. = *ahibhaya-dā* above, L. — **vallī**, f. the plant Betel, L. — **vidvish**, m. (= *-dvish*, q.v.) Garuḍa, L.; Indra, L. — **vishâpahā**, f. 'neutralizing the poison of snakes,' the ichneumon plant, L. — **śushma-sátvan**, m. one whose attendants (the Maruts) hiss like serpents (N. of Indra), RV. v, 33, 5 [the Pada as well as the Saṃhitā Text takes *ahi-śushma* as a voc. by itself, and Sāy. translates accordingly]. — **hátya**, n. = *-ghna* above, RV. — **hán**, m(dat. *-ghné*)f(*ghnī́*)n. killing serpents or Vṛitra, RV.; AV. x, 4, 7. — **hrada**, m., N. of a mythical lake (named in connection with Śālivāhana). **Ahìndra**, m. 'lord of the snakes,' Patañjali (mentioned under this name in Mahīpa's Anekārthatilaka). **Ahī-vatī**, f. 'filled with snakes,' N. of a river (?), Pāṇ. vi, 3, 120. **Ahîśvara**, m. 'lord of the serpents,' i.e. Śesha, L. **Ahy-árshu**, mfn. gliding or shooting like a snake (perhaps N. of a bird), RV. ii, 38, 3.

Áhir budhnyàs, nom. sg. m. (instr. *áhinā budhnyèna*, RV. iv, 55, 6) = ὄφις Πύθων, the serpent of the deep (enumerated in Naigh. v, 4 and Nir. x, 44 among the divinities of the middle region, the abyss in which he lives being that of the region of mist), RV.; VS. x, 19; allegorically identified with Agni Gārhapatya, VS. v, 33; TBr.; AitBr.; in later times:

Ahir-budhnya, *as*, m. (considered as one word and therefore declinable as follows, dat. *ahir-budhnyāya*, PārGṛ.; instr. pl. *ahir-budhnyaiḥ*, MBh. v, 3899; often incorrectly written *ahir-budhna* or *-bradhna*) N. of a Rudra, PārGṛ.; MBh.; Hariv.; (*ās*), m. pl., N. of the Rudras, MBh. v, 3899 (see before); (*am*), n., N. of a hymn of the RV. (i, 186, 5 or vi, 50, 14), KaushBr. — **devatā**, *ās*, f. pl. or **-devatya**, n. 'having Ahirbudhnya as deity,' the Nakshatra Uttara-Bhadrapadā, L.

Ahī́, m. (only gen. sg., nom. and acc. pl. *ahyàs*; gen. pl. *ahīnā́m*) a snake, RV. ix, 77, 3; x, 139, 6; N. of a demon conquered by Indra and his companions, RV. x, 138, 1 & 144, 4; (cf. *ahīśúva* s.v.); (*ī́*), f. a cow, Naigh.; (*ī́*), f. du. heaven and earth, Naigh. — **nara**, m., N. of a prince, VP.

अहिंसक *a-hiṇsaka*, mfn. not hurting, harmless, innocuous, Mn. v, 45; MBh.; R.

Á-hiṇsat, mfn. not hurting, RV. x, 22, 13; VS.; AV.

A-hiṇsā, f. not injuring anything, harmlessness (one of the cardinal virtues of most Hindū sects, but particularly of the Buddhists and Jains; also personified as the wife of Dharma, VāmP.), ChUp.; Nir.; Mn. &c.; security, safeness, ŚBr.; AitBr. — **nirata**, mfn. devoted to harmlessness or gentleness, MBh. iii, 2248.

Á-hiṇsāna, mfn. not hurting, RV. v, 64, 3.

A-hiṇsya, mfn. not to be hurt, MBh. xii, 13088; Ragh. ii, 57.

Á-hiṇsyamāna, mfn. being unharmed, RV. i, 141, 5.

A-hiṇsra, mfn. innocuous, harmless, Kauś.; KātyŚr. &c.; (*am*), n. harmless behaviour, Mn. i, 29; (*ā*), f. the plant Momordica Cochinchinensis Spreng. (commonly called Kūrkavālī), L.; the plant Capparis Sepiaria, L.; Cactus Opuntia, Bhpr.

अहिका *ahikā*, f. the silk-cotton tree (Salmalia Malabarica), L.

अहिण्डुका *a-hiṇḍukā*, f. a kind of small venomous animal, Suśr.

अहित *á-hita*, mfn. unfit, improper, RV. viii, 62, 3; unadvantageous, ŚBr.; KātyŚr.; Mn. iii, 20, &c.; noxious, hostile, Kathās.; (*as*), m. an enemy, Bhag. ii, 36; Ragh.; (*am*), n. damage, disadvantage, evil, Āp.; R. &c.; (*ā*), f., N. of a river, MBh. vi, 328; N. of certain veins (cf. also *hitā*), Yājñ. iii, 108. — **kārin**, mfn. adverse, inimical, noxious, Sāh. — **nāman** (*á-hita-*), mfn. having as yet no name, ŚBr. — **manas**, mfn. not friendly-minded, inimical. **Ahitêcchu**, mfn. wishing evil, malevolent.

अहिम *á-hima*, mf(*ā*)n. without cold, not cold, ŚBr. xiv. — **kara**, m. 'having hot rays,' the sun, L. — **kiraṇa**, m. id., VarBṛS. — **tvish**, m. id. — **dīdhiti**, m. id., Śiś. vi, 41. — **mayūkha**, m. id., Kir. vii, 9. — **raśmi**, m. id., Śiś. xi, 64. — **ruci**, m. id. **Ahimâṇśu**, m. id., Kir. xii, 15.

अहिरण्य *a-hiraṇya*, mfn. without gold, Āp. — **vat** (*á-h°*), mfn. having no gold, AV. xx, 128, 6.

अहिर्बुध्न्य *ahir-budhnya*. See *áhi*.

Ahí. See ib.

अहीन 1. *áhīna, as*, m. (fr. *áhan*, Pāṇ. vi, 4, 145) 'lasting several days,' a sacrifice lasting several days, AitBr.; ĀśvŚr. &c.; (*am*), n. id., Comm. on Mn. xi, 197; (mfn.) only ifc. with numerals (cf. Pāṇ. v, 1, 87 & vi, 4, 145), e.g. *try-ahīna*, *dvy-ahīna*, qq. vv.

अहीन 2. *á-hīna*, mfn. unimpaired, whole, entire, full, ŚBr.; AitBr. &c.; 'not deprived of,' not withdrawing from (instr.), Mn. ii, 183; not defective or inferior, excellent, VarBṛS.; Ragh. xviii, 13; (*as*), m., N. of a prince, VP. — **karman**, mfn. 'not devoted to inferior or vile work' (or 'not neglecting one's regular actions'), Gaut. — **gu**, m., N. of a prince (son of Devānīka), Hariv. 825; Ragh. xviii, 13. — **vādin**, mfn. a witness capable of giving evidence, L.

अहीनर *ahī-nara*. See *ahī́* s.v. *áhi*.

अहीर *ahīra, as*, m. (= *abhīra*) a cowherd, L.

अहीरणि *ahīraṇi, is*, m. (cf. *áhi* and *ahī́*) a two-headed snake, L.

Ahī-vatī. See *áhi*.

Ahīśúva, *as*, m., N. of a demon conquered by Indra, RV. viii, 32, 2 & 26; 77, 2; x, 144, 3.

अहु *ahu*, mfn. only in *paró-'hu*, q.v.

अहुत *á-huta*, mfn. unoffered, not yet offered (as a sacrificial oblation), AV. xii, 4, 53; ŚBr.; Mn. xii, 68; one who has not received any sacrifice, AV. vii, 97, 7; (the fire) through or in which no sacrificial oblation has been offered, Āp.; not obtained by sacrifice, AV. vi, 71, 2; (*as*), m. religious meditation, prayer (considered as one of the five great sacraments, otherwise called Brahma-yajña), Mn. iii, 73 seq. **Ahutâd**, mfn. not eating or not allowed to partake of a sacrifice, AV.; VS.; TS.; ŚBr. **A-hutâśa**, m. not a fire, VarBṛS.

अहुर *ahura, as*, m. the fire in the stomach, MantraBr.; Gobh.

अहूत *á-hūta*, mfn. uncalled, unsummoned, RV. x, 107, 9.

अहृणान *á-hṛiṇāna*, mfn. not being angry, friendly, RV. vii, 86, 2; x, 116, 7.

Á-hṛiṇīyamāna, mfn. id., RV. v, 62, 6; x, 109, 2; AV.; (*am*), ind. willingly, TBr. iii.

अहृत *a-hṛita*, mfn. not captivated or carried away by (instr.), Ragh. viii, 68.

अहृदय *á-hṛidaya*, mfn. without a heart, ŚBr. xiv. — **jña**, mfn. not pleasing to the heart, ChUp.

A-hṛidya, mfn. not pleasing, not being to one's taste (as food), Suśr.

अहे *ahe*, ind. a particle (implying reproach, rejection, separation, L.), TS. iii (only in a sacrificial formula beginning with *áhe daidhishavya* and reoccurring in several other texts).

अहेतु *a-hetu, us*, m. absence of cause or reason, MBh. xii, 10511; not a real or sound argument, Nyāyad.; (in rhetoric) a certain figure of speech. — **tva**, n. (in Buddhist terminology) absence of cause or necessity, Sarvad. — **sama**, m. a particular sophism tending to prove an argument to be untenable, Nyāyad.; Sarvad.

A-hetuka, mf(*ā*, Naish. iv, 105)n. groundless.

A-haituka, mf(*ī*)n. id., Bhag. xviii, 22; causeless, unexpected (as *samṛiddhi*), BhP.; having no motive, disinterested, BhP.; (*am*), ind. without extraneous aid, through one's own ability or power, BhP.

अहेरु *aheru, us*, m. the plant Asparagus Racemosus, L.

अहेळत् *á-heḷat*, mfn. not angry, not displeased, favourable, RV.; VS.

Á-heḷamāna, mfn. id., RV. i, 24, 11; 138, 3 & 4; vi, 41, 1.

Á-heḷayat, mfn. id., RV. x, 37, 5.

अहो 2. aho, ind. a particle (implying joyful or painful surprise) Ah! (of enjoyment or satisfaction) Oh! (of fatigue, discontent, compassion, sorrow, regret) Alas! Ah! (of praise, cf. Pāṇ. viii, 1, 40 seq.) Bravo! (of reproach) Fie! (of calling, Kum. iii, 20) Ho! Halo! (of contempt) Pshaw! Often combined with other particles of similar signification, as *aho dhik* or *dhig aho, aho bata*, &c. **-purushikā**, f. for *āho-pur°*, q. v., L. **-bala**, m., N. of a commentator; N. of a place. **-vīrya**, m., N. of a man, MBh. xii, 8900.

अहोतृ á-hotṛi, mfn. not sacrificing, not competent to sacrifice, AV. ix, 6, 52; ŚBr.

Á-homa, *as*, m. no oblation, ŚBr. xii.

अहोपुरुषिका aho-purushikā, &c. See **2. aho.**

अहोरत्न aho-ratna, &c. See *áhar.*

Aho-rātrá and **aho-rūpa.** See ib.

अहोवीर्य aho-vīrya. See 2. *aho.*

अह्न ahna, only (like *ahá*) ifc. for *áhan* (or *áhar*), q. v., e.g. *aty-ahna, aparâhṇá, pūrvâhṇá*, &c., qq. vv.; (*āya*), dat. ind. formerly, Naigh.; instantly, speedily, MBh.; Kum.; Ragh.

अह्नवाय्य ahnavāyyá(5), mfn. (√*hnu*), not to be denied or set aside, RV. viii, 45, 27.

अह्निज ahni-ja. See *áhan.*

Ahnya, *am*, n. daily course (of the sun), PBr.; BṛĀrUp.; (cf. *rathâhnyá*); (see also *tirô-ahnya.*)

अह्यर्षु ahy-árshu. See *áhi.*

अह्रय á-hraya, mfn. (√*hrī*), not bashful, bold, conscious of one's power, RV.; abundant, RV.

Á-hrayāṇa, mf(*ā*)n. bold, keen, RV. i, 62, 10; iv, 4, 14; vii, 80, 2.

Á-hri, mfn. id., RV.

Á-hrī, mfn. shameless (as a beggar), ŚBr. xi; (*ís*), f. shamelessness, MBh. iii, 8494.

A-hrīka, mfn. 'shameless beggar,' a Buddhist mendicant, L.

अह्रुत á-hruta, mfn. not fluctuating, not stumbling, going in a straight line, RV.; VS. i, 9; not crooked, straight, AV. vi, 120, 3; VS. viii, 29. **-psu** (*áhr°*), mfn. of straight or upright appearance (N. of the Maruts), RV. i, 52, 4; viii, 20, 7.

अह्वला á-hvalā, f. not fluctuating, not stumbling, firmness, ŚBr.; the plant Semecarpus Anacardium, L.

आ Ā.

आ 1. ā, the second vowel of the alphabet corresponding to the *a* in far.

आ 2. ā, ind. a particle of reminiscence, Pāṇ. i, 1, 14, Pat.; also of compassion or pain [more correctly written 1. *ās*, q. v.], and of assent, L. [This particle remains unaltered in orthography even before vowels (which causes it to be sometimes confounded with 1. *ās*), Pāṇ. i, 1, 14.]

आ 3. ā, *ās*, m., N. of Śiva, L.; grandfather, L.; (*ās*), f., N. of Lakshmī, L.

आ 4. á, (as a prefix to verbs, especially of motion, and their derivatives) near, near to, towards (see *ā-√kram* &c.; in the Veda, of course, the prefix is separable from the verb; in a few cases, RV. i, 10, 11 & v, 64, 5, a verb in the imperative is to be supplied; with roots like *gam, yā*, and *i*, 'to go,' and 1. *dā*, 'to give,' it reverses the action; e. g. *ā-gacchati*, 'he comes;' *ā-datte*, 'he takes').

(As a prep. with a preceding acc.) near to, towards, to, RV.; (with a preceding noun in the acc., as *jósham* or *váram*) for, RV.; (with a following acc.) up to .... exclusively, AitBr.; (with a preceding abl.) from, RV.; AV.; out of, from among (e.g. *bahúbhya á*, 'from among many'), RV.; towards (only in *asmád á*, 'towards us'), RV.; (with a following abl., cf. Pāṇ. ii, 1, 13 & 3, 10) up to, to, as far as, RV.; AV. &c.; from, RV. i, 30, 21; (with a preceding loc.) in, at, on, RV.; AV.

(As an adv. after words expressing a number or degree) fully, really, indeed (e. g. *trír á divás*, 'quite or fully three times a day;' *mahimá vām Índrāgnī pánishṭha á*, 'your greatness, O Indra and Agni, is most praiseworthy indeed,' &c.), RV.; (after a subst. or adj.) 'as, like,' (or it simply strengthens the sense of the preceding word), RV., (after a verb) RV. v, 7, 7 & KenaUp.; (as a conjunctive particle) moreover, further, and (it is placed either between the two words connected [rarely after the second, RV. x, 16, 11, or after both, RV. x, 92, 8] or, if there are more, after the last [RV. iv, 57, 1 & x, 75, 5]; see also *ātas ca* s.v.)

In classical Sanskṛit it may denote the limit 'to,' 'until,' 'as far as,' 'from,' either not including the object named or including it (sometimes with acc. or abl. or forming an adv.), e. g. *ā-maraṇam* or *ā-maraṇāt*, 'till death,' Pañcat. (cf. *ā-maraṇânta* &c.); *ā-gopālā dvijātayaḥ*, 'the twice-born including the cowherds,' MBh. ii, 531; *ā-samudram* or *ā-samudrāt*, 'as far as the ocean' or 'from the ocean' (but not including it); *ā-kumāram*, 'from a child' or 'from childhood' or 'to a child' (cf. Lat. *a puero*), MBh. iii, 1403; *ā-kumāram yaśaḥ Pāṇineḥ*, 'the fame of Pāṇini extends even to children;' *ājānu-bāhu*, mfn. 'one whose arms reach down to the knees,' R. i, 1, 12; (see also *ākarṇa-* and *ājanma-*); (cf. *ā-jarasám, ā-vyushám, ā-saptama, ôtsūryám.*)

Prefixed to adj. [rarely to subst.; cf. *ā-kopa*] it implies diminution, Pāṇ. ii, 2, 18, Comm. 'a little,' e. g. *ā-piñjara*, mfn. a little red, reddish, Ragh. xvi, 51; (see also *ā-pakva, ôshṇa*, &c.) Some commentaries (e. g. Comm. on Ragh. iii, 8) occasionally give to *ā* in this application the meaning *samantāt*, 'all through, completely,' as *ā-nīla*, 'blue all round.'

Ā-√i, -√indh, -√inv, -√ish. See *ê, êndh, ênv, êsh.*

Ā-√īksh, -√īr, -√īsh. See *êksh, êr, êsh.*

Ā-√1. uksh, -√ūrṇu. See *ôksh, ôrṇu.*

Ā-√ṛi, -√ṛiñj, -√ṛidh. See *ā-r, ā-rñj, ā-rdh.*

आंश āṇśa, *as*, m. a descendant of Aṇśa, Comm. on Uṇ. v, 21.

Āṇśya, mfn. relating to *áṇśa* (q. v.), (gaṇa *saṃkāśâdi*, q. v.)

आंहस्पत्य āṇhaspatya, mfn. belonging to the dominion of Aṇhaspati (as the intercalary month), Gobh.

आकच् ā-√kac, Ā. (perf. *-cakace*) to tie or fasten on, Bhaṭṭ.

आकण्ठम् ā-kaṇṭham, ind. up to the throat.

Ākaṇṭha (in comp. for *ā-kaṇṭham*). **-tṛipta**, mfn. satiated up to the throat, MBh. iii, 15551.

आकत्थन ā-katthana, mfn. boasting, swaggering, R. vi, 3, 28.

आकत्य ākatya, *am*, n. the being *a-kata*, Pāṇ. v, 1, 121.

आकन् ā-√kan, Intens. (Impv. 2. sg. *-cākandhi*) to be pleased with (loc.), RV. x, 147, 3; (cf. *ā-√kā.*)

आकपिल ā-kapila, mfn. brownish, Kād.

आकम्प् ā-√kamp, Ā. (perf. *-cakampe*) to tremble (as the earth), Kād.: Caus. P. Ā. *-kampayate* (p. *-kampayat*, MBh. i, 1165, &c.) to cause to tremble, ChUp. &c.

Ā-kampa, *as*, m. trembling motion, shaking, R. iii, 62, 31; Vikr.

Ā-kampana, *am*, n. id., Car.; (*as*), m., N. of a Daitya, Kathās.

Ā-kampita, mfn. caused to tremble, shaken, agitated, VarBṛS.; Ragh. ii, 13.

आकर ā-kará, ākarika, &c. See *ā-√1. kṛi.*

आकर्णन ā-karṇana, *am*, n. (fr. *ā-karṇaya* below) hearing, Kathās.

Ā-karṇam, ind. 'up to the ear' or 'from the ear' (generally said of an arrow reaching to or being discharged from the ear in drawing a bow).

Ākarṇa (in comp. for *ā-karṇam*). **-mukta**, mfn. discharged from the ear (as an arrow), R. iii, 69, 16.

Ā-karṇamūlam, ind. up to the ear, R. iv, 9, 106.

Ā-karṇaya, Nom. P. *°yati*, (ind. p. *ā-karṇya*) to give ear to, listen to, hear, R.; BhP.; Śak. &c.

Ākarṇin, mfn. ifc. hearing, Naish. i, 28.

आकर्ष ā-karsha, °rshaka, &c. See *ā-√kṛish.*

आकल् ā-√3. kal, (impf. *ākalayat*) to tie, fasten, Śiś. ix, 45; (ind. p. *-kalayya*) to surrender, transfer, BhP.; to observe, notice, examine, take into consideration, reckon, consider, suppose, take for, BhP.; Śiś. iii, 73; Kathās. &c.

Ā-kalana, *am*, n. fastening, Śiś. v, 42; reckoning, L.; wish, desire, L.

Ā-kalita, mfn. shaken, MBh. iv, 2853; laid hold of, seized, MBh. iv, 762; Śiś. vii, 21 & ix, 72; tied, fastened, Śiś. i, 6; Kathās.; reckoned, L.; observed, examined, considered, L.

आकल्प 1. ā-kalpa, *as*, m. = *kalpana*, q. v., L.; ornament, decoration, MBh. iii, 13373; BhP.; Ragh. &c.

Ā-kalpaka, *as*, m. (= *utkaṇṭhā* or *utkalikā*) remembering with regret, missing, Kād.; (= *mud*) joy, L.; (= *moha*) loss of sense or perception, L.; (= *tamas*) darkness, L.; (= *granthi*) a knot or joint, L.

Ā-kalpam, ind. till the end of the world (lit. of a Kalpa), BhP.; Kathās. &c.

2. **Ākalpa** (in comp. for *ā-kalpam*). **-sthāyin**, mfn. lasting till the end of the world, Kād.

Ā-kalpântam, ind. = *ā-kalpam*, q. v., Ratnāv.

आकल्य ākalya, *am*, n. (fr. *a-kalya*) sickness, L.

आकल्ल ākalla, *as*, m. the plant Anthemis Pyrethrum, L.; (cf. *ākula-kṛit.*)

आकशापेय ākaśāpeya, *as*, m. a descendant of Akaśāpa, (gaṇa *śubhrâdi*, q. v.)

आकष ā-kasha, *as*, m. (√*kash*, 'to rub'), a touchstone, L.; (v. l. for *ākarsha*, Pāṇ. iv, 4, 9, Siddh. & v, 2, 64, Siddh.)

Ā-kashaka and **°shika**, mfn. vv. ll. for *ā-karshaka* and *°rshika*, q. v., s. v. *ā-√kṛish.*

आकस्मिक ākasmika, mf(*ī*)n. (fr. *a-kasmāt*, gaṇa *vinayâdi*, q. v.), causeless, unforeseen, unexpected, sudden, Suśr.; Pañcat. &c.; accidental, casual, BhP.; Sarvad.

आका ā-√kā, (perf. Ā. 1. & 3. sg. *-caké*) to endeavour to obtain, desire, love, RV.: Intens. (Impv. 3. pl. *-cakantu*; cf. *ā-√kan*) to be pleased with (loc.), RV. i, 122, 14.

Ā-kāyya (4), mfn. desirable, RV. iv, 29, 5.

आकाङ्क्ष् ā-√kāṅksh, P. Ā. *-kāṅkshati, °te*, to desire, long for, endeavour to gain (with acc.), AitBr.; Mn. x, 121, &c., (rarely with gen.) Mn. ii, 162; (perf. *-cakāṅksha*, R.; Ragh.) to expect, wait for or till, Lāṭy.; MBh. xiv, 1279, &c.; to endeavour to reach a place, turn to (acc.), Mn. iii, 258; (in Gr.) to require some word or words to be supplied for the completion of the sense, Pāṇ. Sch.

Ā-kāṅksha, mfn. (in Gr.) requiring a word or words to complete the sense, Pāṇ. viii, 2, 96 & 104; (*ā*), f. desire, wish, Suśr.; Sāh. &c.; (in Gr.) need of supplying a word or period for the completion of the sense, Sāh. &c.

Ākāṅkshin, mfn. ifc. wishing, desirous, hoping, expecting, MBh. xii, 4289; R.; Ragh. xix, 57; (see *a-phalâkāṅkshin.*)

Ā-kāṅkshya, mfn. ifc. 'desirable.' See *dṛiśâkāṅkshya.*

आकाय ā-kāya, *as*, m. See *ā-√1. ci.*

आकाय्य ā-kāyyà, mfn. See *ā-√kā.*

आकार ā-kāra, °raṇa, &c. See *ā-√1. kṛi.*

आकाल ā-kālá, *as*, m. 'the right time,' see *án-āk°*; (*é*), loc. just at the time of (gen.), TS. ii.

Ā-kālam, ind. until the same time on the following day, Āp.; Gobh. &c.

1. **Ākālika**, mfn. (fr. *ā-kālam*) lasting until the same time on the following day, Mn. iv, 103 seqq.; Gaut.; (fr. *ā-kālá* [Pāṇ.] or perhaps = 2. *ākālika*) momentary, instantaneous (as lightning), Pāṇ. v, 1, 114 (f. *ī*; also *ā*, Comm.); (*ī*), f. lightning, L.

आकालिक 2. ākālika, mf(*ī*)n. (fr. *a-kāla*) not happening in the right time, unexpected, Mṛicch.; Kum. iii, 34, &c.

आकालिकातीरम् ā-kālikā-tīram, ind. as far as the bank of the Kālikā river, Rājat.

आकाश् ā-√kāś (ind. p. *-kāśya*) to view, recognize, ŚBr. vii.

Ā-kāśá, *as*, m. (Ved.) or (later) *am*, n. (ifc. f. *ā*) a free or open space, vacuity, AitBr.; ŚBr.; MBh. &c.; the ether, sky or atmosphere, Naigh.; ŚBr.; Mn. &c.; (*am*), n. (in philos.) the subtle and ethereal fluid (supposed to fill and pervade the universe and to be the peculiar vehicle of life and of sound), Vedāntas. &c.; Brahma (as identical with ether), L.; = *ākāśa-bhāshita* below, Comm. on Śak.; (*e*), loc. ind. in the air (a stage direction implying something said by or to a person out of sight), Mṛicch.; Śak. &c. **—kakshā**, f. 'girdle of the sky,' the horizon, L. **—ga**, mf(*ā*)n. going through the atmosphere (as the Gaṅgā; see *-gaṅgā*), R.; (*as*), m. a bird, MBh. v, 7287. **—gaṅgā**, f. the Gaṅgā flowing down from the sky, MBh. iii, 10909; R.; Ragh. i, 78. **—gata**, mfn. coming from the air (as a voice), Kathās. **—gati**, f. going through the atmosphere, Pañcat. **—gamana**, n. id. **—garbhi**, m., N. of a Bodhisattva, Buddh. **—camasa**, m. 'a cup or vessel with ether,' the moon, L. **—cārin**, mfn. = *-ga*, mfn. above, Kathās.; (*ī*), m. a bird, MBh. i, 8384. **—ja**, mfn. produced in the sky. **—jananī**, f. a loophole, casement, embrasure, ŚāntiP. 2638. **—dīpa**, m. a lamp or torch lighted in honour of Lakshmī or Vishṇu and elevated on a pole in the air at the Divāli (Dīpāvali) festival, in the month Kārttika, L.; any lántern on a pole, L. **—deśa**, m. an open place, N. **—patha**, m. a way or road through the atmosphere, Kathās. **—pathika**, m. 'sky-traveller,' the sun, Kathās. **—poli**, m., N. of a poet, Śārṅg. **—pratishṭhita**, m., N. of a Buddha. **—pradīpa**, m. = *-dīpa*, q. v., L. **—baddhalaksha**, m. (in theatrical language) fixing the gaze on some object out of sight of the audience, Vikr. **—bhāshita**, n. (in theatrical language) speaking off the stage (to one out of sight), Comm. on Mṛicch. **—máya**, mfn. consisting of ether, ŚBr. xiv (BṛĀrUp.) **—māṃsī**, f. the plant Nardostachys Jaṭāmāṃsī, L. **—mukhin**, *inas*, m. pl., N. of a Śaiva sect (the adherents of which keep their faces turned towards the sky). **—mushṭi-hananāya**, Nom. Ā. °*yate*, to be foolish like one who beats the air with his fist, Sarvad.; (cf. MBh. v, 1334.) **—mūlī**, f. the plant Pistia Stratiotes, L. **—yāna**, n. a car moving through the air, Śak. **—yoginī**, f., N. of a goddess. **—rakshin**, m. a watchman on the outer battlements, L. **—vat**, mfn. spacious, extensive, ChUp.; (said of the fingers) extended, ĀpŚr. **—vartman**, n. = *-patha* above, Hit. **—vallī**, f. the creeper Cassyta Filiformis, L. **—vāṇī**, f. a voice from the air or from heaven, L.; (*īs*), m., N. of the author of a Hanumatstotra. **—śayana**, n. (ifc. f. *ā*) sleeping in open air, R. iii, 16, 12. **—salila**, n. 'water from the atmosphere,' rain, L. **—stha**, mfn. abiding in the sky, aerial. **—sphaṭika**, m. a kind of crystal (supposed to be formed in the atmosphere and of two kinds, Sūrya-kānta and Candra-kānta, q.v.) **Ākāśâtman**, mfn. having the nature of air, aerial, ŚBr. x. **Ākāśânantyâyatana**, n. 'abode of infinity or of infinite space,' N. of a world, Buddh. **Ākāśâstikâya**, m. the ontologic category of space, Jain. **Ākāśêśa**, mfn. 'who has no other possession than the air,' helpless (as a child, woman, pauper, or invalid), Mn. iv, 184; (*as*), m. 'lord of the sky,' Indra, L. **Ākāśôdaka**, n. = *ākāśa-salila*, q. v., L.

Ākāśīya, mfn. relating to the ethereal fluid, Suśr.; atmospherical, aerial.

Ākāśya, mfn. being in the air, (gaṇa *dig-ādi* and *vargyâdi*, q. v.)

आकिंचन्य *ākiṃcanya, am*, n. (fr. *a-kiṃcana*; gaṇa *pṛithv-ādi*, q. v.) want of any possession, utter destitution, MBh. iii, 13994; xii, 6571 seq.; 11901. **Ākiṃcanyâyatana**, n. 'abode of absolute want of any existence,' 'non-existence,' N. of a world with Buddhists, Lalit.

आकिदन्ति *ākidanti, is*, m., N. of a prince [or °*ntī*, f. of a princess, Kāś.], (gaṇa *dāmany-ādi*, q. v.)

Ākidantīya, *ās*, m. pl., N. of the tribe governed by the above prince (or princess), ib.

आकीम् *ā́-kīm*, ind. from (with abl.), RV. i, 14, 9.

आकीर्ण *ā-kīrṇa*. See *ā-√1. kṛī*.

आकुञ्च *ā-√kuñc*, Caus. (Pot. *-kuñcayet*; ind. p. *-kuñcya*) to bend (as a limb), Suśr.

Ā-kuñcana, *am*, n. bending (of a limb), Suśr.

Ā-kuñcita, mfn. bent (as the arm or the knee, &c.), Suśr.; Kum. iii, 70; Ragh. &c.; contracted (as the lips), R. iii, 31, 21; curled (as the hair), MBh. xiii, 882.

आकुण्ठित *ā-kuṇṭhita*, mfn. confounded, abashed, L.

आकुमारम् *ā-kumāram*. See s. v. 3. *ā́*.

आकुर्वती *ā-kurvatī*. See *ā-√1. kṛi*.

आकुल *ā-kula*, mf(*ā*)n. (fr. *ā-√1. kṛī*?) confounded, confused, agitated, flurried, MBh. &c.; confused (in order), disordered, ib.; filled, full, overburdened with (instr. or generally in comp.), eagerly occupied, ib.; (*am*), n. a place crowded with people, R. iii, 43, 34; 'confusion,' see *sâkula*. **—kṛit**, mfn. 'making confused,' the plant Anthemis Pyrethrum (see *ākalla*), Bhpr. **—tā**, f. perplexity, confusion, MBh. iii, 401; Sāh. &c. **—tva**, n. id., Śiś. ix, 42; Kathās. &c.; multitude, crowd, MBh. iii, 13711. **Ākulī-karaṇa**, &c., see below s. v. *ākulī*. **Ākulêndriya**, mfn. confused in mind, R.

Ākulaya, Nom. P. (p. °*yat*) to make disordered, Pañcat.

Ākuli, *is*, m., 'N. of an Asura priest,' see *kilāta*.

Ākulita, mfn. confounded, bewildered, perplexed, MBh. &c.; made muddy (as water), R. iii, 22, 18.

Ākulī (for *ākula* in comp. with √1. *kṛi* and *bhū* and their derivatives). **—karaṇa**, n. confounding, Pāṇ. vii, 2, 54, Sch. **—√1. kṛi**, Pass. (p. *-kriyamāṇa*; aor. *ākuly-akāri*) to be confounded or bewildered, Kād.; Śiś. v, 59. **—kṛita**, mfn. confounded, perplexed, Pañcat.; Kathās.; filled with (instr. or in comp.), R.; VarBṛS. **—bhāva**, m. the becoming perplexed, Sāh. **—bhūta**, mfn. perplexed, Śak.

आकू *ā-√kū*, Ā. *-kuvate*, to intend, ŚBr. iii.

Ā́-kūta, *am*, n. intention, purpose, wish, VS.; ŚBr. &c. (see *cittâkūtá* and *sâkūta*); incitement to activity, Sāṅkhyak.

Ā́-kūti, *is*, f. intention, wish, RV.; AV. &c.; (personified) AV. vi, 131, 2; N. of a daughter of Manu Svāyambhuva and of Śatarūpā, VS.; N. of the wife of Pṛithusheṇa, BhP.; N. of a Kalpa, VāyuP. ii. **—prá**, mfn. accomplishing the wishes, AV. iii, 29, 2.

आकूज् *ā-√kūj* (p. *-kūjat*) to coo (as pigeons), lament, Suśr.

आकूत *ā́-kūta* and *ā́-kūti*. See *ā-√kū*.

आकूपार *ākūpāra, am*, n. (fr. *á-kūp*°, q.v.), N. of different Sāman verses, PBr.; Lāṭy.

Ā-kūvāra, *as*, m. (= *a-kūv*°, q. v.) the sea, L.

आकृ *ā-√1. kṛi*, *-kṛiṇoti* (Impv. 2. sg. P. *-kṛidhi* and Ā. *-kṛiṇushva*; perf. Ā. *-cakre*) to bring near or towards, RV.: Ā. (Subj. 1. pl. *-karāmahe*; impf. *-akṛiṇuta*; perf. *-cakre*, p. *-cakrāṇá*) to drive near or together (as cows or cattle), RV. x: P. (Impv. 2. sg. *-kṛidhi*; ind. p. *-kṛitya*) to drive near, AV.; (perf. 1. pl. *-cakrimá*) to serve or prepare a sacrifice to (dat.), RV. iv, 17, 18; (impf. *ā́karot*) to call near (a deity), MBh. v, 426: Caus. *-kārayati*, to call near, invite to a place, MBh. iii, 15546 seq.; Pañcat.; Daś.; to ask any one (acc.) for anything (acc.), R. ii, 13, 2: Des. *-cikīrshati*, to intend to accomplish, Daś.: Intens. p. *-cárikrat*, attracting repeatedly towards one's self, AV. xi, 5, 6.

1. **Ā-kāra**, *as*, m. (ifc. f. *ā*, R. i, 28, 24; Ragh. xii, 41) form, figure, shape, stature, appearance, external gesture or aspect of the body, expression of the face (as furnishing a clue to the disposition of mind), Mn.; MBh. &c. **—gupti**, f. or **-gūhana** or **-gopana**, n. concealing or suppressing (any expression of the face or any gesture that might show) one's feelings, dissimulation, L. **—mat**, mfn. with √*vah*, 'to behave with a particular behaviour,' affect a gesture or appearance, Rājat. **—vat**, mfn. having a shape, embodied, Kathās.; well-formed, handsome, N. **—varṇa-suślakshṇa**, mfn. delicate in shape and colour.

Ā-kāraṇa, *am*, n. calling, summoning, Pañcat.; (*ā*), f. id., L.

Ā-kāraṇīya, mfn. to be called, Pañcat.

Ākārita, mfn. ifc. having the shape of, Vedāntas.

Ā-kurvatī, mfn. (pr. p. f.), N. of a particular rocky hill, R. ii, 71, 3.

Ā́-kṛita, mfn. arranged, built (as a house), RV. viii, 10, 1; done (as evil or good) to any one, VarBṛS.

Ā́-kṛiti, *is*, f. a constituent part, RV. x, 85, 5 (cf. *dvādaśâkṛiti*); form, figure, shape, appearance, aspect, KātyŚr.; ŚvetUp.; Mn. &c.; a well-formed shape, VarBṛS.; Mṛicch.; kind, species, Suśr.; specimen, RPrāt.; a metre (consisting of four lines with twenty-two syllables each), RPrāt. &c.; (hence in arithm.) the number twenty-two; (*is*), m., N. of a prince, MBh. ii, 126 & 1165 (v.l. *āṃ-kṛiti*). **—gaṇa**, m. a list of specimens, collection of words belonging to a particular grammatical rule (not exhibiting every word belonging to that rule but only specimens, whereas a simple Gaṇa exhibits every word), Pāṇ. Kāś. [Examples of Ākṛiti-gaṇas are *arśa-ādi*, *ādy-ādi*, *kaṇḍv-ādi*, &c.] **—cchattrā**, f. the plant Achyrantes Aspera, L. **—mat**, mfn. (= *ākāra-vat*, q. v.) having a shape, embodied, Kathās. **—yoga**, m. a certain class of constellations, VarBṛS.

Ā-kṛitī, f. (metrically for *ākṛiti*) form, shape, MBh. xv, 698.

Ā-cakrí, mfn. changing one thing (acc.) into another (acc.), RV. vi, 24, 5.

आकृष् *ā-√kṛish*, *-karshati* (ind. p. *-kṛishya*; Inf. *-krashṭum*, Kum. ii, 59) to draw towards one's self, attract, draw away with one's self, MBh. &c.; to draw (a sword), Mṛicch.; Vet. &c.; to bend (a bow), Daś.; Śiś. ix, 40; to take off (as a garment, &c.), MBh. ii, 2291; Mṛicch.; to draw out of (abl.), Vet. &c.; to withdraw, deprive of, take away, MBh. i, 6348; Bhaṭṭ. (fut. 1. sg. *-karkshyāmi*); Kathās.; to borrow from (abl.), Hit.; Pāṇ. iii, 1, 106, Siddh.: Caus. (p. f. *-karshayantī*) to draw near to one's self.

Ā-karsha, *as*, m. drawing towards one's self (as of a rope), BhP.; attraction, fascination or an object used for it, KātyŚr.; MBh. v, 1541; dragging (as of a stone), Car.; bending (of a bow), L.; spasm, L.; playing with dice, MBh. ii, 2116; a die (cf. *ākarsha-phalaka* below), L.; a play-board, L.; an organ of sense, L.; a magnet, L.; N. of a prince, MBh. ii, 1270, ed. Calc.; (*ās*), m. pl., N. of a people, ib., ed. Bomb. **—kārikā**, f., N. of a plant, L. **—krīḍā**, f., N. of a play, Vātsy. **—śva**, m. (fr. *śvan*) = *ākarshaḥ śvêva*, Pāṇ. v, 4, 97, Sch. **Ākarshâdi**, a gaṇa of Pāṇ. (v, 2, 64).

Ā-karshaka, mfn. = *ākarshe kuśala*, Pāṇ. v, 2, 64; (*as*), m. a magnet, VP.; (*ikā*), f., N. of a town, Kathās.

Ā-karshaṇa, *am*, n. pulling, drawing near, attracting, MBh.; Mṛicch. &c.; (in Tāntric texts) attracting an absent person into one's presence by magic formulas; tearing by (as by the hairs; in comp.), MārkP.; Veṇīs. (quoted in Sāh.); bending (of a bow), Car.; (*ī*), f. a crooked stick for pulling down fruit &c., L.

Ākarshika, mf(*ī*)n. = *ākarsheṇa carat*, Pāṇ. iv, 4, 9.

Ā-karshita, mfn. drawn near to one's self, Pañcat.

Ā-karshin, mfn. removing, attracting, see *malâk*°; (*iṇī*), f. = *ā-karshaṇī* above, L.

Ā-kṛishṭa, mfn. drawn, pulled, attracted.

Ā-kṛishṭi, *is*, f. attracting, drawing towards one's self (as of the bow-string in bending the bow), Kap. &c.; (in Tāntric texts) attracting of an absent person into one's presence (by a magic formula), also the formula (*mantra*) used for this purpose. **—mantra**, m. the above formula, Hit.

Ākṛishṭiman, *ā*, m. the being *ā-kṛishṭa*, (gaṇa *dṛiḍhâdi* [Kāś.], q. v.)

Ākṛishṭya, *am*, n. id., ib.

Ā-krashṭavya, mfn. to be dragged towards (acc.), Pat.

आकॄ *ā-√1. kṝī* (2. sg. Subj. *-kirāsi* and Impv. *-kirā*; p. f. *-kirántī*) to scatter or sprinkle over, give abundantly, RV. viii, 49, 4 & ix, 81, 3; AV. iv, 38, 2.

Ā-kará, *as*, m. one who scatters, i. e. distributes abundantly, RV. iii, 51, 3; v, 34, 4; viii, 33, 5; accumulation, plenty, multitude, R.; Suśr. &c.; (ifc. f. *ā*, MBh. iii, 1657; 16215) a mine, Mn.; Yājñ. &c.; a rich source of anything, Sāh.; place of origin, origin; N. of a country (the modern Khandesh), VarBṛS.; N. of a work (quoted in Kamalākara's Śūdradharmatattva); (mfn.) best, excellent, L. **—ja**, mfn. produced in a mine, mineral; (*am*), n. a jewel, L. **—tīrtha**, n., N. of a Tīrtha.

Ākarika, *as*, m. (Pāṇ. iv, 4, 69, Kāś.) a miner, VarBṛS.

Ākarin, mfn. produced in a mine, Kir. v, 7.

Ā-kīrṇa, mfn. scattered, Hit.; overspread, filled, crowded, surrounded, Mn. vi, 51; MBh. &c.; (*e*), loc. ind. in a place filled or crowded with people, Kāvyād. **— tā,** f. or **-tva,** n. fulness, crowd, multitude.

आके *āké*, loc. ind. (fr. 2. *añc* with *ā*, cf. *ápāka*, &c.) 'hitherward,' near, RV. ii, 1, 10, (Naigh. ii, 16); far, Naigh. iii, 26. **— nipá,** mfn. (said of the horses of the Aśvins) protecting in the vicinity, RV. iv, 45, 6; (= *ā* + *kenipá*, q. v., 'wise,' Naigh. iii, 15.)

आकेकर *ā-kekara*, mfn. squinting slightly, Kir. viii, 53; Kād.; Kathās.

आकोकेर *ākokera*, *as*, m. = Αἰγόκερως, the constellation Capricornus.

आकोप *ā-kopa*, *as*, m. a slight anger, Kathās. **— vat,** mfn. slightly angry with (loc.), Śiś. ii, 99.

आकौशल *ākauśala*, *am*, n. (fr. *a-kuśala*, Pāṇ. vii, 3, 30) inexpertness, want of skill, Śiś. xvi, 30.

आक्त *ākta*, mfn. (fr. *añj*) anointed, AV. x, 1, 25; (cf. *sv-ākta*.) **— kha** (*ākta-*), mfn. in whose nave the hole is smeared, TĀr. **Āktâksha,** mfn. whose eyes are anointed, AV. xx, 128, 7 & (*án-ākt°*, neg.) 6.

Āktâkshya, *as*, m. (fr. *āktâksha*), N. of a man, ŚBr. vi.

आक्न *ākna* (fr. *āc*). See *jānv-ākná*.

आक्रन्द् *ā-√krand*, P. *-krandati* (aor. 3. pl. *ākrandishuḥ*, Bhaṭṭ.) to shout out, PārGṛ.; MBh. iii, 11461; to invoke, call for help, Kād.; Kathās.: P. Ā. to cry with sorrow, lament, weep, MBh. iii, 2388; BhP. &c.: Caus. (Impv. 2. sg. *-krandaya*) to inspire (courage) by its sound (as a drum), RV. vi, 47, 30; (p. *-krandáyat*) to shout at, roar at, AV. ii, 36, 6; VS. xvi, 19; ŚBr.; to cry without interruption, L.; to cause to lament or weep, BhP.

Ā-krandá, *as*, m. crying, crying out, Mn. viii, 292; R.; war-cry, AV. xii, 1, 41; lamenting, weeping, MBh. &c.; 'a friend or protector' [only neg. *an-ākranda*, mf(*ā*)n. 'not having on whom to call for help,' 'without a protector,' MBh. i, 6568; iii, 13859]; a king who is the friend of a neighbouring king and checks the attack made on him by another king (called *pārshṇi-grāha*, q. v.), Mn. vii, 207; VarBṛS.; Kām.; (= *saṃgrāma*) war, battle, Naigh.

Ā-krandana, *am*, n. lamentation, Pañcat.

Ā-krandanīya, mfn. to be called for help, Kathās.

Ākrandika, mf(*ī*)n. running to where cries for help are heard, Pāṇ. iv, 4, 38.

Ā-krandita, mfn. invoked, Mṛicch.; (*am*), n. a cry, roar, Ragh. ii, 28; lamentation, BhP.; Vikr.

Ā-krandin, mfn. ifc. invoking in a weeping tone, Kum. v, 26.

आक्रम् *ā-√kram*, P. Ā. (p. P. *-krāmat*, MBh. i, 5018; p. Ā. *-krámamāṇa*, TS.; aor. *-akramīt*, RV.; perf. p. Ā. *-cakramāṇá*, RV. vi, 62, 2; ind. p. *-krámya*, AV. &c.) to step or go near to, come towards, approach, visit, RV.; AV. &c.; to step or tread upon (acc. [RV. x, 166, 5; ŚāṅkhŚr.; Mn. &c.] or loc. [MBh.; BhP.]); (ind. p. *-kramya*) to hold fast with the hands, seize, MBh. i, 5936; R.; to attack, invade, Mṛicch. (Inf. *-kramitum*); Mārk-P.; Hit.; (in astron.) to eclipse, VarBṛS.; to undertake, begin (with Inf.), R. iii, 4, 5: Ā. *-kramate* (Pāṇ. i, 3, 40; fut. p. *-kraṇsyámāna*) to rise, mount, ascend, AV. ix, 5, 1 & 8; ŚBr.; MBh. &c.: Caus. *-kramayati*, to cause to come or step near, TS.; ŚBr.; KātyŚr.; Lāṭy.; to cause any one (instr.) to enter into (acc.), Kum. vi, 52: Desid. *-cikraṇsate*, to wish to ascend, Pāṇ. i, 3, 62, Sch.

Ā-krama, *as*, m. approaching, attaining, obtaining, overcoming, VS. xv, 9; ŚBr. xiv; (cf. *dur-ākr°*.)

Ā-krámaṇa, mfn. approaching, stepping upon, VS. xxv, 3 & 6; (*am*), n. stepping upon, ascending, mounting, AV.; TS. &c.; marching against, invading, subduing, Kathās.; Comm. on Mn. vii, 207; spreading or extending over (loc., *dikshu*), Kathās.

Ā-kramaṇīya, mfn. *an-*, neg., not to be ascended.

Ā-kramya, mfn. *an-*, neg., id.

Ā-krānta, mfn. approached, frequented, visited, Mn.; R.; on which anything lies heavily, pressed by (instr. or in comp.), Mṛicch.; Pañcat. &c.; overcome, overrun, attacked, in the possession of (instr. or in comp.), Pañcat.; Kathās. &c.; overcome or agitated (as by feelings or passions), R.; Kathās. &c.; overspread with (instr.), Hit. &c. **— nāyakā,** f. (in theatrical language) whose lover is won or kept in obedience, Sāh. **— mati,** mfn. mentally overcome, having the mind engrossed or deeply impressed.

Ā-krānti, *is*, f. stepping upon, mounting, Kum. iii, 11; rising, Kathās.; 'overpowering, violence,' *-tas*, ind. from violence, Śiś. v, 41.

आक्रय *ā-krayá* and *ā-krayā́*. See *ā-√krī*.

आक्रष्टव्य *ā-krashṭavya*. See *ā-√kṛish*.

आक्री *ā-krī* (Pass. 3. pl. *-krīyante*) to purchase, obtain, Kām. (v. l. *ā-hāryante*, Pañcat.)

Ā-krayá, *as*, m. trade, commerce, TS. iii; (*ā́*), f. id., VS. xxx, 5.

Ā-krīta, mfn. purchased, Daś.

आक्रीड् *ā-√krīḍ*, Ā. (Pāṇ. i, 3, 21; p. *-krīḍamāna*) to play, sport, MBh. iii, 11095.

Ā-krīḍa, *as*, *am*, m. n. a playing-place, pleasure-grove, garden, MBh.; R.; (*as*), m., N. of a son of Kurūtthāma, Hariv. 1835. **— giri,** m. a pleasure-hill, Daś. **— parvata,** m. id., Kum. ii, 43. **— bhūmi,** f. a playing-place, MBh. i, 4649.

Ā-krīḍin, mfn. sporting, Pāṇ. iii, 2, 142.

आक्रुश् *ā-√kruś* (p. *-krośat*) to cry out at, call out to; *-krósati* (perf. 3. pl. *-cukruśuḥ*, R. ii, 20, 6; ind. p. *-kruśya*) to call to any one in an abusive manner, assail with angry and menacing words, scold at, curse, revile, TS.; ŚBr. &c.

Ā-krushṭa, mfn. scolded, abused, calumniated, Mn. vi, 48; MBh.; (*am*), n. calling out, crying, Suśr.

Ā-krośa, *as*, m. (Nir.; Pāṇ. vi, 2, 158) assailing with harsh language, scolding, reviling, abuse, Yājñ.; Gaut.; Āp. &c.; N. of a prince, MBh. ii, 1188.

Ā-krośaka, mfn. abusing, MBh. v, 1369.

Ā-krośana, *am*, n. scolding &c., L.

Ā-krośayitṛi, mfn. id., Vishṇus.

Ā-krośin, mfn. one who abuses or reviles, MBh. v, 1265.

Ā-kroshṭṛi, *ṭā*, m. id., MBh. i, 3557; xiii, 2196.

आक्लिन्न *ā-klinna*, mfn. 'wet,' i. e. touched with pity (as the mind), BhP.

Ā-kleda, *as*, m. moistening, L.

आक्ली *ā-klī*, ind. joined to √1. *as*, 1. *kṛi*, *bhū*, (gaṇa *ūry-ādi*, q. v.); (cf. *vi-klī*.)

आक्ष *āksha*, mfn. (fr. 1. *áksha*) belonging or referring to terrestrial latitude, Comm. on Sūryas.; (*am*), n. (fr. 2. *akshá*) = *ākshakī*, L.

Ākshakī, f. a kind of spirituous liquor prepared from the seeds of Terminalia Bellerica, Car.

Ākshadyūtika, mfn. (fr. *aksha-dyūta* s. v. 2. *akshá*) effected by gambling, Pāṇ. iv, 4, 19.

Ākshapaṭalika, *as*, m. (fr. *aksha-paṭala* s. v. 3. *aksha*) a keeper of archives or records.

Ākshapāṭika, *as*, m. (= *aksh°* s. v. 3. *aksha*) a judge, L.

Ākshapāda, *as*, m. (fr. *aksh°* s. v. 4. *áksha*) a follower of Akshapāda's (i. e. Gautama's) Nyāya doctrine, L.

Ākshabhārika, mfn. (fr. *aksha-bhāra* s. v. 2. [not 1.] *aksha*)? laden with a burden of Myrobalan fruits, (gaṇa *vaṇśâdi*, q. v.)

Ākshika, mfn. (fr. 2. *akshá*) relating or belonging to a die or to gambling &c., playing or winning or won at dice, Pāṇ. iv, 4, 2; contracted at dice (as a debt), Mn. viii, 159; made of the fruits of Terminalia Bellerica, Suśr.; = *ākshabhārika* above, (gaṇa *vaṇśâdi*, q. v.); (*as*), m. the tree Morinda Tinctoria, L.; (*ī*), f. = *ākshakī* above, Car. (v. l.) &c. **— paṇa,** m. a stake, bet, L.

आक्षर् *ā-√kshar*, Caus. *-kshārayati*, (only for the explan. of *ā-kshāra* below) = *ā-secayati*, ('to besprinkle'), PBr.; (p. *-kshārayat*) to calumniate, accuse (of any great crime), Mn. viii, 275.

Ā-kshāra, *am*, n., N. of a Sāman, PBr. **Ākshārânta,** mfn. 'ending with a calumniation or accusation' (said of a Yaudhājaya Sāman).

Ā-kshāraṇā, f. calumnious accusation (especially of adultery), L.

Ā-kshārita, mfn. calumniated, accused (especially of adultery or fornication), Mn. viii, 354 & (*an-*, neg.) 355.

आक्षरसमाम्नायिक *āksharasamāmnāyika*, mfn. (fr. *aksh°°mnāya*, q. v.) belonging to the alphabet (as a letter), Pat.

आक्षाण *ākshāṇá*, mfn. perf. p. √*aksh*, q. v.

आक्षि *ā-√2. kshi*, cl. 2. *-ksheti* (3. pl. *-kshiyánti* and impf. *ā́kshiyan*; Pot. 1. pl. *-kshiyema*) to abide, dwell in (acc.), inhabit, RV.; AV.; *-ksheti*, to possess, take possession of (acc.), RV.: cl. 6. *-kshiyáti*, to exist, AV. x, 5, 45.

Ā-kshít, mfn. dwelling, RV. iii, 55, 5; (cf. *án-ākshit*.)

आक्षिक *ākshika*. See *āksha*.

आक्षिप् *ā-√kship*, *-kshipati* (ind. p. *-kshipya*) to throw down upon (loc.) or towards (dat.), MBh. &c.; to strike with a bolt, R. vi, 78, 5; to convulse, cause to tremble, Suśr.; to draw or take off or away, withdraw from (abl.), MBh. &c.; to chase or drive out of a place (abl.), disperse, MBh. iii, 539; BhP.; to put into (loc.), Suśr.; to point to, refer to, hint, indicate, Pāṇ. vi, 3, 34, Siddh.; Sāh. &c.; to refuse, object to (acc.), MBh. iii, 16117; Kāvyād. &c.; to insult, deride, Mn. iv, 141; MBh. &c.; to excel so as to put to shame; (perf. *-cikshepa*) to challenge, call to a dispute &c. (dat.), Kathās.: Caus. (perf. *-kshepayām āsa*) to cause to throw down, MBh. iii, 15733.

Ā-kshipta, mfn. cast, thrown down; thrown on the beach (by the sea), Pañcat.; caught, seized, overcome (as the mind, *citta*, *cetas* or *hridaya*) by beauty, curiosity, &c., charmed, transported, BhP.; Kād.; Kathās. &c.; hung out or exposed to view (as flags &c.); put into (loc.), MBh. iii, 3094; pointed or referred to, indicated, Sāh. &c.; refused, left (as the right path), Kām.; insulted, reviled, abused; challenged, called to a dispute (dat.), Kathās.; caused, effected, produced, Kathās.; Comm. on Bād.; (*am*), n. 'absence of mind,' see *sâkshiptam*.

Ā-kshiptikā, f. a particular air or song sung by an actor on approaching the stage, Vikr.

Ā-kshepa, *as*, m. drawing together, convulsion, palpitation, Suśr.; Kum. vii, 95; Kād.; applying, laying (as a colour), Kum. vii, 17; throwing away, giving up, removing, Kum. i, 14, &c.; 'shaking about the hands' or 'turning the hand' (in pronouncing the Svarita), RPrāt.; charming, transporting, Kād. &c.; (in rhetoric) pointing to (in comp.), hinting, Sāh.; Daśar. &c.; (see also *ākshepôpamā* below); reviling, abuse, harsh speech, BhP. &c.; (cf. *sâkshepam*); objection (especially to rectify a statement of one's own), Suśr.; Kāvyād.; Sāh. &c.; challenge, Kathās.; N. of a man, VP. **— rūpaka,** n. a simile, in which the object compared is only hinted at, Kāvyād. **Ākshepôpamā,** f. id., Sāh.

Ā-kshepaka, mfn. pointing to, hinting at, Nyāyam.; reviling, L.; (*as*), m. convulsion, spasm, Suśr.

Ā-kshepaṇa, mf(*ī*)n. charming, transporting, Mālatim.; (*am*), n. throwing, tossing, Suśr.; reviling, Vishṇus.; objecting, Car.

Ā-kshepin, mfn. ifc. applying to, concerning, Yogas.; hinting at, Sāh.

Ā-ksheptṛi, mfn. one who refuses, Kathās.

Ā-kshepya, mfn. to be objected to, Kāvyād.; to be challenged (at play &c.), Kathās.

आक्षीब *ākshība*, *as*, m. (= *aksh°*, q. v.) the plant Hyperanthera Moringa, L.

आक्षील *ākshīla*, *am*, n., N. of a Sāman.

आक्षैत्रज्ञ्य *ākshaitrajñya*, *am*, n. = *a-ksh°*, q. v., Pāṇ. vii, 3, 30; (gaṇa *brāhmaṇâdi*, q. v.)

आक्षोट *ākshoṭa*, *as*, m. = *aksh°*, q. v., L.

आक्षोदन *ā-kshodana*, v. l. for *ā-cchod°*, q. v.

आक्ष्णु *ā-√kshṇu*, *-kshṇauti*, to rub up, polish up, KātyŚr.

आक्ष्यत् *ākshyat* [AitBr.] or *ārkshyát* [ŚBr. xii], mfn. (fut p.) only nom. pl. *°anti* with *áhāni*, certain days for the completion of the ceremony Ayana (performed for the Ādityas and Aṅgirasas).

आख *ā́-kha*, *as*, m. (√*khan*, Pāṇ. iii, 3, 125, Comm.) 'a pitfall' [Comm.], TS. vi (perhaps = *ā-khana* below).

Ā-khana, *as*, m. butt, target, ChUp.; ŚāṅkhŚr.; Lāṭy.

Ā-khana, *as*, m.?, Pāṇ. iii, 3, 125.

Ā-khanika, *as*, m. (= *ā́-kha* above, Pāṇ. iii, 3, 125, Comm.) a digger, ditcher, a miner, underminer, thief, L.; a hog, L.; a mouse, L. **— baka,** m. a stork in relation to a mouse,' (metaphorically) a man who behaves as an oppressor towards a weak person, (gaṇa *pātresamitâdi* and *yuktârohy-ādi*, q. v.)

Ā-khará, *as,* m. (Pāṇ. iii, 3, 125, Comm.) the hole or lair of an animal, RV. x, 94, 5; AV. ii, 36, 4; N. of an Agni, ŚāṅkhGṛ. **Ākhare-shṭhá,** mfn. abiding or dwelling in a hole, VS. ii, 1 (quoted in Kāś. on Pāṇ. vi, 3, 20).

Ā-khā, mfn. or f.?, Pat. on Pāṇ. iii, 2, 101.

Ā-khāna, *as,* m. = *ā-khana,* Pāṇ. iii, 3, 125.

Ā-khú, *us,* m. a mole, RV. ix, 67, 30; VS. &c.; a mouse, rat; a hog, L.; a thief, L.; the grass Lipeocercis Serrata, L.; (*us*), f. a she-mole or she-mouse, Pāṇ. iv, 1, 44, Sch. **-karīshá,** n. a mole-hill, ŚBr.; TBr. **-karṇa-parṇikā,** f. 'Myosotis,' the plant Salvinia Cucullata, L. **-karṇī,** f. id., L. **-kirí,** m. = *-karīshá* above, MaitrS. **-ga,** m. 'riding on a rat,' N. of Gaṇeśa, L. **-ghāta,** m. 'a rat-catcher,' a man of low caste and profession, L. **-parṇikā** or **-parṇī,** f. = *-karṇī* above, L. **-pāshāṇa,** m. a load-stone, L. **-bhuj,** m. 'mouse-eater,' a cat, L. **-ratha,** m. = *-ga* above, L. **-visha-hā** or **-vishâpahā,** f. (= *āhhu,* q. v.) 'destroying a rat's venom,' the grass Lipeocercis Serrata and the grass Andropogon Serratum (both considered as remedies for a rat's bite), L. **-śruti,** f. = *-karṇī* above, L. **Ākhûtkará,** m. a mole-hill, ŚBr.; KātyŚr. **Ākhûttha,** m. the rising up or appearance of rats or moles, a swarm of rats or moles, Pat. on Pāṇ. iii, 2, 4.

आखण्डयितृ *ā-khaṇḍayitṛi, tā,* m. a breaker, destroyer, Nir. iii, 10.

Ā-khaṇḍala, *as,* m. id. (said of Indra), RV. viii, 17, 12 (voc.); (Nir. iii, 10); N. of Indra, Mṛicch.; Śak. &c.; N. of Śiva, SkandaP.; (*ā*), f., i. e. *diś,* 'Indra's region,' the east, VarBṛS. **-cāpa,** m. n. 'Indra's bow,' the rainbow, Kād. **-dhanus,** n. id. **-sūnu,** m. 'Indra's son,' Arjuna, Kir. i, 24.

Ā-khaṇḍi, *is,* m. a kind of artisan, (gaṇa *chāttry-ādi,* q. v.) **-śālā,** f. the workshop of the above artisan, ib.

आखाटीश्वरतीर्थ *ākhāṭîśvara-tīrtha, am,* n., N. of a Tīrtha, ŚivaP.

आखाद् *ā-√khād,* P. (perf. *-cakhāda*) to eat, consume, RV. vi, 61, 1; ŚBr. iii.

आखान *ā-khāna.* See *ā́-kha.*

आखिद् *ā-√khid,* P. *-khidáti* (1. sg. *-khidāmi;* Impv. 2. sg. *-khidā*) to take away, draw to one's self, RV. iv, 25, 7; AV.; ŚBr.

Ā-khidá [MaitrS.] or **ā-khidát** [VS. xvi, 46], mfn. one who draws to himself.

आखिल्य *ākhilya, am,* n. (fr. *a-khila*), the whole, L.

आखु *ā-khú.* See *ā́-kha.*

आखुवग्राम *ākhuva-grāma, as,* m., N. of a village, Rājat.

आखेट *ā-kheṭa, as,* m. (√*khiṭ?*) chase, hunting, Kathās. **-bhūmi,** f. hunting-ground, ib. **-śīrshaka,** v. l. for *ākhoṭa-ś°,* q. v.

Ākheṭaka, *as,* m. = *ā-kheṭa,* Pañcat.; Kathās.; Vet.; a hunter, ib. **Ākheṭakâṭavī,** f. a hunting-forest, Kathās.

Ākheṭika, *as,* m. (also *akh°,* q. v.) a hound, L.; a hunter, L.

आखोट *ākhoṭa, as,* m. (= *akshoṭa,* q. v.) the walnut tree, L. **-śīrshaka,** n. a kind of pavement, L.

Ākhoṭaka-tīrtha, *am,* n., N. of a Tīrtha, VārP.

आख्यस् *ā-khyas.* See 1. *ā-√khyā.*

आख्या 1. *ā-√khyā,* P. (impf. *-akhyat*) to behold, RV. iv, 2, 18; (fut. p. *-khyāsyát;* perf. 3. pl. *-cakhyuḥ*) to tell, communicate, inform, declare, announce, ŚBr. xiii, xiv; Mn.; MBh. &c.; to call (with two acc.), Ragh. x, 22: Pass. *-khyāyate,* to be named or enumerated, ŚBr.; to be called, ŚBr. x, xiv: Caus. P. (2. sg. *-khyāpayasi*) to make known, declare, MBh. i, 7485: Ā. (Pot. *-khyāpayeta*) to cause to tell, AitBr.; ŚāṅkhŚr.

Ā-khyas, *ās,* m. a N. of Prajāpati, L.

2. **Ā-khyā,** f. (ifc. f. *ā,* Kathās.; Sāṃkhyak.) appellation, name, Prāt.; Pāṇ.; Mn. vii, 157, &c.; (= *saṃkhyā*) total amount, Mn. ii, 134; MBh. iii, 12831 (cf. Hariv. 515) & xv, 671; appearance, aspect, R. vii, 60, 12; (*ayā*), instr. ind. 'with the name,' named, Kathās.

Ā-khyāta, mfn. said, told, declared, made known, KātyŚr. (*an-,* neg.) &c.; called, Mn. iv, 6; MBh. &c.; (*am*), n. a verb, Nir. i, 1; Prāt.; (gaṇa *mayūravyaṇsakâdi,* q. v.)

Ā-khyātavya, mfn. to be told, Mn. xi, 17; MBh.

Ā-khyāti, *is,* f. telling, communication, publication of a report, Kathās.; name, appellation, ib.

Ākhyātika, mf(*ī*)n. (Pāṇ. iv, 3, 72) verbal, Comm. on Jaim. and on Nyāyad.

Ā-khyātṛi, *tā,* m. one who tells or communicates, AitBr.; Pāṇ. i, 4, 29, &c.

Ā-khyā́na, *am,* n. telling, communication, Pāṇ.; Kap.; Kathās. &c.; the communication of a previous event (in a drama), Sāh.; a tale, story, legend, ŚBr.; Nir.; Pāṇ. &c.

Ā-khyānaka, *am,* n. a short narrative, Pañcat.; Kād.; (*ī*), f., N. of a metre (being a combination of the Indravajrā and Upendravajrā).

Ākhyānaya, Nom. P. (ind. p. *°nayitvā*) to communicate, MBh. xii, 2452.

Ā-khyāpaka, mfn. making known, L.

Ā-khyāpana, *am,* n. causing to tell, R. v, 72 (colophon).

Ā-khyāpita, mfn. made known, MBh. iii, 11285.

Ā-khyāyikā, f. a short narrative, Pāṇ. iv, 2, 60, Comm.; Sāṃkhyak. &c.; (*°yika,* metrically shortened in comp.) MBh. ii, 453.

Ā-khyāyin, mfn. telling, relating, Mn. vii, 223; Śak.

Ā-khyeya, mfn. to be told or related, to be said or confessed, MBh.; Yājñ. iii, 43, &c.

Ā-cikhyāsā, f. (fr. Desid.) intention of telling or expressing, Nir. vii, 3; Pāṇ. ii, 4, 21.

आग *āga* = *āgas* in *án-āga,* q. v.

आगण्ड *ā-gaṇḍa-,* ind. (in comp. for *ā-gaṇḍam*) as far as the cheeks, Śak.; Megh.

आगम *ā-√gam,* P. *-gacchati* (Impv. *-gacchatāt,* ŚBr. xiv; 2. sg. *-gahi* [frequently in RV.], once *-gadhi* [RV. viii, 98, 4]; perf. *-jagāma,* RV. &c.; Pot. *-jagamyāt,* RV.; Subj. *-gamat;* aor. 3. sg. *-agāmi,* RV. vi, 16, 19; Subj. 2. du. *-gamishṭam,* RV.) to come, make one's appearance, come near from (abl.) or to (acc. or loc.), arrive at, attain, reach, RV.; AV. &c.; (generally with *púnar*) to return, TS.; ŚBr. &c.; to fall into (any state of mind), have recourse to, R.; Pañcat.; to meet with (instr.), MBh. iii, 2688: Caus. (Impv. 2. sg. *-gamaya*) to cause to come near, AV. vi, 81, 2; *-gamayati,* to announce the arrival of (acc.), Pat. on Pāṇ. iii, 1, 26; (Pot. Ā. *-gamayeta;* perf. P. *-gamayām-āsa*) to obtain information about (acc.), ascertain, Gobh.; MBh. v, 132, &c.; to learn from (abl.), MBh. v, 1247; Pāṇ. i, 4, 29, Kāś.; Ragh. x, 72: Ā. *-gamayate* (Pāṇ. i, 3, 21, Comm.) to wait for (acc.), have patience, Lāṭy.: Intens. *-ganīganti,* to approach repeatedly (acc.), RV. vi, 75, 3: Desid. (p. *-jigamishat*) to be about to come, ĀśvGṛ.

Ā́-gata, mfn. come, arrived, RV.; AV. &c.; come to or into (acc. [Mn. iii, 113, &c.] or loc. [Pañcat.; Daś. &c.] or in comp. [Mn. vi, 7; Ragh. iii, 11, &c.]); come from (in comp.), Yājñ. ii, 154; come into existence, born, R. ii, 85, 19; coming from (abl.), Pāṇ. iv, 3, 74; returned, ŚBr.; (with *punar*) Mn. xi, 195 & Hit.; meeting with an obstacle, pushed against (in comp.), Mn. viii, 291; occurred, happened, risen, Mn. ii, 152; MBh. &c.; entered (into any state or condition of mind), MBh.; R.; Kathās.; resulting (from calculation), Sūryas.; walked through (as a path), ŚBr. vi; (*as*), m. a new comer, guest, ŚBr. iii; (*am*), n. anything that has taken place or has fallen to one's share (opposed to *āśā́,* 'anything still expected or hoped for'), ŚBr. ii; (cf. *án-āgata* and *sv-āgata.*) **-kshobha,** mfn. confounded, perplexed. **-tva,** n. origin, Daś. **-nandin** [or **-nardin,** Kāś.], mfn., (gaṇa *yuktârohy-ādi,* q. v.) **-prahārin,** mfn. ib. **-matsya,** mfn. (Kāś. **-matsyā**), ib. **-yodhin,** mfn. ib. **-rohin,** mfn. ib. **-vañcin,** mfn. ib. **-sādhvasa,** mfn. terrified. **Āgatâgama,** mfn. one who has obtained knowledge of (gen.), MBh.

Ā́-gati, *is,* f. arrival, coming, return, RV. ii, 5, 6; VS. &c.; origin, Daś.; rise, origination (as of the world), R. ii, 110, 1.

Ā-gatya, ind. p. having arrived or come.

Ā-gantavya, *am,* n. impers. to be come to (acc. or loc. or adv. of place), R.; Pañcat. &c.

Ā-gantu, mfn. anything added or adhering, VPrāt.; KātyŚr.; adventitious, incidental, accidental, Nir.; Kauś.; Suśr.; (*us*), m. 'arriving,' a new comer, stranger, guest, Ragh. v, 62; Pañcat. &c. **-ja,** mfn. arising accidentally, Suśr.

Āgantuka, mfn. anything added or adhering, ĀśvŚr.; incidental, accidental, adventitious (as pleasure, pain, ornament, &c.), Suśr.; Vishṇus.; arriving of one's own accord, stray (as cattle), Yājñ. ii, 163; interpolated (said of a various reading which has crept into the text without authority), Comm. on Kum. vi, 46; (*as*), m. a new comer, stranger, guest, Kathās.; Hit. &c.

Ā-gantṛí, mfn. (fut. p.) about or intending to come, ŚBr. i.

Ā-gantos, Ved. Inf. 'to return,' ŚBr. xii.

Ā-gama, mf(*ā*)n. coming near, approaching, AV. vi, 81, 2; xix, 35, 3; (*as*), m. (ifc. f. *ā*) arrival, coming, approach, R. &c.; origin, Mn. viii, 401; R. &c.; appearance or reappearance, MBh. ii, 547; course (of a fluid), issue (e. g. of blood), Mn. viii, 252; Suśr.; income, lawful acquisition (of property, *artha, dhana, vitta, draviṇa*), Mn.; MBh. &c.; reading, studying, Pat.; acquisition of knowledge, science, MBh.; Yājñ. &c.; a traditional doctrine or precept, collection of such doctrines, sacred work, Brāhmana, Mn. xii, 105; MBh. &c.; anything handed down and fixed by tradition (as the reading of a text or a record, title-deed, &c.); addition, Nir. i, 4; a grammatical augment, a meaningless syllable or letter inserted in any part of the radical word, Prāt.; Pāṇ. Comm.; N. of a rhetorical figure; (*am*), n. a Tantra or work inculcating the mystical worship of Śiva and Śakti. **-kṛisara,** m. Kṛisara as offered at the arrival (of a guest), Kauś. **-nirapêksha,** mfn. independent of a written voucher or title. **-vat,** mfn. approaching for sexual intercourse, MBh. i, 3025; having an augment or addition of any kind, Comm. on VPrāt. **-śashkulī,** f. Śashkuli as offered on the arrival (of a guest), Kauś. **-śāstra,** n. 'a supplementary manual,' N. of a supplement to the Māṇḍūkyôpanishad (composed by Gauḍa-pāda). **-śruti,** f. tradition, Kathās.

Āgamâpāyin, mfn. 'coming and going,' transient, Bhag. ii, 14.

Ā-gamana, *am,* n. (ifc. f. *ā,* Kathās.) coming, approaching, arriving, returning, KātyŚr.; MBh. &c.; arising, R. iv, 9, 29; confirmation (as of the sense), Sāh. **-tas,** ind. on account of the arrival, MBh. iii, 1839.

Ā-gamita, mfn. learnt from or taught by (in comp.), Śiś. ix, 79; read over, perused, studied, L.; ascertained, learnt, MBh. i, 5434.

Āgamin, mfn. receiving a grammatical augment, Pāṇ. vi, 1, 73, Sch.

Ā́-gamishṭha, mfn. (superl.) coming with pleasure or quickly, RV.; approaching any one (acc.) with great willingness or rapidity, TBr.

Ā-gamya, ind. p. having arrived or come, N.

Ā-gāntu, *us,* m. (= *ā-gantu*) a guest, L.

Āgāmika, mf(*ā*)n. relating to the future, Jain.

Ā-gāmin, mfn. coming, approaching, Nir.; (gaṇa *gamy-ādi,* q. v.); impending, future, MBh. xii, 8244; Kathās. &c.; (with auguries) accidental, changeable (opposed to *sthira,* 'fix'), VarBṛS.

Ā-gā́muka, mfn. (Kāś. on Pāṇ. ii, 3, 69 and iii, 2, 154) coming to or in the habit of, coming to (acc.), MaitrS.; Kāṭh.; ShaḍvBr.

Ā-jigamishu, mfn. intending to come (with neg. *an-*), Pat.

आगर *ā-gará.* See *ā-√1. gṛī.*

आगरव *āgarava,* mfn. (fr. *a-garu*), coming from or formed of Agallochum or Aloe wood, Hcar.

Āgurava, mf(*ī*)n. (fr. *a-guru*), id., Śiś. iv, 52.

आगरिन् *āgarin, ī,* m., N. of a mixed caste, BrahmavP.

आगलित *ā-galita,* mfn. sinking down, drooping (as a flower), falling or flowing down, MBh.; R.; Kād.

आगवीन *āgavīna,* mfn. (fr. *ā-go*), (a servant) who works until the cow (promised as his wages) is given to him, Pāṇ. v, 2, 14.

आगस् *ā́gas,* n. transgression, offence, injury, sin, fault, RV.; AV. &c.; [Gk. ἄγος.] **-kārin,** mfn. evil-doing (with gen.), MBh. i, 4451. **-kṛit,** mfn. id., ib. 4449; Ragh. ii, 32. **-kṛita,** mfn. id.,

MBh. iii, 13701. **Āgo-múc,** mfn. liberating from crimes or sins, MaitrS.

आगस्ती *āgastī*, f. of *āgastya*, q. v.

Āgastīya, mfn. relating to Agastya, Pāṇ. vi, 4, 149, Comm.; (*ās*), m. pl. the descendants of Agastya, ib.

Āgastya, mf(°*stī*)n. (cf. Pāṇ. iv, 1, 114 & gaṇa *saṃkāśâdi*) referring to the Ṛishi Agastya or Agasti, MBh. &c.; coming from the plant Agasti Grandiflorum, Suśr.; (*as*), m. (gaṇa *gargâdi*, q. v.) a descendant of Agasti, AitĀr. &c.; (*ās*), m. pl. (cf. gaṇa *kaṇvâdi*) the descendants of Agasti, MBh. iii, 971; (*āgastī*), f. a female descendant of Agastya, Pāṇ. vi, 4, 149, Comm.

आगा 1. *ā-√1. gā, -jigāti* (Impv. *-jigātu;* aor. *-gāt*, 3. pl. *-guḥ*) to come towards or into (acc.), approach, RV. &c.; to attain, Śiś. v, 41; to overcome, visit (as fear or evil), MBh.

आगाध *ā-gādha*, mfn. 'a little deep,' = *a-gādha*, q. v., L.

आगान्तु *ā-gāntu.* See *ā-√gam.*

Āgāmika, ā-gāmin, ā-gámuka. See ib.

आगार *āgāra*, *am*, n. (=*ag*°, q. v.) apartment, dwelling, house, Mn. vi, 41 & 51; Suśr. &c. **-godhikā**, f. a small house-lizard, Suśr. **-dāha**, m. setting a house on fire, L. **-dāhin**, m. an incendiary, L. **-dhūma**, m., N. of a plant, Suśr.; (cf. *gṛiha-dh*°.)

आगावीय *āgāvīya*, *am*, n. the hymn (RV. vi, 28) which begins with the words *ā́ gâvaḥ*, ĀśvGr.

आगुण्ठित *ā-gunṭhita*, mfn. wrapped up or enveloped in (acc.), R. vii, 59, 23.

आगुर् 1. *ā-√gur*, Ā. *-gurate* (Impv. 2. sg. *-gurasva*) to approve, agree or assent to (acc.), RV. iii, 52, 2; AV. v, 20, 4; TBr.; (Pot. *-gureta*) to pronounce the Āgur (see the next), AitBr.

2. **Ā-gur,** *ūr*, f., N. of applauding or approving exclamations or formularies (used by the priests at sacrificial rites), AitBr.; ĀśvŚr.

Ā-guraṇa, *am*, n. pronouncing the Āgur, Comm. on ĀśvŚr.

Āgūḥ-karaṇa, *am*, n. id., Sāy. on AitBr.

Ā-gūrṇa, *am*, n. id., KātyŚr.

Ā-gūrta, *am*, n. id., Sāy. on ŚBr.

Āgūrtín, mfn. one who pronounces the Āgur, ŚBr. xi, xii.

Ā-gūrya, ind. p. having pronounced the Āgur, AitBr.; ŚāṅkhŚr.; KātyŚr.

आगुरव *āgurava.* See *āgarava.*

आगृ *ā-√1. gṛī* (3. pl. *-gṛiṇánti*) to praise, RV.

Ā-gará, *as*, m.? = *prati-krośá*, q. v.; (cf. also *amā-vāsyà*.)

आगै *ā-√gai* (aor. Ā. 1. sg. *-gāsi*) to sing to, address or praise in singing, RV. viii, 27, 2; (impf. *âgāyat*) to sing in order to obtain anything, ŚBr. xiv; ChUp.; (p. *-gāyat*) to sing in a low voice, TāṇḍyaBr.

2. **Ā-gā,** f. intonation; singing in a low voice, TāṇḍyaBr.; ShaḍvBr.

Ā-gātṛi, *tā*, m. one who sings to obtain anything, ChUp.

Ā-gāna, *am*, n. obtaining by song, ChUp.

Ā-geya, mfn. to be sung or intoned in a low voice, TāṇḍyaBr.

आगोपाल *ā-gopāla*, mfn. See s. v. 3. *ā́*.

आगोमुच् *āgo-múc.* See *ā́gas.*

आग्नापौष्ण *āgnāpaushṇá*, mfn. belonging to Agni and Pûshan, ŚBr. v; KātyŚr.

Āgnāvaishṇavá, mfn. (Pāṇ. vi, 3, 28, Comm.) belonging to Agni and Vishṇu, VS.; ŚBr.; AitBr.; referring to Agni and Vishṇu (as a chapter or a series of hymns), (gaṇa *vimuktâdi*, q. v.)

Āgnika, mf(*ī*)n. belonging to the preparation of the sacrificial fire, KātyŚr.; ĀpŚr.

Āgnidatteya, mfn. relating to Agnidatta, (gaṇa *sakhy-ādi*, q. v.; not in Kāś.)

Āgnipada, mfn., (gaṇa *vyushṭâdi*, q. v.)

Āgnipātnī-vatī, f. (scil. *ṛic*) the verse containing the words *ágne pátnīr* (i. e. RV. i, 22, 9), KaushBr.

Āgnipāvamānī, f. (scil. *ṛic*) the verse containing the words *ágne pavase* (i. e. RV. ix, 66, 19), TāṇḍyaBr.; (cf. *āgneya-pāv*°.)

Āgnimārutá, mf(*ī*)n. (Pāṇ. vi, 3, 28; vii, 3, 21) belonging or referring to Agni and the Maruts, VS. xxiv, 7; Nir.; (*as*), m. (= *agni-māruti*, q. v.) a patron. N. of Agastya, L.; (*am*), n. (i. e. *śastram*) a litany addressed to Agni and the Maruts, ŚBr.; AitBr. &c.

Āgnivāruṇá, mf(*ī́*)n. (Pāṇ. vi, 3, 28; vii, 3, 23) belonging or referring to Agni and Varuṇa, MaitrS.

Ā́gniveśi, *is*, m. a descendant of Agniveśa, RV. v, 34, 9.

Āgniveśyá, mfn. (gaṇa *gargâdi*, q. v.) belonging or referring to Agniveśa; (*as*), m., N. of a teacher (descendant of Agniveśa), ŚBr. xiv (BṛĀr-Up.); TUp.; MBh. xiv, 1903.

Āgniveśyāyana, mfn. descending from Agniveśya (as a family), BhP.; (*as*), m., N. of a grammarian, TPrāt.

Āgniśarmāyaṇa, *as*, m. a descendant of Agniśarman, (gaṇas *naḍâdi* and *bāhv-ādi*, qq. vv.)

Āgniśarmi, *is*, m. id., ib.

Āgniśarmīya, mfn. belonging or referring to Āgniśarmi, (gaṇa *gahâdi*, q. v.)

Āgnishṭomika, mf(*ī*, Pāṇ. v, 1, 95, Comm.)n. (Pāṇ. iv, 3, 68, Comm.) belonging to the Agnishṭoma sacrifice, ŚBr. v.; studying or knowing the ceremonies of the Agnishṭoma, Pāṇ. iv, 2, 60, Comm.

Āgnishṭomīya, mfn. belonging to the Agnishṭoma, ĀpŚr.

Āgnishṭomya, *am*, n. the state or condition of the Agnishṭoma, Lāṭy.

Āgnihotrika, mfn. belonging to the Agnihotra, Comm. on ĀpŚr.

Āgnîdhra, mfn. coming from or belonging to the Agnîdh (i. e. to the priest who kindles the fire), RV. ii, 36, 4; KātyŚr.; (*as*), m. (= *agnī́dh*) the priest who kindles the fire, ŚBr.; AitBr. &c.; fire, BhP.; N. of a son of Manu Svāyambhuva, Hariv. 415; of a son of Priyavrata, BhP.; (*ā*), f. care of the sacred fire, L.; (*am*), n. (Pāṇ. iv, 3, 120, Comm.; v, 4, 37, Comm.) the place where a sacrificial fire is kindled, AitBr.; ŚBr.; KātyŚr.; the function of the priest who kindles the sacred fire, ŚBr.; KātyŚr.

Āgnîdhraka, *as*, m., N. of one of the seven Ṛishis in the twelfth Manvantara, BhP.

Āgnîdhrīya, *as*, m. 'being within the Āgnīdhra or the place where a sacrificial fire is kindled,' the fire (*agni*) within the Āgnīdhra, AitBr.; SBr. &c.; the fire-place (*dhishṇya*) within the Āgnīdhra, ŚBr.; KātyŚr.; ĀśvŚr.

Āgnîdhrya, mf(*ā*)n. belonging to the priest who kindles the sacred fire, Kāṭh. (quoted in Comm. on KātyŚr.)

Āgnîndra, mfn. consecrated to Agni and Indra, MānGṛ.

Āgnêndra, mf(*ī*)n. (Pāṇ. vi, 3, 28; vii, 3, 22) id., AitBr.

Āgneyá, mf(*ī́*)n. (Pāṇ. iv, 2, 8, Comm.) belonging or relating or consecrated to fire or its deity Agni, VS. xxiv, 6; AitBr.; [with *kīṭa*, m. an insect which flies into the fire (applied to a thief who breaks into a room and extinguishes the lamp), Mṛicch.]; belonging or consecrated to Agnāyī (wife of Agni), Pāṇ. vi, 3, 35, Comm.; south-eastern, VarBṛS.; (*as*), m., N. of Skanda, MBh. iii, 14630; of Agastya (cf. *āgnimārutá* above), L.; (*ās*), m. pl., N. of a people, MBh. iii, 15256 (v. l. *āgreya*); (*ī*), f., N. of a daughter of Agni and wife of Ūru, Hariv.; VP.; (= *agnāyī*) the wife of Agni, L.; the south-east quarter (of which Agni is the regent), VarBṛS.; (*am*), n. blood, L.; ghee or clarified butter, L.; gold, L.; the Nakshatra Kṛittikā, VarBṛS.; Sūryas.; N. of a Sāman. **-pāvamānī,** f. = *āgnipāvamānī*, q. v., MaitrS. **-purāṇa,** n. = *agni-purāṇa*, q. v., Sāh. **Āgneyâstra,** n. 'fiery weapon,' N. of a Tāntric formula. **Āgneyâindra,** mfn. belonging to Agni and Indra, DaivBr.; f. *āgneyy-aindrī*, i. e. *ṛic*, a verse addressed to Agni and Indra, TāṇḍyaBr.

Āgneyy-aindrī, f. See *āgneyâindra* above.

Āgnyâdheyika, mf(*ī*)n. belonging to the Agnyâdheya (q. v.), KātyŚr.

आग्रन्थ् *ā-√granth*, P. to twine round.

Ā-grantham, ind. p. twining round, AitBr. v, 15, 10.

आग्रभोजनिक *āgrabhojanika*, mfn. (fr. *agra-bhojana*), one to whom food is first offered, Pāṇ. iv, 4, 66, Comm.

Āgrayaṇá, *as*, m. (fr. *ágra*), the first Soma libation at the Agnishṭoma sacrifice (see *gráha*), VS.; TS. &c.; a form of Agni, MBh. iii, 14188 seqq.; (*ī*), f. (scil. *ishṭi*) an oblation consisting of first-fruits, Comm. on ŚāṅkhGṛ.; (*am*), n. oblation consisting of first-fruits at the end of the rainy season, ŚBr.; AitBr. &c.; Mn. vi, 10, &c. **-pātrá,** n. the vessel used for the Āgrayaṇa libation, ŚBr. iv. **-sthālī́,** f. id., TBr.; ĀpŚr. **Āgrayaṇâgrá,** mfn. beginning with the Āgrayaṇa libation, ŚBr. iv. **Āgrayaṇêshṭí,** f. oblation of the first-fruits (in harvest), ŚBr.; Yājñ. i, 125.

Āgrayaṇaka, *am*, n. oblation consisting of the first-fruits, KātyŚr.; (ifc.) R. iii, 6, 16.

Āgrahāyaṇa, *as*, m. = *agra-hāyaṇa* (q. v.), Pāṇ. v, 4, 36, Comm.; (*ī*), f. (gaṇa *gaurâdi*, q. v.; scil. *paurṇamāsī*) the day of full moon in the month Agrahāyaṇa, ŚāṅkhŚr. &c.; (ifc. ind. °*ṇi* or °*ṇam*, Pāṇ. v, 4, 110); a kind of Pāka-yajña, Gaut.; Bhav-P. i, &c.; N. of the constellation Mṛiga-śiras, L.

Āgrahāyaṇaka, mfn. to be paid (as a debt) on the day of full moon of the month Agrahāyaṇa, Pāṇ. iv, 3, 50.

Āgrahāyaṇika, mfn. id., Pāṇ. iv, 3, 50; containing a full moon of Agrahāyaṇa (as a month or half a month or a year), Pāṇ. iv, 2, 22.

Āgrahārika, mfn. one who appropriates to himself an Agra-hāra or an endowment of lands or villages conferred upon Brāhmans, L.

1. **Āgrāyaṇa,** *as*, m. (gaṇa *naḍâdi*, q. v.) 'descendant of Agra,' N. of a grammarian, Nir.; of a Dārbhāyaṇa, Pāṇ. iv, 2, 102.

2. **Āgrāyaṇa,** *am*, n. (Pāṇ. v, 4, 36, Comm.) = *āgrayaṇa*, n. above, Kāṭh.; ĀpŚr.; (v. l. for *āgray*°, R.; Yājñ. i, 125, &c.)

आग्रस् *ā-√gras*, to devour, BhP.

Ā-grasta, mfn. bored, perforated by (in comp.), Comm. on KātyŚr.

आग्रह् *ā-√grah* (1. sg. Ā. *-gṛibhṇe;* Impv. 2. du. *-gṛihṇītam*) to hold in (as horses), RV. viii, 45, 39; AV.

Ā-graha, *as*, m. insisting on, strong or obstinate inclination for, obstinacy, whim, Kathās.; Śārṅg.; (= *grahaṇa*) seizing, taking, L.; favour, affection, L.; (*āt, eṇa*), abl. instr. ind. obstinately, Kathās.

Ā-jighṛikshu, mfn. intending to seize, Kād.

आग्रहायण *āgrahāyaṇa*, &c. See above.

आग्रेय *āgreya*, v. l. for *āgneya* (N. of a people), q. v.

आग्ला *āglā*, f. (√*glai*), languor?, GopBr. i, 2, 21.

आघट्ट् *ā-√ghaṭṭ*, Caus. *-ghaṭṭayati*, to touch on (as in speaking), Kām.

Ā-ghaṭṭaka, *as*, m. 'causing friction,' the plant Desmochæta Atropurpurea, L.

Ā-ghaṭṭana, *am*, n. friction, rubbing, contact, L.; (*ā*), f. id., Śiś. i, 10.

Ā-ghāṭá, *as*, m. a musical instrument (used for accompanying a dance), cymbal or rattle, AV. iv, 37, 4; boundary, L.; the plant Achyranthes Aspera, L.; ifc. for *ā-ghāta* (see *cārv-āghāṭa* and *dārv-āgh*°), Pāṇ. iii, 2, 49, Comm.

Ā-ghāṭi, *is*, m. f. (= °*ṭá* above) a cymbal or rattle, RV. x, 146, 2.

आघमर्षण *āghamarshaṇa*, *as*, m. a descendant of Agha-marshaṇa (q. v.)

आघर्षण *ā-gharshaṇa*, *am*, n. (√*ghṛish*), rubbing, friction, L.; (*ī*), f. a brush, rubber, L.

आघाट *ā-ghāṭá* and °*ṭi.* See *ā-√ghaṭṭ.*

आघात *ā-ghāta*, *as*, m. (*ā-√han*), ifc. 'a striker, beater' (see *āḍambarāgh*° and *dundubhy-āgh*°); striking; a stroke, blow with or on (in comp.), MBh.; killing, Yājñ. iii, 275; retention (of urine &c.), Suśr., (cf. *mūtrāgh*°); misfortune, pain, L.; place of execution, BhP.; Hit.; a slaughter-house, Mṛicch. **-sthāna,** n. a slaughter-house, VarBṛS.

Ā-ghātana, *am*, n. a slaughter-house, Suśr.; place of execution, Buddh.

Ā-ghnat, mfn. (p. P.), Pāṇ. iii, 1, 108, Pat.

Ā-ghnāna, mfn. (p. Ā.) beating (as with the wings); brandishing (a fire-brand), Bhaṭṭ.

Ā-ghnīya. See *ā-√han.*

आघार *ā-ghārá.* See *ā-√ghṛi.*

आघुष् *ā-√ghush*, P. (Subj. 3. pl. *-ghóshān;*

p. *-ghoshat*) to listen to (acc. or gen.), RV.; (Subj. *-ghoshāt*) to make one's self audible, RV. v, 37, 3; to cry aloud, proclaim, RV. (also Ā. *-ghoshate*, i, 83, 6); VS.: Caus. *-ghoshayati*, to proclaim aloud, Pat.; to complain continually, L.; see also *ā-ghoshāyat*, &c.

Ā-ghosha, *as*, m. calling out to, invocation, Nir.; proclaiming, boastful statement, Sarvad.

Ā-ghoshaṇā, f. public announcement, Pañcat.

Ā-ghoshāyat, mfn. (Caus. p.) causing to sound, RV. x, 76, 6; 94, 4; causing to proclaim aloud, Bhaṭṭ.

Ā-ghoshita, mfn. proclaimed aloud, MBh. iii, 647.

आघूर्ण् *ā-√ghūrṇ, -ghūrṇati* (perf. 3. pl. *-jughūrṇuḥ*, Bhaṭṭ.) to fluctuate, whirl, Mṛicch.; Sāh.

Ā-ghūrṇa, mfn. fluctuating, whirling round, BhP.

Ā-ghūrṇana, *am*, n. fluctuating.

Ā-ghūrṇita, mfn. whirled round, fluctuating, MBh. i, 2850; Hariv.; BhP. &c.

आघृ *ā-√ghṛi, -jigharti* (1. sg. *-jigharmi*) to sprinkle (with fat), RV.; VS.; to throw towards (loc.), RV. iv, 17, 14; v, 48, 3: Caus. *-ghārāyati*, to sprinkle, TS.; ŚBr.; ĀśvGṛ.

Ā-ghārá, *as*, m. sprinkling clarified butter upon the fire at certain sacrifices, TS.; ŚBr.; KātyŚr.; ĀśvGṛ.; clarified butter, L.

आघृणि *ā-ghṛiṇi*, mfn. glowing with heat (N. of Pūshan), RV. **Āghṛiṇi-vasu,** mfn. rich with heat (N. of Agni), RV. viii, 60, 20 (voc.)

आघोष *ā-ghosha*, &c. See *ā-√ghush*.

आघ्नत् *ā-ghnat*. See *ā-ghāta*.

Ā-ghnāna. See ib.

आघ्रा *ā-√ghrā, -jighrati* (p. *-jighrat*; ind. p. *-ghrāya*; Impv. 2. sg. *-jighra*; impf. Ā. *ājighrata*, MBh.; perf. 3. pl. *-jaghruḥ*, Bhaṭṭ.) to smell anything (acc.), AitUp.; ĀśvGṛ.; Mn. &c.; to smell at (acc.), VS.; MBh. &c.; to kiss, kiss on (loc.), MBh.; R. &c.: Caus. *-ghrāpayati*, to cause to smell, KātyŚr.

Ā-ghrāṇa, *am*, n. smelling (the scent of), Gaut.; Kathās.; satiety, L.; (mfn.) satiated, L.

Ā-ghrāta, mfn. smelled at, Śak. (also *an-*, neg.); Hit. &c.; smelling (a scent), Hariv.; smelled, scented, Suśr.; satiated, L.; = *krānta* or *ākrānta*, L.; = *grasta-sandhi*, L.; (*am*), n. (in astron.) one of the ten kinds of eclipses, VarBṛS.

Ā-ghreya, mfn. to be smelled at, MBh. xiv, 610.

आङ्कुशायन *āṅkuśāyana*, mfn., (gaṇa *pakshādi*, q. v.; not in Kāś.)

आंकृति *ām-kriti*, *is*, m., N. of a prince, v. l. for *ā-kṛiti*, q. v.

आङ्क्षी *āṅkshī*, f. a musical instrument, L.

आङ्ग *āṅga*, mfn. (in Gr.) relating to the base (*aṅga*) of a word, Pāṇ. i, 1, 63, Comm.; (*as*), m. a prince of the country Aṅga, (gaṇa *pailādi*, q. v.); (*ī*), f. a princess of that country, MBh. i, 3772; (*am*), n. a soft delicate form or body, L.

Āṅgaka, mfn. relating to the country Aṅga &c., Comm. on Pāṇ. iv, 2, 125 & 3, 100.

Āṅgadī, f., N. of the capital of Aṅgada's kingdom, VP.

Āṅgavidya, mfn. familiar with chiromancy (*aṅga-vidyā*, q. v.), (gaṇa *ṛigayanādi*, q. v.)

Āṅgi, *is*, m. a descendant of Aṅga, N. of Havirdhāna, RAnukr.

Āṅgika, mfn. expressed by bodily action or attitude or gesture &c. (as dramatic sentiment, passion, &c.), Sāh. &c.; a player on a tabor or drum, L.

Āṅgeya, *as*, m. (= *āṅga*, m.) a prince of Aṅga, L.; (*ī*), f. a princess of Aṅga, MBh. i, 3777.

Āṅgya, mfn., (gaṇa *saṃkāśādi*, q. v.)

आङ्गरिष्ठ *āṅgarishṭha*, *as*, m., N. of a man, MBh. xii, 4534 seq.

आङ्गार *āṅgāra*, *am*, n. (fr. *aṅgāra*), a heap of charcoal, (gaṇa *bhikshādi*, q. v.)

Āṅgārika, *as*, m. a charcoal-burner, MBh. xii, 2734.

आङ्गि *āṅgi, āṅgika*. See *āṅga*.

आङ्गिरस *āṅgirasá*, mf(*ī*)n. descended from or belonging or referring to the Aṅgirases or to Aṅgiras, AV.; VS. &c.; (*ás*), m. a descendant of Aṅgiras (as Bṛihatsāman [AV.], Cyavana [ŚBr. iv], Ayāsya [ŚBr. xiv], &c.), RV.; AV. &c.; especially N. of Bṛihaspati, RV.; AV. &c.; the planet Bṛihaspati, i. e. Jupiter; (*ī*), f. a female descendant of Aṅgiras, MBh. i, 6908; iii, 14128. **— pavitra,** n., N. of the verse RV. iv, 40, 5, Āp. **Āṅgirasêśvara-tīrtha,** n., N. of a Tīrtha, ŚivaP. Rev.

Āṅgirasá, mf(*ī*)n. descended from the Aṅgirases or from an Aṅgiras, TBr.

आङ्गुलिक *āṅgulika*, mfn. (fr. *aṅguli*), 'like a finger,' Pāṇ. v, 3, 108.

आङ्गूष *āṅgūshá*, *as*, m. praising aloud, a hymn, RV.; (*ám*), n. id., RV. i, 117, 10; vi, 34, 5.

Āṅgūshyà (4), mfn. praising aloud, sounding, RV. i, 62, 2; ix, 97, 8; (cf. *aṅgoshín*.)

आङ्गेय *āṅgeya, āṅgya*. See *āṅga*.

आच् *āc* (*ā-√ac*). See *ākna, ācya*, and *āñc*.

आच *āca*, *as*, m., N. of a man, Rājat.; see *āca-parāca* and *ācôpaca* ss. vv. **Ācêśvara,** m., N. of a temple built by Āca, Rājat.

आचक्रि *ā-cakrí*. See *ā-√1. kṛi*.

आचक्ष् *ā-√caksh*, Ā. *-cashṭe* (Pot. 2. sg. *-cakshīthās*; perf. *-cacakshe*) to look at, inspect, RV. vii, 34, 10; to tell, relate, make a communication about (acc.), announce, declare, make known, confess, TS. vii; ŚBr. &c.; to acquaint, introduce to (acc.), MBh. xiii, 1986; R.; to address any one (acc.), Daś.; to call, name, ŚBr.; ĀśvGṛ. &c.; to signify, Pāṇ. Sch.

Ā-cakshus, mfn. learned, Uṇ. Comm.

आचतुरम् *ā-caturám*, ind. (Pāṇ. viii, 1, 15, Comm.) till the fourth generation, MaitrS.

आचतुर्य *ācaturya*, *am*, n. (fr. *a-catura*, Pāṇ. v, 1, 121), clumsiness, stupidity, L.

आचन्द्रतारकम् *ā-candra-tārakam*, ind. as long as there are moon and stars, Kathās.

Ā-candram, ind. as long as there is a moon.

आचपराच *āca-parāca*, mf(*ā*)n. (fr. *ā ca parā ca* [cf. e. g. RV. x, 17, 6]; gaṇa *mayūravyaṇsakādi*, q. v.) moving towards and away from, Tāṇḍya-Br.; (cf. *ācôpaca*.)

आचम् *ā-√cam, -cāmati* (Pāṇ. vii, 3, 75) to sip (water) from the palm of the hand for purification (with instr., Mn. ii, 61), ŚBr.; TBr. &c.; (perf. 3. p. *-cemuḥ*) to lap up, lick up, absorb, cause to disappear (as the winds lick up moisture, Ragh. ix, 68; xiii, 20): Caus. (ind. p. *-camayya*) to cause to sip (water) for purification, ŚāṅkhGṛ.; (Pot. *-cāmayet*; p. *-cāmayat*) to cause to sip water, Mn.

Ā-camana, *am*, n. sipping water from the palm of the hand (before religious ceremonies, before meals, &c.) for purification, Āp. &c.; [it is not the custom to spit the water out again; the ceremony is often followed by touching the body in various parts]; the water used for that ceremony, Yājñ.; (*ī*), f. id., Hariv. (v. l.)

Ācamanaka, *am*, n. a vessel for *ā-camana*, Hcar.

Ācamanīya, *as*, m. a vessel used for *ā-camana*, ĀśvGṛ.; (*am*), n. water used for *ā-camana*, ĀśvGṛ.; Kauś.; MBh. &c.

Ācamanīyaka, *am*, n. water used for *ā-camana*, AgP.; Hcat.

Ā-camya, ind. p. having sipped water, Mn.; R.; BhP.

Ā-cānta, mfn. one who has sipped water, ĀśvGṛ.; Gobh.; Mn.; Yājñ. **Ācāntôdaka,** mfn. one who has sipped water (and purified his mouth), Gobh.

Ā-cānti, *is*, f. sipping (water) for purifying the mouth, Bālar.

Ā-cāma, *as*, m. id., L.; the water in which rice has been boiled, KātyŚr.; Yājñ. iii, 322; (mentioned as drunk by Jain ascetics; Prākṛit *āyāma*) Jain.

Ā-cāmaka, mfn. one who sips water, Pāṇ. vii, 3, 34, Sch.

Ācāmanaka, *as*, m. = *ācam°* above, L.

Ā-cāmya, mfn. (impers.) to be sipped, Pāṇ. iii, 1, 126; (*am*), n. = *ā-cānti* above, Bhaṭṭ. vi, 65.

आचय *ā-caya*, *as*, m. (√1. *ci*), (gaṇa *ākarshādi*, q. v.) collection, plenty, Nir.

Ācayaka, mfn. = *acaye kuśala*, (gaṇa *ākarshādi*, q. v.)

आचर् *ā-√car, -carati*, to come near to (acc.), approach, RV.; to lead hither (as a path), TS. ii; to address, apply to (acc.), Pañcat.; to proceed, manage, behave one's self, RPrāt.; Mn. ii, 110, &c.; to use, apply, Āp.; RPrāt.; to examine (a witness), Mn. viii, 102, &c.; (with or without *saha*) to have intercourse with, ChUp.; Mn. xi, 180; to act, undertake, do, exercise, practise, perform, MuṇḍUp.; Mn. (v, 22, impf. *ācarat*, 'has done it'); MBh. &c.; to throw into the fire, KātyŚr.

Ā-cara. See *dur-ācara*.

Ā-cáraṇa, *am*, n. approaching, arrival (as of the dawn), RV. i, 48, 3; undertaking, practising, performing, Kād.; Sāh.; conduct, behaviour, Vedāntas., (cf. *sv-āc°*); a cart, carriage, ChUp. (m., Comm.)

Ā-caraṇīya, mfn. to be done or performed, Pañcat.; Śārṅg.

Ā-carita, mfn. passed or wandered through, frequented by, MBh. iii, 2651; R.; BhP. &c.; observed, exercised, practised, MBh. i, 7259, &c.; (in Gr.) enjoined, fixed by rule, RPrāt.; Pāṇ. i, 4, 51, Comm.; (*am*), n. approaching, arrival, PārGṛ.; conduct, behaviour, BhP.; the usual way (of calling in debts), Mn. viii, 49. **— tva,** n. custom, usage, PārGṛ.

Ā-caritavya, mfn. = *ā caraṇīya*, q. v., MBh. iii, 15120; (impers.) to be acted in a customary manner, Śak. 304, 8.

Ā-carya, mfn. to be approached, Pāṇ. iii, 1, 100, Comm.; = *ā-caraṇīya*, q. v., Pāṇ. vi, 1, 147, Sch.

Ā-cāra, *as*, m. (ifc. f. *ā*, Yājñ. i, 87, &c.) conduct, manner of action, behaviour, good behaviour, good conduct, Mn.; MBh. &c.; custom, practice, usage, traditional or immemorial usage (as the foundation of law), ib.; an established rule of conduct, ordinance, institute, precept; a rule or line, MBh. iii, 166; = *ācārika* below, Suśr.; (with Buddhists) agreeing with what is taught by the teacher, Sarvad.; (*ī*), f. the plant Hingtsha Repens, L. **— cakrin,** *inas*, m. pl., N. of a Vaishṇava sect. **— candrikā,** f., N. of a work on the religious customs of the Śūdras. **— tantra,** n. one of the four classes of Tantras, Buddh. **— dīpa,** m. 'lamp of religious customs,' N. of a work. **— bheda,** m. breaking the rules of traditional usage, Pāṇ. viii, 1, 60, Sch. **— bhrashṭa,** mfn. (= *bhrashṭâcāra*, R. iii, 37, 5) fallen from established usage. **— mayūkha,** m. 'ray of religious customs,' N. of a work. **— vat,** mfn. well-conducted, virtuous, Mn. xii, 126; R. **— varjita,** mfn. out of rule, irregular; outcast. **— viruddha,** mfn. contrary to custom. **— vedī,** f. 'altar of religious customs,' N. of Āryāvarta, L. **— vyapêta,** mfn. deviating from established custom, Yājñ. ii, 5. **— hīna,** mfn. deprived of established ordinances, outcast, Mn. iii, 165. **Ācārâṅga,** n., N. of the first of the twelve sacred books (*aṅga*) of the Jainas. **Ācārâdarśa,** m. 'looking-glass of religious customs,' N. of a work. **Ācārârka,** m. 'sun of religious customs,' N. of a work. **Ā-cārôllāsa,** m., N. of the first part of the Paraśurāma-prakāśa.

Ācārika, *am*, n. habit of life, regimen, diet, Suśr.

Ācārin, mfn. following established practice, L.

Ācāryà, *as*, m. 'knowing or teaching the *ācāra* or rules,' a spiritual guide or teacher (especially one who invests the student with the sacrificial thread, and instructs him in the Vedas, in the law of sacrifice and religious mysteries [Mn. ii, 140; 171]), AV.; ŚBr. &c.; a N. of Droṇa (the teacher of the Pāṇḍavas), Bhag. i, 2; (*ā*), f. a spiritual preceptress, Pāṇ. iv, 1, 49, Siddh. [The title *ācārya* affixed to names of learned men is rather like our 'Dr.'; e. g. *Rāghavâcārya*, &c.] **— karaṇa,** n. acting as teacher, Pāṇ. i, 3, 36. **— jāyā,** f. a teacher's wife, ŚBr. xi. **— tā,** f. the office or profession of a teacher, MBh. i, 5092; VarBṛS. **— tva,** n. id., Yājñ. i, 275. **— deva,** mfn. worshipping one's teacher like a deity, TUp. **— deśīya,** mfn. (cf. Pāṇ. v, 3, 67) 'somewhat inferior to an Ācārya' (a title applied by commentators to scholars or disputants whose statements contain only a part of the truth and are not entirely correct; the term is opposed to 'Ācārya' and 'Siddhāntin'), Kaiyaṭa and Nāyojibhaṭṭa on Pat. **— bhogīna,** mfn. being advantageous or agreeable to a teacher, (gaṇa *kshubhnâdi*, q. v.) **— miśra,** mfn. venerable, honourable, (cf. gaṇa *matallikâdi*.) **— vacasā,** n. the word of the holy teacher, ŚBr. xi. **— vat** (*ācāryà-*), mfn. one who has a teacher, ŚBr. xiv; Vedāntas. **— sava,** m., N. of an Ekāha sacrifice. **Ācāryôpāsana,** n. waiting upon or serving a spiritual preceptor.

Ācāryaka, *am*, n. (Pāṇ. iv, 2, 104, Comm.) the office or profession of a teacher, Pañcat.; Ragh. &c.

Ācāryānī, f. (with dental *n*, Vārtt. on Pāṇ. iv, 1, 49) the wife of an Ācārya, Mcar. 40, 15 (with cerebral *ṇ*).

Ācāryī-√1. kṛi (p. *-kurvat*) to make (one's self, *ātmānam*) a teacher, Pāṇ. i, 3, 36, Comm.

Ā-cīrṇa, mfn. (anom. perf. pass. p.) practised (as Dharma), MBh. xiii, 6454; xiv, 1473; devoured, eaten into, BhP. vii, 13, 15.

आचरण्य *ā-caraṇya*, Nom. P. (Subj. *-caranyāt*) to move or extend towards (acc.), AV. vii, 29, 1 (v. l. Pot. °*ṇyet*, TS. i).

आचल् *ā-√cal*, Caus. *-cālayati*, to remove, move or draw away (from its place, abl.), Kauś.; MBh. xii, 5814; Hariv. 3036; to stir up.

आचान्त *ā-cānta*, &c. See *ā-√cam*.

Ā-cāma, &c. See ib.

आचार *ā-cāra*, &c. See *ā-√car*.

Ācārya, ācāryaka, &c. See ib.

आचि *ā-√1. ci*, P. *-cinoti* [KātyŚr.], Ā. *-cinute* [BhP.] to accumulate; (perf. *-cicāya*, 2. du. Ā. *-cikyāte*) to cover with (instr.), Bhaṭṭ.

Ā-kāya, *as*, m. a funeral pile, L.; (*am*), ind. so as to pile up (the wood), Pāṇ. iii, 3, 41, Comm.

Ā-cita, mfn. collected, AV. iv, 7, 5; accumulated, heaped, Hariv. 12085; filled, loaded with (instr. or in comp.; see *yavâcitá*), covered, overspread, larded with, MBh. &c.; inlaid, set, see *ardhâcita*; (*as* or *am*), m. n. (ifc. f. *ā*, Pāṇ. iv, 1, 22) a cart-load (= twenty Tulās), Gobh. **Ācitâdi**, a gaṇa of Pāṇ. (vi, 2, 146).

Ācitika, mf(*ī*)n. holding or being equal to an Ācita (or cart-load), Pāṇ. v, 1, 53; (also ifc. with numerals, e. g. *dvy-ācitika*) 54.

Ācitīna, mf(*ā*)n. id., ib.

आचिख्यासा *ā-cikhyāsā*. See *ā-√khyā*.

आचित् 1. *ā-√cit* (Impv. 2. sg. *-cikiddhi*; perf. 3. sg. *-ciketa*) to attend to, keep in mind, RV.; (Subj. 1. sg. *-ciketam*; perf. 3. sg. *-ciketa*, p. m. nom. *-cikitvān*) to comprehend, understand, know, RV.; AV. v, 1, 2; to invent, RV. viii, 9, 7; (Subj. *-cetat* or *-ciketat*; perf. Ā. 3. pl. *-cikitre* or *-cikitrire*) to appear, become visible, distinguish one's self, RV.: Desid. (1. pl. *-cikitsāmas*) to wait for, watch clandestinely, lurk, RV. viii, 91, 3.

2. **Ā-cít**, *t*, f. attention to (gen.), RV. vii, 65, 1.

आचीर्ण *ā-cīrṇa*. See *ā-√car*.

आचूषण *ā-cūshaṇa*, *am*, n. suction, sucking out (also said of the application of cupping-glasses to the skin), Suśr.

आचृत् *ā-√cṛit* (Impv. *-cṛitatu*) to fasten, tie, affix, AV. v, 28, 12; Kauś.

आचेश्वर *ācêśvara*. See *āca*.

आचेष्ट् *ā-√cesht*, *-ceshṭate*, to do, perform, Kathās.: Caus. *-ceshṭayati* (v. l. *-veshṭ*°) to cause to move, set in motion, TBr. i.

Ā-ceshṭita, mfn. undertaken, done, Daś.

आचोपच *ācôpaca*, mfn. (fr. *āca upaca*; gaṇa *mayūravyaṇsakâdi*, q. v.) 'moving towards and upwards,' fluctuating, Kāṭh.; (cf. *āca-parāca*.)

आच्छद् 1. *ā-cchad* (√*chad*), *-cchādayati*, to cover, hide, MBh.; R. &c.; to clothe, dress, Kauś.; Gobh.; to present with clothes, MBh.; Mn. &c.: P. Ā. to put on (as clothes), ŚāṅkhGṛ. &c.; MBh.; R.: Ā. to put on clothes, MBh. ii, 1736; to conceal, Hit.; Sarvad.

2. **Ā-cchád**, *t*, f. a cover, VS. xv, 4 & 5. **–vidhāna** (*ācchád-*), n. an arrangement made for defence, means of covering, RV. x, 85, 4.

Ā-cchanna, mfn. clothed, MBh. iii, 2632.

Ā-cchāda, *as*, m. garment, clothes, Mn. vii, 126; R.; Pañcat.

Ā-cchādaka, mfn. concealing, hiding, Sāy. (on RV.); protecting, defending, Vishṇus. **–tva**, n. hiding, Vedāntas.

Ā-cchādana, *am*, n. covering, concealing, hiding, KātyŚr.; cloth, clothes, mantle, cloak, Pāṇ.; Āp.; Mn.; MBh. &c.; a cover for a bed, R. vii, 37, 11; the wooden frame of a roof, L. **–vastra**, n. the lower garment, Pañcat.

Ā-cchādita, mfn. covered, MBh.; R. &c.; clothed, MBh. iii, 1002.

Ā-cchādin, mfn. ifc. covering, concealing, Śak.

Ā-cchādya (and irr. **ā-cchādayitvā**, MBh. iv, 2183), ind. p. having covered, having clothed &c.; covering, clothing &c.

आच्छिद् *ā-cchid* (*ā-√chid*), *-cchinatti* (Impv. 2. sg. *-cchindhi*, AV.; fut. 1. sg. *-cchetsyāmi*, MBh; to tear or cut off, cut or break into pieces, AV.; ŚBr. &c.; to take out of, ŚBr.; KātyŚr.; Daś.; to cut off, exclude or remove from (abl.), MBh. iii, 14710; Comm. on Mn. iv, 219; to snatch away, tear from, rob, MBh. &c.

Ā-cchidya, ind. p. cutting off &c.; interrupting (e.g. a tale, *kathām*), Kathās.; setting aside; in spite of (acc.), notwithstanding, R. ii, 24, 33; 57, 20.

Ā-cchinna, mfn. cut off &c.; removed, destroyed (as darkness), MBh. xiii, 7362.

Ā-cchettṛi, *tā*, m. one who cuts off, TS. i; TBr. iii.

Ā-ccheda, *as*, m. cutting, cutting off, excision, L.

Ā-cchedana, *am*, n. id., L.; exclusion, L.; (*ī*), f., N. of the passage in TBr. (iii, 7, 4, 9, *apām medhyam*,–10, *śaradaḥ śatam*) in which the word *ā-cchettṛi* occurs, ĀpŚr. (by Sāy. called *chedana-mantra*).

आच्छुक *ācchuka*, *as*, m. (=*ākshika*, m.) the plant Morinda Tinctoria, L.

आच्छुरित *ā-cchurita*, mfn. (√*chur*), covered, clothed with (instr.), Kathās.; (*am*), n. making a noise with the finger-nails by rubbing them on one another, L.; a horse-laugh, L.

Ācchuritaka, *am*, n. a scratch with a finger-nail, L.; a horse-laugh, L.

आच्छृद् *ā-cchṛid* (*ā-√chṛid*), *-cchṛiṇatti* (Impv. 3. pl. *-cchṛindantu*) to pour upon, fill, VS. xi, 65; TS.; ŚBr.; (cf. *án-ācchṛiṇṇa*.)

आच्छेतृ *ā-cchettṛí*, &c. See *ā-cchid*.

आच्छो *ā-ccho* (*ā-√cho*), *-cchyati* (Impv. 3. sg. *-cchyatāt*, 3. pl. *-cchyantu*) to skin, flay, VS.; ŚBr.; AitBr.

आच्छोटित *ā-cchoṭita*, mfn. pulled, torn, Jain.; Kād.

आच्छोदन *ā-cchodana*, *am*, n. hunting, the chase, L. (v. l. *ā-kshod*°, q. v.)

आच्य *âcya*. ind. p. (fr. *âc*), bending (the knee), ŚBr.; ĀśvGṛ.

Ắcyā, Ved. ind. p. id., RV. x, 15, 6. **–doha**, n. 'milking while kneeling,' N. of a Sāman, TāṇḍyaBr. (vv.ll. *āci-d*° and *ājyā-d*°, ĀrshBr.)

आच्यु *ā-√cyu*, Caus. P. (1. pl. *-cyāvayāmas* or °*masi*; 2. sg. *-cyāvayasi* and Impv. °*ya*) to cause or induce to come near, RV.; AV. iii, 3, 2; TS. ii; ŚBr.: Intens. P. (impf. *-acucyavīt*, 3. pl. °*vuḥ*) to cause to flow over, pour out, RV.; TS. iii: P. and Ā. (impf. 3. pl. *-acucyavuḥ*: Ā. 1. pl. *-cucyuvīmáhi*, 3. pl. *-cucyavīrata*) to cause or induce to come near, RV.

आच्युतदन्ति *ācyutadanti* and °*tīya*, v. l. for *ācyutanti* and °*tīya* below.

Ācyutanti, *ayas*, m. pl., N. of a warrior-tribe (see *acyuta-danta*), (gaṇa *dāmany-ādi*, q. v.)

Ācyutantīya, *as*, m. a prince of the above tribe, ib.

Ācyutika, mf(*ī*)n. relating to Acyuta, (gaṇa *kāśy-ādi*, q. v.)

Ācyudanti and °**dantīya**, v. l. for °*tanti* and °*tantīya*.

आज् *âj* (*ā-√aj*), *-ájati* (Subj. *ājāti*; Impv. 2. sg. *-aja* or *ájā*, 2. pl. Ā. *-ajadhvam*) to drive towards (as cattle or enemies), RV.; VS.; AitBr.

Ắjani, *is*, f. a stick for driving, AV. iii, 25, 5.

आज *āja*, mfn. (fr. 1. *ajá*), coming from or belonging to goats, produced by goats, ĀśvGṛ.; R.; Suśr.; (*as*), m. a vulture, L.; a descendant of Aja; (*ā́*), f. (only used for the etym. of *ajā́*) = *ajā́*, a she-goat, ŚBr. iii; (*am*), n. the lunar mansion Pūrva-Bhādrapadā (presided over by Aja Ekapād), VarBṛS.; clarified butter, L.

Ājaka, *am*, n. a flock of goats, Pāṇ. iv, 2, 39. **–roṇa**, m., Pāṇ. iv, 2, 78, Kāś.

Ājakrandaka, mfn. belonging to the Ajakranda people, Pāṇ. iv, 2, 125, Kāś.

Ājakrandi, *is*, m. a descendant of an Ājakrandaka man or prince, ib., Pat.

Ājagara, mf(*ī*)n. (fr. *aja-gara*), treating of the boa or large serpent (as a chapter of the MBh.); belonging to a boa, MBh. iii, 12533; Kathās.; proper to a boa, MBh. xii, 6677 seqq.; acting like a boa, BhP.

Ājadhenavi, *is*, m. (fr. *aja-dhenu*), a patronymic, (gaṇa *bāhv-ādi*, q. v.)

Ājapathika, mfn. fr. *aja-patha* (q. v.), Pāṇ. v, 1, 77, Comm.

Ājapāda, *am*, n. (= *āja*, n.) the lunar mansion Pūrva-Bhādrapadā, VarYogay.

Ājabandhavi, *is*, m. (fr. *aja-bandhu*), a patronymic, (gaṇa *bāhv-ādi* in Kāś., q. v.)

Ājamāyava, *am*, n. (fr. *ajá-māyu*), N. of a Sāman, ĀrshBr.

Ājamārya, *as*, m. a descendant of Aja-māra, (gaṇa *kurv-ādi*, q. v.)

Ājamīḍhá or °**mīḷhá**, *as*, m. a descendant of Aja-mīḍha, RV. iv, 44, 6; ĀśvŚr.; N. of a famous king, MBh.

Ājamīḍhaka, mfn. belonging or referring to Aja-mīḍha, Pāṇ. iv, 2, 125, Kāś.

Ājamīḍhi, *is*, m. a descendant of A., ib., Pat.

Ājavasteya, *as*, m. a descendant of an Aja-vasti man or prince, (gaṇa *grishṭy-ādi* and *śubhrâdi*, q. v.)

Ājavāha or °**haka**, mfn. fr. *aja-vāha*, q. v., (gaṇa *kacchâdi*, q. v.)

Ājâdya, *as*, m. a man or chief of the warrior-tribe called *Ajâda*, Pāṇ. iv, 1, 171.

Ājāyana, *as*, m. a descendant of Aja, (gaṇa *naḍâdi*, q. v.)

Ājâvika, mfn. made from the hairs of (*ajâvi*, q. v.) goats and sheep, Kauś.

1. **Ājya**, *as*, m. a descendant of Aja, (gaṇa *gargâdi*, q. v.)

आजकार *ājakāra*, *as*, m. Śiva's bull, L.

Ājagava, *am*, n. = *aj*°, q. v., MBh. iii, 10456.

Ājagāva, *as*, m., v. l. for *aj*°, q. v.

आजक्रन्दक *ājakrandaka*, &c. See *āja*.

आजन् *ā-√jan*, Ā. *-jāyate* (Impv. *-jāyatām* [VS.; AV.; ĀśvGṛ.]; aor. 2. sg. *-janishṭhās*; 3. sg. *-jánishṭa* or *ājani*; Prec. *-janishīshṭa*) to be born, RV. &c.: Caus. (Subj. 2. du. Ā. *-janayāvahai*) to beget, generate, AV. xiv, 2, 71; (Impv. *-janayatu*) to cause to be born, RV. x, 85, 43; (Impv. 2. sg. *-janaya*) to render prolific, RV. i, 113, 19.

Ā-janana, *am*, n. birth, origin, MBh. i, 3756 & 4561.

Ā́-jāta, mfn. born, RV.

Ā-jāti, *is*, f. birth, Mn. iv, 166; viii, 82.

Ā-jāna, *am*, n. birth, descent, VS.; ŚBr. iii; birth-place, Comm. on VS. xxxiii, 72; (*ā*), f. place of conception (as a mother), AitĀr. **–ja**, mfn. ['born in the world of the gods,' Comm.] i. e. *deva*, = *ājāna-deva* below, TUp. **–deva** (*ājāna-*), m. a god by birth (as opposed to *karma-deva*, q. v.), ŚBr. xiv (BṛĀrUp.)

Ā-jāni, *is*, f. birth, descent, RV. iii, 17, 3; noble birth, Comm. on KaushBr. xxx, 5.

Ājāneya, mf(*ī*)n. of noble origin, of good breed (as a horse), KātyŚr.; MBh.; originating or descending from (in comp.), Buddh.; (*as*), m. a well-bred horse, MBh. iii, 15704.

Ājāneyya, mfn. of noble birth, KaushBr. xxx, 5.

आजन्म *ā-janma*, ind. (generally in comp.) from birth, since birth, Ragh. i, 5; Kathās. &c. **–surabhi-pattra**, m., N. of a plant (the leaves of which are fragrant from their first appearance), L.

आजप् *ā-√jap*, to mutter or whisper into (the ear, *kárṇe*), ŚBr. iv; xiii.

आजपथिक *ājapathika*, &c. See *āja*.

आजयन *ā-jayana*. See 2. *ā-√ji*.

आजरसम् *ā-jarasám*, ind. till old age, ŚBr. i; AitBr.

Ā-jarasāya, (dat.) ind. id., RV. x, 85, 43.

आजर्जरित *ā-jarjarita*, mfn. (fr. *jarjara*), torn into pieces, Kād.

आजवन *ā-javana*, *am*, n. (√*ju*), only for the etymol. of *ājí*, q. v., Nir. ix, 23.

आजवस्तेय *ājavasteya*, &c. See *āja*.

आजस्रिक *ājasrika*, mfn. (fr. *á-jasra*), perpetual, occurring every day.

आजातशत्रव *ājātaśatravá*, *as*, m. 'a descendant of Ajāta-śatru,' N. of Bhadrasena, ŚBr. v.

Ājātaśātrava, mf(*ī*)n. belonging to or ruled over by (Ajāta-śatru) Yudhishṭhira, Śiś. ii, 114.

आजाति *ā-jāti.* See *ā-√jan.*

आजाद्य *ājādya.* See *āja.*

आजान *ājāna, ājāni.* See *ā-√jan.*

आजानिक्य *ājānikya, am,* n. (fr. *a-jānika*), the not possessing a wife, (gaṇa *purohitâdi,* q. v.)

आजानु *ā-jānu,* ind. (generally in comp.) as far as the knee. **– bāhu,** mfn.; see s. v. 3. *ā.* **– lambin,** mfn. reaching down to the knee, Kād. **– sama,** mfn. as high as the knee, Suśr.

आजानेय *ājāneya* and °*neyya.* See *ā-√jan.*

आजायन *ājāyana* and *ājâvika.* See *āja.*

आजि 1. *ājí,* m., rarely f., only once in RV. i, 116, 15, (*√aj*), a running-match; a fighting-match, prize-fight, combat, RV.; AV. &c.; [*ājím √aj* or *√i* or *√dhāv* or *√sṛi,* to run with or against any one for a prize, ŚBr.; AitBr. &c.]; war, battle (*ājau,* in battle, MBh.; R.; Ragh. xii, 45, &c.); place for running, race-course, RV. iv, 24, 8; AV. xiii, 2, 4; (= *ākshepa*) abuse, L.; (= *kshaṇa*) an instant, L. **– kṛit,** mfn. fighting or running for a prize, RV. viii, 45, 7. **– ga,** n., N. of a Sāman, TāṇḍyaBr.; LāṭyŚr. **– jityā,** f. victory in a running-match, TāṇḍyaBr. **– túr,** mfn. victorious in battles, RV. viii, 53, 6. **– pati,** m. lord of the battle, RV. viii, 54, 6 (voc.) **– mukha,** n. the front or first line in a battle, Ratnāv. **– śiras,** n. id., MBh. iii, 16479; = *ājy-anta* below, Comm. on TS. **– sṛit,** mfn. = *-kṛit,* q. v., ŚBr. **– hīna,** m. 'defeated in battle,' N. of a man; (*ās*), m. pl. his descendants. **Ājy-anta,** m. the goal in a race-course, Nir. ii, 15.

आजि 2. *ā-√ji* (p. *-jáyat;* impf. 3. du. *âja-yatām*) to conquer, win, RV. ii, 27, 15; AitBr.; TāṇḍyaBr.: Desid. p. *-jigīshamāṇa,* trying or desiring to win, RV. i, 163, 7.

Ā-jayana, *am,* n. (only for the etym. of 1. *āji*) 'conquering,' Nir. ix, 23.

Ā-jigīshu, mfn. wishing to excel or overcome, L.

आजिगमिषु *ā-jigamishu.* See *ā-√gam.*

आजिघृक्षु *ā-jighṛikshu.* See *ā-√grah.*

आजिज्ञासेन्या *ā-jijñāsenyā.* See *ā-√jñā.*

आजिन्व् *ā-√jinv* (2. du. *-jinvathas*) to refresh, RV. iv, 45, 3.

आजिरि *ājiri,* mfn. fr. *ajira,* (gaṇa *sutaṃgamâdi,* q. v.)

Ājireya, *as,* m. a descendant of Ajira, (gaṇa *śubhrâdi,* q. v.)

आजिहीर्षु *ā-jihīrshu.* See *ā-√hṛi.*

आजीकूल *ājī-kūla,* v. l. for *āñjī-k°,* q. v.

आजीगर्त *ājīgarta, am,* n., N. of a Sāman.

Ājīgarti, *is,* m. (gaṇa *bahv-adi,* q. v.) a descendant of Ajīgarta (q. v.), Śunaḥśepa, TS. v; AitBr.

आजीव् *ā-√jīv,* P. (3. pl. *-jīvanti;* ind. p. *-jīvya*) to live by (acc.), subsist through (acc.), MBh. v, 4536; BhP.; (p. *-jīvat;* Pass. p. *-jīvyamāna*) to use, have the enjoyment of (acc.), Yājñ. ii, 67; MārkP.

Ā-jīva, *as,* m. livelihood, ŚvetUp.; Mn. xi, 63; MBh. &c.; = *ājīvika,* q. v., L.

Ājīvaka, *as,* m. = °*vika* below, Lalit.

Ā-jīvana, *am,* n. livelihood, Mn. x, 79; Pañcat.

Ājīvanika, mfn. looking for a livelihood, Kād.

Ā-jīvam, ind. for life, Kathās.

Ājīvika, *as,* m. 'following special rules with regard to livelihood,' a religious mendicant of the sect founded by Gośāla (Makkhaliputra), Jain.; VarBṛ.

Ā-jīvitântam, ind. for life, Vcar. (Śārṅg.)

Ājīvin, *ī,* m. = *ājīvika,* VarBṛ.

Ājīvya, mfn. affording a livelihood, Yājñ. i, 320; MBh. xiv, 1330; (*am*), n. means of living, MBh. iii, 8452; BhP.; (cf. *sv-āj°.*)

आजुर् *ā-jur, ūr,* f. (? *√jṛī*), = *vishṭi,* L.

आज्ञा 1. *ā-√jñā, -jānāti* (Impv. 2. pl. *-jānīta;* perf. *-jajñau;* p. *-jānát*) to mind, perceive, notice, understand, RV. i, 94, 8; 156, 3; ŚBr.; TāṇḍyaBr.; (cf. *án-ājānat*): Caus. *-jñāpayati,* °*te* (Inf. *-jñaptum,* R. iv, 40, 8) to order, command, direct, MBh. &c.; to assure, R. vi, 103, 10.

Ā-jijñāsenyā, *ās,* f. pl. (fr. Desid.) scil. *ṛicas,* 'liable to investigation,' N. of some of the Kuntāpa hymns (of the AV.), AitBr.

Ā-jñapta, mfn. ordered, commanded, Mn. ii, 245; R. &c.

Ā-jñapti, *is,* f. command, Comm. on AitUp.

2. **Ā-jñā,** f. order, command, Mn. x, 56; MBh. &c.; authority, unlimited power, Bālar.; N. of the tenth lunar mansion, VarBṛ.; permission (neg. *an-ājñayā,* instr. ind. without permission of (gen.), Mn. ix, 199). **– kara,** m. 'executing an order,' a servant, R. iv, 9, 4, &c.; (*ī*), f. a female servant, Śak.; (*ājñākara*)*-tva,* n. the office of a servant, Vikr. **– kārin,** mfn. one who executes orders, a minister, L. **– cakra,** n. a mystical circle or diagram (one of the six described by the Tantras.) **– dāna,** n. giving an order, Rājat. **– pattra,** n. a written order, edict, L. **– parigraha,** m. receiving an order, Rājat. **– pālana,** n. 'guarding,' i. e. executing the orders, VP. **– pratighāta,** m. disobedience, insubordination, L. **– bhaṅga,** m. 'breaking,' i. e. not executing an order, Hit.; (*ājñābhaṅga*)*-kara* [Hit.] or *-kārin* [VP.], mfn. not executing an order. **– vaha,** mfn. one who obeys orders, a minister, L. **– sampādin,** mfn. executing orders, submissive, Yājñ. i, 76.

Ā-jñāta, mfn.; see *an-ājñ°.* **– kauṇḍinya,** m., N. of one of the first five pupils of Śākyamuni.

Ā-jñātṛi, *tā́,* m. one who directs, RV. x, 54, 5.

Ā-jñāna, *am,* n. noticing, perceiving, AitUp.

Ā-jñāpaka, mf(*ikā*)n. giving orders, commanding, Hariv. 6518 (v. l. *jñāpaka*).

Ā-jñāpana, *am,* n. ordering, commanding.

Ā-jñāpita, mfn. ordered, commanded, MBh. i, 6310 (loc. *aśane,* 'to eat'); R. &c.

Ā-jñāpya, mfn. to be directed or commanded by (gen.), expecting an order from (gen.), R. i, 66, 3.

Ā-jñāya, ind. p. having noticed or perceived; having heard, MBh.; BhP.; R. &c.

Ā-jñāyin, mfn. perceiving.

आज्य 2. *ā́jya, am,* n. (*√añj,* Vārtt. on Pāṇ. iii, 1, 109), melted or clarified butter (used for oblations, or for pouring into the holy fire at the sacrifice, or for anointing anything sacrificed or offered), RV. x; AV.; VS. &c.; (in a wider sense) oil and milk used instead of clarified butter at a sacrifice; N. of a sort of chant (*śastra*) connected with the morning sacrifice, AitBr.; ŚBr.; KaushBr.; N. of the Sūkta contained in the aforesaid *śastra,* KaushBr.; N. of a Stotra connected with that *śastra,* TāṇḍyaBr. **– graha,** m. a vessel of clarified butter, KātyŚr.; (*ās*), m. pl., N. of certain formulæ, ĀpŚr. **– doha,** n., v. l. for *ā́cyā-d°,* q. v. **– dhanvan,** mfn. having the clarified butter for its bow, AitBr. **– dhānī,** f. receptacle of clarified butter, Kauś. **– pá,** mfn. drinking the clarified butter, VS.; ŚBr.; (*ās*), m. pl. a class of Manes (who are the sons of Pulastya [Mn. iii, 197 seq.] or of Kardama [VP.] and the ancestors of the Vaiśya order). **– pātra,** n. a vessel for clarified butter. **– bhāga** (*ā́jya-*), m. a portion of clarified butter, ŚBr.; (*au*), m. du. the two portions of clarified butter belonging to Agni and Soma, ŚBr.; KātyŚr. &c.; MBh. xiv, 722; (mf(*ā*)n.) partaking of the clarified butter, TS. ii. **– bhuj,** m. 'consumer of clarified butter,' Agni, R. iii, 20, 38. **– lipta** (*ā́jya-*), mfn. anointed with clarified butter, ŚBr. **– lepa,** m. an unguent made of clarified butter, ŚāṅkhGṛ. **– vāri,** m. 'sea of clarified butter,' one of the seven mythical seas, L. **– vilāpanī,** f. the vessel containing the clarified butter, ŚBr. **– sthālī,** f. = *-pātra* above, MānŚr.; MānGṛ. **– havis** (*ā́jya-*), mfn. having an oblation consisting of clarified butter, ŚBr.; AitBr. **– homa,** m. an oblation consisting of clarified butter, Gaut. **Ājyā-doha,** n., v. l. for *ā́cyā-d°,* q. v. **Ājyâhuti,** f. = *ājya-homa* above, ŚBr.; AitBr. &c.

आञ्च् *āñc* (*ā-√añc*), (Impv. *āñcatu*) to bend, curve, AV. xi, 10, 16; (cf. *āc.*)

आञ्छ् *āñch, āñchati* (Pot. *āñchet;* perf. *āñcha* or *anāñcha,* Pāṇ. Siddh.) to stretch, draw into the right position, set (a bone or leg), Suśr.

Āñchana, *am,* n. stretching, drawing, setting (a bone or leg), Suśr.; Bālar.

आञ्ज् *āñj* (*ā-√añj*), (Impv. 2. sg. Ā. *ā́kshva;* ind. p. *ā́jya;* Impv. *-anaktu;* impf. 3. pl. *ā́ āñjan*) to anoint, AV. xix, 45, 5; ĀśvGṛ.; to polish, prepare, RV. vii, 44, 5; to honour, receive respectfully, RV. vi, 63, 3; vii, 43, 3; viii, 60, 1; (cf. *ākta.*)

Ấñjana, *am,* n. ointment (especially for the eyes), AV.; TS.; ŚBr. &c.; fat, RV. x, 18, 7; (mfn.) having the colour of the collyrium used for the eyes, MBh. v, 1708; (*ī*), f. collyrium for the eyes or a box filled with that ointment, R. ii, 91, 70. **– gandhi** (*ā́ñjana-*), mf(acc. °*im*)n. smelling of ointment, RV. x, 146, 6. **– giri,** m., N. of a mountain, Kaṭh.; (cf. *añjana.*) **Āñjanâbhyañjana,** *e,* n. du. ointment for the eyes and for the feet, KātyŚr.; (*ās*), f. pl., N. of a Sattra (which lasts for forty-nine days), Lāṭy. **Āñjanâbhyañjanīya,** *am,* n. sg. [KātyŚr.] or °*nīya, ās,* f. pl. [KātyŚr.; ĀśvŚr.] another N. of the above Sattra. **Ấñjanī-kārī́,** f. a woman who anoints or makes ointments, VS. xxx, 14.

Ấñjanya, mfn. one whose eyes are to be anointed with ointment, TBr.

आञ्जनेय *āñjaneya, as,* m. 'son of Añjanā,' N. of the monkey Hanumat, Mcar.

आञ्जलिक्य *āñjalikya, am,* n. fr. *añjalika,* (gaṇa *purohitâdi,* q. v.)

आञ्जस *āñjasa,* mf(*ī*)n. (fr. *añjasā,* q. v.), immediate, direct, Comm. on Bād.

Āñjasya, *am,* n. (*āt, ena*) abl. instr. immediately, unhesitatingly, Kap.

आञ्जिक *āñjika, as,* m., N. of a Dānava, Hariv. 216.

Āñjiga, *as,* m., N. of a Dānava, ĀrshBr.

आञ्जिनेय *āñjineya, as,* m. a kind of lizard, L.; (cf. *añjanikā.*)

आञ्जीकूल *āñjī-kūla, am,* n. (v. l. *ājī-k°*) N. of a country, (gaṇa *dhūmâdi,* q. v.)

Āñjīkūlaka, mfn. (v. l. *ājīk°*), ib.

आट् *āṭ,* ind. a croak (imitation of the sound uttered by a frog), TāṇḍyaBr.

आट *āṭa,* mfn. (*√aṭ*), going, going after, only ifc., e. g. *kanyâṭa, kshapâṭa, patny-āṭa* &c.; (*as*), m., N. of a Nāga demon, TāṇḍyaBr.; (cf. *āṭaka.*)

Āṭaka, mf(*ikā*)n. going. See *kāraskarâṭikā.*

आटरूष *āṭarūsha, as,* m. = *aṭ°,* q. v., L.

आटविक *āṭavika, as,* m. (fr. *aṭavī*), the inhabitant of a forest, Mn. ix, 257; MBh. &c.; a forester, Sāh.; (mfn.) consisting of inhabitants of the forest (as an army), Kām.

Āṭavin, *ī,* m., N. of a teacher, VāyuP.

Āṭavī, f., N. of a town, MBh. ii, 1175.

Āṭavya, *as,* m., v. l. for *āṭavin,* q. v.

आटि *āṭi, is,* f., N. of the bird Turdus Ginginianus, PārGṛ.; (cf. *āḍi* and *āti.*) **Āṭi-mukha,** n. 'the top of which is like the beak of the *āṭi,*' a surgical instrument employed in blood-letting, Suśr. **Āṭi-meda,** m., N. of a bird, L.

आटिकी *āṭiki,* f., N. of the wife of Ushasti, ChUp. ['marriageable' or 'strolling about (fr. *√aṭ*),' Comm.]

आटीकन *ā-ṭīkana, am,* n. (*√ṭīk*), the leaping motion of a calf, L.; (cf. *āṭīlaka* and *āḍhil°.*)

आटीकर *āṭīkara, as,* m. a bull, L.

आटीमुख *āṭī-mukha,* &c. See *āṭi.*

आटीलक *āṭīlaka, am,* n. = *ā-ṭīkana,* q. v., L.

आटोप *āṭopa, as,* m. puffing, swelling, MBh. iii, 11587; Pañcat. &c.; a multitude, redundancy, BhP.; flatulence, borborygmi, Suśr.; pride, self-conceit, Mṛicch. &c.; (cf. *sâṭopam.*)

आट्टस्थलीक *āṭṭasthalīka,* mfn. fr. *aṭṭa-sthalī,* (gaṇa *dhūmâdi,* q. v., not in Kāś.)

आट्णार *āṭṇārá, as,* m. a descendant of Aṭṇāra, N. of Para, TS. v; ŚBr. xiii; TāṇḍyaBr.; = *aṭana-śīla,* 'fond of wandering' (Comm.), Nir. i, 14.

आडम्बर *āḍámbara, as,* m. a kind of drum, ŚBr. xiv; MBh.; R.; a great noise, Śārṅg.; noisy behaviour, speaking loud or much, bombast, Kathās.; Sāh. &c.; the roaring of elephants, Kād.; the sounding of a trumpet as a sign of attack, L.; ifc. immensity, sublimity, the highest degree of, Uttarar.; Kathās.; Bālar.; pleasure, L.; the eyelid; (the war-drum personified) N. of a being in the retinue of Skanda, MBh. ix, 2541. **– vat,** mfn. making much noise,

Śārṅg. **Āḍambarâghātá,** m. one who beats a drum, VS. xxx, 19.

Āḍambarin, mfn. arrogant, proud, L.

आडारक *āḍāraka, as,* m. (v. l. *aṇḍār°*) N. of a man, (gaṇa *upakâdi,* q. v.)

आडि *āḍi, is,* f. (= *āti,* q. v.) N. of an aquatic bird, MārkP. **— baka,** mfn. (the combat) fought by the birds Āḍi and Baka (into which Vasishṭha and Viśvāmitra had been transformed respectively), MārkP.

Āḍī, f. = *āḍi,* q. v. **— baka,** mfn. = *āḍi-baka,* q. v., Hariv. 11100.

आडीविन् *ā-ḍīvin, ī,* m., N. of a crow, Kathās.

आडु *āḍu.* See *āḍhyāḍu.*

आडू *āḍū, ūs,* m. or f. a raft, Uṇ.

आढक *āḍhaka, as, am,* m. n. (gaṇa *ardharcâdi,* q. v.; ifc. f. *ī,* Pāṇ. iv, 1, 22 & v, 1, 54, Comm.) a measure of grain (= ¼ droṇa = 4 prasthas = 16 kuḍavas = 64 palas = 256 karshas = 4096 māshas; = nearly 7 lbs. 11 ozs. avoirdupois; in Bengal = two mans or 164 lbs. avds.); (*ī*), f. the pulse Cajanus Indicus Spreng., Suśr.; a kind of fragrant earth, Bhpr. **— jambuka,** mfn. Pāṇ. iv, 2, 120, Sch.

Āḍhakika, mf(*ī*)n. holding or containing an Āḍhaka, sown with an Āḍhaka of seed (as a field), &c., Pāṇ. v, 1, 53 seq.

Āḍhakina, mf(*ā*)n. id., ib.

आढीलक *āḍhīlaka* v. l. for *āṭīl°,* q. v.

आढ्य *āḍhyá,* mf(*ā*)n. (? fr. *ārdhya,* √*ṛidh;* or fr. *ārthya,* NBD.), opulent, wealthy, rich, ŚBr. ix; xiv; Mn. &c.; rich or abounding in, richly endowed or filled or mixed with (instr. or in comp.), R.; Pañcat. &c.; (in arithm.) augmented by (instr.) **— kulīna,** mfn. descended from a rich family, Pāṇ. iv, 1, 139, Sch. **— °ṃ-karaṇa,** mf(*ī*)n. enriching, Pāṇ. iii, 2, 56; iv, 1, 15, Pat. **— cara,** mfn. once opulent, Pāṇ. v, 3, 53, Sch. **— tā,** f. opulence, wealth, BhP. **— padi,** ind., (gaṇa *dvidaṇḍy-ādi,* q. v.) **— pūrva,** mfn. formerly rich, Pat. on Pāṇ. i, 1, 29. **— °ṃ-bhavishṇu** or **-°ṃ-bhāvuka,** mfn. becoming rich, Pāṇ. iii, 2, 57; (cf. *an-āḍhyam-bhavishṇu.*) **— roga,** m. rheumatism, gout. **— rogin,** mfn. ill with rheumatism or with gout, Car.; Suśr. **— vāta,** m. a convulsive or rheumatic palsy of the loins, Suśr.

Āḍhyaka, *am,* n. wealth, (gaṇa *manojñâdi.*)

Āḍhyāḍu, mfn. (with affix *āḍu* = *ālu* in *dayālu* &c.) wishing to become rich, Nir. xii, 14.

आणक *āṇaka,* mfn. = *aṇ°,* q. v., Vet.

Āṇava, mfn. (fr. *aṇu*), fine, minute, Up.; = *āṇavīna,* q. v., L.; (*am*), n. exceeding smallness, (gaṇa *pṛithv-ādi,* q. v.)

Āṇavīna, mfn. bearing or fit to bear Panicum Miliaceum, Pāṇ. v, 2, 4.

Āṇí, *is,* m. (cf. *aṇi*) the pin of the axle of a cart, RV. i, 35, 6; 63, 3 ['battle,' Naigh. ii, 17] & v, 43, 8; the part of the leg just above the knee, Suśr.; (*is*), m. f. a linch-pin, L.; the corner of a house, L.; a boundary, L.

Āṇīveya, *as,* m. a descendant of Aṇīva, (gaṇa *śubhrâdi,* q. v.)

आण्ड *āṇḍá, am,* n. (fr. *aṇḍa*), an egg, RV.; AV. &c.; (*aú*), m. du. the testicles, AV. ix, 7, 13; VS. &c.; (*āṇḍyaù*), f. du. (fr. sg. *āṇḍī*) id., AV. vi, 138, 2. **— kapāla,** n. an egg-shell, ChUp. **— kośa,** m. an egg, BhP. **— ja** (*āṇḍá-*), mfn. born from an egg, ChUp.; AitUp.; (*as*), m. a bird, Suparṇ. **Āṇḍâda,** n. 'eating eggs,' N. of a demon, AV. viii, 6, 25. **Āṇḍī-vat,** mfn., (gaṇa *karṇâdi,* q. v.)

Āṇḍāyana, mfn. fr. *aṇḍa,* (gaṇa *pakshâdi.*)

Āṇḍīka, mfn. bearing eggs (i. e. egg-shaped fruits or bulbs), AV. iv, 34, 5; v, 17, 16; Kauś.

Āṇḍīvatāyani, fr. *āṇḍī-vat* above, (gaṇa *karṇâdi,* q. v.)

आत् *ā́t,* ind. (abl. of 4. *a*) afterwards, then (often used in a concluding paragraph antithetically to *yád, yadā́, yádi,* and sometimes strengthened by the particles *ṓha, íd, īm, u*), RV.; AV.; then, further, also, and, RV.; AV. It is sometimes used after an interrogative pronoun (like *u, nú, aṅgá*) to give emphasis to the pronoun, RV.

आत *ā́-ta,* instr. pl. *ā́-tais.* See *ā́-tā* under *ā-*√*tan.*

आतंस् *ā-*√*taṃs,* Caus. (2. du. Ā. *-taṃsayethe*) to bring near, furnish with (acc.), RV. x, 106, 1.

आतक *ātaka, as,* m., N. of a Nāga demon, MBh. i, 2154.

आतक्ष् *ā-*√*taksh* (Impv. 2. pl. *-takshata,* 3. pl. *-takshantu*) to procure, RV.

आतञ्च् *ā-*√*tañc, -tanakti* (KātyŚr.; 1. sg. *-tanacmi,* VS. i, 4; Pot. *-tañcyā́t,* TS. ii; ind. p. *-tácya,* ŚBr.) to cause coagulation (by casting one liquid into another).

Ā-taṅka, *as,* m. disease or sickness of body, Suśr.; fever, L.; (ifc. f. *ā,* MBh. ii, 285) pain or affliction of mind, disquietude, apprehension, fear, Vikr.; Ragh. i, 63, &c.; the sound of a drum, L.; (cf. *nir-āt°.*)

Ā-taṅkya, mfn. See *śritâtaṅkyà.*

Ā-táñcana, *am,* n. that which causes coagulation (as butter-milk which is thrown into fresh milk to turn it), runnet, TS. ii; ŚBr.; KātyŚr.; = *pratīvāpa,* q. v., L.; = *ā-pyāyana,* q. v., L.; = *javana,* q. v., L.

आतन् *ā-*√*tan,* P. (2. sg. *-tanoshi;* impf. *ā́tanot;* perf. *-tatā́na;* p. m. pl. *-tanvā́ntas;* perf. p. m. sg. *-tatanvā́n*) to extend or stretch over, penetrate, spread, overspread (said of the light), illuminate, RV.; (perf. 2. sg. *-tatántha*) to seek to reach, RV. x, 1, 7; to be ready for, wait on (acc.), RV. v, 79, 3; (aor. Subj. *-tanat*) to stop any one, RV. i, 91, 23: P. Ā. (3. pl. *-tanvate;* perf. 1. sg. *-tatane*) to extend (a texture), spread, stretch (a bow for shooting), RV.; AV. &c.: P. to diffuse; to bestow upon, RV.; BhP. &c.; to effect, produce, Hariv. 4635; BhP. &c.: Caus. (Impv. 2. sg. *-tānayā*) to stretch, AV.

Ā-tata, mfn. spread, extended, stretched or drawn (as a bow or bow-string), RV.; long (as a way), ChUp.; fixed on, clinging to (loc.), RV. i, 22, 20; 105, 9; PraśnaUp.; (cf. *án-āt°.*) **Ātatī-karaṇa,** n. drawing (a bow-string), BhP.

Ātatāyín, mfn. having one's bow drawn, VS. xvi, 18; 'one whose bow is drawn to take another's life,' endeavouring to kill some one, a murderer, Mn. viii, 350 seq.; MBh. &c. (in later texts also incendiaries, ravishers, thieves &c. are reckoned among *ātatāyinas*).

Ātatāvín, mfn., v. l. for *°tāyín* (of VS.), TS. iv.

Ā-táni, mfn. penetrating, RV. ii, 1, 10.

Ā́-tā, m. f. the frame of a door, RV. ix, 5, 5 [instr. pl. *ā́-tais;* v. l. *ā-tābhis,* Comm. on Nir. iv, 18] & VS. xxix, 5 (instr. pl. *ā́-tais*); 'the frame,' i. e. a quarter of the sky, RV. (nom. pl. *ā́-tās;* loc. pl. *ā́-tāsu*).

Ā-tāna, *as,* m. an extended cord, string, &c., VS. vi, 12 (voc.); AitBr.; (cf. *ekâhâtānā́.*)

Ā-tāyin, *ī,* m. a falcon, kite, L.; (cf. *ātāpin.*)

आतप् *ā-*√*tap, -tápati* (Impv. *-tapatu;* see *ā-tápat* and *ā-tápas* ss. vv.) to radiate heat, AV.; VS.; Kauś.: Pass. (p. *-tapyamāna*) to suffer pain, be afflicted, BhP.; (with *tapas*) to inflict (austerities) upon one's self, BhP.

Ā-tapá, mfn. causing pain or affliction, RV. i, 55, 1; (*as*), m. (ifc. f. *ā,* R.; Śak.) heat (especially of the sun), sunshine, KaṭhUp.; Mn. &c. **— tra,** n. 'heat-protector' (ifc. f. *ā,* Megh.; Kathās.), a large umbrella (of silk or leaves), MBh. &c.; *ātapatrāyita,* mfn. forming an umbrella (as the branches of a tree), BhP. **— vat,** mfn. irradiated by the sun, Kum. i, 6. **— varshya,** mf(*ā*)n. (water &c.) produced by rain during sunshine, AitBr.; KātyŚr. **— vāraṇa,** n. 'heat-protector,' a parasol, Ragh. iii, 70; ix, 15. **— śushka,** mfn. dried by the sun. **Ātapâtyaya,** m. passing away of the heat, coolness of the evening, Ragh. i, 52. **Ātapâpâya,** m. passing away of the hot season, beginning of the rainy season, R.

Ā-tápat, mfn. (pr. p.) shining (as the sun), loc. *ā-tápati,* while the sun is shining, ŚBr. v; xiv.

Ā-tapana, *as,* m. 'causing heat,' N. of Śiva, MBh. xii, 10374.

Ā-tápas, Ved. Inf. (abl.) from burning or singeing, RV. v, 73, 5 & viii, 73, 8.

Ātapāya, Nom. Ā. *°yate,* to become hot like sunshine, Kād.

Ātapīya, mfn., (gaṇa *utkarâdi,* q. v.)

Ā-tapta, mfn. refined by heat (as gold), Hariv. 15769.

Ātapyà, mfn. being in the sunshine, VS.

Ātāpin, mfn. zealous, Lalit.; (*ī*), m., N. of a Daitya, Kathās.; v. l. for *ā-tāyin,* q. v.

आतम् *ā-*√*tam* (p. Ā. *-tāmyamāna* and P. *-tāmyat*) to faint, become senseless, R. ii, 63, 50; Kād.; to become stiff, Bālar.

आतमाम् *ā-tamā́m,* a superl. form fr. 3. *ā́* (used with √*khyā*), ŚBr. x.

आतर *ā-tara,* &c. See *ā-*√*tṛī.*

आतर्ज् *ā-*√*tarj,* Caus. (impf. *ātarjayat;* Pass. p. *-tarjyamāna*) to scold, abuse, MBh. vii, 7176; Kād.

आतर्द *ā-tarda* and *°rdana.* See *ā-*√*tṛid.*

आतर्पण *ā-tarpaṇa.* See *ā-*√*tṛip.*

आतव *ātava, as,* m., N. of a man, (gaṇa *aśvâdi,* q. v.)

Ātavāyana, *as,* m. a descendant of Ātava, ib.

आतश्च *ātaś ca,* and this for the following reason (used to introduce an argument), Pat.

आता *ā́-tā* and *ā-tāna.* See *ā-*√*tan.*

आतापिन् *ātāpin.* See *ā-*√*tap.*

आताम्र *ā-tāmra,* mf(*ā*)n. reddish, slightly copper-coloured, Kāvyād.; Ratnāv.

आतार *ā-tāra* and *ā-tāryà.* See *ā-*√*tṛī.*

आताली *ātāli,* ind. in comp. with √1. *as,* √*bhū,* and √1. *kṛi,* (gaṇa *ūry-ādi,* q. v.)

आति *ātí, is,* f. (√*at,* Pāṇ. iii, 3, 108, Comm.) an aquatic bird, RV. x, 95, 9; VS. xxiv, 34 (v. l. *ātí,* TS. v); ŚBr. xi; [cf. *āḍi* and Lat. *anas, anati-s*]; = *āṭi,* q. v.) the bird Turdus Ginginianus, L.

आतिच्छन्दस *āticchandasá, am,* n. (fr. *áti-cchandas*), N. of the last of the six days of the Pṛishṭhya ceremony, MaitrS.; KaushBr.

आतिथिग्व *ātithigvá* (5), *as,* m. a descendant of *Atithi-gvá,* RV. viii, 68, 16 seq.

Ātitheya, mf(*ī,* Kum. v, 31)n. Pāṇ. iv, 4, 104 (fr. *atithi*), proper for or attentive to a guest, hospitable, Śak.; Ragh. &c.; (*as*), m. a descendant of Atithi, (gaṇa *śubhrâdi,* q. v.); (*ī*), f. hospitality, Bālar.; (*am*), n. id., Mn. iii, 18.

Ātithyá, mfn. (Pāṇ. v, 4, 26) proper for a guest, hospitable, AitBr.; (*as*), m. a guest, L.; (*ā*), f. (i.e. *ishṭi*) the reception of the Soma when it is brought to the place of sacrifice, KātyŚr.; (*ám*), n. hospitable reception, hospitality, RV.; VS. &c.; the rite also called *ātithyā* (see before), ŚBr.; AitBr.; KātyŚr. **— rūpá,** mfn. being in the place of the Ātithya rite, VS. xix, 14. **— vat,** mfn. mentioning hospitality, AitBr. **— satkāra,** m. [R. iii, 2, 6] or **-satkriyā,** f. [Kathās.] the rites of hospitality. **Ātithyêshṭi,** f. = *ātithyā* before, Comm. on VS. xix, 14.

आतिदेशिक *ātideśika,* mfn. resulting from an *atideśa* or substitution, Pāṇ. iv, 1, 151, Comm.

आतिरश्चीन *ā-tiraścīna,* mfn. a little transverse or across, Daś.

आतिरैक्य *ātiraikya, am,* n. (fr. *ati-reka*), superfluity, redundancy (as of limbs), Mn. xi, 50.

आतिवाहिक *ātivāhika,* mfn. (fr. *ati-vāha*), 'fleeter than wind,' (in Vedānta phil.) N. of the subtle body (or *liṅga-śarīra*), Kap.; Bād. &c.

आतिविज्ञान्य *ātivijñānya,* mfn. (fr. *ati-vijñāna*), surpassing the understanding, ŚBr. i.

आतिशायिक *ātiśayika,* mfn. (fr. *ati-śaya*), superabundant, Śiś. x, 23.

Ātiśayya, *am,* n. excess, quantity, L.

Ātiśāyanika, *as,* m. (in rhetoric) an affix that expresses gradation in an ascending series.

Ātiśāyika, mfn. expressing ascending gradation, Pat.

आतिष्ठ *ātishṭha, am,* n. (fr. *ati-shṭhā*), superiority, AitBr.

आतिष्ठद्गु *ā-tishṭhad-gu,* ind. till the cows stand to be milked or after sunset, Bhaṭṭ. iv, 14.

आतिस्वायन *ātisvāyana,* mfn. (fr. *ati-svan*), (gaṇa *pakshâdi,* q. v.)

आती *ātī.* See *āti.*

आतीषादीय *ātīshādīya, am,* n., N. of a Sāman, TāṇḍyaBr.; Lāṭy.

आतु *ātu, us,* m. = *āḍū,* q. v., L.

आतुच् *ā-túc* (loc. °*ci*), f. growing dusk, evening, RV. viii, 27, 21.

आतुजि *ā-tují*, mfn. (√*tuj*), rushing on, RV. vii, 66, 18.

Ā-túje, Ved. Inf. to bring near, RV. vii, 32, 9.

आतुद् *ā-*√*tud* (p. *-tudát;* perf. *-tutóda;* ind. p. *-tudya*) to strike, push, spur on, stir up, RV. x; Mn. iv, 68; MBh. i, 195.

Ā-tunna, mfn. struck, ŚBr. xiv (v. l. *ā-tṛiṇṇa*).

Ā-todin, mfn. striking, AV. vii, 95, 3.

Ā-todya, *am*, n. 'to be struck,' a musical instrument, Jain. (Prākṛit *āojja*); Ragh.; Kathās.

आतुर *ā́-tura*, mf(*ā*)n. suffering, sick (in body or mind), RV. viii; AV. xi, 101, 2, &c.; diseased or pained by (in comp.), MBh.; R. &c.; desirous of (Inf.); (cf. *an-āturá.*)

आतुल् *ā-*√*tul* (Inf. *-tolayitum*) to lift up, raise, R. i, 34, 10 (v. l.)

आतृद् *ā-*√*trid*, P. *-triṇátti*, to divide, pierce (as the ears), Nir.: Ā. *-tṛintté*, to sever one's self, ŚBr. vii.

Ā-tarda, *as*, m. an opening, hole, Comm. on TS.

Ā-tardana, *am*, n. See *alam-āt°*.

Ā́-tṛiṇṇa, mfn. pierced, TS. v; ŚBr.; Kauś.; wounded, BṛĀrUp. (v. l. *ā́-tunna*, q. v.)

Ā-tṛidas, Ved. Inf. (abl.), (Pāṇ. iii, 4, 17) with *purā́*, 'without piercing,' RV. viii, 1, 12.

आतृप् *ā-*√*trip*, P. (Subj. 3. pl. *-tripán*, Padap. 3. sg. °*pát*) to be satisfied, RV. vii, 56, 10: Caus. (Impv. 2. du. *-tarpayethām*) to satisfy, RV. i, 17, 3.

Ā-tarpaṇa, *am*, n. (= *prīṇana*) satisfying, L.; whitening the wall or floor or seat on festive occasions, pigment used for this purpose, L.

Ā-tṛipya, *as*, m. 'to be enjoyed,' the custard apple tree (Anona Reticulata) and (*am*), n. its fruit, L.

आतृ *ā-*√*tṝi*, P. (impf. *ā́tirat*, 2. sg. °*ras*) to overcome, RV.; (impf. *ā́tirat*, 2. sg. °*ras*, 3. pl. Ā. °*ranta*) to increase, make prosperous, glorify, RV.: Intens. Ā. (3. pl. *-tárushante*) to pass through or over, RV. v, 59, 1.

Ā-tara, *as*, m. crossing over a river, Rājat.; fare for being ferried over a river, Śukasaṃdeśa 10; Buddh.

Ā-tāra, *as*, m. (= *ā-tara*) fare, L.

Ātārya, mfn. relating to landing, TS. iv.

आतोदिन् *ā-todín* and *ā-todya*. See *ā-*√*tud*.

आत्त *ā-tta*. See *ā-*√1. *dā*.

Ā́ttām, aor. 3. du. fr. *ā-*√1. *dā*, q. v. (or fr. √*ad*?).

आत्थ *āttha*, 2. sg. pf. of the defect. √1. *ah*, q. v.

आत्मन् *ātmán*, *ā*, m. (variously derived fr. *an*, to breathe; *at*, to move; *vā*, to blow; cf. *tmán*) the breath, RV.; the soul, principle of life and sensation, RV.; AV. &c.; the individual soul, self, abstract individual [e. g. *ātmán* (Ved. loc.) *dhatte* or *karoti*, 'he places in himself,' makes his own, TS. v; ŚBr.; *ātmanā akarot*, 'he did it himself,' Kād.; *ātmanā vi-*√*yuj*, to lose one's life,' Mn. vii, 46; *ātman* in the sg. is used as reflexive pronoun for all three persons and all three genders, e. g. *ātmānaṃ sā hanti*, 'she strikes herself;' *putram ātmanaḥ sprishṭvā nipetatuḥ*, 'they two having touched their son fell down,' R. ii, 64, 28; see also below s. v. *ātmanā*]; essence, nature, character, peculiarity (often ifc., e. g. *karmâtman*, &c.), RV. x, 97, 11, &c.; the person or whole body considered as one and opposed to the separate members of the body, VS.; ŚBr.; the body, Ragh. i, 14; RāmatUp.; (ifc.) 'the understanding, intellect, mind,' see *nashṭâtman*, *mandâ°*; the highest personal principle of life, Brahma (cf. *paramâtman*), AV. x, 8, 44; VS. xxxii, 11; ŚBr. xiv, &c.; effort, L.; (= *dhṛiti*) firmness, L.; the sun, L.; fire, L.; a son, L.; [Old Germ. *ātum;* Angl. Sax. *ædhm;* Mod. Germ. *Athem*, *Odem;* Gk. ἀϋτμήν, ἀτμός (?).] **— vát**, mfn. animated, having a soul, RV.; AV.; TS. **— vín**, mfn. id., ŚBr. x, xiv.

Ātma (in comp. for *ātmán;* also rarely ifc., e. g. *adhy-ātma*, *adhy-ātmám*). **— karman**, n. one's own act. **— kāma** (*ātmá-*), mf(*ā*)n. loving one's self, possessed of self-conceit, R. ii, 70, 10; loving the supreme spirit, ŚBr. xiv (BṛĀrUp.) **— kāmeya**, *ās*, m. pl., N. of a people, (gaṇa *rājanyâdi*, q. v.); °*yaka*, mfn. inhabited by the Ātmakāmeyas, ib. **— kārya**, n. one's own business, private affairs. **— kṛita** (*ātmá-*), mfn. done or committed against one's self, VS. viii, 13; done of one's self, self-executed, R. ii, 46, 23. **— krīḍa**, mfn. playing with the supreme spirit, NṛisUp. **— gata**, mfn. being on itself, MBh. xi, 566 (ed. Bomb.; see *-ruha* below); (*am*), ind. 'gone to one's self,' (in dram.) aside (to denote that the words which follow are supposed to be heard by the audience only), Śak.; Mālav.; Mṛicch. &c. **— gati**, f. one's own way, R. i, 76, 24; 'course of the soul's existence,' life of the spirit, Nir.; (°*tyā*), instr. ind. by one's own act (without the intervention of another), Śak. **— guṇa**, n. virtue of the soul, Gaut. **— guptā**, f. the plant Mucuna Pruritus Hook, Suśr. **— gupti**, f. the hiding-place of an animal, L. **— grāhin**, mfn. taking for one's self, selfish, L. **— ghāta**, m. suicide, L. **— ghātaka**, m. a suicide. **— ghātin**, m. id., Yājñ. iii, 21; Kād. **— ghosha**, m. 'uttering one's own name,' a crow, L.; a cock, L. **— caturtha**, mfn. being one's self the fourth one with three others (N. of Janārdana respecting his four heads?), Pāṇ. vi, 3, 6. **— cchanda-tīrtha**, n., N. of a Tīrtha, SkandaP. **— ja**, mfn. self-originated, MBh. xii, 12449; (*as*), m. (ifc. f. *ā*, R.) 'born from or begotten by one's self,' a son, Nir.; Mn. &c.; N. of the fifth lunar mansion, VarYogay.; (*ā*), f. a daughter, MBh.; R. &c.; 'originating from intellect,' the reasoning faculty, L. **— janman**, n. the birth (or re-birth) of one's self, i. e. the birth of a son, Kum. vi, 28; (*ā*), m. (= *-ja*, m.) a son, Ragh. i, 33; v, 36. **— jña**, mfn. knowing one's self, MBh. xii, 12440; knowing the supreme spirit, Vedāntas. **— jñāna**, n. self-knowledge, MBh. v, 990 & 1167; knowledge of the soul or supreme spirit, Mn. xii, 85 & 92; MBh.; Vedāntas. **— jyotis**, n. the light of the soul or supreme spirit, MBh. xii, 6509; (*ātmá-jyotis*), mfn. receiving light from one's self, ŚBr. xiv; MBh. xii, 783. **— tattva**, n. the true nature of the soul or of the supreme spirit, ŚvetUp.; (*ātmatattva*)*-jña*, mfn. knowing or versed in the Vedānta doctrines, L. **— tantra**, n. the basis of self, MBh. xiii, 4399; (mfn.) depending only on one's self, independant, BhP.; (cf. *sva-tantra.*) **— tā**, f. essence, nature, BhP. **— tṛipta**, mfn. self-satisfied, Bhag. iii, 17. **— tyāga**, m. self-forgetfulness, absence of mind, Suśr.; suicide, Daś. **— tyāgin**, mfn. committing suicide, Yājñ. iii, 6 [*ātmanas tyāgin*, Mn. v, 89]; MBh. iii, 15156. **— trāṇa**, n. a means of saving one's self, BhP.; (*ātmatrāṇa*)*-parigraha*, m. a body-guard, R. v, 47, 27. **— tva**, n. essence, nature, Sāh. **— dakshiṇa**, mfn. (a sacrifice) in which one offers one's self as Dakshiṇā, TāṇḍyaBr. **— darśa**, m. 'self-shower,' a mirror, Ragh. vii, 65. **— darśana**, n. seeing the soul of or in (in comp.), Yājñ. iii, 157; (cf. Mn. xii, 91.) **— dā́**, mfn. granting breath or life, RV. x, 121, 2. **— dāna**, n. gift of self, self-sacrifice, Kathās. **— dūshi**, mfn. corrupting the soul, AV. xvi, 1, 3. **— devatā**, f. a tutelary deity, Hcat. **— drohin**, mfn. self-tormenting, fretful, L. **— nitya**, mfn. constantly in the heart, greatly endeared to one's self, MBh. i, 6080 [= *sva-vaśa*, Comm.] **— nindā**, f. self-reproach, MBh. ii, 1542. **— nivedana**, n. offering one's self to a deity, BhP. **— nishkrâyaṇa**, mfn. ransoming one's self, ŚBr. xi; KaushBr. **— pa**, mfn. guarding one's self, BhP. **— paksha**, m. one's own party, Hit. **— pañcama**, mfn. being one's self the fifth one with four others, Pāṇ. vi, 3, 5, Pat. Comm. **— parājitá**, mfn. one who has lost himself (at play), AV. v, 18, 2. **— parityāga**, m. self-sacrifice, Hit. **— pāta**, m. 'descent of the soul,' re-birth, BhP. **— pūjā**, f. self-praise, MBh. ii, 1542; Pañcat. **— prakāśa**, mfn. self-shining, self-luminous, NṛisUp.; (*as*), m., N. of a commentary on VP. **— pratikṛiti**, f. one's own reflection or image, MBh. v, 2222; Bhav. P. ii. **— prabodha**, m. 'cognition of soul or supreme spirit,' N. of an Upanishad. **— prabha**, mfn. shining by one's own light, self-illuminated, MBh. (Nala). **— prayojana**, mfn. selfish, Āp. **— pravāda**, m. 'dogmas about the soul or supreme spirit,' N. of the seventh of the fourteen Pūrvas or most ancient sacred writings of the Jainas; (*ās*), m. pl. 'those who assert the dogmas about the supreme spirit,' N. of a philosophical school, Nir. xiii, 9. **— praśaṅsaka**, mfn. self-praising, boasting, MBh. xii, 5400. **— praśaṅsā**, f. self-applause, Āp.; R. **— praśaṅsin**, mfn. = *praśaṅsaka*, q. v., R. **— prīti**, f. strong desire to enjoy anything, Pāṇ. vii, 1, 51. **— bandhu**, m. 'one's own kinsman,' a first cousin or father's sister's son, mother's brother's son, mother's sister's son, L. **— buddhi**, f. self-knowledge, L. **— bodha**, m. 'knowledge of soul or supreme spirit,' N. of a work of Śaṅkarācārya; of one of the Upanishads of the Atharva-veda; the possession of a knowledge of soul or the supreme spirit. **— bhava**, m. becoming or existing of one's self; 'mind-born,' N. of Kāma, Mcar.; (mfn.) produced in or caused by one's self, R. ii, 64, 69. **— bhavāyana**, m., N. of Nārāyaṇa, Hariv. 8819 & 12608. **— bhāva**, m. existence of the soul, ŚvetUp.; the self, proper or peculiar nature, Buddh.; the body, ib. **— bhū**, m. 'self-born,' N. of Brahmā, Śak.; Kum. ii, 53; of Vishṇu, Ragh. x, 21; of Śiva, Śak.; a Brahman, Bhām.; 'mind-born,' N. of Kāma, BhP. **— bhūta**, mfn. 'become another's self,' attached to, faithful, Mn. vii, 217; R. vii, 83, 5. **— bhūya**, n. peculiarity, own nature, AitUp. **— maya**, mf(*ī*)n. issued out from one's own self, Nir. vi, 12. **— māna**, n. the regarding one's self as (e. g. learned &c.), Pāṇ. iii, 2, 83. **— mūrti**, mfn. one whose body is the soul, RāmatUp. **— mūlī**, f. 'striking root in self, self-existent,' the plant Alhagi Maurorum, L. **— °m-bhari**, mfn. self-nourishing, taking care only for one's own person, selfish, Pañcat.; Hit.; °*ri-tva*, n. selfishness, Kathās. **— yājin**, mfn. sacrificing for one's self, ŚBr. xi; one who sacrifices himself, Mn. xii, 91. **— yoga**, m. union with the supreme spirit, MBh. iii, 11245. **— yoni**, m. (= *-bhū*, q. v.) a N. of Brahmā, ŚvetUp.; of Śiva, L.; of Vishṇu, Mudr.; of Kāma, Kum. iii, 70. **— rakshaka**, mfn. 'body-guard,' protector, Jain. [Prākṛit *āya-rakkhaya*]. **— rakshaṇa**, n. taking care of one's self, MBh. xii, 5092. **— rakshā**, f. the plant Trichosanthes Bracteata (a creeper with poisonous fruit), L. **— rati**, mfn. rejoicing in the supreme spirit, NṛisUp. **— ruha**, mfn. growing on itself, MBh. xi, 556 (ed. Calc.) **— lābha**, m. one's own profit, Kāvyād.; acquisition (of the knowledge) of the supreme spirit, Āp.; coming into existence, Comm. on Nyāyad.; birth, Kād. **— vañcaka**, mfn. deceiving one's self, BhP. **— vañcanā**, f. self-delusion. **— vat**, mfn. having a soul, NṛisUp.; self-possessed, composed, prudent, Mn.; Yājñ.; MBh. &c.; ind. like one's self, Hit.; (*ātmavat*)*-tā*, f. self-possession, self-regard, prudence, Mn. xi, 86; Ragh. viii, 83; self-resemblance, proportion, analogy, L. **— vadha**, m. suicide, MBh. i, 6228. **— vadhyā**, f. id., ib. 6227. **— vaśa**, mfn. dependent on one's own will, Mn. iv, 159 seq. **— vikraya**, m. sale of one's self, i. e. of one's liberty, Mn. xi, 59. **— víd**, mfn. knowing the nature of the soul or supreme spirit, ŚBr. xiv; Up.; MBh.; (*ātmavit*)*-tā*, f. = *ātma-vidyā́* below, Ragh. viii, 10. **— vidyā**, f. knowledge of soul or the supreme spirit, ŚBr. x; Mn. vii, 43. **— vidhitsā**, f. selfishness, MBh. v, 1343. **— vivṛiddhi**, f. self-advantage, L. **— vīra**, m. (= *bala-vat*) a mighty man, L.; (= *prāṇa-vat*) a living being, L.; a son, L.; a wife's brother, L.; the jester in a play, L. **— vṛittânta**, m. one's own story, autobiography, L. **— vṛitti**, f. one's own circumstances, Ragh. ii, 33. **— vṛiddhi**, f. = *-vivṛiddhi*, q. v. **— śakti**, f. one's own power or effort, Pañcat. (Hit.) **— śalyā**, f. the plant Asparagus Racemosus Willd., L. **— śuddhi**, f. self-purification, Mn. xi, 164; Bhag. v, 11. **— ślāgha**, mfn. self-praising, boasting, Veṇis.; (*ā*), f. *an-* neg. in comp. with *-kara*, mfn. 'not boasting,' Sāh. **— ślāghin**, mfn. self-praising, BhP. **— saṃyama**, m. self-restraint, Bhag. iv, 27. **— saṃstha**, mf(*ā*)n. based on or connected with the person, Mālav. **— sád**, mfn. dwelling in (my-)self, AV. v, 9, 8. **— sáni**, mfn. granting the breath of life, VS. xix, 48. **— saṃtāna**, m. 'one's own offspring,' a son, Mn. iii, 185. **— saṃdeha**, m. personal risk, Hit. **— sama**, m. equal to one's self; (*ātmasama*)*-tām* √*nī*, to render any one (acc.) equal to one's self, Ratnāv. **— samarpaṇa**, n. = *-nivedana* above, BhP. **— sambhava**, m. (= *-ja*) a son, MBh. i, 6651; R.; Ragh.; N. of Kāma, Kād.; (*ā*), f. a daughter, R. **— sambhāvanā**, f. self-conceit, Kād. **— sammita** (*ātmá-*), mfn. corresponding to the person, ŚBr. vi-x; resembling the soul or supreme spirit, ChUp. **— sācin**, m. one's own companion, Suparṇ. **— sāt**, ind. with √1. *kṛi* (ind. p. *-kṛitvā*) to place upon one's self, Yājñ. iii, 54; *-karoti* (ind. p. *-kṛitvā*, MBh. iii, 493 & 496; *-kṛitya*, BhP.) to make one's own, attract, turn to one's self, acquire or gain for one's self; to cause to become one with the supreme spirit, NṛisUp. **— sukha**, m., N. of a man. **— stava**, m. self-praise, R. iii, 35, 22. **— stuti**, f. id.; (cf. *stutir* [acc. pl.] *ātmanaḥ*, Rājat.) **— spáraṇa**, mfn. saving the person, TS. vi; TBr. ii. **— hatyā**, f. suicide, Prab. **— han**, mfn. one who kills his soul, i. e. does not care about the welfare of his soul, ĪśaUp.; BhP.; (*ā*), m. a suicide, MBh. i, 6839; a priest in a temple attendant upon an idol (the priest subsisting by appropriating to himself offerings to deities for which future punishment is assigned), L. **—hanana,** n. suicide, L. **—hita,** mfn. beneficial to one's self; (*am*), n. one's own profit, L. **—hitāyana,** m. = *-bhavāyana*, q. v., Hariv. 12608. **Ātmâdishṭa,** m. 'self-dictated,' a treaty dictated by the party wishing it himself, L. **Ātmâdhika,** mf(*ā*)n. 'more than one's self,' dearer than one's self, Kathās. **Ātmâdhīna,** mfn. depending on one's own will, Āp.; Śārṅg.; one whose existence depends on the breath or on the principle of animal life, sentient, L.; (*as*), m. a son, L.; a wife's brother, L.; the jester in a play, L.; (cf. *ātma-vīra* and *ātmanīna.*) **Ātmânanda,** mfn. rejoicing in the soul or supreme spirit, NṛisUp. **Ātmânapeksha,** mfn. not regarding one's self, not selfish, Kathās. **Ātmâparādha,** m. one's own offence, personal transgression, R. v, 79, 5; Hit. **Ātmâpahāra,** m. 'taking away self,' concealing of self, dissimulation, see *apa-hāra; -ka*, mfn. self-concealing, dissembling, pretending to belong to a higher class than one's own, Mn. iv, 255. **Ātmâpahārin,** mfn. self-deceiving, self-concealing, dissembling, MBh. i, 3014 (= v, 1611). **Ātmâbhimāni-tā,** f. self-respect, MBh. iii, 17379. **Ātmâbhilāsha,** m. the soul's desire, Megh. **Ātmâmisha,** m. a peace made after having sacrificed one's own army, Kām. **Ātmârāma,** mfn. rejoicing in one's self or in the supreme spirit, BhP. &c. **Ātmârtham,** ind. for the sake of one's self, Kathās. **Ātmârthe,** ind. id., MBh. **Ātmâśin,** m. 'self-eater,' a fish (supposed to eat its young), L. **Ātmâśraya,** m. dependance on self or on the supreme spirit; *ātmâśrayôpanishad*, f., N. of an Upanishad. **Ātmêśvara,** m. master of one's self, Kum. iii, 40. **Ātmôdaya,** m. self-advantage or elevation, L. **Ātmôdbhava,** m. (= *ātma-sambhava*) a son, Ragh. xviii, 11; (*ā*), f. a daughter, L.; the plant Glycine Debilis Roxb., L. **Ātmôpajīvin,** mfn. living by one's own labour, Mn. vii, 138; viii, 362 ['one who lives by his wife,' Comm.]; Gaut. **Ātmôpanishad,** f., N. of an Upanishad. **Ātmôpama,** mfn. like one's self. **Ātmâupamya,** n. 'likeness to self,' instr. °*myena*, by analogy to one's self, Hit.

Ātmaka, mf(*ikā*)n. belonging to or forming the nature of (gen.), MBh. xv, 926; having or consisting of the nature or character of (in comp.), ChUp. [cf. *saṃkalpâtmaka*]; consisting or composed of, Mn.; MBh. &c.; (cf. *pañcâtmaka* &c.)

Ātmakīya, mfn. one's own, MBh. i, 4712.

Ātmanā, instr. of *ātman*, in comp. [but not in a Bahuvrīhi] with ordinals, Pāṇ. vi, 3, 6; (cf. the Bahuvrīhi compounds *ātma-caturtha* and *-pañcama.*) **—tṛitīya,** mfn. 'third with one's self,' being one's self the third, Śak.; Kathās. **—daśama,** mfn. being one's self the tenth, Pat. **—dvitīya,** mfn. being one's self the second, i. e. together with some one else, Hit. **—pañcama,** mfn. being one's self the fifth, R. **—saptama,** mfn. being one's self the seventh, MBh. xvii, 25.

Ātmanīna, mf(*ā*)n. (Pāṇ. v, 1, 9 & vi, 4, 169) appropriate or good or fit for one's self, Prab.; Bhaṭṭ.; (= *ātmâdhīna*, q. v.) sentient, L.; (*as*), m. a son, L.; a wife's brother, L.; the jester in a play, L.

Ātmanīya, mf(*ā*)n. one's own, Lalit.

Ātmane, dat. in comp. for *ātman*, Pāṇ. vi, 3, 7 & 8. **—pada,** n. 'word to one's self,' form for one's self, i. e. that form of the verb which implies an action belonging or reverting to self, the terminations of the middle voice, Pāṇ. i, 4, 100 & 3, 12. **—padin,** mfn. taking the terminations of the middle voice, Pāṇ. Comm. **—bhāsha,** mfn. id., Pat.; (*ā*), f. = *-pada*, q. v., Pāṇ. vi, 3, 7, Kāś.

Ātmanya, mf(*ā*)n. being connected with one's self, TāṇḍyaBr.

Ātmī-√1. kṛi, to make one's own, take possession of, Kād.

Ātmī-bhāva, m. becoming part of the supreme spirit.

Ātmīya, mf(*ā*)n. one's own, Yājñ. ii, 85; R. &c.

Ātmeyá, *ās*, m. pl. a class of divinities also called *Ātmyá* (and named together with the Āpyá), MaitrS.

Ātmyá, *ās*, m. pl. id., TBr.; (cf. *an-* and *etad-*.)

आत्यन्तिक *ātyantika*, mf(ī)n. (fr. *aty-anta*), continual, uninterrupted, infinite, endless, Mn. ii, 242 seq.; Bhag. &c.; entire, universal (as the world's destruction &c.), BhP.; Sarvad.

आत्ययिक *ātyayika*, mfn. (fr. *aty-aya;* gaṇa *vinayâdi*, q. v.), 'having a rapid course,' not suffering delay, urgent, Mn. vii, 165; MBh. &c.; requiring immediate help (as a disease), Suśr.

आत्र *ātra, am*, n. (fr. *átri*), N. of different Sāmans.

Ātreyá, *as*, m. (Pāṇ. iv, 1, 122, Comm.) a descendant of Atri, ŚBr. xiv, &c.; N. of a physician, Bhpr.; a priest who is closely related to the Sadasya (perhaps because this office was generally held by a descendant of Atri), ŚBr. iv; AitBr.; N. of Śiva, L.; chyle, L.; (*ī*), f. a female descendant of Atri, Pāṇ. ii, 4, 65; (with *śākhā*) the Śākhā of the Ātreyas; a woman who has bathed after her courses, ŚBr. i; Mn. xi, 87; Yājñ. iii, 251; N. of a river in the north of Bengal (otherwise called Tistā), MBh. ii, 374; (*am*), n., N. of two Sāmans, ĀśvGṛ. &c.; (*ās*), m. pl., N. of a tribe, MBh. vi, 376; (for *atrayas*, m. pl. of *atri*, q. v.) the descendants of Atri, MBh. iii, 971. **Ātreyī-pútra,** m., N. of a teacher, ŚBr. xiv.

Ātreyāyaṇa, *as*, m. a descendant of an Ātreya, (gaṇa *aśvâdi*, q. v.)

Ātreyikā, f. a woman in her courses, L.

Ātreyīya, mfn. fr. *ātreya*, Pāṇ. iv, 1, 89, Kāś.

आथर्वण *ātharvaṇá*, mf(ī)n. (Pāṇ. iv, 3, 133) originating from or belonging or relating to Atharvan or the Atharvans, AV.; Āp. &c.; (*ás*), m. a descendant of Atharvan or the Atharvans (as Dadhyác), RV.; AV.; TS. v, &c.; a priest or Brahman whose ritual is comprised in the Atharva-veda, a conjurer, MBh. v, 1391, &c.; the Atharva-veda, ChUp. &c.; N. of a text belonging to the Atharva-veda, Comm. on KātyŚr.; (*am*), n., N. of different Sāmans; = *atharvaṇām samūhaḥ*, (gaṇa *bhikshâdi*, q. v.); an apartment (in which the sacrificer is informed by the officiating Brāhman of the happy termination of the sacrifice), L. **—rahasya,** n., N. of a work. **—śiras,** n., N. of an Upanishad (belonging to the Atharva-veda).

Ātharvaṇika, mf(*ī*)n. belonging or relating to the Atharva-veda, Daś. &c.; (*as*), m. (Pāṇ. iv, 3, 133; vi, 4, 174; gaṇa *vasantâdi*, q. v.) a Brāhman versed in the Atharva-veda.

Ātharvaṇīya-rudrôpanishad, *t*, f., N. of an Upanishad.

Ātharvika, mfn. relating to the Atharva-veda, VāyuP. ii.

आद *ā-da*. See *ā-√1. dā.*

आदंश *ā-√daṅś* (impf. *ādaśat*) to bite (as one's lips), BhP.

Ā-daṅśa, *as*, m. a bite, wound caused by biting, Suśr.

Ā-dashṭa, mfn. nibbled, pecked at, MBh. ii, 704; xi, 638.

आदघ् *ā-√dagh*, P. (Subj. *-daghat;* aor. Subj. 2. sg. *-dhak*) to hurt, injure, RV. vi, 61, 14; TS. i; to frustrate (a wish), RV. i, 178, 1; (aor. Subj. 3. sg. *-dhak*) to happen to, befall any one (loc., as misfortune), RV. vii, 1, 21.

आदघ्न *ā-daghná*, mfn. (for *ās-d°*) reaching up to the mouth (as water), RV. x, 71, 7.

आदत् *ádat*, impf. fr. *ā√1. dā*, q. v.

Ā-dadí. See ib.

आदभ् *ā-√dabh*, P. (Subj. *-dabhat;* 3. pl. *-dabhnuvanti*, Subj. *-dabhan* and aor. *-dabhuḥ;* Ved. Inf. *-dábhe*, RV. viii, 21. 16) to harm, hurt, injure, RV.

आदम् *ā-√dam.* See *dáṅsu-patnī.*

आदर *ā-dara*, °*raṇa*, &c. See *ā-√dṛi.*

आदर्दिर *ā-dardirá.* See *ā-√dṝi.*

आदर्श *ā-darśá*, &c. See *ā-√dṛiś.*

आदशस्य *ā-daśasya*, Nom. P. (Impv. 2. sg. *-daśasya*, 2. pl. °*syata*) to honour, be favourable to (acc.), RV. v, 50, 3; vii, 43, 5; (Pot. 2. sg. °*syes*) to present any one with (gen.), RV. vii, 37, 5; viii, 97, 15.

आदह् *ā-√dah*, Caus. Pass. (Pot. *-dāhyeta*) to be burnt, ChUp.

Ā-dáhana, *am*, n. a place where anything is burnt, AV. xii, 5, 48; ĀśvGṛ.; Kauś.

आदा *ā-√1. dā*, Ā. *-datte* (Pāṇ. i, 3, 20), ep. also rarely P. (e. g. 1. sg. *-dadmi* or *-dadāmi*), Ved. generally Ā. [Pot. 1. pl. *-dadīmahi;* impf. 3. sg. *ádatta;* perf. 1. & 3. sg. *-dade;* perf. p. *-dadāná*, RV. iv, 19, 9, or *-dádāna*, RV. x, 18, 9; AV.], but also P. (impf. sg. *ádam, ádas, ádat*, and 1. pl. *ádāma*, aor. 3. du. *áttām*, VS. xxi, 43) 'to give to one's self,' take, accept, receive from (loc., instr. or abl.), RV. &c.; to seize, take away, carry off, rob, ib.; to take back, reclaim, Mn. viii, 222 seq.; to take off or out from (abl.), separate from (abl.), RV. i, 139, 2, &c.; to take or carry away with one's self, KenaUp. (Pot. P. 1. sg. *-dadīyam !*); Mn. ix, 92; MBh.; to seize, grasp, take or catch hold of, RV. &c.; to put on (clothes), RV. ix, 96, 1; ŚvetUp.; to take as food or drink (with gen.), RV. viii, 72, 17 & (perf. Pass. 3. sg. *-dade*) 19, 31; (with acc.) Ragh. ii, 6; to undertake, begin, BhP. &c.; to choose (a path), R.; Ragh. iii, 46; (with *vacanam* &c.) to begin to speak, MBh. &c.; to begin to speak or to recite, TāṇḍyaBr.; Lāṭy. (cf. *punar-ādāyam*); to offer (as oblations), MuṇḍUp. (irreg. pr. p. *-dadāyat*); to perceive, notice, feel, MBh.; Rājat.; to keep in mind, N.; to accept, approve of, MBh. v, 7324; R.; Mālav.; Caus. (ind. p. *-dāpya*) to cause one to take, ŚāṅkhŚr.: Desid. Ā. (impf. 3. pl. *áditsanta*) to be on the point of taking or carrying away from (gen.), TS. i; to be on the point of taking (the hand of), Daś.; to be about to take to one's self, Hcar.

Ā-tta, mfn. (Pāṇ. vii, 4, 47) taken, obtained, ChUp.; Kathās.; taken away or off, withdrawn from, ŚBr.; AitBr. &c.; seized, grasped, ChUp.; Lāṭy. &c.; perceived, felt, Mālav.; undertaken, begun, MBh. xiii, 3567. **—gandha,** mfn. having the pride taken down (according to some = *ārta-kaṇṭha*), Śak.; Ragh. xiii, 7. **—garva,** mfn. whose pride has been taken down, humiliated, L. **—manas** or **-manas-ka,** mfn. whose mind is transported (with joy), Buddh. **—lakshmi,** mfn. stripped of wealth, MBh. iii, 15671. **—vacas** (*átta-*), mfn. destitute of speech, ŚBr. iii.

Ā-dá, mfn. ifc. taking, receiving; (cf. *dāyâdá.*)

Ā-datta, mfn. = *ā-tta*, q. v., Hariv. 11811.

Ā-dadí, mfn. procuring, RV. viii, 46, 8; obtaining, recovering, RV. i, 127, 6; ii, 24, 13.

Ā-dātavya, mfn. seizable; to be taken.

Ā-dātṛi, *tā*, m. a receiver, Mn.; Yājñ.

1. **Ā-dāna,** *am*, n. taking, seizing; receipt, Hit. iv, 94, &c.; receiving, taking for one's self, drawing near to one's self, Ragh. iv, 86; taking away or off; a cause of disease, L.; (for 2. *ā-dāna* see below.) **—vat,** mfn. receiving, obtaining, MBh. **—samiti,** f. a method of (cautious) seizing (so that no creature be hurt), Jain.

Ā-dānī, f., N. of a cucurbitaceous plant, L.

Ā-dāpana, *am*, n. causing to seize, KātyŚr.; ĀśvŚr.

1. **Ā-dāya,** mfn. ifc. taking, seizing.

2. **Ā-dāya,** ind. p. having taken; with, along with, AV. &c. **—cara,** mf(*ī*)n. one who goes away after having taken, Pāṇ. iii, 2, 17.

1. **Ā-dāyamāna** (= *ā-dadāna*), mfn. taking, seizing, MBh.; (for 2. see *ā-√dai.*)

Ā-dāyin, mfn. a receiver, inclined to receive, AitBr.; (ifc.) Mn.; v. l. *ā-dhāyin*, q. v.

Ā-ditsā, f. (fr. Desid.) the wish to take.

Ā-ditsu, mfn. (fr. id.) wishing to take or obtain; greedy of gain, Kād.; Hit.; Kum. &c.

Ā-deya, mfn. to be appropriated; to be received; to be taken away; v. l. for *ā-dheya*, q. v.

आदा *ā-√4. dā*, P. *á-dyati*, to bind on, fasten to, AV.

2. **Ā-dāna,** *am*, n. binding on or to, fettering, AV.; horse-trappings, L.; (for 3. *ā-dāna* see below under *ā-√do.*)

आदादिक *ādādika*, mfn. belonging to the gaṇa *ad-ādi* of the Dhātupāṭha, or to the second class of roots of which the first is *√ad.*

आदि 1. *ādi, is*, m. beginning, commencement; a firstling, first-fruits; ifc. beginning with, et cætera, and so on (e. g. *indrâdayaḥ surāḥ*, the gods beginning with Indra, i. e. Indra &c.; *gṛihâdiyukta*, possessed of houses &c.; *evamādīni vastūni*, such things and others of the same kind; *śayyā khaṭvâdiḥ* [Comm. on Pāṇ. iii, 3, 99], Śayyā means a bed &c.; often with *-ka* at the end, e. g. *dānadharmâdikam* [Hit.], liberality, justice, &c.); *ādau*, ind. in the beginning, at first. **—kara,** m. the first maker, the creator; N. of Brahman, L. **—karṇī,** f. a species of plant, L. **—kartṛi,** m. (cf. *-kara*) the creator, Bhag.; R. **—karman,** n. the beginning of an action (in Gr.) — **kavi**, m. 'the first poet;' N. of Brahman; of Vālmīki, L. — **kāṇḍa**, n. 'first part,' N. of the first book of the Rāmāyaṇa. — **kāraṇa**, n. a primary cause; analysis, algebra. — **kāla**, m. primitive time, R. — **kālīna**, mfn. belonging to primitive time. — **kāvya**, n. 'the first poem,' N. of the Rāmāyaṇa. — **kṛit** (= -*kartṛi*, q. v.), VP. — **keśava**, m. 'the first long-haired one,' N. of Vishṇu, Rājat. — **gadā-dhara**, m. 'the first club-bearer,' N. of an image of Vishṇu, VP. — **jina**, m., N. of Ṛishabha, Jain.; L. — **tas**, ind. from the beginning, from the first, at first, at the head of (with √1. *kṛi*, to put at the beginning, Pat. on Pāṇ. iii, 1, 9; ifc. beginning with). — **tāla**, m. a kind of measure (in music). — **tva**, n. priority, precedence. — **dīpaka**, n., N. of a figure in rhetoric (the verb standing at the beginning of the sentence), Bhaṭṭ. x, 22. — **deva**, m. 'the first god;' N. of Brahman, Vishṇu, Śiva, Gaṇeśa, the sun. — **daitya**, m., N. of Hiraṇyakaśipu, MBh. — **nātha**, m., N. of Ādibuddha; of a Jina; of an author. — **parvata**, m. a principal mountain, Kād. 117, 20. — **parvan**, n. 'the first book,' N. of the first book of the Mahābhārata. — **purāṇa**, n. 'the primitive Purāṇa,' N. of the Brahma-purāṇa; of a Jaina religious book. — **purusha** or -**pūrusha**, m. 'first man,' N. of Hiraṇyakaśipu, MBh.; of Vishṇu, Ragh. x, 6; Śiś.; of Brahman, L. — **pluta**, mfn. (a word) whose first vowel is prolated, Gr. — **bala**, n. 'the primal vigour,' generative power, Suśr. — **buddha**, mfn. 'perceived in the beginning;' m., N. of the chief deity of the northern Buddhists. — **bharata-prastāra**, m., N. of a work. — **bhava**, mfn. 'being at first,' Ragh. &c. — **bhūta**, mfn. being the first of (gen.), VP. iii, 5, 23. — **mat**, mfn. having a beginning, Yājñ. &c.; -*tva*, n. the state of having a beginning, Nyāyad. — **mūla**, n. primitive cause. — **yogâcārya**, m. 'first teacher of Yoga,' N. of Śiva. — **rasa-śloka**, *ās*, m. pl. 'stanzas illustrating the chief sentiment,' N. of a poem supposed to be written by Kālidāsa. — **rāja**, m. [Pāṇ. v, 4, 91] 'first king,' N. of Manu, R.; of Pṛithu, BhP. iv, 15, 4. — **rūpa**, n. 'first appearance,' symptom (of disease). — **lupta**, mfn. (a word) having the first letter cut off, Nir. x, 34. — **vaṅśa**, m. primeval race, primitive family, MBh.; R. — **varāha**, m. 'the first boar,' N. of Vishṇu, Kād.; Hariv.; N. of a poet. — **vārāha**, mfn. relating to the first boar; -*tīrtha*, n., N. of a Tīrtha. — **vipulā**, f., N. of an Āryā metre. — **śakti**, f. the primeval power, N. of Māyā, L. — **śarīra**, n. the primitive body, MBh.; (in phil. = *sūkshma*°, L.) — **śābdika** [NBD.], m. an old grammarian. — **sarga**, m. primitive creation, MBh.; cf. BhP. iv, 10, 12 seqq. — **sūra**, m., N. of a prince. **Ādîśvara**, m., N. of a prince. **Ādy-anta**, n. or *au*, du. pl. beginning and end, Vedāntas. 200; Lāṭy. &c.; ifc. mfn. beginning and ending with, Mn. iii, 205; -*yamaka*, n. 'homophony in the beginning and end of a stanza,' N. of a figure in poetry (occurring in Bhaṭṭ. x, 21; Śiś.; Kir. &c.); -1. *vat*, mfn. 'having beginning and end,' finite, Bhag. v, 22; 2. *vat*, ind. as if it were the beginning and the end, Pāṇ. i, 1, 21. **Ādy-ādi**, m., N. of a gaṇa, Kāty. on Pāṇ. v, 4, 44. **Ādy-udātta**, mfn. having the Udātta accent on the first syllable, Pāṇ. iii, 1, 3; -*tva*, n. the condition of having the Udātta accent on the first syllable, Kāś. on Pāṇ. i, 1, 63.

Ādima, mf(*ā*)n. first, prior, primitive, original, Pāṇ.; Pat.; L. — **tva**, n. the state of being first, &c.

1. **Ādyá**, mf(*ā*)n. [Pāṇ. iv, 3, 54] being at the beginning, first, primitive, KātyŚr.; Hit.; Śak. &c.; ifc. mfn. (= *ādi*, q. v.), Mn. i, 50, 63, &c.; immediately preceding (e. g. *ekādaśâdya*, immediately before the eleventh, i. e. the tenth), earlier, older; being at the head, unparalleled, unprecedented, excellent, AV. xix, 22, 1; MBh.; (*ās*), m. pl. a class of deities, VP. iii, 1, 27; Hariv.; (*ā*), f., N. of Durgā; the earth, L.; (for 2. *ādyà* see s. v.) — **kavi**, m. 'the first poet,' N. of Vālmīki (cf. *ādi-kavi* above), L.; cf. Ragh. xv, 41. — **gaṅgā**, f., N. of a river. — **bīja**, n. a primeval cause, L. — **māshaka**, m., N. of a weight equal to five guñjās, L. — °**rtvij** (-*ṛitvij*), m. chief-priest.

आदि 2. *âdi*, mfn. beginning with *ā*, Rāmat-Up.

आदिग्ध *ā-digdha*. See under *ā-√dih*.

आदितेय *ā-diteyá*, *as*, m. 'son of Aditi,' the sun, RV. x, 88, 11; Nir.; a god, deity, L.

1. **Ādityá** (Pāṇ. iv, 1, 85), mfn. belonging to or coming from Aditi, TS. ii, 2, 6, 1; ŚBr. &c.; m. 'son of Aditi;' (*ās*), m. pl., N. of seven deities of the heavenly sphere, RV. ix, 114, 3, &c.; ŚBr. iii, 1, 3, 3 (the chief is Varuṇa, to whom the N. Āditya is especially applicable; the succeeding five are Mitra, Aryaman, Bhaga, Daksha, Aṅśa; that of the seventh is probably Sūrya or Savitṛi; as a class of deities they are distinct from the *viśve devāḥ*, ChUp.; sometimes their number is supposed to be eight, TS.; Sāy.; and in the period of the Brāhmaṇas twelve, as representing the sun in the twelve months of the year, ŚBr. iv, 5, 7, 2, &c.); N. of a god in general, especially of Sūrya (the sun), RV.; AV.; AitBr.; ŚBr.; Śiś. &c.; N. of Vishṇu in his Vāmana or dwarf *avatāra* (as son of Kaśyapa and Aditi), ChUp.; the plant Calotropis Gigantea, L.; (*au*), m. du., N. of a constellation, the seventh lunar mansion, L.; (*ā*), f.(?) the sun, VS. iv, 21; (*am*), n. = *au* (cf. *punar-vasu*); N. of a Sāman, ChUp. — **kāntā**, f. Polanisia Icosandra (a creeping plant with gold-coloured flowers, growing near the water), L. — **ketu**, m., N. of a son of Dhṛita-rāshṭra, MBh. — **keśava**, m., N. of an image of Vishṇu. — **gati**, f. course of the sun, MBh. — **garbha**, m., N. of a Bodhisattva, L. — **grahá**, m. a particular ladle-full of Soma in the evening-oblation, ŚBr. iv, 3, 5, 16 & 23. — **candrau**, m. du. sun and moon. — **jūta** (*ādityá-*), (fr. √*jū*), mfn. urged by the Ādityas, RV. viii, 46, 5. — **jyotis** (*ādityá-*), mfn. having the light of the sun, ŚBr. — **tīrtha**, n., N. of a Tīrtha. — **tejas**, m. or f. Polanisia Icosandra, L. — **tva**, n. the state of being the sun, MaitrUp. — **darśana**, n. 'showing the sun' (to a child of four months), one of the rites called Saṃskāra, q. v., Vishṇus. xxvii, 10. — **dāsa**, m., N. of a man. — **deva**, m. id. — **devata** (*ādityá-*), mfn. one whose (special) deity is the sun, ŚBr. — **nāman**, n., N. of the sun, ib. — **pattra**, m. Calotropis Gigantea, L. — **parṇikā**, f. [L.], -**parṇin**, m. and -**parṇinī**, f. [Suśr.] Polanisia Icosandra. — **pāka**, mfn. boiled in the sun. — **pātrá**, n. a vessel for drawing off the *āditya-grahá* (q. v.), ŚBr. iv, 3, 5, 6, &c. — **purāṇa**, n., N. of an Upapurāṇa. — **pushpikā**, f. = -*pattra*, L. — **prabha**, m. 'having the splendour of the sun,' N. of a king, Kathās. — **bandhu**, m. 'the sun's friend,' N. of Śākyamuni. — **bhaktā**, f. = -*parṇikā*, L. — **maṇḍalá**, n. the disc or orb of the sun, ŚBr.; Vedāntas. 67. — **yaśas**, m., N. of a man. — **loka**, m. pl. the sun's worlds, ŚBr. xiv, 6, 6, 1. — 1. **vat**, ind. like the sun, MBh. — 2. **vat** (*ādityá-*), mfn. surrounded by the Ādityas, AV. xix, 18, 4; VS.; KātyŚr. — **váni**, mfn. winning (the favour of) the Ādityas, VS. — **varṇa**, mfn. 'having the sun's colour,' ib.; m., N. of a man. — **varman**, m. 'having the sun (the Ādityas?) as protector,' N. of a king, Kathās. — **vallabhā**, f. = -*parṇikā*, L. — **vrata**, n. 'a vow or rite relating to the sun,' Gobh. iii, 1, 28; N. of a Sāman. — **vratika**, mfn. performing the above rite, Kāty. on Pāṇ. v, 1, 94. — **śayana**, n. the sun's sleep; -*vrata*, n. a particular vow or religious observance. — **saṃvatsara**, m. a solar year. — **sūkta**, n. a particular hymn. — **sūnu**, m. 'the sun's son,' N. of Sugrīva (the monkey king), of Yama, of Manu, &c., L. — **sena**, m., N. of a prince, Kathās. — **stotra**, n., N. of a Stotra. — **sthālī**, f. a receptacle from which the *āditya-grahá* is drawn, ŚBr. — **svāmin**, m., N. of a man. — **hṛidaya**, n., N. of a Stotra. **Ādityâcārya**, m., N. of an author. **Ādityânuvartin**, mfn. following the sun, Suśr.

2. **Ādityá**, mfn. (Pāṇ. iv, 1, 85) relating or belonging to or coming from the Ādityas, RV. i, 105, 16; VS.; ŚBr. &c.; relating to the god of the sun.

आदित्सा *ā-ditsā*, *ā-ditsu*. See under *ā-√1. dā*, p. 136, col. 3.

आदिन् *ādin* (√*ad*), mfn. ifc. eating, devouring, Pāṇ. viii, 4, 48; R.; Mn. &c.

आदिनव *ādinavá*, (probably n.) misfortune, want of luck in dice, AV. vii, 109, 4; (cf. *ādīnava*.) — **darśa**, mfn. having in view (another's) misfortune, VS. xxx, 18.

आदिश् 1. *ā-√diś*, P. -*didéshṭi* [Subj. 3. sg. -*dideśati*, AV. vi, 6, 2, &c.], -*diśáti* [3. pl. -*diśanti*, Impv. 2. sg. -*diśa*, impf. 1. sg. *ādiśam*, &c.], rarely -*diśate* [BhP. viii, 24, 51], inf. -*díśe* [RV. ix, 21, 5] and -*deshṭum* (aor. 3. sg. *ādikshat* [Bhaṭṭ. iii, 3, see Pāṇ. iii, 1, 45], fut. 1. pl. -*dekshyāmaḥ*, perf. -*dideśa*) to aim at, have in view; to threaten, RV. ix, 21, 5, &c.; AV.; to hit, RV. ix, 56, 1; to assign, RV. ii, 41, 17, &c.; AV.; BhP.; R.; Ragh. &c.; to point out, indicate; to report, announce, teach, ChUp. iii, 18, 1; BhP.; MBh.; R.; Ragh. &c.; to determine, specify, denominate, ŚBr. iii, 5, 8; ŚāṅkhŚr.; Lāṭy.; BhP.; AitBr. &c.; to declare, foretell, Ratnāv.; Mālav. &c.; to order, direct, command, Gobh.; ĀśvGṛ.; Mn.; MBh.; BhP.; Kathās. &c.; to refer any one to (loc.); to banish, MBh.; Śak.; Kathās. &c.; to undertake, try, MBh.; to profess as one's aim or duty, RV.; Yājñ.: Caus. -*deśayati*, to show, indicate, announce, Ratnāv.; MBh.; Śak.; Mṛicch.: Intens. (p. -*dédiśāna*) to have in view, aim at (acc.), RV. ix, 70, 5.

2. **Ā-díś**, *k*, f. aiming at, design, intention, RV. x, 61, 3, &c.; N. of a particular direction or point of the compass (enumerated with *diś*, *pra*°, *vi*°, and *ud*°), VS. vi, 19; (cf. inf. *ā-díśe* = dat.)

Ā-diśya, ind. p. aiming at, MBh.; announcing, teaching, Ragh. xii, 68; having said, L.

Ā-dishṭa, mfn. directed, assigned, ŚBr. i, 1, 4, 24; announced, ChUp. iii, 18, 1; mentioned, ŚBr.; enjoined, ordered, advised, Śak.; (*am*), n. command, order, instruction, Comm. on Mn. v, 88; N. of a particular kind of treaty (in making peace); fragments or leavings of a meal, L.

Ā-dishṭin, *ī*, m. one who receives (religious) instruction, a student, Brāhman in the first order of his life, Mn. v, 88; MBh.; one who gives instruction, L.

Ā-deśa, *as*, m. advice, instruction, ŚBr. x, 4, 5, 1, &c.; KātyŚr.; ChUp.; TUp.; RPrāt. &c.; account, information, declaration, Mn. ix, 258; Yājñ.; foretelling, soothsaying, Ratnāv.; Mṛicch.; a precept; rule, command, order, R.; Hit.; Pañcat.; Ragh. &c.; a substitute, substituted form or letter, Pāṇ. i, 1, 49; 52, &c.; APrāt. i, 63; Ragh. xii, 58; result or consequence of stellar conjunction, VarBṛ. — **kārin**, mfn. obeying orders.

Ā-deśaka, *as*, m. one who commands, a guide, Kād.

Ā-deśana, *am*, n. the act of pointing out, commanding, instructing, Mn. ii, 173.

Ā-deśin, mfn. ifc. assigning; commanding, directing, Ragh. iv, 68; that (form or letter) for which something is substituted (= *sthānin*, q. v.), Kāty. on Pāṇ. i, 1, 56; (*ī*), m. a fortune-teller, L.

Ā-deśya, mfn. to be said or ordered or commanded, Pañcat.

Ā-deshṭṛi, *tā*, m. one who orders, a teacher, VarBṛ.; an employer of priests, L.

आदिह् *ā-√dih*, only p. p.

Ā-digdha, mfn. ifc. besmeared, anointed, MBh.; Hariv.; BhP.

आदी *ā-√2. dī* (3. sg. impf. *ādidet*, RV. i, 149, 3; 3. sg. aor. *á-dīdayat*, RV. ii, 4, 3) to shine upon, enlighten.

आदीदि *ā-dīdi*. See *ā-√2. dī*.

आदीधि *ā-dīdhi*. See 2. *a-√dhī*.

आदीनव *ādīnava*, *as*, m. distress, pain, uneasiness; fault, L.

आदीप् *ā-√dīp*, Caus. P. -*dīpayati* (2. sg. Subj. *á-dīpayas*, RV. vi, 22, 8) to cause to blaze, kindle, set on fire, illuminate, RV.; ŚBr.; MBh.; R. &c.

Ā-dīpaka, mfn. (Pāṇ. iii, 1, 133) setting on fire, L.; (*as*), m. an incendiary, MBh.

Ā-dīpana, *am*, n. setting on fire, inflaming, Kauś.; BhP.; embellishing, L.; whitening a wall or floor or seat &c. upon festival occasions, L.

Ā-dīpita, mfn. inflamed, R.

Ā-dīpta, mfn. set on fire, blazing up, MBh. &c.

Ā-dīpya, ind. p. having set on fire, TS.; ŚBr.; KātyŚr.

आदीर्घ *ā-dīrgha*, mfn. somewhat long, oval, Bhartṛ. i, 86.

आदु *ā-√1. du* (Ā. 2. sg. Impv. -*dunvasva*, MBh. i, 3289) to feel pain, be consumed by grief.

Ā-dūna, mfn. (Pat. on Pāṇ. viii, 2, 44).

आदुरि *āduri*. See under *ā-√dṛī* below.

आदुह् *ā-√duh*, P. (3. pl. impf. *âduhús*, RV. ix, 72, 2) Ā. (1. sg. pr. *ā-duhe*, RV. ix, 10, 8) to milk near or out.

आदृ *ā-√dṛi* (Pāṇ. vii, 4, 28), Ā. *-driyate*, rarely poet. P. [*ādriyat*, BhP. iv, 4, 7] to regard with attention, attend to, be careful about (acc.), ŚBr.; AitBr.; MBh.; Śak. &c.; to respect, honour, reverence, Pañcat.; BhP.; Ragh.

Ā-dara, *as*, m. respect, regard, notice; care, trouble, Pañcat.; Hit.; Ragh.; Kir. &c.; *ādaram-√1. kṛi*, to exert or interest one's self for; *ādareṇa* and *ādarāt*, adv. respectfully; carefully, zealously. **-vat**, mfn. showing respect, solicitous, Kād.

Ā-daraṇa, *am*, n. showing respect or regard.

Ā-daraṇīya, mf(*ā*)n. to be attended to or regarded, venerable, respectable. **-tva**, n. the state of being venerable.

Ā-dartavya, mfn. = *ā-daraṇīya* above.

Ā-duri, mfn. attentive, NBD. (according to Sāy. on RV. iv, 30, 24 belonging to *ā-√drī* below).

Ā-dṛita, mf(*ā*)n. attentive, careful, zealous, diligent, R.; Pañcat.; BhP.; Ragh. &c.; respected, honoured, worshipped, Mn.; Kathās. &c.

1. **Ā-dṛitya**, mf(*ā*)n. venerable, respectable, R.; Bhaṭṭ.

2. **Ā-dṛitya**, ind. p. having respected, having honoured.

आदृश् *ā-√dṛiś*, Ā. (3. sg. perf. Pass. *-dádṛiśe*, RV. x, 111, 7) to appear, be seen: Caus. *-darśayati*, to show, exhibit.

Ā-darśa, *as*, m. the act of perceiving by the eyes; a looking-glass, mirror, ŚBr.; BṛĀrUp.; MBh.; R. &c.; 'illustrating,' a commentary (often = *darpaṇa*); ideal perfection; a copy, Comm. on VarBṛ.; N. of a son of the eleventh Manu, Hariv.; N. of a country, Comm. on Pāṇ.; of a species of Soma, L.; of a mountain. **-bimba**, m. a round mirror, Kum. vii, 22. **-maṇḍala**, m. 'having mirror-like spots,' N. of a species of serpent, Suśr.; a round mirror, L. **-maya**, mfn. being a mirror, Kād.

Ā-darśaka, mfn. (Comm. on Pāṇ. iv, 2, 124) belonging to the country Ādarśa; (*as*), m. a mirror, R.

Ā-darśita, mfn. shown, pointed out, Ragh. iv, 38.

Ā-drishṭi, f. sight; a glance, look, Daś. **-gocaram**, ind. within range of sight, Kathās. **-prasaram**, ind. id., Amar. 74.

आदृ *ā-√drī*, P. Ā. (2. sg. Subj. *ā́-darshi*, RV. viii, 6, 23, &c.; 3. sg. Subj. aor. *ā́-darshate*, RV. x, 120, 6; 2. sg. Subj. Intens. *ā́-dardarshi*, RV. ii, 12, 15) to crush, force or split open; to make accessible, bring to light: Intens. (2. sg. Impv. *ā́-dardṛihi*, RV. iii, 20, 24) to crack, split open.

Ā-dardirá, mfn. crushing, splitting, RV. x, 78, 16.

Ā-dārá, *as*, m. (according to Sāy. on RV. i, 46, 5 = *ā-dara* fr. *ā-√dṛi* above), N. of a plant that can be substituted for the Soma. **-bimbī**, f. a plant.

Ā-dārin, mfn. breaking open, RV. viii, 45, 13. **-bimbī** (*ā-dāri-*), f., N. of a plant, Suśr.

Ā-dīrya, ind. p. having cracked, ŚBr. xiv, 1, 2, 12.

Ā-duri, m. 'destroyer (of enemies),' N. of Indra, RV. iv, 30, 24 [Sāy.; see also under *ā-√dṛi* above].

आदेय *ā-deya*, mfn. See under *ā-√1. dā* above.

आदेव 1. *ādeva*, mf(*ī*)n. v.l. *adeva*, q.v.

आदेव 2. *ā-deva*, *as*, m. (scil. *jana*) 'all creatures including the gods' (Sāy. on RV. ii, 4, 1); mf(*ī*)n. devoted to the gods [NBD.]

आदेवक *ā-devaka*, mf(*ī*)n. (*√div*), one who sports or plays, L.

Ā-devana, *am*, n. a place for playing, ĀśvGṛ. i, 5, 5; Gobh.; a means of playing, L.; gain in playing, L.

आदै *ā-√dai*, Ā. only p. pr.

2. **Ā-dāyamāna**, mfn. (for 1. see *ā-√1. dā*) examining, proving, MBh.

आदो *ā-√do*, P. *-dāti*, *-dyáti* (Subj. 1. pl. *ā́-dyāmasi*, &c.) to reduce to small pieces, to crush, AV.

3. **Ā-dāna**, *am*, n. reducing to small pieces, crushing, Jaim.; a part; (for 1. and 2. *ādāna* see *ā-√1. dā* and *ā-√4. dā*.)

आद्य 2. *ādyà*, mf(*ā*)n. (*√ad*), to be eaten, edible, AV. viii, 2, 19; (*am*), n. food; grain, L.

आद्युत् *ā-√2. dyut*, Ā. (pf. 3. sg. *-didyóta*) to grow rotten, AV. vi, 24, 2.

आद्यून *ādyūna*, mf(*ā*)n. [etym. doubtful], shamelessly voracious, greedy, MBh.; Rājat.

आद्योत *ā-dyota*, *as*, m. (fr. *√1. dyut*), light, brilliance, L.

आद्रिसार *ādrisāra*, mf(*ī*)n. (fr. *adri-s°*), made of iron, iron, R.

आद्रु *ā-√1. dru*, P. *-dravati*, to run towards, hasten towards, approach running, ŚBr.; VS.; AitBr.; MBh.

Ā-drava (?), *as*, m., N. of a man, VāyuP.

आद्वादशम् *ā-dvādaśám*, ind. up to twelve, RV. x, 114, 6.

आद्वारम् *ā-dvāram*, ind. up to the gate or door, MārkP.

आधमन *ā-dhamana*, *am*, n. (fr. *ā-√dhā*), pledging, Mn. viii, 165.

आधमर्ण्य *ādhamarṇya*, *am*, n. (fr. *adhamarṇa*), the state of being a debtor, Pāṇ. ii, 3, 70, &c.

आधर *ā-dhara*. See under *ā-√dhṛi*.

आधर्मिक *ādharmika*, mf(*ī*)n. (fr. *a-dharma*), unjust, unrighteous, Kāty. on Pāṇ. iv, 4, 41.

आधर्य *ādharya*, *am*, n. (fr. *adhara*), the state of being inferior or of losing a cause (in law), Vishṇus.

आधर्ष *ā-dharsha*, &c. See under *ā-√dhṛish*.

आधव *ā-dhava*, &c. See under *ā-√dhu*.

आधा *ā-√dhā*, P. Ā. *-dadhāti*, *-dhatte* (in the later language usually Ā.), [1. sg. *ā́-dadhāmi*, AV. ii, 10, 5, &c.; Impv. 2. sg. *ā-dhehi*, AV. vi, 26, 1, &c.; pf. 3. pl. *-dadhus*, RV. viii, 103, 1, &c.; aor. 3. pl. *ā́-dhus*, RV. iv, 6, 6, &c.; p. *-dadhāna*, p. Pass. *-dhīyamāna* (in comp., e. g. *ā-dhīyamāna-citta*, Rājat. v, 164); perf. *-dadhau*, &c.; see under *√1. dhā*], (P. and Ā.) to place on, put down, deposit, put; to impregnate, instil (e. g. good sentiments), impress, direct; to apply, appoint; RV.; AV.; ŚBr.; MBh. &c.; to add (fuel to fire), RV.; ŚBr.; ĀśvGṛ.; PārGṛ. &c.; to give or deposit in pledge, stake (money), RV.; to give, supply, lend, deliver, RV.; AV.; PārGṛ.; BhP. &c.; to accept, receive, RV.; AV.; MBh.; BhP. &c.; to make, constitute, effect, Ragh.; Mālav.; Rājat. &c.; (only Ā.) to keep, preserve, appropriate to one's self, hold, possess, take; to conceive (as a woman), get children, RV. &c.: Caus. *-dhāpayati*, to cause to put: Desid. Ā. *-dhitsate*, to wish to kindle (a fire), TBr.: P. (p. *-dhitsat*) to be about to take up (a stick for punishing), MBh. xii, 3170.

Ā-dhātavya, mfn. to be distributed or assigned, Comm. on Nyāyam.

Ā-dhātṛi, m. one who has kindled the sacred fire, Nyāyam.; the giver (of knowledge), a teacher, Mālav.

Ā-dhāna, *am*, n. putting near or upon, depositing, placing, ŚBr.; KātyŚr.; Mn. &c.; lighting, kindling, placing a fire (especially the sacred fire, cf. *agny-ā°* above), ŚBr.; KātyŚr.; ĀśvGṛ. &c.; impregnating (cf. *garbhā°*), Megh. iii, &c.; a ceremony performed before coition; adding, Vām.; causing, effecting, MBh.; Ragh.; Megh. &c.; pledging, depositing, Yājñ.; taking, having, receiving; assigning, attributing, employing; containing, being in possession of; the place in which anything is deposited or rests, ŚBr.; the bit of a bridle, TS. **-kārikā**, f., N. of a work. **-paddhati**, f. id. **-vidhi**, m. id.

Ādhānika, *am*, n. a ceremony performed before conception, L.

Ā-dhāya, ind. p. having placed, Mṛicch.; having given; having delivered, MBh.; having received.

Ā-dhāyaka, mf(*ikā*)n. [Pāṇ. iii, 3, 10] ifc. bestowing, giving; causing, effecting, Sāh. **-tva**, n. the state of giving &c., ib.

Ā-dhāyin, mfn. ifc. = *ā-dhāyaka* above, Rājat. **-tā**, f. the state of causing &c., ib.

1. **Ā-dhi**, *is*, m. (for 2. see p. 139, col. 2) a receptacle, BhP. xi, 13, 33; place, situation, L.; foundation, Nyāyam.; a pledge, deposit, pawn, mortgage, RV.; Mn.; Yājñ.; hire, rent, Āp.; an attribute, title, epithet (cf. *upâdhi*), L. **-tā**, f. the nature or circumstance of a pledge, Comm. on Yājñ. **-bhoga**, m. enjoyment or use of a deposit (use of a horse, cow, &c. when pledged), Gaut. xii, 35.

Ā-dhitsu, mfn. (fr. the Desid.), wishing to receive, Comm. on TBr. i, 58, 3.

Ādhī-√1. kṛi, to pledge, mortgage, pawn, make a deposit, Comm. on Yājñ. **-karaṇa** (*ādhī-*), n. pledging, mortgaging. **-kṛita**, mfn. pledged, pawned, mortgaged. **-kṛitya**, ind. p. having pledged, &c.

Ā-dheya, mf(*ā*)n. to be kindled or placed (as a fire), Comm. on Pāṇ. ii, 3, 69; to be deposited or placed; to be pledged or mortgaged, Yājñ.; to be assigned or attributed or given or conceded, Pañcat. &c.; being contained, comprehended, included, Comm. on Pāṇ. ii, 3, 4; Bālar.; being imputed, Bālar.; (*am*), n. putting on, placing (cf. *agnyā°* above), ĀśvŚr. &c.; an attribute, predicate, Sāh. &c.; to be effected; to be fixed, T.

Ā-hita, mfn. placed on, placed, deposited, put on, Pāṇ. viii, 4, 8; RV.; AV.; MBh. &c.; added (as fuel to the fire); one who has added; deposited, pledged, pawned, Comm. on Yājñ. &c.; given, delivered; conceived; performed, done, effected, MBh.; entertained, felt, L.; comprising, containing. **-klama**, mfn. overcome with fatigue, exhausted. **-lakshaṇa**, mfn. noted or known for good qualities (= *ā-hatal°*, q. v.), L.; one who has laid down his banner, T. **-samit-ka**, mfn. one who has added fuel to the fire or who keeps up a fire. **Āhitâgni**, mfn. one who has placed the sacred fire upon the altar; (*is*), m. sacrificer, a Brāhman who maintains a perpetual sacred fire in a family &c., TS.; ŚBr. &c.; *āhitâgny-ādi*, m. a gaṇa (Pāṇ. ii, 2, 37). **Āhitâṅka**, mfn. marked, spotted, stained.

आधार *ā-dhāra*, &c. See under *ā-√dhṛi*.

आधाव् *ā-√dhāv*, P. *ā́-dhāvati* (Ā. only p. *-dhāvamāna*, MBh.) to flow towards, run near, RV. ix, 17, 4 and ix, 67, 14; to come running, run or hasten towards; to return, RV.; Lāṭy.; ŚBr.; Hariv.

आधि *ā-dhi*. See under *ā-√dhā* and *ā-√dhyai*.

आधिकरणिक *ādhikaraṇika*, *as*, m. (fr. *adhikaraṇa*), a judge, government official, Mṛicch. (see *adhi°*).

Ādhikārika, mf(*ā*)n. (fr. *adhi-kāra*), belonging to a chief matter or principal person, Sāh. &c.; belonging to particular sections or head chapters (*adhikāra*), ŚāṅkhGṛ.; official, relating to any office or duty, Bādar.; (*as*), m. the supreme ruler, the supreme spirit, Bādar.

आधिक्य *ādhikya*, *am*, n. (fr. *adhika*), excess, abundance, superabundance, high degree; overweight, preponderance; superiority, R.; Mn.; Suśr.; Comm. on Pāṇ. &c.

आधिदैविक *ādhidaivika*, mf(*ā*)n. (fr. *adhideva*), relating to or proceeding from gods or from spirits, Mn.; Suśr.; proceeding from the influence of the atmosphere or planets, proceeding from divine or supernatural agencies.

Ādhidaivata, mfn. id. ib.

आधिपत्य *ādhipatya*, *am*, n. [Pāṇ. v, 1, 124] (fr. *adhi-pati*), supremacy, sovereignty, power, RV. x, 124, 5; AV. xviii, 4, 54; VS.; TS.; AitBr.; ŚBr.; Mn.; Yājñ.; Pañcat. &c.

आधिबन्ध *ādhi-bandha*. See under *ā-√dhyai*.

आधिभौतिक *ādhibhautika*, mf(*ī*)n. (fr. *adhibhūta*), belonging or relating to created beings, Suśr.; elementary, derived or produced from the primitive elements, material.

आधिमन्यु *ādhimanyu*, *avas*, m. pl. (fr. *adhimanyu*), febrile heat, L.

आधिरथि *ādhirathi*, *is*, m. (Pāṇ. iv, 1, 95) 'son of Adhi ratha,' N. of Karṇa, MBh.

आधिराज्य *ādhirājya*, *am*, n. (fr. *adhi-rāja*), royalty, royal government, supreme sway, Ragh.; Bālar.

आधिवेदनिक *ādhivedanika*, mfn. (fr. *adhivedana*), belonging to a second marriage, T.; (*am*),

n. (scil. *dānam*) property (gifts &c.) given to a first wife upon marrying a second, Yājñ.; Vishṇus.

आधी 1. *ā-√dhī* (cf. *ā-dhyai*; according to Dhātup. xxiv, 68; Pāṇ. vi, 1, 6, &c., *-dīdhī*), P. (Subj. 3. pl. *ā́-dīdhayan*) to mind, care for, RV. vii, 7, 6: Ā. (Subj. 2. sg. *ā-dīdhīthās*) to meditate on, think about, care for, wish for, AV. viii, 1, 8, &c.; (p. aor. *-dhīshamāṇa*, mfn., RV. x, 26, 6) to wish for, long for.

2. **Ā-dhī́**, f. (for 1. *ā-dhī* see under *ā-√dhā*), eagerness, longing, care, RV.; AV. &c. **-parṇa**, mf(*ā*)n. 'winged with longing,' AV. iii, 25, 2.

Ā́-dhīta, mfn. reflected or meditated upon; (*am*), n. the object of thought, anything intended or hoped for, RV.; VS.; ŚBr.; MaitrS. **-yajús**, n. a sacrificial prayer which is meditated upon.

Ā́-dhīti, *is*, f. thinking about, intending, MaitrS.

आधीन *ādhīna* = *adhīna*, q. v., MBh.

आधु *ā-√dhu* or *-√dhū*, P. (*-dhunoti* [ŚBr.] 1. sg. *ā́-dhūnomi* [VS.], Pot. 3. sg. *-dhūnuyāt* [TBr.]), Ā. (3. pl. *ā́-dhunvate* [RV.], &c.) to stir, agitate.

Ā-dhavá, *as*, m. one who stirs up or agitates, RV.; that which is agitated, mixture, ib.

Ā-dhavana, mfn. stirring, ĀpŚr.; (*am*), n. agitating, moving, L.

Ā-dhavanī́ya, *as*, m. a vessel in which the Soma plant is stirred and cleansed, VS.; TS.; AitBr. &c.

Ā-dhāvá, *ās*, m. pl. that which is agitated or cleansed by stirring, TS.

Ā-dhuta, mf(*ā* & *ī* [T.])n. = the next.

Ā-dhūta, mf(*ā*)n. shaken, agitated, Ragh.; Kathās. &c.; disturbed, trembling, R.

Ā-dhūya, ind. p. having shaken or agitated, TS.; KātyŚr.; MBh. &c.

आधुनय *ā-dhunaya*, Nom. (fr. *dhúni*), Ā. (Impv. 3. pl. *ā-dhunayantām*) to rush towards with violence, RV. iii, 55, 16.

आधुनिक *ādhunika*, mf(*ī*)n. (fr. *adhunā*), new, recent, of the present moment.

आधूपय *ā-dhūpaya*, Nom. (fr. *dhūpa*), P. (Impv. 3. sg. *-dhūpayatu*) to envelop in smoke, TĀr.

Ā-dhūpana, *am*, n. enveloping in smoke or mist, VBr.

आधूमय *ā-dhūmaya*, Nom. (fr. *dhūma*), P. to envelop in smoke.

Ā-dhūmana, *am*, n. = *ā-dhūpana* above, VBr.

Ā-dhūmita, mfn. enveloped in mist, ib.

Ā-dhūmra, mfn. smoke-coloured, ib.

आधृ *ā-√dhṛi*, P. (*-dharati*) to hold, keep, support, R.; Kathās.: Caus. P. (impf. 2. sg. *ā́dhārayas*) to bring, supply, RV. i, 52, 8; ix, 12, 9: Pass. (*-dhriyate*) to be contained, exist in anything (loc.)

Ā-dhara, mfn. ifc. supportable, tenable (cf. *dur°*).

Ā-dhārá, *as*, m. support, prop, stay, substratum; the power of sustaining, or the support given, aid, patronage, AV. xii, 3, 48; MBh.; Suśr.; Vedāntas. &c.; that which contains (a fluid &c.), a vessel, receptacle, Yājñ.; Suśr.; Pañcat. &c.; a dike, dam, Ragh.; a basin round the foot of a tree, L.; a reservoir, pond, L.; (in phil. and Gr.) comprehension, location, the sense of the locative case; ifc. belonging or relating to; the subject in a sentence (of which qualities &c. are affirmed); N. of a lake; of an author. **-kārikā**, f., N. of a Kārikā. **-cakra**, n., N. of a mystical circle on the posterior part of the body, Rasik. **-tā**, f. and **-tva**, n. the state of being a support, &c. **-rūpā**, f. an ornament for the neck. **Ādhārâdheya-bhāva**, m. the relation of the recipient and the thing to be received (as of a mirror and the object reflected), Hit.

Ādhāraka, ifc. a substratum, Suśr.

Ā-dhāraṇa, *am*, n. bearing, holding, supporting.

1. **Ā-dhārya**, mf(*ā*)n. to be located, that to which a location is to be assigned, L.; contained, included, Sāh.

2. **Ā-dhārya**, ind. p. keeping, holding, R.

Ā-dhṛita, mf(*ā*)n. contained (with loc.)

आधृष् 1. *ā-√dhṛish*, P. (perf. 3. sg. *ā́-dadharsha*, Pot. *ā́-dadharshīt*, Subj. aor. 3. sg. *-dadhárshat*, &c.) to assail, attack, injure, overcome, RV.; AV.

Ā-dharsha, mfn. ifc. attackable, assailable (cf. *dur°*); (*as*), m. insulting, assailing, T.

Ā-dharshaṇa, *am*, n. = *ā-dharsha*, T.; conviction of crime or error, L.; refutation, ib.

Ā-dharshita, mf(*ā*)n. convicted, sentenced; refuted in argument, disproved; injured, aggrieved, Yājñ.; Hariv.; MBh.; R.

Ā-dharshya, mfn. to be injured or insulted, assailable, T.; weak, T.; (*am*), n. the state of being assailable, &c.; weakness, ib. (cf. *an°*).

2. **Ā-dhṛish** (only dat. [*°e* used as Inf., RV.; AV. vi, 33, 2] and abl. [*°as*, RV. ii, 1, 9]), assault, attack.

Ā-dhṛishīya, mfn. 'including the *√dhṛish*,' Dhātup.

Ā-dhṛishṭa, mf(*ā*)n. checked, overcome, T. (cf. *an°*).

Ā-dhṛishṭi, *is*, f. assailing, attacking (cf. *an°*).

आधेनव *ā́dhenava*, *am*, n. (fr. *a-dhenu*), want of cows, Comm. on Pāṇ.

आधोरण *ādhoraṇa*, *as*, m. the rider or driver of an elephant, Ragh.; Kathās. &c.

आध्मा *ā-√dhmā*, P. *-dhamati* (Impv. 2. sg. *-dhama*) to inflate, fill with air, blow, Hariv.; to cry out, utter with a loud voice; to sound, TĀr.: Pass. (*-dhmāyati* [irr.], ŚBr. xiv, 6, 2, 12) to swell with wind, puff up, MBh.; Suśr. (in the latter sense sometimes [Suśr. 290, 10] P.): Caus. to blow, inflate.

Ā-dhamana. See s. v.

Ā-dhmāta, mf(*ā*)n. inflated, blown, puffed up; sounded, sounding; heated, burnt.

Ā-dhmāna, *am*, n. blowing, inflation, puffing; Suśr.; boasting; a bellows, L.; intumescence, swelling of the body; N. of certain diseases, Suśr.; N. of a species of sound, T.; (*ī*), f., N. of a fragrant bark.

Ā-dhmāpana, *am*, n. inflating, blowing upon; a method of healing particular wounds (cf. *śalya*), Suśr.; sounding, T.

आध्यक्ष्य *ā́dhyakshya*, *am*, n. (fr. *adhy-aksha*), superintendence, VS.

आध्यश्वि *ādhyaśvi*, *is*, m. (fr. *adhy-aśva*), N. of a place, (gaṇa *gahâdi* on Pāṇ. iv, 2, 138.)

Ādhyaśvīya, mfn. (Pāṇ. iv, 2, 138) belonging to the place Ādhyaśvi.

आध्या *ādhyā*. See under *ā-√dhyai*.

आध्यात्मिक *ādhyātmika*, mf(*ā* & *ī*)n. (fr. *adhy-ātma*), relating to self or to the soul; proceeding from bodily and mental causes within one's self; relating to the supreme spirit, Mn. &c.; spiritual, holy; (*am*), n. (scil. *duḥkham*), N. of a class of diseases, Suśr.

आध्यान *ā-dhyāna*. See under *ā-√dhyai*.

आध्यापक *ādhyāpaka*, *as*, m. a teacher, a religious preceptor (= *adhyāpaka*, q. v.), L.

आध्यायिक *ādhyāyika*, *as*, m. (fr. *adhy-āya*), occupied or employed in reading or studying, TUp.; MBh.

आध्यासिक *ādhyāsika*, mfn. (fr. *adhy-āsa*, q. v.), (in phil.) belonging to or effected by erroneous attribution, T.

आध्यै *ā-√dhyai* (cf. *ā-√dhī*), P. (p. *-dhyāyat* [BhP. ix, 14, 43]; Impv. 2. sg. *-dhyāhi* [MBh.]) to meditate on; to wish or pray for anything for another.

2. **Ā-dhí**, *is*, m. thought, care, anxious reflection, mental agony, anxiety, pain, TS.; MBh.; Yājñ. &c.; reflection on religion or duty, L.; hope, expectation, L.; misfortune, L.; a man solicitous for his family's livelihood, L. **-ja**, mfn. produced by anxiety or pain &c., L. **-jña**, mfn. suffering pain, L. **-bandha**, m. the tie of anxiety (said of a king in relation to his care of his subjects), MBh. **-mlāna**, mf(*ā*)n. withered with anxiety, L.; (for 1. *ā-dhi* see *ā-√dhā*.)

Ā-dhī and **Ā-dhīta**. See under 1. *ā-√dhī*.

Ā-dhyā, f. = the next, L.

Ā-dhyāna, *am*, n. meditating upon, reflecting on, remembering with regret, pensive or sorrowful recollection.

आध्र *ādhrá*, mf(*ā*)n. (according to Sāy. on RV. i, 31, 14 fr. *√dhrai* [?], according to T. fr. *ā-√dhṛi*), poor, destitute, indigent, weak, RV.

आध्वंस् *ā-√dhvaṇs*, p. p.

Ā-dhvasta, mfn. covered, Nir. iv, 3.

आध्वनिक *ādhvanika*, mf(*ī*)n. (fr. *adhvan*), being on a journey, MBh.

आध्वर *ādhvara*, *as*, m., N. of a man.

आध्वरायण *ādhvarāyaṇa*, *as*, m. a descendant of Adhvara (= the second Vasu), gaṇa *naḍâdi* [Pāṇ. iv, 1, 99].

Ā́dhvarika, mf(*ī*)n. (fr. *adhvara*), belonging to the Soma sacrifice, ŚBr.; KātyŚr.; (*as*), m. (scil. *grantha*) a book explaining the Adhvara sacrifice, L.; a man acquainted with the Adhvara sacrifice, L.

Ā́dhvaryava, mf(*ī*)n. (fr. *adhvaryu*), belonging to the Adhvaryu (= Yajur-veda), Pāṇ. iv, 3, 123; VP.; (*am*), n. the office of an Adhvaryu priest, RV. x, 52, 2; VS.; ŚBr. &c.

आध्वस्त *ā-dhvasta*. See under *ā-√dhvaṇs*.

आन *āná*, *as*, m. (fr. *√an*), face [NBD.]; mouth; nose [Sāy.], RV. i, 52, 15; exhaling the breath through the nose, T.; inhalation, breath inspired, breathing, blowing, L.

Ānana, *am*, n. the mouth; the face, R.; Ragh. &c.; entrance, door, L. **Ānanânta**, m. the angle of the mouth, BhP. **Ānanâbja**, n. face-lotus (i. e. lotus-like face).

आनक *ānaka*, *as*, m. (etym. doubtful), a large military drum beaten at one end; a double drum; a small drum or tabor, Bhag.; Hariv.; a thunder-cloud or a cloud to which the thunder is ascribed, L.; (mfn.) energetic, T. **-dundubhi**, m. = *ānaka°*, q. v.; (*is*), m. or (*ī*), f. a large drum beaten at one end, a kettle-drum, L. **-sthalaka**, mfn. belonging to Ānaka-sthalī. **-sthalī**, f., N. of a country.

Ānakāyani, gaṇa *karṇâdi* (Pāṇ. iv, 2, 80).

आनक्ष् *ā-√naksh*, to approach, obtain, reach, present, L.

आनडुह *ā́naḍuha*, mf(*ī*)n. (fr. *anaḍuh*), coming from or belonging to a bull, ŚBr.; KātyŚr. &c.; (*am*), n., N. of a Tīrtha, Hariv.

Ānaḍuhaka, mfn. coming from or belonging to a bull [T.], gaṇa *kulālâdi* (Pāṇ. iv, 3, 118).

Ānaḍuhya, *as*, m. a descendant of the Muni Anaḍuh [T.]

Ānaḍuhyāyana (gaṇa *aśvâdi* [Pāṇ. iv, 1, 110]) and *°ni* (gaṇa *karṇâdi* [Pāṇ. iv, 2, 80]), belonging to Āna-ḍuhya.

आनत *ā-nata*, &c. See under *ā-√nam* next page.

आनद् *ā-√nad*, Caus. P. (p. *-nādayat*) to make resonant, cause to sound, MBh.

आनद्ध *ā-naddha*, &c. See under *ā-√nah*.

आनन *ānana*. See under *āná* above.

आनन्तर्य *ānantarya*, *am*, n. (fr. *an-antara*, Pāṇ. v, 1, 124), immediate sequence or succession, KātyŚr.; Āp.; Mn. &c.; proximity, absence of interval, MBh. &c. **-tṛitīyā**, f. the third day (of a religious rite), BhP.

आनन्त्य *ā́nantya*, mfn. (fr. *an-anta*, Pāṇ. v, 4, 23), infinite, eternal, MBh. &c.; bestowing infinite reward, ĀrshBr.; (*am*), n. infinity, eternity, ŚBr.; Mn.; Yājñ.; MBh. &c.; immortality, future happiness, MBh. &c.

आनन्द् *ā-√nand*, P. *-nandati*, to rejoice, be delighted, Gīt.; Bhaṭṭ.: Caus. P. *-nandayati*, to gladden; to bless, TUp.; Yājñ. &c.: Ā. *-nandayate*, to amuse one's self.

Ā-nandá, *as*, m. happiness, joy, enjoyment, sensual pleasure, RV.; AV.; VS.; R.; Ragh. &c.; (*as*), m. and (*am*), n. 'pure happiness,' one of the three attributes of Ātman or Brahman in the Vedānta philosophy, Vedāntas. &c.; (*as*), m. (in dram.) the thing wished for, the end of the drama [e. g. the VIth Act in the Veṇis.], Sāh. 399; a kind of flute; the sixteenth Muhūrta; N. of Śiva; of a Lokeśvara (Buddh.); of a Bala (Jain.), L.; of several men; of a country; m. and (*am*), n., N. of the forty-eighth year of the cycle of Jupiter; (*ā* and *ī*), f., N. of two plants, L.; (*ā*), f., N. of Gaurī, L.; (*am*), n. a kind of house; (often at the beginning and end of proper names.) **-kanda**, m. 'the root of joy,' N. of an author; of a medical work; of a country. **-kara**, mfn. exhilarating, delighting. **-kalikā,** f., N. of a work. **-kānana-māhātmya,** n., N. of a section of the Vāyu-purāṇa. **-kāvya,** n., N. of a work. **-kośa,** m., N. of a play. **-giri,** m., N. of a pupil of and annotator on Śaṅkarācārya. **-ghana,** mfn. consisting of pure joy, NṛisUp. **-caturdaśī-vrata,** n., N. of a religious rite, BhavP. **-caula,** m., N. of a teacher. **-ja,** mfn. proceeding from joy, T.; *(as),* m., N. of a teacher; *(am),* n. semen virile, L. **-jala,** n. tears of joy, BhP. **-jñāna,** m. = *-giri* above; *-giri,* m. id. **-tā,** f. joyfulness, joy, ŚBr. **-tāṇḍava-pura,** n., N. of a town. **-tīrtha,** m., N. of Madhva, the founder of a Vaishṇava school of philosophy; = *ānanda-giri*(?). **-da,** mfn. = *-kara,* q. v., L. **-datta,** m. membrum virile, L. **-dīpikā,** f., N. of a work. **-deva,** m., N. of a poet. **-nātha,** m., N. of a man. **-nidhi,** m., N. of a commentary. **-paṭa,** m. a bridal garment, L. **-pura,** n., N. of a town. **-pūrṇa,** m., N. of a scholiast. **-prabhava,** m. the seminal fluid, L.; the universe (as proceeding from Ānanda = Brahman, T.) **-prabhā,** f., N. of a celestial woman. **-bāshpa,** m. = *-jala* above. **-bodhêndra,** m., N. of a scholiast. **-bhuj,** mfn. enjoying happiness, MāṇḍUp.; Vedāntas. **-bhairava,** mfn. causing both enjoyment and fear; *(as),* m., N. of Śiva; N. of a teacher; *(ī),* f., N. of Gaurī, T. **-maya,** mf*(ī)*n. blissful, made up or consisting of happiness, TUp.; MāṇḍUp.; Vedāntas.; Kathās.; *(am),* n. (scil. *brahman*) the supreme spirit (as consisting of pure happiness, cf. *ānanda* above); *-kosha,* m. the innermost case of the body, the causal frame enshrining the soul. **-mālā,** f., N. of a work. **-yoga,** m. (in astron.) N. of a particular Yoga. **-rāya,** m., N. of a man. **-rūpa,** mfn. consisting of happiness, NṛisUp. **-lahari** or °**rī,** f. 'wave of enjoyment,' N. of a hymn by Śaṅkarācārya addressed to Pārvatī. **-laharī-stotra,** n., N. of a poem. **-vana,** m., N. of a scholiast; *(am),* n., N. of Kāśī. **-vardhana,** mfn. enhancing enjoyment, R.; *(as),* m., N. of a poet, Rājat. **-vallī,** f., N. of the second part of the Taittirīya-Upanishad. **-vimala,** m., N. of a man. **-veda,** m., N. of several men. **-sambhava,** mfn. = *-prabhava,* q. v. **Ānandâcala,** m. = *-giri,* q. v. **Ānandâtman,** mfn. one whose essence consists in happiness, ŚBr.; *(ā),* m., N. of a teacher. **Ānandâmṛita,** n. 'joy-nectar,' happiness, NṛisUp.; *-rūpa,* mfn. consisting of happiness, ib. **Ānandâśrama,** m., N. of a scholar. **Ānandâśru,** n. = *ānanda-jala* above. **Ānandêśvara-tīrtha,** n., N. of a Tīrtha. **Ānandôtsava,** m. a festival.

Ā-nandaka, mf*(ā)*n. gladdening, rejoicing, Hit.; Kād.; *(am),* n., N. of a lake.

Ā-nandathu, mfn. happy, joyful, L.; *(us),* m. happiness, joy, Bhaṭṭ.

Ā-nandana, *am,* n. delighting, making happy, Hit.; civility, courtesy, courteous treatment of a friend or guest at meeting and parting, L.

Ā-nandayitavya, mfn. to be enjoyed.

Ā-nandayitṛi, *ā,* m. a gladdener, one who makes joyful, Ragh.

Ā-nandi, *is,* m. happiness, enjoyment, pleasure, L.

Ā-nandita, mf*(ā)*n. rejoiced, delighted, happy, Hariv. &c.; N. of a man.

Ā-nandin, mfn. delightful, blissful, happy, cheerful, Kathās.; gladdening, making happy; N. of a man.

आनपत्य *ānapatya,* mfn. (fr. *an-apatya*), proceeding from childlessness, BhP.

आनभिम्लात *ānabhimlāta, as,* m. a descendant of An-abhimlāta, BṛĀrUp.

आनभिम्लान *ānabhimlāna, as,* m. a descendant of An-abhimlāna, Pāṇ.

आनम् *ā-√nam,* P. (3. pl. *ā́-namanti,* RV. &c.; inf. *-námam,* RV. iv, 8, 3), Ā. (Impv. 3. pl. *ā́-namantām,* RV. vi, 49, 4) to bend down, bend, bow, incline, R.; BhP.; Ragh. &c.; to do homage, salute reverently, BhP.; ŚBr. &c.; to condescend; to be propitious (as gods to men), RV. vi, 50, 4; to bring near; to bend towards or near; to subdue, RV.: Caus. *-nāmayati* and *-namayati,* to inflect, bend (a bow), cause to bend, subdue, MBh.; Mālav.; Hariv.

Ā-nata, mfn. bending, stooping, bowed, Ragh.; Kathās.; humbled, submissive, obedient, MBh. &c.; bent or curved inwards (as a bow), ŚBr.; flat, sunk (not elevated), MBh.; R.; pacified, conciliated; saluted reverently. **-ja,** *ās,* m. pl. a class of divine beings (Jain.)

Ā-nati, f. bending, bowing, stooping, VS.; Kathās.; submission, obedience, inferiority, Comm. on KātyŚr. &c.; contentedness, T.; saluting, L.

Ā-nama, *as,* m. bending, stretching (a bow), L.; ifc. to be bent (cf. *dur°*).

Ā-namana, *am,* n. = *ā-nati,* q. v., T.

Ā-námam. See under *ā-√nam.*

Ā-namita and **ā-nāmita,** mfn. (p. of Caus.) bent or bowed down, caused to bend, Bhartṛ.; Mālav.

1. **Ā-namya** and **ā-nāmya,** mfn. to be bent.

2. **Ā-namya** and **ā-natya,** ind. p. having bent.

1. **Ā-namra,** mfn. bent; propitious.

Ā-nāmana, *am,* n. propitiation, gaining (a god's) favour, conciliation.

आनम्र 2. *ā-namra,* mfn. a little bent.

आनय *ā-naya,* &c. See under *ā-√nī.*

आनर्त *ā-narta,* &c. See under *ā-√nṛit.*

आनर्थक्य *ānarthakya, am,* n. (fr. *an-arthaka*), uselessness, unprofitableness, KātyŚr.; Pāṇ. &c.; unfitness, impropriety, L.

आनर्द् *ā-√nard,* to roar.

Ā-nardam, ind. p. roaring, MBh.

Ā-nardita, *am,* n. roaring, R.

आनल *ānala, am,* n. (fr. *anala*), 'belonging to Agni,' N. of the constellation Kṛittikā, VarBṛS.

आनलवि *ānalavi, is,* m., N. of a man.

आनव *ā́nava,* mf*(ī)*n. (fr. 2. *anu,* BRD.), kind to men, RV.; humane, ib.; a foreign man, RV. vii, 18, 13 (according to T. [fr. *ānu* = man], 'belonging to living men').

आनव्य *ānavya,* mfn. = *ā́nava,* T.

आनस *ānasá,* mfn. (fr. *anas*), belonging to a waggon, ŚBr.; belonging to a father, T.

आनह् *ā-√nah,* P. (Impv. 2. sg. *ā́-nahya*) to bind to or on, AV. vi, 67, 3; MBh.: Ā. *-nahyate,* to be stopped up, become stopped, Suśr.

Ā-naddha, mfn. bound to or on, bound, tied, MBh.; costive, Suśr.; *(am),* n. a drum in general, L.; putting on clothes or ornaments, L. **-tva,** n. state of being bound, obstruction. **-vasti-tā,** f. suppression of urine; state of having the bladder obstructed.

Ā-nāha, *as,* m. epistasis, suppression of urine; constipation, Suśr.; MBh.; length, L.

Ānāhika, mf*(ī)*n. to be used in epistasis, Suśr.

आनाकरथवर्त्मन् *ā-nāka-ratha-vartman,* mfn. one the path of whose chariot reaches to the sky, Ragh. i, 5.

आनाथ्य *ānāthya, am,* n. (fr. *a-nātha*), state of being unprotected or without a guardian, orphanage, Kathās.

आनिचेय *āniceya,* mf(ī [Pāṇ. iv, 1, 73])n. (according to T. [fr. *ā-ni-√ci*], to be gathered from every side; more probably) a descendant of Aniceya [NBD.], L.

आनिञ्ज्य *āniñjya, am,* n. (fr. *an* with *√iñj*), immovableness.

आनिधन *ānidhana, am,* n. (scil. *sāman*) N. of a Sāman.

आनिधेय *ānidheya,* mf(ī [Pāṇ. iv, 1, 73])n. a descendant of A-nidheya [NBD.], L.

आनिरुद्ध *āniruddha, as,* m. a descendant of A-niruddha, L.

आनिर्हत *ā́nirhata,* mf*(ī)*n. (fr. *a-nirhata*), of indestructible nature, ŚBr.; VS.; *(ās),* m. pl., N. of a class of principal gods [T.]

आनिल *ānila,* mf*(ī)*n. (fr. *anila*), proceeding from or produced by wind, windy, L.; belonging to Vāyu or Anila, T.; *(as),* m., N. of Hanumat; of Bhīma, L.; *(ī),* f. and *(am),* n., N. of the constellation Svāti.

Ānili, *is,* m. 'a descendant of Anila;' N. of Hanumat; of Bhīma, L.

आनिशम् *ā-niśam,* ind. till night.

आनी *ā-√nī,* P. *-nayati* (1. pl. *ā́-nayāmasi,* AV. v, 25, 8; Impv. 2. sg. *ā́-naya,* 3. sg. *ā́-nayatu;* pf. *ā́-nināya,* AV. v, 17, 2, and *ā-nindruya,* RV. viii, 21, 9; inf. *-netavai,* ŚBr. ii, 1, 14, 16), Ā. (1. sg. *-naye,* R.) to lead towards or near; to bring, carry to a place (acc. or loc.); to fetch, RV.; AV.; SV.; ŚBr.; MBh.; R.; Śak. &c.; (perf. periphr. *-nayāmāsa,* MBh. iii, 2282) to cause to bring or fetch; to bring back or take back, MBh.; R.; to pour in, mix in, RV.; VS.; ŚBr. &c.; to bring any one to, reduce to any state, MBh.; to deduce, calculate; to use, employ, prove: Caus. P. *-nāyayati,* to cause to be brought or fetched or led near, MBh.; R.; Ragh.; Kathās. &c.: Desid. *-ninīshati,* to intend or wish to bring near, BhP. x, 89, 42.

Ā-naya, *as,* m. leading to, T.; leading to a teacher = *upanayana,* q. v.), L.

Ā-nayana, *am,* n. bringing, leading near, VP.; KātyŚr.; MBh.; R. &c.; producing, working; calculating.

Ā-nayitavya, mfn. to be brought or led near, MBh.; to be calculated, Comm. on VarBṛ.

Ā-nāya, *as.* m. a fisherman's net, Pāṇ.

Ānāyāya, Nom. Ā. *(-nāyāyate)* to become a net, form or represent a net.

Ānāyin, *ī,* m. a fisherman, fisher, Ragh.

1. **Ā-nāyya,** mfn. to be brought near; *(as),* m. consecrated fire (taken from the Gārhapatya or household fire, and placed on the south side, where it is called *dakshiṇâgni,* q. v.)

2. **Ā-nāyya,** ind. p. (of the Caus.) having caused to be brought, having caused to be introduced, having brought together.

Ā-nīta, mfn. taken, brought near, &c.

Ā-nīti, *is,* f. the act of leading near, R.

Ā-netavai. See under *ā-√nī.*

Ā-netavya, mfn. = 1. *ā-nāyya,* q. v.

Ā-netṛi, mfn. one who leads or brings near, a bringer, bringing, Kathās.

आनीकवत *ānīkavata,* mfn. (fr. *anīkavat* [= Agni]), relating to Agni, Comm. on KātyŚr.

आनील *ā-nīla,* mf*(ā)*n. darkish, Ragh.; Vikr.; slightly dark or blue; *(as),* m. a black horse, L.; *(ī),* f. a black mare, T.; tin, L.

आनु 1. *ā-√1. nu,* Ā. (aor. 3. pl. *ā́nūshata,* RV. i, 151, 6 & ix, 65, 14) to sound, roar towards or near; (p. *-nuvāna,* Bhaṭṭ.) to cry; to twitter (as birds): Intens. *(ā́-navinot,* RV. vii, 87, 2) to roar towards.

आनु 2. *ānu,* mfn. (fr. *√2. an*), living, human, T.

आनुकल्पिक *ānukalpika,* mfn. (fr. *anu-kalpa,* q. v., gaṇa *ukthâdi,* Pāṇ. iv, 2, 60), one who knows or studies the alternative rules; obtained by alternative rules, T.; *(am),* n. a substitute, T.

आनुकूलिक *ānukūlika,* mfn. (fr. *anu-kūla*), conformable, favourable, inclined to help, Pāṇ. iv, 4, 28.

Ānukūlya, *am,* n. conformity, suitableness, Kathās.; MBh.; Yājñ.; favour, kindness, humouring, Rājat.; agreement of minds, friendliness. **-tas,** ind. conformable to one's wishes, Vātsy.

आनुकृष्ट *ānukṛishṭa,* mfn. (= *anu-kṛishṭa,* q. v.), Vārtt. on Pāṇ. v, 4, 36.

आनुखड्ग्य *ānukhaḍgya,* mfn. (fr. *anu-khaḍga*), being along the sword, Comm. on Pāṇ.

आनुगङ्ग्य *ānugaṅgya,* mfn. (fr. *anu-gaṅga*), being along the Gaṅgā, ib.

आनुगतिक *ānugatika,* mfn. (fr. *anu-gata*), relating to or proceeding from, following, Pāṇ.

Ānugatya, *am,* n. following; acquaintance, familiarity, L.

आनुगादिक *ānugādika,* mfn. (fr. *anu-gādin*), belonging to one who repeats another's words, repeating another's words, Pāṇ.

आनुगुणिक *ānuguṇika,* mfn. (fr. *anu-guṇa*), knowing or studying the Anu-guṇa (i.e. according to T. a manual of the art of keeping within the bounds of one's faculties?), ib.

Ānuguṇya, *am,* n. homogeneousness, Sāh.

आनुग्रामिक *ānugrāmika,* mfn. (fr. *anu-grāma*), belonging or conformable to a village, rustic, rural, Pāṇ.

आनुचारक *ānucāraka*, mfn. (fr. *anu-cāraka*), belonging to an attendant, ib.

आनुजावर *ānujāvará*, mfn. (fr. *anu* and √*jan*), posthumous [BRD.]; common, TS.; TBr.

आनुडुह *ānuḍuha, am*, n., v. l. for *ānaḍuha*, q. v.

आनुतिल्य *ānutilya*, mfn. (fr. *anu-tila*), belonging or conformable to grains of Sesamum, Comm. on Pāṇ.

आनुदृष्टिनेय *ānudṛishṭineya*, m. f. a descendant of Anu-dṛishṭi, q. v., ib.

आनुदृष्टेय *ānudṛishṭeya*, mfn. id., Pāṇ.

आनुदेशिक *ānudeśika*, mfn. belonging to an Anu-deśa (q. v.) rule, L.

आनुनाश्य *ānunāśya*, mfn. (fr. *anu-nāśa*), belonging or conformable to destruction, Pāṇ.

आनुनासिक्य *ānunāsikya, am*, n. (fr. *anu-nāsika*), nasality (of a sound), RPrāt.

आनुपथ्य *ānupathya*, mfn. (fr. *anu-patha*), along the way, Comm. on Pāṇ.

आनुपदिक *ānupadika*, mfn. (fr. *anu-pada*), following, pursuing, tracking; knowing or studying the *anupada* (q. v.) song, ib.

Ānupadya, mfn. being behind any one's steps, ib.

आनुपूर्व *ānupūrva, am*, n. and *ī*, f. (fr. *anu-pūrva*), order, series, succession, MBh.; R. &c.; (in law) direct order of the castes, Mn.; Yājñ. &c.; (generally only instr. *-eṇa* and *-yā*, one after the other, in due order.)

Ānupūrvya, *am*, n. order, succession, KātyŚr.; Mn.; Yājñ. &c.; (generally abl. *-āt*, in due order.)

आनुमत *ānumatá*, mf(*ī*)n. belonging to the goddess Anu-mati (q. v.), TBr.

आनुमानिक *ānumānika*, mf(*ī*)n. (fr. *anu-māna*), relating to a conclusion, derived from inference, subject to inference, inferable, inferred, Āp.; ŚāṅkhŚr.; making conclusions, BhP. **-tva**, n. the state of being inferable, KātyŚr.

आनुमाष्य *ānumāshya*, mfn. (fr. *anu-māsha*), belonging or conformable to kidney-beans, Comm. on Pāṇ.

आनुयव्य *ānuyavya*, mfn. (fr. *anu-yava*), belonging to barley, ib.

आनुयात्रिक *ānuyātrika*, mfn. (fr. *anu-yātra*), belonging to a servant; belonging to a retinue; a servant, ib.

आनुयूप्य *ānuyūpya*, mfn. (fr. *anu-yūpa*), being along or belonging to a sacrificial post, ib.

आनुरक्ति *ānurakti, is*, f. (= *anu-rakti*, q. v.), passion, affection, L.

आनुराहति *ānurāhati, is*, m. f. a descendant of Anu-rahat, Pāṇ. (cf. *ānuhārati*).

आनुरूप्य *ānurūpya, am*, n. (fr. *anu-rūpa*), conformity, suitableness, Sāh.

आनुरोहति *ānurohati, is*, m. f. a descendant of Anu-rohat (according to T., v. l. for °*hārati*, q. v.)

आनुरोहिण *ānurohiṇa*, mf(*ī*)n. belonging to the constellation Rohiṇī.

आनुलोमिक *ānulomika*, mf(*ī*)n. (fr. *anu-loma*), in the direction of the hair, in natural or regular order, in due course; conformable, favourable, benevolent, L.

Ānulomya, mf(*ī*)n. in the direction of the hair, produced in natural or direct order; (*am*), n. a direction similar to that of hairs, natural or direct order, Mn.; Yājñ.; Pāṇ.; the state of being prosperous, doing well, Suśr.; Pāṇ.; bringing to one's right place, Suśr.; favourable direction, fit disposition, favourableness, L.; regular series or succession, L.

आनुवंश्य *ānuvaṇśya*, mfn. (fr. *anu-vaṇśa*), belonging to a race, conformable to a genealogical list (according to T., 'behind a bamboo'), L.

आनुवासनिक *ānuvāsanika*, mfn. (fr. *anu-vāsana*), suitable for an oily enema.

आनुविधित्सा *ānuvidhitsā*, f. (probably for *an-anuvi*°, fr. *anu-vi-* and the Desid. of √*dhā*), ingratitude, L.

आनुवेश्य *ānuveśya*, mfn. (fr. *anu-veśa*, Pāṇ. iv, 3, 59), a neighbour living on the same side, Mn.

आनुशतिक *ānuśatika*, mfn. (fr. *anu-śatika*, Pāṇ. vii, 3, 20), belonging to a person or thing accompanied with or bought for a hundred.

आनुशासनिक *ānuśāsanika*, mfn. (fr. *anu-śāsana*), relating to or treating of instruction, MBh.

आनुशूक *ānuśūka*, mfn. (fr. *anu-śūka*), being with or within the awns (as rice).

आनुश्रव *ānuśrava*, mfn. according to hearing, resting on tradition, derived from the Veda or tradition, BhP.

Ānuśravika and **ānuśrāvika**, mfn. id.

आनुषक् *ānushák*, ind. (fr. *anu-*√*sañj* [gaṇa *svarâdi*]), in continuous order, uninterruptedly, one after the other, RV. v, 16, 2, &c. (cf. *anushak*).

Ānushaṅgika, mf(*ī*)n. (fr. *anu-shaṅga*), closely adherent, following, concomitant, inherent, implied, BhP.; Pañcat.; consistent; lasting, enduring, Rājat.; necessarily following, necessary as a result or consequence, inevitable; occasional, unimportant, secondary, Sāh.; (in Gr.) elliptical, including or agreeing with words not comprised in the sentence. **-tva**, *am*, n. the being occasional, secondary, Siddh. on Pāṇ. ii, 2, 29 (p. 430).

आनुषण्ड *ānushaṇḍa*, mfn. belonging to the country Anu-shaṇḍa (q. v.), L.

आनुषूक *ānushūká*, mfn. (probably fr. *anu-shūka*, 'after-shoot of rice' [according to native interpretation from *anu-*√*sū*]), 'in the manner of the after-shoot of rice,' i. e. shot after, TS. ii, 3, 4, 2.

आनुष्टुभ *ā́nushṭubha*, mf(*ī*)n. consisting of Anu-shṭubhs; formed like the Anu-shṭubh metre (e.g. composed of four divisions), RV. x, 181, 1; VS.; ŚBr.; RPrāt.

Ānushṭubhaushṇiha, mfn. consisting of the two metres Anu-shṭubh and Ushṇih, RPrāt.

आनुसाय्य *ānusāyya*, mfn. (fr. *anu-sāya*), being every evening, Comm. on Pāṇ.

आनुसीत्य *ānusītya*, mfn. (fr. *anu-sīta*), being along the furrow, ib.

आनुसीर्य *ānusīrya*, mfn. (fr. *anu-sīra*), being along the plough, ib.

आनुसुक *ānusuka*, mfn. studying or knowing the work Anusū (q. v.), L.

आनुसूक *ānusūka* = *ānushūka* (?), q. v.

आनुसूय *ānusūya*, mfn. given by Anu-sūyā (Atri's wife), Ragh. xiv, 14.

आनुसृतिनेय *ānusṛitineya*, m. f. a descendant of Anu sṛiti, Pāṇ.

आनुसृष्टिनेय *ānusṛishṭineya*, m. f. a descendant of Anu-sṛishṭi, ib.

आनुहारति *ānuhārati*, m. f. a descendant of Anu-harat, ib.

आनूक *ānūká, am*, n. (fr. *anv-añc*), 'lying close to,' ornament, jewels, RV. v, 33, 9 [according to NBD. *ānūkam*, ind. subsequently; but Sāy. explains the word by *ābharaṇa*].

आनूप *ānūpa*, mfn. (fr. *anūpa*, gaṇa *kacchâdi* [Pāṇ. iv, 2, 133]), belonging to a watery place; wet, watery, marshy, Suśr.; (*as*), m. any animal frequenting watery or marshy places, as fishes, buffaloes, &c. (cf. *anūpa*), ib.; a descendant of Anūpa; (*am*). n., N. of a Sāman, Lāṭy. iv, 6, 1. **-māṇsa**, *am*, n. the flesh or meat of animals frequenting watery or marshy places.

Ānūpaka, mfn. living in marshy places, Pāṇ.

आनृण्य *ānṛiṇya*. *am*, n. (fr. *an-ṛiṇa*), acquittance of debt or obligation, the not being indebted to (gen.), Mn.; MBh.; R.; Ragh.; Pañcat. &c.

आनृत् *ā-*√*nṛit*, P. (aor. 3. pl. *ā́-nṛitus*, RV. v, 52, 12; p. *-nṛítyat*, AV. iv, 37, 7) to dance towards, hasten near, jump near: Caus. (impf. 3. pl. *-nartayan*) to agitate gently, Ṛitus.; Ragh.

Ā-narta, *as*, m. dancing-room, dancing academy, T.; a stage, theatre, L.; war, L.; N. of a king (son of Śaryāti), Hariv.; N. of a country (northern Kāṭhiavāḍ), ib.; (*ās*), m. pl., N. of the inhabitants of the above country; of the kings of that country; (*am*), n. the empire of the Ānartas; water, L.; dancing, T. **-pura**, n. the capital of Ānarta, i. e. Dvāravatī, L.

Ānartaka, mfn. dancing towards, T.; belonging to the inhabitants of Ānarta, (gaṇa *dhūmâdi*, Pāṇ. iv, 2, 127.)

Ā-nartana, *am*, n. the act of dancing towards or near, dancing, ŚāṅkhGṛ. i, 11, 5.

Ā-nartita, mfn. agitated gently, Bhartṛ.

Ānartīya, mfn. belonging to the country (and the people of) Ānarta.

आनृत *ānṛita*, mf(*ī*)n. (fr. *an-ṛita*, gaṇa *chattrâdi*, Pāṇ. iv, 4, 62), untruthful, lying, false.

Ānṛitaka, mfn. belonging to or occupied by liars, L.

आनृशंस *ānṛiśaṇsa, am*, n. (fr. *a-nṛiśaṇsa*), absence of cruelty or harm, absence of injury, mildness, kindness, benevolence, MBh.; Gaut. v, 45.

Ānṛiśaṇsi, m. f. (Pāṇ. iv, 1, 95) the descendant of a benevolent person, T.; a benevolent person, L.

Ānṛiśaṇsīya, mfn. belonging to a benevolent person, (gaṇa *gahâdi*, Pāṇ. iv, 2, 138.)

Ānṛiśaṇsya, mf(*ā*)n. merciful, mild, kind, MBh.; (*am*), n. absence of cruelty or harm, kindness, mercy, compassion, benevolence, MBh.; Mn.; Āp. **-tas**, ind. from harmlessness, through kindness.

आनेमिमग्न *ā-nemi-magna*, mfn. sunk up to the rim or felloe (as a wheel).

आनैपुण *ānaipuṇa, am*, n. (fr. *a-nipuṇa*, Pāṇ. vii, 3, 30), unskilfulness, clumsiness (cf. *a-naipuṇa*).

आनैश्वर्य *ānaiśvarya, am*, n. (fr. *an-īśvara* [Pāṇ. vii, 3, 30]), absence of power or supremacy (cf. *an-aiśvarya*).

आन्त 1. *ānta*. See under 3. *am* (p. 80).

आन्त 2. *ānta*, mfn. final, terminal, relating to the end.

Āntya, *as*, m. one who finishes, personified as Bhauvana, VS.; TS.

Āntyāyaná, *as*, m. a descendant of the above, TS.

आन्तःपुरिक *āntaḥpurika*, mfn. (fr. *antaḥ-pura*), belonging to the women's apartments; (*am*), n. anything done in the women's apartment.

आन्तम् *āntám*, ind. (for *ā-antam*), to the end, completely, from head to foot, ŚBr.; TS.; Gaut.

आन्तर *āntara*, mfn. (fr. *antara*), interior, internal, inward, Bhaṭṭ.; native, indigenous, MBh.; being inside, within (a palace &c.), MBh.; (*as*), m. an intimate friend; (*am*), n. the heart, Naish. **-prapañca**, m. (in phil.) 'the inward expansion;' the fantasies of the soul produced by ignorance.

Āntaratamya, *am*, n. (fr. *antara-tama*), nearest or closest relationship (as of two letters), Siddh.

Āntarya, *am*, n. near relationship (of two letters).

आन्तरागारिक *āntarāgārika*, mfn. (fr. *antarâgāra*), belonging to the inner or women's apartments; (*as*), m. the keeper of a king's wives; (*am*), n. the office of the above

आन्तरायिक *āntarāyika*, mfn. (fr. *antar-āya*), returning at intervals, repeated from time to time.

आन्तराल *āntarāla*, mfn. (fr. *antar-āla*), (in phil.) 'those who know the condition of the soul within the body,' N. of a philosophical sect.

आन्तरिक्ष *āntarikshá* or *āntarīksha*, mf(*ī*)n. (fr. *antariksha*), belonging to the intermediate space between heaven and earth, atmospherical, proceeding from or produced in the atmosphere, VS.; TS.; MBh.; VarBṛS.; Suśr.; (*am*), n. rain-water.

आन्तरीपक *āntarīpaka*, mfn. (fr. *antar-īpa*, gaṇa *dhūmâdi*, Pāṇ. iv, 2, 127, where [in Böhtlingk's edition] *antarīpa* is to be read instead of *antarīya*), belonging to or being in an island.

आन्तर्गणिक *āntargaṇika*, mf(*ī*)n. (fr. *antar-gaṇa*), included or comprehended in a class or troop, L.

आन्तर्गेहिक *āntargehika*, mf(*ī*)n. (fr. *antar-geha*), being inside a house, ib.

आन्तर्वेदिक *āntarvedika*, mfn. (fr. *antarvedika*), being within the place of sacrifice, Comm. on KātyŚr.

आन्तर्वेश्मिक *āntarveśmika*, mf(ī)n. (fr. *antar-veśma*), produced or occurring within a house, L.

आन्तिका *āntikā*, f. (= *antikā*, q. v. [under 2. *anti*]) an elder sister, L.

आन्त्र 1. *āntrá*, *am*, n. (fr. *antra*), the bowels, entrails, RV.; AV.; VS.; ŚBr. **-tanti**, f. a string made from an animal's intestines, gut. **-pāśa**, m. id. **Āntrânucārin**, mfn. being in the bowels, Mantrabr.

Āntrika, mf(ī)n. visceral, within or relating to the bowels, L.

आन्त्र 2. *āntra*, *am*, n. (fr. √*am*), a kind of pipe (for smoking), T.

आन्द *āndá*, *as*, m. (√*and*, Comm. on VS. xxx, 16), one who makes fetters, VS.

आन्दोल *āndola*, *as*, m. swinging; fanning; a swing, L.

Āndolaka, *as*, m. a see-saw, swing.

Āndolana, *am*, n. swinging, a swing; trembling, oscillation, L.; investigation, T.

Āndolaya, Nom. P. *āndolayati*, to swing, agitate, Bālar.

Āndolita, mfn. agitated, shaken, swung, Kāvyād.

आन्धसिक *āndhasika*, mfn. (fr. 2. *andhas*), cooking; (*as*), m. a cook, L.

आन्धीगव *āndhīgava*, *am*, n. (fr. *andhī-gu*), 'seen, i. e. composed by the Ṛishi Andhīgu,' N. of several Sāmans, Lāṭy. iv, 5, 27; TāṇḍyaBr.; Nyāyam.

आन्ध्य *āndhya*, *am*, n. (fr. *andha*, Pāṇ. v, 1, 124), blindness, Suśr.; darkness, Vet.

आन्ध्र *āndhra*, mf(ī)n. (fr. *andhra*), belonging to the Andhra people; (*as*), m. the Andhra country; a king of that country; (*ās*), m. pl. the inhabitants of that country, MBh.; BhP. &c.; (*ī*), f. an Andhra wife.

आन्न *ānna*, *as*, mfn. (fr. *anna*), having food, one who gets food, Pāṇ. iv, 4, 85; relating to food.

आन्यतरेय *ānyatareya*, *as*, m. (fr. *anya-tara*, gaṇa *śubhrâdi*, Pāṇ. iv, 1, 123), N. of a grammarian, APrāt. iii, 74; RPrat. iii, 13 [BRD.], (perhaps rather) belonging to the school [and family] of another [teacher]?.

आन्यभाव्य *ānyabhāvya*, *am*, n. (fr. *anya-bhāva*, gaṇa *brāhmaṇâdi*, Pāṇ. v, 1, 24), the being another thing.

आन्वयिक *ānvayika*, mf(ī)n. (fr. *anv-aya*), of a good family, well born, L.

आन्वाहिक *ānvāhika*, mf(ī)n. (fr. *anv-aha*), daily, Mn.

आन्वीक्षिकी *ānvīkshikī*, f. (fr. *anv-īkshā*), logic, logical philosophy, metaphysics, MBh.; Mn.; Gaut. &c.

आन्वीपिक *ānvīpika*, mfn. (fr. *anv-īpa*), being along (the water); conformable (?), Pāṇ. iv, 4, 28.

आप 1. *āp*, cl. 5. P. *āpnóti* [AV. ix, 5, 22, &c.], (perf. *āpa*, aor. *āpat*, fut. *āpsyati*, inf. *āptum*), Ā. (perf. 3. pl. *āpiré*, RV. ix, 108, 4, p. pf. *āpānd*, RV. ii, 34, 7, but also pres. p. *āpnāna*, RV. x, 114, 7) to reach, overtake, meet with, fall upon, RV.; AV.; ŚBr. &c.; to obtain, gain, take possession of, RV.; AV. &c.; MBh.; Mn. &c.; to undergo, suffer, Mn.; to fall, come to any one; to enter, pervade, occupy; to equal: Pass. *āpyate*, to be reached or found or met with or obtained; to arrive at one's aim or end, become filled, TS. &c.: Caus. P. *āpayati*, to cause to reach or obtain or gain, ChUp. &c.; to cause any one to suffer; to hit, Kathās.: Desid. P. and Ā. *īpsati* and *īpsate* [Pāṇ. vii, 4, 55] to strive to reach or obtain, AV.; ŚBr.; MBh. &c.: Desid. of the Caus. *āpipayishati*, to strive to reach, ŚBr.; [probably connected with 1. *ap*; cf. *apna*; Gk. ἄφενος, ἀφνειός; Lat. *apiscor*, *aptus*, *ops*; Old Germ. *uoban*; Mod. Germ. *üben*.]

1. **Āpa**, *as*, m. obtaining; (mfn.) ifc. to be obtained (cf. *dur°*).

Āpaka, mf(ī)n. one who obtains, L.

Āpana, *am*, n. obtaining, reaching, coming to, BhP.; pepper, L.

Āpaneya, mfn. to be reached or obtained, KaṭhUp.

Āpayitṛi, mfn. one who procures, procuring.

1. **Āpāná**, mfn. one who has reached; (for 2. see *ā*-√1. *pā*.)

Āpí, *is*, m. an ally, a friend, an acquaintance, RV.; VS. (according to Sāy. on RV. ii, 29, 4, from the Caus.) causing to obtain [wealth &c.]; (mfn.) ifc. reaching to, entering. **-tvá**, n. confederation, friendship, RV. viii, 4, 3; 20, 22.

Āptá, mfn. reached, overtaken, met, ŚBr.; received, got, gained, obtained, ŚBr.; Mn.; Hit.; Kathās.; filled up, taken, ŚBr.; come to, Naish.; reaching to, extending; abundant, full, complete; apt, fit, true, exact, clever, trusted, trustworthy, confidential, Mn.; R.; Ragh. &c.; respected; intimate, related, acquainted, MBh.; R.; Ragh. &c.; appointed; divided, Sūryas.; connected, L.; accused, prosecuted, L.; (*as*), m. a fit person, a credible or authoritative person, warranter, guarantee; a friend; an Arhat, Jain.; N. of a Nāga, MBh.; (*ā*), f. = *jaṭā*, q. v., L.; (*am*), n. a quotient; equation of a degree, L. **-kāma**, mfn. one who has gained his wish, satisfied; (in phil.) one who knows the identity of Brahman and Ātman; (*as*), m. the supreme soul, T. **-kārin**, mfn. managing affairs in a fit or confidential manner; (*ī*), m. a trusty agent, a confidential servant, MBh.; Mn. &c. **-garbhā**, f. a pregnant woman. **-garva**, mfn. possessing pride, proud. **-dakshiṇa**, mfn. having proper gifts or furnished with abundant gifts, Mn.; R. **-bhāva**, m. the state of being trustworthy, MBh. **-vacana**, n. speech or word of an authoritative person, Ragh. xi, 42. **-vajra-sūci**, f., N. of an Upanishad. **-varga**, m. 'collection of intimate persons,' intimate persons, friends, Mālav. **-vākya**, *am*, n. = *āpta-vacana*, q. v.; a correct sentence. **-vāc**, f. a credible assertion or the assertion of a credible person, true affirmation, trustworthy testimony; the Veda; the Smṛitis, Itihāsas, Purāṇas, &c., T.; (mfn.) one whose assertion is credible, a Muni, Ragh. **-śruti**, f. a credible tradition; the Veda; the Smṛitis, &c., T. **Āptâgama** = *āpta-śruti*. **Āptâdhīna**, mfn. dependent on credible or trustworthy persons. **Āptôkti**, f. = *āpta-vacana*, q. v.; a word of received acceptation and established by usage only. **Āptôpadeśa**, m. a credible or trusty instruction, Sāh.

Āptavya, mfn. to be reached, obtainable.

Ā́pti, *is*, f. reaching, meeting with, TS.; ŚBr.; BṛĀrUp.; obtaining, gain, acquisition, ŚBr.; R.; MBh. &c.; abundance, fortune, ŚBr.; quotient; binding, connection, L.; sexual intercourse, L.; relation, fitness, aptitude, L.; (*ayas*), f. pl., N. of twelve invocations (VS. ix, 20) the first of which is *āpaye svāhā*.

1. **Āptyá** = *āptavya*, q. v., RV. v, 41, 9; (for 2. *āptya* see below.)

Āpnāna (cf. √1. *āp*), *am*, n. (scil. *tīrtha*) the passage to the place of sacrifice.

1. **Ā́pya**, mfn. to be reached, obtainable, ŚBr.; (*am*), n. confederation, alliance, relationship, friendship, RV. ii, 29, 3, &c.; a friend, RV. vii, 15, 1; (for 2. *āpya* see p. 144, col. 1.)

आप् 2. *āp* (*ā*-√*āp*), pf. *ā́pa*, to arrive at, come towards, RV. x, 32, 8.

आप 2. *āpa*, *as*, m., N. of one of the eight demigods called Vasus, VP.; Hariv.; MBh.; (*ī*), f., N. of a constellation, L.

आप 3. *āpa*, *am*, n. (fr. 2. *ap*, Pāṇ. iv, 2, 37), a quantity of water, Mallinātha on Śiś. iii, 72.

आपकर *āpakara*, mf(ī)n. coming from or native of the (country?) Apakara, Pāṇ. iv, 3, 33.

आपक्व *ā-pakva*, mfn. (√*pac*), half-baked, nearly crude or raw; nearly ripe, not quite ripe; undressed, what is eaten without further preparation (as bread &c.), L.

आपगा *āpagā*, f. (according to Mallinātha on Śiś. iii, 72, fr. 3. *āpa* and √*gā*), a river, a stream, MBh.; R.; Ragh.; Śiś.; N. of a river, MBh.

Āpageya, *as*, m. 'a descendant of the river Āpagā,' N. of Bhīshma, MBh.

आपट् *ā*-√*paṭ*, Caus. *-pāṭayati*, to cause to split, Suśr.

आपटव *āpaṭava*, v. l. for *apāṭava*, q. v.

आपण *āpaṇa*, *as*, m. a market, a shop, MBh.; R.; Kathās.; waves, MBh.; commerce, trade, L. **-devatā**, f. image of a deity placed in the market, R. **-vīthika**, m. and n. a row of stalls (in a market), R. **-vedikā**, f. a shop-counter, R.

Ā-paṇika, mfn. (Uṇ. ii, 45) mercantile, relating to traffic or to a market &c.; (*as*), m. a merchant, dealer, shop-keeper, L.; tax on markets or shops; assize, market-rate, L.

आपत् *ā*-√1. *pat*, P. *-patati* (p. acc. *-patantam*, AV. xii, 4, 47; aor. *ā́-paptata*, RV. i, 88, 1 [Pāṇ. vii, 4, 19]; Pot. perf. *ā́-papatyāt*, AV. vi, 29, 3) to fly towards, come flying; to hasten towards, rush in or on, RV.; AV.; ŚBr.; Hariv.; Ragh. &c.; to fall towards or on, Kathās.; to approach; to assail; to fall out, happen; to appear, appear suddenly; to fall to one's share, to befall, MBh.; R.; Rājat.; BhP.; Pañcat.; Kād. &c.: Caus. P. (3. pl. *-patáyanti*, RV. x, 64, 2) to fly towards; *-pātayati*, to throw down, let fall, cut down; to shed, BhP.; Hariv.; Mn.

Ā-patana, *am*, n. happening, appearing, Sāh.; coming, approaching; reaching; unexpected appearance (as from fate), L.

Ā-pati, *is*, m. incessantly moving (as the wind), VS. v, 5 [Comm.]

Āpatika, mfn. accidental, unforeseen, coming from fate, Comm. on Uṇ. ii, 45; (*as*), m. a hawk, a falcon, ib.

Ā-patita, mfn. happened, befallen; alighted, descended.

Ā-pāta, *as*, m. the falling, descending; rushing upon, pressing against, Mn.; Kum.; Ragh. &c.; forwardness, Kathās.; happening, becoming apparent, (unexpected) appearance, Ragh.; Sāh. &c.; the instant, current moment, Kir.; throwing down, causing to descend, L. **-tas**, ind. unexpectedly; instantly, suddenly, just now, Sāh. **-mātra**, mfn. being only momentary.

Āpātika, mfn. rushing upon, being at hand; (*as*), m., N. of a kind of demigod.

Ā-pātita, mfn. caused to fall down, thrown down, killed, Hariv.

Ā-pātin, mfn. ifc. falling on, happening, Kathās.

Ā-pātya, mfn. (Pāṇ. iii, 4, 68) approaching in order to assault or attack, rushing on, assailing, Śiś. v, 15; to be assaulted or attacked, L.

आपत्काल *āpat-kāla*, &c. See under 1. *ā*-√*pad* below.

आपत्य *āpatya*, mfn. (fr. *apatya*), relating to the formation of patronymic nouns, L.

आपथि *ā́-pathi*, *is*, m. (fr. *pathin* with *ā*), travelling hither or near, RV. v, 52, 10.

Āpathí, f. any impediment in one's way (e. g. a stone, tree, &c.)[?], RV. i, 64, 11.

आपद् 1. *ā*-√*pad*, Ā. *-padyate* (pf. *-pede*, aor. *âpādi*, &c.) to come, walk near, approach, BhP.; to enter, get in, arrive at, go into, ŚBr.; Lāṭy.; R. &c.; to fall in or into; to be changed into, be reduced to any state; to get into trouble, fall into misfortune, AV. viii, 8, 18; xi, 1, 30; ŚBr.; AitBr.; MBh.; Mn. &c.; to get, attain, take possession; to happen, occur, ŚBr.; Mālav. &c.: Caus. *-pādayati* (aor. 1. pl. *ā́-pīpadāma*, AV. x, 5, 42) to cause to enter, bring on, ŚBr.; to bring to any state, Ragh.; to bring into trouble or misfortune, R. &c.; to bring near or towards, fetch, procure, produce, cause, effect, MBh.; Suśr.; Ragh. &c.; to procure for one's self, obtain, take possession, BhP.; to change, transform.

Āpat (in comp. for 2. *āpad* below). **-kalpa**, m. rule of practice in misfortune (cf. *āpad-dharma*), Gaut.; Mn. **-kāla**, m. season or time of distress, Mn.; Pañcat. **-kālika**, mfn. occurring in a time of calamity, belonging to such a time, gaṇa *kāśy-ādi* (Pāṇ. iv, 2, 116).

Ā-patti, *is*, f. happening, occurring; entering into a state or condition, entering into relationship with, changing into, KātyŚr.; APrāt. &c.; incurring, misfortune, calamity, Yājñ.; fault, transgression, L.

2. **Āpad**, f. misfortune, calamity, distress, Mn.; Hit.; Ragh. &c.; (*āpadā*, instr.), through mistake

or error, unintentionally. **-uddharaṇa**, n. bringing out of trouble, Hit. **-gata**, mfn. fallen into misfortune, unhappy. **-grasta**, mfn. seized by misfortune, unfortunate, in misfortune. **-dharma**, m. a practice only allowable in time of distress, Mn.; misfortune, MBh. [NBD.] **-vinīta**, mfn. disciplined or humbled by misfortune, Bālar. 193, 17.

Ā-padā, f. misfortune, calamity, L.

Ā-panna, mfn. entered, got in, ŚBr.; KātyŚr. &c.; afflicted, unfortunate, Śak.; Kathās. &c.; gained, obtained, acquired; having gained or obtained or acquired. **-jīvika**, mfn. having obtained a livelihood, Comm. on Pāṇ. i, 2, 44. **-sattvā**, f. a pregnant woman, Ragh. x, 60; Śak. **Āpannârti-praśamana-phala**, mf(*ā*)n. having as result the relieving of the pains of the afflicted, Megh. 54.

1. **Ā-pāda**, *as*, m. reward, remuneration, ChUp.; arriving at, L.; (for 2. *ā-pāda* see below.)

Ā-pādaka, mfn. causing, effecting.

Ā-pādana, *am*, n. causing to arrive at; bringing any one to any state; producing, effecting, Siddh.

आपदेव *āpadeva*, *as*, m. (fr. 2. *ap*), N. of the god of water (Varuṇa), T.; N. of an author; (*ī*), f., N. of a book written by the above (the Mīmāṅsanyāya-prakāśa).

आपन् *ā-√pan*, Ā. (*ā-pananta*, RV. x, 74, 4), P. (pf. *ā-papana*, RV. viii, 2, 17) to admire, praise.

आपन *āpana*, &c. See under √1. *āp*.

आपभट्ट *āpa-bhaṭṭa*, *as*, m., N. of an author (= Āpa-deva).

आपमित्यक *āpamityaka*, mfn. (fr. *apa-mitya* [Pāṇ. iv, 4, 21], ind. p. of *apa-√mā*), received by barter; (*am*), n. property &c. obtained by barter, L.

आपया *āpayā́* (fr. 3. *āpa* and √*yā*; cf. *āpagā*), a river, L.; N. of a river, RV. iii, 23, 4.

आपरपक्षीय *āparapakshīya*, mfn. (fr. *aparapaksha*), belonging to the second half (of a month), BhP.

आपराधय्य *āparādhayya*, *am*, n. (fr. *aparādhaya*, gaṇa *brāhmaṇâdi*, Pāṇ. v, 1, 124), wronging, offending, L.

आपराह्णिक *āparāhṇika*, mfn. (fr. *aparâhṇa*), belonging to or occurring in the afternoon, Pāṇ.; KātyŚr.

आपर्तुक *āpartuka*, mfn. (fr. *apartu* = *aparitu*), not corresponding to the season.

आपल *āpala*, *am*, n., N. of a Sāman (cf. *āpāla*).

आपव *āpava*, *as*, m., N. of Vasishṭha, MBh.; Hariv. (said to be a patron. fr. *āpu* = Varuṇa?).

आपवर्गिक *āpavargika*, mfn. (fr. *apa-varga*), conferring final beatitude, BhP.

Āpavargya, mfn. id., ib.

आपश् *ā-√paś*, P. *ā́-paśyati* [AV. iv, 20, 1], to look at.

आपस् 1. *ā́pas*, n. (connected with 1. *ap*), a religious ceremony, RV.

आपस् 2. *āpas*, n. (fr. 2. *ap*), water, ChUp.

3. **Āpas**, Nom. (rarely acc.) pl. of 2. *ap*, q. v.

Āpo (in comp. for 2. & 3. *āpas*). **-devata**, mfn. having the water as deity, ĀśvŚr. **-devatya**, mfn. id., ŚāṅkhŚr. **-maya**, mfn. consisting of water, ŚBr.; ChUp.; MBh. **-mātrā**, f. the subtle elementary principle of water. **-mūrti**, m., N. of a son of Manu Svārocisha, Hariv.; N. of one of the seven Ṛishis of the tenth Manvantara. **-'śāna**, mfn. 'taking water' [*āpas* being a rare form of the acc. for *apas*], i. e. sipping water; (*am*), n. sipping water before and after eating. **-hishṭhīya**, mfn. belonging to the hymn x, 9 of the RV. (which begins with *ā́po hi shṭhā́*); (*am*), n., N. of a Sāman.

आपस्तम्ब *āpastamba*, *as*, m., N. of a renowned sage and writer on ritual; (*as*, *ī*), m. f. a descendant of Āpastamba, gaṇa *viḍâdi* [Pāṇ. iv, 1, 104]; (*ās*), m. pl. the pupils of Āpastamba. **-gṛihya**, n., **-dharma**, m., **-śrauta**, n., **-sūtra**, n., &c., N. of works by Āpastamba and his school.

Āpastambi, *is*, m. a descendant of the above.

Āpastambīya, mfn. belonging to or descended from Āpastamba.

आपस्तम्भ *āpastambha*, *as*, m., v. l. for *āpastamba*.

Āpastambhinī, f., N. of a plant, L.

आपा *ā-√1. pā*, P. *-pibati* (Impv. 2. du. *ā́-pibatam*, RV. ii, 36, 6; pf. *-papau*: Pass. *-pīyate*, &c.) to drink in, suck in or up; to sip, RV.; MBh.; Ragh.; to drink in with ears or eyes, i. e. to hear or see with attention, hang on, BhP.; Ragh.; to absorb, take away: Caus. *-pāyayati*, to cause to drink or suck in, BhP.

2. **Ā-pāna**, *am*, n. the act of drinking, a drinking-party, banquet, MBh.; (for 1. *āpāná* see p. 142, col. 2.) **-goshṭhī**, f. a banquet, carouse, Kathās. **-bhūmi**, f. a place for drinking in company, Ragh.; Kum. **-śālā**, f. a tavern, liquor shop, R.

Ā-pānaka, *am*, n. a drinking-bout; drinking liquor, Kād.

Ā-pānta-manyu, mfn. giving zeal or courage when drunk (said of the Soma juice), RV. x, 89, 5.

Ā-pāyin, mfn. fond of drinking, AitBr.

1. **Ā-pīta**, mfn. drunk up, exhausted.

Ā-pīya, ind. p. having drunk in, Hariv.

आपाक 1. *āpāka*, *as*, m. (√*pac*), a baking-oven, potter's kiln; baking, T.; = *puṭapāka*, q. v., T. **Āpāke-sthá**, mfn. standing in an oven, AV. viii, 6, 14.

आपाक 2. *ā-pāka*, *as*, m. slight baking, T.

आपाङ्ग्य *āpāṅgya*, *am*, n. (fr. *apâṅga*), anointing the corners of the eyes, Suśr.

आपाटल *ā-pāṭala*, mf(*ā*)n. reddish, Kād.

आपाटलिपुत्रम् *ā-pāṭaliputram*, ind. as far as or to Pāṭaliputra, L.

आपाण्डु *ā-pāṇḍu*, mfn. slightly pale, palish, pale, VarBṛS. **-tā**, f. paleness.

Ā-pāṇḍura, mfn. palish, pale, white. **-°rī-√bhū**, to become pale, Kum.

आपात *ā-pāta*. See under *ā-√1. pat*.

आपातलिका *āpātalikā*, f., N. of a Vaitālīya metre.

आपाद *ā-pāda*, &c. See under 1. *ā-√pad*.

आपाल *āpāla*, *am*, n., N. of a Sāman (cf. *āpala*).

आपालि *āpāli*, *is*, m. a louse, L.

आपि *āpi*, &c. See under √1. *āp*.

आपिङ्ग *ā-piṅga*, mfn. reddish-brown, Bhaṭṭ.

आपिञ्जर *ā-piñjara*, mfn. somewhat red, reddish, Ragh.; Kād.; (*am*), n. gold, L.

आपिब्द् *ā-√pibd*, p. *ā-píbdamāna*, making a noise, crackling, RV. x, 102, 11 [Sāy.]

आपिश् *ā-√piś*, P. (Impv. 2. pl. *ā́-piṅśata*, RV. x, 53, 7), Ā. (p. *-piśāná*, RV. vii, 57, 3) to decorate, ornament, colour.

आपिशङ्ग *ā-piśaṅga*, mfn. slightly tawny, gold-coloured, Kād.

आपिशर्वर *āpiśarvará*, mfn. (fr. *api-śarvara*), nightly, nocturnal, TS.

आपिशलि *āpiśali*, *is*, m., N. of an ancient grammarian mentioned by Pāṇ. [vi, 1, 92], &c.

Āpiśala, mf(*ī*)n. belonging to or coming from Āpiśali; (*as*), m. a pupil of the same.

आपिष् *ā-√pish*, P. (*ā́-pinashṭi*, AV. xx, 133, 1; pf. *-pipésha*, VS. ix, 11) to press or rub against, to touch.

Ā-pésham, ind. p. having pressed or rubbed against, touching, ŚBr.

आपी *ā-√pī*, &c. See under *ā-√pyai*.

आपीड् *ā-√pīḍ*, Caus. *-pīḍayati*, to press against or out; to press, crush, ĀśvGṛ.; R. &c.; to press hard, give pain, perplex, MBh.

Ā-pīḍa, *as*, m. (ifc. mf(*ā*)n., L.) compressing, squeezing, Suśr.; giving pain, hurting, L.; a chaplet tied on the crown of the head, MBh.; R.; Ragh.; N. of a metre.

Ā-pīḍana, *am*, n. the act of compressing, squeezing, drawing tightly; embracing, clasping; hurting, giving pain, L.

Ā-pīḍita, mfn. compressed, squeezed, R.; Śak.; Prab. &c.; bound tightly, embraced, overlaid, covered, Rājat.; hurt; decorated with chaplets, MBh.

आपीत 2. *ā-pīta*, mfn. yellowish, R.; (*as*), m., N. of a species of tree, Comm.; (*am*), n. filament of the lotus, ib.; a pyritic mineral, L.; (for 1. *ā-pīta* see under *ā-√pā*, and for 3. *ā-pīta* under *ā-√pyai*.)

Ā-pītaya, Nom. P. to make yellowish, dye with any yellow substance, Kād.

आपीन *ā-pīna*. See under *ā-√pyai*.

आपुथ् *ā-√puth*, Caus. *-pothayati*.

Ā-pothya, ind. p. having squeezed or compressed, Suśr.

आपू *ā-√pū*, Ā. (Impv. *ā́-pavasva*, RV. ix, 70, 10; once P. *ā́-pava*, RV. ix, 49, 3; p. *-punāna*) to be pure; to flow towards after purification; to carry towards in its course (as a stream), RV.; VS.

आपूपिक *āpūpika*, mfn. (fr. *apūpa*), relating to cakes (as selling or eating or making cakes), Comm. on Pāṇ.; (*as*), m. a baker, confectioner, L.; (*am*), n. a multitude of cakes, L.

Āpūpya, *am*, n. meal, flour, L.

आपूय् *ā-√pūy*, P. (impf. *ā́pūyat*) to putrify, ŚBr.

Āpūyita, mfn. stinking. See *an-ā-pūyita*.

आपूर *ā-pūra*, &c. See under *ā-√pṛī*.

आपूष *āpūsha*, *am*, n. tin, L.

आपृ 1. *ā-√1. pṛi*, P. (aor. Subj. 2. du. *-parshathas*, RV. x, 143, 4) to give aid, protect.

आपृ 2. *ā-√2. pṛi*, P. (*-priṇoti*) to employ one's self, to be occupied, BhP.

Ā-pṛita, mfn. occupied, engaged, BhP.

आपृच् *ā-√pṛic*, P. (Impv. *ā́-priṇaktu*; pf. *-papṛicus*; Inf. *-pṛíce*, RV. v, 50, 2, and *-pṛícas*, RV. viii, 40, 9) to fill, pervade; to satiate, RV. i, 84, 1; TBr.; to mix with, AitBr.: Ā. (aor. Pot. *ā-pṛicīmahi*) to satiate one's self, RV. i, 129, 7.

Ā-pṛík, ind. in a mixed manner, in contact with, RV. x, 89, 14.

आपृच्छा *ā-pṛicchā*. See under *ā-√prach*.

आपॄ *ā-√pṝī*, P. *-piparti*, *-priṇāti*, and *-priṇati*; to fill up, fulfil, fill, RV.; AV.; VS.; to do any one's desire, satisfy any one's wish, RV.: Ā. *-priṇate*, to surfeit one's self, satiate or satisfy one's self, RV.: Pass. *-pūryate*, to be filled, become full, increase; to be satiated, satisfied, RV.; ŚBr.; BhP.; MBh.; Kathās. &c.: Caus. *-pūrayati*, to fill up, fulfil, fill, ŚBr.; Hariv.; Rājat. &c.; to fill with noise, MBh.; R.; to fill with air, to inflate, R.; to cover; to load anything with, MBh.; R.; Ṛitus.; Kathās.

Ā-pūra, *as*, m. flood, flooding, excess, abundance, Kathās.; Śiś. &c.; filling up, making full, L.; filling a little, T.

Ā-pūraṇa, mfn. making full, filling up, Hit.; (*as*), m., N. of a Nāga, MBh.; (*am*), n. filling, making full, satiating; drawing a bow; flooding.

Ā-pūrita, mfn. filled up, full.

Ā-pūrta, *am*, n. fulfilling; a meritorious work, Kād.

Ā-pūrya, ind. p. having filled, filling.

Ā-pūryamāṇa, mfn. becoming full, increasing. **-paksha**, m. [scil. *candra*] the moon in her increase, the waxing moon, ĀśvGṛ.; PārGṛ.; ŚāṅkhGṛ. &c.

आपेक्षिक *āpekshika*, mfn. (fr. *apekshā*), relative, having relation or reference to, Siddh. (p. 418, l. 10). **-tva**, *am*, n. the state of being relative, Nyāyad.

आपेय *āpeya*, *ās*, m. pl. (fr. 1. *ap*?), a particular class of gods. **-tva**, *am*, n. the being of this class, MaitrS.; (cf. *āpyeya*.)

आपेषम् *āpesham*. See under *ā-√pish*.

आपोक्लिम *āpoklima*, *am*, n. (in astron.) = ἀπόκλιμα.

आपोदेवत *āpo-devata, āpo-maya,* &c. See p. 143, col. 1.

आप्त *āpta,* &c. See under √*āp.*

आप्त्य 2. *āptyá, as,* m., N. of Trita, RV.; N. of Indra, RV. x, 120, 6; (*ās*), m. pl., N. of a class of deities, RV. (ib.); AV.; ŚBr.; KātyŚr.; (for 1. *āptya* see under √*āp.*)

आप्नवान *āpnavāna, as,* m. a descendant of Apnavāna, ĀśvŚr.

आप्य 2. *āpya,* mfn. (fr. 2. *ap*), belonging or relating to water, watery, liquid, Suśr.; consisting of water; living in water; (*as*), m., N. of several asterisms, VarBṛ.; N. of a Vasu; (*ās*), m. pl., N. of a class of deities, BhP.; Hariv.; (*am*), n., N. of a constellation; (for 1. *āpya* see under √*āp.*)

आप्य 3. *āpya, am,* n., N. of a plant, a kind of Costus, L.; (cf. *vāpya.*)

आप्येय *āpyeya, ās,* m. pl. (fr. 1. *ap* ?), N. of a class of deities (= *āpeya*), KapS. **–tva,** *am,* n. = *āpeya-tva,* ib.

आप्यै *ā-√pyai,* Ā. *-pyāyate* (Impv. *ā́-pyāyasva,* AV. vii, 81, 5; aor. Subj. 1. pl. *ā-pyāyishīmahi,* AV. vii, 81, 5) to swell, increase; to grow larger or fat or comfortable; to thrive; to become full or strong; to abound, RV.; AV.; VS.; AitBr.; MBh.; Yājñ. &c.; to make full; to enlarge, strengthen, MBh.: Caus. *ā́-pyāyayati* (AV. iv, 11, 4; aor. Subj. *ā́-pīpayan,* RV. i, 152, 6) to cause to swell; to make full, fill up; to enlarge; to cause to grow, increase; to make fat or strong or comfortable; to confirm, ŚBr.; AitBr.; MBh.; R.; Megh. &c.; to help forward; to cause to increase or get the upper hand (e. g. a disease), Suśr. &c.

Ā-pī, mfn. fat, enlarged, increased, T.

3. **Ā-pīta,** mfn. swollen out, puffed up, distended, full, stout, fat, RV. viii, 9, 19; (for 2. *āpīta* see s. v.)

Ā-pīna, mfn. id., AV. ix, 1, 9; AitBr.; MBh. &c.; (*as*), m. a well, T.; (*am*), n. an udder, Ragh. **–vat,** mfn. containing a form of *ā-√pyai* (as the verse RV. i, 91, 16), AitBr. i, 17, 4; (cf. *āpyāna-vat.*)

Ā-pyāna, mfn. stout, robust, increased; glad, T.; (*am*), n. increasing; stoutness; gladness, T. **–vat** = *ā-pīna-vat,* ŚBr. vii, 3, 1, 12, &c.

Ā-pyāya, *as,* m. becoming full, increasing, Kathās.

Ā-pyāyana, mfn. causing fulness or stoutness, Suśr.; increasing welfare, gladdening, L.; (*ī*), f. an umbilical vein, MārkP.; (*am*), n. the act of making full or fat, Suśr.; satiating; satisfying, refreshing, pleasing, Mn.; increasing, causing to thrive, MBh.; causing to swell (the Soma), ŚBr. &c.; satiety, satisfaction; advancing; anything which causes corpulency or good condition; strengthening medicine, Suśr.; corpulency, growing or being fat or stout; gladness, L. **–vat,** mfn. causing or effecting welfare, increase, MaitrUp. **–śīla,** mfn. capable of satisfying.

Ā-pyāyita, mfn. satisfied, increased, improved, pleased, gratified; stout, fat; grown, spread out (as a disease).

Ā-pyāyin, mfn. causing welfare or increase, Kathās.; (*inī*), f., N. of a Śakti, L.

Ā-pyāyya, mfn. to be satisfied or pleased, MBh.

आप्र 1. *āprá,* mfn. (fr. √1. *āp,* Sāy. on RV. i, 132, 2), getting at [enemies in order to kill them] (?); (for 2. *āpra* see under *ā-√prī.*)

आप्रच्छ् *ā-√prach,* Ā. *-pṛicchate,* rarely P. (Impv. *-pṛiccha,* MBh.) to take leave, bid farewell; to salute on receiving or parting with a visitor, MBh.; R.; Megh.; Ragh.; Kathās. &c.; to call (on a god), implore, Suśr.; to ask, inquire for, BhP.; to extol, L.

Ā-pṛicchā, f. conversation, speaking to or with; address; bidding farewell, saluting on receiving a visitor, asking, inquiring, L.

1. **Ā-pṛicchya,** mfn. (Pāṇ. iii, 1, 123) to be inquired for; to be respected, RV. i, 60, 2; to be praised, laudable, commendable, RV.

2. **Ā-pṛicchya,** ind. p. having saluted or asked or inquired.

Ā-pṛishṭa, mfn. welcomed, saluted, MBh.; asked for, L.

Ā-pṛishṭvā (irr.) = 2. *ā-pṛicchya,* R. i, 72, 20.

Ā-pracchana, *am,* n. expression of civility on receiving or parting with a visitor, welcome, bidding farewell &c.

Ā-prashṭavya, mfn. to be saluted; to be asked, Sāy.

आप्रतिनिवृत् *ā-prati-ni-√vṛit,* to cease completely.

Ā-prati-nivṛitta-guṇormi-cakra, mfn. (scil. *jñāna,* knowledge) through which the whole circle of wave-like qualities (of passion &c.) subside or cease completely, BhP. ii, 3, 12.

आप्रती *ā-prati* (*ā-prati-√i*), P. (Impv. 2. pl. *-ítana,* RV. vi, 42, 2) to go towards any one to meet him.

आप्रथ् *ā-√prath,* Caus. (aor. Subj. 3. pl. *-paprathan,* RV. viii, 94, 9) to spread, extend.

आप्रदिवम् *ā-pradivám,* ind. for ever, ŚBr.

आप्रपदम् *ā-prapadam,* ind. to the end or fore part of the foot, Pāṇ. iv, 2, 8.

Ā-prapadīna, mfn. reaching to the fore part of the foot (as a dress), Kād.

Āprapadīnaka, mfn. id.; (*am*), n. a dress reaching to the end of the foot.

आप्रयम् *ā-pra-√yam,* P. (Impv. *-prá-yaccha,* AV. vii, 26, 8) to hand over, to reach.

आप्रवण *ā-pravaṇa,* mfn. a little precipitous.

आप्रा *ā-√prā,* P. (pf. *ā́-paprau,* AV. xix, 49, 1 & RV.; aor. 2. sg. *ā́prās,* RV. i, 52, 13, &c.), Ā. (pf. *ā-papre,* AV. xi, 2, 27; aor. *ā́prāyi,* AV. xix, 47, 1, &c.) to fulfil; to accomplish any one's desire (*kāmam*).

आप्रावृषम् *ā-prāvṛisham,* ind. until the rainy season, ŚBr.

आप्री 1. *ā-√prī,* P. (*-prīṇāti,* AitBr. ii, 4; aor. Subj. 2. sg. *-piprāyas,* RV. ii, 6, 8) to satisfy, conciliate, propitiate, please, RV.; TS.; ŚBr.; to address or invoke with the Āprī (see below) verses, AitBr.; ŚBr.: Ā. (impf. *ā́prīṇīta*) to amuse one's self, be delighted or pleased, TS.; Lāṭy.

2. **Āpra,** mfn. belonging to or being an Āprī (see below), RAnukr.

2. **Ā-prī,** f. gaining one's favour, conciliation, propitiation; (*-priyas* [AV. xi, 7, 19] and *-pryas* [Nārāy.]), f. pl., N. of particular invocations spoken previous to the offering of oblations (according to ĀśvŚr. iii, 2, 5 seqq. they are different in different schools; e. g. *sámiddho agnír,* RV. v, 28, 1, in the school of Śunaka; *jushásva naḥ,* RV. vii, 2, 1, in that of Vasishṭha; *sámiddho adyá,* RV. x, 110, 1, in that of others; Nārāyaṇa on this passage gives ten hymns belonging to different schools; see also Sāy. on RV. i, 13 [*súsamiddho na ā́ vaha,* the Āprī-hymn of the school of Kaṇva], who enumerates twelve Āprīs and explains that twelve deities are propitiated; those deities are personified objects belonging to the fire-sacrifice, viz. the fuel, the sacred grass, the enclosure, &c., all regarded as different forms of Agni; hence the objects are also called Āprīs, or, according to others, the objects are the real Āprīs, whence the hymns received their names), AV.; TS.; ĀśvŚr. &c.

Ā-prīta, mfn. gladdened, joyous, BhP. x, 62, 27. **–pá,** m. [according to the Comm. on VS. viii, 57, 'guarding those who are propitiated'] guarding when gladdened or propitiated, N. of Vishṇu, VS.; ŚBr.

Ā-prīti-māyu, *us,* m., N. of a place, L.; (*āprītimāyava,* mfn. belonging to the above place, ib.)

आप्रु *ā-√pru* (√*pru* = √*plu*), Ā. *-pravate,* to spring up, jump up.

आप्रुषाय *ā-prushāya,* Nom. P. *ā́-prushāyati,* to besprinkle, bespeckle, RV. x, 26, 3; 68, 4: Ā. (impf. 3. pl. *-prushāyánta*) id., RV. i, 186, 9.

आप्लु *ā-√plu,* Ā. *-plavate* (Pot. *-pluvīta,* ŚāṅkhGṛ. iv, 12, 31 [v. l.], and *-plavet*) to spring or jump towards or over, dance towards or over, AV. xx, 129, 1; AitBr.; MBh.; Hariv. &c.; to bathe, wash, ĀśvGṛ.; ŚāṅkhGṛ. & Śr.; ŚBr.; Mn.; BhP.; MBh. &c.; to immerse one's self, MBh. &c.; to bathe, wash another, MBh.; Ragh. &c.; to water, bedew, inundate; to overrun, MBh.; Hariv.; Pañcat. &c.: Caus. P. *-plāvayati,* to wash or bathe any person or thing, cause to be bathed or washed, ĀśvGṛ.; PārGṛ.; MBh. &c.; to bathe (one's self), MBh.; to inundate, overwhelm, set in commotion, MBh.; Hariv.; Mn. &c.; to dip, steep, Suśr.; VarBṛS.: Ā. *-plāvayate,* id.

Ā-plava, *as,* m. ablution, bathing, Pāṇ.; BhP.; R.; sprinkling with water, L. **–vratin,** m. one whose duty is to perform the Samāvartana ablution (on returning home after completing his studies), an initiated householder, L.

Ā-plavana, *am,* n. immersing, bathing, KātyŚr.; BhP.; MBh.; sprinkling with water, L.

Ā-plāva, *as,* m. (= *ā-plava,* Pāṇ. iii, 3, 50), submerging, wetting; flood, inundation, L.

Ā-plāvita, mfn. inundated, overflowed, Hariv.; Rājat.; Pañcat.

1. **Āplāvya,** mfn. to be used as a bath, serving for bathing, MBh.; bathing (any one), to be washed, bathed; (*am*), n. washing, bathing, Pāṇ.; L.

2. **Ā-plāvya,** ind. p. having washed, wetted or sprinkled.

Ā-pluta, mfn. one who has bathed (himself), bathed, MBh.; BhP.; wetted, sprinkled, overflowed, MBh.; Hariv.; Ragh. &c.; ifc. (used fig.) overrun; afflicted, distressed (*vyasanā°*); one who has sprung or jumped near, Hariv.; MBh.; (*as*), m. (= *ā-plava-vratin*), an initiated householder, L.; (*am*), n. bathing, MBh.; jumping, springing towards, MBh.; Hariv. **–vratin,** m. = *ā-plava-vratin,* q. v., L.

Āplutāṅga, mf(*ī*)n. bathed all over, MBh.

Ā-pluti, *is,* f. bathing, a bath, L.

Ā-plutya, ind. p. having bathed or washed; having jumped up.

आप्लुष्ट *ā-plushṭa,* mfn. a little singed or burnt, Kum. v, 48.

आप्वा *āpvā,* nom. of *āpvan,* m.? (according to Siddh. ii, p. 393, l. 21, fr. √*āp*) wind, air (according to Comm. on Uṇ. i, 154 = *kaṇṭha-sthāna*).

आप्सर *āpsara,* mfn. (fr. *apsaras*), belonging to the Apsaras.

Āpsarasa, mf(*ī*)n. a descendant of an Apsaras, BhP. vi, 4, 16; (*am*), n., N. of a Sāman.

आप्सव *āpsava, as,* m. (fr. *apsu,* loc. pl. of *ap*), N. of a Manu.

आफण् *ā-√phaṇ,* Intens. *-pā́nīphaṇat* (Pāṇ. vii, 4, 65) to skip, jump, RV. iv, 40, 4.

आफलक *ā-phalaka, as,* m. enclosure, palisade, R. i, 70, 3.

आफलोदयकर्मन् *ā-phalódaya-karman,* mfn. persevering in a work until it bears fruit, Ragh. i, 5.

आफल्य *āphalya, am,* n. (fr. *a-phala*), fruitlessness, Nyāyad.

आफीन *āphīna, am,* n. and *āphūka, am,* n. opium, L.; (Hindī *āphīm* and *āphū,* cf. *a-phena.*)

आबध् *ā-√badh.* See *ā-√vadh.*

आबन्ध् *ā-√bandh,* P. *-badhnāti* (impf. *ā́badhnāt,* AV. vi, 81, 3; pf. *-babandha*), Ā. (pf. *-bedhé,* AV. v, 28, 11; Inf. *ā-bádhe,* AV. v, 28, 11) to bind or tie on, tie to one's self, AV.; ŚBr.; ĀśvGṛ.; Lāṭy.; MBh.; Kathās. &c.; to join, bind together, continue, resume, MBh.; Daś.; Kād.; to take hold of, seize, Mn.; to adhere closely to, be constant, Kād.; to fix one's eye or mind on, Kathās.; Ragh.; to effect, produce; to bring to light, show, Megh. &c.

Ā-baddha, mfn. tied on, bound; joined; fixed, effected, produced, shown (cf. the comps.); (*as*), m. affection, L.; (*am*), n. binding fastly, a binding, a yoke, L.; an ornament, cloth, ŚāṅkhGṛ. ii, 1, 25 (L. *as,* m.) **–dṛishṭi,** mfn. having the eyes fixed on, Ragh. **–maṇḍala,** mfn. forming a circle, sitting in a circle, Kād. **–māla,** mfn. forming a wreath, Megh. **Ā-baddhāñjali,** mfn. (= *kṛitāñjali*) joining the palms of the hands, Daś.

Ā-badh, f. binding (cf. Inf. *ā-bádhe* = dat.)

Ā-bandha, *as,* m. a tie or bond; the tie of a yoke (that which fastens the axle to the yoke, or the latter to the plough), L.; ornament, decoration, L.; affection, L.

Ā-bandhana, *am,* n. tying or binding on or round, R.

आबन्धुर *ā-bandhura,* mfn. a little deep.

आबयु ābayu, us, m. (only voc. ā́bayo and ābayo) N. of a plant, AV. vi, 16, 1.

आबर्ह ā-barha, &c. See under ā-√bṛih.

आबल्य ābalya, am, n. (fr. a-bala), weakness, KaushUp.

आबाध ā-√bādh, Ā. -bādhate, to oppress, press on, press hard; to molest, check; to pain or torment, TS. &c.; to suspend, annul, BhP.

Ā-bādhá, as, m. pressing towards, RV. viii, 23, 3; molestation, trouble; m. and (ā), f. pain, distress, MBh.; Mn.; Suśr.; Kir. &c.; (ā), f. (in math.) segment of the base of a triangle; (mfn.) distressed, tormented, T.

आबालम् ā-bālam, ind. down to or including children, beginning with infants, Kathās.

Ā-bālyam, ind. id., ib. & R.

आबिल ābila, mfn. (fr. √bil, 'to split,' T.; cf. āvila), turbid, dirty; confounded, embarrassed, L.; (ám), ind. confusedly, ŚBr. **-kanda**, as, m. a species of bulbous plant, L.

आबुत्त ābutta, as, m. (in dram.) a sister's husband (probably a Prākrit word).

आबुध् ā-√budh, P. (Impv. 2. sg. -bódhā) to attend to, mind, RV. vii, 22, 3.

आबुध्य ābudhya, am, n. (fr. a-budha), want of discernment, foolishness, L.

आबृह् ā-√bṛih, P. -bṛihati (cf. ā-vṛih) to tear up or off or away; to pull off, RV. x, 61, 5; TS.; ŚBr. &c.

Ā-barha, ifc. mfn. tearing out; (as), m. tearing out or away; hurting, violating, L.; (am), ind. so as to tear up, Kāṭh.

Ā-barhaṇa, am, n. the act of tearing off or out, L.

Ā-barhita, mfn. torn out, L.

Ābarhin, mfn. fit for tearing out, ib.

Ā́-bṛiḍha, mfn. torn out or away, ŚBr. ii, 1, 2, 16.

आब्दम् ā́bdam, ind. (for ā-abdam), during a year, BhP.

Ābdika, mfn. annual, yearly, Mn.

आब्रह्म ā-brahma, ind. up to or including Brahman, BhP.

Ā-brahma-sabham, ind. to Brahman's court, Ragh. xviii, 27.

आब्रू ā-brū, Ā. -bruvate, to converse with, Hariv.

आभङ्गिन् ā-bhangin, mfn. (√bhañj), a little curved, Kād.

आभज् ā-√bhaj, P. (Impv. 2. sg. ā́-bhaja; pf. ā́-babhāja; aor. Subj. 2. sg. ā́-bhāg; RV. viii, 69, 8), Ā. (Impv. 2. sg. ā́-bhajasva, &c.) to cause to share or partake; to help any one to anything, let any one have anything, RV.; AV.; AitBr.; ŚBr. &c.; to revere, respect, BhP.: Caus. (Impv. 2. sg. -bhājayasva) to cause to partake, Comm. on Bṛ-ĀrUp. i, 3, 18.

Ā́-bhaga, as, m. one who is to be honoured by a share, RV. i, 136, 4, &c.; AV. iv, 23, 3.

Ā-bhajanīya, mfn. id., Sāy. on RV.

आभण्डन ā-bhaṇḍana, am, n. defining, determining, L.

आभयजात्य ābhayajātya, mf(ī)n. descended from Abhaya-jāta, gaṇa gargâdi (Pāṇ. iv, 1, 105).

Ābhayajāta, mf(ī)n. belonging to Ābhayajātya, gaṇa kaṇvâdi (Pāṇ. iv, 2, 111).

आभर ā-bhara, &c. See under ā-√bhṛi.

आभा 1. ā-√bhā, P. -bhāti (Impv. 2. sg. ā́-bhāhi, RV.; pf. -babhau) to shine or blaze towards, RV.; AV.; to irradiate, outshine, illumine, RV.; AV.; TB.; BhP.; to appear, become visible or apparent, BhP.; MBh.; Hariv.; Rājat. &c.; to look like, Kathās.; MBh. &c.

2. **Ā-bhā**, f. splendour, light; a flash; colour, appearance, beauty, MBh.; Mn.; Suśr.; Pañcat. &c.; a reflected image, outline; likeness, resemblance, MBh.; R.; (mfn.) ifc. like, resembling, appearing, R.; Kāvyād.; Śiś. &c. (e.g. hemâbha, shining like gold); [cf. Hib. avibh, 'likeness, similitude;' avibe, 'neatness, elegance;' avibhcal, 'a spark of fire'?]

Ā-bhāta, mfn. shining, blazing; appearing, visible, MBh.; Mn. &c.

Ā-bhāti, is, f. splendour, light; shade, L.

आभाणक ā-bhāṇaka, as, m. (√bhaṇ), a saying, proverb.

आभाष् ā-√bhāsh, Ā. -bhāshate, to address, speak to, MBh.; R. &c.; to talk, converse with, MBh.; Kathās.; Hariv.; to talk, speak; to communicate; to call, shout, MBh.; Ragh.; to name, Suśr.; to promise, Kathās.

Ā-bhāsha, as, m. speech, talking; addressing, R.; a saying, proverb; introduction, preface, L.

Ā-bhāshaṇa, am, n. addressing, speaking to, conversing with, entertainment, Ragh.

Ā-bhāshita, mfn. addressed; spoken, told, Hariv.

1. **Ā-bhāshya**, mfn. to be addressed, worthy of being spoken to or conversed with, MBh.; Ragh.

2. **Ā-bhāshya**, ind. p. having addressed, having spoken to.

आभास् ā-√bhās, Ā. (pf. -babhāse) to appear, look like, MBh.; Ragh. vii, 40, &c.; Kum.; Kathās.: Caus. P. -bhāsayati, to shine upon, illuminate, Nir.; MārkP.; to throw light upon, exhibit the falsity of anything, Comm. on Bādar.

Ā-bhāsa, as, m. splendour, light, R.; Vedāntas. 195; colour, appearance, R.; Suśr.; Bhag.; semblance, phantom; mere appearance, fallacious appearance, Vedāntas.; ŚāṅkhŚr.; reflection; intention, purpose; (in log.) fallacy, semblance of a reason, sophism, an erroneous though plausible argument (regarded by logicians as of various kind); ifc. looking like, having the mere appearance of a thing, Gaut.; Sāh. &c. **-tā**, f. or **-tva**, n. the being a mere appearance, Sāh. &c.

Ā-bhāsana, am, n. illuminating, making apparent or clear.

Ābhāsin, mfn. ifc. shining like, having the appearance of, Hariv.

Ā-bhāsura, mfn. (Pāṇ. iii, 2, 161) shining, bright, L.; (as), m., N. of a class of deities, L.

Ā-bhāsvara, mfn. (Pāṇ. iii, 2, 175) shining, bright, L.; (as), m., N. of a class of deities, sixty-four in number; N. of a particular set of twelve subjects (ātmā jñātā damo dāntaḥ śāntir jñānaṃ śamas tapaḥ । kāmaḥ krodho mado moho dvādaśâbhāsvarā ime ॥ T.)

आभिकामिक ābhikāmika, mfn. (fr. abhi-kāma), wished for, agreeable, MBh.

आभिचरणिक ābhicaraṇika, mf(ī)n. (fr. abhi-caraṇa), maledictory, imprecatory, serving for incantation or cursing or enchantment, KātyŚr.

Ābhicārika, mf(ī)n. id.; (am), n. spell, enchantment, magic.

आभिजन ābhijana, mfn. (fr. abhi-jana), relating to descent or family, Kum.; (am), n. loftiness of birth.

Ābhijātya, am, n. (fr. abhi-jāta), noble birth, nobility, R.; BhP.; learning, scholarship, L.; beauty, T.

आभिजित ābhijita, mfn. born under the constellation Abhi-jit, Pāṇ.; a descendant of Abhi-jit, ib.

Ābhijitya, mfn. a descendant of Abhi-jit, Pāṇ.

आभिद् ā-√bhid, Pass. -bhidyate, to be divided or torn or cleft.

आभिधा ābhidhā, f. (for abhi-dhā, q.v.), word, name, appellation, L.

Ābhidhātaka, am, n. word, name, L.

Ābhidhānika, mfn. (fr. abhi-dhana), belonging to or contained in a dictionary, lexicographical; (as), m. a lexicographer, Comm. on Mn. viii, 275.

Ābhidhānīyaka, am, n. (fr. abhi-dhānīya), the characteristic of a noun, L.

आभिप्रतारिण ābhipratāriṇa, as, m. a descendant of Abhi-pratārin, AitBr.

आभिप्रायिक ābhiprāyika, mfn. (fr. abhi-prāya), voluntary, optional.

आभिप्लविक ābhiplavika, mfn. relating to the religious ceremony called Abhi-plava, ĀśvŚr.; Lāṭy.; (am), n., N. of a Sāman.

आभिमन्यव ābhimanyava, as, m. a descendant of Abhi-manyu, L.

आभिमानिक ābhimānika, mfn. (in Sāṃkhya phil.) belonging to Abhi-māna or self-conceit.

आभिमुख्य ābhimukhya, am, n. (fr. abhi-mukha), direction towards; being in front of or face to face, presence, Pāṇ.; Pañcat.; Sāh.; wish or desire directed towards anything; the state of being about to do anything.

आभियोगिक ābhiyogika, mfn. (fr. abhi-yoga), done with skill or dexterity.

आभिरूपक ābhirūpaka, am, n. (fr. abhi-rupa), suitableness; beauty, gaṇa manojñâdi, Pāṇ. v, 1, 133.

Ābhirūpya, am, n. suitableness, Lāṭy.; beauty, L.

आभिशस्य ābhiśasya, am, n. (fr. abhi-śas), a sin or offence through which one becomes disgraced, Āp.

आभिषेक ābhisheka, mfn. (fr. abhi-sheka), relating to the inauguration of a king; serving for it, VarYogay.

Ābhishecanika, mfn. id., MBh.; R.

आभिहारिक ābhihārika, mfn. (fr. abhi-hāra), to be presented (especially to a king); (am), n. a respectful present or offering.

आभीक ābhīka, am, n. (fr. abhīka, N. of a Ṛishi?), 'composed by Abhīka' [T.], N. of a Sāman, KātyŚr.

आभीक्ष्ण ābhīkshṇa, mfn. (fr. abhīkshṇa), repeated, frequent, L.; (am), n. continued repetition.

Ābhīkshṇya, am, n. continued repetition, L.

आभीर ābhīra, as, m., N. of a people, MBh.; R.; VP.; a cowherd (being of a mixed tribe as the son of a Brāhman and an Ambashṭha woman), Mn. x, 15, &c.; (ī), f. a cowherd's wife or a woman of the Ābhīra tribe, L.; the language of the Ābhīras; (ī), f. and (am), n., N. of a metre; (mfn.) belonging to the Ābhīra people. **-palli** or **-pallī**, f. a station of herdsmen, village inhabited by cowherds only, abode of cowherds &c., L.

Ābhīraka or **ābhīrika**, mf(ī)n. belonging to the Ābhīra people, L.; (as), m. the Ābhīra people.

आभील ā-bhīla, mfn. (√bhī), formidable, fearful, MBh.; suffering pain, L.; (am), n. bodily pain, misfortune, L.; [cf. Hib. abhéil, 'terrible, dreadful.']

आभीशव ābhīśava, am, n. (fr. abhīśu), 'composed by Abhīśu,' N. of a Sāman, KātyŚr. xxv, 14, 15.

Ābhīśavâdya and **ābhīśavôttara**, am, n. id.

आभु ābhú, mfn. empty, void, RV. x, 129, 3 ('pervading, reaching,' Sāy.); VS.; one whose hands are empty, stingy, RV. x, 27, 1; 4.

Ābhūka, mfn. empty, having no contents; powerless.

आभुग्न ā-bhugna, mfn. (√1. bhuj), a little curved or bent, Ragh.

आभुज् ā-√1. bhuj, P. -bhujati, to bend in, bend down, (paryaṅkam ā-bhujya, bending down in the Paryaṅka (q. v.) posture.)

1. **Ā-bhogá**, as, m. winding, curving, curve, crease, MBh.; R. &c.; a serpent, RV. vii, 94, 12; the expanded hood of the Cobra Capella (used by Varuṇa as his umbrella), MBh.; Hcar.; circuit, circumference, environs, extension, fulness, expanse, Śak.; Bhartṛ. &c.; variety, multifariousness, Bhartṛ.; effort, pains, L.; (for 2. ā-bhoga see s. v.)

1. **Ābhogin**, mfn. curved, bent, Hariv.

आभू 1. ā-√bhū, -bhávati (Impf. 2. sg. ā́-bhavas; pf. ā́-babhūva, &c.) to be present or near at hand; to assist; to exist, be, RV.; AV.; VS.; to continue one's existence, MBh.; to originate, be produced, begin to exist, RV.; AV.; ŚBr.

2. **Ā-bhū**, mfn. present, being near at hand, assisting, helping, RV.; approaching, turning one's self towards (as a worshipper towards the deity), RV. i, 51, 9; (ūs), m. a helper, assistant.

Ā-bhūta, mfn. produced, existing.

Ā-bhūti, is, f. reaching, attaining; superhuman power or strength, RV. x, 84, 6; (is), m., N. of a teacher, ŚBr.

आभूतसंप्लवम् ā-bhūta-samplavam, ind. down to the dissolution or destruction of created things or of the universe, VP.

आभूमिपाल ā-bhūmipāla, mfn. up to the king inclusively, Hariv. 2023.

आभूष् 1. *ā-√bhūsh*, P. *-bhū́shati*, to spread over, reach, AV. vii, 11, 1; xviii, 1, 24; to pass one's existence, pass, RV. x, 11, 7; to go by; to act according to (loc.), obey; to cultivate; to honour or serve, RV.

Ā-bhūshéṇya, mfn. to be obeyed or praised or honoured, RV. v, 55, 4.

आभृ *ā-√bhṛi*, P. *-bhárati* (pf. *ā́-jabhāra*, RV.; aor. P. sg. *ā́bhārsham*, RV. &c.) to bring towards or near; to carry or fetch; to effect, produce, RV.; AV.; VS.; ŚBr. &c.; to fill up, fill, attract (one's attention), BhP.

Ā-bhara, *am*, n., N. of several Sāmans.

Ā-bharaṇa, *am*, n. decorating; ornament, decoration (as jewels &c.), Mn.; Śak.; Hit. &c.; N. of several works (especially ifc.)

Ābharád-vasu, mfn. bringing property or goods, RV. v, 79, 3; (*us*), m., N. of a man. (*Ābharad-vasava*, *am*, n. 'composed by Ābharad-vasu,' N. of a Sāman.)

Ābharita, mfn. (fr. *ā-bharaṇa*), ornamented, decorated, Hariv. 855.

Ā-bhṛita, mfn. brought or carried near, procured, produced, caused to exist, BhP. &c.; filled up, full; firmly fixed, BhP. **Ābhṛitâtman**, mfn. one whose soul is filled with, having the attention fixed or fastened on.

आभेरी *ābherī*, f., N. of one of the Rāgiṇīs or modes of music (personified as a female), L.

आभोग 2. *ā-bhoga*, *as*, m. (√2. *bhuj*), enjoyment, satiety, fulness, completion, L.; N. of a work; (mfn.) ifc. enjoying, eating, TĀr.; (for 1. *ā-bhoga* see *ā-√1. bhuj.*)

Ā-bhogáya, mfn. to be enjoyed, RV. i, 110, 2; [(*as*), m. food, nourishment, NBD.]

Ā-bhogi, *is*, f. food, nourishment, RV. i, 113, 5.

2. **Ābhogin**, mfn. enjoying, eating, T.; (for 1. *ābhogin* see *ā-√1. bhuj.*)

Ā-bhojin, mfn. ifc. eating, consuming, L.

आभ्यन्तर *ābhyantara*, mfn. (fr. *abhy-antara*), being inside, interior, inner, MBh.; Suśr.; (*am*), ind. inside. **-prayatna**, m. internal effort (of the mouth in producing articulate utterance), Comm. on Pāṇ. i, 1, 9; Siddh. p. 10.

Ābhyantarika, mfn. = *ābhyantara*.

आभ्यवकाशिक *ābhyavakāśika*, mfn. (fr. *abhy-avakāśa*), living in the open air, Buddh.

आभ्यवहारिक *ābhyavahārika*, mfn. (fr. *abhy-avahāra*), supporting life, belonging to livelihood, T.

आभ्यागारिक *ābhyāgārika*, mfn. (fr. *abhy-āgāra*), belonging to the support of a family, L.

आभ्याशिक *ābhyāśika*, mfn. (fr. *abhy-āśa*), being near to each other, neighbouring, MBh. (less correctly in this sense written *ābhyāsika*).

आभ्यासिक *ābhyāsika*, mfn. (fr. *abhy-āsa*), resulting from practice, practising, repeating, L.

आभ्युदयिक *ābhyudayika*, mfn. (fr. *abhy-udaya*), connected with the beginning or rising of anything, Mn.; relating to or granting prosperity, Mṛicch.; Uttarar. &c.; (*am*), n., N. of a Śrāddha or offering to ancestors on occasions of rejoicing, ĀśvŚr.; Gaut.; Gobh. &c.

आभ्र *ābhra*, mfn. (fr. *abhra*), made or consisting of talc, Naish.

Ābhrya, m. f. a descendant of Abhra [NBD.], belonging to or being in the air [T.], L.

आभ्राज *ābhrāja*, *am*, n., N. of a Sāman.

आभ्रिक *ābhrika*, mfn. (fr. *abhri*), one who digs with a wooden spade or hoe, L.

आम् *ām*, ind. an interjection of assent or recollection, Mṛicch.; Śak.; Vikr. &c.; (a vocative following this particle is anudātta, Pāṇ. viii, 1, 55.)

आम 1. *āmá*, mf(*ā*)n. raw, uncooked (opposed to *pakva*, q. v.), RV.; AV.; Mn.; Yājñ. &c.; N. of the cow (considered as the raw material which produces the prepared milk), RV. iii, 30, 14, &c.; unbaked, unannealed, AV.; MBh.; VarBṛS. &c.; undressed; unripe, immature, Suśr. &c.; undigested, Suśr.; fine, soft, tender (as a skin), BhP. iii, 31, 27; (*as*), m., N. of a son of Kṛishṇa, VP.; of a son of Ghṛita-pṛishṭha, BhP. v, 20, 21; (*as*), m. or (*am*), n. constipation, passing hard and unhealthy excretions, Suśr.; (*am*), n. state or condition of being raw, Suśr.; grain not yet freed from chaff; [cf. Gk. ὠμός; Lat. *amārus*; Hib. *amh*, 'raw, unsodden, crude, unripe;' Old Germ. *ampher*; Mod. Germ. (*Sauer-*) *ampfer*.] **-kumbha**, m. a water-jar of unbaked clay. **-gandhi**, mfn. smelling like raw meat or smelling musty, L. **-gandhika** and **-gandhin**, mfn. id. ib. **-garbha**, m. an embryo, Bhpr. **-jvara**, m. fever produced by indigestion, Śiś. ii, 54. **-tā**, f. rawness; unpreparedness, Suśr. **-pāka**, m. a method of mellowing or ripening a tumour or swelling, Suśr. **-pācin**, mfn. assisting or causing digestion, Bhpr. **-pātrá**, n. an unannealed vessel, AV. viii, 10, 28; ŚBr. **-pesha**, *ās*, m. pl. grains pounded in a raw (i. e. uncooked) condition, MaitrS.; ĀpŚr. **-bhṛishṭa**, mfn. a little broiled, KātyŚr. v, 3, 2. **-pīnasa**, m. running at the nose, defluxion, Suśr. **-māṉsa**, n. raw flesh. *Āma-māṉsâśin*, m. eater of raw flesh, a cannibal. **-rakta**, m. dysentery. **-rasa**, m. imperfect chyme. **-rākshasī**, f. a particular remedy against dysentery. **-vāta**, m. constipation or torpor of the bowels with flatulence and intumescence, Suśr. **-śūla**, n. cholic pains arising from indigestion, Bhpr. **-śrāddha**, n. a particular Śrāddha offering (of raw flesh). **Āmâtisāra**, m. dysentery or diarrhœa produced by vitiated mucus in the abdomen (the excretion being mixed with hard and fetid matter), Suśr. **Āmâtisārin**, mfn. afflicted with the above disease. **Āmā́d**, mfn. eating raw flesh or food, RV. x, 87, 7; AV. xi, 10, 8; VS.; ŚBr. (*Āmā́dya*, n. the state of eating raw flesh.) **Āmânna**, n. undressed rice. **Āmâśraya**, m. the receptacle of the undigested food, the upper part of the belly as far as the navel, stomach, MBh.; Yājñ.; Suśr.

Āmaka, mfn. raw, uncooked, &c., Suśr.

Āmisha. See s. v.

आम 2. *āma*, m. (probably identical with 1. *āma*), sickness, disease, L.

1. **Āmana**, *am*, n. sickness, disease; (for 2. *āmana* see *ā-√man.*)

Āmaya, *as*, m. sickness, disease, ŚBr.; KātyŚr.; Yājñ.; R. &c.; indigestion, L.; (*am*), n. the medicinal plant Costus Speciosus, Bhpr.

Āmayāvín, mfn. sick, diseased, TS.; KātyŚr.; affected with indigestion, dyspeptic, Mn.; Yājñ. **-°vi-tva**, n. indigestion, dyspepsia, Mn.

आमग्न *ā-magna*, mfn. (p. p. of *ā-√majj*) wholly sunk or submerged, Prab.; Kād.

आमञ्जु *ā-mañju*, mfn. charming, pleasant, Uttarar.

आमण्ड *āmaṇḍa*, *as*, m. and *āmaṇḍaka*, *am*, n. the castor-oil plant, Ricinus Communis, L.; (cf. *amaṇḍa* and *maṇḍa*.)

आमथ् *ā-√math* or *ā-√manth*, P. (pf. *-mamantha*) to whirl round or stir with velocity, agitate, shake about, R.

Ā-mathya or **ā-manthya**, ind. p. having shaken, having twirled or whirled, MBh.

आमध्याह्नम् *ā-madhyâhnam*, ind. to midday.

आमन् *ā-√man*, Ā. (Impv. 2. du. *ā́-manyethām*) to long to be at, wish one's self at, RV. iii, 58, 4 & viii, 26, 5.

2. **Ā́-mana**, *am*, n. friendly disposition, inclination, affection, TS. ii, 3, 9, 1 & 2; MaitrS.; (for 1. *āmana* see under 2. *āma*.) **-homa**, m. an offering at which the above two verses of the TS. are spoken, Nyāyam. iv, 4, 6.

Ā́-manas, mfn. friendly disposed, kind, favourable, AV. ii, 36, 6; TS.; MaitrS.

आमनस्य *āmanasya* and *āmānasya*, *am*, n. (fr. *a-manas*), pain, suffering, L.

आमन्त्र् *ā-√mantr*, Ā. *-mantrayate* (pf. *-mantrayām-āsa* &c.) to address, speak to; to summon, TBr.; KātyŚr. &c.; to call, ask, invite, MBh.; BhP.; Uttarar. &c.; to salute, welcome, R.; MBh. &c.; to bid farewell, take leave, MBh.; R.; BhP.; Kum.; Rājat.; Kathās. &c.

Ā-mántraṇa, *am*, n. addressing, speaking to, calling or calling to, ŚBr.; Sāh. &c.; summoning; inviting, invitation, Yājñ.; MBh. &c.; deliberation, interrogation, AV. viii, 10, 7; KātyŚr.; greeting, courtesy, welcome; bidding adieu, taking leave, L.; the vocative case; (*ā*), f. addressing, calling, L.

Ā-mantraṇīya, mfn. to be addressed or asked, to be asked for advice or consulted, AV. viii, 10, 7; ŚBr.

Ā-mantrayitavya, mfn. to be taken leave of, Veṇīs.

Ā-mantrayitṛi, mfn. asking, inviting, calling; (*tā*), m. an inviter, entertainer (especially of Brāhmans), L.

Ā-mantrita, mfn. addressed, spoken to; called, invited, summoned, MBh.; BhP.; asked; one of whom leave is taken, MBh.; Rājat. &c.; (*am*), n. addressing, summoning; the vocative case, L.

1. **Ā-mantrya**, mfn. to be addressed or called to; to be invited; standing in the vocative case (as a word), L.

2. **Ā-mantrya**, ind. having addressed or saluted; having taken leave; bidding farewell.

आमन्थ् *ā-√manth*. See *ā-√math*, col. 2.

आमन्द्र *ā-mandra*, mfn. having a slightly deep tone, making a low muttering sound (as thunder), Megh.; Kathās. &c.

आमरणम् *ā-maraṇam*, ind. till death, Pañcat.

Ā-maraṇânta or **ā-maraṇântika**, mfn. having death as the limit, continuing till death, lasting for life, Hit.; Mn.; MBh.

आमरीतृ *ā-marītṛí*, *tā*, m. (√*mṛi*), one who hurts or destroys, a destroyer, RV. iv, 20, 7.

आमर्द *ā-marda*, &c. See *ā-√mṛid*.

आमर्श *ā-marśa*. See *ā-√mṛiś*.

आमर्ष *āmarsha*, *as*, m. (for *a-marsha*, q. v., T., with reference to Pāṇ. vi, 3, 137), impatience, anger, wrath, L.

Āmarshaṇa, *am*, n. (for *a-m°*, q. v.), id. ib.

आमलक *āmalaka*, *as*, m. and *ī*, f. (gaṇa *gaurâdi*, Pāṇ. iv, 1, 41) Emblic Myrobalan, Emblica Officinalis Gærtn.; (*am*), n. the fruit of the Emblic Myrobalan, MBh.; Suśr.; ChUp. &c.; (*as*), m. another plant, Gendarussa Vulgaris, L.

Āmalakī-pattra, n. Pinus Webbiana. **-phala**, n. the fruit of the Emblic Myrobalan, Kād.

आमह् *ā-√mah*, Ā. (3. sg. *ā́-mahe*, RV. vii, 97, 2 [= *ā-mahate*, *ā-datte*, Sāy.]) to give, grant (?); to take (?).

आमहीया *āmahīyā*, f. (scil. *ṛic*), N. of the verse *ápāma sómam* (RV. viii, 48, 3), KātyŚr. x, 9, 7.

Āmahīyava, *as*, m. (fr. *amahīyu*?), N. of a Ṛishi; (*am*), n., N. of several Sāmans.

आमा *ā-√2. mā*, P. (Pot. *-mimīyāt*, Kāṭh. xix, 13) to bleat at.

आमात्य *āmātya*, *as*, m. (= *amātya*, q. v.), a minister, counsellor, L.

आमावास्य *āmāvāsya*, mfn. (fr. *amā-vāsyā*, gaṇa *saṃdhivelâdi*, Pāṇ. iv, 3, 16), belonging to the new moon or its festival, ŚBr.; AitBr.; born at the time of new moon, Pāṇ. iv, 3, 30; (*am*), n. the new moon oblation. **-vidha**, mfn. belonging to the new moon, occurring at the time of new moon, ŚBr.

आमि *ā-√mi*. See *ā-√mī*.

आमिक्षा *āmikshā*, f. a mixture of boiled and coagulated milk, curd, AV. x, 9, 13; TS.; VS.; ŚBr. &c.

Āmikshavat, mfn. having the above mixture, TBr. i, 6, 2, 5.

Āmikshīya and **āmikshya**, mfn. suitable for the preparation of Āmikshā, L.; Bhaṭṭ.

आमितौजि *āmitâuji*, *is*, m. a descendant of Amitaujas, (gaṇa *bāhv-ādi*, Pāṇ. iv, 1, 96.)

आमित्र *āmitrá*, mf(*ī*)n. (fr. *a-mitra*), caused or produced by an enemy, inimical, odious, RV.; AV.; ŚBr.

Āmitrāyaṇa, *as*, m., **āmitrāyaṇi**, *is*, m. and **āmitri**, *is*, m. a descendant of A-mitra, Pāṇ.

Āmitrīya, mfn. belonging to Āmitri, Pāṇ.

आमिश्र *ā-miśra*, mfn. mixed, mingled, Pat.

-tva, n. mixedness, ib. -bhūta (āmiśrī-), mfn. mixed, mingled; -tva, n. mixedness.

आमिश्ल ā-miśla, mfn. having a tendency to mix; ā́miśla-tama (superl.), mfn. readily mixing, RV. vi, 29, 4.

आमिष āmisha, am, n. (probably connected with 1. āma; fr. √2. mish, 'to wet,' T.), flesh, MBh.; Mn.; Pañcat.; Hit.; Ragh. &c.; food, meat, prey; an object of enjoyment, a pleasing or beautiful object &c., Mn.; Ragh.; Kathās. &c.; coveting, longing for; lust, desire; a gift, boon, fee, L.; (ī), f., N. of a plant, L. -tā, f. and -tva, n. the state of being a prey or preyed upon, Hit. &c.; -priya, mfn. fond of flesh-meat, carnivorous; (as), m. a heron, L. -bhuj, mfn. carnivorous.

Āmishâśin, mfn. carnivorous, eating flesh and fish, Kathās.

Ā́mis, n. raw flesh, meat; a dead body, RV. vi, 46, 14 [āmishi].

आमी ā-√mī, P. -mināti (RV. vi, 30, 2, &c.) to destroy, neutralize, curtail, RV.; to put aside or away, cause to disappear or vanish, displace; to exchange, RV. i, 92, 10, &c.; to put or push out of place, TBr.: Ā. (impf. ā́minanta) to vanish, disappear, RV. i, 79, 2: Intens. (p. -mémyāna) to change, alter, RV. i, 96, 5.

आमीक्षा āmikshā, f. = amikshā, q. v.

आमील् ā-√mīl, Caus. P. -mīlayati, to close the eyes, Kāvyād.; BhP.; Daś.

Ā-mīlana, am, n. the act of closing the eyes, Kād.; Amar.

आमीव् ā-√mīv, P. -mīvati, to press, push, open by pressure, TBr.; ŚBr.

Ā-mīvat-ká, mfn. pushing, pressing, TS. iv, 5, 9, 2.

Ā́-mīvita, mfn. pressed, opened by pressure, TBr.

आमुकुलित ā-mukulita, mfn. (fr. mukalaya, Nom. with ā), a little open (as a blossom), Kād.

आमुख ā-mukha, am, n. commencement, L.; prelude, prologue, Sāh.; (am), ind. to the face.

Ā-mukhī-√kṛi, to make visible. -√bhū, to become visible.

आमुच् ā-√muc, P. -muñcati, to put on (a garment or ornament &c.), Ragh.; Mālav.; Hariv. &c.; to put off (clothes &c.), to undress, R.; to let go; to throw, sling, cast, MBh.; Megh. &c.

Ā-mukta, mfn. put on (as a garment &c.), dressed, accoutred, MBh.; Rājat.; Śiś. &c.; put off, left off, undressed; let go, discharged, cast, shot off; (am), n. armour, L.

Ā-mukti, f. putting on; cloth, armour, L.

Ā-moka, as, m. putting or tying on, T.

Ā-mocana, am, n. putting or tying on, R.; emitting, shedding, &c., L.

आमुप āmupa, as, m. the cane Bambusa Spinosa Hamilt. Roxb., L.

आमुर् ā-múr and ā-múri, m. (√mṛi), destroying, hurting; destroyer, RV.

आमुष् ā-√mush, P. (impf. ā́mushṇāt, RV. x, 67, 6) to draw or pull towards one's self; to take away, RV.

Ā-moshá, as, m. robbing, stealing, ŚBr. xii.

Ā-moshin, mfn. stealing, a thief, Pāṇ.

आमुष्मिक āmushmika, mf(ī)n. (fr. amushmin, loc. of adas), of that state; being there, belonging to the other world, Suśr.; Sāh.; Daś. &c. -tva, n. the state of being there or belonging to the other world, Nyāyam.

Āmushyakulikā, f. (fr. amushya-kula), the being of that family, Pāṇ. vi, 3, 21, Kāś.

Āmushyaputrikā, f. (fr. amushya-putra), the being the son of that one, ib.

Āmushyāyaṇá, mf(ī)n. (gaṇa naḍâdi, Pāṇ. iv, 1, 99), a descendant of such a one, AV.; ŚBr.; Śāṅkh-Gṛ. &c.; (as), m. a son or descendant of an illustrious person, L.

आमूर्तरयस āmūrtarayasa, as, m. a descendant of Amūrta-rayas, MBh.

आमूर्धान्तम् ā-mūrdhântam, ind up to the crown of the head, Kathās.

आमूलम् ā-mūlam, ind. to the root, by the root, entirely, radically, Kathās.; from the beginning.

आमृज् ā-√mṛij, P. -mṛijati, to wipe away or off; to rub, clean, MBh.; Śak.; BhP. &c.: Intens. (p. -mármṛijat, RV. x, 26, 6) to smooth, polish, clean.

Ā-mṛijya, ind. p. having wiped away or off.

1. **Ā-mṛishṭa**, mfn. wiped off, clean; (for 2. ā-mṛishṭa see under ā-√mṛiś.)

आमृण ā-mṛiṇa, mfn. (√mṛiṇ), violating, hurting; enemy; (cf. an-ā°.)

आमृत ā-mṛita, mfn. (√mṛi), killed, struck by death; (cf. an-ā°.)

आमृद् ā-√mṛid, P. -mṛidnāti, to crush by rubbing; to crumple; to mix together, R.; Suśr.

Ā-marda, as, m. crushing, handling roughly, Śak.; MBh.; pressing, squeezing, Kathās.; N. of a town.

Ā-mardaka, as, m., N. of Kālabhairava.

Ā-mardin, mfn. crushing, pressing, handling roughly, R.

आमृश् ā-√mṛiś, P. -mṛiśati, to touch, MBh.; Śiś.; to touch, taste, enjoy (a woman); to consider, reflect upon, MBh.; Śak.; Kum.; (p. -mṛiśat) to rub off, wipe away, remove, Śiś. vi, 3: Pass. -mṛiśyate, to be eaten, Ragh. v, 9 [Mall. bhakshyate]: Caus. -marśayati, to consider, reflect upon.

Ā-marśa, as, m. touching, L.; contact; nearness, similarity, ĀśvŚr. ii, 2, 13, 32.

Ā-marśana, am, n. touching, wiping off, L.

आमृष् ā-√mṛish, Ā. -mṛishyate, to bear patiently, MBh.: Caus. -marshayati, id., MBh.; R. (for āmarsha see s. v.)

आमेखलम् ā-mekhalam, ind. to the edge (of a mountain), Kum. i, 5.

आमेन्य āmenyá, mfn. to be measured from all sides [Sāy.], RV. v, 48, 1.

आमोक्षण ā-mokshaṇa, am, n. fastening or tying on or to, R.

आमोचन ā-mocana. See under ā-√muc.

आमोद ā-móda, mf(ā)n. (√mud), gladdening, cheering up, ŚBr.; KātyŚr.; (as), m. joy, serenity, pleasure, R.; fragrancy, a diffusive perfume; strong smell, smell, Ragh.; Megh.; Śiś.; Kathās. &c.; Asparagus Racemosus, L. -jananī, f. 'causing a strong smell,' betel, ib.

Ā-modana, am, n. rejoicing, delighting, L.

Ā-modita, mfn. perfumed, Ṛitus.; BhP. &c.

Āmodin, mfn. fragrant; ifc. fragrant or perfumed with, e. g. kadambâmodin, perfumed with Kadambas; (ī), m. a perfume for the mouth made up in the form of a camphor pill &c.

आमोष ā-mosha, &c. See under ā-√mush.

आमोहनिका āmohanikā, f. (√muh, Caus.), a particular fragrant odour, Suśr. ii, 163, 14.

आम्ना ā-√mnā, P. -manati, to utter, mention, allege; to cite, quote; to commit to memory, hand down in sacred texts; to celebrate, KātyŚr.; Lāṭy.; BhP.; Mālav.; Kum. &c.

Ā-mnāta, mfn. mentioned, quoted, committed to memory, handed down in sacred texts; taught; celebrated, KātyŚr.; BhP.; Kum. &c.

Ā-mnātavya, mfn. to be mentioned or quoted, APrāt.

Āmnātin, ī, m. (fr. ā-mnāta), one who has mentioned or quoted, Comm. on Pāṇ. ii, 3, 36.

Ā-mnāna, am, n. mention, handing down by sacred texts, KātyŚr.; study of the sacred texts, T.

Ā-mnāya, as, m. sacred tradition, sacred texts handed down by repetition; that which is to be remembered or studied or learnt by heart; a Veda or the Vedas in the aggregate; received doctrine, VPrāt.; Mn.; MBh. &c.; traditional usage, family or national customs; advice, instruction in past and present usage; a Tantra; a family, series of families, L. -rahasya, n., N. of a work. -sārin, mfn. observing the Vedas and traditional customs, pious; containing the essence of the Veda, L.

Āmnāyin, ī, m. an orthodox Vaishṇava, L.

आम्ब āmbá, as, m. a species of grain, TS.; Kāṭh.

आम्बरीषपुत्रक āmbarīshaputraka, mfn. belonging to or inhabited by the Ambarīsha-putras, (gaṇa rājanyâdi, Pāṇ. iv, 2, 53.)

आम्बष्ठ āmbashṭha, as, m. a man belonging to the Ambashṭha people, Pāṇ.

Āmbashṭhya, as, m. a king of the Ambashṭhas, AitBr. viii, 21, 6; (ā), f., Pāṇ. iv, 1, 74.

आम्बिकेय āmbikeya, as, m. (gaṇa śubhrâdi, Pāṇ. iv, 1, 123), a descendant of Ambikā; N. of Dhṛita-rāshṭra, MBh.; of Kārttikeya, L.; of a mountain, VP. ii, 4, 63.

आम्बुद āmbuda, mfn. (fr. ambu-da), coming from a cloud, Naish.

आम्भस āmbhasa, mfn. (fr. ambhas), consisting of water, being watery, fluid, MBh.

Āmbhasika, mfn. living in water, aquatic; (as), m. a fish, Comm. on Pāṇ. iv, 4, 27.

Āmbhi, mfn. a descendant of Ambhas, (gaṇa bāhvâdi, Pāṇ. iv, 1, 96.)

आम्भृणी āmbhṛiṇī, f. daughter of Ambhṛiṇa, N. of Vāc; (see ambhṛiṇa.)

आम्यक्ष् ā-√myaksh, P. (pf. -mimikshús) to be contained or possessed by (loc.), RV. vi, 29, 2 & 3.

आम्र āmra, as, m. the mango tree, Mangifera Indica, MBh.; R.; Śak. &c.; (am), n. the fruit of the mango tree, Suśr.; ŚBr.; &c.; a particular weight. -kūṭa, m., N. of a mountain, Megh. 17. -gandhaka, m., N. of a plant, L. -gandhi-haridrā, f. Curcuma Reclinata, Bhpr. -gupta, m., N. of a man, Pāṇ. (Āmraguptāyani and °gupti, m. a descendant of Āmra-gupta, ib.) -taila, n. mango oil, L. -niśā, f. Curcuma Reclinata, L. -pañcama, m. a particular Rāga (in music). -pāla, m., N. of a king; (ī), f., N. of a woman. -peśī, f. a portion of dried mango fruit, L. -phala-prapānaka, n. a cooling drink made of mangoes, Bhpr. -maya, mfn. made of mangoes (as sauce), L. -vaṇa (Pāṇ. viii, 4, 5), n. a mango forest, R.; Daś. &c. -vāṭa, -vāṭaka, and -vāṭika, m. the hog-plum, Spondias Mangifera, L. **Āmrâvarta**, m. inspissated mango juice, L. **Āmrâsthi**, n. kernel of the mango fruit, Bhpr.

Āmrāta, as, m. the hog-plum, Spondias Mangifera, Suśr.

Āmrātaka, as, m. the hog-plum, Spondias Mangifera, MBh.; R.; Suśr.; inspissated mango juice, L.; N. of a mountain, R.; (ī), f. a kind of climbing plant, L. **Āmrātakêśvara**, n., N. of a Liṅga.

Āmrāvatī, f., N. of a town, R.

Āmriṅ, mfn. containing mango trees, Comm. on Pāṇ.

Āmriman, ā, m. the state of being a mango tree (?), Pāṇ. v, 1, 123, (gaṇa dṛiḍhâdi.)

Āmrya, am, n. id.

आम्रेड् ā-√mreḍ, Caus. P. -mreḍayati, to repeat, MBh.

Ā-mreḍa, as, m. repetition, Bālar.

Ā-mreḍana, am, n. tautology, reiteration of words and sounds, L.

Ā-mreḍita, mfn. reiterated, repeated; (am), n. repetition of a sound or word; (in Gr.) reduplication, reiteration, the second word in a reiteration, Pāṇ.; APrāt. &c.

आम्ल āmla, as, ā, m. f. (fr. amla), the tamarind tree, Tamarindus Indica, L.; (am), n. sourness, acidity, L. -vallī, f. a species of plant, L. -vetasa, m. the plant Rumex Vesicarius (= amla°).

Āmlikā and **āmlīkā**, f. the tamarind tree; sourness in the mouth, acidity of stomach (= amlīkā), L.

आम्लान ā-mlāna, mfn, v.l. for a-mlāna, q. v., Ragh. xvi, 75.

आय āyá, as, m. (fr. ā-√i), arrival, approach, RV. ii, 38, 10; ChUp.; income, revenue; gain, profit, Pāṇ; Mn.; Yājñ.; MBh.; Hit. &c.; the eleventh lunar mansion, VarBṛS.; a die, Jyot.; the number four, ib.; N. of a kind of formulas inserted at particular occasions of a sacrifice, ŚāṅkhŚr. Comm.;

the guard of the women's apartments, L. **—darśin,** mfn. seeing (i. e. having) revenues, Mṛicch. **—dvāra,** n. the place where revenues are collected. **—vyaya** (*am*), n. or (*au*), m. du. receipt and disbursement, income and expenditure. **—sthāna,** n. a place where revenues are collected, Pān.

1. **Āyat,** mfn. (p. pres.) coming near to. **Āyád-vasu,** mfn. one to whom wealth or property comes, AV. xiii, 4, 54.

1. **Ā-yatī,** f. of the p. **—gavam,** ind. at the time when the cows come home, (gaṇa *tishṭhad-gv-ādi,* Pāṇ. ii, 1, 17), Bhaṭṭ. **—samam,** ind. id., ib.

1. **Áyana,** *am,* n. coming, approaching, RV.; AV.; VS.; (for 2. *āyana* see s. v.)

Âyín, mfn. coming or hastening near, TS. ii, 4, 7, 1.

आयःशूलिक *āyaḥśūlika,* mf(ī)n. (fr. *ayaḥ-śūla,* Pāṇ. v, 2, 76), acting violently, using violence, using forcible means (e. g. a beggar holding a lance to your breast in asking for alms), L.

आयःस्थूण *āyaḥsthūṇá, as,* m. (gaṇa *śivâdi,* Pāṇ. iv, 1, 112), a descendant of Ayaḥ-sthūṇa, ŚBr.

आयक *āyaka,* mfn. (fr. √*i*), going (?), Comm. on Pāṇ. vi, 4, 81.

आयज् *ā-√yaj,* P. (*ā-yajati*) and Ā. (*-yajate*) to make oblations or offer (to gods), RV.; AV.; to do homage, honour, RV.; VS.; to receive or procure through offerings, gain, RV.; VS.; ŚBr.

Ā-yají and **ā-yajin** [TBr.], mfn. procuring or bringing near through offerings, RV. i, 28, 7; viii, 23, 17.

Ā́-yajishṭha, mfn. procuring most or best (superlative of the above), RV. ii, 9, 6; x, 2, 1.

Ā́-yajīyas, mfn. procuring more or better, procuring very much or very well (compar. of *ā-yaji*), TBr.

Ā-yajyú, mfn. = *ā-yajin,* RV. ix, 97, 26.

Ā-yāga, *as,* m. a gift given at a sacrifice, R. **—bhūta,** mfn. obtained by sacrifice.

1. **Éshṭa** (*ā + ishṭa*), mfn. obtained by offerings or oblations, VS. v, 7; (for 2. *eshṭa* see under *ésh* = *ā-√2. ish.*)

आयत् 2. *ā-√yat,* P. (2. du. *ā-yatathas*) Ā. (3. pl. *ā-yatante*) to arrive, enter; to adhere, abide; to attain to, RV.; AV.; ŚBr.; to rest on, depend on; to be at the disposition of, MBh.; R.; Mn.; Megh. &c.; to make efforts, R.; BhP.: Caus. *-yātayati,* to cause to arrive at or reach, ŚBr.; AitBr.

Ā-yátana, *am,* n. resting-place, support, seat, place, home, house, abode, TS.; ŚBr.; ChUp.; AitBr.; Mn.; Yājñ.; Kum. &c.; the place of the sacred fire (= *agny-āyatana*), KātyŚr.; ĀśvŚr. & Gṛ.; an altar; a shed for sacrifices; a sanctuary, ChUp.; R.; Mn.; Pañcat. &c.; a plot of ground, the site of a house; a barn, Yājñ. ii, 154; the cause of a disease, Suśr.; (with Buddhists) the five senses and Manas (considered as the inner seats or Āyatanas) and the qualities perceived by the above (the outer Āyatanas). **—tva,** n. the state of being the site of, &c., Vedāntas. &c. **—vat,** mfn. having a seat or home, TS.; (*ān*), m., N. of the fourth foot of Brahman, ChUp. iv, 8, 4.

Ā-yatta, mfn. adhering, resting on, depending on; being at the disposition of, MBh.; Hariv.; R.; Megh.; Kathās. &c.; exerting one's self, making efforts, BhP.; cautious, circumspect, R.; being ready or prepared, R. **—tā,** f. and **-tva,** n. dependence, Sāh. **—mūla,** mfn. having taken root, TāṇḍyaBr. xx, 16, 1.

Ā-yatti, *is,* f. dependence, subjection, subjecting; affection; power, strength; day; boundary, limit; sleeping; length; majesty, dignity; future time; continuance in the right way, steadiness of conduct, L.

आयथातथ्य *āyathātathya, am,* n. (= *a-yāthātathya,* q. v., Pāṇ. vii, 3, 31), the not being as it should be, wrong application, incorrectness, Śiś. ii, 56.

आयथापुर्य *āyathāpurya, am,* n. (= *a-yāthāpurya,* q. v., Pāṇ. vii, 3, 31), the state of being not as formerly.

Āyathāpūrvya, *am,* n. ib., Daś.

आयन 2. *āyana,* mfn. (fr. *ayana*), belonging to the solstice, Comm. on Sūryas.; (for 1. *āyana* see under *āya.*)

आयम् *ā-√yam,* P. *-yacchati* and (Ved.) *-yamati,* to stretch, lengthen out, extend, RV.; AV.; Lāṭy.; Suśr.; MBh. &c.; to stretch (a bow); to put on (an arrow &c.); to draw near, bring hither; to fetch, procure, RV.; to keep, stop, hold in, draw back, restrain, Mn.; Yājñ.; MBh.; BhP. &c.; to produce, Bhaṭṭ.: Ā. *-yacchate* (cf. Pāṇ. i, 3, 28 & 75) to stretch one's self or be stretched or strained; to grow long, L.; to grasp, possess, L.: Caus. *-yāmayati,* to bring near, draw near; to carry, fetch, RV.; to lengthen, extend, Suśr.; to produce or make visible; to show, MBh.

Ā-yata, mfn. stretched, lengthened, put on (as an arrow); stretching, extending, extended, spread over; directed towards, aiming at; extended, long, future, MBh.; R.; Suśr.; Ragh.; Śiś.; Kirāt. &c.; (*as*), m. an oblong figure (in geometry); (*ā*), f. a particular interval (in music); (*am*) and (*ayā*), ind. without delay, on the spot, quickly, ŚBr. **—catur-asra,** mfn. oblong, ĀśvGṛ. &c.; (*as*), m. an oblong. **—cchadā,** f. 'having long leaves,' the plantain tree, Musa Paradisiaca Lin., L. **—dīrgha-caturasra,** m. = *-caturasra.* **—stū,** m. a panegyrist, Kāty. on Pāṇ. iv, 2, 178. **Āyatâksha,** mf(ī)n. having longish eyes, Bhartṛ. &c. **Āyatâpâṅga,** mf(ī)n. having long-cornered eyes. **Āyatâyati,** f. long continuance, remote futurity, Śiś. **Āyatârdha,** m. (in geom.) half an oblong. **Āyatêkshaṇa,** mfn. long-eyed, having long or large eyes.

Ā-yati, *is,* f. stretching, extending, RV. i, 139, 9; extension, length, Kād.; following or future time; the future, 'the long run,' MBh.; R.; Mn.; Pañcat. &c.; posterity, lineage; descendant, son, Daś.; expectation, hope, Kathās.; Kād.; majesty, dignity, L.; restraint of mind, L.; N. of a daughter of Meru, VP. **—kshama,** mfn. fit or useful for future time, Mn. **—mat,** mfn. long, extended; stately, dignified, L.; self-restrained, L.

2. **Ā-yatī,** f., v. l. for *āyati;* (for 1. see col. 1.)

Ā-yantṛí, *tā,* m. restrainer, ruler (?); one who approaches [Sāy.], RV. viii, 32, 14.

Ā-yamana, *am,* n. stretching (a bow), ChUp.

1. **Ā-yamya,** mfn. to be stretched; to be restrained.

2. **Ā-yamya,** ind. p. having stretched or restrained, MBh. &c.

Ā-yāma, *as,* m. stretching, extending, RPrāt.; Suśr. &c.; restraining, restrained, stopping, Mn.; MBh.; Bhag. &c.; expansion, length (either in space or time), breadth (in mensuration), Suśr.; ĀśvGṛ.; R.; Megh. &c. **—vat,** mfn. extended, long.

Ā-yāmita, mfn. lengthened out, extended; made visible, shown, MBh.

Āyāmin, mfn. long in space or time, Kād.; ifc. restraining, stopping, VP.; Yājñ. &c.

आयल्लक *āyallaka, am,* n. (etym. doubtful), impatience; longing for; missing, regretting, L.

आयव *āyava, am,* n. (fr. *āyu*), N. of a Sāman.

आयवन् *ā́yavan, ā,* m. the dark half of the month, MaitrS.; (cf. *ayava.*)

आयवन *ā-yávana.* See under *ā-√2. yu.*

आयवस् *āyavas,* n. = *ā́yavan* above.

आयवस *āyavasa, as,* m., N. of a king [Sāy.], RV. i, 122, 15.

आयस् *ā-√yas,* P. *-yasyati,* to work hard, exert one's self, weary one's self, MBh.; R.; BhP.; Hariv. &c.; to become exhausted, Hariv.; R. &c.: Caus. P. *-yāsayati,* to weary, worry; to give pain, torment, Suśr.; MBh.; Kathās. &c.: Pass. of Caus. *-yāsyate,* to pine away; to consume by grief, R. &c.

Ā-yasta, mfn. exerted, managed or effected with difficulty; labouring, toiling, making effort or exertion, MBh.; R.; Hariv. &c.; pained, distressed; wearied, vexed, angry, ib.; sharpened, whetted; thrown, cast, L.

Ā-yāsa, *as,* m. effort, exertion (of bodily or mental power), trouble, labour, MBh.; R.; Suśr.; Śak.; Kathās. &c.; fatigue, weariness, MBh.; R.; Daś.

Ā-yāsaka, mfn. causing effort, causing fatigue or weariness, Bhartṛ.

Āyāsin, mfn. making exertion, active, laborious; exhausted by labour, wearied.

आयस *āyasá,* mf(ī)n. (fr. *ayas*), of iron, made of iron or metal, metallic, RV.; ŚBr.; KātyŚr.; MBh.; Yājñ. &c.; iron-coloured, MBh. v, 1709; armed with an iron weapon, L.; (*ī*), f. armour for the body, a breastplate, coat of mail, L.; (*am*), n. iron; anything made of iron, Ragh.; Kum. &c.; a wind-instrument, KātyŚr. xxi, 3, 7. **—maya,** mfn. made of iron, Kād.

Āyasīya, mfn. (fr. *ayas*), belonging to or made of iron, (gaṇa *kṛiśâśvâdi,* Pāṇ. iv, 2, 80.)

आयस्कार *āyaskāra, as,* m. the upper part of the thigh of an elephant; (see also *ayas-kāra.*)

Āyaskāri, *is,* m. a descendant of Ayas-kāra, L.

आया *ā-√yā,* P. *-yāti,* to come near or towards; to arrive, approach, RV.; AV.; ŚBr.; MBh.; Kathās. &c.; to reach, attain, enter, BhP. &c.; to get or fall into any state or condition; to be reduced to, become anything (with the acc. of an abstr. noun), Hariv.; MBh.; R.; BhP.; Ragh. &c.

Ā-yāta, mfn. come, arrived, attained, MBh.; Śak.; Kathās. &c.; (*am*), n. abundance, superabundance, Kirāt.

Ā-yāti, *is,* f. coming near, arrival; (*is*), m., N. of a son of Nahusha, MBh.; Hariv.; VP.

Ā-yā́na, *am,* n. coming, arrival, RV. viii, 22, 18; MBh. &c.; the natural temperament or disposition, L.; (cf. *ayāna.*)

Ā-yāpana, *am,* n. causing to come near, inviting; fetching.

आयाच् *ā-√yāc,* P. (p. *-yācat*) Ā. (p. *-yācamāna*) to supplicate, implore, R.

Ā-yācita, mfn. urgently requested or desired; (*am*), n. prayer, R.

आयु 1. *ā-√2. yu,* Ā. (*ā́-yuvate,* RV. ix, 77, 2; pf. *-yuyuvé,* RV. i, 138, 1; p. *-yuvámāna,* RV. i, 582, and *-yuvāna,* ŚBr. ix, 4, 1, 8) to draw or pull towards one's self; to seize, take possession of, RV.; TBr.; ŚBr.; to procure, provide, produce, TS.; to stir up, agitate, mingle, MānŚr. & Gṛ.: Intens. (p. *-yóyuvāna,* RV. iv, 1, 11) to meddle with.

Ā-yávana, *am,* n. a spoon (or similar instrument) for stirring, AV. ix, 6, 17, &c.

Ā-yuta, mfn. melted, mixed, mingled; ifc. combined with, MBh.; R.; BhP.; (*ā́-yutam*), n. half-melted butter, MaitrS.; AitBr.

आयु 2. *āyú,* mfn. (fr. √*i,* Uṇ. i, 2), living, movable, RV.; VS.; (*us*), m. a living being, man; living beings collectively, mankind, RV.; son, descendant, offspring; family, lineage, RV.; a divine personification presiding over life, RV. x, 17, 4; N. of fire (as the son of Purūravas and Urvaśī), VS.; MBh.; Hariv.; (cf. *ā́yus*); N. of a man persecuted by Indra, RV.; N. of several other men, MBh.; Hariv. &c.; N. of a king of frogs, MBh.; (*u*), n. [and (*us*), m., L.] life, duration of life, RV. iii, 3, 7; ix, 100, 1. **—kṛit,** mfn. making or giving long life, ĀpŚr. **—patnī,** f. ruling over mankind, TāṇḍyaBr. i, 5, 17. **—shák,** ind. (fr. √*sac*), with the co-operation of men, RV. ix, 25, 5; 63, 22.

Āyuḥ- (in comp. for *āyus* below). **—pati,** mf(*inī*)n. presiding over longevity, ĀpŚr.; (cf. *āyushpati.*) **—śesha,** m. remainder of life, Hit.; (mfn.) having still a short space of life left, not yet about to die; *-tā,* f. the state of being not yet about to die, Pañcat. **—shṭoma,** m. a ceremony performed to obtain longevity and forming—together with the Go and Jyotis—part of the Abhi-plava ceremony (cf. *ā́yus*), TS.; ŚBr.; AitBr.; KātyŚr. &c.

Āyur- (in comp. for *āyus* below). **—jñāna,** n., N. of a work. **—dád** or **-dā́** or **-dā́van,** mfn. giving life, giving longevity, AV.; VS.; TS. &c. **—dāya,** m. predicting the length of a man's life from the aspect of the stars. **—dravya,** n. a medicament, L. **—mahôdadhi,** m., N. of a work. **—yúdh,** mfn. struggling for one's life, VS. xvi, 60. **—yoga,** m. a conjunction of planets enabling an astrologer to predict the course of a man's life. **—veda,** m. the science of health or medicine (it is classed among sacred sciences, and considered as a supplement of the Atharva-veda; it contains eight departments: 1. Śalya or (removal of) any substance which has entered the body (as extraction of darts, of splinters, &c.); 2. Śālākya or cure of diseases of the eye or ear &c. by Śalākās or sharp instruments; 3. Kāya-cikitsā or cure of diseases affecting the whole body; 4. Bhūta-vidyā or treatment of mental diseases supposed to be produced by demoniacal influence; 5. Kaumārabhṛitya or treatment of children; 6. Agada-tantra or doctrine of antidotes; 7. Rasāyana-tantra or doctrine of elixirs; 8. Vājikaraṇa-tantra or doctrine of aphrodisiacs, Suśr.; MBh.; Hariv. &c.); *-dṛiś*, m. a physician; *-maya*, mfn. acquainted with medical sciences, R.; *-rasāyana*, n., *-sarvasva*, n., *-saukhya*, n., N. of works. **–vedika**, m. acquainted or familiar with medical science, a physician, L. **–vedin**, m. id. **–hṛit**, mfn. taking away health, obnoxious to health.

Āyush- (in comp. for *āyus* below). **–kara**, mfn. causing or creating long life, Kād. **–kāma**, mfn. wishing for long life or health, ŚBr.; KātyŚr.; Āp. &c. **–kāraṇa**, n. cause of longevity, Sāh. **–kṛit**, mfn. producing or creating long life, AV. **–°ṭoma**, m. for *āyuḥ-shṭoma*, q. v., a particular ceremony. **–tva**(?) **ti**, mf(*tnī*)n. ruling over long life, AV. **–pā**, mfn. preserving life, VS.; TS. **–pratāraṇa**, mfn. prolonging life, AV. iv, 10, 4. **–mat** (*āyush-*), mfn. possessed of vital power, healthy, long-lived; alive, living, AV.; VS.; MBh.; R.; Śak. &c.; lasting, AV. vi, 98, 2; old, aged, ĀśvGṛ.; (*ān*), m. 'life-possessing,' often applied as a kind of honorific title (especially to royal personages and Buddhist monks); the third of the twenty-seven Yogas or divisions of the ecliptic; the Yoga star in the third lunar mansion; N. of a son of Uttānapāda; of Saṃhrāda, VP.; *-purushaka*, mfn. giving long life to men, Pat.

Āyusha, *am*, n. ifc. = *āyus*, duration of life, ŚBr.; Pañcat. &c.

Āyushaya, Nom. to wish long life to any one, L.

Āyushka, *am*, n. the being fond of or depending on life, Jain.

Āyushyà, mfn. giving long life, vital, preservative of life, for the sake of life, relating or belonging to it, ŚBr.; Mn.; MBh.; R.; (*àm*), n. vital power, abundance of life, longevity, AV.; VS.; ŚBr.; Mn.; Pañcat. &c.; a medicament, L.; 'vivifying,' N. of a ceremony performed after a child's birth, PārGṛ. **–vat**, mfn. long-lived, BhP. **–homa**, m., N. of a kind of oblation, MānGṛ.

Ā́yus, n. life, vital power, vigour, health, duration of life, long life, RV.; AV.; TS.; ŚBr.; Mn.; MBh.; Pañcat. &c.; active power, efficacy, RV.; VS.; the totality of living beings [food, Sāy.], RV. ii, 38, 5 & vii, 90, 6; N. of a particular ceremony (= *āyuḥ-shṭoma*, q. v.); N. of a Sāman; of the eighth lunar mansion; food, L.; (*us*), m. the son of Purūravas and Urvaśī (cf. *āyu*), MBh.; Vikr.; VP.; [cf. Dor. αἰές; perhaps also αἰών.] **–tejas**, m., N. of a Buddha.

आयुज् 1. *ā-√yuj*, P. (1. sg. *ā-yunajmi*, RV. iii, 50, 2) Ā. (pf. 3. pl. *-yuyujré*, RV. v, 58, 7) to yoke or join to, RV.; to join, fasten, Śak.; to accommodate with; to appoint, BhP.: Caus. *-yojayati*, to join together; to form, constitute, BhP.; Kum.

Ā-yukta, mfn. joined with, united, applied to; appointed, charged with, L.; burdened with, slightly joined, L.; (*as*), m. a minister, an agent or deputy.

Āyuktaka, *as*, m. an official.

Āyuktin, mfn. a fit official, L.

2. **Ā-yúj**, mfn. uniting, joining, AV. xi, 8, 25.

Ā-yoga, *as*, m. a yoke or team of draft animals, ŚāṅkhŚr.; Kāṭh.; appointment, action, the performance of an action, L.; ornament, decoration, R.; Hariv.; swarm, R. v, 17, 5; presenting or offering flowers, perfumes &c., L.; a shore or bank; a quay to which boats are attached, L.

Ā-yojana, *am*, n. junction, combination; collecting; bringing or carrying near, fetching, L.; N. of particular Mantras, Kauś.

Ā-yojita, mfn. collected together, brought into connexion, Kum.

आयुध् *ā-√yudh*, P. *-yudhyati* (fut. *-yotsyati*, MBh. iii, 15645) to war against, attack, oppose: Caus. *-yodhayati*, id., MBh.; Uttarar. &c.

Ā-yudha, *am*, n. a weapon, RV.; AV.; VS.; R.; Mn.; MBh.; Ragh. &c.; implement, AV. x, 10, 18; AitBr.; Kauś.; gold used for ornaments, L.; (*āni*), n. pl. water, L. **–jīvin**, mfn. living by one's weapons; (*ī*), m. a warrior, Pāṇ. iv, 3, 81. **–dharmiṇī**, f. the plant Sesbania Ægyptiaca (commonly called Jayantī), L. **–pāla**, m. the governor of an arsenal, Hariv. **–bhṛit**, mfn. bearing arms; (*t*), m. a warrior, VarBṛS. **–śālā**, f. an armoury, arsenal, Kād. **–sahāya**, mfn. armed, Veṇīs. **–sâhvaya**, m., N. of a plant, Suśr. ii, 104, 10. **Āyudhâgāra**, n. an armoury, arsenal, Mn.; MBh.; Veṇīs.; *-nara*, m. governor of an arsenal, Hariv. *Āyudhâgārika*, m. governor of an arsenal, Hariv.

Āyudhika, mfn. relating to arms; living by one's weapons; (*as*), m. a warrior, soldier, Pāṇ. iv, 4, 14; MBh.

Āyudhin, m. bearing weapons; (*ī*), m. a warrior, VS. xvi, 36; Kauś.; R.

Āyudhīya, mfn. relating to or living by arms; (*as*), m. a warrior, soldier, Pāṇ. iv, 4, 14; Mn.; Comm. on Yājñ.

Ā-yodhana, *am*, n. war, battle, MBh.; Ragh.; battle-field, MBh.; R.; killing, slaughter, L.

Ā-yodhita, mfn. attacked, MBh.

आयुप् *ā-√yup*, Caus. P. (1. pl. *ā́-yopayāmasi*, RV. x, 134, 7) to blot out, disturb; to sin against.

आयुस् *āyus*. See col. 1.

आये *āye* = *aye*, q. v., L.

आयोग *ā-yoga*. See under 1. *ā-√yuj*.

आयोगव *āyogava*, m. (= *ayogava*, q. v.), a man of mixed tribe (sprung from a Śūdra man and Vaiśya woman; his business is carpentry &c.), ŚBr.; KātyŚr.; Mn.; Yājñ.; (*ī*), f. a woman of this tribe.

आयोजनम् *ā-yojanam*, ind. at the distance of a Yojana, MBh.

आयोद *āyoda*, *as*, m., N. of a Ṛishi, MBh.

आयोध्यक *āyodhyaka*, mfn. belonging to or native of Ayodhyā, VarBṛS.

Āyodhyika, mfn. id., Uttarar. 1, 14.

आर् 1. *ār*, cl. iv, P. *āryanti*, to praise, RV. viii, 16, 6 & x, 48, 3 (perhaps connected with √*ṛi*).

Ārita, mfn. praised, RV. i, 101, 4, &c.

आर् 2. *ār* (*ā-√ṛi*), P. (Subj. 2. sg. *-ṛiṇós*, RV. i, 30, 14 & 15; *ā́-ṛiṇvati*, RV. i, 144, 5; but also Impv. 2. pl. *-iyarta*, RV. viii, 7, 13; aor. *āratām*, &c.) Ā. (3. sg. *ā́-ṛiṇve*, RV. v, 74, 5) to insert, place in, RV.; to excite; to bring near, fetch, RV.; to come; to reach, obtain, fall into (misfortune), RV.; ŚBr.; AitBr. &c.; to inflict, AitBr.: Caus. *ārpayati*, to cause to partake of, ŚBr. iv, 5, 7, 7; to fix, settle, annex; to inflict, injure.

Ārakāt, ind. (with abl.) far from, ŚBr.

Ārā́t and **Āré**. See s. vv.

Ārta, mfn. (optionally also written *ārtta*, whence erroneously derived fr. √*ṛit* or even regarded as irreg. formation fr. √*ard*; see also Weber in ŚBr. p. 339, l. 20 ff.) fallen into (misfortune), struck by calamity, afflicted, pained, disturbed; injured; oppressed, suffering, sick, unhappy, ŚBr.; TS.; Mn.; R.; Śak.; Ragh. &c. **–gala**, m. the plant Barleria Cæruli, Suśr. **–tara**, mfn. extremely pained, disturbed, confounded, R. ii, 77, 19, &c. **–tā**, f. state of affliction, pain, R. ii, 59, 17. **–nāda**, m. and **-svara**, m. a cry of pain, Śak. **–bandhu**, m. friend of the distressed.

1. **Ārti**, *is*, f. painful occurrence, pain, injury, mischief; sickness, AV.; VS.; KātyŚr.; R.; Megh. &c.; (for 2. *ārti* see s. v.) **–mat**, mfn. having or suffering pain, Suśr.; (*ān*), m. a Mantra or spell (against snakes), MBh. i, 21, 88. **–han** or **-hara**, mfn. destroying pain. **Ārty-apaharaṇa**, n. the relieving of distress or pain &c.

Ārpayitṛi, *tā*, m. one who inflicts, injures, ŚBr.

Ārpita, mfn. fastened to, annexed; dependent on, RV.; AV.

आर 1. *āra*, *am*, n. brass, BhP. x, 41, 20; iron, L.; a sting, Comm. on TS.; an angle; a corner; (*as*), m. cavity, Sūryas.; N. of a tree, L.; N. of a lake, KaushUp.; the planet Mars, Ἄρης; the planet Saturn, L.; (*ā*), f. a shoemaker's awl or knife; a bore; a probe, RV.; Suśr. &c.; an aquatic bird. **–kūṭa**, m. n. a kind of brass. **Ārâgra**, n. the point of an awl, ŚvetUp.; the iron thong at the end (of a whip); the edge of a semicircular arrow-head, L.; (mfn.) sharpened, sharp at the top and broad at the bottom like an awl, TS. **Ārā-mukha**, *am*, n. an arrow-head shaped like an awl. **Ārâvalī**, f. 'row of awl-shaped hills,' N. of a chain of mountains (commonly called Aravalli, running for 300 miles in a north-easterly direction through Rājputāna &c., the highest point being Mount Abu 5650 feet high).

आर 2. *āra*, n., v. l. for *ara*, q. v., a spoke, MBh. i, 1498 (ed. Bomb. i, 33, 4 reads *ara*).

आरक्त *ā-rakta*, mfn. reddish, Suśr.; Vikr.; (*am*), n. red sandal-wood, L. **–pushpī**, f., N. of a plant, L.

Ārakti-√bhū, to become or get reddish.

आरक्ष् *ā-√raksh*, P. *-rakshati*, to watch over, defend; to protect from, RV. vii, 50, 1.

Ā-raksha, mfn. preserved, defended, proper or worthy to be defended, L.; (*as*), m. protection, guard, preservation, Mn.; R. &c.; the junction of the frontal sinuses of an elephant, L.; the part of the forehead below this junction, Śiś. v, 5; (*ā*), f. protection, guard.

Ā-rakshaka or **Ā-rakshika**, mfn. who or what guards or protects; (*as*), m. a watchman, patrol; a village or police magistrate, Pañcat.; Daś. &c.

Ā-rakshita, mfn. guarded, protected, MBh.; R.

Ā-rakshin, mfn. guarding, watching, MBh.

Ā-rakshya, mfn. to be preserved or guarded, R.

आरग्वध *ārag-vadha*, *as*, m. the tree Cathartocarpus (Cassia) Fistula, Bhpr.; Suśr.; (*am*), n. its fruit, Suśr.

आरङ्गर *āraṅgará*, *as*, m. (√*rañj*? [Gmn.]), a bee, RV. x, 106, 10.

आरच् *ā-√rac*, Caus. to arrange.

Ā-racayya, ind. p. having prepared or composed; having furnished or provided, Pañcat.

Ā-racita, mfn. arranged, prepared; put on, Daś.

आरट् *ā-√raṭ*, P. (p. *-raṭat*) to shriek, screech, Kathās.; Bhaṭṭ.

Āraṭa, mf(*ī*[gaṇa *gaurâdi*, Pāṇ. iv, 1, 41])n. crying, making a noise; (*as*), m. a mime, T.(?)

Ā-raṭi, *is*, f.(?) noise, roaring (in *muktâraṭi*, 'having uttered a roaring'), Kathās. 52, 123.

Ā-raṭita, *am*, n. a cry, noise, Daś.

आरट्ट *āraṭṭa*, *ās*, m. pl., N. of a people and country in Pañca-nada or the Pañjāb, MBh.; (*as*), m. the ancestor of this people, ib. **–ja**, mfn. born in this country, MBh.; R.

Āraṭṭaka, mfn. belonging to or coming from the country or people of Āraṭṭa.

आरडव *āraḍava*, mfn. belonging to or made of Araḍu tree, Comm. on Pāṇ. iv, 2, 71.

आरण *āraṇa*, *am*, n. (probably connected with *araṇa*) depth, abyss, precipice, RV. i, 112, 6 & viii, 70, 8. **–ja**, m. pl., N. of a class of deities (Jain.)

आरणि *āraṇi*, *is*, m. an eddy, L.

आरणेय *āraṇeya*, mfn. (fr. *araṇi*, q. v.), made of or relating to the Araṇis or two pieces of wood by the attrition of which sacred fire is kindled; (*as*), m., N. of Śuka (as born from Araṇī), MBh.; (*am*), n. a box for Araṇis, MBh. **–parvan**, n., N. of the last section (Adhyāyas 311–314) of the third book of the Mahā-bhārata.

आरण्य *āraṇyá*, mf(*ā*)n. (fr. *araṇya*), being in or relating to a forest, forest-born, wild, RV.; AV.; KātyŚr.; MBh. &c.; (*as*), m. a wild animal, ChUp. **–kāṇḍa**, n., N. of the third book of the Rāmāyaṇa. **–kukkuṭa**, m. a wild cock, Bhpr. **–gāna**, n. one of the four Gānas or hymn-books of the Sāma-veda. **–parvan**, n. the first section (Adhyāyas 1–10) of the third book of the Mahābhārata (= *araṇya°*). **–paśu**, m. a wild or forest animal (as a buffalo, monkey &c.), Mn. &c. **–mudga**, f. a kind of bean, Phaseolus Trilobus Ait., L. **–rāśi**, m. (in the Zodiac) the sign Leo; Aries and Taurus; the former half of Capricorn, L. **Āraṇyôpala**, m. dry cow-dung, Bhpr.

Āraṇyaka, mfn. forest, wild, forest-born, produced in a forest, relating to a forest or a forest animal, (the *āraṇyakam parva* of the Mahā-bhārata is either the whole third book or only the first section of it); (*as*), m. a forester, an inhabitant of the woods, MBh.; Ragh. &c.; (*am*), n., N. of a class of religious and philosophical writings closely connected with the Brāhmaṇas and called Āraṇyakas because either composed in forests or studied there, (the Upanishads are considered to be attached to them.) **–kāṇḍa**, n. N. of the third book of the Rāmāyaṇa and of the fourteenth book of the Śatapatha-brāhmaṇa. **-gāna**, n. = *āraṇya-gāna*, q. v.

आरत *ā-rata*, &c. See *ā-√ram*.

आरड्ड *āraḍḍha as*, m., N. of a man, (gaṇa *tikâdi*, Pāṇ. iv, 1, 154.)

Āraḍḍhāyani, *is*, m. a descendant of the above.

आरद्वत् *āradvat, ān*, m., N. of a king, VP.

आरनाल *āranāla, am*, n. sour gruel made from the fermentation of boiled rice, Suśr.

Āranālaka, *am*, n. id., L.

आरप् *ā-√rap*, P. (p. *-rápat*) to whisper towards, VS. xx, 2.

आरभ् *ā-√rabh*, P. (only pf. 1. pl. *-rara-bhmá*, RV. viii, 45, 20) Ā. *-rabhate* (pf. *-rebhe*, &c.; Inf. *-rábham* and *-rábhe*, RV.) to lay or take hold of, keep fast, cling to, RV.; AV.; ŚBr. &c.; to gain a footing; to enter, reach, attain, RV.; to undertake, commence, begin, TBr.; ŚBr.; MBh.; Ragh.; Kathās. &c.; to make, produce; to form, compose, BhP. &c.: Intens. (pf. *ā-rárabhe*) to cling to, RV. i, 168, 3.

Ā-rabdha, mfn. begun, commenced, undertaken, AitBr.; MBh.; R.; BhP.; Kathās. &c.; one who has begun or commenced, beginning, commencing, R.; BhP.; (*as*), m., N. of a king.

Ā-rabdhavya, mfn. to be begun or undertaken, MBh.

Ā-rabdhi, *is*, f. beginning, commencement, Rājat.

Ā-rabhaṭa, *as*, m. an enterprising man, courageous man, L.; (*ī*), f. boldness, confidence, heroism, Rājat.; (in dram.) the representation of supernatural and horrible events on the stage.

Ā-rabhamāṇa, mfn. beginning, commencing resolutely (with a determination to finish).

1. **Ā-rabhya**, mfn. ifc. = *ā-rabdhavya*, q. v.

2. **Ā-rabhya**, ind. p. having begun; beginning with.

Ā-rabhyamāṇa, mfn. being commenced.

Ā-rambhá, *as*, m. undertaking, beginning, Mn.; Pañcat.; Megh. &c.; a thing begun; beginning, origin, commencement, ŚBr.; KātyŚr.; Megh. &c.; (in dram.) the commencement of the action which awakens an interest in the progress of the principal plot, Sāh. 324 & 325; haste, speed; effort, exertion; pride; killing, slaughter (erroneous for *ālambha*, see Zachariæ, Beiträge, p. 20, l. 9), L. **-tā**, f. the condition of beginning or commencing, Kathās. **-ruci**, mfn. enjoying new undertakings; enterprising; *-tā*, f. spirit of enterprise, Mn. xii, 32. **-siddhi**, f., N. of a work.

Ā-rambhaka, mfn. causing to begin or commence; ifc. commencing, beginning, BhP. &c

Ā-rámbhaṇa, *am*, n. the act of taking hold of, seizing, using; the place of seizing, a handle, ChUp.; AitBr.; KātyŚr.; beginning, undertaking, commencement. **-vat**, mfn. seizable, ŚBr. iv, 6, 1, 2.

Ā-rambhaṇīya, mfn. to be undertaken; that with which one must begin, forming the commencement, AitBr.; ŚBr.; ĀśvGṛ.

Ā-rambhita, mfn. begun, undertaken.

Ārambhin, mfn. enterprising, one who makes many new projects, Yājñ.

Ā-ripsu, mfn. (fr. Desid.), intending to undertake, Nyāyam.

आरम् *ā-√ram*, P. *-ramati* (Pāṇ. i, 3, 83), to pause, stop; to leave off, AitBr.; ĀśvŚr.; Mn.; MBh.; Kathās. &c.; to delight in; to enjoy one's self, take pleasure, Mn.; Daś.; Kathās. &c.

Ā-rata, mfn. ceased, quiet, gentle; (*am*), n. a kind of coitus, Mall. on Kirāt. v, 23.

Ā-rati, *is*, f. stopping, ceasing, L.

Ā-rámaṇa, *am*, n. pleasure, delight, enjoyment, TS.; ŚBr.; sexual pleasure, Gaut. xxiv, 4; cessation, pause; resting-place, L.

Ā-rāmá, *as*, m. delight, pleasure, ŚBr.; TUp.; Bhag.; Bhartṛ.; place of pleasure, a garden, grove, Mn.; Yājñ.; MBh.; R.; Mṛcch.; Kathās. &c.; N. of a particular Daṇḍaka metre; [cf. ἠρέμα and ἔρημος.] **-śītalā**, f., N. of a plant with fragrant leaves, L.

Ārāmika, *as*, m. a gardener, Rājat.

आरम्बण *ā-rambaṇa* (for *ā-lambana*), *am*, n. ifc. support, ChUp.

आरव *ā-rava*. See 1. *ā-√1. ru*.

आरस् *ā-√1. ras*, P. *-rasati*, to roar towards, shout to, Nalod.

Ā-rasa, *as*, m. a scream, shout, Mālav.

Ā-rasita, *am*, n. roaring, screaming, Hariv.

आरस्य *ārasya, am*, n. (fr. *a-rasa*, Pāṇ. v, 1, 121), insipidity; want of flavour or spirit.

आरा *ārā, ārā-mukha*, &c. See 2. *āra*.

आराग *ā-rāga, as*, m. (v.l. for *ā-roga*, q.v.), Comm. on VP. vi, 3.

आराज्ञी *ā-rājñī*, f. (fr. *rājan* with 3. *ā*), N. of a region, (gaṇa *dhūmâdi*, Pāṇ. iv, 2, 127.)

Ārājñaka, mfn. belonging to the above region, ib.

आराड *ārāḍa, as*, m., N. of a teacher of Śākya-muni, Lalit.

आराढि *ārāḍhi* or *ārāḷhi, is*, m. a patronymic of a teacher named Saujāta, AitBr. vii, 22, 1.

आरात् *ārāt*, ind. (abl. of an ideal base *āra* fr. *ā-√ṛi*; cf. *āré*) from a distant place; distant; to a distant place; far from (with abl.), RV.; AV.; Āp.; MBh.; Kathās.; near, Gaut.; Ragh.; directly, immediately, Prab.; Kathās.; Śak. 131·a; (*t*), m., N. of a village, L.

Ārātīya, mfn. remote; near, proximate, L.

Ārātka, mfn. belonging to the village Ārāt, L.

Ārā́t-tāt, ind. from a distant place, RV.

आराति *ā́rāti, is*, m. enemy (=*arāti*, q.v.), MaitrS.

आरात्रिक *ā-rātrika, am*, n. the light (or the vessel containing it) which is waved at night before an idol; N. of this ceremony.

Ārātri-vivāsam, ind. 'till night's departure,' till daybreak, L.

आराध् *ā-√rādh*, Caus. P. *-rādhayati*, to conciliate, propitiate; to strive to obtain the favour of or gain a boon from; to solicit; to honour, worship; to deserve, merit, MBh.; R.; Megh.; Śak.; Kathās. &c.: Pass. *-rādhyate*, to be effected or accomplished, Daś.

Ā-rādha, *as*, m. gratification, paying homage.

Ā-rādhaka, mfn. worshipping, a worshipper, L.

Ā-rādhana, mfn. propitiating, rendering favourable to one's self, Kum.; Kathās.; (*am*), n. gratifying, propitiation, homage, worship, adoration, MBh.; R.; Kathās.; Kum. &c.; effecting, accomplishment, Śak.; acquirement, attainment, L.; cooking, L.; (*ā*), f. worship, adoration, propitiation of the deities, L. **-prakāra**, m., N. of a work.

Ā-rādhanīya, mfn. to be worshipped or adored; to be propitiated or conciliated, Ragh.; Kād.

Ā-rādhaya, mfn. propitiating, doing homage, (gaṇa *brāhmaṇâdi*, Pāṇ. v, 1, 124.)

Ā-rādhayitṛi, mfn. one who propitiates or conciliates, doing homage, Śak. 125, 6.

Ā-rādhayishṇu, mfn. wishing or endeavouring to conciliate, propitiatory, R.

Ā-rādhayya, *am*, n. the act of conciliating or propitiating, Pāṇ. v, 1, 124.

Ā-rādhita, mfn. propitiated, pleased, solicited for a boon; worshipped, honoured, revered; accomplished, effected.

Ā-rādhya, mfn. to be made favourable; to be worshipped, Kathās.; Bhartṛ.; Pañcat.; to be accomplished, Sāh.; Kpr.

Ā-rādhyamāna, mfn. being worshipped, receiving worship; being in course of fulfilment, being accomplished.

Ā-rirādhayishu, mfn. endeavouring to gain one's favour, desirous of worshipping, MBh.

आराल *ārāla*, mfn. (gaṇa *tārakâdi*, Pāṇ. v, 2, 36), a little curved or crooked, T. (?)

Ārālita, mfn. (ib.) id., T.

आरालिक *ārālika, as*, m. (fr. *arāla*, 'crooked, deceitful,' T.), a cook, MBh. xv, 19.

आराव *ā-rāva*. See 1. *ā-√1. ru*.

आरावली *ārāvalī*. See 2. *āra*.

आरिच् *ā-√ric*, P. (Subj. 3. sg. *ā́-riṇak*, RV. ii, 19, 5; pf. *ā́-rireca*, AV. xviii, 3, 41) to give or make over to.

Ā-reka, *as*, m. emptying; doubt, L.

Ā-recita, mfn. emptied; contracted, mixed. **-bhrū**, mfn. having contracted eye-brows, Kum.; Daś.

Ā-recin, mfn. emptying.

आरित्रिक *āritrika*, mf(*ā* and *ī*)n. (fr. *aritra*, gaṇa *kāśy-ādi*, Pāṇ. iv, 2, 116), belonging to or being on an oar.

आरिंदमिक *āriṃdamika*, mf(*ā* and *ī*)n. (fr. *ariṃ-dama*, gaṇa *kāśy-ādi*, Pāṇ. iv, 2, 116), belonging to or being on Ariṃ-dama.

आरिफ् *ā-√riph*, P. (p. *-rephat*) to snore, ŚāṅkhBr. xvii, 19.

आरिश् *ā-√riś*, Ā. (1. pl. *-riśāmahe*) to eat up (grass as a cow in grazing), RV. i, 187, 8 & x, 169, 1; (cf. *ā-liś*.)

आरिष् *ā-√rish*, Caus. (aor. Subj. 2. sg. *ā́-rīrishas*) to hurt, destroy, RV. i, 104, 6.

आरिह् *ā-√rih*, P. *-réḍhi*, to lick up, RV. x, 162, 4; (cf. *ā-lih*.)

Ā-réhaṇa, *am*, n. licking, kissing, AV. vi, 9, 3.

आरी *ā-√rī*, P. (*ā́-riṇanti*, RV. ix, 71, 6) to pour, let drop: Ā. *ā́-rīyate*, to trickle or flow upon; to flow over, RV.

आरु 1. *ā-√1. ru*, P. *-rauti* or *-ravīti* (Impv. *ā́-ruva*, RV. i, 10, 4) to shout or cry towards; to cry out, VarBṛS.; R.; Bhaṭṭ.; to praise, L.: Intens. *-roravīti*, to roar towards or against, RV.

Ā-rava, *as*, m. (Pāṇ. iii, 3, 50) cry, crying, howling; crash, sound, R. &c.; noise; thundering, Śiś. vi, 38; Kathās.; (*ās*), m. pl., N. of a people, VarBṛS. **-ḍiṇḍima**, *as*, m. a kind of drum, Gīt. xi, 7.

Ā-rāva, *as*, m. (Pāṇ. iii, 3, 50) cry, crying out, howling; crash, sound; humming (as bees &c.), N.; MBh.; Hit. &c.

Ā-rāvin, mfn. ifc. tinkling or sounding with, Mālav.; (*ī*), m., N. of a son of Jaya-sena, VP.

Ā-ruta, *am*, n. cry, crying, R.

आरु 2. *āru, us*, m. a hog; a crab; the tree Lagerstrœmia Regina, L.; (*us*), f. a pitcher, L.

आरुक *āruka*, mfn. hurting, injuring, TĀr. i, 5, 2; (*am*), n. the fruit of a medicinal plant growing on the Himālaya mountains, L.

आरुच् *ā-√ruc*, Ā. (Subj. 3. pl. *ā́-rucayanta*, RV. iii, 6, 7) to shine near or towards.

Ā-roká, *as*, m. shining through; small points of light (appearing through the threads of worn cloth &c.), RV.; ŚBr.; an interstice (as between the teeth &c.), MantraBr.

Ā-rocana, mfn. shining, bright, Nir.

आरुज् 1. *ā-√ruj*, P. *-rujati* (Inf. *-rúje*, RV. iv, 31, 2) to break up, loosen; to pull down, tear out; to shatter, demolish, RV.; AV.; MBh.; R. &c.

2. **Ā-ruj**, mfn. ifc. breaking, destroying.

Ā-rujá, mfn. breaking, destroying, RV. viii, 45, 13; (*as*), m., N. of a Rākshasa attendant on Rāvaṇa, MBh.

Ā-rujatnú, mfn. breaking, RV. i, 6, 5.

Ā-roga, *as*, m. one of the seven suns at the end of a period of the world, TĀr.; AitĀr.; (cf. *ā-rāga*.)

आरुण *āruṇa*, mf(*ī*)n. coming from or belonging to Aruṇa; (*ī*), f. a reddish mare [Sāy.], RV. i, 64, 7. **-ketuka**, mfn. belonging to the Aruṇāḥ Ketavaḥ (see under *aruṇa*), TĀr. **-parājin**, *ī*, m., N. of an ancient Kalpa work on the ritual of the Brāhmaṇas.

Āruṇaka, mfn. belonging to the country Aruṇa, (gaṇa *dhūmâdi*, Pāṇ. iv, 2, 127.)

Āruṇi, *is*, m. (fr. *aruṇa*), N. of Uddālaka (a renowned Brāhmaṇa teacher, son of Aruṇa Aupaveśi and father of Śveta-ketu), ŚBr.; AitBr.; MBh.; N. of Auddālaki (= Śveta-ketu), KaṭhUp.; N. of Suparṇeya, a son of Prajāpati, TĀr.; of Vainateya, MBh.; of Taṭāyu, Bālar. **-hotṛi**, mfn. having Āruṇi as Hotṛi priest, TāṇḍyaBr. xxiii, 1, 5.

Āruṇin, *inas*, m. pl., N. of a school derived from Vaiśampāyana Āruṇi, L.

Āruṇīya, mfn. belonging to Āruṇi.

Āruṇeyá, mfn. id.; (*as*), m., N. of Śvetaketu as Āruṇi's son, ŚBr. **-pada**, n., N. of an Āraṇyaka.

Āruṇya, *am*, n. redness, Comm. on Nyāyam.

Āruṇyaka, mfn. belonging to the Aruṇas.

आरुध् *ā-√2. rudh*, P. *-ruṇaddhi* and Ā. (Impv. 3. sg. *ā́-runddhām*, AV. iii, 20, 10; pf. *ā́-rurudhre*, AV. iv, 31, 3) to shut up, lock in, BhP.; to blockade, besiege, Hariv.; to keep off, ward off, RV.; AV.; ŚBr.: Caus. *-rodhayati*, to obstruct, impede, MBh.; R.; Hariv.

Ā-rodha, *as*, m. siege, Hit.

Ā-ródhana, *am*, n. innermost part, secret place [Sāy.]; (fr. √1. *rudh* = √*ruh*), mounting, ascent [Pischel and NBD.], RV.

आरुपित *ārupita*, mfn. = *ā-ropita* [Sāy.?], RV. iv, 5, 7.

आरुष् *ā-√rush*, Caus. to make furious.

Ā-roshita, mfn. made furious, Hariv.

आरुषी *ārúshī*, f. (fr. √*rush*?), hitting, killing [Sāy.], RV. x, 155, 2; N. of a daughter of Manu and mother of Aurva, MBh.

आरुषीय *ārushīya*, mfn. (fr. *arus*), belonging to a wound, (gaṇa *kṛiśāśvâdi*, Pāṇ. iv, 2, 80.)

Ārushkara, *am*, n. the fruit of the Semecarpus Anacardium, Suśr.; (cf. *arush°*.)

आरुह् 1. *ā-√ruh*, P. *-rohati* (aor. *-rukshat* and Ved. *-ruhat* [Pāṇ. iii, 1, 59]; Inf. *-rúham*, RV. x, 44, 6), Ā. (2. sg. *ā́-rohase*, RV. i, 51, 12) to ascend, mount, bestride, rise up, RV.; AV.; ŚBr.; MBh.; R.; Hariv.; Śak.; Kathās. &c.; to arise, come off, result, Kathās.; Kum. &c.; to venture upon, undertake; to attain, gain, RV.; MBh.; Kathās.; Ragh. &c.: Caus. *-rohayati* & *-ropayati*, to cause to mount or ascend; to raise, RV.; KātyŚr.; R.; BhP.; Pañcat. &c.; to string (a bow), MBh.; Hariv.; Kum.; Śak. &c.; to cause to grow; to plant, Kathās. &c.; to place, deposit, fasten, MBh.; R.; BhP.; Yājñ.; to produce, cause, effect, Kathās.; Prab.; MārkP.; to attribute, BhP.; Vedāntas.; Sāh. &c.: Desid. P. *-rurukshati*, to wish to ascend or mount, RV.; BhP.; MBh.

Ā-rurukshu, mfn. desirous to rise or ascend or advance, MBh.; Ragh.; Bhag.; Kād.

2. **Ā-rúh**, mfn. ifc. ascending, RV. i, 124, 7; (*k*), f. excrescence, shoot (of a plant), AV. xiii, 1, 9.

Ā-ruha, ifc. mfn. leaping up, mounting, ascending.

Ā-ruhya, ind. p. having mounted or ascended.

Ā-rūḍha, mfn. mounted, ascended, bestridden (as a horse &c.), MBh.; Hariv.; BhP.; risen; raised up, elevated on high, VarBṛS.; Pañcat.; Hit.; Kathās. &c.; undertaken; reached, brought to (often used in compounds, e. g. *indriyârūḍha*, brought under the cognizance of the senses, perceived), BhP.; having reached or attained, come into (a state), BhP.; Prab.; Sak.; Kathās. &c.; (*am*), n. the mounting, arising. **-vat**, mfn. mounting, rising, N. of a Sāman.

Ā-rūḍhi, *is*, f. ascent, mounting, Śak.

Ā-roḍhavya, mfn. to be ascended or mounted, MBh.; Kathās.; Pañcat.

Ā-roḍhṛi, *ḍhā*, m. one who ascends or rises, Yājñ.

Ā-ropa, *as*, m. imposing (as a burden), burdening with, charging with; placing in or on; assigning or attributing to; superimposition, Vedānt.; Sāh. &c.

Ā-ropaka, mfn. ifc. planting, Mn.; fixing; causing to ascend, L.

Ā-ropaṇa, *am*, n. causing to mount or ascend, Kathās.; raising up, elevating, Kathās.; the act of placing or fixing in or on, R.; Ragh.; Kum.; the stringing of a bow, R.; assigning, attribution, imposition, substitution, Sāh.; planting, L.; trusting, delivering, L.

Ā-ropaṇīya, mfn. to be made to ascend; to be raised or placed, Kathās.; to be planted, L.; to be strung, Pras.; to be inserted or supplied, Comm. on TPrāt. xiv, 9.

Ā-ropita, mfn. raised, elevated, Kum.; fixed, placed, Kād.; made; charged with; strung (as a bow); deposited, intrusted; interposed, supplied; accidental, adventitious, L.

1. **Ā-ropya**, mfn. to be placed or fixed in or on; to be planted, VarBṛS.; to be strung (as a bow), Hariv.; to be attributed, interposed, supplied, Sarvad.

2. **Ā-ropya**, ind. p. having made to ascend or mount &c.

Ā-ropyamāṇa, mfn. being strung (MBh. i, 7032 in the sense of trying to string [Comm.]; perhaps straining at or making great exertions with?).

Ā-roha, *as*, m. one who mounts or ascends, a rider (on a horse &c.), one who is seated in a carriage, R.; ascent, rising, creeping up, mounting, Śak.; Kathās.; R.; haughtiness, pride, Kathās.; elevation, elevated place, altitude, R.; a heap, mountain, R.; increase, Sāh.; a woman's waist, the swell of the body, R.; BrahmaP.; Śiś.; length, L.; a particular measure, L.; descending (= *ava-roha*?), L.

Ā-rohaka, mfn. ascending, rising; raising up; (*as*), m. a rider, Pañcat.; a tree, L.

Ā-róhaṇa, mf(*ī*)n. arising, ascending, MārkP.; (*am*), n. the act of rising, ascending, ŚBr.; KātyŚr.; Śak.; MBh. &c.; a carriage, ŚBr.; KātyŚr.; an elevated stage for dancing, MBh.; a ladder, staircase, L.; the rising or growing of new shoots, growing (of plants), L.; a particular measure, L. **-vāhá**, mfn. drawing a carriage, TS.

Ārohaṇika, mfn. relating to ascent or mounting, MBh.

Ārohaṇīya, mfn. (gaṇa *anupravacanâdi*, Pāṇ. v, 1, 111) helping to ascend or mount.

Ārohin, mfn. ascending, mounting; one who mounts, rides, Pañcat.; VarBṛ.; leading to, helping to attain, Pañcat.

आरु *ārú*, mfn. (√*ṛi* [Uṇ. i, 87]), tawny; (*ūs*), m. tawny (the colour), L.

आरे *āré*, ind. (loc.; see *ārā́t*) far, far from, outside, without, RV.; AV.; near, L. **-agha**, mfn. having evil far removed, RV. vi, 1, 12; 56, 6. **-avadya**, mfn. one from whom blame or insult is far removed, RV. x, 99, 5. **-śatru**, mfn. one whose enemies are driven far away, AV. vii, 8.

आरेहण *ā-rehaṇa*. See *ā-√rih*.

आरोक *ā-roka*. See *ā-√ruc*.

आरोग *ā-roga*. See *ā-√ruj*.

आरोग्य *ārogya*, *am*, n. (fr. *a-roga*), freedom from disease, health, MBh.; R.; Suśr.; Mn.; Gaut.; Āp.; a particular ceremony; (*ā*), f., N. of Dākshāyaṇī; (mfn.) healthy; giving health, L. **-cintā-maṇi**, m., N. of a work. **-tā**, f. health, R. **-pañcaka**, n. a remedy against fever, Bhpr. **-pratipad-vrata**, n. a ceremony for gaining health. **-mālā**, f., N. of a work. **-vat**, mfn. healthy, L. **-vrata**, n. an observance for procuring health. **-śālā**, f. a hospital, L. **Ārogyâmbu**, n. healthful water, Bhpr.

Ārogyaya, Nom. to wish health.

आरोचक *ā-rocaka*. See *ā-√ruc*.

आरोध *ā-rodha*, &c. See *ā-√2. rudh*.

आरोप *ā-ropa*, *ā-roha*, &c. See *ā-√ruh*.

आर्क *ārka*, mfn. (fr. *arka*), belonging or relating to the sun, BhP.; coming from the plant Calotropis Gigantea, VarBṛS.

Ārkalūsha, *as*, m. (fr. *arkalūsha*, gaṇa *vidâdi*, Pāṇ. iv, 1, 104), a descendant of Arkalūsha.

Ārkalūshāyaṇa, *as*, m. (gaṇa *haritâdi*, Pāṇ. iv, 1, 100) a descendant of Ārkalūsha.

Ārkalūshāyaṇi, m. f. (gaṇa *karṇâdi*, Pāṇ. iv, 2, 80) a descendant of Ārkalūsha.

Ārkāyaṇa, mfn. (fr. *arka*, gaṇa *aśvâdi*, Pāṇ. iv, 1, 110) and **ārkāyaṇi**, mfn. (gaṇa *karṇâdi*, Pāṇ. iv, 2, 80) coming from or relating to Arka or the sun; (*as*), m. a ceremony, MBh.

Ārki, *is*, m. a son or descendant of Arka or the sun; N. of the planet Saturn, VarBṛS.; of Yama, T.; of a Manu, T.; of Sugrīva, T.; of Karṇa, T.

आर्कम् *ā́rkam* (for *ā-arkam*), ind. as far as the sun, even to the sun inclusively, BhP. x, 14, 40.

आर्क्ष *ārkshá*, mf(*ī*)n. (fr. *ṛiksha*), stellar, belonging to or regulated by the stars or constellations; (*ás*), m. a son or descendant of Ṛiksha, RV. viii, 68, 16; MBh. **-varsha**, m. a stellar year or revolution of a constellation, L.

Ārkshya, *as*, m. and **ārkshyāyaṇī**, f. (fr. *ṛiksha*, gaṇa *gargâdi*, Pāṇ. iv, 1, 105), a descendant of Ṛiksha.

आर्क्षोद *ārkshoda*, mfn. (fr. *ṛikshoda*), coming from or inhabiting the mountain Ṛikshoda, L.

आर्गयन *ārgayana* (fr. *ṛigayana*, Pāṇ. iv, 3, 73) or *ārgayaṇa* (gaṇa *girinady-ādi*, Kāty. on Pāṇ. viii, 4, 10) contained in or explanatory of the book Ṛigayana, T.

आर्गल *ārgala*, *as*, m. and *ī*, f. a bolt or bar (= *argala*, q. v.), L.

आर्ग्वध *ārgvadha* = *āragvadha*, q. v.

आर्ग्वैदिक *ārgvaidika*, mfn. belonging to the Ṛig-veda, Comm. on KātyŚr. v, 1, 5, &c.

आर्घा *ārghā*, f. a sort of yellow bee, L.

Ārghya, mfn. relating to or coming from the above bee, Suśr.; (*am*), n. its honey, L.

आर्च 1. *ārca*, mfn. (fr. *arcā*, Pāṇ. v, 2, 101) = *arcāvat* (q. v.), worshipping, doing homage.

आर्च 2. *ārca*, mf(*ī*)n. (fr. *ṛic*), relating to the Ṛic or Ṛig-veda.

Ārcāyana, *as*, m. (fr. *ṛic*, gaṇa *naḍâdi*, Pāṇ. iv, 1, 99), a descendant of Ṛic; (mfn.) belonging to the Ṛig-veda [T.]

Ārcika, mfn. relating to the Ṛig-veda or connected with a Ṛic-verse; (*am*), n., N. of the Sāma-veda.

आर्चत्क *ārcatká*, *as*, m. (fr. *ṛicatka*, Sāy.), N. of Śara, RV. i, 116, 22.

आर्चाभिन् *ārcābhin*, *inas*, m. pl., N. of a school founded by Ṛicābha (a pupil of Vaiśampāyana), (gaṇa *kārtakaujapâdi*, Pāṇ. vi, 2, 37), Nir. &c.

आर्चीकपर्वत *ārcīka-parvata*, *as*, m., N. of a mountain, MBh.

आर्छ् *ārch* (*ā-√ṛich*), P. *ārcchati*, to fall into (calamity or mischief), AV. ii, 12, 5; ŚBr. i; AitBr.; to obtain, partake of, ŚBr.; MBh.

आर्जव *ārjava*, mfn. (fr. *ṛiju*, gaṇa *pṛithv-ādi*, Pāṇ. v, 1, 122), straight; honest, sincere, Kathās.; (*as*), m., N. of a teacher, VP.; (*am*), n. straightness, straight direction, Sāh.; rectitude, propriety of act or observance; honesty, frankness, sincerity, ChUp.; Āp.; Gaut.; MBh.; R.; Mn. &c.

Ārjavaka, mfn. straight, direct; (*as*), m., N. of the ninth Sarga or creation, MBh. xii, 11566.

Ārjavin, mfn. having or showing honest behaviour, MBh.

आर्जीक *ārjīká*, mfn. (fr. *ṛijīka* [Sāy.], q. v.), belonging to the country Ṛijīka; (*as*), m. a particular Soma vessel [NBD.], RV.

Ārjīkíya, *as*, m., N. of a country [Sāy.]; a Soma vessel [NBD.], RV. viii, 64, 11; (*ā*), f., N. of a river, RV. x, 75, 5.

आर्जुन *ārjuna*, *as*, m., N. of Indra (= *arjuna*, q. v.), Kāṭh. 34, 3.

Ārjunāyana, *as*, m. (gaṇa *aśvâdi*, Pāṇ. iv, 1, 110) a descendant of Arjuna; (*ās*), m. pl., N. of a people, VarBṛS.

Ārjunāyanaka, mfn. (gaṇa *rājanyâdi*, Pāṇ. iv, 2, 53) inhabited by the Arjunāyanas.

Ārjuni, *is*, m. (fr. *arjuna*, gaṇa *bāhv-ādi*, Pāṇ. iv, 1, 96), a descendant of Arjuna, MBh.

Ārjuneyá, *as*, m. (fr. *ārjuni*), N. of Kutsa, RV

आर्ञ्ज् *ārñj* (*ā-√ṛiñj*), Ā. (only irr. aor. 1. sg. *ā́-ṛiñjase*, RV. v, 13, 6 & x, 76, 1) to strive after, endeavour to obtain, wish to possess.

आर्त *ārta*, &c. See 2. *ār* (*ā-√ṛi*).

आर्तना *ārtanā*, f. [connected with *ārta*, Sāy.] a destructive battle, or *ā́rtana*, mfn. [connected with *ārā́t* and *āré*, BRD.] uncultivated, waste, desert, RV. i, 127, 6.

आर्तपर्ण *ārtaparṇa*, *as*, m. the son of Ṛitaparṇa, N. of Sudāsa, Hariv.

आर्तभाग *ārtubhāga*, *as*, m. and *ī*, f. (fr. *ṛitabhāga*, gaṇa *vidâdi*, Pāṇ. iv, 1, 104), a descendant of Ṛitabhāga, ŚBr. **-°ī-putra**, m., N. of a teacher, ŚBr. xiv.

आर्तव *ārtavá*, mf(*ī*)n. (fr. *ṛitu*), belonging or conforming to the seasons or periods of time, seasonable, R.; Kum.; Ragh.; Vikr. &c.; menstrual, relating to or produced by this discharge, Suśr.; (*as*), m. a section of the year, a combination of several seasons, AV.; TS.; VS. &c.; (*ī*), f. a mare, L.; (*am*), n. the menstrual discharge, ŚBr.; Suśr.; Mn.; the ten days after the menstrual discharge fit for generation, Mn.; Suśr.; fluid discharged by the female of an animal at the time of rut, Suśr.; a flower, L.

Ārtveyī, f. a woman during her courses, L.

आर्तुपर्णि ārtuparṇi (fr. ṛitu-parṇa), v. l. for ārtaparṇa, q. v.

आर्त्नी ártnī, f. the end of a bow, the place where the string or sinew is fastened (κορώνη), RV.; VS.; ŚBr.

आर्त्विजीन ārtvijīna, mfn. (fr. ṛitv-ij, Pāṇ. v, 1, 71), fit for the office of a priest, ŚBr.

Ā́rtvijya, am, n. the office or business of a Ṛitv-ij or sacrificing priest, his rank or order, RV.; AV.; ChUp.; ŚBr. &c.

आर्त्व्य ārtvyá, as, m., N. of the Asura Dvimūrdhan, AV. viii, 10, 22.

आर्थ ā́rtha, mf(ī)n. (fr. artha), relating to a thing or object; material, significant (opposed to śābda, q. v.), Sāh.; resulting from or based on the possession of a thing, Pat. **-tva**, n. significance.

Ārthapatya, am, n. (fr. artha-pati), power or possession of a thing.

Ārthika, mfn. (Pāṇ. iv, 4, 40) significant; wise; rich; substantial, real, pertaining to the true substance of a thing; derivable from the sense of a word, being contained implicitly (not said explicitly), Nyāyam.

आर्द ārda, mf(ī [gaṇa gaurâdi, Pāṇ. iv, 1, 41])n. (√ṛid), pressing hard, tormenting exceedingly, T.

आर्द्र ārdrá, mf(ā)n. (√ard, Uṇ. ii, 18) wet, moist, damp, RV.; TS.; ŚBr.; MBh.; Mn.; Suśr.; Megh. &c.; fresh, not dry, succulent, green (as a plant), living, AV.; ŚBr.; R.; Suśr.; MBh. &c.; fresh, new, Kathās.; soft, tender, full of feeling, warm; loose, flaccid, Kathās.; Megh.; Pañcat. &c.; (as), m., N. of a grandson of Pṛithu, Hariv.; VP.; (ā), f. the fourth or sixth Nakshatra or lunar mansion, AV.; MBh.; VarBṛS.; (am), n. fresh ginger, Vishṇus.; dampness, moisture, Hariv. **-kāshṭha**, am, n. green wood, timber not dry. **-ja**, n. dry ginger, L. **-tā**, f. or **-tva**, n. wetness, moisture; freshness, greenness; softness, tenderness. **-dānu**, mfn. granting or having moisture, AV.; VS.; Kāṭh. **-nayana**, mfn. moist-eyed, weeping, suffused with tears. **-paṭī**, f. a kind of magic ceremony (performed to destroy an enemy), L. **-pattraka**, m. bamboo, L. **-pada**, mf(ī)n. moist-footed, L. **-pavi**, mfn. having moist or dripping fellies (as a carriage), AV. xvi, 3, 4. **-pavitra**, mfn. having a wet strainer (said of the Soma), AV. ix, 6, 27. **-bhāva**, m. wetness, dampness, Kum.; tenderness of heart, Ragh. ii, 11; Kathās. **-mañjarī**, f. a cluster of fresh blossoms, Comm. on Gobh. **-māshā**, f. a leguminous shrub, Glycine Debilis, L. **-mūla**, mf(ā)n. having damp roots, ŚBr. i, 3, 3, 4. **-vastra-tā**, f. the state of having or standing in wet clothes, Gaut. xix, 15. **-śāka**, n. fresh ginger, L. **-hasta**, mf(ā)n. moist-handed, AV. xii, 3, 13. **Ārdrā-lubdhaka**, m. the dragon's tail or descending node, L. **Ārdrâidhâgni**, m. a fire maintained by wet wood, ŚBr. xiv, 5, 4, 10.

Ārdraka, mf(ikā)n. wet, moist, Bhpr.; VarBṛS.; born under the constellation Ārdrā, Pāṇ. iv, 3, 28; (as), m., N. of a king, VP.; (am), n. [and ikā, f., L.] ginger in its undried state, Suśr.

Ārdraya, Nom. P. ārdrayati, to make wet, moisten, Bhartṛ.; to soften, move, Kād.; Bālar.

Ārdrī-√kṛi, to make wet, moisten; to refresh, Kād.; to soften, move, Kād.

Ārdrya, am, n. wetness, dampness, GopBr. i, 1, 1.

आर्ध् ārdh (ā-√ṛidh), P. (Pot. 2. sg. ā́-ṛidhyās, RV. iii, 50, 1) to satisfy, fulfil (a wish): Desid. (p. ī́rtsamāna, AV. vi, 118, 2) to wish to obtain or to collect.

Āraddha, am, n. abundance, Bālar. v, 40.

Ārdhuka, mfn. conducive to success, useful, beneficial, ŚāṅkhBr.; Kāṭh.

आर्ध ārdha-, in comp. optionally for ardha- (q. v.), Pāṇ. vii, 3, 26. **-kaṅsika**, mfn. measuring half a kaṅsa, Comm. on Pāṇ. **-kauḍavika**, mfn. measuring half a kuḍava, ib. **-krośika**, mfn. measuring half a krośa, ib. **-drauṇika**, mfn. measuring or bought with half a droṇa, ib. **-prasthika**, mfn. weighing half a prastha, ib.

Ārdhadhātuka, mf(ā)n. (fr. ardha-dhātu), 'applicable to the shorter form of the verbal base,' a technical N. given to the terminations of the pf. and bened. and to any Pratyaya (q. v.) except the personal terminations of the conjugational tenses in P. & Ā., and except the Pratyayas which have the Anubandha ś, Pāṇ. iii, 4, 114–117; ii, 4, 36, &c.

Ārdhadhātukīya, mfn. belonging or relating to an Ārdhadhātuka, Pat.

Ārdhanārīśvara, am, n. (fr. ardha-nārîśvara, q. v.), the story of the lord (Śiva) in his form as half female (and half male), Bālar.

Ārdhamāsika, mfn. (fr. ardha-māsa), lasting &c. for half a month, Pat.; observing or practising (continence &c.) for a fortnight.

Ārdharātrika, mfn. (fr. ardha-rātra), happening at midnight, midnight, Sūryas.; (ās), m. pl., N. of an astronomical school who reckoned the beginning of the motions of the planets from midnight.

Ārdhika, mfn. sharing half, an equal partner; relating to half; (as), m. one who ploughs the ground for half the crop (cf. ardha-sīrin), Mn.

आर्पयितृ ārpayitṛi. See 2. ār (ā-√ṛi).

आर्बुदि ārbudi, is, m. (fr. arbuda), N. of a Vedic Ṛishi.

आर्भव ārbhava, mf(ī)n. (fr. ṛibhu), belonging or sacred to the Ṛibhus, ŚBr.; KātyŚr.; AitBr.; Lāṭy.; (as), m., N. of a Vedic Ṛishi.

आर्य ā́rya, as, m. (fr. aryá, √ṛi), a respectable or honourable or faithful man, an inhabitant of Āryāvarta; one who is faithful to the religion of his country; N. of the race which immigrated from Central Asia into Āryāvarta (opposed to an-ārya, dasyu, dāsa); in later times N. of the first three castes (opposed to śūdra), RV.; AV.; VS.; MBh.; Yājñ.; Pañcat. &c.; a man highly esteemed, a respectable, honourable man, Pañcat.; Śak. &c.; a master, an owner, L.; a friend, L.; a Vaiśya, L.; Buddha; (with Buddhists [Pāli ayyo or ariyo]) a man who has thought on the four chief truths of Buddhism (see next col.) and lives accordingly, a Buddhist priest; a son of Manu Sāvarṇa, Hariv.; (mf(ā and ā́rī)n.) Āryan, favourable to the Āryan people, RV. &c.; behaving like an Āryan, worthy of one, honourable, respectable, noble, R.; Mn.; Śak. &c.; of a good family; excellent; wise; suitable; (ā), f. a name of Pārvatī, Hariv.; a kind of metre of two lines (each line consisting of seven and a half feet; each foot containing four instants, except the sixth of the second line, which contains only one, and is therefore a single short syllable; hence there are thirty instants in the first line and twenty-seven in the second); [cf. Old Germ. êra; Mod. Germ. Ehre; Irish Erin.] **-kumāra**, m. a noble prince, Pāṇ. vi, 2, 58. **-kulyā**, f., N. of a river, VP. **-kṛita**, mfn. made by a man of the first three castes, Pāṇ.; KātyŚr.; MaitrS. **-gaṇa**, m. (Pāli ayyagaṇo) the whole body of (Buddhist) priests. **-gṛihya**, mfn. taking the side or adhering to the party of the noble ones, Ragh. ii, 33. **-cetas**, mfn. noble-minded, Śiś. xvi, 30. **-jana**, m. Āryans; honest people, Gaut.; Vait. **-jushṭa**, mfn. liked by or agreeable to noble ones, MBh. **-tā**, f. and **-tva**, n. honourable behaviour, Mn.; Rājat. **-duhitṛi**, f. a noble one's daughter (honourable designation of a female friend), Kathās. **-deva**, m., N. of a pupil of Nāgārjuna. **-deśa**, m. a region inhabited by Āryans or followers of the Āryan laws, Rājat. **-deśya**, mfn. belonging to or originated from such a region, ib. **-nivāsa**, m. an abode of Āryans, Pat. **-patha**, m. the path of the honest ones, R. **-putra**, m. [Prākṛit ajja-utta] son of an Āryan or honourable man, (honourable designation of the son of an elder brother or of any person of rank); designation of a husband by his wife (in dram.); of a king by his subjects. **-pravṛitta**, mfn. proceeding in an honest mode or manner, R. **-prāya**, mfn. inhabited for the most part by Āryan people, Mn. vii, 69. **-bala**, m., N. of a Bodhisattva. **-brāhmaṇa**, m. a noble Brāhman, Pāṇ. vi, 2, 58. **-bhaṭa** (or less correctly **-bhaṭṭa**), m., N. of two renowned astronomers and authors. **-bhaṭīya**, n., N. of a work on astronomy by Āryabhaṭa. **-bhāva**, m. honourable character or behaviour, R. **-mārga**, m. the way of the honourable ones. **-miśra**, mfn. distinguished, respectable; (as), m. an honourable person, a gentleman, R.; Prab.; Mṛicch. **-yuvan**, m. an Āryan youth, Kāty. on Pāṇ. **-rāja**, m., N. of a king, Rājat. **-rūpa**, mfn. having only the form or appearance of an Āryan or honest one, Mn. x, 57. **-liṅgin**, mfn. bearing the external semblance of an Āryan or honourable man, Mn. ix, 260. **-varman**, m., N. of a king, Kathās. **-vāc**, mfn. speaking the Āryan language, Mn. x, 45. **-vṛitta**, n. the behaviour of an Āryan or noble man, Mn.; (mfn.) behaving like an Āryan, honest, virtuous, Mn.; Gaut. **-veśa**, mfn. dressed like an Āryan or honest person. **-vrata**, mfn. observing the laws and ordinances of the Āryans or honourable men, behaving like Āryans, MBh. **-śīla**, mfn. having an honest character, MBh. **-saṁgha**, m. the whole body of (Buddhist) priests; N. of a renowned philosopher (founder of the school of the Yogācāras). **-satya**, n. (Pāli ariyasaccam) sublime truth; (with Buddhists the cattari ariyasaccāni or 'four great truths' are, 1. life is suffering, 2. desire of life is the cause of suffering, 3. extinction of that desire is the cessation of suffering, 4. the eightfold path (see below) leads to that extinction.) **-samaya**, m. the law of Āryans or honest men, Āp. **-siṅha**, m., N. of a Buddhist patriarch. **-siddhânta**, m., N. of a work of Āryabhaṭa. **-suta** (= -putra), mfn. a husband, Kathās. **-strī**, f. an Āryan woman or a woman of the first three castes, Āp.; Gaut. **-svāmin**, m., N. of a man. **-halam**, ind. an interjection ('murder!' T.), gaṇa svar-ādi, Pāṇ. i, 1, 37. **-hṛidya**, mfn. beloved by noble ones, L. **Āryâgama**, m. the approaching an Āryan woman sexually, Yājñ. ii, 294. **Āryā-gīti**, f. a variety of the Āryā metre (containing eight equal feet or thirty-two syllabic instants in each verse of the couplet). **Āryā-caṇḍī-tīrtha**, n., N. of a Tīrtha. **Āryâdhishṭhita**, mfn. being under the superintendence of men of the first three castes, Āp. ii, 3, 4. **Āryâvarta**, m. 'abode of the noble or excellent ones;' the sacred land of the Āryans (N. of Northern and Central India, extending from the eastern to the western sea and bounded on the north and south by the Himālaya and Vindhya mountains), Mn.; Rājat. &c.; (ās), m. pl. the inhabitants of that country. **Āryā-vilāsa**, m., N. of a work. **Āryâshṭaśata**, n., N. of a work of Āryabhaṭa, consisting of 108 distichs. **Āryâshṭâṅga-mārga**, m. (Pāli ariyo aṭṭhaṅgiko maggo) 'the holy eightfold path' pointed out by Buddha for escape from the misery of existence: 1. right views, 2. right thoughts, 3. right words, 4. right actions, 5. right living, 6. right exertion, 7. right recollection, 8. right meditation.

Āryaka, as, m. an honourable or respectable man, R.; a grandfather, MBh.; N. of a cowherd who became king, Mṛicch.; of a Nāga, MBh.; (āryakā or āryikā), f. a respectable woman, L.; N. of a river, BhP.; (ikā), f., N. of a Nakshatra, L.; (akam), n. a ceremony performed to the manes, the vessel &c. used in sacrifices made to the manes, L.

Āryava, am, n. honourable behaviour, honesty, Āp.

Āryāṇaka, as, m., N. of a country.

आर्यमण āryamaṇa, mf(ī)n. relating or belonging to Aryaman; (ī), f., N. of the Yamunā, Bālar.

Āryamṇa, am, n., N. of the Nakshatra Uttara-phalgunī (which is presided over by Aryaman), VarBṛS.

आर्श ārśá, mfn. (fr. ṛiśya), belonging to the antelope, AV. iv, 4, 5.

आर्ष ārsha, mf(ī)n. relating or belonging to or derived from Ṛishis (i. e. the poets of the Vedic and other old hymns), archaistic, MBh.; R. &c.; (as), m. a form of marriage derived from the Ṛishis (the father of the bride receiving one or two pairs of kine from the bridegroom), ĀśvGṛ. i, 6, 4; Mn. iii, 21; Yājñ. i, 58; (cf. vivāha); (ī), f. a wife married by the above form of marriage, Vishṇus. xxiv, 31; (am), n. the speech of a Ṛishi, the holy text, the Vedas, Nir.; RPrāt.; Mn.; sacred descent, Comm. on Lāṭy., Yājñ.; the derivation (of a poem) from a Ṛishi author. **-°m-dhara**, n., N. of a Sāman. **Ārshôḍhā**, f. a wife married according to the Ārsha form, L.

Ārsheyá, mf(ī)n. relating or belonging to or

derived from a Ṛishi, of sacred descent; venerable, respectable, RV.; VS.; AV.; ŚBr.; KātyŚr. &c.; (*as*), m., N. of Agni; (*am*), n. sacred descent, AitBr.; KātyŚr.; ŚBr. &c.; N. of several Sāmans. **—vat,** mfn. connected with sacred descent, ŚBr.

आर्षभ *ārshabha*, mf(ī)n. (fr. *ṛishabha*), coming from or produced by a bull, ŚBr.; MBh.; (*as*), m. a descendant of Ṛishabha, BhP.; (*ī*), f., N. of several constellations, VP.; Comm. on BhP.; (*am*), n., N. of a Sāman; a particular metre.

Ārshabhi, *is*, m. a descendant of Ṛishabha Tīrtha-kṛit; N. of the first Cakra-vartin in Bhārata, L.

Ārshabhya, mfn. (Pāṇ. v, 1, 14) to be regarded or used as a full-grown steer; to be castrated, L.

आर्षिक्य *ārshikya*, *am*, n. (fr. *ṛishika*, gaṇa *purohitâdi*, Pāṇ. v, 1, 128), the condition of being a Ṛishika, q. v.

आर्षिणेश्व *ārshiṇeśva*, *as*, m., N. of a king, VP. iv, 31.

आर्ष्टिषेण *ārshṭiohoṇá*, *as*, m. (fr. *ṛishṭi-sheṇa*, Pāṇ. iv, 1, 112 & 104), a descendant of Ṛishṭi-sheṇa, N. of Devāpi, RV. x, 98, 5; 6; 8; N. of a man, MBh.; Hariv.; Comm. on KātyŚr.

आर्ष्यशृङ्ग *ārshyaśṛiṅga*, *as*, m. a descendant of Ṛishya-śṛiṅga, MBh.

आर्हत *ārhata*, mf(ī)n. (fr. *arhat*), belonging to an Arhat or Jaina saint, Prab.; (*as*), m. a Jaina, a follower of Jaina doctrines, Prab.; VP.; a Buddhist, AgniP.; (*am*), n. the Jaina doctrine, Jainism.

Ārhantya, *am*, n. (gaṇa *brāhmaṇâdi*, Pāṇ. v, 1, 124), the state or practice of an Arhat or Jaina saint.

आर्हायण *ārhāyaṇa*, mf(ī)n. (fr. *arha*, gaṇa *aśvâdi*, Pāṇ. iv, 1, 110), a descendant of Arha.

आल *āla*, *am*, n. spawn; any discharge of poisonous matter from venomous animals, Suśr.; Kauś.; yellow arsenic, orpiment, Suśr.; (*as*), m., N. of an ape, Kathās. 57, 136; (mfn.) not little or insignificant, excellent, L. **Ālâkta,** mf(*ā*)n. anointed with poison (as an arrow), RV. vi, 75, 5. **Ālâsya,** m. 'poison-mouthed,' a crocodile, L.

आलक्ष् *ā-√laksh*, Ā. *-lakshayate*, to descry, behold, see, MBh.; R.; BhP.; Pañcat. &c.

Ā-lakshaṇa, *am*, n. perceiving, beholding, observing.

Ā-lakshi, mf(ī)n. beholding, seeing, (gaṇa *gaurâdi*, Pāṇ. iv, 1, 41.)

Ā-lakshita, mfn. beheld, descried, perceived, BhP.; R.

1. **Ā-lakshya,** mfn. to be observed, visible, apparent, MBh.; R.; Ragh. &c.

2. **Ā-lakshya,** ind. p. having observed or beheld, beholding, observing, MBh.; R.; Ragh. &c.

आलक्ष्य 3. *ā-lakshya*, mfn. scarcely visible, just visible, Śak. 181 a.

आलग् *ā-√lag*, P. *-lagati*, to adhere, cling to, Kāvyad.: Caus. *-lagayati*, to affix, Comm. on KātyŚr.

Ā-lagna, mfn. adhered, clung to, Amar.

आलगर्द *ālagarda* and *ālagardha* = *ala°*, q. v.

आलजि *ālaji*, mf(ī)n. speaking to, addressing [T.?], gaṇa *gaurâdi*, Pāṇ. iv, 1, 41.

आलप् *ā-√lap*, to address, speak to, converse, MBh.; Hariv.; Kathās.; Rājat. &c.

Ā-lapana, *am*, n. speaking to, conversation, Kād.

Ā-lapitavya, mfn. to be addressed or spoken to, Kād.

Ā-lapya, ind. p. having addressed, Kathās.

Ā-lāpa, *as*, m. speaking to, addressing; speech; conversation, communication, Pañcat.; Hit.; Kathās.; Śak. &c.; the singing or twittering of birds, Kathās.; statement of the question in an arithmetical or algebraic sum; question; a lesson, Jain.; (*ā*), f. (in music) a particular Mūrcchanā or melody. **—vat,** mfn. speaking, addressing, Amar.

Ā-lāpana, *am*, n. speaking to or with, conversation; a benediction, R. i, 77, 12.

Ā-lāpanīya or **ā-lāpya,** mfn. to be said or spoken; to be spoken to or addressed.

Ā-lāpika-vaṇśa, *as*, m. a kind of flute.

Ālāpin, mfn. speaking or conversing with, Bhartṛ.; (*inī*), f. a lute made of a gourd; (in music) a particular interval.

आलभ् *ā-√labh*, Ā. *-labhate*, to take hold of, touch, handle, RV.; TS.; KātyŚr.; Mn.; MBh. &c.; to kill, sacrifice, AitBr.; ŚBr.; KātyŚr. &c.; to commence, undertake, TS.; to reach, obtain; to conciliate, BhP.; MBh.; Megh. &c.: Caus. *-lambhayati*, to cause to touch, Kauś.; KātyŚr.; to cause to begin, TBr.: Desid. *-lipsate*, to intend or wish to touch, KātyŚr.; to intend to kill or sacrifice, ŚBr.

Ā-labdha, mfn. touched, MBh.; killed, sacrificed; gained, conciliated, BhP.

Ā-labha, *as*, m. touching, grasping.

Ā-labhana, *am*, n. touching, handling, BhP.; VarBṛ.; killing, sacrificing, BhP.

1. **Ā-labhyá,** mfn. to be killed or sacrificed, TS.

2. **Ā-labhya,** ind. p. having grasped or touched, MBh.; having killed or sacrificed, Yājñ.; MBh.; having received or obtained.

Ā-lambha, *as*, m. taking hold of, seizing, touching, ĀśvGṛ.; Mn.; Yājñ.; tearing off, rooting out (plants), Mn.; killing, sacrificing, AitBr.; ŚBr.; MBh.; Megh.

Ā-lambhana, *am*, n. seizure; taking hold of, touching, KātyŚr.; Gaut.; killing, sacrificing, KātyŚr.

Ā-lambhanīya, mfn. to be taken hold of or handled; to be touched, R.

Ā-lambham, ind. p. touching, taking hold of (with acc.), TāṇḍyaBr.

Ālambhin, mfn. ifc. touching, taking hold of.

Ā-lambhya, mfn. to be killed or sacrificed, TBr.

आलमर्थ्य *ālamarthya*, *am*, n. (fr. *alam* and *artha*), the condition of having the sense of *alam*, Pat.

आलम्ब् *ā-√lamb*, Ā. *-lambate*, to hang from, Vikr.; to lay hold of, seize, cling to; to rest or lean upon, MBh.; R.; Kathās.; Pañcat. &c.; to support, hold, R.; Ragh. &c.; to take up; to appropriate; to bring near; to get; to give one's self up to, MBh.; R.; Pañcat.; BhP. &c.; to depend, Sāh.

Ā-lamba, mfn. hanging down, R.; (*as*), m. that on which one rests or leans, support, prop; receptacle; asylum, MBh.; R.; Kathās. &c.; depending on or from; a perpendicular, L.; N. of a Muni, MBh.; (*ā*), f. a species of plant with poisonous leaves, Suśr.; (*am*), ind. holding, supporting, Kāṭh.

Ā-lambana, *am*, n. depending on or resting upon; hanging from, Pāṇ.; supporting, sustaining, Megh.; foundation, base, Prab.; KaṭhUp.; reason, cause; (in rhetoric) the natural and necessary connection of a sensation with the cause which excites it, Sāh.; the mental exercise practised by the Yogin in endeavouring to realize the gross form of the Eternal, VP.; silent repetition of a prayer [W.]; (with Buddhists) the five attributes of things (apprehended by or connected with the five senses, viz. form, sound, smell, taste, and touch; also *dharma* or law belonging to *manas*). **—parīkshā,** mfn., N. of a work. **—vat,** mfn. devoted to the mental exercise called Ālambana, VP.

Ālambāyana, mf(ī)n. a descendant of Ālamba; (*as*), m., N. of a man, MBh. **—°ī-putra,** m., N. of a teacher, ŚBr.

Ālambāyanīya, mfn. belonging to Ālambāyana.

Ā-lambi, mf(*ī* [gaṇa *gaurâdi*, Pāṇ. iv, 1, 41])n.; (*is*), m., N. of a pupil of Vaiśampāyana. **—°ī-putra,** m., N. of a teacher, ŚBr.

Ā-lambita, mfn. pendent, suspended; hanging from or on; supported, upheld; protected.

Ā-lambin, mfn. hanging from, resting or leaning upon; depending on or from, Pañcat.; MBh.; Ragh.; laying hold of, supporting, maintaining, Hit.; wearing, Kum.; (*inas*), m. pl. the school of Ālambi, L.

Ā-lambya, ind. p. having supported; supporting, sustaining; taking by the hand, MBh.; R. &c.

आलय *ā-laya.* See *ā-√lī.*

आलर्क *ālarka*, mfn. (fr. *alarka*), caused by or relating to a mad dog, Suśr.

आलव *ā-lava.* See *ā-√lū.*

आलवण्य *ālavaṇya*, *am*, n. (fr. *a-lavaṇa*, Pāṇ. v, 1, 121), saltlessness; insipidity; ugliness.

आलवाल *ālavāla*, *as*, m. a basin for water round the root of a tree, Ragh.; Vikr.; Śiś. &c.

आलष् *ā-√lash*, Ā. *-lashate*, to desire, lust after, BhP. v, 13, 6.

आलस *ālasa*, mfn. = *a-lasa*, idle, L.: [or fr. *lasa* with 4. *ā* in the sense of diminution, T.] a little active; (fr. *a-lasa*, gaṇa *vidâdi*, Pāṇ. iv, 1, 104), a descendant of A-lasa.

Ālasāyana, *as*, m. (gaṇa *haritâdi*, Pāṇ. iv, 1, 100), a descendant of Ālasa.

Ālasya, *am*, n. idleness, sloth, want of energy, MBh.; Mn.; Yājñ.; Suśr. &c.; (mfn.) idle, slothful, L.

आलाक्त *ālâkta.* See *āla.*

आलाट्य *ā-lāṭyà*, *as*, m. (fr. *√laṭ* = *√raṭ*?), to be cried down, N. of the ocean (?), TS. iv, 5, 8, 2.

आलात *ālāta*, *am*, n. = *alāta*; q. v., L.

आलान *ālāna*, *am*, n. (fr. *ā-√lī*, T.?), the post to which an elephant is tied, Mṛicch.; Ragh. &c.; the rope that ties him; a fetter, tie, rope or string, Ragh.; Kād.; binding, tying, L.; (*as*), m., N. of a minister of Śiva, L.

Ālānika, mfn. serving as a post to which an elephant is tied, Ragh. xiv, 38.

Ālānita, mfn. tied to (as an elephant), Bālar.

आलाप *ā-lāpa*, &c. See *ā-√lap.*

आलाबु *ālābu*, *us*, f. the pumpkin gourd, Cucurbita Pepo, L.

आलावर्त *ālâvarta*, *as*, m. a fan made of cloth, L.

आलि *āli*, *is*, m. (cf. *ali*), a scorpion; Scorpio in the Zodiac, VarBṛS.; a bee, L.; (*is* and *ī*), f. a woman's female friend, Kum.; Sāh.; Amar.; Śiś. &c.; a row, range, continuous line, a swarm (cf. *āvali*), Amar.; Kum.; Ragh.; a ridge or mound of earth crossing ditches or dividing fields &c., L.; a dike, L.; a ditch, L.; a line, race, family, L.; (mfn.) useless, idle, unmeaning, L.; pure, honest, secure, L. **—krama,** m. a kind of musical composition. **—jana,** m. a lady's female friends, Amar.; Prasamar.

Ālin, *ī*, m. a scorpion, L.; (cf. *alin.*)

आलिख् *ā-√likh*, P. *-likhati*, to make a scratch on; to delineate by scratches; to scratch, ŚBr.; KātyŚr.; MBh.; Hariv. &c.; to mark, draw, write, delineate, paint, MBh.; R.; Hariv.; VarBṛS.; Ragh.; Megh.; Mālav. &c.

Ā-likhat, mfn. scratching; (*an*), m., N. of an evil spirit, PārGṛ. i, 16, 23.

Ā-likhita, mfn. delineated by scratches, scratched, ŚBr.; drawn, written, delineated, painted, VarBṛS.; Kathās.; Ragh.; Śak. &c.

Ā-likhya, ind. p. pourtraying, delineating, sketching.

Ā-lekhana, *am*, n. scratching, scraping; marking out by scratches; painting; (*as*), m., N. of a teacher, ĀśvŚr.; (*ī*), f. a brush, pencil, L.

Ā-lekhani, *is*, m., N. of a teacher.

Ā-lekhya, mfn. to be written or delineated or painted; (*am*), n. writing, painting; a picture, portrait, R.; Śak.; Vikr. **—devatā,** f. a painted deity. **—purusha,** m. an image or drawing of a man, Kathās. **—lekhā,** f. painting. **—śesha,** mfn. one of whom there is nothing left but a painting, deceased, Ragh. xiv, 15. **—samarpita,** mfn. fixed on a picture, painted, Ragh. iii, 15.

आलिगव्य *āligavya*, *as*, m. and *āligavyāyanī* (Pāṇ. iv, 1, 18), f. (fr. *aligu*, Pāṇ. iv, 1, 105), a descendant of Aligu.

आलिगी *âligī*, f. a kind of serpent [NBD.?], AV. v, 13, 7.

आलिङ्ग् *ā-√liṅg*, P. *-liṅgati* and *-liṅgayati*, Ā. *-liṅgate*, to clasp, join the limbs closely; to encircle, embrace, MBh.; Kathās.; Pañcat.; Ragh. &c.; to spread out, extend, VarBṛS.

Ā-liṅga, *as*, m. a kind of drum, L.

Ā-liṅgana, *am*, n. clasping, embracing; an embrace, MBh.; Pañcat.; Megh. &c.; (*ā*), f. id., Naish.

Ā-liṅgita, mfn. embraced, Rājat.; Sāh. &c.;

occupied; (*am*), n. an embrace, Megh. **-vat,** mfn. one who has embraced.

Āliṅgin, mfn. embracing; (*ī*), m. a small drum shaped like a barleycorn and carried upon the breast, L.

1. **Ā-liṅgya,** mfn. to be embraced; (*as*), m. a kind of drum, L.

2. **Ā-liṅgya,** ind. p. having embraced.

Āliṅgyāyana, *as,* m. [?], N. of a village or town, (gaṇa *varaṇâdi* on Pāṇ. iv, 2, 82.)

आलिञ्जर *āliñjara, as,* m. a large clay water-jar, L.; (cf. *aliñjara.*)

आलिन्द *ālinda, as,* m. a terrace before a house, a raised place or terrace for sleeping upon, L.; (cf. *alinda.*)

आलिप् *ā-√lip,* P. *-limpati* (aor. *âlipat*) to besmear, anoint, ŚBr.; Hariv.; Suśr.; MBh.; BhP.; Kathās. &c.: Caus. *-limpayati* and *-lepayati,* to besmear, anoint, Kauś.; Suśr.

Ā-lipta, mfn. anointed, smeared, plastered, Mṛicch.; Kathās. &c.

Ā-lipya, ind. p. having besmeared or anointed, MBh.; Kathās. &c.

Ā-limpana, *am,* n. whitening or painting (the floor, wall &c. on festal occasions), L.

Ā-lepa, *as,* m. the act of smearing, plastering, anointing; liniment; ointment, Suśr.; Kathās.

Ā-lepana, *am,* n. smearing, plastering, anointing; liniment; ointment, Suśr.; BhP.

आलिह् *ā-√lih,* P. *-lihati,* to apply the tongue to; to lick, lap, BhP.: Intens. (p. *-lelihāna*) to lick up (as fire), BhP. v, 6, 9.

Ā-līḍha, mfn. licked, lapped by the tongue; licked up, eaten, R.; MBh.; Ragh.; scraped, polished; (*as*), m., N. of a man, (gaṇa *śubhrâdi,* Pāṇ. iv, 1, 123); (*am*), n. a particular attitude in shooting (the right knee advanced, the left leg drawn back), Comm. on Kum.; Ragh.

Āliḍheya, *as,* m. (Pāṇ. iv, 1, 123) a descendant of Ālīḍha.

आली *ā-√lī,* Ā. *-līyate,* to come close to; to settle down upon; to stoop, crouch, MBh.; Hariv.; Ragh. &c.

Ā-laya, *as,* m. and *am,* n. a house, dwelling; a receptacle, asylum, R.; Yājñ.; Kathās. &c.; (often ifc., e.g. *himâlaya,* 'the abode of snow.')

Ā-līna, mfn. having come close to, Kathās.; Hariv.; Ragh.; dwelling or abiding in, Kathās.; crouched, stooped, MBh.; R.

Ālīnaka, *am,* n. tin, (from its close adherence to other metals?), L.

आलु *ālu, us,* m. (*√ṛi,* Comm. on Uṇ. i, 5), an owl, L.; ebony, black ebony, L.; (*us* and *ūs*), f. a pitcher, a small water-jar, L.; (*u*), n. a raft, a float; an esculent root, Arum Campanulatum, L.; (in modern dialects applied to the yam, potatoe, &c.)

Āluka, *as,* m. a kind of ebony, L.; N. of Śesha (the chief of the Nāgas or serpent race); (*ī*), f. a species of root, Bhpr.; (*am*), n. a particular fruit (= *āruka,* q.v.), L.; the esculent root of Amorphophallus Campanulatus.

आलुञ्च् *ā-√luñc,* P. *-luñcati,* to tear in pieces, Suśr.

Ā-luñcana, *am,* n. tearing in pieces, rending, Mṛicch.

आलुड् *ā-√luḍ,* Caus. P. *-loḍayati,* to stir up, mix; to agitate.

Ā-loḍana, *am,* n. mixing, blending, Suśr.; stirring, shaking, agitating.

Ā-loḍita, mfn. stirred up, mixed, blended; shaken, agitated, Suśr.; R.

Ā-loḍya, ind. p. having stirred up or mixed; having agitated, ĀśvGṛ.; MBh.; R.; Suśr. &c.

आलुप् *ā-√lup,* P. *-lumpati,* to tear out or asunder; to dissolve, separate, AV.; ŚBr.; KātyŚr.; AitBr.: Pass. *-lupyate,* to be interrupted, Megh.

Ā-lopa, *as,* m. a morsel, bit, L.

आलुभ् *ā-√lubh,* P. *-lubhyati,* to become disturbed or disordered, ŚBr.: Desid. of Caus. (Subj. 3. sg. *-lulobhayishāt*) to wish to disturb or trouble.

आलुलित *ā-lulita,* mfn. (*√lul*), a little moved or agitated, Mālav.

Ā-lola, mfn. moving gently; trembling slightly; rolling (as an eye), Amar.; Megh.; Śiś.; Kathās.; Kir.; (*as*), m. trembling, agitation; swinging, rocking.

Ā-lolita, mfn. a little shaken or agitated.

आलू *ā-√lū,* P. *-lunāti,* to cut, cut off; to pluck off.

Ā-lava, *as,* m. stubble, Comm. on TS.

Ā-lūna, mfn. cut off, Kum.

आलेखन *ā-lekhana.* See *ā-√likh.*

आलेश *ā-leśá, as,* m. (*√liś = √riś*), grazing, TS. v, 1, 5, 9.

आलोक् *ā-√lok,* Ā. *-lokate,* to look at, Hit.; Sāh.; Kathās.; to descry, behold, Bhaṭṭ.: Caus. *-lokayati,* to see, look at or upon, MBh.; Hariv.; Kathās.; Ragh.; Śak. &c.; to consider; to prove, R.; Mn. &c.; to descry, behold, perceive; to know, MBh.; R.; Hit.; Pañcat. &c.

Ā-loka, *as,* m. looking, seeing, beholding; sight, aspect, vision, Kathās.; Megh.; Mṛicch.; Śak.; Ragh. &c.; light, lustre, splendour; glimmer, R.; MBh.; flattery, praise, complimentary language; panegyric, Ragh.; section, chapter; N. of a work. **-kara,** mfn. spreading or causing light, VarBṛS. **-gadādharī,** f., N. of a commentary on the above work called Āloka. **-patha,** m. and **-mārga,** m. line of sight, range of vision, Ragh. **-vat,** mfn. having light or lustre.

Ālokaka, *as,* m. a spectator, Naish.

Ā-lokana, mfn. looking at; contemplating; (*am*), n. seeing, looking; sight, beholding, Yājñ.; Ragh.; Kum.; Kathās.; Sāh. &c.

Ā-lokanīya, mfn. to be looked at; visible; to be considered, regarded, R. **-tā,** f. the state or condition of being visible, Kum.

Ā-lokita, mfn. seen, beheld.

Ā-lokin, mfn. seeing, beholding; contemplating, Bhartṛ.; Kathās.

Ā-lokya, ind. p. having seen or looked at, beholding.

आलोच् *ā-√loc,* Ā. *-locate,* to consider, reflect upon: Caus. P. Ā. *-locayati, -te,* to make visible, show, MBh.; to behold, view, perceive; to consider, reflect, MBh.; MārkP.; Kathās.; Hit. &c.

Ā-locaka, mfn. causing to see, Suśr.

Ā-locana, *am,* n. seeing, perceiving, Pāṇ.; (*ā, am*), f. n. considering, reflecting, reflection, R.; Sāh.

Ā-locanīya and 1. **ā-locya,** mfn. to be considered or reflected upon, Vedāntas.

Ā-locita, mfn. considered, reflected upon, Kathās.; Hit.; Pañcat.

2. **Ā-locya,** ind. p. having considered, reflecting, MārkP.; Hit.; Kathās. &c.

आलोष्टी *āloshṭī,* ind. hurting (?), gaṇa *ūry-ādi,* Pāṇ. i, 4, 61.

आलोहवत् *ā-lohavat,* mfn. a little reddish, ĀśvGṛ. iv, 8, 6.

Ā-lohita, mfn. reddish, Kathās. **-°ī-√kṛi,** to make reddish, Kād.

आलोहायन *ālohāyana, as,* m. (gaṇa *naḍâdi,* Pāṇ. iv, 1, 99), a descendant of Aloha.

आलोल *ā-lola.* See above.

आव *āvá,* the base of the dual cases of the pronoun of the 1st person; Nom. Acc. *āvām* (Ved. *āvā́m*); Inst. Dat. Abl. *āvābhyām* (Ved. Abl. also *āvā́t*); Gen. Loc. *āváyos.*

आवच् *ā-√vac,* Ā. (aor. 1. sg. *ā́-voce,* RV. vii, 32, 2) to address, invoke.

Ókta (*ā́-ukta*), mfn. addressed, invoked, RV. i, 63, 9.

आवञ्च् *ā-√vañc,* Pass. (Impv. 2. sg. *ā-vacyasva*) to gush or flow towards or near, RV. ix, 2, 2, &c.

आवटिक *āvaṭika, ās,* m. pl., N. of a school.

आवट्य *āvaṭya* (fr. *avaṭa,* gaṇa *gargâdi,* Pāṇ. iv, 1, 105), *as,* m., *ā* (Pāṇ. iv, 1, 75) and *avaṭyāyanī* (Pāṇ. iv, 1, 17), f. a descendant of Avaṭa.

आवत् *ā-vát,* f. proximity, AV. v, 30, 1 (opposed to *parā-vat*).

आवत्सरम् *ā-vatsaram,* ind. for a year, during a year, MārkP.

Ā-vatsarântam, ind. to the end of the year, Kathās.

आवद् *ā-√vad,* P. *-vadati,* to speak to, address; to shout out; to invoke, celebrate, RV.; AV.; VS.; ŚBr.

आवदानिक *āvadānika,* mfn. (fr. *ava-dāna*), offered after being divided into pieces, Vait.

आवध् *ā-√vadh,* P. (aor. 3. sg. *ā́vadhīt,* RV. viii, 72, 4 & viii, 75, 9) to shatter, crush.

आवन् *ā-√van,* Ā. (2. sg. *ā́-vanase,* RV. i, 140, 11; pf. 3. sg. *ā́-vavne,* RV. v, 74, 7; aor. 3. sg. *-ávanishishṭa,* RV. i, 127, 7) to wish, desire, crave for; to procure.

आवनतीय *āvanatīya,* mfn. (fr. *ava-nata,* gaṇa *kṛiśâśvâdi,* Pāṇ. iv, 2, 80.)

आवनेय *āvaneya, as,* m. (fr. *avani*), 'son of the earth,' N. of the planet Mars.

आवन्त *āvanta, as,* m. (fr. *avanti*), a king of Avanti (the district of Oujein), VarBṛS.; N. of a son of Dhṛishṭa, Hariv., (cf. *avanta*); (*ī*), f. the language of Avanti.

Āvantaka, mfn. belonging to or coming from Avanti; (*ās*), m. pl. the inhabitants of Avanti, VarBṛS.

Āvantika, mfn. belonging to or coming from Avanti, VarBṛS.; (*ās*), m., N. of a Buddhist school; (*ā*), f., N. of a woman, Kathās.

Āvantya, mfn. coming from or being in the country Avanti, Suśr.; (*as*), m. a king or inhabitant of Avanti, MBh.; Hariv.; (according to Manu x, 21 the Āvantyas are offsprings of degraded Brāhmans.)

आवन्दन *ā-vandana, am,* n. (*√vand*), salute, L.

आवप् *ā-√2. vap,* P. *-vapati,* to throw or scatter into; to mix with; to put together, AV.; ŚBr.; KātyŚr.; ĀśvGṛ.; MārkP.; to insert, AitBr.; ŚBr.; Lāṭy. &c.; to pour out; to fill up, VarBṛS.; to present, afford, supply; to offer, MBh.: Caus. P. *-vāpayati,* to mix with, Suśr.; to comb, smooth; to shave, MBh.

Ā-vápana, *am,* n. the act of sowing, throwing, scattering, placing upon, ŚBr.; KātyŚr.; Gaut.; instilling, inserting, ŚBr.; KātyŚr.; capacity, MBh.; a vessel, jar, ewer, MaitrS.; BhP.; sowing seed, weaving, L.; a hempen cloth. L.; (*ī*), f. a vessel, jar, AV. xii, 1, 61.

Ā-vapantaka, mf(*ikā́*)n. scattering, AV. xii, 2, 63.

Ā-vāpa, *as,* m. scattering, throwing; sowing seed, MBh.; Comm. on Yājñ.; insertion, Śulb.; casting, directing; (in med.) throwing additional ingredients into any mixture in course of preparation; mixing, inserting; setting out or arranging vessels, jars, &c., L.; a kind of drink, L.; a bracelet, L.; a basin for water round the root of a tree, L.; uneven ground, L.; hostile purpose, intention of going to war, Sāh.; Śiś. &c.; a vessel; principal oblation to fire, Gobh.

Āvāpaka, *as,* m. a bracelet of gold &c., L.

Ā-vāpana, *am,* n. a loom, an implement for weaving; a reel or frame for winding thread, L.

Āvāpika, mfn. additional, inserted, supplementary, Nir.

आवभृत्य *āvabhṛitya, as,* m. a king of Avabhṛiti; (*ās*), m. pl., N. of a dynasty of kings, BhP.

आवभृथ *āvabhṛitha,* mfn. belonging to Avabhṛitha, q. v., BhP.

आवय *āvayá, am,* n. (fr. 2. *a-vi,* cf. *avi*), pangs of childbirth, painful childbirth (?), AV. viii, 6, 26; (*as*), m. arrival, T.; one who arrives, T.; N. of a country, L.

Āvayaka, mfn. belonging to the country Āvaya, L.

आवयस् *ā-vayas, ās,* m. perhaps 'the youthful one' (cf. *abhi-vayas*), RV. i, 162, 5.

आवयास् *āvayās,* m. (f.?) pl. water, Nigh. i, 12.

आवरक *ā-varaka,* &c. See 1. *ā-√vṛi.*

आवरसमक *āvarasamaka,* mfn. (fr. *avara-*

sama, Pāṇ. iv, 3, 49), to be paid in the following year (as a debt).

आवर्जक *ā-varjaka*, &c. See *ā-√vṛij.*

आवर्त *ā-varta*, &c. See *ā-√vṛit.*

आवर्ष *āvarsha.* See *ā-√vṛish.*

आवर्ह *ā-varha*, &c. See *ā-√vṛih.*

आवलि *āvali, is* and *ī*, f. (*√val*, T.), a row, range; a continuous line; a series; dynasty, lineage, Vikr.; BhP.; Prab.; Hit. &c. — **°ī-kanda**, m. a kind of bulbous plant, L.

Āvalikā, f. = *āvali*, q. v., coriander, L.

आवल्ग *ā-√valg*, Ā. *-valgate*, to spring, jump, leap up, MBh.

Ā-valgita, mfn. springing, jumping, MBh.; Hariv.

Ā-valgin, mfn. id.

आवल्गुज *āvalguja*, mfn. (fr. *a-valgu-ja*), coming or produced from the plant Vernonia Anthelminthica, Suśr.

आवशीर *āvaśīra, ās*, m. pl., N. of a people, MBh.

आवश्यक *āvaśyaka*, mfn. (fr. *avaśya*), necessary, inevitable, Comm. on Kum. and Ragh.; (*am*), n. necessity, inevitable act or conclusion, Pāṇ.; religious duty, Jain.; a call of nature, Mn. — **tā**, f. necessity, inevitability, Hit. — **bṛihad-vṛitta**, *am*, n., N. of a Jaina work.

आवस् *ā-√5. vas*, P. *-vasati*, to abide, dwell; to spend (time), RV.; MBh.; MārkP.; to enter, inhabit; to take possession of, Mn.; Yājñ.; MBh.; R.; BhP.; VarBṛS. &c.; to sleep with, Mn.: Caus. *-vāsayati*, to cause or allow any one to dwell or abide; to receive hospitably, R.; Rājat.; to inhabit, settle in a place, MBh.; Hariv.; R.; Kathās. &c.

Ā-vasati, *is*, f. shelter, night's lodging, TBr.; night (i. e. the time during which one rests).

Ā-vasathá, *as*, m. (Uṇ. iii, 114) dwelling-place, abode, habitation, night's lodging, AV. ix, 6, 7; ŚBr.; ChUp.; Mn.; R.; Hit.; Ragh. &c.; a dwelling for pupils and ascetics; a village; a particular religious observance, L.; a treatise on Āryā metres, T.

Āvasathika, mf(*ī*)n. dwelling in a house; household, domestic, Pāṇ. iv, 4, 74; (*as*), m. a householder (who keeps a domestic fire), T.

Āvasathya and **āvasathīya** [TBr. iii, 7, 4, 6], mfn. being in a house; (*as*), m. [scil. *agni*] a domestic fire, MBh.; Vait.; m. and (*am*), n. a night's lodging, dwelling for pupils and ascetics, L.; (*am*), n. establishing or keeping a domestic fire, L.

Ā-vasathyâdhāna, n. establishing a domestic fire, PārGṛ.

Ā-vāsa, *as*, m. abode, residence, dwelling, house, MBh.; R.; Pañcat.; Ragh. &c.

Āvāsin, mfn. ifc. abiding or dwelling in.

Ā-vāsya, mfn. ifc. to be inhabited by, full of, BhP. viii, 1, 10.

आवसान *āva-sāna*, mf(*ī*)n. (fr. *ava-sāna*, gaṇa *takshaśilâdi*, Pāṇ. iv, 3, 93), dwelling or living on the boundaries of a village &c., T.

Āvasānika, mf(*ī*)n. being at the end, L.

आवसायिन् *āvasāyin*, mfn. (fr. *avasa* and *āyin*), going after or procuring a livelihood, AitBr. vii, 29, 2.

आवसित *āvasita* = *avasita* (q. v.), L.

आवस्थिक *āvasthika*, mfn. (fr. 2. *ava-sthā*), being in accordance with or adapted to the circumstances; suitable, Suśr.

आवह् *ā-√vah*, P. Ā. *-vahati, -te*, to drive or lead near or towards; to bring; to fetch, procure, RV.; AV.; ŚBr.; MBh.; R.; BhP.; Pañcat. &c.; to bring home (a bride), MBh.; Hariv.; to pay, Yājñ. ii, 193; to carry away, MBh.; to bear, R.; Hariv.; to use, MārkP.: Caus. *-vāhayati*, to cause to drive or come near; to invite, invoke, ŚBr.; ŚāṅkhŚr.; ĀśvŚr.; MBh.; R. &c.

Ā-vaha, mf(*ā*)n. bringing, bringing to pass, producing; what bears or conveys, Mn.; Bhag.; R.; Pañcat. &c.; (*as*), m., N. of one of the seven winds or bands of air (that which is usually assigned to the *bhuvar-loka* or atmospheric region between the *bhūr-loka* and *svar-loka*), Hariv.; one of the seven tongues of fire.

Ā-vahana, *am*, n. bringing near.

Ā-vahamāna, mfn. bringing near, bearing along, followed or succeeded by, bringing in succession.

Ā-vāha, *as*, m. inviting, invitation, MBh.; marrying, L.; N. of a son of Śvaphalka, Hariv.

Ā-vāhana, *am*, n. sending for, inviting, calling, Yājñ.; VP.; VarBṛS.; invocation, invitation; (*ī*), f. a particular position of the hands (the palms being placed together, and the thumbs turned towards the root of the ring-finger), L.

Ā-vāhita, mfn. invoked, invited.

Ā-vāhya, mfn. to be invoked or invited, Nyāyam.

आवा *ā-√vā*, P. *-vāti*, to blow towards or upon, RV.; TBr.; BhP.; Kirāt.; Bhaṭṭ.

आवाधा *ā-vādhā.* See *ā-bādhā.*

आवाप *ā-vāpa*, &c. See *ā-√vap.*

आवार *ā-vāra*, &c. See 1. *ā-√vṛi.*

आवाल *āvāla, as*, m. a basin of water round the foot of a tree (= *ālavāla*, q. v.), L.

आवास् *ā-√vās*, Caus. *-vāsayati*, to perfume, R. ii, 103, 40.

आवास *ā-vāsa.* See *ā-√5. vas*, col. 1.

आवि *āvi, is* and *ī́*, f. (perhaps *√vī*), pain, suffering, Suśr.; TS.; (*yas*), f. pl. pangs of childbirth, Suśr.

आविक *āvika*, mf(*ī*)n. (fr. *avi*), relating to or coming from sheep, MBh.; Mn.; Yājñ.; Gaut.; Suśr.; woollen, Mn.; Suśr.; (*ī*), f. and (*am*), n. a sheepskin, R.; Āp.; (*am*), n. [and (*as*), m., L.] a woollen cloth or blanket, ŚBr.; KātyŚr.; Mn. &c. — **sautrika**, mfn. made of woollen threads, Mn.

Āvikya, *am*, n. (gaṇa *purohitâdi*, Pāṇ. v, 1, 128), the state of being or belonging to a sheep.

आविक्षित *āvikshitá, as*, m. a descendant of A-vikshit, N. of Marutta, ŚBr.; AitBr.; MBh.; Hariv.

आविग्न 1. *āvigna* = *avigna*, q. v.

आविज् *ā-√vij*, Caus. *-vejayati*, to stir up, confuse, R.

2. **Ā-vigna**, mfn. agitated, confused, MBh.; Hariv.; Kathās.

आविज्ञान्य *ā́vijñānya*, mfn. (fr. *a-vijñāna*), undistinguishable, ŚBr. i, 6, 3, 39.

आवितन् *ā-vi-√tan*, Ā. (p. *-tanvāna*) to spread over (as rays of light), BhP. v, 20, 37.

आविद् 1. *ā-√1. vid*, P. (pf. *ā́-veda*, RV. x, 114, 9) to know well or thoroughly: Caus. (1. sg. *-vedayāmi*) to address, invite, RV.; ŚBr.; to make known, report, declare, announce, MBh.; Hariv.; Śak.; Vikr.; BhP.; Kathās. &c.; to offer, present, MBh.; Kathās.

2. **Ā-víd**, *t*, f. knowledge, the being or becoming known, ŚBr.; TS.

Ā-vidvás, mfn. acquainted with, knowing thoroughly, skilled in, RV. iv, 19, 10.

Ā-vedaka, mfn. ifc. making known, reporting, announcing; (*as*), m. an appellant, a suitor; one who makes known, an informer.

Ā-vedana, *am*, n. announcing, informing, AitBr.; stating a complaint; addressing or apprising respectfully.

Ā-vedanīya, mfn. to be declared or reported or announced, Kād.; Pañcat.

Ā-vedita, mfn. made known, communicated, represented, Ragh.; Comm. on Yājñ. &c.

Ā-vedin, mfn. ifc. announcing, declaring.

1. **Ā-vedya**, mfn. = *ā-vedanīya* above.

2. **Ā-vedya**, ind. p. having made known &c.

Ā-vedyamāna, mfn. being made known, being stated or represented.

आविद् 3. *ā-√2. vid*, P. (Subj. 1. sg. *ā́-vidam*, RV. ii, 27, 17; Inf. *-víde*, RV. x, 113, 3) Ā. (Subj. 1. sg. *ā́-vide*, RV. viii, 45, 36; aor. 1. sg. *ā́vitsi*, RV. x, 15, 3; 97, 7) to reach, obtain; to get into: Pass. *-vidyate*, to exist, RV. iii, 54, 4.

Ā-vitta, mfn. existing, being, VS. x, 9.

4. **Ā-víd**, *t*, f. technical designation of the formulas (in VS. x, 9) beginning with *āvis* and *āvitta*, ŚBr.

Ā-vinna, mfn. existing, being, TBr. i, 7, 6, 6.

आविदूर्य *āvidūrya, am*, n. (fr. *a-vidūra*), proximity, Pāṇ.

आविद्ध *ā́-viddha.* See *ā-√vyadh.*

आविभा *ā-vi-√bhā*, P. *ā́-vi-bhāti*, to shine near or towards [Gmn.]; to kindle on all sides [Sāy.], RV. i, 71, 6.

आविर् *āvír-.* See *āvís* below.

आविल *āvila*, mfn. (also written *ā-bila*, q. v.) turbid (as a fluid), foul, not clear, Suśr.; Ragh.; Kum.; MBh. &c.; confused; (ifc.) polluted by or mixed with. — **kanda**, m. a kind of bulbous plant, L.; (for *āvalī-kanda*, q. v.)

Āvilaya, Nom. P. *āvilayati*, to make turbid; to blot, Śak. 122 a.

आविश् *ā-√viś*, P. Ā. *-viśati, -te* (inf. *ā-víśam*, RV. ii, 24, 6) to go or drive in or towards; to approach, enter; to take possession of, RV.; AV.; VS.; ŚBr.; MBh.; BhP.; R.; Mn. &c.; to sit down, settle, MBh.; to get or fall into; to reach, obtain; to become, RV.; MBh.; R.; BhP. &c.: Caus. *-veśayati*, to cause to enter or approach; to cause to reach or obtain; to deliver, offer, present; to make known, RV.; AV.; AitBr.; MBh.; BhP.; Ragh.; Bhag. &c.

Ā-vishṭa, mfn. entered, BhP.; Kathās. &c.; being on or in, BhP.; R.; intent on, L.; possessed (by a demon &c.); subject to, burdened with; possessed, engrossed; filled (by any sentiment or feeling), MBh.; AitBr.; Hariv.; Kathās.; Pañcat. &c. — **tva**, n. the state of being possessed or burdened, Vām. — **liṅga**, mfn. 'having a fixed gender,' (in Gr.) a word which does not change its gender.

Ā-veśa, *as*, m. joining one's self, KātyŚr.; entering, entrance, taking possession of, MBh.; Śak.; Prab. &c.; absorption of the faculties in one wish or idea, intentness, devotedness to an object, BhP.; demoniacal frenzy, possession, anger, wrath, Bālar.; Kād.; pride, arrogance, L.; indistinctness of idea, apoplectic or epileptic giddiness, L.

Ā-veśana, *am*, n. entering, entrance, L.; possession by devils &c., Sāh.; passion, anger, fury, L.; a house in which work is carried on, a workshop, manufactory, &c., Mn.; the disk of the sun or moon, L.; (for *ā-veshaṇa.*)

Ā-veśika, mfn. own, peculiar; inherent; (*as*), m. a guest, a visitor; (*am*), n. entering into; hospitable reception, hospitality, L.

आविष् *āvísh-.* See *āvís.*

आविष्टित *ā́-vishṭita.* See *ā-√vesht.*

आविस् *āvís*, ind. (said to be connected with *vahis* and *ava*; or fr. *ā-vid*, BRD.; cf. Gk. ἐξ; Lat. *ex*?), before the eyes, openly, manifestly, evidently, RV.; AV.; VS. — **tarā́m**, ind. in a more manifest or very manifest way, ŚBr. (very often joined to the roots *as*, *bhū*, and 1. *kṛi*).

Āvír- (in comp. for *āvís*). — **ṛijīka**, mfn. having manifest means [Sāy.], RV. iv, 38, 4. — **bhāva**, m. manifestation, becoming visible, presence, ŚBr.; ChUp.; Sāh. — **√bhū**, to be or become apparent or visible; to appear, become manifest, be present before the eyes, RV.; AV.; ŚBr.; Śak.; Megh. &c. — **bhūta**, mfn. become apparent, visible, manifest. — **bhūti**, f. = *-bhāva*, q. v. — **maṇḍala**, mfn. manifesting the form of a circle, Kir. xiv, 65. — **mukha**, mfn. having a visible or manifest aperture; (*ī*), f. an eye, BhP. — **mūla**, mfn. having the root laid bare, eradicated (as a tree), AitĀr. ii, 3, 6, 10. — **hita** (*√dhā*), mfn. made visible, BhP. — **hotra**, m., N. of a man, BhP.

Āvísh- (in comp. for *āvís*). — **karaṇa**, n. and **-kāra**, m. making visible, manifestation, Sāh. — **√1. kṛi**, to make apparent; to reveal, uncover; to show, RV.; AV.; ŚBr.; Sāh. &c. — **kṛita**, mfn. made visible, revealed; uncovered; evident, manifest; known, Mn.; Ragh.; Kum. &c.

Āvishṭya, mfn. apparent, manifest, RV.

आविहन् *ā-vi-√han*, P. *-hanti*, to hew at, MBh. iii, 10654.

आवी *ā-√vī*, P. *-véti* (but also *-váyati*, Nigh. ii, 8; pf. *-vivāya*, &c.) to undertake; to hasten near, approach, RV.; to grasp, seize, AitUp.; to drive on or near, RV.: Intens. (Pot. 3. pl. *ā-vevīran*, TS. iii, 2, 9, 5) to tremble, be agitated; (for the noun *āvī* see *āvi*, and for *āvī*, f. see *āvya.*)

आवीज् *ā-√vij*, Caus. *-vījayati*, to fan, Hariv. 4444.

आवीत *ā-vīta* and *āvītin.* See *ā-√vye.*

आवीरचूर्ण **āvīra-cūrṇa**, *am*, n. a kind of red powder, L.

आवुक **āvuka**, *as*, m. (in dram.) father, L.

आवृ 1. *ā-√1. vṛi*, P. *-vṛiṇoti*, to cover, hide, conceal; to surround, enclose, shut, comprehend, hem in; to keep off, MBh.; R.; BhP.; Śak.; Kathās. &c.: Caus. *-vārayati*, to cover, enclose; to ward off, keep off, MBh.; R.; BhP.; VarBṛS.

Ā-varaka, mfn. covering, concealing, darkening, Sāh.; Sarvad.

Ā-varaṇa, mfn. covering, hiding, concealing, Ragh.; (*am*), n. the act of covering, concealing, hiding, Suśr.; Ragh.; shutting, enclosing; an obstruction, interruption, Mn.; Suśr.; Ragh.; a covering, garment, cloth, MBh.; Kirāt.; Śak.; Ragh.; anything that protects, an outer bar or fence; a wall; a shield; a bolt, lock, MBh.; R.; Ragh. &c.; (in phil.) mental blindness, Jain. **-śakti**, f. the power of illusion (that which veils the real nature of things), Vedāntas.

Āvaraṇin, *inas*, m. pl., N. of a Buddhist sect.

Āvaraṇīya, mfn. belonging to Āvaraṇa or mental blindness, Jain.

Ā-varikā, f. a shop, stall, L.

Ā-vāra, *as*, m. shelter, defence; ifc. enclosing, keeping out.

Ā-vāri, *is*, f. a shop, stall, L.

Ā-vārya, ind. p. having covered or concealed, BhP.; MBh.; R.; warding off, keeping off, MBh.

Ā́-vṛita, mfn. covered, concealed, hid; screened, RV.; AV.; ŚBr.; Kathās.; MBh.; BhP. &c.; enclosed, encompassed, surrounded (by a ditch, wall, &c.), Mn.; R.; Rājat.; Pañcat. &c.; invested, involved; spread, overspread, overcast; filled with, abounding with; (*ás*), m. a man of mixed origin (the son of a Brāhman by a woman of the Ugra caste), Mn. x, 15.

Ā-vṛiti, *is*, f. covering, closing, hiding.

1. **Ā-vṛitya**, ind. p. having covered &c., Śak.; MBh. &c.

आवृ 2. *ā-√2. vṛi*, Ā. (*ā́-vṛiṇe*, RV. i, 17, 1, &c.; 1. pl. *-vṛiṇīmáhe*) P. (*-várat*, RV. i, 143, 6, &c.) to choose, desire, prefer, RV.; AV.; to fulfil, grant (a wish), RV.; MBh.

आवृज् *ā-√vṛij*, Ā. *-vṛiṅkte* (Subj. *-várjate*, RV. i, 33, 1; aor. *ā́vṛikta*, RV. viii, 90, 16; also P. aor. 1. sg. *ā́vṛiksham*, RV. x, 159, 5) to turn or bring into the possession of, procure for, bestow, give, RV.; to turn or bring into one's own possession; to appropriate, RV.; ŚBr.; BhP.; to be propitiated, favour, BhP.: Caus. P. *-varjayati*, to turn over, incline, bend, Hariv.; Śak.; Vikr.; Ragh.; Megh. &c.; to pour out, Ragh.; Kum.; to deliver, BhP.; Ragh. &c.; to cause to yield, overcome; to gain one's favour, propitiate, attract, Kathās.; Daś. &c.

Ā-varjaka, mfn. attracting, propitiating, Rājat.

Ā-varjana, *am*, n. attracting, propitiating, Sāh.; overcoming, victory; bending or bringing down, Lalit. **-°ī-√1. kṛi**, to bring down, humble, Lalit.

Ā-varjita, mfn. inclined, bent down, prone, MBh.; Ragh. &c.; poured out, made to flow downwards, Kum.; overcome, humbled, Kathās. &c.; (*am*), n. a particular position of the moon, VarBṛS.

Ā-varjya, ind. p. bending, turning down, &c.

आवृत् 1. *ā-√vṛit*, P. (only pf. in RV., *-vavárta*) Ā. *-vartate* (aor. 3. sg. *ā́vṛitsata*, RV. viii, 1, 29; Inf. *-vṛ́te*, RV. iii, 42, 3) to turn or draw round or back or near, RV.; ŚāṅkhŚr.; to turn or go towards; to turn round or back, return, revolve, RV.; AV.; VS.; ŚBr.; ChUp.; MBh.; Kathās.; R. &c.: Caus. P. *-vartayati* (Ved. Subj. *-vavártati*, Pot. *-vavṛityāt*, &c.), Ā. *-vartayate* (Ved. Pot. *-vavṛitīta*, &c.) to cause to turn, roll; to draw or turn towards; to lead near or towards; to bring back; to turn round or back, RV.; AV.; VS.; TBr.; MBh.; BhP. &c.; to repeat, recite, say repeatedly; to pray, ĀśvŚr.; KātyŚr.; Kathās.; R.; Hariv. &c.: Intens. *-varīvartti*, RV. i, 164, 31; AV. ix, 10, 11, &c., to move quickly or repeatedly.

Ā-varta, *as*, m. turning, winding, turning round, revolving, R.; Sāh.; Suśr.; whirl, gulf, whirlpool, ŚBr.; Megh.; MBh.; Ragh. &c.; deliberation, revolving (in the mind), L.; a lock of hair that curls backwards (especially on a horse considered lucky), a curl, R.; Śiś. &c.; the two depressions of the forehead above the eyebrows, Suśr.; a crowded place where many men live close together; a kind of jewel, L.; N. of a form of cloud personified; (*ā*), f., N. of a river, L.; (*am*), n. a mineral substance, pyrites, marcasite, L.

Ā-vartaka, *as*, m. a kind of venomous insect, Suśr.; N. of a form of cloud personified, Kum.; Ragh.; a depression above the frontal ridge or over the eyebrows; whirlpool; revolution; excitement of the mind from the influence of the senses; a curl of hair; (*ī*), f., N. of a creeping plant, L.

Ā-vártana, mfn. turning round or towards; revolving, TS.; (*am*), n. turning, turning round, returning, RV. x, 19, 4; 5; circular motion, gyration, churning, stirring anything in fusion; melting metals together, alligation, L.; the time when the sun begins to cast shadows towards the east or when shadows are cast in an opposite direction, noon; year, MBh.; repeating, doing over again; study, practising, L.; (*as*), m., N. of an Upa-dvīpa in Jambu-dvīpa, BhP.; (*ī*), f. a crucible, L.; a magic art, R. **-maṇi**, m. a gem of secondary order (generally known as Rājāvarta), L.

Ā-vartanīya, mfn. to be turned round or whirled; to be reversed; to be repeated, Comm. on Nyāyam.

Ā-vartamāna, mfn. going round, revolving; advancing, proceeding.

Ā-vartita, mfn. turned round, stirred round, Hariv.; BhP. &c.

Āvartin, mfn. whirling or turning upon itself; returning; (*ī*), m. a horse having curls of hair on various parts of his body (considered as a lucky mark); (*inī*), f. a whirlpool; N. of the plant Odina Pinnata &c.; (*i*), n., N. of particular Stotras, Lāṭy.

2. **Ā-vṛ́t**, f. turning towards or home, entering, RV.; turn of path or way, course, process, direction, AV.; VS.; TS.; ŚBr.; progress of an action, occurrence, a series of actions, ŚBr.; AitBr. &c.; doing an act without speaking or silently (cf. *agnihotrā́vṛit*), ŚBr.; KātyŚr.; ĀśvŚr. &c.; order, method, ŚBr. **-vat**, mfn. turning or turned towards, RV. viii, 45, 36.

Ā-vṛitta, mfn. turned round, stirred, whirled; reverted, averted; retreated, fled; (*am*), n. addressing a prayer or songs to a god.

Ā-vṛ́tti, *is*, f. turning towards, entering, turning back or from, reversion, retreat, flight; recurrence to the same point, TS.; ŚBr.; Bhag.; Kathās. &c.; repetition, KātyŚr.; repetition (as a figure of rhetoric), Kāvyād.; turn of a way, course, direction; occurrence; revolving, going round, ŚBr.; KātyŚr. &c.; worldly existence, the revolution of births, Kap.; use, employment, application. **-dīpaka**, n. (in rhetoric) enforcing a statement by repeating it, Kuval.

2. **Ā-vṛitya**, ind. p. having turned, turning towards, &c.

आवृध् *ā-√vṛidh*, Ā. (Subj. 3. pl. *ā́-vardhanta*; pf. *-vāvṛidhe*) P. (pf. 3. pl. *-vāvṛidhus*) to grow up, increase, RV.

Ā-vṛiddha-bālakam, ind. from childhood to old age.

आवृष् *ā-√vṛish*, P. (pf. *-vavarsha*) to pour over; to cover (with arrows), MBh. iv, 1688: Ā. *-varshate*, to pour in for one's self, RV.

Ā-varsha, *as*, m. pouring, raining.

Ā-vṛishṭi, *is*, f. id. (both only in comp. with *nis*).

आवृह् *ā-√vṛih*, P. *-vṛihati*, to pull or tear out or off; to eradicate.

Ā-varhá, *as*, m. tearing out or off, cutting out, AV. iii, 9, 2; (*as*), m. tearing out, L.

Ā-varham, ind. p. tearing up, Kāṭh.

Ā-varhita, mfn. eradicated, plucked up by the roots, L.

Āvarhin, mfn. fit to be torn out, L.

आवे 1. *ā-√ve*, P. *-vayati*, to weave on to; to interweave, string; to sew loosely, AV.; TBr.; ŚBr.; KātyŚr. &c.

Ōta (*ā-uta*), mfn. interwoven, BhP.; MuṇḍUp. **-prōta**, mfn. sewn lengthwise and crosswise, MBh. v, 1789.

आवे 2. *ā́ve* (*ā-ava-√i*), P. (3. pl. *ā́va-yanti*, RV. v, 41, 13) to rush down upon (acc.)

आवेग *ā-vega*, *as*, m. (*√vij*), hurry or haste produced by excitement; flurry, agitation, Śak.; Mṛicch.; Kathās.; Kirāt. &c.; (*ī*), f., N. of the plant Argyreia Speciosa, L.

आवेणिक *āveṇika*, mf(*ī*)n. (fr. *a-veṇi*), not connected with anything else, independent, Buddh.

आवेदक *ā-vedaka*, &c. See *ā-√1. vid*.

आवेध *ā-vedha*, &c. See *ā-√vyadh*.

आवेश *ā-veśa*, &c. See *ā-√viś*.

आवेष्ट् *ā-√vesht*, Ā. *-veshṭate*, to spread over, ŚBr.: Caus. *-veshṭayati*, to envelop, cover, ŚBr.; Suśr.; to keep together; to close (the hand), MBh.: Pass. *-veshṭyate*, to be twisted (as a rope), Hit.

Ā́-vishṭita (p. p. from an earlier form of the root), mfn. enveloped, surrounded, covered, RV. x, 51, 1; AV. v, 18, 3 & 28, 1; TS. iii, 4, 1, 4.

Ā-veshṭa, *as*, m. surrounding, covering with (clothes); to strangle, throttle, Yājñ. ii, 217.

Ā-veshṭaka, *as*, m. a snare, Comm. on KātyŚr. vi, 5, 19: a wall, fence; an enclosure, L.

Ā-veshṭana, *am*, n. wrapping round; binding, tying; a wrapper, bandage, envelope, enclosure, Kauś.; Pañcat.

Ā-veshṭita, mfn. surrounded, enveloped, &c.

Ā-veshṭya, ind. p. having surrounded &c.

आव्य *āvyá*, mf(*āvī*)n. (fr. *avi*), belonging to sheep, TS.; woollen, ĀśvGṛ.

Āvī-sūtra, *am*, n. a woollen thread, Āp.; HirGṛ.

आव्यक्तिक *āvyaktika* (fr. *a-vyakta*), mfn. not perceivable, immaterial, Comm. on Nyāyas.

आव्यञ्ज् *ā-vy-√añj*.

Ā-vy-akta, mfn. quite clear or intelligible, R. vii, 88, 20.

आव्यध् *ā-√vyadh*, P. *-vidhyati*, to throw in, fling away, ŚBr.; KātyŚr.; to drive or scare away; to push away or out, R.; MārkP.; to shoot at, wound, TS.; ŚBr.; Lāṭy. &c.; to hit, pierce, break; to pin on, R.; Ragh. &c.; to swing, MBh.; BhP.; Hariv. &c.; to stir up, excite, agitate, BhP.

Ā́-viddha, mfn. cast, thrown, sent, Mn.; pierced, wounded, TS.; Ragh.; swung, whirled, Suśr.; disappointed, L.; crooked; false, fallacious, L.; stupid, foolish, L.; (*am*), n. swinging; a particular manner of fencing, Hariv. **-karṇa**, mfn. having the ears pierced; (*ī*), f., N. of a plant, L.

Ā-vidha, *as*, m. an awl, a drill; a kind of gimlet worked by a string, L.

Ā-vidhya, ind. p. having pierced &c.

Ā-vedha, *as*, m. swinging, shaking, MBh.

Ā-vedhya, mfn. to be pierced or pinned on; to be put on.

Ā-vyādhá, *as*, m. the act of piercing or making an incision; breaking into for the first time, TBr.

Āvyādhin, mfn. shooting, attacking, wounding, VS.; ŚBr.; (*inyas*), f. pl. a band of robbers, MaitrS.

आव्यात्त *ā-vyātta* (*√1. dā*), mfn. a little open, VarBṛS.

आव्युषम् *ā-vyusham*, ind. till the dawn, AV. iv, 5, 7.

आव्ये *ā-√vye*, P. (Pot. 1. sg. *ā-vyayeyam*, RV. ii, 29, 6; aor. 2. pl. *-ávyata*, RV. i, 166, 4) Ā. (aor. 3. sg. *-avyata*, RV. ix, 101, 14; 107, 13) to cover or hide one's self; to take refuge.

Ā-vīta, mfn. covered, invested (especially with the sacred thread).

Āvītin, *ī*, m. (a Brāhman) who has the sacred thread on (in the usual manner over the left shoulder and under the right arm, cf. *prācīnā́vītin*), ŚBr.; KātyŚr.; ĀśvGṛ.; ŚāṅkhGṛ. &c.

आव्रज् *ā-√vraj*, P. *-vrajati*, to come near, proceed to, ŚBr.; Lāṭy.; Mn.; Yājñ.; MBh. &c.; to come back or home, return, R.; BhP.; Suśr.; MBh. &c.

Ā-vrajita, mfn. come near, come home.

आव्रश्च् *ā-√vraśc*, P. *-vṛiścati*, to tear off, cut off; to separate, remove, ŚBr.; Kāṭh.; TBr.: Ā. *-vṛiścate*, AV. xii, 4, 6, &c. (aor. 1. sg. *-vṛikshi*, RV. i, 27, 13; TS.; ŚāṅkhŚr.) to cut off, take away: Pass. *-vṛiścyate*, to be torn or cut off, RV.; AV.; TBr.

Ā-vráścana, *am*, n. the stump of a tree, TS.; ŚBr.; KātyŚr.; Nyāyam.

Ā-vraska, *as*, m. (cf. *an°*), the being torn off or dropping down.

आव्रीडक *āvrīḍaka*, mfn. (fr. *a-vrīḍa*, gaṇa *rājanyâdi*, Pāṇ. iv, 2, 53), inhabited by shameless people.

आश् *âś* (*ā-√1. aś*), P. (aor. 3. sg. *-ānaṭ*, RV. i, 71, 8) to reach, obtain.

1. **Āśa**, *as*, m. (*√1. aś*), reaching, obtaining; (cf. *dur°*.)

Āśiná, mfn. aged (having reached old age), RV. i, 27, 13 [eating, T.]

आश 2. *āśa*, *as*, m. (*√2. aś*), food; eating, ŚBr.; KātyŚr. &c.; (cf. *prātar-āśa*, *sāyam-āśa*, &c.; *hutâśa*, *āśrayâśa*, &c.)

Āśaka, mfn. eating; (cf. *an°*.)

Āśayitṛi (fr. the Caus. of *√2. aś*), mfn. feeding; protecting; (*tā*), m. a feeder, protector.

1. **Āśi**, *is*, f. eating, Kauś.

Ā́śita, mfn. (p. p. of the Caus. of *√2. aś*) fed, boarded, satiated, RV.; KātyŚr.; HirGṛ.; R. &c.; given to eat (as food); (*am*), n. food, RV. **-°ṃ-gavīna**, mfn. (a meadow &c.) where cattle have been fed, Pāṇ. v, 4, 7. **-°ṃ-bhava**, mfn. (rice &c.) by which one can be fed, satiating, Pāṇ. iii, 2, 45; (*am*), n. and (*as*), m. satiety, L.

Āśitimán, *ā*, m. satiety, TS. vii, 1, 17, 1.

Āśitri, mfn. eating greedily, voracious, gluttonous, L.

Āśin, mfn. ifc. eating, consuming.

1. **Āśira**, *as*, m. (Uṇ. i, 53) fire; a Rākshasa; (mfn.) eating, voracious, L.; (for 2. *āśira* see *āśír*.)

आशंस् *ā-√śaṅs*, P. *-śaṇsati* (aor. 1. sg. *-śaṇsisham*, RV. x, 44, 5), Ā. *-śaṇsate*, to hope for, expect; to wish to attain, desire; to suspect, fear, RV.; AV.; AitBr.; ĀśvGṛ.; R.; MBh.; Kathās.; Śak.; BhP.; Mn. &c.; to ask, MBh.; BhP.; to praise, extol, BhP.; to tell, speak, recite; to announce, Śak.; Kum.; BhP.; Daś.: Caus. (Impv. *ā́-śaṇsaya*, RV. i, 29, 1 & [with Wh. and Ro.] AV. xix, 64, 4) to excite, hope for.

Ā-śaṇsana, *am*, n. wishing for another, wishing, Sāh.

Ā-śaṇsā, f. hope, expectation, desire, wish, Pāṇ.; Ragh.; Vikr.; Sāh.

Ā-śaṇsita, mfn. hoped, expected; suspected, feared; told, announced, R.; Kir.; BhP.; Ragh.

Ā-śaṇsitṛi, mfn. one who wishes or expects, L.; (*tā*), m. one who announces, an announcer.

Ā-śaṇsin, mfn. ifc. announcing, promising, R.; Śak.; ĀśvGṛ.

Ā-śaṇsu, mfn. wishing, hoping, desiring, Pāṇ.; Kauś.; Bhaṭṭ.

Ā-śás, f. (earlier form for 1. *āśā́*) wish, desire, hope (praise [Sāy.]), RV.; AV. vii, 57, 1.

Ā-śasta. See *an-ā°*.

1. **Ā-śā́**, f. wish, desire, hope, expectation, prospect, AV.; ŚBr.; ChUp.; R.; Śak.; Kathās.; Pañcat. &c.; Hope personified as the wife of a Vasu, Hariv.; as the daughter-in-law of Manas, Prab.; (for 2. *āśā* see s. v.) **-kṛita**, mfn. 'formed into expectation,' attended with the expectation (of being gratified) or with hope of success, R. **-°nvita** (*āśânvita*), mfn. having hope. **-piśācikā**, f. fallacious hopes, Pañcat. **-prāpta**, mfn. successful, possessing the object hoped for. **-bandha**, m. band of hope, confidence, trust, expectation; a spider's web, Megh. 10. **-bhaṅga**, m. disappointment. **-vat**, mfn. hoping, having hope, trusting, Hit.; Mn.; Suśr. **-vaha**, m. bringing hope; N. of the sun, MBh.; of a Vṛishṇi, MBh. **-vibhinna**, mfn. disappointed in expectation. **-hīna**, mfn. one who has lost all hope, desponding, despairing.

आशक् *ā-√śak*, P. (only RV.; aor. Subj. *ā́-śakat*, viii, 32, 12; pf. 3. pl. *ā́-śekus*, x, 88, 17, &c.) to stimulate; to bring near, invite; to aid, help; to give a share of, let partake: Desid. Ā. *-śikshate*, to let partake; to give, bestow, confer, RV. & TBr.

Ā-śakta, mfn. very powerful or mighty, able, L.

Ā-śakti, *is*, f. might, power, ability, L.

Ā-śikshā́, f. desire of learning, VS. xxx, 10.

आशङ्क् *ā-√śaṅk*, Ā. *-śaṅkate* (seldom P. *-śaṅkati*) to suspect, fear, doubt, hesitate, MBh.; R.; Kathās.; Hit. &c.; to expect, suppose, conjecture, think, imagine, Ragh.; Kathās.; Pañcat. &c.; (in grammatical and philosophical discussions) to object, state a possible objection; to mistrust, Bhaṭṭ.

Ā-śaṅkanīya, mfn. to be suspected or doubted; to be feared, Vedântas.; questionable.

Ā-śaṅkā, f. fear, apprehension; doubt, uncertainty; distrust, suspicion; danger; objection, Kathās.; R.; Śiś. &c. (often ifc., e. g. *vigatâśaṅka*, mfn. 'fearless; doubtless;' *baddhâśaṅka*, mfn. 'filled with anxiety'); (*am*), n. (as the last word of a Tatpurusha compound, Pāṇ. vi, 2, 21, e. g. *vacanâśaṅkam*, 'fear of speaking,' &c.) **Āśaṅkânvita**, mfn. apprehensive, doubting; uncertain; afraid.

Ā-śaṅkita, mfn. feared, dreaded; doubted &c.

Ā-śaṅkitavya, mfn. = *ā-śaṅkanīya*, q. v.

Āśaṅkin, mfn. fearing, R.; Ragh.; Prab. &c.; suspecting, Kathās.; imagining to be, thinking, Kād.; doubting, hesitating.

Ā-śaṅkya, ind. p. having suspected &c.

आशद् *ā-√śad*, to go, Vop. on Dhātup. xx, 25.

आशन 1. *āśana*, *as*, m. (fr. *aśani*, gaṇa *pārśvâdi*, Pāṇ. v, 3, 117), a king of the Aśanis.

आशन 2. *āśana* = 2. *asana*, Terminalia Tomentosa, L.

आशय *āśaya*, &c. See 3. *ā-√śī*.

आशर *ā-śara*, *as*, m. (*√śṛī*), fire, L.; a Rākshasa, L.

Ā́-śarīka, *am*, n. rheumatic pains, AV. xix, 34, 10.

आशरीरम् *ā-śarīram*, ind. to or as far as the body, (all things) including the body, Kathās. 90, 18.

आशव *āśava*. See p. 158, col. 1.

आशसन *ā-śásana*, *am*, n. (*√śas*), cutting up (a killed animal), RV.; AV.; ŚBr.

आशा 2. *āśā́*, f. (*√1. aś*; for 1. *āśā́* see *ā-√śaṅs*), space, region, quarter of the heavens, RV.; AV.; TS.; R.; MBh.; Ragh. &c. **-gaja**, m. elephant of the quarter; (one of the supposed four [or eight] mythical elephants which support the world, standing in the quarters [and intermediate points] of the compass), R. **-cakravāla**, n. the whole horizon, Kād. **-dāman**, m., N. of a king. **-°ditya** (*āśâditya*), m., N. of a commentator. **-pati**, m. (Naish.) and **-pālá**, m. guardian or lord of the regions or quarters, AV.; TS.; VS.; ŚBr. &c. **-parā**, f., N. of a goddess. **-pura**, n., N. of a town; *-guggulu* and *-sambhava*, m. a kind of bdellium, L. **-vāsas**, mfn. having the sky's regions as a garment = naked, Bhartṛ. **-vijaya**, m. conquering the world, Kād. **-saṃśita** (*√śi*), mfn. sharpened by the quarters of the sky, AV. x, 5, 29.

आशाढ *āśāḍha* = *āshāḍha*, q. v., L.

आशार *ā-śāra*, *as*, m. (*√śṛi*), shelter, refuge. **Āśārâishin**, mfn. seeking shelter, AV. iv, 15, 6.

आशास् *ā-√śās*, Ā. *-śāste* (aor. 1. pl. *ā́-śiṣhāmahi*, RV. viii, 24, 1) to desire, wish, ask, pray for; to hope, expect, RV.; AV.; TS.; ŚBr.; AitBr.; BhP.; MBh. &c.; to instruct, order, command, Kathās.; Bhaṭṭ.; to subdue, RV. ii, 28, 9 [*ā́-śādhi* = '*anuśishṭān kuru*,' Sāy.]

Ā-śāsana, *am*, n. asking, praying or craving for, Comm. on Nyāyam.

Ā-śāsanīya, mfn. to be wished or craved for, Comm. on Nyāyas.

Ā-śāsya, mfn. to be wished, desirable, Comm. on Kum.; Mālav.; (*am*), n. wish, benediction, Ragh.

1. **Āśis**, *īs*, f. asking for, prayer, wish, RV.; AV.; VS.; TS.; ŚBr. &c.; blessing, benediction; wishing for any other, R.; Ragh.; Kum.; Śak. &c.; a particular medicament; (for 2. *āśis* see s. v.)

1. **Āśī**, f. = 1. *āśis*, L.; (for 2. *āśī* see 2. *āśis*.)

Āśīr- (in comp. for 1. *āśis*). **-ukti**, f. benediction, Prasannar. **-geya**, n. song together with benediction, R. **-grahaṇa**, n. accepting a benediction. **-dā́** and **-dāyā́**, f. fulfilment of a benediction or wish, VS.; TS. **-vacana**, n. a blessing, benediction; *āśīr-vacanâkshepa*, m. a deprecatory benediction [e. g. if a wife wishes 'a happy journey' to her departing husband though deprecating his departure], Kāvyâd. **-vācaka**, mfn. expressing a wish, Comm. on Mn. **-vāda** [*āśīrvāda*, Nir.], m. benediction, MBh.; Pañcat. &c.; *āśīrvādâbhidhāna-vat*, mfn. containing a word which expresses benediction (as a name), Mn. ii, 33.

आशि 2. *ā-√śi*, P. (Impv. *ā́-śiśīhi*) to sharpen [Sāy.], i. e. to make zealous, RV. vii, 16, 6; viii, 21, 8 [to bestow, let partake, BRD.]; (for 1. *āśi* see 2. *āśa*.)

आशिक्षा *ā-śikshā́*. See *ā-√śak*.

आशिखम् *ā-śikham*, ind. as far as the top lock of hair inclusively, Hariv.

आशिञ्ज् *ā-√śiñj*.

Ā-śiñjita, mfn. tinkling (as of the ornaments worn on the hands and feet), Kum.; (*am*), n. tinkling, R.; Viddh.

आशित *āśita*, &c. See 2. *āśa*, col. 1.

आशिन *āśiná*. See *âś*, col. 1.

आशिमन् *āśiman*. See p. 158, col. 1.

आशिर् *āśír*, f. See *ā-√śrī*, p. 158, col. 3.

आशिरःपदम् *ā-śiraḥ-padam*, ind. from the foot up to the head, Kathās.

आशिस् 2. *āśis*, f. a serpent's fang; (for 1. *āśis* see *ā-√śās*.) **Āśīr-visha**, m. a venomous snake, L.

2. **Āśī**, f. = 2. *āśis*, L. **-visha**, m. a kind of venomous snake, BhP.

आशी 3. *ā-√śī*, Ā. (irr. *-śáye* [3. sg.], RV.; AV.: Impv. 3. sg. *ā-śayām*, AV. v, 25, 9; 3. pl. *-śerate*, Vikr.) to lie or rest on or round: P. (impf. 3. pl. *āśayan*) to wish, BhP. ix, 1, 37 [perhaps this form is rather a Nom. from 1. *āśā*?]: Caus. (impf. *ā́śiśayat*) to lay or put upon, R.

Ā-śaya, *as*, m. resting-place, bed; seat, place; an asylum, abode or retreat, ŚBr.; MBh.; Pañcat.; Bhag. &c.; a receptacle; any recipient; any vessel of the body (e. g. *raktâśaya*, 'the receptacle of blood,' i. e. the heart; *āmâśaya*, the stomach &c.), Suśr.; the stomach; the abdomen, Suśr.; the seat of feelings and thoughts, the mind, heart, soul, Yājñ.; R.; Kathās. &c.; thought, meaning, intention, Prab.; Kathās.; Pañcat.; disposition of mind, mode of thinking; (in Yoga phil.) 'stock' or 'the balance of the fruits of previous works, which lie stored up in the mind in the form of mental deposits of merit or demerit, until they ripen in the individual soul's own experience into rank, years, and enjoyment' (Cowell's translation of Sarvad. 168, 16 ff.); the will; pleasure; virtue; vice; fate; fortune; property; a miser, niggard, L.; N. of the plant Artocarpus Integrifolia, L. **Āśayâgni**, m. the fire of digestion, Daś. **Āśayâśa**, m. fire, L.; (v. l. for *āśrayâśa*, q. v.)

Ā-śáyāna, mfn. lying round, surrounding, RV. i, 21, 11, &c. (said of Vṛitra, who surrounds the water = ὠκεανός; see Kaegi, Der Ṛigveda, p. 177, l. 28 ff.)

आशु *āśú*, mfn. (*√1. aś*, Uṇ. i, 1), fast, quick, going quickly, RV.; AV.; ŚBr. &c.; (*us*), m. Ved. the quick one, a horse, RV.; AV.; (*us* or *u*), m. n. rice ripening quickly in the rainy season, ŚBr.; KātyŚr.; L.; (*u*), n., N. of a Sāman; (*u*), ind. quickly, quick, immediately, directly, Suśr.; Megh.; Pañcat. &c.; [cf. Gk. ὠκύς, ὤκιστος; Lat. *acu* in *acupedius*, *ôcissimus*: of the same origin may be the Lat. *aquila* and *accipiter*.] **-kārin**, mfn. doing anything quickly, smart, active, Kād.; (in med.) operating speedily, Suśr.; (*ī*), m. a kind of fever, Bhpr. **-kopin**, mfn. easily provoked, irritable. **-kriyā**, f. quick procedure, Suśr. **-klānta**, mfn. quickly faded, Śak. 71 a. **-gá**, mf(*ā*)n. going or moving quickly, swift, fleet, TBr. i, 2, 1, 26; Mn.; MBh.; R.; (*as*), m. the wind, L.; the sun, L.; an arrow, MBh.; Ragh. &c.; N. of one of the first five followers of Śākya-muni, L. **-gati-tva**, n. the going or moving quickly, Nyāyas. **-gāmin**, mfn. going or moving quickly; (*ī*), m., N. of the sun, MBh. **-°ṃ-ga**, m., N. of an animal, perhaps a bird [BRD.], AV. vi, 14, 3. **-tosha**, mfn. easily pleased or appeased, BhP.; (*as*), m., N. of Śiva. **-tva**, n. quickness. **-pattrī**, f. a tree which yields frankincense, Boswellia Serrata, L. **-pátvan**, m. flying quickly, RV. **-phala**, m. a kind of weapon, L. **-bodha**, m. 'easily understood,' 'teaching quickly,' N. of a grammar. **-bhāvin**, mfn. proceeding quickly, Sāh. **-mat**, mfn. quick; (*át*), ind. quickly, AV. vi, 105, 1; 2; 3. **-ratha**, mfn. possessing a fast chariot, VS. **-rathīya**, n., N. of a Sāman. **-vikrama**, mfn. having a quick step, R. **-vṛitti-tva**, n. the proceeding quickly, Comm. on Nyāyas. **-vrīhi**, m. rice ripening quickly in the rainy season. **–śushka-tva,** n. getting dry quickly, Kām. **–śravas,** m., N. of a mythical horse, Kathās. **–sheṇa,** mfn. having swift arrows, VS.; MaitrS. **–saṃdheya,** mfn. easy to be joined together or reconciled, Hit.; Pañcat. **–heman,** m. urged to fast course, running on quickly; inciting his horses (N. of Agni, especially when regarded as Apām-napāt), RV.; TS. **–heshas,** mfn. having neighing horses; having quick horses or quickly praised [Sāy.]; N. of the Aśvins, RV. viii, 10, 12. **Āśv-āpas,** mfn. acting quickly, RV. **Āśv-aśva,** mfn. possessed of quick horses; N. of the Maruts, RV. (*Āśvāśvya, am,* n. possession of quick horses, RV.)

Āśava, *am,* n. (gaṇa *prithv-ādi,* Pāṇ. v, 1, 122) quickness, rapidity.

Āśiman, *ā,* m. (ib. v, 1, 123), id.

Ā́śishṭha, mfn. (superl.) quickest, very quick, RV.

Ā́śīyas, mfn. (compar.) quicker, very quick, RV.

Āśuyā́, ind. (Ved. instr. of the fem.) quickly, RV. iv, 4, 2; vi, 46, 14.

आशुच् *ā-√śuc,* P. (Impv. *ā́-śuśugdhi,* RV. i, 97, 1) to procure or bestow by shining forth.

Ā-śuśukshaṇi, mfn. gleaming or shining forth or round (said of fire), RV. ii, 1, 1; (*is*), m. fire, Kād.; Bālar.; wind, air, L.

आशुष् *ā-√śush* (*√śush* = *√śvas* [BRD.] = *√1. aś,* Sāy.), Ā. (1. sg. *ā́-śushe,* RV. viii, 93, 16) to strive after [BRD.]; to incite, stimulate [Gmn.]; to reach, obtain [Sāy.]

Ā-śushāṇá, mfn. striving after [BRD.]; inciting, stimulating [Gmn.]; reaching, obtaining [Sāy.], RV.

आशृत *ā-śrita,* mfn. (*√śrā*), slightly cooked, ŚāṅkhŚr. iv, 3, 7.

आशेकुटिन् *āśekuṭin, ī,* m., N. of a mountain, L.

आशोका *āśokā,* f., N. of a woman, (gaṇa *śubhrâdi,* Pāṇ. iv, 1, 123.)

1. **Āśokeya,** mf(*ī*), a descendant of Āśokā, ib.

आशोकेय 2. *āśokeya,* mfn. (fr. *a-śoka,* gaṇa *sakhy-ādi,* Pāṇ. iv, 2, 80), belonging to or coming from the Aśoka tree.

आशौच *āśauca, am,* n. (fr. *a-śuci,* Pāṇ. vii, 3, 30), impurity, Gaut.; Mn.; Yājñ. **–nirṇaya,** m., N. of a work.

Āśaucin, mfn. impure.

आश्चर्य 1. *āścarya,* mfn. (said to be fr. *√car* with *ā* and a sibilant inserted, Pāṇ. vi, 1, 147), appearing rarely, curious, marvellous, astonishing, wonderful, extraordinary, KaṭhUp.; Prab.; Śak.; Ragh.; (*am*), ind. rarely, wonderfully, Nir.; (*am*), n. strange appearance; a wonder, miracle, marvel, prodigy; wonder, surprise, astonishment, R.; Bhag.; Śak. &c. **–tā,** f. or **-tva,** n. wonderfulness, wonder, astonishment. **–bhūta,** mfn. having a marvellous appearance, wonderful, R. **–maya,** mfn. wonderful, marvellous, miraculous, Kathās.; Bhag. **–ratnamālā,** f., N. of a work. **–rūpa,** mfn. being of marvellous appearance, strange, wonderful, NṛisUp.

2. **Āścarya,** Nom. P. *āścaryati,* to be marvellous or strange, L.

आश्चुत् *ā-√ścut* (or *-√ścyut*), Caus. (inf. *-ścotayitavai,* ŚBr. ii, 3, 1, 16) to sprinkle, let drop on.

Ā-ścutita, mfn. trickled, dripped, ŚBr.

Ā-ścotana (or **ā-ścyotana**), *am,* n. aspersion, sprinkling; applying (ghee &c.) to the eyelids, Suśr.

आश्म *āśma,* mfn. (fr. *aśman,* Kāty. on Pāṇ. vi, 6, 144), stony, made of stone.

Āśmana, mfn. stony, Bhaṭṭ.; (*as*), m., N. of Aruṇa (the sun's charioteer), L.

Āśmabhāraka, mf(*ikā*)n. (fr. *aśma-bhāra*), belonging to or burdened with a mass of stones, Pāṇ.

Āśmarathya, *as,* m. (fr. *aśma-ratha*), N. of a teacher, ŚāṅkhŚr.; (*āśma-ratha,* mf(*ī*), a descendant of Āśmarathya, Pāṇ.)

Āśmarika, mfn. (fr. *aśmarī*), suffering from gravel (in the bladder), Suśr.

Āśmāyana, *as,* m. a descendant of Aśman, Pāṇ.

Āśmika, mfn. stony, ib.

Āśmeya, *as,* m. a descendant of Aśman, ib.

आश्यै *ā-√śyai,* Ā. *-śyāyate,* to become dry, dry up, shrink in drying, Ragh.

Ā-śyāna, mfn. dried up, shrunk in drying, Ragh.; Kum.; almost dried or shrunk up, Kād.

आश्रपण *ā-śrapaṇa, am,* n. (*√śrā*), cooking slightly, Nir.

आश्रम *ā-śrama, as, am,* m. n. (*√śram*), a hermitage, the abode of ascetics, the cell of a hermit or of retired saints or sages, Mn.; R.; Daś.; Ragh.; Megh. &c.; a stage in the life of a Brāhman (of which there are four corresponding to four different periods or conditions, viz. 1st, Brahmacārin, 'student of the Veda;' 2nd, Gṛiha-stha, 'householder;' 3rd, Vāna-prastha, 'anchorite;' and 4th, Saṃnyāsin, 'abandoner of all worldly concerns,' or sometimes Bhikshu, 'religious beggar:' in some places the law-givers mention only three such periods of religious life, the first being then omitted), Mn.; R.; Suśr.; Ragh. &c.; a hut built on festal occasions, VarBṛS.; a college, school; a wood or thicket, L.; (*as*), m., N. of a pupil of Pṛithvī-dhara. **–guru,** m. the head of a religious order, a principal preceptor. **–dharma,** m. the special duty of each period of life. **–pada,** n. a hermitage; a period in the life of a Brāhman, R.; Śak.; Vikr. **–parvan,** n. the first section of the fifteenth book of the Mahā-bhārata. **–bhrashṭa,** mfn. fallen or apostatizing from a religious order. **–maṇḍala,** n. a group or assemblage of hermitages, R.; BhP. **–vāsika,** mfn. relating to residence in a hermitage; (*āśramavāsikam parva,* the fifteenth book of the Mahā-bhārata.) **–vāsin** or **-sad,** m. an inhabitant of a hermitage, an ascetic, Śak. **–sthāna,** n. the abode of hermits, a hermitage, R. **Āśramâlaya,** m. an inhabitant of a hermitage, an ascetic, Ragh. **Āśramôpanishad,** f., N. of an Upanishad.

Āśramika or **āśramin,** mfn. belonging to one of the four periods of religious life; belonging to a hermitage, a hermit, anchorite, &c., Mn.; Kathās.

आश्रय *āśraya,* &c. See *ā-√śri.*

आश्रव *ā-śrava.* See *ā-√śru.*

आश्रवस्य *ā-śravasya,* Nom. P. (fr. 2. *śravas*), to approach with haste, hasten towards, RV. v, 37, 3.

आश्रि 1. *ā-√śri,* P. *-śrayati,* to affix; to apply anything, AV. xi, 10, 10: Ā. *-śrayate,* to attach one's self to; to join, MBh.; BhP.; Kathās.; Pañcat. &c.; to adhere, rest on, Mn.; MBh.; to betake one's self to, resort to; to depend on; to choose, prefer; to be subject to, keep in mind; to seek refuge in, enter, inhabit; to refer or appeal to, MBh.; Kathās.; Śak.; Ragh.; Prab.; R. &c.

Ā-śraya, *as,* m. that to which anything is annexed or with which anything is closely connected or on which anything depends or rests, Pāṇ.; R.; Ragh.; Suśr.; a recipient, the person or thing in which any quality or article is inherent or retained or received; seat, resting-place, R.; Kathās.; Suśr. &c.; dwelling, asylum, place of refuge, shelter, R.; Śiś. &c.; depending on, having recourse to; help, assistance, protection, Pañcat.; Ragh. &c.; authority, sanction, warrant; a plea, excuse, L.; the being inclined or addicted to, following, practising; attaching to, choosing, taking; joining, union, attachment; dependance, contiguity, vicinity, RPrāt.; Yājñ.; Mn. &c.; relation; connection; appropriate act or one consistent with the character of the agent; (in Gr.) the subject, that to which the predicate is annexed; (with Buddhists) the five organs of sense with *manas* or mind (the six together being the recipients of the *āśrita* or objects which enter them by way of their *ālambana* or qualities); source, origin; ifc. depending on, resting on, endowed or furnished with (e. g. *ashṭa-guṇâśraya,* see under *ashṭa*). **–tas,** ind. in consequence of the proximity. **–tva,** n. the state of *ā-śraya* above, Suśr.; Comm. on Nyāyam. **–bhuj,** m. fire; see *āśrayâśa.* **–bhūta,** mfn. one who is the refuge or support of another person, protecting, supporting, Hit.; Nyāyam. &c. **–liṅga,** mfn. (a word) the gender of which must agree with the gender of the word to which it refers, an adjective. **–vat,** mfn. having help or support, MBh.; Comm. on Nyāyad. **Āśrayâśa,** m. 'consuming everything with which it comes in contact,' fire, Hit.; Mn. &c.; a forfeiter of an asylum, one who by misconduct &c. loses patronage or protection. **Āśrayâsiddha,** mfn. (an argument) in which the existence of the subject is not established, Tarkas.

Ā-śrayaṇa, mf(*ī*)n. having recourse to, resorting or applying to, seeking refuge or shelter from, Kum.; relating to, concerning, Vikr.; (*am*), n. betaking one's self or applying to; joining, accepting, choosing; refuge, asylum, means of protection or security, ŚvetUp.; TS. &c.

Āśrayaṇīya, mfn. to be applied or resorted to, Hit.; to be followed or practised, Sarvad. **–tva,** n. the state of being a refuge, Ragh. xvii, 60.

Ā-śrayitavya, mfn. to be applied to, Comm. on Nyāyam.

Āśrayin, mfn. joining, attaching one's self to; following, Suśr.; Jaim.; dwelling in, resting on, inhabiting, Ragh.; Śak.; Ratnāv.; Sāh.

Ā-śrita, mfn. attaching one's self to, joining; having recourse to, resorting to as a retreat or asylum, seeking refuge or shelter from; subject to, depending on, MBh.; Kathās.; Rājat.; Kum. &c.; relating or belonging to, concerning, R.; Hariv.; BhP.; MārkP. &c.; inhabiting, dwelling in, resting on, being anywhere, taking one's station at, MBh.; R.; Yājñ.; VarBṛS. &c.; following, practising, observing; using, employing; receiving anything as an inherent or integral part, Mn.; MBh.; BhP.; Kum.; Pañcat. &c.; regarding, respecting, Bhag.; R.; taken or sought as a refuge or shelter, Kathās.; BhP.; Rājat.; inhabited, occupied, Kathās.; Pañcat.; Ragh.; BhP.; chosen, preferred, taken as rule, Kathās.; Rājat.; (*as*), m. a dependant, subject, servant, follower, Kum.; Hit.; Yājñ. &c.; (*am*), n. (with Buddhists) an object perceived by the senses and *manas* or mind. **–tva,** n. dependance.

Ā-śritya, ind. p. having sought or obtained an asylum; having recourse to, employing, practising, &c.

आश्रि 2. *āśri, is,* f. the edge of a sword (= *aśri,* q.v.), L.; (= *ā-aśri,* a very sharp edge, T.)

आश्री *ā-√śrī,* P. (3. pl. *-śriṇanti,* RV. ix, 71, 4) Ā. (impf. *ā́śrīṇīta,* RV. x, 61, 3) to mix, shuffle; to boil.

Ā-śir, f. mixing, a mixture; especially the milk which is mixed with the Soma juice to purify it, RV.; AV.; TS.; KātyŚr. &c. **Āśír-vat,** mfn. mixed with milk (as the Soma), RV.; KātyŚr.

2. **Āśira** (= *āśir*), n. (?) the milk mixed with the Soma. **–dugh,** mfn. milking for a mixture with Soma, ĀśvŚr.

आश्रु *ā-√śru,* P. *-śriṇoti,* Ā. *-śriṇute,* to listen to; to hear; to perceive (with the ear), RV.; AV.; TS.; ŚBr.; BhP. &c.; to accept, promise, Pāṇ. i, 4, 40; R.; Yājñ.; L.: Caus. *-śrāvayati* [but *ā-śravayatam,* RV. vii, 62, 5; aor. *-aśuśravus,* RV. x, 94, 12], to cause to hear; to announce, make known, tell, RV.; ĀśvŚr.; MBh.; to address, speak to, call to (especially at particular rites), RV.; AV.; TS.; ŚBr.; ChUp.; TUp.; KātyŚr. &c.: Desid. *-śuśrūshati* [only P., Pāṇ. i, 3, 59], to wish to hear; to listen.

1. **Ā-śrava,** mfn. listening to, obedient, compliant, Ragh.; Daś.; L.; (*as*), m. promise, engagement, L.

Ā-śrāvaṇa, *am,* n. causing to listen, calling out (especially with the words *om, svadhā,* &c.), ŚBr.

Ā-śrāvya, *as,* m., N. of a Muni, MBh.

Ā-śrut, mfn. listening. **–karṇa,** mfn. having listening ears, listening attentively, RV. i, 10, 9.

Ā́-śruta, mfn. listened to, heard; audible, TS.; promised, agreed, Yājñ.; (*am*), n. a calling (at rites, see *ā-śrāvaṇa*), KātyŚr.; TS.

Ā́-śruti, *is,* f. hearing, range of hearing, VS.; promising, L.

आश्रेष *ā-śresha* (*√śrish* = *√ślish,* see below), one who embraces; N. of an evil spirit or goblin, AV. viii, 6, 2; (*ā*), f. = *āśleshā,* q. v., TBr.

आश्लथ *ā-√ślath,* Ā. *-ślathate,* to become loose, BhP. v, 5, 9.

आश्लिष् *ā-√ślish* (cf. *ā-śresha* above), P. *-ślishyati* (but also *-ślishati,* BhP.; R.) and Ā. *-ślishyate* (MBh. i, 3040) to adhere or cling to, TS.;

MBh.; to embrace, Mn.; MBh.; BhP.; Śak.; R.; Pañcat.; Kathās. &c.: Caus. *-śleshayati*, to affix, stick on, Lāṭy.; KātyŚr.; to embrace (see *ā-śleshita*).

Ā-ślishṭa, mfn. adhering, clung to, ŚBr.; Kathās.; embracing, Hariv.; R.; Śiś.; embraced, surrounded; twisted round, MBh.; Kathās.; Ragh. &c.

Ā-ślesha, *as*, m. intimate connection, contact; slight contact, L.; embracing, embrace; intwining, MBh.; BhP.; Megh.; Amar. &c.; adherence, clinging to, Nyāyam.; (*ā́*), f. and (*ā́s*), f. pl., N. of the seventh Nakshatra, AV.; TS.; Suśr.; MBh.; VarBṛS.

Ā-śleshaṇa, *am*, n. adherence, hanging on, Nyāyam.

Ā-śleshita, mfn. embraced, R. v, 13, 58.

आश्व *āśva*, mf(ī)n. (fr. *aśva*), belonging to a horse, equestrian, Nir.; Suśr.; drawn by horses (as a chariot), Comm. on Pāṇ.; (*am*), n. a number of horses, Pāṇ.; the state or action of a horse, Comm. on Pāṇ.; N. of several Sāmans.

Āśvaghná, m. (fr. *aśva-ghna*), N. of a man, RV. x, 61, 22.

Āśvatara, m. (fr. *aśva-tara*), N. of Buḍila or Bulila, AitBr. *Āśvatarâśvi*, m. id., ŚBr.; ChUp.

Āśvattha (or °tthi or °tthika), mf(*ī́*, gaṇa *gaurâdi*, Pāṇ. iv, 1, 41) n. belonging to the Aśvattha tree (Ficus Religiosa), AitBr.; TS.; KātyŚr.; ŚBr. &c.; relating to the fruit-bearing season of this tree, Comm. on Pāṇ.; belonging to the Nakshatra Aśvattha, L.; (*am*), n. the fruit of the Ficus Religiosa, Pāṇ. & L.

Āśvapata, mfn. belonging to Aśva-pati, Pāṇ.

Āśvapālika, m. f. a descendant of Aśva-pāli, Pāṇ.

Āśvapeyin or °pejin, m. followers or pupils of Aśva-pey(j)in, Pāṇ.

Āśvabala, mf(ī)n. coming from or made of the plant Aśva-balā, Suśr.

Āśvabhārika, mfn. (fr. *aśva-bhāra*), carrying a horse-load, Pāṇ.

Āśvamedhá, m. a descendant of Aśva-medha, RV. viii, 68, 15 & 16.

Āśvamedhika, mfn. (fr. id.), belonging to a horse-sacrifice, ŚBr.; KātyŚr.; Āp.; (*āśva-medhikam parva* is the N. of the fourteenth book of the Mahā-bhārata.)

Āśvayuj, m. (fr. *aśva-yuj*), the month Āśvinā, MBh.

Āśvayuja, mf(ī)n. (fr. id.), born under the constellation Aśvayuj, Pāṇ. iv, 3, 36; belonging to or occurring in the month Āśvina, VarBṛS.; (*as*), m. the month Āśvina, Suśr.; Mn.; (*ī*), f. (sc. *paurṇamāsī*) day of full moon in that month, ĀśvGṛ.; PārGṛ.; KātyŚr. **—karman** (*āśva-yujī-*), n. a Pākayajña or 'small sacrifice' [see Indian Wisdom, p. 197, note] to be performed on the day called Āśvayujī, ĀśvGṛ.; ŚāṅkhGṛ.; Gaut.

Āśvayujaka, mfn. sown on the day called Āśvayujī, Pāṇ. iv, 3, 45.

Āśvaratha, mfn. (fr. *aśva-ratha*), belonging to a chariot drawn by horses, Comm. on Pāṇ.

Āśvalakshaṇika, mfn. (fr. *aśva-lakshaṇa*), knowing the marks of horses, Comm. on Pāṇ.

Āśvavāra and °**vāla,** mfn. made of the cane Aśva-vār(l)a, ŚBr.; KātyŚr.; MaitrS.

Āśvasūkta, n., N. of a Sāman, = *aśva-*°, q. v.

Āśvasūkti, m. a descendant of Aśva-sūktin, TāṇḍyaBr.

Āśvāyana, *as*, m. a descendant of Aśva, Pāṇ. iv, 1, 110.

Āśvika, mfn. equestrian; relating to a horse; carrying a load of horses, Pāṇ.

1. **Āśvina,** mf(ī)n. like riders or horsemen, RV. ix, 86, 4; (*am*), n. a day's journey for a horseman, AV. vi, 131, 3.

2. **Āśviná,** mfn. (fr. *aśvin*), belonging or devoted to the Aśvins, VS.; TS.; ŚBr.; KātyŚr.; ĀśvŚr.; (*as*), m., N. of a month in the rainy season (during which the moon is near to the constellation Aśvinī); (*ī*), f., N. of a kind of brick (*ishṭakā*), ŚBr.; KātyŚr.; (*am*), n. the Nakshatra Aśvinī, VarBṛS. **—cihnita,** n. the autumnal equinox, L. **—pātrá,** n. the vessel belonging to the Aśvins, ŚBr. iv, 1, 5, 19.

Āśvineya, *as*, m. (fr. *aśvin*), N. of Nakula; of Saha-deva, MBh.; (fr. *aśvinī*), N. of either of the two Aśvins, Naish.

Āśvīna, mfn. as much as can be passed over by a horse in one day (as a way or road), Pāṇ. v, 2, 19; (*am*), n. a day's journey for a horse, AitBr.; TāṇḍyaBr.

Āśveya, *as*, m. (gaṇa *śubhrâdi*, Pāṇ. iv, 1, 123), a descendant of Aśva.

आश्वपस् *āśv-apas*, &c. See under *āśu*.

आश्वलायन *āśvalāyana*, *as*, m. (fr. *aśvala*, gaṇa *naḍâdi*, Pāṇ. iv, 1, 99), N. of a pupil of Śaunaka's, author of Sūtra or ritual works (relating to the Ṛig-veda) and founder of a Vedic school; (mf(ī)n.) relating or belonging to Āśvalāyana; (*ās*), m. the school of Āśvalāyana. **—gṛihya-kārikā,** f. and **-brāhmaṇa,** n., N. of works. **—śākhā,** f. the school of Āśvalāyana. (*Āśvalāyanaśākhin*, mfn. belonging to the school of Āśvalāyana.)

आश्वस् *ā-√śvas*, P. *-śvasiti* and *-śvasati* (Impv. 2. sg. *-śvasihi* and *-śvasa* [MBh. vi, 490]; impf. *-aśvasīt* [Bhaṭṭ.] and *-aśvasat* [Kathās. xxxiii, 129]), Ā. *-śvasate*, to breathe, breathe again or freely; to take or recover breath, take heart or courage; to revive, MBh.; R.; Kathās.; BhP. &c.: Caus. *-śvāsayati*, to cause to take breath; to encourage, comfort; to calm, console, cheer up, MBh.; Suśr.; Ragh.; Kum. &c.

Ā-śvasya, ind. p. taking heart or confidence, MBh.

Ā-śvāsa, *as*, m. breathing again or freely, taking breath; recovery, Suśr.; cheering up, consolation; relying on, Kathās.; a chapter or section of a book, Sāh.

Ā-śvāsaka, mfn. causing to take breath or courage, consolatory, comforting, L.

Ā-śvāsana, *am*, n. causing to revive, refreshing, reviving; consoling, encouraging, cheering up, MBh.; R.; Pañcat.; Kathās.; refreshment, recreation, consolation, comfort, Bālar.; Veṇīs. &c.

Ā-śvāsanīya, mfn. to be refreshed or cheered up, Uttarar.

Ā-śvāsita, mfn. encouraged, animated, comforted, consoled, Daś.; BhP.; Pañcat. &c.

Āśvāsin, mfn. breathing freely, reviving, becoming cheerful, Śak. 35 a.

Ā-śvāsya, mfn. to be acquiesced in, Megh.

आषाढ *āshāḍha*, *as*, m. (fr. *a-shāḍhā*), N. of a month (corresponding to part of June and July) in which the full moon is near the constellation Ashāḍhā, Suśr.; VarBṛS.; Megh.; Kathās. &c.; a staff of the wood of the Palāśa (carried by an ascetic during certain religious observances in the month Āshāḍha), Pāṇ. v, 1, 110; Kum. &c.; N. of a prince, MBh.; the Malaya mountain, L.; a festival (of Indra), Āp. i, 11, 20; (*ā*), f. (for *a-shāḍhā*, q. v.) the twenty-first and twenty-second lunar mansions (commonly compounded with *pūrva* and *uttara*), L.; (*ī*), f. the day of full moon in the month Āshāḍha, KātyŚr.; Vait.; (mfn.) belonging to the month Āshāḍha, VarBṛS. **—pura,** n., N. of a mythical mountain, Kathās. **—bhava,** mfn. produced in the month Ashāḍha; (*as*), m. the planet Mars, L. **—bhūti,** m., N. of a man, Pañcat. **Āshāḍhâdri-pura,** n., N. of a mythical mountain, Kathās. **Āshāḍhābhū,** m. produced in the month Āshāḍha; the planet Mars, L.

Āshāḍhaka, *as*, m. the month Āshāḍha, L.; N. of a man, Kathās.; (*ikā*), f., N. of a Rākshasī, R.

Āshāḍhi, *is*, m. a descendant of Ashāḍha, ŚBr.

Āshāḍhīya, mfn. born under the constellation Ashāḍhā, Kāty. on Pāṇ. iv, 3, 34.

आष्टक *āshṭaka*, *am*, n., N. of a district, Pat. on Kāty. Vārt. 31 on Pāṇ. iv, 2, 104.

Āshṭakīya, mfn. belonging to or coming from the above country, ib.

आष्टम *āshṭama*, *as*, m. (fr. *ashṭama*), the eighth part, Pāṇ.

Āshṭamika, mfn. taught in the eighth (book of Pāṇini), Pat.

आष्ट्र *āshṭra*, *am*, n. (fr. √1. *aś*, Uṇ. iv, 159), ether, sky, atmosphere; (*ā*), f. a prick or goad for driving cattle (= *ashṭrā*, q. v.), Kāṭh.; (*ī*), f. an extensive forest [Sāy.], RV. x, 165, 3.

आष्ठा *āshṭhā*, f. region, quarter, L.

आस् 1. *ās*, ind. (an interjection implying joy, anger, menace, pain, affliction, recollection) Ah! Oh! &c.

आस् 2. *ās*, cl. 2. Ā. *āste* (and *āsate*, AV. xi, 8, 32, &c.; Impv. 2. sg. *ās-sva*, *āsva*, and *āsasva*; 2. pl. *ādhvam*; p. *āsāná*, *āsat* [R.], and *āsīna* [see below]; *āsām-cakre* [Pāṇ. iii, 1, 87]; *āsishyate*; *āsishṭa*; *āsitum*) to sit, sit down, rest, lie, RV.; AV.; ŚBr.; Mn.; MBh.; Śak. &c.; to be present; to exist; to inhabit, dwell in; to make one's abode in, RV.; AV.; VS.; MBh. &c.; to sit quietly, abide, remain, continue, RV.; AV. &c.; to cease, have an end, Pañcat.; Daś.; Hit. &c.; to solemnize, celebrate; to do anything without interruption; to continue doing anything; to continue in any situation; to last; (it is used in the sense of 'continuing,' with a participle, adj., or subst., e. g. *etat sāma gāyann āste*, 'he continues singing this verse;' with an indeclinable participle in *tvā*, *ya*, or *am*, e. g. *uparudhya arim āsīta*, 'he should continue blockading the foe;' with an adverb, e. g. *tūshṇīm āste*, 'he continues quiet;' *sukham āsva*, 'continue well;' with an inst. case, e. g. *sukhenâste*, 'he continues well;' with a dat. case, e. g. *āstām tushṭaye*, 'may it be to your satisfaction'): Caus. *āsayati*, to cause any one to sit down, Comm. on Pāṇ.: Desid. Ā. *āsisishate*, ib.; [cf. Gk. ἧ(σ)-μαι, ἧσ-ται: Lat. *āsa* changed to *āra*; *â-nus* for *âs-nus*.]

1. **Āsa,** *as*, m. seat (in *sv-āsa-sthá*, q. v.), RV.; TS.; ŚBr. &c.; the lower part of the body behind, posteriors, ChUp.

1. **Āsana** (but *āsaná*, ŚBr.), *am*, n. sitting, sitting down, KātyŚr.; Mn.; sitting in peculiar posture according to the custom of devotees, (five or, in other places, even eighty-four postures are enumerated; see *padmâsana*, *bhadrâsana*, *vajrâsana*, *vīrâsana*, *svastikâsana*: the manner of sitting forming part of the eightfold observances of ascetics); halting, stopping, encamping; abiding, dwelling, AV. xx, 127, 8; Mn.; Yājñ.; Hit. &c.; seat, place, stool, KātyŚr.; ŚBr. xiv; Kum.; Mn. &c.; the withers of an elephant, the part where the driver sits, L.; maintaining a post against an enemy; (*ā*), f. stay, abiding, L.; (*ī*), f. stay, abiding, sitting, L.; a shop, a stall, L.; a small seat, a stool, Kauś. **—bandha,** m. the act of sitting down, Ragh. ii, 6. **—mantra,** m. a Mantra or sacred formula to be spoken at taking a seat, T. **—vidhi,** m. the ceremony of offering a seat to a visitor. **—stha,** mfn. abiding on a seat, sitting, Mn.; Ratnāv. **—°ī-√1. kṛi,** to make a seat of anything (e. g. of a lotus), Kād.

Āsikā, f. turn or order of sitting, Comm. on Pāṇ.; sitting, ib.

Āsita, mfn. seated, being at rest; one who has sat down, one who is seated or dwells, Kathās.; R. &c.; (*am*), n. sitting, sitting down, Sāh.; MBh.; a seat; a place where one has lived, an abode, R.; way or manner of sitting (cf. *dur-*°); N. of several Sāmans.

Āsitavya, only *am*, n. (used impersonally) to be seated, BhP.

Āsīna, mfn. sitting, seated. **—pracalāyita,** n. nodding when seated, falling asleep on a seat, Rājat.

Āsyā, f. sitting, Suśr.; abiding, abode; state of rest, L.

आस् 3. *ās* (*ā-√2. as*), P. *āsyati*, to throw upon, lay or put upon, TBr.; Kāṭh.: Ā. (Impv. 2. pl. *āsyadhvam*) to cause to flow in, pour in, RV. x, 30, 2; ŚBr. i; to put or throw on for one's self, MaitrS.

आस् 4. *ās*, n. (?) mouth, face, (only in abl. & instr.) *āsás* (with the prep. *ā*), from mouth to mouth, in close proximity, RV. vii, 99, 7; *āsā́* and *āsayā́* (generally used as an adv.), before one's eyes; by word of mouth; personally; present; in one's own person; immediately, RV. vi, 16, 9, &c. **—pātra,** n. a vessel fit for the mouth, a drinking vessel, ŚBr.

1. **Āsán,** n. (defective, Pāṇ. vi, 1, 63), mouth, jaws, RV.; AV.; VS.; ŚBr.; TBr. **—ishu** (*āsánn-*), mfn. having arrows in the mouth, RV. i, 84, 16. **—vát,** mfn. having a mouth (?); showing the mouth; present, AV. vi, 12, 2.

Āsanyà, mfn. being in the mouth, ŚBr. xiv, 4, 1, 8.

Āsyà, *am*, n. [ifc. mf(*ā*)n.] mouth, jaws, RV.; AV.; VS.; MBh. &c.; face, Yājñ.; (mfn.) belonging to the mouth or face, belonging to that part of the mouth which is the organ of uttering sounds or letters, Pāṇ.; Siddh.; Kāś. &c. **-daghna,** mfn. reaching to the mouth, Kāṭh. -°**m-dhaya,** mf(*ī*)n. sucking the mouth, kissing the mouth. **-pattra,** n. 'leaf-faced,' lotus, L. **-modaka,** n. a mythical weapon, MBh. v, 3491. **-lāṅgala,** m. 'having a plough-like face;' a hog, boar, L. **-loman,** n. the hair of the face, beard, L. **-sravaṇa,** n. watering the mouth, Car. **Āsyâsava,** m. spittle, saliva, L. **Āsyâsukha,** mfn. disagreeable to the mouth, tasting ill, Car. **Āsyôpalepa,** m. obstruction of the mouth by phlegm, Suśr.

आस 2. *ā́sa, as,* m. (√2. *as*), ashes, dust, AV. ix, 8, 10; ŚBr.; (*am*), n. a bow, L.

2. **Āsana** = 2. *asana,* Terminalia Tomentosa.

आसंसारम् *ā-saṃsāram,* ind. (√*sṛi*), from the beginning of the world, ever, Kathās.; Bhartṛ.; Kāvyād.; till the end of the world, for ever, Rājat.

आसंगत्य *āsaṃgatya, am,* n. (fr. *a-saṃgata,* Pāṇ. v, 1, 121), non-union, non-relation.

आसंग्रह् *ā-sam-√grah* (Impv. 2. sg. *-sáṃgribhāya,* RV. viii, 81, 1) to seize.

आसच् *ā-√sac,* Ā. *-sacate,* to seek for, RV. i, 136, 3, &c.

आसञ्ज् *ā-√sañj,* P. *-sajati,* to fasten on, attach, fix; to fasten on one's self, put on (as dress, armour, &c.), RV.; AV.; KātyŚr.; R.; Kum. &c.; to fix one's self to, adhere to, Kir. xiii, 44; to take up, MBh. &c.; to take hold of, cling to, AV.; MBh.; ŚBr.; BhP. &c.: Caus. *-sañjayati,* to cause to attach or put or fix on, ŚāṅkhŚr.; Ragh.; to employ, MBh.: Pass. *-sajyate,* to adhere, cohere, be attached: Desid. *-sisaṅkshati,* to wish to attach, ŚBr. i, 6, 1, 12; 15.

Ā-sakta, mfn. fixed or fastened to; attached to, lying on or upon, ŚBr.; Kum.; R.; Kathās. &c.; attached strongly to, intent on; zealously following or pursuing, MBh.; VarBṛ.; Kathās.; Pañcat. &c.; wound round, encircled; accompanied or furnished with, following directly, immediately proceeding from (acc.), MBh. **-citta, -cetas,** and **-manas,** mfn. having the mind deeply engaged in or fixed upon (any object), intent on, devoted to, absorbed in. **-bhāva,** mfn. having one's affection fixed on, being in love with, Daś.

Ā-sakti, *is,* f. the act of adhering or attaching one's self firmly behind; placing behind; waylaying, RV.; devotedness, attachment; diligence, application; (*i*), ind. uninterruptedly, wholly, throughout, ŚBr.

Ā-saṅgá, *as,* m. the act of clinging to or hooking on, association, connection, Śak.; Kum.; BhP. &c.; attachment, devotedness, Sāh.; Kathās. &c.; waylaying, RV.; ŚBr.; N. of a man, RV. viii, 1, 32; 33; of a son of Śva-phalka, BhP. ix, 24, 15; (*am*), n. a kind of fragrant earth, L.; (mfn.) uninterrupted, L.; (*am*), ind. uninterruptedly, L.

Āsaṅgin, mfn. clinging to, attached, Kād.; (*inī*), f. a whirlwind, L.

Ā-saṅgima, *as,* m. (in surgery) a kind of bandage, Suśr.

Ā-sajá, mfn. clinging to; dragging (a wheel), RV. v, 34, 6.

Ā-sajya, ind. p. having attached one's self or clinging to, Kir. &c.

Ā-sañjana, *am,* n. the act of clinging to, being hooked on; adherence, fixing, fastening to, AitBr.; KātyŚr.; a handle, hook, ŚBr.; attaching (an Anubandha to an affix), Pat. **-vat,** mfn. having a handle &c., KātyŚr.

Ā-sañjita, mfn. fastened on, put on.

आसंज्ञित *ā-saṃjñita,* mfn (fr. *sam-jñā*), one with whom one has agreed or concerted, Kām.

आसद् *ā-√sad,* P. *-sīdati* (Ved. also *-sadati;* Inf. *-sádam* and *-sáde,* RV.; pf. *-sasāda;* fut. *-satsyati*), Ā. (Ved. aor. 1. sg. *-satsi* and 3. sg. *-sādi*) to sit, sit down, sit near, RV.; AV.; ŚBr.; ŚāṅkhŚr.; to preside over, RV. viii, 42, 1; to lie in wait for, RV. x, 85, 32; to go to, go towards, approach; to meet with, reach, find; to encounter, attack; to commence, undertake, AV.; MBh.; R.; BhP.; Kum.; Ragh. &c.: Caus. *-sādayati,* to cause to sit down; to set down, put down, place, RV.; TS.; ŚBr.; BhP. &c.; to cause, effect, BhP.; to approach, meet with, find, reach, obtain, MBh.; R.; Megh.; Kathās.; Pañcat. &c.

Ā-satti, *is,* f. vicinity, proximity; intimate union; uninterrupted sequence (of words = *sam-nidhi,* q.v.), continual succession, Sāh.; Nyāyak.; Ragh. &c.; embarrassment; perplexity, MBh.; reaching, obtaining; gain, profit, L.

Ā-sada, *as,* m. approaching, meeting (see *dur-*°).

Ā-sadana, *am,* n. sitting down; a seat, KātyŚr.; reaching, L.

Ā-sanna, mfn. seated down, set down, AV.; ŚāṅkhŚr.; KātyŚr.; AitBr.; near, proximate, MBh.; R.; Ragh.; Megh.; Kathās. &c.; reached, obtained, occupied, BhP.; (*am*), n. nearness, vicinity, proximity, R.; Kathās. &c.; end, death, L. **-kāla,** m. the hour of death; (mfn.) one who has reached his time or hour (of death). **-kshaya,** mfn. one whose ruin is near. **-cara,** mfn. moving round about in the proximity, Kum. **-tara,** mfn. nearer; *-tā,* f. greater nearness, Hit. **-nivāsin,** mfn. living in the vicinity, a neighbour, L. **-prasavā,** f. a female (of an animal) whose (time of) parturition is near or who is about to bring forth (young ones), Hit. **-vartin,** mfn. being or abiding in the neighbourhood or vicinity, Kathās.

Ā-sādá, *as,* m. a footstool, cushion, AV. xv, 3, 8; TāṇḍyaBr.

Ā-sādana, *am,* n. putting or laying down, KātyŚr.; reaching, getting possession of, MBh.; Ratnāv.

Ā-sādayitavya, mfn. accessible, attainable; to be attacked or encountered, R.; Ragh.

Ā-sādita, mfn. put down; reached &c.

1. **Ā-sādya,** mfn. = *ā-sādayitavya* above.

2. **Ā-sādya,** ind. p. having put down; reaching.

Ā-sisādayishu, mfn. (fr. Desid. of the Caus.), being about or wishing to attack, R.

आसन् 2. *ā-√san,* P. (Impv. 2. sg. *ā-sanuhi,* AV. xiv, 2, 70) to gain, obtain; (for 1. *āsan* and *ā-sanya* see under 3. *ās.*)

आसन *āsana.* See 2. √*ās.*

आसन्द *āsanda, as,* m. (probably fr. √*sad*), N. of Vishṇu, L.; (*ī*), f. a chair or stool (generally made of basket work), AV.; VS.; ŚBr.; KātyŚr.; TS. &c. **-vat** (*āsandī-*), m., N. of a country, Pāṇ.; AitBr. **-sád** (*āsandī-*), mfn. sitting on a chair, ŚBr. xii, 8, 3, 4.

Āsandikā, f. a little chair, Kād.

आसपिण्डक्रियाकर्म *ā-sapiṇḍa-kriyā-karma,* ind. till the Śraddha or funeral ceremony of which the Sapiṇḍas (q.v.) partake, Mn. iii, 247.

आसप्तम *ā-saptama,* mfn. reaching or extending to the seventh, MuṇḍUp.; Yājñ.; R.

आसमञ्ज *āsamañja, as,* m. a descendant of Asamañja, R. i, 42, 9.

आसमुद्रान्तम् *ā-samudrântam,* ind. as far as the shore of the ocean (including it), R.

आसंबाध *ā-sambādha,* crowded, blocked up, R.

आसया *āsayā.* See 4. *ās.*

आसात् *āsā́t,* ind. (fr. an ideal base *āsa*), from or in the proximity, near, RV.

आसाद *āsāda,* &c. See *ā-√sad.*

आसायम् *ā-sāyam,* ind. till evening.

आसार *ā-sāra,* &c. See *ā-√sṛi.*

आसि *ā-√si,* P. (pf. *ā́-sishāya,* RV. x, 28, 10) to wrap or pack up.

आसिक *āsika,* mfn. (fr. *asi*), combating with a sword, Comm. on Pāṇ.

आसिका *āsikā.* See 2. √*ās.*

आसिच् 1. *ā-√sic,* P. Ā. *-siñcati, -te,* to pour in, fill up, RV.; AV.; ŚBr.; ŚāṅkhGṛ.; KātyŚr. &c.; to pour on, besprinkle, water, wet, BhP.; Kathās. &c.: Caus. *-secayati,* to pour in or on, ĀśvGṛ. & Śr.; Mn.

Ā-sikta, mfn. poured in or on, AV.; ŚBr. &c.; sprinkled.

2. **Ā-síc,** *k,* f. pouring in or towards; an oblation of Soma or butter (poured out towards or for the gods), RV. ii, 37, 1 & vii, 16, 11.

Ā-seka, *as,* m. wetting, sprinkling, watering, MBh.; Kathās.

Āsekya. See s. v.

1. **Ā-sécana,** *am,* n. pouring into, wetting, sprinkling, KātyŚr.; a reservoir or vessel for fluids, RV.; ŚBr.; KātyŚr.; (*ī*), f. a small vessel, L. **-vat,** mfn. serving for sprinkling, ĀśvGṛ. iv, 3, 16; KātyŚr.

आसिध् *ā-√2. sidh,* Caus. *-sedhayati,* to imprison, Comm. on Yājñ.

Ā-siddha, mfn. put under restraint, imprisoned, Comm. on Yājñ.

Ā-seddhṛi, *ā,* m. one who confines, imprisons, ib.

Ā-sedha, *as,* m. arrest, custody, legal restraint of four kinds, (*kālâsedha,* limitation of time; *sthānâsedha,* confinement to a place; *pravāsâsedha,* prohibition against removal or departure; *karmâsedha,* restriction from employment), ib.

आसिधार *āsidhāra,* mfn. (fr. *asi-dhārā*), relating to or being like the edge of a sword (e.g. °*ṃ vratam,* a vow as difficult as standing on the edge of a sword, Ragh. xii, 67), Kathās.

आसिनासि *āsināsi, is,* m. (fr. *ási-nāsa,* gaṇa *taulvaly-ādi,* Pāṇ. ii, 4, 61), a descendant of Asināsa.

आसिबन्धिक *āsibandhika, as,* m. (fr. *asi-bandha,* ib.), a descendant of Asi-bandha.

आसिव् *ā-√siv,* P. *-sīvyati,* to sew together.

Ā-sīvana, *am,* n. sewing together or on, Kāṭh.

Ā-syūta, mfn. sewn together, Bhartṛ.

आसीतकी *āsītakī,* f. a kind of plant, Lalit.

आसीमान्तम् *ā-sīmântam,* ind. extending to the boundary, Kathās. lvi, 306.

आसु *ā-√3. su,* P. *-sunóti* (Subj. 2. pl. *-sunótā,* AV. xx, 127, 7 and *ā́-sotā,* RV. ix, 108, 7) to press out (Soma juice); to distil, RV.; AV.; ŚBr.; ChUp.

1. **Ā-sava,** *as,* m. distilling, distillation, L.; decoction; rum, spirit distilled from sugar or molasses, spirituous liquor in general; juice, MBh.; Suśr.; Vikr.; Prab.; Yājñ. &c.; the nectar or juice of a flower, Śiś. vi, 7; the nectar or juice of the lips (of a woman), Śāntiś. **-dru,** m., N. of the Palmyra tree Borassus Flabelliformis (its juice, on fermenting, affords a spirituous liquor, L.)

Ā-sāva, *as,* m. (a priest) who presses out the Soma juice, RV. viii, 103, 10.

Ā-sāvya (Pāṇ. iii, 1, 26), mfn. to be pressed out.

Ā-sut, mfn. pressing out, distilling, (gaṇa *gahâdi,* Pāṇ. iv, 2, 138.)

Ā-suta, *am,* n. a manner of pressing the Soma, ChUp. v, 12, 1; a mixture, Bhpr.

1. **Ā-suti,** *is,* f. a brew, mixture, RV.; AV.; distillation, L. **-mat,** mfn. (gaṇa *madhv-ādi,* Pāṇ. iv, 2, 86) mixed with liquors(?). **Āsutī-vala** (Pāṇ. v, 2, 112), a priest (who prepares the Soma); one who prepares or sells spirituous liquors, a distiller, brewer, L.

आसुक *āsuka, am,* n., N. of a Sāman.

आसुर 1. *āsurá,* mf(*ī*)n. (fr. *asura*), spiritual, divine, RV.; VS.; AV.; belonging or devoted to evil spirits; belonging or relating to the Asuras, RV.; AV.; VS.; KātyŚr.; Prab.; Daś. &c.; infernal, demoniacal; (*as*), m. an Asura or demon, AV.; AitBr.; Pāṇ.; a form of marriage (in which the bridegroom purchases the bride from her father and paternal kinsmen), ĀśvGṛ. i, 6, 6; Mn. iii, 31; (cf. *vivāha*); (*ās*), m. pl. the stars of the southern hemisphere, Sūryas. &c.; a prince of the warrior-tribe Asura, Pāṇ.; (*ī*), f. a female demon; a division of medicine (surgery, curing by cutting with instruments, applying the actual cautery); N. of the plant Sinapis Ramosa, L.; the urethra, BhP.; (*am*), n. blood; black salt, L.

2. **Āsura,** mfn. belonging to Āsuri (below).

Āsurāyaṇá, *as,* m. (fr. *āsuri* below), a descendant of Āsuri, ŚBr.; BṛĀrUp.; MBh.; (*ās*), m. pl., N. of a school.

Āsurāyaṇīya, mfn. (fr. *āsurāyaṇa*), belonging to or coming from Āsurāyaṇa.

Āsuri, *is,* m. [*ī,* f., L.], (fr. *asura*), N. of a teacher, ŚBr.; BṛĀrUp. &c. **-vāsin,** m., N. of Prāśnī-putra, ŚBr. **Āsurī-kalpa,** m., N. of a Tantra.

Āsurīya, mfn. (fr. *āsuri*), Pat. on Kāty. on Pāṇ. iv, 1, 19.

आसू *ā-√1. sū,* P. *ā́-suvati* (p. *-suvānā́*) to

excite towards; to throw to, send off towards; to assign to, to bring quickly, procure; to yield, grant, RV.; AV.; ŚBr.

2. **Ā-savá**, *as*, m. exciting, enlivening, VS.

Ā-savitṛi, *tā*, m. exciting, exciter, ŚBr.

2. **Ā-sutí**, *is*, f. exciting, enlivening, RV. i, 104, 7; vii, 97, 7.

आसूत्रय *ā-sūtraya*, Nom. (fr. *sūtra*).

Ā-sūtrita, mfn. tied on or round, forming or wearing a garland.

आसृ *ā-√sṛi*, P. *-sarati*, to hasten towards, come running, RV.; AV.: Caus. Pass. *-sāryate*, to be undertaken or begun, Hariv.

Ā-sāra, *as*, m. surrounding an enemy; incursion, attack, L.; a hard shower, MBh.; Megh.; Ragh.; Mālav.; Kathās. &c.; a king whose dominions are separated by other states and who is an ally in war, Kām. **-śarkarā**, f. pl. hailstorm, BhP.; a particular metre.

Ā-sāraṇa, *as*, m., N. of a Yaksha, BhP.

आसृज् *ā-√sṛij*, P. (Impv. 2. sg. *ā́-sṛija*) Ā. (pf. 3. pl. *ā́-sasṛijire*) to pour out upon, pour in, RV.; to admit (a stallion to a mare), RV. ix, 97, 18; to adorn, decorate, RV. v, 52, 6; to carry near; to procure, KātyŚr.

आसेक्य *āsekya*, *as*, m. (fr. *a-seka*), impotent, a man of slight generative power, Suśr. i, 318, 8.

आसेचन 2. *āsecana* and *āsecanaka* = *a-secana* and *a-secanaka*, qq. v., L.; (for 1. *ā-secana* see *ā-√sic*.)

आसेद्धृ *ā-seddhṛi*, &c. See *ā-√2. sidh*.

आसेव् *ā-√sev*, (rarely P.) Ā. *-sevati*, *-te*, to frequent; to abide in, inhabit, dwell on, R.; BhP.; Kāvyād.; to attend to, serve; to honour; to take the part of, side with, BhP. &c.; to enjoy (sexual intercourse); to indulge in, like; to perform assiduously, practise, MBh.; Suśr.; Megh.; Kum. &c.

Ā-sevana, *am*, n. abiding in, Rājat.; assiduous practice or performance of anything, Pāṇ.

Ā-sevā, f. id., ib.

Ā-sevita, mfn. frequented; practised assiduously.

Ā-sevin, mfn. frequenting, inhabiting, Kathās.; zealously cultivating or performing anything, Rājat.

Ā-sevya, mfn. to be frequented or visited, Kāvyapr.

आस्कन्द् *ā-√skand*, P. *-skandati*, to leap, skip (see *ā-skándam*); to invade, attack, assault, Mālatīm.; Kathās.; BhP.

Ā-skandá, *as*, m. ascending, mounting, jumping upon, Kathās.; attack, assault, Rājat. &c.; a die (especially the fourth), VS.; TS.; a manner of recitation, Lāṭy.

Ā-skandana, *am*, n. going towards; assailing, attack; battle, combat, Kathās.; reproach, abuse, L.; drying, L.

Ā-skándam, ind. p. leaping, skipping, VS.

Ā-skandita, mfn. subject to or burdened with; (*am*) and (°*akam*), n. a horse's gallop, L.

Ā-skandin, mfn. jumping upon, Ragh.; assailing; causing to jump away, giving away, granting, Kathās.; a robber, L.

आस्कभ् *ā-√skabh*, P. (*-skabhnā́ti*, RV. x, 6, 3) to fix firmly into, stick into.

आस्कु *ā-√sku*, P. (*-skauti*, ŚBr. and *-skunóti*, AV. xii, 4, 6) to pull, pluck, tear.

आस्क्र *ā́skra*, mfn. (*√kram*, Sāy., fr. *skṛi* = *√1. kṛi*, BRD.), attacking, assaulting [Sāy.]; joined, united [BRD.], RV. i, 186, 2, &c.

आस्तर *ā-stara*, &c. See *ā-√stṛi*.

आस्तायन *āstāyana*, mfn. (fr. *asti*, 'existent,' gaṇa *pakshâdi*, Pāṇ. iv, 2, 80), belonging to something existent.

आस्ताव *ā-stāvá*, *as*, m. (*√stu*), the place where a particular Stotra is sung, TS.; ŚBr.; KātyŚr.; ĀśvŚr.

आस्तिक *āstika*, mf(ī)n. (fr. *asti*, 'there is or exists,' Pāṇ. iv, 2, 60), one who believes in the existence (of God, of another world, &c.); believing, pious, faithful, MBh.; Yājñ.; Suśr.; (*as*), m. = *āstīka*, q. v. **Āstikârtha-da**, *as*, m. 'granting Āstika's request,' N. of the king Janamejaya (who at the request of the sage Āstika [see *āstīka*] excepted the Nāga Takshaka from the destruction to which he had doomed the serpent-race), L.

Āstikya, *am*, n. (fr. *āstika*), belief in God, piety, faithfulness; a believing nature or disposition, MBh.; Bhag.; BhP.

Āsteya, mfn. (Pāṇ. iv, 3, 56) belonging to something existent.

आस्तीक *āstīka*, *as*, m., N. of a Muni (the son of Jaratkāru and Bhaginī Jaratkāru), MBh.; Hariv.; (mfn.) relating to or treating of the Muni Āstīka; (*āstīkam parva*, a section of the first book of the Mahā-bhārata.)

आस्तुभ् *ā-√stubh*, P. *-stobhati*, to receive or attend with shouts of joy; to huzza to, ŚāṅkhŚr.

आस्तृ *ā-√stṛi*, P. Ā. *-stṛiṇoti*, *-stṛiṇute*, *-starati*, *-te* (generally ind. p. *ā-stīrya*, q. v.) to scatter over, cover, bestrew, spread, R.; VarBṛ.; KātyŚr. &c.

Ā-stara, *as*, m. covering; a coverlet, blanket, carpet; a bed, cushion, Śāntiś.; Kathās.; N. of a man.

Ā-stáraṇa, *am*, *ī*, n. f. the act of spreading; a carpet, rug; a cushion, quilt, bed-clothes; a bed; a layer of sacred grass spread out at a sacrifice, AV. xv, 3, 7; AitBr.; ĀśvGṛ.; MBh.; Pañcat. &c.; an elephant's housings, a painted cloth or blanket worn on his back. **-vat**, mfn. covered with a cloth or carpet, R.; MBh.

Āstaraṇika, mfn. resting on a cloth or carpet, R.

Ā-stāra, *as*, m. spreading, strewing, scattering. **-paṅkti**, f., N. of a metre (the first verse of which consists of two Pādas of eight syllables each, the second of two Pādas of twelve syllables each), RAnukr.

Ā-stāraka, *as*, m. a fire-receptacle, grate, Bhpr.

Ā-stīrṇa, mfn. spread, strewed, scattered, KātyŚr.; Kathās.; Ragh.; covered, MBh.; R.; Suśr. &c.

Ā-stīrya, ind. p. having scattered over or strewed; covering, spreading, ŚBr.; ĀśvGṛ.; Lāṭy.; Kauś.

Ā-stṛita, mfn. = *ā-stīrṇa* above, VS.; VP.; BhP. &c.

आस्त्रबुध्न *āstrabudhná*, *as*, m., N. of a man, RV. x, 171, 3.

आस्था 1. *ā-√sthā*, P. Ā. *-tishṭhati*, *-te*, to stand or remain on or by; to ascend, mount; to stay near, go towards, resort to, RV.; AV.; ŚBr.; ĀśvGṛ.; MBh.; R.; BhP.; Kum. &c.; to act according to, follow, R.; BhP.; to undertake, perform, do, carry out, practise, use, MBh.; R.; Hariv.; BhP.; Kathās. &c.; to side or take part with, be of the opinion of; to maintain, affirm, Pat.; to acknowledge; to take care for, have regard for, MBh.; Sarvad. &c.: Caus. *-sthāpayati*, to cause to ascend, Kauś.; to cause to stay or stop; to arrest, stop, RV.; Kauś.; to fix into, put into, AitBr.; BhP.; Kathās.; to hurt, RV.; to constipate; to strengthen, Suśr.; to introduce, Sāh.

2. **Ā-sthā**, f. consideration, regard, care, care for (with loc., e.g. *mayy āsthā*, care for me), Hit.; Ragh.; Kathās. &c.; assent, promise, L.; confidence, hope; prop, stay, support, L.; place or means of abiding, L.; an assembly, L.; state, condition, L.

Ā-sthātṛi, mfn. standing on, mounting on, RV. vi, 47, 26.

Ā-sthāna, *am*, n. place, site, ground, base, VS.; AV.; ŚBr.; an assembly; a hall of audience, Kathās.; L.; (*ī*), f. an assembly, Ratnāv. **-gṛiha**, n. an assembly-room, L. **-maṇḍapa**, m. & n. a hall of audience, Hariv.; Kād.

Āsthānīya, mfn. belonging to an assembly; (*as*), m. chamberlain, Rājat.

Ā-sthāpana, *am*, n. placing, fixing, causing to stay or remain; a strengthening remedy; an enema of oil, ghee, &c., Suśr.

Ā-sthāpita, mfn. placed, fixed, &c.; (*am*), n. (gaṇa *âcitâdi*, Pāṇ. vi, 2, 146), a particular Sandhi, RPrāt.; APrāt.

Ā-sthāya, ind. p. having recourse to, using, employing; having ascended; standing, standing by.

Ā-sthāyikā, f. access, audience; (e.g. *āsthāyikām dā*, to give an audience.)

Ā-sthita, mfn. staying or sitting on, dwelling on, abiding, MBh.; R.; BhP.; Kathās. &c.; come or fallen into; one who has undertaken or performed, MBh.; R.; Mn.; Śiś. &c.; being, existing, BhP.; Hit.; acknowledging, believing, Sarvad.; stayed, dwelt, inhabited; ascended, Ragh.; BhP.; undertaken, performed, MBh.; R.; brought, carried to, BhP.

Ā-stheya, mfn. to be approached; to be seized; to be applied or practised, R.; to be regarded as; to be acknowledged or adopted (as an opinion), Sarvad.

आस्नान *ā-snā́na*, *am*, n. (*√snā*), water for washing, a bath, AV. xiv, 2, 65.

आस्नेय *ā́sneya*, mf(ī)n. (fr. *asan*), bloody, being in blood, AV. xi, 8, 28.

आस्पद *āspada*, *am*, n. (ifc. mf[ā]n. fr. *pada* with *ā* prefixed, *s* being inserted), place, seat, abode, Śak.; Kathās.; Mṛicch.; Bhartṛ.; Daś. &c.; the tenth lunar mansion, VarBṛ.; business, affair; dignity, authority; power, L. **-tā**, f. and **tva**, n. the state of being the place or abode of.

आस्पन्द् *ā-√spand*, Ā. *-spandate*, to palpitate, quiver, R.

Ā-spandana, *am*, n. trembling, quivering, BhP.

आस्पात्र *ās-pātra*. See 3. *ās*.

आस्पृ *ā-√spṛi*, P. *-spṛiṇoti*, to procure for one's self, ŚBr.

आस्पृश् *ā-√spṛiś*.

Ā-spṛiśya, ind. p. having touched softly, BhP.

Ā-spṛishṭa, mfn. touched softly or gently, ŚBr.

आस्फल् *ā-√sphal*, Caus. *-sphālayati*, to cause to flap; to rock, shake, throw, Hariv.; Ragh.; Uttarar. &c.; to tear asunder, BhP.

Ā-sphāla, *as*, m. causing to flap or move; striking; flapping, clapping; rebounding, recoiling, Naish.; the flapping motion of an elephant's ears towards each other, L.

Ā-sphālana, *am*, n. rubbing, stirring, flapping; striking; clashing, colliding, collision, MBh.; Śak.; Hit.; Ragh.; Śiś. &c.; pride, arrogance, L.

Ā-sphālita, mfn. struck gently; stirred; caused to move; flapped, clapped, struck together.

आस्फाय् *ā-√sphāy*, Ā. *-sphāyate*, to grow, increase, Bhaṭṭ.

आस्फार *ā-sphāra*, *as*, m. (fr. *√sphar* = *√sphal*?), a dice-board, Sāy. on RV. x, 34, 1 & 8.

आस्फुजित् *āsphujit* = Ἀφροδίτη, N. of the planet Venus.

आस्फुट् *ā-√sphuṭ*, Caus. *-sphoṭayati*, to split open, crush, grind, Kathās.; to move, agitate quickly; to shake, MBh.; Mn.; BhP. &c.

Ā-sphoṭa, *as*, m. (and *ā*, f., L.) moving or flapping to and fro; quivering, trembling, shaking; the sound of clapping or striking on the arms (as made by combatants, wrestlers, &c.), MBh.; a species of plant, L.

Ā-sphoṭaka, *as*, m. a species of plant, L.

Ā-sphoṭana, *am*, n. shaking, moving to and fro, R.; MBh.; slapping or clapping the arms or the noise made by it; stretching, VarBṛ.; Suśr.; blowing, expanding, L.; closing, sealing, L.; (*ī*), f. a gimlet or auger, L.

Ā-sphota, *as*, m. (probably for *ā-sphoṭa* above), N. of several plants, viz. Calotropis Gigantea (Suśr.), Bahinia Variegata, Echites Dichotoma, L.; (*ā*), f., N. of several plants, viz. Jasminum Sambac (Suśr.), Clitoria Ternatea (of two kinds, with white and blue flowers, Bhpr.), Echites Frutescens, Echites Dichotoma, L.

Ā-sphotaka, *as*, m. Calotropis Gigantea, L.

आस्फुल् *ā-√sphul* = *ā-√sphal* above.

आस्माक *āsmākā*, mf(ī)n. (fr. *asmākam*, Pāṇ. iv, 3, 1 & 2), our, ours, VS.; Sāh.

Āsmākīna, mfn. (Pāṇ. iv, 3, 1 & 2), id.

आस्य *āsyà*, &c. See 4. *ās*.

आस्यन्द् *ā-√syand*, Ā. *-syandate* (p. *-syándamāna*), to stream or flow towards or near, AV. iii, 12, 3; ŚāṅkhGṛ. and Śr.

Ā-syandana, *am*, n. flowing near, Nir.

आस्यहात्य *āsyahātya*, mfn. (fr. *asy-a-hatya*, gaṇa *vimuktâdi*, Pāṇ. v, 2, 61), containing the word *asy-a-hatya*, 'non-killing with a sword' (as a chapter) or (gaṇa *anutatikâdi*, Pāṇ. vii, 3, 20) belonging to a non-massacre [*asi-hatya* and *āsihātya*, Kāś.]

आस्या *āsyā*, f. See √2. *ās.*

आस्यूत *ā-syūta.* See *ā-√siv.*

आस्रंस् *ā-√srans.*

Ā-srasta, mfn. fallen off, loose, MBh.

आस्रप *āsrapa, as,* m. (fr. *asra-pa*), the nineteenth lunar mansion (presided over by the Rākshasa Asra-pa), L.; = *asra-pa* (q. v.), T.

आस्रु 1. *ā-√sru,* P. *-sravati,* to flow near or towards; to flow, stream, flow from, BhP.; Sarvad.; to spring a leak; to flow off, go off, deteriorate, AV. v, 19, 8; ii, 29, 7: Caus. *-srāvayati* and *-sravayati,* to cause to flow; to bleed, cup, Kām.; to impel, Sarvad.

Ā-srava, *as,* m. the foam on boiling rice, L.; a door opening into water and allowing the stream to descend through it, Sarvad.; (with Jainas) the action of the senses which impels the soul towards external objects (one of the seven Sattvas or substances; it is twofold, as good or evil), Sarvad.; distress, affliction, pain, L.

Ā-srāvá, *as,* m. flow, issue, running, discharge, Suśr.; suppuration, MBh.; pain, affliction; a particular disease of the body, AV. i, 2, 4; ii, 3, 3-5; (*ās*), m. pl. the objects of sense, Āp. **-bheshajá,** n. a medicament, medicine, AV. vi, 44, 2.

Ā-srāvin, mfn. flowing, emitting fluid, discharging humour (as an elephant who emits fluid from his temples during the rutting time), MBh.; suppurating, festering, Suśr.

2. **Ā-sru,** mfn. flowing or streaming in abundance. **-payas,** mfn. one whose milk is streaming away in abundance (as a cow), BhP. x, 13, 30.

आस्वद् *ā-√svad,* P. *-svadati,* to eat, consume, MBh.: Caus. *-svādayati,* to taste, enjoy, eat with a relish, MBh.; R.; BhP.; VarBṛ.; Suśr.; Pañcat. &c.

Ā-svāda, *as,* m. eating with a relish, tasting, enjoying (also metaphorically), Mn.; Kathās.; Sāh.; Yājñ. &c.; flavour, taste, R.; Pañcat.; Megh. &c. **-vat,** mfn. having a good taste, palatable; delicious in flavour, Ragh.

Ā-svādaka, mfn. tasting, enjoying, Sāh.

Ā-svādana, *am,* n. the act of eating, tasting, enjoying, Pañcat.; Hit.

Ā-svādita, mfn. tasted, enjoyed, eaten.

Ā-svādya, mfn. to be eaten; to be tasted or enjoyed, MBh.; Kathās.; having a good taste, palatable, delicious. **-toya,** mf(*ā*)n. having sweet or palatable water (as a stream), Hit.

आस्वन् *ā-√svan,* P. (pf. 3. pl. *-svenus,* Bhaṭṭ.) to resound.

Ā-svanita and **ā-svānta,** mfn. (Pāṇ. vii, 2, 28) sounded, resounded.

आस्विद् *ā-√svid,* Ā. (p. pf. *-sishvidānā,* RV. x, 106, 10) to sweat, perspire.

आह 1. *āha,* ind. an interjection; a particle implying reproof; severity; command; casting; sending, L.

आह 2. *āha,* perf. 3. sg. of the defect. √1. *ah,* q. v.

आहक *āhaka, as,* m. a peculiar disease of the nose, inflammation of the Schneiderian membrane.

आहंकारिक *āhaṃkārika,* mfn. (fr. *ahaṃkāra*), belonging to Ahaṃ-kāra or self-consciousness, MBh.

Āhaṃkārya, erroneously for *ahaṃkārya,* q. v.

आहन् *ā-√han,* P. *-hanti* (Impv. *ā́-jahi,* AV. &c.; pf. *ā́-jaghāna,* RV. &c.), Ā. *-hate* (only if no object follows, Pāṇ. i, 3, 28, or if the object is a part of one's own body, Kāty.; Pot. 1. sg. *-ghnīya,* Pat. on Pāṇ. i, 1, 62, Daś.) to strike at, hit, beat; to attack, assault, RV.; TS.; ĀśvGṛ.; MBh.; Kathās. &c.: (Ā.) to strike one's self (or any part of one's body), BhP.; Pāṇ. & Comm.; Bhaṭṭ.; to make away with one's self, Daś. 91, 15; to fasten, AV.; ŚBr.; to beat or cause to sound (a drum &c.), TS.; ŚBr.; Kathās.; Bhaṭṭ. &c.: Intens. *ā́-janghanti,* RV. vi, 75, 13, to strike at or beat violently.

Ā́-hata, mfn. struck, beaten, hit, hurt, R.; Ragh.; Kum.; Kathās.; VarBṛ. &c.; fastened, fixed, RV.; AV.; beaten, caused to sound (as a drum &c.), MBh.; Hariv.; Ragh. &c.; crushed, rubbed, Śiś.; rendered null, destroyed, frustrated, BhP.; VarBṛS.; multiplied, VarBṛS.; hit, blunted (said of a Visarga, when changed to *o*), Sāh.; uttered falsely, L.; known, understood, L.; repeated, mentioned, L.; (*as*), m. a drum, L.; (*am*), n. old cloth or raiment, L.; new cloth or clothes, L.; assertion of an impossibility, L. **-lakshana,** mfn. one whose marks or characteristics are mentioned, famed, reputed, L. **-visarga-tā,** f. the deadening of a Visarga or its change into *o,* Sāh.

Ā-hati, *is,* f. hitting, striking; a blow, hit, Kathās.; Ratnāv.; Kpr. &c.; (in arith.) a product, Āryabh.; Bījag.

Ā-hatya, ind. p. having struck or beaten, striking, hitting. **-vacana,** n. and **-vāda,** m. an explicit or energetic explanation.

Ā-hánana, *am,* n. the act of striking at, beating, KātyŚr.; killing (an animal), AV.; a stick for beating a drum, AV. xx, 133, 1. **-prakāra,** mfn. fit for beating, ĀpŚr.

Āhananyà, mfn. (fr. *ā-hanana*), being in the act of beating (a drum &c.), VS. xvi, 35.

Ā-hanás, mfn. to be beaten or pressed out (as Soma); to be skimmed (as milk), RV.; to be beaten (as an unchaste woman); unchaste, wanton; obscene, lascivious, profligate, RV. v, 42, 13; x, 10, 6. 8.

Ā-hanasya, *am,* n. unchasteness, lasciviousness, AitBr.; lascivious words, obscenity, ŚBr.; (*ās*), f. pl. (scil. *ṛicas*) verses of a lascivious character; a chapter of the Kuntāpa hymns in the Atharva-veda, AitBr.; ĀśvŚr. &c.; (with *an*°, mfn. chaste, decent, ŚāṅkhGṛ.; HirGṛ.)

आहर *ā-hara,* &c. See *ā-√hṛi.*

आहर्य *ā-√hary,* P. (p. *-háryat,* RV. x, 105, 1) Ā. (p. *-háryamāṇa,* RV. x, 96, 11) to like; to foster.

आहलक् *āhálak* [VS.] and *āhálam* [TS.], ind. a smacking sound.

आहव *ā-hava,* &c. See *ā-√hu* & *ā-√hve.*

आहस्पत्य *āhaspatya,* mfn. (fr. *ahas-pati*), belonging to the lord of the day or to the sun, MantraBr; Gobh.

आहार *ā-hāra,* &c. See *ā-√hṛi.*

आहाव *ā-hāva,* &c. See *ā-√hu* & *ā-√hve.*

आहि *ā-√hi,* Ā. (3. pl. *ā́-hinvire,* RV. ix, 74, 8) to carry near; to procure.

आहिंस् *ā-√hins,* Ā. *-hinsate,* to attack, make war upon, TāṇḍyaBr.

आहिंसि *āhinsi, is,* m. a descendant of A-hinsa.

Āhinsāyana, *as,* m. (fr. *āhinsi,* gaṇa *taulvalyādi,* Pāṇ. ii, 4, 61), a descendant of Āhinsi.

आहिक *āhika, as,* m. (fr. *ahi*), the descending node, L.; N. of Pāṇini, L.

आहिच्छत्र *āhicchattra,* mfn. (fr. *ahi-cchattra* or °*ā*), coming from the country Ahicchattra or its city, Kathās.; Pat.

Āhicchattrika, *as,* m. an inhabitant of the country Ahicchattra or its city.

आहिण्डक *āhiṇḍaka* and *āhiṇḍika, as,* m. a man of mixed origin (the son of a Nishāda father and a Vaidehī mother, Mn. x, 37; employed as a watchman outside gaols &c., Comm. on Mn.); a traveller [in Prākṛit], Mṛicch.

आहित *ā-hita* and *ā-hiti.* See *ā-√dhā.*

आहितुण्डिक *āhituṇḍika, as,* m. (fr. *ahi-tuṇḍa*), 'one (who plays) with a snake's mouth,' a snake-catcher, juggler, Pañcat.; Mudr.

आहिमत *āhimata,* mfn. (fr *ahi-mat*), belonging to (a country) abounding in snakes, Comm. on Pāṇ.

आहिर्बुध्न्य *āhirbudhnya, am,* n., N. of the Nakshatra Uttara-bhadra-padā (presided over by Ahir-budhnya).

आहु *ā-√hu,* P. Ā. *-juhoti, -juhute* (p. *-júhvāna*) to sacrifice, offer an oblation; to sprinkle (with butter), RV.; AV.; TS.; Hariv.

1. **Ā-hava,** *as,* m. sacrificing, sacrifice, L.; (for 2. *ā-hava* see *ā-√hve.*)

Ā-hávana, *am,* n. offering an oblation, offering sacrifice, a sacrifice, RV. vii, 1, 17; 8, 5.

Ā-havanīya, mfn. to be offered as an oblation; (*āhavanīya*), m. (scil. *agni*) consecrated fire taken from the householder's perpetual fire and prepared for receiving oblations; especially the eastern of the three fires burning at a sacrifice, AV.; ŚBr.; KātyŚr.; ĀśvŚr.; ChUp. &c. **-tas,** ind. from the Āhavanīya fire, ĀpŚr.

Āhavanīyaka, *as,* m. = *āhavanīya* above.

1. **Ā-hāvá,** *as,* m. a trough, pail, vessel, RV.; a trough near a well for watering cattle, Pāṇ.; (for 2. *ā-hāva* see *ā-√hve.*)

Ā́-huta, mfn. offered as an oblation, sacrificed, RV.; AV.; ŚāṅkhŚr.; laid in the fire (as a corpse), RV. x, 16, 5; offering made to men, hospitality (= *manushya-yajña,* q. v.), L.; nourishment of all created beings (considered as one of the five principal sacrifices of the Hindūs; cf. *bhūta-yajña*), L.

1. **Ā́-huti,** *is,* f. offering oblations with fire to the deities; any solemn rite accompanied with oblations, RV.; AV.; TS.; AitBr.; ŚBr.; MBh. &c.; (*is*), m., N. of a son of Babhru, MBh.; Hariv.; VP. **-kṛita,** mfn. offered as an oblation, ŚBr. vi, 6, 4, 2. **-bhāga,** mf(*ī*)n. one whose share is a sacrifice, AitBr. **-bhāj,** mfn. one who partakes of a sacrifice or oblation, MaitrS. **-máya,** mfn. consisting of oblations, ŚBr. **-vat** (*ā́huti*°), mfn. accompanied with oblations, ŚBr. **Āhutishṭakā́,** f. pl. a kind of brick, TS.; (for 2. *ā-huti* see *ā-√hve.*)

Āhutī (in comp. for 1. *ā́-huti*). **-√1. kṛi,** to offer as an oblation, Ratnāv.; Bālar. **-√bhū,** to become or be an oblation, Bālar. **-vṛidh,** mfn. delighting in sacrifices, RV. ix, 67, 29.

आहुक *āhuka, as,* m., N. of a king (great-grandfather of Kṛishṇa, a son or grandson of Abhijit), MBh.; Hariv.; VP.; (*ī*), f. a sister of that king, Hariv.; VP.; (*ās*), m. pl., N. of a people, MBh.

आहुल्य *āhulya, am,* n. the leguminous shrub Tabernæmontana Coronaria, L.

आहू *ā-hū,* &c. See *ā-√hve.*

आहूर्य *ā-hūrya.* See *ā-√hvṛi.*

आहृ *ā-√hṛi,* P. *-harati* (aor. 1. sg. *-ahārsham,* RV.; AV.; pf. *-jahāra,* Inf. *-hartavai,* ŚBr. xiii, 8, 3, 10); seldom Ā. (pf. *-jahre,* Hariv.) to fetch, bring, bring near; to offer, reach forth, deliver, give, RV.; AV.; TS.; ŚBr.; MBh.; R.; BhP.; Śak. &c.; to fetch for one's self, take away, take, receive, get, AV.; ĀśvGṛ.; Mn.; Yājñ.; MBh.; Kathās. &c.; to conceive (as a woman), Mn.; to bring home (a bride), R.; Kathās.; Kum.; to put on; to take for one's self, use, enjoy, MBh.; Kathās.; R. &c.; to manifest, utter, speak, MBh.; BhP.; R. &c.: Caus. P. Ā. *-hārayati, -te,* to cause to fetch; to procure, ŚBr.; AitBr.; TBr.; to cause to bring, collect (taxes), Mn.; MBh.; to take for one's self, enjoy, eat, MBh.; R.; to manifest, utter, MBh.; R.; Hariv.: Desid. P. Ā. *-jihīrshati, -te,* to wish or intend to procure, ŚBr.; to seek to get, MBh.

Ā-jihīrshu, mfn. (fr. Desid.), being about to bring near or fetch, MBh. iii, 11078.

1. **Ā-hara,** mfn. ifc. bringing, fetching, Ragh.; (*as*), m. taking, seizing; accomplishing, offering (a sacrifice), MBh.; Kād.; drawing in breath, inhaling; inhaled air; breath inspired, inspiration, L.

2. **Ā-hara** (2. sg. Impv. forming irregular Tatpurusha compounds with the following words): **-karaṭā** (i. e. *ā-hara karaṭa! ity-ucyate yasyāṃ kriyāyāṃ sā*), **-ceṭā, -nivapā, -nishkirā, -vanitā, -vasanā, -vitanā, -senā,** gaṇa *mayūra-vyansakâdi,* Pāṇ. ii, 1, 72.

Ā-haraṇa, mfn. ifc. taking away, robbing; (*am*), n. taking, seizing, bringing, fetching, KātyŚr.; Śak. &c.; extracting, removing, Suśr.; accomplishing, offering (a sacrifice), MBh.; battle, combat, L.; causing, inducing, L.

Āharaṇi-√1. kṛi, to offer, give as a present, Ragh.

Ā-hartṛi, *tā,* m. one who brings or fetches; one who procures, TS.; ŚBr.; MBh.; R.; one who takes or seizes; one who takes away or removes, Yājñ.; causing, inducing, an originator, MBh.; Vikr.; an offerer (of a sacrifice), MBh.; one who takes for himself or enjoys, Lalit.

Ā-hāra, mf(*ī*)n. ifc. bringing near, procuring; being about to fetch, going to fetch, MBh.; (*as*),

m. taking; fetching, bringing near, KātyŚr.; R.; employing, use, KātyŚr.; taking food; food [e. g. *ā-hāram* √1. *kṛi*, to take food, eat, MBh. &c.]; livelihood, Hit.; Pañcat.; R.; Mn.; Suśr. &c. **-niḥsaraṇa-mārga**, m. 'the place of the exit of food,' the posterior part of the body, Bhartṛ. **-nirgama-sthāna**, n. id. **-pāka**, m. 'food-maturing,' digestion, Bhpr. **-bhūmi**, f. eating-place, Kathās. **-yojana**, n. dressing food, MBh. **-viraha**, m. want of food. **-vṛitti**, f. livelihood, Pañcat. **-śuddhi**, f. purity in food, ChUp. **-sambhava**, m. the juice produced by food, chyle, lymph, serum, L. **Āhārârthin**, mfn. seeking or begging for food.

Āhāraka, mfn. bringing near, procuring, fetching, Comm. on Pāṇ.; (cf. *kṛitâhāra-ka.*)

Āhāraya, Nom. (fr. *ā-hāra*) P. *ā-hārayati*, to take food, eat, dine, Vet.

Āhārika, *as*, m. (with Jainas) one of the five bodies belonging to the soul (a minute form, issuing from the head of a meditative sage to consult an omniscient saint and returning with the desired information, Colebrooke).

Ā-hārin, mfn. taking together, collecting.

Ā-hārya, mfn. to be taken or seized; to be fetched or brought near, ĀśvŚr.; KātyŚr.; Mn.; to be extracted or removed, Suśr.; to be taken or eaten; what may be removed, adventitious, accessory, incidental, L.; (*as*), m. a kind of bandage, Suśr.; (*am*), n. any disease to be treated by the operation of extracting; extraction, Suśr.; a vessel, AV. ix, 1, 23; 6, 18; the decorative part of a drama (the press, decorations, &c.), L. **-śobhā**, f. adventitious beauty (not natural but the effect of paint, ornaments, &c.)

Ā-hṛita, mfn. brought near, fetched, procured, Mn.; Ragh.; Yājñ.; MārkP. &c.; taken, seized, captivated, Kathās.; Yājñ.; MBh. &c.; taken (as food), eaten, R. &c.; uttered, spoken, R.; BhP. &c. **-yajña-kratu** (*ā́hṛita-*), mfn. intending to accomplish a prepared sacrifice, AV. ix, 6, 27.

Ā-hṛiti, *is*, f. bringing or drawing near, VarBṛS.

Ā-hṛitya, ind. p. having fetched or brought &c.

आहृष् *ā-√hṛish*, P. (p. *-hṛishyat*) to shudder, shiver, BhP. x, 82, 14.

आहेय *āheya*, mfn. (fr. *ahi*, Pāṇ. iv, 3, 56), belonging to or coming from a snake, Pañcat.

आहो *ā́ho*, ind. (gaṇa *câdi*, Pāṇ. i, 4, 57) an interjection of asking and of doubt, 'Is it so?' ŚBr.; TUp.; Śak.; Bhag. **-purushikā** (gaṇa *mayūra-vyaṅsakâdi*, Pāṇ. ii, 1, 72), f. boasting of one's manliness or military prowess; vaunting of one's power, Bhaṭṭ. **-svit**, ind. an interrogative particle (often after *kim*, e.g. *kim īśvarânapêkshikam āho svid īśvarâpêksham*, 'is it independent of God or dependent on God?')

आह्न *āhná*, *am*, n. (fr. *ahan*), a series of days, many days, ŚBr.; Pāṇ.

Āhnika, mfn. performed or occurring in the daytime, diurnal, MBh.; performed or done or occurring every day, daily, R. &c.; (*am*), n. a religious ceremony to be performed every day at a fixed hour, MBh.; R.; a day's work; what may be read on one day; division or chapter of a book; constant occupation, daily work; daily food &c., L.; N. of several works. **-candrikā**, f., **-tattva**, n., **-dīpaka**, m., **-pradīpa**, m., **-prayoga**, m., **-mañjarī**, f., **-sāra**, m., N. of works. **Āhnikâcāra**, m. daily observance (the diurnal prayers and practices necessary for bodily and mental purification); *-tattva*, n., N. of a work.

आह्नेय *āhneyá*, *as*, m. (fr. *ahni*, *is*, f.), N. of Sauca, TĀr. ii, 12, 2.

आह्रुत *ā-hruta*. See *ā-√hvṛi*.

आह्लाद् *ā-√hlād*, Caus. *-hlādayati*, to refresh, revive, gladden, MBh.; Ragh.; Rājat. &c.

Ā-hlāda, *as*, m. refreshing, reviving; joy, delight, Pañcat. **-kara**, mfn. causing or conferring delight, Kād.; Ratnāv. **-kārin**, **-dugha**, mfn. id.

Ā-hlādaka, mfn. causing delight, refreshing, reviving, Kathās.

Ā-hlādana, *am*, n. the act of gladdening, refreshing, R.

Ā-hlādanīya, mfn. to be refreshed or gladdened, Kād.

Ā-hlādita, mfn. delighted, rejoiced.

Ā-hlādin, mfn. causing joy or delight, Ratnāv.

आह्वृ *ā-√hvṛi*, Ā. (Subj. 2. sg. *ā́-juhūrthās*, RV. vii, 1, 19) to make crooked; to hurt, injure.

Ā-hūrya, mfn. one to whom homage is to be paid; to be made favourable, RV. i, 69, 4

Ā-hruta, mfn. stooped, crooked; hurt, wounded. **-bheshajá**, mf(*ī*)n. curing anything wounded or hurt, AV. xix, 2, 5.

Ā-hvara, mfn. crooked, T. **-kantha**, n., N. of a town of the Uśīnaras, Kāś. on Pāṇ. ii, 4, 20.

Ā-hvaraka, *ās*, m. pl., N. of a school, TPrāt.

Ā-hvāraka, *ās*, m. pl. id., ib.

Ā-hvṛiti, mfn. crooked, cunning, Hariv.; (*is*), m., N. of a king, MBh.

आह्वे *ā-√hve*, P. *-hvayati* (but also Pot. 1. sg. *ā-huvema*, AV. vii, 85, 1), Ā. *-hvayate* (but also 1. sg. *ā-huve*, RV.; aor. 3. pl. *ā́hūshata*, RV. i, 14, 2, &c.; Inf. *-huvádhyai*, RV. vi, 60, 13, and *-hvayitavaí*, ŚBr. ii, 5, 3, 18) to call near, invoke, invite, summon, cite, RV.; ŚBr.; TS.; MBh.; Mṛicch.; BhP.; Pañcat. &c.; to provoke, challenge, emulate (in this sense only Ā., Pāṇ. i, 3, 31), RV.; ŚBr.; R.; Kathās. &c.; to call to (especially in rites said of the Hotṛi, who addresses the Adhvaryu by the Ā-hāva or Ā-hvāna; see below), AitBr.; ĀśvŚr.; KātyŚr.; ŚāṅkhBr. & Sr.; to proclaim, AitBr.; ŚBr.; KātyŚr.; ĀśvŚr.: Caus. *-hvāyayati*, to cause to call near, send for; to cause to summon or challenge or invite, R.; Ragh.; Bhaṭṭ.: Desid. *-juhūshati*, to wish to call near, to be about to call near: Intens. *ā́-johavīti*, RV. vii, 56, 18, to call near zealously.

2. **Ā-havá**, *as*, m. challenge, provoking; war, battle, RV.; MBh.; Mn.; R.; Bhag. &c. **-kāmyā**, f. desire of war. **-bhūmi**, f. battle-field, Kathās. (For 1. *ā-hava* see *ā-√hu.*)

2. **Ā-hāva**, *as*, m. a particular invocation (*śoṅsāvom* corrupt from *śaṅsāva*, 'let us two pray!') by which the Hotṛi addresses the Adhvaryu, AitBr.; ĀśvŚr. (cf. *ā-hvāna*); battle, war, L.; (for 1. *ā-hāva* see *ā-√hu.*)

2. **Ā-huti**, *is*, f. calling, invoking [sometimes with this sense in the oldest Vedic texts, but see the more correct form *ā-hūti*]; (for 1. *ā-huti* see *ā-√hu.*)

Ā-húva, mfn. to be invoked (Sāy.), RV. viii, 32, 19.

Ā-hū́, f. calling, invoking (BRD.), ib.

Ā-hūta, mfn. called, summoned, invoked, invited. **-prapalāyin**, m. a defendant or witness absconding or not appearing when summoned, Yājñ. **Āhūtâdhyāyin**, mfn. one who studies only after having been called (by the teacher).

Ā-hūtavya[?], mfn. to be called, Kathās. cx, 141.

Ā-hūti, *is*, f. calling, invoking, AitBr.

Ā-hūya, ind. having invited &c.

Ā-hva, mfn. a caller, crier; (ifc.) named, called; (*ā*), f. a name, appellation, Suśr.

Ā-hvaya, *as*, m. a lawsuit arising from a dispute about games with animals (as cock-fighting &c.), Mn. viii, 7; appellation, name (generally ifc., e.g. *rāmāyaṇâhvayam kāvyam*, &c.), MBh.; Ragh.; Suśr.; Kathās. &c.

Ā-hvayana, *am*, n. appellation, name, R.

Ā-hvayitavya, mfn. to be summoned or invited, MBh.

Ā-hvāna, *am*, n. calling, invitation, a call or summons, MBh.; Pañcat.; Hit.; invocation of a deity, Mn.; MBh.; challenge, R.; legal summons, Mṛicch.; Comm. on Yājñ.; an appellation, a name, L.; a particular calling in rites = 2. *ā-hāva*, q. v. **-darśana**, n. a day of trial.

Āhvānaya, Nom. P. *āhvānayati*, (in law) to summon, Comm. on Yājñ.

Ā-hvāya, *as*, m. a summons; a name, L.

Āhvāyaka, *as*, m. a messenger, courier, MBh.; (*ikā*), f. a female messenger.

Ā-hvāyitavya, mfn. to be called before a tribunal, Mṛicch.

इ I.

इ 1. *i*, the third vowel of the alphabet, corresponding to *i* short, and pronounced as that letter in *kill* &c. **-kāra**, **-varṇa**, m. the letter or sound *i*.

इ 2. *i*, ind. an interjection of anger, calling, sorrow, distress, compassion, &c., (gaṇa *câdi*, Pāṇ. i, 4, 57, &c.)

इ 3. *i*, base of Nom. & Acc. sing. du. & pl. of the demonstrative pronoun *idam*, 'this' or 'that;' [cf. *itara*, *itas*, *iti*, *id*, *idā́*, *iyat*, *iva*, *iha:* cf. also Lat. *id;* Goth. *ita;* Eng. *it:* Old Germ. *iz;* Mod. Germ. *es.*]

इ 4. *i*, *is*, m., N. of Kāmadeva, L.

इ 5. *i*, cl. 2. P. *éti* (Impv. 2. sg. *ihí*) & 1. P. Ā. *áyati*, *ayate* [cf. √*ay*], (pf. *iyā́ya* [2. sg. *iyátha*, AV. viii, 1, 10, & *iyétha*, RV.], fut. *eshyati*; aor. *aishīt*; inf. *etum*, *étave*, RV. & AV., *étavaí*, RV., *étos*, RV., *ityaí*, RV. i, 113, 6; 124, 1) to go, walk; to flow; to blow; to advance, spread, get about; to go to or towards (with acc.), come, RV.; AV.; ŚBr.; MBh.; R.; Hit.; Ragh. &c.; to go away, escape, pass, retire, RV.; AV.; ŚBr.; R.; to arise from, come from, RV.; ChUp.; to return (in this sense only fut.), MBh.; R.; (with *punar*) to come back again, return, MBh.; R.; Pañcat. &c.; to succeed, Mn. iii, 127; to arrive at, reach, obtain, RV.; AV.; ŚBr.; Śak.; Hit. &c.; to fall into, come to; to approach with prayers, gain by asking (cf. *ita*); to undertake anything (with acc.); to be employed in, go on with, continue in any condition or relation (with a part. or instr., e.g. *asura-rakshasāni mṛidyamānāni yanti*, 'the Asuras and Rakshases are being continually crushed,' ŚBr. i, 1, 4, 14; *gavāmayanenêyuḥ*, 'they were engaged in the [festival called] Gavāmayana,' KātyŚr. xxv, 5, 2); to appear, be, KaṭhUp.: Intens. Ā. *īyate* (RV. i, 30, 18; p. *iyāná*, RV.; inf. *iyádhyai*, RV. vi, 20, 8) to go quickly or repeatedly; to come, wander, run, spread, get about, RV.; AV.; VS.; to appear, make one's appearance, RV.; AV.; BṛĀrUp.; to approach any one with requests (with two acc.), ask, request, RV.; AV.: Pass. *īyate*, to be asked or requested, RV.: Caus. *āyayati*, to cause to go or escape, Vop.; [cf. Gk. εἶ-μι, ἴ-μεν; Lat. *e-o*, *ī-mus*, *i-ter*, &c.; Lith. *ei-mì*, 'I go;' Slav. *i-dû*, 'I go,' *i-ti*, 'to go;' Goth. *i-ddja*, 'I went.']

1. **It**, ifc. going, going towards; cf. *arthêt;* (for 2. *it* see s. v.)

Ita, mfn. ifc. gone; returned; obtained (cf. *an-ita*, *ud-ita*, &c.); remembered, L.; (*ám*), n. way, ŚBr. **Itasu**, mfn. one whose animal spirits have departed, TS.

1. **Iti**, f., *ityaí* (dat.), see √*i* above; (for 2. *iti* see s. v.)

Itya, mfn. to be gone to or towards, Pāṇ. iii, 1, 109; Bhaṭṭ.; (*ā́*), f. going, stepping, VS. xii, 62; RV.; ŚBr.; a litter, palanquin, Pāṇ. Comm.

Ityaka, *as*, m. a door-keeper, chamberlain, Kathās.

Itvan, mf(*arī*)n. going. See *agrêtvan* and *prātar-itvan.*

Itvará, mf(*ī*)n. going, walking, RV. x, 88, 4; travelling; a traveller; cruel, harsh, L.; poor, indigent, L.; low, vile, condemned, Pañcad.; (*as*), m. a bull or steer allowed to go at liberty (v. l. *itcara*, q. v.), L.; (*ī*), f. a disloyal or unchaste woman, Rājat.

इक्कट *ikkaṭa*, *as*, m. a kind of reed, L. See *itkaṭa* and *utkaṭa.*

इक्कवाल *ikkavāla*, in astrology = اقبال *iqbāl*, good fortune, prosperity.

इक्षु *ikshú*, *us*, m. (√2. *ish*, Uṇ. iii, 157), the sugar-cane, AV. i, 34, 5; Kauś.; ĀśvGṛ.; Mn. &c.; (twelve species of it are enumerated, Suśr.); the stem of the sugar-cane, Mn.; eyelash, VS.; TS. &c.; N. of a king, VP. **-kāṇḍá**, n. the stem or cane of the Saccharum Officinale, the sugar-cane, Suśr.; R.; (*as*), m., N. of two different species of sugar-cane, Saccharum Munja Roxb. and Saccharum Spontaneum, L. **-kuṭṭaka**, m. a gatherer or reaper of sugar-cane, Un. **-kshetra**, n. a field of sugar-cane, Pañcad. **-gandha**, m. Saccharum Spontaneum; a kind of Asteracantha Longifolia; (*ā*), f. Saccharum Spontaneum, Asteracantha Longifolia, Capparis Spinosa, Batatas Paniculata, L. **-gandhikā**, f. Batatas Paniculata, L. **-ja**, mfn. coming from sugar-cane, Suśr. **-tulyā**, f. Saccharum Spontaneum, L. **-daṇḍa**, n. the stem or cane of the Saccharum Officinale. **-darbhā**, f. a kind of grass or sugar-cane, L. **-dā**, f., N. of a river; see *ikshulā*, *ikshumālinī*, *ikshu-mālavī*. **-netra**, n. a kind of sugar-cane, L. **—pattra,** m. the grain Penicillaria Spicata, L.; (*ī*), f. Acorus Calamus, Nir. **—parṇī,** f. Acorus Calamus, ib. **—pāka,** m. molasses, L. **—pra,** m. the plant Saccharum Sara, L. **—bālikā,** f. Saccharum Spontaneum, = *-tulyā*, L. **—bhakshikā,** f. a meal of sugar or molasses, Comm. on Pāṇ. **—bhakshita,** m.f(*ā* & *ī*). chewing sugar-cane, Vop. **—matī,** f., N. of a river in Kurukshetra, MBh.; Hariv.; R. **—mālavī** or **-mālinī,** f., N. of a river, MBh.; see *ikshu-dā*. **—mūla,** n. a kind of sugar-cane; the root of sugar-cane. **—meha,** m. diabetes or diabetes mellitus; see *madhu-meha*; (*°mehin*, mfn. suffering from diabetes, Suśr.) **—yantra,** n. a sugar-mill. **—yoni,** m. Saccharum Officinarum, L. **—rasa,** m. the juice of the sugar-cane; molasses, unrefined sugar, Suśr.; Pañcat.; the cane Saccharum Spontaneum, L.; *-kvātha*, m. raw or unrefined sugar, molasses, L.; *-kvāthôda*, m. the sea of syrup L. **—vaṇa,** n. (Pāṇ. viii, 4, 5) a sugar-cane wood. **—vallarī** and **-vallī,** f. Batatas Paniculata, L. **—vāṭikā** or **-vāṭī,** f. Saccharum Officinarum (the common yellow cane), L. **—vāri,** n. the sea of syrup (one of the seven seas), L. **—vikāra,** m. 'change of sugar-cane,' sugar, molasses; any sweetmeat, Suśr. **—veshṭana,** m. a kind of sugar-cane, L. **—śākaṭa** or **-śākina,** n. a field of sugar-cane, L. **—samudra,** m. the sea of syrup (one of the seven seas), L. **—sāra,** m. molasses, raw or unrefined sugar, L. **Ikshvārī** (for *ikshu-vārī*?), m. Saccharum Spontaneum. **Ikshvālikā,** m. (for *ikshu-vālikā*?), Saccharum Spontaneum; (*ā*), f. another sort, Saccharum Fuscum (native reed-pens are made from its stem), L.

Ikshuka, *as*, m. sugar-cane, Suśr.

Ikshukīya, mfn. (Pāṇ. iv, 2, 31) abounding in sugar-cane (as a country or region).

Ikshura, *as*, m. Capparis Spinosa; Asteracantha Longifolia; Saccharum Spontaneum, L.

Ikshuraka, *as*, m. Capparis Spinosa; Saccharum Spontaneum, L.

Ikshulā, f., N. of a river, MBh. See *ikshu-dā*.

इक्ष्वाकु *ikshvākú* [RV.] and *íkshvāku* [AV.], *us*, m., N. of a man, RV. x, 60, 7; AV. xix, 39, 9; of a son of Manu Vaivasvata (father of Kukshi and first king of the solar dynasty in Ayodhyā), MBh.; R.; Bhag.; Hariv.; VP.; a descendant of Ikshvāku, R.; Ragh.; (some Buddhists as well as the Jainas derive their Cakravartins and many of their Arhats from Ikshvāku); (*avas*), m., N. of a warrior-tribe descended from Ikshvāku, VarBṛS.; (*us*), f. a bitter gourd; according to some, the Coloquintida (Citrillus Colocynthis), the fruit of a wild species of Lagenaria Vulgaris, Suśr. **—kula-ja,** mfn. born in the family of Ikshvāku.

इख् *ikh*, cl. 1. P. *ekhati, iyekha, ekhishyati, ekhitum*, to go, move, Dhātup. v, 26 & 27; [cf. Gk. εἴκω, οἴχομαι?]

इङ्कार *iṅ-kāra* and *iṅ-kṛita* = *hiṅ-kāra, hiṅkṛita*, q.v.

इङ्ख् *iṅkh*, cl. 1. P. *iṅkhati, iṅkhām-cakāra, iṅkhishyati, iṅkhitum*, to go, move, Dhātup. v, 26 & 27; [cf. Hib. *imchim*, 'I go on, proceed, march?']

इङ्ग् *iṅg*, cl. 1. P., ep. Ā. *iṅgati, -te* (Dhātup. v, 46), to go, go to or towards; to move or agitate, MBh.; Bhag.: Caus. P. *iṅgayati*, to move, agitate, shake, RV. i, 167, 45; ŚBr.; (in Gr.) to divide or separate the members of a compound word, use a word or bring it into such a grammatical relation that it is considered *iṅgya*, see below, RPrāt.; [cf. Hib. *ing*, 'a stir, a move.']

Iṅga, mfn. movable, locomotive, MBh.; surprising, wonderful, L.; (*as*), m. a hint or sign, an indication of sentiment by gesture, knowledge, L.; (*ā*), f. (with Buddh.) a manner of counting, Lalit.

Iṅgana, *am*, n. shaking, KātyŚr.; (in Gr.) separation of one member of a compound from another; separation by the *ava-graha* or mark of tmesis, Comm. on RPrāt.

Iṅgita, *am*, n. palpitation; change of the voice, internal motion, motion of various parts of the body as indicating the intentions; hint, sign, gesture; aim, intention, real but covert purpose, Mn.; R.; MBh.; Suśr.; Hit.; Ragh. &c. **—kovida** or **-jña,** mfn. understanding signs, acquainted with the gesture of another, skilled in the expression or interpretation of internal sentiments by external gesture. **Iṅgitâdhyāsita,** n. play of features, MBh.

Iṅgya, mfn. movable from its place (in the Prātiśākhyas a term for those words or rather parts of a compound word which in certain grammatical operations may be separated from the preceding part), a word which in the Pada-pāṭha is divided by the *ava-graha* or mark of tmesis, RPrāt.; APrāt.

इङ्गिड *iṅgiḍa*, *as*, m., N. of a plant, Kauś.

इङ्गुद *iṅguda*, *as, ī*, m. f. the medicinal tree Terminalia Catappa (in Bengal confounded with Putrañjīva Roxburghii Wall.), MBh.; R.; Suśr.; Śak.; Ragh.; (*am*), n. the nut of the tree Terminalia Catappa, MBh.

Iṅgula, *as, ī*, m. f. Terminalia Catappa, L.

इचिकिल *icikila*, *as*, m. a pond; mud, mire, L.

इच्छक 1. *icchaka*, *as*, m. the citron, Citrus Medica, L.

इच्छक 2. *icchaka, icchā*, &c. See p. 169, col. 1.

इज्जल *ijjala*, *as*, m. a small tree growing in wet and saline soil (or on low grounds near the sea), Barringtonia Acutangula Gærtn., L.

इज्य *ijya*, mfn. (irr. fut. pass. p. of √*yaj*), to be revered or honoured, RāmatUp.; BhP. &c.; (*as*), m. a teacher, BhP.; a deity, god, BhP.; N. of Bṛihaspati (the teacher or Guru of the gods); of the planet Jupiter; (*ā*), f. a sacrifice, making offerings to the gods or manes, Pāṇ. iii, 3, 98; KātyŚr.; MBh.; Bhag.; Suśr.; Ragh. &c.; a gift, donation; worship, reverence; meeting, union, L.; a cow, L.; a bawd or procuress, L. **—śīla,** mfn. sacrificing frequently, L.

इञ्चाक *iñcāka*, *as*, m. a shrimp, prawn.

इञ्जना *iñjanā*, f. (fr. *iñj* = √*iṅg*?), movement, Lalit.

इट् *iṭ*, cl. 1. P. *eṭati, eṭitum* (Dhātup. ix, 31), to go; to go to or towards; (p. *iṭát*, RV. x, 171, 1) to make haste; to err [NBD.]

इट *íṭa*, *as*, m. a kind of reed or grass; a texture woven from it, a mat, AV. vi, 14, 3; ix, 3, 18; N. of a Ṛishi (author of RV. x, 171), RAnukr. **—sūná,** n. a texture formed of reed, a mat, ŚBr.

इट्चर *iṭ-cara*, *as*, m. (fr. 4. *ish* and *cara*), a bull or steer allowed to go at liberty, L.

इठिमिका *iṭhimikā*, f., N. of a section of the Kaṭhaka recension of the Yajur-veda.

इड् *iḍ* (fr. √1. *ish*; connected with *írā*, q.v.; only in inst., gen., abl. sing., and acc. pl. *iḍā́* and *iḍás*; or, according to the spelling of the Ṛig-veda, *iḷā́* and *iḷás*), a refreshing draught, refreshment, libation offered to the gods, RV.; the flow of speech, the stream of sacred words and worship, prayer; (Sāy.) the earth, food, RV.; VS.; (*iḍas* or *iḷas*), pl. the objects of devotion (a particular form of Agni addressed in the fourth verse of the Āprī hymn RV. i, 13), RV. iii, 4, 3; (erroneously also referred to in the Brāhmaṇas &c. as if etymologically connected with the words *īḍya, īḍita, īḷita*, 'the praiseworthy,' 'the praised,' which are used in other passages as the designation of the same object of worship), VS.; AitBr.; ŚBr.; ĀśvŚr. &c.

Iḍá, *as*, m., N. of Agni (who is to be addressed with prayers, or invoked with the stream or flow of praise), VS. ii, 3; N. of a king (a son of Kardama or Manu), VP.; (cf. *ila*.) **—viḍa,** m., N. of a son of Daśaratha, VP.; (*ā*), f., N. of a daughter of Tṛiṇabindu and mother of Kuvera, VP.; BhP.; a species of she-goat, BhP.

Iḍás or **Iḷas** (gen. of *iḍ* above). **—páti,** 'Lord of refreshment,' N. of Pūshan, RV. vi, 58, 4; of Bṛihaspati, RV. v, 42, 14; of Vishṇu, BhP. vi, 5, 27. **—padé,** in the place of sacred libation, i.e. at the altar or place of offering, RV.

Íḍā, f. or (in Ṛig-veda) **Iḷā,** (not to be confounded with the inst. case of *iḍ* above), refreshing draught, refreshment, animation, recreation, comfort, vital spirit, RV.; AV.; AitBr.; offering, libation (especially a holy libation, offered between the Pra-yāja and Anu-yāja, and consisting of four preparations of milk, poured into a vessel containing water, and then partially drunk by the priest and sacrificers; personified in the cow, the symbol of feeding and nourishment), ŚBr. i, 8, 1, 1, &c.; AitBr.; KātyŚr.; Kauś.; (metaphorically, cf. *iḍ*) stream or flow of praise and worship (personified as the goddess of sacred speech and action, invoked together with Aditi and other deities, but especially in the Āprī hymns together with Sarasvatī and Mahī or Bhāratī), RV.; AV.; VS. &c.; the earth, food, Sāy.; a cow; the goddess *Iḍā* or *Iḷā* (daughter of Manu or of man thinking on and worshipping the gods; she is the wife of Budha and mother of Purū-ravas; in another aspect she is called Maitrāvaruṇī as daughter of Mitra-Varuṇa, two gods who were objects of the highest and most spiritual devotion); N. of Durgā; of a daughter of Daksha and wife of Kaśyapa; of a wife of Vasudeva and of the Rudra Ṛita-dhvaja; speech, BhP.; heaven, L.; earth, MBh.; a particular artery on the left side of the body; a tubular vessel (one of the principal channels of the vital spirit, that which is on the right side of the body), L. **—camasa,** m. a vessel for the Iḍā oblation, Kauś. **—jāta,** m. a species of Agallochum, L. **—daḍha** (*iḷā°, iḍā°*, and *iḷā°*), n., N. of a particular Ishṭy-ayana or sacrificial observance, AitBr.; ĀśvŚr. **—pātra,** n. and **-pātrī,** f. a vessel for the Iḍā oblation. **—prajas** (*asas*), f. pl. the descendants of Iḍā. **—°yás-padé** (*iḷāyā́s-padé*), ind. at the place of Iḷā, i.e. of worship and libation, earth, RV.; AV. **—vat** (*iḍā°*), mfn. refreshing, granting fresh vital spirits; possessed of refreshment, refreshed; possessed of sacrificial food [Sāy.], RV.; containing the word *iḍā*, TāṇḍyaBr.; (in music) a particular time.

Iḍācikā, f. (fr. *iḍā*?), a wasp, L.

Iḍikā, f. the earth, L.

Iḍīya, mfn. (gaṇa *utkarâdi*, Pāṇ. iv, 2, 90), belonging to *iḍā*.

इडिक्क *iḍikka*, *as*, m. a wild goat, L.

इड्वर *iḍvara*, *as*, m. a bull fit to be set at liberty, L. See *iṭ-cara*.

इण्डरी *iṇḍarī* or *iṇḍalī*, f. a kind of cake, L.

इण्ड्व *iṇḍvá*, *e*, n. du. two coverings for the hands (made of Muñja grass) to protect them in removing the Ukhā (from the fire), ŚBr.; KātyŚr. [T. reads *iṇḍra*].

इण्वेरिका *iṇverikā*, f. a kind of cake, L.

इत् 2. *it*, (in Gr.) an indicatory letter or syllable attached to roots &c. (= *anubandha*, q.v.)

इत् 3. *it* for the Ved. particle *id*, q.v.

इतर *í-tara*, mf(*ā*)n. (the neuter is *ad* in classical Sanskṛit, but *am* [*ad*, ŚBr.] in Ved., Pāṇ. vii, 1, 25. 26; comparative form of pronom. base 3. *i*; cf. Lat. *iterum*; Hib. *iter*), the other (of two), another; (pl.) the rest; (with abl.) different from, RV.; AV.; ŚBr.; MBh.; R.; Mn.; Ragh.; Hit. &c.; low, vile, Kād.; expelled, rejected, L.; (*ā*), f. said to be a N. of the mother of Aitareya; (*ad*), ind. whereas, whilst, Subh.; *itara, itara*, the one—the other, this—that. (*Itara* connected antithetically with a preceding word often signifies the contrary idea, e.g. *vijayāya itarāya vā* [MBh.], to victory or defeat; so in Dvandva compounds, *sukhêtareshu* [ŚvetUp.], in happiness and distress; it sometimes, however, forms a Tat-purusha compound with another word to express the one idea implied in the contrary of that word, e.g. *dakshiṇêtara*, the left hand.) **—janá,** m. an ordinary man, Śārṅg.; (*ās*), m. pl. 'other men;' a euphemistic name of certain beings who appear to be considered as spirits of darkness (Kuvera belongs to them), AV.; VS.; TS.; MaitrS.; GopBr. **—jātīya,** mfn. ordinary, common-place. **—tas,** ind. otherwise than, different from; from or to another direction, KātyŚr.; ŚBr. &c.; (*itaścêtaratasca*, hither and thither, R.) **—tra,** ind. elsewhere, BhP.; on the other hand, else, Yogas. **—thā,** ind. in another manner, in a contrary manner; perversely; on the other hand, else, ŚBr.; KātyŚr.; Śiś. &c. **—pāṇi,** m. the left hand, ĀśvGṛ. iv, 7, 13. **Itarâṅga,** mfn. being a means to another, ancillary to another, Sāh. 266. **Itarêtara,** mfn. (occurring chiefly in oblique cases of sing. and in comp.; perhaps for *itaras-itara*; cf. *anyo'nya, paras-para*), one another, one with another, mutual, respective, several; (*am*), n. or adv. mutually, &c., KātyŚr.; MBh.; Ragh. &c.; *-kāmyā*, f. respective or several fancies or inclinations; *-pratyaya*, mfn. dependent on each other; *-pratyaya-tva*, n. mutual dependance, Bādar.; *-yoga*, m. mutual connexion or relation (of the simple members, as in a

Dvandva compound), Siddh. i, p. 431. **Itarêtarâśraya,** mfn. taking refuge with or depending on each other, concerning mutually; (*as*), m. a particular logical error, circular reasoning, Sarvad. **Itarêtarôpakṛiti-mat,** mfn. helping each other, Śiś. ix, 33.

Itare-dyus, ind. on another or different day, Pāṇ. v, 3, 22.

इतस् *i-tás*, ind. (fr. 3. *i* with affix *tas*, used like the abl. case of the pronoun *idam*), from hence, hence, here (opposed to *amu-tas* and *amu-tra*), RV.; AV.; ŚBr.; Śak. &c.; from this point; from this world, in this world, ŚBr.; ChUp.; Prab. &c.; (*itas, itas*, here—there; *itaścêtaśca*, hence and thence, hither and thither, here and there, to and fro); from this time, now, RV.; AV.; MBh. &c.; therefore, R. **Itá-ūti,** mfn. extending or reaching from hence; existing or lasting longer than the present time, future; one who has obtained help [Sāy.], RV. **Itáḥ-pradāna,** mfn. offering from hence, i. e. from this world, TS.; ŚBr. **Itas-tatas,** ind. here and there, hither and thither, R.; Hit. &c.

इति 2. *iti*, ind. (fr. pronominal base 3. *i*), in this manner, thus (in its original signification *iti* refers to something that has been said or thought, or lays stress on what precedes; in the Brāhmaṇas it is often equivalent to 'as you know,' reminding the hearer or reader of certain customs, conditions, &c. supposed to be known to him).

In quotations of every kind *iti* means that the preceding words are the very words which some person has or might have spoken, and placed thus at the end of a speech it serves the purpose of inverted commas (*ity uktvā*, having so said; *iti kṛitvā*, having so considered, having so decided). It may often have reference merely to what is passing in the mind, e.g. *bālo 'pi nâvamantavyo manushya iti bhūmipaḥ*, a king, though a child, is not to be despised, saying to one's self, 'he is a mortal,' (Gr. 928.) In dram. *iti tathā karoti* means 'after these words he acts thus.'

Sometimes *iti* is used to include under one head a number of separate objects aggregated together (e.g. *ijyâdhyayanadānāni tapaḥ satyaṃ kshamā damaḥ | alobha iti mārgo 'yam*, 'sacrificing, studying, liberality, penance, truth, patience, self-restraint, absence of desire,' this course of conduct, &c.)

Iti is sometimes followed by *evam, iva*, or a demonstrative pronoun pleonastically (e.g. *tām brūyād bhavatîty evam*, her he may call 'lady,' thus).

Iti may form an adverbial compound with the name of an author (e. g. *iti-pāṇini*, thus according to Pāṇini). It may also express the act of calling attention (lo! behold!) It may have some other significations, e. g. something additional (as in *ity-ādi*, et cætera), order, arrangement specific or distinctive, and identity. It is used by native commentators after quoting a rule to express 'according to such a rule' (e.g. *anudāttaṅita ity ātmanepadam bhavati*, according to the rule of Pāṇini i, 3, 12, the Ātmane-pada takes place). *Kim iti* = *kim*, wherefore, why? (In the Śatapatha-brāhmaṇa *ti* occurs for *iti*; cf. Prākṛit *ti* and *tti*.) **–katha,** mfn. unworthy of trust, not fit to be credited; wicked, lost; (*ā*), f. unmeaning or nonsensical discourse; (for *atikatha*, q.v.), L. **–karaṇa,** n. or **-kāra,** m. the word *iti*, RPrāt. **–karaṇīya** [Kir. vii, 17] or **-kartavya** or **-kārya** or **-kṛitya,** mfn. proper or necessary to be done according to certain conditions; (*am*), n. duty, obligation, MBh.; R.; Mn.; *-tā*, f. any proper or necessary measure, obligation. *Itikartavyatā-mūḍha*, mfn. embarrassed, dumb-foundered, wholly at a loss what to do, Hit. **–thá,** mf(*ī*)n. Ved. such a one, such, ŚBr. i, 8, 1, 4 & xi, 6, 3, 11. **–nāman,** mfn. having such a name, Hariv. **–para,** mfn. followed by *iti* (as a word), TPrāt. **–pāṇini,** ind. thus according to Pāṇini's very words, Comm. on Pāṇ. **–mātra,** mfn. of such extent or quality. **–vat,** ind. in the same manner, Sāh.; Comm. on Ragh. **–vṛitta,** n. occurrence, event, R.; Sāh.; Vām. &c. **–hari,** ind. thus according to Hari's very words, Vop. **Ity-anta,** mfn. ending thus, Comm. on Pāṇ. **Ity-artha,** mfn. having such a sense or meaning; (*am*), ind. for this purpose, R. **Ity-ādi,** mfn. having such (thing or things) at the beginning, thus beginning, and so forth, et cætera, Hit.; Vet.; Vedāntas. &c. **Ity-ālikhitá,** mfn. so scratched or marked, ŚBr. **Ity-ukta,** n. 'so said,' information, report. **Ity-unmṛiśya,** mfn. to be touched in this manner, ŚBr. **Ity-etan-nāmaka,** mfn. having those names (as aforesaid), Vedāntas. **Ity-evam-ādi,** ind. and so forth, VP.; Kāvyād.

Itiśa, *as*, m., N. of a man, (gaṇa *naḍâdi*, Pāṇ. iv, 1, 99.)

Iti-ha, ind. thus indeed, according to tradition. **Iti-hâsa,** *as*, m. (*iti-ha-āsa*, 'so indeed it was'), talk, legend, tradition, history, traditional accounts of former events, heroic history, ŚBr.; MBh.; Mn. &c.

इतीक *itīka*, *as*, m., N. of a people (cf. *ijika*).

इत्कट *itkaṭa*, *as*, m. a kind of reed or grass. See *ikkaṭa*.

इत्किला *itkilā*, f., N. of a perfume, L. See *rocanā*.

इत्थ *ittha*, *am*, n. in astron. = ἰχθύς, VarBṛS.

इत्थम् *itthám*, ind. (fr. *id*, q.v.; Pāṇ. v, 3, 24), thus, in this manner, RV.; AV.; TS.; R.; Śak. &c.; [cf. Lat. *item*.] **–vidha** (*itthaṃ°*), mfn. of such a kind, endowed with such qualities, Bhartṛ. **–kāram,** ind. in this manner, Pāṇ. iii, 4, 27. **–bhāva,** m. the being thus endowed. **–bhūta,** mfn. become thus, being thus or in such manner; so circumstanced, Pāṇ.; Śak.; Megh. &c.

इत्थशाल *itthaśāla* (fr. Arabic اِتِّصال), N. of the third Yoga in astronomy.

इत्था *itthā́*, ind. Ved. thus; (often used in the Ṛig-veda, and sometimes only to lay stress on a following word; therefore by native etymologists [Nir.] considered as a particle of affirmation.) *Itthā* is often connected with words expressing devotion to the gods &c. in the sense of thus, truly, really; especially with *dhī* as an adjective. Hence *itthā-dhī* = such, i.e. true (*satyā*) or real worship. Similarly, *itthā-dhī*, mfn. so devout, so pious, i. e. very devout; performing such or true works [Sāy.], RV.; AV.; KaṭhUp.

इत्थात् *itthā́t*, ind. (= *ittham*), Ved. thus, in this way.

इत्य *itya*, &c., *itvan*, &c. See p. 163, col. 3.

इद् *id*, ind. Ved. (probably the neut. form of the pronom. base *i*, see 3. *i*; a particle of affirmation) even, just, only; indeed, assuredly (especially in strengthening an antithesis, e.g. *yáthā váśanti devā́s tátheˊd asat*, as the gods wish it, thus indeed it will be, RV. viii, 28, 4; *dípsanta íd ripávo nā́ha debhuḥ*, the enemies wishing indeed to hurt were in nowise able to hurt, RV. i, 147, 3).

Id is often added to words expressing excess or exclusion (e.g. *viśva it*, every one indeed; *śaśvad it*, constantly indeed; *eka it*, one only). At the beginning of sentences it often adds emphasis to pronouns, prepositions, particles (e.g. *tvam it*, thou indeed; *yadi it*, if indeed, &c.)

Id occurs often in the Ṛig-veda and Atharva-veda, seldom in the Brāhmaṇas, and its place is taken in classical Sanskṛit by *eva* and other particles.

इदम् 1. *idám*; *ayám, iyám, idám* (fr. *id*, Uṇ. iv, 156; gaṇa *sarvâdi*, Pāṇ. i, 1, 27; Vop.; a kind of neut. of the pronom. base 3. *i* with *am* [cf. Lat. *is, ea, id*, and *idem*]; the regular forms are partly derived from the pronom. base *a*; see Gr. 224; the Veda exhibits various irregular formations, e.g. fr. pronom. base *a*, an inst. *enā́, ayā́* [used in general adverbially], and gen. loc. du. *ayós*, and perhaps also *avós*, in RV. vi, 67, 11; vii, 67, 4; x, 132, 5 [BRD.]; fr. the base *ima*, a gen. sing. *imásya*, only RV.; the RV. has in a few instances the irregular accentuation *ásmai*, v, 39, 5, &c.; *ásya*, iv, 15, 5, &c.; *ā́bhis*, vi, 25, 2, &c.: the forms derived fr. *a* are used enclitically if they take the place of the third personal pronoun, do not stand at the beginning of a verse or period, and have no peculiar stress laid upon them), this, this here, referring to something near the speaker; known, present; (opposed to *adas*, e.g. *ayaṃ lokaḥ* or *idaṃ viśvam* or *idaṃ sarvam*, this earthly world, this universe; *ayam agniḥ*, this fire which burns on the earth; but *asāv agniḥ*, that fire in the sky, i. e. the lightning: so also *idam* or *iyam* alone sometimes signifies 'this earth;' *ime smaḥ*, here we are.)

Idam often refers to something immediately following, whereas *etad* points to what precedes (e.g. *śrutvâitad idam ūcuḥ*, having heard that they said this).

Idam occurs connected with *yad, tad, etad, kim*, and a personal pronoun, partly to point out anything more distinctly and emphatically, partly pleonastically (e.g. *tad idaṃ vākyam*, this speech here following; *so 'yaṃ vidūshakaḥ*, this Vidūshaka here).

Idád-vasu, mfn. rich in this and that, AV. xiii, 4, 54.

2. Idám, ind. [Ved. and in a few instances in classical Sanskṛit] here, to this place; now, even, just; there; with these words, RV.; AV.; ŚBr.; AitBr.; ChUp.; in this manner, R. ii, 53, 31; Śak. (v.l. for *iti* in *kim iti josham āsyate*, 202, 8). **–yu** (*idaṃ°*), desiring this, Nir. **–yuga,** n. = *etad yugam* [T.], gaṇa *pratijanâdi*, Pāṇ. iv, 4, 99. **–rūpa** (*idáṃ°*), mfn. having this shape, ŚBr. **–vid,** mfn. knowing this or conversant with this, AitĀr.; Nir. **–kāryā,** f. the plant Hedysarum Alhagi, L. **–tana** mfn. being now, living in this time, Comm. on Mn. ix, 68. **–tā,** f. the being this, identity, Sarvad. **–tṛitīya,** mfn. doing this for the third time, Comm. on Pāṇ. vi, 2, 162. **–dvitīya,** mfn. doing this for the second time, ib. **–prakāram,** ind. in this manner, Vop. **–prathama,** mfn. doing this for the first time; having this as the first or best; being by this the first, Comm. on Pāṇ. vi, 2, 162. **–madhu** (*idáṃ°*), n. a particular hymn, TS. vii, 5, 10, 1. **–madhura,** n. id., Kāṭh. 34, 5. **–máya,** mf(*ī*)n. made or consisting of this, ŚBr. xiv, 7, 2, 6.

इदा *i-dā́*, ind. (fr. pronom. base 3. *i*, Pāṇ. v, 3, 20), Ved. now, at this moment; (often connected with a gen. of *ahan*, e. g. *idā́ cid áhnaḥ* or *ahna idā*, this present day, 'now-a-days;' and with *hyas*, e.g. *idā hyaḥ*, only yesterday), RV. **–°dika** (*idâdika*), mfn. beginning now or with this moment. **–vatsará,** m. (originally perhaps) 'the present or current year;' one of the names given to the single years of a period of five years; one of the five years in which gifts of clothes and food are productive of great rewards, AV.; VS.; MaitrS. &c. (*Idāvatsarīya*, mfn. belonging to such a year, Comm. on Pāṇ. *Idu-vatsara* and *id-vatsara* = *idā-vatsara* above. *Id-vatsarīya* = *idāvatsarīya* above.)

I-dāni, *i*, n. a measure of time (the fifteenth part of an Etarhi), ŚBr. xii, 3, 2, 5.

I-dā́nīm, ind. now, at this moment, in this case, just, even (with gen. of *ahan*, e.g. *idānīm ahnaḥ*, this present day, 'now-a-days;' *idānīm eva*, just now; immediately; *idānīm api*, in this case too; *tata idānīm*, thereupon, then), RV; ŚBr.; Ait.; Ragh.; (in rare cases it is an expletive, affecting but slightly the sense). **Idānīṃtana,** mf(*ī*)n. present, modern, momentary, of the present moment, Sāh.; *-tva*, n. the being momentary, Comm. on Mn.

इद्ध *iddhá*, इध्म *idhmá*, &c. See √*indh*.

इन् *in*. See √*inv*.

इन *iná*, mfn. (fr. √*i*, Uṇ. iii, 2; or fr. *in* = √*inv*), able, strong, energetic, determined, bold; powerful, mighty; wild; glorious, RV.; (*as*), m. a lord, master; a king, BhP.; N. of an Āditya; the sun; the lunar mansion Hasta, L. **–sabha,** n. a royal court or assembly. **Inôdaya,** m. sunrise.

इनक्ष् *inaksh* (said to be a Desid. of √*naś*; 2. sg. *ínakshasi*, RV. x, 75, 4; Subj. *ínakshat*, i, 132, 6; p. *ínakshat*, i, 51, 9; x, 45, 7), to endeavour to reach, strive to obtain, RV.

इनानी *inānī*, f., N. of a plant (= Vaṭapattrī), L.

इनु *inu*, *us*, m., N. of a Gandharva, L.

इन्थिहा *inthihā*, f. (fr. Arabic اِنْتِهَا), an astrological term.

इन्द् *ind*, cl. 1. P. *indati, aindat, indām-babhūva, inditum*, to be powerful; 'to see' [Goldst.]; perhaps = √*und*, 'to drop?' (the meaning 'to be powerful' seems to be given by native lexicographers merely for the etymology of the word *indra*, q.v.), Dhātup. iii, 26; Nir.; Vop.

इन्दम्बर *indambara*, *am*, n. the blue lotus, Nymphæa Cærulea, L. See *indī-vara*.

इन्दिन्दिरा *indindirā*, f. a large bee, Prasannar.

इन्दिरा *indirā*, f., N. of Lakshmī, wife of Vishṇu, Kathās.; BhP.; beauty, splendour. **–mandira,** m. 'the home of Lakshmī;' N. of Vishṇu, L.

Indirâlaya, n. 'the abode of Indirā or Lakshmī,' the blue lotus, Nymphæa Stellata and Cyanea (the goddess Indirā issued at the creation from its petals), L.

इन्दीवर *indī-vara* or *indī-vāra* or *indi-vara, as, am,* m. n. the blossom of a blue lotus, Nymphæa Stellata and Cyanea, MBh.; R.; Suśr.; Prab. &c.; (*as*), m. a bee, Gīt.; (*ī*), f. the plant Asparagus Racemosus; (*ā*), f. another plant, L. **–dala,** n. the petal of a blue lotus, Bhartṛ. **–prabhā,** f., N. of a daughter of Kaṇva, Kathās. **Indīvarâksha,** m. 'lotus-eyed,' N. of a man, Kathās.

Indīvariṇī, f. a blue lotus, a group of blue lotuses, L.

इन्दु *índu, us,* m. (√*und,* Uṇ. i, 13; probably fr. *ind* = √*und,* 'to drop' [see p. 165, col. 3, & cf. *índra*]; perhaps connected with *bindu,* which last is unknown in the Ṛig-veda, BRD.), Ved. a drop (especially of Soma), Soma, RV.; AV.; VS.; a bright drop, a spark, TS.; the moon; (*avas*), m. pl. the moons, i. e. the periodic changes of the moon; time of moonlight, night, RV.; MBh.; Śak.; Megh. &c.; (*us*), m. camphor, Bhpr.; the point on a die, AV. vii, 109, 6; N. of Vāstoshpati, RV. vii, 54, 2; a symbolic expression for the number 'one;' designation of the Anusvāra; a coin, L. (In the Brāhmaṇas *indu* is used only for the moon; but the connexion between the meanings 'Soma juice' and 'moon' in the word *indu* has led to the same two ideas being transferred in classical Sanskṛit to the word *Soma,* although the latter has properly only the sense 'Soma juice.') **–kakshā,** f. the radiating circle all round the moon. **–kamala,** n. the blossom of the white lotus, L. **–kara,** m., N. of a man. **–kalaśa,** m. id., Kathās. **–kalā,** f. a digit of the moon; N. of several plants, Cocculus Cordifolius, Sarcostema Viminale, Ligusticum Ajowan, L. **–kalikā,** f. the plant Pandanus Odoratissimus, L. **–kānta,** m. 'moon-loved,' the moon-stone, Kād.; (*ā*), f. night, L. **–kirīṭa,** m. 'moon-crested,' N. of Śiva, Prasannar. **–kesarin,** m., N. of a king, Kathās. **–kshaya,** m. wane of the moon; new moon. **–ja,** m. 'son of the moon,' N. of the planet Mercury, VarBṛS.; (*ā*), f. the river Revā or Narmadā in the Dekhan, L. **–janaka,** m. 'father of the moon,' the ocean (the moon being produced at the churning of the ocean), L. **–dala,** n. a portion of the moon, a digit, crescent. **–dina,** n. a lunar day. **–nandana** and **-putra,** m., N. of the planet Mercury. **–pushpikā,** f. the plant Methonica Superba, L. **–prabha,** m., N. of a man, Kathās. **–phala,** m. Spondias Mangifera, L. **–bimba,** n. the disk of the moon, Śārṅg. **–bha,** n., N. of the Nakshatra Mṛigaśiras; (*ā*), f. a group of lotuses. **–bhavā,** f., N. of a river. **–bhṛit,** m. 'bearing the crescent on his forehead,' N. of Śiva. **–maṇi,** m. the moon-stone. **–maṇḍala,** n. the orb or disc of the moon. **–mat** (*índu°*), m. (in liturgical language) N. of Agni (because in the verses in which he is addressed the word *indu* occurs), VS. xxvi, 13; SBr.; (*tī*), f. day of full moon, L.; N. of the sister of Bhoja and wife of Aja, Ragh.; N. of a river, R.; of a commentary. **–mitra,** m., N. of a grammarian. **–mukha,** mf(*ī*)n. moon-faced, Hāsy. **–mauli,** m., N. of Śiva, Prab.; Bālar. **–ratna,** n. a pearl, L. **–rāja,** m., N. of a man. **–rekhā,** f. a digit of the moon. **–lekhā,** f. a digit of the moon; the plant Menispermum Glabrum; the moon-plant Asclepias Acida; a kind of lovage, Ligusticum Ajwæn, L. **–loka,** m. = *candraloka,* q.v. **–lohaka,** n. silver, L. **–vadana,** mf(*ā*)n. moon-faced, Mālav.; (*ā*), f. a metre of four verses (each of which contains fourteen syllables). **–vallī,** f. the plant Sarcostemma Viminale, L. **–vāra,** m. in astrology = the Arabic إِدْبار. **–vrata,** n. a religious observance depending on the age of the moon (diminishing the quantity of food by a certain portion daily, for a fortnight or a month, &c.), MBh.; (cf. *cāndrāyaṇa.*) **–śakalā,** f. Vernonia Anthelminthica, L. **–śapharī,** f. Bauhinia Tomentosa, L. **–śekhara,** m. 'moon-crested,' N. of Śiva, Kathās.; of a Kiṃnara. **–suta** and **-sūnu,** m., N. of the planet Mercury.

Induka, *as,* m., N. of a plant, = *aśmantaka,* L.

इन्दूर *indūra, as,* m. a rat, a mouse [cf. *undura, unduru*], L.

इन्द्र *índra, as,* m. (for etym. as given by native authorities see Nir. x, 8; Sāy. on RV. i, 3, 4; Uṇ. ii, 28; according to BRD. fr. *in* = √*inv* with suff. *ra* preceded by inserted *d,* meaning 'to subdue, conquer;' according to Muir, S. T. v, 119, for *sindra* fr. √*syand,* 'to drop;' more probably from √*ind,* 'to drop,' q.v., and connected with *indu* above), the god of the atmosphere and sky; the Indian Jupiter Pluvius or lord of rain (who in Vedic mythology reigns over the deities of the intermediate region or atmosphere; he fights against and conquers with his thunderbolt [*vajra*] the demons of darkness, and is in general a symbol of generous heroism; *Indra* was not originally lord of the gods of the sky, but his deeds were most useful to mankind, and he was therefore addressed in prayers and hymns more than any other deity, and ultimately superseded the more lofty and spiritual Varuṇa; in the later mythology *Indra* is subordinated to the triad Brahman, Vishṇu, and Śiva, but remained the chief of all other deities in the popular mind), RV.; AV.; ŚBr.; Mn.; MBh; R. &c. &c.; (he is also regent of the east quarter, and considered one of the twelve Ādityas), Mn.; R.; Suśr. &c.; in the Vedānta he is identified with the supreme being; a prince; ifc. best, excellent, the first, the chief (of any class of objects; cf. *surêndra, rājêndra, parvatêndra,* &c.), Mn.; Hit.; the pupil of the right eye (that of the left being called Indrāṇī or Indra's wife), ŚBr.; BṛĀrUp.; the number fourteen, Sūryas; N. of a grammarian; of a physician; the plant Wrightia Antidysenterica (see *kuṭaja*), L.; a vegetable poison, L.; the twenty-sixth Yoga or division of a circle on the plane of the ecliptic; the Yoga star in the twenty-sixth Nakshatra, γ Pegasi; the human soul, the portion of spirit residing in the body; night, L.; one of the nine divisions of Jambu-dvipa or the known continent, L.; (*ā*), f. the wife of Indra, see *indrāṇī;* N. of a plant, L.; (*ī*), f., N. of an attendant of Devī. **–ṛishabhā** (*índra°*), f. 'having Indra as a bull, or impregnated by Indra,' the earth, AV. xii, 1, 6. **–karman,** m. 'performing Indra's deeds;' N. of Vishṇu, R. **–kavi,** m., N. of a poet. **–kārmuka,** n. rainbow, VarBṛS. **–kīla,** m., N. of a mountain, MBh.; a bolt, cross-beam, AVPar.; Suśr. **–kukshi,** m. 'Indra's belly,' N. of particular Soma sacrifices, TāṇḍyaBr. **–kuñjara,** m. Indra's elephant (see *airāvata*), L. **–kūṭa,** m., N. of a mountain, Hariv. **–kṛishṭa,** mfn. 'ploughed by Indra,' growing in a wild state, MBh. **–ketu,** m. Indra's banner, Lalit.; N. of a man, BhP. **–kośa** or **-kosha** or **-koshaka,** m. a platform; a scaffold; a projection of the roof of a house, a kind of balcony or terrace; a pin or bracket projecting from the wall, R. & L. **–krośa,** m., N. of a place, TāṇḍyaBr. **–giri,** m., N. of a mountain, Rājat. **–gupta** (*índra°*), mf(*ā*)n. guarded or protected by Indra, AV. xii, 1, 11; (*as*), m., N. of a Brāhman. **–guru,** m. teacher of Indra, N. of Kaśyapa. **–gopa,** or *ā,* mfn. Ved. having Indra as one's protector, RV. viii, 46, 32; (*as*), m. the insect cochineal of various kinds; a fire-fly (in this sense also *indra-gopaka*). **–ghoshá,** m. 'having the name Indra,' N. of a particular deity, VS.; MaitrS. **–candana,** n. = *hari-candana,* L. **–cāpa,** m. n. Indra's bow, the rainbow, MBh.; Megh.; VarBṛS. **–cirbhiṭī,** f., N. of a plant, L. **–cchanda,** m. a necklace consisting of 1008 strings, VarBṛS.; Pañcad. **–ja,** m., N. of the ape Vālin, L. **–jatu,** n. bitumen, Nir. **–janana,** n. Indra's birth. (*Indrajananīya* [gana *indra-jananâdi,* Pāṇ. iv, 3, 88], mfn. treating of Indra's birth.) **–jā,** mfn. descended from Indra, AV. iv, 3, 7. **–jānu,** m., N. of a monkey, R. **–jālá,** n. the net of Indra, AV. viii, 8, 8; a weapon employed by Arjuna, MBh.; sham, illusion, delusion, magic, sorcery, juggle; the art of magic &c., Kathās.; Ratnāv.; Prab.; Vedāntas.; Sāh. &c.; *-jña,* m. knowing the art of magic, a juggler, sorcerer, VarBṛS.; *-paricaya,* m. knowledge of magic art, Kshem.; *-purusha,* m. a phantom of a man, Daś.; *-vidyā,* f. the science of magic art. **–°jālika,** m. a juggler, a conjurer. **–°jālin,** m. a juggler, sorcerer, Kathās.; N. of a Bodhi-sattva, Lalit. **–jit,** m. 'conqueror of Indra,' N. of the son of Rāvaṇa, R.; Ragh.; of a Dānava, Hariv.; of the father of Rāvaṇa and king of Kāśmīra, Rājat.; of a king and protector of Keśava-dāsa. *Indrajid-vijayin,* m. 'conqueror of Indra-jit,' N. of Lakshmaṇa, L. **–jūta** (*índrá-*), mfn. promoted or excited or procured by Indra, RV. & AV. **–jyeshṭha** (*índra-*), mfn. one whose chief is Indra, led by Indra, RV.; AV.; TS. **–tanū,** f., N. of a kind of bricks, TS. **–tama,** mfn. most Indra-like, RV.; VS. **–taru,** m. Terminalia Arjuna, VarBṛS.; Nir. **–tā,** f. power and dignity of Indra. **–tāpana,** m., N. of a Dānava, MBh.; Hariv. **–tūrīya,** n. a particular rite, TBr.; ŚBr. **–tūla** or **-tūlaka,** n. a flock of cotton or a flocculent seed &c. blown about in the air, L. **–tejas,** n. Indra's thunderbolt, BhP. **–toyā,** f., N. of a river, MBh. **–tva,** n. Indra's power and dignity; kingship. **–tvôta** (*índra°*), mfn. 'favoured or protected by thee, O Indra,' RV. i, 132, 1; viii, 19, 16. **–datta,** m., N. of a Brāhman, Kathās. **–damana,** m., N. of an Asura. **–dāru,** m. the tree Pinus Devadāru, Bhpr. **–devī,** f., N. of the wife of king Megha-vāhana; *-bhavana,* n., N. of the monastery built by the above, Rājat. **–dyumna,** m., N. of several men; (*am*), n., N. of a lake, MBh.; Hariv. **–dru,** m. the trees Terminalia Arjuna and Wrightia Antidysenterica, L. **–druma,** m. Terminalia Arjuna, L. **–dvishṭa** (*índra°*), mfn. hated by Indra, RV. ix, 73, 5; MBh. **–dvīpa,** m. one of the nine Dvīpas or divisions of the known continent, VP. **–dhanús,** n. Indra's bow, the rainbow, AV. xv, 1, 6. **–dhruva,** m., N. of a man. **–dhvaja,** m. Indra's banner, VarBṛS.; N. of a Tathāgata; of a Nāga, L. **–nakshatrá,** n. Indra's lunar mansion; N. of Phalgunī, ŚBr. ii, 1, 2, 11. **–nīla,** m. a sapphire, Ragh.; Megh.; Śiś.; BhP.; *-ka,* m. an emerald, L. **–patnī,** f. the wife of Indra, RV.; VS. **–pada,** m. = *indra-tā.* **–parṇī,** f., N. of a plant (perhaps Methonica Superba), Suśr. **–parvata,** m., N. of a mountain, MBh. **–pātama,** mfn. most worthy to be drunk by Indra, RV. ix, 99, 3. **–pāna,** mfn. worthy to be Indra's drink, RV. **–pāla,** m., N. of a king. **–pālita,** m. 'protected by Indra,' N. of a king, VP.; also of a Vaiśya, Comm. on Pāṇ. viii, 2, 83. **–pīta** (*índra°*), mfn. drunk by Indra, RV.; KātyŚr. **–putrā,** f. 'having Indra as son,' Indra's mother, AV. iii, 10, 13. **–purogama,** mfn. preceded or led on by Indra, having Indra as leader. **–purohitā,** f. the asterism Pushya, L. **–pushpa,** m., **-pushpā, -pushpikā,** and **-pushpī,** f. the medicinal plant Methonica Superba, Bhpr.; Suśr.; L. **–pramati,** m. a pupil of Paila and author of some verses of the Ṛig-veda, RAnukr.; BhP.; VP.; AgP. **–pramada,** m., N. of a man. **–prasūta** (*índra°*), mfn. caused or impelled by Indra, RV. x, 66, 2. **–prastha,** n. 'Indra's place,' N. of a city (now called Delhi, the residence of the Pāṇḍavas), MBh. **–praharaṇa,** n. Indra's weapon, the thunderbolt, L. **–phala,** n. = *indra-yava,* q. v., L. **–bāhu,** m. du. Indra's arms, R. v, 21, 32. **–bīja,** n. = *indra-yava,* q.v. **–brāhmaṇa,** m., N. of a man. **–bhaginī,** f. 'Indra's sister,' N. of Parvatī, L. **–bhājaná,** n. a substitute for Indra, ŚBr. iii, 4, 2, 15. **–bhū,** m., N. of a teacher, VBr. **–bhūti,** m., N. of one of the eleven Gaṇadhipas of the Jainas. **–bheshaja,** n. dried ginger, L. **–makha,** m. a sacrifice to Indra. **–mada,** m. a disease to which fish and leeches are liable, Suśr. **–mantrin,** m., N. of Bṛihaspati (the planet Jupiter), Comm. on VarBṛS. **–maha,** m. a festival in honour of Indra, MBh.; Hariv. &c.; *-karman* or *-kamuka,* m. a dog, L. **–mahôtsava,** m. a great festival in honour of Indra. **–mādana,** mfn. animating or delighting Indra, RV. vii, 92, 4. **–mārga,** m., N. of a Tīrtha, MBh.; (*ā*), f., N. of a river, R. **–medin** (*índra°*), mfn. one whose friend or ally is Indra, AV. v, 20, 8. **–yajña,** m. a sacrifice for Indra, PārGṛ. **–yava,** n. Indra's grain; the seed of the Wrightia Antidysenterica, Suśr. **–yashṭi,** m., N. of Nāga. **–yāga,** m. = *indra-yajña.* **–yogá,** m. Indra's union or uniting power, AV. x, 5, 3. **–rājan,** mfn. having Indra as king, TBr. i, 5, 6, 4. **–lupta,** m. n. or **-luptaka,** n. morbid baldness of the head; loss of beard. **–loká,** m. Indra's world; Svarga or paradise, ŚBr.; Mn.; R. &c.; *-°lokâgamana,* n. '(Arjuna's) journey to Indra's world,' N. of a section of the third book of the Mahā-bhārata; *-°lokêśa,* m. the lord of Indra's world, i. e. Indra; a guest (as conferring paradise on his host). **–vaṇśā,** f. a metre of four lines (each of which contains twelve syllables). **–vajra,** n. Indra's thunderbolt, VarBṛS.; N. of a Sāman; (*ā*), f. a metre of four lines occurring frequently in epic poetry (each line contains eleven syllables). **–vat** (*índra°*), or in some cases (RV. iv, 27, 4 & x, 101, 1) *índrā-vat,* mfn. associated with or accompanied by Indra, RV.; AV. v, 3, 3; AitBr. **–vana,** n., N. of a place. **–varman,** m., N. of a warrior. **–vallarī** or **-vallī,** f. the plant Cucumis Colocynthis, L. **–vasti,** m. the calf (of the leg), Suśr. **–váh** (in strong cases *°vāh*), mfn. conveying Indra (said of his horses), RV. **–vātatama,** mfn. much desired by Indra, RV. x, 6, 6. **–vāyū,** m. du. Indra and Vāyu, AV. iii, 20, 6; RV. **–vāruṇikā** or **-vāruṇī,** f. Colocynth, a wild bitter gourd, Cucumis

Colocynthis; the favourite plant of Indra and Varuṇa, Comm. on KātyŚr.; L. **-vāh**, see *-vah.* **-vāha**, m., N. of a man, BhP. **-vāhana**, n. Indra's chariot, Vām. **-vīja**, see *-bīja.* **-vīrudh**, f. Indra's snare, PārGṛ. **-vṛiksha**, m. = *indra-dru*, q. v., Suśr.; Nir. **-°vṛikshīya** [gaṇa *utkarâdi*, Pāṇ. iv, 2, 90], belonging to or coming from the above. **-vṛiddhā**, f. a kind of abscess, Suśr. **-vṛiddhika**, m. a kind of horse, L. **-vaidūrya**, n. a kind of precious stone, Suśr. **-vairin**, m. Indra's enemy, a Daitya, L. **-vrata**, n. 'Indra's rule of conduct,' one of the duties of a king (to distribute benefits, as Indra pours down rain), Mn. ix, 304. **-śakti**, f. Indrāṇī the wife or personified energy of Indra. **-śatru** (*índra°*), mfn. one whose enemy or conqueror is Indra, conquered by Indra, RV. i, 32, 6; TS.; ŚBr.; (*as*), m. 'Indra's enemy,' N. of Prahlāda, Ragh. vii, 32; BhP. vi, 9, 11 (with both the meanings). **-śarman**, m., N. of a man. **-śalabha**, m., N. of a man. **-śaila**, m., N. of a mountain. **-śreshṭha** (*índra°*), mfn. having Indra as chief, led by Indra (cf. *indra-jyeshṭha*), ŚBr. **-sakhi** (*índra°*), mf(*ā*)n. one whose ally or companion is Indra, RV.; AV. **-saṃjaya**, n., N. of a Sāman, ĀrshBr. **-saṃdhā**, f. connexion or alliance with Indra, AV. xi, 10, 9. **-savá**, m. a particular Soma sacrifice, MaitrS.; Kāṭh. **-sārathi** (*índra°*), mfn. Indra's companion, N. of Vāyu, RV. iv, 46, 2 & 48, 2. **-sāvarṇi**, m., N. of the fourteenth Manu, BhP. **-sāhva**, n. = *indra-yava*, q. v. **-siṇha**, m., N. of a poet. **-suta**, m. 'son of Indra,' N. of the monkey-king Vālin; of Arjuna; of Jayanta, L. **-surasa**, m. a shrub (the leaves of which are used in discutient applications), Vitex Negundo, L. **-surā**, f. a species of Colocynth, Suśr. **-surisa**, m. = *-surasa.* **-sūnu**, m. 'the son of Indra,' N. of the monkey-king Vālin. **-sena**, m., N. of several men; N. of a Nāga; of a mountain, BhP.; (*ā́*), f. Indra's army, RV. x, 102, 2; N. of a goddess; of several women; *-dvitīya*, mfn. attended by Indrasena. **-stút** or **-stoma**, m. 'praise of Indra;' N. of particular hymns to Indra in certain ceremonies, ŚBr.; ĀśvŚr.; KātyŚr. **-sthāna**, n. the place of Indra's banner, VarYogay. **-°s-vat** (*índras-vat*), mfn. similar to Indra; accompanied by Indra, possessed of power (?) [Sāy.], RV. iv, 37, 5. **-havá**, m. invocation of Indra, RV. ix, 96, 1. **-hasta**, m. a kind of medicament, L. **-hū**, m., N. of a man. **-hūti** (*índra°*), f. invocation of Indra, RV. vi, 38, 1. **Indrā-kutsa**, *ā*, m. du. Indra and Kutsa, RV. v, 31, 9. **Indrâgní**, *ī*, m. du. Indra and Agni, RV.; AV.; TāṇḍyaBr.; *-devatā*, f. the sixteenth lunar mansion; *-daiva*, mfn. having Indra and Agni as deities, VarBṛS.; *-daivata*, n. the Nakshatra Viśākhā, ib.; *-dhūma*, m. frost, snow, L. **Indrâṅka**, m. a species of crab, L. **Indrâditya**, m., N. of a man. **Indrânuja**, m. 'the younger brother of Indra,' N. of Vishṇu or Kṛishṇa. **Indrā-parvata**, *ā*, m. du. Indra and Parvata, RV. **Indrā-pūshan** or **-pūshan**, *ṇā*, m. du. Indra and Pūshan, RV.; AV. **I'ndrā-bṛihaspáti**, *ī*, m. du. Indra and Bṛihaspati, RV. **Indrā-brahmaṇaspati**, *ī*, m. du. Indra and Brahmaṇaspati, RV. **Indrâbha**, m., N. of a son of Dhṛitarāshṭra, MBh.; a species of fowl. **Indrā-marut**, *tas*, m. pl. Indra and the Maruts, RV. **I'ndrâyatana**, mfn. depending on Indra, ŚBr. **Indrâyudha**, n. 'Indra's weapon,' the rainbow, MBh.; VarBṛS.; Ragh.; diamond, L.; (*as*), m. a horse marked with black about the eyes; (*ā*), f. a kind of leech (marked with rainbow tints), Suśr.; *-maya*, mfn. consisting of rainbow, Kād.; *-śikhin*, m., N. of a Nāga. **Indrâri**, m. Indra's enemy, an Asura or demon, L. **Indrāvat**, see *índra-vat.* **Indrâvaraja**, m. 'the younger brother of Indra,' N. of Vishṇu or Kṛishṇa, VP. **I'ndrā-váruṇa**, *ā*, m. du. Indra and Varuṇa, RV.; AV. **I'ndrā-víshṇu**, *ū*, m. du. Indra and Vishṇu, RV. **Indrâśana**, m. hemp (dried and chewed); the shrub which bears the seed used as a jeweller's weight, Abrus Precatorius, L. **Indrâsana**, n. the throne of Indra, any throne; a foot of five short syllables. **I'ndrā-sóma**, *ā*, m. du. Indra and Soma, RV.; AV. **-°somíya**, mfn. consecrated to Indra and Soma, TBr. i, 7, 23. **Indrâhva**, n. = *indra-yava*, q. v. **Indrêjya**, m., N. of Bṛihaspati, the preceptor of the gods, L. **Indre-nata**, mf(*ā*)n. naturally curved (as a reed), TāṇḍyaBr. xv, 5, 20; Lāṭy. iv, 1, 7. **Indrêśvara**, m., N. of a Tīrtha; *-liṅga*, n., N. of a Liṅga. **I'ndrêshita**, mfn. sent or driven or instigated by Indra, RV.; AV. **Indrôtá**, m. 'upheld or promoted by Indra,' N. of a teacher, RV.; ŚBr.; MBh. **Indrôtsava**, m. a festival in honour of Indra, Kathās.

Indraka, *am*, n. an assembly-room, a hall, L.

Indraya, Nom. Ā. *indrayate*, to behave like Indra, RV. iv, 24, 4.

Indrayú, mfn. longing for or wishing to approach Indra, RV. ix, 2, 9; 6, 9; 54, 4.

Indrāṇikā, f. the plant Vitex Negundo, L.

Indrāṇī́, f. the wife of Indra, RV.; AV.; VS.; TS.; MBh. &c.; N. of Durgā, Hariv., (reckoned as one of the eight mothers [*mātṛikā*] or divine energies); the pupil of the left eye (cf. *indra*), ŚBr.; a kind of coitus, L.; the plant Vitex Negundo, L.; a species of Colocynth, Nir. **-karman**, n. a particular rite. **-tantra**, n., N. of a Tantra. **-śāka**, n. a species of vegetables. **-sāman**, n., N. of a Sāman, ĀrshBr.

Indriyá, mfn. fit for or belonging to or agreeable to Indra, RV.; AV.; VS.; (*as*), m. a companion of Indra (?), RV. i, 107, 2; AV. xix, 27, 1; (*am*), n. power, force, the quality which belongs especially to the mighty Indra, RV.; AV.; VS.; TS.; AitBr.; ŚBr.; exhibition of power, powerful act, RV.; VS.; bodily power, power of the senses; virile power, AV.; VS.; ŚBr.; semen virile, VS.; KātyŚr.; MBh. &c.; faculty of sense, sense, organ of sense, AV.; Suśr.; Mn.; Ragh.; Kir. &c.; the number five as symbolical of the five senses. (In addition to the five organs of perception, *buddhîndriyāṇi* or *jñānêndriyāṇi*, i. e. eye, ear, nose, tongue, and skin, the Hindūs enumerate five organs of action, *karmêndriyāṇi*, i. e. larynx, hand, foot, anus, and parts of generation; between these ten organs and the soul or *ātman* stands *manas* or mind, considered as an eleventh organ; in the Vedānta, *manas*, *buddhi*, *ahaṃkāra*, and *citta* form the four inner or internal organs, *antar-indriyāṇi*, so that according to this reckoning the organs are fourteen in number, each being presided over by its own ruler or *niyantṛi*; thus, the eye by the Sun, the ear by the Quarters of the world, the nose by the two Aśvins, the tongue by Pracetas, the skin by the Wind, the voice by Fire, the hand by Indra, the foot by Vishṇu, the anus by Mitra, the parts of generation by Prajāpati, manas by the Moon, buddhi by Brahman, ahaṃkāra by Śiva, citta by Vishṇu as Acyuta; in the Nyāya philosophy each organ is connected with its own peculiar element, the nose with the Earth, the tongue with Water, the eye with Light or Fire, the skin with Air, the ear with Ether; the Jainas divide the whole creation into five sections, according to the number of organs attributed to each being.) **-kāma** (*indriyá°*), mfn. desiring or endeavouring to obtain power, KātyŚr.; TS.; Āp. **-kṛita**, mfn. performed or done with the organs of sense. **-gocara**, mfn. being within the range of the senses, perceptible, capable of being ascertained by the senses. **-grāma**, m. the assemblage of the organs, the senses or organs of sense collectively, Vedāntas. 232; Mn.; MBh. **-ghāta**, m. weakness of the organs of sense, Sāṃkhyak. **-jñāna**, n. the faculty of perception, sense, consciousness. **-tva**, n. the state or condition of being an organ of sense, Kap. **-nigraha**, m. restraint of the organs of sense. **-prasaṅga**, m. sensuality. **-buddhi**, f. perception by the senses, the exercise of any sense, the faculty of any organ. **-bodhana** and **-bodhin**, mfn. arousing the bodily powers, sharpening the senses, Suśr.; (*am*), n. any excitement of sense, an object of perception, a stimulus, &c. **-mocana**, n. abandonment of sensuality, Gobh. **-vat**, mfn. having senses, BhP.; (see also *indriyā-vat.*) **-varga**, m. the assemblage of organs, the organs of sense collectively. **-vipratipatti**, f. perversion of the organs, erroneous or perverted perception. **-vishaya**, m. any object of the senses. **-vṛitti**, f. sensitive faculty, Kap. **-śakti**, f. power of the senses, Bhartṛ.; Kap. **-saṃyama**, m. restraint of the senses. **-svāpa**, m. sleep of the senses, unconsciousness, insensibility; the end of the world, L. **Indriyâgocara**, mfn. imperceptible by the senses. **Indriyâtman**, m. 'having the senses for soul,' identical or one with the senses; N. of Vishṇu, VP. v, 18, 50. **Indriyâyatana**, n. the residence of the senses; the body, L. **Indriyârtha**, m. an object of sense (as sound, smell, &c.), anything exciting the senses, Mn.; MBh.; Pañcat.; Ragh. &c. **Indriyā́-vat** (the Vedic lengthening of the *a* according to Pāṇ. vi, 3, 131; but also once [AV. xv, 10, 10] *indriyá-vat*), mfn. powerful, mighty, TS.; VS.; ŚBr.; KātyŚr. **Indriyā-vín**, mfn. id., TS. **Indriyâsaṅga**, m. non-attachment to sensual objects, stoicism, philosophy, Mn.

इन्ध् **indh**, cl. 7. Ā. *inddhé*, *indhām-cakre* or *īdhé*, *indhishyate*, *aindhishṭa*, *indhitum*, to kindle, light, set on fire, RV.; AV.; ŚBr. &c. (p. *índhāna*, RV.; AV. v, 3, 1; xix, 55, 3; 4, kindling, lighting; *ídhāna*, RV., kindled, lighted, flaming): Pass. *idhyáte*, to be lighted; to blaze, flame, RV.; SV.; MBh.; [cf. Gk. αἴθω, ἰθαρός; αἰθήρ, Αἴτνη; Ἥφ-αισ-τος; Lat. *æs-tus*, *æs-tas*; Old. Germ. *eit*, 'fire.']

Iddhá, mfn. kindled, lighted, alight; shining, glowing, blazing, RV.; Mn.; ChUp.; Ratnāv. &c.; clean, clear, bright; wonderful, L.; (*am*), n. sunshine, light, heat; a wonder, L. **-tejas**, m., N. of a man. **-dīdhiti**, m. 'kindling rays,' fire, Śiś. xvi, 35. **-manyu**, mfn. having the anger excited or kindled. **Iddhâgni**, mfn. one whose fire is kindled, RV. i, 83, 4; viii, 27, 7.

Idh, ifc. lighting; [cf. *agnídh.*]

Idhmá, *as*, m. (*am*, n., L.) fuel in general; fuel as used for the sacred fire, RV.; AV.; ŚBr.; KātyŚr.; ĀśvGṛ.; MBh. &c.; (*as*), m., N. of an Āṅgirasa, GopBr.; [cf. Zend *aesma*; Hib. *adhmad.*] **-citi**, f. a pile of wood, ĀśvGṛ. iv, 2, 14. **-jihva**, m. 'the fuel's tongue,' fire, BhP. v, 1, 25; (also N. of a son of Priya-vrata, ib.) **-parivāsana**, n. chip of wood, MānŚr. **-pravraścana**, m. 'wood-cutter,' an axe, L. **-bhṛiti** (*idhmá°*), mfn. bringing fuel, RV. vi, 20, 13. **-vat** (*idhmá°*), mfn. furnished or provided with fuel, TBr. ii, 1, 3, 8 [misprinted *idhya°*]. **-vāha**, m., N. of a son of Agastya, MBh.; BhP. **-vraścana**, m. = *-pravraścana*, AgP. **-saṃnahana**, n. a string for fastening fuel together, ŚBr. **Idhmābarhis** [Pāṇ. ii, 4, 14], n. sg. & (*ishī*) du. fuel and grass.

I'ndha, mfn. lighting, kindling, ŚBr.; (*as*), m., N. of a Ṛishi, (gaṇa *naḍâdi*, Pāṇ. iv, 1, 99.)

Indhana, *am*, n. kindling, lighting, [cf. *agnîndhana*]; fuel; wood, grass &c. used for this purpose, Mn.; MBh.; R.; Yājñ.; Śiś. &c. **-vat**, mfn. possessed of fuel. **I'ndhan-van**, mfn. possessed of fuel; flaming, RV. ii, 34, 5.

Indhanī-√1. kṛi, to make into fuel, Kād.

इन्धूक *indhūka*, *as*, m., N. of a man.

इन्व् **inv**, cl. 6. P. *ínvati*, RV.; AV.; or *in*, cl. 8. P. *inóti*, RV.; 2. sg. Impv. *inú* & *inuhí*; impf. *°ainot*, RV; (also once [SV. ii, 2, 2, 4, 2] cl. 9. P. 1. pl. *inīmasi*) Ā. perf. 3. pl. *invire*, to advance upon, press upon, drive; to infuse strength, invigorate, gladden; to use force, force; to drive away; to keep back, remove; to have in one's power, take possession of, pervade; to be lord or master of anything, have the disposal of, RV.; AV.; SV.; Dhātup.; Nir.

Inva, mfn. pervading. See *viśvam-inva.*

Invaka, *am*, n., N. of a Sāman; (*ā́s*), f. pl., N. of the Nakshatra Mṛigaśirsha, TBr.

Invagā, f. = *invakā́s* above, MaitrS.

इभ *íbha*, *as*, m. (? √*i*, Uṇ. iii, 153) servants, dependants, domestics, household, family, RV. [BRD.]; fearless [Sāy.]; an elephant, Mn.; Bhartṛ.; Ragh. &c.; the number eight; N. of a plant, L.; (*ī*), f. a female elephant, L.; [cf. Gk. ἐλ-έφας; Lat. *ebur.*] **-kaṇā**, f. a plant with an aromatic seed, Scindapsus Officinalis, L. **-keśara**, m. the tree Mesua Roxburghii, Suśr. **-gandhā**, f., N. of a poisonous fruit, L. **-dantā**, f. the plant Tiaridium Indicum, L. **-nimīlikā**, f. smartness, shrewdness, sagacity (like that of an elephant), L. **-pa** and **-pālaka**, m. the driver or keeper of an elephant, VarBṛS. **-potā**, f. a young elephant, a cub. **-°m-acala** (*ibham-acala*), m. a lion, L. **-yuvati**, f. an elephant's cub. **Ibhâkhya**, m. the plant Mesua Roxburghii, L. **Ibhâri**, m. 'enemy of the elephant,' a lion, L. **Ibhôshaṇā**, f. a kind of aromatic plant, L.

I'bhya, mfn. belonging to one's servants or attendants, RV. i, 65, 7 [BRD.]; (*as*), m. an enemy [Sāy.]; wealthy, opulent, having many attendants, ChUp.; Daś.; Pañcad. &c.; (*ā*), f. a female elephant, L.; the Olibanum tree, Boswellia Serrata. **-tilvila**, mfn. abundantly possessed of household requisites, ŚBr.

इम् *ím*, interj., MaitrS.

इम *imá*, the base of some cases of the demonstrative pronoun *idám*, q. v. (acc. sg. m. *imám*,

f. *imám*; nom. pl. m. *imé*, &c.; irregular gen. sg. *imásya*, RV. viii, 13, 21 [once]).

Imaka, mfn. diminutive of *ima*, Comm. on Pāṇ.

Imáthā, ind. in this way or manner, RV. v, 44, 1.

इयक्ष् iyaksh (anom. Desid. of √*yaj*), P. *íyakshati* (Subj. 3. pl. *íyakshān*, RV. x, 50, 3; p. *íyakshat*), Ā. (p. *íyakshamāṇa*, RV. i, 123, 10; VS. xvii, 69) to go towards, approach; to request, endeavour to gain; to long for, seek, RV.; VS.

Iyakshú, mfn. Ved. longing for, seeking to gain, RV. x, 4, 1.

इयत् íyat, mfn. (fr. pronominal base 3. *i*), so large, only so large; so much, only so much; of such extent, RV.; TS.; ŚBr.; AitBr.; Pañcat.; Ragh. &c.; [cf. the syllable *iens* or *ies* in such Lat. words as *totiens*, *toties*, *quotiens*, *quoties*, and in numeral adverbs as *quinquies*.] **—°c-ciram** (*iyac-ciram*), ind. so long, such a time, Kathās. **—taká** (*iyat°*), mf(*ikā*)n. so small, so little, RV. i, 191, 11; 15. **—tā**, f. or **-tva**, n. the state of being of such extent, quantity, fixed measure or quantity, so much, Ragh.; Kād. &c.

इयम् iyám, f. nom. sg. of the demonstrative pronoun *idám*, q. v.

इयस्य iyasya (anom. Intens. of √*yas*), Ā. *iyasyate*, to relax, weaken; to vanish, ŚBr.

Iyasā́, f. lassitude, shrinking, ŚBr.

Iyasitá, mfn. shrunk, ŚBr.; (*ám*), n. shrinking, ib.

इर् ir, cl. 6. P. *irati*, to go [cf. *il*], Nir.

इरज्य irajya (anom. Intens. of √*raj*), P. rarely Ā. *irajyati*, *-te*, to order, prepare, arrange; to lead; to dispose; to be master of; to grow [Sāy.], RV.

Irajyú, mfn. busy with preparations for the sacrificial rite, RV. x, 93, 3.

इरण iraṇa, desert; salt or barren (soil); = *iriṇa*, q. v., L.

Iraṇyà, mfn. perhaps = *iriṇyà*, q. v., MaitrS. ii, 9, 8.

इरध् iradh (anom. Intens. of √*rādh*), Ā. (3. pl. *iradhanta*, RV. i, 129, 2), P. *iradhyati*, Nir. to endeavour to gain; to worship [Sāy.] (The inf. *irádhyai* (RV. i, 134, 2) is by BRD. referred to this form, and regarded as a shortened form for *irádhadhyai*; but Sāy. refers it to √*ir*.)

इरंमद iram-madá, *as*, m. (Pāṇ. iii, 2, 37) delighting in drink; N. of Agni (in the form of lightning and Apām-napāt), VS. xi, 76; a flash of lightning or the fire attending the fall of a thunderbolt, Kād.; submarine fire, L.

Iram-mád, *t*, m. id., MaitrS. i, 5, 3.

इरस् iras, n. ill-will, anger, hostility, (gaṇa *kaṇḍv-ādi*, Pāṇ. iii, 1, 27.)

Irasya, Nom. P. *irasyáti*, to show enmity to, be angry or envious, RV.; [cf. Lat. *ira*, *irasci*.]

Irasyā́, f. enmity, malevolence, RV. v, 40, 7.

इरा írā (also *irā́*, AV. xv, 2, 3), f. (closely allied to *iḍā* and *iḷā*), any drinkable fluid; a draught (especially of milk), RV.; AV.; ŚBr. &c.; food, refreshment; comfort, enjoyment, AV.; ŚBr.; AitBr.; N. of an Apsaras (a daughter of Daksha and wife of Kaśyapa), Hariv.; VP.; water, L.; ardent spirits, Bhpr.; the earth, L.; speech, L.; the goddess of speech, Sarasvatī, L.; [cf. *iḍā*.] **—kshīra** (*írā°*), mfn. one whose milk is a refreshment or enjoyment, AV. 10, 6. **—cara**, n. hail, L.; (mfn.) earth-born, terrestrial; aquatic, L. **—ja**, m. 'born from water,' N. of Kāma, god of love. **—mukha**, n., N. of a city of the Asuras near Meru. **—vat** (*írā°*), mfn. possessing food, full of food; granting drink or refreshment, satiating, giving enjoyment; endowed with provisions; comfortable, RV.; AV.; AitBr.; MBh. &c.; (*ān*), m., N. of a son of Arjuna, VP.; the ocean; a cloud; a king, L.; (*tī*), f., N. of a plant, L.; N. of Durgā (the wife of Rudra), BhP.; of a daughter of the Nāga Suśravas, Rājat.; N. of a river in the Pañjāb (now called Rāvi), MBh.; Hariv.; VP. **Irêśa**, m., N. of Vishṇu, L.; a king, sovereign; Varuṇa, L.; Brahman, BhP.

इरिका irikā, f., N. of a plant or tree, L. **—vana**, n. a grove of such trees, L.

इरिण íriṇa, *am*, n. (√*ṛi*, 'to go,' Uṇ. ii, 51; connected with *irā*), a water-course; a rivulet, well, RV.; any excavation in the ground, a hollow, hole, AV.; TS.; ŚBr.; KātyŚr.; a dice-board, RV. x, 34, 1; a desert, an inhospitable region; a bare plain, barren soil; salt soil, Mn.; Yājñ.; MBh. &c.

Iriṇyà, mfn. belonging or relating to a desert, VS.

इरिन् írin, mfn. (connected with *ina*?), powerful, violent; a tyrant; an instigator [Sāy.], [cf. *irasya* &c.], RV. v, 87, 3.

इरिमेद irimeda, *as*, m., N. of a plant, = *ari-meda*.

इरिम्बिठि irimbiṭhi, *is*, m., N. of a Ṛishi of the family of Kaṇva (author of several hymns of the Ṛig-veda), RAnukr.

इरिविल्ला irivillā or **irivellikā**, f. pimples or pustules on the head, Suśr.; Bhpr.

इर्गल irgala (= *argala*), n. a bolt, (gaṇa *apûpâdi*, Pāṇ. v, 1, 4).

Irgalīya and **irgalya**, mfn. fit for a bolt (as wood), belonging to a bolt &c.

इर्य írya, mfn. active, powerful, energetical; N. of Pūshan and of the Aśvins; instigating; destroying enemies [Sāy.]; a lord, RV.; AV.

इर्वारु irvāru, *us*, m. f. a kind of cucumber, Cucumis Utilissimus; another kind, Cucumis Colocynthis (see *irvālu*, *īrvāru*, *urvāru*, *ervāru*), L. **—śuktikā**, f. a kind of melon (commonly Sphuti or Sphut), Cucumis Momordica, L.

Irvālu, *us*, m. f. Cucumis (see above), L.

इल् il, cl. 6. P. *ilati* (*iyela*, *elishyati*, *ailīt*, *elitum*, Dhātup. xxviii, 65) to come, Hariv.; VP.; to send, cast, L.; to sleep, L.: cl. 10. P. *ilayati* (Impv. 2. pl. *iláyatā*, AV. i, 17, 4) or *elayati* (Pāṇ. iii, 1, 51), aor. *aililat* or *ailayīt*, to keep still, not to move; to become quiet, AV.; TS.; ŚBr. &c.; [a various reading has the form *iḷ*: cf. Old Germ. *īllu*, *īllo*, for *īlju*; Mod. Germ. *Eile*; Cambro-Brit. *il*, 'progress, motion;' Gk. ἐλάω.]

इल ila, ilā. See *iḍa*, *iḍā*, p. 164, col. 2, and *ilā* below.

इलव ilava (*iḷava*, Sāy.), *as*, m. a ploughman, boor, AitBr. v, 25, 5.

इलविल ilavila, *as*, m. = *iḍaviḍa*, q. v., N. of a son of Daśaratha; (*ā*), f., N. of a daughter of Tṛiṇa-bindu (wife of Viśravas and mother of Kuvera), VP.

इला ilā, f. (closely connected with *íḍā* and *írā*, qq. v.) flow; speech; the earth, &c.; see *iḍā*. **—gola**, n. the earth, globe, L. **—tala**, n. the fourth place in the circle of the zodiac; the surface of the earth. **—dadha**, m., N. of a particular sacrifice, ĀśvŚr. &c.; see *iḍā-dadha*. **—durga**, n., N. of a place. **—°m-da** (*ilām-da*), n. 'granting refreshment or food;' N. of a Sāman, MaitrS.; Tāṇḍya-Br.; Lāṭy. &c. **—°vṛita** (*ilâvṛita*), *as*, m., N. of a son of Āgnīdhra (who received the Varsha Ilāvṛita as his kingdom); (*am*), n. one of the nine Varshas or divisions of the known world (comprehending the highest and most central part of the old continent, cf. *varsha*), MBh.; BhP.; MārkP.; VP. &c. **—sutā**, f., N. of Sītā. **Ilâspada**, n., N. of a Tīrtha, MBh.

Ilikā, f. the earth, L.

इलिना ilinā, f., N. of a daughter of Yama, VP.; (*ī*), f., N. of a daughter of Medhātithi, Hariv.

इलिविल ilivila, *as*, m., N. of a son of Daśaratha, VP.; (cf. *idaviḍa*.)

इली ilī, f. a cudgel, a stick shaped like a sword or a short sword, L. See *īlī*.

इलीबिश ilībiśa, *as*, m., N. of a demon conquered by Indra, RV. i, 33, 12.

इलीश ilīśa, *as*, m. (said to be fr. *il*, 'to go'), a kind of fish (commonly called the hilsa or sable, Clupea Alosa), [cf. *illiśa*], L.

इलुवर्द iluvárda, *as*, m. the first year in a cycle of five years [Sāy.?], TBr. iii, 8, 20, 5.

इलूष ilūsha, *as*, m., N. of the father of Kavasha. See *ailūsha*.

इल्य ilya, *as*, m., N. of a mythical tree in the other world, KaushUp.

इल्लक illaka, *as*, m., N. of a man, Kathās.

इल्लल illala, *as*, m. a species of bird, L.

इल्लिश illiśa, *as*, m. the fish Clupea Alosa [cf. *ilīśa*], L.

इल्लिस illisa, *as*, m. id., Bhpr.

इल्वका ilvakā, *ās*, f. pl. the five stars in Orion's head, L. See *ilvala*.

इल्वल ilvala, *as*, m. a kind of fish, L.; N. of a Daitya (the brother of Vātāpi), MBh.; Hariv.; VP.; (*ās*), f. pl., N. of the five stars in Orion's head, L. **Ilvalâri**, m. 'Ilvala's enemy,' N. of Agastya, L.

इळस्पति iḷás-pati, &c. See *iḍás-pati*, p. 164, col. 2.

इव iva, ind. (fr. pronominal base 3. *i*), like, in the same manner as (in this sense = *yathā*, and used correlatively to *tathā*); as it were, as if (e. g. *pathêva*, as if on a path); in a certain manner, in some measure, a little, perhaps (in qualification or mitigation of a strong assertion); nearly, almost, about (e. g. *muhūrtam iva*, almost an hour); so, just so, just, exactly, indeed, very (especially after words which involve some restriction, e. g. *īshad iva*, just a little; *kiṃcid iva*, just a little bit: and after a negation, e. g. *na cirād iva*, very soon). *Iva* is connected vaguely, and somewhat pleonastically, with an interrogative pronoun or adverb (e. g. *kim iva*, what? *katham iva*, how could that possibly be? *kvêva*, where, I should like to know?). In the Pada texts of the Ṛig, Yajur, and Atharva-veda, and by native grammarians, *iva* is considered to be enclitic, and therefore compounded with the word after which it stands, RV.; AV. &c. &c. **Ivôpamā**, f. a kind of simile (in which *iva* is employed), Bhaṭṭ. x, 30.

इवीलक ivīlaka, *as*, m., N. of a son of Lambodara, VP.

इशीका iśīkā, f. an elephant's eyeball, L. See *ishīkā*.

इष् 1. ish, cl. 1. P. *eshati* (see *anu*-√1. *ish* and *pari*-√1. *ish*), Ā. *eshate*, to seek, search, BhP.: cl. 4. P. *ishyati* & 9. P. Ā. *ishṇāti* (p. *ishṇát*, RV. i, 181, 6, & *ishṇāná*, RV. i, 61, 13; pf. 3. pl. *īshus*, RV., & *īshiré*, AV.; *aishīt*; inf. *isháddhyai*, RV. vii, 43, 1) to cause to move quickly, let fly, throw, cast, swing, RV.; to send out or off, stream out, pour out, discharge; to deliver (a speech), announce, proclaim, AV.; ŚBr.; to impel, incite, animate, promote, RV.; AV.; VS.; ŚBr.

2. Ish, ifc. mfn. moving quickly, speedy. See *aram-ish*.

Ishaṇaya, Nom. Ā. (3. pl. *ishaṇayanta*, RV. x, 67, 8) to move, excite.

Ishaṇya, Nom. P. *ishaṇyati* (p. *ishaṇyát*, RV. iii, 61, 7) to cause to make haste, excite, drive, RV.

Ishaṇyā́, f. instigation, impulse, RV. viii, 60, 18.

Ishán, n. (loc. *isháṇi*, RV. ii, 2, 9) streaming out, pouring out, giving (wealth).

Ishavyà, mfn. (fr. *íshu* below), skilled in archery, VS. xx, 22 (cf. *anishavyà*).

Ishikā, f. (= *ishīkā* below) a brush, L.; the eyeball of an elephant, L.

Ishitá, mfn. moved, driven, tossed, sent out or off, discharged, RV.; AV.; Kauś.; caused, excited, animated, RV.; ŚBr.; AitBr. &c.; quick, speedy, AV. **—tvátā**, ind. by impulse or excitement, RV. x, 132, 2. **—sena**, m., N. of a man, Nir.

Ishīka, *ās*, m. pl., N. of a people (= *aishīka*), VP.; (*ā*), f. (*ishī́kā*) a reed, rush, stem or stalk of grass used as an arrow, AV. vii, 56, 4; xii, 2, 54; ŚBr.; Kauś.; MBh.; R.; Ragh. &c.; a sort of sugar-cane, Saccharum Spontaneum, L.; a brush, L.; a small stick of wood or iron (used for trying whether the gold in a crucible is melted), L.; the eyeball of an elephant; see *ishikā*, *īshikā*, *īshīkā*, *iśīkā*. **Ishīka-tūla** (Pāṇ. vi, 3, 65) and **ishīkā°**, n. the point or upper part of a reed, Kauś.; ChUp. **Ishīkâṭavī**, f. a bed of reeds, BhP.

I'shu, *us*, m. f. an arrow, RV.; AV.; VS.; MBh.; Ragh.; Śak. &c.; (in mathematics) a versed sine; N. of a Soma ceremony, KātyŚr.; the number five, Sāh.; N. of a particular constellation, VarBṛ. xii, 7. [According to Dayānanda *ishu* may mean 'ray of light;' cf. Gk. ἰός; Zd. *ishu*.] **—kāmaśamī**, f., N. of a region, Comm. on Pāṇ. ii, 1, 50. **—kārá** or **-kṛit** (1. *ishu-kṛit*, for 2. see s. v.), m. an arrow-maker, RV.; AV.; MBh.; Kap. &c. **—kshepa**, m. (the distance of) an arrow shot, Lalit. **—dhanvá** (TĀr.) or **-dhanvan**, n. (sg.) arrow and bow. **—dhanvín**, m. an archer, TĀr. **—dhara**, m. an archer. **—dhí**, m. (√*dhā*), a quiver, RV.; AV.; VS.; R. &c.; -*mat*, mfn. possessed of a quiver, VS. **—pa**, m., N. of an Asura (who appeared on earth as king Nagnajit), MBh. **—patha**, m. the range of an arrow, L. **—pushpā**, f., N. of a plant. **—bala** (*íshu°*), mfn. powerful by arrows, RV. vi, 75, 9. **—bhṛít**, mfn. carrying arrows, an archer, AV.; Bhaṭṭ. **—mat** (*íshu°*), mfn. possessed of arrows, RV.; VS.; TS.; AV.; Daś. **—mātrá**, n. the length of an arrow, Āp. i, 15, 19; (mfn.) having the length of an arrow (about three feet), ŚBr.; KātyŚr.; (*ám*), ind. as far as the range of an arrow, ŚBr.; TS.; ŚāṅkhBr. **—mārga**, m. 'arrow-path,' the atmosphere, L. **—vadhá**, m. death by an arrow, ŚBr. v, 4, 2, 2. **—sâhva**, m., N. of a plant, Hariv. 3843. **—°s-trikāṇḍā** (*ishus-trikāṇḍā*), f. 'the threefold arrow,' N. of a constellation (perhaps the girdle of Orion), AitBr. **—hata**, mfn. killed by an arrow, TāṇḍyaBr. xxii, 14, 3. **—hasta**, mfn. 'arrow-handed,' carrying arrows in the hand. **Ishv-agra**, n. the point of an arrow, AV. xi, 10, 16; °*agrīya*, mfn. [gaṇa *gahâdi*, Pāṇ. iv, 2, 138] belonging to the point of an arrow. **Ishv-anīka**, n. the point of an arrow; °*anīkīya*, mfn. [gaṇa *gahâdi*] belonging to the point of an arrow. **Ishv-asana** or **ishv-astra**, n. 'arrow-thrower,' a bow, Ragh.; R. **Ishv-āyudhá**, n. arrow and weapons, AV. v, 31, 7. **Ishv-āsá**, mfn. throwing arrows; (*as*), m. a bow; an archer; a warrior, AV. xv, 5, 1-7; MBh.; R. &c.

Ishuka, mfn. arrow-like, gaṇa *sthūlâdi*, Pāṇ. v, 4, 3; ifc. = *íshu* (e.g. *tríshukam dhanus*, KātyŚr.); (*ā́*), f. an arrow, AV. i, 3, 9; (*ā*), f., N. of an Apsaras, VP.

1. **Ishudhya**, Nom. (fr. *ishu-dhi*) P. Ā. *ishudhyati*, -*te*, to be a quiver, contain arrows, gaṇa *kaṇḍv-ādi*, Pāṇ. iii, 1, 27; (for 2. *ishudhya*, also for *ishudhyā* and *ishudhyu*, see next col.)

1. **Ishṭi**, *is*, f. impulse, acceleration, hurry; invitation; order; despatch, RV.

Ishma, *as*, m. (Uṇ. i, 144), N. of Kāma; the spring, L.

Ishmin, mfn. going quickly, speedy, impetuous (said of the winds), RV.

इष् 3. *ish*, cl. 6. P., ep. & Ved. also Ā. *icchāti* (Subj. *icchāt*, RV.; AV.), *icchate* (AV. xi, 5, 17; impf. *aicchat*, *iyesha* and *īshe*, *eshishyate*, *aishīt*, *eshitum* or *eshṭum*) to endeavour to obtain, strive, seek for, RV.; AV.; ŚBr.; AitBr.; to endeavour to make favourable; to desire, wish, long for, request; to wish or be about to do anything, intend, RV.; AV.; ŚBr.; R.; Hit.; Śak. &c.; to strive to obtain anything (acc.) from any one (abl. or loc.); to expect or ask anything from any one, MBh.; Mn.; Śak.; Ragh.; Hit. &c.; to assent, be favourable, concede, KātyŚr.; Mn.; Kathās.; to choose, Mn.; to acknowledge, maintain, regard, think, Pāṇ. Comm.: Pass. *ishyate*, to be wished or liked; to be wanted, MBh.; Hit.; Śak. &c.; to be asked or requested; to be prescribed or ordered, Mn.; R.; to be approved or acknowledged; to be accepted or regarded as, MBh.; Prab.; Yājñ.; Mn. &c.; to be worth; to be wanted as a desideratum, see 2. *ishṭi*: Caus. *eshayati*, (in surg.) to probe, Suśr. ii, 7, 15: Desid. *eshishishati*; [with *ish* cf. Old Germ. *eiscôm*, 'I ask;' Mod. Germ. *heische*; Angl. Sax. *âscian*: cf. also Gk. ἴσ-της, ἵμερος; Lith. *jěskóti*; Russ. *iskate*, 'to seek.']

Icchaka, mfn. wishing, desirous of (cf. *yathêcchakam*); (*as*), m. Citrus Medica, L.; (in arithm.) the sum or result sought, L.

Iccha-tā, f. or **iccha-tva**, n. desire, wishfulness, L.

Icchā, f. wish, desire, inclination, K.; Mn.; Yājñ.; Pañcat.; Ragh. &c.; (in math.) a question or problem; (in gram.) the desiderative form, APrāt.; (*icchayā*, ind. according to wish or desire, Pañcat.; Hit.; Megh. &c.; *icchām ni √grah*, to suppress one's desire.) **—kṛita**, mfn. done at pleasure. **—dāna**, n. the granting or gratification of a wish. **—nivṛitti**, f. suppression or cessation of desire. **—°nvita** (*icchânvita*), mfn. having a desire, wishing, wishful. **—phala**, n. (in math.) result or solution of a question or problem. **—°bharaṇa** (*icchâbharaṇa*), m., N. of a man, Kathās. **—rāma**, m., N. of an author. **—rūpa**, n. Desire (as personified by the Śāktas), the first manifestation of divine power (cf. *svêcchā-maya*). **—vat**, mfn. wishing, wishful, desirous, L. **—vasu**, m. 'possessing all wished-for wealth,' N. of Kuvera, L. **—śakti-mat**, mfn. having the power of wishing, Vedântas. **—sampad**, f. fulfilment or attainment of a wish, Hit.

Icchu, mfn. wishing, desiring (with acc. or inf.), KātyŚr.; Pañcat.; R.; Kathās.

4. **Ish**, mfn. ifc. seeking for (see *gav-ish*, *paśv-ish*, &c.); *ṭ*, f. wish, Hariv. [cf. *iṭ-cara*].

1. **Isha**, mfn. seeking (see *gav-isha*).

Ishaṇi. See *ishan*, p. 168, col. 3.

2. **Ishudhya**, Nom. P. *ishudhyáti*, to implore, request, crave for (dat.), RV.; [cf. Zd. *ishud*, 'prayer;' *ishûidyāmahi*, 'we will pray.']

Ishudhyā́, f. imploring, request, RV. i, 122, 1.

Ishudhyú, mfn. imploring, requesting, RV. v, 41, 6.

Ishūya, P. *ishūyati* (dat. of the pres. p. *ishūyaté*, RV. i, 128, 4) to strive for, endeavour to obtain.

1. **Ishṭá**, mfn. (for 2. see s. v.), sought, ŚBr.; wished, desired; liked, beloved; agreeable; cherished, RV.; ŚBr.; KātyŚr.; Mn.; Pañcat.; Śak. &c.; reverenced, respected; regarded as good, approved, Mn.; Sāṃkhyak.; valid; (*as*), m. a lover, a husband, Śak. 83 c; the plant Ricinus Communis, L.; (*ā*), f., N. of a plant, L.; (*am*), n. wish, desire, RV.; AV.; AitBr.; Mn.; R.; (*am*), ind. voluntarily. **—karman**, n. (in arithm.) rule of supposition, operation with an assumed number. **—kāma-duh**, *dhuk*, f. 'granting desires,' N. of the cow of plenty, Bhag. **—gandha**, mfn. having fragrant odour, Suśr.; (*as*), m. any fragrant substance; (*am*), n. sand, L. **—jana**, m. a beloved person, man or woman; a loved one, Śak. **—tama**, mfn. most desired, best beloved, beloved, dearest. **—tara**, mfn. more desired, more dear, dearer. **—tas**, ind. according to one's wish or desire. **—tā**, f. or **-tva**, n. desirableness, the state of being beloved or reverenced. **—darpaṇa**, m., N. of a work. **—deva**, m. (L.) or **-devatā**, f. a chosen tutelary deity, favourite god, one particularly worshipped (cf. *abhîshṭa-devatā*). **—yāman** (*ishṭá°*), mfn. going according to desire, RV. ix, 88, 3. **—raśmi** (*ishṭá°*), mfn. one who wishes for reins or bridles, RV. i, 122, 13. **—vrata**, mfn. that by which good (*ishṭa*) works (*vrata*) succeed [Sāy.], RV. iii, 59, 9. **—sampādin**, mfn. effecting anything desired or wished for, Kathās. **Ishṭârtha**, m. anything desired or agreeable; (mfn.) one who has obtained a desired object, MBh.; R.; °*rthôdyukta*, mfn. zealous or active for a desired object. **Ishṭā́-vat**, mfn. possessing a desired object (?), AV. xviii, 3, 20 [perhaps belonging to 2. *ishṭa*]. **Ishṭâśva**, mfn. one who wishes for horses, RV. i, 122, 13. **Ishṭâhotrīya** or **°hotrya**, n., N. of a Sāman, Lāṭy.; MaitrS.

2. **Ishṭí**, *is*, f. seeking, going after, RV.; endeavouring to obtain; wish, request, desire, RV.; VS. &c.; any desired object; a desired rule, a desideratum, a N. applied to the statement of grammarians who are considered as authoritative.

Ishṭu, *us*, f. wish, desire, L.

इष् 5. *ish*, *ṭ*, f. anything drunk, a draught, refreshment, enjoyment; libation; the refreshing waters of the sky; sap, strength, freshness, comfort, increase; good condition, affluence, RV.; AV.; VS.; AitBr. **Ishaḥ-stut**, mfn. praising comfort or prosperity, RV. v, 50, 5.

2. **Ishá**, mfn. possessing sap and strength; well-fed, strong; sappy, juicy, fertile, RV.; (*as*), m., N. of the month Āśvina (September–October), VS.; ŚBr.; Suśr.; VP.; N. of a Ṛishi, BhP. **—vat** (*ishá°*), mfn. vigorous, RV. i, 129, 6.

Ishaya, Nom. P. Ā. *isháyati*, -*te* (inf. *ishayádhyai*, RV. i, 183, 3, &c.) to be sappy; to be fresh or active or powerful, RV.; ĀśvŚr.; to refresh, strengthen, animate, RV.

Ishayú, mfn. fresh, strong, powerful, RV. i, 120, 5.

Ishí, f. (only dat. sing. *isháye*, RV. vi, 52, 15, and nom. pl. *isháyas*, SV. i, 6, 2, 2, 2) = 5. *ish*, q.v.

Ishídh, f. (only nom. pl. *ishídhas*, RV. vi, 63, 7) libation, offering.

Ishirá, mfn. refreshing, fresh; flourishing; vigorous, active, quick, RV.; AV.; VS.; (*as*), m., N. of Agni, L.; (*am*), ind. quickly, RV. x, 157, 5; [cf. Gk. ἱερός, especially in Homer (e.g. Il. xvi, 404).]

Ishetvaka, mfn. containing the words *ishé tvā* (VS. i, 1), gaṇa *goshadâdi*, Pāṇ. v, 2, 62.

Ishovṛidhīya, *am*, n., N. of a Sāman, Lāṭy. iii, 4, 16.

इषु *ishu*, *ishu-dhi*, &c. See 1. *ish*.

इषुकृत् 2. *ishu-kṛit*, mfn. (only RV. i, 184, 3) = *ish-kṛit*, preparing, arranging [NBD.]; (fr. √*kṛit*, 'to cut'), hurting like an arrow [Gmn.]; Sāy. reads *ishu-kṛita*, and explains it by 'made quick as an arrow.'

इष्कृ *ish*-√1. *kṛi* (√1. *kṛi* with *is* [= *nis*, BRD.]), P. (impf. 1. sg. *ish-karam*, RV. x, 48, 8) Ā. (Impv. 2. pl. *ish-kṛiṇudhvam*, RV. x, 53, 7) to arrange, set in order, prepare, RV.

Ish-kartṛí, mfn. arranging, preparing, setting in order.

Ísh-kṛita, mfn. arranged, set in order, RV. **Íshkṛitâhāva**, mfn. one whose Soma vessel is prepared or ready, RV. x, 101, 6.

Ísh-kṛiti, *is*, f. healing, RV. x, 97, 9.

इष्ट 2. *ishṭá*, mfn. (p. p. fr. √*yaj*; for 1. *ishṭá* see col. 2) sacrificed, worshipped with sacrifices, VS.; ŚBr.; KātyŚr.; AitBr. &c.; (*as*), m. sacrifice, MārkP. xiii, 15; (*am*), n. sacrificing, sacrifice; sacred rite, sacrament, L. **—kṛit**, mfn. performing a sacrifice, Comm. on KātyŚr. **—yajus** (*ishṭá°*), mfn. one who has spoken the sacrificial verses, VS.; TS. **—svishṭakṛit**, mfn. one to whom a Svishṭakṛit sacrifice has been offered, ŚBr. **Ishṭā-kṛita**, n. for *ishṭīkṛita* (q. v.), MBh. iii, 10513 (ed. Calc.; ed. Bomb. iii, 129, 1 reads *ishṭi°*). **Ishṭâpūrtá**, n. 'filled up or stored up sacrificial rites,' or the merit of sacred rites &c. stored up in heaven, RV.; AV.; VS.; ŚBr.; R. &c. (see Muir v, 293; according to Banerjea's translation of Brahma-sūtras, p. 19, *ishṭa* means personal piety, *pūrta* works for the benefit of others). **Ishṭâpūrti** (or *ishṭá°*), f. id., BrahmUp. **Ishṭâpūrtin**, mfn. one who has stored up sacrificial rites, or one who has performed sacrifices for himself and good works for others.

Ishṭaka-cita (for the shortening of the *ā* see Pāṇ. vi, 3, 65), mfn. overlaid or covered with bricks, Yājñ. i, 197.

Íshṭakā, f. a brick in general; a brick used in building the sacrificial altar, VS.; AitBr.; ŚBr.; KātyŚr.; Mṛicch. &c. **—gṛiha** (*ishṭakā*), n. a brick-house, Hit. **—citi**, f. putting bricks in layers or rows, ŚBr. x, 1, 3, 8. **—nyāsa**, m. laying the foundation of a house. **—patha**, n. the root of the fragrant grass Andropogon Muricatus, Bhpr.; (°*thaka* and °*thika*, n. id., L.) **—paśu**, m. sacrificing an animal during the preparation of bricks, Comm. on VS. **—maya**, mfn. made of bricks. **—mātrā́**, f. size of the bricks, ŚBr. **—rāśi**, m. a pile of bricks. **—vat**, mfn. possessed of bricks, Pāṇ. **—sampad**, f. completeness of the bricks, ŚBr. **Íshṭakâika-śata-vidha**, mfn. corresponding to the 101 bricks, ŚBr. x, 2, 6, 11.

3. **Íshṭi**, *is*, f. sacrificing, sacrifice; an oblation consisting of butter, fruits, &c., opposed to the sacrifice of an animal or Soma, RV. i, 166, 14; x, 169, 2; ŚBr.; ĀśvŚr.; Yājñ.; Mn.; Śak.; Ragh. &c. **—tva**, n. the being an Ishṭi sacrifice, AitBr.; Jaim. **—paca** or **-mush**, m. an Asura, demon, L. **—yā́juka**, mfn. one who offers an Ishṭi sacrifice, ŚBr. **—śrāddha**, n. a particular funeral rite, VP. **—hautra**, n. the office of an Hotṛi at an Ishṭi sacrifice, Comm. on TBr. iii, 5, 1. **Ishṭy-ayana**, n. a sacrifice lasting a long time, ĀśvŚr.

Ishṭikā, f. = *íshṭakā*, q. v., L.

Ishṭin, mfn. (Pāṇ. v, 2, 88) one who has sacrificed, TS.; Kāṭh.

Ishṭi-kṛita, *am*, n. a particular sacrifice or festive rite, MBh.

Ishṭvā, ind. p. having sacrificed or worshipped.

इष्टनि *ishṭani*, mfn. (fr. √*yaj*), to be worshipped, RV. i, 127, 6 [Sāy.]; (for *ni-shṭani* fr. √*stan*) rustling [NBD.]

इष्टर्ग *ishṭárga*, *as*, m. (etym. doubtful), the Adhvaryu priest [Sāy.], TS. & TBr.

इष्य *ishya*, *as*, m. the spring, L. (= **ishma**, col. 1).

इस् *is*, ind. an interjection of anger or pain or sorrow, L.; (according to BRD. *is* Ved. = *nis*, cf. *ish*-√1. *kṛi* above.)

इह *ihá*, ind. (fr. pronom. base 3. *i*), in this place, here; to this place; in this world; in this book or system; in this case (e.g. *tenêha na*, 'therefore not in this case,' i.e. the rule does not apply here); now, at this time, RV. &c. &c.; [cf.

Zend *idha*, 'here;' Gk. ἰθᾶ or ἰθαι in ἰθα-γενής and ἰθαι-γενής; Goth. *ith*; perhaps Lat. *igi-tur*.] **-kāra**, m. the word *iha*, Lāṭy. **-kāla**, m. this life. **-kratu** or **-citta** (*ihá°*), mfn. one whose intentions or thoughts are in this world or place, AV. xviii, 4, 38. **-tra**, ind. here, in this world. **-dvitīyā**, f., **-pañcamī**, f. being here (in this place, world, &c.) the second or fifth woman, (gaṇa *mayūra-vyaṇsakâdi*, Pāṇ. ii, 1, 72.) **-bhojana** (*ihá°*), mfn. whose goods and gifts come hither, AV. xviii, 4, 49. **-loka**, m. this world, this life; (*e*), ind. in this world, MBh.; Mn.; Pañcat. &c. **-vat**, n., N. of several Sāmans. **-samaye**, ind. here, now, on the present occasion, at such a time as this. **-stha**, mfn. standing here, Ratnāv.; Bālar. &c. **-sthāna**, mfn. one whose place or residence is on the earth; (*e*), ind. in this place. **Ihâgata**, mfn. come or arrived hither. **Ihâmutra**, ind. here and there, in this world and in the next, Vedāntas. &c. **Ihéha**, ind. here and there, now and then, repeatedly; *-mātṛi*, m. one whose mother is here and there, i. e. everywhere, RV. vi, 59, 1.

Ihatya, mfn. being here, Kathās.; Daś. &c.

Ihatyaka, mf(*ikā*)n. id., Pāṇ. Comm.

ई Ī.

ई 1. *ī*, the fourth letter of the alphabet, corresponding to *i* long, and having the sound of *ee* in *feel*. **-kāra**, m. the letter or sound *ī*.

ई 2. *ī*, *is*, m., N. of Kandarpa, the god of love, L.; (*ī* or *īs*), f., N. of Lakshmī, L. [also in MBh. xiii, 1220 according to Nīlak. (who reads *puṇyacañcur ī*)].

ई 3. *ī*, ind. an interjection of pain or anger; a particle implying consciousness or perception, consideration, compassion.

ई 4. *ī* for √*i*. See 5. *i*.

ईक्ष् *īksh*, cl. 1. Ā. *īkshate*, *īkshāṃ-cakre* (Pāṇ. i, 3, 63), *īkshishyate*, *aikshishṭa*, *īkshitum*, to see, look, view, behold, look at, gaze at; to watch over (with acc. or rarely loc.), AV.; AitBr.; ŚBr.; Mn.; Kathās. &c.; to see in one's mind, think, have a thought, ŚBr.; ChUp.; MBh.; Bhag. &c.; to regard, consider, Kum.; to observe (the stars &c.), VarBṛS.; to foretell for (dat.; lit. to observe the stars for any one), Pāṇ. i, 4, 39: Caus. *īkshayati*, to make one look at (with acc.), ĀśvGṛ. (This root is perhaps connected with *akshi*, q. v.)

Ī'ksha, mf(*ī*)n. ifc. seeing, looking, visiting (see *tiryag-īksha*, *vadhv-īksha*); (*ā*), f. sight, viewing; considering, BhP.; Nyāyad.; (*am*), n. anything seen, ŚBr. vii, 1, 2, 23 (merely for the etym. of *antariksha*).

Ī'kshaka, *as*, m. a spectator, beholder, ŚBr.; ĀśvGṛ.; Gobh.

Īkshaṇa, *am*, n. a look, view, aspect, sight, KātyŚr.; Lāṭy.; Kathās.; Pañcat.; Ratnāv. &c.; regarding, looking after, caring for, Mn.; eye, MBh.; R.; Suśr.; Śak. &c.

Īkshaṇika, *as*, *ā*, m. f. and **Īkshaṇīka**, m. a looker into the future, a fortune-teller, VarBṛS.

Īkshaṇīya, mfn. to be seen or perceived.

Īkshamāṇa, mfn. looking at, surveying, VS.; R.

Īkshita, mfn. seen, beheld, regarded; (*am*), n. a look, Śak. 45 a; Prab.

Īkshitṛi, mfn. seeing, beholding, a beholder, Mn.; Prab. &c.

Īkshéṇya, mfn. deserving to be seen, curious, RV. ix, 77, 3.

Īkshyamāṇa, mfn. being beheld, being viewed.

ईख् *īkh* or *ikh*, cl. 1. P. *ekhati*, *iyekha*, or *īkhati*, *īkhāṃ-cakāra*, *ekhitum* or *īkhitum*, to go, move, Dhātup. v, 28.

ईङ्ख् *īṅkh* or *iṅkh*, cl. 1. P. (*iṅkhati*, *iṅkhāṃ-cakāra*, or *īṅkhati*, *īṅkhāṃ-cakāra*, *iṅkhitum* or *īṅkhitum*) to go, move, Dhātup. v, 28: Caus. *īṅkháyati*, to move backwards and forwards, move up and down, swing, RV.; AitBr.

Īṅkhana, *am*, n. swinging, BhP.

Īṅkhaya, mfn. moving, causing to flow or go.

ईज् *īj* or *īñj*, cl. 1. P. *ījati*, *ījāṃ-cakāra*, *ījitum* or *īñjati*, &c., to go; to blame or censure, Dhātup. vi, 24; (cf. *apêj* and *sam-īj*.)

ईजान *ījāná*, mfn. (pf. p. of √*yaj*, q. v.) one who has sacrificed, RV.; AV.; ŚBr. &c.

Ījitum (irr. inf. of √*yaj*, q. v.) = *yashṭum*.

ईजिक *ījika*, *ās*, m. pl., N. of a people, VP.; MBh.

ईड् 1. *īḍ*, cl. 2. Ā. *ī́ṭṭe* (2. sg. pres. *īḍishe*, Ved. *īḷishe*, pf. *īḍé*, fut. *īḍishyate*, aor. *aiḍishṭa*, inf. *īḍitum*, Ved. *īḷe*, &c.) to implore, request, ask for (with two acc.); to praise, RV.; AV.; VS.; R.; BhP. &c.: Caus. P. *īḍayati*, to ask; to praise, BhP.

2. **Īḍ**, *ṭ*, f. praise, extolling, RV. viii, 39, 1.

Īḍana, *am*, n. the act of praising, L.

Īḍā, f. praise, commendation, L.

Īḍita or ** īḷitá**, mfn. implored, requested, RV.

Īḍitṛí, mfn. one who praises, AV. iv, 31, 4.

Īḍénya or **īḷenya** or **īḍya**, mfn. to be invoked or implored; to be praised or glorified, praiseworthy, laudable, RV.; AV.; VS.; ŚBr.; Ragh. &c.

Īḍyamāna, mfn. being praised.

ईति 1. *īti*, *is*, f. (fr. 4. *ī*?), plague, distress, any calamity of the season (as drought, excessive rain, swarm of rats, foreign invasion, &c.); infectious disease, MBh.; R.; Suśr. &c.; an affray, L.; travelling in foreign countries, sojourning, L.

ईति 2. *īti*, ind. = *iti*, R. vii, 32, 65.

ईदृक्ष *īdṛiksha*, mf(*ī*)n. (fr. *id*, neut. of pronom. base 3. *i*, and *dṛiksha*, √*dṛiś*, dropping one *d* and lengthening the preceding *i*; cf. *tadṛiksha* from *tad*, &c.), of this aspect, of such a kind, endowed with such qualities, such-like, VS.; Kathās. &c.

Ī-dṛíś, *k* (Ved. *ṅ*, Pāṇ. vii, 1, 83), mfn. endowed with such qualities, such, VS.; TS.; ŚBr.; Śak.; Pañcat. &c.; (*k*), f. such a condition, such occasion, RV.; AV. **-Īdṛik-tā**, f. quality, Ragh.; Daś.

Īdṛiśa, mf(*ī*)n. or **Īdṛiśaka**, mf(*ikā*)n. endowed with such qualities, such, ŚBr.; ChUp.; Mn; R.; Bhag.; Śak. &c.; [with the final syllables *dṛiś* and *dṛiśa* of these words cf. the Gk. λικ in ὁμῆλιξ, λικο in τηλίκο-ς, &c.; Goth. *leika* in *hvêleiks*, 'which one,' *svaleik-s*, 'such;' Mod. Germ. *welcher*, *solcher*; Slav. *liko*, nom. *lik*, e. g. *tolik*, 'such;' Lat. *li* in *tâlis*, *quâlis*.]

ईन्त् *īnt*, cl. 1. P. *īntati*, *īntitum*, to bind [cf. *ant* and *and*], Vop. on Dhātup. iii, 25.

ईप्स् *īps* (Desid. of √*āp*, q. v.), to wish to obtain.

Īpsana, *am*, n. desiring or wishing to obtain, L.

Īpsā, f asking, desire or wish to obtain, MBh.; R.

Īpsita, mfn. wished, desired; (*am*), n. desire, wish, MBh.; R.; Ragh.; Kathās. **-tama**, mfn. most desired, immediately aimed at (as the object of an action), Pāṇ. i, 4, 49.

Īpsu, mfn. striving to obtain; wishing to get or obtain, desirous of (with acc.), Mn.; MBh.; Ragh.; R. &c. **-yajña**, m. a particular Soma sacrifice, KātyŚr.

ईम् *īm*, ind. (fr. pronominal base 3. *i*), Ved. a particle of affirmation and restriction (generally after short words at the beginning of a period, or after the relative pronouns, the conjunction *yad*, prepositions and particles such as *āt*, *uta*, *atha*, &c.) *Īm* has also the sense 'now' (= *idānīm*), and is by Sāy. sometimes considered as an acc. case for *enam*, RV.; VS.

ईयक्षमाण *īyakshamāṇa* = *iyakshamāṇa* (fr. *iyaksh*), q. v., MaitrS. ii, 10, 6.

ईयचक्षस् *īya-cakshas*, mfn. (*īya* fr. √*i*), of pervading or far-reaching sight, RV. v, 66, 6.

ईयिवस् *īyivas* (*īyivān*, *īyushī*, *īyivat*), mfn. (pf. p. of √*i*) one who has gone; one who has obtained &c.

ईर् *īr*, cl. 2. Ā. *ī́rte* (3. pl. *ī́rate*, AV.; RV.), *īraṃ-cakre*, *īrishyati*, *airishṭa*, *īritum*; Ved. inf. *irádhyai*, RV. i, 134, 2, to go, move, rise, arise from, RV.; to go away, retire, AV. xix, 38, 2; to agitate, elevate, raise (one's voice), RV.: Caus. P. *īráyati* (cf. √*īl*), to agitate, throw, cast; to excite, RV.; AV.; MBh.; R. &c.; to cause to rise; to bring to life; to raise one's voice, utter, pronounce, proclaim, cite, RV.; ChUp.; Ragh.; Suśr. &c.; to elevate, RV.; VS.; TS.; ŚBr.: Ā. to raise one's self, AV.; VS.

Īra, m. wind. **-ja**, m. 'wind-born,' N. of Hanumat. **-pāda**, m. a snake, AitBr. **-putra**, m. 'wind-son,' N. of Hanumat.

Īraṇa, mfn. agitating, driving, L.; (*as*), m. the wind, Suśr.; (*am*), n. uttering, pronouncing, BhP.; painful and laborious evacuation of the bowels, Bhpr.

Īrita, mfn. sent, despatched; said, uttered. **Īritâkūta**, *am*, n. declared purpose or intention.

Īrṇa, mfn. See *ud-īrṇa*.

Īrya, mfn. to be excited. **-tā** (*īryá°*), f. the condition of one who is to be excited, VS.; AitĀr.

Īryā, f. wandering about as a religious mendicant (i. e. without hurting any creature). **-patha**, m. the observances of a religious mendicant; the four positions of the body (viz. going, standing upright, sitting and lying down), Buddh. & Jain.; (cf. *airyāpathikī*.)

ईरामा *īrāmā*, f., N. of a river, MBh.

ईरिण *īriṇa*, mfn. desert; (*am*), n. salt and barren soil (see *iriṇa*), MBh.

ईरिन् *īrin*, *ī*, m., N. of a man; (*iṇas*), m. pl. the descendants of this man, MBh.

ईर्क्ष्य् *īrkshy*. See *īrshy*.

ईर्त्स् *īrts* (Desid. of √*ṛidh*, q. v.), P. *īrtsati*, to wish to increase, Pāṇ. vii, 4, 55; Vop.

Īrtsā, f. the wish to increase anything, L.

Īrtsu, mfn. wishing to increase anything, Bhaṭṭ.

ईर्म 1. *īrmá* or *īrmā́*, ind. in this place, here, to this place; going constantly, or instigating [Sāy.], RV.

ईर्म 2. *īrmá*, *as*, m. the arm, the fore-quarter of an animal, AV. x, 10, 21; ŚBr.; TāṇḍyaBr.; (*am*), n. a sore or wound, TāṇḍyaBr. iv, 2, 10 [Sāy.]

Īrman, m. = 2. *īrmá* above, Bhaṭṭ.

ईर्मान्त *īrmánta*, mfn. (fr. *īrma* = *īrita* with *anta*, Sāy.), full-haunched (lit. full-ended); thin-haunched; (perhaps) having the biggest (or quickest?) horses on both sides of the team; N. of a team of horses or of the horses of the sun's car, RV. i, 163, 10.

ईर्वारु *īrvāru*, *us*, m. a cucumber, Cucumis Utilissimus, L. See *irvāru*.

ईर्ष्य् *īrshy* or *īrkshy*, cl. 1. P. *īrshyati* (p. *īrshyat*, TS.), *īrshyāṃ-cakāra*, *īrshyitum* or *īrkshyati*, Pāṇ.; Vop.; Dhātup.; to envy, feel impatient at another's prosperity (with dat.): Desid. *īrshyishishati* or *īrshyiyishati*, Comm. on Pāṇ.

Īrshā, f. impatience, envy of another's success (more properly read *īrshyā*), MBh.; R. &c.

Īrshālu, mfn. = *īrshyālu*, q. v., L.

Īrshita, mfn. envied; (*am*), n. envy (v. l. for *īrshyita*, q. v.), Hit.

Īrshitavya, mfn. to be envied (v. l. for *īrshyitavya*, q. v.), Prab.

Īrshu, mfn. envious, jealous (v. l. for *īrshyu*, q. v.), MBh.; Hit.

Īrshya, mfn. envious, envying, L.; (*á*), f. envy or impatience of another's success; spite, malice; jealousy, AV.; Mn.; MBh.; Kathās. &c. **Īrshyâbhirati**, **Īrshyā-rati**, and **Īrshyā-shaṇḍha**, m. a kind of semi-impotent man, = *īrshyaka*, q. v., Car.; Nār. **-vat**, mfn. envious, spiteful. **-vaśa**, mfn. overcome with envy.

Īrshyaka, mfn. envious, envying; (*as*), m. a particular kind of semi-impotent man whose power is stimulated through jealous feelings caused by seeing others in the act of sexual union, Suśr.

Īrshyamāṇa, mfn. envying, envious.

Īrshyālu, mfn. envious, jealous.

Īrshyita, n. envy, jealousy.

Īrshyin, mfn. envious, spiteful.

Īrshyú, mfn. jealous, AV. vi, 18, 2; MBh.; Hit.

ईल् *īl*, Caus. P. *īláyati*, to move, TS. vi, 4, 2, 6; (cf. *īr*, Caus.)

ईलिन *īlina*, *as*, m., N. of a son of Taṃsu and father of Dushyanta, MBh.; (*ī*), f., N. of a daughter of Medhātithi, Hariv.

ईली *īlī* or *ili*, *is*, f. a kind of weapon (sometimes considered as a cudgel and sometimes as a short sword or stick shaped like a sword), L.

ईळ् *iḷ, iḷā*, &c. See under √*iḍ*.

ईवत् *ī-vat*, mfn. (fr. pronominal base 3. *i*), so large, so stately, so magnificent, so much, RV.; going, moving [Sāy.]

ईश् 1. *īś*, cl. 2. Ā. *īshṭe*, or Ved. *īśe* (2. sg. *īśishe* and *īkshe*, RV. iv, 20, 8; vi, 19, 10; Pot. 1. sg. *īśīya*, pf. 3. pl. *īśire*, *īśishyati*, *īśitum*) to own, possess, RV.; MBh.; Bhaṭṭ.; to belong to, RV.; to dispose of, be valid or powerful; to be master of (with gen., or Ved. with gen. of an inf., or with a common inf., or the loc. of an abstract noun), RV.; AV.; TS.; ŚBr.; MBh.; Ragh. &c.; to command; to rule, reign, RV.; AV.; ŚBr. &c.; to behave like a master, allow, KaṭhUp.; [cf. Goth. *aigan*, 'to have;' Old Germ. *eigan*, 'own;' Mod. Germ. *eigen*.]

2. **Īś**, *ṭ*, m. master, lord, the supreme spirit, VS. &c.; N. of Śiva. **Īśâdhyāya**, m., N. of the Īśā-upanishad. **Īśā-vāsya** or **īśâvāsya**, n. 'to be clothed or pervaded by the Supreme,' N. of the Īśopanishad (q. v.) which commences with that expression. **Īśôpanishad**, f., N. of an Upanishad (so called from its beginning *īśā* [VS. xl, 1]; the only instance of an Upanishad included in a Saṃhitā).

Īśá, mfn. owning, possessing, sharing; one who is completely master of anything; capable of (with gen.); powerful, supreme; a ruler, master, lord, Mn.; ŚBr.; MBh.; Kum. &c.; (*as*), m. a husband, L.; a Rudra; the number 'eleven' (as there are eleven Rudras); N. of Śiva as regent of the north-east quarter, MBh.; Hariv.; R.; Śak. &c.; N. of Śiva; of Kuvera; (*ā*), f. faculty, power, dominion, AV.; VS.; ŚBr. **-gītā**, f. pl., N. of a section of the Kūrma-purāṇa. **-tva**, n. supremacy, superiority. **-saṃstha**, mfn. appearing as lord, ŚvetUp. **-sakhi**, m. Śiva's friend, N. of Kuvera. **-saras**, n., N. of a lake.

Īśana, *am*, n. commanding, reigning, ŚvetUp.

Ī́śāna (& **īśāná**), mfn. owning, possessing, wealthy; reigning, RV.; AV.; VS.; ŚBr. &c.; (*as*), m. a ruler, master, one of the older names of Śiva-Rudra, AV.; VS.; ŚBr.; MBh.; Kum. &c.; one of the Rudras; the sun as a form of Śiva; a Sādhya; N. of Vishṇu; N. of a man; (*ā*), f., N. of Durgā; (*ī*), f. the silk-cotton tree, Bombax Heptaphyllum, L.; (*am*), n. light, splendour, L. **-kalpa**, m., N. of a Kalpa. **-kṛit**, mfn. acting like a competent person, making use of one's possessions or faculties; rendering one a master or able [Sāy.], RV. **-candra**, m., N. of a physician, Rājat. **-ja**, *ās*, m. pl. a class of deities forming a section of the Kalpa-bhavas, L. **-devī**, f., N. of a woman. Rājat. **-bali**, m. a particular sacrifice, VS. **Īśānâdhipa**, mfn. one whose lord is Śiva; (*ā*), f. (scil. *diś*) the north-east.

Īśānya, *am*, n., N. of a Liṅga.

Īśitavya, mfn. to be reigned or ruled over, BhP.

Īśitṛi, *tā*, m. a master, owner, proprietor; a king, ŚvetUp.; Prab.

Īśin, mfn. commanding, reigning; (*inī*), f. supremacy, Mn. **Īśi-tā**, f. or **-tva**, n. superiority, supremacy, one of the eight attributes of Śiva, MBh.; BhP.

Īśvará, mfn. able to do, capable of (with gen. of Vedic inf., or with common inf.), liable, exposed to, AV.; TS.; ŚBr.; AitBr.; Kum.; Hit. &c.; (*as, ī*), m. f. master, lord, prince, king, mistress, queen, AV.; ŚBr.; Ragh.; Mn. &c.; (*as*), m. a husband, MBh.; God; the Supreme Being, Mn.; Suśr.; Yājñ. &c.; the supreme soul (*ātman*); Śiva; one of the Rudras; the god of love; N. of a prince; the number 'eleven;' (*ā* or *ī*), f., N. of Durgā; of Lakshmī; of any other of the Śaktis or female energies of the deities; N. of several plants, L. **-krishṇa**, m., N. of the author of the Sāṃkhya-kārikā. **-gītā**, f. pl. a section of the Kūrma-purāṇa. **-tā**, f. or **-tva**, n. superiority, supremacy, Prab.; MBh.; Hariv.; Mṛicch. **-tīrthâcārya**, m., N. of a teacher. **-datta**, m., N. of a prince. **-nishedha**, *as*, m. denial of God, atheism. **-nishṭha**, mfn. trusting in God. **-pūjaka**, mfn. pious. **-pūjā**, f. worship of God. **-praṇidhāna**, n. devotion to God, Vedāntas. **-prasāda**, m. divine grace. **-bhāva**, m. royal or imperial state. **-varman**, m., N. of a man, Kathās. **-vāda**, m., N. of a work. **-sadman**, n. a temple. **-sabha**, n. a royal court or assembly. **-sūri**, m., N. of a teacher. **-sena**, m., N. of a king, VP. **-sevā**, f. the worship of God. **Īśvarâdhīna**, mfn. subject to a king, dependant on a master or on God; **-tā**, f. or **-tva**, n. dependance upon God, subjection to a ruler. **Īśvarânanda**, m., N. of a scholiast.

Īśvarī-√1. kṛi, to make any one a lord or master. **Īśvarī-tantra**, n., N. of a work.

ईष् 1. *īsh*, cl. 1. Ā. (with prep. also P.) *īshate, -ti* (p. *īshamāṇa*, RV.; AV.; *īshé*, *īshitum*) to go; to fly away, escape, RV.; AitBr.; to attack, hurt, TS.; to glean, collect a few grains; to look, Dhātup.

Īshaṇa, mfn. hastening; (*ā*), f. haste, L.

Īshaṇin, mfn. hastening, L.

1. **Īshat**, mfn. (pres. p.) attacking, hurting.

ईष् 2. *īsh*, ind. a Nidhana or concluding chorus at the end of a Sāman, ĀrshBr.

ईष *īsha*, *as*, m. the month Āśvina, see *isha*; a son of the third Manu; a servant of Śiva.

ईषत् 2. *īshát*, ind. (gaṇa *svar-ādi*, Pāṇ. i, 1, 37; for the use of *īshat* see Pāṇ. iii, 3, 126, &c.) little, a little, slightly, ŚBr.; R.; Suśr. &c. **-°c-chvāsa** (*īshac-chvāsa*), mfn. slightly resounding. **-°j-jala** (*īshaj-jala*), n. shallow water, a little water. **-kara** (*īshat*), mf(*ī*)n. doing little; easy to be accomplished, Prab. **-kārya**, mfn. connected with slight effort. **-pāṇḍu**, m. a pale or light brown colour. **-pāna**, mfn. that of which a little is drunk; easy to be drunk; (*am*), n. a little draught. **-purusha**, m. a mean man. **-pralambha**, mfn. to be deceived easily. **-spṛishṭa**, mfn. uttered with slight contact of the organs of speech (said of the semi-vowels), APrāt.; Siddh. &c.

Īshad- (in comp. for *īshat*). **-asamāpta**, mfn. a little incomplete, not quite complete, almost complete. **-asamāpti**, f. almost completeness or perfection, little defectiveness or imperfection, Pāṇ. v, 3, 67. **-āḍhyam-kara**, mfn. easy to be enriched, Comm. on Pāṇ. **-āḍhyam-bhava**, mfn. easy to become rich, ib. **-upadāna**, mfn. easy to be ruined, Kāś. on Pāṇ. vi, 1, 50. **-ushṇa**, mfn. slightly warm, tepid. **-ūna**, mfn. slightly defective. **-guṇa**, mfn. of little merit. **-darśana**, n. a glance, a slight inspection. **-dhāsa** (*īshat-hāsa*), mfn. slightly laughing, smiling. **-dhāsya** (°*t-hā*°), mfn. id.; (*am*), n. slight laughter, a smile. **-bījā**, f. a species of grape (having no kernel), Nir. **-rakta**, mfn. pale red. **-vivṛita**, mfn. uttered with slight opening of the organs of speech. **-vīrya**, m. almond tree, Nir.

Īshan- (in comp. for *īshat*). **-nāda**, mfn. slightly sounding (applied to unaspirated soft consonants). **-nimaya**, mfn. exchanged for a little, L. **-marsha** or **-marshaṇa**, mfn. easy to be endured, tolerable, L.

Īshal-labha (*īshat-labha*), mfn. to be obtained for a little, L.

ईषा *īshā́*, f. (said to be fr. 1. *īsh*), the pole or shafts of a carriage or plough; (*e*), f. du. the double or fork-shaped pole, RV. iii, 53, 17; viii, 5, 29; AV. viii, 8, 23; xi, 3, 9; ŚBr.; KātyŚr.; MBh. &c.; a plank, board, VarBṛS.; a particular measure, Śulb. **-daṇḍa**, m. the handle of a plough, VP. **-danta**, mfn. having tusks as long as a pole; (*as*), m. an elephant with a large tusk, MBh.; R. **Īshâdhāra**, m., N. of a Nāga.

ईषिका *īshikā*, f. an elephant's eyeball; a painter's brush, &c.; a weapon, a dart or arrow, L. Cf. *ishīkā* and *īshīkā*.

ईषिर *īshira*, *as*, m. fire, L. See *ishira*.

ईषीका *īshī́kā*, f. a reed, cane, MaitrS.; an arrow, R.; a painter's brush or a fibrous stick used as one; an ingot-mould; a dipping rod or something cast into a crucible to examine if the metal it contains is in fusion, L. See *ikshikā*.

ईष्म *īshma* and 1. *īshva*, *as*, m., N. of Kāmadeva; spring, L. See *ishma* and *ishva*.

ईष्व 2. *īshva*, *as*, m. a spiritual teacher, L.

ईसराफ *īsarāpha*, *as*, m. (fr. the Arab.), N. of the fourth Yoga (in astrol.)

ईह् *īh*, cl. 1. Ā. *īhate*, *īhām-cakre*, *īhishyate*, *īhitum*, rarely P. *īhati*, &c., to endeavour to obtain; to aim at, attempt; to long for, desire; to take care of; to have in mind, think of (with acc.), MBh.; R.; BhP.; Bhag.; Pañcat. &c.: Caus. *īhayati*, to impel.

Īha, *as*, m. attempt (see *ūrdhvêha*); (*ā*), f. effort, exertion, activity, Mn.; MBh.; R. &c.; request, desire, wish, R.; Sāh.; MBh. &c. **-tas**, ind. diligently, energetically, by or with labour or exertion. **Īhāmṛiga**, m. a wolf, MBh.; R.; a kind of drama, Sāh. **Īhârthin**, mfn. aiming at any object, seeking wealth. **Īhâvṛika**, m. a wolf, L.

Īhita, mfn. sought, attempted, striven for; wished, desired; (*am*), n. desire, request, wish, effort, Hit.; Kathās.; Prab. &c.

उ U.

उ 1. *u*, the fifth letter and third short vowel of the alphabet, pronounced as the *u* in *full*. **-kāra**, m. the letter or sound *u*.

उ 2. *u*, ind. an interjection of compassion, anger, L.; a particle implying assent, calling, command, L.

उ 3. *u*, ind. an enclitic copula used frequently in the Vedas; (as a particle implying restriction and antithesis, generally after pronominals, prepositions, particles, and before *nu* and *su*, equivalent to) and, also, further; on the other hand (especially in connexion with a relative, e. g. *ya u*, he on the contrary who &c.)

This particle may serve to give emphasis, like *id* and *eva*, especially after prepositions or demonstrative pronouns, in conjunction with *nu, vai, hi, cid*, &c. (e. g. *ayám u vām purutámo . . . johavīti* [RV. iii, 62, 2], this very person [your worshipper] invokes you &c.) It is especially used in the figure of speech called Anaphora, and particularly when the pronouns are repeated (e. g. *tám u stusha índram tám gṛiṇīshe* [RV. ii, 20, 4], him I praise, Indra, him I sing). It may be used in drawing a conclusion, like the English 'now' (e. g. *tád u táthā ná kuryāt* [ŚBr. v, 2, 2, 3], that now he should not do in such a manner), and is frequently found in interrogative sentences (e. g. *ká u tác ciketa* [RV. i, 164, 48], who, I ask, should know that?)

Pāṇini calls this particle *uñ* to distinguish it from the interrogative *u*. In the Pada-pāṭha it is written *ūṃ*.

In the classical language *u* occurs only after *atha*, *na*, and *kim*, with a slight modification of the sense, and often only as an expletive (see *kim*); *u—u* or *u—uta*, on the one hand—on the other hand; partly—partly; as well—as.

उ 4. *u*, cl. 5. P. *unoti* (see *vy-u*, RV. v, 31, 1): cl. 2. Ā. (1. sg. *uvé*, RV. x, 86, 7): cl. 1. Ā. *avate*, Dhātup.; to call to, hail; to roar, bellow (see also *ôta* = *ā-uta*).

उ 5. *u*, *us*, m., N. of Śiva; also of Brahman, L.

उक *uka*, ind., gaṇa *cādi*, Pāṇ. i, 4, 57.

उकण *ukaṇa*, v. l. for *uṇaka*, q. v., Kāś. on Pāṇ. iv, 1, 41.

उकनाह *ukanaha*, *as*, m. a horse of a red and yellow or red and black colour, a bay or chestnut horse, L.

उकुण *ukuṇa*, *as*, m. a bug, L.; v. l. *utkuṇa*.

उक्त *ukta*, mfn. (p. p. of √*vac*, q. v.), uttered, said, spoken; (*as*), m., N. of a divine being (v. l. for *uktha*, q. v.), Hariv.; (*am*), n. word, sentence, Śiś. &c.; (*am, ā*), n. f. a stanza of four lines (with one syllabic instant or one long or two short syllables in each); [cf. Zend *ukhta*.] **-tva**, n. the being spoken or uttered, Sāh. **-nirvāha**, m. maintaining an assertion. **-puṇska**, a (feminine or neuter) word of which also a masculine is mentioned or exists (and whose meaning only differs from that of the masculine by the notion of gender; e. g. the word *Gaṅgā* is not *ukta-puṇska*, whereas such words as *śubhra* and *grāma-ṇī* are so; cf. *bhāshita-puṇska*), Vop. iv, 8. **-pūrva**, mfn. spoken before or formerly, MBh. **-pratyuktá**, n. speech and reply, discourse, conversation, ŚBr. xi, 5, 1, 10; a kind of anthem or alternate song, Sāh. **-vat**, mfn. one who has spoken (see √*vac*). **-varjam**, ind. except the cases mentioned. **-vākya**, mfn. one who has given an opinion, R.; (*am*), n. a dictum, decree, L. **Uktânukta**, mfn. spoken and not spoken. **Uktânuśāsana**, mfn. one who has received an order, ŚBr. xiv, 7, 3, 25. **Uktôpanishatka**, mfn. one who has been taught the Upanishads, ŚBr. xiv, 6, 11, 1. **Uktôpasam-**

kāra, m. any brief or compendious phrase or description.

Ukti, *is*, f. sentence, proclamation, speech, expression, word, Mn.; Pañcat.; Kathās. &c.; a worthy speech or word, BhP.

Uktvā, ind. p. having spoken or said (see √*vac*).

Ukthá, *am*, n. a saying, sentence, verse, eulogy, praise, RV.; AV.; VS.; (in the ritual) a kind of recitation or certain recited verses forming a subdivision of the Śastras (they generally form a series, and are recited in contradistinction to the Sāman verses which are sung and to the Yajus or muttered sacrificial formulas), AitBr.; TS.; ŚBr.; ChUp. &c.; (the *Mahad-uktham* or *Bṛihad-uktham*, 'great Uktha,' forms a series of verses, in three sections, each containing eighty Tṛicas or triple verses, recited at the end of the Agni-cayana); N. of the Sāma-veda, ŚBr.; (*ā*), f. a kind of metre (four times one long or two short syllables); (*as*), m. a form of Agni, MBh.; N. of a prince, VP.; N. of a divine being belonging to the Viśve Devās, Hariv. 11542. **—°m-vāc**, f. a particular part of a Śastra, ĀśvŚr. **—doha**, m. a particular final part of a Śastra, AitĀr. **—pattra**, mfn. having verses as wings, VS. xvii, 55. **—pātra**, n. vessels of libation offered during the recitation of an Uktha, Nir. **—bhṛit**, mfn. offering verses, RV. vii, 33, 14. **—mukha**, n. the beginning of an Uktha recitation, AitBr.; AitĀr.; ŚāṅkhBr. **—vat**, mfn. connected with an Uktha, AitBr. **—várdhana**, mfn. having hymns as a cause of refreshment, one who is refreshed or delighted by praise, RV. viii, 14, 11. **—vāhas** (*ukthá°*), mfn. offering verses, RV. viii, 12, 13; one to whom verses are offered, RV. **—vid**, mfn. conversant with hymns of praise, ŚBr. **—vidha**, mfn. verse-like, ŚBr. **—vīrya**, n. a particular part of a Śastra, AitĀr. **—śaṇsin**, mfn. praising, RV. vi, 45, 6; viii, 103, 4; uttering the Ukthas. **—śás** (in strong cases °*śās*), mfn. and **-śasá**, mfn. uttering a verse, praising, Pāṇ. iii, 2, 71; RV.; AitBr.; TS.; KātyŚr.; ŚBr. &c. **—śāstra**, n., N. of a work. **—śushma** (*ukthá°*), mfn. loudly resonant with verses, moving on with the sound of verses (as with the roaring of waters), accompanied by sounding verses; one whose strength is praise [Sāy.], RV. **—sampad**, f. a particular concluding verse of a Śastra, AitĀr. **Ukthâdi**, m., N. of a gaṇa, (Pāṇ. iv, 2, 60.) **Ukthā-madá**, n. praise and rejoicing, AV. v, 26, 3; AitBr.; Kāṭh.; TĀr.; MaitrS. **Ukthârká**, n. recitation and hymn, RV. vi, 34, 1. **Ukthā-vī**, mfn. fond of verses, VS. **Ukthā-śastrá**, n. recitation and praise, VS.

Ukthāyú, mfn. eager for praise, TS.; MaitrS.

Ukthin, mfn. uttering verses, praising, lauding; accompanied by praise or (in ritual) by Ukthas, RV.; VS.; AitBr.

Ukthyà, mfn. accompanied by verse or praise, consisting of praise, deserving praise, skilled in praising, RV.; AV.; accompanied by Ukthas, ŚBr.; KātyŚr.; (*as*), m. a libation (*graha*) at the morning and midday sacrifice, TS.; ŚBr.; KātyŚr.; (scil. *kratu*) N. of a liturgical ceremony (forming part of the Jyotishṭoma &c.), AV.; TS.; ĀśvŚr. &c.; a Soma-yajña, Lāṭy.; R. **—pātrá**, n. a vessel for the libation during an Uktha recitation, ŚBr. **—sthālí**, f. a jar for the preparation of an Uktha libation, ŚBr.

उक्ष् 1. *uksh*, cl. 1. P. Ā. *uksháti*, *ukshate* (p. *úkshat*, RV. i, 114, 7, and *ukshamāṇa*, AV. iii, 12, 1; RV. iv, 42, 4, &c.; *ukshām-cakāra* [Bhaṭṭ.; for *vavāksha* &c. see √*vaksh*]; *aúkshat* and *aúkshīt*, *ukshitum*) to sprinkle, moisten, wet, RV.; AV.; ŚBr.; MBh. &c.; to sprinkle or scatter in small drops; to emit; to throw out, scatter (as sparks), RV.; AV. &c.; to emit seed (as a bull); to be strong, RV. i, 114, 7; x, 55, 7, &c.: Caus. Ā. *ukshayate*, to strengthen, RV. vi, 17, 4; [cf. Lith. *ūkana*: Hib. *uisg*, *uisge*, 'water, a river;' *uisgeach*, 'aquatic, watery, fluid, moist, pluvial:' Gk. ὑγρός, ὑγρότης, ὑγραίνω: Lat. *ūveo* (for *ugveo*), *ūmor*, &c.]

2. **Uksh**, mfn. ifc. dropping, pouring, see *bṛihad-uksh*; becoming strong, see *sākam-uksh*.

Uksha, mfn. large, Nir.; ifc. = *ukshán* below (see *jātôksha*, *bṛihad-uksha*, &c.)

Ukshaṇa, *am*, n. sprinkling, consecrating, BhP., VarBṛS.; Ragh. &c.

Ukshaṇya, Nom. P. *ukshaṇyáti*, to wish for bulls &c.; to desire one who pours down riches [Sāy.], RV. viii, 26, 9.

Ukshaṇyāyana, *as*, m. a descendant of Ukshaṇya, RV. viii, 25, 22.

Ukshaṇyú, mfn. wishing for bulls &c.; desirous of one who pours down riches [Sāy.], RV. viii, 23, 16.

Ukshán, *ā*, m. an ox or bull (as impregnating the flock; in the Veda especially as drawing the chariot of Ushas or dawn), RV.; AV.; TS.; KātyŚr.; MBh.; Kum. &c.; N. of the Soma (as sprinkling or scattering small drops); of the Maruts; of the sun and Agni, RV.; one of the eight chief medicaments (*ṛishabha*), L.; N. of a man; (mfn.) large, L.; [cf. Zend *ukhshan*; Goth. *auhsa* and *auhsu*; Armen. *eṣn*.]

Ukshá (in comp. for *ukshán*). **—tara**, m. a small or young bull, Pāṇ. v, 3, 91; a big bull, L. **—vaśa**, m. sg. & du. a bull and a barren cow, TS.; ŚBr. **—vehát**, m. an impotent bull, ŚBr. **—sena**, m., N. of a king, MaitrUp. **Ukshânna**, mfn. one whose food is oxen, RV. viii, 43, 11.

Ukshitá, mfn. sprinkled, moistened, AV. v, 5, 8; MBh.; Ragh.; Kum. &c.; strong, of full growth, RV.

उख् *ukh*, cl. 1. P. *okhati*, *uvokha*, *okhitum*, to go, move, Dhātup.; Vop.

उख *ukhá*, *as*, m. (fr. rt. *khan* with 1. *ud*?), a boiler, caldron, vessel, AV. xi, 3, 18; N. of a pupil of Tittiri, Pāṇ.; TAnukr.; a particular part of the upper leg, Lāṭy.; (*ā́*), f. a boiler; any saucepan or pot or vessel which can be put on the fire, RV.; AV. xii, 3, 23; TS.; Suśr. &c.; a particular part of the upper leg, Pāṇ.; Car. &c. **—cchid** (*ukhá°*), mfn. fragile as a pot [NBD.], RV. iv, 19, 9. **Ukhā-sambharaṇa**, n. 'preparing the caldron,' N. of the sixth book of the Śatapatha-brāhmaṇa.

U'khya, mfn. being in a caldron, VS.; ŚBr.; KātyŚr. &c.; boiled or cooked in a pot (as flesh &c.), Pāṇ. &c.; (*as*), m., N. of a grammarian.

उखर्वल *ukharvala* or *ukhala*, *as*, m. a kind of grass (a sort of Andropogon), L.

उगण *úgaṇa*, mfn. (corrupted fr. *ud-gaṇa* or *uru-gaṇa*?), consisting of extended troops (used in connexion with *senā*, an army), VS.; SV.

उग्र *ugrá*, mfn. (said to be fr. √*uc* [Uṇ. ii, 29], but probably fr. a √*uj* or √*vaj*, fr. which also *ojas*, *vāja*, *vajra* may be derived; compar. *ugratara* and *ójīyas*; superl. *ugratama* and *ójishṭha*), powerful, violent, mighty, impetuous, strong, huge, formidable, terrible; high, noble; cruel, fierce, ferocious, savage; angry, passionate, wrathful; hot, sharp, pungent, acrid, RV.; AV.; TS.; R.; Śak.; Ragh. &c.; (*as*), m., N. of Rudra or Śiva, MBh.; VP.; of a particular Rudra, BhP.; N. of a mixed tribe (from a Kshatriya father and Śūdra mother; the Ugra, according to Manu x, 9, is of cruel or rude [*krūra*] conduct [*ācāra*] and employment [*vihāra*], as killing or catching snakes &c.; but according to the Tantras he is an encomiast or bard), Mn.; Yājñ. &c.; a twice-born man who perpetrates dreadful deeds, Comm. on Āp. i, 7, 20; Āp.; Gaut.; the tree Hyperanthera Moringa, L.; N. of a Dānava, Hariv.; a son of Dhṛita-rāshṭra, MBh.; the Guru of Narendrāditya (who built a temple called Ugreśa); a group of asterisms (viz. *pūrva-phālgunī*, *pūrvâshāḍhā*, *pūrva-bhādrapadā*, *maghā*, *bharaṇī*); N. of the Malabar country; (*ā*), f., N. of different plants, Artemisia Sternutatoria, Coriandrum Sativum, &c.; (*ī*), f. a being belonging to the class of demons, AV. iv, 24, 2; (*am*), n. a particular poison, the root of Aconitum Ferox; wrath, anger; [cf. Zend *ughra*: Gk. ὑγι-ής, ὑγίεια: Lat. *augeo* &c.: Goth. *auka*, 'I increase:' Lith. *ug-is*, 'growth, increase;' *aug-u*, 'I grow,' &c.] **—karṇika**, mfn. having an exceedingly big ornament for the ear, R. (ed. Gorr.) iv, 40, 29. **—karman**, mfn. fierce in action, violent, MBh. **—kāṇḍa**, m. a sort of gourd, Momordica Charantia, L. **—kālī**, f. a form of Durgā. **—gandha**, mfn. strong-smelling; (*as*), m. the plant Michelia Champaca; garlic; (*ā*), f. orris root; a medicinal plant; Artemisia Sternutatoria; Pimpinella Involucrata; the common caraway (Carum Carui &c.); Ligusticum Ajowan; (*am*), n. Asa Fœtida, L. **—gandhikā**, f. a species of caraway, L. **—gandhin**, mfn. strong-smelling, stinking, Vishṇus. **—gādha**, m. any unfathomable or dangerous depth (of a river &c.), TāṇḍyaBr. **—caṇḍā**, f., N. of a goddess, KālikāP. **—caya**, m. strong desire. **—cārin**, mfn. moving impetuously (said of the moon), BhP.; (*iṇī*), f., N. of Durgā. **—jāti**, mfn. base-born. **—jit**, f., N. of an Apsaras, AV. vi, 118, 1. **—tapas**, m., N. of a Muni. **—tā**, f. and **-tva**, n. violence, passion, anger; pungency, acrimony, MBh.; Sāh. &c. **—tārā**, f., N. of a goddess, KālikāP. **—tejas**, mfn. endowed with great or terrible energy, R.; (*ās*), m., N. of a Nāga, MBh.; of a Buddha; of another divine being, Lalit.; **—daṇshṭra**, mfn. having terrific teeth. **—daṇḍa**, mfn. 'stern-sceptred or holding a terrible rod;' relentless, remorseless, severe, VarBṛS.; Pañcat. &c. **—danta**, mfn. having terrific teeth, L. **—darśana**, mfn. of a frightful appearance, frightful, terrible, MBh. **—duhitṛi**, f. daughter of a powerful man, Kāty. on Pāṇ. vi, 3, 70. **—deva**, m., N. of a man, TĀr.; TāṇḍyaBr. **—dhanvan** (*ugrá°*), m. having a powerful bow, N. of Indra, RV. x, 103, 3; AV. viii, 6, 18; xix, 13, 4. **—nāsika**, mfn. large-nosed, L. **—paśyá**, mfn. frightful, hideous, fierce-looking; malignant, wicked (said of dice), AV. vii, 109, 6; (*ā*), f., N. of an Apsaras, AV.; TĀr. **—putra**, *as*, m. son of a powerful man, ŚBr.; (*ī*), f. = *-duhitṛi* above; (mfn.) having mighty sons, RV. viii, 67, 11. **—bāhu**, mfn. one whose arms are large or powerful, RV.; AV. **—bhaṭa**, m., N. of a king, Kathās. **—bhairava**, m., N. of a Kāpālika. **—maya**, m., N. of a demon causing diseases, Hariv. **—retas**, m. a form of Rudra, BhP. **—vīra**, mfn. having powerful men. **—vīrya**, mfn. terrible in might, MBh. **—vega**, mfn. of terrible velocity, MBh. **—vyagra**, m., N. of a Dānava, Hariv. **—śakti**, m. 'of terrible might,' N. of a son of king Amaraśakti. **—śāsana**, mfn. severe in command, strict in orders. **—śekharā**, f. 'crest of Śiva,' N. of the Gaṅgā. **—śoka**, mfn. sorely grieving. **—śravaṇa-darśana**, mfn. terrible to hear and see. **—śravas**, m., N. of a man, MBh. **—sena**, m., N. of several princes, e. g. of a brother of Janam-ejaya, ŚBr.; MBh. &c.; (*ī*), f., N. of the wife of Akrūra, VP.; *-ja*, m., N. of Kaṇsa (the uncle and enemy of Kṛishṇa). **—senānī**, m., N. of Kṛishṇa, MBh. **—sevita**, mfn. inhabited by violent beings, R. **Ugrâcārya**, m., N. of an author. **Ugrâdeva**, m. 'having mighty deities,' N. of a Ṛishi, RV. i, 36, 18. **Ugrâyudha**, mfn. having powerful weapons, AV. iii, 19, 7; (*as*), m., N. of a prince. **Ugrêśa**, m. the mighty or terrible lord, N. of Śiva; N. of a sanctuary built by Ugra, Rājat.

Ugraka, *as*, m., N. of a Nāga, MBh.

उङ्कार *uṅ-kāra*, *as*, m., N. of a companion of Vishṇu, Hariv.

उङ्कुण *uṅkuṇa*, *as*, m. a bug, L. See *ut-kuṇa*.

उङ्ख् *uṅkh*, cl. 6. P. *uṅkhati*, *uṅkhām-cakāra*, &c., to go, move, Dhātup.

उच् *uc*, cl. 4. P. *ucyati* (pf. 2. sg. *uvócitha*, RV. vii, 37, 3), Ā. (pf. 2. sg. *ūcishé*, RV.) to take pleasure in, delight in, be fond of, RV.; to be accustomed; to be suitable, suit, fit.

Ucita, mfn. delightful, pleasurable, agreeable; customary, usual; proper, suitable, convenient; acceptable, fit or right to be taken, R.; Pañcat.; Hit.; Suśr. &c.; known, understood, Śiś.; intrusted, deposited; measured, adjusted, accurate; delighting in; used to, MBh.; Suśr.; Ragh. &c. **—jña**, mfn. knowing what is becoming or convenient. **—tva**, n. fitness, MBh.

उचथ *ucátha*, *am*, n. (fr. √*vac*), verse, praise, RV.

Ucathya, mfn. deserving praise, RV. viii, 46, 28; (*as*), m., N. of an Āṅgirasa (author of some hymns of the Ṛig-veda).

उच्च *ucca*, mfn. (said to be fr. *ca* fr. √*añc* with 1. *ud*), high, lofty, elevated; tall, MBh.; Kum.; Śiś.; Kathās. &c.; deep, Caurap.; high-sounding, loud, Bhartṛ.; VarBṛS.; pronounced with the Udātta accent, RPrāt.; VPrāt. &c.; intense, violent, R.; (*as*), m. height, MBh.; the apex of the orbit of a planet, Kālas.; R. &c.; compar. *ucca-tara*, superl. *ucca-tama*; [cf. Hib. *uchdan*, 'a hillock;' Cambro-Brit. *uched*, 'cleve.'] **—gir**, mfn. having a loud voice; proclaiming, Śiś. xiv, 29. **—taru**, m. the cocoa-nut tree, L.; any lofty tree. **—tā**, f. or **-tva**, n. height, superiority, MBh.; the apex of the orbit of a planet, Sūryapr. **—tāla**, n. music and dancing at feasts, drinking parties, &c., L. **—deva**, m., N. of Vishṇu or Kṛishṇa, L. **—devatā**, f. the time personified, L. **—dhvaja**, m., N. of Śākya-muni (as teacher of the gods among the Tushitas, q.v.) **—nīca**, mfn. high and low, variegated, heterogeneous, MBh.; (*am*), n. the upper and lower station of the planets; change of accent. **—pada**, n. a high situation, high office. **-bhāshaṇa,** n. speaking aloud. **-bhāshin,** mfn. speaking with a loud voice, shouting, brawling. **-lalāṭā** or °**ṭikā,** f. a woman with a high or projecting forehead, L. **-śas,** ind. upwards, GopBr.

Uccâvaca, mfn. high and low, great and small, variegated, heterogeneous; various, multiform, manifold; uneven, irregular, undulating, ŚBr.; TS.; MBh.; R.; Mn. &c.

Uccakaiḥ (for *uccakais* below) √1. **kṛi,** to make high, set up in a high place, Kir. ii, 46.

Uccakais, ind. (sometimes used as an indeclinable adjective) excessively lofty; tall; loud, Pañcat, &c.

Uccā́, ind. above (in heaven), from above, upwards, RV.; AV. xiii, 2, 36. **-cakra** (*uccā́°*), mfn. having a wheel above (said of a well), RV. viii, 61, 10. **-budhna** (*uccā́°*), mfn. having the bottom upwards, RV. i, 116, 9.

Uccaiḥ (in comp. for *uccais* below). **-kara,** mfn. making acutely accented, TPrāt. **-kāram,** ind. with a loud voice, Comm. on Pāṇ. iii, 4, 59. **-kula,** n. exalted family, high family, Śak. 97 a; (mfn.) of high family. **-pada,** n. a high situation, Kum. v, 64. **-paurṇamāsī,** f. a particular day of full moon (on which the moon appears before sunset), Gobh. i, 5, 10. **-śabdam,** ind. with a loud voice, Prab. **-śiras,** mfn. carrying one's head high, a man of high rank, Kum. **-śravas,** m. 'long-eared or neighing aloud,' N. of the horse (of Indra, L.) produced at the churning of the ocean (regarded as the prototype and king of horses), MBh.; Hariv.; Bhag.; Kum. &c. **-śravasa,** m. id., L.; N. of a horse of the god of the sun, R. **-sthāna,** n. a high place, Śārṅg.; (mfn.) of high place; of high rank or family, Mn. **-stheya,** n. loftiness, firmness (of character).

Uccair (in comp. for *uccais* below). **-gotra,** n. high family or descent. **-ghushṭa,** n. making a loud noise, clamour, L. **-ghosha** (*uccair°*), mfn. sounding aloud, crying, neighing, roaring, rattling, AV. ix, 1, 8; v, 20, 1; VS.; AitBr. **-dvish,** mfn. having powerful enemies, Kum. **-dhāman,** mfn. having intense rays. **-bhāshaṇa** and **-bhāshya,** n. speaking aloud. **-bhuja,** mfn. having the arms outstretched or elevated, Megh. **-manyu,** m., N. of a man. **-mukha,** mfn. having the face upreared.

Uccaís, ind. (sometimes used adjectively) aloft, high, above, upwards, from above; loud, accentuated; intensely, much, powerfully, RV.; AV. iv, 1, 3; ŚBr.; Kum.; Pañcat. &c. **-taṭa,** n. a steep declivity. **-tamām,** ind. exceedingly high; on high; very loudly, aloud, Comm. on Pāṇ.; L. **-tara,** mfn. higher, very high; loftier, Pañcat.; Kum. &c.; louder, very loud; (*ām*), ind. higher, louder, Āp.; pronounced with a higher accent, Pāṇ. **-tva,** n. height, loudness, &c.

उच्चक् *uc-cak* (*ud-√cak*), P. *-cakati,* to look up steadfastly or dauntlessly, BhP. vi, 16, 48; to look up perplexedly, L.

Uc-cakita, mfn. looking up perplexedly or in confusion, Kād.

उच्चक्षुस् *uc-cakshus* (*ud-cakshus*), mfn. having the eyes directed upwards, Daś.

Uccakshū-√1. **kṛi,** to cause any one to raise the eyes, Kāś. on Pāṇ. v, 4, 51. **-√bhū** or **-√1. as,** to raise one's eyes.

उच्चघन *uccaghana,* n. laughter in the mind not expressed in the countenance, W.

उच्चट् *uc-caṭ* (*ud-√caṭ*), P. *-caṭati* (pf. *-cacāṭa*) to go away, disappear, BhP. v, 9, 18: Caus. P. *-cāṭayati,* to drive away, expel, scare, Pañcat.; BhP.; Bhartṛ.

Uc-cāṭa, *as,* m. ruining (an adversary), causing (a person) to quit his occupation by means of magical incantations, Mantram.

Uc-cāṭana, mf(*ī*)n. ruining (an adversary); (*as*), m., N. of one of the five arrows of Kāma, Vet.; (*am*), n. eradicating (a plant); overthrow, upsetting, BhP.; causing (a person) to quit (his occupation by means of magical incantations), Prab. &c.

Uc-cāṭanīya, mfn. to be driven away, Naish.

Uc-cāṭita, mfn. driven away, BhP. v, 24, 27.

उच्चटा *uccaṭā,* f. (etym. doubtful), pride, arrogance, L.; habit, usage, L.; a species of cyperus, Suśr.; a kind of garlic, L.; Abrus Precatorius, L.; Flacourtia Cataphracta, L.

उच्चण्ड *uc-caṇḍa* (*ud-ca°*), mfn. very passionate, violent; terrible, mighty, Bālar.; Prasannar.; quick, expeditious, L.; hanging down, L.

उच्चन्द्र *uc-candra* (*ud-ca°*), *as,* m. the moonless period of the night, the last watch of the night, L.

उच्चय *uc-caya.* See *uc-ci.*

उच्चर् *uc-car* (*ud-√car*), P. Ā. *-carati, -te* [Pāṇ. i, 3, 53], to go upwards, ascend, rise (as the sun), issue forth, go forth, RV.; AV.; VS.; ŚBr.; Ragh. &c.; to let the contents (of anything) issue out; to empty the body by evacuations, ŚBr.; BhP.; to emit (sounds), utter, pronounce, MBh.; Ragh.; Sāh. &c.; to quit, leave, Naish.; Bhaṭṭ.; to sin against, be unfaithful to (a husband); to trespass against, MBh.: Caus. P. *-cārayati,* to cause to go forth; to evacuate the body by excretion, discharge feces, Suśr.; to emit, cause to sound, utter, pronounce, declare, MBh.; R.; BhP.; Mṛicch. &c.

Uc-caraṇa, *am,* n. going up or out; uttering, articulating.

Uccaraṇya, Nom. P. *uccaraṇyati,* to move out, stretch out to.

Uc-carita, mfn. gone up or out, risen; uttered, articulated; (*am*), n. excrement, dung, BhP.; Suśr.; Mn.; Hit.

Uc-cārá, mfn. rising, TS. ii, 3, 12, 2; (*as*), m. feces, excrement; discharge, Suśr.; Mn.; Gaut.; Hit. &c.; pronunciation, utterance. **-prasravaṇa,** n. excrement, Jain. **-prasrāva-sthāna,** n. a privy, Kāraṇḍ.

Uc-cāraka, mfn. pronouncing, making audible.

Uc-cāraṇa, *am,* n. pronunciation, articulation, enunciation; making audible, MBh. **-jña,** m. a linguist, one skilled in utterances or sounds, Śiś. iv, 18. **-sthāna,** n. the part of the throat whence certain sounds (such as nasals, gutturals &c.) proceed.

Uccāraṇârtha, mfn. useful for pronunciation; necessary for pronunciation, a redundant letter &c. (only used to make pronunciation easy), Vop.

Uc-cāraṇīya, mfn. to be pronounced.

Uc-cārayitṛi, mfn. one who utters or pronounces, Comm. on Nyāyam.

Uc-cārita, mfn. pronounced, uttered, articulated, L.; having excretion, one who has had evacuation of the bowels, Gaut.; Suśr.; (*am*), n. evacuation of the bowels, Suśr.

Uc-cārin, mfn. emitting sounds, uttering, L.

1. **Uc-cārya,** mfn. to be spoken, to be pronounced, Sāh.

2. **Uc-cārya,** ind. p. having spoken or uttered.

Uc-cāryamāṇa, mfn. being uttered or pronounced.

उच्चल् *uc-cal* (*ud-√cal*), P. *-calati,* to go or move away from; to free or loosen one's self from, BhP.; Hariv.; Ragh.; Śak. &c.; to set out, Kathās.; to spring or jump up.

Uc-cala, *as,* m. the mind, understanding, L.; N. of a king, Rājat.

Uc-calana, *am,* n. going off or out, moving away, L.

Uc-calita, mfn. gone up or out, setting out, Ragh.; Kathās. &c.; springing or jumping up, L.

उच्चि *uc-ci* (*ud-√1. ci*), P. *-cinoti,* Ā. (pf. 3. pl. *-cikyire,* Bhaṭṭ. iii, 38) to gather, collect.

Uc-caya, *as,* m. gathering, picking up from the ground, Śak. 139, 5; adding to, annumeration, KātyŚr.; collection, heap, plenty, multitude, MBh.; R.; Daś.; Śak.; Sāh. &c.; the knot of the string or cloth which fastens the lower garments round the loins tied in front, L.; the opposite side of a triangle, L. **Uccayâpacaya,** *au,* m. du. prosperity and decline, rise and fall.

Uc-cita, mfn. gathered, collected, Kathās.

Uc-ceya, mfn. to be picked up or gathered, Kād.

उच्चिङ्गट *ucciṅgaṭa, as,* m. a passionate or angry man; a kind of crab; a sort of cricket, L.; (see *ucciṭiṅga, ciṅgaṭa, cicciṭiṅga.*)

उच्चिटिङ्ग *ucciṭiṅga, as,* m. a small venomous animal living in water; a crab, Suśr.; [cf. the last.]

उच्चुम्ब् *uc-cumb* (*ud-√cumb*), P.

Uc-cumbya, ind. p. having lifted up and kissed, Kād.

उच्चुलुम्प् *uc-culump* (*ud-√culump*), to sip up, Mcar.

उच्चूड *uc-cūḍa* (*ud-cū°*), *as,* m. the flag or pennon of a banner; an ornament tied on the top of a banner, L.

उच्च्यु *uc-cyu* (*ud-√cyu*), Caus. P. *-cyāvayati,* to loosen, make free from, liberate, AitBr.

उच्छंस् *uc-chaṇs* (*ud-√śaṇs*), P. (Impv. 2. sg. *úc-chaṇsa,* RV. v, 52, 8) to extol, praise.

उच्छद् *uc-chad* (*ud-√chad,* sometimes also incorrectly for *ut-sad,* q. v.), Caus. P. *-chādayati,* to uncover (one's body), undress.

Uc-channa, mfn. uncovered, undressed; (for *ut-sanna,* q. v.) lost, destroyed &c., Suśr.; Mudrār.

Uc-chādana, *am,* n. cleaning or rubbing the body with oil or perfumes, R.

Uc-chādya, ind. p. having undressed, R.

उच्छल् *uc-chal* (*ud-√śal*), P. *-chalati* (p. *-chalat*) to fly upwards or away, jerk up, spring upwards, Amar.; Śiś.; Kathās. &c.

Uc-chalita, mfn. jerked up, moved, waved, waved above, Pañcat.; Vikr.; Kathās. &c.

उच्छास् *uc-chās* (*ud-√śās*), P. (Impv. 2. sg. *úc-chaśādhi,* RV. vii, 1, 20 & 25) to lead up (to the gods).

उच्छास्त्रवर्तिन् *uc-chāstra-vartin* (*ud-śā°*), mfn. deviating from or transgressing the law-books, Mn. iv, 87; Yājñ.; Kathās.; BhP.

उच्छिंहन *uc-chiṇhana* = *uc-chiṅkhana* below.

उच्छिख *uc-chikha* (*ud-śi°*), mfn. having an upright comb (as a peacock), Uttarar.; having the flame pointed upwards; flaming, blazing up, Ragh.; Prab.; radiant; 'high-crested,' N. of a Nāga, MBh.

उच्छिखण्ड *uc-chikhaṇḍa* (*ud-śi°*), mfn. having an upright tail (as a peacock), Mālatīm.

उच्छिङ्खन *uc-chiṅkhana* (*ud-śi°*), n. breathing through the nostrils, snuffing, snoring, Suśr.

उच्छिद् *uc-chid* (*ud-√chid*), P. *-chinatti* (Impv. 2. sg. *-chindhi,* AV.; inf. *-chettum,* Śak.; *-chettavai,* ŚBr. i, 2, 5, 10, &c.) to cut out or off, extirpate, destroy, AV. vii, 113, 1; ŚBr.; MBh.; R.; Ragh.; Śak. &c.; to interfere, interrupt, stop, MBh.; Mn.; Sāh. &c.; to analyze, resolve (knotty points or difficulties); to explain [W.]: Caus. P. *-chedayati,* to cause to extirpate or destroy, Pañcat.: Pass. *-chidyate,* to be cut off; to be destroyed or extirpated, MBh.; to be interrupted or stopped; to cease, be deficient, fail, MBh.; Mn.

U'c-chitti, *is,* f. extirpation, destroying, destruction, ŚBr.; Kathās.; Suśr.; Ratnāv.; decaying, drying up, VarBṛS.

Uc-chidya, ind. p. having cut off or destroyed, having interrupted &c.

Uc-chinna, mfn. cut out or off; destroyed, lost; abject, vile, Mṛicch.; (*as*), m. (scil. *saṃdhi*) peace obtained by ceding valuable lands, Hit. &c.

Uc-chettṛi, *tā,* m. an extirpator, destroyer, R.

Uc-cheda, *as,* m. cutting off or out; extirpation, destruction; cutting short, putting an end to; excision, MBh.; Pañcat.; Hit.; Prab. &c.

Uc-chedana, *am,* n. cutting off; extirpating, destroying, destruction, MBh.; Pañcat.; R.

Uc-chedanīya, mfn. to be cut off, Mālatīm.

Uc-chedin, mfn. destroying, resolving (doubts or difficulties), Hit.

Uc-chedya, mfn. to be cut off or destroyed, Pañcat.; Prab.

उच्छिरस् *uc-chiras* (*ud-śi°*), mfn. having the head elevated, with upraised head, Kum.; N. of a mountain also called Urumuṇḍa.

उच्छिलीन्ध्र *uc-chilīndhra* (*ud-śi°*), mfn. covered with sprouting mushrooms, Megh. 11.

उच्छिष् *uc-chish* (*ud-√śish*), P. (2. sg. *-chishas,* RV.; AV.; 3. pl. *-chiṇshanti,* TBr.; Kāṭh.) to leave as a remainder, RV.; AV.; TBr.; Kāṭh. &c.: Ā. (Subj. 3. sg. *-śishātai,* AV. ii, 31, 13) to be left remaining: Pass. *-śishyate* (aor. *úc-cheshi,* AV. xi, 9, 13) to be left remaining, TāṇḍyaBr.; ŚBr.; AitBr. &c.

U'c-chishṭa, mfn. left, rejected, stale; spit out of the mouth (as remnants of food), TS.; ChUp.; ŚBr.; MBh.; Yājñ. &c.; one who has still the remains of food in the mouth or hands, one who has not washed his hands and mouth and therefore is considered impure, impure, Gaut.; Mn.; (*am*), n. that which is spit out; leavings, fragments, remainder (especially of a sacrifice or of food), AV.; ŚBr.; KātyŚr.; Mn.; ĀśvGṛ. &c. **-kalpanā,** f. a stale invention. **-gaṇapati** or **-gaṇêśa,** m. (opposed to *śuddha-gaṇapati*), Gaṇeśa as worshipped by the Ucchishṭas (or men who leave the remains of food in their mouth during prayer), Tantras. &c. **-cāṇḍālinī,** f., N. of a goddess, Tantras. **-tā,** f. and **-tva,** n. the being left, state of being a remnant or remainder, Comm. on Mn.; Pañcat. **-bhāj,** mfn. receiving the remainder, Gobh. iv, 3, 28. **-bhoktṛi,** mfn. one who eats leavings, Mn. iv, 212; a mean person. **-bhojana,** n. eating the leavings of another man, Mn.; (*as*), m. one who eats another's leavings; the attendant upon an idol (whose food is the leavings of offerings), L. **-bhojin,** mfn. or **-modana,** n. wax, L. **Ucchishṭânna,** n. leavings, offal. **Ucchishṭâśana,** n. eating leavings, Gaut. ii, 32.

Uc-chishya, mfn. to be left, Pāṇ. iii, 1, 123.

Uc-chesha, mfn. left remaining, Kathās.; remainder, leavings, BhP.; MBh.

Uc-chéshana, *am*, n. remainder, leavings, TS.; Mn.

Uccheshaṇī-√1. kṛi, to leave as a remainder, Das.

उच्छी **uc-chī** (*ud-√śī*), Ā. (3. du. *-chyāte*, ŚBr. iv, 5, 7, 5) to be prominent, stand out, stick out.

उच्छीर्षक **uc-chīrshaka** (*ud-śī°*), mfn. one who has raised his head, Suśr.; (*am*), n. 'that which raises the head,' a pillow.

उच्छुच् **uc-chuc** (*ud-√śuc*), Caus. P. (p. *-chocáyat*) to inflame, AV. v, 22, 2.

Uc-chócana, mfn. burning, AV. vii, 95, 1.

उच्छुष् **uc-chush** (*ud-√1. śush*), P. *-chushyati*, to dry up, ChUp. iv, 3, 2: Caus. *-choshayati*, to cause to dry up; to parch, MBh.; R.; Sārṅg.

Uc-chushka, mfn. dry, dried up, withered, Mṛicch.; Kathās.; Rājat.

Uc-choshaṇa, mfn. making dry, parching, Bhag.; (*am*), n. drying up, R.; making dry, parching, R.

Uc-chóshuka, mfn. drying up, withering, ŚBr.; GopBr.

उच्छुष्म **uc-chushma** (*ud-śushma* [√2. *śush*]), mfn. one whose crackling becomes manifest (said of Agni), TS.; AVPar.; N. of a deity, Buddh. **-kalpa,** m., N. of a section of the Atharva-veda-pariśishṭa. **-bhairava,** n., N. of a work. **-rudra,** m. pl., N. of a class of demons, AVPar.; of a Śaivite sect.

उच्छून **uc-chūna.** See *uc-chvi*, col. 2.

उच्छृङ्खल **uc-chṛiṅkhala** (*ud-śṛi°*), mfn. unbridled, uncurbed, unrestrained; perverse, self-willed; irregular, desultory, unmethodical, Pañcat.; Hit.; Kathās. &c.

उच्छृङ्गित **uc-chṛiṅgita** (*ud-śṛi°*), mfn. (fr. *śṛiṅga*), having erected horns, Śiś. v, 63.

उच्छोचन **uc-chocana.** See *uc-chuc*.

उच्छोषण **uc-choshaṇa.** See *uc-chush*.

उच्छ्रथ् **uc-chrath** (*ud-√śrath*), Caus. P. (Impv. 2. sg. *-śrathāya*, RV. i, 24, 15) to untie.

उच्छ्रि **uc-chri** (*ud-√śri*), P. *-chrayati* (aor. *úd-aśret*, RV. vii, 62, 1 & 76, 1) to raise, erect, extol, RV.; VS.; ŚBr.; AitBr.; Lāṭy.; MBh.; R. &c.: Ā. *-chrayate* (Impv. 2. sg. *-chrayasva*, RV. iii, 8, 3) to rise, stand erect, RV.; VS.; AitBr. &c.: Pass. *-chrīyate* (pf. *-chiśriye*) to be erected, AitBr.; ŚBr.; MBh.; Prab.: Caus. *-chrāpayati*, to raise, erect, VS. xxiii, 26.

Uc-chraya, *as*, m. rising, mounting, elevation; rising of a planet &c.; elevation of a tree, mountain, &c.; height, MBh.; R.; Yājñ.; Mṛicch.; growth, increase, intensity, Suśr.; the upright side of a triangle. **Ucchrayôpêta,** mfn. possessing height, high, lofty, elevated.

Uc-chrayaṇa, *am*, n. raising, erecting, KātyŚr.; ĀśvGṛ.; VarBṛS.

Uc-chrāya, *as*, m. (Pāṇ. iii, 3, 49) rising upwards, elevation, height, MBh.; Yājñ.; Suśr.; Pañcat.; growth, increase, intensity, Kir.; Suśr.; (*ī*), f. an upraised piece of wood, plank, KātyŚr.; ŚBr.

Ucchrāyin, mfn. high, raised, lofty, W.

Uc-chrita, mfn. raised, lifted up, erected, ŚBr.; ŚāṅkhŚr.; R.; Ragh.; Kathās. &c.; rising, arising, mounting, MBh.; Hariv.; MārkP.; VarBṛS.; high, tall, R.; BhP.; Kir.; Suśr.; VarBṛS. &c.; advancing, arisen, grown powerful or mighty, MBh.; Kathās.; Mn.; Hit. &c.; wanton, luxuriant, Hariv.; R. &c.; excited, Suśr.; increased, grown, enlarged, large, huge, Prab.; Ragh.; born, produced, L.; (*as*), m. Pinus Longifolia, L. **-pāṇi,** mfn. with outstretched hand.

Uc-chriti, *is*, f. rising upwards, elevation, MārkP.; increase, intensity, Mn.; the upright side of a triangle; the elevation or height of a figure.

Uc-chritya, ind. p. having erected or raised, MBh.

Uc-chreya, mfn. high, lofty, W.

उच्छ्लख **uc-chlakhá** (*ud-śl°*), *au*, m. du. a particular part of the human body, AV. x, 2, 1.

उच्छ्वञ्च् **uc-chvañc** (*ud-√śvañc*), Ā. (Impv. 2. sg. *úc-chvañcasva*, RV. x, 18, 11 & 142, 6) to gape, cleave open.

Uc-chvaṅká, *as*, m. gaping, cleaving open, forming a fissure, ŚBr. v, 4, 1, 9.

उच्छ्वस् **uc-chvas** (*ud-√śvas*), P. Ā. *-chvasiti* (p. *-chvasat*, *-chvasamāna*; Pot. *-chvaset*, *-chvasīta*) to breathe hard, snort; to take a deep breath, breathe; to breathe again, get breath, recover, rest, Gobh.; MBh.; BhP.; Suśr.; MārkP.; ŚvetUp. &c.; to sigh, pant, respire, Bhaṭṭ.; to rise, Vikr.; to unfasten one's self, BhP.; to open, begin to bloom, Vikr.; Mālav.; to heave: Caus. *-chvāsayati*, to cause to breathe again or recover; to gladden, BhP.; to raise, lift, elevate; to untie (cf. *uc-chvāsita* below).

Uc-chvasat, mfn. breathing &c. (see above); (*an*), m. a breathing being, R.

Uc-chvasana, *am*, n. breathing, taking breath; sighing; swelling up, Comm. on Bādar.

Uc-chvasita, mfn. heaving, beating, breathed, inspired; recovered, calm; revived, refreshed, gladdened, Kum.; Mālav.; Kathās.; Ragh. &c.; heaving, swelling up, raised, lifted, Ragh.; Kathās.; Megh. &c.; expanded, burst, unfastened, untied; blooming, BhP.; Mālatīm.; (*am*), n. breathing out, respiration; exhalation; breath; throbbing, sighing, Sāh.; Ragh.; Kum.; Śak.; bursting; unfastening, untying, Megh.; Ragh.

Uc-chvāsá, *as*, m. breathing out; breath, deep inspiration, KātyŚr.; Suśr.; Śak.; Prab. &c.; expiration, death, KātyŚr.; sigh, MBh.; Megh.; Amar.; froth, yeast, foam, RV. ix, 86, 43; swelling up, rising, increasing; consolation, encouragement, W.; pause in a narration, division of a book (e. g. of the Daśakumāra-carita); an air-hole, L.

Uc-chvāsita, mfn. caused to recover, gladdened, Ṛitus.; Kathās.; raised, lifted up, R.; Megh.; unfastened, untied, loosened, released, Megh.; breathless, out of breath; much, excessive, L.; desisted from; disjointed, divided, L.

Uc-chvāsin, mfn. breathing out, expiring, ŚBr.; breathing, Suśr.; sighing, Megh.; swelling up, rising, coming forward, Vikr.; Kum. &c.; pausing [MW.]

उच्छ्वि **uc-chvi** (*ud-√śvi*).

Uc-chūna, mfn. swollen up, swollen, bloated, Megh.; Kathās. &c.; increased, Sarvad.

Uc-chotha, *as*, m. bloatedness, Mālatīm.

उछ् **1. uch,** cl. 1. P. *ucchati*, RV. See √3. *vas*.

उछ् **2. uch,** cl. 1. P. *ucchati*, *ucchām-cakāra*, *ucchitum*, &c., to finish; to bind; to abandon, transgress, Dhātup.

उज्जन् **uj-jan** (*ud-√jan*), only RV.: P. (pf. *-jajāna*, iii, 1, 12) to beget, produce: Ā. (impf. 3. pl. *ud-ájāyanta*, iv, 18, 1; aor. *-ajani*, i, 74, 3; precative of the aor. *-janishīshṭa*, vii, 8, 6) to be born or produced, originate.

उज्जयन **uj-jayana,** &c. See *uj-ji*, col. 3.

उज्जस् **uj-jas** (*ud-√jas*), Caus. P. *-jāsayati*, to destroy, extirpate, kill (with gen., Pāṇ. ii, 3, 56), Bhaṭṭ.; Śiś.

Uj-jāsana, *am*, n. killing, slaughter, L.

उज्जागृ **uj-jāgṛi** (*ud-√jāgṛi*), P. (pf. *-jagāra* [?], Hcar. 140, 3) to pass (time) waking: Caus. *-jāgarayati*, to awake, call up, Sāh.; to excite; to effect, cause, Kāvyād.

Uj-jāgara, mfn. excited, irritated, Kād.

उज्जानक **uj-jānaka,** *as*, m., N. of a Tīrtha, MBh.; Hariv.

उज्जालुक **ujjāluka,** *as*, m., N. of a place, MBh.

उज्जि **uj-ji** (*ud-√ji*), P. *-jayati* (pf. *-jigāya*, &c.) to win, conquer, acquire by conquest, AV.; TS.; ŚBr.; TBr. &c.; to be victorious, AV.; TBr.: Caus. *-jāpayati*, to assist any one to win; to cause to conquer (with two acc.), Kāṭh.; TāṇḍyaBr. &c.: Desid. *-jigīshati*, to wish to conquer, ŚāṅkhŚr.

Uj-jayana, *as*, m., N. of a man, MBh.; (*ī*), f. Ujjayinī (see below) or Oujein.

Uj-jayanta, *as*, m., N. of a mountain in Surāshṭra (in the west of India, part of the Vindhya range), MBh.; (see *raivata*.)

Uj-jayinī, f. the city Oujein (the Gk. Ὀζήνη, a city so called in Avanti or Mālava, formerly the capital of Vikramāditya; it is one of the seven sacred cities of the Hindūs, and the first meridian of their geographers, from which they calculate longitude; the modern Oujein is about a mile south of the ancient city), Hit.; Megh.; Rājat. &c.

Ú-jiti, *is*, f. victory, VS.; TBr.; KātyŚr.; N. of the verses VS. ix, 31 sqq. (so called because the words *údajayat tam újjesham* occur in them), ŚBr.; KātyŚr.

Uj-jeshá, mf(*ā*)n. victorious, AV. iv, 17, 1 (voc. fem. *új-jeshe*); ŚBr. **-vat** (*uj-jeshá-*), mfn. containing the word *ujjesha*, ŚBr.

Ujjeshin, *ī*, m., N. of one of the seven Maruts, VS. xvii, 85.

उज्जिहान **uj-jihāna.** See 2. *ud-dhā*.

उज्जिहीर्षा **uj-jihīrshā,** f. (fr. Desid. of √*hṛi* with *ud*), wishing to take or seize [see also 2. *ud-dhṛi*].

उज्जीव् **uj-jīv** (*ud-√jīv*), P. *-jīvati*, to revive, return to life, Bhaṭṭ.; MBh.: Caus. P. *-jīvayati*, to restore to life, animate, Comm. on Kum.

Uj-jīvin, *ī*, m., N. of a counsellor of Meghavarṇa (king of the crows), Pañcat.

उज्जूटडिम्ब **ujjūṭa-ḍimba,** *am*, n., N. of a place, Rājat. (v. l. *ujjhaṭa°*)

उज्जूटित **uj-jūṭita,** mfn. one who wears the hair twisted together and coiled upwards, Rājat.

उज्जृम्भ् **uj-jṛimbh** (*ud-√jṛimbh*), Ā. *-jṛimbhate*, to gape; to open, part asunder, BhP.; to show one's self, become visible, come forth, break forth, expand, arise, Prab.; Naish.; Dhūrtas.

Uj-jṛimbha, mfn. gaping, Sāh.; parting asunder, open, apart; blown, expanded, L.

Uj-jṛimbhaṇa, *am*, n. the act of gaping, opening the mouth, Suśr.; coming forth, arising, Bālar.; (*ā*), f. coming forth, arising, Bālar.

Uj-jṛimbhita, mfn. opened, stretched; expanded, blown; (*am*), n. effort, exertion, L.

उज्जेन्द्र **ujjendra,** *as*, m., N. of a man, Rājat.

उज्ज्य **uj-jya,** mfn. (fr. *jyā* with *ud*), having the bow-sinew loosened, BṛĀrUp.; KātyŚr.

उज्ज्वल् **uj-jval** (*ud-√jval*), P. *-jvalati*, *-jvaliti* (Pāṇ. vii, 2, 34), to blaze up, flame, shine, TS.; ŚBr.; R.; BhP.: Caus. P. *-jvalayati*, to light up, cause to shine, illuminate, ŚBr.; Rājat.; Śiś. &c.

Uj-jvala, mfn. blazing up, luminous, splendid, light; burning; clean, clear; lovely, beautiful, Suśr.; MBh.; Kathās.; Sāh. &c.; glorious; full-blown, L.; expanded; (*as*), m. love, passion, L.; (*am*), n. gold, L.; (*ā*), f. splendour, clearness, brightness; a form of the Jagatī metre. **-tā,** f. or **-tva,** n. splendour, radiance; beauty. **-datta,** m., N. of the author of a commentary on the Uṇādi-sūtras. **-nara-siṅha,** m., N. of a Tīrtha. **-nīlamaṇi,** m., **-bhāshya,** n., **-rasakaṇā,** f., N. of works.

Uj-jvalana, *am*, n. burning, shining; fire, gold (?), R.

Uj-jvalita, mfn. lighted, shining, flaming, &c. **-tva,** n. the state of being lighted, Kap.

Uj-jvālana, *am*, n. lighting up, Car.

उज्झ् **ujjh,** cl. 6. P. *ujjhati*, *ujjhām cakāra*, *aujjhīt*, *ujjhitum*, &c. (probably a contraction from *ud-√2. hā* [*-jahāti*]) to leave, abandon, quit, Ragh.; Pañcat.; MBh. &c.; to avoid, escape, Ragh.; Śiś.; to emit, discharge, let out.

Ujjha, mfn. quitting, abandoning, Mn.

Ujjhaka, *as,* m. a cloud; a devotee, L.

Ujjhana, *am,* n. removing, Comm. on Yājñ.; abandoning, leaving, HYog.

Ujjhita, mfn. left, abandoned; free from, MBh.; R.; Śak. &c.; left off, discontinued; emitted, discharged (as water), Kir. v, 6. **-vat,** mfn. one who has emitted or discharged, Śiś. v, 36.

Ujjhiti, *is,* f. abandoning (the world), TāṇḍyaBr. xviii, 6, 10.

Ujjhitṛi, mfn. one who leaves.

उज्झटडिम्ब and उज्झटित *ujjhaṭa-ḍimba* and *ujjhaṭita,* vv. ll. for *ujjūṭa-ḍimba* and *ujjūṭita,* qq. v.

उञ्चदेश *uñca-deśa, as,* m., N. of a country.

उञ्छ् *uñch,* cl. 1. 6. P. *uñchati,* to gather, glean, ŚāṅkhGṛ.; Mn.; MBh. &c.

Uñcha, *as,* m. gleaning, gathering grains, Mn.; MBh.; R. **-vartin** or **-vṛitti,** mfn. one who lives by gleaning, a gleaner, MBh. **-śila,** n. the gleaning, gathering, L.; (cf. *śilôñcha.*) **Uñchâdi,** m., N. of a gaṇa (Pāṇ. vi, 1, 160).

Uñchana, *am,* n. gleaning, gathering grains of corn in market-places &c., BhP. &c.

उट *uṭa, as,* m. leaves, grass &c. (used in making huts, thatches &c.), L. **-ja,** *as, am,* m. n. a hut made of leaves (the residence of hermits or saints), MBh.; R.; Ragh.; Śak. &c.; a house in general, L.

उट्टङ्कन *uṭ-ṭaṅkana* (*ud-ṭa°*), *am,* n. the act of stamping, characterizing, Sāh.

उठ् *uṭh* or *ūṭh,* cl. 1. P. *oṭhati* or *ūṭhati,* to strike or knock down, Dhātup. ix, 54.

उडु *uḍu, us, u,* f. n. a star, Ragh.; BhP.; Mālav. &c.; (*u*), n. a lunar mansion or constellation in the moon's path, VarBṛS. &c.; water, L. **-gaṇâdhipa,** m. 'the lord of the stars,' the moon; *uḍu-gaṇâdhiparksha* (°*pa-ṛi*), n., N. of the Nakshatra Mṛigaśiras. **-nātha,** *as,* m. the moon, VarBṛS. **-pa,** m. n. a raft or float, MBh.; Ragh. &c.; a kind of drinking vessel covered with leather, Comm. on Ragh. i, 2; (*as*), m. the moon (the half-moon being formed like a boat), MBh.; Mṛicch. &c. **-pati** or **-rāj,** m. the moon, MBh.; R.; Kum. &c.; the Soma, Suśr. **-patha,** m. 'the path of the stars,' the ether, firmament. **-loman,** m., N. of a man, L. **Uḍū-pa,** m. n. a raft, float; (*as*), m. the moon, L.

उडुम्बर *uḍumbára, as,* m. (in Ved. written with *d,* in Class. generally with *ḍ*), the tree Ficus Glomerata, AV.; TS.; AitBr.; ŚBr.; MBh.; R.; Suśr. &c.; a species of leprosy with coppery spots, Car.; the threshold of a house, VarBṛS.; a eunuch, L.; a kind of worm supposed to be generated in the blood and to produce leprosy, L.; membrum virile, L.; (*ās*), m. pl., N. of a people, VarBṛS.; (*ī*), f. Ficus Oppositifolia, Suśr.; (*am*), n. a forest of Uḍumbara trees, TāṇḍyaBr.; the fruit of the tree Ficus Glomerata, ŚBr.; copper, VarBṛS.; a karsha (a measure of two tolas), ŚārṅgS. **-dalā** or **-parṇī,** f. the plant Croton Polyandrum. **Uḍumbarā-vatī,** f., N. of a river; see also *udumbara* and *udumbala.*

उड्डमर *uḍ-ḍamara* = *uḍ-ḍāmara* below.

Uḍḍamarita, mfn. stirred up, excited.

उड्डयन *uḍ-ḍayana.* See *uḍ-ḍī.*

उड्डामर *uḍ-ḍāmara,* mfn. (fr. *ud-ḍa°* ?), excellent, respectable, of high rank or consequence, Prab.; Bālar. &c. **-tantra,** n., N. of a Tantra.

Uḍḍāmarin, mfn. one who makes an extraordinary noise, Bālar.

उड्डियाण *uḍḍiyāṇa, as,* m., N. of a place.

उड्डियान *uḍḍiyāna, am,* n. a particular position of the fingers.

उड्डी *uḍ-ḍī* (*ud-√ḍī*), Ā. *-ḍayate* or *-ḍīyate,* to fly up, soar, Hit.; Pañcat.; MBh. &c.: Caus. *-ḍāpayati,* to cause to fly up, scare.

Uḍ-ḍayana, *am,* n. flying up, flying, soaring, Pañcat.

Uḍ-ḍīna, mfn. flown up, flying up, MBh.; Kathās.; (*am*), n. flying up, soaring, Pañcat.

Uḍ-ḍīyana, *am,* n. flying up, soaring, MBh.

Uḍ-ḍīyamāna, mfn. flying up, soaring, one who soars, Hit.

उड्डीयकवि *uḍḍīya-kavi, is,* m., N. of a poet.

उड्डीश *uḍḍīśa, as,* m., N. of Śiva, L.; N. of a Tantra work (containing charms and incantations), L.

उड्र *uḍra, ās,* m. pl., N. of a people, MBh.; VarBṛS. &c.

उणक *uṇaka,* mf(*ī* [gaṇa *gaurâdi,* Pāṇ. iv, 1, 41]) n. removing [? T.]

उणादि *uṇ-ādi* (according to some *uṇṇ-ādi;* but see Kielhorn, Mahābhāshya, vol. i, preface, p. 9 f.), *ayas,* m. pl. the class of Kṛit-affixes which begin with *uṇ.* **-sūtra,** n. pl. the Sūtras (Pāṇ. iii, 3, 1–4, 75) treating of the Uṇādi-affixes; *-vṛitti,* f. a commentary on the Uṇādi-sūtras.

उण्डुक *uṇḍuka, as,* m. a texture; a net; the stomach, Suśr.

उण्डेरक *uṇḍeraka, as,* m. a ball of flour, a roll, loaf. **-sraj,** f. a string of rolls, balls of meal or flour upon a string, Yājñ.

उत् *ut,* ind. a particle of doubt or deliberation (= 2. *uta,* q. v.), L.; (for the prep. *ud* see 1. *ud*)

उत 1. *uta,* mfn. (fr. √*ve,* q. v.), sewn, woven.

उत 2. *utá,* ind. and, also, even, or, RV.; AV.; ŚBr.; ChUp. &c.; often used for the sake of emphasis, especially at the end of a line after *iti* or a verb (e. g. *sarva-bhūtāni tam pārtha sadā paribhavanty uta,* all creatures, O king, certainly always despise him, MBh. iii, 1026), MBh.; Bhag. &c.

(As an interrogative particle, generally at the beginning of the second or following part of a double interrogation) or, utrum-an (e. g. *katham nirṇīyate kiṃ syān nishkāraṇo bandhur uta viśvāsa-ghātakaḥ,* how can it be decided whether he be a friend without a motive or a violator of confidence? Hit.), Kum.; Kathās.; Bhartṛ.; Sāh. &c.; in this sense it may be strengthened by *āho* (e. g. *kaccit tvam asi mānushī utâho surâṅganā,* art thou a mortal woman or divine? Nala), or by *āho-svit* (e. g. *Śālihotraḥ kiṃ nu syād utâhosvid rājā Nalaḥ,* can it be Śālihotra or king Nala?) Rarely *kim* is repeated before *uta* used in this sense (e. g. *kiṃ nu svargāt prāptā tasyā rūpeṇa kimutânyâgatā,* has she arrived from heaven or has another come in her form? Mṛicch.), Amar.; MBh. &c.

(As a particle of wishing, especially at the beginning of a sentence followed by a potential) would that! utinam! (e. g. *utâdhīyīta,* would that he would read!)

(*Uta* preceded by *kim*) on the contrary, how much more, how much less (e. g. *samartho 'si sahasram api jetuṃ kimutâkam,* thou art able to conquer even a thousand, how much more one, R.), Śak.; Vikr.; Ragh. &c.

(*Uta* preceded by *prati*) on the contrary, rather (e. g. *esha pṛishṭo 'smābhir na jalpati hanti praty-uta pāshāṇaiḥ,* this one questioned by us does not speak, but rather throws stones at us), Kathās.; Pañcat. &c.; *uta vā,* or else, and (e. g. *samudrād uta vā purīshāt,* from the sea or from the moisture in the air); *vā—uta vā* or *utâho vâpi—vā,* either—or; *uta—uta,* both—and (e. g. *uta balavān utâbalaḥ,* both the strong and the weak); *kim—uta vā,* whether—or else.

उतङ्क *utaṅka, as,* m., N. of a Ṛishi, MBh; (see also *uttaṅka.*) **-megha,** *as,* m. a kind of cloud named after that Ṛishi, MBh.

उतथ्य *utathya, as,* m., N. of a son of Aṅgiras and elder brother of Bṛihaspati, MBh.; VP. &c. **-tanaya,** m. 'a descendant of Utathya,' N. of Gautama, Mn. iii, 16. **Utathyânuja,** m. 'Utathya's younger brother,' N. of Bṛihaspati (regent of the planet Jupiter), L.

उताहो *utâho* and *utâho-svid.* See 2. *utá* above.

उतूल *utūla, as,* m. a servant, ParGṛ. iii, 7, 1 & 2; HirGṛ.; (*ās*), m., N. of a people, MBh.; VP.; (see also *ulūta* and *kulūta.*)

उत्क *utka,* mfn. (fr. 1. *ud,* Pāṇ. v, 2, 80), excited by the desire of obtaining anything; wishing for (with inf.), desirous of, longing for; regretting, sad, sorrowful; absent, thinking of something else, Kathās.; Megh.; Śiś. &c.; (*as, am*), m. n. desire, Kathās.; opportunity, occasion, L. **-tā,** f. a state of longing or regret, Kathās.; the plant Pothos Officinalis having aromatic seeds, L.

Utkaya, Nom. P. *utkayati,* to cause to long for, cause longing or regret, Śiś. i, 59.

Utkāya, Nom. Ā. *utkāyate,* to long for, Comm. on Bhaṭṭ. v, 74.

उत्कच *ut-kaca,* mfn. hairless, MBh.; full blown, BhP. iii, 23, 38.

Utkacaya, Nom. P. *utkacayati,* to coil the hair upwards, Sāh.

उत्कच्छा *ut-kacchā,* f. a metre of six verses (each verse containing eleven syllabic instants).

उत्कञ्चुक *ut-kañcuka,* mfn. having no coat of mail, without bodice or jacket, Bhartṛ.

उत्कट *ut-kaṭa,* mfn. (fr. 1. *ud* with affix *kaṭa,* Pāṇ. v, 2, 29), exceeding the usual measure, immense, gigantic, R.; Prab.; Pañcat. &c.; richly endowed with, abounding in, MBh.; R.; Pancat. &c.; drunk, mad, furious, MBh.; R.; excessive, much; superior, high, proud, haughty; uneven; difficult; (*as*), m. fluid dropping from the temples of an elephant in rut, L.; the plant Saccharum Sara, or a similar kind of grass, Suśr.; intoxication, pride, L.; (*ā*), f. the plant Laurus Cassia, L.; N. of a town; (*am*), n. the fragrant bark of Laurus Cassia.

उत्कटिका *utkaṭikā,* f. a manner of sitting (the legs being outstretched and forming a right angle), Yogaś. **Utkaṭikâsana,** n. id., ib.; (cf. *utkuṭaka.*)

उत्कटुक *utkaṭuka,* v. l. for *utkuṭaka,* q. v., Suśr.

उत्कणिका *utkaṇikā,* f. desire, longing (v. l. for *utkalikā,* q. v.), MārkP.

उत्कण्टकित *utkaṇṭakita,* mfn. one whose (thorn-like) short hairs are erected (through joy or emotion), Kād.

Utkaṇṭakin, mfn. id., ib.

उत्कण्ठ 1. *ut-kaṇṭha,* mfn. having the neck uplifted (on the point of doing anything), Ragh.; having the throat open (as in crying), BhP.; longing for; (*as*), m. longing for; a kind of sexual union, L.; (*ā*), f. longing for (a beloved person or thing); regretting or missing anything or a person, MBh.; Bhartṛ.; Pañcat.; Amar. &c. **-māhātmya,** n., N. of a work.

2. **Utkaṇṭha,** Nom. Ā. *utkaṇṭhate,* to raise the neck; to long for, regret, sorrow for, R.; Śiś.; Bhaṭṭ. &c.: Caus. *utkaṇṭhayati,* to cause any one to lift up the neck; to excite longing, inspire with tender emotions, Bhartṛ.; Kāvyād. &c.

Utkaṇṭhaka, mfn. exciting desire, VarBṛS.

Utkaṇṭhita, mfn. lifting up the neck; longing for, regretting, sorrowing for, R.; Daś.; Vikr. &c.; in love, Mālav.; (*ā*), f. a woman longing after her absent husband or lover.

उत्कन्द् *ut-kand* (for *ut-√skand,* Kāty. on Pāṇ. viii, 4, 61), to leap, jump over.

Utkandaka, *as,* m. a kind of disease.

उत्कन्धर *ut-kandhara,* mfn. having the neck erect or uplifted, Śiś.; Pañcat.; Rājat. &c.

उत्कम्प् *ut-kamp* (*ud-√kamp*), Ā. *-kampate,* to tremble, shudder, Kathās.; Gīt.: Caus. P. *-kampayati,* to cause to tremble; to shake up, rouse; to agitate, ŚBr.; KātyŚr.

Ut-kampa, mfn. trembling, shuddering, MBh.; Kathās.; Prab. &c.; (*as*), m. tremor, agitation, Suśr.; Bhartṛ.; Megh.; Kathās. &c.

Ut-kampana, *am,* n. the act of trembling, shuddering, agitation.

Utkampin, mfn. shuddering, trembling; agitated, Bhartṛ.; Kād.; Ratnāv. &c.; (ifc.) causing to tremble, agitating, R.

उत्कर *ut-kara,* &c. See *ut-√kṛī.*

उत्कर्कर *utkarkara, as,* m. a kind of musical instrument, L

उत्कर्ण *ut-karṇa,* mfn. having the ears erect, Ragh.; Śiś. **-tāla,** mfn. flapping with erected ears (as an elephant), Kathās. xii, 19.

उत्कर्तन *ut-kartana*, &c. See 1. *ut-kṛit*.

उत्कर्ष *ut-karsha*, &c. See *ut-kṛish*.

उत्कल् 1. *ut-kal* (*ud-√1. kal*), P. *-kalayati*, to unbind, loosen.

Ut-kalikā, f. longing for, regretting, missing any person or thing, Amar.; Kathās.; Mālatīm.; Ratnāv. &c.; wanton sportfulness, dalliance, L.; a bud, unblown flower, Ratnāv.; a wave, Mālatīm.; MārkP.; Śiś. **-prāya**, mfn. abounding in compound words (a kind of prose), Sāh.; Vām. &c.

Ut-kalita, mfn. unbound, loosened, BhP.; opened, blossoming; brilliant, bright, BhP.; appearing, coming forth, becoming visible, BhP.; regretting, longing for, L.; prosperous, rising, increasing, L

उत्कल् 2. *ut-kal* (*ud-√2. kal*), P. *-kālayati*, to drive out, expel, Comm. on KātyŚr.

Ut-kala, *as*, m. (perhaps fr. *ud-√1. kal*?), N. of the country Orissa (see Oḍra; the word is interpreted to mean 'the glorious country' [Hunter]; or 'lying beyond, the outlying strip of land' [Beames]; according to others it merely means 'the country of bird-catchers'); N. of a son of Dhruva, BhP.; of Su-dyumna, Hariv.; VP. &c.; a porter, one who carries a burden or load, L.; a fowler, bird-catcher, L.; (*ās*), m. pl. the inhabitants of the above country. **-khaṇḍa**, n., N. of a section of the Skanda-purāṇa. **-deśa**, m. the country of Orissa.

उत्कलाप *ut-kalāpa*, mfn. having the tail erect and expanded (as a peacock), Ragh.; Mṛicch.

उत्कलापय *ut-kalāpaya* (said to be a Caus. fr. *ud-√1. kal* above), Nom. P. *-kalāpayati*, to take leave of, bid farewell, Pañcat.; to bring one's wife home from her father's house; to marry, Vet.

Ut-kalāpana, *am*, n. marrying, Vet.

उत्कष् *ut-kash* (*ud-√kash*), P. *-kashati*, to dye, paint (e.g. the teeth), VarBṛS.; to tear up, L.

Ut-kashaṇa, *am*, n. tearing or ploughing up, drawing through (as a plough), Megh. 16.

उत्कस् *ut-kas* (*ud-√kas*), P. (Impv. 3. pl. *út-kasantu*, AV. xi, 9, 21) to gape asunder, open.

उत्काका *utkākā*, f. a cow calving every year.

उत्काकुद् *ut-kākud* (fr. *kākuda* with *ud*, Pāṇ. v, 4, 148), having an elevated or high palate.

उत्कान्ति *ut-kānti*, *is*, f. excessive splendour, Sāh.

उत्काय *utkāya*. See *utka*.

उत्कार *ut-kāra*, &c. See *ut-kṛī*.

उत्काश् *ut-kāś* (*ud-√kāś*), Ā. (pf. *-cakāśe*, BhP. i, 11, 2) to shine forth, flash.

Ut-kāśa, *am*, n. going out, coming forth, ŚāṅkhBr.

Ut-kāśana, *am*, n. giving orders, commanding, L.

उत्कास् *ut-kās* (*ud-√kās*), Ā. *-kāsate*, to cough up, hawk; to expectorate, Car.

Ut-kāsana, *am*, n. coughing up; clearing the throat of mucus, expectorating, Suśr.

उत्कास *utkāsa*, *as*, m. (gaṇa *yaskâdi*, Pāṇ. ii, 4, 63) N. of a man; (*ās*), m. pl. (Pāṇ. ii, 4, 63) the descendants of the above.

उत्किर *ut-kira*, *ut-kīrṇa*. See under *ut-kṛī*, col. 3.

उत्कीर्तन *ut-kīrtana*, &c. See *ut-kṛīt*.

उत्कील् *ut-kīl* (*ud-√kīl*).

Ut-kīlita, mfn. unfastened, opened (by drawing out the peg), Kād. ii.

उत्कील *utkīla*, *as*, m., N. of a Ṛishi, Comm. on VS. & RV. (v. l. *atkīla*, q. v.)

उत्कीलक *utkīlaka*, *as*, m., N. of a mountain.

उत्कुच् *ut-kuc* (*ud-√kuc*), *-kucati*, to bend upwards or asunder, crook, Kauś.; to open (as a flower): Caus. *-kocayati*, to cause to bend or to open (e.g. a flower).

Ut-kuñcikā or **ut-kuñcitā**, f. the plant Nigella Indica, L.

Ut-koca, *as*, m. winding off, unbinding, Comm. on TBr.; bribery, corruption, Yājñ. i, 339.

Utkocaka, mfn. receiving a bribe, Mn. ix, 258; (*am*), n., N. of a Tīrtha, MBh.

Utkocin, mfn. corruptible, to be bribed, MBh.

उत्कुट् *ut-kuṭ* (*ud-√2. kuṭ*), Caus. *-koṭayati*, to bend upwards, Kāś. on Pāṇ. i, 2, 1.

Ut-kuṭa, mfn. lying stretched out on the back, lying with the face upwards, sleeping with the head erect, L.

Ut-kuṭaka, mfn. sitting upon the hams, squatting, Suśr. **Utkuṭakâsana**, n. the sitting upon the hams, Suśr.

Utkuṭuka, v. l. for above.

उत्कुण *ut-kuṇa*, *as*, m. a bug; a louse, L.; (cf. *matkuṇa*.)

उत्कुतुक *ut-kutuka*, mfn. (ifc.) amusing one's self by, Prasannar.

उत्कुमुद *ut-kumuda*, mfn. having lotus flowers on the surface, Kāvyād.

उत्कुल *ut-kula*, mf(*ā*)n. fallen from or disgracing one's family, an outcast from the family, Śak. 128 b.

उत्कूज् *ut-kūj* (*ud-√kūj*), P. *-kūjati*, to utter a wailing monotonous note or coo (as a bird), Kathās.; Ṛitus.; Kād.

Ut-kūja, *as*, m. a cooing note (as of the kokila), R.

Ut-kūjita, *am*, n. id., Ṛitus.

उत्कूट *ut-kūṭa*, *as*, m. an umbrella or parasol, L.

उत्कूर्द् *ut-kūrd* (*ud-√kūrd*), P. Ā. *-kūrdati*, *-te*, to jump up, spring upwards, Pañcat.

Ut-kūrdana, *am*, n. jumping up, springing upwards, Pañcat.

उत्कूल *ut-kūla*, mfn. passing beyond the bank (as water), overflowing, Kād.; being on an elevation, going up-hill; (*ám*), ind. up-hill, AV. xix, 25, 1. **-gāmin**, mfn. passing beyond the bank, Kād. **-nikūlá**, mfn. going up and down, VS.; Lalit.

Utkūlita, mfn. brought to the bank or shore, thrown up on a bank, stranded, Sāh.

उत्कृ *ut-kṛi* (*ud-√1. kṛi*), P. *-karoti*, to do away with, extirpate, MaitrS.: Ā. *-kurute*, to inform against (?), Kāś. on Pāṇ. i, 3, 32; to promote, help.

Ut-kartṛi-tva, *am*, n. the being a helper, the state of being conducive to, NṛisUp.

Ut-kṛiti, *is*, f. a metre of four times twenty-six syllables; the number twenty-six.

उत्कृत् 1. *ut-kṛit* (*ud-√1. kṛit*), P. *-kṛintati*, to cut out or off, tear out or off; to cut up, cut in pieces, carve, butcher, ŚBr.; Mn.; Yājñ.; MBh.; Ragh. &c.; to destroy, ruin, extirpate: Pass. *-kṛityate*, to perish, AitBr. vi, 23, 7.

Ut-kartana, *am*, n. cutting up, cutting to pieces, cutting off, Suśr.

Ut-kártam, ind. p. cutting off, ŚBr. xiii, 7, 1, 9.

Ut-kṛitya, ind. p. having cut off or up, having cut out, MBh.; R.

Ut-kṛityamāna, mfn. being cut to pieces, being cut up.

उत्कृत् 2. *ut-kṛit* (*ud-√2. kṛit*), P. *-kṛiṇatti*, to continue spinning, RV. x, 130, 2.

उत्कृष् *ut-kṛish* (*ud-√kṛish*), P. sometimes Ā. *-karshati*, *-te*, to draw or drag or pull up; to raise; to draw or take out; to extract; to pull or put off, MāṇḍUp.; MBh.; Ragh.; Suśr.; R. &c.; to put off, delay, Nyāyam.; to bend (a bow); to tear asunder: Caus. *-karshayati*, to elevate, raise, increase, Sāh.: Pass. *-kṛishyate*, to be lifted or drawn up; to be raised, rise, become powerful, become eminent, MBh. &c. (cf. *ut-kṛishṭa*).

Ut-karsha, mfn. superior, eminent; much, excessive, L.; exaggerated, boastful, Yājñ.; attractive; (*as*), m. pulling upwards, drawing, pulling; elevation, increase, rising to something better, prosperity; excellence, eminence, Mn.; R.; Pañcat.; Hit.; Kathās. &c.; excess, abundance; self-conceit; boasting, Yājñ.; excepting, omitting, Comm. on KātyŚr.; putting off, delaying, Nyāyam. **-sama**, m. a kind of fallacy (attributing similar qualities to two objects because they have one quality in common; e.g. affirming that a sound has a shape like a jar because both are perishable), Sarvad.; Nyāyad.; Nyāyak.

Ut-karshaka, mfn. drawing upwards, raising, increasing, Sāh.

Ut-karshaṇa, *am*, n. the act of drawing upwards, taking off, Suśr.; pulling off (a dress), MBh.; (*ī*), f., N. of a Śakti.

Ut-karshita, mfn. drawn upwards, elevated.

Utkarshin, mfn. superior, better; more excellent or eminent, Kāvyād.; (*iṇī*), f., N. of a Śakti, RāmatUp.

Ut-kṛishṭa, mfn. (opposed to *apa-kṛishṭa* and *ava-kṛishṭa*), drawn up or out; attracted; extracted; taking a high position; excellent, eminent; superior, best; (ifc., e.g. *jñānôtkṛishṭa*, mfn. eminent in knowledge); much, most, excessive, Mn.; MBh.; Pañcat. &c. **-tā**, f. or **-tva**, n. excellence, superiority, eminence. **-bhūma**, m. a good soil. **-vedana**, n. marrying a man of a higher caste, Mn. iii, 44. **Utkṛishṭôpādhitā**, f. state of having something superior as an indispensable condition, Vedântas. 42.

Ut-krashṭavya, mfn. to be delayed, Nyāyam.

Ut-krashṭṛi, *ṭā*, m. one who draws up, Mn.

उत्कॄ *ut-kṝī* (*ud-√kṝī*), P. *-kirati*, to scatter upwards; to pile up, heap up, Ragh.; R.; to dig up or out, excavate, VS.; ŚBr.; KātyŚr.; MBh.; Suśr. &c.; to engrave, Vikr.; Ragh.

Ut-kara, *as*, m. anything dug out or scattered upwards, rubbish, AitBr.; ŚBr.; KātyŚr.; ĀśvŚr.; Mṛicch. &c.; a heap, multitude, MBh.; R.; Kathās. &c.; sprawling, Bhpr. i, 138. **Utkarâdi**, m., N. of a gaṇa (Pāṇ. iv, 2, 90).

Ut-karikā, f. a sort of sweetmeat (made with milk, treacle, and ghee [W.]), Comm. on Mn.

Utkarīya, mfn. relating or belonging to a heap &c., Pāṇ. iv, 2, 90.

Ut-kāra, *as*, m. piling up (corn), Pāṇ.; Bhaṭṭ.

Ut-kārikā, f. a poultice, Suśr. **Utkārikôpanāha**, m. id., Car.

Ut-kira, mfn. (ifc.) piling up, heaping up, Ragh. i, 38; Kum. &c.

Ut-kīrṇa, mfn. heaped up, scattered, Ragh.; covered with, Kād.; dug out, perforated, KātyŚr.; Suśr. &c.; pierced; engraved, carved; cut out, Vikr.; Kāvyād.

उत्कृत् *ut-kṝit* (*ud-√kṝit*), P. *-kīrtayati*, to proclaim, celebrate, praise, promulgate.

Ut-kīrtana, *am*, n. crying out, proclaiming; reporting, promulgating, Sāh.; praising, celebrating.

Ut-kīrtita, mfn. proclaimed, promulgated; praised, celebrated, L.

Ut-kīrtya, ind. p. having celebrated or praised, Ragh. x, 32; having proclaimed &c.

उत्क्लृप् *ut-kḷip* (*ud-√kḷip*), Caus. P. (impf. 3. pl. *-ákalpayan*, AV. xii, 4, 41) to form, fashion, create.

उत्कोच *ut-koca*, &c. See *ut-kuc*.

उत्कोटि *ut-koṭi*, mfn. ending in a point or edge, Kād.

उत्कोठ *ut-koṭha*, *as*, m. a kind of leprosy, Bhpr.

उत्कोरकय *utkorakaya*, Nom. P. *utkorakayati*, to abound with opening buds, Kād.

उत्कोशय *utkośaya*, Nom. P. *utkośayati*, to draw (a sword) out of its scabbard, Vet.

उत्क्रम् *ut-kram* (*ud-√kram*), P. (and rarely Ā.) *-krāmati*, *-kramati* (Ved. impf. 3. pl. *-akraman*, AV. iv, 3, 1), *-te* (pf. 3. pl. *-cakramus*, ŚBr.) to step up, go up, ascend, AV.; VS.; TS.; ŚBr.; KātyŚr.; R.; Kathās. &c.; to step out, go out or away; to pass away, die, ŚBr.; Mn.; Nir.; Kād. &c.; to go over, pass over, omit; not to notice; to neglect, transgress, MBh.; R. &c.: Caus. P. *-kramayati* and *-krāmayati*, to cause to go up or ascend, TS.; ŚBr.; Kauś. &c.: Desid. *-cikramishati* or *-cikramishyati*, to wish to go up or out, ŚBr.; ChUp.

Ut-kramá, *as*, m. going up or out, VS.; ŚBr. &c.; inverted order, Sūryas.; progressive increase; going astray, acting improperly, deviation, transgression, L. **-jyā**, f. (in geom.) the versed sine, Sūryas.

Ut-krámaṇa, *am*, n. going up or out, soaring aloft, flight; stepping out, VS.; ChUp. &c.; KātyŚr.; surpassing, exceeding; departing from life, dying, death, KaṭhUp.; (cf. *prāṇôtkr°*.)

Ut-kramaṇīya, mfn. to be abandoned or given up, MBh.

Ut-kramayya, ind. p. (of Caus.) having caused to ascend, Lāṭy.

Ut-kramya, ind. p. having gone up, stepping up &c.; having neglected, MBh.

Ut-krānta, mfn. gone forth or out; gone over or beyond, passed, surpassed; trespassing, exceeding. **-medha** (*út-krānta°*), mfn. sapless, powerless, ŚBr. vii, 5, 2, 37. **-śreyas**, mfn. abandoned by fortune, Vait.

Ut-krānti, *is*, f. stepping up to, VS.; SBr.; going out; passing away, dying, Kathās.

Utkrāntin, mfn. passing, passing away, gone, departed, L.

Ut-krāma, *as*, m. going from or out, going above, surpassing, deviating from propriety, transgression; opposition, contrariety, L.

उत्क्रष्टव्य *ut-krashṭavya, ut-krashṭṛi.* See *ut-kṛish*, p. 176, col. 3.

उत्क्री *ut-krī, is*, m., N. of a particular Soma sacrifice, ŚāṅkhŚr. xiv, 42, 8.

उत्क्रुश् *ut-kruś* (*ud-√kruś*), P. *-krośati*, to cry out, scream, MBh.; R.; MārkP.; to call to (with acc.), MBh.; to exclaim; to proclaim, W.

Ut-krushṭa, mfn. crying out, speaking out or aloud; (*am*), n. the act of crying out, MBh.; calling, exclaiming.

Ut-krośa, *as*, m. clamour, outcry, L.; a sea eagle, Suśr.

Utkrośīya, mfn. (gaṇa *utkarâdi*, Pāṇ. iv, 2, 90), relating or belonging to a clamour &c.

उत्क्रोद *ut-krodá, as*, m. (*√krud=√kūrd?* BRD.), jumping up, exulting, exultation, TS. vii, 5, 9, 2.

Ut-krodin, mfn. exulting, MaitrS. ii, 5, 7.

उत्क्लिश् *ut-kliś* (*ud-√kliś*), P. *-kliśnāti*, to feel uneasy, be uncomfortable or distressed: Caus. P. *-kleśayati*, to excite, stir up, Suśr.; to expel.

Ut-kliśya, ind. p. having become uneasy, Suśr.

Ut-klishṭa, mfn. distressed, Car.

Ut-kleśa, *as*, m. excitement, disquietude; disorder or corruption of the humors (of the body), Suśr.; sickness, nausea.

Ut-kleśaka, *as*, m. a kind of venomous insect, Suśr.

Ut-kleśana, mfn. exciting, stirring up, causing disorder (cf. *kaphôt°*), Suśr.

Ut-kleśin, mfn. id.

उत्क्लेद *ut-kleda, as*, m. (*√klid*), the becoming wet or moist, Suśr.

Utkledin, mfn. wet, Suśr.; wetting, Car.

उत्क्वथ् *ut-kvath* (*ud-√kvath*), P. *-kvathati*, to boil out, extract by boiling &c., Suśr.: Pass. *-kvathyate*, to be boiled; to be consumed (by the ardour of love), Kād. 176, 3: Caus. *-kvāthayati*, to boil out, Suśr.

उत्क्षिप् *ut-kship* (*ud-√kship*), P. Ā. *-kshipati, -te*, to throw up, raise, set up, erect, Mn.; MBh.; Kathās. &c.; to throw away, reject, get rid of, vomit up, BhP.

Ut-kshipta, mfn. thrown upwards, tossed, raised, MBh.; Kathās. &c.; thrown out, ejected; vomited; rejected, dismissed; (*as*), m. the thorn apple (Datura Metel and Fastuosa), L.

Ut-kshipti, *is*, f. raising, lifting up, Priy.

Utkshiptikā, f. an ornament in the shape of a crescent worn in the upper part of the ear, L.

Ut-kshepa, *as*, m. throwing or tossing up, raising, lifting up, Megh.; Suśr. &c.; throwing away; sending, despatching; bringing up, vomiting; expanding (the wings), Suśr.; N. of a country; also of a man, L.; (*au*), m. du. the region above the temples, Suśr.; (*ā*), f., N. of a woman, Kāś. on Pāṇ. iv, 1, 112.

Ut-kshepaka, mfn. throwing up, a thrower; who or what elevates or raises; one who sends or orders, L.; (*as*), m. a stealer of clothes, Yājñ. ii, 274.

Ut-kshepaṇa, *am*, n. the act of throwing upwards, tossing, KātyŚr.; Śak. 30 a; sending, sending away, Suśr.; vomiting, taking up; a kind of basket or bowl used for cleaning corn, L.; a fan, L.; a measure of sixteen paṇas, L.

Ut-kshepam (*bāhût°*), ind. p. having thrown up (the arms), Śak. 131 b.

उत्क्ष्विद् *ut-kshvid* (*ud-√kshvid*), P. *-kshvedati*, to creak, MaitrS. iii, 2, 2.

उत्खच् *ut-khac* (*ud-√khac*).

Ut-khacita, mfn. intermixed with, Ragh.

उत्खन् *ut-khan* (*ud-√khan*), P. *-khanati* (pf. *-cakhāna*) to dig up or out, to excavate; to tear out by the roots, root up, ŚBr.; AitBr.; Ragh.; Kathās. &c.; to draw or tear out, Kauś.; Kathās.; Bhaṭṭ.; to destroy entirely, Ragh.; Rājat.; Pañcat.

Ut-khāta, mfn. dug up; excavated, eradicated, pulled up by the roots; destroyed, annihilated; (*am*), n. a hole, cavity; a deepening, uneven ground; undermining, hollowing out; destroying, extirpating, Mudrār.

Utkhātin, mfn. having cavities or holes, uneven, Śak. 10, 6; destructive.

Ut-khānam, ind. p. digging out, Lāṭy.

Ut-khāya, ind. p. having dug up; having torn out, Ragh.; Śiś. v, 59.

उत्खला *utkhalā*, f. a kind of perfume, L.

उत्खलिन् *utkhalin, ī*, m., N. of a Buddhist deity.

Utkhalī and **utkhālī**, f., N. of a Buddhist goddess.

उत्खिद् *ut-khid* (*ud-√khid*), P. *-khidáti*, to draw out, extract, TS.; AV.; AitBr.; ŚBr.; KātyŚr.; ĀśvGṛ.

उत्त *utta*. See p. 183, col. 1.

उत्तंस *ut-taṇsa, as*, m. (*√tan*), a crest, chaplet; a wreath worn on the crown of the head, Sāh.; Rājat.; an earring, L.; (figuratively) an ornament, VarBṛS.; Bālar.

Ut-taṇsaka, *as*, m. id., VarBṛS.

Uttaṇsaya, Nom. P. *uttaṇsayati*, to adorn with a crest, Veṇīs.

Uttaṇsika, *as*, m., N. of a Nāga, L.

Uttaṇsita, mfn. used as crest or ornament for the head, Bhartṛ.; crested, Prasannar.

उत्तक्ष् *ut-taksh* (*ud-√taksh*), P. (Impv. 2. du. *út-takshatam*, RV. vii, 104, 4) to form (anything) out of (any other thing), [BRD.]; to take out of (anything), [Sāy.]

उत्तङ्क *uttaṅka* and *uttaṅka-megha*, vv. ll. for *utaṅka* and *utaṅka-megha*, qq. v.

उत्तट *ut-taṭa*, mfn. overflowing its banks (as a river), Ragh. xi, 85.

उत्तथ्य *uttathya, as*, m., N. of a son of Devaputra, BhP.; VP.; (cf. *utathya*.)

उत्तन् *ut-tan* (*ud-√tan*), Ā. (aor. 3. pl. *-atnata*, RV. i, 37, 10) to stretch one's self upwards, endeavour to rise; to stretch out.

U't-tata, mfn. stretching one's self upwards, rising upwards, AV. ii, 7, 3; vii, 90, 3.

Ut-tāná, mfn. stretched out, spread out, lying on the back, sleeping supinely or with the face upwards, RV.; AV.; VS.; upright, ŚBr.; KātyŚr. &c.; turned so that the mouth or opening is uppermost (as a vessel), concave, TS.; ŚBr.; KātyŚr.; BhP. &c.; spreading out over the surface, Suśr.; shallow; open, Śak.; (*as*), m., N. of an Āṅgirasa, TBr.; Kāṭh. **-kūrmaka**, n. a particular posture in sitting. **-pattraka**, m. a species of Ricinus, Bhpr. **-pad** (*uttānâ°*), f. one whose legs are extended (in parturition); N. of a peculiar creative agency, RV. x, 72, 4; vegetation, the whole creation of upward-germinating plants, [Sāy.] **-parṇa** (*uttānâ-*), mfn. having extended leaves, RV. x, 145, 2. **-parṇaka**, m. a species of plant, L. **-pāṇi-dvaya**, mfn. having the two hands with the palms turned upwards. **-pāda**, *as*, m. the star β in the little bear (personified as son of Vīra or Manu Svāyambhuva and father of Dhruva), Hariv.; VP. &c.; *-ja*, m. a N. of Dhruva (or the polar-star), L. **-barhis**, m., N. of a prince, BhP. **-recita**, m. (sc. *hasta*) a particular position of the hands. **-śaya**, mfn. lying on the back, sleeping with the face upwards; (*as*), m. a little child, L. **-śāyin**, mfn. lying on the back. **-śīvan**, mf(*arī*)n. lying extended, stagnant (as water), AV. iii, 21, 10. **-haya**, m., N. of a son of Śatājit, VP. **-hasta** (*uttānâ°*), mfn. having the hands extended, extending them in prayer, RV.; KātyŚr.; Vait.; (*au*), m. du. the two hands with the fingers stretched out (but with the backs towards the ground), W. **-hṛidaya** (Prākṛit *uttāṇahiaa*), open-hearted, Śak. 204, 6.

Uttānârtha, mfn. superficial, shallow, Subh.

Uttānaka, *as*, m. a species of Cyperus grass, L.; (*ikā*), f., N. of a river, R.

Uttānita, mfn. wide open (as the mouth), Kād.

Uttānī-√1. kṛi, to open wide (the mouth), Ratnāv. **-√bhū**, to spread, extend, Kād.

उत्तप् *ut-tap* (*ud-√tap*), P. *-tapati*, to make warm or hot; to heat thoroughly, Rājat.; Lāṭy. &c.; to pain, torment, press hard, Rājat.; Śiś. &c.: Ā. *-tapate*, to shine forth, give out heat, Pāṇ. i, 3, 27; to warm one's self or a part of one's body, Kāty. on Pāṇ. i, 3, 27: Caus. *-tāpayati*, to warm up, heat, MBh.; to excite, urge on, Sāh.

Ut-tapana, *as*, m. a particular kind of fire.

Ut-tapta, mfn. burnt; heated, red hot, glowing, Śārṅg.; pained, tormented, pressed hard, Rājat.; bathed, washed, L.; anxious, excited, W.; (*am*), n. dried flesh, L.; great heat, T.

Ut-tāpa, *as*, m. great heat, glow; ardour, effort, excessive energy, Hit.; Bālar.; affliction, distress; excitement, anxiety, L.

Ut-tāpita, mfn. heated, made hot; pained, distressed; excited, roused.

उत्तब्ध *út-tabdha*, &c. See *ut-tambh*, p. 179, col. 1.

उत्तम् *ut-tam* (*ud-√tam*), P. *-tāmyati*, to be out of breath or exhausted; to lose heart, faint, R.; Rājat.; Daś.

उत्तम *ut-tamá*, mfn. (superlative fr. 1. *ud*; opposed to *avama*, *adhama*, &c.; cf. *an-uttama*), uppermost, highest, chief; most elevated, principal; best, excellent, RV.; AV.; AitBr.; Mn.; Pañcat. &c. (often ifc., e. g. *dvijôttama*, best of the twice-born, i. e. a Brāhman, Mn.); first, greatest; the highest (tone), ĀśvŚr.; KātyŚr.; the most removed or last in place or order or time, RV.; ŚBr.; MBh. &c.; (*ám*), ind. most, in the highest degree, R.; at last, lastly, ŚBr. iii, 2, 1, 21; (*as*), m. the last person (=in European grammars the first person), Pāṇ.; Kāty.; Kāś. &c.; N. of a brother of Dhruva (son of Uttāna-pāda and nephew of Priya-vrata), VP.; of a son of Priya-vrata and third Manu; of the twenty-first Vyāsa, VP.; (*ās*), m. pl., N. of a people, VP.; MBh.; (*ā*), f. a kind of Piḍakā or pustule, Suśr.; the plant Oxystelma Esculentum (Asclepias Rosea Roxb.), Suśr.; an excellent woman (one who is handsome, healthy, and affectionate), L. **-gandhâḍhya**, mfn. possessing abundantly the most delicate scent or delicious fragrance. **-jana**, m. pl. excellent men, Bhartṛ. (Hit. &c.) **-tā**, f. or **-tva**, n. excellence, superiority; goodness, good quality. **-tejas**, mfn. having extraordinary splendour, very glorious, MBh. **-darśana**, mfn. of excellent appearance, MBh. **-pada**, n. a high office. **-purusha**, m. the last person in verbal conjugation, i. e. 'I, we two, we' (=in European grammars the first person, our third person being regarded in Hindū grammars as the *prathama-purusha*, q. v.; cf. also *madhyama-purusha*), Nir.; Kāś. &c.; the Supreme Spirit, ChUp.; Gaut. &c. **-pūrusha**, m. =*-purusha* above; the Supreme Spirit; an excellent man, L. **-phalinī**, f. the plant Oxystelma Esculentum (Asclepias Rosea Roxb.), L. **-bala**, mfn. of excellent strength, very strong, Car. **-maṇi**, m. a kind of gem, L. **-°rṇa** (*uttama-ṛiṇa*), m. a creditor, Pāṇ. i, 4, 35; Mn. &c.; (*ās*), m. pl., N. of a people, VP.; MārkP. **-°rṇika**, m. a creditor, Mn.; Yājñ. **-°rṇin**, m. a creditor, L. **-lābha**, m. great profit, a double return. **-vayasá**, n. the last period of life, ŚBr. xii, 9, 1, 8. **-varṇa**, mfn. having an excellent colour (also being of the best caste), Hit. **-vesha**, m. 'having the most excellent dress,' N. of Śiva. **-śākha**, m., N. of a region, (gaṇa *gahâdi*, Pāṇ. iv, 2, 138.) **-°śākhīya**, mfn. belonging to that region. **-śruta**, mfn. possessing the utmost learning, R.

-śloka (*uttamá°*), m. the most excellent renown, TS. v, 7, 4, 3; (mfn.) possessing the most excellent fame, highly renowned, illustrious, BhP.; *-tīrtha*, m., N. of a teacher. **-saṃgraha**, m. intriguing with another man's wife, addressing her privately, casting amorous looks &c. **-sāhasa**, n. the highest of the three fixed mulcts or fines (a fine of 1000 or of 80,000 paṇas; capital punishment, branding, banishment, confiscation, mutilation, and death). **-sukha**, m., N. of a man. **-strī-saṃgrahaṇa** = *-saṃgraha* above. **Uttamâṅga**, n. the highest or chief part of the body, the head, Mn.; MBh.; Bhag.; Suśr.; Mṛicch. &c. **Uttamâdhama**, mfn. high and low; *-madhyama*, mfn. good, bad, and indifferent; high, low, and middling. **Uttamâmbhas**, n. (in Sāṃkhya phil.) one of the nine kinds of Tushṭi, q. v., Sāṃkhya-kaumudī (quoted by T.) **Uttamâraṇī**, f. the plant Asparagus Racemosus, L. **Uttamârdhá**, m. the last half or part, ŚBr.; Lāṭy.; the best half. **Uttamârdhya**, mfn. relating to or connected with the last part or the best half, Pāṇ. iv, 3, 5. **Uttamâha**, m. the last or latest day, a fine day (?), a lucky day (?), L. **Uttamôttama**, mfn. the best among the best, the very best. **Uttamôttarīya**, m., N. of a grammarian. **Uttamôpapada**, mfn. one to whom the best term is applicable, best, good. **Uttamâujas**, m. 'of excellent valour,' N. of one of the warriors of the Mahā-bhārata. **Uttamâudārya**, mfn. very noble-hearted, R.

Uttamáyya, mfn. (fut. pass. p. of a Nom. *uttamāya*?) to be raised or celebrated, RV. ix, 22, 6.

Uttamīya, mfn. (gaṇa *gahâdi*, Pāṇ. iv, 1, 138) belonging to anything excellent or best or last &c.

1. **U'ttara**, mfn. (compar. fr. 1. *ud*; opposed to *adhara*; declined Gram. 238. *a*), upper, higher, superior (e. g. *uttare dantās*, the upper teeth), RV.; AV.; TS.; ChUp.; Ragh. &c.; northern (because the northern part of India is high), AV.; Mn.; Suśr.; Pañcat. &c.; left (opposed to *dakshiṇa* or right, because in praying the face being turned to the east the north would be on the left hand), AV.; KātyŚr.; MBh. &c.; later, following, subsequent, latter, concluding, posterior, future, RV.; AV.; KātyŚr.; MBh.; Ragh.; Hit. &c. (opposed to *pūrva*, &c., e. g. *uttaraḥ kālaḥ*, future time; *uttaram vākyam*, a following speech, answer, reply; *phalam uttaram*, subsequent result, future consequence; *varshôttareshu*, in future years); followed by (e. g. *smôttara*, mfn. followed by '*sma*,' Pāṇ. iii, 3, 176); superior, chief, excellent, dominant, predominant, more powerful, RV.; AV.; gaining a cause (in law); better, more excellent, RV.; (*as*), m., N. of a son of Virāṭa, MBh.; of a king of the Nāgas, L.; N. of a mountain, Kathās.; of several men; (*ās*), m. pl., N. of a school; (*ā*), f. (scil. *diś*) the northern quarter, the north, Kathās. &c.; N. of each of the Nakshatras that contain the word '*uttara*' (cf. *uttara-phalgunī*, &c.); N. of a daughter of Virāṭa and daughter-in-law of Arjuna, MBh.; of a female servant, Lalit.; (*e*), f. du. the second and third verse of a Tṛica (or a stanza consisting of three verses); (*ās*), f. pl. the second part of the Sāma-saṃhitā; (*am*), n. upper surface or cover, MBh.; Ragh.; Daś. &c.; the north, R.; Dhūrtas.; the following member, the last part of a compound; answer, reply, Ragh.; R.; Prab. &c.; (in law) a defence, rejoinder, a defensive measure; contradiction, Car.; (in the Mīmāṇsā philosophy) the answer (the fourth member of an adhikaraṇa or case); superiority, excellence, competency, R.; Pañcat.; Kathās. &c.; result, the chief or prevalent result or characteristic, what remains or is left, conclusion, remainder, excess, over and above, (often ifc., e. g. *bhayôttara*, attended with danger, having danger as the result; *dharmôttara*, chiefly characterized by virtue; *shashty-uttaram sahasram*, one thousand with an excess of sixty, i. e. 1060; *saptôttaram śatam*, 107); remainder, difference (in arithmetic); N. of a song, Yājñ.; N. of each of the Nakshatras that contain the word '*uttara*;' a particular figure in rhetoric; N. of the last book of the Rāmāyaṇa; (*am*), ind. at the conclusion, at the end, e. g. *bhavad-uttaram*, having the word '*bhavat*' at the end; *asrôttaram īkshitā*, looked at with tears at the close, i. e. with a glance ending in tears; afterwards, thereafter; behind, MBh. &c.; in the following part (of a book); [cf. Gk. ὕστερος.] **-kalpa**, m., N. of a work. **-kāṇḍa**, n. following or concluding book; the seventh book of the Rāmāyaṇa; also the last book of the Adhyātma-rāmāyaṇa. **-kāmâkhya-tantra**, n., N. of a work. **-kāya**, m. the upper part of the body, Ragh. **-kāla**, m. future time; time reckoned from full moon to full moon; (*am*) or (*atas*), ind. afterwards, after; (mfn.) future, MBh. **-kuru**, m. n. one of the nine divisions of the world (the country of the northern Kurus, situated in the north of India, and described as the country of eternal beatitude). **-kośalā**, f. the city Ayodhyā (the modern Oude), L. **-kriyā**, f. the last (sacred) action, funeral rites, obsequies. **-khaṇḍa**, n. last section; the concluding book of the Padma-purāṇa; also of the Śiva-purāṇa and of other works. **-khaṇḍana**, n. cutting off a reply, refutation. **-ga**, mfn. flowing towards the north, R. **-gītā**, f., N. of a section of the sixth book of the Mahābhārata. **-grantha**, m., N. of a supplement of the Yoni-grantha. **-°ṃ-ga** (1. *uttaraṃ-ga*; for 2. see s. v.), n. a wooden arch surmounting a door frame, L. **-cchada**, m. a cover thrown over anything, MBh.; R.; Daś.; Ragh. **-ja**, mfn. born in the latter (or last-mentioned kind of wedlock), Yājñ. i, 59; born subsequently or afterwards. **-jyā**, f. the versed sine of an arc, the second half of the chord halved by the versed sine, L. **-jyotisha**, n., N. of a country, MBh. **-tantra**, n. 'concluding doctrine,' N. of a supplementary section in the medical manual of Suśruta; also of supplementary portions of several other works. **-tara**, mfn. (compar. fr. *uttara*), still further removed, still more distant, still higher, ŚvetUp. **-tás**, ind. at the top, above; from the north, northward, AV.; VS.; MBh.; ChUp. &c.; to the left (opposed to *dakshiṇa-tas*), ŚBr.; AitBr.; PārGṛ. &c. (in some cases it is not to be decided whether 'northward' or 'to the left' is meant); afterwards; behind; *°ḥ-paścāt*, ind. north-westward (with gen., Pāṇ. ii, 3, 30), AitBr.; ŚBr. &c. **-tāpanīya**, n., N. of the second part of the Nṛisiṇha-tāpanīyôpanishad. **-tra**, ind. in what follows, after, subsequently, later, further on, beyond, below (in a work), Pāṇ.; northward, (*pūrvatra*, in the first case or place; *uttaratra*, in the second), Sāh. **-danta**, m. a tooth of the upper mandible, Comm. on TPrāt. **-dāyaka**, mfn. replying, giving an answer, impertinent, Hit. **-dik-stha**, mfn. situated in the north, northern. **-dig-īśa**, m., N. of Kuvera. **-diś**, f. the north quarter. **-deśa**, m. the country towards the north, the up-country. **-drú**, m. an upper beam (?), AV. vi, 49, 2. **-dharma**, m., N. of a teacher (Buddh.) **-dhāraya**, mfn. one who has to give an answer, Naish. **-dhurīṇa**, mfn. yoked on the left pole of a carriage (as a horse), Kāś. on Pāṇ. iv, 4, 78. **-dheya**, mfn. to be done or applied subsequently. **-nābhí**, f. the cavity on the north of the sacrificial fire, ŚBr., Comm. on Śulbas. **-nārāyaṇá**, m. the second part of the Nārāyaṇa- or Purusha-hymn (RV. x, 90), ŚBr. **-paksha**, m. the northern or left wing (side), KātyŚr.; second or following part of an argument, the reply, refutation; the answer to the first or objectionable argument (cf. *pūrva-paksha*); the right argument, demonstrated truth, or conclusion; the minor proposition in a syllogism; *-tā*, f. or *-tva*, n. conclusion, demonstration, reply. **-paṭa**, m. an upper garment, MBh. **-patha**, m. the northern way, the way leading to the north; the northern country, Pāṇ. v, 1, 27, &c. **-°pathika**, mfn. inhabiting the northern country, Prab. **-pada**, n. the last member of a compound word, Pāṇ. &c.; *°dârtha-pradhāna*, mfn. (a compound) in which the sense of the last member is the chief one (said of Tatpurusha compounds), Kāś. on Pāṇ. ii, 1, 22. **-°padika** or **°padakīya**, mfn. relating to or studying the last word or term, Pāṇ. Comm. **-parvata**, m. the northern mountain, R. **-paścârdha**, m. the north-western half. **-paścima**, mfn. north-western, ĀśvGṛ.; (*ā*), f. (scil. *diś*) the north-west. **-pāda**, m. a division of legal practice (that part which relates to the reply or defence, four divisions being admitted in every suit). **-purastāt**, ind. north-eastward (with gen.), ĀśvGṛ. **-purāṇa**, n., N. of a Jaina work. **-pūrva**, mfn north-eastward, KātyŚr.; one who takes the north for the east, Siddh.; (*ā*), f. (scil. *diś*) the north-east. **-pracchada**, m. a coverlid, quilt, L. **-pratyuttara**, n. 'reply and rejoinder,' a dispute, altercation, discussion; the pleadings in a lawsuit. **-proshṭhapadā**, f., **-phalgunī** or **-phālgunī**, f., N. of lunar mansions; (cf. *proshṭhapadā*, *phalgunī*.) **-barhis**, n. the sacrificial grass on the north of the fire. **-bhaktika**, mfn. employed after eating, Car. **-bhadrapadā** or **-bhādrapadā**, f., N. of a lunar mansion; (cf. *bhādrapadā*.) **-bhāga**, m. the second part. **-mati**, m., N. of a man. **-mandrā** (*úttara°*), f. a loud but slow manner of singing, ŚBr.; KātyŚr.; *-°rāyā*, f. a particular Mūrchanā (in music). **-mātra**, n. a mere reply, only a reply. **-mānasa**, n., N. of a Tīrtha. **-mārga**, m. the way leading to the north. **-mīmāṇsā**, f. the Vedānta philosophy (an inquiry into the Jñāna-kāṇḍa or second portion of the Veda; opposed to *pūrva-mīmāṇsā*; see *mīmāṇsā*). **-mūla** (*úttara°*), mfn. having the roots above, ŚBr. i, 2, 4, 16. **-yuga**, n. a particular measure (= 13 Aṅgulas), Śulbas. **-rahita**, mfn. devoid of reply, having no answer. **-rāma-carita** (or *°caritra*), n. 'the further or later deeds of Rāma,' N. of a drama of Bhava-bhūti. **-rūpa**, n. the second of two combined vowels or consonants, Comm. on APrāt. **-lakshaṇa**, n. the indication of an actual reply; (mfn.) marked on the left side, KātyŚr. **-lakshman**, mfn. marked above or on the left side, Kap. **-loman** (*úttara°*), mfn. having the hairs turned upwards or outwards, ŚBr.; KātyŚr.; ĀśvGṛ. **-vayasa**, n. the latter or declining years of life, ŚBr. **-vallī**, f., N. of the second section of the Kāṭhakôpanishad (when divided into two Adhyāyas). **-vasti**, f. a small syringe, a urethra injection pipe, Suśr. **-vastra**, n. an upper garment. **-vādin**, m. a replicant; a defendant; one whose claims are of later date than another's, Yājñ. **-vāsas**, n. an upper garment, R. **-vīthi**, f. (in astron.) the northern orbit, VarBṛS. **-vedí**, f. the northern altar made for the sacred fire, VS.; ŚBr.; AitBr. &c. **-śānti**, f. final consecration, ŚāṅkhGṛ. vi, 2, 7. **-śaila**, m. pl., N. of a Buddhist school. **-saktha**, n. the left thigh, Pāṇ. v, 4, 98. **-saṃjñita**, mfn. designated in the reply (a witness &c.); learnt from report, hearsay evidence. **-sākshin**, m. witness for the defence; a witness testifying from the report of others. **-sādhaka**, mfn. effective of a result, assisting at a ceremony, befriending; an assistant, helper, friend; establishing a reply, Vet. **-hanú**, f. the upper jawbone, AV. ix, 7, 2. **Uttarâṇsa**, m. the left shoulder (the clavicle ?), MBh. **Uttarâgāra**, n. an upper room, garret, Hariv. **Uttarâṅga**, n. the last sound of combined consonants, Comm. on VPrāt. **Uttarâdri**, m. 'northern mountain,' the Himālaya, L. **Uttarâdhará**, mfn. superior and inferior, higher and lower, ŚBr.; (*am*), n. upper and under lip, Kum.; the lips (see *adharôttara*); *-vivara*, n. the mouth, Daś. 73, 11. **Uttarâdhikāra**, m. right to property in succession to another person, heirship; *-tā*, f. or *-tva*, n. right of succession. **Uttarâdhikārin**, mfn. n heir or claimant subsequent to the death of the original owner, an heir who claims as second in succession, L. **Uttarā-patha**, m. the northern road or direction, the northern country, north, Pañcat.; Hit.; Kathās. &c. **Uttarâbhāsa**, m. a false or indirect or prevaricating reply; *-tā*, f. or *-tva*, n. inadequacy of a reply, the semblance without the reality. **Uttarâbhimukha**, mfn. turned towards the north. **Uttarâmnāya**, m., N. of a sacred book of the Śāktas. **Uttarâyaṇa**, n. the progress (of the sun) to the north; the period of the sun's progress to the north of the equator, the summer solstice, Mn.; Bhag.; VarBṛS.; Pañcat. &c. **Uttarâraṇi**, f. the upper *araṇi* (q. v.) which is also called Pramantha or churner, ŚBr. **Uttarârka**, m., N. of one of the twelve forms of the sun, SkandaP. **Uttarârcika**, n., N. of the second part of the Sāmaveda-saṃhitā (also called *uttarāgrantha*). **Uttarârtha**, mfn. (done &c.) for the sake of what follows, Lāṭy.; Kāś. &c. **Uttarârdhá**, n. the upper part (of the body), Ragh.; the northern part, ŚBr.; KātyŚr.; the latter half, Śrut.; the further end; *-pūrvârdha*, n. the eastern part of the northern side (of the fire), ŚBr.; HirGṛ. **Uttarârdhyà** (fr. *uttarârdha*), mfn. being on the northern side, TS.; ŚBr. **Uttarā-vat**, mfn. being above, TBr.; victorious, overpowering, AV.; ŚBr. **Uttarâśā**, f. the northern quarter; *°śâdhipati*, m. 'lord of the north,' N. of Kuvera. **Uttarâśman**, mfn. having high rocks, Rājat.; (*ā*), m., N. of a country, (gaṇa *ṛiśyâdi*, Pāṇ. iv, 2, 80); *°maka*, mfn. belonging to the above country, ib. **Uttarâśramin**, m. (a Brāhman) who enters into the next Āśrama (or period of religious life), Comm. on ŚāṅkhGṛ. i, 1, 2. **Uttarâśrita**, mfn. having gone to or being in the northern direction, Bhpr. **Uttarâshāḍhā**, f., N. of a lunar mansion (cf.

ashāḍhā), L. **Uttarâsaṅga**, m. an upper or outer garment, MBh.; R.; Pañcat. &c. **Uttarā-sád**, mfn. seated northward or on the left, VS. ix, 35 & 36. **Uttarâha**, m. the following day, Kāty. on Pāṇ. iv, 2, 104. **Uttarêtarā**, f. (scil. *diś*) 'other or opposite to the northern,' the southern quarter, L. **Uttarôttara**, mfn. more and more, higher and higher, further and further; always increasing, always following, Yājñ.; Suśr.; Pañcat.; Kap. &c.; each following, Paribh. 38; (*am*), ind. higher and higher, more and more, in constant continuation, one on the other, MBh.; Hit.; Suśr.; Gaut. &c.; (*am*), n. reply to an answer, reply on reply; a rejoinder; conversation, MBh.; Hit.; R. &c.; excess, exceeding quantity or degree; succession, gradation; descending; *-pracchalā*, f., N. of a section of the Sāmaveda-cchalā; *-vaktṛi*, m. one who never fails to answer, MBh. **Uttarottarin**, mfn. one following the other; constantly increasing, AitBr.; Śāṅkh-Br.; RPrāt. &c. **Uttarôshṭha** or **uttarâushṭha**, m. the upper lip, Suśr.; the upper part of a pillar, VarBṛS. 53, 29.

Uttaraya, Nom. P. *uttarayati*, to reply; to defend one's self.

Uttarā, ind. north, northerly; northward (with gen. or abl.), Pāṇ.; Vop.; (*uttarā-patha*, &c., see p. 178, col. 3.)

Uttarắt, ind. from the left; from the north, RV.; AV.; VS. &c. **-sád**, mfn. = *uttarā-sad* above, MaitrS. ii, 6, 3.

Uttarắttāt, ind. from the north, RV.

Uttarắhi, ind. northerly, from the north, ŚBr.; Daś. (with abl., Pāṇ.)

Uttarin, mfn. increasing, becoming more and more intense, Vait.

Uttarīya, *am*, n. an upper or outer garment, KātyŚr.; PārGṛ.; HirGṛ.; MBh.; Pañcat. &c.; a blanket, Car. **-tā**, f. the state of being an upper garment, Gobh. i, 2, 21.

Uttarīyaka, *am*, n. an upper or outer garment, Kathās.; VP. &c.

U'ttareṇa, ind. (with gen., abl., acc., or ifc.) northward; on the left side of, KātyŚr.; ŚBr.; ĀśvGṛ.; MBh.; Megh. &c.

Uttare-dyús, ind. on a subsequent day, on the day following, to-morrow, TS.; Pāṇ.

उत्तमर्ण *uttamarṇa*, &c.. See under **uttama**.

उत्तम्भ् *ut-tambh* (*ud-√stambh*, Pāṇ. viii, 4, 61; the radical *s* appears in augmented and reduplicated forms and if [in Veda] the preposition is separated from the verb), P. *-(s)tabhnāti* (Impv. 2. sg. *-(s)tabhāná*, impf. *úd-astabhnāt*, aor. *-astāmpsīt*, TBr. iii, 2, 10, 1, and *-astambhīt*, RV. iii, 5, 10) to uphold, stay, prop; to support, RV.; VS.; TBr.; TāṇḍyaBr. &c.: Caus. *-tambhayati*, to lift up, raise, erect, Hariv.; BhP. &c.; to bring up; to irritate, excite, Kir. ii, 48; BhP.; Uttarar.; to raise in rank; to honour, make respectable.

U't-tabdha, mfn. upheld; erected, ŚBr.

U't-tabdhi, *is*, f. support, upholding, MaitrS.

U't-tabhita, mfn. upheld, uplifted, supported, RV.; ŚBr.; BhP. &c.

Ut-tambha, *as*, m. support, prop, upholding, L.

Ut-támbhana, *am*, n. a prop, stay, VS.; KātyŚr.

Ut-tambhita, mfn. supported, upheld; raised; excited, Uttarar.

Ut-tambhitavya, mfn. to be supported or upheld &c., Pāṇ. Comm.

उत्तर 1. *úttara*, &c., see p. 178, col. 1; for 2. see *ut-trī*, col. 2.

उत्तरंग 2. *ut-taraṃga* (for 1. see p. 178, col. 2), a high wave, Kathās. 123, 196; (mfn.) rough with high waves, washed over by waves; inundated, flooded, Ragh.; Kum. &c.

3. **Uttaraṃga**, Nom. Ā. *uttaraṃgate*, to surge; to break or burst (like a wave), Kād.

Uttaraṃgaya, Nom. P. *uttaraṃgayati*, to cause to wave or undulate, to move to and fro, Prasannar.

उत्तरल *ut-tarala*, mf(*ā*)n. trembling, shuddering, quivering, Bālar.; Kād.

Uttaralāya, Nom. Ā. *uttaralāyate*, to shudder, quiver, tremble, Kād.

Uttaralita, mfn. caused to tremble, excited, Bālar.

Uttaralī-√1. kṛi, to cause to quiver; to cause to skip, let leap, Sāh.

उत्तर्जन *ut-tarjana*, *am*, n. (*√tarj*), violent threatening, Sāh.

उत्तान *ut-tāná*. See *ut-tan*.

उत्ताप *ut-tāpa*. See *ut-tap*.

उत्तार 1. *ut-tāra* (fr. *tārā* with 1. *ud* in the sense of 'apart'), mfn. (an eye) from which the pupil is taken out, BhP. vi, 14, 46; (for 2. *ut-tāra* &c. see *ut-trī*.)

उत्ताल *ut-tāla*, mfn. great, strong, high, elevated, Śiś.; impetuous, violent, Viddh.; formidable, horrid, Kathās.; Pañcad.; abundant, plentiful, Bālar.; best, excellent, Gīt.; tall, loud, L.; swift, speedy, L.; (*as*), m. an ape, L.; (*am*), n. a particular number (Buddh.)

Uttālī-bhavana, n. impetuous proceeding.

उत्तिङ्ग *uttiṅga*, *as*, m. a species of insect, Kalpas.; Jain.

उत्तिज् *ut-tij* (*ud-√tij*), Caus. P. *-tejayati*, to excite, stimulate, incite, instigate, animate, encourage, Kathās.; Mṛicch. &c.

Ut-tejaka, mfn. instigating, stimulating, L.

Ut-tejana, *am*, *ā*, n. f. incitement, instigation, encouragement, stimulation, exciting, animating, R.; Sāh.; sending, despatching; urging, driving; whetting, sharpening, furbishing, polishing, Śiś.; an inspiring or exciting speech, L.; an incentive, inducement, stimulant, L.

Ut-tejita, mfn. incited, animated, excited, urged; sent, despatched; whetted, sharpened, furbished, polished; (*am*), n. an incentive, inducement; sidling, one of a horse's five paces; moderate velocity in a horse's pace, L.

उत्तीर्ण *ut-tīrṇa*. See col. 3.

उत्तु *ut-tu* (*ud-√tu*), P. *út-tavīti* (RV. x, 59, 1), to effect, bring about; to prosper, increase [Say.]

उत्तुङ्ग *ut-tuṅga*, mfn. lofty, high, tall; swollen (as a stream), MBh.; Pañcat.; Kathās.; Prab. &c. **-tā**, f. or **-tva**, n. height, loftiness, elevation.

उत्तुण्डित *ut-tuṇḍita*, *am*, n. the head of a thorn &c. which has entered the skin [W.]

उत्तुद् *ut-tud* (*ud-√tud*), P. *-tudati*, to push up, tear up; to push open, AV. iii, 25, 1; AitĀr.; to stir up, urge on.

Ut-tudá, mfn. one who stirs up, AV. iii, 25, 1.

उत्तुल् *ut-tul* (*ud-√tul*), P. *-tolayati*, to take up (a sword), Tantras.; to erect, set up, Comm. on Prab.; to raise up (by means of a counterpoise); to weigh; to raise, excite (anger &c.)

Ut-tolana, *am*, n. lifting up, raising, elevating (by means of a counterpoise or balance), L.

Ut-tolita, mfn. raised, lifted up, L.

उत्तुष *ut-tusha*, *as*, m. fried grain (freed from the husks), L.

उत्तृद् *ut-tṛid* (*ud-√tṛid*), P. *-tṛiṇatti*, to split or cut through, TBr.; Kāṭh.: Desid. (p. *-titṛitsat*) to wish to split or cut through, Kāṭh. xiii, 3.

उत्तॄ *ut-tṝ* (*ud-√tṝ*), P. *-tarati* and *-tirati* (Ved.) to pass out of (especially *jalāt*, water, with abl.); to disembark; to come out of, ĀśvGṛ.; MBh.; Hariv.; Śak.; Mṛicch. &c.; to escape from (a misfortune, affliction, &c.), BhP.; Kathās.; to come down, descend, alight, put up at, Vet.; to pass over; to cross (a river, with acc.); to vanquish, MBh.; R.; Ragh.; Hariv.; Kathās. &c.; to give up, leave, MBh.; to elevate, strengthen, increase, RV.; VS.; SV.; Śāṅkh-Śr.: Caus. *-tārayati*, to cause to come out; to deliver, assist, rescue, MBh.; R.; Hariv.; Pañcat. &c.; to make any one alight, take down, take off, Pañcat.; Vet.; to cause to pass over; to convey or transport across, land, disembark, Pañcat.; to vomit up: Desid. *-titīrshati*, to wish to cross, MBh.

2. **U't-tara**, mfn. (for 1. see p. 178, col. 1) crossing over; to be crossed (cf. *dur-uttara*).

Ut-táraṇa, mfn. coming out of, crossing over, VS. &c.; (*am*), n. coming forth or out of (especially out of water), VarBṛS.; landing, disembarking; crossing rivers &c., Pañcat.

Ut-tarikā, f., N. of a river, R.

2. **Ut-tāra** (for 1. see s. v. above), *as*, m. transporting over, Prab.; landing; delivering, rescuing, MBh.; ejecting, getting rid of; vomiting; passing away, instability; (mfn.) surpassing others, excellent, pre-eminent, L.

Ut-tāraka, *as*, m. 'a deliverer,' N. of Śiva.

Ut-tāraṇa, mfn. transporting over, MBh.; bringing over, rescuing; (*am*), n. the act of landing, delivering; rescuing; helping to cross over or escape; transportation, R. &c.

Ut-tārin, mfn. transporting across; unsteady, inconstant, changeable, tremulous; sick, L.

1. **Ut-tārya**, mfn. to be made to land; to be ejected; to be thrown up by vomiting, Mn. xi, 160.

2. **Ut-tārya**, ind. p. having caused to come out &c.

Ut-titīrshu, mfn. about to pass out of (water), wishing to land, MBh.

Ut-tīrṇa, mfn. landed, crossed, traversed; rescued, liberated, escaped; released from obligation; thrown off; one who has completed his studies, experienced, clever. **-vikṛiti**, mfn. one who has escaped any change, NṛisUp.

Ut-tīrya, ind. p. having crossed, having landed &c.

उत्तेरित *utterita*, *am*, n. (said to be fr. *ut-trī*), one of the five paces of a horse, L.

उत्तोरण *ut-toraṇa*, mfn. decorated with raised or upright arches, Ragh.; Kum. &c. **-patāka**, mfn. decorated with raised arches and flags, Kathās. x, 210.

उत्तोलन *ut-tolana*. See *ut-tul*, col. 2.

उत्त्यज् *ut-tyaj* (*ud-√tyaj*).

Ut-tyakta, mfn. thrown upwards; left, abandoned; free from worldly passion, L.

Ut-tyāga, *as*, m. throwing up; abandonment, quitting; secession from worldly attachments, L.

उत्त्रस् *ut-tras* (*ud-√tras*), Caus. P. *-trāsayati*, to frighten, alarm, Hariv.

Ut-trasta, mfn. frightened, Hariv.; Rājat.

Ut-trāsa, *as*, m. fear, terror, L.

Ut-trāsaka, mfn. frightening, alarming, Sāh.

उत्त्रिपद *ut-tripada*, *am*, n. an upright tripod, L.

उत्त्रुट् *ut-truṭ* (*ud-√truṭ*).

Ut-truṭita, mfn. torn, broken, Kād.

उत्था *ut-thā* (*ud-√sthā*, Pāṇ. viii, 4, 61; cf. *ut-tambh*, col. 1), P. Ā. (but not Ā. in the sense of 'rising, standing up,' Pāṇ. i, 3, 24) *-tishṭhati*, *-te* (pf. *-tasthau*, aor. *-asthāt* &c.) to stand up, spring up, rise, raise one's self, set out, RV.; AV.; ŚBr.; Ragh.; Śak.; Bhag. &c.; to rise (from the dead), BhP.; to rise (from any occupation), leave off; to finish, AitBr.; ŚBr.; TāṇḍyaBr. &c.; to come forth, arise, appear, become visible, result; to spring, originate from, RV.; AV.; ŚBr.; TS.; MBh.; Kathās. &c.; to come in (as revenues), Śak.; to rise (for the performance of any action); to be active or brave; to make efforts, take pains with, strive for; to excel, MBh.; R. &c.: Caus. *-thāpayati* (aor. 1. sg. *úd-atishṭhipam*, AV. vii, 95, 2) to cause to stand up, raise, rouse, start, AV.; AitBr.; TBr.; ŚBr.; MBh.; Daś.; BhP. &c.; to set up, lift up, erect, Gobh.; MBh.; R.; Hit. &c.; to get out, Hit.; to drive out, send out, push out, AitBr.; Kathās.; BhP.; to excite; to produce, Ragh.; Sāh.; to arouse, awaken, raise to life, make alive, animate; to stir up, agitate, ŚBr.; KaushUp.; Hariv.; R.; Kathās. &c.: Desid. *-tishṭhāsati*, to wish or intend to stand up, ŚBr. xi, 1, 6, 5; to intend to leave off (a sacrifice), Nyāyam.

Ut-tishṭhāsā, f. the intention to leave off; the wish to leave (a sacrifice &c.) unfinished, Nyāyam.

Ut-tha, mfn. (generally ifc.) standing up, rising, arising, MBh.; Ragh.; Caurap. &c.; coming forth, originating, derived from, Bhag.; Kathās.; Rājat.; Pañcat. &c.; (*as*), m. arising, coming forth, L.; [cf. Zend *usta*.]

Ut-thātavya, mfn. (impers.) to be stood up, Kād.; to be set out, BhP.; to be active, MBh.

Ut-thātṛi, *tā*, m. one who rises, ChUp.; reviving, AV. ix, 4, 14.

Ut-thāna, *am*, n. the act of standing up or rising, ŚBr.; Suśr.; Gaut.; ŚāṅkhGṛ.; Bhartṛ. &c.; rising (of the moon &c.), BhP.; Ragh. &c.; resurrection, MBh.; Pañcat.; rising up to depart; leaving off, ŚBr.; TS.; KātyŚr. &c.; starting on a warlike expedition, Mn.; MBh.; R. &c.; coming forth, appearing, Kap.; bursting open, Jaim.; tumult, sedition, Rājat.; rise, origin, Suśr.; effort, exertion; manly exertion, manhood, MBh.; Rājat.; Āp. &c.; evacuating (by stool &c.), Suśr.; Kauś.; an army, L.; joy, pleasure, L.; a book, L.; a court-yard, L.; a shed where sacrifices are offered, L.; a term, limit, L.; business of a family or realm, the care of subjects or dependants, L.; reflection, L.; proximate cause of disease, L.; (mfn.) causing to arise or originate, MBh. **–yukta,** mfn. and **-vat,** mfn. possessed of effort or energy, ready for action, zealous, diligent, MBh. **–vīra,** m. a man of action, one who makes efforts, MBh. **–śīla** or **-śīlin,** mfn. active, zealous, diligent. **–hīna,** mfn. inactive, lazy, MBh. **Utthānâikādaśī,** f. the eleventh day in the light or former half of the month Kārttikā (when Vishṇu rises from his sleep).

Utthānīya, mfn. belonging to the completion, forming the conclusion, TāṇḍyaBr.; Comm. on Lāṭy.

Ut-thāpaka, mfn. lifting up, causing to get up, who or what raises &c.; exciting, animating; *(as),* m. a waiting-man, Car.; a particular composition, Sāh.

Ut-thāpana, *am,* n. causing to rise or get up; raising, elevating, KātyŚr.; causing to leave (a house &c., with acc. of the person made to leave), Vet.; causing to come forth, bringing forth, Suśr.; exciting, instigating; bringing about; causing to cease, finishing; (in math.) the finding of the quantity sought, answer to the question, substitution of a value, Bījag.; *(ī),* f. (scil. *ṛic*) a concluding verse, Kauś.

Ut-thāpanīya, mfn. to be raised or made to get up; able to raise or arouse, MaitrS.

Ut-thāpayitṛi, *tā,* m. one who raises or erects.

Ut-thāpita, mfn. caused to stand up; raised, lifted up, elevated; made to get up or out; aroused, instigated, &c.

1. **Ut-thāpya,** mfn. to be raised; to be sent away, AitBr. vii, 29, 4; (in math.) to be brought out (as a result) by substitution, Bījag. 45.

2. **Ut-thāpya,** ind. p. having raised or caused to rise, having roused or instigated &c.

Ut-thāya, ind. p. having risen (from a seat &c.), having risen (in rank &c.), standing up &c. **Utthāyôtthāya,** ind. every time one rises (from one's bed), Hit.

Ut-thāyam, ind. p. having risen, Kāś. on Pāṇ. iii, 4, 52.

Ut-thāyin, mfn. rising (from one's bed), MBh.; coming forth, becoming visible, MBh.; exerting one's self, active, Kām. **Utthāyi-tva,** n. exertion, energy, activity, Kām.

Ut-thita, mfn. risen or rising (from a seat &c.), MBh.; Hariv.; BhP.; Kathās. &c.; risen (from a sickness), Hariv.; elevated, high, VarBṛS.; Ragh. &c.; come forth, arisen; born, produced, originated, RV.; Mn.; MBh.; BhP. &c.; come in (as revenue), Hit.; endeavouring, striving, exerting one's self, active, MBh.; R.; Kām. &c.; happened, occurring; advancing, increasing; extended; high, lofty, eminent (said of a Pragātha consisting of ten Pādas), RPrāt.; *(am),* n. *(út-thitam)* rising, arising, AV. iii, 15, 4. **–tā,** f. state of activity or readiness to serve, MBh. **Utthitâṅguli,** m. the palm of the hand with the fingers extended, L.

Ut-thiti, *is,* f. elevation, rising up, L.

उत्पक्ष *ut-paksha, as,* m., N. of a son of Sva-phalka, Hariv.; BhP.; (v. l. *upeksha,* q. v.)

उत्पक्ष्मन् *ut-pakshman,* mfn. with upturned eyelashes, Śak. 95 a; Kathās.

Ut-pakshmala, mfn. id., Vikr. 32.

उत्पच् *ut-pac (ud-√pac),* Caus. P. *-pācayati,* to boil thoroughly, heat.

Utpaca-nipacā, f. any act in which it is said '*utpaca! nipaca!*' (i.e. 'cook thoroughly and well!'), gaṇa *mayūravyaṇsakâdi,* Pāṇ. ii, 1, 72.

Ut-pacishṇu, mfn. easily ripening, apt to ripen or become cooked, Pāṇ. iii, 2, 136.

Ut-pācita, mfn. boiled or heated thoroughly, Suśr. ii, 67, 2.

उत्पट् *ut-paṭ (ud-√paṭ),* Caus. *-pāṭayati,* to tear up or out, pluck, pull out, break out, ŚāṅkhŚr.; Gaut.; Susr.; Mn.; Pañcat. &c.; to draw out (a sword from its scabbard), Prasannar.; to open (the eyes &c.), Daś.; Kathās. &c.; to root up, eradicate, extirpate, R.; Rājat. &c.; to drive away, banish; to dethrone, R.; Rājat. &c.: Pass. of the Caus. *-pāṭyate,* to be cleft; to part asunder, split, Suśr.

U't-paṭa, *as,* m. sap issuing from the cleft of a tree, ŚBr. xiv, 6, 9, 31.

Ut-pāṭa, *as,* m. pulling up by the roots, destroying, L.; a disease of the external ear, Suśr. ii, 149, 10 & 17 [BRD.; see *ut-pāta*]. **–yoga,** m. a particular Yoga (in astrology).

Ut-pāṭaka, *as,* m. the above disease, Suśr.; *(ut-pāṭikā),* f. the external bark of a tree, ŚBr. xiv, 6, 9, 30.

Ut-pāṭana, mfn. tearing out; destroying, banishing, L.; *(am),* n. the act of tearing out or up; pulling up by roots, eradicating; driving away, banishing; dethronement, Suśr.; R.; Kathās. &c.

Ut-pāṭita, mfn. pulled up by the roots, eradicated, torn out; driven away; banished, dethroned.

Ut-pāṭin, mfn. ifc. tearing out, pulling up, Kathās.

Ut-pāṭya, ind. p. having plucked up &c.

उत्पत् *ut-pat (ud-√pat),* P. *-patati* (p. *-pátat,* RV. ii, 43, 3; AV. xix, 65, 1; aor. *-apaptat,* RV. i, 191, 9; p. fut. *-patishyát,* AV. xviii, 4, 14) to fly or jump up, fly upwards; to ascend, rise, RV.; AV.; AitBr.; TBr.; Hariv.; Megh.; Ragh.; Kathās. &c.; to rise (from one's bed), MBh.; to shoot up, ChUp.; to start from, leave, run away, AitBr.; MBh.; to jump out, hasten out, come out, Hariv.; R.; Hit. &c.; to rise, be produced, originate, MBh.; BhP.: Caus. P. *-pātayati,* to cause to fly up or to rise, RV.; AV.: Desid. (impf. *-apipatishat,* ŚBr. x, 2, 1, 1) to wish or intend to fly up.

Ut-pata, *as,* m. 'flying upwards,' a bird, L.

Ut-patana, mf(*ī*)n. flying upwards, (*utpatanī vidyā,* a spell by means of which one is able to fly upwards or to rise, Kathās. lxxxvi, 158); *(am),* n. flying or jumping up, rising, ascending, going up, R.; Pañcat.; Kathās.; birth, production, L.

Utpata-nipatā, f. any act in which it is said '*utpata! nipata!*' (i. e. 'fly up and down!'), gaṇa *mayūravyaṇsakâdi,* Pāṇ. ii, 1, 72.

Ut-patita, mfn. springing up, risen, ascended.

Ut-patitavya, mfn. (impers.) to be flown upwards, Pañcat.

Ut-patitṛi, mfn. jumping up, rising, going upwards, L.

Ut-patishṇu, mfn. jumping up or rising constantly; being about to jump up or to rise, Ragh.; Bhaṭṭ.; Pañcat.

Ut-pāta, *as,* m. flying up, jumping up; a spring, jump, MBh.; R.; Car.; rising, arising, Hit.; a sudden event, unexpected appearance; an unusual or startling event boding calamity; a portent, prodigy, phenomenon; any public calamity (as an earthquake, meteor &c.), AV. xix, 9, 7; MBh.; GopBr.; Gaut.; Ragh.; Suśr.; Pañcat. &c.; a disease of the external ear (erroneously for *ut-pāṭa* above, BRD.)

Ut-pātaka, mfn. causing misfortune or calamity, T.; flying upwards, T.; *(as),* m. a kind of animal (= *ut-pāda,* W.?), MBh. xviii, 44; *(am),* n., N. of a Tīrtha.

Ut-pātika, mfn. (Prākṛit *uppāiya*) supernatural, Jain.

Ut-pitsu, mfn. (fr. Desid.), desirous of rising or ascending, Śiś.; being about to come forth or to arise.

उत्पताक *ut-patāka,* mfn. with raised flags; with uplifted banners, Ragh.; Rājat.; *(ā),* f. a raised banner or flag, Kathās. **Ut-patākā-dhvaja,** mfn. with raised banner and flags, Kathās.

उत्पथ *ut-patha, as,* m. wrong road, bad way, Kāś.; error, evil, R.; MBh.; Pañcat.; Prab.; (mfn.) one who is come off from the right way, lost, stray, BhP. **–vārika,** mfn. keeping back or preserving from the bad way, NṛisUp.

उत्पद् *ut-pad (ud-√pad),* Ā. *-padyate,* to arise, rise, originate, be born or produced; to come forth, become visible, appear; to be ready, ŚBr.; MBh.; R.; Mn.; Yājñ.; Kathās.; BhP.; Prab. &c.; to take place, begin, Kāś. on Pāṇ. iii, 3, 111: Caus. P. *-pādayati* (rarely Ā. *-te*), to produce, beget, generate; to cause, effect; to cause to issue or come forth, bring forward, Hariv.; MBh.; Yājñ.; Mn.; Kathās.; Hit. &c.; to mention, quote (see *ut-panna*).

Ut-pattavya, mfn. (impers.) to be produced or born, Kād.

Ut-patti, *is,* f. arising, birth, production, origin, Suśr.; MBh.; Yājñ. &c.; resurrection, Mn.; production in general, profit, productiveness, Rājat.; producing as an effect or result, giving rise to, generating as a consequence; occurrence, the being mentioned or quoted (as a Vedic passage), Jaim. **–kāla,** m. time of birth or origin; °*lâvacchinnatva,* n. exact limitation of the time of origin (e. g. of a jar), Nyāyak. **–kālīna,** mfn. taking place at the time of birth. **–ketana,** n. birth-place, Kathās. **–krama,** m. the successive stages of creation (e. g. in TUp., 'from Brahman arose ether, from ether wind, from wind fire, from fire water, from water earth, from earth plants, from plants food, from food seed, from seed man'). **–dhāman,** n. birth-place, Kathās. **–prakaraṇa,** n., N. of a work. **–prayoga,** m. production by the joint operation of cause and effect; purport, meaning, W. **–mat,** mfn. produced, born, Ragh. viii, 82. **–vākya,** n. a sentence quoted from the Veda, an authoritative sentence, Nyāyam.; Comm. on Nyāyam. & Jaim. **–vidhi,** m. id. **–vyañjaka,** m. a type of birth (as investiture, a mark of the twice-born), Mn. **–śishṭa,** mfn. taught by a passage occurring in the Veda, taught authoritatively, Comm. on MBh.

Ut-panna, mfn. risen, gone up; arisen, born, produced, R.; Mn.; Kathās. &c.; come forth, appeared; ready, Yājñ.; mentioned, quoted (esp. fr. the Veda), Jaim. **–tantu,** mfn. having a line of descendants. **–tva,** n. origin, production. **–bala,** mfn. one in whom strength or power is produced, strong, powerful, L. **–buddhi,** mfn. one in whom wisdom is produced, wise, VP. **–bhakshin,** mfn. 'eating what has just been produced,' living from hand to mouth. **–vināśin** and **utpannâpavargin,** mfn. perishing as soon as produced.

1. **Ut-pāda** (for 2. see s.v.), *as,* m. coming forth, birth, production, Yājñ.; Prab. &c. **–pūrva,** n., N. of the first of the fourteen Pūrvas (or older sacred writings of the Jainas).

1. **Utpādaka** (for 2. see p. 181, col. 1), mfn. bringing forth, producing; productive, effective, Mn.; Hit.; Kathās.; *(as),* m. a producer, generator, Mn.; *(ikā),* f. a species of insect (perhaps the white ant?), L.; Enhydra Hingtsha, Hariv.; Basilla Rubra, L.; *(am),* n. origin, cause, L.

Ut-pādana, mfn. bringing forth, producing, productive, MBh.; Kathās.; *(am),* n. the act of producing or causing, generating, begetting, ChUp.; MBh.; Suśr.; Hit. &c.

Ut-pādayitavya, mfn. to be produced, Comm. on Jaim.

Ut-pādayitṛi, *tā,* m. a producer, generator, Pat.

Ut-pādita, mfn. produced, effected; generated, begotten.

Utpādin, mfn. produced, born, Hit.; (ifc.) bringing forth, producing, Yājñ.

1. **Ut-pādya,** mfn. to be produced or brought forth, Nyāyam.; produced, brought forth, invented (by a poet), BhP.; Sāh.; Sarvad. &c. **Utpādyôtpādaka-tā,** f. the relation between that which is to be produced and that which produces, Pratāpar.

2. **Ut-pādya,** ind. p. having produced, having begotten &c.

Ut-pādyamāna, mfn. being produced or generated.

उत्पल 1. *ut-pala, am,* n. (& *as,* m., L.), (*√pal,* 'to move,' T; fr. *pal = √paṭ,* 'to burst open,' BRD.), the blossom of the blue lotus (Nymphæa Cærulea), MBh.; R.; Suśr.; Ragh.; Megh. &c.; a seed of the Nymphæa, Suśr.; the plant Costus Speciosus, Bhpr.; VarBṛS.; any water-lily; any flower, L.; a particular hell (Buddh.); *(as),* m., N. of a Nāga; of an astronomer; of a lexicographer; of several other men; *(ā),* f., N. of a river, Hariv. 9511; *(ī),* f. a kind of cake made of unwinnowed corn, L. **–gandhika,** n. a species of sandal (of the colour of brass and very fragrant), L. **–gopā,** f. Ichnocarpus Frutescens, Nigh. **–cakshus,** mfn. 'lotus-eyed,' fine-eyed. **–pattra,** n. the leaf of a Nymphæa, L.; a wound on the breast &c. of a woman (caused by the finger-nail of her lover), L.; a Tilaka (or mark on the forehead, made with sandal &c. by the Hindūs), L.; a broad-bladed knife or lancet, L. **–pattraka,** m. a broad-bladed knife or lancet used by surgeons, Suśr. **–pura,** n., N. of a town built by Utpala, Rājat. **-bhedyaka,** m. a kind of bandage, Suśr. **-mālā,** f. a wreath of lotus-flowers; N. of a dictionary compiled by Utpala; *-bhārin* (*utpala-mālā°*, Pāṇ. vi, 3, 65), wearing a wreath of lotus-flowers, Kāś. on Pāṇ. vi, 3, 65. **-rāja,** m., N. of a poet. **-vana,** n. a group of lotuses, Kathās. **-varṇā,** f., N. of a woman. **-śāka,** n., N. of a plant, Rājat. **-śrigarbha,** m., N. of a Bodhisattva. **-shaṭka,** n., N. of a medicament, Comm. on Suśr. **-sārivā,** f. the plant Ichnocarpus Frutescens, Suśr. **Utpalâksha,** mf(*ī*)n. 'lotus-eyed;' (*as*), m., N. of a king, Rājat.; (*ī*), f., N. of a goddess, MatsyaP. **Utpalâcārya,** m., N. of an author. **Utpalâpīḍa,** m., N. of a king, Rājat. **Utpalâbha,** mfn. lotus-like, resembling a lotus. **Utpalā-vatī,** f., N. of a river, MBh.; of an Apsaras. **Utpalā-vana,** n., N. of an abode of the Pañcālas, MBh. **Utpalâvartaka,** m.(?), N. of a place, MatsyaP.

Utpalaka, *as*, m., N. of a Nāga, L.; of a man, Rājat.

Utpalin, mfn. abounding in lotus-flowers, R.; (*inī*), f. an assemblage of lotus-flowers; a lotus (Nymphæa), MBh.; a particular metre; N. of a river, MBh.; of a dictionary.

उत्पल 2. *ut-pala* (fr. *pala*, 'flesh,' with 1. *ud* in the sense of 'apart'), fleshless, emaciated, L.; (*am*), n., N. of a hell, L.

उत्पवन *ut-pávana*, &c. See *ut-pū*, col. 2.

उत्पश् *ut-paś* (*ud-√paś*), P. *-paśyati* (p. *-pâśyat*: Pass. *ud-dṛiśyate*) to see or descry overhead, RV. i, 50, 10; AitBr. ii, 31; to descry before or in the future; to foresee, expect, Ragh.; Megh.; Bhaṭṭ.; to behold, perceive, descry, Megh.; Śiś.

Ut-paśya, mfn. looking up or upwards, L.

उत्पा 1. *ut-pā* (*ud-√1. pā*), P. (3. pl. *-pibanti*) to drink out, sip out; to drink up, devour, ŚBr. v, 2, 4, 7 & 11.

Ut-piba, mfn. drinking out, Vop.

उत्पा 2. *ut-pā* (*ud-√5. pā*), Ā. *-pípīte* (p. *-pipāna*) to rise against, rebel; to show enmity, AV. v, 20, 7; xiii, 1, 31; TS. iii, 2, 10, 2; (cf. *anût-√5. pā*.)

उत्पाद 2. *ut-pāda* (for 1. see p. 180, col. 3), mfn. having the legs stretched out, standing on the legs. **-śayāna,** m. 'sleeping while standing on the legs,' a species of fowl, L.

2. **Utpādaka** (for 1. see p. 180, col. 3), *as*, m. the fabulous animal called Śarabha, L.; (cf. *ūrdhva-pāda*.)

उत्पार *ut-pāra*, mfn. endless, boundless. **-pāram,** ind. to the bottom of the boundless (ocean), BhP. iii, 13, 30.

उत्पारण *ut-pāraṇa*. See *ut-pṛi*, col. 2.

उत्पाली *ut-pālī*, f. (fr. the Caus. of √2. *pā*, T.?), health, L.

उत्पाव *ut-pāva*. See *ut-pū*, col. 2.

उत्पिञ्ज *ut-piñja*, *as*, m.(?) sedition, revolt, Rājat.

Ut-piñjara, mfn. uncaged, set free, L.; out of order, extremely confused; let loose, unfolded, expanded.

Utpiñjarī-bhūta, mfn. let loose, unfolded, Comm. on Śiś. iv, 6.

Ut-piñjala, mfn. let loose, unfolded, unrolled, Śiś. iv, 6.

Ut-piñjalaka, mfn. disordered, tumultuous (as a battle), MBh.; Hariv.

उत्पिण्ड *ut-piṇḍa*, *am*, n.(?) any morsel eaten with the food, L.

Ut-piṇḍita, mfn. swollen up, swelled, Car.

उत्पित्सु *ut-pitsu*. See p. 180, col. 2.

उत्पिब *ut-piba*. See 1. *ut-pā* above

उत्पिष् *ut-pish* (*ud-√pish*).

Ut-pishṭa, mfn. crushed, bruised, MBh.; Ratnāv.; (*am*), n. (in surgery) a kind of dislocation, Suśr.

उत्पीड् *ut-pīḍ* (*ud-√pīḍ*), P. *-pīḍayati*, to press upwards or against, squeeze, Kum.; to press out of, Suśr.

Ut-pīḍa, *as*, m. pressing against, squeezing, pressure, Prab.; Kād.; bursting out (as a stream or tears), R.; Hariv.; Megh.; Uttarar.; Kād.; a wound, MBh. iii, 825.

Ut-pīḍana, *am*, n. the act of pressing against or out, VarBṛS.; Ṛitus.; rooting out, Car.

Ut-pīḍita, mfn. pressed upwards or against, squeezed, Ragh.

Ut-pīḍya, ind. p. having pressed against, having squeezed, MBh.

उत्पीन *ut-pīna*. See *ut-pyai* below.

उत्पुंसय *utpuṇsaya*, Nom. (etym. doubtful; erroneously for *utpāṇsaya*, NBD.?) P. *utpuṇsayati*, to slip away, Kathās. lxxii, 323.

उत्पुच्छ *ut-puccha* (*ud-pu°*), mfn. above the tail (?); one who has raised the tail (as a bird), Pāṇ. vi, 2, 196.

Utpucchaya, Nom. P. Ā. *utpucchayati*, *-te*, to raise or cock the tail, Kāś. on Pāṇ. vi, 2, 196.

उत्पुञ्जय *ut-puñjaya*, Nom. (fr. *puñja*) P. *utpuñjayati*, to lay up, heap, Comm. on KātyŚr.; Kād.

उत्पुट *ut-puṭa*, mfn. one whose fold is open [T.]?, gaṇa *saṃkalâdi*, Pāṇ. iv, 2, 75, and *utsaṅgâdi* [not in the Kāś.], Pāṇ. iv, 4, 15.

Ut-puṭaka, m. a disease of the external ear, Suśr.

उत्पुलक *ut-pulaka*, mfn. having the hairs of the body raised (through joy or rapture), BhP.; Rājat.; (*am*), n. erection of the hairs of the body (through rapture), BhP.

उत्पू *ut-pū* (*ud-√pū*), P. Ā. *-punāti*, *-punīte*, to cleanse, purify, AV. xii, 1, 30; VS. i, 12; TBr.; ŚBr.; KātyŚr.; Gobh. &c.; to extract (anything that has been) purified, TBr. iii, 7, 12, 6.

Ut-pávana, *am*, n. cleaning, cleansing, Kauś.; Comm. on Nyāyam.; straining liquids for domestic or religious uses; any implement for cleaning, ŚBr. i, 3, 1, 22; the act of sprinkling clarified butter or other fluids on the sacrificial fire (with two blades of Kuśa grass, the ends of which are held in either hand and the centre dipped into the liquid), L.

Ut-pavitṛī, mfn. purifying; a purifier, ŚBr. i, 1, 3, 6.

Ut-pāva, *as*, m. purifying ghee &c., Pāṇ. iii, 3, 49.

Ut-pūta, mfn. cleaned, cleansed, ĀśvŚr.; AitBr. &c.

उत्पृ *ut-pṛi* (*ud-√1. pṛi*), Caus. *-pārayati* (aor. 1. sg. *-apīparam*, AV.) to transport over, conduct out of (the ocean), RV. i, 182, 6; to save, AV. viii, 1, 17; 18; 19, & viii, 2, 9.

Ut-pāraṇa, *am*, n. transporting over, AV. v, 30, 12.

उत्पॄ *ut-pṝi* (*ud-√pṝi*), Caus. (pf. Pot. 2. sg. *út-pupūryās*, RV. v, 6, 9) to fill up.

उत्पोषध *ut-poshadha*, *as*, m., N. of an ancient king (Buddh.)

उत्प्यै *ut-pyai* (*ud-√pyai*).

Ut-pīna, mfn. swollen, Kathās. lxiii, 185.

उत्प्रभ *ut-prabha*, mfn. flashing forth or diffusing light, shining, L.; (*as*), m. a bright fire, L.

उत्प्रवाल *ut pravāla*, mfn. having sprouting branches or trees (as a forest), Kāvyād.

उत्प्रवेष्टृ *ut-praveshṭṛi* (*√viś*), mfn. one who enters or penetrates. **-tva,** n. the state or condition of penetrating, NṛisUp.

उत्प्रसव *ut-prasava* (*√4. su*), *as*, m. abortion, W.

उत्प्रास *ut-prâsa* (*√2. as*), *as*, m. hurling, throwing afar, L.; violent burst of laughter; derision, jocular expression, Sāh.

Ut-prâsana, *am*, n. derision, jocular expression, Sāh.

उत्प्रु *ut-pru* (*ud-√pru* connected with *√plu*), Ā. (aor. 2. sg. *-proshṭhās*, ĀśvŚr. iii) to spring, leap.

उत्प्रुष् *ut-prúsh*, *t*, f. (*√prush*), that which bubbles up, a bubble, VS. p. 58, l. 18; Kauś. 6.

उत्प्रेक्ष् *ut-prêksh* (*ud-pra-√īksh*), Ā. *-prêkshate*, to look up to (with attention, as a pupil to his teacher who occupies an elevated seat), R.; to observe, regard; to look out or at, Kād.; to expect, Bālar.; to reflect on the past, Amar.; to use (a word) figuratively; to transfer (with loc.), Sāh.; Kāvyād.; to take anything for another, compare one thing with another, illustrate by a simile; to fancy, imagine, Kād.; Veṇis.; to ascribe, impute.

Ut-prêkshaka, mfn. observing, considering, BhP.

Ut-prêkshaṇa, *am*, n. looking into; observing, L.; foreseeing, anticipating, L.; comparing, illustrating by a simile, Sāh.

Ut-prêkshaṇīya, mfn. to be expressed by a simile, Sāh.

Ut-prêkshā, f. the act of overlooking or disregarding; carelessness, indifference, Veṇis.; observing, L.; (in rhetoric) comparison in general, simile, illustration, metaphor; a parable; an ironical comparison, Sāh.; Vām.; Kpr. **Utprêkshâvayava,** m. a kind of simile, Vām. **Utprêkshā-vallabha,** m., N. of a poet.

Ut-prêkshita, mfn. compared (as in a simile). **Utprêkshitôpamā,** f. a kind of Upamā or simile, Kāvyād.

1. **Ut-prêkshya,** mfn. to be expressed by a simile, Sāh.

2. **Ut-prêkshya,** ind. p. having looked up &c.

उत्प्लु *ut-plu* (*ud-√plu*), Ā. *-plavate* (rarely P. *-ti*), to swim upwards, emerge, Suśr.; ShaḍvBr.; Kād.; to draw near, approach (as clouds), Kāṭh.; to spring up, jump up or upwards, jump out, leap up, Mn.; Hariv.; Hit.; Pañcat. &c.; to jump over; to bound, Comm. on Mn.; to spring upon; to rise, arise, R.; Kathās.

Ut-plava, *as*, m. a jump, leap, bound, L.; (*ā*), f. a boat, L.

Ut-plavana, *am*, n. jumping or leaping up, springing upon, BhP.; skimming off (impure oil or ghee, or any dirt floating on a fluid by passing two blades of Kuśa grass over it, Kull.), Mn. v, 115.

Ut-pluta, mfn. jumped up or upon or over, sprung upon suddenly.

Ut-plutya, ind. p. having sprung up or jumped upon &c.

उत्फण *ut-phaṇa*, mfn. having an expanded hood (as a snake).

उत्फल् *ut-phal* (*ud-√phal*), P. *-phalati*, to spring open, burst, expand; to jump out, Bālar.: Caus. *-phālayati*, to open, open wide (the eyes), MBh.

Ut-phāla, *as*, m. a spring, jump, leap; gallop, Kathās.

Ut-phulla, mfn. (Kāty. on Pāṇ. viii, 2, 55) blown (as a flower), Kir.; Kathās.; Śiś.; wide open (as the eyes), R.; Pañcat.; Hit. &c.; swollen, increased in bulk, bloated, puffed up, Kathās.; Bālar.; Śārṅg.; sleeping supinely, L.; looking at with insolence, insolent, impudent, Pat.; (*am*), n. a kind of coitus, L.

उत्फल *ut-phala*. See *prôt-phala*.

उत्फुलिङ्ग *ut-phuliṅga* (for *ut-sphuliṅga*), mfn. emitting sparks, sparkling.

उत्स *útsa*, *as*, m. (*√ud*, Uṇ. iii. 68), a spring, fountain (metaphorically applied to the clouds), RV.; AV.; VS.; TBr.; Suśr.; Daś. **-dhí,** m. the receptacle of a spring, a well, RV. i, 88, 4. **Utsâdi,** m., N. of a gaṇa, Pāṇ. iv, 1, 86.

Utsyà, mfn. coming from a well or fountain (as water), AV. xix, 2, 1.

उत्सक्थ *út-saktha*, mf(*ī*)n. lifting up the thighs (as a female at coition), VS. xxiii, 21.

उत्सङ्ग *ut-saṅga* (*√sañj*), *as*, m. the haunch or part above the hip, lap, MBh.; R.; Suśr.; Pañcat. &c.; any horizontal area or level (as a roof of a house &c.), Ragh.; Megh.; Bhartṛ. &c.; the bottom or deep part of an ulcer, Suśr.; embrace, association, union, L.; a particular position of the hands, PSarv.; Hastar.; (*am*), n. a high number (= 100 Vivāhas), Lalit. **-vat,** mfn. having depth, deep-seated, Suśr. **Utsaṅgâdi,** m., N. of a gaṇa, Pāṇ. iv, 4, 15.

Utsaṅgaka, *as*, m. a particular position of the hands, Nastar.

Utsaṅgita, mfn. associated, combined, joined, made coherent, Śiś. iii, 79.

Utsaṅgin, mfn. having depth, deep-seated (as an ulcer), Suśr.; R.; Car.; associating or combining with, coherent, Mall. on Śiś. iii, 79; an associate, partner, L.; (*ī*), m. an ulcer, deep sore, L.; (*inī*), f. pimples on the inner edge of the eyelid, Suśr.

Ut-sañjana, *am*, n. raising up, lifting up, Pāṇ. i, 3, 36.

उत्सद् ut-sad (*ud-√sad*), P. Ā. *-sīdati, -te* (Ved. 3. pl. *út-sadan*) to sit upwards; to raise one's self or rise up to (acc.), [Gmn.], RV. viii, 63, 2; to withdraw, leave off, disappear; to sink, settle down, fall into ruin or decay, be abolished, TS.; ŚBr.; MBh.; Bhag.; BhP. &c.: Caus. *-sādayati*, to put away, remove, ŚBr.; ĀśvŚr.; AitBr. &c.; to abolish, destroy, annihilate, MBh.; Hariv.; R.; Mn.; Kathās. &c.; to anoint, rub, chafe, Yājñ.; MBh.

Ut-satti, *is*, f. vanishing, fading, absence, Pat.

Ut-sanna, mfn. raised, elevated (opposed to *ava-sanna*), Suśr.; vanished, abolished, decayed, destroyed; in ruins; disused, fallen into disuse, ŚBr.; TBr.; ŚāṅkhŚr.; Hariv.; BhP. &c. **–yajñá,** m. an interrupted or suspended sacrifice, ŚBr.

Ut-sādá, *as*, m. ceasing, vanishing; ruin, MBh. i, 4364; one who disturbs or destroys, VS. xxx, 20; a particular part of a sacrificial animal, VS.

Ut-sādaka, mfn. destroying, overturning, gaṇa *yājakâdi*, Pāṇ. ii, 2, 9 (in the Kāś.)

Ut-sādana, *am*, n. putting away or aside; suspending, interrupting, omitting, ŚBr.; KātyŚr.; ĀśvŚr.; destroying, overturning, MBh.; R.; Bhag.; rubbing, chafing, anointing, Mn.; Suśr.; ŚāṅkhGṛ.; causing a sore to fill up, healing it, Suśr.; a means of healing a sore, Car.; going up, ascending, rising, L.; raising, elevating, L.; ploughing a field twice or thoroughly, L.

Utsādanīya, mfn. to be destroyed &c., L.; (*am*), n. any application, applied to a sore producing granulations, Suśr.

Ut-sādayitavya, mfn. to be destroyed &c.

Ut-sādita, mfn. destroyed, overturned, MBh. &c.; rubbed, anointed, Yājñ.; raised, elevated, L.

Utsādin, mfn. See *agny-utsādin*.

Ut-sādya, mfn. = *ut-sādayitavya* above.

उत्सर ut-sara, &c. See *ut-sṛi*, col. 2.

उत्सर्ग ut-sargá, &c. See col. 3.

उत्सर्ज् ut-sarj (*ud-√sarj*), P. *-sarjati*, to rattle, creak, TS.; ŚBr.

उत्सर्जन ut-sarjana. See col. 3.

उत्सर्प ut-sarpa, &c. See *ut-sṛip*, col. 3.

उत्सव ut-savá, &c. See *ut-sū*, col. 2.

उत्सह् ut-sah (*ud-√sah*), Ā. *-sahate* (inf. *-sáham*, TBr. i, 1, 6, 1) to endure, bear, TBr.; AitBr. iii, 44, 5; ŚBr. i, 3, 3, 13; to be able, be adequate, have power (with inf. or dat. of abstr. noun); to act with courage or energy, MBh.; R.; Śak.; Pañcat. &c.: Caus. *-sāhayati*, to animate, encourage, excite, MBh.; Kathās.: Desid. of the Caus. (p. *-sisāhayishat*) to wish to excite or encourage, Bhaṭṭ. ix, 69.

Ut-saha. See *dur-utsaha*.

Ut-sāha, *as*, m. power, strength; strength of will, resolution; effort, perseverance, strenuous and continuous exertion, energy; firmness, fortitude, R.; Mn.; Suśr.; Śak.; Hit. &c.; joy, happiness, Vet.; a thread, L. **–yoga,** m. bestowing energy, exercising one's strength, Mn. ix, 298. **–vat** (gaṇa *balâdi*, Pāṇ. v, 2, 136), mfn. active, energetic, persevering, Pañcat. **–vardhana,** mfn. increasing energy, L.; (*as*), m. (scil. *rasa*) the sentiment of heroism, L.; (*am*), n. increase of energy, heroism, L. **–śakti,** f. strength of will, energy, Pañcat. **–śaurya-dhana-sāhasa-vat,** mfn. having boldness and wealth and heroism and energy, VarBṛ. xiii, 7. **–sampanna,** mfn. endowed with energy.

Utsāhaka, mfn. active, persevering, gaṇa *yājakâdi*, Pāṇ. ii, 2, 9; (the Kāś. reads *utsādaka*.)

Ut-sāhana, *am*, n. causing energy or strength, T.

Utsāhin, mfn. powerful, mighty, Pañcat.; firm, steady; active, energetic, Sāh.

उत्सि ut-si (*ud-√si*), P. *-sinâti*, to fetter, chain, RV. i, 125, 2.

Ut-sita, mfn. fettered, entangled, AV. vi, 112, 2; 3.

उत्सिच् ut-sic (*ud-√sic*), P. Ā. *-siñcati, -te*, to pour upon, make full; to cause to flow over, RV. vii, 16, 11; x, 105, 10; VS. xx, 28; ŚBr.; ŚāṅkhŚr.; KātyŚr.; Kauś.; to make proud or arrogant (see the Pass.): Pass. *-sicyate*, to become full, flow over, foam over, BhP.; to be puffed up, become haughty or proud, Ragh. xvii, 43.

Ut-sikta, mfn. overflowing, foaming over; puffed up, superabundant, Car.; BhP.; Rājat.; drawn too tight (as a bow), Hariv. 1876; elevated, raised; haughty, proud; wanton; rude; crack-brained, disordered, disturbed in mind, MBh.; BhP.; Mn.; Kathās. &c.

Ut-seka, *as*, m. foaming upwards, spouting out or over, showering; overflow; increase, enlargement, superabundance, MBh.; R.; Suśr.; Megh.; haughtiness, pride, MBh.; R.; Pañcat. &c.

Utsekin, mfn. See *an-utsekin*.

Ut-sekya, mfn. to be filled up or made full, Viddh.

Ut-secana, *am*, n. the act of foaming or spouting upwards, boiling or foaming over, L.

उत्सिध् ut-sidh (*ud-√2. sidh*), P. *-sedhati*, to drive off or aside, TāṇḍyaBr.; to drive or push upwards.

Ut-sedhá, *as*, m. height, elevation, altitude, ŚBr.; Car.; thickness, bigness, MBh.; Suśr.; Kum.; Śiś. &c.; excelling; sublimity, R.; the body, R. vii, 116, 19 [Comm.]; Kāś. on Pāṇ. v, 2, 21; (*am*), n. killing, slaughter, L.; N. of several Sāmans. **–vistāratas,** ind. by altitude and latitude, Car.

उत्सिव् ut-siv (*ud-√siv*).

Ut-syūtá, mfn. sewed up; sewed to, TS.; Lāṭy.; ŚāṅkhŚr. &c.

उत्सुक utsuka, mfn. (fr. *su*, 'well,' with 1. *ud* in the sense of 'apart,' and affix *ka*), restless, uneasy, unquiet, anxious, R.; MBh. &c.; anxiously desirous, zealously active, striving or making exertions for any object (cf. *jayôtsuka*), R.; Pañcat.; Śak.; Megh. &c.; eager for, fond of, attached to; regretting, repining, missing, sorrowing for, Ragh.; Vikr.; Śak. &c.; (*am*), n. sorrow; longing for, desire (see *nir-utsuka*). **–tā,** f. and **-tva,** n. restlessness, uneasiness, unquietness, Pañcat.; zeal, desire, longing for, Śiś.; Vikr.; attachment, affection; sorrow, regret, L.

Utsukāya, Nom. Ā. *utsukāyate*, to become unquiet; to long for &c., (gaṇa *bhṛiśâdi*, Pāṇ. iii, 1, 12), Bhaṭṭ.

उत्सू ut-sū (*ud-√2. sū*), P. *-suvati*, to cause to go upwards, Kāṭh. xix, 5; (*-sunoti*), to stir up, agitate, BhP. iii, 20, 35.

Ut-savá, *as*, m. enterprise, beginning, RV. i, 100, 8; 102, 1; a festival, jubilee; joy, gladness, merriment, MBh.; Ragh.; Kathās.; Amar. &c.; opening, blossoming, BhP.; height, elevation; insolence, L.; passion, wrath, L.; wish, rising of a wish, L. **–pratāna,** m., N. of a work. **–vidhi,** m. id. **–saṃketa,** *ās*, m. pl., N. of a people, MBh.; VP.; Ragh.

उत्सूत्र ut-sūtra, mfn. (fr. *sūtra* with 1. *ud* in the sense of 'apart'), unstrung; out of rule, deviating from or disregarding rules (of policy and grammar), Śiś. ii, 112; anything not contained in a rule, Pat.; loose, detached, L.

उत्सूर ut-sūra, *as*, m. (scil. *kāla*) the time when the sun sets, the evening, L.

Ut-sūrya. See *ôtsūryám*.

उत्सृ ut-sṛi (*ud-√sṛi*), P. *-sarati*, to hasten away, escape, AV. iii, 9, 5; MBh.: Caus. *-sārayati*, to expel, turn out, drive away, put or throw away, leave off, MBh.; Hariv.; Kathās.; BhP.; to send away, Rājat.; to cause to come out, MBh.; to challenge, MBh.

Ut-sara, *as*, m. a species of the Ati-śakvarī metre (consisting of four verses of fifteen syllables each); N. of the month Vaiśākha, L.

Ut-saraṇa, *am*, n. going or creeping upwards, L.

Ut-saryā, f. a cow when grown up and fit to take the bull, L.

Ut-sāraka, *as*, m. one who drives away (the crowd from a person of rank), a door-keeper, porter, L.

Ut-sāraṇ , *am*, n. the act of causing to move, driving away (the crowd), R.; (*ā*), f. id., Mudrār.

Ut-sāraṇīya and **ut-sārya,** mfn. to be driven away or removed, MBh.

Ut-sārita, mfn. caused to move, driven away &c.

Ut-sṛita, mfn. high, Hariv. 3926 (v.l. *uc-chrita*).

उत्सृज् ut-sṛij (*ud-√sṛij*), P. Ā. *-sṛijati, -te*, to let loose, let off or go; to set free; to open, RV.; AitBr.; ĀśvGṛ. & Śr.; KātyŚr.; MBh.; Śak. &c.; to pour out, emit, send forth, ĀśvGṛ.; MBh. &c.; to sling, throw, cast forth or away; to lay aside, MBh.; R.; Mṛicch. &c.; to quit, leave, abandon, avoid, eschew, Mn.; Yājñ.; MBh. &c.; to discontinue, suspend, cease, leave off, TS.; TBr.; TāṇḍyaBr.; KātyŚr. &c.; to send away, dismiss, discharge, AitBr.; ŚāṅkhŚr.; MBh.; to drive out or away, ŚBr.; to hand out, deliver, grant, give, AV. xii, 3, 46; BhP.; R.; Mālatīm.; to bring forth, produce, create, AV. vi, 36, 2; R.: Desid. *-sisṛikshati*, to intend to let loose, PārGṛ.; to intend to leave, BhP.

Ut-sargá, *as*, m. pouring out, pouring forth, emission, dejection, excretion, voiding by stool &c., R.; Mn.; Megh.; Suśr. &c.; Excretion (personified as a son of Mitra and Revatī), BhP. vi, 18, 5; laying aside, throwing or casting away, Gaut.; Kum.; loosening, setting free, delivering (N. of the verses VS. xiii, 47–51), ŚBr.; KātyŚr.; PārGṛ; MBh. &c.; abandoning, resigning, quitting, retiring from, leaving off; suspending; end, close, KātyŚr.; ĀśvŚr. & Gṛ.; MBh.; Mn. &c.; handing over, delivering; granting, gift, donation, MBh.; oblation, libation; presentation (of anything promised to a god or Brāhman with suitable ceremonies); a particular ceremony on suspending repetition of the Veda, Mn. iv, 97; 119; Yājñ. &c.; causation, causing, Jaim. iii, 7, 19; (in Gr.) any general rule or precept (opposed to *apa-vāda*, q. v.), Kum.; Kāś.; Siddh. &c. **–tas,** ind. generally (i. e. without any special limitation). **–nirṇaya,** m., **-paddhati,** f., **-mayūkha,** m., N. of works. **–samiti,** f. carefulness in the act of excretion (so that no living creature be hurt, Jain.), Sarvad.

Utsargin, mfn. leaving out or off, KātyŚr.; omitting, abandoning, quitting.

Ut-sarjana, mfn. expelling (the feces, said of one of the muscles of the anus), Bhpr.; (*am*), n. letting loose, abandoning, leaving, KātyŚr.; suspending (a Vedic lecture), Lāṭy.; ĀśvGṛ.; Kauś.; (with *chandasām*) a ceremony connected with it, Mn. iv, 96; gift, donation, oblation, L. **–prayoga,** m., N. of a work.

Ut-sárjam, ind. p. letting loose, setting free, ŚBr. v, 2, 3, 7.

Ut-sisṛikshu, mfn. (fr. Desid.), being about or intending to leave off or give up, BhP.

Ut-sṛijya, ind. p. having let loose, having abandoned &c.

Ut-sṛishṭa, mfn. let loose, set free; poured forth, cast into; left, abandoned; given, presented &c. **–paśu,** m. a bull set at liberty (on particular occasions, as on a marriage &c., and allowed to go about at will). **–vat,** mfn. one who has let fall, who has shed (a tear &c.) **Utsṛishṭâgni,** mfn. one who has given up fire-worship, Gaut. xv, 16.

Ut-sṛishṭi, *is*, f. abandonment, letting go, emission, TS. **–kârika,** m. a drama in a single act, Sāh. 519.

Ut-srashṭavya, mfn. to be excreted, Tattvas.; to be dismissed, Kād.

Utsrashṭu-kāma, mfn. wishing to let go or put down.

उत्सृप् ut-sṛip (*ud-√sṛip*). P. *-sarpati*, to creep out or upwards; to rise up, glide or soar upwards, AV. vi, 134, 2; ŚBr.; KātyŚr.; BhP.; Ragh. &c.; to glide along, move on slowly, TBr.; ĀśvŚr.; KātyŚr.; Gobh. &c.: Desid. *-sisṛipsati* (p. *-sisṛipsat*) to wish to get up, RV. viii, 14, 14; BhP.

Ut-sarpa, *as*, m. going or gliding upwards, L.; swelling, heaving, L.; (*am*), n., N. of a Sāman.

Ut-sarpaṇa, *am*, n. gliding upwards, rising, sun-rise, Nir.; going out, Comm. on ĀśvŚr.; stepping out or forwards, BhP.; swelling, heaving, L.

Utsarpin, mfn. moving or gliding upwards, jumping up, Ragh. xvi, 62; coming forth, appearing, Kād.; soaring upwards, mounting upwards, Śak. 283, 8; causing to increase or rise, VP.; (*iṇī*), f. 'the ascending cycle' (divided into six stages beginning with bad-bad time and rising upwards in the reverse order to *ava-sarpiṇī*, q. v.), Āryabh.; Jain.

उत्सेक ut-seka. See col. 2.

उत्सेध ut-sedhá. See *ut-sidh*.

उत्स्तन ut-stana, mf(*ī*)n. having prominent breasts, VarBṛS.

उत्स्थल *ut-sthala*, *am*, n., N. of an island, Kathās.

उत्स्ना *ut-snā* (*ud-√snā*), P. *-snāti* and *-snāyati*, to step out from the water, emerge, come out, ŚBr.; TBr.

Ut-snāta, mfn. one who has emerged from the water, Kāś. on Pāṇ. viii, 4, 61; Nir.

Ut-snāna, *am*, n. stepping out or emerging from the water.

Ut-snā́ya, ind. p. having emerged, stepping out from the water, RV. ii, 15, 5.

उत्स्नेहन *ut-snehana*, *am*, n. (*√snih*), sliding, slipping away; deviating.

उत्स्पृश् *ut-spriś* (*ud-√spriś*), P. (impf. 3. pl. *-aspriśan*) to reach upwards, AV. v, 19, 1.

उत्स्मि *ut-smi* (*ud-√smi*), P. *-smayati*, to begin smiling, smile at; to deride, MBh.; BhP.

Ut-smaya, *as*, m. a smile, L.; (mfn.) open, blooming (as a flower), BhP.; wide open, ib.

Ut-smayitvā, (irr.) ind. p. having smiled at, deriding, R. i, 1, 65.

Ut-smita, *am*, n. a smile, BhP.

उत्स्य *utsyà*. See *útsa*.

उत्स्रोतस् *ut-srotas*, mfn. having the flow of life or current of nutriment upward (opposed to *arvāk-srotas*, q. v.; cf. also *ūrdhva-srotas*), BhP.

उत्स्वन *ut-svana*, *as*, m. a loud sound, BhP.

उत्स्वप्न *ut-svapna*, mfn. 'out of sleep,' talking in one's sleep, starting out of sleep, T.

Utsvapnāya, Nom. Ā. *utsvapnāyate*, to talk in one's sleep, start out of sleep, Mālav.; Mṛicch.

Utsvapnāyita, *am*, n. the act of starting out of sleep, dreaming uneasily, Sāh. 219.

उद् 1. *ud*, a particle and prefix to verbs and nouns. (As implying superiority in place, rank, station, or power) up, upwards; upon, on; over, above. (As implying separation and disjunction) out, out of, from, off, away from, apart. (According to native authorities *ud* may also imply publicity, pride, indisposition, weakness, helplessness, binding, loosing, existence, acquisition.)

Ud is not used as a separable adverb or preposition; in those rare cases, in which it appears in the Veda uncompounded with a verb, the latter has to be supplied from the context (e. g. *úd útsam śatá-dhāram*, AV. iii, 24, 4, out (pour) a fountain of a hundred streams).

Ud is sometimes repeated in the Veda to fill out the verse, Pāṇ. viii, 1, 6 (*kim na ud ud u harshase dātavā u*, Kāś. on Pāṇ.)

[Cf. Zend *uz*; Hib. *uas* and in composition *os*, *ois*, e. g. *os-car*, 'a leap, bound,' &c. See also *ut-tamá*, 1. *úttara*, &c.]

उद् 2. *ud* or *und*, cl. 7. P. *unátti* (RV. v, 85, 4): cl. 6. P. *undati* (p. *undát*, RV. ii, 3, 2; Impv. 3. pl. *undantu*, AV. vi, 68, 1; 2), Ā. *undáte* (AV. v, 19, 4; *undām cakāra*, *undishyati* &c., Dhātup. xxix, 20) to flow or issue out, spring (as water); to wet, bathe, RV.; AV.; ŚBr.; Kāty-Śr.; ĀśvGṛ.; PārGṛ. &c.: Caus. (aor. *aundidat*, Vop. xviii, 1): Desid. *undidishati*, Kāś. on Pāṇ. vi, 1, 3; [cf. Gk. ὕδωρ; Lat. *unda*; Goth. *vat-o*; Old High Germ. *waz-ar*; Mod. Eng. *wat-er*; Lith. *wand-ū*.]

Utta, mfn. moistened, wet, L.; (cf. *unna*, col. 3.)

Uda, *am*, n. (only at the beginning or end of a compound) water. **-kamaṇḍalú**, m. a water-jar, ŚBr. **-kīrṇa** or **-kīrya**, m. the tree Galedupa Piscidia (the bark of which is ground and scattered on water to stupefy fishes), Bhpr. **-kīryā**, f. a species of the Karañja tree [NBD.], Car. **-kumbhá**, m. a water-jar, a jar with water, ŚBr.; Kāty-Śr.; Mn. &c. **-koshṭha**, m. a water-jar, Car. **-grābhá**, m. holding or surrounding water, RV. ix, 97, 15. **-ghosha**, m. the roaring of water, Lāṭy. iii, 5, 14. **-camasá**, m. a cup holding water, ŚBr.; KātyŚr. **-ja** (for 1. *udaja*; for 2. see *ud-√aj*), mfn. produced in or by water, aquatic, watery; (*am*), n. a lotus, BhP. x, 14, 33. **-jña**, v. l. for *udanya*, q. v. **-tantu**, m. 'water-thread,' a continuous gush. **-taulika**, m. a particular measure. **-dhāna**, mfn. holding water, Kauś.; (*am*), n. a reservoir for water, Āp.; Gobh. **-dhārā**, f. a flow or current of water. **-dhí**, mfn. holding water, AV. i, 3, 6; VS.; (*is*), m. 'water-receptacle,' a cloud; river, sea; the ocean, RV.; AV.; VS.; TS.; R.; Śak.; Mn. &c. (in classical Sanskṛit only the ocean); *-kumāra*, *ās*, m. pl. a class of deities (belonging to the Bhavanâdhīśas, Jain.), L.; *-krā*, m. (*√kram*), a navigator, mariner, Vop.; *-jala-maya*, mfn. made or formed out of sea-water, Kād.; *-mala*, m. cuttle-fish bone, L.; *-mekhalā*, f. 'ocean-girdled,' the earth, BhP.; *-rāja*, m. the ocean-king, ocean-god, R.; *-vastrā*, f. 'ocean-clothed,' the earth, L.; *-sambhava*, n. 'ocean-born,' sea-salt, L.; *-sutā*, f. 'daughter of the ocean,' N. of Lakshmī; of Dvārakā (Kṛishṇa's capital), W.; *-sutā-nāyaka*, m. 'husband of the ocean's daughter,' N. of Kṛishṇa, Prasannar. **-nemi**, mfn. rimmed by the ocean, Comm. on Nyāyad. **-pa**, mfn. helping out of the water (as a boat), Comm. on Uṇ. ii, 58. **-pātrá**, n. a water-jar, a vessel with water, TS.; ŚBr.; KātyŚr.; MBh.; BhP.; (*ī*), f. id. **-pāna**, m. n. a well, ChUp.; MBh.; Mn.; Bhag. &c.; *-maṇḍūka*, m. 'frog in a well,' a narrow-minded man who knows only his own neighbourhood, Pāṇ. **-pīti**, f. a place for drinking water, Kād. **-purá**, n. a reservoir for water, TS. iv, 4, 5, 1. **-pū́**, mfn. cleansing one's self with water, purified by water, AV. xviii, 3, 37. **-pesham** (ind. p. of *√pish*), ind. by grinding in water, Pāṇ. vi, 3, 58; PārGṛ. **-prút**, mfn. causing water to flow [Sāy.], swimming or splashing in water [BRD.], RV.; AV. **-plava**, m. water-flood, BhP. **-plutá**, mfn. swimming in water, AV. x, 4, 3 & 4. **-bindu**, m. a drop of water, Kum. **-bhāra**, m. 'water-carrier,' a cloud, Pāṇ. vi, 3, 60. **-mantha**, m. a particular mixture, Suśr.; ŚāṅkhGṛ. **-maya**, mfn. consisting of water, BhP.; (*as*), m., N. of a man, AitBr. **-māna**, m. a particular measure (the 50th part of an Āḍhaka), T. **-meghá**, m. a watery cloud; a shower of rain, RV. i, 116, 3; N. of a man, Kāś. on Pāṇ. vi, 3, 57. **-mehin**, mfn. having watery urine or diabetes, Car. **-lāvaṇika**, mfn. prepared with brine, L. **-vajra**, m. a thunder-like crash of water, a water-spout, Śiś. viii, 39; Pāṇ. vi, 3, 60. **-vāsa**, m. residence in water, Pāṇ. vi, 3, 58; MBh.; Kum.; (*am*), n. a house on the margin of a stream or pond, a marine grotto &c., W. **-°vāsin**, mfn. living in water, Kād. **-vāhá**, m. bringing water, RV. i, 38, 9; v, 58, 3 (said of the Maruts); AV. xviii, 2, 22. **-vāhana**, mfn. bringing water, Pāṇ. vi, 3, 58; (*am*) n. a cloud, W. **-vindu**, see *-bindu*. **-vīvadha**, m. a yoke used in carrying water, Pāṇ. vi, 3, 60. **-vraja** (*udá°*), m., N. of a place [Sāy.], RV. vi, 47, 21. **-śarāva**, m. a jar filled with water, ChUp. **-śuddha**, m., N. of a man. **-śocā**, f., N. of a witch, Vīrac. **-śvit**, n. a mixture (consisting of equal parts of water and buttermilk), MaitrS. ii, 1, 6; Suśr.; *-vat*, mfn. having the above mixture, Kāś. **-saktu**, m. barley-water, Pāṇ. vi, 3, 60. **-stoká**, m. a drop of water, ŚBr. **-sthāna**, n., N. of a place. **-sthālī**, f. a caldron, a kettle with water, ŚBr. **-háraṇa**, n. a vessel for drawing water, ŚBr.; KātyŚr. **-hārá**, mf(*ī*)n. fetching or carrying water, AV. x, 8, 14; VS.; Kauś.; intending to bring water, Daś.; (*as*), m. 'water-carrier,' a cloud, W. **Udâśaya**, m. n. a lake, tank. **Udâudana**, m. rice boiled with water, ŚBr.; Pāṇ. vi, 3, 60.

Udaká, *am*, n. water, RV.; AV.; KātyŚr.; ŚBr.; MBh. &c.; the ceremony of offering water to a dead person, Gaut.; (*udakam √dā* or *pra-√dā* or *√1. kṛi*, to offer water to the dead [with gen. or dat.], Yājñ.; Mn.; R. &c.; cf. *upa-√spriś*); ablution (as a ceremony, see *udakârtha*); a particular metre, RPrāt. **-karman**, n. presentation of water (to dead ancestors as far as the fourteenth degree), PārGṛ. **-kārya**, n. id., R.; ablution of the body, MBh. **-kumbha**, m. a water-jar, Comm. on Uṇ. **-kriyā**, f. = *-karman* above, Gaut. xiv, 40; Mn.; Yājñ. &c. **-krīḍana**, n. sporting about in water, MBh. **-kshveḍikā**, f. sprinkling water (on each other), a kind of amorous play, Vātsy. **-gāha**, mfn. diving into water, Pāṇ. vi, 3, 60. **-giri**, m. a mountain abounding in water, Kāś. on Pāṇ. vi, 3, 57. **-ghāta**, m. 'beating the water' (at bathing?), one of the 64 Kalās or arts, Vātsy. **-candra**, m. (?) a kind of magic (Buddh.), L. **-tarpaṇa**, n. 'satisfying by water,' a libation of water, Gaut.; Sāmav-Br. **-da**, mfn. a giver of water, yielding water, offering water to the dead, L.; (*as*), m. an heir, a kinsman, L. **-dātṛi**, mfn.; (*tā*), m. id., ib. **-dāna**, n. gift of water (especially to the manes), Gaut.; Prab.; a particular festival, Kathās. **Udakadānika**, mfn. relating to the above rite, MBh. **-dāyin**, mfn. = *-da*, Mn. **-dhara**, m. 'water-holder,' a cloud, Comm. on Uṇ. **-dhārā**, f. a gush or flow of water. **-parīkshā**, f. 'water-trial,' a kind of ordeal, Comm. on Yājñ. **-parvata**, m. = *-giri*, col. 2, Kāś. on Pāṇ. vi, 3, 59. **-pūrva**, mfn. preceded by pouring out water (into the extended palm of a recipient's right hand as preparatory to or confirmatory of a gift or promise), Āp. ii, 9, 8; preceded by ablution, ĀśvGṛ. **-°pūrvakam**, ind. preceded by the above ceremony. **-pratikâśa**, mfn. water-like, watery fluid, W. **-bindu**, m. a drop of water, Pāṇ. vi, 3, 60. **-bhāra**, m. a water-carrier, ib. **-bhūma**, v. l. for *udag-bhūma*, q. v. **-mañjarī**, f., N. of a work on medicine; *-rasa*, m. a particular decoction used as a febrifuge, Bhpr. **-mantha**, m. a mixture of water and meal stirred together, Pāṇ. vi, 3, 60. **-maya**, mfn. consisting of water, Kād. **-meha**, m. 'watery urine,' a sort of diabetes. **-°mehin**, mfn. suffering from the above, Suśr. **-vajra**, m. = *uda-vajra*, q. v., Pāṇ. **-vat** (*udaká°*), mfn. supplied or filled with water, ŚBr. **-vādya**, n. 'water-music' (performed by striking cups filled with water), one of the 64 Kalās or fine arts, Vātsy.; (cf *jala-taraṅgiṇī*.) **-vindu**, see *-bindu*. **-vīvadha**, m. = *uda-vī°*, q. v., Pāṇ. vi, 3, 60. **-śāka**, n. any aquatic herb, W. **-śānti**, f. sprinkling consecrated water (over a sick person) to allay fever; *-prayoga*, m., N. of a work. **-śīla**, mfn. practising the Udaka-ceremony, MBh. **-śuddha**, mfn. cleansed by ablution; (*as*), m., N. of a man (?), gaṇa *anuśatikâdi*, Pāṇ. vii, 3, 20. **-saktu**, m. = *uda-sa°*, q. v., Pāṇ. vi, 3, 60. **-sādhu**, mfn. helping out of the water, Gobh. iii, 2, 28. **-sparśa**, mfn. touching different parts of the body with water; touching water in confirmation of a promise, Kāś. **-sparśana**, n. the act of touching water, ablution, Āp. **-hāra**, m. a water-carrier, Pāṇ. vi, 3, 60. **Udakâñjali**, m. a handful of water, VP. **Udákâtman**, mfn. having water for its chief substance, AV. viii, 7, 9. **Udakâdhāra**, m. a reservoir, cistern, well. **Udakânta**, m. margin of water, bank, shore, ĀśvŚr.; PārGṛ.; Śak.; (*am*), ind. to the water's edge, MBh. **Udakârṇava**, m. 'water-reservoir,' the ocean, R. **Udakârtha**, m. a ceremony with water, PārGṛ.; (*am*), ind. for the sake of water or of the Udaka ceremony, MBh. **Udakârthin**, mfn. desirous of water, thirsty. **Udakâhāra**, mfn. one who carries or fetches water. **Udake-cará**, mfn. moving in or inhabiting water, ĀśvŚr.; ŚBr. **Udake-viśīrṇa**, mfn. dried in water (i. e. uselessly), Pāṇ. ii, 1, 47. **Udake-śaya**, mfn. lying in or inhabiting water, R. **Udakôdañjana**, n. a water-jar. **Udakôdara**, n. 'water-belly,' dropsy. **Udakodarin**, mfn. dropsical, Suśr. **Udakôpasparśana**, n. touching or sipping water; ablution, Gaut.; Āp. **Udakôpasparśin**, mfn. one who touches or sips water, Gaut. **Udakâudana**, n. rice boiled with water, Pāṇ. vi, 3, 60.

Udakala, mfn. containing water, watery, Pāṇ.

Udakila, mfn. id., ib.

Udakīya, Nom. P. *udakīyati*, to wish for water, Kāś. on Pāṇ. vii, 4, 34.

Udakya, mfn. being in water, Kauś.; Pāṇ.; wanting water (for purification); (*ā*), f. a woman in her courses, KātyŚr.; Lāṭy.; Mn.; Yājñ. &c. **Udakyâgamana**, n. connection with a woman during her courses, Gaut. xxiii, 34.

Udadhīya Nom. (fr. *uda-dhi*) P. *udadhīyati*, to mistake (anything) for the ocean, VarYogay.

1. **Udán** (for 2. see s. v.), n. Ved. (defective in the strong cases, Pāṇ. vi, 1, 63) a wave, water, RV.; AV.; TS.; Kāṭh. **-vát**, mfn. wavy, watery, abounding in water, RV. v, 83, 7; vii, 50, 4; AV. xviii, 2, 48; xix, 9, 1; (*ān*), m. the ocean, Ragh.; Kum.; Bhartṛ. &c.; N. of a Ṛishi, Kāś. on Pāṇ. viii, 2, 13.

Udani-mát, mfn. abounding in waves or water, RV. v, 42, 14.

1. **Udanya**, Nom. P. *udanyati* (p. *udanyát*) to irrigate, RV. x, 99, 8; to be exceedingly thirsty, Pāṇ. vii, 4, 34.

2. **Udanyà**, mfn. watery, RV. ii, 7, 3; (*ā*), f. want or desire of water, thirst, ChUp.; Rājat.; Bhaṭṭ. **-já**, mfn. born or living in water, RV. x, 106, 6.

Udanyú, mfn. liking or seeking water, RV. v, 57, 1; pouring out water, irrigating, RV. v, 54, 3; ix, 86, 27.

Undana, *am*, n. wetting, moistening, PārGṛ.

Unna, mfn. wetted, wet, moistened, moist, Kāty-Śr. &c.; kind, humane, L.

उदक् *udak*, &c. See below.

उदग्र *ud-agra*, mfn. having the top elevated or upwards, over-topping, towering or pointing upwards, projecting; high, tall, long, R.; Kathās.; Ragh. &c.; increased, large, vast, fierce, intense, Ragh.; Vikr.; Śak. &c.; haughty, Prasannar.; advanced (in age), Suśr.; excited, enraptured, R.; Ragh. &c.; loud, R. **–dat**, mfn. having projecting teeth, large-toothed; (*an*), m. an elephant with a large tusk. **–pluta-tva**, n. lofty bounding, Śak. 7 d.

उदङ्गुलीक *ud-aṅgulīka*, mfn. having the fingers upraised, Viddh.

उदज् *ud-√aj*, P. Ā. *-ajati*, *-te* (impf. *-ājat*, RV. ii, 12, 3, &c., and *úd-ājat*, RV. ii, 24, 3) to drive out, expel, RV.; BṛĀrUp.; to fetch out of, RV. i, 95, 7.

2. **Ud-aja**, m. (for 1. see under *uda*) driving out or forth (cattle), Pāṇ. iii, 3, 69.

Ud-āja, m. leading out (soldiers to war), marching out, MaitrS. i, 10, 16.

उदजलक *udajalaka*, *as*, m., N. of a wheelwright, Pañcat.

उदजिन *ud-ajina*, mfn. one who has passed beyond (the use of) a skin (as his covering), gaṇa *nirudakâdi*, Pāṇ. vi, 2, 181.

उदञ्च् 1. *ud-√añc*, P. *-acati* [Ved.] and *-añcati*, to elevate, raise up, lift up, throw up, RV. v, 83, 8; VS.; ŚBr. &c.; to ladle out, AV.; Comm. on Pāṇ.; to cause, effect, Prasannar.; to rise, arise, Bālar.; Sāh.; to resound, Rājat.: Pass. *-acyate*, to be thrown out; to come forth, proceed, BṛĀrUp. v, 1: Caus. *-añcayati*, to draw up, raise, elevate, Daś.; Bālar.; to send forth, utter, cause to resound (see *ud-añcita*).

1. **U'dak** (in comp. for *údac* below; for 2. see col. 2). **–kūla**, mfn. directed towards the north (as grass with the tops), Gobh. iv, 5, 16. **–tás**, ind. from above, from the north, AV. viii, 3, 19. **–tāt** (*údak°*), ind. from above, from the north, RV. **–patha**, m. the northern country, Rājat. **–pāda**, mf(*ī*)n. having one's feet turned towards the north, Kauś. **–pravaṇa** (*údak°*), mfn. sloping towards the north, ŚBr.; KātyŚr.; ChUp. &c. **–prasravaṇa**, mfn. flowing off towards the north, Kauś.; (*am*), n. an outlet or drain towards the north; *°ânvita*, mfn. having an outlet towards the north, MBh. **–saṃstha**, mfn. ending in the north, ĀśvGṛ. **–samāsa**, mfn. being united or tied in the north, Lāṭy. ii, 6, 4. **–sena**, m., N. of a king, VP.

Ud-akta, mfn. raised or lifted up, drawn up, Siddh.; Vop. &c.

Udag (in comp. for *údac* below). **–agra**, mfn. having the points turned to the north (as grass), KātyŚr.; Lāṭy.; HirGṛ. &c. **–adri**, m. 'the northern mountain,' N. of the Himālaya, L. **–apavargam**, ind. ending to the north, Āp. **–ayaná**, n. the sun's progress north of the equator; the half year from the winter to the summer solstice, ŚBr.; Kauś.; ĀśvGṛ. &c.; (mfn.) being on the path of the sun at its progress north of the equator, BhP. **–āyata**, mfn. extending towards the north, ĀśvGṛ. **–āvṛitti**, f. (the sun's) turning to the north, Ragh. **–gati**, f. = *-ayaná* above. **–dakshiṇa**, mfn. northern and southern, L. **–daśa** (*údag°*), mfn. having the border turned upwards or to the north, ŚBr.; ĀśvGṛ. **–dvāra**, mfn. having the entrance towards the north, ŚāṅkhGṛ.; (*am*), ind. north of the entrance, MBh. **–bhava**, mfn. being in the northern quarter, north, L. **–bhūma**, m. fertile soil (turned upwards or towards the north), Kāś. on Pāṇ. v, 4, 75.

Udaṅ (in comp. for *údac* below). **–īsha** (*udaṅ-ṅīsha*), mfn. having the pole turned to the north (as a carriage), Comm. on KātyŚr. vii, 9, 25. **–mukha**, mf(*ī*)n. turned upwards, Bālar.; facing the north, KātyŚr.; ChUp.; Mn.; Suśr. &c. **–mṛittika**, m. = *udag-bhūma*, q. v., L.

Ud-aṅká, *as*, m. a bucket or vessel (for oil &c. but not for water), Pāṇ. iii, 3, 123; (*ás*), m., N. of a man, ŚBr.; (*ās*), m. pl. the descendants of Udaṅka, gaṇa *upakâdi*, Pāṇ. ii, 4, 69; (*ī*), f. a bucket, MānŚr. i, 1, 2.

Udaṅkya, *as*, m., N. of a demon, Kauś.

U'd-ac or 2. **úd-añc** (*ud-2. añc*), mf(*īcī*)n. turned or going upwards, upper, upwards (opposed to *adharâñc*), RV. ii, 15, 6; x, 86, 22; ChUp. &c.; turned to the north, northern (opposed to *dakshiṇa*), AV.; VS.; ŚBr.; Megh.; Ragh. &c.; subsequent, posterior, L.; (*udīcī*), f. (scil. *diś*) the northern quarter, the north; (2. *údak*; for 1. see col. 1), ind. above; northward, RV.; VS.; ŚBr.; KātyŚr.; Mn. &c.; subsequently, L.

Ud-añcana, *am*, n. a bucket, pail (for drawing water out of a well), RV. v, 44, 13; AitBr.; KātyŚr. &c.; a cover or lid, L.; directing or throwing upwards; rising, ascending, W.

Ud-añcita, mfn. raised up, lifted, elevated; thrown up, tossed, Hpar.; uttered, caused to resound, Gīt.; worshipped, W.

Ud-añcu, *us*, m., N. of a man, gaṇa *bāhv-ādi*, Pāṇ. iv, 1, 96.

Ud-ácam, ind. p. lifting up, raising, ŚBr. iii, 3, 2, 14, &c.

Udīcīna, mfn. turned towards the north, northern, AV.; AitBr.; ŚBr. **–pravaṇa**, mfn. sloping towards the north, ŚBr.

Udīcya, mfn. being or living in the north, Pāṇ. iv, 2, 101; AV.; ŚBr.; KātyŚr.; (*as*), m. the country to the north and west of the river Sarasvatī, the northern region, MBh.; (*ās*), m. pl. the inhabitants of that country, MBh.; R.; Ragh.; VarBṛS. &c.; N. of a school, VāyuP.; a kind of perfume, Suśr.; Bhpr. **–vṛitti**, f. the custom of the Northerners, Āp. ii, 17, 17; a species of the Vaitālīya metre.

उदञ्ज् *ud-√añj*, P. *-anakti*, to adorn, trim, RV. iv, 6, 3.

उदञ्जलि *ud-añjali*, mfn. hollowing the palms and then raising them, Daś.

उदञ्जि *úd-añji*, mfn. erect and unctuous (said of the membrum virile), TS. vii, 4, 19, 1.

उदण्डपाल *ud-aṇḍa-pāla*, mfn. a species of fish, L.; of snake, L.

उदधि *uda-dhí*, &c. See *uda*.

उदन् 2. *ud-√an* (for 1. see p. 183, col. 3), P. *-aniti* (& *āniti*, BṛĀrUp. iii, 4, 1; cf. *vy-√an*; p. *-anát*, ŚBr.; aor. 3. pl. *-ānishus*, AV. iii, 13, 4) to breathe upwards, emit the breath in an upward direction; to breathe out, breathe, AV.; ŚBr.; BṛĀrUp.

Ud-āna, *as*, m. breathing upwards; one of the five vital airs of the human body (that which is in the throat and rises upwards), Vedāntas. 97; AV. xi, 8, 4; VS.; ChUp.; ŚBr.; MBh.; Suśr. &c.; the navel, L.; an eyelash, L.; a kind of snake, L.; joy, heart's joy (Buddh.)

Udānaya, Nom. P. *udānayati*, to disclose (the joy of one's heart), Lalit.

उदन्त *úd-anta*, mfn. reaching to the end or border, running over, flowing over, ŚBr.; KātyŚr.; TBr.; good, virtuous, excellent, L.; (*am*), ind. to the end or border, AitBr.; (*as*), m. (*ud-antá*) end of the work, rest; harvest time, TBr. i, 2, 6, 2; 'telling to the end,' full tidings, intelligence; news, Ragh.; Megh.; Kathās.; Śak. 226, 6; one who gets a livelihood by a trade &c., W.; by sacrificing for others, L.

Ud-antaka, *as*, m. news, tidings, intelligence, L.; (*ikā*), f. satisfaction, satiety, L.

Udantya, mfn. living beyond a limit or boundary, AitBr.

उदन्य *udanya*, &c. See p. 183, col. 3.

उदपास् *ud-apâs* (*ud-apa-√2. as*), P. to throw away, give up entirely, BhP. x, 14, 3.

उदभी *ud-abhí* (*ud-abhi-√i*), P. (2. sg. *-eshi*) to rise over (acc.), RV. viii, 93, 1.

उदय *ud-ayá*, &c. See p. 186, col. 1.

उदर *udára*, *am*, n. (*√dṛī*, Uṇ. v, 19; *√ṛi*, BRD. & T.), the belly, abdomen, stomach, bowels, RV.; AV.; ŚBr.; Suśr.; MBh.; Kathās. &c.; the womb, MBh.; VP.; Car.; a cavity, hollow; the interior or inside of anything (*udare*, inside, in the interior), Pañcat.; Śak.; Ragh.; Mṛicch. &c.; enlargement of the abdomen (from dropsy or flatulence), any morbid abdominal affection (as of the liver, spleen &c.; eight kinds are enumerated), Suśr.; the thick part of anything (e. g. of the thumb), Suśr.; Comm. on Yājñ.; slaughter, Naish. **–kṛimi** or **-krimi**, m. 'worm in the belly,' an insignificant person, gaṇa *pātre-sammitâdi*, Pāṇ. ii, 1, 48. **–granthi**, m. 'knot in the abdomen,' disease of the spleen (a chronic affection not uncommon in India). **–trāṇa**, n. a cuirass or covering for the front of the body, L.; a girth, belly-band, L. **–dārá**, m. a particular disease of the abdomen, AV. xi, 3, 42. **–pātra**, n. the stomach serving as a vessel, BṛĀrUp. 5. **–piśāca**, m. 'stomach-demon,' voracious, a glutton, one who devours everything (flesh, fish &c.), L. **–pūram**, ind. till the belly is full, Pāṇ. iii, 4, 31. **–poshaṇa**, n. feeding the belly, supporting life. **–bharaṇa-mātra-kevalêcchu**, mfn. desirous only of the mere filling of the belly, Hit. **–°m-bhara**, mfn. nourishing only one's own belly, selfish, voracious, gluttonous, BhP. **–°m-bhari**, mfn., Kāś. **–randhra**, n. a particular part of the belly of a horse, Kād. **–roga**, m. disease of the stomach or bowels, VarBṛS. **–vat**, mfn. having a large belly, corpulent, Pāṇ. v, 2, 117. **–vyādhi**, m. = *-roga* above, Rājat. **–śaya**, mfn. lying or sleeping on the belly, Kāty. on Pāṇ. iii, 2, 15. **–śāṇḍilya**, m., N. of a Ṛishi, ChUp.; VBr. **–sarpin**, mfn. creeping on the belly. **–sarvasva**, mfn. one whose whole essence is stomach, a glutton, epicure, L. **–stha**, m. 'being in the stomach,' the fire of digestion, MaitrUp. **Udarâksha**, m., N. of a demon causing diseases, MBh. ix, 2565 (v. l. *udarâksha*, q. v.) **Udarâgni**, m. 'stomach-fire,' the digestive faculty, VarBṛS. **Udarâṭa**, m. 'wandering in the bowels,' a species of worm, Car. **Udarâdhmāna**, n. puffing of the belly, flatulence, Suśr. **Udarâmaya**, m. disease of the bowels, dysentery, diarrhœa, Suśr. **Udarāmayin**, mfn. suffering from the above, Suśr. **Udarâvarta**, m. 'stomach-coil,' the navel, L. **Udarâveshṭa**, m. tapeworm, W.

Udaraka, mfn. abdominal, W.

Udarika, mfn. having a large belly, corpulent, Pāṇ. v, 2, 117.

Udarin, mfn. id., ib.; having a large belly (from flatulence), Suśr.; (*iṇī*), f. a pregnant woman.

Udarila, mfn. corpulent, Pāṇ. v, 2, 117.

Udarya, mfn. belonging to or being in the belly, ŚBr.; Car.; (*am*), n. contents of the bowels, that which forms the belly, VS. xxv, 8.

उदरथि *udarathi*, *is*, m. (*√ṛi*, Uṇ. iv, 88), the ocean, L.; the sun, L.

उदर्च् *ud-√arc*, P. (pf. 3. pl. *-ānṛicús*) to drive out, cause to come out, AV. xii, 1, 39.

Ud-arká, *as*, m. arising (as a sound), resounding, RV. i, 113, 18; the future result of actions, consequence, futurity, future time, MBh.; R.; Daś.; Kathās.; Mn. &c.; a remote consequence, reward; happy future, MBh.; conclusion, end, ŚBr.; TS.; AitBr.; repetition, refrain, Pāṇ.; Kāṭh.; ŚāṅkhŚr.; elevation of a building, a tower, look-out place, MBh.; the plant Vanguiera Spinosa.

Ud-ṛic, *k*, f. remainder, conclusion, end, VS.; TS.; ŚBr.; ĀśvŚr. &c.; (*ṛici*), ind. lastly, at last, finally, RV. i, 53, 11; x, 77, 7; AV. vi, 48, 1; 2; 3.

उदर्चिस् *ud-arcis*, mfn. flaming or blazing upwards, brilliant, resplendent, Ragh.; Kum.; (*is*), m. fire, Śiś. ii, 42; N. of Śiva, L.; of Kandarpa, L.

उदर्द *ud-√ard*, P. *-ardati*, to swell, rise; to undulate, wave, ŚBr. v, 3, 4, 5; 6.

Ud-arda, *as*, m. (in medic.) erysipelas, Bhpr.

उदर्द्ध *ud-arddha*, *as*, m. (*√ṛidh*), scarlet fever, W.

उदर्ष *ud-arshá*, *as*, m. (*√1. ṛish*), overflowing, overflow, TBr. iii, 7, 10, 1.

उदल *udala*, *as*, m., N. of a man.

उदलाकाश्यप *udalākāśyapa*, *as*, m., N. of a goddess of agriculture, PārGṛ.

उदवग्रह *ud-avagraha*, mfn. having the Udātta on the first part of a compound which contains an Ava-graha, VPrāt.

उदवसो *ud-ava-√so*, P. *-áva-syati*, to leave off, go away; to finish, end, AV. ix, 6, 54; AitBr.; ŚBr.; to go away to (another place, with loc.), ĀśvGṛ. iv, 1, 1.

Ud-avasātṛi, *tā*, m. one who goes away after concluding (a sacrifice), Nyāyam.

Ud-avasāna, *am*, n. the act of leaving the place of sacrifice (see above), BhP.; Nyāyam.

Udavasānīya, mfn. forming the end (of a sacrifice), concluding, final, ŚBr.; AitBr.; MaitrS.; (*ā*), f. the end or conclusion (of a sacrifice), ŚBr.

Ud-avasāya, ind. p. ending, concluding, ŚBr.; KātyŚr.

Ud-avasita, *am,* n. a house, dwelling, Mṛicch.

Ud-avasya, ind. p. concluding, BhP. iv, 7, 56.

उदश् *ud-√1. aś,* P. *-aśnoti* (Subj. *-aśnavat,* RV. v, 59, 4; pf. *-ānaṇśa,* RV. viii, 24, 12; aor. *-ānaṭ* and *-ānaṭ,* &c.), Ā. (3. du. *-aśnuvāte,* ŚBr. iv, 2, 1, 26) to reach, attain, arrive at, ŚBr.; to reach, be equal; to overtake, surpass; to master, rule, RV.

उदश्रु *ud-aśru,* mfn. one whose tears gush forth, shedding tears, weeping, Ragh.; BhP.; Kathās. &c.; (*u*), ind. with tears gushing forth, Sāh.; (cf. *ud-asra* below.)

Udaśraya, Nom. P. *udaśrayati,* to shed tears; to cause to weep, Kāvyād.

Udaśrayaṇa, *am,* n. the act of causing to weep, Comm. on Kāvyād.

उदस् *ud-√2. as,* P. *-asyati,* to cast or throw up; to raise, erect, elevate, ŚBr.; MBh.; to throw out, expel, ŚBr. ii, 6, 2, 16; KātyŚr.; to throw (a weapon), Naish.

Ud-asana, *am,* n. throwing up; raising, erecting.

Ud-asta, mfn. thrown or cast up; raised, thrown &c.

Ud-asya, ind. p. having thrown or cast up &c.

1. **Ud-āsa** (for 2. see col. 3), *as,* m. throwing out; extending, protracting, TāṇḍyaBr.; casting out; (with *garbhasya*) abortion, VarBṛS. 51, 38.

उदस्तात् *udastāt,* ind. above (with gen.), BhP. iii, 18, 8.

उदस्र *ud-asra,* mfn. shedding tears, weeping, Naish. viii, 34.

उदाकृ *ud-ā-√1. kṛi,* P. Ā. *-karoti, -kurute* (impf. *-ākar,* RV. x, 67, 4) to expel, drive out; to fetch out of, RV.; ŚBr.; TS.; to select, choose, AV. xii, 4, 41; ŚBr. iii, 3, 1, 14; (only Ā.; Pāṇ. i, 3, 32) to prick, Kāś. on Pāṇ. i, 3, 32; to revile, abuse, ib.

उदाख्या *ud-ā-√khyā.*

Ud-ākhyāya, ind. p. having related aloud; enunciating, ŚBr. iii, 3, 3, 4.

उदागा *ud-ā-√1. gā,* P. (aor. 1. sg. *-āgām*) to come up or out towards (with acc.), AV. xiv, 2, 44.

उदाचक्ष् *ud-ā-√caksh,* Ā. *-ācashṭe,* to declare or say aloud, ŚBr. iii, 3, 3, 4.

उदाचर् *ud-ā-√car,* P. (impf. *-ācarat*) to rise out of (the ocean), RV. vii, 55, 7.

Ud-ācāra, *as,* m. a place for walking, Āp.

उदाज *ud-āja.* See *ud-√aj.*

उदाजन् *ud-ā-√jan,* Ā. (aor. *-ájanishṭa*) to arise from, RV. v, 31, 3.

उदातन् *ud-ā-√tan,* P. *-tanoti,* to spread, extend, TāṇḍyaBr. xx, 14.

उदादा *ud-ā-√1. dā,* P. to lift up, elevate.

Ud-ātta, mfn. (for *ud-ā-datta*) lifted up, upraised, lofty, elevated, high, R.; BhP.; arisen, come forth, Prab.; highly or acutely accented, Pāṇ.; Nir.; RPrāt.; APrāt. &c.; high, great, illustrious; generous, gentle, bountiful; giving, a donor, Daś.; Sāh.; haughty, pompous, Rājat.; dear, beloved, L.; (°*tara,* compar. more elevated, more acute); (*as*), m. the acute accent, a high or sharp tone, RPrāt.; APrāt.; Pāṇ. &c.; a gift, donation, L.; a kind of musical instrument; a large drum, L.; an ornament or figure of speech in rhetoric, L.; work, business, L.; (*am*), n. pompous or showy speech, Kāvyād.; Sāh.; Pratāpar. **—tā,** f. pompousness, Pratāpar. **—tva,** n. the state of having the acute accent, Comm. on Pāṇ. **—maya,** mfn. similar to the high tone or accent, Udātta-like, VPrāt. **—rāghava,** n., N. of a drama. **—vat,** mfn. having the Udātta, VPrāt.; Pāṇ. **—śruti,** f. pronounced or sounding like the Udātta, APrāt.; *-tā,* f. the state of being pronounced so, RPrāt.

Udāttaya, Nom. P. *udāttayati,* to make high or illustrious; to make honourable or respectable, Bālar.

उदाद्यन्त *ud-ādy-anta,* mfn. preceded and followed by an Udātta, VPrāt.

उदाद्रु *ud-ā-√2. dru,* P. *-dravati,* to run out, run upwards, ŚBr.; TBr.

उदान *ud-āna.* See 2. *ud-√an.*

उदानी *ud-ā-√nī,* P. *-nayati,* to lead up or out of (water), ŚBr.; Lāṭy.: Ā. *-nayate,* to raise, elevate, Bhaṭṭ. viii, 21.

उदाप् *ud-√āp,* P. (pf. 3. pl. *-āpus*) to reach up to, reach, attain, ŚBr.

उदापि *ud-āpi, is,* m., N. of a son of Sahadeva, Hariv.; N. of Vasu-deva, VP. (v.l. *udāyin,* q.v.)

उदाप्यम् *ud-āpyàm,* ind. up the stream, against stream, AV. x, 1, 7.

उदाप्लु *ud-ā-√plu.*

Ud-āpluta, mfn. overflowed, inundated, BhP. iii, 8, 10.

उदामन्त्रण *ud-ā-mantraṇa, am,* n. addressing loudly, calling out to, Āp.

उदायम् *ud-ā-√yam,* P. (Impv. *-āyacchatu*) to bring out, fetch out, get off, AV. v, 30, 15: Ā. (aor. 3. sg. *-āyata,* du. *-āyasātām,* pl. *-āyasata*) to show, exhibit, make known, Pāṇ. i, 2, 15; (but also aor. *-āyaṇsta,* in the sense to bring out, get off, Kāś. on Pāṇ. i, 2, 15.)

उदायस *udāyasa, as,* m., N. of a prince.

उदाया *ud-ā-√yā,* P. *-yāti,* to go up to, Kauś. 17.

उदायिन् *ud-āyin, ī,* m., N. of Vasu-deva (v.l. *ud-āpi,* q.v.), VP.; of Kūṇika, VP.

उदायु *ud-ā-√2. yu,* P. *-yauti,* to stir up, whirl, Kauś.; Gobh.

उदायुध *ud-āyudha,* mfn. with uplifted weapon, raising up weapons, MBh.; R.; Ragh.; Kathās.

उदार *ud-ārá,* mf(*ā* and *ī* [*gaṇa bahv-ādi,* Pāṇ. iv, 1, 45])n. (√*ṛi*), high, lofty, exalted; great, best; noble, illustrious, generous; upright, honest, MBh.; Śak.; Śiś. &c.; liberal, gentle, munificent; sincere, proper, right; eloquent; unperplexed, L.; exciting, effecting, RV. x, 45, 5; active, energetic, Sarvad.; (*as*), m. rising fog or vapour (in some cases personified as spirits or deities), AV.; AitBr.; a sort of grain with long stalks, L.; a figure in rhetoric (attributing nobleness to an inanimate object). **—kīrti,** mfn. highly renowned, illustrious. **—carita,** mfn. of generous behaviour, noble-minded, noble, Hit.; Śārṅg. &c.; (*as*), m., N. of a king, Kathās. **—cetas,** mfn. high-minded, magnanimous. **—tā,** f. or **-tva,** n. nobleness, generousness, liberality; energy, Kathās.; Daś.; Sarvad. &c.; elegance of speech or expression, Vām.; Sāh. **—darśana,** mfn. of noble appearance, R.; Kum. **—dhishaṇa,** m., N. of an astronomer. **—dhī,** mfn. highly intelligent, wise, sagacious, R.; Suśr.; Ragh. &c.; (*īs*), m., N. of a man, VP. **—bhāva,** m. noble character, generosity. **—mati,** mfn. noble-minded, highly intelligent, wise, Ragh. **—vikrama,** mfn. highly brave, heroic, Kām. **—vīrya,** mfn. of great power. **—vṛittârtha-pada,** mfn. of excellent words and meaning and metre, R. i, 2, 45. **—śobha,** mfn. of great or excellent splendour. **—sattva,** mfn. of noble character, generous-minded, R.; °*vâbhijana,* of noble character and descent, R. iv, 47, 19.

Udārâksha, m., N. of a demon that causes diseases, MBh. (ed. Bombay ix, 45, 63; v.l. *udarâksha,* q.v.)

Udārârtha, mfn. of excellent meaning.

Udāraka, *as,* m. honorific name of a man, Daś.

उदारथि *ud-ārathi,* mfn. (√*ṛi*), rising, arising, RV. i, 187, 10; AV. iv, 7, 3; (*is*), m., N. of Vishṇu, L.

उदारुह् *ud-ā-√ruh,* P. (aor. 1. sg. *-āruham,* VS. xvii, 67; 3. pl. *-āruhan,* AV. xviii, 1, 61) to rise up to.

उदावत्सर *udāvatsara,* v.l. for *idā-vatsara,* q.v.

उदावस् *ud-ā-√5. vas,* P. *-vasati,* to remove or migrate out to, MBh.: Caus. *-vāsayati,* to cause to remove out, turn out, BhP.

उदावसु *udāvasu, as,* m., N. of a son of Janaka (king of Videha), R.; VP.

उदावह् *ud-ā-√vah,* P. *-vahati,* to lead away, carry or draw away, ŚBr.; MBh.; to marry, MBh.; R.; to extol, praise, W.

उदावृत् *ud-ā-√vṛit,* Caus. *-vartayati,* to cause to go out, excrete, Suśr.; to secrete; to retain (see the next).

Ud-āvarta, *as,* m. a class of diseases (marked by retention of the feces), disease of the bowels, iliac passion, Suśr.; TS. vi, 4, 1, 1; (*ā*), f. painful menstrual discharge (with foamy blood), Suśr.

Ud-āvartaka, mfn. retaining (the feces), Bhpr.

Ud-āvartana, *am,* n. retention, retarding, Car.

Udāvartin, mfn. suffering from disease of the bowels, Suśr.

उदाव्रज् *ud-ā-√vraj,* P. *-vrajati,* to go or move onwards, go forwards, Kauś.

उदाशंस् *ud-ā-√śaṇs,* Ā. *-śaṇsate,* to wish for, ŚBr. v, 2, 3, 5; xi, 1, 4, 2.

उदास् *ud-√ās,* Ā. *-āste,* to sit separate or away from, sit on one side or apart; to abstain from participating in; to take no interest in, be unconcerned about, be indifferent or passive, MBh.; BhP.; Śiś. &c.; to pass by, omit, Sarvad.

2. **Ud-āsa** (for 1. see *ud-√2. as*), *as,* m. indifference, apathy, stoicism, L.

Ud-āsitṛi, mfn. indifferent, disregarding, stoical; void of affection or concern, Śiś. i, 33.

Udāsin, mfn. indifferent, disregarding; one who has no desire nor affection for anything; (*ī*), m. a stoic, philosopher; (in popular acceptation) any religious mendicant (or one of a particular order), W.

Ud-āsīna, mfn. (pres. p.) sitting apart, indifferent, free from affection; inert, inactive; (in law) not involved in a lawsuit, MBh.; Yājñ.; Bhag. &c.; (*as*), m. a stranger, neutral; one who is neither friend nor foe; a stoic, philosopher, ascetic. **—tā,** f. indifference, apathy, Pañcat.

उदास्था *ud-ā-√sthā,* P. (aor. 1. pl. *-asthāma,* AV. iii, 31, 11) to rise again.

Ud-āsthita, mfn. set over, L.; (*as*), m. an ascetic who instead of fulfilling his vow is employed as a spy or emissary, Comm. on Mn. vii, 154; a superintendent, L.; a door-keeper, L.

उदास्यपुच्छ *ud-āsya-puccha,* mfn. having the tail and head upraised, BhP. x, 13, 30.

उदाहन् *ud-ā-√han,* P. (impf. 3. pl. *-aghnan*) to strike at; to cause to sound (the lyre), ŚBr.

उदाहित *ud-āhita,* mfn. (√*dhā*), elevated. **—tara,** mfn. more elevated, higher, ŚBr. vii, 5, 1, 38.

उदाहृ *ud-ā-√hṛi,* P. *-ā-harati,* to set up, put up, ŚBr. i, 1, 1, 22; to relate, declare, announce; to quote, cite, illustrate; to name, call, ŚBr.; Gobh.; ĀśvŚr.; Baudh.; MBh.; RPrāt. &c.: Pass. *-hriyáte,* to be set up or put up, TS. vi, 2, 9, 4.

Ud-āharaṇa, *am,* n. the act of relating, saying, declaring, declaration, Gaut.; Kum.; Vikr.; referring a general rule to a special case, an example, illustration, Sāh.; Kāś. &c.; (in log.) the example, instance (constituting the third member in a fivefold syllogism), Tarkas. 41; Nyāyad.; Nyāyak.; exaggeration, Sāh. **—candrikā,** f., N. of a work. **Udāharaṇânugama,** m., N. of a work.

Ud-āharaṇīya, mfn. to be quoted as example, to be referred (as a general rule to a special case), Comm. on Nyāyam.

Ud-āharin, mfn. relating, saying, calling, BhP.

Ud-āhāra, *as,* m. an example or illustration, L.; the beginning of a speech, L.

Ud-āhārya, mfn. = *ud-āharaṇīya* above.

Ud-āhṛita, mfn. said, declared, illustrated; called, named, entitled, MBh.; BhP.; VarBṛS. &c.

Ud-āhṛiti, *is,* f. an example, illustration; exaggeration, Pratāpar.

Ud-āhṛitya, ind. p. bringing forward an example, illustrating &c.

उदि *ud-√i,* P. *-éti, -etum* (and *úd-etos,* Maitr. i, 6, 10) to go up to, proceed or move up, proceed, RV.; AV.; VS.; to rise (as the sun or a star &c.), RV.; VS.; ŚBr.; ChUp.; VarBṛS. &c.; to come up (as a cloud), Mṛicch.; R.; to start up, rise up against, march off, AV. iii, 4, 1; MBh.; Kum.; to rise, raise one's self; to increase, be enhanced; to be conceited or proud, R.; Ragh.; Śiś. ii, 33; RPrāt. &c.; to go out of; to come out or arise from, RV.; AV.; ŚBr.; Ragh. &c.; to escape, ChUp.; Śak. &c.: Pass. (impers. -*īyate*) to be risen, Subh.

Ud-ayá, *as*, m. going up, rising; swelling up, R.; rising, rise (of the sun &c.), coming up (of a cloud), ŚBr.; KātyŚr.; Mn.; Śak. &c.; the eastern mountain (behind which the sun is supposed to rise), MBh.; Hariv.; Kathās. &c.; going out, R.; coming forth, becoming visible, appearance, development; production, creation, RV. viii, 41, 2; R.; Ragh.; Yājñ.; Śak.; Kum. &c.; conclusion, result, consequence, MBh.; Ragh.; Mn.; that which follows; a following word, subsequent sound, Pāṇ. viii, 4, 67; RPrāt.; APrāt. &c.; rising, reaching one's aim, elevation; success, prosperity, good fortune, Kathās.; Ragh. &c.; profit, advantage, income; revenue, interest, R.; Yājñ.; Mn. &c.; the first lunar mansion; the orient sine (i. e. the sine of the point of the ecliptic on the eastern horizon), Sūryas.; N. of several men. **-kara**, m., N. of an author. **-giri**, m. the eastern mountain (see above), Hit.; VP. &c. **-gupta**, m., N. of a man, Rājat. **-jit**, m., N. of a son of Guṇala, Rājat. **-jyā**, f. the orient sine (see above), Sūryas. **-taṭa**, m. the slope of the eastern mountain (see *udaya*), Ratnāv. **-tuṅga**, m., N. of a king, Kathās. **-dhavala**, m., N. of a king. **-parvata**, m. = *-giri* above, Hariv.; Kathās. **-pura**, n., N. of the capital of Marwar. **-prastha**, m. the plateau of the eastern mountain. **-prāṇa**, m. pl. a particular measure of time (reckoned by the number of respirations till the rising of a particular constellation), Sūryas. **-rāja**, m., N. of a man, Rājat. **-rāśi**, m. the constellation in which a planet is seen when on the horizon, VarBṛ. iv, 6. **-°rksha** (*udaya-ṛi°*), n. id., ib.; the lunar mansion in which a star rises heliacally, VarBṛS. vi, 1. **-vat**, mfn. risen (as the moon &c.), Śiś.; (*tī*), f., N. of a daughter of Udaya-tuṅga, Kathās. **-śaila**, m. = *-giri* above, Kathās. **-siṅha**, m., N. of a king. **Udayâcala** and **udayâdri**, m. = *-giri* above. **Udayâditya**, m., N. of several men. **Udayânta**, mfn. ending with sunrise, MBh. **Udayântara**, n. (in astron.) a particular correction for calculating the real time of a planet's rising, SiddhŚir. **Udayâśva**, m., N. of a grandson of Ajāta-śatru, VP. **Udayâsu**, m. pl. = *-prāṇa* above, Sūryas. **Udayônmukha**, mf(*ī*)n. about to rise; expecting prosperity, Pañcad. **Udayôrvī-bhṛit**, m. = *-giri* above, Ratnāv.

Ud-áyana, *am*, n. rise, rising (of the sun &c.), RV. i, 48, 7; ŚBr.; R. &c.; way out, outlet, AV. v, 30, 7; exit; outcome, result, conclusion, end, TS.; ŚBr.; TāṇḍyaBr.; means of redemption, Car.; (*as*), m., N. of several kings and authors. **-carita**, n., N. of a drama. **-tas**, ind. finally, TāṇḍyaBr. xiii, 12, 1. **Udayanâcārya**, m., N. of a philosopher and author of several works. **Udayanôpâdhi**, m., N. of a work.

Udayanī́ya, mfn. belonging to an end or conclusion, finishing (as a ceremony), ŚBr.; AitBr.; KātyŚr. &c.

Udayin, mfn. rising, ascending; prosperous, flourishing, L.; (*ī*), m., N. of a grandson of Ajāta-śatru (= Udayâśva). **Udayi-bhadra**, m. id.

Ud-āyá, *as*, m. emerging, coming forward; see *try-ud°*.

1. **U'd-ita** (for 2. see s. v.), mfn. risen, ascended; being above, high, tall, lofty, RV.; ChUp.; Mn. &c.; conceited, proud, boasting, MBh.; elevated, risen; increased, grown, augmented, R.; Kir. &c.; born, produced, Bhartṛ.; apparent, visible, RV. viii, 103, 11; incurred, experienced. **-homin**, mfn. sacrificing after sunrise, AitBr.; ŚBr. **Uditâdhāna**, n. kindling fire after sunrise, Comm. on ĀpŚr. v, 13, 2. **Uditânudita**, mfn. 'risen and not risen,' not quite risen, ĀpŚr. xv, 18, 13.

U'd-iti, *is*, f. ascending or rising (of the sun), RV.; AV. vii, 5, 3; iii, 16, 4; going away or down, setting of the sun, RV. v, 69, 3; 76, 3; vii, 41, 4; conclusion, end (of a sacrifice, through the fire going out, Gmn.), RV. vi, 15, 11; AV. x, 2, 10.

Ud-itvara, mfn. risen, Naish.; surpassing, exceeding, extraordinary, NṛisUp.

Ud-īta, mfn. = 1. *ud-ita*, Naish. i, 83; vi, 52; 74.

Ud-eshyat, mfn. about to rise or mount upwards, about to increase, Śiś. ii, 76.

उदिङ्ग् *ud-√iṅg*, Caus. -*iṅgayati*, to impart a tremulous motion, vibrate, swing, RV. iv, 57, 4; ŚBr.; to cause (a sound) to vibrate, pronounce, RPrāt. xvii, 8.

Ud-iṅgana, *am*, n. swinging, oscillating, vibrating, Comm. on KātyŚr.

उदित 2. *udita* (p. p. of √*vad*, q. v.; for 1. see col. 1) said, spoken, AitBr.; Kathās.; Ragh.; Śiś. &c.; spoken to, addressed, BhP.; Śiś. ix, 61; Kathās.; communicated, proclaimed, declared, Mn.; Kathās.; BhP.; Rājat. &c.; (especially) proclaimed by law, taught, handed down; authoritative, right, ŚāṅkhBr.; Mn.; Yājñ. i, 154; indicated, signified, VarBṛS.; [a form *udita* occurs, incorrectly spelt for *ud-dita*, p. 188, col. 1.] **Uditânuvādin**, mfn. one who repeats what is said by others, AitBr. ii, 15. **Uditôdita**, mfn. (fr. 2. *udita* with 1. *ud-ita*), conversant with what has been handed down by tradition, learned, Yājñ.

उदिनक्ष् *ud-inaksh* (anom. Desid. of √*naksh*), P. (p. -*inakshat*) to wish or endeavour to obtain or reach; to strive after, pretend to, RV. x, 8, 9; 45, 7.

उदीक्ष् *ud-√īksh*, Ā. -*īkshate* (once P. p. -*īkshat*, BhP. xi, 30, 44) to look up to, ŚBr.; R.; to look at, regard, view, behold, ŚBr. xiv, 9, 1, 1; MBh.; Mn. &c.; to wait, delay, hesitate; to expect, MBh.; R.; Mn.

Ud-īkshaṇa, *am*, n. the act of looking up, seeing, beholding, L.

Ud-īkshā, f. id., BhP.; expecting, waiting, Comm. on Bādar.

Ud-īkshita, mfn. looked at, beheld &c.

Ud-īkshya, ind. p. having looked at or beheld &c.

उदीचीन *udīcī́na*, &c. See p. 184, col. 2.

उदीप *ud-īpa*, mfn. (fr. 2. *ap* with *ud*; cf. Pāṇ. vi, 3, 97), inundated, flooded; (*as*), m. high water, inundation, Rājat.

उदीर् *ud-√īr*, Ā. -*īrte* (3. pl. -*ī́rate*, RV.; AV.; Impv. 2. sg. -*īrshva*, RV. x, 18, 8; AV.; impf. -*airata*, RV. vii, 39, 1; p. -*īrāṇa*, AV. xii, 1, 28; RV.), P. (Subj. 3. sg. -*īrat*, RV. iv, 2, 7; aor. 2. du. -*airatam*, RV. i, 118, 6) to bring or fetch out of, RV. i, 118, 6; to rise, start off (in order to go or to come), RV.; AV.; ŚBr.; to move upwards, ascend; to arise, originate, RV.; AV.; to honour, respect, RV. iv, 2, 7; (in class. Sanskṛit only *ud-īrṇa* occurs): Caus. -*īrayati*, to bring or fetch out of, RV. i, 112, 5; x, 39, 9; to cause to rise or move; to raise, rouse, excite, RV.; MBh.; R.; Ragh.; Daś.; to throw or cast upwards; to cast, discharge, drive forward, R.; Ragh. &c.; to cause to come forth or appear, Kum.; to raise one's voice; to utter, speak, RV.; Yājñ.; Mn. &c.; to procure, cause, effect, RV. i, 48, 2; x, 39, 2; TS.; Suśr.; to excite, raise, enhance, multiply, increase, Suśr.; Kum. &c.; to extol, glorify, RV. v, 42, 3; MBh.; to stir up, urge, stimulate, RV.; R.; to rise, start off, RV. v, 55, 5; viii, 7, 3: Pass. -*īryate*, to be cast or thrown upwards, R.; to be excited, be roused or stirred up, MBh.; R.; Suśr.; Kum. &c.; to be uttered or announced or enunciated; to pass for, VP.; Kum.; Kathās.; Pañcat.; Suśr. &c.; to sound; to issue forth.

Ud-īraṇa, *am*, n. the act of throwing, casting, discharging (a missile), MBh.; throwing out; exciting, stirring up, Car.; saying, speaking, communicating, Kum.; Kathās.; Sāh.

Ud-īrita, mfn. excited, stirred up; animated, agitated; increased, augmented; said, uttered, enunciated. **-dhī**, mfn. one whose mind is active, acute-minded, Prab. **Udīritêndriya**, mfn. one whose senses are excited, Kum. iv, 41.

Ud-īrṇa, mfn. issued out, excited, increased, elevated, MBh.; R.; Suśr.; Kum. &c.; self-conceited, proud, MBh. **-tā**, f. excitement, activity, agility, Suśr. **-dīdhiti**, mfn. intensely bright. **-varāha-tīrtha**, n., N. of a Tīrtha. **-vega**, mfn. impetuous in its course (as a torrent), violent.

1. **Ud-īrya**, mfn. to be raised; to be uttered &c.
2. **Ud-īrya**, ind. p. having uttered &c.

उदीष् *ud-√īsh*, P. -*ishati*, to rise, mount, Kāṭh.; MaitrS.

U'd-īshita, mfn. risen, elevated, RV. x, 119, 12.

उदुक्ष् *ud-√uksh*, P. -*ukshati*, to sprinkle upwards or outwards, ŚBr.; KātyŚr.; ĀśvŚr.

उदुत *ud-uta*. See p. 192, col. 3.

उदुब्ज् *ud-√ubj*, P. -*ubjati*, to open by bending or breaking, TS. vi, 5, 9, 1; to set up, erect, AV. xi, 1, 7.

उदुम्बर *udumbára*, Ved. for *uḍumbara*, q. v., the tree Ficus Glomerata.

1. **Udumbála**, *as*, m. = *udumbára* [T.?], AV. viii, 6, 17.

उदुम्बल 2. *udumbalá*, mfn. of widely-reaching power (for *uru-bala*, Sāy.; said of the two dogs, the messengers of Yama), RV. x, 14, 12; AV. xviii, 2, 13, [copper-coloured, BRD.]

उदुम्भर *udumbhára*, m. (fr. √*bhṛi* with *ud*), a word coined for the etymological explanation of *udumbára*, ŚBr. vii, 5, 1, 22.

उदुष् *ud-√ush*, P. -*oshati*, to heat, make red-hot; to torment by heat, AV. xii, 5, 72; ŚBr.; ŚāṅkhŚr.

U'd-ushṭa, mfn. red-hot; red. **-mukha**, mfn. having a red mouth (as a horse), ŚBr. vii, 3, 2, 14.

उदुह *uduhá*, *as*, m.? misprint for *udūhá* below.

उदूखल *udū́khala*, *am*, n. a wooden mortar (used for pounding rice and separating the husk); any mortar, Suśr.; bdellium, L.

उदूढ *ud-ūḍha*. See *ud-√vah*.

उदूह् *ud-√1. ūh*, P. Ā. -*ūhati*, -*te*, to push or press upwards, move or bear upwards; to throw or turn out, sweep out, push out, AV. xi, 1, 9; ŚBr.; KātyŚr.; Comm. on TBr. iii, 8, 4, 3; BhP. &c.; to bring out of, Vait.; to heighten (an accent), SaṃhUp. iii, 3.

Ud-ūhá, *as*, m.(?) a besom, broom, TBr. iii, 8, 4, 3; the highest acute (accent), SaṃhUp. iii, 4.

उदृ *ud-√ṛi*, P. -*iyarti* (pf. 2. sg. -*ārithā*, RV. ii, 9, 3; aor. -*ārat*, RV. iv, 58, 1), Ā. (aor. -*ārta*, RV. vii, 35, 7) to start up, rise, come up; to move up, raise, excite, RV. i, 113, 17; iii, 8, 5, &c.: Caus. -*arpayati*, to cause to rise or prosper, RV. ii, 33, 4; KātyŚr.

उदृच् *ud-ṛíc*. See *ud-√arc*.

उदृष् *ud-√2. ṛish*, P. (p. -*ṛishát*) to perforate, pierce, RV. x, 155, 2.

उदे *ud-é* (*ud-ā-√i*), P. -*éti* (Impv. 2. sg. *ud-éhi*, AV. v, 30, 11, &c.) to go up, rise, arise from, come up, move upwards, RV. vi, 5, 1; AV.; ŚBr.; ChUp.; to move out, come out of, go out, ŚBr.; VS.; to arise, be produced.

Udêyivas, mfn. (p. p. P.) that has come up, produced, originated, born, BhP. x, 31, 4.

उदेज् *ud-√ej*, P. -*ejati*, to move upwards, rise, AV. iv, 4, 2; to shake, tremble: Caus. -*ejayati*, to cause to tremble, shake, Kāś. on Pāṇ. iii, 1, 138.

Ud-ejaya, mfn. shaking, causing to tremble, Pāṇ. iii, 1, 138.

उदोजस् *úd-ojas*, mfn. exceedingly powerful or effective, RV. v, 54, 3; x, 97, 7.

उद्गद्गदिका *ud-gadgadikā*, f. sobbing, Kād. ii, 99, 15.

उद्गन्धि *ud-gandhi*, mfn. (Pāṇ. v, 4, 135) giving forth perfume, fragrant, Ragh.

उद्गम् *ud-√gam*, P. -*gacchati* (Ved. impf. 1. pl. -*aganma*) to come forth, appear suddenly, become visible, RV. i, 50, 10; R.; Ragh.: Vikr. &c.; to go up, rise (as a star), ascend, start up, MBh.; VarBṛS.; Ratnāv. &c.; to go out or away, disappear, R.; BhP.; Bhartṛ. &c.; to spread, extend, Ragh.: Caus. -*gamayati*, to cause to rise, Pat.; to cause to come out or issue (as milk from the mother's breast), suck.

Ud-gata, mfn. gone up, risen, ascended, Ṛitus.; MBh. &c.; come or proceeded forth, appeared, Ratnāv.; Ragh. &c.; gone, departed; extended, large, Ragh.; vomited, cast up, L.; (*ā*), f., N. of a metre (consisting of four lines, with ten syllables in the first three, and thirteen in the last; occurring e. g. in Śiś. xv). **-śriṅga,** mfn. one whose horns are just appearing (as a calf), Kāś. on Pāṇ. vi, 2, 115. **Udgatâsu,** mfn. one whose life is gone, deceased, dead.

Ud-gati, *is,* f. coming forth, Kathās.; going up, rising, ascent, L.; bringing up; vomiting, L.

Ud-gántṛi, *tā,* m. one who leads out, MaitrUp. vi, 31.

Ud-gama, *as,* m. going up, rising (of a star &c.), ascending, elevation (of a mountain), R.; Suśr.; Hit.; VarBṛS. &c.; coming forth, becoming visible, appearing, production, origin, Suśr.; Ragh.; Vikr.; Ratnāv. &c.; going out or away, R.; Kathās.; Bhartṛ.; shooting forth (of a plant), Kir.; Kāvyād.

Ud-gamana, *am,* n. the act of rising (of a star &c.), ascending, Pāṇ. i, 3, 40; the act of coming forth, becoming visible, R.

Ud-gamanīya, mfn. to be gone up or ascended, L.; cleansed, clean, Kum. vii, 11; Hcar.; *(am),* n. a clean cloth or garment, Daś.; a pair of bleached cloths or sheets, L.

उद्गर्ज् *ud-√garj,* P. *-garjati,* to burst out roaring; to cry out loudly, Kathās.

उद्गर्भ *ud-garbha,* mfn. pregnant, Vām.

उद्गल् *ud-√gal,* P. *-galati,* to trickle out, ooze out, issue in drops, BhP.

उद्गल *ud-gala,* mfn. raising the neck, BhP.

उद्गा *ud-√gā,* Ved. P. (aor. or impf. *-agāt*) to rise (as the sun &c.), come up, RV.; AV.; TS.; TBr.; to come forth, begin, Kāś. on Pāṇ. ii, 4, 3.

उद्गातृ *ud-gātṛí,* &c. See col. 2.

उद्गार *ud-gāra,* &c. See *ud-√gṛī* below.

उद्गाह् *ud-√gāh,* Ā. (pf. 3. pl. *-jigāhire* [irr.], KātyŚr. xiii, 3, 21) to emerge.

Ud-gāḍha, mfn. flowing over, excessive, violent, much, Prab.; Sāh.; Bhartṛ. &c.; *(am),* ind. excessively, much, L.

उद्गुर् *ud-√gur,* P. *-gurate* (p. *-gurámāṇa,* VS. xvi, 46) to raise one's voice in a threatening manner; to raise (a weapon &c.), lift up, Bhaṭṭ.

Ud-gūrayitṛi, mfn. threatening, Vishṇus. v, 60.

Ud-gūrṇa, mfn. raised, lifted, held up, Veṇis.; Pañcat. &c.; erected, excited, W.; *(am),* n. the act of raising (a weapon), threatening, Yājñ. ii, 215.

Ud-goraṇa, *am,* n. the act of raising (a weapon), threatening, Comm. on Yājñ. ii, 215.

उद्गुह् *ud-√guh,* P. Ā. *-gūhati, -te,* to wind through, twist through, ŚBr.; KātyŚr.

Ud-gūhana, *am,* n. the act of twisting or winding through, Comm. on KātyŚr. ii, 7, 2.

उद्गृभाय *ud-gṛibhāya.* See *ud-√grah.*

उद्गॄ *ud-√gṛī,* P. *-girati,* to eject (from the mouth), spit out, vomit out or up, belch out; to pour out, discharge, spout, MBh.; R.; Mṛicch.; Pañcat. &c.; to force out (a sound), utter; to breathe out; to raise from, Rājat.; Kathās. &c.: Caus. P. *-girayati* (irr.), to raise (sounds), utter, Pañcat.

Ud-gāra, *as,* m. (Pāṇ. iii, 3, 29) the act of discharging, spitting out, ejecting (from the mouth), vomiting, belching, eructation, R.; Suśr.; Ragh.; Megh. &c.; relating repeatedly, Hit.; spittle, saliva, MBh.; Suśr.; Gaut.; flood, high water, R.; Kāś. on Pāṇ. iii, 3, 29; roaring, hissing, a loud sound, MBh.; Śāntiś. &c. **-cūḍaka,** m. a species of bird, Car. **-śodhana,** m. black caraway, Bhpr.

Ud-gārin, mfn. (ifc.) ejecting, spitting, vomiting; discharging, thrusting out, R.; Mṛicch.; Ragh.; Rājat. &c.; uttering, causing to sound, Bālar.; *(ī),* m. the 57th year of the Jupiter cycle, VarBṛS. viii, 50.

Ud-giraṇa, *am,* n. the act of vomiting, ejecting (from the mouth), spitting out, slobbering, slavering, Suśr.; Vedāntas. &c.

Ud-gīrṇa, mfn. vomited forth, ejected, Suśr. &c.; cast forth, fallen out of, VarBṛS.; caused, effected, Gīt. i, 36.

Ud-girya, ind. p. having omitted or ejected &c.

उद्गेही *udgehī,* f. a kind of ant, L.

उद्गै *ud-√gai,* P. *-gāyati* (*-gāti,* ŚāṅkhBr. xvii, 7) to begin to sing; to sing or chant (applied especially to the singing or chanting of the Sāma-veda, cf. *ud-gātṛí*), RV. x, 67, 3; AV. ix, 6, 45-48; AitBr.; ŚBr.; TS.; Lāṭy. &c.; to sing out loud, Śiś. vi, 20; to announce or celebrate in song, sing before any one (with acc.); to fill with song, ŚvetUp.; MBh.; Ragh. &c.

Udgātu-kāma, mfn. wishing to sing.

Ud-gātṛi, *tā,* m. one of the four chief-priests (viz. the one who chants the hymns of the Sāma-veda), a chanter, RV. ii, 43, 2; TS.; AitBr.; ŚBr.; KātyŚr.; Suśr.; Mn. &c. **-damana,** n., N. of several Sāmans. **Udgātr-ādi** (°*tṛi-ā*°), m., N. of a gaṇa, Pāṇ. v, 1, 129.

Ud-gāthā, f. a variety of the Āryā metre (consisting of four lines, containing alternately twelve and eighteen instants).

Ud-gīta, mfn. sung; announced, celebrated; *(am),* n. singing, a song, MBh.

Ud-gīti, *is,* f. singing, singing loud; chanting; a variety of the Āryā metre (consisting of four lines of twelve, fifteen, twelve, and eighteen instants).

Ud-gīthá, *as,* m. (Uṇ. ii, 10) chanting of the Sāma-veda (especially of the exact Sāma-veda without the additions, the office of the Udgātṛi), AV. xi, 7, 5; xv, 3, 8; TS.; ŚBr.; Lāṭy. &c.; the second part of the Sāma-veda; N. of a son of Bhuva, VP.; of a son of Bhūman (the same?), BhP.; of a commentator of Vedic texts, Sāy.; the syllable *Om* (the triliteral name of God), L.

Ud-gīya, ind. p. having sung or chanted &c.

Ud-geya, mfn. to be sung, TāṇḍyaBr.

उद्ग्रन्थ् *ud-√granth,* P. *-grathnāti* or *-granthati,* to bind up, tie into bundles, tie up, truss, AitBr.; TBr.; ĀśvŚr. &c.; to fasten, wind, MBh.; Kauś.; to unbind, loosen, BhP.: Caus. *-grathayati,* to unbind, loosen, BhP. iv, 22, 39.

Ud-grathana, *am,* n. (v. l. for *ā-grathana,* Ragh. xix, 41) the act of winding round.

Ud-grathita, mfn. tied up; fastened, wound, interlaced; unbound, loosened.

Ud-grathya and **ud-granthya,** ind. p. having tied up; having wound &c.

Ud-grantha, *as,* m. section, chapter, L.; N. of a man (Buddh.)

उद्ग्रन्थि *ud-granthi,* mfn. untied, free (from worldly ties), BhP.

उद्ग्रह् *ud-√grah,* P. Ā. *-gṛihṇāti* (or Ved. *-gṛibhṇāti*), *-ṇīte* (Impv. 2. sg. *-gṛibhāya,* RV. v, 83, 10; p. *-gṛihṇát,* AV. ix, 6, 47) to lift up, keep above, TS.; ŚBr.; KātyŚr.; to set up, erect, raise, elevate, VS.; TS.: (Ā.) to raise one's self, ŚBr. iii, 1, 4, 1; vi, 6, 1, 12; to take out, draw out; to tear away, take away, AV. iv, 20, 8; TBr.; ŚBr.; MBh.; to take away from, preserve, save, AV. viii, 1, 2; 17; to intercept, cause (the rain) to cease, RV. v, 83, 10; to break off, discontinue (speaking), AV. ix, 6, 47; VS.; ŚBr.; ChUp.; Lāṭy.; to concede, grant, allow, BhP. xi, 22, 4: Caus. *-grāhayati,* to cause to take up or out, cause to pay, NṛisUp.; Yājñ.; to bespeak, describe, set forth, Śiś. ii, 75; Bhaṭṭ.

Ud-gṛihīta, mfn. lifted up, taken up, turned up, upraised, Megh. &c.

Ud-gṛihya, ind. p. having lifted up; having taken out, ŚBr.

Ud-grabhaṇa, *am,* n. the act of taking up, raising, KātyŚr. xvi, 5, 11.

Ud-gráhaṇa, *am,* n. the act of taking out, ŚBr.; recovering (a debt, cf. *ṛiṇôdgr*°); taking up, lifting up; describing.

Udgrahaṇikā, f. replying in argument, objection, Comm. on BhP. v, 11, 1.

Ud-grābhá, *as,* m. taking up, raising, elevating, TS.; VS.

Ud-grāha, *as,* m. (Pāṇ. iii, 3, 35) taking up, reception, Uttarar.; 'taking away,' N. of a Sandhi rule (which causes the change of *aḥ, e,* and *o,* to *a* before a following vowel), RPrāt. 133; replying in argument, objection, L.; (in music) the introductory part of a piece. **-pada-vṛitti,** f. the Udgrāha Sandhi before a long vowel, RPrāt. 134. **-vat,** n. a kind of Sandhi (causing the change of *ā* and *a* to *ă* before *ṛi*), RPrāt. 136.

Ud-grāhaṇikā, f. and **ud-grāhiṇī,** f. replying in argument, objection, L.

Ud-grāhita, mfn. taken away, lifted up; deposited, delivered; seized; bound, tied; described, set forth; excellent, exalted; recalled, remembered, recited, L.

उद्ग्रासक *ud-grāsaka,* mfn. (√*gras*), devouring, NṛisUp. 203.

उद्ग्रीव *ud-grīva,* mfn. one who raises or lifts up the neck (in trying to see anything), Amar.; Rājat. &c.; having the neck turned upwards (as a vessel), Kād.

Udgrīvin, mfn. raising or lifting up the neck, Śāntiś.

उद्घ *ud-gha,* &c. See *ud-dhan,* p. 188, col. 3.

उद्घट् *ud-√ghaṭ,* Caus. *-ghāṭayati,* to open, unlock, unfasten, unveil; to peel, shell, MBh.; Kathās.; Mṛicch.; VarBṛS. &c.; to expose; to betray, Pañcat.; Kathās.; to commence, begin, Hit.; to rub over, stroke; to tickle.

Ud-ghaṭita, mfn. unlocked, Kum. vii, 53.

Ud-ghāṭa, *as,* m. the act of exposing or showing (the teeth), Śubh.; a watch or guard-house, L.

Ud-ghāṭaka, *as,* m. a key, Mṛicch.; *(am),* n. a leather bucket used for drawing up water, L.

Ud-ghāṭana, mfn. opening, unlocking, Hit.; *(am),* n. the act of opening, unlocking; revealing, manifesting, MārkP.; Sāy.; the act of unveiling, exposing, uncovering, Sarvad.; a leather bucket used for drawing up water, L.; hoisting, raising, lifting up, L.

Ud-ghāṭanīya, mfn. to be opened, Kathās.

Ud-ghāṭita, mfn. opened, manifested; undertaken, commenced; raised, hoisted, lifted up; done with effort, exerted; stroked, tickled, Suśr. **-jña,** mfn. wise, intelligent, Daś. **Udghāṭitâṅga,** mfn. 'having the limbs exposed,' naked, L.; wise, intelligent, W.

Ud-ghāṭin, mfn. one who opens or unlocks, Prasannar.; commencing, L.

उद्घट्ट् *ud-√ghaṭṭ,* Caus. *-ghaṭṭayati* and *-ghāṭṭayati,* to unlock, open, L.; to stir up, Car.

Ud-ghaṭṭaka, *as,* m. a kind of time (in music), L.

Ud-ghaṭṭana, *am,* n. striking against, a stroke, Megh.; outbreak (of violence or passion), Kathās.; Bālar.; opening, opening upwards (as a lid), L.

Ud-ghaṭṭita, mfn. opened, unlocked, L.

उद्घस *ud-ghasa,* *as,* m. (√*ghas*), flesh, L.

उद्घात *ud-ghāta,* &c. See *ud-dhan,* p. 188, col. 3.

उद्घुष् *ud-√ghush,* P. *-ghoshati,* to sound; to cry out, MBh.; to fill with cries; to proclaim aloud, Sarvad.: Caus. *-ghoshayati,* to cause to sound aloud, Rājat.; to declare aloud, proclaim, noise abroad, Mṛicch.; Kathās.; Rājat.

Ud-ghushṭa, mfn. sounded out, VarBṛS.; filled with cries, R.; proclaimed, noised abroad; *(am),* n. sound, noise, R.

Ud-ghosha, *as,* m. the act of announcing or proclaiming aloud; popular talk, general report. **-ḍiṇḍima,** m. a drum beaten by a town-crier (to attract attention in the streets), Kathās.

Udghoshaka, *as,* m. one who makes a proclamation, a town-crier, Kathās.

Ud-ghoshaṇa, *ā,* f. and *am,* n. proclamation, publication, Sāh.; Kathās.; Sarvad.

उद्घूर्ण *ud-ghūrṇa,* mfn. (√*ghūrṇ*), wavering, unsteady, Kād.

उद्घृष् *ud-√ghṛish,* P. *-gharshati,* to rub up, rub together, grind, comminute by rubbing; to rub over; to strike at, toll (a bell); see *ud-ghṛishṭa.*

Ud-gharsha, *as,* m. rubbing (the skin with hard substances), Car.

Ud-gharshaṇa, *am,* n. id., Suśr.; rubbing up, scratching, Suśr. ii, 149, 13; striking, beating, blows, Mṛicch.

Ud-ghṛishṭa, mfn. rubbed, ground, pulverized, Ragh.; struck at, tolled (as a bell), Rājat.

उद्घोण *ud-ghoṇa,* mfn. having the nose or snout erected (as a boar), Kād.

उद्दंश *ud-daṅśa* and *uddaṅśaka,* *as,* m. a bug, L.; a mosquito, gadfly, L.

उद्दण्ड *ud-daṇḍa,* mfn. one who holds up a staff (said of a doorkeeper), Kuval.; having a stick or staff or stalk raised or erect, Hit.; Prab.; Ragh.;

Kathās.; prominent, extraordinary, Daś.; (*as*), m. a kind of time (in music). **-pāla**, m. = *udaṇḍa-pala*, q. v.

Ud-daṇḍita, mfn. raised up, elevated, Kathās.

उद्दन्तुर *ud-dantura*, mfn. large-toothed, having projecting teeth; high, tall, L.; terrific, formidable, L.

उद्दम् *ud-√dam*, Caus. *-damayati*, to subdue, overpower, become master of.

Ud-dama, *as*, m. the act of subduing, taming, L.

Ud-damya, ind. p. having subdued, MBh. xii, 6596.

Ud-dānta, mfn. humble; energetic; elevated, L.

उद्दर्शन *ud-darśana*. See *ud-√driś*.

उद्दल् *ud-√dal*, Caus.

Ud-dala, *as*, m., N. of a pupil of Yājñavalkya's.

Ud-dalana, mfn. tearing out, Kād.; (*am*), n. the act of splitting, causing to burst, Jain.

Ud-dāla, *as*, m. the plant Paspalum Frumentaceum, Suśr.; Cordia Myxa or Latifolia, L.

Ud-dālaka, *as*, m. = *ud-dāla* above, Suśr.; N. of a teacher, ŚBr.; (*am*), n. a kind of honey, L. **-pushpa-bhañjikā**, f. 'breaking Uddālaka flowers,' a sort of game (played by people in the eastern districts), Kāś. **-vrata**, n. a particular vow, Comm. on ĀśvGṛ. i, 19, 6.

Uddālakāyana, *as*, m. a descendant of the teacher Uddālaka.

Ud-dālana, *am*, n. a means of tearing away or removing, Car.

Uddālin, *ī*, m. = *ud-dala*, q. v., VP.

Ud-dālya, ind. p. having caused to burst, having split, MBh.

उद्दा 1. *ud-√1. dā*.

Ud-dāya, ind. p. having taken out or away, having extorted, BhP. iii, 1, 39.

उद्दा 2. *ud-√4. dā*, P.

Ud-dāna, *am*, n. the act of binding on, fastening together, stringing, MBh.; taming, subduing, L.; the middle, waist, L.; a fire-place, L.; submarine fire, L.; entrance of the sun into the sign of the zodiac, L.; contents, L.; tax, duty, L.; (*as*), m., N. of a man, Rājat.

Ud-dita, mfn. bound, tied, L.

उद्दाम *ud-dāma*, mfn. (fr. *dāman* with 1. *ud*), unrestrained, unbound, set free; self-willed; unlimited, extraordinary; violent, impetuous, fiery; wanton; proud, haughty; large, great, MBh.; Megh.; Rājat. &c.; (*as*), m. a particular metre; 'one whose noose is raised,' N. of Yama, L.; of Varuṇa, L.; (*am*), ind. in an unrestrained manner, without any limits, Sāh.; Kād.

Uddāmaya, Nom. P. *uddāmayati*, to unfetter, cause to come forth, Kād. ii.

उद्दास *ud-dāsa*, *as*, m., gaṇa *balâdi*, Pāṇ. v, 2, 136.

Uddāsin, mfn., gaṇa *grāhy-ādi*, Pāṇ. iii, 1, 134.

उद्दिधीर्षा *ud-didhīrshā*. See p. 189, col. 2.

उद्दिन *ud-dina*, *am*, n. midday, W.

उद्दिश् 1. *ud-√diś*, P. Ā. *-diśati*, *-te*, to show or direct towards, ŚāṅkhŚr.; TBr.; to point out, signify, declare, determine, R.; Mn.; Megh.; Śak. &c.; to speak of; to say, enunciate, prophesy, R.; Śak.; to mean, point at, take for; to aim at, intend, destine, MārkP.; Kathās. &c.; to explain, instruct, teach, Bhartṛ.

Ud-diśya, ind. p. having shown or explained; stipulating for, demanding; (used as a preposition) aiming at, in the direction of; with reference to; towards; with regard to, for, for the sake of, in the name of &c. (with acc.), MBh.; BhP.; Śak. &c.

Ud-dishṭa, mfn. mentioned, particularized; described; promised; (*am*), n. a kind of time (in music).

Ud-deśa, *as*, m. the act of pointing to or at, direction; ascertainment; brief statement; exemplification, illustration, explanation; mentioning a thing by name, MBh.; Bhag.; Suśr.; Pañcat. &c.; assignment, prescription; stipulation, bargain, MBh.; R.; quarter, spot, region, place; an object, a motive; upper region, high situation, MBh.; Pañcat.; Śak. &c.; (in Nyāya phil.) enunciation of a topic (that is to be further discussed and elucidated), Nyāyak.; (*ena* & *āt*), ind. (ifc.) relative to, aiming at, Kathās.; Suśr. &c. **-tas**, ind. pointedly, distinctly; by way of explanation; briefly, Bhag. &c. **-pādapa**, *as*, m. a tree planted for a particular purpose, L. **-vidheya-vicāra**, m., N. of a work. **-vṛiksha**, m. = *-pādapa* above.

Ud-deśaka, mfn. illustrative, explanatory, L.; (*as*), m. an illustration, example; an illustrator, guide, L.; (in math.) a question, problem, Comm. on Āryabh. **-vṛiksha**, m. = *uddeśa-pādapa*, q.v.

Ud-deśana, *am*, n. the act of pointing to or at, Comm. on TBr.

Ud-deśin, mfn. pointing at or to, Vām.

Ud-deśya, mfn. to be illustrated or explained; anything to which one refers or which one has in view, Vedāntas.; Comm. on Gobh.; Siddh.; that which is said or enunciated first, Sāh.; Kpr.; Comm. on KātyŚr.; destined for, Āp.; to be mentioned by name only, Comm. on Nyāyam.; (*am*), n. the end in view, an incentive. **-pādapa**, m. = *uddeśa-pādapa*, q. v.

Uddeśyaka, mfn. pointing at or to, Comm. on R.

Ud-deshṭṛi, mfn. pointing out &c.; one who acts with a certain scope or design.

उद्दिश् 2. *ud-diś*, *k*, f. a particular point or direction of the compass (cf. 2. *ā-diś*), VS. vi, 19; ĀśvGṛ.

उद्दिह् *ud-√dih*, P. *-degdhi* (3. pl. *-dihanti*) to throw or heap up, TĀr. v, 2, 8.

Ud-dehika, *ās*, m. pl., N. of a people, VarBṛ.; (*ā*), f. the white ant.

उद्दीप् *ud-√dīp*, Ā. *-dīpyate*, to flame, blaze up, be kindled, AitBr.; ŚBr.; TāṇḍyaBr.; Kauś.: Caus. *-dīpayati*, to light up, inflame, AV. xii, 2, 5; Kauś.; Hariv.; to illuminate, Mṛicch.; to animate, excite, irritate, provoke, MBh.; BhP.; Sāh. &c.

Ud-dīpa, *as*, m. the act of inflaming, lighting; an inflamer; animating, L.; (*am*), n. a gummy and resinous substance, bdellium, L.

Ud-dīpaka, mfn. inflaming, exciting, rendering more intense, Sāh.; Comm. on Kāvyād.; lighting, setting alight, L.; (*as*), m. a kind of bird, MBh.; (*ikā*), f. a kind of ant.

Ud-dīpana, mfn. inflaming, exciting, VarBṛS.; affecting violently (as poison), Daś. 12, 10; (*am*), n. the act of inflaming, illuminating; lighting up, VarBṛS.; inflaming (a passion), exciting, animating, stimulating, R.; Ṛitus.; Sāh. &c.; an incentive, stimulus; any aggravating thing or circumstance (giving poignancy to feeling or passion), Sāh.; burning (a body &c.), L.

Ud-dīpta, mfn. lighted, set on fire or alight, shining, L.; inflamed, aggravated (as passion), L.

Ud-dīpti, *is*, f. the being inflamed or excited, Sāh.

Ud-dīpra, *am*, n. bdellium, L.

उद्दीश *uddīśa*, *as*, m. (= *uḍḍīśa*, q. v.), N. of Śiva, L.

उद्दुष् *ud-√dush*, P. *-dūshayati*.

Ud-dūshya, ind. p. having publicly calumniated or discredited, Śiś. ii, 113.

उद्दृंह् *ud-√dṛiṇh*, P. (Impv. 2. sg. *úd-dṛiṇha*) to erect and fortify, VS. xvii, 72.

उद्दृश् *ud-√dṛiś*. See *ut-paś*, p. 181, col. 1.

Ud-darśana, *as*, m., N. of a king of the Nāgas, L.

Ud-darśita, mfn. made visible, come forth, appearing, Vikr.

U'd-dṛishṭa, mfn. descried, visible; (*am*), n. the appearance or becoming visible of the moon, ŚBr.; KātyŚr.; TBr.; TāṇḍyaBr.

Ud-drashṭṛi, *ṭā*, m. one who descries, NṛisUp.

उद्दॄ *ud-dṝi*, P.

Ud-dīrṇa, mfn. torn out, Daś. (v. l. *ud-īrṇa*).

उद्द्युत् *ud-√1. dyut*, P. Ved. (impf. *-a-dyaut*) Ā. *-dyotate*, to blaze up, shine, shine forth, RV. iii, 5, 9; Hariv.: Caus. P. *-dyotayati*, to cause to shine or shine forth, Prab.; Ragh.: Intens. Ved. (Subj. *-dávidyutat*) to shine intensely, RV. vi, 16, 45.

Ud-dyota, mfn. flashing up, shining, R.; (*as*), m. the act of flashing up, becoming bright or visible, revelation, Kathās.; Subh. &c.; light, lustre, MBh.; Sārṅg. &c.; a division of a book, chapter; N. of Nāgojibhaṭṭa's Comm. on Kaiyaṭa's Bhāshyapradīpa. **-kara** and **-kārin**, mfn. causing light, enlightening, illuminating. **-karâcārya**, m., N. of a teacher. **-mayūkha**, m., N. of a work.

Ud-dyotaka, mfn. enlightening, emblazoning; inflaming, stimulating, Comm. on Sāṃkhyak.

Ud-dyotana, *am*, n. the act of enlightening, illumination. **-sūri**, m., N. of a teacher (Jain.)

Ud-dyotita, mfn. caused to shine, lighted up, bright, MBh.

Uddyotin, mfn. shining upwards, VarBṛS. 30, 10.

उद्द्रु *ud-√dru*, P. to run up or out or through; to recite quickly.

Ud-drāvá, mfn. running away, VS. xxii, 8; TS.; (*as*), m. going upwards; flight, retreat, Pāṇ. iii, 3, 49.

U'd-druta, mfn. running away, VS. xxii, 8.

Ud-drutya, ind. p. running up or away, TBr.; Kāṭh.; reciting quickly (cf. *anu-√dru*), ŚāṅkhGṛ. iv, 17, 5.

उद्धन् *ud-dhan* (*ud-√han*), P. *-dhanti* (Ved. impf. 3. sg. *-ahan*, RV. x, 102, 7; Impv. *-hantu*, iii, 33, 13, 2; du. *-hatam*, i, 184, 2, &c.), Ā. (3. pl. *uj-jighnante*, RV. i, 64, 11; Ved. inf. *-dhantavai*, ŚBr. xiii, 8, 1, 20) to move or push or press upwards or out, lift up, throw away, RV.; ŚBr.; to root up or out, BhP.; to turn up (the earth), dig, throw open, TS.; ŚBr.; TBr. &c.: (Ā.) to kill one's self, hang one's self, R.; Pañcat.

Ud-gha, *as*, m. excellence; a model, pattern, Pāṇ. iii, 3, 86; happiness; the hollow hand; fire; organic air in the body, L.

Ud-ghana, *as*, m. a carpenter's bench, a plank on which he works, Pāṇ. iii, 3, 80.

Ud-ghāta, *as*, m. the act of striking, wounding, inflicting a hurt; a wound, blow, Kathās.; slipping, tripping, L.; raising, elevation, R.; beginning, commencement; a thing begun, Ragh.; Kum.; Kathās.; breathing through the nostrils (as a religious exercise), VāyuP.; a club, mallet; a weapon, L.; a division of a book, chapter, section, L.

Ud-ghātaka and **ud-ghātya**, *am*, n. a dialogue carried on in short abrupt but significant words, Pratāpar.; Daśar.

Ud-ghātana, *am*, n. a bucket for drawing (water), L.

Udghātin, mfn. having elevations, uneven, rough (v. l. for *ut-khātin*), Śak. 10, 6.

Ud-ghātyaka, *as*, m. abrupt interruption in the prologue of a drama (where an actor suddenly strikes in with an irrelevant remark caused by his having mistaken a word uttered by another actor), Sāh. 289.

Ud-dhata, mfn. raised (as dust), turned up, R.; Śak. 8 c; Kathās.; lifted up, raised, elevated, high, ŚBr.; TBr.; KātyŚr.; Suśr. &c.; struck (as a lute), KātyŚr. xxi, 3, 7; enhanced; violent, intense, BhP.; Pañcat.; Kathās. &c.; puffed up, haughty, vain, arrogant; rude, ill-behaved, R.; BhP.; Sāh. &c.; exceeding, excessive; abounding in, full of, MBh.; Pañcat.; Kathās. &c.; stirred up, excited, agitated, MBh.; Ragh. &c.; (*as*), m. a king's wrestler, L.; N. of a certain donkey, Pañcat. **-tva**, n. pride, arrogance, MaitrUp. iii, 5. **-manas**, mfn. high-minded; haughty, proud, R. **-manaska**, mfn. id., L.; *-tva*, n. pride, arrogance, L. **Uddhatârṇava-nisvana**, mfn. making a noise like that of the agitated sea.

Ud-dhati, *is*, f. a stroke, shaking, Śak. (*nir-uddhatis* v. l. for *nir-undhatas*, 174 c); elevation; pride, haughtiness, L.

Ud-dhanana, *am*, n. the act of throwing up or turning up, Comm. on Nyāyam.

उद्धम *ud-dhama*. See *ud-√dhmā*.

उद्धय *ud-dhaya*, mfn. (√*dhe*), sucking out, drinking, Vop.

उद्धर *ud-dhara*, &c. See 2. *ud-dhṛi*.

उद्धर्म *ud-dharma*, *as*, m. unsound doctrine, heresy.

उद्धर्ष 1. *ud-dharsha* (for 2. see p. 189, col. 3), *as*, m. (√*dhṛish*), courage to undertake anything, R.

1. **Ud-dharshaṇa** (for 2. see p. 189, col. 3), mfn. animating, encouraging, R.; (*am*), n. the act of animating or encouraging, MBh.

उद्धव *ud-dhava*, *as*, m. (√*hu*), sacrificial fire,

L.; a festival, holiday, L.; joy, pleasure, L.; N. of a Yādava (Kṛishṇa's friend and counsellor), MBh.; Hariv.; VP.; BhP. **-dūta** and **-saṃdeśa**, m., N. of two poems.

उद्धस् *ud-dhas* (*ud-√has*), P. *-dhasati*, to break out into laughter (said of the lightning); to flash, BhP. iii, 12, 6.

उद्धस्त *ud-dhasta*, mfn. (*hasta* with *ud*) extending the hands, raising the hands, Suśr. ii, 533, 10.

उद्धा 1. *ud-dhā* (*ud-√dhā*), P. (Subj. 2. pl. *-dadhātana*) to erect (*kapṛithám*), RV. x, 101, 12; to expose (an infant), ŚBr. iv, 5, 2, 13.

Ud-dhí, *is*, m. the seat of a carriage, AV. viii, 8, 22; ŚBr. xii, 2, 2, 2; TBr.; an earthen stand on which the Ukhā rests, ŚBr.; Kāṭh.

U'd-dhita, mfn. erected, raised, built up, AV. ix, 3, 6; ix, 42, 2; ŚBr.; exposed, RV. viii, 51, 2; AV. xviii, 2, 34.

उद्धा 2. *ud-dhā* (*ud-√1. hā*), Ā. *-jihīte* (p. *uj-jihāna*, RV. v, 5, 1 = AV. xiii, 2, 46; see also below) to go upwards, move upwards, rise up, RV.; AV. viii, 7, 21; VS.; TBr.; BhP. &c.; to open (as a door), RV. ix, 5, 5; to go out or away, start from, leave, RV. v, 5, 1; Daś.; Naish. &c.

Uj-jíhāna, mfn. (pres. p., see above); (*ās*), m. pl., N. of a people, VarBṛS. 14, 2; (*ā*), f., N. of a town, R. ii, 71, 12.

उद्धान 1. *ud-dhāna*, *am*, n. (√2. *hā*), the act of leaving, abandonment, TāṇḍyaBr.

उद्धान 2. *uddhāna*, mfn. (corrupted from *ud-vānta*, *ud-dhmāta*, *ud-dhmāna*, BRD.) ejected, vomited, L.; corpulent, inflated, L.; (*am*), n. the act of ejecting, vomiting, L.; a fire-place, L.

Uddhānta, mfn. (see above), ejected, vomited, L.; (*as*), m. an elephant out of rut (from whose temples the juice ceases to flow), L.

उद्धार *ud-dhārá*, &c. See 2. *ud-dhṛi*.

उद्धी *ud-√dhī*, P. (impf. 3. pl. *-ádīdhayus*) to look upwards with desire, RV. vii, 33, 5.

उद्धुर *ud-dhura*, mfn. (fr. *dhur* with *ud*; cf. Pāṇ. v, 4, 74), freed from a yoke or burden, unrestrained, wild, lively, cheerful, Śiś. v, 64; Ragh.; Kathās. &c.; heavy, thick, gross, firm, Śiś.; Daś. &c.; high, L.

उद्धुषण *ud-dhushaṇa*, *am*, n. (corrupted from *ud-dharshaṇa*?) erection of the hair, L.

उद्धू *ud-√dhū*, P. Ā. *-dhūnoti* and *-dhunoti*, *-nute*, to rouse up, shake up, move, cause to rise (dust), RV. x, 23, 4; MBh.; R.; Ragh.; VarBṛS. &c.; to throw upwards, lift up, MBh.; Kathās. &c.; to kindle; to disturb, excite, MBh. &c.; to shake off, throw off; to expel.

Ud-dhūta (sometimes *ud-dhuta*), mfn. shaken up, raised, caused to rise, MBh.; Ragh.; Kum. &c.; thrown upwards, tossed up, scattered above, MBh.; R.; Prab.; kindled (as fire), Ragh. vii, 45; Kathās.; excited, agitated, Hariv.; R.; Kathās.; shaken off, fallen from or off, thrown off or away, Hariv.; BhP.; exalted; high, loud, MBh.; Hariv.; (*am*), n. (*ud-dhūta*) stamping, Hariv.; turning up, digging, Hariv.; roaring (of the ocean), MBh. **-pāpa**, mfn. one who has shaken off his sins, Megh. 56.

Ud-dhūnana, *am*, n. the act of shaking, jolting, Veṇis. 90, 4; a kind of powder, L.

उद्धूपन *ud-dhūpana*, *am*, n. (fr. Nom. *dhūpaya* with *ud*) fumigation, Suśr.

उद्धूलय *ud-dhūlaya*, Nom. (fr. *dhūli* with *ud*) P. *-dhūlayati*, to powder, sprinkle with dust or powder, Kathās.; Kād.

Ud-dhūlana, *am*, n. the act of sprinkling with dust or powder, Bālar. 185, 19.

उद्धूषण *ud-dhūshaṇa*, *am*, n. (for *ud-dharshaṇa*?) erection of the hair, L.; (cf. *ud-dhushaṇa*.)

Ud-dhūshita, mfn. having the hairs erect (through joy), Pañcat.

उद्धृ 1. *ud-√dhṛi*, P. Ā. *-dharati*, *-te* (in many cases not to be distinguished from 2. *ud-dhṛi* below; the impf. and pf. are the only forms clearly referable to this root), to bring out of, draw out, MBh.; R.; to raise up, elevate, honour (see also 2. *ud-dhṛi* below): Desid. *-didhīrshati*, to wish to draw out, Caṇḍak.; Siddh.

Ud-didhīrshā, f. desire to remove, Comm. on Nyāyad.

Ud-didhīrshu, mfn. wishing to draw or bring out, Siddh.

उद्धृ 2. *ud-dhṛi* (*ud-√hṛi*, in some cases not to be distinguished from 1. *ud-√dhṛi*), P. Ā. *-dharati*, *-te* (p. *-dhárat*, RV.; pf. 3. pl. *új-jahārus*, AV. iii, 9, 6; aor. *-ahārsham*, AV.) to take out, draw out, bring or tear out, pull out, eradicate; to extricate, RV. x, 68, 4; AV. viii, 2, 15; xx, 136, 16; ĀśvGṛ.; KātyŚr.; MBh.; Śak. &c.; to draw, ladle up, skim, AV.; ŚBr.; Lāṭy.; R.; to take away (fire, or anything from the fire), TS.; AitBr.; ŚBr.; KātyŚr. &c.; to raise, lift up, TS.; ĀśvGṛ.; MBh.; Mn. &c.; to rescue (from danger &c.), deliver, free, save, AV. viii, 2, 28; MaitrUp.; MBh.; Vikr. &c.; to put away or off, remove; to separate, MBh.; BhP.; Suśr. &c.; to leave out, omit; to except (see *ud-dhṛitya*); to select, choose: Ā. to take for one's self, AV. iii, 9, 6; TS.; AitBr.; ŚBr.; MBh.; Mn. &c.; to extend, elevate, raise; to make strong or brisk or quick, MBh.; Suśr.; MārkP. &c.; to present, offer, Yājñ. i, 159; BhP. iv, 30, 47; to root out, destroy, undo, MBh.; Ragh.; Prab. &c.; to divide (in math.): Caus. *-dhārayati*, to raise, uplift, MBh.; to take for one's self, MBh. xiv, 1928; Desid. *uj-jihīrshati*, to wish to draw out or to rescue, Mn. iv, 251; MBh.

1. **Ud-dhara**, *as*, m., N. of a Rakshas, L.; mfn. v. l. for *ud-dhura*, q. v., MBh. iii, 11188.

2. **Ud-dhara** (2. sg. Impv. forming irregular Tatpurusha compounds). **Uddharâvasṛijā**, **uddharôtsṛijā**, f. any act in which it is said *uddhara! avasṛija!* [or *utsṛija!*], gaṇa *mayūra-vyaṃsakâdi*, Pāṇ. ii, 1, 72.

Ud-dharaṇa, *am*, n. (in some meanings perhaps from 1. *ud-√dhṛi*, q. v.), the act of taking up, raising, lifting up, MBh.; Śārṅg.; the act of drawing out, taking out, tearing out, Mn.; MBh.; Suśr. &c.; means of drawing out, Vet.; taking off (clothes), Suśr.; taking away, removing, Vām.; putting or placing before, presenting, treatment, KātyŚr. iv, 1, 10; extricating, delivering, rescuing, Hit.; Ragh. &c.; taking away (a brand from the Gārhapatya-fire to supply other sacred fires), KātyŚr.; eradication; extermination; the act of destroying; vomiting, bringing up; vomited food; final emancipation, L.; (*as*), m., N. of the father of king Śantanu (the author of a commentary on a portion of the Mārkaṇḍeya-purāṇa).

Ud-dharaṇīya, mfn. to be raised or taken up; to be extracted, W.; to be separated, Comm. on Nyāyam.

Ud-dhartavya, mfn. to be drawn out, Kathās.; to be separated, Comm. on Nyāyam.

Ud-dhartṛi, mfn. one who raises or lifts up; a sharer, co-heir; one who recovers property, W.; (*tā*), m. a destroyer, exterminator, Yājñ.; redeemer, deliverer, Kathās.

Ud-dhārá, *as*, m. (in some senses perhaps from 1. *ud-√dhṛi*), the act of raising, elevating, lifting up; drawing out, pulling out, Gaut.; MBh.; Comm. on BṛĀrUp.; removing, extinction, payment (of a debt); taking away, deduction; omission, Mn.; Comm. on Yājñ.; selection, a part to be set aside, selected part; exception, TS.; ŚBr.; AitBr.; Mn. &c.; selecting (a passage), selection, extract (of a book), Comm. on Kir. x, 10; extraction, deliverance, redemption, extrication, MBh.; Prab. &c.; a portion, share; a surplus (given by the Hindū law to the eldest son beyond the shares of the younger ones), W.; the first part of a patrimony, W.; the sixth part of booty taken in war (which belongs to the prince), W.; a debt (esp. one not bearing interest), KātyDh.; obligation, Daś.; recovering property; refutation, Car.; Comm. on Nyāyad.; (*ā*), f. the plant Cocculus Cordifolius, L.; (*am*), n. a fire-place, L. **-kośa**, m., N. of a work. **-vibhāga**, m. division of shares, partition.

Uddhāraka, mfn. one who raises or lifts, drawing out, L.; paying, giving out, affording. **-vidhi**, m. mode of giving out or paying, Pañcat. ii, 38, 18 (ed. Bühler).

Ud-dhāraṇa, *am*, n. the act of raising, elevating; drawing out, BhP.; the act of giving out or paying, Pañcat. 138, 14 (ed. Kosegarten).

Ud-dhārita, mfn. taken out, drawn forth, extricated; released.

Ud-dhārya, mfn. to be removed or expelled, Āp.; to be cured, Car.; to be delivered.

U'd-dhṛita, mfn. drawn up or out (as water from a well &c.); extracted, pulled up or out, eradicated, broken off, MBh.; R.; Suśr. &c.; drawn up or out, ladled out, skimmed, AV. xii, 5, 34; xv, 12, 1; ŚBr. &c.; raised, elevated, lifted up, thrown up or upwards, MBh.; Rājat. &c.; separated, set apart, taken away, removed, BhP.; Mn. &c.; chosen, selected, taken from or out of, Mn. &c.; raised, made strong or famous, Hit.; recovered; uncovered; dispersed, scattered; holding, containing; vomited, L. **-sneha**, mfn. having the oil extracted (as the refuse of seeds ground for oil), Mn. iv, 62. **Uddhṛitâri**, mfn. one who has extirpated his enemies. **Uddhṛitôddhāra**, mfn. that from which the thing to be excepted is excepted, Mn. x, 85.

Ud-dhṛiti, *is*, f. the act of drawing out, extraction, Suśr.; Rājat.; Śiś.; taking away or out, removing (the fire), Nyāyam.; abstract, extract, L.; delivering, rescue.

Ud-dhṛitya, ind. p. having raised up or drawn &c.; having excepted, excepting; with the exception of, ŚBr.; Lāṭy.; ĀśvŚr. &c.

उद्धृष् *ud-dhṛish* (*ud-√hṛish*), Ved. Ā. *-[d]harshate*, to be excited with joy, rejoice; to do anything with joy or pleasure, RV. iv, 21, 9; AV. iii, 19, 6; (in class. lang.) P. *-dhṛishyati*, to be merry or in high spirits; to flare upwards, AitBr. iii, 4, 5; to open (as a calyx), BhP.: Caus. *-dharshayati* (3. pl. *-dharsháyanti*, RV.) to make merry or in high spirits, rejoice, cheer, RV. v, 21, 5; x, 103, 10; AV. v, 20, 8; to make brisk, encourage, MBh.; MārkP.

2. **Ud-dharsha**, mfn. (for 1. see s. v.) glad, pleased, happy, BhP.; (*as*), m. the flaring upwards (of the fire), Sāy. on AitBr. iii, 4, 5; great joy; a festival (especially a religious one), L.

2. **Ud-dharshaṇa**, mfn. (for 1. see p. 188, col. 3) causing joy, gladdening; (*ī*), f. a kind of metre; (*am*), n. erection of the hair (through rapture), L.

Uddharshin, mfn. one whose hair is erect (through joy), AV. viii, 6, 17; (*iṇī*), f. a kind of metre (consisting of four verses, of fourteen syllables each).

उद्ध्मा *ud-√dhmā*, P. *-dhamati*, to blow out, breathe out, expire (see *ud-dhmāya* below); to inflate, make known by blowing (a trumpet &c.), TĀr. i, 12, 1.

1. **Ud-dhama**, mfn. one who blows, Vop.; (*as*), m. breathing hard, panting; blowing, sounding, L.

2. **Ud-dhama** (2. sg. Impv. forming irregular Tatpurusha compounds). **-vidhamā**, f. any act in which it is said *udhama! vidhama!*, gaṇa *mayūra-vyaṃsakâdi*, Pāṇ. ii, 1, 72.

Ud-dhmāna, *am*, n. a fire-place, stove, L.

Ud-dhmāya, ind. p. having breathed out, expiring, ŚBr. i, 4, 3, 18; (the MSS. read *udhnāya*; Sāy. *udmāya*; Weber conjectures *ud-dhmāya*.)

उद्ध्य *uddhya*, *as*, m. (√*ujjh*, Kāś. on Pāṇ. iii, 1, 115) a river, Ragh. xi, 8; N. of a river, Bhaṭṭ.; L.

उद्ध्वंस् *ud-√dhvaṃs*, Ā. *-dhvaṃsate*, to be affected or attacked (by disease &c.), Car.: Caus. P. *-dhvaṃsayati*, to attack, cause to befall, affect, MBh.; Car.

Ud-dhvaṃsa, *as*, m. destruction, Car. ii, 2, 8; affection (of the throat), hoarseness, Suśr.; Car.; the state of being attacked (by infectious disorders &c.), an epidemic, Car. iii, 3.

Ud-dhvaṃsana, *am*, n. affection (of the throat), Car.; an epidemic, Car. iii, 3.

उद्ध्वे *ud-dhve* (*ud-√hve*), P. *-dhvayati* (impf. 1. sg. *-ahvam*, AV.) to call out, entice, AV. x, 10, 22; xviii, 2, 23; AitBr.

उद्बन्ध् *ud-bandh*, Ā. (Pot. *-badhnīta*) to tie up, hang one's self, ŚBr. xi, 5, 1, 8.

Ud-baddha, mfn. tied up or upwards, MBh.; Kum.; hung, hung up, MBh. iv, 13, 12; checked, interrupted; annulled, BhP. x, 85, 43; compact, firm (as the leg of a man), MBh.; VarBṛS.

Ud-badhya, ind. p. having tied up or hanged one's self, hanging one's self, Rājat.; Kathās.; Pañcat.

1. **Ud-bandha** (for 2. see s. v.), *as*, m. hanging one's self, Kathās.; VarBṛS.

Udbandhana, mf(*ī*)n. serving for hanging up (as a string), R. ii, 12, 80; (*am*), n. hanging, hanging one's self, MBh.; Kathās.; Gaut.

Ud-báudhuka, mfn. one who hangs up, TS. ii, 5, 17.

उद्बन्ध 2. *ud-bandha* (fr. *bandha* with *ud* in sense of apart), mfn. unbound, loosened, united (as hair), Ragh. xvi, 67 (ed. Calc.)

उद्बर्हिस् *ud-barhis*, mfn. having sacrificial grass above, MaitrS. ii, 2, 3.

उद्बल *ud-bala*, mfn. strong, powerful; (cf. *upôdbalaya*.)

उद्बाध् *ud-√bādh*, Ā. *-bādhate*, to burst forth, break forth, ŚBr.

उद्बाष्प *ud-bāshpa*. See *ud-vāshpa*.

उद्बाहु *úd-bāhu*, mfn. having the arms raised; extending the arms, ŚBr.; Ragh. i, 3.

Ud-bāhuka, mfn. id., ĀśvGṛ. iv, 1, 9.

उद्बिल *ud-bila*, mfn. emerged from a hole, (an animal) that has quitted its hole, R.

उद्बुद्बुद *ud-budbuda*, mfn. bubbling out or forth, Mcar.

उद्बुध् *ud-√budh*, Ā. *-budhyate* (aor. 3. pl. *-abudhran*, RV.) to awake, RV. vii, 72, 3; x, 101, 1; VS.

Ud-buddha, mfn. roused up, awaked; come forth, appearing, Sāh.; blown, budded, L.; excited; reminded, made to think of, recalled, W. **—saṃskāra**, m. association of ideas, recalling anything to remembrance.

Ud-bodha, *as*, m. awaking; coming forth, appearing, Sāh.; Rājat.; fumigation, VarBṛS.; reminding; incipient knowledge, W.

Ud-bodhaka, mfn. exciting, calling forth, Sāh.; reminding; one who reminds or calls to remembrance; discovering, exhibiting, W.

Ud-bodhana, *am*, n. awaking, arousing; recalling, reminding, W.

उद्बुध्न्य *ud-budhnya*, Nom. (fr. *-budhna*), P. *-budhnyati*, to come out of the deep, come or spring up, MaitrUp.

उद्बृंहण *ud-bṛiṇhaṇa*, mfn. (√*bṛih*), increasing, strengthening, BhP.

उद्ब्रू *ud-√brū*, Ā. *-bruvate*, to extol, praise (see RTL. p. 424), TBr. i, 7, 10, 6; ŚBr. v; ii, 2, 4 (to renounce, give up, NBD.)

उद्भञ्ज् *ud-√bhañj*. See forms below.

Ud-bhagna, mfn. burst, torn, Suśr.

Ud-bhaṅga, *as*, m. the act of breaking off, leaving off.

उद्भट *udbhaṭa*, mfn. excellent, eminent, exalted, magnanimous, extraordinary, Bhar.; Viddh.; vehement, passionate, Gīt.; (*as*), m. a tortoise, L.; a fan for winnowing corn, L.; N. of an author. **—tva**, n. weight, importance (of a contradiction), Sarvad.

उद्भर्त्स् *ud-√bharts*, P. (impf. 2. pl.? *-abhartsata*, ŚāṅkhŚr. xii, 23, 1; *-abhartsatha*?, AV. xx, 134, 1 [MSS.]) to use roughly?

उद्भव *ud-bhava*. See *ud-√bhū*.

उद्भस *udbhasa*, *ās*, m. pl., N. of a people, MBh.

उद्भा *ud-√bhā*, P. *-bhāti*, to become visible, appear, Mn.; BhP.

उद्भास् *ud-√bhās*, P. Ā. *-bhāsati*, *-te*, to come forth or appear brightly, shine, MBh.; R.; Kathās.; to become visible, strike, MBh. v, 728: Caus. P. Ā. *-bhāsayati*, *-te*, to illuminate, light up, Hariv.; VP.; VarBṛS.; Kathās.; to make apparent or prominent, cause to come forth, Bhartṛ.; Comm. on Kum. i, 2; to render brilliant or beautiful, Mṛicch.; Ragh.

Ud-bhāsa, *as*, m. radiance, splendour, gaṇa *balâdi*, Pāṇ. v, 2, 136 (not in the Kāś.) **—vat**, mfn. shining, radiant, ib.

Ud-bhāsita, mfn. come forth, appeared; lighted up, illuminated, splendid; ornamented, graced, beautiful.

Udbhāsin, mfn. shining, radiant, Kum.; Bhartṛ.; coming forth, appearing, Rājat.; Daśar.; giving or causing splendour, Mṛicch.

Ud-bhāsura, mfn. shining, radiant, Amar.

उद्भिद् 1. *ud-√bhid*, P. *-bhinatti* (Subj. *-bhinádat*, RV.; Pot. 1. sg. *-bhideyam*, AV.) to break or burst through, break out; to appear above, become visible, rise up, RV. x, 45, 10; AV. ix, 2, 2; iv, 38, 1; TāṇḍyaBr.; ŚBr.; to pierce, Vedāntas.; BhP.: Pass. *-bhidyate*, to spring open, burst forth, MBh.; to shoot open or up, break out, appear, Daś.; BhP. &c.

Ud-bhij- (in comp. for 2. *ud-bhíd* below). **—ja**, mfn. sprouting, germinating (as a plant), ChUp.; AitUp.; MBh.; Mn. &c.

2. **Ud-bhíd**, mfn. penetrating, bursting through; coming or bursting forth, pouring, overflowing; abounding with, RV.; AV. v, 20, 11; VS.; breaking forth (from the earth), sprouting, germinating, MBh.; (*t*), m. a kind of sacrifice, KātyŚr.; ĀśvŚr. &c.; (*t*), f. a sprout or shoot of a plant, a plant; a spring, fountain, Suśr.; (with *indrasya*) N. of a Sāman. **—vidyā**, f. the science of plants, botany.

Ud-bhida, mfn. sprouting, germinating, MBh.; (*as*), m., N. of a son of Jyotishmat; of the Varsha ruled over by him, VP.; (*am*), n. a fountain, spring, L.; a kind of salt, L.; N. of a Sāman.

U'd-bhinna, mfn. burst forth, opened, burst; having broken through, come forth, appeared; made to appear, brought to light, Kull.; appearing above, AV. x, 5, 36; xvi, 8, 1 seqq.; Mālav.; Pañcat. &c.; discovered, betrayed, Sāh.; provided or abounding with, BhP.; Pañcar.

Ud-bheda, *as*, m. the act of breaking through or out, becoming manifest or visible, appearing, sprouting, Śak. 85 d; Kum.; Bhartṛ.; Sāh. &c.; (in dram.) the first manifestation of the germ (*bīja*) of the plot, Sāh.; Daśar.; Pratāpar.; a sprout or shoot of a plant, L.; a spring, fountain, R.; MBh.; treachery, Kathās.; mentioning, Prasannar.

Ud-bhedana, *am*, n. the act of breaking through or out, coming forth, MBh.; Car.

उद्भू 1. *ud-√bhū*, P. *-bhavati*, to come up to, reach, be equal, ŚBr.; TBr.; to rise, rise against, Kathās.; to come forth, arise, exist, spring from, MBh.; Kathās.; Hariv.; Rājat. &c.; to shoot forth, increase, grow larger, thrive, MaitrUp.; Naish.: Caus. *-bhāvayati*, to cause to exist, produce, Ragh. ii, 62; Vedāntas.; to make apparent, show, explain, MBh.; Sāh. &c.; to speak of, mention, Prasannar.; Comm. on Bādar.; to consider, think (with two acc.), Vcar. ix, 19.

Ud-bhava, *as*, m. existence, generation, origin, production, birth; springing from, growing; becoming visible, Yājñ.; Mn.; Kathās.; Pañcat. &c.; birthplace, ŚvetUp.; Kāvyād.; N. of a son of Nahusha, VP.; a sort of salt, L.; (ifc.) mfn. produced or coming from, MBh.; Mn. &c. **—kara**, mfn. productive. **—kshetra**, n. the place of origin, Daś.

Ud-bhāva, *as*, m. production, generation, gaṇa *balâdi*, Pāṇ. v, 2, 136; rising (of sounds), Pushpas. ix, 4, 22.

Ud-bhāvana, *am*, n. the act of raising up, elevation, MBh. xiii, 2913; Lalit.; passing over, inattention, neglect, disregard, MBh.; announcement, communication, Naish.; making visible, manifestation, Karaṇḍ.

Ud-bhāvayitṛi, mfn. one who raises upwards or elevates, Daś.

Ud-bhāvita, mfn. caused to exist, created, produced, Sāh.

Udbhāvin, mfn. (Pāṇ. v, 2, 136) coming forth, becoming visible &c.

2. **Ud-bhū**, mf(*bhvī*)n (*bhū́*) 'being up to what is wanted,' sufficient; having persistency, persevering, AV. ix, 2, 16; xviii, 4, 26; VS. xv, 1.

Ud-bhūta, mfn. come forth, produced, born; grown, MaitrUp.; MBh.; R.; Kathās. &c.; raised, elevated, increased, R.; Ṛitus.; visible, perceptible, distinct, positive, Bhāshāp. **—tva**, n. the state of being increased, MaitrUp. v, 2. **—rūpa**, n. visible form or shape; (mfn.) having a visible shape. **—sparśa-vat**, mfn. having distinct or positive tangibility, tangible, Bhāshāp. 55.

Ud-bhūti, *is*, f. coming forth, existence, appearance, Kap.; elevation, increase, Kum.; Vikr.

उद्भृ *ud-√bhṛi*, P. Ā. *-bharati*, *-te* (pf. *-jabhāra*, pres. p. *-bhárat*; but *-bibhrat*, Gīt. i, 16) to take or carry away or out, RV.; AV.; ŚBr.; to take for one's self, choose, select, RV.; AV.; VS.; to raise up, elevate, RV. viii, 19, 23; to carry above, raise up, Gīt.

उद्भ्यस *ud-bhyasá* (√*bhyas* connected with √*bhī*), trembling, AV. xi, 9, 17.

उद्भ्रम् *ud-√bhram*, P. *-bhramati*, *-bhrāmyati*, to whirl or move upwards, start or jump up; to rise, ascend, raise one's self, R.; Gīt.; MārkP.; BhP. &c.: Caus. *-bhrāmayati*, to wave, swing, MBh.; to excite, R.

Ud-bhrama, *as*, m. whirling; excitement, L.; intoxication, L.; N. of a class of beings attending on Śiva, SkandaP.

Ud-bhramaṇa, *am*, n. the act of moving or whirling upwards, rising, ascending, Comm. on Śak. 263, 1.

Ud-bhrānta, mfn. risen, ascended, gone or jumped up, turned upwards, MBh.; R.; Ragh.; Pañcat. &c.; come forth or out of (the earth), Kathās.; run away, disappeared, Rājat.; wandering about, roaming, MBh.; agitated, excited, bewildered, distressed, MBh.; R.; VarBṛS. &c.; whirled, flourished; waved (as a sword); (*am*), n. the act of waving (a sword), MBh.; the rising (of the wind), Hariv.; excitement, agitation, Sāh.

Udbhrāntaka, mfn. wandering about, roaming, NṛisUp.; (*am*), n. whirling upwards, rising, ascending, Śak. 263, 1.

उद्भ्रू *ud-bhrū*, mfn. having the brows drawn up, Bālar. 36, 1.

उद्मन् *údman*, *a*, n. (√*ud*), surging, flooding, VS.; MaitrS.

उद्य *udya*, mfn. (√*vad*, q. v.), to be spoken; (*udyá*, ŚBr. xiv, 6, 8, 2, erroneous for *uj-jyá*, q.v.; *udya*, L., erroneous for *uddhya*, q.v.)

उद्यत् *ud-yat*, mfn. (fr. *ud-√i*, q. v.), rising &c.; (*an*), m. a star, PārGṛ.; (*tī*), f. a particular manner of recitation, TāṇḍyaBr.; Lāṭy. **—parvata** and **udyad-giri**, m. the eastern mountain (cf. *udaya-giri*), MBh.; R.

उद्यम् *ud-√yam*, P. *-yacchati* (aor. *-ayān*, RV. vi, 71, 5), Ā. (if the result of the action returns to the agent, Pāṇ. i, 3, 75) *-yacchate* (aor. *-ayaṃsta* & *-yamishṭa*); Subj. *-yaṃsate*, RV. i, 143, 7; inf. *-yámam*, MaitrS. ii, 4, 3) to lift up, raise, RV. v, 32, 7; vi, 71, 1 & 5; AV.; AitBr.; ŚBr.; Lāṭy.; Śak. &c.; to raise, set up, elevate; to put up or higher, carry or bring upwards, RV. iv, 53, 1; i, 143, 7; TS.; ŚBr.; KātyŚr. &c.; to hold out, present, offer (a sacrifice to gods, or any other thing to men), RV.; AV.; TS.; MBh.; BhP.; R. &c.; to shake up, rouse, RV. i, 10, 1; i, 56, 1; x, 119, 2; AV. xiv, 1, 59; to raise (one's voice, or rays, or light), RV.; to undertake, commence; to be diligent, strive after (only P., e. g. *udyacchati cikitsām vaidyaḥ*, 'the physician strives after the science of medicine,' Kāś. on Pāṇ. i, 3, 75; with dat. or acc. or without any object), MBh; Hariv.; Ragh.; Kathās.; Rājat. &c.; to rein, curb; to guide, MBh.; to keep away or off, restrain, check, TS. vi, 3, 4, 6; TBr. iii, 3, 1, 3: Intens. *-yamyamīti*, to raise, stretch out (the arms), RV. i, 95, 7.

U'd-yata, mfn. raised, held up, elevated, high, MBh.; R.; BhP.; Ragh.; Kathās. &c.; hold out, offered, presented, RV.; AV.; MBh.; R.; BhP. &c.; undertaken, commenced, begun, R.; undertaking, commencing; ready or eager for; prepared, intent on; trained, exercised, disciplined; active, persevering, labouring diligently and incessantly (with dat. or loc. or inf. or without any object), MBh.; R.; Kathās.; Ragh.; Yājñ.; MārkP.; Rājat. &c.; (*as*), m. a kind of time (in music), L.; a section, division of a book, chapter. **—kārmuka**, mfn. with raised bow. **—gada**, mfn. with uplifted mace. **—śūla**, mfn. with raised spear. **—sruc** (*údyata-*), mfn. one who has raised a ladle (to offer a libation), RV. i, 31, 5.

Udyatâyudha or **udyatâstra**, mfn. having an uplifted weapon, MBh.; R.; BhP. &c.

U'd-yati, *is*, f. raising, elevation, RV. i, 190, 3; TS.; ŚBr.; AitBr.

Ud-yantṛi, mfn. one who raises or elevates, RV. i, 178, 3.

Ud-yama, *as,* m. the act of raising or lifting up, elevation, R.; Yājñ.; Pañcat. &c.; undertaking, beginning; the act of striving after, exerting one's self, exertion, strenuous and continued effort, perseverance, diligence, zeal, R.; Kum.; Pañcat.; VarBṛS. &c. **— bhaṅga,** m. frustration of effort, discouragement, dissuasion; desisting. **— bhṛit,** mfn. bearing or undergoing exertion, Bhartṛ.

Ud-yamana, *am,* n. raising, elevation, Pāṇ.; Sarvad.; effort, exertion, Daś.

Ud-yamita, mfn. excited, instigated, Kir. ix, 66.

Udyamin, mfn. undertaking, persevering; making effort, active, Yājñ.; Kathās.; Bhartṛ.

U'dyamīyas, mfn. raising more or excessively, RV. x, 86, 6.

1. **Ud-yamya,** mfn. to be undertaken with exertion, W.

2. **Ud-yamya,** ind. p. having lifted or taken up; having made exertion.

Ud-yāmá, *as,* m. the act of erecting or stretching out, ŚBr. viii, 5, 1, 13; a rope, cord, TS.; ŚBr.; KātyŚr.

उद्या ud-√yā, P. *-yāti,* to rise (as the sun), RV. x, 37, 3; to go out or away, start from, ŚBr. xiv, 5, 4, 1; Ragh.; to raise one's self, rise, Gīt.; Kathās.; to rise, originate from, Rājat.; Naish.; to excel, surpass (acc.), MārkP.

Ud-yāna, *am,* n. the act of going out, AV. viii, 1, 6; walking out; a park, garden, royal garden, Yājñ.; R.; Megh.; Śak.; Pañcat. &c.; purpose, motive, L.; N. of a country in the north of India. **— pāla, -pālaka,** m., **-pālikā, -pālī,** f. a gardener, superintendent or keeper of a garden, Kum.; Kathās. &c. **— mālā,** f. a row of gardens, Kāvyād. **— rakshaka,** m. a gardener.

Udyānaka, *am,* n. a garden, park, R.

Ud-yāpana, *am,* n. the act of bringing to a conclusion, finishing, accomplishment.

Ud-yāpanikā, f. return home from a journey, Hpar.

Ud-yāpita, mfn. brought to a conclusion, finished, accomplished, MW.

उद्याव ud-yāva. See *ud-√2. yu.*

उद्यास ud-yāsá, *as,* m. (*√yas*), exertion, effort, VS. xxxix, 11.

उद्यु ud-√2. yu, P. Ā. *-yauti* (1. pl. *-yuvāmahe*) to draw up or upwards, RV. vi, 57, 6; TS. ii, 6, 5, 5; to join, mix; to confound.

Ud-yāva, *as,* m. the act of mixing, joining, Pāṇ.

U'd-yuta, mfn. mixed with, MaitrS.; confounded, mad, AV. vi, 111, 2.

उद्युज् 1. ud-√yuj, P. Ā. *-yunakti, -yuṅkte* (inf. *-yujé,* AV.) to join, be in contact with, AV. vi, 70, 2; to get off or away, go away, ŚBr. iv, 1, 5, 7; Lāṭy.; to go near, undergo, prepare; to make efforts, be active, MBh.; Kathās.; Daś.: Caus. *-yojayati,* to excite, incite, make active or quick, stimulate to exertion, MBh.; Hariv.; R.

Ud-yukta, mfn. undergoing, undertaking; prepared or ready for, zealously active, labouring for some desired end, MBh.; R.; Kathās. &c.

Ud-yugá, *am,* n. a particular disease [BRD.], AV. v, 22, 11.

2. **Ud-yuj,** *k,* f. endeavour, striving after, MānGṛ.

Ud-yoga, *as,* m. the act of undertaking anything, exertion, perseverance, strenuous and continuous endeavour; active preparation, Yājñ.; Kathās.; Hit. &c. **— parvan,** n., N. of the fifth book of the Mahābhārata; also of a section of the fifth book (chapters 45–47) of the Rāmāyaṇa. **— samartha,** mfn. capable of exertion.

Udyogin, mfn. one who makes effort, active, laborious, persevering, energetic.

Ud-yojita, mfn. excited, raised, gathered (as clouds), Prab.

उद्युध् ud-√yudh, P. *-yodhati,* to bubble up (as water), AV. xii, 3, 29; to fly into a passion, show enmity or hatred against, TāṇḍyaBr.

उद्र udrá, *as,* m. (*√ud,* Uṇ. ii, 13), a kind of aquatic animal (a crab, Comm on VS.; an otter, Uṇ. & L.), VS. xxiv, 37; (*am*), n. water; see *anudrá* and *udrín.* **— pāraka,** m., N. of a Nāga, MBh.

Udraka, *as,* m., N. of a Ṛishi.

Udrín, mfn. abounding in water, RV.

उद्रङ्क udraṅka and **udraṅga,** *as,* m. a town, L.; N. of Hariścandra's city (floating in the air), L.

उद्रञ्ज् ud-√rañj, Intens. P. *-rārajīti,* to become agitated, fly into a passion, AV. vi, 71, 2.

उद्रथ ud-ratha, *as,* m. the pin of the axle of a carriage, L.; a cock, L.

उद्रम् ud-√ram, P. (impf. *-aramat*) to cease, leave off (speaking), ŚBr. vii, 4, 1, 39.

उद्रश्मि ud-raśmi, mfn. radiating upwards, sending rays of light upwards, Śiś. iii, 62.

उद्राव ud-rāva, *as,* m. (*√ru*), a loud noise, W.

उद्रिच् ud-√ric, Pass. *-ricyate* (pf. *-ririce,* RV.) to be prominent, stand out, exceed, excel, preponderate, RV. i, 102, 7; vii, 32, 12; to increase, abound in: Caus. *-recayati,* to enhance, cause to increase, Rājat.

Ud-rikta, mfn. prominent, standing out, R.; increased, augmented, abundant, abounding, excessive; superfluous, left, remaining, TS. vii; ĀśvŚr.; MBh.; Mn. &c. **— citta,** n. a mind abounding in (goodness &c.), Pañcar. i, 6, 12; (mfn.) having a lofty mind, proud, arrogant, Kathās. xci, 55. **— cetas,** mfn. high-minded, Kathās. xxxii, 73; intoxicated, L.

Ud-reka, *as,* m. abundance, overplus, excess, preponderance, superiority, predominance, MBh.; Suśr.; VarBṛS. &c.; (*ā*), f. the plant Melia Sempervirens, L.

Udrekin, mfn. excessive, violent, Sāh.; (ifc.) abounding in, giving preponderance, Suśr.

Udrecaka, mfn. enhancing or augmenting exceedingly, Rājat. iv, 526.

उद्रुच् ud-√ruc, Ā. (impf. 2. sg. *-arocathās*) to shine forth, AV. xiii, 3, 23.

उद्रुज ud-ruja, mfn. (*√ruj*), destroying, breaking down; undermining, rooting up, Pāṇ.; Ragh.; (cf. *kūlam-udruja.*)

उद्रुध् ud-√2. rudh, P. (aor. *-arautsīt*) to push away, turn out, ŚBr. xiv, 7, 1, 41.

उद्रोधन ud-rodhana, *am,* n. (*√1. rudh* = *√ruh*), rising, growing, AitBr. iv, 14, 5.

उद्वंश ud-vaṇśa, mfn. of high descent, Hcat.; (*as*), m., N. of a Ṛishi; (*am*), n., N. of a Sāman, TāṇḍyaBr.

Udvaṇśīya, *am,* n., N. of a Sāman. **Udvaṇśīyôttara,** *am,* n. id., TāṇḍyaBr.

उद्वक्त्र ud-vaktra, mfn. having the face uplifted.

उद्वत् ud-vát, *t,* f. (fr. 1. *ud*), height, elevation, RV.; AV. xii, 1, 2; Kauś.; (mfn.) containing the word *ud,* TāṇḍyaBr.; (*t*), n., N. of a Sāman, Lāṭy.

उद्वत्सर ud-vatsará, *as,* m. the last year of a cycle, MaitrS.; Kāṭh.; VarBṛS.

Udvatsarīya, mfn. belonging to the above year, VarBṛS.

उद्वद् ud-√vad, P. *-vadati* (inf. *úd-vaditos,* MaitrS. i, 4, 10) to raise one's voice, utter, speak, pronounce, RV. x, 166, 5; AV. v, 20, 11; MaitrS.; ŚBr.; TBr.: Caus. *-vādayati,* to cause to proclaim; to cause to resound, ŚBr.

Ud-vādana, *am,* n. the act of crying aloud, proclaiming, KātyŚr.; Vait.

उद्वध् ud-√vadh, P. (aor. Subj. *-vadhīt*) to tear to pieces, lacerate, RV. ii, 42, 2; VS. xiii, 16.

उद्वन ud-vana, mfn. steep, precipitous, Kāṭh.; (cf. *pravaṇa.*)

उद्वप् ud-√2. vap, P. *-vápati* (pf. 2. du. *-ūpáthus* and *-ūpathus,* RV.) to pour out, take out; to scrape, dig up; to throw away, destroy, annul, RV.; AV.; VS.; ŚBr.; KātySr.; ĀśvŚr.; Kauś.: Caus. *-vāpayati,* to cause to pour out or away, ŚāṅkhGṛ. iii, 1, 3; to cause to dig up, ŚBr.

Ud-vapana, *am,* n. the act of pouring out, shaking out; (*ī*), f., see *pishṭôd°.*

Ud-vāpa, *as,* m. the act of throwing out, removing, Comm. on Nyāyam.; ejection, KātyŚr.; Kauś.; (in logic) non-existence of a consequent resulting from the absence of an antecedent, W.

Ud-vāpana, *am,* n. the act of putting out (the fire), Comm. on ĀpŚr.

उद्वम् ud-√vam, P. *-vamati,* to vomit out, spit out; to give out, emit, shed (tears), throw (arrows, glances &c.), TS.; MBh.; Ragh. &c.

Ud-vamana, *am,* n. the act of giving out, emitting, shedding (e. g. tears), Pāṇ. iii, 1, 16.

Ud-vamita, mfn. vomited, ejected, L.

Ud-vānta, mfn. id.; (*as*), m. an elephant out of rut, L.

Ud-vānti, *is,* f. the act of giving out, emitting, Vop.

Ud-vāmin, mfn. ifc. vomiting out, Car.

उद्वयस् úd-vayas, mfn. one by whom corn is produced or ripened [Mahīdh.], VS. ix, 3.

उद्वर्ग ud-varga. See *ud-√vṛij.*

उद्वर्त ud-varta, &c. See *ud-√vṛit.*

उद्वर्त्मन् ud-vartman, *a,* n. a wrong road, MaitrUp. vi, 30.

उद्वर्धन ud-vardhana. See *ud-√vṛidh.*

उद्वस् ud-√5. vas, P. *-vasati,* to live away, MW.: Caus. P. Ā. *-vāsayati, -te,* to cause to live away; to banish, expel; to remove, separate, VS.; ŚBr.; AitBr.; KātyŚr.; BhP. &c.; to root out (trees), ĀśvGṛ.; to destroy, lay waste, Hariv.; Pañcat.

1. **Ud-vāsa** (for 2. see s.v.), *as,* m. banishment, exile; abandonment; setting free, dismission, gaṇa *balâdi,* Pāṇ. v, 2, 136; BhP.; carrying out for slaughter, killing, L. **— vat,** mfn., Pāṇ. v, 2, 136.

Ud-vāsana, *am,* n. the act of taking out or away (from the fire), KātyŚr.; Kauś.; quitting, abandoning; expelling, banishing; taking out in order to kill, killing, slaughter, L.

Udvāsin, mfn., gaṇa *balâdi,* Pāṇ. v, 2, 136.

Udvāsī-kārin, mfn. making (a country) inhabited, TBr. i, 2, 6, 7.

Ud-vāsya, mfn. to be taken off; to be put away, BhP., relating to the killing of a sacrificial animal, R.

उद्वस ud-vasa, mfn. (cf. *dur-vasa*) uninhabited, empty, Rājat.; disappeared, gone, Viddh.; (*am*), n. solitude, Śatr.

उद्वह् ud-√vah, P. Ā. *-vahati, -te,* to lead or carry out or up, draw out, save, RV. i, 50, 1; vii, 69, 7; AV.; AitBr.; TāṇḍyaBr.; Hariv. &c.; to bear up, lift up, elevate, MBh.; BhP.; to take or lead away (a bride from her parents' house), lead home, marry, PārGṛ.; Gobh.; Yājñ.; Ragh.; Kathās. &c.; to lead to or near, bring, BhP.; to bear (a weight or burden), wear (clothes &c.), MBh.; R.; Kum.; Śiś. &c.; to support (the earth), rule, govern, Rājat.; Kathās. &c.; to wear, have, possess; to show, BhP.; VarBṛS.; Rājat.; Sāh.; Pañcat. &c.: Caus. *-vāhayati,* to cause to marry, marry, MBh.; Pañcat.

Ud-ūḍha, mfn. borne up, raised up; carried; sustained; recovered, acquired, MW.; married; coarse, gross, heavy, fat, L.; material, substantial; much, exceeding, L.

Ud-vahá, mfn. carrying or leading up, AV. xix, 25, 1; carrying away, taking up or away, ŚBr.; Pāṇ.; continuing, propagating, MBh.; R.; Kathās.; eminent, superior, best, L.; (*as*), m. the act of leading home (a bride), marriage, BhP.; son, offspring, MBh.; R.; Ragh.; chief offspring, Ragh. ix, 9; the fourth of the seven winds or courses of air (viz. that which supports the Nakshatras or lunar constellations and causes their revolution), Hariv.; the vital air that conveys nourishment upwards; one of the seven tongues of fire; N. of a king, MBh.; (*ā*), f. daughter, L.

Ud-vahana, *am,* n. the act of lifting or bringing up, Suśr.; Ragh.; carrying, drawing, driving; being carried on, riding (inst.), Pañcat.; Ragh.; Kum.; Mn. &c.; leading home (a bride), wedding, marriage, PārGṛ.; BhP.; possessing, showing, Rājat.; the lowest part of a pillar, pediment, Comm. on VarBṛS.

Ud-vāha, *as,* m. the act of leading home (a bride), marriage, wedding, MBh.; Kathās.; VarBṛS. &c. **— karman,** n. the marriage ceremony, Mn. iii, 43. **— tattva,** n., N. of a work of Raghu-nandana on marriage ceremonies. **Udvāharksha,** n. (°*a* + *ṛi*°) 'marriage Nakshatra,' one held to be auspicious for a marriage, BhP. x, 53, 4.

Ud-vāhana, mf(*ī*)n. dr wing up, lifting up, L.; (*am*), n. anything which raises or draws up, L.; ploughing a field twice, L.; anxiety, anxious regret, L.; marriage, L.; (*ī*), f. a cord, rope, L.

Udvāhika, mfn. relating to a marriage, matrimonial, Mn. ix, 65.
Ud-vāhita, mfn. raised, lifted or pulled up, eradicated.
Udvāhin, mfn. one who raises or draws up, L.; one who marries, relating to marriage, L.; (*inī*), f. a rope, L.
Udvoḍhu-kāma, mfn. desirous of marrying.
Ud-voḍhṛi, *ḍhā*, m. a husband, T. (quoted from the Mahā-nirṇaya-tantra).

उद्वह्नि *ud-vahni*, mfn. emitting sparks or gleams (as an eye), Śiś. iv, 28. **-jvāla**, mfn. sending flames upwards, shining upwards, Kathās. cxviii, 76.

उद्वा *ud-√vā*, P. *-vāti*, to be blown out, go out, AitBr. viii, 28, 10; Kauś.; (cf. *ud-√vai*.)
1. **Ud-vāna**, *am*, n. the going out, being extinguished, Nyāyam.

उद्वाचन *ud-vācana*, mfn. causing to cry out (?), AV. v, 8, 8.

उद्वादन *ud-vādana*. See *ud-√vad*.

उद्वान 2. *ud-vāna*, mfn. (probably corrupted fr. *ud-vānta*), ejected, vomited, L.; (*am*), n. the act of ejecting, vomiting, L.; a stove, L.

उद्वार *úd-vāra*, mfn. (fr. 1. *vāra* = *vāla*), having the tail raised, TS. i, 8, 9, 2; TBr. i, 7, 3, 6.

उद्वालवत् *udvāla-vat*, *ān*, m., N. of a Gandharva, ŚBr. xi, 2, 3, 9; Comm. on VS.

उद्वाश् *ud-√vāś*, Ā. *-vāśyate*, to address in a weeping voice or while uttering lamentations, Bhaṭṭ. iii, 32.

उद्वाष्प *ud-vāshpa*, mfn. shedding tears, Kathās. **-tva**, n. the act of shedding tears, Vikr. 29.

उद्वास 2. *ud-vāsa*, mf(*ā*)n. (for 1. see *ud-√5. vas*) one who has put off clothes (said of a woman who has put off her soiled clothes after her period of impurity), Kauś.
Ud-vāsas, mfn. id., ŚBr.

उद्विकासिन् *ud-vikāsin*, mfn. (√*kas*), blown, expanded, open, Kād.

उद्विघुष् *ud-vi-√ghush*, Caus. P. *-ghoshayati*, to cause to sound loud; to declare or proclaim aloud, BhP.

उद्विचक्ष् *ud-vi-√caksh*, Ā. *-cashṭe*, to perceive, BhP. xi, 23, 44.

उद्विज् *ud-√vij*, Ā. *-vijate* (rarely *-vejate* in MBh.), P. *-vijati* (rarely), to gush or spring upwards, AV. iv, 15, 3; to be agitated, grieved or afflicted; to shudder, tremble, start; to fear, be afraid of (with gen., abl. or instr.), MBh.; BhP.; Pañcat. &c.; to shrink from, recede, leave off, Śatr.; Bhaṭṭ.; to frighten, MBh. ii, 178: Caus. P. *-vejayati*, to frighten, terrify, intimidate, MBh.; Kathās.; Mṛicch.; Pañcat. &c.; to cause to shudder, Vāgbh.; to revive a fainting person (by sprinkling water), Suśr.; to tease, molest, Kum.; Prab.; Śārṅg.
Ud-vigna, mfn. shuddering, starting, frightened, terrified, MBh.; R.; Suśr.; Ragh. &c.; sorrowful, anxious, grieving for (an absent lover), MBh.; Daś.; Bhag. &c. **-citta**, **-cetas**, **-manas**, or **-hṛidaya**, mfn. having the mind or soul agitated by fright, depressed in mind; sorrowful, anxious, distressed, MBh.; BhP.; MārkP. &c. **-dris**, f. and **-locana**, n. a frightened glance; (mfn.) one who looks frightened, BhP.
Ud-vega, mfn. going swiftly; an express messenger, a runner, courier, &c., L.; steady, composed, tranquil, L.; ascending, mounting, going up or upwards, L.; an ascetic whose arms by long habit continue always raised above the head, L.; (*as*), m. trembling, waving, shaking; agitation, anxiety; regret, fear, distress (occasioned by separation from a beloved object), MBh.; Ragh.; Pañcat. &c.; the being offended, Kāvyād.; admiration, astonishment, L.; (*udvegam* √1. *kṛi*, to disturb; to be disturbed in mind, R.; Sāh.; Pañcat. &c.); (*am*), n. the fruit of the Areca Faufel; the Areca nut (called betel nut because eaten with the betel leaf), L. **-kara**, **-kāraka**, **-kārin**, mfn. causing anxiety or agitation or distress, Pañcat. **-vāhin**, mfn. bringing or causing agitation, disquieting, troubling, Kathās.
Udvegin, mfn. suffering distress, anxious, unhappy, L.; causing anxiety or agitation of mind, Pañcat.
Ud-vejaka, mfn. agitating, distressing, annoying, causing pain or sorrow, Śārṅg.
Ud-vejana, mfn. id., Kathās.; Kām.; (*am*), n. shudder, shuddering, Suśr.; agitation, fear; the act of terrifying, causing to shudder, Daśar.; Sāh. **-kara**, mfn. causing to shake with horror, causing excitement or pain, Mn.
Ud-vejanīya, mfn. to be feared; to be shrunk from, MBh.; R.; Pañcat.; Suśr.
Ud-vejayitṛi, mfn. terrifying; a terrifier, MW.
Ud-vejita, mfn. caused to shudder; grieved, pained, afflicted.
Ud-vejin, mfn. causing anxiety or agitation of mind, causing shudder or horror, Kathās.

उद्विदॄ *ud-vi-√dṝi*, Caus. P. *-dārayati*, to dig up, turn or tear up, BhP. x, 68, 71.

उद्विद्ध *ud-viddha*, mfn. See *ud-√vyadh*.

उद्विवर्हण *ud-vivarhaṇa*, *am*, n. (√*vṛih*), the act of plucking out, tearing out, BhP.

उद्विसृज् *ud-vi-√sṛij*, P. *-sṛijati*, to leave, abandon, BhP. iv, 31, 32.

उद्वीक्ष् *ud-vīksh* (*ud-vi-√īksh*), Ā. *-vīkshate*, to look up or upwards, look at, view; to perceive, Śak.; Ratnāv.; Amar. &c.; to consider, examine, Pañcat.
Ud-vīkshaṇa, *am*, n. the act of looking up or upwards; look, view, MBh.; Ragh.
Ud-vīkshita, mfn. looked at; perceived, MBh.; Ragh.
Ud-vīkshya, ind. p. having looked upwards &c.

उद्वीज् *ud-√vij*, Pass. *-vijyate*, to be blown upon or against, MBh. iii, 1757.

उद्वृ *ud-√1. vṛi*.
Ud-vṛitya, ind. p. having opened, opening wide (the eyes), MBh.

उद्वृ *ud-√2. vṛi*, Ā. (Impv. 2. sg. *-varasva*) to elect, select, choose, R. (ed. Schlegel) ii, 11, 9; (v. l. *-dharasva*, ed. Bombay.)

उद्वृंहण *ud-vṛiṇhaṇa*. See *ud-bṛiṇhaṇa*.

उद्वृज् *ud-√vṛij*, P. (Impv. 2. sg. *-vṛiṅgdhi*) to tear out, pluck out, root up (figuratively), KaushUp. ii, 7: Intens. (p. *-várīvṛijat*) to stretch out, extend, RV. vi, 58, 2.
Ud-varga, *as*, m. one who roots up, a destroyer, KaushUp. ii, 7.

उद्वृत् *ud-√vṛit*, P. (pf. *-vavarta*) to go asunder, burst open, ŚBr. iv, 4, 3, 4: Ā. *-vartate*, to go upwards, rise, ascend, swell; to bubble up, overflow, Hariv.; BhP.; Suśr.; to be puffed up with pride, become arrogant or extravagant; to proceed from, originate, ŚBr. xiv, 5, 1, 5; to fall down, BhP.: Caus. P. *-vartayati*, to beat to pieces, split, burst, RV. viii, 14, 13; TBr.; MBh.; Hariv.; to swing or throw out, Kauś.; to cause to swell up.
Ud-varta, mfn. superfluous, redundant, plentiful; left over as a remainder, L.; (*as*), m. a remainder, surplus, L.
Ud-vartaka, mfn. causing to rise, increasing, MW.; (ifc.) rubbing, Pāṇ.; (*as*), m. (in math.) the quantity assumed for the purpose of an operation.
Ud-vartana, mfn. causing to burst, Hariv. 9563; (*am*), n. the act of rising, going up, ascending, jumping up, Megh.; Kathās.; VarBṛS.; the springing up of plants or grain &c.; swelling up, overflowing, Car.; drawing out metal, laminating, W.; grinding, pounding; rubbing or kneading the body, rubbing and cleansing it with fragrant unguents; the unguents used for that purpose (or to relieve pains in the limbs &c.), Yājñ.; Mn.; Suśr.; Kathās. &c.; bad behaviour, bad conduct, L.
Ud-vartita, mfn. caused to come out or swell up, Kathās. xxix, 80; raised, elevated, Suśr.; perfumed, scented, rubbed, kneaded, shampooed, Pañcat.; Subh.
Ud-vartin, mfn. ifc. rubbing or kneading with.
Ud-vṛitta, mfn. swollen up, swelling; prominent, Suśr.; MBh.; Hariv.; Bhartṛ.; excited, agitated, waving, MBh.; Ragh.; BhP.; Suśr. &c.; extravagant, ill-behaved, ill-mannered, proud, arrogant, MBh.; R.; Rājat. &c.; turned up; opened, opened wide (as eyes), MBh. vii, 5405; ix, 432; MārkP. xiv, 62 (erroneous for *ud-vṛita*, BRD.); (*as*), m. a particular position of the hands in dancing; (*am*), n. (in astron.) the east and west hour circle or six o'clock line (cf. *un-maṇḍala*).
Ud-vṛitya, mfn. turning round or about, BhP. x, 13, 56.

उद्वृध् *ud-√vṛidh*. See *ud-vṛiddha* below.
Ud-vardhana, *am*, n. sly or suppressed laughter, L.
Ud-vṛiddha, mfn. grown up, come forth, appearing, Rājat. i, 252.

उद्वृष् *ud-√vṛish*, Ā. (Impv. 2. sg. *-vāvṛishasva*, RV. viii, 50, 7; p. *-vāvṛishāṇá*, RV. iv, 20, 7; 29, 3) to pour out, distribute plentifully.

उद्वृषभयज्ञ *ud-vṛishabha-yajña*, *as*, m. a particular sacrifice, Comm. on Jaim.; Comm. on Nyāyam.

उद्वृह् *ud-√vṛih*, P. *-vṛihati*, to draw up, pull out by the roots, eradicate, RV. iii, 30, 17; vi, 48, 17; TS.; ŚBr.; KātyŚr.; MBh.; to draw out (e. g. a sword from the scabbard), MBh.; Bhaṭṭ.
Ud-vṛiḍha, mfn. drawn or pulled out, eradicated, KātyŚr.

उद्वे *ud-√ve*, P. *-vayati*, to weave or fasten to or up, AitBr. iv, 19, 3; TBr. i, 2, 4, 2.
Ud-uta, mfn. bound up, tied on, ŚBr. v, 5, 4, 28.

उद्वेग *ud-vega*, *ud-vejaka*, &c. See cols. 1 & 2.

उद्वेदि *ud-vedi*, mfn. furnished with an elevated altar, Ragh. xvii, 9.

उद्वेप् *ud-√vep*, Ā. *-vepate*, to tremble, be agitated or frightened, AV. v, 21, 2; TBr.; Kāṭh.; MBh.: Caus. P. *-vepáyati*, to cause to tremble, agitate, frighten, AV.
Ud-vepa, *as*, m. the act of trembling, agitation, T.; (mfn.) trembling, agitated, T.; gaṇa *saṃkalâdi*, Pāṇ. iv, 2, 75 (not in the Kāś.)

उद्वेल *ud-vela*, mfn. running over the brim or bank, overflowing, Kathās.; BhP.; Ragh.; AgP.; excessive, extraordinary, Kād.; loosened, free from, Prasannar.
Udvelaya, Nom. P. *udvelayati*, to cause to run over or overflow, Prasannar.
Udvelita, mfn. caused to overflow, Hcat.

उद्वेल्ल् *ud-√vell*, P. *-vellati*, to toss up; to raise one's self, rise, Mālatīm. 140, 3; Kathās. lix, 42.
Ud-vellita, mfn. tossed up, elevated, high, Kathās.

उद्वेष्ट् *ud-√vesht*, Ā. *-veshṭate*, to wind or twist upwards, writhe, MBh.: Caus. P. *-veshṭayati*, to untwist, Kathās.; to open, unseal (a letter), Mālav.
Ud-veshṭa, mfn. investing, enveloping, surrounding, L.; (*as*), m. the act of surrounding, enclosing, tying together, Car.; investing a town, besieging or surrounding it, W.
1. **Ud-veshṭana** (for 2. see s.v.), *am*, n. the act of surrounding, wrapping, tying together; contraction; convulsion (of the heart), straitening; pain in the back of the body, Suśr.
Ud-veshṭanīya, mfn. to be unbound or unfastened, Megh. 95.
Ud-veshṭita, mfn. surrounded, invested, enclosed.

उद्वेष्टन 2. *ud-veshṭana*, mfn. freed from bonds or ties, unbound, unfettered, Ragh.; Kum.

उद्वै *ud-√vai*, P. *-vāyati* (aor. *-avāsīt*, ŚBr. x, 3, 3, 8) to become weak or languish, faint, be extinguished, go out (as fire), die, TS.; TBr.; ŚBr.; ChUp.: Caus. *-vāpayati*, to cause to extinguish or go out, TBr. i, 4, 4, 7.

उद्वोढृ *ud-voḍhṛi*. See col. 1.

उद्व्यध् *ud-√vyadh*.
Ud-viddha, mfn. tossed upwards, high, elevated, MBh.; R.

उद्व्युदस् *ud-vy-ud-√2. as*, P. *-asyati*, to give up wholly or completely, BhP. iv, 7, 44.

उद्व्रज् *ud-√vraj*, P. *-vrajati*, to go away or

out of (the house); to leave, abandon (one's house), TāṇḍyaBr.; ChUp.

उधन् udhán, a, n. = ūdhan, an udder, MaitrS. i, 3, 26; see also try-udhan.

Udhas, n. = ūdhas, q. v., L.

उध्रस् 1. udhras, cl. 9. P. udhrasnāti, u-dhrasām-babhūva or -cakāra or -āsa, audhrāsīt, to gather, glean, Dhātup.; Vop.

उध्रस् 2. udhras, cl. 10. P. Ā. udhrāsayati, -te, aor. audidhrasat, -ta, to glean; to throw or cast upwards, Dhātup.; Vop.

उन्द् und, undana. See 2. ud.

उन्दरु undaru = the next, L.

उन्दुर undura, as, m. a rat, mouse, Suśr. **-karṇikā** (Suśr.) and **-karṇī** (L.), f. the plant Salvinia Cucullata.

Unduru, us, m. a rat, mouse.

उन्न unna. See 2. ud.

उन्नट् un-naṭ, Caus. -nāṭayati, to jump towards; to injure (with gen.), Kāś. on Pāṇ. ii, 3, 56.

उन्नद् un-nad (ud-√nad), P. -nadati, to cry out, roar, make a noise, MBh.; R.; BhP.; Kum.; Pañcat.

Un-nāda, as, m. crying out, clamour, MBh.; N. of a son of Kṛishṇa, BhP.

उन्नभ् un-nabh (ud-√nabh), Caus. (Impv. 2. sg. -nambhaya) to tear open, open, TS.

उन्नम् un-nam (ud-√nam), P. -namati, to bend upwards, raise one's self, rise, ascend, Prab.; Mṛicch.; Pañcat.; Bhartṛ. &c.; to raise up, lift up, Pañcat.: Caus. -namayati or -nāmayati, to bend upwards, raise, erect, elevate, MBh.; R.; Śak.; Kathās. &c.

Un-natá, mfn. bent or turned upwards, elevated, lifted up, raised, high, tall, prominent, projecting, lofty, MBh.; Śak.; Hit. &c.; (figuratively) high, eminent, sublime, great, noble, Kathās.; Bhartṛ.; Sāh. &c.; having a large hump, humpbacked (as a bull), VS.; TS.; Lāṭy.; (as), m. a boa (aja-gara), L., N. of a Buddha, Lalit.; of one of the seven Ṛishis under Manu Cākshusha, VP.; of a mountain, VP.; (am), n. elevation, ascension; elevated part, TS.; means of measuring the day, SiddhŚir.; Sūryas. **-kāla**, m. a method of determining the time from the shadow, SiddhŚir. **-kokilā**, f. a kind of musical instrument. **-caraṇa**, mfn. with uplifted feet or paws; rampant, Hit. **-tva**, n. height, sublimity, majesty, Ragh. **-nābhi**, mfn. 'having a projecting navel,' corpulent. **-śiras**, mfn. holding up the head, carrying the head high, with head upraised. **Unnatânata**, mfn. elevated and depressed, uneven; undulating, wavy, L.

Un-nati, is, f. rising, ascending, swelling up; elevation, height; increase, advancement, prosperity, Pañcat.; Bhartṛ.; Kathās. &c.; N. of a daughter of Daksha and wife of Dharma, BhP.; of the wife of Garuḍa, L. **-mat**, mfn. elevated, projected; high, sublime, of rank, respectable, Kathās.; Amar.; Śiś. &c. **Unnatîśa**, m. 'the lord of Unnati,' N. of Garuḍa.

Un-namana, am, n. the act of bending upwards; raising, lifting up, Suśr.; increase, prosperity, Prasannar.

Un-namayya, ind. p. having raised, Kum.

Un-namita, mfn. caused to rise, raised, elevated, lifted or pulled up; heightened, increased, Suśr.; Ragh.; Śak.; Hit. &c.

Un-namya, ind. p. having raised, raising, elevating; causing to increase &c., Yājñ.; Kathās.; BhP.; VarBṛS. &c.

Un-namra, mfn. ascending, rising; erect, upright, elevated, lofty, high. **-tā**, f. ascension, ascent, rising, Rājat.

Un-nāma, as, m. the act of bending one's self upwards, raising one's self, rising, Pañcat.

Un-nāmita, mfn. = un-namita above.

Un-nāmya, ind. p. = un-namya above.

उन्नय un-naya. See col. 2.

उन्नयन 1. un-nayana (ud-na°; for 2. see col. 2), mfn. having upraised eyes. **-paṅkti**, mfn. having the line of the eyes upraised, Ragh. iv, 3.

उन्नश् un-naś (ud-√1. naś), P. (Subj. -naśat) to reach, obtain, RV. i, 164, 22; ii, 23, 8.

उन्नस un-nasa, mfn. having a prominent nose, BhP.; Kāś.

उन्नह् un-nah (ud-√nah), P. -nahyati, to tie up, bind up; to free from fetters or ties, push out, Suśr.; Kauś.; to free one's self from fetters, rush out, get out, MBh.

Un-naddha, mfn. tied or bound up, Ragh.; swollen, increased, BhP.; Gīt.; unbound, excessive, BhP.; arrogant, impudent, haughty, self-conceited, MBh.; BhP.; Rājat.

Un-nāha, as, m. excess, abundance, BhP. xi, 19, 43; impudence, haughtiness, BhP.; sour gruel (made from the fermentation of rice), L.

उन्नहन un-nahana (fr. nahana with ud in the sense of 'apart'), freed from fetters, unfettered, unbound, BhP. xi, 1, 4.

उन्नाभ un-nābha, as, m., N. of a king, Ragh.

उन्नाय un-nāya. See below.

उन्नाल un-nāla (ud-nā°), mfn. having an upraised stalk, Bālar.; Kād.

उन्निद्र un-nidra, mfn. (fr. nidrā with ud), sleepless, awake, Śak. 137 b; Megh.; expanded (as a flower), budded, blown, Kathās.; Śiś.; Kāvyād. &c.; shining (as the moon, supposed to be awake when others are asleep; or as the rising sun), Prab.; Prasannar.; bristling (as hair), Naish. **-tā**, f. sleeplessness.

Unnidraka, am, n. sleeplessness, Kathās.

Unnidraya, Nom. P. unnidrayati, to make sleepless, awaken.

उन्निधा un-ni-dhā (ud-ni-√dhā), Ā. -dhatte, to hold above, BhP.

उन्नी 1. un-nī (ud-√nī), P. Ā. -nayati, -te, to lead up or out, lead upwards or up to; to bring or fetch out of, free from, help, rescue, redeem; to raise, set up, erect, promote, RV.; AV.; ŚBr.; KātyŚr.; MBh. &c.; to draw up, fill up a vessel by drawing (a fluid out of another vessel), RV. ii, 14, 9; VS.; TS.; ŚBr. &c.; to raise up, lift up (only Ā., Pāṇ. i, 3, 36); to put up, lay up, MBh.; to press or squeeze out (e. g. pus), MBh. v, 2776; to lead away (e. g. a calf from its mother), TS.; ŚāṅkhŚr.; KātyŚr.; to lead aside, separate, MBh.; BhP.; to stroke, smooth, Gṛihyas.; to raise, cause, BhP.; to intone, BhP. x, 33, 10; to find out, discover by inference, infer, MBh.; Rājat.; Daś.; Bālar. &c.: Desid. Ā. -ninīshate, to intend or wish to lead out, KaushUp.

Un-naya, as, m. the act of leading up, raising, elevating, hoisting, L.; conclusion, induction, inference, Sāh.; Kāś.

2. **Un-nayana**, am, n. (for 1. see s.v. col. 1) the act of raising, elevating, lifting up, BhP.; taking out of, drawing out (a fluid), KātyŚr.; the vessel out of which a fluid is taken, KātyŚr.; making a straight line, or parting the hair (of a pregnant woman) upwards (see sīmantônnayana); conclusion, induction, inference.

Un-nāya, as, m. the act of raising, elevating, Pāṇ. iii, 3, 26.

2. **Un-nī**, mfn. bringing or leading upwards, Kāś. on Pāṇ. vi, 4, 82.

U'n-nīta, mfn. led up; drawn out (as Soma), RV. ix, 81, 1; TS.; ŚBr. &c.; led away or apart, separated, BhP.; (am), n. the act of drawing out; filling up, AitBr. **-śikha**, mfn. having the locks of hair parted upwards (from the forehead), Suparṇ. **-śushma** (únnīta), mfn. one whose breath goes upwards, MaitrS. i, 1, 11.

Unnītin, mfn. one who has drawn out or filled up, AitBr.

Un-nīya, mfn. to be led upwards, Ved. by Pāṇ. iii, 1, 123.

Un-nīyam, ind. p. pouring or sprinkling upwards, ŚāṅkhGṛ. iv, 14, 4.

Un-netavya, mfn. to be inferred, Comm. on Nyāyam.

Un-netṛi, mfn. one who draws out; (tā), m. the priest who pours the Soma juice into the receptacles, AitBr.; ŚBr.; KātyŚr.; ĀśvŚr. &c.

Unnetra, am, n. the office of the Unnetṛi.

Un-neya, mfn. to be inferred or ascertained by analogy, Comm. on Nyāyam.

उन्मकर un-makara (ud-ma°), as, m. 'a rising Makara,' a kind of ornament for the ears (so shaped), BhP. v, 21, 13.

उन्मज्ज् un-majj (ud-√majj), P. -majjati, to emerge, AV. x, 4, 4 (-májya); TBr.; MBh.; Śak.; Śiś. &c.; to dive, ĀśvGṛ. iv, 4, 10: Caus. -majjayati, to cause to emerge, bear on the surface (Kullūka), Mn. viii, 115.

Un-majjana, am, n. the act of emerging, emergence, MBh.; (as), m., N. of a demon causing fever, Hariv.

उन्मणि un-maṇi (ud-ma°), is, m. a gem lying on the surface, BhP. x, 27, 26.

उन्मण्डल un-maṇḍala (ud-ma°), am, n. (in astron.) the east and west hour circle or six o'clock line, Sūryas. &c.

उन्मत्त ún-matta, &c. See un-mad.

उन्मथ् un-math or -manth (ud-√ma[n]th), P. -mathnāti, to shake up, disturb, excite, MBh.; BhP.; PārGṛ.; to stir up, rouse, MBh.; BhP.; Pañcar.; to press hard upon, treat with blows, act violently, beat, MBh.; Hariv.; R.; to shake or tear or cut off; to pluck out, root up, rub open; to strike, kill, annul, MBh.; R.; BhP.; Prab. &c.; to refute, confute, Comm. on Bādar.; to mix, mingle: Caus. -mathayati, to shake, agitate, excite, BhP.

Un-mathana, am, n. the act of shaking off, MBh.; Suśr.; throwing off or down, Ragh.; stirring up, churning, BhP. xi, 4, 18; rubbing open, Car.; slaughter, L.

Un-mathay (derived fr. the simple root), P. -mathāyati, to shake up, rouse, AV. xx, 132, 4.

Un-mathita, mfn. shaken, agitated, &c.; mixed, mingled, Suśr.

Un-mathya, ind. p. having shaken, shaking, &c.

Un-mantha, as, m. agitation, L.; killing, slaughter, L.; a disease of the outer ear, Suśr.

Un-manthaka, mfn. shaking up or off, agitating, stirring, L.; throbbing, beating, L.; (as), m. a disease of the outer ear, Suśr.

Un-manthana, am, n. the act of shaking, agitating; beating, throbbing, L.; a means of beating, a stick, staff, cane, T.

Un-mātha, as, m. the act of shaking, Prab.; killing, slaughter, L.; a snare, trap, MBh.; murderer, L.; N. of an attendant of Skanda, MBh. ix, 2532.

Un-māthin, mfn. ifc. shaking, agitating, Prab.; Nāg.; destroying, annulling, Bālar.

उन्मद् un-mad (ud-√mad), P. -mādyati, to become disordered in intellect or distracted, be or become mad or furious, TS.; TBr.; TāṇḍyaBr.; ŚBr.; MBh.; Kathās.: Caus. -madayati or -mādayati, to excite, agitate, AV. vi, 130, 4 (see also ún-madita); to make furious or drunk, inebriate, madden, TS.: MBh.; R.; Daś.; (cf. un-mand, next page.)

U'n-matta, mfn. disordered in intellect, distracted, insane, frantic, mad, AV. vi, 111, 3; AitBr.; Yājñ.; MBh. &c.; drunk, intoxicated, furious, MaitrUp.; MBh.; Śak. &c.; (as), m. the thorn-apple, Datura Metel and Fastuosa, Suśr.; Pterospermum Acerifolium, L.; N. of a Rakshas, R.; of one of the eight forms of Bhairava. **-kīrti**, m., N. of Śiva. **-gaṅgam**, ind. where the Gaṅgā roars, Pat.; (am), n., N. of a place, Siddh. on Pāṇ. ii, 1, 21. **-tara**, mfn. more furious or mad, R. **-tā**, f. or **-tva**, n. insanity, intoxication. **-darśana**, mfn. maniac-like, mad. **-pralapita**, n. the chatter of a madman, Kāś. on Pāṇ. vi, 2, 149. **-bhairava**, m. a form of Bhairava; (ī), f. a form of Durgā; -tantra, n., N. of a work. **-rāghava**, n., N. of a work. **-rūpa**, mfn. maniac-like, mad. **-liṅgin**, mfn. feigning madness. **-vat**, ind. like a madman, as if mad. **-vesha**, m. 'dressed like a madman,' N. of Śiva. **Unmattâvanti**, m., N. of a king, Rājat.

Unmattaka, mfn. insane, mad; drunk, MBh.; Yājñ.; Kād.; (as), m. the thorn-apple, L.

Un-mada, mfn. mad, furious; extravagant; drunk, intoxicated, Pañcat.; Kathās.; Ragh.; Prab. &c.; causing madness, intoxicating, Śiś. vi, 20; (as), m. insanity, intoxication, W.

Un-madana, mfn. inflamed with love, Kum.

U'n-madita, mfn. excited, wrought up into an exstatic state; mad, RV. x, 136, 6; AV. vi, 111, 3; (cf. án-unmadita.)

Unmadishṇu, mfn. (Pāṇ. iii, 2, 136) insane, crazed, intoxicated, Kāvyād.; causing madness, intoxicating, Naish.

Un-māda, mfn. mad, insane, extravagant, BhP.; (*as*), m. insanity, madness; mania (as illness); intoxication, MBh.; Suśr.; Sāh. &c. **–vat**, mfn. mad, insane, wild, extravagant, Kathās.

Un-mādaka, mfn. causing madness, maddening; intoxicating, BhP.; Sāh.

Un-mādana, mfn. id., Kathās.; (*as*), m., N. of one of Kāma's five arrows, Vet.

Un-mādayitṛi, mfn. causing to go mad or be intoxicated, Śak. 46, 2; (Prākṛit *ummādaïttaaṃ*.)

Un-mādin, mfn. insane, mad, intoxicated, Kathās.; causing madness, bewitching; (*ī*), m., N. of a merchant, Kathās.; (*inī*), f., N. of a princess, Kathās. **Unmādi-tā**, f. insanity, madness, Hcar.

Un-māduka, mfn. fond of drinking, TS.; MaitrS.

उन्मन unmana, *as*, m. a particular measure of quantity (= *droṇa*), Śārṅg S.

उन्मनस् un-manas (*ud-ma°*), mfn. excited or disturbed in mind, perplexed, Pāṇ. v, 2, 80; Ragh.; Kathās.; Vikr.; longing or wishing for, eagerly desirous, Bhartṛ.; Śiś.; (*ās*), m. (with Śāktas) one of the seven Ullāsas or mystical degrees.

Unmanaya, Nom. P. *unmanayati*, to excite, make perplexed, Kāvyād.

Unmanaska, mfn. disturbed, perplexed, Mṛicch. **–tā**, f. perplexedness, Śak. (v. l.)

Unmanāya, Nom. Ā. *unmanāyate*, to become perplexed or excited, gaṇa *bhṛiśādi*, Pāṇ. iii, 1, 12; Daś.

Unmanī-√as, to become perplexed or excited; to become absent in mind, Kāś. on Pāṇ. v, 4, 51; Kathās. **Unmanī-√kṛi**, to make perplexed or excited, Kāś.; Prab. **Unmanī-bhāva**, m. absence of mind, BrahmUp. **Unmanī-√bhū** = -√1. *as* above.

उन्मन्द् un-mand (*ud-√1. mand*), P. (Impv. 3. pl. *-mandantu*, RV. viii, 64, 1; pf. *-mamanda*, ii, 33, 6; aor. 3. pl. *-amandishus*, i, 82, 6, and *-ámandishus*, ix, 81, 1) to cheer, delight, amuse.

उन्मयूख un-mayūkha (*ud-ma°*), mfn. shining forth, radiant, Ragh.; Megh.; Kād.

उन्मर्द un-marda. See *un-mṛid*, col. 3.

उन्मा 1. un-mā (*ud-√3. mā*).

2. **Un-má**, f. measure (of altitude), VS.; MaitrS.

Un-māna, *am*, n. measure, measure of altitude or longitude, VarBṛS.; VarBṛ.; Comm. on Pāṇ.; weight; value, price, worth, ŚBr.; Suśr.; (*as*), m. a particular measure of quantity (= *unmana*, q. v.), ŚārṅgS.

Un-mita, mfn. ifc. measuring, having the measure of, Suśr.

Un-miti, *is*, f. measure of altitude, Comm. on Āryabh.; measure; value, price.

Un-meya, mfn. to be weighed, L.; (*am*), n. weight, burden, L.

उन्मार्ग un-mārga (*ud-mā°*), mfn. taking a wrong way, going wrong or astray, BhP.; overflowing, Hariv.; (*as*), m. deviation from the right way, wrong way (lit. and fig.), Pañcat.; MBh.; Hit. &c. **–gata, -gāmin, -yāta, -vartin, -vṛitti**, mfn. going on a wrong road, going wrong, erring (lit. and fig.), MBh.; Rājat.; Kathās. &c. **–gamana**, n. the act of going aside, finding an outlet, Suśr. **–jala-vāhin**, mfn. carrying water by a wrong way.

Unmārgin, mfn. going astray; finding an outlet, Suśr.

उन्मार्जन un-mārjana. See *un-mṛij*, col. 3.

उन्मि un-mi (*ud-√1. mi*), P. (3. pl. *-minvanti*) to set upright (e. g. a post), AitBr. ii, 2, 7.

उन्मिश्र un-miśra (*ud-mi°*), mfn. ifc. mixed with, variegated, Suśr.; MBh.; R. &c.

उन्मिष् un-mish (*ud-√1. mish*), P. *-mishati* (but once Ā., p. *-mishamāṇa*, MBh. ix, 3280) to open the eyes, draw up the eyelids, MBh.; BhP.; Bhag.; Kathās.; to open (as eyes or buds), Hariv.; to come forth, rise, originate, Rājat.; Kathās. &c.; to shine forth, become brilliant, BhP.; Daś.; Rājat.

Un-misha, *as*, m. the act of opening the eyes, L.

Un-mishita, mfn. opened (as an eye), Kum. iv, 2; blown, expanded (as a flower), L.; open (as the face, i. e.) smiling, Hariv.; (*am*), n. the opening (of the eyes), Ragh. v, 68; Kum. v, 25.

Un-mesha, *as*, m. the act of opening the eyes, looking at; winking, twinkling or upward motion of the eyelids, R.; MBh.; flashing, Megh. 84; blowing or blossoming (of a flower), Kum.; coming forth, becoming visible, appearing, Śāntiś.; Prab.; Bhartṛ. &c.

Un-meshaṇa, *am*, n. the coming forth, becoming visible, appearing, Sāh.; Prab.

उन्मी un-mī (*ud-√mī*), P. (Pot. *-mimīyāt*, RV. x, 10, 9) Ā. (or Pass.?) *-mīyate* (ChUp. viii, 6, 5), to disappear.

उन्मील् un-mīl (*ud-√mīl*), P. *-mīlati*, to open the eyes; to open (as an eye), ShaḍvBr.; Hariv.; R.; Hit.; Bhaṭṭ.; to become visible, come forth, appear, Bhartṛ.; Gīt.; Uttarar.; Prab.: Caus. *-mīlayati*, to cause to open, open, MBh.; BhP.; Mṛicch. &c.; to cause to appear, make visible, show, Prab.; Daś.; Comm. on Lāṭy.

Un-mīla, *as*, m. becoming visible, appearance, Kauś.

Un-mīlana, *am*, n. the act of opening the eyes, raising the eyelids, MBh.; the becoming visible, coming forth, appearance, Prab.; Sūryas.

Un-mīlita, mfn. opened (as an eye or a flower), caused to come forth, made visible; (*am*), n. (in rhet.) unconcealed or open reference or allusion to, Kuval.

उन्मुख un-mukha (*ud-mu°*), mf(*ī*)n. raising the face, looking up or at, Suśr.; Megh.; Kum.; Kathās.; Pañcat. &c.; waiting for, expecting, R.; Kum.; Kathās. &c.; near to, about to, Vikr.; Bhartṛ.; VarBṛS. &c.; (*as*), m., N. of an antelope (supposed to have been a Brāhman and hunter in former births), Hariv. 1210. **–tā**, f. the state of having the face raised; state of watching or expectancy, Kathās. **–darśana**, n. looking at with upraised face or with eager expectation, Mudrār.

Unmukhī-karaṇa, n. or -**°kāra**, m. the causing to look at, excitement of attention, Daś.; Sāh.

उन्मुखर un-mukhara (*ud-mu°*), mfn. loud-sounding, noisy, Prab.

उन्मुग्ध un-mugdha. See 1. *un-muh* below.

उन्मुच् un-muc (*ud-√muc*), P. Ā. *-muñcati*, *-te* (Impv. 2. sg. *-mumugdhi*, RV. i, 25, 21; aor. 2. sg. *-amukthās*, AV. ii, 10, 6) to unbind, unfasten, RV. i, 25, 21; AV.; to unfasten one's self, get loose (only Ā.), AV. xiv, 1, 57; ii, 10, 6; ŚBr.; to pull off, take off (clothes &c.), AitBr.; PārGṛ.; Kathās. &c.; to unseal (a letter), Rājat.; to liberate, set free, R.; Kathās.; Pañcat. &c.; to send away, throw off; to sling; to give out, utter, Hariv.; Pañcat.: Caus. *-mocayati*, to unbind, unfasten, set free, MBh.; R.; Kathās.

Un-mukta, mfn. taken off, laid aside, Kathās.; thrown out, uttered, R.; (ifc.) free from; deprived of, wanting, VarBṛS.

Ú n-mukti, *is*, f. deliverance, MaitrS.

Un-mukshá, f. id., ib.

Un-muca, *as*, m., N. of a Ṛishi, MBh.

Un-mucu, *us*, m. id., ib.

Un-mocana, *am*, n. the act of unfastening, unbinding; giving up or away, Kād. **–pramocaná**, *e*, n. du. unfastening and loosening, unfastening completely, AV. v, 30, 2–4.

Un-mocanīya, mfn. to be unfastened, Megh. 95; (v. l. *udveshṭanīya*.)

उन्मुद् un-mud (*ud-√mud*).

Un-mudita, mfn. exulting, rejoicing, BhP.

उन्मुद्र un-mudra (*ud-mu°*), mfn. unsealed; opened, blown (as a flower), L.; unbound, unrestrained, wild (through joy), Prasannar.

उन्मूर्छ् un-murch (*ud-√murch*), P. *-mūrchati*, to become weak, faint, Kuv.; Mcar.

उन्मुष् un-mush (*ud-√mush*).

Un-mushita, mfn. stolen, VarBṛS.

उन्मुह् 1. un-muh (*ud-√muh*).

Un-mugdha, mfn. confounded, confused, Siddh.; silly, stupid, Kathās.

2. **Un-muh** (*k* or *ṭ*, Pāṇ. viii, 2, 33), mfn. confounded, silly.

उन्मूल 1. un-mūla (*ud-mū°*), mfn. eradicated, pulled up by the root, AitBr.; R.; Prab.

2. **Unmūla**, Nom. P. *unmūlati*, to be eradicated, ShaḍvBr.: Caus. P. *unmūlayati*, to eradicate, pull up by the roots; to destroy, extirpate, MBh.; Pañcat.; Kathās.; Prab. &c.

Unmūlana, mfn. eradicating, destroying, Kathās. lxvii, 14; (*am*), n. the act of pulling up or out, Ragh.; Pañcat.; destroying, extirpation, Prab.; Rājat.

Unmūlanīya, mfn. to be eradicated or pulled up by the roots, HYog.

Unmūlita, mfn. eradicated, pulled up by the roots; destroyed, R.; Vikr.

उन्मृज् un-mṛij (*ud-√mṛij*), Ā. (*-mṛijate*, aor. 3. pl. *-amṛikshanta*, RV. i, 126, 4) to pull or draw near to one's self; to receive, get, RV. v, 52, 17; x, 167, 4; AV. xviii, 3, 73; TS. iii, 2, 3, 1; P. Ā. *-mārshṭi*, *-mṛishṭe*, to stroke, make smooth; to rub off, wipe off, polish; to efface, blot out, AV. viii, 6, 1; TBr.; ŚBr.; Kauś.; Yājñ. &c.: Caus. *-mārjayati*, to polish, cleanse.

Un-mārjana, mfn. rubbing or wiping off, effacing, Prab.

Un-mārjita, mfn. polished, clean, ib.

Unmṛijâvamṛijā, f. any act in which it is said *un-mṛija! ava-mṛija!* ('rub up and down;' with irr. Impv.), gaṇa *mayūra-vyaṇsakâdi*, Pāṇ. ii, 1, 72.

Ú n-mṛishṭa, mfn. stroked, TBr.; rubbed or wiped off, effaced, blotted out, Ragh.; Yājñ. &c.

उन्मृद् un-mṛid (*ud-√mṛid*), P. *-mṛidati*, to rub, mash together, mingle, KātyŚr.; Lāṭy.: Caus. *-mardayati*, to rub (the body).

Un-marda, *as*, m. rubbing off, rubbing (the body), BhP.

Un-márdana, *am*, n. id., KātyŚr.; Gaut.; Suśr.; BhP.; a fragrant essence used for rubbing, ŚBr.; KātyŚr.; ĀśvGṛ.

Un-mardita, mfn. rubbed, rubbed off, Suśr.

उन्मृश् un-mṛiś (*ud-√mṛiś*), P. *-mṛiśati*, to touch from above, ŚBr. vi, 3, 3, 12: Ā. (Impv. *-mṛiśasva*) to lift up (after having touched), RV. viii, 70, 9.

Un-mṛiśya, mfn. to be touched (see *ity-u°*).

उन्मेदा un-medā, f. (√*mid*), corpulence, fatness, W.

उन्मेय un-meya. See col. 1.

उन्मेष un-mesha, &c. See col. 2.

उप úpa, ind. (a preposition or prefix to verbs and nouns, expressing) towards, near to (opposed to *apa*, away), by the side of, with, together with, under, down (e. g. *upa-√gam*, to go near, undergo; *upa-gamana*, approaching; in the Veda the verb has sometimes to be supplied from the context, and sometimes *upa* is placed after the verb to which it belongs, e. g. *āyayur upa* = *upâyayuḥ*, they approached).

(As unconnected with verbs and prefixed to nouns *upa* expresses) direction towards, nearness, contiguity in space, time, number, degree, resemblance, and relationship, but with the idea of subordination and inferiority (e. g. *upa-kanishṭhikā*, the finger next to the little finger; *upa-purāṇam*, a secondary or subordinate Purāṇa; *upa-daśa*, nearly ten); sometimes forming with the nouns to which it is prefixed compound adverbs (e. g. *upa-mūlam*, at the root; *upa-pūrva-rātram*, towards the beginning of night; *upa-kūpe*, near a well) which lose their adverbial terminations if they are again compounded with nouns (e. g. *upakūpa-jalâśaya*, a reservoir in the neighbourhood of a well); prefixed to proper names *upa* may express in classical literature 'a younger brother' (e. g. *Upêndra*, 'the younger brother of Indra'), and in Buddhist literature 'a son.'

(As a separable adverb *upa* rarely expresses) thereto, further, moreover (e. g. *tatrôpa brahma yo veda*, who further knows the Brahman), RV.; AV.; ŚBr.; PārGṛ.

(As a separable preposition) near to, towards, in the direction of, under, below (with acc., e. g. *upa āśāḥ*, towards the regions); near to, at, on, upon; at the time of, upon, up to, in, above (with loc.,

e. g. *upa sānushu*, on the tops of the mountains); with, together with, at the same time with, according to (with inst., e. g. *upa dharmabhiḥ*, according to the rules of duty), RV.; AV.; ŚBr.

Upa, besides the meanings given above, is said by native authorities to imply disease, extinction; ornament; command; reproof; undertaking; giving; killing; diffusing; wish; power; effort; resemblance, &c.; [cf. Zd. *upa;* Gk. ὑπό; Lat. *sub;* Goth. *uf;* Old Germ. *oba;* Mod. Germ. *ob* in *Obdach, obliegen,* &c.]

Upaka, *as*, m. a diminutive for all proper names of men beginning with *upa*, Pāṇ. v, 3, 80. **Upakâdi**, m. a gaṇa, Pāṇ. ii, 4, 69.

Upaḍa, *as*, m. = *upaka*, Pāṇ. v, 3, 80.

उपऋ *upa-√ṛi*. See *upār*.

उपकक्ष *upa-kakshá*, mfn. reaching to the shoulder, RV. x, 71, 7; Nir.; being under the armpit; (*am*), n. (scil. *loman*) the hair under the armpit, GopBr. i, 3, 9.

उपकण्ठ *upa-kaṇṭha*, mfn. being upon the neck or near the throat; being in the proximity of, proximate, near, Kum.; Pañcat.; Ragh.; (*am*), n. proximity, neighbourhood, contiguous space, Kathās.; Rājat. &c.; space near a village or its boundary, L.; a horse's gallop, L.; (*am*), ind. towards the neck, round the neck, Śiś. iii, 36.

उपकथा *upa-kathā*, f. a short story, tale; a subordinate narrative.

उपकनिष्ठिका *upa-kanishṭhikā*, f. (scil. *aṅguli*) the finger next to the little finger, the last finger but one, ĀśvGṛ.; ŚāṅkhGṛ.; HirGṛ. &c.

उपकन्या *upa-kanyā* = *upa-gatā kanyām*, Pāṇ. vi, 2, 194. **-puram** (*upa-kanyāpuram*), ind. near the women's apartments, Daś.

उपकरण *upa-karaṇa*, &c. See *upa-√1. kṛi*.

उपकर्णम् *upa-karṇam*, ind. near the ear, close to the ear, Pāṇ.

Upakarṇikā, f. that which goes from ear to ear, rumour, report, W.

उपकर्षण *upa-karshaṇa*. See col. 3.

उपकलापम् *upa-kalāpam*, ind. near the girdle, down to the girdle, gaṇa *parimukhâdi*, Kāty. on Pāṇ. iv, 3, 59 (Kāś.)

उपकल्प *upa-kalpa*, &c. See *upa-√klṛip*.

उपकान्तम् *upa-kantam*, ind. near a friend, near a lover or a loved one, Kir. i, 19.

उपकार *upa-kāra*, &c. See *upa-√1. kṛi*.

उपकाल *upa-kāla*, *as*, m., N. of a king of the Nāgas, L.

Upa-kālikā, f. Nigella Indica, Bhpr.

उपकाश *upa-kāśa*, *as*, m. aurora, dawn, ĀpŚr.; ifc. aspect, appearance (cf. *nīlôpakāśa*).

उपकिरण *upa-kiraṇa*. See *upa-√kṛī*.

उपकीचक *upa-kīcaka*, *as*, m. a follower of Kīcaka, MBh.

उपकुञ्चि *upa-kuñci*, *is*, f. Nigella Indica, L.

Upa-kuñcikā, f. id., Suśr.; small Cardamoms, L.

उपकुम्भ *upa-kumbha*, *am* or *ena* or *e*, ind. near the water-jar, Kāś.; (*āt*), ind. from the water-jar; (*ā*), f. Croton Polyandrum, Nigh.

उपकुरङ्ग *upa-kuraṅga*, *as*, m. a species of antelope, Nigh.

उपकुर्वाण *upa-kurvāṇa*. See *upa-√1. kṛi*.

उपकुल *upa-kula*, *am*, n. 'secondary family or class,' N. of particular Nakshatras.

उपकुल्या *upa-kulyā*, f. Piper Longum, Suśr.; a canal, trench, ditch, L.

उपकुश *upa-kuśa*, *as*, m. a gum-boil, Suśr.; Car.; N. of a son of Kuśa, L.

उपकूज् *upa-√kūj*.

Upa-kūjita, mfn. made to resound with cooing, MBh.; BhP.

उपकूप *upa-kūpa*, *as*, m. a small well, L.; (*e*), ind. near a well, L. **-jalâśaya**, m. a trough near a well for watering cattle.

उपकूल *upa-kūla*, mfn. being or growing on the shore or bank, BhP.; Kād.; Kāś. on iv, 3, 59; (*am* and *tas*), ind. on the shore, Ragh.; BhP.

Upa-kūlaka, *as*, m., N. of a man.

उपकृ *upa-√1. kṛi*, P. Ā. *-karoti*, *-kurute*, to bring or put near to, furnish with, provide, Mn.; Vikr.; Ratnāv.; to assist, help, favour, benefit, cause to succeed or prosper, R.; Mn.; Megh. &c.; to foster, take care of; to serve, do homage to (with acc.; only Ā. by Pāṇ. i, 3, 32; but see MBh. i, 6408), ŚBr.; Rājat. &c.; to undertake, begin, set about, R.; to scold, insult, Vop. xxiii, 25; *upa-s-kṛi* (*s* inserted or perhaps original), Ā. *-skurute*, to add, supply, Pāṇ.; Vop.; Siddh.; to furnish with; to prepare, elaborate, arrange, get ready; to adorn, decorate, ornament; to deform, disfigure, derange, disorder, spoil; to take care for, Pāṇ.; Bhaṭṭ.; Kāś.; to bring together, assemble.

Upa-karaṇa, *am*, n. the act of doing anything for another, doing a service or favour, helping, assisting, benefiting, Pañcat.; Sāh.; Subh. &c.; instrument, implement, machine, engine, apparatus, paraphernalia (as the vessels at a sacrifice &c.), KātyŚr.; ŚāṅkhGṛ.; Yājñ.; Mn. &c.; anything added over and above, contribution, expedient; means of subsistence, anything supporting life; any object of art or science; anything fabricated, Mn.; Suśr.; Kathās.; Car. &c.; the insignia of royalty, W.; the attendants of a king, L. **-vat** (*upakaraṇâ°*), mfn. furnished with means or instruments or implements, competent to do anything, ŚBr.; Car. **Upakaraṇârtha**, mfn. suitable (as a meaning), requisite, Car.

Upa-karaṇī-√1. kṛi, to cause to be an instrument, make dependent, Hit.; Hcar.; Kād. **Upakaraṇī-√bhū**, to become an instrument, become or be dependent, Kād.

Upa-karaṇīya, mfn. to be helped or assisted &c.

Upa-kartṛi, mf(*trī*)n. one who does a favour, one who benefits, a helper, MBh.; Ragh.; Hit.; Sāh.

Upa-kāra, *as*, m. help, assistance, benefit, service, favour; use, advantage, MBh.; Yājñ.; Hit.; Vikr. &c.; (*upakāre √vṛit*, to be of service to another, R.); preparation, ornament, decoration, embellishment (as garlands suspended at gateways on festivals, flowers &c.), Suśr.; L.; (*ī*), f. a royal tent; a palace; a caravansera, L. **-para**, mfn. intent on doing benefits or good, beneficent. **Upakārâpakāra**, *au*, m. du. kindness and injury.

Upa-kāraka, mf(*ikā*)n. doing a service or favour, assisting, helping, benefiting; suitable, requisite, Hit.; Kathās.; Sarvad. &c.; subsidiary, subservient; accessory, Sarvad.; (*ikā*), f. a protectress, L.; a female assistant, L.; a palace, a caravansera, L.; a kind of cake, L. **-tva**, n. the state of being helpful or assisting, Sarvad.

Upa-kārin, mfn. helping, assisting, doing a favour; a benefactor; subsidiary, subservient, requisite, MBh.; Pañcat.; Śak.; Vedāntas. &c. **Upakāri-tva**, n. aid, succour, protection, Bhartṛ.

Upa-kārya, mfn. to be helped or assisted, deserving or requiring assistance or favour, Sarvad.; Sāh.; KapS.; (*ā*), f. a royal tent, R.; Ragh.; a king's house, palace; a caravansera; a cemetery, L.

Upa-kurvāṇa (p. of the Ā. of *upa-√1. kṛi*, see above), *as*, m. a Brahmacārin or student of the Veda who honours his religious teacher by a gift on completing his studies and becoming a Gṛihastha (opposed to the Naishṭhika, who stays with his teacher till death), BhP.; Comm. on ChUp. &c.

Upakurvāṇaka, *as*, m. id., Comm. on Mn. ix, 94; Comm. on BhP. &c.

Upa-kṛita, mfn. helped, assisted, benefited; rendered as assistance, done kindly or beneficently &c.; ifc. gaṇa *kṛitâdi*, Pāṇ. ii, 1, 59; (*am*), n. help, favour, benefit, Śak. 165 a; Sāh.

Upa-kṛiti, *is*, f. assistance, help, favour, kindness, Kathās.; Rājat.; Prab. **-mat**, mfn. one who does a favour, helping, assisting, Śiś.

Upakṛitin, mfn. one who has done or does a favour, a helper &c., gaṇa *ishṭâdi*, Pāṇ. v, 2, 88.

Upa-kriyā, f. the act of bringing near to; favour, assistance, help, benefit, service, Mn. ii, 149; Rājat.; means, expedient; remedy, Car.

Upa-cikīrshu, mfn. wishing or intending to do a service or favour, Kathās.; Bālar.

1. **Upa-s-kara** (for 2. see below), *as*, m. (*am*, n., MBh. v, 7234) any utensil, implement or instrument; any article of household use (as a broom, basket &c.), appurtenance, apparatus, MBh.; Suśr.; Mn. &c.; an ingredient, condiment, spice, L.; N. of a Ṛishi, BrahmaP.; ornament, decoration, T.; blame, censure, W.

1. **Upa-s-karaṇa** (for 2. see below), *am*, n. the act of decorating, embellishing, ornamenting; ornament, embellishment, T.

Upa-s-kāra, *as*, m. anything additional, a supplement, Kir.; Comm. on Ragh. 7, &c.; decoration, decorating, T.

Upa-s-kṛita, mfn. furnished with, Suśr.; BhP.; added, supplied, Siddh.; prepared, arranged, elaborated; ornamented, embellished, decorated, adorned, MBh.; R.; Mn.; Bhartṛ. &c.; deformed, deranged, spoiled, Pāṇ.; MBh.; Mn.; assembled, Siddh.; blamed, censured, W.

Upa-s-kṛiti, *is*, f. the act of preparing, adorning &c., Comm. on Pāṇ.; a supplement, anything additional, W.

उपकृत् *upa-√1. kṛit*, P. *-kṛintati*, to hurt, violate, R.

उपकृष् *upa-√1. kṛish*, P. *-karshati*, to draw towards or near one's self, Suśr.; BhP.; to draw with one's self, draw or drag away, R.; to remove, give up, MBh.

Upa-karshaṇa, *am*, n. the act of drawing or dragging near, Pat.

Upa-karsham, ind. drawing near or towards one's self, seizing, Pāṇ. iii, 4, 49.

उपकृष्ण *upa-kṛishṇa*, mfn. = *upagataḥ kṛishṇam*, gaṇa *gaurâdi*, Pāṇ. vi, 2, 194.

Upakṛishṇaka, *as*, m., N. of a being in Skanda's retinue, MBh.

उपकॄ *upa-√kṛī*, P. *-kirati*, to scatter or throw down, scatter upon; to pour upon, besprinkle, bestrew, ŚBr.; KātyŚr.; MBh. &c.; *upa-s-kṛī* (with *s* inserted or perhaps original), P. *-skirati*, to cut up, split; to hurt, Pāṇ.; Vop.; Kāś.

Upa-kiraṇa, *am*, n. the act of scattering or throwing over, covering up (with earth), burying, KātyŚr.

U'pa-kīrṇa, mfn. besprinkled; strewed with, covered, ŚBr. ix, 1, 3, 14; MBh.

2. **Upa-s-kara**, *as*, m. the act of hurting, violating, T.

2. **Upa-s-karaṇa**, *am*, n. id., ib.

उपक्लृप् *upa-√klṛip*, Ā. *-kalpate*, to be fit for, be ready at hand, become, ŚBr.; BhP.; to serve as, lead to (with dat.), R. v, 25, 21; to take the shape or form of, become, be, BhP.; Mn.: Caus. P. *-kalpayati* (inf. *-kalpayitavai*, ŚBr. iv, 5, 2, 2) to prepare, make ready, equip; to procure, bring near, fetch, ŚBr.; KātyŚr.; Lāṭy.; MBh. &c.; to allot, asign, MBh.; R.; Yājñ.; Kathās.; to put or set up, turn towards; to arrange, BhP.; Pañcat.; Prab.; to impart, communicate, BhP.; to assume, suppose, Sāh.

Upa-kalpa, *as*, m. an appurtenance, BhP.

Upa-kalpana, *am*, n. the act of preparing, preparation, KātyŚr.; (*ā*), f. preparing (articles of food or medicine), fabricating, making, Suśr.; substituting, L.

Upakalpanīya, mfn. to be prepared or procured or fetched, Car.; treating of preparation &c. (as a chapter), ib.

Upa-kalpayitavya, mfn. to be prepared or made, Suśr.

Upa-kalpita, mfn. prepared, procured, fetched; arranged &c.

Upa-kalpya, ind. p. having prepared or procured &c.

U'pa-klṛipta, mfn. ready, prepared, ŚBr.; AitBr.; KātyŚr.; Mn. &c.; equipped, adapted, fitted for, brought near, MBh.; R. &c.; produced, formed, BhP.

उपकेतु *upa-ketu*, *us*, m., N. of a man, Kāth.

उपकेरु *úpa-keru*, *us*, m., N. of a man, MaitrS.

उपकोण *upa-koṇa*, *as*, m. an intermediate point of the compass, Bālar.

उपकोशा *upa-kośā*, f., N. of a daughter of Upa-varsha and wife of Vara-ruci, Kathās.

उपकोसल *upa-kosala, as*, m., N. of a man, ChUp.

उपक्रम् *upa-√kram*, P. *-krāmati* (rarely *-kramati*), Ā. *-kramate*, to go near, approach, come to, RV. viii, 1, 4; 21, 2; 81, 7; MBh.; R.; Megh.; to rush upon, attack (only P. by Kāś. on Pāṇ. i, 3, 39 & 42), MBh. xiii; to approach with any object, have recourse to, set about, undertake, begin (with acc., dat. or inf. only Ā. by Pāṇ. i, 3, 39 & 42), Lāṭy.; MBh.; Ragh. &c.; to treat, attend on (as a physician), MBh.; Suśr. &c.

Upa-krantṛi, mfn. one who undertakes, a beginner, Vop.

Upa-krama, *as*, m. the act of going or coming near, approach, MBh.; R.; setting about, undertaking, commencement, beginning, Lāṭy.; KātyŚr.; BhP.; Sāh.; Sarvad. &c.; enterprise, planning, original conception, plan, Ragh.; Rājat.; Pañcat. &c.; anything leading to a result; a means, expedient, stratagem, exploit, MBh.; Yājñ.; Mālav. &c.; remedy, medicine, Suśr.; attendance (on a patient), treatment, practice or application of medicine, physicking, Suśr. &c.; the rim of a wheel, Hcat.; a particular ceremony preparatory to reading the Vedas, W.; trying the fidelity &c. of a counsellor or friend, ib.; heroism, courage, L. **-parākrama**, m., N. of a work.

Upa-kramaṇa, mf(*ī*)n. approaching; complying with, granting, Kathās.; (*am*), n. attendance (on a patient), treatment, Suśr. &c.

Upa-kramaṇīya, mfn. to be approached or gone to; to be undertaken or commenced, L.; to be treated (as a patient), Suśr. &c.; (*upakramaṇīya*), mfn. treating of attendance (on a patient).

Upa-kramitavya, mfn. to be undertaken or commenced, R.

1. **Upa-kramya**, mfn. to be attended or treated (as a patient), Suśr.; Vikr. &c.

2. **Upa-kramya**, ind. p. having approached; having undertaken or commenced &c.

Upa-krānta, mfn. approached, MBh.; undertaken, commenced, begun, MBh.; Mālav. &c.; treated, attended on, cured, Daś.; Suśr. &c.; previously mentioned, MW.

Upa-krāmya, mfn. = 1. *upa-kramya* above.

उपक्री *upa-√krī.*

Upa-krīya, ind. p. having bought or purchased, Hit.

उपक्रीड् *upa-√krīḍ*, P. *-krīḍati*, to play or dance around, MBh. xiii, 3832.

Upa-krīḍā, f. place for playing, play-ground, R.; (a kind of circus for public sports common in Malabār, Burnell.)

उपक्रुश् *upa-√kruś*, P. *-krośati*, to scold, blame: Caus. *-krośayati*, to cause to cry or lament, BhP.

Upa-kruśya, ind. p. having scolded, blaming, chiding, Hit.

Upa-krushṭa, mfn. chid, scolded at; (*as*), m. a person of low caste, a carpenter, [Comm.] ĀśvŚr. ii, 1, 13.

Upa-krośa, *as*, m. reproach, censure, MBh.; R.; Ragh.; Daś.

Upa-krośana, *am*, n. the act of censuring, blaming, Daś. **-kara**, mfn. causing reproach, disgracing, dishonouring, Hariv.

Upa-kroshṭṛi, mfn. one who scolds or censures; making a noise, braying; (*tā*), m. an ass, BhP.

उपक्लिद् *upa-√klid*, P. to become wet; to rot, putrefy: Caus. *-kledayati*, to make wet, soak, Car.

Upa-klinna, mfn. wet, moist, Car.; rotten, putrid, ib.

उपक्लेश *upa-kleśa, as*, m. (with Buddh.) a lesser Kleśa (q. v.) or cause of misery (as conceit, pride &c.), Sarvad.

उपक्वण *upa-kvaṇa* or *upa-kvāṇa, as*, m. (*√kvaṇ*), the sound of a lute, L.

उपक्वस *upa-kvasa, as*, m. (voc. *úpa-kvasa*) a kind of worm, AV. vi, 50, 2.

उपक्षत्र *upa-kshatra, as*, m., N. of a king, VP.

उपक्षय 1. *upa-kshaya* (for 2. see col. 2), *as*, m. 'a secondary or intermediate destruction of the world,' N. of Śiva [Nīlak.], MBh. xii, 10368.

उपक्षर् *upa-√kshar*, P. *-ksharati*, to flow or stream towards, RV. i, 124, 4; v, 62, 4; AitBr.; to pour over, TBr.

उपक्षि 1. *upa-√1. kshi*, Pass. *-kshīyate*, to waste away, decay, be consumed or exhausted, TBr.

Upa-kshapayitṛi, mfn. (fr. the Caus.), one who destroys, a destroyer, Sāy. on RV.

2. **Upa-kshaya** (for 1. see col. 1), *as*, m. decrease, decline, decay, waste, Hit.; Comm. on VS. &c.

Upa-kshita. See *án-upakshita.*

Upa-kshīṇa, mfn. exhausted, consumed, KātyŚr.; absorbed, lost in, Comm. on BṛĀrUp.; vanished, disappeared, Sāh.; Kathās.

उपक्षि 2. *upa-√2. kshi*, P. *-ksheti* (RV.; 3. pl. *-kshiyanti*, AV. iv, 30, 4; RV.; Pot. 1. pl. *-kshayema*, AV. xix, 15, 4) to stay or dwell near or at, abide, dwell on (lit. and fig.), RV.; AV.

Upa-kshít, mfn. dwelling near; clinging to, adhering, RV. viii, 19, 33.

Upa-kshetṛi, mfn. one who dwells or stays near at, RV. iii, 1, 16.

उपक्षिप् *upa-√kship*, P. *-kshipati*, to throw at, hurl against, BhP.; Sāh.; to beat, strike, ŚBr.; to strike with words, insult, accuse, insinuate, R.; to allude, hint at, Sāh.; Mṛicch.; Daś.; to speak of, describe, define, Sāh.; Sarvad.; to commence, set about (a work), Mall.

Upa-kshepa, *as*, m. throwing at; threatening, L.; mention, allusion, hint, Sāh.; Kathās.; Daśar.; Viddh. &c.; poetical or figurative style in composition, W.

Upa-kshepaka, mfn. alluding, suggesting; see *arthôpakshepaka.*

Upa-kshepaṇa, *am*, n. throwing at or down, L.; allusion, hint, suggestion, Sāh.; putting a Śūdra's food into a Brāhman's house (where it is cooked), Śambupurāṇa (T.)

उपक्षुद्र *upa-kshudra*, mfn. somewhat small, TāṇḍyaBr.

उपखातम् *upa-khātam*, ind. near the ditch, Daś.

उपखिल *upa-khila, am*, n. a sub-supplement, supplement to a supplement, Hariv.; VāyuP.

उपख्या *upa-√khyā*, Pass. *-khyāyate*, to be seen or perceived, ŚBr. iv, 1, 2, 13.

उपगण *upa-gaṇa*, mfn. constituting a small class or number less than a troop, Kāś. on Pāṇ. v, 4, 73; (*as*), m., N. of a man (Buddh.)

उपगम् *upa-√gam*, P. *-gacchati* (inf. *-gantavaí*, RV. x, 160, 5) to go near to, come towards, approach, arrive at, reach, attain, visit (with acc. and rarely dat.), RV.; ŚBr.; MBh. &c.; to come upon, attack; to press hard upon, RV. i. 53, 9; MBh.; Mṛicch. &c.; to occur, happen, present itself, R.; Megh.; Pañcat. &c.; to undertake, begin, ŚBr.; R.; to approach (a woman sexually), MBh.; Mn.; to enter any state or relation, undergo, obtain, participate in, make choice of, suffer, MBh.; Yājñ.; Kum.; Mālar. &c.; to admit, agree to, allow, confess: Caus. *-gamayati*, to cause to come near or approach, Daś.: Desid. *-jigamishati*, to wish to approach, desire to go, BhP.

Upa-ga, mfn. ifc. approaching, going towards, Āp.; being or staying in or on, BhP.; VarBṛS.; Śiś.; following, belonging to; fit for, conducive to, MBh.; Car.; approached; furnished with, MBh.; R.; Mn.; covered (as a female), L.

Upa-gata, mfn. gone to, met, approached (esp. for protection or refuge, Kām.), MBh.; Śak. &c.; attained, obtained; arrived, occurred, happened; undergone, experienced, MBh.; Śiś.; Pañcat. &c. furnished with, MBh.; agreed, allowed, Mn.; MBh.; promised, L.; near at hand; approximate, Vop.; L.; passed away, dead, L.; (*am*), n. receipt, acquittance, Yājñ. ii, 93. **-vat**, mfn. one who has gone to or approached; possessing; feeling, suffering (e.g. sorrow); one who has undertaken or promised, W.

Upa-gati, *is*, f. approach, going near, Śiś. ix, 75; undergoing, L.

Upa-gatya, ind. p. = 2. *upa-gamya.*

Upa-gama, *as*, m. approach, coming to, approximation, R.; Megh.; Ragh.; Sarvad. &c.; entering (into any state or condition), obtaining, acquiring, having, Śak. 14 c; approaching respectfully, veneration, BhP.; coming near to, perceiving, Comm. on Daśar.; acquaintance, society; intercourse (as of the sexes), L.; undergoing, suffering, feeling, L.; agreement, promise, L.; a particular number (Buddh.)

Upa-gamana, *am*, n. the act of going towards, approaching, attaining, MBh.; R.; the act of coming near, perceiving, Daśar.; Sāh.; undertaking, addicting one's self to.

1. **Upa-gamya**, mfn. to be approached, approachable, obtainable, Mṛicch.

2. **Upa-gamya**, ind. p. having approached, approaching &c.

Upa-gāmin, mfn. coming near, approaching, arriving, Kathās.

Upa-jigamishu, mfn. (fr. Desid.), wishing or desiring to go near, Megh. 43.

उपगहन *upa-gahana, as*, m., N. of a Ṛishi, MBh.

उपगा 1. *upa-√1. gā* (for 2. see *upa-√gai*), P. *-gāti* (Subj. *-gāt*; 3. pl. *-gus*; aor. 1. sg. *-gesham*, VS. v, 5) to go near to, arrive at; to come into, undergo, RV. i, 164, 4; vii, 93, 3; AV.; to go, walk (*pathā́*, a way), RV. i, 38, 5; VS.; ŚBr.

1. **Upa-geya** (for 2. see p. 197, col. 1), mfn. to be approached; to be observed or kept, Kāś. on Pāṇ. iii, 1, 86.

उपगातृ *upa-gātṛí*, &c. See p. 197, col. 1.

उपगाह् *upa-√gāh*, P. (p. *-gāhat*) to penetrate, force one's way into, R.

उपगिरम् *upa-giram*, ind. near or at a mountain, Pāṇ. v, 4, 112.

Upa-giri, *i*, ind. id., ib.; (*is*), m. the country near a mountain, MBh.

उपगीति *upa-gīti*, &c. See p. 197, col. 1.

उपगु *upa-gu, us*, m., N. of a king, TāṇḍyaBr.; VP. (v. l. *upa-guru*); (*u*), ind. near a cow, Pāṇ.

उपगुध *upa-gudha* (v. l. *upa-guḍa*, Kāś.), Pāṇ. vi, 2, 194.

उपगुप् *upa-√gup.*

Upa-gupta, mfn. hidden, concealed; (*as*), m., N. of a king. **-vitta**, mfn. of concealed resources, BhP.

उपगुरु *upa-guru, us*, m., N. of a king, VP. (v. l. *upa-gu*); an assistant teacher, W.; (*u*), ind. near a teacher.

उपगुह् *upa-√guh*, P. *-gūhati*, to hide, cover, conceal, ŚBr.; KātyŚr.: P. Ā. to clasp, embrace, press to the bosom, MBh.; R.; BhP.; Ragh. &c.

Upa-guhya, ind. p. having hidden, hiding, concealing; having embraced, embracing.

Upa-gūḍha, mfn. hidden, concealed, covered, VarBṛS.; BhP.; clasped round, embraced, R.; BhP.; Ragh.; Śiś. &c.; (*am*), n. the act of embracing, pressing to the bosom, an embrace, Megh.; Bhartṛ.; Veṇis. &c. **-vat**, mfn. one who has embraced, Hit.

Upa-gūhana, *am*, n. the act of hiding, concealing, KātyŚr.; pressing to the bosom, embrace, VarBṛS.; (in dram.) the occurrence of any wonderful event, Sāh.; Daśar.

Upa-gūhya, ep. = *upa-guhya* above.

Upa-gohya, mfn. to be hidden; (*as*), m. a kind of fire considered as impure, PārGṛ.; MantraBr.

उपगॄ 1. *upa-√1. gṝi*, P. (1. pl. *-gṛiṇīmasi*, 3. p. *-gṛiṇánti*) to approach with praise, revere, worship, RV. i, 48, 11; ii, 34, 14.

उपगॄ 2. *upa-√2. gṝi*, P. (Pot. *-gilet*) to swallow down, Suśr. ii, 237, 8.

उपगै *upa-√gai*, P. *-gāyati* (Impv. 2. pl. *-gāyatā́*, RV.) to sing to any one (dat. or acc.); to join in singing, accompany a song; to sing before, sing, praise in song, celebrate, 'fill with song,' RV. viii, 32, 17; ix, 11, 1; AV. iv, 15, 4; TS.; ŚBr. &c.; MBh.; BhP. &c.; to sing near: Pass. *-gīyate* (p. *-gīyámāna*, RV.; MBh.; and *-gīyat* [irr.], MBh. xv, 883) to be sung or praised in song; to be sung before, RV. viii, 70, 5; MBh.

2. **Upa-gā**, f. accompaniment of a song, KātyŚr.; Lāṭy.; Jaim.

Upa-gātṛi, *tā*, m. one who accompanies the song of the Ud-gātṛi, a chorister, TS.; ŚBr.; AitBr.

Upa-gāna, *am*, n. an accompanying song, Mālav.

Upa-gāyana, *am*, n. singing, BhP.

Upa-gīta, mfn. sung to or before, sung, celebrated, proclaimed, MBh.; R.; Ragh.; one who has begun to sing near, Śiś. iv, 57.

Upa-gīti, *is*, f. a kind of Āryā metre (consisting of four lines of alternately twelve and fifteen instants).

Upa-gīthá, *am*, n. id., MaitrS. ii, 13, 14.

Upa-geya, mfn. to be sung or celebrated; (*am*), n. song, BhP. v, 26, 38.

उपग्रन्थ् *upa-√granth*, P. (1. sg. *-granthāmi* for *-grathnāmi?*) to intwine or wind round, Comm. on TS. i, 2, 7.

Upa-grantha, *as*, m. 'minor work,' a class of writings.

उपग्रस् *upa-√gras*, P. (impf. *upâgrasat*) to swallow down, devour (as Rāhu the sun); to eclipse, MBh. ii, 2693.

उपग्रह् *upa-√grah*, P. *-gṛihṇāti* (aor. *-agrabhīt*, AV.) to seize from below; to hold under, put under; to support, AV. vii, 110, 3; ŚBr.; KātyŚr.; PārGṛ. &c.; to collect a fluid (by holding a vessel under), TS.; to seize, take possession of, take, obtain; to subdue, become master of, MBh.; R.; BhP.; Mn.; Pañcat. &c.; to draw near (to one's self); to conciliate, propitiate; to take as one's ally, ChUp.; to comprehend, BhP. iii, 22, 21; to take up again, renew, MBh. xii, 5206; to accept, approve, MBh. xii, 6977.

Upa-gṛihīta, mfn. held from below, supported, ĀśvGṛ. iv, 7, 10; subdued, mastered, Prab.

Upa-gṛihya, ind. p. having held under or seized from below; having obtained, obtaining &c.

1. **Upa-graha**, *as*, m. (for 2. see s. v.) seizure, confinement, L.; a prisoner, L.; a handful (of Kuśa grass), Kāty.; adding, addition (of a sound), Comm. on Pāṇ.; an *e* used as Nidhana (q. v.) at the end of a Sāman, Lāṭy. vii, 8, 11; alteration, change, SaṃhUp. ii, 3; propitiation, conciliation, coaxing, Daśar.; a kind of Sandhi or peace (purchased by the cession of everything), Kām.; Hit.; the Pada or voice of a verb, Comm. on Pāṇ.; a kind of demon causing diseases (supposed to preside over the planets), Hariv. 9562.

Upa-grahaṇa, *am*, n. the act of seizing from below, holding under, supporting, KātyŚr. i, 10, 6; comprehending, learning, R. i, 4, 4; the taking any one prisoner, seizure, capture, L.

Upa-grāha, *as*, m. a complimentary gift, present to a superior, MBh. ii, 1898.

Upa-grāhya, *am*, n. id., L.

उपग्रह 2. *upa-graha*, *as*, m. (fr. *graha* with *upa* implying inferiority), a minor planet or any heavenly body of a secondary kind, a comet, meteor, falling star &c., MBh. &c.

उपघट्ट् *upa-√ghaṭṭ*, to stir up, Car.

उपघात *upa-ghāta*, *as*, m. (fr. *upa-√han*, q. v.), a stroke, hurt, violation; injury, damage, offence, wrong, MBh.; R.; Mn.; Śak. &c.; weakness, sickness, disease, morbid affection (cf. *puṃstvôpa°*, *svarôpa°*), Suśr.; a kind of oblation or sacrifice, Gṛihyas. ii, 7.

Upa-ghātaka, mfn. striking, hurting; injuring, damaging offending, MBh.; Car.; (*as*), m. injury, offence, damage, MBh. xiii, 3610.

Upa-ghātam, ind. p. See *upa-√han*.

Upa-ghātin, mfn. one who does damage, hurting, injuring, Suśr.; MBh.

Upa-ghna, *as*, m. contiguous support, resting-place, shelter, refuge, Pāṇ.; Bhaṭṭ. **— taru**, m. a supporting tree, a tree which supports a climbing plant, Ragh. xiv, 1.

उपघुष् *upa-√ghush*.

Upa-ghushṭa, mfn. caused to resound, resounding with, MBh.; BhP.

Upa-ghoshaṇa, *am*, n. proclamation, publication, Daś.

उपघ्रा *upa-√ghrā*, P. *-jighrati* (*-jíghrati*, AV.) to smell at; to touch (with the mouth), AV. xii, 4, 5; ŚBr.; Lāṭy.; MBh. &c.; to smell, MBh.; Ragh.; to kiss, MBh. vii, 4357; Ragh. xiii, 70; R.: Caus. *-ghrāpayati*, to cause to smell at, TS. v, 2, 8, 1.

Upa-ghrāta, mfn. smelled at, touched by the mouth (of a cow), Mn. iv, 209; Gaut. xvii, 12.

Upa-ghrā́yam, ind. p. smelling at, MaitrS. ii, 1, 3.

Upa-jighraṇa, *am*, *ā*, n. f. the act of smelling at, Car.

उपच *upaca*, mfn. See *ācôpaca*.

उपचक्र *upa-cakra*, *as*, m. a species of duck (cf. *cakra* and *cakra-vāka*), MBh.

उपचक्षुस् *upa-cakshus*, n. a superhuman or divine eye (= *divya-cakshus*), L.; spectacles (Beng. *casamā*), T.

उपचतुर *upa-catura*, mfn. (pl.) almost four, nearly four, Kāty. on Pāṇ. v, 4, 77.

उपचय *upa-caya*. See *upa-√1. ci*.

उपचर् *upa-√car*, P. *-carati*, to go towards, come near, approach, RV. vii, 46, 2; TS. v, 7, 6, 1; ŚBr.; R.; to come near, wait upon, serve, attend, assist, bear a hand, ŚBr.; MBh.; Mṛicch.; Daś. &c.; to approach, set about, undertake, perform, TS. iii, 1, 6, 1; ŚBr.; to attend on (a patient), physic (a person), treat, tend, nurse, Suśr.; Pañcat.; to use figuratively or metaphorically, apply figuratively (generally Pass. *-caryate*), VarBṛS.; Sāh.; Sarvad. &c.

Upa-cára, mfn. accessory, supplementary, ŚāṅkhBr.; (*as*), m. access, approach, ŚBr. ii, 3, 4, 30; attendance, cure, Suśr.; (cf. *sûpacara*.)

Upa-caraṇá, *am*, n. approach. See *sûpacaraṇá*.

Upa-caraṇīya, mfn. to be approached; to be attended; to be applied or attributed, Sāy. on TBr. i, 3, 2, 3.

Upa-carita, mfn. approached, attended; applied &c.; (*am*), n. a particular rule of Sandhi (cf. *upacāra*), VPrāt.

Upa-caritavya, mfn. to be attended or waited upon, Bhartṛ.; to be treated, Car.; to be respected or revered or treated with attention, MBh.; R.; Mn.; Pañcat. &c.; (*ā*), f. service, attendance; attendance on a patient; practice of medicine.

1. **Upa-carya**, mfn. id.

2. **Upa-carya**, ind. p. having approached, having attended &c.

Upa-cārá, *as*, m. approach, service, attendance, Hcat. i, 111, 2 seqq.; act of civility, obliging or polite behaviour, reverence, ŚBr.; MBh.; Śak. &c. (64 Upacāras are enumerated in the Tantra-sāra, quoted by T.); proceeding, practice; behaviour, conduct; mode of proceeding towards (gen.), treatment, ŚBr.; MBh.; Āp.; Mn. &c.; attendance on a patient, medical practice, physicking, Suśr.; Pañcat.; Vikr.; a ceremony, Kum. vii, 86; present, offering, bribe; solicitation, request, L.; ornament, decoration, Kum.; Ragh. vii, 4; a favourable circumstance, Sāh. 300; usage, custom or manner of speech, Nyāyad.; a figurative or metaphorical expression (*upacārāt*, ind. metaphorically), metaphor, figurative application, Sāh.; Sarvad.; Comm. on Śiś. &c.; pretence, pretext, L.; a kind of Sandhi (substitution of *s* and *sh* in place of Visarga), Kāś. on Pāṇ. viii, 3, 48; N. of a Pariśishṭa of the Sāma-veda. **— karaṇa** or **-karman**, n. or **-kriyā**, f. (Mn. viii, 357) act of courteousness, politeness, civility. **— cchala**, n. a kind of fallacious inference (to be refuted by reference to the real sense of a word used metaphorically, e. g. if any one from the sentence 'the platform cries' were to conclude that the platform really cries and not persons on the platform), Nyāyad.; Nyāyak. **— pada**, n. a courteous or polite word, a mere compliment, Kum. iv, 9. **— para**, mfn. intent on service or politeness. **— paribhrashṭa**, mfn. devoid of civility, destitute of kindness, churlish, uncourteous, Hit. **— parita**, mfn. full of politeness. **— vat**, mfn. polite; furnished with ornaments, decorated, Ragh. vi, 1.

Upacāraka, mf(*ikā*)n. ifc. for *upa-cāra*, Kathās.; (*as*), m. courteousness, politeness, Hcat.

Upacārika, mfn. ifc. serving for, belonging to, MBh. iv, 1621.

Upacārin, mfn. attending upon, serving; revering, R.; MaitrUp.; ifc. using (a remedy), Car.

Upa-cārya, mfn. to be attended upon, to be treated with attention, Pañcat.: (*ā*), f. practice of medicine, L.

Upa-cīrṇa, mfn. attended upon, assisted, MBh. (= *vañcita*, 'deceived,' Nīlak.)

उपचर्म *upa-carma*, ind. near or on the skin, Comm. on Pāṇ.

उपचाकु *upacāku*, *us*, m., N. of a man, gaṇa *bāhv-ādi*, Pāṇ. iv, 1, 96 (not in the Kāś.)

उपचायिन् 1. *upa-cāyin* (for 2. see below), mfn. (√*2. ci*), honouring, revering, MBh.

उपचारु *upa-cāru*, *us*, m., N. of a Cakravartin. **— mat**, m. id. (Buddh.)

उपचि *upa-√1. ci*, P. *-cinoti*, to gather together, TS. i, 1, 7, 2; to heap up, collect, hoard up, accumulate; to increase, strengthen, MBh.; Kum.; Suśr.; Megh. &c.; to pour over, cover, overload: Pass. *-cīyate*, to be heaped together or accumulated; to increase, become strong, MBh.; Suśr.; Rājat.; Hit. &c.; to gain advantage, succeed, be prosperous, Mn. viii, 169; to be covered with; to cover one's self, furnish one's self with, MBh.; Suśr.

Upa-caya, *as*, m. accumulation, quantity, heap; elevation, excess; increase, growth, prosperity, MBh.; Suśr.; Hit. &c.; (*upacayam* √*1. kṛi*, to promote or advance the prosperity of, help, assist, Kām.); addition, KātyŚr.; the third, sixth, tenth, and eleventh of the zodiacal signs, VarBṛS. &c. **Upacayâpacaya**, *au*, m. du. prosperity and decay, rise and fall, Suśr. **Upacayâvaha**, mfn. causing prosperity or success, Kām.

2. **Upa-cāyin**, mfn. ifc. causing to increase or succeed, MBh.

Upa-cāyya, *as*, m. a particular sacrificial fire, Pāṇ.; L.; a place for holding sacrificial fire, an altar, hearth, Bhaṭṭ.; L.

Upacāyyaka, *as*, m. id.

Upa-cít, *t*, f. a particular disease, a kind of swelling, VS. xii, 97, (*śvayathu-guḍa-ślīpadâdayaḥ*, Comm.)

Upa-cita, mfn. heaped up, increased; thriving, increasing, prospering, succeeding, MBh.; BhP.; Megh.; Ragh. &c.; big, fat, thick, Suśr.; Car.; covered over, furnished abundantly, possessing plentifully, MBh.; Hariv.; Pañcat. &c.; plastered, smeared; burnt, L. **— rasa**, mfn. one whose (appetite or) desire is increased, Megh. 115.

Upa-citi, *is*, f. accumulation, increase; augmentation, Śāntiś.; gain, advantage; a heap, pile, MBh. iii, 15144; (in arithm.) progression, Āryabh. ii, 21.

Upaciti-√bhū, to increase, grow, Gīt. xii, 27.

Upa-ceya, mfn. to be collected or heaped up.

उपचिकीर्षु *upa-cikīrshu*. See *upa-√1. kṛi*.

उपचित्र *upa-citra*, mfn. variegated, coloured; (*as*), m., N. of a man, MBh.; (*ā*), f., N. of particular metres (viz. 1. a variety of Mātrāsamaka, consisting of four lines of sixteen instants each; 2. a metre of four lines of eleven instants each; in two varieties); the plants Salvinia Cucullata and Croton Polyandrum, L.

Upacitraka, *am*, n. a particular metre (consisting of four lines of eleven instants each).

उपचूडन *upa-cūḍana* or *upa-cūlana*, *am*, n. singeing, searing, heating, Parāś.; Comm. on Yājñ. &c.

उपचृत् *upa-√cṛit*, P. *-cṛitati*, to fasten, tie or bind on, Kauś.

उपच्छद् *upa-cchad* (*upa-√chad*).

Upa-cchanna, mfn. covered, MBh. i, 5005; concealed, hidden, secret, MBh. i, 6006; Mn.

उपच्छन्द् *upa-cchand* (*upa-√chand*), Caus. *-cchandayati*, to conciliate (privately by flattering or coaxing language), coax, entice; to seduce, Prab.; Rājat.; Kathās.; to supplicate, beg, Ragh. v, 58.

Upa-cchanda, *as*, m. anything necessary or needful, a requisite, MBh. xiii, 3300.

Upa-cchandana, *am*, n. persuasion, conciliation by coaxing, enticing, Daś.; Bālar.; Kāś. on Pāṇ. i, 3, 47.

Upa-cchandita, mfn. persuaded, coaxed, enticed, Śak. 207, 2, (Prākṛit *uba-cchandido*.)

उपच्छल् *upa-cchal* (*upa-√chal*), P. *-cchalayati*, to deceive, overreach, Prab.

उपच्यव *upa-cyavá*, *as*, m. (√*cyu*), the act of pressing or moving towards (said of a woman in sexual intercourse), RV. i, 28, 3, (= *śālā-prāpti*, Sāy.)

उपज 1. *upa-já* (for 2. see p. 198, col. 1), mfn. (√*jan*), additional, accessory, ŚBr. i, 1, 1, 10 (Sāy. reads *upa-cám* [√*1. ci*]; see Weber's extracts from the Comm. on the above passage, where T.

reads correctly *tricatura-māsād āropitam* instead of *tricaturān mākhābapitam* [?]).

उपजगती *upa-jagatī*, f. a particular metre (a variety of the Trishṭubh; three Pādas containing twelve instants instead of eleven), RPrāt.

उपजन् *upa-√jan*, Ā. *-jāyate*, to be produced or originate in addition; to be added or put to, RV. i, 25, 8; TāṇḍyaBr.; ĀśvŚr.; ŚāṅkhŚr.; RPrāt. &c.; to follow (as a consequence), Sarvad.; to be born, originate, come forth, appear, become visible, happen, MBh.; BhP.; Mn.; Hit.; Suśr. &c.; to be born again, MBh. xiii, 6689; Yājñ. iii, 256; Bhag.; to exist, be, Pañcat.; Hit.: Caus. *-janayati*, to generate, produce; to cause, effect, TāṇḍyaBr. Prab.; Mālav.; Sarvad.

2. **Upa-ja** (for 1. see s.v.), mfn. produced or coming from, Gaut. xii, 36, &c.; (*as*), m., N. of a deity.

Upa-jana, *as*, m. addition, increase; appendage, ĀśvŚr.; ChUp.; Comm. on Nyāyam. &c.; addition of a letter (in the formation of a word), letters or syllables or affixes added, RPrāt.; APrāt.; Nir.; Sāy. &c.

Upa-janana, *am*, n. generation, procreation, MānGṛ. i, 14.

Upa-jā, f. distant or not immediate posterity, AV. xi, 1, 19.

Upa-jāta, mfn. added, additional, APrāt. &c.; produced, engendered, aroused, originated, MBh.; Daś. &c. **-kopa** or **-krodha**, mfn. one whose anger is aroused, provoked, excited, Prab. **-kheda**, mfn. suffering from exhaustion, faint, feeble, Mṛicch. **-viśvāsa**, mfn. inspired with confidence, confident, trusting, believing, Hit.

Upa-jāti, *is*, f. a mixed metre (esp. a combination of Indra-vajrā and Upendra-vajrā, or of Vaṅśa-stha and Indra-vaṅśā).

Upajātikā, f. id.

उपजनम् *upa-janam*, ind. near the people, Kir. iv, 1.

उपजन्धनि *upa-jandhani*, *is*, m., N. of a man, SkandaP.

उपजप् *upa-√jap*, P. *-japati*, to whisper (*karṇe* or *karṇam*, into anybody's ear), MBh.; R.; to bring over to one's own party (by secretly suggesting anything into the ear); to instigate to rebellion or treachery, MBh. xii, 2633; Mn. vii, 197; Daś.; Kathās. &c.

Upa-japta, mfn. brought over or instigated to rebellion (by whispering into the ear &c.)

Upa-japya, mfn. to be brought over or instigated to rebellion (cf. the last), Mn. vii, 197; Bhaṭṭ.

Upa-jāpa, *as*, m. the act of rousing to rebellion or bringing over to one's own party (see above), Hit.; Pañcat.; Daś.; Śiś. &c.

Upa-jāpaka, mfn. one who brings over to his party or one who rouses to rebellion (by whispering into the ear &c.), Mn. ix, 275.

उपजरसम् *upa-jarasam*, ind. towards or near old age, cf. Pāṇ. v, 4, 107.

उपजला *upa-jalā*, f., N. of a river, MBh.

उपजल्प् *upa-√jalp*.

Upa-jalpita, *am*, n. talk, R. ii, 60, 14.

Upajalpin, mfn. talking to a person, giving advice, MBh. i, 5396.

उपजानु *upa-jānu*, ind. in or near the knee, Pāṇ. iv, 3, 40.

उपजि *upa-√ji*, P. *-jayati*, to acquire by conquest, gain, obtain, GopBr. ii, 2, 16.

उपजिगमिषु *upa-jigamishu*. See *upa-√gam*.

उपजिघ्रण *upa-jighraṇa*. See *upa-√ghrā*.

उपजिज्ञासु *upa-jijñāsu*. See *upa-√jñā*.

उपजिहीर्षा *upa-jihīrshā*, f. See *upa-√hṛi*.

उपजिह्वा *upa-jihvā*, f. the epiglottis, Yājñ. iii, 97; an abscess on the under side of the tongue, Suśr.; a kind of ant, L.

Upa-jihvikā, f. a kind of ant, RV. viii, 102, 21; the epiglottis, Car.; an abscess (see above), Suśr.

उपजीक *upa-jīka*, *as*, m. (*ā*, f.?) a water deity, AV. ii, 3, 4; vi, 100, 2.

उपजीव् *upa-√jīv*, P. *-jīvati* (3. pl. *-jīvanti*) to live or exist upon (food), subsist, support one's self on, be supported by, RV. i, 190, 5; AV; TS.; ŚBr.; TBr.; MBh.; Pañcat. &c.; to derive profit from, make use of (with acc.), Yājñ.; BhP.; MārkP. &c.; to live under, be dependent on, serve, MBh.; BhP.; Śiś. &c.; to live for a profession, practice, Mn.; MBh.; BhP. &c.: Caus. *-jīvayati*, to use, make the most of, Kathās. lxi, 268.

Upa-jīvá, mfn. probably not very different in meaning from *jīvá*, q. v., AV. xix, 69, 2; (*ā́*), f. subsistence, TBr. i, 5, 6, 4.

Upa-jīvaka, mfn. living upon, subsisting by (with instr. or ifc.), MBh.; R.; Kathās.; Comm. on Mn.; living under, depending upon, subject to, a dependant, servant, Kathās.; (*am*, *ikā*), n. f. subsistence, livelihood, L.

Upa-jīvana, *am*, n. livelihood, subsistence, ŚBr.; Mn. ix, 207; Yājñ. iii, 236; MBh.; Pañcat. &c.; dependance, submissiveness, Prasannar.

Upajīvanīya, mfn. affording or serving for livelihood, AV. viii, 10, 22-29; TS.; ŚBr.

Upa-jīvin, mfn. living on, subsisting by (with acc. or gen. or ifc.), MBh.; Mn.; Yājñ. &c.; living in dependence, dependent, subject, MBh.; Ragh.; Rājat. &c.; submissive, humble, Ratnāv.

1. **Upa-jīvya**, mfn. that by which one lives, affording or serving for a livelihood, MBh.; Yājñ. &c.; that on which one depends or rests, Daś.; Sāh.

2. **Upa-jīvya**, ind. p. having lived upon; depending on, because of (with acc.)

उपजुष् *upa-√jush*, P. (pf. 3. pl. *-jujushus*) to excite pleasure, gladden, RV. viii, 23, 9.

Upa-josha, *as*, m. desire, pleasure, liking, see *yathôpajosham*; (*am*), ind. according to one's desire or liking, L.; silently, quietly, Śak. 202, 8, v.l.

Upa-joshaṇa, *am*, n. enjoyment, use; taking (food), BhP. v, 16, 19.

उपज्ञा 1. *upa-√jñā*, Ā. *-jānīte* (3. pl. *-jānate*, AV.) to ascertain, excogitate, invent, find out, hit upon, AV. iv, 36, 8; ŚBr.

Upa-jijñāsu, mfn. (fr. Desid.), wishing to know or to become acquainted with, MBh. xii, 3884.

Upa-jijñāsya, mfn. to be excogitated or found out; enigmatical, ŚBr. iii, 2, 1, 24.

2. **Upa-jñā**, f. knowledge found out or invented by one's self (not handed down by tradition), untaught or primitive knowledge, invention, Pāṇ.; L.; (mfn. ifc.) invented or first taught by, unknown before, Ragh. xv, 63; Kāś. and Siddh. on Pāṇ. ii, 4, 21 & vi, 2, 14; Bhaṭṭ.

U'pa-jñāta, mfn. excogitated, invented, found out; ascertained by one's self, unknown before, ŚBr.; Pāṇ.

उपज्मन् *úpa-jman*, *ā*, m. (*√gam*), way, path [NBD.], SV. i, 4, 1, 5, 6.

उपज्योतिष *upa-jyotisha*, *am*, n. a compendium of astronomy, VarBṛS.

उपज्रि *upa-√jri*, P. *-jrayati*, to go near to, RV. ix, 71, 5.

उपज्वल् *upa-√jval*.

Upa-jvalita, mfn. lighted up (with *an*° neg.), ŚBr. xi, 8, 3, 7.

उपड *upaḍa*, *as*, m. a diminutive for all proper names of men which begin with *upa*, Pāṇ. v, 3, 80.

उपढौक् *upa-√ḍhauk*, Caus. P. *-ḍhaukayati*, to fetch, bring, prepare; to offer, present, Hit.; Comm. on KātyŚr. vii, 2, 2; Kāraṇḍ.

Upa-ḍhaukana, *am*, n. a respectful present (made to a king), L.

Upa-ḍhaukita, mfn. prepared, arranged, Pañcat.

उपतक्ष *upa-taksha* or *upatakshaka*, *as*, m. N. of a Nāga, Kauś.; R.

उपतटम् *upa-taṭam*, ind. near the slope, Megh. 58; near the bank, Kād.

उपतप् *upa-√tap*, P. *-tapati* (p. *-tápat*, see col. 3) to make warm, heat, ŚBr.; to afflict (as an illness; with gen. or acc. of the afflicted person), ŚBr.; ChUp.; to feel pain, become sick, ĀśvGṛ. iv, 1, 1: Pass. *-tapyate*, to be made warm or heated; (with *tapas*) to undergo bodily mortification, AV. vii, 61, 1, 2; to be afflicted with pain, be tormented, feel pain, become ill, KātySr.; MBh.; BhP.; Suśr. &c.: Caus. *-tāpayati* (aor. Subj. 2. sg. *-tītapāsi*, AV.) to ignite, burn, consume, AV. vi, 32, 1; to cause pain, mortify, torment, hurt, oppress, MBh.; BhP.; Comm. on Mn.

Upa-tápat, *t*, n. interior heat, disease, ŚBr.; TBr. iii, 9, 17, 1.

Upa-tapta, mfn. heated, hot, MBh. iii, 71; R.; sick, ill, KātyŚr. xxii, 3, 23; distressed, afflicted.

Upa-taptṛi, mfn. heating, burning; (*tā*), m. interior heat, disease, L.

Upa-tāpa, *as*, m. heat, warmth; heating, Suśr.; L.; pain, trouble; paining, Śak. 122, 2 (v.l. for *anu-tāpa*), Suśr.; sickness, disease, hurt, ĀśvGṛ.; MBh.; Suśr &c.; haste, hurry, L.

Upa-tāpaka, mfn. causing pain, paining.

Upa-tāpana, mfn. id., BhP.

Upa-tāpin, mfn. heating, inflaming; causing pain, paining, MBh.; Kāvyād. &c.; (*upatāpin*), suffering heat or pain, sick, ill, ŚBr.; ChUp.; Kauś.; Mn.

उपतल्प्य *upa-talpya*, *as*, m. a kind of wooden seat or stool, Sāy. on TBr. iii, 8, 14.

उपतारक *upa-tāraka*, mfn. (*√tṛī*), overflowing, Kauś.

उपतिष्ठासु *upa-tishṭhāsu*. See *upa-√sthā*.

उपतिष्य *upa-tishya*, *as*, m., N. of a son of Tishya.

उपतीरम् *upa-tīram*, ind. on the shore, Kāś. on Pāṇ. vi, 2, 121.

उपतीर्थ *upa-tīrtha*. See *sûpatīrtha*.

उपतुष् *upa-√tush*, Caus.

Upa-toshya, ind. p. having satisfied; contenting, satisfying, ĀśvGṛ. i, 6.

उपतूलम् *upa-tūlam*, ind. near or on the panicle (of a plant), Kāś. on Pāṇ. v, 2, 121.

उपतृण्य *upa-tṛiṇya* (voc. *úpa-tṛiṇya*), *as*, m. 'lurking in the grass,' a kind of snake, AV. v, 13, 5.

उपतृद् *upa-√tṛid*, P. *-tṛiṇátti* (Pot. *-tṛindyā́t*) to pierce, cleave, TS. vi, 3, 9, 3.

उपतैल *upa-taila*, mfn. (gaṇa *gaurâdi*, Pāṇ. vi, 2, 194) = *abhyakta-taila*, T.

उपतैष *upataisha* v.l. for *upa-naisha* (Kāś.), gaṇa *gaurâdi*, Pāṇ. vi, 2, 194 (ed. Böhtl.)

उपत्यका *upatyakā*, f. land at the foot of a mountain or hill, low-land, Pāṇ.; Ragh.; Śak.; Śiś. &c.; a vale, valley, L.

उपत्सर् *upa-√tsar*.

Upa-tsárya, ind. p. having approached stealthily, creeping near, ŚBr. i, 6, 3, 28.

उपदंश् *upa-√daṅś*.

Upa-daṅśa, *as*, m. anything eaten in addition (to excite thirst or appetite), a relish, spice, R.; Kathās.; Suśr.; Daś.; a kind of venereal disease, Suśr.; the tree Moringa Hyperanthera (the scraped root of which is used for horse-radish), L.; a kind of shrub, L.

Upa-daṅśaka, *as*, m. a particular plant, L.

Upa-daṅśam, ind. p. having taken an additional bit or morsel of (with instr. or ifc.), Pāṇ. iii, 4, 47; Kāś. on Pāṇ. ii, 2, 21.

Upadaṅśin, mfn. afflicted with the Upadaṅśa (q. v.) disease, L.

Upa-daśya, ind. p. = *upa-daṅśam* above.

उपदम्भ् *upa-√dambh*, Caus. P. (3. pl. *-dambhayanti*) to lessen, diminish, destroy, ŚBr. xiii, 8, 1, 1.

उपदर्शक *upa-darśaka*, &c. See *upa-√dṛiś*.

उपदश *upa-daśa*, mfn. nearly ten, almost ten, Comm. on Pāṇ.; Vop.

उपदस् *upa-√das*, P. *-dasyati* (Subj. *-dasat*, RV. i, 139, 5; AV. v, 30, 15) to fail, be wanting, be extinguished or exhausted, dry up, RV.; AV. iii, 29, 2, 6; v, 30, 15; TS. i, 6, 3, 3; ŚBr.; TāṇḍyaBr.; GopBr.; Kauś.; to want, lose, be deprived of (instr.), AV. xii, 4, 2: Caus. *-dāsayati*, to cause to fail or cease, extinguish, AV. xii, 5, 27; 52; TBr.; Nir.

Upa-dasta, &c. See *an-upadasta*, p. 34, col. 2.

Upa-dāsuka, mfn. failing, TS.

उपदह् *upa-√dah*, P. *-dahati* (aor. *-adhā-*

kshīt, MBh. iii, 546) to burn, set fire to, ŚBr.; Gobh.; MBh.

Upa-dagdha, mfn. burnt, set on fire, ŚBr.; Kauś.

उपदा 1. *upa-√1. dā*, P. *-dadāti*, to give in addition, add; to give, grant, offer, RV. vi, 28, 2; AV. iv, 21, 2; xix, 34, 8; R.; to take upon one's self: Pass. (irr. p. *-dadyámāna*) to be offered or granted (as protection), RV. vi, 49, 13.

Upa-dā́dya, ind. p. having taken or taking upon one's self, AV. x, 8, 18 (=xiii, 3, 14).

2. **Upa-dā́**, mfn. giving a present, VS. xxx, 9; (*ā*), f. a present, offering (esp. a respectful present to a king or person of rank); a bribe, Pāṇ.; Ragh.; Śatr. &c.

1. **Upa-dātṛi** (for 2. see col. 2), mfn. one who gives or grants or confers, Pañcat. iv, 107 (ed. Bombay).

1. **Upa-dāna** (for 2. see col. 2) or **upa-dānaka**, *am*, n. a present, offering, = 2. *upa-dā* above, L.

Upadī-kṛita, mfn. offered as a present, Śiś.

उपदानवी *upa-dānavī*, f., N. of a daughter of the Dānava Vṛisha-parvan, Hariv.; of a daughter of Vaiśvānara, BhP.

उपदासुक *upa-dā́suka.* See *upa-√das.*

उपदिग्ध *upa-digdha.* See *upa-√dih.*

उपदिश् 1. *upa-√diś*, P. Ā. *-diśati, -te*, to point out to, ŚBr. x, 6, 1, 11; to indicate, specify, explain, inform, instruct, teach, ŚBr.; ĀśvŚr. & Gṛ.; MBh.; Mṛicch.; Ragh. &c.; to advise, admonish, BhP.; Hit.; to mention, exhibit, speak of, BhP.; Mn.; Mṛicch.; VPrāt. &c.; to settle, prescribe, command, dictate, govern, MBh.; Mn.; Kum.; Pañcat. &c.; to name, call, MBh.; BhP.; Mn. &c.: Pass. *-diśyate*, to be taught, &c.

Upa-didikshā, f. (fr. Desid.), the wish or intention to teach or inform, Comm. on Bādar. iii, 4, 8.

2. **Upa-diś** (for 3. see s. v.), mfn. (ifc.) pointing out to, showing; see *mārŏpadiś.*

Upa-diśa, *as*, m., N. of a son of Vasu-deva, Hariv.

Upa-diśya, ind. p. having indicated or taught &c.; indicating, teaching &c.

Upa-dishṭa, mfn. specified, particularized; taught, instructed; mentioned; prescribed, commanded &c.; initiated, W.; (*am*), n. counsel, advice, (in dram.) a persuasive speech in conformity with the prescribed rules, Sāh. 449 &c.

Upa-deśa, *as*, m. pointing out to, reference to, Pāṇ. i, 4, 70; Kap.; Bādar.; Jaim. &c.; specification, instruction, teaching, information, advice, prescription, TUp.; MBh.; Mn.; Suśr.; Śak.; Hit. &c.; plea, pretext (= *apa-deśa*), Mn. ix, 268; Ragh.; Kathās.; initiation, communication of the initiatory Mantra or formula, KātyŚr.; (in Gr.) original enunciation (i. e. the original form [often having an Anubandha] in which a root, base, affix, augment, or any word or part of a word is enunciated in grammatical treatises), Pāṇ.; Kāś.; Siddh. &c.; N. of a class of writings (Buddh.); a name, title, MW. **-karṇikā**, f., N. of a work. **-tā**, f. the being a precept or rule, Kum. v, 36. **-pañcaka**, n., **-mālā**, f., **-ratna-mālā**, f., **-rasāyana**, n., **-sāhasrī**, f., N. of certain works. **Upadeśâmṛita**, n., N. of a work. **Upa-deśârtha-vākya**, n. 'a tale for the sake of instruction,' a parable.

Upa-deśaka, mfn. giving instruction, instructing, instructive, didactic, Sarvad.; teacher, instructor, L.

Upa-déśana, *am*, n. the act of advising; instruction, information, doctrine, TBr.; Sāh.; (*ā*), f. id., Pañcat. **-vat**, mfn. furnished with advice, TāṇḍyaBr.

Upa-deśin, mfn. advising, teaching, informing; (*ī*), m. a teacher, adviser, Hit.; Kathās.; (*upadeśin*), mfn. (in Gr.) a word or affix &c. used in an Upa-deśa (q. v.), Comm. on Pāṇ.

Upa-deśyà, mfn. to be taught; taught, AV. xi, 8, 23; Kap.

Upa-deshṭavya, mfn. to be taught or advised; fit or proper to be taught, Hit.; Mṛicch.

Upa-deshṭṛi, *ṭā*, m. one who teaches, a teacher, adviser; a Guru or spiritual guide, MBh.; BhP.; Pañcat.; Sarvad. **-tva**, n. the state of being a teacher, Kap.

उपदिश् 3. *upa-diś*, *k*, f. an intermediate region or point of the compass.

Upa-diśam, ind. between two regions, in an intermediate region, L.

Upa-diśā, f. id., ŚBr.

उपदिह् *upa-√dih.*

Upa-digdha, mfn. smeared, covered, Suśr.; fat, VarBṛS. 67, 1. **-tā**, f. the state of being smeared or covered, Kām.

1. **Upa-deha** (for 2. see s. v.), *as*, m. a cover, liniment, ointment, Comm. on Car.

Upa-dehikā, f. a species of ant, L.

उपदी 1. *upa-√3. dī* (*kshaye*, Dhātup. xxvi, 25).

Upa-dātavya, mfn., Pāṇ. vi, 1, 50.

2. **Upa-dātṛi**, mfn. ib.

2. **Upa-dāna**, *am*, n. ib.

उपदी 2. *upadī*, f. a parasitical plant, L.

उपदीक *upadīka*, *as*, *ā*, m. f. a species of ant, ŚBr.; TBr.; TĀr.

उपदीक्ष् *upa-√dīksh*, Caus.

Upadīkshin, mfn. one who has been initiated in addition to, KātyŚr. xxv, 14, 3; 4.

Upa-dīkshya, ind. p. having initiated in addition to, KātyŚr. xxv, 13, 28.

उपदीप् *upa-√dīp*, Caus. *-dīpayati*, to kindle, set fire to, MBh.; Hariv.

Upa-dīpayitvā, (irr.) ind. p. having kindled, MBh. iii, 10230.

उपदुष् *upa-√dush*, P. *-dushyati*, to become corrupt or depraved (as a woman), Hariv. 11264.

उपदुह् *upa-duh*, °*dhuk*, m. (*√duh*), a milk-pail, MBh.

Upadoha, *as*, m. id., ib.

Upa-dohana, *am*, n. id., ib.

उपदृश् 1. *upa-√dṛiś*, P. (aor. Subj. 2. du. *-darśathas*, RV.) to descry, perceive, RV. viii, 26, 4; to look at or regard (with indifference), MBh.: Pass. *-dṛiśyate* (aor. *-adarśi*; 3. pl. *-adṛiśran*, RV.) to be perceived, be or become visible, appear, RV. i, 124, 4; vii, 67, 2; TāṇḍyaBr.; BhP.: Caus. *-darśayati*, to cause to see, show, exhibit, MBh.; Ragh.; Kathās.; Prab. &c.; to cause to appear, present a false show, deceive, illude, Kathās. xix, 75; Rājat.; to explain, illustrate, Yājñ. ii, 8.

Upa-darśaka, *as*, m. one who shows the way, a door-keeper, L.

Upa-darśana, *am*, n. the act of exhibiting, representing, Sāh.; a commentary, L.

Upa-darśita, mfn. caused to appear, shown; perceived, distinguished; explained.

2. **Upa-dṛiś**, *k*, f. aspect, look, appearance, RV. viii, 102, 15; ix, 54, 2.

Upa-dṛishṭi, *is*, f. id., L.

Upa-drashṭṛi, *ṭā*, m. a looker-on, spectator; a witness, AV. xi, 3, 59; TS.; ŚBr.; ĀśvŚr.; Kāṭh.; BhP. &c.; (*upa-drá́shṭṛikā*), f. a female witness, MaitrS. iii, 2, 4. **-mát**, mfn. having witnesses; (*máti*, loc. ind. before witnesses, TBr. ii, 2, 1, 3; 5.)

उपदृषद् *upa-dṛishad*, *t*, ind. near or on a mill-stone, Pāṇ. v, 4, 111.

Upa-dṛishadam, ind. id., ib.

उपदेव *upa-deva*, *as*, m. an inferior or secondary deity (as a Yaksha, Gandharva, Apsaras, &c.), BhP.; N. of several men, Hariv.; VP.; (*ā*, *ī*), f., N. of a wife of Vasu-deva, Hariv.; VP. **-°tā**, f. a minor or inferior deity, L.

उपदेश *upa-deśa*, &c. See *upa-√diś.*

उपदेह 2. *upa-deha*, *as*, m. (for 1. see *upa-√dih*) 'a secondary growth of the body,' a kind of excrescence, Suśr. **-vat**, mfn. having the above excrescence, ib.

उपदोह *upa-doha.* See *upa-duh.*

उपद्रु *upa-√dru*, P. *-dravati* (aor. *-ádudrot*, RV.) to run near or towards; to run at, rush at, oppress, assault, attack, RV. ii, 30, 3; iv, 16, 1; AV. vii, 73, 6; xviii, 2, 23; TS.; ChUp.; to sing the Upa-drava or fourth of the five parts of a Sāman stanza, AitĀr. ii, 3, 4, 3.

Upa-drava, *as*, m. that which attacks or occurs suddenly, any grievous accident, misfortune, calamity, mischief, national distress (such as famine, plague, oppression, eclipse, &c.); national commotion, rebellion; violence, outrage, MBh.; R.; Śak.; VarBṛS. &c.; a supervenient disease or one brought on whilst a person labours under another, Suśr.; the fourth of the five parts of a Sāman stanza, ShaḍvBr.; Comm. on TĀr. &c.

Upa-dravin, mfn. attacking suddenly, falling on; tyrannical, violent; factious; (*ī*), m. a tyrant, oppressor; a rebel, L.

Upa-druta, mfn. run after, persecuted, attacked, oppressed, visited (by calamities), tyrannized over, Hariv.; R.; Kathās.; Hit.; Suśr. &c.; (in astrol.) eclipsed = boding evil, inauspicious, VarBṛS.; (*am*), n. a kind of Sandhi, ŚāṅkhŚr.

उपद्वार *upa-dvāra*, *am*, n. a side-door, AgP.; (cf. *sūpadvāra.*)

उपद्वीप *upa-dvīpa*, *as*, m. a small adjacent island, minor island, BhP.; Pañcar.

उपधमन *upa-dhamana.* See *upa-√dhmā.*

उपधर्म *upa-dharma*, *as*, m. a minor or subordinate duty; a by-law, Mn. ii, 237; iv, 147; a false faith, heresy, BhP.

उपधा 1. *upa-√dhā*, P. Ā. *-dadhāti, -dhatte*, to place or lay upon, place near to, put on or into; to place, lay, put, RV. x, 87, 3; 145, 6; AV.; ŚBr.; KātyŚr.; Mn.; Ragh. &c.; to put to, yoke (horses), RV. iv, 29, 4; to give or make over, hand over (knowledge), teach, Ragh.; to impose, lay upon, commit, consign, Ragh.; to place under one's self, lie down upon, R.; to place in addition, add, connect, AitBr.; ŚBr.; Lāṭy. &c.; to communicate, cause to share in; to use, employ; (in Gr.) to lie or be placed close to, precede without the intervention of another syllable, RPrāt. &c.; to cause to rest upon or depend on, BhP.

2. **Upa-dhā**, f. imposition, forgery, fraud, deceit, trick, false pretence, MBh.; Mn.; R.; trial or test of honesty (of four kinds, viz. of loyalty, disinterestedness, continence, and courage), Kām.; Bhaṭṭ.; Śiś. &c.; (in Gr.) a penultimate letter, Pāṇ.; RPrāt.; APrāt.; Nir. &c.; condition, reservation, L. **-bhṛita**, m. a kind of servant (engaged under particular conditions), L. **-lopa**, m. elision of the penultimate letter. **-°lopin**, mfn. subject to the above (as a Bahuvrīhi compound ending in *an*), Pāṇ. iv, 1, 28. **-śuci**, mfn. of approved virtue, approved, tried, Hit.

Upa-dhāna, mfn. placing upon, employed or used in placing upon (as a Mantra in the setting up of the sacrificial bricks), Pāṇ. iv, 4, 125; (*am*), n. the act of placing or resting upon, KātyŚr.; Kauś.; that on which one rests, a pillow, cushion, AV. xiv, 2, 65; ŚBr.; KātyŚr.; MBh.; Suśr. &c.; cover, lid, Car.; Hcat.; peculiarity, singularity, excellence (cf. *premŏpa*°), Bālar.; Siddh.; affection, kindness; religious observance; poison, L.; (*ī*), f. a pillow, cushion; footstool (see *pādŏpa*°), MBh. **-vidhi**, m., N. of a work.

Upadhānaka, *am*, n. a pillow, cushion, Hcat.

Upa-dhānīya, mfn. to be put under; (*am*), n. a pillow, cushion, Pañcat.

Upa-dhāya, ind. p. having placed or rested upon &c.

Upa-dhāyin, mfn. ifc. placing under, Kum.

Upa-dhí, *is*, m. the act of putting to, adding, addition, Lāṭy.; the part of the wheel between the nave and the circumference, RV. ii, 39, 4; AV. vi, 70, 3; Kāṭh.; fraud, circumvention, MBh.; R.; Yājñ.; Kir. &c.; condition; peculiarity, attribute (Buddh.; see *upâ-dhi*); support, MW.

Upadhika, *as*, m. a cheat, knave (especially one who imposes by threats), Mn. ix, 258; (Kull. reads *aupadhika*, and probably *cŏupadhikā* is to be read for *cŏpadhikā* in the text.)

Upa-dheya, mfn. to be placed upon, being placed upon.

1. **Upa-hita** (for 2. see s. v.), mfn. put on or upon, placed, deposited, put into, KātyŚr.; MBh.; Hariv.; Ragh. &c.; joining, connected with; mixed, ŚBr.; Mālav.; Suśr.; (in Gr.) immediately preceded by, RPrāt.; resting or depending upon, having as a condition, Vedāntas.; Sarvad.; used, employed for, MBh.; Ragh.; brought near, handed over, given, MBh.; R.; Mṛicch. &c.; misled, deceived, MBh.

U'pa-hiti, *is*, f. the putting or placing upon, Nyāyam.; devotedness to, TS. ii.

उपधातु *upa-dhātu, us,* m. a secondary mineral, semi-metal (seven are specified: *svarṇa-mākshika,* pyrites; *tāra-mākshika,* a particular white mineral; *tuttha,* sulphate of copper; *kāṇsya,* brass; *rīti,* calx of brass; *sindūra,* red lead; *śilā-jatu,* red chalk), Bhpr.; secondary secretions and constituents of the body (viz. the milk, menses, adeps, sweat, teeth, hair, and lymph), ŚārṅgS. &c.

उपधारण *upa-dhāraṇa.* See *upa-√dhṛi.*

उपधाव् *upa-√dhāv,* Ā. (p. *-dhā́vamāna*) to run; to soar, RV. viii, 3, 21: P. *-dhāvati,* to run near, approach hastily; to have recourse to for assistance, TS.; ŚBr.; TāṇḍyaBr.; MBh.; R.; BhP. &c.

Upa-dhāvana, *as,* m. a follower, W.

उपधि *upa-dhí.* See p. 199, col. 3.

उपधूपय *upa-dhūpaya,* Nom. (fr. *dhūpa*) P. *-dhūpayati,* to fumigate, envelop in smoke; to envelop in mist; to darken, cover, Kauś.

Upa-dhūpita, mfn. fumigated, enveloped in smoke, MBh.; R.; near death, dying, L.; (*ā*), f. (scil. *diś*) = the next.

उपधूमिता *upa-dhūmitā,* f. (scil. *diś,* fr. *upa-dhūmaya*), 'enveloped in haze,' the quarter of the heavens to which the sun is proceeding (opposed to *dagdhā, dīptā,* and the five *śāntā*), Vasantarāja, T.; (cf. *pra-dhūmitā, sam-dhū°.*)

उपधृ *upa-√dhṛi,* Caus. P. *-dhārayati,* to hold up, support, bear, MBh.; Suśr.; to hold as, consider as, regard, think, MBh.; R.; Mn.; BhP. &c.; to hold in the mind, reflect or meditate on, MBh.; to perceive, comprehend, hear, experience, learn, Suśr.; MBh.; BhP.

Upa-dhāraṇa, *am,* n. the act of considering, consideration, reflection, MBh.

1. **Upa-dhārya,** mfn. to be comprehended, Car.

2. **Upa-dhārya,** ind. p. having taken or held up &c.

Upa-dhṛiti, *is,* f. a ray of light, L.

उपधृष् *upa-√dhṛish,* P. (pf. *-dadharsha*) to venture to undertake, ŚBr. ix, 5, 2, 1.

उपधे *upa-√dhe,* Caus. Ā. (3. du. *-dhāpayete*) to suckle, rear by suckling, RV. i, 95, 1.

उपध्मा 1. *upa-√dhmā,* P. *-dhámati,* to blow or breathe at or upon, RV. v, 9, 5; ŚBr.; TāṇḍyaBr.; ShaḍvBr.; MānŚr.; Mn.

Upa-dhamana, *am,* n. the act of blowing at, blowing, Gaut. ix, 32.

2. **Upa-dhmā,** f. id.; the effort of the voice which produces the sound *upadhmānīya.*

Upa-dhmā́na, mf(*ī*)n. breathing or blowing upon, AV. viii, 8, 2.

Upa-dhmānīya, *as,* m. the Visarga (q.v.) as pronounced before the letters *p* and *ph,* Pāṇ.; VPrāt. &c.

उपध्यै *upa-√dhyai.*

Upa-dhyāta, mfn. remembered, thought of, MBh.

उपध्वंस् *upa-√dhvaṇs,* Pass. *-dhvasyate,* to be afflicted or attacked, Suśr.

Upa-dhvastá, mfn. speckled, spotted, VS.; TS.; ŚBr.; KātyŚr.; (cf. *dhvasta.*)

उपनक्ष् *upa-√naksh,* Ā. (Impv. 2. sg. *-nakshasva*) to come near to, RV. viii, 54, 7.

उपनक्षत्र *upa-nakshatrá, am,* n. a secondary star, minor constellation, ŚBr.

उपनख *upa-nakha, am,* n. a particular disease of the finger-nails, whitlow, agnail (also called *cippa;* one of the twenty-four Kshudra-rogas or slight diseases), Suśr.

उपनगर *upa-nagara, am,* n. a suburb, L.; (*am*), ind. near the city. **— bhava,** mfn. being near the city, near the city, Daś.

उपनति *úpa-nati.* See *upa-√nam.*

उपनद् *upa-√nad,* Caus.

Upa-nādita, mfn. caused to resound, R.

उपनदम् *upa-nadam,* ind. (fr. *nadī,* Pāṇ. v, 4, 110), near the river, on the river.

Upa-nadi, ind. id., ib.

उपनद्ध *upa-naddha,* &c. See *upa-√nah.*

उपनन्द *upa-nanda, as,* m., N. of a Nāga; of several men, VP.; BhP. &c.

Upa-nandaka, *as,* m., N. of a son of Dhṛita-rāshṭra; of a being attendant on Skanda, MBh.

Upa-nandana, *as,* m. a form of Śiva, VP.

उपनम् *upa-√nam,* P. *-namati,* to bend towards or inwards; to tend towards, approach, come to, arrive at; to fall to one's share or lot, become one's property, share in (with acc., dat., or gen.), VS.; ŚBr.; TBr.; ChUp.; Rājat. &c.; to come to one's mind, occur, TS.; TBr. i, 1, 2, 8; to attend upon any one (acc.) with (instr.); to gain the favour of any one (acc.), BhP. vi, 19, 16: Caus. *-nāmayati,* to put or place before (gen.), Gobh. ii, 1, 7; to lead towards or into the presence of, present any one (gen.), Lalit.; to reach, hand to, ib.; to offer, present, ib.; Kāraṇḍ.

U'pa-nata, mfn. bent towards or inwards, ŚBr.; KātyŚr.; Kāṭh.; subdued, subjected, surrendered; dependent on (for protection &c.), Āp.; MBh.; Ragh. &c.; brought near to, approached, near (either in form or space); fallen to one's share; brought about, produced, existing, being, BhP.; Megh. &c.

U'pa-nati, *is,* f. inclination, affection, VS. xx, 13; the falling to one's share, Kathās.

Upa-namra, mfn. coming to, being present, Naish.

Upa-nā́muka, mfn. bending towards, approaching, ŚBr.

उपनय *upa-naya, upa-nayana.* See p. 201, col. 2.

उपनर *upa-nara, as,* m., N. of a Nāga, L.

उपनह् *upa-√nah,* P. *-nahyati,* to tie or bind to or up, bind together; to make up into a bundle, TS.; AitBr.; ŚBr.; KātyŚr.; ĀśvŚr.: Caus. *-nāhayati,* to tie up, wrap, dress (a wound), Suśr.; Car.

Upa-naddha, mfn. covered with, Suśr.; inlaid, BhP.

Upa-naddhavya, mfn. to be wrapped or covered with, Car.

Upa-nahana, *am,* n. anything fit for binding up or wrapping (as a cloth), ŚBr.; KātyŚr.

Upa-nāhá, *as,* m. a bundle, AV. ix, 4, 5; TS.; a plaster, unguent (applied to a wound or sore); a cover, poultice, Suśr.; inflammation of the ciliary glands, stye, Suśr.; the tie of a lute (the lower part of the tail-piece where the wires are fixed), L.; continual enmity, L. **— sveda,** m. (in med.) perspiration caused by a kind of poultice.

Upa-nāhana, *am,* n. the act of putting a plaster upon, applying an unguent; plaster; cover; poultice, Suśr.

उपनागर *upa-nāgara, as,* m. (scil. *apabhranśa,* q. v.) a particular Prākṛit dialect.

Upa-nāgarikā, f. a kind of alliteration, Kpr.

उपनाथ् *upa-√nāth,* P. *-nāthati,* to ask, entreat, Kāś. on Pāṇ. ii, 3, 55.

उपनामन् *upa-nāman, a,* n. a surname, nickname, W.

उपनाय *upa-nāyá,* &c. See p. 201, col. 2.

उपनायक *upa-nāyaka, as,* m. (in dram.) a secondary hero, Sāh.

उपनासिक *upa-nāsika, am,* n. the part surrounding the nose, that which is near the nose, Suśr.

उपनिःश्रि *upa-niḥ-śri* (*upa-nis-√śri*).

Upa-niḥśritya, ind. p. having gone out to, Lalit.

उपनिक्षिप् *upa-ni-√kship,* P. *-kshipati,* to throw down; to put or place down, Mn. iii, 224; to deposit.

Upa-nikshepa, *as,* m. a deposit (sealed or covered up so that the contents are unknown); any article intrusted to one's keeping, Yājñ. ii, 25.

उपनिगम् *upa-ni-√gam,* P. *-gacchati,* to meet with, fall upon, get, ŚBr.; AitBr.

उपनिग्रह् *upa-ni-√grah,* P. Ā. *-gṛihṇāti, -ṇīte,* to press down upon, TS.; to bring or push near to, AitBr.; ĀpŚr.

उपनिधा *upa-ni-√dhā,* P. Ā. *-dadhāti, -dhatte,* to put or place down near to, put or place before, ŚBr.; TāṇḍyaBr.; TBr.; Lāṭy.; ChUp.; ĀśvGṛ.; to place down, conceal; to deposit, intrust; to bring near, lead near to, Gīt.; to produce, cause, Bhaṭṭ.

Upa-nidhātṛi, mfn. one who puts or places down, ŚBr.

Upa-nidhāna, *am,* n. the act of putting down near to, putting by the side of, Comm. on Lāṭy.; a deposit, W.

Upa-nidhā́ya, ind. p. having put down near to &c.

Upa-nidhi, *is,* m. a deposit, pledge, property put under the care of a creditor, friend &c. (generally a sealed deposit, but also any article intrusted to a friend which he may use whilst in his keeping), Mn. viii, 145, &c.; Yājñ. ii, 25; MBh.; a ray of light, L.; N. of a son of Vasu-deva, VP.

Upa-nihita, mfn. placed or put down near to, placed or put before, ĀśvGṛ.; ChUp.; put down, kept; deposited, intrusted, Mn. viii, 37; 196; BhP.

उपनिपत् *upa-ni-pat,* P. *-patati,* to fly down to, ChUp.; to take place in addition, accede, exist or be in addition, Suśr.; Comm. on Bādar.: Caus. *-pātayati,* to cause to lie down, ŚāṅkhŚr.; ĀśvŚr.

Upa-nipāta, *as,* m. acceding, accession, Sarvad.; taking place, occurring, Comm. on Bādar.; a sudden occurrence or event, breaking forth, Mudrār.; Kād.; a sudden and unexpected attack, Comm. on Pāṇ. v, 3, 106.

Upa-nipātana, *am,* n. occurring or taking place suddenly, Comm. on Nyāyad.

Upa-nipātin, mfn. rushing in, Śak. 237, 5; attacking suddenly.

उपनिपद् *upa-ni-√pad,* Ā. (p. *-pádyamāna*) to lie down at the side of, RV. i, 152, 4: Caus. *-pādayati,* to cause to lie down at the side of, ŚBr.; to lay down at, ib.

उपनिपीड् *upa-ni-√pīḍ,* Caus.

Upa-nipīḍita, mfn. afflicted, troubled, MBh.

उपनिप्लु *upa-ni-√plu,* Ā. (3. pl. *-plavante*) to approach, reach, AitBr. iv, 26, 3.

उपनिबन्ध् *upa-ni-√bandh,* P. to write, compose; to explain.

Upa-nibaddha, mfn. adhering to, Comm. on Nyāyad.; written, composed, arranged, Bālar.; Uttarar.; Comm. on Mn., on Pat. &c.; spoken of, discussed, Comm. on KātyŚr. &c.

Upa-nibandha, *as,* m. obligation, oath, Mcar.

Upa-nibandhana, mfn. manifesting, explaining, BhP.; Sarvad.; (*am*), n. description, Sāh.

उपनिभ *upa-nibha,* mfn. ifc. similar, equal, RPrāt.

उपनिमज्ज् *upa-ni-√majj,* P. (impf. *-amajjat*) to dive near, TBr. i, 1, 3, 6.

उपनिमन्त्र् *upa-ni-√mantr,* P. to invite; to offer, MBh.; R.; to consecrate, inaugurate, L.

Upa-nimantraṇa, *am,* n. invitation, Veṇis.; inauguration, L.

उपनिमन्द् *upa-ni-√2. mand,* P. *-madati,* to restrain, stop, ŚBr.

उपनिम्रेड् *upa-ni-√mreḍ,* Ā. *-mreḍate,* to make happy, gladden, ChUp.

उपनियुज् *upa-ni-√yuj,* Ā. to tie or join to, Kāṭh.

उपनिरुध् *upa-ni-√rudh,* P. to shut up, ŚBr.

उपनिर्गम *upa-nirgama, as,* m. a main or royal road, L.

उपनिर्वृत् *upa-nir-vṛit* (*upa-nis-√vṛit*), Caus. *-vartayati,* to cause to appear (e.g. a disease), Suśr.

उपनिवप् *upa-ni-√2. vap,* P. *-vapati,* to throw or pour down in addition, ŚBr.

Upa-nivapana, *am,* n. the act of throwing or pouring down upon, KātyŚr.

उपनिविश् *upa-ni-√viś,* P., see *upa-nivishṭa:* Caus. P. *-veśayati,* to cause to encamp, R.; to lay the foundation of, Ragh.

Upa-nivishṭa, mfn. besieging, R.; occupying, inhabiting, MBh.; occupied, inhabited, VāyuP.

Upa-niveśin, mfn. adherent, belonging to, Vārtt. on Pāṇ. i, 4, 1.

उपनिवृ *upa-ni-√vṛi*, P. to restrain, keep off, R.

उपनिवृत् *upa-ni-√vṛit*, Ā. *-vartate*, to come again, be repeated, AitBr.; ŚāṅkhBr.; RPrāt.: Caus. P. *-vartayati*, to bring or fetch again, AitBr. vii, 5, 5.

उपनिवेश *upa-niveśa, as*, m. a suburb, Hariv. 8962.

उपनिवेष्ट् *upa-ni-√vesht*, Ā. *-veshṭate*, to surround, ŚBr. v, 3, 4, 11.

उपनिशम् *upa-ni-√śam*.

Upa-niśamya, ind. p. having perceived, perceiving, MBh. viii, 1738.

उपनिश्रि *upa-ni-√śri*, P. *-śrayati*, to go near or to the side of, ŚBr. xiv, 4, 2, 23: Ā. *-śrayate*, to cling to, lean against, ŚBr.; ŚāṅkhBr. & Śr.

उपनिषद् 1. *upa-ni-shad* (*upa-ni-√sad*), P. (pf. *-ní-shedus*) to sit down near to; to approach, set about, AV. xix, 41, 1; ŚBr.; Kauś.

2. **Upa-nishád,** *t*, f. (according to some) the sitting down at the feet of another to listen to his words (and hence, secret knowledge given in this manner; but according to native authorities *upanishad* means 'setting at rest ignorance by revealing the knowledge of the supreme spirit'); the mystery which underlies or rests underneath the external system of things (cf. IW. p. 35 seqq.); esoteric doctrine, secret doctrine, mysterious or mystical meaning, words of mystery &c., ŚBr.; ChUp. &c.; a class of philosophical writings (more than a hundred in number, attached to the Brāhmaṇas [but see Īśopanishad]; their aim is the exposition of the secret meaning of the Veda, and they are regarded as the source of the Vedānta and Sāṃkhya philosophies; for the most important of the Upanishads, see IW. p. 37 seq.) **—°t-√1. kṛi** (*upanishat-√1. kṛi*), to treat anything as a mystery (?), Pāṇ. i, 4, 79. **—brāhmaṇa,** n., **-ratna,** n., **-vivaraṇa,** n., N. of works.

Upa-nishada, *am*, n. = 2. *upa-nishád* above (esp. occurring ifc.)

Upa-nishādín, mf(*inī*)n. staying or sitting near at hand, ŚBr. ix, 4, 3, 3.

उपनिषेव् *upa-ni-shev* (*upa-ni-√sev*), Ā. to devote one's self to, MBh.

उपनिष्कर *upa-nish-kara, as*, m. (√*kṛi*), a main road, highway, L.

उपनिष्क्रम् *upa-nish-kram* (*upa-nis-√kram*), P. *-krāmati*, to go out towards, ŚBr.

Upa-nishkramaṇa, *am*, n. the act of going or stepping out towards, PārGṛ.; taking a child in the fourth month of its age for the first time into the open air (usually called *nishkramaṇa*, q.v., one of the Saṃskāras or religious rites; cf. Mn. ii, 34), Hcat.; L.; a main road, road, Gaut. ix, 65; L.

Upa-nishkramya, ind. p. having gone or going out towards, stepping out, going out, ŚBr.; ŚāṅkhŚr.; MBh.

Upa-nishkrānta, mfn. one who has gone out of, R.

उपनिहन् *upa-ni-√han*, P. *-hanti*, to hammer or ram down (a stake) by the side of, ŚBr.; KātyŚr.

उपनी 1. *upa-√nī*, P. Ā. *-nayati, -te* (Ā. Pot. *-nayīta*, HirGṛ. i, 1, 2; p. *-nayamāna*, AV.) to lead or drive near, bring near, bring, adduce, offer, RV. ii, 3, 10; iii, 35, 3; ŚBr.; TBr.; MBh.; Mn.; Ragh.; to bring information, communicate; to lead or bring near to one's self, take possession of, R.; Kathās.; to lead, guide, MBh.; BhP.; to lead or draw towards one's self (said of the Guru who, in the ceremony of initiation, draws the boy towards himself); to initiate into one of the twice-born classes by investing with the sacred thread &c. (only Ā., Pāṇ. i, 3, 36), AV. xi, 5, 3; ŚBr.; ĀśvGṛ.; ŚāṅkhGṛ. &c.; Mn. &c.; to bring about, produce, cause, Gīt.; Prab.; Sāh.; to bring into any state, reduce to, R.; Hariv.; Kām. &c.; to take into one's service (only Ā., Pāṇ. i, 3, 36): Caus. *-nāyayati*, to cause to initiate (a pupil), Mn. xi, 191.

Upa-naya, *as*, m. the bringing near, procuring, MBh.; attaining, obtaining, obtainment, BhP.; employment, application, R.; application (the fourth member in a fivefold syllogism), Sarvad.; Tarkas, &c.; introduction (into any science), VarBṛS.; initiation = the next, L.

Upa-nayana, *am*, n the act of leading to or near, bringing, R.; BhP.; Vikr.; employment, application, Car.; introduction (into any science), Prab.; leading or drawing towards one's self; that ceremony in which a Guru draws a boy towards himself and initiates him into one of the three twice-born classes (one of the twelve Saṃskāras or purificatory rites [prescribed in the Dharma-sūtras and explained in the Gṛihya-sūtras] in which the boy is invested with the sacred thread [different for the three castes] and thus endowed with second or spiritual birth and qualified to learn the Veda by heart; a Brāhman is initiated in the eighth year [or seventh according to Hiraṇyakeśin; or eighth from conception; according to Śāṅkhāyana &c.], a Kshatriya in the eleventh, a Vaiśya in the twelfth; but the term could be delayed); see IW. p. 201; RTL. p. 360 seqq.; ĀśvGṛ. i, 19–22; ŚāṅkhGṛ. ii, 1–6; PārGṛ. ii, 2–5; Gobh. ii, 10; HirGṛ. i, 1 seqq.; Mn. ii, 36; Yājñ. i, 14. **—cintāmaṇi,** m., **-lakshaṇa,** n., N. of works.

Upa-nāyá, *as*, m. leader, RV. ix, 91, 4; initiation, = *upa-nayana*, L.

Upa-nāyana, *am*, n. initiation, = *upa-nayana* above.

Upanāyika, mfn. fit or belonging to an offering, Hariv. 4417 (v. l. *aupanāyaka*).

Úpa-nīta, mfn. led near, brought near, RV. i, 129, 2; MBh.; Mṛicch.; VarBṛS. &c.; led to a man, married (?), RV. x, 109, 4 = AV. v, 17, 6; adduced; presented &c.; initiated, BhP.; Mn. ii, 49; Ragh. &c.; (*as*), m. a boy brought near to a Guru and initiated into one of the twice-born classes (by investiture with the sacred thread and other ceremonies).

Upa-nīti, *is*, f. initiation, = *upa-nayana* above, Nyāyam.

Upa-netavya, mfn. to be brought near; to be applied, R.; L.

Upa-netṛi, mf(*trī*)n. one who brings near, Kum. i, 61; (*tā*), m. the spiritual preceptor, Pañcat.

उपनी 2. *upa-ní* (*upa-ni-√i*), P. *-ny-eti*, to enter into, move towards, ŚBr.

उपनुद् *upa-√nud*.

Upa-nunna, mfn. driven near, wafted, Śiś. iv, 68.

उपनृत् *upa-√nṛit*, P. Ā. *-nṛityati, -te*, to dance before, dance round (acc.), MBh.; Hariv.; R.

Upa-nṛitta, mfn. any person before or round whom it is danced, MBh. v, 4100.

Upa-nṛitya, *am*, n. a place for dancing, R.

उपन्यस् *upa-ny-√2. as*, P. *-asyati*, to place down, put down, R.; to announce, MBh.; to speak of, mention; to explain; to hint, allude, suggest, Kir.; Kāvyapr.

Upa-nyasta, mfn. mentioned, explained, brought forward, hinted at, alluded, Yājñ.; Śak. 200, 2; Hit.

Upa-nyasya, ind. p. having put down &c.

Upa-nyāsa, *as*, m. putting down, placing near to, juxta-position, Comm. on Pāṇ.; bringing or procuring (requisites), MBh.; bringing forward, speaking of, mention; statement, suggestion, hint; quotation, reference, Mn.; Mālav.; Sāh.; Daśar. &c.; pretext, Amar. 23; proof, reason, Sāh.; a particular kind of treaty or alliance, Kām.; Hit.; (in dram.) propitiation, gratifying, Sāh.; a deposit, pledge, pawn, W.

Upa-nyāsya, mfn. to be adduced or stated, W.

उपन्याचर् *upa-ny-ā-√car*, P. *-cárati*, to enter into, penetrate, ŚBr. vi, 5, 4, 10.

उपन्याप्लु *upa-ny-ā-√plu*, Ā. *-plavate*, to swim near, ŚBr.

उपन्याहृ *upa-ny-ā-√hṛi*, to bring near, offer (a present to a teacher), Gobh. iii, 4, 2.

उपपक्ष *upa-pakshá, as*, m. the armpit; (*au*), m. du. the hair under the armpits, TBr. **—daghná,** mfn. reaching to the armpit, ŚBr.

Upapakshyà, mfn. being on the shoulder, AV. vii, 76, 2.

उपपक्ष्म *upa-pakshma*, ind. (fr. *-pakshman*), on the eye-lash, Suśr.

उपपत् *upa-√pat*, P. *-patati*, to fly near, hasten towards, RV.; BhP.

Upa-pāta, *as*, m. accident, occurrence, misfortune, KātyŚr.

Upa-pātin, mfn. ifc. falling to, hastening towards.

उपपतनीय *upa-patanīya, am*, n. a smaller sin, minor offence, = *upa-pātaka*, q. v., SāmavBr. i, 5, 14.

उपपति *upa-patí, is*, m. a paramour, gallant, VS. xxx, 9; Mn.; Yājñ.; Kathās.

उपपथ *upa-patha, as*, m. appendix [Aufrecht], BrahmaP.; (*am*), ind. on the way or road, Vop.

उपपद् 1. *upa-√pad*, Ā. *-padyate*, (rarely P.) *-ti*, to go towards or against, attack, AV. iv, 18, 2; to approach, come to, arrive at, enter, MBh.; Pañcat.; VarBṛS.; Kāraṇḍ.; to approach or come to a teacher (as a pupil), MBh.; to approach for succour or protection; to approach or join with in speech, AitBr. vii, 17, 5; to reach, obtain, partake of; to enter into any state, MBh.; R.; Hariv.; to take place, come forth, be produced, appear, occur, happen; to be present, exist, Lāṭy.; to be possible, be fit for or adequate to (with loc.), ĀśvGṛ.; Kauś.; Mn.; MBh. &c.; to be regular or according to rules; to become, be suitable, MBh.; R.; Suśr.; Śak. &c.: Caus. P. *-pādayati*, to bring to any state (with two acc.); to cause anything (acc.) to arrive at (loc. or dat.), cause to come into the possession of, offer, present, MBh.; MārkP.; Mn.; Yājñ.; Ragh. &c.; to cause to come forth or exist; to accomplish, effect, cause, produce, Lāṭy.; MBh.; Megh. &c.; to get ready, prepare, make fit or adequate for, make conformable to, MBh.; R.; to furnish or provide or endow with, MBh.; Kām. &c.; to make anything out of, Prab.; to examine; to find out, ascertain, R.; Mn. &c.; to prove, justify, Sarvad.; Comm. on Prab., on Kap. &c.; to attend on a patient, physic, Suśr. i, 56, 20; Car.

Upa-patti, *is*, f. happening, occurring, becoming visible, appearing, taking place, production, effecting, accomplishing, MBh.; BhP.; Bhag.; Ragh. &c.; proving right, resulting; cause, reason; ascertained or demonstrated conclusion, proof, evidence, argument, Sarvad.; Sāh.; Vedāntas.; Naish.; Rājat. &c.; fitness, propriety, possibility, KātyŚr.; MBh. &c. (instr. *upa-pattyā*, suitably, in a fit manner); association, connection, possession; religious abstraction, L. **—parityakta,** mfn. destitute of argument or proof, unproved, unreasonable, Rājat. **—mat,** mfn. demonstrated, proved. **—yukta,** mfn. id. **—sama,** m. (in log.) a kind of contradiction in which both the contradicting assertions are supposed to be demonstrable (e. g. sound is uneternal, because it is produced; it is eternal, because it is not tangible), Nyāyad.; Nyāyak.

2. **Upa-pad,** *t*, f. the act of happening, occurring, taking place.

Upa-panna, mfn. one who has approached a teacher (as a pupil), Suśr.; Vedāntas.; one who has approached for protection, R.; one who has obtained or reached, MBh.; R.; Kāś. on Pāṇ. iv, 2, 13; obtained, reached, gained; happened, fallen to one's share, produced, effected, existing, being near at hand, MBh.; Yājñ.; Ragh. &c.; endowed with, possessed of, furnished with, MBh.; Mn. &c.; fit, suited for the occasion, adequate, conformable, Śak.; Vikr.; Rājat. &c.

Upa-pāda, *as*, m. happening; effecting, accomplishing; see *dur-upapāda* and *yathopapādam*.

Upa-pādaka, mfn. causing to occur or happen, producing, effecting, making visible, Sāh.

Upa-pādana, mfn. id.; (*am*), n. the act of causing to appear, effecting, doing, MBh.; bringing near, BhP.; giving, delivering, presenting; proving or establishing by argument, Sarvad.; explaining, examining, L.

Upa-pādanīya, mfn. to be treated medically, Car.

Upa-pādita, mfn. effected, accomplished, performed, done; given, delivered, presented; proved, demonstrated; treated medically, cured.

1. **Upa-pāduka** (for 2. see below), mfn. self-produced; (*as*), m. a superhuman being, a god, demon &c., L.

Upa-pādya, mfn. to be effected or done; to be shown or proved; being produced, coming into existence.

उपपद *upa-pada*, *am*, n. a word standing near or accompanying another to which it is subordinate (either a subordinate word in a compound [but not in a Bahu-vrīhi compound] generally forming the first member, or a discriminative appellation at the end of proper names, as *varman*, *śarman* &c.; or a preposition, particle &c. prefixed to a verb or noun; or a secondary word of any kind which is governed by or limits the general idea contained in the principal word), Pāṇ.; VPrāt.; Sarvad.; (*vṛikshāḥ kalpôpapadāḥ*, 'those trees which have the word *kalpa* as accompanying word,' = *kalpa-vṛikshāḥ*, Śiś. iii, 59; cf. Ragh. xvi, 40); a bit, little, L. – **samāsa**, m. a compound containing an Upa-pada (e. g. *kumbha-kāra*).

उपपरामृश *upa-parā-√mṛiś*. See *upôpa-parā-√mṛiś*.

उपपरासृ *upa-parā-√sṛi*.

Upa-parāsṛitya, ind. p. having crept near or towards, ŚBr. xiv, 1, 1, 9.

उपपरीक्ष *upa-parîksh* (*upa-pari-√îksh*), Ā. to find out, learn, Lalit.; to examine, inquire into.

Upa-parîkshaṇa, *am*, n. inquiring into, investigation, examination, L.

Upa-parîkshā, f. id., Nir.

उपपरे *upa-parê* (*upa-parā-√i*), P. -*párâiti*, to go towards, go near, approach, ŚBr.

उपपर्चन *upa-parcana*. See *upa-√pṛic*.

उपपर्यावृत् *upa-pary-ā-√vṛit*, P. (pf. -*ā-vavarta*) to turn round towards, ŚBr.; Kāṭh.

उपपर्वन् *upa-parvan*, *a*, n. the day before the Parvan or change of the moon, ŚāṅkhGṛ. vi, 1, 11.

उपपर्शुका *upa-parśukā*, f. a false rib, N.

उपपली *upa-pali* (*upa-pali* [for *pari*]-√*i*).

Upa-paly-áyya, ind. p. turning back or round, ŚBr.

उपपल्वलम् *upa-palvalam*, ind. on the pool, Naish.

उपपा *upa-√1. pā*, Caus. -*pāyayati*, to give to drink, MānŚr. & Gṛ.

Upa-pāyana, *am*, n. the act of giving to drink, ib.

उपपात *upa-pāta*, *upa-pātin*. See *upa-√pat*.

उपपातक *upa-pātaka*, *am*, n. a secondary crime, minor offence (as killing kine, forgetting the Veda, breaking a vow of chastity, offending a Guru, selling the Soma plant &c.), Gaut. xxi, 11, &c.; Baudh. ii, 2, 12–14, &c.; Mn. xi, 66, &c.; Hariv. &c. (see also Yājñ. ii, 210; iii, 225; 242).

Upapātakin, mfn. one who has committed an Upa-pātaka or minor offence, Mn. xi, 107; 117.

उपपादुक 2. *upa-pāduka* (for 1. see above), mfn. having shoes, shod, W.

उपपाप *upa-pāpa*, *am*, n. a minor offence, = *upa-pātaka*, Yājñ. iii, 286.

उपपार्श्व *upa-pārśva*, *as*, m. a shoulder; flank, MBh.; a lesser rib; the opposite side, L.

उपपीड् *upa-√pīḍ*, Caus. -*pīḍayati*, to press on or to; to press down, oppress, check, Kām.; to cause pain, disturb, distress, Mn.; Kām.; (in astron.) to eclipse, R.; VarBṛS.

Upa-pīḍana, *am*, n. the act of pressing down, oppressing; causing pain, tormenting, torture, Mn.

Upa-pīḍam, ind. p. (Pāṇ. iii, 4, 49) pressing, pressing on or to, Śiś. x, 47; Naish.

Upa-pīḍita, mfn. pressed down, oppressed; tortured, pained, distressed.

उपपुर *upa-pura*, *am*, n. 'near the city,' a suburb, L.

Upa-purī, f. the environs of a city, BhP. iv, 25, 26.

Upapaurika, mfn. being near or in the environs of a city, Daś.

उपपुराण *upa-purāṇa*, *am*, n. a secondary or minor Purāṇa (eighteen are enumerated; the following is the list in the Kūrma-purāṇa: 1. Sānat-kumāra, 2. Nārasiṇha (fr. Nṛisiṇha), 3. Bhāṃda, 4. Śiva-dharma, 5. Daurvāsasa, 6. Nāradīya, 7. Kāpila, 8. Vāmana, 9. Auśanasa, 10. Brahmāṇḍa, 11. Vāruṇa, 12. Kālikā-purāṇa, 13. Māheśvara, 14. Śāmba, 15. Saura, 16. Pārāśara, 17. Mārīca, 18. Bhārgava).

उपपुष्पिका *upa-pushpikā*, f. yawning, gaping, L.

उपपूर्वरात्रम् *upa-pūrvarātram*, ind. about the first part of the night, Pāṇ. vi, 2, 33, Comm.

उपपूर्वाह्णम् *upa-pūrváhṇam*, ind. about fore-noon, ib.

उपपृच् 1. *upa-√pṛic*, P. Ā. (Impv. 2. sg. -*pṛindhi*, RV. ii, 24, 15; -*pṛiñca*, AV. ix, 4, 23; inf. -*prakshé*, RV. v, 47, 6) to add, RV.; to enlarge, increase, RV. i, 40, 8; to approach, come near, AV. xviii, 4, 50; to mix, couple, RV. v, 47, 6; vi, 28, 8; AV. ix, 4, 23.

Upa-párcana, *am*, n. coition, impregnation, RV. vi, 28, 8; AV. ix, 4, 23; (mfn.) being in close contact, closely touching, Nir.

2. **Upa-pṛic**, mfn. (Nom. *k*) adhering to, holding fast to (with gen.), RV. i, 32, 5.

उपपॄ *upa-√pṝi*, Ā. (Impv. 2. pl. -*pṛiṇadhvam*) to fill up, RV. vii, 16, 11.

उपपौरिक *upa-paurika*. See *upa-pura*.

उपपौर्णमासम् *upa-paurṇamāsam* and °*māsi*, ind. (Pāṇ. v, 4, 110) at the time of full moon.

उपप्रक्षे *upa-prakshé*, Ved. inf. of 1. *upa-√pṛic* above.

उपप्रगा *upa-pra-√gā*, P. (impf. or aor. -*prâgāt*) to step near to, approach, RV. i, 162, 7; 163, 12; 13; AV. i, 28, 1; vi, 37, 1; VS. vi, 7.

उपप्रछ् *upa-√prach*, Ā. (1. pl. -*pṛicchāmahe*) to ask (a person, acc.) about anything, consult, MBh.

उपप्रजन् *upa-pra-√jan*, Ā. -*jāyate*, to be born after or in addition to, Kāṭh.

उपप्रजिन्व् *upa-pra-√jinv*, P. (Subj. 3. pl. -*jinvan*) to please or gratify in approaching [Sāy.], RV. i, 71, 1; to impel, stir up [BRD.]

उपप्रतिग्रह् *upa-prati-√grah*, P. to conciliate again, MaitrS.

उपप्रतॄ *upa-pra-√tṝi*, Caus. (Impv. 2. sg. -*prá-tāraya*) to convey or transport across, AV. ii, 36, 5.

उपप्रदा *upa-pra-√1. dā*, P. to deliver over, present or give away to, ŚBr. i.

Upa-pradāna, *am*, n. the act of giving away to; presenting, a present, VP.; Pañcat.; Kathās. &c.

उपप्रदृश् *upa-pra-√dṛiś*, Caus. -*darśayati*, to point out to or towards, Comm. on TUp. & Bādar.

Upa-pradarśana, *am*, n. the act of pointing out, showing, indication, Comm. on AitUp.

उपप्रभिद् *upa-pra-√bhid*, P. (impf. -*prâbhinat*) to crumble and scatter, TBr. i, 1, 3, 5.

Upa-prábhinna, mfn. crumbled, TBr. i, 2, 13.

उपप्रभू *upa-pra-√bhū*, P. (aor. 3. pl. -*prâbhūvan*) to be present for help, help, assist, ŚBr. xii, 4, 2, 10; 4, 2.

उपप्रभूष् *upa-pra-√bhūsh*, P. (Subj. 3. pl. -*bhūshan*) to attend to, observe, RV. iii, 55, 1.

उपप्रयम् *upa-pra-√yam*, P. -*yacchati*, to present in addition, ŚBr.

उपप्रया *upa-pra-yā*, P. -*yāti*, to go towards, approach; to proceed towards, RV. i, 82, 6; TS. ii, 2, 1, 2; 3; ŚāṅkhBr.

उपप्रलोभन *upa-pra-lobhana*, *am*, n. (√*lubh*) the act of seducing, alluring, Daś.

उपप्रवद् *upa-pra-√vad*, P. (Impv. 2. sg. -*právada*) to join in, AV. iv, 15, 14.

उपप्रवृत् *upa-pra-√vṛit*, Caus. P. -*vartayati*, to throw or push down, TS.; Kāṭh.

उपप्रवृह् *upa-pra-√vṛih*, Ā. (Impv. 2. sg. -*varhasva*) to tear out and bring near to one's self, ŚBr. iii, 9, 4, 22.

उपप्रश्रि *upa-pra-√śri*, P. to lay or lean against, Kāṭh.

उपप्रसद् *upa-pra-√sad*, P. (1. sg. -*sīdāmi*) to enter (a house), inhabit, AV. iii, 12, 9.

उपप्रसृ *upa-pra-√sṛi*, Intens. Ā. (pf. 3. sg. -*sarsré*) to move towards, reach, RV. ii, 35, 5.

उपप्रस्तॄ *upa-pra-√stṛi*, Ā. -*stṛiṇīte*, to lie down upon, RV. vi, 67, 2.

उपप्रहि *upa-pra-√hi*, P. (Impv. 2. pl. -*hinuta*, AV. xviii, 4, 40; pf. 3. pl. -*jighyus* [Sāy. reads -*jigyus*, but explains it by *prêshitavantaḥ*], ŚBr. xi, 5, 1, 10) to send away to (acc.)

उपप्राण *upa-prāṇa*, *as*, m. a secondary vital air belonging to the body, W.

उपप्राप् *upa-prâp* (*upa-pra-√āp*).

Upa-prâpta, mfn. approached, come near, R.

उपप्राया *upa-prâ-√yā*, P. (Impv. 2. du. -*yātam*) to come near, RV. vii, 70, 6.

उपप्रुत् *upa-prút*, mfn. (fr. √*pru* = √*plu*, BRD.) flowing or rushing near, RV. ix, 71, 2; approaching [Sāy.]

उपप्रे *upa-pré* (*upa-pra-√i*), P. -*eti*, to go or come near to, approach, rush upon; to set about, undertake, begin, RV.; AV.; ŚBr.; Kenop.: Ā. -*plâyate* (for -*prâyate*) to rush upon, MaitrS. i, 10, 14; 16.

उपप्रेक्ष *upa-prêksh* (*upa-pra-√îksh*), P. (2. sg. -*prêkshasi*) to overlook, pass over unnoticed, disregard, MBh.

Upa-prêkshaṇa, *am*, n. the act of overlooking, looking at without interest, disregarding, MBh.

उपप्रेष् *upa-prêsh* (*upa-pra-√1. ish*), P. -*prêshyati* (Impv. 2. du. -*preshyatam*) to impel, AV. xviii, 2, 53; to invite, summon (said of the Adhvaryu priest who summons the Hotṛi priest to sacrifice), AitBr. ii, 5, 6; 8.

Upa-praisha, *as*, m. invitation, summons (see the preceding), AitBr. ii, 5, 7; 8.

उपप्ले *upa-plê* (*upa-pla-√i*) for *upa-prê*, q.v.

उपप्लु *upa-√plu*, P. -*plavati*, to overflow, inundate; to assault, invade, afflict; to eclipse, Kauś.; to rush upon, assail, MBh.: Ā. -*plavate*, to swim on the surface (as a light object), Comm. on Pāṇ. iii, 2, 126; to hang over, move aloft, TāṇḍyaBr.; Kāṭh.: Caus. -*plāvayati*, to irrigate, flood, water, BhP.; to float near (?), ŚBr. xiii, 1, 2, 9.

Upa-plava, *as*, m. affliction, visitation, invasion, inundation; any public calamity, unlucky accident, misfortune, disturbance; a portent or natural phenomenon (as an eclipse &c.), MBh.; Suśr.; Vikr.; Kum.; Kathās. &c.; N. of Rāhu (who is supposed to cause eclipses), L.; N. of Śiva, L.

Upaplavin, mfn. afflicted or visited by a calamity, Ragh.; under an eclipse, Kād.; flooded.

Upa-plavya, mfn. to be overflowed; to be afflicted, L.; (*am*), n., N. of the capital of the Matsyas, MBh.

Upa-pluta, mfn. overflowed; invaded, afflicted, visited; distressed, pained; marked by prodigies; swallowed (as sun and moon by Rāhu), eclipsed, R.; BhP.; Mn.; Ragh. &c.; (*ā*), f. (with *yoni*) a particular disease of the female organ, ŚārṅgS.; Car.

Upaplutêkshaṇa, mfn. having overflowing eyes, weeping, Hariv.

उपबन्ध् *upa-√bandh*, P. (3. pl. -*badhnanti*) to tie up, fasten, ŚBr. ii, 1, 4, 3; Comm. on Bādar.

U'pa-baddha, mfn. tied up, fastened, AV. i, 7, 7; ŚBr. xi, 5, 1, 2; connected.

Upa-bandha, *as*, m. union, connexion, KātyŚr.; tie, bond, rope, BhP.; quotation, TPrāt.; application, employment, use (of a word &c.), Bādar.; a particular manner of sitting, Caurap.; an affix, Nir.

उपबहु *upa-bahu*, mfn. tolerably numerous, a good many, Kāś. on Pāṇ. v, 4, 73.

उपबाहु *upa-bāhu*, *us*, m. the lower arm

(from the elbow to the wrist), VarBṛS.; N. of a man, gaṇa *bāhv-ādi*, Pāṇ. iv, 1, 96.

उपबिन्दु *upa-bindu*, *us*, m., N. of a man, gaṇa *bāhv-ādi*, Pāṇ. iv, 1, 96.

उपबिल *upa-bila*, mfn. near the aperture, Comm. on KātyŚr.

उपबृह् *upa-bṛih*, Intens. P. (Subj. *-bárbṛi-hat*; Impv. 2. sg. *-barbṛihi*) to press with the arms or cling closely (to a man, dat.); to embrace closely or passionately, RV. v, 61, 5; x, 10, 10; Nir.; (cf. *upa-√vṛiṅh*.)

Upa-barha, *as*, m. a pillow, L.

Upa-bárhaṇa, *am*, n. a cushion, pillow, RV. x, 85, 7; AV.; AitBr.; ŚBr.; TBr. &c.; (*ī*), f. id., RV. i, 174, 7; (*as*), m., N. of the Gandharva Nārada, BhP.; VP.; Pañcar. &c. (*Upabarhaṇa*), mf(*ā*)n. having a cushion, furnished with a pillow, Vait. 36, 7.

Upa-barhiṇa, *as*, m., N. of a mountain, BhP. v, 20, 21.

Upa-bṛiṅhaṇa, **°bṛiṅhin**. See *upa-vṛiṅhaṇa*, *°vṛiṅhin* under *upa-√vṛiṅh*.

उपब्द *upabdá*, *as*, m. noise, sound, rattling, clanking, RV. vii, 104, 17 (= AV. viii, 4, 17).

Upabdí, *is*, m. id., RV.; ŚBr.; (voc. *úpabde*) a particular venomous animal [NBD.], AV. ii, 24, 6. **—mát**, mfn. noisy, loud, TS.; AitBr.

उपब्रू *upa-brū*, Ā. *-brūte* (once P., impf. 1. sg. *-abravam*, RV. viii, 24, 14) to speak to, address; to invoke for, entreat, ask for; to persuade, RV.; AV.; ŚBr.; MBh.

उपब्लय *upa-blaya*, *as*, m. the region round the clavicle, Lāṭy. i, 5, 7.

उपभक्ष् *upa-√bhaksh*.

Upa-bhakshita, mfn. eaten up, consumed, Suśr.

उपभङ्ग *upa-bhaṅga*, *as*, m. (√*bhañj*), a division of a stanza, Vikr.

उपभज् *upa-√bhaj*, Ā. (aor. *-dbhakta*) to obtain, take possession of (acc.), RV. ix, 102, 2.

उपभाषा *upa-bhāshā*, f. a secondary dialect, Dhūrtas.

उपभुज् *upa-√2. bhuj*, Ā. *-bhuṅkte* (ep. also *-bhuñjate*) to enjoy, eat, eat up, consume, MBh.; Yājñ.; Pañcat. &c.; to enjoy, make use of, partake of; to experience (happiness or misfortune &c.), MBh.; Hariv.; Mn.; BhP. &c.; to enjoy (a woman), Hariv.; Kathās.; Pañcat. &c.; to receive as a reward, Mn. xii, 8; R. vi, 98, 29: P. (1. pl. *-bhuñjāmas*) to be useful, ChUp. iv, 11, 2: Caus. *-bhojayati*, to cause to take (medicine), Suśr.

Upa-bhukta, mfn. enjoyed, eaten, consumed; used, possessed &c. **—dhana**, mfn. one who has enjoyed or made use of his riches; (*as*), m., N. of a merchant's son, Pañcat. (also in the former meaning).

Upa-bhukti, *is*, f. enjoyment, use, T.; (in astron.) the daily course of a star (= *bhukti*, q. v.)

Upa-bhoktṛi, mfn. one who enjoys or makes use of, an enjoyer, possessor, ŚvetUp.; VarBṛS.

Upa-bhoga, *as*, m. enjoyment, eating, consuming; using, usufruct, MBh.; Mn.; Śak. &c.; pleasure, enjoyment; enjoying (a woman or a lover), VP.; Ragh. &c.; (with Jain.) enjoying repeatedly. **—kshama**, mfn. suited to enjoyment, Śak.

Upabhogin, mfn. ifc. enjoying, making use of.

Upa-bhogya, mfn. to be enjoyed or used; anything enjoyed or used, BhP.; Kum.; Pañcat. &c.; (*am*), n. object of enjoyment, MBh.; Mṛicch. **—tva**, n. the state of being enjoyable, R.

Upa-bhojin, mfn. eating, enjoying, Suśr.

Upa-bhojya, mfn. ifc. serving for food, causing enjoyment, MBh.

उपभू *upa-√bhū*, P. (pf. Pot. 2. sg. *-babhūyās*; aor. Subj. 2. sg. *-bhuvas*) to come near to, approach, RV. x, 183, 2; to help, assist, RV. i, 138, 4: Intens. *-bubhūshati*, to wish to help, MBh. xii, 3514.

उपभूष् *upa-√bhūsh*, P. *-bhūshati*, to approach (in order to revere), RV. x, 104, 7; to regard, be careful, pay attention to, observe, obey, RV.

उपभूषण *upa-bhūshaṇa*, *am*, n. secondary ornament or decoration; implement.

उपभृ *upa-√bhṛi*, P. Ā. (p. *-bibhrat*; Impv. 2. sg. *-bharasva*) to bring or convey near, RV. i, 166, 2; AV. v, 20, 4; to bear, Kir. v, 12.

Upa-bhṛit, *t*, f. a sacrificial vessel or ladle made of wood, AV. xviii, 4, 5; 6; VS.; TS.; ŚBr.; KātyŚr. &c.

Upa-bhṛita, mfn. brought near, procured for (dat.); destined to (dat.), BhP. **Upabhṛitôpaśama**, mfn. one to whom calmness of mind is brought, calm, quiet, BhP. v, 7, 10.

उपभेद *upa-bheda*, *as*, m. a subdivision, MatsyaP.

उपभ्रम् *upa-√bhram*, P. (pf. *-babhrāma*) to saunter or move slowly towards, BhP.

उपम 1. *upamá*, mf(*ā*)n. uppermost, highest; most excellent, eminent, best, RV.; AV.; nearest, next, first, RV.; Nigh. **—śravas** (*upamá°*), mfn. of highest fame, highly renowned; (*ās*), m., N. of a son of Kuru-śravaṇa and grandson of Mitrātithi, RV. x, 33, 6; 7; *-tama*, mfn. highly renowned, illustrious, RV. ii, 23, 1.

1. **Upamá** (for 2. see below, and for 3. see col. 3), ind. (Ved. instr. of the above) in the closest proximity or neighbourhood, RV. i, 31, 15; viii, 69, 13.

Upamám, ind. in the highest degree, RV. v, 34, 9; AV. viii, 3, 65; SV.

उपम 2. *upama*, mfn. ifc. for 3. *upa-mā*, q. v.

उपमज्ज् *upa-√majj*, P. Ā. *-majjati*, *-te*, to dive, sink, ŚBr.; Lāṭy.; ŚāṅkhŚr.; Comm. on KātyŚr.

Upa-majjana, *am*, n. ablution, bathing, a bath, BhP.

उपमथ् *upa-√math*, P. *-manthati*, to whirl around, RV. x, 136, 7; to stir, churn, mix, TBr. i, 6, 8, 4; 5.

Upa-mathita, mfn. stirred, churned, mixed, ŚBr. ii, 6, 1, 6; Kauś.

Upa-mathya, ind. p. having stirred; churning, mixing, Kauś.; ChUp.

Upa-manthaní, f. a staff for stirring, ŚBr.

Upa-manthitṛi, mfn. one who stirs or churns (butter &c.), VS. xxx, 12.

उपमद् *upa-√1. mad*, P. *-madati*, to cheer up, encourage, ŚBr. i, 4, 2, 1.

Upa-máda, *as*, m. enjoyment, amusement, RV. iii, 5, 5.

उपमद्गु *upa-madgu*, *us*, m., N. of a younger brother of Madgu, Hariv.; VP.

उपमध्यमा *upa-madhyamā*, f. (scil. *aṅguli*) the finger next to the middle finger, the last finger but one, ĀpŚr. iii, 1, 2.

उपमन्त्र् *upa-√mantr*, P. Ā. *-mantrayati*, *-te*, to call near or towards one's self, call hither, induce to come near, TS.; ŚBr.; to summon, invite, persuade, MBh.; Kām.; BhP.; to address.

Upa-mantraṇa, *am*, n. the art of persuading, coaxing (= *rahasy upa-cchandanam*, Kāś.), Pāṇ. i, 3, 47.

U'pa-mantrita, mfn. called near or hither, ŚBr.; ChUp. &c.; summoned, invited, persuaded, MBh.; Hariv.; addressed, Daś.

1. **Upa-mantrin**, mfn. persuading, inciting, impelling, RV. ix, 112, 4.

उपमन्त्रिन् 2. *upa-mantrin*, *ī*, m. a subordinate counsellor, BhP.

उपमन्थनी *upa-manthanī*. See above.

उपमन्यु *upa-manyú*, mfn. striving after, zealous [BRD.], RV. i, 102, 9; (knowing, understanding, intelligent, Sāy.); (*us*), m., N. of a Ṛishi (pupil of Āyoda-dhaumya, who aided Śiva in the propagation of his doctrine and received the ocean of milk from him), MBh.; LiṅgaP.; Kathās. &c.; (*avas*), m. pl. the descendants of the above, ĀśvŚr.; (cf. *aupamanyava*.)

उपमर्द *upa-marda*, &c. See *upa-√mṛid*.

उपमा 2. *upa-√mā*, P. Ā. (Impv. 2. sg. *-mimīhi*, *-māhi*, and *-māsva*; Subj. 2. sg. *-māsi*) to measure out to, apportion to, assign, allot, grant, give, RV.: Ā. *-mimīte*, to measure one thing by another, compare, MBh.; Hariv.; Caurap. &c.

3. **Upa-má**, f. comparison, resemblance, equality, similarity; a resemblance (as a picture, portrait &c.), ŚBr.; MBh.; Kum. &c.; a particular figure in rhetoric, simile, comparison (a full simile must include four things; see *pūrṇôpama*, *luptôpamā*, &c.), Sāh.; Kāvyād.; Vām. &c.; a particle of comparison, Nir.; a particular metre, RPrāt.; (mfn. ifc.) equal, similar, resembling, like (e. g. *amarôpama*, mfn. resembling an immortal), MBh.; Ragh.; Daś.; Hit. &c. **—dravya**, n. any object used for comparison, Kum. **—rūpaka**, n. (in rhet.) a particular figure combining comparison and metaphor, Vām. **—vyatireka**, m. (in rhet.) a particular figure combining comparison and contrast, Kāvyād. **Upamêta**, m. the tree Vatica Robusta, L.; (*vṛikshāṇām madhye tasya sarvôccatvād anyasyôpomānatām prāptatvāt tathātvam*, T.)

1. **U'pa-māti** (for 2. see s. v.), *is*, f. comparison, similarity [Sāy.], RV.; (*is*), m. 'assigning or granting' (wealth), N. of Agni [Sāy.], RV. viii, 60, 11; (BRD. derives both 1. and 2. *upa-māti* fr. *upa-√man*, 'to address.')

1. **Upa-mātṛi** (for 2. see s. v.), mfn. one who compares, Naish.; an image-maker, portrait-painter, L.

Upa-māna, *am*, n. comparison, resemblance, analogy, MBh.; Suśr.; Kathās. &c.; simile; the object with which anything is compared, Pāṇ.; Sāh.; Kum. &c.; a particle of comparison, Nir.; (in log.) recognition of likeness, comparison (the third of the four Pramāṇas or means of correct knowledge); (mfn. ifc.) similar, like, Kathās. **—cintā-maṇi**, m., N. of a philosophical work. **—tā**, f., **-tva**, n. similarity, Kathās.; the state of being an object of comparison, Sāh.; Vām. **—vat**, mfn. similar, like, Śatr.

Upamānôpameya-bhāva, m. the connection between the thing to be compared and the object with which it is compared.

1. **Upa-mita** (for 2. see *upa-√mi*), mfn. compared, illustrated by comparison, Pāṇ.; Bhartṛ. &c.; similar.

Upa-miti, *is*, f. comparison; resemblance, likeness, similarity, Sāh.; analogy; knowledge of things derived from analogy or resemblance, Sarvad.

Upa-meya, mfn. to be compared, comparable with (with instr. or ifc.), Megh.; Kum. &c.; (*am*), n. that which is compared, the subject of comparison (opposed to *upa-māna*, the object with which anything is compared), Sāh.; Comm. on Pāṇ. **Upameyôpamā**, f. the resemblance of any object to that compared with it; reciprocal comparison (as of a moon to a beautiful face), Vām.; Kpr.

उपमात् *upa-mắt*, f. a prop, support, = *upamít* below [Sāy.], RV. vi, 67, 6.

उपमाति 2. *upa-māti*, *is*, f. (√1. *mī*, Sāy.), destroying, killing. **—váni**, mfn. engaged in killing enemies, destroyer of enemies [Sāy.], RV. v, 41, 16; (fr. *upa-√man*, one who receives addresses in a friendly way, BRD.)

उपमातृ 2. *upa-mātṛi*, *tā*, f. 'second mother,' foster-mother, nurse, L.; a near female relative, L.

उपमाद *upa-māda*. See *upa-√mad*.

उपमारण *upa-māraṇa*. See *upa-√mṛi*.

उपमालिनी *upa-mālinī*, f. a particular metre.

उपमालिनीतीरम् *upa-mālinī-tīram*, ind. near the banks of the Mālinī, Śak. 16, 7.

उपमास्य *úpamāsya*, mfn. (fr. *upa-māsam*), occurring every month, monthly, AV. viii, 10, 19.

उपमि *upa-√1. mi*, P. *-minoti*, to stick or fasten on, put into, Kāṭh.

Upa-mít, *t*, f. a prop, stay, RV. i, 59, 1; iv, 5, 1; AV. ix, 3, 1.

2. **Upa-mita** (for 1. see above), mfn. stuck or fastened on, put into, Vait.

उपमित्र *upa-mitra*, n. a minor friend, not an intimate friend, Nilak.

उपमिह् *upa-√mih*, Caus. *-mehayati*, to wet, BhP. vi, 16, 32.

उपमीमांसा *upa-mīmāṅsā* (fr. Desid. of √*man*), deliberation, investigation, consideration, ŚBr. xi, 4, 2, 12; 15.

उपमुखम् *upa-mukham*, ind. on the mouth, Lāṭy. iv, 2, 6.

उपमुच् *upa-√muc*, Ā. *-muñcate*, to put on (e. g. shoes), TS.; TBr.; KātyŚr.; Kauś.

उपमूलम् *upa-mūlám*, ind. on or at the root, ŚBr.; KātyŚr.; Kauś.; Gobh.

उपमृ *upa-√mṛi*, Caus. *-mārayati*, to throw into water, plunge, immerse, ŚBr.; Comm. on KātyŚr.; (with *apsu*), ĀpŚr. viii, 8, 12.

Upa-māraṇa, *am*, n. the act of throwing into water, submerging, KātyŚr. xx, 8, 22.

Úpa-mṛita, mfn. died, dead, TS. vi, 2, 8, 6.

उपमृज् *upa-√mṛij*, P. *-mārshṭi* (3. pl. *-mṛijanti*, RV. ix, 15, 7) to stroke; to touch, sweep, wipe, cleanse, TBr.; ŚBr.; KātyŚr.; ŚāṅkhŚr.

उपमृद् *upa-√mṛid*, P. *-mṛidnāti*, to graze in passing (said of a heavenly body in its transit), VarBṛS.; to crush, destroy, annul, Naish.; Comm. on BṛĀrUp.: Caus. *-mardayati*, to destroy, devastate, annul, annihilate, BhP.; Comm. on ChUp. & BṛĀrUp.

Upa-marda, *as*, m. friction, rubbing down; pressure, Sāh.; Kathās.; injury, violation; destruction, MBh.; Comm. on BṛĀrUp. & Nyāyad.; suppression (of a sound), Nyāyad. ii, 2, 59.

Upa-mardaka, mfn. destroying, annulling, oppressing, Hariv.; Kathās.; Sarvad.

Upa-mardana, *am*, n. the act of injuring, violation; suppression, oppression, Comm. on KātyŚr.

Upa-mardin, mfn. ifc. destroying, annulling, BhP.

उपमृष् *upa-√mṛish*, Caus.

Upa-marshita, mfn. borne patiently, tolerated; granted, not begrudged, MBh.

उपमॄ *upa-√mṛī*, Pass. (p. *-mūryámāṇa*) to be worn away or destroyed, ŚBr. i, 7, 3, 21; 4, 12.

उपमेखलम् *upa-mekhalam*, ind. about or on the slopes or sides (of a mountain), Kir. vii, 32.

उपम्लुच् *upa-√mluc*, P. (pf. *-mumloca*) to hide one's self among (with gen.), ŚBr. i, 2, 5, 8.

उपम्लुप् *upa-√mlup.*

Úpa-mlupta, mfn. hidden, concealed, TBr. iii, 2, 9, 4.

उपयज् 1. *upa-√yaj*, P. Ā. *-yajati, -te*, to sacrifice in addition to, TS.; ŚBr.; KātyŚr.; PārGṛ.; Comm. on VS. vi, 21.

2. **Upa-yáj**, *ṭ*, f. (Pāṇ. iii, 2, 73) N. of eleven additional formulas at an animal sacrifice (enumerated in VS. vi, 21), TS.; MaitrS.; ŚBr.

Upa-yashṭrí, *ṭā*, m. the priest who utters the above formulas, ŚBr. iii, 8, 5, 5.

1. **Upa-yāja** (for 2. see s. v.), *as*, m. = 2. *upa-yáj*, AitBr. ii, 18, 8; Kāś. on Pāṇ. vii, 3, 62.

उपयत् 1. *upa-√yat*, Ā. *-yatate*, to befall, ŚBr. viii, 5, 1, 7.

उपयत् 2. *upa-yat*. See *upé*.

उपयन्त् *upa-yantr*, P.

Upa-yantrita, mfn. solicited or compelled to do anything, allured, Mn. xi, 177 (erroneous for *upa-ma°*, BRD.)

उपयन्त्र *upa-yantra*, *am*, n. a minor or secondary instrument or implement (esp. in surg.), Suśr.; a secondary application of any kind (as cautery, escharotics &c.), W.

उपयम् *upa-√yam*, P. Ā. *-yacchati, -te*, to seize, lay hold of, touch (P. if not in the sense of appropriating, Pat. on Pāṇ. i, 3, 56), RV. viii, 35, 21; AV. xii, 3, 19; ŚBr. &c.; to reach forth, offer (Pass. aor. *-ayāmi*), RV. vii, 92, 1; to put under, prop, stay, ŚBr.; KātyŚr.; Kauś.; to take for one's self, receive, appropriate; to take as one's wife, marry (only Ā., Pāṇ. i, 3, 56; but see Gobh. ii, 1, 8; Gaut. xxviii, 20; Kathās. xiv, 67), ĀśvGṛ.; Mn. iii, 11; MBh.; Śak. &c.; to sleep with (a woman), Mn. xi, 172.

Upa-yantṛi, *tā*, m. a husband, Ragh. vii, 1; Kum.

Upa-yama, *as*, m. (Pāṇ. iii, 3, 63) appropriation, taking possession of; marrying, marriage, Sāh.; kindling a fire, (*kanyâgny-upayama*, taking a wife and kindling the domestic fire, Gaut. xviii, 18); a support, stay, ĀpŚr. xv, 9, 10.

Upa-yamana, mfn. serving as support (as grass), PārGṛ.; (*ī*), f. (*upa-yámanī*) any support (of stone, clay, gravel &c. for holding fire-wood), ŚBr. iii, 5, 2, 1; KātyŚr.; a ladle (used at sacrifices), ŚBr.; AitBr.; KātyŚr.; (*am*), n. a support, stay, ĀśvŚr.; the taking a wife, marrying, Pāṇ.; sleeping with (a woman), Kād.

Upa-yāmá, *as*, m. (Pāṇ. iii, 3, 63) a particular vessel for ladling out; a ladle (used at sacrifices), VS. vii, 4, &c.; N. of a deity, VS. xxv, 2; N. of the verses (VS. vii, 4 seqq.) uttered in ladling out the Soma juice, ŚBr.; KātyŚr.; marrying, marriage, L. **–vat**, mfn. furnished with a ladle, gaṇa *balâdi*, Pāṇ. v, 2, 136.

Upayāmin, mfn. (fr. *upa-yāma*, gaṇa *balâdi*, Pāṇ. v, 2, 136), furnished with a ladle.

उपया *upa-√yā*, P. *-yāti* (inf. *-yaí*, opposed to *ava-yaí*, see *ava-√yā*) to come up, RV. viii, 47, 12; to come near, go near or towards, approach (for protection), visit, frequent, RV.; AV.; ĀśvGṛ.; MBh.; BhP.; Kathās. &c.; to approach (a woman for sexual intercourse), MBh.; R. &c.; to arrive at, reach, obtain; to get into any state or condition, MBh.; VarBṛS.; Ragh. &c., to occur, befall, Hit.; to give one's self up to, VP.

Upa-yāta, mfn. approached, visited, frequented; one who has approached or come near; one who has obtained; approached sexually (as a woman); (*am*), n. arrival.

Upa-yāna, *am*, n. coming near, approach, arrival, R.; Kum.; Sāh.

Upa-yāpana, *am*, n. the act of causing to come near, leading near, BhP.

Upa-yāyin, mfn. coming towards, approaching, R.

उपयाच् *upa-√yāc.*

Upa-yācaka, mfn. one who asks, begging, soliciting, L.

Upa-yācana, *am*, n. the act of soliciting, approaching with a request or prayer, R.

Upa-yācita, mfn. requested, solicited, Ragh. xiii, 53; Kād.; asked for, begged, VarBṛS.; Sarvad. &c.; (*am*), n. a prayer, request; a gift or oblation offered to deities for the fulfilment of a prayer or work, Pañcat.; Kathās.

Upayācitaka, *am*, n. a prayer, request, L.

उपयाज 2. *upa-yāja* (for 1. see *upa-√yaj*), *as*, m., N. of a younger brother of Yāja, MBh.

उपयुज् *upa-√yuj*, only Ā. (Pāṇ. i, 3, 64) *-yuṅkte* (but also rarely P., e. g. impf. *-ayunak*, RV. x, 102, 7) to harness to, RV.; AV. iv, 23, 3; ŚBr. v; to take for one's self, appropriate, RV. i, 165, 5; MBh.; Mn. viii, 40; to follow, attach one's self to, be devoted; to undertake, MBh.; to use, employ, apply, ŚBr.; AitBr.; MBh.; BhP.; to have the use of, enjoy (e. g. food or a woman or dominion &c.), ĀśvGṛ.; Lāṭy.; MBh. &c.: Pass. *-yujyate*, to be employed or applicable, be useful or fit or proper, MBh.; Pañcat.; Kathās. &c.: Caus. *-yojayati*, to use, employ, Suśr.; to cause to eat, MānGṛ.; to come into contact, BhP.

Upa-yukta, mfn. enjoyed, eaten, consumed, MBh.; R.; employed, applicable; suitable, fit, appropriate, useful, Kathās.; Rājat.; Prab. &c.; proper, right; serviceable; worthy, Śak.; Hit.; Pat. &c.

Upa-yuyukshu, mfn. (fr. the Desid.), about to employ or apply, Suśr.

Upa-yoktavya, mfn. to be employed; to be enjoyed, MBh.

Upa-yoktṛi, mfn. one who employs; one who enjoys (food), Car.

Upa-yoga, *as*, m. employment, use, application, MBh.; Suśr.; Prab.; (*upayogam √gam* or *√vraj*, to be employed, Kum.; Śārṅg.); enjoyment, consuming, taking, Suśr.; any act tending to a desired object; an engagement, compact, agreement, Pāṇ. i, 4, 29; use, fitness; acquisition (of knowledge), Gaut. vii, 1; good conduct, observing established practices, L.

Upayogin, mfn. serving for use or application, suitable, fit, useful, convenient, Kathās.; Sāh. &c.; appropriate; favourable, propitious; (ifc.) using, employing, Daś.; touching, in contact with, L. **Upayogi-tā**, f. or **-tva**, n. the state of being applicable; usefulness, suitableness, Naish.; Kathās.

Upa-yogya, mfn. to be employed or used, Bālar.

Upa-yojana, *am*, n. the act of harnessing (a horse by the side of another), AitBr. v, 30, 6; a team, Nir.

Upa-yojya, mfn. to be employed or used or applied, Suśr.

उपयुत *upa-yuta*, *as*, m., N. of a king, VP.

उपयोषम् *upa-yosham*, ind. v. l. for *upa-josham*, q. v.

उपर *úpara*, mfn. (fr. *upa*), situated below, under; posterior, later; nearer, approximate, RV.; (*as*), m. the lower stone on which the Soma is laid (that it may be ground by means of another stone held in the hand), RV. i, 79, 3; x, 94, 5; 175, 3; AV.; the lower part of the sacrificial post, VS.; ŚBr.; KātyŚr.; a cloud, L.; region, L. **–tāti** (*upa-rá°*), ind. in the proximity; a circumference, RV. i, 151, 5; vii, 48, 3.

उपरक्षण *upa-rakshaṇa*, *am*, n. a guard, outpost, L.

उपरच् *upa-√rac*, Caus. P. *-racayati*, to construct, form, make, prepare, effect, Kād.

Upa-racita, mfn. constructed, formed, made, prepared, BhP.; Bhartṛ.; Kād.

उपरञ्ज् *upa-√rañj*, Caus. P. *-rañjayati*, to influence, affect, Sarvad.

Upa-rakta, mfn. dyed, coloured, coloured red; heated, inflamed, ŚBr.; Sāh.; afflicted, distressed (esp. by Rāhu; said of sun and moon), eclipsed, R.; VarBṛS. &c.; influenced or affected by, BhP.; Sarvad.

Upa-rajya, ind. p. having dyed or coloured; darkening, obscuring, BhP. iv, 29, 69.

Upa-rañjaka, mfn. dyeing; affecting, influencing, Sarvad.; Kap.; Sāh.

Upa-rañjya, mfn. to be dyed; to be affected or influenced, Kap.

Upa-rāga, *as*, m. the act of dyeing or colouring, colour, Ragh.; Kathās. &c.; darkening, eclipse (of sun and moon, caused by Rāhu), Śak. 186 b; MBh.; VarBṛS.; influence, affecting, Sarvad.; Kap.; Prab. &c.; misbehaviour, ill-conduct, L.; reproach, abuse, L.; Rāhu, L.

उपरत्न *upa-ratna*, *am*, n. a secondary or inferior gem, Bhpr.

उपरध् *upa-√radh*, Caus. P. *-randhayati*, to pain, torment, BhP.

उपरन्ध्र *upa-randhra*, *am*, n. a minor hole or cavity; N. of a particular part of the body of a horse (probably a hollow place or depression on the flanks or ribs; cf. *randhra*, Śiś. v, 4).

उपरम् *upa-√ram*, P. Ā. (Pāṇ. i, 3, 85) *-ramati, -te*, to cease from motion, stop, TS.; TBr.; ŚBr.; ŚāṅkhŚr.; to cease from action, be inactive or quiet (as a quietist), BhP.; Bhag.; to pause, stop (speaking or doing anything), ŚBr.; ŚāṅkhŚr.; ĀśvGṛ.; Pañcat. &c.; to leave off, desist, give up, renounce (with abl.), MBh.; R.; BhP.; Comm. on BṛĀrUp.; Daś.; to await, wait for, ŚBr. ii, 2, 1, 2; iii, 8, 2, 29; to cause to cease or stop; to render quiet, Pāṇ. i, 3, 84: Caus. *-ramayati*, to cause to cease or stop; to render quiet, Nir.; Kāś.

Upa-rata, mfn. ceased, stopped, quiet, indifferent, patient, ŚBr.; MBh.; BhP. &c.; dead, ŚāṅkhGṛ.; R.; Pañcat. &c.; ceasing to exist, disappeared, non-existing, PārGṛ.; Mn.; BhP. &c.; withdrawn or retired from, left off, given up, R. **–rāsa**, mfn. ceasing to play or dance. **–vishayâbhilāsha**, mfn. one whose desire after worldly things has ceased. **–śoṇitā**, f. (a woman) whose menses have ceased, Gobh. ii, 5, 8. **–spṛiha**, mfn. one in whom desire has ceased, free from desire. **Uparatâri**, mfn. one whose foes are quiet; having no foe, being at peace with all.

Upa-rati, *is*, f. cessation, stopping, MārkP.; Suśr.; death, Kād.; desisting from sensual enjoyment or any worldly action, quietism, Vedāntas.

Upa-rama, *as*, m. cessation, stopping, expiration, MBh.; R.; leaving off, desisting, giving up, Suśr.; Sāṃkhyak.; death, Kād. **–tva**, n. the state of ceasing from (all worldly desires and actions), Vedāntas.

Upa-ramaṇa, *am*, n. the abstaining from worldly actions or desires, Vedāntas.; ceasing, discontinuance.

Upa-rāma, *as,* m. ceasing, stopping, desisting.

उपरम्भ् *upa-√rambh,* P. *-rambhati,* to cause to resound, BhP. x, 35, 12.

उपरव *upa-rava, as,* m. (√*ru*), a hole (over which the Soma is ground; so called from its increasing the sound of the grindstones), TS.; ŚBr.; KātyŚr.

Upa-rāva, *as,* m. a near sound [T.], Pāṇ. iii, 3, 22.

उपरस *upa-rasa, as,* m. a secondary mineral (as red chalk, bitumen &c.), Bhpr.; a secondary feeling or passion, L.; a secondary flavour, L.

उपराज *upa-rāja,* m. a viceroy, gaṇa *kāśy-ādi,* Pāṇ. iv, 2, 116.

उपराजम् *upa-rājam,* ind. near a king, Pāṇ. v, 4, 108; Kāś.

उपराधय *upa-rādhaya,* mfn. (√*rādh*), propitiating, doing homage, gaṇa *brahmaṇâdi,* Pāṇ. v, 1, 124.

उपरामम् *upa-rāmam,* ind. near Rāma, T.

उपरि *upári,* ind. (as a separable adverb) above, upon, on, upwards, towards the upper side of (opposed to *adhas* and *nīcā,* e. g. *upari* √*yā,* to go upwards; sometimes written with a following word as if compounded with it, see below); besides, in addition to, further (*sahasraṃ śatāny upari câshṭau,* 1000 and 800 in addition); afterwards (e. g. *upari payaḥ pibet,* he should drink milk afterwards); *upary upari,* higher and higher; repeatedly, continuously, RV. &c.

(As a separable preposition, with acc., loc., or gen.) over, above, upon, on, at the head of, on the upper side of, beyond (e. g. *upari śailam* √*gam,* to go over the mountain; *upari Laṅkāyām samprāptaḥ saḥ,* he arrived over Laṅkā; *upary upari sarveshām atishṭhat,* he stood at the very head of all; *ātmānaṃ tasya upari kshiptvā,* having thrown himself upon him); in connection with, with reference to, with regard to, towards (with gen., e. g. *mamôpari vikāritaḥ,* changed in feeling with regard to me; *putrasyôpari kruddhaḥ,* enraged towards his son); after (with abl., e. g. *muhūrtād upari,* after a minute; see also *tad-upari* &c.), RV. &c.; [cf. Zend *upairi;* Goth. *ufar;* Old Germ. *obar;* Mod. Germ. *über;* Eng. *over;* Gk. ὑπέρ; Lat. *super.*]

Upari may stand first in a compound, as in the following examples: **–kāṇḍa,** n. the third division of the Maitrāyaṇī Saṃhitā. **–kuṭī,** f. an upper room, L. **–ga,** mfn. moving or soaring above, BhP. **–gata,** mfn. gone up, ascended, BhP. **–cara,** mfn. moving or walking above or in the air; (*as*), m., N. of the king Vasu, MBh.; VP.; a bird, T. **–cita,** mfn. piled over or above. **–cihnita,** mfn. marked or sealed above, Yājñ. **–ja,** mfn. growing upwards or out, protuberant, Suśr. **–jānu,** ind. above the knee, Āp. **–tala,** n. the upper surface, Mṛicch.; Daś. **–tas,** ind. over, above, Hcat. **–°daṇshṭrin,** mfn. having large teeth in the upper jaw, VarBṛS. **–daśa,** mfn. (fr. *daśā*), having the fringes turned upwards, Lāṭy. ii, 6, 4. **–nābhi,** ind. above the navel, ŚBr. vi. **–nihita** and **-nyasta,** mfn. put down or laid over. **–pātra,** n. upper-plate, upper-cup (used as a lid for the real vessel; cf. *ūrdhva-pātra*), Hcat. **–purusha,** m. a man standing above, Daś. **–prút,** mfn. (√*pru* = √*plu*), coming from above, VS. vii, 3. **–babhrava,** m., N. of a Ṛishi, Kauś. **–buddhi,** mfn. of lofty intellect. **–budhna** (*upári-*), mfn. raised above the ground, RV. x, 73, 8. **–bṛihatī,** f. a variety of the Bṛihatī (q. v.) metre (having twelve instants in the second line, and eight instants in each of the other three lines; cf. *uparishṭād-bṛihatī* and *purastād-bṛihatī*). **–bhakta,** mfn. eaten or taken after (i. e. after a meal), Car. **–bhāga,** m. the upper portion or side, Hcat.; Comm. on TS. &c. **–bhāva,** m. the state of being higher or above, Nir. **–bhūmi,** ind. above the ground, ŚBr. **–martya** (*upári-*), mfn. more than human, RV. viii, 19, 12. **–mekhala,** m., N. of a man, gaṇa *yaskâdi,* Pāṇ. ii, 4, 63; (*ās*), m. pl. the descendants of the above, ib. **–yāna,** n. the going upwards, ascending (into heaven), Naish. **–śaya,** mfn. lying above or over, Comm. on ĀpŚr. **–śayaná,** n. an elevated resting-place, AV. ix, 6, 9. **–śayyā,** f. id., Āp.; Gobh. **–śāyin,** mfn. resting on an elevated bed, GopBr. **–śreṇika,** mfn. being in the upper series. **–shad,** mfn. sitting above (= *-sád* below), TāṇḍyaBr. **–shadya,** n. the sitting above (= *-sádya* below), ib. **–shṭha,** mfn. staying above (= *-stha* below), R.; Daś.; Vet. **–sád,** mfn. sitting or being above, VS. ix, 35; 36; (v. l. *-shád.*) **–sádya,** n. the sitting above, ŚBr. v. **–stha,** mfn. standing above, MaitrUp.; MBh.; Hcat. &c. **–sthāpana,** n. the act of placing upon or above, Comm. on Pāṇ. **–sthāyin,** mfn. standing higher, prominent, Comm. on TPrāt. **–sthita,** mfn. staying above. **–spṛiś,** mfn. reaching above, elevated, high, RV. x, 128, 9; AV. v, 3, 10. **–hasta,** m. an elevated hand, Hcat. **Uparitaka,** m. (scil. *sṛiṅgāra-bandha*) a kind of coitus, Rati-mañjarī, T. **Upary-āsana,** n. the sitting on high or above, KātyŚr. **Upary-āsīna,** mfn. sitting above, AitĀr.

Uparitana, mf(*ī*)n. upper (opposed to *adhastana*), Mṛicch.; Comm. on VS. & TāṇḍyaBr.; following, further on, subsequent (in a book), Comm. on Mn., on VPrāt., on Nyāyam.

Uparishṭāj (in comp. for *upárishṭāt* below). **–jyotishmatī,** f., N. of a variety of the Jyotishmatī (q. v.) metre (having twelve instants in the last line, and eight instants in each of the three preceding lines). **–jyotis,** n. id.

Upárishṭāt, ind. (as an adverb) above, from above, on the upper part, RV. ix, 91, 4; AV. iv, 40, 7; viii, 8, 13; ŚBr.; ChUp. &c.; behind (opposed to *purastāt*), TS.; ŚBr.; further on, later, below (in a book), Nir.; Suśr.; afterwards, ChUp.; Yājñ.; (as a preposition) over, upon, down upon (with acc. and gen.), ŚBr.; MBh. &c.; behind (with gen.), TS.; ŚBr.; Suśr.; with reference to, about (with gen.), Daś. **–svāhā-kāra** and **-svāhā-kṛiti,** mfn. followed by the exclamation 'Svāha!' ŚBr.; TBr.

Upárishṭād (in comp. for *upárishṭāt* above). **–udarka,** mfn. ending in a burden (as a song), Sāy. on AitBr. v, 2, 17. **–upayāma,** mfn. followed by the Upa-yāma (q. v.) verses. **–dhoma-bhāj** (for *°ād-ho°*), mfn. partaking afterwards of the oblations, Comm. on ĀpŚr. vii, 20, 9. **–bṛihatī,** f., N. of a variety of the Bṛihatī (q. v.) metre (having twelve syllables in the last Pāda, and eight syllables in each of the three preceding lines; cf. *purastād-bṛi°*). **–vātá,** m. wind coming from above, MaitrS.

Upárishṭāl (in comp. for *upárishṭāt* above). **–lakshaṇa** and **-lakshman,** mfn. marked on the upper side, ŚBr. i; MaitrS.

उपरुच् *upa-√ruc,* Ā. (pf. *-ruruce*) to approach shining, RV. vii, 77, 1.

उपरुध् *upa-√2. rudh,* P. Ā. *-ruṇaddhi, -runddhe,* and *-rundhati, -te* (also *-rodhati,* R. vii, 74, 7) to lock in, shut up, besiege, blockade, TBr.; ŚBr.; ChUp.; Mn.; Śiś. &c.; to keep, hold back, stop, obstruct, hinder, interrupt, MBh.; Mn.; Śak.; to molest, trouble, importune, annoy, R.; Ragh. &c.; to cover, conceal, Ragh. vii, 36; R.: Caus. *-rodhayati,* to injure, Vātsyāy.

Upa-ruddha, mfn. locked in, shut up, besieged, blockaded, BhP.; Kathās.; Kām.; hindered, obstructed, prevented, R.; molested, troubled, R.; (*as*), m. a captive, Ragh. xviii, 17.

Upa-rudhya, ind. p. having locked in, having obstructed or kept in check &c.

Upa-rodha, *as,* m. besieging, obstruction, blockading, impediment, check, MBh.; Suśr.; Prab. &c.; trouble, disturbance, injure, damage, PārGṛ.; Mn.; Śak.; disunion, quarrel, VarBṛS.; regard, respect, Kathās. **–kārin,** mfn. causing trouble or disturbance, Śak.

Uparodhaka, *am,* n. an inner room, private apartment, L.

Upa-rodhana, *am,* n. the act of besieging or blockading, Sāh.; obstruction, impediment, R.

Upa-rodham, ind. p. besieging, shutting up, Pāṇ. iii, 4, 49 (with loc. or abl. or ifc., Kāś.)

Upa-rodhin, mfn. ifc. obstructing, impeding, Ragh.; (*uparodhin*), having an impediment, impeded, obstructed.

उपरुह् *upa-√ruh,* P. *-rohati,* to grow over or together, heal over (as a wound), Suśr.: Caus. *-rohayati,* to cause to heal over, cicatrize, Suśr.

Upa-rūḍha, mfn. healed over, cicatrized, Suśr.; 'grown out of shape,' altered, changed, Mālav.

उपरूप *upa-rūpa, am,* n. (in med.) inferior or insignificant symptom, Car.

उपरूपक *upa-rūpaka, am,* n. 'minor Rūpaka,' a drama of an inferior class (eighteen of which are enumerated), Sāh. 276; cf. Sāh. 539 seqq.

उपल *upala, as,* m. a rock, stone, MBh.; Suśr.; Śak. &c.; a precious stone, jewel, Yājñ. iii, 36; Śiś. iii, 48; Kir.; a cloud, L.; (*ā*), f. (*úpalā*) the upper and smaller mill-stone (which rests on the *dṛishad*), ŚBr.; KātyŚr.; ĀśvGṛ.; = *śarkarā,* L.; [cf. Gk. ὄπαλος; Lat. *opalus?*] **–prakshin,** mf(*iṇī*)n. grinding (grain) upon mill-stones, miller, RV. ix, 112, 3. **–bhedin,** m., N. of a plant, L. **–hasta,** m. 'stone-hand,' N. of a Caṇḍāla, Kathās.

Upalaka, *as,* m. a stone, Suśr.

उपलक्ष् *upa-laksh,* P. Ā. *-lakshayati, -te,* to look at, observe, behold, perceive, ĀśvŚr.; Śāṅkh-Śr.; MBh.; Suśr. &c.; to pay attention to, regard, MBh.; Kām.; to regard or value as, MBh.; R.; to distinguish, mark; to distinguish by a secondary or unessential mark; to imply in addition, designate implicitly, Sāy.: Pass. *-lakshyate,* to be observed &c.; to be implied, BhP.; Comm. on Mn.; Sarvad. &c.

Upa-lakshaṇa, *as,* m. distinction, distinguishing (see *dur-upa°*).

Upa-lakshaka, mfn. observing closely or with attention; implying; designating by implication, Comm. on Pāṇ. & TPrāt.

Upa-lakshaṇa, *am,* n. the act of observing, Śak. 142, 4; designation, KātyŚr.; Comm. on Pāṇ.; the act of implying something that has not been expressed, implying any analogous object where only one is specified; using a term metaphorically or elliptically or in a generic sense; synecdoche (of a part for the whole, of an individual for the species, or of a quality for that in which it resides), VPrāt.; Comm. on Pāṇ.; Sāh.; Nyāyak. &c.; a mark, Vikr.; Kathās. **–tā,** f. or **-tva,** n. the being implied or expressed elliptically, Vedāntas.; Sarvad. &c.

Upa-lakshayitavya, mfn. to be observed or regarded, MBh.; Suśr.

Upa-lakshita, mfn. beheld, perceived, looked at, R.; BhP.; Daś. &c.; observed; valued or regarded for, R.; characterized, marked, distinguished, MārkP.; Yājñ.; Mn.; Kathās. &c.; included, implied, expressed by implication or elliptically, understood.

Upa-lakshya, mfn. to be implied or understood by implication, inferable, BhP.

उपलधि *upaladhi,* err. for *vāladhi,* q. v.

उपलभ् *upa-√labh,* Ā. *-labhate,* to seize, get possession of, acquire, receive, obtain, find, MBh.; R.; Mn.; Mṛicch. &c.; (with *garbham*) to conceive, become pregnant, R.; to perceive, behold, hear [cf. Gk. ὑπολαμβάνω]; to understand, learn, know, ascertain, MBh.; BhP.; Pañcat.; VarBṛS. &c.: Caus. P. *-lambhayati,* to cause to obtain or take possession, BhP. viii, 15, 36; to cause to hear or learn or know, Pat. on Vārtt. 2 on Pāṇ. i, 4, 52; to cause to be known or distinguished, BhP. iv, 1, 25: Desid. (p. *-lipsamāna,* AV. vi, 118, 11) to wish to catch or grasp.

Upa-labdha, mfn. obtained, received; conceived; perceived, heard, understood, learnt, known, guessed. **–sukha,** mfn. one who has experienced pleasure. **Upalabdhârtha,** mf(*ā*)n. (a statement, tale &c.) the meaning or plot of which is known; true, probable, L.

Upa-labdhavya, mfn. to be perceived, KaṭhUp.

Upa-labdhi, *is,* f. obtainment, acquisition, gain, MBh.; Vikr.; Ragh.; (with *garbhasya*) conception, R.; observation, perceiving, perception, becoming aware, understanding, mind, knowledge, MBh.; Suśr.; Tarkas.; Sarvad. &c.; perceptibility, appearance, TPrāt.; [cf. Gk. ὑπόληψις.] **–mat,** mfn. perceiving, understanding; perceptible, intelligible, TPrāt.; *-tva,* n. the condition or faculty of perceiving, Tattvas. **–sama,** m. (in log.) a kind of sophistical refutation of an argument (e. g. the argument, 'sound is uneternal because it is produced by some effort,' is refuted by saying that sound is also produced by wind), Sarvad.; Nyāyad.; Nyāyak.

Upa-labdhṛi, mfn. one who perceives, NṛisUp.; Comm. on Bādar.

1. **Upa-labhya**, mfn. obtainable, Ragh.; perceivable, to be understood, VP.

2. **Upa-labhya**, ind. p. having obtained; having perceived &c.

Upa-lambha, *as*, m. obtainment, R.; Śiś.; perceiving, ascertaining, recognition, Ragh.; Śak.; Sarvad.; Nyāyak. &c.

Upa-lambhaka, mfn. perceiving, BhP.; (from the Caus.) causing to perceive, reminding, Bhāshāp.

Upa-lambhana, *am*, n. apprehension, perceiving; the capacity of perceiving, intelligence, BhP.

Upa-lambhya, mfn. worthy to be acquired, Pāṇ. vii, 1, 66.

Upa-lābha, *as*, m. grasping, catching (see *án-upalābha*).

Upa-lipsā, f. (fr. Desid.), wish to obtain, Śāntiś.

Upa-lipsu, mfn. (fr. id.), wishing to learn or hear, Daś.

उपलल् *upa-√lal*, Caus. *-lālayati*, to treat with tenderness, caress, fondle, BhP.; Śak. 292, 8; Mālav.

Upa-lālana, *am, ā*, n. f. the act of caressing, fondling, BhP.; Comm. on R.

Upa-lālita, mfn. caressed, fondled, BhP.

उपलिख् *upa-√likh*, to encircle with lines or trenches.

Upa-likhya, ind. p. having encircled with lines or trenches, MBh. xii.

उपलिङ्ग *upa-liṅga*, n. a portent, natural phenomenon considered as boding evil, L.

उपलिप् *upa-√lip*, P. *-limpati*, to defile, besmear (esp. with cow-dung), smear, anoint, Āśv-Gṛ.; ŚāṅkhGṛ.; Gobh.; MBh. &c.; to cover, overlay, Suśr. i, 262, 7; Vāgbh.: Caus. *-lepayati*, to besmear (esp. with cow-dung), smear, anoint, Mn. iii, 206; R.

Upa-lipta, mfn. besmeared, anointed.

Upa-lipya, ind. p. having besmeared or anointed.

Upa-lepa, *as*, m. the act of besmearing (with cow-dung), BhP.; obstruction (by phlegm), Suśr. i, 115, 15; bluntness, dullness, Suśr.

Upa-lepana, *am*, n. the act of besmearing (with cow-dung), Pañcat.; PSarv. &c.; a means of besmearing, cow-dung, Car.

Upa-lepin, mfn. obstructing, Suśr.; smearing, anointing; (*upalepin*), serving as ointment, Suśr. ii, 353, 15.

उपलिप्सा *upa-lipsā*, &c. See *upa-√labh*.

उपली *upa-√lī*, Ā. *-līyate*, to lie close to, cling to, MBh. viii.

उपलुभ् *upa-√lubh*, Caus. *-lobhayati*, to cause to wish, excite the desire of (acc.), allure, PārGṛ.; Kām.

उपलेख *upa-lekha*, *as*, m. 'subordinate writing,' N. of a grammatical work connected with the Prāti-śākhyas. **-pañjikā**, f., **-bhāshya**, n., N. of commentaries on the above work.

उपलेट *upa-leṭa*, Pāṇ. vi, 2, 194.

उपलोट *upa-loṭa*, ib.

उपलोह *upa-loha*, n. a secondary metal.

उपवङ्ग *upa-vanga*, *as*, m. pl., N. of a people, VarBṛS.

उपवच् *upa-√vac*, A. (pf. 3. pl. *-ūciré*, AV. v, 8, 6; aor. Subj. 1. sg. *-vóce*, RV. v, 49, 4; 3. pl. *-vócanta*, RV. i, 127, 7) to address, praise; to animate by the voice, rouse, impel.

Upa-vaktṛí, *tā*, m. one who rouses or animates or impels, RV. iv, 9, 5; vi, 71, 5; ix, 95, 5; ŚāṅkhBr.; a kind of priest, ĀśvŚr.; Sāy. on TBr. ii, 2, 1, 1, &c.

1. **Upa-vāká** (for 2. see s. v.), *as*, m. addressing, praising, RV. i, 164, 8; AV. ix, 9, 8.

Upa-vākyà, mfn. to be addressed or praised, RV. x, 69, 12.

Upa-vácya, mfn. id., RV. i, 132, 2; iv, 54, 1.

उपवञ्च् *upa-√vañc*.

Upa-vañcana, *am*, n. the act of crouching or lying close to (see *sûpavañcanā*).

Upa-vañcita, mfn. deceived, disappointed, R. ii, 52, 19.

उपवट *upa-vaṭa*, *as*, m. the tree Buchnania Latifolia, L.

उपवत् *úpa-vat*, mfn. containing the word *upa*; (*tī*), f. (scil. *ṛic*) a verse beginning with *upa* (e. g. RV. ix, 19, 6; 11, 1, &c.), ŚBr. ii; TāṇḍyaBr. xi, 1, 1; Lāṭy.

उपवत्स्यत् *upa-vatsyat*. See below.

उपवद् *upa-√vad*, P. *-vadati*, to speak ill of, decry, abuse, curse, AV. xv, 2, 1; TBr.; AitBr. ii, 31, 5; ŚāṅkhBr.; Lāṭy.; to speak to, address, AitBr. iii, 23, 1; Pañcat.: Ā. *-vadate*, to talk over, conciliate; to flatter; to cajole, court secretly, Pāṇ. i, 3, 47; Kop.; Bhaṭṭ.

Upa-vāda, *as*, m. censure, blame, KātyŚr.; ShaḍvBr.

Upa-vādin, mfn. censuring, blaming, ŚBr. xi; ChUp.

उपवध् *upa-√vadh*, P. (aor. *upávadhīt*) to strike at or upon, AV. xx, 136, 2; to strike dead, kill, MBh. xii.

उपवन *upa-vana*, *am*, n. a small forest or wood, grove, garden, MBh.; Mn.; Megh. &c.; a planted forest, L. **-vinoda**, m., N. of a work.

उपवनम् *upa-vanam*, ind. near a wood, in the wood, Śiś. vi, 62.

उपवप् *upa-√2. vap*, P. *-vapati* (Pot. *upópet*, Lāṭy. v, 3, 2) to fill up, choke (with earth), strew over; bury under, TS.; ŚBr.; TBr.; TāṇḍyaBr.; Lāṭy.: Pass. *-upyate*, to be buried &c.

Upa-vapana, *am*, n. the act of strewing over, ĀpŚr.

उपवर्ण् *upa-√varṇ*, P. *-varṇayati*, to tell fully, describe particularly or minutely, communicate, relate, MBh.; BhP.; Hit. &c.

Upa-varṇana, *am*, n. description, minute description, delineation, Yājñ.; Suśr.; Hcat. &c.; glorification, praise, Bālar.

Upa-varṇanīya, mfn. to be described.

Upa-varṇita, mfn. described minutely, delineated, MBh.; Kathās. &c.

उपवर्त *upa-varta*, *-vartana*. See *upa-√vṛit*.

उपवर्ष *upa-varsha*, *as*, m., N. of a younger brother of Varsha (and son of Śaṃkara-svāmin; author of writings on the Mīmāṃsa philosophy), Kathās. &c.

उपवर्ह *upa-varha*. See *upa-barha*.

उपवल्लिका *upa-vallikā*, f., N. of a plant (= *amṛitasrava-latā*).

उपवल्ह् *upa-√valh* (√*valh* connected with √*vṛih*?), P. Ā. *-valhati*, *-te*, to ask earnestly, importune with a question, VS. xxiii, 51; ŚBr. xi, xii.

Upa-valhá, *as*, m. impetuosity, superiority (?), ŚBr. xi, 4, 1, 1.

उपवस् *upa-√5. vas*, P. *-vasati*, to abide or dwell with or at; to stay, wait, wait for, TS.; TBr.; AitBr.; ŚBr.; to abide in a state of abstinence, abstain from food, fast, Kāty. on Pāṇ. i, 4, 48; TS. i, 6, 7, 3; ŚBr. i, 6; xi; KātyŚr.; ŚāṅkhGṛ.; Mn. &c.; to encamp (with acc.), Pāṇ. i, 4, 48; to dwell on, give one's self up to, apply one's self to, MārkP.; MuṇḍUp.: Caus. to cause to abide or wait, TS.; to cause to fast, PārGṛ.; MBh.; R.

Upa-vatsyat, mfn. (fut. p.) **= °d-bhakta**, n. food taken before fasting, Kauś.; Vait.

Upa-vasathá, *as*, m. a fast-day (esp. the day preceding a Soma sacrifice), the period of preparation for the Soma sacrifice, AitBr.; ŚBr.; KātyŚr.; Kauś.; a place of abiding, village, L.

Upavasathīya, mfn. belonging to the Upavasatha day or to the preparation for a Soma sacrifice, ŚBr. ix; AitBr.

Upavasathya, mfn. id.

Upa-vasana, *am*, n. a fast, fasting (see *payo-'pavasana*); the state of abiding or being near (see *pīvo'pavasana*; both with irr. Sandhi).

Upavasanīya, mfn. belonging to a fast, Jyot.

Upa-vasta, *am*, n. a fast, fasting, L.

Upa-vastavya, mfn. to be celebrated by fasting (as the end of a fortnight), Gobh. i, 5, 5; Jyot.

Upa-vastṛi, *tā*, m. one who fasts, Pat. on Pāṇ. v, 1, 97. **Upavastr-ādi**, m., N. of a gana (including besides *upavastṛi*, *prāśitṛi*), ib.

Upa-vāsa, *as*, m. (*am*, n., L.) a fast, fasting (as a religious act comprising abstinence from all sensual gratification, from perfumes, flowers, unguents, ornaments, betel, music, dancing &c.), Gaut.; ĀśvGṛ.; Mn. ii, 183; xi, 195; 212; Yājñ. iii, 190; MBh. &c.; abstinence from food &c. in general, Suśr.; R.; Pañcat. &c.; kindling a sacred fire; a fire altar, W. **-°vratin**, mfn. one who observes a vow of fasting, Naish.

Upavāsaka, mfn. belonging to a fast or fasting, MBh.; Yājñ.

Upavāsin, mfn. one who observes a fast, fasting, MBh.; Dhūrtas.

Upôshaṇa, *am*, n. a fast, fasting.

Uposhaya, Nom. P. *uposhayati*, to celebrate or pass (time) by fasting.

Upôshita, mfn. one who has fasted, fasting, MBh.; Yājñ.; Ragh. &c.; (*am*), n. a fast, fasting, MārkP.; Mn. v, 155, &c.

1. **Upôshya**, mfn. to be celebrated or passed by fasting (as time).

2. **Upôshya**, ind. p. having fasted, fasting, MBh.; Yājñ. &c.

उपवस्ति *upavasti*, gaṇa *vetanâdi*, Pāṇ. iv, 4, 12; (Kāś. reads *upasti*.)

उपवह् *upa-√vah*, P. *-vahati*, to bring or lead or convey near, RV.; MBh.; to bring near, procure, MBh. xiii; BhP.; to adduce, R.; (cf. *upôḍh*.)

Upa-vahá, *am*, n. a piece of wood placed on the neck of an ox under the yoke (to raise it to the right level for a yoke-fellow of greater height), ŚBr. i, 4, 4, 7; (v. l. *úpa-vahas*.)

Upa-vāha, *as*, m. driving, riding, L.; (*ās*), m. pl., N. of a people, VP.

Upa-vāhana, *am*, n. the act of bringing or carrying near, L.

Upa-vāhin, mfn. flowing or streaming towards, MBh. i, 2367.

Upa-vāhya, mfn. to be brought near, R.; (*upavāhya* fr. *upa-vāha*), serving for driving or riding, serving as a vehicle, VarBṛS.; (*as*), m. an animal for riding, ib.; a king's elephant, any royal vehicle, L.

1. **Upôḍha** (in some cases not to be distinguished from 2. *upôḍha*, q. v. under *upôh*), mfn. brought near, effected, appeared, Rājat.; Daś. &c.; near (in time and space), Mālav.; Kum.; (*ā*), f. 'brought home in addition to,' a second or inferior but favourite wife, R. i, 13, 37 (ed. Schlegel; *vāvātā* [q. v.] ed. Bombay i, 14, 35).

उपवा 1. *upa-√vā*, P. *-vāti*, to blow upon, ŚBr. xiii, 3, 8, 6.

2. **Upa-vā́**, f. the act of blowing upon, AV. xii, 1, 51.

1. **U'pa-vāta** (for 2. see *upa-√vai*), mfn. blown upon, ŚBr. iv, 1, 3, 7.

उपवाक 2. *upa-vāka* (for 1. see col. 1), *as*, *ā*, m. f. Indra-grain (cf. *indra-yava*), VS.; ŚBr.; KātyŚr.

उपवाजय *upa-vājaya*, Nom. (fr. *vāja*) P. *-vājayati*, to impel, accelerate, ŚBr. v; to fan, kindle, inflame, TS.; TBr.; KātyŚr.

Upa-vājana, *am*, n. a fan, KātyŚr.

उपवाद *upa-vāda*, &c. See *upa-√vad*.

उपवासन *upa-vāsana*, *am*, n. (√*4. vas*), a dress, garment, cover, AV. xiv, 2, 49; 65.

उपविगुल्फ् *upa-vi-√gulph*, Caus. (Pot. 3. pl. *-gulphayeyus*) to add abundantly, ĀśvŚr. ii, 6, 8, 33.

उपविचार *upa-vi-cāra*, *as*, m. environs, neighbourhood, L.

उपविद् *upa-vid*, *t*, f. (√*1. vid*), ascertaining, learning, RV. viii, 23, 3 [Sāy.; fr. √*2. vid*, investigating, finding out, inquiring into, BRD.]

Upa-vedana, *am*, n. ascertainment, learning, Sāy. on RV. viii, 23, 3.

Upa-vedanīya, mfn. to be learnt or found out, Comm. on Nyāyad.

उपविद्या *upa-vidyā*, f. inferior knowledge, profane science.

उपविध् *upa-√1. vidh*, P. (3. pl. *-vidhán*) to honour, worship, RV. i, 149, 1.

उपविन्दु *upa-vindu*. See *upa-bindu*.

उपविन्ध्य *upa-vindhya, as*, m. the land near the Vindhya mountain, L.

उपविपाशम् *upa-vipāśam* (fr. *vipāś*, gaṇa *śarad-ādi*, Pāṇ. v, 4, 107) near the (river?) Vipāś.

उपविमोकम् *upa-vi-mokam*, ind. p. (fr. *upa-vi-√muc*), unharnessing, i. e. changing (the oxen), AitBr. iv, 27, 4.

उपविश् *upa-√viś*, P. *-viśati*, to go or come near, approach, RV. viii, 96, 6; to sit down, take a seat (as men), lie down (as animals), AitBr.; ŚBr.; MBh.; Śak.; Hit. &c.; to enter; to stop, settle one's self, MBh. iii; to sit near to, MBh. i, 573; R. ii; to set (as the sun), Kathās.; to apply or devote one's self to, cultivate, BhP.: Caus. P. *-veśayati*, to cause to sit down, summon or invite to sit down, AitBr.; ĀśvGṛ.; Gobh.; MBh.; Suśr. &c.; to cause to settle, BhP.; R.

Upa-viśya, ind. p. having sat down, sitting down &c.

Upa-vishṭa, mfn. seated, sitting, KātyŚr.; MBh. &c.; come to, arrived, entered (into any state or condition); ifc. having obtained, R.; Daś. &c.; occupied with, engaged in, MBh.; Pañcat.; Bhaṭṭ.

Upavishṭaka, mfn. 'firmly settled' (said of a fœtus which remains in the womb beyond the usual time), Car.

Upa-veśá, *as*, m. the act of sitting down, sitting, resting, TS.; KātyŚr.; the act of applying one's self to or being engaged in, MBh.; R.; stool, motion, L.; N. of a Ṛishi.

Upa-veśana, *am*, n. the act of sitting down, ĀśvŚr.; Kauś.; a seat, Ragh.; the being devoted to or engaged in, MBh.; Pañcat.; evacuation or motion of the bowels, Car.; causing to sit down, L.

Upa-veśi, *is*, m., N. of a Ṛishi, ŚBr. xiv, 9, 4, 33.

Upa-veśita, mfn. caused to sit down, seated; caused to settle.

Upa-veśin, mfn. ifc. devoting or applying one's self to, MBh.; (*upaveśin* fr. *upa-veśa*), one who has a motion of the bowels, Car.

उपविश्रम्भ् *upa-vi-√śrambh*, Caus.

Upa-viśrambhayya, ind. p. having inspired with confidence, BhP. v, 26, 31; (v. l. *anu-vi-śrambhayya*.)

उपविष् *upa-√vish*, P. *-viveshṭi* (RV.; *-ve-veshṭi*, ŚBr.; Impv. 2. sg. *-viḍḍhi*, TBr.) to be active for; to obtain or gain by activity, RV. x, 61, 12; to perform service, be effective or useful for (esp. said of the Upa-vesha below), ŚBr. i, 2, 1, 3; TBr. iii, 3, 11, 1.

Upa-veshá, *as*, m. a stick (of green wood) used for stirring the sacrificial fire, TS.; TBr.; VS.; ŚBr.; KātyŚr.

उपविष *upa-visha, am*, n. factitious poison, a narcotic, any deleterious drug (as opium, datura, &c.); (*ā*), f. the plant Aconitum Ferox, L.

उपविष्ठा *upa-vi-shṭhā* (*upa-vi-√sthā*), Ā. *-tishṭhate*, to be or stand here and there, ŚBr. vii, 4, 1, 14.

उपवी *upa-√vī*, P. (2. sg. *-veshi*, RV. viii, 11, 4; Impv. *-vetu*, RV. v, 11, 4; x, 16, 5) to hasten near, come near, attain, obtain.

उपवीक्ष् *upa-√vīksh* (*upa-vi-√īksh*), Ā. *-vī-kshate*, to look at or towards, R.; to regard as fit or proper, Bhpr.

उपवीज् *upa-√vīj*, P. *-vījati*, to blow upon, fan, MBh.: Caus. P. *-vījayati*, to fan, Śak. 105, 4; Comm. on KātyŚr.

Upa-vījita, mfn. blown upon, fanned, MBh. i, 1308; Mṛicch.

उपवीणय *upa-vīṇaya*, Nom. (fr. *vīṇā*, Pāṇ. iii, 1, 25), to play on a lute before or in the presence of, Ragh.; Kād. &c.

उपवीत *upa-vīta*, &c. See *upa-√vye*.

उपवीर *upa-vīra, as*, m. a kind of demon, PārGṛ. i, 16, 23.

उपवृंह् *upa √vṛiṅh*, Caus. *-vṛiṅhayati*, to make strong or powerful, promote, BhP.; MārkP. &c.; (see also *upa-√bṛih*.)

Upa-vṛiṅhaṇa, *am*, n. the act of making strong, invigorating, promoting, R.; BhP.

Upa-vṛiṅhita, mfn. made strong or powerful, invigorated, supported, promoted; (ifc.) increased or supported or aided by, accompanied by, MBh.; BhP.; Kathās.; Daś. &c.

Upa-vṛiṅhin, mfn. invigorating, supporting, Kathās.

उपवृत् *upa-√vṛit*, Ā. *-vartate*, to step or walk upon, ĀśvŚr. ii, 4, 8, 3; to move or come near, approach, fall to, R.; BhP.; to return: Caus. Ā. *-vartayate*, to cause to move up; to stroke upwards, TBr.; to cause to recover, Kathās.

Upa-varta, *as*, m. a particular high number, L.

Upa-vartana, *am*, n. (fr. the Caus.), the act of bringing near, Sarvad.; a place for exercise; a country (inhabited or not), L.

Upa-vṛitta, mfn. come near, approached; come back, brought back (from exhaustion &c.), recovered, MBh.; (in geom.) a circle in a particular position relatively to another one.

Upa-vṛitti, *is*, f. motion towards (one's place), Prab.

उपवे *upa-√ve*, P. to bring into close contact with, enclose, enfold, wrap.

Upa-vāya, ind. p., Pāṇ. vi, 1, 41; Kāś.

Upôta, mfn. put into, wrapped, enveloped (in armour or mail), Lāṭy. viii, 5, 8; ŚāṅkhŚr.

उपवेणा *upa-veṇā*, f., N. of a river, MBh.

उपवेद *upa-veda, as*, m. 'secondary knowledge,' N. of a class of writings subordinate or appended to the four Vedas (viz. the *Āyur-veda* or science of medicine, to the Ṛig-veda; the *Dhanur-veda* or science of archery, to the Yajur-veda; the *Gāndharva-veda* or science of music, to the Sāma-veda; and the *Śastra-śāstra* or science of arms, to the Atharva-veda; this is according to the Caraṇa-vyūha, but Suśr. and the Bhpr. make the Āyur-veda belong to the Atharva-veda; according to others, the *Sthāpatya-veda* or science of architecture, and *Śilpa-śāstra* or knowledge of arts, are reckoned as the fourth Upa-veda).

उपवेष *upa-veshá*. See *upa-√vish*.

उपवेष्ट् *upa-√veshṭ*, Caus.

Upa-veshṭana, *am*, n. the act of wrapping up, swathing.

Upa-veshṭita, mfn. wrapped in, surrounded, Mṛicch.; Kathās.

Upaveshṭitin, mfn. one who has wrapped himself round the loins in a cloth, Āp.

उपवै *upa-√vai*, P. *-vāyati*, to dry up, shrink in drying, TāṇḍyaBr.; ŚāṅkhŚr.; Kāṭh.

2. **Upa-vāta** (for 1. see *upa-√vā*), mfn. dried up; dry, ĀśvGṛ.; Kauś.

उपवैणव *upavaiṇava, am*, n. (fr. *upa-veṇu*?), the three periods of the day (viz. morning, midday, and evening), L.

उपव्यध् *upa-√vyadh*, P. (2. sg. *-vidhyasi*) to throw at or on, hit, MBh. vii, 6534 (ed. Calc.)

उपव्याख्यान *upa-vyākhyāna, am*, n. (*√khyā*), explanation, interpretation, ChUp.; MuṇḍUp.

उपव्याघ्र *upa-vyāghra, as*, m. the small hunting leopard, L.

उपव्युषम् *upa-vyushám*, ind. about dawn, TBr.; TāṇḍyaBr.

Upa-vyushasam, ind. id., KātyŚr.; Āp.; Car.

उपव्ये *upa-√vye*, Ā. *-vyayate*, to put on or invest one's self with the sacred thread, TS. ii, 5, 11, 1.

U'pa-vīta, mfn. invested with the sacred thread; (*am*), n. the being invested with the sacred thread; the sacred thread or cord (worn by the first three classes over the left shoulder and under the right arm), TS.; ŚBr.; Mn. ii, 44; 64; iv, 66; Yājñ. i, 29; Hariv.; Ragh. &c.; (cf. *yajñôpavīta*.)

Upavītaka, *am*, n. the sacred thread, Kathās.; BhP.

Upavītin, mfn. wearing the sacred cord in the usual manner (over the left shoulder and under the right arm), VS. xvi, 17; KātyŚr.; ĀśvŚr.; Mn. ii, 63; (cf. *yajñôpavītin*.)

Upa-vīya, ind. p. having put on the sacred thread, TBr. i, 6, 8, 2; Kāṭh.; BhP.

उपव्रज् *upa-√vraj*, P.

Upa-vrájya, ind. p. having gone towards, coming near, approaching, TBr. iii, 10, 11, 3; BhP.; going behind, following, R. v.

उपव्रजम् *upa-vrajam*, ind. near a cattle pen, BhP.

उपव्रतय *upa-vrataya*, Nom. (fr. *vrata*) Ā. (Pot. 3. pl. *-vratayeran*) to eat (anything) together with the food prescribed for a Vrata or fast, ĀśvŚr. ii, 6, 8, 39.

उपव्लय *upa-vlaya*. See *upa-blaya*.

उपशक् *upa-√śak*, P. (pf. 1. pl. *-śekima*) to be able to bring into one's power, master, be superior, AV. vi, 114, 2; 3 [= TBr. ii, 4, 4, 9]: Desid. P. *-śikshati*, to endeavour to bring into one's power, master or subdue; to bring or draw near, call near, allure; to bring into one's possession, RV.; AV. vii, 12, 1; xi, 8, 17; TBr.; TāṇḍyaBr.: Ā. *-śikshate*, to try, undertake, ŚāṅkhBr.; to endeavour to help or serve, offer one's service, MBh.; to learn, inquire into, MBh.; BhP.: Caus. of Desid. P. *-śi-kshayati*, to teach, train, BhP.

Upa-śāká, *as*, m. a helper, companion, RV. i, 33, 4.

Upa-śikshá, f. desire of learning, VS. xxx, 10; learning, acquisition, Mṛicch.; Kathās.

Upa-śikshita, mfn. learnt, studied; trained, MBh.; BhP.

उपशङ्क् *upa-√śaṅk*, Ā. to suspect, suppose, think, MBh.; R.

उपशद *upa-śada, as*, m. (perhaps fr. *√2. śad*, 'to excel') a particular Ekāha or sacrifice during one day, ĀśvŚr.; Vait.; removal of an impediment to get children, Sāy. on TāṇḍyaBr. xix, 3, 1.

उपशफ *upa-śapha, as*, m. a hind hoof, Sāy. on TBr. ii, 6, 4.

उपशम् *upa-√śam*, P. Ā. *-śāmyati, -te*, to become calm or quiet; to cease, become extinct, AitBr.; Kauś.; ĀśvGṛ.; ChUp.; MBh. &c.: Caus. *-śamayati* and ep. *-śāmayati*, to make quiet, calm, extinguish; to tranquillize, appease, pacify, mitigate, MBh.; VarBṛS.; Daś. &c.

Upa-śama, *as*, m. the becoming quiet, assuagement, alleviation, stopping, cessation, relaxation, intermission, MāṇḍUp.; Prab.; Pañcat. &c.; tranquillity of mind, calmness, patience, MBh. iii; Bhartṛ.; Śāntiś.; (in astron.) N. of the twentieth Muhūrta. **-kshaya**, m. (with Jainas) the destruction (of activity &c.) through quietism, Sarvad. **-vat** and **-śīla**, mfn. placid, calm, tranquil. **Upaśamâyana**, mfn. going to or obtaining tranquillity of mind, BhP. v, 1, 29.

Upa-śamana, mf(*ī*)n. calming, appeasing, BhP.; (*am*), n. the becoming extinct, ceasing, Nir.; calming, appeasing, mitigation, MBh.; BhP.; Suśr.; Pañcat.; an anodyne.

Upa-śamanīya, mfn. to be appeased or made quiet, Sāh.; (*upaśamanīya* fr. *upa-śamana*), serving as an anodyne, calming, appeasing, Car.

Upa-śānta, mfn. calmed, appeased, pacified; calm, tranquil, BhP.; Kathās.; ceased, extinct, intermitted, R.; PraśnUp. **-vaira**, mfn. one whose enmity has ceased, reconciled, pacified, VarBṛS.

Upaśāntâtman, mfn. one whose mind is pacified, placid, BhP.

Upa-śānti, *is*, f. cessation, intermission, remission, Suśr.; Ragh.; Hit. &c.; tranquillity, calmness.

Upaśāntin, mfn. appeased, tranquil, calm; tame; (*ī*), m. a tame elephant, L.

Upa-śāmaka, mfn. calming, quieting, affording repose, making patient, Lalit.

उपशय *upa-śaya*. See *upa-√śī*.

उपशरदम् *upa-śaradam*, ind. (fr. *śarad*, gaṇa *śarad-ādi*, Pāṇ. v, 4, 107), at or near the autumn.

उपशल्य *upa-śalya, as*, m. a small spear or lance tipped with iron, MBh. iii, 641; (*am*), n. a neighbouring district, environs, the ground near a village, Daś.; Ragh.; the ground at the base or edge of a mountain, Śiś. v, 8.

Upa-śalyaka, *am*, n. a small piece of ground near a village, Kād.

उपशाखा *upa-śākhā*, f. a smaller branch of a tree, little branch, BhP. iv, 31, 14; Sāy.

उपशान्त्व् *upa-√śāntv.* See *upa-√sāntv.*

उपशाय *upa-śāya*, &c. See *upa-√śī.*

उपशाल *upa-śāla*, *am*, n. a place or court in front of a house, Kauś.

Upa-śālam, ind. (fr. *śālā*, Pāṇ. vi, 2, 121), near a house.

उपशास्त्र *upa-śāstra*, *am*, n. a minor science or treatise, L.

उपशिक्षा *upa-śikshā.* See *upa-√śak.*

उपशिङ्घ् *upa-√śiṅgh*, P. *-śiṅghati*, to smell at, kiss, Bhaṭṭ.

Upa-śiṅghana, *am*, n. (in med.) anything given to smell at, Suśr. ii, 515, 11; (*-śiṅhana*, *-siṅhana* are wrong readings.)

उपशिरस् *upa-śiras*, ind. upon the head, Kauś. 86.

उपशिव *upa-śiva*, *as*, m., N. of a man.

उपशिष्य *upa-śishya*, *as*, m. the pupil of a pupil, Prab.

उपशी *upa-√śī*, Ā. *-śete*, to lie near or by the side of (acc.), RV. x, 18, 8; ŚBr.; Kauś.; MBh.; to lie by the side of (for sexual intercourse), ŚBr.; TS.; Kāṭh.; MBh. xiii; to lie upon (loc.), R. vi; to do good, be suitable or useful, Car.

Upa-śayá, mfn. lying near at hand or close by, lying ready for use, ŚBr.; ŚāṅkhŚr.; (*as*), m. one of the Yūpas (or posts to which the sacrificial animal is tied), TS. vi, 6, 4, 4; the lying near or by the side of; a kind of hole in the ground (placed near the track of wild animals, for a hunter to conceal himself in, Mall. on Śiś. ii, 80); (in med.) the allaying (of diseases) by suitable remedies, suitableness, usefulness, advantageous medicine, Car.; the liking, predilection (of a sick person as for coolness &c.), ib.; diagnosis by the effect of certain articles of food or medicine, W.; (*ā́*), f. (scil. *mṛid*) a piece of clay prepared and ready for use, ŚBr.; KātyŚr. **–tvá**, n. the being a particular sacrificial post, TS. vi, 6, 6, 4. **–stha**, mfn. lying in ambush (as a hunter), Śiś. ii, 80.

Upa-śāya, *as*, m. (ifc.) the turn for lying down or sleeping with, Pāṇ. iii, 3, 39; (cf. *rājôpaśāya.*)

Upaśāyaka, mf(*ikā*)n. sleeping alternately with, Bhaṭṭ.; (*as*), m., N. of a man, VārP.

Upa-śāyin, mfn. lying near to or by the side of, KātyŚr.; lying, sleeping, R.; lying down, going to bed, MBh.; allaying, tranquillizing, anything that calms &c.; (in med.) composing, narcotic, W.

Upaśāyi-tā, f. or **-tva**, n. tranquillization, calming; means of allaying disease (as diet &c.), W.

Upa-śīvan, mf(°*varī*)n. lying near or by the side of, MaitrS. ii, 13, 16; Kāṭh.

उपशीर्षक *upa-śīrshaka*, *am*, n. a kind of disease of the head, ŚārṅgS.

उपशुनम् *upa-śunam* (fr. *śvan*), ind. near a dog, Pāṇ. v, 4, 7, 7.

उपशुभ् *upa-√śubh*, Ā. *-śobhate* (p. *-śumbhamāna*, BhP.) to be beautiful or brilliant, BhP. v, 17, 13; Hit.: Caus. P. *-śobhayati*, to adorn, ornament, MBh.; VarBṛS. &c.

Upa-śobhana, *am*, n. the act of adorning, ornamenting, R.; BhP.

1. **Upa-śobhā** (for 2. see s. v.), f. ornament, Śiś. xiii, 36.

Upa-śobhikā, f. ornament, decoration, AgP.

Upa-śobhita, mfn. adorned, ornamented, decorated, MBh.; MārkP.; Suśr.; Pañcat. &c.

Upaśobhin, mfn. of beautiful appearance, brilliant, Kathās.

उपशुष् *upa-√śush*, P. *-śushyati*, to dry up, TS. iii, 1, 10, 3; Suśr.; Car.: Caus. *-śoshayati*, to cause to dry up or shrink, make dry or withered, Āp.; MBh.; Kathās.

Upa-śoshaṇa, mfn. the act of causing to dry up or shrink, Suśr.; Prab.

Upa-śoshita, mfn. made dry, dried, dry, MBh.; Suśr.

उपशोभा 2. *upa-śobhā* (for 1. see col. 1), f. secondary ornament or decoration, AgP.; Hcat.

उपश्च्युत् *upa-√ścyut* or *-√ścut*, P. *-ścyotati*, to ooze or trickle down, fall in drops, MW.

उपश्रम् *upa-√śram*, P. *-śrāmyati*, to rest, repose, Kauś.

उपश्रि *upa-√śri*, P. *-śrayati*, to lean (anything) against, TBr. i, 6, 6, 2; ŚBr. xiv; KātyŚr.: Ā. *-śrayate* (p. of the pf. *-śiśriyāṇā*) to lean against, support, prop, RV. x, 18, 12; to cling to, fit closely (as an ornament), RV. vii, 56, 13; to place one's self near to, go towards, MBh.; BhP.; to accommodate one's self to, ChUp. vi, 8, 2.

U'pa-śrita, mfn. placed near, brought to the attention of, RV. vii, 86, 8; leaning towards or upon, TS.; VS.; KātyŚr.

Upa-śrī, f. an over-garment (fitting closely), KaushUp.

उपश्रु *upa-√śru*, P. *-śriṇoti*, to listen to, give ear to, hear, RV.; AV. xii, 4, 27; xx, 27, 1; ŚBr.; TāṇḍyaBr.; TBr.; ChUp.; MBh. &c.

Upa-śruta, mfn. listened to, heard, MBh.; Hariv.; BhP.; promised, agreed, L.

U'pa-śruti, *is*, f. giving ear to, listening attentively, RV. i, 10, 3; viii, 8, 5; 34, 11; AV. ii, 16, 2; xvi, 2, 5; range of hearing, ŚBr.; ŚāṅkhŚr.; hearing, BhP.; rumour, report, MBh. v, 30, 5 (ed. Bomb.; *apa-śruti*, ed. Calc. v, 871); a kind of supernatural oracular voice (answering questions about future events, and supposed to be uttered by an idol after mystic invocations, Vidhāna-pārijāta, T.), MBh.; Kād. &c., (cf. *śakunôpa*°); (*is*), m., N. of an evil spirit, PārGṛ. i, 16, 23

Upa-śrútya, ind. p. having listened to; listening to, hearing, AV. xii, 4, 28; MBh.; BhP. &c.

Upa-śrotṛi, *tā*, m. a listener, hearer, RV. vii, 23, 1; TS.; ŚāṅkhŚr.; Vait.

उपश्लाघा *upa-ślāghā*, f. boasting, brag, swagger, GopBr.

उपश्लिष् *upa-√ślish*, P. *-ślishyati*, to come near to or into close contact with, cling to, MBh.; Daś.: Caus. *-śleshayati*, to bring near or into close contact, Vikr.

U'pa-ślishṭa, mfn. brought near or into close contact, contiguous, adjoining, TBr. iii, 8, 17, 4; Pañcat.

Upa-ślesha, *as*, m. close contact, contiguity, Pat.; embrace, Prab.

Upa-śleshaṇa, *am*, n. the act of joining or fixing on, sewing together, Sarvad.

उपश्लोक *upa-śloka*, *as*, m., N. of the father of the tenth Manu, BhP. viii, 13, 21.

उपश्लोकय *upa-ślokaya*, Nom. (fr. *śloka*, Pāṇ. iii, 1, 25) P. *-ślokayati*, to praise in Ślokas.

उपश्वस् *upa-√śvas*, Caus. (Impv. 2. sg. *-śvāsaya*) to fill with roarings or noise, RV. vi, 47, 29.

Upa-śvasá, *as*, m. breeze, draught of air, AV. xi, 1, 12.

उपष्टम्भ *upa-shṭambha*, &c. See *upa-stambha.*

उपष्टुत् *upa-shṭút.* See *upa-√stu.*

उपस् *upás*, only loc. *upási* [=*upasthe*, Nir.; Sāy.], 'in the lap,' RV. v, 43, 7; x, 27, 13.

उपसंयम् *upa-saṃ-√yam.*

Upa-saṃyata, mfn. closely joined or fixed together, wedged in, Suśr. 101, 7.

Upa-saṃyama, *as*, m. bringing into close contact, wedging in, L.

Upa-saṃyamana, *am*, n. the act of fixing one thing to another; a means of fastening together, L.

उपसंया *upa-saṃ-√yā*, P. (Impv. 2. pl. *-yāta*) to come in a body towards, AV. vi, 73, 1.

उपसंयुज् *upa-saṃ-√yuj*, Caus. *-yojayati*, to furnish with, MBh. xiii.

उपसंयोग *upa-saṃyoga*, *as*, m. a secondary or subordinate connection, modification, Nir.

उपसंरुध् *upa-saṃ-√2. rudh*, P. (impf. 3. pl. *-arundhan*; fut. 2. pl. *-rotsyatha*) to throng towards, ŚBr. i, 2, 4, 11; 12.

उपसंरुह् *upa-saṃ-√ruh*, P. *-rohati*, to grow over or together, cicatrize, Suśr.

Upa-saṃroha, *as*, m. growing over or together, cicatrizing, ib.

उपसंवाद *upa-saṃ-vāda*, *as*, m. (√*vad*), agreeing together, agreement, Pāṇ. iii, 4, 8.

उपसंविश् *upa-saṃ-√viś*, P. *-viśati*, to gather round, environ (in order to attend), TBr.; to lie down by the side of, KātyŚr.: Caus. *-veśayati*, to cause to lie or sit down by the side of, Kauś.; MBh.

उपसंव्ये *upa-saṃ-√vye*, Ā. (Impv. 2. sg. *-sáṃ-vyayasva*) to wrap up or envelop one's self in (acc.), AV. ii, 13, 3; xix, 24, 5.

Upa-saṃvīta, mfn. wrapped up, covered, MBh. xv.

Upa-saṃvyāna, *am*, n. an under garment, Pāṇ. i, 1, 36.

उपसंव्रज् *upa-saṃ-√vraj*, P. *-vrajati*, to step into, enter, Mn. vi, 51.

उपसंशंस् *upa-saṃ-√śaṇs*, P. *-śaṇsati*, to recite in addition, add, ŚBr. xiii, 5, 1, 8.

Upa-saṃśasya, ind. p. having recited in addition, adding, ĀśvŚr.; ŚāṅkhŚr.

उपसंश्रि *upa-saṃ-√śri*, P. Ā. *-śrayati*, *-te*, to join, attach one's self to, TBr. i; ŚBr. ii; to devote one's self to, serve, attend, MBh. xiii

उपसंश्लिष् *upa-saṃ-√ślish.*

Upa-saṃślishṭa, mfn. united, joined, coherent. **–tva**, n. coherency, MaitrUp.

उपसंसृ *upa-saṃ-√sṛi.*

Upa-saṃsṛitya, ind. p. having stepped near to, approaching, BhP. iii, 21, 47.

उपसंसृज् *upa-saṃ-√sṛij.*

Upa-saṃsṛishṭa, mfn. united with; burdened, afflicted, blasted (by a curse), BhP. xi, 30, 2; joined together; effected, produced, BhP

उपसंसृप् *upa-saṃ-√sṛip.*

Upa-saṃsṛipya, ind. p. having crept towards, ŚBr. iv.

उपसंस्कार *upa-saṃskāra*, *as*, m. a secondary or supplementary Saṃskāra (q. v.), Sāy. on TBr. ii, 1, 4.

उपसंस्कृ *upa-saṃ-s-√1. kṛi.*

Upa-saṃskṛita, mfn. prepared, dressed, cooked (as food), MBh.; Suśr. 335, 14; Car.; prepared, arranged, adorned, Suśr.

उपसंस्था *upa-saṃ-√sthā.*

Upa-saṃsthita, mfn. one who has stopped, Hariv. 9700.

उपसंहित *upa-saṃ-hita.* See *upa-saṃ-√dhā.*

उपसंहृ *upa-saṃ-√hṛi*, P. Ā. *-harati*, *-te*, to draw together, bring together, contract, collect, ŚBr.; MBh.; Pañcar.; TPrāt.; to summarize, sum up, Comm. on BṛĀrUp., on Mn., on BhP.; to withdraw, take away, withhold, MBh. xiv; BhP.; Śak. 267, 7; to stop, interrupt, suppress, MBh. vii; Kathās.; Pat. &c.; to make away with, absorb, MBh. i; MārkP.: Desid. (p. *-jihīrshat*) to wish to destroy or annul, BhP. v, 25, 3.

Upa-saṃharaṇa, *am*, n. the act of withdrawing &c., L.

Upa-saṃhartavya, mfn. to be brought near, Lalit.

Upa-saṃhāra, *as*, m. the act of withdrawing, withholding, taking away, MBh.; drawing towards one's self, bringing near, TPrāt.; summarizing, summing up, résumé, Vedāntas.; Nyāyak.; conclusion, end, epilogue, Kathās.; Sāh.; Sarvad. &c.; N. of the concluding chapters in several books; suppression, subduing; end, death, destruction, L. **–prakaraṇa**, n., N. of a work.

Upa-saṃhārin, mfn. comprehending; exclusive, Tarkas.; Bhāshāp. (with *an*° neg.)

Upa-saṃhṛita, mfn. drawn near, brought into contact, TPrāt.; withheld, drawn back; stopped, interrupted, suppressed, BhP.; Kathās.; Comm. on Mn.; absorbed, destroyed, NṛisUp.; MBh.; BhP.; Sarvad. &c.; dead; comprehended; excluded, L.

Upa-saṃhṛiti, *is*, f. comprehension; conclusion; (in dram.) the end or conclusion, the catastrophe (= *nir-vahaṇa*), Sāh. 332; Daśar.

उपसंक्लृप् *upa-saṃ-√klṛip*, Caus. P. *-kalpayati*, to put upon, set, cause to settle, MBh.; to appoint, elect for, Gṛihyas.

Upa-saṃklṛipta, mfn. put above, being above, BhP. iv, 9, 54.

उपसंक्रम् *upa-saṃ-√kram*, P. Ā. *-krāmati*, *-kramate*, to step or go to the other side (or other world &c.), ŚBr. iv, xii; TUp.; Daś. &c.: Caus. *-kramayati*, to cause to go to the other side, ŚBr. vi.

Upa-saṃkramaṇa, *am*, n. the act of going over towards, Lalit.; gaṇa *vyushṭâdi*, Pāṇ. v, 1, 97.

Upa-saṃkrānta, mfn. turned to, changed into (another meaning; as a word employed in another meaning), Pat.

Upa-saṃkrānti, *is*, f. the being conveyed across, reaching the other side, VarBṛS.; Rājat.

उपसंक्षेप *upa-saṃ-kshepa*, *as*, m. (√*kship*), a concise abridgment or summary, an abstract compendium, R.

उपसंख्यान *upa-saṃ-khyāna*, *am*, n. (√*khya*), the act of adding, annumeration, further enumeration, Kāty.; Pat.; reckoning along with.

Upa-saṃkhyeya, mfn. to be added or enumerated in addition to (loc.), Pat.

उपसंगम् *upa-saṃ-√gam*, Ā. *-gacchate*, to approach together, join in approaching, ŚBr.; BhP.; to unite, join, MBh.; to go or come near, MBh.; BhP.; Bhag.; to enter into any condition or state, MBh. xiii.

Upa-saṃgata, mfn. come together, assembled, BhP.; united, joined (*mithunāya*, for sexual intercourse), MBh. i, 6897.

Upa-saṃgamana, *am*, n. the act of coming together, sexual union, Gaut. iv, 13.

उपसंग्रह् *upa-saṃ-√grah*, Desid. P. *-jighṛikshati*, to wish or intend to embrace (the feet of), Āp. i, 8, 19.

Upa-saṃgṛihīta, mfn. seized, taken into custody, Pañcat.

Upa-saṃgṛihya, ind. p. taking hold of, clasping, embracing, ŚBr.; ŚāṅkhGṛ.; ĀśvGṛ.; Mn.; embracing (especially *pādau* or *pādayoḥ*, the feet of a revered person; the word *pādau* being not unfrequently omitted), PārGṛ.; Āp.; MBh.; Suśr. &c.; partaking of, receiving, accepting, MBh.; R.; getting or entering into, experiencing, MBh. xii; winning over, conciliating, propitiating, Daś.

Upa-saṃgraha, *as*, m. the act of clasping round, embracing, embrace (esp. of the feet of a revered person), Pañcat.; Kathās.; respectful salutation, polite address (performed by touching the feet of the addressed person with one's hands), L.; clasping (a woman, see *dārôpa°*); bringing together, collecting, joining, R.; Nir.; a pillow, cushion, MBh. iv, 517.

Upa-saṃgrahaṇa, *am*, n. the act of clasping round, embracing (e. g. the feet), respectful salutation (by embracing the feet), Āp.; Gaut.; Mn.

Upa-saṃgrāhya, mfn. (one whose feet are) to be embraced; to be saluted reverentially, respectable, venerable, Āp.; Mn.

उपसंघात *upa-saṃ-ghāta*, *as*, m. (√*han*), the act of collecting (one's ideas), Comm. on Nyāyad.

उपसच् *upa-√sac*, Ā. (3. pl. *-sácante*, impf. 3. pl. *-asacanta*) to follow closely, RV. i, 190, 2; AV. xviii, 4, 40; to pursue, AitBr. vi, 36, 2.

उपसंचर् *upa-saṃ-√car*, P. *-carati*, to approach, enter, AV. iii, 12, 1; to approach (*bhartāram*, a husband sexually), VarBṛS.

Upa-saṃcāra, *as*, m. access, entrance, Gobh. iv, 2, 7.

उपसञ्ज् *upa-√sañj*, Ā. *-sajjate*. to be attached to, fond of (loc.), BhP. xi, 26, 22.

Upa-sakta, mfn. attached to, depending on (worldly desires), R.

उपसंजन् *upa-saṃ-√jan*, Ā. (fut. p. *-janishyamāṇa*) to present one's self, appear, Paribh. 64.

Upa-saṃjāta, mfn. appeared, present, ib.

उपसद् 1. *upa-√sad*, P. *-sīdati* (Ved. Pot. 1. pl. *-sadema*; impf. *-asadat*) to sit upon (acc.), RV. vi, 75, 8; to sit near to, approach (esp. respectfully), revere, worship, RV.; AV.; TS.; ŚBr. &c.; MBh.; Ragh. &c.; to approach (a teacher in order to become his pupil), Kathās.; to approach asking, request, crave for, RV. i, 89, 2; vii, 33, 9; TS. ii; ŚBr. ii; to approach in a hostile manner, BhP. vi, 3, 27; to possess, RV. viii, 47, 16; AV. iii, 14, 6; to perform the Upasad ceremony (see below), TS. vi, 2, 3, 4: Caus. *-sādayati*, to place or put upon or by the side of, TS.; TBr.; ŚBr. &c.; to cause to approach, lead near (see *upa-sādita*).

Upa-sat (in comp. for 2. *upa-sád* below). **-tvá**, n. the being an Upasad ceremony (see below), MaitrS. iii, 8, 1. **-pathá**, m. the path or way of the Upasad ceremony (see below), ŚBr. v, 4, 5, 17.

Upa-satti, *is*, f. connection with, union, L.; service, worship, L.; gift, donation, W.

Upa-sattṛi, *tā*, m. one who has seated himself near or at (esp. at the domestic fire), any person who is domiciled, the inhabitant of a house (with and without *gṛiha*), AV. ii, 6, 2; iii, 12, 16; vii, 82, 3; VS. xxvii, 2; 4; ChUp.

2. **Upa-sád**, mfn. approaching (respectfully), worshipping, serving, AV.; VS. xxx, 9; (*t*), m., N. of a particular fire (different from the Gārhapatya, Dakshiṇâgni, and Āhavanīya), VahniP.; (*t*), f. attendance, worship, service, RV. ii, 6, 1; settlement (?), AV. vi, 142, 3; siege, assault, ŚBr. iii; AitBr.; Kāṭh.; N. of a ceremony or sacrificial festival preceding the Sutyā or pressing of the Soma (it lasts several days, and forms part of the Jyotishṭoma), VS. xix, 14; TS.; ŚBr.; KātyŚr. &c. **-rūpá**, n. (*eṇa*, instr.) in the form of an Upasad ceremony, ŚBr. xi, 2, 7, 27. **-van**, mfn. receiving reverence or worship, ĀśvŚr. ii, 5, 9 (in a Mantra). **-vrata**, n. a particular observance prescribed for the Upasad ceremony (consisting principally of drinking milk in certain quantities), Comm. on BṛĀrUp. **-°vratin**, mfn. performing the above observance, ŚBr. xiv; BṛĀrUp.

Upa-sada, mfn. one who goes near, W.; (*as*), m. the Upasad ceremony (see above), ChUp.; approach, W.; gift, donation, W.; (*ī*), f. (*úpa°*) continuous propagation, ŚBr. xiv, 9, 4, 23 (= *saṃtati*, Comm.)

Upa-sadana, *am*, n. the act of approaching (respectfully), respectful salutation, MBh. i; approaching (a work), setting about, undertaking, Gaut.; approaching or going to (a teacher [gen.] to learn any science or art [loc.]), MBh. iii, 17169; performing (a ceremony or sacrifice), R.; neighbouring abode, neighbourhood, R.

Upa-sádya, mfn. to be respectfully approached; to be revered or worshipped, RV.; AV.; ŚāṅkhŚr.

Upa-sanna, mfn. put or placed upon, being on, TBr. ii; AitBr.; KātyŚr.; come near, approached (for protection or instruction or worship &c.), Kauś.; PārGṛ.; MuṇḍUp.; BhP.; placed near to, given, bestowed upon, MBh.

Upa-sādana, *am*, n. the act of placing or putting upon, Sāy. on TBr. ii, 1, 3, 6; approaching respectfully, reverence, respect, BhP.

Upa-sādita, mfn. caused to come near, led near, conveyed to, BhP.

Upa-sādya, ind. p. having caused to approach towards one's self, having obtained, BhP. x, 45, 32.

उपसंतन् *upa-saṃ-√tan*, P. *-tanoti*, to bring into close connection or accompaniment with, recite immediately after, ĀśvŚr.; Vait.

Upa-saṃtāna, *as*, m. close accompaniment or connection or junction (in reciting Mantras &c.), ĀśvŚr. v, 9, 14; 18.

उपसंधा *upa-saṃ-√dhā*, P. Ā. *-dadhāti*, *-dhatte*, to put to, add, annex, increase, Kauś.; ŚāṅkhBr.; to put together, join, connect, ŚāṅkhŚr.; RPrāt.; to bring together with, cause to partake of, Kām.; to place before one's self, aim at, take into consideration.

Upa-saṃhita, mfn. connected or furnished with, accompanied or surrounded by, having, possessing, MBh.; placed before one's self, taken into consideration, ib.; attached to, devoted, Car.

Upa-saṃdhāya, ind. p. having added, adding &c.; placing before one's self, aiming at, with regard to, ŚāṅkhŚr.; MBh.; directing towards, AitBr. ii, 38, 13.

उपसंध्यम् *upa-saṃdhyam*, ind. (fr. *saṃdhyā*), about twilight, Śiś. ix, 5.

उपसंनह् *upa-saṃ-√nah*.

Upa-sáṃnaddha, mfn. tied on or to, ŚBr. ii, iii; KātySr.

उपसंनुद् *upa-saṃ-√nud*, P. (Impv. 2. sg. *-sáṃ-nuda*) to impel near or towards, bring near, procure, TBr. iii, 1, 1, 8; TĀr. iv, 39, 1.

उपसंन्यास *upa-saṃ-ny-āsa*, *as*, m. (√2. *as*), abandonment, leaving off, giving up, MBh.

उपसपत्नि *upa-sapatni*, ind. (fr. *sapatnī*), towards or near a fellow-wife, Śiś. x, 45.

उपसमश् *upa-sam-√1. aś* (aor. *-ānaṭ*) to reach, obtain, RV. iv, 58, 1.

उपसमस् *upa-sam-√2. as*.

Upa-samásya, ind. p. placing or putting upon, ŚBr. vi; adding, Śulbas.

उपसमाकृ *upa-sam-ā-√1. kṛi*, P. (3. pl. *-ā-kurvanti*) to combine together, connect, ŚBr. iv.

उपसमाधा *upa-sam-ā-√dhā*, P. *-dadhāti*, to put on, add (esp fuel to a fire); to kindle (a fire), ŚBr.; ĀsvGṛ.; Āp.; Gaut. &c.; to put upon, place in order, Daś.

Upa-samādhāna, *am*, n. the act of placing upon, accumulation, Pāṇ. iii, 3, 41.

Upa-samādhāya, ind. p. having added (fuel to a fire), having kindled (a fire).

Upa-samāhita, mfn. placed, kindled (as fire), ChUp.; SaṃhUp.

उपसमावृत् *upa-sam-ā-√vṛit*, Ā. *-vartate*, to return home, TBr. iii, 2, 1, 5; ŚBr. iii.

उपसमाहृ *upa-sam-ā-√hṛi*, P. *-harati*, to bring together, Kauś.

Upa-samāhārya, mfn. to be brought together; to be prepared or arranged, ib.

उपसमि *upa-sam-i*, P. *-eti* (Impv. 3. pl. *-sáṃ-yantu*) to approach together, AV. iii, 8, 4; ŚBr. xii; ChUp.

उपसमिधम् *upa-samidham*, ind. (fr. *sam-idh*, Pāṇ. v, 4, 111), near the fuel.

Upa-samit, ind. id., ib.

उपसमिन्ध् *upa-sam-√indh*, Ā. *-inddhe*, to kindle, TBr. ii, 1, 4, 8.

Upa-samindhana, *am*, n. the act of kindling, Sāy. on TBr.

उपसमूह् *upa-sam-√1. ūh*, P. Ā. *-ūhati*, *-te*, to draw together, contract, draw near to one's self, bring near, TS.; ŚBr.

Upa-samūhana, *am*, n. the act of drawing together or in, Comm. on KātyŚr.

उपसमे *upa-sam-ê* (*upa-sam-ā-√i*), P. *-samâiti*, to come together with, meet with, meet, ŚBr.; ChUp.

उपसंपद् *upa-saṃ-√pad*, Ā. *-padyate*, to come to, arrive at, reach, obtain, ChUp.; MBh.; to come up to, be equivalent to, TāṇḍyaBr. xiii, 10, 16: Caus. P. *-pādayati*, to bring near to, lead near to, procure, give, MBh.; R.; to receive into the order of monks, ordain, Buddh.

Upa-sampatti, *is*, f. the approaching or reaching or entering into any condition, Pāṇ. vi, 2, 56; coming up to, Sāy. on TāṇḍyaBr.

Upa-sampadā, f. the act of entering into the order of monks, Buddh.

Upa-sampanna, mfn. arrived at, reached, obtained, L.; one who has reached, MBh.; Comm. on BṛĀrUp.; furnished with, R.; MBh.; Mn.; familiar with, MBh. xiii; staying or dwelling in the same house, Gaut. xiv, 22; Mn. v, 81; finished; prepared, dressed, cooked, L.; enough, sufficient, L.; dead, deceased, L.; immolated, sacrificed (as a victim), L.

Upa-sampādana, *am*, n. the act of causing to come up with, making equivalent, Sāy. on TāṇḍyaBr.

उपसंपराणी *upa-saṃ-parā-ṇī* (*upa-saṃ-parā-√nī*), P. (Subj. *-ṇayāt*) to lead away collectively towards, AV. xviii, 4, 50.

उपसंप्रछ् *upa-saṃ-√prach*, P. (inf. *-prashṭum*) to question about, MBh.

उपसंप्रया *upa-saṃ-pra-√yā*, P. (Impv. 2. pl. *-yāta*) to go near or approach to, VS. xv, 53.

उपसंप्राप् *upa-saṃ-prâp* (*upa-sam-pra-√āp*).

Upa-samprâpta, mfn. one who has obtained or experienced or drawn down upon himself, MBh.; approached, come near, ib.

Upa-samprâpya, ind. p. having arrived at, ib.

उपसंबन्ध् *upa-sam-√bandh.*

Upa-sámbaddha, mfn. tied on, TBr. iii, 8, 4, 3.

उपसंभाषा *upa-saṃ-bhāshā,* f. (*√bhāsh*), talking over, friendly persuasion, Pāṇ. i, 3, 47.

उपसंभिद् *upa-sam-√bhid,* P. (Impv. 2. sg. *-bhinddhi*) to join, unite, Lāṭy. v, 1, 4.

उपसंभृ *upa-sam-√bhṛi.*

Upa-sambhṛita, mfn. brought together, prepared, arranged, Suśr.

उपसर *upa-sara,* &c. See *upa-√sṛi.*

उपसर्ग *upa-sarga, upa-sarjana.* See col. 2.

उपसर्प *upa-sarpa,* &c. See *upa-√sṛip.*

उपसादन *upa-sādana,* &c. See *upa-√sad.*

उपसाध् *upa-√sādh,* Caus. P. *-sādhayati,* to subdue, Pañcat.; to prepare, dress, cook, BhP.; MārkP.; Suśr.

Upa-sādhaka, mfn. preparing, dressing (see *bhaktôpasādhaka*).

उपसान्त्वय *upa-sāntvaya,* Nom. (fr. *sāntva*) P. *-sāntvayati,* to appease, tranquillize, soothe, coax, persuade, Kāś. on Pāṇ. i, 3, 47.

Upa-sāntvana, *am,* n. the act of appeasing, soothing, ib.; kind words, Kād.

Upa-sāntvita, mfn. appeased, made quiet, R.

Upa-sāntvya, ind. p. having appeased, appeasing, MBh.

उपसिच् *upa-√sic,* P. *-siñcati,* to pour upon, sprinkle, RV. iv, 57, 5; AV. iii, 17, 7; vi, 57, 2; ŚBr.; KātyŚr.; Kauś.

Upa-sikta, mfn. sprinkled with, Pāṇ. iv, 4, 26.

Upa-sicya, ind. p. pouring on, sprinkling, AV. ix, 6, 40-41.

Upa-seka, *as,* m. sprinkling upon, infusion, MW.

Upa-sektṛi, *tā,* m. one who pours upon or sprinkles, VS. xxx, 12.

Upa-sécana, mfn. pouring upon or sprinkling, serving for sprinkling, RV. vii, 101, 4; (*ī*), f. a ladle or cup for pouring, RV. x, 21, 2; 105, 10; (*am*), n. the act of pouring upon, sprinkling, RV. x, 76, 7; KātyŚr.; PārGṛ.; anything poured over or upon, infusion, juice, AV. xi, 3, 13; KaṭhUp.; (cf. *anupa°* and *kshīrôpa°*.)

उपसिध् *upa-√2. sidh,* P. (impf. *-asedhat*) to keep off, MBh. vii, 1748.

उपसीम *upa-sīma,* ind. (fr. *sīman*), near the boundary (of a field), Kir. iv, 2.

उपसीरम् *upa-sīram,* ind. near or on a plough, gaṇa *parimukhâdi,* Pāṇ. iv, 3, 59, Comm.

उपसुन्द *upa-sunda, as,* m. 'the younger brother of Sunda,' N. of a Daitya, MBh.; VP.; Hit.

उपसुपर्णम् *upa-suparṇam,* ind. upon Suparṇa or Garuḍa, BhP. viii, 5, 29.

उपसूच् *upa-√sūc.*

Upa-sūcaka, mfn. indicating, betraying, Daśar.

Upa-sūcita, mfn. made manifest, indicated, MBh.

उपसूतिका *upa-sūtikā,* f. a midwife, VarBṛS.

उपसूर्यक *upa-sūryaka, as,* m. a kind of beetle or glow-worm (?), L.; (*am*), n. halo of the sun, L.

उपसृ *upa-√sṛi,* P. *-sarati,* to go towards, step near, approach, visit, TBr. & Up.; AitBr.; MBh.; Ragh.; Vikr. &c.; to approach (sexually), MBh. iii; to set about, undertake, ŚāṅkhBr.; ChUp.

Upa-sara, *as,* m. approach, Bhaṭṭ.; the approach (of a male to a female); covering (a cow), impregnation, Pāṇ. **-ja,** mfn. produced by impregnation, the young of an animal (?), Pat. on Pāṇ. vi, 2, 83.

Upa-saraṇa, *am,* n. the act of coming near, approaching, approach, Megh.; going or flowing towards; (in med.) accumulation of blood, congestion, Suśr.; a refuge, shelter, ChUp.

Upa-sártavya, mfn. to be approached for help or protection; to be had recourse to, ŚBr.; Comm. on ChUp.; to be set about or undertaken, Nir.

Upa-saryā, f. to be covered or impregnated (as a female), Pāṇ. iii, 1, 104.

Upa-sārya, mfn. to be approached, Kāś. on ib.

U'pa-sṛita, mfn. one who has approached, come near (esp. for protection), TBr. i, 4, 6, 1; BhP.; approached, applied to, TS. ii, 1, 4, 6; asked for, ŚāṅkhBr.; furnished with, having, BhP. iv. **-vat,** mfn. one who has approached, R.

Upa-sṛitya, ind. p. having approached, approaching, &c.

उपसृज् *upa-√sṛij,* P. Ā. *-sṛijati, -sṛijate* (aor. Ā. 1. sg. *-sṛikshi,* RV. ii, 35, 1: Pass. 3. sg. *-sarji,* RV. ix, 69, 1) to let loose upon or towards; to let stream upon, pour on, shed forth, RV. vi, 36, 4; x, 98, 12; VS. xi, 38; TS. v; TBr. i; ŚBr. iii; to emit towards, cause to go near, bring or lead near, RV.; BhP.; to admit (a calf to its mother), RV. viii, 72, 7; ix, 69, 1; VS.; ŚBr.; ŚāṅkhŚr. &c.; to add, subjoin, increase, AitBr.; ĀśvŚr.; APrāt. &c.; to visit, afflict, plague, trouble, ŚBr. xiv; to come together or into contact with, Car.; to cause, effect, BhP. iv, 19, 19: Caus., see *upa-sarjita.*

Upa-sarga, *as,* m. (gaṇa *nyaṅkv-ādi,* Pāṇ. vii, 3, 53) addition, AitBr. iv, 4, 1; 2; RPrāt.; misfortune, trouble, a natural phenomenon (considered as boding evil), R.; Prab.; Ratnāv.; Daś. &c.; an eclipse (of a star), Comm. on Mn. iv, 105; (in med.) a fit, paroxysm (supposed to be possession by an evil spirit), Suśr.; a disease superinduced on another, Suśr. ii, 429, 13; change occasioned by any disease, L.; indication or symptom of death, L.; a Nipāta or particle joined to a verb or noun denoting action, a preposition (see also *gati* and *karma-pravacanīya;* they are enumerated Pāṇ. i, 4, 58; in the Veda they are separable from the verb), Pāṇ. i, 4, 59; vi, 3, 97; 122; Kāty.; Pat.; RPrāt.; APrāt. &c. **-vāda,** m., **-hāra-stotra,** n., N. of several works.

Upasargaya, Nom. (fr. the above) P. *upasargayati,* to cause trouble, plague.

Upa-sargin, mfn. adding, one who adds, Lāṭy. iv, 8, 21.

Upa-sarjana, *am,* n. (ifc. mf[*ā*]n.) the act of pouring upon, KātyŚr.; infusion, Car.; an inauspicious phenomenon, eclipse, Mn. iv, 105; anything or any person subordinate to another, Mn.; a substitute, representation, Nyāyam. &c.; (in Gr.) 'subordinate, secondary' (opposed to *pradhāna*), any word which by composition or derivation loses its original independence while it also determines the sense of another word (e.g. the word *rājan* in *rāja-purusha,* 'a king's servant or minister,' and the word *Apiśali* in *Āpiśala,* Pāṇ. i, 2, 43, &c.; vi, 2, 36; in a Bahu-vrīhi compound both members are *upa-sarjana;* in other compounds generally the first member, Pāṇ. ii, 2, 30; for exceptions, see Pāṇ. ii, 2, 31); (*ī*), f. (*upa-sárjanī*) infusion, ŚBr. i; KātyŚr.

Upa-sarjita, mfn. sent off or out, BhP. i, 12, 27.

Upa-sṛijya, ind. p. having added, adding &c.

Upa-sṛishṭa, mfn. let loose towards; sent or thrown off, BhP. i, 12, 1; admitted (as the calf to its mother; also applied to the milk at the time of the calf's sucking), TBr. ii, 1, 7, 1; KātyŚr.; increased; furnished with, ŚāṅkhŚr.; furnished with an Upasarga or preposition (e.g. *√dā* with *ā* is said to be *upasṛishṭa*), Pāṇ. i, 4, 38; Nir.; APrāt. &c.; visited, afflicted, burdened with, plagued, R.; Suśr.; BhP. &c.; obscured (by Rāhu, as the sun), eclipsed, MBh.; Mn. iv, 37; possessed (by a god or demon), Yājñ. i, 271; R.; (*am*), n. coition, sexual intercourse, L.

उपसृप् *upa-√sṛip,* P. Ā. *-sarpati, -te,* to creep towards, approach stealthily or softly or gently, RV. x, 18, 10; 99, 12; AV.; ŚBr.; AitBr.; MBh.; Śak. &c.; to approach (a woman for intercourse), MBh. i; to meet with, Kāś. on Pāṇ. i, 4, 40; to draw near, approach slowly (as sunset, misfortune, &c.), MBh.; BhP.; Hit.

Upa-sarpa, *as,* m. approaching, approach, sexual approach, MBh. iii, 2513 (= *upa-sasarpa,* Nilak.; erroneous for *upa-sṛipya,* BRD.)

Upa-sarpaṇa, *am,* n. the act of approaching softly, advancing towards, Suśr.; Vikr.; Kap.; going or stepping out softly, KātyŚr.; Yājñ.

Upasarpitaka, *am,* n. approach, advancing towards, Bālar.

Upa-sarpin, mfn. creeping near, approaching, MBh.; Mn.

Upa-sṛipta, mfn. approached, come near to.

Upa-sṛipya, mfn. to be approached, Bādar.

उपसेक्तृ *upa-sektṛí, upa-sécana.* See *upa-√sic.*

उपसेन *upa-sena, as,* m., N. of a pupil of Śākya-muni, L.

उपसेव् *upa-√sev,* Ā. *-sevate,* to frequent, visit, abide or stay at (a place), MBh. xiii; R.; Kām.; to stay with a person, attend on, serve, do homage, honour, worship, MBh.; Mn.; Kathās. &c.; to have sexual intercourse with (acc.), Suśr.; to practise, pursue, cultivate, study, make use of, be addicted to, ChUp.; MBh.; MārkP. &c.

Upa-sevaka, mfn. ifc. doing homage; courting (e.g. the wife of another), Yājñ. iii, 136.

Upa-sevana, *am,* n. the act of doing homage; courting (e.g. the wife of another), Mn. iv, 134; service, worship, honouring, MBh.; addiction to, using, enjoying, MBh.; Suśr.; experiencing, suffering, R.

Upa-sevā, f. homage, worship, courting, MBh.; Mn.; addiction to, use, enjoyment, employment, Hit.; Car.

Upa-sevin, mfn. ifc. serving, doing homage, worshipping, Mn.; R.; Kathās.; addicted or devoted to, MBh.; Suśr.; Pañcat.

उपसोम *upa-soma, as,* m. one who has approached the Soma, a Soma sacrificer, [T.]; Kāś. on Pāṇ. vi, 2, 194; (*am*), ind. near the Soma, T.

उपस्कम्भ् *upa-√skambh,* P. (irr. pf. 2. du. *-skambháthus*) to support, prop, RV. vi, 72, 2.

उपस्कृ *upa-s-√kṛi* and its derivations, see under *upa-√1. kṛi,* p. 195, cols. 2 & 3.

उपस्तम्भ् *upa-√stambh,* P. *-stabhnāti* (1. sg. *-stabhnomi,* TBr. iii, 7, 10, 1) to set up, erect, prop, stay, support, ŚBr.; KātyŚr.: Caus. P. (Subj. *-stabhāyat*) to raise, erect, set up, stay, support, RV.; *-stambhayati,* id.

Upa-stabdha, mfn. supported, stayed, Car.

Upa-stambha, *as,* m. (less correctly written *upa-shṭambha*) stay, support, strengthening, Hit.; Comm. on ChUp.; encouragement, incitement; excitement, Comm. on Sāṃkhyak.; base, basis, ground, occasion; support of life (as food, sleep, and government of passions), Car.

Upa-stambhaka, mfn. (less correctly written *upa-shṭa°*) supporting, promoting, encouraging, Sāṃkhyak.; Comm. on BṛĀrUp.

Upa-stámbhana, *am,* n. a support, stay, TS.; ŚBr.; KātyŚr.

उपस्ति *úpa-sti* and *upa-stí* (AV.), mfn. (fr. *s-ti* [*√1. as*] with *upa,* cf. *abhi-shṭi;* fr. *√styai,* Comm. on VS. xii, 101), being lower or inferior, subordinate, subject, submissive, RV. x, 97, 23 = VS. xii, 101 = AV. vi, 15, 1; AV. iii, 5, 6; 7; TS.; TBr.; Kāṭh. **-taram,** ind. more inferior, more subject, TS. vi, 5, 8, 2.

उपस्तु *upa-√stu,* P. *-stauti,* to invoke, celebrate in song, praise, RV.; AV. iii, 15, 7; TBr. iii; (esp. said of the Hotṛi), ŚBr.: Pass. *-stūyate,* to be praised or celebrated in song, BhP. iii, 13, 45; Sāy.

Upa-shṭút, mfn. praised, invoked (= *upa-stūyamāna,* Sāy.), RV. ix, 87, 9.

Upa-stava, *as,* m. praise, SaṃhUp.

U'pa-stuta, mfn. invoked, praised, RV.; AV. xix, 5, 1; (*as*), m. (*upa-stutá*), N. of a Ṛishi, RV.; (*ās*), m. pl. the family of the above, ib.

U'pa-stuti, *is,* f. celebration, invocation, praise, RV.

Upa-stútya, mfn. to be praised, RV. i, 136, 2; 163, 1; vi, 61, 13.

उपस्तृ *upa-√stṛi,* P. Ā. *-stṛiṇāti, -stṛiṇīte* (Ā. 1. sg. *-stire,* RV. ii, 31, 5; inf. *-stire,* RV. v, 85, 1, &c.; inf. used as Impv. *-stṛiṇīshaṇi,* RV. vi, 44, 6 [cf. *gṛiṇīshaṇi* under *√1. gṛī*]) to spread over, cover with, clothe, wrap up, RV. i, 162, 16; viii, 73, 3; ŚBr. xiii; ŚāṅkhŚr.; to spread out under, spread or lay under, scatter under, RV.; AV.; ŚBr.; to scatter round, surround (the Āhavanīya and Gārhapatya fire with grass), TBr. iii, 7, 4, 18; TS.; (at sacrifices) to pour out (esp. clarified butter), pour out so as to form a lower layer or substratum, TS.; AitBr.; ŚBr.; Kauś.; Gobh. &c.

Upa-stára, *as*, m. anything laid under, a substratum, AV. xiv, 2, 21.

Upa-stáraṇa, *am*, n. the act of spreading over, a cover, RV. ix, 69, 5; AV. v, 19, 12; the act of spreading out under, anything laid under, an under-mattress, pillow, ĀśvGṛ.; Āp.; BhP. &c.; the act of pouring under, ŚāṅkhGṛ. i, 13, 16; pouring out so as to form a substratum, a substratum (said of the water which is sipped before taking food; cf. *amṛitôpa°*), ĀśvGṛ. i, 24, 12; HirGṛ. &c.; scattering grass (round the Āhavanīya and Gārhapatya fire, accompanied with the Mantra *ubhāv agnī upa-stṛiṇate*), Comm. on TS. i, 6, 7, 2, &c.

Upa-stāra, *as*, m. anything poured under, Nyāyam. x, 2, 2.

Upa-stir, f. anything spread over, a cover, RV. ix, 62, 28; (dat. *upa-stire* used as inf., see last col.)

U'pa-stīrṇa, mfn. spread or scattered over; clothed, wrapped; poured out, poured under.

Upa-stīrya, ind. p. having covered &c.

उपस्त्री *upa-strī*, f. a subordinate wife, a concubine, L.

उपस्था *upa-√sthā*, P. Ā. *-tishṭhati, -te* (irr. aor. Pot. 3. pl. *-stheshus*, AV. xvi, 4, 7) to stand or place one's self near, be present (Ā. if no object follows, Pāṇ. i, 3, 26); to stand by the side of, place one's self near, expose one's self to (with loc. or acc.), RV.; AV.; KātyŚr.; Gobh.; MBh.; Mn. &c.; to place one's self before (in order to ask), approach, apply to, RV.; AV.; ŚBr.; ĀśvGṛ.; Ragh. &c.; to come together or meet with, become friendly with, conciliate (only Ā., Vārtt. on Pāṇ. i, 3, 25); to lead towards (as a way, only Ā.; ib.); to go or betake one's self to, Pañcat.; R.; to stand near in order to serve, attend, serve, MBh.; Kathās. &c.; to attend on, worship (only Ā., Kāty. on Pāṇ. i, 3, 25, e.g. *arkam upatishṭhate*, he worships the sun; but *arkam upatishṭhati*, he exposes himself to the sun, Pat.), MBh.; BhP.; Ragh. &c.; to serve with, be of service or serviceable by, attend on with prayers (e.g. *aindryā gārhapatyam upatishṭhate*, he attends on the Gārhapatya with a Ṛic addressed to Indra; but *bhartāraṃ upatishṭhati yauvanena*, (she) attends on her husband with youthfulness, Kāś.), MBh.; Ragh.; Daś. &c.; to stand under (in order to support), approach for assistance, be near at hand or at the disposal of, RV.; AV.; TS.; MBh.; Śak. &c.; to fall to one's share, come to the possession of, MBh.; R. &c.; to rise against, RV. vii, 83; to start, set out, Hariv.; Daś.: Caus. *-sthāpayati*, to cause to stand by the side of, place before, cause to lie down by the side of (e.g. a woman), AitBr.; ĀśvŚr.; KātyŚr. &c.; to cause to come near, bring near, procure, fetch, MBh.; R.; Śak. &c.; (in Gr.) to add *iti* after a word (in the Pada-pāṭha), RPrāt. 842 (cf. *upa-sthita*).

Upa-tishṭhāsu, mfn. (fr. Desid.), wishing or being about to betake one's self to, Daś.

1. **Upá-stha**, *as*, m. 'the part which is under,' lap, middle or inner part of anything, a well-surrounded or sheltered place, secure place, RV.; AV.; VS.; AitBr.; ŚBr. &c.; (*upasthaṃ √kṛi*, to make a lap, sit down with the legs bent, AitBr. viii, 9, 5; ĀśvGṛ.; ŚāṅkhŚr.; *upasthe √kṛi*, to take on one's lap, ŚBr. iii); (*as, am*), m. n. the generative organs (esp. of a woman), VS. ix, 22; ŚBr.; MBh.; Mn.; Yājñ. &c.; the haunch or hip; the anus, L. **–kṛita**, mfn. one who has formed a lap by sitting down, seated with the legs bent down, ŚBr. iv; ĀśvŚr. **–daghná**, mfn. reaching to the lap, ŚBr. xiii. **–nigraha**, m. restraint of sexual desire, Yājñ. iii, 314. **–pattra**, m. the Indian fig tree, L. **–padā**, f. a particular artery leading to the generative organs (of a male), Sāy. on AitBr. iii, 37, 6. **–pāda**, mfn. sitting with the legs bent down (so as to form a lap), ŚāṅkhGṛ. iv. **–sád**, mfn. sitting in the lap or in the centre of, RV. x, 156, 5.

2. **Upa-sthá**, mfn. standing upon, AV. xii, 1, 62; standing by the side of, being near at hand, near, L.

Upasthaka, *am*, n. membrum virile, L.

Upa-sthātavya, mfn. to be attended upon with, Śak. 4, 4; to be obliged to appear (in person), Bālar.

Upa-sthātṛi, mfn. one who is near at hand, an attendant, servant, waiter, nurse, Car.; one who makes his appearance, Comm. on Yājñ.

Upa-sthāna, *am*, n. the act of placing one's self near to, going near, approach, access (*upa-sthānam √kṛi*, to give access or scope for, ŚBr. i); coming into the presence of, going near to (in order to worship), worshipping, waiting on, attendance, ŚBr.; KātyŚr.; ĀśvŚr.; MBh. &c.; standing near, presence, proximity, nearness, Yājñ.; Hcat.; staying upon or at, abiding, a place of abiding, abode, Nir.; assembly, MBh.; R.; BhP.; any object approached with respect, a sanctuary, abode (of a god), PārGṛ.; a particular part of the Saṃdhyā, MW. **–gṛiha**, n. an assembly-room, MBh. i, 5003. **–śālā**, f. the assembly-room (of a monastery), Buddh. **–sāhasrī**, f., N. of a work.

Upa-sthānīya, mfn. to be attended on or served, Pāṇ. iii, 4, 68; (*upasthānīya*), one who is to attend on (gen.), ib.

Upa-sthāpaka, mfn. causing to turn one's attention (to a past event or one of a former birth), causing to remember, T.

Upa-sthāpana, *am*, n. the act of placing near, having ready for, see *an-upa°*; (*ā*), f. the act of ordaining (a monk), Jain.; the causing to remember, calling to mind, T.

Upa-sthāpayitavya, mfn. to be brought near or fetched or procured, R.

Upasthāpya, mfn. to be produced or effected, Comm. on Pāṇ. ii, 3, 65.

Upa-sthāya, ind. p. having approached, standing by the side of; attending on &c.

Upa-sthāyaka, *as*, m. a servant, Buddh.

Upa-sthāyam, ind. p. standing near, keeping one's self fast to, RV. i, 145, 4.

Upasthāyika, *as*, m. a servant, Nāṭyaś.; a keeper, nurse, L.

Upa-sthāyin, mfn. one who makes his appearance, arriving, Gaut.

Upa-sthāyuka, mfn. going near to, approaching, Kāṭh.

Upa-sthāvan, mfn. standing near or at hand, ŚāṅkhŚr.

Upa-sthāvara, mfn. id., VS. xxx, 16.

Upa-sthita, mfn. come near, approached, arisen, arrived, appeared, ĀśvGṛ.; MBh.; Mn.; Yājñ. &c.; present, near at hand, ready for, R.; BhP.; Kum. &c.; near, impending, Mn. iii, 187; MBh. &c.; fallen to one's share, received, gained, obtained, Śak.; Ragh. &c.; accomplished, happened; lying or being upon, Suśr.; turned towards, R.; approached, come near to, visited, MBh.; Ragh. &c.; caused, occasioned; felt; known; clean, cleansed, L.; (in the Prātiśākhyas) followed by *iti* (as a word in the Pada-pāṭha), RPrāt.; VPrāt.; Pāṇ.; (*as*), m. a door-keeper, porter, L.; (*ā, am*), f. n., N. of several metres; (*am*), n. (scil. *pada*) a word followed by *iti* (in the Pada-pāṭha; cf. *sthita* and *sthitôpa-sthita*), RPrāt.; VPrāt. **–pracupita**, n., N. of a particular metre. **–vaktṛi**, m. a ready speaker, an eloquent man. **–samprahāra**, mfn. being about to engage in battle, having battle at hand.

Upa-sthiti, *is*, f. standing near, approach; presence, proximity, Sāh.; accomplishing, completeness, see *an-upa°*; obtaining, getting; remaining, L.; the faculty of remembering, memory, T.

Upa-stheya, mfn. to be attended on or worshipped, KātyŚr.; R.

उपस्थूणम् *upa-sthūṇam*, ind. on a post, gaṇa *parimukhâdi*, Kāty. on Pāṇ. iv, 3, 58.

उपस्निह् *upa-√snih*, Ā. *-snihyate*, to become wet, become smooth, Suśr.: Caus. *-snehayati*, to conciliate, gain the favour of, Uttarar.

Upa-snihiti, *is*, f. the becoming wet, moistening, Pat. on Pāṇ. vii, 2, 9.

Upa-sneha, *as*, m. the moistening; becoming wet, attracting moisture, Suśr.; R.

उपस्नु *upa-√snu*.

Upa-snuta, mfn. caused to flow, streaming forth, Kir. i, 18.

उपस्पिजम् *upa-spíjam*, ind. with emulation, emulatively, RV. x, 88, 18 [*upaspijam iti spardhā-yuktaṃ vacanam*, Sāy.]

उपस्पृश् 1. *upa-spriś*, P. *-spriśati*, to touch above, reach up to, touch, RV.; AV.; to touch softly, caress, ŚBr.; AitBr.; ĀśvŚr.; KātyŚr.; MBh. &c.; (with or without *apaḥ* or *jalam* &c.) to touch water (for ablution), wash, bathe (as a religious ceremony); to sip water (from the palm of the hand; it is not the custom to spit out the water after sipping it), ŚBr.; ĀśvŚr. & Gṛ.; MBh.; Yājñ.; Mn. &c.; to touch certain parts of one's body (acc.) with water (instr.), Mn. iv, 143; (also without the instr.) Mn. v, 138; (or without the acc.) MBh.: Caus. *-sparśayati*, to cause to touch water or wash the hands, ŚBr. iii.

Upa-sparśa, *as*, m. touching, contact, L.; washing, bathing, ablution (as a religious act), L.; sipping water (from the palm of the hand and swallowing it as a ceremonial), L.

Upa-sparśana, *am*, n. the act of touching, KātyŚr. v, vi; SaṃhUp.; ablution, bath, MBh.; R.; sipping water, KātyŚr.; ŚāṅkhŚr.; (cf. *udakôpa°*.)

Upa-sparśin, mfn. ifc. touching; bathing in, BhP.; (cf. *udakôpa°*.)

2. **Upa-spríś**, mfn. touching, AV. xx, 127, 2; (*k*), f. (scil. *stuti*) 'the touching or affecting verse,' N. of the verse RV. x, 22, 13.

Upa-spriśya, ind. p. having touched or sipping water &c.

Upa-sprishṭa, mfn. touched (as water), sipped, Mn. iii, 208; MBh.; R.; BhP.

उपस्मि *upa-√smi*, Ā. (pf. p. *-sishmiyāṇá*) to smile upon, RV. x, 123, 5.

उपस्मृ *upa-√smṛi*, P. *-smarati*, to remember, ŚBr. ii; KātyŚr.; Comm. on ChUp.

Upa-smāram, ind. p. having remembered, remembering. See *yathôpa°*.

उपस्मृति *upa-smṛiti*, *is*, f. a minor law-book (the following authors of such books are named Jābāli, Nāciketa, Skanda, Laugākshin, Kaśyapa, Vyāsa, Sanatkumāra, Śatarju, Janaka, Vyāghra, Kātyāyana, Jātūkarṇya, Kapiñjala, Baudhāyana, Kaṇāda, and Viśvāmitra), Hcat. i, 528, 21 ff.

उपस्रु *upa-√sru*, P. (Impv. 3. pl. *-sravantu*) to stream or flow upon or towards, VS. xxxv, 20.

Upa-sravaṇa, *am*, n. the flowing out; termination of the periodical flow of a woman, KātyŚr. xxv, 11, 13.

उपस्रोतस् *upa-srotas*, ind. on the river.

उपस्वत्व *upa-svatva*, *am*, n. the produce or profit of property (as corn &c.), L.

उपस्वावत् *upa-svāvat*, *ān*, m., N., of a son of Satrājit, Hariv.; (v. l. *upa-svāya*.)

उपस्विद् *upa-√svid*, Caus. *-svedayati*, (in med.) to cause to sweat (by applying sudorifics), Suśr.

Upa-sveda, *as*, m. moisture, sweat, vapour, MBh.; Car.

Upa-svedana, *am*, n. the causing to sweat (by sudorifics), Car.

उपस्वृ *upa-√svṛi*, P. *-svarati*, to join in singing, Lāṭy. i, 8, 9.

उपहदन *upa-hadana*, *am*, n. the act of discharging excrement upon, VarBṛS.

उपहन् *upa-√han*, P. *-hanti*, Ā. *-jighnate*, to beat, hit at, strike, touch, RV. vi, 75, 13; ŚBr. vi, xiv; Lāṭy.; ĀśvGṛ.; MBh. ii; to stick on, put on, force in, ram, TS. ii; TBr. i; ŚBr.; ŚāṅkhŚr.; to take hold of, seize, take out; to hit, hurt, damage, visit, afflict, impede, spoil, TBr. iii; AitBr.; MBh.; Mn. &c.; to make a mistake in reciting, blunder, AitBr. iii, 35, 3; ŚāṅkhBr.: Pass. *-hanyate*, ib., TS. vii, 3, 1, 1; 2.

Upa-ghāta, &c. See p. 197, col. 1.

Upa-ghātam, ind. p. taking out, drawing out; ladling out, ŚBr.; Gobh.; PārGṛ.

U'pa-hata, mfn. hit, hurt, damaged, injured, visited, afflicted, pained, infected, ŚBr.; MBh.; R.; Śak. &c.; affected, transported (with passion), BhP.; seduced, misled, Śāntiś.; distressed, weakened, discouraged, MBh.; R.; Hit.; Kathās.; killed, Uttarar.; scattered over, covered, Comm. on Mn. iii, 208. **–dhī**, mfn. affected in mind, infatuated.

Upahatâtman, mfn. id., Kathās.; Car.

Upahataka, mfn. ill-fated, unfortunate, unlucky, L.

Upa-hati, *is*, f. hurt, damage, injure, oppression,

Kap.; Naish.; (= *ava-kara*) a dust-heap, Sāy. on TāṇḍyaBr. i, 6, 5.

Upa-hatnú, mfn. hitting, hurting, destroying (enemies), RV. ii, 33, 11 = AV. xviii, 4, 40.

Upa-hatyá, f. hurt, damage, morbid affection (as of the eyes), AV. v, 4, 10.

Upa-hantavya, mfn. to be killed, Kathās.

Upa-hantṛi, mfn. one who hurts or destroys, a destroyer, Sāy. on RV. ii, 33, 11; pernicious, unwholesome, Suśr.

उपहव्य *upa-hávya*. See *upa-√hu*.

उपहस् *upa-√has*, P. *-hasati*, to laugh at, deride, ridicule, MBh.; L.; Mṛicch.; Pañcat. &c.; to smile: Caus. *-hāsayati*, to deride, ridicule, BhP.; Kathās.

Upa-hasita, mfn. laughed at, derided, Kathās.; (*am*), n. laughter accompanied by shaking the head (*sa-śiraḥ-kampam*), Daśar. iv, 70.

Upa-hásvan, mfn. laughing at, deriding, mocking, RV. viii, 45, 23.

Upa-hāsá, *as*, m. laughter, derision, mockery, jeer, Kathās.; Ragh.; Sāh.; ridiculousness, VarBṛS.; fun, play, jest, sport, ŚBr.; PārGr.; MBh. &c. **-gir**, f. a joke, jest, L. **Upahāsâspada**, n. a laughing-stock.

Upa-hāsaka, mfn. ridiculing others, jocose, L.; (*as*), m. a jester, L.; (*am*), n. drollery, fun, BhP. x, 18, 15.

Upa-hāsin, mfn. ifc. deriding, ridiculing, Sāh.; Veṇis.

Upa-hāsya, mfn. to be laughed at or derided, ridiculous, Mṛicch.; Kathās. **-tā**, f. the state of being to be laughed at or derided, ridiculousness; (*upahāsyatām √gam*, to expose one's self to laughter, become ridiculous, Ragh. i, 3.)

उपहस्त *upa-hasta*, *as*, m. the act of taking with the hand, receiving [T.], gaṇa *vetanâdi*, Pāṇ. iv, 4, 12, (not in Kaś.)

Upahastaya, Nom. P. *upahastayati*, to take with the hand, receive, T.

Upahastikā, f. a box for betel or condiments, Daś.

उपहा 1. *upa-√2. hā*, Ā. (Pot. 2. sg. *-jihīthās*) to descend, come down upon, Śiś. i, 37.

उपहा 2. *upa-√3. hā*, Pass. *-hīyate*, to diminish, wane, MBh. xiii, 2028.

उपहालक *upa-hālaka*, *ās*, m. pl., N. of a people (= *kuntala*), L.

उपहिंस् *upa-√hiṇs*, P. Ā. *-hiṇsati*, *-te*, to hurt, wound, injure, damage, MBh.; R.; Mn.

उपहित 2. *upa-hita* (for 1. see p. 199, col. 3), mfn. good in a secondary degree, somewhat good; (*am*), n. a secondary good, MBh. xii, 5219.

उपहु *upa-√hu*, P. *-juhoti*, to sacrifice or offer a libation in addition to, KātyŚr.; ŚāṅkhŚr.; Bhag.

Upa-hávya, *as*, m. a secondary or supplementary libation or sacrifice, N. of a particular religious act, AV. xi, 7, 15; KātyŚr. xxii, 8; ĀśvŚr. &c.

उपहृ *upa-√hṛi*, P. *-harati*, to bring near, reach forth, proffer, offer, place before, give to taste (esp. food), AV.; TBr.; ŚBr.; ĀśvŚr. & Gr.; KātyŚr.; MBh.; Suśr. &c.; to put together, gather, collect, MBh.; BhP.; to apply (medicine), Suśr.; to take away; to destroy, MBh. ii: Ā. *-harate*, to accept, receive, TS. v: Caus. *-hārayati*, to place before, proffer, offer, MBh.; R.; Suśr.: Desid. *-jihīrshati*, to wish to offer, MBh. ii, 862.

Upa-jihīrshā, f. the wish or intention to take away or to rob, MBh.

Upa-harana, *am*, n. the act of bringing near, proffering, offering, BhP.; presenting victims; distributing or serving out food; taking, seizing, L.

Upa-haraṇīya, mfn. to be offered or presented, Mālatim.; Kathās.

Upa-hartavya, mfn. id.

Upa-hartṛi, mfn. one who offers or presents, one who serves out (food), a host, Mn. v, 51.

Upa-hāra, *as*, m. offering, oblation (to a deity); complimentary gift, present (to a king or superior), MBh.; Megh.; Kathās. &c.; (*upahāram vi-√dhā*, to offer an oblation to a god [acc.], sacrifice to any one, Kathās.); a particular kind of alliance (purchased through a gift), Kām.; Hit. &c.; food (distributed to guests &c.); (with the Pāśupatas) a kind of religious service (consisting of laughter, song, dance, muttering *huḍuk*, adoration and pious ejaculation), Sarvad. 77, 22. **-tā**, f., **-tva**, n. the state of being an oblation or offering, Kum.; Kathās. **-paśu**, m. a victim, Kathās. **-varman**, m., N. of a man, Daś.

Upahāraka, *as*, *ikā*, m. f. an offering, oblation, gift, present, BhP.; Kathās.

Upa-hārin, mfn. offering, presenting; sacrificing.

Upa-hārī-√kṛi, P. Ā. to offer (as an oblation or sacrifice), Kathās.; Hit. **Upahārī-cikīrshu**, mfn. intending to sacrifice any one, Kathās.

Upa-hārya, mfn. to be offered as an oblation; to be presented, BhP.; (*am*), n. an offering, oblation, MBh.; BhP.

Upa-hṛita, mfn. brought near, offered, presented; immolated, sacrificed (as a victim); served out (as food); taken; collected, gathered.

Upa-hṛitya, ind. p. having brought near &c.

उपहोम *upa-homá*, *as*, m. an additional or supplementary sacrifice, ŚBr. xi.

उपह्वृ *upa-√hvṛi*, Ā. *-hvárate*, to approach by windings and turnings, reach an end after many deviations or errors, RV. i, 141, 1.

Upa-hvará, *as*, m. a winding or circuitous course full of turnings, uneven or rough ground, slope, declivity &c., RV. i, 62, 6; 87, 2; viii, 6, 28; a car, carriage, L.; (*am*), n. (generally *e* loc.) proximity, nearness, RV. viii, 69, 6; MBh.; a solitary or private place, RV. viii, 96, 14; MBh.

Upa-hvartavya, mfn. to be approached by windings and turnings, Sāy.

उपह्वे *upa-√hve*, only Ā. (Pāṇ. i, 3, 30) *-hvayate* (rarely P., Kathās.; BhP.) to call near to, invite, RV.; AV.; TS.; ŚBr. &c.; to call up, invoke, AV. vi, 23, 1; VS. iii, 42; to call to, cheer, encourage, AitBr. iii, 20, 1; ĀśvŚr. ii, 16, 18: Desid. *-juhūshati*, to wish to call near, ŚāṅkhBr.

Upa-havá, *as*, m. calling to, inviting, invitation, (*upa-havám √ish*, to desire an invitation to [loc.], wish to be invited to, e. g. *tásminn índra upahavám aicchata*, Indra wished to be invited to that [sacrifice], TS. ii, 4, 12, 1), TS.; ŚBr.; ĀśvŚr.; KātyŚr.

Ú'pa-hūta, mfn. called near, invited, AV.; TBr.; ŚāṅkhŚr.; MBh. &c.; that to which one invites, TS. i; ŚBr. i; KātyŚr. iii; summoned, invoked, AV. vii, 60, 4; 5; VS. xx, 35; (*as*), m., N. of Śakalya, Kāś. on Pāṇ. vi, 2, 146; (*ās*), m. pl., N. of particular manes, L.

Upa-hūti, *is*, f. calling (to fight), challenging, challenge, Śiś.

Upa-hūya, ind. p. having called near or invited &c.

Upa-hvāna, *am*, n. the act of inviting, invitation, KātyŚr.

उपा *upā*, ind. a particular Nidhana or concluding chorus at the end of a Sāman, Lāṭy. vii, 10, 1 ff.; Sāy. on TāṇḍyaBr.

उपांशु *upāṇśu*, *u*, ind. (fr. *√aṇś*, 'to divide,' with *upa* and affix *u*, T.(?), gaṇa *svar-ādi*, Pāṇ. i, 1, 37), secretly, in secret, RV. x, 83, 7; MBh.; Ragh. &c.; in a low voice, in a whisper, ŚBr.; AitBr.; (*as*), m. a prayer uttered in a low voice (so as not to be overheard), Mn. ii, 85; MārkP. &c.; a particular Soma oblation, = *upāṇśu-graha* below, VS.; TS.; ŚBr.; KātyŚr. &c. **-krīḍita**, m. a person jested with privately, the companion of (a king's) private amusements, Hit. **-graha**, m. the first Graha or ladle-full of Soma pressed out at a sacrifice, TS.; ŚBr. &c. **-tā**, f. and **-tva**, n. the being uttered in a low voice or whisper, ŚāṅkhŚr.; Comm. on Nyāyam. **-daṇḍa**, n. a punishment inflicted in private, R. **-pātrá**, n. the vessel or ladle for the Upāṇśu-graha, q. v., ŚBr. iv; KātyŚr. **-yājá**, m. a sacrifice offered silently or with muttered prayers, ŚBr. i. &c.; TS.; ŚāṅkhŚr. &c. **-vadha**, m. a clandestine murder, Mudrār. **-vrata**, n. a vow made secretly or privately, Hariv. **-sávana**, mfn. (used for) pressing out the Upāṇśu-graha, q. v. (said of stones so used), ŚBr.; KātyŚr.; Lāṭy. &c. **-havis**, mfn. (a sacrifice) at which the offerings are made silently, ŚāṅkhŚr. **Upāṇśv-antaryāmá**, *au*, m. du., N. of two particular ladles-full of Soma (offered with the breath held and inaudible), ŚBr. iv. **Upāṇśv-āyatana**, mfn. having a silent abode, kept inaudible (as the breath), ŚBr. x.

उपाक *úpāka*. See *upāñc*.

उपाकर्णय *upâkarṇaya*, Nom. (fr. *ā-karṇa*).

Upâkarṇya, ind. p. hearing, learning, Bhp.

उपाकृ *upâ-√1. kṛi*, P. Ā. *-karoti*, *-kurute* (Ved. impf. 1. sg. *-akaram*, 3. sg. *-akar*) to drive or bring near or towards, fetch, RV.; TS. vii; ŚBr.; ĀśvGṛ.; MBh. iii; to commit to, deliver, make over, give, bestow, grant (*kāmam*, a wish), MBh.; R.; to procure for one's self, obtain, MBh. iii, 10278; to bring or set about, make preparations (for a sacred ceremonial), undertake, begin, TS.; AitBr.; ŚBr. xiv; Lāṭy.; Mn. &c.; to consecrate, Mn. v, 7; Yājñ. i, 171.

Upâ-karaṇa, *am*, n. the act of bringing near, fetching, ŚBr.; PārGṛ. &c.; setting about, preparation, beginning, commencing, Āp.; ĀśvŚr. & Gṛ.; KātyŚr. &c.; commencement of reading the Veda (after the performance of preparatory rites, as initiation &c.), ŚāṅkhGṛ. iv, 5, 1; N. of a particular Stotra or prayer at sacrifices, KātyŚr. iii. **-vidhi**, m., N. of a work.

Upâ-karman, *a*, n. preparation, setting about, commencement (esp. of reading the Veda), PārGṛ. ii; Mn. iv, 119; Yājñ. **-prayoga** (*upâkarma°*), **-vidhi**, m., N. of works.

Upấ-kṛita, mfn. brought or driven near, fetched, AV. ii, 34, 2; prepared, undertaken, begun; attended with evil omens, disastrous, calamitous, L.; (*as*), m. a sacrificial animal (killed during the recitation of particular prayers), L.; disaster, calamity, L.

Upâ-kṛiti, *is*, f. setting about, beginning, L.

Upâkṛitin, mfn. one who prepares or begins, gaṇa *ishṭâdi*, Pāṇ. v, 2, 88.

Upâ-cikīrshu, mfn. (fr. Desid.), one who is about to undertake or commence, Comm. on BṛĀrUp.

उपाक्रम् *upâ-√kram*, P. *-krāmati*, to fall upon, attack, MBh.

उपाक्ष *upâksha*, *as*, m. (fr. 1. *aksha*), a particular part of a car (supporting the axletree), Comm. on Lāṭy. i, 9, 23.

Upâkshaka, *as*, m. id.

उपाक्षम् *upâksham*, ind. (fr. *akshi*, Pāṇ. vi, 2, 121), on or near the eye.

उपाख्या 1. *upâ-√khyā*, Ā. (fut. 1. sg. *-khyāsye*) to give an account about (anything), relate, BhP. ii, 9, 45.

Upâ-khya, mfn. discernible, observable by the eye; (cf. *an-upâ°* & *nir-upâ°*.)

1. **Upâ-khyāna**, *am*, n. account, relation, repetition of an event, BhP.

उपाख्या 2. *upâkhyā*, f. (fr. *ā-khyā* with *upa*), a secondary name, surname, epithet, BhP. xi, 4, 7, &c.

2. **Upâkhyāna**, *am*, n. (fr. *ā-khyāna* with *upa*), a subordinate tale or story, an episode, MBh.; Hit. &c.; (cf. *nalôpâ°*.)

Upâkhyānaka, *am*, n. id.

उपागम् *upâ-√gam*, P. *-gacchati* (Ved. Impv. 2. sg. *-gahi*) to come near, come towards, step near, approach, RV.; AV. vii, 48, 2; xix, 4, 3; MBh.; Pañcat. &c.; to come back, return, Kathās.; to approach, come or enter into any state or condition, be subject to, MBh.; Mn.; Yājñ. &c.; to occur, come or fall to one's share, Yājñ. ii, 143.

Upâ-gata, mfn. approached, arrived, come to (for protection); entered into any state or condition, subject to, burdened with; occurred, happened, fallen to one's share; promised, agreed, L.

Upâ-gatya, ind. p. = *upâ-gamya* below.

Upâ-gama, *as*, m. arrival, approach; occurrence, L.; promise, agreement, L.

Upâ-gamya, ind. p. having approached &c.

उपागा *upâ-√gā*, P. *-gāti*, to come near, go towards, rush upon, RV. iii, 56, 2; x, 73, 5; ChUp.; Kathās.

उपाग्नि *upâgni*, ind. on the fire, Kāś. on Pāṇ. i, 1, 41.

Upâgnikā, f. (scil. *bhāryā*) a wife given away in presence of the sacred fire or with due observance of the fire-ritual, a properly married wife, MBh. xiii, 2460.

उपाग्र *upâgra, am,* n. the part which is next to the end or top, Comm. on Pāṇ.; a secondary member, L.

Upâgrya, *am,* n. a secondary member, L.

उपाग्रह् *upâ-√grah.*

Upâ-gṛihya, ind. p. having taken with, together with, BhP. x, 58, 55.

Upâ-grahaṇa, *am,* n. commencement of reading the Veda (after the performance of initiation &c., see *upâ-karaṇa*), L.

उपाग्रहायणम् *upâgrahāyaṇam,* ind. (fr. *āgrahāyaṇī* with *upa,* Pāṇ. v, 4, 110), near the day of full moon in the month A-grahāyaṇa.

Upâgrahāyaṇi, ind. id.

उपाघ्रा *upâ-√ghrā,* P. *-jighrati* (and *-ghrāti,* Ā. *-jighrate,* ep.) to smell at; to kiss, apply the lips to (loc.), MBh.; R.; Ragh.

उपाङ्क्य *upâṅkya,* mfn. (*√aṅk*), to be marked or stamped. **–pṛishṭha,** m., N. of an Ekāha (q. v.) sacrifice, ŚāṅkhŚr.

उपाङ्ग 1. *upâṅga* (for 2. see *upâñj*), *am,* n. a minor limb or member of the body, MārkP.; Sarvad.; a subdivision; a supplementary or additional work, secondary portion of a science, MBh.; Hariv. &c. (such as the Purāṇas, the Nyāya, Mīmāṃsā, and the Dharma-śāstras); N. of a class of sacred writings of the Jainas (eight are enumerated, the last of which includes four subdivisions); a sectarial mark (made with sandal &c.) on the forehead, L.; (in mus.) a particular drum-like instrument. **–gīta,** n. a kind of song, Rājat. **–lalitā-vrata,** n. a particular observance.

उपाचर् *upâ-√car,* P. *-carati,* to come near to, approach, RV. i, 46, 14; 187, 3; ŚBr. ii, iv; to attend upon, wait on, serve, be obedient, RV.; MBh. ii, 408; to physic, Suśr.

Upâ-carita, *as,* m. (in Gr.) a particular Sandhi rule (by which a Visarga in the Pada-pāṭha becomes *s* before *k* and *p* in the Saṃhitā, e. g. *yás pátiḥ,* RV. x, 24, 3), RPrāt. 260, &c.

Upâ-cāra, *as,* m. proceeding, procedure, ŚāṅkhŚr.; established use (of a word), Nir. i, 4; a particular Sandhi (see above), APrāt. iv, 74; RPrāt.

Upâ-cīrṇa, mfn. deceived, MBh. xviii.

उपाच्युतम् *upâcyutam,* ind. in the proximity of A-cyuta or Kṛishṇa, BhP. x.

उपाज् *upâj* (*upa-√aj*), P. (Impv. *upâjatu,* RV. x, 19, 2) Ā. (1. sg. *úpâje,* AV. v, 11, 2; impf. *úpâjata,* RV. i, 161, 6) to drive near or towards.

Upāje, ind. so as to help or support (optionally to be regarded as a *gati* [q. v.] in connection with *√kṛi,* Pāṇ. i, 4, 73; *upāje-kṛitya* or *upāje kṛitvā,* ind. p. having helped, supporting, Kāś. on Pāṇ.)

उपाजिनम् *upâjinam,* ind. on a skin, Pāṇ. vi, 2, 194.

उपाञ्च् *upâñc* (*upa-√añc*), P. *-acati,* to draw up (e. g. water), ŚBr. xiii.

U'pāka, mf(*ā*)n. brought near to each other, joined, approximate, (only *e*) f. du. (said of night and morning), RV. i, 142, 7; iii, 4, 6; x, 110, 6; (*upāké*) AV. v, 12, 6; 27, 8; (*e*), ind. (*upāké*) in the next neighbourhood, in the presence of, before (with gen.), RV. **–cakshas** (*upākâ°*), mfn. standing present before the eyes, to be seen from near at hand, RV. viii, 6, 25.

उपाञ्ज् *upâñj* (*upa-√añj*), P. *-anakti,* to smear or anoint (with butter), grease (e. g. a wheel), TS. ii, 6, 3, 4; iii.

Upâkta, mfn. anointed, greased, TS. ii, 6, 3, 3.

2. **Upâṅga** (for 1. see above), *as,* m. the act of smearing, anointing, Car.

Upâñjana, *am,* n. the act of anointing, smearing, KātyŚr.; besmearing (the ground with cow-dung &c. for purification), Mn. v, 105, &c.

उपातङ्क्य *upâtaṅkyà, am,* n. (*√tañc*), runnet for coagulating milk, TBr. iii, 7, 4, 2.

उपाती *upâti* (*upa-ati-√i*), P. *-eti,* to be added as a surplus, ŚBr. xii; to pass over, neglect.

Upâty-aya, *as,* m. transgressing, neglect or disobedience of customs, Pāṇ. iii, 3, 38.

उपादा *upâ-√1. dā,* Ā. *-datte* (once P., pf. 3. pl. *-dadus,* BhP. i, 8, 12) to receive, accept, gain, acquire, appropriate to one's self, take away, carry off, steal, MBh.; BhP.; Mālav. &c.; to take with; to take in addition, include, comprise; to take as help, use, employ, apply, BhP.; Pat. (cf. *upâ-dāya*); to seize, lay hold of, gather, take up, draw up, MBh.; Ragh.; Kum. &c.; to assume (a form or meaning), BhP.; MārkP.; Pat. &c.; to cling to; to feel, perceive, experience, MBh. vii; Śiś. vi, 23; Ṛitus. &c.; to consider, regard, MBh. xii; to mention, enumerate; to set about, undertake, begin, Hariv.; Kum. &c.: Caus. P. *-dāpayati,* to cause to use or employ, Comm. on KātyŚr.: Desid. P. *-ditsati,* to strive to acquire, BhP. v, 14, 7.

Upâ-tta (contracted fr. *upâ-datta;* cf. *ā-tta*), mfn. received, accepted, acquired, gained, obtained; appropriated; taken away; seized, gathered; shaped; felt, perceived, regarded; comprised; employed, used; begun; enumerated; allowed in argument, granted, conceded; (*as*), m. an elephant out of rut, L. **–raṅhas,** mfn. acquiring speed, quick, fleet. **–vidya,** mfn. one who has acquired knowledge, learned, Kathās. **–śastra,** mfn. one who has taken up arms, armed.

Upâ-dāna, *am,* n. the act of taking for one's self, appropriating to one's self, MBh.; Mn. &c.; perceiving, noticing, learning, acquiring (knowledge), Hit.; Vop.; accepting, allowing, including; employment, use, Sāh.; Sarvad.; Kap.; saying, speaking, mentioning, enumeration, Vedāntas.; Kāś.; Siddh.; abstraction, withdrawing (the organs of sense from the outer world), L.; (with Buddh.) grasping at or clinging to existence (caused by *tṛishṇā,* desire, and causing *bhava,* new births); (with Rāmānujas) preparation (of perfumes, flowers &c. as one of the five elements of worship), Sarvad.; cause, motive, material cause; material of any kind, Sāṃkhyak.; Vedāntas.; Kap. &c.; offering, present, L. **–kāraṇa,** n. a proximate cause. **–tā,** f., **–tva,** n. the state of being a material cause, Kap. **–lakshaṇā,** f. implied signification (beyond the literal meaning, e. g. *kuntāḥ praviśanti,* 'spears pierce,' where *kuntāḥ* implies *kuntinaḥ,* 'spearmen'), Sāh. 14; Sarvad.

Upâ-dāya, ind. p. having received or acquired &c.; receiving, acquiring &c.; taking with, together with, MBh.; Hariv.; Kathās. &c.; including, inclusive of, BhP.; Comm. on RPrāt. &c.; by help of, by means of (acc.), MBh.

Upâ-ditsā, f. (fr. Desid.), wish or readiness to accept, Sarvad.

Upâ-deya, mfn. to be taken or received; not to be refused; to be allowed, admissible, acceptable, Śāntiś.; Sarvad.; Kap. &c.; to be included, included, Sāh.; to be chosen or selected, excellent, admirable. **–tva,** n. selection, choice, preference.

उपादिक *upâdika, as,* m. a kind of insect, L.

उपादिश् *upâ-√diś,* P. *-diśati,* to advise, show, point out, prescribe, command, MBh.; BhP.; to indicate, inform, declare, BhP. i.

उपादीप् *upâ-√dīp.*

Upâ-dīpta, mfn. blazing, flaming, ŚBr. vii.

उपाद्य *upâdya,* mfn. next to the first, the second, ĀśvŚr. v, 6, 27.

उपाद्रु *upâ-√dru,* P. (Impv. 2. sg. *-drava*) to run or hasten near to, RV. vi, 48, 16.

उपाधा *upâ-√dhā,* P. Ā. *-dadhāti, -dhatte,* to place upon, put on, ŚBr. x; BhP.; to seize, lay hold of, take up, MBh.; to keep, hold back, TBr. ii; to seduce (a woman), R.

Upâ-dhāya, ind. p. taking up or with, together with, ŚBr. iv.

1. **Upâ-dhi** (for 2. see s. v.), *is,* m. that which is put in the place of another thing, a substitute, substitution, R.; anything which may be taken for or has the mere name or appearance of another thing, appearance, phantom, disguise (said to be applied to certain forms or properties considered as disguises of the spirit, W.), Prab.; Bhāshāp.; Sāh. &c.; anything defining more closely, a peculiarity; an attribute (*asty-upâdhi,* having 'is' as an attribute); title, discriminative appellation, nickname; limitation, qualification (e.g. *an-upâdhi-rāmaṇīya,* beautiful without limitation, i. e. altogether beautiful); (in log.) a qualifying term added to a too general middle term to prevent ativyāpti; that which is placed under, supposition, condition, postulate, Sarvad.; Vedāntas.; Tarkas.; BhP. &c.; deception, deceit, MBh. iii, 13017; species. **–khaṇḍana,** n., N. of a work. **–tas,** ind. in consequence of any qualification or condition. **–dūshakatā-bīja,** n., **-nyāya-saṃgraha,** m., N. of works. **–mātrāyām,** ind. for the sake of mere appearance, Kauś. **–vivṛiti,** f., **-siddhânta-grantha,** m., N. of works.

Upâ-hita, mfn. put or placed on, deposited; set out, proposed (as a prize), ŚBr. xi; caused, effected, produced, Bhartṛ.; Gīt.; joined, annexed, L.; agreed upon, made or done mutually, L.; (*as*), m. outbreak of fire, fire, Gaut. xvi, 34.

उपाधाव् *upâ-√dhāv,* P. *-dhāvati,* to run towards, BhP.: Caus. *-dhāvayati,* to carry or convey towards, ŚBr. x.

उपाधि 2. *upâ-dhi* (for 1. see col. 2), *is,* m. (*√dhyai*), point of view, aim, Car.; reflection on duty, virtuous reflection, L.; a man who is careful to support his family, L.

उपाधिक *upâdhika,* mfn. exceeding, supernumerary.

उपाधिरुह् *upâdhi-√ruh,* P. *-rohati,* to ascend or mount up to, ŚBr. iii, vi.

उपाध्मा *upâ-√dhmā,* P. (aor. *-adhmāsīt*) to blow into, MBh.; Hariv.

उपाध्याय *upâdhy-āya, as,* m. (*√i*), a teacher, preceptor (who subsists by teaching a part of the Veda or Vedāṅgas, grammar &c.; he is distinguished from the Ācārya, q. v.), Mn. iv, 141, &c.; Yājñ. i, 35; MBh.; Śak. &c.; (*ā* or *ī*), f. a female teacher, Kāty. on Pāṇ. iii, 13, 21; (*ī*), f. the wife of a teacher, Kāty. on Pāṇ. iv, 1, 49. **–sarvasva,** n., N. of a grammar (frequently referred to by the Comm. on Uṇ.)

Upâdhyāyānī, f. the wife of a teacher, Kāty. on Pāṇ. iv, 1, 49.

Upâdhyāyī-√1. kṛi, to choose as teacher, appoint as teacher, Bālar.; N.

उपाध्वर्यु *upâdhvaryu, us,* m. a second Adhvaryu (in place of the true Adhvaryu), MBh. xiii.

उपानस *upânasá,* mfn. (fr. *anas* with *upa*), being or standing on a carriage, RV. x, 105, 4; (*am*), n. the space in a carriage, AV. ii, 14, 2.

Upânasyaka, *as,* m., N. of Indra, ĀpŚr.

उपानह् *upā-náh, t,* f. (fr. *√nah* with *upa* [not *upâ*], Pāṇ. vi, 3, 116), a sandal, shoe, TS.; ŚBr.; Mn.; MBh. &c. (ifc. with affix *-ka, upānatka;* cf. *an-upā°, sôpā*).

Upā-nad (in comp. for *upā-náh* above). **–gūḍha,** mfn. covered with a shoe, Hit. **–yuga,** n. a pair of shoes, ĀśvGṛ. iii, 8, 1.

Upā-naha, *as,* m. (in comp.) = *upā-náh,* MBh.; Pāṇ. v, 4, 107.

Upānahin, mfn. having shoes, shoed, Āp.

उपानी *upâ-√nī,* P. Ā. *-nayati, -te,* to convey or bring or lead near, MBh.; BhP.; R. &c.; to draw near, MBh. iii; BhP. viii; to lead away or off, carry off, R.; BhP.; to lead near, introduce to; to imitate, MBh. v, 1339.

Upâ-nayana, *am,* n. the act of leading near or home (a wife), BhP.

उपानुवाक्य *upânuvākyà,* mfn. to be invoked with Anuvākyās (q. v.); (*as*), m., N. of Agni, TĀr. i, 22, 11; (*am*), n., N. of a particular section of the Taittirīya-saṃhitā.

उपान्त *upântá,* mfn. near to the end, last but one; (*am*), n. proximity to the edge or margin; border, edge, TS. vi; Ragh.; Pañcat.; Kir. &c.; the last place but one, VarBṛS.; immediate or close proximity, nearness, Kathās.; Rājat.; Megh. &c.; (*e*), ind. in the proximity of, near to; (*am, āt*), ind. (ifc.) near to, towards; the last letter but one, L.; the corner of the eye, W. **–bhāga,** m. border, edge, Kum. **–sarpin,** mfn. creeping or coming near.

Upântika, *am,* n. vicinity, proximity, MBh.; Pañcat. &c.; (*am*), ind. near to, towards; (*āt*), ind. from the neighbourhood; (mfn.) near, proximate, neighbouring, L.

Upântima, mfn. the last but one, Bījag.

Upântya, mfn. id., VarBṛS.; Śrutab.

उपान्वारुह् *upânv-ā-√ruh,* P. *-rohati,* to mount (a carriage) after and by the side of another one, MBh. v, 4745.

उपाप् *upâp* (*upa-√1. āp*), P. *-āpnoti,* to

arrive at, reach, obtain, TS. vi; ŚBr.; AitBr.; Ait-Âr.; TUp.: Desid. P. *upêpsati*, to endeavour to win over or conciliate, MaitrS. ii, 1, 11; Kauś.; Gobh. i, 9, 5.

Upâpa, *as*, m. the act of obtaining, acquirement. See *dur-upâpa*.

Upâpti, *is*, f. reaching; obtainment, ŚBr.; Ait-Âr.

Upêpsâ, f. desire to obtain, MaitrS. ii, 9, 8; ŚBr.

उपापत् *upâ-√pat*, P. (Impv. 2. du. *-patatam â ... úpa*, RV. v, 78, 1) to fly near to or upon.

उपाप्रछ् *upâ-√prach*, P. *-pṛicchati*, to take leave of, R.

उपाभिगद *upâbhigada*, mfn. (√*gad*), unable to speak much, KaushUp. ii, 15.

उपाभूष् *upâ-√bhûsh*, P. (Impv. 2. sg. *-bhûsha*) to come near to, RV. vii, 92, 1.

उपाभृति *upâ-bhṛiti*, *is*, f. (√*bhṛi*), the act of bringing near, RV. i, 128, 2.

उपामन्त्र् *upâ-√mantr*.

Upâ-mantrita, mfn. addressed, called upon, summoned, BhP.

Upâ mantrya, ind. p. having addressed, addressing, summoning, R.; BhP.; taking leave, bidding adieu, MBh.; Hariv.

उपाय *upâya*, &c. See p. 215, col. 2.

उपाया *upâ-√yā*, P. *-yāti*, to come near or towards, approach, RV.; MBh.; BhP.; Kathās. &c.; to come into any state or condition, undergo, MārkP.; Kir.

Upâ-yâta, mfn. approached; (*am*), n. arrival.

उपायुज् *upâ-√yuj*, P. (1. sg. *-yunajmi*) to put to, harness, RV. iii, 35, 2.

उपार् *upâr* (*upa-√ṛi*), P. (pf. 1. pl. *-ārimá*; aor. Subj. 2. du. *-aratam*; 1. pl. *-arāma*) to go near to, RV. viii, 5, 13; to hasten near (for help), RV. x, 40, 7; to grieve, offend; to err, make a mistake, RV. x, 164, 3; AV.: Caus., see *upârpya*.

Upârá, *as*, m. offence, sin, RV. vii, 86, 6.

Upâraṇa, *am*, n. id., RV. viii, 32, 21.

Upârpya, ind. p. having caused to come near, bringing near, ŚBr. viii.

उपारम् *upâ-√ram*, P. Â. *-ramati*, *-te*, to rest, cease, MBh.; BhP. &c.; to cease, leave off, give up, MBh.; R.; BhP.; Kum.

Upâ-rata, mfn. resting, lying upon, fixed upon, BhP.; ceasing, turning back, returning, Kir. iv, 10; leaving off, giving up, free from, BhP.; Ragh. &c.

Upâ-rama, *as*, m. the act of ceasing, BhP.

Upâ-râma, *as*, m. rest, repose, GopBr.

उपाराध् *upâ-√rādh*.

Upâ-râdhya, ind. p. having waited upon, waiting upon, serving, Mn. x, 121.

उपारुद् *upâ-√rud*, P. (pf. *-ruroda*) to bewail, deplore (with acc.), Bhaṭṭ. ii, 4.

उपारुह् 1. *upâ-√ruh*, P. *-rohati* (aor. *-aruhat*) to ascend or go up to, mount, ĀśvGṛ.; MBh.; R.; Sarvad.; to arrive at, reach, R.

2. **Upâ-rúh**, *k*, f. 'that which goes up or comes forth,' a shoot, sprout, RV. ix, 68, 2.

Upâ-rûḍha, mfn. mounted, ascended; one who has arrived, approached, R.; Ragh.; Mālav. &c.

उपार्छ् *upârch* (*upa-√ṛich*), P. *upârcchati*, to molest, importune, TS. i, 5, 9, 6.

उपार्ज् *upârj* (*upa-√arj*), P. *-arjati*, to admit, ŚBr. xiv: Caus. P. Â. *-arjayati*, *-te*, to convey near, procure, acquire, gain, Kām.; Pañcat.

Upârjaka, mfn. acquiring, obtaining, earning, gaining, L.

Upârjana, *am*, *ā*, n. f. the act of procuring, acquiring, gaining, R.; Pañcat.

Upârjita, mfn. procured, acquired, gained, MBh.; Hit. &c.

Upârjya, mfn. to be acquired or earned, Kathās.

उपार्ध् *upârdh* (*upa-√ṛidh*), Desid. P. *upêrtsati*, to wish to accomplish, persevere, ŚBr. ii, xi.

उपार्ध *upârdha*, *am*, n. the first half, Comm. on ŚāṅkhGṛ. vi, 1, 11; the half, Lalit.

उपार्ष् *upârsh* (*upa-√ṛish*), P. *uparsháti* (against Pāṇ. vi, 1, 91; see APrāt. iii, 47) and *upârshati* (ŚBr. v), to pierce, prick, goad, AV. ix, 8, 14; 15; 16.

उपालक्ष् *upâ-√laksh*.

Upâ-lakshya, ind. p. having beheld, beholding, descrying, BhP.

उपालभ् *upâ-√labh*, Â. *-labhate*, to touch, ŚBr.; to lay hold of, seize (a sacrificial animal in order to kill it), kill, slaughter; to censure, reproach, revile, scold, ChUp.; MBh.; Śak.; Śiś. &c.

Upâ-labdha, mfn. reproached, reviled.

Upâ-labdhavya, mfn. to be reviled, blamable, censurable, Kād.

Upâ-labhya, mfn. id., Pañcat.

Upâ-lambha, *as*, m. reproach, censure, abuse, finding fault with, MBh.; Hit.; Kathās. &c.; prohibition, interdict, Nyāyad.

Upâ-lambhana, *am*, n. reproach, censure, Śak. 187, 5.

Upâ-lambhya, mfn. to be laid hold of or seized (as a sacrificial animal); to be slain, KātyŚr.; ŚāṅkhŚr.

उपालाल्य *upâ-√lālya*, mfn. (√*lal*), to be fondled.

उपालि *upâli*, *is*, m., N. of one of Buddha's most eminent pupils (mentioned as the first propounder of the Buddhist law and as having been formerly a barber).

उपाव् *upâv* (*upa-√av*), P. *-avati*, to cherish, behave friendly towards, encourage by approval, approve, consent, RV.; AV. i, 16, 2; ŚBr. iii.

Upâvî, mfn. cherishing, pleasing, VS. vi, 7.

उपावधा *upâva-√dhā*.

Upâva-hita, mfn. placed or put down close by, TBr. ii, 7, 18, 4.

उपावनम् *upâva-√nam*.

Upâva-nata, mfn. bent in, ĀpŚr.

उपावरम् *upâva-√ram*, Â. to sport, take one's pleasure; to prance about (as a horse), TāṇḍyaBr. vi.

उपावरुह् *upâva-√ruh*, P. *-rohati*, to descend upon, come out towards, VS. vi, 26; TS. vii; TBr.; ŚBr.; TāṇḍyaBr.; ŚāṅkhGṛ.: Caus. *-rohayati*, to cause (the fire) to come out (of the two Araṇis), kindle through friction, ŚāṅkhŚr.; Kauś.

Upâva-rohaṇa, *am*, n. the act of causing (fire) to come out (of the two Araṇis), kindling through friction, ŚāṅkhGṛ. v, 1, 7.

उपावर्तन *upâ-vartana*, &c. See col. 3.

उपावश्रि *upâva-√śri*, Â. *-śrayate*, to betake one's self to, ŚBr. iv, 6, 9, 5.

उपावसु *úpā-vasu*, mfn. bringing near or procuring riches, RV. v, 56, 6; ix, 84, 3; 86, 33.

उपावसृज् *upâva-√sṛij*, P. *-sṛijati* (aor. *-asrāk*, TS. i, 6, 11, 3) to dismiss towards; to reach over, give, bestow, RV. i, 142, 11; iii, 4, 10; x, 110, 10; to let loose, shoot off, TS. vi; to let go towards, admit (a calf to its mother), TS.; TBr.; ŚBr.; AitBr.

Upâva-sṛishṭa, mfn. admitted (as a calf to its mother); (*am*), n. the milk of a cow at the time when its calf is admitted (cf. *upa-sṛishṭa*), AitBr. v, 26, 6.

उपावसृप् *upâva-√sṛip*, P. *-sarpati*, to creep towards, approach creeping, ŚBr.

उपावसो *upâva-√so*, P. *-syati*, to settle near at (acc.), TS. ii.

Upâvasâyin, mfn. attaching one's self to; submissive, compliant, ŚBr.

Upâvasita, mfn. settled or abiding near by, ŚBr. iii.

उपावह् *upâ-√vah*, P. *-vahati*, to bring or convey near, RV. i, 74, 6; iii, 35, 2.

उपावहृ *upâva-√hṛi*, P. *-harati*, to fetch or bring or take down, cause to let down (e. g. the arms), VS. viii, 56; TBr.; ŚBr.; AitBr.; ŚāṅkhŚr.

Upâva-haraṇa, *am*, n. the act of taking or bringing down, KātyŚr. ix.

उपावि *upâvi*, *is*, m., N. of a Ṛishi, AitBr. i, 25, 15.

उपाविश् *upâ-√viś*, P. *-viśati*, to enter, enter into any state, MBh.; R.; BhP.; (the augmented forms might also be referred to *upa-√viś*.)

उपावृ *upâ-√vṛi*.

Upâ-vṛita, mfn. covered, veiled, Hariv.

उपावृत् 1. *upâ-√vṛit*, Â. (rarely P.) *-vartate*, *-ti* (Impv. 2. pl. *-vavṛidhvam* [for *-vavṛiddhvam*], RV.) to turn towards, go towards, approach, stand by the side of, RV. viii, 20, 18; TS.; TBr.; ŚBr.; AitBr.; MBh. &c.; to apply one's self to, approach for protection, MBh.; BhP.; to fall to one's share, MBh.; BhP.; to return, come back, MBh.; R.; Śak. &c.: Caus. P. *-vartayati*, to cause to turn or go towards, ŚBr.; KātyŚr.; to lead near or back, bring back, MBh.; R.; Daś.; to draw back, divert, cause to desist from, Suśr.; MBh.; to cause to get breath (e. g. horses), MBh. vii.

Upâ-vartana, *am*, n. the act of coming back, return, Ragh. viii, 52; R.; Vātsy.

Upâ-vartitṛi, mfn. one who will turn towards (periphrastic fut.), TBr. i, 6, 7, 3.

2. **Upâ-vṛít**, f. return, AV. vi, 77, 3; VS. xii, 8.

Upâ-vṛitta, mfn. turned towards, approached or come to, come near, ŚBr.; MBh.; BhP.; returned, come back, MBh.; Śak.; Ragh. &c.; (*as*), m. a horse rolling on the ground, L.; (*ās*), m. pl., N. of a people, MBh. vi; VP.

Upâ-vṛitti, *is*, f. return, TāṇḍyaBr.

Upâ-vṛitya, ind. p. having turned towards, going near; applying one's self to &c.

उपावे *upâvê* (*upa-ava-√i*), P. *upâvâiti*, to go or come down, descend, AV. ix, 6, 53; TBr. ii; to join (in calling), assent, consent, ŚBr.

उपावेक्ष् *upâvêksh* (*upa-ava-√īksh*), Â. *-īkshate*, to look down upon, ŚBr.

उपाव्याध *upâ-vyādhá*, *as*, m. (√*vyadh*), a vulnerable or unprotected spot, TS. vii, 2, 5, 4.

उपाव्रज् *upâ-√vraj*, P. *-vrajati*, to betake one's self to, BhP.

उपाश् 1. *upâś* (*upa-√1. aś*), P. Â. *-aśnoti*, *-aśnute*, to reach, obtain, meet with, MBh.; Mn.

उपाश् 2. *upâś* (*upa-√2. aś*), P. *-aśnāti*, to eat, taste, enjoy, MBh.

उपाशंसनीय *upâ-śaṅsanīya*, mfn. (√*śaṅs*), to be expected or hoped for, Nir.

उपाशार *upâ-śāra*, *as*, m. (√*śṛi*=*śri*), shelter, refuge, Kāṭh.

उपाश्रि *upâ-√śri*, P. *-śrayati*, to lean against, rest on, Mn.; to go or betake one's self towards, R.; to take refuge or have recourse to, seek shelter from, give one's self up to, abandon one's self to, Hariv.; R.; Bhag. &c.

Upâśraya, *as*, m. leaning against, resting upon, Kathās.; Kāvyād.; any support for leaning against, a pillow, cushion, Car.; shelter, refuge, recourse, MBh.; Bhartṛ.

Upâ-śrayitvā, (irr.) ind. p. taking refuge with, relying upon, R. vii, 17, 36.

Upâ-śrita, mfn. lying or resting upon, leaning against, clinging to, ŚāṅkhGṛ.; KaṭhUp.; R.; having recourse to, relying upon, taking refuge with, MBh.; Bhag.; Kathās. &c.; taking one's self to; approached, arrived at, abiding in, MBh.; BhP.; VarBṛS. &c.; anything against which one leans or upon which one rests, Uttarar.

उपाश्लिष् *upâ-√ślish*, to embrace, MārkP.

Upâ-ślishṭa, mfn. one who has clasped or laid hold of, MBh. i, 1125.

उपास् 1. *upâs* (*upa-√1. as*), P. (Pot. 1. pl. *-syāma*) to be near to or together with (acc.), RV. ii, 27, 7.

उपास् 2. *upâs* (*upa-√2. as*), P. *-asyati*, to throw off, throw or cast down upon, throw under, AV. vi, 42, 2; ŚBr.; KātyŚr.: Â. *-asyate*, to throw (anything) under one's self, TS. i, 6, 10, 1; MaitrS. ii, 1, 1.

1. **Upâsana**, *am*, n. the act of throwing off (arrows), exercise in archery, MBh.

उपास् 3. *upâs* (*upa-√ās*), Ā. *-āste*, to sit by the side of, sit near at hand (in order to honour or wait upon), AV.; ŚBr.; ChUp.; Mn. &c.; to wait upon, approach respectfully, serve, honour, revere, respect, acknowledge, do homage, worship, be devoted or attached to, RV.; AV.; VS.; ŚBr.; MBh. &c.; to esteem or regard or consider as, take for, AV.; VS.; ŚBr.; to pay attention to, be intent upon or engaged in, perform, converse or have intercourse with, RV. x, 154, 1; AV.; MBh.; Suśr. &c.; to sit near, be in waiting for, remain in expectation, expect, wait for, RV. i, 162, 12; ŚBr.; KātyŚr.; MBh.; to sit, occupy a place, abide in, reside, R.; Mn. ii, v; to be present at, partake of (e.g. a sacrifice), Mn. iii, 104; MBh. xiv; to approach, go towards, draw near (e.g. an enemy's town), arrive at, obtain, ŚBr.; MBh.; Yājñ.; Bhaṭṭ.; to enter into any state, undergo, suffer, Mn. xi, 183; MBh. iii; R.; to remain or continue in any action or situation (with pres. p. or ind. p.), ŚBr.; R.; Bhag. &c.; to employ, use, make subservient, Suśr.; Sāh.

Upâsaka, mfn. serving, a servant, Kauś.; Kathās.; worshipping, a worshipper, follower, Mṛicch.; intent on, engaged or occupied with, Kap.; a Buddhist lay worshipper (as distinguished from the Bhikshu, q.v.), Sarvad.; Lalit.; Prab. &c.; a Śūdra, L.; (*ikā*), f. a lay female votary of Buddha (as distinguished from a Bhikshuṇī, q.v.) **-daśa**, *ās*, m. pl., N. of one of the Aṅgas or chief Jaina sacred writings.

2. **Upâsana**, *am*, *ā*, n. f. the act of sitting or being near or at hand; serving, waiting upon, service, attendance, respect, Āp.; Gaut.; Mn.; Yājñ. &c.; homage, adoration, worship (with Rāmānujas, consisting of five parts, viz. Abhigamana or approach, Upādāna or preparation of offering, Ijyā or oblation, Svādhyāya or recitation, and Yoga or devotion), Sarvad.; Vedāntas. &c.; (*am*), n. a seat, Vait.; the being intent on or engaged in, Mṛicch.; R.; domestic fire, Yājñ. iii, 45. **Upâsanā-khaṇḍa**, n., N. of the first section of the Gaṇeśa-purāṇa. **Upâsanā-candrâmṛita**, n., N. of a work. **Upâsanârtha**, mfn. worthy of attendance.

Upâsanīya, mfn. to be attended on, worthy to be engaged in.

Upâsā, f. homage, adoration, worship, MuṇḍUp.; Bādar.; Kathās. &c.

Upâsita, mfn. served, honoured, worshipped &c.; one who serves or pays worship.

Upâsitavya, mfn. to be revered or honoured, MBh.; TUp.; RāmatUp.; to be attended on; to be accomplished, Suśr.

Upâsitṛi, mfn. one who reveres or pays homage, R.; Car.

Upâsīna, mfn. sitting near to, ŚBr. i; that to which one sits near, R. ii; abiding at; waiting for; attending on, serving &c.

Upâsti, *is*, f. adoration, worship, BhP.; RāmatUp.; Sarvad. &c.

1. **Upâsya**, mfn. to be revered or honoured or worshipped, MBh.; Śāntiś.; Sarvad. &c.; to be attended on; to be performed, TUp.; to be had recourse to, Sāh.

2. **Upâsya**, ind. p. having served or worshipped.

उपासङ्ग *upâ-saṅga*, *as*, m. (*√sañj*), a quiver, MBh.

उपासद् *upâ-√sad*, P. (Ved. inf. *-sádam*) to sit down upon (acc.), RV. viii, 1, 8; to approach, walk along, Kir. iv, 1.

Upâ-sādita, mfn. met with, approached, gaṇa *ishṭâdi*, Pāṇ. v, 2, 88.

Upâsāditin, mfn. one who has met or approached, ib.

Upâ-sādya, ind. p. (fr. Caus.), meeting with, approaching, BhP. vii, 10, 55; accepting (an order), BhP. iv, 24, 71.

उपासृज् *upâ-√sṛij*, Ā. (aor. 1. sg. *-ásṛikshi*) to make, perform, compose (e.g. a song), RV. viii, 27, 11.

उपास्तमनवेला *upâstamana-velā*, f. the time about sunset, MBh. x, 1.

U'pâstamayam, ind. about the time of sunset, ŚBr.; KātyŚr.

उपास्तॄ *upâ-√stṛi*, P. (Pot. *-staret*) to spread (e.g. a skin, acc.) over (loc.), VarBṛS.

उपास्त्र *upâstra*, *am*, n. a secondary or minor weapon, MBh.; Suśr.

उपास्था *upâ-√sthā*, Ā. *-tishṭhate*, to betake one's self to, approach, set about, devote one's self to, ŚāṅkhŚr.; R.; to approach (sexually), MBh.

Upâ-sthita, mfn. one who has mounted, standing or being (in a carriage), ŚBr. v; one who has devoted himself to, R.

उपास्नात *upâ-snāta*, *am*, n. (*√snā*), N. of a Tīrtha, Pat.

उपास्यन्द् *upâ-√syand*, Caus. *-syandayati*, to cause to flow towards, convey towards (as a river), BhP. v, 16, 20.

उपाहन् *upâ-√han*, Ā. (p. *-ghnāná*) to beat upon, ŚBr. ii.

उपाहित *upâ-hita*. See *upâ-√dhā*, p. 213.

उपाहृ *upâ-√hṛi*, P. Ā. *-harati*, *-te*, to bring near to, bring near for, reach over, offer, give, TBr. iii; ŚBr.; Lāṭy.; MBh.; Yājñ. &c.; to bring near to one's self, take before one's self, take to task, undertake, prepare, accomplish, MBh.; Nir.; to subdue, make subject, Prab.; BhP.; to propitiate, BhP. x; to take away, draw away, separate, MBh.; BhP.; Car.

Upâ-hṛita, mfn. brought, offered, given, VarBṛS.; BhP. &c.; prepared, undertaken, AV. x, 1, 19.

उपाह्वे *upâ-√hve*, Ā. *-hvayate*, to call near, invite, summon; to challenge, Kauś.; MBh.; Bhaṭṭ.

उपिक *upika*, *as*, m. a diminutive for all proper names of men beginning with *upa*, Pāṇ. v, 3, 80.

Upiya and **upila**, *as*, m. id., ib.

उपित *upita*, mfn. See *√2. vap*.

उपे 1. *upé* (*upa-√i*), P. *-eti*, to go or come or step near, approach, betake one's self to, arrive at, meet with, turn towards, RV.; AV.; TS.; ŚBr.; MBh.; Śak. &c.; to approach (any work), undergo, set about, undertake, perform (a sacrifice), devote one's self to, RV. ii, 2, 11; AV. ix, 6, 4; VS.; AitBr.; ŚBr.; to come near to, reach, obtain, enter into any state, fall into; undergo, suffer, RV. iv, 33, 2; ŚBr.; AitBr.; Ragh.; Pañcat. &c.; to approach sexually, TS. ii, v; Mn. ix, 4; xi, 172; MBh.; Suśr.; Kathās.; to approach a teacher, become a pupil, ŚBr. x, xi; BṛĀrUp.; ChUp.; to occur, be present, make one's appearance, RPrāt.; R.; to happen, fall to one's share, befall, incur, RV. i, 167, 1; vii, 84, 3; Hit.; Bhag. &c.; to join (in singing), ŚāṅkhŚr.; to regard as, admit, acknowledge, Sāh.; Comm. on Nyāyam.; to comprehend, understand, Sarvad.: Intens. Ā. (1. pl. *-īmahe*) to implore (a god), RV. x, 24, 2.

2. **Upa-yat** (for 1. see s. v.), mfn. going near, approaching &c.; flowing into, attached, Kir. vi, 16 (said of rivers and female friends); entering any state, serving for, Kir. vi, 26.

Upâya, *as*, m. coming near, approach, arrival, Bhartṛ.; that by which one reaches one's aim, a means or expedient (of any kind), way, stratagem, craft, artifice, MBh.; Mn.; Yājñ.; Pañcat. &c.; (esp.) a means of success against an enemy (four are usually enumerated, sowing dissension, negotiation, bribery, and open assault); joining in or accompanying (in singing), ŚāṅkhŚr. **-catushṭaya**, n. the above four expedients against an enemy, Hit. &c. **-cintā**, f. devising an expedient, thinking of a resource. **-jña**, mfn. knowing or fertile in expedients, contriving, provident. **-tas**, ind. by some means or expedient, in a clever way, Kathās. **-turīya**, n. 'the fourth means, violence, Pañcat. **-tva**, n. the state of being provided with means. **-yoga**, m. application of means or combination of expedients. **-vat**, mfn. (any Stobha, q.v.) marked by the joining in or accompaniment (of other Stobhas), Lāṭy. vii, 6, 5. **-śrībhadra**, m., N. of a Buddhist student. **Upâyâkshepa**, m. (in rhet.) deprecatory speech making mention of the remedy (against the evil deprecated), Kāvyād. ii, 151 seq. **Upâyântara**, n. 'another means,' a remedy.

Upâyana, *am*, n. the act of coming near, approach, RV. ii, 28, 2; going to a teacher, becoming a pupil, initiation, ŚBr. xiv; Āp. i, 1, 5; engaging (in any religious observance), undertaking, ŚBr. xi; KātyŚr.; an offer, present, gift, MBh.; BhP.; Śak. &c.

Upâyanī-√kṛi, to offer as a present, Daś.; to communicate respectfully, Prasannar. 10, 3. **-kṛita**, mfn. offered as a present, Kathās.

Upâyin, mfn. going near, one who approaches, KātyŚr. iii; one who reaches, RāmatUp.; approaching sexually, KātyŚr.; expert in the use of means, L.

Upâyú, mfn. approaching, TS. i, 1, 1, 1; ŚBr. i; KātyŚr.

Upêta, mfn. one who has come near or approached, one who has betaken himself to, approached (for protection), arrived at, abiding in, MBh.; VarBṛS. &c.; one who has obtained or entered into any state or condition, one who has undertaken (e.g. a vow), MBh.; Ratnāv.; Sāh. &c.; come to, fallen to the share of, Prab.; (a pupil) who has approached (a teacher), initiated, Yājñ. iii, 2; ĀśvGṛ. i, 22, 21; 22; PārGṛ. iii, 10, 10; accompanied by, endowed with, furnished with, having, possessing, MBh.; R.; Bhag; Hit. &c.; one who has approached (a woman sexually), T.

Upêtavya, mfn. to be set about or commenced, Comm. on TāṇḍyaBr. iv, 10, 3.

U'pêti, *is*, f. approach, approximation, RV.

Upêtṛi, mfn. one who sets about or undertakes, Mn. vii, 215.

1. **Upêtya**, mfn. to be set about or commenced, TāṇḍyaBr. iv, 10, 3; 4.

2. **Upêtya**, ind. p. having approached, approaching &c.

Upeya, mfn. to be set about or undertaken, a thing undertaken, Mn. vii, 215; Mālav.; to be approached sexually, Mn. xi, 172; to be striven after or aimed at, that which is aimed at, aim, Naish.; Comm. on VarBṛS.

Upêyivas, mfn. one who has approached &c.

उपे 2. *upê* (*upa-ā-√i*), P. *-eti*, to approach, come near or towards, RV.; AV.; ŚBr.; to apply to, implore, RV. viii, 20, 22; (with *śaraṇam*) to approach for protection; to approach sexually, MBh.; to reach, obtain, strive to obtain, Bhartṛ.

उपेक्ष् *upêksh* (*upa-√īksh*), Ā. *-īkshate* (rarely P.) to look at or on, ŚBr.; MBh.; to perceive, notice, R.; to wait on patiently, expect, Suśr.; to overlook, disregard, neglect, abandon, MBh.; R.; Śak.; Pañcat. &c.; to connive at, grant a respite to, allow, MBh. v; to regard, Pañcat.

Upêksha, *as*, m., N. of a son of Śva-phalka, Hariv.; (*ā*), f. overlooking, disregard, negligence, indifference, contempt, abandonment, MBh.; Ragh.; Hit. &c.; endurance, patience; dissent; trick, deceit (as one of the minor expedients in war), L.; regard, L.

Upêkshaka, mfn. overlooking, disregarding, indifferent, BhP.; Mn.; Sāṃkhyak.

Upêkshaṇa, *am*, n. the act of disregarding, overlooking, disregard, indifference, connivance, MBh.; Hit.; Sarvad. &c.; not doing, omission, Lāṭy. i, 1, 26; care, circumspection, Car.

Upêkshaṇīya, mfn. to be overlooked or disregarded, unworthy of regard, any object of indifference, R.; Ragh.; Comm. on Nyāyad. &c.

Upêkshita, mfn. looked at; overlooked, disregarded &c.

Upêkshitavya, mfn. to be looked at; to be regarded or paid attention to, Nir.; R.; to be overlooked or disregarded, Śārṅg.

1. **Upêkshya**, mfn. id., Suśr.; R.; Pañcat. &c.

2. **Upêkshya**, ind. p. having looked at, looking at; overlooking &c.

उपेडकीय *upêḍakīya* or *upaiḍakīya*, Nom. (fr. *eḍaka*) P. *upêḍakīyati* or *upaiḍ°*, to behave as a sheep towards, Kāś. on Pāṇ. vi, 1, 94.

उपेन् *upén* (*upa-√in*).

U'pênita, mfn. driven in, pressed or pushed in, ŚBr.

उपेन्द्र *upéndra*, *as*, m. 'younger brother of Indra,' N. of Vishṇu or Kṛishṇa (born subsequently to Indra, especially as son of Aditi, either as Āditya or in the dwarf Avatāra), MBh.; Hariv.; R.; VP. &c.; N. of a Nāga, L.; (*ā*), f., N. of a river, MBh.; VP. **-gupta**, **-datta**, **-bala**, m., N. of various men. **-vajrā**, f., N. of a metre (consisting of four lines of eleven instants each). **-śakti**, m., N. of a merchant.

उपेन्ध्य *upéndhya*, mfn. (√*indh*), to be kindled or inflamed, Pat.

उपेप्सा *upêpsā́*, f. See p. 214, col. 1.

उपेष् 1. *upésh* (*upa*-√1. *ish*), P. to tend towards, endeavour to attain, MaitrS. i, 2, 14.

उपेष् 2. *upêsh* (*upa*-√*īsh*), P. (inf. *upêshé*, RV. i, 129, 8) to rush upon.

उपेष् 3. *upêsh* (*upa-ā*-√*ish*), Ā. (1. sg. *-īshe*) to approach (with prayers), apply to, implore, RV. i, 186, 4; v, 41, 7.

उपेष् 4. *upesh* (*upa*-√*esh*; for the Sandhi, see Pāṇ. vi, 1, 94), P. *upeshati*, to creep near, approach creeping, AV. vi, 67, 3.

Upéshat, *an*, m., N. of an evil demon [NBD.], AV. viii, 6, 17.

उपैध् *upâidh* (*upa*-√*edh*), Ā. *upâidhate*, to thrive or prosper in addition (?), Pāṇ. vi, 1, 89; Kāś.

उपोक्तवती *upókta-vatī*, f. (scil. *ṛic*) a verse containing any form of *upa*-√*vac*, ĀśvŚr. ii, 17, 19.

उपोक्ष् *upôksh* (*upa*-√*uksh*), P. *-ukshati*, to sprinkle in addition, ŚBr.; KātyŚr.

उपोढ *upôḍha*. For 1. see *upa*-√*vah*, p. 206, col. 3; for 2. see *upôh*, next col.

उपोत *upóta*. See *upa*-√*ve*.

उपोती *upotī*, f., v. l. for *upodikā* below, L.

उपोत्क्रम् *upót-kram* (*upa-ud*-√*kram*), P. (impf. 3. pl. *upód-akrāman*) to go up or ascend towards (acc.), ŚBr. i, iii, iv.

उपोत्तम *upóttamá*, mfn. last but one, AV. xix, 22, 11; KātyŚr.; ŚāṅkhŚr.; RPrāt. &c.; (*am*), n. (with or without *akshara*) the last vowel but one, RPrāt. 990; Pāṇ.; Kāty. &c.

उपोत्था *upót-thā* (*upa-ud*-√*sthā*), P. *-tishṭhati*, to stand up or rise towards, advance to meet, approach, TS.; ŚBr.; AitBr.; ĀśvŚr. &c.; to rise or set out towards, TBr. i.

Upôtthāya, ind. p. having risen towards, advancing to meet &c.

Upôtthita, mfn. risen up towards, approached, come near, VS. viii, 55; VPrāt. vi, 29.

उपोत्सद् *upót-sad* (*upa-ud*-√*sad*), P. to set out or depart towards, ŚBr.

उपोत्सिच् *upót-sic* (*upa-ud*-√*sic*), P. *-siñcati*, to pour out upon, ŚBr. iii.

उपोद् *upôd* (*upa*-√*ud*), P. *-unatti*, to wet, moisten, ŚBr. i.

U'pôtta, mfn. moistened, wet, TS. iv.

उपोदक *úpódaka*, mfn. near to water, VS. xxxv, 6; ŚBr. xiii; (*ī*, *ikā*), f., (*am*), n. Basella Cordifolia, Suśr.

Upodikā, v. l. for *upôdikā*.

उपोदयम् *upódayam*, ind. about the time of sunrise, ŚāṅkhŚr.

उपोदासृप् *upód-ā*-√*sṛip*, P. (impf. *-âsarpat*) to creep out towards, AitBr. i, 6, 1; 3.

Upôdásṛipta, mfn. crept out towards, ŚBr. vii.

उपोदाहृ *upód-ā*-√*hṛi*, P. *-harati*, to quote in addition, mention a further quotation, PārGṛ.

उपोदि *upód*-√*i*, P. *-eti*, to go towards, advance to meet, AitBr. viii, 24, 6.

Upodita, *as*, m., N. of a man, Sāy. on TS. i, 7, 2, 1.

Upoditi, *is*, m., N. of a Ṛishi (son of Gopāla), TāṇḍyaBr.

उपोद्ग्रह् *upód*-√*grah*, P. *-gṛihṇāti*, to bring near (to the mouth) after (others have done so), AitBr. vii, 33, 2; to perceive, know [Comm.], ChUp. iv, 2, 4.

Upôdgṛihya, ind. p. holding together and holding upwards, Gobh. ii, 2, 16.

उपोद्धन् *upód-dhan* (*upa-ud*-√*han*), Caus. *-ghātayati*, to speak of at the beginning, introduce, begin, commence, Sāy. on ŚBr. xi, 7, 2, 8; Mall. on Śiś. i, 40; 42; Comm. on BṛĀrUp.

Upôd-ghāta, *as*, m. an introduction, preface, commencement, beginning, Sāy. on ŚBr.; Sarvad.; Nyāyam. &c.; any observation or episodical narrative inserted by the way, Kathās.; anything begun; an example, opposite argument or illustration, W.; analysis, the ascertainment of the elements of anything, W. **–pāda**, m., N. of the third part of the Vāyu-purāṇa.

उपोद्बलय *upódbalaya*, Nom. (fr. *bala*) *upôdbalayati*, to help, promote, Comm. on Yājñ.; to assert, confirm, ratify, Comm. on ŚBr.

Upôdbalaka, mfn. helping, promoting, Mall. on Kir.; confirming, asserting, Pat.; Sāy. on ŚBr.; Comm. on Nyāyam. &c.

Upôdbalana, *am*, n. the act of confirming, assertion, ratification, Comm. on Kap.

Upôdbalita, mfn. confirmed, asserted, Nīlak.

उपोद्यम् *upód*-√*yam*, P. *-yacchati*, to erect by supporting or propping, ĀśvŚr.; ŚāṅkhŚr.; MānŚr.

उपोन्नी *upón-nī* (*upa-ud*-√*nī*), P. *-nayati*, to lead up towards, ŚBr. ii.

उपोपधा *upópa*-√*dhā*, Ā. (Pot. *-dadhīta*) to bring near or procure in addition to, RV. viii, 74, 9.

उपोपपरामृश् *upópa-parā*-√*mṛiś*, P. (Impv. 2. sg. *-mṛiśa*) to touch closely, RV. i, 126, 7.

उपोपया *upópa*-√*yā*.

Upôpayāta, mfn. approached, come near, MBh. iii.

उपोपविश् *upópa*-√*viś*, P. *-viśati*, to sit down or take a seat by the side of, sit down near to (acc.), ŚāṅkhŚr.; Gobh.; ChUp.; MBh. &c.

उपोलप *upólapá*, mfn. nearly of the character of a shrub, shrub-like, MaitrS. i, 7, 2.

उपोष् *upósh* (*upa*-√*ush*), P. *uposhati* (but Pot. *úpâushet*, TS. iii, 3, 8, 4, against Pāṇ. vi, 1, 94) to burn down, burn, ĀśvGṛ. ii, 4, 9; Vait.

उपोषण *upôshaṇa*, &c. See *upa*-√5. *vas*.

उपोषध *uposhadha*, *as*, m., N. of a man (Buddh.)

उपोह् *upôh* (*upa*-√1. *ūh*; cf. *upa*-√*vah*), P. *upôhati*, to push or pull or draw near, R.; to drive near, impel towards, BhP.; to push under, insert, KātyŚr.; to add, accumulate; to bring near, cause to appear, produce: Pass. *upôhyate*, to draw near, approach (as a point of time), MBh.

2. **Upôḍha**, mfn. (in some cases not to be distinguished from 1. *upôḍha*, p. 206, col. 3) pushed or driven near, near; brought near, caused to appear, produced, Śak. 177 a; Vikr. &c.; brought about, advanced, commenced; heaped up, accumulated, gathered, Śak. 111 a.

Upôhá, *as*, m. the act of accumulating, heaping up, AV. iii, 24, 7.

Upôhya, ind. p. having pushed near &c.

उप्त *upta*, *upti*, &c. See √2. *vap*.

उब्ज् *ubj*, cl. 6. P. *ubjáti* (*ubjām-cakāra*, *ubjitā*, *ubjishyati*, *aubjīt*, Dhātup. xxviii, 20) to press down, keep under, subdue, RV.; AV. viii, 4, 1; 8, 13; to make straight, Dhātup.; to make honest, Sāy. on RV. i, 21, 5: Caus. *ubjayati*, *aubjijat*, Vop.: Desid. *ubjijishati*, Kāś. on Pāṇ. vi, 1, 3.

उभ् *ubh*, cl. 9. P. *ubhnāti* (impf. 2. sg. *ubhnās*) to hurt, kill, RV. i, 63, 4: cl. 6. P. *ubhati*, *umbhati*, *umbhām-cakāra*, *umbhitā*, *aumbhīt*, to cover over, fill with, Dhātup. xxviii, 32; Vārtt. on Pāṇ. vii, 1, 59; Bhaṭṭ. &c.

उभ *ubhá*, *au* (Ved. *ā*), *e*, *e*, mfn. du. (gaṇa *sarvâdi*, Pāṇ. i, 1, 27) both, RV.; AV.; ŚBr.; Mn. &c.; [cf. Zd. *uba*; Gk. ἄμφω; Lat. *ambo*; Goth. *bai*; Old High Germ. *beidê*; Slav. *oba*; Lith. *abhù*.]

Ubháya, mf(*ī*)n. (only sg. and pl.; according to Hara-datta also du., see Siddh. vol. i, p. 98) both, of both kinds, in both ways, in both manners, RV.; AV.; TS.; ŚBr.; AitĀr.; Mn. &c.; (*ī*), f. a kind of bricks, Śulbas. **–kāma**, mfn. wishing both, ŚBr. ix. **–guṇa**, mfn. possessed of both qualities. **–°m-kará**, mfn. doing or effecting both, RV. viii, 1, 2. **–cara**, mfn. 'moving in or on both,' living in water and on land or in the air, amphibious. **–cārin**, mfn. going or moving in both (night and day), VarBṛS. **–cchannā**, f. (in rhet.) a kind of enigma, Kāvyād. **–dat**, mfn. (Ved. Pāṇ. v, 4, 142, Kāś.) having teeth in both (jaws). **–dyús**, ind. on both days, on two subsequent days, AV. **–pad** (nom. m. *pāt*), mfn. having both feet, with both feet, ChUp. **–°padin**, mfn. (fr. *ubhaya-pada*), having both Parasmai-pada and Ātmane-pada. **–bhāga**, mfn. having part in both (night and day); *-hara*, mfn. taking two shares or parts; applicable to two purposes; (*am*), n. a medicine that acts in two ways (as an emetic and a purge). **–bhāj**, mfn. acting in two ways (as a medicine, cf. the last), Car. **–mukha**, mf(*ī*)n. 'having a face towards either way,' 'two-faced,' a pregnant female (so called because the embryo has its face turned in an opposite direction to that of the mother), BhavP. **–°vaṅśya**, mfn. (fr. *ubhaya-vaṅśa*), belonging to both families or lineages, BhP. **–vat**, mfn. furnished with or containing both, VPrāt.; Nir. **–vāsin**, mfn. living or abiding in both (places), Pat. **–vidyā**, f. the two-fold science (i. e. religious knowledge and acquaintance with worldly affairs, MW.) **–vidha**, mfn. of two kinds or forms, Nir.; Comm. on Nyāyam. **–vipulā**, f., N. of a metre. **–vetana**, mfn. 'receiving wages from both,' a spy who seemingly enters the enemy's service, Śiś. ii, 113; a perfidious or treacherous servant, Pañcat.; *-tva*, n. the state of receiving wages from both, Bālar. **–vyañjana**, n. having the marks of both sexes, a hermaphrodite, L. **–śiras**, mfn. 'having a head towards both ways' or 'two-headed,' a pregnant female (cf. *-mukha* above), Hcat. **–saptamī**, f., N. of a particular day, BhavP. **–sambhava**, m. the possibility of both cases, a dilemma, W.; (mfn.) having its origin in both. **–sāman**, mfn. (a day) on which both Sāmans (viz. Bṛihat and Rathaṃtara) are sung, AitBr.; Lāṭy.; ĀśvŚr. **–stobha**, n., N. of several Sāmans. **–snātaka**, mfn. one who has performed the prescribed ablutions after finishing both (his time of studying and his vow), Comm. on Mn. iv, 31. **–sprishṭi**, f., N. of a river, BhP. **Ubhayâtmaka**, mfn. of both natures or kinds, Mn.; Sāṃkhyak.; Viddh. **Ubhayânumata**, mfn. agreed to or accepted on both sides. **Ubhayâyin**, mfn. tending towards or fit for both (worlds), BhP. **Ubhayârtham**, ind. for a double purpose (e. g. for prosperity on earth and happiness in heaven). **Ubhayâlaṃkāra**, m. (in rhet.) a figure of speech which sets off both the sense and the sound. **Ubhayâvṛitti**, f. (in rhet.) recurrence of a word both with the same sound and sense, Kāvyād.

Ubhayáta (in comp. for *ubhayátas* below). **–ukthya**, mfn. 'having Ukthya sacrifices on both sides,' between two Ukthya sacrifices, ŚBr. xiii. **–eta**, mf(*enī*)n. variegated on both sides, TS. vii; Kāṭh.

Ubhayátaḥ (in comp. for *ubhayátas* below). **–kālam**, ind. at both times (i. e. before and after a meal), Car. **–kshṇút**, mfn. two-edged, ŚBr. vi; TāṇḍyaBr.; Lāṭy. **–paksha**, mfn. being on both sides. **–pad**, mfn. (nom. m. *°pād*) having or using both feet, AitBr. v, 33, 4. **–parigṛihītá**, mfn. enclosed on both sides, ŚBr. ii. **–pāśa**, mfn. having a loop or knot on both sides (as a rope), Sarvad. **–praüga**, mfn. having a Praüga (q. v.) on both sides, TS. v; ŚBr. vi; Kāṭh.; KātyŚr. **–prajña**, mfn. (fr. *prajñā*), one whose cognizance is directed both inwards and outwards, MāṇḍUp. **–prāṇa**, mfn. having vital air on both sides, TāṇḍyaBr. **–śīrshan**, mf(*śīrshṇī*)n. having a head towards either way, two-headed, VS. iv, 19; *°śīrsha-tvá*, n. the state of having two heads, MaitrS. iii. **–saṃśvāyin**, mfn. swelling on both sides, TS. ii. **–sasya**, mfn. yielding a crop in both seasons (as a field), ĀśvGṛ. **–sujāta**, mfn. well-born both by the paternal and maternal side, ŚāṅkhGṛ. **–stobha**, mfn. having a Stobha both at the beginning and end (as a Sāman), TāṇḍyaBr.

Ubhayataś (in comp. for *ubhayátas* below). **–cakra**, mfn. having wheels on both sides, two-wheeled, AitBr. v, 33, 4.

Ubhayátas, ind. from or on both sides, to both sides (with gen. or acc.); in both cases, RV.; VS.; ŚBr.; MBh. &c. **–tīkshṇa**, mfn. sharp on both sides (as a spear), Mn. viii, 315.

Ubhayáto (in comp. for *ubhayátas* above).

-'ṅga (°*tas-aṅga*), mfn. having a part on both sides. **-jyotis,** mfn. having light on both sides, ŚBr. xii, xiii; 'having a Jyotiḥ-shṭoma, sacrifice on both sides,' being between two Jyotiḥ-shṭoma sacrifices, AitBr. iv, 15, 5. **-'ti-rātra** (°*tas-ati*°), mfn. being between two Ati-rātra sacrifices, Vait. **-dat,** mfn. having teeth in both jaws, MaitrS. ii; Mn. &c. **-danta,** mf(*ā*)n. id., ŚBr. i. **-dvāra,** mfn. having a door on both sides, ŚBr. iii. **-namas-kāra,** mfn. having the word *namas* on both sides, ŚBr. ix. **-nābhi,** mfn. having a nave on both sides (as wheels), BhP. **-bārhatam,** ind. on both sides accompanied by Bṛihat-sāman songs, SBr. xi. **-bhāga-hara,** mfn. = *ubhaya-bhāga-hara,* q. v., Suśr. **-bhāj,** mfn. id., Car. **-bhāsha,** mfn. occurring both in the Parasmai-bhāshā (= Parasmai-pada) and Ātmane-bhāshā (= Ātmane-pada), Dhātup. xxx, B. **-mukha,** mf(*ī*)n. = *ubhaya-mukha,* q. v., Yājñ.; Hcat. &c.; having a spout on both sides (as a pitcher), ŚBr. iv. **-hrasva,** mfn. having a short vowel on both sides, produced by two short vowels (as a vowel accented with a Svarita), VPrāt.

Ubhayátra, ind. in both places, on both sides; in both cases or times, RV. iii, 53, 5; ŚBr.; MBh.; Mn. &c.

Ubhayáthā, ind. in both ways, in both cases, ŚBr.; Pāṇ.; Vikr. &c.

1. **Ubhayā́,** ind. in both ways, RV. x, 108, 6. **-da** (? AV. v, 19, 2) and **-dat,** mfn. having teeth in both jaws, RV. x, 90, 10; AV. v, 31, 3; xix, 6, 12; TS.

2. **Ubhayā** (in comp. for *ubhaya* above). **-karṇi, -°ñjali** (*ubhayâñjali*), **-danti, -pāṇi, -bāhu,** ind., gaṇa *dvidaṇḍy-ādi,* Pāṇ. v, 4, 128. **-hasti,** ind. in both hands, with both hands, ib.; RV. v, 39, 1. **-hastyā́,** ind. id., RV. i, 81, 7.

Ubhayāvin, mfn. being on both sides, partaking of both, RV. viii, 1, 2; x, 87, 3; AV. viii, 3, 3; v, 25, 9.

Ubhayīya, mfn. belonging to both.

Ubhaye-dyus, ind. on both days, on two subsequent days, AitBr. v, 29, 3; Pāṇ. v, 3, 22.

Ubhā (in comp. for *ubha* above). **-karṇi, -°ñjali** (*ubhâñjali*), **-danti, -pāṇi, -bāhu, -hasti,** ind., gaṇa *dvidaṇḍy-ādi,* Pāṇ. v, 4, 128.

उम् *um,* ind. an interjection of anger; a particle implying assent; interrogation, L.

उम *uma, as,* m. a city, town, L.; a wharf, landing-place, L.

उमा *úmā,* f. (perhaps fr. √*ve*, BRD.) flax (Linum Usitatissimum), ŚBr. vi; Kauś.; Pāṇ.; turmeric (Curcuma Longa), Car.; N. of the daughter of Himavat (wife of the god Śiva; also called Pārvatī and Durgā; the name is said to be derived from *u mā,* 'O [child], do not [practise austerities]!' the exclamation addressed to Pārvatī by her mother), Hariv. 946; ŚivP.; Kum. i, 26; R.; Ragh. &c.; N. of several women; splendour, light, L.; fame, reputation, L.; quiet, tranquillity, L.; night, L. **-kaṭa,** n. the pollen of Linum Usitatissimum. **-kānta,** m. 'Umā's loved one,' N. of Śiva, MBh. xiii. **-guru,** m. 'Umā's Guru or father,' N. of Himavat; *-nadī,* f., N. of a river, Hariv. **-caturthī,** f. the fourth day in the light half of the month Jyaishṭha. **-nātha,** m. 'Umā's husband,' N. of Śiva. **-pati,** m. id., TĀr.; MBh.; Kathās. &c.; N. of a grammarian; *-datta,* m., N. of a man; *-dhara,* m., N. of a poet; *-sevin,* mfn. worshipping Śiva. **-pariṇayana,** n. 'Umā's wedding,' N. of a work. **-mahêśvara-vrata,** n., N. of a particular observance, BhavP. **-vana,** n., N. of the town Vana-pura or Devī-koṭa (Devi Cote), L. **-saṃhitā,** f., N. of a work. **-sahāya,** m. 'Umā's companion,' N. of Śiva. **-suta,** m. 'Umā's son,' N. of Skanda. **Umêśa,** m. 'Umā's lord,' N. of Śiva; 'Umā and Śiva,' N. of an idol (representing Śiva joined with Umā), MatsyaP.

Umya, *am,* n. a flax-field, L.; a turmeric-field, L.

उम्बर *umbara, as,* m. the upper timber of a door frame, L.; N. of a Gandharva, Hariv.

Umbura, *as,* m. id., L.

उम्बी *umbī,* f. fried stalks of wheat or barley (considered as a tonic), Bhpr.; (cf. *ulumbā.*)

Umbikā, f. id., Nigh.

उम्बेक *umbeka, as,* m., N. of a man.

उम्भ् *umbh.* See *ubh.*

उम्लोचा *umlocā,* f., N. of an Apsaras, MBh.

उरःकपाट *uraḥ-kapāṭa,* &c. See *úras.*

उरग *urá-ga, as,* m. (fr. *ura* = *uras* [Kāty. on Pāṇ. iii, 2, 48] and *ga,* 'breast-going'), a serpent, snake; a Nāga (semi-divine serpent usually represented with a human face), Suparṇ. viii, 5; Suśr.; Ragh. &c.; N. of the Nakshatra Āślesha (presided over by the Nāgas); lead, L.; (*ā*), f., N. of a town, MBh.; (*ī*), f. a female snake, Prab. **-bhūshaṇa,** n. 'snake-ornamented,' N. of Śiva, L. **-yava,** n. a barleycorn (used as a measure), Buddh. **-rāja,** m. the king of snakes, N. of Vāsuki; a large or excellent snake, Śiś. **-sāra-candana,** n. a kind of sandal-wood, Lalit.; *-cūrṇa,* n. the powder of the above, ib.; *-maya,* mfn. made of sandal-wood, ib. **-sthāna,** n. 'abode of the snakes,' N. of Pātāla (q. v.), L. **Uragâri,** n. 'enemy of snakes,' N. of Garuḍa; *-ketana,* m. 'having Garuḍa as symbol,' N. of Vishṇu, VP. **Uragâśana,** m. 'having serpents as food,' N. of Garuḍa, Śiś. v, 13; a species of crane, L. **Uragâsya,** n. 'snake's mouth,' a kind of spade, Daś. **Uragêndra,** m. = *uraga-rāja* above, Śiś.

Uraṃ-ga, *as,* m. a snake, BhP.

Uraṃ-gama, *as,* m. id.

उरण *úraṇa, as,* m. (√*ṛi*, Uṇ. v, 17; fr. √1. *vṛi*; cf. √*ūrṇu, ūrṇā*), a ram, sheep, young ram, ŚBr. xi; MBh. &c.; N. of an Asura (slain by Indra), RV. ii, 14, 4. **Uraṇâksha, °ka, uraṇâkhya, °ka,** m. Cassia Alata or Tora, L.

Uraṇaka, *as,* m. a ram, sheep, BhP. **-vatsa,** m. a young ram, ib.

Ura-bhra, *as,* m. a ram, sheep, Suśr. (cf. *aurabhra*); N. of a plant, = *dadrughna,* L. **-sārikā,** f. a kind of poisonous insect, Suśr. ii, 287, 14.

U'rā, f. a ewe, RV. viii, 34, 3; x, 95, 3. **-máthi,** mfn. killing sheep (as a wolf), RV. viii, 86, 8 [BRD.]

उररी *urarī,* ind. (in one sense connected with *uru* [col. 3] and in the other with *úras* below) a particle implying extension or expansion; assent or admission (only in comp. with √*kṛi* and its derivations; cf. *urasi kṛitvā*; also *urī-*√*kṛi* and *aṅgī-*√*kṛi*). **-karaṇa,** n. the act of admitting, adopting, admission, Sarvad. **-kāra,** m. id., L. **-√kṛi,** to make wide, extend; to admit, allow, assent, adopt, Sāh.; Comm. on ChUp.; to adopt, assume, Śiś. x, 14; to accept, receive, Daś.; to promise, agree, Naish. **-kṛita,** mfn. extended; admitted, adopted; promised, agreed.

उरल *urala,* mfn. gaṇa *balâdi,* Pāṇ. iv, 2, 80.

उरश *uraśa, as,* m., N. of a sage, gaṇa *bhargâdi,* Pāṇ. iv, 1, 178 (v.l. *urasa*); (*ā*), f., N. of a city, Rājat.

उरस् *úras,* n. (√*ṛi*, Uṇ. iv, 194), the chest, breast, bosom, RV.; AV.; ŚBr.; MBh.; Śak. &c. (*urasi kṛitvā* or *urasi-kṛitya,* ind. having assented or adopted, but only *urasi kṛitvā* in the sense of having put upon the breast, Pāṇ. i, 4, 75); the best of its kind, L.; (*ās*), m., N. of a man, gaṇa *tikâdi,* Pāṇ. iv, 1, 154 (in the Kāś.) **-kaṭa,** m. the sacred thread hung round the neck and upon the breast (as sometimes worn), L. **-tas,** ind. from the breast, out of the breast, Pāṇ. iv, 3, 114; TāṇḍyaBr. vi. **-tra** and **-trāṇa,** n. breastplate, cuirass, coat of mail, L. **-vat,** mfn. broad-chested, full-breasted, strong, L.

Uraḥ (in comp. for *úras* above). **-kapāṭa,** m. a door-like chest, a broad or strong chest, Kād. **-kshata,** mfn. 'chest-injured,' suffering from disease of the lungs; *-kāsa,* m. a consumptive cough, ŚārṅgS. **-kshaya,** m. disease of the chest, consumption. **-śūla,** n. 'chest-dart,' shooting pain in the chest. **-°śūlin,** mfn. suffering from the above, Car. **-sūtrikā,** f. a pearl necklace hanging on the breast, L. **-stambha,** m. oppression of the chest, asthma. **-sthala,** n. the breast, bosom.

Uraś (in comp. for *úras* above). **-chada,** m. breastplate, cuirass, armour, mail, R.

Urasa, mfn. having a strong or broad breast, Pāṇ. v, 2, 127; (*as, ā*), m. f., vv. ll. for *uraśa* and °*śā* above; (*am*), n. the best of its kind, Pāṇ. v, 4, 93.

Urasi (in comp. for *úras* above). **-kṛitya,** see *úras* above. **-ja,** m. 'produced on the chest,' the female breast, R.; Śiś. **-ruha,** m. id. **-loman,** mfn. having hair on the breast, Comm. on Pāṇ.

Urasila, mfn. having a full or broad breast, broad-chested, gaṇa *picchâdi,* Pāṇ. v, 2, 100.

Uraska, ifc. = *úras,* breast; see *vyūḍhôraska.*

1. **Urasya,** mfn. pectoral, belonging to or coming from the chest, requiring (exertion of) the chest, Pāṇ. iv, 3, 114; v, 3, 103; Suśr.; produced from one's self, belonging to one's self (as a child), Pāṇ. iv, 4, 94; (*as*), m. the female breast, VarBṛS.; (in Gr.) N. of the *h* and Visarga, RPrāt. 41.

2. **Urasya,** Nom. P. *urasyati,* to be strong-chested, be strong, Pāṇ. iii, 1, 27.

Uro (in comp. for *úras* above). **-gama** (*urô*°), m. serpent, snake, Suparṇ.; (cf. *uraṃ-ga.*) **-graha,** m. 'chest-seizure,' pleurisy, ŚārṅgS. **-ghāta,** m. pain in the chest, W. **-ja,** m. the female breast, Bhām. (cf. *urasi-ja*). **-bṛihatī,** f., N. of a metre. **-bhūshaṇa,** n. an ornament of the breast, L. **-vibandha,** m. oppression of the chest, asthma, Car. **-hasta,** n. a mode of boxing or wrestling (*bāhuyuddha-bheda*), T.

उरा *úrā.* See under *úraṇa,* col. 2.

उराण *urāṇá,* mfn. (= *uru kurvāṇa,* Sāy.) making broad or wide, extending, increasing, RV.; [pres. p. of √2. *vṛi,* BRD.]

उराह *urāha, as,* m. a horse of pale colour with dark legs, L.

उरी 1. *urī,* ind. (probably connected with *úras,* see *urarī,* col. 2) a particle implying assent or admission or promise. **-√kṛi,** to adopt, assume, Naish.; to promise, agree, allow, grant, Ragh.; Mālav. &c.; to accept, receive, take part of, Sāh.

उरी 2. *urī,* f., N. of a river, ŚivaP.

उरु *urú,* mf(*vī́*)n. (√1. *vṛi*; √*ūrṇu,* Uṇ. i, 32), wide, broad, spacious, extended, great, large, much, excessive, excellent, RV.; AV.; MBh.; Ragh.; (*us*), m., N. of an Āṅgirasa, ĀrshBr.; of a son of the fourteenth Manu, BhP.; VP.; (*vī*), f. the earth; see *urvī́,* p. 218, col. 1; (*u*), n. wide space, space, room, RV. (with √*kṛi,* to grant space or scope, give opportunity, RV.); (*u*), ind. widely, far, far off, RV.; (*uruyā́,* MaitrS.; 1. *urvyā́* and *urviyā́,* instr. of the fem.), ind. far, far off, to a distance, RV.; VS.; TS.; compar. *varīyas,* superl. *varishṭha*; [cf. Gk. εὐρύς, εὐρύνω, &c.: Hib *ur,* 'very;' *uras,* 'power, ability.'] **-kāla** and **kālaka,** m. the creeper Cucumis Colocynthis, L. **-kīrti,** mfn. of far-reaching fame, Ragh. vi, 74. **-kṛit,** mfn. causing to extend or spread out, increasing, RV. viii, 75, 11. **-kramá,** mfn. far-stepping, making wide strides (said of Vishṇu), RV.; TUp.; (*as*), m. (Vishṇu's) wide stride, MaitrS. i, 3, 9; N. of Vishṇu, BhP.; of Śiva. **-ksháya** (*urú-kshaya,* AV.), mfn. occupying spacious dwellings, RV. i, 2, 9 (said of Varuṇa); AV. vii, 77, 3 (said of the Maruts); (*as*), m. a spacious dwelling, wide habitation, RV. x, 118, 8; N. of a king, VP. **-kshití,** f. spacious dwelling or habitation, RV. vii, 100, 4; ix, 84, 1. **-gavyūti** (*urú*°), mfn. having a wide domain or territory, RV. ix, 90, 4; ŚBr.; ŚāṅkhŚr. **-gāyá,** mfn. making large strides, wide-striding [fr. √*gā,* Nir. ii, 7; also according to Sāy., 'hymned by many, much-praised,' fr. √*gai*], RV.; AV.; VS.; TBr. &c. (said of Indra, Vishṇu, the Soma, and the Aśvins); spacious for walking upon, wide, broad (as a way), AitBr. vii, 13, 13; (*am*), n. wide space, scope for movement, RV.; ŚBr.; KaṭhUp.; *-vat,* mfn. offering ample space for motion, unconfined, ChUp. **-gū́lā,** f. a kind of serpent, AV. v, 13, 8. **-grāhá,** m. far-spreading sickness (?), AV. xi, 9, 12. **-cakrá,** mfn. having wide wheels (as a carriage), RV. ix, 89, 4. **-cákri,** mfn. (fr. √*kṛi*), doing or effecting large work or great wealth, granting ample assistance, RV. ii, 26, 4; v, 67, 4; viii, 18, 5; (*is*), m., N. of a descendant of Atri. **-cákshas,** mfn. far-seeing, RV.; AV. xix, 10, 8; VS. iv, 23 (said of Varuṇa, Sūrya, and the Ādityas). **-jman,** mfn. (only voc.) having a wide path or range, AV. vi, 4, 3. **-jráyas** and **-jrí,** mfn. moving in a wide course, extending over a wide space, RV. (said of Agni and Indra). **-tā,** f. wideness, TPrāt. **-tāpa,** m. great heat. **-tva,** n. wideness; magnitude, vastness. **-drápsu,** mfn. having large drops, TS. iii. **-dhāra** (*urú*°), mf(*ā*)n. giving a broad stream, streaming abundantly, RV.; VS.; KātyŚr.; ŚāṅkhŚr. **-dhishṇya**, m. 'exceedingly full of thoughts,' N. of a sage in the eleventh Manv-antara. **-pushpikā**, f. a species of plant, Nigh. **-práthas** (and *urú-prathas*), mfn. wide-spreading, widely extended, far-spreading, VS. **-bindu**, m., N. of a flamingo, Hariv. (Langlois' transl.) **-bilá**, mf(ī)n. having a wide opening (as a jar), ŚBr. vi, ix. **-bilvā**, f., N. of the place to which the Buddha retired for meditation and where he obtained supreme knowledge (afterwards called Buddha-Gayā); *-kalpa*, m., N. of a place, Lalit.; *-kāśyapa*, m., N. of a descendant of Kaśyapa, ib. **-'bja**, mfn. (fr. *uru*, 2. *ap*, and *ja*, Sāy.?), producing or causing much milk, RV. ix, 77, 4; [for *uru-ubja*, 'widely opened,' BRD.] **-māṇa**, m. Cratæva Religiosa, Car. **-mārga**, m. a long road. **-muṇḍa**, m., N. of a mountain. **-yuga** (*urú°*), mfn. furnished with a broad yoke, RV. viii, 98, 9. **-rātri**, f. the latter portion of the night, late at night, Comm. on Gobh. **-loka** (*urú°*), mfn. visible to a distance, ample, vast, RV. x, 128, 2. **-valka**, m., N. of a son of Vasu-deva, BhP. **-vas**, m., N. of a man, VP. **-vāsa**, m., N. of a Buddhist monastery. **-vikrama**, mfn. of great strength or bravery, valiant, brave, MBh.; Veṇīs. **-vilvā**, see *-bilvā* above. **-vyácas**, mfn. occupying wide space, widely extending, widely capacious, RV.; AV.; VS. xxvii, 16; (*ās*), m., N. of a Rakshas, L. **-vyáñc** (*°vyáṅ*, *urūcī*, *°vyák*), mfn. extending far, capacious; far-reaching (as a sound), RV.; AV.; VS. xxi, 5; (*urūcī*), f. the earth, RV. vii, 35, 3. **-vraja**, mfn. (only loc.) having a wide range, having ample space for movement, RV. viii, 67, 12. **-śáṇsa**, mfn. to be praised by many, praised by many, RV. (said of Varuṇa, Pūshan, Indra, the Soma, and the Ādityas). **-śarman** (*urú°*), mfn. finding refuge everywhere throughout the universe, widely pervading, VS. x, 9. **-śriṅga**, m. 'having high peaks,' N. of a mountain, BhP. **-śravas**, m. 'of far-reaching fame,' N. of a man, VP. **-shā**, mfn. (√*san*), granting much, producing abundantly, RV. v, 44, 6. **-sattva**, mfn. magnanimous, of a generous or noble nature. **-svana**, mfn. of strong voice, stentorian. **-hāra**, mfn. a valuable necklace. **Urū-ṇasá**, mfn. broad-nosed, RV. x, 14, 12; AV. xviii, 2, 13 (said of Yama's dogs). **Urv-aṅga**, m. 'large-bodied,' a mountain, L.; the ocean, L. **Urv-ájra**, m. an extensive field, RV. x, 27, 9.

Urudhā, ind. in many ways, BhP.

Uruvu, *us*, **uruvuka** and **uruvūka**, *as*, m. Ricinus Communis, Suśr.

Urví, f. (cf. *urú*), 'the wide one,' the wide earth, earth, soil, RV. i, 46, 2; ii, 4, 7; Śak.; Mn. &c.; (*ví*), f. du. 'the two wide ones,' heaven and earth, RV. vi, 10, 4; x, 12, 3; 88, 14; (*vyás*), f. pl. (with and without *shash*) the six spaces (viz. the four quarters of the sky with the upper and lower spaces), RV.; AV.; (also applied to heaven, earth, day, night, water, and vegetation) ŚāṅkhŚr.; (also to fire, earth, water, wind, day and night) ŚBr. i, 5, 1, 22; rivers, Nir. **-tala**, n. the surface of the earth, ground, Ratnāv. **-dhara**, m. a mountain, L.; N. of Śesha, L. **-pati**, m. 'lord of the earth,' a king, Naish.; Rājat. **-bhuj**, m. 'earth-enjoyer,' a king, sovereign, Prasannar. **-bhṛit**, m. a mountain, Rājat.; Amar. &c. **-ruha**, m. 'growing on the earth,' a tree, plant. **Urvīśa** and **urvīśvara**, m. 'lord of the earth,' a king, sovereign, BhP.; Kathās.

2. **Urvyā́**, f. (for 1. see *úru*) amplitude, vastness, ŚBr. i, 5, 1, 17.

Urvy-ūti (fr. *ūti* with *urvī*=*urvyā*?), mfn. granting extensive protection, RV. vi, 24, 2.

उरुञ्जिरा *uruñjirā*, f., N. of the river Vipāś, Nir.

उरुण्ड *úruṇḍa*, *as*, m. a kind of demon, AV. viii, 6, 15; N. of a man.

उरुरी *ururī*=*urarī*, q. v., L.

उरुष्य *urushya*, Nom. (fr. *uru*, BRD.; perhaps an irr. fut. or Desid. of √1. *vṛi*?) P. *urushyáti* (Ved. Impv. 2. sg. *urushyā́*, Pāṇ. vi, 3, 133) to protect, secure, defend from (abl.), RV.; AV. vi, 3, 3; 4, 3; VS. vii, 4.

Urushyā́, ind. (instr.) with desire to protect, RV. vi, 44, 7.

Urushyú, mfn. wishing to protect, RV. viii, 48, 5.

उरूक *urūka*, *as*, m. a kind of owl [*ulūkākhya-pakshi-sadṛiśa*, Sāy.], AitBr. ii, 7, 10; Nyāyam.

उरूची *urūcī*. See *uru-vyáñc*, col. 1.

उरूणस *urū-ṇasá*. See col. 1.

उरोगम *uro-gama*, &c. See p. 217, col. 3.

उर्ज् *urj*, &c. See *ūrj*, &c.

उर्जिहाना *urjihānā*, f., N. of a city, R. (Gorresio; v. l. *ujjihānā*).

उर्ण *urṇa*, &c. See *ūrṇa*, &c.

उर्द् *urd*. See *ūrd*.

उर्दि *urdi*, *is*, m., N. of a man, Pat.

उर्द्र *urdra*, *as*, m.=*udra*, an otter, L.

उर्मिला *urmilā*=*ūrmilā*, q. v.

उर्व् *urv*. See *ūrv*.

उर्व *urva*, *as*, m., N. of a man, gaṇa *vidâdi*, Pāṇ. iv, 1, 104; (*urvá*, AV. xvi, 3, 3, perhaps erroneous for *ukha*, BRD.)

उर्वट *urvaṭa*, *as*, m. year, L.

उर्वरा *urvárā*, f. (probably connected with *urú*), fertile soil, field yielding crop, RV.; AV.; TS.; ŚBr. &c.; land in general, soil, the earth, Bālar.; Śārṅg. &c.; N. of an Apsaras, MBh. **-jit**, mfn. acquiring fertile soils, RV. ii, 21, 1. **-pati**, m. (only voc.) lord of the fields under crop, RV. viii, 21, 3. **-sā́**, mfn. (√*san*), procuring or granting fertile land, RV. iv, 38, 1; vi, 20, 1.

Urvaryà (VS. xvi, 33) and **urvárya** (MaitrS. ii, 9, 6), mfn. belonging to a fertile soil &c.

उर्वरित *urvarita*, mfn. left, left over, BhP. (=*avaśishṭa*, Comm.)

उर्वरी *urvárī* (f. of *urvan*, fr. √*ṛi*, T.), f. 'super-added,' a wife presented together with many others for choice, AV. x, 4, 21 (*ādhikyaprāptā strī*, T.) **-vat**, mfn. 'having many wives for choice,' N. of a Ṛishi, VP.

उर्वशी *urvaśī*, f. (fr. *uru* and √1. *aś*, 'to pervade,' see M.M., Chips, vol. ii, p. 99), 'widely extending,' N. of the dawn (personified as an Apsaras or heavenly nymph who became the wife of Purū-ravas), RV.; AV. xviii, 3, 23; VS.; ŚBr.; Vikr. &c.; N. of a river, MBh. xii. **-tīrtha**, n., N. of a Tirtha, MBh. **-nāma-mālā**, f., N. of a lexicon by an anonymous author. **-ramaṇa** and **-vallabha**, m. 'beloved by Urvaśī,' N. of Purū-ravas, L. **-sahāya**, m. 'Urvaśī's companion,' N. of Purū-ravas, L.

उर्वारु *urvāru*, *us* (L.), *ūs*, m. f. a species of cucumber, Cucumis Usitatissimus, AV. vi, 14, 2; (*u*), n. the fruit of Cucumis Usitatissimus, TāṇḍyaBr.; (cf. *irvāru*.)

Urvāruka, *am*, n. id., Hcat.

उर्विया *urviyā́*, ind. See *urú*, p. 217, col. 3.

उल् *ul*, P. *olati*, to burn (a Sautra [q. v.] root).

उल *ulá*, *as*, m. a kind of wild animal, AV. xii, 1, 49; VS.; MaitrS.; half-ripe pulses fried over a slight fire, Nigh.; N. of a Ṛishi.

उलड् *ulaḍ*, cl. 10. P. *ulaṇḍayati*, *auliulaṇḍat*, to throw out, eject, Dhātup. xxii, 9; (see *olaḍ*.)

उलन्द *ulanda*, *as*, m., N. of a king [T.], gaṇa *arīhaṇâdi*, Pāṇ. iv, 2, 80.

Ulandaka, *as*, m., N. of Śiva, L.

उलप *úlapa*, *as*, m. (√*val*, Uṇ. iii, 145), a species of soft grass, RV. x, 142, 3; AV. vii, 66, 1; KātyŚr.; MBh.; Śiś. &c.; N. of a pupil of Kalāpin, Kāś. on Pāṇ. iv, 3, 104; (*ā*), f. a species of grass, Bālar. **-rāji** or **-rājikā** or **-rājī**, f. a bundle of grass, Lāṭy.; Nyāyam. &c.

Ulapin, *ī*, m. a kind of guinea-pig, L.

Ulapyà [VS.] and **ulapyá** [MaitrS.], mfn. abiding in or belonging to the Ulapa grass; (*as*), m., N. of a Rudra, T.

Ulupa, *as*, *am*, m. n. a kind of grass, =*ulapa*, L.

Ulupin or **ulūpin**, *ī*, m.=*ulapin*, L.

Ulupya, mfn.=*ulapya*.

उलभ *ulabha*, *as*, m., gaṇa *dāmany-ādi*, Pāṇ. v, 3, 116 (Kāś.)

उलिन्द *ulinda*, *as*, m., N. of a country, L.; N. of Śiva, L.

उलुम्बा *ulumbā*, f. the stalks of wheat or barley fried over a fire of wet grass, Nigh.; (cf. *umbī*.)

उलुलि *ululí*, *is*, m. an outcry indicative of prosperity, AV. iii, 19, 6.

उलूक *úlūka*, *as*, m. (√*val*, Uṇ. iv, 41), an owl, RV. x, 165, 4; AV. vi, 29, 1; VS.; TS.; MBh.; Mn. &c.; N. of Indra, Vām.; of a Muni (in the VāyuP. enumerated together with Kaṇāda, but perhaps identical with him, as the Vaiśeshika system is called Aulūkya-darśana in the Sarvad.); of a Nāga, Suparṇ.; of a king of the Ulūkas; (*ās*), m. pl., N. of a people, MBh.; Hariv.; (*ī*), f., N. of the primeval owl, Hariv. 222; VP.; (*am*), n. a kind of grass (=*ulapa*), L.; [cf. Lat. *ulula*; Gk. ὀλ-ολυγ-αία; Old High Germ. *ūla*; Angl. Sax. *ūle*; Mod. Germ. *Eule*; Eng. *owl*; Fr. *hulotte*.] **-ceṭī**, f. a species of owl, VarBṛS. **-jit**, m. 'conquering the owl,' the crow, Nigh.; 'conqueror of Indra,' N. of a man (=Indra-jit), Vām. ii, 1, 13. **-paksha**, mf(ī)n. having the shape of the wing of an owl, Pat. **-pāka**, m. the young of an owl, gaṇa *nyaṅkv-ādi*, Pāṇ. vii, 3, 53. **-puccha**, mf(ī)n. having the shape of the tail of an owl, Pat. **-yātu** (*úlūka°*), m. a demon in the shape of an owl, RV. vii, 104, 22; AV. viii, 4, 22.

उलूखल *ulūkhala*, *am*, n. a wooden mortar, RV. i, 28, 6; AV.; TS.; ŚBr.; ĀśvŚr. &c.; N. of a particular kind of cup for holding the Soma (shaped like a mortar), Comm. on KātyŚr.; a staff of Uḍumbara wood (carried on certain occasions), L.; bdellium, L.; (*as*), m., N. of an evil spirit, PārGṛ. i, 16, 23; of a particular ornament for the ear, MBh. iii, 10520. **-budhna**, mfn. forming the base or pedestal of a mortar, TS. vii, 2, 1, 3. **-musalá**, *e*, n. du. mortar and pestle, AV. ix, 6, 15; ŚB.; KātyŚr.; **-rūpá-tā**, f. the state of having the shape of a mortar, ŚBr. vii. **-suta**, mfn. pressed out or pounded in a mortar (as the Soma), RV. i, 28, 1–4. **Ulūkhalâṅghri**, m. the base of a mortar, BhP.

Ulūkhalaka, *am*, n. a small mortar, mortar, RV. i, 28, 5 (voc.); bdellium, L.; (*as*), m., N. of a Muni, VāyuP.

Ulūkhalika, mfn. pounded in a mortar, L.; (ifc.) using as a mortar; (see *dantôlūkhalika*.)

Ulūkhalin, mfn. ifc. id.

उलूट *ulūṭa*, *ās*, m. pl., N. of a people, VP.; (cf. the next, and *utūla*.)

उलूत *ulūta*, *as*, m. the boa, L.; (*ās*), m. pl., N. of a people, MBh.; (*ī*), f., N. of a wife of Garuḍa, L. **Ulūtîśa**, m. 'Ulūtī's husband,' N. of Garuḍa, L.

उलूप *ulūpa*, *as*, m. a species of plant (cf. *ulapa*); (*ī*), f., N. of a daughter of the Nāga Kauravya (married to Arjuna), MBh.

उलूलि *ulūli*, mfn. crying aloud, noisy, ChUp. iii, 19, 3; (cf. *ululi*.)

Ulūlu, mfn. id., Lāṭy. iv, 2, 9.

उल्क *ulka*, *as*, m., N. of a king, Hariv.

उल्का *ulkā́*, f. (√*ush*, Uṇ. iii, 42), a fiery phenomenon in the sky, a meteor, fire falling from heaven, RV. iv, 4, 2; x, 68, 4; AV. xix, 9, 9; MBh.; Yājñ.; Suśr. &c.; a firebrand, dry grass &c. set on fire, a torch, ŚBr. v; R.; Kathās. &c.; (in astrol.) one of the eight principal Daśās or aspect of planets indicating the fate of men, Jyotisha (T.); N. of a grammar. **-cakra**, n. (in astrol.) a particular position of the stars, Rudrayāmala (T.) **-jihva**, m. 'fire-tongued,' N. of a Rakshas, R. **-dhārin**, mfn. a torch-bearer. **-navamī**, f. the ninth day of the light half of the month Aśvayuj; *-vrata*, n. a particular observance to be performed on that day, Hcat. ii, 895 seqq. **-nirhata**, mfn. struck down by a fiery meteor, AV. xix, 9, 9. **-°mālin**, m. 'wearing a wreath of firebrands,' N. of a demon causing diseases, Hariv. **-mukha**, m. 'fire-mouthed,' a particular form of demon (assumed by the departed spirit of a Brāhman who eats ejected food), Mn. xii, 71; Kathās.; Mālatim.; N. of a descendant of Ikshvāku; of an ape, R.; of a Rakshas, R. vi, 87, 12; (*ī*), f. a fox, L.

Ulkushī́, f. a brilliant phenomenon in the sky, a meteor, ŚBr. xi; KātyŚr. iii; a firebrand, ŚBr.; KātyŚr. — **mat**, mfn. accompanied by fiery phenomena, AV. v, 17, 4. **Ulkushy-ànta**, mfn. taking place at the end or after a fiery phenomenon, ŚBr. xi, 2, 7, 25.

U'lmuka, *am*, n. (Uṇ. iii, 84) a firebrand, a piece of burning charcoal used for kindling a fire, ŚBr.; AitBr.; KātyŚr.; ĀśvGṛ. &c.; (*as*), m., N. of a son of a Bala-rāma, MBh.; Hariv.; of a son of Manu Cākshusha, VP. — **mathyā**, mfn. to be produced out of a firebrand (as fire), ŚBr. xii, 4, 3, 3.

Ulmukyā, mfn. coming from or produced out of a firebrand (as fire), ŚBr. xii.

उल्ब *úlba* or *úlva* (rarely *as*, m.), *am*, n. (√*uc*, 'to accumulate,' Uṇ. iv, 95; more probably fr. √1. *vṛi*, BRD.), a cover, envelope, esp. the membrane surrounding the embryo, RV. x, 51, 1; AV. iv, 2, 8; VS.; TS.; ŚBr. &c.; the vulva, womb, VS. xix, 76; a cave, cavity, L.; [cf. Lat. *alvus, vulva*; Lith. *urwā, ūla*.]

Ulbáṇa or **ulváṇa**, *am*, n. the membrane enveloping the embryo, TĀr. i, 10, 7; (*ulbaṇá*), mfn. anything laid over in addition, superfluous, abundant, excessive, much, immense, strong, powerful, TS. iii; MBh.; BhP.; Suśr. &c.; singular, strange, AitĀr.; manifest, evident, L.; (ifc.) abundantly furnished with, MBh.; Suśr. &c.; (*as*), m. a particular position of the hands in dancing; N. of a son of Vasishṭha, BhP.; (*ā*), f. a particular dish (consisting of milk mixed with the juice of melons, bananas &c.), Nigh.

Ulbaṇishṇu, mfn. somewhat strange, rather strange, AitĀr.

U'lbya, mfn. being inside the membrane enveloping the embryo, (with *āpaḥ*) the fluid surrounding the embryo, ŚBr.; KātyŚr.; (*am*), n. excess and vitiation of any of the three humors of the body (bile, phlegm, or wind), MW.; any calamity, MW.

उल्ल *ulla*, *as, ī*, m. f. a species of Arum, Nigh.

उल्लकसन *ullakasana*, *am*, n. erection of the hair of the body (through joy), L.

उल्लग्न *ul-lagna* (*ud-la°*), *am*, n. (in astron.) the Lagna (q. v.) of any particular place, W.

उल्लङ्घ *ul-laṅgh* (*ud-√laṅgh*), Caus. P. *-laṅghayati*, to leap over, pass over or beyond, overstep, transgress, Megh.; Kathās.; Rājat. &c.; to pass (time), Kathās. lxvii, 106; lxxii, 707; to pass over, escape, Kathās. lii, 211; Pañcar.; to transgress, exceed, violate, spurn, trespass, offend, MārkP.; BhP.; Daś. &c.

Ul-laṅghana, *am*, n. the act of leaping or passing beyond or over, Mall. on Kum.; transgression, trespass, offence, sin, Kathās.

Ul-laṅghanīya, mfn. to be transgressed; to be passed over; to be trespassed against, Pañcat.

Ul-laṅghita, mfn. jumped or passed over; exceeded, transgressed, violated, trespassed against. — **śāsana**, mfn. one by whom orders are transgressed, rebellious, disobedient. **Ullaṅghitâdhvan**, mfn. one who has passed over a road.

1. **Ul-laṅghya**, mfn. = *ul-laṅghanīya* above, Kathās.

2. **Ul-laṅghya**, ind. p. having leapt over, springing over, passing beyond; transgressing &c.

उल्लप *ul-lap* (*ud-√lap*), Caus. *-lāpayati*, to flatter, coax, caress, MārkP.

Ul-lāpa, *as*, m. a coaxing or complimentary speech, Bhartṛ.; calling out in a loud voice; change of voice in grief or sickness &c. (= *kāku*, q. v.), W.

Ullāpaka, *am*, n. a coaxing or flattering speech, Car.

Ul-lāpana, *am*, n. the act of coaxing, flattering, MārkP.; (mfn.) transitory, perishable, Lalit.

Ullāpika, *am*, n.(?) a kind of cake, MBh.

Ullāpin, mfn. calling out in a coaxing or complimentary manner, Amar.

Ullāpya, *am*, n. a kind of drama (in one act), Sāh. 545.

उल्लम्फन *ul-lamphana* (*ud-la°*), *am*, n. a jump, L.

उल्लम्ब *ul-lamb* (*ud-√lamb*), Caus. P. *-lambayati*, to hang up, hang, Kathās.

Ul-lambita, mfn. hanging, hovering, Mṛicch.

Ul-lambin, mfn. ifc. hanging on, Kathās.

उल्लल् *ul-lal* (*ud-√lal*), P. *-lalati*, to jump up, spring up, Śiś. v, 47: Caus. *-lalayati*, to jump up, spring up, Śiś. v, 7; Pañcat. (ed. Bühler) ii, 40, 22.

Ul-lala, mfn. shaking, trembling, W.

Ul-lāla, *as*, m.(?), N. of a metre (four verses of alternately fifteen and thirteen instants).

उल्लस् *ul-las* (*ud-√las*), P. Ā. *-lasati, -te*, to shine forth, beam, radiate, be brilliant, BhP.; Pañcar.; Śiś. &c.; to come forth, become visible or perceptible, appear, BhP.; Kathās. &c.; to resound, Kathās.; Rājat.; to sport, play, dance, be wanton or joyful, Amar.; Chandom.; to jump, shake, tremble, be agitated, BhP.; Pañcar. &c.: Caus. *-lāsayati*, to cause to shine or radiate, make brilliant, Pañcar.; Prab.; to cause to come forth or appear, cause to resound, Sāh.; to divert, delight, Śatr.; Hit.; to cause to dance or jump, agitate, cause to move, Kathās.; Rājat.; Hit. &c.

Ul-lasa, mfn. bright, shining; sporting, merry, happy; going out, issuing, W. — **tā**, f. splendour, brilliancy; mirth, happiness; going out, issuing, W.

Ul-lasat, mfn. (pres. p.) shining forth, beaming; coming forth &c. (see above). — **phala**, m. poppy, Nigh.

Ul-lasita, mfn. shining, bright, brilliant, Pañcar.; coming forth, rising, appearing, Śiś.; Sāh.; ejected, brought out; drawn, unsheathed (as a sword), Śiś. vi, 51; merry, happy, joyful, Kathās.; moving, trembling.

Ul-lāsa, *as*, m. light, splendour, L.; the coming forth, becoming visible, appearing, Kathās. xiv, 13; Sāh.; Kap. &c.; joy, happiness, merriness, Kathās.; Amar. &c.; increase, growth, BhP. vii, 1, 7; (in rhet.) giving prominence to any object by comparison or opposition, Kuval.; chapter, section, division of a book (e. g. of the Kāvya-prakāśa).

Ul-lāsana, *am*, n. the act of shining forth, radiating, Rājat. v, 343; (*ā*), f. causing to come forth or appear, Bālar.

Ul-lāsita, mfn. caused to shine, caused to come forth, &c.

Ullāsin, mfn. playing, sporting, dancing.

उल्लाघ *ul-lāgha*, mfn. (fr. √*lāgh*, 'to be able,' with *ud*, Kāś. on Pāṇ. viii, 3, 55), recovered from sickness, convalescent; dexterous, clever, L.; pure, L.; wicked, L.; happy, merry, L.; (*as*), m. black pepper, L. — **tā**, f. wholesomeness, health, Rājat.

Ullāghaya, Nom. P. *ullāghayati*, to cause to recover or revive, resuscitate, Rājat.

उल्लाङ्गूल *ul-lāṅgūla* (*ud-lā°*), mfn. with upraised tail.

उल्लाप *ul-lāpa*, &c. See *ul-lap*.

उल्लाल *ul-lāla*. See *ul-lal*.

उल्लिख् *ul-likh* (*ud-√likh*), P. *-likhati*, to make a slit or incision or line, tear, mark by scratching; to furrow, ŚBr.; KātyŚr.; Suśr.; to scratch, scrape, cut, make lines upon, MBh.; BhP.; Suśr. &c.; to make a scratch or incision, cut into, ShaḍvBr.; Gobh.; ĀśvGṛ. &c.; to chip, chisel, Kum.; Kathās.; to delineate, shape, make visible or clear, Sarvad.; to polish, grind away by polishing, Śak. 139 d; Ragh.; to stir up, cause to come up (e. g. phlegm), Suśr.: Caus. *-lekhayati*, to stir up, cause to come up, ŚārṅgS.

Ul-likhana, *am*, n. an emetic, Bhpr.

Ul-likhita, mfn. slit, torn; scratched, polished, &c.

Ul-lekha, *as*, m. causing to come forth or appear clearly, Prasannar.; bringing up, vomiting, Car.; mentioning, speaking of, description, intuitive description, Sāh. 486; Kathās.; Rājat. &c.; (in rhet.) description of an object according to the different impressions caused by its appearance, Sāh.; Kuval.; (*ā*), f. stroke, line, L.; (*am*), n. (scil. *yuddha*) (in astron.) a conjunction of stars in which a contact takes place, Sūryas. vii, 18; VarBṛS.

Ul-lekhana, mfn. delineating, making lines, making visible or clear, Sarvad.; (*am*), n. the act of marking by lines or scratches, furrowing, KātyŚr.; scratching open or up, scraping, Mn.; Yājñ.; bringing up, vomiting; an emetic, Suśr.; mentioning, speaking of, L.

Ul-lekhin, mfn. scratching, touching, Kād.; delineating, making visible or clear, Sarvad.

Ul-lekhya, mfn. to be scraped or pared; to be written, Kathās.; to be delineated; to be made visible or clear, Sarvad.

उल्लिङ्गय *ul-liṅgaya* (*ud-li°*), Nom. (fr. *liṅga*).

Ulliṅgita, mfn. made manifest by marks or characteristics, Kir. xiv, 2.

उल्लिह् *ul-lih* (*ud-√lih*).

Ul-līḍha, mfn. ground, polished, Bhartṛ.

उल्ली *ul-lī* (*ud-√lī*), Caus. P. *-lāpayati*, to cause to lie down, put to bed (?), Kāś. on Pāṇ. i, 3, 70: Ā. *-lāpayate*, to humiliate, subdue, ib.; to deceive, not to keep one's promise to, ib.

उल्लुञ्च् *ul-luñc* (*ud-√luñc*).

Ul-luñcana, *am*, n. the act of pulling or tearing out, plucking out (e. g. the hair), BhP.; Yājñ.

Ul-luñcita, mfn. plucked, Kathās. lxii, 71.

उल्लुठ् *ul-luṭh* (*ud-√2. luṭh*), P. *-luṭhati*, to roll, wallow, Kuval.

उल्लुण्ठा *ul-luṇṭhā* (*ud-lu°*), f. (√*luṇṭh*), irony, Sāh.

उल्लुप् *ul-lup* (*ud-√lup*).

U'l-lupta, mfn. taken out or away, drawn up, AV. v, 28, 14; ix, 33, 2; 46, 6; Kauś.; Suśr.

Ul-lopam, ind. p. having taken out, taking out, drawing up, Kauś.

Ul-lopya, *am*, n. a kind of song, Yājñ.

उल्लू 1. *ul-lū* (*ud-√lū*).

2. **Ul-lū**, mfn. cutting off, cutting, Comm. on Pāṇ. vi, 4, 83.

Ul-lūna, mfn. cut off, cut (as grass), ŚāṅkhŚr.

उल्लोच *ul-loca* (*ud-lo°*), *as*, m. (√*loc*), an awning, canopy, L.

उल्लोल *ul-lola* (*ud-lo°*), mfn. (√*lul*), dangling, waving, Comm. on MBh.; (*as*), m. a large wave, L.

उल्व *úlva*, &c. See *úlba*, col. 1.

उवट *uvaṭa*, *as*, m., N. of a commentator on the Ṛigveda-prātiśākhya.

उवे *uvé*, ind. an interjection, RV. x, 86, 7.

उशंगव *uśaṃgava*, *as*, m., N. of a king, MBh. ii.

उशत् 1. *uśat*, *an*, or *uśata*, *as*, m., N. of a king, Hariv.

उशत् 2. *uśát*, mfn. (pres. p. of *vaś*, q. v.) wishing, desiring.

Uśá-dah, *dhak*, m. burning with desire or intensely, N. of Agni, RV. iii, 6, 7; 34, 3; vii, 7, 2.

Uśánas, *ā* (Pāṇ. vii, 1, 94; Ved. acc. *ām*; Ved. loc. and dat. *e*; voc. *as, a*, and *an*, Kāś. on Pāṇ.), m., N. of an ancient sage with the patronymic Kāvya, RV.; AV. iv, 29, 6; Kauś. (in later times identified with Śukra, the teacher of the Asuras, who presides over the planet Venus); N. of the planet Venus, MBh.; Yājñ.; Pañcat. &c.; N. of the author of a Dharma-śāstra, Hcat. i, 5; (*uśanasaḥ stoma*, m., N. of a verse (RV. v, 29, 9) to be muttered by one who thinks himself poisoned, ĀśvŚr. v, 9, 1.)

Uśánā, ind. with desire or haste, zealously, RV.; (*ā*), f., N. of a wife of Rudra.

Uśānā́, f. (cf. *uśānā* under √*vaś*), N. of a plant, ŚBr. iii, iv.

Uśika, *as*, m., N. of a king, BhP.

Uśíj, mfn. (Uṇ. ii, 71) wishing, desiring, striving earnestly, zealous, RV.; desirable, amiable, lovely, charming, VS.; TS.; ŚāṅkhŚr.; BhP.; (*k*), m. fire, Uṇ.; boiled butter, ghee, ib.; (*k*), f., N. of the mother of Kakshīvat.

Uśija, *as*, m., N. of the father of Kakshīvat, Comm. on TāṇḍyaBr.

Uśī, f. wish, L. — **nara**, *ās*, m. pl. (Comm. on Uṇ. iv, 1), N. of an ancient people in Central India, AitBr.; Pāṇ.; MBh. &c.; (*as*), m. a king of that people, MBh.; Hariv.; VP. &c.; (*°nārāṇī*), f. a queen of that people, [N. of a plant, Say.], RV. x, 59, 10; *-giri*, m., N. of a mountain, Kathās.

Uśīra, *as, am*, m. n. (Uṇ. iv, 31), the fragrant root of the plant Andropogon Muricatus, Suśr.; Śak.;

Hcat. &c.; (*ī*), f. a species of grass, L. — **giri**, m., N. of a mountain. — **bīja**, m., N. of a mountain, MBh.; Hariv.

Uśīraka, *am*, n. the above root, L.

Uśīrika, mf(*ī*)n. trading in or selling Uśīra, Pāṇ. iv, 4, 53.

Uśenya, mfn. to be wished or longed for, desirable, RV. vii, 3, 9.

उशती *uśatī*, f., incorrect for *ruśatī*, q. v.

उश्रायुस् *uśrāyus*, *us*, m., N. of a son of Purūravas, VP.

उष् 1. *ush*, cl. 1. P. (connected with 3. *vas*, q. v.) *oshati, oshām-cakāra*, and *uvosha* (Pāṇ. iii, 1, 38; 3. pl. *ūshuḥ*, Kāś. on Pāṇ. vi, 4, 78), *oshitā, oshishyati, aushit*, Dhātup. xvii, 45: cl. 9. P. (p. *ushṇát*, RV. ii, 4, 7) to burn, burn down (active), RV.; AV.; ŚBr.; Mn. iv, 189; Śiś.; to punish, chastise, Mn. ix, 273: Pass. *ushyate, oshām-cakre*, to burn (neuter), Suśr.; Car.; Bhaṭṭ.

2. **Ush**, f. (only *ás*, gen. sg.) early morning, dawn, RV.; AV. xvi, 6, 6; (*ushás tisráḥ*, f. pl. morning, midday, and evening, RV. viii, 41, 3.)

1. **Usha**, *as*, m. (for 2. see s. v.) early morning, dawn, daybreak, L.; bdellium; saline earth, L.; (*ā*), f., see below; (*am*), n. fossile salt, L.; (cf. *ūsha*.) — °**m-gu**, *us*, m., N. of a Ṛishi, MBh. xiii, 7667; of a king, MBh.; of Śiva, MBh. xiii, 1219.

Ushaḥ (in comp. for *ushás* below). — **kala**, m. 'crying at daybreak,' a cock, L.

Ushaṇa, *am*, n. black pepper; the root of Piper Longum; (*ā*), f. Piper Longum; Piper Chaba; dried ginger; (cf. *ūshaṇa*.)

Ushat, *an*, m., N. of a son of Su-yajña, Hariv.; (*tī*), f. (scil. *vāc*) a harsh speech (v. l. *uśatī*; erroneous for *ruśatī*?), MBh. **Ushad-gu**, *us*, m., N. of a son of Svāhi, Hariv.; VP. **Ushad-ratha**, *as*, m., N. of a son of Titikshu, ib.

Ushapa, *as*, m. fire, L.; the sun, L.; Ricinus Communis, L.

Ushar (in comp. for *ushás* below). — **búdh** (nom. -*bhut*), mfn. awaking with the morning light, early awaked (a N. esp. applied to Agni as kindled in the early morning), RV. — **búdha**, mfn. id., RV. iii, 2, 14; vi, 15, 1; fire, L.; a child, L.; Ricinus Communis, L.

Ushás, *ās*, f. (nom. pl. *ushā́sas* and *ushásas*; instr. pl. *ushádbhis*, RV. i, 6, 3; see Kāś. on Pāṇ. vii, 4, 48) morning light, dawn, morning (personified as the daughter of heaven and sister of the Ādityas and the night), RV.; AV.; ŚBr.; Śak. &c.; the evening light, RV. x, 127, 7; N. of a wife of Bhava (= Φοῖβος) or Rudra, VP.; (*ushā́sau*, °*ā́sā*, and °*ásā*), f. du. night and morning, RV.; VS. &c.; (*sī*), f. the end of day, twilight, L.; (*as*), n. daybreak, dawn, twilight, Uṇ. iv, 233; L.; the outer passage of the ear, L.; the Malaya range, L.; [cf. Gk. ἠώς; Lat. *aurora*; Lith. *ausz-ra*; Old High Germ. *ôs-tan*.]

1. **Ushasyà**, mfn. sacred to the dawn (Pāṇ. iv, 2, 31), VS. xxiv, 4; ĀśvŚr.

2. **Ushasya**, Nom. (fr. *ushas*, gaṇa *kaṇḍv-ādi*, Pāṇ. iii, 1, 27 [not in Kāś.]) P. *ushasyati*, to grow light, dawn.

Ushā́, f. morning light, dawn, morning, RV.; AV. xii, 2, 45; VS. &c.; night, VP.; Car.; a cow, L.; N. of a daughter of Bāṇa and wife of A-niruddha, AgP.; burning, scorching, Suśr.; (*ā*), ind. at daybreak, L.; at night, L. — **kara**, m. 'night-maker,' the moon, VarBṛS. — **kala**, m. a cock; (cf. *ushaḥ*°.) — **pati**, m. 'Ushā's husband,' N. of A-niruddha, AgP. — **ramaṇa**, m. id., L. — **rāgôdaya**, m. 'appearance of the morning light,' N. of a drama. **Ushêśa**, m. 'the night's husband,' the moon, VarBr.; 'Ushā's husband,' N. of A-niruddha, L.

Ushā́sā (in Dvandva comp. for *ushás* above, Pāṇ. vi, 3, 31). — **naktā**, f. du. dawn and night, RV.; AV. — **sūrya**, n. dawn and sun, Kāś. on Pāṇ. vi, 3, 31.

1. **Ushita** (for 2. see s. v.), mfn. burnt; quick, expeditious, L.

Usho (in comp. for *ushás* above). — **jala**, n. pl. 'the Dawn's tears,' dew, Kathās. — **devatya**, mfn. one whose deity is the dawn. — **rāga**, m. the morning light, dawn, Daś.

Ushṭa, mfn. burnt, L.

Ushṇá, mf(*ā*, rarely *ī*)n. (Uṇ. iii, 2) hot, warm; ardent, passionate, impetuous, RV. x, 4, 2; AV. vi, 68, 1; viii, 9, 17; ŚBr.; ChUp.; Suśr.; Mn. &c.; pungent, acrid; sharp, active, L.; (*as*), m. onion, L.; N. of a man, VP.; (*as, am*), m. n. heat, warmth, the hot season (June, July), Mn. xi, 113; Śak.; Daś. &c.; any hot object, MBh.; N. of certain positions in the retrograde motion of the planet Mars, VarBṛS.; N. of a Varsha, VP.; (*ā*), f. heat, L.; consumption, L.; bile, L.; N. of a plant, Nigh.; (*am*), ind. hotly, ardently, R.; (*ushṇam kṛitvā* or *ushṇam-kṛitya*, ind. p. having made hot or heated, Pāṇ. i, 4, 74.) — **kara**, m. 'hot-rayed,' the sun, Kād. — **kāla**, m. the hot season, Suśr.; Pañcat.; Hit. — **kiraṇa**, m. 'hot-rayed,' the sun, VarBṛS. — **kṛit**, m. 'causing heat,' the sun, L. — **ga**, m. (with and without *kāla*) the hot season, R. — **gandhā**, f., N. of a plant. — **gu**, m. 'hot-rayed,' the sun, BhP. — **ghna**, n. 'heat-destroyer,' a parasol, L. — °**m-karaṇa**, mfn. causing heat, heating, Vārtt. on Pāṇ. vi, 3, 70. — **tā**, f., -**tva**, n. heat, warmth. — **tīrtha**, n., N. of a Tīrtha. — **dīdhiti**, m. 'hot-rayed,' the sun, L. — **nadī**, f. 'the hot river,' N. of Vaitaraṇī the river of hell, L. — **pa**, see *ūshma-pa*. — **phalā**, f. a species of plant, Nigh. — **bhās, -bhṛit, -mahas, -raśmi, -ruci**, m. the sun, MBh.; Ragh.; Kum.; Kir. &c. — **vāta**, m. a particular disease of the bladder, ŚārṅgS. — **vāraṇa**, n. 'keeping off the heat,' a parasol, chattar, Kum. — **vidagdhaka**, m. a particular disease of the eyes, ŚārṅgS. — **vīrya**, mfn. possessing warming power, Car.; Delphinus Gangeticus, L. — **vetālī**, f., N. of a witch, Hariv. — **samaya**, m. the hot season. — **sundara**, m., N. of several plants. — **sparśa-vat**, mfn. anything which feels hot (as fire), Tarkas. **Ushṇâṅśu**, m. 'hot-rayed,' the sun. **Ushṇâgama**, m. approach of the heat, beginning of the hot season, L. **Ushṇânta**, m. end of the hot season, R. **Ushṇâbhigama**, m. approach or beginning of the hot season, L. **Ushṇâbhiprāya**, mfn. tending to heat (as a fever), Car.; °*prāyin*, mfn. suffering from the above fever, ib. **Ushṇâsaha**, m. (scil. *kāla*) 'the time in which heat is tolerable,' the winter, L. **Ushṇôdaka**, n. hot water, water boiled and so reduced in quantity (said to be wholesome to drink and healing when used for bathing), Bhpr. **Ushṇôpagama**, m. the beginning of the hot season, L. **Ushṇôshṇa**, mfn. very hot, Śiś. v, 45.

Ushṇaka, mfn. hot, warm; sick of fever, feverish, L.; sharp, smart, active, L.; warming, heating, L.; (*as*), m. heat, hot season (June and July), L.; fever, L.; blight, blast, L.; the betel-nut, Nigh.

Ushṇaya, Nom. P. *ushṇayati*, to make hot, heat.

Ushṇālu, mfn. suffering from heat, Kāty. on Pāṇ. v, 2, 122; Vikr.

Ushṇi, mfn. burning; see *ā́sny-ushṇi*, p. 114, col. 1.

Ushṇikā, f. (Pāṇ. v, 2, 71) rice-broth, L.

Ushṇiman, *ā*, m. heat, ChUp.

Ushṇī (in comp. for *ushṇa*). — √**kṛi**, to make warm or hot, heat, Suśr.; Mṛicch. — **kṛita**, mfn. heated, hot, boiled, Subh. — **gaṅga**, n., N. of a Tīrtha, MBh. iii, 10698. — **nābha**, m., N. of a divine being, MBh.

Ushṇīsha, *as, am*, m. n. (*ushṇam īshate hinasti*, *śakandhv-ādi* [Vārtt. on Pāṇ. vi, 1, 94] *para-rūpam*, T.) anything wound round the head, turban, fillet, AV. xv, 2, 1–4; ŚBr.; ĀśvŚr.; KātyŚr.; MBh. &c.; a diadem, crown, L.; a kind of excrescence on the head of Buddha. — **paṭṭa**, m. a turban, fillet, Ratnāv. — **bhājaná**, n. anything serving for a turban, ŚBr. iii. **Ushṇīshârpaṇā**, f., N. of a goddess (Buddh.)

Ushṇīshin, mfn. furnished with or wearing a turban, VS. xvi, 22; R.; N. of Śiva, MBh. xiii.

1. **Ushma**, *as*, m. heat, L.; the hot season, L.; spring, L.; passion, anger, L.; ardour, eagerness, L.

2. **Ushma** (in comp. for *ushman* below). — **ja**, mfn. produced from vapour. — **tā**, f. heat, MBh. — **pa**, see *ūshma-pa*. — **vat**, mfn. heated, burning, smoking, Suśr. — **sveda**, m. a vapour bath, Suśr. **Ushmâgama**, m. beginning of the hot season, L. **Ushmânvita**, mfn. filled with rage, L. **Ushmâyaṇa**, n. the hot season. **Ushmôpagama**, m. beginning of the hot season, L.

Ushmaka, m. the hot season, L.

Ushman, *ā*, m. heat, ardour, steam, Mn.; MBh.; Suśr. &c. (in many cases, where the initial *u* is combined with a preceding *a*, not to be distinguished from *ūshmán*, q. v.); the hot season, L.; anger, wrath, L.

Ushmāya, Nom. Ā. *ushmāyate*, = *ūshmāya*, q. v.

उष 2. *usha* (for 1. see col. 1), *as*, m. (probably for *uśa*, fr. √*vaś*; cf. *uśa-dah*), a lover, L.

उषस्त *ushastá*, *as*, m., N. of a Ṛishi, ŚBr.

Ushasti, *is*, m. id., ChUp.

उषिज *ushija*, *as*, m., N. of a son of Ūru, VP.

उषित 2. *ushita* (for 1. see col. 1), mfn., p. of √5. *vas*, q. v.

Ushitavya, ushitvā, ushṭvā. See √5. *vas*.

उषीर *ushīra*, v. l. for *uśīra*, q. v.

उष्ट्र *ushṭrí* (RV.) and *úshṭri*, *ṭā*, m. (probably fr. √*uksh* and connected with *ukshán*), a bull drawing a plough, RV. x, 106, 2; TS. v; KātyŚr.; Kauś.

U'shṭra, *as*, m. (√*ush*, Uṇ. iv, 161; but probably connected with the above), a buffalo, RV.; AV. xx, 127, 2; 132, 13; VS.; ŚBr.; AitBr.; a camel, MBh.; Mn.; Pañcat. &c.; a cart, waggon, L.; N. of an Asura, Hariv.; (*ī*), f. a she-camel, Suśr.; Pañcat. &c.; an earthen vessel in the shape of a camel, L.; N. of a plant, Nigh. — **karṇika**, *ās*, m. pl., N. of a people, MBh. — **kāṇḍī**, f. Echinops Echinatus, L. — **krośin**, mfn. making a noise like a camel, Kāś. on Pāṇ. iii, 2, 79. — **khara**, n. camel and donkey, gaṇa *gavâśvâdi*, Pāṇ. ii, 4, 11. — **grīva**, m. hemorrhoids, Suśr. — **jihva**, m., N. of a being attending on Skanda, MBh. — **tva**, n. the state of being a camel, Hcat. — **dhūsara-pucchikā** or °**cchī**, f. the plant Tragia Involucrata, L. — **nishadana**, n. a particular posture among Yogins, Sarvad. — **pādikā**, f. Jasminum Sambac, L. — **pāla**, m. a driver of camels, L. — **bhakshā** or °**kshikā**, f., N. of a plant, L. — **yāna**, n. a camel-carriage, vehicle drawn by camels, L. — **vāmi**, n. (?), Kāś. on Pāṇ. vi, 2, 40. — **vāmī-śata**, n. a hundred of camels and mares, Ragh. v, 32. — **vāhin**, mfn. drawn by camels (as a car). — **śaśa**, n. camel and hare, Pāṇ. ii, 4, 11. — **śirodhara**, n. hemorrhoids. — **sādi**, n. (?), Kāś. on Pāṇ. vi, 2, 40. — **sthāna**, n. a stable for camels; (mfn.) born in a stable for camels, Comm. on Pāṇ. iv, 3, 35. **Ushṭrâkṛiti**, m. 'having the shape of a camel,' the fabulous animal called Śarabha, L. **Ushṭrâksha**, m. 'camel-eyed,' N. of a man.

Ushṭrikā, f. a she-camel, Pañcat.; an earthen vessel shaped like a camel, L.; N. of a plant, L.

उष्णिह् *ushṇíh*, *k*, f. (fr. √*snih* with *ud*, Kāś. on Pāṇ. iii, 2, 59), N. of a Vedic metre (consisting of twenty-eight syllabic instants, viz. two Pādas with eight instants, and one with twelve; the varieties depend on the place of the twelve-syllabled Pāda), RPrāt. 888 ff.; AV. xix, 21, 1; VS.; a brick sacred to the above metre, KātyŚr.; N. of one of the Sun's horses, VP.

Ushṇig (in comp. for *ushṇih* above). — **garbhā**, f. (with *gāyatrī*) N. of a Vedic metre (consisting of three Pādas of six, seven, and eleven instants), RPrāt. 887.

Ushṇíhā, f. the Ushṇih metre, RV. x, 130, 4; VS.; (*ās*), f. pl. the nape of the neck, RV. x, 163, 2; AV.

उष्य *ushya*. See √5. *vas*.

उष्यल *úshyala*, *am*, n. a frame of a bed [BRD.], AV. xiv, 1, 60.

उस्र् *usrí*, f. (√2. *vas*), morning light, daybreak, day (acc. pl. *usrás*), RV. vii, 15, 8; viii, 41, 3; (instr. *usrā́*), RV. iv, 45, 5.

Usrá, *ā*, f. (Uṇ. ii, 13) morning light, daybreak, brightness, RV.; (personified as a red cow); a cow, RV.; AV. xii, 3, 73; MBh. xiii; Nir. &c.; N. of a plant, L.; (*as*), m. a ray of light, RV. i, 87, 1; Ragh.; Kir. &c.; the sun; day; an ox, bull, RV. vi, 12, 4; VS. iv, 33; N. of the Aśvins, RV. ii, 39, 3; iv, 62, 1; vii, 74, 1. — **yāman**, mfn. moving towards brightness or the day, RV. vii, 74, 1.

U'sri, *is*, f. morning light, brightness, RV. ix, 65, 1; 67, 9.

Usriká, *as*, m. a small ox, RV. i, 190, 5.

Usríya, mfn. reddish, bright (said of a cow and bull), RV.; (*as*), m. a bull, RV.; (*ā*), f. light, brightness; a cow, RV.; AV.; any product of the cow (as milk), RV.; AV. **Usriyā-tvá**, n. the state of being a cow, MaitrS.

Usrīya, Nom. P. *usrīyati*, to wish for a cow, Comm. on Pāṇ. vi, 1, 95.

उह् *uh*, cl. 1. P. *ohati, uvoha, auhīt*, &c., to give pain, hurt, kill, L.; (cf. 1. *ūh*.)

उहान *uhāna, as*, m., N. of a country, L.

उहुवायिवासिष्ठ *uhuvāyi-vāsishṭha, am*, n., N. of a Sāman.

उहू *uhū́*, mfn. (√*vah*), bearing, carrying, RV. iv, 45, 4.

Uhyamāna. See √*vah*.

Uhra, *as*, m. a bull, L.

उह्यगान *uhya-gāna*, v.l. for *ūhya-gāna*, q. v.

ऊ Ū.

ऊ 1. *ū*, the sixth letter of the alphabet (corresponding to *u* long, and having the sound of that letter in the word *rule*). **–kāra, -varṇa,** m. the letter or sound *ū*, TPrāt.; VPrāt. **–bhāva,** m. the becoming *ū*, TPrāt.

ऊ 2. *ū*, ind. an interjection of calling to; of compassion; a particle implying promise to protect, L.; a particle used at the beginning of a sentence.

ऊ 3. *ū*, mfn. (√*av*, Pāṇ. vi, 4, 20), helping, protecting, L.; (*ūs*), m. the moon, L.; N. of Śiva, L.

1. **Ūta,** mfn. (p. p. of √*av*, q. v.) favoured; loved; promoted, helped; protected.

1. **Ūtí,** *is*, f. help, protection, promoting, refreshing favour; kindness, refreshment, RV.; AV.; means of helping or promoting or refreshing, goods, riches (also plur.), RV.; AV.; ŚBr. xii; enjoyment, play, dalliance, BhP. viii, 5, 44; = *ksharaṇa*, T. **–matī,** f. (scil. *ṛic*) N. of a Ṛic (RV. i, 30, 7) which contains the word *ūti*, MaitrS.

Ū'ma, *as*, m. (Uṇ. i, 143) a helper, friend, companion, RV.; AV. v, 2, 1; 3; AitBr.; ŚāṅkhŚr.; (*am*), n., N. of a town or place, Comm. on Uṇ.; Siddh.

ऊ 4. *ū*, mfn. (√*ve*, Vop. xxvi, 73), weaving, sewing.

2. **Ūta,** mfn. (p. p. of √*ve*, q. v.) woven, sewed.

2. **Ūti,** *is*, f. the act of weaving, sewing, L.; red texture; tissue, BhP. ii, 10, 1; a mole's hole, TBr. i, 1, 3, 3.

ऊँ *ūṃ*, a mode of designating 3. *u* (q. v.) in the Pada-pāṭha followed by *iti*.

ऊखर *ūkhara, ās*, m. pl., N. of a Śaiva sect.

ऊठ् *ūṭh, ūṭhati*, = *uṭh*, q. v.

ऊढ 1. *ūḍha* (for 2. and 3. see 1. and 2. *uh*), mfn., p. p. of √*vah*, q. v.; (*ā*), f. a married woman, wife; (cf. *an-ūḍhā*.)

Ūḍhi, *is*, f. the act of bearing, carrying, Rājat.

ऊणि *ūṇí, is*, f. a particular Soma vessel, TS. i, 2, 6; (cf. *oṇi*.)

ऊणीतेजस् *ūṇī-tejas, ās*, m. (etym. doubtful), N. of a Buddha, L.

ऊति 3. *ūti, is*, m. (for 1. and 2. see 3. and 4. *ū* above), N. of a Daitya, SkandaP.

ऊतीक *ūtīka, as*, m., N. of a plant which can be substituted for the Soma (cf. *pūtīka*), Kāṭh.; TāṇḍyaBr.

ऊदक *ūdaka*. See *an-ūdaka*.

ऊदल *ūdala, am*, n., N. of a Sāman, Lāṭy.

ऊधस् *ū́dhas*, (in Veda also) *ū́dhan, ū́dhar* (see Whitney's Gr. 430 b; in classical Sanskrit the stem *ūdhan* appears only in the fem. of an adj. compound, e.g. *kuṇḍódhnī* &c.), *as, ar*, n. (√*vah*, Comm. on Uṇ. iv, 192; √*ud*, T.) the udder of any female, breast, bosom, RV.; AV.; ŚBr.; MBh. &c.; figuratively applied to the clouds, RV.; the night, Nir.; N. of a passage in the Mahānāmnī (q. v.) verses, Lāṭy.; [cf. Gk. οὖθαρ; Lat. *über*; Angl.Sax. *úder*; Old High Germ. *ūtar*; Mod. Germ. *Euter*; Mod. Eng. *udder*; Gaël. *uth*.] **–vatī,** f. (a female) with full udders, BhP.

Ūdhanyà, mfn. (Pāṇ. v, 1, 2) contained in or coming from the udder, MaitrS.; Kāṭh.

Ūdhasya, mf(*ā*)n. milking, giving milk, Hcat.; coming from the udder; (*am*), n. milk, Ragh.

ऊन *ūná*, mfn. (√*av*, Uṇ. iii, 2; ? cf. Zd. *ūna*), wanting, deficient, defective, short of the right quantity, less than the right number, not sufficient; less (in number, size, or degree), minus, fewer, smaller, inferior, AV. x, 8, 15; 44; xii, 1, 61; TS.; ŚBr.; Mn.; Ragh. &c.; less than (with abl., e. g. *lakshād ūna*, less than a Laksha, Kathās. liii, 10; or ifc., e. g. *tad-ūna*, inferior to that one, Mn. ix, 123), less by (with instr., e. g. *dvābhyām ūna*, less by two, ŚBr. xi; or ifc., e. g. *alpôna*, less by a little, a little less, Mn.; *pañcôna*, less by five &c.); less by one (prefixed to decimals from twenty up to one hundred, e.g. *ūna-viṇśa* = *ekôna-viṇśa*, the twentieth minus one, the nineteenth). **–koṭi-liṅga,** n., N. of a Liṅga. **–tā,** f., **-tva,** n. deficiency, inferiority, Hcat. **–rātra,** m., **-rātri,** f. 'defective by a night,' a N. applied to a particular lunar day (which is omitted if two lunar days end in one solar day), Sūryas. i, 40; 50; VarBṛS. **Ūnâkshara,** mfn. defective by a syllable, Lāṭy. **Ūnâtiriktá,** mfn. too little or too much, VS.

Ūnaka, mfn. not sufficient, defective, less, inferior, ŚāṅkhŚr.

Ūnaya, Nom. P. *ūnayati* (aor. Subj. 2. sg. *ūnayīs*) to leave deficient, not to fulfil, RV. i, 53, 3; to deduct or lessen, Pāṇ.; Vop. &c.

Ūnita, mfn. lessened, reduced, fewer, less by (with instr.)

Ūnī-√kṛi, to reduce or lessen by subtraction, subtract, Comm. on Sūryas.

ऊबध्य *ū́badhya* or *ū́vadhya, am*, n. (etym. doubtful) undigested grass &c. in the stomach or bowels (of an animal killed for sacrifice), RV. i, 162, 10; AV.; TS.; ŚBr.; KātyŚr. &c. **–gohá,** m. any hole in the ground where the above is concealed, MaitrS.; AitBr. ii, 6, 16; ĀśvŚr. & Gṛ. &c.

ऊम् *ūm*, ind. an interjection of anger, L.; of reproach, L.; of envy, L.; a particle of interrogation, L.

ऊम *ū́ma*. See 3. *ū*.

ऊय् *ūy*, cl. 1. Ā. *ūyate, ūyām-āsa, ūyitā, ūyishyate, ūyishṭa*, to weave, sew, = *ve*, q. v., Dhātup. xiv, 2.

ऊररी *ūrarī*, ind. = *urarī*, q. v., L.

Ūrī, ind. = *urī*, q. v., Śiś. **Ūry-ādi,** m., N. of a gaṇa, Pāṇ. i, 4, 61.

ऊरु *ūrú, us*, m. [the f. may be *ū* at the end of compounds in comparison, Pāṇ. iv, 1, 69], (fr. √*ūrṇu*, Uṇ. i, 31) the thigh, shank, RV.; AV.; VS.; TS.; ŚBr.; MBh.; Mn. &c.; N. of an Āṅgirasa and author of a Vedic hymn; N. of a son of Manu Cākshusha. **–graha,** m. paralysis of the thigh, Car. **–°grahin,** mfn. suffering from the above, ib. **–glāni,** f. weakness of the thigh. **–ja,** mfn. born from the thigh, MBh.; (*as*), m. a Vaiśya (supposed to be born from Brahmā's thigh, see RV. x, 90, 12; Mn. i, 31, &c.), L.; N. of the Ṛishi Aurva (q.v.) **–janman,** m. 'born from the thigh,' N. of Aurva (q.v.), Mālav. **–daghná,** mf(*ī*)n. reaching to the thighs, ŚBr. xii, xiii. **–dvayasa,** mf(*ī*)n. id., Kāś. on Pāṇ. iv, 1, 15. **–parvan,** m. n. joint of the thigh, knee, L. **–phalaka,** n. the thigh-bone, hip-bone, Yājñ. iii, 87. **–bhinna,** mf(*ī*)n. having a rent in the thigh, Kāś. on Pāṇ. iv, 1, 52. **–mātra,** mf(*ī*)n. reaching to the thigh, Kāś. on Pāṇ. iv, 1, 15. **–shkambha,** m. paralysis of the thigh, Car. **–sāda,** m. weakness of the thigh, ib. **–skambhá,** m. paralysis of the thigh; *-grihīta*, mfn. afflicted by the above, MaitrS. **–stambha,** m. paralysis of the thigh, Suśr.; Kathās.; (*ā*), f. the plantain tree, L. **Ūrūdbhava,** mfn. sprung from the thigh. **Ūrû-papīḍam,** ind. pressing upon the thigh, Daś. **Ūrv-aṅga,** n. 'having a thigh-like body,' fungus, mushroom, L. **Ūrv-ashṭhīvá,** n. sg. (Pāṇ. v, 4, 77), *é*, n. du. (VS. xviii, 23), *ā́ni*, n. pl. (ŚBr. viii) thigh and knee. **Ūrv-asthá,** n. thigh-bone, ŚBr. viii; *-mātrá*, mf(*ī*)n. reaching to the thigh-bone, ib.

Ūravya, *as*, m. 'born from the thigh (of Brahmā),' a Vaiśya (see *ūru-ja*), L.

1. **Ūrva** (for 2. see s. v.), *as*, m., N. of the Ṛishi Aurva (from whose thigh sprang the submarine fire which is also called Aurva, q.v.), TāṇḍyaBr.; MBh.; Hariv. &c.; the submarine fire [Sāy.], RV.

Ūrvī, f. the middle of the thigh, Suśr.

Ūrvyá, mfn. (fr. 1. *ūrva*?), being in the submarine fire [Mahīdhara], VS. xvi, 45.

ऊरुरी *ūrurī*, ind. = *urarī*, q. v.

ऊर्ज् 1. *ūrj* (connected with √*vṛij*), Caus. P. *ūrjayati* (p. *ūrjáyat*), to strengthen, invigorate, refresh, RV.; ŚBr.: Ā. *ūrjayate* (p. *ūrjáyamāna*), to be strong or powerful, be happy, RV. x, 37, 11; VS.; ĀśvŚr.; ŚāṅkhŚr.; to live, L.; [cf. Gk. ὀργάω; Lat. *urge-o*; Goth. *vrik-a*; Lith. *verz-iù*.]

2. **Ū'rj,** *k*, f. strength, vigour; sap, juice; food, refreshment, RV.; AV.; VS.; ŚBr.; BhP. &c.

Ūrjá, mfn. strong, powerful, eminent, BhP.; Śiś.; invigorating, strengthening; (*as*), m., N. of a month (= *kārttika*), TS. i; VS.; ŚBr.; Suśr. i, 19, 9; BhP. &c.; power, strength, vigour, sap, MBh.; Mn. ii, 55; BhP. &c.; life, breath, L.; effort, exertion, L.; N. of several men; (*ā*), f. strength, vigour, sap, RV. x, 76, 1; AV.; SV.; Suśr. &c.; N. of a daughter of Daksha and wife of Vasishṭha, VP.; BhP.; (*am*), n. water, L. **–medha,** mfn. of eminent intelligence, very wise, Hcat. **–yoni,** m., N. of a son of Viśvāmitra, MBh. **–vaha** and **-vāha,** m., N. of a king, VP. **–sani** (voc.), mfn. granting strength, N. of Agni, RV. vi, 4, 4. **–stambha,** m., N. of a Ṛishi in the second Manv-antara, BhP. **Ūrjâd** (3), mfn. consuming food, RV. x, 53, 4. **Ūrjā-vat,** mfn. powerful, strong, PārGṛ. i, 15, 6; MBh. **Ūrjā́huti,** mfn. worshipped with strengthening sacrifices, RV. viii, 39, 4; VS.

Ūrjayat, mfn. pres. p. of √*ūrj*, q. v.; (*an*), m., N. of a teacher, VBr.

Ūrjavyà, mfn. abounding in strength, sappy, strengthening, RV. v, 41, 20.

Ūrjas, *as*, n. vigour, strength, power, Sāh. **–kara,** mfn. causing strength, MBh. **–vat** (*ū́rjas°*), mfn. sappy, juicy, vigorous, RV.; AV.; ŚBr.; AitBr. &c.; powerful, strong, BhP.; (*tī*), f., N. of several women. **–vala,** mfn. powerful, strong, mighty, Pāṇ. v, 2, 114; Ragh. &c.; (*as*), m., N. of a Ṛishi in the second Manv-antara, VP. **–vin,** mfn. powerful, strong, mighty, Pāṇ. v, 2, 114; MBh. &c.; violent; (*inī*), f. (in rhet.) description of violence.

Ūrjā́nī, f. strength personified [BRD.; *sūryasya duhitri*, Sāy.], RV. i, 119, 2.

Ūrjita, mfn. endowed with strength or power, strong, mighty, powerful, excellent, great, important, gallant, exceeding, MBh.; Bhag.; Ragh.; Hit. &c.; proud, bragging; (*am*), n. strength, power, valour; (*am*), ind. excellently. **–citta,** mfn. of powerful mind, MBh. **Ūrjitâśraya,** m. an abode of bravery, a hero, Kirāt.

Ūrjin, mfn. possessing food or strength, faithful.

ऊर्णु *ūrṇu* (connected with √1. *vṛi*), cl. 2. P. Ā. *ūrṇoti* and *ūrṇauti* (Pāṇ. vii, 3, 90), *ūrṇute, aurṇot* (Pāṇ. vii, 3, 91; AV.), *ūrṇunāva, ūrṇunuve, ūrṇavitā*, and *ūrṇuvitā* (Pāṇ. i, 2, 3), *ūrṇuvishyati, -te, aurṇavīt, aurṇāvīt*, and *aurṇuvīt* (Pāṇ. vii, 2, 6), *aurṇavishṭa*, to cover, invest, hide, surround, AV. vii, 1, 2; x, 2, 18; xviii, 4, 59; Bhaṭṭ.: Ā. to cover one's self, BhP.: Desid. P. *ūrṇunūshati, ūrṇunavishati, ūrṇunuvishati*, Pāṇ. vii, 2, 49; Vop.: Intens. Ā. *ūrṇonūyate*, Pat.

Ūrṇa, *am*, n. (in some compounds = *ū́rṇā* below) wool; (*as*), m., N. of a Yaksha, BhP. **–nābha,** m. 'having wool on the navel,' a spider, ŚvetUp. &c.; a particular position of the hands; N. of a son of Dhṛita-rāshṭra, MBh.; of a Dānava, Hariv.; (*ās*), m. pl., N. of a people, gaṇa *rājanyâdi*, Pāṇ. iv, 2, 53. **–nā́bhi,** m. a spider (see above), TBr.; BṛĀr-Up.; BhP. &c. **–nābhī,** f. id. **–paṭa,** m. 'having a woollen covering,' a spider, BhP. **–mradas** (*ū́rṇa°*), mfn. soft as wool, RV. v, 5, 4; x, 18, 10; AV. xviii, 3, 49; VS. **–vā́bhi,** m. (fr. an obsolete √*vabh* [= Gk. ὑφ-αίνω; Old High Germ. *web-an*, 'to weave'], Aufrecht) a spider (= *ūrṇa-nābhi*, Sāy.), ŚBr. xiv, 5, 1, 23.

Ū'rṇā (less correctly spelt *urṇā*), f. (Uṇ. v, 47) wool, a woollen thread, thread, RV. iv, 22, 2; v, 52, 9; ŚBr.; KātyŚr.; Mn. &c.; cobweb, BhP.; a circle of hair between the eyebrows, Kād.; Lalit.; N. of several women; [cf. *ūraṇa, úrā, ura-bhra*; also Gk. ἔρ-ι-ον; Lat. *vell-us, vill-us*; Lith. *vilna*; Goth. *vulla* (for *vulna*); Russ. *volna*; Mod. Germ. *Wolle*; Eng. *wool*.] **–piṇḍa,** m. a ball of wool. **–maya,** mfn. made of wool, woollen, Kum.

vii, 25. **-vat**, mfn. abounding in wool, having wool, woolly, RV. vi, 15, 16; x, 75, 8; (*ān*), m. a spider, ŚāṅkhBr.; N. of a man, Pāṇ. v, 3, 118; (*atī*), f. a ewe, RV. viii, 56, 3. **-valá**, mfn. having wool, woolly, ŚBr. vii. **-sūtrá**, n. a thread of wool, VS.; ŚBr. &c. **-stukā**, f. a tuft of wool, AitBr.; ĀśvGṛ. &c. **Ūrṇôdara**, m., N. of a teacher.

Ūrṇuta, mfn. covered, invested, Vop.; Kāś.

ऊर्द् *ūrd* or *urd*, cl. 1. Ā. *ūrdate*, *ūrdām-cakre*, *ūrditā*, *ūrdishyate*, *aurdishṭa*, Dhātup. ii, 19, to measure, L.; to play, be cheerful, L.; to taste, L.

Ūrda, mf(*ī*)n. sportful, cheerful [T.], gaṇa *gaurâdi*, Pāṇ. iv, 1, 42; (v.l. *kūrda*, Kāś.)

ऊर्दर *ū́rdara*, *as*, m. (etym. doubtful; fr. √*dṛī* with *ūrj*, Uṇ. v, 40) a granary [Sāy.], RV. ii, 14, 11; a hero, Comm. on Uṇ.; a Rakshas, ib.

ऊर्ध *ūrdha*, *ūrdhaka*, an incorrect spelling for *ūrdhva*, *ūrdhvaka* below.

ऊर्ध्व *ūrdhvá*, mf(*ā*)n. (√*vridh*, BRD.; perhaps fr. √*ṛi*), rising or tending upwards, raised, elevated, erected, erect, upright, high, above, RV.; AV.; VS.; ŚBr.; AitBr. &c. (in class. Sanskṛit occurring generally in compounds); (*am*), n. height, elevation, L.; anything placed above or higher (with abl.), L.; (*am*), ind. upwards, towards the upper part, aloft, above, in the upper regions, higher (with abl.), AV. xi, 1, 9; ŚBr. xii; KātyŚr.; MBh.; Mn. &c.; (*ūrdhvam* √*gam*, to go upwards or into heaven, die); in the sequel, in the later part (e.g. of a book or MS.; because in Sanskṛit MSS. the later leaves stand above), subsequent, after (with abl.), ŚBr.; ŚāṅkhŚr.; Suśr.; Mn. &c.; (*ata ūrdhvam* or *ita ūrdhvam*, henceforward, from that time forward, after that passage, hereafter, ŚBr.; ŚāṅkhŚr.; Yājñ. &c.; *ūrdhvam saṃvatsarāt*, after a year, Mn. ix, 77; *ūrdhvaṃ dehāt*, after life, after death, MBh. i, 3606); after, after the death of (with abl., e.g. *ūrdhvaṃ pituḥ*, after the father's death, Mn. ix, 104); in a high tone, aloud, BhP.; [cf. Gk. ὀρθός; Lat. *arduus*; Gaël. *ard.*] **-kaca**, m. 'having the hair raised,' the descending node, L. **-kaṇṭha**, *ās*, m. pl., N. of a people, VBṛS.; (*ā*), f. a species of asparagus, L. **-kaṇṭhaka**, m., N. of a plant; (*ā*), f. a species of asparagus, L. **-kapāla**, mf(*ā*)n. having a lid or cover (as a vessel), MaitrS. i, 8, 3; KātyŚr. iv, 14, 1. **-kara**, m. an upper hand (of Vishṇu), Hcat.; (mfn.) having the hands raised upwards (and also casting rays of light upwards), Ratnāv. **-karṇa**, mfn. having the ears erect, Śak. 8 b; N. of a place. **-karman**, n. motion or action tending upwards, Pāṇ. i, 3, 24; (mfn.) one whose actions tend upwards, L.; (*ā*), m., N. of Vishṇu, L. **-kāya**, m. the upper part of the body, Naish. **-kṛita**, mfn. turned or directed upwards, Kathās. **-kṛiśana** (*ūrdhvá°*), mfn. (a beverage) whose pungent or strong part is on the surface (said of the Soma), RV. x, 144, 2; (or N. of a Ṛishi, Sāy.) **-ketu**, m., N. of a man, BhP. **-keśa**, mfn. having the hair erect; (*as*), m., N. of a man; (*ī*), f., N. of a goddess. **-kriyā**, f. motion or action tending upwards. **-ga**, mfn. going upwards, ascending, hovering, MBh.; Suśr. &c.; being above, high; (*as*), m., N. of a son of Kṛishṇa, BhP.; *-pura*, n. the city of Hariścandra (who with his subjects is supposed to be suspended in the atmosphere), W.; *°âtman*, m. 'one whose soul tends upwards,' N. of Śiva, MBh. **-gati**, f. the act of going or tending upwards, Suśr.; the act of skipping, bounding, Pañcat.; (mfn.) going or tending upwards, reaching the heaven, MBh.; R. &c.; (*is*), m. fire, L. **-gamana**, n. the act of going or tending upwards or to the heaven, Naish.; rising (of a star), Vop.; rising (of the voice), VPrāt.; rising, promotion, Tattvas.; *-vat*, mfn. moving or tending upwards, Vedāntas. **-gāmin**, mfn. going or tending upwards, Suśr. **-guda**, m. a particular disease in the mouth, ŚārṅgS. **-grāvan** (*ūrdhvá°*), mfn. one who has raised the stone for pressing the Soma, RV. iii, 54, 12; (*ā*), m., N. of a Ṛishi, RAnukr. **-caraṇa**, mfn. having the feet upwards; (*as*), m. a kind of ascetic or devotee, T.; N. of the fabulous animal Śarabha (which has four of its eight feet upwards), T. **-cít**, mfn. heaping or piling up, VS. **-ja**, mfn. being higher, upper, Suśr. i, 82, 8. **-jatru**, mfn. being above the collar-bone, ib. **-jānu**, **-jānuka**, mfn. raising the knees (in sitting), ŚāṅkhŚr. **-jña** (L.) and **jñu** (*ūrdhvá°*), mfn. (Pāṇ. v, 4, 130), id., MaitrS.; AitĀr. &c. **-jyotis**, mfn. one whose light tends upwards, MaitrS. **-°m-jānu**, mfn. being above the knee, SāmavBr. **-taraṇa**, n. breaking out, overflowing (of a river), VarBṛS. **-tas**, ind. upwards, Hcat. **-tā**, f. = *-tva* below. **-tāla**, m. a kind of time (in music). **-tilaka**, n. an upright or perpendicular sectarian mark on the forehead. **-°tilakin**, mfn. having the above mark. **-tva**, n. height, elevation. **-daṇshṭra-keśa**, m. 'one whose teeth and hair are erect,' N. of Śiva, MBh. **-diś**, f. the point of the sky overhead, the region above, zenith, L. **-dṛiś**, mfn. looking or seeing upwards, Kathās.; (*k*), m. a crab, L. **-drishṭi**, f. a glance or look upwards; (mfn.) looking upwards. **-deva**, m., N. of Vishṇu, L. **-deha**, m. a body gone above or into heaven, a deceased one, R.; (cf. *aurdhvadehika.*) **-dvāra**, n. the gate opening into heaven, AmṛitUp. **-nabhas**, mfn. being above the clouds, VS. vi, 16. **-nayana**, mfn. having eyes turned upwards; N. of the fabulous animal Śarabha, L. **-nāla**, mfn. with upraised stalk. **-°m-dama**, mfn. erect, raised, Pat. on Pāṇ. iv, 3, 60; (cf. *aurdhvaṃdamika.*) **-patha**, m. 'the upper path,' the ether, R. **-pavitra**, mfn. pure above, TUp. **-pāṭha**, m. that which will be read (or is told) further on, Comm. on TĀr. **-pātana**, n. the act of causing (mercury) to rise, sublimation (of mercury), Bhpr.; *-yantra*, n. an apparatus for sublimation (of mercury). **-pātra**, n. the lid of a vessel, HirGṛ.; Yājñ. i, 182; Hcat. **-pāda**, m. the top of the foot, Hcat.; (mfn.) having the feet upward, R.; (*as*), m. the fabulous animal Śarabha (see *-caraṇa* above). **-puṇḍra** or **-puṇḍraka**, n. = *-tilaka* above. **-pūram**, ind. p. so as to become full to the brim, Pāṇ. iii, 4, 44. **-pṛiśni**, mfn. spotted above, VS.; MaitrS. **-pramāṇa**, n. height, altitude, Śulbas. **-barhis**, mfn. being over the sacrificial grass, VS. xxxviii, 15. **-bāhu**, mfn. having the arms lifted up, TS. v; ŚBr. v; KātyŚr.; BhP. &c.; a kind of ascetic or devotee; N. of several Ṛishis. **-budhna**, mfn. turned with the bottom upwards (as a vessel), AV. x, 8, 9; ŚBr. xiv. **-bṛihatī**, f., N. of a Vedic metre (three lines with twelve syllabic instants in each), RPrāt. 906. **-°bhaktika**, mfn. effective upwards, causing to come up, emetic, Car. **-bharam**, ind. carrying upwards, lifting up, TāṇḍyaBr. **-bhāga**, m. upper part, higher part, subsequent part, Hcat.; Comm on Pāṇ.; (mfn.) effective towards the upper part, emetic, Car. **-°bhāgika**, mfn. id., ib. **-bhāj**, mfn. tending upwards, MaitrUp.; MBh. iii (also N. of Agni); emetic, Car. **-bhās**, mfn. one whose splendour rises (see *anū°*). **-bhāsin**, mfn. flaming or radiating upwards, MBh. **-bhūmi**, f. upper floor or story, Pañcad. **-maṇḍalin**, m. a particular position of the hands in dancing. **-manthin**, mfn. 'keeping the semen (*manthin*) above,' abstaining from sexual intercourse, living in chastity, TĀr. ii, 7, 1; BhP. **-māna**, n. height, altitude. **-māyu**, mfn. giving forth a loud noise, AV. v, 20, 4. **-māruta**, n. pressure of the wind (of the body) upwards (so as to cause vomiting), Suśr. **-mukha**, mfn. having the mouth or opening turned upwards, turned upwards, Kum.; Ragh. &c. **-muṇḍa**, mfn. being bald above, having a bald crown (of the head), VP. **-muhūrta**, n. the immediately following moment. **-°mauhūrtika**, mfn. happening immediately afterwards or after a short interval, Pāṇ. **-°raktin**, mfn. one whose blood rises towards the head, Bhpr. **-rāji**, f. a line running from below upwards, Suśr. **-rekhā**, f. id., Ragh.; Pañcad.; Naish. **-retas** or **-reta** (TĀr. x, 12), mfn. keeping the semen above, living in chastity, Gaut.; MBh.; Hariv.; Kathās. &c.; (*ās*), m., N. of Śiva, MBh. xiii; of Bhīshma, L.; *-tīrtha*, n., N. of a Tīrtha. **-roman**, mfn. having the hair of the body erect, MBh.; BhP.; (*ā*), m., N. of a mountain, BhP. v, 20, 15. **-liṅga** and **°liṅgin**, mfn. having the membrum above (i.e. chaste); (*ī*), m., N. of Śiva, MBh.; Hcat. **-loka**, m. the upper world, world above, heaven. **-vaktra**, *ās*, m. pl. 'having the face above,' N. of a class of deities, VP. **-vayas**, n. of eminent vigour, MaitrS. **-vartman**, n. 'the path above,' the ether, W. **-vāc**, mfn. having a loud voice. **-vāta**, m. = *-māruta* above. **-vāla**, mfn. with the hair turned upwards or outwards, Gaut. xxiii, 18; PārGṛ. **-vāsya**, n. a particular dress of women, ĀpŚr. **-vṛita**, mfn. put on or wound round from below upwards (as the sacred thread), Mn. ii, 44. **-veṇī-dhara**, mfn. wearing the hair tied together on the crown, MBh.; (*ā*), f., N. of a woman in the retinue of Skanda. **-śāyin**, m. 'lying with the face upwards, supine,' N. of Śiva, MBh. iii. **-śocis**, mfn. one whose splendour rises upwards, flaming upwards (said of Agni), RV. vi, 15, 2. **-śodhana**, n. 'purifying or emptying upwards,' vomiting, W. **-śosham**, ind. p. so as to dry above, Pāṇ. iii, 4, 44; Bhaṭṭ. **-śvāsa**, m. 'breathing above,' shortness of breath, a kind of asthma, Suśr.; Bhpr. **-saṃhanana**, m. 'of tall and robust frame,' N. of Śiva, MBh. xiii. **-sad**, mfn. sitting or being above or on high, ĀpŚr. **-sadman**, m., N. of an Āṅgirasa. **-°sadmana**, n., N. of a Sāman composed by the above, TāṇḍyaBr.; (cf. the more correct form *aurdhva-sa°*.) **-sasya**, mf(*ā*)n. having high spikes of corn, MBh. **-sāná**, mfn. high, superior, victorious, RV. x, 99, 7. **-sānu**, mfn. having a high back (as a horse), high, surpassing, RV. i, 152, 5; having an elevated edge, ĀpŚr. **-stana**, mf(*ī*)n. high-breasted, Suśr. **-stoma**, mfn. celebrated with continually increasing Stomas (as a Daśa-rātra festival), ŚBr. xii; Vait. **-sthiti**, f. standing upright, rearing (of a horse); a horse's back; the place where the rider sits, W.; elevation, superiority, L. **-srotas**, n. 'having the current upwards,' N. of a particular creation, MārkP.; (*asas*), m. pl., N. of particular animals whose stream of life or nutriment tends upwards, MBh.; BhP.; VP. &c.; (*ās*), m. (= *ūrdhva-retas*), N. of Śiva, L.; a kind of Yogin, T. **-svapna**, mfn. sleeping upright (said of trees), AV. vi, 44, 1. **Ūrdhvâṅga**, n. the upper part of the body, i.e. the part above the collar-bone. **Ūrdhvâṅguli**, mfn. with raised fingers, MBh. **Ūrdhvâmnāya**, m. 'a subsequent or further sacred tradition,' N. of a sacred writing of the Śāktas; also of a certain Vaishṇava sect. **Ūrdhvâyana**, n. going or rising up, flying up, Naish.; (*ās*), m. pl., N. of the Vaiśyas in Plakshadvīpa, BhP. **Ūrdhvâroha**, m. rising upwards, Rājat. **Ūrdhvâvarta**, m. rearing of a horse, L. **Ūrdhvâsin**, eating upright, Sarvad. **Ūrdhvâsita**, m. Momordica Charantia. **Ūrdhvêḍa**, m., N. of a Sāman, TāṇḍyaBr. **Ūrdhvêha**, m. wish or effort to raise one's self, Vop. **Ūrdhvôcchvāsin**, mfn. breathing one's last, ŚBr. xiv.

Ūrdhvaka, mfn. raised, lifted up, SaṃnyUp.; (*as*), m. a kind of drum, Naish.

Ūrdhváthā, ind. upwards, erect, RV. x, 23, 1.

Ūrdhvāya, Nom. Ā. *ūrdhvāyate*, to rise, go upwards, Bhpr.

Ūrdhvī-√kṛi, P. to raise aloft, elevate.

ऊर्मि *ūrmí*, *is*, m. f. (√*ṛi*, Uṇ. iv, 44), a wave, billow, RV.; AV.; VS.; KātyŚr.; MBh.; Ragh. &c.; (figuratively) wave of pain or passion or grief &c., R.; Prab. &c.; 'the waves of existence' (six are enumerated, viz. cold and heat [of the body], greediness and illusion [of the mind], and hunger and thirst [of life], Subh.; or according to others, hunger, thirst, decay, death, grief, illusion, Comm. on VP.; W.); speed, velocity, TBr. ii, 5, 7, 1; Śiś. v, 4; symbolical expression for the number six, RāmatUp.; a fold or plait in a garment, L.; line, row, L.; missing, regretting, desire, L.; appearance, becoming manifest, L.; [cf. Lith. *vil-ni-s*; Old High Germ. *wella*; Mod. Germ. *Welle*; Engl. *well.*] **-mat**, mfn. wavy, undulating, billowy, R.; plaited, curled (as hair), MBh.; (*ān*), m. the ocean, MBh. i; crooked, L.; *-tā*, f. undulation; crookedness, L. **-mālā**, f. 'a garland of waves,' row of waves; N. of a metre (consisting of four lines of eleven syllables each), VarBṛS. **-°mālin**, mfn. wreathed with waves, having waves, MBh.; R.; (*ī*), m. the ocean, Ragh. v, 61. **-shaṭkâtiga**, mfn. one who has surpassed or overcome the six waves of existence, BrahmaP.

Ūrmikā, f. a wave, L.; a finger ring, Rājat.; a plait or fold in a garment, L.; humming (of bees), L.

Ūrmin, mfn. undulating, wavy, RV. ix, 98, 6; TS. i; MBh. &c.

Ū́rmya, mfn. undulating, wavy, VS. xvi, 31; (*ā*), f. night, RV.

ऊर्मिला *ūrmilā*, f., N. of several women, MBh.; Ragh. &c.

ऊर्व् *ūrv* or *urv*, cl. 1. P. *ūrvati*, *ūrvāṃcakāra*, &c., to kill, hurt, Dhātup. xv, 60.

ऊर्व 2. *ūrvá* (for 1. see p. 221, col. 2), mfn. (probably connected with *uru*), broad, extensive, great, excessive, much, RV.; (*as*), m. the ocean, RV.

ऊर्वरा *ūrvarā*, f., v.l. for *urvarā*, q.v.

ऊर्वशी *ūrvaśī*, f., v.l. for *urvaśī*, q.v.

ऊर्वष्ठीव *ūrv-ashṭhīvá*, &c. See under *ūrú*.

ऊर्वी *ūrvī*, &c. See p. 221, cols. 2 & 3.

ऊर्षा *ūrshā*, f. Andropogon Serratum, L.

ऊलुपिन् *ūlupin*, ऊलूक *ūlūka*, ऊवट *ūvaṭa*, vv.ll. for *ulupin*, *ulūka*, *uvaṭa*, qq. v.

ऊवध्य *ū́vadhya*. See *ū́badhya*.

ऊष् *ūsh*, cl. 1. P. *ūshati*, *ūshām-cakāra*, *ūshitā*, &c., to be sick or ill, Dhātup. xvii, 32.

ऊष *ū́sha*, *as*, m. (√*ush*, BRD.; √*ūsh*, T.), salt ground, soil impregnated with saline particles, TS.; AitBr. iv, 27, 9; ŚBr.; Mn. v, 120; Suśr. &c. (according to the Brāhmaṇas also 'cattle'); a cleft, hole, L.; the cavity of the ear, L.; the Malaya mountain, L.; dawn, daybreak, L. (in the latter sense also n., W.); (*ā* and *ī*), f. soil impregnated with saline particles, sterile soil, KātyŚr.; BhP.; (*ā*), f., N. of a daughter of Bāṇa and wife of Aniruddha (v.l. *ushā*, q.v.) **-puṭá**, m. a case of salt, pieces of salt put into a wrapper, MaitrS.; ŚBr.; KātyŚr. **-vat**, mfn. containing salt, consisting of saline soil, L. **-sikatá**, n. granular salt, ŚBr. vi; MānGṛ.

Ūshaka, *am*, n. salt or pepper, Suśr.; daybreak, dawn, L.

Ūshaṇa, *am*, n. black pepper, Suśr.; (*ā*), f. long pepper, Suśr.

Ūshará, mf(*ā*)n. impregnated with salt, containing salt; (*am*), n. saline soil, ŚBr.; KātyŚr.; MBh.; Mn. &c. **-ja**, n. a kind of fossil salt, L.

Ūsharāya, Nom. Ā. *ūsharāyate*, to become a saline or sterile soil, Pañcat.

ऊष्मन् *ūshmán*, *ā*, m. (√*ush*, cf. *ushman*), heat, glow, ardour, hot vapour, steam, vapour, AV. vi, 18, 3; VS.; ŚBr.; KātyŚr.; BhP. (also figuratively said of passion or of money &c.); the hot season, L.; (in Gr.) N. applied to certain sounds (viz. the three sibilants, *h*, Visarga, Jihvāmūlīya, Upadhmānīya, and Anusvāra), RPrāt. 11, &c.; APrāt.; VPrāt.; Kāś. &c. (the TPrāt. omits Visarga and Anusvāra).

Ūshmá (in comp. for *ūshmán* above). **-ja**, mfn. produced from vapour (as animals of low order), Kap. **-tva**, n. (in Gr.) the state of being an Ūshman (see above), Comm. on TPrāt. **-pa**, mfn. imbibing the steam of hot food, Kād.; (*as*), m. fire, BhP.; (*ās*), m. pl., N. of a class of manes, MBh.; Bhag.; Hariv. &c. **-para**, mfn. followed by an Ūshman sound, see above. **-pura**, n., N. of a Buddhist temple. **-prakṛiti**, mfn. produced from an Ūshman, RPrāt. 406. **-bhāga** (*ūshmá*°), mfn. one whose portion is vapour, TBr. i. **-vat**, mfn. hot, steaming, Suśr. **Ūshmânta**, mfn. ending in an Ūshman. **Ūshmântaḥstha**, *ās*, m. pl. the Ūshmans and the Antaḥsthas or semivowels. **Ūshmâpaha**, m. 'removing heat,' the winter, L. **Ūshmâyaṇa**, n. the hot season, L. **Ūshmôpagama**, m. the approach of the hot season, L.

Ūshmaka, *as*, m. the hot season, L.

Ūshmaṇyà, mfn. giving forth hot vapour, steaming, RV. i, 162, 13.

Ūshmā, f. vapour, steam, MBh. xiii.

Ūshmāya, Nom. Ā. *ūshmāyate*, to emit heat or hot vapour; to steam, Pāṇ. iii, 1, 16; Hcar. &c.

ऊह् 1. *ūh*, cl. 1. P. Ā. *ūhati*, *-te*, *ūhām-cakāra* and *-cakre*, *ūhitā*, *auhīt*, *auhishṭa* (connected with √*vah*, q.v., and in some forms not to be distinguished from it), to push, thrust, move, remove (only when compounded with prepositions); to change, alter, modify, ŚāṅkhŚr.; Comm. on Nyāyam.

2. **Ūḍha**, mfn. (for 1. see s.v. and √*vah*) pushed, thrust, moved; changed, modified.

1. **Ūha**, *as*, m. removing, derangement, transposition, change, modification, Lāṭy.; ŚāṅkhŚr.; Pat. &c.; adding, addition, Car. **-gāna**, n. and **-gīti**, f., N. of the third Gāna or hymn-book of the Sāma-veda. **-cchalā**, f., N. of a chapter of the Sāmaveda-cchalā.

1. **Ūhana**, *am*, n. transposition, change, modification, Nyāyam.; (*ī*), f. a broom, L.

1. **Ūhanīya**, mfn. to be changed or modified, Nyāyam.

Ūhita, mfn. changed, modified.

Ūhitavya, mfn. id., ib.; Comm. on Lāṭy.

Ūhinī, f. a broom, L.

1. **Ūhya**, mfn. to be changed or modified, Nyāyam. **-gāna**, n., N. of the fourth Gāna or hymn-book of the Sāma-veda. **-cchalā**, f., N. of a chapter of the Sāmaveda-cchalā.

ऊह् 2. *ūh*, cl. 1. P. Ā. *ūhati*, *-te* (Ved. *ohate*), *ūhām-cakāra*, &c. (by native authorities not distinguished from 1. *ūh* above), to observe, mark, note, attend to, heed, regard, RV.; AV. xx, 131, 10; to expect, hope for, wait for, listen for, RV.; to comprehend, conceive, conjecture, guess, suppose, infer, reason, deliberate upon, MBh.; BhP.; Nyāyam.; Bhaṭṭ. &c.: Caus. *ūhayati* (aor. *aujihat*), to consider, heed, MBh.; to cause to suppose or infer, Bhaṭṭ.

3. **Ūḍha**, mfn. concluded, inferred; (cf. *abhyūḍha*.)

2. **Ūha**, *as*, m. the act of comprehending, conceiving; consideration, deliberation, examination; supposition, conclusion, inference, MBh.; BhP.; Mn. &c.; (*ā*), f. id., L. **-vat**, mfn. comprehending easily, Gaut.; MBh.

2. **Ūhana**, *am*, n. deliberation, reasoning.

2. **Ūhanīya**, mfn. to be deliberated upon; to be inferred or concluded, Sarvad.

2. **Ūhya**, mfn. id., VarBṛS.

ऊहिवस् *ūhivas*, perf. p. of √*vah*, q.v.

ऋ ṚI.

ऋ 1. *ṛi*, the seventh vowel of the Sanskṛit alphabet and peculiar to it (resembling the sound of *ri* in *merrily*). **-kāra**, m. the letter or sound *ṛi*, TPrāt.; APrāt. &c. **-varṇa**, m. the sounds *ṛi*, *ṛī*, and pluta *ṛī*, APrāt. i, 37, &c. (see also Siddh. vol. i, p. 17).

ऋ 2. *ṛi*, ind. an interjection expressing laughter, L.; a particle implying abuse, L.; a sound inarticulate or reiterated as in stammering, W.

ऋ 3. *ṛi*, m. heaven, L.; f., N. of Aditi, L.

ऋ 4. *ṛi*, cl. 1. 3. 5. P. *ṛicchati*, *iyarti*, *ṛiṇoti*, and *ṛiṇvati* (only Ved.); *āra*, *arishyati*, *ārat*, and *ārshīt*, to go, move, rise, tend upwards, RV.; Nir. &c.; to go towards, meet with, fall upon or into, reach, obtain, RV.; AV.; ŚBr.; ChUp.; MBh. &c.; to fall to one's share, occur, befal (with acc.), RV.; AitBr.; ŚBr.; Mn. &c.; to advance towards a foe, attack, invade, ŚBr.; MBh.; Mn.; to hurt, offend, ŚBr. vii; to move, excite, erect, raise, (*iyarti vācam*, he raises his voice, RV. ii, 42, 2; *stómān iyarmi*, I sing hymns, RV. i, 116, 1), RV.; AV. vi, 22, 3: Caus. *arpayati*, to cause to move, throw, cast, AV. x, 9, 1; Ragh. &c.; to cast through, pierce, AV.; to put in or upon, place, insert, fix into or upon, fasten, RV.; Śak.; Kum.; Bhag. &c.; to place on, apply, Kathās.; Ratnāv.; Ragh. &c.; to direct or turn towards, R.; Bhag. &c.; to deliver up, surrender, offer, reach over, present, give, Yājñ.; Pañcat.; Vikr. &c.; to give back, restore, Mn. viii, 191; Yājñ.; Śak. &c.: Ved. Intens. *alarti*, RV. viii, 48, 8; (2. sg. *alarshi*, RV. viii, 1, 7; Pāṇ. vii, 4, 65); to move or go towards with speed or zeal: Class. Intens. Ā. *arāryate* (Pāṇ. vii, 4, 30), to wander about, haste towards, Bhaṭṭ.; Pat.; Kāś.; [cf. Gk. ὄρ-νυ-μι, ἐρ-έ-της, ἀρό-ω, &c.: Zend √*ir*: Lat. *or-ior*, *re-mus*, *aro*: Goth. *argan*: Angl. Sax. *ār*: Old High Germ. *ruo-dar*, *ar-an*: Lith. *ir-ti*, 'to row;' *ar-ti*, 'to plough.']

Árpita, mfn., see p. 92, col. 3.

Ṛitá, mf(*ā*)n. met with, afflicted by (with instr.), TS. v; proper, right, fit, apt, suitable, able, brave, honest, RV.; VS. xvii, 82; true, MBh.; BhP.; Mn. viii, 82; 87; Bhag. &c.; worshipped, respected, L.; enlightened, luminous, L.; (*as*), m., N. of a Rudra, MBh.; of a son of Manu Cākshusha, BhP. iv, 13, 16; of a son of Vijaya, VP.; (*am*), n. fixed or settled order, law, rule (esp. in religion); sacred or pious action or custom, divine law, faith, divine truth (these meanings are given by BRD. and are generally more to be accepted than those of native authorities and marked L. below), RV.; AV.; VS.; ŚBr. &c.; truth in general, righteousness, right, RV.; AV.; MBh.; Mn. viii, 61; 104; Pañcat. &c.; figuratively said of gleaning (as the right means of a Brāhman's obtaining a livelihood as opposed to agriculture, which is *anṛita*), Mn. iv, 4 ff.; promise, oath, vow, TāṇḍyaBr.; Lāṭy.; truth personified (as an object of worship, and hence enumerated among the sacred objects in the Nir.); water, L.; sacrifice, L.; a particular sacrifice, L.; the sun, L.; wealth, L.; (*ám*), ind. right, duly, properly, expressly, very, RV.; BhP.; (*ṛitam* √*i*, to go the right way, be pious or virtuous, RV.); (*éna*), ind. right, duly, properly, regularly, lawfully, according to usage or right, RV.; AV.; truly, sincerely, indeed, RV.; MBh. i. **-cít**, mfn. conversant with or knowing the sacred law or usage (at sacrifices &c.), RV. **-já**, mfn. 'truly-born,' of a true nature, RV. iv, 40, 5; well made, excellent, RV. iii, 58, 8. **-jāta**, mfn. of true nature; well made, proper, RV.; AV. v, 15, 1-11; xviii, 2, 15; *-satya* (*ṛitá-jāta-satya*), mfn. appearing at the proper time and true or constant (said of the Ushases), RV. iv, 51, 7. **-jít**, mfn. gaining the right [BRD.], VS. xvii, 83; (*t*), m., N. of a Yaksha, VP. **-júr**, mfn. grown old in (observance of the) divine law, RV. x, 143, 1. **-jña**, mfn. knowing or conversant with the sacred law or usage (at sacrifices &c.), RV.; AV. **-jya** (*ṛitá*°), mfn. one whose string is truth, truth-strung (said of Brahmaṇas-pati's bow), RV. ii, 24, 8. **-°m-jaya**, m., N. of a Vyāsa, VāyuP. **-dyumna** (voc.), mfn. brilliant or glorious through divine truth, RV. ix, 113, 4. **-dhāman** (*ṛitá*°), mfn. one whose abode is truth or divine law, abiding in truth, VS. v, 32; xviii, 38; (*ā*), m., N. of Vishṇu, R.; of a Manu, VP.; of Indra in the twelfth Manv-antara, BhP. **-dhī**, mfn. of right intelligence or knowledge, BhP. **-dhīti** (*ṛitá-dhīti*), mfn. worshipped with true devotion, praised or adored sincerely, RV. **-dhvaja**, m., N. of a Rudra, BhP.; of several men. **-ní** (Ved. for °*nī*), mfn. leader of truth or righteousness, RV. ii, 27, 12. **-nidhana**, n. 'having proper Nidhanas' (q.v.), N. of a Sāman, TāṇḍyaBr. **-parṇa**, m. = *ṛitu-parṇa*, q.v. **-pā́**, mfn. guarding divine truth, RV. **-pātra**, n. a properly adjusted sacrificial vessel, TāṇḍyaBr. i, 2, 3. **-peya**, m. a particular Ekāha (q.v.), Lāṭy.; KātyŚr.; ĀśvŚr. &c. **-peśas**, mfn. having a perfect shape [BRD.], RV. v, 66, 1; (looking like water, Sāy.) **-prajāta**, mfn. of true nature, well made, proper, apt, RV.; (produced or come forth from water, Sāy.); (*ā*), f. a woman delivered (of a child) at proper time, AV. i, 11, 1. **-pravīta**, mfn. invested or surrounded with divine truth (as Agni), RV. i, 70, 4. **-psu** (voc.), mfn. one whose appearance is truth or one who consumes the sacrificial food [Sāy.], RV. i, 180, 3 (said of the Aśvins). **-bhāga**, m., N. of a man; (*ās*), m. pl. the descendants of the above. **-bhuj**, mfn. enjoying (the fruit of) one's righteousness or pious works, MaitrUp. **-°m-bhara**, mfn. bearing the truth in one's self; (*as*), m., N. of Vishṇu, BhP. vi, 13, 17; (*ā*), f. (with and without *prajñā*) intellect or knowledge which contains the truth in itself, Prab.; Sarvad. &c.; N. of a river, BhP.; *-prajña*, mfn. possessing the above knowledge (said of a class of Yogins), Sarvad. **-yukti**, mfn. well applied, proper (as a word or hymn), RV. x, 61, 10. **-yuj**, mfn. properly harnessed, RV.; united with divine law, RV. vi, 39, 2. **-vat**, mfn. being right, saying the truth, BhP. **-vāká**, m. a true or right speech, RV. ix, 113, 2. **-vādín**, mfn. saying right, speaking the truth, VS. v, 7; MBh. **-vīrya**, m., N. of a man. **-vrata**, mfn. one whose vow is truth, truthful, BhP. **-satyá**, *e*, n. du. right and truth, ŚBr. xi. **-sád**, mfn. seated or dwelling in truth [BRD.], RV. iv, 40, 5; TS. iii; (seated at sacrifice, Sāy.) **-sádana**, n. and °*nī*, f. the right or proper seat, VS. iv, 36. **-sáp** (in strong forms °*sā́p*), mfn. connected with or performing worship or pious works (as men), connected with or accepting worship or religious acts (as gods), RV. **-sāta**, mfn. filled with truth or righteousness, AV. xviii, 2, 15. **-sāman**, n., N. of a Sāman, ĀrshBr. **-sena**, m., N. of a Gandharva, BhP. **-stúbh**, m. 'praising properly or duly,' N. of a Ṛishi, RV. i, 112, 20. **-sthā́**, mfn. standing right, AV. iv, 1, 4. **-°s-pati** (voc. *ṛitaspate*), m. lord of pious works (as sacrifice &c.; N. of Vāyu), RV. viii, 26, 21. **-spṛiś,** mfn. connected with pious works or worship, RV. v, 67, 4 (N. of the Ādityas); i, 2, 80; iv, 50, 3 (N. of Mitra-varuṇa); (touching water, Sāy.) **Ṛitânṛita,** n. truth and falsehood. **Ṛitâyus,** m., N. of a son of Purū-ravas. **Ṛitá-van,** mf(*arī*)n. keeping within the fixed order or rule, regular, proper (as inanimated objects); performing (as men) or accepting (as gods) sacred works or piety, truthful, faithful, just, holy, RV.; AV.; TS.; VS. **Ṛitā-vasu** (voc.), mfn. one whose wealth is piety, pious, faithful, RV. viii, 101, 5. **Ṛitā-vṛídh,** mfn. increasing or fostering truth or piety (said of gods), RV.; VS. **Ṛitā-shah,** *shāṭ,* mfn. maintaining the sacred law, VS. xviii, 38; TS. iii, 4, 7. **Ṛite-karmám,** ind. while (Indra) pours down rain, during the rain [Sāy.], RV. x, 55, 7; (see also *ṛité,* p. 226, col. 1.) **Ṛite-jā́,** mfn. produced or come forth at the time of sacrifice [Sāy.], RV. i, 113, 12; vi, 3, 1; vii, 20, 6. **Ṛitódya,** n. true speech, truth, AV. xiv, 1, 31.

Ṛitaya, Nom. P. (p. *ṛitayát*) Ā. *ṛitayate,* to observe the sacred law, be regular or proper [BRD.]; to wish for sacrifice [Sāy.], RV. viii, 3, 14; v, 12, 3; 43, 7.

Ṛitayā́, ind. in the right manner [BRD.], [through desire of reward of pious actions, Sāy.], RV. ii, 11, 12.

Ṛitayú, mfn. observing the sacred law [BRD.]; wishing for sacrifice [Sāy.], RV. viii, 70, 10.

Ṛitavyà, mfn. (fr. *ṛitú* below), relating or devoted to the seasons, Pāṇ. iv, 2, 31; (*ā*), f. (scil. *ishṭakā*), N. of particular sacrificial bricks, TS.; ŚBr.; KātyŚr. &c. **-vat,** mfn. furnished with the above bricks, ŚBr. x. **Ṛitavyā-tva,** n. state of being the above brick, Kāṭh.

Ṛitāya, Nom. P. (p. *ṛitāyát*) to wish for speech, RV. vii, 87, 1; to maintain the sacred law [BRD.]; to wish for sacrifice [Sāy.], RV.

Ṛitāyin, mfn. truthful, RV. x, 5, 3.

Ṛitāyú, mfn. = *ṛitayú* above, RV.

Ṛiti or *ṛīti, is,* f. going, motion, L.; assault, attack [BRD.], AV. xii, 5, 25; VS. xxx, 13; envy, emulation, L.; reproach, abuse, L.; path, way, L.; prosperity, felicity, L.; aversion, L.; remembrance, memory, L.; protection, L.; misery, L.; pain, T.; (*is*), m., N. of a god to be worshipped by human sacrifice, VS. xxx, 13 [T.]; an assailant, enemy, AV. xii, 5, 25 [T.] **-°m-kara,** mfn. causing pain [T.], Pāṇ. iii, 2, 43.

Ṛitī (in comp. for *ṛiti* above). **-sháh** (strong cases *shāh* and *shah*), mfn. subduing or conquering assailants or enemies [Sāy.], RV.; (enduring an assault, BRD.)

Ṛitīya. See √*ṛit.*

Ṛitú, *us,* m. (Uṇ. i, 72) any settled point of time, fixed time, time appointed for any action (esp. for sacrifices and other regular worship), right or fit time, RV.; AV.; VS.; an epoch, period (esp. a division or part of the year), season (the number of the divisions of the year is in ancient times, three, five, six, seven, twelve, thirteen, and twenty-four; in later time six seasons are enumerated, viz. Vasanta, 'spring;' Grīshma, 'the hot season;' Varshās (f. nom. pl.), 'the rainy season;' Śarad, 'autumn;' Hemanta, 'winter;' and Śiśira, 'the cool season;' the seasons are not unfrequently personified, addressed in Mantras, and worshipped by libations), RV.; AV.; VS. &c.; MBh.; Mn. &c.; symbolical expression for the number six, VarBṛS.; Sūryas. &c.; the menstrual discharge (in women), the time after the courses (favourable for procreation; according to Bhpr. sixteen days after their appearance), Suśr.; MBh.; Mn. &c.; sexual union at the above time, Mn. ix, 93; MBh.; fixed order, order, rule [BRD.], RV. i, 162, 19; light, splendour, L.; a particular mineral, L.; N. of a Ṛishi; of the twelfth Manu. **-kāla,** m. the fit or proper season, MBh. iii, 14763; the time of a woman's courses, the time after the courses (favourable for procreation, see above), ŚāṅkhŚr.; Mn. iii, 45; v, 153; MBh.; Pañcat. **-gaṇa,** m. the seasons collectively. **-gāmin,** mfn. approaching (a woman sexually) at the fit time (i. e. after her courses), R.; BhP. **-grahá,** m. a libation offered to the Ṛitus or seasons, ŚBr.; KātyŚr. **-caryā,** f., N. of a work. **-jit,** m., N. of a king of Mithilā, VP. **-jush,** f. a woman enjoying intercourse at the time fit for procreation, Kathās. cxx, 35. **-dhāman,** m. (probably for *ṛita-dh°*), N. of Vishṇu, VP. **-nātha,** m. 'lord of the seasons,' the spring, T. **-páti,** m. lord of the times fit for sacrifices, lord of the proper times, N. of Agni, RV. x, 2, 1; of other deities, AV. iii, 10, 9; xi, 6, 17; the spring, T. **-parṇa,** m., N. of a king of Ayodhyā, MBh. (v.l. *ṛita-p°*). **-paryāya,** m. the revolution of the seasons. **-paśú,** m. an animal to be sacrificed at a particular season, ŚBr. xiii; Vait. **-pā́,** mfn. drinking the libation at the right time, RV. **-pātrá,** n. a vessel for the libation to the Ṛitus or seasons, ŚBr.; KātyŚr.; Vait. **-prāpta,** mfn. that which has approached its own season (as a fruit-bearing tree), L. **-praisha,** m., N. of particular invocations spoken before the sacrifice to the seasons, AitBr. v, 9, 3; 4. **-bhāga,** m. the sixth part, Hcat. **-bhāj,** mfn. partaking of a season (said of a sacrificial brick), ŚBr. x, 4, 4, 4. **-mát,** mfn. coming at regular or proper times, VS. xix, 61; TāṇḍyaBr. xiv; enjoying the seasons, ChUp.; (*tī*), f. 'having courses,' a girl at the age of puberty, marriageable girl, Mn. ix, 89 ff.; Pañcat. &c.; a woman during her courses or just after them (during the period favourable for procreation), Gobh. ii, 5, 6; MBh. &c.; (*at*), n., N. of Varuṇa's grove, BhP. **-máya,** mfn. consisting of seasons, ŚBr. viii. **-múkha,** n. beginning or first day of a season, ŚBr. i; KātyŚr.; R. **-°mukhin,** mfn. taking place on the first day of a season, Comm. on TBr. **-yāja,** m. 'offering to the seasons,' a particular ceremony, AitBr.; ĀśvŚr.; KātyŚr. &c. **-yājín,** mfn. sacrificing at the beginning of every season, MaitrS. **-yājyā,** f. = *-yāja* above, Vait. **-rāja,** m. 'the king of the seasons,' the spring, Kathās. **-liṅga,** n. characteristic of a season, Mn. i, 30; sign of menstruation, W. **-lokā,** f., N. of particular bricks, ŚBr. x. **-vṛitti,** f. revolution of the seasons, a year, L. **-velā,** f. the time of or after menses (fit for procreation), ŚāṅkhGṛ. i, 19, 1. **-śás,** ind. at the proper or due time, at the very time, RV.; AV. ix, 5, 13; VS. **-śānti,** f., N. of a work. **-shāman** (for *-sāman*), n., N. of a Sāman. **-shṭhā́** (for *-sthā*), mfn. being in season or in the seasons, VS. xvii, 3; MaitrS. iii, 3, 4; *-yajñāyajñīya,* n., N. of a Sāman, Lāṭy. i, 5, 15; ĀrshBr. **-saṃhāra,** m. 'collection of the seasons,' N. of a poem ascribed to Kālidāsa. **-saṃdhi,** m. junction of two seasons, transition from one season to the next one, PārGṛ.; GopBr. &c.; junction of two fortnights, the days of new and full moon (as the junction of the dark and light half of the month, and reversely), T. **-samaya,** m. the period of or after the menses (fit for procreation), VarBṛS.; Pañcat. **-sahasrá,** n. a thousand seasons, ŚBr. x. **-sātmya,** n. diet &c. suited to a season. **-sevya,** mfn. to be taken or applied at certain seasons (as particular medicines or food &c.), T. **-sthalā,** f., N. of an Apsaras. **-sthā́,** f. = *-shṭhā* above, TS. v. **-snātā,** f. a woman who has bathed after her courses (and so prepared herself for sexual intercourse), Suśr.; MBh.; Ragh. &c. **-snāna,** n. the act of bathing after menstruation. **-hārikā,** f. 'taking away or obstructing the menses,' N. of a female demon. **-homa,** m. a particular sacrifice, Vait. **Ṛitv-anta,** m. the close of a season, Mn. iv, 26; the termination of menstruation, W.; (mfn.) forming the close of a season (as a day), Mn. iv, 119. **Ṛitv-ik** (in comp. for *ṛitvij* below); *-tva,* n. the state of being a Ṛitvij or priest, TāṇḍyaBr.; *-patha,* m. the path of the priest on the sacrificial ground, Lāṭy.; *-phala,* n. the reward of a priest, Jaim. **Ṛitv-ij,** mfn. (fr. √*yaj*), sacrificing at the proper time, sacrificing regularly; (*k*), m. a priest (usually four are enumerated, viz. Hotṛi, Adhvaryu, Brahman, and Udgātṛi; each of them has three companions or helpers, so that the total number is sixteen, viz. *Hotṛi,* Maitrāvaruṇa, Acchāvāka, Grāva-stut; *Adhvaryu,* Prati-prasthātṛi, Neshṭṛi, Un-netṛi; *Brahman,* Brāhmaṇācchaṇsin, Agnīdhra, Potṛi; *Udgātṛi,* Prastotṛi, Pratihartṛi, Subrahmaṇya, ĀśvŚr. iv, 1, 4-6), RV.; AV.; TS.; ŚBr.; KātyŚr. &c.

Ṛituthā́, ind. at the due or proper time, regularly, properly, RV.; AV.; VS. &c.

Ṛité, ind. See √*ṛit.*

Ṛitva, *am,* n. (fr. *ṛitú*), timely or matured semen, TāṇḍyaBr. x, 3, 1; proper time, time fit for generation, Āp. ii, 5, 17.

Ṛitvíya, mfn. (fr. *ṛitú*), being in proper time, observing or keeping the proper time, regular, proper, RV.; AV. iii, 20, 1; vii, 72, 1; VS.; (*ā*), f. (voc. *ṛitviye*) a woman in or after her courses, a woman during the time favourable for procreation, AV. xiv, 2, 37; (*am*), n. (*ṛítviya*) the time after the courses (favourable for procreation), AV. xii, 3, 29; TS. ii, 5, 1, 5. **-vat,** mfn. having courses, being at the period fit for generation, TBr. i. **Ṛitvíyā-vat,** mfn. in proper time, regular, proper, RV.

Ṛitvya, mfn. belonging to the time fit for generation, RV. x, 183, 2.

ऋक् *ṛik, ṛik-chas, ṛik-tas,* and *ṛik-śas.* See under 2. *ṛic,* p. 225, col. 1.

ऋक्ण 1. *ṛikṇa,* mfn. = *vṛikṇa,* Sāy. **-vaha,** mf(*ī*)n. having the shoulders wounded or rubbed (by the yoke; said of an animal used for drawing vehicles), AitBr. v, 9, 4.

ऋक्ण 2. *ṛikṇa* = the next, L.

ऋक्थ *ṛiktha,* mfn. (for *riktha* [q. v.], fr. √*ric*), property, wealth, possession, effects (esp. left at death), Mn. ix, 132; 144, &c.; Yājñ. ii, 117; Śak. &c.; gold, L. **-grahaṇa,** n. inheriting property. **-grāha,** mfn. one who inherits or receives property, Yājñ. ii, 87; (*as*), m. inheritance of property, L. **-bhāgin,** mfn. one who inherits or receives property, Mn. ix, 188. **-bhāj,** mfn. id., Mn. ix, 155. **-hara,** mfn. id., Mn. ix, 185. **Ṛikthâda,** m. 'receiver or inheritor of property,' a son.

Ṛikthin, mfn. receiving or inheriting property, an inheritor, heir, Yājñ.

ऋक्व *ṛikva,* &c. See p. 225, col. 1.

ऋक्ष 1. *ṛikshá,* mfn. (etym. doubtful) bald, bare, TS.; MaitrS.

ऋक्ष 2. *ṛíksha,* mfn. (√2. *ṛish,* Uṇ. iii, 66; 67; probably fr. √*ṛiś*), hurting, pernicious, RV. viii, 24, 27; (*as*), m. a bear (as a ravenous beast), RV. v, 56, 3; VS. xxiv, 36; Mn.; Suśr. &c.; a species of ape, Kathās.; Bignonia Indica, L.; N. of several men, RV. viii, 68, 15; MBh. &c.; of a mountain, VP.; MBh.; (ifc.) the best or most excellent, L.; (*ās*), m. pl. the seven stars, the Pleiades, the seven Ṛishis, RV. i, 24, 10; ŚBr. ii; TĀr.; (*ā*), f., N. of a wife of Ajamīḍha, MBh. i; of a woman in the retinue of Skanda, MBh. ix; (*ī*), f. a female bear, MBh.; R.; Kathās.; m. and (*am*), n. a star, constellation, lunar mansion, Mn.; MBh.; R. &c.; (*am*), n. the twelfth part of the ecliptic; the particular star under which a person happens to be born, VarBṛS.; Sūryas. &c.; [cf. Gk. ἄρκτος; Lat. *ursus;* Lith. *loky-s* for *olkys.*] **-gandhā,** f. Argyreia Argenteia, L.; Batatas Paniculata, L. **-gandhikā,** f. Batatas Paniculata, L. **-giri,** m. the mountain called Ṛiksha. **-grīva,** m. 'bear-necked,' a kind of demon, AV. viii, 6, 2. **-jihva,** n. (scil. *kushṭha*) 'like a bear-tongue,' a kind of leprosy, Car. **-nātha,** m. 'lord of the stars,' the moon. **-pati,** m. lord of the bears, R.; a planet presided over by a lunar mansion, VarBṛS. **-mantra,** m. a Mantra or text addressed to the lunar mansions. **-rāj** and **-rāja,** m. the lord of the bears (or apes?), Hariv.; R.; BhP.; 'lord of the stars,' the moon, Vikr. **-vat,** m., N. of a mountain, R.; Ragh. v, 44. **-vanta,** n., N. of a town, Hariv. **-viḍambin,** m. 'deceiving by means of the stars,' a fraudulent astrologer, VarBṛS. **-vibhāvana,** n. observation of the stars. **-hariśvara,** m. lord of the bears and apes, N. of Sugrīva, Ragh. xiii, 72. **Ṛikshêśa,** m. 'lord of the stars,' the moon, L. **Ṛikshêshṭi,** f. offering to the stars, Mn. vi, 10. **Ṛikshôda,** m., N. of a mountain, Kāś. on Pāṇ. iv, 3, 91.

Ṛikshīkā, f., N. of an evil spirit, AV. xii, 1, 49; VS. xxx, 8; ŚBr. xiii.

ऋक्ष 3. *ṛiksha,* mfn. cut, pierced, L.

ऋक्षम *ṛík-shama.* See p. 225, col. 1.

ऋक्षर *ṛikshara, as,* m. (probably fr. √*ṛiś*) a thorn (see *an-ṛikshará*); a priest, Uṇ. iii, 75 (fr. √*ṛish*); (*am*), n. a shower, L.

ऋक्षला *ṛikshálā,* f. the part of an animal's leg between the fetlock joint and the hoof, VS. xxv, 3; (cf. *ṛicchárā.*)

ऋग् *ṛig.* See p. 225, col. 1.

ऋघा *ṛíghā,* f. violence, passion. **-vat** and **-van,** mfn. raving, impetuous, violent, RV.; [cf. Zd. *ĕrĕghant;* Mod. Germ. *arg.*]

Ṛighāya, Nom. P. Ā. *ṛighāyati, -te,* to be passionate or impetuous, rave, rage, RV.; to tremble, RV. ii, 25, 3; iv, 17, 2.

ऋङ्ग *ṛiṅga.* See *ṛiñj.*

ऋच् 1. *ṛic*, cl. 6. P. *ṛicati, ānarca, arcitā*, &c., = 1. *arc*, p. 89, col. 3; to praise, Dhātup. xxviii, 19; (cf. *arká.*)

Ṛik (by Sandhi for 2. *ṛic* below). **-chas** and **-śas**, ind. verse by verse, one Ṛic verse after the other, AitBr.; ŚāṅkhŚr.; Gobh. &c. **-tantra**, n., N. of a work; *-vyākaraṇa*, n., N. of a Pariśishṭa of the Sāma-veda. **-tás**, ind. from a Ṛic, with reference to a Ṛic, AitBr.; ŚBr. &c. **-thā**, mfn. erroneous for *-sthā* below. **-vat**, see *ṛikvá* below. **-śas**, see *-chas* above. **-shama** (*ṛíkshama*, TS. iv, 3, 2, 2), n. 'similar to a Ṛic,' N. of a Sāman. **-saṃśita**, mfn. sharpened by Ṛic verses (cf. *āśā-saṃśita*), AV. x, 5, 30. **-saṃhitā**, f. the Saṃhitā (q. v.) of the Ṛig-veda, Mn. xi, 262. **-sama** = *-shama* above, VS. xiii, 56. **-sāmá**, *e*, n. du. the Ṛic verses and the Sāmans, RV. x, 114, 6; AV. xiv, 1, 11; VS.; ŚBr. &c.; *-śriṅga*, m., N. of Vishṇu, R. **-sāman**, n., N. of a Sāman (= *ṛikshama*?). **-sthā**, mfn. consisting of Ṛic verses, TāṇḍyaBr. xvi, 8, 4.

Ṛikvá, *ṛíkvan*, and *ṛik-vát*, mfn. praising, jubilant with praise, RV.; AV. xviii, 1, 47.

Ṛig (by Sandhi for 2. *ṛic* below). **-ayana**, n. (not *-ayaṇa*, Pat. on Pāṇ. viii, 4, 3) going through the Veda, study of the complete Veda, a book treating on the study of the Veda, T.; *-°ādi*, m., N. of a gaṇa, Pāṇ. iv, 3, 73. **-artha-sāra**, m., N. of a work. **-ātmaka**, mfn. 'consisting of Ṛicas,' Ṛic-like, Comm. on Pāṇ. vii, 4, 38. **-āvānam**, ind. p. (√*ve*), connecting one Ṛic with another, not interrupting their continuance, ĀśvŚr. **-uttama**, mfn. ending in a Ṛic, MaitrS. **-gaṇa**, *ās*, m. pl. the whole body of the Ṛig-veda. **-gāthā**, f. a song consisting of Ṛic-like stanzas, Yājñ. iii, 114. **-brāhmaṇa**, n. the Brāhmaṇa which belongs to the Ṛig-veda, the Aitareya-Brāhmaṇa. **-bhāj**, mfn. partaking of Ṛic verses, praised in Ṛic verses (as a deity). **-bhāshya**, n., N. of a commentary on the Ṛig-veda by Mādhava, W. **-mat**, mfn. having or praised in Ṛic verses, Nir. **-yajuḥ-sāma-veda**, *ās*, m. pl. the Ṛig-, Yajur-, and Sāma-vedas; *-°din*, mfn. conversant with the above three Vedas. **-yajusha**, n. the Ṛig- and Yajur-vedas, Gaut. **-vid**, mfn. knowing the Ṛig-veda, Vait. **-vidhāna**, n. employing Ṛic verses, AgP.; N. of a work. **-virāma**, m. the pause in a verse, TPrāt. **-vedá**, *as*, m. 'Hymn-Veda' or 'Veda of praise,' the Ṛig-veda, or most ancient sacred book of the Hindūs (that is, the collective body of sacred verses called Ṛicas [see below], consisting of 1017 hymns [or with the Vālakhilyas 1028] arranged in eight Ashṭakas or in ten Maṇḍalas; Maṇḍalas 2-8 contain groups of hymns, each group ascribed to one author or to the members of one family; the ninth book contains the hymns sung at the Soma ceremonies; the first and tenth contain hymns of a different character, some comparatively modern, composed by a greater variety of individual authors; in its wider sense the term Ṛig-veda comprehends the Brāhmaṇas and the Sūtra works on the ritual connected with the hymns), AitBr.; ŚBr.; Mn. &c.; *-prātiśākhya*, n. the Prātiśākhya of the Ṛig-veda; *-bhāshya*, n., N. of treatises and commentaries on the Ṛig-veda; *-vid*, mfn. knowing the Ṛig-veda; *-saṃhitā*, f. the continuous text of the Ṛig-veda arranged according to the Saṃhitā-pāṭha, q.v.; *°ânukramaṇikā*, f. the Anukramaṇikā or index of the Ṛig-veda. **-vedin**, mfn. conversant with the Ṛig-veda. **-°vedīya**, mfn. belonging to the Ṛig-veda.

Ṛigma, mfn. having the beginning of a Ṛic, beginning like a Ṛic [Sāy.], AitBr. v, 9, 6.

Ṛigmin, mfn. praising, jubilant with praise, RV. i, 100, 4; ix, 86, 46.

Ṛigmiya and *ṛígmiya*, mfn. to be celebrated with Ṛic verses; to be praised, RV.; consisting of Ṛic verses, TS. vi.

Ṛigmya, mfn. consisting of Ṛic verses, Kāṭh.

Ṛiṅ (by Sandhi for 2. *ṛic* below). **-máya**, mfn. consisting of Ṛic verses, AitBr.; ŚBr.

2. **Ṛíc**, *k*, f. praise, verse, esp. a sacred verse recited in praise of a deity (in contradistinction to the Sāman [pl. Sāmāni] or verses which were sung and to the Yajus [pl. Yajūṃshi] or sacrificial words, formularies, and verses which were muttered); sacred text, RV.; AV.; VS.; ŚBr. &c.; Mn. &c.; the collection of the Ṛic verses (sg., but usually pl. *ṛicas*), the Ṛig-veda, AitBr.; ĀśvŚr. & Gṛ.; Mn. i, 23, &c. (cf. *ṛig-veda* above); the text of the Pūrvatāpanīya, RāmatUp.

Ṛica, ifc. = 2. *ṛic*, verse, sacred verse (cf. *try-ṛica*, &c.); (*as*), m., N. of a king, VP.

Ṛicī-shama, *as*, m. 'Ṛic-like' [Nir.], N. of Indra, RV.

ऋचाभ *ṛicābha*, *as*, m., N. of a pupil of Vaiśampāyana, Kāś.

ऋचीक *ṛicīka*, *as*, m., N. of Jamad-agni's father, MBh.; of a country, Daś.

ऋचीष *ṛicīsha*, *am*, n. a frying-pan, L.; a particular hell, L.; [cf. 2. *ṛijīsha.*]

ऋचेयु *ṛiceyu*, *as*, m., N. of a Ṛishi, MBh.; of a son of Raudrāśva, Hariv.; VP.; (see *ṛiteyu.*)

ऋच्छरा 1. *ṛiccharā* (= *ṛikshálā*, q. v.), f. the part of an animal's leg between the fetlock joint and the hoof, AV. x, 9, 23.

ऋच्छा *ṛicchā*, f. See *yad-ṛicchā.*

ऋछ् *ṛich*, cl. 6. P. *ṛicchati, ānarcha, ṛicchitā*, &c., to be stiff; to be infatuated or foolish; to go, move, Dhātup. xxviii, 15; [cf. 4. *ṛi.*]

Ṛicchaka (?), Kāś. on Pāṇ. vi, 1, 91.

2. **Ṛiccharā**, f. (Uṇ. iii, 131) a harlot, courtezan.

ऋज् *ṛij*, cl. 1. P. Ā. *arjati, -te, ānṛije, arjitā, arjishyate, ārjishṭa*, to go; to stand or be firm; to obtain, acquire; to be strong or healthy: Caus. *arjayati*, to obtain, get, acquire, Dhātup. vi, 16; [cf. *arj*, p. 90, col. 1.]

ऋजिप्य *ṛijipyá*, mfn. (fr. *ṛiju* and √*āp*, Sāy.?), going straight upwards, moving upwards, RV.; [cf. Zd. *ĕrĕzifya.*]

Ṛijīpín, mfn. id., RV. iv, 26, 6.

ऋजिमन् *ṛijiman.* See col. 3.

ऋजिश्वन् *ṛijíśvan*, *ā*, m., N. of a king (protected by Indra), RV.

ऋजिष्ठ *ṛijishṭha.* See *ṛijú.*

ऋजीक *ṛijīka* (√*ṛij*, Uṇ. iv, 22; v, 51), mfn. (= *upa-hata*) hid, concealed; removed, obviated?; (*as*), m. smoke; Indra; (*am*), n. a means, expedient, according to Sāy. in *āvir-ṛijīka*, q. v.

ऋजीति *ṛijīti*, mfn. (fr. *ṛiju* and √*i*, Sāy.), going or tending upwards, RV.

ऋजीयस् *ṛijiyas.* See *ṛijú.*

ऋजीष 1. *ṛijīshá*, *as*, m. (√*ṛij*), expeller (of enemies), N. of Indra [Sāy.], RV. i, 32, 6.

ऋजीष 2. *ṛijīsha*, *am*, n. (√*arj*, Uṇ. iv, 28), the sediment or residue of Soma, the Soma plant after the juice has been pressed out, AV. ix, 6, 16; VS. xix, 72; TS. vi; ŚBr.; KātyŚr. &c.; the juice produced by the third pressure of the plant, Sāy.; a frying-pan, Uṇ.; a particular hell, Mn. iv, 90.

Ṛijīshita, mfn. possessed of the residue of Soma, gaṇa *tārakâdi*, Pāṇ. v, 2, 36.

Ṛijīshin, mfn. receiving the residue of Soma or the juice produced by the third pressure of the plant [Sāy.], N. of Indra and of the Maruts, RV.; having or consisting of the residue, TS.

ऋजु *ṛijú*, mf(*jvī́*)n. (√*arj*, Uṇ. i, 28; probably fr. √2. *ṛiñj*, col. 3, BRD.), tending in a straight direction, straight (lit. and fig.; opp. to *vṛijiná*), upright, honest, right, sincere, RV.; AV. xiv, 1, 34; TS. &c.; Mn.; MBh. &c.; (*ú*), ind. in the right manner, correctly, RV. ii, 3, 7; v, 46, 1; x, 67, 2; AitBr. iii, 3, 10; in a straight line, straight on, Suśr. &c.; compar. *ṛijīyas*, RV. vii, 104, 12; AV. v, 14, 12; viii, 4, 12, and *rajīyas*, Pāṇ. vi, 4, 162; superl. *ṛijishṭha*, Pāṇ., and *rájishṭha*, RV.; [observe that the metaphorical meaning of this word is more common in Vedic, and the literal meaning in classical literature]; (*us*), m., N. of a son of Vasu-deva, BhP.; (*jvī*), f. (scil. *gati*) the straight stage or duration in the course of a planet, VarBṛS.; [cf. Zd. *ĕrĕzu*; Gk. ὀρέγω; Lat. *rectus*; Goth. *raihts*; Eng. *right.*] **-kāya**, mfn. having a straight body, BhP.; N. of Kaśyapa, L. **-kratú**, mfn. one whose works are right or honest, N. of Indra, RV. i, 81, 7. **-gá**, mfn. going straight on, AV. i, 12, 1; TS. iii, 1, 10, 2; (*as*), m. an arrow, T. **-gātha**, mfn. (voc.) celebrated with right praises or songs, RV. v, 44, 5. **-tā**, f., **-tva**, n. straight direction, straightness, Kum. iv, 23; uprightness, sincerity, honesty, Amar.; HYog. **-dāru-maya**, mf(*ī*)n. made of straight wood, Hcat. **-dāsa**, m., N. of a son of Vasu-deva, VP. **-dṛiś**, mfn. seeing right, Naish. **-dhā́**, ind. in straight direction, straight on, TBr. ii; in right manner, correctly, AitBr. i, 28, 28. **-nīti**, f. right guidance, RV. i, 90, 1. **-paksha**, mfn. having straight wings (said of the fire-receptacle when shaped like a bird). **-pālikā**, f., N. of a river. **-buddhi** or **-mati**, mfn. of honest mind, sincere, R.; Dhūrtas. **-mitāksharā**, f., N. of a commentary on Yājñavalkya's law-book (composed by Vijñāneśvara, and generally called Mitāksharā). **-mushká**, mfn. having strong testicles; strong and muscular [Sāy.], (said of Agni's horses), RV. iv, 2, 2; 6, 9. **-raśmi**, mfn. having straight traces or reins (as a chariot), AV. iv, 29, 7. **-rohita**, n. the straight red bow of Indra, L. **-lekha**, mfn. rectilinear, Śulbas. **-lekhā**, f. a straight line, Comm. on ŚBr. **-váni**, mfn. granting rightly or liberally (said of the earth), RV. v, 41, 15. **-sarpa**, m. a species of snake, Suśr. **-hásta**, mf(*ā*)n. 'good-handed,' bestowing liberally (said of the earth), RV. v, 41, 15.

Ṛijiman, *ā*, m. straightness, gaṇa *pṛithv-ādi*, Pāṇ. v, 1, 122.

Ṛijū (in comp. for *ṛijú* above). **-karaṇa**, n. the act of straightening, Suśr. **-√kṛi**, to straighten; to set right, correct, Comm. on RPrāt. **-kṛita**, mfn. made straight. **-nas** (*ṛijū°*), m. 'straight-nosed,' N. of a man, RV. viii, 52, 2. **Ṛijv-áñc**, mfn. moving or tending straightforward, RV. iv, 6, 9. **Ṛijv-ālikhitá**, mfn. scratched with straight lines, ŚBr. x. **Ṛijv-āhva**, m., N. of a Ṛishi.

Ṛijūka, *as*, m., N. of a country (in which the river Vipāśā rises), Nir.

Ṛijūya, Nom. P. (p. *ṛijūyat*) to walk straightforward, be right or honest, RV.: Ā. (p. *ṛijūyámāna*) to tend straight upwards, RV. x, 88, 9.

Ṛijūyā́, ind. in a straight line, RV. i, 183, 5.

Ṛijūyú, mfn. upright, honest, RV. i, 20, 4.

1. **Ṛijrá**, mf(*ā*)n. going straightforward, moving on, quick (as horses), RV. **Ṛijrāśva**, m. 'having quick horses,' N. of a man, RV.

ऋज्र 2. *ṛijrá*, mfn. (fr. √*rañj*), red, reddish, ruddy; [cf. *árjuna*; Gk. ἀργός, ἄργυρος; Lat. *argentum.*]

ऋज्र 3. *ṛijra*, *as*, m. (√*ṛij*, Uṇ. ii, 28), a leader.

ऋञ्ज् 1. *ṛiñj*, cl. 1. Ā. *ṛiñjate, ṛiñjām-cakre, ṛiñjitā*, &c., to fry, Dhātup. vi, 17.

1. **Ṛiñjasāna**, *as*, m. (Uṇ. ii, 87) a cloud.

ऋञ्ज् 2. *ṛiñj*, cl. 6. P. (p. *ṛiñját*) Ā. *ṛiñjate*: cl. 4. P. Ā. (see *abhy-ṛiñj*): cl. 7. Ā. (3. pl. *ṛiñjate*) to make straight or right, make proper, arrange, fit out, decorate, ornament; to make favourable, propitiate; to gain, obtain, RV.; [cf. Gk. ὀρέγω; Lat. *rego*; Goth. *rak-ja.*]

Ṛiṅga, *as*, m. = *prasādhana*, Sāy.; see *manaṛiṅga.*

2. **Ṛiñjasāná**, mfn. to be made favourable or propitiated (by songs); to be celebrated, RV.

ऋण् *ṛiṇ*, cl. 8. P. Ā. *ṛiṇoti* or *arṇoti*, *-ṇute, ānarṇa, ānṛiṇe*, &c., to go, move, Dhātup. xxx, 5; (cf. 4. *ṛi.*)

Ṛiṇá, mfn. going, flying, fugitive (as a thief), RV. vi, 12, 5; having gone against or transgressed, guilty [cf. Lat. *reus*]; (*am*), n. anything wanted or missed; anything due, obligation, duty, debt (a Brāhman owes three debts or obligations, viz. 1. Brahmacarya or 'study of the Vedas,' to the Ṛishis; 2. sacrifice and worship, to the gods; 3. procreation of a son, to the Manes, TS. vi, 3, 10, 5; Mn. vi, 35, &c.; in later times also, 4. benevolence to mankind and 5. hospitality to guests are added, MBh. &c.), RV.; AV. &c.; Mn.; MBh. &c.; a debt of money, money owed, MBh.; Mn.; Yājñ.; (*ṛiṇam* √*kṛi*, to get into debt, Yājñ. ii, 45; *°m* √*prâp*, to become indebted, Mn. viii, 107; *°m* √*dā* or √*nī* or *pra*-√*yam*, to pay a debt, MBh.; Mn. &c.; *°m* √*yāc*, to ask for a loan, Kathās.; *°m parîps*, to call in a debt, Mn. viii, 161); guilt; a negative quantity, minus (in math.); water, L.; a fort, stronghold, L.; [cf. Zd. *arena.*] **-kartṛi**, mfn. one who contracts a debt, indebted, MBh. xiii. **-kāti**, m. one to whom praise is due, RV. viii, 61, 12. **-graha**, mfn. getting into debt, borrowing, W.; (*as*), m. the act of borrowing, W. **-grāhin**, mfn. borrowing; (*ī*), m. a borrower, W. **-cít**, mfn. 'giving heed to worship' (paid as a debt by men to gods), N. of Brahmaṇas-pati, RV. ii, 23, 17. **-ccheda**, m. payment of a debt. **-cyút**, mfn. inciting to fulfilment of obligations (to the gods &c.),

RV. vi, 61, 1. **–jya**, m., N. of a Vyāsa, VP. **–°m-caya**, m., N. of a king, RV. v, 30, 12; 14; of an Āṅgirasa (author of the end of RV. ix, 108), RAnukr. **–tā**, f. the state of being under obligations or in debt. **–da** or **-dātṛi** or **-dāyin**, mfn. one who pays a debt. **–dāna**, n. payment of a debt. **–dāsa**, m. 'debt-slave,' one who pays his debt by becoming his creditor's slave, Comm. on Yājñ. **–nirmoksha**, m. discharge or acquittance of debt (to ancestors &c.), Ragh. x, 2. **–pradātṛi**, m. a money-lender, Hit. **–bhaṅgâdhyāya**, m., N. of a work. **–matkuṇa**, m. money given as security, bail (sticking to the debtor like an insect), L. **–mārgaṇa**, m. security, bail, L. **–mukti**, f., **-moksha**, m. discharge of a debt, paying a debt. **–mocana**, n. id.; *-tīrtha*, n., N. of a Tīrtha. **–yā́**, mfn. going after or demanding (fulfilment of) obligations, RV. **–yā́t**, mfn. striving for or demanding (fulfilment of) obligations, TS. i, 5, 2, 5. **–yā́van**, mfn. relieving from debt or obligations, RV. i, 87, 4. **–lekhya**, n. a bond, note of hand. **–vat**, mfn. one who is in debt, indebted, Hit.; VarBṛS.; [cf. Zd. *erenava*.] **–vā́n**, mfn. being in debt, indebted, TS. vi. **–śodhana**, n. payment or discharge of a debt, W. **–samuddhāra**, m. id. **Ṛiṇâdāna**, n. recovery of a debt, receipt of money &c. lent (as one of the eighteen titles or subjects of judicial procedure), Mn. viii, 4; Comm. on Yājñ. ii, 5. **Ṛiṇântaka**, m. 'terminator of debts,' N. of the planet Mars, L. **Ṛiṇâpakaraṇa, ṛiṇâpanayana, ṛiṇâpanodana**, n. discharge or payment of debt. **Ṛiṇārṇa** (fr. *ṛiṇa-ṛiṇa*, Kāty. on Pāṇ. vi, 1, 89), n. a loan borrowed for the payment of a previous debt. **Ṛiṇā-van**, mfn. being under obligation, indebted, RV. i, 169, 7; x, 34, 10. **Ṛiṇôdgrahaṇa**, n. recovering a debt in any way from a creditor (by friendly or legal proceedings, by strategem or arrest), W. **Ṛiṇôddhāra**, m. payment or discharge of a debt.

Ṛiṇika, *as*, m. a debtor, Yājñ. ii, 56; 93; [cf. Lat. *reus*.]

Ṛiṇin, mfn. one who is in debt or indebted, MBh.; (*ī*), m. a debtor, Yājñ. ii, 86; R.; Kathās. &c.

ऋत् *ṛit* (a Sautra root), Ā. *ṛitīyate*, to go; to hate, abhor, avoid, shun, Saddh.; to hate each other, quarrel, ŚBr.

Ṛitīyā, f. loathing, horror; scorn, contempt, L.

Ṛité, ind. (according to BRD. loc. case of the p. p. of √*ṛi*) under pain of, with the exclusion of, excepting, besides, without, unless (with abl. or acc. or a sentence beginning with *yatas*), RV.; AV. &c.; MBh.; Pañcat. &c. **–karmám**, ind. without work [BRD.], RV. x, 55, 7; (cf. under *ṛitá*, p. 224, col. 1.) **–barhishka**, mfn. without the formula on the Barhis (q. v.), ŚāṅkhŚr. **–mūla**, mfn. without roots, MaitrS. i. **–yajñám**, ind. outside the sacrifice, MaitrS. i. **–rakshas**, mfn. performed with exclusion of the Rakshases (as a sacrifice), AitBr. ii, 7, 2.

ऋत *ṛita*, **ऋति** *ṛiti*, **ऋतु** *ṛitu*. See p. 223, col. 2—p. 224, col. 1.

ऋतक *ṛitaka*. See *lṛitaka*.

ऋतेयु *ṛiteyu*, *us*, m., N. of a Ṛishi; of a son of Raudrâśva, (v. l. *ṛiceyu*, q. v.)

ऋत्विज् *ṛitv-ij*. See p. 224, col. 2.

ऋत्विय *ṛitviya*, &c. See ib.

ऋदूदर *ṛidū́dara*, mfn. (fr. *ṛidu*=*mṛidu* and *udára*), having a soft or pleasant inner nature, RV. ii, 33, 5; iii, 54, 10; viii, 48, 10.

Ṛidū (in comp. for *ṛidu*=*mṛidu*). **–pá́**, mfn. drinking what is sweet or pleasant, RV. viii, 77, 11. **–vṛidh**, mfn. increasing sweetness or pleasantness, ib.

ऋध् *ṛidh*, cl. 6. 2. 4. 5. 7. P. (Pot. 1. pl. *ṛidhema*, AV.; Subj. 3. sg. *ṛidhat*, RV.; pres. p. *ṛidhát*; cf. *ṛidhád* below) *ṛidhyati*; *ṛidhnoti*; *ṛiṇaddhi*; *ānardha, ardhitā, ardhishyati*, &c., to grow, increase, prosper, succeed, RV.; AV.; ŚBr.; MBh.; Mn. &c.; to cause to increase or prosper, promote, make prosperous, accomplish, RV.; AV.; VS.; ŚBr.: Pass. *ṛidhyate*, to be promoted, increase, prosper, succeed, ŚBr.: BṛĀrUp.: Caus. *ardhayati*, to satisfy, AV. vii, 80, 4; Nir.: Desid. *ardidhishati* or *īrtsati*; [cf. √*rādh* and *vṛidh*.]

Ṛiddha, mfn. increased, thriving, prosperous, abundant, wealthy, Kum.; Ragh.; Kathās. &c.; filled with (voices), made to resound; (*am*), n. stored grain, L.; a demonstrated conclusion, distinct result, L.

Ṛiddhi, *is*, f. increase, growth, prosperity, success, good fortune, wealth, abundance, VS.; TS.; ŚBr.; ĀśvGṛ. &c. (personified as Kuvera's wife, MBh.; Hariv.); accomplishment, perfection, supernatural power, BhP.; Lalit. &c.; magic; a kind of medicinal plant, Bhpr.; Car.; N. of Pārvatī, L.; of Lakshmī, L. **–kāma**, mfn. desiring prosperity or wealth, KātyŚr. **–pāda**, m. one of the four constituent parts of supernatural power, Lalit. **–mat**, mfn. being in a prosperous state, prosperous, wealthy, MBh.; R.; Ragh. &c.; bringing or bestowing prosperity or wealth, Suśr.

Ṛiddhita, mfn. (p. p. of a Nom. *ṛiddhaya*) caused to increase, made to prosper, (*asi-ṛiddhita*, made to prosper by the power of the sword, MBh. xviii, 105.)

Ṛiddhila, *as*, m., N. of a man (Buddh.)

Ṛidhád (by Sandhi for *ṛidhat*, pres. p. of *ṛidh*, cl. 6). **–rī** (√*rī*), mfn. one whose speed is increasing or excessive, exceedingly swift (as horses), RV. viii, 46, 23. **–vāra**, mfn. one whose wealth is increasing or abundant, abounding in wealth (said of Agni), RV. vi, 3, 2.

Ṛidhmuka, mfn. causing increase or prosperity, ĀśvGṛ. iv, 8, 9.

ऋधक् *ṛidhak* (and *ṛidhák*, SV.), ind. (related to *ardha*, BRD.), separately, aside, apart; singly, one by one; in a distinguished manner, particularly, RV.

Ṛídhaṅ (in comp. for *ṛidhak*). **–mantra**, mfn. one who is destitute of speech [BRD.], AV. v, 1, 7.

ऋधुक *ṛidhuka*, mfn. short, L.

ऋफ् *ṛiph* and *ṛimph*, cl. 6. P. *ṛiphati, ṛimphati, ānarpha, ṛimphām-cakāra*, &c., to hurt, kill; to reproach, Dhātup. xxviii, 30.

ऋबीस *ṛibīsa*, *am*, n. an abyss, chasm (in the earth, from which hot vapours arise), RV.; warmth of the earth, KātyŚr. **–pakva**, mfn. matured by warmth of the earth, ĀpŚr.

ऋभु *ṛibhú*, mfn. (√*rabh*), clever, skilful, inventive, prudent (said of Indra, Agni, and the Ādityas, RV.; also of property or wealth, RV. iv, 37, 5; viii, 93, 34; of an arrow, AV. i, 2, 3); (*us*), m. an artist, one who works in iron, a smith, builder (of carriages &c.), N. of three semi-divine beings (Ṛibhu, Vāja, and Vibhvan, the name of the first being applied to all of them; thought by some to represent the three seasons of the year [Ludwig, RV. vol. iii, p. 187], and celebrated for their skill as artists; they are supposed to dwell in the solar sphere, and are the artists who formed the horses of Indra, the carriage of the Aśvins, and the miraculous cow of Bṛihaspati; they made their parents young, and performed other wonderful works [Sv-apas]; they are supposed to take their ease and remain idle for twelve days [the twelve intercalary days of the winter solstice] every year in the house of the Sun [Agohya]; after which they recommence working; when the gods heard of their skill, they sent Agni to them with the one cup of their rival Tvashṭṛi, the artificer of the gods, bidding the Ṛibhus construct four cups from it; when they had successfully executed this task, the gods received the Ṛibhus amongst themselves and allowed them to partake of their sacrifices &c.; cf. Kaegi, RV. p. 53 f.), RV.; AV. &c.; they appear generally as accompanying Indra, especially at the evening sacrifice; in later mythology Ṛibhu is a son of Brahman, VP.; a deity, L.; (*avas*), m. a class of deities; [cf. Gk. ἀλφεῖν; Lat. *labor*; Goth. *arb-aiths*; Angl. Sax. *earfod*; Slav. *rab-ŭ*.] **–mát**, mfn. clever, skilful, prudent, RV. i, 111, 2; accompanied by or connected with the Ṛibhus, RV.; VS. xxxviii, 8; AitBr. ii, 20, 14; KātyŚr. **–shṭhira** (voc.), mfn. clever and wise (said of Indra), RV. viii, 77, 8.

Ṛibhuksha, *as*, m. Indra, L.; (Indra's) heaven, Comm. on Uṇ. iv, 12; Indra's thunderbolt, L.; (this word appears to owe its origin to the next.)

Ṛibhukshin, *ās*, m. (see Gr. 162; Pāṇ. vii, 1, 85 ff.), N. of the above Ṛibhus, and esp. of the first of them, RV.; N. of Indra (as the lord of the Ṛibhus, Nir.), RV.; of the Maruts, RV. viii. 7, 9; xx, 2; great, best [Sāy.], RV. viii, 93, 34.

Ṛibhukshīṇa, Nom. P. *ṛibhukshīṇati*, to behave like Ṛibhukshin, Siddh.

Ṛíbhva, ṛibhvan, and **ṛíbhvas**, mfn. clever, skilful, prudent, wise (N. of Indra, Tvashṭṛi, Agni, &c.), RV.; AV. v, 2, 7.

ऋल्लक *ṛillaka, ṛillarī, ṛillīsaka*, probably wrong readings for *jhallaka*, &c., qq. v.

ऋश *ṛíśa*, *as*, m. the male of a species of antelope = the next, AV. iv, 4, 7.

Ṛiśya or (in later texts) **ṛishya**, *as*, m. the male of a species of antelope, the painted or white-footed antelope, RV. viii, 4, 10; AV. v, 14, 3; VS.; AitBr.; Suśr. &c.; N. of a Ṛishi, ĀrshBr.; of a son of Devâtithi, BhP.; (*am*), n. hurt, violation, T. (for the explanation of *ṛiśya-da*); [cf. *riśya*.] **–ketana** and **-ketu**, m., N. of A-niruddha, L. **–gatā**, f. Asparagus Racemosus, L. **–gandhā**, f. a species of plant, Car. **–jihva**, n. a kind of leprosy, Car.; Suśr. **–dá**, n. a pit (for catching antelopes, BRD.; as hurting what falls into it, T.) **–proktā**, f., N. of several plants. **–mūka**, m., N. of a mountain, VP.; R.; Pañcat. &c. **–lobha**, m., N. of a man. **–śṛiṅga**, m., N. of several men. **Ṛiśyâṅka**, m., N. of A-niruddha, L. **Ṛiśyâdi**, m., N. of a gaṇa, Pāṇ. iv, 2, 80.

Ṛiśyaka, mfn. ifc. having the colour of or looking like the white-footed antelope, R.

ऋष् 1. *ṛish*, cl. 1. P. *arshati, ānarsha, arshitā*, to flow, flow quickly, glide, move with a quick motion, RV.; AV.; VS.; to bring near by flowing, RV.; [cf. Gk. ἔρσῃ (?); ἄψ-oρρος, 'flowing back;' παλίν-ορσος, 'darting back.']

Ṛishabhá, *as*, m. (fr. √2. *ṛish*, Uṇ. ii, 123), a bull (as impregnating the flock; cf. *vṛishabha* and *ukshan*), RV.; AV.; VS.; ChUp.; BhP. &c.; any male animal in general, ŚBr.; the best or most excellent of any kind or race (cf. *purusharshabha*, &c.), MBh.; R. &c.; the second of the seven notes of the Hindū gamut (abbreviated into Ṛi); a kind of medicinal plant, Suśr.; Bhpr.; a particular antidote, Suśr. ii, 276, 7; a particular Ekâha (q. v.), KātyŚr.; the fifteenth Kalpa; N. of several men; of an ape; of a Nāga; of a mountain; of a Tīrtha; (*ās*), m. pl. the inhabitants of Krauñca-dvīpa, BhP. v, 20, 22; N. of a people, VarBṛS.; (*ī*), f. a woman with masculine peculiarities (as with a beard &c.), L.; a widow, L.; Carpopogon Pruriens, Car.; another plant, L.; [cf. Zd. *arshan*; Gk. ἄρσην.] **–kūṭa**, m., N. of the Hema-kūṭa, MBh. iii. **–gajavilasita**, n., N. of a metre. **–tara**, m. a small bull, Pāṇ. v, 3, 91. **–tā**, f. the state of being the best, eminence, superiority, TāṇḍyaBr. **–dāyin**, mfn. bestowing bulls, AV. ix, 4, 20. **–deva**, m., N. of a Tīrtham-kara or Arhat (Jain.) **–dvīpa**, m., N. of a place. **–dhvaja**, m., N. of Śiva, L.; of an Arhat (Jain.) **–pañcāśikā**, f., N. of a work. **–pūjā**, f. 'veneration of the bull,' a particular observance, Gobh. iii, 6, 12. **–vat**, mfn. containing the word *ṛishabha*, TāṇḍyaBr. **–stava**, m., N. of a work. **Ṛishabhânana**, m., N. of a Jina.

Ṛishabhaka, *as*, m. a bull, Nigh.; a kind of medicinal plant, Suśr.; Car.; Bhpr.; N. of a king, Kathās.; of a mountain, Kathās. cx, 148.

ऋष् 2. *ṛish*, cl. 6. P. *ṛishati, ānarsha, arshitā*, to go, move, Dhātup. xxviii, 7; to stab, kill, AV. ix, 4, 17; to push, thrust.

Ṛishad-gu, *us*, m., N. of a man, MBh.

Ṛishṭa, mfn. pushed, thrust.

Ṛishṭi, *is*, f. a spear, lance, sword, RV.; AV. iv, 37, 8; 9; viii, 3, 7; [cf. O. Pers. *arstis*; Zd. *arsti*.] **–mát**, mfn. furnished with spears (as the Maruts), RV. **–vidyut** (*ṛishṭí°*), mfn. glancing or glittering with swords (as the Maruts), RV. i, 168, 5; v, 52, 13. **–sheṇa**, m., N. of a man; (cf. *rishṭi*.)

Ṛishṭika, *ās*, m. pl., N. of a people, R.

ऋषि *ṛíshi*, *is*, m. (√2. *ṛish*, Comm. on Uṇ. iv, 119; *ṛishati jñānena saṃsāra-pāram*, T.; perhaps fr. an obsolete √*ṛish* for √*dṛiś*, 'to see?' cf. *ṛishi-kṛit*), a singer of sacred hymns, an inspired poet or sage, any person who alone or with others invokes the deities in rhythmical speech or song of a sacred character (e. g. the ancient hymn-singers Kutsa, Atri, Rebha, Agastya, Kuśika, Vasishṭha, Vy-aśva), RV.; AV.; VS. &c.; the Ṛishis were regarded by later generations as patriarchal sages or saints, occupying the same position in Indian history as the heroes and patriarchs of other countries, and constitute a peculiar class of beings in the early mythical system, as distinct from gods, men, Asuras, &c., AV. x, 10, 26; ŚBr.; AitBr.; KātySr.; Mn. &c.; they are the authors or rather seers of the Vedic hymns, i. e. according to orthodox Hindū ideas they are the inspired personages to whom these hymns were revealed, and such an expression as 'the Ṛishi says' is equivalent to 'so it stands in the sacred text;' seven Ṛishis, *sapta ṛishayaḥ* or *saptaṛishayaḥ* or *saptarshayaḥ*, are often mentioned in the Brāhmaṇas and later works as typical representatives of the character and spirit of the pre-historic or mythical period; in ŚBr. xiv, 5, 2, 6 their names are given as follows, Gotama, Bharadvāja, Viśvā-mitra, Jamadagni, Vasishṭha, Kaśyapa, and Atri; in MBh. xii, Marīci, Atri, Aṅgiras, Pulaha, Kratu, Pulastya, Vasishṭha are given as the names of the Ṛishis of the first Manv-antara, and they are also called Prajāpatis or patriarchs; the names of the Ṛishis of the subsequent Manv-antaras are enumerated in Hariv. 417 ff.; afterwards three other names are added, viz. Pracetas or Daksha, Bhṛigu, and Nārada, these ten being created by Manu Svāyambhuva for the production of all other beings including gods and men, ĀśvŚr.; MBh.; VP. &c.; in astron. the seven Ṛishis form the constellation of 'the Great Bear, RV. x, 82, 2; AV. vi, 40, 1; ŚBr.; ĀśvGṛ.; MBh. &c.; (metaphorically the seven Ṛishis may stand for the seven senses or the seven vital airs of the body, VS. xxxiv; ŚBr. xiv; KātyŚr.); a saint or sanctified sage in general, an ascetic, anchorite (this is a later sense; sometimes three orders of these are enumerated, viz. Devarshis, Brahmarshis, and Rājarshis; sometimes seven, four others being added, viz. Maharshis, Paramarshis, Śrutarshis, and Kāṇḍarshis), Mn. iv, 94; xi, 236; Śak.; Ragh. &c.; the seventh of the eight degrees of Brāhmans, Hcat.; a hymn or Mantra composed by a Ṛishi; the Veda, Comm. on MBh. and Pat.; a symbolical expression for the number seven; the moon; an imaginary circle; a ray of light, L.; the fish Cyprinus Rishi, L.; [cf. Hib. *arsan*, 'a sage, a man old in wisdom;' *arrach*, 'old, ancient, aged.'] **-kalpa**, m. 'almost a Ṛishi,' 'similar to a Ṛishi;' the sixth of the eight degrees of Brāhmans, Hcat. **-kulyā**, f. 'the river of the Ṛishis,' a sacred river, N. of Sarasvatī (also denoting 'the river of Ṛishis, i.e. sacred hymns,' Sarasvatī being the goddess of speech), BhP. iii. 16, 13; 22, 27; N. of a river, MBh.; VP.; MārkP. &c.; of a wife of Bhūman, BhP. v, 15, 5. **-kṛit**, mfn. causing to see (Sāy.), enlightening (said of Agni), RV. i, 31, 16; enlightening (the mind), inspiring (said of the Soma), RV. ix, 96, 18. **-gaṇa**, m. the company or number of sages, host of patriarchal sages. **-giri**, m., N. of a mountain in Magadha, MBh. **-gupta**, mfn. N. of a Buddha, Lalit. **-cāndrāyaṇa**, n. a particular observance or penance. **-códana**, mfn. animating or inspiring the Ṛishis, RV. viii, 51, 3. **-cchandas**, n., N. of particular metres, RPrāt. **-jāṅgalikī**, f., N. of a plant, L. **-tarpaṇa**, n. a handful of water presented as libation to the Ṛishis, T.; cf. Mn. ii, 176; N. of a work. **-tīrtha**, n., N. of a Tīrtha. **-tva**, n. the state of a Ṛishi, MBh. **-deva**, m., N. of a Buddha. **-deśa**, m. the country inhabited by the Ṛishis, Hcat. **-droṇa**, m., N. of a place. **-dvísh**, mfn. hating the Ṛishis, RV. i, 39, 10. **-pañcamī**, f. the fifth day in the light half of the month Bhādrapada. **-patana**, m., N. of a forest near Benares, Lalit. **-putra**, m. the son of a Ṛishi, MBh.; N. of an author. **-putraka**, m. Artemisia Vulgaris. **-praśishṭa**, mfn. instructed by the Ṛishis, AV. xi, 1, 15. **-proktā**, f. Glycine Debilis, L. **-bandhu**, mfn. related to the Ṛishis, RV. viii, 100, 6. **-brāhmaṇa**, n., N. of a work. **-maṇḍala**, n., N. of a work. **-manas**, mfn. of far-seeing or enlightened mind, RV. ix, 96, 18. **-mukha**, n. the beginning of a Ṛishi or hymn. **-yajña**, m. sacrifice to the Ṛishis, i.e. study of the Veda, Mn. iv, 21. **-loka**, m. the world of the Ṛishis (cf. *deva-loka*, *brahma-l°*), MBh. **-vát**, ind. like a Ṛishi, RV. x, 66, 14; Mn. ii, 189. **-śṛiṅga**, m., N. of a man; (cf. *ṛiśya-śṛ°*.) **-śrāddha**, n. 'funeral oblation for the Ṛishis' (consisting of a mere handful of water), a figurative expression for insignificant acts which are preceded by great preparations, Śārṅg. **-shah** (nom. *-shāṭ*), mfn. overcoming the Ṛishi (said of the Soma), RV. ix, 76, 4. **-shāṇa**, mfn. (√*san*), presented or offered by the Ṛishis (to the gods; said of the Soma), RV. ix, 86, 4. **-shṭuta**, mfn. praised by the Ṛishis, RV. viii, 75, 5; viii, 13, 25; AV. vi, 108, 2; ŚBr. &c. **-saṃhitā**, f. the Saṃhitā of the Ṛishis, Saṃh-Up. **-sattama**, m. the best or most excellent of the sages. **-sâhvaya**, n. 'having Ṛishi as an appellation,' N. of the forest Ṛishi-patana above, Lalit. **-stoma**, m. a particular sacrifice, ĀśvŚr. **-svará**, mfn. praised by Ṛishis, RV. v, 44, 8. **-svādhyāya**, m. repetition of the Veda, ŚāṅkhGṛ. **Ṛishí-vat**, mfn. (m. voc. °*vas*) associated with the Ṛishis, RV. viii, 2, 28; (*vatī*), f., Kāś. on Pāṇ. viii, 2, 11. **-vaha**, mfn., Kāś. on Pāṇ. vi, 3, 121.

Ṛishika, *as*, m. a Ṛishi of lower degree; N. of the king of the Ṛishikas; (*ās*), m. pl., N. of a people, MBh.; Hariv. &c.; (*ā*), f. the wife of an inferior Ṛishi; N. of a river, MBh.; VP.

Ṛishīka, *as*, m. a species of grass, Nigh.

ऋषु *ṛishú*, *us*, m. (√2. *ṛish*?), glow, flame(?), BRD.; (according to Sāy., moving constantly; approaching; great; mighty; knowing; a Ṛishi), RV.

ऋष्टि *ṛishṭí*. See under √2. *ṛish*, p. 226.

ऋष्य *ṛishya*, &c., vv.ll. for *ṛiśya*, &c., qq.v.

ऋष्व *ṛishvá*, mf(*ā*)n. (√2. *ṛish*?), elevated, high, RV.; AV.; VS.; sublime, great, noble (as gods), RV. **-vīra**, mfn. inhabited by sublime heroes (as the sky), RV. i, 52, 13. **Ṛishvâñjas**, mfn. having sublime power (as Indra), RV. x, 105, 6.

ऋहत् *ṛihát*, mfn. (√*rah*, T.), small, weak, powerless, RV. x, 28, 9.

ॠ ṜĪ.

ॠ 1. *ṝi*, the eighth vowel of the alphabet (the corresponding long vowel to *ṛi* and resembling the sound of *ri* in *marine*, but after labials more like *ru*; it generally only appears in some forms of nouns in *ṛi*, viz. in the gen. pl. of all genders, in the acc. pl. m. and f., and in nom. acc. and voc. pl. n.) **-kāra**, m. the letter or sound *ṝi*, TPrāt.

ॠ 2. *ṝi*, ind. an interjection of terror, L.; a particle implying reproach; warding off, L.; a particle used at the beginning of a sentence, L.

ॠ 3. *ṝi*, *ṝis*, m. a Bhairava, L.; a Dānava, L.; f. the mother of the gods; of the demons, L.; recollection; going, motion, L.; n. a breast, L.

ॠ 4. *ṝi* for 4. *ṛi*, q.v.

ऌ LṚI.

ऌ 1. *lṛi*, the ninth vowel of the alphabet (resembling the sound *lry* in *revelry*; it only appears in some forms of √*klṛip*). **-kāra**, **-varṇa**, m. the sound *lṛi*, RPrāt.; APrāt.; TPrāt.

ऌ 2. *lṛi*, *lṛis*, m. a mountain, L.; the earth, the mother of the gods, L.

ऌतक *lṛitaka*, *as*, m., N. of a man, mispronunciation of Ṛitaka, Pat. and Kāś. on Śivasūtra 2.

ॡ LṜĪ.

ॡ 1. *lṝi*, the tenth vowel of the alphabet (the corresponding long vowel to *lṛi*, entirely artificial and only appearing in the works of some grammarians and lexicographers).

ॡ 2. *lṝi*, *lṝis*, m. Śiva, L.; f. the mother of the cow of plenty; the mother of the Dānavas; wife of a Daitya; mother; divine female; female nature.

ए E.

ए 1. *e*, the eleventh vowel of the alphabet (corresponding to the letter *e* as pronounced in *prey*, *grey*). **-kāra**, m. the letter or sound *e*, TPrāt. &c.

ए 2. *e*, ind. an interjection, MaitrS.; a particle of recollection; addressing; censure; contempt; compassion, L.

ए 3. *e*, *es*, m. Vishṇu, L.

ए 4. *ê* (*ā*-√*i*), P. *-eti*, to come near or towards, go near, approach, RV.; AV.; ŚBr. &c.; (with and without *punar*) to come back, come again to, AitBr.; MBh.; Kathās. &c.; to reach, attain, enter, come into (a state or position), Mn. xii, 125; Megh.; Prab. &c.; to submit, fall to one's share, ChUp. v, 14, 1 (*āyayanti*?); KaṭhUp.: Intens. Ā. (3. du. *-iyāte*; 1. pl. *-īmahe*) to hasten near, RV. vii, 39, 2; to request, VS. iv, 5.

Āya, &c. See p. 147, col. 3.

1. **É'ta** (for 2. see s.v.), mfn. come near, approached, RV.; Nir. &c.

É'ti, *is*, f. arrival, approach, RV. x, 91, 4; 178, 2.

É'tya, ind. p. having come near &c., RV. x, 66, 14; AV.; Mn.; Ragh. &c.

एक *éka*, mfn. (√*i*, Uṇ. iii, 43, probably fr. a base *e*; cf. Zd. *ae-va*; Gk. *οἰ-ϝ-ός*, *οἶος*; Goth. *ai-n-s*; also Lat. *aequu-s*; gaṇa *sarvâdi*, Pāṇ. i, 1, 27; see Gr. 200), one (*eko 'pi* or *ekaś-cana*, with *na* preceding or following, no one, nobody; the words *ekayā na* or *ekān na* are used before decade numerals to lessen them by one, e.g. *ekān na triṇśat*, twenty-nine), RV. &c.; (with and without *eva*) alone, solitary, single, happening only once, that one only (frequently ifc.; cf. *dharmâika-raksha*, &c.), RV. &c.; the same, one and the same, identical, ŚBr. v; KātyŚr.; Mn. &c.; one of two or many (*eka—eka*, *eka—dvitīya*, the one—the other; esp. pl. *eke*, some, *eke—apare*, some—others, &c.), ŚBr.; KātyŚr.; MBh.; Hit. &c.; (*eka* repeated twice, either as a compound [cf. *ekâika*] or uncompounded, may have the sense 'one and one,' 'one by one,' RV. i, 20, 7; 123, 8; v, 52, 17; R.; BhP. &c.); single of its kind, unique, singular, chief, pre-eminent, excellent, Ragh.; Kathās.; Kum. &c.; sincere, truthful, MW.; little, small, L.; (sometimes used as an indefinite article), a, an, R.; Śak.; Vet. &c. (the fem. of *eka* before a Taddhita suffix and as first member of a compound is *eka* not *ekā*, Pāṇ. vi, 3, 62); (*as*), m., N. of a teacher, Āp.; of a son of Raya, BhP.; (*ā*), f., N. of Durgā; (*am*), n. unity, a unit (ifc.), Hcat. **-ṛitú**, m. the only time, only season, AV. viii, 9, 25; 26. **-ṛishi**, m. the only or chief Ṛishi, AV. viii, 9, 25; 26; x, 7, 14; N. of a Ṛishi, ŚBr. xiv. **-kaṇṭaka**, m. a species of Silurus, L. **-kaṇṭha**, mfn. 'having one throat,' uttering simultaneously. **-kapāla**, mfn. contained in one cup, one cup-full, AitBr. iii, 48, 2; ŚBr. **-kara**, mf(*ī*)n. doing or effecting one, Pāṇ. iii, 2, 21; mf(*ā*)n. one-handed, one-rayed, L. **-karma-kāraka**, mfn. doing the same thing, having the same profession. **-kalpa**, mfn. having the same method of performing ceremonial, observing the same ritual (as priests). **-kārya**, n. the same business or work, MBh.; mfn. executing the same work, performing the same business, Pañcat. **-kāla**, m. happening at the same time, simultaneous, BhP.; (*am*), ind. at one time only, once a day, Mn. vi, 55. **-°kālikam**, ind. once a day, Mn. xi, 123. **-°kālin**, mfn. happening only once a day, MārkP. **-kuṇḍala**, m. 'having one ear-ring or ring,' N. of Kuvera, L.; of Śesha, L.; of Bala-rāma, L. **-kushṭha**, n. a kind of leprosy, Suśr.; Car. **-kṛishṭa**, mfn. once ploughed, L. **-kshīra**, n. the milk of one and the same cow, Kāś. on Pāṇ. vi, 3, 62. **-khura**, m. a one-hoofed animal, Āp. ii, 16, 16. **-gu**, m. a particular Agni-shṭoma (q.v.), GopBr. **-guru** or **-°guruka**, m. having the same teacher, pupil of the same preceptor. **-grāma**, m. the same village, gaṇa *gahâdi*, Pāṇ. iv, 2, 138; SāmavBr. **-°grāmīṇa**, mfn. inhabiting the same village, ŚāṅkhGṛ. ii, 16, 5; Mn. iii, 103. **-°grāmīya**, mfn. id., Pāṇ. **-cakra**, mf(*ā*)n. having one wheel (said of the sun's chariot), RV. i, 164, 2; AV. ix, 9, 2; x, 8, 7; possessing only one army, governed by one king (as the earth), BhP.; (*as*), m., N. of a Dānava, MBh.; VP. &c.; (*ā*), f., N. of a town of the Kicakas, MBh.; *-varti-tā*, f. the state of revolving on one wheel (said of the sun); the state of being sole master, supremacy (of a king), Kathās. xviii, 70. **-cakshus**, mfn. one-eyed (said of an animal or of a needle). **-catvāriṇśa**, mf(*ī*)n. the forty-first. **-catvāriṇśat**, f. forty-one. **-candrā**, f., N. of one of the mothers in the retinue of Skanda, MBh. **-cará**, mf(*ā*)n. wandering or living alone, not living in company, solitary, segregarious, MBh.; BhP.; (said of certain animals), Mn. v, 17; BhP. v, 8, 15; (N. of a thief), Kathās.; moving at the same time, ŚBr. iii, 8, 3, 17; 18; N. of Śiva-Rudra, Gaut.; of Bala-deva, L.; (*as*), m. a rhinoceros, L. **-caraṇa**, mfn. one-footed; (*ās*), m. pl., N. of a fabulous race, VarBṛS. **-cārin**, mfn. living alone, solitary, MBh.; (*ī*), m. a Pratyeka-buddha, L.; (*iṇī*), f. a woman who goes after one man only, a faithful woman, Daś. **-citi**, mfn. having one layer (of wood or bricks &c.), Jaim. **-citika**, mfn. id., ŚBr. ix. **-citīka**, mfn. id., TS.; V.; Śulbas.; *-tva*, n. the state of having one layer, Comm. on Śulbas. **-citta**, n. fixedness of thought on one single object, Prab.; one and the same thought, unanimity, R.; Kathās.; (mfn.) thinking of one thing only, intent upon, absorbed in, Kap.; Hit.; Pañcat.;

having the same mind, agreeing, concurring; *-tā,* f. unanimity, agreement, Bhartṛ. **– citti-√bhū,** to become unanimous, Hit. **– cintana,** n. unanimous or joint consideration, MBh. **– cin-maya** (*cit-m°*), mfn. consisting of intelligence only, RāmatUp. **– cūrṇi,** m., N. of an author. **– cetas,** mfn. of one mind, unanimous, BhP. **– codana,** n. a rule concerning one act only, KātyŚr. iv, 3, 11; v, 6, 8; (mfn.) having one and the same rule, KātyŚr. **– cchattra,** mfn. having only one (royal) umbrella, ruled by one king solely, BhP.; Hcat. &c. **– cchannā,** f. a kind of riddle, Kāvyād. **– cchāya,** mfn. having shadow only, quite darkened, MBh. iv, 1858; 1878. **– cchāyâśrita,** mfn. involved in similarity (of debt) with one debtor (said of a surety who binds himself to an equal liability with one debtor, i. e. to the payment of the whole debt, Mit.), Yājñ. ii, 56; KātyDh. **– já,** mfn. born or produced alone or single, solitary, single, alone of its kind, RV. i, 164, 15; x, 84, 3; AV.; KātyŚr. &c. **– jaṭa,** m., N. of a being in the retinue of Skanda, MBh.; (*ā*), f., N. of a goddess, Tantras. [T.] **– janman,** m. 'once-born,' a Śūdra, L.; 'having pre-eminent birth,' a king, L. **– jāta,** mfn. of one parentage, born of the same parents, Mn. ix, 148; 182. **– jāti,** mfn. once-born (as a Śūdra), Gaut. x, 50; Mn. x, 4; of the same species or kind (as animals), Suśr.; (*is*), m. a Śūdra, Mn. viii, 270. **– jātīya,** mfn. of the same species, Suśr.; of the same family, Dāyabh. **– jīva-vāda,** m. (in phil.) the assertion of a living soul only. **– jyā,** f. the cord of an arc; sine of 30° or of the radius, W. **– jyotis,** n. 'the only light,' N. of Śiva. **– tatpara,** mfn. solely intent on, Kathās. **– °tantrikā** or **-°tantrī,** f. a lute with one chord. **– tamá,** mfn. (n. *-at*) one of many, one (used sometimes as indef. article), Pāṇ. v, 3, 94; ŚBr.; MBh. &c. **– tara,** mfn. (n. *am,* not *at* by Vārtt. on Pāṇ. vii, 1, 26) one of two, either, other, MBh.; Pañcat. &c.; (rarely) one of many, Dāy.; Kād. **– tas,** see p. 230, col. 3. **– tā,** f. oneness, unity, union, coincidence, identity, ŚBr.; ChUp.; MBh. &c.; (*ekatām api-√yā,* to become one with [instr.], VP.) **– tāna,** mfn. directed to one object only, having the mind fixed on one object only, closely attentive, Kathās.; Daś.; of the same or equal extent, L.; (*as*), m. attention fixed on one object only, BhP.; harmonious tone or song (cf. *tāna*), L. **– tāla,** m. harmony, unison (of song, dance, and instrumental music); accurate adjustment; (*ī*), f. a particular time (in mus.); an instrument for beating time; any instrument having but one note, W.; (mfn.) having a single palm tree (as a mountain), Ragh. xv, 23. **– tālikā,** f. a particular time (in mus.) **– °tīrthin,** mfn. inhabiting the same hermitage, Yājñ. ii, 137. **– tumba,** mf(*ī*)n. having a single bottle-gourd (for a sounding-board). **– triṇśa,** mf(*ī*)n. the thirty-first. **– triṇśaka,** mfn. consisting of thirty-one elements. **– triṇśat,** f. thirty-one; *°d-akshara,* mf(*ā*)n. consisting of thirty-one syllables, ŚBr. iii. **– tejana,** mfn. having a single shaft (as an arrow), AV. vi, 57, 1. **– trika,** m., N. of a particular Ekāha sacrifice, KātyŚr.; ĀśvŚr. &c. **– tva,** n. oneness, unity, union, coincidence, identity, KātyŚr.; MBh.; Suśr. &c.; (in Gr.) the singular number, Kāś.; singleness, soleness, HYog. **– daṇshṭra,** m. 'single-tusked,' N. of Gaṇeśa, L.; a kind of fever, L. **– °daṇḍin,** m. 'bearing one staff,' N. of a class of monks, Comm. on TāṇḍyaBr.; RāmatUp.; (*inas*), m., N. of a Vedāntic school; *ekadaṇḍi-saṃnyāsa-vidhi,* m., N. of a work. **– danta,** m. 'one-toothed,' N. of Gaṇeśa, L. **– diś,** mfn. being in the same quarter or direction, Pāṇ. iv, 3, 112. **– dīksha,** mfn. (a sacrificial observance) at which only one Dīkshā or consecration takes place, Lāṭy. viii, 5, 19. **– duḥkha,** mfn. having the same sorrows, MBh.; *-sukha,* mfn. having the same sorrows and joys, sympathizing. **– dugdha,** n. = *-kshīra* above. **– dṛiś,** mfn. one-eyed, L.; a crow, L.; N. of Śiva, L.; = *tattva-jña,* T. **– dṛiśya,** mfn. alone worthy of being beheld, sole object of vision, Kum. vii, 64; Naish. **– dṛishṭi,** f. gaze fixed upon one object, Pañcat.; (mfn.) one-eyed, L.; (*is*), m. a crow, Nigh. **– deva,** m. the only God, supreme Lord, T. **– devata,** mfn. devoted or offered to one deity, directed to one deity, KātyŚr.; ŚāṅkhŚr. **– devatyà,** mfn. id., TS. iii; ŚBr. **– deśa,** m. one spot or place, one passage, a certain spot or passage, some place, MBh.; Pañcat.; Sāh. &c.; a part, portion or division of the whole, KātyŚr.; Mn. &c.; one and the same place, Kap.; (mfn.) being in the same place, KātyŚr. xvi, 7, 17; *-tva,* n. the state of being a part or portion of the whole, Jaim.; *-vikāra,* m. change of only a part (of a word); *-vikṛita,* mfn. changed in only a part; *-vibhāvita,* mfn. convicted of one part of a charge, Yājñ. ii, 20; *-vivartin,* mfn. extending or relating to one part only, partial, Sāh.; Kpr.; *-stha,* mfn. situated in the same place; standing or occurring in a certain place or passage. **– °deśin,** mfn. consisting of single parts or portions, divided into parts (as a whole), Pāṇ. ii, 2, 1; Comm. on Bādar.; a sectary, Sarvad.; Comm. on Kap. &c.; (*ī*), m. a disputant who knows only part of the true state of a case. **– deha,** mfn. having a similar body or descended from the same person (as a family), Hariv. 2532; having as it were one body, Hariv. 3439; (*au*), m. du. husband and wife, T.; (*as*), m. 'having a singular or beautiful form,' N. of the planet Mercury, L. **– dyū,** m., N. of a Ṛishi, RV. viii, 80, 10. **– dravya,** n. a single object, KātyŚr. i, 10, 6; one and the same object, KātyŚr. i, 7, 9. **– dhaná,** n. a choice portion of wealth, ŚBr. xi, 4, 1, 1; Āp. ii, 13, 13; (*éka-dhana*), 'put down in an odd number,' N. of particular water-vessels by means of which water is taken up at certain sacrificial observances, ŚBr.; KātyŚr. &c.; (*ās*), f. pl. (scil. *āpas*) the water taken up by means of those vessels, AitBr. ii, 20, 5; KātyŚr. &c.; *-vid,* mfn. obtaining the chief portion of wealth, VS. v, 7. **– °dhanin,** mfn. carrying the above water-vessels, ŚBr. iii; having one part of wealth, having the choice portion of wealth, L. **– dharma, -°dharmin,** mfn. of the same properties or kind, Kāvyād. **– dhātu,** mfn. consisting of one part or element. **– dhāra,** m. a single or uninterrupted current, TāṇḍyaBr. xiv, 4, 7. **– dhāraka,** m., N. of a mountain. **– dhishṇya,** mfn. having the same place for the sacred fire, ŚBr. iv. **– dhura** or **-dhurā-vaha** or **-dhurīṇa,** mfn. bearing the same burden, fit for the same burden, equal, apt, Pāṇ. iv, 4, 79; Naish. **– dhenu,** f. a unique or excellent cow, RV. vii, 38, 5. **– nakshatrá,** n. a lunar mansion consisting of only one star, or one whose name occurs but once, ŚBr.; KātyŚr. **– naṭa,** m. the principal actor in a drama, the manager (who recites the prologue), L. **– nayana,** m. the planet Venus, L. **– navata,** mfn. the ninety-first. **– navati,** f. ninety-one; *-tama,* mfn. the ninety-first. **– nātha,** m. 'having one master,' N. of an author; (*ī*), f., N. of his work. **– nāyaka,** m. 'the only Ruler,' N. of Śiva. **– nipāta,** m. a particle which is a single word. **– niścaya,** m. one and the same resolution, common resolution, MBh. i, 7625; (mfn.) having the same intention or resolution, MBh. i, 7624. **– nīḍa,** mfn. having a common abode, VS. xxxii, 8; having only one seat, BhP. **– netra,** m. 'one-eyed,' N. of Śiva; (with Śaivas) one of the eight forms of Vidyeśvara, Sarvad. **– netraka,** m. id. **– nemi,** mfn. having one felly, AV. x, 8, 7; xi, 4, 22. **– paksha,** m. one side or party, the one case or alternative, the one side of an argument; (*e*), ind. in one point of view; (mfn.) being of the same side or party, siding with, an associate, L.; partial, taking one view only, L. **– pakshī-bhāva,** m. the state of being the one alternative, Comm. on Nyāyam. **– pakshī-√bhū,** to be only one side or alternative, Pat. **– pañcāśa,** mfn. the fifty-first. **– pañcāśat,** f. fifty-one; *-tama,* mfn. the fifty-first. **– pati,** m. one and the same husband, BhP. iv, 26, 27. **– patika,** mfn. having the same husband, Comm. on Mn. ix, 183. **– pattra,** m., N. of a plant, L. **– pattrikā,** f. Ocimum Gratissimum, L. **– patni-tā,** f. the state of having the same wife, (with *bahūnām*) polyandry, MBh. **– patnī** (*éka-*), f. a woman who has only one husband or lover, a faithful wife, one devoted to her husband or lover, P. iv, 1, 35; AV. x, 8, 39; MBh.; Mn. &c.; (*yas*), f. pl. women who have the same husband, Mn. ix, 183; a single wife, an only wife, BhP. **– patnīka,** mfn. having only one wife. **– pád** (*pāt, padī, pat* and *pāt*), mfn. having only one foot, limping, lame, RV.; AV.; VS.; AitBr. &c.; incomplete, ŚBr. xiv; (with 1. *aja,* N. of one of the Maruts, RV.); (*pāt*), m., N. of Vishṇu, MBh. iii; of Śiva, L.; of a Dānava, MBh. i; (*padī*), f. a foot-path, MBh.; Daś. &c. **– pada,** n. one and the same place or spot; the same panel, AgP.; a single word, VPrāt.; Śiś.; a simple word, a simple nominal formation, Nir.; one and the same word, VPrāt. i, 111; (*e*), ind. on the spot, in one moment, at once, R.; Ragh.; Vikr. &c.; mf(*ā* & *ī* [ĀśvGṛ.])n. taking one step, ĀśvGṛ. i, 7, 19; having only one foot, ŚBr.; BhP.; occupying only one panel, Hcat.; consisting of a single word, named with a single word, MBh.; VPrāt.; APrāt. &c.; (*as*), m. a kind of coitus; (*ā*), f. (scil. *ṛic*) a verse consisting of only one Pāda or quarter stanza, ŚBr.; RPrāt.; N. of the twenty-fifth lunar mansion (= *pūrva-bhādra-padā*), VarBṛS.; (*ās*), m. pl., N. of a fabulous race, VarBṛS.; *-vat,* ind. like one word; *-stha,* mfn. being in the same word. **– °padi,** ind. upon or with only one foot, gaṇa *dvidaṇḍy-ādi,* Pāṇ. v, 4, 128. **– °padika,** mfn. occupying only one panel, Hcat. **– pará,** mfn. of singular importance, more important than any other, first of all (said of dice), RV. x, 34, 2. **– pari,** ind. with exception of one (die), Pāṇ. ii, 1, 10. **– parṇā,** f. 'living upon one leaf,' N. of a younger sister of Durgā, Hariv.; N. of Durgā, L. **– parṇikā,** f., N. of Durgā, DevīP. **– parvataka,** m., N. of a mountain, MBh. **– palāśa,** m. a tree with one leaf, gaṇa *gahâdi,* Pāṇ. iv, 2, 138. **– °palāśīya,** mfn. being on or belonging to the above tree, ib. **– paśuka,** mfn. having the same victim, ĀśvŚr. iii. **– pākôpajīvin,** mfn. living on food prepared by the same cooking (as a family), Comm. on Gobh. i, 4, 24. **– pāṭalā,** f. 'living upon a single blossom,' N. of a younger sister of Durgā, Hariv.; N. of Durgā, L. **– pāṇa,** m. a single wager or stake. **– pāta,** mfn. happening at once, sudden, rapid; (*as*), m. the Pratīka or first word of a Mantra, Sāy. on AitBr. ii, 19, 9. **– °pātin,** mfn. having a common or the same appearance, appearing together, belonging to each other, RPrāt.; ĀśvŚr. &c.; having a single or common Pratīka or first word, quoted together as one verse (as Mantras), AitBr. i, 19, 9; ĀśvŚr. v, 18, 11. **– pātra,** mfn. being in one and the same vessel, TS. vi. **– pāda,** m. a single foot, MBh.; BhP.; one quarter, MBh. xii; the same Pāda or quarter stanza, RPrāt. 100; (mfn.) having or using only one foot, AV. xiii, 1, 6; MBh.; (*ās*), m. pl., N. of a fabulous people, MBh. ii; (*am*), n., N. of a country; (cf. *eka-pád,* col. 2.) **– pādaka,** *ās,* m. pl., N. of a fabulous people, R.; (*ikā*), f. a single foot, Naish.; N. of the second book of the Śatapatha-brāhmaṇa. **– pārthiva,** m. sole ruler or king, Ragh. iii, 31. **– piṅga** or **-piṅgala,** m. 'having a yellow mark (in the place of one eye),' N. of Kuvera, R.; Daś. &c.; *-°lâcala,* m. 'Kuvera's mountain,' N. of the Himavat, Daś. **– piṇḍa,** mfn. = *sa-piṇḍa,* q. v., L. **– pīta,** mfn. quite yellow, Ratnāv. **– puṇḍarīka,** n. 'the only lotus,' i. e. the only or very best, ŚBr. xiv, 9, 3, 14. **– putra,** mfn. having only one son; (*as*), m. an only son. **– putraka,** m. a species of bird, VarBṛS. **– purusha,** m. the one supreme Spirit, Prab.; one man only; a unique or excellent man, L.; (mfn.) having or consisting of only one man, BhP. vi, 5, 7. **– puroḍāśa,** mfn. receiving the same sacrificial cake, ŚBr. iv. **– pushkala,** m. (*-pushkara,* ed. Bombay) a kind of musical instrument (= *kāhala,* Nīlak.), MBh. v, 3350. **– pushpā,** f. 'producing only one blossom,' N. of a plant, L. **– pṛithak-tva,** n. unity and distinctness. **– prakāra,** mfn. of the same kind or manner. **– prakhya,** mfn. having the same appearance, similar. **– pratihāra,** mfn. having only one Pratihāra (q. v.) syllable, Lāṭy. vi. **– pradāna,** mfn. receiving the offerings at the same time or sacrifice (as deities), ĀśvŚr. i, 3, 18. **– prabhu-tva,** n. the sovereignty of one, monarchy. **– prayatna,** m. one effort (of the voice). **– prastha,** m. 'having one table-land,' N. of a mountain [T.], gaṇa *mālâdi,* Pāṇ. vi, 2, 88. **– prahārika,** mfn. (killed) by one blow. **– prāṇa-bhāva,** m. the act of breathing once, TPrāt. **– prāṇa-yoga,** m. union (of sounds) in one breath, VPrāt. **– prādeśa,** mf(*ā*)n. one span long, ŚBr. vi. **– phalā,** f. producing only one fruit, N. of a plant, L. **– buddhi,** mfn. of one mind, unanimous, Kathās.; 'having only one idea,' N. of a fish, Pañcat. **– bhakta,** mf(*ā*)n. devoted or faithful to only one (husband), faithful, Mn. viii, 363; (*am*), n. the eating only one meal (a day), Kauś.; Yājñ. iii, 319; MBh. &c. **– bhakti,** f. id. **– °bhaktika,** mfn. eating only one meal (a day), Gaut. **– bhaksha,** m. sole food. **– bhāga,** m. one part, one-fourth, Pancar. **– bhāva,** m. the being one, oneness, BhP.; simplicity, sincerity, Pañcat.; (mfn.) of the same nature, agreeing, MBh.; simple, sincere, Pañcat. **– bhāvin,** mfn. becoming one, being combined, RPrāt. **– bhūta,** mfn. become one, concentrated (as the mind), BhP. **– bhūmika,** mfn. one-storied, Hcat. **– bhūya,** n. the becoming one, union, KaushUp. **– bhojana,** n. the eating only one meal (a day), MBh.; eating together, MBh. xiii, 6238. **—bhojin,** mfn. eating only one meal (a day), Subh. **—mati,** f. concentration of mind, BhP.; (mfn.) unanimous, MBh.; Suśr.; Pañcat. **—manas,** mfn. fixing the mind upon one object, concentrated, attentive, MBh.; R.; Ratnâv. &c.; unanimous, AitBr. viii, 25, 4. **—maya,** mf(*ī*)n. consisting of one, uniform, Kathās. **—mātra,** mfn. consisting of one syllabic instant, APrāt. **—mukha,** mfn. having one mouth, Hcat.; having the face turned towards the same direction, AV. ix, 4, 9; having one chief or superintendent, Yājñ. ii, 203; belonging to the same category, Sāy. on TBr. **—mūrdhan,** mf(*dhnī*)n. having the head or face turned towards the same direction, AV. viii, 9, 15. **—mūla,** mfn. having one root, ĀśvGṛ.; (*ā*), f. Linum Usitatissimum, L.; Desmodium Gangeticum, L. **—yakāra,** mfn. containing only one *ya*. **—yajña,** m. a sacrifice offered by one person, KātyŚr. xxv. **—yama,** mfn. monotonous, TPrāt. **—yashṭi** or **-yashṭikā,** f. any ornament consisting of a single pearl, L. **—yávan,** m., N. of a king, TBr. ii; TāṇḍyaBr. **—yūpá,** m. one and the same sacrificial post, MaitrS. iii, 4, 8; TāṇḍyaBr. **—yoga,** m. one rule (opposed to *yoga-vibhāga*, q. v.) **—yoni,** f. the same womb; (mfn.) of the same mother, ĀśvŚr.; of the same origin or caste, Mn. ix, 148. **—raja,** m. Verbesina Scandens, L. **—ratha,** m. an eminent warrior, MBh. iii. **—rada,** m. 'one-tusked,' N. of Gaṇeśa, L. **—rasa,** m. the only pleasure, only object of affection, R. i; (mfn.) having only one pleasure or object of affection, relishing or finding pleasure in only one thing or person, R. iii; Ragh. &c.; having (always) the same object of affection, unchangeable, Uttarar. **—rāj,** mfn. shining alone, alone visible, BhP. iii, 5, 24; (*ṭ*), m. the only king or ruler, monarch, RV. viii, 37, 3; AV. iii, 4, 1; AitBr. &c.; the king alone, KātyŚr. xxii, 11, 33. **—rājá,** m. the only king, monarch, TBr.; MBh. **—rājñī,** f. the only queen, absolute queen. **—rātra,** n. duration of one night, one night, one day and night, PārGṛ.; Mn. iii, 102, &c.; (*as*), m. a particular observance or festival, AV. xi, 7, 10; MBh. xiii; (mfn.) during one night. **—rātrika,** mfn. lasting for one night; lasting for one day and night (as food), Mn. iv, 223; staying one night, MBh. **—rātrīṇa,** mfn. during one night, Lāṭy. viii, 4, 3. **—rāśi,** f. one heap, a quantity heaped together; *-gata* or *-bhūta*, mfn. heaped or collected together, mingled. **—°rikthin,** mfn. sharing the same heritage, co-heir, Mn. ix, 162. **—rudra,** m. Rudra alone; (with Śaivas) one of the eight forms of Vidyeśvara, Hcat. **—rūpa,** n. one form, one kind, Sāṃkhyak.; (mfn.) having the same colour or form, one-coloured, of one kind, uniform, RV. x, 169, 2; AV.; ŚBr. &c.; (*am*), n., N. of a metre; *-tas*, ind. in one form, unalterably; *-tā*, f. uniformity, invariableness, Pañcat. **—rūpya,** mfn. descended from one and the same man or woman, Comm. on Pāṇ. vi, 3, 62. **—°rcá** (*eka-ṛica*), m. n. a single verse, gaṇa *ardharcâdi*, Pāṇ. ii, 4, 31 [T.]; (mfn.) consisting of only one verse, ŚBr.; (*am*), n. a Sūkta of only one verse, AV. xix, 23, 20. **—°rtú,** see *-ṛitú*, p. 227, col. 3. **—°rshi,** see *-ṛishi*, ib. **—lakshya-tā,** f. the state of being the only aim, Daś. **—lavya,** m., N. of a son of Hiraṇya-dhanus and king of the Nishādas, MBh.; (*ā*), f., N. of a town. **—liṅga,** n. (scil. *kshetra*) a field or place in which (for the distance of five Krośas) there is but one Liṅga or landmark, T.; 'having a singular Śiva-liṅga (q. v.),' N. of a Tīrtha; (*as*), m., N. of Kuvera, L. **—lū,** m., N. of a Ṛishi, gaṇa *gargâdi*, Pāṇ. iv, 1, 105. **—vaktra,** m. 'one-faced,' N. of a Dānava, Hariv.; (*ā*), f., N. of a mother in the retinue of Skanda, MBh., (v. l. *-candrā*); (*am*), n. a kind of berry, T. **—vaktraka,** mfn. one-faced, Hcat. **—vacaná,** n. the singular number, ŚBr.; Pāṇ. &c. **—vat,** ind. like one, simple; as one, as in the case of one, Āp.; Pāṇ. &c.; *-°d-bhāva*, m. the being or becoming like one, aggregation, Comm. on KātyŚr. &c. **—varṇa,** m. a single sound or letter, RPrāt.; VPrāt. &c.; (mfn.) of one colour, one-coloured, uniform, PārGṛ.; MBh.; BhP. &c.; having one caste only, being all one caste, MBh. iii; consisting of one sound only, RPrāt. 110; VPrāt. i, 151; (*ī*), f. a kind of musical instrument, L.; *-samīkaraṇa*, n. equalization of two uniform quantities, a kind of equation (in math.) **—°varṇaka,** mfn. consisting of one syllable. **—vartman,** n. a by-way, path, Naish. **—varshikā,** f. a heifer one year old, L. **—vastra,** mfn. having but a single garment, clothed in only one garment, Āp.; PārGṛ.; Hcat. &c.; *-tā*, f. the state of having but a single garment, MBh.; *-snāna-vidhi*, m., N. of a work. **—vākya,** n. a single expression or word; a single sentence, Comm. on Jaim.; the same sentence, an identical sentence (either by words or meanings), T.; a speech not contradicted, unanimous speech, Ragh.; *-tā*, f. unanimity; (in Gr.) the being one sentence. **—vācaka,** mfn. denoting the same thing, synonymous, Comm. on VarBṛS. **—vāda,** m. a kind of drum, L.; (with Vedântins) a particular theory (establishing the identity of all objects with Brahman), T. **—vādyá,** f. a kind of spirit or demon [BRD], AV. ii, 14, 1. **—vāram,** ind. only once, at one time, Comm. on Mn.; Pañcat.; at once, suddenly, Pañcat. **—vāre,** ind. id., L. **—vāsa,** mfn. living on the same place. **—vāsas,** mfn. clothed in only one garment, Āp.; MBh. **—viṇśá,** mf(*ī*)n. the twenty-first, TS.; ŚBr. &c.; consisting of twenty-one parts (as the Ekaviṇśa-stoma), VS.; ŚBr.; AitBr. &c.; (*as*), m. the Ekaviṇśa-stoma, AV. viii, 9, 20; VS.; ŚBr. &c.; N. of one of the six Pṛishṭhya-stomas, KātyŚr. xx, 6, 26; xxiii, 1, 18; *-vat*, mfn. accompanied with the Ekaviṇśa-stoma, ŚBr. viii; *-sampád*, f. accomplishing the number twenty-one, ŚBr.; *-stoma*, m. a Stoma (q. v.) consisting of twenty-one parts, TS. v; ŚBr. xiii. **—viṇśaka,** mf(*ikā*)n. the twenty-first, Mn. iii, 37; Hcat.; consisting of twenty-one (syllables), RPrāt. 880; (*am*), n. the number twenty-one, Yājñ. iii, 224. **—viṇśat,** f. twenty-one, R. **—viṇśati,** f. twenty-one, a collection or combination of twenty-one, TS.; ŚBr.; *-tama*, mfn. the twenty-first; *-dhā́*, ind. twenty-one-fold, in twenty-one parts, ŚBr.; *-vidha*, mfn. twenty-one times, twenty-one-fold, MaitrS. **—viṇśatka,** n. the number twenty-one, Kām. **—viṇśinī,** f. id., TāṇḍyaBr. **—vidha,** mfn. of one kind, simple, ŚBr.; Sāṃkhyak.; identical, Sāh. **—vibhakti,** mfn. that (member of a compound) which (when the compound is resolved) appears throughout in one and the same case, Pāṇ. i, 2, 44. **—vilocana,** *ās*, m. pl. 'one-eyed,' N. of a fabulous people, VarBṛS. **—°vishayin,** mfn. having one common object or aim, a rival. **—vīrá,** m. a unique or pre-eminent hero, RV. x, 103, 1; AV. xix, 13, 2; xx, 34, 17; MBh. &c.; a species of tree, L.; (*ā*), f., N. of a daughter of Śiva; a species of gourd, Nigh.; *-kalpa*, m., N. of a work. **—vīrya,** mfn. of equal strength, TāṇḍyaBr. **—vṛika,** m. a solitary wolf, Comm. on TĀr. **—vṛiksha,** m. an isolated tree, MānGṛ.; VarYog.; one and the same tree, Subh.; a country or place in which (for the distance of four Krośas) there is but one tree, L. **—°vṛikshīya,** mfn. belonging to an isolated tree or to one and the same tree, belonging to a country like the above, gaṇa *gahâdi*, Pāṇ. iv, 2, 138. **—vṛít,** mfn. 'being one,' simple, AV.; TS.; ŚBr. &c. **—vṛitta,** n. the same metre, Sāh. **—vṛinda,** m. a particular disease of the throat, Suśr. **—vṛishá,** m. the chief bull, the best or most excellent of a number, AV.; (*am*), n., N. of a Sāman. **—veni** or **-veṇī,** f. a single braid of hair (worn by women, as a sign of mourning, when their husbands are dead or absent for a long period), Śak.; R.; Megh.; a woman wearing her hair in the above manner. **—veśmán,** n. a unique building, ŚBr. i, 3, 2, 14; one and the same house, Mn. iii, 141; a solitary house or room, Mn. xi, 176. **—vyavasāyin,** mfn. following the same employment. **—vyākhyāna,** mfn. having the same explanation, ŚBr. **—vyāvahārika,** *ās*, m. pl. 'living solitary (?),' N. of a Buddhist school. **—vrata,** mfn. obedient or devoted to one person only, ĀśvGṛ. i, 21, 7; keeping a fast in which food is taken only once a day, TS. vi. **—vrātyá,** m. the only or supreme Vrātya (q. v.), AV. xv, 1, 6. **—śata,** n. 101; mf(*ā*)n. the 101st, MBh. iii, 101; *-tamá*, mf(*ī*)n. the 101st; *-dhā́*, ind. 101-fold, in 101 parts; *-vidha*, mfn. 101-fold. **—śapha,** mfn. whole-hoofed, not cloven-hoofed, solidungulate, VS.; TS. &c.; (*as*), m. a whole-hoofed animal (as a horse &c.); (*am*), n. the race of solidungulate animals, AV. v, 31, 3; ŚBr.; Mn. &c. **—śarīra,** mfn. descended from one body, consanguineous, W.; *°rânvaya*, m. consanguineous descent, W.; *°rârambha*, m. beginning of consanguinity (by union of father and mother), W.; *°râvayava*, m. a descendant in right line, kinsman by blood, W.; *°râvayava-tva*, n. consanguineous descent or connexion. **—śalākā́,** f. a single staff, ŚBr. ii. **—śas,** see p. 231, col. 1. **—śākha,** mfn. being of the same branch or school (as a Brāhman), W.; having but one branch (as a tree), T.; gaṇa *gahâdi*, Pāṇ. iv, 2, 138. **—°śākhīya,** mfn. belonging to the above, ib. **—śāyin,** mfn. sleeping alone, chaste, MBh. xiii, 355. **—śālā,** f. a single hall or room, Pāṇ. v, 3, 109; N. of a place, ŚivP.; (*am*), n. a house consisting of one hall, MatsyaP.; N. of a town, R. ii. **—°śālika,** mfn. like a single hall or room, Pāṇ. **—śiti-pad** (*pāt, padī, pat*), mfn. having one white foot, TS. ii; VS. **—śilā,** f., N. of a town. **—śīrshan,** mfn. having the face turned towards the same direction, AV. xiii, 4, 6. **—śīla,** mfn. of one and the same nature or character, MBh. **—śuṅga,** mfn. having but one sheath (as a bud), AV. viii, 7, 4. **—śulka,** n. one and the same purchase-money (given to the parents of a bride), Mn. viii, 204. **—śṛiṅga,** mfn. having but one horn, unicorn, L.; having but one peak (as a mountain), T.; being of singular eminence, pre-eminent; (*as*), m., N. of Vishṇu, L.; (*ās*), m. pl. a class of Manes, MBh. ii; (*ā*), f., N. of the first wife of Śuka, Hariv. 987. **—śepa,** m., N. of a man. **—śesha,** m. the only remainder, Naish.; Veṇīs.; Kathās.; 'the remaining of one,' (in Gr.) a term denoting that of two or more stems (alike in form and followed by the same termination) only one remains (e. g. the plural *vṛikshās* is the only remainder of *vṛikshas* + *vṛikshas* + *vṛikshas* + ...), Pāṇ. i, 2, 64 ff. **—śruta-dhara,** mfn. keeping in mind what one has heard once, Kathās. **—śruti,** f. an only Śruti or Vedic passage, the same Śruti; an enunciation in the singular, Lāṭy. i, 1, 4; Jaim.; the hearing of only one sound, monotony, Comm. on Pāṇ. i, 2, 33; Comm. on Nyāyam.; the neutral accentless tone; (mfn.) of only one sound, monotonous, Pāṇ. i, 2, 33; KātyŚr.; ĀśvŚr.; *-mūla-tva*, n. the state of being based on the same Vedic passage; *-°ty-upadeśa*, m., N. of a work. **—śrushṭi,** mfn. obedient to one command, AV. iii, 30, 7. **—shashṭá,** mfn. (fr. the next), the 61st; connected or together with 61, ŚBr. &c. **—shashṭi,** f. 61; *-tama*, mfn. the 61st. **—saṃvatsará,** m. duration of one year, MaitrS. i, 9, 7. **—saṃśraya,** mfn. keeping together, closely allied, Vikr.; Pañcat. **—satī,** f. the only Satī or faithful wife, Naish. **—saptata,** mfn. the 71st. **—saptati,** f. 71; *-tama*, mfn. the 71st. **—°saptatika,** mfn. consisting of 71. **—sabhá,** n. the only meeting-place or resort, ŚBr. xiv. **—sarga,** mfn. closely attentive, having the mind intent upon one object, L. **—sahasra,** n. 1001; ([*v*]*ṛisha-bhâikasahasram* [MBh. xii] or *°hasrās* scil. *gāvas*, a thousand cows and one bull, Gaut. xxii, 14; Mn. xi, 127.) **—sākshika,** mfn. witnessed by one. **—sârtha-prayāta,** mfn. going after one and the same object, having the same aim, MBh.; Rājat. **—sāla,** n., N. of a place (v. l. for *-śāla*), R. ed. Bombay. **—sūtra,** n. a small double drum (played by a string and ball attached to the body of it), L. **—sūnu,** m. an only son. **—sṛika,** m. a kind of jackal (having solitary habits), Āp. **—stambha,** mfn. resting upon one pillar, MBh. **—stoma,** mfn. accompanied or celebrated by only one Stoma, Lāṭy.; Jaim. **—sthá,** mfn. standing together, remaining in the same place, conjoined, combined, assembled, ŚBr.; MBh.; Kum. &c.; standing in or occupying only one panel, AgP. **—sthāna,** n. one place, one and the same place; (*e*, loc.) ind. together, Hit.; (mfn.) having the same place of production, uttered by the same organ of speech, Comm. on TPrāt. **—sphyā,** f. (scil. *lekhā*) a line scratched with one piece of wood, ŚBr. iii, ix. **—haṇsá,** m. 'the only destroyer of ignorance' [Śaṇkara on ŚvetUp. vi, 15; cf. *haṇsa*], the Supreme Soul, ŚBr. xiv; (*am*), n. 'inhabited by a solitary or unique swan,' N. of a Tīrtha, MBh. iii. **—halya,** mfn. once ploughed, L. **—hasta,** mfn. one hand long, AgP.; Hcat. **—hāyana,** mf(*ī*)n. one year old, TS.; Mn.; (*ī*), f. a heifer one year old, Kāṭh.; (*am*), n. the duration or period of one year, TS. vi, 6, 3, 1. **—hārya,** mfn., v. l. for *ekāhārya*, q. v. **—helā,** f. (*ayā*, instr.) ind. by one stroke, at once, Pañcat. **Ekâṇśa,** m. a single part, one part, MBh.; Mn. ix, 150; Ragh. &c. 1. **Ekâksha,** mfn. (fr. 1. *aksha* with *eka*), having only one axle, BhP. iv, 26, 1. 2. **Ekâksha,** mfn. (fr. *akshi* with *eka*), one-eyed, VarYog.; having an excellent eye, L.; (*as*), m. a crow, L.; N. of Śiva; of a Dānava; of a being attending on Skanda. **Ekâksharà,** n. the sole imperishable thing, AV. v, 28, 8; a single syllable, Subh.; a monosyllabic word, VS.; ŚBr.; RPrāt. &c.; the sacred monosyllable *om*, Mn. ii, 83; MBh. &c.; N. of an Upanishad; (mfn.)

monosyllabic; *-kośa*, m., N. of a vocabulary of monosyllabic words; *-gaṇapati-stotra*, n. a hymn in honour of Gaṇeśa (a portion of the Rudrayāmala); *-nāmamālā*, f., *-nighaṇṭa*, m., *-mālikā*, f., °*râbhidhānakośa*, m., N. of vocabularies of monosyllabic words. **Ekâksharī-bhāva**, m. 'the becoming one syllable,' contraction of two syllables into one, RPrāt. **Ekâgni**, m. one and the same fire, Lāṭy. iv, 9, 2; (mfn.) keeping only one fire, Āp. ii, 21, 21; *-kāṇḍa*, n., N. of a section of the Kāṭhaka. **Ekâgnika**, m. one and the same fire, Hcat. **Ekâgra**, mfn. one-pointed, having one point, fixing one's attention upon one point or object, closely attentive, intent, absorbed in, MBh.; Mn. i, 1; BhP.; Bhag. &c.; undisturbed, unperplexed; known, celebrated, L.; (*am*), n. (in math.) the whole of the long side of a figure which is subdivided; (*am*), ind. with undivided attention, MBh.; *-citta*, mfn. having the mind intent on one object; *-tas*, ind. with undivided attention, Vet.; *-tā*, f., *-tva*, n. intentness in the pursuit of one object, close and undisturbed attention; *-drishṭi*, mfn. fixing one's eyes on one spot, Suśr.; *-dhī*, mfn. fixing one's mind on one object, closely attentive, BhP.; *-mati*, mfn. id.; (*is*), m., N. of a man, Lalit.; *-manas*, mfn. fixing one's mind on one object, closely attentive, MBh.; Pañcat. **Ekâgrya**, mfn. closely attentive, L.; (*am*), n. close attention, L. **Ekâṅga**, n. a single member, single part, MBh.; R. &c.; the most excellent member of the body, the head, T.; sandal-wood, L.; (*as*), m. 'having a unique or beautiful shape,' N. of the planet Mercury, L.; of the planet Mars, L.; of Vishṇu, L.; (*au*), m. du. 'forming a single body,' a married couple, T.; (*ās*), m. pl. 'constituting one body,' body-guard, Rājat.; (*ī*), f. a particular perfume, Bhpr.; (mfn.) relating to or extending over one part only, incomplete; *-rūpaka*, n. an incomplete simile, Kāvyād. **Ekâñjali**, m. a handful. **Ekâṇḍa**, m. 'having only one testicle,' a kind of horse, T. **Ekâtapatra**, mfn. having only one royal umbrella, ruled by one king only, Vikr. **Ekâtman**, m. the one spirit, MāṇḍUp.; (mfn.) depending solely on one's self, being without any friend, only, alone, MBh.; having the same nature, of one and the same nature, BhP.; °*ma-tā*, f. the unity of spiritual essence, the doctrine of one universal spirit. **Ekâtmya**, mfn. only, alone, MāṇḍUp.; homogeneous, BhP.; (cf. *aikātmya*.) 1. **Ekâdaśá**, mf(*ī*)n. the eleventh, RV. x, 85, 45; ŚBr.; Mn. &c.; ([*v*]*rishabhâikādaśā gāvas*, 'cows that have a bull as the eleventh,' i. e. ten cows and one bull, Gaut.; Mn. &c.); together with eleven, plus eleven, Vop.; consisting of eleven, lasting eleven (e. g. months), RV.; AV. v, 16, 11; MBh. &c.; (*ī*), f. the eleventh day of a fortnight (on which fasting is considered an indispensable observance and very efficacious), MBh.; Kathās. &c.; presentation of offerings to Pitṛis or deceased ancestors on the eleventh day after their death (on which occasion Brāhmans are fed, and the period of impurity for a Brāhman terminates); (*am*), n. the number eleven, ŚBr. 2. **É'kādaśa** (in comp. for *ékādaśan* below); *-kapāla*, mfn. distributed in eleven dishes, VS. xx, 16; *-kṛitvas*, ind. eleven times, KātyŚr.; *-cchadi*, mfn. having eleven roofs, TS. vi; *-tva*, n. the number eleven, BhP.; *-dvāra*, mfn. having eleven doors, KaṭhUp.; *-mārikā*, f. 'killing eleven,' N. of a woman, Kathās. lxvi, 97; *-rātra*, n. duration of eleven nights (and days; the period of a Kshatriya's impurity through the death of a relative), Gaut. xiv, 2; *-rāśika*, n. (in math.) the rule of eleven, Līl.; *-vidha*, mfn. eleven-fold, BhP.; *-vishṇu-gaṇa-śrāddha*, n. a particular Śrāddha; *-skandhârthanirūpaṇa-kārikā*, f., N. of a Kārikā on the BhP.; °*śâksha*, m., N. of a man, GopBr.; °*śâkshara*, mfn. consisting of eleven syllables, VS.; °*śâratni*, mfn. eleven cubits long, ŚBr.; °*śâha*, n. duration or period of eleven days, R.; (*as*), m. a sacrifice lasting eleven days; °*śôttama*, m. 'chief among (the) eleven (Rudras),' N. of Śiva, L. **Ekādaśaka**, mfn. the eleventh, Kap.; Sāṃkhyak.; onsisting of eleven, MBh.; (*am*), n. the number eleven, Vop. **Ekādaśadhấ**, ind. eleven-fold, in eleven parts, ŚBr. x. **É'kādaśan**, mfn. eleven. **Ekādaśama**, mfn. the eleventh. **Ekādaśin**, mfn. consisting of eleven; (*inī*), f. the number eleven, TS.; ŚBr.; Yājñ. **Ekādaśī-vrata**, n. fasting on the eleventh day of a fortnight. **Ekâdeśa**, m. substitution of one sound for two or more; the one sound substituted for two or more (as in contraction of vowels &c.), APrāt.; Pāṇ. &c. **Ekâdhipati**, m. a sole monarch. **Ekâdhyâyin**, m. a single pupil, Āp. i, 16, 24. **Ekânaṅśâ**, f. (scil. *kalā*) 'the single portionless one,' N. of Kuhū or the new moon, MBh. iii, 14129; personified as Durgā, Hariv.; VarBṛS.; N. of Durgā, Kathās. **Ekânartha**, mfn. having the same evils, MBh. **Ekânugāna**, n., N. of a Sāman, ĀrshBr. **Ekânudishṭa**, n. (scil. *śrāddha*) a funeral ceremony having reference to only one ancestor recently dead, Mn. iv, 111. **Ekânṛica**, Atharva-veda xix, 23. **Ekâneka-svarūpa**, mfn. simple yet manifold, VP. i, 2, 3. **Ekânta**, m. a lonely or retired or secret place, (*e*, ind. in a lonely or solitary place, alone, apart, privately), MBh.; Mn.; Śak. &c.; a single part, part, portion, Pat.; the only end or aim, exclusiveness, absoluteness, necessity, R.; Suśr. &c.; devotion to one object, worship of one Being, monotheistic doctrine, MBh.; BhP.; (*am, ena, āt*), ind. solely, only, exclusively, absolutely, necessarily, by all means, in every respect, invariably, MBh.; Megh.; Bhartṛ.; Kap. &c.; (mfn.) directed towards or devoted to only one object or person, BhP.; R. &c.; *-karuṇa*, mfn. wholly and solely compassionate, wholly charitable, Hit.; *-grahaṇa*, n. partial comprehension, Car.; *-grāhin*, mfn. comprehending partially, ib.; *-tas*, ind. lonely, alone; solely, exclusively, invariably, &c.; *-tā*, f., *-tva*, n. exclusive worship, BhP.; the state of being a part or portion, Pat.; *-duḥshamā*, f. 'containing only bad years,' (with Jainas) N. of two spokes in the wheel of time (the sixth of the Avasarpiṇī and the first of the Utsarpiṇī, qq.v.); *-bhāva*, m. devotedness to only one object, MBh.; *-bhūta*, mfn. one who is alone or solitary, BhP.; *-mati*, mfn. having the mind fixed on one object; *-rahasya*, n., N. of a work; *-rāj*, m., N. of a Bodhi-sattva; *-vihārin*, mfn. wandering alone; *-śīla*, mfn. fond of loneliness, MBh.; *-sushamā*, f. 'containing only good years,' (with Jainas) N. of two spokes in the wheel of time (the first of Avasarpiṇī and the sixth of Utsarpiṇī, qq. v.); *-sthita*, mfn. staying or remaining alone or apart. **Ekântara**, mfn. separated by one intermediate (caste), Gaut. iv, 16; next but one, one removed from, Śak. 191 d. **Ekāntika**, mfn. devoted to one aim or object or person or theory. **Ekāntin**, mfn. id., MBh.; BhP.; -°*ti-tva*, n. devotion to only one object or thing, BhP. **Ekânna**, n. one and the same food; only one meal; food given by only one person; (mfn.) having or eating the same food, a messmate; *-nakta-bhojana*, mfn. taking one's only meal at night, Hcat.; *-bhojin*, mfn. taking food but once a day, Hcat.; -°*nâdin*, mfn. eating food given by only one person, Mn. ii, 188. **Ekānna-pañcāśadrātra**, m. n. a sacrifice lasting 49 nights (and days), KātyŚr. **Ekān-na-vinsa**, m. a Stoma consisting of 19 parts, Lāṭy. **Ekān-na-vinśatidhấ**, ind. 19-fold, in 19 parts, ŚBr. x. **Ekânvaya**, mfn. of the same family, Śak. 292, 13. **Ekâpacaya**, m. diminution (of one's food) by one (mouthful), Gaut. xxvii, 12. **Ekâpāya**, m. diminution by one. **Ekâbdā**, f. a heifer one year old. **Ekâmra-nātha**, m. 'matchless lord of the mango,' N. of Śiva as worshipped at Kāñjīvaram. **Ekâmra-vaṇa**, n. 'matchless mango grove,' N. of a sacred grove. **Ekâyaná**, n. a narrow way or path accessible for only one person, MBh.; R.; the only way or manner of conduct, worldly wisdom, ChUp. vii, 1, 2; meeting-place, centre of union, ŚBr.; absorption in one, absolute devotedness to one, unity, MBh.; ChUp.; (mfn.) passable for only one (as a foot-path), MBh.; fixing one's thoughts on one object, closely attentive, absorbed in, L.; *-gata*, mfn. walking on a foot-path only wide enough for one, MBh. i; one who has fixed all his thoughts on one object, L. **É'kâyu**, mfn. affording excellent food or the chief vigour of life, RV. i, 31, 5. **É'kâratni**, mfn. one cubit long, ŚBr. xi. **Ekârāmá**, mfn. having but one object of pleasure, Yājñ. iii, 58; *-tā*, f. the state of the above, ŚBr. xi. **Ekârṇava**, m. only one ocean, nothing but ocean, general inundation, VS. **Ekârtha**, m. one and the same object, MBh.; Rājat.; one and the same purpose; one and the same meaning; (mfn.) having the same purpose or aim, KātyŚr.; MBh. i, iii; R. &c.; having the same meaning, denoting the same thing, synonymous, Nir.; (in rhet.) tautological (as a sentence), Vām. ii, 2, 11; Kāvyād.; expressing one thing, forming only one notion (as a compound); (*as*), m., N. of a glossary of synonymous words; *-tā*, f., *-tva*, n. the state of having the same object or purpose, KātyŚr.; Mit.; the act of expressing only one thing or notion, Pat.; *-nāma-mālā*, f., N. of a glossary of synonymous words; *-samupeta*, mfn. arrived at one object. **Ekârthī-bhāva**, m. the act of conveying only one idea, Comm. on Pāṇ. **Ekâlāpaka**, mfn. having one sound, sounding as one (but expressing more than one thing), Bālar. vi, 1. **Ekâvama**, mfn. inferior or less by one, diminishing by one, RPrāt. **Ekâvayava**, mfn. made up of the same members or constituent parts. **Ekâvarta**, mfn. forming one whirl, Vāgbh. **Ekâvali** or °*ī*, f. a single row, single string of pearls or beads or flowers, &c., Vikr.; Naish.; Kād. &c.; (in rhet.) a series of sentences where the subject of each following sentence has some characteristic of the predicate of the preceding one, Kpr. x, 45; Sāh. &c.; N. of a work on rhetoric; *-tarala*, *-prakāśa*, m., N. of commentaries on the above works. **Ekâvāñc**, mfn. diminishing by one. **Ekâśin**, mfn. eating alone, Suśr. **Ekâśīta**, mfn. the 81st. **Ekâśīti**, f. 81; *-tama*, mfn. the 81st. **Ekâśrama**, m. a solitary hermitage. **Ekâśraya** and **ekâśrita**, mfn. resting upon or clinging to one object or person (cf. *an-ekâśr*°), Bhāshap.; *-guṇa*, m. a simple attribute or predicate (as form, smell, taste, &c.) **Ekâshṭakấ**, f. the eighth day after full moon (esp. of the month Māgha; personified as Śacī, T.), AV. iii, 10, 5; 8; 12; TS.; TāṇḍyaBr. &c. **Ekâshṭī**, f. a pod or seed of cotton, W. **Ekâshṭhīla**, m. 'having one kernel,' Agati Grandiflora, L; (*ā*), f. a species of Calotropis, Car.; Clypea Hernandifolia, L. **Ekâsanika**, mfn. having only one seat. **Ekâsya**, mfn. one-faced, Hcat. **Ekâhá**, m. the period or duration of one day, Pāṇ. v, 4, 90; Mn.; a ceremony or religious festival lasting one day; a Soma sacrifice in which Soma is prepared during one day only (as the Agnishṭoma &c.), ŚBr. iv, vi, xii, xiii; AitBr. vi; ĀśvŚr. ii, 3; KātyŚr. &c.; (*am* and °*hnā*), ind. during one day; *-gama*, m. a day's journey, Pāṇ. v, 2, 19. **Ekâhatāná**, n. the continued series of Ekāhas, ŚBr. xiii. **Ekâhāra**, m. a single meal during the day; (mfn.) taking food only once a day, MBh. **Ekâhārya**, mfn. having but one kind of food, eating anything, making no difference between allowed and forbidden food [Nīlak.], MBh. (ed. Bombay) iii, 190, 41. **Ekêkshaṇa**, m. 'one-eyed,' N. of Śukra or Venus (the teacher of the Asuras), T. **Ekêndriya**, mfn. having but one organ of sense, L. **É'kêsha**, mfn. furnished with only one pole, RV. x, 135, 3. **É'kêshṭaka**, mfn. (fr. the next), having but one sacrificial brick, ŚBr. vi, x. **Ekêshṭakấ**, f. a single sacrificial brick, ŚBr. ii. **É'kâika**, mfn. one by one, single, every single one, AV. iii, 28, 1; ŚBr.; MBh.; Mn. &c.; (*am*), ind. singly, one by one, R. &c.; *-tara*, mfn. one by one (out of many), BhP.; *-vṛitti*, mfn. existing in only one object, Bhāshāp.; *-śas*, ind. one by one, severally, seriatim, Suśr.; Mn. &c. **Ekaikaśya**, n. single state, severalty, MBh.; (*ena*), ind. seriatim, severally, BhP. **Ekâiśvarya**, n. sole monarchy, Mālav. **Ekâishikā**, f., N. of a medicinal plant, Suśr. **Ekôkti**, f. a single expression, single word. **Ekôccaya**, m. increase (of food) by one (mouthful), Gaut. xxvii, 13. **É'kôti**, mfn. having one and the same object of desire or aim (course), tending to one single purpose, ŚBr. xii, 2, 2, 4; *-bhāva*, m. state of concentration on one single object, tranquillity, blissful serenity (state of mind, following after conversion), (Buddh.) **É'kôttara**, mfn. greater or more by one, increasing by one, ŚBr.; Suśr.; RPrāt. &c. **Ekôttarikā**, f., N. of the fourth Āgama or sacred book of the Buddhists; -°*āgama*, m. id. **Ekôdaka**, mfn. offering water as funeral oblation to the same deceased ancestor, a kind of relative, Mn. v, 71. **Ekôdātta**, mfn. having one Udātta accent, VPrāt. **Ekôddishṭa**, n. (scil. *śrāddha*) a funeral ceremony having reference to one individual recently dead (not including ancestors generally), ĀśvGṛ. iv, 7, 1; Mn. iv, 110; VP. &c.; *-śrāddha-paddhati*, f., N. of a work. **Ekôna**, mfn. less by one, minus one (used in comp. with *vinśati* and the succeeding decade numerals, thus *ekôna-vinśati*, f. nineteen &c.) **É'kônnata**, mfn. having one elevation, TS. vi. **Ekôlmuká**, n. a single fire-brand, MaitrS. **Ekâugha**, m. a single flight (of arrows), Śiś. xviii, 55; *-bhūta*, mfn. collected into one mass, heaped or crowded together.

Ekaká, mf(*ā, ikā*)n. single, alone, solitary, RV. x, 59, 9; AV. xx, 132, 1. **–śata**, n. one per cent.

Ekatá, *as,* m., N. of one of the three Āptyas, VS. i, 23; ŚBr. i; Kāṭh. &c.; of a Brāhman, MBh.

E'kataya, mfn. single, one by one, MaitrS. ii, 2, 1.

Ekatas, ind. from one, from one and the same, Rājat.; from one view, from one side, on one side, on one part, on the one hand, AitBr.; MBh. &c.; (the correlative to *ekatas* is either *ekatas* repeated or *aparatas* or *anyatas* or *vā*, e. g. *ekatas—ekatas* or *ekatas—aparatas*, on the one hand—on the other); in one body, all together, MBh. xiii, 2230; Suśr.

Ékato (by Sandhi for *ekatas*). **-dat,** mfn. having teeth in only one (i. e. the lower) jaw, Mn. v, 18.

Ekatra, ind. in one, in one and the same, MBh.; Kathās.; Pañcat. &c.; in one place, in the same place, in a single spot (with the force of the locative), MBh.; Yājñ.; Mṛicch. &c.; on the one side; (the correlative is *aparatra* or sometimes *anyasmin*, on the one side—on the other side, here—there); in one and the same place, all together, Kathās.; Suśr. &c.

Ekadā, ind. at the same time, at once, Sāh.; sometimes, once, one time, some time ago, MBh.; Pañcat.; Hit. &c.

Ekadhā́, ind. simply, singly; in one way, together, at once, AV.; TS. &c.; MBh. &c. **-bhū́ya,** n. the becoming one or simple, ŚBr. xiv.

Ekala, mfn. alone, solitary, ChUp.; BhP. &c.; (in mus.) a solo singer.

Ekaśas, ind. one by one, singly, KātyŚr.; R. &c.

Ekākín, mfn. (Pāṇ. v, 3, 52) alone, solitary, AV. xix, 56, 1; ŚBr.; MBh. &c.

Ekāyanī-√bhū (cf. *ekâyana*), to become the centre of union, become the only object (of affection &c.), Mālav.

Ekin, mfn. simple, consisting of one, Lāṭy.

Ekí (in comp. for *eka*). **-karaṇa,** n. the act of making one, uniting, combination, Comm. on TPrāt. **-√kṛi,** to unite, combine, associate, R.; RāmatUp. **-bhāva,** m. the becoming one, coalition, Vedāntas.; RPrāt. &c. **-°bhāvin,** mfn. relating to coalition or blending (of vowels), RPrāt. **-√bhū,** to become one, be blended or combined, ŚBr.; MBh.; RPrāt. &c.

Ekīya, mfn. belonging to or proceeding from or resting upon one, Gṛihyas.; belonging to the same party, a partisan, associate, companion.

एक्ष् *êksh* (*ā-√īksh*).

Êkshya, ind. p. having looked at, looking at, MBh. ii, 2389.

एज् *ej,* cl. 1. P. *éjati,* to stir, move, tremble, shake, RV.; AV.; ŚBr.; BhP.: cl. 1. Ā. *ejate, ejām-cakre, ejitā,* to shine, Dhātup. vi, 20: Caus. P. Ā. *ejayati, -te,* to agitate, shake, ŚBr.; BhP.

E'jat, mfn. (pres. p. of the above); (*t*), n. anything moving or living, RV.; AV.

Ejatká, mfn. trembling, moving (the head), BhP. ix, 6, 42; (*as*), m. a kind of insect, AV. v, 23, 7.

Ejáthu, *us,* m. trembling, motion, shaking (of the earth), AV. xii, 1, 18.

Ejaya, mfn. causing to shake or tremble (forming irr. compounds with preceding acc., Pāṇ. iii, 2, 28; cf. *janam-ejaya*).

Eji, *is,* m., N. of a man, gaṇa *kurv-ādi,* Pāṇ. iv, 1, 151 (not in Kāś.)

Ejitavya, mfn. to be shaken.

Ejitṛi, mfn. a shaker, causing to tremble.

एज्य *éjya,* mf(*ā*)n. (irr. fut. pass. p. fr. *ā-√yaj*) to be offered (as an oblation), ŚBr. i, 7, 3, 14.

एठ् *eṭh,* cl. 1. Ā. *eṭhate, eṭhām-cakre, eṭhitā,* &c., to be a rogue or rascal; to cheat, Dhātup. viii, 14.

एड *eḍa,* *as,* m. a kind of sheep, KātyŚr.; (*ī*), f. a female sheep, ewe, MW.; N. of a woman in the retinue of Skanda, MBh.; (mfn.) deaf, L. **-gaja,** m. the plant Cassia Tora or Alata (used for the cure of ringworm), Car. **-mūka,** m. deaf and dumb, L.; blind, L.; wicked, perverse, L.

Eḍaka, *as,* m. a kind of sheep, ram, wild goat MBh.; Bhpr. &c.; a kind of medicinal plant, Suśr.; (*ā*, gaṇa *ajâdi,* Pāṇ. iv, 1, 4, and *ikā*), f. the female of the above sheep, a ewe, Bhpr.; (cf. *aiḍaka.*)

Eḍikâkshī, f., N. of a certain plant (= *eḍa-gaja?*), Comm. on VarBṛS.

Eḍakīya, Nom. P. *eḍakīyati,* to behave like a sheep, Kāś. on Pāṇ. vi, 1, 94.

एडूक *eḍūka* (and *eḍuka,* L.), *as,* m. (*am,* n., L.) a building constructed of or enclosing rubbish or bones or hard substances resembling bones, a Buddhist shrine (filled with relics), MBh.; (cf. *buddhâḍūka.*)

Eḍoka, *am,* n. id., L.; (mfn.) deaf, L.

एण *eṇa,* *as, ī,* m. f. a species of deer or antelope (described as being of a black colour with beautiful eyes and short legs), AV. v, 14, 11; VS. xxiv, 36; Mn. iii, 269; MBh. &c.; (*as*), m. (in astron.) Capricorn. **-jaṅgha,** m. 'deer-legged,' N. of a running messenger, Daś. **-tilaka,** m. 'deer-marked,' the moon, L. **-dṛiś,** f. the eye of an antelope, Naish.; (*k*), m. (in astron.) Capricorn. **-netra,** mf(*ā*)n. deer-eyed. **-bhṛit,** m. 'bearing an antelope,' the moon, L. **-mada,** m. the juice of the antelope, musk, Naish. **-vilocana,** mf(*ā*)n. deer-eyed. **-śiras,** n., N. of the Nakshatra Mṛigaśiras. **Eṇâksha,** mf(*ī*)n. deer-eyed, Śāntiś.; Viddh. **Eṇâṅka,** m. 'deer-marked,' the moon, BhP.; *-maṇi,* m. the moon-gem, Kuval. **Eṇâjina,** n. deer-skin. **Eṇêkshaṇa,** mf(*ā*)n. deer-eyed, Naish.; Viddh.

Eṇaka, *as,* m. a species of deer (= *eṇa* above), VarBṛS.; (*ikā*), f., N. of a woman.

Eṇī, f., see *eṇa* above. **-dāha,** m. a kind of fever, Bhpr. **-dṛiś,** mfn. deer-eyed, Bālar.; Prasannar.; Viddh. **-nayana,** mf(*ā*)n. id. **-pacana,** *ās,* m. pl. 'cooking antelopes for food,' N. of a tribe. **-°pacanīya,** mfn. belonging to the above tribe, Kāś. on Pāṇ. i, 1, 75. **-pada,** m. a kind of snake, Suśr.; (*ī*), f. a kind of poisonous insect, ib.

एत 2. *éta* (for 1. see 4. *ê*), mf(*ā* & *énī*, Pāṇ. iv, 1, 39)n. (√*i*, Uṇ. iii, 86), 'rushing,' 'darting;' of a variegated colour, varying the colour, shining, brilliant, RV.; AV.; TS.; VS. &c.; (*as*), m. a kind of deer or antelope, RV.; the hide of the same, RV.; variegated colour, T.; (*ā*), f. a hind, MBh. iii, 8384; (*enī*), f. a river, Nigh. **-gva,** mfn. of variegated colour, shining (said of horses), RV. i, 115, 3; vii, 70, 2; viii, 70, 7.

Etaka, mf(*ikā, enikā*)n. = *éta* above, Pat.

E'taśa and **etaśá,** mfn. of variegated colour, shining, brilliant (said of Brahmaṇas-pati), RV. x, 53, 9; (*as*), m. a horse of variegated colour, dappled horse (esp. said of the Sun's horse), RV.; N. of a man (protected by Indra), RV.; a Brāhman, Uṇ. iii, 149.

Etaśas, *ās,* m. a Brāhman, Uṇ.

एतद् *etád,* mfn. (Gr. 223; gaṇa *sarvâdi,* Pāṇ. i, 1, 27) this, this here, here (especially as pointing to what is nearest to the speaker, e. g. *esha bāṇaḥ,* this arrow here in my hand; *esha yāti panthāḥ,* here passes the way; *esha kālaḥ,* here, i. e. now, is the time; *etad,* this here, i. e. this world here below); sometimes used to give emphasis to the personal pronouns (e. g. *esho 'ham,* I, this very person here) or with omission of those pronouns (e. g. *esha tvām svargam nayāmi,* I standing here will convey thee to heaven; *etau pravishṭau svaḥ,* we two here have entered); as the subject of a sentence it agrees in gender and number with the predicate without reference to the noun to be supplied (e. g. *etad eva hi me dhanam,* for this [scil. cow] is my only wealth, MBh.); but sometimes the neuter sing. remains (e. g. *etad gurushu vṛittiḥ,* this is the custom among Gurus, Mn. ii, 206); *etad* generally refers to what precedes, esp. when connected with *idam,* the latter then referring to what follows (e. g. *esha vai prathamaḥ kalpaḥ | anukalpas tv ayam jñeyaḥ,* this before-mentioned is the principal rule, but this following may be considered a secondary rule, Mn. iii, 147); it refers also to that which follows, esp. when connected with a relative clause (e. g. *esha câiva gurur dharmo yam pravakshyāmy ahaṃ tava,* this is the important law, which I will proclaim to you, MBh.). RV. &c. &c.; (*ád*), ind. in this manner, thus, so, here, at this time, now (e. g. *ná vā́ u etán mriyase,* thou dost not die in this manner or by that, RV. i, 162, 21), AV.; VS. &c.; [cf. Zd. *aêta;* Old Pers. *aita;* Armen. *aid;* Osk. *eiso.*] **-atirikta,** mfn. besides this. **-anta,** mfn. terminating with this, ending thus, Mn. i, 50. **-artham,** ind. on this account, for this end, therefore, Kathās.; Pañcat. &c.; (*etad-artham yad,* to this end—that, R.) **-avadhi,** ind. to this limit, so far. **-avastha,** mfn. of such a state or condition, Vikr.; Ratnāv. **-ātmya,** n., ChUp. vi, 8, 7, misprint for *aitadātmya* (q.v.; cf. Śaṃkara's Comm. on the passage). **-ādi,** mfn. beginning with this, and so forth. **-dā́,** mfn. granting or bestowing this, ŚBr. ix. **-devatyà,** mfn. having this as deity, ŚBr. viii. **-dvitīya,** mfn. doing this for the second time, Pāṇ. vi, 2, 162. **-yoni,** mfn. of this origin, Bhag. **-vat,** ind. like this, thus.

Etaj (in comp. for *etad*). **-ja,** mfn. arising from this.

Etat (in comp. for *etad*). **-kālam,** ind. now. **-°kālīna,** mfn. belonging to or happening in the present time. **-kshaṇāt,** ind. from this moment, henceforth; (*e*), ind. in this moment, now. **-tulya,** mfn. similar to this. **-tṛitīya,** mfn. doing this for the third time, Pāṇ. vi, 2, 162. **-para,** mfn. intent on or absorbed in this, Comm. on Mn. **-prathama,** mfn. doing this for the first time, Pāṇ. vi, 2, 162. **-sama,** mfn. equal to this. **-samīpa,** n. presence of this one.

Etadīya, mfn. belonging or relating to this (person or thing), Kathās.; Hcat. &c.

Etan (by Sandhi for *etad*). **-máya,** mf(*ī*)n. made or consisting of this, of such a kind, ŚBr.; AitBr.

Etárhi, ind. now, at this time, at present, now-a-days, TS.; ŚBr.; AitBr. &c.; then (correlating to *yárhi*), ib.; (*i*), n. a measure of time (fifteen Idānis, or the fifteenth part of a Kshipra), ŚBr. xii, 3, 2, 5.

Etādṛiksha, **°dṛiś,** and **°dṛiśa,** mf(*ī*)n. such, such like, so formed, of this kind, similar to this, RV. viii, 102, 19; x, 27, 24; VS.; ŚBr. &c.

Etāvac (by Sandhi for *etā́vat* below). **-chás** (°*t-śas*), ind. so many times, so often, MaitrS. i, 9, 8.

Etā́vat, mfn. so great, so much, so many, of such a measure or compass, of such extent, so far, of such quality or kind, RV.; AV.; ŚBr.; MBh. &c.; (often in connection with a relative clause, the latter generally following; *etāvān eva purusho yaj jāyâtmā prajā,* a man is of such measure as [i. e. made complete by] his wife, himself, and his progeny, Mn. ix, 45), R.; BhP.; Hit. &c.; (*at*), ind. so far, thus far, so much, in such a degree, thus, RV. vii, 57, 3; ŚBr.; Hit. &c. **-tva,** n. the being so great or so much, quantity, number, size, Pāṇ. ii, 4, 15; BhP. &c.; (with following *yad,* such a state or quantity &c., that.)

Etāvad (by Sandhi for *etā́vat*). **-dhā́,** ind. so many fold, TS. vi.

Etāvan (by Sandhi for *etā́vat*). **-mātrá,** mfn. of this measure, of this quantity, so great, such, ŚBr.; MBh.

एतन *etana,* *as,* m. expiration, breathing out, discharging air from the lungs, L.; the fish Silurus Pelorius, L.

एतृ *etṛí* (*etárī,* Padap. *etári,* loc., Sāy.), m. (√*i*), one who goes or approaches (for anything); asking, requesting, RV. v, 41, 10; vi, 12, 4; (mfn.), ifc. one who goes; (cf. *párâparâitṛi* &c.)

E'ma, *am, éman, a,* n. course, way, RV.; VS.; [cf. Gk. οἶμος, οἴμη; Lith. *eisme.*]

एदिधिषुःपति *edidhishuḥ-pati,* m. the husband of a younger sister whose elder sister has not yet been married, VS. xxx, 9; (cf. *agre-didhishu* and *didhishu.*)

एध् *edh,* cl. 1. Ā. *édhate* (rarely P. *-ti*), *edhām-cakre, edhitā, edhishyate, aidhishṭa,* to prosper, increase, become happy, grow strong, RV.; AV.; VS.; ŚBr.; Mn.; to grow big with self-importance, become insolent; to become intense, extend, spread, gain ground (as fire or passions), MBh.; BhP.; to swell, rise (as waters), BhP.: Caus. *edhayati,* to cause to prosper or increase, wish for the welfare or happiness (of any one), bless, BhP.; Kum. vi, 90; Bhaṭṭ.

1. **Edhatú** (for 2. see p. 232, col. 1), *us,* m. f. prosperity, happiness, RV. viii, 86, 3; AV.; ŚBr. &c.; (*us*), m. man, Uṇ. i, 79; (mfn.) increased, grown, L.

Edhanīya, mfn. to be increased or enlarged.

Edhamāna, mfn. (pres. p. of √*edh*). **-dvish,** mfn. hating those who have become insolent or impious (through prosperity), RV. vi, 47, 16.

1. **Edhas,** *as,* n. happiness, prosperity, ŚāṅkhGṛ. v, 1, 8; MBh.

Edhā, f. id., L.

Edhita, mfn. grown, increased, enlarged, made big, made to spread, filled up, MBh.; Śak. &c.

Edhitṛi, mfn. one who increases &c.

एध *édha,* *as,* m. (√*indh*), fuel, RV. i, 158,

4; x, 86, 18; VS; ŚBr.; Ragh. &c.; (mfn.) ifc. kindling, see *agny-edha*; [cf. Gk. αἰθός, αἶθος; Hib. *aodh*; O.H.G. *eit*; Angl. Sax. *âd*.] **-vat**, mfn. kept up with fuel (as fire), Ragh. xiii, 41.

Edhôdaka, n. fuel and water, Mn. iv, 247.

2. **Edhatu** (for 1. see p. 231, col. 3), m. fire, L.; [cf. Lat. *aestus*.]

2. **E'dhas**, n. fuel, AV. vii, 89, 4; xii, 3, 2; Mn.; Śak. &c.

एन 1. *ena*, a pronom. base (used for certain cases of the 3rd personal pronoun, thus in the acc. sing. du. pl. [*enam, enām, enad*, &c.], inst. sing. [*enena, enayā*], gen. loc. du. [*enayos*, Ved. *enos*]; the other cases are formed fr. the pronom. base *a*, see under *idam*), he, she, it; this, that, (this pronoun is enclitic and cannot begin a sentence; it is generally used alone, so that *enam purusham*, 'that man,' would be very unusual if not incorrect. Grammarians assert that the substitution of *enam* &c. for *imam* or *etam* &c. takes place when something is referred to which has already been mentioned in a previous part of the sentence; see Gr. 223 & 836); [cf. Gk. ἕν, οἶος; Goth. *ains*; Old Pruss. *ains*; Lat. *oinos, unus*.]

एन 2. *ena* and *enā*, Ved. instr. of *idam*, q.v.

Ená, ind. here, there; in this manner, thus; then, at that time, RV.; AV.; (*enā parás*, ind. further on, RV. x, 27, 21; 31, 8; *parā enā*, ind. beyond here; there; beyond [with instr.], RV. x, 125, 8; *yátra—enā*, whither—thither.)

एन 3. *ena* (cf. *eṇa*), a stag. See *an-ena*.

Enī, f. See under 2. *éta*.

एनस् *énas, as*, n. (√*i*, Uṇ. iv, 197; √*in*, BRD.), mischief, crime, sin, offence, fault, RV.; AV.; ŚBr.; Mn. &c.; evil, unhappiness, misfortune, calamity, RV.; AV.; censure, blame, L.; [cf. Zd. *aenaṅh*; Gk. αἰνός.] **-vat, -vín**, mfn. wicked, sinful, a sinner, RV.; AitBr.; ŚBr.; Mn.

Enasyà, mfn. produced by sin; counted a sin or crime, wicked, sinful, AV. vi, 115, 2; viii, 7, 3; ŚBr.

Eno (in comp. for *enas*). **-múc**, mfn. rescuing from sin or evil, MaitrS. iii, 15, 11.

एन्ध् *endh* (ā-√*indh*), Ā. (Subj. *-idhate* and *-inddhate*; pf. *īdhe*) to inflame, kindle, RV.; to be inflamed, flame, RV. vii, 36, 1.

एन्व् *ênv* (ā-√*inv*), P. *-invati*, to drive near; to procure, bestow, RV. ix, 20, 2.

एम *éma, éman*. See p. 231, col. 3.

एमुषम् *emushám* (acc. sg. of the perf. p. of 3. *am*, p. 80, col. 1).

Emûshá, *as*, m. (formed fr. the above) N. of the boar which raised up the earth, ŚBr. xiv, 1, 2, 11; Kāṭh.

एर् *êr* (ā-√*ir*), Caus. P. Ā. *-irayati, -te* (pf. 3. pl. *érire* and *îrire*) to bring near, cause to obtain, procure, RV.; AV.; VS.; to procure for one's self, obtain, RV. i, 6, 4; iii, 60, 3; to raise (as the voice in singing), RV. iii, 29, 15; x, 122, 2.

एरक *eraka, as*, m., N. of a Nāga, MBh. i, 2154; (*ā*), f. a kind of grass of emollient and diluent properties, MBh.; VP.; Bhpr. &c.; [cf. Gk. αἶρα]; (*ī*), f. a species of plant; N. of a river; (*am*), n. a woollen carpet (Buddh.)

एरङ्ग *eraṅga, as*, m. a kind of fish, Bhpr.

एरण्ड *eraṇḍa, as*, m. the castor-oil plant, Ricinus Communis or Palma Christi, Suśr.; Pañcat. &c.; (*ā*), f. long pepper, L. **-taila**, n. castor-oil, Suśr. **-pattraka**, m. Ricinus Communis, L.; (*ikā*), f. Croton Polyandron, L. **-phalā**, f. id., L. **Eraṇḍa-tîrtha**, n., N. of a Tîrtha.

Eraṇḍaka, *as*, m. Ricinus Communis, L.

एरमत्तक *eramattaka, as*, m., N. of a man, Rājat.

एरु *éru*, mfn. (fr. ā-√*ir*) = *gantṛi*, T.(?); AV. vi, 22, 3.

एर्वारु *ervāru, us*, m. f. Cucumis Utilissimus, Yājñ. iii, 142; Suśr.; (*u*), n. the fruit of the above plant.

Ervāruka, *as*, m. Cucumis Utilissimus, Suśr.

एल *ela* and *elada, am*, n. a particular number (Buddh.)

एलक *elaka* = *eḍaka*, q. v., L.

एलङ्ग *elaṅga* = *eraṅga*, col. 1, L.

एलवालु *elavālu, u*, n. the fragrant bark of Feronia Elephantum, Suśr.; a granular substance (apparently a vegetable of a reddish-brown colour; used as a drug and perfume).

Elavāluka, *am*, n. the above fragrant bark, Suśr.

एलविल *elavila, as*, m., N. of Kuvera, L.; (cf. *ailavila*.)

एला 1. *elā*, f. any species of Cardamom, Suśr.; Kathās.; N. of a metre (consisting of four lines of fifteen syllables each); N. of a river, Hariv.; (v. l. *arlā*.) **-gandhika**, n. the fragrant bark of Feronia Elephantum. **-pattra**, m., N. of a Nāga, MBh. **-parṇī**, f. Mimosa Octandra. **-pura**, n., N. of a town. **-phala**, n. = *elavālu*. **Elâvali**, f. a species of plant, L.

Elāka, *as*, m., N. of a man, gaṇa *gargâdi*, Pāṇ. iv, 1, 105; (*am*), n. = *elā* above. **-pura**, n., N. of a town.

Elikā, f. small Cardamom, L.

एला 2. *elā*, f. sport, pastime, merriness, gaṇa *kaṇḍv-ādi*, Pāṇ. iii, 1, 27.

Elāya, Nom. P. *elāyati*, to be wanton or playful, be merry.

एलान *elāna*, n. orange, Nigh.

एलु *elu, u*, n. a particular number, Buddh.

एलुक *eluka, am*, n. a kind of fragrant substance, Suśr.

एल्वालुक *elvavāluka, am*, n. = *elavālu*, L.

Elvālu, n., **elvāluka**, *am*, n. id., Bhpr.; Car.

एव 1. *evá* (in the Saṃhitā also *evā́*), ind. (√*i*, Uṇ. i, 152; fr. pronom. base *e*, BRD., probably connected with 2. *éva*), so, just so, exactly so (in the sense of the later *evam*), RV.; AV.; indeed, truly, really (often at the beginning of a verse in conjunction with other particles, as *id, hi*), RV.; (in its most frequent use of strengthening the idea expressed by any word, *eva* must be variously rendered by such adverbs as) just, exactly, very, same, only, even, alone, merely, immediately on, still, already, &c. (e. g. *tvam eva yantā nânyo 'sti pṛithivyām*, thou alone art a charioteer, no other is on earth, i. e. thou art the best charioteer, MBh. iii, 2825; *tāvatīm eva rātrim*, just so long as a night; *evam eva* or *tathâiva*, exactly so, in this manner only; in the same manner as above; *tenâiva mantreṇa*, with the same Mantra as above; *apaḥ sprishṭvâiva*, by merely touching water; *tān eva*, these very persons; *na cirād eva*, in no long time at all; *japyenâiva*, by sole repetition; *abhuktvâiva*, even without having eaten; *iti vadann eva*, at the very moment of saying so; *sa jīvann eva*, he while still living, &c.), RV. &c.; MBh. &c.; (sometimes, esp. in connection with other adverbs, *eva* is a mere expletive without any exact meaning and not translatable, e. g. *tv eva, câiva, eva ca*, &c.; according to native authorities *eva* implies emphasis, affirmation, detraction, diminution, command, restraintment); [cf. Zd. *aeva*; Goth. *aiv*; Old Germ. *eo, io*; Mod. Germ. *je*.]

Evá thā, ind. so, just so, like, RV. viii, 24, 15.

एव 2. *éva*, mfn. (√*i*), going, moving, speedy, quick, TBr. iii; Uṇ.; (*as*), m. course, way (generally instr. pl.), RV.; the earth, world, VS. xv, 4; 5 [Mahīdh.]; a horse, RV. i, 158, 3 [Sāy.]; (*ās*), m. pl. way or manner of acting or proceeding, conduct, habit, usage, custom, RV.; [cf. Gk. αἰές, αἰών; Lat. *aevu-m*; Goth. *aivs*; O.H.G. *êwa* and Angl. Sax. *êu, êo*, 'custom,' 'law;' Germ. *Ehe*.] **-yā́**, mfn. going quickly (said of Vishṇu), RV. i, 156, 1; (of the Maruts), RV. v, 41, 16; *-marut*, m. 'accompanied or protected by the quick Maruts,' N. of a Ṛishi, RV. v, 87, 1 ff.; N. of a hymn (RV. v, 87), AitBr. vi, 30, 1 ff.; ŚaṅkhŚr. &c. **-yā́van**, mf(*arī*)n. going quickly (said of Vishṇu and the Maruts), RV.

एवम् *evám*, ind. (fr. pronom. base *e*, BRD.; probably connected with 1. *evá*), thus, in this way, in such a manner, such, (it is not found in the oldest hymns of the Veda, where its place is taken by 1. *evá*, but occurs in later hymns and in the Brāhmaṇas, especially in connection with √*vid*, 'to know,' and its derivatives [e. g. *ya evaṃ veda*, he who knows so; cf. *evaṃ-vid*, col. 3]; in classical Sanskṛit *evam* occurs very frequently, especially in connection with the roots *vac*, 'to speak,' and *śru*, 'to hear,' and refers to what precedes as well as to what follows [e. g. *evam uktvā*, having so said; *evam evâitat*, this is so; *evam astu* or *evam bhavatu*, be it so, I assent; *asty evam*, it is so; *yady evam*, if this be so; *kim evam*, how so? what is the meaning of it? what does this refer to? *mâivam*, not so! *evam—yathā* or *yathā—evam*, so—as), Mn.; Śak. &c.; (it is also often used like an adjective [e. g. *evaṃ te vacane rataḥ*, rejoicing in such words of thine; where *evam* = *evaṃ-vidhe*]), MBh.; Śak. &c.; sometimes *evam* is merely an expletive; according to lexicographers *evam* may imply likeness (so); sameness of manner (thus); assent (yes, verily); affirmation (certainly, indeed, assuredly); command (thus, &c.); and be used as an expletive. **-yuktam** (°*m-yuktam*), ind. in such a manner, Pat. **-rūpa**, mf(*ā*)n. of such a form or kind, ŚBr.; MBh. &c. **-vid**, mfn. knowing so or thus, well instructed, familiar with what is right, ŚBr.; AitBr.; TUp. **-vidvas** (once *-vidvás*, ŚBr. xiv, 8, 6, 2), id. **-vidha**, mfn. of such a kind, in such a form or manner, such, MBh.; R.; Suśr. &c. **-viśeshaṇa**, mfn. having such an attribute, thus defined, Comm. on Nyāyam. **-vishaya**, mfn. having such an object, referring to that, Comm. on Mn. **-vīrya**, mfn. strong in that respect, ŚBr. xiii; possessed of such a power, BhP. **-vṛitta** and **-vṛitti**, mfn. acting or behaving in such a manner, of such a kind, Mn.; BhP. &c. **-vrata**, mfn. fulfilling such duties, SāmavBr.; of such a behaviour, acting thus, BhP. xi, 2, 40. **-saṃsthitika**, mfn. of such a nature or kind, MBh. iii. **-saṃjñaka**, mfn. having such a name or term, named thus, Pat. **-samṛiddha**, mfn. so complete, ŚBr. v. **-kāram**, ind. in this manner, Pāṇ. iii, 4, 27. **-kārya**, mfn. having such an aim, aiming at that, Car. **-kāla**, mfn. containing so many syllabic instants, Kāś. on Pāṇ. i, 2, 27. **-kratú**, mfn. thus minded, ŚBr. x. **-gata**, mfn. being in such a condition or state, so circumstanced, of such kind, MBh.; R.; (*e*), ind. under such circumstances, MBh. iii, 15109; Daś. **-guṇa**, mfn. possessing such qualities or good qualities, MBh.; BhP. &c.; *-jātīya, -sampanna*, °*nôpeta*, mfn. id., MBh.; Śak. &c. **-jātīya**, mfn. of such a kind or nature, such, Lāṭy.; Gobh. **-°tarkin**, mfn. concluding, reasoning thus, Śak. **-dravya**, mfn. consisting of such substances, Car. **-nāman**, mfn. so called, ŚBr. v. **-nyaṅga**, mfn. having such a characteristic, of such a kind, AitBr. vi, 14, 2. **-nyāya**, mfn. following this manner or rule of performance, ĀśvŚr. ii, 5, 1, 13. **-abhyanûkta**, mfn. so stated or spoken about, ŚBr. viii. **-°arthīya**, mfn. relating to that, Nir. **-avastha**, mfn. so situated, Prab. **-ākṛiti**, mfn. so shaped, Daś. **-ācāra**, mfn. behaving or acting in such a manner, Gaut. **-ātmaka**, mf(*ikā*)n. of such a nature, so conditioned, Pat. **-ādi** and **-ādya**, mfn. beginning with such a one, of such qualities or kind, such, Mn.; Śak. &c. **-pūrva**, mfn. preceded by this, Kāś. **-prakāra** and **-prāya**, mfn. of such a kind, such, ĀśvŚr.; MBh.; Mn. &c. **-prabhāva**, mfn. possessed of such power, R. **-bhūta**, mfn. of such a quality or nature, such, MBh.; *-vat*, mfn. furnished with anything of this kind.

एवार *evā́ra, as*, m. (etym. doubtful), N. of a kind of Soma [Sāy.], RV. viii, 45, 38.

एवावद *evāvada, as*, m. (fr. 1. *eva* and *ā-√vad*, T.?), N. of a Ṛishi [Sāy.], RV. v, 44, 10.

एष् 1. *esh* (probably connected with 3. *ish*), cl. 1. P. Ā. *eshati* (Impv. *éshatu*, p. *éshat*, inf. *éshe*), *-te, eshāṃ-cakre, eshitā*, &c., to go, move, Dhātup. xvi, 17; to creep, glide, RV. x, 89; 14; AV. vi, 67, 3; to glide or hasten towards, attain, obtain, RV. v, 41, 5; 66, 3; 86, 4.

1. **Eshá**, mfn. gliding, running, hastening, RV.

एष् 2. *êsh* (ā-√*ish*), P. Ā. *-ishati, -te*, to hasten near or towards, fly at; to endeavour to reach or obtain; to desire, request, RV.

1. **Êshaṇa**, *am, ā*, n. f. impulse, ardent desire, BhP.

Ê'shṭa, mfn. (or fr. ā-√3. *ish*), that which is desired or asked for, RV. i, 184, 2.

Êshṭávya, mfn. (see above) to be striven after, desirable, wished for, ŚBr.; MBh. &c.; to be approved, Sarvad.

Ê'shṭi, *is*, f. (see above) seeking to go towards, wish, desire, RV. vi, 21, 8; VS.

1. **Êshya**, mfn. (see the last) to be striven after, to be sought for, AV. xii, 2, 39; 4, 16; TāṇḍyaBr.

एष 2. *eshá* (nom. m. of *etád*, q. v.) **-vīra**, m., N. of a despised Brāhmanic family, Sāy. on ŚBr. xi, 2, 7, 32.

Eshakā or **eshikā**, f. sg. of the dimin. of *etad*, Pāṇ. vii, 3, 47.

एष 3. *ésha*, mfn. (fr. √3. *ish*), ifc. seeking, ŚBr. xiii; (*as*), m. the act of seeking or going after, RV. x, 48, 9; (*eshá*), wish, option, RV. i, 180, 4, (cf. *svâishá*); (*ā*), f. wish, L.; [cf. Zd. *aêsha*; O. H. G. *ërā*.] **Eshâishya**, mfn. to be sought for, desirable, RV. x, 102, 11.

2. **E'shaṇa**, mfn. seeking for, wishing, Nir.; (*as*), m. an iron arrow, L.; (*ā*), f. seeking with, desire, begging, solicitation, request, ŚBr.; Pāṇ.; Rājat. &c.; (with Jainas) right behaviour when begging food, Sarvad. 39, 9; (*ī*), f. an iron or steel probe, Suśr.; a goldsmith's scale, L.; (*am*), n. the act of seeking, begging, solicitation, MBh.; medical examination, probing, Suśr. **Eshaṇā-samiti**, f. correct behaviour when begging food, HYog.

Eshaṇikā, f. a goldsmith's scale, L.

Eshaṇin, mfn. seeking, striving, Nir.

Eshaṇīya, mfn. to be sought or aimed at, desirable, Kum.; ifc. belonging to the medical examination of, Suśr.

Eshitavya, mfn. to be sought, Comm. on Bādar.; to be approved, Comm. on Nyāyam.

Eshitṛi, mfn. one who seeks or strives after, desiring, Bhaṭṭ.

Eshin, mfn. (generally ifc.) going after, seeking, striving for, desiring, AitBr.; MBh.; Ragh. &c.

Eshṭṛi = *eshitṛi* above, Bhaṭṭ.

2. **Eshya**, mfn. (fr. the Caus.), to be examined medically or probed, Suśr.

एष्य 3. *eshya*, mfn. (√*i*, fut.), what is to come, future, Sūryas.

Eshyat, mfn. (fut. p. of √*i*), id. **-kālīya**, mfn. belonging to future time, future.

एह *ehá*, mf(*ā*)n. desirous, wishing, AV. xiii, 3, 33.

Ehas, *as*, n. anger, Nigh.; emulation, rivalry; (cf. *an-ehás*.)

एहि 1. *êhi* (Impv. 2. sg. of *ā*-√*i*), come near! **-kaṭā**, f., **-dvitīyā**, f. &c., gaṇa *mayūra-vyaṇsakâdi*, Pāṇ. ii, 1, 72. **-vat**, mfn. containing the word *êhi*, TāṇḍyaBr.

2. **Ehi**, *is*, m., N. of a man, gaṇa *śārṅgarava-âdi*, Pāṇ. iv, 1, 73.

एहिमाय *êhi-māya* (RV. i, 3, 9), mfn. erroneous for *áhi-māya* [BRD.], of all-pervading intelligence; [*yad vā saucikam agnim apsu pravishṭam 'êhi mā yāsīr!' iti yad avocan, tadanukaraṇahetuko 'yam viśveshām devānām vyapadeśa ehimāyāsa iti*, Sāy.]

ऐ AI.

ऐ 1. *ai*, the twelfth vowel of the alphabet and having the sound of *ei* in *height*. **-kāra**, m. the letter or sound *ai*.

ऐ 2. *ai*, ind. an interjection, MaitrS.; a particle of addressing; summoning; remembering, L.

ऐ 3. *ai*, *ais*, m., N. of Śiva, L.

ऐक *aika*, mfn. (fr. *eka*), belonging or relating to one (?), gaṇa *gahâdi*, Pāṇ. iv, 2, 138 (not in Kāś.)

Aikakarmya, *am*, n. (fr. *eka-karman*), unity of action, Jaim.

Aikakālya, *am*, n. (fr. *eka-kāla*), unity of time, Jaim.

Aikagavika, mfn. (fr. *eka-gava*), possessing but one cow, Pat. on Pāṇ. v, 2, 118.

Aikaguṇya, *am*, n. (fr. *eka-guṇa*), the value of a single unit, simple unity, MBh.

Aikadhya, *am*, n. (fr. *ekadhā*), singleness of time or occurrence; (*am*), ind. at once, together, Pāṇ. v, 3, 44; KātyŚr.; Suśr. **-tas**, ind. id., Suśr.

Aikapatya, *am*, n. (fr. *eka-pati*), sovereignty of one, absolute monarchy, BhP.

Aikapadika, mfn. (fr. *eka-pada*), belonging to a simple word, Nir.; consisting of single words, Nir. iv, 1.

Aikapadya, *am*, n. (see the last) unity of words, the state of being one word, Kāś. on Pāṇ. ii, 1, 25.

Aikabhāvya, *am*, n. (fr. *eka-bhāva*, gaṇa *brāhmaṇâdi*, Pāṇ. v, 1, 124), the state of being one, singleness.

Aikabhautika, mfn. (fr. *eka-bhūta*), consisting of one element, Kap.

Aikamatya, n. (fr. *eka-mata*), unanimity, conformity or sameness of opinions, MBh.; Ragh.; Rājat. &c.; (mfn.) having conformity of opinions, conforming, agreeing, R. v.

Aikarājya, *am*, n. (fr. *eka-rāj*), sole monarchy, ĀśvŚr. v.

Aikarātrika, mfn. (fr. *eka-rātra*), staying one night, Gaut.

Aikarūpya, *am*, n. (fr. *eka-rūpa*), the being of one sort, identity, Sāh.

Aikalava, mf(*ī*)n. (fr. *aikalavya*, Pāṇ. iv, 2, 111), belonging to a descendant of Eka-lū.

Aikalavya, *as*, *vī*, m. f. a descendant of Eka-lū, gaṇa *gargâdi*, Pāṇ. iv, 1, 105.

Aikavarṇika, mfn. (fr. *eka-varṇa*), relating to one caste, MBh.

Aikaśatika, mfn. (fr. *eka-śata*), possessing 101, Kāś. on Pāṇ. v, 2, 118.

Aikaśapha, mfn. (fr. *eka-śapha*), coming from or relating to an animal with uncloven hoofs, Gaut. xvii, 24; Mn. v, 8; Yājñ.; Suśr.

Aikaśabdya, *am*, n. (fr. *eka-śabda*), sameness or identity of words, Jaim.

Aikaśālika, mfn. = *eka-śālika*, q. v., Pāṇ. v, 3, 110.

Aikaśrutya, *am*, n. (fr. *eka-śruti*, q. v.), sameness of tone or accent, monotony, ĀśvŚr.; Kāś.

Aikasahasrika, mfn. (fr. *eka-sahasra*), possessing 1001.

Aikasvarya, *am*, n. (fr. *eka-svara*), the state of having but one accent (as of a compound), Kāś. on Pāṇ. ii, 1, 25; sameness of tone, monotony, ŚāṅkhŚr.

Aikāgārika, *as*, *ī*, m. f. (fr. *ekâgāra*; *ekam asahāyam āgāram prayojanam asya*, whose object is a solitary house), a thief, Pāṇ. v, 1, 113; Daś.; Śiś.

Aikāgnika, mfn. (fr. *ekâgni*), relating to or performed with a single fire.

Aikāgrya, *am*, n. (fr. *ekâgra*), intentness or concentration on one object, MBh.; BhP.; Vedântas.

Aikāṅkāyana, m. a descendant of Ekâṅka.

Aikāṅga, *as*, m. (fr. *ekâṅga*), a soldier who acts as body-guard, Rājat.

Aikātmya, *am*, n. (fr. *ekâtman*), unity of the soul, unity of being, oneness, identity, MBh.; BhP.; oneness with the Supreme Spirit, L.

Aikādaśâksha, *as*, m. a descendant of Ekādaśâksha.

Aikādaśinā, mf(*ī*)n. (fr. *ekādaśa*), belonging to a collection of eleven (e. g. animals), ŚBr.

Aikādhikaraṇya, *am*, n. (fr. *ekâdhikaraṇa*), the state of having but one object of relation, Bhāshāp.

Aikāntika, mf(*ī*)n. (fr. *ekânta*), absolute, necessary, complete, exclusive, BhP.; Suśr.; Sāṃkhyak. &c.

Aikāntya, *am*, n. (fr. id.), exclusiveness, absoluteness, Sarvad.

Aikānyika, mfn. (*ekam anyad viparītam vṛittam adhyayane 'sya*) one who commits a single error in reciting, Pāṇ. iv, 4, 63.

Aikāyana, *as*, m. a descendant of Eka, gaṇa *naḍâdi*, Pāṇ. iv, 1, 99.

Aikārthya, *am*, n. (fr. *ekârtha*), oneness of aim or intention, Daśar.; oneness or unity of an idea, Pat.; sameness of meaning, Jaim.

Aikāśramya, *am*, n. the existence of one order only, Gaut. iii, 36; Comm. on Nyāyam.

Aikāhika, mf(*ī*)n. (fr. *ekâha*), lasting one day, ephemeral, quotidian (as fever), AgP.; belonging to an Ekāha (q. v.) sacrifice, ŚBr.; AitBr.; ĀśvŚr. &c.

Aikāhya, *am*, n. (fr. id.), the state of an Ekāha (q. v.) sacrifice, ŚāṅkhŚr.

Aikya, *am*, n. (fr. *eka*), oneness, unity, harmony, sameness, identity, MBh.; Ragh.; Sarvad. &c.; identity of the human soul or of the universe with the Deity, MW.; an aggregate, sum, Sūryas.; (in math.) the product of the length and depth of excavations differing in depth. **Aikyâropa**, m. equalization, Kuv.

ऐक्षव *aikshavá* and *aikshavyà*, mf(*ī*)n. (fr. *ikshu*), made of or produced from the sugar-cane, TS. vi; ŚBr.; KātyŚr.; Hcat.; (*am*), n. sugar, Suśr.

Aikshuka, mfn. suitable for sugar-cane, gaṇa *guḍâdi*, Pāṇ. iv, 4, 103; bearing sugar-cane, gaṇa *vaṇśâdi*, Pāṇ. v, 1, 50; (fr. *ikshukīyā*), being in a country which abounds in sugar-cane, gaṇa *bilvakâdi*, Pāṇ. vi, 4, 153.

Aikshubhārika, mfn. (fr. *ikshu-bhāra*), carrying a load of sugar-canes.

ऐक्ष्वाक *aikshvākâ*, *as*, *ī*, m. f. a son or descendant of Ikshvāku, ŚBr. xiii; MBh.; R.; Ragh. &c.

Aikshvāku, ep. for *aikshvākâ* above.

ऐङ्गुद *aiṅguda*, mf(*ī*)n. coming from the plant Iṅguda, Suśr.; R.; (*am*), n. the fruit of that plant, L.

ऐच्छिक *aicchika*, mfn. (fr. *icchā*), optional, arbitrary, at will, Comm. on Pāṇ.; Kuv. &c.

ऐटत *aiṭata*, *am*. n. (fr. *iṭata*), N. of several Sāmans, ĀrshBr.; TāṇḍyaBr.

ऐड 1. *aiḍá*, mf(*ī*)n. (fr. *iḍā*), containing anything that refreshes or strengthens, VS. xv, 7; ending in or containing the word *iḍā* (as a Sāman), VS.; TāṇḍyaBr.; Kāṭh. &c.; descended from Iḍā, VP.; (*as*), m., N. of Purūravas, RV. x, 95, 18 (*ailá*); ŚBr. &c.; (*ās*), m. pl. the descendants or family of Purūravas, VP.; (cf. *aila*.) **-kāva**, **-kautsa**, **-krauñca**, **-yāma**, **-vāsishṭha**, **-śuddhāśuddhīya**, **-saindhukshita**, **-sauparṇa**, n., N. of certain Sāmans.

Aiḍâdadha = *iḍā-dadha*, p. 164, col. 3, ĀpŚr.

ऐड 2. *aiḍa*, mfn. (fr. *eḍa*), coming from the sheep Eḍa, MBh. viii.

Aiḍaká, mf(*ī*)n. id., ŚBr.; KātyŚr.; (*as*), m. a species of sheep, ŚBr. xii.

ऐडविड *aiḍaviḍa*, *as*, m. a descendant of Iḍa-viḍā, N. of Kuvera, BhP.; Rājat.; of a son of Daśaratha, BhP. ix; (cf. *ailavila*.)

ऐडूक *aiḍūka*, n. = *eḍūka*, q. v.

ऐण *aiṇa*, mf(*ī*)n. (fr. *eṇa*), produced from or belonging to the male black antelope, Yājñ. i, 258; Kāś. on Pāṇ. iv, 3, 159.

Aiṇika, mfn. hunting black antelopes, L.

Aiṇikīya, mfn. = *aiṇa*?, Pat. on Pāṇ. iv, 2, 141.

Aiṇīpacana, mfn. = *eṇīpacanīya*, q. v., Siddh. on Pāṇ. i, 1, 75.

Aiṇeya, mfn. (fr. *eṇī*), produced or coming from the female black antelope, Pāṇ. iv, 3, 159; ĀśvGṛ.; Suśr.; BhP. &c.; (fr. *aiṇeya*) belonging to anything which is produced from the female black antelope, Kāś. on Pāṇ. iv, 3, 155; (*as*), m. the black antelope; (*am*), n. a kind of coitus.

ऐतदात्म्य *aitadātmya*, *am*, n. (fr. *etad-ātman*), the state of having the nature or property of this, ChUp. vi, 8, 7; 16, 3 (= Vedântas. 200).

ऐतर *aitara*, mfn. (fr. *itara*), gaṇa *saṃkalâdi*, Pāṇ. iv, 2, 75.

Aitareya, *as*, m. a descendant of Itara or Itarā, N. of Mahidāsa (author of a Brāhmaṇa and Āraṇyaka called after him); (mfn.) composed by Aitareya. **-brāhmaṇa**, n., N. of the Brāhmaṇa composed by Aitareya (attached to the Ṛig-veda and prescribing the duties of the Hotṛi priest; it is divided into forty Adhyāyas or eight Pañcikās). **Aitareyâraṇyaka**, n., N. of the Āraṇyaka composed by Aitareya (consisting of five books or Āraṇyakas, the second and third books of which form the Upanishad). **Aitareyôpanishad**, f., N. of either the second and third books of the Aitareya-āraṇyaka or of the four last sections of the second book only; *-bhāshya*, n., N. of a treatise and commentary on the last.

Aitareyaka, *am*, n. the Aitareya-brāhmaṇa.

Aitareyin, *iṇas*, m. pl. the school of Aitareya, ĀśvŚr.

ऐतश *aitaśa*, *as*, m., N. of a Muni. **-pralāpa**, m., N. of a section of the Atharva-veda by the above Muni (coming after the Kuntāpa hymns, Sāy.), AitBr. vi, 33, 1; Vait.

Aitaśâyana, *as*, m. a descendant of Aitaśa, AitBr. vi, 33, 3.

ऐतिकायन *aitikāyana*, *as*, m. a descendant of Itika, gaṇa *naḍâdi*, Pāṇ. iv, 1, 99.

Aitikāyanīya, mfn. belonging to the above.

ऐतिशायन *aitiśāyana, as,* m. a descendant of Itiśa, gaṇa *naḍâdi*, Pāṇ. iv, 1, 99; Jaim.

ऐतिह *aitiha, am,* n. = the next, ŚāṅkhŚr.

Aitihya, *am,* n. (fr. *iti-ha*), traditional instruction, tradition, TĀr. i, 2, 1; MBh.; R.

ऐतिहासिक *aitihāsika,* mf(*ī*)n. (fr. *iti-hāsa*), derived from ancient legends, legendary, historical, traditional, Sāy.; Prab.; (*as*), m. one who relates or knows ancient legends; an historian.

ऐदंयुगीन *aidaṃyugīna,* mfn. (fr. *idam-yuga;* gaṇa *pratijanâdi*, Pāṇ. iv, 4, 99), suitable for or belonging to this Yuga or age, Comm. on ChUp. i, 9, 1.

ऐदंपर्य *aidamparya, am,* n. (fr. *idam-para*), chief object or aim, chief end, Mālatīm.; Comm. on Bādar.

ऐध *aidhá, am,* n. (fr. 2. *edhas*, Sāy.), flame, splendour; ardour, power, RV. i, 166, 1.

ऐन *aina, ās,* m. pl., N. of a people, MBh. (ed. Calc.) xiii; (v. l. *aila.*)

ऐनस *ainasa, am,* n. (fr. *enas*, gaṇa *prajñâdi*, Pāṇ. v, 4, 38 [not in Kāś.]), = *enas.*

ऐन्दव *aindava,* mf(*ī*)n. (fr. *indu*), relating to the moon, like the moon, lunar, Prab.; Kathās.; (*as*), m. the planet Mercury, VarBṛS.; (*ī*), f. Serratula Anthelminthica, L.; (*am*), n. the Nakshatra Mṛigaśiras, VarBṛS.; (with and without *śodhana*) the observance called Cāndrāyaṇa (q. v.), Mn. xi, 125; Parāś.

Aindumateya, *as,* m. a descendant of Indumatī, N. of Daśaratha, Bālar.

Ainduśekhara, mfn. (fr. *indu-śekhara*), belonging to or treating of the moon-crested one, i. e. Śiva, Bālar.

ऐन्द्र *aindrá,* mf(*ī*)n. (fr. *indra*), belonging to or sacred to Indra, coming or proceeding from Indra, similar to Indra, AV.; TS.; VS.; ŚBr.; Mn. &c.; (*as*), m. (scil. *bhāga*) that part of a sacrifice which is offered to Indra, R.; (*ī*), f. (scil. *ṛic*) a verse addressed to Indra, ŚBr. iv; ĀśvŚr. vi; Nir. &c.; (scil. *diś*) Indra's quarter, the east, VarBṛS.; (scil. *tithi*) the eighth day in the second half of the month Mārgaśirsha; (scil. *śakti*) Indra's energy (personified as his wife and sometimes identified with Durgā), MārkP.; DevībhP. &c.; N. of the lunar mansion Jyeshṭhā, L.; a species of cucumber, Bhpr.; Car.; Cardamom, L.; misfortune, L.; (*am*), n. the lunar mansion Jyeshṭhā, VarBṛS.; N. of several Sāmans; of a country in Bhāratavarsha, VP.; wild ginger, L. **–turīyá,** m. (scil. *graha*) a libation the fourth part of which belongs to Indra, ŚBr. iv, 1, 3, 14.

Aindrajāla, *am,* n. (fr. *indra-jāla*), magic, sorcery, Vātsyāy.

Aindrajālika, mf(*ī*)n. familiar with or relating to magic, magical, Prab.; (*as*), m. a juggler, magician, Kathās.; Ratnāv.

Aindradyumna, mfn. relating to or treating of Indradyumna, MBh. i.

Aindradyumni, *is,* m. a descendant of Indradyumna, N. of Janaka, MBh. iii.

Aindranīla, mf(*ī*)n. (fr. *indra-nīla*), made of sapphire, Kuv.

Aindramahika, mfn. serving for an Indra-maha festival, Kāś. on Pāṇ. v, 1, 109.

Aindramāruta, mfn. relating to Indra and the Maruts, TāṇḍyaBr. xxi, 14, 12.

Aindralājya, mfn. a descendant of Indralājī, gaṇa *kurv-ādi*, Pāṇ. iv, 1, 151 (Kāś. reads *indrajāli*).

Aindraluptika, mfn. (fr. *indra-lupta*), afflicted with morbid baldness of the head, L.

Aindravāyavá, mfn. belonging or relating to Indra and Vāyu, TS.; ŚBr.

Aindraśira, m. (fr. *indra-śira*, N. of a country, Comm.), a species of elephant, R. ii, 70, 23.

Aindraseni, *is,* m. a descendant of Indrasena, Hariv.

Aindrahava, mfn. belonging to Aindrahavya, Pāṇ. iv, 2, 111.

Aindrahavya, *as,* m. a descendant of Indrahū, gaṇa *gargâdi*, Pāṇ. iv, 1, 105.

Aindrāgná, mf(*ī*)n. sacred or belonging to or coming from Indra and Agni, AV. viii, 5, 19; xi, 7, 6; VS.; TS.; ŚBr.; MBh.; (*am*), n. the Nakshatra Viśākhā, VarBṛS. **–kulāya,** m. a particular Ekāha (q. v.), KātyŚr. xxii, 11, 13.

Aindrāgnya, mfn. v. l. for *aindrāgna*, MBh. (ed. Calc.) xii, 2307.

Aindrājāgata, mfn. addressed to Indra and composed in the Jagatī metre (as a prayer), Vait.; GopBr. ii, 6, 16.

Aindrādṛiśa, mfn. made of Indrādṛiśa or the cochineal insect [T.], gaṇa *tālâdi*, Pāṇ. iv, 3, 152.

Aindrānairṛita, mfn. belonging to Indra and Nirṛiti, Kāṭh.

Aindrāpaushṇá, mfn. belonging to Indra and Pūshan, ŚBr.; KātyŚr.

Aindrābārhaspatyá, mfn. belonging to Indra and Bṛihaspati, MaitrS.; ŚBr.; AitBr. &c.

Aindrāmāruta, mfn. belonging to Indra and the Maruts, KātyŚr.

Aindrāyaṇa, *as,* m. a descendant of Indra; (*ī*), f., N. of a woman.

Aindrāyaṇaka, mfn. belonging or relating to Aindrāyaṇa, gaṇa *arīhaṇâdi*, Pāṇ. iv, 2, 80.

Aindrāyudha, mfn. (fr. *indrâyudha*, gaṇa *tālâdi*, Pāṇ. iv, 3, 152), made of (?) or relating to Indra's rainbow.

Aindrārbhava, mfn. relating to Indra and the Ṛibhus, AitBr.

Aindrāliśa, mfn. made of Indrāliśa or the cochineal insect [T.], gaṇa *tālâdi*, Pāṇ. iv, 3, 152.

Aindrāvaruṇa, mfn. relating to Indra and Varuṇa, AitBr.; Vait.

Aindrāvasāna, mf(*ī*)n. (fr. *indrâvasāna*, gaṇa *utsâdi*, Pāṇ. iv, 1, 86), inhabiting a desert [= *marubhava*, T.]

Aindrāvāruṇa, mfn. = *aindrāvaruṇa* above, TāṇḍyaBr.

Aindrāvaishṇavá, mf(*ī*)n. relating to Indra and Vishṇu, ŚBr.; AitBr.; TāṇḍyaBr.

Aindrāsaumyá, mfn. belonging to Indra and Soma, ŚBr.; KātyŚr.

Aindri, *is,* m. a descendant of Indra; N. of Jayanta, Hariv.; of Arjuna, MBh.; of the monkey-king Vālin, L.; a crow, Ragh. xii, 22.

Aindroti, *is,* m. a descendant of Indrota, TāṇḍyaBr.; VBr.

ऐन्द्रिय *aindriya,* mfn. (fr. *indriya*), relating to the senses, sensual, BhP.; Comm. on Nyāyad.; (*am*), n. sensual pleasure, world of senses, BhP.

Aindriye-dhī, mfn. one whose mind is fixed upon sensual pleasure only, BhP. v, 18, 22.

Aindriyaka, mfn. relating to the senses, sensual, Car.; VP. **–tva,** n. the state of relating to senses, Comm. on Nyāyad.

ऐन्धन *aindhana,* mfn. (fr. *indhana*), produced from fuel (as fire), MBh. iii, 149.

ऐन्धायन *aindhāyana, as,* m. a descendant of Indha, gaṇa 1. *raḍâdi*, Pāṇ. iv, 1, 99 (not in Kāś.)

ऐन्य *ainya, as,* m. (with *indrasya*), N. of a Sāman, ĀrshBr.

ऐन्वक *ainvaka, am,* n., N. of a Sāman, ib.

ऐभ *aibha,* mf(*ī*)n. (fr. *ibha*), belonging to an elephant, Murdār.; Śiś.; (*ī*), f. a kind of pumpkin, L.

Aibhāvatá, *as,* m. a descendant of Ibhāvat, N. of Pratīdarśa, ŚBr. xii.

ऐयत्य *aiyatya, am,* n. (fr. *iyat*), quantity, number, value.

ऐर *airá,* mfn. (fr. *írā*), relating to or consisting of water or refreshment or food, TS. ii; TāṇḍyaBr.; Comm. on ChUp. viii, 5, 3; (*am*), n. a heap or plenty of food or refreshment; (with *madīya*) N. of a lake in Brahman's world, ChUp. viii, 5, 3.

Airammada, mfn. (fr. *iram-mada*), coming from sheet-lightning, Bālar.; a descendant of Agni, N. of Devamuni (author of a Vedic hymn), RAnukr.

Airāvaṇa, *as,* m. (fr. *irā-van*), N. of Indra's elephant, MBh.; Hariv.; Lalit.; N. of a Nāga, MBh. ii; (cf. the next.)

Airāvatá, *as,* m. (fr. *irā-vat*), a descendant of Irā-vat; N. of a Nāga or mythical serpent, AV. viii, 10, 29; TāṇḍyaBr.; MBh.; Hariv. &c.; 'produced from the ocean,' N. of Indra's elephant (considered as the prototype of the elephant race and the supporter of the east quarter; cf. *nāga*, which means also elephant and serpent), MBh.; Ragh.; Megh. &c.; a species of elephant, R. ii, 70, 23; the tree Artocarpus Lacucha; the orange tree, L.; N. of a particular portion of the moon's path; of a form of the sun, VP.; MBh.; (*as, am*), m. n. a kind of rainbow, MBh.; Ragh. &c.; (*ī*), f. the female of Indra's elephant; N. of a river, MBh.; lightning, L.; a species of fern, Suśr.; (*ī, ā*), f. a particular portion of the moon's path (including the lunar mansions Punarvasu, Pushya, and Āślesha), VarBṛS.; (*am*), n. the fruit of Artocarpus Lacucha, Suśr.; N. of a Varsha, MBh.

Airāvataka, *as,* m., N. of a mountain; (*am*), n. the fruit of Artocarpus Lacucha, Car.

Aireya, *am,* n. (fr. *irā*), an intoxicating beverage, MānGṛ.

ऐरिण *airiṇa, am,* n. (fr. *iriṇa*), fossil or rock salt, L.; N. of a Sāman.

ऐर्म्य *airmya, am,* n. (fr. 2. *īrma*), 'fit for a sore,' an ointment, plaster, Suśr. ii, 86, 2.

ऐल *aila, as,* m. (fr. *ilā* = *iḍā*), a descendant of Ilā, N. of Purūravas (cf. 1. *aiḍá*), Hariv.; MBh.; N. of the planet Mars, T.; (*ās*), m. pl. the descendants or family of Purūravas, MBh. xiii; (*ā*), f., N. of a river (v. l. *elā*), Hariv.; (*am*), n. plenty or abundance of food or refreshment; a particular number (Buddh.) **–dhāna,** m., N. of a place, R. ii, 71, 3; (*ī*), f., N. of a river, Comm. on R. ib. **–bridá,** mfn. bringing or procuring plenty of food, VS. xvi, 60; TS. iv. **–mṛiḍá,** mfn. id. (?), MaitrS. ii, 9, 9.

1. **Aileya,** *as,* m., N. of the planet Mars, T.

ऐलक *ailaka,* mfn. coming rom the sheep called Eḍaka, Āp.

ऐलब *ailabá, as,* m. noise, cry, roaring, AV. vi, 16, 3; xii, 5, 47–49. **–kārá,** mfn. making a noise, roaring (said of Rudra's dogs), AV. xi, 2, 30.

ऐलवालुक *ailavāluka* = *elavālu*, q. v., L.

ऐलविल *ailavila* or *ailaviḍa* (cf. *aiḍaviḍa*), *as,* m. a descendant of Ilavila, N. of Dilīpa, MBh. vii, 2263; a descendant of Ilavilā, N. of Kuvera, MBh.; Hariv.; Bālar.

ऐलाक *ailāka,* mfn. belonging to Ailākya, gaṇa *kaṇvâdi*, Pāṇ. iv, 2, 111.

Ailākya, *as,* m. a descendant of Elāka, gaṇa *gargâdi*, Pāṇ. iv, 1, 105.

ऐलिक *ailika, as,* m. a descendant of Ilinī, N. of Jaṃsu (father of Dushyanta), Hariv.

ऐलूष *ailūsha, as,* m. a descendant of Ilūsha, N. of Kavasha (author of a Vedic hymn), AitBr. ii, 19, 1.

ऐलेय 2. *aileya, am,* n. = *elavālu*, q. v., L.

ऐश *aiśa,* mfn. (fr. *īśa*), relating to or coming from Śiva, Śiva-like, BhP.; AgP.; Ragh.; divine, supreme, regal.

Aiśika, mfn. relating to Śiva &c., R. i, 56, 6 (v. l. *aishīka*).

Aiśya, *am,* n. supremacy, power, BhP.

ऐशान *aiśāna,* mf(*ī*)n. (fr. *īśāna*), relating to or coming from Śiva, RāmatUp.; Vikr.; belonging to Śiva's quarter, north-eastern, VarBṛS.; (*ī*), f. (scil. *diś*) Śiva's quarter, north-east, VarBṛS. **–ja,** *ās,* m. pl. = *īśānaja*, q. v.

ऐश्वर *aiśvara,* mf(*ī*)n. (fr. *īśvara*), relating to or coming from a mighty lord or king, mighty powerful, majestic, MBh.; BhP.; Kathās. &c.; belonging to or coming from Śiva, Ragh. xi, 76; Kathās. cxvi, 10; (*am*), n. supremacy, power, might, BhP. x; (*ī*), f., N. of Durgā, T.

Aiśvari, *is,* m. a descendant of Īśvara, N. of a Ṛishi.

Aiśvarya, *am,* n. the state of being a mighty lord, sovereignty, supremacy, power, sway, ŚBr. xiii; MBh.; Mn. &c.; dominion, Kathās.; superhuman power (either perpetual or transient, consisting, according to some, of the following eight: *aṇiman, laghiman, mahiman, prāpti, prākāmya, vaśitva, īśitva,* and *kāmâvasāyitva*, qq. v.; or, according to others, of such powers as vision, audition, cogitation, discrimination, and omniscience; and of active powers such as swiftness of thought, power of assuming forms at will, and faculty of expatiation, Sarvad. &c.) **–vat,** mfn. possessing power or supremacy, MBh.;

possessed of or connected with superhuman powers. **-vivaraṇa**, n., N. of a work.

ऐष *aisha, am*, n., N. of several Sāmans.

ऐषमस् *aishámas*, ind. (Pāṇ. v, 3, 22) in this year, in the present year, ŚBr. iii. **-°tana, -°tya**, mfn. occurring in or relating to this year, of this year, Pāṇ. iv, 2, 105.

ऐषावीर *aishāvīrá, as*, m. belonging to the despised Brāhmanic family called Eshavīra [Sāy.], ŚBr. ix, xi.

ऐषिर *aishira, am*, n., N. of several Sāmans.

ऐषीक *aishīka* (or *aishika*), mfn. (fr. *ishīkā*), consisting of stalks, KātyŚr.; made of reeds or cane (as a missile), MBh.; R.; treating of missiles made of reeds; (*aishīkam parva*, N. of a section [Adhyāyas 10–18] of the tenth book of the Mahābhārata); (*ās*), m. pl., N. of a people, VP.

ऐषीरथि *aishīrathi, is*, m., N. of Kuśika (author of a Vedic hymn), Sāy. on RV. i, 10, 11.

ऐषुकारि *aishukāri, is*, m. a descendant of Ishu-kāra, Pāṇ. iv, 2, 54. **-bhakta**, mfn. inhabited by Aishukāris (as a country), ib. **Aishukāry-ādi**, m., N. of a gaṇa, ib.

Aishumata, *as*, m. a descendant of Ishu-mat, N. of Trāta, VBr.

ऐष्टक *aishṭaká*, mfn. (fr. *ishṭakā*), made of bricks (as a house), Hcat.; (*am*), n. the sacrificial bricks collectively, ŚBr.; putting up the bricks, Śulbas.

ऐष्टिक *aishṭika*, mf(*ī*)n. (fr. *ishṭi*), belonging or relating to an Ishṭi sacrifice, relating to sacrifice, ĀśvŚr.; Comm. on VS.; Hcat. &c.; to be performed in the manner of an Ishṭi sacrifice, Comm. on KātyŚr. **-paurtika**, mfn. connected with sacrifices and with doing good works (not included under the head of sacrifices), Mn. iv, 227, (*antarvedikaṃ bahirvedikaṃ ca*, Kull.)

ऐहिक *aihika*, mfn. (fr. *iha*), of this place, of this world, worldly, local, temporal, BhP.; Vedāntas. &c.

Aihalaukika, mf(*ī*)n. (fr. *iha-loka*), of this world, happening in this world, terrestrial &c., gaṇa *anuśatikādi*, Pāṇ. vii, 3, 20; MBh.

ओ O.

ओ 1. *o*, the thirteenth vowel of the alphabet (corresponding to English *o*). **-kāra**, m. the letter or sound *o*, Lāṭy.; APrāt.

ओ 2. *o*, ind. an interjection, L.; a particle of addressing; calling; reminiscence; of compassion, L.

ओ 3. *o, oś*, m., N. of Brahmā, L.

ओ 4. *ô* (*ā-√u*).

1. **Ô'ta** (for 2. see col. 3), mfn. addressed, invoked, summoned, AV.

ओक *oka, as*, m. (√*uc*, Comm. on Uṇ. iv, 215), a house, refuge, asylum (cf. *an-oka-śāyin*); a bird, L.; = *vṛishala*, T.; conjunction of heavenly bodies, L. **-ja**, mfn. born in the house, bred at home (as cows), Hcat.

O'kas, *as*, n. house, dwelling, place of abiding, abode, home, refuge, asylum, RV.; AV.; MBh.; BhP. &c.; (cf. *divâúkas, vanâúkas*, &c.) **Okaḥsārin**, mfn. going after or frequenting an abode, AitBr. **Oko-nidhana**, n., N. of a Sāman.

Okivas, mfn. (irr. p. p. P. of √*uc*) accustomed to, used to, having a liking for, RV. vi, 59, 3.

Okyà, mfn. fit for or belonging to a home, RV. ix, 86, 45; (*am*), n. = *ókas* above, RV.

ओकण *okaṇa, as, okaṇi, is*, m. a bug, L.

Okodanī, okkaṇī, f. id., L.

ओकुल *okula, as*, m. wheat fried slightly, L.

ओक्ष् *ôksh* (*ā-√uksh*), P. *-ukshati*, to sprinkle over or upon, RV.

ओख् *okh*, cl. 1. P. *okhati, okhām-cakāra, okhitā*, &c., to be dry or arid; to be able, suffice; to adorn; to refuse, ward off, Dhātup. v, 7.

ओगण *ogaṇá*, mfn. assembled, united [Sāy.], RV. x, 89, 15.

ओगीयस् *ogīyas* (= *ójīyas*), compar. of *ugrá*, p. 172, col. 2, BṛĀrUp.

ओघ *ogha, us*, m. (ifc. f. *ā*); (√*vah*) flood, stream, rapid flow of water, MBh.; Megh.; Śak. &c.; heap or quantity, flock, multitude, abundance, MBh.; BhP.; Kathās. &c.; quick time (in music), L.; uninterrupted tradition, L.; instruction, L.; (cf. *augha*.) **-niryukti**, f., N. of a work. **-ratha**, m., N. of a son of Oghavat, MBh. xiii. **-vat**, mfn. having a strong stream (as a river), MBh. iii; (*ān*), m., N. of a king, MBh. xiii; BhP.; (*tī*), f., N. of a daughter (MBh.) or sister (BhP.) of Oghavat; N. of a river, VP.

ओज् *oj*, cl. 1. 10. P. *ojati, ojayati*, to be strong or able; to increase, have vital power, Dhātup. xxxv, 84.

ओज *oja*, mfn. odd (as the first, third, fifth, &c. in a series), RPrāt.; Sūryas.; VarBṛS.; (*as*), m., N. of a son of Kṛishṇa, BhP.; = *ójas*, L.

ओजस् *ójas, as*, n. (√*vaj* or *uj*; cf. *ugra*), bodily strength, vigour, energy, ability, power, RV.; AV.; TS.; AitBr.; MBh. &c.; vitality (the principle of vital warmth and action throughout the body), Suśr. &c.; (in rhet.) elaborate style (abounding with compounds); vigorous or emphatic expression, Sāh.; Vām.; water, L.; light, splendour, lustre, L.; manifestation, appearance, L.; support, L.; (*ās*), m., N. of a Yaksha, BhP.; [cf. Zd. *avjaṅh*, 'power;' Gk. ὑγ-ιές, αὐγ-ή, ἐρι-αυγής; Lat. *vigēre, augere, augur, augus-tus, auxilium*; Goth. *aukan*; Eng. *eke*.] **-tara**, mfn. = *ójīyas*, Comm. on BṛĀrUp. **-°vat**, mfn. vigorous, powerful, strong, energetic, RV. viii, 76, 5; AV. viii, 5, 4; 16; VS. **-°vín**, mfn. id., TS.; ŚBr.; MBh. &c.; (*ī*), m., N. of a son of Manu Bhautya, VP.; (*ojasvi*)*-tā*, f. an energetic or emphatic manner of expression or style, Sāh.

Ojasína, mfn. having strength, powerful, TS. iv; Pāṇ.

Ojasyà, mfn. vigorous, powerful, MaitrS. ii; Pāṇ.

Ojāya, Nom. Ā. *ojāyate* (p. *ojāyámāna*) to exhibit strength or energy, make effort, RV. i, 140, 6; ii, 12, 11; iii, 32, 11; Pat. on Pāṇ. iii, 1, 11; Bhaṭṭ.

Ojāyita, *am*, n. stout-heartedness, courageous behaviour.

O'jishṭha, mfn., superl. of *ugrá*, q. v.; (*as*), m., N. of a Muni, BrahmP.; (*ās*), m. pl. the descendants of the same, ib.; [cf. Zd. *aojista*.]

O'jīyas, mfn., compar. of *ugrá*, q. v.

Ojo (in comp. for *ójas* above). **-dā́**, mfn. granting power, strengthening, RV. viii, 3, 24; TS. v; [cf. Zd. *aogazdâo*]; *-tama*, granting great power, very strengthening, RV. viii, 92, 17; [cf. Zd. *aogazdaçtema*.] **-pati** (with irr. Sandhi), m., N. of a deity of the Bodhi tree, Lalit. **-balā**, f., N. of a goddess of the Bodhi tree, ib. **-mānī**, f., N. of a plant, Kauś.

Ojmán, *ā*, m. power, vigour, energy, speed, velocity, RV. vi, 47, 27; AV.; [cf. Lat. *augmentu-m*; Lith. *augmů*.]

ओड *oḍa, as*, m., N. of a man, Rājat.

ओडव *oḍava* (*oḍaka*, W.), *as*, m. (in mus.) a mode which consists of five notes only (omitting Ṛishabha and Pañcama).

ओडिका *oḍikā, oḍi*, f. wild rice, L.; (cf. *odaná*.)

ओड्र *oḍra, as*, m., N. of a country (the modern Orissa; see Lassen, IA. i, 224, note 2); (*ās*), m. pl. the inhabitants of that country, Hariv.; Mn. x, 44; R. &c.; the China rose, L. **-deśa**, m., N. of the country Orissa. **-pushpa**, n. the flower of the China rose, L. **Oḍrâkhyā**, f. the China rose, L.

ओढ *ôḍha*, mfn. (p. p. of *ā-√vah*, q. v.) brought or carried near.

ओण् *oṇ*, cl. 1. P. *oṇati, oṇām-cakāra, oṇitā*, &c., to remove, take away, drag along, Dhātup. xiii, 11.

Oṇí, *is*, m. (or f.?) protection (from misfortune), shelter [Sāy.], RV. i, 61, 14; (*ī*), m. (or f.?) du. 'the two protectors,' the parents, RV. ix, 101, 14; (metaphorically) heaven and earth, RV. ix, 16, 1; 65, 11; AV. vii, 14, 1 (= VS. iv, 25).

ओण्ड्र *oṇḍra, as*, m., N. of a king, Bālar.

ओत 2. *ốta* (for 1. see 4. *ô*), p. p. of *ā-√ve*, p. 156, col. 2. **-prota**, see id.

ओतु 1. *ótu, us*, m. (√*ve*), the woof or cross-threads of a web, RV. vi, 9, 2; AV. xiv, 2, 51; TS. vi; Kauś.; (*u*), n., N. of a Sāman, ĀrshBr.

O'tave, ótavai, Ved. inf.

ओतु 2. *otu, us*, m. f. (√*av*, Uṇ. i, 70), a cat, Comm. on Pāṇ. vi, 1, 94.

ओत्सूर्यम् *ôtsūryám*, ind. until the sun rises, AV. iv, 5, 7.

ओदक *oduká, am*, n. (probably irr. for *audaka*) an animal living in water, TĀr. i, 26, 7.

ओदती *ódatī*, f. (pres. p. of √*ud*) 'sprinkling or refreshing,' N. of Ushas or the dawn, RV. i, 48, 6; viii, 69, 2.

Odaná, *as, am*, m. n. (√*ud*, Uṇ. ii, 76), grain mashed and cooked with milk, porridge, boiled rice, any pap or pulpy substance, RV.; AV.; ŚBr.; MBh. &c.; (*as*), m. cloud, Nigh.; (*ī*), f. Sida Cordifolia, L. **-pacana**, m., N. of the fire on the southern altar, Kaṭh. **-pākī**, f. (Pāṇ. iv, 1, 64) Barleria Cærulea, Bhpr.; Nigh. **-pāṇiniya**, m. one who becomes a pupil of or studies the work of Pāṇini only for the sake of getting boiled rice, Kāś. on Pāṇ. vi, 2, 69; Pat. on Pāṇ. i, 1, 73. **-bhojikā**, f. eating boiled rice, Kāś. on Pāṇ. iii, 3, 111. **-vat**, mfn. provided with boiled rice, TS. ii. **-sava**, m. a particular oblation, Comm. on TBr. ii, 7, 7. **Odanâhvayā** and **odanâhvā**, f., N. of a plant, L.

Odanika, mf(*ī*)n. receiving boiled rice, Kāś. on Pāṇ. iv, 4, 67; (*ā*), f. Sida Cordifolia, L.

1. **Odanīya**, Nom. P. *odanīyati*, to wish for boiled rice, Comm. on KātyŚr.

2. **Odanīya**, mfn. consisting of or belonging to boiled rice, gaṇa *apūpâdi*, Pāṇ. v, 1, 4.

Odanya, mfn. id., ib.

Odma, *as*, m. the act of wetting, moistening, Pāṇ. vi, 4, 29.

O'dman, *a*, n. flowing, flooding, VS. xiii, 53; Kāś. on Pāṇ. vi, 1, 94; [cf. *olla* (= *od-la*); also Zd. *aodha*, pl. 'waters,' 'flood.']

ओधस् *odhas, as*, n. = *ūdhas*, q. v., L.

ओपद्रु *ôpa-√dru*, P. (Impv. 2. sg. *-drava*) to hasten near to, RV. vi, 48, 16.

ओपश *opaśá, as*, m. (fr. *upa-√śī*), that on which any one rests, a cushion, pillow, RV. ix, 71, 1; x, 85, 8; AV. ix, 3, 8; xiv, 1, 8; top-knot, plume (perhaps for *avapaśa*, √*paś*); (*am*), n. a support, stay, pillar, RV. i, 173, 6; viii, 14, 5.

Opaśin, mfn. provided with or lying upon cushions or pillows, effeminate, AV. vi, 138, 1; 2.

ओप्य *ôpya* (*ā-upya*), ind. p. of *ā-√2. vap* (q. v.), having scattered or thrown into, pouring down, ŚBr.; ĀśvGṛ. &c.

ओम् *óm*, ind. (√*av*, Uṇ. i, 141; originally *om* = *ām*, which may be derived from *ā*, BRD.), a word of solemn affirmation and respectful assent, sometimes translated by 'yes, verily, so be it' (and in this sense compared with Amen; it is placed at the commencement of most Hindū works, and as a sacred exclamation may be uttered [but not so as to be heard by ears profane] at the beginning and end of a reading of the Vedas or previously to any prayer; it is also regarded as a particle of auspicious salutation [Hail!]; *om* appears first in the Upanishads as a mystic monosyllable, and is there set forth as the object of profound religious meditation, the highest spiritual efficacy being attributed not only to the whole word but also to the three sounds *a, u, m*, of which it consists; in later times *om* is the mystic name for the Hindū triad, and represents the union of the three gods, viz. *a* (Vishṇu), *u* (Śiva), *m* (Brahmā); it may also be typical of the three Vedas; *om* is usually called *praṇava*, more rarely *akshara* or *ekākshara*, and only in later times *oṃkāra*), VS.; ŚBr.; ChUp. &c.; (Buddhists place *om* at the beginning of their *vidyā shaḍakshari* or mystical formulary in six syllables [viz. *om maṇi padme hūṃ*]; according to T. *om* may be used in the following senses: *praṇave, ārambhe, svīkāre, anumatau, apâkṛitau, asvīkāre, maṅgale, śubhe, jñeye, brahmaṇi*; with preceding *a* or *ā*, the *o* of *om* does not form Vṛiddhi (*au*), but Guṇa (*o*), Pāṇ.

vi, 1, 95.) — **kāra** (*oṃ-k°*), m. the sacred and mystical syllable *om*, the exclamation *om*, pronouncing the syllable *om*, Mn. ii, 75; 81; Kathās.; Bhag. &c., (cf. *vijayoṃkāra*, *kṛitoṃkāra*); a beginning, prosperous or auspicious beginning of (e.g. a science), Bālar.; N. of a Liṅga; (*ā*), f. a Buddhist Śakti or female personification of divine energy, L.; *-grantha*, m., N. of a work of Nārāyaṇa; *-tīrtha*, n., N. of a Tīrtha; *-pīṭha*, n., N. of a place; *-bhaṭṭa*, *as*, m., N. of a man. — **°kārīya**, Nom. P. *oṃkārīyati*, to be an Oṃkāra(?), Comm. on Pāṇ. vi, 1, 95. — **kṛita**, mfn. having an uttered *om*; accompanied by *om*.

Oma (*omāsas*, voc. pl.), m. (√*av*), a friend, helper, protector, RV. i, 3, 7.

Omán, *ā*, m. help, protection, favour, kindness, RV.; (*ómān*, *ā*, m.) a friend, helper, protector, RV. v, 43, 13. — **vat** (*óman-*), mfn. helping, useful, RV. x, 39, 9; favourable, propitious, MaitrS. iv, 3, 9; ŚBr. i.

O'mātrā, f. protection, favour, readiness to help, RV. x, 50, 5.

Omyā́, f. id., MaitrS. i, 8, 9; ŚāṅkhŚr. — **vat**, mfn. helping, useful, favourable, RV. i, 112, 7; 20.

ओमला *omalā*, f., N. of a Śakti, NṛisUp.; (v. l. *aupalā*.)

ओमिल *omila*, *as*, m., N. of a man.

ओरिमिका *orimikā*, f., N. of a section of the Kāṭhaka recension of the Yajur-veda.

ओल *ola* or *olla*, mfn. wet, damp, L.; (*am*), n. Arum Campanulatum, L.

ओलण्ड् *olaṇḍ*, cl. 1. 8. 10. P. *olaṇḍati*, *olaṇḍayati*, *olaṇḍām-* or *olaṇḍayām-babhūva*, *aulaṇḍīt*, to throw out, eject, Dhātup. xxxii, 9; (cf. *ulaḍ*.)

Olaj, **olj**, vv. ll. for the above.

ओवा *ovā*, f. a particular exclamation at sacrifices, Lāṭy. vii, ix.

ओविली *ovilī* or *ovīlī*, f. that in which the upper part of the churning-stick turns, Comm. on KātyŚr.; (vv. ll. *aupavīlī* and *auvīlī*.)

ओष *osha*, *as*, m. (√*ush*), burning, combustion, Suśr.; (*oshá*) mfn. burning, shining, RV. x, 119, 10; (*ám*), ind. with ardour or vehemence, eagerly, quickly, AV.

Oshaṇa, *as*, m. pungent taste, sharp flavour, pungency, L.; (*ī*), f. a kind of vegetable, L.

O'sham, ind. p. while burning, ŚBr. ii, 2, 4, 5.

Oshishṭha, mfn. (superl. of *oshá* above). — **dā́van**, mfn. giving eagerly or immediately, TS. i, 6, 12, 3. — **hán**, mfn. killing vehemently or suddenly.

ओषधि *ósha-dhi*, *is*, f. (etym. doubtful; probably fr. *osha* above, 'light-containing,' see ŚBr. ii, 2, 4, 5; Nir. ix, 27) a herb, plant, simple, esp. any medicinal herb, RV.; AV.; ŚBr.; MBh. &c.; an annual plant or herb (which dies after becoming ripe), Mn. i, 46, &c.; Suśr. i, 4, 16; 18; Yājñ. &c.; a remedy in general, Suśr. i, 4, 15. — **garbha**, m. 'producer of herbs,' the moon, L.; the sun, T. (with reference to RV. i, 164, 52). — **jā́**, mfn. born or living amongst herbs (as snakes), AV. x, 4, 23; produced from plants (as fire), Kir. v, 14. — **pati**, m. 'lord of herbs,' the moon, Śiś.; Kād. &c.; the Soma plant; camphor, T.; 'master of plants,' a physician. — **prastha**, n., N. of the city of Himālaya, Kum. — **loká**, m. the world of plants, ŚBr. xiii. — **vanaspatí**, n. herbs and trees, ŚBr. vi; (*ayas*), m. pl. id., AitUp. **Oshadhīśa**, m. 'lord of herbs,' the moon, L. **Oshadhy-anuvāka**, m. a particular Anuvāka.

O'shadhī, f. (only Ved. and not in nom. c., Pāṇ. vi, 3, 132; but occasional exceptions are found) = *ósha-dhi* above. — **pati**, m. 'lord of herbs,' the moon, MBh.; the Soma plant, Suśr. — **mat**, mfn. provided with herbs, AV. xix, 17, 6; 18, 6. — **saṃśita**, mfn. sharpened by herbs (used in a formula), AV. x, 5, 32. — **sūkta**, n., N. of a hymn.

ओष्टृ *oshṭṛi*, v. l. for *ushṭṛi*, q. v., KātyŚr. v, 11, 13.

ओष्ठ *óshṭha*, *as*, m. (etym. doubtful; √*ush*, Un. ii, 4) the lip (generally du.), RV. ii, 39, 6; AV. x, 9, 14; xx, 127, 4; VS.; ŚBr.; Mn. &c.; the forepart of an Agnikuṇḍa, q. v., Hcat.; (*ī*), f. the plant Coccinia Grandis (to whose red fruits lips are commonly compared), L.; (in a compound the *o* of *oshṭha* forms with a preceding *a* either Vṛiddhi *au* or Guṇa *o*, Kāty. on Pāṇ. vi, 1, 94); [cf. Zd. *aoshtra*; O. Pruss. *austa*, 'mouth;' O. Slav. *usta*, 'mouth.'] — **karṇaka**, *ās*, m. pl., N. of a people, VP.; R. — **kopa**, m. disease of the lips, Suśr. — **ja**, mfn. produced by the lips, labial. — **jāha**, n. the root of the lips (?), Pāṇ. v, 2, 24. — **pallava**, n. 'lip-bud,' a lip. — **puṭa**, m. the space between the lips, MBh.; Śak. &c. — **prakopa**, m. = *-kopa* above. — **phalā**, f. bearing lip-like fruits, the plant Coccinia Grandis, Nigh. — **roga**, m. = *-kopa* above. **Oshṭhâdhara**, *au*, m. du. the upper and lower lip. **Oshṭhâpidhāna**, mfn. covered by the lips, MantraBr.; AitĀr. **Oshṭhôpama-phalā**, f. = *oshṭha-phalā* above, L.

Oshṭhaka, ifc. = *óshṭha*, lip; (mfn.) taking care of the lips, Pāṇ. v, 2, 66.

Oshṭhya, mfn. being at the lips, belonging to the lips, Suśr. &c.; esp. produced by the lips, labial (as certain sounds), RPrāt.; APrāt.; Comm. on Pāṇ. &c.; (*as*), m. a labial sound, PārGṛ. iii, 16. — **yoni**, mfn. produced from labial sounds. — **sthāna**, mfn. pronounced with the lips.

ओष्ण *óshṇa* (fr. *ushṇa* with 4. *ā* in the sense of diminution), mfn. a little warm, tepid.

ओह *óha*, *as*, m. (fr. √*vah* or *ā*-√*vah*; fr. √2. *ūh*, BRD.), a vehicle, means, RV. i, 180, 5; (mfn.) bringing near, causing to approach, RV. iv, 10, 1; worthy to be approached, excellent, RV. i, 61, 1 [Sāy.]; (attention, consideration, NBD.) — **brahman**, m. (a priest) possessing or conveying Brahman or sacred knowledge (*uhyamānam brahma .... yeshāṃ te*, Sāy.), RV. x, 71, 8.

O'has, *as*, n. a vehicle, means (fig. said of a Stotra, Sāy.), RV. vi, 67, 9.

ओहल *ohala*, *as*, m., N. of a man.

औ AU.

औ 1. *au*, the fourteenth vowel of the alphabet (having the sound of English *ou* in *our*). — **kāra**, m. the letter or sound *au*, TPrāt.; APrāt.

औ 2. *au*, ind. an interjection; a particle of addressing; calling; prohibition; ascertainment, L.

औ 3. *au*, *aus*, m., N. of Ananta or Śesha, L.; a sound, L.; the Setu or sacred syllable of the Śūdras, KālikāP. [T.]; (*aus*), f. the earth, L.

औक्थिक *aukthika*, mfn. one who knows or studies the Ukthas, Pāṇ. iv, 3, 129.

Aukthikya, *am*, n. the tradition of the Aukthikas, ib.

औक्थ्य *aukthya*, *as*, m. a descendant of Uktha, gaṇa *gargâdi*, Pāṇ. iv, 1, 105; (*am*), n., see *mahad-aukthya*.

Auktha, *as*, m. a descendant or pupil of Aukthya, gaṇa *kaṇvâdi*, Pāṇ. iv, 2, 111.

औक्ष *aukshá* (fr. *ukshan*), mf(*ī*)n. coming from or belonging to a bull, AV. ii, 36, 7; Kauś.; Pāṇ. vi, 4, 173; (*am*), n. a multitude of bulls, L. — **gandhi**, f., N. of an Apsaras, AV. iv, 37, 3.

Aukshaka, *am*, n. a multitude of bulls, Pāṇ. iv, 2, 39.

Aukshaṇa, *as*, m. a descendant of Ukshan.

Aúkshṇa (ŚBr. i) and **aukshṇá** (ŚBr. xiv), mfn. relating to or coming from a bull; (*as*), m. a descendant of Ukshan, Kāś. on Pāṇ. vi, 4, 173.

औखीय *aukhīya*, *ās*, m. pl. the descendants or pupils of Ukha.

Aukheya, *ās*, m. pl. id.

Aukhya, mfn. (fr. *ukhā*), boiled or being in a caldron, L.

Aukhyeyaka, mfn. = *ukhyā-jāta*, gaṇa *kattry-ādi*, Pāṇ. iv, 2, 95.

औग्रसेनि *augraseni*, *is*, m. a descendant of Ugra-sena, BhP.

Augrasenya, *as*, m. id., Pat. on Vārtt. 7 on Pāṇ. iv, 1, 114.

Augrasainya, *as*, m. id., N. of Yudhāṃśraushṭi, AitBr. viii, 21, 7.

औग्रेय *augreya*, *as*, m. a descendant of Ugra, gaṇa *śubhrâdi*, Pāṇ. iv, 1, 123.

Augrya, *am*, n. (fr. *ugra*), horribleness, dreadfulness, fierceness, Sāh.

औघ *aughá*, *as*, m. (fr. *ogha*; √*vah*), flood, stream, ŚBr.; (cf. *ogha*.)

औचथ्य *aucathyá*, *as*, m. a descendant of Ucathya, N. of Dīrghatamas, RV. i, 158, 1; 4; ĀśvŚr. (= *autathya* below, Sāy.)

औचिती *aucitī*, f. (fr. *ucita*), fitness, suitableness, decorum, Sāh.; Naish.; Rājat. &c.

Aucitya, *am*, n. fitness, suitableness, decorum, Sāh.; Kathās.; Kshem. &c.; the state of being used to, habituation, Kathās. xxiv, 95; Suśr. &c. **Aucityâlaṃkāra**, m., N. of a work.

औच्च्य *auccya*, *am*, n. (fr. *ucca*), height, distance (of a planet), Sūryas.

Auccāmanyava, *as*, m. a descendant of Uccāmanyu, TāṇḍyaBr.

Auccaiḥśravasá, *as*, m. (fr. *uccaiḥ-śravas*), N. of Indra's horse, AV. xx, 128, 15; 16; a horse, Nigh.

औजस *aujasa*, *am*, n. (fr. *ojas*), gold, L.

Aujasika, mfn. energetic, vigorous, Pāṇ. iv, 4, 27.

Aujasya, mfn. conducive to or increasing vitality or energy, Suśr.; (*am*), n. vigour, energy, Sāh.

औज्जयनक *aujjayanaka*, mfn. relating to or coming from the town Ujjayanī, gaṇa *dhūmâdi*, Pāṇ. iv, 2, 127.

Aujjayanika, *as*, m. a king of Ujjayanī, VarBṛS.

औज्जिहानि *aujjihāni*, *is*, m. a descendant of Ujjihāna, gaṇa *pailâdi*, Pāṇ. ii, 4, 59.

औज्ज्वल्य *aujjvalya*, *am*, n. (fr. *uj-jvala*), brightness, brilliancy, Mālatīm.; splendour, beauty, Sāh.; Vām.; Daśar. &c.

औडव 1. *auḍava*, mf(*ī*)n. (fr. *uḍu*), relating to a constellation, Kād.

औडव 2. *auḍava*, *as*, m. (in mus.) a mode which consists of five notes only; (*ā*), f. a particular Rāgiṇī, q. v.; (cf. *oḍava*.)

औडवि *auḍavi*, *ayas*, m. pl., N. of a warrior tribe, gaṇa *dāmany-ādi*, Pāṇ. v, 3, 116 (not in Kāś.)

Auḍavīya, *as*, m. a king of the Auḍavis, ib.

औडायन *auḍāyana*, *as*, m. a descendant of Uḍa (?) or of Auḍa [T.?], gaṇa *aishukāry-ādi*, Pāṇ. iv, 2, 54. — **bhakta**, mfn. inhabited by Auḍāyanas (as a country), ib.

औडुप *auḍupa*, mfn. (fr. *uḍupa*), relating to a raft or float, gaṇa *saṃkalâdi*, Pāṇ. iv, 2, 75.

Auḍupika, mfn. carrying over in a boat, gaṇa *utsaṅgâdi*, Pāṇ. iv, 4, 15.

औडुम्बर *auḍumbara*. See *aúdumbara*.

औडुलोमि *auḍulomi*, *is*, m. a descendant of Uḍu-loman, N. of a philosopher, Bādar.

औड्र *auḍra*, v. l. for *oḍra*, q. v.

औतङ्क *autaṅka*, v. l. for *auttaṅka* below.

औतथ्य *autathya*, *as*, m. a descendant of Utathya, N. of Dīrghatamas, MBh. (cf. *aucathyá* above). **Autathyêśvara**, n., N. of a Liṅga.

औत्कण्ठ्य *autkaṇṭhya*, *am*, n. (fr. *ut-kaṇṭha*), desire, longing for, BhP.; intensity, BhP. x, 13, 35. — **vat**, mfn. desirous, longing for, BhP.

औत्कर्ष *autkarsha*, *am*, n. (fr. *ut-karsha*), excellence, superiority, Priy.

Autkarshya, *am*, n. id., L.

औत्क्य *autkya*, *am*, n. (fr. *ut-ka*), desire, longing for, Vop.

औत्क्षेप *autkshepa*, *as*, *ī*, m. f. a descendant of Ut-kshepa, gaṇa *śivâdi*, Pāṇ. iv, 1, 112; (Kāś. reads *ut-kshipā*.)

औत्तङ्क *auttaṅka*, mf(*ī*)n. relating or belonging to Uttaṅka, MBh. xiv.

औत्तमि *auttami*, *is*, m. a descendant of Uttama, N. of the third Manu, Mn. i, 62; Hariv.; VP.

Auttamika, mfn. (fr. *uttama*), relating to the gods who are in the highest place (in the sky), Nir.

Auttameya, *as*, m. a descendant of Auttami, Hariv.

औत्तर *auttara*, mfn. (fr. 1. *uttara*), living in the northern country, MBh.

Auttarapathika, mfn. (fr. *uttara-patha*), coming from or going towards the northern country, Pāṇ. v, 1, 77.

Auttarapadika, mfn. (fr. *uttara-pada*), belonging to or occurring in the last member of a compound, Pat.

Auttarabhaktika, mfn. (fr. *bhakta* with *uttara*), employed or taken after a meal, Car.

Aúttaravedika, mfn. (fr. *uttara-vedi*), relating to or performed on the northern altar, ŚBr. vii.

Auttarādharya, *am* n. (fr. *uttarâdhara*), the state of being below and above; the state of one thing being over the other; confusion, Pāṇ. iii, 3, 42.

Auttarārdhika, mfn. (fr. *uttarârdha*), being on or belonging to the upper or northern side, Pat.

Auttarāha, mfn. (fr. *uttarâha*), of or belonging to the next day, Vārtt. on Pāṇ. iv, 2, 104.

Auttareya, *as*, m. a descendant of Uttarā, BhP.

औत्तानपाद *auttānapāda*, *as*, m. a descendant of Uttāna-pāda, N. of Dhruva (or the polar star), MBh.; BhP. &c.

Auttānapādi, *is*, m. id.

औत्थानिक *autthānika*, mfn. (fr. *ut-thāna*), relating to the getting up or sitting up (of a child), BhP.

औत्पत्तिक *autpattika*, mf(ī)n. (fr. *ut-patti*), relating to origin, inborn, original, natural, Lāṭy.; BhP. &c.; *à priori*; inherent, eternal, Jaim. i, 1, 5.

औत्पात *autpāta*, mfn. (fr. *ut-pāta*, gaṇa *ṛigayanâdi*, Pāṇ. iv, 3, 73), treating of or contained in a book which treats of portents, T.

Autpātika, mf(ī)n. astounding, portentous, prodigious, calamitous, MBh.; Ragh. &c.; (*as*), m., N. of the third act of the Mahānāṭaka.

औत्पाद *autpāda*, mfn. (fr. *ut-pāda*, gaṇa *ṛigayanâdi*, Pāṇ. v, 3, 73), knowing or studying a book on birth or production; contained in such a book, T.

औत्पुट *autpuṭa*, mfn. (fr. *ut-puṭa*, gaṇa *saṃkalâdi*, Pāṇ. iv, 2, 75) = *utpuṭena nirvṛitta*.

Autpuṭika, mfn. (fr. id., gaṇa *utsaṅgâdi*, Pāṇ. iv, 4, 15) = *utpuṭena hāraka*.

औत्र *autra*, mfn. (etym. unknown; perhaps fr. *ut-tara*, BRD.), superficial, rough, inexact (in math.)

औत्स *autsa*, mf(ī)n. (fr. *utsa*), produced or being in a well, Pāṇ.

Autsāyana, *as*, m. a descendant of Utsa, gaṇa *aśvâdi*, Pāṇ. iv, 1, 110.

औत्सङ्गिक *autsaṅgika*, mf(ī)n. (fr. *utsaṅga*, gaṇa *utsaṅgâdi*, Pāṇ. iv, 4, 15) = *utsaṅgena hāraka*.

औत्सर्गिक *autsargika*, mfn. (fr. *ut-sarga*), belonging to or taught in a general rule, general, not particular or special, generally valid, Kāś.; Siddh. &c.; terminating, completing, belonging to a final ceremony by which a rite is terminated; abandoning, leaving; natural, inherent; derivative, W. **— tva**, n. generality (of a rule &c.), Comm. on Pāṇ.

औत्सुक्य *autsukya*, *am*, n. (fr. *ut-suka*), anxiety, desire, longing for, regret, MBh.; R.; Ragh. &c.; eagerness, zeal, fervour, officiousness, Pañcat.; Kathās.; impatience, Sāh.; Pratāpar. **— vat**, mfn. impatient, waiting impatiently for (dat.), Kathās.

औदक *audaka*, mf(ī)n. (fr. *udaka*), living or growing in water, relating to water, aquatic, watery, Lāṭy.; Mn.; MBh.; Suśr. &c.; (*ā*), f. a town surrounded by water, Hariv. 6874. **— ja**, mfn. coming from aquatic plants, Suśr.

Audaki, *is*, m. a descendant of Udaka, gaṇa *bāhv-ādi*, Pāṇ. iv, 1, 96; (*ayas*), m. pl., N. of a warrior tribe, gaṇa *dāmany-ādi*, Pāṇ. v, 3, 116.

Audakīya, *as*, m. a king of the Audakis, ib.

औदङ्कि *audaṅki*, *is*, m. a descendant of Udaṅka, gaṇa *bāhv-ādi*, Pāṇ. iv, 1, 96; (*ayas*), m. pl., N. of a warrior tribe, gaṇa *dāmany-ādi*, Pāṇ. v, 3, 110.

Audaṅkīya, *as*, m. a king of the Audaṅkis, ib.

औदज्ञायनि *audajñāyani*, *is*, m. a descendant of Udajña [Kāś. reads *udanya*], gaṇa *tikâdi*, Pāṇ. iv, 1, 154.

औदञ्चन *audañcana*, mfn. (fr. *ud-añcana*), contained in a bucket, BhP.

Audañcanaka, mfn. relating to a bucket, gaṇa *arīhaṇâdi*, Pāṇ. iv, 2, 80.

औदञ्चवि *audañcavi*, *is*, m. a descendant of Udañcu, gaṇa *bāhv-ādi*, Pāṇ. iv, 1, 96.

औदनिक *audanika*, mf(ī)n. (fr. *odana*), one who knows how to cook mashed grain, gaṇa *saṃtāpâdi*, Pāṇ. v, 1, 101.

औदन्य *audanyá*, *as*, m. (fr. *udanya*), N. of the Ṛishi Muṇḍibha, ŚBr. xiii.

Audanyavá, *as*, m. (fr. *udanyu*), id., TBr. iii.

Audanyāyani, *is*, m. a descendant of Udanya, gaṇa *tikâdi* [Kāś.], Pāṇ. iv, 1, 154.

Audanyi, *is*, m. id., gaṇa *pailâdi*, Pāṇ. ii, 4, 59 [not in Kāś.]

औदन्वत *audanvata*, mfn. (fr. *udanvat*), relating to the sea, marine, Bālar.; (*as*), m. a descendant of Udanvat, Kāś. on Pāṇ. viii, 2, 13.

औदपान *audapāna*, mf(ī)n. (fr. *uda-pāna*), raised from wells or drinking fountains (as a tax &c.); belonging or relating to a well; coming from the village Udapāna, gaṇas on Pāṇ.

औदबुद्धि *audabuddhi*, *is*, m. a descendant of Udabuddha, gaṇa *pailâdi*, Pāṇ. ii, 4, 59.

औदभृज्जि *audabhṛijji*, *is*, m. a descendant of Uda-bhṛijja, ib.

औदमज्जि *audamajji*, *is*, m. a descendant of Uda-majja, ib.

औदमेघ *audamegha*, *ās*, m. pl. the school of Audameghyā, Pat.

औदमेघि *audameghi*, *is*, m. a descendant of Uda-megha, ib.

Audameghīya, mfn. belonging to Audameghi [v.l. *audameyi*, Kāś.], gaṇa *raivatakâdi*, Pāṇ. iv, 3, 131.

Audameghyā, f. of *audameghi* above, Pat.

औदयक *audayaka*, *ās*, m. pl. (fr. *ud-aya*), a school of astronomers (who reckoned the first motion of the planets from sunrise).

Audayika, mfn. to be reckoned from sunrise; relating to or happening in an auspicious time, prosperous, T.; (with *bhāva*, the state of the soul when actions arise, Sarvad.)

औदयन *audayana*, mfn. relating to or coming from (the teacher) Udayana, Sarvad.

औदर *aúdara*, mfn. (fr. *udara*), being in the stomach or belly, Suparṇ.; gastric (as a disease), Hcat.

Audarika, mf(ī)n. gluttonous, a belly-god, glutton, Pāṇ.; MBh.; Suśr. &c.; greedy; fit for or pleasant to the stomach (as food), Lalit.; dropsical, Hcat.

Audarya, mfn. being in the stomach or belly; being in the womb, BhP.

औदल *audala*, *as*, m. a descendant of Udala, ĀśvŚr.; (*am*), n., N. of a Sāman, Lāṭy.

औदवापि *audavāpi*, *is*, m. a descendant of Uda-vāpa, gaṇa *raivatikâdi*, Pāṇ. iv, 3, 131 (Kāś. reads *audavāhi*).

Audavāpīya, mfn. relating to Audavāpi, ib.

औदवाहि *audavāhí*, *is*, m. a descendant of Uda-vāha, ŚBr.; ĀśvGṛ.

औदव्रज *audavraja*, mf(ī)n. composed by Uda-vraja.

Audavraji, *is*, m. a descendant of Uda-vraja, VBr.

औदशुद्धि *audaśuddhi*, *is*, m. a descendant of Uda-śuddha, gaṇa *pailâdi*, Pāṇ. ii, 4, 39.

औदश्वित *audaśvita* and *audaśvitka*, mfn. (fr. *uda-śvit*), dressed with or made of buttermilk, like buttermilk, Pāṇ.

औदस्थान *audasthāna*, mfn. (fr. *uda-sthāna*), accustomed to stand in water; relating to one who stands in water, gaṇas on Pāṇ.

औदात्त्य *audāttya*, *am*, n. (fr. *udātta*), the state of having the high tone or accent.

औदारिक *audārika*, *as*, m. (fr. *udāra*), (with Jainas) the gross body which invests the soul, Sarvad.; HYog.

Audārya, *am*, n. generosity, nobility, magnanimity, MBh.; R.; Daś. &c.; liberality, Kathās.; noble style, Sāh. **— tā**, f. liberality, Pañcad.

औदासीन्य *audāsīnya*, *am*, n. (fr. *ud-āsīna*), indifference, apathy, disregard, R.; Daś.; Ragh. &c.

Audāsya, *am*, n. (fr. 2. *ud-āsa*), id., Naish.; Śāntiś. &c.

औदीच्य *audīcya*, mfn. (fr. *udīcī*, f. of 2. *udañc*), coming from or relating to the northern country, northern, Comm. on MBh.; Comm. on Pat. **— prakāśa**, m., N. of a work.

औदुम्बर *aúdumbara* (in class. Sanskṛit commonly written *auḍu°*), mf(ī)n. (fr. *ud[d]umbára*), coming from the tree Udumbara or Ficus Religiosa, made of its wood, AV.; ŚBr.; Mn. ii, 45; Yājñ.; MBh. &c.; made of copper, SāmavBr. ii, 5, 3; (*as*), m. a region abounding in Udumbara trees, Kāś. on Pāṇ. iv, 2, 67; a kind of worm, Car.; N. of Yama; (*ās*), m. pl., N. of a race, MBh.; of a class of ascetics, Hariv. 7988; BhP. iii, 12, 43; (*ī*), f. (with and without *śākhā*) a branch of the Udumbara tree, ŚBr.; Lāṭy.; Nyāyam. &c.; a kind of musical instrument; (*am*), n. an Udumbara wood, KātyŚr.; a piece of Udumbara wood, PārGṛ.; the fruit of the Udumbara tree, AitBr.; a kind of leprosy, Suśr.; copper, L. **— cchada**, m. Croton Polyandrum, Nigh. **— tā**, f., **-tva**, n. the state of being made of the Udumbara tree, Nyāyam.

Audumbaraka, *as*, m. the country inhabited by the Udumbaras, gaṇa *rājanyâdi*, Pāṇ. iv, 2, 53.

Audumbarāyaṇa, *as*, m. a descendant of Udumbara, N. of a grammarian.

Audumbarāyaṇi, *is*, m. a descendant of the last.

Audumbari, *is*, m. a king of the Udumbaras, Comm. on Pāṇ.

औद्गात्र *audgātra*, mfn. relating to the Udgātṛi priest, KātyŚr.; Comm. on BṛĀrUp. &c.; (*am*), n. the office of the Udgātṛi priest, Pāṇ. v, 1, 129. **— sāra-saṃgraha**, m., N. of a work.

औद्गाहमानि *audgāhamāni*, *is*, m. a descendant of Udgāhamāna, Gobh.

औद्ग्रभण *audgrabhaṇá*, *am*, n. (fr. *ud-grabhaṇa*), N. of a particular offering, MaitrS.; ŚBr.; KātyŚr. **— tva**, n. the being such an offering, MaitrS.

Audgrahaṇá, *am*, n. id., TS. vi.

औद्दण्डक *auddaṇḍaka*, mfn. (fr. *ud-daṇḍa*), relating to one who holds up a staff, gaṇa *arīhaṇâdi*, Pāṇ. iv, 2, 80.

औद्दालक *auddālaka*, *am*, n. (fr. *ud-dālaka*), a kind of honey (taken from certain bees which live in the earth), Bhpr.; Suśr.; N. of a Tīrtha, MBh. iii.

Auddālakāyana, *as*, m. a descendant of Auddālaki, Pat.

Aúddālaki, *is*, m. a descendant of Uddālaka, N. of several men, TS.; ŚBr.; KaṭhUp.; MBh.

औद्देशिक *auddeśika*, mfn. (fr. *ud-deśa*), pointing out, indicative of, showing, enumerating, Nir.; prepared for the sake of (mendicants; said of alms), Jain.

औद्धत्य *auddhatya*, *am*, n. (fr. *ud-dhata*), arrogance, insolence, overbearing manner, disdain, Kathās.; Sāh.

औद्धव *auddhava*, *ās*, m. pl. (fr. *ud-dhava*), grass left over of the sacrificial straw, ĀpŚr. viii, 14, 4; mf(ī)n. consisting of such grass, ĀpŚr. viii, 14, 5; coming from or spoken by Uddhava, relating to Uddhava, Śiś. ii, 118. **— maya**, mfn. id., Comm. on ib.

औद्धारिक *auddhārika*, mfn. (fr. *ud-dhāra*), belonging to or forming the part to be set aside, Mn. ix, 150.

औद्बिल्य *audbilya*, *am*, n. (fr. *ud-bila*), excessive joy, Buddh.

औद्भट **audbhaṭa**, *ās*, m. pl. the pupils of Ud-bhaṭa, Daśar.

औद्भारि **aúdbhāri**, *is*, m. a descendant of Ud-bhāra, N. of Khaṇḍika, ŚBr. xi.

औद्भिज्ज **audbhijja**, mfn. (fr. *udbhij-ja*), coming forth from the earth, Hariv. 11122; (*am*), n. fossil salt, L.

औद्भिद **aúdbhida**, mfn. (fr. 2. *ud-bhid*), coming forth, springing forth, breaking through, issuing from, MBh.; Suśr.; forcing one's way towards an aim, victorious, VS. xxxiv, 50; (*am*), n. (with and without *lavaṇa*) fossil salt, Suśr.; (scil. *udaka*) water breaking through (the earth and collecting in a mine, L.), Suśr. i, 170, 12.

Aúdbhidya, *am*, n. forcing one's way to an aim, success, victory, VS. xviii, 9; TBr. ii.

Aúdbhettra, *am*, n. (fr. *ud-bhettṛi*), id., MaitrS. ii, 11, 4.

Audbhettriya, *am*, n. id., ĀpŚr.

औद्याव **audyāva**, mf(*ī*)n. (fr. *udyāva*, gaṇa *ṛigayanâdi*, Pāṇ. iv, 3, 73), treating of the art of mixing or joining (?).

औद्वाहिक **audvāhika**, mfn. (fr. *ud-vāha*), relating to or given at marriage, Mn. ix, 206; Yājñ. ii, 118.

औद्वेप **audvepa**, mfn. (fr. *ud-vepa*, gaṇa *saṃkalâdi*, Pāṇ. iv, 2, 75), resulting from tremor or trembling (?).

औधस **audhasa**, mfn. (fr. *ūdhas*), being or contained in the udder (as milk), BhP.

औधेय **audheya**, *ās*, m. pl., N. of a family; of a school (belonging to the White Yajur-veda), Caraṇavy.

औन्नत्य **aunnatya**, *am*, n. (fr. *un-nata*), elevation, height, Kathās.

औन्नेत्र **aunnetra**, *am*, n. the office of the Un-netṛi priest, gaṇa *udgātṛ-ādi*, Pāṇ. v, 1, 129.

औन्मुख्य **aunmukhya**, *am*, n. (fr. *un-mukha*), expectancy, Rājat.

औपकर्णिक **aupakarṇika**, mfn. (fr. *upa-karṇa*), being on or near the ears, Pāṇ. iv, 3, 40.

औपकलाप्य **aupakalāpya**, mfn. (fr. *upa-kalāpa*, gaṇa *parimukhâdi*, Kāty. on Pāṇ. iv, 3, 58), being on or near the girdle (?).

औपकायन **aupakāyana**, *as*, m. a descendant of Upaka, N. of an author, Hcat.

औपकार्या **aupakāryā**, f. = *upa-kāryā*, q. v., R.

औपकुर्वाणक **aupakurvāṇaka** = *upakurvāṇaka*, q. v., BhP.

औपगव **aupagava**, mf(*ī*)n. coming from or composed by Upagu; (*am*), n., N. of two Sāmans, Lāṭy.; (*as*, *ī*), m. f. a descendant of Upagu, Kāś. on Pāṇ. iv, 2, 39.

Aupagavaka, *am*, n. an assemblage of Aupagavas, ib.; (*as*), m. an admirer or worshipper of Upagu, Kāś. on Pāṇ. iv, 3, 99.

Aupagavi, *is*, m. a descendant of Aupagava, N. of Uddhava, BhP.

Aupagavīya, *as*, m. a pupil of Aupagavi, Pat.

औपगात्र **aupagātra**, *am*, n. the state of an Upa-gātṛi, q. v., ŚāṅkhBr.

औपग्रस्तिक **aupagrastika**, *as*, m. (fr. *upa-grasta*), the sun or moon in eclipse, L.

औपग्रहिक **aupagrahika**, *as*, m. (fr. *upa-graha*), id., W.

औपचन्धनि **aupacandhani**, v. l. for *aupajandhani*, col. 2.

औपचारिक **aupacārika**, mf(*ī*)n. (fr. *upa-cāra*), honorific, complimentary (as a name or title), Comm. on TāṇḍyaBr. xiv, 2, 6; not literal, figurative, metaphorical, Sarvad.

औपच्छन्दसिक **aupacchandasika**, mfn. (fr. *upa-cchandas*), conformable to the Veda, Vedic, VarBṛS.; (*am*), n., N. of a metre (consisting of four lines of alternately eleven and twelve syllabic instants, see Gr. 969).

औपजन्धनि **aúpajandhani**, *is*, m. a descendant of Upa-jandhani, N. of a teacher, ŚBr. xiv.

औपजानुक **aupajānuka**, mfn. (fr. *upa-jānu*), being on or near the knees, Pāṇ. iv, 3, 40; Bhaṭṭ.

औपतस्विनि **aúpatasvini**, *is*, m. a descendant of Upatasvina, N. of a Ṛishi, ŚBr. iv.

औपदेशिक **aupadeśika**, mf(*ī*)n. living by teaching, gaṇa *vetanâdi*, Pāṇ. iv, 4, 12 (not in Kāś.); depending on or resulting from a special rule, Comm. on KātyŚr. & ĀśvŚr.; (in Gr.) denoting or relating to an originally enunciated grammatical form (see *upadeśa*), Paribh. cxx, 2. **–tva**, n. the state of resulting from a special rule, Comm. on KātyŚr. v, 11, 21.

औपद्रविक **aupadravika**, mfn. (fr. *upa-drava*), relating to or treating of symptoms, Suśr.

औपद्रष्ट्र्य **aúpadrashṭrya**, *am*, n. (fr. *upa-drashṭṛi*), the state of being an eye-witness, superintendence, VS. xxx, 13.

औपधर्म्य **aupadharmya**, *am*, n. (fr. *upa-dharma*), false doctrine, heresy, BhP.

औपधिक **aupadhika**, mfn. (fr. *upa-dhi*), deceitful, deceptive; (*as*), m. an impostor, cheat, Car.; an extortioner of money, Mn. ix, 258, (*cópadhikā* misprint for *cáupadhikā*.)

Aupadheya, mfn. serving for the Upadhi (a particular part of the wheel of a carriage), Pāṇ. v, 1, 13; (*am*), n. the part of a wheel called Upadhi, Kāty. on ib.

औपधेनव **aupadhenava**, *as*, m. a descendant of Upadhenu, N. of a physician, Suśr.

औपनायिक **aupanāyika**, mfn. (fr. *upa-nāya*), belonging to or serving for an offering, Hariv.

Aupanāyanika, mfn. (fr. *upa-nāyana*), relating to or fit for the ceremony called Upanayana, q. v., Mn. ii, 68; Yājñ. i, 37.

औपनासिक **aupanāsika**, mfn. (fr. *nāsā* with *upa*), being on or near the nose, Suśr.

औपनिधिक **aupanidhika**, mfn. (fr. *upa-nidhi*), relating to or forming a deposit, Yājñ. ii, 65.

औपनिषत्क **aupanishatka**, mfn. (fr. *upanishad*, gaṇa *vetanâdi*, Pāṇ. iv, 4, 12), subsisting by teaching an Upanishad.

Aupanishadá, mf(*ī*)n. contained or taught in an Upanishad, ŚBr. xiv; MuṇḍUp.; ŚāṅkhGṛ.; Mn. vi, 29, &c.; a follower of the Upanishads, a Vedāntin, Comm. on Bādar. ii, 2, 10.

Aupanishadika, mfn. Upanishad-like, Vātsy.

औपनीविक **aupanīvika**, mfn. (fr. *upa-nīvi*), on or near the Nīvi (q. v.), Pāṇ. iv, 3, 40; Śiś. x, 60.

औपपक्ष्य **aúpapakshya**, mfn. (fr. *upa-paksha*), being in the armpit (as hair), ŚBr. xi.

औपपत्तिक **aupapattika**, mfn. (fr. *upa-patti*), present, ready at hand, fit for the purpose, MBh.

औपपत्य **aupapatya**, *am*, n. (fr. *upa-pati*), intercourse with a paramour, adultery, BhP. x, 29, 26.

औपपातिक **aupapātika**, mfn. (fr. *upa-pātaka*, irr.), one who has committed a secondary crime, Nār.; (fr. *upa-pāta*), *am*, n., N. of the first Jaina Upāṅga.

औपपादुक **aupapāduka**, mfn. (fr. *upa-pāduka*), self-produced, Lalit.; Car.

Aupapādika, mfn. id., Car.

औपबाहवि **aupabāhavi**, *is*, m. a descendant of Upa-bāhu, gaṇa *bāhv-ādi*, Pāṇ. iv, 1, 96.

औपबिन्दवि **aupabindavi**, *is*, m. a descendant of Upa-bindu, ib.

औपभृत **aupabhṛita**, mfn. belonging to or being in the ladle called Upa-bhṛit, KātyŚr.; Jaim.

औपमन्यव **aúpamanyava**, *as*, m. a descendant of Upa-manyu, ŚBr.; ChUp.; Nir.; (*ās*), m. pl., N. of a school belonging to the Yajur-veda.

औपमानिक **aupamānika**, mfn. (fr. *upa-māna*), derived by analogy, Comm. on Nyāyad.

Aupamika, mfn. (fr. 3. *upa-mā*), serving for or forming a comparison, Nir.

Aupamya, *am*, n. (ifc. f. *ā*) the state or condition of resemblance or equality, similitude, comparison, analogy, MBh.; BhP.; Bhag. &c.; (cf. *an-aup°*, *ātmáup°*, &c.)

औपयज **aupayaja**, mfn. belonging to the verses called Upayaj, q. v., KātyŚr.; ĀśvŚr.

औपयिक **aupayika**, mf(*ī*)n. (fr. *upâya*, gaṇa *vinayâdi*, Pāṇ. v, 4, 34; with shortening of the *ā*, Kāś. on ib.), answering a purpose, leading to an object, fit, proper, right, MBh.; BhP. &c.; belonging to, VarBṛS.; obtained through a means or expedient, L.; (*am*), n. a means, expedient, Kir. ii, 35. **–tā**, f., **-tva**, n. fitness, properness, Sarvad.; Comm. on KātyŚr. &c.

औपयौगिक **aupayaugika**, mfn. (ifc.) relating to the application of (a remedy &c.), Suśr.

औपर **auparâ**, *as*, m. a descendant of Upara, N. of Daṇḍa, TS.; MaitrS.

औपरव **auparava**, mfn. relating to the hole called Upa-rava, q. v., Comm. on KātyŚr. viii, 5, 7.

औपराजिक **auparājika**, mf(*ī* and *ā*)n. (fr. *upa-rāja*, gaṇa *kāśy-ādi*, Pāṇ. iv, 2, 116), relating to a viceroy.

औपराधय्य **auparādhayya**, *am*, n. (fr. *upa-rādhaya*, gaṇa *brāhmaṇâdi*, Pāṇ. v, 1, 124), the state of being serviceable or officious.

औपरिष्ट **auparishṭa**, mfn. (fr. *uparishṭāt*, Kāty. on Pāṇ. iv, 2, 104), being above.

Auparishṭaka, *am*, n. (scil. *rata*) a kind of coitus, Vātsy.

औपरोधिक **auparodhika**, mfn. (fr. *upa-rodha*), relating to a check or hindrance, L.; a staff of the wood of the Pīlu tree, L.

औपल **aupala**, mfn. (fr. *upala*), made of stone, stony, Mn. iv, 194; raised from stones (as taxes), gaṇa *suṇḍikâ*, Pāṇ. iv, 3, 76; (*ā*), f., N. of a Śakti, NṛisUp.; (v. l. *omalā*.)

औपवसथिक **aupavasathika**, mfn. designed for or belonging to the Upa-vasatha (q. v.) ceremony, ĀśvŚr.; Gobh. &c.; (*am*), n., N. of a Pariśishṭa of the Sāma-veda.

Aupavasathya, mfn. = *aupavasathika* above, AitBr.; ĀśvŚr.; KātyŚr.

औपवस्त **aupavasta**, *am*, n. (fr. *upa-vasta*), fasting, a fast, Āp. ii, 1, 5.

Aupavastra, *am*, n. fasting, L.

Aupavastraka, *am*, n. food suitable for a fast, L.

Aupavastha, *am*, n. = *aupavasta* above.

औपवास **aupavāsa**, mf(*ī*)n. (fr. *upa-vāsa*, gaṇa *vyushṭâdi*, Pāṇ. v, 1, 97), given during fasting, relating to fasting.

Aupavāsika, mf(*ī*)n. fit or suitable for a fast, gaṇa *guḍâdi*, Pāṇ. iv, 4, 103; able to fast, gaṇa *saṃtāpâdi*, Pāṇ. v, 1, 101.

Aupavāsya, *am*, n. fasting, R.

औपवाह्य **aupavāhya**, mfn. (fr. *upa-vāha*), designed for driving or riding (as a carriage or elephant &c.), R.; (*as*), m. a king's elephant, any royal vehicle.

औपवीतिक **aupavītika**, *am*, n. (fr. *upa-vīta*), investiture with the sacred thread, VāmP.

औपवीली **aupavīlī**, f., v. l. for *ovilī*, q. v.

औपवेशि **aúpaveśi**, *is*, m. a descendant of Upa-veśá, N. of Aruṇa, TS.; ŚBr.

औपवेषिक **aupaveshika**, mfn. (fr. *upa-vesha*, gaṇa *vetanâdi*, Pāṇ. iv, 4, 12), living by entertainment (?).

औपश **aupaśa**. See *sv-aupaśá*.

औपशद **aupaśada**, *as*, m. (fr. *upa-śada*), N. of an Ekâha, KātyŚr.; Lāṭy.; TāṇḍyaBr.

औपशमिक *aupaśamika*, mfn. (fr. *upa-śama*), (with Jainas) resulting from the ceasing (of the effects of past actions), Sarvad.

औपशाल *aupaśāla*, mfn. (fr. *śālā* with *upa*), near the house or hall, Pat.

औपशिवि *aupaśivi*, *is*, m. a descendant of Upa-śiva, N. of a grammarian.

औपश्लेषिक *aupaśleshika*, mfn. (fr. *upa-ślesha*), connected by close contact, Siddh.

औपसंक्रमण *aupasaṃkramaṇa*, mf(ī)n. (fr. *upa-saṃkramaṇa*), that which is given or proper to be done on the occasion of passing from one thing to another, gaṇa *vyushṭâdi*, Pāṇ. v, 1, 97.

औपसंख्यानिक *aupasaṃkhyānika*, mfn. (fr. *upa-saṃkhyāna*), depending on the authority of any addition or supplement, mentioned or occurring in one; supplementary, Comm. on Pāṇ.

औपसद *aupasada*, mfn. occupied with or relating to the Upa-sad (q. v.) ceremony, ĀśvŚr.; (an Adhyāya or Anuvāka) in which the word *upasad* occurs, gaṇa *vimuktâdi*, Pāṇ. v, 2, 61; (*as*), m. a particular Ekāha (incorrect v. l. for *aupaśada*, p. 238, col. 3).

औपसंध्य *aupasaṃdhya*, mfn. (fr. *saṃdhyā* with *upa*), relating to dawn, Naish.

औपसर्गिक *aupasargika*, mfn. (fr. *upa-sarga*), superior to adversity, able to cope with calamity, gaṇa *saṃtāpâdi*, Pāṇ. v, 1, 101; superinduced, produced in addition to (or out of another disease), Suśr.; infectious (as a disease), Suśr. i, 271, 13; connected with a preposition, prepositive; portentous; relating to change &c., W.; (*as*), m. irregular action of the humors of the body (producing cold sweat &c.), L.

औपसीर्य *aupasīrya*, mfn. (fr. *upa-sīra*, gaṇa *parimukhâdi*, Kāty. on Pāṇ. iv, 3, 58), being on or near a plough.

औपस्थान *aupasthāna*, mf(ī)n. (fr. *upasthāna*), one whose business is to serve or wait on or worship, gaṇa *chattrâdi*, Pāṇ. iv, 4, 62.

Aupasthānika, mf(ī)n. one who lives by waiting on or worshipping, gaṇa *vetanâdi*, Pāṇ. iv, 4, 12.

Aupasthika, mf(ī)n. (fr. *upa-stha*), living by the sexual organ (i. e. by fornication), ib.

Aupasthya, *am*, n. cohabitation, sexual enjoyment, BhP.

औपस्थूण्य *aupasthūṇya*, mfn. (fr. *upa-sthūṇa*, gaṇa *parimukhâdi*, Kāty. on Pāṇ. iv, 3, 58), being near or on a post.

औपस्वस्ती *aupasvastī*, f., N. of a woman. **-putra**, m., N. of a teacher, BṛĀrUp.

औपहस्तिक *aupahastika*, mfn. (fr. *upa-hasta*, gana *vetanâdi*, Pāṇ. iv, 4, 12 [not in Kāś.]), living by presents (? *pratigraheṇa jīvati*, T.)

औपहारिक *aupahārika*, mfn. (fr. *upa-hāra*), fit for an offering; (*am*), n. that which forms an oblation, an oblation, offering, MBh. xiii.

औपाकरण *aupākaraṇa*, mfn. (fr. *upâkaraṇa*), relating to the preparatory ceremony before beginning the study of the Veda; (*am*), n. the time of that ceremony, Āp. i, 10, 2.

औपादानिक *aupādānika*, mfn. (fr. *upâdāna*), effected by assuming or adopting.

औपाधिक *aupādhika*, mfn. (fr. *upâdhi*), relating to or depending on special qualities, limited by particular conditions, valid only under particular suppositions, Sarvad.; Comm. on RV. & ŚBr. &c.

औपाध्यायक *aupādhyāyaka*, mfn. (fr. *upâdhyāya*), coming from a teacher, Kāś. on Pāṇ. iv, 3, 77.

औपानह्य *aupānahya*, mfn. (fr. *upā-nah*), serving or used for making shoes, Pāṇ. v, 1, 14 (as grass or leather, Kāś.)

औपानुवाक्य *aupānuvākya*, mfn. (fr. *upânuvākya*), contained in the portion of the TS. called Upānuvākya, Jaim. v, 3, 15. **-kāṇḍa**, n. = *upânuvākya*, Comm. on TS.

औपायिक *aupāyika*, mfn. = *aupayika*, q.v., MBh. v, 7019.

औपावि *aúpāvi*, *is*, m. a descendant of Upāva, N. of Jānaśruteya, ŚBr. v.

औपासन *aupāsana*, *as*, m. (scil. *agni*), (fr. *upâsana*), the fire used for domestic worship, ŚBr. xii; KātyŚr.; PārGṛ. &c.; (scil. *piṇḍa*) a small cake offered to the Manes, ŚāṅkhBr. & Śr.; mf(*ā*)n. relating to or performed at an Aupāsana fire (as the evening and morning oblations), Yājñ. iii, 17; HirGṛ. **-prayoga**, m. the manner of performing the rites at the Aupāsana fire, Comm. on ĀśvŚr.

Aupāsanika, *as*, m. the Aupāsana fire, Comm. on ĀśvŚr.

औपोदिति *aúpoditi*, *is*, *ī*, m. f. a descendant of Upodita; (*is*), m., N. of Tumiñja, TS. i.

Aupoditeyá, *as*, m. a descendant of Aupoditi, ŚBr. i.

औपोद्घातिक *aupodghātika*, mfn. (fr. *upôdghāta*), occasioned, occasional, Comm. on ShaḍvBr.

औम् *aum*, ind. the sacred syllable of the Śūdras (see 3. *au*).

औम 1. *auma*, mf(ī)n. (fr. *umā*), made of flax, flaxen, Pāṇ. iv, 3, 158.

Aumaka, mfn. id., ib.

Aumika, mf(ī)n. relating to flax, gaṇa *aśvâdi*, Pāṇ. v, 1, 39.

Aumīna, *am*, n. a field of flax, Pāṇ. v, 2, 4.

औम 2. *auma*, mfn. relating to the goddess Umā, Paraś.

Aumāpata, *am*, n. (fr. *umā-pati*), relating to or treating on Umā's husband or Śiva, Bālar.

औम्भेयक *aumbheyaka*, mfn. (fr. *umbhi*, gaṇa *kattry-ādi*, Pāṇ. iv, 2, 95), relating to one who fills up (T.?)

औरग *auraga*, mfn. (fr. *ura-ga*), relating or belonging to a snake, serpentine, MBh.; Naish.; (*am*), n., N. of the constellation Āśleshā, L.

औरभ्र *aurabhra*, mfn. (fr. *ura-bhra*), belonging to or produced from a ram or sheep, Mn. iii, 268; MBh.; Suśr. &c.; (*as*), m. a coarse woollen blanket, L.; N. of a physician, Suśr.; (*am*), n. mutton, the flesh of sheep; woollen cloth, W.

Aurabhraka, *am*, n. a flock of sheep, Pāṇ. iv, 2, 39.

Aurabhrika, mfn. relating to sheep, W.; (*as*), m. a shepherd, Mn. iii, 166.

औरव *aurava*, *am*, n. (fr. *uru*), width, dimension, extension, spaciousness, gaṇa *pṛithv-ādi*, Pāṇ. v, 1, 122; (*as*), m. a descendant of Uru, N. of the Ṛishi Arga.

औरश *auraśa*, v. l. for 2. *aurasa* below.

औरस 1. *aurasa*, mf(ī)n. (fr. *uras*), belonging to or being in the breast, produced from the breast, MBh.; innate, own, produced by one's self, Suśr.; (*as*), m. a sound produced from the breast, PārGṛ. iii, 16; an own son, legitimate son (one by a wife of the same caste married according to the prescribed rules), Mn. ix, 166, &c.; Yājñ. ii, 128, &c.; Hit.; R. &c.; (*ī*), f. a legitimate daughter, Dāy.; Naish.

Aurasāyani, *is*, m. a descendant of Uras, gaṇa *tikâdi*, Pāṇ. iv, 1, 154; a descendant of Aurasa, ib.

Aurasi, *is*, m. a descendant of Uras (?).

Aurasika, mfn. like a breast, gaṇa *aṅguly-ādi*, Pāṇ. v, 3, 108.

Aurasya, mfn. belonging to or produced from the breast (as a sound); produced by one's self, own, legitimate; (cf. 1. *aurasa*.)

औरस 2. *aurasa*, mfn. coming from or belonging to Urasā, gaṇa *sindhv-ādi*, Pāṇ. iv, 3, 93.

औरा *aurā*, f., N. of a woman.

औरिण *auriṇa*, *am*, n. = *airiṇa*, q. v., L.

औरुक्षय *aurukshaya*, *am*, n. (fr. *uru-kshaya*), N. of a Sāman.

Aurukshayasa, *as*, m. a descendant of Urukshayas, ĀśvŚr.

और्जस्य *aurjasya*, *am*, n. (fr. *ūrjas*), a particular style of composition, Pratāpar.

Aurjitya, *am*, n. (fr. *ūrjita*), strength, vigour, Comm. on Kāvyād.

और्ण *aurṇa*, mf(ī)n. (fr. *ūrṇā*), made of wool, woollen, Yājñ. ii, 179; MBh.; Pāṇ.

Aurṇaka, mf(ī)n. id., Pāṇ. iv, 3, 158.

Aurṇanābha, *as*, m. a descendant of Ūrṇanābha, gaṇa *śivâdi*, Pāṇ. iv, 1, 112.

Aurṇanābhaka, mfn. inhabited by the Ūrṇanābhas (as a country), gaṇa *rājanyâdi*, Pāṇ. iv, 2, 53.

Aurṇavābhá, *as*, m. a descendant of Ūrṇavābhi, N. of a demon, RV. ii, 11, 18; viii, 32, 26; 77, 2; N. of a grammarian, Nir.; of several other men, ŚBr. &c.

Aurṇāyava, *am*, n. (fr. *ūrṇāyu*), N. of a Sāman, TāṇḍyaBr. &c.

Aurṇāvatya, *as*, m. (nom. pl. °*vatās*), a descendant of Ūrṇāvat, Pāṇ. v, 3, 118.

Aurṇika, mf(ī)n. woollen, gaṇa *aśvâdi*, Pāṇ. v, 1, 39.

और्दायनी *aurdāyanī*, f. a descendant of Urdi, Pat. on Pāṇ. iv, 2, 99.

और्ध्व *aurdhva* (fr. *ūrdhva*, q. v.), in the following compounds:

Aurdhvakālika, mf(*ā* & *ī*)n. (fr. *ūrdhva-kāla*), relating to subsequent time, gaṇa *kāśy-ādi*, Pāṇ. iv, 2, 116.

Aurdhvadeha, mfn. (fr. *ūrdhva-deha*), relating or referring to the state after death, relating to future life, R. ii, 83, 24.

Aurdhvadehika, mfn. id.; relating to a deceased person, performed in honour of the dead, funereal, funeral; (*am*), n. the obsequies of a deceased person, any funeral ceremony; whatever is offered or performed on a person's decease (as burning of the body, offering cakes, distributing alms &c.), Mn. xi, 10; MBh.; R.; Ragh. &c. **-kalpavalli**, f., **-nirṇaya**, m., **-paddhati**, f., **-prayoga**, m., N. of works.

Aurdhvadaihika, mfn. = *aurdhvadehika*, L.

Aurdhvaṃdamika, mfn. (fr. *ūrdhvaṃ-dama*), belonging to an elevated or upright person or thing, Pat. on Pāṇ. iv, 3, 60.

Aurdhvabhaktika, mfn. (fr. *ūrdhva-bhakta*), used or applied after a meal, Car.

Aurdhvasadmana, *am*, n. (fr. *ūrdhva-sadman*), N. of a Sāman, TāṇḍyaBr.; Lāṭy.

Aurdhvasrotasika, *as*, m. (fr. *ūrdhva-srotas*), a Śaiva (q. v.), L.

और्मिलेय *aurmileya*, *as*, m. a descendant of Urmilā, Uttarar.

और्म्य *aurmya*, *as*, m. (fr. *ūrmi*?), a particular personification, SāmavBr.

और्व 1. *aurva*, *as*, m. a descendant of Ūrva, N. of a Ṛishi, RV. viii, 102, 4; TS. vii; AitBr.; MBh. &c.; (in later mythology he is called Aurva Bhārgava as son of Cyavana and grandson of Bhṛigu; he is the subject of a legend told in MBh. i, 6802; there it is said that the sons of Kṛitavīrya, wishing to destroy the descendants of Bhṛigu in order to recover the wealth left them by their father, slew even the children in the womb; one of the women of the family of Bhṛigu, in order to preserve her embryo, secreted it in her thigh [*ūru*], whence the child at its birth was named Aurva; on beholding whom, the sons of Kṛitavīrya were struck with blindness, and from whose wrath proceeded a flame that threatened to destroy the world, had not Aurva at the persuasion of the Bhārgavas cast it into the ocean, where it remained concealed, and having the face of a horse; Aurva was afterwards preceptor to Sagara and gave him the Āgneyâstram, with which he conquered the barbarians who invaded his possessions; cf. *vaḍavā-mukha*, *vaḍavâgni*); N. of a son of Vasishṭha, Hariv.; (*ās*), m. pl., N. of a class of Pitṛis, TāṇḍyaBr.; Lāṭy.; (*ī*), f. a female descendant of Ūrva, Kāś. on Pāṇ. iv, 1, 73; (mfn.) produced by or relating to the Ṛishi Aurva, MBh. i, 387, &c.; (*as*), m. the submarine fire (cast into the ocean by Aurva Bhārgava, cf. above). **-dahana**, m. the submarine fire, Rājat. **Aurvâgni**, m. id., Prab.; Śiś. **Aurvânala**, m. id., Kād.

Aurvāya, Nom. Ā. *aurvāyate*, to behave like the submarine fire, Veṇīs.

और्व 2. *aurva*, mf(*ī*)n. (fr. *urvī*), relating to the earth, of the earth, VarBṛS.; (*am*), n. fossil salt, L.

Aurvara, mfn. (fr. *urvarā*), relating to or coming from the earth, coming from the ground (as dust), Śiś. xvi, 27.

और्वश *aurvaśa*, mfn. containing the word *urvaśī* (as an Adhyāya or Anuvāka), gaṇa *vimuktâdi*, Pāṇ. v, 2, 61.

Aurvaśeya, m. a descendant of Urvaśī, Vikr.; N. of Agastya, L.

औल *aula, as*, m. Arum Campanulatum (=*ola*), Nigh.

औलपि *aulapi, ayas*, m. pl. (fr. *ulapa*), N. of a warrior-tribe, gaṇa *dāmany-ādi*, Pāṇ. v, 3, 116.

Aulapin, *inas*, m. pl. the school of Ulapa, Kāś. on Pāṇ. iv, 3, 104.

Aulapiya, *as*, m. a king of the Aulapis above.

औलभीय *aulabhīya, as*, m. a king of the Ulabhas, gaṇa *dāmany-ādi*, Pāṇ. v, 3, 116.

औलान *aulānā, as*, m., N. of Śantanava [Sāy.], RV. x, 98, 11.

औलुण्ड्य *auluṇḍya, as*, m. a descendant of Uluṇḍa, N. of Supratīta, VBr.

औलूक *aulūka, as*, m. (fr. *ulūka*), N. of a village; (*am*), n. a number of owls, gaṇa *khaṇḍikâdi*, Pāṇ. iv, 2, 45.

Aulūkīya, mfn. (fr. *aulūka*), Pat. on Vārtt. 2 on Pāṇ. iv, 2, 104.

Aulūkya, *as*, m. a descendant of Ulūka, gaṇa *gargâdi*, Pāṇ. iv, 1, 105; a follower of the Vaiśeshika doctrine (cf. *ulūka*). **-darśana**, n., N. of the Vaiśeshika system, Sarvad. 103 seqq. (erroneously printed *aulukya-d°*).

औलूखल *aulūkhalá*, mfn. (fr. *ulūkhala*), coming from a mortar, ground or pounded in a mortar, ŚBr.; KātyŚr.; (*au*), m. du. mortar and pestle, MaitrS. i, 4, 10.

औल्वण्य *aulvaṇya, am*, n. (fr. *ulvaṇa*), excess, superabundance (?).

औवीली *auvīlī*, f., v. l. for *ovīlī*, q. v.

Auvelī, f. id.

औवेणक *auveṇaka, am*, n. a kind of song (*gītaka*), Yājñ. iii, 113.

औशत *auśata, as*, m. a descendant of Uśata, Hariv.

औशन *auśana*, mf(*ī*)n. (fr. *uśanas*), = *auśanasa* below, Kāś. on Pāṇ. iv, 2, 8; (*am*), n., N. of several Sāmans, Comm. on Nyāyam.

Auśanasa, mf(*ī*)n. relating to or originating from Uśanas, peculiar to him, ĀśvGṛ.; MBh.; BhP. &c.; (*as, ī*), m. f. a descendant of Uśanas, MBh. i, 3376; BhP. vii, ix; (*am*), n. (scil. *śāstra*) the law-book of Uśanas, Pañcat.; N. of an Upa-purāṇa, KūrmaP.; N. of a Tīrtha, MBh. iii, 7005.

Auśanasya, mfn. originating from Uśanas, Mudr.

औशान *auśānā*, mfn (perhaps pres. p. of *ā-√vaś*, NBD.) wishing for, desirous (*somena saha miśrī-bhāvam kāmayamāna*, Sāy.), RV. x, 30, 9.

औशिज *auśijá*, mfn. (fr. *uśij*), desirous, zealous, wishing, RV.; N. of Kakshīvat and other Ṛishis, RV.; TS.; ĀśvŚr. &c.

औशीनर *auśīnara*, mf(*ī*)n. belonging to the Uśīnaras, MBh.; Hariv. &c.; (*ī*), f., N. of a wife of Purūravas, Vikr.

Auśīnari, *is*, m. a king of the Uśīnaras, MBh.

औशीर *auśīra*, mfn. made of Uśīra, MBh. xii, 2299; (*as, am*), m. n. the stick which serves as a handle to the cow's tail used as a fan or chowri, L.; the cow's tail used as a fan, the chowri, W.; (*am*), n. an unguent made of Uśīra, Mṛicch.; a bed (used also as a seat), L.; a seat, chair, stool, L.; = *uśīra*, q. v., W.

Auśīrikā, f. the shoot (of a plant), L.; a basin, bowl, L.

औषण *aushaṇa, am*, n. (fr. *ushaṇa*), pungency, L. **-śauṇḍī**, f. black pepper, L.

औषत *aushata*, incorrect for *auśata*, q. v.

औषदश्वि *aushadaśvi, is*, m. a descendant of Oshad-aśva, N. of Vasumat, MBh. i, 3664.

औषध *aushadhá*, mf(*ī*)n. (fr. *oshadhi*), consisting of herbs, ŚBr. vii; (*ī*), f., N. of Dākshāyaṇī, MatsyaP.; (*am*), n. herbs collectively, a herb, ŚBr.; AitBr.; KātyŚr. &c.; herbs used in medicine, simples, a medicament, drug, medicine in general, Mn.; MBh.; Ragh. &c.; a mineral, W.; a vessel for herbs. **-peshaka**, m. one who grinds or pounds medicaments, Car. **Aushadhâvali**, f., N. of a medical work composed by Prāṇa-kṛishṇa.

Aushadhi, *is* or *ī*, f. = *oshadhi*, q. v.

Aushadhī-√kṛi, to make into a medicament, Mṛicch.

Aushadhīya, mfn. medicinal, W.; consisting of herbs, herby.

औषर *aushara, am*, n. (fr. *ūshara*), fossil salt, L.; iron stone, L.

Ausharaka, *am*, n. fossil salt, L.

औषस *aushasá*, mf(*ī*)n. (fr. *ushas*), relating to dawn, early, matutinal, TBr. ii; (*ī*), f. daybreak, morning, ŚBr. vi; (*am*), n., N. of several Sāmans.

Aushasika, mfn. walking out at daybreak; early, matutinal &c., T.

Aushika, mfn. (fr. 2. *ush*), id., Pat. on Pāṇ. vii, 3, 51.

औषस्त्य *aushastya*, mfn. relating to or treating of the sage Ushasti.

औषिज *aushija*, incorrect for *auśija*, q. v.

औष्ट्र *aushṭra*, mfn. (fr. *ushṭra*), relating to or coming from a camel, Gaut. xvii, 24; Mn. v, 8; Yājñ.; Suśr. &c.; abounding in camels or buffaloes (as a country), Comm. on Pāṇ. iv, 2, 69; (*am*), n. the skin of a buffalo, Vait.; the camel genus; camel-nature, W.

Aushṭraka, mfn. coming from a camel, Pāṇ. iv, 3, 157; (*am*), n. a herd or multitude of camels, Pāṇ. iv, 2, 39.

Aushṭraratha, mfn. (fr. *ushṭra-ratha*), belonging to a carriage drawn by camels (as a wheel), Kāś. on Pāṇ. iv, 3, 122.

Aushṭrākshi, *is*, m. a descendant of Ushṭrāksha, N. of a teacher, VBr.

Aushṭrāyaṇa, *as*, m. a descendant of Ushṭra, gaṇa *arīhaṇâdi*, Pāṇ. iv, 2, 80.

Aushṭrāyaṇaka, mfn. relating to the above, ib.

Aushṭrika, mfn. coming from a camel (as milk), Suśr.; an oil-miller (*tailika*, Nīlak.), MBh. viii, 2095.

औष्ठ *aushṭhá*, mfn. (fr. *oshṭha*), lip-shaped, ŚBr. iv; KātyŚr.

औष्णिह *aúshṇiha*, mfn. in the Ushṇih metre, beginning with an Ushṇih, VS.; ŚBr.; ŚāṅkhŚr. &c.; (*am*), n. = *ushṇih*, gaṇa *prajñâdi*, Pāṇ. v, 4, 38.

औष्णिक *aushṇika, ās*, m. pl., N. of a people, MBh.

औष्ण्य *aushṇya, am*, n. (fr. *ushṇa*), heat, warmth, burning, Yājñ. iii, 77; Suśr. &c.

Aushmya, *am*, n. (fr. *ushman*), id., Ragh. xvii, 33.

क KA.

क 1. *ka*, the first consonant of the alphabet, and the first guttural letter (corresponding in sound to *k* in *keep* or *king*). **-kāra**, m. the letter or sound *ka*, TPrāt. **-vat**, mfn. having the word *ka*, NBD. **-varga**, m. the gutturals (of which *ka* is the first letter), TPrāt.; Siddh.; (cf. *vargá*.)

क 2. *ká, kas, kā, kim*, interrog. pron. (see *kim* and 2. *kad*, and cf. the following words in which the interrogative base *ka* appears, *katama, katara, kati, katham, kadā, karhi, kā*, &c.), who? which? what? In its declension *ka* follows the pronoun *tad* except in nom. acc. sing. neut., where *kim* has taken the place of *kad* or *kat* in classical Sanskṛit; but the old form *kad* is found in the Veda (see Gram. 227); [cf. Zd. *ka, kô, kâ, kat;* Gk. *πόθεν, πῶς* (Ion. *κόθεν, κῶς*), *τίς, τί*; Lat. *quis, quid;* Lith. *kas, kà;* Goth. *hvas, hvô, hva;* Angl. Sax. *hwā, hwaet;* Eng. *who, what*.]

The interrogative sentence introduced by *ka* is often terminated by *iti* (e. g. *kasya sa putra iti kathyatām*, let it be said, 'whose son is he?'), but *iti* may be omitted and the sentence lose its direct interrogative character (e. g. *kasya sa putro na jñāyate*, it is not known whose son he is). *Ka* with or without √1. *as* may express 'how is it possible that?' 'what power have I, you, they, &c.?' (e. g. *ke mama dhanvino 'nye*, what can the other archers do against me? *ke āvām paritrātum*, what power have we to rescue you?) *Ka* is often connected with a demonstrative pron. (e. g. *ko 'yam āyāti*, who comes here?) or with the potential (e. g. *ko Hariṃ nindet*, who will blame Hari?) *Ka* is sometimes repeated (e. g. *kaḥ ko 'tra*, who is there? *kān kān*, whom? whom? i. e. which of them? cf. Gram. 54), and the repetition is often due to a kind of attraction (e. g. *keshāṃ kiṃ śāstram adhyayanīyam*, which book is to be read by whom? Gram. 836. *a*). When *kim* is connected with the inst. c. of a noun or with the indecl. participle it may express 'what is gained by doing so, &c.?' (= *ko 'rthas*); (e. g. *kiṃ vilambena*, what is gained by delay? *kim bahunā*, what is the use of more words? *dhanena kiṃ yo na dadāti*, what is the use of wealth to him who does not give? with inst. and gen., *nīrujaḥ kim aushadhaiḥ*, what is the use of medicine to the healthy?)

Ka is often followed by the particles *iva, u, nāma, nu, vā, svid*, some of which serve merely to generalize the interrogation (e. g. *kim iva etad*, what can this be? *ka u śravat*, who can possibly hear? *ko nāma jānāti*, who indeed knows? *ko nv ayam*, who, pray, is this? *kiṃ nu kāryam*, what is to be done? *ko vā devād anyaḥ*, who possibly other than a god? *kasya svid hṛidayaṃ nāsti*, of what person is there no heart?)

Ka is occasionally used alone as an indefinite pronoun, especially in negative sentences (e. g. *na kasya ko vallabhaḥ*, no one is a favourite of any one; *nânyo jānāti kaḥ*, no one else knows; *kathaṃ sa ghātayati kam*, how does he kill any one?) Generally, however, *ka* is only made indefinite when connected with the particles *ca, caná, cid, vā*, and *ápi*, in which case *ka* may sometimes be preceded by the relative *ya* (e. g. *ye ke ca*, any persons whatsoever; *yasyai kasyai ca devatāyai*, to any deity whatsoever; *yāni kāni ca mitrāṇi*, any friends whatsoever; *yat kiṃca*, whatever). The particle *cana*, being composed of *ca* and *na*, properly gives a negative force to the pronoun (e. g. *yasmād Indrād ṛite kiṃcana*, without which Indra there is nothing), but the negative sense is generally dropped (e. g. *kaścana*, any one; *na kaścana*, no one), and a relative is sometimes connected with it (e. g. *yat kiṃcana*, anything whatsoever). Examples of *cid* with the interrogative are common; *vā* and *api* are not so common, but the latter is often found in classical Sanskṛit (e. g. *kaścid*, any one; *kecid*, some; *na kaścid*, no one; *na kiṃcid api*, nothing whatsoever; *yaḥ kaścid*, any one whatsoever; *kecit—kecit*, some—others; *yasmin kasmin vā deśe*, in any country whatsoever; *na ko 'pi*, no one; *na kimapi*, nothing whatever).

Ka may sometimes be used, like 2. *kad*, at the beginning of a compound. See *ka-pūya*, &c.

क 3. *ká, as*, m. (according to native authorities) N. of Prajāpati or of a Prajāpati, VS. xx, 4; xxii, 20; TS. i; ŚBr. &c.; of Brahman, MBh. i, 32; BhP. iii, 12, 51; xii, 13, 19; 20; of Daksha, BhP. ix, 10, 10; of Vishṇu, L.; of Yama, L.; of Garuḍa; the soul, Tattvas.; a particular comet, VarBṛS.; the sun, L.; fire, L.; splendour, light, L.; air, L.; a peacock, L.; the body, L.; time, L.; wealth, L.; sound, L.; a king, L.; = *kāma-granthi* (?); (*am*), n. happiness, joy, pleasure, ChUp. iv, 10, 5; Nir. &c.; water, MaitrS. i, 10, 10; ŚBr. x; Yājñ. &c.; the head; hair, a head of hair, L.; (also regarded as ind.; cf. 1. *kam*.) **-ja**, mfn. produced in or by water, watery, aquatic; (*am*), n. a lotus, AgP.; -°*âsana*, m. 'sitting on a lotus,' N. of Brahmā, Hcat. **-da**, m. 'water-giver,' a cloud, L.

क 4. *ka*, a Taddhita affix (much used in forming adjectives; it may also be added to nouns to express diminution, deterioration, or similarity, e. g. *putraka*, a little son; *aśvaka*, a bad horse or like a horse).

कंय *kaṃya*, &c. See 1. *kam*.

कंवूल *kaṃvūla, am,* n. (in astrol.) N. of the eighth Yoga, = Arabic قبول.

कंश *kanśa* = *kansá* below.

कंस् *kans,* cl. 2. Ā. *kanste, cakanse, kansitā,* &c., to go; to command; to destroy, Dhātup. xxiv, 14.

कंस *kansá, as, am,* m. n. (√*kam,* Uṇ. iii, 62), a vessel made of metal, drinking vessel, cup, goblet, AV. x, 10, 5; AitBr.; ŚBr. &c.; (a noun ending in *as* followed by *kansa* in a compound does not change its final, cf. *ayas-kansa,* &c., Pāṇ. viii, 3, 46); a particular measure (= two Āḍhakas, Car.; = one Āḍhaka, L.); a metal, tutanag or white copper, brass, bell-metal; (*as*), m., N. of a king of Mathurā (son of Ugra-sena and cousin of the Devakī who was mother of Kṛishṇa [Ugra-sena being brother of Devaka, who was father of Devakī]; he is usually called the uncle, but was really a cousin of Kṛishṇa, and became his implacable enemy because it had been prophesied to Kansa that he would be killed by a child of Devakī; as the foe of the deity he is identified with the Asura Kālanemi; and, as he was ultimately slain by Kṛishṇa, the latter receives epithets like *Kansa-jit,* conqueror of Kansa, &c.), MBh.; VP.; BhP. &c.; N. of a place, gaṇa *takshaśilâdi,* Pāṇ. iv, 3, 93; (*ā*), f., N. of a sister of Kansa, Hariv.; BhP.; VP. **-kāra,** m. a worker in white copper or brass, bell-founder (considered as one of the mixed castes), BrahmavP. **-kṛish,** m. 'punisher of Kansa,' N. of Kṛishṇa, Śiś. i, 16. **-keśi-nishūdana,** m. the destroyer or conqueror of Kansa and Keśin, N. of Kṛishṇa, MBh. iii, 623. **-jit,** m., N. of Kṛishṇa, L. **-nishūdana,** m. id., MBh. iii, 15528. **-pātra,** n. a particular measure (= one Āḍhaka), ŚārṅgS. **-mardana,** m., N. of Kṛishṇa, L. **-mākshika,** m. a metallic substance in large grains, a sort of pyrites. **-yajña,** m. a particular sacrifice. **-vaṇij,** m. a brazier or seller of brass vessels. **-vatī,** f., N. of a sister of Kansa and Kansā. **-vadha,** m. 'killing of Kansa,' N. of a drama by Śesha-Kṛishṇa. **-vidrāvaṇakarī,** f. 'driver away of Kansa,' N. of Durgā, MBh. iv, 180. **-śatru,** m., N. of Kṛishṇa. **-sthāla,** n. a vessel made of metal, Lāṭy. **-han,** m., N. of Kṛishṇa. **-hanana,** n. the slaying of Kansa. **Kansârāti,** m. 'enemy of Kansa,' N. of Kṛishṇa. **Kansâri,** m. id.; N. of a king, Kshit. **Kansâsthi,** n. tutanag, white copper, any alloy of tin and copper, L. **Kansôdbhavā,** f. a fragrant earth, L.

Kansaka, *as,* m. a vessel made of metal, goblet, cup, Pat.; (*am*), n. a kind of unguent applied to the eyes, L.

Kansika, mf(*ī*)n. relating to or made of bell-metal, Pāṇ. v, 1, 25.

Kansīya, mfn. id., Pāṇ. iv, 3, 168; (*am*), n. bell-metal.

कंसार *kaṃ-sāra,* mfn. having a hard centre (said of rice), BRD.; AitBr. ii, 9, 2, (but Aufrecht divides according to Sāy., *yatkiṃcitkaṃ sāram.*)

कक् *kak,* cl. 1. Ā. *kakate, cakake, kakitā,* &c., to be unsteady; to be proud; to wish, Dhātup. iv, 16.

ककजाकृत *kakajā-kṛita,* mf(*ā*)n. mutilated, torn to pieces [BRD.], AV. xi, 10, 25.

ककन्द *kakanda, as,* m. gold, L.; N. of a king, L.

ककर *kákara, as,* m. a kind of bird, VS. xxiv, 20; MaitrS. iii, 14, 1.

ककर्दु *kakárdu, us,* m. destruction of enemies [Sāy.], RV. x, 102, 6.

ककाट *kakāṭa,* mfn. whirling up. See *reṇu-ka°.*

ककाटिका *kakāṭikā,* f. a particular part of the frontal bone, AV. x, 2, 8; the back of the neck, T.; (cf. *kṛikāṭikā.*)

ककुञ्जल *kakuñjala, as,* m. the bird Cātaka, L.; (cf. *kapiñjala.*)

ककुठ *kakuṭhá, as,* m. a kind of bird, MaitrS. iii, 14, 13; (cf. *kakkaṭa.*)

ककुत्सल *kakutsala, am,* n. (perhaps) an expression of endearment applied to a child [BRD.], AV. xviii, 4, 66, (= *kakut-sthala, jāmayo navôḍhāḥ kakut-sthalam vastreṇa yathôrṇuvanti tathâiva mana ācchādaya, ity-arthaḥ,* T.)

ककुत्स्थ *kakut-stha.* See below.

ककुद् *kakúd, t,* f. a peak or summit (Lat. *cacumen*); chief, head, RV. viii, 44, 16; AV. vi, 86, 3; TS.; ŚBr.; any projecting corner or projection (as of a plough), BhP. v, 25, 7; the hump on the shoulders of the Indian bullock, AV.; TS.; BhP. &c.; the hump (of a man), Kathās.; N. of a metre (= *kakúbh*), TS.; an ensign or symbol of royalty (as the white parasol &c.); N. of a daughter of Daksha and wife of Dharma; (cf. *tri-kakud, sthūla-kakud,* &c., where the form *kakud* is said to be substituted for *kákuda* below, Pāṇ. v, 4, 146; 147.) **-druma,** m., N. of a jackal, Pañcat. **-mat,** mfn. having a projection or elevation, possessing a hump, RV. x, 8, 2; 102, 7; VS. ix, 6; Ragh.; Pañcat. &c.; (*ān*), m. a mountain, Ragh. xiii, 47; a bullock with a hump on his shoulders, Kum. i, 57; N. of a medicinal plant, L.; (*tī*), f. the hip and loins, L.; N. of a metre; N. of the wife of Pradyumna, VP. **-man,** mfn. high, lofty, Hariv. **-mi** (in comp. for *-min*), *-kanyā,* f. 'mountain-daughter,' a river, L.; N. of Revatī (wife of Bala-rāma), Śiś. ii, 20. **-min,** mfn. peaked, humped, MBh.; VarBṛS.; (*ī*), m. a mountain, L.; a bullock with a hump on his shoulders, BhP.; N. of Vishṇu, Hariv.; of a king of the Ānartas, Hariv. 644; BhP. ix, 3, 29; VP.; (*inī*), f., N. of a river, PadmaP. **-vat,** mfn. having a hump; (*ān*), m. a bullock with a hump on his shoulders, R.; (*tī*), f., N. of the wife of Pradyumna (v. l. *kakudmatī*), VP.

Kakut (in comp. for *kakúd* above). **-stha,** m. 'standing on a hump,' N. of a son of Śaśāda and grandson of Ikshvāku, MBh.; Hariv.; BhP. &c. (so called because in a battle he stood on the hump of Indra who had been changed into a bull; according to the R. he is a son of Bhagīratha).

Kákuda, *as, am,* m. n. a peak, summit (of a mountain &c.); chief, head, pre-eminent, AV. x, 10, 19; ŚBr.; Ragh. &c.; the hump on the shoulders of the Indian bullock, MBh.; a species of serpent, Suśr.; an ensign or symbol of royalty (as the white parasol &c.), Ragh.; (*as*), m., N. of a king, VP. **-kātyāyana,** m., N. of a Brāhman (who was a violent adversary of Śākyamuni). **-°rūpin,** mfn. shaped like a hump, DaivBr. **-vat,** mfn. hump-backed, VarBṛ. **Kakudâksha,** m., N. of a man, gaṇa *revaty-ādi,* Pāṇ. iv, 1, 146. **Kakudâvarta,** m. a kind of curl on the coat (of a horse). **Kakudāvartin,** m. a horse having the above curl, L.

Kakún (in comp. for *kakúd* above). **-mat,** mfn. = *kakúd-mat,* q. v., TS.

ककुन्दर *kakundara, am,* n. (connected with *kakud*?) the cavities of the loins, Yājñ. iii, 96; Bhpr.

ककुभ् *kakúbh, p,* f. (cf. *kakud*) a peak, summit, RV.; space, region or quarter of the heavens, BhP.; Mṛicch.; Kathās. &c.; N. of a metre of three Pādas (consisting of eight, twelve, and eight syllables respectively; so called because the second Pāda exceeds the others by four syllables), RPrāt. 889; AV. xiii, 1, 15; VS.; ŚBr. &c.; unornamented hair or the hair hanging down like a tail, L.; a wreath of Campaka flowers, L.; splendour, beauty, L.; a Śāstra or science, L.; a Rāgiṇī or mode of music, L.; N. of a daughter of Daksha and wife of Dharma (as a personified quarter of the sky), BhP. **-vat,** mfn. having an elevation, rising to a peak, MaitrS. i, 11, 1.

Kakup (in comp. for *kakúbh*). **-kāram,** ind. p. accompanied by rendering into Kakubh metres, ŚāṅkhBr. **-pradāha,** m. 'a glowing of the quarters of the sky,' unusual redness of the horizon, VarBṛS.

Kakub (in comp. for *kakúbh*). **-jaya,** m. conquest of the quarters or of the world, Rājat. **-bhaṇḍá,** m. a mythical being, Suparṇ.

Kakubhá, mfn. lofty, excelling, distinguished, VS.; TS.; (*as*), m. a kind of evil spirit, AV. viii, 6, 10; a kind of bird, Svapnac.; the tree Terminalia Arjuna, MBh.; Suśr. &c.; a part of the Indian lute called the belly (a wooden vessel covered with leather placed under its neck to render the sound deeper, or a crooked piece of wood at the end of the lute), L.; (in mus.) a particular Rāga or mode; a kind of disease, L.; N. of a man, gaṇa *tika-kitavâdi,* Pāṇ. ii, 4, 68; of a mountain, BhP.; (*ā*), f. space, region, L.; (in mus.) a particular Rāgiṇī; (*am*), n. the flower of Terminalia Arjuna, Kāvyād. **-maya,** mfn. made of the wood of Terminalia Arjuna, VarBṛS. **Kakubhâkāra,** m. a kind of bird (cf. *kakubha*), L. **Kakubhâdinī,** f. 'tasting like Kakubha' [T.], a kind of perfume, L.; (cf. *nalī.*)

Kakum (by Sandhi for *kakúbh*). **-matī,** f., N. of a metre, ChandS. iii, 56.

Kakuhá (= *kakubhá*), mfn. lofty, high, eminent, great, RV.

Kakuhastinā, v. l. for *kakuhá,* Nigh.

ककुयष्टिका *kakuyashṭikā,* f. a kind of bird, Car.

ककेरुक *kakeruka, as,* m. a worm in the stomach, Car.; ŚārṅgS.

कक्क् *kakk,* v. l. for *kakh,* q. v.

कक्कट *kakkaṭá, as,* m. a species of animal (offered at a sacrifice to the goddess Anumati), VS. xxiv, 32; TS. v.

कक्कराज *kakka-rāja, as,* m., N. of a king.

कक्कल *kakkala, as,* m., N. of a man.

कक्कुल *kakkula, as,* m., N. of a Buddhist Bhikshu, Lalit. (v. l. *vakula*).

कक्कोल *kakkola, as,* m. a species of plant (bearing a berry, the inner part of which is waxy and aromatic), Suśr.; R. &c.; (*ī*), f. id., Pañcad.; (*am*), n. a perfume prepared from the berries of this plant, Suśr.

Kakkolaka, *am,* n. the above perfume, Suśr.

Kakkolikā, f. a species of plant, L.

कक्ख् *kakkh,* v. l. for *kakh,* q. v.

कक्खट *kakkhaṭa,* mfn. hard, solid, L.; (*ī*), f. chalk, L. **-pattraka,** m. Corchorus Olitorius (rope is made from its fibre), L.

कक्वल *kakvala, as,* m., N. of a man (vv. ll. *kakkvala, kakvalla*).

कक्ष *káksha, as,* m. (√*kash,* Uṇ. iii, 62; cf. √*kac*), lurking-place, hiding-place, RV. x, 28, 4; VS. xi, 79; a wood, large wood (?), RV. vi, 45, 31; a forest of dead trees, a dry wood, underwood (often the lair of wild beasts), VS.; TS.; TāṇḍyaBr.; Mn. &c.; an inner recess, the interior of a forest; grass, dry grass; a spreading creeper, climbing plant, L.; side or flank, L.; sin, L.; a gate, W.; a buffalo, L.; Terminalia Bellerica, W.; (*as, ā*), m. f. the armpit (as the most concealed part of the human body), region of the girth, AV. vi, 127, 2; Suśr.; Mṛicch. &c.; [cf. Lat. *coxa,* 'hip;' O. H. G. *hahsa;* Zd. *kasha;* cf. Sk. *kaccha*]; a girdle, zone, belt, girth, MBh.; BhP. &c.; the end of the lower garment (which, after the cloth is carried round the body, is brought up behind and tucked into the waistband); hem, border, lace, BhP. ix, 10, 37; the scale of a balance, Kāvyād.; Vcar.; (*ā*), f. painful boils in the armpit, Suśr.; a surrounding wall, a wall, any place surrounded by walls (as a court-yard, a secluded portion of a building, a private chamber or room in general), MBh.; BhP.; Mn. &c.; the orbit of a planet, VarBṛS.; Sūryas. &c.; the periphery, circumference, Sūryas. xii, 65; balance, equality, similarity, resemblance, MBh. xii, 7269; VarBṛS. 26, 6; emulation, rivalry, object of emulation, Naish.; the jeweller's weight called Retti, L.; objection or reply in argument, L.; a particular part of a carriage, L.; (*ās*), m. pl., N. of a people, MBh.; VP. **-dhara,** m. the part of the body where the upper arm is connected with the shoulder, the shoulder-joint, Suśr. **-pa,** m. one of the nine treasures of Kuvera; (cf. *kacchapa.*) **-puṭa,** m. the armpit; N. of a work on magic. **-ruhā,** f. a fragrant grass, Cyperus, L. **-loman,** n. the hair under the armpit, R. **-śaya,** m. 'sleeping upon dry grass' [T.], a dog, L.; (cf. *kaṅka-śāya.*) **-sena,** m., N. of a Rājarshi, MBh. **-stha,** mfn. situated on the side, seated on the heap or flank. **Kakshâgni,** m. fire in dry wood or grass, MBh. iii, 14757. **Kakshâdhyāya,** m., N. of a part of a commentary by Bhū-dhara on the Sūrya-siddhānta. **Kakshântara,** n. an inner or private apartment. **Kakshā-paṭa** or **-°puṭa,** m. a cloth passed between the legs to cover the privities, Pañcat. **Kakshāputi,** m., N. of a physician (wrong for *kākshaputi*?). **Kakshâvêkshaka,** m. overseer of the inner apartments, L.; keeper of a royal garden, door-keeper, L.; a poet, L.; a debauchee, L.; a player, painter, L.; warmth of feeling, strength of sentiment, W. **Kakshâśrita**, n. 'being in the arm-pit,' the hair under the armpit, L. **Kakshôtthā**, f. a species of Cyperus, L. **Kakshôdaka**, n. moisture in a thicket, AitĀr. v, 3, 3, 18.

Kakshaka, as, m., N. of a Nāga, MBh.

Kakshatu, us, m., N. of a plant, Kāś. on Pāṇ. iv, 2, 71.

Kakshas, asī, n. du. (perhaps) the depressions on both sides of the wrist, AitĀr. i, 2, 6, 20.

Kakshāya, Nom. Ā. kakshāyate, to wait for any one in a hidden place, lie in ambush; to intend anything wicked, Kāty. on Pāṇ. iii, 1, 14.

Kakshin, mfn. having or furnished with a kaksha, gaṇa sukhâdi, Pāṇ. v, 2, 131 (not in Kāś.)

Kakshī (in comp. for kaksha). — **karaṇa**, n. the act of admitting or assenting, Sarvad. — **kartavya**, mfn. to be adopted or admitted (as an opinion), ib. — **kāra**, m. adoption, admission, holding (as of an opinion), ib. — √**kṛi**, 'to put anything under the arm,' accept, assent to, hold (as an opinion), admit, recognize (cf. aṅgī-√kṛi, urarī-√kṛi, &c.), Sarvad. — **kṛita**, mfn. assented, held, promised, admitted.

Kakshīvat, ān, m. (for kakshyā-vat, Kāś. on Pāṇ. viii, 2, 12), N. of a renowned Ṛishi (sometimes called Pajriya; he is the author of several hymns of the Ṛig-veda, and is fabled as a son of Uśij and Dīrgha-tamas), RV.; AV.; ŚāṅkhŚr. &c.; (antas), m. pl. the descendants of Kakshīvat, RV. i, 126, 4.

Kaksheyu, us, m., N. of a son of Raudrāśva and Ghṛitācī, MBh.; Hariv.; VP.

Kákshya, mfn. being or abiding in shrubs or dry grass, VS. xvi, 34; (kakshyà, fr. kakshyà), filling out the girth, well fed [Sāy.], RV. v, 44, 11; (kakshyā̀), f. girth (of an animal), girdle, zone, RV.; AV. viii, 4, 6; xviii, 1, 15; MBh. &c. (cf. baddha-kakshya); the enclosure of an edifice (either the wall &c. so enclosing it, or the court or chamber constituting the enclosure, the inner apartment of a palace), MBh.; R. &c.; the orbit of a planet, Āryabh.; the scale of a balance, Pat.; an upper garment, L.; similarity, equality, L.; effort, exertion, L.; a shrub yielding the black and red berry (that serves as a jeweller's weight), the Retti or Guñja, Abrus Precatorius, L.; (ās), f. pl. the fingers, Nigh.; (am), n. the scale of a balance, Comm. on Yājñ.; a part of a carriage, R.; a girdle, girth. — **prá**, mfn. filling out the girth, well fed, RV. i, 10, 3. **Kakshyā-vat**, mfn. furnished with a girth; (ān), m. = kakshīvat, Kāś. on Pāṇ. viii, 2, 12. **Kakshyâvekshaka**, m. = kakshâvekshaka, q.v., L. **Kakshyā-stotra**, n., N. of a Stotra.

कख् kakh, cl. 1. P. kakhati, cakākha, kakhitā, &c., to laugh, laugh at or deride: Caus. kakhayati, to cause to laugh, Dhātup. v, 6; xix, 22; [cf. Lat. cachinnare; Gk. καχάζω, καγχάζω; O.H.G. huoch; Germ. häher, heher; Eng. cackle.]

कख्या kakhyā, incorrect for kakshyā, q.v., L.

कग् kag, cl. 1. P. kagati, to act, perform (?), Dhātup. xix, 29.

कगित्थ kagittha, v.l. for kapittha, q. v., L.

कङ्क् kaṅk, cl. 1. Ā. kaṅkate, cakaṅke, kaṅkitā, &c., to go, Dhātup. iv, 20; [cf. Hib. cichet, 'walking;' Lith. kankù, 'to come to.']

कङ्क kaṅká, as, m. (fr. the above according to T.), a heron (the first heron is supposed to be a son of Surasā, MBh. i, 2633), VS. xxiv, 31; SV.; MBh.; Mṛicch. &c.; a kind of mango, L.; N. of Yama, L.; of several men, MBh.; Hariv.; BhP. &c.; a N. assumed by Yudhishṭhira (before king Virāṭa, when in the disguise of a Brāhman), MBh. iv; a false or pretended Brāhman, L.; a man of the second or military tribe, L.; one of the eighteen divisions of the continent, W.; (ās), m. pl., N. of a people, MBh.; BhP.; VarBṛS.; (ā), f. a kind of sandal, L.; the scent of the lotus, L.; (ā & ī), f., N. of a daughter of Ugrasena (and sister of Kaṅka), BhP.; VP. — **cit**, mfn. collected into a heap resembling a heron, TS. v; ŚBr.; Śulbas. &c. — **tuṇḍa**, m., N. of a Rakshas, R. — **troṭa**, m. a kind of fish, Esox Kankila, L. — **troṭi**, m. id., L. — **pattra**, n. a heron's feather (fixed on an arrow), R.; Ragh.; (mfn.) furnished with the feathers of a heron (as an arrow), MBh.; (as), m. an arrow furnished with heron's feathers. — °**pattrin**, mfn. furnished with heron's feathers, MBh.; R. — **parvan**, m. a kind of serpent, AV. — **pṛishṭhī**, f. a species of fish, L. — **mālā**, f. beating time by clapping the hands, W. — **mukha**, mfn. shaped like a heron's mouth (said of a sort of forceps), Suśr. — **rola**, m. Alangium Hexapetalum, L. — **latā**, f. a species of plant, L. — **loḍya**, v. l. for aṅga-loḍya, q. v. — **vadana**, n. 'heron's mouth,' a pair of tongs, Veṇīs. — **śatru**, m. Desmodium Gangeticum, L. — **śāya**, m. 'sleeping like a heron' (?), a dog, L.; (cf. kaksha-śāya.)

कङ्कट kaṅkaṭa, as, m. (√kaṅk, Uṇ. iv, 81), armour, mail, R.; Ragh.; Veṇīs.; an iron hook (to goad an elephant), L.; boundary, limit; (ās), m. pl., N. of a people, VarBṛ.

Kaṅkaṭaka, as, m. armour, mail, L.

Kaṅkaṭika, mfn. relating to armour, gaṇa kumudâdi, Pāṇ. iv, 2, 80.

Kaṅkaṭin, mfn. furnished with armour, gaṇa prekshâdi, ib.; (ī), m. a chamberlain, Hcar. 121, 24.

Kaṅkaṭila, mfn. armed with mail, gaṇa kāśâdi, Pāṇ. iv, 2, 80.

कङ्कटेरी kaṅkaṭerī, f. turmeric, W.

कङ्कण kaṅkaṇa, am, n. (as, m., L.), (√kai, Comm. on Uṇ. iv, 24), a bracelet, ornament for the wrist, ring, MBh.; Bhartṛ.; Hit. &c.; a band or ribbon (tied round the wrist of a bride or bridegroom before marriage), Mcar.; an annual weapon, MBh.; an ornament round the feet of an elephant, MBh. iii, 15757; any ornament or trinket; a crest; (as), m., N. of a teacher; (ā), f., N. of one of the mothers in the retinue of Skanda, MBh. ix, 2634; (ī), f. an ornament furnished with bells, L.; (cf. kakshā; kiṅkiṇī.) — **dhara**, m. a bridegroom, Mcar.; (ā), f. a bride, ib. — **pura**, n., N. of a town, Rājat. — **priya**, m., N. of a demon causing fevers, Hariv. — **bhūshaṇa**, mfn. adorned with tinkling ornaments, L. — **maṇi**, f. a jewel in a bracelet, Comm. on Uṇ. iv, 117. — **varsha**, mfn. 'raining down bracelets,' a magician, Rājat. iv, 246; N. of a king, Rājat. — **varshi-tā**, f. the state of being the above, ib. — **hārikā**, f. a kind of bird, Comm. on PārGṛ.

Kaṅkaṇin, mfn. ornamented with a bracelet, Kathās.

Kaṅkaṇīka, as, m., N. of a Nāga, VP.; (ā), f. an ornament furnished with bells, L.; a string tied round the wrist, L.

कङ्कत káṅkata, as, m. (ī, am, f. n., L.) a comb, hair-comb, AV. xiv, 2, 68 (v. l. kaṇṭaka); TBr.; PārGṛ. &c.; a slightly venomous animal [Sāy.], RV. i, 191, 1; N. of a teacher; (ī), f. Sida Rhombifolia.

Kaṅkatikā, f. a comb; Sida Rhombifolia, Bhpr.

Kaṅkatīya, ās, m. pl., N. of a family.

कङ्कर kaṅkara, mfn. vile, bad, L.; (am), n. buttermilk mixed with water, L.; a particular high number, Lalit.

कङ्काल kaṅkāla, as, am, m. n. a skeleton, MBh.; Kathās. &c.; (as), m. a particular mode in music. — **ketu**, m., N. of a Dānava. — **bhairava**, n., N. of a work; -tantra, n. id. — **māla-bhārin**, m. 'wearing a necklace of bones,' N. of Śiva. — °**mālin**, m. id. — **musala**, n., N. of a mythical weapon, R.

Kaṅkālaya, as, m. the human body, T.; N. of an author.

Kaṅkālin, ī, m., N. of a Yaksha, BrahmaP.; (inī), f., N. of a form of Durgā, Kathās. lxxviii, 92.

कङ्कु kaṅku, us, m. a kind of Panic seed (= kaṅgu), VarBṛS.; N. of a son of Ugra-sena (erroneous for kaṅka).

कङ्कुष्ठ kaṅkushṭha, as, m. a medicinal earth (described as of two colours, one of silvery and one of a gold colour, or one of a light and one of a dark yellow), Suśr.

कङ्कूष káṅkūsha, ās, m. pl. a particular part of the head, [NBD.], AV. ix, 8, 2 (= ābhyantara-deha, T.)

कङ्केरु kaṅkeru, us, m. a kind of crow, L.

कङ्केलि kaṅkeli, is, m. the tree Jonesia Asoka, Bālar.

Kaṅkella, as, m. id., L.

Kaṅkelli, is, ī, m. f. id., Vām.

कङ्कोल kaṅkola, as, m. a kind of plant, Bhartṛ.; N. of a Nāga, RāmatUp.; of an author; (am), n. cubeb, Bhpr.

Kaṅkolaka, am, n. cubeb, L.

कङ्ख kaṅkha, am, n. (perhaps a combination of ka and kha), enjoyment, fruition, L.

कङ्गनील kaṅganīla, as, m., N. of a Nāga, VP.

कङ्गु kaṅgu, us, f. a kind of Panic seed (several varieties are cultivated as food for the poor), VarBṛS.; Comm. on ŚBr. &c.

Kaṅguka, as, ā, m. f. id., Suśr.

Kaṅgunī, f. Celastrus Paniculatus, Bhpr.; = kaṅgu, L. — **pattrā**, f. Panicum Verticillatum, L.

Kaṅgū, f. = kaṅguka, L.

कङ्गुल kaṅgula, as, m. a particular position of the hand, PSarv.

कच् kac, cl. 1. P. kacati, to sound, cry, Vop.: Ā. kacate, cakace, kacitā, &c., to bind, fetter; to shine, Dhātup. vi, 8; [cf. kañc; Lat. cingere; Lith. kinkau.]

Kaca, as, m. the hair (esp. of the head), Ragh.; Bhartṛ. &c.; a cicatrix, a dry sore, scar, L.; a band, the hem of a garment, L.; a cloud, L.; N. of a son of Bṛihaspati, MBh.; BhP.; Rājat.; N. of a place; (ā), f. a female elephant, L.; beauty, brilliancy, L.; (cf. a-kaca, ut-kaca, &c.) — **graha**, m. seizing or grasping the hair, MBh.; Ragh. &c. — **grahaṇa**, n. id., BhP. — **dugdhikā**, f. Cucurbita Hispida, Nigh. — **pa**, m. 'cloud-drinker,' grass; a leaf, W.; (am), n. a vessel for vegetables, L. — **paksha**, m. thick or ornamented hair. — **pāśa**, m. id., Naish.; (cf. keśa-pāśa.) — **bhāra**, m. id., Śārṅg. — **māla**, m. smoke (kacaṃ kaca-kāntiṃ malate, T.; v. l. khatamāla), L. — **ripuphalā**, f. = śamī, q.v., L. — **hasta**, m. thick or ornamented hair, beautiful hair, L. **Kacā-kaci**, ind. hair against hair, pulling each other's hair, Kāś. on Pāṇ. v, 4, 127; MBh.; Bālar.; (cf. keśā-keśi.)

Kacâcita, mfn. having long or dishevelled hair, W.

Kacâmoda, n. a fragrant ointment for the hair, L.

Kacêśvara, n., N. of a temple.

Kacaka, as, m. a kind of mushroom, Nigh.

Kacela, am, n. a string or cover containing and keeping together the leaves of a manuscript, L.; (cf. kācana.)

कचङ्गल kacaṅgala, am, n. the ocean, L; a free market (a place of sale paying no duty or custom), L.; N. of a region.

कचाकु kacāku, mfn. ill-disposed, wicked, L.; difficult to be borne, intolerable, difficult to be approached, L.; (us), m. a snake, L.

कचाटुर kacāṭura, as, m. a kind of gallinule, L. (see dātyūha).

कचु kacu, us, f. Arum Colocasia (an esculent root cultivated for food; cf. kacvī). — **rāya**, m., N. of a man.

कचोर kacora, as, m. Curcuma Zerumbet, Nigh.

कच्चट kaccaṭa, am, n. an aquatic plant (= jalapippalī).

कच्चर kaccara, mfn. dirty, foul, spoiled by dirt, L.; vile, wicked, bad, L.; (am), n. buttermilk diluted with water; (cf. kaṅkara, kaṭura, &c.)

कच्चिद् kac-cid. See under 2. kad.

कच्छ kaccha, as, m. (ā, am, f. n., L.) a bank or any ground bordering on water, shore; [cf. Zd. kasha, voura-kasha, the 'wide-shored,' the Caspian Sea; cf. kaksha]; a mound or causeway; watery soil, marshy ground, marsh, morass, MBh.; Megh.; Pañcat.; N. of several places, e.g. Cutch, Pāṇ.; VarBṛS.; Cedrela Toona (the timber of which is used for making furniture &c.), L.; Hibiscus Populneoides, L.; a particular part of a tortoise, L.; a particular part of a boat, L.; (ās), m. pl., N. of a people (v. l. for kaksha), VP.; (as, ā), m. f. the hem or end of a lower garment (tucked into the girdle or waistband), L., (probably a Prākrit form for kaksha); (ā), f. a cricket, L.; N. of a plant, L.; girdle, girth (v. l. for kakshā), Nilak. on MBh. (ed. Bomb.) iv, 13, 22. — **jā**, f. a species of Cyperus, L. — **deśa**, m., N. of a place. — **nīra**, m., N. of a Nāga; -bila, n., N. of a place. — **pa**, m. 'keeping or inhabiting a marsh,' a turtle, tortoise, MBh.; Gaut.; Mn. &c.; a tumour on the palate,

Suśr. i, 306, 8; an apparatus used in the distillation of spirituous liquor, a flat kind of still, L.; an attitude in wrestling, L.; Cedrela Toona, L.; one of the nine treasures of Kuvera, L.; N. of a Nāga, MBh.; of a son of Viśvā-mitra, Hariv.; of a country, Kathās.; (*ī*), f. a female tortoise or a kind of small tortoise, L.; a cutaneous disease, wart, blotch, Suśr.; a kind of lute (so named from being similar in shape to the tortoise; cf. *testudo*); *-deśa*, m., N. of a country. — **°paka**, m. a tortoise, VarBṛS.; (*ikā*), f. a kind of small tortoise; a pimple, blotch, wart, Suśr.; a wart accompanying gonarrhœa, W. — **puṭa**, m. a box with compartments, VarBṛS. — **bhū**, f. marshy ground, swamp, morass, W. — **ruhā**, f. 'marsh-growing,' a kind of grass. W. — **vihāra**, m., N. of a marshy region. **Kacchâdi**, m., N. of a gaṇa, Pāṇ. iv, 2, 133. **Kacchânta**, m. the border of a lake or stream; *-ruhā*, f. Dūrvā grass, L. **Kacchâlaṃkāra**, m. a kind of reed (used for writing), Nigh. **Kacchêśvara**, m., N. of a town; (cf. *kaceśvara.*) **Kacchêshṭa**, m. the tortoise, L.

Kacchaṭikā, f. the end or hem of a lower garment or cloth (gathered up behind and tucked into the waistband), L.

Kacchāṭikā, kacchāṭī, f. id., L.

Kacchāra, *ās*, m. pl., N. of a people, VarBṛS.

Kacchiya, *ās*, m. pl., N. of a people, VP.

Kacchoṭikā, f. = *kacchaṭikā*, L.

कच्छु *kacchu* = *kacchū* below, L.; a species of plant, L. — **ghna**, m. Trichosanthes Diœca, L.; (*ī*), f. a species of Hapushā (q. v.), L.

Kacchura, mfn. (fr. the next), scabby, itchy, affected by a cutaneous disease, Kāś. on Pāṇ. v, 2, 107; unchaste, libidinous; (*as, am*), m. n. a species of turmeric, L.; (*ā*), f. Alhagi Maurorum, Suśr.; Carpopogon Pruriens, L.; a species of turmeric, L.

Kacchū, f. (√*kash*, Uṇ. i, 86), itch, scab, any cutaneous disease, Suśr. — **matī**, f. Carpopogon Pruriens (said to cause itching on being applied to the skin), L. — **rākshasa**, n. (scil. *taila*) a kind of oil (applied in cutaneous diseases), Bhpr.

Kacchora, *am*, n. a kind of turmeric, L.

कच्वी *kacvī*, f. Arum Colocasia (a plant with an esculent root, cultivated for food). — **vana**, n., N. of a forest, Kshit.

कज् *kaj*, cl. 1. P. *kajati*, to be happy; to be confused with joy or pride or sorrow, Dhātup. vii, 58; to grow (in this sense a Sautra root).

कज *ka-ja.* See under 3. *ka.*

कजिङ्ग *kajiṅga*, *ās*, m. pl., N. of a people, VP.

कज्जल *kajjala*, *as*, m. a cloud (in this sense perhaps for *kad-jala*), L.; (*ā, ī*), f. a species of fish, L.; (*ī*), f. Æthiops Mineralis, L.; ink, L.; (*am*), n. lampblack (used as a collyrium and applied to the eyelashes or eyelids medicinally or as an ornament); sulphuret of lead or antimony (similarly used), Suśr.; Kathās. &c.; (fig.) dregs, BhP. vi, 2, 27. — **dhvaja**, m. a lamp, L. — **maya**, mfn. consisting of lampblack, Hcar. — **rocaka**, m. n. the wooden stand or tripod on which a lamp is placed, a candlestick, L. **Kajjalī-tīrtha**, n., N. of a Tīrtha.

Kajjalikā, f. powder (esp. made of mercury), Bhpr.

Kajjalita, mfn. covered with lampblack or with a collyrium prepared from it, gaṇa *tārakâdi*, Pāṇ. v, 2, 36; blackened, soiled, Hcar.

कज्ज्वल *kajjvala, kajvala*, vv. ll. for *kajjala* above.

कञ्च् *kañc*, cl. 1. Ā. *kañcate, cakañce, kañcitā*, &c., to bind; to shine, Dhātup. vi, 9; [cf. *kac* and *kāñc, kaksha*; Lat. *cingere.*]

कञ्चट *kañcaṭa*, *as*, m. Commelina Salicifolia and Bengalensis, L.

Kañcaḍa, *as*, m. Commelina Bengalensis, Bhpr.

कञ्चार *kañcāra*, *as*, m. the sun, L.; = *arka-vṛiksha*, T.

कञ्चिका *kañcikā*, f. a small boil; the branch of a bamboo, L.

कञ्चिदेक *kañcideka*, *am*, n., N. of a village, MBh. v, 934.

Kañcidevā, f. id., MBh. v, 2595.

कञ्चुक *kañcuka*, *as, ī* (ifc. f. *ā*), *am*, m. f. n. (fr. √*kañc*?) a dress fitting close to the upper part of the body, armour, mail; a cuirass, corselet, bodice, jacket, BhP.; Ratnāv.; Kathās. &c.; (*as*), m. the skin of a snake, Pañcat.; husk, shell, Bhpr.; cover, cloth, envelope, Bhpr.; (fig.) a cover, disguise, Hcat.; = *karabha*, L.; (*ī*), f. Lipeocercis Serrata, L. **Kañcukôshṇishin**, mfn. having armour and a turban, R. vi, 99, 23.

Kañcukālu, *us*, m. a snake, L.

Kañcukita, mfn. furnished with armour or mail, gaṇa *tārakâdi*, Pāṇ. v, 2, 36; (cf. *pulakakañcukita.*)

Kañcukin, mfn. furnished with armour or mail; (ifc.) covered with, wrapped up in, Bhartṛ.; (*ī*), m. an attendant or overseer of the women's apartments, a chamberlain, Śak.; Vikr.; Pañcat. &c.; a libidinous man, a debauchee, L.; a snake, L.; N. of several plants (Agallochum, barley, Cicer Arietinum, Lipeocercis Serrata), L. **Kañcuki-recaka**, *au*, m. du. the chamberlain and the forester.

Kañcukīya, *as*, m. a chamberlain, Nāṭyaś.

Kañcula, *as*, m. a partridge, L.; (*ī*), f. a bodice, jacket &c., L.

Kañculikā, f. a bodice, corset, Amar.

Kañcūla, *as, am*, m. n. id., L.

कंज *kaṃ-ja*, *as*, m. (fr. *kam* = 3. *ka* and *ja*), 'produced from the head,' the hair, L.; 'produced from water,' N. of Brahmā, L.; (*am*), n. a lotus, R.; BhP.; Amṛita, the food of the gods, L. — **ja**, m. 'born from a lotus,' N. of Brahmā, L. — **nābha**, m. 'lotus-naveled,' N. of Vishṇu, BhP. iii, 9, 44. — **bāhu**, m. 'having hairy arms,' N. of an Asura, Hariv. — **vadana**, n. a lotus-face; (cf. *vadanakaṃja.*) — **sū**, *ūs*, m. the god of love, L.

कञ्जक *kañjaka*, *as*, m. the bird Gracula Religiosa, L.

Kañjana, *as*, m. id., L.; N. of Kāma, the god of love, L.

Kañjala, *as*, m. the bird Gracula Religiosa, L.

Kañjinī, f. a courtezan, L.

कञ्जर *kañjara*, *as*, m. the belly; an elephant; the sun; N. of Brahmā, L.

Kañjāra, *as*, m. a peacock; the belly; an elephant; a Muni, hermit; the sun; N. of Brahmā; = *vyañjana*, L.

कञ्जिका *kañjikā*, f. Siphonantus Indica, Pañcat.

कट् 1. *kaṭ*, cl. 1. P. *kaṭati* or *kaṇṭati*, to go, Dhātup. ix, 33.

कट् 2. *kaṭ*, cl. 1. P. *kaṭati, cakāṭa, kaṭitā*, &c., to rain; to surround; to encompass, cover, screen; to divide, Dhātup. ix, 6; (cf. √*cat.*)

Káṭa, *as*, m. (perhaps for *karta* fr. √3. *kṛit*) a twist of straw or grass, straw mat, a screen of straw, TS.; ŚBr.; KātyŚr.; Mn. &c.; the hip, MBh. (cf. *kaṭi*); the hollow above the hip or the loins, the hip and loins; the temples of an elephant, Ragh.; a glance or side look, BhP. x, 32, 6 (cf. *kaṭâksha*); a throw of the dice in hazard, Mṛicch.; a corpse, L.; a hearse or any vehicle for conveying a dead body, L.; a burning-ground or place of sepulture, L.; a time or season, L.; excess, superabundance, L.; (*kaṭa* ifc. is considered as a suffix, cf. *ut-kaṭa, pra-kaṭa*, &c.); an annual plant, L.; grass, L.; Saccharum Sara, L.; a thin piece of wood, a plank, L.; agreement, L.; environs, L.; N. of a Rakshas, R.; (*ī*), f. long pepper, L.; (*am*), n. (ifc.) dust of flowers (considered as a suffix, Kāty. on Pāṇ. v, 2, 29). — **kaṭa**, m., N. of Śiva, MBh. xii, 10364. — **kuṭi**, m. a straw hut, BhP. x, 71, 16. — **kṛit**, m. a plaiter of straw mats, BhP. — **kola**, m. a spittoon, L. — **kriyā**, f. plaiting straw mats. — **khādaka**, mfn. eating much, voracious, L.; (*as*), m. a jackal, L.; a crow, L.; a glass vessel, tumbler, bowl, L. — **ghosha**, m., N. of a place in the east of India, Kāś. on Pāṇ. iv, 2, 139. — **°ghoshīya**, mfn. belonging to the above place, ib. — **ṃ-kaṭa**, m., N. of Siva, MBh.; Yājñ.; of Agni, AgP. — **ṃ-kaṭerī**, f. turmeric, Suśr. — **cchu**, f. (?) a spoon, VarBṛS. — **°jaka**, m., N. of a man, Pat. on Vārtt. 3, on Pāṇ. i, 1, 23. — **nagara**, n., N. of a place in the east of India, Kāś. on Pāṇ. iv, 2, 139. — **°nagarīya**, mfn. belonging to the above place, ib. — **palli-kuñcikā**, f. a straw hut (*-pari-k°* and *-pali-k°* vv. ll.) — **palvala**, m., N. of a place, Kāś. on Pāṇ. iv, 2, 139. — **°palvalīya**, mfn. belonging to the above place, ib. — **pūtana**, *as, ā*, m. f. a kind of Preta (q. v.) or demon (a form assumed by the deceased spirit of a Kshatriya who when alive neglected his duties), Mn. xii, 71; Mālatīm. — **prū**, m. a worm, L.; a player with dice, gambler, L.; N. of Śiva, L.; a Rakshas, L.; a Vidyā-dhara, L. — **bhaṅga**, m. plucking or gleaning corn with the hands, L.; destruction of a prince, royal misfortune, L. — **bhī**, f. Cardiospermum Halicacabum, Suśr.; N. of several other plants, L. — **bhū**, f. the cheek or region of the temples of an elephant, Śiś. v, 46. — **marda**, m., N. of Śiva, L. — **mālinī**, f. any vinous liquor. — **ṃ-bhara**, m. Bignonia Indica, L.; (*ā*), f. a female elephant, L.; red arsenic, L.; N. of several plants. — **vraṇa**, m., N. of Bhīmasena, L. — **śarkarā**, f. a species of sugar-cane (?), Suśr.; Guilandina Bonducella, L. — **saṃghāta**, m. a frame of wicker-work, Comm. on AitĀr. — **sthala**, n. the hip and loins; an elephant's temples. — **sthāla**, n. a corpse, L. **Kaṭâksha**, m. a glance or side look, a leer, MBh.; BhP.; Megh. &c.; *-kshetra*, n., N. of a country; *-māhātmya*, n., N. of a work; *-mushṭa*, mfn. caught by a glance; *-viśikha*, m. an arrow-like look of love, Bhartṛ.; *-°kshâvêkshaṇa*, n. casting lewd or amorous glances, ogling. **Kaṭâkshita**, mfn. looked at with a side glance, leered at, Kathās. lxxi, 9. **Kaṭâkshipya**, ind. p. (of an irr. compound verb *kaṭâkship*), having looked at with a side glance, BhP. x, 36, 10. **Kaṭâkshepa**, m. a side glance, leer, BhP. **Kaṭâgni**, m. fire kept up with dry grass or straw; straw placed round a criminal (according to Kull. the straw is wound round his neck and then kindled), Mn. viii, 377; Yājñ. ii, 282; MBh. **Kaṭôdaka**, n. libation of water offered to a dead person, BhP. vii, 2, 17.

Kaṭaka, *as*, m. (Comm. on Uṇ. ii, 32 & v, 35) a twist of straw, a straw mat, Comm. on KātyŚr.; (*as, am*), m. n. a string, Kād.; a bracelet of gold or shell &c., Śak.; Mṛicch. &c.; a zone; the link of a chain; a ring serving for a bridle-bit, Suśr.; a ring placed as ornament upon an elephant's tusk; the side or ridge of a hill or mountain; a valley, dale, Ragh.; Kathās.; Hit.; a royal camp, Kathās.; Hit. &c.; an army, L.; a circle, wheel, W.; a multitude, troop, caravan, Daś.; collection, compilation, Kād. 40, 11; sea-salt, L.; N. of the capital of Orissa (Cuttack); (*ikā*), f. a straw mat, Comm. on KātyŚr. — **gṛiha**, m. a lizard, L. — **°valayin**, mfn. ornamented with a bracelet and an armlet, Kāś. on Pāṇ. v, 2, 128. — **vārāṇasī**, f., N. of a town.

Kaṭakin, *ī*, m. a mountain, L.

Kaṭakīya, mfn. belonging to a mat or string &c., gaṇa *apūpâdi*, Pāṇ. v, 1, 4.

Kaṭakya, mfn. id., ib.

Kaṭamba, *as*, m. (Uṇ. iv, 82) a kind of musical instrument; an arrow, L.

Kaṭambarā, f. Helleborus Niger, L.

Kaṭasī, f. a cemetery, L.

Kaṭâṭaṅka, *as*, m., N. of Śiva, L.

Kaṭâyana, *am*, n. Andropogon Muricatus, L.

Kaṭâra, *as*, m. a libidinous man, lecher, L. — **malla**, m., N. of a man.

Kaṭāla, mfn. (fr. *kaṭā*), gaṇa *sidhmâdi*, Pāṇ. v, 2, 97.

Kaṭālu, *us*, m. Solanum Melongena, L.

Kaṭāha, *as*, m. (rarely *ī*, f., *am*, n.) a frying-pan; a boiler, caldron, saucepan (of a semi-spheroidal shape and with handles), MBh.; Suśr.; Sūryas. &c.; a turtle's shell, L.; anything shaped like a caldron (as the temple of an elephant), Śiś. v, 37; a well, L.; a winnowing basket, W.; a mound of earth; hell, the infernal regions, L.; a cot, L.; a young female buffalo whose horns are just appearing, L.; N. of a Dvīpa, Kathās.

Kaṭāhaka, *am*, n. a pan, caldron, pot, L.

Kaṭi, *is, ī*, f. the hip, buttocks, MBh.; Mn.; Suśr. &c.; the entrance of a temple, VarBṛS.; an elephant's cheek, L.; long pepper, L. — **karpaṭa**, n. a ragged garment wrapped round the hip, Kathās. — **kushṭha**, n. a kind of leprosy. — **kūpa**, m. the hollow above the hip, the loins, L. — **taṭa**, n. the loins, the hip, L. — **tra**, n. anything to protect the hips, a cloth tied round the loins, a girdle, zone, BhP. vi, 16, 30; armour for the hips or loins, Comm. on Uṇ. iv, 172; an ornament of small bells worn round the loins. — **deśa**, m. the loins. — **nāḍikā**, f. a zone, girdle, L. — **protha**, m. the buttocks, L.; (cf. *kaṭa-pr°.*) — **bandha**, m. a zone, girdle, L. — **mālikā**, f. id., ib. — **rohaka**, m. the rider on an elephant (as sitting behind and not, like the driver, sitting in front), L. — **vāsa**, m. a cloth worn round the loins, Hcat. — **śīrshaka**, m. the hip (as projecting like a head), L.; the hip and loins or the hollow above the hip, W. **–śūla,** m. sciatic pain, stitch in the side; pleurisy, Bhpr. **–śṛiṅkhalā,** f. a girdle of small bells, L. **–sūtra,** n. a zone or waistband, girdle, BhP.; Pañcad.

Kaṭika, ifc. = *kaṭi*, the hip, Suśr.; (*ā*), f. the hip, MBh.

Kaṭin, mfn. matted, screened; having handsome loins; (*ī*), m. an elephant, L.

Kaṭilla, *as*, m. Momordica Charantia, Car.

Kaṭillaka, *as*, m. id., L.

Kaṭī, f. = *kaṭi* above. **–tala,** n. a crooked sword, sabre, scymitar, L. **–nivasana,** n. a cloth worn round the hip, Kathās. **–paṭa,** m. id., Rājat.

Kaṭīka, ifc. = *kaṭī* above. **–taruṇa,** *e*, n. du. a particular part of the hip-bone, Suśr.

Kaṭīra, *as*, *am*, m. n. the cavity of the loins or the iliac region, L.; a cave, indentation, L.; (*as*), m. Mons Veneris, L.

Kaṭīraka, *am*, n. the hip, Śiś. xiii, 34.

Kaṭu, mf(*vī* & *us*)n. (Uṇ. i, 9; cf. √2. *kṛit*) pungent, acrid, sharp (one of the six kinds of flavour, *rasa*, q.v.), MBh.; Suśr.; Bhag. &c.; pungent, stimulating (as smell), strong-scented, ill-smelling, MBh. xiv; Ragh. v, 48; R. &c.; bitter, caustic (as words), displeasing, disagreeable (as sounds); fierce, impetuous, hot, envious, Ragh. vi, 85; Pañcat. &c.; (*us*), m. pungency, acerbity (as of a flavour), L.; [cf. Lith. *kartus*, 'bitter']; Trichosanthes Dioeca, Suśr.; Michelia Campaka, L.; N. of several other plants, L.; a kind of camphor, L.; (*us* & *vī*), f., N. of several plants; (*u*), n. an improper action, an act which ought not to have been done; blaming, reviling, scandal, W. **–kanda,** m. ginger, L.; garlic, L.; Hyperanthera Moringa, L. **–karañja,** m. Guilandina Bonducella, L. **–kīṭa,** m. a gnat or musquito, L. **–kīṭaka,** m. id. **–kvāṇa,** m. 'making a piercing noise,' a species of chicken (Parra Jacana or Goensis), L. **–granthi,** m. dried ginger, L.; the root of long pepper, L. **–cāturjātaka,** n. an aggregate of four acid substances (cardamoms, the bark and leaves of Laurus Cassia, and black pepper), L. **–cchada,** m. Tabernæmontana Coronaria, L. **–ja,** mfn. produced from or made of acid substances (as a kind of drink), MBh. **–tā,** f. sharpness, pungency, Śārṅg.; strong scent or smell, Bhām.; harshness, coarseness, Hariv. **–tikta,** m. a species of plant, L. **–tiktaka,** m. Cannabis Sativa, R.; Gentiana Cherayta, L.; (*ā*), f. a kind of gourd, L. **–tuṇḍikā,** f., N. of a plant, L. **–tuṇḍī,** f. id., ib. **–tumbinī,** f. a particular plant, L. **–tumbī,** f. a kind of bitter gourd, Suśr. **–taila,** m. white mustard, L. **–traya,** n. an aggregate of three pungent substances or spices (as ginger, black and long pepper), L. **–trika,** n. id., Suśr. **–tva,** n. pungency, acerbity, Subh. **–dalā,** f. Cucumis Utilissimus, L. **–nishpāva,** m. Lablab Vulgaris, L. **–pattra,** m. Oldenlandia Biflora, L.; white basil, L. **–pattraka,** m. white basil, L.; (*ikā*), f., N. of a plant, L. **–padra,** m., N. of a place (?). **–pāka,** mfn. producing acrid humors in digestion, Suśr. **–°pākin,** mfn. id., ib. **–phala,** m. Trichosanthes Dioeca, L.; (*ā*), f. Luffa Fœtida, Car.; (*am*), n. a species of plant. **–badarī,** f., N. of a plant and of a village called after it, Comm. on Pāṇ. i, 2, 51. **–bījā,** f. long pepper, L. **–bhaṅga,** m. dried ginger, L. **–bhadra,** m. id., Car. **–bhāshi-tā,** f. sarcastic speech, Prasannar. **–mañjarikā,** f. Achyranthes Aspera. **–mūla,** n. the root of long pepper, L. **–moda,** n. a particular perfume, L. **–°m-bharā,** f., N. of a plant, L. **–rava,** m. a frog, L. **–rohiṇikā,** f. Helleborus Niger. **–rohiṇī,** f. id., Suśr. **–vallī,** f. Gærtnera Racemosa, L. **–vārttākī,** f. a species of Solanum, L. **–vipāka,** mfn. = *-pāka* above, Suśr. **–śṛiṅga,** n. a particular vegetable, L. **–śṛiṅgāṭa,** n. id., ib. **–sneha,** m. Sinapis Dichotoma, L. **Kaṭûtkaṭa,** n. dried ginger, L. **Kaṭûtkaṭaka,** n. id., ib. **Kaṭûshaṇa,** n. dried ginger, L.; the root of long pepper; (cf. *ūshaṇa*.)

Káṭuka, mf(*ā* & *ī*)n. sharp, pungent, bitter; fierce, impetuous, hot, bad, RV. x, 85, 34; MBh.; Kathās. &c.; (*as*), m., N. of several plants, L.; N. of a man; (*ā*, *ī*), f., N. of several plants, L.; (*am*), n. pungency, acerbity, MBh. ii; (ifc. in a bad sense, e.g. *dadhi-kaṭuka*, m. bad coagulated milk, Pāṇ. vi, 2, 126); N. of a plant, L.; an aggregate of three pungent substances (see *-traya*), L. **–tā,** f. pungency, acerbity, Subh. **–traya,** n. an aggregate of three pungent substances (long and black pepper, and ginger), Suśr. **–tva,** n. = *-tā* above, Suśr. **–phala,** n., N. of a plant (= *kakkolaka*), L. **–bhakshin,** mfn., N. of a man. **–rohiṇī,** f. Helleborus Niger, Suśr. **–vallī,** f., N. of a plant, L. **–viṭapa,** *ās*, m. pl., N. of a species of plant, VarBṛS. **Kaṭukâñjanī,** f. Helleborus Niger, L. **Kaṭukârohiṇī,** f. id., Car. **Kaṭukâlābu,** m. Trichosanthes Dioeca, L. **Kaṭukôdaya,** mfn. leading to disagreeable consequences, having bad results, MBh.

Kaṭukita, mfn. (Prākṛit *kaḍuida*) spoken to sharply or bitterly, treated harshly, Ratnāv.

Kaṭukiman, *ā*, m. sharpness, Nir. v, 4.

Kaṭura, *am*, n. buttermilk mixed with water, L.

Kaṭora, *as*, *ā*, m. f. a kind of cup or vessel.

Kaṭola, mfn. (Uṇ. i, 67) pungent, acrid, sharp; (*as*), m. a Caṇḍāla. **–pāda,** mfn. footed like a Caṇḍāla, gaṇa *hasty-ādi*, Pāṇ. v, 4, 138. **–vīṇā,** f. a kind of lute played by Caṇḍālas.

Kaṭolaka, *as*, m. a Caṇḍāla. **–pāda,** mfn. having feet like a Caṇḍāla, gaṇa *hasty-ādi*, Pāṇ. v, 4, 138.

Kaṭ-phala, *as*, m. (for *kaṭu-phala*, but different in meaning from it), N. of a small tree (found in the north-west of Hindūstān, the aromatic bark and seeds of which are used in medicine; the fruit is eaten; the common name is Kāyaphal), Suśr.; (*ā*), f., N. of several plants.

Kaṭvara, *am*, n. (Uṇ. iii, 1; cf. *kaṭura*) buttermilk mixed with water, Suśr.; a sauce, condiment, Comm. on Uṇ.; (mfn.) despised, L.

कटकटा *kaṭakaṭā*, ind. an onomatopoetic word (supposed to represent the noise of rubbing), MBh.; Dhūrtas.; [cf. *kiṭakiṭāya*.]

Kaṭakaṭāpaya, Nom. P. °*payati*, to rub two substances together, produce a creaking or grating noise, R.

कटन *kaṭana*, *am*, n. the roof or thatch of a house, W.

कटुङ्कता *kaṭuṅka-tā*, f. (for *kaṭuka-tā*?, but cf. *khaṭunka*) harshness, L.

कटेरकग्राम *kaṭeraka-grāma*, m., N. of a village.

कट्ट् *kaṭṭ*, cl. 10. P. *kaṭṭayati*, to heap, cover with earth, Kṛishis.

Kaṭṭana, *am*, n. the act of heaping, covering with earth, ib.

कट्टरिनृत्य *kaṭṭari-nṛitya*, *am*, n. a kind of dance.

कट्टार *kaṭṭāra*, *as*, m. a weapon, dagger, W.

Kaṭṭāraka, *as*, *ikā*, m. f. id., Rājat.; Comm. on KātyŚr.

कट्फल *kaṭ-phala*. See above.

कट्वर *kaṭvara*. See above.

कट्वाङ्ग *kaṭvāṅga*, a wrong reading for *khaṭvāṅga*, q.v., BhP. (ed. Burnouf).

कठ् *kaṭh*, cl. 1. P. *kaṭhati*, to live in distress, Dhātup. ix, 48.

1. **Kaṭha** (for 2. see s. v.), *am*, n. distress (?). **–marda,** m. 'dissipating distress' (?), N. of Śiva, L.; (cf. *kaṭa-marda*.)

Kaṭhara, mfn. hard, L.; (cf. *kaṭhina*.)

Kaṭhalya, *am*, n. gravel, Buddh.

Kaṭhalla, *am*, n. id., ib.

Kaṭhāku, *us*, m. (Uṇ. iii, 77) a bird or a particular bird.

Kaṭhāhaka, *as*, m. a kind of fowl, L.

Kaṭhikā, f. chalk, W.; (cf. *kaṭhinī*.)

Kaṭhiñjara, *as*, m. Ocimum Sanctum (commonly called Tulasi), L.

Kaṭhina, mfn. (Comm. on Uṇ. ii, 49) hard, firm, stiff (opposed to *mṛidu*); difficult, Megh.; Suśr.; Pañcat. &c.; harsh, inflexible, cruel, Kum.; Amar. &c.; violent (as pain), Vikr.; (*ā*), f. crystallized sugar, a sweetmeat made with refined sugar, L.; a species of betel, L.; (*ī*), f. chalk, Pañcat.; Hit.; (*am*), n. an earthen vessel for cooking, MBh.; R.; a strap or pole for carrying burdens, Pāṇ. iv, 4, 72 (cf. *vaṃśa-kaṭhina*); a shovel, scoop, L. **–citta,** mfn. hard-hearted, cruel, unkind. **–tā,** f., **-tva,** n. hardness, firmness, harshness, severity, Śāntiś.; BhP. &c.; difficulty, obscurity, W. **–pṛishṭha,** m. 'hard-backed,' a tortoise, L. **–pṛishṭhaka,** m. id., ib. **–phala,** m. Feronia Elephantum, L. **–hṛidaya,** mfn. = *-citta* above. **Kaṭhinâvadāna,** n., N. of a Buddhist legend. **Kaṭhinêkshu,** m. a kind of sugar-cane, L.

Kaṭhinaka, *as*, m. a shovel, scoop, L.; (*ikā*), f. chalk, L.

Kaṭhinaya, Nom. P. *kaṭhinayati*, to harden, indurate, render hard, Viddh.

Kaṭhinī-√kṛi, id., Car.

Kaṭhinī-√bhū, to become hard. **–bhūta,** mfn. hardened, indurated.

Kaṭhilla, *as*, m. Momordica Charantia, L.; gravel; (cf. *kaṭhalya*.)

Kaṭhillaka, *as*, m. Momordica Charantia, L.; Ocimum Sanctum, L. (cf. *kaṭhiñjara*); Bœrhavia Diffusa, L.

Kaṭhura, mf(*ā*)n. hard, cruel, VCāṇ.

Kaṭhera, *as*, m. (Uṇ. i, 59) a needy or distressed man, pauper.

Kaṭheru, *us*, m. = *cāmara-vāta*, T.

Kaṭhora, mf(*ā*)n. (Uṇ. i, 65) hard, solid, stiff, offering resistance, BhP.; Prab. &c.; sharp, piercing, BhP.; Pañcat. &c.; hard, severe, cruel, hard-hearted, Pañcat.; Sāh.; full, complete, full-grown (as the moon), Comm. on Uṇ.; Comm. on Śiś.; luxuriant, rank, Mṛicch. **–giri,** m., N. of a mountain, BrahmāṇḍaP. **–citta,** mfn. hard-hearted, cruel, Śārṅg. **–tā,** f., **-tva,** n. hardness, firmness; rigour, severity. **–tārâdhipa,** m. 'full-star-lord,' full moon, Śiś. i, 20. **–hṛidaya,** mfn. = *-citta* above, Sāh.

Kaṭhoraya, Nom. P. *kaṭhorayati*, to cause to thrive, make luxuriant, Mālatīm.

Kaṭhorita, mfn. made to thrive, strengthened, Hcar.

Kaṭhorī-√bhū, to grow strong, become hard or intense, Hcar.

Kaṭhola, mfn. = *kaṭhora*, L.

कठ 2. *kaṭha*, *as*, m., N. of a sage (a pupil of Vaiśampāyana and founder of a branch of the Yajur-veda, called after him), MBh. &c.; (*as*), m. a pupil or follower of Kaṭha (esp. pl.); a Brāhman, L.; (*ī*), f. a female pupil or follower of Kaṭha, Comm. on Pāṇ.; the wife of a Brāhman, L. **–kalāpa,** *am* or *ās*, n. or m. pl. the schools of Kaṭha and Kalāpin, R. ii, 32, 18; gaṇa *kārtakaujapâdi*, Pāṇ. vi, 2, 37. **–kauthuma,** *am* or *ās*, n. or m. pl. the schools of Kaṭha and Kuthumin, ib. **–dhūrta,** m. a Brāhman skilled in the Kaṭha branch of the Yajur-veda, W. **–vallī,** f., N. of an Upanishad; (cf. *kaṭhôpanishad*.) **–śākhā,** f. the Kaṭha branch of the Yajur-veda. **–śāṭha,** m. Kaṭha and Śāṭha [Kāś.], gaṇa *śaunakâdi*, Pāṇ. iv, 3, 106. **–°śāṭhin,** *inas*, m. pl. the schools of Kaṭha and Śāṭha, ib. **–śruti,** f., N. of an Upanishad; (cf. *kaṭhôpanishad*.) **–śrotriya,** m. a Brāhman who has studied the Kaṭha branch, W. **Kaṭhâdhyāpaka,** m. a teacher of the above branch. **Kaṭhôpanishad,** f., N. of an Upanishad (generally said to belong to the Atharva-veda, but in some MSS. and books ascribed to the Black Yajur-veda, probably because the story of Naciketas occurs also in TBr. iii, 1, 8); *-bhāshya*, n., N. of a commentary on the Kaṭhôpanishad; *-bhāshya-ṭīkā*, f., N. of a commentary on the last; *-bhāshyaṭīkā-vivaraṇa*, n., N. of a commentary on the last.

कठेरणि *kaṭheraṇi*, *is*, m., N. of a man, gaṇa *upakâdi*, Pāṇ. ii, 4, 69.

कड् *kaḍ*, cl. 1. P. *kaḍati*, to be confused or disturbed by pleasure or pain; to be elated or intoxicated, Dhātup.: cl. 6. P. *kaḍati*, to eat, consume, Vop.: Caus. *kāḍayati*, to break off a part, separate, divide; to remove the chaff or husk of grain &c.; to preserve, Dhātup. xxxii, 44; (cf. *kaṇḍ*.)

Kaḍá, mfn. dumb, mute, ŚBr. xiv; ignorant, stupid, L. **–°m-kara,** m. straw, the stalks of various sorts of pulse &c., Pāṇ. v, 1, 69. **–°m-karīya,** mfn. to be fed with straw, ib. **–°m-gara,** v.l. for *kaḍaṃ-kara* above. **–°m-garīya,** mfn. = *kaḍaṃ-karīya*, Ragh. v, 9.

Kaḍaka, *am*, n. sea-salt (obtained by evaporation), L.

Kaḍaṅga, *as*, m. a spirituous liquor, a kind of rum, L.

Kaḍaṅgaka = *nishpāva*, L.

कडच्छक *kaḍacchaka*, *as*, m. a kind of spoon, ladle.

कडत् *kaḍat*, ind. an onomatopoetic word expressive of noise. **–kāra,** m. a noise, Bālar.

कडत्र *kaḍatra*, *am*, n. (fr. √*gaḍ*, Uṇ. iii, 106?) = *kalatra*, Comm. on Uṇ.; a kind of vessel. L.

कडन्दिका *kaḍandikā*, f. science, L.; (cf. *kalandikā, kalindikā.*)

कडम्ब *kaḍamba*, *as*, m. (Uṇ. iv, 82) an end or point, Comm. on Uṇ.; the stalk of a pot-herb, L.; Convolvulus Repens, Car.; (*ī*), f. id., L.

कडवक *kaḍavaka*, *am*, n. a section of a great poem written in an Apabhraṇśa dialect, Sāh. 562.

कडार *kaḍāra*, mfn. (fr. √*gad*, Uṇ. iii, 135?), tawny, Śiś. v, 3; (*as*), m. tawny (the colour), L.; a servant, slave, L. **Kaḍārâdi**, m., N. of a gaṇa, Pāṇ. ii, 2, 38.

कडितुल *kaḍitula*, *as*, m. a sword, scymitar; a sacrificial knife, L.

कडुली *kaḍulī*, f. a kind of drum.

कडेर *kaḍera*, m., N. of a people, Pat. on Pāṇ. iv, 1, 195.

कड्ड *kaḍḍ*, cl. 1. P. *kaḍḍati*, to be hard or rough; to be harsh or severe, Dhātup. ix, 65.

कण *kaṇ*, cl. 1. P. *kaṇati*, *cakāṇa*, *kaṇishyati*, *akaṇīt* or *akāṇīt*, *kaṇitā*, to become small; to sound, cry, Dhātup. xiii, 6; to go, approach, Dhātup. xix, 32: cl. 10. P. *kāṇayati*, to wink, close the eye with the lids or lashes, Dhātup. xxx, 41: Caus. *kāṇayati* (aor. *acīkaṇat* and *acakāṇat*, Pat. on Pāṇ. vii, 4, 3), to sigh, sound; [cf. √*can* and √*kvan*.]

Káṇa, *as*, m. (Nir. vi, 30; related to *kanā, kanishṭha, kanīyas, kanyā*, in all of which smallness is implied, BRD.), a grain, grain of corn, single seed, AV. x, 9, 26; xi, 3, 5; KātyŚr.; Mn. &c.; a grain or particle (of dust), Ragh. i, 85; Vikr.; flake (of snow), Amar.; a drop (of water), Śak. 60 a; Megh.; BhP. &c.; a spark (of fire), Pañcat.; the spark or facet of a gem; any minute particle, atom, Prab.; Śāntiś.; (*ā*), f. a minute particle, atom, drop; long pepper, Suśr.; cummin seed, L.; a kind of fly (= *kumbhīra-makshikā*), L.; (*ī*), f. = *kaṇikā* below, L.; (*am*), n. a grain, single seed, Kathās.; (cf. *kanishṭha.*) — **guggulu**, m. a species of bdellium, L. — **ja**, m. a particular measure, Hcat. — **jīra**, m. a white kind of cummin seed, L. — **jīraka**, n. id., L. — **dhūma**, m. a kind of penance, MatsyaP. — **pa** (*kaṇān, lohagulikāḥ pibati*), m. a kind of weapon, MBh.; Daś. &c. — **pāyin**, m. id., MBh. viii, 744. — **priya**, m. 'fond of seeds,' a sparrow, L. — **bha**, m. 'shining like a grain' (*kaṇa iva bhāti*), a kind of fly with a sting, Suśr. — °**bhaka**, m. id., ib. — **bhaksha**, m. = *kaṇâda* below. — **bhakshaka**, m. a kind of sparrow, L. — **bhuj**, m. = *kaṇâda* below. — **lābha**, m. a whirlpool, L. — **śas**, ind. in small parts, in minute particles, Kum.; Bālar. &c. **Kaṇâda**, *as*, m. 'atom-eater,' N. given to the author of the Vaiśeshika branch of the Nyāya philosophy (as teaching that the world was formed by an aggregation of atoms; he is also called Kāśyapa, and considered as a Devarshi; see also *ulūka*), Prab.; Sarvad. &c.; a goldsmith (= *kalāda*), L.; -*rahasya-saṃgraha*, m., N. of a work. **Kaṇânna**, mfn. one whose food consists of grains (of rice); -*tā*, f. the state of the above, Mn. xi, 167. **Kaṇâhvā**, f. a kind of white cummin seed, L.

Kaṇika, *as*, m. a grain, ear of corn; a drop, small particle, VarBṛS.; the meal of parched wheat, the heart of wheat, L.; an enemy, L.; a purificatory ceremony (= *nīrājana*, q. v.), L.; N. of a minister of king Dhṛita-rāshṭra, MBh. i; (*ā*), f. an ear of corn, Comm. on BhP.; a drop, atom, small particle, Prab.; Megh. &c.; a small spot, Kād.; the meal of parched wheat; Premna Spinosa or Longifolia, L.; a kind of corn, Pañcad.

Kaṇita, *am*, n. crying out with pain, L.

Kaṇiśa, *as*, m. an ear or spike of corn, Kād. — **kiṃśāru**, m. the beard of corn, L.

Kaṇīka, mfn. small, diminutive, L.; (*ā*), f. a grain, single seed, MBh. xii.

Kaṇīci, *is*, *ī*, f. (Uṇ. iv, 70) a sound; a creeper in flower; Abrus Precatorius; a cart, L.; (cf. *kanīci.*)

Kaṇīyas, mfn. very small, young, younger, L.; = *kanīyas*, q. v.

Kaṇūkaya, Nom. P. (pres. p. f. *kaṇūkayántī*) to desire to utter words (of blame or censure), RV. x, 132, 7.

कणाटीन *kaṇāṭīna*, *as*, m. a wagtail, L.

Kaṇāṭīra, °**raka**, *as*, m. id., ib.

कणाद *kaṇâda*. See under *káṇa*

कणे *kaṇe*, ind., considered as a *gati* in the sense of 'satisfying a desire,' Pāṇ. i, 4, 66, (e. g. *kaṇe-hatya payaḥ pibati*, he drinks milk till he is satiated, Kāś.)

कणेर *kaṇera*, *as*, m. Pterospermum Acerifolium, L.; (*ā*), f. a she-elephant, L.; a courtezan, L. **Kaṇeru**, *us*, m. = *kaṇera*; cf. *kareṇu*.

कण्ट *kaṇṭ*, cl. 1. P. *kaṇṭati*, to go, move, Nir.; (cf. *kaṭ*.)

कण्ट *kaṇṭa*, *as*, m. (thought by some to be for original *karnta*, fr. √2. *kṛit*) a thorn, BhP. ix, 3, 7 (cf. *tri-kaṇṭa, bahu-kaṇṭa*, &c.); the boundary of a village, L.; [cf. Gk. κεντέω, κεστός, κέστρον?] — **kāra**, m. a particular plant, L.; (*ī*), f. Solanum Jacquini, Suśr.; Bombax Heptaphyllum, L.; Flacourtia Sapida, L. — **kāraka**, m. a kind of Solanum, L.; (*ikā*), f. Solanum Jacquini, Suśr. — **kārī-traya**, n. the aggregate of three sorts of Solanum, L. — **kāla**, m. Artocarpus Integrifolia, L. — **kuraṇṭa**, m. Barleria Cristata, L. — **tanu**, f. a sort of Solanum, L. — **dalā**, f. Pandanus Odoratissimus, L. — **pattra**, m. Flacourtia Sapida, L.; -*phalā*, f. a particular plant, L. — **pattrikā**, f. Solanum Melongena, L. — **pāda**, m. Flacourtia Sapida, L. — **puṅkhikā**, f. Solanum Jacquini, L. — **phala**, m., N. of several plants (Asteracantha Longifolia; bread-fruit tree; Datura Fastuosa; Guilandina Bonduc; Ricinus Communis), L.; (*ā*), f. a sort of Cucurbita, L. — **vallī**, f. Acacia Concinna, L. — **vṛiksha**, m. Guilandina Bonduc, L. **Kaṇṭā-phala**, m. Asteracantha Longifolia, L. **Kaṇṭârtagalā**, f. Barleria Cærulea, L. **Kaṇṭâlu**, m. Solanum Jacquini, L.; another species of Solanum, L.; a bamboo, L. **Kaṇṭâhvaya**, n. the tuberous root of the lotus, L

Káṇṭaka, *as*, m. (*am*, n., L.) a thorn, ŚBr. v; MBh.; Yājñ. &c.; anything pointed, the point of a pin or needle, a prickle, sting, R.; a fish-bone, R. iii, 76, 10; Mn. viii, 95; a finger-nail (cf. *karaka*°), Naish. i, 94; the erection of the hair of the body in thrilling emotions (cf. *kaṇṭakita*); unevenness or roughness (as on the surface of the tongue), Car.; any troublesome seditious person (who is, as it were, a thorn to the state and an enemy of order and good government), a paltry foe, enemy in general (cf. *kshudra-śatru*), Mn. ix, 253, &c.; BhP.; R. &c.; a sharp stinging pain, symptom of disease, Suśr.; a vexing or injurious speech, MBh. i, 3559; any annoyance or source of vexation, obstacle, impediment, R.; Hit.; the first, fourth, seventh, and tenth lunar mansions, VarBṛS. & VarBṛ.; a term in the Nyāya philosophy implying refutation of argument, detection of error &c., L.; a bamboo, L.; workshop, manufactory, L.; boundary of a village, L.; fault, defect, L.; N. of Makara (or the marine monster, the symbol of Kāma-deva), L.; of the horse of Śākya-muni, Lalit. (wrong reading for *kaṇṭhaka*, BRD.); of an Agrahāra, Rājat.; of a barber, Hariv. (v. l. *kaṇḍuka*); (*ī*), f. a species of Solanum, Suśr. — **traya**, n. an aggregate of three sorts of Solanum, L. — **dalā**, f. Pandanus Odoratissimus, L. — **druma**, m. a tree with thorns, a thorn bush, BhP.; Mṛicch.; Bombax Heptaphyllum, L. — **prāvṛitā**, f. Aloe Perfoliata, L. — **phala**, m. Artocarpus Integrifolia, L.; Ruellia Longifolia, L.; (the term is applicable to any plant the fruit of which is invested with a hairy or thorny coat, W.; cf. *kaṇṭaki-phala*.) — **bhuj**, m. 'eating thorns,' a camel, Hit. — **yukta**, mfn. having thorns, thorny. — **latā**, f. Capparis Zeylanica, Nigh. — **vat**, mfn. id.; covered with erect hair. — **vṛintākī**, f. Solanum Jacquini, L. — **śreṇī**, f. id., ib.; a porcupine, W. — **sthalī**, f., N. of a country, VarBṛS. **Kaṇṭakâkhya**, m. Trapa Bispinosa. **Kaṇṭakâgāra**, m. 'dwelling among thorns,' a kind of lizard, L.; a porcupine, W. **Kaṇṭakâḍhya**, mfn. full of thorns, thorny, VarBṛS. **Kaṇṭakâluka**, m. Hedysarum Alhagi, L. **Kaṇṭakâśana**, m. 'whose food is thorns,' a camel, L. **Kaṇṭakâshṭhīla**, m. 'having sharp bones,' a kind of fish, L. **Kaṇṭakôddharaṇa**, n. weeding or extracting thorns &c.; removing annoyances, extirpating thieves or rogues or any national and public nuisance, Mn. ix, 252; R. &c. **Kaṇṭakôddhāra**, m., N. of a work.

Kaṇṭaki (in comp. for *kaṇṭakin*, col. 3). — **kshīrin**, m. pl. thorn-plants and milk-plants. — **ja**, mfn. produced from or grown upon a thorny plant, Vishṇus.; produced from a fish, W. — **phala**, m. = *kaṇṭaka-phala*, q. v., L. — **latā**, f. a gourd, L. — **vṛiksha**. m. a sort of tree, Suśr.

Kaṇṭakita, mfn. thorny, MBh.; Kathās. &c.; covered with erect hairs, having the hair of the body erect, Śak. 68 b; Kum.; Kād. &c.

Kaṇṭakin, mfn. thorny, prickly, ĀśvGṛ.; MBh.; Suśr. &c.; vexatious, annoying; (*ī*), m., N. of several plants (viz. Acacia Catechu; Vanguiera Spinosa; Ruellia Longifolia; Zizyphus Jujuba; bamboo), L.; a fish, L.; (*inī*), f. Solanum Jacquini, L.; a kind of date-palm; red amaranth, L.; N. of a mother in the retinue of Skanda, MBh.

Kaṇṭakila, *as*, m. Bambusa Spinosa, L.

Kaṇṭala, *as*, m. Mimosa Arabica (commonly called Vāvalā; a tree yielding a species of Gum Arabic: the branches are prickly, whence the name, W.), L.

Kaṇṭārikā, f., N. of a plant, L.

Kaṇṭālikā, f. Solanum Jacquini, L.

Kaṇṭin, mfn. thorny; (*ī*), m., N. of several plants (viz. Achyranthes Aspera; Acacia Catechu; Ruellia Longifolia; a species of pea), L.

कण्ठ *kaṇṭh*, cl. 1. P. Ā. *kaṇṭhati*, -*te*: cl. 10. P. *kaṇṭhayati*, to mourn; to long for, desire (cf. 2. *ut-kaṇṭha*), Dhātup. viii, 11; xxxiv, 40.

कण्ठ *kaṇṭhá*, *as*, m. (√*kaṇ*, Uṇ. i, 105), the throat, the neck (cf. *ā-kaṇṭha-tripta*; *kaṇṭhe* √*grah*, to embrace, Kathās.); the voice (cf. *sannakaṇṭha*), MBh.; BhP. &c.; sound, especially guttural sound, W.; the neck (of a pitcher or jar), the narrowest part (e. g. of the womb; of a hole in which sacrificial fire is deposited; of a stalk &c.), Suśr.; Hcat.; Kathās. &c.; immediate proximity, Pañcat.; Vanguiera Spinosa, L.; N. of a Maharshi, R.; (*ī*), f. neck, throat, L.; a rope or leather round the neck of a horse, L.; a necklace, collar, ornament for the neck, L. — **kubja**, m. a kind of fever (cf. *adhara-kaṇṭha*, 1. *ut-kaṇṭha*, &c.); -*pratīkāra*, m. the cure of the preceding disease. — **kūṇikā**, f. the Vīṇā or Indian lute, L. — **kūpa**, m. cavity of the throat. — **ga**, mf(*ā*)n. reaching or extending to the throat, Mn. ii, 62. — **gata**, mfn. being at or in the throat, reaching the throat, R.; Pañcat.; Ratnāv. &c. — **graha**, m. 'clinging to the neck,' embracing, embrace, Kathās.; Ratnāv.; Mṛicch. — **grahaṇa**, n. id., Amar. — **coheda**, m. cutting off the neck. — **taṭa**, m. n. the side of the neck. — **talāsikā**, f. the leather or rope passing round the neck of a horse, L. — **tas**, ind. from the throat; distinctly; singly. — **daghná**, mfn. reaching to the neck, ŚBr. xii. — **dvayasa**, mfn. id. — **dhāna**, *ās*, m. pl., N. of a people, VarBṛS. — **nāla**, n. 'neck-stalk,' the throat compared to a lotus-stalk, Ragh. xv, 52; the neck, Prab.; Bālar.; (*ī*), f. throat, neck, Prasannar. — **nīḍaka**, m. Falco Cheela, L.; a kite, W. — **nīlaka**, m. a torch, whisp of lighted straw &c. (= *ulkā*), L. — **paṇḍita**, m., N. of a poet. — **pāśaka**, m. a halter, a rope passing round an elephant's neck, L.; an elephant's cheek, L. — **pīṭha**, n. gullet, throat, Bālar.; (*ī*), f. id., Prasannar. — **pīḍā**, f. sharp pains in the throat, Bhpr. — **prāvṛita**, n. covering the throat, Gaut. ii, 14. — **bandha**, m. a rope tied round an elephant's neck, L. — **bhaṅga**, m. 'break of the voice,' stammering. — **bhūshaṇa**, n. an ornament for the neck, collar, necklace, Hcat. — **bhūshā**, f. id., L. — **maṇi**, m. a jewel worn on the throat, L.; a dear or beloved object; thyroid cartilage, L. [NBD. Nachtrag 2]. — **mūla**, n. the deepest part of the throat. — °**mūlīya**, mfn. being in the deepest part of the throat, Comm. on TS. xxiii, 17. — **rava**, m., N. of an author. — **rodha**, m. stopping or lowering the voice (see *sa-ka*°). — **lagna**, mfn. fastened round the throat; clinging to, embracing. — **latā**, f. a collar, necklace. — **vartin**, mfn. being in the throat (as the vital air), about to escape, Ragh. xii, 54. — **vibhūshaṇa**, n. ornament for the neck, L. — **śālūka**, n. hard tumour in the throat, Suśr. — **śuṇḍī**, f. swelling of the tonsils, ib. — **śosha**, m. dryness of the throat, a dry throat, ŚārṅgS. — **śruti**, f., N. of an Upanishad (belonging to the Atharva-veda). — **sañjana**, n. hanging on or round the throat. — **sūtra**, n. a particular mode of embracing, Ragh. xix, 32. — **stha**, mfn. staying or sticking in the throat; being in or upon the throat; guttural; being in the mouth ready to be repeated by rote, learnt by heart and ready to be recited, W. — **sthalī**, f. throat. **Kaṇṭhâgata**, mfn. come to the throat (as the breath or soul of a dying person), W. **Kaṇṭhâgni**, m. 'digesting in the throat or gizzard,' a bird, L. **Kaṇṭhâbharaṇa**, n. an ornament for the neck, necklace; a shorter N. of the work called Sarasvatī-kaṇṭhābharaṇa (cf. also *kavika°*); *-darpaṇa, -mārjana*, n., N. of two commentaries on the above work. **Kaṇṭhâvasakta,** mfn. clinging to the neck, embracing. **Kaṇṭhâślesha,** m. the act of embracing, embrace, Bhartṛ.; Ratnāv. **Kaṇṭhe-kāla,** m. 'black on the neck,' N. of Śiva, L. **Kaṇṭhe-viddha,** m., N. of a man; (cf. *kāṇṭheviddhi.*) **Kaṇṭhêśvara-tīrtha,** n., N. of a Tīrtha. **Kaṇṭhôkta,** mfn. spoken of or enumerated singly or one by one, Comm. on TPrāt. **Kaṇṭhôkti,** f. speaking of or enumerating one by one, ib.

Kaṇṭhaka, *as*, m. an ornament for the neck, Kathās.; N. of the horse of Śākyamuni, Lalit.; (*ikā*), f. a necklace of one string or row, L.; ornament for the neck, Kathās.

Kaṇṭhā-rava = *kaṇṭhī-rava* below.

Kaṇṭhin, mfn. belonging to the throat.

Kaṇṭhī-rava, *as*, m. 'roaring from the throat,' a lion, Pañcat.; an elephant in rut, L.; a pigeon, L.; (*ī*), f. Gendarussa Vulgaris, L.

Káṇṭhya, mfn. being at or in the throat, VS. xxxix, 9; Suśr. ii, 130, 13; suitable to the throat, Suśr.; belonging to the throat, pronounced from the throat, guttural (as sounds; they are, according to the Prātiśākhyas, *a, ā, h*, and the Jihvāmūlīya [or Visarjanīya]; according to the Comm. on Pāṇ. i, 1, 9, *a, ā, k, kh, g, gh, ṅ*, and *h*; according to Vop. also *e*); (*as*), m. a guttural sound or letter, PārGṛ. **-varṇa,** m. a guttural sound or letter. **-svara,** m. a guttural vowel (i. e. *a* and *ā*).

कण्ठला **kaṇṭhalā**, f. a basket made of canes, L.; (cf. *kaṇḍola.*)

कण्ठाल **kaṇṭhāla**, *as*, m. a boat, ship, L.; a hoe, spade, L.; war, L.; Arum Campanulatum, L.; a camel, L.; a churning-vessel, L.; (*ā*), f. a churning-vessel, L.

Kaṇṭhīla, *as*, m. a camel, L.; (*as, ī*), m. f. a churning-vessel, L.

कण्ड **kaṇḍ**, cl. 1. P. Ā. *kaṇḍati, -te*, to be glad or wanton: cl. 10. P. *kaṇḍayati*, to separate (the chaff from the grain), Dhātup.; (cf. *kad.*)

Kaṇḍana, *am*, n. the act of threshing, separating the chaff from the grain in a mortar, Hcat.; that which is separated from the grain, chaff, Suśr.; (*ī*), f. a wooden bowl or mortar (in which the cleaning or threshing of grain is performed), Mn. iii, 68.

Kaṇḍarā, f. a sinew (of which sixteen are considered to be in the human body), Suśr.; Bhpr. &c.; a principal vessel of the body, a large artery, vein &c., W.

Kaṇḍikā, f. a short section, the shortest subdivision (in the arrangement of certain Vedic compositions); [cf. *kāṇḍa* and *kāṇḍikā.*]

Kaṇḍī-√kṛi, to pound, bray, Car.

Kaṇḍīra, *as*, m. a sort of vegetable, Car.; (cf. *gaṇḍīra.*)

Kaṇḍu, *us*, f. = *kaṇḍū* below, Suśr.; (*us*), m., N. of a Ṛishi, VP.; BhP. &c.

Kaṇḍuka, *as*, m., N. of a barber, Hariv.

Kaṇḍura, mf(*ā*)n. scratching; itching, Suśr.; (*as*), m. Momordica Charantia, L.; a species of reed, L.; (*ā*), f. Mucuna Pruritus, L.; a species of creeper, L.

Kaṇḍula, mfn. itching, Car.

Kaṇḍū, *ūs*, f. itching, the itch, Suśr.; Kum. &c.; scratching, Śāntiś.; (cf. *sa-kaṇḍūka.*) **-karī,** f. Mucuna Pruritus, L. **-ghna,** m. Cathartocarpus Fistula, L.; white mustard, L. **-jush,** mfn. feeling a desire to scratch, itching, Hcar. 44, 7. **-makā,** f. a kind of insect whose bite is poisonous, Suśr. **-mat,** mfn. scratching, itching, Suśr. **Kaṇḍv-ādi,** m., N. of a gaṇa, Pāṇ. iii, 1, 27.

Kaṇḍūti, *is*, f. scratching; itching, the itch, BhP.; Sāh. &c.; (fig.) sexual desire (of women), Rājat.; N. of one of the mothers in the retinue of Skanda, MBh. ix.

Kaṇḍūna, mfn. feeling a desire to scratch, itching, desiring or longing for, Sāh.

Kaṇḍūya, Nom. P. Ā. *kaṇḍūyáti, -te*, to scratch, scrape, rub, TS.; ŚBr.; Mn. &c.; to itch, Śārṅg.: Pass. *kaṇḍūyate*, to be scratched, VarBṛS.: Desid. *kaṇḍūyiyishati*, Vārtt. on Pāṇ. vi, 1, 3; Vop.

Kaṇḍūyana, *am*, n. the act of scratching, scraping, rubbing; itching, the itch, KātyŚr.; Suśr.; Ragh. &c.; (*ī*), f. a brush for scraping or rubbing, KātyŚr.

Kaṇḍūyanaka, mfn. serving for scratching or tickling (as a straw), Pañcat. (Hit.)

Kaṇḍūyā, f. scratching, itching, Comm. on Pāṇ.; Vop.

Kaṇḍūyita, *am*, n. id.

Kaṇḍūyitṛi, mfn. scratching, a scratcher, Ragh. xiii, 43.

Kaṇḍūra, *as*, m. Amorphophallus Campanulatus, Car.; (*ā*), f. Mucuna Pruritus, L.

Kaṇḍūla, mfn. having or feeling a desire to scratch, itchy, Uttarar.; Bālar.; (*ā*), f. Amorphophallus Campanulatus, L. **-bhāva,** m. the itch, a state of eager desire for (loc.), Naish.

कण्डरीक **kaṇḍarīka**, *as*, m., N. of a man, Hariv.

कण्डानक **kaṇḍānaka**, *as*, m., N. of a being attendant on Śiva, L.

कण्डोल **kaṇḍola**, *as*, m. a basket for holding grain (made of bamboo or cane), Comm. on Mn.; a safe, any place in which provisions are kept, W.; a camel (cf. *kaṇṭhāla*), L.; (*ī*), f. the lute of a Caṇḍāla (cf. *kaṭola, gaṇḍola*), L. **-pāda,** mfn. camel-footed (?), gaṇa *hasty-ādi*, Pāṇ. v, 4, 138 (not in Kāś.) **-vīṇā,** f. the lute of a Caṇḍāla, a common lute, L.

Kaṇḍolaka, *as*, m. a basket, safe, store-room, L.

कण्डोष **kaṇḍosha**, *as*, m. a scorpion, tarantula, L.

कण्व **káṇva**, *as*, m. (√*kaṇ*, Uṇ. i, 151), N. of a renowned Ṛishi (author of several hymns of the Ṛig-veda; he is called a son of Ghora and is said to belong to the family of Aṅgiras), RV.; AV.; VS.; KātyŚr. &c.; (*ās*), m. pl. the family or descendants of Kaṇva, ib. (besides the celebrated Ṛishi there occur a Káṇva Nārshadá, AV. iv, 19, 2; Káṇva Śrāyasa, TS. v, 4, 7, 5; Kaṇva Kāśyapa, MBh.; Śak. &c.; the founder of a Vedic school; several princes and founders of dynasties; several authors); a peculiar class of evil spirits (against whom the hymn AV. ii, 25 is used as a charm), AV. ii, 25, 3; 4; 5; (mfn.) deaf, KātyŚr. x, 2, 35; praising, a praiser, L.; one who is to be praised, T.; (*am*), n. sin, evil, Comm. on Uṇ. **-jámbhana,** mf(*ī*)n. consuming or destroying the evil spirits called Kaṇva, AV. ii, 25, 1. **-tama,** m. the very Kaṇva, a real Kaṇva, RV. i, 48, 4; x, 115, 5. **-bṛihat,** n., N. of several Sāmans. **-mat,** mfn. prepared by the Kaṇvas (as the Soma, NBD.); united with the praisers or with the Kaṇvas (as Indra, Sāy.), RV. viii, 2, 22. **-rathaṃtara,** n., N. of several Sāmans. **-vát,** ind. like Kaṇva, RV. viii, 6, 11; AV. ii, 32, 3. **-veda,** m., N. of a work. **-sakhi,** *ā*, m. having the Kaṇvas as friends, friendly disposed to them, RV. x, 115, 5. **-sūtra,** n., N. of a work. **-hotṛi,** mfn. one whose Hotṛi priest is a Kaṇva, RV. v, 41, 4. **Kaṇvâdi,** m., N. of a gaṇa, Pāṇ. iv, 2, 111. **Kaṇvâśrama,** m., N. of a Tīrtha, Vishṇus. **Kaṇvôpanishad,** f., N. of an Upanishad.

Kaṇvāya, Nom. Ā. *kaṇvāyate*, to do mischief (cf. *kaṇva*, n.), Pāṇ. iii, 1, 17.

Kaṇvīya, mfn. relating to or performed by Kaṇva. **-saṃhitā-homa,** m., N. of a work.

कत **kata**, *as*, m. Strychnos Potatorum (cf. the next), L.; N. of a Ṛishi, Pāṇ. **-phala,** n. = the next.

Kataka, *as*, m. Strychnos Potatorum or the clearing nut plant (its seeds rubbed upon the inside of water-jars precipitate the earthy particles in the water, W.), Mn. vi, 67; Suśr.; N. of a commentator on the Rāmāyaṇa.

कतम **katamá**, *as, ā, at*, mfn. (superlative of 2. *ka*; declined as a pronom., Gram. 236), who or which of many? (e. g. *katamena pathā yātās te*, by which road have they gone?); it is often a mere strengthened substitute for *ka*, the superlative affix imparting emphasis; hence it may occasionally be used for 'who or which of two?' (e. g. *tayoḥ katamasmai*, to which of these two?); it may optionally be compounded with the word to which it refers (e. g. *katamaḥ Kaṭhaḥ* or *katama-kaṭhaḥ*, which Kaṭha out of many?); when followed by *ca* and preceded by *yatama* an indefinite expression is formed equivalent to 'any whosoever,' 'any whatsoever,' &c. (e. g. *yatamad eva katamac ca vidyāt*, he may know anything whatsoever). In negative sentences *katama* with *cana* or *katama* with *api* = not even one, none at all (e. g. *na katamaccanâhaḥ*, not even on a single day, on no day at all); in addition to the above uses *katama* is said to mean 'best,' 'excessively good-looking' (cf. 3. *ka*), RV. &c. **Katamôraga,** m., N. of a man.

Katará, *as, ā, at*, mfn. (comparative of 2. *ka*; declined as a pronom., Gram. 236), who or which of two? whether of two? Analogously to *katama* above *katara* may occasionally be used to express 'who or which of many?' (e. g. *katarasyāṃ diśi*, in which quarter?), and may optionally be compounded with the word to which it refers (e. g. *kataraḥ Kaṭhaḥ* or *katara-kaṭhaḥ*); in negative sentences *katara* with *cana* = neither of the two (e. g. *na kataraś-cana jigye*, neither of the two was conquered, RV. &c.; [cf. Zd. *katāra*; Gk. πότερος, κότερος; Goth. *hvathar*; Eng. *whether*; Lat. *uter*; Old Germ. *huedar*; Slav. *kotoryi.*] **-tas,** ind. on which of the two sides? ŚBr. vi.

1. **Káti** (fr. 2. *ka*, declined in pl. only, Gram. 227 *a*; all the cases except the nom. voc. and acc. taking terminations, whereas the correlative *iti* has become fixed as an indeclinable adverb), how many? *quot?* several (e. g. *kati devāḥ*, how many gods? *kati vyāpādayati kati vā tāḍayati*, some he kills and some he strikes). In the sense of 'several,' 'some,' *kati* is generally followed by *cid* or *api* (e. g. *katicid ahāni*, for several or some days); it may be used as an adverb with *cid* in the sense of 'oftentimes,' 'much,' 'in many ways' (e. g. *katicit stutaḥ*, much or often praised), RV. &c.; [cf. Zd. *caiti*; Gk. πόσος; Lat. *quot*; cf. Sk. *tati* and Lat. *tot.*] **-kṛitvas,** ind. how many times? Vop.; (cf. *káti, kṛítvas*, ŚBr. xii, 3, 2, 7.) **-bheda,** mfn. of how many divisions or kinds? Car. **-vidha,** mfn. of how many kinds? **-śas,** ind. how many at a time? Kum. **-saṃkhya,** mfn. how many in number? Pañcat. **-hāyana,** mfn. how many years old? Bālar.

1. **Katika** (for 2. see below), mfn. how many? Car.; bought for how much? Pat.

Katititha, mfn. with following *cid* or *ca*, the so-maniest, Bālar.

Katithá, mfn. the how-maniest? Pāṇ. v, 2, 51; with *cid*, the so-maniest, RV. x, 61, 18 (= *katipayānāṃ pūraṇaḥ*, Sāy.); to such and such a point; [cf. Gk. πόστος; Lat. *quotus.*]

Katidhá, ind. how many times? how often? in how many places? in how many parts? RV. &c.; with *cid*, everywhere, RV. i, 31, 2.

Katipayá, mf(*ī, ā* [only BhP. ix, 18, 39])n. (m. pl. *e* and *ās*) several, some; a certain number, so many (e. g. *katipayenâhar-gaṇena*, after some days; also *katipayair ahobhiḥ, katipayâhasya*, &c.), ŚBr. &c.; (*am*), n. a little, some (at the end of Tatpurusha compounds, e. g. *udaśvit-katipayam*, a little Udaśvit), Pāṇ. ii, 1, 65; (*ena* or *āt*), ind. with some exertion, with difficulty, narrowly, Pāṇ. ii, 3, 33.

Katipayatha, mfn. somewhat advanced, somaniest, Kāṭh.; Pāṇ. v, 2, 51.

कतमाल **katamāla**, *as*, m. fire, L.; (incorrect for *khatamāla*, BRD.; cf. *kacamāla, karamāla.*)

कति 2. **kati** (for 1. see above), *is*, m., N. of a sage (son of Viśvā-mitra and ancestor of Kātyāyana), Hariv.

2. **Katika** (for 1. see above), *am*, n., N. of a town, Rājat.

कतीमुष **katīmusha**, *as*, m., N. of an Agrahāra, Rājat.

कत्ताशब्द **kattā-śabda**, *as*, m. the rattling sound of dice, Mṛicch.

कत्तृण **kat-tṛiṇa**, &c. See 2. *kad*.

कत्थ् **katth**, cl. 1. Ā. *katthate, cakatthe, katthitā*, &c. (Dhātup. ii, 36), to boast, MBh.; R.; BhP.; to mention with praise, praise, celebrate, MBh. iii, 1252; xvi; R.; to flatter, coax, W.; to abuse, revile, BhP. viii.

Katthaka, *as*, m., N. of a man.

Katthana, mfn. boasting, praising, MBh.; R.; (*am*), n. the act of boasting, MBh.; R.; Suśr.; (*ā*), f. id., Comm. on Bhaṭṭ.

Katthita, *am*, n. boasting, MBh. i, 5995.

Katthitavya, mfn. to be boasted, Car.

कत्पय **kat-payá**, mfn. (fr. 2. *kad* and *paya* fr. √*pyai*, BRD.), swelling, rising, RV. v, 32, 6;

(=*sukha-payas*, Nir. vi, 3; and accordingly=*sukha-karaṃ payo yasya*, Sāy.)

कत्र् katr, cl. 10. P. *katrayati*, to loosen, slacken, remove, Dhātup. xxxv, 60; (cf. *kart, kartr.*)

कत्सवर katsavara, *as*, m. the shoulder, shoulder-blade, L.

कथ् kath, cl. 10. P. (ep. also Ā.) *kathayati* (*-te*), aor. *acakathat* (Pāṇ. vii, 4, 93, Kāś.) and *acīkathat* (Vop.), to converse with any one (instr., sometimes with *saha*), MBh.; to tell, relate, narrate, report, inform, speak about, declare, explain, describe (with acc. of the thing or person spoken about), MBh.; R.; Śak. &c.; to announce, show, exhibit, bespeak, betoken, Mn. xi, 114; Śak. 291, 4; Suśr. &c.; to order, command, Pañcat. 57, 22; to suppose, state, MBh. iii, 10668; Mn. vii, 157: Pass. *kathyate*, to be called, be regarded or considered as, pass for, Pañcat.; Hit. &c.; [fr. *katham*, 'to tell the how;' cf. Goth. *qvithan*; Old High Germ. *quethan* and *quedan*; Eng. *quoth* and *quote*.]

Kathaka, mfn. relating, reciting, Śāntiś.; (*as*), m. a narrator, relater, one who recites a story (or who publicly reads and expounds the Purāṇas &c.), one who speaks or tells, a professional story-teller, MBh.; Kathās. &c.; the speaker of a prologue or monologue, chief actor, L.; N. of a man; of a being in the retinue of Skanda.

Kathana, mfn. telling, talkative, W.; (*am*), n. the act of telling, narration, relating, informing, Suśr.; Bhartṛ.; Pañcat. &c.

Kathanika, *as*, m. a narrator, story-teller, Hcar.

Kathanīya, mfn. to be said or told or declared, worthy of relation or mentioning, MBh.; BhP. &c.; to be called or named, Śrutab.

Kathayāna, mfn. (ep. pres. p.) relating, telling, MBh. iii, 2906.

Kathayitavya, mfn. to be told or mentioned; to be communicated, Śak. 233, 4.

1. **Kathā** (for 2. see col. 3), f. conversation, speech, talking together, ĀśvGṛ.; MBh.; Mn. &c.; talk, mention; (*kā kathā* [with gen. or more commonly with loc. and sometimes with *prati*], what should one say of? how should one speak of? e.g. *eko 'pi kṛicchrād varteta bhūyasāṃ tu kathaîva kā*, even one person would live with difficulty, what should one say of many? i.e. how much more many? Kathās. iv, 123; *kā kathā bāṇa-saṃdhāne*, what mention of fitting the arrow? i.e. what necessity for fitting the arrow? Śak. 53 a); story, tale, fable, MBh.; R.; Hit. &c.; a feigned story, tale (as one of the species of poetical composition), Sāh. 567; Kāvyād.; Story (personified), Kathās.; (in log.) discussion, disputation, Sarvad. **-kośa**, m., N of a work. **-kautuka**, n., N. of a work. **-krama**, m. uninterrupted progress of conversation, continuous conversation, Kathās. **-caṇa**, mfn. famous by report, far renowned, Sarvad. 99, 6. **-chala**, n. or °*cchala*, the device or artifice or guise of fables, Hit. **-java**, m., N. of a pupil of Bāshkali, VP. **-°di** (*kathâdi*), m., N. of a gaṇa, Pāṇ. iv, 4, 102. **-°nurāga** (*kathânu°*), m. taking pleasure in a story, attention to a discourse. **-°nta** (*kathânta*), m. end of a conversation. **-°ntara** (*kathântara*), n. the course of a conversation, Mṛicch.; Kathās. **-pīṭha**, n. 'pedestal of Story,' N. of the first Lambaka or book of the Kathā-sarit-sāgara. **-prabandha**, m. a continuous narrative, the connection or course of a narrative, tale, composed story, fiction. **-prasaṅga**, m. occasion to speak or talk; course of conversation, Naish.; Hit.; (*ena* or *āt*), ind. on the occasion of a conversation, in the course of conversation, Kathās.; Comm. on Kāvyād.; (mfn.) talkative, talking much, half-witted, L.; a conjurer, dealer in antidotes &c. **-prāṇa**, m. an actor, the speaker of a prologue or monologue, the introducer of a drama; a professed story-teller, L. **-mātra**, n. a mere story, nothing but a narrative; (mfn.) one of whom nothing but the narrative is left, i.e. deceased, dead, BhP. xii, 2, 44; *-°trâvaśishṭa*, mfn. id., BhP. xii, 2, 36; *-°trâvaśeshita*, mfn. id., MBh. xv, 988; (cf. *kathâvaśesha* and *kathā-śesha*.) **-mukha**, n. the introduction to a tale, Pañcat.; N. of the second Lambaka or book of the Kathā-sarit-sāgara. **-°mṛita-nidhi** (*kathâmṛi°*), m., N. of a work. **-yoga**, m. conversation, talk, discourse, MBh.; Hariv.; Hit. **-°rambha** (*kathâra°*), m. beginning of a story or tale, story-telling; *-kāla*, m. story-beginning-time, Hit. **-°rāma** (*kathârā°*), m. garden of fable. **-°rṇava** (*kathârṇa°*), m., N. of a work. **-lakshaṇa**, n., N. of a work. **-°lāpa** (*kathâlā°*), m. speech, conversation, discourse, Kathās.; Hit. **-°vatāra**, m. incarnation of Kathā or Story. **-°valī** (*kathâva°*), f. a string or collection of stories, Kathās. **-°vaśesha** (*kathâva°*), m. a narrative as the only remainder, (°*ṃ* √*gam*, to enter into a state in which nothing is left but the story of one's life, i.e. to die, Naish.); (mfn.) one of whom nothing remains but his life-story, i.e. deceased, dead; *-tā*, f. the state of the above, (*kathâvaśeshatāṃ gataḥ*, deceased, dead, Prab.) **-°vaśeshī-√bhū** (*kathâva°*), to die, Kād.; (cf. the last.) **-virakta**, mfn. disliking conversation, reserved, taciturn. **-śesha**, mfn.=*kathâvaśesha* above, Rājat. **-saṃgraha**, m. a collection of tales or fables. **-sarit-sāgara**, m. 'the ocean of rivers of stories,' N. of a work by Soma-deva. **Kathôdaya**, m. the beginning of or introduction to a tale, BhP. **Kathôdghāta**, m. the beginning of a tale, Ragh. iv, 20; (in dram.) the opening of a drama by the character that first enters overhearing and repeating the last words of the Sūtradhāra or manager (cf. *udghātyaka*), Sāh. 290; Daśar. **Kathôpakathana**, n. conversation, talking together, conference, narration. **Kathôpâkhyāna**, n. narration, narrative, relation, telling a story.

Kathānaka, *am*, n. a little tale, Vet.; Hcat. &c.

Kathāpaya, Nom. P. *kathāpayati*, to tell, relate, recite.

Kathika, mfn. a narrator, relater, story-teller by profession, W.

Kathita, mfn. told, related, reckoned, Mn. vii, 157; (*am*), n. conversation, discourse, MBh.; Śak.; narration, tale, Ragh. xi, 10. **-pada**, n. repetition, tautology, W.

Kathī-√kṛi, to reduce to a mere tale. **Kathīkṛita**, mfn. reduced to a mere tale, i.e. deceased, dead (e.g. *kathī-kṛitam vapuḥ*, a body reduced to a mere tale, a dead body, Kum. iv, 13).

Kathya, mfn. to be spoken about or told, fit to be mentioned, R.; to be related, Daś.

कथम् kathám, ind. (fr. 2. *ka*), how? in what manner? whence? (e.g. *katham etat*, how is that? *katham idānīm*, how now? what is now to be done? *katham mārâtmake tvayi viśvāsaḥ*, how can there be reliance on thee of murderous mind? *katham utsṛijya tvāṃ gaccheyam*, how can I go away deserting you? *katham buddhvā bhavishyati sā*, how will she be when she awakes? *katham mṛityuḥ prabhavati vedavidām*, whence is it that death has power over those that know the Veda? *katham avagamyate*, whence is it inferred?); sometimes *katham* merely introduces an interrogation (e.g. *katham ātmānam nivedayāmi kathaṃ vâtmâpahāraṃ karomi*, shall I declare myself or shall I withdraw?)

Katham is often found in connection with the particles *iva*, *nāma*, *nu*, *svid*, which appear to generalize the interrogation (how possibly? how indeed? &c.); with *nu* it is sometimes=*kimu* or *kutas* (e.g. *kathaṃ nu*, how much more! *na kathaṃ nu*, how much less!)

Katham is often connected, like *kim*, with the particles *cana*, *cid*, and *api*, which give an indefinite sense to the interrogative (e.g. *kathaṃ cana*, in any way, some how; scarcely, with difficulty; *na kathaṃ cana*, in no way at all; *kathaṃcit*, some how or other, by some means or other, in any way, with some difficulty, scarcely, in a moderate degree, a little; *na kathaṃcit*, not at all, in no way whatever; *na kathaṃcid na*, in no way not, i.e. most decidedly; *yathā kathaṃcit*, in any way whatsoever; *kathaṃcid yadi jīvati*, it is with difficulty that he lives; *katham api*, some how or other, with some difficulty, scarcely a little; *katham api na*, by no means, not at all), RV. &c.; according to lexicographers *katham* is a particle implying amazement; surprise; pleasure; abuse.

Katham (in comp. for *katham*; at the beginning of an adjective compound it may also have the sense of *kim*). **-ruru**, m., N. of a Rājarshi, Sāy. on RV. iv, 16, 10. **-rūpa**, mfn. of what shape? R. **-vīrya**, mfn. of what power? R. iii, 73, 9. **-kathika**, mfn. one who is always asking questions, an inquisitive person, L.; *-tā*, f. questioning, inquiring, inquisitiveness, L. **-karman**, mfn. how acting? **-kāram**, ind. in what manner? how? Naish.; Śiś. ii, 52. **-jātīyaka**, mfn. of what kind? Pat. **-tarām**, ind. still more how or why? (used in emphatic questions), Sarvad. 105, 12. **-tā**, f. 'the how,' the what state? Yogas. **-pramāṇa**, mfn. of what measure? R. **-bhāva**, m.=*-tā* above, Comm. on KātyŚr. **-bhūta**, mfn. how being, of what kind? Caurap.

2. **Kathā́** (for 1. see col. 1), ind. (Ved. for *kathám*, Pāṇ. v, 3, 26) how? whence? why? RV.; AV. viii, 1, 16; TS. &c.; (*yathā́ kathā́ ca*, in any way whatsoever, ŚBr. iv); sometimes merely a particle of interrogation (e.g. *kathā́ śṛiṇoti ... I'ndraḥ*, does Indra hear? RV. iv, 23, 3; *kathā́—kathā́*, whether—or? TS. ii, 6, 1, 7).

कद् 1. kad, cl. 1. Ā. *kadate*, *cakāda* (R. ed. Gorresio vi, 65, 23; but ed. Bomb. vi, 86, 24 reads *cakāra*), to be confused, suffer mentally; to grieve; to confound; to kill or hurt; to call; to cry or shed tears, Dhātup. xix, 10.

Kadana, *am*, n. destruction, killing, slaughter, MBh.; R.; Pañcat. &c. **-pura**, n., N. of a town, L. **-priya**, mfn. loving slaughter, BhP. vii, 12, 13.

Kadamba, *as*, m. (Uṇ. iv, 82) Nauclea Cadamba (a tree with orange-coloured fragrant blossoms), MBh.; Suśr.; Megh. &c.; white mustard, L.; Andropogon Serratus, L.; turmeric, L.; a particular mineral substance, L.; a particular position of the hand; (in astron.) the pole of the ecliptic, Comm. on Sūryas.; an arrow (cf. *kādamba*), L.; N. of a dynasty; (*ī*), f., N. of a plant, L.; (*am*), n. a multitude, assemblage, collection, troop, herd, Git.; Sāh. &c. **-da**, m. Sinapis Dichotoma, L. **-pushpā**, f., N. of a plant (the flowers of which resemble those of the Kadamba, commonly called Muṇḍeri), L.; (*ī*), f., N. of a plant, Suśr. **-bhrama-maṇḍala**, n. (in astron.) the polar circle of the ecliptic. **-yuddha**, n. a kind of amorous play or sport, Vātsy. **-vallarī**, f., N. of a medicinal plant, L. **-vāyu**, m. a fragrant breeze. **-vṛitta**, n.=*-bhrama-maṇḍala* above. **Kadambânila**, m. a fragrant breeze; 'accompanied by fragrant breezes,' the rainy season, Kir. iv, 24.

Kadambaka, *as*, m. Nauclea Cadamba, VarBṛS.; Sinapis Dichotoma, L.; Curcuma Aromatica; (*ikā*), f. a particular muscle in the nape of the neck (cf. *kalambikā*), L.; (*am*), n. multitude, troop, herd, Śak.; Kir.; Śiś.

Kadambakī-√kṛi, to transform into flowers of the Kadambaka, MBh. vii, 6276.

कद् 2. kád, ind. (originally the neuter form of the interrogative pronoun *ka*), a particle of interrogation (=Lat. *nonne*, *num*), RV.; anything wrong or bad, BhP. vii, 5, 28 (cf. below); =*sukha*, Nigh.; *kad* is used, like *kim*, with the particles *cana* and *cid*, 'sometimes, now and then;' *kac-cana* with the negation *na*, 'in no way or manner,' RV.; *kac-cid* is also used, like the simple *kad*, as a particle of interrogation (e.g. *kaccid dṛishṭā tvayā rājan Damayantī*, was Damayantī seen by thee, O king?), MBh., or *kaccid* may be translated by 'I hope that;' at the beginning of a compound it may mark the uselessness, badness or defectiveness of anything, as in the following examples. **-akshara**, n. a bad letter, bad writing, L. **-agni**, m. a little fire, Vop. **-adhvan**, m. a bad road, L. **-anna**, n. bad food or little food, BhP.; Śārṅg.; (mfn.) eating bad food, VarBṛS.; *-tā*, f. the state of bad food, VCāṇ. **-apatya**, n. bad posterity, bad children, BhP. **-artha**, m. a useless thing; (mfn.) having what purpose or aim? RV. x, 22, 6; useless, unmeaning, W. **-°arthana**, *am*, *ā*, n. f. (fr. *kadarthaya* below), the act of tormenting, torture, trouble, Daś.; Kathās. **-°arthanīya**, mfn. (fr. the next), to be tormented or troubled, Naish.; Hcar. **-°arthaya**, Nom. (fr. *kad-artha*) P. *kadarthayati*, to consider as a useless thing, estimate lightly, despise, Bhartṛ.; Vcar.; to torment, torture, trouble, Pañcat.; Kathās.; Naish. &c. **-°arthita**, mfn. rendered useless; despised, disdained, rejected. **-°arthī-√kṛi**, to disdain, disregard, despise, overlook, MBh.; BhP.; to torment, torture. **-°arthī-kṛiti**, f. contempt, disdain; tormenting, torture, Hcar. **-arya**, mfn. avaricious, miserly, stingy, niggardly, Gaut.; ChUp.; Mn. iv, 210, 224; Yājñ. &c.; little, insignificant, mean, W.; bad, disagreeable, W.; (*as*), m. a miser; *-tā*, f., *-tva*, n. the state or condition of the above, MBh.; *-bhāva*, m. id., ib. **-aśva**, m. a bad horse, Comm. on Pāṇ. **-ākāra**, mfn. ill-formed, ugly, L. **-ākhya**, mfn. having a bad name, T.; (*am*), n. Costus Speciosus, L. (commonly called Kushṭha).

—ācāra, m. bad conduct; (mfn.) of bad conduct, wicked, abandoned, W. **—āhāra,** m. bad food, Car.; (mfn.) taking bad food, ib. **—indriya,** *āṇi,* n. pl. bad organs of sense, BhP.; (mfn.) having bad organs of sense, BhP. viii, 3, 28; *-gaṇa,* m. & mfn. id., BhP. x, 60, 35. **—ushṭra,** m. a bad camel, Comm. on Pāṇ. **—ushṇa,** mfn. tepid, lukewarm, Pāṇ.; Suśr. &c.; harsh, sharp (as a word), Naish. ix, 38; (*am*), n. slight warmth, lukewarmness, W.; (cf. *kavôshṇa, kôshṇa.*) **—ratha,** m. a bad carriage, ŚāṅkhŚr.; Pāṇ. **—vat,** mfn. containing the word *ka,* ŚBr. vi; ŚāṅkhŚr. **—vada,** mfn. speaking ill or inaccurately or indistinctly, Pāṇ. vi, 3, 102; Vop. &c. (with neg. *a°,* Śiś. xiv, 1); contemptible, vile, base, L. **—vara,** n. whey or buttermilk mixed with water, L.; (cf. *kaṅkara, kaṭvara,* &c.)

Kat (in comp. for 2. *kad* above). **—tṛiṇa,** n. a fragrant grass, Suśr.; Pistia Stratiotes, L. **—toya,** n. an intoxicating drink, wine or vinous spirit, L. **—tri,** mfn. pl. three inferior (persons or articles &c.), Vārtt. on Pāṇ. vi, 3, 101. **—try-ādi,** m., N. of a gaṇa, Pāṇ. iv, 2, 95; (cf. *kāttreyaka.*)

Kal (in comp. for 2. *kad*). **—lola,** m. a wave, surge, billow, Pañcat.; Bhartṛ. &c.; an enemy, foe, L.; joy, happiness, pleasure, L.; *-jātaka,* n., N. of an astrological work. **—°lolita,** mfn. surging, billowy, gaṇa *tārakâdi,* Pāṇ. v, 2, 36. **—lolinī,** f. a surging stream, river in general, Prab.

कद *ka-da.* See 3. *ka.*

कदक *kadaka, as,* m. an awning, L.; (cf. *kandaka.*)

कदम्ब *kadamba.* See under 1. *kad.*

कदर *kadara, as,* m. a saw, L.; an iron goad (for guiding an elephant), L.; a species of Mimosa (= *śveta-khadira;* cf. Gk. κέδρος), Bhpr.; Comm. on KātyŚr.; (*as, am*), m. n. a corn, callosity of the feet (caused by external friction), Suśr.; (*am*), n. coagulated milk, L.; (cf. *kaṅkara, kaṭura,* &c.)

कदल *kadala, as, ī* (*ā,* L.), m. f. the plantain or banana tree, Musa Sapientum (its soft, perishable stem is a symbol of frailty), Suśr.; R.; Megh.; (*ā*), f., N. of several plants (Pistia Stratiotes, Bombax Heptaphyllum, Calosanthes Indica), L.; (*ī*), f. the plantain tree, Bhpr.; a kind of deer (the hide of which is used as a seat), MBh.; Suśr.; a flag, banner, flag carried by an elephant, L.; (*am*), n. the banana, Suśr.

Kadalaka, *as,* m. Musa Sapientum, L.; (*ikā*), f. id., Śiś. v, 2; a flag carried by an elephant, Kād.

Kadalin, *ī,* m. a kind of antelope, L.

Kadalī, f. (see above). **—kanda,** m. the root of the plantain, Bhpr. **—kshatā,** f. a sort of cucumber, W.; a fine woman, W. **—garbha,** m. the pith of the plantain tree, MaitrUp.; Kathās. &c.; (*ā*), f., N. of a daughter of Maṅkaṇaka, Kathās. xxxii, 104. **—sukham,** ind. as easily as a plantain tree (= *kadalīvat sukham,* Mall.), Ragh. xii, 96. **—skandha,** m. a particular form of illusion (Buddh.), L.

कदा *kadā́,* ind. (fr. 2. *ka*), when? at what time? (with following fut. or pres. tense, Pāṇ. iii, 3, 5), RV.; MBh.; Pañcat. &c.; at some time, one day, RV. viii, 5, 22; how? RV. vii, 29, 3; with a following *nu khalu,* when about? MBh. iii; with a following *ca* and preceding *yadā,* whenever, as often as possible (e.g. *yadā́ kadā́ ca sunávāma sómam,* let us press out the Soma as often as may be or at all times, RV. iii, 53, 4); with a following *canā́,* never at any time, RV.; AV.; TUp.; Hit. &c.; (irr. also) at some time, one day, once, MBh. xiii; Kathās. &c.; *na kadā́,* never, RV. vi, 21, 3; Subh.; *na kadā cana,* never at any time, RV.; AV. &c.; *kadā cit,* at some time or other, sometimes, once; *na kadā cit,* never; *kadâpi,* sometimes, now and then; *na kadâpi,* never; [cf. Zd. *kadha;* Gk. κότε and πότε; Lat. *quando;* Lith. *kadà;* Slav. *kŭda.*] **—matta,** *as,* m., N. of a man, gaṇa *upakâdi,* Pāṇ. ii, 4, 69.

कदूहि *kadūhi, is,* m., N. of a man.

कद्रु *kádru,* mfn. (etym. doubtful; fr. √*kav,* Comm. on Uṇ. iv, 102) tawny, brown, reddish-brown, TS.; KātyŚr. &c.; (*us*), m. tawny (the colour), W.; (*us, ūs*), f. a brown Soma-vessel, RV. viii, 45, 26; N. of a daughter of Daksha (wife of Kaśyapa and mother of the Nāgas), MBh.; BhP. &c.; (*ū́s*), f. a particular divine personification (described in certain legends which relate to the bringing down of the Soma from heaven; according to the Brāhmaṇas, 'the earth personified'), TS. vi; ŚBr. iii, vi; Kāṭh. &c.; N. of a plant (?). **—ja,** m. 'Kadru's son,' a serpent, L. **—putra,** m. id., Hariv. **—suta,** m. id., L.

Kadruka. See *tri-ka°.*

Kadruṇa, mfn. (fr. *kadru,* gaṇa *pāmâdi,* Pāṇ. v, 2, 100), tawny.

Kadrūṇa, mfn. (fr. *kadrū,* ib.), id.

कद्रूक *kadrūka, am,* n. the hump on the back of the Indian bullock, Hcat. i, 399, 6; (cf. *gadrūka.*)

कद्र्यञ्च् *kadryañc,* mf(*kadrī́cī*)n. (fr. 2. *añc* and 2. *ka,* Pāṇ. vi, 3, 92), turned towards what? RV. i, 164, 17.

कद्वत् *kadvat,* &c. See under 2. *kad.*

कधप्रिय *kadha-priya,* mfn. ever pleased or friendly [NBD.]; fond of praise [Sāy.], RV. i, 30, 20; (*kadha* = *kadā;* cf. Zd. *kadha;* cf. also *adha-priya.*)

Kadha-prī, mfn. id., RV. i, 38, 1.

कधि *ka-dhi, is,* m. the ocean; (cf. *kaṃ-dhi.*)

कन् *kan* (*kā* in Veda), cl. 1. P. *kanati, cakāna, cake, akānīt, kanitā,* &c., Dhātup. xiii, 17; (aor. 1. sg. *akānisham,* 2. sg. *kānishas,* RV.), to be satisfied or pleased, RV. iv, 24, 9; to agree to, accept with satisfaction, RV. iii, 28, 5; to shine; to go, Dhātup.: Intens. P. (Subj. *cā́kanat;* Pot. *cākanyāt;* pf. 1. sg. *cākana*); Ā. (Subj. 3. pl. *cā́kananta* & *cakánanta,* RV. i, 169, 4), to be satisfied with, like, enjoy (with loc., gen., or instr.), RV.; to please, be liked or wished for (with gen. of the person), RV. i, 169, 4; v, 31, 13; viii, 31, 1; to strive after, seek, desire, wish (with acc. or dat.), RV.; [cf. *kā, kai, kam, kvan,* and *can:* cf. also Zd. *kan;* Gk. καναχή; Angl. Sax. *hana;* Lat. *canus, caneo, candeo, candela* (?); Hib. *canu,* 'full moon.']

Kánaka, *am,* n. (Comm. on Uṇ. ii, 32) gold, MBh.; Suśr.; Śak. &c.; (*as*), m. thorn-apple, Suśr.; Mesua Ferrea, Bhartṛ.; several other plants (Michelia Campaka, Butea Frondosa, Bauhinea Variegata, Cassia Sophora, a kind of bdellium, a kind of sandal-wood), L.; a kind of decoction, Car.; N. of particular Grahas or Ketus, AVpar.; N. of several men; (*ās*), m. pl., N. of a people, VarBṛS.; (*ā*), f. one of the seven tongues of fire, L.; (mfn.) of gold, golden, SaṃhUp. 44, 1. **—kadalī,** f. a species of plantain, Megh. 77. **—kalaśa,** m., N. of a man, Kathās. **—kāra,** m. a goldsmith. **—kuṇḍalā,** f., N. of the mother of the Yaksha Harikeśa. **—ketakī,** f. a species of Pandanus with yellow blossoms, L. **—kshāra,** m. borax, L. **—kshīrī,** f. Cleome Felina, L. **—giri,** m., N. of the founder of a sect; = *kāñcana-giri,* L. **—°gairika,** n. a species of ochre, Suśr.; (cf. *kāñcana-gai°.*) **—gaura,** n. saffron, Caurap. **—candra,** m., N. of a king. **—campaka,** m. a species of Campaka, Caurap. **—ṭaṅka,** m. a golden hatchet. **—tālâbha,** mfn. bright as a golden palm tree. **—daṇḍa,** n. 'golden-sticked,' a royal parasol, Gīt. **—datta,** m., N. of a man, Vet. **—dhvaja,** m., N. of a son of Dhṛita-rāshṭra, MBh. **—pattra,** n. a particular ornament for the ear, Caurap. **—parāga,** m. gold-dust. **—parvata,** m. the mountain Meru, MBh. xii. **—pala,** m. a Pala (a weight of gold and silver equal to sixteen Māshakas, or about 280 grains troy), L. **—piṅgala,** n., N. of a Tīrtha, Hariv. **—pura,** n., N. of several towns. **—purī,** f. id. **—pushpikā,** f. Premna Spinosa, Nigh. **—pushpī,** f. a species of Pandanus with yellow blossoms, L. **—°prabha,** mfn. bright as gold; (*ā*), f. Cardiospermum Halicacabum, L.; N. of a metre (consisting of four lines of 13 syllables each); N. of a princess, Kathās. **—prasavā,** f. = *-pushpī* above. **—prasūna,** m. Dalbergia Ougeinensis, L. **—phala,** n. the seed of Croton Tiglium. **—bhaṅga,** m. a piece of gold. **—mañjarī,** f., N. of a woman, Kathās. **—maya,** mf(*ī*)n. consisting or made of gold, golden, Pañcat.; Ratnāv. &c. **—mālā,** f., N. of a woman, Pañcad. **—muni,** m., N. of a Buddha, Lalit. **—rambhā,** f. a species of Musa, L. **—rasa,** m. fluid gold, a golden stream, Śak. 279, 4; yellow orpiment, L. **—rekhā,** f., N. of a woman, Kathās. **—latā,** f., N. of a plant (to which the slender figure of a woman is compared), Kuv. **—latikā,** f. id., Kpr. **—vatī,** f., N. of a town; of a woman, Kathās. **—varṇa,** m., N. of a king (supposed to be a former manifestation of Śākya-muni). **—varman,** m., N. of a merchant, Kathās. **—varsha,** m., N. of a king, ib. **—vāhinī,** f. 'gold stream,' N. of a river, Rājat. **—vigraha,** m., N. of a king of Viśālapurī. **—śaka,** *ās,* m. pl., N. of a people, VarBṛS. **—śakti,** m. 'the golden-speared one,' N. of Kārttikeya, Mṛicch. **—°śikharin,** m. 'golden-crested,' N. of the mountain Meru, Kād. **—sūtra,** n. a golden cord or chain, Hit. **—sena,** m., N. of a king, Pañcad. **—stambha,** m. a golden column or stem &c.; (*ā*), f. 'having a golden stem,' a species of Musa, L.; *-rucira,* mfn. shining with columns of gold, Hit. **—sthalī,** f. a gold mine, golden soil, W. **Kanakâkara,** m. id., Suśr. **Kanakâksha,** m. 'gold-eyed,' N. of a being attendant on Skanda, MBh.; of a king, Kathās. **Kanakâṅgada,** n. a golden bracelet, Śiś.; (*as*), m., N. of a son of Dhṛita-rāshṭra, MBh.; of a Gandharva, Bālar. **Kanakâcala,** m. 'the golden mountain,' N. of Meru; a piece of gold shaped like a mountain (cf. *hema-parvata*). **Kanakâdri,** m. the mountain Meru; *-khaṇḍa,* n., N. of a section of the Skanda-purāṇa. **Kanakâdhyaksha,** m. the superintendent of gold, treasurer. **Kanakântaka,** m. Bauhinia Variegata, L. **Kanakâpīḍa,** m., N. of a being attending on Skanda, MBh. **Kanakâbhá,** mfn. similar to gold, like gold, TĀr. i, 4, 1. **Kanakâyu** or **°yus,** m., N. of a son of Dhṛita-rāshṭra, MBh. (v.l. *karakâyu*). **Kanakâraka,** m. Bauhinia Variegata, L.; (cf. *kanakântaka* above.) **Kanakâlukā,** f. a golden jar or vase, L. **Kanakâvalī,** f. a golden chain, Pañcad. **Kanakâhva,** n. the blossom of Mesua Ferrea, L. **Kanakâhvaya,** m. the thorn apple, L.; N. of a Buddha, Lalit. **Kanakêśvara-tīrtha,** n., N. of a Tīrtha.

Kanakā-vatī, f., N. of one of the mothers in the retinue of Skanda, MBh.; *-mādhava,* m., N. of a work, Sāh.

Kanala, mfn. shining, bright [T.], gaṇa *ari-haṇâdi,* Pāṇ. iv, 2, 80.

कन *kana,* mfn. (substituted for *alpa,* 'little, small,' in forming its comparative and superlative, see below; cf. *kaṇa;* according to Gmn. fr. √*kan,* 'to shine, be bright or merry,' originally meaning 'young, youthful'). **—kalôdbhava,** m. resin of the plant Shorea Robusta, L. **—khala,** n., N. of a Tīrtha, MBh.; Hariv.; AgP.; (*ās*), m. pl., N. of mountains, MBh. iii. **—deva,** m., N. of a Buddhist patriarch. **—pa,** n. = *kaṇapa,* q.v., MBh. iii, 810; N. of a man.

Kanaya, Nom. P. *kanayati,* to make less or smaller, diminish, Bhaṭṭ. xviii, 25.

Kanā́, f. a girl, maid, RV. x, 61, 5; 10; 11; 21.

Kanā́nakā, f. the pupil of the eye, TS. v, 7, 12, 1; (cf. *kanī́nakā* below.)

Kanishṭhá and **kánishṭha,** mfn. the youngest, younger born (opposed to *jyeshṭha* and *vṛiddha*), RV. iv, 33, 5; AV. x, 8, 28; AitBr.; KātyŚr. &c.; the smallest, lowest, least (opposed to *bhūyishṭha*), TS.; ŚBr. &c.; (*as*), m. a younger brother, L.; (scil. *ghaṭa*) the descending bucket of a well, Kuv.; (*ās*), m. pl., N. of a class of deities of the fourteenth Manvantara, VP.; (*ā*), f. (with or without *aṅguli*) the little finger, Yājñ. i, 19; R.; Suśr.; a younger wife, one married later (than another), Mn. ix, 122; an inferior wife, Vātsy.; (cf. *kana* and *kanyā.*) **—ga,** m. a Jina, L. **—tā,** f., **-tva,** n. the state of being younger or smaller. **—pada,** n. least root (that quantity of which the square multiplied by the given multiplicator and having the given addend added or subtrahend subtracted is capable of affording an exact square root), Colebr. **—prathama,** mfn. having the youngest as the first. **—mūla,** n. id., ib. **Kanishṭhâtreya,** m. 'the younger Ātreya,' N. of an author on medicine.

Kanishṭhaka, mf(*ikā́*)n. the smallest, AV. i, 17, 2; (*kanishṭhikā*), f. the little finger (*aṅguli*), ŚBr.; KātyŚr. &c.; subjection, obedience, service, VCāṇ.; (*am*), n. a sort of grass, L.

Kanī́, f. a girl, maiden, RV. (only gen. pl. *kanī́nām*); Pañcad.; Kāvyād.

Kanīna, mfn. young, youthful, RV.; ŚāṅkhŚr.; (*ī*), f. the pupil of the eye, L.; the little finger, L.

Kanīnaká, *as,* m. a boy, youth, RV. x, 40, 9; (*kanī́naka*), the pupil of the eye, VS.; ŚBr.; Suśr.; the caruncula lacrymalis, W.; (*ā́*), f. a girl, maiden, virgin, RV. iv, 32, 23; (*kanī́nakā* and *kanī́nikā*), the pupil of the eye, AV. iv, 20, 3; TS.; ŚBr. &c.; the little finger, L.

Kanīnika, *am,* n., N. of several Sāmans.

Kánīyas, mfn. younger, a younger brother or

sister, younger son or daughter (opposed to *jyāyas*), RV. iv, 33, 5; AitBr.; MBh. &c.; smaller, less, inferior, very small or insignificant (opposed to *bhūyas* and *uttama*), RV.; AV. iii, 15, 5; xii, 4, 6; TS.; ŚBr. &c.; (*yasī*), f. the younger sister of a wife, L. **-tva**, n. the state of being smaller or less, Hcat. **-vin**, mfn. less, inferior, TāṇḍyaBr.

Kanīyasa, mfn. younger, MBh.; Hariv. &c.; smaller, less, MBh. xiii, 2560; (*am*), n. 'of less value,' copper, L.

Kanya, mf(*ā*)n. the smallest (opposed to *uttama* and *madhyama*), Hcat. i, 302, 8 ff.; (*ā*), f., see *kanyā* below; [cf. Zd. *kainin*; Hib. *cain*, 'chaste, undefiled.'] **-kubja**, n. (*ā*, f., L.), N. of an ancient city of great note (in the north-western provinces of India, situated on the *Kālī nadī*, a branch of the Gaṅgā, in the modern district of Farrukhabad; the popular spelling of the name presents, perhaps, greater variations than that of any place in India [e. g. *Kanauj, Kunnoj, Kunnouj, Kinoge, Kinnoge, Kinnauj, Kanoj, Kannauj, Kunowj, Canowj, Canoje, Canauj*, &c.]; in antiquity this city ranks next to Ayodhyā in Oude; it is known in classical geography as Canogyza; but the name applies also to its dependencies and the surrounding district; the current etymology [*kanyâ*, 'a girl,' shortened to *kanya*, and *kubja*, 'round-shouldered or crooked'] refers to a legend in R. i, 32, 11 ff., relating to the hundred daughters of Kuśanābha, the king of this city, who were all rendered crooked by Vāyu for non-compliance with his licentious desires; the ruins of the ancient city are said to occupy a site larger than that of London), MBh.; Kathās. &c.; *-deśa*, m. the country round Kanyakubja. **-kumārī**, f., N. of Durgā, TĀr.

Kanyaka, mfn. the smallest, Hcat. i, 302, 16; (*ā*), f. a girl, maiden, virgin, daughter, MBh.; Śak.; Yājñ. &c.; the constellation Virgo in the zodiac, VarBṛS.; N. of Durgā, BhP. x, 2, 12; Aloe Indica, L.; (*ikā*), f. a girl, maiden, daughter, L. **Kanyakâgāra**, n. the women's apartments, BhP. **Kanyakā-guṇa**, *ās*, m. pl., N. of a people, VP. **Kanyakā-chala**, n. or °*cchala*, beguiling a maiden, seduction, Yājñ. i, 61. **Kanyakā-jāta**, m. the son of an unmarried woman, Yājñ. ii, 129. **Kanyakā-pati**, m. a daughter's husband, son-in-law, L.

Kanyánā, f. a maiden, girl, RV. viii, 35, 5.

Kanyálā, f. id., AV. v, 5, 3; xiv, 2, 52.

Kanyasa, mf(*ā* & *ī*)n. younger, MBh.; R.; smaller, the smallest, Hcat.; (*ā*), f. the little finger, L.

Kanyā̀, f. (√*kan*, Uṇ. iv, 111), a girl, virgin, daughter, RV.; AV. &c.; MBh. &c. (*kanyām* √*dā* or *pra*-√*dā* or *pra*-√*yam* or *upa*-√*pad*, Caus. to give one's daughter in marriage, Mn. viii, ix; *kanyām prati*-√*grah* or √*hṛi* or √*vah*, to receive a girl in marriage, marry, Mn. ix); the sign of the zodiac Virgo, VarBṛ. & BṛS. &c.; the female of any animal, Mṛicch.; N. of Durgā, MBh. iii, 8115; N. of a tuberous plant growing in Kaśmīra, Suśr.; Aloe Perfoliata, L.; several other plants, L.; N. of a metre (of four lines, each of them containing four long syllables). **-kāla**, m. the time of maidenhood, T. **-kubja**, *am*, *ā*, n. f. = *kanya-kubja* above, L. **-kumārī**, f. = *kanya-ku*°. **-kūpa**, m., N. of a Tīrtha, MBh. **-gata**, mfn. inherent in or pertaining to a virgin; the position of a planet in the sign Virgo. **-garbha**, m. the offspring of an unmarried woman, MBh. xii, 49. **-grahaṇa**, n. taking a girl in marriage. **-ja**, m. the son of an unmarried woman, L. **-jāta**, m. id., ib. **-°ṭa** (*kanyâṭa*), mfn. following after young girls, L.; (*as*), m. the women's apartments, L. **-tīrtha**, n., N. of a Tīrtha, MBh. **-tva**, n. virginity, maidenhood, MBh. **-dātṛi**, m. (a father) who gives a girl in marriage, Mn. ix, 73. **-dāna**, n. giving a girl in marriage, Mn. iii, 35; (*kanyâ-dāna*, receiving a girl in marriage, W.) **-dūshaka**, m. the violator of a virgin, Mn. iii, 164; the calumniator of a girl, W. **-dūshaṇa**, n. defilement of a virgin; calumniating a maiden. **-dūshayitṛi**, m. the defiler of a maiden, MārkP. **-dūshin**, m. id., Yājñ. i, 223. **-dosha**, m. a blemish in a virgin (as disease, bad repute &c.) **-dhana**, n. a girl's property, portion, dowry, R.; (if a girl dies unmarried her property falls to her brother's share, T.) **-pati**, m. a daughter's husband, son-in-law, L. **-pāla**, m. the protector or father of a girl, L.; a dealer in slave girls, W.; a dealer in spirituous liquors (for *kalyā-pāla*), L. **-putra**, m. the offspring of an unmarried woman, L. **-pura**, n. the women's apartments, BhP.; Daś. &c. **-pradāna**, n. giving a daughter in marriage, Mn. iii, 29 ff. **-bhartṛi**, m. (= *kanyābhiḥ prârthanīyo bhartā*, T.), N. of Kārttikeya, MBh. iii; a daughter's husband, son-in-law, L. **-bhāva**, m. virginity, maidenhood, MBh. **-bhaiksha**, n. begging for a girl, MBh. **-maya**, mfn. consisting of a girl (as property &c.), being a girl or daughter, Ragh. vi, 11; xvi, 86. **-ratna**, n. 'girl-jewel,' an excellent maiden, a lovely girl. **-°rāma** (*kanyârāma*), m., N. of a Buddha. **-rāśi**, m. the sign Virgo. **-°rthika** (*kanyârthika*), mfn. wanting or desiring a girl. **-°rthin** (*kanyârthin*), mfn. id., MBh. **-vat**, mfn. possessing a daughter; (*ān*), m. the father of a girl, Gaut. iv, 8. **-vedin**, m. a son-in-law, Yājñ. i, 261. **-vrata-sthā**, f. a woman in her monthly state, Kathās. xxvi, 55. **-śulka**, n. = *-dhana* above. **-°śrama** (*kanyâśrama*), m., N. of a hermitage, MBh. **-saṃvedya**, n., N. of a Tīrtha, MBh. iii. **-samudbhava**, mfn. born from an unmarried woman, Mn. ix, 172. **-sampradāna**, n. the giving away a maiden in marriage. **-svayaṃvara**, m. the voluntary choice of a husband by a maiden. **-haraṇa**, n. carrying a girl off forcibly, rape, W. **-hrada**, m., N. of a Tīrtha, MBh.

Kanyikā. See under *kanyaka*.

कनक *kanaka*. See under √*kan*.

कनक्नक *kanáknaka*, mfn. an epithet given to a kind of poison [BRD.], AV. x, 4, 22.

कनखल *kana-khala, kana-deva*. See *kana*.

कनटी *kanaṭī*, f. red arsenic (= *kunaṭī*).

कनवक *kanavaka*, *as*, m., N. of a son of Śūra, Hariv.

कना *kanā́*. See p. 248, col. 3.

कनाठ *kanāṭha*, *as*, m., N. of a man.

कनिक्रद *kanikradá*, mfn. (√*krand*, Intens.), neighing, VS. xiii, 48.

कनिष्क *kanishka*, *as*, m., N. of a celebrated king of Northern India (whose reign began in the first century of our era and who, next to Aśoka, was the greatest supporter of Buddhism; his empire seems to have comprised Afghānistān, the Panjāb, Yarkand, Kashmīr, Ladak, Agra, Rājputāna, Gujarāt, and Sindh), Rājat. **-pura**, n., N. of a town founded by him.

कनिष्ठ *kanishṭha*, &c. See p. 248, col. 3.

कनीचि *kanīci*, *is*, f. (cf. *kaṇīci*) a cart, L.; a creeping plant with blossoms, L.; Abrus Precatorius, L.

कनेरा *kanerā*, f. (cf. *kaṇerā*) a female elephant, W.; a harlot, W.

कन्त *kanta*, mfn. (fr. 1. *kam*, ind.), happy, Pāṇ v, 2, 138.

Kanti, mfn. id., ib.

Kantu, mfn. id., ib.; (*us*), m. (fr. √*kam*, Uṇ. i, 28; 73), love, the god of love; the mind, heart, Comm. on Uṇ.; a granary, L.

Kantvà, *am*, n. happiness, prosperity, MaitrS. i, 10, 10.

कन्थक *kanthaka*, *as*, m., N. of a man, gaṇa *gargâdi*, Pāṇ. iv, 1, 105; (*ā*), f. a species of Opuntia, L.

Kantharī, f. a species of Opuntia, L.

Kanthārikā, °*rī*, f. id.

कन्था *kanthā*, f. a rag, patched garment (especially one worn by certain ascetics), Bhartṛ.; Pañcat.; [cf. Gk. κέντρων; Lat. *centon*; O. H. G. *hadara*; Germ. *hader*]; a wall, L.; a species of tree, L.; a town, L.; (a Tatpurusha compound ending in *kanthā* is neuter if it imply a town of the Uśīnaras, Pāṇ. ii, 4, 20.) **-dhāraṇa**, n. wearing a patched garment (as practised by certain Yogins). **-dhārin**, m. 'rag-wearer,' a Yogin, religious mendicant, Bhartṛ. **Kanthêśvara-tīrtha**, n., N. of a Tīrtha, ŚivP.

कन्द् *kand*, cl. 1. P. *kandati, cakanda*, to cry, utter lamentations: Ā. *kandate*, to be confounded, confound, Dhātup. iii, 33; (cf. 1. *kad*, *krand*.)

कंद *kaṃ-da*. See p. 252, col. 1.

कन्द *kanda*, *as*, *am*, m. n. (√*kan*, Comm. on Uṇ. iv, 98), a bulbous or tuberous root, a bulb, MBh.; BhP.; Suśr. &c.; the bulbous root of Amorphophallus Campanulatus, L.; garlic, L.; a lump, swelling, knot, Suśr. i, 258, 9; [cf. Gk. κόνδος, κονδύλος; O. H. G. *hnūtr, hnuta*]; an affection of the female organ (considered as a fleshy excrescence, but apparently prolapsus uteri, W.); N. of a metre (of four lines of thirteen syllables each); (in mus.) a kind of time; (*ī*), f., see *māṇsa-k*°. **-guḍūcī**, f. a species of Cocculus, L. **-ja**, mfn. growing or coming from bulbs, Suśr. **-da**, mfn. giving or forming bulbs, MBh. xii, 10403 (v. l. *kakuda*, ed. Bomb.) **-phalā**, f., N. of a cucurbitaceous plant, L. **-bahulā**, f., N. of a bulbous plant, L. **-mūla**, n. a radish, L. **-mūlaka**, n. id., L. **-rohiṇī**, f., N. of a plant, L. **-latā**, f., N. of a plant with a bulbous root, L. **-vat**, m. a species of the Soma plant, Suśr. ii, 168, 14. **-vardhana**, m. the esculent root of Amorphophallus Campanulatus. **-valli**, f., N. of a medical plant, L. **-śāka**, n. a kind of vegetable, Bhpr. **-śūraṇa**, m. Amorphophallus Campanulatus. **-saṃjña**, n. prolapsus uteri (cf. *kanda*), L. **-sambhava**, mfn. growing from bulbs, Suśr. **-sāra**, n. Indra's garden, L. **-sāraka**, n. id., ib. **Kandâḍhya**, m. a kind of tuberous plant, L. **Kandâmṛitā**, f. a species of Opuntia, L. **Kandârha**, m. Amorphophallus Campanulatus, L. **Kandâlu**, m., N. of several tuberous plants, L. **Kandâśana**, mfn. living upon bulbs, Bālar. 298, 12. **Kandêkshu**, m. a sort of grass, Nigh. **Kandôttha**, n. the blue lotus, L.; (cf. *kandoṭa*.) **Kandôdbhavā**, f. a species of Cocculus, L. **Kandâushadha**, n. a sort of Arum, L.

Kandaṭa, m. the white esculent water-lily, L.

Kandin, *ī*, m. Amorphophallus Campanulatus, L.

Kandirī, f. Mimosa Pudica, L.

Kandila, m. a kind of tuberous plant, L.

Kandoṭa, m. Nymphæa Esculenta, L.; the blue lotus, L.

Kandota, m. Nymphæa Esculenta, L.

कन्दर *kandara*, *ā*, *am*, f. n. (*as*, m., L.), (√*kand*, Comm. on Uṇ. iii, 131; *kam*, *jalena dīryate*, T.), 'great cliff,' an artificial or natural cave, glen, defile, valley, R.; Pañcat.; Megh. &c.; (*as*), m. a hook for driving an elephant, L.; (*ā*), f. the lute of the Caṇḍālas, L.; N. of a mother in the retinue of Skanda, MBh.; BhP.; (*am*), n. ginger, L. **-vat**, mfn. containing caves or valleys, R. **Kandarâkara**, m. a mountain, L. **Kandarântara**, n. the interior of a cave, L.

Kandarāla, *as*, m., N. of several plants (Hibiscus Populneoides; Ficus Infectoria; the walnut tree), L.

Kandarālaka, *as*, m. Ficus Infectoria, L.

कन्दर्प *kandarpa*, *as*, m. (etym. doubtful; according to some fr. *kam-darpa*, 'inflamer even of a god,' see 3. *ka*, or 'of great wantonness'), N. of Kāma (q. v.), love, lust, MBh.; Bhag.; Suśr. &c.; (in mus.) a particular Rāga (q. v.); a kind of time; membrum virile, L.; N. of a man, Kathās.; (*ā*), f. one of the divine women attending on the fifteenth Arhat (Jain.) **-kūpa**, m. 'a well of love,' pudendum muliebre, L. **-ketu**, m., N. of a prince, Hit. **-keli**, m., N. of a work. **-cūḍā-maṇi**, m., N. of a work. **-jīva**, m., N. of a plant (= *kāma-vriddhi*). **-jvara**, m. passion, desire, L. **-dahana**, n. a section of the Śiva-purāṇa. **-mathana**, m., N. of Śiva, L. **-mātṛi**, f., N. of Lakshmī, L. **-musala**, m. membrum virile, L. **-śṛiṅkhala**, m. a kind of coitus, Ratim. **-siddhânta**, m., N. of a commentator. **-senā**, f., N. of a woman, Kathās.; of a Surâṅganā.

कन्दल *kandala*, *as*, *ā*, *am*, m. f. n. the cheek (or the cheek and temple), W.; girth, girdle, L.; a new shoot or sprig, L.; a low soft tone, L.; a portent (as an eclipse, supposed to forbode evil), L.; reproach, censure, L.; (*as*), m. gold, L.; war, battle, Subh.; (*ī*), f. a species of deer (the hide of which is useful), L.; N. of a plant with white flowers (which appear very plentifully and all at once in the rainy season), Suśr.; Ṛitus.; Bālar.; lotus seed, L.; a flag, banner, L.; N. of a work; (*am*), n. the flower of the Kandalī tree, Ragh.; Bhartṛ. &c. **Kandalânta**, m. a species of serpent, L.

Kandalaya, Nom. P. *kandalayati*, to bring forth or produce in abundance or simultaneously, Bālar.; Prasannar.

Kandalāyana, *as*, m., N. of an ancient sage, Sarvad.

Kandalita, mfn. put forth or emitted in abundance or simultaneously, Bālar.

Kandalin, mfn. covered with Kandalī flowers,

Bhartṛ.; (ifc.) abounding with, full of, Kād.; (ī), m. a kind of deer, L.

Kandalī, f., see above. – **kāra**, m., N. of an author. – **kusuma**, n. the flower of Kandalī, L.; a mushroom, L.

कन्दु **kandu**, *us*, m. f. (√*skand*, Uṇ. i, 15), a boiler, saucepan, or other cooking utensil of iron, Suśr.; Mālav.; Comm. on KātyŚr.; an oven, or vessel serving for one, W.; a kind of fragrant substance, L.; (*us*), m., N. of a man. – **gṛiha**, n. a cookery, Comm. on KātyŚr. – **pakva**, mfn. parched or roasted (as grain) or fried in a pan, dressed without water, W. – **śālā**, f. = *-gṛiha*, L.

Kanduka, *as*, m. a boiler, saucepan, Comm. on KātyŚr.; a ball of wood or pith for playing with, MBh.; Bhartṛ.; Ragh.; a pillow, Bhartṛ. iii, 93, (*am*, n., v.l.); a betel-nut, L.; a kind of time in music. – **gṛiha**, n. a place for cooking, Comm. on KātyŚr. – **prastha**, n., N. of a town, gaṇa *karky-ādi*, Pāṇ. vi, 2, 87 (not in Kāś.) **Kandukêśa**, n., N. of a Liṅga. **Kandukêśvara-liṅga**, n. id.

Kandukāya, Nom. Ā. *kandukāyate*, to be like a playing ball, Bālar.

Kandūraka, *as*, m. a kind of fragrant substance, L.

कन्दोट **kandoṭa**, &c. See p. 249, col. 3.

कंध **kam-dha**, *as*, m. (fr. *kam*, water, and *dha* fr. √*dhā*), a cloud, L.; (cf. *kam-da*.)

Kam-dhara, *as*, *ā*, m. f. (fr. *kam*, head, and *dhara* fr. √*dhṛi*), the neck, Yājñ.; Kathās.; Ragh. &c.; (*as*), m. (*kam* = water) a cloud, L. (cf. the last); Ameranthus Oleraceus, L.

Kam-dhi, *is*, m. (fr. *kam*, water, and *dhi* fr. √*dhā*), the ocean, L.; (*kam* = head), the neck, L.

कन्न **kanna**, *as*, m., N. of a Ṛishi, R. (ed. Gorresio) v, 91, 7, (v.l. *kaṇva*); (*am*), n. fainting, falling in a fit or state of insensibility, L.; sin, L.; (v.l. *kalla*.)

कन्य **kanya**, *kanyaka*, *kanyā*, &c. See p. 249, col. 1.

कन्युष **kanyusha**, *am*, n. the hand below the wrist.

कप् **kap**, v.l. for *krap*, q.v., Dhātup. xix, 9.

कप **kapa**, *ās*, m. pl., N. of a class of deities, MBh.

कपट **kapaṭa**, *as*, *am*, m. n. (√*kamp*, Comm. on Uṇ. iv, 81), fraud, deceit, cheating, circumvention, MBh.; Bhartṛ.; Pañcat. &c.; (*as*), m., N. of a Dānava, MBh. i, 2534; (*ī*), f. a measure equal to the capacity of the hollows of the two hands joined, L.; N. of a tree, Nigh. – **cīḍā**, f., N. of a tree, Nigh. – **tā**, f., **-tva**, n. deceitfulness. – **tāpasa**, m. one who deceitfully pretends to be an ascetic, Kathās. – **daitya**, m., N. of a Daitya, or one who pretends to be a Daitya, GaṇP.; *-vadha*, m., N. of a section of the Gaṇeśa-purāṇa. – **nāṭaka**, m., N. of a man. – **prabandha**, m. continued series of frauds, machination, cunning contrivance, fraud, plot, trick, Hit. – **lekhya**, n. a forged document, false or fraudulent statement, W. – **vacana**, n. deceitful talk. – **veśa**, m. disguise; (mfn.) assuming a false dress or appearance, masked, disguised, W. – °**veśin**, mfn. disguised, in masquerade, L. **Kapaṭêśvara**, n., N. of a particular shrine, Kathās.; (*ī*), f., N. of a plant, L.

Kapaṭika, mfn. acting deceitfully, fraudulent, dishonest, a rogue, cheat, L.

Kapaṭin, mfn. id., L.; (*inī*), f. a kind of perfume, L.

कपना **kapanā**, f. (√*kamp*, Nir. vi, 4), a worm, caterpillar, RV. v, 54, 6; [cf. κάμπη.]

कपर्द **kaparda**, *as*, m. a small shell or cowrie (of which eighty = one paṇa, used as a coin or as a die in gambling, Cypræa Moneta), Comm. on VS.; Comm. on Pāṇ.; braided and knotted hair (esp. that of Śiva, knotted so as to resemble the cowrie shell), L.; (cf. *cátush-kaparda*.) – **yaksha**, m., N. of a Yaksha, Śatr.

Kapardaka, *as*, m. the cowrie shell (= *kaparda*), Comm. on ŚBr.; Hit. &c.; braided and knotted hair, L.; (*ikā*), f. Cypræa Moneta, Comm. on VS.; Pañcat.

Kapardín, mfn. wearing braided and knotted hair (like the cowrie shell), RV.; VS. (said of Rudra, Pūshan, &c.); shaggy, RV. x, 102, 8; (*ī*), m., N. of Śiva, Gaut.; MBh. &c.; of one of the eleven Rudras, VP.; of a Yaksha, Śatr.; of an author, Sāy. on RV. i, 60, 1; (*inī*), f., N. of a goddess, BrahmaP. **Kapardi-kārikā**, *ās*, f. pl., N. of a work. **Kapardi-bhāshya**, n., N. of a work. **Kapardi-svāmin**, m., N. of an author. **Kapardîśa-liṅga**, n., N. of a Liṅga. **Kapardîśvara-tīrtha**, n., N. of a Tīrtha.

कपल **kapala**, *am*, n. a half, part, ŚāṅkhŚr. & Br.

कपाट **kapāṭa**, *as*, (*ī*, L.) *am*, m. (f.) n. a door, the leaf or panel of a door, MBh.; BhP.; Pañcat.; Mṛicch. &c. – **ghna**, mfn. one who breaks a door, a house-breaker, thief, Pāṇ. iii, 2, 54. – **toraṇa-vat**, mfn. furnished with doors surmounted by ornamental arches, R. – **vakshas**, mfn. having a door-like chest, broad-chested, Ragh. iii, 34. – **saṃdhi**, m. the junction of the leaves of a door; a mode of multiplying (in which the multiplicand is placed in a peculiar manner under the multiplier). – °**saṃdhika**, mfn. a term used for a kind of bandage, Suśr.; (similarly *ardha-kapāṭasaṃdhika*.) **Kapāṭôdghāṭana**, n. a door-key.

Kapāṭaka, *as*, *ikā*, m. f. = *kapāṭa*, MBh.; BhP.

Kapāṭita, mfn. (p. p. of a Nom. *kapāṭaya*) locked up, Rājat. viii, 321.

कपाल **kapāla**, (*as*, m., L.), *am*, n. (√*kamp*, Uṇ. i, 117), a cup, jar, dish (used especially for the Puroḍāśa offering), TS.; ŚBr.; Suśr. &c.; (cf. *tri-kapāla*, *pañca-kapāla*, &c.); the alms-bowl of a beggar, Mn. vi, 44; viii, 93; R. &c.; a fragment of brick (on which the oblation is placed), ŚBr. vi, xii; KātyŚr.; Suśr. &c.; a cover, lid, ĀśvGṛ. iv, 5, 8; Bhāshāp. &c.; the skull, cranium, skull-bone, AV. ix, 8, 22; x, 2, 8; ŚBr. i; Yājñ. &c.; the shell of an egg, ŚBr. vi, 1, 3; Kathās. &c.; the shell of a tortoise, ŚBr. vii, 5, 1, 2; the cotyla of the leg of an animal, any flat bone, AitBr.; Suśr.; a kind of leprosy, Suśr. i, 268, 1; 13; multitude, assemblage, collection, L.; (*as*), m. a treaty of peace on equal terms, Kām. ix, 2; (cf. *kapāla-saṃdhi* below); N. of an intermediate caste; N. of several men; (*ās*), m. pl., N. of a school; (*ī*), f. a beggar's bowl, Bhartṛ.; (*am*), n., N. of a Tantra; [Gk. κωπή, 'handle;' Lat. *capere*; Hib. *gabhaim*; Goth. *hafyan*; Angl. Sax. *haban*, *haefene*, *hafoc*; Eng. *haven*, *hawk*; cf. Gk. κεφαλή; Lat. *caput*; Goth. *haubith*; Angl. Sax. *heafud*.] – **ketu**, m., N. of a comet, VarBṛS. – °**khaḍgin**, mfn. bearing a skull and a sword, Hcat. – **nālikā**, f. a sort of pin or spindle (for winding cotton, thread &c.), L. – **pāṇi-tva**, n. the state of bearing a skull in the hand (as Śiva does), Kathās. ii, 14. – °**pāśin**, mfn. bearing a skull and a snare, Hcat. – **bhātī**, f. a particular sort of penance (consisting in alternate suppression and emission of the breath). – **bhṛit**, m. 'bearing a skull,' N. of Śiva, L. – **mālā**, f., N. of a being in the retinue of Devī. – °**mālin**, mfn. bearing a garland of skulls, MBh.; Kathās.; Hcat. – **mocana**, n., N. of a Tīrtha, MBh. iii, 7007; Hariv. &c. – °**vajrin**, mfn. bearing a skull and a thunderbolt, Hcat. – **vat**, mfn. having or bearing a skull, Bālar. – **śakti-hasta**, mf(*ā*)n. bearing a skull and spear in hand, Hcat. – **śiras**, m. (*kapālam śirasi yasya*, T.), N. of Siva, R. ii, 54, 31; (the larynx, NBD.) – °**śūla-khaṭvāṅgin**, mfn. 'bearing a skull, a spear, and a club,' N. of Śiva, Hcat. – **saṃdhi**, m. a treaty of peace on equal terms, Kām. ix, 8 (= Hit. iv, 114). – **sphoṭa**, m. 'splitting the skull,' N. of a Rakshas, Kathās. **Kapālêśvara-tīrtha**, n., N. of a Tīrtha.

Kapālaka, mfn. shaped like a bowl (cf. *kāpālika*), Pañcat.; (*as*), m. a cup, jar, bowl, Hcat.; (*ikā*), f. a potsherd, MBh.; Mn. &c.; the tartar of the teeth, Suśr. i, 205, 9; ii, 128, 13.

Kapāli, *is*, m., N. of Śiva (cf. the next).

Kapālin, mfn. bearing a pot (to receive food, as a beggar), Nār.; furnished with or bearing skulls, Yājñ. iii, 243; BhP.; Kum.; (*ī*, *inī*), m. f. a man or woman of low caste (son or daughter of a Brāhman mother and a fisherman father); the follower of a particular Śaiva sect (carrying skulls of men as ornament and eating and drinking from them; cf. *kāpālika*), Prab.; Kathās. &c.; (*ī*), m., N. of Śiva, MBh. i; Bālar. &c.; of one of the eleven Rudras, MBh. ii; Hariv. &c.; of a demon causing diseases, Hariv. 9557; of a teacher; (*inī*), f. a form of Durgā (as the wife of Śiva-kapālin), Hariv.; Kathās.; of a being attending on Devī.

Kapālina, mfn. relating to Kapālin, VāmP.

कपि **kapí**, *is*, m. (√*kamp*, Uṇ. iv, 143), an ape, monkey, RV. x, 86, 5; AV.; Mn.; Suśr. &c.; an elephant, L.; Emblica Officinalis, L.; a species of Karañja, L.; Olibanum, L.; the sun, L.; N. of Vishṇu or Kṛishṇa, MBh. xiii, 7045; N. of several men; (*ayas*), m. pl., N. of a school; (*i*, *ī*), f. a female ape, L.; (mfn.) brown, Comm. on Uṇ.; [cf. Gk. κῆπος, κεῖπος, κῆβος; Old Germ. *affo*; Angl. Sax. *apa*; Eng. *ape*.] – **kacchu**, *us* & *ūs*, f. Mucuna Pruritus, VarBṛS.; *-phalôpamā*, f. a kind of creeping plant, L. – **kacchurā**, f. Mucuna Pruritus, L. – **kanduka**, n. 'a playing-ball for monkeys,' the skull, cranium, L. – **ketana**, m. 'having a monkey as symbol,' N. of Arjuna (the third son of Pāṇḍu), MBh. – **keśa**, mfn. brown-haired, L. – **koli**, m. a species of Zizyphus. – **cūḍa**, *as*, *ā*, m. f. Spondias Mangifera. – **cūta**, m. id., L. – **ja**, mfn. born of a monkey, L.; (*as*), m. 'produced from the tree Kapi,' the oil of Olibanum; incense, benzoin, L. – **jaṅghikā**, f. a species of ant, L. – **tīrtha**, n., N. of a Tīrtha, ŚivP. – **taila**, n. benzoin, storax, liquid ambar, Bhpr. – **tva**, n. the state of an ape, apishness. – **dhvaja**, m., N. of Arjuna (cf. *-ketana* above), MBh. – **nāmaka**, m. storax, liquid ambar, Bhpr. – **nāman**, m. id., L. – **nāśana**, n. an intoxicating beverage, L. – **nāsa**, m. a kind of musical instrument. – **nāsikā**, f. id. – **nṛitta**, f. a kind of medicinal substance, L. – **pati**, m. 'lord of apes,' N. of Hanumat, Comm. on Prab. – **pippalī**, f. Scindapsus Officinalis, L.; another plant, L. – **prabhā**, f. Mucuna Pruritus, L. – **prabhu**, m. 'master of the monkeys,' N. of Rāma, L. – **priya**, m. Spondias Mangifera, L.; Feronia Elephantum, L. – **bhaksha**, m. 'food of apes,' N. of a sweet substance, R. – **ratha**, m., N. of Rāma (cf. *-prabhu* above), L.; of Arjuna, T. – **rasâḍhyā**, f. Spondias Mangifera, L. – **roma-phalā**, f. Mucuna Pruritus, L. – **roma-latā**, f. id. – **loma-phalā**, f. id. – **lolā**, f. Piper Aurantiacum, L. – **loha**, n. 'monkey-coloured metal,' brass, L. – **vaktra**, m. 'monkey-faced,' N. of Nārada (a saint and philosopher, and friend of Kṛishṇa), L. – **vana**, m., N. of a man. – **vallikā**, f. Scindapsus Officinalis, L. – **vallī**, f. id. – **śāka**, m. n. a cabbage, L. – **śiras**, n. the upper part or coping of a wall, L. – **śīrsha**, n. id., Vcar. – **śīrshṇī**, f. a kind of musical instrument, Lāṭy. – **shṭhala**, m., N. of a Ṛishi, Pāṇ.; VarBṛS. &c.; (*ās*), m. pl. the descendants of the above, gaṇa *upakâdi*, Pāṇ. ii, 4, 69; *-saṃhitā*, f., N. of a work. – **skandha**, m., N. of a Dānava, Hariv.; of a being in the retinue of Skanda, MBh. – **sthala**, n. the abode of an ape, Kāś. on Pāṇ. viii, 3, 91. – **svara**, m., N. of a man. **Kapī-kacchu**, m. = *kapi-ka*° above. **Kapîjya**, m. 'to be revered by monkeys,' Mimusops Kauki, L.; N. of Sugriva, T. **Kapîndra**, m. 'lord of monkeys,' N. of Vishṇu, MBh. xiii, 7002; of Jāmbavat (the father-in-law of Kṛishṇa), MBh. xiii, 629; of Sugrīva, RāmatUp.; of Hanumat, R. **Kapī-vat**, m., N. of a sage, Hariv.; (*tī*), f., N. of a river, R. **Kapîśvara**, m. 'lord of the apes,' N. of Sugriva, RāmatUp. **Kapîshṭa**, m. Feronia Elephantum, L. **Kapy-ākhya**, n. incense, L. – **Kapy-āsa**, n. the buttocks of an ape, ChUp. i, 6, 7, (*as*, m. Comm.)

Kapikā, f. Vitex Negundo.

Kapittha, *as*, m. (*ttha* = *stha*) 'on which monkeys dwell,' Feronia Elephantum, MBh.; Suśr. &c.; a particular position of the hands and fingers; (*am*), n. the fruit of Feronia Elephantum, Suśr.; VarBṛS. &c. – **tvac**, f. the bark of Feronia Elephantum, Bhpr. – **parṇī**, f., N. of a plant, L. – **phala**, m. a species of Mango tree, L. **Kapitthâsya**, m. 'having a face like a wood apple,' a species of monkey, L.

Kapitthaka, *as*, m. Feronia Elephantum; (*am*), n. the fruit of it, R.

Kapitthānī, f., N. of a plant (= *kapittha-parṇī*), L.

Kapitthinī, f. a region abounding in Kapitthas, gaṇa *pushkarâdi*, Pāṇ. v, 2, 135.

Kapiraka = *kapilaka*, q.v., Vārtt. on Pāṇ. viii, 2, 18.

Kapilá, mf(*ā*)n. (√*kam*, Uṇ. i, 56; more probably connected with *kapi*, BRD.), 'monkey-coloured,' brown, tawny, reddish, RV. x, 27, 16; ŚBr.; R. &c.; red-haired, Mn. iii, 8; (*as*), m. the brown or tawny or reddish colour, Suśr.; a kind of mouse; a kind of ape, Kathās.; a (brown) dog, L.; incense, L.; N. of an ancient sage (identified by some with Vishṇu and considered as the founder of the Sāṃkhya system of philosophy), MBh.; Bhag. &c.; N. of several other men; of a Dānava, Hariv. 197; BhP.; of a Nāga, MBh. iii, 8010; Hariv. &c.; of a Varsha in Kuśa-dvīpa, VP. ii, 4, 37; of several mountains; a form of fire, MBh. iii, 14197; N. of the sun, MBh. iii, 154; (*ās*), m. pl., N. of a people, VarBṛS.; of the Brāhmans in Śālmala-dvīpa, VP. ii, 4, 31; (*ā*), f. a brown cow, Yājñ. i, 205; MBh. &c.; a fabulous cow celebrated in the Purāṇas, W.; a kind of leech, Suśr. i, 40, 20; a kind of ant, Suśr. ii, 296, 12; Dalbergia Sissoo, L.; Aloe Perfoliata, L.; a sort of perfume, L.; a kind of medicinal substance, L.; a kind of brass, L.; N. of a daughter of Daksha, MBh.; of a Kiṃnara woman, Kāraṇḍ.; of a river, MBh. iii, 14233; VP.; N. of the female of the elephant Puṇḍarīka (q. v.), L. **-gītā**, f., N. of a work. **-jaṭa**, m., N. of a Muni, Kathās. **-deva**, m., N. of the author of a Smṛiti. **-dyuti**, m., N. of the sun, L. **-drākshā**, f. a vine with brown or tawny-coloured grapes, L. **-druma**, m. Cytisus Cajan, L. **-dhārā**, f., N. of the Gaṅgā, L.; N. of a Tīrtha, L. **-dhūsara**, mfn. brownish grey, Kathās. **-pañcarātra**, n., N. of a work. **-pura**, n. = *-vastu* below. **-phalā**, f. = *-drākshā* above. **-bhadrā**, f., N. of a woman. **-bhāshya**, n., N. of a commentary on Kapila's Sāṃkhya-pravacana. **-rudra**, m., N. of a poet. **-°rshi** (*kapila-ṛishi*), m. the Ṛishi Kapila. **-loha**, m. a kind of brass, Nigh. **-vastu**, n., N. of the town in which Śākyamuni or Buddha was born. **-śarman**, m., N. of a Brahman, Kathās. **-śiṅśapā**, f. a variety of Śiṅśapā with reddish flowers, L. **-saṃhitā**, f., N. of an Upa-purāṇa. **-sāṃkhya-pravacana**, n., N. of a work (= *sāṃkhya-pravacana*); *-bhāshya*, n., N. of a commentary on the above. **Kapilâkshā**, f. a variety of Śiṅśapā (with reddish flowers), L.; (*ī*), f. id.; a species of Colocynth, L. **Kapilâcārya**, m. the teacher Kapila. **Kapilâñjana**, m. 'using a brown collyrium,' N. of Śiva, L.; (cf. *kapiśāñjana*.) **Kapilā-tīrtha**, n., N. of a Tīrtha (any one bathing and performing worship there obtains a thousand brown cows), MBh. iii, 6017 f. **Kapilâdhikā**, f. a kind of ant, Nigh. **Kapilā-pati**, m., N. of Drupada, L. **Kapilâvaṭa**, m., N. of a Tīrtha, MBh. **Kapilâśrama**, m., N. of a hermitage, VP. **Kapilâśva**, m. 'having brown horses,' N. of Indra, L.; N. of a man, MBh.; BhP. &c. **Kapilā-shashṭhī**, f. the sixth day in the dark half of the month Bhādrapada. **Kapilā-hrada**, m., N. of a Tīrtha, MBh. **Kapileśvara-tīrtha**, n., N. of a Tīrtha. **Kapileśvara-deva**, m., N. of a king.

Kapilaka, mf(*ikā*)n. reddish, Suśr.; (*ikā*), f., N. of a woman, gaṇa *śivâdi*, Pāṇ. iv, 1, 112.

Kapilāya, Nom. Ā. *kapilāyate*, to be somewhat brown or reddish, Hcar. 40, 20.

Kapilī-√kṛi, to colour brown or reddish, MBh.; R.; Kād.

Kapiśa, mf(*ā*)n. 'ape-coloured,' brown, reddish-brown, MBh.; BhP. &c.; (*as*), m. brown or reddish colour; incense, L.; the sun, L.; N. of Śiva, L.; (*ā*, *ī*), f. a spirit, sort of rum, L.; (*ā*), f., N. of the mother of the Piśācas, W.; N. of a river, Ragh. iv, 38; (*am*), n. a sort of rum, L. **-bhrū**, f., N. of a woman, Kathās. **Kapiśâñjana**, m., N. of Śiva; (cf. *kapilâñjana*.) **Kapiśā-putra**, m. a Piśāca, an imp or goblin, W. **Kapiśâvadāna**, n. N. of a Buddhist work.

Kapiśaya, Nom. P. *kapiśayati*, to redden, embrown, Śiś. iv, 24; Prasannar. &c.

Kapiśita, mfn. embrowned, made brown or dusky red, Mall. on Śiś. &c.

Kapiśikā, f. a sort of rum, L.

Kapiśī-√kṛi, to make brown or red.

Kapīta, *as*, m., N. of a tree, L.

Kapītaka, *am*, n. Berberis Asiatica, Bhpr.

Kapītana, *as*, m. Spondias Mangifera; Thespesia Populnea; Acacia Sirisa; Ficus Religiosa; Areca Faufel; Ægle Marmelos, Suśr.

कपिङ्गल *kapiṅgala*, v. l. for the next, L.

कपिञ्जल *kapiñjala*, *as*, m. (etym. doubtful) the francoline partridge, heathcock, VS.; TS.; ŚBr.; Suśr. &c.; Cuculus Melanoleucus (= *caṭaka*), L.; N. of a Vidyādhara, Bālar.; of a man, Kād.; of a sparrow, Pañcat.; (*ā*), f., N. of a river, VP. **Kapiñjalâda**, m., N. of a man; (cf. *kāpiñjalādi*.) **Kapiñjalârma**, n., N. of an old city (cf. *arma*), Kāś. on Pāṇ. vi, 2, 90.

कपुच्छल *kapúcchala*, *am*, n. a tuft of hair on the hind part of the head (hanging down like a tail), Gobh. ii, 9, 18; the fore-part of a sacrificial ladle (i. e. the part with which the fluid is skimmed off), ŚBr.

Kapútsala, v. l. for the above.

Kapushṭikā, f. = the next, L.

Kapushṇikā, f. a tuft of hair on each side of the head, Gobh. ii, 9, 19.

कपूय *kapūya*, mf(*ā*)n. smelling badly, stinking, ChUp. v, 10, 7; Nir.

कपृथ् *kápṛith*, *t*, m. (fr. 4. *ka* and √*prī*, Sāy.), 'causing or increasing pleasure,' membrum virile, RV. x, 86, 16; 17; N. of Indra [Sāy.], RV. x, 101, 12.

Kapṛithá, *as*, m., N. of Indra [Sāy.], RV. x, 101, 12.

कपोत *kapóta*, *as*, m. (√*kav*, Uṇ. i, 63; fr. 2. *ka* + *pota*?), a dove, pigeon, (esp.) the spotty-necked pigeon (in the Vedas often a bird of evil omen), RV.; AV.; VS.; MBh. &c.; a bird in general, L.; a frieze, cornice; a particular position of the hands, Comm. on Śak.; PSarv. &c.; the grey colour of a pigeon, Suśr. ii, 280, 1; the grey ore of antimony, Suśr. ii, 84, 10; (*ī*), f. the female of a pigeon, Pañcat. **-caraṇā**, f. a kind of perfume, Bhpr. **-pāka**, m. the young of a pigeon, gaṇa *nyaṅkv-ādi*, Pāṇ. vii, 3, 53; (*ās*), m. pl., N. of a mountain-tribe, Kāś. on Pāṇ. v, 3, 113; (*ī*), f. a princess of this tribe, ib. **-pāda**, mfn. pigeon-footed, gaṇa *hasty-ādi*, Pāṇ. v, 4, 138 (Kāś. reads *kaṭola*). **-pāli**, f. frieze, cornice, VarBṛS. **-pālikā**, f. a dove-cot, pigeon-house, aviary, L. **-pālī**, f. id. **-bāṇā**, f. a kind of perfume, L. **-retasa**, m., N. of a man. **-roman**, m., N. of a king, MBh.; Hariv. &c. **-vakra**, n. a particular plant, L. **-vaṅkā**, f., N. of a medicinal plant (used as a remedy for the stone), Suśr. **-varṇa**, mfn. pigeon-coloured, lead-grey, Suśr.; (*ī*), f. small cardamoms, L. **-vallī**, f., N. of a plant, Bhpr. **-vegā**, f. Ruta Graveolens, L. **-sāra**, m. the grey ore of antimony, L. **-hasta**, m. a particular position of the hands. **-hastaka**, m. id. **Kapotâṅghri**, f. a kind of perfume, L. **Kapotâñjana**, n. ore of antimony, L. **Kapotâbha**, mfn. pigeon-coloured, lead-grey, Suśr.; (*as*), m. a pale or dirty white colour, W. **Kapotâri**, m. 'enemy of the pigeons,' a hawk, falcon, L.

Kapotaka, mf(*ikā*)n. pigeon-coloured, lead-grey, Pat.; (*as*), m. a small pigeon or dove, MBh.; VarBṛS.; Pañcat. &c.; a particular position of the hands; (*ikā*), f. the female of a pigeon, Pañcat.; (*ī*), f. a kind of bird (= *śyāmā*), VarBṛS.; (*am*), n. ore of antimony, Car.

Kapotakīya, mf(*ā*)n. abounding in or relating to pigeons, gaṇa *naḍâdi*, Pāṇ. iv, 2, 91.

Kapotin, mfn. pigeon-shaped, ŚBr. xi, 7, 3, 2; having pigeons, L.

कपोल *kapola*, *as*, m. (ifc. f. *ā*), (√*kap*, Uṇ. i, 67) the cheek (of men or elephants &c.), Suśr.; Yājñ.; Ragh. &c.; (*ās*), m. pl., N. of a school belonging to the white Yajur-veda; (*ī*), f. the fore-part of the knee, knee-cap or pan, L. **-kavi**, m., N. of a poet. **-kāsha**, m. any object against which the cheeks or temples are rubbed, Kir.; the elephant's temples and cheeks, W. **-tāḍana**, n. striking the cheeks (as a token of confession of fault), MW. **-pattra**, n. a mark painted on the cheek, Naish. vii, 60. **-pāli**, *is*, *ī*, f. the side of a cheek, Kād. **-phalaka**, n. (ifc. f. *ā*), the cheek-bone, Amar. **-bhitti**, f. id., Bhartṛ.; Śiś. **-rāga**, m. colour or flush in the cheek.

कप्फिण *kapphiṇa*, *as*, m., N. of a man (Buddh.)

Kapphilla, **kaphina**, **kaphila**, **kamphilla**, vv. ll. for the above.

कप्लक *káplaka*, mfn. = *kapivad-gamana-samartha*, Sāy., TBr. ii, 7, 18, 4 (the text has the reading *kálpaka*).

कफ *kapha*, *as*, m. phlegm (as one of the three humors of the body, see also *vāyu* and *pitta*), Suśr.; watery froth or foam in general; (cf. *abdhi-k°*, *megha-k°*, &c.) **-kara**, mfn. producing phlegm; occasioning cold. **-kūrcikā**, f. saliva, spittle, L. **-kshaya**, m. pulmonary consumption. **-gaṇḍa**, m. a particular disease of the throat, ŚārṅgS. **-gulma**, m. a disease of the belly. **-ghna**, mf(*ī*)n. removing phlegm, antiphlegmatic, curing colds (said of several plants), Suśr.; (*ī*), f. a particular plant, L. **-ja**, mfn. arising from or produced by phlegm, Suśr. **-jvara**, m. fever arising from excess of phlegm. **-da**, mfn. = *-kara* above. **-nāśana**, mfn. = *-ghna* above. **-prāya**, m. phlegmatic, Suśr. **-vardhaka**, mfn. exciting or increasing phlegm. **-vardhana**, mfn. id.; (*as*), m. a species of Tabernæmontana. **-°vātika**, mfn. (fr. *kapha-vāta*), one in whom phlegm and wind prevail. **-virodhin**, mfn. obstructing the phlegm; (*ī*), n. black pepper, L. **-vairin**, m. id., L. **-sambhava**, mfn. arising from phlegm, Suśr. **-hara**, mfn. removing phlegm, antiphlegmatic, ib. **-hṛit**, mfn. id., ib. **Kaphâtmaka**, mfn. phlegmatic, Suśr. **Kaphântaka** or **°ika**, m., N. of a plant, L. **Kaphâri**, m. dry ginger, L.

Kaphala, mfn. phlegmatic, Suśr.

Kaphin, mfn. id., L.; (*ī*), m. an elephant, L.; v. l. for *kapphiṇa*, q. v.; (*inī*), f., N. of a river, L.

Kaphelū, *ūs*, m. Cardia Latifolia, Comm. on Uṇ. i, 95.

कफणि *kaphaṇi*, *is*, m. f. the elbow, L.

Kaphoṇi, *is*, m. f. the elbow, L. **-guḍa**, m. a ball on the elbow (as a symbol of unsteadiness or uncertainty). **-ghāta**, m. a stroke with the elbow, L.

Kaphoṇiguḍāya, Nom. Ā. *°āyate*, to be like a ball on the elbow, i. e. to be unsteady or uncertain, Sarvad. 116, 12.

कफौड *kaphauḍá*, *as*, m. the elbow (? BRD.), AV. x, 2, 4.

कब् *kab*, cl. 1. Ā. *kabate*, *cakabe*, *kabitā*, &c., to colour, tinge with various hues, Dhātup. x, 17; to praise, Vop.; (cf. *kav*.)

कबन्ध *kábandha*, *as*, *am*, m. n. (sometimes written *kávandha*) a big barrel or cask, a large-bellied vessel (metaphorically applied to a cloud), RV.; AV. ix, 4, 3; x, 2, 3; (ep.) the clouds which obscure the sun at sunset and sunrise (sometimes personified), MBh.; the belly, Nir.; a headless trunk (shaped like a barrel; esp. one retaining vitality, W.), R.; Pañcat.; Ragh. &c.; (*as*), m., N. of the Rākshasa Danu (son of Śrī; punished by Indra for insolently challenging him to combat; his head and thighs were forced into his body by a blow from the god's thunderbolt, leaving him with long arms and a huge mouth in his belly; it was predicted that he would not recover his original shape until his arms were cut off by Rāma and Lakshmaṇa), R. iii, 69, 27 ff.; Hariv.; Ragh. &c.; N. of Rāhu, L.; N. of certain Ketus (96 in number), VarBṛS.; N. of an Ātharvaṇa and Gandharva, ŚBr. xiv (*kabándha*); VP. &c.; (*am*), n. water, Sāy. & L. **-tā**, f., **-tva**, n. headlessness, decapitation, Śiś. **-muni**, m., N. of a sage, VāyuP. **-vadha**, m. 'the slaying of Kabandha,' N. of a chapter of the Padma-purāṇa.

Kabandhin, mfn. 'bearing huge vessels of water or clouds' ('endowed with water,' Sāy.), N. of the Maruts, RV. v, 54, 8; (*ī*), m., N. of a Kātyāyana, PraśnUp.

कबर *kabara*. See *kavara*.

कबित्थ *kabittha* = *kapittha*, q. v., L.

कबिल *kabila* = *kapila*, q. v., L.

कबुलि *kabuli*, *is*, f. the hinder part of an animal, L.

कब्रु *kábru*, *u*, n. (perhaps erroneous for *kambu* and = *kambūka*, NBD.), AV. xi, 3, 6.

कम् 1. *kám*, ind. (Gk. κεν) well (opposed to *a-kam*, 'ill'), TS.; ŚBr. &c.; a particle placed after the word to which it belongs with an affirmative sense, 'yes,' 'well' (but this sense is generally so weak that Indian grammarians are perhaps right in enumerating *kam* among the expletives, Nir.; it is often found attached to a dat. case, giving to that case a stronger meaning, and is generally placed at the end of the Pāda, e. g. *ájījana óshadhīr bhójanāya kám*, thou didst create the plants for actual food, RV. v, 83, 10), RV.; AV.; TS. v; *kam* is also used as an enclitic with the particles *nu*, *su*, and *hi* (but is treated in the Pada-pāṭha as a separate word; in this connection *kam* has no accent but once, AV. vi, 110, 1), RV.; AV.; a particle of interrogation (like *kad* and *kim*), RV. x, 52, 3; (sometimes, like *kim* and *kad*, at the beginning of compounds) marking the strange or unusual character of anything or expressing reproach, L.; head, L.; food, Nir.; water, Nir.; Nigh.; happiness, bliss, L. **Káṃ-vat,** mfn. blissful, ŚBr. xiii. **Kaṃ-da,** m. 'water-giver,' a cloud, L.

Kamya, mfn. happy, prosperous, L.

Kaṃyu, kaṃyya, kaṃyyu, kaṃva, mfn. id., ib.

Kanta, kanti, kantu, mfn. id., T.

Kambha, mfn. id., L.

कम् 2. *kam*, cl. 1. Ā. (not used in the conjugational tenses) *cakame, kamitā, kamishyate, acakamata,* Dhātup. xii, 10; to wish, desire, long for, RV. v, 36, 1; x, 117, 2; AV. xix, 52, 3; ŚBr.; Ragh. &c.; to love, be in love with, have sexual intercourse with, ŚBr. xi; BhP.: Caus. Ā. (ep. also P.) *kāmayate, -ti, kāmayām-cakre, acīkamata,* &c.; to wish, desire, long for (with acc. or inf. or Pot., Pāṇ. iii, 3, 157; e.g. *kāmaye bhuñjīta bhavān,* I wish your worship may eat; *kāmaye dātum,* I wish to give, Kāś.), RV.; AV.; TS.; MBh. &c.; to love, be in love with, have sexual intercourse with, RV. x, 124, 5; 125, 5; ŚBr.; MBh. &c.; to cause any one to love, Ṛitus. (in that sense, P.; Vop.); (with *bahu* or *aty-artham*) to rate or value highly, R.: Desid. *cikamishate* and *cikāmayishate*: Intens. *caṃkamyate;* [cf. Lat. *comis;* also *amo,* with the loss of the initial, for *camo; cā-rus* for *cam-rus:* Hib. *caemh,* 'love, desire; fine, handsome, pleasant;' *caomhach,* 'a friend, companion;' *caomhaim,* 'I save, spare, protect:' Armen. *kamim.*]

Kamaka, *as,* m., N. of a man; (*ās*), m. pl. the descendants of this man, gaṇa *upakâdi,* Pāṇ. ii, 4, 69.

Kamaṭha, *as,* m. (Uṇ. i, 102) a tortoise, BhP.; Pañcat. &c.; a porcupine, L.; a bamboo, L.; N. of a king, MBh.; of a Muni; of a Daitya; (*as* or *am*), m. or n. a water-jar (esp. one made of a hollow gourd or cocoa-nut, and used by ascetics), L.; (*ī*), f. a female tortoise, a small one Śāntiś. **-pati,** m. the king of tortoises. **Kamaṭhâsura-vadha,** m. 'the slaying of the Asura Kamaṭha,' N. of a section of the Gaṇeśa-purāṇa.

Kama-dyū́, *ūs,* f. (= *kāmasya dīpanī,* Sāy.), N. of a woman, RV. x, 65, 12.

Kamana, mf(*ā*)n. wishing for, desirous, libidinous, L.; beautiful, desirable, lovely, BhP.; (*as*), m., N. of Kāma, L.; of Brahmā, L.; Jonesia Asoka, L. **-cchada,** m. 'having beautiful plumage,' a heron, L.

Kamanīya, mfn. to be desired or wished for, desirable, Kum. i, 37; lovely, pleasing, beautiful, Śak. 62 b; Bhartṛ. &c. **-tā,** f., **-tva,** n. desirableness, loveliness, beauty.

Kamara, mfn. (Uṇ. iii, 132) desirous, lustful, L.

Kámala, mfn. (Comm. on Uṇ. i, 106) pale-red, rose-coloured, TS. vii, 3, 18, 1; (*kamálā*) AV. viii, 6, 9 (desirous, lustful, BRD.); (*as*), m. a species of deer, L.; the Indian crane (Ardea Sibirica), L.; N. of Brahmā, L.; of a pupil of Vaiśampāyana, Kāś.; of an Asura, GaṇP.; (in mus.) a particular Dhruvaka (q. v.); (*as, am*), m. n. a lotus, lotus-flower, Nelumbium, Suśr.; Śak.; Bhartṛ. &c.; (*ā*), f., N. of Lakshmī, BhP.; Sāh.; Kathās.; wealth, prosperity, Subh.; N. of Dākshāyaṇī, MatsyaP.; of one of the mothers in the retinue of Skanda, MBh.; of the wife of Jayāpīḍa, Rājat.; an excellent woman, L.; an orange, Tantras.; (*ī, am*), f. n., N. of a metre (four times three short syllables); (*am*), n. a particular constellation, VarBṛ.; water, Kir. v, 25; copper, L.; the bladder, L.; a medicament, drug, L.; N. of a town built by Kamalā, Rājat.; a particular number, Buddh. **-kīṭa, -kīra,** m. (?), N. of two villages, gaṇa *palady-ādi,* Pāṇ. iv, 2, 110 (Kāś.) **-khaṇḍa,** n. a group of lotuses, Kāś. on Pāṇ. iv, 2, 51. **-garbha,** mfn. 'offspring of the lotus,' N. of Brahmā, Kathās.; the lotus-cup. **-garbhâbha,** mfn. bright as the lotus-cup. **-ja,** m., N. of Brahmā, VarBṛS.; Kathās.; (cf. the last.) **-deva,** m., N. of a man; (*ī*), f., N. of the wife of king Lalitāditya (and mother of king Kuvalāpīḍa). **-nayana,** m. 'lotus-eyed,' N. of a king. **-nābha,** m. 'lotus-naveled,' N. of Vishṇu, BhP.; Kād. **-netra,** mfn. lotus-eyed, Dhūrtas. **-pattra,** n. leaf of the lotus-flower. **-pattrâksha,** mfn. having eyes like leaves of the lotus-flower, R. &c. **-bāndhava,** m. 'the friend of the lotus,' the sun, Kād. **-bāla-nāla,** n. the stalk of a young lotus. **-°bālanālaya,** Nom. Ā. °*yate,* to be like the stalk of a young lotus, Siṇhās. **-bhava,** m. 'sprung from the lotus,' N. of Brahmā, VarBṛS. **-bhavana,** m. id. **-bhidā,** f., N. of a village, gaṇa *palady-ādi,* Pāṇ. iv, 2, 110. **-bhū,** m. 'rising out of a lotus,' N. of Brahmā, Viddh. **-mati,** m., N. of a man, Kathās. **-maya,** mfn. consisting of lotus-flowers, Hcar.; Kād. **-yoni,** m. 'lotus-born,' N. of Brahmā, VarBṛS.; Hcat. **-locana,** mf(*ā*)n. lotus-eyed; (*ā*), f., N. of a woman, Kathās. **-vatī,** f. = *-devī* above, Rājat.; N. of a princess, Kathās. **-vadana,** mf(*ā*)n. lotus-faced, Śrutab. **-vana,** n. a cluster of lotuses; *-maya,* mfn. consisting of masses of lotuses, nothing but lotuses, Kād. **-vardhana,** m., N. of a king of Kampana, Rājat. **-varman,** m., N. of a king, Kathās. **-śīla,** m., N. of a scholar, Buddh. **-shashṭhī-vrata,** n., N. of a particular religious observance, BhavP. **-saptamī-vrata,** n. id., MatsyaP. **-saṃbhava,** m., N. of Brahmā. **Kamalâkara,** m. a mass of lotuses; a lake or pool where lotuses abound, R.; Ratnāv. &c.; N. of the author of a commentary on the Mitāksharā, and of several other authors and men; *-tīrtha-yātrā,* f., N. of a work. **Kamalā-keśava,** m., N. of a shrine built by Kamalavatī, Rājat. **Kamalâksha,** mf(*ī*)n. lotus-eyed; (*ī*), f., N. of a mother in the retinue of Skanda, MBh.; (*am*), n., N. of a town, MatsyaP. **Kamalâgrajā,** f. 'born before Lakshmī,' N. of A-lakshmī or Bad Luck. **Kamalā-chāyā,** f. (or °*cchāyā*), N. of an Apsaras, VP. **Kamalā-tīrtha,** n., N. of a Tīrtha, SkandaP. **Kamalâdi,** m., N. of a gaṇa, Comm. on Pāṇ. iv, 2, 51. **Kamalânandana,** n. 'Kamalā's joy,' N. of Miśra-dinakara. **Kamalā-pati,** m., N. of a man. **Kamalāpāta,** m., N. of a man. **Kamalā-bhakta,** m. id. **Kamalâyatâksha,** mfn. having large lotus-eyes. **Kamalâyudha,** m., N. of a poët. **Kamalâlaya,** m., N. of a country, MatsyaP.; (*ā*), f. 'abiding in a lotus,' N. of Lakshmī, R. **Kamalâsana,** n. a lotus-flower serving as a seat, RāmatUp.; a particular manner of sitting; (*as*), m. 'having a lotus as seat,' N. of Brahmā, MBh.; BhP.; Kum. &c.; *-stha,* m. id. **Kamalā-haṭṭa,** m., N. of a market-place (founded by Kamalavatī), Rājat. 1. **Kamalâhāsa,** m. the 'smiling,' i. e. opening or shutting of a lotus. 2. **Kamalāhāsa,** Nom. (fr. the above) P. °*sati,* to smile like a lotus, Dhūrtas. **Kamalêkshaṇa,** mf(*ā*)n. lotus-eyed, MBh.; R. &c. **Kamalôttara,** n. safflower (Carthamus Tinctorius), L. **Kamalôtpalamālin,** mfn. having garlands of Kamala and Utpala lotuses, MBh. iii. **Kamalôdaya,** m., N. of a man, Kathās. **Kamalôdbhava,** m., N. of Brahmā, Kathās.

Kamalaka, *am,* n., N. of a town, Rājat.

Kamalinī, f. the lotus plant, Kathās.; a number of lotus plants; a pool or place abounding with them, MBh.; Ragh. &c. **-kānta,** m. 'the lover of the lotus,' N. of the sun, Kathās. **-bandhu,** m. id.

Kamalikā, f. a small lotus, Kād.

Kamā, f. loveliness, beauty, radiance, L.

Kamitṛi, mfn. lustful, desirous, cupidinous, Naish.; the male, husband, Hcar.

Kamra, mf(*ā*)n. (Pāṇ. iii, 2, 167) loving, being in love, desirous, L.; desirable, beautiful, lovely, Kāvyād.; (*ā*), f. a kind of musical instrument.

Kānta, &c. See s. v.

Kāma, &c. See s. v.

कमण्डलु *kamaṇḍalu, us, u,* m. n. (in the Veda *ūs,* f. according to Pāṇ. iv, 1, 71) a gourd or vessel made of wood or earth used for water (by ascetics and religious students), a water-jar, MBh.; BhP.; Yājñ. &c.; a kind of animal, ĀśvŚr.; (*us*), m. Ficus Infectoria, L.; (*ūs*), f. a kind of animal, Pāṇ. iv, 1, 72.

कमन्तक *kamantaka, as,* m., N. of a man; (*ās*), m. pl., N. of his descendants, gaṇa *upakâdi,* Pāṇ. ii, 4, 69.

कमन्दक *kamandaka, as,* m.; (*ās*), m. pl. id., ib.

कमन्ध *kamandha, am,* n. water, L.; (cf. *kabandha.*)

कमल *kamala.* See col. 1.

कमुञ्जा *kamuñjā,* f. a tuft or lock of hair.

Kamuñja, f. id., Parāś.

कम्प् *kamp,* cl. 1. Ā. (ep. also P.) *kampate (-ti), cakampe, kampishyate, a-kampishṭa, kampitā* (Dhātup. x, 13), to tremble, shake, MBh.; BhP.; Pañcat. &c.: Caus. P. Ā. *kampayati, -te,* to cause or make to tremble, shake, MBh.; R. &c.; to pronounce in a tremulous manner (i. e. with a thrill or shake): Desid. *cikampishate:* Intens. *caṃkampyate, caṃkampti;* [cf. Gk. *κάμπτω;* Hib. *cabhōg,* 'hastening.']

Kampa, *as,* m. trembling, tremor, trembling motion, shaking, MBh.; Suśr. &c.; earthquake (cf. *bhūmi-kampa, mahī-k°,* &c.); tremulous or thrilling pronunciation (a modification of the Svarita accent which may take place if the Svarita syllable is followed by an Udātta syllable), Nir. &c.; a kind of time (in mus.); N. of a man. **-rāja,** m., N. of a man. **-lakshman,** m. air, wind, L. **Kampâṅka,** m. id., L. **Kampânvita,** mfn. affected with trembling, agitated.

Kampana, mf(*ā*)n. trembling, shaken, unsteady; causing to tremble, shaking, MBh.; (*as*), m. a kind of weapon, MBh. i, 2836; R.; a kind of fever, Bhpr.; the cool or dewy season (from about the middle of January to that of March), L.; N. of a king, MBh. ii, 117; of a country near Kāśmīra, Rājat.; (*ā*), f., N. of a river, MBh.; VP.; (*am*), n. trembling, quivering, Suśr.; an earthquake, MBh. v, 7239; quivering or thrilling pronunciation (see *kampa*), Comm. on RPrāt.; the act of shaking, swinging, KātyŚr.; Suśr. i, 85, 9; Tarkas. &c.

Kampanīya, mfn. to be shaken, movable, vibratory.

Kampāka, a wrong reading for *kampâṅka* above.

Kampāya, Nom. Ā. *kampāyate,* to tremble, shake, Comm. on VarBṛS.

Kampikā, f. a kind of musical instrument.

Kampita, mfn. trembling, shaking, MBh.; Ṛitus.; caused to tremble, shaken, swung, MBh. iv, 1290; Tattvas.; (*am*), n. trembling, a tremor.

Kampin, mfn. trembling, quivering, Kathās.; (ifc.) causing to tremble, shaking; (cf. *śiraḥ-kampin.*)

Kampila, *as,* m., N. of a man, Buddh.; = the next, L.

Kampilya, *as,* m., N. of a pigment (produced from the plant Rottleria Tinctoria), L.

Kampilyaka, m. (Car.), **kampilla,** m. (Suśr.), **kampillaka,** m. (Suśr.), **kampilvaka,** m. (Car.), and **kampīla,** n. (L.), id.

Kampya, mfn. to be shaken or made to tremble (cf. *a-kampya*); to be moved away from one's place; to be pronounced in a quivering or trilling manner.

Kampra, mf(*ā*)n. trembling, shaken, Pāṇ.; Bālar.; movable; agile, quick, KātyŚr.; Lāṭy.; unsteady, uncertain, Naish.

कम्फिल्ल *kamphilla, as,* m., v. l. for *kapphiṇa,* q. v.

कम्ब् *kamb,* cl. 1. P. *kambati,* to go, move; (v. l. *karb.*)

कम्बर *kambara,* mfn. variegated, spotted, L.; (*as*), m. variegated colour, L.

कम्बल *kambalá, as, am,* m. n. (√*kam,* Comm. on Uṇ. i, 108), a woollen blanket or cloth or upper garment, AV. xiv, 2, 66; 67; MBh.; Hit. &c.; (*as*), m. a dew-lap, VarBṛS.; Hcat.; a small worm or insect, L.; a sort of deer with a shaggy hairy coat, L.; N. of a teacher; of a man; of a Nāga, MBh.; MārkP. &c.; (*am*), n. water (cf. *kamala*); N. of a Varsha in Kuśa-dvīpa, MBh. vi, 454. **-kāraka,** m. a woollen-cloth manufacturer. **-cārāyaṇīya,** *ās,* m. pl. a nickname of a school of the Cārāyaṇas, Pat. on Kāty., on Pāṇ. i, 1, 73; (cf. *odana-pāṇinīya.*) **-dhāvaka,** m. one who cleans woollen clothes. **-barhisha,** m., N. of a man, Hariv.; BhP.; VP. **-vāhya** or **-vāhyaka,** m. = *kambali-vāhyaka* below. **-hāra,** m., N. of a man; (*ās*), m. pl. the descendants of this man, gaṇa *yaskâdi,* Pāṇ. ii, 4, 63. **Kambalārṇa** (for *kambala-ṛiṇa,* Vārtt. on Pāṇ. vi, 1, 89), n. a debt consisting of a woollen blanket or garment. **Kambalâlukā,** f. a kind of vegetable, L.

Kambalaka, *as,* m. a woollen cloth or garment, Suśr.; (*ikā*), f., gaṇa *pakshâdi,* Pāṇ. iv, 2, 80.

Kambalin, mfn. covered with a woollen cloth or blanket, wearing a woollen garment, Jain.; (*ī*), m. 'having a dew-lap,' an ox, L. **Kambali-vāhyaka,** n. a carriage drawn by oxen.

Kambalīya, mf(*ā*)n. fit for woollen blankets &c., Kāś. on Pāṇ. v, 1, 3.

Kambalya, *am*, n. (ifc. f. *ā*, Pāṇ. iv, 1, 22) one hundred Palas of wool (necessary for making a woollen blanket), Pāṇ. v, 1, 3.

कम्बलायिन् *kambalāyin*, *ī*, m. a sort of kite, W. (?)

कम्बि *kambi*, *is*, f. a ladle or spoon, L.; a shoot or branch or joint of a bamboo, L.

कम्बु *kambu*, *us*, m. (*u*, n., L.) a conch; a shell, MBh. iv, 255; BhP.; Kathās. &c.; (*us*), m. a bracelet or ring made of shells, MBh.; a bracelet in general, L.; three lines or marks in the neck (indicative of good fortune), VarBṛS.; the neck, L.; an elephant, L.; a tube-shaped bone, L.; a vein or tubular vessel of the body, W.; a sort of Curcuma, L. — **kaṇṭha**, mf(*ī*)n. 'shell-neck,' having folds in the neck like a spiral shell (cf. above), Kathās. — **kaṃdhara**, mfn. id., BhP. — **kāshṭhā**, f. Physalis Flexuosa, L. — **grīva**, mf(*ā*)n. = *-kaṇṭha* above, MBh.; R. &c.; (*as*), m. 'shell-neck,' N. of a tortoise, Pañcat.; (*ā*), f. a shell-like neck (i. e. one marked with three lines, cf. above), L. — **ja**, m. a kind of drum. — **pushpī**, f. Andropogon Aciculatus, L. — **mālinī**, f. id., L. **Kambv-āṭāyin**, m. the bird Falco Cheela, L.

Kambuka, *as*, m. a conch, shell, L.; a mean person, W.; (*ā*), f. Physalis Flexuosa, L.; (*am*), n., N. of a town, Kathās.

Kambū, *ūs*, m. (√*kam*, Uṇ. i, 95), a thief, plunderer; a bracelet, W.

Kambūka, *as*, m. the husk of rice, AV. xi, 1, 29; Gṛihyas.

Kamboja, *ās*, m. pl., N. of a people and its country; (*as*), m. the king of this people, Pāṇ. iv, 1, 175; a shell, L.; a species of elephant, L.; (cf. *kāmboja*.) — **muṇḍa**, mfn. bald like a Kamboja, gaṇa *mayūra-vyaṅsakâdi*, Pāṇ. ii, 1, 72; (cf. Hariv. 780.) **Kambojâdi**, m., N. of a gaṇa, Kāty on Pāṇ. iv, 1, 175.

कम्भ *kambha*. See p. 252, col. 1.

कम्भारी *kambhārī*, f. Gmelina Arborea, L.

कम्भु *kambhu*, *u*, n. the fragrant root of Andropogon Muricatus.

कम्वत् *kam-vat*. See p. 252, col. 1.

कय *káya* (Ved. for 2. *ka*; only gen. sg. with *cid*), every one (e. g. *nú shū́ namâtimatiṃ káyasya cit*, bow well down the haughtiness of every one, RV. i, 129, 5), RV. i, 27, 8; viii, 25, 15; [cf. Zd. *kaya*; Armen. *ui*.]

Káyā, ind. (inst. fem. of 2. *ka*) in what manner? RV.

कयस्था *kayasthā*, f. a medicinal plant, L.; (v. l. for *vayaḥsthā*.)

कयाद् *kayâd*, v. l. for *kravyâd*, q. v., SV.

कयाधु *kayādhu*, *us* (*ūs*, v. l.), f., N. of Hiraṇyakaśipu's wife, BhP. vi, 18, 12; Comm. on TBr.

कय्य *kayya*, *as*, m., N. of a prince (founder of a shrine and a Vihāra called after him), Rājat.

Kayyaka, *as*, m., N. of a man, Rājat.

कय्यट *kayyaṭa*, *as*, m. = *kaiyyaṭa*, q. v.

कर 1. *kará* (for 2. see p. 254, col. 3), mf(*ī*, rarely *ā*)n. (√1. *kṛi*), a doer, maker, causer, doing, making, causing, producing (esp. ifc.; cf. *duḥkha-kara*, *bhayam-k°*, *sampat-k°*, &c.; cf. Lat. *cerus*, 'creator'), AV. xii, 2, 2; Mn.; Pañcat. &c.; helping, promoting, RV. i, 116, 13; (*as*), m. the act of doing, making &c. (ifc.; cf. *īshat-kara*, *su-k°*, *dush-k°*, &c.); 'the doer,' the hand, RV. x, 67, 6; MBh.; Mn. &c.; a measure (the breadth of twenty-four thumbs); an elephant's trunk, MBh.; Pañcat. &c.; the claws of a crab, Hit.; symbolical expression for the number two; the lunar mansion Hasta, VarBṛS. — **kacchapikā**, f. a particular position of the fingers. — **kaṭa**, m. an elephant's temple (cf. *karaṭa*); Centropus Pyropterus, Nigh. — **kaṇṭaka**, m. 'hand-thorn,' a finger-nail, L. — **kamala**, n. 'hand-lotus,' the hand (esp. of a lover or a mistress), Ṛitus.; (cf. *-padma*, *-paṅkaja*, &c. below.) — **karṇa**, m., N. of a man, Buddh. — **kalaśa**, m. the hand hollowed to receive water, W. — **kisalaya**, m. n. 'hand-bud,' the hand closed in the form of a bud, L.; 'hand-shoot,' the finger, Ṛitus.; Daś. — **kudmala**, n. 'hand-bud' (cf. above), the finger, W. — **kṛitâtman**, mfn. 'living from hand to mouth,' destitute, MBh. xiii, 1625. — **kosha**, m. the hand hollowed to receive water; (cf. *-kalaśa*.) — **gṛihīti**, f. the act of taking the hand, Hcar. — **graha** (1. *kara-graha*; for 2. see p. 254, col. 3), m. taking the hand (of the bride; one part of the ceremony being the placing of the bride's right hand with the palm uppermost in the right hand of the bridegroom), marriage, Kathās. — **grahaṇa** (1. *kara-grahaṇa*; for 2. see p. 254, col. 3), n. id., MBh. ii, 900; Pañcad. &c.; (cf. *pāṇi-gr°*.) — **grāham**, ind. p. so as to take the hand, Kāś. on Pāṇ. iii, 4, 39. — **grāhin** (1. *kara-grāhin*; for 2. see p. 254, col. 3), mfn. taking the hand, W.; a bridegroom, T. — **gharshaṇa**, m. a churning-stick, W.; (n.) the act of rubbing the hands together, W. — **gharshin**, m. a churning-stick, W. — **ghāṭa**, m. a kind of poisonous tree, Suśr. ii, 251, 14; 252, 2. — **cchada**, m. Trophis Aspera, Bhpr.; (*ā*), f. a species of tree (commonly called *sindūra-pushpī-vṛiksha*), L. — **ja**, m. 'produced in or from the hand,' a finger-nail, Mn.; MBh.; Suśr. &c.; Pongamia Glabra (= *karañja*), L.; (*am*), n. a kind of perfume (resembling a nail in appearance, = *vyāghra-nakha*), L.; *-vardhana*, m., N. of a prince; *-°jâkhya*, n. a perfume (= *-ja*), L. — **japya**, m., N. of a man; (*ās*), m. pl., N. of his tribe, Hariv. — **jyoḍi**, m., N. of a tree (= *hasta-jyoḍi*), L. — **tala**, m. the palm of the hand, R.; Suśr.; BhP. &c.; (*ā*), f. a knife, Kathās.; *-gata*, mfn. being in the hand or in one's possession, Pañcat.; Śak.; *-tāla*, m. clapping the hands, Gīt.; *-dhṛita*, mfn. held in the hand, W.; *-stha*, mfn. resting in the palm of the hand, W.; *-°âmalaka*, n. 'a myrobalan lying in the hand,' anything quite clear to all eyes. — **talī-√kṛi**, to take in the palm of the hand, BhP. viii, 7, 42. — **talī-kṛita**, mfn. taken in the open hand, lying open. — **tas**, ind. from the hand, out of the hand. — **tāla**, *as*, *ī*, m. f. a musical instrument, a cymbal, L.; (*am*), n. beating time by clapping the hands, Bālar. — **tālaka**, n. a cymbal; (*ikā*), f. clapping the hands, Naish.; beating time by clapping, Kathās.; a kind of cymbal, L. — **tṛiṇa**, n. Pandanus Odoratissimus, Nigh. — **toyā**, f., N. of a river in the north-east of Bengal (said to have originated from the water poured into the hand of Śiva at his marriage with Pārvatī, and thrown by him on the ground), MBh.; VP. — **toyinī**, f., N. of a river (probably = the last), MBh. xiii, 4887. — **da** (1. *kara-da*; for 2. see p. 254, col. 3), mfn. one who gives his hand, W. — **daksha**, mfn. handy, dexterous, ready, W. — **druma**, m., N. of a poisonous tree (= *kāra-skara*), L. — **dvish**, m. pl., N. of a tribe or school, TāṇḍyaBr. ii, 15, 4; iii, 6, 4. — **dvīpa**, m. Guilandina Bonducella, Nigh. — **dhṛita**, mfn. held or supported by the hand, Megh. — **nihita**, mfn. held in the hand, W. — **°m-dhama**, m., N. of two princes, MBh.; VP. &c. — **°m-dhaya**, mfn. sucking the hand, Vop. — **nyasta-kapolântam**, ind. the end of the cheek held in the hand. — **nyāsa**, m. marking the hand with mystical figures, BhP. — **paṅkaja**, m. = *-kamala* above. — **pattra**, n. a saw, Suśr.; Hit.; splashing water about while bathing, playing or gamboling in water, L.; (*ā*), f. a species of fig-tree, L.; *-vat*, m. Borassus Flabelliformis (the leaves being compared to a saw), L. — **pattraka**, n. a saw, L.; (*ikā*), f. playing in water; (cf. *-pattra*.) — **padma**, m. n. = *-kamala* above. — **parṇa**, m. Abelmoschus Esculentus, L.; a kind of Ricinus, L. — **pallava**, m. 'hand-shoot,' a finger, MārkP.; = *-kisalaya* above, T. — **pātra**, n. splashing water about while bathing (cf. *-pattra* above), L.; the hand hollowed so as to hold anything, W.; (*ī*), f. a cup made of leather, L. — **pāla** (1. *kara-pāla*; for 2. see p. 254, col. 3), m. 'hand-protecting,' a sword, scymitar, L. — **pālaka**, m. id., L.; (*ikā*), f. a cudgel, short club or wooden sword, a sword or one-edged knife, L. — **pāli**, m. a kind of sword, L. — **puṭa**, m. joining the palms of the hands in token of respect, W.; the hands joined and hollowed to receive anything, W.; a box, chest with a lid, MBh. xiv, 1928; *-°âñjali*, m. cavity made in joining the palms of the hands, R. — **puṭī**, f. the hollow of the hand, Śārṅg. — **pṛishṭha**, n. the back of the hand, W. — **praceya** (1. *kara-praceya*; for 2. see p. 254, col. 3), mfn. to be held or taken hold of by the hand, W. — **prada** (1. *kara-prada*; for 2. see p. 254, col. 3), mfn. giving the hand &c. — **prâpta**, mfn. held in the hand, obtained, possessed, Hit. — **baka**, m. a species of bird, VarBṛS. — **badara**, n. 'a jujube lying in the hand,' anything quite clear to all eyes, Vāsav. — **bāla**, see *-vāla* below. — **bhañjaka**, *ās*, m. pl., N. of a people, MBh. — **bhañjika**, v. l. for the above, VP. — **bhājana**, m., N. of a Brāhman, BhP. — **bhū**, m. a finger-nail. — **bhūshaṇa**, n. a hand-ornament, bracelet. — **maṇḍalin**, m. Achyranthes Aspera, L. — **madhya**, m. a particular measure (= *karsha*), ŚārṅgS. — **manda**, m., N. of a man. — **marda**, m. Carissa Carandas, MBh.; Suśr. &c.; (*ā*), f., N. of a river, ŚivP.; (*ī*), f. Carissa Carandas, L. — **mardaká**, m. id.; (*am*), n. the fruit of Carissa Carandas, Suśr. i, 210, 18. — **mālā**, f. the hand used as a rosary (the joints of the fingers corresponding to the beads), Tantras. &c. — **mukta**, n. (scil. *astra*) a missile, weapon thrown with the hand; a dart, javelin &c., L.; *-°têśvara*, n., N. of a temple. — **moksha**, m. the act of setting free the hand (of the bride by her father when the wedding is finished; cf. Kathās. xvi, 82), Pañcad. — **mocana**, n. id., ib. — **ruddha**, mfn. stopped by the hand, held tight or fast. — **ruha**, m. 'growing from the hand,' a finger-nail, Śak.; Bhartṛ. &c.; Unguis Odoratus, L.; *-pada*, n. a scratch with the finger-nail, Megh. 95. — **°rddhi** (*kara-ṛiddhi*) = *-tālī* above, L.; indication of luck by the hand, T. — **vartam**, ind. p. whilst turning the hand, Kāś. on Pāṇ. iii, 4, 39. — **vallī**, f. a kind of plant, L. — **vāraka**, m., N. of Skanda, L. — **vāri**, n. water from the hand. — **vāla**, m. a sword, scymitar, MBh.; BhP. &c. (cf. *-pāla* above); a finger-nail, L.; *-putrī*, f. a knife, Virac. — **vāli**, m. a kind of sword, L. — **vālikā**, f. = *-pālika* above, L. — **vinda**, m., N. of an author. — **°vindīya**, n. (fr. the last), the work of Karavinda. — **vimukti**, f., N. of a Tīrtha. — **vīra**, m. Oleander (Nerium Odorum), MBh.; Suśr.; Mṛicch.; VarBṛS.; a species of Soma, Suśr. ii, 164, 15; a sword, L.; a particular spell (for recovering a missile of mystic properties after its discharge), R.; the thumb; a cemetery, L.; N. of a Nāga, MBh. i, 1557; of a Daitya, L.; of a town on the river Veṇvā (founded by Padma-varṇa), Hariv. 5230 (cf. *kara-vīra-pura* below); of a town on the river Dṛishadvatī (the residence of Candra-śekhara), KapS.; of a mountain, BhP.; (*ā*, f. red arsenic, L.; (*ī*), f. a woman who has borne a son, a mother, L.; a good cow, L.; N. of Aditi, T.; (*am*), n. the flower of Oleander, L.; *-kanda-saṃjña*, m. a species of onion; a bulb (= *taila-kanda*), L.; *-karambhin*, n., N. of a wood, Hariv. 8954 (v. l. *karavīrākara*); *-pura*, n., N. of a town founded by Padma-varṇa (cf. *karavīra*), MBh.; *-bhujā*, f. Cajanus Indicus, L.; *-bhūshā*, f. = *-bhujā*, T.; *-māhātmya*, n., N. of a work; *-vrata*, n. a certain rite; *-°râkara*, n., N. of a wood, Hariv. — **vīraka**, m. the poisonous root of Oleander, L.; Terminalia Arjuna, L.; a sword, L.; a cemetery, L.; a particular part of the face, VarBṛS.; N. of a Nāga, Hariv.; (*ā*), f. red arsenic, Nigh.; (*am*), n. the flower of Oleander, L. — **vīrya**, m., N. of a physician, Suśr. i, 18. — **vraṇa**, m., N. of Bhīmasena, L. — **śākhā**, f. a finger, L. — **śīkara**, m. water expelled by an elephant's trunk, L. — **śuddhi**, f. cleansing the hands with fragrant flowers, Tantras. — **śūka**, m. 'hand-spicule,' a finger-nail, L. — **sāda** (1. *kara-sāda*; for 2. see p. 254, col. 3), m. languor of the hands, Pañcat. — **sūtra**, n. an auspicious string (tied to the hand at marriage &c.), T. — **stha**, mfn. lying in the hand, Naish. — **sthālin**, m. 'using the hands for a jar,' N. of Śiva, MBh. xiii, 1243. — **sthī-√kṛi**, to lay on the hand. — **spanda**, m. trembling of the hands. — **sphoṭa**, m. extending the hands, Pañcat. — **svana**, m. sound produced by clapping the hands, R. — **svāmin**, m., N. of a Tīrtha. — **hati**, f. a blow with the hand.

1. **Karâgra** (for 2. see p. 254, col. 3), n. the tip of an elephant's trunk, L.; tip of the finger, Śiś.; *-pallava*, m. 'hand-shoot,' a finger; *-ja*, m. a finger-nail. **Karâghāta**, m. a blow with the hand, Bhartṛ. **Karâṅgaṇa**, m. a much-frequented market, L. **Karâṅguli**, f. a finger of the hand, Kathās. **Karâmarda**, m. = *kara-marda*. **Karâmalaka**, n. = *karatalâmalaka*. **Karâmbuka**, m. Carissa Carandas, L. **Karâmla**, °ka, m. id., L. **Karâroṭa**, m. finger-ring. **Karâroha**, m. id., L. **Karârgala**, n. a lute, L. **Karârpita**, mfn. placed in hand. **Karâlamba**, m. a support of the hand, means of safety, Hit.; (mfn.) stretching out one's hand to support or raise another, W. **Karâlambana**, n. the act of supporting the hand, helping, sustaining. **Karênduka**, m. a sort of grass, L. **Karôtpala**, n. a lotus-hand; (cf. *-kamala* above.)

Karôdaka, n. water held in or poured into the hand, W.

1. **Karaka** (for 2. see col. 3), *as*, m. a water-vessel (esp. one used by students or ascetics), MBh.; R.; a species of bird, L.; hand (?), L.; N. of several plants (the pomegranate tree, Pongamia Glabra, Butea Frondosa, Bauhinia Variegata, Mimusops Elengi, Capparis Aphylla), L.; a cocoa-nut shell, L.; (*as, am*), m. n. a cocoa-nut shell hollowed to form a vessel; (*ās*), m. pl., N. of a people, MBh.; VP.; (*am*), n. fungus, mushroom, L.; (*ikā*), f. a wound caused by a finger-nail, Śiś. iv, 29. **—caturthī**, f. the fourth day in the dark half of the month Āśvina. **—toya**, m. the cocoa-nut tree, L. **—pātrikā**, f. a leather vessel for holding water. **Karakâmbu**, m. the cocoa-nut tree, L. **Karakâmbhas**, m. id., L.

Kárana (once *karaṇá*, RV. i, 119, 7), mf(*ī*)n. doing, making, effecting, causing (esp. ifc.; cf. *anta-karaṇa, ushṇam-k°*, &c.), R. &c.; clever, skilful, RV. i, 119, 7; (*as*), m. a helper, companion, AV. vi, 46, 2; xv, 5, 1-6; xix, 57, 3; a man of a mixed class (the son of an outcast Kshatriya, Mn. x, 22; or the son of a Śūdra woman by a Vaiśya, Yājñ. i, 92; or the son of a Vaiśya woman by a Kshatriya, MBh. i, 2446; 4521; the occupation of this class is writing, accounts &c.); a writer, scribe, W.; (in Gr.) a sound or word as an independent part of speech (or as separated from the context; in this sense usually n.), Kāś. on Pāṇ. iii, 1, 41; Pat.; Comm. on RPrāt.; (in mus.) a kind of time, Kum. vi, 40; (*ī*), f. a woman of the above mixed tribe, Yājñ. i, 95; (with *sutā*) an adopted daughter, R. (ed. Gorr.) i, 19, 9; (in arithm.) a surd or irrational number, surd root; the side of a square, Śulbas.; Comm. on VS.; a particular measure, Comm. on Kāty-Śr.; a particular position of the fingers; (*am*), n. the act of making, doing, producing, effecting, ŚBr.; MBh. &c. (very often ifc., e.g. *mushti-k°, virūpa-k°*); an act, deed, RV.; an action (esp. a religious one), Yājñ. i, 250; R.; the special business of any tribe or caste, L.; a calculation (esp. an astronomical one), VarBṛS.; an astrological division of the day (these Karaṇas are eleven, viz. *vava, valava, kaulava, taitila, gara, vaṇija, vishṭi, śakuni, catushpada, kintughna*, and *nāga*, two being equal to a lunar day; the first seven are called *a-dhruvāṇi* or movable, and fill, eight times repeated, the space from the second half of the first day in the moon's increase to the first half of the fourteenth day in its wane; the four others are *dhruvāṇi* or fixed, and occupy the four half-days from the second half of the fourteenth day in the wane of the moon to the first half of the first day in its increase), VarBṛS.; Suśr. &c.; pronunciation, articulation, APrāt.; (in Gr.) a sound or word as an independent part of speech, separated from its context, Pāṇ.; Kāś. &c., (*karaṇa* may be used in this way like *kāra*, e.g. *iti-karaṇa*, ŚāṅkhŚr.); the posture of an ascetic; a posture in sexual intercourse; instrument, means of action, Śvet-Up.; Yājñ.; Megh.; an organ of sense or of speech, VPrāt.; PārGṛ.; (in law) an instrument, document, bond, Mn. viii, 51; 52; 154; (in Gr.) the means or instrument by which an action is effected, the idea expressed by the instrumental case, instrumentality, Pāṇ. i, 4, 42; ii, 3, 18; iii, 2, 45; cause (= *kāraṇa*); a spell, charm, Kathās. (cf. *karaṇa-prayoga*); rhythm, time, Kum.; body, Megh.; Kum.; Kād.; N. of a treatise of Varāha-mihira on the motion of the planets; of a work belonging to the Śiva-darśana; a field, L.; the mind, heart, W. (cf. *antaḥ-karaṇa*); grain, W. **—kutūhala**, n., N. of a work on practical astronomy by Bhāskara. **—kesarin**, m., N. of a work. **—grāma**, m. the senses collectively, L. **—tā**, f. instrumentality, the state of being an instrument, Kāś. on Pāṇ. ii, 3, 33. **—trāṇa**, n. 'protecting the organs of sense,' the head, L. **—tva**, n. instrumentality, mediate agency, KapS. **—niyama**, m. repression or restraint of the organs of sense. **—neri** and **-nerika**, m. a kind of dance. **—paddhati**, f., N. of a work. **—prakāśa**, m., N. of a work. **—prabodha**, m., N. of a work. **—prayoga**, m. spell, charm, Kathās. xliv, 151; xlix, 147. **—yati**, f. a kind of time (in mus.) **—vat**, mfn. articulated, TPrāt. **—vinyaya**, m. manner of pronunciation, TPrāt. **—vyāpāra**, m. action of the senses, T. **—sāra**, m., N. of a work on practical astronomy by Bhāskara. **—sūtra**, n., N. of a work, Līl. **—sthāna-bheda**, m. difference of articulation or organ of pronunciation. **Karaṇâṭṭa**, n., N. of a place. **Karaṇâdhikāra**, m. a chapter on the subject of pronunciation. **Karaṇâdhipa**, m. 'lord of the organs,' the principle of life, living soul, T.; the god presiding over each sense (e.g. the sun is the lord of the eye &c.), T. **Karaṇâbda**, *ās*, m. pl. the years used in astronomical calculations, i.e. years of the Sāka era, Comm. on VarBṛS.

Karaṇi, *is*, f. doing, making (cf. *a-karaṇi*); form, aspect, Bālar. &c.

Karaṇin, mfn. having instruments, VP.; (*ī*), m., N. of a teacher.

Karaṇīya, mfn. to be done or made or effected &c., MBh.; R. &c.

Karaṇḍa, *as*, (*ī*, L.), *am*, mfn. (Uṇ. i, 128) a basket or covered box of bamboo wicker-work, BhP.; Bhartṛ. &c.; a bee-hive, honey-comb, L.; (*as*), m. a sword, L.; a sort of duck, L.; a species of plant (= *dalāḍhaka*), L.; (*am*), n. a piece of wood, block, Bhpr. **—phalaka**, m. Feronia Elephantum, L. **—vyūha**, m., N. of a Buddhist work.

Karaṇḍaka, *as, ikā*, m. f. a basket, Kathās. **—nivāpa**, m., N. of a place near Rājagṛiha. **—vat**, ind. like a basket, Kāraṇḍ.

Karaṇḍin, *ī*, m. (*karaṇḍas tad-ākāro 'sty asya*, T.) a fish, L.

1. **Karabha** (for 2. see col. 3), *as*, m. (√*kṛī*, Uṇ. iii, 122; but more probably connected with 1. *kara*), the trunk of an elephant, MBh.; Śak. &c.; a young elephant, BhP.; a camel, MBh.; Suśr. &c.; a young camel, Pañcat.; the metacarpus (the hand from the wrist to the root of the fingers), Sāh.; Comm. on Uṇ. &c.; (in mus.) a singer who wrinkles the forehead when singing; a kind of perfume, L.; a wall, L.; N. of Danta-vakra (king of the Karūshas), MBh. ii, 577; (*ā*), f. a particular plant, L.; (*ī*), f. a she-camel, L.; Tragia Involucrata, L. **—kāṇḍikā**, f. Echinops Echinatus, L. **—grāma**, m., N. of a village, Kathās. **—grīva**, m., N. of a fortress in the Vindhya mountain, Kathās. **—priya**, m. a sort of tree, L.; (*ā*), f. a sort of Alhagi, L. **—vallabha**, m. Feronia Elephantum. **Karabhâdanī**, f. a species of Alhagi (= *-priyā* above). **Karabhâshṭaka**, n., N. of a work. **Karabhôrū**, f. a woman whose thighs resemble the trunk of an elephant, Śak.; Naish. &c.

Karabhaka, *as*, m., N. of a messenger, Śak.; of a village, Kathās.; (cf. *karabha-grāma* above.)

Karabhin, *ī*, m. 'having a trunk,' an elephant, L.

Káras, *as*, n. a deed, action, RV. iv, 19, 10.

Karásna, *as*, m. the fore-part of the arm, RV.; a finger-nail, ŚāṅkhŚr.

1. **Kari**, mfn. (ifc.) causing, accomplishing (cf. *śakṛit-k°*); (*is*), m. the hand, L.

2. **Kari** (in comp. for *karin*, col. 3). **—kaṇā**, f. Piper Chaba; *-vallī*, f. id. **—kumbha**, m. the frontal globe of an elephant. **—kusumbha**, m. a fragrant powder prepared from the flowers of Nāgakeśara, L. **—kusumbhaka**, m. id. **—kṛit**, m. Pongamia Glabra, L. **—kṛishṇā**, f. Piper Chaba, Nigh. **—garjita**, n. the roaring of elephants, L. **—carman**, n. an elephant's hide. **—ja**, m. a young elephant, L. **—danta**, m. an elephant's tusk, W.; ivory, W. **—dāraka**, m. a lion, L. **—nāsā**, f. the trunk of an elephant, L. **—nāsikā**, f. a kind of musical instrument, W. **—pa**, m. the keeper of an elephant [T.], gaṇa *cūrṇâdi*, Pāṇ. vi, 2, 134. **—pattra**, n., N. of a plant; (cf. *tālīśa-pattra*.) **—patha**, m. the way of an elephant, gaṇa *deva-pathâdi*, Pāṇ. v, 3, 108. **—pippalī**, f. Pothos Officinalis, L.; Piper Chaba, L. **—pota**, m. a young elephant, L. **—bandha**, m. the post to which an elephant is tied, L. **—makara**, m. a fabulous monster, L. **—maṇḍita**, n., N. of a wood, Kathās. lxx, 40. **—mācala**, m. 'destroyer of elephants,' a lion, L. **—muktā**, f. a pearl (said to be found sometimes in an elephant's head), L. **—mukha**, m. 'elephant-faced,' N. of Gaṇeśa, L. **—yādas**, n. a water-elephant, hippopotamus, W. **—rata**, n. 'elephant's coitus,' a kind of coitus, Kir. v, 23. **—vara**, m. an excellent elephant. **—vaijayantī**, f. a flag carried by an elephant, L. **—śāvaka**, m. a young elephant under five years old, L. **—sundarikā**, f. a gauge, water-mark, L. **—skandha**, m. a herd of elephants, Kāś. on Pāṇ. iv, 2, 51. **—hasta**, m. a particular position of the hands. **Karîndra**, m. a large elephant, a war or state elephant; Indra's elephant, W.

Karika, m. ifc. (= *karin*) an elephant, Śiś. iv, 29; (*karikā*, f., see 1. *karaka*.)

Kariṇī, f. (fr. the next), a female elephant, Bhartṛ.; Vikr.; Kathās.; *-sahāya*, m. the mate of the female elephant.

Karin, mfn. doing, effecting &c.; Kāś. on Pāṇ. ii, 3, 70; (*ī*), m. 'having a trunk,' an elephant, MBh.; BhP.; Pañcat. &c.; (*iṇī*), f., see above.

Kárishṭha, mfn. (superl.) doing most, doing very much, RV. vii, 97, 7.

Karishṇu, mfn. (ifc.) doing, accomplishing, Daś.

Karishyá, mfn. to be done [= *kartavya*, Sāy.], RV. i, 165, 9.

Karishyat, mfn. (fut. p. of √1. *kṛi*, q. v.) about to do; future, AitBr.

Karīyas, mfn. (compar.) one who does more, W. (?)

Kareṭa, *as*, m. a finger-nail, L.

Kareṇu, *us*, m. (Uṇ. ii, 1) an elephant, MBh.; Pañcat. &c.; Pterospermum Acerifolium, L.; (*us* [and *ūs*, L.]), f. a female elephant, MBh.; Suśr.; Ragh. &c.; a sort of plant, Suśr. ii, 171, 16; 173, 7; the Svarabhakti (q. v.) between *r* and *h*, Comm. on TPrāt. **—pāla**, m. 'keeper of an elephant,' N. of a man. **—bhū**, m., N. of Pālakāpya, L. **—matī**, f., N. of the wife of Nakula (and daughter of a king of the Cedis), MBh. **—varya**, m. a large or powerful elephant. **—suta**, m. = *-bhū* above.

Kareṇuka, *am*, n. the poisonous fruit of the plant Kareṇu, Suśr. ii, 251, 18; (*ā*), f. a female elephant, Pañcat.

कर 2. *kara* (for 1. see p. 253, col. 1), m. (√*kṛī*), a ray of light, sunbeam, moonbeam, R.; Megh.; Pañcat. &c.; hail, L.; royal revenue, toll, tax, tribute, duty, Mn.; Yājñ.; MBh. &c. **—graha** (2. *kara-graha*; for 1. see p. 253, col. 2), m. levying or gathering taxes; a tax-gatherer. **—grahaṇa** (2. *kara-grahaṇa*), n. levying or gathering taxes. **—grāhin** (2. *kara-grāhin*), mfn. levying a tax, a tax-collector. **—jāla**, n. a pencil of rays, a stream of light, W. **—da**, mfn. paying taxes, subject to tax, tributary, MBh.; *°dī-√kṛi*, to render tributary, Hcar.; *°dī-kṛita*, mfn. made tributary, subjugated, MBh. i, 4462. **—paṇya**, n. a commodity given as tribute, MBh. ii, 1052. **—pāla** (2. *kara-pāla*; for 1. see p. 253, col. 2), m. chief tax-gatherer, Pañcat. **—praceya**, mfn. to be collected by taxes. **—prada** (2. *kara-prada*), mfn. paying taxes, tributary, MBh. iii, 14774. **—rudh**, mfn. ray-obstructing. **—vat**, mfn. paying tribute. **—sāda** (2. *kara-sāda*; for 1. see p. 253, col. 3), m. the fading away of rays, Pañcat. **—spanda** (2. *kara-spanda*; for 1. see p. 253, col. 3), m. trembling of rays. **—sphoṭa** (2. *kara-sphoṭa*; for 1. see p. 253, col. 3), m. extending the rays. **—hāra**, mfn. taking tribute, BhP. 2. **Karâgra** (for 1. see p. 253, col. 3), n. point of a ray. **Karôtkara**, m. a bundle of rays; a heavy tax, W.

2. **Karaka** (for 1. see col. 1), m. hail; toll, tax, tribute. **Karakâbhighāta**, m. shower of hail, Śārṅg. 1. **Karakāsāra**, m. a shower of hail. 2. **Karakāsāra**, Nom. P. *karakāsārati*, to pour or shower down like hail, Dhūrtas.

2. **Karabha** (for 1. see col. 2), *am*, n. the lunar mansion called Hasta, Hcat.

Karī-√kṛi, to offer as a tribute, Kathās. xix, 114.

करकायु *karakāyu*, *us*, m., N. of a son of Dhṛitarāshṭra (cf. *kanakāyu*), MBh. i, 6982.

करङ्क *karaṅka*, *as*, m. the skull, head, Kathās.; Mālatīm.; a cocoa-nut hollowed to form a cup or vessel, L.; a kind of sugar-cane (cf. the next), L.; any bone of the body, L.; [cf. Gk. κάρυον, κέρας, καρκίνος; Lat. *carina, cornu, cancer*; Eng. *horn*; cf. *karka*.] **—śāli**, m. a sort of sugar-cane.

Karaṅkiṇī, f., N. of a Yoginī, Hcat.

करङ्गण *karaṅgaṇa* (v. l. for *karāṅgaṇa*), m. a market, fair, W.

करचुलि *karaculi*, *is*, m., N. of a country, Viddh.

करञ्ज *kárañja*, *as*, m. the tree Pongamia Glabra (used medicinally), Āp.; Suśr.; MBh. iii; N. of an enemy of Indra (slain by this god), RV. i, 53, 8; (*ī*), f. Galedupa Piscidia, Bhpr. **—phalaka**, m. Feronia Elephantum, L. **—há**, mfn. pernicious to Karañja, RV. x, 48, 8.

Karañjaka, *as, ikā*, m. f. Pongamia Glabra, MBh.; R.; Suśr.; Verbesina Scandens, L.

करट karaṭa, as, m. an elephant's temple, MBh.; Bhartṛ. &c.; the spot between the forehead and ear of a bird, VarBṛS.; a crow, BhP. v, 14, 29; Śāntiś. &c.; a kind of drum, Comm. on VarBṛS.; a man of a low or degraded profession, L.; a bad Brāhman, L.; an atheist, unbeliever, impugner of the doctrines of the Veda, L.; a kind of funeral ceremony, L.; Carthamus Tinctorius, L.; (*ās*), m. pl., N. of a people, MBh. vi, 370; VP.; of a royal dynasty; (*ā*), f. an elephant's temple; a cow difficult to be milked, L.; (*ī*), f. a crow, L.; (mfn.) dark-red, VarBṛS. 61, 2; 6. **Karaṭā-mukha**, n. the spot where an elephant's temple bursts, MBh.

Karaṭaka, *as*, m. a crow, L.; N. of a jackal, Pañcat.; Hit. &c.

Karaṭin, *ī*, m. an elephant, Subh. **Karaṭi-kautuka**, n., N. of a work treating on elephants.

करटु karaṭu, us, m. the Numidian crane, L.; (cf. *kareṭavyā, kareṭu*, &c.)

करण karaṇa, &c. See p. 254, col. 1.

करण्ड karaṇḍa. See p. 254, col. 2.

करथ karatha, as, m., N. of a physician, BrahmavP.

करन्थ karantha, ās, m. pl., N. of a people, VP.

करफु karaphu, a particular high number, L. (Buddh.)

करभ karabha, &c., for 1. see p. 254, col. 2; for 2., p. 254, col. 3.

करम karama, as, m. (= *kalama*) a reed for writing with, Kāraṇḍ.

करमट्ट karamaṭṭa, as, m. the betel-nut tree, L.

करमरी karamarī, f. a prisoner, L.

करमाल karamāla, as, m. smoke (probably a corruption of *khatamāla*).

करम्ब karamba, mfn. (√1. *kṛi*, Uṇ. iv, 82), mixed; set, inlaid, W.; (*as*), m. a kind of gruel.

Karambita, mfn. intermingled, mixed, Gīt.; Naish.; Viddh. &c.; pounded, reduced to grains or dust, W.; set, inlaid, W.

करम्भ karambhá, as, m. groats or coarsely-ground oats &c.; a dish of parched grain, a cake or flour or meal mixed with curds, a kind of gruel (generally offered to Pūshan as having no teeth to masticate hard food), RV.; AV.; VS. &c.; a mixture; N. of a poisonous plant, Suśr.; of a son of Śakuni and father of Devarāta, Hariv.; of the father of Asura Mahisha; of a monkey, R.; of a brother of Rambha; (*ā*), f. Asparagus Racemosus, L.; fennel; N. of the daughter of a king of Kaliṅga and wife of Akrodhana, MBh. i, 3775; (mfn.) mixed (as an odour), BhP. **-pātrá**, n. a dish of gruel, ŚBr. **-bhāga**, mfn. one who receives gruel for his part, ŚāṅkhBr. **-vālukā**, *ās*, f. nom. pl. hot sand as gruel (a certain punishment in hell), MārkP.; MBh.; *-tāpa, ās*, m. pl. the pains caused by this punishment, Mn. xii, 76. **Karambhâd**, mfn. eating groats or gruel, RV. vi, 56, 1.

Karambhaka, *as*, m. a kind of Achyranthes, Nigh.; N. of a man, Kathās.; (*ās*), m. pl., N. of a people, MārkP.; (*am*), n. groats, coarsely-ground oats &c., Rājat.; a document drawn up in different dialects, Sāh.

Karambhi, *is*, m., N. of a son of Śakuni and father of Devarāta, BhP.; VP.; (*ayas*), pl. the lineage of Karambhi.

Karambhin, mfn. possessing gruel, RV.

करर्द्धि kararddhi, f. a cymbal, L.

करवी karavī, f. the leaf of the plant Asa Fœtida, Suśr.; (cf. *karvarī, kavarī, kāvarī*.)

करवीक karavīka, as, m., N. of a mountain.

करवीर kara-vīra. See p. 253, col. 3.

करस् káras. See under 1. *kará*.

करस्न karásna. See under 1. *kará*.

करहञ्चा karahañcā, f., N. of a metre of four lines (each consisting of seven syllables).

करहाट karahāṭa, as, m. the tree Vangueria Spinosa, Suśr.; the fibrous root of a lotus, L.; N. of a region.

Karahāṭaka, *as*, m. Vangueria Spinosa, Suśr.; N. of an heretical prince, MBh. ii, 1173; a series of six ślokas with one sentence running through, Comm. on Kāvyād.

कराङ्गण karāṅgaṇa. See under 1. *kará*, p. 253, col. 3.

कराट karā́ṭa, as, m., N. of Gaṇeśa, MaitrS.

करायिका karāyikā, f. a bird, a small kind of crane, Pañcat.

करारिन् karārin, i, m. (°*riṇas*, pl.), N. of a sect worshipping Devī.

कराल karāla, mfn. opening wide, cleaving asunder, gaping (as a wound), Mṛicch.; Pañcat.; R. &c.; having a gaping mouth and projecting teeth, BhP.; R.; Prab.; formidable, dreadful, terrible, MBh.; R.; Suśr.; (*as*), m. a species of animal, musk-deer, Suśr.; Nigh.; a mixture of oil and the resin of Shorea Robusta, L.; N. of a region, Rājat.; of an Asura; of a Rakshas; of a Deva-gandharva; (*ā*), f. Hemidesmus Indicus, L.; N. of Durgā, Mālatīm.; of a procuress, Hit.; (*ī*), f. one of the seven tongues and nine Samidhs of Agni, MuṇḍUp.; Gṛihyas.; a sword; (*am*), n. a sort of basil, Car.; a kind of Ocimum, L. **-kara**, mfn. having a powerful arm or hand; having a large trunk (as an elephant). **-kesara**, m., N. of a lion, Pañcat. **-janaka**, m., N. of a prince (also called Janaka), MBh. **-tripuṭā**, f. a species of corn, L. **-daṇshṭra**, mfn. having terrific teeth, BhP. **-bhairava**, n., N. of a Tantra, KūrmaP. [T.] **-mukha**, mfn. having a terrible mouth, Pañcat. **-locana**, mfn. terrific. **-vaktra**, mfn. having a terrible mouth, BhP.; Pañcat. **-vadana**, mfn. id., Bhag.; R.; BhP.; (*ā*), f., N. of Durgā. **Karālâksha**, m. 'having terrible eyes,' N. of a follower of Skanda, MBh. **Karālânana**, mfn. having a terrific face.

Karālaka, *am*, n. a kind of Ocimum.

Karālika, *as*, m. a tree, L.; a sword, L.; (*ā*), f., N. of Durgā.

Karālita, mfn. rendered formidable, afraid of, alarmed at; magnified, intensified, Kād.

Karālin, mfn. singing with a gaping and distorted mouth; (*ī*), m. a tree, L.

करि kari, &c. See p. 254, col. 2.

करिक्रत karikrata, as, m., N. of the author of RV. x, 130, 5.

करिभ karibha, as, m. Ficus Religiosa, L.

करिर karira, as, am, m. n. the shoot of a bamboo; (cf. *karīra*.)

करिष्ठ kárishṭha, &c. See p. 254, col. 3.

करीति karīti, m., ayas, pl., N. of a people, VP.

करीर karī́ra, as, am, m. n. the shoot of a bamboo, Suśr.; Hcat.; (*as*), m. a water-jar, L.; Capparis Aphylla (a thorny plant growing in deserts and fed upon by camels), ŚBr.; MBh.; Suśr.; (*ā* or *ī*), f. the root of an elephant's tusk, L.; a cricket, small grasshopper, L.; (*am*), n. the fruit of Capparis Aphylla. **-kuṇa**, m. the fruit-season of Capparis Aphylla. **-prastha**, m., N. of a town; (v. l. *karīri-prastha*.) **-vatī**, f., N. of a woman.

Karīrikā, f. the root of an elephant's tusk, L.

करीरक karīraka, am, n. fight, battle, L.

करीलदेश karīla-deśa, as, m., N. of a country.

करीष kárīsha, as, am, m. n. (√1. *kṛī*, Uṇ. iv, 26), rubbish, refuse; dung, dry cow-dung, ŚBr. ii; Mn. viii, 250; R. &c.; N. of a mountain. **-gandhi**, m., N. of a man, Comm. on Pāṇ. **-°ṃ-kasha**, mf(*ā*)n. sweeping away dung, Pāṇ. iii, 2, 42. **Karīshâgni**, m. a fire of dry cow-dung (this substance is very generally used as fuel in Hindūstān), L. **Karīshôttha**, m. (scil. *agni*) id., L.

Karīshaka, *ās*, m. pl., N. of a people, VP.

Karīshin, mfn. abounding in dung, AV. iii, 14, 3; xix, 31, 3; (*iṇī*), f., N. of a river, MBh.; VP.; a region abounding in dung, gaṇa *pushkarâdi*, Pāṇ. v, 2, 135.

करुण karúṇa, mf(*ā*)n. (√1. *kṛī*, Uṇ. iii, 53; but in some of its meanings fr. √1. *kṛī*), mournful, miserable, lamenting, MBh.; Daś. &c.; compassionate, BhP.; (*am*), ind. mournfully, wofully, pitifully, in distress, MBh.; Pañcat.; Vet. &c.; (*as*), m. 'causing pity or compassion,' one of the Rasas or sentiments of a poem, the pathetic sentiment, Sāh. &c.; Citrus Decumana, L.; a Buddha, L.; N. of an Asura, Hariv.; (*ā*), f. pity, compassion, BhP.; Ragh.; Pañcat. &c.; one of the four Brahma-vihāras (Buddh.); the sentiment of compassion (cf. above), L.; a particular tone (in mus.); (*ī*), f. a particular plant, L.; (*am*), n. an action, holy work, RV. i, 100, 7; AV. xii, 3, 47; TS. i. **-dhvani**, m. a cry of distress, Vikr. **-puṇḍarīka**, n., N. of a Buddhist work. **-mallī**, f. Jasminum Sambac. **-vedi-tva**, n. compassion, sympathy, Mn. vii, 211; R. **-vedin**, mfn. compassionate, sympathising, Car.; R. **Karuṇâkara**, m., N. of a Brāhman. **Karuṇā-kalpa-latā**, f., N. of a work. **Karuṇâtman**, mfn. miserable, mournful, Bālar. **Karuṇânanda-kāvya**, n., N. of a poem. **Karuṇā-para**, mfn. compassionate, tender, L. **Karuṇā-maya**, mfn. 'consisting of compassion,' compassionate, Bālar. **Karuṇā-mallī**, f. = *-mallī* above, W. **Karuṇârambha**, mfn. engaging in deplorable actions, R. **Karuṇârdra**, mfn. tender with pity, tender-hearted, sensitive. **Karuṇā-vat**, mfn. being in a pitiful state, pitiable, R.; pitiful, compassionate; (*vatī*), f., N. of a Surāṅganā, Jain. **Karuṇā-vipralambha**, m. grief of separation with the uncertainty of meeting again; sorrowful events occurring during separation, W. **Karuṇā-vṛitti**, mfn. disposed to pity. **Karuṇā-veditā**, f. charitableness, kindliness, sympathy, W. **Karuṇêśvara**, n., N. of a Liṅga, SkandaP.

Karuṇāya, Nom. P. (MBh.) Ā. (Pāṇ.) *karuṇāyati, -te*, to be compassionate, pity.

Karuṇin, mfn. (fr. *karuṇā*, gaṇa *sukhâdi*, Pāṇ. v, 2, 131), being in a pitiful condition, pitiable; compassionate, pitiful.

करुत्थाम karutthāma, as, m., N. of a son of Dushyanta (and father of Ākrīḍa), Hariv.; (v. l. *karūtthāma*.)

करुन्धक karundhaka, as, m., N. of a son of Śūra (and brother of Vasu-deva), VP.

करुम karúma, as, m. a kind of demon, AV. viii, 6, 10.

करूकर karū́kara, am, n. the joint of the neck and the back-bone, AV. xi, 9, 8; ŚBr. xii.

करूळतिन् kárūḷatin, mfn. one whose teeth are decayed and broken, having gaps in the teeth, RV. iv, 30, 24; Nir.

करूष karūsha, ās, m. pl., N. of a people, MBh.; Hariv. &c.; (*as*), m., N. of Danta-vakra (a king of that people), MBh. ii, 577; N. of a son of Manu Vaivasvata (the founder of the above people), Hariv.; BhP. &c. **-ja**, m., N. of Danta-vakra (or Danta-vaktra), BhP. vii, 10, 37.

Karūshaka, *as*, m., N. of a son of Manu Vaivasvata, BhP. ix, 1, 12 (cf. above); (*am*), n., N. of a species of fruit, MBh. iii, 10039.

करेट kareṭa. See p. 254, col. 3.

करेटव्या kareṭavyā, f. the Numidian crane, L.

Kareṭu, *us*, m. id., L.

Kareḍuka, *as*, m. id., L.; (cf. *karaṭu*, &c.)

करेणु kareṇu, &c. See p. 254, col. 3.

करेनर karenara, as, m. benzoin, storax, W.

करेवर karevara, as, m. Olibanum, L.

करोट karoṭa, as, m. a basin, cup, L.; the bones of the head, the skull, L.

Karoṭaka, *as*, m., N. of a Nāga, MBh. i, 1553; (cf. *karkoṭaka*.)

Karoṭi, *is, ī*, f. a basin, cup; the skull, Rājat. &c.

Karoṭika, ifc. (= *karoṭi*) the skull, Rājat. v, 417.

करोत्कर karótkara, &c. See under 1. and 2. *kara*.

कर्क् kark (a Sautra root), to laugh.

कर्क karká, mf(*ī*)n. (√*kṛi*, Uṇ. iii, 40; cf. *karaṅka*), white, AV. iv, 38, 6; 7; good, excellent, W.; (*as*), m. a white horse, MBh.; a crab, L.; the sign Cancer; a water-jar, L.; fire, L.; a mirror, L.; a younger brother of the father, L.; beauty, L.; a particular gem, L.; N. of a plant (= *karkaṭa*), L.; N. of a commentator; (*ā*), f. a white mare, Kathās. cxxi, 278. **–khaṇḍa,** *ās,* m. pl., N. of a people, MBh. **–candrêśvara-tantra,** n., N. of a Tantra. **–cirbhiṭā,** f. a species of cucumber, L. **–phala,** n., N. of a plant, L. **–rāja,** m., N. of a man. **–vallī,** f. Achyranthes Aspera, L. **–sāra,** n. flour or meal mixed with curds, L. **–svāmin,** m., N. of a man. **Karkâksha,** mfn. 'white-eyed' (said of the owl), Pañcat. (ed. Bombay). **Karkâhva,** m., N. of a plant, L.

Karkaṭa, *as,* m. a crab, Suśr.; Pañcat. &c.; the sign Cancer, VarBṛS.; VarBṛ. &c.; a particular bird, L.; N. of several plants; the fibrous root of a plant, L.; the curved end of the beam of a balance (to which the strings supporting the scale are attached), Mit.; a pair of compasses in a particular position; a particular position of the hands; a kind of fever, Bhpr.; a kind of coitus, L.; (*ā*), f. Momordica Mixta, L.; (*ī*), f. a female crab, MBh.; Cucumis Utilissimus, a kind of cucumber, Comm. on Tāṇḍya-Br.; a small water-jar, Pañcat.; the fruit of Bombax Heptaphyllum, L.; N. of a Rākshasī; [cf. Gk. καρκίνος; Lat. *cancer.*] **–pura,** n., N. of a town. **–vallī,** f. Achyranthes Aspera, L.; Piper Chaba, L.; Carpopogon Pruriens, L. **–śriṅga,** n. the claw of a crab. Mit.; (*ī*), f. gall-nut (an excrescence on Rhus Succedana), Suśr.; (*ikā*), f. id. **Karkaṭâksha,** m. Cucumis Utilissimus, L. **Karkaṭâkhyā,** f. gall-nut, Suśr. **Karkaṭâṅgā,** f. id., L. **Karkaṭâsthi,** n. the shell or crust of a crab, Suśr. ii, 389, 17. **Karkaṭâhva,** m. Ægle Marmelos, L.; (*ā*), f. gall-nut (cf. *-śriṅgī* above), Bhpr. **Karkaṭêśa,** m., N. of a sanctuary, Rājat. **Karkaṭêśvara-tīrtha,** n., N. of a Tīrtha, ŚivP.

Karkaṭaka, *as,* m. a crab, Suśr.; Pañcat. &c.; the sign Cancer, VarBṛS.; a pair of tongs, Daś.; a pair of compasses (cf. *karkaṭa*); a kind of plant, Suśr.; a particular position of the hands; N. of a Nāga, R.; (*ikā*), f. a sort of plant, Suśr. ii, 276, 3; Pañcat.; a kernel, L.; (*am*), n. a kind of poisonous root, Suśr.; a particular fracture of the bones, Suśr. i, 301, 5. **Karkaṭakâsthi,** n. the shell or crust of a crab, Suśr.

Karkaṭi, *is,* f. Cucumis Utilissimus, L.

Karkaṭinī, f. Curcuma Xanthorrhiza, L.

Karkaṭu, *us,* m. the Numidian crane; (cf. *karaṭu,* &c.)

Karki, *is,* m. the sign Cancer.

Karkin, *ī,* m. id., VarBṛS. **Karki-prastha** or **karkī-prastha,** m., N. of a town, Pāṇ. vi, 2, 87. **Karky-ādi,** m., N. of a gaṇa, ib.

कर्कन्धु *karkándhu, us, ūs,* m. f. (fr. *karka* and √*dhā,* Comm. on Uṇ. i, 95; according to others fr. *karka* and *andhu,* 'a well'), Zizyphus Jujuba; (*u*), n. the fruit of this tree, the jujube berry, VS.; ŚBr.; KātyŚr.; Suśr. &c.; (*us*), m. a well without water, one dried up, Comm. on Uṇ. i, 28; N. of a man, RV. i, 112, 6; (*ūs*), f. a term or name applied to a fetus which is ten days old, BhP. iii, 31, 2. **–kuna,** m. the fruit-season of the jujube tree, gaṇa *pīlvâdi,* Pāṇ. v, 2, 24. **–prastha,** m., N. of a town, gaṇa *karky-ādi,* Pāṇ. vi, 2, 87. **–mati,** f., N. of a woman, gaṇa *madhv-ādi,* Pāṇ. iv, 2, 86. **–rohita,** mfn. red like a berry of the jujube tree, VS. xxiv, 2. **–saktú,** *avas,* m. pl. flour of jujube berries, ŚBr. xii.

Karkandhūká, f. a small berry of the jujube tree (?), AV. xx, 136, 3.

कर्कर *karkara,* mf(*ā*)n. (perhaps connected with *karka*) hard, firm, Git.; Mālatīm.; Amar.; (*as*), m. a bone, L.; a hammer, L.; a mirror, L. (cf. *karphara*); N. of a Nāga, MBh. i, 1561; (*as, am*), m. n. stone, limestone (esp. the nodule found in Bengal under the name of Kaṅkar, W.), Satr.; a species of date, L.; [cf. *karaṅka, śarkara;* Gk. κρόκη, κροκάλη; Lat. *hallus, calx;* Hib. *carraice;* Gael. *carraig;* W. *careg.*] **–cchadā,** f., N. of a plant, L. **Karkarâksha,** m. a wagtail, L. **Karkarâṅga,** m. id., L. **Karkarândhaka** or °**ndhuka,** m. a blind well (one of which the mouth is overgrown with grass &c. so as to be hidden; cf. *karkándhu* and *andhakūpa*), L. **Karkarâhvā,** f., N. of a plant, L.

कर्कराटु *karkarāṭu, us,* m. a glance, side-look, L.

कर्कराटुक *karkarāṭuka, as,* m. the Numidian crane, L.

Karkareṭu, *us,* m. id., L.

Karkareḍu, *us,* m., °**ḍuka,** *as,* m. id., L.

कर्करि *karkarí, is, ī,* f. a kind of lute, RV. ii, 43, 3; AV. iv, 37, 4; xx, 132, 8; ŚāṅkhŚr.; (*ī*), f. a water-jar, Bhartṛ.; AgP. &c.; a kind of plant, L. **–karṇá,** mf(*ī*)n. having ears like a lute, MaitrS.

Karkariká, *as,* m. a kind of lute, AV. xx, 132, 3.

Karkarīkā, f. a small water-jar, Comm. on Uṇ. iv, 20.

कर्करेट *karkareṭa* (connected with *karka* ?), m. the hand curved like a claw for the purpose of grasping anything, L.

कर्कश *karkaśa,* mf(*ā*)n. (perhaps connected with *karka* and *karkara*) hard, firm, rough, harsh (lit. and metaph.), Suśr.; Mṛicch.; Bhartṛ. &c.; (*as*), m. a sword, scymitar, L.; Cassia or Sennia Esculenta; a species of sugar-cane; = *guṇḍorocanī,* L.; (*ā*), f. Tragia Involucrata, L.; N. of an Apsaras, MārkP.; (*ī*), f. the wild jujube, L. **–cchada,** m. Trophis Aspera, L.; Trichosanthes Diœca, L.; (*ā*), f. Luffa Acutangula, L.; = *dagdhā,* L. **–tva,** n. hardness; harshness, rough manners, MBh.; Kum. **–dala,** m. Trichosanthes Diœca, L.; (*ā*), f. = *dagdhā,* L.

Karkaśikā, f. wild jujube, L.

कर्कारु *karkāru, us,* m. Beninkasa Cerifera (a species of gourd), Suśr.; (*u*), n. the fruit of this plant, L.

Karkāruka, *as,* m. Beninkasa Cerifera, Suśr.; (*am*), n. its fruit, L.

कर्कि *karki,* &c. See col. 1.

कर्केणत *karkeṇata, as,* m. a species of quartz, Car.

Karketana, karketila, m. id., L.

कर्कोट *karkoṭa, as,* m., N. of one of the principal Nāgas of Pātāla, VP.; Rājat. &c.; (*ās*), m. pl., N. of a people, VarBṛS.; (*ī*), f., N. of a plant with a bitter fruit; (*am*), n., N. of a plant, Suśr. **–vāpī,** f., N. of a reservoir of water in Benares, SkandaP.

Karkoṭaka, *as,* m. Momordica Mixta, Suśr.; Ægle Marmelos, L.; the sugar-cane, L.; N. of a Nāga, MBh.; Hariv. &c.; (*ās*), m. pl., N. of a people, MBh. viii, 2066; (*ikā*), f. Momordica Mixta, L.; (*ī*), f., N. of a plant with yellow flowers, Bhpr.; Car.; Momordica Mixta, L.; (*am*), n. the fruit of Momordica Mixta, Suśr. i, 222, 1. **–visha,** n. the poison of Karkoṭaka, MW.

Karkoṭaki, *is,* m., N. of a Nāga (cf. above), Bālar. 225, 5.

कर्चरिका *karcarikā,* f. a kind of pastry or cake; (Beng. *kacurī.*)

Karcarī, f. a kind of medicinal substance, Bhpr.

Karcūṭikā, f. a kind of pastry, L.

कर्चूर *karcūra, as,* m. turmeric, L.; (*am*), n. an orpiment, Śiś. iii, 11; gold, L.; (cf. *karbura, karbūra.*)

Karcūraka, *as,* m. turmeric, L.; (cf. *karbūraka.*)

कर्ज् *karj,* cl. 1. P. *karjati, cakarja,* &c., to pain, torment, Dhātup. vii, 53.

कर्ण् *karṇ,* cl. 10. P. *karṇayati,* to pierce, bore, Dhātup. xxxv, 71; (*ā-karṇaya,* p. 126, col. 2, is a Nom. fr. the next.)

कर्ण *kárṇa, as,* m. (√*kṛit,* Nir.; √1. *kṝ,* Uṇ. iii, 10), the ear, RV.; AV.; TS.; Suśr. (*ápi kárṇe,* behind the ear or back, from behind, RV. [cf. *api-karṇá*]; *karṇe,* [in dram.] into the ear, in a low voice, aside, Mṛicch.; Mālav.; *karṇam* √*dā,* to give ear to, listen to, Śak.; Mṛicch.; *karṇam ā-*√*gam,* to come to one's ear, become known to, Ragh. i, 9); the handle or ear of a vessel, RV. viii, 72, 12; ŚBr. ix; KātyŚr. &c.; the helm or rudder of a ship, R.; (in geom.) the hypothenuse of a triangle or the diagonal of a tetragon, Hcat. &c.; the diameter of a circle, Sūryas; (in prosody) a spondee; Cassia Fistula, L.; Calotropis Gigantea, L.; N. of a king of Aṅga (and elder brother by the mother's side of the Pāṇḍu princes, being the son of the god Sūrya by Pṛithā or Kuntī, before her marriage with Pāṇḍu; afraid of the censure of her relatives, Kuntī deserted the child and exposed it in the river, where it was found by a charioteer named Adhi-ratha and nurtured by his wife Rādhā; hence Karṇa is sometimes called Sūta-putra or Sūta-ja, sometimes Rādheya, though named by his foster-parents Vasu-sheṇa), MBh.; BhP. &c.; N. of several other men; (mfn. *karṇá*), eared, furnished with ears or long ears, AV. v, 13, 9; VS.; TS.; furnished with chaff (as grain), TS. i, 8, 9, 3. **–kaṇḍū,** f. painful itching of the ear, Suśr. **–karṇikā,** f. a kind of colocynth, L. **–kashāya,** m. dirt in the ears, BhP. ii, 6, 45. **–kiṭṭa,** n. the wax of the ear, Nigh. **–kīṭā, -kīṭī,** f. Julus Cornifex (an insect or worm with many feet and of reddish colour), L. **–kutūhala,** n., N. of a work, L. **–kubja,** n., N. of an imaginary town, Vet. **–kumārī,** f., N. of Bhavānī. **–kuvalaya,** n. a lotus flower stuck into the ear (as an ornament), Daś. **–krośa,** m. an affection of the ear, singing in the ears, Gobh. iii, 3, 27. **–kshveḍa,** m. id., Suśr. **–kharaka, -kharika,** m., N. of a Vaiśya, Comm. on Pāṇ. **–ga,** mfn. touching the ear, hanging on it, next to the ear, extending to it, W. **–giri,** m., N. of a mountain. **–gūtha,** m. n. ear-wax; (*as*), m. hardening of the wax of the ear, Suśr. **–gūthaka,** m. id. **–gṛihītá,** mfn. seized by the ear, TS. vi, 1, 7, 6. **–gṛihyā** (Padap. *-gṛíhya*), ind. p. seizing by the ear, RV. viii, 70, 15. **–gocara,** m. the range of hearing, anything perceptible by the ear, T. **–grāha,** m. a helmsman, gaṇa *revaty-ādi,* Pāṇ. iv, 1, 146; *-vat,* mfn. furnished with a helmsman (as a ship), R. **–cāmara,** n. a cowrie as ornament for the ear of an elephant, Kād. **–cchidra,** n. the outer auditory passage, Suśr. **–ja,** m. ear-wax, L. **–japa,** m. 'ear-whisperer,' an informer, Kathās. **–jalūkā,** f. = *-kīṭā* above, L. **–jalaukas,** n., **-jalaukā,** f. id., L. **–jāpa,** m. the act of whispering in the ear; tale-bearing, calumniating, Pañcat. **–jāha,** n. the root of the ear, Pāṇ. v, 2, 24; Mālatīm. **–jit,** m. 'the conqueror of Karṇa,' N. of Arjuna (Karṇa having taken the part of the Kurus, was killed by Arjuna in one of the great battles between them and the Pāṇḍus, cf. MBh. viii, 4798 f.), L. **–jyoti,** f. Gynandropsis Pentaphylla, Nigh. **–jvara,** m. affection of the ears. **–tás,** ind. away from or out of the ear, AV. ix, 8, 3. **–tā,** f. the being an ear, Amar. **–tāla,** m. the flapping of an elephant's ears, Ragh.; Śiś.; *-latā,* f. the flap of the ear of an elephant, HYog. **–darpaṇa,** m. a particular ornament for the ear, L. **–dundubhi,** f. 'a drum in the ear,' a kind of worm, = *-kīṭā* above, L. **–deva,** m., N. of a king. **–dhāra,** m. a helmsman, pilot, Suśr.; BhP. &c.; a sailor, seaman, Kathās. xviii, 300; (*ā*), f., N. of an Apsaras, Kāraṇḍ.; *-tā,* f. the office of a helmsman, Kathās. xxvi, 8. **–dhāraka,** m. a helmsman, L. **–dhāriṇī,** f. a female elephant, L. **–dhvanana,** n. singing in the ear. **–nāda,** m. id. **–nāsā,** *e,* f. du. ear and nose, R. iii, 18, 21. **–nīlôtpala,** n. a blue lotus-flower stuck into the ear, Kuv. **–pa,** m., N. of a man, Rājat. **–pattraka,** m. the lobe of the ear, Yājñ. iii, 96. **–pattrabhaṅga,** m. ornamenting the ears (one of the 64 Kalās), Vātsyāy. **–patha,** m. the compass or range of hearing, (°*m ā-*√*yā,* to come within the range of or reach the ear, be heard, Śak. 232, 11; °*m upa-*√*i,* id., BhP. ii, 3, 19); -°*thâtithi,* m. 'a visitor in the compass of the ear,' anything heard of or learnt, Rājat. **–param-parā,** f. the going from one ear to another, Pañcat.; Kathās. **–parâkrama,** m., N. of a work. **–parvan,** n., N. of the eighth book of the Mahābhārata. **–pāka,** m. inflammation of the outer ear, Suśr. **–pāli,** f. the lobe of the ear, the outer ear, Suśr.; (*ī*), f. id., ib.; a particular ornament for the ear, L.; N. of a river; -°*lyāmaya,* m. a particular disease of the outer ear (produced from piercing the ear), Suśr. **–pitṛi,** m. 'Karṇa's father,' N. of Sūrya, L. **–piśācī,** f., N. of a goddess, Tantras. **–pīṭha,** n. the concha or outer end of the auditory passage, Suśr. **–puṭa,** n. the auditory passage of the ear, BhP. **–puṭraka,** m. the concha of the ear, Car.; (*ikā*), f. id., L. **–pur,** *ūr,* f. 'the capital of Karṇa,' Campā (the ancient N. for Bhagalpur), L. **–purī,** f. id., ib. **–pushpa,** m. blue Amaranth, Nigh. **–pūra,** m. n. an ornament (esp. of flowers) worn round the ears, MBh.; Ragh.; Kād. &c.; a blue lotus-flower, L.; Acacia Sirissa, L.; Jonesia Asoka, L.; N. of the father of Kavicandra and author of the Alaṃkāra Kaustubha. **–pūraka,** m. Nauclea Cadamba, L.; N. of a servant, Mṛicch. **–pūraṇa,** m., N. of an author (= *-pūra* above); the act of filling the ears (with cotton &c.); any substance used for that purpose, Suśr. **–pūrī-**√**kṛi,** to make (anything) an ornament for the ear, Kād.; Hcar. **-prakāśa**, m., N. of a work. **-pratināha**, m. a particular disease of the ear (suppression of its excretion or wax, which is supposed to have dissolved and passed out by the nose and mouth), Suśr. **-pratīnāha**, m. id., ib. **-prayāga**, m., N. of the confluence of the rivers Gaṅgā and Pindur. **-prādheya**, *ās*, m. pl., N. of a people. **-prânta**, m. the lobe of the ear, L. **-prāvaraṇa**, mf(*ā*)n. using the ears for a covering, R. v, 17, 5; (*ās*). m. pl., N. of a fabulous people, MBh.; R. &c.; (*ā*), f., N. of one of the mothers attending on Skanda, MBh. ix, 2643. **-prāveya**, *ās*, m. pl., N. of a people. **-phala**, m. a sort of fish (Ophiocephalus Kurrawey), L. **-bhūshaṇa**, n. an ornament for the ear. **-bhūshā**, f. id.; the art of ornamenting the ears (one of the 64 Kalās). **-madgura**, m. a sort of fish, Silurus unitus, L. **-mala**, n. the excretion or wax of the ear, L. **-mukura**, m. a particular ornament for the ear, L. **-mukha**, mfn. headed by Karṇa, having Karṇa as leader. **-muni**, m., N. of a man. **-mūla**, n. the root of the ear, Suśr.; BhP. &c. **-°mūlīya**, mfn. belonging to the root of the ear. **-moṭā**, f. Acacia arabica, L. **-moṭī**, f., N. of Durgā in her form as Cāmuṇḍā, L. **-moṭī**, id., L. **-yoni** (*kárṇa°*), mfn. having the ear as a source or starting-point, going forth from the ear (said of arrows, because in shooting the bow-string is drawn back to the ear), RV. ii, 24, 8. **-randhra**, m. the orifice or auditory passage of the ear, BhP. **-roga**, m. disease of the ear, Suśr.; *-pratishedha*, m. cure of a disease of the ear; *-vijñāna*, n. diagnosis of any disease of the ear. **-latā**, f. the lobe of the ear, L.; *-maya*, mfn. representing the lobe of an ear, Naish. vii, 64. **-latikā**, f. the lobe of the ear, L. **-vaṇśa**, m. an elevated platform of bamboo. **-vat** (*kárṇa°*), mfn. having ears, RV. x, 71, 7; R.; long-eared; furnished with tendrils or hooks, Suśr.; having a helm. **-varjita**, m. 'earless,' a snake, L. **-vallī**, f. the lobe of the ear, L. **-viṭka**, n. (fr. *-vish* below), excretion or wax of the ear, Suśr. **-vivara**, n. the auditory passage of the ear, BhP. **-vish**, f. ear-wax, Mn. v, 135. **-visha**, n. 'ear-poison' (any bad precept), Pañcat. **-vishayī-kṛita**, mfn. made an object of hearing, made known, Kathārṇ. **-vedha**, m. 'ear-boring' (a religious ceremony sometimes performed as a saṃskāra or to prevent a woman from dying if the birth of a third son be expected), PSarv.; piercing the ear to receive ear-rings. **-vedhanikā**, f. an instrument for piercing the ear of an elephant, L. **-vedhanī**, f. id., L. **-veshṭa**, m. an ear-ring, R.; N. of a king, MBh. i, 2696. **-veshṭaka**, m. an ear-ring, PārGṛ. **-°veshṭakiya**, **-°veshṭakya**, mfn. belonging or relating to an ear-ring, gaṇa *apūpâdi*. **-veshṭana**, n. an ear-ring, L. **-vyadha**, m. piercing the ear (to receive ear-rings), Suśr. **-śashkulikā**, f. the auditory passage of the ear, Car. **-śashkulī**, f. id. **-śirīsha**, n. a Śirīsha-flower fastened to the ear (as an ornament), Śak. **-śūnya**, mfn. deaf, L. **-śūlá**, n. ear-ache, AV. ix, 8, 1; 2; Suśr. **-°śūlin**, mfn. having ear-ache, Suśr. **-śóbhana**, n. an ornament for the ear, RV. viii, 78, 3. **-śrava**, mfn. perceptible by the ears, audible, Mn. iv, 102. **-śravas**, m., N. of a man, TāṇḍyaBr.; MBh. iii. **-śrāvin**, mfn. audible, Gaut. **-śrut**, m., N. of a Vedic author, RAnukr. **-saṃsrāva**, m. running of the ear, discharge of pus or ichorous matter from the ear, Suśr. **-sakha**, m. 'Sakha's friend,' N. of Jarāsaṃdha, L. **-sundarī**, f., N. of a drama. **-subhaga**, mfn. pleasant to the ear, pleasant to be heard, Veṇīs. **-sū**, m. 'Karṇa's father,' N. of Sūrya, L. **-sūci**, f. a kind of insect. **-sphoṭā**, f. Gynandropsis pentaphylla, L. **-srāva**, m. = *-saṃsrāva* above, Suśr. **-srotas**, n. the auditory passage of the ear, Hariv. 2921; VarBṛS.; the wax of the ear, MBh. vi. **-hallikā**, f. a particular disease of the ear, ŚārṅgS. **-hīna**, mfn. deaf; (*as*), m. 'earless,' a snake, T. **Karṇākarṇi**, ind. from ear to ear, whispering into each other's ear, R.; (cf. *keśākeśi*, &c.) **Karṇâkhya**, m. white amaranth, Npr. **Karṇâñjali**, m. the ears pricked up, BhP. iii, 13, 50. **Karṇâtarda**, m. a hole on both sides of a chariot into which the poles are fixed, ĀpŚr.; Comm. on TS. **Karṇâdarśa**, m. an ear-ring, L. **Karṇâdi**, m., N. of a gaṇa, Pāṇ. v, 2, 24. **Karṇânuja**, m. 'Karṇa's younger brother,' N. of Yudhishṭhira, L. **Karṇântika-cara**, mfn. going close to the ear, Śak. **Karṇându**, f. an ornament for the ear, L.; an ear-ring, L. **Karṇândū**, f. id., L. **Karṇâbharaṇa**, n. an ornament for the ear, Ratnāv. **Karṇâbharaṇaka**, m. Cathartocarpus fistula, L. **Karṇâmṛita**, n. nectar for the ears, ŚārṅgP.; N. of a work. **Karṇârā**, f. an instrument for perforating the ear of an elephant, L. **Karṇâri**, m. 'Karṇa's enemy,' N. of Arjuna, L.; Terminalia Arjuna, L. **Karṇârdha**, m. n. (?) the radius of a circle, Sūryas. **Karṇârpaṇa**, n. applying the ear, giving ear, paying attention, listening to. **Karṇârśas**, n. a particular disease of the ears, ŚārṅgS. **Karṇâlaṃkaraṇa**, n. an ornament for the ear. **Karṇâlaṃkāra**, m. id. **Karṇâlaṃkṛiti**, f. id. **Karṇâvataṇsa**, m. n. (?) id., Vām.; Kpr. &c.; °*ṇsī-√kṛi*, to make (anything) an ornament for the ear, Kād. **Karṇâvadhāna**, n. giving ear to, listening to, attention (°*dhānam ava-dhā*, to pay attention, attend). **Karṇâśva**, m., N. of a man. **Karṇâsphāla**, m. the flapping to and fro of an elephant's ears, L. **Karṇe-curacurā** or **-curucurā**, f. whispering into the ear, tale-bearing, gaṇa *pātre-samitâdi*. **Karṇe-japa**, m. an ear-whisperer, tale-bearer, informer, Pāṇ.; Bhaṭṭ. **Karṇe-ṭiṭṭibha**, m., **-ṭiriṭirā**, f. whispering into the ear, tale-bearing, gaṇa *pātre-samitâdi*. **Karṇêndu**, f. = *karṇându*, q. v., L. **Karṇôtpala**, n. a lotus-flower fastened to the ear (as an ornament), Ragh. vii, 23; (*as*), m., N. of a poet; of a king. **Karṇôdaya**, m., N. of a work. **Karṇôpakarṇikā**, f. the going from one ear to the other, Pañcat. **Karṇôrṇa**, m. an animal with wool on the ears, BhP. iv, 6, 21.

Kárṇaka, *as*, m. (ifc. f. *ā*) a prominence or handle or projection on the side or sides (of a vessel &c.), a tendril, ŚBr.; KātyŚr.; a rime, ring, Car.; a kind of fever; a particular defect of wood, Comm. on KātyŚr.; N. of a man; (*ās*), m. pl. the descendants of this man, gaṇa *upakâdi*; (*au*), m. du. the two legs spread out, AV. xx, 133, 3; (*ikā*), f. (Pāṇ. iv, 3, 65) an ear-ring or ornament for the ear, Kathās.; Daś. &c.; a knot-like tubercle, Suśr.; a round protuberance (as at the end of a reed or a tube), Suśr.; the pericarp of a lotus, MBh.; BhP. &c.; central point, centre, Car.; Bālar.; the tip of an elephant's trunk, L.; the middle finger, L.; chalk, L.; a pen, small brush, L.; Premna spinosa or longifolia, L.; Odina pinnata, L.; a bawd, L.; N. of an Apsaras, MBh. **-vat** (*kárṇaka-*), mfn. having prominences or handles &c., furnished with tendrils, MaitrS.; Kāṭh. **Kárṇakā-vat**, mfn. id., TS.; ŚBr.

Karṇakita, mfn. having handles, furnished with tendrils &c., gaṇa *tārakâdi*.

Karṇandu, f. = *karṇându*, q. v., L.

Karṇala, mfn. furnished with ears, gaṇa *sidhmâdi*.

Karṇi, *is*, m. a kind of arrow (the top being shaped like an ear), L. (cf. *karṇika*, n.); the act of splitting, breaking through, T.

Karṇika, mfn. having ears, having large or long ears, W.; having a helm, W.; (*as*), m. a steersman, W.; a kind of fever, Bhpr.; N. of a king in Potāla; (*ās*), m. pl., N. of a people, VP.; (*as*, *am*), m. n. the pericarp of a lotus, MBh.; (*am*), n. a kind of arrow (the top being shaped like an ear), Śārṅg.

Karṇikā, see *kárṇaka*. **Karṇikâcala**, m. 'the central mountain' [*karṇikāyām sthito 'calaḥ*, T.], N. of Meru, L.; (cf. BhP. v, 16, 7.) **Karṇikâdri**, m. id., L.

Karṇikāra, mfn. (fr. *karṇikā*, BRD.; *karṇiṃ bhedanam karoti*, T.), Pterospermum acerifolium, MBh.; Suśr. &c.; Cathartocarpus fistula, L.; (*am*), n. the flower of Pterospermum acerifolium, Ṛitus.; the pericarp of a lotus, Hcat.; Rājat. **-priya**, m. 'fond of Karṇikāra,' N. of Śiva.

Karṇikāraka, *as*, m. Pterospermum acerifolium, L.

Karṇikikā, f. a heifer, L.

Karṇikin, *ī*, m. an elephant, L.

Karṇín, mfn. having ears, AV. x, 1, 2; TS. vii; relating to the ears; (ifc.) having (a ring &c.) attached to the ear, MBh. xiii; furnished with flaps or anything similar (said of shoes), KātyŚr. xxii; barbed, furnished with knots &c. (as a missile), Mn. vii, 90; MBh.; Suśr. &c.; having a helm, W.; (*ī*), m. a missile, arrow; the side of the neck, the part near the ear, W.; a steersman, Kathās.; N. of one of the seven principal ranges of the mountains dividing the universe, L.; (*inī*), f. (scil. *yoni*) a disease of the uterus (prolapsus or polypus uteri), Suśr. ii, 397, 7; 398, 11. **Karṇī-ratha** (for *karṇi-ratha*), m. a kind of litter, Ragh. xiv, 13; Rājat. vii, 479.

Karṇī, f. of °*ṇa*, ifc. (e.g. *ayas-k°* & *payas-k°*), Pāṇ. viii, 3, 46; 'N. of Kaṇsa's mother,' in comp. **-ratha**, see s. v. *karṇin*. **-suta**, m., N. of Kaṇsa, L.; of the author of a thieves' manual, Kād.

Kárṇya, mfn. being in or at the ear, AV. vi, 127, 3; suitable to the ear, Comm. on Pāṇ.

कर्णाट *karṇāṭa*, *ās*, m. pl., N. of a people and the country they inhabit (the modern Karnatic; the name, however, was anciently applied to the central districts of the peninsula, including Mysore), VarBṛS.; Rājat.; Kathās. &c.; (*as*), m. a king or inhabitant of Karṇāṭa, Kathās.; (in mus.) a particular Rāga; (*ī*), f. a queen of Karṇāṭa, Rājat. iv, 152; a kind of Mimosa, L.; (in mus.) a particular Rāgiṇī. **-gauḍa**, m. (in mus.) a particular Rāga. **-deśa**, m. the country of Karṇāṭa. **-bhāshā**, f. the language spoken in Karṇāṭa, Sarvad.

Karṇāṭaka, *ās*, m. pl., N. of a people and the country they inhabit, VP.; BhP. &c.; (*ikā*), f. (in mus.) a particular Rāgiṇī. **-deśa**, m. the Karṇāṭa country. **-bhāshā**, f. the dialect of Karṇāṭa.

कर्त् *kart*, v. l. for *kartṛ*, q. v.

कर्त *kartá*, *as*, m. (√1. *kṛit*; a more recent form is 2. *gárta*), a hole, cavity, RV.; AV. iv, 12, 7; AitBr. &c.; separation, distinction, BhP. **-patya**, n. falling or tumbling into a hole, TāṇḍyaBr. **-praskanda**, m. id., ib.

1. **Kartana**, *am*, n. the act of cutting off, excision, Yājñ.; Hit. &c.; the act of extinguishing, extinction, Vīrac.; (*ī*), f. scissors, W.

Kartari, *is*, f. scissors, a knife, or any instrument for cutting, Suśr.; Hcat.

Kartarikā, f. id., Hit.; Hcat.

Kartarī, f. id., Hcat.; the part of an arrow to which the feathers are attached, L.; a kind of dance. **-phala**, n. the blade of a knife, Hcat. **-mukha**, m. a particular position of the hands, PSarv. **Kartary-āsya**, m. id.

Kartarīya, *am*, n. (?) a kind of poisonous plant, Suśr.

Karttavya, mfn. to be cut off; to be destroyed or extinguished, MBh.

1. **Karttṛi**, mfn. one who cuts off; one who extinguishes, a destroyer, Vīrac.

Karttṛikā, f. = *kartari*, Tantras.

Karttrikā, **karttrī**, f. id.

Kartya, mfn. to be cut off or down, Mn. viii, 367.

कर्तन 2. *kartana*, *am*, n. (√2. *kṛit*), the act of spinning cotton or thread, L. **-sādhana**, n. a spindle, L.

2. **Karttṛi**, mfn. one who spins, a spinner, MBh. viii.

कर्तवे *kártave* [RV. and AV.] and *kártavaí* [Naigh.; ŚBr.], Ved. inf. of √1. *kṛi*, to do, q. v.

Kártavya and **kartavyà**, mfn. (fut. pass. p. of √1. *kṛi*, q. v.) to be done or made or accomplished &c., TS.; ŚBr.; AitBr.; Mn. &c.; (*am*), n. that which ought to be done, obligation, duty, task, MBh.; Pañcat.; Kathās. &c. **-tā**, f., **-tva**, n. the state of being necessary to be done or accomplished, Sāh.; necessity, obligation, task, Yājñ.; Hit. &c.; the possibility or suitableness of being done, Tattvas.

Kartu (for *kartum* inf. of √1. *kṛi*, q.v.) **-kāma**, mfn. desirous or intending to do.

Kartṛi, mfn. one who makes or does or acts or effects, a doer, maker, agent, author (with gen. or acc. or ifc., cf. *bhaya-kartṛi*, &c.), RV.; AV. &c.; MBh.; Mn. &c.; doing any particular action or business, applying one's self to any occupation (the business or occupation preceding in the compound, cf. *suvarṇa-kartṛi*, *rājya-k°*, &c.); one who acts in a religious ceremony, a priest, ŚBr.; ĀśvGṛ. &c.; (*tā*), m. the creator of the world, ŚBr. xiv; Yājñ. iii, 69; N. of Vishṇu, Pañcat.; of Brahman, L.; of Śiva, L.; (in Gr.) the agent of an action (who acts of his own accord [*sva-tantra*]), the active noun, the subject of a sentence (it stands either in the nom. [in active construction], or in the instr. [in passive construction], or in the gen. [in connection with a noun of action]; it is opposed to ***karman***, the object), Pāṇ. &c.; one who is about to do, one who will do (used as periphr. fut.), MBh. **-kara**, mfn.?, Pāṇ. iii, 2, 21. **-ga**, mfn. going towards or falling to the share of the agent, Comm. on Pāṇ. **-gāmin**, mfn. id., ib. **-gupta**, n. (a kind of artificial sentence) in which the subject or agent is hidden, Śārṅg. **—guptaka**, n. id., ib. **—tā**, f. the state of being the agent of an action, Sāh. **—tva**, n. id., Kāś.; the state of being the performer or author of anything, MBh.; BhP. &c. **—pura**, n., N. of a town. **—bhūta**, mfn. that which has become or is the agent of an action, Kāś. **—mat**, mfn. having a *kartṛi*, Comm. on Pāṇ. **—vācya**, n. the active voice, W. **—stha**, mfn. standing or being or contained in the agent of an action, Pāṇ. i, 3, 37; *-kriyaka*, mfn. (any root &c.) whose action is confined to the agent; *-bhāvaka*, mfn. (any root &c.) whose state stands within the agent.

Kartṛika, mfn. ifc. = *kartṛi*. **—tva**, n. agency, action.

Kártos, Ved. inf. of √1. *kṛi*, q. v.

Kártra, *am*, n. a spell, charm, AV. x, 1, 19 & 32.

Kartrīya, Nom. (fr. *kartṛi*) P. °*yati*, to be an agent, Vop. xxi, 2.

Kártva, mfn. to be done or accomplished, RV.; (*am*), n. obligation, duty, task, ib.

कर्त्तव्य *karttavya*, &c. See p. 257, col. 3.

कर्त् *kartr*, cl. 10. P. *kartrayati*, to unloose, remove, Dhātup. xxxv, 60 (perhaps connected with √1. *kṛit*).

कर्द् *kard*, cl. 1. P. *kardati*, to rumble (as the bowels), Dhātup. iii, 22; to caw (as a crow), ib.; to make any unpleasant noise, ib.; (cf. *pard*.)

Karda, *as*, m. mud, clay, L.; (cf. *kardama*.)

Kardaṭa, *as*, m. mud, dirt, L.; the fibrous root of the lotus, L.; any aquatic weed (as Vallisneria &c.; = *paṅkāra*), L.

Kardana, *am*, n. rumbling of the bowels, borborygm, L.; (*as*), m., N. of a prince, Daś.; (*ī*), f. = *kūrdanī*, q. v.

Kardama, *as*, m. (Uṇ. iv, 84) mud, slime, mire, clay, dirt, filth, MBh.; Yājñ.; Ragh. &c.; sin, Comm. on Uṇ.; shade, shadow (in Veda according to BrahmavP.); N. of a Prajāpati (born from the shadow of Brahmā, husband of Devahūti and father of Kapila), MBh.; a kind of rice, Suśr.; a kind of poisonous bulb; N. of Pulaka (a son of Prajāpati), VP.; of a Nāga, MBh. i, 1561; (*ī*), f. a species of jasmine; (*am*), n. flesh, L.; Civet, L.; (mfn.) covered with mud or mire or dirt, dirty, filthy, Suśr. **—rāja** or **-rājan**, m., N. of a man (a son of Kshema-gupta), Rājat. **—visarpa**, m. a kind of erysipelas, Car. **Kardamâkhya**, m. a kind of poisonous bulb, Suśr. ii, 253, 4. **Kardamâṭaka**, m. a receptacle for filth, a sewer &c. **Kardamêśvara-māhātmya**, n., N. of a work. **Kardamôdbhava**, m. marsh-produced kind of rice, L.

Kardamaka, *as*, m. a kind of rice, Suśr.; a kind of poisonous bulb, Suśr.; a kind of snake, Suśr.; a kind of erysipelas, Car.

Kardamita, mfn. muddy, dirty, soiled, Kathās.; Mālatīm.

Kardaminī, f. a marshy region, gaṇa *pushkarâdi*.

Kardamila, *am*, n. (gaṇa *kāśâdi*), N. of a place, MBh. iii, 10692.

कर्पट *karpaṭa*, *am*, n. (*as*, m., L.) old or patched or ragged garments, a patch, rag, Pañcat.; Kathās. &c.; N. of a mountain, KālP. **—dhārin**, m. 'wearing rags or a rag,' a beggar, L.

Karpaṭika, mfn. covered with patched or ragged garments, clothed in a beggar's raiment, L.

Karpaṭin, mfn. id., ib.

कर्पण *karpaṇa*, *as*, m.(?) a kind of lance or spear, Daś.

कर्पर *karpara*, *as*, m. a cup, pot, bowl, Pañcat.; Kathās. &c.; the skull, cranium, L.; the shell of a tortoise; a kind of weapon, L.; Ficus glomerata, L.; N. of a thief, Kathās. lxiv, 43 ff.; (*ī*), f. a kind of collyrium, L.; (*am*), n. a pot, potsherd, Pañcat. **Karparâṇśa**, m. a potsherd.

Karparaka, *as*, m., N. of a thief, Kathās. lxiv, 52; (*ikā*), f. a kind of collyrium, L.

Karparāla, *as*, m., v. l. for *kandarāla*, q. v.

Karparāśa, *as*, m. sand, gravel, a sandy soil, W.; (erroneous for *karparâṇśa*, BRD.)

कर्पास *karpāsa*, *as*, *ī*, *am*, m. f. n. the cotton tree, cotton, Gossypium Herbaceum, Suśr.; [cf. Gk. κάρπασος; Lat. *carbasus*.] **—dhenu-māhātmya**, n., N. of a work.

Karpāsakī, f. the cotton tree, Bhpr.

कर्पूर 1. *karpūra*, *as*, *am*, m. n. (√*kṛip*, Comm. on Uṇ. iv, 90), camphor (either the plant or resinous exudation or fruit), Suśr.; Pañcat. &c.; (*as*), m., N. of several men; of a Dvīpa, Kathās. lvi, 61 f.; (*ā*), f. a kind of yellowish pigment, Bhpr.; mf(*ā*)n. made of camphor, Hcat. **—keli**, m., N. of a flamingo, Hit. **—gaura**, n. 'yellowish-white like camphor,' N. of a lake, Hit. **—tilaka**, m., N. of an elephant, Hit.; (*ā*), f., N. of Jayā (one of Durgā's female friends), L. **—taila**, n. camphor liniment, L. **—dvīpa**, m., N. of a Dvīpa, Viddh. **—nālikā**, f. a kind of food prepared with camphor (rice dressed with spices and camphor and ghee), Bhpr. **—paṭa**, m., N. of a dyer, Hit. **—prakaraṇa**, n., N. of a Jaina work. **—mañjarī**, f., N. of a daughter of Karpūra-sena, Kathārṇ.; of a daughter of the flamingo Karpūra-keli, Hit.; of a drama by Rāja-śekhara. **—maṇi**, m. a kind of white mineral, L. **—maya**, mfn. made of camphor, like camphor, Kād. **—rasa**, m. camphorated mixture. **—varsha**, m., N. of a king, Viddh. **—vilāsa**, m., N. of a washerman, Hit. **—saras**, n., N. of a lake or pond, Hit. **—sena**, m., N. of a king, Kathārṇ. **—stava**, m., N. of a work. **—stotra**, n. id. **—haridrā**, f. Curcuma Amada. **Karpūrâśman**, m. crystal, L.

2. **Karpūra**, Nom. P. *karpūrati*, to be like camphor, Dhūrtas.; Kuval.

Karpūraka, *as*, m. Curcuma Zerumbet, L.

Karpūrin, mfn. having camphor, gaṇa *suvâstvādi*.

Karpūrila, mfn. id., gaṇa *kāśâdi*.

कर्फर *karphara*, *as*, m. a mirror, L.; (cf. *karkara*.)

कर्ब् *karb*, cl. 1. P. *karbati*, to go, move, approach, Dhātup. xi, 26.

कर्बर *karbara*. See 2. *karvara*.

Karbu, mfn. variegated, spotted, Yājñ. iii, 166. **—dāra**, m. Bauhinia candida, Suśr.; Car.; Bauhinia variegata, L.; Barleria cærulea, L. **—dāraka**, m. Cordia latifolia, L.

Karbuka, *ās*, m. pl., N. of a people, R.

Karbura, mf(*ā*)n. variegated, of a spotted or variegated colour, Suśr.; Hit.; Kum. &c.; (*as*), m. sin, L.; a Rakshas, L.; Curcuma Amhaldi or Zerumbet, L.; a species of Dolichos, L.; (*ā*), f. a venomous kind of leech, Suśr. i, 40, 10; Bignonia suaveolens, L.; = *barbarā*, L.; (*ī*), f., N. of Durgā, L.; (*am*), n. gold, L.; thorn-apple, L.; water, L. **—phala**, m. a particular plant, L. **Karburâṅgā**, f. a species of fly or bee, L.

Karburaka, mfn. variegated, spotted, VarBṛS.

Karbūra, *as*, m. a Rakshas, L.; Curcuma Amhaldi or Zerumbet, L.; (*ā*), f. a kind of venomous leech, L.; (*am*), n. gold, L.; a yellow orpiment, L.

Karbūraka, *as*, m. a kind of Curcuma, L.

Karbūrita, mfn. variegated, many-coloured, W.

कर्बेल *karbela*, *as*, m., N. of the copyist Vishṇu-bhaṭṭa.

कर्मन् *kárman*, *a*, n. (*ā*, m., L.), (√*kṛi*, Uṇ. iv, 144), act, action, performance, business, RV.; AV.; ŚBr.; MBh. &c.; office, special duty, occupation, obligation (frequently ifc., the first member of the compound being either the person who performs the action [e.g. *vaṇik-k*°] or the person or thing for or towards whom the action is performed [e.g. *rāja-k*°, *paśu-k*°] or a specification of the action [e.g. *śaurya-k*°, *prīti-k*°]), ŚBr.; Mn.; Bhartṛ. &c.; any religious act or rite (as sacrifice, oblation &c., esp. as originating in the hope of future recompense and as opposed to speculative religion or knowledge of spirit), RV.; AV.; VS.; Ragh. &c.; work, labour, activity (as opposed to rest, *praśānti*), Hit.; RPrāt. &c.; physicking, medical attendance, Car.; action consisting in motion (as the third among the seven categories of the Nyāya philosophy; of these motions there are five, viz. *ut-kshepaṇa*, *ava-kshepaṇa*, *ā-kuñcana*, *prasāraṇa*, and *gamana*, qq. vv.), Bhāshāp.; Tarkas.; calculation, Sūryas.; product, result, effect, Mn. xii, 98; Suśr.; organ of sense, ŚBr. xiv (or of action, see *karmêndriya*); (in Gr.) the object (it stands either in the acc. [in active construction], or in the nom. [in passive construction], or in the gen. [in connection with a noun of action]; opposed to *kartṛi* the subject), Pāṇ. i, 4, 49 ff. (it is of four kinds, viz. a. *nirvartya*, when anything new is produced, e.g. *kaṭaṃ karoti*, 'he makes a mat;' *putraṃ prasūte*, 'she bears a son:' b. *vikārya*, when change is implied either of the substance and form, e.g. *kāshṭhaṃ bhasma karoti*, 'he reduces fuel to ashes;' or of the form only, e.g. *suvarṇaṃ kuṇḍalaṃ karoti*, 'he fashions gold into an ear-ring:' c. *prāpya*, when any desired object is attained, e.g. *grāmaṃ gacchati*, 'he goes to the village;' *candraṃ paśyati*, 'he sees the moon:' d. *anīpsita*, when an undesired object is abandoned, e.g. *pāpaṃ tyajati*, 'he leaves the wicked'); former act as leading to inevitable results, fate (as the certain consequence of acts in a previous life), Pañcat.; Hit.; Buddh., (cf. *karma-pāka* and *-vipāka*); the tenth lunar mansion, VarBṛS. &c.

Karma (in comp. for *kárman* above). **—kara**, mf(*ī*)n. doing work, a workman, a hired labourer, servant of any kind (who is not a slave, W.), mechanic, artisan, MBh.; BhP.; Pañcat. &c.; (*as*), m., N. of Yama, L.; (*ī*), f. Sanseviera zeylonica, L.; Momordica monadelpha, L. **—karī-bhāva**, m. the state of being a female servant, Kathās. **—kartṛi**, m. (in Gr.) 'an object-agent' or 'object-containing agent,' i. e. an agent which is at the same time the object of an action (this is the idea expressed by the reflexive passive, as in *odanaḥ pacyate*, 'the mashed grain cooks of itself'), Pāṇ. iii, 1, 62 (cf. Gr. 461, iii); (*ārau*), m. du. the work and the person accomplishing it. **—kāṇḍa**, n. that part of the Śruti which relates to ceremonial acts and sacrificial rites, Pāṇ. iv, 2, 51, Kāś.; Prab.; N. of a Jaina work. **—kāra**, mfn. = doing work (but without receiving wages, according to native authorities), Kāś. on Pāṇ. iii, 2, 22; Pañcat. &c.; (*as*), m. a blacksmith (forming a mixed caste, regarded as the progeny of the divine artist Viśva-karman and a Śūdra woman), BrahmavP.; a bull, L.; (*ī*), f. = *-karī* above, L. **—kāraka**, mfn. one who does any act or work. **—°kārāpaya**, Nom. P. °*yati*, to cause any one to work as a servant, Saddh-P. **—kārin**, mfn. (ifc.) doing or accomplishing any act or work or business; (cf. *tat-k*°, *śubha-k*°.) **—kārmuka**, m. a strong bow, W.(?) **—kāla**, m. the proper time for action; *-nirṇaya*, m., N. of a work. **—kīlaka**, m. a washerman, L. **—kṛit**, mfn. performing any work, skilful in work, AV. ii, 27, 6; VS. iii, 47; TBr. &c. (cf. *tīkshṇa-k*°); one who has done any work, Pāṇ. iii, 2, 89; (*t*), m. a servant, workman, labourer, Rājat.; Kām. &c. **—kṛita-vat**, m. the director of a religious rite, reciter of Mantras, W.(?) **—kṛítya**, n. activity, the state of active exertion, AV. iv, 24, 6. **—kaumudī**, f., N. of a work. **—kriyā-kāṇḍa**, n., N. of a work by Soma-śambhu (q. v.) **—kshama**, mfn. able to do an action, Ragh. i, 13. **—kshaya**, m. annihilation or termination of all work or activity, ŚvetUp. **—kshetra**, n. the place or region of (religious) acts, BhP. v, 17, 11; (cf. *-bhūmi* below.) **—gati**, f. the course of Fate, Kathās. lix, 159. **—gupta**, n. a kind of artificial sentence which has the object hidden, Śārṅg. **—grantha**, m., N. of a Jaina work. **—granthi-prathama-vicāra**, m. id. **—ghāta**, m. annihilation or termination of work or activity, L.; (cf. *-kshaya* above.) **—caṇḍāla**, m. 'a Caṇḍāla by work' (as opposed to a born Caṇḍāla), a contemptible man, T.; N. of Rāhu, T. **—candra**, m., N. of several princes. **—cārin**, mfn. engaged in work. **—cit**, mfn. collected or accomplished by work, ŚBr. x. **—ceshṭā**, f. active exertion, activity, action, Mn. i, 66; MBh.; Daś. &c. **—codanā**, f. the motive impelling to ritual acts, W. **—ja**, mfn. 'act-born,' resulting or produced from any act (good or bad), Mn. xii, 3 & 101; Daś. &c.; (*as*), m. Ficus religiosa; the Kali-yuga (q. v.); a god, L.; *-guṇa*, m. a quality or condition resulting from human acts (as separation, reunion &c.), W. **—jit**, mfn., N. of a king, BhP. **—jña**, mfn. skilled in any work; acquainted with religious rites, W. **—tattva-pradīpikā**, f., N. of a work. **—tā**, f., **-tva**, n. the state or effect of action &c., Car.; Sarvad. &c.; activity; the state of being an object, Comm. on TPrāt. **—tyāga**, m. abandonment of worldly duties or ceremonial rites, W. **—dīpa**, m., N. of a work. **—dushṭa**, mfn. corrupt in action, wicked in practice, immoral, disreputable. **—deva** (*kárma*°), m. a god through religious actions (*ye 'gnihotrâdiśrautakarmaṇā devalokaṃ prâpnuvanti te karmadevāḥ*, Comm. on ŚBr. xiv, 7, 1, 35), ŚBr.; TUp. &c. **—dosha**, m. a sinful work, sin vice, Mn.; error, blunder, W.; the evil consequence of human acts, discreditable conduct or business, W. **–dhāraya**, m., N. of a class of Tatpurusha (q. v.) compounds (in which the members would stand in the same case [*samānâdhikaraṇa*] if the compound were dissolved), Pāṇ. i, 2, 42 (see Gr. 735, iii; 755 ff.) **–dhvaṇsa**, m. loss of benefit arising from religious acts, W.; destruction of any work, disappointment, W. **–nāmán**, n. a name in accordance with or derived from actions, ŚBr. xiv, 4, 2, 17; a participle, APrāt. iv, 29. **–nāśā**, f. 'destroying the merit of works,' N. of a river between Kāśī and Vihāra, Bhāshāp. **–nibandha**, m. necessary consequence of works. **–nirṇaya**, m., N. of a work. **–nirhāra**, m. removal of bad deeds or their effects. **–nishṭha** (Ved. *-nishṭhá*), mfn. diligent in religious actions, engaged in active duties, RV. x, 80, 1; Mn. iii, 134; (*as*), m. a Brāhman who performs sacrifices &c., W. **–nyāsa**, m. the giving up of active duties, Āp. **–patha**, m. the way or direction or character of an action, MBh.; Kāraṇḍ. **–paddhati**, f., N. of a work. **–pāka**, m. 'ripening of acts,' matured result of previous acts or actions done in a former birth, BhP.; Pañcat.; (cf. *-vipāka* below.) **–pāra-dā**, f., N. of a goddess, BrahmaP. **–prakāśa**, m., **-prakāśikā**, f., **-prakāśinī**, f., **-pradīpa**, m., **-pradīpikā**, f., N. of several works. **–pravacanīya**, mfn. 'employed to denote an action;' (*as*), m. (scil. *śabda*; in Gr.) a term for certain prepositions or particles not connected with a verb but generally governing a noun (either separated from it or forming a compound with it; a Karma-pravacanīya never loses its accent, and exercises no euphonic influence on the initial letter of a following verb; see also *upa-sarga*, *gati*, and *nipāta*), Pāṇ. i, 4, 83–98; ii, 3, 8, &c. **–pravāda**, m., N. of a Jaina work. **–phala**, n. the fruit or recompense of actions (as pain, pleasure &c., resulting from previous acts or acts in a former life), Āp.; the fruit of Averrhoa Carambola, L.; °*lôdaya*, m. the appearance of consequences of actions, Mn. xi, 231. **–bandha**, m. the bonds of action (i. e. transmigration or repeated existence as a result of actions), Bhag. ii, 39. **–bandhana**, n. id.; (mfn.) bound by bonds of actions (as worldly existence), Bhag. **–bāhulya**, n. much or hard work. **–bīja**, n. the seed of works. **–buddhi**, f. the mental organ of action, Manas (q. v.), MBh. xi. **–bhū**, f. tilled or cultivated ground, L. **–bhūmi**, f. the land or region of religious actions (i. e. where such actions are performed, said of Bhārata-varsha), R.; VP. &c., (cf. *-kshetra* above; cf. also *phala-bhūmi*); the place or region of activity or work, Kāraṇḍ. **–bhūya**, n. the becoming an action, (°*ṃ-√bhū*, to assume the peculiar characteristic of any action, Comm. on Bādar. iv, 1, 6.) **–bheda-vicāra**, m., N. of a work. **–máya**, mf(*ī*)n. consisting of or resulting from works, ŚBr. x; MBh. &c. **–mārga**, m. the course of acts, activity, VP. vi, 6, 9; the way of work (a term used by thieves for a breach in walls &c.), Mṛicch. **–māsa**, m. the calendar month of thirty days. **–mīmāṇsā**, f. = *pūrva-mīmāṇsā*, q. v. **–mūla**, n. Kuśa grass (as essential part in many religious acts), L. **–yuga**, n. the Kali-yuga (q. v.), L. **–yoga**, m. performance of a work or business (esp. of religious duties), Bhag.; Mn. &c.; active exertion, industry; agriculture and commerce [Kull.], Mn. x, 115; practical application, Sarvad.; connection with a sacrifice, KātyŚr.; Lāṭy.; Āp. **–yoni**, f. source of an action, Tattvas. **–raṅga**, m. Averrhoa Carambola, R.; (cf. *-phala* above.) **–ratnâvalī**, f., N. of a work. **–°rgha** (*karma+ṛigha* fr. *ṛighā*), m., N. of a teacher. **–locana**, n., N. of a work. **–vacana**, n. (with Buddh.) the ritual. **–vajra**, mfn. 'whose power (thunderbolt) is work' (said of Śūdras), MBh. i, 6487. **–vat**, mfn. busy with or employed in any work, MBh. **–vaśa**, m. the necessary influence of acts, fate (considered as the inevitable consequence of actions done in a former life); (mfn.) being in the power of or subject to former actions, MBh. xiii. **–°vaśi-tā**, mfn. the condition of having power over one's works (as a quality of a Bodhi-sattva), Buddh. **–vāṭī**, f. 'demarcation or regulation of religious actions,' a lunar day. **–vighna**, m. an impediment to work, obstruction. **–vidhi**, m. rule of actions or observances, mode of conducting ceremonies, Mn. **–viparyaya**, m. perversity of action, perverse action, mistake, Hit. **–vipāka**, m. 'the ripening of actions,' i. e. the good or evil consequences in this life of human acts performed in previous births (eighty-six consequences are spoken of in the Śātātapa-smṛiti), MBh.; Yājñ. &c.; N. of several works; *-saṃgraha*, m., N. of a work; *-sāra*, m. id. **–virodhin**, mfn. disturbing or preventing any one's works, Sāy. **–viśesha**, m. variety of acts or actions, W. **–vyatihāra**, m. reciprocity of an action, Pāṇ. **–śataka**, n., N. of a Buddhist work. **–śalya**, n. an impediment of action, Nāṭyaś. **–śālā**, f. workshop, the hall or room where daily work is done, sitting-room, MBh.; R **–śālī**, f., N. of a river in Caturgrāma. **–śīla**, mfn. assiduous in work, L.; one who perseveres in his duties without looking to their reward, W.; (*as*), m., N. of a man, Buddh. **–śūra**, m. a skilful or clever workman, L.; (mfn.) assiduous, laborious, L. **–śauca**, n. humility, L. **–śreshṭha**, m., N. of a son of Pulaha by Gati, BhP.; VP. **–saṃvatsara**, m. the calendar year of 360 days. **–saṃgraha**, m. assemblage of acts (comprising the act, its performance, and the performer), W. **–saciva**, m. an officer, assistant, L. **–saṃnyāsika**, mfn. one who has given up works, an ascetic, L. **–samāpta**, mfn. one who has performed all religious actions, Āp. **–sambhava**, mfn. produced by or resulting from acts. **–sākshin**, m. 'the witness of all acts,' the sun, L. **–sādhaka**, mfn. accomplishing a work. **–sādhana**, n. implement, means; articles essential to the performance of any religious act. **–sārathi**, m. a companion, assistant, BhP. **–siddhi**, f. accomplishment of an act, success, Mālav.; Kum. **–sena**, m., N. of a king, Kathās. **–°senīya**, mfn. belonging to that king, ib. **–stava**, m., N. of a work. **–stha**, mfn. contained or being in the object. **–sthāna**, n. public office or place of business, Rājat.; a stage or period in the life of an Ājīvika (q. v.), T. **–hasta**, mfn. clever in business, L. **–hīna**, *ās*, m. pl., N. of a Vaishṇava sect. **–hetu**, mfn. caused by acts, arising from acts. **Karmâkshama**, mfn. incapable of business. **Karmâṅga**, n. part of any act, part of a sacrificial rite. **Karmâjīva**, m. livelihood earned by work, trade, profession, VarBṛS. **Karmâtman**, mfn. one whose character is action, endowed with principles of action, active, acting, Mn. i, 22 & 53; Tattvas. &c. **Karmâditya**, m., N. of a king. **Karmâdhikāra**, m. the right of action, MW. **Karmâdhyaksha**, m. overseer or superintendent of actions, ŚvetUp. vi, 11. **Karmânubandha**, m. connection with or dependance upon acts, W. **Karmânubandhin**, mfn. connected with or involved in works, ib. **Karmânurūpa**, mfn. according to action, according to function or duty, W.; *-tas*, ind. conformably to act or function, ib. **Karmânushṭhāna**, n. the act of practising one's duties, discharging peculiar functions, W. **Karmânushṭhāyin**, mfn. practising duties, performing rites &c., W. **Karmânusāra**, m. consequence of or conformity to acts, W.; *-tas*, ind. according to one's deeds, W. **Karmânta**, m. end or accomplishment of a work, Mṛicch.; Subh.; end or conclusion of a sacred action, SāmavBr.; Karmapr.; work, business, action, management, administration (of an office), MBh.; Mn.; Yājñ. &c.; tilled or cultivated ground, L. **Karmântara**, n. interval between religious actions, suspense of such an action, MBh.; R.; another work or action, BhP. x, 9, 1; Nyāyam. &c. **Karmântika**, mfn. completing an act, W.; (*as*), m. a labourer, artisan, R.; *-loka*, m. labourers, Kād. **Karmâbhidhāyaka**, mfn. enjoining or prescribing duties or acts, W. **Karmâbhidhāyin**, mfn. id., ib. **Karmârambha**, m. commencement of any act, W. **Karmârha**, mfn. fit for work, able to perform a sacrificial rite, Jyot.; (*as*), m. a man, L. **Karmâśaya**, m. receptacle or accumulation of (good and evil) acts, Sarvad.; Comm. on Bādar.; on Nyāyad. &c. **Karmâśrita-bhakta**, *ās*, m. pl., N. of a Vaishṇava sect. **Karmêndriya**, n. an organ of action (five in number like the five organs of sense, viz. hand, foot, larynx, organ of generation, and excretion), MBh.; Mn. ii, 91; Vedāntas. 91, &c. **Karmôdāra**, n. any honourable or valiant act, magnanimity, prowess, W. **Karmôdyukta**, mfn. actively labouring, busily engaged, W. **Karmôdyoga**, m. activity in work, W. **Karmôpakaraṇa**, mfn. one who gives aid by work.

Karmaka, ifc. = *karman*, work, action &c.; (cf. *a-k°*, *sa-k°*, &c.)

Karmaṭha, mfn. capable of work, skilful or clever in work, clever, Pāṇ.; Bhaṭṭ.; working diligently, eagerly engaged in sacred actions or rites, Rājat. &c.; (*as*), m. the director and performer of a sacrifice, W.

Karmaṇi, mfn. connected with or being in the action, ŚBr. vi, 6, 4, 9.

Karmaṇyà, mfn. skilful in work, clever, diligent, RV. i, 91, 20; iii, 4, 9; AV. vi, 23, 2; TS. &c.; proper or fit for any act, suitable for a religious action, Gaut. &c.; (ifc.) relating to any business or to the accomplishment of anything, Suśr.; (*ā*), f. wages, hire, L.; (*am*), n. energy, activity, W. **–tā**, f. cleverness; activity, VarYog. **–bhuj**, mfn. receiving wages, working for hire, L. **Karmaṇyā-bhuj**, mfn. id., L.

Karmanda, *as*, m., N. of a man (author of a Bhikshu-sūtra), Pāṇ. iv, 3, 111.

Karmandin, *ī*, m. one who studies Karmanda's work, ib.; a beggar (= *bhikshu*), L.

Karmara, *as*, m. Averrhoa Carambola (cf. *karmāra*), L.; (*ī*), f. the manna of the bamboo, L.

Karmaraka, *as*, m. id.; (cf. *karma-raṅga*.)

Karmaśa, *as*, m., N. of a son of Pulaha (= *karma-śreshṭha*), VP.

Karmasa, *as*, m., v. l. for the last.

Karmā́ra, *as*, m. an artisan, mechanic, artificer; a blacksmith &c., RV. x, 72, 2; AV. iii, 5, 6; VS.; Mn. iv, 215 &c.; a bamboo, L.; Averrhoa Carambola, L. **–vana**, n., N. of a place, gaṇa *kshubhnâdi*.

Karmāraka, *as*, m. Averrhoa Carambola, L.

Karmika, mfn. active, acting, gaṇas *vrīhy-ādi* and *purohitâdi*.

Karmin, mfn acting, active, busy; performing a religious action, engaged in any work or business, ĀśvŚr.; MBh.; BhP. &c.; belonging or relating to any act, W.; (*ī*), m. performer of an action, Sarvad.; labourer, workman, VarBṛS.; Butea frondosa, Nigh.

Karmishṭha, mfn. (superl. of the last) very active or diligent, L.

Karmīṇa, mfn. only ifc., cf. *anushṭup-karmīṇa*, *alam-karmīṇa*.

कर्मष *karmasha* = *kalmasha*, q. v.

कर्मीर *karmīra* = *kirmīra*, q. v.

कर्व् *karv*, cl. 1. P. *karvati*, to be proud, boast, Dhātup. xv, 72; (cf. *kharv*, *garv*.)

कर्व *karva*, *as*, m. (√1. *kṛī*, Uṇ. i, 155), love, L.; a mouse, rat, L.

कर्वट *karvaṭa* (*as*, m., L.), *am*, n. declivity of a mountain, L.; a village, market-town, the capital of a district (of two or four hundred villages, W.; cf. *kāvaṭa*), Yājñ. ii, 167; Hcat. &c.; (*ās*), m. pl., N. of a people, MBh. ii, 1098; VarBṛS.; (*ī*), f., N. of a river, R.

Karvaṭaka, *am*, n. (?) declivity of a mountain, L.

कर्वर 1. *kárvara*, mfn. (√1. *kṛi*), a deed, action, RV. vi, 24, 5; x, 120, 7; AV.

कर्वर 2. *karvara* or *karbara*, mfn. (√1. *kṛī*, Uṇ. ii, 123), variegated, spotted, L.; (*as*), m. sin, L.; a Rakshas, L.; a tiger, L.; a particular medicament, L.; (*ī*), f. night, L.; a Rākshasī, L.; a tigress, L.; the leaf of Asa fœtida, L.; N. of Durgā, L.; (*am*), n. red lead, L.; (cf. *karbu*, *karbura*, &c.; *karavī*; *kāravī*.)

कर्विणी *karviṇī*, f. a term for the Svarabhakti between *l* and *h*, Comm. on TPrāt.

कर्शन *karśana*, mfn. (√*kṛiś*), rendering lean, attenuating, causing emaciation, Suśr.; troubling, hurting, MBh. xiii, 6307 (cf. *karshaṇa*); (*am*), n. the act of rendering lean, causing emaciation, Car.

Karśanīya, mfn. serving for emaciation, Car.

Karśita, mfn. emaciated, thin, R.; Suśr.; Ragh.; Kum. &c.

Karśya, m. turmeric plant, L.

कर्शफ *karśapha*, *as*, m. a class of imps or goblins, AV. iii, 9, 4.

कर्ष *karsha*, *as*, m. (√*kṛish*), the act of drawing, dragging, Pāṇ.; (with and without *halasya*) ploughing, agriculture, Āp.; Yājñ. ii, 217; 'anything scratched off,' see *kshāma-karsha-miśrá*; (*as*, *am*), m. n. a weight of gold or silver (= 16 Māshas = 80 Rettis = ¼ Pala = $\frac{1}{400}$ of a Tulā = about 176 grains troy; in common use 8 Rettis are given to the Māsha, and the Karsha is then about 280 grains troy'), Suśr.; VarBṛS. &c.; Terminalia Bellerica (also called aksha, q.v.), L.; a boat, L. **— phala,** m. Terminalia Bellerica, L.; (*ā*), f. Emblica officinalis, L. **Karshârdha,** n. = *tolaka*, L.

Karshaka, mfn. pulling to and fro, dragging, tormenting, vexing, AgP.; ploughing, one who ploughs or lives by tillage, a husbandman, Gaut.; MBh.; Yājñ. &c.

Karshaṇa, mfn. pulling to and fro, dragging, tormenting, vexing (v. l. *karśana*), MBh.; R. &c.; extending (in time), APrāt.; the act of drawing or dragging near, Śak. (v. l.); drawing out, pulling off; tugging, pulling (cf. *keśa-k°*), drawing to and fro, removing, hurting, injuring, tormenting, Mn. vii, 112; MBh.; Suśr. &c.; drawing back, bending (a bow), Ragh. xi, 46 (cf. *dhanush-k°*); prolonging (a sound), SaṃhUp.; ploughing, cultivating the ground, Mn. iv, 5; MBh.; BhP.; cultivated land, MBh. iii, 10082; erroneous for *karśana*, q.v., Car.; (*ī*), f., N. of a plant (= *kshīriṇī*), L.

Karshaṇi, *is*, f. an unchaste woman ('attracting men,' BRD.); erroneous for *dharshaṇi*, T.), L.

Karshaṇīya, mfn. to be drawn or pulled &c.; (*am*), n. (?) a kind of defensive weapon, Hariv. 14459.

Karshi, mfn. drawing, furrowing, Kapishṭh.; (cf. *kārshi*.)

Karshita, mfn. ploughed, L.

Karshin, mfn. drawing along, pulling, dragging, Ragh.; Mṛicch. &c.; attractive, inviting, Ragh. xix, 11; ploughing, furrowing; (*as*), m. a ploughman, peasant, husbandman, Kathās.; (*iṇī*), f. the bit of a bridle, L.; a particular plant (= *kshīriṇī*), L.

Karshū, *ūs*, f. (Uṇ. i, 82) a furrow, trench, incision, ŚBr.; KātyŚr. &c.; a river, canal, Comm. on Uṇ.; (*ūs*), m. a fire of dried cow-dung, ib.; agriculture, L.; livelihood, L. **— śaya,** mfn. lying in a trench (*karshū-śayasya śaśasya vratam*, a kind of vow, ĀrshBr. 72, 3). **— sveda,** m. causing sweat by (putting hot coals in) a trench-like receptacle (underneath the bed of a sick person), Car.

कर्षापण *karshāpaṇa* = *kārshāpaṇa*, q.v.

कर्हि *kárhi*, ind. (fr. 2. *ka*), when? at what time? Pāṇ. v, 3, 21; (with *svid* or *cid* or *api* [BhP. v, 17, 24]) at any time, RV.; MBh.; BhP. &c.; (with *cid* and a particle of negation) never, at no time, Mn.; Pañcat. &c.; [cf. Goth. *hvar*, 'where?' Eng. *where?*]

कल् 1. *kal*, cl. 1. Ā. *kalate*, to sound, Dhātup. xiv, 26; to count, ib.; [cf. Lat. *calculo*.]

कल् 2. *kal*, cl. 10. P. (rarely Ā.) *kālayati* (°*te*), to push on, drive forward, drive before one's self or away, carry off, MBh.; BhP.; to go after (with hostile intention), persecute, R. iii, 41, 26; to count, tell over, MBh. iii, 14853; to throw, L.; to announce the time (?).

कल् 3. *kal*, P. (rarely Ā.) *kalayati* (°*te*), to impel, incite, urge on, MBh.; BhP. &c.; to bear, carry, Gīt.; Śāntiś. &c.; to betake one's self to, Naish. ii, 104; to do, make, accomplish, Bhartṛ. iii, 20; Sāh.; to utter a sound, murmur, Naish.; Śiś. &c.; (sometimes in connection with nouns merely expressing the verbal conception, e.g. *mūrchām* √*kal*, to swoon, Bālar.; *culukam jalasya* √*kal*, to take a draught of water, ib.); to tie on, attach, affix, Gīt.; to furnish with; to observe, perceive, take notice of; to consider, count, take for, Gīt.; Bālar.; Ratnāv.; (see 1. *kalaya*, col. 3.)

Kalana, mf(*ā*)n. (ifc.) effecting, causing, Bhartṛ.; (*as*), m. Calamus Rotang, L.; (*ā*), f. the act of impelling, inciting, Sūryas. i, 10; doing, making, effecting, Comm. on MBh.; behaving, behaviour, Kathās.; touching, contact, VarBṛS.; tying on, putting on, Śiś. iii, 5; (according to Mall. also letting loose, shedding, *āmocanam avamocanaṃ vā*); the state of being provided with or having, Bālar.; calculation, Jyot.; (*am*), n. the act of shaking, moving to and fro, Prasannar.; murmuring, sounding, W.; an embryo at the first stage after conception, L. (cf. *kalaka*); a spot, stain, fault, defect, L.; (cf. *kalaṅka*.)

Kalita, mfn. impelled, driven &c. (cf. √3. *kal*); made, formed, Śiś. iii, 81; furnished or provided with, Vikr.; Bhpr. &c.; divided, separated, L.; sounded indistinctly, murmured, W.

कल *kala*, mf(*ā*)n. (etym. doubtful) indistinct, dumb, BṛĀrUp.; ChUp.; (ifc., *bāshpa* or *aśru* preceding) indistinct or inarticulate (on account of tears), MBh.; R. &c.; low, soft (as a tone), emitting a soft tone, melodious (as a voice or throat), R.; BhP.; Vikr. &c.; a kind of faulty pronunciation of vowels, Pat.; weak, crude, undigested, L.; (*as*), m. (scil. *svara*) a low or soft and inarticulate tone (as humming, buzzing &c.), L.; Shorea robusta, L.; (in poetry) time equal to four Mātras or instants, W.; (*ās*), m. pl. a class of manes, MBh.; (*am*), n. semen virile, L.; Zizyphus Jujuba; (*ā*), f., see *kalā* below. **— kaṇṭha,** m. a pleasing tone or voice, L.; 'having a pleasant voice,' the Indian cuckoo, L.; a dove, pigeon, L.; a species of goose, L.; (*ī*), f. the female of that goose, Prasannar.; N. of an Apsaras, Bālar. **— kaṇṭhikā,** f. the female of the Indian cuckoo, Śārṅg. **— kaṇṭhin,** m. the Indian cuckoo, Bālar. **— kala,** m. any confused noise (as a tinkling or rattling sound, the murmuring of a crowd &c.), Mṛicch.; Śiś.; Ratnāv. &c.; the resinous exudation of Shorea robusta, L.; a N. of Śiva, MBh. xii, 10378; *-rava*, m. a confused noise, Bhartṛ.; *-vat*, mfn. tinkling, rattling, Amar.; °*lârava*, m. a confused noise, Pañcat.; °*leśvara-tīrtha*, n., N. of a Tīrtha, ŚivP. **— kīṭa,** m., N. of a village, gaṇa *palady-ādi*. **— kūjikā,** f. a wanton, lascivious wife, W. **— kūṭa,** *ās*, m. pl., N. of a warrior-tribe, Pāṇ. iv, 1, 173. **— kūṇikā,** f. = *-kūjikā* above, L. **— ghosha,** m. the Indian cuckoo, L. **— °m-kasha,** m. a lion, L.; a cymbal, L. **— °m-kura,** m. an eddy, whirlpool, L. **— curi,** m., N. of a royal family, Bālar. **— cūri,** m. id. **— ja,** m. a cock, Bhpr. **— tā,** f., *-tva*, n. melody, music, W. **— tūlikā,** f. a wanton or lascivious woman, L.; (cf. *-kūṇikā* above.) **— dhūta,** n. silver, L. **— dhauta,** n. gold and silver, MBh.; Śiś.; Prasannar. &c.; (*as, am*), m. n. a low or pleasing tone, L.; (mfn.) golden, R.; *-maya*, mfn. golden, Hcat.; *-lipi*, f. (?) a streak of gold, illumination of a MS. with gold, Gīt. **— dhvani,** m. a low and pleasing tone, L.; (in mus.) a particular time; 'having a pleasing voice,' the Indian cuckoo, L.; a pigeon, L.; a peacock, L. **— nātha,** m., N. of an author. **— nāda,** m. a kind of goose, L.; (cf. *-haṃsa* below.) **— bhava,** m. the thorn-apple tree, L. **— bhāshaṇa,** n. the act of speaking in a low voice. **— bhāshin,** mfn. speaking with a pleasing voice, Mālav. **— bhairava,** m. or n. (?), N. of a deep ravine in the mountain between the rivers Tāpī and Narmadā. **— mūka,** mfn. deaf and dumb (cf. *kalla-mūka*), L. **— rava,** m. a low sweet tone, Bhartṛ.; 'having a sweet voice,' the Indian cuckoo, L.; a pigeon, L. **— vacas,** mfn. speaking sweetly, singing, L. **— vikarṇī,** f., N. of a form of Durgā, Hcat. **— vikala,** m., N. of an Asura; *-vadha*, m., N. of a chapter of the Gaṇeśa-purāṇa. **— vyāghra,** m. a mongrel breed between a tigress and panther, L. **— svana,** mfn. having a charming voice (as a bird), L. **— svara,** n. a low musical sound, W. **— haṃsa,** m., N. of several species of the Haṃsa bird or goose, MBh.; R.; Pañcat. &c.; an excellent king, L.; Brahma or the Supreme Spirit, L.; a particular metre (consisting of four lines of thirteen syllables each); (*ī*), f. the female of the Kala-haṃsa above, Ragh. viii, 58. **— haṃsaka,** m. a kind of duck or goose, Kād. **Kalânunādin,** m. 'giving out a low note,' a sparrow, L.; the Cātaka bird, L.; a kind of bee, L. **Kalâlāpa,** m. a sweet sound, pleasing voice, Kathās.; 'having a low voice,' a bee, L. **Kalôttāla,** mf(*ā*)n. sweet and loud (as a voice), Gīt. i, 47.

कलक *kalaka*, *as*, m. a sort of fish, L.; a kind of prose, L.; (*am*), n. the root of Andropogon Muricatus, L.

कलङ्क *kalaṅka*, *as*, m. (etym. doubtful) a stain, spot, mark, soil; defamation, blame, Kathās.; Mṛicch. &c. **— kara,** mfn. causing stains, soiling; censorious, calumniating, defaming. **— kalā,** f. a digit of the moon in shadow, Gīt. **— maya,** mfn. full of stains, spotted; calumniated, defamed. **— lekhā,** f. a line of spots, spotted streak, Ragh. xiii, 15. **— hṛit,** m., N. of Śiva. **Kalaṅkâṅka,** m. the spots or marks of the moon, R.

Kalaṅkaya, Nom. P. *kalaṅkayati*, to spot, soil, Kād.; to defame, disgrace, Daś.

Kalaṅkita, mfn. spotted, soiled, stained, disgraced, defamed, Bhartṛ.; Kathās. &c.

Kalaṅkin, mfn. id., Kāvyād.; Naish. &c.

कलङ्कुर *kalaṃ-kura*. See *kala*.

कलञ्ज *kalañja*, *as*, m. Calamus Rotang; tobacco; a particular weight (= 10 Rūpakas), Bhpr.; an animal (struck with a poisonous weapon), L.; (*am*), n. the flesh of such an animal, Nyāyam.

कलट *kalaṭa*, n. the thatch of a house, L.; (cf. *kuṭala*.)

कलत *kalata*, mfn. bald-headed, L.; (cf. *khalati*.)

कलत्र *kalatra*, *am*, n. a wife, consort, MBh.; Bhartṛ.; Hit. &c.; the female of an animal, Vikr.; the hip and loins, L.; pudendum muliebre, L.; a royal citadel, a stronghold or fastness, W.; (in astron.) the seventh lunar mansion, VarBṛ. **— tā,** f. the state of being a wife or consort, Ratnāv. **— vat,** mfn. having a wife, united with one's wife, BhP.; Mṛicch. &c. **Kalatrī-√kṛi,** to make any one one's wife, Viddh.

Kalatrin, mfn. having a wife, Ragh. viii, 82.

कलन्तक *kalantaka* = the next.

कलन्दक *kalandaka*, *as*, m. a squirrel (or a kind of bird?), Buddh.; a particular vessel used by Śramaṇas, Buddh.; (*ikā*), f. = *kalindikā*, q. v.

Kalandana, *as*, m., N. of a man.

कलन्दर *kalandara*, *as*, m. a man of a mixed caste, BrahmavP.

कलन्धु *kalandhu*, *us*, m. a kind of vegetable (= *gholi*), L.

कलभ *kalabha*, *as*, m. (√3. *kal*, Uṇ. iii, 122), a young elephant (one thirty years old), Ragh.; Mṛicch.; Pañcat. &c.; a young camel, Pañcat. iv; Datura Fastuosa (= *dhustūra*), L.; (*ī*), f. a sort of vegetable, L. **— vallabha,** m., N. of a tree, L.

Kalabhaka, *as*, m. the young of an elephant, Kād.

कलम *kalama*, *as*, m. (√1. *kal*, Uṇ. iv, 84), a sort of rice (sown in May and June and ripening in December or January), Suśr.; Ragh. &c.; a reed for writing with; [cf. Lat. *calamus*; Gk. κάλαμος; and Arab. قلم]; a thief, L. **— gopa-vadhū,** f. a woman employed to guard a rice-field, Śiś. vi, 49. **— gopī,** f. id., Bālar. **— sthāna,** n. an ink-stand, L. **Kalamôttama,** m. fragrant rice, L.

Kalamba, *as*, m. the stalk of a pot-herb, L.; Convolvulus repens, L.; Nauclea Cadamba, L.; an arrow, L.; (*ī*), f. Convolvulus repens, Hariv.; (*am*), n. a panicle of flowers (?), Car.; Calumba-root, W.; (cf. *kadamba, kadamba*.)

Kalambaka, *as*, m. a species of Kadamba, L.; (*ikā*), f. Convolvulus repens, L.; (*ike*), f. du. the nape of the neck, L.

Kalambukā, f. Convolvulus repens, Jain.

Kalambū, *ūs*, f. id., L.

कलम्बुट *kalambuṭa*, *am*, n. fresh butter, L.

कलय 1. *kalaya*, Nom. P. (fr. *kali*) *kalayati*, to take hold of the die called Kali, Kāś. on Pāṇ. iii, 1, 21.

कलय 2. *kalaya*, v.l. for *kala-ja*, q. v.

कलयज *kalayaja* = *kalalaja* below, Npr.

कलल *kalala*, *am*, n. (*as*, m., L.) the embryo a short time after conception, Suśr.; BhP.; (cf. *kalana*.)

कललज *kalalaja*, *as*, m. the resinous exudation of the Shorea robusta, L.; (cf. *kala-kala*.)

Kalalajôdbhava, m. Shorea robusta, L.

कलविङ्क *kalaviṅka*, *as*, m. a sparrow, VS.; TS. &c.; Mn. &c.; the Indian cuckoo, Kāraṇḍ.; a spot, stain (cf. *kalaṅka*), L.; a white Cāmara, L.; N. of a plant (= *kaliṅgaka*), L.; N. of a top of a Tīrtha, MBh. **— svara,** m. a kind of Samādhi (q. v.), Kāraṇḍ.

कलश *kaláśa*, *as*, m. (*am*, n., L.) a water-pot, pitcher, jar, dish, RV. &c.; Śak.; Hit. &c. (the breasts of a woman are frequently compared to jars, cf. *stana-k°* & *kumbha*); (*as*), m. a butter-tub, churn, MBh.; a particular measure (= *droṇa*), ŚārṅgS.; a round pinnacle on the top of a temple (esp. the pinnacle crowning a Buddhist Caitya or Stūpa), Kād.; N. of a man, RV. x, 32, 9; of a poet; of a Nāga, MBh. v; (*ī*), f. a pitcher &c., Bālar.; a churn, L.; Hemionitis cordifolia, Suśr.; N. of a Tīrtha, MBh.; [cf. Gk. κάλιξ; Lat. *calix*.] **— janman,** m., N. of Agastya, SkandaP. **— dir,** mfn. one whose pitcher is broken, ŚBr. iv. **— pura,** n., N. of a town, Kathās. **—potaka,** m., N. of a Nāga, MBh. **—bhū,** m.'jar-born,' N. of Agastya, Bālar. **—yoni,** m. id., Kād.; N. of Droṇa, Hcar. **Kalaśôdara,** m., N. of an attendant in Skanda's retinue, MBh.; of a Daitya, Hariv.; (*ī*), f., N. of a great river, Kāraṇḍ. **Kalaśôdbhava,** m., N. of Agastya, Bālar.

Kalaśi, *is,* f. a water-pot, pitcher, jar, L.; a churn, Śiś. xi, 8; Hemionitis cordifolia, L.

Kalaśī, f. of *kalaśa.* **—kaṇṭha,** m., N. of a man, and (*ās*), m. pl. his descendants, gaṇa *upakâdi.* **—padī,** f. a woman with feet like a water-jar, gaṇa *kumbhapady-ādi.* **—mukha,** m. a sort of musical instrument, L. **—suta,** m., N. of Agastya, L.

कलस *kalasa,* v. l. for *kalaśa* above.

Kalasi, v. l. for *kalaśi* above.

कलह 1. *kalaha, as,* m. (*am,* n., L.) strife, contention, quarrel, fight, MBh.; Mn. &c.; the sheath of a sword, L.; a road, way, W.; deceit, falsehood, W.; violence without murderous weapons, abuse, beating, kicking, W.; (*ā*), f., N. of a woman. **—kandala,** m., N. of an actor. **—kāra,** mf(*ī*)n. quarrelsome, turbulent, contentious, pugnacious, Pāṇ.; Hit.; N. of the wife of Vikrama-caṇḍa, Kathās. **—kārikā,** f. a species of bird, VarBṛS. **—kārin,** mfn. quarrelsome, contentious. **—nāśana,** m. Guilandina Bonduc, L. **—priya,** mf(*ā*)n. fond of contention, quarrelsome, turbulent, R.; N. of Nārada, MBh.; of a king, L.; (*ā*), f. Gracula religiosa, L. **—vat,** mfn. having a quarrel, quarreling with, Pañcat. **Kalahâkulā,** f. Gracula religiosa, L. **Kalahâṅkura,** m., N. of a man. **Kalahântaritā,** f. a heroine separated from her lover in consequence of a quarrel, Sāh.; Gīt. &c. **Kalahâpahṛita,** mfn. taken away by force, W.

2. **Kalaha,** Nom. P. *kalahati,* to quarrel, MBh. xii, 5349.

Kalahāya, Nom. Ā. °*yate,* to quarrel, contend, Pāṇ. iii, 1, 17.

Kalahin, mfn. contentious, quarrelsome, ĀśvGṛ.; ChUp. &c.

कलहु *kalahu, us,* m. (f.?) a particular high number, Lalit.; (cf. *karahu.*)

कला *kalā́,* f. (etym. doubtful) a small part of anything, any single part or portion of a whole, esp. a sixteenth part, RV. viii, 47, 17; TS.; ŚBr.; Mn. &c.; a digit or one-sixteenth of the moon's diameter, Hit.; Kathās.; (personified as a daughter of Kardama and wife of Marīci, BhP.); a symbolical expression for the number sixteen, Hcat.; interest on a capital (considered as a certain part of it), Śiś. ix, 32; a division of time (said to be $\frac{1}{900}$ of a day or 1·6 minutes, Mn. i, 64; Hariv.; or $\frac{1}{1800}$ of a day or 0·8 minutes, Comm. on VP.; or 2 minutes and 26$\frac{54}{201}$ seconds, Suśr.; or 1 minute and 35$\frac{205}{301}$ seconds, or 8 seconds, BhavP.); the sixtieth part of one-thirtieth of a zodiacal sign, a minute of a degree, Sūryas.; (in prosody) a syllabic instant; a term for the seven substrata of the elements or Dhātus of the human body (viz. flesh, blood, fat, phlegm, urine, bile, and semen; but according to Hemacandra, *rasa,* 'chyle,' *asthi,* 'bone,' and *majjan,* 'marrow,' take the place of phlegm, urine, and bile), Suśr.; an atom (there are 3015 Kalās or atoms in every one of the six Dhātus, not counting the *rasa,* therefore in all 18090); (with Pāśupatas) the elements of the gross or material world, Sarvad.; an embryo shortly after conception (cf. *kalana*); a designation of the three constituent parts of a sacrifice (viz. *mantra, dravya,* and *śraddhā,* Nīlak. on MBh. [ed. Bomb.] xiv, 89, 3); the menstrual discharge, L.; any practical art, any mechanical or fine art (sixty-four are enumerated in the Śaivatantra [T.]; the following is a list of them: *gītam, vādyam, nṛityam, nāṭyam, ālekhyam, viśeshaka-cchedyam, taṇḍula-kusuma-bali-vikārāḥ, pushpâstaranam, daśana-vasanâṅga-rāgāḥ, maṇi-bhūmikā-karma, śayana-racanam, udaka-vādyam, udaka-ghātaḥ, citrā yogāḥ, mālya-granthana-vikalpāḥ, keśa-śekharâpīḍa-yojanam, nepathya-yogāḥ, karṇa-pattra-bhaṅgāḥ, gandha-yuktiḥ, bhūshaṇa-yojanam, indra-jālam, kaucumāra-yogāḥ, hasta-lāghavam, citra-śākâpūpa-bhakshya-vikāra-kriyā, pānaka-rasa-rāgâsava-yojanam, sūcīvāpa-karma, vīṇā-ḍamaruka-sūtra-krīḍā, prahelikā, pratimā, durvacaka-yogāḥ, pustaka-vācanam, nāṭakâkhyāyikā-darśanam, kāvya-samasyā-pūraṇam, paṭṭikā-vetra-bāṇa-vikalpāḥ, tarkū-karmāṇi, takshaṇam, vāstu-vidyā, rūpya-ratna-parīkshā, dhātu-vādaḥ, maṇi-rāga-jñānam, ākara-jñānam, vṛikshâyur-veda-yogāḥ, mesha-kukkuṭa-lāvaka-yuddha-vidhiḥ, śuka-sārikā-pralāpanam, utsādanam, keśa-mārjana-kauśalam, akshara-mushṭikā-kathanam, mlechitaka-vikalpāḥ, deśa-bhāshā-jñānam, pushpa-śakaṭikā-nimitta-jñānam, yantra-mātṛikā, dhāraṇa-mātṛikā, sampātyam, mānasī kāvya-kriyā, kriyā-vikalpāḥ, chalitaka-yogāḥ, abhidhāna-kosha-cchando-jñānam, vastra-gopanāni, dyūta-viśeshaḥ, ākarshaṇa-krīḍā, bālaka-krīḍanakāni, vaināyikīnām vidyānām jñānam, vaijayikīnām vidyānām jñānam;* see also Vātsy. i, 3, 17), R.; Pañcat.; Bhartṛ. &c.; skill, ingenuity; ignorance; a low and sweet tone, Bālar.; a boat, L.; a N. given to Dākshāyaṇī in the region near the river Candrabhāgā, MatsyaP.; N. of a grammatical commentary. **—°ṇśa** (*kalâṇśa*), m. the part of a part, BrahmavP. **—kanda,** n.(?) a particular metre. **—kuśala,** mfn. skilled in the arts (enumerated above). **—keli,** m. amorous play, Bālar.; 'frolicsome,' N. of Kāma, L. **—°ṅkura** (*kalâṅk*°), m., N. of Mūladeva or Kaṇsa (the author of a book on the art of stealing, T.); the bird Ardea Sibirica, L. **—jājī,** f., N. of a tree, T. **—jña,** mf(*ā*)n. skilled in arts, Subh.; (*as*), m. an artist. **—°tman** (*kalât*°), f. a particular ceremony of ordination. **—°da** (*kalâda?*), m. a goldsmith, Jain. **—dīkshā,** f., N. of a work. **—dhara,** mfn. bearing or skilled in an art; (*as*), m. 'having digits,' the moon; 'bearing a digit of the moon,' N. of Śiva. **—nātha,** m. 'lord of the digits,' the moon, Subh.; N. of an author of Mantras. **—nidhi,** m. 'a treasure of digits,' the moon, Dhūrtas. **—°ntara** (*kalântara*), n. interest, Rājat. **—nyāsa,** m. tattooing a person's body with particular mystical marks, Tantras. **—°pa** (*kalâpa,* fr. √*āp*), m. 'that which holds single parts together,' a bundle, band (cf. *jaṭā-k*°, *muktā-k*°, *raśanā-k*°), MBh.; Kum. &c.; a bundle of arrows, a quiver with arrows, quiver, MBh.; R. &c.; (once n., MBh. iii, 11454); a peacock's tail, MBh.; Pañcat. &c.; an ornament in general, Mālav.; a zone, a string of bells (worn by women round the waist), L.; the rope round an elephant's neck, L.; totality, whole body or collection of a number of separate things (esp. ifc.; cf. *kriyā-k*°, &c.); the moon, L.; a clever and intelligent man, L.; N. of a grammar also called Kātantra (supposed to be revealed by Kārttikeya to Śarvavarman); N. of a village (cf. *kalāpa-grāma*), VP.; a poem written in one metre, W.; (*ī*), f. a bundle of grass, KātyŚr.; ĀśvŚr.; *-khañja,* m. a particular disease (said to be St. Vitus's dance; v. l. *kalāya-khañja*), Bhpr.; *-grāma,* m., N. of a village, Hariv.; BhP.; VP.; *-cchanda,* m. an ornament of pearls consisting of twenty-four strings, L.; *-tattvârṇava,* m., N. of a commentary on the grammar called Kalāpa; *-dvīpa,* m., v. l. for *kalāpa-grāma* above; *-varman,* m., N. of a man, Kād.; *-śas,* ind. in bundles, bundle by bundle, MBh. xiii; *-śiras,* m. N. of a man (v. l. *kapāla-śiras*), R. **—°paka** (*kalâpaka*), m. a band, bundle, Śiś.; a kind of ornament, MBh.; a string of pearls, L.; the rope round an elephant's neck, L.; a sectarian mark on the forehead, L.; (*am*), n. a series of four stanzas in grammatical connection (i. e. in which the government of noun and verb is carried throughout, contrary to the practice of closing the sense with each stanza, e. g. Kir. xvi, 21–24), Sāh. 558; *= candraka,* L.; a debt to be paid when the peacocks spread their tails (*kalāpini* [see *kalāpin* below] *kāle deyam ṛiṇam,* Kāś.), Pāṇ. iv, 3, 48. **—°pin** (*kalâpin*), mfn. furnished with a bundle of arrows, bearing a quiver with arrows, KātyŚr.; MBh.; spreading its tail (as a peacock), MBh. iii, 11585; (with *kāla,* the time) when peacocks spread their tails, Pāṇ. iv, 3, 48; (*ī*), m. a peacock, Ragh.; Pañcat. &c.; the Indian cuckoo, L.; Ficus infectoria, L.; N. of an ancient teacher, Pāṇ. iv, 3, 104; (*inī*), f. a peahen, Śatr.; night, L.; the moon, L.; a species of Cyperus, L. **—pūra,** *am, ā,* n. f. a kind of musical instrument, L. **—pūrṇa,** mfn. filled up or counterbalanced by the sixteenth part of (gen.), (*na kalā-pūrṇo mama,* he is not equal to the sixteenth part of myself, i. e. he is far under me), MBh. iv, 1299; (*as*), m. 'full of digits,' the moon, L. **—bāhya,** n. a kind of fault in singing, L. **—bhara,** m. 'possessing the arts,' an artist, mechanic, Gaut. **—bhṛit,** m. id.; 'digit-bearer,' the moon, L. **—°yana** (*kalâyana*), m. a tumbler, dancer (esp. one who dances or walks on the edge of a sword &c.), L. **—rūpa,** n. a particular ceremony; (*ā*), f., N. of one of the five Mūla-prakṛitis. **—°rṇava** (*kalârṇava*), m., N. of a dancing-master, Comm. on Pratāpar. **—vat,** m. 'having digits,' the moon, Kum.; (*ī*), f. a mystical ceremony (the initiation of the Tantrika student in which the goddess Durgā is supposed to be transferred from the water-jar to the body of the novice), Tantras.; (in mus.) a particular Mūrchanā; the lute of the Gandharva Tumburu, L.; N. of an Apsaras; of a daughter of the Apsaras Alambushā, Kathās. cxxi, 111 ff.; of several other women. **—vāda,** n., N. of a Tantra. **—vikala,** m. a sparrow, L.; (cf. *kalaviṅka.*) **—vid,** mfn. knowing or conversant with arts; (*t*), m. an artisan, VarBṛS.; a Vidyā-dhara, L. **—vidvas,** m. id., ib. **—vidhi,** m. the practice of the sixty-four arts; *-tantra,* n., N. of a Tantra. **—vilāsa,** m., N. of a work on rhetoric. **—śas,** ind. in single parts, part by part. **—śāstra,** n., N. of a work by Viśākhila. **—ślāghya,** m., N. of Śiva, Sarvad. 95, 19. **—sāra,** n., N of a Tantra.

Kalikā, f. the sixteenth part of the moon, Bhartṛ.; a division of time (= *kalā,* q. v.); an unblown flower, bud, Śak. Ragh. &c.; the bottom or peg of the Indian lute (made of cane), L.; N. of several metres; a kind of artificial verse (cf. *kānta-k*°); N. of a work on medicine. **Kalikâpūrva,** n. an unforeseen event (as birth &c.) partly resulting from an act and leading to totally unforeseen consequences (as heaven &c.; *paramâpūrvajanako 'ṅgajanyâpūrvabhedaḥ,* T.), Nyāyak.

कलाकुल *kalākula, am,* n. a kind of poison, L.; (cf. *halāhala.*)

कलाङ्गल *kalāṅgala,* (ifc. f. *ā*) a kind of weapon [BRD.], MBh. iii, 642; [according to T. *saśataghnīkalāṅgalā* is thus to be resolved: *śataghnyā sahitam saśataghnīkam tādṛiśam lāṅgalam yatra;* in that case *kalāṅgala* is no word.]

कलाचिक *kalācika, as,* m. (?) a ladle, spoon, L.; (*ā*), f. the fore-arm, L.

Kalācī, f. the fore-arm, L.

कलाटीन *kalāṭīna, as,* m. the white water-wagtail, L.

कलाण्डी *kalāṇḍī,* f., N. of a plant, L.

कलाधिक *kalādhika, as,* m. (fr. *kala* and *adhika?*), a cock, L.; (cf. *kalāvika.*)

कलानक *kalānaka, as,* m., N. of one of the attendants of Śiva, L.

कलाप *kalâpa,* &c. See *kalā.*

कलामक *kalāmaka, as,* m. a kind of rice (ripening in the cold season), L.; (cf. *kalama.*)

कलाम्बि *kalāmbi, is,* f. lending, usury, L.

Kalāmbikā, f. id., ib.

कलाय *kalāya, as,* m. a sort of pea or pulse, MBh.; Suśr. &c.; a kind of plant with dark-coloured flowers, Śiś. xiii, 21; (*ā*), f. a species of Dūrvā-grass, L. **—khañja,** m. = *kalāpa-khañja,* q. v., ŚārṅgS. **—sūpa,** m. pea-soup, L.

कलाविक *kalāvika, as,* m. = *kalādhika,* q. v.

कलाविकल *kalā-vikala.* See *kalā.*

कलाशुरि *kalāśuri, is,* m., N. of a royal family, L.; (cf. *kalacuri.*)

कलाहक *kalāhaka, as,* m. a kind of musical instrument, L.; (cf. *kāhala.*)

कलि *káli, is,* m. (√1. *kal,* Comm. on Uṇ. iv, 117), N. of the die or side of a die marked with one dot, the losing die, AV. vii, 109, 1; ŚBr. &c. (personified as an evil genius in the episode of Nala); symbolical expression for the number 1; Terminalia Bellerica (the nuts of which in older times were used as dice), L.; N. of the last and worst of the four Yugas or ages, the present age, age of vice, AitBr.; Mn. i, 86; ix, 301 f.; MBh. &c. (the Kali age contains, inclusive of the two dawns, 1200 years of the gods or 432,000 years of men, and begins the eighteenth of February, 3102 B.C.; at the end of this Yuga the world is to be destroyed; see *yuga*); strife, discord, quarrel, contention (personified as the son of *Krodha,* 'Anger,' and *Hiṅsā,* 'Injury,' and as generating with his sister *Durukti,* 'Calumny,' two children, viz. *Bhaya*, 'Fear,' and *Mṛityu*, 'Death,' BhP. iv, 8, 3; 4), MBh.; Hit. &c.; the worst of a class or number of objects, MBh. xii, 361; 363; a hero (or an arrow, *śūra* or *śara*), L.; N. of Śiva, MBh. xiii, 1192; N. of an Upanishad (= *kali-saṃtaraṇa*); (*is*), m., N. of a class of mythic beings (related to the Gandharvas, and supposed by some to be fond of gambling; in epic poetry Kali is held to be the fifteenth of the Deva-gandharvas or children of the Munis), AV. x, 10, 13; MBh.; Hariv.; N. of a man, RV.; (*is, ī*), f. an unblown flower, bud, L. **–kāra**, m. (in all its meanings, L.) the fork-tailed shrike; Loxia philippensis; a kind of chicken; Pongamia glabra; Guilandina Bonduc; N. of Nārada; (*ī*), f. Methonica superba, L. **–kāraka**, m., N. of Nārada, L.; Cæsalpina Bonducella, L.; (*ikā*), f., N. of a plant. **–kāla**, m. the Kali age, Kathās. **–kuñcikā**, f. a younger sister of a husband, L. **–kṛit**, mfn. contentious, quarreling. **–cchandas**, n. a kind of metre. **–dru**, m. 'tree of strife,' Terminalia Bellerica (supposed to be the haunt of imps), Bhpr. **–druma**, m. id., Comm. on Uṇ. i, 108. **–dharma-nirṇaya**, m., N. of a work. **–dharma-sāra-saṃgraha**, m., N. of a work. **–nātha**, m., N. of a writer on music. **–prada**, m. a liquor-shop, Nigh. **–priya**, mfn. fond of quarreling, quarrelsome, mischievous; (*as*), m., N. of Nārada, an ape, L. **–māraka**, m. Cæsalpina Bonducella, L. **–mālaka, -mālya**, m. id., ib. **–yuga**, n. the Kali age (see above), Mn. i, 85; MBh. &c. **–vināśinī**, f., N. of a goddess, BrahmaP. **–vṛiksha**, m. Terminalia Bellerica, L. **–śāsana**, m. a Jina, L. **–saṃtaraṇa**, n., N. of an Upanishad. **–saṃśraya**, m. the act of betaking one's self to Kali. **–stoma**, m. a particular Stoma. **–hārī**, f. Methonica Superba, Bhpr.

कलिक *kalika*, *as*, m. a curlew, W.

कलिका *kalikā*. See p. 261, col. 3.

कलिकाता *kalikātā*, f. the town Calcutta.

कलिङ्ग *kaliṅga*, *ās*, m. pl., N. of a people and their country (the N. is applied in the Purāṇas to several places, but especially signifies a district on the Coromandel coast, extending from below Cuttack [Kaṭaka] to the vicinity of Madras), MBh.; Hariv.; VP. &c.; (*as*), m. an inhabitant of Kaliṅga, Sāh.; N. of a king of Kaliṅga (from whom the Kaliṅga people are said to have originated; he is sometimes mentioned as a son of Dīrghatamas and Sudeshṇā, sometimes identified with Bali), MBh.; Hariv. &c.; N. of a being attending on Skanda, MBh. (ed. Bomb.) ix, 45, 64 (v.l. *kalinda*, ed. Calc.); N. of several authors; the fork-tailed shrike, L.; Cæsalpina Bonducella, L.; Wrightia antidysenteria, L.; Acacia Sirissa, L.; Ficus infectoria, L.; (*ā*), f. a beautiful woman, L.; Opomea Turpethum; (*am*), n. the seed of Wrightia antidysenteria, Suśr.; (mfn.) clever, cunning, L. **–bīja**, n. the seed of Wrightia antidysenteria, L. **–yava**, m. id., Npr. **–senā**, f., N. of a princess, Kathās.

Kaliṅgaka, *as*, m. the country of the Kaliṅgas; the seed of Wrightia antidysenteria, Car.; (*ā*), f. a particular plant, L.

कलिञ्ज *kaliñja*, *as*, m. a mat, L.; (*am*), n. wood, L.; (cf. *kiliñja*.)

कलिञ्जर *kaliñjara*, *as*, m., N. of a king (?), Rājat. vii, 1268.

कलित *kalita*. See √3. *kal*.

कलिनी *kalini*, f. pea-plant, pulse, L.

कलिन्द *kalinda*, *as*, m. Terminalia Bellerica, L.; the sun, L.; N. of a mountain on which the river Yamunā rises; N. of a being attending on Skanda, MBh. (ed. Calc.) ix, 2566 (v.l. *kaliṅga*, ed. Bomb.); (*ās*), m. pl., N. of a people, MBh. (ed. Calc.) xiii, 2104 (v.l. *kaliṅga*, ed. Bomb.); (*ā*), f., N. of a river, R.; (*ī*), f., N. of the river Yamunā (= *kālindī*, q. v.), R. **–kanyā**, f. 'Kalinda's daughter,' N. of the river Yamunā, Ragh. **–tanayā, -nandinī, -śaila-jātā, -sutā**, f. id., Bālar.; Kād. &c. **Kalindâtmajā**, f. id.

कलिन्दिका *kalindikā*, f. science, L.; (v.l. *kalandikā*.)

कलिल *kalila*, mfn. (√1. *kal*, Uṇ. i, 55), mixed with, Śiś. xix, 98; full of, covered with, MBh.; BhP. &c.; impenetrable, impervious; (*am*), n. a large heap, thicket, confusion, ŚvetUp.; Bhag. &c.

कलुक्क *kalukka*, *as*, m. a cymbal, L.; (*ā*), f. a tavern, L.; a meteor, L.

कलुष *kalusha*, mf(*ā*)n. (√3. *kal*, Uṇ. iv, 75), turbid, foul, muddy, impure, dirty (lit. and fig.), Mn.; Suśr.; Kathās. &c.; hoarse (as the voice), Śak.; (ifc.) unable, not equal to, Ragh. v, 64; (*as*), m. a buffalo, L.; a sort of snake, Suśr.; (*ā*), f. the female of a buffalo, L.; (*am*), n. foulness, turbidness, dirt, impurity (lit. and fig.), MBh.; R. &c.; sin, wrath, L. **–cetas**, mfn. of impure mind, bad, wicked, R. **–tā**, f., **-tva**, n. foulness, turbidness &c. **–mati**, mfn. = *-cetas* above. **–mañjarī**, f. Odina Wodier, Nigh. **–yoni**, f. impure origin; *-ja*, mfn. of impure origin, Mn. x, 57; 58. **Kalushâtman**, mfn. of impure mind, bad, wicked, Kathās. **Kalushī-√kṛi**, to make turbid or unclean, dirty, defile, MBh.; R.; Prabh. &c. **Kalushī-√bhū**, to become troubled or agitated, MW.

Kalushaya, Nom. P. *kalushayati*, to make unclean or dirty, dirty, Viddh.

Kalushāya, Nom. Ā. *kalushāyate*, to become turbid or unclean, Mṛicch.

Kalushita, mfn. foul, impure, W.; defiled, contaminated, W.; wicked, W.

Kalushin, mfn. id., ib.

कलूतर *kalūtara*, v.l. for *kulūna*, q.v.

कलेवर *kalevara*, *as, am*, m. n., the body, MBh.; R. &c.; [cf. Lat. *cadāver*]; (*as*), m. Olibanum, L.

कल्क *kalka*, *as*, m. (*am*, n., L.), (√3. *kal*, Uṇ. iii, 40), a viscous sediment deposited by oily substances when ground, a kind of tenacious paste, Suśr.; Yājñ. &c.; dirt, filth; the wax of the ear; ordure, fæces, L.; impurity, meanness, falsehood, hypocrisy, deceit, sin, MBh.; BhP. &c.; Terminalia Bellerica, L.; Olibanum, L.; (mfn.) sinful, wicked, L.; (cf. *kalusha, kalmasha, kilbisha*.) **–phala**, m. the pomegranate plant, L. **Kalkâlaya**, m., N. of a man. **Kalkī-√kṛi**, to knead, render doughy (by kneading), Suśr. **Kalkī-√bhū**, to become doughy, Rājat. vii, 1544 (*śalkī*, ed.)

Kalkana, *am*, n. meanness, wickedness, BhP.

Kalki, *is*, m., N. of the tenth incarnation of Vishṇu when he is to appear mounted on a white horse and wielding a drawn sword as destroyer of the wicked (this is to take place at the end of the four Yugas or ages), MBh. &c. **–dvādaśī-vrata**, n., N. of a particular observance. **–purāṇa**, n., N. of a Purāṇa.

Kalkin, mfn. foul, turbid, having sediment, dirty, W.; wicked, W.; (*ī*), m. = *kalki* above.

कल्कल *kalkala*, *ās*, m. pl., N. of a people, VP.

कल्कुषी *kalkushī́*, f. or n. du. wrist and elbow, ŚBr. x, 2, 6, 14.

कल्प 1. *kálpa*, mf(*ā*)n. (√*kḷip*), practicable, feasible, possible, ŚBr. ii, 4, 3, 3; proper, fit, able, competent, equal to (with gen., loc., inf., or ifc.; e.g. *dharmasya kalpaḥ*, competent for duty; *svakarmaṇi na kalpaḥ*, not competent for his own work; *yadā na śāsituṃ kalpaḥ*, if he is not able to rule), BhP.; (*as*), m. a sacred precept, law, rule, ordinance (= *vidhi, nyāya*), manner of acting, proceeding, practice (esp. that prescribed by the Vedas), RV. ix, 9, 7; AV. viii, 9, 10; xx, 128, 6-11; MBh.; (*prathamaḥ kalpaḥ*, a rule to be observed before any other rule, first duty, Mn. iii, 147; MBh. &c.; *etena kalpena*, in this way; cf. *paśu-k°*, &c.); the most complete of the six Vedāṅgas (that which prescribes the ritual and gives rules for ceremonial or sacrificial acts), MuṇḍUp.; Pāṇ. &c.; one of two cases, one side of an argument, an alternative (= *paksha*; cf. *vikalpa*), Sarvad.; investigation, research, Comm. on Sāṃkhyak.; resolve, determination, MW.; (in medic.) treatment of the sick, manner of curing, Suśr. ii; the art of preparing medicine, pharmacy, Car.; the doctrine of poisons and antidotes, Suśr. i; (ifc.) having the manner or form of anything, similar to, resembling, like but with a degree of inferiority, almost (e.g. *abhedya-kalpa*, almost impenetrable; cf. *prabhāta-k°*, *mṛita-k°*, &c.; according to native grammarians, *kalpa* so used is an accentless affix [Pāṇ. v, 3, 67], before which a final *s* is left unchanged, and final *ī* and *ū* shortened, Pāṇ.; Vop.; *kalpam*, ind., may be also connected with a verb, e.g. *pacati-kalpam*, he cooks pretty well, Kāś. on Pāṇ. viii, 1, 57); a fabulous period of time (a day of Brahmā or one thousand Yugas, a period of four thousand, three hundred and twenty millions of years of mortals, measuring the duration of the world; a month of Brahmā is supposed to contain thirty such Kalpas; according to the MBh., twelve months of Brahmā constitute his year, and one hundred such years his lifetime; fifty years of Brahmā's are supposed to have elapsed, and we are now in the *Śveta-vārāha-kalpa* of the fifty-first; at the end of a Kalpa the world is annihilated; hence *kalpa* is said to be equal to *kalpânta* below, L.; with Buddhists the Kalpas are not of equal duration), VP.; BhP.; Rājat. &c.; N. of Mantras which contain a form of √*kḷip*, TS. v; ŚBr. ix; a kind of dance; N. of the first astrological mansion, VarBṛS.; N. of a son of Dhruva and Bhrami, BhP. iv, 10, 1; of Śiva, MBh. xii, 10368; the tree of paradise; = *-taru* below, L.; (with Jainas) a particular abode of deities (cf. *-bhava* and *kalpâtīta* below); (*am*), n. a kind of intoxicating liquor (incorrect for *kalya*), L. **–kāra**, m. an author of rules on ritual or ceremonies. **–kedāra**, m., N. of a medical work by Kāliśiva. **–kshaya**, m. the end of a Kalpa, destruction of the world, Kathās. **–gā**, f., N. of a river, ŚivP. **–cintā-maṇi**, m., N. of a work. **–tantra**, n., N. of a work. **–taru**, m. one of the five trees (cf. *pañca-vriksha*) of Svarga or Indra's paradise fabled to fulfil all desires (cf. *saṃkalpa-vishaya*), the wishing tree, tree of plenty, Hit.; Pañcat.; Ragh. i, 75; xvii, 26; any productive or bountiful source, BhP. i, 1, 3; (fig.) a generous person, MW.; N. of various works; *-parimala*, m., N. of a work; *-rasa*, m. a particular kind of mixture, Bhpr. **–tā**, f. fitness, ability, competency, BhP. xi. **–dūshya**, n. cloth produced by the Kalpa-taru, Buddh. **–dru**, m. = *-taru* above; N. of various works; *-kalikā*, f., N. of a work by Lakshmī Vallabha expounding the Kalpa-sūtra of the Jainas. **–druma**, m. = *-taru* above, Rājat.; Daś.; Kum. ii, 39; Pañcat. iii, 10; N. of various works [cf. *kavi-k°* and *śabda-k°*]; *-tantra*, n., N. of a work; *-kalikā*, f. = *-dru-kalikā* above; *-tā*, f. state of possessing the qualities of a Kalpa-druma, Ragh. xiv, 48; *kalpadrumâvadāna*, n., N. of a Buddhist work. **–drumī-√bhū**, to become a Kalpa-druma, Kathās. **–dvīpa**, m. a particular Samādhi, Kāraṇḍ. **–dhenu**, f., N. of the cow of plenty. **–nṛitya**, n. a particular kind of dance. **–pādapa**, m. = *-taru* above, Naish. **–pāla**, m. 'order-preserver,' a king, Rājat. [*-pālyā*, Calc. ed. for *-pālī*]; mf(*ī*). a distiller or seller of spirituous liquors, Rājat.; (see *kalya-pāla*.) **–pradīpa**, m., N. of a work. **–pradīpikā**, f., N. of a work. **–bhava**, *ās*, m. pl., N. of a class of deities among the Jainas. **–mahīruh** (*ṭ*), **-mahīruha**, m. = *-taru*, Rājat. i, 1; Kathās. **–mātra**, m., N. of Śiva, MBh. xii, 10368. **–yukti**, f., N. of a work. **–latā**, f. a fabulous creeper granting all desires, Śak.; Bhartṛ. ii, 38; N. of various works [cf. *kavi-k°*]; *-tantra*, n., N. of a Tantra; *-prakāśa*, m., N. of a comm. on the Vishṇu-bhakti-latā. **–latâvatāra**, m., N. of a comm. of Kṛishṇa on the Vīja-gaṇita. **–latikā**, f. = *-latā*, Bhartṛ. i, 89; a kind of magical pill. **–vaṭa**, n., N. of a Tīrtha, KapSaṃh. **–varsha**, m., N. of a prince (son of Vasu-deva and Upa-devā). **–vallī**, f. = *-latā*, Kathās. i, 66; lii, 21. **–vāyu**, m. the wind that blows at the end of a Kalpa, W. **–viṭapin**, m. = *-taru*, Kathās. xxii, 29; lxxxvi, 77. **–vidhi**, m. a rule resembling a ceremonial injunction, MW. **–vivaraṇa**, n., N. of a work. **–vṛiksha**, m. = *-taru*, MBh.; Śak.; Kum. vi, 6; Megh.; Mṛicch.; *-latā*, f., N. of a work by Lollaṭa. **–śata**, Nom. Ā. *°tāyate*, to appear as long as a hundred Kalpas. **–śākhin**, m. = *-taru*. **–siddhānta**, m., N. of a Jaina work. **–sūtra**, n., N. of various ceremonial guides or manuals containing short aphoristic rules for the performance of Vedic sacrifices; N. of a medicinal work; N. of a Jaina work giving the life of Mahāvīra; *-vyākhyā*, f., N. of a commentary on the Jaina Kalpa-sūtra. **–sthāna**, n. the art of preparing drugs, Car. vii; the science of poisons and antidotes, Suśr. **Kalpâgni**, m. the destroying fire at the end of a Kalpa, Veṇīs. 153. **Kalpâṅka**, m. a kind of plant, L. **Kalpâtīta**, *ās*, m. pl., N. of a class of deities among the Jainas. **Kalpâdi**, m. the beginning of a Kalpa, W. **Kalpâdhikārin**, m. the regent of a Kalpa, W. **Kalpânupada**, n., N. of a work belonging to the Sāma-veda. **Kalpânta**, m. the end of a Kalpa, dissolution of all things, L.; (cf. *pralaya*); *-vāsin*, mfn. living at the end of a Kalpa, R. iii, 10, 4; *-sthâyin*, mfn. lasting to the end of time, Hit. i, 50; BhP. **Kalpântara**, n. another Kalpa. **Kalpêtara**, mf(*ā*)n. having or requiring a different kind of treatment, Suśr. ii, 216, 8. **Kalpôtthāyin**, mfn., MBh. v, 135, 35, misprint for *kalyôtthāyin*. **Kalpôpanishad**, f. 'science of medicine,' pharmacology, Car. i, 4.

2. **Kalpa**, Nom. Ā. °*pāyate*, to become a Kalpa, to appear as long as a Kalpa, Hcar.

Kálpaka, mfn. conforming to a settled rule or standard, BhP. i, 8, 6; ix, 11, 1; adopting, Hariv.; (*as*), m. a rite, ceremony, MBh. [TBr. ii, 7, 18, 4 of doubtful meaning, Comm. *kaplaka*]; a barber (cf. *kalpanī*; Lith. *kerpikas*), L.; a kind of Curcuma (commonly *karcūra*), L. **-taru**, m. = *kalpa-taru* above.

Kalpana, *am*, n. forming, fashioning, making, performing, L.; 'forming in the imagination, inventing,' composition of a poem, Prab.; cutting, clipping, working with edge-tools, VarBṛS.; N. of a religious ceremony; anything put on for ornament, MBh. xiii, 2784; (*ā*), f. making, manufacturing, preparing, Suśr.; BhP.; practice, Car.; fixing, settling, arranging, Mn. ix, 116; Yājñ.; creating in the mind, feigning, assuming anything to be real, fiction, KapS. &c.; hypothesis, Nyāyam.; caparisoning an elephant, Daś.; form, shape, image; a deed, work, act, Mṛicch.; (*ī*), f. a pair of scissors or sheers, L. **-vidhi**, m. a particular method of preparing (food), Bhpr. **Kalpanā-śakti**, f. the power of forming ideas, MW.

Kalpanīya, mfn. to be accomplished, practicable, possible, Sch. on ŚBr. ii, 4, 3, 3; to be assumed, to be supposed, Sarvad.; Comm. on Nyāyam. and Bādar.; to be arranged or settled, VarBṛS.

Kalpayitavya, mfn. to be assumed, to be supposed, to be conceived, Comm. on Bādar. ii, 2, 13.

Kalpika, mfn. fit, proper, Buddh.

Kalpita, mfn. made, fabricated, artificial; composed, invented; performed, prepared; assumed, supposed; inferred; regulated, well arranged, Yājñ.; having a particular rank or order, MBh.; Mn. ix, 166; caparisoned (as an elephant), L.; (*as*), m. an elephant armed or caparisoned for war, W.; (*ā*), f. a kind of allegory, Vām. iv, 2, 2. **-tva**, n. the existing merely as an assumption or in the imagination, Comm. on Vām. iv, 2, 2.

Kalpín, mfn. forming plans, contriving, designing (applied to a gambler), VS. xxx, 18.

Kalpya, mfn. (Pāṇ. iii, 1, 110; Vop. xxvi, 17, 18) to be formed from (inst.), Naish. viii, 21; to be performed, to be prescribed; to be settled or arranged, VarBṛS.; to be conceived or imagined, VarBṛS.; to be substituted, W.; relating to ritual, W.

कल्मन् *kalman*, *a*, n. = *karman*, Kāś. on Pāṇ. viii, 2, 18; cf. Pat. (K.), vol. i, p. 336, and vol. iii, p. 398, gaṇa *kapilakâdi*.

कल्मलि *kalmalí*, *is*, m. (√3. *kal* + *mala*, 'dispelling darkness,' T.) splendour, brightness, sparkling, AV. xv, 2, 1.

Kalmalīka, n. (artificially formed to serve as source of the next) = *tejas*, Sāy. on RV. ii, 33, 8.

Kalmalīkin, mfn. (Naigh. i, 17) flaming, burning, RV. ii, 33, 8.

कल्मष *kalmasha*, *am*, n. (*as*, m., BhP. viii, 7, 43 = *karmasha* fr. *karma* + √*so*, 'destroying virtuous action,' Kāś. on Pāṇ. viii, 2, 18) stain, dirt; dregs, settlings (cf. *jala-k*°); darkness; moral stain, sin, MBh.; R.; BhP.; Mn. iv, 260; xii, 18, 22; ifc. f. *ā*, Bhag. iv, 30 &c.; mf(*ā*)n. dirty, stained, L.; impure, sinful, L.; (*am*), n. the hand below the wrist, L.; (*as*), m. or (*am*), n. a particular hell, L. **-dhvaṇsa**, m. destruction of darkness or sin; *-kārin*, mfn. causing the destruction of darkness or sin, preventing the commission of crime, Comm. on Hit. i, 17.

कल्माष *kalmâsha*, mf(*ī*)n. (Pāṇ. iv, 1, 40, gaṇa *gaurâdi*, Pāṇ. iv, 1, 41) variegated, spotted, speckled with black, VS.; TS.; ŚBr.; ĀśvGṛ.; MBh.; black, L.; (*as*), m. a variegated colour (partly black, partly white), L.; a Rakshas, L.; a species of fragrant rice, L.; N. of a Nāga, MBh.; a form of Agni, Hariv.; N. of an attendant on the Sun (identified with Yama), L.; a kind of deer, T.; N. of Śākya-muni in a former birth; (*ī*), f. the speckled cow (of Jamad-agni, granting all desires), MBh.; R.; N. of a river (the Yamunā), MBh. i, 6360; (*am*), n. a stain, ŚBr. vi, 3, 1, 31; N. of a Sāman. **-kaṇṭha**, m. 'having a stained neck,' N. of Śiva; (cf. *nīla-kaṇṭha.*) **-grīva** (*kalmâsha-*), mfn. having a variegated neck, AV. iii, 27, 5; xii, 3, 59, TS. v. **-tantura**, m., N. of a man. **-tā**, f. spottedness, the state of being variegated, BhP. **-pāda**, mfn. having speckled feet, R.; (*as*), m., N. of a king of Saudāsa (descendant of Ikshvāku transformed to a Rākshasa by Vasishṭha), MBh.; R.; Hariv.; VP.; *-carita*, n., N. of a work. **-puccha**, mfn. having a speckled tail, Up. **Kalmāshâṅghri**, m., N. of a king (= °*sha-pāda*), BhP. **Kalmāshâbhibhava**, n. sour boiled rice, L.

Kalmāshita, mfn. speckled, bespotted with (inst.), Kād.

कल्य *kalya*, mf(*ā*)n. (√3. *kal*, T.) well, healthy, free from sickness (cf. *a-k*°, Gaut. ix, 28); hale, vigorous, MBh. ii, 347; Naish.; Yājñ. i, 28; sound, perfect, strong, MBh.; clever, dexterous, L.; ready or prepared for (loc. or inf.), MBh.; agreeable, auspicious (as speech), L.; instructive, admonitory, L.; deaf and dumb (cf. *kala* and *kalla*), L.; (*am*), n. health, L.; dawn, morning, L.; yesterday, L.; (*am*, *e*), ind. at day-break, in the morning, to-morrow, MBh.; Nal. xxiv, 14; R.; BhP.; (*am*, *ā*), n. f. spirituous liquor, L. (cf. *kadambarī*); (*ā*), f. praise, eulogy, T.; good wishes, good tidings, L.; Emblic Myrobalan (*harītakī*, q.v.), [cf. Gk. καλός.] **-jagdhi**, f. 'morning-meal,' breakfast, L. **-tā**, f., **-tva**, n. health, convalescence, Hit. **-pāla**, mf(*ī*). or **-pālaka**, mf. a distiller or seller of spirituous liquors, Rājat. v, 202; [cf. *śaṇḍika.*] **-varta**, m. a morning meal, any light meal, L.; (*am*), n. anything light, a trifle, trivial matter, Mṛicch.; (Prākrit *kalla-vatta.*) **Kalyôtthāyin**, mfn. rising at day-break, MBh. v, 4616.

Kalyāṇa, mf(*ī*)n. (gaṇa *bahv-ādi*) beautiful, agreeable, RV.; ŚBr. &c.; illustrious, noble, generous; excellent, virtuous, good (*kalyāṇa*, voc. 'good sir;' *kalyāṇi*, 'good lady'); beneficial, salutary, auspicious; happy, prosperous, fortunate, lucky, well, right, RV. i, 31, 9; iii, 53, 6; TS.; AV.; ŚBr.; Nir. ii, 3; MBh.; R.; (*as*), m. a particular Rāga (sung at night); N. of a Gandharva; of a prince (also called Bhaṭṭa-śrī-kalyāṇa); of the author of the poem Gītā-gaṅgā-dhara; (*ī*), f. a cow, L.; the plant Glycine Debilis, L.; red arsenic, L.; a particular Rāgiṇī; N. of Dākshāyaṇī in Malaya; N. of one of the mothers attending on Skanda, MBh. ix, 2625; N. of a city in the Dekhan and of one in Ceylon; a river in Ceylon; (*am*), n. good fortune, happiness, prosperity; good conduct, virtue (opposed to *pāpa*), ŚBr.; Bhag.; R.; Ragh.; Pañcat.; Mn. iii, 60, 65; Suśr.; a festival, Mn. viii, 292; gold, L.; heaven, L.; N. of the eleventh of the fourteen Pūrvas or most ancient writings of the Jainas, L.; a form of salutation ('Hail!' 'May luck attend you!'), Śāntiś. **-kaṭaka**, m., N. of a place, Hit. **-kara**, **-kāra**, mf(*ī*)n. causing prosperity or profit or good fortune. **-kāraka**, mfn. id., Yājñ. ii, 156; (*as*), m., N. of a Jaina work by Ugrâdityâcārya. **-kīrti**, mfn. having a good reputation, AitĀr. **-kṛit**, mfn. doing good, virtuous; propitious, Bhag. vi, 40. **-giri**, m. 'mountain of good conduct,' N. of an elephant, Kathās. **-candra**, m., N. of an astronomer in the twelfth century; of a king. **-cāra**, mf(*ī*)n. following virtuous courses. **-tara**, mfn. more agreeable, ŚBr. xiv, 7, 2, 5. **-devī**, f., N. of the wife of Jayâpīḍa, Rājat. **-dharman**, mfn. of virtuous character or conduct. **-pañcaka-pūjā**, f., N. of a Jaina work. **-pañcamīka**, mfn. (scil. *paksha*) any fortnight the fifth lunar day of which is lucky, W. **-puccha**, mf(*ī*)n. having a beautiful tail, Pāṇ. iv, 1, 55. **-pura**, n., N. of a town, Rājat. **-bīja**, m. = *-vīja*, q.v. **-bhaṭṭa**, m., N. of a man. **-mandira**, n. temple or abode of health or prosperity; N. of a work; *-ṭīkā*, f. the commentary on it; *-stotra*, n., N. of a Jaina work. **-maya**, mfn. abounding in blessings, prosperous, Kathās. **-malla**, m., N. of a prince; of the author of the work Anaṅga-raṅga; of a son of Gaja-malla (author of the comm. called Mālatī). **-mitra**, n. a friend of virtue; a well-wishing friend, Kāraṇḍ. lxvii, 1; a good counsellor (opposed to *pāpa-mitra*), Buddh.; N. of Buddha; °*tra-tā*, f. the perfect life of Buddhism; °*tra-sevana*, n. the becoming a disciple of Buddha. **-rāja-caritra**, n. 'the life of king Kalyāṇa' by Madana. **-rāya**, m., N. of a man. **-vacana**, n. friendly speech, good wishes. **-vat**, mfn. happy, lucky, L.; (*ī*), f., N. of a princess. **-vartman**, m. 'walker on a noble path,' N. of a king; f., N. of a princess who erected an image of Vishṇu (see *kalyāṇa-svāmi-keśava*). **-vardhana**, m. 'increase of prosperity,' N. of a man, Buddh. **-varman**, m., N. of an astronomer; of a man, Kathās. **-vīja**, m. a sort of lentil (Ervum Hirsutum, = *masūra*), L. **-vṛitta**, mfn. of virtuous conduct. **-śarman**, m., N. of a commentator on Varāha-mihira. **-sattva**, mfn. of noble character. **-saptamī**, f. an auspicious seventh day; *-vrata*, n. a religious observance on that day. **-sūtra**, m., N. of a Brāhman. **-sena**, m., N. of a king. **-svāmi-keśava**, n., N. of an image of Vishṇu, Rājat. **Kalyāṇâcāra**, mfn. following good practices, W. **Kalyāṇâbhijana**, mf(*ī*)n. of illustrious birth, Nal.; R. **Kalyāṇâbhiniveśin**, mfn. intent on virtue or on benefiting others, Kād. 153.

Kalyāṇaka, mf(*ikā*)n. auspicious, prosperous, happy; efficacious; (*ikā*), f. red arsenic, L. **-guḍa**, m. a particular drug, Suśr. **-ghṛita**, n. a kind of clarified butter, Suśr. **-lavaṇa**, n. a kind of salt, Suśr.

Kalyāṇin, mfn. happy, lucky, auspicious, prosperous; illustrious; virtuous, good, Kathās.; (*inī*), f. the aquatic plant Sida cordifolia, L.

Kalyāṇī, in comp., gaṇa *priyâdi*. **-daśama**, mfn. having the tenth night lucky, Kāś. on Pāṇ. v, 4, 116. **-pañcama**, mfn. having the fifth lucky; (*ās*), f. pl. (scil. *rātrayas*) nights of which the fifth is lucky, Vop. vi, 15. **-pañcamīka**, mfn. (scil. *paksha*) a fortnight having the fifth night lucky, Vop. vi, 16. **-priya**, mfn. having a beloved one worthy of honour, Pāṇ. v, 4, 116; Sch. on Vop. vi, 15. **-stotra**, n., N. of a work. **Kalyāṇy-ādi**, m. a gaṇa of Pāṇ. (iv, 1, 126).

कल्यापाल *kalyā-pāla* = *kalya-pāla*, q.v., L.

कल्ल् *kall*, cl. 1. Ā. *kallate*, to utter an indistinct sound, Dhātup. xiv, 27; to be mute, ib.

Kalla, mfn. deaf, L.; also v. l. for *kanna*, q. v. **-tā**, f., **-tva**, n. stammering, hoarseness, L.; a sound, L.; deafness, L. **-mūka**, mfn. deaf and dumb, L. **-vīra-tantra**, n., N. of a Buddhist work (also called Caṇḍā-mahā-roshaṇa-tantra). **Kallârya**, m., N. of an author.

कल्लट *kallaṭa*, *as*, m., N. of a king, Rājat. iv, 461; of a pupil of Vasu-gupta (q. v.) and father of Mukula (q. v.), Rājat. v, 66 (*śrī-k*°).

कल्लाट *kallāṭa*, *ās*, m. pl. (probably) N. of a tribe, Inscr.

कल्लार्य *kallârya*, m. See *kalla*.

कल्लालेश *kallāleśa*, *as*, m., N. of a god (Lakshmī-kānta).

कल्लि *kalli*, ind. to-morrow, W.

कल्लिनाथ *kallinātha*, *as*, m., N. of a writer on music.

कल्लोल *kallola*, *as*, m. (1. *kam*, water, + *lola*, T., but according to Uṇ. i, 67 fr. √*kall*) a wave, billow, Bhartṛ. iii, 37; Pañcat.; gambol, recreation, L.; an enemy, L.; mfn. hostile, L.

Kallolita, mfn. surging, billowing (gaṇa *tārakâdi*).

Kallolinī, f. a surging stream, river, Prab. (gaṇa *pushkarâdi*).

कल्हण *kalhaṇa*, *as*, m. (also spelt *kahlaṇa*), N. of the author of the Rāja-taraṅgiṇī.

कल्हार *kalhāra*, v. l. for *kahlāra*, q.v.

कल्होडीगङ्गेश्वरतीर्थ *kalhoḍī-gaṅgêsvara-tīrtha*, *am*, n., N. of a Tīrtha.

कव् *kav*, cl. 1. Ā. *kavate*, to describe (as a poet), W.; to praise, T.; to paint, picture, W.: cl. 10. P. Ā. *kāvayati*, °*te*, to compose (as a poet), W.; [cf. √*kab*.]

Kavayitṛi, *tā*, m. a poet, Viddh. ix, 12; Comm. on Kum.

कव 1. *kava*, a form substituted for *ka*, *kā*, and 1. *ku*, to express depreciation or deficiency, Pāṇ. vi, 3, 107, 108; Vop. vi, 97. **-patha**, m. a bad way, Pāṇ. vi, 3, 108. **Kavâgni**, m. a little fire, Vop. vi, 97. **Kavôshṇa**, mfn. slightly warm, tepid; (*am*), n. slight warmth; *-tā*, f. slight warmth, Kād.

कव 2. *kava*, mfn. (√1. *ku*) 'miserly' (perhaps originally 'provident'), 'selfish,' in *á-kava*, q.v., and *kavā-sakhá* below; [cf. *kavatnú* and *kavā́rī*.]

कवक *kavaka, am,* n. a fungus, mushroom, Mn.; Yājñ.; Hcat.; a mouthful, L.

कवच *kávaca, as, am,* m. n. (√3. *ku,* Uṇ. iv, 2; Nir. v, 25) gaṇa *ardharcâdi,* armour, cuirass, a coat of mail, ŚBr. xii, 2, 2, 7; KātyŚr. xiii, 3, 10; MBh.; R. &c.; any covering; a corset, jacket, Kāth. xxxiv, 5 [ifc. f. *ā*]; Pāṇ. iii, 2, 129; bark, rind, Śārṅg.; (*as*), m. a war-drum, a kettle-drum, L.; (*am*), n. a piece of bark or birch-leaf or any substance inscribed with mystical words and carried about as an amulet, any amulet, charm, W.; a mystical syllable (such as *hum* or *hūm*) forming part of a Mantra used as an amulet [cf. *bīja*], W.; (*as*), m. the tree Oldenlandia herbacea, Bhpr.; the tree Hibiscus populneoides, L. **-dhara,** mfn. = *-hara* below. **-pattra,** n. a birch-leaf, L.; a species of birch, L.; (cf. *bhūrja-pattra.*) **-pāśá,** m. the fastening of a coat of mail, AV. xi, 10, 22. **-hara,** mfn. wearing a coat of mail or jacket, W.; wearing an amulet, W.; (*as*), m. a Kshatriya youth when arrived at the age suitable for martial training, Kāś. on Pāṇ. iii, 2, 10.

Kavacita, mfn. covered with armour, Lalit.

Kavacin, mfn. covered with armour, mailed, AV. xi, 10, 22; VS. xvi, 35; ŚBr.; MBh.; R.; (*ī*), f., N. of Śiva; of a son of Dhṛita-rāshṭra, MBh.

कवटी *kavaṭī,* f. (= *kavāṭa*) the leaf or panel of a door, L.

कवड *kavaḍa, as,* m. a mouthful of water &c., water for rinsing the mouth, Suśr.; [cf. *kavala.*]

कवत् *ka-vat,* mfn. having the word *ka,* TāṇḍyaBr.

कवत्नु *kavatnú,* mfn. (fr. 2. *kava*), avaricious, stingy, RV. vii, 32, 9.

कवन *kavana, as,* m., N. of a man; (*am*), n. water, Nir. x, 4.

कवन्तक *kavantaka, as,* m., N. of a man; (*ās*), m. pl. his descendants, gaṇa *upakâdi.*

कवन्ध *kávandha* and *kavandhín.* See *kában°.*

कवपथ *kava-patha.* See 1. *kava.*

कवयितृ *kavayitri.* See √*kav.*

कवयी *kavayī,* f. the fish Cojus Cobojus (commonly Kavay or Kay, said to go by land from one piece of water to another), L.; (cf. *kavikā.*)

कवर *kavara,* mf.(*ā*)n. (√3. *ku,* Uṇ. iv, 154) mixed, intermingled, variegated, Śiś. v, 19; (*as*), m. a lecturer, L.; (*as, ī*), m. f. (Pāṇ. iv, 1, 42; Vop. iv, 26; also n. according to a Sch.) a braid, fillet of hair, BhP.; Gīt.; Sāh.; Śiś.; (*am*), n. salt, L.; sourness, acidity, L.; (*ā*), f. (Sch. on Pāṇ. iv, 1, 42) the plant Ocimum gratissimum, L.; (*ī*), f. id., L.; Acacia arabica or another plant, Npr. **-puccha,** mf(*ī*)n. having a twisted tail or one resembling a braid, Pāṇ. iv, 1, 55, Vārtt. 2. **-bhāra,** m. a fine head of hair, BhP. v, 2, 6.

Kavarī (f. of °*ra,* q. v.) **-bhara,** m. a fine head of hair, Gīt. xii, 26. **-bhāra,** m. id., Pañcar. **-bhṛit,** mfn. wearing a fillet of hair, Śiś.

कवरकी *kavarakī,* f. a captive, a prisoner, L.; (cf. *vandi.*)

कवर्ग *ka-varga, as,* m. the class of guttural letters, TPrāt.; (cf. *varga.*)

कवल *kavala, as,* m. (*am,* n. ?) a mouthful (as of water &c.); a morsel, MBh.; R.; Ragh.; Mn.; Bhartṛ.; a wash for cleansing the mouth, gargle, Suśr.; a kind of fish (commonly Baliya), L. **-graha,** m. the taking a mouthful of water for swallowing; water for rinsing the mouth, Bhpr.; a weight = *karsha,* ŚārṅgS. **-grāha,** m. water enough for swallowing or for rinsing the mouth, gargle, Car. **-tā,** f. the state of being a mouthful, a morsel, Vcar. **-prastha,** m., N. of a town, gaṇa *karkyâdi.* **Kavalī-√kṛi,** to swallow or eat up, devour, Nāg.; Bālar.

Kavalana, mfn. swallowing by the mouthful; (*am*), n. swallowing, gulping down, eating, Vām.; putting into the mouth, Bālar.

Kavalaya, Nom. P. °*yati,* to swallow or gulp down, devour, Hcar. &c.

Kavalikā, f. a piece of cloth over a sore or wound, a bandage, Suśr.

Kavalita, mfn. swallowed by the mouthful, eaten, devoured, Pañcat.; Kathās.

Kavalī-√kṛi. See *kavala.*

कवष् *kavásh,* mfn. (according to Mahīdhara fr. √3. *ku*) 'emitting sound,' 'creaking' (said of the leaves of a door), open, yawning (faulty?), VS. xxix, 5 = MaitrS. iii, 16, 2. (Instead of *kavá-shas* the TS. v, 11, 1, 2 (cf. *kaví*) and the Kāṭh. have *kaváyas.*)

Kavásha, mf(*ī*)n. opened (as the legs), AitBr.; (*as*), m. a shield, L.; (or *Kavasha Ailūsha*) N. of a Ṛishi (son of Ilūsha by a slave girl, and author of several hymns in the tenth Maṇḍala of the Ṛig-veda; when the Ṛishis were performing a sacrifice on the banks of the Sarasvatī he was expelled as an impostor and as unworthy to drink of the water, being the son of a slave; it was only when the gods had shown him special favour that he was re-admitted to their society), RV. vii, 18, 12; AitBr. ii, 19; N. of a Muni, BhP.; N. of the author of a Dharma-śāstra.

Kavashin, *ī,* m., N. of a Ṛishi, R. vii, 1, 4.

कवस *kavasa, as,* m. (fr. √3. *ku,* Uṇ. iv, 2) armour, mail, L.; a prickly shrub; (cf. *kávaca.*)

कवाग्नि *kavâgni.* See 1. *kava* above.

कवाट *kavāṭa, as, ī, am,* mfn. (for *kapāṭa*) the leaf or panel of a door, a door, R.; Naish. &c.; (ifc. *kavāṭaka*; cf. *kavaṭī.*) **-ghna,** m. 'door-breaking,' a thief. **-vakra,** n., N. of a plant (commonly *kavāṭa-veṭu* or *kavāḍa-venṭuyā*), L.

Kavāṭaka, ifc. = *kavāṭa,* Kathās.

कवातिर्यञ्च् *kávā-tiryañc* (fr. 1. *kava*+*ti°*), mfn. arranged or directed a little across, TS.; TĀr.

कवार *kavāra, as,* m. the bird Tantalus falcinellus, W.; (*am*), n. a lotus, L.; [cf. *kavela.*]

कवारि *kavārí,* mfn. (fr. 2. *kava*), selfish, stingy, RV. x, 107, 3.

Kavā-sakhá, mfn. 'having a selfish man for companion, being the companion of a selfish man,' selfish, RV. v, 34, 3; Nir. vi, 19.

कवि *kaví,* mfn. (√1. *kū,* cf. 2. *kava, ákūta, ákūti, kāvya,* Naigh. iii, 15; Nir. xii, 13; Uṇ. iv, 138) gifted with insight, intelligent, knowing, enlightened, wise, sensible, prudent, skilful, cunning; (*is*), m. a thinker, intelligent man, man of understanding, leader; a wise man, sage, seer, prophet; a singer, bard, poet (but in this sense without any technical application in the Veda), RV.; VS.; TS.; AV.; ŚBr. i, 4, 2, 8; KaṭhUp. iii, 14; MBh.; Bhag.; BhāgP.; Mn. vii, 49; R.; Ragh.; N. of several gods, (esp.) of Agni, RV. ii, 23, 1; x, 5, 4, 3; iii, 5, 1; i, 31, 2; 76, 5; of Varuṇa, Indra, the Aśvins, Maruts, Ādityas; of the Soma; of the Soma priest and other sacrificers; (probably) N. of a particular poet; cf. *A'ṅgiras* (Mn. ii, 151) and *Uśánas* (Bhag. x, 37); of the ancient sages or patriarchs (as spirits now surrounding the sun); of the Ṛibhus (as skilful in contrivance); of Pūshan (as leader or guider); N. of a son of Brahmā, MBh. xiii, 4123, 4142-4150; of Brahmā, W.; of a son of Bhṛigu and father of Śukra, MBh. i, 2606 (cf. 3204; BhāgP. iv, 1, 45 and Kull. on Mn. iii, 198); that of Śukra (regent of the planet Venus and preceptor of the demons), Rājat. iv, 495; of the planet Venus, NBD.; of the sons of several Manus, Hariv.; BhāgP.; VP.; of a son of Kauśika and pupil of Garga, Hariv.; of a son of Ṛishabha, BhāgP.; of Vālmīki, L.; a keeper or herd, RV. vii, 18, 8; (fig.) N. of the gates of the sacrificial enclosure, TS. v, 11, 1, 2 (cf. *kavásh*); the sun, W.; of various men; the soul in the Sāṃkhya philosophy, Comm.; a cunning fighter, L.; an owl, L.; (*is* or *ī,* W.), f. the bit of a bridle, L.; the reins (cf. *kavikā*), W.; a ladle (cf. *kambi*), L. **-kaṇṭha-hāra,** m. 'poet's necklace,' N. of a work on rhetoric, L. **-kamala-sadman,** m. 'lotus-seat of poets,' N. of Brahmā (cf. *kamala*) as the supporter of poets, Prasannar. **-karṇa-pūrṇa,** m., N. of a poet. **-karpaṭī,** f., N. of a work on prosody. **-kalpa-druma,** m., N. of a metrical collection of roots written by Vopa-deva. **-kalpa-latā,** f., N. of a work on rhetoric by Devêndra. **-kratu** (*kaví-*), mfn. having the insight of a wise man, full of discernment, wise (said of Agni and the Soma), RV.; VS.; AV.; one who possesses wisdom or sacrifices, Sāy. **-cakra-vartin,** m., N. of Pūrṇânanda. **-candra,** m., N. of various authors (of the Kāvya-candrikā; of the Dhātu-candrikā; of the Ratnāvalī; of the Rāmacandra-campū; of the Śānti-candrikā; of the Sārala-harī grammar; of a book named Stavāvali). **-cchád,** mfn. delighting (cf. √*chad*) in wise men ['causing pleasure to the wise,' Sāy.], RV. iii, 12, 15. **-jana-vinoda,** m. 'delight of wise men,' N. of a work. **-jyeshṭha,** m. 'oldest of poets,' N. of Vālmīki (author of the Rāmāyaṇa), L. **-tama** (*kaví-*), mfn. wisest, RV. **-tara** (*kaví-*), mfn. wiser, RV.; AV. **-tā,** f. poetry, ornate style (whether of verse or prose), Bhartṛ.; Prasannar.; a poem, W.; °*tâmrita-kūpa,* m. 'well of nectar of poetry,' N. of a modern collection of verses; *-rahasya,* n. 'the secret of style,' N. of a work on rhetoric; *-vedin,* mfn. 'understanding poesy,' wise, learned; a poet, genius, W.; *-śakti,* f. poetic talent, MW. **-tārkika-siṇha,** m. 'lion of poets and philosophers,' N. of Veṅkaṭa-nātha. **-tri,** v. l. for *kavayitri,* L. **-tvá,** n. intelligence, RV. x, 124, 7; poetic skill or power or gift, Daś.; Sāh.; Vet.; *-ratnâkara,* m. 'jewel-mine of poesy,' N. of a modern work on rhetoric. **-tvaná,** n. wisdom, RV. viii, 40, 3. **-darpaṇa,** m. 'poet's mirror,' N. of a work by Raghu. **-putra,** m., N. of a dramatic author, Mālav. **-praśastá,** mfn. esteemed or praised by sages, RV. v, 1, 8. **-priyā,** f., N. of a work on rhetoric by Keśava-dāsa. **-bhaṭṭa,** m., N. of a poet. **-bhūma,** m., N. of a man. **-bhūshaṇa,** m., N. of the son of Kavi-candra. **-maṇḍana,** m., N. of Sambhu-bhaṭṭa. **-ratna-purushôttama-miśra,** m., N. of a man. **-ratha,** m., N. of a prince (son of Citra-ratha). **-rahasya,** n. 'secret of the learned,' N. of a collection of roots by Halāyudha. **-rāja,** m. a king of poets, Vām. iv, 1, 10; N. of the author of the Rāghavapāṇḍavīya, Bālar. viii, 20; *-kautuka,* m., N. of a work; *-bhikshu,* m., N. of a man; *-yati,* m., N. of a man; *-vasumdhara,* m., N. of a man. **-rāmāyaṇa,** m., N. of Vālmīki (for *rāmâyaṇa-kavi*). **-lāśikā** (W.) or **-lāsikā** (L.), f. a kind of lute. **-vallabha,** m., N. of the son of Kavi-candra. **-vṛidhá,** mfn. prospering the wise, RV. viii, 63, 4. **-vṛishan,** m. an eminent poet, Bālar. vii, 7. **-śastá** (and °*vi-śasta,* ŚBr. i, 4, 2, 8), mfn. (gaṇa *pravṛiddhâdi*) pronounced by wise men, RV.; praised by wise men, RV.; AV. **-śikshā,** m. instruction for poets. **Kavîndu,** m. 'moon of poets,' N. of Vālmīki, Śārṅg. **Kavîndra,** m. a prince among poets, Prasannar.; *-kalpa-taru,* m., N. of a work. **Kavîśvara,** m. 'lord among poets,' N. of a poet.

Kavika, *am,* n. the bit of a bridle or the reins, L.; (*ā*), f. the bit of a bridle, Mudr.; N. of a flower (= *kevikā-pushya*), L.; a sort of fish (commonly Kay), Bhpr.; [cf. *kavayī.*]

Kaviṭa, *as,* m., N. of a Ṛishi.

Kaviya, *as, am,* m. n. the bit of a bridle or the reins, W.

Kavila, gaṇa *pragady-ādi* (for *kaliva* according to Kāś.)

Kavīya, *as, am,* m. n. the bit of a bridle or the reins, W.; [cf. *kaviya.*]

Kavīyát, mfn. (pr. p. P.) acting like a wise man, RV. ix, 94, 1.

Kavīyámāna, mfn. (pr. p. Ā.) making pretension to wisdom, RV. i, 164, 18.

Kávīyas, mfn. compar. (= *kavítara*) wiser, v. l. of SV. for RV. ix, 94, 1; (see *kavīyát* above.)

1. **Kavyá,** mfn. (= *kavi,* Kāś. on Pāṇ. v, 4, 30) wise, RV. x, 15, 9 (at VS. xxii, 2 read *kavyáḥ*); a sacrificer, sacrificial priest, RV. ix, 91, 2; N. of a class of deities associated with Aṅgiras and Ṛikvan [Gmn.; a class of manes], RV. x, 14, 3; AV.; N. of one of the seven sages of the fourth Manv-antara, Hariv.; (*am*), n. (generally in connection with *havya,* see *havya-kavya*) 'what must be offered to the wise,' an oblation of food to deceased ancestors, MBh.; Mn. **-tā** (*kavyá-*), f. the state of a sage, wisdom, RV. i, 96, 2. **-bhuj, -bhojana,** m. pl. 'oblation-eaters,' the manes or a class of manes, L. **-vah,** nom. *vāṭ,* **-vāḍa,** mfn. = *-vāhana* below. **-vāla,** mfn. a corrupted form of *-vāḍa,* which is derived fr. the nom. *-vāṭ* of *-vah.* **-vâhana,** mfn. (Pāṇ. iii, 2, 65) conveying oblations to the manes (said of fire), RV. x, 16, 11 [Sāy.]; VS.; TS.; AV.;

ŚBr.; ĀśvŚr.; (as), m. fire (= Agni), W.; N. of Śiva, W.; [cf. kravya-v°, havya-v°, vahni.]

2. Kavya, Nom. P. kavyati, to be wise, Pāṇ. vii, 4, 39.

कविट kaviṭa, kaviya. See kaví.

कवूल kavūla, am, n. (in astrol.) = Arabic قبول; (cf. kaṃvūla.)

कवेरकन्या kavera-kanyā, f. (= kāverī), N. of a river in the Dekhan.

कवेल kavela, am, n. a lotus flower, L.; (cf. kavāra.)

कवोष्ण kavóshṇa. See 1. kava.

कश् kaś, cl. 1. P. kaśati, to go, move, Comm. on TBr. i; to sound, Dhātup. xvii, 75; to strike, punish, hurt, kill (v.l. for kaṇs, kas, jhash, śaś. See √kash.

Káśa, as, m. a species of rodent animal, VS.; TS. (cf. kaśīkā); a whip, thong, MBh. (cf. pra-kaśá); (ās), m. pl., N. of a people, BhP. (ed Bomb.) **-kṛitsna**, m., N. of a man (v.l. for kāśa-kṛitsna, q.v.), gaṇa arīhaṇādi. **-plaká**, au, m. du. 'parts struck by the whip,' the hinder parts (originally of beasts of burden), [Gmn.; 'pudenda muliebria,' BRD.], RV. viii, 33, 19; (cf. plaka.)

Káśā, f. (Naigh. i, 11; Nir. ix, 19) a whip, RV.; AV.; ŚBr.; MBh.; R. &c. (also written kashā, R.; BhP.); a rein, bridle, Śiś.; whipping, flogging, W.; a string, rope, thong, L.; face, mouth, L.; quality, L. **-ghāta**, m. stroke of a whip, Pañcat. **-traya**, n. three modes of whipping (a horse), W. **-nipāta**, m. blow or stroke with a whip, R. **-vat** (°śá-), mfn. furnished with a whip, RV. **-Kaśârha**, mfn. deserving a whipping, L.

Kaśya, mfn. (gaṇa daṇḍâdi) deserving the whip, L.; (am), n. a horse's flank, L.; a spirituous liquor (cf. kāśya), L.

कशकु kaśaku, Coix Barbata (= gavedhukā), Comm. on KātyŚr.

कशम्बूक kaśambūká, as, m. a particular mythical being, Suparṇ. xxiii, 5.

कशस् kaśas, n. moving, motion, TBr. i, 4, 8, 3; water, Naigh. i, 12 (v.l. śaka, q.v.; cf. kaśo-jú).

कशा káśā, &c. See √kaś.

कशाय kaśāya, as, m., N. of a preceptor, Kāś. on Pāṇ. iv, 3, 106 (v.l. kashāya).

कशारि kaśāri, is, f., N. of the Uttara-vedi, Kāṭh. xxv, 6.

कशिक kaśika and -pāda, gaṇa hasty-ādi.

कशिपु kaśipú, us, u, m. n. a mat, pillow, cushion, mattress, AV.; ŚBr.; KātyŚr.; Kauś.; Vait.; BhP.; a couch, BhP.; (us), m. food, L.; clothing, L.; (ū), m. du. food and clothing, L.; (sometimes spelt kasipu.) **Kaśipûpabarhaṇá**, n. the cover of a pillow, covering, cloth, AV. ix, 6, 10; Vait.

कशीका kaśīkā, f. (= nakulī) a weasel (Sāy.), RV. i, 126, 6; (cf. káśa, kashīkā, and √kash.)

कशु kaśu, us, m., N. of a man, RV. viii, 5, 37.

कशेरक kaśeraka, as, m., N. of a Yaksha, MBh. ii, 397.

कशेरु kaśeru, u, n., us, m. (fr. ka, water or wind, + √śṛi, Uṇ. i, 90; also written kaseru) the back-bone, L.; (ūs), f. (Uṇ. i, 90) and (u), n. the root of Scirpus Kysoor (a kind of grass with a bulbous root), Suśr.; (us), m. one of the nine divisions of Bhārata-varsha, Hariv. 6793; VP.; Rājat.; (ū), f., N. of the daughter of Tvashṭṛi, Hariv. 6793 (v.l.) **-mat**, m., N. of a Yavana king, MBh. iii, 491; Hariv. **-yajña**, m. a kind of oblation, Pat.; (cf. kāśeruyajñika.)

Kaśeruka, ā, am, f. n. (Uṇ. i, 90) = kaśeru, the back-bone, L.; (as), m. [ā, am, f. n., L.] the root of Scirpus Kysoor, Suśr.; (sometimes spelt kaseruka.)

Kaśerus, n. = kaśeru above, L.

Kaśerū, see s.v. kaśeru. **-mat**, m., N. of a division of Bhārata-varsha, VP.

कशोक kaśóka, ās, m. pl., N. of a class of demons, AV. v, 2, 4 (= yātu-dhánās of RV.)

कशोजू kaśojú, ūs (acc. úvam), m. 'hastening to the water' (káśas; Sāy.), 'impelling with the whip' (káśas = káśā; Gmn.), N. of Divodāsa, RV. i, 112, 14; [cf. √kash.]

कश्चन kaś-cana, &c. See 2. ká.

कश्मल kaśmala, mf(ā or ī)n. foul, dirty, impure, Dhūrtas.; timid, pusillanimous; (am), n. dirt, filth, Subh.; impurity, sin, L.; (as, am), m. n. (ifc. f. ā) consternation, stupefaction, faintheartedness, pusillanimity, MBh.; dejection of mind, weakness, despair, MBh.; BhP. **-cetas**, mfn. debased or dejected in mind. **-maya**, mfn. filled with or producing distress of mind, Comm. on R. (ed. Bomb.) ii, 42, 22.

कश्मश káśmaśa, as or am, m. or n.? stupefaction?, AV. v, 21, 1.

कश्मीर kaśmīra, ās, m. pl. (ifc. f. ā; √kaś? perhaps contraction of kaśyapa-mīra; cf. Rājat. i, 25; R. i, 70, 19), N. of a country and of the people inhabiting it (cf. kāśmīra), gaṇa bhargâdi, Pāṇ. iv, 1, 178; saṅkāśâdi, iv, 2, 80; kacchâdi, iv, 2, 133; sindhv-ādi, iv, 3, 93; Rājat. **-janman**, n. 'produced in Kaśmīr,' saffron, L.

कश्य kaśya. See √kaś.

कश्यत kaśyata, as, m., N. of a man, VP.

कश्यप kaśyápa, mfn. (fr. kaśya + 2. pa) having black teeth, Comm. on KātyŚr. x, 2, 35; (as), m. a tortoise (kacchapa), VS. xxiv, 37; AitBr.; ŚBr.; a sort of fish, W.; a kind of deer (cf. kāśyapa), L.; a class of divine beings associated with Prajāpati, AV.; TS.; VS.; (ās), m. pl. a class of semi-divine genii connected with or regulating the course of the sun, AV. xiii, 1, 23; TĀr. i, 8; PārGṛ. ii, 9, 13; N. of a mythical Ṛishi, AitBr.; ŚBr.; of an ancient sage, VS.; AV. &c., (a descendant of Marīci and author of several hymns of the Ṛig-veda, RV.; AV.; ŚBr.; he was husband of Aditi and twelve other daughters of Daksha, MBh. i, 2598; Mn. ix, 129; by Aditi he was father of the Ādityas [cf. kāśyapeya], TS.; ŚBr.; and of Vivasvat, R.; and of Vishṇu in his vāmana avatāra, R.; BhP.; VP.; by his other twelve wives he was father of demons, nāgas, reptiles, birds, and all kinds of living things; from the prominent part ascribed to him in creation he is sometimes called Prajā-pati; he is one of the seven great Ṛishis and priest of Paraśu-rāma and Rāma-candra; he is supposed by some to be a personification of races inhabiting the Caucasus, the Caspian, Kaśmīr, &c.); a patronymic from Kaśyapa, ŚBr.; the author of a Dharma-śāstra called Kaśyapôllara-saṃhitā; the constellation Cancer (cf. Pers. kashaf), VP.; (ās), m. pl. the descendants of Kaśyapa, AitBr.; ĀśvŚr.; (ā), f. a female Ṛishi (authoress of a verse in the White Yajur-veda). **-grīva**, n., N. of a Sāman, ĀrshBr. **-tuṅga**, m., N. of a place. **-dvīpa**, m., N. of a Dvīpa (v.l. kāśyapa-dvīpa). **-nandana**, m. 'son of Kaśyapa,' N. of Garuḍa (bird of Vishṇu), L. **-puccha**, n., N. of a Sāman. **-bhāskara**, m., N. of the author of a commentary called Paribhāshā-bhāskara. **-vrata**, n., N. of a Sāman. **-saṃhitā**, f., N. of a work. **-sūnu-jyeshṭha**, m. 'eldest of the sons of Kaśyapa,' N. of Hiraṇyāksha, L. **-smṛiti**, f., N. of a work. **-Kaśyapâpatya**, n. a descendant of Kaśyapa, Comm. on Pat.; N. of a Daitya, L.; of Garuḍa, L. **-Kaśyapêśvara**, and -tīrtha, n., N. of a Tīrtha. **-Kaśyapôttara-saṃhitā**, f., N. of a Dharma-śāstra.

कष् kash, cl. 1. P. Ā. kashati, °te, to rub, scratch, scrape, Pāṇ. iii, 4, 34; Naish.: Ā. to rub or scratch one's self, ChUp. (pr. p. Ā. kasha-māṇa); Vait.; to itch (Ā.), BhP.; to rub with a touchstone, test, try, Kāś. on Pāṇ. vii, 2, 22; to injure, hurt, destroy, kill, Dhātup. xvii, 34; to leap, ib. xvii, 77 (v.l.): Caus. P. kāshayati, to hurt, ib. xxxii, 121 (v.l.); [cf. Gk. κεωρέω, κάσσα.]

Kasha, mfn. (ifc.) rubbing, scraping, rubbing away; (as), m. rubbing, Naish.; a touchstone, assay (nikasha), Kāś. on Pāṇ. iii, 3, 119; Mṛicch.; (ā), f. (for kaśā, q.v.) a whip, R. vi, 37, 41; BhP. **-paṭṭikā**, f. a touchstone. **-pāshāṇa**, m. a touchstone, Naish **Kashôtka**, m., TĀr., = paramêśvara (Comm.)

Kashā, f., see before s.v. kasha. **-putra**, m. a Rākshasa, L.; (cf. nikashâtmaja.) **Kashâghāta** (or kashā-gh°), m. a cut or stroke with a whip (v.l. for kaśā-ghāta, q.v.)

Kashaṇa, mfn. (ifc.) rubbing one's self on, adapting one's self to, BhP. x, 90, 49; unripe, immature, L.; (am), n. rubbing, scratching, Kād.; Kir.; shaking, Śiś.; marking, W.; the touching or testing of gold by a touchstone.

Kashan-mukha, as, m. (pres. p. of √kash + mukha), N. of a man, Rājat. vi, 319 (ed. Calc. kashaṇ-mukha).

Kashāku, us, m. fire, Uṇ.; the sun, ib.

Kashi, mfn. hurtful, injurious, Uṇ. iv, 139.

Kashita, mfn. rubbed; tested; hurt, injured.

Kashīkā, f. a kind of bird, Uṇ. iv, 16.

Káshkasha, as, m. a kind of noxious insect or worm, AV. v, 23, 7.

1. Kashṭi, is, f. test, trial, W.

कषाय kashāya, mfn. astringent, MBh. xiv, 1280 & 1411; R.; Suśr.; Pañcat.; BhP.; fragrant, Megh. 31; red, dull red, yellowish red (as the garment of a Buddhist Bhikshu), MBh.; Hariv.; Mṛicch.; Yājñ.; (as, am), m. n. (gaṇa ardharcâdi) an astringent flavour or taste, Suśr.; a yellowish red colour, Yājñ. i, 272; Kāś. on Pāṇ. iv, 2, 1; an astringent juice, extract of juice, ŚBr.; KātyŚr.; Mn. xi, 153; a decoction or infusion, Suśr. (the result of boiling down a mixture consisting of one part of a drug and four or, according to some, eight or sixteen parts of water until only one quarter is left, Suśr.); any healing or medicinal potion, Bhpr.; exudation from a tree, juice, gum, resin, L.; ointment, smearing, anointing, L.; colouring or perfuming or anointing the person with cosmetics, MBh.; dirt, filth; stain or impurity or sin cleaving to the soul, ChUp.; BhP.; dulness, stupidity, Vedāntas.; defect, decay, degeneracy (of which, according to Buddhists, there are five marks, viz. āyus-k°, dṛishṭi-k°, kleśa-k°, sattva-k°, kalpa-k°); attachment to worldly objects, W.; (as), m. red, redness; a kind of snake, Suśr. ii, 265, 14; emotion, passion (rāga, of which the Jainas reckon four kinds, HYog. iv, 6 & 77); the Kali-yuga, L.; the tree Bignonia Indica, R. ii, 28, 21; N. of a teacher (v.l. kaśāya), gaṇa śaunakâdi; (as, ā, am), m. f. n. the tree Grislea tomentosa, L.; (ā), f. a thorny shrub, a species of small Hedysarum, L.; (am), n. a dull or yellowish red garment or robe, MBh. ii, 675; (cf. kāshāya, pañca-kashāya; a-nishkashāya, full of impure passions, MBh. xii, 568.) **-kṛit**, m. the tree Symplocos racemosa (its bark is used in dyeing), L. **-citra**, mfn. dyed of a dull-red colour, W. **-tā**, f. contraction (of the mouth), Suśr. **-danta**, m. 'having red teeth,' a kind of mouse, Suśr. **-daśana**, m. id., ib. **-pāṇa**, ās, m. pl. 'drinkers of astringent liquids,' N. of the Gāndhāras, Kāś. on Pāṇ. viii, 4, 9. **-pāda**, m. a decoction of a kind of drug, Suśr. **-yāva-nāla**, m. a sort of grain, L. **-vaktra-tā**, f. contraction of the mouth, ŚārṅgS. **-vasana**, n. the yellowish-red garment of Buddhist mendicants (forming with head-shaving their distinctive badge, cf. kashāya, n. above, and kāshāya-v°), Yājñ. i, 272. **-vastra**, n. id., Mṛicch. **-vāsas**, n. id. **-vāsika**, m. a kind of venomous insect, Suśr. **Kashāyânvita**, mfn. having astringent properties, styptic; harsh, W. **Kashāyī √-kṛi**, to make red. **Kashāyī-kṛita**, mfn. made red, reddened; -locana, mfn. having reddened eyes, MBh.; R. **Kashāyī-bhūta**, mfn. become red, reddened.

Kashāyaka, as, m. the shrub Acacia Catechu, L.

Kashāyita, mfn. reddened, red, Bālar.; Viddh.; coloured, Prab.; spotted, soiled; prepared for dyeing or colouring, W.; ifc. permeated with, rendered full of, Bālar.; Kād.; dimmed, cloaked (with envy, īrshyā), Sarvad. 121, 6.

Kashāyin, mfn. yielding a resinous exudation, astringent, dyed of a red colour; worldly-minded, W.; (ī), m. the plant Shorea robusta (śāla), L.; Artocarpus Lakucha, L.; the wild date-palm (kharjūrī), L.

Kashāyī-√kṛi, &c. See kashāya.

कषि kashi, &c. See √kash.

Kashīkā. See ib.

कषेरुका kasherukā, f. the back-bone, spine (v.l. for kaśer°, q.v.), L.

कष्कष káshkasha. See √kash.

कष्ट kashṭa, mfn. (perhaps p.p. of √kash, Pāṇ. vii, 2, 22; Vop. 26, 111; Kāś. on Pāṇ. vi, 2,

47), bad, R.; ill, evil, wrong, Mn.; MBh.; R.; Suśr. &c.; painful, Suśr.; grievous, severe, miserable, Mn. xii, 78; Yājñ. iii, 29; Bhartṛ.; difficult, troublesome, Mn. vii, 186 & 210; worst, Mn. vii, 50 & 51; pernicious, noxious, injurious, Suśr.; dangerous (= *kṛicchra*), Pāṇ. vii, 2, 22; Nal. xiii, 16; inaccessible (= *gahana*), Pāṇ. vii, 2, 22; boding evil, Comm. on Pāṇ. iii, 2, 188; (*as*), m., 'N. of a man,' see *kāshṭāyana*; (in rhetoric) offending the ear, Vām. ii, 1, 6; forced, unnatural; (*am*), n. a bad state of things, evil, wrong; pain, suffering, misery, wretchedness; trouble, difficulty; bodily exertion, strain, labour, toil, fatigue, weariness, hardship, uneasiness, inquietude (mental or bodily), R.; Kathās.; Pañcat.; Śak.; Hit.; *kashṭāt-kashṭam* or *kashṭataram*, worse than the worst; *kashṭena* or *kashṭāt*, with great difficulty, Pañcat.; (*am*), ind. an exclamation of grief or sorrow; ah! woe! alas! MBh.; R.; Mṛicch. **-kara**, mf(*ī*)n. causing pain or trouble, W. **-kāraka**, mfn. causing trouble, L.; (*as*), m. the world, L. **-guggula**, m. a kind of perfume, Comm. on VarBṛS. **-tapas**, m. one who practises severe austerities, Śak. 282, 2. **-tara**, mfn. worse, more pernicious, Mn. vii, 53; more difficult, MW.; (*am*), n. a worse evil. **-tā**, f. and **-tva**, n. (in rhetoric) state of being forced or unnatural. **-bhāgineya**, m. a wife's sister's son, L. **-mātula**, m. a brother of a step-mother, L. **-labhya**, mfn. difficult to be obtained, Hit. (v. l. *kashṭatara-labhya*). **-śrita**, mfn. undergoing pain or misfortune or hardships, performing penance, Sch. on Pāṇ. vi, 2, 47. **-sādhya**, mfn. to be accomplished with difficulty, painful, toilsome, MW. **-sthāna**, n. a bad situation, disagreeable place or site, W. **Kashṭâgata**, mfn. arrived with difficulty, Viddh. **Kashṭâdhika**, mf(*ā*)n. more than bad, = worse; excessively bad, wicked. **Kashṭârtha**, mfn. giving a forced or unnatural meaning; *-tva*, n. state of having a forced meaning, Sāh. 227, 18.

Kashṭāya, Nom. Ā. *kashṭāyate*, to have wicked intentions, Pāṇ. iii, 1, 14; and Vārtt.; Vop. xxi, 10.

2. **Kashṭi**, *is*, f. pain, trouble, W.; (for 1, see p. 265, col. 3.)

कष्फिल *kashphila*, m., N. of a Bhikshu, Lalit. (*kasphila*, ed. Calc.)

कस् 1. *kas*, cl. 1. P. *kasati* (Dhātup. xx, 30), to go, move, approach, Naigh. ii, 14; (perf. *cakāsa* = *śuśubhe*, Comm.) to beam, shine, Nalod. ii, 2: Intens. *canīkasīti*, *canīkasyate*, Pāṇ. vii, 4, 84; Vop. xxi, 10; (cf. *kaś*, *kaṇs*, *niḥ-kas*, and *vi-kas*.)

1. **Kasa**, mfn., Pāṇ. iii, 1, 140.

Kasvara, mfn., Pāṇ. iii, 2, 175.

कस् 2. *kas*, *kaste*, v. l. for *kaṇs*, *kaṇste*, Dhātup. xxiv, 14.

कस् 3. *kas*, in the Bhāshā = √*kṛish*, Pat.

कस 2. *kasa*, *as*, m. (= *kasha*) a touchstone, Sch. on L.; (*ā*), f. (= *kaśā*) a whip, Sch. on L.

कसन *kasana*, *as*, m. cough (= *kāsa*), T.; (*ā*), f. a kind of venomous snake (or spider, *lūtā*, T.), Suśr. **Kasanôtpāṭana**, *as*, m. 'cough-relieving,' the plant Gendarussa vulgaris, L.

कसर्णीर *kasarṇīra* or *kasarṇila*, *as*, m. a kind of snake, AV. x, 4, 5; (personified) TS. i, 5, 4, 1.

कसाम्बु *kásāmbu*, n. a heap of wood (?), AV. xviii, 4, 37.

कसार *kasāra*, *am*, n. (v. l. *kaṇsāra* or *kaṃsāra*) = *kṛisara*, q. v., Gal.

कसारस् *kasāras*, *ās*, m. ? a kind of bird, MBh. xiii, 736.

कसिपु *kasipu*, *us*, m. food (= *kaśipu*), L.

कसीय *kasīya*, *am*, n. brass (*kāṇsya*), Gal.

कसुन् *kasun*, the *kṛit* suffix *as* forming in the Veda an indeclinable (*avyaya*, Pāṇ. i, 1, 40) infinitive with abl. sense, Pāṇ. iii, 4, 13 & 17; (cf. *vi-sṛipas*, *ā-tṛidas*.)

कसेतु *kasetu*, *us*, m. (= *kaseru*), N. of a part of Bhārata-varsha, VP.

कसेरु *kaseru*, &c. See *kaśeru*, &c.

कस्कादि *kaskâdi*, a gaṇa (Pāṇ. viii, 3, 48).

कस्तम्भी *ka-stambhí*, f. (fr. *ka*, 'head'? + *stambha*) the prop of a carriage-pole, piece of wood fastened on at the extreme end of the pole serving as a prop or rest (popularly called 'sipoy' in Western India, and in English 'horse'), ŚBr. i, 1, 2, 9.

कस्तीर *kastīra*, *am*, n. (said to be from √*kāś*, 'to shine'), tin, L.; (cf. *kāstīra*; κασσίτερος.)

कस्तूरिका *kastūrikā* (or *kasturikā*?), f. musk-deer, T.; musk, the animal perfume (supposed to come out of the navel of the musk-deer, and brought from Kaśmīr, Nepāl, Western Assam or Butan, the latter being the best), VarBṛS.; Pañcat.; Kathās. &c.; (cf. Gk. κάστωρ.) **-kuraṅga**, m. the musk-deer, Kād. **-mada**, m. musk. **-mṛiga**, m. the musk-deer; (*ī*), f. the female musk-deer, Kād. **Kastūrikâṇī**, f. the female musk-deer, Bālar.

Kastūrī, f. musk, Sāh. 337, 3; Bhpr. &c.; the plant Hibiscus Abelmoschus, L.; the plant Amaryllis zeylanica, L. **-mallikā**, f. a species of jasmine, L. **-mṛiga**, m. the musk-deer, Comm. on Kum. i, 55.

कस्फिल *kasphila*, *as*, m., N. of a Buddhist Bhikshu (v. l. for *kashphila*).

कस्मल *kasmala* for *kaśmala*, q. v.

कस्मात् *kásmāt*, ind. (abl. fr. 2. *ká*, AV. &c.) where from? whence? why? wherefore? MBh.; R.; Śak.; Pañcat. &c.; (cf. *a-kasmāt*.)

कस्वर *kasvara*. See √1. *kas*.

कहय *kahaya*, *as*, m., N. of a man, gaṇa *śivâdi*.

कहिक *kahika*, *as*, m. a family N. for Kahoḍa, Pāṇ. v, 3, 83, Pat.

कहूय *kahūya* (or *kahūsha*, Kāś.), *as*, m., N. of a man, gaṇa *śivâdi*.

कहोड *kahóḍa*, *as*, m. (gaṇa *śivâdi*), N. of a man with the patr. *kaushītaki* or *kaushītakeya*, ŚBr.; MBh.

Kahola, *as*, m. id., BṛĀrUp.; (*am*), n., N. of a work by Kahoḍa or Kahola, ĀśvGṛ. iii, 4, 4.

कह्लण *kahlaṇa*, for *kalhaṇa*, q. v.

कह्लार *kahlāra*, *am*, n. the white esculent water-lily (Nymphæa Lotus), MBh.; Suśr.; Ṛitus. &c.; (cf. *kalhāra*.)

कह्व *kahva*, *as*, m. a kind of crane (Ardea nivea), L.

का 1. *kā*, onomat. imitation of the cry of the ass, BhP. x, 15, 30.

का 2. *kā* = 2. *kád* and 1. *ku* in comp. to express depreciation, e. g. *kâksha*, *kā-patha*, *kā-purusha*, *kôshṇa*, qq. vv., Pāṇ. vi, 3, 104; Vop. vi, 93.

का 3. *kā* = √*kan* (perf. *cake*, *cakāná*; see *kā́yamāna* s. v.), to seek, desire, yearn, love (with acc. and dat.), RV.; to like, enjoy, be satisfied with (loc., gen. or inst.), RV.: Intens. (p. *cā́kát*) to please, be sought after, be wished for, satisfy, RV. x, 29, 1; (cf. *anu-*, *ā-*, *sam-*√3. *kā*, *kāti*.)

कांशि *kāṇśi*, *is*, m. a cup, Kauś.; (cf. *kāṇsya*.)

कांस् *kāṇs*, cl. 1. Ā. *kāṇsate*, to shine, glitter, Dhātup. xvi, 46 (v. l. for *kāś*).

कांस *kāṇsa*, mf(ī)n. born in Kaṇsa, gaṇa *takshaśilâdi*.

कांसीकृ *kāṇsī-*√1. *kṛi*. See *kāṇsya*.

कांसीय *kāṇsīya*, for *kaṇs*°, q. v., W.

Kāṇsya, mf(*ā*)n. (fr. *kaṇsa*) consisting of white-copper or bell-metal or brass, KātyŚr.; MBh. xiii, 94, 91; R.; Mn. iv, 65; (*am*), n. white-copper or bell-metal or brass, queen's metal, any amalgam of zinc and copper, Mn. v, 114; xi, 167; xii, 62; Yājñ. i, 190; Suśr.; a drinking vessel of brass, goblet, ŚāṅkhŚr.; MBh.; R.; (ifc. f. *ā*) Hcat.; (cf. AV. xviii, 3, 17); a kind of musical instrument (a sort of gong or plate of bell-metal struck with a stick or rod), L.; a particular measure of capacity, L. **-kāra**, mf(*ī*). a brass-founder, worker in white or bell-metal, Comm. on Yājñ. **-kośī**, f. a kind of musical instrument, Hcar. **-ghana**, m. a kind of cymbal. **-ja**, mfn. made of brass, Suśr. **-tāla**, m. a cymbal, Rājat.; Bālar. **-doha**, mf(*ā*)n. having a copper milk-pail, MBh. xiii, 71, 33. **-dohana**, mf(*ā*)n. id., MBh. ii, 53, 2; R. i, 72, 23. **-nīla**, mfn. 'dark as copper,' N. of a monkey, R. iv, 39, 23 (occasionally written *kāṇsya-nīla*); (*am*), n. = (*ī*), f., L.; (*ī*), f. blue vitriol (considered as a collyrium), Suśr. ii, 380, 4; (°*la*, ifc.) Suśr. ii, 109, 1; 512, 10. **-pātra**, n., **-pātrī**, f. a copper or brazen vessel, Suśr. **-bhājana**, id., ib. **-makshika**, n. a metallic substance (probably a kind of pyrites), Suśr. **-maya**, mfn. consisting of brass, Hcat. **-mala**, n. verdigris, Suśr. **Kāṇsyâbha**, mfn. coloured like copper or brass, Suśr. **Kāṇsyôpadoha**, mf(*ā*)n. = *kāṇsya-doha*, MBh. iii, 186, 11 & 13; xviii, 6, 13. **Kāṇsyôpadohana**, mf(*ā*)n. id., MBh. xiii, 64, 33.

Kāṇsī-√1. **kṛi**, to make the measure called *kāṇsya*, Naish. (v. l. for *kaṇs*°.)

Kāṇsyaka, *am*, n. copper, brass, L.; (mfn.) consisting of brass, Hcat.

काक *kāka*, *as*, m. (onomat. imitation of the cawing of the crow, cf. √*kai*, Nir. iii, 18; Uṇ.), a crow, AdbhBr.; Mn.; MBh.; R.; Suśr.; Hit.; (metaphorically, as an expression of contempt, e. g. *na tvāṃ kākaṃ manye*, I rate thee less than a crow, Pāṇ. ii, 3, 17, Pat.; cf. *tīrtha-kāka*, Comm. on Pāṇ. ii, 1, 42); an impudent or insolent fellow, L.; a lame man, a cripple, W.; washing the head, bathing by dipping the head only in water (after the manner of crows), L.; a sectarial mark (*tilaka*), L.; a particular measure, L.; the plant Ardisia Humilis, L.; N. of a Dvīpa or division of the world, L.; (*ās*), m. pl., N. of a people, VP.; Nal.; (*ī*), f. a female crow, Pāṇ. vi, 3, 42, Pat. on Vārtt. 2; Pañcat.; Kathās.; personified as a daughter of Kaśyapa by Tāmrā and mother of crows (Hariv. 222) and owls (MBh. i, 2620); the plant Kākolī, L.; N. of one of the seven mothers of Śiśu; (*ā*), f. the plant Abrus precatorius, L.; Leea Hirta, L.; Solanum indicum, L.; Ficus oppositifolia, L.; the plant Kākolī, L.; the plant Raktikā, L.; (*am*), n. a multitude or assembly of crows, Kāś. on Pāṇ. iv, 2, 37; a modus coeundi, L. **-kaṅgu**, f. a kind of panic grass (Panicum miliaceum), L. **-kaṅgunī**, f. id., Gal. **-kadalī**, f. a particular plant, Comm. on ŚāṅkhGṛ. i, 23. **-karkaṭī**, f. a kind of small date, Npr. **-kalā**, f. the plant Leea Hirta (*kāka-jaṅghā*), L. **-kāshṭha**, n. a position in the game Catur-aṅga. **-kulāya-gandhika**, mfn. having the smell of a crow's nest, AitĀr. **-kūrma-mṛigâkhu**, *avas*, m. pl. the crow, tortoise, deer, and mouse, Hit. **-kūrmâdi**, *ayas*, m. pl. the crow, the tortoise, and the rest, Hit. **-khara**, *ās*, m. pl., N. of a people. **-guha**, mfn. 'crow-concealing,' gaṇa *mūla-vibhujâdi*, Pāṇ. iii, 2, 5, Kāś. **-ghnī**, f. a kind of Karañja (Galedupa arborea, *mahā-karañja*), L. **-caṇḍīśvara**, m., N. of a man. **-caṇḍêśvarī**, f., N. of a work. **-ciñcā**, **-ciñci**, f. Abrus precatorius, L. **-ciñcika**, m. or n. (?) a particular soft substance, Lalit. 29, 11; RLM.; (vv. ll. *kācilindi* & °*dika*, the down on the pod of the Abrus precatorius). **-ciñcī**, f. = *ciñcā*, Bhpr. **-cchada**, m. a wagtail, L.; side-locks of hair (*kāka-paksha*), W. **-cchadi**, v. l., **-cchardi**, m. a wagtail, L.; a crow's vomit, W. **-jaṅghā**, f. the plant Leea Hirta, Suśr.; Abrus precatorius, L. **-jambu**, f. the plant Ardisia humilis, L. **-jambū**, f. another kind of Jambu, L. **-jāta**, m. 'crow-born,' the Indian cuckoo (*pika*), L. **-tā**, f. the state of a crow, Mn. xi, 25. **-tālīya**, mfn. after the manner of the crow and the palm-fruit (as in the fable of the fruit of the palm falling unexpectedly at the moment of the alighting of a crow and killing it), unexpected, accidental, R. iii, 45, 17; Comm. on Pāṇ. v, 3, 106 (cf. Pat. and Kaiy.); (*am*), ind. unexpectedly, suddenly, MBh. xii, 6596; (*am*), n. the fable of the crow and the palm-fruit; *-vat*, ind. as in the fable of the crow and the palm-fruit, unexpectedly, suddenly, Hit. **-tālukin**, mfn. having the palate of a crow, contemptible, Comm. on Pāṇ. v, 2, 128. **-tiktā**, f. Abrus precatorius, L. **-tindu**, **-tinduka**, m. a kind of ebony (Diospyros tomentosa), L. **-tuṇḍa**, m. the dark Agallochum, BhP. v, 14, 12; (*ī*), f. Asclepias Curassavica, L.; Xanthochymus pictorius, L.; a kind of brass,

L. — **tuṇḍaka**, m. a kind of water-fowl, Car.; (*ikā*), f. the plant Xanthochymus Pictorius, L. — **tulya**, mfn. like a crow, crow-like, crafty, MW. — **tva**, n. the state of a crow, Kathās. — **danta**, m. 'crow's tooth,' anything impossible or not existing, chimera (cf. *śaśa-vishāṇa*), Jyot. &c.; -*vicāra*, m. a discussion about nothing, Comm. on Nyāyam. — **dantaki**, *ayas*, m. pl., N. of a warrior-tribe, gaṇa *dāmany-ādi*. — °**dantakīya**, m. a prince of the Kāka-dantakis, ib. — **danti**, m. id., ib., Kāś. — °**dantīya**, m. id., ib., Kāś. — **dhvaja**, m. submarine fire (personified in Hindū mythology, cf. *aurva*), L. — **nāman**, m. the plant Agati Grandiflora, L. — **nāsa**, m. the plant Asteracantha Longifolia, L.; (*ā*), f. the plant Leea Hirta, Suśr. — **nāsikā**, f. the plant Leea Hirta, L.; the red-blossomed Trivṛit, L. — **nidrā**, f. 'crow's sleep,' light slumber (easily broken). — **nīlā**, f. = -*jambū*. — **paksha**, m. 'crow's wing,' side-locks of hair on the temples of young men (three or five locks on each side left when the head is first shaved and allowed to remain there, especially in persons of the military caste); -*dhara*, mfn. wearing side-locks, R.; Ragh. xi, 1 & 42. — **pakshaka**, mfn. (ifc.) id., Ragh. iii, 28 & xi, 31. — **pada**, n. the mark of a crow's foot or a similar mark or figure, Suśr.; VarBṛS.; marks or lines in the skin similar to a crow's foot, Suśr.; the foundation or base of anything so shaped, Jyot.; the sign V in MSS. marking an omission; a particular flourish of the pen indicating an oft-recurring word; (*as*), m. a modus coeundi, L. — **parṇī**, f. the plant Phaseolus trilobus, Bhpr. — **pīlu**, m. the plant Diospyros tomentosa (*kāka-tinduka*), L.; Xanthochymus pictorius (*kāka-tuṇḍī*), L.; a variety of Abrus precatorius (*śvetc-guñjā*), Bhpr. — **pīluka**, m. the plant Diospyros tomentosa (*kāka-tinduka*), L. — **puccha**, for -*pushṭa*, L. — **pushṭa**, m. 'crow-nourished,' the Kokila or Indian cuckoo (said to leave its eggs in the nest of the crow &c.), L. — **pushpa**, m. a kind of plant, Bhpr. — **peya**, mfn. 'crow-drinkable,' full to the brim or to the brink with water so that a crow may drink, Comm. on Pāṇ. ii, 1, 33; (cf. Pāli *kāka-peyya* in Mahāparinibbāna Sutta.) — **phala**, m. the tree Azadirachta Indica (*nimba*), L.; (*ā*), f. a kind of Jambū, L. — **bandhyā**, for -*vandhyā*. — **bali**, m. 'crow-offering,' N. of the Bali-karaṇa or offerings of food for crows and other animals, RTL. p. 329. — **bījaka**, m. the plant Diospyros tomentosa, Gal. — **bhāṇḍī**, f. a species of Karañja, L. — **bhīru**, m. 'afraid of crows,' an owl (cf. *kākâri*), L. — **madgu**, m. a water-hen, gallinule (*dātyūha*, resembling a crow in colour), MBh. — **marda** and -**mardaka**, m. a kind of gourd (Cucumis colocynthis, *mahā-kāla*), L. — **mācikā**, f. the plant Solanum indicum (commonly Gūrkamai), L. — **mācī**, f. id., Suśr. — **mātā**, f. id., L. — **mārin**, m. Menispermum Cocculus. — **mukha**, *ās*, m. pl. 'crow-faced,' N. of a mythical people, W. — **mudgā**, f. the wild bean Phaseolus trilobus, L. — **mṛiga**, *au*, m. du. the crow and the deer, Hit.; -*go-carita*, mfn. following the manner of the crow in drinking, of the deer in eating, and of the cow in making water, BhP. v, 5, 34. — **meshī**, f. Vernonia anthelminthica, L. — **yava**, m. barren corn (the ear of which has no grains), MBh.; Pañcat. — **rakta**, n. crow's blood. — **ranti**, *ayas*, m. pl., N. of a warrior-tribe, gaṇa *dāmany-ādi*. — °**rantīya**, m. a prince of the Kāka-rantis, ib., Kāś. — **rava**, mfn. crying out like a crow, cowardly; a coward, Pañcat. (ed. Bomb.) i, 7, 16 (v.l. *kākaruka*). — **rudra-saṃvāda**, m., N. of a work on omens. — **ruhā**, f. a parasitic plant (Epidendrum tesseloides, &c.), L. — **vaktra**, m. 'crow-faced,' a kind of duck, L.; (*ī*), f., N. of a Buddhist goddess, Buddh. — **vat**, ind. like a crow, in the manner of a crow. — **vandhyā**, f. a woman that bears only one child, Comm. on Gobh. iii, 5, 7. — **varṇa**, m., N. of a prince, VP. — **varṇin**, m., N. of a prince (or descendant of Bimbisāra), Buddh. — **vartaka**, *au*, m. du. the crow and the quail. — **vallabhā**, f. a particular plant (= *kāka-jambū*) L. — **vallarī**, f. a kind of creeper, Bhpr.; Abrus precatorius, Bhpr. — **vāśika**, mfn. crying *kāka*, MBh. viii, 41, 58. — **vairin**, m. 'crow's enemy,' an owl, Mahīdh. on VS. xxiv, 23. — **vyāghra-gomāyu**, *avas*, m. pl. the crow, the tiger, and the jackal. — **śabda**, m. the cawing of a crow. — **śāva**, m. a young crow, Pat. on Pāṇ. vi, 3, 42, Vārtt. 2. — **śimbī**, f. the plant Xànthochymus pictorius, L. — **śīrsha**, m. the tree Agati grandiflora, L. — **śīrshi**, m., N. of a man (probably a patronymic), L. — **sampāta**, m. the flight of a crow, Kauś. 31 & 34. — **strī**, f. = -*śīrsha*, W. — **sparśa**, m. the touching of a crow, Nilak. on MBh. xii, 177, 11; a ceremony performed on the tenth day after a death consisting in the offering of rice to crows. — **sphūrja**, m. the plant Diospyrus tomentosa, L. — **svara**, m. a shrill tone. — **hrada-tīrtha**, n., N. of a Tīrtha, ŚivaP. **Kākâkshi**, n. the eye of a crow (crows are supposed to have but one visual orb which, as occasion requires, moves from the cavity on one side into that on the other), AgP. ix, 13; -*nyāyena*, -*nyāyāt*, and -*vat*, ind. in the manner of a crow's eye (said of a word which follows two rules), on this side and that, in such a way as to belong both to the preceding and subsequent, Comm. on Lāṭy.; on Mn. iv, 83 &c.; Comm. on Naish. i, 11 (°*kshi-golaka-nyāyāt*). **Kākâṅgā**, °**ṅgī**, f. the plant Leea Hirta, L. **Kākâñcī**, f. id., ib.; an esculent vegetable (Solanum indicum), W. **Kākâṇḍa**, m. a kind of bean, Suśr.; Diospyros tomentosa, L.; Melia Bukayun, L.; (*ā*), f. a kind of spider, Suśr.; Carpopogon pruriens, L.; (*ī*), f. a kind of plant, L. **Kākâṇḍaka**, m. Diospyros tomentosa, MBh.; (*ā*), f. a kind of spider, Suśr. **Kākâṇḍolā**, f. a plant similar to the Carpopogon pruriens, Car. **Kākâtanī**, f. the gourd Cucumis colocynthis, ŚāṅkhGṛ. i, 23 (v.l. for the next). **Kākâdanī**, f. id., gaṇa *gaurâdi*, Pāṇ. iv, 1, 41; a white variety of the Abrus precatorius, Suśr.; the plant Capparis sepiaria. **Kākâyu**, m. a kind of creeping plant, Bhpr. **Kākâri**, m. 'enemy of crows,' an owl, L. **Kākâsyā**, f. 'crow-faced,' N. of a Buddhist goddess, Buddh. **Kākâhvānā**, f. 'named after the crow,' (sc. *udumbarī*) the Ficus oppositifolia, Suśr. **Kākêkshu**, m. a kind of reed (Saccharum spontaneum, *kāśa*), L. **Kākêndu**, m. a kind of ebony (Diospyros tomentosa), L. **Kākêshṭa**, m. the tree Melia Azadirachta, L.; -*phalā*, f. a kind of plant, Gal. **Kākôcchvāsa**, mfn. breathing quickly like a crow (in fear), Hariv. 4510; Suśr. **Kākôḍumbara**, m., (*ī*), f. and °**rikā**, f. the opposite-leaved fig-tree (Ficus oppositifolia), Suśr. **Kākôdara**, m. 'crow-bellied,' a serpent, L. **Kākôdumbara**, m. = *kākôḍumbara*. **Kākôlūka**, n. the crow and owl (as natural enemies), Comm. on Pāṇ. ii, 4, 9. **Kākôlūkikā**, f. the natural enmity between the owl and the crow, Pāṇ. iv, 3, 125, Kāś.; iv, 2, 104, Pat. on Vārtt. 21. **Kākôlūkīya**, n. 'the story of the crow and the owl,' N. of the third book of the Pañcatantra. **Kākoshṭhaka** and **kākâushṭhaka**, mfn. shaped like the beak of a crow (said of a bandage), Suśr.

Kākakāyani, *is*, m. a patr. fr. *kāka*, gaṇa *vākinâdi*.

Kākaṇa, *am*, n. (gaṇa *gaurâdi*, Pāṇ. iv, 1, 41) a kind of leprosy with black and red spots (so called from its similarity to the black and red seed of the plant Abrus precatorius); a small coin (= *kākaṇi*), L. **Kākaṇâhvā**, f. Abrus precatorius, Car. vii, 7.

Kākaṇaka, *am*, n. a kind of leprosy, Suśr.

Kākaṇantikā, f. the plant Abrus precatorius, Suśr.

Kākaṇi and **kākaṇī**, f. a small coin (= *kākiṇī*), L.; (Pāṇ. iv, 1, 41.)

Kākati, f., N. of a household deity of the prince of Ekaśilā (a form of Durgā), Pratāpar.

Kākatīya, mfn. a worshipper of Kākati; (*ās*), m. pl., N. of a people, Pratāpar. — **rudra**, m., N. of a king of Nāgapura.

Kākanantī, f. = *kākaṇantikā*, Suśr.

Kākani and °**nī**, f. a small coin (= *kākiṇī*), L.

Kākandaka, mfn. fr. *kakandī*, Comm. on Pāṇ. iv, 2, 123.

Kākandi, *ayas*, m. pl., N. of a warrior-tribe, gaṇa *dāmany-ādi*.

Kākandī, f., N. of a land or town, Comm. on Pāṇ. iv, 2, 123; Uṇ. iv, 98; Emblic myrobalan, W.

Kākandīya, *as*, m., N. of a prince of the Kākandi tribe, gaṇa *dāmany-ādi*.

Kākambīra, *as*, m. 'crow-bearer' (Sāy.), N. of a tree, RV. vi, 48, 17.

काकरुक **kākaruka**, mfn. faint-hearted, cowardly, timid; a coward, craven, Pañcat. ix, 15; naked, L.; poor, indigent, L.; (*as*), m. a hen-pecked husband (governed by his wife), L.; an owl, L.; deceit (*dambha*), L.; (cf. *kāka-rava*.)

Kākarūka, v.l. for *kākaruka*.

काकल **kākala**, m.(?) n.(?) the thyroid cartilage, Car. i, 18; a jewel worn upon the neck, W.; (*as*), m. a raven.

Kākalaka, *am*, n. the larynx, thyroid cartilage, Pat. (vol. i, p. 61); Suśr.; an ornament of the neck, W.; a kind of rice, Suśr.

काकलि **kākali**, *is*, f. a soft sweet sound (*kala*), Kathās.; Ṛitus.; N. of an Apsaras, L.

Kākalikā, f., N. of an Apsaras, VP.

Kākalī, f. a low and sweet tone, Bhartṛ. i, 35; a musical instrument with a low tone (for ascertaining whether a person is asleep or not), Daś. 71, 1; a kind of grape without a stone, L. — **drākshā**, f. a kind of grape without a stone or with a very small one, L. — **rava**, m. the Kokila or Indian cuckoo, L.; (cf. *kala-rava*.)

Kākalika (?) = *kākali*.

काका **kākā**, onomat. from the cawing of the crow. — **kṛit**, mfn. uttering that cry, MBh. viii, 1932 (v.l.)

काकायु **kākâyu**. See *kāka*.

काकार **kâkāra**, *as*, *ī*, *am*, m. f. n. scattering water, W.

काकाल **kākāla**, *as*, m. a raven, Vet. iv, 18; (cf. *kāka* and *kākola*.)

काकि **kāki**, m. a son or descendant of Kāka, gaṇa *vākinâdi*.

काकिणि **kākiṇi**, *is*, m. = *kākiṇī*, BhP. xi, 23, 20.

Kākiṇika, mfn. worth a Kākiṇī, BhP. xii, 3, 41; (*ā*), f. = *kākiṇī*, BhP. v, 14, 26.

Kākiṇī, f. a small coin or a small sum of money equal to twenty Kapardas or cowries, or to a quarter of a Paṇa, Pañcat.; Daś.; a seed of the Abrus precatorius used as a weight, L.; the shell Cypræa moneta or a cowrie used as a coin, L.; a cubit, the fourth part of a Daṇḍa or short pole, L.; a Daṇḍa, L.; a part of a measure (*unmānasyâṅśaka*), L.

Kākiṇīka, mfn. worth a Kākiṇī, Pat. on Pāṇ. v, 1, 33, Vārtt. 3.

Kākinī, f the fourth part of a Paṇa, Hit.; a quarter of a Māna, L.; the seed Abrus precatorius, L.; the shell Cypræa moneta, L.; a kind of Svarabhakti, Māṇḍūkī Śikshā ix, 13; N. of a goddess.

काकिल **kākila**, *as*, m. the larynx (= *kākala*), L.; a jewel worn upon the neck, W.

काकु **kāku**, f. a peculiar tone or change of the voice resulting from distress or fear or anger or grief &c., Uṇ. i, 1; Sāh.; a cry of sorrow, complaint, lamentation, Vikr. 42; stress, emphasis, Naish.; the tongue, L.; muttering, murmuring, W.; (cf. *sevā-kāku*.) — **vāc**, f. a cry of sorrow, L.; (*as*), m. Ardea Sibirica, L.

काकुत्स्थ **kākutstha**, *as*, m. (gaṇa *śivâdi*, Pāṇ. iv, 1, 112) a descendant of Kakutstha, R. ii, 110, 28; Rājat.; N. of Anenas, MBh. iii, 13516; of Aja, Ragh. vi, 2; of Daśa-ratha, R. i, 23, 3; of Rāma, i, 24, 18; Ragh. xii, 46; of Lakshmaṇa, R. iii, 49, 22; N. of a sovereign (also Puraṃjaya), L.; (*au*), m. du. Rāma and Lakshmaṇa, R. ii, 99, 3; Ragh. xii, 30.

काकुद् **kākúd**, *t*, f. the hollow of the mouth, the palate (cf. *kakud*, Lat. *cacūmen*), RV. i, 8, 7; vi, 41, 2 & viii, 69, 12; (Naigh. i, 11; Nir. v, 26.)

Kākuda, *am*, n. id., L.

Kākudâkshika, *as*, m. a son or descendant of Kakudâksha, gaṇa *revaty-ādi*.

Kākudra, mfn. palatable, AitBr. vii, 1 ('the palate,' Sāy.)

Kākubh, v. l. for *kākud*, Naigh. i, 11.

काकुदीक **kākudīka**, *am*, n. a particular mythical weapon, MBh. v, 3490.

काकुभ 1. **kākubha**, mfn. consisting of Kakubh verses, gaṇa *utsâdi*, Pāṇ. iv, 1, 86; RPrāt. xviii, 1, 2; ŚāṅkhŚr. (cf. *pragātha*). — **bārhata**, m. a species of Pragātha, RPrāt. xviii, 10.

2. **Kākubha**, *as*, m. a son or descendant of Kakubh, gaṇa *śivâdi*, Pāṇ. iv, 1, 112.

काकुलीमृग **kākulī-mṛiga**, *as*, m. an animal belonging to the class of Bhūmi-śayas, Car. i, 27.

काकेची **kākecī**, f. a kind of fish, L.

Kākocika, *as*, m. the fish Cyprinus Cachius, L.
Kākocin, *ī*, m. id., L.
Kākocī, f. id., L.

काकोल **kākola**, *as*, m. a raven, Mn. v, 14; Yājñ. i, 174 &c. (cf. *kāka* and *kākāla*); a boar, L.; a snake, L.; a potter (cf. *kulāla*), L.; the plant Kākolī, L.; (*as, am*), m. n. a kind of poison, L.; a poisonous substance of a black colour or the colour of a raven (perhaps the berry of the Cocculus indicus), W.; (*am*), n. a division of hell, Yājñ. iii, 223.
Kākoli, f. a medicinal plant, Suśr.
Kākolī, f. id., Car. vi, 13; viii, 10.

काक्वशेय **kākvaśeya**, for *kārkaśeya*.

काक्ष 1. **kâksha**, mfn. (fr. 2. *kā*+*aksha*) frowning, looking scornfully or in displeasure, Siddh. on Pāṇ. vi, 3, 104; Sch. on Bhaṭṭ. v, 24; (*as, am*), m. n. a glance, wink, leer, Pāṇ. vi, 3, 104; Bhaṭṭ. v, 24; Vop. vi, 93; (cf. *kaṭâksha*.)

काक्ष 2. **kāksha**, *as*, m. a kind of plant, gaṇa *plakshâdi* in the Kāś.; (*am*), n. the fruit of the same, ib.; (*ī*), f. the plant Cytisus Cajan, L.; a kind of fragrant earth, perfume (*kacchī, saurāshṭra-mṛittikā*), L.

काक्षतव **kākshatava**, mfn. fr. *kakshatu*, Comm. on Pāṇ. iv, 2, 71; (*am*), n. the fruit of the Kakshatu, gaṇa *plakshâdi*.

काक्षसेनि **kākshaseni**, *is*, m. 'son of Kakshasena,' N. of Abhipratārin, TāṇḍyaBr. x; xiv; ChUp. iv, 3, 5.

काक्षि **kākshi**, *is*, m., N. of a man.

काक्षीव **kākshīva**, *as*, m. the plant Hyperanthera Moringa, L.; (patr. fr. *kakshīvat*) N. of a son of Gautama and Auśinarī, MBh. ii, 802.
Kākshīvaka, *as*, m. the plant Hyperanthera Moringa, L.
Kākshīvat = *kakshīvat*, MBh.; BhP.
Kākshīvata, mf(*ī*)n. composed by or relating to Kakshīvat (scil. *sūkta*), ŚāṅkhŚr. ix, 20, 12; *ākhyāna*, xvi, 11, 4; (*as*), m. (patr. fr. *kakshīvat*), N. of Nodhas, TāṇḍyaBr. vii; of Kauravya; of Śabara; (*ī*), f. a female descendant of Kakshīvat, MBh. i, 4695; (*am*), n., N. of different kinds of Sāman, TāṇḍyaBr. xiv.

काग **kāga**, *as*, m. (cf. *kāka*) a crow (in Prākrit dialects 'a raven'), L.

कागद **kāgada**, *am*, n. paper (Hindūstānī *kāghaz*).

काग्नि **kâgni**, *is*, m. (fr. 2. *kā*+*agni*) a little fire, Vop. vi, 96.

काङ्कत **kāṅkata**, *ās*, m. pl. the school of Kaṅkata, Pat.

काङ्कायन **kāṅkāyana**, *as*, m. 'descendant of Kaṅka,' N. of a physician.

काङ्क्ष् **kāṅksh** (connected with √*kam*), cl. 1. P. *kāṅkshati* (*cakāṅksha, akāṅkshīt*, Dhātup. xvii, 16), ep. also Ā. °*te*, to wish, desire, long for, hope for (with acc.), expect, wait for, await (with acc.), strive to obtain, look for anything (dat.), ĀśvŚr.; Mn.; MBh.; R.; Bhag.; Megh.; Suśr.: Caus. *kāṅkshayati, acakāṅkshat*, Pat. on Pāṇ. vii, 4, 1, Vārtt. 1: Desid. *cikāṅkshishati*: Intens. *cākāṅkshyate* and *cākāṅshṭi*.
Kāṅkshaṇīya, mfn. to be desired, Kād. 102, 17.
Kāṅkshat, mfn. wishing, desiring; hoping, expecting.
Kāṅkshamāṇa, mfn. id.
Kāṅkshā, f. (ifc.) wish, desire, inclination, R.; Nal.; Suśr.; Pañcat.
Kāṅkshita, mfn. wished, desired, longed for; expected, MBh.; R.; Ragh.; considered, thought upon (dat., acc. ed. Bomb.), R ii, 25, 43; (*am*), n. wish, desire, R. v, 29, 9.
Kāṅkshin, mfn. desiring, longing for, expecting, waiting for (acc. or in comp.), MBh.; R.; Bhag.; Pañcat.; waiting, R. v, 33, 27; Pañcat. iii, 134. **-tā**, f. wish, desire, R. ii, 34, 28.

काङ्क्षी **kāṅkshī**, f. a kind of fragrant earth, L.; (cf. *kākshī* and *kacchī*.)

काङ्क्षोरु **kāṅkshoru**, *us*, m. a heron, L.; (also written *kāṅkshāru*?.)

काङ्गा **kāṅgā**, f. Orris root (=*varāṭikā*), L.

काङ्गुक **kāṅguka**, *am*, n. a kind of corn, Suśr.; (cf. *kaṅgu*.)

काच **kācá**, *as*, m. (√*kac*) glass, Suśr.; Pañcat.; Kathās.; (pl. glass pearls) ŚBr. xiii, 2, 6, 8; crystal or quartz (used as an ornament), W.; alkaline ashes, any salt of potash or soda in a crystalline state, W.; a class of diseases of the eye (especially an affection of the optic nerve or gutta serena), Suśr.; a loop, a string fastened to each end of a pole with a net in which burdens &c. are held or suspended, a yoke to support burdens &c. (=*śikya*), L.; the string of the scale of a balance, L.; a Dviśālaka having one room on the north side and another on the south; (*am*), n. alkaline salt, block salt, L.; wax, L.; (mfn.) having the colour of glass. **-kāmala**, n. a kind of disease of the eyes. **-kāmalin**, mfn. afflicted with the preceding disease. **-kūpī**, f. a glass bottle, W. **-ghaṭī**, f. a glass ewer, W. **-tilaka**, n. black salt, L. **-baka-yantra**, n. a glass retort, L. **-bhājana**, n. a vessel of glass or crystal, cup, goblet, L. **-maṇi**, m. a 'glass-jewel,' crystal, quartz, Hit. **-mala**, n. the impurity secreted by the eye in the disease *kāca*; black salt or soda, L. **-mācī**, f. a spirituous liquor, L. **-mālī**, f. = *mālatī*, L. **-māsha**, m. Dolichos Catjang, L. **-lavaṇa**, n. black salt (a medicinal salt prepared by calcining fossil salt and the fruit of the Emblic myrobalan together; it consists chiefly of muriate of soda with a small quantity of iron, lime, and sulphur, and is a tonic aperient, W.), L. **-vakayantra** = *-baka-yantra* above. **-sambhava**, n. 'produced from alkaline ashes,' black salt, L. **-sauvarcala**, n. black salt, L. **-sthālī**, f. the trumpet flower (Bignonia suaveolens), L. **Kācâksha**, m. 'glass-eyed,' N. of an aquatic bird, Suśr. i, 205, 14.
Kācaka, *as*, m. glass, W.; stone, W.; alkaline ashes &c., W.
Kācana or **kācanaka**, *am*, n. a string or tape or wrapper which ties or keeps together a parcel or bundle of papers or leaves of a manuscript &c., L.; (cf. *kacela*.)
Kācanakin, *ī*, m. a writing, manuscript, L.
Kācara, mfn. 'consisting of glass,' glass-like (said of a cat's eyes), Kathās.
Kācita, mfn. suspended by a swing or in a loop, carried in the basket hanging from each end of a yoke or pole, L.

काचलिन्दि **kācalindi**, v.l. for *kāka-ciñcika*, Lalit.

काचिघ **kācigha**, *as*, m. a mouse, rat, L.; gold, L.; a legume, W.

काचिञ्चिक **kāciñcika**, v.l. for *kāka-ciñcika*, Lalit. xix, 3.

काचित **kācita**. See *kācá*.

काचित्कर **kācit-kará**, mfn. (fr. *kā-cid* = *kāni-cid*) doing everything, doing various things, serving various purposes, very active, RV. x, 86, 13.

काचिम **kācima**, *as*, m. a sacred tree (growing near a temple), L.

काचिलिन्दि **kācilindi** and *kācilindika*, vv.ll. for *kāka-ciñcika*, Lalit.

काच्छ **kāccha** and *kācchaka*, mfn. (fr. *kaccha*) being on the bank of a river (not applicable to human beings), Pāṇ. iv, 2, 133 & 134; (*ī*), f. a kind of fragrant earth (cf. *kākshī*), L.
Kācchika, mf(*ī*)n. being on the bank of a river (?), W.; a preparer of perfumes, VarBṛS.

काच्छप **kācchapa**, mf(*ī*)n. (fr. *kacchapa*) relating or belonging to a tortoise.

काच्छिक **kācchika**. See *kāccha*.

काच्छिम **kācchima**, mfn. (=*accha*) clear (as water), L.

काज **kāja**, *am*, n. a wooden hammer, Āp.; R. ii, 55, 17.

काजल **kā-jala**, *am*, n. (see 2. *kā*) a little water, Vop. vi, 95; (mfn.) waterless, Caraka vi, 2.

काञ्च् **kāñc**, cl. 1. Ā. *kāñcate*, to shine, Dhātup. vi, 10; to bind, ib.; (cf. *kac, kañc*.)
Kāñcana, *am*, n. gold, Naigh. i, 2; Mn.; Yājñ.; Nal.; Suśr.; Hit.; money, wealth, property, W.; the filament of the lotus, L.; (mf(*ī*)n.) golden, made or consisting of gold, MBh.; R.; Mn.; Megh.; Śak.; BhP.; (*as*), m., N. of several edible plants (Mesua ferrea, L.; Michelia Champaca, L.; Ficus glomerata, L.; Bauhinia variegata, L.; Datura fastuosa, L.; Rottleria tinctoria, L.); a covenant binding for the whole life, Kām. (=Hit.); a particular form of temple, Hcat.; N. of the fifth Buddha, L.; N. of a son of Nārāyaṇa (author of the play Dhanañjaya-vijaya); N. of a prince (cf. *kāñcana-prabha*); (*ī*), f. turmeric, L.; a kind of Asclepias (*svarṇakshīrī*), L.; a plant akin to the Premna spinosa, L.; a kind of yellow pigment. **-kadalī**, f. a variety of the plant Musa sapientum, L. **-kandara**, m. a gold mine, W. **-kānti**, mfn. shining like gold, Daś. xii, 5. **-kāriṇī**, f. the plant Asparagus Racemosus, L. **-kshīrī**, f. a kind of Asclepias, (ifc. °*rya*, mfn.) Suśr. ii, 62, 5. **-garbha**, R. iii, 53, 33 (probably for *-varṇa*, ed. Bomb. iii, 47, 27). **-giri**, m. 'golden-mountain,' N. of Meru, BhP. v, 16, 28; of an elephant, Kathās. **-gairika**, n. a kind of ochre, Suśr. **-caya**, m. a heap of gold, W. **-daṇshṭra**, m., N. of a prince, Kathās. **-pura**, n., N. of a town, Kathās.; Vet. **-purī**, f. id., Kathās. **-pushpaka**, n. the plant Tabernæmontana coronaria, L. **-pushpī**, f. a plant akin to the Premna spinosa, L. **-prabha**, mfn. glittering with gold, R.; (*as*), m., N. of a prince (son of Bhīma and father of Suhotra), Hariv.; VP.; (*ā*), f., N. of a Vidyā-dhara princess, Kathās. **-bhū**, f. gold-dust, a golden or yellow soil, W. **-bhūshā**, f. ochre, Npr. **-maya**, mf(*ī*)n. made of gold, R.; Pañcat. **-mālā**, f. 'having a golden garland,' N. of the daughter of Kṛikin and wife of Kuṇāla (son of Aśoka), Buddh.; N. of another woman, Kathās.; N. of an Apsaras, Kāraṇḍ. iii, 14. **-ruci**, mfn. shining like gold. **-vapra**, m. a hill or mound of gold. **-varman**, m. 'golden-armoured,' N. of a prince, MBh. v, 189, 20. **-vega**, m., N. of a Vidyā-dhara, Kathās. **-śṛiṅga**, n., N. of a mythical town, ib. **-śṛiṅgin**, mfn. golden-peaked, Hcat. **-saṃdhi**, m. a treaty of friendship between two parties on equal terms, Hit. iv. **-saṃnibha**, mfn. like gold. **Kāñcanâksha**, m. 'gold-eyed,' N. of an attendant of Skanda, MBh. ix; N. of a Dānava, Hariv.; (*ī*), f., N. of the river Sarasvatī, Gal. **Kāñcanâṅga**, mf(*ī*)n. golden-bodied. **Kāñcanâṅgadin**, mfn. wearing a golden bracelet (*aṅgada*) on the upper arm, MBh. xii, 4, 9. **Kāñcanâcala**, m. 'golden mountain,' N. of mount Meru, MBh. i, 67, 30. **Kāñcanâcārya**, m., N. of the author of the Dhanañjaya-vijaya. **Kāñcanâdri**, m. 'golden mountain,' N. of mount Meru. **Kāñcanâbhā**, f. 'golden splendour,' N. of a town, Kathās. **Kāñcanâbhidhāna-saṃdhi**, m. the alliance called golden (see *-saṃdhi* above), Hit. iv. **Kāñcanâhva**, mfn. called after gold; (*am*), n. (scil. *gairika*) a kind of ochre, Suśr. **Kāñcanêshudhi**, m. 'golden-quiver,' N. of a prince, Hariv. 1683.
Kāñcanaka, mfn. golden; m. the fruit of rice or grain, L.; the mountain ebony (Bauhinia variegata), L.; (*ā*), f., N. of a town, VP.; (*ikā*), f. a plant related to the Premna Spinosa, L.; N. of a servant, Vāsav.; (*am*), n. yellow orpiment, L.
Kāñcanāra, *as*, m. mountain ebony (Bauhinia variegata), Bhpr.; Bālar.
Kāñcanāraka, °**nāla**, *as*, m. id., L.
Kāñcanīya, mf(*ā*)n. golden, MBh.; (*ā*), f. a yellow pigment (*go-rocana*), L.

काञ्चि **kāñci**, *ayas*, m. pl., N. of a people, MBh. i, 6684; (*is*), f. = *kāñcī*, Comm. on Uṇ. iv, 117; (ifc. °*ci*, ind.) Śiś. ix, 82. **-purī**, f., N. of a town (= *kāñcī-pura*), W.

काञ्चिक **kāñcika**, *am*, n. sour gruel (*kāñjika*), L.

काञ्ची **kāñcī**, f. (fr. √*kac*; cf. *kāñci*) a girdle (especially a woman's zone or girdle furnished with small bells and other ornaments, *rasanā*), R.; Ragh.; Megh.; BhP.; Suśr.; the plant Abrus precatorius, L.; N. of an ancient city (one of the seven sacred cities of the Hindūs, now Koñjīvaram, not very far from Madras, = *kāñcī-varam, -puram*, RTL. p. 446), VarBṛS.; BhP. &c. **-kalāpa**, m. (ifc. *ā*) a girdle, Bhartṛ. i, 66. **-kshetra**, n., N. of the district round Kāñcī. **-guṇa-sthāna**, n. the hips, haunches, Kum. i, 37; Vām. xvi, 3; (cf. *kāñcī-pada*.) **-nagara**, n., N. of a town (Kāñcī). **-pada**,

n. the hips, haunches (= *-guṇa-sthāna*), L. **-pura**, n., N. of a town (Kāñcī), Kāś. on Pāṇ. vi, 2, 99; (*ī*), f. id., PadmaP. **-puraka**, mfn. of or belonging to Kāñcī-pura, Pat. **-prastha**, m., N. of a town, gaṇa *mālâdi*. **-yamaka**, n. a kind of paronomasia or punning, e.g. Bhaṭṭ. x, 8.

काञ्चुकिन् *kāñcukin*, mfn. = *kañcukin*, clad in armour, Āp.

Kāñcukīya, *as*, m. = *kañc°*, Lalit. 241, 17.

काञ्जिक *kāñjika*, *am*, n. sour gruel, water of boiled rice in a state of spontaneous fermentation, Suśr.; (*ā*), f. id., L.; a medicinal plant, L.; an edible legume, L.; a kind of creeping plant, L. **-pūjā**, f., N. of a Jaina work. **-vaṭaka**, m. a dish consisting of sour gruel, meal, and several condiments, Bhpr.

Kāñjī, f. sour gruel (*kāñjika*), L.; N. of a plant (*mahā-droṇa*), L.

Kāñjika, *am*, n. sour gruel (*kāñjika*), L.

काट *kāṭá*, *as*, m. (= *kartá* from which it is derived, Naigh. iii, 23) deepness, hole, well (Sāy.), RV. i, 106, 6; AV. xii, 4, 3; MaitrS. iii, 12, 12; ĀpŚr. xvii, 2.

Kāṭya, mfn. being in a hole, VS. xvi, 37 & 44.

काटयवेम *kāṭayavema*, *as*, m., N. of a commentator on Kālidāsa's Śakuntalā.

काटव *kāṭava*, *am*, n. (fr. *kaṭu*) sharpness, Vām.

काटवेम *kāṭavema*, for *kāṭayavema*.

काटाक्ष *kāṭāksha*, *as* or *am*, m. or n. (?) (cf. *kāṭá*), a sort of vessel for holding liquid, Kaṭh. xl, 4.

काटिप्य *kāṭipya*, mfn. fr. *kaṭipa*, gaṇa *saṃkāśâdi*.

काटुक *kāṭuka*, *am*, n. (fr. *kaṭuka*) acidity, gaṇa *yuvâdi*.

काठ *kāṭha*, mf(*ī*)n. proceeding from or composed by Kaṭha, Pāṇ. iv, 3, 107, Kāś.; (*as*), m. a rock, stone, L.

Kāṭhaka, mf(*ī*)n. relating to Kaṭha, according to the Kaṭhaka school of the Black Yajur-veda, Pat.; Sarvad.; (*am*), n., N. of one of the recensions of the Black Yajur-veda, Nir.; Pāṇ.; Pat. **-gṛihya-sūtra**, n., N. of a work. **Kāṭhakôpanishad**, f. the Kaṭhôpanishad, q.v.

Kāṭhaśāṭhin, *inas*, m. pl. the pupils of Kaṭha-śāṭha, gaṇa *śaunakâdi*, Pāṇ. iv, 3, 106; or of Kaṭha and Śāṭha, ib., Kāś.

काठिन *kāṭhina*, *am*, n. (fr. *kaṭhina*) hardness, sternness, W.; (*as*), m. the date fruit, W.

Kāṭhinya, *am*, n. hardness, rigidity, stiffness, sternness, severity (N. of a disease), ŚārṅgS.; firmness of character, difficulty, obscurity (of style), Comm. on Pāṇ. vi, 1, 24; Vop. xiii, 1; Śak. 63; Kum.; BhP.; error for *kaṭhilla*, Lalit. xliv, 7. **-phala**, n. the plant Feronia Elephantum (*kapittha*), L.

काठेरणि *kāṭheraṇi*, *is*, m. (fr. *kaṭheraṇi*), N. of a man, gaṇa *gahâdi*.

Kāṭheraṇīya, mfn. relating to Kāṭheraṇi, gaṇa *gahâdi*.

काण *kāṇá*, mf(*ā*)n. (etym. doubtful; gaṇa *kaḍārâdi*) one-eyed, monoculous (*akshṇā kāṇaḥ*, blind of one eye, Comm. on Pāṇ. ii, 1, 30 & 3, 20), RV. x, 155, 1; AV. xii, 4, 3; TS. ii, 5, 1, 7; Mn.; MBh.; pierced, perforated (as a cowrie perforated or broken by insects), Comm. on Pāṇ. ii, 3, 20; Hit.; Pañcat.; Bhartṛ. iii, 5; 'having only one loop or ring' and 'one-eyed,' Pañcat.; (*as*), m. a crow, L. **-tva**, n. one-eyedness, Sāh. **-deva**, m., N. of a man, Buddh. **-bhūti**, m., N. of a Yaksha, Kathās. i, 59; (cf. *á-kāṇa*, *ekâksha*, and *kāṇūka*.)

Kāṇeya, *as*, m. the son of a one-eyed woman, Comm. on Pāṇ. iv, 1, 131; one-eyed, W. **-vidha**, n. a country inhabited by Kāṇeyas, gaṇa *bhaurikyādi*.

Kāṇera, *as*, m. = *kāṇeya*, Comm. on Pāṇ. iv, 1, 131.

Kāṇeri, *is*, or **°rin**, *ī*, m., N. of a teacher (v.l. *kānerin*).

काणभुज *kāṇabhuja*, mf(*ī*)n. descended from Kana-bhuj or Kaṇâda (q.v.), composed by or relating to Kaṇâda, Comm. on Bādar.; (*as*), m. a follower of Kaṇâda, ib.; Hcar.

Kāṇāda, mf(*ī*)n. composed by or relating to Kaṇâda.

काणिकेर *kāṇikera*, *as*, m. a metron. fr. *kaṇikā*, Pat.

काणुक *kāṇuká*, mfn. an adj. qualifying *saras*, RV. viii, 77, 4 (Nir. v, 11).

काणूक *kāṇūka*, *as*, m. (√*kaṇ*, Uṇ. iv, 39) a crow (wrongly written *kānūka*, cf. *kāṇá*), Uṇ.; the bird which makes a hanging nest on the Tāl tree, W.; a cock, W.; a species of goose, W.

काणेरि *kāṇeri*. See *kāṇá*.

काणेलीमातृ *kāṇelī-mātṛi* (perhaps connected with *kāṇera* above), *ā*, m. a bastard (a name of reproach occurring generally in the voc. case and according to native Comm. designating one whose mother was an unmarried woman), Mṛicch.

काण्टक *kāṇṭaka*, mf(*ī*)n. (fr. *kaṇṭaka*) consisting of thorns, ĀpŚr. xv, 1.

Kāṇṭakamardanika, mfn. (from *kaṇṭaka-mardana*) effected by or resulting from the treading down or crushing of thorns or enemies, gaṇa *aksha-dyūtâdi*.

काण्टकार *kāṇṭakāra*, mfn. made of the wood of Kaṇṭakāra, gaṇa *rajatâdi*.

काण्ठेविद्धि *kāṇṭheviddhi*, *is*, m. (Pāṇ. iv, 1, 81) a descendant of Kaṇṭhe-viddha, VBr.; Pravar.; (*°ddhī* or *°ddhyā*), f. a female descendant of Kaṇṭhe-viddha, Pat.

काण्ड *kāṇḍa* [or *kāṇḍá*, TS. vii], *as*, *am*, m. n. (ifc. f. *ā* or *ī*) [cf. *khaṇḍa*, with which in some of its senses *kāṇḍa* is confounded] a single joint of the stalk or stem of a plant, such as a bamboo or reed or cane (i.e. the portion from one knot to another, cf. *tri-k°*), any part or portion, section, chapter, division of a work or book (cf. *tri-k°*), any distinct portion or division of an action or of a sacrificial rite (as that belonging to the gods or to the manes), AV.; TS.; VS.; a separate department or subject (e.g. *karma-kāṇḍa*, the department of the Veda treating of sacrificial rites, Kāś. on Pāṇ. iv, 2, 51), AV.; TS.; ŚBr.; R.; a stalk, stem, branch, switch, MBh.; R.; Mn. i, 46, 48; Kauś.; Suśr.; the part of the trunk of a tree whence the branches proceed, W.; a cluster, bundle, W.; a multitude, heap, quantity (ifc.), Pāṇ. iv, 2, 51, Kāś.; an arrow, MBh. xiii, 265; Hit.; a bone of the arms or legs, long bone (cf. *kāṇḍa-bhagna* & *puccha-kāṇḍá*), Suśr.; a rudder (?), R. ii, 89, 19; a kind of square measure, Pāṇ. iv, 1, 23; Vop. vii, 55; a cane, reed, Saccharum Sara (*śara*), L.; water, L.; opportunity, occasion (cf. *a-kāṇḍa*), L.; a private place, privacy, L.; praise, flattery, L.; (ifc. implying depreciation) vile, low, Pāṇ. vi, 2, 126; *-kāṇḍa-syâvayavo vikāro vâ*, gaṇa *bilvâdi*; (*ī*), f. a little stalk or stem, Rājat. vii, 117. **-ṛishi**, m. the Ṛishi of a particular Kāṇḍa of the Veda, TĀr. i, 32, 2. **-kaṭu** and **-kaṭuka**, m. the plant Momordica Charantia, L. **-kaṇṭa**, m. a kind of plant, Gal. **-kāṇḍaka**, m. the grass Saccharum spontaneum, L. **-kāra**, m. the Areca or betel-nut tree, L.; the betel-nut, W. **-kīlaka**, m. the tree Symplocos racemosa, L. **-guṇḍa**, m. a species of grass, L. **-gocara**, m. an iron arrow, L. **-tikta**, **-tiktaka**, m. a kind of gentian (Gentiana Chirayita), Bhpr. **-dhāra**, m., N. of a country, gaṇa *takshaśilâdi*, Pāṇ. iv, 3, 93; (mfn.) coming from or relating to that country, ib. (v.l. *kāṇḍa-vāraṇa*). **-nīla**, m. the plant Symplocos racemosa, L. **-paṭa**, m. an outer tent, screen surrounding a tent, curtain, Daś.; Kād. ii, 121, 14; (*ī*), f. id., L. **-paṭaka**, m. id., Śiś. **-patita**, m., N. of a serpent-king, Kāṭh. **-pattra**, m. a kind of sugar-cane, L. **-pāta**, m. an arrow's fall or flight, Hit. **-puṅkhā**, f. the plant Galega purpurea, L. **-pushpa**, n. the flower of the Artemisia indica, L.; (*ā*), f. the plant Artemisia indica, Pāṇ. iv, 1, 64, Vārtt. 1; gaṇa *ajâdi*, Pāṇ. iv, 1, 4; Vop. iv, 15. **-pṛishṭha**, m. 'arrow-backed,' a Brāhman who lives by making arrows and other weapons, MBh. (cf. *kāṇḍa-spṛishṭa*); a soldier, W.; the husband of a courtezan; an adopted or any other than a natural son, W.; (*am*), n. the bow of Karṇa, L.; the bow of Kāma, W. **-phala**, m. the plant Ficus glomerata, L. **-bhagna**, n. a fracture or dislocation of the bones, Suśr.; *-tva*, n. the state of having a fractured limb, Suśr. **-maya**, mfn. consisting of reed or cane, L.; (*ī*), f. a kind of lute (= *kāṇḍa-vīṇā*), Lāṭy. **-ruhā**, f. the plant Helleborus niger, Bhpr. i, 173. **-°rshi**, m. = *kāṇḍa-ṛishi* above, Comm. on Bādar. 301, 7. **-lāva**, mfn. cutting canes or twigs, Comm. on Pāṇ. iii, 2, 1; 3, 12. **-vat**, mfn. armed with arrows, an archer, Pāṇ. v, 2, 111. **-vastra**, n. a curtain, Caurap. **-vāraṇa**, n. the warding off of arrows, Bālar.; N. of a country (v.l. for *kāṇḍa-dhāra*); (mfn.) coming from or relating to that country, gaṇa *takshaśilâdi*, Kāś. on Pāṇ. iv, 3, 93. **-vāriṇī**, f., N. of Durgā, DeviP. **-vīṇā**, f. a kind of lute composed of joints of reed, Kāṭh.; Lāṭy.; KātyŚr.; ŚāṅkhŚr.; (said to be played by Cāṇḍālas, L.; cf. *kāṇḍola-vīṇā*.) **-śākhā**, f. a kind of Soma-vallī, L. **-sandhi**, m. a joint in the stem of a tree or of a reed, L. **-spṛishṭa**, m. a Brāhman who lives by making weapons (cf. *-pṛishṭha*), Hariv. **-hīna**, n. 'without knots,' the grass Cyperus pertenuis, L. **Kāṇḍâgnaka**, mfn. relating to *kāṇḍâgni*, Kāś. on Pāṇ. iv, 2, 126. **Kāṇḍâgni** (v.l. *kuṇḍâgni*), m., N. of a particular locality, ib. **Kāṇḍânukrama**, m., **°maṇikā** or **°maṇī**, f. an index of the kāṇḍas of the Taittirīya-Saṃhitā. **Kāṇḍânusamaya**, m. the performance of all prescribed acts of ritual in orderly succession for a particular object before performing the same acts in the same order for a second object, Comm. on ĀśvGṛ. i, 24, 7; on KātyŚr. i, 5, 9 & 11; viii, 8, 14; 15; 17; on Nyāyam. v, 2, 1 (cf. *padârthânusamaya*). **Kāṇḍêkshu**, m. the plant Saccharum spontaneum, Bhpr. ii, 64, 9; Car. iii, 8; the plant Asteracantha longifolia, L. **Kāṇḍe-ruhā**, f. = *kāṇḍa-ruhā*, L.

Kāṇḍanī, f. the plant Sūkshma-parṇī, L.

Kāṇḍāra, *as*, m. a kind of mixed caste, BrahmavP.

Kāṇḍāla, *as*, m. a reed-basket (cf. *kāṇḍola*), L.

Kāṇḍikā, f. a part or division of a book, Comm. on ŚBr. xiii, 2, 5, 1; a kind of corn (cf. *laṅkā*), L.; a kind of gourd (Cucumis utilissimus), L.

Kāṇḍín, mfn. reed-shaped, grass-like, hollow, AV. viii, 7, 4; TBr. ii.

Kāṇḍīra, mfn. (Pāṇ. v, 2, 110; Vop. vii, 32 & 33) armed with arrows, an archer, L.; (*as*), m. the plant Achyranthes aspera, L.; the plant Momordica Charantia, L.; (*ā* and *ī*), f. the plant Rubia Munjista, L.

Kāṇḍera, *as*, m. the plant Amaranthus polygonoides, Bhpr. i, 282; (*ī*), f. the plant Tiaridium indicum, L.; (cf. *kīḍera*.)

Kāṇḍola, *as*, m. = *kāṇḍāla*, L.

काण्डमायन *kāṇḍamāyana*, *as*, m. (fr. *kāṃdama*?), N. of a grammarian, TPrāt.

काण्व *kāṇvá*, mfn. relating to or worshipping Kaṇva, Pāṇ. iv, 2, 111; (*as*), m. a descendant of Kaṇva, RV.; TāṇḍyaBr.; ŚāṅkhŚr.; a worshipper of Kaṇva, Comm. on Pāṇ. iv, 2, 111; (*ās*), m. pl. (Pāṇ. iv, 2, 111) the school of Kāṇva; N. of a dynasty, VP.; (*am*), n., N. of several Sāmans. **-deva**, m., N. of a man. **-śākhā**, f. the Kāṇva branch or school of the White Yajur-veda. **-°śākhin**, m. a follower of the Kāṇva branch of the Veda.

Kāṇvaka, mfn. pertaining to Kaṇva, Pāṇ. iv, 2, 104, Vārtt. 23; (*am*), n., N. of a Sāman, Lāṭy. vi, 11, 4.

Kāṇvāyana, m. a descendant of Kaṇva; (*ās*), m. pl. the descendants or followers of Kaṇva, RV. viii, 55, 4; N. of a dynasty, BhP. xii, 1, 19.

Kāṇvāyani, m. a descendant of Kaṇva, ShaḍvBr. according to Sāy. on RV. i, 51, 1 (*kaṇv°* in printed text) & viii, 2, 40; Comm. on Nyāyam. ix, 1, 21.

Kāṇvī-putra, *as*, m., N. of a teacher, BṛĀrUp. vi, 5, 1.

Kāṇvīya, mfn. fr. *kaṇva*, Comm. on Pāṇ. iv, 2, 111.

Kāṇvya, *as*, m. (gaṇa *gargâdi*) a descendant of Kaṇva, TāṇḍyaBr.; (cf. *kāṇva*.)

Kāṇvyāyana, *as*, m. a descendant of Kāṇva, ShaḍvBr.; (*ās*), m. pl., Hariv. i, 32, 5; N. of a dynasty, VP. iv, 24, 12.

Kāṇvyāyanīya, *ās*, m. pl. the school of Kāṇvyāyana, Pat.

कात् *kāt*, ind. a prefix implying contempt (cf. 2. *kad*), only in comp. with **-√kṛi**, 'to insult,' dishonour,' p. p. *kāt-kṛita*, mfn. insulted, dishonoured, BhP. vi, 7, 11.

कातन्त्र *kā-tantra*, *am*, n., N. of a grammar, also called *Kalāpaka* or °*pa-sūtra* or *Kaumāra-vyākaraṇa* (composed by Śrī-śarvavarman 'after the Sūtra composed by Bhagavat-Kumāra, and at his command;' (*ās*), m. pl. the followers of the Kātantra grammar. **–kaumudī**, f., N. of a comm. on the above by Go-vardhana. Other similar works are: *-gaṇa-dhātu*, *-catushṭaya-pradīpa*, *-candrikā*, *-dhātu-ghoshā*, *-pañjikā*, *-pariśishṭa*, *-pariśishṭa-prabodha*, *-laghu-vṛitti*, *-vibhrama-sūtra*, *-vistara* or *-vistāra*, *-vṛitti*, *-vṛitti-ṭīkā*, *vṛitti-pañjikā*, *-śabda-mālā*, *-shaṭ-kāraka*, and *kātantrôṇādi-vṛitti*.

कातर *kātara*, mf(*ā*)n. (etym. doubtful, perhaps from *katara*, 'uncertain as to which of the two,' BRD.), cowardly, faint-hearted, timid, despairing, discouraged, disheartened, confused, agitated, perplexed, embarrassed, shrinking, frightened, afraid of (loc. or inf. or in comp.), R.; Mṛicch.; Ragh.; Megh.; Śak.; Pañcat.; Hit.; (*as*), m. a kind of large fish (Cyprinus Catla, *kātala*), L.; N. of a man (see *kātarāyaṇa*); (*am*), n. (in *sa-kātara*) 'timidity, despair, agitation.' **–tā**, f. or **-tva**, n. cowardice, timidity, agitation, Śak.; Megh.; Pañcat.

Kātarāyaṇa, *as*, m. a descendant of Kātara, gaṇa *naḍâdi*.

Kātarya, *am*, n. cowardice, timidity, dejection, agitation, fear, MBh.; R.; Ragh.

कातल *kātala*, *as*, m. a kind of large fish (Cyprinus Catla, cf. *kātara*), L.; N. of a man, gaṇa *naḍâdi*.

Kātalāyana, *as*, m. a descendant of Kātala, gaṇa *naḍâdi*; (cf. *kātarāyaṇa*.)

काति *kāti*, mfn. (fr. √3. *kā*), 'wishing, desiring' (only in comp., see *ṛiṇá-kāti* and *kā́ma-kāti*, cf. *ṛiṇa-cít*); (*ayas*), m. pl., N. of a school.

कातीय *kātīya*, mfn. (fr. *kātya*), composed by Kātya. **–kalpa-sūtra**, n., N. of a work. **–gṛihya-sūtra**, n., N. of a work by Pāraskara (belonging to the White Yajur-veda). **–sūtra**, n., N. of a work.

कातीर *kā-tīra*, *am*, n. a bad shore, Pāṇ. vi, 1, 155, Kāś.

कातु *kā́tu*, *us*, m. = *kūpa*, Naigh. iii, 23; (cf. *kāṭá*.)

कातृण *kā-tṛiṇa*, *am*, n. 'bad grass,' a particular kind of grass (Rohisha-tṛiṇa), L.; (cf. *kat-tṛiṇa*.)

कात्कृ *kāt-√kṛi*. See *kāt*.

कात्त्रेयक *kāttreyaka*, mfn. (fr. 2. *kád* + *tri*), produced from or pertaining to any combination of three inferior articles, Pāṇ. iv, 2, 95.

कात्थक *kātthaka*, *as*, m. 'descendant of Katthaka,' N. of a commentator, Nir.

कात्य *kātya*, *as*, m. = *kātyāyana*, gaṇa *gargâdi*, Pāṇ. iv, 1, 105.

Kātyāyana, *as*, m. 'descendant of Kati' (see 2. *kati*), N. of the author of several treatises on ritual, grammar, &c., Hariv. 1461 & 1768; R. ii, 67, 2; VPrāt.; Yājñ. i, 4 (he is also author of the Vārttikas or critical annotations on the aphorisms of Pāṇini, of the Yajur-veda Prātiśākhya, and of the Śrauta-sūtras, and is identified with Vara-ruci, the author of the Prākṛita-prakāśa); (*ī*), f., N. of one of the two wives of Yājñavalkya, ŚBr.; of a Pravrājikā, Kathās.; of Durgā, Hariv.; Lalit.; Prab.; a middle-aged widow dressed in red clothes, L.; mf(*ī*)n. composed by Kātyāyana. **–tantra**, n., N. of a work. **–māhātmya**, n., N. of a work. **–sūtra**, n. the Śrauta-sūtras of Kātyāyana; *-paddhati*, f. a commentary on the same by Yājñika-deva; *-bhāshya*, n. a commentary on the same by Karka.

Kātyāyanêśvara, n., N. of a Liṅga, SkandaP.

Kātyāyanikā, f. a widow in middle age, L.

Kātyāyanī, f. of °*yana*, q. v. **–kalpa**, m., N. of a Kalpa. **–putra**, m., N. of a teacher, BṛĀrUp. vi, 5, 1.

Kātyāyanīya, *ās*, m. pl. the school of Kātyāyana; (*am*), n., N. of several works; (mfn.) composed by Kātyāyana (e. g. *-śāstra*, the law-book composed by Kātyāyana); (*as*), m. a pupil of Kātyāyana, W.

काथक *kāthaka*, *as*, m. a son or descendant of Kathaka, Pravar.

Kāthakya, *as*, m. id., gaṇa *gargâdi*.

Kāthakyāyanī, f. of Kāthakya, gaṇa *lohitâdi*.

काथञ्चित्क *kāthañcitka*, mf(*ī*)n. (fr. *katham-cid*), accomplished with difficulty, gaṇa *vinayâdi*.

काथिक *kāthika*, mf(*ī*)n. (fr. 1. *kathā*), belonging to a tale, told in a tale, W.; knowing stories, Pāṇ. iv, 4, 102; (*as*), m. a narrator of stories, W.

कादम्ब *kādamba*, *as*, m. (Uṇ. iv, 84) a kind of goose with dark-grey wings (*kala-haṅsa*), MBh.; R.; Ragh.; Suśr.; an arrow, L.; the plant Nauclea Cadamba, L.; (*ā*), f. a kind of plant, L.; (*am*), n. the flower of the Nauclea Cadamba, Suśr.

Kādambaka, *as*, m. an arrow, L.

Kādambinī, f. a long line or bank of clouds, Prasannar. iv, 20; N. of a daughter of Takshaka, Vīrac.

कादम्बर *kādambara*, *as*, *am*, m. n. the surface or skim of coagulated milk, sour cream, L.; (*am*, *ī*), n. f. (n., L.) a spirituous liquor distilled from the flowers of the Cadamba, Kād. 102, 19; the rain water which collects in hollow places of the tree Nauclea Cadamba when the flowers are in perfection (it is supposed to be impregnated with honey), L.; wine, L.; spirituous liquor (in general), L.; the fluid which issues from the temples of a rutting elephant, L.; (*ī*), f. the female of the Kokila or Indian cuckoo, L.; the preaching-crow, L.; N. of Sarasvatī, L.; of a daughter of Citra-ratha and Madirā; of a celebrated story by Bāṇa named after her.

Kādambarī, f. of °*bara*, q. v. **–kathā-sāra**, m., N. of a work by Abhinanda (q. v.) **–bīja**, n. any cause of fermentation, ferment, yeast, L. **–locanânanda**, m. 'the pleasure of Kādambarī's eyes,' N. of the moon, Kād. ii. 133, 7.

Kādambarya, *as*, m. the tree Nauclea Cadamba (*kādamba*), L.

कादलेय *kādaleya* (fr. *kadala*), gaṇa *sakhy-ādi*.

कादाचित्क *kādācitka*, mf(*ī*)n. (fr. *kadā-cid*; Vop. vii, 15), appearing now and then, produced sometimes, occasional, incidental, Comm. on Bādar. ii, 3, 18 & iii, 2, 10. **–tā**, f. and **-tva**, n. the state of occurring occasionally, Sāh.

कादिक्रमस्तुति *kādi-krama-stuti*, *is*, f., N. of a work attributed to Śaṅkarācārya.

Kādi-mata, *am*, n., N. of a Tantra work, L.

काद्रव *kādrava*, mfn. dark yellow, reddish brown, MBh. v, 1708.

Kādraveyá, *as*, m. (fr. *kadrū*, Pāṇ. vi, 4, 147; gaṇa *śubhrâdi*, Pāṇ. iv, 1, 123; Vop. vii, 6), N. of certain Nāgas or serpent-demons supposed to people the lower regions, e.g. of Arbuda, AitBr. vi, 1; ŚBr. xiii, 4, 3, 9; ŚāṅkhŚr. xvi, 2, 14; ĀśvŚr. x, 7; of Kasarṇira, TS. i, 5, 4, 1; MBh.; Hariv.; BhP.; a serpent (?), L.

कानक *kānaka*, mfn. (fr. *kanaka*), golden, Suśr. i, 99, 5; (*am*), n. the seed of Croton Jamalgota, L.

कानच् *kānac*, the suffix *āna*; (forming perf. p. Ā.)

कानडा *kānaḍā*, f. a particular Rāgiṇī.

कानद *kānada*, *as*, m., N. of a son of Dhīmarana.

कानन 1. *kānana*, *am*, n. (said to be fr. √*kan*) a forest, grove (sometimes in connection with *vana*), R.; Nal.; Ragh.; Pañcat.; Suśr.; (ifc. f. *ā*, R.; Ragh.); a house, L. **Kānanânta**, n. the skirts or neighbourhood of a forest, wooded district, forest, R.; (cf. *vanânta*.) **Kānanâri**, m. 'forest-enemy,' a species of the Mimosa-tree (*śamī*), L. **Kānanâukas**, m. 'forest-dweller,' a monkey, R.; (cf. *vanâukas*.)

कानन 2. *kânana*, *am*, n. (fr. 3. *ka* + *ānana*), the face of Brahmā, L.

कानलक *kānalaka*, mfn. (fr. *kanala*), gaṇa *arīhaṇâdi*, Pāṇ. iv, 2, 80; (v. l. *kālanaka*.)

कानायन *kānāyana* (?), *as*, m. a patronymic, Pravar.

कानिष्ठिक *kānishṭhika*, mfn. (fr. *kanishṭhikā*), gaṇa *śarkarâdi*.

Kānishṭhineyá, *as*, m. (gaṇa *kalyāṇy-ādi*) a son of the youngest or of a younger wife, TBr. ii, 1, 8, 1; (pl.) Comm. on Mn. ix, 123 (*kanish°* printed text).

Kānishṭhya, *am*, n. the position of the youngest or a younger, Hariv. 113.

कानीत *kānītá*, *as*, m. a patr. of Pṛithu-śrávas, RV. viii, 46, 21 & 24; ŚāṅkhŚr. xvi, 11, 23.

कानीन *kānīná*, mf(*ī*)n. (fr. *kanīna*), born of a young wife, Pāṇ. iv, 1, 116; Mn. ix, 160 & 172; Yājñ. ii, 129; MBh.; Hariv.; BhP.; (*as*), m., N. of Vyāsa, Comm. on Pāṇ. iv, 1, 116 (cf. MBh. i, 3802); of Karṇa, Comm. on Pāṇ. iv, 1, 116 (cf. Hariv. 4057; BhP. ix, 23, 13); of Agniveśya, BhP. ix, 2, 21; (mfn.) suitable to or designed for the eyeball (cf. *kanīnaka*), Suśr. ii, 353, 13.

कानीयस *kānīyasá*, *ās*, m. pl. (fr. *kanīyas*), less in number, ŚBr. xiv, 4, 1, 1.

कानेरिन् *kānerin*, m. = *kāṇerin*, q. v.

कान्त 1. *kānta*, mf(*ā*)n. (fr. √2. *kam*), desired, loved, dear, pleasing, agreeable, lovely, beautiful; (*as*), m. any one beloved, a lover, husband; the moon, L.; the spring, L.; the plant Barringtonia Acutangula, L.; iron, L.; a stone (cf. *sūrya-k°*, &c.), L.; N. of Kṛishṇa, L.; of Skanda, MBh. iii, 14631; of a son of Dharma-netra, Hariv. i, 33, 3; (*ā*), f. a beloved or lovely woman, wife, mistress, Kathās.; a charming wife, L.; the earth, L.; N. of certain plants, L.; large cardamoms, L.; a kind of perfume (*reṇukā*, Piper aurantiacum), L.; N. of a metre of four lines of seventeen syllables each; a kind of Śruti; (*am*), n. saffron, L.; a kind of iron, L.; a magnet, Buddh.; a kind of house, L. **–kalikā**, f. a particular kind of artificial verse. **–tva**, n. loveliness, beauty, agreeableness, MBh. iii, 14437. **–pakshin**, m. 'lovely-bird,' a peacock, L. **–pāshāṇa**, m. the iron-stone, loadstone, L. **–pushpa**, m. the mountain-ebony (Bauhinia variegata), L. **–miśra**, m., N. of an author. **–loha**, n. the loadstone, L. **–lauha**, n. cast-iron (cf. *loha-kānta*), L. **Kāntânuvṛitta**, m. compliance with a beloved one. **Kāntâyasa**, n. the iron-stone, loadstone, magnet, L.; (cf. *-pāshāṇa*, *-loha*, and *ayas-kānta*.) **Kāntôtpīḍā**, f., N. of a metre consisting of four lines of twelve syllables each.

Kāntaka, *as*, m., N. of a man, Daś.

Kāntalaka, *as*, m. the tree Cedrela Toona (commonly *tunna*, the wood of which resembles mahogany), L.

Kāntā, f. of *kānta*, q. v. **Kāntâṅghri-dohada** and **kāntā-caraṇa-d°**, m. 'having a longing desire for contact with the foot of a beautiful woman' (to hasten its blossoms), the tree Jonesia Asoka, L. **Kāntā-purī**, v. l. for *kānti-purī*, VP.

Kāntāya, Nom. Ā. °*yate*, to behave like a lover, Bhartṛ. i, 50.

Kānti, *is*, f. desire, wish, L.; loveliness, beauty, splendour, female beauty, personal decoration or embellishment, Nal.; Śak.; Megh.; Pañcat.; Suśr.; Kathās.; a lovely colour, brightness (especially of the moon), Kathās.; (ifc. f. *ī*) Caurap.; (in rhetoric) beauty enhanced by love, Vām. iii, 1, 22; xxii, 14; Sāh.; a lovely or desirable woman personified as wife of the moon, Hariv. 5419; N. of Lakshmī, BhP. x, 65, 29; of Durgā, DevīP. **–kara**, mfn. causing beauty, beautifying, illuminating, W. **–kosala**, *ās*, m. pl., N. of a people, MBh. vi, 9, 40. **–da**, mfn. giving beauty, beautifying, adorning, W.; (*ā*), f. the plant Serratula anthelminthica (*vākucī*), L.; (*am*), n. bile, bilious humor, L. **–dāyaka**, mf(*ikā*)n. granting beauty, beautifying, adorning, W.; (*am*), n. a fragrant wood (a kind of Curcuma from the root of which a yellow dye is prepared; C. Zanthorrhiza, cf. *kālīyaka*), L. **–pura**, n., N. of a town in Nepal, VarBṛS.; (*ī*), f., N. of a town, PadmaP. **–mat**, mfn. lovely, splendid, R.; Kum.; Suśr.; (*ī*), f., N. of a metre; N. of a woman; *-tā*, f. loveliness, beauty, Kum. **–rāja**, m., N. of a prince. **–vrata**, n. a kind of ceremony. **–hara**, mfn. destroying beauty, making ugly, dulling, dimming, W.

Kāntika, *ās*, m. pl., N. of a people, VP.

Kānti, f., N. of a town. **-nagarī**, f., N. of a city in the north (for *kānti-nagarī*, cf. *kānti-pura*).

कान्तार *kāntāra, as, am*, m. n. a large wood, forest, wilderness, waste, MBh.; R.; Yājñ. ii, 38; Kathās.; Pañcat.; a difficult road through a forest, forest-path, L.; a hole, cavity, L.; (*as*), m. a red variety of the sugar-cane, Suśr.; a bamboo, L.; the mountain ebony (Bauhinia variegata), L.; (in music) a kind of measure, (*ī*), f. a kind of sugar-cane, L.; (*am*), n. a national calamity, calamity, Kāraṇḍ. xlvii, 15 & 20; the blossom of a kind of lotus, lotus, L.; a symptom or symptomatic disease, W. **-ga**, mfn. wood-going. **-patha**, m. a path through a forest, Daś. **-°pathika**, mfn. going on or conveyed on forest-roads, Pāṇ. v, 1, 77, Vārtt. 1. **-bhava**, m. a dweller in the woods, VarBṛS. **-vāsinī**, f. 'wood-dwelling,' N. of Durgā, MBh. vi, 23, 11. **Kāntārêkshu**, m. a kind of sugar-cane, Bhpr. ii, 64.

Kāntāraka, *as*, m. a kind of sugar-cane, L.; (*ās*), m. pl., N. of a people, MBh. ii, 1117; (*ikā*), f. a kind of bee, Suśr.

कान्तोत्पीडा *kāntôtpīḍā.* See *kānta.*

कान्थक *kānthaka, am*, n. 'coming from the town Kanthā,' a particular substance, Pāṇ. iv, 2, 103.

Kānthika, mfn. (fr. *kanthā*), Pāṇ. iv, 2, 102.

कान्थक्य *kānthakya, as*, m. a descendant of Kanthaka, gaṇa *gargâdi*; *°kyâyanī*, f., gaṇa *lohitâdi*.

कान्द *kānda*, gaṇa *aśmâdi*.

Kāndakāyana, *as*, m. a descendant of Kāndaki, gaṇa *taulvaly-ādi*, Kāś.

Kāndaki, *is*, m. a patr., gaṇa *taulvaly-ādi*, Kāś.

कान्दम *kāṃdama, as*, m. a patr. of Ekayāvan, TBr. ii, 7, 11, 2; (cf. *gām-damā*.)

कान्दर्प *kāndarpa, as*, m. descended from or relating to Kandarpa, gaṇa *bidâdi*.

Kāndarpika, *am*, n. 'treating of aphrodisiaca,' N. of the seventy-sixth Adhyāya of VarBṛS.

कान्दव *kāndava*, mfn. (fr. *kandu*), roasted or baked in an iron pan or oven (as bread cakes &c.), W.

Kāndavika, mfn. employed in baking, L.; (*as*), m. a baker, Pañcad.

कान्दाविष *kāndā-vishá, am*, n. a species of poison, AV. x, 4, 22.

कांदिश् *kāṃdiś, k*, mfn. (fr. *kām diśam*, 'to which region shall I fly?'), put to flight, running away, flying, MBh. xii, 6320; (cf. MBh. iii, 11113.)

Kāṃdig-bhūta, mfn. run away, MBh. v, 1870; MārkP.

Kāṃdiśī-, ind. with $\sqrt{}$*bhū*, to take to flight, L.

Kāṃdiśīka, mfn. running away, MBh. ix, 134; Rājat. &c.

कान्दुला *kāndulā*, f. a particular Rāgiṇī.

कान्दूरा *kāndūrā*, f. a kind of plant, Gal.

कान्यकुब्ज *kānyakubja, am*, n., N. of a city (= *kanya-kubja*, q. v.), MBh.; R.; BhP. &c.; (mf(*ī*)n.) belonging to or dwelling in Kānyakubja; (*ī*), f. a princess or a female inhabitant of Kānyakubja, Comm. on Pāṇ. iv, 1, 78. [In Kathās. lxi, 219 wrongly printed Kānyākubja.]

कान्यजा *kānyajā*, f. a kind of perfume, L.

कापट *kāpaṭa*, mf(*ī*)n. (fr. *kapaṭa*), addicted to deceit or fraud, dishonest, VarBṛS.

Kāpaṭika, mf(*ī*)n. fraudulent, dishonest, wicked, perverse, bad, L.; (*as*), m. a flatterer, parasite, W.; a student, scholar, L.

Kāpaṭya, *am*, n. deceit, fraud, dishonesty, wickedness, W.

कापटव *kāpaṭava, as*, m. (gaṇa *śārṅgaravâdi*) a son or descendant of Kāpaṭu, VBr.; (*ī*), f. a female descendant of Kapaṭu, Comm. on Pāṇ. iv, 1, 78.

Kāpaṭavaka, mfn. coming from Kāpaṭava or from his family, Comm. on Pāṇ. iv, 3, 80.

कापथ *kā-patha, as*, m. (fr. 2. *kā*+*patha*), a bad road, bad ways, erring or evil course, Pāṇ. vi, 3, 104 & 108; Vop. vi, 94; MBh. v, 4193; R. ii, 108, 7; v, 86, 2; (*as*), m., N. of a Dānava, Hariv. 14287; (*am*), n. the fragrant root of Andropogon muricatus, L.

कापा *kā́pā*, f. a carriage (Gmn.), RV. x, 40, 3.

कापाटिक *kāpāṭika*, mfn. = *kapāṭikêva*, gaṇa *śarkarâdi* (*kāpālika*, Kāś.); also v. l. for *kārpaṭika*, L.

कापाल *kāpāla*, mf(*ī*)n. (fr. *kapāla*), relating to the skull or cranium, R. i, 29, 13; VarBṛS. (= Pañcat.); made of skulls, Prasannar. lxxviii, 15; (*as*), m. a follower of a particular Śaiva sect of ascetics (see *kāpālika*); the plant Cucumis utilissimus, L.; (*ās*), m. pl. the school of Kapālin; (*ī*), f. the Embelia Ribes, L.; a clever woman, L.; (*am*), n. a kind of leprosy, Car. vi, 7.

Kāpāli, *is*, m., N. of a Siddha, Sarvad.

Kāpālika, mf(*ī*)n. relating to or belonging to a skull (= *kapālikêva*), gaṇa *śarkarâdi*, Pāṇ. v, 3, 107; (*as*), m. a kind of Śaiva ascetic who carries a human skull and uses it as a receptacle for his food (he belongs to the left-hand sect), VarBṛS.; Bhartṛ. i, 64; Prab. liii, 5; Kathās. &c.; N. of a mixed class (*kapālin*), L.; N. of a teacher; (*am*), n. a kind of leprosy; (mfn.) peculiar to a Kāpālika, Prab.; Pañcat.

Kāpālin, *ī*, m. 'adorned with skulls,' N. of Śiva, MBh. xiii, 1217 (cf. *kapālin*); N. of a mixed caste, BrahmavP.; N. of a son of Kṛishṇa and Yaudhishṭhirī, Hariv. 9196.

कापिक *kāpika*, mf(*ī*)n. (fr. *kapi*), shaped or behaving like a monkey, gaṇa *aṅguly-ādi*.

कापिञ्जल *kāpiñjala*, mfn. (fr. *kap°*), coming from the francoline partridge, Kauś. 46; (*as*), m. a patr. fr. *kap°* (v. l. *kup°*), gaṇa *śivâdi*.

Kāpiñjalāda, *ās*, m. pl. the school of Kāpiñjalādya, Pat.

Kāpiñjalādi, *is*, m. a patr. fr. *kapiñjalâda*, gaṇa *kurv-ādi*.

Kāpiñjalādya, *as*, m. a patr. fr. *°lādi*, ib.

Kāpiñjali, *is*, m. a patr. fr. *kapiñjala*, Pat.

कापित्थ *kāpittha*, mfn. (fr. *kapittha*), belonging to the tree Feronia elephantum, Pāṇ. iv, 3, 140.

Kāpitthaka, *as*, m. (?) N. of a place, Comm. on VarBṛ.

Kāpitthika, mfn., N. of certain ascetics, Hariv. 7988; (*ā*), f. (perhaps) the tree Feronia elephantum, Hariv. 7984.

कापिल *kāpila*, mf(*ī*)n. (fr. *kapila*), peculiar or belonging to or derived from Kapila, MBh.; R.; of a tawny or brownish colour, L.; (*as*), m. a follower of the teacher Kapila, follower of the Sāṅkhya system of philosophy (founded by Kapila), MBh. xii; Kāvyād.; Hcar.; a tawny colour, L.; (*am*), n., N. of a work by Kapila (= *sāṅkhya*, or according to others an Upa-purāṇa), Pañcar.; (with *tīrtha*) N. of a Tīrtha, SkandaP.; KapSaṃh. **-purāṇa**, n., N. of a work. **-bali**, m., N. of a man, Car.

Kāpilêśvara-tīrtha, n., N. of a Tīrtha, ŚivaP.

Kāpilika, *as*, m. a metron. fr. *kapilikā*, gaṇa *śivâdi*.

Kāpileya, mfn. derived from Kapila, Pañcar.; (*as*), m. a patr. fr. *kapila* or a metron. fr. *kapilā*, AitBr. vii, 17; MBh.

Kāpilya, mfn. fr. *kapila*, gaṇa *saṃkāśâdi*.

कापिवन *kāpivana, as*, m. (fr. *kapi-v°*), N. of a festival lasting two days, KātyŚr.; ĀśvŚr.; Vait.

कापिश *kāpiśa, am*, n. (fr. *kapiśa*), a kind of spirituous liquor, L.; (*ī*), f., N. of a place, Pāṇ. iv, 2, 99.

Kāpiśāyana, mf(*ī*)n. coming from Kāpiśī (e. g. *madhu*, honey, or *drākshā*, grape, W.), Pāṇ. iv, 2, 99; (*as*), m. a patr. or metron., Pravar.; (*am*), n. a kind of spirituous liquor, Śiś. x, 4; a deity, L.

Kāpiśeya, *as*, m. (fr. *kapiśā*), a Piśāca, imp, goblin, L.

कापिष्ठल *kāpishṭhala, as*, m. a son or descendant of Kapishṭhala, Comm. on Nir. iv, 14; (*ās*), m. pl., N. of a people (cf. Καμβισθολοί), VarBṛS. **-kaṭha**, m. pl., N. of a school of the Yajur-veda.

Kāpishṭhalāyana, mfn. (fr. *kāpishṭhala*), Pāṇ. viii, 3, 91, Pat.

Kāpishṭhali, *is*, m. a son or descendant of Kapishṭhala, gaṇa *kraudy-ādi*: Pāṇ. viii, 3, 91, Vārtt.; (*°lyā*), f. of *°li*, gaṇa *kraudy-ādi*.

कापी *kāpī*, f. a patr. fr. *kāpya*; N. of a river, MBh. vi, 9, 24; VP. **-putra**, m., N. of a teacher, BṛĀrUp.

Kāpīyakānika, *as*, m., N. of a Muni, VāyuP.

Kāpeya, mf(*ī*)n. (fr. *kapi*), belonging or peculiar to a monkey, R. vi, 111, 19; (*as*), m. a descendant of Kapi, Comm. on Pāṇ. iv, 1, 107; (pl.) Tāṇḍya-Br.; (*am*), n. monkey tricks, Pāṇ. v, 1, 127.

1. **Kāpya**, *as*, m. (Pāṇ. iv, 1, 107; gaṇa *gargâdi*) a descendant of Kapi, BṛĀrUp.

Kāpyāyanī, f. of *kāpya*, gaṇa *lohitâdi*.

कापुरुष *kā-purusha, as*, m. (fr. 2. *kā*; Pāṇ. vi, 3, 106; Vop. vi, 94), a contemptible man, coward, wretch, R.; Pañcat.; Hit.; (mf(*ā*)n.) unmanly, cowardly, miserable, Hariv.; R. vi, 88, 13. **-tā**, f. and **-tva**, n. unmanliness, cowardliness.

Kāpurushya, *am*, n. unmanliness, meanness, cowardice, gaṇa *brāhmaṇâdi*.

कापोत *kāpota*, mf(*ī*)n. (fr. *kapota*, Pāṇ. iv, 3, 135, Sch., 154, Sch.), belonging to or coming from a pigeon, MBh.; BhP.; Pat.; of the colour of a pigeon, of a dull white colour, grey, VarBṛS.; (*as*), m. natron, fossil alkali, L.; antimony, a collyrium or application for the eyes, W.; (*ī*), f. a kind of plant, Suśr. ii, 173, 12; (*am*), n. a flock of pigeons, Comm. on Pāṇ. iv, 2, 44; antimony, L.; N. of two Sāmans, ĀrshBr. **Kāpotâñjana**, n. antimony, a collyrium for the eyes, L.

Kāpotaka, mfn. fr. *kapotakīya*, gaṇa *bilvakâdi*.

Kāpotapākya, *as*, m. a prince of the Kapotapākas, Pāṇ. v, 3, 113, Kāś.

Kāpotaretasa, *as*, m. a patr. fr. *kapota-r°*, Comm. on ŚāṅkhBr. iii, 2.

Kāpoti, *is*, m. (Pat.) a patr. fr. *kapota*, MBh. xiv, 2712.

कापोल *kāpola, ās*, m. pl., N. of a school of the Sāma-veda.

काप्य 1. *kāpya.* See *kāpi.*

काप्य 2. *kāpya*, only in comp. **-kara**, mfn. confessing sin, L. **-kāra**, mfn. confessing sin, L.; (*as*), m. confession of sin, L.

काफल *kā-phala, as*, m. = *kaṭphala*, L.

काबन्ध *kābandha* (fr. *kab°*). See *kāv°*.

Kābandhya, *am*, n. the state of being a trunk.

काबव *kābavá, as*, m., N. of certain evil spirits, AV. iii, 9, 3-5.

काभर्तृ *kā-bhartṛi, ā*, m. a bad husband or lord or master, Sāh.

काम् *kām*, ind. an interjection used in calling out to another, L.

काम *kā́ma, as*, m. (fr. $\sqrt{}$2. *kam*; once *kāmá*, VS. xx, 60), wish, desire, longing (*kāmo me bhuñjīta bhavān*, my wish is that you should eat, Pāṇ. iii, 3, 153), desire for, longing after (gen., dat., or loc.), love, affection, object of desire or of love or of pleasure, RV.; VS.; TS.; AV.; ŚBr.; MBh.; R. &c.; pleasure, enjoyment; love, especially sexual love or sensuality; Love or Desire personified, AV. ix; xii; xix (cf. RV. x, 129, 4); VS.; PārGṛ.; N. of the god of love, AV. iii. 25, 1; MBh.; Lalit.; (represented as son of Dharma and husband of Rati [MBh. i, 2596 ff.; Hariv.; VP.]; or as a son of Brahmā, VP.; or sometimes of Saṃkalpa, BhP. vi, 6, 10; cf. *kāma-deva*); N. of Agni, SV. ii, 8, 2, 19, 3; AV.; TS.; KātyŚr.; ŚāṅkhŚr.; of Vishṇu, Gal.; of Baladeva (cf. *kāma-pāla*), L.; a stake in gambling, Nār. xvi, 9; a species of mango tree (= *mahā-rāja-cūta*), L.; N. of a metre consisting of four lines of two long syllables each; a kind of bean, L.; a particular form of temple, Hcat.; N. of several men; (*ā*), f. 'wish, desire' (only instr. *kāmayā*, q. v.); N. of a daughter of Pṛithuśravas and wife of Ayuta-nāyin, MBh. i, 3774; (*am*), n. object of desire, L.; semen virile, L.; N. of a Tīrtha, MBh. iii, 5047; (*am*), ind., see s. v.; (*ena*), ind. out of affection or love for; (*āya* or *e*), ind. according to desire, agreeably to the wishes of, out of love for (gen. or dat.), RV.; AV.; TS.; ŚBr.; ChUp.; (*āt*), ind. for one's own pleasure, of one's own free will, of one's own accord, willingly, intentionally, Mn.; R.; (*kāmá*), mfn. wishing, desiring, RV. ix, 113, 11; (ifc.) desirous of, desiring, having a desire or intention; (cf. *go-k°*, *dharma-k°*; frequently with inf. in *tu*, cf. *tyaktu-k°*.) **-kandalā**, f., N. of a woman. **-karśana** in *á-kāma-k°*, q. v. **-kalā**, f., N. of Rati (wife of Kāma), L.; *°lâṅganā-vilāsa*, m., N. of a work; *°lā-tantra*, n. another work; *°lā-bīja*, n. the essential letter or syllable of a charm or spell. **— kalikā**, f., N. of a Surâṅganā. **— kākurava**, m. a dove, Gal. **— kāti** (*kā́ma-*), mfn. requesting the fulfilment of a wish, RV. viii, 92, 14. **— kāntā**, f. the plant Jasminum Sambac, L. **— kāma** and **-kāmin**, mfn. 'wishing wishes,' having various desires or wishes, following the dictates of passion, TĀr. i, 31, 1; MBh. iii, 11256; Bhag. **— kāra**, mfn. fulfilling the desires of any one (gen.), R. vii, 63, 8; (*as*), m. the act of following one's own inclinations, spontaneous deed, voluntary action, acting of one's own free will, free will, Mn.; MBh.; R.; Bhag.; *°raṃ √kṛi*, to act as one likes; *°reṇa* and *°rāt* and *°ra-tas*, ind. according to one's desires or inclinations, willingly, spontaneously, Mn.; MBh. &c. **— kuṇḍa**, n., N. of a Liṅga, SkandaP. **— kūṭa**, m. the paramour of a harlot, L.; wanton caresses, L. **— kṛita**, mfn. done intentionally or knowingly, Āp. ii, 28, 12. **— klṛipti**, f. arranging to one's liking, Vait. **— keli**, m. 'love-sport,' amorous sport, sexual intercourse, L.; the Vidūshaka of the drama, L.; (mfn.) having amorous sport, wanton, L.; *-rasa*, m. a kind of aphrodisiac. **— kôshṇī**, f., N. of a river, BhP. **— krīḍā**, f. amorous sport; N. of a metre consisting of four lines of fifteen long syllables each. **— khaḍga-dalā**, f. the plant Pandanus Odoratissimus (cf. *svarṇa-ketakī*), L. **— ga**, mfn. going or coming of one's own accord; moving or acting as one pleases, MBh.; R.; following one's impulses, indulging one's passions, running after men or women, Yājñ. iii, 6 (of a woman = *kulaṭā*, Comm.); (*as*), m. one who comes accidentally or unexpectedly, casual visitor, one who travels about without any specific purpose, Nal. xviii, 23; (*ā*), f. a female Kokila, L. **— gati**, mfn. going or coming of one's own accord, Ragh. xiii, 76. **— gama**, mf(*ā*)n. id., MBh.; R.; (*ās*), m. pl. a class of deities of the eleventh Manvantara, VP. **— gavī**, f. = *-dhenu*. **— gāmin**, mfn. = *-gati*, L. **— giri**, m., N. of a mountain, VP. **— guṇa**, m. 'quality of desire,' affection, passion; satiety, perfect enjoyment; an object of sense; (*ās*), m. pl. the objects of the five senses, sensual enjoyments, Lalit. 225, 4. **— go**, f. = *-dhenu*. **— °ṃ-gāmin**, mfn. = *-gati*, L. **— cakra**, n. a kind of mystical circle. **— candra**, m., N. of a prince, Buddh. **— cara**, mf(*ī*)n. moving freely, following one's own pleasure, unrestrained, MBh.; (*ī*), f., N. of one of the mothers attending on Skanda, MBh. ix. 2641; *-tva*, n. the state of being free to move or act as one likes, Kathās. **— caraṇá**, n. free or unchecked motion, ŚBr. vi, 7, 3, 3. **— cāra**, mf(*ā*)n. moving freely, following one's own pleasure, unrestrained, MBh.; (*ás*), m. free unrestrained motion, independent or spontaneous action; the following one's own desires, sensuality, selfishness, ŚBr.; ChUp.; Yājñ. ii, 162; Kathās.; Comm. on Pāṇ. i, 4, 96; Ragh.; *-tas*, ind. according to one's inclination, voluntarily, Mn. ii, 220; (*eṇa*), ind. at pleasure, at will, Comm. on TPrāt.; *-vāda-bhaksha*, mfn. following one's inclinations in behaviour and speech and eating, Gaut. ii, 1. **— cārin**, mfn. moving or acting at pleasure, acting unrestrainedly, MBh.; R.; Megh.; indulging the desires, behaving libidinously (*para-strī-kāma-cārin*, lusting after the wife of another), MBh. xiii, 2265; (*as*), m., N. of a Yaksha, Kathās.; a sparrow (*caṭaka*), L.; N. of Garuḍa, L.; (*iṇī*), f., N. of Dākshāyaṇī in mount Mandara, MatsyaP.; an Artemisia, Npr.; *°ri-tva*, n. moving or acting at pleasure, Kād. ii, 130, 18; lewdness, KapS. **— cālana**, n. an erotic term. **— ja**, mfn. produced or caused by passion or desire, arising from lust, Mn. vii, 46. 47. 50; begotten or born of desire or lust, Mn. ix, 107. 143. 147; (*as*), m. 'born of Kāma,' N. of Aniruddha, W.; (*ās*), m. pl. = *kāma-gamās*, VP. **— jananī**, f. betel-pepper, Npr. **— jani**, m. the Indian cuckoo, L. **— jāna**, m. id., L. **— jāla**, m. = *-tāla*, W. **— jit**, m. 'conquering desire,' N. of Skanda, MBh. **— jyeshṭha** (*kā́ma-*), mfn. having the god Desire at the head, led by Kāma, AV. ix, 2, 8. **— tantra**, n., N. of a work. **— taru**, m. the god of love considered as a tree (cf. *-vṛiksha*), Śak.; the plant Vanda Roxburghii, Npr. **— tas**, ind. according to wish or affection, passionately, from passion or feeling (opposed to *dharma-tas*); of one's own accord, of one's own free will, willingly, intentionally, by consent, Mn.; Yājñ.; MBh.; R.; (cf. *a-kāma-tas*.) **— tāla**, m. the Indian cuckoo (considered as an incentive to love), L. **— tīrtha**, n., N. of a Tīrtha. **— da**, mf(*ā*)n. giving what is wished, granting desires, R.; Kathās. &c.; N. of the sun, MBh. iii, 154; of Skanda, MBh. iii, 14631; (*ā*), f. = *-dhenu*, R. i, 53, 20; betel-pepper, Npr.; the yellow Myrobalan, Npr.; a Sanseviera, Npr.; N. of one of the mothers in attendance on Skanda, MBh. ix, 2645; of a daughter of Śata-dhanvan; *-tva*, n. the granting desires. **— dattā**, f., N. of a work. **— dattikā**, f., N. of a daughter of Śata-dhanvan, Hariv. 2037. **— dantikā**, f., v.l. for *-dattikā*, Hariv. i, 38, 6. **— daminī**, f. 'taming love,' N. of a libidinous woman, Pañcat. **— darśana**, mfn. having the look of a charming person, looking lovely, Hariv. **— dahana**, n. 'the burning up of the god of love by Śiva,' N. of a chapter of the LiṅgaP.; a particular festival on the day of full moon in the month Phālguna. **— dāna**, n. a gift to one's satisfaction, Hcat. i, 14, 7; a kind of ceremony among prostitutes, BhavP. **— dúgha**, mf(*ā*)n. (Pāṇ. iii, 2, 70, Kāś.) 'milking desires,' yielding objects of desire like milk, yielding what one wishes, VS.; TS.; AV.; ŚBr.; MBh. &c.; Bālar.; (*ā*), f. = *-dhenu*. **— duh**, mfn. (nom. sg. *-dhuk*), id., MBh. &c. **— duha**, mf(*ā*)n. id., MBh.; (*ā*), f. the cow of plenty, W. **— dūtikā**, f. the plant Tiaridium Indicum, L. **— dūtī**, f. the female of the Indian cuckoo, W.; the plant Bignonia suaveolens, Bhpr. **— deva**, m. the god of love (see *kāma* above; according to some, son of Sahishṇu and Yaśo-dharā, VP.); N. of Vishṇu (as the god who creates, preserves, or destroys at will), Vishṇ. xcviii, 10; (cf. BhP. v, 18, 15); of Śiva, L.; of a poet; of a king of Jayantī-purī; N. of the author of the Prāyaścitta-paddhati; *-tva*, n. the being the god of love, Kathās.; *-maya*, mfn. representing the god of love, AgP. **— dohanā**, f. yielding milk easily, yielding desires, Hcat. **— dohinī**, f. 'yielding desires,' = *-dhenu*, Hcat. **— dhara**, m., N. of a lake in Kāma-rūpa, KālP. **— dhāraṇa**, n. the procuring of desires, fulfilment of desire, VS. iii, 27; xii, 46. **— dharma**, m. amorous behaviour. **— dhātu**, m. the region of the wishes, seat of the Kāmâvacara, Buddh. **— dhenu**, f. the mythical cow of Vasishṭha which satisfies all desires, cow of plenty (= *surabhi*), Kathās.; BrahmavP.; N. of a goddess, BrahmaP.; N. of several works; *-gaṇita*, n., N. of a work; *-tantra*, n., N. of a work on the mystical signification of the letters of the alphabet. **— dhvaṇsin**, m. 'subduing the god of love,' N. of Śiva, L. **— nāśaka**, mfn. destroying irregular desires, subduing sensual appetite. **— nīḍā**, f. musk, L. **— °ṃ-dhamin**, m. a brazier (= *kāraṃ-dhamin*), L. **— pati**, m. the lord of desire. **— patnī**, f. the wife of Kāma (viz. Rati), Hariv. **— parṇikā, -parṇī**, f. Trichodesma Zeylanicum, Npr. **— pāla**, m. 'gratifier of human desires,' N. of Vishṇu, Vishṇ.; of Śiva, L.; of Baladeva, L.; of a man, Daś. **— pālaka**, m., N. of Baladeva, Gal. **— pīḍita**, mfn. tormented with lust or irregular desires. **— pūra**, mfn. fulfilling wishes, gratifying desires, BhP. **— pra**, mfn. id., RV.; AV.; ŚBr.; (*ám*), n. the fulfilment of desire, AV.; Kauś.; ŚāṅkhŚr. **— prada**, mfn. granting desires; (*as*), m. a kind of coitus, L. **— pradīpa**, m., N. of a work. **— praśná**, m. questioning as one pleases, asking unrestrainedly, ŚBr. **— prastha**, m., N. of a town, gaṇa *mālâdi*. **— °prasthīya**, mfn. relating to that town, gaṇa *gahâdi*, Pāṇ. iv, 2, 138. **— pri**, m. one whose wishes are fulfilled [Sāy.; 'son of Kāma-pra,' N. of Marutta, BRD.], AitBr. viii, 21. **— priyakarī**, f. Physalis Flexuosa, L. **— phala**, m. a species of mango tree, L. **— baddha**, mfn. bound by love; (*am*), n. a wood, W. **— bala**, n. force of desire, sexual power, Bhpr. **— bāṇa**, m. an arrow of the god of love. **— bindu**, m. 'wish-drop,' anything dropped into the fire to procure the fulfilment of a wish, drop of melted butter, BhP. **— bhaksha** (ed. *-bhakshya*), m. eating according to one's inclinations, Comm. on Yājñ. **— bhāj**, mfn. partaking of sensual enjoyment, enjoying all desires, KaṭhUp. i, 24. **— bhoga**, *ās*, m. pl. gratification of desires, sensual gratification, Nal.; R.; BhP. **— mañjarī**, f. 'love-bud,' N. of a woman, Daś. **— máya**, mf(*ī*)n. consisting of desire, ŚBr.; BṛArUp.; answering all desires, R. iv, 33, 6. **— mardana**, m. 'destroyer of the god of love,' N. of Śiva, L. **— maha**, m. the festival of the god of love (on the day of full moon in the month Caitra or March-April), L. **— mālin**, m., N. of Gaṇêśa. **— mūḍha**, mfn. infatuated by lust, MW. **— mūta** (*kā́ma-*), mfn. strongly affected or impelled by love, RV. x, 10, 11. **— moha**, m. infatuation of lust. **— mohita**, mfn. infatuated by desire or love or passion. **— ratna**, n., N. of a Tantra. **— rasa**, m. enjoyment of sexual love, MBh. **— rasika**, mfn. libidinous, Bhartṛ. **— rāja**, m., N. of a prince; of a poet. **— rūpa**, n. a shape assumed at will; (mfn.) assuming any shape at will, protean, MBh.; R.; Megh.; (*as*), m. a god, L.; (*ās*), m. pl., N. of a people and of their country (east of Bengal and in the west part of Assam), Ragh.; Kathās. &c.; *-tīrtha*, n., N. of a Tīrtha; *-dhara*, mfn. assuming any shape at will, protean, MBh.; R.; *-dhara-tva*, n. the state of assuming any form at will, R.; *-nibandha*, m., N. of a work; *-pati*, m., N. of an author; *-yātrā-paddhati*, f., N. of a work; *°pôdbhavā*, f. a kind of musk, Npr. **— rūpin**, mfn. assuming any shape at will, protean, ŚBr.; TUp.; MBh.; R.; Suśr.; (*as*), m. a pole-cat, L.; a boar, L.; a Vidyā-dhara (a kind of subordinate deity), L.; (*iṇī*), f. the plant Physalis Flexuosa, L. **— rūpīya-nibandha**, m. = *-rūpa-nibandha*. **— rekhā**, f. a harlot, courtezan (cf. *-lekhā*), L. **— latā**, f. membrum virile, penis, L.; the plant Ipomæa (Quamoclit Pennata). **— lekhā**, f. a harlot, courtezan (cf. *-rekhā*), L. **— lola**, mfn. overcome with desire or passion, W. **— vat** (*kā́ma-*), mfn. being in love, enamoured, wanton, MBh.; R.; containing the word *kāma*, ŚBr.; (*tī*), f. a species of Curcuma (Curcuma Aromatica, *dāru-haridrā*); N. of a town. **— vatsa** (*kā́ma-*), mf(*ā*)n. having the wish for a calf, having the wish in place of a calf, TBr. iii, 12, 3, 2. **— vara**, m. a gift chosen at one's own liking or will, BhP. **— varshin**, mfn. raining according to one's wishes. **— vallabha**, m. 'love's favourite,' spring, W.; a species of mango tree, L.; the cinnamon tree; (*ā*), f. moonlight, L. **— vaśa**, m. subjection to love, MW. **— vaśya**, mfn. being in subjection to the god of love, enamoured, MBh. **— vasati**, f. an erotic term. **— vāda**, m. speech at will, Comm. on Yājñ.; (cf. Gaut. ii, 1.) **— vāsin**, mfn. dwelling where one pleases, choosing or changing one's residence at will, Nal. **— viddha**, mfn. wounded by the god of love; (*as*), m., N. of a man, gaṇa *kārtakaujapâdi*; (*ās*), m. pl. his descendants, ib. **— vivarjita**, mfn. freed from all desires, Up. **— vihantṛi**, mfn. disappointing desires, W. **— vīrya**, m. 'displaying heroism at will,' N. of Garuḍa, MBh. i, 1240; iii, 14360. **— vṛiksha**, m. a parasitical plant (*vandāka*, Vanda Roxburghii), L. **— vṛitta**, mfn. eating licentiously, dissipated, Mn. v, 154; MBh.; R. **— vṛiddhi**, f. increase of sexual desire or passion, L.; (*is*), m. a shrub of supposed aphrodisiac properties (called Kāma-ja in the Karṇāṭaka), L. **— vṛintā**, f. the trumpet flower (Bignonia suaveolens). **— veraṇi**, v.l. in gaṇa *gahâdi* in the Kāś. **— °veraṇīya**, mfn. fr. the preceding, ib. **— vyāhārin**, mfn. singing sweetly. **— śara**, m. 'love's shaft,' an arrow of the god of love, Pañcat.; the mango tree, L.; *°rônmādinī*, f., N. of a Surâṅganā. **— śalya** (*kā́ma-*), mf(*ā*)n. having love for a shaft, AV. iii, 25, 2. **— śāsana**, m. 'punisher of Kāma,' N. of Śiva, Daś. **— śāstra**, n. a treatise on pleasure or sexual love, MBh.; = *-sūtra*, N. of several erotic works. **— śaila**, m., N. of a mountain, R. (ed. Bomb.) iv, 43, 28. **— saṃyoga**, m. attainment of desired objects, W. **— sakha**, m. 'Kāma's friend,' spring, L.; the month Caitra, L.; the mango tree, L. **— saṃkalpa**, mfn. having all kinds of wishes, BrahmabUp. **— sani**, mfn. fulfilling wishes, TāṇḍyaBr. **— samūha**, m., N. of a work of Ananta. **— suta**, m. Aniruddha (the son of Kāma-deva), L. **— sū**, mfn. gratifying wishes, Ragh.; (*ūs*), f., N. of Rukmiṇī, L. **— sûkta**, n. a kind of hymn, Hcat. **— sūtra**, n., N. of a treatise on sexual love by Vātsyāyana. **— sena**, m., N. of a king of Rāmavatī; (*ā*), f. the wife of Nidhipati. **— hāni**, m., N. of a teacher. **— haituka**, mfn. caused or produced by mere desire, of one's own accord, Bhag. **Kāmâkshā**, f. a form of Dākshāyaṇī; *-tantra*, n., N. of a work. **Kāmâkshī**, f. a form of Durgā; N. of a district sacred to Durgā in Assam. **Kāmâkhya**, n., N. of a Tīrtha, MBh.; (*ā*), f. a form of Durgā, VP.; N. of a Tantra; *-tantra*, n., N. of a Tantra. **Kāmâgni**, m. the fire of love, passion, lust; *-saṃdīpana*, n. kindling the fire of lust, excitement of sexual love. **Kāmâṅkuśa**, m. the pointed hook by which the god of love excites or inflames lovers; a finger nail (which plays an important part in erotic acts), L.; membrum virile, L. **Kāmâṅga**, m. the mango tree, Magnifera indica, L.; (*ā*), f. a particular Śruti, L. **Kāmâtura**, mfn. love-sick, affected by love or desire; (*as*), m., N. of a man, Pañcat. **Kāmâtman**, mfn. 'whose very essence is desire,' consisting of desire, indulging one's desires, given to lust, sensual, licentious, MBh.; Mn. vii, 27; desiring, wishing for, W.; °*tma-tā*, f. passion, lust, Mn. ii, 2; R. ii, 21, 57. **Kāmâdhikāra,** m. the influence of passion or desire, W.; that part of a Śāstra that relates to human wishes or desires, W. **Kāmâdhishṭhita,** mfn. influenced or dominated by love, W. **Kāmânala,** m. the fire of love, passion, lust, W. **Kāmândha,** mfn. blinded through love, blind with lust, Mn. vii, 27 (v.l.); Subh.; (*as*), m. 'blind from love,' the Indian cuckoo, L.; the falcon, L.; (*ā*), f. musk, L. **Kāmânnin,** mfn. having as much food as one likes, TUp. iii, 10, 5. **Kāmâbhikāma,** mfn. lustful, MW. **Kāmâbhivarshaṇa,** n. granting of desires, BhP. **Kāmâyudha,** m. a species of the mango tree, L.; (*am*), n. the weapon or arrow of the god of love; membrum virile, W. **Kāmâyus,** m. a vulture, L.; N. of Garuḍa, L. **Kāmâraṇya,** n. a pleasure grove or wood, L. **Kāmâri,** m. 'love's adversary,' N. of Śiva, R. vii, 6, 31; Prasannar.; a mineral substance used in medicine, a sort of pyrites (= *vita-mā-shika*), L. **— Kāmârta,** mfn. afflicted by love or passion, in love, W. **Kāmârthin,** mfn. desirous of pleasure or love, amorous, MW.; °*rthi-nagara*, n., N. of a town. **Kāmâvacara,** *ās*, m. pl. the spheres or worlds of desire (six in number, also called *deva-loka*, q.v), Buddh.; the gods or inhabitants of the worlds of desire (1. *cāturmahārāja-kāyikās*; 2. *trāyastriṇśās*; 3. *tushitās*; 4. *yāmās*; 5. *nir-māṇa-ratayas*; 6. *paranirmitavaśa-vartinas*), ib. **Kāmâvatāra,** m., N. of a metre consisting of four lines of six syllables each; N. of a work. **Kāmâvasāya,** m. suppression of the passions. **Kāmâvasāyitṛi,** mfn. one who or anything that suppresses or destroys passion or desire, L. **Kāmâvasāyin,** mfn. suppressing desire, W.; °*yi-tā*, f., °*yi-tva*, n. the power of suppressing desire (one of the eight supernatural faculties of Śiva), L.; (cf. *yatra-kām*°.) **Kāmâśana,** n. eating at will, unrestrained eating, ŚBr. vi. **Kāmâśaya,** m. the seat of desire, BhP. **Kāmâśoka,** m., N. of a king, Buddh. **Kāmâśrama,** m. the hermitage of the god of love, R. i, 25, 17; *-pada*, n. id., ib. **Kāmâsakta,** mfn. intent on gratifying desire, engrossed with love, deeply in love, W. **Kāmâsakti,** f. addiction to love, W. **Kāmêpsu,** mfn. desirous of sensual objects, SāmavBr. **Kāmêśvara,** m., N. of Kubera, TĀr.; (*ī*), f., N. of a goddess; (*am*), n., N. of a Tīrtha, SkandaP.; *-tīrtha*, n., N. of a Tīrtha; *-moda-ka*, m. or n. a kind of plant with aphrodisiac properties. **Kāmêshṭa,** m. 'desired by Kāma,' the mango tree, Npr. **Kāmôtthāpya,** mfn. to be sent away at will, AitBr. vii, 29. **Kāmôda,** m. a particular Rāga; (*ī*), f. the plant Phaseolus trilobus, L.; a particular Rāgiṇī (also *kāmôdā*). **Kāmôdaka,** n. a voluntary oblation of water to deceased friends &c. (exclusive of those for whom it is obligatory), PārGṛ. iii, 10; Yājñ. iii, 4. **Kāmônmatta,** mfn. mad with love, Daś. **Kāmônmādinī,** f., N. of a Surâṅganā. **Kāmôpahata,** mfn. overcome with passion or desire, W.; *-cittâṅga*, mfn. one whose mind and body are overcome with love, W.

Kāmana, mfn. lustful, sensual, lascivious, L. [cf. O. Pers. *kamana*, 'loving, true, faithful']; (*ā*), f. wish, desire, L.; the plant Vanda Roxburghii, Npr.

Kāmanīyaka, n. loveliness, beauty, Naish.

Kā́mam, ind. (acc. of *kā́ma*, gaṇa *svarâdi*, not in Kāś.) according to wish or desire, according to inclination, agreeably to desire, at will, freely, willingly, RV.; TS.; AitBr.; ŚBr.; ChUp.; MBh.; R. &c.; with pleasure, readily, gladly, MBh. iii, 298; Ragh.; (as a particle of assent) well, very well, granted, admitted that, indeed, really, surely, MBh. iii, 17195; R. v, 24, 4; Śak.; Bhartṛ.; well and good, in any case, at any rate, MBh. iii, 310, 19; R. iv, 9, 105; v, 53, 11; Śak.; Dhūrtas.; (with *na*, 'in no case,' R. iii, 56, 17); granted that, in spite of that, notwithstanding, R. iv, 16, 50; Pañcat. &c.; though, although, supposing that (usually with Impv.), R. vi, 95, 49 & 56; Ragh. ii, 43; Śāntiś. (*kāmaṃ—na* or *na tu* or *na ca*, rather than, e.g. *kāmam ā maraṇāt tishṭhed gṛihe kanyā—na enām prayacchet tu guṇa-hīnāya*, 'rather should a girl stay at home till her death, than that he should give her to one void of excellent qualities,' Mn. ix, 89; the negative sentence with *na* or *na-tu* or *na ca* may also precede, or its place may be taken by an interrogative sentence, e.g. *kā-maṃ nayatu māṃ devaḥ kim ardhenâtmano hi me*, 'rather let the god take me, what is the use to me of half my existence?' BhP. vii, 2, 54; *kāmam—tu* or *kiṃ tu* or *ca* or *punar* or *athâpi* or *tathâpi*, well, indeed, surely, truly, granted, though—however, notwithstanding, nevertheless, e.g. *kāmaṃ tvayā parityaktā gamishyāmi—imaṃ tu bālaṃ saṃtyaktuṃ nârhasi*, 'granted that forsaken by thee I shall go—this child however thou must not forsake,' MBh. i, 3059; or the disjunctive particles may be left out, R.; Ragh. ii, 43; Śāntiś.; *yady-api -kāmaṃ tathâpi*, though—nevertheless, Prab.) **Kāmaṃ-gāmin,** see *kāma*.

Kāmayā, ind. (instr. of *kāmā*, q. v.) only used with *brūhi* or *pra-brūhi* (e.g. *kāmayā me brūhi deva kas tvam*, 'for love of me, say, O god, who thou art,' MBh.)

Kāmayāna, mfn. (irreg. pr. p., Caus. √*kam*) desiring, lusting after, MBh.; BhP. x, 47, 17.

Kāmayitṛi, mfn. libidinous, lustful, desirous, L.

Kāmala, mfn. libidinous, lustful, L.; (*as*), m. the spring, L.; dry and sterile soil, desert, L.; (*as, ā*), m. f. a form of jaundice, Suśr.; Hcat.; excessive secretion or obstruction of bile, W.; (*ā*), f., N. of an Apsaras, L.; (*ī*), f., N. of a daughter of Reṇu (also called Reṇukā), Hariv. 1453.

Kāmalakīkara, mfn. fr. *kamala-kīkara*, gaṇa *palady-ādi*.

Kāmalakīṭa, mfn. fr. *kamala-kīṭa*, ib.

Kāmalabhida, mfn. fr. *kamala-bhidā*, ib.

Kāmalāyana, *as*, m. a descendant of Kamala, N. of Upakosala, ChUp. iv, 10, 1.

Kāmalāyani, *is*, m. a descendant of Kamala, Pravar.

Kāmali, *is*, m. a descendant of Kamala, N. of a pupil of Vaiśampāyana, Pāṇ. iv, 3, 104, Kāś.; gaṇa *taulvaly-ādi* in the Kāś.

Kāmalika, mfn. customary in (or symptomatic of) jaundice, Car. vi, 18.

Kāmalin, mfn. suffering from jaundice, Suśr.; (*inas*), m. pl. the school of Kamala, Pāṇ. iv, 3, 104, Kāś.

Kāmāyanī, f. a patr. of Śraddhā, RAnukr.

1. **Kāmi,** *is*, m. a lustful or libidinous man, L.; (*is*), f., N. of a Rati (wife of Kāma), L.

2. **Kāmi** (in comp. for *kāmin*). **— jana,** m. a lover. **— tā,** f. or **-tva,** n. the state of a lover, love, desire. **— maha,** m. = *kāma-maha*, L. **— vallabha,** m. Ardea sibirica, L.

Kāmika, mfn. desired, wished for, MBh. xiii, 6025; satisfying desires, MBh. iii, 13860; (ifc.) relating to or connected with a desire or wish; (*as*), m. a wild duck (*kāraṇḍava*), L.; N. of an author of Mantras; (*ā*), f. a mystical N. of the letter *t*; (*am*), n., N. of a work, Hcat.

Kāmita, mfn. wished, desired; (*am*), n. a wish, desire, longing, MBh. i, 58, 22; Kir. x, 44.

Kāmin, mfn. desirous, longing after (acc. or in comp.); loving, fond, impassioned, wanton; amorous, enamoured, in love with (acc. or with *saha* or *sârdham*), RV.; AV.; ŚāṅkhŚr.; MBh.; R.; Śak. &c.; (*ī*), m. a lover, gallant, anxious husband; the ruddy goose (*cakra-vāka*), L.; a pigeon, L.; Ardea Sibirica, L.; a sparrow, L.; N. of Śiva, L.; (*inī*), f. a loving or affectionate woman, Mn. viii, 112; R.; Megh.; Hariv.; Ragh. &c.; a timid woman, L.; a woman in general, L.; a form of Devī, Hcat.; the plant Vanda Roxburghii, L.; the plant Curcuma aromatica, L.; a spirituous liquor, L.

Kāminī (f. of *kāmin*, q.v.) **— kānta,** n. a metre consisting of four lines of six syllables each. **— priyā,** f. a kind of spirituous liquor, Npr. **Kāminīśa,** m. the plant Hyperanthera Moringa, L.

Kāmīna or **kāmīla,** *as*, m. the plant Areca Triandra, L.

Kā́muka, mf(*ā*)n. wishing for, desiring, longing after (in comp.), R.; BhP.; loving, enamoured or in love with (acc.), TS. vi; (f. *ī*), desirous, lustful, Pāṇ. iv, 1, 42; (*as*), m. a lover, gallant, R.; Ragh. xix, 33 &c.; (with gen.) Vārtt. on Pāṇ. ii, 3, 69; a sparrow, L.; the plant Jonesia Aśoka, L.; the creeping plant Gærtnera racemosa, L.; a bow (v. l. for *kārmuka*), W.; a kind of pigeon, L.; N. of an author of Mantras; (*ā*), f., N. of Dākshyāyaṇī in Gandha-mādana; a woman desirous of wealth &c., W.; (*ī*), f. a lustful woman, cf. Pāṇ. iv, 1, 42, and Vop. iv, 26; a kind of crane, L. **— kāntā,** f. the plant Gærtnera racemosa, L. **— tva,** n. desire, Megh.; Comm. on Mṛicch.

Kāmukāya, Nom. Ā. °*yate*, 'to act the part of a lover,' p. °*yita*, n. the actions or behaviour of a lover, Kathās. civ, 89.

Kāmukāyana, *as*, m. (gaṇa 1. *naḍâdi*) 'a descendant of Kāmuka,' N. of a teacher, Jaim.

1. **Kāmya,** Nom. P. °*yati*, to have a desire for (only ifc., e.g. *putra-kāmyati*, to have a desire for children), Pāṇ. iii, 1, 9; Comm. on Pāṇ. viii, 3, 38 & 39; Vop. xxi, 1; Śāntiś.; Bhaṭṭ. ix, 59.

2. **Kā́mya,** mf(*ā*)n. desirable, beautiful, amiable, lovely, agreeable, RV.; VS.; R. ii, 25, 9; v, 43, 13; Ragh. vi, 30; Śāntiś. ii, 7; Bhartṛ. iii, 40; to one's liking, agreeable to one's wish, KātyŚr. iv, 5, 1; ŚāṅkhŚr. iii, 11, 5; ĀśvGṛ. iv, 7; optional (opposed to *nitya* or indispensable observance), performed through the desire of some object or personal advantage (as a religious ceremony &c.), done from desire of benefit or from interested motives, KātyŚr. xii, 6, 15; ĀśvŚr. ii, 10; ĀśvGṛ. iii, 6; Kauś. 5; ChUp. v, 2, 9; Mn. ii, 2; MBh. &c.; (*ā*), f., N. of an Apsaras, MBh. i, 4820; Hariv.; of several women, VP. **— karman,** n. any act or ceremony done from interested or selfish motives. **— gir,** f. a pleasing sound, agreeable speech. **— tā,** f. loveliness, beauty, MBh. **— tva,** n. the state of being done from desire or from interested motives, selfishness, Jaim. v, 3, 34. **— dāna,** n. a desirable gift; voluntary gift. **— maraṇa,** n. voluntary death, suicide, W. **— vrata,** n. a voluntary vow. **Kāmyâbhiprāya,** m. self-interested motive or purpose. **Kāmyâshṭamī,** f. a particular eighth day, Hcat. **Kāmyêshṭi,** f., N. of a work; *-tantra*, n. id.

Kāmyaka, m., N. of a forest, MBh. iii, 218; 242 sqq.; of a lake, ib. ii, 1877.

Kāmyā, f. wish, desire, longing for or striving after (gen. or in comp., e.g. *putra-kāmyayā*, through desire for a son, R. i, 13, 36; Ragh. i, 35); will, purpose, intention (e.g. *yat-kāmyā*, irreg. instr. 'with which intention,' ŚBr. iii, 9, 3, 4), Mn.; MBh.; R.; Ragh. &c.; [cf. Zd. *khshathrō-kāmya*, 'wish for dominion.']

कामठ *kāmaṭha*, mfn. (fr. *kamaṭha*), peculiar or belonging to the tortoise, R. i, 45, 30.

Kāmaṭhaka, m., N. of a Nāga, MBh. i, 2157.

कामण्डलव *kāmaṇḍalava*, mfn. (fr. *kamaṇ-ḍalu*), contained in a water-pot, Hcar.; (*am*), n. the business or trade of a potter, gaṇa *yuvâdi*.

Kāmaṇḍaleya, *as*, m. a metron. fr. *kamaṇḍalū*, Pāṇ. iv, 1, 135, Kāś.; vii, 1, 2; (*ī*), f., gaṇa *śārṅga-ravâdi*.

कामन्द *kāmanda*, *as*, m., N. of a Ṛishi, MBh. xii, 4535 ff.

Kāmandaka, *as*, m. = *kāmanda*, ib. 4534; (*ī*), f., N. of a Buddhist priestess, Mālatim.; N. of a town, Kathās.; (*am*), n., N. of a work, Comm. on Uṇ. iv, 75.

Kāmandaki, *is*, m. 'son of Kamandaka,' N. of the author of a *nīti-śāstra* called Nīti-sāra (in which are embodied the principles of his master Cāṇakya).

Kāmandakīya, mfn. relating to or composed by Kāmandaki, Daś.

कामेरी *kāmerī*, f., N. of a locality.

काम्पिल *kāmpila*, *as*, m., N. of a country (believed to be situated in the north of India), L.; (*ī*), f. its capital, W.

Kāmpilya, *as*, m., N. of a country, L.; of one of the five sons of Hary-aśva or Bharmyâśva (called collectively Pañcālas), VP.; BhP.; of a plant (probably a Crinum, cf. *kampila* and *kāmpīla*), L.; a perfume (commonly Sunda Rocanī), L.; (*ā, am*), f. n., N. of a city of the Pañcālas, MBh.; R.; Kathās.; VP.

Kāmpilyaka, *as*, m. an inhabitant of Kāmpilya, Pat.; N. of a plant (= *kāmpilya*), Mālatim. (ed. Bomb. v. l.)

Kāmpilla, *as*, m. (= *kāmpilya*), N. of a country (said to be in the north-west of India), L.; of a plant, L.; of a perfume and drug, L.

Kāmpillaka, *as*, m. (= *kāmpilya*), N. of a plant, Mālatim.; (*ikā*), f. id., L.; a drug (commonly called Sunda Rocanī), L.; a perfume, L.; (*am*), n. a kind of medicinal substance (*śuṇḍā-rocanikā*), Suśr.

Kāmpīla, *as*, m. (= *kāmpilya*), N. of a plant, Kauś.; (mf(*ī*)n.), coming from that plant, ib.; (*am*), n., N. of a town, Comm. on VS. xxiii, 18. **— vāsin,** mfn. dwelling in that town, VS. xxiii, 18.

काम्बल *kāmbala*, mfn. (fr. *kambala*), covered with a woollen cloth or blanket (as a carriage), L.

T

Kāmbalika, *as,* m. sour milk mixed with whey and vinegar, gruel, barley-water, Car.; Suśr.

Kāmbalikāyana, mfn. (fr. *kambalikā*), gaṇa *pakshâdi.*

काम्बविक *kāmbavika, as,* m. (fr. *kambu*), a dealer in shells, maker or vendor of shell ornaments, L.

Kāmbukā, f. (= *kamb°*) Physalis flexuosa, L.

काम्बुव *kāmbuva, as,* m., N. of a locality (? *ḍhakka*), Rājat. iii, 227.

काम्बोज *kāmboja,* mfn. (fr. *kamboja,* gaṇas *sindhv-ādi* & *kacchâdi*), born in or coming from Kamboja (as horses), R. v, 12, 36 &c.; (*as*), m. a native of Kamboja (a race who, like the Yavanas, shave the whole head; originally a Kshatriya tribe, but degraded through its omission of the necessary rites, W.); a prince of the Kambojas, MBh. i, 6995; a horse of the Kamboja breed, W.; (*ās*), m. pl., N. of a people = Kamboja, Mn. x, 44; MBh.; R.; Ragh.; BhP.; Rājat.; the plant Rottleria tinctoria (commonly Punnag), L.; a kind of white Mimosa, L.; (*ī*), f. the plant Glycine debilis, L.; a kind of Mimosa, L.; the tree Abrus precatorius, L.; the plant Serratula anthelminthica, L.

Kāmbojaka, mfn. born in or coming from Kamboja, gaṇa *kacchâdi,* Pāṇ. iv, 2, 134; (*ikā*), f. the white Abrus, Npr.

Kāmboji, *is,* f. (metrically for *kāmbojī*) the plant Glycine debilis, Suśr.

Kāmbojinī, f., N. of an attendant on Devī.

काम्ल *kāmla,* mfn. (fr. 2. *kā* + *amla*), slightly acid, acidulous, W.

काय 1. *kāyá,* mf(*ī*)n. (fr. 3. *ka,* Pāṇ. iv, 2, 25), relating or devoted to the god Ka (Prajā-pati, RV. x, 121), VS.; TS.; ŚBr. &c.; (*as*), m. one of the eight modes of marriage (= Prājāpatya, see *vivāha*), Mn. iii, 38; Yājñ. i, 60; (*am*), n. part of the hand sacred to Prajā-pati, the root of the little finger, Mn. ii, 58 & 59.

काय 2. *kāya, as,* m. (√*ci,* Pāṇ. iii, 3, 41), the body, KātyŚr.; Mn. &c.; the trunk of a tree, R.; the body of a lute (the whole except the wires), L.; assemblage, collection, multitude, SaddhP.; principal, capital, Nār.; Bṛihasp.; a house, habitation, L.; a butt, mark, L.; any object to be attained, L.; natural temperament, L. **– kāraṇa-kartṛi-tva,** n. activity in performing bodily acts. **– kleśa,** m. bodily suffering, toil, Mn.; MBh. iii, 1472. **– cikitsā,** f. 'body-cure,' treatment of bodily diseases, Suśr. **– daṇḍa,** m. complete command over one's body, Mn. xii, 10. **– bandhana,** n. 'body-fastening,' a girdle, Buddh. **– vat,** mfn. embodied, Mcar. **– vadha,** m., N. of an Asura, VP. **– valana,** n. 'body-fence,' armour, L. **– śuddhi,** f. = *-cikitsā,* VP. **– stha,** m. 'dwelling in the body,' the Supreme Spirit, L.; a particular caste or man of that caste, the Kāyath or writer caste (born from a Kshatriya father and Śūdra mother), Yājñ.; Mṛicch. &c.; (*ā*), f. a woman of that caste, L.; Myrobalanus Chebula, L.; Emblica officinalis, Bhpr.; Ocimum sanctum, L.; a drug (commonly Kākolī), L.; cardamoms, L.; (*ī*), f. the wife of a Kāyath or writer, L. **– sthālī,** f. a red variety of Bignonia, Npr. **– sthikā,** f. (= *-sthā*) a drug (commonly Kākolī), Npr. **– sthita,** mfn. situated in the body, corporeal. **Kāyâgni,** m. 'body-fire,' the digestive secretion, Car. **Kāyârohaṇa** and **Kāyâvarohaṇa,** n. two names of places. **Kāyôtsarga,** m. a kind of religious austerity, Jain.

Kāyaka, mf(*ikā*)n. belonging or relating to the body, &c., corporeal, L.; (*as*), m. ifc. = *kāya,* body, Sarvad.; (*ikā*), f. (with or without *vṛiddhi*), interest obtained from capital, &c., Mn. viii, 153; Gaut. xii, 35. [*Kāyikā vṛiddhi,* f. interest consisting in the use of an animal or any capital stock pawned or pledged; service rendered by the body of an animal (as a cow, &c.) pledged and used by the person to whom it is pledged; or (according to some) interest of which the payment does not affect the principal.]

Kāyika, mf(*ī*)n. performed with the body, Mn. xii, 8; MBh. xviii, 303; corporeal, Suśr. &c.; (ifc.) belonging to an assemblage or multitude, Buddh.

कायमान 1. *kāyamāna, am,* n. a hut made of grass or thatch, Kād.; Vāsav.

Kāyamānika-niketana, *am,* n. id., Vāsav.

कायमान 2. *kāyamāna,* mfn. (pr. p. Ā. √3. *kā*?) shunning, avoiding, RV. iii, 9, 2.

कायव्य *kāyavya, as,* m., N. of a man, MBh. xii, 4854 ff.

कार 1. *kāra,* mf(*ī*)n. (√1. *kṛi,* Pāṇ. iii, 2, 23), making, doing, working, a maker, doer (ifc., see *kumbha-k°, yajña k°, suvarṇa-k°*); an author (e. g. *vārttika-k°*); (*as*), m. (ifc.) an act, action (see *kāma-k°, purusha-k°*); the term used in designating a letter or sound or indeclinable word (e. g. *a-k°, ka-k°,* qq. vv.; *eva-k°,* the word *eva; phūt-k°,* q. v.), Prāt.; Mn. &c., effort, exertion, L.; determination, L.; religious austerity, L.; a husband, master, lord, L.; (*as* or *ā*), m. or f. act of worship, song of praise, Divyâv.; (*ī*), f., N. of a plant (= *kārikā, kāryā,* &c.), L. **– kara,** mf(*ī*)n. doing work, acting as agent (?), Pāṇ. iii, 2, 21. **Kārâvara,** m. a man of a mixed and low caste (born from a Nishāda father and Vaidehī mother, working in leather and hides), Mn. x, 36 = MBh. xiii, 2588.

1. **Kāraka,** mf(*ikā*)n. (generally ifc.) making, doing, acting, who or what does or produces or creates, MBh. &c. (cf. *siṇha-k°, kṛitsna-k°, śilpa-k°*); intending to act or do, Pāṇ. ii, 3, 70, Sch.; (*am*), n. 'instrumental in bringing about the action denoted by a verb (= *kriyā-hetu* or *-nimitta*),' the notion of a case (but not co-extensive with the term case; there are six such relations accord. to Pāṇ., viz. *karman, karaṇa, kartṛi, sampradāna, apâdāna, adhikaraṇa,* qq. vv. The idea of the genitive case is not considered a *kāraka,* because it ordinarily expresses the relation of two nouns to each other, but not the relation of a noun and verb). **– gupti,** f. a sentence with a hidden subject, Sāh. **– parīkshā,** f., N. of a work on the cases. **– vat,** mfn. (Pāṇ. v, 2, 115, Vārtt. 2) relating to one who is active in anything, W.; instrumental, causal, W. **– vāda,** m. a treatise on the cases by Rudra. **– vicāra,** m., N. of a work. **– hetu,** m. the efficient cause. **Kārakânvitā,** f. = *kriyā,* Gal.

Kāraja, mfn. (fr. *kar°*), of or relating to the finger-nail, W.; (*as*), m. (for *°ruja*) a young elephant, W.

1. **Kāraṇa,** *am,* n. cause, reason, the cause of anything (gen., also often loc.), KātyŚr.; MBh.; Mn. &c.; instrument, means; motive; origin, principle; a cause (in phil., i. e. that which is invariably antecedent to some product, cf. *samavâyi-k°, asamavâyi-k°, nimitta-k°*); an element, elementary matter, Yājñ. iii, 148; Bhag. xviii, 13; the origin or plot of a play or poem, Sāh.; that on which an opinion or judgment is founded (a sign, mark; a proof; a legal instrument, document), Mn.; MBh. &c.; an organ of sense, Ragh. xvi, 22 &c.; an action, MBh. xii, 12070; agency, instrumentality, condition, Kathās. cxii, 178; 'the cause of being,' a father, W.; 'cause of creation,' a deity, W.; the body, L.; a kind of musical instrument, L.; a sort of song, L.; a number of scribes or Kāyasthas, W.; (*ā*), f. pain, agony, Daś.; an astronomical period, W. [*Kāraṇāt,* from some cause or reason, RPrāt. iii, 13; Mn. viii, 355; *kasmāt kāraṇāt,* from what cause? *mama kāraṇāt,* for my sake, R. &c.; *a-kāraṇena,* without a reason, Yājñ. ii, 234; *yena kāraṇena,* because; *yasmin kāraṇe,* from which motive, wherefore.] **– kāraṇa,** n. a primary cause, elementary cause, atom, W. **– kāritam,** ind. in consequence of, R. ii, 58, 24. **– gata,** mfn. referred to a cause, resolved into first principles, W. **– guṇa,** m. 'a quality of cause,' an elementary or causal property, Sāṃkhyak. 14; *°ṇôdbhava-guṇa,* m. a secondary or derivative property (as form, taste, smell, &c. produced by combinations of elementary or causal particles), Bhāshāp. 95. **– tas,** ind. fr. a certain reason (cf. *kārya-k°*), Ragh. x, 19. **– tā,** f. causality, causation, Kum. ii, 6; *-vāda,* m., N. of a work. **– tva,** n. = *-tā,* MBh. xiii, 38; BhP. &c. **– dhvaṇsa,** m. removal of a cause. **– dhvaṇsaka,** mf(*ikā*)n. removing a cause. **– dhvaṇsin,** mfn. id. **– bhūta,** mfn. become a cause. **– mālā,** f. 'a series or chain of causes,' a particular figure in rhet., Sāh. **– vat,** mfn. having a cause, Nyāyad. **– vādin,** m. 'cause-declarer,' a complainant, plaintiff, W. **– vāri,** n. primeval water, the water produced and created (from which as from an original reservoir the Hindūs suppose all the water in the universe to be supplied), W. **– vihīna,** mfn. destitute of a cause or reason, unreasonable. **– śarīra,** n. 'causal body,' the original embryo or source of the body existing with the Universal impersonal Spirit and equivalent to A-vidyā (equivalent also to Māyā, and when investing the impersonal Spirit causing it to become the Personal God or Īśvara, RTL., p. 35 & 36), Vedântas. **Kāraṇâkshepa,** m. (in rhet.) an objection raised to the cause of a phenomenon, Kāvyād. **Kāraṇâkhyā,** f. (with the Pāśupatas) a N. of the organs of perception and action, of Buddhi, Ahaṃkāra, and Manas. **Kāraṇânvita,** mfn. possessed of a cause or reason, following as an effect fr. its cause. **Kāraṇâbhāva,** m. absence of cause. **Kāraṇôttara,** n. answer to a charge, denial of the cause (of complaint; e. g. acknowledgment that a debt was incurred, but assertion that it has been repaid, &c.)

Kāraṇaka, ifc. = 1. *kāraṇa,* cause, Sāh.

Kāraṇika, mfn. (gaṇa *kāśy-ādi*) 'investigating, ascertaining the cause,' a judge, Pañcat.; a teacher, MBh. ii, 167.

Kāram (√1. *kṛi*), adv. ind. p. ifc. (see *svāhā-k°,* ŚBr.; *namas-k°; cauraṃ-k° ākrośati,* he abuses a person by calling him a thief, Pāṇ. iii, 4, 26, Sch.; *svādum-k°,* ib., Kāś. &c.)

Kārayat, *°yamāṇa,* pr. p. Caus. √*kṛi,* q. v.

Kārayitavya, mfn. to be caused or effected or made to do, R.; Pañcat. xxiv. **– daksha,** mfn. clever at performing what has to be done, Kum. vii, 27.

Kārayitṛi, mfn. causing or instigating to act or do, Mn. xii, 12; MBh.; performer of a religious ceremony, Hcat.

Kārayishṇu, mfn. causing to act or perform, Vop.

1. **Kāri,** *is,* m. f. an artist, artificer, mechanic, Pāṇ. iv, 1, 152; (*is*), f. action, act, work (only used in questions), Pāṇ. iii, 3, 110.

Kārikā (f. of *kāraka*), a female dancer, L.; a business, L.; trade, L.; concise statement in verse of (esp. philos. and gramm.) doctrines, MBh. ii, 453 &c.; torment, torture, L.; interest, L.; N. of a plant, L.; (*ās*), f. pl. or more commonly *Hari-kārikās,* the Kārikās of Bhartṛi-hari, i. e. the verses contained in his gramm. work Vākya-padīya (q. v.) **– nibandha,** m., N. of a work. **Kārikâvalī,** f., N. of a work.

Kārita, mfn. ifc. caused to be made or done, brought about, effected, Mn.; MBh. &c.; (*ā*), f. (scil. *vṛiddhi*) forced to be paid, interest exceeding the legal rate of interest, Gaut.; Comm. on Mn. viii, 153; (*am*), n. the Caus. form of a verb, Nir. i, 13. **– vat,** mfn. one who has caused to be made or done.

Kāritânta, mfn. ending with a Caus. affix, APrāt.

1. **Kārin,** mfn. (Pāṇ. v, 2, 72) doing, making, effecting, producing, acting, an actor, Yājñ.; MBh. &c. (mostly ifc., ŚBr.; Mn. &c.); (*ī*), m. a mechanic, tradesman, L.

कार 2. *kāra, as,* m. (= 2. *kara*) tax, toll, royal revenue, Pāṇ. vi, 3, 10; a heap of snow or a mountain covered with it, L.; (mfn.) produced by hail, Suśr. **– kukshīya,** m., N. of the country of king Sālva on the skirts of the Himālaya ridge in the N.W of Hindūstān, L.; (*ās*), m. pl. the people of this country, L. **– mihikā,** f. camphor (?), L.

2. **Kāraka,** *am,* n. hail-water, L.

कार 3. *kārá, as,* m. (√2. *kṛi*), a song or hymn of praise, RV.; a battle song, RV.

2. **Kārí,** mfn. raising hymns of praise, VS. xxx, 6 & 20.

2. **Kārín,** mfn. rejoicing, praising, RV.

कार 4. *kāra, as,* m. (√2. *kṝi*), killing, slaughter, L.

2. **Kāraṇa,** *am,* n. killing, injury, L.

कारञ्ज *kārañja,* mfn. produced by or coming fr. the tree Karañja (Pongamia glabra), Suśr.; (*ī*), f. a kind of pepper, L.

कारण्ड *kāraṇḍa, as,* m. a sort of duck, R. vii, 31, 21; (cf. *karaṇḍa.*) **– vatī,** f. 'abounding in Kāraṇḍavas,' N. of a river, gaṇa *ajirâdi;* Comm. on Pāṇ. vi, 1, 220. **– vyūha,** m., N. of a Buddha, L.; of a Buddhist work; (cf. *karaṇḍa-vy°.*)

Kāraṇḍava, *as,* m. = *kāraṇḍa,* MBh.; R. &c.

कारतन्तविका *kāratantavikā* or *°kī,* f., fr. *kara-tantu,* Pāṇ. iv, 2, 104, Vārtt. 3 & 24, Pat.

कारंधम *kāraṃdhama, as,* m. (fr. *karaṃ-dh°*), a patr. of Avikshit, MBh. xiv, 63 & 80; (*am*), n., N. of a Tīrtha, MBh. i, 7841.

Kāraṃdhamin, *ī,* m. a brazier, worker in mixed or white metal, L.; an assayer, L.

कारपचव *kārapacava,* N. of a region near the Yamunā, TāṇḍyaBr.; ĀśvŚr.; KātyŚr.; ŚāṅkhŚr. &c.

कारपथ *kārapatha.* See *kārāp°.*

कारभ *kārabha,* mfn. (fr. *kar°*), produced by or coming fr. a camel, Car.; Suśr.

कारमिहिका *kāra-mihikā.* See 2. *kāra.*

कारम्भा *kārambhā*, f. (cf. *kar°*), N. of a plant bearing a fragrant seed (commonly Priyaṃgu), L.

कारव *kā-rava*, *as*, m. 'making the sound *kā*,' a crow, L.; N. of a man, Saṃskārak.

कारवल्ली *kāravallī*, f. Momordica Charantia, Car.; (cf. *kāravella* and *kāṇḍīra*.)

कारवी *kāravī*, f. the Asa fœtida plant or its leaf (= Hiṅgu-parṇī), L.; Celosia cristata, L.; a kind of anise (Anethum Sowa), L.; Nigella indica, Bhpr.; a kind of fennel, ib.; a small kind of gourd, L.; Carum Carvi, Bhpr.

कारवेल्ल *kāravella*, *as*, m. the gourd Momordica Charantia, Suśr.; (*ī*), f. id., Bhpr.; (*am*), n. its fruit, L.

Kāravellaka, *as*, m. and **°llikā**, f. id., Suśr.

कारव्य *kāravya.* See 2. *kārú.*

कारस्कर *kāraskara*, *as*, m. (Pāṇ. vi, 1, 156), N. of a poisonous medicinal plant, BhP. v, 14, 12; a tree in general, L.; (*ās*), m. pl., N. of a people, MBh. ii, 1804; viii, 2066; (vv. ll. *kāraskāra* and *kāraskṛita*.) **Kāraskarâṭikā**, f. (√*aṭ*), a centipede or worm resembling it, L.

कारा *kārā*, f. (√1. *kṛi?*), a prison, Vikr.; Das.; binding, confinement, gaṇa *bhidâdi*; the part of a lute below the neck (for deadening the sound), L.; pain, affliction, L.; a female messenger, L.; a female worker in gold, L.; a kind of bird, L. **– °gāra** (*kārâg°*), n. a gaol or place of confinement, Daś.; Bālar. **– gupta**, mfn. 'prison-confined,' imprisoned. **– gṛiha**, n. a prison-house, Ragh. &c. **– pāla**, m. prison-guard. **– bhū**, Pāṇ. vi, 4, 84, Kāś. **– vāsa**, m. a prison, Daś. **– veśman**, n. id., Bālar. **– stha**, mfn. imprisoned, Kathās.

काराधुनी *kārādhuni*, f. a kind of musical instrument (Sāy.; 'battle-cry,' NBD.), RV. i, 180, 8.

कारापथ *kārāpatha*, *as*, m., N. of a country, Ragh. xv, 90; (v.l. *kārup°*, R. vii; *kārap°*, VP.)

कारायिका *kārāyikā*, f. = *karāy°*, L.

कारीर *kārīra*, mfn. (gaṇa *palāśâdi*) made of the shoots of reed, Lalit.; Pāṇ. iv, 3, 135, Kāś.; (*ī*), f. (scil. *ishṭi*) 'connected with the fruit of the plant Capparis aphylla,' a sacrifice in which this fruit is used, MaitrS.; Kāṭh. &c.

Kārīrya, mfn. connected with the sacrifice called *karīrī*, ĀtrAnukr.

कारीष *kārīsha*, mfn. (fr. *kar°*), produced from or coming from dung, Suśr.; (*am*), n. a heap of dung, L.; (Hariv. 4355 misprinted for *kar°*.)

Kārishi, *is*, m., N. of a man, MBh. xiii, 254; (*ayas*), m. pl., N. of a family, Hariv.

कारु 1. *kāru*, *us*, m. f. (fr. √1. *kṛi*), a maker, doer, artisan, mechanic, Mn.; Yājñ. &c.; (*us*), m. 'architect of the gods,' N. of Viśva-karman, L.; an art, science, L.; mfn. (only etymological) horrible, MBh. i, 1657. **– caura**, m. 'mechanical thief,' burglar, L. **– ja**, m. anything produced by an artist or mechanic, any piece of mechanism or product of manufacture, L.; a young elephant, L.; an ant-hill, L.; froth, foam, L.; sesamum growing spontaneously, L.; the tree Mesua ferrea, L.; red orpiment, L. **– hasta**, m. the hand of an artisan, Mn. v, 129.

Kāruka, *as*, *ā*, m. f. an artisan, artificer, Mn.; MBh.; VarBṛS. **– siddhântin**, *inas*, m. pl., N. of a Śaiva sect, Comm. on Bādar. ii, 2, 37.

कारु 2. *kārú*, *us*, m. (fr. √2. *kṛi*), one who sings or praises, a poet, RV.; AV.; (*avas*), m. pl., N. of a family of Ṛishis, GopBr. **– dveshin**, mfn. hating the singer, MaitrS. **– dhāyas** (*kārú-*), mfn. favouring or supporting the singer, RV.

Kāravya, mfn. 'relating to the singer,' (*ās*), f. pl. (scil. *ṛicas*), N. of certain verses of the AV. (xx, 127, 11–14), AitBr. vi, 32.

1. **Kāruṇya**, mfn. praiseworthy [Comm.], TBr. ii.

कारुणिक *kāruṇika*, mfn. (fr. *karuṇa*), compassionate, MBh. &c. **– tā**, f. compassion, BhP.

2. **Kāruṇya**, *am*, n. compassion, kindness, MBh.; R. &c. **– dhenu**, m. 'compassion-cow,' N. of Buddha, Divyâv. **– vedin**, mfn. compassionate, R. &c.; °*ditva*, n. compassion, R. **– sūtra**, n., N. of a Sūtra.

कारुण्डिका *kāruṇḍikā*, °*ṇḍī*, f. a leech, L.

कारुपथ *kārupatha.* See *kārāp°.*

कारुविदा *kāruvidā*, f. ? GopBr. i, 2, 21.

कारूष *kārūsha*, *as*, m. (gaṇa *bhargâdi*) a prince of the Kārūshas, Hariv. 4964; BhP.; (*ās*), m. pl. (= *kar°*), N. of a country, MBh. ii, 1864; of a people, MBh.; BhP.; VP.; (*as*), m. (= *kar°*), N. of a son of Manu, MBh.; an intermediate caste or man of that caste, Mn. x, 23.

Kārūshaka, mfn. reigning over the Kārūshas, MBh. i, 2700.

कारेणव *kāreṇava*, mfn. (fr. *kareṇu*), drawn from a female elephant (as milk), Suśr.; a patr. of Pālakāpya, L.

Kāreṇupālāyana, *as*, m. a descendant of Kāreṇupāli, gaṇa *taulvaly-ādi.*

Kāreṇupāli, *is*, m. a son or descendant of Kareṇu-pāla, ib.

कारोतर *kārotará*, *as*, m. a filtering vessel or a cloth used to purify the liquor called Surā, RV. i, 116, 7; VS.; ŚBr. &c.

Kārottama, *as*, m. the froth of Surā, L.

1. **Kārottara**, *as*, m. id., L.; a well, L.

कारोती *kā́rotī*, f., N. of a river or of a locality, ŚBr. ix, 5, 2, 15.

कारोत्तर 2. *kārôttara*, mfn. followed by *kāra*, TPrāt.

कार्कट्य *kārkaṭya*, *as*, m., N. of a man, gaṇa *vākinâdi* (Kāś.)

Kārkaṭyāyani, *is*, m. a patr. fr. °*ṭya*, ib.

कार्कण *kārkaṇa*, mf(*ī*)n. (fr. *kṛikaṇa*), relating to a pheasant, Pāṇ. iv, 2, 145; gaṇa *śuṇḍikâdi.*

कार्कन्धव *kārkandhava*, mf(*ī*)n. coming from or belonging to the plant Karkandhū (q.v.), gaṇa *bilvâdi.*

कार्कलासेय *kārkalāseya*, *as*, m. (fr. *kṛikalāsá*), N. of a man, gaṇa *śubhrâdi.*

कार्कवाकव *kārkavākava*, mf(*ī*)n. (fr. *kṛikavāku*), relating to a cock, W.

कार्कश्य *kārkaśya*, *am*, n. (fr. *karkaśa*), roughness, hardness, Suśr. &c.; rough labour, MBh. xiii, 5551; firmness, sternness, Pañcat. &c.

कार्कष *kārkasha*, v. l. for *kārkaṭya*, q. v.

कार्कीक *kārkīka*, mfn. (fr. *karka*), resembling a white horse, Pāṇ. v, 3, 110.

कार्कोट *kārkoṭa*, *as*, m., N. of a serpent-demon, Kathās.

Kārkoṭaka, *as*, m. id., ib.; (*am*), n., N. of a town, ib.

कार्ण *kārṇa*, mfn. (fr. *kárṇa*), relating to the ear, L.; a patr. fr. *karṇa*, gaṇa *śivâdi*; (*am*), n. ear-wax, W.; an ear-ring, W.

Kārṇakharaki, *is*, m. a patr. fr. *karṇa-kharaka*, Pāṇ. ii, 4, 58, Pat.

Kārṇacchidrika, mfn. (fr. *karṇa-cchidraka*), (a well) shaped like the opening of the ear, Pāṇ. iv, 2, 79, Kāś.

Kārṇaveshṭakika, mf(*ī*)n. (fr. *karṇa-veshṭaka*), ornamented with or fit for ear-rings, Pāṇ. v, 1, 99, Kāś.

Kārṇaśravasa, *am*, n. (fr. *karṇa-śravas*), N. of a Sāman, TāṇḍyaBr.; ĀrshBr.; Lāṭy.

Kārṇāyani, mfn. fr. *kárṇa*, Pāṇ. iv, 2, 80.

Kārṇi, mfn. id., gaṇa *sutaṃ-gamâdi.*

Kārṇika, mf(*ī*)n. relating to the ear, W.

कार्णाटभाषा *kārṇāṭa-bhāshā*, f. the dialect of Karṇāṭa.

कार्त 1. *kārta*, mfn. (fr. 1. *kṛit*), relating to or treating of the *Kṛit* suffixes, Pāṇ. iv, 3, 66, Kāś.

कार्त 2. *kārta*, *as*, m. (fr. *kṛitá*), N. of a son of Dharma-netra, Hariv. 1845; a patr. in the compound **kārta-kaujapau**, nom. du. m., which begins a Gaṇa of Pāṇ. (vi, 2, 37).

Kārtayaśa, *am*, n. (irreg. fr. *kṛita-yaśas*), N. of a Sāman, TāṇḍyaBr.; ĀrshBr.; Lāṭy.

Kārtayuga, mfn. relating to the Kṛita age, MBh. i, 3600; xii, 2681.

Kārtavīrya, *as*, m. 'son of Kṛita-vīrya,' N. of Arjuna (a prince of the Haihayas, killed by Paraśu-rāma), MBh. &c.; N. of one of the Cakravartins (emperors of the world in Bhārata-varsha), Jain.

Kārtasvara, *am*, n. (fr. *kṛita-sv°*), gold, MBh.; BhP.; the thorn-apple, W.

Kārtântika, *as*, m. an astrologer, Daś.

Kārtârthya, *am*, n. (fr. *kṛitârtha*), the attainment of an object, Sāh.

Kārti, *is*, m. (Pāṇ. viii, 2, 42, Vārtt. 3) a son or descendant of Kṛita, Hariv. 1082; (*ayas*), m. pl., N. of his family, ib. **– siṃha-deva**, m., N. of a man.

कार्त्तिक *kārttika*, *as*, m. (fr. *kṛittikā*, q.v.; with or without *māsa*), N. of a month corresponding to part of October and November (the twelfth month of the year, when the full moon is near the Pleiades), Pāṇ.; Lāṭy.; MBh. &c.; N. of Skanda (see *kārttikeya*), BrahmavP.; of a Varsha; of a medical author; (*as* or *am*), m. n., N. of the first year in Jupiter's period of revolution, VarBṛS.; Sūryas.; (*am*), n., N. of a Tīrtha, MatsyaP. **– kuṇḍa**, m., N. of a physician, Comm. on Suśr. **– mahiman**, m. 'the greatness of Kārttika,' N. of a treatise on the festivals of that month. **– māhātmya**, n., N. of a section of the PadmaP. **– śāli**, m. rice ripening in the month Kārttika (forming the principal harvest in India), W. **– siddhânta**, m., N. of a scholiast on the Mugdha-bodha. **Kārttikôtsava**, m. a festival on the day of full moon in the month Kārttika, L.

Kārttikika, mfn. taking place in Kārttika, Vām.; (*as*), m. the month Kārttika, Pāṇ. iv, 2, 23.

Kārttikī, f. of *kārttika* above, (with or without *rātri*) the night of full moon in the month Kārttika, the day on which the moon stands in the constellation Kṛittikā, KātyŚr.; ŚāṅkhŚr.; MBh. &c.; the night of new moon in the month Kārttika, Jain.; the *śakti* of Kārttikeya, BrahmaP. **– vrata**, n., N. of a particular religious observance.

Kārttikeya, *as*, m., N. of a son of Śiva and Pārvatī (popularly regarded as god of war, because he leads the Gaṇas or hosts of Śiva against the demon hosts, see RTL. p. 213; accord. to one legend he was son of Śiva without the intervention of Pārvatī, the generative energy of Śiva being cast into the fire and then received by the Ganges, whence he is sometimes described as son of Agni and Gaṅgā; when born he was fostered by the six Kṛittikās, q. v., and these offering their six breasts to the child he became six-headed; he is also called Kumāra, Skanda, and Subrahmaṇya; his N. Kārttikeya may be derived from his foster mothers or from the month Kārttika as the best for warfare: in the Mṛicch. and elsewhere he is regarded as presiding over thieves), MBh. &c. **– prasū**, f. 'mother of Kārttikeya,' N. of Pārvatī.

कार्त्स्न *kārtsna*, *am*, n. (fr. *kṛitsná*; probably for the next), the whole, totality, Suśr.

Kārtsnya, *am*, n. id., MBh. &c.; (*ena*), ind. in full, entirely, Mn. iii, 183.

कार्दम *kārdama*, mf(*ī*)n. (fr. *kardama*), made of mud, muddy, filled or covered with mud, R. v, 27, 16; Pāṇ. iv, 2, 2, Kāś.; belonging to Prajāpati Kardama, BhP. iii, 24, 6.

Kārdami, *is*, m. a son of Kardama (see *Iḍa*), R. vii, 87, 29.

Kārdamika, mf(*ī*, Pāṇ. iv, 2, 2, Vārtt.)n. muddy, Daś.

Kārdameya, *as*, m. = *kārdami*, R. vii.

कार्पट *kārpaṭa*, *as*, m. (fr. *karpaṭa*), 'one dressed in ragged garments,' a beggar, petitioner, suitor, L.; lac, L.

Kārpaṭika, *as*, m. a pilgrim, Kathās.; a caravan of pilgrims, W.; a deceiver, rogue, BhavP.; a trusty follower, Hcar.; an experienced man of the world, L.; N. of a pilgrim, Kathās.

कार्पणी *kārpaṇī*, f. gladness, Npr.

कार्पण्य *kārpaṇya*, *am*, n (fr. *kṛipaṇa*), poverty, pitiful circumstances, MBh. &c.; R.; poorness of spirit, weakness, ib.; parsimony, niggardliness, Hit. &c.; compassion, pity, BhP. v, 8, 10.

कार्पाण *kārpāṇá*, *am*, n. (fr. *kṛipāṇa*), a sword-fight [Sāy.], RV. x, 22, 10.

कार्पास *kārpāsa*, mf(*ī*, L.)n. (fr. *karpāsa*;

gaṇa *bilvâdi*), made of cotton, cottony, ĀśvŚr.; Lāṭy.; Mn.&c.; (*as, am*), m. n. cotton, cotton cloth, &c., Mn.; MBh. &c.; paper, W.; (*ī*), f. the cotton plant, Suśr. **—tāntava,** n. texture made of cotton, Mn. xii, 64. **—nāsikā,** f. a spindle, L. **—sautrika,** n. = *-tāntava*, Yājñ. ii, 179. **Kārpāsâsthi,** n. the seed of the cotton plant, Mn. iv, 78.

Kārpāsaka, mfn. made of cotton, W.; (*ikā*), f. the cotton plant, L.

Kārpāsika, mf(*ī*)n. made of cotton, MBh. &c.

कार्पूर *kārpūra*, mfn. (fr. *karpūra*), made of camphor, Hcat.

Kārpūriṇa, mfn. fr. *karpūrin*, gaṇa *suvāstv-ādi*.

Kārpūreya, mfn., N. of a man, gaṇa *śubhrâdi*.

कार्म 1. *kārma*, mf(*ī*)n. (fr. *kárman*; gaṇa *chattrâdi*), active, laborious, Pāṇ. vi, 4, 172.

Kārmaṇa, mf(*ī*)n. relating to or proceeding from a work or action, W.; finishing a work, W.; performing anything by means of magic; (*am*), n. magic, sorcery, witchcraft, Pāṇ. v, 4, 36; Rājat. **—tva,** n. magic, sorcery, Śiś. x, 37.

Kārmaṇeyaka, *ās*, m. pl., N. of a people, VarBṛS.

Kārmārá, *as*, m. = *karmā́ra*, a mechanic, smith, RV. ix, 112, 2; a patr. fr. Karmāra, gaṇa *śivâdi*.

Kārmāraka, *am*, n. smith's work, gaṇa *kulāl-âdi*.

Kārmārāyaṇi, *is*, m. a patr. fr. Karmāra, Pāṇ. iv, 1, 155.

Kārmika, *ās*, m. pl. 'engaged in action,' N. of a Buddh. philos. school; (*am*), n. 'manufactured, embroidered,' any variegated texture, Yājñ. ii, 180.

Kārmikya, *am*, n. (fr. *karmika*), activity, industry, gaṇa *purohitâdi*.

1. **Kārmuka,** mfn. (Pāṇ. v, 1, 103) efficacious (as a medicine), Car.; (*as*), m. a bamboo, L.; the plant Melia sempervirens, Bhpr.; the white Khadira tree, L.; Smilax China, Npr.; a kind of honey (v. l. *gārmuta*, q. v.), L.

कार्म 2. *kārma*, mfn. (fr. *kṛimi*), belonging to a worm, Comm. on Uṇ. iv, 121. **—raṅga,** mfn. deep red, crimson, Hcar.

कार्मुक 2. *kārmuka*, mf(*ī*)n. consisting of the wood *kṛimúka*, ŚBr.; KātyŚr.; (*am*), n. (ifc. f. *ā*, MBh.) a bow, ŚāṅkhŚr.; Mn. &c.; a bow-shaped instrument, L.; a geometrical arc, Sūryas.; the rainbow, VarYogay.; Sagittarius, VarBṛS.; a particular constellation, VarBṛ. **—bhṛit,** mfn. bearing a bow, Veṇīs.; (*t*), m. Sagittarius, VarBṛ. **Kārmukôpanishad,** f. the secret of the art of shooting, Bālar.

Kārmukāya, Nom. Ā. °*kāyate*, to form or represent a bow, Śṛiṅgār.

Kārmukin, mfn. armed with a bow, R. iii.

कार्य *kāryà*, mfn. (fut. p. p. √1. *kṛi*), to be made or done or practised or performed, practicable, feasible, AV. iii, 24, 5; TS.; Mn. &c.; to be imposed (as a punishment), Mn. viii, 276 & 285; to be offered (as a libation), Mn. &c.; proper to be done, fit, right; (*am*), n. work or business to be done, duty, affair, Mn.; MBh. &c.; a religious action or performance, Mn. &c.; occupation, matter, thing, enterprise, emergency, occurrence, crisis; conduct, deportment; occasion, need (with inst., e.g. *tṛiṇena kāryam*, there is need of a straw; *na bhūmyā kāryam asmākam*, we have no business with the earth, R. i, 13, 50); lawsuit, dispute; an operation in grammar (e.g. *sthāny-āśrayaṃ kāryam*, an operation resting on the primitive form as opposed to the *ādeśa* or substitute), Kāś. on Pāṇ.; an effect, result, MBh.; Sāṃkhyak.; Vedāntas.; motive, object, aim, purpose (e.g. *kiṃ kāryam*, for what purpose? wherefore?), Mn.; R. &c.; cause, origin, L.; the denouement of a drama, Sāh.; (*ā*), f. (= *kārī*, °*rikā*), N. of a plant, L. **—kara,** mfn. efficacious, Suśr. **—kartṛi,** m. one who works in the interest of (gen.), Pañcat. **—kāraṇa,** n. a particular or special cause (*tat-kārya-kāraṇāt*, in consequence of that), Pañcat.; Kathās.; *-tas*, ind. from some special cause, with a particular design or motive, Hit. i, 33; *-tva*, n. the state of both cause and effect, Sarvad.; *-bhāva*, m. state or relation of cause and effect. **—kārin,** mfn. performing a work. **—kāla,** m. time for action, appointed time, season, opportunity, R. i, 30, 12 &c. **—kuśala,** mfn. skilful in work. **—kshama,** mfn. fit for a work. **—guru-tā,** f. importance of any act. **—guru-tva,** n. id. **—gaurava,** n. id., Nal. xx, 22. **—cintaka,** m. 'taking care of a business,' manager of a business, Yājñ. ii, 191; prudent, cautious. **—cintā,** f. prudence in action, caution. **—cyuta,** mfn. removed from office, out of work. **—tama,** mfn. most proper to be done, MBh.; R. v, 77, 16. **—tas,** ind. consequently, necessarily, actually. **—tā,** f. the being an effect, the relation or state of an effect, KapS. **—tva,** n. id., BhP.; Vedântas.; Sāh. **—darśana,** n. inspection of work, revision, Mn. viii, 9 & 23. **—darśin,** m. an inspector or superintendent of affairs. **—nirṇaya,** m. ascertainment of a fact, settlement or decision of an affair, Yājñ. ii, 10. **—nirvṛitti,** f. the result of an action, Suśr. **—paricheda,** m. right estimate of a case, discrimination, Hit. xxxii, 22. **—puṭa,** m. one who does useless things, L.; a crazy or hair-brained man, L.; an impudent fellow, L.; an idler, L. **—pradvesha,** m. 'hatred of work,' idleness, L. **—preshya,** m. a person sent on any business, messenger, Sāh. **—bhāj,** mfn. undergoing or subject to a grammatical operation, Comm. on TPrāt.; *-(bhāk)-tva*, n. the state of being so, ib. **—bhājana,** n. any one fit for business. **—bhrashṭa,** mfn. = *-cyuta*. **—vat,** mfn. having any business or duty, engaged in a business, Mn. ix, 74; MBh. &c.; having a cause or motive, R. vii, 53, 26; pursuing a certain purpose, R. v, 8, 9 (*-tā*); the state of being engaged in a work; *-tā*, f. any business or affair, MBh. i, 1789; R.; *-tva*, n. id. **—vaśa,** m. 'the force of a reason,' (*āt*), abl. ind. for some reason, Pañcat. **—vastu,** n. anything that has to be done, aim, object, W. **—vinimaya,** m. mutual engagement to do something, Mālav. **—vinirṇaya,** m. = *-nirṇaya*, Mn. i, 114; viii, 8. **—vipatti,** f. failure of an action, reverse, Hit. **—vṛittânta,** m. a matter of fact, actual occurrence, MBh. **—vyasana,** n. failure of an affair, Kām. **—śesha,** m. the remainder of a business, Mn. vii, 153 & 179; Ratnāv. **—saṃdeha,** m. uncertainty about a work, embarrassment, W. **—sama,** m. (in Nyāya phil.) a particular sophistical objection (ignoring that similar effects may result from dissimilar circumstances), Nyāyad. v, 1, 37; Sarvad. **—sāgara,** m. "ocean of business,' mass or weight of affairs, W. **—sādhaka,** mfn. effective of any work, accomplishing any object, agent, W. **—siddhi,** f. accomplishment of a work, fulfilment of an object, success, Mudr. **—sthāna,** n. a place of business, office, W **—hantṛi,** m. one who obstructs an affair, mar-plot, Hit. **Kāryâkārya,** n. what is to be done and not to be done; *-vicāra*, m. deliberation on what is to be done or not. **Kāryâkshama,** mfn. unfit for work, Hit. **Kāryâkshepa,** m. (in rhet.) a denial of the results stated to follow on a particular condition of things, Kāvyād. **Kāryâkhyā,** f. (with the Pāśupatas) N. of the five elements and the five Guṇas. **Kāryâtipāta,** m. neglect of business, Śak. **Kāryâtipātin,** mfn. neglecting business, Comm. on Yājñ. **Kāryâdhikārin,** m. a superintendent of affairs, minister, Hit. **Kāryâdhipa,** m. a dominant or presiding planet determining any matter (in astrol.), VarBṛ. **Kāryânta,** m. the end of a business. **Kāryântara,** n. interval of business, leisure, Hariv. 4339; another affair, Comm. on Yājñ.; *-saciva*, m. the associate of a prince in his leisure hours, Mālav. **Kāryâpêkshin,** mfn. pursuing a particular object, Kathās. lvi, 134. **Kāryârtha,** m. the object of a business or enterprise; any object or purpose; application for employment; (*am*), ind. for the sake of any business or for any particular object, Mn.; *-siddhi*, f. the accomplishment of any object or purpose, Mn. vii, 167. **Kāryârthin,** mfn. making a request, seeking for business, applying for employment; pleading a cause in court, going to law, Mṛicch.; Comm. on Mn. vii, 124. **Kāryêkshaṇa,** n. superintendence of public affairs, Mn. vii, 141. **Kāryêśa** & °**śvara,** m. = *kāryâdhipa*. **Kāryôdyukta,** mfn. engaged in any business, intent upon any object. **Kāryôdyoga,** m. active engagement in any business. **Kāryôpêkshā,** f. neglect of duty, Hit.

Kāryika, mfn. (Pāṇ. v, 2, 115, Pat.) pleading a cause in court, Mn. vii, 124.

Kāryin, mfn. (Pāṇ. v, 2, 115, Pat.) one who transacts business, assiduous; seeking for employment; having an object; a party to a suit either as plaintiff or defendant, Mn. viii, ix; (in Gr.) subject to the operation of a grammatical rule, requiring an affix, &c., Pāṇ. Pat. & Kāś.

कार्वटिक *kārvaṭika*, *as*, m. the chief of a village (*karvaṭa*), Divyâv.

कार्श *kārśa*, *as*, m. Curcuma Zedoaria, L.

कार्शकेयीपुत्र *kārśakeyī-pútra*, *as*, m. (the first part fr. *kṛiśaka* ?), N. of a teacher, ŚBr. xiv.

कार्शन *kārśaná*, mfn. (fr. *kṛiśana*), consisting of pearl or mother-of-pearl, AV. iv, 10, 7 [MSS. *karśaná*.]

कार्शानव *kārśānava*, mfn. (fr. *kṛiśānu*), fiery, hot, glaring, Bālar.

कार्शाश्वीय *kārśāśvīya*, *am*, n. (Pāṇ. iv, 2, 80) the Sūtra of Kṛiśāśva, [NBD.]

कार्श्मरी *kārśmarī*, f., N. of a plant (= *kārshmaryà*, *kāśmarī*), L.

कार्श्य 1. *kārśya*, *as*, m., N. of a plant (= *kārshya*, *kārshmaryà*), L.; another plant (= *karcūra*), L.; the plant Artocarpus Lacucha, L.

कार्श्य 2. *kārśya*, *am*, n. (fr. *kṛiśá*, gaṇa *dṛiḍhâdi*), emaciation, thinness, Suśr.; BhP.; Kathās. &c.; 'smallness (of property),' see *artha-k°*.

कार्ष *kārsha*, *as*, m. (√*kṛish*; gaṇa *chattrâdi*), 'one who ploughs,' a peasant, husbandman, Divyâv.; (*ī*), f., see *gomaya-k°*.

Kārshaka, *as*, m. id., Kathās.; Rājat. v, 169.

Kārshâpaṇa, *as, am*, m. n. (gaṇa *ardharcâdi*; cf. *karsh*) 'weighing a Karsha,' a coin or weight of different values (if of gold, = 16 Māshas, see *karsha*; if of silver, = 16 Paṇas or 1280 Kowries, commonly termed a Kahān; if of copper, = 80 Raktikās or about 176 grains; but accord. to some = only 1 Paṇa of Kowries or 80 Kowries), Mn. viii, 136; 336; ix, 282; (ifc.) worth so many Kārshāpaṇas, Pāṇ. v, 1, 29; (*am*), n. money, gold and silver, L.; (*ās*), m. pl., N. of a warrior-tribe, gaṇa *parśv-ādi*; (*as*), m. the chief of this tribe, ib. & iv, 1, 177, Vārtt. 2. **Kārshāpaṇâvara,** mfn. having the value of at least one Kārshāpaṇa (as a fine), Mn. viii, 274 & x, 120.

Kārshâpaṇaka, *as, am*, m. n. a weight or measure = *kārshâpaṇa*, L.

Kārshâpaṇika, mf(*ī*)n. worth one Kārshāpaṇa, bought &c. with one Kārshāpaṇa, Pāṇ. v, 1, 25, Vārtt. 2; ifc. id. v, 1, 29.

Kā́rshi, mfn. (cf. *karshī*) drawing, ploughing, VS. vi, 28 [v. l. *kārshin*, MaitrS.; Kāṭh.]; (*is*), m. fire, Comm. on Uṇ. iv, 128; (*is*), f. drawing, ploughing, cultivation, W.

Kārshika, mfn. (gaṇa *chedâdi*) weighing a Karsha, Mn. viii, 136; Yājñ. i, 364; Suśr.; (*as*), m. a coin (= *kārshâpaṇa*), L.; = *kārshaka*, cf. *tila-k°*

Kārshin, mfn. See *kā́rshi*.

Kā́rshīvaṇa, *as*, m. (fr. *kā́rshi* with *i* lengthened), one who ploughs a field, husbandman, AV. vi, 116, 1.

Kārshuka, mfn. = °*shaka*, Gal.

Kā́rshman, *a*, n. the goal of a race-course (a line like a furrow), RV. i, 116, 17; ix, 36, 1 & 74, 8.

कार्ष्ण *kā́rshṇa*, mf(*ī*)n. (fr. *kṛishṇá*), coming from or belonging to the black antelope, made of the skin of the black antelope, TS. v, 4, 4, 4; Lāṭy.; Mn. ii, 41; belonging to the dark half of a month; belonging to the god Kṛishṇa or to Kṛishṇa-dvaipāyana or composed by him &c. (e.g. *kārshṇa veda*, i.e. the Mahā-bhārata, MBh. i, 261 & 2300), Ragh. xv, 24; belonging to a descendant of Kṛishṇa, gaṇa *kaṇvâdi*; (*ī*), f. the plant Asparagus racemosus, L.; (*am*), n. the skin of the black antelope, AV. xi, 5, 6; N. of two Sāmans, ĀrshBr.

Kārshṇakarṇa, mfn. fr. *kṛishṇa-k°*, gaṇa *suvāstv-ādi*.

Kārshṇasundari, *ayas*, m. pl. the descendants of Kṛishṇa-sundara, Pāṇ. ii, 4, 68, Kāś.

Kārshṇâjina, mfn. (fr. *krishṇâjiná*), made from the skin of the black antelope, ĀpŚr. xv, 5.

Kārshṇâjini, *is*, m. (Pāṇ. ii, 4, 68, Kāś.) 'a son or descendant of Kṛishṇâjina,' N. of a teacher, KātyŚr. i, 6, 23; of a philosopher, Jaim.; Bādar.; of an author on law.

Kārshṇâyana, *as*, m. a descendant of Kṛishṇa, gaṇa 1. *naḍâdi*.

Kārshṇâyasa, mf(*ī*)n. (fr. *kṛishṇâyas*), made

of black iron, ChUp. vi, 1, 6; Mn. xi, 133; MBh. &c.; (*am*), n. iron, Mn. x, 52; R. i, 38, 20.

Kārshṇi, *is*, m. (gaṇa *bāhv-ādi;* Gaṇar. 34, Comm.) a son or descendant of Kṛishṇa, MBh.; BhP.; N. of Viśvaka; of a Deva-gandharva, MBh.; Hariv.; of the god of love, L.; (cf. Hariv. 9209.)

Kārshṇya, *as*, m. a son or descendant of Kṛishṇa, gaṇa *gargâdi;* (*am*), n. (gaṇa *dṛiḍhâdi;* ifc. f. *ā*) blackness, black colour, darkness, MBh. i, 4236, Suśr.; Rājat.; iron filings, L.

कार्ष्मन् *kārshman*. See *kārsha*.

कार्ष्मर्य *kārshmaryà*, *as*, m. (=*kāśm°*) the tree Gmelina arborea, TS.; ŚBr.; KātyŚr. **–máya,** mf(*ī*)n. made of that tree, ib.

कार्ष्य *kārshya*, *as*, m. the tree Shorea robusta, L.; the tree Artocarpus Lacucha, L. **–vaṇa,** n. a forest of Shorea robusta, Pāṇ. viii, 4, 5.

काल् 1. *kāla*, mf(*ī*, Pāṇ. iv, 1, 42)n. (fr. √3. *kal?*), black, of a dark colour, dark-blue, MBh.; R. &c.; (*as*), m. a black or dark-blue colour, L.; the black part of the eye, Suśr.; the Indian cuckoo, L.; the poisonous serpent Coluber Nāga (=*kāla-sarpa*), Vet.; the plant Cassia Sophora, L.; a red kind of Plumbago, L.; the resin of the plant Shorea robusta, L.; the planet Saturn; N. of Śiva; of Rudra, BhP. iii, 12, 12; of a son of Hrada, Hariv. 189; of the prince Kāla-yavana, BhP. iii, 3, 10; of a brother of king Prasena-jit, Buddh.; of a future Buddha; of an author of Mantras (=Aśva-ghosha), Buddh.; of a Nāga-rāja, Buddh.; of a Rakshas, R. vi, 69, 12; of an enemy of Śiva, L.; of a mountain, R. iv, 44, 21; Kāraṇḍ.; of one of the nine treasures, Jain.; a mystical N. of the letter *m;* (*ā*), f., N. of several plants (Indigofera tinctoria, L.; Piper longum, L.; (perhaps) Ipomœa atropurpurea, Suśr.; Nigella indica, L.; Rubia Munjista, L.; Ruellia longifolia, L.; Physalis flexuosa, L.; Bignonia suaveolens, Bhpr.); the fruit of the Kālā, gaṇa *harītaky-ādi;* N. of a *śakti*, Hcat.; of a daughter of Daksha (the mother of the Kāleyas or Kālakeyas, a family of Asuras), MBh. i, 2520; Hariv.; N. of Durgā, L.; (*ī*), f. black colour, ink or blacking, L.; abuse, censure, defamation, L.; a row or succession of black clouds, L.; night, L.; a worm or animalcule generated in the acetous fermentation of milk (=*kshīra-kīṭa* or *kshāra-kīṭa*), L.; the plant Kālāñjanī, L.; Ipomœa Turpethum, L.; a kind of clay, L.; Bignonia suaveolens, L.; one of the seven tongues or flames of fire, MuṇḍUp. i, 2, 4; a form of Durgā, MBh. iv, 195; Hariv.; Kum.; one of the Mātṛis or divine mothers, L.; N. of a female evil spirit (mother of the Kālakeyas), Hariv. 11552; one of the sixteen Vidyā-devīs, L.; N. of Satyavatī, wife of king Śāntanu and mother of Vyāsa or Kṛishṇa-dvaipāyana (after her marriage she had a son Vicitra-vīrya, whose widows were married by Kṛishṇa-dvaipāyana, and bore to him Dhṛita-rāshṭra and Pāṇḍu, MBh.; Hariv.; according to other legends Kālī is the wife of Bhīmasena and mother of Sarvagata, BhP.); (with or without *gaṅgā*) N. of a river; (*am*), n. a black kind of Agallochum, L.; a kind of perfume (*kakkolaka*), L.; iron, L. **–kacu,** f. Arum Colocasia, L. **–kañjá,** *ās*, m. pl., N. of a race of Asuras [or Dānavas, MBh. &c.], (some of whom ascended into heaven and there shine as stars), TBr.; Kāṭh. &c.; (*as*), m., N. of an Asura, Hariv. 12940. **–kañjya** =*-kañjá*, KaushUp. **–kaṭaṅkaṭa,** m., N. of Śiva, MBh. xiii, 1172. **–kaṇī,** f. a kind of Rākshasī. **–kaṇṭaka,** m. a gallinule, L. **–kaṇṭha,** m. a peacock, L.; a gallinule, L.; a wagtail, L.; a sparrow, L.; =*pīta-śāla*, *-sāra* (Terminalia tomentosa, W.), L.; N. of Śiva; of a being in Skanda's retinue, MBh. ix, 2571. **–kaṇṭhaka,** m. a sparrow, Bhpr.; a gallinule, L. **–kandaka,** m. a water-snake, L. **–karṇikā,** f. misfortune (predicted as the consequence of having black ears), L. **–karṇī,** f. id., L.; N. of Lakshmī, NṛisUp.; of a Yoginī, Hcat. **–kalāya,** m. Phaseolus Max., L. **–kavi,** m., N. of Agni, Hcat. **–kastūrī,** f. Hibiscus Abelmoschus (the seeds smelling of musk when rubbed), W. **–kāñjá,** *ās*, m. pl. =*-kañjá*, AV. vi, 80, 2; MaitrS. **–kīrti,** m., N. of a king identified with the Asura Suparṇa, MBh. i, 2673. **–kuñja,** m., N. of Vishṇu, L. **–kushṭha,** m. a kind of earth brought from mountains, L. **–1.-kūṭa,** m. (n., L.) a poison (contained in a bulbous root or tube), MBh. iii, 540; Pañcat.; a poison (produced at the churning of the ocean, swallowed by Śiva and causing the blueness of his neck), MBh. i, 1152; BhP. &c.; poison (in general), BhP. iii, 2, 23. **–kūṭaka,** m. a poison (contained in a bulbous root), MBh. i, 5008 ff.; N. of a poisonous plant, L. **–kūṭīya,** n. the legend of Śiva and the poison Kāla-kūṭa, Bālar. **–koṭi,** f., N. of a locality, MBh. iii, 8513; VarBṛS. **–klītaka,** n. the indigo plant, ŚāṅkhGṛ. **–khañja,** *ās*, m. pl. =*-kañjá*, MBh. ii, iv; (*am*), n. the liver, L. **–khañjana,** n. the liver, L. **–khaṇḍa,** n. id., Bālar.; *-han*, m., N. of Arjuna, L. **–gaṅgā,** f., N. of a river in Ceylon. **–gaṇḍikā,** f., N. of a river, Rājat. **–gandha,** m. =*-kandaka*, W. **–ghaṭa,** m., N. of a Brahman, MBh. i, 2048. **–jihva,** m. 'having a black tongue,' N. of a Yaksha, Kathās. lxx, 35. **–1.-tā,** f. blackness, Kpr.; (for 2. *kāla-tā*, see p. 278, col. 2.) **–tāla,** m. Xanthochymus pictorius (=*tamāla*), L. **–tinduka,** m. a kind of ebony, Bhpr. **–tīrtha,** n., N. of a Tirtha, MBh. iii, 8153. **–dantaka,** m., N. of a Nāga (a son of Vāsuki), MBh. i, 2147. **–1.-nara,** m., N. of a son of Sabhā-nara (a son of Anu), BhP. ix, 23, 1; (cf. *kālânala.*) **–nābha,** m. (fr. *nābhi*), N. of an Asura, Hariv. 199; BhP.; of a son of Hiraṇyâksha, Hariv. 195; VP.; of a son of Hiraṇya-kaśipu, BhP. vii, 2, 18; of a son of Vipra-citti and Siṇhikā, Hariv. 216; VP. **–niryāsa,** m. a fragrant and resinous exudation from the plant Amyris Agallocha, L. **–netra,** mf(*ā*)n. black-eyed, Kauś. 106. **–parṇa,** m. Tabernæmontana coronaria, L.; (*ī*), f. a dark kind of Ipomœa, Npr.; N. of Nirṛiti. **–parvata,** m., N. of a mountain, MBh. iii, 15998. **–pātrika,** m. a kind of mendicant whose alms-dish is painted black, Buddh. **–pālaka,** n. a kind of earth, L.; (cf. *-kushṭha*, *kaṅkushṭha.*) **–pīluka,** m. a kind of ebony, L. **–puccha, -pucchaka,** m. a species of animal living in marshes, Suśr. (cf. *asita-pucchaka*); a kind of sparrow, Npr. **–pushpa,** n., N. of a plant (=*kalāya*), Comm. on Śiś. xiii, 21. **–pṛishṭha,** m. 'having a black back,' a species of antelope, L.; a heron, L.; a bow, L.; Karṇa's bow, L. **–peśikā,** f. Rubia Munjista, Npr. **–peśī,** f., N. of a plant (=*śyāmā*), L. **–bījaka,** m. a Diospyros, L. **–bhāṇḍikā,** f. Rubia Munjista, L. **–bhairava,** m. a form of Bhairava. **–bhogin,** m. Coluber Naga, Daś. **–mallikā,** f. an Ocimum, L. **–masī,** f., N. of a river, R. iv, 40, 24; (v. l. *-mahī*, Hariv. 12828.) **–mahī,** f. =*-masī*. **–māna,** m. =*-māla*, L. **–māla,** m. Ocimum sanctum, Car.; Suśr. **–mālaka,** m. id., Car. **–mukha,** mfn. black-faced, dark-faced, Pat.; (*as*), m. a kind of monkey, MBh. iii, 16613; R.; N. of a fabulous people, MBh. ii, 1171; R.; (*ā*), f., N. of a woman, Pāṇ. iv, 1, 58, Kāś. **–mushkaka,** m., N. of a plant, L. **–mūla,** m. the plant Plumbago, L. **–megha,** m. a black cloud, R.; Kād.; N. of an elephant, Kathās. **–meśikā** or **-meshikā,** f. Rubia Munjista, L.; Ipomœa atropurpurea (?), L. **–meshī,** f. =*-meshikā;* Vernonia anthelminthica, L. **–yavana,** m., N. of a prince of the Yavanas, Hariv.; VP.; of a tyrannical Asura (the foe of Kṛishṇa, destroyed by him by a stratagem), ib.; N. of a Dvipa, Daś. **–1.-rātri,** f., **-rātrī,** f. a dark night, W.; (for 2. *-rātri*, see p. 278, col. 3.) **–lavaṇa,** n. a kind of black factitious and purgative salt (commonly called *viḍ-lavaṇa*), L. **–locana,** m. 'black-eyed,' N. of a Daitya, Hariv. 12941. **–loha,** n. iron, Daś. **–lauha,** n. id., L. **–vadana,** m. 'black-faced,' N. of a Daitya, Hariv. 14291; (v. l. *śāla-v°*, ib. 2288.) **–varāṭaka,** m., N. of a man, Kathās. lxxiv, 179. **–vāla,** n. a kind of black earth, Npr.; (cf. *-pālaka.*) **–vāluka,** n. id., ib. **–vāhana,** m. a buffalo, Npr. **–visha,** n. (probably) the venom of Coluber Nāga, MBh. iii, 141, 14. **–vṛiksha,** m. a kind of vetch (Dolichos biflorus; cf. *kulattha*), W. **–°vṛikshīya,** m., N. of a Ṛishi, Hariv. 9570. **–vṛinta,** m. =*-vṛiksha*, L.; (*ī*), f. the trumpet flower (Bignonia suaveolens), L.; *°tikā*, f. id., Npr. **–velā,** f. 'the time of Saturn,' a particular time of the day at which any religious act is improper (half a watch in every day), L. **–śambara,** m., N. of a Dānava, Hariv. 9210. **–śāka,** n. the pot-herb Ocimum sanctum, Mn. iii, 272; MBh. &c.; Corchorus capsularis, L. **–śāli,** m. a black kind of rice, L. **–śibi,** m., N. of a man, Pravar. **–śaila,** m., N. of a mountain, MBh. iii, 10820 ff. **–sarpa,** m. the black and most venomous variety of the Cobra, Coluber Nāga, Gīt. x, 12; Vet. **–sāra,** mfn. having a black centre or pupil, Naish. vi, 19; (*as*), m. the black antelope, ib.; a sort of sandal-wood, Bhpr.; N. of a Prākṛit poet. **–siṇha,** m., N. of a Prākṛit poet. **–sūkarikā,** f., N. of a woman, Jain. **–skandha,** m. the plant Diospyros embryopteris, Suśr.; the Jamāla tree (bearing dark blossoms, Xanthochymus pictorius), L.; Ficus glomerata, L.; a kind of Acacia (Catechu), L.; another plant (=*jīvaka*), L. **–skandhin,** m. Ficus glomerata, L. **–hasti-pura,** n., N. of a town. **–hasti-śaila,** n., N. of a Tirtha. **–hastîśvara,** n., N. of a Tirtha. **Kālâguru,** m. (n., L.) a kind of black aloe wood or Agallochum, MBh.; R. &c. **Kālâṅga,** mfn. having a dark-blue body (as a sword with a dark-blue edge), MBh. iv, 231. **Kālâjājī,** f. a kind of cummin, L. **Kālâjina,** *ās*, m. pl., N. of a people, VarBṛS. **Kālâñjana,** n. a black unguent, Kum. vii, 20; (*ī*), f. a small shrub (used as a purgative), L. **Kālâṇḍaja,** m. 'the black bird,' Indian cuckoo, Daś. **Kālânusāraka,** n., N. of the powder called *tagara*, q. v., L.; yellow sandal, L. **Kālânusārin,** m. benzoin or benjamin, Suśr.; (*iṇī*), f. id., Car. **Kālânusārivā,** f. id., Suśr. **Kālânusārya,** m., n. id., L.; (*ā*), f. id., Suśr.; (*as* or *am*), m. n. a yellow fragrant wood, L.; Dalbergia Sissoo, L.; (*am*), n. the powder *tagara*, q. v., L. **Kālânusāryaka,** n. gum benzoin or benjamin, L. **Kālā-mukha,** *ās*, m. pl., N. of a Śaiva sect; (cf. *kālī-m°*.) **Kālâmra,** m., N. of a Dvipa, Hariv. 8653. **Kālâyasa,** n. (fr. *áyas*), iron, R.; Hariv. &c.; (mfn.) made of iron, R. vii, 8, 15; *-maya*, mf(*ī*)n. id., R. v, 49, 32. **Kālâśoka,** m., N. of a king (probably N. of the celebrated king Candra-gupta, q. v.) **Kālâsuhṛid,** m. 'an enemy of Kāla,' N. of Śiva, L. **Kālī-√kṛi,** to blacken, Kād.; Hcar. **Kālôdaka,** n., N. of a Tīrtha, MBh. xiii, 1746; of an ocean, R. iv, 40, 36. **Kālôdāyin,** m. 'the black Udāyin,' N. of a pupil of Śākya-muni, Buddh.

1. **Kālaka,** mfn. (Pāṇ. v, 4, 33) dark-blue, black, Lalit.; freckled (? or 'dark,' as with anger), Pat.; (*as*), m. a freckle (? 'black colour'), Pat.; the black part of the eye, Suśr.; a water-snake, L.; a kind of grain, Suśr.; (in alg.) the second unknown quantity, Bījag.; N. of a Rakshas, R. iii, 29, 30; of an Asura, Hariv.; (*ās*), m. pl., N. of a people, VarBṛS.; of a dynasty, VP.; (*kālakā*), f. a kind of bird, VS. xxiv, 35; (gaṇa *sthūlâdi*) N. of a female evil spirit (mother of the Kālakeyas; daughter of Daksha, R.; also of Vaiśvānara, Hariv. & BhP.), MBh. &c.; (*kālikā*), f. blackness or black colour, L.; ink or blacking, L.; a dark spot, rust, VarBṛS.; a fault or flaw in gold, L.; change of complexion, L.; the liver, Comm. on Yājñ.; a particular blood-vessel in the ear, Suśr.; the line of hair extending from the pudenda to the navel, L.; a multitude of clouds, R. ii; Ragh. xi, 15; snow, L.; fog, L.; the female of the bird Aṅgāraka, Pat.; a female crow, L.; the female of the bird Turdus macrourus (commonly *śyāmā*), L.; a scorpion, L.; a small worm or animalcule formed by the fermentation of milk, L.; N. of several plants (Vṛiścika-pattra, Valeriana Jaṭāmāṇsī, a kind of Terminalia, a branch of Trichosanthes diœca), L.; a kind of fragrant earth, L.; a N. or form of Durgā, L.; a girl of four years old who personates the goddess Durgā at a festival held in honour of that deity, L.; a kind of female genius, MBh. ii, 457; Hariv. 9532; one of the mothers in Skanda's retinue, MBh. ix, 2632; N. of a Vidyādharī, Kathās. cviii, 177; of a Kiṃnarī, L.; of a Yoginī, L.; of an attendant of the fourth Arhat, Jain.; of a river, MBh. iii, 8134; (*am*), n. a worm-hole (in wood), VarBṛS.; the liver, L.; N. of a pot-herb, Bhpr. **–vana,** m., N. of a mountain, Pāṇ. ii, 4, 10, Pat. **–°vṛikshīya,** m., N. of a Ṛishi, MBh. ii, 299; xii, 3059 & 3849; (cf. *kāla-v°*.) **Kālakâkranda,** m., N. of two Sāmans. **Kālakâksha,** m. 'black-eyed,' N. of an Asura, Hariv. 14289; of an attendant in Skanda's retinue, MBh. ix, 2571. **Kālakâcārya,** m., N. of a Jaina teacher and astronomer. **Kālakêndra,** m., N. of a prince of the Dānavas, R.

Kālakeya, *as*, m. (a metron. fr. *kālakā*), N. of an Asura, Hariv. 2286; (*ās*), m. pl., N. of a Dānava race, MBh.; Hariv.; R. vii, 12, 2.

Kālala, mfn., gaṇa *sidhmâdi*.

1. **Kālika,** *as*, m. a species of heron (Ardea jaculator), L. (v. l. *kālīka*); N. of a king of the Nāgas, Lalit.; of a prince, Pañcad. **Kālikâcārya,** m., v. l. for *kālakâc°*, q. v. **Kālikârya,** m. =*kālakâcārya*.

1. **Kālikā** (f. of 1. *kālaka*, q. v.) **–krama,** m., N. of a work (=*kālī-kr°*). **–guru,** *avas*, m. pl., N. of certain authors of mystical prayers. **–grantha,** m. a medical work. **–tantra,** n., N. of a Tantra. **–purāṇa,** n. 'the Purāṇa of Kālikā (i. e.

of Durgā),' N. of an Upa-purāṇa. **-mukha**, m., N. of a Rakshas, R. iii, 29, 30. **-rahasya**, n., N. of a work. **-vrata**, n., N. of a ceremony, KālP. **Kālikâśrama**, m., N. of a hermitage, MBh. xiii, 1710. **Kālikā-stotra**, n., N. of a Stotra. **Kālikôpanishad**, f., N. of an Upanishad. **Kālikôpapurāṇa**, n. = *kālikā-pur°*.

Kālikeya, mfn. relating to Kālikā, BrahmaP.

Kāli-tarā, f. (compar.), Pāṇ. v, 3, 55, Pat.

Kāliman, *ā*, m. blackness, Śiś. iv, 57; Hit. &c.

Kālim-manyā, f. thinking oneself to be Kālī, Pāṇ. vi, 3, 66, Kāś.

Kāliya, *as*, m., N. of a Nāga (inhabiting the Yamunā, slain by Kṛishṇa, also written *kālīya*, VP.), MBh.; Hariv. &c. **-jit**, m. 'destroyer of Kāliya,' N. of Kṛishṇa or Vishṇu, L. **-damana**, m. id., L.

Kāliyaka, *am*, n. (= *kālīyaka*) a yellow fragrant wood (perhaps sandal-wood or Agallochum), L.

Kālila, mfn., gaṇa *picchâdi*.

Kālī (f. of 1. *kāla*, q. v.) **-kula-sarvasva**, n., N. of a work. **-krama**, m. = *kālikā-kr°*. **-tattva**, n., N. of a work. **-tanaya**, m. 'son (or favourite) of Durgā,' a buffalo, L.; (cf. *haṇsa-kālī-t°*.) **-tantra**, n., N. of a Tantra. **-purāṇa**, n. 'the Purāṇa of Kālī,' N. of an Upa-purāṇa. **-manu**, *avas*, m. pl., N. of certain mystical prayers. **-māhātmya**, n. = *devī-māh°*. **-mukha**, *ās*, m. pl., N. of a religious sect; (cf. *kālā-m°*.) **-yantra**, n., N. of a Yantra. **-rahasya**, n., N. of a work. **-vilāsa-tantra**, n. id. **-vilāsin**, m. 'the husband of Kālī,' a form of Śiva, Daś. **-samasta-mantra**, m., N. of a Mantra. **-sahasra-nāman**, n., N. of a work. **-sāra-tantra**, n. id. **-hṛidaya**, n. id. **Kāly-upanishad**, f., N. of an Up.

Kālīya, *as*, m. = *kāliya*; (*am*), n. a dark kind of sandal-wood, Suśr. **-damana**, m. = *kāliya-jit*, Gal. **-mardana**, m. id., Gal.

Kālīyaka, *am*, n. = *kāliyaka*, MBh.; R.; Suśr. &c.; (*as, am*), m. n. a kind of turmeric (Curcuma xanthorrhiza), L.; (*as*), m., N. of a Nāga (different fr. Kāliya), MBh. i, 1555.

1. **Kāleya**, *am*, n. (fr. 1. *kāla*), the liver, L.; a yellow fragrant wood, Kum. vii, 9; saffron, L.

2. **Kāleya**, *as*, m. (metron. fr. *kālā*), N. of a Nāga (= Kāliya), L.; (*ās*), m. pl., N. of a family of Daityas, MBh. iii; BhP.

Kāleyaka, *as*, m. the plant Curcuma xanthorrhiza, L.; a particular part of the intestines (different fr. the liver), Suśr.; a disease like jaundice, Suśr.; a dog (for *kaul°*), Hcar.; (*am*), n. a fragrant wood, R.

काल 2. *kālá*, *as*, m. (√3. *kal*, 'to calculate or enumerate'), [ifc. f. *ā*, RPrāt.], a fixed or right point of time, a space of time, time (in general), AV. xix, 53 & 54; ŚBr. &c.; the proper time or season for (gen., dat., loc., in comp., inf., or Pot. with *yad*, e. g. *kālaḥ prasthānasya* or *°nāya* or *°ne*, time for departure; *kriyā-kāla*, time for action, Suśr.; *nâyam kālo vilambitum*, this is not the time to delay, Nal.; *kālo yad bhuñjīta bhavān*, it is time for you to eat, Pāṇ. iii, 3, 168, Kāś.), ŚBr.; MBh. &c.; occasion, circumstance, MBh. xii, 2950; Mṛicch.; season, R. &c.; meal-time (twice a day, hence *ubhau kālau*, 'in the morning and in the evening,' MBh. i, 4623; *shashṭhe kāle*, 'in the evening of the third day,' MBh.; *shashṭhânna-kāla*, 'one who eats only at the sixth meal-time, i. e. who passes five meals without eating and has no meal till the evening of the third day,' Mn. xi, 200; or without *anna*, e. g. *caturtha-kālam*, 'at the fourth meal-time, i. e. at the evening of the second day,' Mn. xi, 109); hour (hence *shashṭhe kāle 'hnaḥ*, 'at the sixth hour of the day, i. e. at noon,' Vikr.); a period of time, time of the world (= *yuga*), Rājat.; measure of time, prosody, Prāt.; Pāṇ.; a section, part, VPrāt.; the end, ChUp.; death by age, Suśr.; time (as leading to events, the causes of which are imperceptible to the mind of man), destiny, fate, MBh.; R. &c.; time (as destroying all things), death, time of death (often personified and represented with the attributes of Yama, regent of the dead, or even identified with him: hence *kālam* √*i* or *kālam* √*kṛi*, 'to die,' MBh. &c.; *kāla* in this sense is frequently connected with *antaka*, *mṛityu*, e. g. *abhy-adhāvata prajāḥ kāla ivântakaḥ*, 'he attacked the people like Time the destroyer,' R. iii, 7, 9; cf. *kālântaka*; *kāla* personified is also a Devarshi in Indra's court, and a son of Dhruva, MBh. i, 2585; Hariv.; VP.); (*am*), acc. ind. for a certain time (e. g. *mahântam kālam*, for a long time, Pañcat.); *nitya-k°*, constantly, always, Mn. ii, 58 & 73; *dīrgha-k°*, during a long time, Mn. viii, 145; (*ena*), instr. ind. in the course of time, Mn. ix, 246; MBh. &c.; with *gacchatā*, id., VP.; *dīrgheṇa kālena*, during a long time, MBh.; after a long time, R. i, 45, 40; *kālena mahatā* or *bahunā*, id.; (*āt*), abl. ind. in the course of time, Mn. viii, 251; *kālasya dīrghasya* or *mahataḥ*, id., Mn.; MBh. &c.; *kasya-cit kālasya*, after some time, MBh. i, 5299; Hariv.; (*é*), loc. ind. in time, seasonably, RV. x, 42, 9; ŚBr.; (cf. *a-kāle*); *kāle gacchati*, in the course of time; *kāle yāte*, after some time; *kāle kāle*, always in time, MBh. i, 1680; Ragh. iv, 6; [cf. κήρ; Lat. *calen-dæ*; Hib. *ceal*, 'death and everything terrible.'] **-karaṇa**, n. appointing or fixing a time. **-karman**, n. 'Time's act,' death, R. vi, 72, 11. **-kalpa**, mfn. like death, fatal, deadly. **-kāra**, mfn. making or producing time, ŚvetUp. **-kārita**, mfn. effected or brought about by or in time; (cf. *kāla-kṛita*.) **-kuṇṭha**, m., N. of Yama, L. **-2.-kūṭa**, m. id., L.; (for 1. & 3. see p. 277, col. 1, and p. 279, col. 2.) **-kṛit**, m. 'producing the times, i. e. seasons,' the sun, L. **-kṛita**, mfn. produced by time, Suśr.; appointed (as to time), lent or deposited (by a giver) for a certain time, Yājñ. ii, 58; (*kāla-kārita*) Mn. viii, 348; (*as*), m. (= *-kṛit*) the sun, L.; time, L. **-kaumudī**, f., N. of a work. **-krama**, m. lapse of time, Kathās.; (*eṇa*), instr. ind. in process of time; (*āt*), abl. ind. id., Pañcat.; Kathās. **-kriyā**, f. 'fixing the times,' N. of a chapter of the Sūrya-siddhânta; death, Buddh. **-kshepa**, m. allowing time to pass away, delay, loss of time, Megh.; Pañcat. &c.; *a-kālakshepam*, ind. without delay, Śak. **-gata**, mfn. dead, Lalit. **-gati**, f. lapse of time, W. **-gupta**, m., N. of a Vaiśya, Daś. **-granthi**, m. 'a joint of time,' year, L. **-ghātin**, mfn. (said of a poison) killing in the course of time (i. e. by degrees, slowly), Suśr. **-cakra**, n. the wheel of time (time represented as a wheel which always turns round), MBh.; Hariv. &c.; a given revolution of time, cycle [according to the Jainas, the wheel of time has twelve Aras or spokes and turns round once in 2000,000,000,000,000 Sāgaras of years; cf. *ava-sarpiṇī* and *ut-s°*]; the wheel of fortune (sometimes regarded as a weapon), R.; N. of a Tantra, Buddh.; (*as*), m., N. of the sun, MBh. iii, 151; *-jātaka*, n., *-prakāśa*, m., N. of works. **-codita**, mfn. summoned by Death; *-karman*, mfn. acting under the influence of fate. **-joshaka**, *ās*, m. pl., N. of a people (v. l. *°shika* and *-toyaka*), MBh. vi, 353; VP. **-jña**, mfn. knowing the fixed times or seasons, Mn. vii, 217; Ragh. xii, 33; (*as*), m. an astrologer, W.; a cook, L. **-jñāna**, n. knowledge of the fixed times or seasons, Jyot.; VP.; N. of several medical works (by Malladeva, Śambū-nātha, and others). **-jñānin**, mfn. knowing the fixed times or seasons, L. **-tattvârṇava**, m. 'ocean of the truth of time,' N. of a work. **-tantra-kavi**, m. an astrologer. **-tara**, m. (compar.), Pāṇ. v, 3, 55, Pat. **-taraṅga**, m. the first part of the Smṛity-artha-sāgara by Nṛi-siṇha. **-tas**, ind. in the course of time, Kathās. vi, 101. **-2.-tā**, f. seasonableness, timeliness, Ghaṭ. **-tulya**, mfn. like death, deadly. **-toyaka**, see *-joshaka*. **-traya**, n. the three times, i. e. past, present, and future. **-tritaya**, n. id. **-daṇḍa**, m. the staff of death, death, MBh.; R. &c. **-damanī**, f. 'conquering Kāla,' N. of Durgā. **-dāsa**, m. = *tintiḍa* (?), L. **-divākara**, m., N. of a work. **-dūta**, m. the angel of death, Hcat.; an omen pointing to death, Kād. **-deśa-vibhāga**, m. the difference of time and locality, Suśr. **-dharma**, m. the law or rule or operation of time, death, dying, MBh.; Hariv.; R.; line of conduct suitable to any time or season; influence of time, seasonableness; effects suited to the time or season. **-dharman**, m. the law or operation of time, death, MBh.; Hariv. **-dhāraṇā**, f. 'prolongation of time,' a pause, RPrāt. **-2.-nara**, m. 'a time-man,' i. e. (in astrol.) the figure of a man's body on the various limbs of which the twelve signs of the zodiac are distributed for the purpose of foretelling future destinies, Comm. on VarBṛ. **-nātha**, m. 'the lord of time,' N. of Śiva, MBh. xii, 10368. **-nidhi**, m., N. of Śiva. **-niyoga**, m. 'time's ordinance,' fate, destiny, W. **-nirūpaṇa**, n. chronology. **-nirṇaya**, m. 'determination or fixing of times,' N. of a work (composed 1336 A.D., also called *kāla-mādhavīya*, by Mādhavâcārya); *-candrikā*, *-dīpikā*, f., *-prakasa*, m., *-śikshā*, f., *-siddhânta*, m., N. of works. **-nirvāha**, m. providing for daily wants. **-nemi**, m. 'felly of the wheel of time,' N. of an Asura (slain by Kṛishṇa, identified with Kaṇsa), MBh.; Hariv. &c.; N. of a Rakshas, R. vi, 82, 64; N. of a son of the Brāhman Yajña-soma, Kathās. x, 7; *-purāṇa*, n., N. of a legendary work; *-ripu*, *-han*, *-hara*, *-(nemy-)ari*, m. 'destroyer of Kāla-nemi,' N. of Kṛishṇa or Vishṇu, L. **-nemin**, mfn. having the fellies of Kāla as a weapon, Hariv. 2640; (*ī*), m. = *-nemi*, ib. seqq. **-pakva**, mfn. ripened or matured by time, i. e. naturally (opposed to *agni-p°*), Mn. vi, 17 & 21; Yājñ. iii, 49; 'ripe for death,' destined to die, MBh. vii. **-patha**, m., N. of a son of Viśvā-mitra, MBh. xiii, 249. **-paripāka**, m. 'time-ripening,' the change of times, Bālar. **-parivāsa**, m. standing for a time (so as to become stale or fermented), W. **-paryaya**, m. the revolution or course of time; (*āt*), abl. ind. in the course of time, Hcat. **-pāśa**, m. Yama's noose or death, Kād.; *-parīta*, mfn. destined to death, Car. **-°pāśika**, m. 'having Yama's noose,' an executioner, Mudr. **-purusha**, m. = *-nara*, time personified, VarBṛS.; a servant of the god of death, Kād. **-pūga**, m. 'a time-heap,' a long time, *°gasya mahataḥ*, after a long time, MBh. ii, 1329. **-prabodhin**, mfn. awakening in time (as a Mantra), Kathās. xcii, 68. **-prabhāta**, n. 'the dawning of the best season,' the two months following the rainy season, autumn, L. **-prarūḍha**, mfn. too long developed, overgrown, overripe. **-priya**, N. of a place consecrated to the sun; *-nātha*, m., N. of a Liṅga in Ujjayinī (= Mahākāla), Uttarar.; Mālatīm.; Mcat. **-bhaksha**, m. 'time-devourer,' N. of Śiva. **-bhāga**, m. a degree of time, Sūryas. **-bhṛit**, m. (cf. *-kṛit*), the sun, L. **-mayūkha**, m. = *tithi-m°* or *samaya-m°*, qq.vv. **-mahiman**, m. the power of time. **-mādhava**, m., N. of a work on jurisprudence; *-kārikā*, f. a metrical version of the same work. **-mārtāṇḍa**, m., N. of a work. **-māhātmya**, n. = *-mahiman*. **-mūrti**, f. time personified. **-yāpa**, m. allowing time to pass, delaying, procrastination, Hit. **-yāpana**, n. id., ib. **-yukta**, m. n. the fifty-second year in the sixty years' cycle of Jupiter. VarBṛS. **-yoga**, m. connection with or consequence of fate or destiny, MBh. iii; Hariv. **-yogin**, m. 'reigning over destiny,' N. of Śiva, MBh. xiii, 1162. **-2.-rātri**, **-rātrī**, f. the night of all-destroying time, night of destruction at the end of the world (often personified and identified with Durgā or with one of her Śaktis), MBh.; R. &c.; the night of a man's death, Pañcad.; a particular night in the life of a man (on the seventh day of the seventh month of the seventy-seventh year, after which period a man is exempt from attention to the usual ordinances), L.; N. of a Brāhman woman (skilled in magic), Kathās. xx, 104. **-rudra**, m. Rudra regarded as the fire that is to destroy the world, DevībhP. **-rūpa-dhṛish**, mfn. wearing the form of Yama or death. **-rūpin**, m. id., N. of Śiva. **-vat**, mfn. connected with time or with the future (as hope), MBh. i, 5629; R.; (*tī*), f., N. of a daughter of Kāla-jihva, Kathās. cx, 34. **-vikrama**, m. power of time, death. **-vid**, mfn. knowing the times, R. iv, 32, 13. **-vidyā**, f. knowledge of the calendar. **-vidvas**, mfn. (perf. p. P.) 'knowing the seasons,' a maker of calendars, VarBṛS. **-vidhāna**, m., N. of a work. **-vidhṛiti**, f. lapse of time, Bhpr. **-vidhvaṇsana**, m. (scil. *rasa*) N. of a particular drug or medicine. **-viprakarsha**, m. interval of time, APrāt.; Prab. **-vibhakti**, f. a section or part of time, Mn. i, 24. **-vibhāga**, m. id., MBh.; Pāṇ. iii, 3, 137. **-viveka**, m., N. of a work (by Jīmūta-vāhana). **-vṛiddhi**, f. periodical interest (payable monthly, &c.), Mn. viii, 153; Gaut.; (cf. 2. *kālaka*.) **-vega**, m., N. of a Nāga (a son of Vāsuki), MBh. i, 2147. **-vyāpin**, mfn. filling all time, everlasting. **-vrata**, n., N. of a ceremony. **-śakti**, f. the Śakti or all-destroying time, Vcar. **-saṃrodha**, m. remaining for a long time (in the possession of any one), Mn. viii, 143. **-saṃhitā**, f., N. of an astronomical work (written in Jaina Prākrit, by Kālakâcārya). **-saṃkarshā**, f. a girl nine years old who personates Durgā at a festival in honour of this goddess. **-saṃkarshin**, mfn. shortening time (as a Mantra), Kathās. lxviii, 65. **-saṃkhyā**, f. fixing or calculating the time, Pañcat. **-saṃgraha**, m. period of time, term, R. iv, 31, 8. **-sadṛiśa**, mfn. 'conformable to time,' seasonable; death-like. **-samanvita**, mfn. 'possessed by death,' dead, R. ii, 65, 16. **-samāyukta**, mfn. id., R. vi, 93, 23. **-sampanna**, mfn. effected by time; dated, bearing a date. **—sâhvaya**, m. (scil. *niraya*, a hell) named after Kāla (= *kāla-sūtra*), MBh. xiii, 2479. **—siddhânta**, m., N. of a work. **—sûkta**, n., N. of a hymn, Hcat. **—sūtra**, n. the thread of time or death, MBh. iii, 11495; (*as, am*), m. n. one of the twenty-one hells, Mn. iii, 249; iv, 88; VP. &c. **—sūtraka**, n., N. of the hell Kāla-sūtra, Yājñ. iii, 222. **—sūrya**, m. the sun at the end of the world, MBh. vii, 633. **—svarūpa**, mfn. having the very form of death (applied to any terrific object). **—hāra**, m. loss of time, Kathās. cii, 119; profit of time, Kathās. xxxi, 75 ff., xxxii, 10. **Kālâṇsa**, m. = *kāla-bhāga*, Sūryas. **Kālâkāṅkshin**, mfn. expecting (quietly) the coming time, R.; Kathās. cvii, 8. **Kālâkṛishṭa**, mfn. led to death or destruction, drawn to or by one's fate; produced or brought about by time. **Kālâksharika**, m. a pupil who has begun to read. **Kālâgni**, m. the fire that is to destroy the world, conflagration at the end of time; *-bhairava*, n., N. of a Tantra; *-rudra*, m. = *kāla-rudra*; (scil. *rasa*) N. of a particular drug or medicine; *-rudra-tīrtha*, n., N. of a Tīrtha, ŚivP.; *-rudrôpanishad*, f., N. of several Upanishads. **Kālâtikramaṇa**, n. lapse of time, loss or destruction by lapse of time, Pañcat. **Kālātipāta**, m. delay of time, Kād.; Prasannar. **Kālâtīta**, mfn. elapsed, passed away, become unseasonable, MBh. xii; R. iv, 28, 16. **Kālâtmaka**, mfn. depending on time or destiny, MBh. xiii, 52 ff. **Kālâtyaya**, m. passing away of time, Mn. viii, 145; R.; °*yâpadishṭa*, mfn. invalidated by lapse of time (term for a vain argument [*hetv-ābhāsa*], also called *atīta-kāla* and *bādhita*), Bhāshāp.; Sarvad.; Comm. on Nyāyam. (wrongly spelt °*tyayôpad*°). **Kālâdarśa**, m. 'the mirror of time,' N. of a work. **Kālâdika**, m. (scil. *māsa*) the month Caitra, L. **Kālâdhyaksha**, m. 'the overseer or ruler of time,' the sun, MBh. iii, 152. **Kālânayana**, n. calculation of time, Comm. on VarBṛ. **Kālânala**, m. = *kālâgni*, R. iii, 69, 19; Bhag.; N. of a son of Sabhā-nara (also called *kālânara*, VP.), Hariv. 1669; VP.; of another man; *-rasa*, m., N. of a medical drug. **Kālântaka**, m. time regarded as the god of death, MBh. iii, 11500; R.; *-yama*, m. all-destroying time in the form of Yama, MBh. iii; R. **Kālânta-yama**, m. id., R. vi, 86, 3; (cf. *yamântaka*.) **Kālântara**, n. 'interval, intermediate time,' (*eṇa, āt*), ind. after some time, MBh.; Pañcat.; 'another time,' opportunity, Pañcat.: *-kshama*, mfn. able to bear an interval of delay, Mālav.; *-visha*, m. 'venomous at certain times,' an animal venomous only when enraged or alarmed (as a rat, &c.), L.; *kālântarâvṛita*, mfn. hidden or concealed by time; °*râvṛitti-śubhâśubha*, *āni*, n. pl. good and evil things occurring within the revolutions of time. **Kālâpahāra**, m. waste of time, delay, Rājat. viii, 127. **Kālâbhyāgamana**, n., N. of R. iii, chapter 97. **Kālâvadhi**, m. a fixed period of time. **Kālâvara**, mfn. later in time, Vop. iii, 37. **Kālâvyavāya**, m. absence of pause, RPrāt. **Kālâśuddhi**, f. a season of ceremonial impurity (as at the birth of a child, the death of a relation, &c., when it is considered unlawful to perform any religious rites). **Kālâśauca**, n. id. **Kālo-ja**, mfn. born or produced in due season, Pāṇ. vi, 3, 15. **Kālêśvara**, n., N. of a Liṅga, SkandaP.; *-māhātmya*, n., N. of a work. **Kālêhikā**, f., N. of one of the mothers in Skanda's retinue, MBh. ix, 2641. **Kālôttara**, n., N. of a work, Hcat.; *-śaiva-śāstra*, n. id., ib. **Kālôtpādita**, mfn. produced in due season. **Kālôpta**, mfn. sown in due season, Mn. ix, 39.

2. **Kālaka**, mf(*ikā*)n. to be paid monthly (as interest, *vṛiddhi*).

Kālaya, Nom. P. °*yati*, to show or announce the time, Dhātup. xxxv, 28 (v. l.)

2. **Kālika**, mf(*ī*, Pāṇ. v, 1, 108)n. relating to or connected with or depending on time, Bhāshāp.; fit for any particular season, seasonable, MBh. iii, 868; lasting a long time, Pāṇ. v, 1, 108; (often ifc., e. g. *āsanna-k*°, relating to a time near at hand, impending, Pāṇ. v, 4, 20, Sch.; *māsa-k*°, monthly, MBh. ii, 2080). **—tā**, f. time, date, season. **—tva**, n. id.

Kālin, *ī*, m., N. of a son of Caidyôparicara, Hariv. 1806; (*inī*), f. 'bringing death,' N. of the sixth lunar mansion, L.

Kālīna, mfn. (only ifc.) belonging or relating to any particular time.

Kālya, mf(*ā*)n. timely, seasonable, Pāṇ. v, 1, 107; being in a particular period, gaṇa *aṅg-ādi*; ifc., gaṇa *vargyâdi*; pleasant, agreeable, auspicious (as discourse, cf. *kalya*), L.; (*ā*), f. (with *prajane*) a cow fit for the bull, Pāṇ. iii, 1, 104; (*am*), n. 'day-break,' (*am, e*), acc. loc. ind. at day-break, R.; Suśr.

Kālyaka. See *kālpaka*.

कालकञ्ज *kāla-kañja*, &c. See 1. *kāla*.

कालकीट *kālakīṭa*, mfn. fr. *kal*°, gaṇa *palady-ādi*.

कालकील *kālakīla*, *as*, m. a confused or mingled sound, tumult, L.; (cf. *kalakala*.)

कालकुञ्ज *kāla-kuñja*. See 1. *kāla*.

कालकूट 3. *kālakūṭa*, *ās*, m. pl. (1. fr. *kalak*°), N. of a country near the Himālaya and of the people inhabiting it, MBh.; mfn. relating to that country, gaṇa *palady-ādi*. **—pati**, m., N. of a Vidyā-dhara, Kathās. cviii, 177.

Kālakūṭi, *is*, m. a prince of the Kalakūṭas, Pāṇ. iv, 1, 173.

कालङ्कत *kālaṅkata*, *as*, m. the plant Cassia Sophora, Car. iii, 8.

कालञ्जर *kālañjara*, *as*, m., N. of a sacred mountain in Bundalkhand (the modern Kalliñjer, a spot adapted to practices of austere devotion), MBh., Hariv. &c.; (pl.) N. of the people living near that mountain, Pāṇ. iv, 2, 125, Kāś.; an assembly or meeting-place of religious mendicants, L.; N. of Śiva, L.; (*ā*), f., N. of Durgā, L.; (*ī*), f. id., L.

Kālañjaraka, mfn., Pāṇ. iv, 2, 125, Kāś.

कालद *kālada*. See *kālava*.

कालबव *kālabava*, *as*, m. a patr. of Ārya-mabhūti, VBr.; (*ās*), m. pl. his family, ĀśvŚr. xii.

Kālabavin, *inas*, m. pl., N. of a school.

कालब्धी *kālabdhī*, f. a female descendant of Ka-labdha (accord. to Śākaṭ.), Gaṇar. 48, Comm.

कालम्ब्य *kālambya*, *as*, m., N. of a caravansery, Rājat. iii, 480.

कालव *kālava*, *ās*, m. pl., N. of a people, MBh. vi, 370 (v. l. *kālada*).

Kālaveya, *ās*, m. pl., N. of a school of the SV.

कालशेय *kālaśeya*, *am*, n. (fr. *kalaśī*, Pāṇ. iv, 3, 56), buttermilk, Daś.

कालानर *kālânara*. See *kālânala*.

कालानुनादिन् *kālânunādin* for *kal*°, q. v.

कालाप *kālāpa*, *as*, m. (fr. *kalâpa*), a serpent's hood, L.; a demon, imp or goblin, L.; a student of the Kalāpa grammar, L.; (fr. *kalāpin*) a pupil of Kalāpin, Pāṇ.; MBh. ii, 113; N. of Ārāḍa (a teacher of Śākya-muni), Buddh. (v. l. *kālāma*); (*ās*), m. pl. the school of Kalāpin (often named together with the Kaṭhas, q. v.)

Kālāpaka, *am*, n. the school of Kalāpin, Pāṇ. iv, 3, 104, Kāś.; the Veda recension of this school, ib. 101, Vārtt. 1, Pat.; Sarvad.; N. of the Kātantra grammar, Kathās. vii, 13.

कालाम *kālāma*. See *kālāpa*.

कालामुख *kālā-mukha*. See 1. *kāla*.

कालायन *kālāyana*, mfn. fr. *kalā*, gaṇa *pakshâdi*; (*ī*), f., N. of Durgā, L.

Kālāyani, *is*, m., N. of a teacher (a pupil of Bāshkali), VP.

कालायसूपिक *kālāyasūpika*, mfn. fr. *kalā-ya-sūpa*, Pāṇ. v, 1, 19, Vārtt. 3, Pat.

कालिक 1. & 2. *kālika*. See col. 1 & p. 277, col. 3.

Kālikā. See p. 277, col. 3.

Kālikeya. See p. 278, col. 1.

कालिङ्ग *kāliṅga*, *as*, m. 'produced in or belonging to the Kaliṅga country,' a Kaliṅga man, VP.; (Pāṇ. iv, 1, 170) a prince of the Kaliṅgas, Hariv.; Ragh. iv, 40 &c.; (pl.) the Kaliṅgas, MBh.; VP.; an elephant, L.; a snake, L.; a species of cucumber (Cucumis usitatissimus), L.; Beninkasa cerifera; a poisonous plant, L.; a sort of iron; (*as, am*), m. n. the plant Wrightia antidysenterica, Bhpr.; (*ī*), f. a princess of the Kaliṅgas, MBh. i, 3775 ff.; a kind of gourd, L.; (*am*), n. the water-melon.

Kāliṅgaka, *as*, m. a prince of the Kaliṅgas, MBh. ii, 1270; the plant Wrightia antidysenterica, Bhpr.; (*ikā*), f. Ipomœa Turpethum, L.

कालिञ्जर *kāliñjara*, *as*, m. (cf. *kālañj*°), N. of a mountain, Kathās. cxi, 70 & 81; of a country, Rājat. viii, 917; (*ī*), f., N. of Gaurī, L.

कालितरा *kāli-tarā*. See p. 278, col. 1.

Kāli-dāsa, *as*, m. (fr. *kālī*, the goddess Durgī, and *dāsa*, a slave, the final of *kālī* being shortened; cf. Pāṇ. vi, 3, 63), N. of a celebrated poet (author of the Śakuntalā, Vikramôrvaśī, Mālavikâgnimitra, Megha-dūta, and Raghu-vaṇśa; described as one of the nine gems of Vikramâditya's court, and variously placed in the first, second, third, and middle of the sixth century A. D.; the name is, however, applied to several persons, especially to two others who may have written the Nalôdaya and Śruta-bodha [hence the N. is used to denote the number 'three'], and seems, in some measure, to have been used as an honorary title).

Kālidāsaka, *as*, m. = preceding, L.

कालिन् *kālin*. See col. 1.

कालिन्द *kālinda*, *am*, n. the water-melon, Suśr.; (*ī*), f. a sort of vessel, L.; a sort of Trivṛit with red flowers, L.; N. of a wife of Kṛishṇa (a daughter of Sūrya, BhP.), Hariv.; VP.; N. of the wife of Asita and mother of Sagara, R.; a patr. of the river Yamunā, MBh.; Hariv. &c.; (mfn.) connected with or coming from the river Yamunā, Lāṭy.

Kālindaka, *am*, n. a water-melon, Suśr.; (*ikā*), f. (= *kal*°) science, L.

Kālindī (f. of °*nda*, q. v.) **—karshaṇa**, m. 'diverting the Yamunā stream,' N. of Bala-rāma (who diverted the Yamunā into a new and devious channel marked out by his ploughshare), L. **—pati**, m. 'the lord of Kālindī,' N. of Kṛishṇa, L. **—bhedana**, m. = *-karshaṇa*, L. **—māhātmya**, n., N. of a work. **—sū**, m. 'generator of Kālindī,' N. of Sūrya, L.; (*ūs*), f. 'giving birth to Kālindī,' N. of one of Sūrya's wives, L. **—sôdara**, m. 'brother of Yamunā,' N. of Yama, L.

कालिमन् *kāliman*, &c. See p. 278, col. 1.

Kālim-manyā, kāliya, &c. See ib.

कालिव्य *kālivya*, mfn. fr. *kaliva*, gaṇa *pragady-ādi*; (v. l. *kāvilya* fr. *kavila*.)

काली *kālī*. See p. 278, col. 1.

Kālīka, v. l. for 1. °*lika*, q. v.

कालीची *kālīcī*, f. (fr. 2. *kāla* and *añc*?), the judgment-hall of Yama (judge of the dead), L.

कालीन *kālīna*. See col. 1.

कालीय *kālīya*. See p. 278, col. 1.

कालुष्य *kālushya*, *am*, n. (fr. *kalusha*), foulness, dirtiness, turbidness, opacity, Kathās. xix, 95; Kām.; disturbance or interruption of harmony, Rājat. v, 63; Sarvad.

कालेज *kāle-ja*. See 2. *kāla*.

कालेय 3. *kāleya*, *am*, n. (fr. 1. *kali* [see s. v. *kāli*], Pāṇ. iv, 2, 8), the Sāman of Kali, ŚāṅkhŚr.; ĀrshBr.; Lāṭy.; (*ās*), m. pl., N. of a school of the black Yajur-veda; (mfn.) belonging to Kali or the Kali age, &c., Pāṇ. iv, 2, 8, Pat.

कालेयक *kāleyaka*. See p. 278, col. 1.

कालेश्वर *kāleśvara*, &c. See 2. *kāla*.

Kālôdaka, kālôdāyin. See 1. *kāla*.

कालोल *kā-lola*, *as*, m. (= *mahā-l*°) a crow, Npr.

काल्प *kālpa*, mfn. (fr. *kálpa*), preceptive, ritual, W.; relating to a period called Kalpa, W.; (*as*), m. the plant Curcuma Zerumbet, L.

Kālpaka, *as*, m. Curcuma Zerumbet, L. (v. l. *kālyaka*).

Kālpanika, mfn. (fr. *kalpanā*), existing only in fancy, invented, fictitious, Sāh.; Sarvad.; artificial, fabricated. **—tā**, f. fictitiousness. **—tva**, n. id.

Kālpasūtra, *as*, m. (fr. *kalpa-s*°), one who is familiar with the Kalpa-sūtras, Pāṇ. iv, 2, 60, Kāś.

काल्य *kālya*. See 2. *kāla*.

काल्याणक *kālyāṇaka*, *am*, n. the state of being *kalyāṇa* (q. v.), gaṇa *manojñâdi*.

Kālyāṇineya, *as*, m. the son of a virtuous or fortunate woman (*kalyāṇī*), Pāṇ. iv, 1, 126.

काल्वाल *kālvālá*, mfn. 'bald (?),' only *kālvālī-kṛita*, mfn. made bald (?), ŚBr. ii, 2, 4, 3.

काव *kāva*, *am*, n. (fr. *kaví*), N. of a Sāman, TāṇḍyaBr.; Lāṭy.

कावचिक *kāvacika*, *am*, n. (fr. *kávaca*), a multitude of men in armour, Pāṇ. iv, 2, 41.

कावट *kāvaṭa*, *am*, n. a district containing 100 Grāmas, L. (cf. *karvaṭa*).

Kāvaṭikā, f. a district of 200 Grāmas, L.

कावन्ध *kāvandha*, mf(ī)n. (fr. *káv°*), having the appearance of a headless trunk, Śiś. xix, 51.

कावष *kāvasha*, *am*, n. (fr. *kavásh*), N. of a Sāman.

Kāvasheyá or **kā́v°**, *as*, m. a patr. of Tura, ŚBr. ix, x, xiv; AitBr. viii, 21; BhP.

कावार *kârāra*, *am*, n. the aquatic plant Vallisneria, L.; (*ī*), f. 'keeping off the water,' an umbrella (esp. one without a stick), L.

काविराज् *kā-virāj*, *ṭ*, f. a metre consisting of 9 + 12 + 19 syllables, RPrāt.

काविल्य *kāvilya*. See *kālivya*.

कावृक *kā-vṛika*, *as*, m. a gallinaceous fowl (= *kukkuṭa*, *kṛikavāku*), L.; the ruddy goose (Anas Casarca, = *koka*), L.; a small singing bird (Loxia philippensis), L.

कावेर *kāvera*, *am*, n. saffron, L; (*ī*), f. turmeric, L.; a courtezan, harlot, L.; N. of a river in the Dekhan (accord. to a legend [Hariv. 1421 f.; 1761 f.] daughter of Yuvanāśva and wife of Jahnu, changed by her father's curse from one half of the Gaṅgā into the river Kāverī, therefore also called Ardha-gaṅgā or -jāhnavī), MBh.; Hariv.; R. &c.

Kāveraká, *as*, m. a patr. of Rajata-nābhi, AV. viii, 10, 28; (*ikā*), f., N. of the river Kāverī.

Kāverani, gaṇa *gahâdi*.

Kāveranīya, mfn. fr. °*rani*, ib.

काव्य *kāvyá*, mfn. (fr. *kaví*), endowed with the qualities of a sage or poet, descended or coming from a sage, prophetic, inspired, poetical, RV. i, 117, 12; viii, 8, 11; VS.; AV.; [*kā́vya*, mfn. id., RV. v, 39, 5; x, 144, 2; VS.]; mf(*ā*)n. coming from or uttered by the sage Uśanas, Parāś.; MBh. ii, 2097; (*ás*), m. (gaṇa *kurv-ādi*) a patr. of Uśanas, RV.; TS. &c.; of the planet Śukra, VarBṛS.; Sarvad.; (*ās*), m. pl. poems, MBh. ii, 453; a class of Manes, ŚāṅkhŚr.; Lāṭy.; Mn. iii, 199; the descendants of Kavi, VP.; (*ā*), f. intelligence, L.; N. of a female fiend (= *pūtanā*), L.; (*kā́vyam*), n. wisdom, intelligence, prophetic inspiration, high power and art (often in pl.), RV.; AV.; ŚBr. xi; a poem, poetical composition with a coherent plot by a single author (opposed to an Itihāsa), R.; Sāh. &c.; term for the first tetrastich in the metre Shaṭ-pada; a kind of drama of one act, Sāh. 546; a kind of poem (composed in Sanskṛit interspersed with Prākṛit), Sāh. 563; happiness, welfare, L. **–kartṛi**, m. a poet, Subh. **–kalpa-latā**, f., N. of a work on artificial poems; *-vṛitti*, f. a Comm. by Amara-candra on the last work; *-vṛitti-parimala*, m. another Comm. on the preceding work. **–kāma-dhenu**, f., N. of a Comm. by Vopa-deva on his work called Kavi-kalpadruma. **–goshṭhī**, f. a conversation on poetry, Kād. **–candrikā**, f., N. of a work on artificial poems by Kavi-candra; another work on the same subject by Nyāya-vāgīśa. **–caura**, m. a robber of other poems, plagiarist, L. **–tā**, f. the being a poetical composition, Sāh. **–tva**, n. id., ib. **–devī**, f., N. of a princess who erected a statue of Śiva called Kāvya-deviśvara. **–prakāśa**, m. 'illustration of poetry,' N. of a work on rhetoric or the composition of artificial poems by Mammaṭa; *-ṭīkā*, *-dīpikā*, f., *-nidarśana*, n., *-pradīpa*, m., *-mañjarī*, f., *-saṃketa*, m., N. of commentaries on Mammaṭa's work. **–pradīpa**, m., N. of a Comm. on the Kāvya-prakāśa. **–mīmāṅsaka**, m. a rhetorician, Comm. on Śak. **–mīmāṅsā**, f. theory of poetry, Sarvad.; N. of a work on it. **–rasa**, m. the flavour or sweetness of poetry, ŚārṅgP. **–°rasika**, mfn. having a taste for poetical compositions, Śrut. **–rākshasa**, n., N. of an artificial poem. **–lakshaṇa**, n. illustration of poetry or rhetoric. **–liṅga**, n. a kind of Alaṃkāra or figure of rhetoric in which a statement is explained or made clearer by giving the reason for it, Kpr. x, 28. **–vilāsa**, m., N. of a work. **–śāstra**, n., N. of a short work on poetics. **–saṃhāra**, m. the benediction pronounced at the end of a play, Sāh. **–saṃjīvanī**, f., **-sāra-saṃgraha**, m., N. of works. **–sudhā**, f., N. of a Comm. on a work on artificial poems. **–hāsya**, n. a farce. **Kāvyâdarśa**, m., N. of a work on poetics by Daṇḍin; *-mārjana*, n., N. of a Comm. on it. **Kāvyâmṛita**, m., N. of a work. **Kāvyâlaṃkāra**, m., N. of a work on poetics by Vāmana; *-vṛitti*, f., N. of Vāmana's Comm. on it. **Kāvyâloka**, m., N. of a work on poetics, Comm. on Pratāpar. lxiii, 19. **Kāvyâshṭaka**, n., N. of a work by Sūrya. **Kāvyôdaya**, m., N. of a work.

Kāvyāyana, *as*, m. a patr. fr. *kāvya*, gaṇa 1. *naḍâdi*; (cf. Gaṇar. 233 & 236.)

काश् *kāś*, cl. 1. Ā. *kāśate* (perf. *cakāśe*, 3. pl. °*śire*), to be visible, appear, MBh. &c.; to shine, be brilliant, have an agreeable appearance, ib.: cl. 4. *kāśyate*, Dhātup. xxvi, 53: Intens. P. Ā. *cākaśīti*, *cākaśyáte*, to shine brightly, ŚBr. ii; KātyŚr.; to see clearly, survey, ŚBr. xi; Pāṇ. vii, 3, 87, Vārtt. 1, Pat.

1. **Kāśa**, *as*, m. 'the becoming visible, appearance,' only in *sa-k°*, q. v.; N. of a man, gaṇa *aśvâdi*; of a prince (the son of Suhotra and father of Kāśi-rāja), Hariv.; VP.; a species of grass (Saccharum spontaneum, used for mats, roofs, &c.; also personified, together with the Kuśa grass, as one of Yama's attendants), Kauś.; R.; Kum. &c.; (*ā*, *ī*), f. id., L.; (*am*), n. id., L. **–kṛitsna**, m. (gaṇas *upakâdi* and *arīhaṇâdi*) N. of a grammarian (quoted by Kaiy. & others); N. of a philosopher, Bādar.; (mf(*ī*)n.) taught by Kāśakṛitsni, Pat.; (mf(*ā*)n.) studying Kāśakṛitsni's doctrines, Pat. **–°kṛitsnaka**, mfn. relating to Kāśa-kṛitsna, gaṇa *arīhaṇâdi*. **–°kṛitsni**, m., N. of a teacher, KātyŚr.; of a philosopher, Pat. **–ja**, mfn., Pāṇ. vi, 2, 82. **–pauṇḍra**, *ās*, m. pl., N. of a people, MBh. viii, 2084. **–maya**, mfn. consisting of the grass Saccharum spontaneum, Lāṭy.; BhP. **Kāśâdi**, a Gaṇa of Pāṇ. (iv, 2, 80; Gaṇar. 296).

Kāśaka, *as*, m. the grass Saccharum spontaneum, L.; N. of the prince Kāśa, Hariv. 1733 (v. l. °*śika*).

Kāśaya, *as*, m., N. of a son of Kāśa or Kāśi, Hariv. 1734; of the country of the Kāśis, Comm. on Uṇ. iv, 117.

Kāśi, *is*, m. 'shining,' the sun, L.; the clenched hand, fist, handful, RV. iii, 30, 5; vii, 104, 8; viii, 78, 10; Kauś.; N. of a prince (the ancestor of the kings of Kāśi, of the family of Bharata, son of Suhotra and grandfather of Dhanvantari, Hariv. 1734; the son of Kāśya and grandson of Suhotra, BhP. ix, 17, 4); (*áyas*), m. pl. the descendants of this prince, BhP. ix, 17, 10; N. of the people of Kāśi, ŚBr. xiii; MBh. &c.; (*is*), f. 'the splendid,' N. of a celebrated city and place of pilgrimage (the modern Benares, usually written Kāśī, q. v.), Uṇ. iv, 119; fine cotton or silk (from Kāśi), Divyâv. **–kanyā**, f. a girl or virgin from Kāśi, MBh. v. **–°kosalīya**, mfn. connected with or coming from Kāśi and Kosala, Pat. **–khaṇḍa**, n. the section of the Skanda-purāna treating of Benares. **–nagara**, n. 'the city of the Kāśis,' Benares, MBh. v. **–nātha**, m., N. of a man. **–pa**, m. a sovereign of the Kāśis, MBh. i, 1809; VarBṛS. **–pati**, m. id., MBh. i, 4083; Bhag.; N. of Divo-dāsa Dhanvantari (a king of Benares, author of certain medical works and teacher of the Āyur-veda; he is often confounded with the celestial namesake, the physician of the gods), Suśr. **–purī**, f. = *-nagara*, MBh. xiii, 7785. **–manuja**, m. a man from Kāśi, VarBṛS. **–rāja**, m. = *-pa*, MBh.; Hariv.; BhP.; N. of the Dānava Dīrgha-jihva, MBh. i, 2676; of Divo-dāsa Dhanvantari, Suśr.; of Pratardana Daivodāsi, RAnukr.; of a grandfather of Dhanvantari, VP.; of a prince who has been killed by his wife, VarBṛS. **–rājan**, m. = *-pa*, MBh. v. **–rāma**, m., N. of a scholiast (who commented on the Tithitattva and several other works). **–vilāsa**, m. = *kāśī-vil°*. **Kāśîśa**, m. 'the lord of the Kāśis,' N. of Divo-dāsa, W.; N. of Śiva, W.; (*am*), n. wrongly spelt for *kāsīsa*, q. v. **Kāśîśvara**, m. a sovereign of the Kāśis, MBh. iii, 6027; N. of a grammarian. **Kāśy-ādi**, a Gaṇa of Pāṇ. (iv, 2, 116).

Kāśika, mf(*ā*, *ī*, Pāṇ. iv, 2, 116)n. coming from Kāśi, Pat.: Lalit.; silken, Divyâv.; (*as*), m., N. of a prince (see *kāśaka*); (*ā*), f. (scil. *purī*) 'the city of the Kāśis,' Benares; (with or without *vṛitti*) 'the Comm. composed or used in Kāśi,' N. of a Comm. on Pāṇ. by Vāmana and Jayâditya. **–vastra**, n. fine cotton from Kāśi, Kāraṇḍ. **–sūkshma**, n. id., L.

Kāśikā (f. of *kāśika*, q. v.) **–tilaka**, n., N. of a poem by Nīla-kaṇṭha. **–nyāsa**, see *-vivaraṇa-pañjikā*. **–priya**, m. 'dear to the Kāśikā city,' N. of the king Divo-dāsa, L. **–vivaraṇa-pañjikā**, f., N. of a Comm. on the *Kāśikā vṛitti* by Jinêndra-buddhi (also called °*kā-nyāsa* or °*kā-nyāsa-pañjikā*).

Kāśin, mfn. (only ifc.) shining, appearing, having the semblance of (e.g. *jita-k°*, appearing or behaving like a conqueror, MBh.; *jaya-k°*, id., BhP. iv, 10, 15); (*ī*), m., N. of a man (as son of Brahman Kavi), MBh. xiii, 4150.

Kāśila, mfn., Pāṇ. iv, 2, 80.

Kāśishṇu, mfn. shining, brilliant, BhP. iv, 30, 6.

Kāśī, f. = *kāśi*, Benares, q. v.; N. of the wife of Sudeva and mother of Supārśva, Hariv. 9204; VP. **–khaṇḍa**, n. = *kāśi-kh°*. **–nātha**, m. 'lord of Benares,' N. of Śiva, L.; of several men; *-bhaṭṭa*, m., N. of a man. **–pati**, m. a sovereign of Benares, R. i, 12, 22 [*kāśi-p°*, ed. Bomb. i, 13, 23]; N. of a dramatist. **–prakāśa**, **-praghaṭṭaka**, m., N. of works. **–māhātmya**, n. 'the glory of Benares,' a section of the BrahmavP. **–moksha**, m., N. of a work. **–rāja**, m. a sovereign of Benares, MBh. iv, 2351 (*kāśi-r°*, ed. Bomb.) **–vilāsa**, m., N. of a work. **–setu**, m., N. of a work. **–stotra**, n., N. of a panegyric poem on Benares.

Kāśīya, mfn. fr. *kāśa*, gana *utkarâdi*; fr. *kāśi*, Pāṇ. iv, 2, 113; (*as*), m., N. of a prince (v. l. for *kāśi-rāja*), VP.

Kāśeya, *as*, m. (fr. *kāśi*), a prince of the Kāśis, R. vii, 38, 19; (*ās*), m. pl., N. of a dynasty, VP.; (*ī*), f. a princess of the Kāśis, MBh. i, 3785.

1. **Kāśya**, *as*, m. 'belonging to the Kāśis, ruling over the Kāśis,' a king of Kāśi (as Dhṛitarāshṭra, ŚBr. xiii; or Ajāta-śatru, ib. xiv), ŚBr.; ŚāṅkhŚr.; MBh. &c.; N. of a king (the father of Kāśyapa and ancestor of Kāśi-rāja Dhanvantari, Hariv. 1521; the son of Suhotra [cf. *kāśa*], BhP. ix, 17, 3; the son of Senā-jit, Bh. ix, 21, 23; VP.); (*ā*), f. (Gaṇar. 37, Comm.) a princess of Kāśi, MBh.; Hariv.

Kāśyaka, *as*, m. a king of Kāśi, Hariv. 1520.

Kāśyāyana, *as*, m. a patr. fr. 1. *kāśya*, gaṇa 1. *naḍâdi*.

काश 2. *kāśa*, wrongly spelt for *kāsa*, q. v.

काशफरी *kāśapharī*, f., gaṇa *nady-ādi*.

Kāśaphareya, mfn. fr. °*pharī*, ib.

काशब्द *kā-śabda*, *as*, m. the sound *kā*.

काशाल्मलि *kā-śālmali*, *is*, f. a kind of silk-cotton tree, Bombax heptaphyllum, L.

काशि *kāśi*, *kāśika*. See col 2.

Kāśin, **kāśishṇu**, **kāśī**. See above.

काशीत *kāśīta*, *am*, n., N. of a Sāman, Lāṭy.

काशू *kāśū*, *ūs*, f. = *vikala-dhātu*, Comm. on Uṇ. i, 87; an iron spear (= *kāsū*), ib. **–kāra**, m. the Areca or betel-nut tree, W.

काशेय *kāśeya*. See above.

काशेरुयज्ञिक *kāśeruyajñika*, mfn. fr. *kaśeru-yajña*, Pat.

काश्मरी *kāśmarī*, f. the plant Gmelina arborea (Gambhārī), MBh.; R.; Suśr.; Mālatīm.

Kāśmarya, *as*, m. (= *kārshm°*) id., MBh.; Suśr.

काश्मल्य *kāśmalya*, *am*, n. (fr. *kaśmala*), dejection of mind, weakness, despair, Mcar.

काश्मीर *kāśmīra*, mf(ī)n. (gaṇas *kacchâdi* and *sindhv-ādi*) born in or coming from Kaśmīra, MBh. iv, 254; (*as*), m. a king of Kaśmīra, Mudr.; Kathās.; the country Kaśmīra, MBh. &c.; (*ās*), m. pl. the inhabitants of Kaśmīra, ib.; the country Kaśmīra, ib.; (*ā*), f. a sort of grape, L.; (*ī*), f. = *kāśmarī*, Bhpr.; the tree Ficus elastica, L.; (*am*), n. the tuberous root of the plant Costus speciosus, L.; saffron, Bhartṛ.; Git.; L.; = *ṭaṅka*, L. **–ja**, n. 'coming from Kāśmīra,' saffron, Naish. xxii, 56; Bhām.; the tuberous root of the plant Costus speciosus; (*ā*), f. birch (or Aconitum ferox?), L. **–janman**, n. saffron, L. **–jīrakā**, f. a sort of cummin, L. **–deśa**, m. the country Kaśmīra. **–pura**, n. the city of the Kaśmīras. **–maṇḍala**, n. = *-deśa*. **–liṅga**, n., N. a Liṅga. **–vṛiksha**, m., N. of a tree with oily seeds, Npr. **–sambhava**, n. saffron, L.

Kāśmīraka, mfn. (gaṇa *kacchâdi*) born or produced in Kaśmīra, relating to Kaśmīra, MBh.; Rājat.: (*as*), m. a prince of Kaśmīra, VarBṛS.; (*ās*), m. pl. the inhabitants of Kaśmīra, MBh. iii, 1991; (*ikā*), f. a princess of Kaśmīra, Rājat. vi, 254.

Kāśmīrika, mfn. born or produced in Kaśmīra, Rājat. **— nivāsa,** m. the residence of the Kaśmīras, Rājat. iii, 480.

Kāśmīrya, mfn., gaṇa *saṃkāśâdi.*

काश्य 2. *kāśya, am,* n.=*kaśya,* a spirituous liquor, L.

काश्यप *kāśyapa,* mf(*ī*)n. belonging to Kaśyapa, relating to or connected with him (e.g. *kāśyapī devī,* the earth, Hariv. 10645; see *kāśyapī* below), MBh. &c.; (gaṇa *bidâdi*) a patr. fr. Kaśyapa (designating an old grammarian [VPrāt.; Pāṇ. viii, 4, 67] and many other persons, including some whose family-name was unknown [Comm. on KātyŚr.]; many subdivisions of Kāśyapa families are known, e.g. *Urubilvā-k°, Gayā-k°, Daśabala-k°, Nadī-k°, Mahā-k°, Hasti-k°*); N. of Aruṇa (the sun), VP. iii, 12, 41; of Vishṇu, L.; a sort of deer, L.; a fish, L.; (*ī*), f. a female descendant of Kaśyapa, VarBṛS.; the earth (according to a legend of the Purāṇas, Paraśu-rāma, after the destruction of the Kshatriya race and the performance of an Aśvamedha sacrifice, presented the sovereignty of the earth to Kaśyapa), MBh. viii, 3164; Hcar.; (*am*), n., N. of different Sāmans, ĀrshBr. **— dvīpa,** m., N. of a Dvipa, MBh. vi. **— nandana,** *ās,* m. pl. 'the children of Kaśyapa,' N. of the gods, MBh. xiii, 3330. **— parivarta,** m., N. of a section of the Ratnakūṭa-text, Buddh. **— smṛiti,** f., N. of a work.

Kāśyapaka, mf(*ikā*)n. relating to or connected with Kaśyapa, VāyuP.

Kāśyapāyana, *as,* m. a patr. fr. Kāśyapa, gaṇa 1. *naḍâdi.*

Kāśyapi, *is,* m. id., N. of Tārkshya, Kathās. xc, 110; of Garuḍa, L.; of Aruṇa, L.

Kāśyapin, *inas,* m. pl. the school of Kāśyapa, Pāṇ. iv, 3, 103.

Kāśyapī (f. of *kāśyapa,* q.v.) **— bālākyā-māṭharī-pútra,** m., N. of a teacher, ŚBr. xiv. **— bhuj,** m. 'enjoying the earth,' a king, Rājat. i, 45.

Kāśyapīya, *ās,* m. pl. the school of Kāśyapa, Buddh.

Kāśyapeya, *as,* m. a patr. of the twelve Ādityas, MBh. xiii, 7094; of Garuḍa, MBh. i, 1247; of Aruṇa (the sun), L.

काश्यायन *kāśyāyana.* See p. 280, col. 3.

काश्वरी *kāśvarī,* f.=*kāśmarī,* L.

काष *kāsha.* See *kapola-k°.*

Kāshaṇa, mfn. unripe, Divyâv.

काषाय *kāshāya,* mfn. (fr. *kash°*), brown-red, dyed of a reddish colour, ĀśvGṛ.; Kauś.; MBh. &c.; (*ī*), f. (with *makshikā*) a sort of fly or wasp, Suśr.; (*am*), n. a brown-red cloth or garment, MBh.; R.; Yājñ. iii, 157. **— grahaṇa,** n., N. of a Caitya, Lalit. **— dhāraṇa,** n. wearing a brown-red garment, MBh. xii, 11898. **— vasana,** mf(*ā*)n. = *-vāsas,* Nal. xxiv, 9; (*ā*), f. a widow, L. **— vāsas,** mfn. wearing a brown garment, MBh.; Hariv. **— vāsika,** m. (= *kash°*) a kind of poisonous insect, Suśr.

Kāshāyaṇá, *as,* m. (a patr. fr. *kashāya* or *kāsh°*), N. of a teacher, ŚBr. xiv.

Kāshāyin, *ī,* m. 'wearing a brown-red garment,' a Buddhist monk, Car.; Vishṇ.; (*inas*), m. pl. the school of Kashāya, gaṇa *śaunakâdi.*

काषिन् *kāshin.* See *pat-k°.*

Kāsheya, *ās,* m. pl., N. of a dynasty, VP.

काष्टायन *kāshṭāyana, as,* m. a patr. fr. *kashṭa,* Pravar.

काष्ठ *kāshṭha, as,* m., N. of one of Kubera's attendants, MBh. ii, 415; (*ám*), n. a piece of wood or timber, stick, ŚBr.; KātyŚr.; Mn. &c.; wood or timber in general; an instrument for measuring lengths; a kind of measure, SaddhP.; [*kāshṭha-,* in comp., or *kāshṭham,* ind. with a verb expresses excellence or superiority, Pāṇ. viii, 1, 67 & 68.] **— kadalī,** f. the wild plantain, L. **— kīṭa,** m. a small insect or worm found in decayed wood, L. **— kuṭṭa,** m. a sort of woodpecker (Picus bengalensis), Pañcat. **— kuddāla,** m. a kind of wooden shovel or scraper (used for baling water out of a boat, or for scraping and cleaning its bottom), L.; (vv.ll.*-kudāla* and *-kūddāla.*) **— kūṭa,** m. = *-kuṭṭa,* Pañcat. **— khaṇḍa,** n. a stick, spar, piece of wood, Megh.; Śiś.; Hit. **— garbha,** mfn. woody in the interior, Bhpr. **— ghaṭana,** m. framing and joining timber. **— ghaṭita,** mfn. framed or formed of wood, wooden. **— citā,** f. a funeral pile, Pañcad. **— jambū,** f. the plant Premna herbacea, L. **— taksh,** m. 'cutting and framing timber,' a carpenter, L. **— takshaka,** m. id., L. **— tantu,** m. a caterpillar (which secretes itself in wood and there passes into a chrysalis), L.; a small worm found in timber, W. **— dāru,** m. the tree Pinus Deodora, L. **— dru,** m. the plant Butea frondosa, L. **— dhātrī-phala,** n. the fruit of the plant Emblica officinalis, L. **— paṭṭa,** m. a wooden board, Bhpr. **— pattrôpajīvin,** mfn. living by working on wood and leaves, Sāh. **— pāṭalā,** f., N. of a plant (= *sita-pāṭalikā*), L. **— pāshāṇa-vāsas,** *āṃsi,* n. pl. wood, stone, and clothes. **— puttalikā,** f. a wooden image. **— pushpa,** *āṇi,* n. pl. a kind of flower, Kāraṇḍ. **— pradāna,** n. piling up wood, forming a funeral pile, Pañcat. **— bhakshaṇa,** n. 'devouring of wood (of the funeral pile),' = *°shṭhâdhirohaṇa,* Pañcad. **— bhāra,** m. a particular weight of wood, Hariv. 4356; R. i, 4, 21. **— °bhārika,** mfn. a wood-carrier, bearer of wood, Kathās. vi, 42. **— bhid,** mfn. cleaving wood, Pāṇ. iii, 2, 61, Kāś. **— bhūta,** mfn. one who has become wood or stands stock still (as an ascetic), R. i, 65, 3; (*as*), m., N. of a demon who causes diseases, Hariv. 9559. **— bhṛit,** see s. v. *kāshṭhā.* **— bheda,** m. cleaving of wood, Pāṇ. vi, 2, 144, Kāś. **— maṭhī,** f. a funeral pile, L. **— maya,** mf(*ī*)n. made of wood, wooden, consisting of pieces of wood, Mn. ii, 157; MBh. &c. **— malla,** m. a bier or plank &c. on which dead bodies are carried, L. **— rajanī,** f. = *dāru-haridrā,* L. **— rajju,** f. a cord for binding together a load of wood, R. i, 4, 20. **— lekhaka,** m. a small worm found in wood, L. **— loshṭa-maya,** mfn. made of wood or clay, Mn. viii, 289. **— lohin,** m. a club, short cudgel (especially if bound with iron), L. **— vat,** mfn. having wood for fuel, &c.; (*t*), ind. like a piece of wood, like a stick (as when petrified with fear, &c.) **— vallikā,** f., N. of a plant (= *kaṭukā*), L. **— vallī,** f. id., L. **— vāṭa,** m. a wall made of wood, Rājat. vi, 202. **— vāstuka,** n. a sort of spinage, Npr. **— vivara,** n. the hollow of a tree, Comm. on Śak. **— sārivā,** f. the plant Ichnocarpus frutescens, L. **— stambha,** m. a beam of wood, Hit. **Kāshṭhâgāra,** m. a wooden house, L. **Kāshṭhâguru,** m. Agallochum, L. **Kāshṭhâdi,** a Gaṇa of Pāṇ. (viii, 1, 67). **Kāshṭhâdhirohaṇa,** n. ascending the funeral pile, Pañcad. **Kāshṭhâmbu-vāhinī,** f. a wooden bucket or baling vessel, L. **Kāshṭhâluka,** n. a species of Āluka, Suśr.; Hcar. **Kāshṭhī-√bhū,** to stand stock still or become immovable like a piece of wood, Bhpr. **Kāshṭhī-rasa,** m. the wild plantain, Musa sapientum, L.; (cf. *kâshṭhīlā.*) **Kāshṭhêkshu,** m. a kind of sugar-cane, L.

1. **Kāshṭhaka,** *as,* m. a kind of wheat, L.; (*ikā*), f. a small piece of wood, Pañcat.; Kathās.; wild Pisang, L.; (*am*), n. aloe wood or Agallochum, L.

Kāshṭhika, *as,* m. a bearer of wood, Kād.; Kathās.; (*ā*), f., see *°shṭhaka.*

Kāshṭhin, mfn. wooden, W.; having wood, W.

काष्ठा *kâshṭhā,* f. a place for running, race-ground, course (also the course, path or track of the wind and clouds in the atmosphere), RV.; the mark, goal, limit, VS.; TS.; ŚBr. &c.; the highest limit, top, summit, pitch, Kum.; Daś. &c.; a quarter or region of the world, cardinal point, Naigh.; Nir.; MBh. &c.; the sixteenth part of the disk of the moon, BhP. i, 12, 31; a measure of time ($=\frac{1}{30}$ Kalā, Mn. i, 64; Suśr.; $=\frac{1}{15}$ Kalā, Jyot.; $=\frac{1}{15}$ Laghu, $=\frac{1}{225}$ Nāḍikā, $=\frac{1}{450}$ Muhūrta, BhP. iii, 11, 7), MBh. i, 1292 &c.; form, form of appearance, BhP. iii, 28, 12; vii, 4, 22; the sun, Nir. ii, 15; water, ib.; the plant Curcuma xanthorrhiza, L.; N. of a daughter of Daksha and wife of Kaśyapa (mother of the solidungulous quadrupeds), BhP. vi, 6, 25 ff.; N. of a town. **Kāshṭha-bhṛit,** mfn. leading to a mark or aim, ŚBr. xi.

2. **Kāshṭhaka,** mfn. relating to *kāshṭhakīya,* gaṇa *bilvâdi.*

Kāshṭhakīya, *am,* n. [Kāś.], *ā,* f. fr. *kāshṭhā* (a mark, goal), gaṇa 2. *naḍâdi.*

काष्ठील *kâshṭhīla, as,* m. a large kind of Calotropis, L.; (*ā*), f. a plantain, Musa sapientum, L.

कास् 1. *kās,* cl. 1. Ā. *kāsate* (perf. *kāsām cakre,* Pāṇ. iii, 1, 35 (see also Comm. on Bhaṭṭ. v, 105); *cakāse* or *kāsām āsa,* Vop.), to cough, Suśr. (once P. Pot. *kāset*).

2. **Kās,** f. cough, AV. i, 12, 3; v, 22, 10 & 11.

1. **Kāsa,** *as,* m. id., Suśr.; BhP.; (*ā*), f. id., AV. vi, 105, 1–3. **— kanda,** m. a species of root (= *kāsālu*), L. **— kara,** mfn. producing cough or catarrh. **— kuṇṭha,** mfn. 'afflicted with cough,' N. of Yama. **— ghna,** mf(*ī*)n. removing or alleviating cough, pectoral, Suśr.; (*ī*), f. a sort of prickly nightshade (Solanum Jacquini), L. **— jit,** f. 'removing cough,' Clerodendrum siphonanthus, L. **— nāśinī,** f., N. of a thorny plant (= *karkaṭa-śṛiṅgī*), L. **— marda,** m. 'cough-destroying,' Cassia Sophora, Suśr.; a remedy against cough (an acid preparation, mixture of tamarinds and mustard), L. **— mardaka,** m. Cassia Sophora, L. **— mardana,** m. Trichosanthes dioeca, L. **— vat,** mfn. having a cough, Car.; Suśr. **Kāsāri,** m. 'enemy of cough,' Cassia Sophora, L. **Kāsālu,** m. an esculent root (sort of yam), L.

Kāsikā, f. cough, AV. v, 22, 12; xi, 2, 22.

Kāsin, mfn. having a cough, Suśr.

Kāsundī-vaṭikā, f. a remedy against cough (= *kāsa-marda*), L.

कास 2. *kāsa, as, am,* m. n. for *kāśa* (the grass Saccharum spontaneum), L.; (*as*), m. the plant Moringa pterygosperma, L.

कास 3. *kāsa,* mfn. fr. √*kas,* Pāṇ. iii, 1, 140.

Kāsaka, *ās,* m. pl., N. of a dynasty, VP.

कासक्तिक *kā-saktika.* mfn. wearing a turban (or = *baddha-parikara kañcukin*), Gobh. i, 2, 25.

कासर *kā-sara, as,* m. (cf. *kā-sṛiti*) a buffalo, L.

कासार *kāsāra, as,* m. [*am,* n., L.] a pond, pool, Hariv.; Daś.; Bhartṛ.; Gīt.; N. of a teacher, BhP. xii, 6, 59.

कासिका *kāsikā, kāsin.* See √*kās.*

कासीस *kāsīsa, am,* n. green vitriol, green sulphate of iron, Car.; Suśr.

कासुन्दीवटिका *kāsundī-vaṭikā.* See √*kās.*

कासू *kāsū, ūs,* f. (cf. *kāśū*) a sort of spear or lance, Pāṇ. v, 3, 90; Uṇ. i, 85; indistinct speech, L.; speech in general, L.; light, lustre, L.; disease, L.; devotion, W.; understanding, L. **— tarī,** f. a short spear, javelin, L.

कासृति *kā-sṛiti, is,* f. a by-way, secret path, L.

कासेरुयज्ञिक *kāseruyajñika.* See *kaś°.*

कास्तम्बर *kāstambara, as,* m., N. of a man, (pl.) his family, Saṃskārak.

कास्तीर *kāstīra, am,* n., N. of a village of the Bāhīkas, Pāṇ. vi, 1, 155.

Kāstīrika, mf(*ikā, ikī*)n., Pāṇ. iv, 2, 104, Pat.

कास्तूरिक *kāstūrika.* mf(*ā*)n. (fr. *kastūrikā*), made or consisting of musk, Hcat.

काहका *kāhakā,* f. (cf. *kāhalā*) a kind of musical instrument, L.

काहन् *káhan, káhas,* n. (fr. 3. *ká*), a day of Brahmā (or one thousand Yugas, see *kalpa*), Āryabh.

काहय *kāhaya, as,* m. a patr. fr. *kahaya,* gaṇa *śivâdi.*

काहल *kāhala,* mfn. speaking unbecomingly, HYog.; speaking indistinctly, L.; mischievous, L.; large, excessive, L.; dry, withered, L.; (*as*), m. a large drum, Pañcat.; a sound, L.; a cat, L.; a cock, L.; N. of an author; (*ā*), f. a kind of musical instrument, Rājat. v, 464; N. of an Apsaras, L.; (*ī*), f. a young woman, L.; N. of Varuṇa's wife, L.; (*am*), n. unbecoming speech, SāmavBr.; a kind of musical instrument, L. **Kāhalā-pushpa,** n. a thorn-apple (Datura Metel, = *dhustūra*), L.

Kāhali, *is,* m., N. of Śiva, MBh. xiii, 1179.

Kāhalin, *ī,* m., N. of a Ṛishi, Tantr.

काहस् *káhas.* See *káhan.*

काहाबाह *kāhābāha, am,* n. a rumbling noise in the bowels, AV. ix, 8, 11.

काहारक *kā-hāraka, as,* m. a bearer of a palanquin.

काही *kāhī,* f. the plant Wrightia antidysenterica, L.

काहूजी *kāhūjī,* m., N. of the author of an astronomical work (father of the writer Mahā-deva).

काहूय *kāhūya, as,* m. a patr. fr. *kahūya,* gaṇa *śivâdi* (*kāhūsha,* Kāś.)

काहूष *kāhūsha.* See *kāhūya.*

काहोड *kāhoḍa, as,* m. a patr. fr. *kahoḍa,* gaṇa *śivâdi.*

Kāhoḍi, *is,* m. id., Kāṭh. xxv, 7.

काह्लार *kāhlāra,* mfn. (fr. *kahl°*), coming from the white water-lily, Kuval.

कि 1. *ki,* a pronominal base, like 2. *ká* and 1. *ku,* in the words *kím, kíyat, kis, ki-dṛiksha, kī-dṛiś, kī-dṛiśa, kívat.*

कि 2. *ki,* cl. 3. P. *cikéti.* See √*ci.*

किंयु *kim-yú, kim-rāja,* &c. See *kím.*

Kim-śāru, kim-śilá. See ib.

Kim-śuka, &c., **kim-s-tu-ghna.** See ib.

किंस्त्य *kiṃstya, am,* n. a kind of fruit (?), Kauś.

किकि *kiki, is,* m. a blue jay, L.; the cocoa tree (Nārikela), L. **-diva, -divi,** m. a blue jay, L. **-dīvi,** m. id., RV. x, 97, 13; a partridge, TS. v, 6, 22, 1.

Kikin, *ī,* m. a blue jay, L.

Kikī, f. id., L. **-diva, -divi, -dīvi,** m. id., L.

किकिरा *kikirā́,* ind. with √1. *kṛi,* to tear into pieces, rend into rags and tatters, RV. vi, 53, 7 & 8.

किक्किटा *kikkiṭā́,* ind. a particular exclamation, TS. iii, 4, 2, 1; Kāṭh. **-kāram,** ind. p. with the exclamation *kikkiṭā,* TS. iii.

किक्किश *kikkiśa, as,* m. a kind of worm (pernicious to the hair, nails, and teeth), Suśr.

Kikkisa, *as,* m. id., Car. **Kikkisâda,** m. 'eating the Kikkisa,' a species of snake, Suśr.

किक्नस *kiknasa, as,* m. particles of ground corn, bruised grain, groats, AitBr. ii, 9.

किक्विश *kikviśa,* v.l. for *kikkiśa.*

किखि *kikhi, is,* m. a monkey, L.; *(is),* f. a small kind of jackal or fox, L.

किङ्कणी *kiṅkaṇī,* v.l. for *kiṅkiṇī.*

किंकर *kim-kara,* &c. See *kím.*

किङ्किण *kiṅkiṇa, as,* m. a kind of drum, L.; N. of a son of Bhajamāna, BhP. ix, 24, 7; *(ī),* f. a small bell, MBh.; Hariv. &c.; N. of an acid sort of grape (= Vikaṅkata), L.; N. of a goddess, Tantras.

Kiṅkiṇi, *is,* f. (= °*ṇī*) a small bell, L.

Kiṅkiṇikā, f. id., Śiś. v, 58; Hcat.

Kiṅkiṇī (f. of *kiṅkiṇa,* q.v.) **-jāla-mālin,** mfn. having a circlet of small bells, MBh.; Hcat. **-sāyaka,** m. an arrow ornamented with small bells, MBh. iv, 1336.

Kiṅkiṇīka, id., Kum. vii, 49. **Kiṅkiṇīkâśrama,** m., N. of an hermitage, MBh. xiii, 1709.

Kiṅkiṇīkin, mfn. decorated with small bells, MBh.; Hariv. 2023.

किङ्किर *kiṅkira, as,* m. a horse, L.; the Indian cuckoo (Kokila or Koïl), L.; a large black bee, L.; the god of love, L.; *(ā),* f. blood, L.; *(am),* n. the frontal sinus of an elephant, L.

Kiṅkirāta, *as,* m. (or *kim-k°*; gaṇa *kimśukâdi*) a parrot, L.; the Indian cuckoo; the god of love, L.; Jonesia Aśoka, L.; red or yellow amaranth, Kād.

Kiṅkirāla, *as,* m., N. of a plant (= *varvūra*), L.

Kiṅkirin, *ī,* m. the plant Flacourtia sapida, L.

किंकृते *kim-kṛite.* See *kím.*

Kim-kshaṇa, &c., **kim-ca,** &c. See ib.

किञ्चिलिक *kiñcilika, as,* m. an earth-worm, L.

Kiñculaka, *as,* m. id., Bhpr.

Kiñculuka, *as,* m. id., ib.

किंज *kim-ja, -jopya.* See *kím.*

किञ्जल *kiñjala, as,* m. = °*jalka,* L.

Kiñjalka, *as, am,* m. n. (or *kim-j°*; gaṇa *kimśukâdi*) the filament of a plant (especially of a lotus), ĀśvŚr.; MBh.; R. &c.; *(am),* n. the flower of Mesua ferrea, L.

Kiñjalkin, mfn. having filaments, Devīm.

किट् *kiṭ,* cl. 1. P. *keṭati,* to go or approach, Dhātup.; to alarm or terrify, ib.; to fear, ib.

किट *kiṭa, as,* m. a kind of ape, Gal.

Kiṭaka, *am,* n. See *kiṭika.*

किटकिटापय *kiṭakiṭāpaya,* Nom. P. °*yati,* to gnash the teeth, Car.

Kiṭakiṭāya, Nom. Ā. °*yate,* id., Suśr.

किटि *kiṭi, is,* m. (cf. *kira, kiri*) a hog, Kauś. 25; Batatas edulis, Npr. **-mūlaka,** m., **-mūlâbha,** m. Batatas edulis, Npr. **-vara-vadanā,** f., N. of a deity, Buddh.

Kiṭika, *am,* n. (v.l. °*ṭaka*), a kind of weapon (?), Pāṇ. ii, 4, 85, Vārtt. 3, Pat.

किटिभ *kiṭibha, as,* m. a bug, L.; a louse, L.; *(am),* n. a kind of exanthema, Suśr.

Kiṭibhaka, *as,* m. a louse, Divyâv.

Kiṭima, *am,* n. a kind of leprosy, Suśr.

किट्ट *kiṭṭa, am,* n. secretion, excretion, Suśr.; dirt, rust (of iron), ib.; (cf. *tila-k°, taila-k°.*) **-varjita,** n. 'free from any impurity,' semen virile, L.

Kiṭṭāla, *as,* m. rust of iron, L.; a copper vessel, L.

Kiṭṭima, *am,* n. unclean water, L.

किण *kiṇa, as,* m. a corn, callosity, MBh.; Mṛicch.; Śak. &c.; a scar, cicatrix, Bhpr.; Hcar.; an insect found in wood, L. **-kṛita,** mfn. (for *kṛita-kiṇa*) callous, MBh. iv, 53. **-jāta,** mfn. (for *jāta-kiṇa*), id., ib. iii, 11005. **-vat,** mfn. id., MBh. iv, 633 & 639.

किणि *kiṇi, is,* f. Achyranthes aspera, L.

Kiṇihī, f. id., Suśr.

किण्व *kiṇva* [*as,* m., L], *am,* n. ferment, drug or seed used to produce fermentation in the manufacture of spirits from sugar, bassia, &c., Āp.; Mn. viii, 326; Suśr.; (cf. *taṇḍula-k°*); *(am),* n. sin, Uṇ. i, 150.

Kiṇvin, *ī,* m. a horse, L.; (cf. *kindhin.*)

Kiṇvīya, mfn., fr. *kiṇva,* gaṇa *apūpâdi.*

Kiṇvya, mfn. id., ib.

कित् *kit,* cl. 3. *cíketti.* See 2. *cit* & *ketaya.*

कित *kita, as,* m., N. of a man, gaṇa *aśvâdi.*

कितव *kitavá, as,* m. (gaṇa *śauṇḍâdi* [also *vyāghrâdi,* but not in Kāś. and Gaṇar.]) a gamester, gambler, RV.; VS.; AV. &c.; a cheat, fraudulent man, BhP. viii, 20, 3; Megh.; Amar.; (also ifc., e.g. *yājñika-k°,* Pāṇ. ii, 1, 53, Kāś.); (= *matta*) a crazy person, L.; thorn-apple (cf. *dhūrta* and *unmatta*), L.; a kind of perfume (commonly Rocana), Bhpr.; N. of a man, gaṇas *tikâdi, utkarâdi, aśvâdi*; *(ās),* m., N. of a people, MBh. ii, 1832; *(ī),* f. a female gambler, ĀśvGṛ.

Kitavīya, mfn., gaṇa *utkarâdi.*

किदर्भ *kidarbha, as,* m., N. of a man, gaṇa *bidâdi* (vv. ll. *kim-d°, vid°,* &c.; cf. Gaṇar. 243).

किनाट *kínāṭa, am,* n. the inner part of a tree, ŚBr. xiv.

किनारिलिपि *kināri-lipi, is,* f. a kind of writing, Lalit.

किंतनु *kim-tanu, -tu-ghna,* &c. See *kím.*

किन्दुबिल्व *kindu-bilva,* N. of the place where Jaya-deva was born and where his family resided, Gīt. iii, 10 (vv. ll. *kinduvilla, kenduvilla,* and *tinduvilla*).

किंदेव *kim-deva,* &c. See *kím.*

किन्धिन् *kindhin, ī,* m. a horse, L. (v.l. for *kilkin*).

किंनर *kim-nara,* &c. See *kím.*

Kim-nu. See s. v. *kím.*

किप्प *kippa, as,* m. a kind of worm, Suśr. (v.l. *kishya*).

किम् *kím,* ind. (fr. 1. *ki,* originally nom. and acc. sg. n. of 2. *ká,* q.v.), what? how? whence? wherefore? why?

Kim is much used as a particle of interrogation like the Lat. *num, an,* sometimes translatable by 'whether?' but oftener serving only like a note of interrogation to mark a question (e.g. *kim vyādhā vane 'smin samcaranti,* 'do hunters roam about in this wood?' In an interrogation the verb, if uncompounded with a preposition, generally retains its accent after *kim,* Pāṇ. viii, 1, 44). To this sense may be referred the *kim* expressing inferiority, deficiency, &c. at the beginning of compounds (e.g. *kim-rājan,* what sort of king? i.e. a bad king, Pāṇ. ii, 1, 64; v, 4, 70); also the *kim* prefixed to verbs with a similar meaning (e.g. *kim-adhīte,* he reads badly, Pāṇ. viii, 1, 44, Kāś.) *Kim—uta* or *kim—uta-vā* or *kim—athavā—uta,* whether—or—or, R.; Śak.; Bhartṛ. &c.; (cf. *utá.*)

Kim is very frequently connected with other particles, as follows: *kím aṅgá,* wherefore then? RV.; *atha kim,* see *átha*; *kim api,* somewhat, to a considerable extent, rather, much more, still further, Śak.; Megh. &c.; *kim iti,* why? Śak.; Kum.; Pañcat. &c.; *kim-iva,* what for? Śiś. xvi, 31; *kím-u* or *kím-utá,* how much more? how much less? RV.; ŚBr.; MBh. &c.; *kim kila,* what a pity! (expressing dissatisfaction), Pāṇ. iii, 3, 146; *kim-ca,* moreover, further, Pañcat.; Kathās. &c.; what more (expressing impatience), Śak.; *kim-cana* (originally *-ca na,* negative = 'in no way'), to a certain degree, a little, Kathās.; (with a negation) in no way, not at all, MBh. i, 6132; *kim-cid,* somewhat, a little, MBh.; R. &c.; *kim tarhi,* how then? but, however, Pāṇ. ii, 2, 4, Pat.; iv, 1, 163, Kāś.; *kim-tu,* but, however, nevertheless (bearing the same relation to *tu* that *kim-ca* bears to *ca*), MBh.; R. &c.; *kim-nu,* whether indeed? (a stronger interrogative than *kim* alone), MBh.; R. &c.; how much more? how much less? Bhag. i, 35; *kim nu khalu,* how possibly? (a still stronger interrogative), Śak.; *kim punar,* how much more? how much less? R.; Bhag. ix, 33 &c.; however, Bālar.; but, ib.; *kim vā,* whether? or whether? Śak.; Pañcat. &c.; or (often a mere particle of interrogation); *kím svid,* why? Kathās. xxvi, 75; a stronger interrogative than *kim* alone, RV.; MBh.; Kathās.

1. **Kim** (in comp. for *kím*). **-yú,** mfn. what wishing? RV. iii, 33, 4. **-rāja,** m. whose sovereign? Pāṇ. v, 4, 70, Pat. **-rājan,** see s. v. *kím.* **-rūpa,** mf(*ā*)n. of what shape? MBh. i, 1327; Pañcat.; Hcat. **-lakshaṇaka,** mfn. distinguished by what marks? Comm. on Bādar. **-vat,** mfn. having what? Pāṇ. i, 1, 59, Pat.; *(t),* ind. like what? Sarvad. **-vadanta,** m., N. of an imp (inimical to children), PārGṛ. i, 16; *(ī),* f. (Uṇ. iii, 50) 'what do they say?' the common saying or rumour, report, tradition, tale, Prab.; Dhūrtas.; Hit. **-vadanti,** *is,* f. = *-vadantī* before, L. **-varāṭaka,** m. one who says 'what is a cowrie?' i. e. a spendthrift who does not value small coins, Hit. ii, 87. **-varṇa,** mfn. of what colour? MBh.; BhP. **-vid,** mfn. what knowing? ŚāṅkhBr. **-vidya,** mfn. possessing the science of what? MBh. xii. **-vidha,** mfn. of what kind? Bālar. **-vibhāga,** mf(*ā*)n. having what subdivisions? Sūryas. **-viśeshaṇa,** mfn. distinguished by what? Comm. on Nyāyad. **-vishayaka,** mfn. relating to what? Comm. on Bādar. **-vīrya,** mfn. of what power? R.; BhP. **-vṛitta,** m. who says 'what is an event?' i. e. who does not wonder at any event (N. of the attendants of a lion), Pañcat.; *(am),* n. any form derived from the pron. *ká,* Pāṇ. iii, 3, 6 & 144; viii, 1, 48. **-vyāpāra,** mfn. following what occupation? Śak. **-śāru** [m., Uṇ.], n. the beard of corn, AitBr. ii, 9; *(us),* m. an arrow, L.; a heron, L. **-śilá,** mfn. (land) having small stones or gravelly particles, VS.; TS.; MaitrS.; Kāṭh. **-śīla,** mfn. of what habits? in what manner generally existing or living? MBh. **-śuka,** m. the tree Butea frondosa (bearing beautiful blossoms, hence often alluded to by poets), MBh. &c.; *(am),* n. the blossom of this tree, R.; Suśr.; (cf. *palāśá* & *sukimśuká*); °*kâdi,* a Gaṇa of Bhoja (Gaṇar. 107); °*kôdaka,* n. a decoction made from the blossoms of the tree Butea frondosa, Suśr. **-śulaka,** m. a variety of the tree Butea frondosa, Pāṇ. vi, 3, 117; °*lakā-giri,* m., N. of a mountain, ib.; °*lakâdi,* a Gaṇa of Pāṇ., ib. **-śuluka,** v.l. for *-śulaka,* q.v. **-sa,** mfn. = *kim syati,* Pāṇ. viii, 3, 110, Kāś. **-sakhi,** nom. *ā,* m. (Pāṇ. ii, 1, 64, Kāś.) a bad friend, Kir. i, 5. **-samniśraya,** mf(*ā*)n. having what support or substratum? Comm. on Bādar. **-samācāra,** mfn. of what behaviour? MBh. xii. **-sādhana,** mfn. hav-

ing what proof? Comm. on Nyāyad. **—suhṛid**, m. = *-sakhi*, Hit. **—s-tu-ghna**, m.n. = *kiṃ-tu-ghna* (below), Jyot.; VarBṛS.; Sūryas. **—svarūpa**, mf(*ā*)n. of what characteristics? Comm. on Sūryas.

2. **Kiṃ** (in comp. for *kim*). **—kara**, m. (Pāṇ. iii, 2, 21) a servant, slave, MBh.; R. &c.; (probably) a particular part of a carriage, AV. viii, 8, 22; a kind of Rākshasa, MBh.; R.; N. of one of Śiva's attendants, Kathās. cxviii, 5; (*ās*), m. pl., N. of a people, R. iv, 44, 13; (*ā*), f. a female servant, Pāṇ. iii, 2, 21, Vārtt.; (*ī*), f. the wife of a servant, ib.; a female servant, MBh. iv, 634; BhP.; Kathās.; *-tva*, n. the condition of a servant or slave, Pañcat.; *-pāṇi*, mfn. (fr. *kiṃ karavāṇi*, 'what am I to do?'), having hands ready to attend any one, MBh. iii, 303; *kiṃkarī-√bhū*, to become a slave, Comm. on Naish. vi, 81; *kiṃkarīya*, Nom. P. °*yati*, to think (any one) to be a slave, HYog. **—karāla**, m. the tree Acacia arabica, L. **—kartavya-tā**, f. any situation or circumstances in which one asks one's self what ought to be done? Daś.; (cf. *iti-kart°*.) **—karman**, mfn. of what occupation? R. iii, 73, 9. **—kala**, m., N. of a man, gaṇa 1. *naḍâdi*. **—kāmya**, Nom. P. °*yati*, to wish what? Pāṇ. iii, 1, 9, Siddh. **—kāmyā́**, (old instr.) ind. from a desire for what? ŚBr. i, 2, 5, 25. **—kāraṇa**, mfn. having what reason or cause? ŚvetUp. **—kārya-tā**, f. = *-kartavya-tā*, Kathās. x, 101; lxxx, 50. **—kirāta**, see s. v. *kiṅkira*. **—kṛite**, loc. ind. what for? Kathās. lxxi, 79. **—kshaṇa**, m. who says 'what is a moment?' i.e. a lazy fellow who does not value moments, Hit. ii, 87. **—gotra**, mfn. belonging to what family? Kauś. 55. **—cana**, see 2. *ká* and *kím* above; (*as*), m. (= *kiṃ-śuka*) Butea frondosa, L.; *-tā*, f. something, somewhat. **—canaka**, m., N. of a Nāga demon, Buddh. **—°canya**, n. property, MBh. xii, 11901; (cf. *a-kiṃcana*.) **—cid**, n. (see 2. *ká*) 'something,' N. of a particular measure (= eight handfuls), Comm. on ŚāṅkhGṛ.; (*kiṃcic*)*-cirita-pattrikā*, f. the plant Beta bengalensis (= *cīrita-cchadā*), Npr.; *-chesha* (°*cid-ś°*), mf(*ā*)n. of which only a small remainder is left, MBh. ix, 34 & 1442; Kathās.; (*kiṃcij*)*-jña*, mfn. knowing a little, a mere smatterer; (*kiṃcit*)*-ka*, mfn. (with the pron. *ya* preceding) whatever, AitBr. ii, 9; *-kara*, mfn. significant, Pāṇ. i, 2, 27, Vārtt. 6, Pat.; [*a-kiṃc°*, mfn. not able to do anything, insignificant, Pañcat.; Veṇis.]; *-pare*, loc. ind. a little after; *-pāṇi*, m., N. of a particular weight (= *karsha*), ŚārṅgS.; *-prâṇa*, mfn. having a little life left; (*kiṃcin*)*-mātra*, n. only a little. **—chandas**, mfn. conversant with which Veda? ŚāṅkhBr.; having what metre? TāṇḍyaBr. **—ja**, mfn. of low origin, Bhaṭṭ. vi, 133; (*am*), n. the blossom of Mesua ferrea, L. **—japya**, n., N. of a Tīrtha, MBh. iii, 6049; (cf. *kiṃ-dāna*.) **—jyotis** (*kím-*), mfn. having which light? ŚBr. xiv. **—tanu**, m. an insect (described as having eight legs and a very slender body), a species of spider, L. **—tamām**, ind. whether? whether of many? **—tarām**, ind. whether? whether of two? **—tā**, f. 'the state of whom?' any despicable state or condition, contemptibleness; (*ayā*), instr. ind. contemptibly. **—tu-ghna**, m. 'destroying all but,' one of the eleven periods called Karaṇa; (cf. *kiṃ-s-tu-ghna* before.) **—tvá**, mfn. (fr. *kím tvám*, 'what thou?'), questioning impudently (as a drunken man), VS. xx, 28. **—datta**, m., N. of a sacred well, MBh. iii, 6069 (v. l. °*data*). **—dama**, m., N. of a Muni, MBh. i, 4585; Kād. **—darbha**, v. l. for *kidarbha*, q. v. **—dāna**, n., N. of a Tīrtha, MBh. iii, 6049. **—dāsa**, m., N. of a man, gaṇa *bidâdi*. **—deva**, m. an inferior god, demi-god, BhP. xi, 14, 6. **—devata** (*kím-*), mfn. having what deity? ŚBr. xiv. **—devatyà**, mfn. belonging to or devoted to what deity? TS.; ŚBr. **—dharmaka**, mfn. of what nature or character? Comm. on Nyāyad. **—nara**, m. 'what sort of man?' a mythical being with a human figure and the head of a horse (or with a horse's body and the head of a man, Śiś. iv, 38; originally perhaps a kind of monkey, cf. *vā-nara*; in later times (like the Naras) reckoned among the Gandharvas or celestial choristers, and celebrated as musicians; also attached to the service of Kubera; (with Jains) one of the eight orders of the Vyantaras), Mn.; MBh. &c.; N. of a prince, VP.; of Nara (a son of Vibhīshaṇa), Rājat. i, 197; of the attendant of the fifteenth Arhat of the present Avasarpiṇī, Jain.; N. of a locality, gaṇa *takshaśilâdi*; (*ā*), f. a kind of musical instrument, L.; (cf. κινύρα); (*ī*), f. a female Kiṃnara, R.; Megh. &c.; a female Kimpurusha, R. vii, 89, 3; the lute of the Caṇḍālas, L.; *-kaṇṭha*, mfn. singing like a Kiṃnara, Viddh.; *-nagara*, n. a town of the Kiṃnaras, Divyâv.; *-pati*, m. 'the lord of the Kiṃnaras,' N. of Kubera, Bālar.; *-varsha*, m. a division of the earth (said to be north of the Himālaya mountains); *kiṃnarêśa*, °*śvara*, m. 'the lord of the Kiṃnaras,' N. of Kubera, L. **—nāmaka**, mf(*ikā*)n. having what name? Sāh. **—nāmadheya**, mfn. id., Pañcat. **—nāman**, mfn. id., Śāntiś.; Kuval. **—nimitta**, mfn. having what cause or reason? Mālav.; BhP.; (*am*), ind. from what cause? for what reason? why? R. &c.

Kim (in comp.) **—adhikaraṇa**, mf(*ā*)n. referring to what? Śāntiś. **—antara**, mf(*ā*)n. being at what distance from each other? Sūryas. **—abhidhāna**, mfn. having what name? Kād.; Sāh. **—artha**, mfn. having what aim? AitĀr.; MBh. &c.; (*kim-ártham*), ind. from what motive? what for? wherefore? why? ŚBr. xiv; MBh. &c. **—avastha**, mfn. being in what condition (of health)? Pat. on Pāṇ. i, 3, 1, Vārtt. 11. **—ākāra**, mf(*ā*)n. of what shape? Sūryas. **—ākhya**, mfn. how named? Śak. **—ācāra**, mfn. being of what conduct or behaviour? R. vii, 62, 1. **—ātmaka**, mf(*ikā*)n. of what particularity? Comm. on Sūryas. **—ādhāra**, mfn. referring to what? Śāntiś. **—āyus**, mfn. reaching what age? R. vii, 51, 9. **—āśraya**, mf(*ā*)n. being supported by what? Sūryas. **—āhāra**, mfn. taking what food? R. vii, 62, 1. **—icchaka**, n. what one wishes or desires, anything desired, MBh. xii, xiii; (*as*), m., N. of a particular form of austerity (by which any object is obtained), MārkP. **—utsedha**, mf(*ā*)n. of what height? Sūryas. **—paca**, mfn. 'who cooks nothing,' miserly, avaricious, L. **—pacāna**, mfn. id., L. **—parākrama**, mfn. of what power? MBh.; R. **—parivāra**, mfn. having what attendance? Daś. **—paryantam**, ind. to what extent? how far? how long? **—pāka**, mfn. not mature, childish, ignorant, stupid, L.; (*as*), m. a Cucurbitaceous plant (of a very bad taste, Trichosanthes palmata), Bhartṛ.; MārkP.; Strychnos nux vomica, L., (*am*), n. the fruit of Trichosanthes palmata, R. ii, 66, 6; Jain.; Prasannar. **—punā**, f., N. of a river, MBh. ii, 373; iii, 12910. **—purushá** [ŚBr. vii] or **-púrusha** [ŚBr. i], m. 'what sort of a man?' a mongrel being (according to the Brāhmaṇas an evil being similar to man; perhaps originally a kind of monkey [cf. BhP. xi, 16, 29]; in later times the word is usually identified with *kiṃ-nara*, though sometimes applied to other beings in which the figure of a man and that of an animal are combined; these beings are supposed to live on Hema-kūṭa and are regarded as the attendants of Kubera; with Jains the Kimpurushas, like the Kiṃnaras, belong to the Vyantaras); N. of one of the nine sons of Āgnīdhra (having the Varsha Kimpurusha as his hereditary portion), VP.; a division of the earth (one of the nine Khaṇḍas or portions into which the earth is divided, and described as the country between the Himâcala and Hema-kūṭa mountains, also called *kimpurusha-varsha*, Kād.), VP.; BhP.; MatsyaP. &c.; (*ī*), f. a female Kimpurusha, R. vii, 88, 22; *kimpurushī-√1. kṛi*, to change into a Kimpurusha, ib.; *kimpurushêśa*, m. 'lord of the Kimpurushas,' N. of Druma, MBh. ii, 410; Hariv. 5014 = 5495; °*shêśvara*, m., N. of Kubera, L. **—°purushīya**, n. story about a Kimpurusha, R. **—pūrushá**, m. 'what sort of a man?' (probably) a low and despicable man, VS. xxx, 16; a mongrel being (= *-purushá*), BhP. &c.; (*am*), n., N. of the Kimpurusha-varsha, L. **—prakāram**, ind. in what manner? Vop. vii, 110. **—prabhāva**, mfn. possessing what power? Pañcat. **—prabhu**, m. a bad lord or master, Hit. **—pramāṇa**, n. what circumference? R. vii, 51, 9; mf(*ā*)n. of what circumference? R.; Sūryas.; Hcat. **—phala**, mfn. giving what kind of fruit? Daś. **—bala**, mfn. possessing what strength or power? BhP. vii, 8, 7. **—bharā**, f. a kind of perfume (commonly called Nalī), L. **—bhūta**, mfn. being what? Comm. on VS., on Ragh. &c.; (*am*), ind. how? in what manner or degree? like what? **—bhṛitya**, m. a bad servant, Hit. **—mantrin**, m. a bad minister, Hit. **—máya**, mfn. consisting of what? RV. iv, 35, 4. **—mātra**, mf(*ī*)n. of what circuit? Sūryas.

Kimīya, mfn. belonging to whom or what? Daś.

किमीदिन् *kimīdín, ī*, m., N. of a class of evil spirits, RV. vii, 104, 2 & 23; x, 87, 24; AV.; (*inī*), f. id., AV. ii, 24, 5–8.

किम्पल *kimpala* (= κύμβαλον?), a kind of musical instrument, Lalit.

कियत् *kíyat*, mfn. (fr. 1. *ki*, Pāṇ. v, 2, 40; vi, 3, 90), how great? how large? how far? how much? of what extent? of what qualities? RV.; AV. &c. (Ved. loc. *kíyāti* with following *ā́*, how long ago? since what time? RV. i, 113, 10; ii, 30, 1; *kiyaty adhvani*, at what distance? how far off? MBh. xiv, 766; *kiyad etad*, of what importance is this to (gen.), Kathās. iii, 49; *tena kiyān arthaḥ*, what profit arises from that? BhP.; *kiyac ciram*, ind. how long? Kathās.; *kiyac cireṇa*, in how long a time? how soon? Śak.; *kiyad dūre*, how far? Pañcat. iii, 4; *kiyad rodimi*, what is the use of my weeping? Kād.; *kiyad asubhis*, what is the use of living? BhP. i, 13, 22); little, small, unimportant, of small value (often in comp., e.g. *kiyad-vakra*, a little bent, Comm. on Yājñ.; *kiyad api*, how large or how far soever, Pañcat.; *yâvat kiyac ca*, how large or how much soever, of what qualities soever, AV. viii, 7, 13; ŚBr.); (*kíyat*), ind. how far? how much? how? RV.; AV.; ŚBr.; a little, Pañcat.; Hit. **—kālam**, ind. how long? some little time ago.

Kiyad (in comp. for *kiyat*). **—etikā** or **-ehikā**, f. effort, vigorous or persevering exertions according to one's strength, L. **—dūra**, n. 'what distance?' see *-dūre* above s.v. *kiyat*; 'some small distance,' (*e*, *am*, or in comp.), ind. not far, a little way, Hit.

Kiyan (in comp. for *kiyat*). **—mātra**, mfn. of little importance, Pañcat.; (*am*), n. trifle, small matter, Kathās. lxv, 139.

Kiyedhā́, mfn. (for *kiyad-dhā́*) containing or surrounding much (N. of Indra), RV. i, 61, 6 & 12 (Nir. vi, 20).

कियाम्बु *kiyā́mbu, u*, n. a kind of aquatic plant (= *kyāmbū*), RV. x, 16, 13.

कियाह *kiyāha, as*, m. a chestnut-coloured horse, L.

कियेधा *kiyedhā́*. See *kíyat*.

किर् *kir*, mfn. (√1. *kṛī*) ifc. pouring out, Viddh.

Kira, mf(*ā*)n. scattering, &c., Pāṇ. iii, 1, 135; (cf. *mṛit-kirā*); (*as*), m. a hog, L.; (cf. *kiṭi*, *kiri*.)

Kiraka, *as*, m. a scribe, L.; (*ikā*), f. ink-stand, Gal.

Kiráṇa, *as*, m. dust, very minute dust, RV.; a rein (a meaning drawn probably fr. RV. iv, 38, 6), Naigh. i, 5; a ray or beam of light, a sun- or moon-beam, MBh.; Suśr. &c.; (perhaps) thread, RV. x, 106, 4; AV. xx, 133, 1 & 2; N. of a kind of Ketu (of which twenty-five are named), VarBṛS.; the sun, L.; N. of a Śaiva work, Sarvad.; (*ā*), f., N. of a river, SkandaP. **—pati**, m. 'the lord of rays,' the sun, VarBṛS. **—pāṇi**, m. 'whose hands are rays,' the sun, ShaḍvBr. **—maya**, mfn. radiant, bright. **—mālin**, m. 'garlanded with rays,' the sun, L. **Kiraṇâkhya-tantra**, n., N. of a work on architecture, Comm. on VarBṛS. **Kiraṇâvalī**, f., N. of a Comm. by Udayana; of another Comm. by Dādābhāi on the Sūryas.; *-ākāśa*, m., *-prakāśa-vyākhyā*, f., N. of comments on the preceding commentaries.

Kirat, mfn. (pr. p.) scattering, spreading; pouring out, Amar.; throwing (as arrows), MBh.; strewing, pouring over, filling with, MBh. &c.

Kiri, *is*, m. 'a pile,' see *ākhu-kiri*; a hog (= *kiṭi*), Uṇ. iv, 144; Batatas edulis, Npr.; for *giri*, q. v.

Kiriká, mfn. sparkling, beaming, VS. xvi, 46 (cf. *gir°*); (*ā*), f., see *kiraka*.

Kiryāṇī, f. a wild hog, L.

किराट *kirāṭa, as*, m. a merchant, Rājat. viii, 132; (cf. *kirīṭa*.)

किरात *kirā́ta, ās*, m. pl., N. of a degraded mountain-tribe (inhabiting woods and mountains and living by hunting, having become Śūdras by their neglect of all prescribed religious rites; also regarded as Mlecchas; the Kirrhadæ of Arrian), VS. xxx, 16; TāṇḍyaBr.; Mn. x, 44; MBh. &c.; (*as*), m. a man of the Kirāta tribe; a prince of the Kirātas, VarBṛS. xi, 60; a dwarf, L.; (cf. *kubja-k°*); a groom, horseman, L.; the plant Agathotes Chirayta (also called *kirāta-tikta*), L.; N. of Śiva (as a mountaineer opposed to Arjuna, described in Bhāravi's poem Kirātârjunīya); (*ī*), f. a woman of the Kirāta tribe; a low-caste woman who carries a fly-flap or anything to keep off flies, Ragh. xvi, 57; a bawd, procuress, L.; N. of the goddess Durgā, Hariv. 10248; of the river Gaṅgā, L.; of the celestial Gaṅgā as river of Svarga, L. **—kula**, mf(*ī*)n. belonging to the Kirāta tribe, TāṇḍyaBr.; (see *kilāta*.) **—tikta**, m. the plant

Agathotes Chirayta (a kind of gentian), Suśr. **-tiktaka**, m. id., ib. **-vallabha**, n. a kind of sandal-wood, Gal. **Kirātârjunīya**, n., N. of a poem by Bhāravi (describing the combat of Arjuna with the god Śiva in the form of a wild mountaineer or Kirāta; this combat and its result is described in the MBh. iii, 1538–1664). **Kirātâśin**, m. 'swallowing the Kirātas,' N. of Vishṇu's bird Garuḍa, L.

Kirātaka, *as*, m. ifc. a man of the mountain-tribe of the Kirātas; Agathotes Chirayta, L.

Kirāti, *is*, f. (= *kirātī*), N. of Gaṅgā, L.

Kirātinī, f. Indian spikenard (Nardostachys Jaṭāmāṇsi), L.

किरि *kiri*, *kiriká*. See *kir*.

किरिट *kiriṭa*. See *áti-kir°*.

Kiriṭi, *i*, n. the fruit of the marshy date tree (Phœnix paludosa), L.

किरिश *kiriśa*, *as*, m. the ancestor of Kairiśi, q. v.

किरीट *kirīṭa*, mfn., see *ati-kir°*; (*am*), n. [*as*, m., gaṇa *ardharcâdi*], a diadem, crest, any ornament used as a crown, tiara, MBh.; R. &c.; N. of a metre of four lines (each containing twenty-four syllables); (*as*), m. (= *kirāṭa*) a merchant, BhP. xii, 3, 35; (*ī*), f. Andropogon aciculatus, L. **-dhāraṇa**, n. wearing a diadem, assuming the crown. **-dhārin**, mfn. crowned, having a tiara; (*ī*), m. a king. **-bhṛit**, m. 'wearing a diadem,' N. of Arjuna, MBh. xiv, 2436. **-mālin**, m. ornamented with a diadem, Hariv. 13018; N. of Arjuna, MBh.; BhP.

Kirīṭin, mfn. decorated with a diadem, MBh. &c.; (*ī*), m., N. of Indra, MBh. i, 1525; xiii, 765; of Arjuna, MBh.; Bhag.; Pañcat.; of Nara [according to the Comm.], MBh. i; of an attendant of Skanda, MBh. ix, 2573; of an attendant of Śiva, Comm. on Kum. vii, 95.

किरोडाट्य *kiroḍāṭya*, Nom. P. *°ṭyati*, to cheat, gaṇa *kaṇḍv-ādi*.

किर्बिर *kirbira*, mfn. variegated, Gal.

Kirmirá, mfn. id., VS. xxx, 21; (cf. *karbara*.)

Kirmīra, mfn. id., Hcar.; (*as*), m. a variegated colour, L.; the orange tree, L.; N. of a Rākshasa conquered by Bhīma-sena, MBh. iii, 368 ff. **-jit**, m. 'conquering the Rākshasa Kirmīra,' N. of Bhīma-sena, L. **-tvac**, m. 'having a variegated rind,' the orange tree, L. **-nishūdana**, **-bhid**, m. = *-jit*, L. **-sūdana**, m. id., Gal. **Kirmīrâri**, m. 'the enemy of Kirmīra,' N. of Bhīma-sena, L.

Kirmīrita, mfn. 'variegated,' mingled with (in comp.), Naish. vi, 97; variegated, spotted, Prab.

किर्मी *kirmī*, f. a hall, L.; an image of gold or iron, L.; (= *karmin*) the Palāśa tree (Butea frondosa), L.

किर्मीर *kirmīra*. See *kirbira*.

किर्याणी *kiryāṇī*. See *kir*.

किल् *kil*, cl. 6. P. *kilati*, to be or become white (or 'to freeze'), Dhātup. xxviii, 61; to play, ib.: cl. 10. P. *kelayati*, to send, throw, Dhātup. xxxii, 64.

1. **Kila**, *as*, m. play, trifling, L. **-kiñcita**, n. amorous agitation (such as weeping, laughing, being angry, merry, &c. in the society of a lover), Sāh.; Daśar. ii, 30 & 37.

किल 2. *kíla*, ind. (a particle of asseveration or emphasis) indeed, verily, assuredly, RV.; AV. &c.; (or of explanation) namely, ŚBr. &c.; 'so said,' 'so reported,' pretendedly, VarBṛS.; Kād.; (*kila* is preceded by the word on which it lays stress, and occurs very rarely at the beginning of a sentence or verse [R. iv, 14, 14; Pañcat. lxxxix, 4]; according to native lexicographers *kila* may be used in communicating intelligence, and may imply 'probably,' 'possibly,' 'agreement,' 'dislike,' 'falsehood,' 'inaccuracy,' and 'reason.')

किल 3. *kila*, *as*, m., N. of a man, Pravar.

किलकिल *kilakila*, *as*, m., N. of Śiva, MBh. xii, 10365; (*ās*), m. pl., N. of a Yavana tribe, VP.; (cf. *kilikila*); (*ā*), f. (an onomatopoetic word), sounds or cries expressing joy, or the expression of joy by any sound or cry, MBh.; R.; Mcar.; Bālar.

Kilakilāya, Nom. P. Ā. *°yati*, *°yate*, to raise sounds expressing joy, Bhaṭṭ. vii, 102; Kāraṇḍ.; to cry, give a shriek, Kāraṇḍ.

Kilikilaya, Nom. P. *°yati*, to raise sounds expressing joy, Bālar.

Kilikilāya, Nom. Ā. *°yate*, id., Hcar.

Kilikilita, *am*, n. sounds expressing joy, Bālar.

किलञ्ज *kilañja*, *as*, m. (= *kiliñja*) a mat, Comm. on KātyŚr.

किलाट *kilāṭa*, *as*, m. inspissated milk, Hariv. (v. l. *kilāda*); Suśr.; Bhpr.; (*ī*), f. id., L.

Kilāṭin, *ī*, m. 'having white juice like *kilāṭa* milk,' a bamboo, L.

किलात *kilāta*, *as*, m. (= *kír°*) a dwarf, L.; (gaṇa *bidâdi*), 'N. of an Asura priest,' only in comp. **Kilātâkulī**, m. du. the two Asura priests Kilāta and Ākuli, ŚBr. i, 1, 4, 14 (v. l. *kirāta-kulyau*, f. du., TāṇḍyaBr.)

किलास *kilā́sa*, mfn. leprous, VS. xxx, 21; Kāṭh.; TāṇḍyaBr.; (*ī́*), f. a kind of spotted deer (described as the vehicle of the Maruts), RV. v, 53, 1; (*am*), n. a white leprous spot, AV. i, 23, 1 & 2; 24, 2; (in med.) a species of leprosy (resembling the so-called white leprosy in which the skin becomes spotted without producing ulcers), KātyŚr.; Suśr. **-ghna**, m. 'removing leprosy,' a sort of gourd (Momordica Mixta), L. **-tva**, n. the state of being leprous, TāṇḍyaBr. **-nā́śana**, mfn. removing leprosy, AV. i, 24, 2. **-bheshajá**, n. a remedy against leprosy, ib. **-maya**, mfn. scabby (as a dog), Kauś. 13.

Kilāsin, mfn. leprous, ŚāṅkhBr.; Gaut.; Pāṇ. v, 2, 128, Kāś.

किलिकिल *kilikila*, *ās*, m. pl., N. of a people, VP.; (*ā*), f., N. of a town, BhP. xii, 1, 30; (= *°lak°*) cries expressing joy, Divyâv.

किलिकिलय *kilikilaya*, &c. See *kilakila*.

किलिञ्च *kiliñca*, *as*, m. a thin plank, board, L.; (= *vaṇśa*) a bamboo, L.

Kiliñcana, *as*, m. a sort of fish, Npr.

Kiliñja, *as*, m. a thin plank of green wood, L.; a mat, Suśr. **-hastin**, m. an elephant formed by mats, Sāh.

Kiliñjaka, *as*, m. a mat, L.

किलिम *kilima*. *am*, n. a kind of pine (Pinus Deodar, cf. *deva-dāru*), Car.; (*as*), m. id., L.

किल्किन् *kilkin*, *ī*, m. (= *kindhin*) a horse, L.

किल्बिष *kílbisha*, *am*, n. (ifc. f. *ā*) fault, offence, sin, guilt, RV. v, 34, 4; AV.; VS. &c. (once *as*, m., BhP. iii, 28, 11); injustice, injury, MBh. i, 882; disease, L. **-spṛít**, mfn. removing or avoiding sins, RV. x, 71, 10; AitBr. i, 13.

Kilbishin, mfn. one who commits an offence, wicked, culpable, sinful, Mn.; MBh. &c. (often ifc., e. g. *artha-k°*, q. v., *rāja-k°*, who as a king commits an offence, MBh. i, 1703).

किल्विन् *kilvin*, *ī*, m. (= *°lkin*) a horse, L.

किशर *kiśara*, *as*, m. a fragrant article for sale, Pāṇ. iv, 4, 53 (v. l. *kisara*); (*ā*), f., gaṇa *madhv-ādi*. **Kiśarâdi**, a Gaṇa of Pāṇ. (iv, 4, 53; Gaṇar. 387). **Kiśarā-vat**, mfn., gaṇa *madhv-ādi*.

Kiśarika, *as*, *ī*, m. f. selling Kiśara, Pāṇ. iv, 4, 53.

किशल *kiśala*, v. l. for *kisala*, L.

किशोर *kiśorá*, *as*, m. a colt, AV. xii, 4, 7; Hariv.; R.; a youth, lad, BhP.; the sun, L.; Benjamin or Styrax Benzoin (= *taila-parṇy-oshadhi*), L.; N. of a Dānava, Hariv.; (*ī*), f. (Pāṇ. vi, 1, 107, Pat.) a female colt, R.; a maiden, BhP.

Kiśoraka, *as*, m. a colt, L.; the young of any animal, Daś.; Kād.; Prasannar.; Kathās.; (*ikā*), f. 'a female colt' or 'a maiden,' gaṇa *śubhrâdi*.

किष्क् *kishk*, cl. 10. Ā. *°shkayate*, to injure, kill, Dhātup. xxxiii, 12.

Kishkin. See *śva-kishkin*.

किष्किन्ध *kishkindha*, *as*, m., N. of a mountain (in the south of India, in Oḍra, containing a cave, the residence of the monkey-prince Vālin who was slain by Rāma; the territory which is said to be in the northern part of Mysore, near the sources of the Pampā river, was transferred after the conquest by Rāma to Su-grīva, brother of Vālin and rightful king), VarBṛS.; (*ās*), m. pl., 'N. of a people,' see *-gandika*; (*ā*), f. (gaṇas *pāraskarâdi* and *sindhv-ādi*), N. of the cave contained in the mountain Kishkindha (the city of Vālin and Su-grīva), MBh.; R.; N. of the mountain Kishkindha. **-gandika**, n. (v. l. *°ndhika*), Pāṇ. ii, 4, 10, Pat. **Kishkindhā-kāṇḍa**, n., N. of the fourth book of the Rāmāyaṇa. **Kishkindhâdhipa**, m. 'the ruler of Kishkindha,' N. of Vālin, L.

Kishkindhaka, *ās*, m. pl., N. of a people, Hariv. 784.

Kishkindhya, *as*, m. incorrect reading for *°ndha*; (*ā*), f. likewise for *°ndhā*.

किष्किश *kishkiśa*, v. l. for *kikk°*.

किष्कु *kishku*, *us*, m. [f., L.] the fore-arm, R. v, 32, 11; the handle (of an axe), TāṇḍyaBr.; a kind of linear measure (= *hasta* or *kara* = twenty-four thumbs' breadths = $\frac{1}{400}$ of a Nalva), MBh. &c.; gaṇa *pāraskarâdi*; mfn. contemptible, bad, L. **-parvan**, m. a bamboo, L.; sugar-cane, L.; Arundo tibialis, L.

किस् *kís*, ind. (fr. 1. *ki*, cf. *nákis*, *mā́kis*), a particle of interrogation, 'whether' [= *kartṛi*, 'a doer,' Nir. vi, 34], RV. x, 52, 3.

किस *kisa*, *as*, m., N. of an attendant of the sun, L.

किसर *kisara*, &c. See *kiśara*.

किसल *kisala*, *as*, *am*, m. n. = 1. *kisalaya*, L.

1. **Kisalaya**, *am*, n. [*as*, m., L.] a sprout or shoot, the extremity of a branch bearing new leaves, Gaut.; R.; Śak. &c. **-karā**, f. (a woman) having hands as tender as buds, Gaṇar. 43, Comm.

2. **Kisalaya**, Nom. P. *°yati*, to cause to shoot or spring forth, Prasannar.

Kisalayita, mfn. (gaṇa *tārakâdi*) furnished with leaf-buds or young shoots, Bhartṛ.; ŚārṅgP.

कीकट *kī́kaṭa*, *as*, m., N. of a son of Ṛishabha, BhP. v, 4, 10; of a son of Saṃkaṭa, BhP. vi, 6, 6; a horse (perhaps originally a horse of the Kīkaṭas), L.; (*ās*), m. pl., N. of a people not belonging to the Āryan race, RV. iii, 53, 14; BhP.; (mfn.), poor, L.; avaricious, L.

Kīkaṭaka, *as*, m. a horse, Npr.

Kīkaṭin, *ī*, m. a hog, Npr.

कीकस *kīkasa*, mfn. hard, firm, L.; (*as*), m. the breast-bone and the cartilages of the ribs connected with it (cartilagines costarum), ĀrshBr.; a kind of worm (= *kikkiśa*?), L.; (*kī́kasā*), f. Ved. vertebra or a rib (of which six are enumerated), RV. x, 163, 2; AV.; TS. &c.; (*am*), n. id., VS. xxv, 6; a bone, L.; (cf. *kaikasa*.) **-mukha**, m. 'having a mouth of bone,' a bird, L. **Kīkasâsthi**, n. vertebra, L. **Kīkasâsya**, m. = *kīkasa-mukha*, L.

कीकि *kīki*, *is*, m. (= *kiki*) the blue jay, L.

कीचक *kīcaka*, *as*, m. (√*cīk*, Uṇ. v, 36) a hollow bamboo (whistling or rattling in the wind, Arundo Karka), MBh.; R. &c.; N. of a chief of the army of king Virāṭa (conquered by Bhīma-sena), MBh. i, 328; iv, 376 ff.; Pañcat.; N. of a Daitya, L.; of a Rākshasa, L.; (*ās*), m. pl., N. of a people (a tribe of the Kekayas), MBh. **-jit**, m. 'conquering Kīcaka,' Bhīma-sena, L. **-nishūdana**, m. id., L. **-bhid**, m. id., L. **-vadha**, m. 'the killing of Kīcaka,' N. of a poem. **-sūdana**, m. = *-jit*, Gal.

कीज *kī́ja*, *as*, m. a kind of instrument ['spur,' Gmn.], RV. viii, 66, 3.

कीट् *kīṭ*, cl. 10. P. *kīṭayati*, to tinge or colour, Dhātup. xxxii, 98; to bind, ib.

कीट *kīṭa*, *as*, m. (ifc. f. *ā*, Hcat.) a worm, insect, ŚBr. xiv; ĀśvŚr. &c.; the scorpion in the zodiac, VarBṛS.; (ifc.) an expression of contempt (cf. *śūra-k°*), Mcar.; (*ī*), f. a worm, insect, L.; (*am*), n. id., L.; (= *kiṭṭa*) feces, L. **-gardabhaka**, m., N. of a particular insect, Suśr. **-ghna**, m. 'killing insects,' sulphur, L. **-ja**, n. 'coming from insects,' silk, Mn. xi, 168; MBh. ii, 1847; (*ā*), f. an animal dye of red colour, lac, L. **-nāman**, the plant Cissus pedata, Npr. **-pakshôdgama**, m. the change from chrysalis or pupa to butterfly, W. **-pakshôdbhava**, m. id., W. **-pataṃgá**, *ās*, m. pl. Kīṭa worms and pilsers, ŚBr. xiv. **-pādikā**, f. = *-nāman*, L. **-maṇi**, m. a glow-worm, ŚārṅgP. **-mātṛi**, f. a female bee, Gal.; the plant Cissus pedata, Bhpr. **-mārī**, f. = *-nāman*, L. **-yoni**, f. (= *-mātṛi*) a female bee, Gal. **-śatru**,

m. 'enemy of worms,' the plant Embelia Ribes, Suśr. **Kīṭāri,** m. id., ib.; sulphur, Gal. **Kīṭâvapanna,** mfn. anything on which an insect has fallen, Kapishṭh.; MānŚr.; (cf. *keśa-kīṭâvapatita.*) **Kīṭôt-kara,** m. an ant-hill, Kathās. ci, 290.

Kīṭaka, *as,* m. a worm, insect, R.; BhP.; MārkP.; a kind of bard, panegyrist (descended from a Kshatriya father and Vaiśya mother), L.; N. of a prince, MBh. i, 2696; (mfn.), hard, harsh, L.

कीडेर *kīḍera, as,* m. the plant Amaranthus polygonoides, L.

कीदृक्ष *kīdṛiksha,* mf(*ī*, Gr.)n. (fr. 1. *ki* or *kid* and *dṛiksha,* √*dṛiś,* cf. *īdṛiksha*), of what kind? of what description? of what qualities?

Kīdṛig (in comp. for *kīdṛiś*). **–ākāra,** mfn. of what appearance? Pañcad. **–rūpa,** mfn. of what shape? MBh. xiii, 4086. **–varṇa,** mfn. of what colour? ib. **–vyāpāra-vat,** mfn. of what occupation? Hit.

Kīdṛiś, mfn. (Pāṇ. vi, 3, 90) of what kind? who or what like? RV. x, 108, 3; MBh.; Pañcat. &c.; *yādṛik-kīdṛik-ca,* of whatsoever kind, Comm. on KātyŚr.

Kīdṛiśa, mf(*ī*, Gr.)n. (Pāṇ. vi, 3, 90) of what kind? what like? MBh.; Pañcat. &c.; of what use? i. e. useless, Bhartṛ.

कीन *kīna, am,* n. flesh, L.; (cf. *kīra.*) .

कीनार *kīnāra, as,* m. (perhaps =*kīnāśa*) a cultivator of the soil ['a vile man,' Sāy.], RV. x, 106, 10.

Kīnāśa, *as,* m. (√*kliś,* Uṇ. v, 56) a cultivator of the soil, RV. iv, 57, 8; VS. xxx, 11; AV. &c.; niggard, MBh.; Daś.; BhP.; Kathās.; N. of Yama, Naish. vi, 75; Bālar.; (= *kīśa*) a kind of monkey, L.; a kind of Rākshasa, L.; (mfn.), killing animals (or 'killing secretly'), L.

कीम् *kīm,* ind. See *ā́-kīm, mā́-kīm.*

कीर *kīra, as,* m. a parrot, Vet. &c.; (*ās*), m. pl., N. of the people and of the country of Kaśmīr, VarBṛS.; Mudr.; (*am*), n. flesh, L. **–varṇaka,** n. a kind of perfume (= *sthauṇeyaka*), L. **Kīrêshṭa,** m. the tree Mangifera indica, L.; the walnut tree, L.; another plant (= *jala-madhūka*), L. **Kīrôdbhūta,** mfn. coming from the Kīra country (as a horse), Gal.

Kīraka, *as,* m. a kind of tree, L.; gaining, obtaining (*prâpaṇa*), L.; a Jain ascetic (*kshapaṇaka*), L.

कीरि *kīrí, is,* m. (√2. *kṛī*) a praiser, poet, RV. **–códana,** mfn. exciting the praiser, RV. vi, 45, 19.

Kīrín, mfn. praising, RV. v, 4, 10 & 40, 8; (*ī́*), m. a praiser, RV. i, 100, 9; v, 52, 12.

कीरेष्ट *kīrêshṭa,* &c. See *kīra.*

कीर्ण 1. *kīrṇa,* mfn. (√1. *kṛī*) scattered, thrown, cast, R. &c.; filled with, full of (instr.), ib.; covered, hidden, Śak.; Pañcat. &c.; stopped up (as the ears), Rājat. iv, 34; given (= *datta*), L. **–pushpa,** m. 'having scattered blossoms,' N. of a creeper, L.

Kīrṇi, *is,* f. scattering, throwing, Pāṇ. viii, 2, 44, Vārtt. 2; covering, concealing, ib.

Kīrya. See *uda-k°.*

Kīryamāṇa, mfn. (pr. p. Pass.) being covered or strewed, MBh. &c.; being scattered or thrown.

Kīrvi, mfn. = *kīrṇi,* Vop. xxvi, 167.

कीर्ण 2. *kīrṇa,* mfn. (√2. *kṛī*) injured, hurt, L.

कीर्त *kīrt,* cl. 10. P. *kīrtáyati* (rarely Ā. °*yate*), aor. *acīkīrtat* or *acīkṛitat* (Pāṇ. vii, 4, 7, Kāś.), to mention, make mention of, tell, name, call, recite, repeat, relate, declare, communicate, commemorate, celebrate, praise, glorify (with gen., AV.; TS.; ŚBr.; AitBr.; with acc., ŚBr.; AitBr.; ĀśvGṛ.; Mn. &c.)

Kīrtana, *am,* n. mentioning, repeating, saying, telling, MBh.; Pañcat. &c.; (*ā*), f. id., Suśr.; fame, L.

Kīrtanīya, mfn. to be mentioned or named or celebrated, MBh.; Ragh.

Kīrtanya, mfn. deserving to be mentioned or related, BhP.

Kīrtayat, mfn. (pr. p.) mentioning, relating, &c.

Kīrti, *is,* f. (Pāṇ. iii, 3, 97; fr. √2. *kṛī*) mention, making mention of, speech, report, RV. x, 54, 1; AV.; ŚBr. &c.; good report, fame, renown, glory, AV.; ŚBr.; TUp.; Mn. &c.; Fame (personified as daughter of Daksha and wife of Dharma), MBh.; Hariv.; VP.; (in music) a particular measure or time; extension, expansion, L.; lustre, L.; = *prasāda* (favour) or *prāsāda* (a palace), L.; (fr. √1. *kṛī*), dirt, L.; N. of one of the Mātṛikās (or personified divine energies of Kṛishṇa), L.; (*is*), m., N. of a son of Dharma-netra, VP. **–kara,** mf(*ī*)n. conferring fame, Hit. **–dhara,** m., N. of an author. **–pratāpa-bala-sahita,** mfn. attended with or possessed of fame and majesty and power. **–bhāj,** m. 'receiving fame, famous,' N. of Droṇâcārya (military preceptor of the Pāṇḍus and Kurus), L. **–mat,** mfn. praised, famous, ChUp.; R. &c.; (*ān*), m., N. of one of the Viśve Devās, MBh. xiii, 4356; of a son of Uttāna-pāda and Sūnṛitā, Hariv. 62; of a son of Vasu-deva and Devakī, Bh. ix, 24, 53; VP.; of a son of Aṅgiras, VP.; (*atī*), f., N. of Dākshāyaṇī, MatsyaP. **–maya,** mf(*ī*)n. consisting of fame, R.; BhP. **–mālinī,** f. 'garlanded with fame,' N. of a woman, SkandaP. **–yuta,** mfn. famous, Hit. **–ratha,** m., N. of a prince of the Videhas (son of Pratīndhaka; also called Kṛitti ratha, son of Prasiddhaka), R. i, 71, 9 & 10. **–rāja,** *ās,* m. pl., N. of certain Ṛishis. **–rāta,** m., N. of a prince of the Videhas (son of Mahândhraka; also called Kṛiti-rāta, son of Andhaka), R. i, 71, 11 & 12. **–varman,** m., N. of a prince, Prab. **–vāsa,** m., N. of an author; of an Asura, SkandaP. **–śesha,** m. 'the leaving behind of nothing but fame,' death, L.; (cf. *ālekhya-ś°, nāma-ś°, yaśaḥ-ś°.*) **–sāra,** m., N. of a man, Daś. **–siṇha-deva,** m., N. of a man. **–sena,** m., N. of a nephew of the serpent-king Vāsuki, Kathās. vi, 13. **–soma,** m., N. of a man, Kathās. lxi, 300. **–stambha,** m. a column of fame, Bālar.

Kīrtita, mfn. said, mentioned, asserted; celebrated; known, notorious.

Kīrtitavya, mfn. to be praised, BhP. i, 2, 14.

Kīrtényа, mfn. deserving to be named or praised, RV. i, 103, 4 & 116, 6.

Kīrtti, *is,* f. incorrectly for *kīrti.*

Kīrtya, mfn. (Pāṇ. iii, 1, 110, Kāś.) 'to be recited,' see *divā-k°.*

कीर्मि *kīrmi,* f. a house for straw (?), W.

कीर्य *kīrya,* mfn. See *uda-k°.*

Kīryamāṇa, kīrvi. See 1. *kīrṇa.*

कीर्शा *kīrśā,* f. a species of bird, TS. v.

कील् *kīl,* cl. 1. *kīlati,* to bind, fasten, stake, pin, Dhātup. xv, 17.

Kīla, *as,* m. (ifc. f. *ā*), a sharp piece of wood, stake, pin, peg, bolt, wedge, &c., MBh. &c.; a post, post in a cow-house to which cows are fastened, pillar, L.; a gnomon, L.; handle, brace, Suśr.; the elbow, VP.; a kind of tumour (having the form of a stake), Suśr.; a position of the fœtus impeding delivery, Suśr.; N. of the inner syllables of a Mantra, RāmatUp.; N. of Vita-rāga Maheśa (= *kīleśvara*); = *bandha,* Comm. on VS. ii, 34; a weapon, L.; flame, lambent flame, L.; a minute particle, L.; a blow with the elbow (= *kīlā*), L.; (*ā*), f. a stake, pin, L.; the elbow, L.; a weapon, L.; flame, L.; a minute particle, L.; a blow with the elbow (or 'a blow in copulation'), Vātsyāy.; (*am*), n. (= *kīna*), flesh, Gal. **–pādikā,** f., v. l. for *kīṭa-p°,* L. **–saṃsparśa,** m., N. of the plant Diospyros glutinosa (commonly called Gāva, a plant the fruit of which yields a substance like turpentine used to cover the bottom of boats), L. **Kīlêśvara,** m., N. of Vita-rāga Maheśa.

Kīlaka, *as,* m. a pin, bolt, wedge, Pañcat.; Hit.; a splint (for confining a broken bone), Suśr.; a kind of tumour (having the form of a pin), L.; (= *śivaka*) a kind of pillar for cows &c. to rub themselves against, or one to which they are tied, L.; N. of the forty-second year of the sixty years' cycle of Jupiter, VarBṛS.; (*ās*), m. pl., N. of certain Ketus, ib.; (*ikā*), f. a pin, bolt, Pañcat.; Hcat.; (*am*), n., N. of the inner syllables of a Mantra. **–vivaraṇa,** n., N. of a work.

Kīlana, *am,* n. fastening, staking.

Kīlanīya, mfn. to be fastened or staked.

Kīlita, mfn. staked, impaled; set up as a stake or pole, Kād.; pinned, fastened by a stake, &c.; bound, tied, confined, Mālatīm.; Kathās.; (*as*), m., N. of a Mantra, Sarvad.

कीलाल *kīlā́la, as,* m. a sweet beverage (also a heavenly drink similar to Amṛita, the food of the gods), AV.; VS.; Kauś.; (*ám*), n. id., Naigh. ii, 7; blood, Prab.; water, L. **–ja,** n. flesh, MBh. iii, 15341. **–dhi,** m. 'receptacle of water,' the ocean, L. **–pa,** mfn. drinking blood, MBh. iii, 13241; (*as*), m. a Rākshasa (sort of goblin), L. **–pá,** mfn. (Pāṇ. iii, 2, 74, Kāś.) drinking the beverage *kīlāla* (N. of Agni), RV. x, 91, 14. **–peśas** (*kī́l°*), mfn. ornamented with the beverage *kīlā́la,* MaitrS. **Kīlālôdhan,** mfn., f. °*dhnī,* (a cow) who carries the beverage *kīlā́la* in her udder, AV. xii, 1, 59. **Kīlālaûshadhi,** f. a kind of herb used to prepare the beverage *kīlā́la,* Āp.

Kīlālin, *ī,* m. a lizard, chameleon, Npr.

कीलित *kīlita.* See √*kīl.*

कीवत् *kī́vat,* mfn. (fr. 1. *ki*; cf. *kíyat*), only in the expression *ā́ kī́vatas,* how long? how far? RV. iii, 30, 17 (Nir. vi, 3).

कीश *kīśa,* mfn. naked, L.; (*as*), m. an ape, BhP.; Pañcat.; (cf. *ambu-k°*); a bird, L.; the sun, L. **–parṇa,** m. the tree Achyranthes aspera (= *apā́mārgá*), L.; (*ī*), f. id., L.; (cf. *keśa-p°.*)

कीश्मील *kiśmīla, as,* m., N. of a disease, AV.Paipp. xix, 8, 4.

कीस्त *kīstá, as,* m. (=*kīrí*) a praiser, poet RV. i, 127, 7; vi, 67, 10.

कु 1. *ku,* a pronom. base appearing in *kú-tas, kútra, kuvíd, kúha, kvà,* and as a prefix implying deterioration, depreciation, deficiency, want, littleness, hindrance, reproach, contempt, guilt; originally perhaps *ku* signified 'how (strange!);' as a separate word *ku* occurs only in the lengthened form 3. *kū́,* q. v. **–kathā,** f. a bad or miserable tale, BhP. iii, 15, 23. **–kanyakā,** f. a bad girl, Kathās. xxvi, 58. **–kara,** mfn. having a crooked or withered hand, L. **–karman,** n. a wicked deed, Pañcat.; (ifc.) Rājat.; (mfn.), performing evil actions, wicked, BhP. i, 16, 22; (*kukarma*)-*kārin,* mfn. wicked, depraved. **–kalatra,** n. a bad wife, ŚārṅgP. **–kavi,** m. a bad poet, poetaster. **–kārya,** n. a bad action, wickedness. **–kāvya,** n. a bad poem, Śāntiś. **–kīrti,** f. ill-repute. **–kuṭumbinī,** f. a bad house-wife, Kathās. xxiii, 27. **–kuṇḍaka,** n. the fruit of Chattrāka. **–ku-dru,** n. Blumea lacera, Npr. **–ku-vāc,** m. 'having a very disagreeable voice,' jackal, Npr. **–kṛita,** mfn. badly made, VarBṛS.; one who has acted badly, Divyâv. **–kṛitya,** n. an evil deed, wickedness, Pañcat.; Hit. **–kriyā,** f. a bad action; (°*ya*), mfn. wicked. **–khāṭi,** f. (= *asad-graha*) wantonness, Comm. on Uṇ. iv, 124. **–khyāti,** f. evil report, infamy; bad reputation. **–gaṇin,** mfn. belonging to an evil set of people, Lalit. **–gati,** f. 'wrong path,' deviation from the path of righteousness, Buddh. **–gehinī,** f. = *-kuṭumbinī,* Kathās. **–go,** m. a miserable or weak bull, R. vi, 112, 6. **–graha,** m. an unpropitious planet (five are reckoned, viz. Maṅgala, Ravi, Śani, Rāhu, and Ketu), Subh. **–grāma,** m. a petty village (without a Rājā, an Agnihotrin, a physician, a rich man, or a river), **–caṇḍikā,** f. the plant Aletris hyacinthoides (= *mūrvā*), L. **–candana,** n. red sanders (Pterocarpus santalinus), Suśr.; sappan or log-wood (Cæsalpina Sappan, cf. *pattrâṅga*), W.; a leguminous plant (Adenanthera pavonina), W.; saffron, L. **–cará,** mfn. roaming about, RV. i, 154, 2; x, 180, 2; TBr. iii; following evil practices, wicked, MBh. xiv, 1070ff.; speaking ill of any one, detracting, L.; (*as*), m. a wicked man, Gaut. **–caritra,** n. evil conduct, VarBṛ. **–caryā,** f. id., Mn. ix, 17. **–cāṅgerī,** f. a kind of wood sorrel (Rumex vesicarius, = *cukrikā*), L. **–cīrā,** f., N. of a river (v. l. *ku-vīrā,* VP.), MBh. vi, 334. **–cela,** n. a bad garment, Mn. vi, 44; rag, Car.; (mfn.), badly clothed, dressed in dirty or tattered garments, MBh. v, 1132; (*ā*), f., N. of a plant (= *avi-karṇī* or *viddha-parṇī*), L.; (*ī*), f. the plant Clypea hernandifolia (or accord. to Haughton 'Cissampelos hexandra'), L. **–ceshṭā,** f. a wicked contrivance. **–caila,** mf(*ā*)n. badly clothed, BhP. x, 80, 7. **–cailin,** mfn. id. **–codya,** n. an unsuitable question. **–jana,** m. a bad or wicked man, BhP.; vulgar people. **–jananī,** f. a bad mother, R. vi, 82, 118. **–1.-janman,** mfn. of inferior origin, BhP.; (*ā*), m. a low-born man, slave. **–jambha,** m., N. of a Daitya (younger brother of Jambha and son of Prahlāda or Prahrāda, a son of Hiraṇya-kaśipu), Hariv. **–jīvikā,** f. a miserable kind of living, MBh. v, 2698. **–jñāna,** n. imperfect or defective knowledge. **–tanaya,** m. a degenerate son, Pañcat. **—tanu,** m. 'deformed,' N. of Kubera (this deity being of a monstrous appearance, having three legs and but eight teeth), L. **—tantrī,** f. tail, MBh. xii, 5355 & 5363. **—tapa,** mfn. slightly hot, W.; (*as, am*), m. n. (gaṇa *ardharcâdi*) a sort of blanket (made of the hair of the mountain goat), Gaut.; Mn.; Yājñ.; VarBṛS.; (*as*), m. the Kuśa grass (Poa cynosuroides), Hcat.; the eighth Muhūrta or portion of the day from the last Daṇḍa of the second watch to the first of the third or about noon (an eligible time for the performance of sacrifices to the Manes), MBh. xiii, 6040; MatsyaP.; grain, L.; a daughter's son, L.; a sister's son, L.; a twice-born man (one of the first three classes), L.; a Brāhman, L.; a guest, L.; the sun, L.; fire, L.; an ox, L.; a kind of musical instrument, L.; *-saptaka*, n. a Śrāddha in which seven constituents occur (viz. noon, a horn platter, a Nepāl blanket, silver, sacrificial grass, Sesamum, and kine), W.; *-sauśruta*, m., N. of a man, gaṇa *pārthivâdi*. **—tapasvin,** m. a wicked or bad ascetic, Pañcat. **—tarka,** m. fallacious argument, sophistry, BhP.; MārkP.; a bad logician, KapS. vi, 34; *-patha*, m. 'the way of sophists,' a sophistical method of arguing, Rājat. v, 378. **—tāpasa,** m. a wicked ascetic, Kathās.; (*ī*), f. a wicked female ascetic, ib. **—tārkika,** m. a bad logician. **—tittiri,** m. a species of bird resembling the partridge, Suśr. **—tīrtha,** m. a bad teacher. **—tumbuka,** m. a kind of pot-herb, Car. **—tumburu,** n. a bad fruit of the plant Diospyros embryopteris, Pāṇ. vi, 1, 143, Kāś. **—tṛiṇa,** n. water houseleek (Pistia Stratiotes), L. **—daṇḍa,** m. unjust punishment, L. **—darśana,** n. a heterodox doctrine. **—1. -dāra,** mfn. having a bad wife, VarBṛ.; *-dāra, ās*, m. pl. a wife who is a bad wife, Suśr. **—1. -dina,** n. an evil day; a rainy day. **—dishṭi,** f. a measure of length (longer than a Dishṭi, shorter than a Vitasti), Kauś. 85. **—dṛiśya,** mfn. ill-favoured, ugly. **—dṛishṭa,** mfn. seen wrongly or indistinctly, Pañcat. **—dṛishṭi,** mfn. having bad eyes; (*is*), f. weak sight; a heterodox philosophical doctrine (as that of the Sāṃkhyas, &c.), Mn. xii, 95; Kād. **—dṛishṭin,** mfn. one who has adopted a heterodox doctrine, Kād. **—deśa,** m. a bad country (where it is difficult to obtain the necessaries of life), Kathās. &c.; a country subject to oppression. **—deha,** m. a miserable body, BhP. v, 12, 2. **—dravya,** n. bad riches. **—dvāra,** n. backdoor, Gaut. **—dharma,** m. a bad practice. **—dharman,** n. bad or no justice, MBh. iii, 10571. **—dhānya,** n. an inferior kind of grain, Suśr. **—dhī,** mfn. foolish; (*īs*), m. a fool, Pañcat.; BhP. **—nakha,** mfn. having ugly nails or claws, VarBṛS.; (*am*), n. a disease of the nails, Suśr. **—nakhin,** mfn. having bad or diseased nails, AV.; TS.; Kāṭh. &c.; (*ī*), m., N. of a man; of a work belonging to the AV. **—naṭa,** m. a sort of trumpet flower (Bignonia, *śyonāka*), L.; (*ās*), m. pl., N. of a people, VarBṛS. (v. l. *kunatha*); (*ī*), f. a kind of coriander (Coriandrum sativum), L.; red arsenic, Bhpr. **—nadikā,** f. a small river, MBh. v, 4502; Pañcat. **—nadī,** f. id. **—nannamá,** mfn. (√*nam*) inflexible, RV. x, 136, 7. **—naraka,** m. a bad hell. **—narêndra,** m. a bad king, Subh. **—nalin,** m. the plant Agati grandiflora, L. **—nātha,** m. a bad protector, BhP. ix, 14, 28; (mfn.), having a bad leader, ib. v, 14, 2. **—nādīkā,** for *-nadikā*. **—nāman,** m. 'having a bad name,' N. of a man, gaṇas *bāhv-ādi* & *kāśy-ādi*; (*a*), n. a bad name, ill repute. **—nāyaka,** mfn. having a bad leader, BhP. v, 13, 2. **—nārī,** f. a bad woman, VarBṛ. **—nāśaka,** m. the plant Alhagi Maurorum, L. **—nāsa,** m. 'ugly-nosed,' a camel, Npr. **—nishañja,** m., N. of a son of the tenth Manu, Hariv. 474. **—nīta,** m. bad leading, Mudr. **—nīti,** f. ill conduct, W.; corrupt administration, W.; a low state of morals, W. **—nīlī,** f., N. of a shrub. **—nṛipa,** m. a bad prince, VarBṛS. **—nṛipati,** m. id., Veṇīs. **—netraka,** m., N. of a Muni, VāyuP. **—paṅka,** m. a slough, heap of filth and mud. **—paṭa,** m. or n. a miserable garment, BhP. v, 9, 11; (*as*), m. 'covered with a miserable garment,' N. of a Dānava, MBh. i, 2534. **—paṭu,** mfn. stupid, Hcar. **—paṇḍita,** m. a bad scholar. **—1. -pati,** m. a bad husband, Kād.; a bad king, ib. **—patha,** m. a bad road, evil way, BhP.; bad conduct; heterodox doctrine; (mfn.), walking in a wrong road; (*as*), m., N. of an Asura or Dānava, MBh. i, 2664; Hariv.; (*ās*), m. pl., N. of a people, VP.; *-ga, -gāmin, -cara*, mfn. going in a wrong road, wicked. **—°pathya,** mfn. belonging to a bad way (lit. and fig.); unwholesome (as diet, regimen, &c.), improper. **—parijñāta,** mfn. badly understood, Pañcat. **—parîkshaka,** mfn. making a wrong estimate, not valuing rightly, Bhartṛ. **—parîkshita,** mfn. badly examined, Pañcat. **—pāka,** m. 'not digestive,' Strychnos nux vomica, L. **—pāṇi,** mfn. having a deformed or maimed hand, L. **—pātra,** n. an unfit recipient. **—pātraka,** n. a bad vessel, MBh. xii, 227, 15. **—piñjala,** m., N. of a man, gaṇa *śivâdi*. **—pitṛi,** m. a bad father, MārkP. **—pīlu,** m. a sort of ebony tree (= *kāraskara*), Bhpr.; = *-pāka*, L. **—putra,** m. (gaṇa *manojñâdi*) a bad or wicked son; a son of an inferior degree (as an adopted son, &c.), Mn. ix, 161; Pañcat. **—purusha,** m. a low or miserable man, Pāṇ. vi, 3, 106; MBh. &c.; a poltroon, MBh. v, 5493; (cf. *kā-pur°*); *-janitā*, f., N. of a metre (consisting of four lines of eleven syllables each). **—pūya,** mfn. inferior, low, contemptible, L.; (cf. *ka-p°*.) **—prabhu,** m. a bad lord, Kathās. lix, 69. **—prâvaraṇa,** mfn. wearing a bad mantle, L. **—prâvṛita,** mfn. badly dressed, R. i, 6, 8. **—priya,** mfn. disagreeable, contemptible, L. **—plava,** m. a weak or frail raft, Mn. ix, 161. **—bandha,** m. a disgraceful stigma, Yājñ. ii, 294; (cf. *aṅka-bandha*.) **—bandhu,** m. a bad relative. **—bāhula,** m. camel, L. **—bimba,** m. n. (?), L. **—buddhi,** mfn. having vile sentiments, Pañcat.; Hcat.; stupid, BhP.; (*is*), f. a wrong opinion. **—brahma, -brahman,** m. a degraded or contemptible Brāhman, Pāṇ. v, 4, 105. **—brāhmaṇa,** m. id., Pat. **—bhartṛi,** m. a bad husband, Kathās. cxx, 65. **—bhārya,** mfn. having a bad wife, BhP.; (*ā*), f. a bad wife, MārkP.; Kathās. **—bhikshu,** m. a bad mendicant, Kathās. **—bhukta,** n. bad food, Vet. **—bhukti,** f. id. **—bhūmi,** f. bad (i. e. barren) ground, VarBṛ. **—bhṛitya,** m. a bad servant, Pañcat. **—bhoga,** m. bad pleasure, Kathās. **—bhojana,** n. = *-bhukta*. **—bhojya,** n. id. **—bhrātṛi,** m. a bad brother, Kathās. **—mata,** n. a bad doctrine, Subh. **—mati,** f. vile sentiment; weak intellect, folly, Daś.; BhP.; (mfn.), of slow intellect, foolish, BhP. **—manas** (*kú-*), mfn. displeased, angry, MaitrS. iv, 2, 13. **—manîsha, shin,** mfn. of slow intellect, BhP. **—mantra,** m. a bad advice, BhP.; a bad charm, Kathās. **—mantrin,** m. a bad counsellor, BhP. **—mārga,** m. a bad way (lit. and fig.), Pañcat. &c. **—mitra,** n. a bad friend, ib. **—mukha,** m. a hog, L. **—mud,** mfn. unfriendly, L.; avaricious, L.; (see also s. v.) **—muda,** see s. v. **—mudvin,** mfn. unfriendly, BhP. x, 20, 47. **—muhūrta,** m. a fatal hour, Kathās. **—medhas,** mfn. of little intellect, BhP. **—meru,** m. the southern hemisphere or pole (region of the demons and Titans), W. **—modaka,** m., N. of Vishṇu, L.; (cf. *kaumodakī*.) **—yajvin,** m. a bad sacrificer, BhP. iv, 6, 50. **—yava** (*kú-*), mfn. causing a bad harvest (N. of a demon slain by Indra), RV.; (*as*), m., N. of another demon, RV. i, 103, 8 (& 104, 3); (*am*), n. a bad harvest (?), see *kú-y°*. **—yoga,** m. an inauspicious conjunction of planets or signs or periods, &c. **—yogin,** m. a bad Yogin, impostor, BhP. **—yoni,** f. a base womb, womb of a low woman, MārkP. **—rava,** mfn. having a bad voice, W.; (*as*), m. a kind of dove, L.; (*ī*), f. a species of pepper, L.; [see also s. v. *kuraba*, which is sometimes written *kurava*.] **—rasa,** mfn. having bad juice or flavour or essence, W.; (*as*), m. spirituous or vinous liquor, L.; (*ā*), f. a wild creeping plant (species of hieracium, = *go-jihvā*), L. **—rājan,** m. a bad king, Pañcat. **—rājya,** n. a bad dominion, Pāṇ. vi, 2, 130, Vārtt. **—rūpa,** mfn. ill-shaped, deformed, ugly, Pañcat.; Kathās.; *-tā*, f., *-tva*, n. ugliness. **—rūpin,** mfn. ill-shaped, ugly. **—rūpya,** n. 'bad silver,' tin, L. **—lakshaṇa,** mf(*ā*)n. having fatal marks on the body, Kathās. xci, 17 & 19. **—liṅga,** m. 'having bad marks, kind of mouse, Suśr.; the fork-tailed shrike, MBh. i, 2239; Suśr.; BhP.; a sparrow, Bhpr.; (*ā*), f. a kind of oak-apple, L.; N. of a town (or of a river), R. ii, 68, 16; (*ī*), f. the female of the fork-tailed shrike, BhP.; N. of a plant (= *karkaṭaśṛiṅgī*), L.; *kuliṅgâkshī*, f., N. of a plant (= *peṭikā, kuberâkshī*), L. **—liṅgaka,** m. a sparrow (v. l. *kuliṅkaka*), L.; N. of a bird of prey, Car. **—luñcá,** m. one who plucks out hairs, VS. xvi, 22. **—vakra,** mfn. slightly bent, ŚāṅkhBr. **—vaṅga,** n. (= *vaṅga*) lead, L. **—vaca,** mfn. using bad language, abusive, L. **—vajraka,** m. a stone resembling a diamond, L. **—vaṇij,** m. a bad merchant, Kathās. ci, 266. **—vada,** mfn. = *-vaca*, W. **—vadhū,** f. a bad wife, Kathās. xix, 39. **—vapus,** mfn. ill-shaped. **—vartman,** n. 'a bad road,' bad doctrine, MBh. iii, 10571 (ed. Bomb.); Sarvad. **—varsha,** m. a sudden and violent shower of rain, R. vi, 89, 15. **—vastra,** n. a bad garment, Subh. **—vākya,** n. injurious or censorious language, Pañcat. **—vāc,** f. id., BhP. iv, 3, 15. **—vāda,** mfn. detracting, censorious, L. **—vādika,** m. 'crying unpleasantly,' a charletan, quack, Kād. **—vikrama,** m. bravery exhibited in the wrong place, Naish. i, 132. **—vidambanā,** f. cheat or deceit of a very low kind, Sarvad. **—vivāha,** m. degrading or improper marriage, Mn. iii, 63. **—vīṇā,** f. the lute of the Cāṇḍālas, L. **—vṛitti,** f. bad living; *-kṛit*, m. the plant Cæsalpina Bonducella (= *pūtika*), L. **—vṛishala,** m. a bad Śūdra, Pat. **—veṇā,** f. (= *-veṇī*) a fish-basket, L.; N. of a river (v. l. *tuṅga-v°*), VP. **—veṇī,** f. a badly braided tress of hair, W.; a woman with her hair badly braided, W.; a fish-basket, L. **—vedhas,** m. bad fate, Kathās. lxx, 232. **—vaidya,** m. a bad physician, Suśr.; Subh. **—vyāpāra,** m. a bad occupation, HYog. **—śaṅku,** m., N. of a prince, VP. **—śara** (*kú-*), m. a kind of reed, RV. i, 191, 3. **—śarīra,** n. a bad body, BhP. v, 26, 17; (mfn.), ill-shaped, MārkP.; N. of a Muni, VāyuP.; *-bhṛit*, mfn. furnished with a body that is miserable in comparison with the soul, BhP. x, 87, 22. **—śālmalī,** f. the plant Andersonia Rohitaka, Npr. **—1. -śāsana,** n. a bad doctrine, heterodoxy. **—śiṅśapā,** f. a kind of Sisu tree (Dalbergia Sisu, = *kapila-śiṅśapā*), L. **—śimbi,** f., N. of a plant, Suśr. **—śimbī,** f. id., L. **—śishya,** m. a bad pupil, Kathās. **—śīla,** n. a bad character, Kathās. xxxii, 153. **—śruta,** mfn. indistinctly heard, Pancat.; ignorant in (in comp.), Bālar. lxxvi, 7; (*am*), n. a bad rumour, Vet. (= Subh.) **—śvabhra,** n. a small hole, L. **—shaṇḍa,** m., N. of a priest, TāṇḍyaBr.; Lāṭy. **—sakhī,** f. a bad female friend, Kathās. **—saṃgata,** n. a bad connection, MBh. v, 1362. **—saciva,** m. a bad minister, Mudr.; Rājat. **—sambandha,** m. a bad relation, MBh. xii, 5226 (= Hariv. 1160). **—sarit,** f. a shallow stream, Pañcat. **—sahâya,** m. a bad companion, L. **—sārathi,** m. a bad charioteer, BrahmaP.; MārkP. **—sṛiti,** f. a by-way, secret way, Āp.; evil conduct, wickedness; cheating, trickery, jugglery, Kathās.; (mfn.), going evil ways, wicked, BhP. viii, 23, 7. **—sauhṛida,** m. a bad friend. **—strī,** f. (gaṇa *yuvâdi*) a bad wife, VarBṛS.; Kathās. **—strī-ka,** mfn. having a bad wife, VarBṛ. **—sthāna,** n. a bad place. **—smaya,** Nom. Ā. *°yate*, to smile improperly, Dhātup. xxxiii, 37; to see mentally, guess, ib.; to perceive, imagine, ib. **—smayana,** n. smiling improperly, ib. **—smita,** n. a fart, Gal. **—svapna,** m. a bad dream, nightmare. **—svāmin,** m. a bad master, Pañcat. **—hārīta,** m., N. of a man, Pravar. **—huṃkāra,** m., N. of a particular noise, Viddh. **—hvāna,** n. a disagreeable noise, BhP. i, 14, 14. **Kûdara,** m. 'sprung from a bad womb,' the offspring of a Brāhman woman (by a Ṛishi) begotten during menstruation, BrahmavP. **Kū-manas,** see s. v.

कु 2. **ku,** *us*, f. the earth, Āryabh.; VarBṛS.; VarBṛ.; BhP. vi, 1, 42; the ground or base of a triangle or other plane figure, Comm. on Āryabh.; the number 'one.' **—kīla,** m. 'a pin or bolt of the earth,' mountain, L. **—ja,** m. 'born from the earth,' a tree, L.; 'the son of the earth,' N. of the planet Mars, VarBṛS.; of the Daitya Naraka (conquered by Kṛishṇa), BhP.; (*ā*), f. 'earth-daughter,' Durgā, L.; of Sītā, W.; (*am*), n. the horizon (= *kshiti-ja*); *-dina*, n. 'the day of Mars,' i. e. Tuesday, VarBṛS.; *-pa*, m. 'whose protector is Mars,' N. of the ancestor of Kaujapa. **—2. -janman,** m. (= *-ja*) the planet Mars. **—jyā,** f. = *kshiti-jyā*. **—2. -dina,** n. (= *kshiti-d°*) a civil day, Āryabh. **—dhara,** m. 'earth-supporter,' a mountain, L. **—dhra,** m. id., gaṇa *mūla-vibhujâdi*. **—nābhi,** m. 'having the earth for its navel,' the air, atmosphere, L.; the collective treasures of Kubera, L. **—2. -pati,** m. 'lord of the earth,' a king, VarBṛS.; Rājat. **—papa** or **-papi** or **-papī,** m. the sun, MBh. xiii, 93, 90. **—prada,** mfn. making gifts consisting in land, Comm. on Nir. ii, 7. **—bhṛit,** m. = *-dhara*; (hence) the number 'seven.' **—ruha,** m. 'growing from the earth,' a tree, L. **—valaya,** n. the orb, BhP. v, 16, 5 & 7; *kuvalayêśa*, m. 'ruler of the earth,' a king, Rājat. iv, 372. **—suta,** m. (= *-ja*) the planet Mars, Comm. on VarBṛ. **—sū,** m. 'earth-born,' an earth-worm, L.

कु 3. *ku*. See √1. *kū*.

कुंश् *kuṉś* or *kuṉs*, cl. 1. or 10. P. *kuṉśati*, *°śayati* or *kuṉsati*, *°sayati*, 'to speak' or 'to shine,' Dhātup. xxxiii, 90 & 92.

Kuṇsa, kuṇsa. See *bhṛik°, bhrak°, bhru-k°, bhrū-k°.*

कुंस् *kuns.* See √*kuṇś.*

Kunsa. See *kuṇsa.*

कुक् *kuk,* cl. 1. Ā. *kokate,* to take, accept, seize, Dhātup. iv, 17.

Kuka, mfn. taking, accepting, W.

कुकथा *ku-kathā,* &c. See 1. *ku.*

कुकभ *kukabha, am,* n. a kind of spirituous liquor, L.

कुकर *ku-kara,* &c. See 1. *ku.*

कुकुट *kukuṭa, as,* m. (= *kukkuṭa*), N. of a pot-herb (= *sitāvara,* commonly called *sushaṇi-śāka,* Marsilea quadrifolia), L.

कुकुटुम्बिनी *ku-kuṭumbinī,* &c. See 1. *ku.*

कुकुद *kukuda* = *kūkuda,* q. v., L.

कुकुद्रु *ku-ku-dru.* See 1. *ku.*

कुकुन्दनी *kukundanī,* f. the plant Cardiospermum halicacabum, Bhpr.

कुकुन्दर *kukundara, e,* n. du. [*au,* m. du., L.] = *kakundara,* q. v., Suśr.; VarBṛS. (ifc. f. *ā*); (*as*), m. = *ku-ku-dru,* q. v., Bhpr.

Kukundura, *am,* n. = *kakundara,* L.

कुकुन्ध *kukúndha, as,* m., N. of a kind of evil spirit, AV. viii, 6, 11.

कुकुभा *kukubhā,* f. one of the female personifications of music or Rāgiṇīs, L.

कुकुर *kukura, as,* m. (Uṇ. i, 41) = *kukkura* (a dog), L.; N. of a plant and perfume (= *granthi-parṇī*), L.; N. of a prince (son of Andhaka), MBh. xiii, 7679; Hariv.; BhP.; (*ās*), m. pl. the descendants of that prince, Hariv. 2030; N. of a people (branch of the Yadu race), MBh.; R. &c. (often named in connection with the Andhakas or Andhas); the country of the Kukura people. **–jihvā,** f. a species of fish (Acheiris Kookur Zibha), L.; the plant Leea staphylea, L.; the plant Ixora undulata, L. **Kukurâdhinātha,** m. 'lord of the Yādavas,' N. of Kṛishṇa.

कुकुवाच् *ku-ku-vāc.* See 1. *ku.*

कुकूटी *kukūṭī,* f. (= *kukkuṭī*) the plant Salmalia malabarica, L.

कुकूणक *kukūṇaka, as,* m. a kind of disease of the eyes in infants, Suśr.

कुकूनन *kukūnána,* mf(*ā*)n. (onomat.) gargling, VS. viii, 48.

कुकूरभ *kukūrabha, as,* m. a kind of evil spirit, AV. viii, 6, 11.

कुकूल *kukūla, as* or *am,* m. or n. chaff, Prab.; conflagration or fire made of chaff, L.; (*am*), n. a hole filled with stakes, L.; armour, mail, L. **–murmura,** m. a fire made of chaff, Bālar. **Kukūlâgni,** m. id., Kathās. cxvii, 92.

कुकूवाच् *kukū-vāc, k,* m. = *kukku-vāc,* Gal.; (cf. *ku-ku-vāc.*)

कुकृत *ku-kṛita,* &c. See 1. *ku.*

कुकोल *kukola, as,* m. the jujube (Zizyphus Jujuba), L.; (cf. *koli.*)

कुक्कुट् *kukkuṭ,* ind. an onomatopoetic word imitating the cock's cry, Pāṇ. i, 3, 48, Pat.

Kukkuṭá, *as,* m. (ifc. f. *ā,* Pāṇ. iv, 1, 14, Kāś.) a cock, VS. i, 16; Mn.; MBh. &c.; a wild cock (Phasianus gallus); (= *kukuṭa*) the plant Marsilea quadrifolia, L.; a whisp of lighted straw or grass, L.; a firebrand, spark of fire, L.; the offspring of a Nishāda by a Śūdra woman (cf. *kukkura*), L.; (*ī*), f. (Pāṇ. iv, 4, 46) a hen, VarBṛS. lxiii, 3; a small house-lizard, L.; the plant Dolichos pruriens, Suśr.; (= *kukūṭī*) the plant Salmalia malabarica (or the silk-cotton tree Bombax heptaphyllum), Suśr.; hypocrisy (cf. *kaukkuṭika*), L.; (*am*), n. = *kukkuṭâsana,* Tantras. **–kantha,** n., N. of a town, gaṇa *cihaṇâdi.* **–dhvani,** m. the crowing of a cock, cackling of fowls. **–nāḍī-yantra,** n., N. of an instrument. **–pakshaka,** m. a knife shaped like the wing of a cock, L. **–pāda,** m. 'cock-foot,' N. of a mountain, Buddh. **–mañjarī,** f. a sort of pepper (Piper Chaba), Npr. **–maṇḍapa,** m., N. of a sanctuary in Benares (standing on the right side of a statue of Śiva, a place where final emancipation may be attained), SkandaP.; (cf. *mukti-maṇḍapa.*) **–mardaka,** m., N. of a plant (with fragrant leaves), L.; (*ikā*), f. id., L. **–mardana,** m. id., L. **–mastaka,** m. = *-mañjarī,* L. **–miśra,** m. a fictitious nickname ('Mr. Cock'), Sāh. **–vrata,** n. a religious observance (worship of Śiva, on the seventh of the light fortnight of the month Bhādra, by women, especially for the sake of offspring), BhavP. **–śikha,** m. 'cockscomb,' safflower (Carthamus tinctorius), L. **Kukkuṭa-giri,** m., N. of a mountain, gaṇa *kiṃśulakâdi.* **Kukkuṭâṇḍa,** n. (Pāṇ. vi, 3, 42, Vārtt.) a fowl's egg, Suśr.; (*as*), m. a species of rice, Gal.; *-sama,* m., N. of a plant (having a white fruit), Npr. **Kukkuṭâṇḍaka,** m. a species of rice, Suśr.; Bhpr. **Kukkuṭâbha,** m. 'resembling a fowl,' a kind of snake, L. **Kukkuṭârāma,** m., N. of a grove (celebrated hermitage near Gayā), Buddh. **Kukkuṭârma,** n., N. of a place, Pāṇ. vi, 2, 90, Kāś. **Kukkuṭâsana,** n. a particular posture of an ascetic in religious meditation. **Kukkuṭâhi,** m. = °*ṭâbha,* L. **Kukkuṭêśvara,** m., N. of a Mantra; (*am*), n., N. of a Liṅga, SkandaP.; *-tantra,* n., N. of a Tantra. **Kukkuṭôraga,** m. = °*ṭâhi,* Npr.

Kukkuṭaka, *as,* m. a wild cock (Phasianus gallus), L.; the offspring of a Nishāda by a Śūdra woman, Mn. x, 18; (*ikā*), f., N. of one of the mothers in Skanda's retinue, MBh. ix, 2633.

Kukkuṭi, *is,* f. hypocrisy, L.

Kukkuṭī, f. of °*ṭa,* q. v. **–markaṭī-vrata,** n. a religious observance (in honour of Śiva and Durgā), BhavP.; (cf. *kukkuṭa-vrata.*) **–vrata,** n. id., ib.

Kukkuṭy-ādi, N. of a Gaṇa (Pāṇ. vi, 3, 42, Kāś.; Gaṇar. 140[b]).

Kukkubha, *as,* m. the wild cock (Phasianus gallus), MBh. xiii, 2835; varnish, oily gloss, W.

कुक्कुर *kukkura, as,* m. (Uṇ. i, 41; fr. *kurkurá*), a dog, Mṛicch.; PSarv.; Hit.; a despicable man of a mixed caste (= *kukkuṭa*), Kāraṇḍ.; N. of a Muni, MBh. ii, 113; of a prince (son of Andhaka), VP.; of an author, Tantr.; (*ās*), m. pl., N. of a people, MBh. ii, 1872; vi, 368; VP.; VarBṛS.; (*ī*), f. a bitch, VarBṛS.; (*am*), n. a vegetable perfume, L. **–dru,** m. the plant Blumea lacera, L.

कुक्कुवाच् *kukku-vāc, k,* m. (fr. *kukku,* an onomatopoetic word), a kind of deer (= *sāraṅga-mṛiga*), L.; (cf. *kukū-vāc* and *ku-ku-v°.*)

कुक्रिया *ku-kriyā.* See 1. *ku.*

कुक्ष *kuksha, am,* n. the belly, Uṇ. iii, 67; (*ī*), f. id., VarBṛS.

Kukshi, *is,* m. [f., L.] the belly, cavity of the abdomen (in the earlier language generally used in du., RV.; VS.; AV.); the interior of anything, W.; the womb, R.; Ragh. x, 60 &c.; a cavity in general (e. g. *adri-kukshi,* cavity of a mountain, Ragh. ii, 38), MBh. iii, 10694 &c.; a valley, Kathās. lxv, 214; (with *sāgara* or *samudra*) an ocean-cavity, i. e. a bay, gulf, MBh.; Pañcat.; the sheath of a sword, L.; steel, L.; N. of a son of Priya-vrata and Kāmyā, Hariv. 59; of Bali, Hariv. 191; of a king, MBh. i, 2692; of a son of Ikshvāku and father of Vikukshi, R.; of a teacher, BhP.; of a region, gaṇa *dhūmâdi;* (*is*), f., N. of a daughter of Priya-vrata and Kāmyā, VP.; [cf. Lat. *coxa, coxendix;* Gk. κοχώνη? Old Germ. *bûh;* Mod. Germ. *Bauch.*] **–gata,** mfn. being in the belly; °*tī-*√1. *kṛi,* to devour, Naish. ii, 83. **–ja,** m. 'born from the womb,' son, Ragh. xv, 15. **–bheda,** m., N. of one of the ten ways in which darkness terminates, VarBṛS. **–°m-bhari,** mfn. one who nourishes only his belly, filling or pampering the belly, gluttonous, Pāṇ. iii, 2, 26, Vārtt. **–randhra,** m. a kind of reed (Amphidonax Karka), L. **–randhraka,** m. id., Gal. **–śūla,** m. n. belly-ache, colic, Suśr. **Kukshyāmaya,** m. disease of the belly, VarBṛS.

कुक्षिल *kukshilá, as,* m. a species of evil spirit, AV. viii, 6, 10.

कुक्षेयु *kuksheyu,* v. l. for *kaksh°,* BhP.

कुखाटि *ku-khāṭi.* See 1. *ku.*

Ku-khyāti, -gaṇin, &c. See ib.

कुङ्कुण *kuṅkuṇa,* N. of a locality, AV. Pariś.

कुङ्कुम *kuṅkuma, am,* n. saffron (Crocus sativus, the plant and the pollen of the flowers), Suśr.; Ragh.; Bhartṛ. &c. **–tāmra,** mfn. red, coppery red. **–paṅka,** m. saffron used as an unguent, Bhartṛ. **–reṇu,** f. the pollen of saffron. **Kuṅkumâkṛiti,** m. 'resembling saffron,' a kind of rice, Gal. **Kuṅkumâkta,** mfn. dyed with saffron, orange. **Kuṅkumâṅka,** mfn. marked or dyed with saffron, orange. **Kuṅkumâruṇa,** mfn. red, ruddy.

कुङ्गनी *kuṅgani,* f., N. of a plant (= *mahā-jyotishmatī*), L.

कुच *kuc,* cl. 1. P. *kocati,* to sound high, utter a shrill cry (as a bird), Dhātup.; to polish, ib.; to go, ib. vii, 2; to connect, mix, ib.; to bend, make curved, ib.; to be curved or crooked, ib.; to oppose, impede, ib.; to mark with lines, write, ib. xx, 27: cl. 6. P. *kucati,* to contract, Dhātup. xxviii, 75; to be or make small, ib. vii, 3; (cf. √*kuñc.*)

Kuca, *as,* m. (generally du. *au;* ifc. f. *ā*), the female breast, teat, Suśr.; Śak. &c. **–kumbha,** m. the female breast. **–taṭa,** n. id.; °*ṭâgra,* n. 'point of the breast,' a nipple. **–phala,** m. 'having fruits shaped like the female breast,' the pomegranate, L.; the plant Feronia elephantum, L. **–mukha,** n. 'breast-top,' a nipple, L. **–harā,** f., N. of an evil spirit who deprives women of their breasts, MārkP.

Kucâgra, n. a nipple, L.

Kucita, mfn. contracted, Dhātup. vii, 3; small, Uṇ. iv, 187.

कुचण्डिका *ku-caṇḍikā.* See 1. *ku.*

Ku-candana, -cará, &c. See ib.

कुचिक *kucika, as, ā,* m. f. a kind of fish (in shape like an eel, commonly Kuñciya, Unibranchapertura Cuchiya, or Muræna apterygia synbrache; the Hindūs affirm that its bite is mortal to cows, though perfectly harmless to men), L.; (*ās*), m. pl. (v. l. for *kuśika*), N. of a people, VarBṛS.; (*ā*), f., N. of a plant, L. **–ṛṇa** (°*ka-ṛiṇa*), m., N. of a man, HYog.

कुचीरा *ku-cīrā.* See 1. *ku.*

कुचुण्टक *kucuṇṭaka, as,* m. a kind of pot-herb, Npr.

कुचुमार *kucumāra, as,* m., N. of the author of the Aupanishadâdhikaraṇa.

कुचेल *ku-cela,* &c. See 1. *ku.*

कुच्छ *kuccha, am,* n. the white water-lily, L.

कुच्छिला *kucchilā,* f., N. of a river, VP.

कुज् *kuj,* cl. 1. P. *kojati,* to steal, Dhātup. vii, 19: cl. 6. P. *kujati,* to be crooked, Nir. vii, 12.

कुज *ku-ja.* See 2. *ku.*

कुजन *ku-jana,* &c. See 1. *ku.*

कुजम्भल *kujambhala, as,* m. a thief who breaks into a house, L. (vv. ll. °*mbhira* and °*mbhila;* cf. *kumbhila*).

कुज्जिश *kujjiśa, as,* m. a sort of fish, L.; (cf. *kudiśa.*)

कुज्झटि *kujjhaṭi, is,* f. a fog or mist, L.

Kujjhaṭikā, °*ṭī,* f. id., L.

कुज्या *ku-jyā.* See 2. *ku.*

कुञ्च् *kuñc,* cl. 1. P. *kuñcati,* to make crooked, Dhātup.: to bend or curve, move crookedly, Suśr.: Caus. *kuñcayati,* to curl, crisp, frounce, Comm. on Uṇ. iv, 117; [cf. Hib. *cuachaim,* 'I fold, plait;' *cuach,* 'a curl;' *cuachach,* 'curled.']

Kuñcana, *am,* n. curving, bending, contracting; contraction (of a vein), Suśr.; a particular disease of the eyes (contracting the eyelids).

Kuñca-phalā, f. a kind of gourd (Beninkasa cerifera), L.

Kuñci, *is,* f. a measure of capacity (equal to eight handfuls, = *kim-cid*), Hcat.; Comm. on Mn. vii, 126.

Kuñcikā, f. a key, Bhartṛ.; Prasannar.; N. of a fish (= *kucika,* q. v.), L.; a plant bearing a red and black seed used as a weight (Abrus precatorius), L.; fennel-flower seed (Nigella indica), Car.; a reed (Trigonella fœnum græcum), L.; the branch or shoot of a bamboo, L.; a bawd, Gal.; 'key,' N. of a commentary on the Mañjūshā; (cf. *keli-k°.*)

Kuñcita, mfn. crooked; curved, bent, contracted, R. &c.; curled, MBh.; Suśr.; BhP.; (*ā*), f. (scil. *sirā*) an unskilful way of opening a vein, Suśr.; (*am*), n. the plant Tabernæmontana coronaria, L. **Kuñcitâṅguli,** mfn. with bent or curved fingers.

Kuñcī, f. cummin, Bhpr.; (= *kuñcikā*) Trigonella fœnum græcum, L.

कुञ्ज् *kuñj*, cl. 1. P. *kuñjati*, to murmur (= √*kūj*), Hcar.

कुञ्ज *kuñja, as*, m. [*am*, n., L.] a place overrun with plants or overgrown with creepers, bower, arbour, MBh. &c.; (with *sarasvatyās*) 'the bower of Sarasvatī,' N. of a Tīrtha, MBh. iii, 6078 ff.; the lower jaw, L.; an elephant's tusk or jaw, Pāṇ. v, 2, 107, Vārtt.; a tooth, L.; N. of a man, Pāṇ. iv, 1, 98. **– kuṭīra,** m. a bower, arbour, Mālatīm.; Gīt. **– vallarī,** f., N. of a plant similar to Mimosa concinna, L. **– vallī,** f. id., Gal. **Kuñjâdi,** a Gaṇa of Pāṇ. (iv, 1, 98; Gaṇar. 245).

Kuñjikā, f. = *kuñja-vallarī*, L.; fennel-flower seed (= *kuñcikā*, Nigella indica), Car.

कुञ्जर *kuñjara, as*, m. (ifc. f. *ā*, MBh.; R.) an elephant, Mn. iii, 274; MBh. &c.; anything pre-eminent in its kind (generally in comp., e.g. *rāja-k°*, 'an eminent king,' MBh.; Kathās.; cf. Pāṇ. ii, 1, 62 and gaṇa *vyāghrâdi*); the number 'eight' (there being eight elephants of the cardinal points), Sūryas.; a kind of temple, VarBṛS.; a kind of step (in dancing to music); the tree Ficus religiosa, L.; N. of a Nāga, MBh. i, 1560; of a prince (of the Sauvīraka race), MBh. iii, 15597; of a mountain, Hariv.; R.; of a locality; (*ā*), f. a female elephant, L.; the plant Bignonia suaveolens, L.; the plant Grislea tomentosa; (*ī*), f. a female elephant, L. **– kara,** m. an elephant's trunk. **– kshāra-mūla,** n. a kind of radish (= *mūlaka*), L. **– graha,** m. an elephant-catcher, R. ii, 91, 55. **– tva,** n. the state of an elephant, MBh. xii, 4282. **– darī,** f. 'elephant's cave,' N. of a locality, VarBṛS. **– pādapa,** m. the plant Ficus benjamina, Npr. **– pippalī,** f. the plant Gaja-pippalī (described as bearing a fruit resembling long pepper, Scindapsus officinalis), L. **– rūpin,** mfn. elephant-shaped. **Kuñjarânīka,** n. the division of an army consisting of elephants, elephant-corps. **Kuñjarârāti,** m. 'the enemy of elephants,' a lion, L.; the Śarabha (a fabulous animal with eight legs), L. **Kuñjarâroha,** m. a driver mounted on an elephant's back, R. vi, 19, 10. **Kuñjarâluka,** n. a species of esculent root, L. **Kuñjarâśana,** n. 'elephant's food,' the holy fig tree (Ficus religiosa), L.

कुञ्जल *kuñjala, as*, m., N. of one of Skanda's attendants, MBh. ix, 2578; (*am*), n. sour gruel (cf. *kāñjika*), L.

कुञ्जिका *kuñjikā.* See *kuñja.*

कुट् *kuṭ*, cl. 6. P. *kuṭati*, to become crooked or curved, bend, curve, curl, Dhātup. xxviii, 73; ?Nir. vi, 30; to be dishonest, cheat, Dhātup.: cl. 4. P. *kuṭyati*, or cl. 10. Ā. *koṭayate*, to break into pieces, tear asunder, divide, Dhātup. xxxiii, 25; to speak indistinctly, ib.; to be warm, burn, ib.; (cf. √*kuṭṭ* and √*kuṇṭ*.)

Kúṭa, *as* or *am*, m. n. a house, family (cf. *kuṭi*), RV. i, 46, 4 [? = *kṛita*, Nir. v, 24]; a water-pot, pitcher, L.; (*as*), m. a fort, stronghold, L.; a hammer, mallet for breaking small stones, ax, L.; a tree, L.; a mountain, L.; N. of a man, gaṇas *aśvâdi* and *kurv-ādi* [also RV. i, 46, 4, accord. to Gmn.]; (*ī*), f., gaṇa *gaurâdi* (Gaṇar. 47). **– kārikā,** f. a female servant (bringing the water-jar). **– ja,** m. Wrightia antidysenterica (having seeds used as a vermifuge; cf. *indra-yava*), MBh.; R. &c.; 'born in a pitcher,' N. of the sage Agastya (cf. Nir. v, 13 & 14), L.; of Droṇa, L.; *-malli*, f. a kind of plant, L. **– jīva,** m. the plant Putramjīva Roxburghii, L. **– hārikā,** f. = *-kārikā*, Hcar. **Kuṭâmoda,** m. civet, L.

Kuṭaka, *as*, m. a kind of tree, Kauś. 8 (v. l. *kuṭuka*); = *kuṭhara*, q. v., L.; (*ās*), m. pl., N. of a people, BhP. v, 6, 8 & 10; (*ikā*), f. a hut, Divyâv.; N. of a river, R. ii, 71, 15 (v. l. *kuṭilā*); (*am*), n. a plough without a pole, L. **Kuṭakâcala,** m., N. of a mountain, Bh. v, 6, 8.

Kuṭan (in comp. for *kuṭat*, pr. p.) **– naka,** m., v. l. for *-naṭa*, Bhpr. **– naṭa,** m. the fragrant grass Cyperus rotundus, Bhpr.; Calosanthes indica, Suśr.

Kuṭi, *is*, f. 'a curvature, curve,' see *bhṛik°, bhru-k°*; a hut, cottage, hall, shop (= *kuṭī*, q. v.), Uṇ. iv, 144; (*is*), m. a tree, L.; the body, L. **– cara,** m. a crocodile, L. **– pārthiva,** m., N. of a man.

Kuṭika, mfn. bent, crooked, MBh. iii, 13454; (*ā*), f., see *kuṭaka.*

Kuṭita, mfn. crooked, bent, Uṇ. iv. 187.

Kuṭitṛi, mfn. (Pāṇ. i, 2, 1) making crooked; acting dishonestly; being bent.

Kuṭira, *am*, n. (= *kuṭīra*) a hut, L.

Kuṭila, mf(*ā*)n. bent, crooked, curved, round, running in curved lines, crisped, curled, KātyŚr.; MBh. &c.; dishonest, fraudulent, Pañcat.; Vet. &c.; (*as*), m. a he-goat with particular marks, VarBṛS.; (*ā*), f. (scil. *gati*) a particular period in the retrograde course of a planet, Sūryas.; N. of a magic power; of a river (v. l. for *kuṭikā*), R.; of the river Sarasvatī, L.; (*ā, am*), f. n., N. of a metre (containing four lines of fourteen syllables each); (*am*), n., N. of a plant (= *tagara, kuñcita, vakra*), L.; a kind of perfume, L.; tin, W. **– kīṭaka,** m. a kind of spider, L. **– gati,** mfn. being in a particular period of the retrograde course (as a planet); (*is*), f. a species of the Ati-jagatī metre (= *candrikā*). **– gā,** f. 'going crookedly,' a river; *kuṭilageśa*, m. 'the lord of rivers,' the ocean, VarBṛS. **– gāmin,** mfn. going crookedly, tortuous, Nir. ix, 26; -(*gāmi*)-*tva*, n. the state of being capricious, Sāh. **– tā,** f. crookedness, guile, dishonesty. **– tva,** n. id.; deviation from (in comp.), Vām. **– pakshman,** mfn. having curved eyelashes or brows, Śak. **– pushpikā,** f. Trigonella corniculata, Npr. **– mati,** mfn. crooked-minded, deceitful, Mudr. **– manas,** mfn. id. **– svabhāva,** mfn. id. **Kuṭilâṅgī,** f., N. of a magical faculty. **Kuṭilâśaya,** mf(*ā*)n. 'going crookedly' and 'ill-intentioned, deceitful,' Kathās. xxxvii, 143. **Kuṭilī-√kṛi,** to distort (the brows), Ratnāv.

Kuṭilaka, mfn. bent, curved, crisped, Pañcat.; (*ikā*), f. (Pāṇ. iv, 4, 18) crouching, coming stealthily (like a hunter on his prey; a particular movement on the stage), Vikr.; a tool used by a blacksmith, Pāṇ. iv, 4, 18, Kāś.

Kuṭī, f. 'a curvature, curve,' see *bhṛik°, bhru-k°*; a hut, cottage, house, hall, shop, MBh.; R. &c.; a room with openings used for fumigations, Car.; Suśr.; a bawd, L.; a nosegay, bundle or tuft of flowers or vegetables, L.; a kind of perfume (commonly Murā), or = *surā* (spirituous liquor), L. **– kuṭa,** n., gaṇa *gavâśvâdi.* **– kṛita,** n. 'twisted, frizzled,' anything (as woollen cloth) curled or twisted, MBh. ii, 1847. **– gata,** mfn. inside the house. **– gu,** m., N. of a man, gaṇa *gargâdi.* **– caka,** m. 'delighting in staying in the house,' a kind of religious mendicant (who lives at his son's expense), MBh. xiii, 6478; BhP. iii, 12, 43. **– cara,** m. id., ĀruṇUp.; Bālar.; (= *bahish-kuṭ°*) crawfish, Gal. **– nivātam,** ind. so as to be protected in a hut against wind, Pāṇ. vi, 2, 8, Kāś. **– praveśa,** m. 'entering a hut,' settling in a cottage, Car. **– maya,** mfn., gaṇa *śarâdi.* **– maha,** m. a festival held in a Vihāra, Buddh. **– mukha,** m., N. of one of the attendants of Kubera, MBh. ii, 415.

Kuṭīkā, f. a small house (cf. Hariv. 15829).

Kuṭīya, Nom. P. °*yati*, to imagine one's self in a hut, Pāṇ. iii, 1, 10, Sch. (not in Kāś.)

Kuṭīra, *as* or *am*, m. n. (Pāṇ. v, 3, 88) a cottage, hut, hovel, Bhartṛ.; Vcar.; (cf. *kuñja-k°*); N. of a plant, gaṇa *bilvâdi*; (*am*), n. sexual intercourse, L.; = *kevala* (exclusiveness?), L.

Kuṭīraka, *as*, m. a hut, Vet.; = *kuṭī-caka.*

कुटङ्क *kuṭaṅka, as*, m. a roof, thatch, L.

Kuṭaṅga, *as*, m., N. of a locality, Romakas.

Kuṭaṅgaka, *as*, m. = *kuṭuṅg°*, q. v.

Kuṭala, *am*, n. = *kuṭaṅka*, L.

कुटच *kuṭaca*, v. l. for *kuṭa-ja* (Wrightia antidysenterica), L.

कुटज *kuṭa-ja, as*, m. See s. v. *kúṭa.*

कुटन्नक *kuṭan-naka* & *-naṭa.* See √*kuṭ.*

कुटप *kuṭapa, as*, m. a measure of grain, &c. (= *kuḍava*), Jyot.; Uṇ. iii, 141; (*as*), m. a divine sage or Muni, L.; a garden or grove near a house (= *nishkuṭa*), L.; (*am*), n. a lotus, L.

Kuṭapinī, f. (= *kamalinī*) a lotus plant, Npr.

कुटर *kuṭara*, v. l. for *kuṭhara*, q. v.

कुटरु *kuṭáru, us*, m. a cock, VS. xxiv, 23; MaitrS.; TS. v; a tent, L.

कुटरुणा *kuṭaruṇā*, f. the plant Ipomœa Turpethum (commonly Teōri).

कुटल *kuṭala.* See *kuṭaṅka.*

कुटहारिका *kuṭa-hārikā.* See √*kuṭ.*

Kuṭi, kuṭika, &c. See ib.

कुटिकुटी *kuṭikuṭī*, ind. (onomat.) only in comp. with **-√kṛi,** to fill with warbling or twittering, Hcar.

कुटिकोष्टिका *kuṭikoshṭikā*, f., N. of a river, R. ii, 71, 10.

कुटिञ्जर *kuṭiñjara, as*, m. a kind of Chenopodium, Car.

कुटिल *kuṭila.* See col. 2.

Kuṭī, &c., **kuṭīra,** &c. See ib.

कुटुक *kuṭuka*, v. l. for *kuṭaka*, q. v.

कुटुङ्गक *kuṭuṅgaka, as*, m. an arbour or bower formed of creeping plants, L.; a creeper winding round a tree; a thatch, roof (cf. *kuṭaṅka*), L.; a hut, cottage, L.; a granary, store-room, L.

कुटुम्ब *kuṭumba, am*, n. a household, members of a household, family, ChUp.; Āp.; Mn. &c.; the care of a family, house-keeping (hence metaphorically care or anxiety about anything; ifc., BhP. i, 9, 39); N. of the second astrological mansion (= *artha*), VarBṛ.; (*as, am*), m. n. name, L.; race, L.; a relation (by descent, or by marriage from the mother's side), L.; offspring, progeny, L. **– kalaha,** m. n. domestic dissension. **– vyāpṛita,** m. an attentive father of a family. **Kuṭumbârtham,** ind. for the support or on account of a family. **Kuṭumbaukas,** n. apartments &c. appropriated to the accommodation of relations. &c.

Kuṭumbaka, *am*, n. a household, family, Daś.; Hit. &c.; the duties and cares of a householder; (*as*), m., N. of a grass (= *bhū-triṇa*), L.

Kuṭumbaya, Nom. P. °*yati*, to support a family, Dhātup. xxxiii, 5.

Kuṭumbika, mfn. taking care of a household, MBh. xiii, 4401; (*as*), m. a home-slave, L.

Kuṭumbin, *ī*, m. a householder, Āp.; Mn. iii, 80; Yājñ. &c.; ifc. (metaphorically) one who takes care of anything, R. vi, 89, 19; a member of a family, any one (also a servant) belonging to a family, Pañcat.; Kathās.; Śāntiś.; a peasant, Inscr.; (*inī*), f. the wife of a householder, mother of a family, MBh.; Ragh. &c.; a female servant of a house, Comm. on Yājñ.; a large household, gaṇa *khalâdi*; a small shrub used in med. (*kshīriṇī*, a kind of moon-plant), L.; (*inau*), m. pl. the householder and his wife, Āp.

Kuṭumbi-tā, f., **-tva,** n. the state of being a householder or a member of a family; family connection or union, living as one family.

कुट्ट् *kuṭṭ*, cl. 10. *kuṭṭayati* (Dhātup. xxxii, 23), to crush, bruise, Bhpr.; AV.Pariś.; to grind or pound, paw (the ground), VarBṛS.; to strike slightly, Bālar.; Comm. on KātyŚr.; to multiply; to censure, abuse, Dhātup.; to fill, ib.

Kuṭṭa, mfn. ifc. breaking or bruising, grinding, &c., cf. *aśma-k°, śilā-k°*; (*as*), m. a multiplier such that a given dividend being multiplied by it and a given quantity added to (or subtracted from) the product, the sum (or difference) may be measured by a given divisor. **– pracaraṇa,** *ās*, m. pl., N. of a people, VP. **– prâvaraṇa,** *ās*, m. pl. id., ib. **– hārikā,** f. for *kuṭa-hār°*, q. v., L. **Kuṭṭâkāra,** m., N. of the mathematical operation relative to a multiplier called *kuṭṭa*, Comm. on Āryabh. **Kuṭṭâparânta,** *ās*, m. pl., N. of a people, MBh. vi, 356 (v. l. *kundâp°*).

Kuṭṭaka, mfn. ifc. cutting, breaking, bruising, grinding, &c., cf. *aśma-k°; ikshu-k°*; (*as*), m. a grinder, pulveriser; a multiplier (= *kuṭṭa*, q. v.); a buck-goat with particular marks, VarBṛS.; a kingfisher, W. **– vyavahāra, kuṭṭakâdhyāya,** m. that branch or chapter of arithmetic (treated by Brahmagupta) which treats of the multiplier called *kuṭṭaka.*

Kuṭṭana, *am*, n. cutting; pounding, grinding, beating, threshing, BhP. &c.; (cf. *śilā-k°*); abusing; (*ī*), f. a kind of spear, Gal.; a bawd, Kathās.; Hit.

Kuṭṭantī, f. a kind of dagger, L.

Kuṭṭāka, mf(*ī*, Pāṇ. iii, 2, 155) n. ifc. cutting, breaking, splitting, Mālatīm.

Kuṭṭita, mfn. bruised, Bhpr.; pounded, flattened; (*ā*), f. (scil. *sirā*) unskilful opening of a vein (the latter being cut to pieces by repeated application of the knife), Suśr.

Kuṭṭin, mfn. cutting, pounding; (*inī*), f. (= *kuṭṭanī*) a bawd, Prab.

Kuṭṭima, mf(*ā*)n. plastered or inlaid with small stones or with mosaic, L.; (*as, am*), m. n. (gaṇa *ardharcâdi*) an inlaid or paved floor, pavement, ground paved with mosaic, ground smoothed and plastered, MBh.; R. &c.; ground prepared for the site of a mansion, W.; a cottage, L.; the pomegranate, L.

कुट्टमित *kuṭṭamita, am*, n. affected repulse of a lover's caresses (one of the ten blandishments of women; v. l. *kuṭṭum°*), Sāh.

कुट्टार *kuṭṭāra, as*, m. a mountain, L.; (*am*), n. 'sexual intercourse' or 'pleasure,' L.; a woollen cloth, L.; = *kevala* (exclusiveness?), L.; (cf. *kuṭīra*.)

Kuṭṭīra, *as*, m. a mountain, L.

कुट्टुमित *kuṭṭumita*. See *kuṭṭam°*.

कुट्मल *kuṭmala*. See *kuḍmala*.

कुठ *kuṭha, as*, m. a tree (cf. *kuṭa*), L.

कुठर *kuṭhara, as*, m. the post round which the string of the churning-stick winds, L.; (*as*), m., N. of a Nāga, MBh. i, 1560 (v. l. *kuṭara*).

कुठाकु *kuṭhāku, us*, m. the wood-pecker (Picus bengalensis, commonly Kāṭhṭhākro), L.

कुठाटङ्क *kuṭhā-ṭaṅka, as, ā*, m. f. an axe, L.

Kuṭhāra, *as*, m. an axe, R.; Bhartṛ. &c.; a sort of hoe or spade, W.; a tree (= *kuṭha*), L.; N. of a man, gaṇa *śivâdi*; of a Nāga, MBh. i, 2156; (*ī*), f. an axe, L.

Kuṭhāraka, *as*, m. an axe, VarBṛS.; (*ikā*), f. a small axe, Bhartṛ. iii, 23; a similarly shaped instrument (used in surgery for scarification), Suśr.; N. of a woman, gaṇa *śubhrâdi*.

Kuṭhārika, *as*, m. a wood-cutter, Rājat.

Kuṭhāru, *us*, m. a tree, L.; a monkey, L.; an armourer, L.

कुठि *kuṭhi*, mfn. 'leafless, bare' or 'crooked, wry' (Comm.; said of a tree), ShaḍvBr.; (*is*), m. a tree, L.; a mountain, L.

Kuṭhika, *as*, m. the plant Costus speciosus or arabicus, L.

कुठुमि *kuṭhumi, is*, m., N. of a teacher (author of a law-book).

कुठेर *kuṭhera, as*, m. the plant Ocimum pilosum, Car.; Bhpr.; fire, L. **-ja**, m. (= *kuṭheraka*) a kind of Basilicum, L.

Kuṭheraka, *as*, m. a kind of Basilicum (Ocimum sanctum or Ocimum gratissimum), Suśr.; Cedrela Toona, L.

कुठेरु *kuṭheru, us*, m. the wind produced by a fan or chowrie, L.

कुड् *kuḍ*, cl. 6. P. *kuḍati*, to play or act as a child, trifle, Dhātup. xxviii, 89; to eat, ib.; to heap, ib.; to plunge, dive, ib. 101.

कुडङ्ग *kuḍaṅga, as*, m. (found in Prākṛit) = *kuṭaṅga*(*ka*), a bower, L.

कुडप *kuḍapa, as, am*, m. n. a measure of grain, &c. (= *kuḍava*), gaṇa *ardharcâdi*.

Kuḍava, *as, am*, m. n. a measure of grain or of wood or of iron &c. (4th part of a Prastha, described by some as a vessel four fingers wide and as many deep and containing 12 Prakṛitis or handfuls; also said to contain 13½ cubic Aṅgulas, or to contain 64 cubic Aṅgulas [ŚārṅgS.], or to be a finger and a half deep and three fingers each in length and breadth; in med. it is equal to two Prakṛitis or thirty-two Tolakas), MBh.; Jyot.; VarBṛS. &c.

कुडायिका *kuḍāyikā*, f. (in music) N. of a particular Rāga.

Kuḍāyī, f. id.

कुडालगाच्छि *kuḍālagācchi*, N. of a village (v. l. *kuḍālig°*.)

कुडि *kuḍi, is*, m. (= *kuṭi*) the body, Uṇ.

Kuḍikā, f. (= *kuṭa*) a water-pot (used by ascetics), W.; (perhaps for *kuṇḍikā*.)

कुडिश *kuḍiśa, as*, m. a kind of fish (commonly Kūrchi, Cyprinus Curchius), L.

कुडी *kuḍī*, f. (a wrong reading) for *kuṭī*, q. v., MBh. xiii, 6471.

कुडुक्क *kuḍukka, as*, m. (in music) N. of a measure or time.

कुडुप *kuḍupa, as*, m. the clasp or fastening of a necklace or bracelet, W.

कुडूहुञ्ची *kuḍūhuñcī*, f. (a Mahratti N. of) Solanum trilobatum, Npr.

कुड्मल *kuḍmala*, mfn. filled with buds, MBh. iv, 393; R.; Ragh. xviii, 36; (*as* or *am*), m. or n. a bud (sometimes written *kuṭmala*), Mṛicch.; Ragh.; BhP. &c.; (cf. *stana-k°*); (*am*), n. a particular hell, Mn. iv, 89; Yājñ. iii, 222. **-tā**, f. the state of being shut like a bud. **-dantī**, f., N. of a metre (= *anukūlā*). **Kuḍmalâgra-dat, -danta**, mfn. one whose teeth look like buds, Pāṇ. v, 4, 145, Kāś.

Kuḍmalāya, Nom. Ā. °*yate*, to (look i. e. to) be shut like a bud, Bālar.

Kuḍmalita, mfn. (gaṇa *tārakâdi*) filled with buds, Bālar.; shut like a bud, W.

कुड्य *kuḍya, am*, n. a wall, Yājñ.; MBh. &c.; plastering (a wall), L.; curiosity, L.; (*ā*), f. (gaṇa *kattry-ādi*) a wall, BhP. vii, 1, 27. **-cchedin**, m. a housebreaker, thief, L. **-cchedya**, n. a hole in the wall, breach, L. **-pucchā**, f. a house-lizard, Npr. **-matsī**, f. id., L. **-matsya**, m. id., VarBṛS. **-lepa**, m. a plasterer, Pāṇ. iii, 2, 1, Vārtt. 6, Pat.

Kuḍyaka, *am*, n. a wall, L.

कुण् *kuṇ*, cl. 6. P. *kuṇati*, to sound, Dhātup. xxviii, 45; to support or aid (with gifts, &c.), ib.; to be in pain (?), ib.: cl. 10. P. *kuṇayati*, to converse with, address, invite, Dhātup. xxxv, 41; [cf. Lat. *cano*.]

Kuṇitâhi, *is*, m., N. of an author of a Dharmaśāstra, Parāś.

कुण *kuṇa, as*, m. a kind of insect living in clothes; dirt on the navel, Gal.; (ifc. with *aśvattha, pīlu*, and other names of trees or flowers) the time when a plant bears fruit, Pāṇ. v, 2, 24.

Kuṇaka, *as*, m. a young animal just born (ifc. e. g. *eṇa-k°*, a young antelope just born), BhP. v, 8, 4–6.

कुणञ्जी *kuṇañjī*, f. orach, L.

Kuṇañja, m., °*ñjara*, n. id., L.

कुणप *kúṇapa, am*, n. [*as*, m., gaṇa *ardharcâdi*] a dead body, corpse, AV.; TS.; ŚBr.; Mn. &c.; (said contemptuously of) the living body, BhP.; dung; (*as*), m. a spear, MBh.; R.; (*ās*), m. pl., N. of a people, VarBṛS.; (*ī*), f. a small bird (Maina or Salik, cf. *viṭ-sārikā*); (*kuṇápa*), mfn. mouldering, smelling like a carcase, ŚBr.; Suśr. **-gandhá**, m. the smell of a dead body, ŚBr. iv. **-gandhi**, mfn. smelling like a dead body, Suśr. **Kuṇapâṇḍya**, m. 'having dead testicles,' N. of a man. **Kuṇapâśana**, mfn. eating dead bodies, Śak.

कुणरवाडव *kuṇara-vāḍava, as*, m., N. of a grammarian, Pāṇ. iii, 2, 14 & vii, 3, 1, Pat.

कुणारु *kúṇāru*, mfn. having a withered arm (cf. *kuṇi*; 'crying out,' fr. √*kuṇ*, Sāy.), RV. iii, 30, 8.

कुणाल *kuṇāla, as*, m. a kind of bird, Lalit.; N. of a son of Aśoka (whose eyes were put out in consequence of a rivalry between Aśoka's wives); N. of a place, Uṇ. iii, 75.

कुणावी *kuṇāvī*, f., N. of a plant (?), Suśr.

कुणि *kuṇi*, mfn. having a crooked or withered arm or an arm without a hand or finger, MBh. iii, 1270; Suśr.; (*is*), m. a whitlow, W.; the tree Cedrela Toona (= *tunna*), L.; N. of a prince (son of Jaya), BhP. ix, 24, 13; of the author of a Comm. on Pāṇ., Bhartṛ. Comm. on Pat.; of a man, TāṇḍyaBr. xiii, 4, 11, Sch.; of a Ṛishi, VāyuP.; of Garga, MBh. ix, 2981 f.; of the author of a Dharma-śāstra, Parāś. **-tva**, n. the state of being maimed, mutilation, lameness, Sāṃkhyak.; Tattvas. **-padī**, f., gaṇa *kumbhapady-ādi*. **-bāhu**, m. 'having a withered arm,' N. of a Muni, VāyuP.

Kuṇika, *as*, m., N. of a teacher, Āp.

कुणिन् *kuṇin, ī*, m. a kind of savage (= *kaṇabha*), Suśr.

कुणिन्द *kuṇinda, as*, m. (√*kuṇ*) sound, Uṇ. iv, 86.

कुण्ट् *kuṇṭ* = √*kuṇḍ*, q. v.

कुण्टक *kuṇṭaka*, mfn. fat, corpulent, L.

कुण्ठ् *kuṇṭh*, cl. 1. P. *kúṇṭhati*, to be lame or mutilated or blunted or dulled, Dhātup. ix, 57; to be lazy or stupid, ib.: cl. 10. *kuṇṭhayati*, to cover, conceal (cf. √*guṇṭh*), Dhātup. xxxii, 46; (cf. *avakuṇṭhana*.)

Kuṇṭha, mfn. (gaṇa *kaḍārâdi*) blunt, dull, MBh. i, 1178; R. &c.; stupid, indolent, lazy, foolish. **-tā**, f. bluntness, dulness (of a part of the body), Suśr.; indolence. **-tva**, n. indolence, stupidity, Rājat. iv, 618. **-dhī**, mfn. 'dull-minded,' foolish, Gol. **-manas**, mfn. weak-minded, BhP. iii, 32, 17. **-rava**, m., N. of a man, Comm. on AitĀr.

Kuṇṭhaka, mfn. stupid, L.; (*as*), m., N. of a pupil of Luṇṭaka; (*ās*), m. pl., N. of a people (v. l. *kuṇḍala*), MBh. vi, 370; VP.

Kuṇṭhita, mfn. blunted, dulled, (*a-k°*, neg.) Ragh. xi, 74; blunt, Kathās. lxviii, 3; weak, of no vigour, Rājat. v, 138; stupid; grasped, held, encircled, W.; (cf. *vi-*.) **Kuṇṭhitâśri**, mfn. having the edge or corners blunted, Kum. ii, 20.

कुण्ड् *kuṇḍ*, cl. 1. P. *kuṇḍati*, to mutilate, Dhātup. ix, 37: cl. 1. Ā. *kuṇḍate*, to burn, ib. viii, 17: cl. 10. *kuṇḍayati*, to protect, ib. xxxii, 45.

कुण्ड *kuṇḍa, am*, n. [*as*, m., L.], a bowl-shaped vessel, basin, bowl, pitcher, pot, water-pot, KātyŚr.; MBh. &c.; a vessel for coals, R. v, 10, 16 &c.; a round hole in the ground (for receiving and preserving water or fire, cf. *agni-kuṇḍa*), pit, well, spring or basin of water (especially consecrated to some holy purpose or person), MBh.; R. &c.; (*as*), m. an adulterine, son of a woman by another man than her husband while the husband is alive, Mn. iii, 174; (see *-gola* and *-golaka* below); N. of Śiva, MBh. xii, 10358; of a Nāga, MBh. i, 4828; of a son of Dhṛita-rāshṭra, MBh. i, 4550; (*ā*), f. (√*kuṇḍ*) mutilation, Pāṇ. iii, 3, 103, Kāś.; N. of Durgā, L.; (*ī*), f. (Pāṇ. iv, 1, 42) a bowl, pitcher, pot, Hcat.; Prasannar.; (*am*), n. ifc. a clump (e. g. *darbha-k°*, a clump of Darbha grass), Pāṇ. vi, 2, 136; a particular measure, L.; N. of certain mystical figures; a particular appearance of the moon (surrounded by a circle), VarBṛS. iv, 15. **-karṇa** (*kuṇḍá-*), m. 'pot-eared,' N. of a mythical being, Suparṇ. **-kalpa-druma**, m., **kalpa-latā**, f., N. of works. **-kīṭa**, m. the son of a Brāhman woman born in adultery with a man of an inferior caste, L.; a keeper of concubines, L.; a follower of the Cārvāka doctrine, L. **-kīla**, m. a low or vile man (*nāgara*), W. **-kaumudī**, f., N. of a work by Viśva-nātha. **-gola**, m. sour rice, gruel, W.; (*au*), m. du. an adulterine (*kuṇḍa*) and the son of a widow (*gola*), Yājñ. i, 222. **-golaka**, n. sour rice, gruel, L.; (*au*), m. du. = *kuṇḍa-golau*, Mn. iii, 156 & 174; MBh. iii, 13366. **-ja**, m. 'pitcher-born,' N. of a son of Dhṛita-rāshṭra, MBh. i, 2740. **-jaṭhara**, m. 'pitcher-bellied,' N. of an old sage, MBh. i, 2048; iii, 8263; (cf. *kuṇḍôdara*.) **-dhāra**, m., N. of a Nāga, MBh. ii, 361; of a son of Dhṛita-rāshṭra, MBh. i, 4546 ff. **-nadī**, f., N. of a river, Hariv. (v. l. *luṇṭha-n°*). **-pāyin**, mfn. drinking out of pitchers (°*yinām ayana*, n. a particular religious ceremony), TāṇḍyaBr.; ĀśvŚr.; KātyŚr.; (cf. *kauṇḍapāyina*.) **-pāyya**, mfn. (scil. *kratu*, &c., a ceremony or sacrifice) at which ewers or pitchers are used for drinking, Pāṇ. iii, 1, 130; (*as*), m., N. of a man, RV. viii, 17, 13. **-prastha**, m., N. of a town, Pāṇ. vi, 2, 87, Sch. **-bhedin**, mfn. 'breaking pots,' clumsy, Car.; (*ī*), m., N. of a son of Dhṛita-rāshṭra, MBh. i. **-maṇḍapa-kaumudī**, f., °**pa-saṃgraha**, m., N. of works. **-maṇḍapa-siddhi**, f., N. of a work by Viṭṭhala-dīkshita. **-mārtaṇḍa**, m., N. of a work. **-ratnâkara**, m., N. of a work by Viśva-nātha. **-vāsinī**, f. 'pitcher-dwelling,' Gautama's tutelar deity, BrahmaP. **-vidhāna**, n., N. of a work. **-śāyin**, m., N. of a son of Dhṛita-rāshṭra, MBh. i, 4549. **-siddhi**, f., N. of a work.

Kuṇḍâgni, m., 'N. of a locality,' see *kauṇḍâgnaka*. **Kuṇḍârka**, m., N. of a work. **Kuṇḍā-vṛisha**, mfn. adulterous, Hariv. 11162; (cf. *kuṇḍīvisha*.) **Kuṇḍâśin**, mfn. one who is supported by an adulterine, Gaut.; Mn. iii, 158; Yājñ. i, 224; MBh. xiii; (*ī*), m. a pander, L.; N. of a demon causing fever, Hariv. 9563; of a son of Dhṛita-rāshṭra, MBh. i, 4553. **Kuṇḍī-vṛisha**, v. l. for °*ṇḍā-v*°. **Kuṇḍêśvara-tīrtha**, n., N. of a Tīrtha, ŚivaP. **Kuṇḍôda**, m., N. of a mountain, MBh. iii, 8321. **Kuṇḍôdara**, mfn. having a belly like a pitcher, Pāṇ. vi, 2, 108, Kāś.; (*as*), m., N. of a Nāga, MBh. i, 1561; of a son of Janamejaya and brother of Dhṛita-rāshṭra, ib. 3744; of a son of Dhṛita-rāshṭra, ib. 2732; °*dareśvara*, n., N. of a Liṅga, SkandaP. **Kuṇḍôddyota-darśana**, n., N. of a work by Śaṃkara-bhaṭṭa. **Kuṇḍôdhnī**, f. a cow with a full udder, Ragh. i, 84; a woman with a full bosom. **Kuṇḍôpadhānīyaka**, m. 'using a pitcher as a pillow,' N. of Pūrṇa, Buddh. **Kuṇḍôparatha**, m., 'N. of a man,' see *kauṇḍôparatha*.

Kuṇḍaka, m. or n. a pot, Kathās. iv, 47; (*as*), m., N. of a son of Dhṛita-rāshṭra, MBh. i, 6983; N. of Kshudraka, VP.; (*ikā*), f. (ifc., Pāṇ. viii, 3, 45, Kāś.) a pot, student's water-pot, Up.; Pat. on Pāṇ. i, iii, vi; Hariv. 14836 &c.; N. of an Up.

Kuṇḍanī, f., N. of a utensil, Hcat.

Kuṇḍika, *as*, m., N. of a son of Dhṛita-rāshṭra, MBh. i, 3747; (*ā*), f., see *kuṇḍaka*.

Kuṇḍin, mfn. furnished with a pitcher, MBh.; Hcat.; (*ī*), m. a kind of vessel (v. l. *kuṇḍinī*), MBh. ii, 2061; a horse (= *kindhin*), L.; a pander, L.; (*inī*), f. a kind of vessel, MBh. ii, 2061; (with the Yogins) matter (as opposed to spirit), RāmatUp.; N. of a woman, Pat.

Kuṇḍina, *as*, m., N. of a son of Dhṛita-rāshṭra, MBh. i, 3747; of an author; of a Ṛishi, Comm. on Uṇ. ii, 49; (*ās*), m. pl. the descendants of Kuṇḍina, Pāṇ. ii, 4, 70; ĀśvŚr. &c.; the descendants of Kuṇḍinī, Pat.; (*am*), n. (Uṇ. ii, 50), N. of the capital of Vidarbha (ruled over by Bhīma, the father-in-law of Nala, apparently the modern Kondavir in Berar), Nal.; Hariv.; Ragh. vii, 30.

कुण्डल **kuṇḍala**, *am*, n. (ifc. f. *ā*; gaṇas *sidhmâdi* and *ardharcâdi*) a ring, ear-ring, Āśv-Gṛ.; Lāṭy.; Mn. &c.; a bracelet, Śiś. vi, 27; a fetter, tie, L.; the coil of a rope, L.; a particular disease of the bladder, Car.; (*as*), m. (in music) a kind of measure; N. of a Nāga, MBh. i, 2154; (*ās*), m. pl., N. of a people (v. l. *kuṇṭhaka*), MBh. vi; (*ā*), f., N. of a woman, MārkP.; (*ī*), f. a kind of drum (perhaps *kuṇḍalī*, nom. sg. fr. °*lin*, m.); a particular dish (curds boiled with ghee and rice); N. of a Śakti; mountain ebony (Bauhinia variegata), L.; Cocculus cordifolius, Bhpr.; Mucuna pruritus (= *kapi-kacchu*), L.; N. of two other plants (Sarpiṇī-vṛiksha and Kuṇḍali-cālana), L.; N. of a river, MBh. vi, 9, 21. **–dhāraṇa**, n. the wearing of ear-rings. **Kuṇḍalâkāra**, mfn. shaped like an ear-ring, circular. **Kuṇḍalôddyotitânana**, mfn. having his face radiant with glittering pendants.

Kuṇḍalanā, f. drawing a circle round a word which is to be left out in a MS., Naish. i, 14.

Kuṇḍalikā, f., N. of a metre in Prākṛit poetry; (cf. *vāta-k*°.) **–tva**, n. the state of being circular, Comm. on KātyŚr. **–mata**, n., N. of a Tantra.

Kuṇḍalita, mfn. annulated, Sāh.

Kuṇḍalin, mfn. decorated with ear-rings, MBh.; R. &c.; circular, annulate, Hariv. 4664; (*ī*), m. a snake, Rājat. i, 2; the spotted or painted deer, L.; a peacock, L.; the tree Bauhinia variegata, Bhpr.; N. of Śiva; of Varuṇa, L.; (*inī*), f. the plant Coccus cordifolius, L.; a particular dish (curds boiled with ghee and rice), Bhpr.; a Śakti or form of Durgā.

Kuṇḍalī, ind. for °*la*. **–karaṇa**, n. bending a bow so as to form a circle, Hcar. **–kṛita**, mfn. forming a ring, curled, moving in circles, Nal.; Suśr. **–bhūta**, mfn. id., BhP.; having the disease of the bladder called Kuṇḍala, Car.

Kuṇḍalikā, f. a circle, Hcat.

कुण्डावृष **kuṇḍā-vṛisha**. See *kuṇḍa*.

कुण्डीर **kuṇḍīra**, mfn. strong, powerful, L.; (*as*), m. a man, L.

कुण्डीविष **kuṇḍīvisha**, *ās*, m. pl., N. of a people, MBh. vi, 2083; (cf. *kuṇḍī-vṛisha*, *kauṇḍī-*.)

कुण्ड्रणाची **kuṇḍriṇācī**, f. a house-lizard [= *kuṭila-gati*, Sāy.], RV. i, 29, 6; VS. xxiv, 37.

कुत् **kut**, a Sautra root (i. e. one found in grammatical Sūtras only), to spread.

कुत **kuta**, *as*, m., N. of one of the eighteen attendants of the sun (identified with the god of the ocean), L.

कुतनय **ku-tanaya**. See 1. *ku*.

Ku-tanu, **ku-tapa**, &c. See ib.

कुतस् **kútas**, ind. (fr. 1. *ku*), from whom? (for the abl. case of 2. *ká*), RV. i, 164, 18; AV. viii, 9, 4; (*kutaḥ kālāt*, since what time? VP.); from where? whence? RV. &c.; whereto? in which direction? BhP. viii, 19, 34; (*ā kutas*, up to where? Pat.); where? R. vii, 23, 3; wherefore? why? from what cause or motive? because, Lāṭy. &c. (often in dramas before verses giving the reason of what precedes); how? in what manner? ChUp. &c.; how much less? much less, ChUp.; MuṇḍUp.; MBh. &c. In *a-kutas*, which occurs in comp., *kutas* has an indefinite sense (e. g. *a-kuto-mṛityu*, not fearing death from any quarter, BhP. iii, 17, 19; cf. *a-kuto-bhaya*); *kutas* is also indefinite when connected with the particles *api*, *cid*, *cana* (e. g. *kuto 'pi*, from any quarter, from any cause, Pañcat.; *kuto 'pi kāraṇāt*, from any cause, Prab.; *kutaś-cid*, from any one, from anywhere, RV.; KaṭhUp. &c.; (cf. *a-kutaścid-bhaya*); *kutaś cana*, (with a negation preceding) from no side, RV.; TS.; TUp. &c.; to no side, R. v, 74, 21; *yataḥ kutaś-cid*, from any person soever, Comm. on KātyŚr.) **–tarām**, ind. how? in what manner? KapS. i, 80. **–tya**, mfn. coming from where? Uttarar.; Prasannar.; (with *api*) of unknown origin, Uttarar.

Kuto (in comp. for *kutas*). **–nimitta**, mfn. having what cause or reason? R. ii, 74, 17. **–mūla**, mfn. having what origin? MBh. i, 6205; Car.

कुतस्त **kutasta**, *as*, m. (for °*tas-tya*?), N. of a man, Comm. on TāṇḍyaBr.; (cf. *kautasta*.)

कुतापस **ku-tāpasa**, &c. See 1. *ku*.

कुतीपाद **kutīpāda**, *as*, m., N. of one of the Ṛishis of the Sāma-veda, ĀrshBr.

कुतुक **kutuka**, *am*, n. (gaṇa *yuvâdi*) curiosity, Rājat. viii, 1613; eagerness, desire for (in comp.), Gīt. i, 42; (cf. *kautuka*.)

Kutukita, mfn. curious, inquisitive, Prasannar.

Kutukin, mfn. id., Naish. ii, 35.

कुतुप **kutupa**, *as*, m. a small *kutū* or leathern oil-bottle, Pāṇ. v, 3, 89; (*as*, *am*), m. n. the eighth Muhūrta of the day (= *ku-tapa*, q. v.), L.

Kutū, *ūs*, f. a leathern oil-bottle, Pāṇ. v, 3, 89

कुतुम्बुक **ku-tumbuka**, &c. See 1. *ku*.

कुतूणक **kutūṇaka** = *kukūṇ*°, L.

कुतूहल **kutūhala**, *am*, n. (fr. *kutas* and *hala*, 'calling out'?), curiosity, interest in any extraordinary matter, Sāh. &c.; inclination, desire for (*prati*, loc. or in comp.), Śak. &c.; eagerness, impetuosity; what excites curiosity, anything interesting, fun, Pañcat.; (mfn.) surprising, wonderful, W.; excellent, celebrated, W.; (cf. *kautūhala*.) **–kṛit**, mfn. exciting curiosity, Hcar. **–vat**, mfn. curious, taking interest in anything, Mālav.

Kutūhalita, mfn., gaṇa *tārakâdi*.

Kutūhalin, mfn. curious, highly interested in anything, Mn. iv, 63 &c.; eager, impatient.

कुतृण **ku-tṛiṇa**. See 1. *ku*.

कुत्थ **kuttha**, (in astron.) the fifteenth Yoga, VarBṛ.

कुत्र **kútra**, ind. (fr. 1. *ku*), where? whereto? in which case? when? RV. &c.; wherefore? Pañcat.; Hit.; *kutra—kva*, where (this)—where (that), i. e. how distant or how different is this from that, how little is this consistent with that? BhP. vii, 9, 25. *Kutra* becomes indefinite when connected with the particles *api*, *cid*, e. g. *kutrâpi*, anywhere, somewhere, wherever, to any place, wheresoever, Pañcat.; MārkP.; *kútrā cid* [RV.] or *kutra cid* [R. &c.], anywhere, somewhere, wheresoever; *na kutra cid*, nowhere, to no place whatsoever, MBh.; Pañcat.; = *kasmiṇś-cid*, e. g. *kutra cid araṇye*, in a certain wood, Pañcat.; *kutra cid—kutra cid*, in one case—in the other case, sometimes—sometimes, Mn. ix, 34; *yatra kutra cid*, wherever it be, here or there, Comm. on KapS. i, 69. **–tya**, mfn. where living or residing? BhP.; Daś.

कुत्स् **kuts** (perhaps related to *kútas*), cl. 10. P. *kutsayati* [also Ā. °*yate*, Dhātup.; rarely cl. 1. P. *kutsati*, MBh. ii, 2298 & 2303; once cl. 4. P. *kutsyati*, R. vii, 43, 18], to despise, abuse, revile, contemn, Mn.; Yājñ. &c.; [cf. Lith. *kussinu*.]

Kutsana, *am*, n. abuse, reviling, reproach, Pāṇ.; Mn. iv, 163; reproachful or abusive expression, Pāṇ. ii, 1, 53; (*ā*), f. an expression of contempt, Nir. ii, 3.

Kutsā, f. reproach, contempt, Pāṇ.; MBh.; (*ayā*), instr. ind. contemptuously, Kathās. lxi, 298.

Kutsita, mfn. despised, reviled, contemptible, vile, Nir.; Pāṇ.; MBh. &c.; (*am*), n. the grass Cyperus, L.

Kutsī-√bhū, to become subject to reproach, Comm. on Nir. vi, 30.

1. **Kutsya**, mfn. blamable, Bhartṛ.

कुत्स **kútsa**, *as*, m., N. of a Ṛishi (called Ārjuneya, author of several hymns of the RV.; when attacked by the demon Śushṇa, Indra defended him and killed the demon; but in other hymns [RV. i, 53, 10; ii, 14, 7; iv, 26, 1; viii, 53, 2] Kutsa is represented as persecuted by Indra), RV.; AV. iv, 29, 5; TāṇḍyaBr.; N. of a descendant of Aṅgiras (author of the hymns RV. i, 94–98; 100–115; ix, 97, 45 seqq.), ĀśvŚr.; lightning, thunderbolt, Naigh.; Nir.; (*ās*), m. pl. (Pāṇ. ii, 4, 65) the descendants or the family of Kutsa, RV. vii, 25, 5; Lāṭy.; (*am*), n. the plant Costus speciosus or arabicus, L.; (cf. *kaútsa*, *puru-kútsa*, &c.) **–kuśikikā**, f. the intermarriage of the Kutsa and Kuśika families, Pāṇ. iv, 3, 125, Kāś. **–putrá**, m. a son of Kutsa, RV. x, 105, 11. **–vatsá**, m. id., ib.

Kutsāyana, *as*, m., N. of a man, MaitrUp.; (cf. *kautsāyana*.)

2. **Kutsyá**, *as*, m., N. of the Ṛishi Kutsa, RV. iv, 16, 12.

कुत्सला **kutsalā**, f. the indigo plant, L.

कुत्सव **kutsava**. See *puru-k*°.

कुत्सार **ku-tsāra** (fr. 2. *ku*), a fissure in the earth, Comm. on KātyŚr. xv, 1, 10.

कुत्स्य 1. & 2. **kutsya**. See √*kuts* & *kútsa*.

कुथ् **kuth**, cl. 4. *kuthyati*, to stink, become putrid, Dhātup. xxvi, 11: Caus. P. *kothayati*, to cause to putrify, Suśr.

Kuthita, mfn. stinking, Suśr. (also *a-k*°, neg.)

कुथ **kutha**, *as*, *ā*, m. f. [*am*, n., L.] a painted or variegated cloth (serving as an elephant's housings), MBh.; R. &c.; (*as*), m. sacrificial or Kuśa grass (Poa cynosuroides), L.; Śākya-muni in one of his former thirty-four births, L. **Kuthôdarī**, f., N. of a daughter of Nikumbha, KalkiP.

Kuthaka, *as*, m. a variegated cloth, Car.

कुथुम **kuthuma**, *ās*, m. pl. the family of Kuthumin, VāyuP.

Kuthumi, *is*, m. = °*thumin*, VāyuP.

Kuthumin, *ī*, m., N. of a teacher, Pāṇ. vi, 4, 144, Vārtt.; (cf. *kuṭhumin*.)

कुद् **kud**, cl. 10. P. *kodayati*, to tell a lie, Dhātup. xxxii, 6; (v. l. for √*kundr*.)

कुदार 2. **kudāra**, *as*, m. mountain-ebony (Bauhinia variegata), L.; [for 1. *ku-dāra*, see 1. *ku*.]

Kudāla, *as*, m. id., L.; (cf. *kuddāla*.)

कुदिन **ku-dina**. See 2. *ku*.

कुदृश्य **ku-dṛiśya**, *-deśa*, &c. See 1. *ku*.

कुद्दल **kuddala**, *as*, m. = 2. *kudāra*, L.

Kuddāla, *as*, m. id., L.; (*as*, *am*), m. n. a kind of spade or hoe, L. **–khāta**, n., N. of a town, Pāṇ. vi, 2, 146, Kāś. **–pāda**, mfn., gaṇa *hasty-ādi*.

Kuddālaka, *as* or *am*, m. or n. (?) a spade or hoe, L.; (*am*), n. a copper pitcher, L. **–khāta**, v. l. for *kuddāla-kh*°, q. v.

कुद्मल **kudmala**, for *kuḍm*°, q. v.

कुद्य **kudya**, for *kuḍya*, q. v.

कुद्रङ्क **kudraṅka**, *as*, m. a watch-house ('a dwelling raised on a platform or scaffold,' W.), L.

Kudraṅga, *as*, m. id., L.

कुद्रव **kudrava** = *kodrava*, q. v., L.

कुद्रि *kudri, is,* m., N. of a man, g. *grishty-ādi; (ayas),* m. pl. his descendants, g. *yaskâdi.*

Kudryâkshi, *is,* m., N. of a man, Pravar.

कुद्वार *ku-dvāra.* See 1. *ku.*

कुधर *ku-dhara.* See 2. *ku.*

कुधर्म *ku-dharma,* &c. See 1. *ku.*

कुधि *kudhi, is,* m. (=*kuvi*) an owl, Gal.

कुधी *ku-dhī.* See 1. *ku.*

कुध्र *ku-dhra.* See 2. *ku.*

कुनक *kunaka, ās,* m. pl., N. of a people, VP.

कुनख *ku-nakha,* &c. See 1. *ku.*

Ku-nannamá, -naraka, &c. See ib.

Ku-nalin, ku-nātha, &c. See ib.

कुनाभि *ku-nābhi.* See 2. *ku.*

कुनामन् *ku-nāman,* &c. See 1. *ku.*

कुनाल *kunāla, as,* m. a kind of bird (living on the Himālaya), Buddh.; N. of a son of king Aśoka (named after the eyes of that bird), ib.; (cf. *kuṇāla.*)

Kunālika, *as,* m. the Indian cuckoo, L.

कुनाशक *ku-nāśaka, -nāsa.* See 1. *ku.*

कुनिषञ्ज *ku-nishañja.* See 1. *ku.*

Ku-nīta, -nīti, -nīlī, &c. See ib.

कुन्त *kunta, as,* m. a spear, lance [cf. Lat. *contus;* Gk. *κοντός*], R. &c.; a small animal, insect, L.; a species of grain (Coix barbata), L.; passion, L.; the god of love, Gal. **–prâvaraṇa,** *ās,* m. pl., N. of a people, MārkP. lvii, 57. **–vanamaya,** mfn. consisting of a forest of spears, Kād.

Kuntara, *as,* m. (=*kuntala*) the hair, Gal.

Kuntala, *as,* m. (ifc. f. *ā,* Gīt. ii, 15) the hair of the head, lock of hair, BhP.; Sāh. &c.; a particular head-dress, L.; a drinking cup, L.; a plough, L.; barley, L.; a kind of perfume (=*hrīvera*), L.; (in music) a certain Dhruvaka; (*ās*), m. pl., N. of a people, MBh.; VP. &c.; (*as*), m. a prince of that people, MBh. ii, 1270; VarBṛS. **–vardhana,** m. the plant Eclipta prostrata, L. **–svātí-karṇa,** m., N. of a prince, VP. **Kuntalôśīra,** n. a perfume, L.

Kuntalikā, f. a species of plant, Suśr.; butter knife or scoop, L.

कुन्ताप *kúntāpa, am,* n., N. of certain organs or glands (twenty in number, supposed to be in the belly), ŚBr. xii, xiii; N. of a section of the AV. (xx, 127 & 128 according to Sāy. on AitBr. vi, 32; or xx, 127–136 according to the MSS.), ŚāṅkhBr.; ŚāṅkhŚr.; ĀśvŚr.

कुन्ति *kunti, ayas,* m. pl., N. of a people, Kāṭh.; Pāṇ. iv, 1, 176; MBh. &c.; (*is*), m. a prince of that people (also called Kunti-bhoja), Hariv. &c.; N. of a son of Dharma-netra, VP.; of a son of Netra and grandson of Dharma, BhP. ix, 23, 21 ff.; of a son of Kratha, BhP. ix, 24, 3; VP.; of a son of Vidarbha and father of Dhṛishṭa, Hariv.; of a son of Supārśva and grandson of Sampati and great-grandson of Garuḍa, MārkP.; of a son of Kṛishṇa, BhP. x, 61, 13. **–jit,** m. 'conqueror of Kunti,' N. of a prince, VP. **–nandana,** for *kuntī-n°,* q. v. **–bhoja,** m., N. of a Yādava prince (king of the Kuntis, who adopted Kuntī), MBh.; Hariv. &c.; (*ās*), m. pl., N. of a people, VarBṛS. x, 15. **–rājan,** m. king Kunti, i. e. Kunti-bhoja, MBh. i, iii. **–surāshṭra,** *ās,* m. pl. the Kuntis and the inhabitants of Surāshṭra, g. *kārtakaujapâdi.*

Kuntika, *ās,* m. pl., N. of a people, VP.

Kuntī, f., N. of Pṛithā (daughter of a Yādava prince named Śūra [or Vasu, Hariv. 5255], who gave her to his childless cousin Kunti or Kunti-bhoja, by whom she was adopted; she afterwards became one of the wives of Pāṇḍu; on one occasion before her marriage she paid such respect to the powerful sage Durvāsas that he taught her an incantation or charm, by virtue of which she was to have a child by any god she liked to invoke; out of curiosity she invoked the Sun, by whom she had a child, cf. *karṇa;* but the Sun afterwards restored to her her maidenhood: soon after his marriage Pāṇḍu retired to the woods to indulge his passion for hunting; there he killed a male and female deer, who turned out to be a Ṛishi and his wife in the form of these animals; the sage cursed Pāṇḍu and predicted that he would die in the embrace of one of his wives; hence Pāṇḍu lived apart from Kuntī, but with his approval she made use of her charm and had three sons, Yudhishṭhira, Bhīma, and Arjuna, by the three deities Dharma, Vāyu, and Indra respectively; cf. *mādrī*), Pāṇ.; MBh. &c.; N. of a Rākshasī, Buddh.; of a river, VP.; the wife of a Brāhman, L.; the plant Boswellia thurifera, L.; a fragrant resin (=*guggulu*), L. **–nandana,** m. either of the three elder Pāṇḍava princes. **–bhoja,** a wrong spelling for *kunti-bh°,* q. v., MBh. iii, 17067. **–mātṛi,** m. 'having Kuntī as his mother,' N. of Arjuna, MBh. i, 8665. **–suta,** m. a son of Kuntī.

कुन्थ् *kunth,* cl. 1. *kunthati,* to hurt, injure, Dhātup. iii, 6; to suffer pain, want, &c., ib.: cl. 9. *kuthnāti,* to cling to, twine round, embrace, Dhātup. xxxi, 42; to injure, ib.; [cf. Lat. *quatio, percutio.*]

Kuntha. See *bāhu-k°.*

Kunthana, *am,* n. =*stanana,* L.

Kunthita, *am,* n. id., L.

कुन्थु *kunthu, us,* m., N. of the sixth Jaina Cakravartin or emperor in Bhārata; of the seventeenth Arhat of the present Avasarpiṇī.

कुन्द *kunda, as,* m. (Uṇ. iv, 101) a kind of jasmine (Jasminum multiflorum or pubescens), MBh. &c.; fragrant oleander (Nerium odorum, *karavīra*), L.; Olibanum (the resin of the plant Boswellia thurifera), L.; a turner's lathe, L.; one of Kubera's nine treasures (N. of a *guhyaka,* Gal.), L.; the number 'nine,' W.; N. of Vishṇu, MBh. xiii. 7036; of a mountain, BhP. v, 20, 10; (*am*), n. the jasmine flower. **–kara,** m. a turner, W. **–kundâcārya,** m., N. of a Jain teacher (author of the Pañcâstikāya-saṃgraha-sūtra). **–caturthī,** f. the fourth day in the light half of the month Māgha. **–pushpa,** m. fragrant oleander (Nerium odorum), Gal. **–mālā,** f., N. of a work. **–sama-danta,** mfn. one whose teeth are like the jasmine. **Kundâparânta** = *kuṭṭâp°,* q. v.

Kundaka, *as,* m. the resin of the plant Boswellia thurifera, L.

Kundinī, f. an assemblage of jasmines, L.

कुन्दम *kundama, as,* m. a cat, gaṇa *cūrṇâdi.*

कुन्दर *kundara, as,* m. a kind of grass, L.; N. of Vishṇu, MBh. xiii, 7036.

Kundarikā, f. the plant Boswellia thurifera, L.

Kundu, *us,* m. a mouse, rat, L.; (*us*), f. (=*kunda*) Olibanum, L.

Kundura, *as,* m. Olibanum, L.

Kunduru, *us,* m. f. Boswellia thurifera, VarBṛS. lvii, 5; the resin of that plant (Olibanum).

Kunduruka, *as,* m. Olibanum, Suśr.; VarBṛS.; (*ā*), f. id., L.; (*ī*), f. Boswellia thurifera, L.

Kundurūka, *as,* m. Olibanum, VarBṛS. lvii, 3.

कुन्द्र् *kundr,* cl. 10. P. *kundrayati,* to tell a lie, Dhātup. xxxii, 6; (cf. √*kud* and √*gundr.*)

कुप् 1. *kup,* cl. 4. P. Ā. *kupyati, °te* (perf. *cukopa*), to be moved or excited or agitated, Suśr.; BhP.; to swell, heave or boil with rage or emotion, be angry, be angry with (dat.; also gen., once [R. i, 49, 7] acc.; or with *upari* and gen., e. g. *tasmai* or *tasya* or *tasyôpari cukopa,* he was angry with him), MBh. &c.: Caus. P. *kopáyati,* to move, shake, agitate, RV. i, 54, 4; v, 57, 3; x, 44, 8; Suśr.; P. Ā. *kopayati, °te,* to cause to swell with anger, provoke, make angry, MBh. &c.; [cf. Lat. *cupio;* Engl. *hope;* Germ. *hoffe.*]

Kupá, *as,* m. the beam or lever of a pair of scales, ŚBr.; KātyŚr.; field-lark, Npr.

Kupana, *as,* m., N. of an Asura, Hariv. 2284.

Kúpaya, mfn. heaving, swelling with emotion ['to be guarded,' Sāy. fr. √*gup*], RV. i, 140, 3.

Kupāyú, mfn. inclined to be angry, AV. xx, 130, 8.

Kupita, mfn. provoked, incensed, offended, angry. **–vāyu,** m. aggravated flatulence, hypochondria, W. **Kupitântaka,** m. imminent death, W.

Kupya, mfn. to be excited, MBh. xv, 821 (*a-k°,* neg.); (*am*), n. base metal, any metal but silver and gold, copper, brass, &c., zinc, lapis calaminaris, pewter, tutenag, Mn. vii, 96; x, 113; xi; Yājñ. &c.; (*as*), m., N. of a man, Rājat. vi, 264. **–dhauta,** n. silver, L. **–śālā,** f. a braziery, place where metallic vessels &c. are made or sold or kept, L.

Kupyaka, *am,* n. ifc. (=*kupya*) a vile metal, Yājñ. 1, 262.

कुप् 2. *kup,* cl. 10. P. *kopayati,* 'to speak' or 'to shine. Dhātup. xxxiii, 106; [cf. Hib. *cubhas,* 'word, promise,' Lat. *nun-cupo;* Goth. *huf,* 'to lament.']

कुपङ्क *ku-paṅka,* &c. See 1. *ku.*

कुपत *kupata,* mfn. excellent, W.

कुपति *ku-pati.* See 1. *ku* and 2. *ku.*

कुपथ *ku-patha,* &c. See 1. *ku.*

कुपन *kupana.* See √1. *kup.*

कुपप *ku-papa,* &c. See 2. *ku.*

कुपय *kúpaya.* See √1. *kup.*

कुपरिज्ञात *ku-parijñāta,* &c. See 1. *ku.*

कुपायु *kupāyú.* See √1. *kup.*

कुपिञ्जल *ku-piñjala,* &c. See 1. *ku.*

कुपिनिन् *kupinin, ī,* m. a fisherman, L.

Kupinī, f. a net for catching small fish (made of bamboos or rushes), L.

कुपिन्द *kupinda, as,* m. a weaver, Uṇ.

कुपीलु *ku-pīlu,* &c. See 1. *ku.*

कुप्य *kupya.* See √1. *kup.*

कुप्रद *ku-prada.* See 2. *ku.*

कुप्रभु *ku-prabhu,* &c. See 1. *ku.*

कुबेर *kúbera,* or in later Sanskṛit *kuvera, as,* m. (originally) N. of a chief of the evil beings or spirits of darkness having the N. Vaiśravaṇa, AV. viii, 10, 28; ŚBr. &c.; (afterwards) the god of riches and treasure (regent of the northern quarter which is hence called *kubera-guptā diś,* Kum. iii, 25), Mn.; MBh. &c.; (he is regarded as the son of Viśravas by Iḍaviḍā [BhP.], the chief of the Yakshas, and a friend of Rudra [Hariv. 13131]; he is represented as having three legs and only eight teeth; with Jainas he is the attendant of the nineteenth Arhat of the present Avasarpiṇī); N. of a prince of Devarāshṭra; of the great-grandfather of Bāṇa-bhaṭṭa (author of the Kādambarī); of the author of the Datta-candrikā; the tree Cedrela Toona; (mfn.), deformed, monstrous, L.; slow, lazy, L. **–giri,** m. 'Kubera's mountain,' the Himālaya, Gal. **–tīrtha,** n., N. of a Tīrtha, ŚivaP. **–datta,** m., N. of a mythical being, Kathās. **–nalinī,** f., N. of a Tīrtha, MBh. iii, 10894. **–bāndhava,** m. 'a relation of Kubera's,' N. of Śiva. **–vana,** n. 'the forest of Kubera,' N. of a place, gaṇa *kshubhnâdi.* **–vallabha,** m. 'Kubera's favourite,' N. of a Vaiśya, Daś. **–hṛidaya** or **-hṛidya,** n., N. of a hymn, VarBṛS. **Kuberâksha,** m., N. of a plant (=*vallī-karañja*), Gal.; (*ī*), f. the plant Bignonia suaveolens, Suśr.; the plant Guilandina Bonduc, L.; also N. of other plants, L. **Kuberâcala,** m. 'Kubera's mountain,' N. of the Kailāsa mountain, L. **Kuberâdri,** m. id., L.

Kuberaka, *as,* m. a kind of pot-herb, Car.; the tree Cedrela Toona (= *tunna*), L.; (*ikā*), f., N. of a woman, gaṇa *śubhrâdi.*

Kuberin, *ī,* m., N. of a mixed caste.

कुब्ज *kubjá,* mf(*ā*)n. hump-backed, crooked, VS. xxx, 10; ShaḍvBr.; MBh. &c.; (*as*), m., N. of a person born under certain constellations and being an attendant of the model man Haṃsa, VarBṛS.; a curved sword, L.; a sort of fish (Bola Cuja), W.; the plant Achyranthes aspera (=*apâmārga*), L.; (*ā*), f. a kind of musical instrument; [cf. *nyubja* and *kanya-kubja;* cf. also Lith. *kupra, kupotas;* Gk. *κυφός, κύπτω;* Lat. *gibbus, gibba, gibber.*] **–kaṇṭaka,** m. a white species of Mimosa, L. **–kirāta,** n. sg. a hump-backed person and a dwarf, gaṇa *gavâśvâdi.* **–tā,** f. the state of being hump-backed, Car. **–pushpa,** n. the flower of Trapa bispinosa, L. **–līḍha,** m., N. of the founder of a sect (v. l. *kubjâl°*). **–vāmana,** n. =*-kirāta,* gaṇa *gavâśvâdi.* **Kubjâmra,** n., N. of a Tīrtha, Vishṇus. **Kubjâmraka,** n. id., MBh. iii, 8018; MatsyaP.; VārP. **Kubjâlīḍha,** see *kubja-l°.* **Kubjī-karaṇa,** n. curving (as of a stalk), Tattvas.

Kubjaka, mfn. hump-backed, crooked, Pañcat.; Vet.; (*as*), m. the plant Rosa moschata, L.; the aquatic plant Trapa bispinosa, L.; (*ikā*), f. a girl eight years old (personating the goddess Durgā at a festival of this deity).

Kubjikā (f. of *kubjaka*, q.v.) **-tantra**, n., N. of a Tantra.

Kubjita, mfn. crooked, curved.

Kubji-mat, mfn. id., TāṇḍyaBr.

कुब्र *kubra*, *am*, n. a forest, Uṇ. ii, 29; a hole for sacrificial fire, L.; a ring, ear-ring, L.; a thread, L.; a cart, L.

कुब्रह्म *ku-brahma*, &c. See 1. *ku*.

कुभन्यु *kubhanyú*, mfn. desirous of water [Sāy.; said of the poets], RV. v, 52, 12.

कुभा *kúbhā*, f. the Kabul river (Κωφήν, a river falling into the Indus), RV. v, 53, 9; x, 75, 6.

कुभार्य *ku-bhārya*, &c. See 1. *ku*.

कुभृत् *ku-bhṛit*. See 2. *ku*.

कुभृत्य *ku-bhṛitya*, &c. See 1. *ku*.

कुभ्र *kubhrá*, *as*, m. a hump-backed bull, MaitrS. ii, 5, 3; (*unnatá*, TS. ii, 1, 5, 2.)

कुम् *kum*, ind. an interjection, gaṇa *câdi*.

कुमत *ku-mata*, *-mati*, &c. See 1. *ku*.

कुमार *kumārá*, *as*, m. (fr. 1. *ku*+*māra*, √*mri*? 'easily dying;' fr. √2. *kam*, Uṇ. iii, 138) a child, boy, youth, son, RV.; AV. &c.; a prince, heir-apparent associated in the kingdom with the reigning monarch (especially in theatrical language), Ragh.; Mālav. &c.; a groom, L.; N. of Skanda (or Kārttikeya, q.v.; represented as a beautiful youth; also as the author of certain grammatical Sūtras, cf. *kalâpa;* also as causing certain diseases, Suśr.), MBh.; Hariv. &c.; N. of a son of Agni (who is the author of some Vedic hymns), RAnukr.; one of the nine names of Agni, ŚBr. vi; N. of a Prajāpati, VāyuP.; of Mañju-śrī, Buddh.; of a river, VP.; of the Sindhu river, L.; of the author of a Dharma-śāstra; of the attendant of the twelfth Arhat of the present Avasarpiṇī, Jain.; a parrot, L.; the tree Capparis trifoliata (cf. *kumāraka*); (*ās*), m. pl., N. of a people, MBh. ii, 1075 & 1870 (cf. *kumālaka*); (*ī*), f. a young girl, one from ten to twelve years old, maiden, daughter, AV.; AitBr. &c.; or (in the Tantras) any virgin up to the age of sixteen or before menstruation has commenced; N. of certain flags (set up along with Indra's banner), VarBṛS.; N. of the wife of Bhīma-sena (son of Parīkshit), MBh. i, 3796; of a daughter of Vasu-deva by Rohiṇī, Hariv. 1952; of Sītā (Rāma's wife), L.; of the goddess Durgā, Hariv. 9425; of Dākshāyaṇī (in Māyā-purī), MatsyaP.; of a metre (a kind of Śakvarī, consisting of four lines of sixteen syllables each); the bird commonly called Śyāmā, L.; the plant Aloe perfoliata, L.; the plant Clitoria ternatea (=*a-parājitā*), L.; the plant Jasminum Sambac, L.; the plant commonly called *bandhyā-karkoṭakī*, L.; the blossom of the plants Taruṇī and Modinī, L.; great cardamoms, L.; the most southerly of the nine portions of the known continent or of Jambū-dvīpa (the southern extremity of the peninsula, whence the modern name Cape Comorin [Kumārī]), W.; the central part of the universe (according to Hindū geography, Jambū-dvīpa or India), L.; N. of a river flowing from the mountain Śuktimat, MBh.; Hariv.; VP.; of another river, Hcat.; (when a name is given to a pupil to indicate his attachment to any particular master, *kumārī* may be prefixed to denote that the pupil's object is to gain the affections of the master's daughter, e.g. *kumārī-dāksha*, q.v. s.v. *kumārī*); (*am*), n., N. of a Varsha governed by Kumāra (the son of Bhavya), VP.; pure gold, L. **-kulaṭā**, f. unchaste while still a girl, gaṇa *śramaṇâdi*. **-kuśala**, mfn. skilful while still a boy, ib. **-garbhiṇī**, f. pregnant while still a girl, ib. **-gupta**, m. 'protected by the god of war,' N. of several princes, Daś.; Hcar. &c. **-ghātin**, m. the slayer of a boy or child, Pāṇ. iii, 2, 51. **-capala**, mfn. giddy while still a boy, gaṇa *śramaṇâdi*. **-jīva**, m. the plant Putram-jīva Roxburghii, Car. **-tāpasī**, f. an ascetic while still a girl, gaṇa *śramaṇâdi*. **-tva**, n. boyhood, youth, Ragh. xvii, 30. **-datta**, m. 'given by the god of war,' N. of a son of Nidhipati, Kathās. **-darśana**, m., N. of a prince of the Gandharvas, Kāraṇḍ. **-dāsa**, m., N. of a poet; (*ī*), f. a slave while still a girl, gaṇa *śramaṇâdi*. **-devī**, f., N. of the mother of Samudra-gupta. **-deshṇa** (°*rá-*), mfn. granting perishable gifts ['granting children,' Sāy.], RV. x, 34, 7. **-dhārā**, f., N. of a river, MBh. iii, 8127; Kathās. **-nipuṇa**, mfn. = *-kuśala*, gaṇa *śramaṇâdi*. **-paṭu**, mfn. id., ib. **-paṇḍita**, m. a scholar while still a boy, ib. **-pāla**, m., N. of a king (= *Śāli-vāhana*, W.); N. of a king of Guzerat, W. **-pravrajitā**, f. religious while still a girl, gaṇa *śramaṇâdi*. **-bandhakī**, f. = *-kulaṭā*, ib. **-bhaṭṭa**, m., N. of a poet. **-bhṛityā**, f. care of a young child or of a pregnant or lying-in woman, midwifery, Ragh. iii, 12. **-lalitā**, f. 'boy's play,' N. of a metre (consisting of four lines of eight syllables each). **-vana**, n. Kumāra's (i.e. Kārttikeya's) grove. **-vāri-dhārā**, f. = *-dhārā*, Kathās. **-vāhin**, m. 'carrying Skanda,' a peacock (as being Skanda's usual vehicle), L. **-vrata**, n. a vow of eternal chastity, Vikr. **-śiras**, m., N. of the physician Bharadvāja, Car. **-śramaṇā**, f. = *-tāpasī*, gaṇa *śramaṇâdi*. **-sambhava**, m. the birth of Skanda or Kārttikeya, R. i, 38, 31; N. of a poem by Kālidāsa. **-siṇha**, m., N. of an astronomer. **-sū**, m. 'the father of the god of war,' N. of Agni, MBh. ii, 1148; (*ūs*), f. 'the mother of the god of war,' N. of the river Gaṅgā, L.; of Durgā, L. **-sena**, m., N. of a minister, Rājat. iii, 382. **-svāmin**, m., N. of the author of a Comm. on the Mīmāṇsā-bhāshya. **-hāritá**, m., N. of a teacher, ŚBr. xiv. **Kumārâgāra**, m. 'child's room,' nursery, Car. iv, 8. **Kumārâdhyāpaka**, m. a teacher while still a youth, gaṇa *śramaṇâdi*. **Kumārâbhirūpaka**, mfn. instructed while still a boy, ib. **Kumārâbhisheka**, m. 'inauguration of Kumāra,' N. of Kum. xiii. **Kumārêśvara-tīrtha**, n., N. of a Tīrtha, ŚivaP.

Kumāraká, *as*, m. a little boy, boy, youth, RV. viii, 30, 1; 69, 15; ŚBr.; MBh. &c.; (also ifc., e.g. *ṛishi-k°*, a young Ṛishi, Śak.; *nāga-k°*, a young Nāga, Kathās.); the pupil of the eye, ŚBr. iii; N. of a Nāga, MBh. i, 2154; the plant Capparis trifoliata, L.; (*ikā*), f. a girl from ten to twelve years old, virgin, AV.; TāṇḍyaBr.; MBh. &c.; a female servant, VarBṛS.; N. of certain flags (=*kumārī*), VarBṛS.; an insect (Sphex asiatica), L.; double jasmine (Jasminum Sambac), L.; large cardamoms, L.; N. of a part of Bhārata-varsha (a division of the known continent), VP.; N. of a river, Hcat.

Kumāraya, Nom. P. °*yati*, to play (as a child), Dhātup. xxxv, 25.

Kumārayu, *us*, m. a prince, Comm. on Uṇ.

Kumāri (shortened for °*rī*, q.v.; cf. Pāṇ. vi, 3, 63). **-tamā**, f. (superl.), Pāṇ. i, 1, 22, Kāś. **-tarā**, f. (compar.), ib. **-datta**, m., N. of a man, Kathās. li, 123. **-dā**, mfn. Ved. 'granting children,' v.l. for *-dārā*, q.v. **-dārā**, f. 'being a wife while still a girl' (?), Pāṇ. vi, 3, 63, Kāś.

Kumārika, mfn. furnished with or abounding in girls, gaṇa *vrīhy-ādi*.

Kumārikā, f. of °*raká*, q.v. **-kshetra**, n., N. of a part of Bhārata-varsha. **-khaṇḍa**, n. id.; N. of a section of the SkandaP.

Kumārin, mfn. (gaṇa *vrīhy-ādi*) having children, RV. viii, 31, 8; granting children, SāmavBr.

Kumārila, *as*, m., N. of a renowned teacher of the Mīmāṇsā philosophy. **-bhaṭṭa** or **-svāmin**, m. id.

Kumārī, f. of °*rá*, q.v.; (mfn.) desirous of a daughter, Pāṇ. i, 4, 3, Pat. **-kalpa**, m., N. of a work. **-krīḍanaka**, n. a plaything for girls, gaṇa *yāvâdi*. **-tantra**, n., N. of a Tantra. **-dāksha**, *ās*, m. pl. the Dākshas desirous of a girl, Pāṇ. vi, 2, 69, Kāś. **-pāla**, m. the guardian of a virgin or bride, Kauś. 75 & 76. **-putrá**, m. (gaṇa *sthūlâdi*) the child of an unmarried woman, VS. xxx, 6. **-°putraka**, mfn. fr. *-putra*, gaṇa *sthūlâdi*. **-pura**, n. a part of the gynæceum in which the girls are kept, MBh. iv, 309; Daś.; Kād. **-pūjā**, f. the worship of Kumārī or Durgā (a ceremony performed at the great Durgā festival, when a girl between ten and twelve years old is placed on a pedestal as the representative of the goddess, and fed with offerings made to the idol). **-śvaśura**, m. the father-in-law of a maiden, gaṇa *sthūlâdi*. **-°śvaśuraka**, mfn. fr. °*śura*, ib.

कुमार्ग *ku-mārga*. See 1. *ku*.

कुमालक *kumālaka*, *ās*, m. pl., N. of a people, L.

कुमालन *kumālana*, *as*, m., N. of a man, Āp.

कुमालय *kumālaya*, v.l. for °*māraya*, q.v.

कुमित्र *ku-mitra*, *-mukha*, &c. See 1. *ku*.

कुमुद् *ku-mud*, mfn., see 1. *ku*; (*t*), n. (=*kumuda*) the white water-lily, BhP. iii, 23, 38. **-vat** (*kúmud-*), mfn. (Pāṇ. iv, 2, 87) abounding in lotuses, Ragh. iv, 19; BhP.; (*ān*), m. the moon, BhP. x, 29, 3; N. of a wind, MaitrS. iv, 9, 8; (*atī*), f. an assemblage of lotuses, place or pond filled with them, Kauś.; Śak. &c.; the flexible stalk of a water-lily, W.; N. of a plant bearing a poisonous fruit (Villarsia indica), Suśr.; N. of a sister of the serpent-king Kumuda and wife of Kuśa, Ragh.; of the wife of the Kirāta king Vimarshaṇa, SkandaP.; of the wife of Pradyumna, VP.; of a river, ib.; *kumudvatīśa*, m. 'lord of the lotuses,' N. of the moon, L.

Kú-muda, *am*, n. [*as*, m., L.], 'exciting what joy,' the esculent white water-lily (Nymphæa esculenta), AV. iv, 34, 5; Suśr.; Śak. &c.; the red lotus (Nymphæa rubra), L.; (*as*), m. camphor, Bhpr.; (in music) N. of a Dhruvaka; N. of a particular comet, VarBṛS.; of a Nāga, MBh.; Ragh.; of an attendant of Skanda [MBh. ix, 2558] or of Vishṇu [BhP.]; of the elephant of the south-west or southern quarter, L.; of a Daitya, L.; of a son of Gada by Bṛihatī, Hariv. 9193; of a confidant of king Unmattâvanti, Rājat.; of a monkey-hero, MBh.; R.; of a poet; of a pupil of Pathya, BhP. xii, 7, 2; of a mountain, BhP.; VP.; of one of the smaller Dvīpas, VP.; (*ā*), f. a form of Durgā, BhP. x, 2, 12; MatsyaP.; the plant Gmelina arborea, L.; the plant Pistia Stratiotes, L.; the plant Desmodium gangeticum, L.; the plant Grislea tomentosa, L.; another plant (commonly Kaṭphala), L.; (*ī*), f. the plant Kaṭphala (Myrica sapida); (*am*), n. camphor, L.; silver, L. **-khaṇḍa**, n. an assemblage of Kumudas, gaṇa *kamalâdi*. **-ghnī**, f. 'pernicious to the Kumudas,' N. of a plant containing a poisonous milky juice, Suśr. **-candra**, m., N. of the astronomer Siddha-sena. **-nātha**, m. 'lord of the lotuses,' the moon, Kād. **-pattrâbha**, mfn. resembling the leaves of the white water-lily. **-pushpā**, f., N. of a Gandharva girl, Kāraṇḍ. **-bandhu**, m. 'friend of the lotus' (the white esculent lotus expanding its petals during the night and closing them in the day-time), the moon, L. **-bāndhava**, m. id., L. **-maya**, mfn. consisting of white lotus flowers, Kād. **-vatī**, f. an assemblage of Kumudas, place abounding in them, L. **-vana**, n. id. **-suhṛid**, m. = *-bandhu*, L. **Kumudâkara**, m. a number of water-lilies, Viddh.; Kathās.; *-bândhava*, m. = °*da-bandhu*, Comm. on VarBṛ. **Kumudâksha**, m. 'lotus-eyed,' N. of a Nāga, MBh. i, 1560; of an attendant of Vishṇu, BhP. viii, 21, 16. **Kumudâdi**, m., N. of a teacher, VP. **Kumudâvāsa**, mfn. abounding in lotuses, L. **Kumudêśa**, m. = °*da-nātha*, L. **Kumudôttara**, m., N. of a Varsha, MBh. vi, 425. **Kumudôtpalin**, mfn. richly furnished with Kumudas and Utpalas, R. iii, 78, 26.

Kumudika, mf(*ī*)n. abounding with Kumudas, Pāṇ. iv, 2, 80; (*ā*), f., N. of a woman, Kathās.; N. of the plant Kaṭphala, L.; of a small tree (the seeds of which are aromatic), W.

Kumudinī, f. (gaṇa *pushkarâdi*) an assemblage of Kumudas or a place abounding in them, Pañcat.; Śiś. &c.; N. of the daughter of a Daitya, Kathās.; of the mother of Raghu-deva. **-nāyaka**, m. (=*kumuda-bandhu*) the moon, Hit. **-pati**, m. id., L. **-vadhū-vara**, m. id., Kād. **-vanitā**, f. a loved woman fancifully represented as an assemblage of lotus flowers.

कुमुहूर्त *ku-muhūrta*, &c. See 1. *ku*.

कुम्प् *kump*, v.l. for √*kumb*, q.v.

कुम्प *kumpa*, mfn. crooked-armed, L.

कुम्ब् *kumb*, cl. 6. and 10. P. *kumbati*, °*bayati*, to cover, Pāṇ. iii, 3, 105; Dhātup.

कुम्ब *kúmba*, *as* or *am*, m. or n. (ifc. f. *ā*) a kind of head-dress for women, AV. vi, 138, 3; the thick end (of a bone or of a club), TS.; (*ā*), f. (Pāṇ. iii, 3, 105) a thick petticoat, L.; an enclosure round a place of sacrifice, L. **-kurīra**, m. a kind of head-dress for women, ĀpŚr.

कुम्ब्या *kúmbyā* or *kumbyā́*, f. a precept in form of a verse or formula, ŚBr. xi; AitĀr.

कुम्भ् *kumbh*, v.l. for √*kumb*, q.v.

कुम्भ *kumbhá*, *as*, m. a jar, pitcher, water-pot, ewer, small water-jar [often ifc. (f. *ā*), e.g. *chidra-k°*, a perforated pitcher, R.; *āma-k°*, a jar of unbaked clay, Pañcat.; *hema-k°*, a golden ewer, Ragh. ii, 36; Amar.; *jala-k°*, a water-pot, Pañcat.], RV.; AV. &c.; an urn in which the bones of a dead person are collected, ĀśvGṛ.; KātyŚr.; ŚāṅkhŚr.; the sign of the zodiac Aquarius, Jyot.; VarBṛS. &c.; a measure of grain (equal to twenty Droṇas, a little more than three bushels and three gallons; commonly called a comb; some make it two Droṇas or sixty-four Seers), Mn. viii, 320; Hcat.; the frontal globe or prominence on the upper part of the forehead of an elephant (there are two of these prominences which swell in the rutting season), MBh.; Bhartṛ. &c.; a particular part of a bed, VarBṛS.; N. of a plant (and also of its fruit), BhP. x, 18, 14; the root of a plant used in medicine; a religious exercise, viz. closing the nostrils and mouth so as to suspend breathing, L.; the paramour of a harlot, bully, flash or fancy man, L.; N. of a Mantra (pronounced over a weapon), R. i; N. of a Dānava (a son of Prahlāda and brother of Nikumbha), MBh. i, 2527; Hariv.; of a Rākshasa (son of Kumbhakarṇa), R.; BhP.; of the father of the nineteenth Arhat of the present Avasarpiṇī, Jain.; of a monkey, R. iv, 33, 14; one of the thirty-four Jātakas or former births of Śākya-muni, L.; N. of a work, Sāh.; (*ā*), f. a harlot, L.; the plant Tiaridium indicum, L.; (fr. √*kumbh*) covering, Vop.; (*ī*), f. a small jar or pot, earthen cooking vessel, VS.; AV.; TS. &c.; N. of a hell, Kāraṇḍ.; of a plant, Bālar.; a small tree (the seeds of which are used in medicine, commonly Kaṭphala), L.; Bignonia suaveolens, L.; Pistia Stratiotes, L.; another plant (commonly Romaśa), L.; the plant Croton polyandrum, L.; the plant Myrica sapida, L.; (*am*), n. the plant Ipomœa Turpethum, L.; a fragrant resin (*gúggulu*), or the plant which bears it, L.; gold, Gal.; [cf. Gk. κύμβη; Lat. *cymba*.] **-karṇa**, m. 'pot-eared,' N. of a Rākshasa (the brother of Rāvaṇa, described in R. vi as sleeping for six months at a time and then waking to gorge himself, MBh. iii; R.; Ragh. xii, 80; BhP.; N. of a Daitya, Hariv.; of a Muni, VāyuP.; of a locality; of Śiva, MBh. xii, 10350; *-vadha*, m. 'the slaughter of Kumbhakarṇa,' N. of a section of the PadmaP. **-kāmalā**, f. a bilious affection (sort of jaundice together with swelling of the joints, Suśr.; cf. *kumbha-pāda*). **-kāra**, m. a potter (being according to some authorities the son of a Brāhman by a wife of the Kshatriya caste), Yājñ. iii, 146; MBh. &c.; a serpent, L.; a wild fowl (Phasianus gallus), L.; (*ī*), f. the wife of a potter, Pāṇ. iv, 1, 15, Kāś.; N. of a girl, Lalit.; a mineral substance used as an application to strengthen the eyes and beautify the eyelashes, L.; red arsenic, L. **-kāraka**, m. a potter, W.; (*ikā*), f. the wife of a potter, woman of the potter caste, Kathās.; a sort of collyrium, L.; *-kukkuṭa*, m. a wild fowl (Phasianus gallus), L. **-ketu**, m., N. of a son of Śambara, Hariv. 9254. **-ghoṇa-tīrtha**, n., N. of a Tīrtha. **-janman**, m. 'born in a pitcher,' N. of Agastya, Ragh. xii, 31. **-tāla**, m. (in music) a kind of measure. **-tumbī**, f. a kind of large round gourds, L. **-dāsa**, m.?, Rājat. iii, 456; (*ī*), f. a harlot, Hcar.; a bawd, L. **-dhara**, m. 'pot-holder,' the sign Aquarius; N. of a Mantra (pronounced over a weapon), R. i. **-dhānya**, mfn. having grains only to fill a single pot, MBh. xii. **-nābha**, m., N. of a son of Bali, Hariv. **-padī**, f. of *-pāda*, q.v. **-pāda**, mf(*-padī*)n. having swollen legs bulging like a pitcher, Pāṇ. v, 4, 139. **-phalā**, f. the plant Cucurbita Pepo, L. **-bāhu**, m., N. of a Daitya, Hariv. **-bila**, n., Pāṇ. vi, 2, 102. **-bījaka**, m. a kind of Karañja, L. **-bhava**, m. (= *-janman*) the star Canopus (= Agastya). **-bhū**, m. = *-janman*, Hcar. **-maṇḍūka**, m. 'a frog in a pitcher,' i.e. an inexperienced man, gaṇas *pātresamitâdi* and *yuktârohy-ādi*; (cf. *kūpa-maṇḍūka*.) **-mushka** (*°bhá-*), mfn. having a jar-shaped scrotum (N. of demons), AV. **-mūrdhan**, m. 'pot-headed,' a particular demon causing diseases, Hariv. 9560. **-yoni**, m. 'born in a water-jar,' N. of Agastya, MBh.; Ragh.; BhP.; of Droṇa (the military preceptor of the Kurus and Pāṇḍus), L.; of Vasishṭha, L.; (*is*), f. the plant Phlomis ceylanica (commonly *droṇa-pushpī*), L.; 'having a jar-shaped pudendum,' N. of an Apsaras, MBh. iii, 1785. **-rāśi**, m. the sign Aquarius. **-retas**, n. semen virile deposited in a Kumbha, MBh. xiii, 7372; (*ās*), m. a form of Agni, MBh. iii, 14139. **-lagna**, n. that time of day in which Aquarius rises above the horizon. **-vaktra**, m., N. of an attendant of Skanda, MBh. ix, 2577. **-śālā**, f. a pottery, L. **-saṃdhi**, m. the hollow on the top of an elephant's head between the frontal globes, L. **-sambhava**, m. (= *-yoni*), N. of Agastya, R. vii, 80, 1; BhP.; of Nārāyaṇa, Hariv. 11426. **-sarpis**, n. butter placed in a jar, Suśr. **-stanī**, f. (Pāṇ. iv, 1, 54) having breasts like jars, BhP. **-hanu**, m. 'having a chin shaped like a Kumbha,' N. of a Rākshasa, R. vi, 32, 15. **Kumbhâṇḍa**, *ās*, m. pl. (perhaps a Prākrit form for *kushmāṇḍa*, q.v., but cf. *kumbhá-mushka*) 'having testicles shaped like a Kumbha,' a class of demons (at whose head stands Rudra), Buddh.; (*as*), m., N. of a minister of the Asura Bāṇa, BhP.; (*ī*), f. a pumpkin gourd (v.l. for *kushmāṇḍī*), L. **Kumbhâṇḍaka**, *ās*, m. pl. the class of demons called Kumbhâṇḍa, Buddh.; N. of an attendant of Skanda, MBh. ix, 2571 (v.l. *kumbhâṇḍakôdara*). **Kumbhêśvara-tīrtha**, n., N. of a Tīrtha, ŚivaP. **Kumbhêshṭakā**, f., N. of a particular brick, ApŚr. **Kumbhôdara**, m., N. of an attendant of Śiva, Ragh. ii, 35. **Kumbhôdbhava**, m. (= *kumbha-sambh°*), N. of Agastya. **Kumbhôdbhūta**, m. id. **Kumbhôlūka**, m. a kind of owl, MBh. xiii, 5499.

Kumbhaka, *as*, m. ifc. a pot, Kathās.; a measure (of grain, &c.), Jyot.; the prominence on the upper part of an elephant's forehead, MBh. xii, 4280; (*as, am*), m. n. stopping the breath by shutting the mouth and closing the nostrils with the fingers of the right hand (a religious exercise), BhP.; Vedântas.; Sarvad. &c.; (*as*), m. the base of a column, Buddh.; N. of an attendant of Skanda, MBh. ix, 2577; (*ikā*), f. a small pot or pitcher, Kathās. vi, 41; the plant Myrica sapida, Bhpr.; the plant Pistia Stratiotes, L.; Bignonia suaveolens, L.; a small shrub (= *droṇa-pushpī*), L.; a disease of the eyes (= *kumbhīkā*); N. of one of the mothers in Skanda's retinue, MBh. ix, 2633. **-paddhati**, f., N. of a work.

Kumbhi (in comp. for *°bhin*, q.v.) **-naraka**, m., N. of a hell, L. **-mada**, m. the juice that exudes from an elephant's temples at certain seasons, L.

Kumbhin, mfn. having a jar, RV. i, 191, 14; Lāṭy.; Vait.; shaped like a jar, W.; (*ī*), m. 'having on his forehead the prominence called *kumbha*,' an elephant; (hence) the number 'eight;' a crocodile, L.; a kind of poisonous insect, Suśr.; a sort of fragrant resin (*gúggulu*) or the plant bearing it, L.; N. of a demon hostile to children, PārGṛ. i, 16; (*inī*), f. the earth, Gal.

Kumbhinī (f. of *°bhin*, q.v.) **-bīja**, n. the croton-nut (Croton Jamalgota), L.

Kumbhila, *as*, m. a thief who breaks into a house (often in Prākrit *kumbhīlaa*, Mṛicch.; Vikr. &c.), L.; a plagiarist, L.; a wife's brother, L.; a child begotten at undue seasons or a child of an imperfect pregnation, W.; a kind of fish (the gilt-head, Ophiocephalus Wrahl), L.

Kumbhī (f. of *°bha*, q.v.) **-dhānya**, m. one who has grain stored in jars sufficient for six days or (according to others) for one year's consumption, Pat. on Pāṇ. i, 3, 7, Vārtt. 5. **-dhānyaka**, m. id., Mn. iv, 7; (cf. Yājñ. i, 128.) **-nása**, m. 'jar-nosed,' a kind of large venomous snake, TS. v, 5, 14, 1; a kind of venomous insect, Suśr.; (*ī*), f., N. of the wife of the Gandharva Aṅgāra-parṇa, MBh. i, 6469; of a Rākshasī (mother of Lavaṇa), R. v, 78, 8; Ragh. xv, 15. **-nasi**, m., N. of a demon, MBh. xiii, 2238. **-pāka**, m. the contents of a cooking vessel, Kauś. 6; a kind of fever, Bhpr.; (*as, ās*), m. sg. or pl. a hell in which the wicked are baked like potter's vessels or cooked like the contents of a cooking vessel, Mn. xii, 76; Yājñ. iii, 224; MBh. &c. **-bīja**, n. = *kumbhinī-b°*, q.v., L. **-māhātmya**, n., N. of a work. **-mukha**, n., N. of a particular wound, Car.

Kumbhīka, *as*, m. a pathic, catamite, Suśr.; the plant Rottleria tinctoria or perhaps Pistia Stratiotes (the bark of which furnishes a yellow dye), Suśr.; (*ā*), f. id., ib.; a swelling of the eyelids (similar to a seed or grain of the Kumbhika; hordeolum or stye), Suśr.; a kind of demon, AV. xvi, 6, 8. **-piḍakā**, f. the eye-disease called Kumbhikā, Suśr.

Kumbhīkin, mfn. similar to a seed of the Kumbhīka, Suśr.

Kumbhīra, *as*, m. a crocodile of the Ganges (the long-nosed alligator), MBh. xiii, 5457; Suśr.; N. of a Yaksha; of a plant, Gal. **-makshikā**, f. a sort of fly (Vespa solitaria), L.

Kumbhīraka, *as*, m. a thief, W.

Kumbhīla, *as*, m. (= *°bhīra*) a crocodile, L.

कुम्भरी *kumbharī*, f. a form of Durgā, L.

कुम्भला *kumbhalā*, f. a plant the flowers of which are compared to those of Nauclea Cadamba (Sphæranthus Hirtus), L.

कुम्भिल *kumbhila*, &c. See *kumbhá*.

कुयज्विन् *ku-yajvin*, &c. See 1. *ku*.

कुयवाच् *kúya-vāc*, mfn. (*kuya* = 1. *ku*), speaking ill, abusing (N. of a demon slain by Indra), RV. i, 174, 7; (cf. RV. v, 29, 10 & 32, 8.)

कुयोग *ku-yoga*, &c. See 1. *ku*.

कुर् *kur*, cl. 6. P. *kurati*, to utter a sound, Dhātup. xxviii, 51.

कुरका *kurakā*, f. the olibanum tree (Boswellia thurifera), L.

कुरङ्कर *kuraṅkara*, *as*, m. the Indian crane (Ardea sibirica), L.

Kuraṅkura, *as*, m. id., L.

कुरङ्ग *kuraṅga*, *as*, m. (√1. *kṛī*, Uṇ. i, 120), a species of antelope, antelope or deer (in general), Suśr.; Pañcat. &c.; (hence like *mṛiga*) the spot in the moon, Prasannar.; N. of a mountain, MBh. xiii, 1699; BhP. v, 16, 27; (*ī*), f. a female antelope, Gīt.; N. of a daughter of Prasena-jit, Kathās. **-nayanā**, f. 'fawn-eyed,' a handsome woman, Caurap. **-nābhi**, m. musk (formed in a bag attached to the belly of the deer above the navel), Naish.; Prasannar. **-netrā**, f. = *-nayanā*, ib. **-lāñchana**, m. 'deer-spotted,' the moon, Dhūrtan. **-locanā**, f. = *-nayanā*, Prasannar. **-vadhū**, f. a female antelope, ib. **Kuraṅgâkshī**, f. = *kuraṅga-nayanā*, Prasannar.; N. of a woman, Hcar.

Kuraṅgaka, *as*, m. an antelope, Kād.; N. of a man, Viddh.; (*ikā*), f. a kind of bean (= *mudga-parṇī*), L.; N. of a female servant, Viddh.

Kuraṅgama, *as*, m. an antelope, L.

Kuraṅgāya, Nom. Ā. *°yate*, to take the shape of an antelope, Bhartṛ.

कुरचिल्ल *kuracilla*, for *kuru-c°*, q.v., L.

कुरट *kuraṭa*, *as*, m. a shoemaker, leather-seller, L.; (*ās*), m. pl., N. of a people (v.l. for *kar°*).

कुरण्ट *kuraṇṭa*, *as*, m. yellow amaranth (*pītâmlāna*), L.; the plant Marsilea quadrifolia, L.

Kuraṇṭaka, *as*, m. yellow amaranth, L.; a yellow kind of Barleria, L.; (*ikā*), f. id., Suśr.; (*am*), n. the blossom of that plant, ib.

Kuraṇḍa, *as*, m. the plant commonly called *sā-kuruṇḍa*, L.; enlargement of the testicles or rather of the scrotum (including inguinal hernia &c.), L.

Kuraṇḍaka, *as*, m. yellow amaranth, L.; a yellow kind of Barleria, L.

Kuraba, *as*, m. a red kind of Barleria, L.; a kind of tree ['the Sesam tree,' Comm.], BhP. iii, 15, 19.

Kurabaka, *as*, m. red amaranth (or a red kind of Barleria), MBh.; Suśr.; Ragh. &c.; a species of rice, Suśr.; (*am*), n. the blossom of red amaranth (or of a red kind of Barleria), Śak.; Mālav.; Vikr. &c.

कुरयाण *kurayāṇa*, *as*, m. (probably) N. of a man, see *kauray°*

कुरर *kurara*, *as*, m. (fr. √3. *ku*, Uṇ. iii, 133) an osprey, Yājñ. i, 174; MBh. &c.; also another species of eagle, W.; the plant Capparis aphylla, Gal.; N. of a mountain, BhP. v, 16, 27; (*ī*), f. a female osprey, MBh. &c.; an ewe, L. **Kurarâṅghri**, m. a kind of mustard (= *deva-sarshapa*), L.

Kurarāva, mfn. abounding with ospreys (as a place), Pāṇ. v, 2, 109, Pat.

Kurarin, *ī*, m., N. of a mountain, VP.

Kurarī (f. of *°ra*, q.v.) **-gaṇa**, m. a flight of ospreys.

Kurala, *as*, m. an osprey, AV. Pariś.; = *kurula*, q.v., L. **-prastha**, m., N. of a town, gaṇa *karky-ādi*, Kāś.

कुरव *ku-rava*, &c. See 1. *ku*.

Ku-rājan, -rājya. See ib.

कुरी *kurī*, f. a kind of grass or corn, L.

कुरीर *kurī́ra*, *am*, n. (√1. *kṛi*, Uṇ. iv, 33), a kind of head-dress for women, RV. x, 85, 8; AV. vi, 138, 3; GopBr.; copulation, Uṇ.

Kurīrin, mfn. decorated with the head-dress called *kurīra*, AV. v, 31, 2; vi, 138, 2.

कुरु *kúru*, *avas*, m. pl., N. of a people of India and of their country (situated near the country of the Pañcālas; hence often connected with Pañcāla or Pāñcāla [see *kuru-pañc°* below]: the *uttarā-kuravaḥ* or *uttarāḥ kuravaḥ* are the northern Kurus, the most northerly of the four Mahā-dvīpas or principal divisions of the known world [distinguished from the *dakshiṇāḥ kuravaḥ* or southern Kurus, MBh. i, 4346], by other systems regarded as one of the nine divisions or Varshas of the same; it was probably a country beyond the most northern range of the Himālaya, often described as a country of everlasting happiness [AitBr.; MBh. &c.], and considered by some to be the ancient home of the Āryan race); = *ṛitvijas* (priests), Naigh.; = *kartāras* ('doers,' fr. √1. *kṛi*), Comm. on ChUp.; (*us*), m., N. of the ancestor of the Kurus (son of Saṃvaraṇa and Tapatī, daughter of the sun [MBh. i, 3738 ff.; Hariv. 1799 &c.]; Kuru is the ancestor of both Pāṇḍu and Dhṛita-rāshṭra, though the patronymic derived from his name is usually applied only to the sons of the latter, the sons and descendants of the former being called Pāṇḍavas); N. of a son of Āgnīdhra and grandson of Priya-vrata, VP.; BhP.; boiled rice, L.; the plant Solanum Jacquini (= *kaṇṭakārikā*), L.; (*ūs*), f. a princess of the Kuru race, Pāṇ. iv, 1, 66 & 176; (cf. *kaurava*, &c.) — **kata**, m., N. of a man, gaṇas *gargâdi* and *anuśatikâdi*. — **kandaka**, n. horse-radish (Raphanus sativus), L. — **kuru-kshetra**, n. the country of the Kurus and Kuru-kshetra, Pāṇ. ii, 4, 7, Kāś. — **kuru-jāṅgala**, n. the country of the Kurus and Kuru-jāṅgala, ib. — **kshetrá**, n. 'the field of the Kurus,' N. of an extensive plain near Delhi (the scene of the great battles between the Kurus and Pāṇḍus), AitBr.; ŚBr. &c.; (*ās*), m. pl. the inhabitants of that country (renowned for their bravery), Mn. vii, 193. — **kshetraka**, *ās*, m. pl. the inhabitants of the Kuru-kshetra, VarBṛS. — **kshetrin**, mfn. (with *yoga*) a solar day, in the course of which three lunar days, three asterisms, and three yogas occur. — **gārhapata**, n.?, Pāṇ. vi, 2, 42. — **cara**, mf(*ī*)n. ifc. f. *ā*, Pāṇ. iv, 1, 14 & 15, Pat. — **cilla**, m. a crab, L. — **jāṅgala**, n., N. of a country, MBh.; R. &c.; (*ās*), m. pl. the inhabitants of that country, MBh.; BhP.; VarBṛS. — **tīrtha**, n., N. of a Tīrtha, MBh. iii, 7036 ff. — **nadikā**, f. = *ku-nad°*, Comm. on Lāṭy. — **nandana**, m. a descendant of Kuru (as Arjuna, Yudhishṭhira, &c.), Bhag. &c. — **pañcālā**, *ās*, m. pl. the Kurus and Pañcālas, Kāṭh.; AitBr.; ŚBr.; MBh.; -*trā*, ind. as among the Kurus and Pañcālas, ŚBr. iii. — **patha**, m., 'N. of a man,' see *kaurupathi*. — **pāṇḍava**, *au*, *ās*, m. du. & pl. the descendants of Kuru (i. e. of Dhṛita-rāshṭra) and of Pāṇḍu, MBh. i, 2234; Rājat. — **piśaṅgila**, mf(*ā*)n.?, VS. xxiii, 55 f. — **puṃgava**, m. a Kuru chief (in the Draupadī-haraṇa applied to the Pāṇḍu princes). — **bāhu**, m. a kind of bird, L. — **bilva**, m. a ruby, L. — **bilvaka**, m. = *kulmāsha*, L. — **rāj**, m. 'lord of the Kurus,' N. of Duryodhana, L. — **rāja**, m., N. of Yudhishṭhira, MBh. xvi, 7. — **rājya**, n. the Kuru realm. — **vaṅśa**, m., N. of a prince, VP. — **vaṅśaka**, m. id., ib. — **vatsa**, m., N. of a prince (v.l. for -*vaśa*). — **varṇaka**, *ās*, m. pl., N. of a people, MBh. vi, 364. — **vaśa**, m., N. of a prince, BhP. ix, 24, 5. — **vājapeya**, m. a particular kind of Vājapeya, ŚāṅkhŚr.; Lāṭy. — **vista**, m. a Pala of gold (in weight equal to about 700 troy grains), Hcat. — **vṛiddha**, m., N. of Bhīshma, Bhag. i, 12. — **śrávaṇa**, m., N. of a prince, RV. x, 32, 9 & 33, 4. — **śreshṭha**, m., N. of Arjuna, Bhag. — **sattama**, m. id., ib. — **suti**, m., N. of a Vedic poet (author of RV. viii, 76–78). — **hāra**, m., N. of an Agra-hāra, Rājat. i, 88.

Kuruka, *as*, m., N. of a prince (v. l. for *ruruka*), VP.

कुरुकुल्ला *kurukullā*, f. (fr. °*ru-kulyā*, 'belonging to the Kuru race'?), N. of a Buddh. deity.

कुरुङ्ग *kuruṅgá*, *as*, m., N. of a prince, RV. viii, 4, 19.

कुरुट *kuruṭa*, *as*, m. a kind of pot-herb (Marsilea quadrifolia), L.; (cf. *kuraṇṭa*.)

Kuruṭin, *ī*, m. a horse, L.

कुरुण्ट *kuruṇṭa*, *as*, m. yellow amaranth, L.; yellow Barleria, L.; (*ī*), f. a doll, puppet made of wood, L.; the wife of a Brāhman, L.

Kuruṇṭaka, *as*, m. yellow amaranth or Barleria, Suśr.; (*ikā*), f. id., ib.

Kuruṇṭha, *as*, m. yellow amaranth or Barleria, Lalit.

कुरुण्डि *kuruṇḍi*, *is*, m., N. of a Ṛishi in the third Manv-antara, VP.

कुरुत *kuruta*, ? gaṇa *hasty-ādi* (v. l.); (*ā*), f. a particular high number, Lalit. — **pāda**, mfn., gaṇa *hasty-ādi*, v. l.

कुरुम्ब *kurumba*, *as*, m. a kind of orange (= *kula-pālaka*), L.; (*ā*), f. the plant Phlomis ceylanica (commonly Droṇa-pushpi), L.; (*ī*), f. a kind of pepper, L.

Kurumbikā, f. the plant Phlomis ceylanica, L.

कुरुरी *kururī*, for *kurarī*, q. v.

कुरुल *kurula*, *as*, m. a curl or lock of hair (especially on the forehead), L.

कुरुवक *kuruvaka*, for *kurabaka*, q. v.

कुरुविन्द *kuruvinda*, *as*, m. a kind of barley, Suśr.; Comm. on Śiś. ix, 8; a fragrant grass (Cyperus rotundus), L.; the plant Terminalia Catappa, L.; the bud of a flower, L.; = *kulmāsha* (cf. *kuru-bilvaka*), L.; (*as*, *am*), m. n. a ruby, Suśr.; Daś.; Śiś. ix, 8; (*am*), n. black salt, L.; cinnabar, L.

Kuruvindaka, *as*, m. a wild variety of Dolichos biflorus, L.

कुरूटिन् *kurūṭín*, mfn. perhaps = *kirīṭin*, AV. x, 1, 15.

कुरूप *ku-rūpa*, &c. See 1. *ku*.

कुरूरु *kurū́ru*, *us*, m. a species of worm, AV. ii, 31, 2 & ix, 2, 22.

कुर्कुट *kurkuṭa*, *as*, m. (= *kukk°*) a cock, Pañcat. **Kurkuṭâhi**, m. a kind of serpent, L.; (cf. *kukkuṭâhi*.) **Kurkuṭī-vrata**, n. = *kukk°*, q. v., BhavP.

कुर्कुर *kurkurá*, *as*, m. (= *kukk°*) a dog, AV.; VarBṛS.; Pañcat.

Kurkurīya, Nom. P. °*yati*, to behave like a dog, Pāṇ. viii, 2, 78, Pat.

कुर्चिका *kurcikā*, f. (= *kūrc°*) the milky juice of a bulbous root, L.; a needle, L.

कुर्णज *kurṇaja*, *as*, m., N. of a plant (commonly *kulañjana*), L.

कुर्द *kurd*, °*rdana*, for *kūrd*, &c., q. v.

कुर्पर *kurpara*, for *kūrp°*, q. v.

कुर्पास *kurpāsa*, for *kūrp°*, q. v.

कुर्मल *kurmala*. See *kúlmala*.

कुर्वत् *kurvat*, mfn. (pr. p. P., √1. *kṛi*) doing, acting, &c.; acting as a servant, agent, servant, L.; present, actual, AitBr. iv, 31, 3. **Kurvad-rūpa**, n. cause (according to the Cārvākas), W.

Kurvāṇa, mfn. (pr. p. Ā.) doing, making; acting as a servant, agent, L.

कुल् *kul*, cl. 1. *kolati*, to accumulate, collect, Dhātup. xx, 12; to be of kin, behave as a kinsman, ib.; to proceed continuously or without interruption, ib.; to count, ib.

कुल *kúla*, *am*, n. (ifc. f. *ā*) a herd, troop, flock, assemblage, multitude, number, &c. (of quadrupeds, birds, insects, &c., or of inanimate objects, e. g. *go-kula*, a herd of cows, R. &c.; *mahishi-k°*, a herd of female buffaloes, Ṛitus.; *ali-k°*, a swarm of bees, Śiś.; Git. &c.; *alaka-k°*, a multitude of curls, BhP.); a race, family, community, tribe, caste, set, company (e. g. *brāhmaṇa-k°*, the caste of the Brāhmans, BhP.; *padātīnām kula*, infantry, Rājat. v, 247); (ifc. with a gen. sg.) a lot, gang (e. g. *caurasya-k°*, a gang of thieves), Pāṇ. vi, 3, 21, Kāś.; the residence of a family, seat of a community, inhabited country (as much ground as can be ploughed by two ploughs each drawn by six bulls, Comm. on Mn. vii, 119); a house, abode, MBh.; a noble or eminent family or race, Mn.; MBh. &c.; high station (in comp. 'chief, principal,' cf. *kula-giri*, &c.); the body, L.; the front, forepart, W.; a blue stone, L.; (with Śāktas) N. of Śakti and of the rites observed in her worship; (cf. *kaula*); = *kula-nakshatra*, q. v., Tantras.; (*as*), m. the chief of a corporation or guild, L.; = *kula-vāra*, q. v., Tantras.; N. of a man, R. vii, 43, 2; (*ā*), f. 'a principal day,' N. of the 4th and 8th and 12th and 14th day in a *paksha* or half-month, Tantras.; (*ī*), f. a wife's elder sister, L.; the plant Solanum Jacquini or Solanum longum, L. — **kajjala**, m. disgrace of the family. — **kaṇṭaka**, m. 'a thorn in a family,' a bad member of a family, Comm. on MBh. i, 170, 15. — **kanyakā**, f. a girl of good family, R. — **kanyā**, f. id. — **kara**, m. the founder of a family, ancestor, MBh. — **karkaṭī**, for *kulaka-kark°*, q. v. — **kartṛi**, m. the founder of a family or race, ancestor, MBh. xv, 988. — **karman**, n. the peculiar or proper duty of a family, any observance peculiar to a family, W. — **kalaṅka**, m. 'a family stain,' any one who disgraces his family, W.; -*kārin*, mfn. disgracing one's family, Pañcat. — **kalaṅkita**, mfn. causing disgrace to a family, Kathās. xxii, 216. — **kuṇḍalinī**, f., N. of a particular Śakti. — **kūṇī**, f. a harlot, Gal. — **kauśika**, m., N. of an author of Mantras. — **kshaya**, m. decay of a race or family, MBh. iii, 13231; (*ā*), f. a sort of cowach (Mucuna pruritus), L. — **gariman**, m. family pride or dignity. — **giri**, m. a chief mountain-range (any one of the seven principal ranges supposed to exist in each Varsha or division of a continent; those of Bhārata-varsha are Mahendra, Malaya, Sahya, Śuktimat, Ṛiksha, Vindhya, and Pāripātra or Pāriyātra), BhP. — **guru**, m. the head of a family, family preceptor, VP. — **gṛiha**, n. a noble house, Ṛitus. vi, 21. — **gopá**, m. the protector of a domicile, TS. vi. — **gaurava**, n. family importance. — **ghna**, mf(*ā*, MBh. xiii, 2397; *ī*, R. ii, 35, 6)n. destroying a family. — **m-kula**, mfn. visiting houses one after the other, ŚāṅkhGṛ.; Gaut. — **candra**, m., N. of the author of a Comm. on the Kāt.; of the author of the Durgā-vākya-prabodha. — **cūḍāmaṇi**, m., N. of a Tantra. — **cyuta**, mfn. expelled from a family. — **ja**, mf(*ā*)n. born in a noble family, well-born, of good breed, Mn. viii, 179; Pañcat.; Sāh. &c.; (*am*), n. sour gruel, Gal. — **jana**, m. a person belonging to a noble family, Mṛicch. — **jāta**, mfn. born in a noble family, R. i, 71, 2. — **tattva-vid**, mfn. knowing the true state of a family. — **tantu**, m. 'the thread coming down from a race,' the last representative of a family, MBh. i. — **tas**, ind. by birth. — **tithi**, f. = *kulā*, q. v., L. — **tilaka**, m. the glory of a family. — **damana**, mfn. subduing a family, holding it in subjection, gaṇa *nandy-ādi*. — **dīpa**, m. the lamp or light or glory of a race or family; *kula-dīpôtsava*, m., N. of a festival. — **dīpikā**, f., N. of a work (treating on the noble families of Bengāl). — **duhitṛi** (Pāṇ. vi, 3, 70, Vārtt. 9), f. the daughter of a noble family, high-born maiden, Karaṇḍ. — **dūshaṇa**, mfn. disgracing one's family, Mṛicch. — **deva**, m. the family deity, BrahmaP.; (*ī* or metrically shortened *i*), f. 'principal goddess,' N. of Durgā, BhP. x, 52, 42. — **devatā**, f. the family deity, Kum. vii, 27; VP. &c.; = -*devī*, f., N. of Durgā, W. — **daiva**, n. family destiny, BhP. ix, 5, 9; the family deity, BhP. ix, 9, 43. — **daivata**, n. the family deity, R. i, 72, 14. — **dhara**, m. 'upholder of his family,' N. of a prince, Kathās. lx, 3. — **dharma**, m. practice or observance peculiar to a tribe or family, peculiar duty of caste or race, ĀśvGṛ.; Āp.; Mn. &c.; peculiar practice or duty of the Kaulas. — **dhāraka**, m. 'upholder of the family,' a son, L. — **dhurya**, mfn. one who is able to support a family (as a grown-up son), Ragh. vii, 68. — **nakshatra**, n. any Nakshatra or lunar mansion distinguished above others, any auspicious asterism, Tantras. — **nandana**, m., *ā*, f. a boy or girl causing joy or doing honour to a family, Pañcat.; BhP.; Vet. — **nāga**, m. a chief of the Nāgas, RāmatUp. — **nāyikā**, f. a girl worshipped at the celebration of the orgies of the left-hand Śāktas. — **nārī**, f. a woman of good family, high-bred virtuous woman, Hit. — **nāśa**, m. 'destroying its family,' a camel, L.; a reprobate, outcast, W. — **nindā**, f. family disgrace. — **nimnagā**, f. a principal river, Rājat. iv, 308.

—**m-dhara,** mfn. upholding one's family, BhP. i, 13, 15. —**pañcāśikā,** f., N. of a work. —**patana,** n. decay or disgrace of a family, Pañcat. —**pati,** m. the head or chief of a family, MBh.; R.; Mṛicch. &c. —**paramparā,** f. the series of generations comprising a race. —**parvata,** m. = *-giri,* q. v. —**pā́,** m. f. the chief of a family or race or tribe, RV. x, 179, 2; AV. —**pāṇsukā,** f. an unchaste woman, W. —**pāta,** for *kūla-p°,* MBh. xii, 12059. —**pālaka,** mfn. protecting or providing for a family; (*as*), f. a kind of orange (= *kurumba*), L.; (*ikā*), f. a virtuous high-born woman; N. of a woman, Daś. —**pāli, -pālī,** f. 'family-protectress,' a high-born virtuous woman, L. —**putra,** m. a son of a noble family, respectable youth, MBh.; Mṛicch.; Daś. &c.; the plant Artemisia indica, L.; (*ī*), f. the daughter of a good family, high-born or respectable girl (= *-duhitṛi*), Pāṇ. vi, 3, 70, Vārtt. 9; (*kula-putra-*)*jana,* m. a son of a noble family, Mṛicch. —**putraka,** m. a son of a noble family, Kathās.; the plant Artemisia indica, Bhpr. —**purusha,** m. a man of good family, noble or respectable man, Bhartṛ. i, 91; an ancestor, family progenitor, W. —**pūrvaka,** m. an ancestor, R. ii, 73, 24 (ifc. f. *ā*). —**pūrva-ga,** v. l. for *-pūrvaka,* q. v. —**prakāśa,** m., N. of a work. —**pradīpa,** m. the lamp or light or glory of a family, Hcar. —**prasūta,** mfn. born in a noble family, Pañcat. —**bālikā,** f. (= *-pālikā*) a virtuous high-born woman, L. —**bīja,** m. the head or chief of a guild, Gal. —**bhava,** mfn. born in a noble family. —**bhavana,** n. the chief residence, Kād. —**bhāryā,** f. a virtuous or noble wife, Pāṇ. i, 3, 47, Kāś. —**bhū-bhṛit,** m. = *-giri,* Ragh. xvii, 78; Kathās.; an excellent prince, Kathās. ic, 7. —**bhūshaṇa,** mfn. 'family-adorning,' a family ornament. —**bhṛityā,** f. the nursing of a pregnant woman, L.; a midwife, nurse, W.; (cf. *kumāra-bhṛityā.*) —**bheda-kara,** m. one who causes discord in a family. —**bhrashṭa,** mfn. expelled from a family. —**maryādā,** f. family honour or respectability. —**mātṛikā,** f. a kind of spear, Gal. —**mārga,** m. the best or principal way, way of honesty; the doctrine of the Kaulas; *-tantra,* n. a collective N. for 64 Tantras. —**mitra,** n. a friend of the family, W.; (*as*), m. = *-bīja,* Gal. —**m-puna,** n. 'purifying a family,' N. of a Tīrtha, MBh. iii, 6074; (*ā*), f., N. of a river, MBh. xiii, 7646. —**m-bhara,** mfn. carrying or upholding a family (with *anaḍ-vah,* a bull kept for breeding), MBh. xiii, 4427; (*as*), m., v. l. for *kujambhala* (a thief), L. —**yukti,** f., N. of a work. —**yoshit,** f. a virtuous high-born woman, Mn. iii, 245; Kathās. —**rakshaka,** mfn. preserving a family. —**ratnamālā, °likā,** f., N. of two works. —**ṛddhika** (*ṛiddh°*), m. the son of a cousin, Gal. —**vat,** mfn. (*gaṇa balâdi*) belonging to a noble family, R.; Kathās. —**vadhū,** f. a virtuous wife, respectable woman, KapS. iii, 70; *-tā,* f. virtue in a wife. —**varṇā,** f. a species of the plant Convolvulus with red blossoms (= *rakta-trivṛit*), L. —**vartman,** n. (= *-mārga*) the doctrine of the Kaulas. —**vardhana,** mfn. increasing or advancing or propagating a family, R. —**vāra,** m. 'a principal day,' Tuesday or Friday, Tantras. —**vidyā,** f. knowledge handed down in a family, Mālav. —**vipra,** m. a family priest, L. —**vṛiddha,** m. the oldest member or head of a family, BhP. —**vṛiddhi,** f. family advancement. —**vyāpin,** mfn. attaching or applicable to tribe or caste. —**vrata,** n. a family vow, traditional custom or manners in a family, Śak.; Mālav.; Ragh. iii, 70. —**śikharin,** m. = *-giri,* Bhartṛ. —**śīla,** n. character or conduct honourable to a family; *-vat,* mfn. endowed with a noble character or disposition, Hcat.; *-samanvita,* mfn. id. —**śulka,** n. the present to be given to the father-in-law for his daughter before marriage, L. —**śekhara,** m., N. of the author of the Mukunda-mālā. —**śaila,** m. = *-giri,* Kathās. cxix, 16. —**śreshṭhin,** mfn. of good family, eminent in family; (*ī*), m. the chief of a guild, L. —**sa,** mfn. (√*so*) ruining a family, Comm. on MBh. i, 170, 15. —**saṃkhyā,** f. ranking or being reckoned as a family, family respectability, Mn. iii, 66. —**sattra,** n. a family sacrifice, KātyŚr. —**saṃtati,** f. propagation of a family, descendants, Mn. v, 159; MBh. —**saṃnidhi,** m. the presence of a number of persons or of witnesses, Mn. viii, 194 & 201. —**samudbhava,** mfn. born in a noble family, Hit. —**sambhava,** mfn. id., L. —**sāra,** n., N. of a Tantra. —**sundarī,** f., N. of a deity, BrahmaP. —**sūtra,** n., N. of a work. —**sevaka,** m. an excellent attendant or servant, Pañcat. —**saurabha,** n., N. of a plant (= *maruvaka*), L. —**strī,** f. a woman of good family, respectable or virtuous woman, MBh.; R. &c. —**sthiti,** f. custom observed in a family, Kād.; antiquity or prosperity of a family, W. —**haṇḍaka,** for *kūla-h°,* q. v. —**hīna,** mfn. of low origin, Mudr. **Kulâkula,** mfn. excellent and not excellent, middling, W.; of mixed character or origin, W.; (*as*), m. (or *kulâkula-vāra,* m.) Wednesday, Tantras.; (cf. *kula-vāra*); N. of a Dānava (v. l. *°li*), Hariv. 12936; (*am*), n. (or *kulâkula-tithi,* f.) the second, sixth, and tenth lunar day in a half-month, Tantras.; (*am*), n. (or *kulâkula-nakshatra,* n.) 'an asterism of mixed character,' N. of the lunar mansions Ārdrā, Mūlā, Abhijit, and Śatabhishā, Tantras.; *-tithi,* f., *-nakshatra,* n., *-vāra,* m., see before. **Kulâkuli,** m., N. of a Dānava (v. l. for *kulâkula,* q. v.) **Kulâṅkura,** m. offspring of a family, Śak. **Kulâṅganā,** f. a respectable or virtuous woman, MBh. &c. **Kulâṅgāra,** m. 'a family fire-brand,' a man who foments domestic dissensions or ruins his family, Pañcat.; BhP.; Prasannar.; (*ī*), f. a woman who ruins her family, Hariv. 9940. **Kulâcala,** m. = *kula-giri,* BhP.; Kathās.; N. of a Dānava (v. l. for *kulâkula*), Hariv. **Kulâcāra,** m. the peculiar or proper duty of a family or caste. **Kulâcārya,** m. a family teacher, family priest, BhP.; VP.; a person well versed in pedigrees and customs of different families and employed to contract marriages between them, L.; a genealogist, W. **Kulâdya,** see *adhivājya-k°.* **Kulâdri,** m. = *kula-giri,* BhP.; Rājat. iii, 341. **Kulâdhāraka,** m. 'upholder of a family,' a son, L.; (cf. *kula-dhār°.*) **Kulânanda,** m. 'the joy of his family,' N. of an author of Mantras. **Kulânala,** m. 'a family fire-brand (cf. *kulâṅgāra*),' N. of a man. **Kulânta-karaṇa,** mfn. one who ruins his family, MBh. **Kulânvaya,** m. noble descent, MBh. v, 1136; xii, 4300. **Kulânvita,** mfn. sprung from a noble family, Pañcat. **Kulâpīḍa,** m. the glory of a family, Ragh. xviii, 28. **Kulâbhimāna,** n. family pride. **Kulâbhimānin,** mfn. proud of birth or of family descent. **Kulâmṛita,** n., N. of a work. **Kulâmbā,** f. 'mother of a family,' family deity, BrahmaP. **Kulârṇava,** m., N. of a Tantra work; *-tantra,* n. id. **Kulâlambin,** mfn. supporting or maintaining a family, W. **Kulâshṭamī,** f. (with Śāktas) N. of a particular eighth day. **Kulecara,** a kind of plant, Suśr. **Kuleśāna,** m., N. of an author of Tantras. **Kuleśvara,** m. the lord or chief of a family, L.; 'the lord κατ' ἐξοχήν,' N. of Śiva, L.; of an author of Mantras; (*ī*), f., N. of Durgā; *°śvarī-tantra,* n., N. of a Tantra. **Kulôtkaṭa,** mfn. excellent by birth, L.; (*as*), m. a horse of good breed, L. **Kulôtkarsha,** m. family eminence. **Kulôtpanna,** mfn. sprung from a good family, well-born; belonging to a family (as property, &c.) **Kulôdgata,** mfn. sprung from a noble family, Mn. vii. **Kulôddeśa,** n., N. of a Tantra. **Kulôdbhava,** mfn. = *kulôdgata,* L. **Kulôdbhūta,** mfn. id. **Kulôdvaha,** mfn. propagating the family of, descendant of (gen. or in comp.), MBh. iii, 676; R. **Kulôpakula,** n. 'excellent and less excellent,' N. of certain lunar mansions, Sūryapr. **Kulôpadeśa,** m. family name, W.

Kulaka, *am,* n. ifc. a multitude, BhP. v, 7, 11; the stone of a fruit, Car.; a sort of gourd (Trichosanthes dioeca), L.; a collection of three or four [Rājat.] or five [Sāh.] stanzas in which the government of verb and noun is carried throughout (contrary to the practice of closing the sense with each verse); a kind of prose composition with few compound words; (*as*), m. the chief of a guild, L.; any artisan of eminent birth, L.; an ant-hill, mole-hill, L.; a sort of mouse; a green snake, L.; a kind of ebony (Diospyros tomentosa), L.; another species of ebony (commonly Ku-pīlu), Bhpr.; another plant (commonly *maruvaka, śukla-pushpa, tilaka*), L.; (*ās*), m. pl., N. of the Śūdras in Kuśa-dvīpa, BhP. v, 20, 16. —**karkaṭī,** f. a species of gourd, L.

Kulara, mfn., g. *aśmâdi* (not in Kāś.)

Kulāyana, *as,* m., N. of a man, Pravar.

Kulika, mfn. of good family, W.; (*as*), m. a kinsman, Yājñ. ii, 233; the chief or head man of a guild, L.; any artisan of eminent birth, L.; a hunter, BhP. x, 47, 19; a thorny plant (Ruellia longifolia or Asteracantha longifolia), L.; (= *kula-vāra*) Tuesday or Friday; one of the eight chiefs of the Nāgas or serpent-race (described as having a half-moon on the top of his head and being of a dusky-brown colour), MBh. i, 2549; BhP.; Rāmat-Up.; N. of a prince, VP.; a kind of poison, Gal. —**velā,** f. certain portions of each day on which it is improper to begin any good business.

Kulin, mfn. belonging to a noble family, *gaṇa balâdi;* (*inī*), f. the plant Impatiens balsamina, L.

Kulīna, mf(*ā,* Pāṇ. iv, 1, 139)n. belonging to the family of (in comp.), ŚBr.; ChUp.; MBh.; R.; of high or eminent descent, well-born, Mn.; Yājñ. &c.; of good breed (as horses or elephants), R. v, 12, 31; (*as*), m. a horse of good breed, L.; a Brāhman of the highest class in Bengāl (i. e. a member of one of the eight principal families of the Vārendra division or of one of the six chief families of the Rāḍha or Rāṛh division as classified by Balāl Sen, Rāja of Bengāl, in the twelfth century; common names of the latter families are Mukharjea, Banarjea, Chatarjea, &c.); a worshipper of Śakti accord. to the left-hand ritual, W.; (*ā*), f. a variety of the Āryā metre; (*am*), n. a disease of the nails, Suśr. —**tā,** f. rank, family respectability. —**tva,** n. id., Bhartṛ. i, 61.

Kulīnaka, mfn. of good family, W.; (*as*), m. a kind of wild kidney-bean (Phaseolus trilobus), L.

Kulīya, mfn. belonging to the family of (in comp.), Pañcad.

Kuleya, mfn. ifc. id., MBh. i, 6804.

1. **Kulya,** mf(*ā*)n. relating to a family or race, Bhartṛ. iii, 24 (ifc.); BhP. vii, 6, 12; x, 57, 1; (cf. *rāja-k°*); belonging to a congregation or corporation, W.; of good family, well-descended, Pāṇ. iv, 1, 140; (*as*), m. a respectable man, L.; N. of a teacher (the pupil of Paushpañji), BhP. xii, 6, 79; 1. (*ā*), f. (perhaps) custom or habit of a family, AV, xi, 3, 13; a virtuous or respectable woman, L.; the medicinal plant Celtis orientalis (= *jīvantikâushadhi*), L.; the plant Solanum longum, L.; (*am*), n. friendly inquiry after family affairs or domestic accidents (condolence, congratulation, &c.), W.

कुलक्क *kulakka, as,* m. a cymbal (beating time in music), L.

कुलङ्ग *kulaṅgá, as,* m. (= *kuraṅga*) an antelope, MaitrS.; (*ī*), f., v. l. for *kuliṅgī,* q. v.

कुलञ्ज *kulañja, as,* m. the plant Alpinia Galanga, L.

Kulañjana, *as,* m. id., L.

कुलट *kulaṭa, as,* m. (fr. *kula* and √*aṭ,* Pāṇ. iv, 1, 127, Kāś.), any son except one's own offspring (an adopted son, bought son, &c.), W.; (*ā*), f. (*gaṇa śakandhv-ādi*) an unchaste woman, Ap.; Yājñ. &c.; (cf. *kumāra-k°*); an honourable female mendicant, Pāṇ. iv, 1, 127, Kāś. **Kulaṭā-pati,** m. the husband of an unchaste woman, cuckold, W.; (*ī*), f. (= *kunaṭī*) red arsenic, L.

कुलत्थ *kulattha, as,* m. (fr. *kula?,* cf. *aśvattha, kapittha*), a kind of pulse (Dolichos uniflorus), Pāṇ. iv, 4, 4; MBh. &c.; (*ās*), m. pl., N. of a people, MBh. vi, 373; VP.; (*ā*), f. a kind of Dolichos (Glycine labialis), L.; a blue stone used in medicine and applied as a collyrium to the eyes and as an astringent to sores, &c., L.; a species of metre.

Kulatthikā, f. a kind of Dolichos (cf. *araṇya-k°*), Suśr.; a blue stone used as a collyrium &c., L.

कुलभ *kulabha, as,* m., N. of a Daitya (v. l. *sulabha*), Hariv. 12940.

कुलाक्षुता *kulākshutā,* f. a bitch, W.

कुलाट *kulāṭa, as,* m. a kind of small fish, L.

कुलाभि *kulābhi,* v. l. for *ku-nābhi,* L.

कुलाय *kulā́ya, am,* n. (in later language also *as,* m., Pañcat. &c.) a woven texture, web, nest (of a bird), case or investing integument, receptacle, home, AV.; TS.; ŚBr. &c.; the body as the dwelling-place of the soul, AV.; ŚBr. xiv; BhP.; the kennel or resting-place of a dog, Pāṇ. i, 3, 21, Vārtt. 4; a place, spot in general, L.; (with *agneḥ,* Vait.; or with *indrâgnyoḥ,* TāṇḍyaBr.; ĀśvŚr. &c.) N. of a particular Ekâha; (cf. *aindrâgna-k°.*) —**nilāya,** m. the act of sitting in a nest, hatching, brooding. —**nilāyin,** mfn. sitting in a nest, brooding; *-(nilāyi-)tā,* f. the act of hatching, &c. —**stha,** m. 'nest-dweller,' a bird, L.

Kulāyayat, mfn. (pr. p. P.) building nests or a resting-place, RV. vii, 50, 1.

Kulāyikā, f. a bird-cage, aviary, L.

Kulāyín, mfn. forming a nest, shaped like a nest, RV. vi, 15, 16; VS.; TS.; (*inī*), f. an aviary, Gal.; N. of a liturgical service, TāṇḍyaBr.; Lāṭy.; Comm. on Nyāyam.

कुलायन *kulāyana*. See *kúla*.

कुलाल *kúlāla*, *as*, m. (fr. √*kul*, Uṇ. i, 117), a potter, VS. xvi, 27; Pāṇ.; Bhartṛ. &c.; a wild cock (Phasianus gallus), L.; an owl, L.; N. of a prince, VP.; (*ī*), f. the wife of a potter, Rājat. viii, 138; (= *kulatthā*) the plant Glycine labialis, L.; a blue stone applied as a collyrium to the eyes, L. — **kukkuṭa**, m. a wild cock (Phasianus gallus), VarBṛS. — **kṛita** (*kúl°*), mfn. made by a potter, MaitrS. i, 8, 3. — **cakra**, n. a potter's disk, BhP. v, 22, 2. — **vat**, ind. like a potter. — **śālā**, f. a potter's workshop, JābālaUp.

कुलालिका *kulālikā*, for *°lāyikā*, q.v.

कुलाह *kulāha*, *as*, m. a horse of a light-brown colour with black knees, L.

Kulāhaka, *as*, m. a lizard, chamelion, L.; the plant Celsia coromandelina, L.

कुलाहल *kulāhala*, *as*, m., N. of a plant (= *alambusha*, *gocchāla*, *bhū-kadamba*, commonly Kokaśimā, Coryza terebinthina or Celsia coromandelina [see *kulāhaka*], a plant which dogs are fond of smelling before they expel urine), Suśr.

कुलि *kuli*, *is*, m. the hand, L.; (*is*), f. (= *°lī*) Solanum Jacquini (prickly nightshade), L.

कुलिक *kulika*. See *kúla*.

कुलिङ्कक *kuliṅkaka*. See *°liṅgaka*.

कुलिङ्ग *ku-liṅga*, *°ṅgaka*. See 1. *ku*.

कुलिज *kulija*, *am*, n. a particular vessel, Kauś. 12 & 43; a sort of measure, Pāṇ. v, 1, 55 (ifc. f. *ā* [Kāś.] or *ī*).

Kulijika, mf(*ī*)n. ifc. fr. *kulija*, Pāṇ. v, 1, 55.
Kulijīna, mf(*ā*)n. id., ib.

कुलिन् *kulin*. See *kúla*.

कुलिन्द *kulinda*, *ās*, m. pl., N. of a people, MBh.; (*as*), m. a prince of the Kulindas, ib. **Kulindôpatyaka**, *ās*, m. pl., N. of a people, MBh. vi, 363.

कुलिर *kulira*, for *°līra*, q.v., L.

कुलिश *kúliśa*, *as*, m. (fr. 1. *ku* and *liśa* for *riśa* fr. √*riś*), an axe, hatchet, RV. i, 32, 5 & iii, 2, 1; AV.; MBh.; (*am*), n. [*as*, m., Naigh.; Nir. & L.] the thunderbolt of Indra, MBh.; Ragh.; Bhartṛ. &c.; (= *vajra*) a diamond, Megh.; Rājat. vi, 273; (*as*), m. a sort of fish, Suśr.; (*as*, *am*), m. n. the plant Heliotropium indicum, L.; (*ī*), f., N. of a river (supposed to be in the middle region of the sky), RV. i, 104, 4. — **druma**, m. a sort of Opuntia tree, Npr. — **dhara**, m. 'holding the thunderbolt,' N. of Indra, VarBṛS. — **nāyaka**, m. a kind of coitus. — **pāṇi**, m. = *-dhara*, Śiś. xi, 43. — **bhṛit**, m. = *-dhara*, VarBṛS. — **lepa**, m. = *vajra-l°*, q.v., VarBṛS. **Kuliśâṅkuśā**, f., N. of one of the sixteen Vidyā-devīs, L. **Kuliśâsana**, m. 'having a diamond seat,' N. of Śākya-muni, L.

Kuliśāya, Nom. Ā. *°yate*, to be equal to the thunderbolt or to a diamond (in hardness), Hcar.

कुलिशासन *kuliśāsana* = *kuliśâsana*, q.v. (s.v. *kúliśa*) or = *kuli-śāsana*, 'one who commands with his hand (*kuli*),' N. of Śākya-muni, L.

कुली *kulī*. See *kúla*.

कुलीकय *kulīkáya*, *as*, m. a kind of aquatic animal, TS. v, 5, 13, 1; (*kulīpáya*) VS. xxiv, 21 & 35.

Kulīkā, f. a kind of bird, VS. xxiv, 24.

कुलीन *kulīna*, &c. See *kúla*.

कुलीनस *kulīnasa*, *am*, n. water, L.

कुलीपय *kulīpáya*. See *°līkáya*.

कुलीर *kulīra*, *as*, m. a crab, Suśr.; Pañcat.; the sign of the zodiac Cancer, R. i, 19, 8; VarBṛ. — **vishāṇikā**, f. a kind of oak-apple, Bhpr. — **śṛiṅgī**, f. id., ib. **Kulīrâd**, m. 'eating i.e. destroying crabs,' a young crab (the old crab being supposed to perish on producing young), L.

Kulīraka, *as*, m. a small crab, Pañcat.

कुलीश *kulīśa*, *as*, *am*, m. n. (= *kuliśa*) Indra's thunderbolt, L.

कुलुक *kuluka*, *am*, n. the fur or foulness of the tongue, L. (v. l. *kulvaka*).

कुलुक्कगुञ्जा *kulukka-guñjā*, f. (for *ulkā-g°*?) a firebrand, L.

कुलुङ्ग *kuluṅgá*, *as*, m. (= *kulaṅgá*) an antelope, VS. xxiv; TS. v.

कुलुञ्च *ku-luñcá*. See 1. *ku*.

कुलूत *kulūta*, *ās*, m. pl., N. of a people, VarBṛS.; Kād. &c.

Kulūtaka, *ās*, m. pl. id., VarBṛS.; (*as*), m. sg. a Kulūta man, Pratāpar.

कुलून *kulūna*, N. of a place, gaṇa *kacchâdi* (Kāś.)

कुलेचर *kule-cara*, &c. See *kúla*.

कुल्फ *kulphá*, *as*, m. (= *gulphá*; √3. *kal*, Uṇ.) the ancle, RV. vii, 50, 2; ŚBr. xi; (*as*, *am*), m. n. a disease, L. — **daghná**, mfn. reaching down to the ancle, ŚBr. xii.

कुल्मल *kúlmala*, *am*, n. the part of an arrow or spear by which the head is attached to the shaft, MaitrS.; AV. (once *kúrmala*); ŚBr. iii; sin, Uṇ. iv, 189. — **barhisha**, m., N. of a Vedic poet (author of RV. x, 126), RAnukr. — **barhis**, m. id., TāṇḍyaBr. xv.

कुल्माष *kulmāsha*, *as*, m. (also *ās*, m. pl.) sour gruel (prepared by the spontaneous fermentation of the juice of fruits or of boiled rice), Suśr.; an inferior kind of grain, half-ripe barley, ChUp.; BhP. v, 9, 12; Bhpr.; (*as*), m. a kind of disease, L.; (*am*), n. sour gruel, L.; forced rice, L.; a sort of Phaseolus (= *rāja-māsha*), L.; a species of Dolichos (= *yāvaka*), L.; (*ī*), f., N. of a river, Hariv. 9507. — **khāda**, mfn. eating sour gruel, Pāṇ. iii, 2, 81, Kāś. **Kulmāshâbhishuta**, n. sour gruel, L.

कुल्मि *kulmí*, *is*, m. or f. a herd, TS. ii.

कुल्य 1. *kulya*, 1. *kulyā́*. See *kúla*.

कुल्य 2. *kúlya*, mfn. (fr. 2. *kulyā́*), presiding over a river (as a deity), VS. xvi, 37.

2. **Kulyā́**, f. a small river, canal, channel for irrigation, ditch, dyke or trench, RV.; VS.; AV. &c.; (ifc. f. *ā*) Ragh. vii, 46; N. of a river, MBh. xiii, 1742.

Kulyāya, Nom. Ā. *°yate*, to become a river, Bhartṛ. ii, 78.

कुल्य 3. *kulya*, *am*, n. a receptacle for bones (left from a burnt corpse), MBh. i, 150, 13; Hariv. 2098; a bone, L.; flesh, L.; a winnowing basket, L.; a measure of eight Droṇas, L.

कुल्लूक *kullūka*, *as*, m., N. of a celebrated commentator on Manu (he was born in Gaur, and lived about 300 years ago); (*ā*), f. (with Śāktas) N. of certain syllables preceding a Mantra. — **bhaṭṭa**, m. title given to the commentator Kullūka.

कुल्व *kulva*, mfn. bald, KātyŚr.; (cf. *áti-k°*,) [Lat. *calvus*.]

कुल्वक *kulvaka*. See *kuluka*.

कुल्हरिका *kulharikā*, f. a pot, Bhpr.

Kulharī, f. id., ib.

कुव *kuva*, *am*, n. a water-lily, lotus, L.; (cf. *kuvala*, &c.)

कुवकालुका *kuvakālukā*, f., N. of a vegetable (= *gholī-śāka*), L.

कुवक्र *ku-vakra*, &c. See 1. *ku*.

कुवम *kuvama*, *as*, m. the sun [Comm.], MBh. xiii, 4486.

कुवय *kuváya*, *as*, m. (= *kváyi*) a kind of bird, MaitrS. iii, 14, 20.

कुवर *kuvara*, mfn. (= *tuv°*) astringent in flavour, L.; (*ī*), f. a sort of fish, Gal.

कुवर्त्मन् *ku-vartman*, &c. See 1. *ku*.

कुवल *kúvala*, *as*, *ī*, m. f. (gaṇa *gaurâdi*) the jujube tree (Zizyphus Jujuba), L.; (*am*), n. the fruit of that tree, Kāṭh.; VS.; ŚBr.; KātyŚr.; (= *kuvalaya*) the water-lily, Kathās. liii, 88; a pearl, L. — **kuṇa**, m. the time when the tree Zizyphus Jujuba bears fruits, gaṇa *pīlv-ādi*. — **prastha**, m., N. of a town, gaṇa *karky-ādi* (v. l. for *kurala-pr°*). — **saktú**, *avas*, m. pl. Jujuba fruits and barley grains, ŚBr. xii. **Kuvalâśva**, m., N. of the prince Dhundhumāra, MBh. iii, 13486; Hariv. 671; (vv. ll. *kubal°*, *kuvalayâśva* and *°śvaka*, q.v.) **Kuvaleśaya**, m. 'resting on a water-lily,' N. of Vishṇu, MBh. xiii, 7012.

कुवलय 1. *kuvalaya*, *am*, n. the water-lily (especially the blue variety, the flower of which opens at night), MBh.; Suśr.; Megh. &c.; (ifc. f. *ā*) Kathās.; (*as*), m., N. of the horse of Kuvalayâśva, MārkP.; (cf. *kuvala*.) — **dṛiś**, f. 'lotus-eyed,' a handsome woman, Bhartṛ.; Śāntiś. &c. — **nayanā**, f. id., Mālav. — **pura**, n., N. of a town. — **maya**, mf(*ī*)n. consisting of blue water-lilies, Prasannar. — **mālā**, f., N. of a mare, Kathās. — **vatī**, f. 'possessing water-lilies,' N. of a princess, Kathās. lxx, 215. **Kuvalayâditya**, m., N. of a prince (= *°yâpīḍa*), Rājat. iv, 355. **Kuvalayânanda**, m., N. of a work on rhetoric by Apya-dīkshita. **Kuvalayâpīḍa**, m., N. of a prince (= *°yâditya*), Rājat. iv, 362 ff.; N. of a Daitya (who, changed to an elephant, became the vehicle of Kaṇsa), Hariv.; Gīt.; N. of an elephant, Kathās. cxiii, 19. **Kuvalayâvalī**, f., N. of a princess, Kathās. xx, 49. **Kuvalayâśva**, m., N. of the prince Dhundhumāra, VP.; N. of the prince Pratardana, MārkP. (v. l. *kubal°*); BhP. ix, 17, 6; *-caritra*, n. 'the adventures of Kuvalayâśva,' N. of a Prākṛit poem (composed by Viśvanātha Kavi-rāja), Sāh. **Kuvalayâśvaka**, m., N. of the prince Dhundhumāra, BhP. ix, 6, 21. **Kuvalayâśvīya**, n. the story of Kuvalayâśva, MārkP.

Kuvalayita, mfn. (gaṇa *tārakâdi*) decorated with water-lilies, Ragh. xi, 93.

Kuvalayinī, f. an assemblage of water-lilies, place abounding with them, L.

कुवलय 2. *ku-valaya*. See 2. *ku*.

कुवस्त्र *ku-vastra*, &c. See 1. *ku*.

कुवाट *kuvāṭa*, *as*, m. = *kav°*, L.

Kuvāṭaka, *as*, m. id., Gal.

कुवाद *ku-vāda*, &c. See 1. *ku*.

कुवित्स *kuvít-sa*; m. (fr. *kuvíd*), any one, an unknown person, RV. vi, 45, 24.

Kuvíd, ind. (fr. 1. *ku* and *id*; gaṇa *cādi*), if, whether (a particle of interrogation used in direct and indirect questions), RV.; AV.; ŚBr.; 'where, where at all' ['often, frequently,' Sāy.], RV. iv, 51, 4; (a verb following this particle does not lose its accent, Pāṇ. viii, 1, 30); = *bahu*, Naigh. iii, 1.

कुविन्द *kuvinda*, *as*, m. (= *kupinda*) a weaver, Kathās.; Comm. on Bādar.

Kuvindaka, *as*, m. id., BrahmavP.; (in music) a kind of measure.

कुविवाह *ku-vivāha*, &c. See 1. *ku*.

कुवीरा *kuvīrā*, f., N. of a river, MBh. vi, 9, 27.

कुवृत्ति *ku-vritti*, &c. See 1. *ku*.

कुवेर *kuvera*, &c. See *kubera*.

कुवेल *kuvela*, *am*, n. (= *kuvalaya*) a blue water-lily, L.

कुवैद्य *ku-vaidya*, &c. See 1. *ku*.

कुश् *kuś*, cl. 4. P. *kuśyati*, to embrace, enfold, Dhātup. xxvi, 109 (v. l. *kus*).

कुश *kuśá*, *as*, m. grass, ŚBr.; ŚāṅkhŚr.; KātyŚr.; ĀśvGṛ.; (the Brāhmaṇas commonly call it *darbhá*); the sacred grass used at certain religious ceremonies (Poa cynosuroides, a grass with long pointed stalks), Mn.; Yājñ.; MBh. &c.; a rope (made of Kuśa grass) used for connecting the yoke of a plough with the pole, L.; N. of a son of Vasu Uparicara, Hariv. 1806; of the founder of Kuśathalī, SkandaP.; of a son of Balākâśva (grandson of Balāka, father of Kuśāmba or Kuśa-nābha), R.; BhP. ix, 19, 4; of a son of Suhotra (cf. *kāśa*), BhP.; of a son of Vidarbha, ib.; of a son of Rāma (cf. *kuśīlava*), Hariv. 822; BhP.; Ragh. xvi, 72; of a son of Lava (king of Kaśmira), Rājat. i, 88; one of the great Dvīpas or divisions of the universe (surrounded by the sea of liquified butter), BhP. v, 1, 32; VP.; (*ā*), f. (Pāṇ. viii, 3, 46) a small pin or piece of wood (used as a mark in recitation), Lāṭy. ii, 6, 1 & 4; a cord (cf. *kāśā*), L.; a horse's bridle (cf. *kāśā*), L.; N. of a plant (commonly Madhu-karkaṭikā), L.; (*ī*), f. (= *kuśā*) a small pin (used as a mark in recitation and consisting of wood [MaitrS. iv] or of metal [TBr. i; ŚBr. iii]); a ploughshare, L.; a pod of cotton, L., (*am*), n. water; (mfn.) wicked, depraved, L.; mad, inebriate, L. **–kāśa-maya,** mfn. made of the Kuśa and Kāśa grass, BhP. iii, 22, 31. **–ketu,** m., N. of Brahmā, Gal. **–cīra,** n. a garment made of Kuśa grass, R. ii, 37, 10; (*ā*), f. 'covered with a garment of Kuśa grass,' N. of a river, MBh. vi, 9, 23. **–ja,** *ās,* m. pl., N. of a people (v. l. *kuśala*), VP. **–dūrvā-maya,** mfn. made of the Kuśa and Dūrvā grass, Hcat. **–dvīpa,** m., N. of one of the seven large Dvīpas or divisions of the universe, MBh. xiii, 673; BhP.; MatsyaP. **–dhārā,** f., N. of a river, MBh. vi, 9, 24. **–dhvaja,** m., N. of a prince (a son of Hrasva-roman), R.; BrahmavP.; (a grandson of Hrasva-roman) BhP. **–nagara,** n., N. of the town in which Śākya-muni died, Buddh. **–nābha,** m., N. of a son of Kuśa, Hariv.; R.; BhP.; Kathās. **–nāman,** for *śiśu-n°,* q. v., L. **–nāra,** v. l. for *-dhārā.* **–netra,** m., N. of a Daitya, Hariv. 12944. **–pushpa,** n. a kind of oak-apple, L.; N. of a plant (= *granthi-parṇa*) or of a perfume so called, L. **–pushpaka,** n. a kind of poison, Car. vi, 23. **–plava,** m., N. of a hermitage, R. i, 46, 8 (ed. Bomb.) **–plavana,** n., N. of a Tīrtha, ib.; MBh. iii, 8179. **–bindu,** *avas,* m. pl., N. of a people, MBh. vi, 9, 56. **–mushṭi,** m. f. a handful of sacred grass, KātyŚr.; MBh. &c.; (mfn.) having the hand full of sacred grass. **–rajju,** f. a string made of Kuśa grass, Gobh. **–lava,** *au,* m. du. the two sons of Rāma called Kuśa and Lava. **–vat,** mfn. covered with Kuśa grass, MBh. iii, 10553; Ragh. xiv, 28; (*tī*), f., N. of a town (= *-sthalī*), MBh. iii, 11792; (cf. *kuśā-vatī.*) **–vāri,** n. water in which Kuśa grass has been soaked, Mn. xi, 148. **–vīrā,** v. l. for *-cīrā,* q. v. **–stamba,** m. a bundle of Kuśa grass, KātyŚr.; ĀśvGṛ.; BhP.; VP.; (*am*), n., N. of a Tīrtha, MBh. xiii, 1714. **–sthala,** n., N. of the town Kānyakubja, Hcar.; (*ī*), f., N. of the town Dvārakā, MBh. ii, 614; Hariv.; BhP.; Bālar. **–hasta,** mfn. having Kuśa grass in the hand or in the paw (as applied to the tiger), Hit. **Kuśâkara,** m. fire (the sacrificial fire being made on a bundle of Kuśa grass), L. **Kuśâksha,** m. 'having sharp eyes,' a monkey, L. **Kuśâgra,** n. the sharp point of a blade of the Kuśa grass, MBh. iii, 11023; N. of a prince (the son of Bṛihad-ratha), Hariv. 1807; BhP.; (mfn.) sharp, shrewd, W.; *-buddhi,* mfn. one whose intelligence is as sharp as the point of Kuśa grass, shrewd, intelligent, Ragh. v, 4; (*is*), f. shrewdness, W. **Kuśâgrīya,** mfn. sharp as the point of Kuśa grass, penetrating, Pāṇ. v, 3, 105; *-mati,* mfn. of subtle intellect, possessing mental acumen, L. **Kuśâṅkura,** m. a blade of Kuśa grass, W. **Kuśâṅgurīya,** n. a ring of Kuśa grass (worn at religious ceremonies), W. **Kuśâṅgurīyaka,** n. id., ib. **Kuśâraṇi,** m. 'one who may be irritated by a Kuśa blade,' N. of the sage Durvāsas (famous for his irascibility), L. **Kuśâ-vatī,** f., N. of a town (residence of Kuśa son of Rāma), R.; Mṛicch.; Ragh.; Divyâv. **Kuśâvarta,** m., N. of a Tīrtha or passage of the Ganges, Vishṇ.; MBh. xiii, 1700; BhP.; ŚivaP.; N. of a son of Ṛishabha, BhP. v, 4, 10; of a Muni, BrahmaP.; (*ās*), m. pl. the family of that Muni, ib. **Kuśâvaleha,** m. a kind of electuary. **Kuśâśva,** m., N. of a prince (v. l. *kriśâśva*), R. i. 47, 16; (also v. l. for *kuśâmba,* q. v.) R. 2. **Kuśâsana,** n. a small mat of sacred grass (on which a Brahman sits when performing his devotion); for 2. see 1. *ku* (*ku-śāsana*). 1. **Kuśī-lava,** *au,* m. du. = *kuśa-lava,* R. i. **Kuśe-śaya,** mfn. lying in Kuśa grass, MBh. xiii, 1698; (*as*), m. a kind of tree (Pterospermum Acerifolium), L.; the Indian crane, L.; N. of a mountain in Kuśa-dvīpa, VP.; (*am*), n. 'lying in water,' a water-lily, MBh.; R. &c.; [once (*ā*), f., Hariv. 8428]; *-kara,* m. 'having rays like water-lilies,' the sun, W.; *-bhū,* m., N. of Brahmā, Bālar.; *-maya,* mf(*ī*)n. consisting of water-lilies, R. vii, 36, 10; *-locanā,* f. a lotus-eyed woman, Bhām.; *kuśeśayâksha,* mfn. lotus-eyed, Ragh. xviii, 3; Rājat. **Kuśôdaka,** n. = *kuśa-vāri,* Mn. xi, 212; Yājñ. iii, 315; (*ā*), f., N. of Dākshāyaṇī in Kuśa-dvīpa, MatsyaP. **Kuśôrṇā,** *ās,* f. pl. wool made of grass, ŚBr. ii, 5, 21, 15.

Kuśi (in comp. for *kuśin*). **–grāmaka,** m., N. of a village of the Mallas, Buddh. **–nagara,** n., N. of the capital of the Mallas, Buddh.; (*ī*), f. id., ib.

Kuśikā, f. a piece of wood used as a splint for a broken leg, Car. viii, 23.

Kuśita, mfn. mixed or combined with water (v. l. *kushita*), L.

Kuśin, mfn. furnished with Kuśa grass, MBh. xiii, 973; (*ī*), m., N. of Vālmīki (so called with reference to Kuśa the son of Rāma), L.

कुशङ्कु *ku-śaṅku.* See 1. *ku.*

कुशण्ड *kuśaṇḍa, ās,* m. pl. (= *ku-shaṇḍa?*), N. of a people, VP.; (*ī*), f. = *kuśaṇḍikā.*

Kuśaṇḍikā, f. consecration of the sacred fire, Jyot.

कुशप *kuśapa, as,* m. a drinking vessel, L.; (v. l. *°śaya.*)

Kuśayá, *as,* m. a cistern, Naigh. iii, 23.

कुशर *kú-śara,* &c. See 1. *ku.*

कुशल *kúśala,* mf(*ā*)n. (gaṇas *sidhmâdi, śreṇy-ādi,* and *śramaṇâdi*) right, proper, suitable, good (e. g. *kuśalam* √*man,* to consider good, approve, AitBr.; ŚāṅkhŚr.); well, healthy, in good condition, prosperous, R. &c.; fit for, competent, able, skilful, clever, conversant with (loc. [Pāṇ. ii, 3, 40; ChUp.; Mn. &c.], gen. [Pāṇ. ii, 3, 40; Yājñ. ii, 181], inf. [MBh.], or in comp. [gaṇa *śauṇḍâdi;* Gaut.; Mn. &c.]); (*ās*), m. pl., N. of a people, MBh. vi, 359; N. of the Brāhmans in Kuśa-dvīpa, BhP. v, 20, 16; (*as*), m., N. of Śiva; of a prince, VP.; of a grammarian (author of the Pañjikā-pradīpa); (*ā*), f., N. of a woman, gaṇa *bāhv-ādi;* (*ī*), f. the plant Oxalis Corniculata (= *aśmantaka*), L.; the plant *kshudrâmlikā,* L.; (*am*), n. welfare, well-being, prosperous condition, happiness, TUp.; Gaut.; Āp.; MBh. &c. [*kuśalam* √*pracch,* to ask after another's welfare, to say 'how do you do?' Mn.; MBh. &c.; *kuśalaṃ te* (optionally with dat., Pāṇ. ii, 3, 73), 'hail to thee!' (used as a salutation, especially in greeting a Brāhman), MBh. &c.]; benevolence, R. ii, 34, 22; virtue, L.; cleverness, competence, ability, Pañcat.; N. of a Varsha governed by Kuśala, VP.; (*am*), ind. well, in a proper manner, properly, ChUp.; (in comp.) gaṇa *vispashṭâdi;* happily, cheerfully, (with √*as,* 'to be well'), BhP.; (*ena*), ind. in due order, Gobh. (also in comp. *kuśala-*). **–kāma,** mfn. desirous of happiness; (*as*), m. desire for happiness. **–tā,** f. cleverness, ability, conversancy with (loc.), Mṛicch.; acuteness of sensation, Mn. xii, 73. **–tva,** n. cleverness, skilfulness. **–praśna,** m. friendly enquiry after a person's health or welfare, salutation, saying 'how do you do?' MBh.; Hit.; Vet.; BhP. **–buddhi,** mfn. wise, able, intelligent. **–vat,** mfn. well, healthy, Kathās. cxx, 129. **–vāc,** mfn. eloquent, Subh. **–sāgara,** m., N. of a scribe (pupil of Lāvaṇya-ratna). **Kuśali-**√1. **kṛi,** to make right or proper, arrange in due order, ĀśvGṛ.: Caus. *-kārayati,* 'to cause to make right,' to cause to shave (the head), Gobh.

Kuśalin, mfn. healthy, well, prosperous, MBh. &c.; auspicious, favourable, Sāh.; clever; virtuous, W.

Kuśalya, *ās,* m. pl., N. of a people, MBh. vi, 9, 40.

कुशाम्ब *kuśāmba, as,* m. (gaṇa *śubhrâdi;* cf. *kūś°*), N. of a son of Vasu Uparicara, MBh. i, 2363; BhP.; N. of a son of Kuśa (who was the founder of the town Kauśāmbī, R. i, 34, 3), Hariv. 1425.

Kuśāmbu, v. l. for *°ba* (the son of Kuśa), BhP.

कुशाल *kuśāla, as,* m., N. of a prince, VP.

कुशाल्मली *ku-śālmalī,* &c. See 1. *ku.*

कुशि *kuśi, is,* m. an owl, L.

कुशिक *kuśiká,* mfn. squint-eyed, L.; (*ás*), m., N. of the father [or grandfather, MBh.; Hariv.] of Viśvā-mitra, RV. iii, 33, 5; MBh. &c.; of the father of Gāthin or Gādhin or Gādhi (the latter being sometimes identified with Indra, who is called Kauśika or Kuśikôttama, MBh. xiii, 800; Gādhi is also regarded as the father of Viśva-mitra, MBh.; R.); (*ās*), m. pl. the descendants of Kuśika, RV.; AitBr. &c.; N. of a people, VarBṛS.; (*as*), m., N. of the thirteenth Kalpa, VāyuP.; the sediment of oil, L.; the plant Shorea Robusta, L.; the plant Terminalia Bellerica, L.; the plant Vatika Robusta, L.; (*as, am*), m. n. a ploughshare, L.; (*ā*), f., see the top of the col. **–m-dhara,** m., N. of a Muni, VāyuP. **–sūtra,** n., N. of a Sūtra belonging to the AV. (generally called Kauśika-sūtra, cf. IW. p. 157).

कुशित *kuśita.* See col. 2.

कुशिम्बि *ku-śimbi,* &c. See 1. *ku.*

कुशीति *kuśīti, is,* m., N. of a teacher, VāyuP.

Kuśīda, *as,* m. id., BhP. xii, 6, 79; (see *kúsida* & *kusīdin.*)

कुशीरक *kuśīraka,* gaṇa *sakhy-ādi* (also Gaṇar. 273; *uśīra,* Kāś.)

कुशील *ku-śīla.* See 1. *ku.*

कुशीलव 2. *kuśīlava, as,* m. (fr. *ku-śīla?*), a bard, herald, actor, mime, Mn.; MBh.; Mṛicch.; Mālatim.; a newsmonger, L.; N. of Vālmīki (cf. *kuśin*), L.; (*au*), m. du., see *kuśá.*

Kuśīvaśa, *as,* m., N. of Vālmīki, L.

कुशूल *kuśūla.* See *kusūla.*

कुशेशय *kuśe-śaya,* &c. See *kuśá.*

कुश्रि *kuśrí* or *kúśri, is,* m., N. of a teacher, ŚBr. x, xiv.

कुश्रुत *ku-śruta,* &c. See 1. *ku.*

कुष् *kush,* cl. 9. P. *kushṇāti* (ind. p. *kushitvā,* Pāṇ. i, 2, 7; aor. *akoshīt,* Pāṇ. Sch.), to tear asunder, Bhaṭṭ.; to pinch, Car. i, 8; VP. iii, 12, 9; to force or draw out, extract, Bhaṭṭ.; to knead, Comm. on KātyŚr. (perf. p. *kushita*); to test, examine (?); to shine (?): cl. 6. *kushati,* to gnaw, nibble, BhP. iii, 16, 10: Pass. *kushyati* and *°te,* 'to weigh, balance' [NBD.], Pāṇ. iii, 1, 90.

कुषण्ड *ku-shaṇḍa.* See 1. *ku.*

कुषल *kushala,* for *kuśala,* q. v., L.

कुषवा *kusháva,* f. (perhaps) N. of a river, RV. iv, 18, 8 ('N. of a Rākshasī,' Sāy.)

कुषाकु *kushāku,* mfn. burning, scorching, L.; wicked, detestable, W.; (*us*), m. (= *kash°*) fire, Uṇ. iii, 76; the sun, ib.; a monkey, L.

कुषारु *kushāru, us,* m., 'N. of a man,' see *kaushārava.*

कुषिक *kushika, as,* m., N. of a prince, MBh. ii, 8, 10 (v. l. *kuśika*).

कुषित *kushita.* See *kuśita* and √*kush.*

कुषीतक *kushītaka, as,* m. a kind of bird, TS. v; N. of a man, TāṇḍyaBr.; Pāṇ. iv, 1, 124; Comm. on BṛĀrUp.; (*ās*), m. pl. the descendants of that man, gaṇa *upakâdi.*

कुषीद *kushīda,* mfn. indifferent, apathetic, W.; (*am*), n. for *kusīda,* q. v., L.

Kushīdin, *ī,* m., N. of a teacher (for *kuśīti*), W.

कुषुभ्य *kushubhya,* Nom. P. *°bhyati,* 'to throw' or 'to despise,' gaṇa *kaṇḍv-ādi.*

कुषुम्भ *kushúmbha, as,* m. the venom-bag of an insect, AV. ii, 32, 6; (cf. *kusumbha.*)

Kushumbhaká, *as,* m. id., RV. i, 191, 15; a venomous insect ['an ichneumon,' Sāy.], ib. 16.

कुष्ट *kushṭa,* mf(*ā*)n. being of a particular colour, TāṇḍyaBr. xxi, 1, 7. **–cit,** gaṇa *kathâdi,* Kāś. (vv. ll. *-vid* and *kushṭha-vid*).

कुष्ठ *kúshṭha, as, am,* m. n. (fr. 1. *ku* + *stha,* Pāṇ. viii, 3, 97) the plant Costus speciosus or arabicus (used as a remedy for the disease called *takmán*), AV.; Kauś. 35; R. ii, 94, 23; Suśr.; the plant Saussurea auriculata; (*as*), m. (= *kakundara*) cavity of the loin [Comm.; but perhaps = *kúshṭhikā*], VS. xxv, 6; (*ā*), f. the prominent part of anything, mouth or opening (of a basket), TāṇḍyaBr. xxi; PārGṛ.; Comm. on KātyŚr.; = *kúshṭhikā* (taken as measure equal to 'one-twelfth'), MaitrS. iii, 7, 7; (*am*), n. leprosy (of which eighteen varieties are enumerated, i. e. seven severe and eleven less so), Suśr.; Bhartṛ. i, 89; Kathās.; a sort of poison, L. **–kaṇṭaka,** m. the tree Acacia Catechu, Npr. **–kanda,** m. the plant Trichosanthes dioeca, Gal. **–ketu,** m., N. of a shrub akin to the Cassia auriculata, L. **–gandhi,** n. the fragrant bark of the plant Feronia elephantum, L. **–gala,** mfn. having a leprous throat, Caurap. **–ghna,** m. 'curing leprosy,' N. of the medicinal plant Hiyāvalī (= *hitâvalī*), L.;

N. of a remedy for leprosy, Suśr.; (*ī*), f. an esculent root (Solanum indicum, = *kāka-mācī*), W.; the tree Ficus oppositifolia, L.; the plant Vernonia anthelminthica, Bhpr. **-cikitsita**, n. the cure of leprosy. **-ja**, mfn. produced by leprosy, Suśr. **-nāśana**, m. 'curing leprosy,' the root of Dioscorea, L.; white pepper or mustard, L.; the tree Lipeocercis serrata (= *kshīrīśa-vṛiksha*), L. **-nāśinī**, f. 'curing leprosy,' the plant Vernonia anthelminthica, L.; the plant Proralia corylifolia (commonly Hākuca), L. **-nodana**, m. 'curing leprosy,' the red Khadira tree, L. **-maya**, mfn. full of leprosy, leprous. **-roga**, m. the disease called leprosy. **-vid**, mfn., see *kushṭa-cit*. **-sūdana**, m. 'subduing leprosy,' the Cassia tree (Cassia or Cathartocarpus Fistula), L. **-hantṛi**, m. 'removing leprosy,' a kind of bulbous plant, L.; (*trī*), f. = *-nāśinī*, L. **-hara**, m. = *-sūdana*, Gal. **-hṛit**, m. = *-kaṇṭaka*, L. **Kushṭhâṅga**, mfn. having leprous limbs, Vet. **Kushṭhânvita**, mfn. afflicted with leprosy. **Kushṭhâri**, m. 'enemy of leprosy,' sulphur, L.; the plant Acacia Catechu, L.; the plant Acacia Farnesiana, L.; = *kushṭha-kanda*, L.; a sort of Helianthus (*āditya-pattra* or *arka-p°*), L.

Kushṭhaka. See *aṅgāra-k°*.

Kúshṭhikā, f. a dew-claw, spur [considered worthless for sacrificial purposes; 'the contents of the entrails,' Sāy.], AV.; AitBr. ii, 11.

Kushṭhita, mfn. leprous, Suśr.

Kushṭhin, mfn. id., ĀśvGṛ.; Mn.; MBh. &c.

कुष्ठल *ku-shṭhala, am*, n., Pāṇ. viii, 3, 96.

कुष्ठिका *kúshṭhikā*, &c. See *kúshṭha*.

कुष्मल *kushmala, am*, n. a leaf, Uṇ.

कुष्माण्ड *kushmāṇḍa, as*, m. (cf. *kūshm°*) a kind of pumpkin-gourd (Beninkasa cerifera), MBh. xiii, 4364 (*kūśm°*, ed. Bomb.); Suśr.; = *bhrūṇāntara* (a state of the womb in gestation, W.), L.; false conception (?); (*am*), n., N. of the verses VS. xx, 14 ff., TĀr. (*kūśm°*); MBh. xiii, 6236 ff. (*kūśm°*, ed. Bomb.); (*ās*), m. pl. a class of demons (or of demi-gods attached to Śiva; cf. *kumbhāṇḍa*), BhP. x; VP. (*kūshm°*); Kathās.; (*as*), m., N. of a demon causing disease, Hariv. 9560 (v. l. *kūshm°*); (*ī*), f. the gourd Beninkasa Cerifera, L.; N. of the verses VS. xx, 14 ff. (see *kūshm°*), L.; N. of Durgā, Hariv. 10245 (v. l. *kūshm°*).

Kushmāṇḍaka, *as*, m. the gourd Beninkasa Cerifera, Bhpr.; Car. (*kūshm°*); N. of a Nāga, MBh. i, 1556 (*kūśm°*, ed. Bomb.); N. of an attendant of Śiva, L. (v. l. *kūshm°*).

कुस् *kus*, v. l. for √*kuś*, q. v.

कुसखी *ku-sakhī*, &c. See 1. *ku*.

कुसल *kusala*, for *kuśala*, q. v.

कुसहाय *ku-sahāya*, &c. See 1. *ku*.

कुसित *kusita, as*, m. (fr. √*kus* = *kuś*?), an inhabited country, Uṇ.; a kind of demon, Pāṇ. iv, 1, 37; (*ā́*), f. = *kusitāyī*, MaitrS. iii, 2, 6; (*kústā*) iv, 2, 3.

Kusitāyī, f. a kind of demon, MaitrS.

Kusida, *as*, m. id., Pāṇ. iv, 1, 37.

Kusidāyī, f. (Pāṇ. iv, 1, 37) id., Kāṭh. x, 5; the wife of a money-lender, L.

कुसिन्ध *kúsindha, am*, n. a trunk, AV.; Kāṭh.; ŚBr.

कुसिम्बी *ku-simbī*, f. = *-śimbī*, L.

कुसीद *kúsīda*, mfn. (fr. 1. *ku* and √*sad*?; cf. *kushīda*), lazy, inert (?), TS. vii; (*am*), n. any loan or thing lent to be repaid with interest, lending money upon interest, usury, TS. iii; Gobh.; Gaut.; Pāṇ. &c.; red sandal wood, L.; (*as, ā*), m. f. a money-lender, usurer, L. **-patha**, m. usury, usurious interest, Mn. viii, 152. **-vṛiddhi**, f. usurious interest on money, Gaut.; Mn. viii, 151.

Kusīdāyī, f. the wife of a usurer, Vop. iv, 25.

Kusīdika, *as, ī*, m. f. a usurer, Pāṇ. iv, 4, 31.

Kusīdin, *ī*, m. id., Nir.; ŚBr. xiii; ĀśvŚr.; ŚāṅkhŚr.; Gaut.; (see *kuṣīti*) N. of a descendant of Kaṇva (author of RV. viii, 81–83), RAnukr.; of a teacher, VP.

कुसुत *ku-suta*. See 2. *ku*.

कुसुम *kusuma, am*, n. (fr. √*kus*, Uṇ.; gaṇa *ardharcâdi*), a flower, blossom, Mn. xi, 70; R. &c. (ifc. f. *ā*), Mālav. & Ratnāv.; N. of the shorter sections of Deveśvara's Kavi-kalpa-latā (the longer chapters being called *stabaka*); fruit, L.; the menstrual discharge, L.; a particular disease of the eyes, L.; (*as*), m. a form of fire, Hariv. 10465; N. of an attendant of the sixth Arhat of the present Avasarpiṇī, L.; N. of a prince, Buddh. **-kārmuka**, m. 'having flowers for his bow,' Kāma (the god of love), Śiś. vi, 16. **-ketu**, m. id., Vāsav.; *-maṇḍalin*, m., N. of a Kiṃnara, Buddh. **-komala**, mfn. tender as a flower, W. **-cāpa**, m. = *-kārmuka*, Ragh.; Ṛitus.; Ratnāv. **-cita**, mfn. heaped with flowers. **-jaya**, m., N. of a prince, Buddh. **-danta**, m. (= *pushpa-d°*), N. of a mystical being, VarBṛS. **-deva**, m., N. of an author. **-druma**, m. a tree full of blossom, Ragh. xvi, 36. **-dhanus**, m. = *-kārmuka*, Viddh. **-dhanvan**, m. id., Ratnāv. **-dhvaja**, m. = *-pura*, GārgīS. **-naga**, m., N. of a mountain, VarBṛS. **-nagara**, n. = *-pura*, Caṇḍak. **-pura**, n., N. of the town Pāṭali-putra, Āryabh.; Mudr.; Kathās. &c. **-phala**, m. the plant Croton Tamalgota, Npr. **-bāṇa**, m. 'flower-arrowed,' N. of the god of love, L.; the flower-arrow of the god of love, Śak. (v. l.); Pañcat. **-madhya**, n., N. of a tree bearing a large acid fruit (commonly Cālitā Gāc, Cordia Myxa or Dillenia Indica), L. **-maya**, mf(*ī*)n. consisting of flowers, Viddh.; Kād.; Prab. **-mārgaṇa**, m. (= *-bāṇa*) the god of love, Kād. **-lakshman**, m. 'having flowers as a symbol,' Pradyumna, Śiś. xix, 22. **-latā**, f. a creeper in blossom, Śak. **-vat**, mfn. furnished with flowers, in flower, W.; (*tī*), f. a female during menstruation, W.; = *kusuma-pura*, W. **-vicitra**, mf(*ā*)n. having various flowers; (*ā*), f., N. of a metre consisting of four lines of twelve syllables each. **-śayana**, n. a couch of flowers, Śak.; Vet. **-śara**, m. = *-bāṇa*, Kathās.; Gīt.; *-tva*, n. the state of one who has flowers for arrows, Śak.; *°râsana*, m. = *-kārmuka*, Gīt. xi, 4. **-śekhara-vijaya**, m., N. of a play, Sāh. **-sanātha**, mfn. possessed of flowers, having flowers. **-sambhava**, m., N. of the tenth month, Sūryapr. **-sāyaka**, m. = *-bāṇa*, Daś. **-sāra**, m., N. of a merchant, Kathās. lxvii, 36. **-stabaka**, m. a bunch of flowers, nosegay, bouquet, Bhartṛ. ii, 25; N. of a metre. **Kusumâkara**, m. a quantity of flowers or place abounding with them, L.; a nosegay, L.; spring, Bhag. x, 35. **Kusumâñjana**, n. the calx of brass (used as a collyrium), L. **Kusumâñjali**, f. a handful of flowers (properly as much as will fill both hands), Ratnāv.; N. of a philosophical work (written by Udayana Ācārya to prove the existence of a Supreme Being, and consisting of seventy-two Kārikās divided into five chapters), Sarvad.; *-kārikā-vyākhyā, -ṭīkā*, f., *-prakāśa, -prakāśa-makaranda, -makaranda*, m., *-vṛitti, -vyākhyā*, f., N. of commentaries on the preceding work. **Kusumâtmaka**, n. saffron. **Kusumâdhipa**, m. 'the prince of flowers,' the Campa (a tree which bears a yellow fragrant flower, Michelia Campaka), L. **Kusumâdhirāj**, m. id., L. **Kusumâyudha**, m. 'flower-armed,' N. of Kāma (the god of love, his arrows being tipped with flowers), Śak.; Bhartṛ. &c.; N. of a Brāhman, Kathās. **Kusumâvacaya**, m. gathering flowers, Mṛicch.; Śak.; Kathās. **Kusumâvataṃsaka**, n. a chaplet, crown of flowers. **Kusumâvalī**, f., N. of a medicinal work. **Kusumâsava**, n. 'flower-liquor,' honey. **Kusumâstra**, m. = *kusumâyudha*, Ragh. vii, 58. **Kusumêśvara-tīrtha**, n., N. of a Tīrtha, ŚivaP. **Kusumêshu**, m. = *°ma-bāṇa*, Pañcat.; Kād.; Śiś. viii, 70; (*u*), n. the bow of Kāma, W. **Kusumôjjvala**, mfn. brilliant with blossoms. **Kusumôda**, m., N. of a prince, VP.; (*am*), n. 'flower-sea,' N. of the Varsha governed by that prince, ib.

Kusumaya, Nom. P. *°yati*, to produce flowers, Viddh.; to furnish with flowers, Śiś. vi, 62.

Kusumita, mfn. (gaṇa *tārakâdi*) furnished with flowers, in flower, MBh.; Mṛicch. &c. **-latā** or **-latā-vellikā**, f., N. of a metre consisting of four lines of eighteen syllables each.

Kusumya, Nom. P. *°yati*, to begin to flower (?), gaṇa *kaṇḍv-ādi*.

कुसुमाल *kusumāla, as*, m. a thief, L.

कुसुम्बक *kusumbaka, as, am*, m. n. a kind of vegetable, Car. i, 27.

Kusumbha, *as*, m. [*am*, n., L.] safflower (Carthamus tinctorius), Suśr.; VarBṛS.; Śiś. &c.; saffron (Crocus sativus), L.; 'the water-pot of the student and Saṃnyāsin,' see *-vat*; (*as*), m. outward affection (compared with the colour of safflower), Sāh.; N. of a mountain, BhP. v, 16, 27; (*ī*), f. = *manthara*, L.; (*am*), n. gold, L. **-rāga**, m. the colour of safflower, Ṛitus.; (mfn.) 'resembling the colour of safflower,' outward (as affection), Sāh. **-vat**, mfn. furnished with a water-pot, Mn. vi, 52.

Kusumbhalā, f. a kind of Curcumā, Npr.

कुसुरुबिन्द *kusurubínda, as*, m., N. of a descendant of Uddālaka, TS. vii; TāṇḍyaBr.; Shaḍv-Br. **-daśa-rātra**, n., N. of particular observances (lasting ten days).

Kusurubindu, *as*, m. = *°nda* (author of VS. viii, 42 & 23). **-tri-rātra**, n., N. of particular observances (lasting three days), ŚāṅkhŚr.

कुसू *ku-sū*. See 2. *ku*.

कुसूल *kusū́la, as*, m. (also written *kuśūla*) a granary, store-room (in which rice or other grain is kept), BhP.; a frying-pan, L.; pulse, L.; a kind of goblin, AV. viii, 6, 10. **-dhānya**, n. grain stored for three years' consumption, W.; (mfn.) having grain stored for three years' consumption, Yājñ. i, 128. **-dhānyaka**, m. a householder &c. who has three years' grain in store, Mn. iv, 7. **-pāda**, mfn., gaṇa *hasty-ādi*. **-pūraṇâḍhaka**, mfn. being (like to mere empty) measures filling a granary, Hit. **-bila**, n., Pāṇ. vi, 2, 102.

कुसृति *ku-sṛiti*, &c. See 1. *ku*.

कुस्ता *kústā*. See *kusita*.

कुस्तुक *kustuka, as*, m., N. of a teacher, VBr.

कुस्तुभ *kustubha, as*, m. (derived fr. *kaustubha*), N. of Vishṇu, L.

कुस्तुम्बरी *kustumbarī*, f. the plant coriander, Suśr.; (cf. *tumburī*.)

Kustumburu, *us*, m. id., Suśr.; (*sa-k°*) VarBṛS.; (*u*), n. the seed of coriander, Pāṇ. vi, 1, 143.

कुस्तुम्बुरु *kustumbaru, us*, m., N. of one of Kubera's attendants, MBh. ii, 397.

कुस्त्री *ku-strī*, &c. See 1. *ku*.

कुह् 1. *kuh*, cl. 10. Ā. *kuhayate*, to surprise or astonish or cheat by trickery or jugglery, Dhātup. xxxv, 47.

1. **Kuha**, *as*, m. (Pāṇ. vi, 1, 216) N. of Kubera, L.; a rogue, cheat, R. ii, 109, 27 (*a-k°*, 'no deceiver').

1. **Kuhaka**, *as*, m. (Uṇ. ii, 38) a cheat, rogue, juggler, MBh.; BhP.; Kām.; an impostor, Āp.; a kind of frog, Suśr.; N. of a Nāga prince, BhP.; (*am*), n. juggling, deception, trickery, Hit.; BhP. &c.; (*ā*), f. id., MBh. v, 5461. **-kāra**, mfn. practising jugglery, cheating. **-kāraka**, mfn. id.; (*ikā*), f. a bawd, Gal. **-cakita**, mfn. afraid of a trick, suspicious, cautious, Hit. **-jīvaka**, m. one who lives by slight-of-hand, juggler, cheat, VarBṛS. **-jīvin**, m. id., MBh. **-jña**, m. 'knowing jugglery,' cheat, juggler, VarBṛS. **-vṛitti**, f. juggling, slight-of-hand; hypocrisy.

Kuhana, mfn. envious, hypocritical, L.; (*as*), m. a mouse, rat, L.; a snake, L.; N. of a man, MBh. iii, 15598; (*am, ā*), f. hypocrisy, assumed and false sanctity, interested performance of religious austerities, L.; (*ā*), f. envy, Gal.; (*am*), n. a small earthen vessel, L.; a glass vessel, L.

Kuhanikā, f. jugglery, L.; hypocrisy, L.

कुह् 2. *kuh*. See *vishū-k°*.

कुह 2. *kúha*, ind. (fr. 1. *ku*), where? RV. **-cid** (*kúha-*), ind. wherever, RV. i, 184, 1; to any place, RV. i, 24, 10; *kuhacid-vid*, mfn. wherever being, RV. vii, 32, 19. **-°śrutīya**, mfn. belonging to the hymn that begins with *kúha śrutáḥ* (RV. x, 22), ŚāṅkhBr. xxii, 8.

Kuhayā́, ind. where? RV. viii, 24, 30. **-kṛiti**, mfn. where active? ib. (voc.)

कुहक 2. *kuhaka*, ind. onomat. from the cry of a cock, &c., only in comp. **-svana**, m. a wild cock (Phasianus gallus), L. **-svara**, m. id., L. **Kuhakârāva**, m. neighing, HPariś.

Kuhakuhārāva, *as*, m. the clamour or cries of Dātyūha, Bālar. xxviii, 13.

कुहक्क *kuhakka, as*, m. (in music) a kind of measure.

कुहन *kuhana*, &c. See √*kuh*.

कुहर *kuhara, as*, m. (fr. √*kuh* = *guh*?), N. of a serpent belonging to the Krodha-vaśa race, MBh. i, 2701; Hariv. 229; (*am*), n. a cavity, hollow, hole, Bhartṛ.; Hit.; Prab. &c.; a small window(?), VarBṛS.; the ear, L.; the throat or larynx, L.; a guttural sound, L.; proximity, L.; copulation, Daś.

Kuharita, *am*, n. noise, sound, L.; the song or cry of the Kokila or Indian cuckoo, L.; a sound uttered in copulation, L.

कुहलि *kuhali, is*, m. the leaf of the Piper Betel (commonly called Pān) with small pieces of the Areca-nut and Catechu and a little lime (chewed by persons in the East and especially offered to the persons at a matrimonial ceremony), L.

कुहा *kuhā*, f. a kind of Zizyphus tree, Bhpr. — **vatī**, f., N. of Durgā, L.

कुहारीत *ku-hārīta*. See 1. *ku*.

कुही *kuhī*, f. a mist, fog, Gal.

कुहु 1. *kuhu, us*, m., N. of a particular weight, Hcat.; (*uś*), f. (= 1. *kuhū*) the new moon, Pāṇ.; Siddh.

कुहु 2. *kuhu*, ind. onomat. from the cry of the Kokila, &c., only in comp.; cf. 2. *kuhū*. — **rava**, m. the cry of the Kokila, MBh. xv, 724.

कुहुकुहाय *kuhukuhāya* (fr. *kuhu-kuha* for *kuha-kuha*, where? where?), Nom. Ā. °*yate*, to show one's admiration, MBh. iii, 14129.

कुहुंकार *ku-huṃkāra*. See 1. *ku*.

कुहू 1. *kuhū́, ūs*, f. (fr. √*kuh* = *guh*?), the new moon (personified as a daughter of Aṅgiras), AV.; Kāṭh.; TS.; AitBr. &c.; the first day of the first quarter (on which the moon rises invisible), W.; N. of one of the seven rivers of Plaksha-dvīpa, VP.; BhP. v, 20, 10. — **pāla**, m. the king of turtles (supposed to uphold the world), W.

कुहू 2. *kuhū*, ind. = 2. *kuhu*. — **kaṇṭha**, m. the Kokila or Indian cuckoo (κόκκυ), Sāh. — **mukha**, m. id., L. — **rava**, m. id., L.; = *kuhu-rava*, Naish. ix, 38.

Kuhūs, ind. = 2. *kuhu*, Gīt. i, 47.

कुहूल *kuhūla, am*, n. a pit filled with stakes, L.

कुहेडिका *kuheḍikā*, f. fog, mist, L.

Kuheḍī, f. id., L.

Kuhelikā, f. id., L.

कुह्वान *ku-hvāna*. See 1. *ku*.

कू 1. *kū* or *ku*, cl. 2. P. *kauti* (Ved. *kavīti*, Pāṇ. vii, 3, 95), or cl. 1. Ā. *kavate* (Dhātup. xxii, 54), or cl. 6. *kuvate* (ib. xxviii, 108), or cl. 9. P. Ā. *kūnāti, kūnāte* (perf. 3. pl. *cukuvur*, Bhaṭṭ.), to sound, make any noise, cry out, moan, cry (as a bird), coo, hum (as a bee) &c., Bhaṭṭ.: cl. 1. *kávate*, to move, Naigh. ii, 14: Intens. Ā. *kokūyate* (Nir.; Pāṇ.), P. Ā. *kokavīti* and *cokūyate* (Pāṇ. vii, 4, 63, Kāś.), to cry aloud, Bhaṭṭ.; [cf. Gk. κωκύω.]

कू 2. *kū́*, ind. (= *kvà*) where?, RV. v, 74, 1. — **cid** (*kū́*-), ind. anywhere, RV. ix, 87, 8; (*kū́cid*)-*arthin*, mfn. striving to get anywhere [‘seeking oblations from any quarter,’ Sāy.], RV. iv, 7, 6.

कू 3. *kū, ūs*, f. a female Piśāca or goblin, L.

कूकुद *kūkuda, as*, m. one who gives a girl in marriage with due ceremony and suitable decorations, Hcat.

कूच *kūca, as*, m. (= *kuca*) the female breast (especially that of a young or unmarried woman), Comm. on Uṇ. iv, 91; an elephant, ib.

कूचका *kūcakā*, f. the milky juice of a bulbous plant (= *kūrcikā*), L.

कूचक्र *kū́-cakra, am*, n. (for *kūpa-c*°?) a wheel for raising water from a well [NBD.; ‘the female breast,’ Gmn.], RV. x, 102, 11.

कूचवार *kūcavāra, as*, m., N. of a locality, Pāṇ. iv, 3, 94; of a man, gaṇa *biḍâdi*.

कूचिका *kūcikā*, f. a small brush or hair-pencil, L.; a key, L.; (cf. *kūrcikā*.)

Kūcī, f. (Uṇ. iv, 93) a paint brush, pencil, Suśr.

कूचिदर्थिन् *kūcid-arthín*. See 2. *kū́*.

कूची *kūcī*. See *kūcikā*.

कूचीका *kūcīkā*, f. a sort of animal (belonging to the division called *bhūmi-śaya*), Car. i, 27.

कूच्छलिङ्ग *kūcchaliṅga, au*, m. du. = *kukundara*, L.

कूज *kūj*, cl. 1. P. *kū́jati* (perf. *cukūja*, Kum. iii, 32 &c.), to make any inarticulate or monotonous sound, utter a cry (as a bird), coo (as a pigeon), caw (as a crow), warble, moan, groan, utter any indistinct sound, AV. vii, 95, 2; MBh.; R. &c.; ‘to fill with monotonous sounds,’ &c., see *kūjita*; to blow or breathe (the flute), BhP. x, 21, 2.

Kūja, *as*, m. (Pāṇ. vii, 3, 59, Kāś.) cooing, murmuring, warbling, &c., MBh. i, 4916; R. ii, 59, 10; rumbling (as of the bowels, &c.), Suśr.

Kūjaka, mf(*ikā*)n. ‘cooing, warbling,’ &c.; see *kala-k*°.

Kūjana, *am*, n. the uttering of any inarticulate sound, cooing, moaning; the rattling of wheels, Pāṇ. i, 3, 21, Vārtt.; rumbling of the bowels, Suśr.

Kūjita, mfn. uttered inarticulately, cooed, &c., Vikr. &c.; filled with monotonous sounds, &c., R. iii, 78, 27; Vet.; (*am*), n. the cry of a bird, cooing, warbling, cackling, &c., R.; Mālav.; Vikr. &c.

Kūjitavya, *am*, n., only (*e*), loc. ind. when answer is to be given, MBh. xii, 109, 15.

Kūjin, mfn. warbling, &c.; making a rumbling sound in the bowels, Suśr.

Kūjya, mfn. (p. fut. Pass.), Pāṇ. vii, 3, 59, Kāś.

कूट् *kūṭ*, cl. 10. P. *kūṭayati*, to burn, Dhātup. xxxv, 38; to give pain, ib.; to be distressed, ib.; to counsel, advise, ib.: Ā. *kūṭayate*, to avoid or decline giving, Dhātup. xxxiii, 28; to render indistinct or unintelligible, render confused or foul, ib.; to be distressed, despair, ib.

कूट *kū́ṭa, am*, n. the bone of the forehead with its projections or prominences, horn, RV. x, 102, 4; AV.; ŚBr.; AitBr.; a kind of vessel or implement, Kauś. 16; (*as, am*), m. n. any prominence or projection (e. g. *aṃsa-k*°, *akshi-k*°, qq. vv.); summit, peak or summit of a mountain, MBh. &c.; summit, head, i. e. the highest, most excellent, first, BhP. ii, 9, 19; a heap, multitude (e. g. *abhra-k*°, a multitude of clouds), MBh.; R.; BhP.; part of a plough, ploughshare, body of a plough, L.; an iron mallet, MBh. xvi, 4, 6; a trap for catching deer, concealed weapon (as a dagger in a wooden case, sword-stick, &c.), R.; Pañcat.; (*as*, L.; *am*), m. n. illusion, fraud, trick, untruth, falsehood, L.; a puzzling question, enigma, BhP. vi, 5, 10 & 29; (*as*), m. a kind of hall (= *maṇḍapa*), Hcat.; N. of a particular constellation, VarBṛ. xii, 8 & 16; a subdivision of Graha-yuddha, Sūryas.; a mystical N. of the letter *ksha*, RāmatUp.; N. of Agastya (cf. *kuṭaja*), L.; of an enemy of Vishṇu, R.; BhP. x; (*as, am*), m. n. uniform substance (as the etherial element, &c.), L.; a water-jar, Hcar.; a kind of plant, L.; (*as, ī*), m. f. a house, dwelling (cf. *kuṭa* and *kuṭī*), L.; (*kūṭá*), mf(*ā́*)n. not horned or cornuted (as an animal with incomplete continuations of the bone of the forehead), AV. xii, 4, 3; TS. i; Kāṭh. &c.; false, untrue, deceitful, Mn.; Yājñ.; Kathās. &c.; base (as coins), Yājñ. ii, 241; (*as*), m. an ox whose horns are broken, L.; (*am*), n. counterfeited objects (of a merchant), VarBṛ. xiv, 3. — **karman**, n. fraudulent act, trick, Daś. — **kāra**, m. a cheat, false witness, W. — **kāraka**, m. id., Mn. iii, 158 (= MBh. xiii, 4276). — **kṛit**, m. a cheat, briber, falsifier of (gen.), Yājñ.; a Kāyastha or man of the writer-caste, L.; N. of Śiva, L. — **khaḍga**, m. a hidden sword, sword-stick, R. vi, 80, 4. — **grantha**, m., N. of a work (attributed to Vyāsa). — **cchadman**, m. a rogue, cheat, Pañcat. — **ja**, m. (= *kuṭ*°) the tree Wrightia antidysenterica, R. iv, 29, 10. — **taksh**, mfn., Pāṇ. vii, 1, 84, Vārtt. 2; Pat. — **tā**, f. falsehood. — **tāpasa**, m. a pretended ascetic, Kathās. — **tulā**, f. a false pair of scales, Pañcat. — **tva**, n. = -*tā*. — **dharma**, mfn. (a country) where falsehood is considered a duty, BhP. — **parva**, v. l. for -*pūrva*, q. v., L. — **pākala**, m. a bilious fever (of men), Bhpr.; fever in an elephant, Mālatīm. — **pālaka**, m. a potter's kiln, L., v. l. for -*pākala*, q. v. — **pāśa**, m. a trap, Pañcat.; Kād. — **pūrī**, f. (= *karāyikā*) a kind of crane, VarBṛS. (metrically also °*ri*). — **pūrva**, m. fever in an elephant, L. — **bandha**, m. = -*pāśa*, Ragh. xiii, 19; (*am*), ind. p., Pāṇ. iii, 4, 41, Kāś. — **māna**, n. false measure or weight, MBh. — **mudgara**, m. a concealed weapon similar to a hammer, MBh.; Hariv.; R.; MārkP.; N. of a work. — **mohana**, m. ‘baffling or bewildering rogues,’ N. of Skanda, MBh. iii, 14632. — **yantra**, n. a trap or snare, L. — **yuddha**, n. a treacherous or unfair battle, Ragh. xvii, 69; (mfn.) fighting treacherously, R. i, 22, 7. — **yodhin**, mfn. fighting unfairly or treacherously, R. — **racanā**, f. artifice, trick, Kathās. lvii, 115; a laid trap, Pañcat. — **lekha**, m. a falsified document, Kathās. cxxiv, 198. — **lekhya**, n. id., Pañcat. (ed. Bomb.) — **vyavahārin**, m. a deceitful merchant, Vishṇ. — **śas**, ind. in heaps, by crowds, MBh. — **śālmali**, m. f. the plant Andersonia Rohitaka, L.; a fabulous cotton plant with sharp thorns (with which the wicked are tortured in the world of Yama), MBh. (also °*lika*, m.); R. (°*lī*, f.); Ragh. xii, 95; N. of a hell, PadmaP. — **śālmalika**, m., °**lī**, f., see -*śālmali*. — **śāsana**, n. a forged grant or decree, Mn. ix, 232. — **śaila**, m., N. of a mountain, VP. — **saṃkrānti**, f. the entrance of the sun into another zodiacal sign after midnight, L. — **saṃghaṭita-lakshaṇa**, n., N. of a work. — **saṃdoha**, m. id. — **sâkshin**, m. a false witness, Gaut.; Yājñ. ii, 77; MārkP. — **sākshya**, n. a false testimony, HYog. ii, 54. — **stha**, mfn. standing at the top, keeping the highest position, Comm. on ŚBr. i, 4, 2, 4; standing in a multitude of or in the midst of (in comp.), BhP. i, 11, 36; (in phil.) immovable, uniform, unchangeable (as the soul, spirit, space, ether, sound, &c.), Up.; Pat.; Bhag. vi, xii; BhP. iii, &c. (Pāli *kūṭaṭṭha*, Sāmaññaphala-sutta); (*as, ām*), m. n. a kind of perfume (a species of dried shell-fish, commonly Nathi), L.; (*am*), n. the soul, W.; -*tā*, f. unchangeableness, uniformity; -*tva*, n. id., Comm. on KapS.; -*dīpa*, m., N. of a treatise forming part of the Pañcadaśī. — **svarṇa**, n. alloyed or counterfeit gold, Yājñ. ii, 297; Hcat. — **heman**, n. id., Naish. xxii, 52.

Kūṭâksha, m. loaded or false dice, Yājñ. ii, 202. **Kūṭâkhyāna**, n. = *kūṭakâkhy*°, q. v. **Kūṭâgāra**, m. n. an upper room, apartment on the top of a house, R.; Mṛicch.; Car. &c.; -*śālā*, f. id., Buddh.; Jain. **Kūṭâyu**, m. a Moringa with red blossoms, L. **Kūṭârtha**, m. ambiguity of meaning, fiction; -*bhāshitā*, f. (scil. *kathā*) = *kūṭakâkhyāna*, q. v., L. **Kūṭôpâya**, m. trick, fraud, stratagem, W.

Kūṭaka, mfn. base (as a coin), Yājñ. ii, 241; (*as*), m. a braid or tress of hair, L.; N. of a fragrant plant, L.; of a mountain, BhP. v, 19, 16; (*am*), n. elevation, prominence, projection, L. (see *akshi-k*°); ‘a ploughshare,’ or ‘the body of a plough (i. e. the wood without the ploughshare and pole),’ L.

Kūṭakâkhyāna, n. a tale containing passages of ambiguous meanings.

Kūṭī-√kṛi, to heap, Comm. on MBh. v, 48, 24.

कूटी *kūṭi*, v. l. for *kūḍi*.

कूड् 1. *kūḍ*, cl. 6. P. *kūḍati*, to eat, graze, Dhātup. xxviii, 88; to become firm or fat or solid, ib. (v. l. *kriḍ*).

कूड् 2. *kūḍ* (= 2. *kūl*), cl. 10. P. *kūḍayati* (subj. 3. du. *kūḷayātas*), to burn, scorch, RV. viii, 26, 10; (impf. *akūlayat*) AitBr. iv, 9; Kapishṭh. iv, 2.

कूड्य *kūḍya, am*, n. (= *kuḍya*) a wall, L.

कूण् *kūṇ*, cl. 1. *kūṇati*, to contract, shrink, shorten, Kpr.: Caus. P. Ā. *kūṇayati*, °*te*, to draw together, contract, close, Dhātup. xxxiii, 15; xxxv, 42.

Kūṇita, mfn. contracted, shut, closed, Suśr. **Kūṇitêkshaṇa**, m. ‘having the eyes shut,’ a hawk, L.

कूणकुच्छ *kūṇakuccha, as*, m., N. of one of Śiva's attendants, L.; (cf. *kauṇakutsya*.)

कूणि *kūṇi*, mfn. (= *kuṇi*) crooked-armed, L.; (*is*), m. a sort of bird, Gal.

कूणिक *kūṇika, as*, m., N. of a prince of Campā, HPariś.; (*kūnika*) VP.; (*a*), f. the horn of any animal, L.; the peg of a lute (= *kalikā*), L.

कूतना *kūtanā, ās*, f. pl., N. of particular waters, Kāṭh. xxx, 6; (*kótanā*) TS. iii, 3, 3, 1.

कूदर *kúdara.* See 1. *ku.*

कूदी *kūdī*, f. a bunch of twigs, bunch (v. l. *kūṭī*), AV. v, 19, 12; Kauś. **— maya**, mfn. consisting of a bunch, Kauś. 21.

कूद्दाल *kūddāla, as*, m. (= *kudd°*) mountain ebony (Bauhinia variegata), L.

कूप् *kūp*, cl. 10. P. *kūpayati*, to be weak, weaken, Dhātup. xxxv, 17.

कूप *kū́pa, as*, m. (fr. 1. *ku* and *áp*?; cf. *anūpá, dvīpá*), a hole, hollow, cave, RV. i, 105, 17; AV.; ŚBr. &c.; a pit, well, ŚāṅkhGṛ.; Mn.; Mṛicch. &c.; a post to which a boat or ship is moored, L.; a mast, L.; a tree or rock in the midst of a river, L.; a leather oil vessel, L.; = *mṛin-māna*, L.; (*ī*), f. a small well, W.; the navel, W.; a flask, bottle, W.; [cf. Gk. κύπη.] **— kacchapa**, m. 'a tortoise in a well,' a man without experience (who has seen nothing of the world), gaṇas *pātresamitâdi* and *yuktârohy-ādi*. **— kandara**, m., N. of a man, GaṇP. **— karṇa**, m., N. of a man, BhP. x, 63, 8 & 16. **— kāra**, m. a well-digger, R. ii, 80, 3. **— kūrma**, m. = *-kacchapa*. **— khā**, m. Ved. a well-digger, Kāś. on Pāṇ. iii, 2, 67 & vi, 4, 41. **— khānaka**, m. id., Kathās. lxvi, 134. **— cakra**, n. a wheel for raising water from a well, Up. **— ja**, m. 'produced from pores,' hair, L. **— jala**, n. well-water, spring-water; *°lôdvāhana*, n. = *kūpa-cakra*, Gal. **— dardura**, m. = *-kacchapa*, MBh. v, 5509; Pañcat. **— bila**, n., Pāṇ. vi, 2, 102. **— maṇḍūka**, m. (gaṇa *pātresamitâdi*) = *-kacchapa*, Prasannar.; Hit.; (*ī*), f. id., Bhaṭṭ. v, 85. **— yantra**, n. = *-cakra*, Mṛicch. **— rājya**, n., N. of a country. **— śaya**, mfn. hidden in a well, MBh. v, 160, 102. **Kūpâṅka**, m. bristling or erection of the hairs of the body, L. **Kūpâṅga**, v. l. for *kūpâṅka*. **Kūpe-piśācaka**, *ās*, m. pl., Pāṇ. ii, 1, 44, Kāś. **Kūpôdaka**, n. well-water.

Kūpaka, *as*, m. (gaṇa *prekshâdi*) a hole, hollow, cave, L.; the hollow below the loins, L.; a pore, VarBṛS.; a small well; a hole dug for water in the dry bed of a rivulet, L.; a stake &c. to which a boat is moored, L.; the mast of a vessel, L.; a rock or tree in the midst of a river, L.; a funeral pile (or 'a hole dug under a funeral pile'), L.; a leather oil vessel, L.; = *a-cyutā*, L.; (*ikā*), f. a stone or rock in the middle of a stream, L.; = *a-cyutā*, L.

Kūpāya, Nom. Ā. *°yate*, to become a well, Bhartṛ. ii, 78.

Kūpika, mfn. fr. *kūpa*, gaṇa *kumudâdi*; (*ā*), f., see *kūpaka*.

Kū́pya, mf(*ā*)n. (gaṇa *gav-ādi*) being in a hole or well, VS.; TS.; TBr.; ŚBr.; KātyŚr.

कूपत् *kūpat*, ind., gaṇa *cādi*.

कूपद *kūpada, as*, m. = *kūkuda*, L.

कूपार *kūpāra, as*, m. (= *akūp°*) the ocean, L.

कूपुष *kūpusha, am*, n. the bladder, L.

कूबर *kū́bara, as* or *am*, m. or n. the pole of a carriage or the wooden frame to which the yoke is fixed, MaitrS.; Gobh.; MBh. &c. (ifc. f. *ā*, Hcat.); (*ī*), f. id., ŚBr.; ŚāṅkhBr. &c.; a carriage drawn by oxen, L.; (*as*), m. a hump-backed man, L.; (mfn.) beautiful, agreeable, L. **— sthāna**, n. the seat on a carriage, Sāy. on RV. iii, 14, 3.

Kūbarin, *ī*, m. a carriage, W.

कूम *kūma, am*, n. a lake, pond, L.

कूमनस् *kū-manas*, mfn. (1. *ku*) Ved. wicked-minded, Pāṇ. vi, 3, 133, Kāś.

कूयव *kú-yava, am*, n., N. of particular grains, MaitrS. ii, 11, 4; Kapishṭh. xxviii, 9; (*kú-y°*) VS. xviii, 10; (*ās*), m. pl. id., TS. iv.

कूर *kūra, am*, n. boiled rice, Bhpr.

कूर्कुर *kūrkura, as*, m., N. of a demon who persecutes children (perhaps cough or some similar disease personified), PārGṛ. i, 16.

कूर्च *kūrcá, as*, m., rarely *am*, n. (gaṇa *ardharcâdi*) a bunch of anything, bundle of grass, &c. (often used as a seat), TS. vii; ŚBr. &c.; a fan, brush, NarasP.; a handful of Kuśa grass or peacock's feathers, Comm. on MBh.; (*as*), m. (*am*, n., L.) 'ball, roll,' N. of certain parts of the human body (as the hands, feet, neck, and the membrum virile), Suśr.; the upper part of the nose (the part between the eyebrows), L.; (*as*, L.; *am*), m. n. the beard, Kād.; Rājat.; BhavP.; (beard of a buck) Comm. on KātyŚr.; (Prākṛit *kucca*) Śak.; the tip of the thumb and middle finger brought in contact so as to pinch &c., W.; deceit, fraud, hypocrisy, L.; false praise, unmerited commendation either of one's self or another person, boasting, flattery, L.; hardness, solidity, L.; (*as*), m. the head, L.; a store-room, L.; the mystical syllable *huṃ* or *hrūṃ*. **— parṇī**, f. 'beard-leaved,' the plant Gymnema sylvestre, Npr. **— śiras**, n. the upper part of the palm of the hand and foot, Suśr. **— śīrsha**, m., N. of a plant (commonly Jīvaka, one of the eight principal medicaments), L. **— śīrshaka**, m. id., L. **— śekhara**, m. the cocoa-nut tree, L. **Kūrcā-mukha**, m., N. of a Ṛishi, MBh. xiii, 252.

Kūrcaka, *as*, m. a bunch, bushel, Jain. Comm.; a brush for cleaning the teeth, painter's brush &c.; Suśr.; Kād.; N. of certain parts of the human body (see *kūrca*), Suśr.; (ifc.) the beard; = *kūrca-śīrsha*, Npr.; (*ikā*), f. a painting brush or pencil, L.; a key, L. (cf. *kūcikā*); a needle, L.; a bud, blossom, L.; inspissated milk, Suśr.; (*am*), n., see *tri-k°*.

Kūrcakin, mfn. stuffed, puffy, Suśr.

Kūrcala, mfn. bearded (as an animal), Comm. on ŚāṅkhŚr. and KātyŚr.

Kūrcin, mfn. having a long beard, VarBṛ.

कूर्द् *kūrd*, cl. 1. P. Ā. *kūrdati, °te* (perf. *cukūrda*, Hariv.; aor. *akūrdishṭa*, Bhaṭṭ.), to leap, jump, MBh. vi, 101; Hariv.; Bhaṭṭ.: Ā. *kūrdate*, to play, Dhātup. ii, 20.

Kūrda, *as*, m. 'a jump,' *prajāpateḥ k°*, 'Prajāpati's jump,' N. of a Sāman.

Kūrdana, *am*, n. leaping, Pañcat.; Comm. on VS.; playing, sport, L.; (*ā*), f. the day of full moon in the month Caitra (a festival day in honour of Kāma-deva or the god of love), Gal.; (*ī*), f. id., L.

कूर्प *kūrpa, am*, n. the space between the eyebrows, L. **— dṛiś**, mfn. one whose eyes are formed in a particular manner, BhP. x, 87, 18 ('having sand in the eyes,' Comm.)

Kūrpaka, *am*, n. = *kūrpa*, Gal.

कूर्पर *kūrpara, as*, m. the elbow, Suśr.; Daś.; Bālar.; Comm. on KātyŚr.; the knee, L.; N. of a village; (*ā*), f. the elbow, L.

Kūrparita, mfn. struck by the elbow, Bālar.

कूर्पस *kūrpasa, am*, n. the inner part of a cocoa-nut, Gal.

कूर्पास *kūrpāsa, as*, m. a cuirass or quilted jacket (worn as armour), L.; (= *cola*) a jacket, Comm. on Naish. xxii, 42.

Kūrpāsaka, *as*, m. a bodice, jacket (with short sleeves worn next the body, especially by women), Ṛitus; a cuirass, corselet, Hcat.; Śiś. v, 23.

कूर्म *kūrmá, as*, m. a tortoise, turtle, VS.; TS. &c. (ifc. f. *ā*, MBh. iv, 2016); the earth considered as a tortoise swimming on the waters (see *-vibhāga*); (hence) N. of the fourteenth Adhyāya of VarBṛS., VarYogay. ix, 4; a particular figure or intertwining of the fingers (*mudrā*), Tantras.; one of the outer winds of the body (causing the closing of the eyes), Vedântas.; N. of a deity, Rasik.; of a serpent or Kādraveya king, MBh. i, 2549; of a Ṛishi (son of Gṛitsa-mada, author of RV. ii, 27–29), RAnukr.; Vishṇu's second incarnation (descent in the form of a tortoise to support the mountain Mandara at the churning of the ocean), NarasP. &c.; (*ī*), f. a female tortoise; [cf. κλέμμυς, χέλυς, χελώνη.] **— kalpa**, m., N. of a particular Kalpa or period of time, Hcat. **— cakra**, n., N. of a mystical diagram. **— dvādaśī**, f. the twelfth day in the light (or dark?) half of the month Pausha, VarP. **— nātha**, m., N. of an author of Mantras. **— pati**, m. the king of turtles (who upholds the earth), Subh. **— pitta**, n. the bilious humor of a tortoise, Suśr.; a vessel with water, PārGṛ. i, 14. **— purāṇa**, n. 'Purāṇa of the tortoise incarnation,' the 15th of the eighteen Purāṇas. **— pṛishṭha**, n. the back or shell of a tortoise; (*as*), m. globe-amaranth (Gomphrena globosa), L.; N. of a Yaksha, BrahmaP.; *°shṭhâsthi*, n. tortoise-shell; *°shṭhônnata*, mfn. raised or elevated like the back of a tortoise, MBh. **— pṛishṭhaka**, n. the cover of a dish, lid, L. **— ramaṇī**, f. a female tortoise, Naish. xii, 106. **— rāja**, m. the king of turtles (who upholds the world), L. **— lakshaṇa**, n., N. of a work. **— vibhāga**, m. division of the globe or semi-globe of the earth, AV. Pariś.; VarBṛS. **Kūrmâṅga**, n. the globe of the earth, VarYogay. **Kūrmâvatāra**, m. the tortoise incarnation (of Vishṇu). **Kūrmâsana**, n. a particular posture in sitting (practised by ascetics).

Kūrmikā, f. a kind of musical instrument.

कूर्मि *kūrmi* and *°rmin*. See *tuvi-k°*.

कूल् 1. *kūl*, cl. 1. P. *kūlati*, 'to cover, hide,' or 'to keep off, obstruct' (derived from *kūla*), Dhātup. xv, 18.

कूल् 2. *kūl* = √2. *kūḍ*, q. v.

Kūlita, mfn. burnt, scorched, Suśr.

कूल *kū́la, am*, n. a declivity, slope, RV. viii, 47, 11; a shore, bank, ŚBr. xiv; Nir.; Mn. &c. (ifc., Pāṇ. vi, 2, 121; 129 & 135; f. *ā*, MBh. xiv, 1163); a heap, mound, tope, Car.; a pond or pool, L.; the rear of an army, L.; N. of a locality, gaṇa *dhūmâdi*; [cf. *aja-kūlā, anu-kūla, ut-k°*, &c.; cf. also Hib. *cul*, 'custody, guard, defence, back part of anything;' *col*, 'an impediment;' Lat. *collis*?] **— m-kasha**, mf(*ā*)n. (Pāṇ. iii, 2, 42) carrying or tearing away the bank, Śak.; (*am*), n. the ocean, sea, L.; the stream or current of a river, W.; (*ā*), f. a river, L. **— cara**, mfn. frequenting the banks of rivers, grazing there &c., Suśr. **— jāta**, mfn. growing on the bank, Pañcat. **— taṇḍula**, m. breakers, surges, L. **— m-dhaya**, mf(*ī*)n., Vop. xxvi, 53. **— bhū**, f. a bank, land upon the bank or shore, L. **— m-udruja**, mf(*ā*)n. (Pāṇ. iii, 2, 31) breaking down banks (as a river &c.), Ragh. iv, 22. **— m-udvaha**, mfn. carrying or tearing away the bank (as a river &c.), Pāṇ. iii, 2, 31. **— vat**, mfn. furnished with shores, gaṇa *balâdi*; (*tī*), f. a river, L. **— haṇḍa**, m. = *-taṇḍula*, L. **— haṇḍaka**, m. id., L. **Kūle-cara**, mfn. = *kūla-c°*, Bhpr.

Kūlaka, *as, am*, m. n. a bank, shore, L.; a mound, heap, tope, L.; (*as*), m. an ant-hill, L.; N. of a mountain, Divyâv.; (*am*), n. the plant Trichosanthes dioeca, L.; (*ikā*), f. bottom part of the Indian lute (cf. *kūṇikā*), W.

Kūlin, mfn. furnished with banks or shores, gaṇa *balâdi*; (*inī*), f. a river, Rājat. v, 68.

Kūlya, mfn. belonging to a bank, VS. xvi, 42.

कूलास *kūlāsa*, gaṇa *saṃkalâdi*.

कूलि *kūli, is*, m., N. of a Brāhman, Kathārṇ.

कूलिक *kūlika, as*, m., N. of a prince, Mcar.; (*ā*), f., see *kūlaka*.

कूलिन् *kūlin*, &c. See *kū́la*.

कूल्बज *kúlbaja*?, AV. xii, 5, 12 & 53.

कूल्व *kūlva*, mfn. 'bald,' only in *áti-k°*, v. l. for *áti-kulva*, q. v.

कूवर *kūvara*, for *kūbara*, q. v.

कूवार *kūvāra* = *kūpāra*, q. v., L.

कूशाम्ब *kūśāmba, as*, m. (cf. *kuś°*) N. of a man, TāṇḍyaBr. viii, 6, 8.

कूश्म *kūśmá, as*, m. (probably) N. of an imp or goblin, VS. xxv, 7; (*kūshmá*) MaitrS. iii, 15, 9.

कूश्माण्ड *kūśmāṇḍa*, v. l. for *kushm°*, q. v.

Kūśmāṇḍaka, v. l. for *kushm°*, q. v.

कूष्म *kūshmá*, v. l. for *kūśmá*, q. v.

कूष्माण्ड *kūshmāṇḍa*, v. l. for *kushm°*, q. v.; (*ā*), f., N. of Durgā; (*ī*), f. id. (see *kushm°*); (*yas*), f. pl., N. of the verses VS. xx, 14–16 (spoken in a certain rite for penance or expiation), Yājñ. iii, 304; (*am, āni*), n. sg. and pl. id., Gaut.; Mn. viii, 106. **— dīpikā**, f., N. of a work. **— rāja-putra**, m., N. of a demon.

Kūshmāṇḍaka, v. l. for *kushm°*, q. v.

Kūshmāṇḍinī, f., N. of a goddess.

कूहना *kūhanā*, f. (= *kuh°*) hypocrisy, L.

कूहा *kūhā*, f. (= *kuhī*) a fog, L.

कृ 1. *kṛi*, Ved. I) cl. 2. P. 2. sg. *kárshi*, du. *kṛithás*, pl. *kṛithá*; Ā. 2. sg. *kṛishé*;

impf. 2. & 3. sg. *ákar*, 3. sg. rarely *ákat* (ŚBr. iii, xi); 3. du. *ákartām*; pl. *ákarma*, *ákarta* (also BhP. ix), *ákran* (aor., according to Pāṇ. iv, 2, 80, Kāś.); Ā. *ákri* (RV. x, 159, 4 & 174, 4), *ákṛithās* (RV. v, 30, 8), *ákṛita* (RV.); *akrātām* (ŚāṅkhŚr.), *ákrata* (RV.; AV.): Impv. *kṛidhí* (also MBh. i, 5141 & BhP. viii), *kṛitám*, *kṛitá*; Ā. *kṛishvá*, *kṛidhvám*; Subj. 2. & 3. sg. *kar*, pl. *kárma*, *kárta* & *kartana*, *kran*; Ā. 3. sg. *kṛita* (RV. ix, 69, 5), 3. pl. *kránta* (RV. i, 141, 3): Pot. *kriyāma* (RV. x, 32, 9); pr. p. P. (nom. pl.) *krántas*, Ā. *krāṇá*. II) cl. 1. P. *kárasi*, *kárati*, *kárathas*, *káratas*, *káranti*; Ā. *kárase*, *kárate*, *karāmahe*: impf. *ákaram*, *ákaras*, *ákarat* (aor., according to Pāṇ. iii, 1, 59): Impv. *kára*, *káratam*, *káratām*: Subj. *káram*, *kárāṇi*, *káras*, *kárat*, *kárāma*, *káran*; Ā. *karāmahai*; pr. p. (f.) *kárantī* (Naigh.) III) cl. 5. P. *kṛiṇómi*, °*nóshi*, °*nóti*, *kṛiṇuthás*, *kṛiṇmás* & *kṛiṇmasi*, *kṛiṇuthá*, *kṛiṇvánti*; Ā. *kṛiṇvé*, *kṛiṇushé*, *kṛiṇuté*, 3. du. *kṛiṇvaíte* (RV. vi, 25, 4); pl. *kṛiṇmáhe*, *kṛiṇváte*: impf. *ákṛiṇos*, *ákṛiṇot*, *ákṛiṇutam*, *ákṛiṇuta* & °*notana* (RV. i, 110, 8), *ákṛiṇvan*; Ā. 3. sg. *ákṛiṇuta*, pl. *ákṛiṇudhvam*, *ákṛiṇvata*: Impv. *kṛiṇú* or *kṛiṇuhí* or *kṛiṇutāt*, *kṛiṇótu*, *kṛiṇutám*, *kṛiṇutām*, 2. pl. *kṛiṇutá* or *kṛiṇóta* or *kṛiṇótana*, 3. pl. *kṛiṇvántu*; Ā. *kṛiṇushvá*, *kṛiṇutām*, *kṛiṇváthām*, *kṛiṇudhvám*: Subj. *kṛiṇávas*, °*ṇávat* or °*ṇávāt*, *kṛiṇávāva*, °*ṇávāma*, °*ṇávātha*, °*ṇávatha*, °*ṇávan*; Ā. *kṛiṇávai* (once °*ṇavā*, RV. x, 95, 2), *kṛiṇavase* (also ŚvetUp. ii, 7, v. l. °*ṇvase*), *kṛiṇavate*, *kṛiṇávāvahai*, *kṛiṇávāmahai*, 3. pl. *kṛiṇávanta* (RV.) or *kṛiṇavante* or *kṛiṇvata* (RV.): Pot. Ā. *kṛiṇvītá*; pr. p. P. *kṛiṇvát* (f. °*vatī*), Ā. *kṛiṇvāṇá*. IV) cl. 8 (this is the usual formation in the Brāhmaṇas, Sūtras, and in classical Sanskṛit), P. *karómi* (ep. *kurmi*, MBh. ii, 10943; R. ii, 12, 33); *kurvás*, *kuruthás*, *kurutás*, *kurmás* [*kulmas* in an interpolation after RV. x, 128], *kuruthá*, *kurvánti*; Ā. *kurvé*, &c., 3. pl. *kurváte* (Pāṇ. vi, 4, 108–110): impf. *akaravam*, *akaros*, *akarot*, *akurva*, &c.; Ā. 3. sg. *akuruta*, pl. *akurvata*: Impv. *kuru*, *karotu* (in the earlier language 2. & 3. sg. *kurutāt*, 3. sg. also BhP. vi, 4, 34), *kuruta* or *kurutana* (Nir. iv, 7); Ā. *kurushva*, *kurudhvam*, *kurvātām*: Subj. *karavāṇi*, *karavas*, °*vāt*, °*vāva* or °*vāvas* (Pāṇ. iii, 4, 98, Kāś.), °*vāma* or °*vāmas* (ib.), °*vātha*, °*van*; Ā. *karavai*, *kuruthās*, *karavāvahai* (TUp.; °*he*, MBh. iii, 10762), *karavaithe*, °*vaite* (Pāṇ. iii, 4, 95, Kāś), °*vāmahai* (°*he*, MBh.; R. i, 18, 12): Pot. P. *kuryām*, Ā. *kurvīya* (Pāṇ. vi, 4, 109 & 110); pr. p. P. *kurvát* (f. °*vatī*); Ā. *kurvāṇá*: perf. P. *cakā́ra*, *cakártha*, *cakṛivá*, *cakṛimá*, *cakrá* (Pāṇ. vii, 2, 13); Ā. *cakré*, *cakriré*; p. *cakṛivas* (acc. *cakrúsham*, RV. x, 137, 1); Ā. *cakrāṇa* (Vop.): 2nd fut. *karishyáti*; Subj. 2. sg. *karishyás* (RV. iv, 30, 23); 1st fut. *kartā́*: Prec. *kriyāsam*: aor. P. Ved. *cakaram* (RV. iv, 42, 6), *acakrat* (RV. iv, 18, 12), *ácakriran* (RV. viii, 6, 20); Ā. 1. sg. *kṛishe* (RV. x, 49, 7); Class. *akārshīt* (Pāṇ. vii, 2, 1, Kāś.; once *akārashīt*, BhP. i, 10, 1); Pass. aor. reflex. *akāri* & *akṛita* (Pāṇ. iii, 1, 62, Kāś.): Inf. *kártum*, Ved. *kártave*, *kártavai*, *kártos* (see ss. vv.); ind. p. *kṛitvā́*, Ved. *kṛitvī́* [RV.] & *kṛitvā́ya* [TS. iv, v]; to do, make, perform, accomplish, cause, effect, prepare, undertake, RV. &c.; to do anything for the advantage or injury of another (gen. or loc.), MBh.; R. &c.; to execute, carry out (as an order or command), ib.; to manufacture, prepare, work at, elaborate, build, ib.; to form or construct one thing out of another (abl. or instr.), R. i, 2, 44; Hit. &c.; to employ, use, make use of (instr.), ŚvetUp.; Mn. x, 91; MBh. &c.; to compose, describe, R. i; to cultivate, Yājñ. ii, 158 (cf. Mn. x, 114); to accomplish any period, bring to completion, spend (e. g. *varshāṇi daśa cakruḥ*, 'they spent ten years,' MBh. xv, 6; *kshaṇam kuru*, 'wait a moment,' MBh.; cf. *kṛita-kshaṇa*); to place, put, lay, bring, lead, take hold of (acc. or loc. or instr., e. g. *ardhám* √*kṛi*, to take to one's own side or party, cause to share in (gen.; see 2. *ardhá*); *haste* or *pāṇau* √*kṛi*, to take by the hand, marry, Pāṇ. i, 4, 77; *hṛidayena* √*kṛi*, to place in one's heart, love, Mṛicch.; *hṛidi* √*kṛi*, to take to heart, mind, think over, consider, Rājat. v, 313; *manasi* √*kṛi*, id., R. ii, 64, 8; Hcar.; to determine, purpose [ind. p. °*si kṛitvā* or °*si-kṛitya*], Pāṇ. i, 4, 75; *vaśe* √*kṛi*, to place in subjection, become master of, Mn. ii, 100); to direct the thoughts, mind, &c. (*mánas* [RV.; Mn.; MBh. &c.] or *buddhim* [Nal. xxvi, 10] or *matim* [MBh.; R.] or *bhāvam* [ib.], &c.) towards any object, turn the attention to, resolve upon, determine on (loc., dat., inf., or a sentence with *iti*, e. g. *mā śoke manaḥ kṛithāḥ*, do not turn your mind to grief, Nal. xiv, 22; *gamanāya matim cakre*, he resolved upon going, R. i, 9, 55; *alābum samutsrashṭum manaś cakre*, he resolved to create a gourd, MBh. iii, 8844; *drashṭā tavâsmīti matim cakāra*, he determined to see him, MBh. iii, 12335); to think of (acc.), R. i, 21, 14; to make, render (with two acc., e. g. *ādityam kāshṭhām akurvata*, they made the sun their goal, AitBr. iv, 7), RV.; ŚBr. &c.; to procure for another, bestow, grant (with gen. or loc.), RV.; VS.; ŚBr. &c.; Ā. to procure for one's self, appropriate, assume, ŚBr.; BṛĀrUp.; Mn. vii, 10 &c.; to give aid, help any one to get anything (dat.), RV.; VS.; to make liable to (dat.), RV. iii, 41, 6; ŚBr. iv; to injure, violate (e. g. *kanyām* √*kṛi*, to violate a maiden), Mn. viii, 367 & 369; to appoint, institute, ChUp.; Mn.; to give an order, commission, Mn.; R. ii, 2, 8; to cause to get rid of, free from (abl. or *-tas*), Pāṇ. v, 4, 49, Kāś.; to begin (e. g. *cakre śobhayitum purīm*, they began to adorn the city), R. ii, 6, 10; to proceed, act, put in practice, VS.; ŚBr.; AitBr. &c.; to worship, sacrifice, RV.; ŚBr.; Mn. iii, 210; to make a sound (*svaram* or *śabdam*, MBh. iii, 11718; Pāṇ. iv, 4, 34; Hit.), utter, pronounce (often ifc. with the sounds *phaṭ*, *phut*, *bhāṇ*, *váshaṭ*, *svadhā́*, *svā́hā*, *him*), pronounce any formula (Mn. ii, 74 & xi, 33); (with numeral adverbs ending in *dhā*) to divide, separate or break up into parts (e. g. *dvidhā* √*kṛi*, to divide into two parts, ind. p. *dvidhā kṛitvā* or *dvidhā-kṛitya* or *-kāram*, Pāṇ. iii, 4, 62; *sahasradhā* √*kṛi*, to break into a thousand pieces); (with adverbs ending in *vat*) to make like or similar, consider equivalent (e. g. *rājyam tṛiṇa-vat kṛitvā*, valuing the kingdom like a straw, Vet.); (with adverbs ending in *sāt*) to reduce anything to, cause to become, make subject (see *ātma-sāt*, *bhasma-sāt*), Pāṇ. v, 4, 52 ff.

The above senses of √*kṛi* may be variously modified or almost infinitely extended according to the noun with which this rt. is connected, as in the following examples: *sakhyam* √*kṛi*, to contract friendship with; *pūjām* √*kṛi*, to honour; *rājyam* √*kṛi*, to reign; *sneham* √*kṛi*, to show affection; *ājñām* or *nideśam* or *śāsanam* or *kāmam* or *yācanām* or *vacaḥ* or *vacanam* or *vākyam* √*kṛi*, to perform any one's command or wish or request &c.; *dharmam* √*kṛi*, to do one's duty, Mn. vii, 136; *nakhāni* √*kṛi*, 'to clean one's nails,' see *kṛita-nakha*; *udakam* [Mn.; Yājñ.; R.; Daś.] or *salilam* [R. i, 44, 49] √*kṛi*, to offer a libation of water to the dead; to perform ablutions; *astrāṇi* √*kṛi*, to practise the use of weapons, MBh. iii, 11824; *darduram* √*kṛi*, to breathe the flute, Pāṇ. iv, 4, 34; *daṇḍam* √*kṛi*, to inflict punishment &c., Vet.; *kālam* √*kṛi*, to bring one's time to an end, i. e. to die; *ciram* √*kṛi*, to be long in doing anything, delay; *manasā* (for °*si*, see above) √*kṛi*, to place in one's mind, think of, meditate, MBh.; *śirasā* √*kṛi*, to place on the head; *mūrdhnā* √*kṛi*, to place on one's head, obey, honour.

Very rarely in Veda (AV. xviii, 2, 27), but commonly in the Brāhmaṇas, Sūtras, and especially in classical Sanskṛit the perf. forms *cakāra* and *cakre* are auxiliarily used to form the periphrastical perfect of verbs, especially of causatives, e. g. *āsām cakre*, 'he sat down;' *gamayām cakāra*, 'he caused to go' [see Pāṇ. iii, 1, 40; in Veda some other forms of √*kṛi* are used in a similar way, viz. pr. *karoti*, ŚāṅkhŚr.; impf. *akar*, MaitrS. & Kāṭh.; 3. pl. *akran*, MaitrS. & TBr.; Prec. *kriyāt*, MaitrS. (see Pāṇ. iii, 1, 42); according to Pāṇ. iii, 1, 41, also *karotu* with √*vid*].

Caus. *kārayati*, °*te*, to cause to act or do, cause another to perform, have anything made or done by another (double acc., instr. & acc. [see Pāṇ. i, 4, 53], e. g. *sabhām kāritavān*, he caused an assembly to be made, Hit.; *rāja-darśanam mām kāraya*, cause me to have an audience of the king; *vāṇijyam kārayed vaiśyam*, he ought to cause the Vaiśya to engage in trade, Mn. viii, 410; *na śakshyāmi kimcit kārayitum tvayā*, I shall not be able to have anything done by thee, MBh. ii, 6); to cause to manufacture or form or cultivate, Lāṭy.; Yājñ. ii, 158; MBh. &c.; to cause to place or put, have anything placed, put upon, &c. (e. g. *tam citrapaṭam vāsa-gṛihe bhittāv akārayat*, he had the picture placed on the wall in his house, Kathās. v, 30), Mn. viii, 251. Sometimes the Caus. of √*kṛi* is used for the simple verb or without a causal signification (e. g. *padam kārayati*, he pronounces a word, Pāṇ. i, 3, 71, Kāś.; *mithyā k*°, he pronounces wrongly, ib.; *Kaikeyīm anu rājānam kāraya*, treat or deal with Kaikeyī as the king does, R. ii, 58, 16): Desid. *cikīrshati* (aor. 2. sg. *acikīrshīs*, ŚBr. iii), ep. also °*te*, to wish to make or do, intend to do, design, intend, begin, strive after, AV. xii, 4, 19; ŚBr.; KātyŚr.; Mn. &c.; to wish to sacrifice or worship, AV. v, 8, 3: Intens. 3. pl. *karikrati* (pr. p. *kárikrat*, see Naigh. ii, 1 & Pāṇ. vii, 4, 65), to do repeatedly, RV.; AV.; TS.; Class. *carkarti* or *carikarti* or *carīkarti* [Pāṇ. vii, 4, 92, Kāś.], also *carkarīti* or *carikarīti* or *carīkarīti* or *cekrīyate* [ib., Sch.; Vop.]; [cf. Hib. *caraim*, 'I perform, execute;' *ceard*, 'an art, trade, business, function;' *sucridh*, 'easy;' Old Germ. *karawan*, 'to prepare;' Mod. Germ. *gar*, 'prepared (as food);' Lat. *creo*, *ceremonia*; κραίνω, κρόνος.]

1. **Kṛit**, mfn. only ifc. (Pāṇ. vi, 1, 182) making, doing, performing, accomplishing, effecting, manufacturing, acting, one who accomplishes or performs anything, author (see *su-k*°, *karma-k*°, *pāpa-k*°, &c.); (*t*), m. an affix used to form nouns from roots, VPrāt.; Pāṇ. iii, 1, 93; 4, 67; vi, 1, 71; vii, 2, 8 & 11; 3, 33; viii, 4, 29; a noun formed with that affix, Nir.; PārGṛ.; Gobh.; Pāṇ. **-tattva-bodhinī**, f., N. of a grammatical treatise. **-paṭala**, m., N. of a treatise on Kṛit affixes. **Kṛid-anta**, m. a word ending with a Kṛit affix (such a word would be called by Pāṇ. simply *kṛit*). **Kṛil-lopa**, m. the rejection of a Kṛit affix.

1. **Kṛitá**, mfn. done, made, accomplished, performed, RV.; AV. &c.; prepared, made ready, ib.; obtained, gained, acquired, placed at hand, AV. iii, 24, 5; well done, proper, good, ŚBr. iv; cultivated, Mn. x, 114; appointed (as a duty), Yājñ. ii, 186; relating or referring to, Yājñ. ii, 210; (*as*), m., N. of one of the Viśve Devās, MBh. xiii, 4356; of a son of Vasu-deva, BhP. ix, 24, 45; of a son of Saṃnati and pupil of Hiraṇya-nābha, Hariv. 1080; BhP. xii, 6, 80; of a son of Kṛita-ratha and father of Vibudha, VP.; of a son of Jaya and father of Haryavana, BhP. ix, 17, 17; of a son of Cyavana and father of Upari-cara, VāyuP.; (*am*), n. (with *saha* or with instr.) 'done with,' away with, enough of, no need of, &c. (e. g. *kṛitam saṃdehena*, away with doubt, Śak.; *k*° *parihāsena*, enough of joking, ib.); the past tense, AitBr. v, 1; (*ám*), n. deed, work, action, RV.; AV.; ŚvetUp.; Mn. &c.; service done, kind action, benefit (cf. *kṛita-jña* & *-ghna*), MBh. v, 1692; Pañcat.; magic, sorcery, SāmavBr.; consequence, result, L.; aim, Vop. i, 2; stake at a game, RV.; AV.; prize or booty gained in battle, ib.; N. of the die or of the side of a die marked with four points or dots (this is the lucky or winning die), VS. xxx, 18; TS.; ŚBr. &c.; (also the collective N. of the four dice in opposition to the fifth die called *kali*, Comm. on VS. x, 28); (hence) the number 'four,' VarBṛS.; Sūryas.; N. of the first of the four ages of the world (also called *satya* or 'the golden age,' comprehending together with the morning and evening dawn 4800 years of men [Mn.; MBh.; Hariv.] or according to the later conception [BhP. &c.; Comm. on Mn. i, 69] 4800 years of the gods or 1,728,000 years of men); (*e*), loc. ind. on account of, for the sake of, for (with gen. or ifc., e. g. *mama kṛite* or *mat-kṛite*, on my account, for me), Yājñ. i, 216; MBh.; R. &c.; (*ena*), instr. ind., id., MBh.; R. i, 76, 6 & vi, 85, 10. **-kapaṭa**, mfn. deceiving, beguiling. **-kara**, m., N. of Śiva, Gal. **-kartavya**, mfn. one who has performed what was to be done, one who has done or discharged his duty, Prab. **-karman**, n. an act that has been accomplished, Subh.; (*kṛitá-k*°), mfn. one who has done his work or duty, ŚBr.; MBh.; R.; Ragh. ix, 3; clever, able, L. **-kalpa**, mfn. one who knows the customary rites, R. ii, 1, 16; *-taru*, m., N. of a work. **-kāma**, mf(*ā*)n. one whose desire is attained, satisfied, R. **-kārin**, mfn. doing again what has been done already, Pat.; doing any work, MBh. i, 5551 (= xii, 5307). **-kārya**, n. an attained object, Śak.; (mfn.) one who has obtained his object, Yājñ. ii, 189; R.; Kathās.; one who has no need of another person's aid (instr.), MBh. xiii, 3862; *-tva*, n. the state of having obtained one's

object, Kathās. **-kāla,** m. appointed time, Yājñ. ii, 184; (mfn.) 'fixed or settled as to time,' sent, deposited &c. for a certain time, Nār.; one who has accomplished a certain time, who has waited a certain time, MBh. ii, 1875. **-kūrcaka,** mfn. tied up as a small bundle or brush. **-kṛitya,** n. what has been done and what is to be done, Up.; (mfn.) one who has done his duty or accomplished a business, R.; one who has attained any object or purpose, contented, satisfied with (loc., R. vii, 59, 3), AitUp.; Mn.; MBh. &c.; *-tā,* f. the full discharge of any duty or realisation of any object, accomplishment, success, Mn.; MBh.; KapS. &c.; *-bhāva,* m. id., Naish. vi, 106. **-koṭi,** m., N. of a Kāśyapa, L.; of Upavarsha, L. **-kopa,** mfn. one who shows anger, angry, indignant. **-kautuka,** mfn. one who engages in sport, playful. **-kraya,** m. one who makes a purchase, a purchaser. **-kriya,** mfn. one who has accomplished any act, W.; one who has fulfilled his duty, W.; one who has performed a religious ceremony, Mn. v, 99; ix, 102. **-krudha,** mfn. one who shows anger, angry, resentful. **-kshaṇa,** mfn. one who waits for the right moment, one who waits impatiently for a person or thing (loc., or acc. with *prati,* or inf., or in comp.; e.g. *kṛita-kshaṇâhaṃ te gamanaṃ prati,* I am waiting impatiently for thy going, R. ii, 29, 15; *te bhūmiṃ gantuṃ kṛita-kshaṇāḥ,* they are waiting for the time to proceed to the earth, MBh. i, 2505); having leisure, Car. viii, 3; ready at hand, not tarrying or lingering, Car. iii, 8; liable to (in comp.), Comm. on ChUp.; (*as*), m., N. of a prince, MBh. ii, 122. **-ghāta-yatna,** mfn. one who makes efforts to slay, trying to kill. **-ghna,** mf(*ā*)n. 'destroying past services or benefits, unmindful of (services) rendered, ungrateful, Mn.; R. &c.; BrahmavP. (sixteen kinds of ungrateful men are enumerated); defeating or rendering vain all previous measures, W.; *-tā,* f. ingratitude, Pañcat.; Sāh.; *-tva,* n. id., MārkP.; *kṛitaghnī-kṛiti,* f. representing as ungrateful, Naish. vi, 85. **-cihna,** mfn. marked, MBh. iii, 280, 35. **-cūḍa,** m. a boy on whom the ceremony of tonsure has been performed, Mn. v, 58 & 67. **-cetas,** m., N. of a Brāhman, MBh. iii, 985. **-cchandas,** *ānsi,* n. p., N. of a class of metres. **-cchidra,** mfn. having a hole, BhP. iii, 11, 9; (*ā*), f. the plant Luffa acutangula, L. **-janman,** mfn. born, produced, generated. **-jña,** mf(*ā*)n. knowing what is right, correct in conduct, MBh. xii, 104, 6; acknowledging past services or benefits, mindful of former aid or favours, grateful, Mn.; Yājñ. &c.; (*as*), m. a dog, L.; N. of Śiva, L.; *-tā,* f. gratitude, R.; Pañcat.; *-tva,* n. id.; *-śīla,* m., N. of a Prākrit poet. **-m-jaya,** m. 'conquering the Kṛita age,' N. of the seventeenth Vyāsa, VāyuP.; of a prince, BhP. ix, 12, 12. **-tanū-trāṇa,** mfn. covered with armour, mailed. **-tīrtha,** mfn. one who has visited holy places, who frequents them, W.; an adviser, one fertile in expedients, W.; 'furnished with a passage,' rendered accessible or easy, Kir. ii, 3. **-trāṇā,** f. the tree Ficus heterophylla, L. **-tva,** n. the state of being effected, KātyŚr.; Jaim. iii, 4, 40. **-tvara,** mf(*ā*)n. making haste, hurrying, Ratnāv. **-dāra,** mfn. married, Mn.; MBh.; R.; (cf. *dāra-kriyā.*) **-dāsa,** m. one who offers himself as a servant for a certain time. **-deśa,** mfn. one whose place is fixed, Jaim. **-dyuti,** f., N. of the wife of king Citra-ketu, BhP. vi, 14, 30. **-dvishṭa** (*kṛitá-*), mfn. one who has shown anger (at the doings of another person), AV. vii, 113, 1. **-dhanvan,** v.l. for *-varman,* q.v. **-dharma,** m. 'one who performs his duty,' N. of a man, VP. **-dharman,** m. id., ib. **-dhī,** mfn. of formed mind, prudent, considerate, Mudr.; learned, educated, Sāh.; determined, resolved on (inf.), Mudr.; Bh. xi, 6, 39. **-dhvaṃsa,** mfn. defeated, overpowered, W.; injured, destroyed, W.; (= *-ghna*) destroying past transactions, W. **-dhvaj** (*kṛitá-*), mfn. furnished with banners, RV. vii, 83, 2. **-dhvaja,** m., N. of a prince (son of Dharmadhvaja), BhP. ix, 13, 19 & 20. **-dhvasta,** mfn. lost after being once possessed or acquired, W. **-nakha,** mfn. one who has cleaned his nails, Kauś. 54. **-nandana,** m., N. of a prince, VP. **-nāmaka,** mfn. named, Hariv. 3436. **-nāśaka,** mfn. (= *-ghna*) ungrateful, Hit. **-nāśana,** mfn. id. **-nitya-kriya,** mfn. one who has duly performed his daily religious observances. **-nirṇejana,** mfn. one who has performed penance or made expiation, Mn. xi, 190. **-niścaya,** mfn. determined or resolved on (dat., loc., inf. or in comp.), R. iii, 50, 16; Bhag. ii, 37 &c.; resolute (as speech), Kād.; one who has ascertained anything, sure, certain. **-niścayin,** mfn. one who has formed a resolution, determined, resolved, Pañcat. **-paṇa,** mf(*ā*)n. one who has laid a wager (with loc. of the stake), MBh. i, 1203 & 1206. **-parva,** n. (= *-yuga*) the golden age of the world, ShaḍvBr. **-paścāttāpa,** mfn. one who has performed penance, showing regret or penitence. **-puṅkha,** mfn. 'one who has fixed the feathers of his arrows,' skilled in archery, L. **-puṇya,** mf(*ā*)n. one who has accomplished meritorious acts in a former life, happy, R.; MārkP. **-pūrva,** mfn. done formerly, Daś.; *-nāśana,* n. the forgetting of past services, ingratitude, Hit. **-pūrvin,** mfn. one by whom anything (acc.) was formerly done, Kāś. on Pāṇ. v, 2, 87 & ii, 3, 65. **-paurusha,** mfn. one who does a manly act, behaving gallantly. **-prajña,** mfn. wise, prudent, MBh. v, 1246; Kathās. **-praṇāma,** mfn. making obeisance, saluting. **-pratikṛita,** n. assault and counter-assault, attack and resistance, MBh. iv, 351; Ragh. xii, 94; retaliation for an assault, R. vi, 91, 10. **-pratijña,** mfn. one who fulfils a promise or agreement. **-prayatna,** mfn. one who makes effort, active, persevering, Pañcat. (= Hit.) **-prayojana,** mfn. one who has attained his object, Kathās. xiii, 158. **-praharaṇa,** mfn. one who has practised the use of weapons, MBh. v, 5733. **-priya,** mfn. one who has been favoured or pleased, MBh. iii, 166, 14. **-phala,** mfn. 'fruitful,' successful, W.; (*ā*), f., N. of a plant (= *kola-śimbī*), L.; (*am*), n. consequence of an act, result, W.; N. of a poisonous substance, L. **-bandhu,** m., N. of a prince, MBh. i, 231. **-bāhu,** mfn. laying hands upon, grasping, touching, W. **-buddhi,** mfn. of formed mind, learned, wise, VarBṛS.; KapS. v, 50; (*a-k°*) Bhag. xviii, 16; one who has made a resolution, resolved (with dat. [Vikr.] or inf. [Hariv.]), Mn. i, 97 (cf. MBh. v, 110) & vii, 30; Yājñ. i, 354; MBh. &c.; informed of one's duty, one who knows how religious rites ought to be conducted, W. **-brahman** (*kṛitá-*), mfn. one who has performed his devotions, RV. ii, 25, 1; (a deity) towards whom devotion is performed, RV. vi, 20, 3; (a sacrifice) in which prayers are duly offered, RV. vii, 70, 6. **-bhaga,** m., N. of a man (pl. his family), Saṃskārak. **-bhaya,** mfn. alarmed, apprehensive. **-bhāva,** mfn. one whose mind is directed towards anything (loc.), R. vi, 70, 12. **-bhūtamaitra,** mfn. friendly to all. **-bhūmi,** f. a place ready made, Āp. **-bhojana,** mfn. one who has dined or made a meal. **-maṅgala,** mf(*ā*)n. blessed, consecrated, ŚāṅkhGṛ. i, 12; Suśr.; Kathās.; MārkP. **-mati,** mfn. one who has taken a resolution, who has resolved upon anything, MBh. xiii, 2211. **-manoratha,** mfn. one whose wishes are fulfilled, R. v, 50, 1. **-mandāra,** m., N. of a man, Rājat. v, 35. **-manyu,** mfn. indignant. **-mārga,** mfn. having a road or path made. **-māla,** m. the spotted antelope, Suśr.; the tree Cassia fistula, Suśr.; (*ā*), f., N. of a river, BhP. v, 19, 18; x, 79, 16. **-mālaka,** m. the spotted antelope, Gal.; the tree Cassia fistula, L. **-mukha,** mfn. skilled, clever, L. **-mūlya,** mfn. of a fixed price, Yājñ. ii, 63. **-maitra,** mfn. one who performs friendly acts, friendly. **-yajus** (*kṛitá-*), mfn. one who has uttered the sacrificial formulas, TS. i, 5, 2, 4. **-yajña,** m., N. of a son of Cyavana and father of Upari-cara, Hariv. 1803; VP. **-yaśas,** m., N. of a descendant of Aṅgiras (author of RV. ix, 108, 10 & 11), RAnukr. **-yuga,** n. the first of the four ages of the world, golden age, Mn.; MBh.; Hariv.; Sūryas. (see *kṛita* above); *kṛitayugāya,* Nom. Ā. *°yate,* to resemble the golden age, Pratāpar. **-yūsha,** m. the juice of pulses prepared with salt and fat, L. **-yogya,** mfn. joining in combat. **-ratha,** m., N. of a grandson of Maru, BhP. ix, 13, 16. **-rava,** mfn. making a cry, sounding, singing. **-ruc,** mfn. splendid, brilliant. **-rusha,** mfn. angry, displeased. **-lakshaṇa,** mf(*ā*)n. marked, stamped, branded, Gobh.; MBh.; (*a-k°*) Lāṭy.; noted for good qualities, excellent, amiable; stigmatized, Mn. ix, 239; caused by (in comp.), R. vi, 95, 19; relating to (in comp.), MBh. xiii, 16, 23; Hariv. 5031; (*as*), m., N. of a man, Hariv. 1940. **-lavaṇa,** n. factitious salt, Vishṇ. **-vat,** mfn. perf. p. P. √*kṛi,* one who has done or made anything; one who holds the stake at a game (?), Nir. v, 22; (*tī*), f., N. of a river, VP. **-varman,** m., N. of several princes, especially of a son of Hṛidika and of a son of Kanaka or Dhanaka, MBh.; Hariv. &c.; N. of the father of the thirteenth Arhat of the present Avasarpiṇī, L. **-vasati,** mfn. one who has taken up his abode, dwelling, Megh.; Pañcat.; Śāntiś. **-vāpa,** m. a penitent who has shaven his head and chin, Mn. xi, 108. **-vāpana,** m. id., Mn. xi, 78. **-vikāra,** mfn. any one or anything that has undergone change, altered, changed. **-vikrama,** mfn. displaying valour, making vigorous efforts. **-vikriya,** mfn. = *-vikāra.* **-vidya,** mfn. one who has acquired knowledge, well informed, learned, MBh.; R.; Pañcat. **-vilāsa,** m., N. of a man, Śaṅkar. **-vivāha,** mfn. one who has contracted marriage, married. **-vismaya,** mfn. astonished; astonishing. **-vīrya** (*kṛitá-*), mfn. one who is strong or powerful, AV. xvii, 1, 27; (*as*), m., N. of a prince (son of Kanaka or Dhanaka and father of Arjuna; cf. *kārtavīrya*), MBh.; Hariv.; BhP.; of a medical teacher, Suśr. **-vṛiddhi,** mfn. (a word) whose (first syllable) has been vṛiddhied. **vega,** m., N. of a prince, MBh. ii, 320. **-vetana,** mfn. one who receives wages (as a hired servant or labourer), Yājñ. ii, 164. **-vedin,** mfn. (= *-jña*) one who acknowledges past benefits or services, grateful, Mudr.; Lalit.; observant of propriety, W. **-vedhaka,** m. a sort of Ghoshā with white flowers, L. **-vedhana,** m. id., Suśr.; (*ā*), f. = *-cchidrā,* L. **-vepathu,** mfn. trembling. **-vesha,** mfn. one who has assumed clothing, attired, decorated, Gīt. xi, 1; (*as*), m., 'N. of a man,' see *kārtavesha.* **-vyadhana,** mf(*ī*)n. skilled in piercing, AV. v, 14, 9. **-vyalīka,** mfn. annoyed, vexed. **-vrata,** m., N. of a pupil of Loma-harshaṇa. **-śakti,** mfn. one who puts forth his strength or displays courage. **-śarman,** m., N. of a prince, VP. **-śastra-niḥśrama,** mfn. exercised in arms, MBh. i, 5443. **-śilpa,** mfn. one who has learned his art or is skilled in his own trade, Yājñ. ii, 184. **-śobha,** mfn. splendid, brilliant, beautiful, W.; dexterous, W. **-śauca,** mfn. one who has performed purification, purified, free from bodily impurities, Mn.; MBh.; R.; (*as* or *am*), m. or n., N. of a locality, MatsyaP. **-śrama,** mfn. one who has made great exertions, painstaking, laborious (with loc. or ifc.), MBh.; R. &c.; (*as*), m., N. of a Muni, MBh. ii, 109. **-śrāma,** for *-śrama,* R. i, 21, 6. **-saṃsarga,** mfn. brought into contact, united. **-saṃskāra,** mfn. one who has performed all the purificatory rites, initiated, Mn. ix, 326; Ragh. x, 79; prepared, adorned. **-saṃkalpa,** mfn. one who has formed a resolution. **-saṃketa,** mfn. one who has made an agreement or appointment. **-saṃjña,** mfn. one to whom a sign has been given, Rājat. iv, 221; (pl.) having agreed upon special signs, Mn. vii, 190; initiated (into a plan), MBh. xiv, 588 (*a-k°,* neg.) **-saṃnāha,** mfn. cased in armour. **-saṃnidhāna,** mfn. = *-saṃsarga.* **-sapatnikā,** f. a woman whose husband has taken another wife, superseded wife, L. **-sampuṭa,** mfn. = *°tâñjali-puṭa,* VārP. **-sambandha,** mfn. connected, allied. **-savya,** mfn. one who has the sacred thread over the left shoulder, Comm. on KātyŚr. **-sāpatnikā, °tnī, °tnīkā,** f. = *-sapatnikā,* L. **-stoma,** m., N. of certain Stomas. **-sthalā,** f., N. of an Apsaras, TS. iv; MaitrS. ii, 8, 10; (*°lī*) VP. **-sthiti,** mfn. one who has taken up an abode. **-sneha,** mfn. one who shows affection, affectionate. **-smara,** m., N. of a mountain, VP.; *-carita,* n., N. of a work. **-svara,** mfn. having the original accent, Lāṭy. **-svasty-ayana,** mf(*ā*)n. blessed or commended to the protection of gods previous to any journey or undertaking, MBh.; R.; BhP. **-svecchâhāra,** mfn. one who feeds or eats at pleasure. **-hasta,** mfn. one who has exercised his hands, dexterous, skilled (especially in archery), Hariv.; *-tā,* f. dexterity, MBh. iv, 1976; *-vat,* ind. in a clever way, MBh. iv, 1843. **Kṛitâkṛita,** mfn. done and not done, done in part but not completed, MBh. xii, 6542 (= 9946); prepared and not prepared, manufactured and not manufactured, MBh. xiii, 2794; Yājñ. i, 286; optional, ĀśvŚr.; ĀśvGṛ.; indifferent, MBh. xiii, 7612; (*ám, é*), n. sg. & du. what has been done and what has not been done, AV. xix, 9, 2; ŚBr. xiv, 7, 2, 27; KaṭhUp. ii, 14; *-prasaṅgin,* mfn. in Gr. = *nitya.* **Kṛitâkṛityasama,** *ās,* m. pl. 'indifferent as to what has been done and what ought to be done,' N. of a sect. **Kṛitâgama,** mfn. one who has made progress, advanced. **Kṛitâgas,** mfn. one who has committed an offence, criminal, sinful, AV. xii, 5, 60 & 65; MBh.; Amar.; (*a-k°,* neg.) R. i, 7, 13. **Kṛitâ-**

gas-ka, mfn. id., BhP. x, 88, 29. **Kṛitâgni,** m., N. of a son of Kanaka or Dhanaka, Hariv. 1850; BhP. ix, 23, 22. **Kṛitâgni-kārya,** m. a Brāhman who has offered the usual fire-oblation. **Kṛitâṅka,** mfn. marked, branded, Mn. viii, 281; R. ii, 15, 37; numbered, W. **Kṛitâñjali,** mfn. one who joins the hollowed palms in reverence or to solicit a favour (holding the hollowed palms together as if to receive alms or an offering), standing in a reverent or respectful posture, Mn.; MBh.; R.; (*as*), m. a shrub used in medicine and in magical potions, L.; *-puṭa,* mf(*ā*)n. joining the palms of the hands for obeisance or for holding offerings of water &c., R. i, 39, 9. **Kṛitâtithya,** mf(*ā*)n. one who has practised hospitality; one who has received hospitality, regaled, R. iii, 7, 1; Daś. **Kṛitâtman,** mfn. one whose spirit is disciplined, MuṇḍUp.; Mn.; MBh. &c. **Kṛitâdara,** mf(*ā*)n. one to whom regard or attention has been paid, Kathās. **Kṛitânati,** mfn. one who bends in reverence, bowing, paying homage or respect; one to whom homage is paid, Rājat. v, 215. **Kṛitânana,** mfn. possessing a great experience, Gal. **Kṛitânukara,** mfn. imitating what has been done by another, following another's example, not independent, ŚBr.; KātyŚr. **Kṛitânukūlya,** mfn. compliant, kind, favouring. **Kṛitânukṛita-kārin,** mfn. doing anything before and after, R. vi, 91, 28. **Kṛitânuvyādha,** mfn. mixed, combined, W. **Kṛitânusāra,** m. established practice, custom. **Kṛitânta,** mfn. causing an end, bringing to an end, leading to a decisive termination, BhP. ix, 6, 13; whose end is action, W.; (*as*), m. 'the inevitable result of actions done in a past existence,' destiny, fate, R.; Pañcat.; Megh.; Vet.; death personified, N. of Yama (god of death), MārkP.; Hit.; a demonstrated conclusion, dogma, Bhag. xviii, 13; a conclusion, MBh. xii, 218, 27; (in Gr.) a fixed form or name (?), Pat. Introd. (on Vārtt. 1) & on Pāṇ. i, 1, 1, Vārtt. 4; a sinful or inauspicious action, L.; 'closing the week,' Saturday, L.; (*ā*), f. a kind of medicinal drug or perfume (= *reṇukā*), L.; *-kālâsura,* m., N. of an Asura, GaṇP.; *-janaka,* 'father of Yama,' N. of the sun, L.; *-saṃtrāsa,* m., N. of a Rākshasa, Kathās. lxxxvi, 137. **Kṛitântara,** mfn. one who has prepared a passage to any object (gen.), Kād. **Kṛitânná,** n. prepared or cooked food, ŚBr. xiii; KātyŚr.; Lāṭy.; Mn.; Suśr.; digested food, excrement; (mfn.) eating, W. **Kṛitâpakāra,** mfn. injured, wronged, discomfited, overpowered; doing wrong, offending. **Kṛitâpakṛita,** mfn. done for and against, done well and done wrong, gaṇa *śāka-pārthivâdi.* **Kṛitâpadāna,** mfn. one who has completed a great or noble work. **Kṛitâparādha,** mfn. one who has committed an offence against (gen.), guilty, culpable, Vikr.; Mālav. **Kṛitâbhaya,** mfn. saved from danger or fear, W. **Kṛitâbharaṇa,** mfn. adorned. **Kṛitâbhisheka,** mfn. one who has performed a religious ablution, R. i, 44, 30; consecrated, inaugurated; (*as*), m. a prince who has been inaugurated; (*ā*), f. the consecrated wife of a prince, Gal. **Kṛitâbhisaraṇa-vesha,** mfn. attired in the dress of a maiden who goes to meet her lover, Vikr. **Kṛitâbhyāsa,** mfn. trained, exercised, practised. **Kṛitâya,** m. the die called Kṛita, Comm. on ChUp. (in the text *kṛitâya* is dat. of °*ta*). **Kṛitâyāsa,** mfn. labouring, suffering. **Kṛitârgha,** mfn. received or welcomed by the Argha offering, PārGṛ.; (*as*), m., N. of the nineteenth Arhat of the past Utsarpiṇī, L. (v. l. *kṛitârtha*). **Kṛitârta-nāda,** mfn. one who makes cries of pain. **Kṛitârtha,** mf(*ā*)n. one who has attained an end or object or has accomplished a purpose or desire, successful, satisfied, contented, MuṇḍUp.; ŚvetUp.; MBh. &c.; clever, Comm. on L.; (*as*), m., v. l. for *kṛitârgha,* q. v.; *-tā,* f. accomplishment of an object, success, Ragh. viii, 3; Gīt. v, 19; Kathās.; *-tva,* n. id., Sāh.; *kṛitârthī-√kṛi,* to render successful, content, satisfy, Kathās. lxxiv, 125; °*rthī-karaṇa,* mfn. rendering successful, Kathās.; °*rthī-kṛita,* mfn. rendered successful, Dhūrtas.; Amar.; °*rthī-√bhū,* to become successful, be contented, Mālatīm.; °*rthī-bhūta,* mfn. become successful. **Kṛitârthanīya,** mfn. to be rendered successful, Naish. ix, 51. **Kṛitârthaya,** Nom. P. °*yati,* to render successful, content, satisfy, Mālatīm.; Kād.; Śiś.; Naish.; Viddh. **Kṛitâlaka,** m., N. of one of Śiva's attendants, Comm. on L. **Kṛitâlaya,** mfn. one who has taken up his abode in any place (loc. or in comp., e. g. *svarga-k°,* an inhabitant of heaven), R. &c.; (*as*), m. a dog, L. **Kṛitâloka,** mfn. supplied with light, lighted, W. **Kṛitâvadhāna,** mfn. one who takes care, careful, cautious, attentive. **Kṛitâvadhi,** mfn. having a fixed limit, fixed, appointed, agreed upon; bounded, limited. **Kṛitâvamarsha,** mfn. one who has effaced from recollection; intolerant. **Kṛitâvaśyaka,** mfn. one who has done all that is necessary. **Kṛitâvasakthika,** mfn. seated on the hams with the knees tied together or the hips and knees surrounded by a cloth, KātyŚr. **Kṛitâvastha,** mfn. settled, received (as a guest), Āp.; Mn. viii, 60. **Kṛitâvāsa,** m. a lodging, W.; (mfn.) lodging. **Kṛitâśa,** mfn. one who forms hopes, hoping for anything ['despairing,' Comm.], MBh. iii, 31, 37. **Kṛitâśaṇsa,** mfn. one who forms hopes or expectations, hoping, Kād. **Kṛitâśana,** mfn. one who makes a meal, feeding upon. **Kṛitâśana-parigraha,** mfn. one who has taken a seat. **Kṛitâskandana,** mfn. one who has made an attack, assailing, attacking; effacing from recollection (?), W. **Kṛitâstra,** mfn. one who has exercised himself in throwing arrows or other weapons, skilled in archery, MBh.; R.; armed; (*as*), m., N. of a warrior, MBh. ii, 127; *-tā,* f. consummate skill or proficiency in the use of arms, MBh. i, 5156. **Kṛitâspada,** mfn. one who takes up a station or residence or abode; supporting, resting on; governed, ruled. **Kṛitâhaka,** mfn. (fr. *ahan*), one who has performed the daily ceremonies or devotions. **Kṛitâhāra,** °**raka,** mfn. one who has eaten food or made a meal. **Kṛitâhvāna,** mfn. summoned, called, challenged. **Kṛitêrshya,** mfn. envious, jealous. **Kṛitoṃkāra,** mfn. (cf. Pāṇ. vi, 1, 95) one who has pronounced the holy syllable *om,* Vet. v, 1. **Kṛitôccais,** ind. raised on high (?), cf. gaṇa *svar-ādi* and Pāṇ. v, 4, 57. **Kṛitôtsāha,** mfn. one who has made effort, striving. **Kṛitôdaka,** mfn. one who has performed his ablutions, MBh. iii, 8141; one who has offered a libation of water to the dead, MBh.; R. **Kṛitôdvāha,** mfn. performing penance by standing with uplifted arms, W.; married, MBh.; R.; Kathās. **Kṛitônmāda,** mfn. one who feigns to be insane, Kathās. xviii, 250. **Kṛitôpakāra,** mf(*ā*)n. assisted, befriended, Kum. iii, 73; one who has rendered a service, giving aid, friendly. **Kṛitôpacāra,** mfn. served, waited upon. **Kṛitôpanayana,** m. one who has been invested with the sacrificial cord, Mn. ii, 108 & 173. **Kṛitôpabhoga,** mfn. used, enjoyed. **Kṛitâujas,** m., N. of a son of Kanaka or Dhanaka, Hariv. 1850; BhP. ix, 23, 22.

Kṛitaka, mfn. artificial, factitious, done artificially, made, prepared, not produced spontaneously, Nir.; MBh. &c.; not natural, adopted (as a son), MBh. xiii, 2630; Megh.; assumed, simulated, false, MBh.; Pañcat.; Ragh. xviii, 51 &c.; (*am* or *a-* in comp.), ind. in a simulated manner, Śiś. ix, 83; Kathās.; (*as*), m., N. of a son of Vasu-deva, BhP. ix, 24, 47; of a son of Cyavana, VP.; (*am*), n. a kind of salt (= *viḍ-lavaṇa*), L.; sulphate of copper, L.

Kṛitaya, Nom. P. °*yati* (aor. *acīkṛitat* or *a-cak°,* Vop.), to take the die called Kṛita, Pāṇ. iii, 1, 21.

Kṛitânta, kṛitârtha, &c. See *kṛitá.*

Kṛitâvin, mfn. skilled, Divyâv.

1. **Kṛiti,** *is,* f. the act of doing, making, performing, manufacturing, composing, ŚBr. x; ChUp.; Pañcat.; Kāś. &c.; action, activity, MBh. iii, 12480; Bhāshāp.; Tarkas.; creation, work, Vop.; literary work, Mālav.; Ragh.; Pāṇ. vi, 2, 151, Kāś.; a house of relics, Divyâv.; 'magic,' see *-kara;* a witch (cf. *kṛityā*), Devīm.; a kind of Anushṭubh metre (consisting of two Pādas of twelve syllables each and a third Pāda of eight syllables), ṚPrāt.; another metre (a stanza of four lines with twenty syllables in each), RPrāt.; (hence) the number twenty, VarBṛ.; a collective N. of the metres *kṛiti, prak°, āk°, vik°, saṃk°, abhik°,* and *utkṛiti;* a square number, VarBṛ.; (in dram.) confirmation of any obtainment, Sāh.; Daśar.; Pratāpar.; N. of the wife of Saṃhrāda and mother of Pañca-jana, BhP. vi, 18, 13; (*is*), m., N. of several persons, MBh. ii, 320 & 1882; Hariv.; BhP.; MārkP.; of a pupil of Hiraṇya-nābha, VāyuP. **-kara,** m. 'practising magic or enchantment,' N. of Rāvaṇa, L.; (cf. *kṛityā-rāvaṇa.*) **-mat,** m., N. of a prince (son of Yavī-nara), BhP. ix, 21, 27. **-ratha,** m., N. of a prince, VP. **-rāta,** m., N. of a prince, R.; VP.; BhP. **-roman,** m., N. of a son of Kṛiti-rāta, R. i, 73, 10 & 11. **-sādhya-tva,** n. the state of being accomplished by exertion.

Kṛitin, mfn. one who acts, active, MBh. xii, 8682; xiii, 305; expert, clever, skilful, knowing, learned (with loc. or ifc.), MBh.; Ragh.; Bhartṛ. &c.; good, virtuous, L.; pure, pious, L.; obeying, doing what is enjoined, W.; one who has attained an object or accomplished a purpose, satisfied, Śak.; Ragh.; Vikr. &c.; (*ī*), m., N. of a son of Cyavana and father of Upari-cara, BhP. ix, 22, 5; N. of a son of Saṃnatimat, ib. 21, 28. **Kṛiti-tva,** n. the state of one who has attained any object, Kathās.

Kṛitī, in comp. for °*ti.* **-suta,** m. 'the son of Kṛitī (= Kṛiti),' N. of Ruci-parvan, MBh. vii, 1177.

Kṛite, kṛitena, loc. instr. ind., see s. v. *kṛitá.*

Kṛiteyu, *us,* m., N. of a son of Raudrâśva, VP.

Kṛiteyuka, *as,* m. id., BhP. ix, 20, 4.

Kṛitnú, mfn. working well, able to work, skilful, clever, an artificer or mechanic, artist, RV.; (*us*), m., N. of a Ṛishi (author of RV. viii, 79), RAnukr.

Kṛitya, mfn. 'to be done or performed,' (*am*), n. ind. anybody (gen.) is concerned about (instr.), Mṛicch.; practicable, feasible, W.; right, proper to be done, MBh.; R. &c.; one who may be seduced from allegiance or alliance, who may be bribed or hired (as an assassin), Rājat. v, 247; (in med.) to be treated or attended with (in comp.), Suśr.; (*as*), m. (scil. *pratyaya*) the class of affixes forming the fut. p. Pass. (as *tavya, anīya, ya, elima,* &c.), Pāṇ.; a kind of evil spirit (named either with or without the addition of *yaksha, mānusha, asura,* &c.), Buddh. (perhaps v. l. for °*tyā* below); (*ā*), f. (Pāṇ. iii, 3, 100) action, act, deed, performance, achievement, AV. v, 9, 8; Mn. xi, 125; MBh. xii, 3837; (with gen. *rujas*) ill usage or treatment, Mn. xi, 67; magic, enchantment, AV. &c.; (especially personified) a kind of female evil spirit or sorceress, RV. x, 85, 28 & 29; VS. &c.; a female deity to whom sacrifices are offered for destructive and magical purposes, L.; N. of a river, MBh. vi, 9, 18; (*am*), n. what ought to be done, what is proper or fit, duty, office, Mn.; R. &c.; action, business, performance, service, Śak.; Sarvad. &c.; purpose, end, object, motive, cause, MBh. &c. **-kalpa-taru,** m., N. of a work on jurisprudence. **-kalpa-druma,** m. id. **-kalpa-latā,** f., N. of a work by Vācaspati-miśra. **-kaumudī,** f., N. of a work. **-cintā,** f. thinking of any possibility, Nyāyam. **-cintāmaṇi,** m., N. of a work by Śiva-rāma. **-jña,** mfn. one who knows what is to be done, learned. **-tattva,** n. 'the true nature of duty or obligation,' N. of a work. **-°tama,** n. anything most proper or fit, MBh. **-tā,** f. seduction from allegiance or alliance, Suśr. **-pradīpa,** m., **-mañjarī,** f., **-mahârṇava,** m., **-ratna,** n., **-ratnâkara,** m., **-ratnâvalī,** f., **-rāja,** m., N. of works. **-vat,** mfn. having any business, engaged in any occupation, MBh. i, 5153 ff.; having any request, MBh. iii, 270, 6; wanting, longing for (instr.), R. vii, 92, 15; having the power to do something (loc.), R. iii, 75, 66. **-vartman,** n. the right way or manner in which any object is to be effected. **-vid,** mfn. knowing duty, Daś. **-vidhi,** m. the way to do anything, rule, precept. **-śesha,** mfn. one who has left some work to be done, who has not finished his task, BhP. iii, 2, 14. **-sāra,** m. 'essence of what is to be done,' N. of a work. **Kṛityâkṛitya,** n. what is to be done and what is not to be done, right and wrong, Suśr.; Pañcat.; Sāh.

Kṛityakā, f. an enchantress, witch, woman who is the cause of injury or destruction, Nal. xiii, 29.

Kṛityā́, f. of *kṛitya,* q. v. **-kṛit,** mfn. practising magic or sorcery, bewitching, AV. **-dū́shaṇa,** mf(*ī*)n. counteracting magic, destroying its effect, AV. **-dū́shi,** mfn. id., AV. ii, 4, 6. **-rāvaṇa,** m., N. of a work, Sāh. **-rūpa** (°*tyā́-*), mfn. looking like a phantom, ŚBr. iv. **Kṛityâstra,** n., N. of a Mantra, Tantr.

Kṛitrima, mf(*ā*)n. made artificially, factitious, artificial, not naturally or spontaneously produced, RV.; AV. &c.; falsified, Yājñ. ii, 247; Kathās.; not natural, adopted (as a son), Mn.; Yājñ. ii, 131; MBh.; Kathās.; assumed, simulated; not necessarily connected with the nature of anything, adventitious, Pañcat.; (*as*), m. incense, olibanum, L.; an adopted son, L.; (*am*), n. a kind of salt (the common Bit Noben, or Bit Lavan [*viḍ-lavaṇa*], obtained by cooking), L.; a kind of perfume (= *javādi*), L.; sulphate of copper (used as a collyrium), L.; (*ā*), f. a channel, Gal. **-tā,** f. shrewdness, cunningness, Mcar. **-tva,** n. the being made, factitiousness. **-dhūpa,** m. incense, olibanum, L. **-dhūpaka,** m. compound perfume (containing ten or eighteen ingredients). **-putra,** m. an adopted son, W. **-pu-**

traka, m. a doll, Kum. i, 29; (*ikā*), f. id., Kathās. xxiv, 29. **-bhūmi,** f. an artificial floor, W. **-mitra,** n. an acquired friend (on whom benefits have been conferred or from whom they have been received), Yājñ., Sch. **-ratna,** n. 'false jewel,' glass, Npr. **-vana,** n. a plantation, park. **-śatru,** m. an acquired enemy, W. **Kṛitrimâri,** m. id., Comm. on Yājñ. **Kṛitrimârti,** mfn. feigning to be low-spirited, Daś. **Kṛitrimôdâsīna,** m. an acquired neutral, Comm. on Yājñ.

Kṛitrimaka, *as,* m. olibanum, Gal.

Kṛítvan, mf(*varī*)n. causing, effecting (ifc.), Lāṭy.; active, busy, RV. viii, 24, 25; ix, 65, 23; x, 144, 3; (*īs*), Ved. f. pl. (= *kṛityás*) the magic powers, AV. iv, 18, 1.

Kṛitvarī, f. of *kṛítvan,* q. v.

Kṛitvas, ind. at the end of a numeral or numeral adjective, = fold, times (e. g. *daśa-kṛitvas,* ten times; *bahu-k°,* many times; *pañca-k°,* fivefold, Pāṇ. ii, 3, 64). In the Veda *kṛitvas* is used as a separate word (e. g. *bhū́ri k°,* many times, RV. iii, 18, 4; *pā́ñca k°,* TS. vi), but according to Pāṇ. v, 4, 17 & 20 (Vop. vii, 70) it is only an affix, and it is so used in classical Sanskrit; it was originally an acc. pl. fr. *kṛitu,* formed by the affix *tu* fr. √1. *kṛi;* (cf. also *krit* in *sakṛit.*)

Kṛitvā́, ind. p. having done, see s. v. √1. *kṛi.*

Kṛitvā́ya, 1. kṛitvī́, ind. p. See ib.

2. **Kṛitvī,** f., N. of a daughter of Śuka (wife of Aṇuha [Nīpa] and mother of Brahma-datta), Hariv. 981 & 1242; BhP. ix, 21, 25.

Kṛitvya, mfn. one who is able to perform anything, strong, efficacious, RV.; having accomplished many deeds, exerting one's power, RV.

Kriyamāṇa, mfn. (pr. Pass. p.) being done &c.

कृ 2. *kṛi,* cl. 3. P. p. *cakrát* (Pot. 2. sg. *cakriyās;* aor. 1. sg. *akārsham* [AV. vii, 7, 1] or *akārisham* [RV. iv, 39, 6]), to make mention of, praise, speak highly of (gen.), RV.; AV.: Intens. (1. sg. *carkarmi,* 1. pl. *carkirāma,* 3. pl. *carkiran;* Impv. 2. sg. *carkṛitát* & *carkṛidhi;* aor. 3. sg. Ā. *cárkṛishe*), id., RV.; AV.; (cf. *kārú, kīrí, kīrtí.*)

कृ 3. *kṛi,* to injure, &c. See √2. *kṛī.*

2. **Kṛita,** mfn. injured, killed, L.; (cf. 2. *kīrṇa.*)

2. **Kṛiti,** *is,* f. hurt, hurting, injuring, L.; (*is*), m. or f. a kind of weapon, sort of knife or dagger, RV. i, 168, 3.

कृक *kṛika, as,* m. the throat, larynx, L. (cf. *kṛikāṭa*); the navel, Comm. on Uṇ. i, 6. **-dāśū́,** m. or f. a kind of evil spirit ['one who hurts or injures,' Sāy.], RV. i, 29, 7.

कृकण *kṛikaṇa, as,* m. a kind of partridge (commonly Kaër, Perdrix sylvatica, cf. *kṛikara* & *krakara*), L.; a worm, L.; = *āya-sthāna,* gaṇa *śuṇḍikâdi;* N. of a man, VP.; of a locality, Pāṇ. iv, 2, 145.

Kṛikaṇīya, mfn. coming from Kṛikaṇa, Pāṇ. iv, 2, 145.

Kṛikaṇeyu, *us,* m., N. of a son of Raudrâśva, MBh. i, 3700; Hariv.

कृकण्ठक *kṛikaṇṭhaka, as,* m., N. of a venomous animal, Car. vi, 23.

कृकदाशू *kṛika-dāśū.* See *kṛika.*

कृकर *kṛikara, as,* m. a kind of partridge (= *kṛikaṇa,* q. v.), SāmavBr.; R. iv, 50, 2; a kind of pepper (Piper Chaba), L.; the fragrant oleander tree (?), L.; one of the five vital airs (that which assists in digestion), Vedântas.; N. of Śiva, L.; (*ā*), f. long pepper, L.

Kṛikala, *as,* m. (= °*kara*) a kind of partridge, R. vii, 53, 19; one of the five vital airs; (*ā*), f. (= *kṛikarā*) long pepper, L.

कृकलास *kṛikalāsá, as,* m. a lizard, chameleon, MaitrS.; VS.; ŚBr. &c. **-tīrtha,** n., N. of a Tīrtha, SkandaP. **-tva,** n. the state of a chameleon, MBh. xiii, 332. **-dīpikā,** f., N. of a mystical work.

Kṛikalāsaka, *as,* m. = °*lāsa,* MBh. xiii, 736; Suśr.

कृकवाकु *kṛikavā́ku, us,* m. a cock, VS.; AV.; MaitrS. &c.; a peacock, R. ii, 28, 10; a lizard, chameleon (= *kṛikalāsa*), L.; (*us*), f. a hen, Pāṇ. iv, 1, 66, Vārtt. **-dhvaja,** m. 'having a cock in his banner,' N. of Kārttikeya, L.

कृकषा *kṛikashā,* f. a kind of bird (= *kaṅkaṇa-hārikā*), PārGṛ. i, 19.

कृकाट *kṛíkāṭa, am,* n. the joint of the neck, AV. ix, 7, 1; (*ī*), f. id., VarBṛS. li, 9.

Kṛikāṭaka, *am,* n. the neck, L.; a part of a column, R.; VarBṛS.; (*ikā*), f. the joint of the neck, Suśr.

कृकालिका *kṛikālikā,* f. a kind of bird, Pañcat.

कृकिन् *kṛikin, ī,* m., N. of a mythical king, Buddh.

कृकुलास *kṛikulāsa,* v. l. for *kṛikal°,* L.

कृच्छ्र *kṛicchrá,* mf(*ā*)n. (perhaps fr. √*kṛiś,* and connected with *kashṭa*), causing trouble or pain, painful, attended with pain or labour, MBh.; R.; Pañcat.; Suśr.; being in a difficult or painful situation, R. ii, 78, 14; bad, evil, wicked, W.; (*am*), ind. miserably, painfully, with difficulty, R. iv, 22, 7; (*as, am*), m. n. difficulty, trouble, labour, hardship, calamity, pain, danger (often ifc., e. g. *vana-vāsa-k°,* the difficulties of living in a forest; *mūtra-k°,* q. v.; *artha-kṛicchreshu,* in difficulties, in a miserable situation, MBh. iii, 65; Nal. xv, 3; *prāṇa-kṛicchra,* danger of life, MBh. ii, 6; BhP.), RV. x, 52, 4; Nir.; AitBr. &c.; ischury (= *mūtra-k°*), L.; bodily mortification, austerity, penance, Gaut.; Mn. &c.; a particular kind of religious penance, Mn.; Yājñ.; (*as*), m., N. of Vishṇu, MBh. xii, 12864; (*eṇa* or *a-* in comp.), instr. ind. with difficulty, with great exertion, painfully, hardly, scarcely, Pāṇ. ii, 3, 33; R.; Suśr. &c. (*alpa-kṛicchreṇa,* 'easily,' SaddhP.); (*āt*), abl. ind. id., MBh.; R. &c.; (in comp. with a perf. Pass. p., Pāṇ. ii, 1, 39; vi, 3, 2.) **-karman,** n. a difficult act, difficulty, labour, Kathās. **-kāla,** m. a season of difficulty or of danger, MBh. i. **-kṛit,** mfn. undergoing a penance, Yājñ. iii, 328. **-gata,** mfn. undergoing trouble or misery, suffering pain, distressed, MBh.; R.; Bhartṛ.; undergoing a penance, MBh. **-tas,** ind. with difficulty, MBh. iii, 2036. **-tā,** f. painful or dangerous state (especially in disease), Suśr. **-dvādaśa-rātra,** m., N. of a penance lasting twelve days, Āp. **-patita,** mfn. fallen into distress, Kathās. **-prāṇa,** mfn. one whose life is in danger, hardly supporting life, MBh.; R.; BhP.; breathing with difficulty, W. **-bhāj,** mfn. encompassed with pain and distress, MBh. ii, 15, 2. **-bhojin,** mfn. undergoing austerities, MBh. xii, 1247. **-mūtra-purīsha-tva,** n. difficulty in evacuating the bladder and intestines, Suśr. **-rūpa,** mfn. being in difficulties, MBh. iii, 34, 13. **-śas,** ind. with difficulty, scarcely, Kāṭh. xxv, 2. **-saṃvatsara,** m., N. of a penance lasting one year, Āp. **-sādhya,** mfn. to be done with difficulty, Mcar.; curable with difficulty, Suśr. **Kṛicchrâtikṛicchra,** m., N. of a penance (taking no sustenance but water for 3, 9, 12, or 21 days), Gaut. xxvi, 20; Yājñ. iii, 321; (*au*), m. du. the ordinary and the extraordinary penance, Gaut. xix, 20; Mn. xi, 208. **Kṛicchrân-mukta,** mfn. freed from trouble, Pāṇ. ii, 1, 39 & vi, 3, 2, Kāś. **Kṛicchrâpta,** mfn. gained with difficulty. **Kṛicchrâbda,** m. = *kṛicchra-saṃvatsara,* Gaut. **Kṛicchrâri,** m. 'enemy of pain,' removing ischury, N. of a plant (a species of Bilva), L. **Kṛicchrârdha,** m. an inferior penance lasting only six days, Āp. **Kṛicchrī-√bhū,** to become embarrassed, ChUp. v, 3, 7. **Kṛicchre-śrít,** mfn. undergoing danger, RV. vi, 75, 9. **Kṛicchrônmīla,** m. a disease of the eye-lids, ŚārṅgS.

Kṛicchrāya, Nom. Ā. °*yate* (gaṇa *sukhâdi*), to feel pain &c., ĀpŚr.; to have wicked designs, Pāṇ. iii, 1, 14, Kāś.; (Bhaṭṭ. xvii, 76.)

Kṛicchrin, mfn. encompassed with difficulties, being in trouble, feeling pain, gaṇa *sukhâdi;* (*a-k°,* Pāṇ. iii, 2, 130.)

कृड् *kṛiḍ,* v. l. for 1. *kūḍ,* q. v.

कृणञ्ज *kṛiṇañja,* for *kuṇ°,* q. v.

कृणु *kṛiṇu, us,* m. a painter, L.

कृणुष्वपाजवती *kṛiṇushva-pāja-vatī, yas,* f. pl., N. of the verses RV. iv, 4, 1 ff., ĀpŚr.

Kṛiṇushva-pājīyā, *ās,* f. pl. id., ib., Comm.

कृत् 2. *kṛit,* cl. 6. P. *kṛintáti,* ep. also Ā. °*te* and cl. 1. P. *kartati* (perf. *cakarta,* 2nd fut. *kartsyati* or *kartishyati,* 1st fut. *kartitā,* Pāṇ. vii, 2, 57; Subj. *kṛintát;* aor. *akartīt,* Ved. 2. sg. *akṛitas*), to cut, cut in pieces, cut off, divide, tear asunder, destroy, RV.; AV.; AitBr.; MBh. &c.: Caus. *kartayati,* id., Pañcat.: Desid. *cikartishati* or *cikṛitsati,* Pāṇ. vii, 2, 57; [cf. κείρω, κάρσις; Lith. *kertu,* inf. *kirsti,* 'to cut;' Slav. *korjŭ,* 'to split;' Lat. *curtus, culter;* Hib. *cearlaighim,* 'I prune, trim, cut;' *cuirc,* 'a knife.']

Kṛitā, f. an abyss, RV. ii, 35, 5.

1. **Kṛitta,** mfn. cut, cut off, divided, MBh. &c. (*á-kṛitta-nābhi,* 'one whose navel string is not cut,' ŚBr. xiv). **-ruhā,** f. the plant Cocculus cordifolius, L.

Kṛitti, *is,* f. skin, hide, RV. viii, 90, 6; VS.; AV.; a garment made of skin (fr. √3. *kṛit* ?), Nir. v, 22; the hide or skin on which the religious student sits or sleeps, &c. (usually the skin of an antelope), W.; the birch tree, L.; the bark of the birch tree (used for writing upon, for making hooka pipes, &c.), W.; (= *kṛíttikā*) one of the lunar mansions (the Pleiads), L.; a house, Naigh. iii, 4 (probably with reference to RV. viii, 90, 6; but cf. *kuṭī*); food, Nir. v, 22; fame (*yaśas*), ib.; [cf. Hib. *cart;* Lat. *cortex.*] **-pattrī,** f. a species of Karañja, Gal. **-ratha,** m., N. of a prince, R. i, 73, 8 & 9. **-vāsa,** m. = *-vāsas,* in comp. °*sêśvara-liṅga,* n., N. of a Liṅga, SkandaP. **-vāsas** (*kṛítti-*), m. 'covered with a skin,' N. of Rudra-Śiva, VS. iii, 61; MBh.; Kum.; Mālav.; (*ās*), f., N. of Durgā, Hariv. 3285.

Kṛitty-adhīvāsá, m. a skin used as a garment, TBr. iii, 9, 20, 1.

Kṛíttikā, *ās,* f. pl. (rarely sg., MBh. iii, 14464; BhP. vi, 14, 30), N. of a constellation (the Pleiads, originally the first, but in later times the third lunar mansion, having Agni as its regent; this constellation, containing six stars, is sometimes represented as a flame or as a kind of razor or knife; for their oldest names see TS. iv, 4, 5, 1; in mythol. the six Kṛittikās are nymphs who became the nurses of the god of war, Kārttikeya), AV.; TS.; ŚBr. &c.; white spots, VarBṛS. lxv, 5, Sch.; a vehicle, cart, ŚBr. xiii, Sch. **-ñji** (°*kâñ*), mfn. having white spots, ŚBr. xiii, 4, 2, 4; KātyŚr. **-piñjara,** mfn. red with white spots, Hcar. **-bhava,** m. 'being in the lunar mansion Kṛittikā,' N. of the moon, L. **-sambhava,** m. id., Gal. **-suta,** m. 'son of the Kṛittikās,' N. of Skanda or Kārttikeya (the nymphs called Kṛittikās being his foster-mothers), L.

Kṛintátra, *am,* n. a section, shred, chip, RV. x, 27, 23; AitBr.; (ifc. °*trá,* ŚBr. xii); (= *kṛitā*) an abyss (?), RV. x, 86, 20; ŚāṅkhBr.; a plough, Uṇ. iii, 108.

Kṛintana, *am,* n. cutting, cutting off, dividing, BhP. iii, 30, 28 & vi, 2, 46; (cf. *tantu-, śiraḥ-.*)

Kṛintta-vicakshaṇā, f. (Impv. 2. pl. fr. √2. *kṛit*), gaṇa *mayūra-vyaṃsakâdi.*

Kṛinddhi-vicakshaṇā, f. (Impv. 2. sg.), ib.

कृत् 3. *kṛit,* cl. 7. P. *kṛiṇátti* (impf. 3. pl. *ákṛintan*), to twist threads, spin, AV.; TS. ii; ŚBr. iii; MaitrS. = TāṇḍyaBr. (Nir. iii, 21); to wind (as a snake), AV. i, 27, 2 (pr. p. f. *kṛintatī*); to surround, encompass, attire, Dhātup. xxix, 10.

Kṛitád-vasu, mfn. distributing goods (?), RV. viii, 31, 9.

2. **Kṛitta,** mfn. surrounded, attired, L.

कृता *kṛitā.* See √2. *kṛit.*

कृतान्त *kṛitánta, kṛitârtha.* See p. 303, col. 2.

Kṛitāvin, kṛiti, °*tin,* &c. See ib.

कृत्त 1. & 2. *kṛitta.* See √2. & 3. *kṛit.*

कृत्ति *kṛ́itti, kṛíttikā.* See √2. *kṛit.*

कृत्नु *kṛitnú, kṛitya.* See √1. *kṛi.*

Kṛitríma, kṛítvan, kṛítvas, &c. See ib.

कृत्स *kṛitsa, am,* n. entire, whole, L.; water, Uṇ. iii, 66.

Kṛitsná, mf(*ā*)n. (rarely used in pl., R. iv, 43, 64) all, whole, entire, ŚBr.; Mn. &c.; (*as*), m., N. of a man; (*am*), n. water, L.; the flank or hip, W.; the belly, L. **-kāraka,** mfn. what everybody is able to do, MBh. iii, 283, 25. **-gata,** m., N. of a Samādhi, Kāraṇḍ. **-°tara,** mfn. more complete in number, AitĀr. **-tā** (*kṛitsná-*), f. totality, completeness, ŚBr. **-tva,** n. id., Kathās. **-vid,** mfn. omniscient, Bhag. iii, 29. **-vītá,** mfn. completely covered or mailed, TS. iv. **-vṛita,** mfn. completely covered, ŚBr. iii. **-śas,** ind. wholly, entirely, altogether, Mn.

vii, 215; MBh. &c. — **hṛidaya**, n. the whole heart, VS. xxxix, 8. **Kṛitsnâkarā**, f., N. of an Apsaras, Kāraṇḍ. **Kṛitsnâgata**, m., N. of a fabulous mountain, ib. **Kṛitsnâyatá**, mfn. stretched out to its full length, VS. xvi, 20.

Kṛitsnaka, mfn. all, every, ŚāṅkhŚr. xvi, 29, 9.

कृथ *kṛitha.* See *tanū-* & *putra-kṛithá.*

कृदन्त *kṛid-anta.* See 1. *kṛit*, p. 301.

कृदर *kṛídara*, *am*, n. a store-room, VS. xxix, 1 (Nir. iii, 20); (*as*), m. id., Uṇ. v, 41.

कृधु *kṛidhú*, mfn. shortened, mutilated, small, deficient, RV. iv, 5, 14; VS. xxiii, 28; (superl. *kradhishṭha* & compar. *kradhīyas*) Kāṭh. — **kárṇa**, mfn. having short ears (as a sort of imp), AV. xi, 9, 7 & 10, 7; hearing badly, RV. x, 27, 5.

Kṛidhuka, mfn. = *kṛidhú*, Naigh. iii, 2 (v. l.)

कृन्तत्र *kṛintátra*, °*ntana*, &c. See √2. *kṛit.*

कृप 1. *kṛíp*, f. (only instr. *kṛipā́*) beautiful appearance, beauty, splendour, RV.; VS. iv, 25. **Kṛipá-nīla**, mfn. (for *kṛipā-n*°) one whose home is splendour, dwelling in splendour (N. of Agni), RV. x, 20, 3 ['the support of sacred rites,' Sāy.] **Kṛipā-nīla**, m., N. of a man, Saṃskārak.

कृप 2. *kṛip*, cl. 6. Ā. *kṛipate* (impf. *akṛipanta*; aor. 3. pl. *akṛipran* & *cakṛipánta*, 3. sg. *akṛapishṭa*; pr. p. *kṛípamāṇa*), to mourn, long for (acc.), RV.; to lament, implore, RV.; AV. v, 19, 3: cl. 10. P. *kṛipayati* (impf. *akṛipayat*; p. *kṛipáyat*, gen. sg. m. *kṛipayatás*, RV. viii, 46, 16), to mourn, grieve, lament (with acc.), RV.; to pity, BhP. viii, 7, 40; to be weak, Dhātup. xxxv, 17; (cf. *kṛipāya* & √*krap.*)

Kṛipa, *as*, m., N. of a man (described as a friend of Indra), RV. viii, 3, 12 & 4, 2; (*as*), m. and (*ī*), f., N. of the son and daughter of the sage Śaradvat (who performed severe penance; the jealous Indra therefore sent a nymph to tempt him, but without success; however, twin sons were born to the sage in a clump of grass [*śara-stambe*], who were found by king Śāntanu and out of pity [*kṛipā*] taken home and reared; the daughter, Kṛipī, married Droṇa, and had by him a son called Aśvatthāman; the son, Kṛipa, became one of the council at Hastināpura, and is sometimes called Gautama, sometimes Śāradvata; according to Hariv. and VP., Kṛipa and Kṛipī were only distant descendants of Śaradvat; according to others, Kṛipa = Vyāsa or = a son of Kṛishṇa), MBh. &c.; (*ā*), f., see s. v. below. — **nīla**, see s. v. 1. *kṛip.* **Kṛipâcārya**, m., N. of Gautama, Gal.

1. **Kṛipaṇá**, mf(*ā́*; *ī*, g. *bahv-ādi*)n. (gaṇas *śreṇy-ādi* & *sukhâdi*; Pāṇ. viii, 2, 18, Pat.) inclined to grieve, pitiable, miserable, poor, wretched, feeble, ŚBr. xi, xiv; MBh. &c.; resulting from tears, AV. xi, 8, 28; low, vile, W.; miserly, stingy, Pañcat.; Hit.; (*as*), m. a poor man, VarBṛS.; a scraper, niggard, Pañcat.; ŚārṅgP.; a worm, L.; N. of a man, VP.; (*am*), ind. miserably, pitiably, MBh.; Pañcat.; Daś.; (*kṛipáṇam*), n. wretchedness, misery, RV. x, 99, 9; AitBr. vii, 13; ŚāṅkhŚr.; Mn. iv, 185 &c.; (*sa kṛipaṇam*, 'miserably, pitiably'), Śāntiś.; (cf. *kārpaṇya.*) — **kāśin**, mfn. looking suppliantly or desirous, TS. iii, 4, 7, 3. — **tva**, n. misery, wretchedness, MBh. ii, 1361. — **dhī**, mfn. little-minded, W. — **nindā**, f. 'censure of the miser,' N. of a chapter of ŚārṅgP. — **buddhi**, mfn. = *-dhī*, W. — **vatsala**, mfn. kind to the poor, W. — **varṇa**, mfn. looking miserably, Daś.

2. **Kṛipaṇa**, Nom. Ā. (3. pl. *kṛipáṇanta*) to long for, desire, RV. x, 74, 3.

Kṛipaṇāya, Nom. Ā. °*yate*, to lament, gaṇa *sukhâdi.*

Kṛipaṇin, mfn. miserable, being in misery, ib.

Kṛipaṇya, Nom. P. °*yáti*, to wish, desire, pray for, RV. viii, 39, 4; = √*arc*, Naigh. iii, 14.

Kṛipaṇyú, mfn. 'one who praises' (= *stotṛi*), Naigh. iii, 16.

Kṛipaya, Nom. P. p. °*yát*, only gen. sg. m. °*yatás*, see s. v. √2. *kṛip.*

Kṛipā, f. (g. *bhidâdi*) pity, tenderness, compassion (with gen. or loc.; *kṛipām* √*kṛi*, to pity [with loc.], Nal. xvii; R.), MBh. &c.; N. of a river (v. l. *rūpā*), VP. **Kṛipâkara**, m. 'a mine of compassion,' extremely compassionate, Hcat. **Kṛipā-drishṭi**, f. a look with favour, kind look, W. **Kṛipâdvaita**, m. 'unrivalled in compassion,' N. of a Buddha, L. **Kṛipā-nīla**, see s. v. 1. *kṛip.* **Kṛipânvita**, mfn. pitiful, merciful, compassionate. **Kṛipā-maya**, mfn. id. **Kṛipā-miśra**, m., N. of a son of Deva-miśra. **Kṛipā-vat**, mfn. = *-maya*, Kum. v, 26. **Kṛipâvishṭa**, mfn. id., MBh. ii, 333. **Kṛipā-sāgara**, m. 'an ocean of compassion,' = *kṛipâkara.* **Kṛipā-sindhu**, m. id., Sarvad. **Kṛipā-hīna**, mfn. pitiless, unfeeling.

Kṛipāya, Nom. Ā. °*yate* (Pot. °*yīta*), to mourn, grieve, lament, Nir. ii, 12; to have pity, MBh.: P. °*yáti*, to praise (cf. *kṛipaṇyú*), Naigh. iii, 14.

Kṛipāyita, *am*, n. lamenting, MBh. iii, 337. — **vat**, mfn. lamenting, mourning, ib. (ed. Bomb.)

Kṛipālu, mfn. pitiful, compassionate (with gen.), MBh.; BhP.; Daś. — **tā**, f. compassion, Kathās.; Subh.

Kṛipī, f. of *kṛipa*, q. v. — **pati**, m. 'husband of Kṛipī,' N. of Droṇa, L. — **putra**, m. 'son of Kṛipī,' N. of Aśvatthāman, L. — **suta**, m. id., L.

कृपनीळ *kṛipá-nīḷa.* See 1. *kṛip.*

कृपाण *kṛipāṇa*, *as*, m. (Pāṇ. viii, 2, 18, Pat.) a sword, Daś.; Prab.; a sacrificial knife, W.; (*ī*), f. a pair of scissors, dagger, knife, Kād.; (cf. *ajā-kṛipāṇīya.*) — **ketu**, m. 'having a pair of shears in his banner,' N. of a Vidyā-dhara, Bālar.

Kṛipāṇaka, *as*, m. a sword, scimitar, L.; (*ikā*), f. a dagger, Kathās. lii (ifc.); liii, 91; lxxviii, 10.

Kṛipāṇi, *is*, m., N. of a man, Vātsyāy. ii, 7, 32.

कृपानील *kṛipā-nīla.* See 1. *kṛip.*

कृपीट *kṛípīṭa*, *am*, n. (Pāṇ. viii, 2, 18, Pat.) underwood ['fuel,' Gmn.], RV. x, 28, 8; wood, forest, L.; fuel, L.; water, Naigh. i, 12; Uṇ.; the belly, Uṇ. — **pāla**, m. a rudder or large oar used as one, L.; the ocean, L.; wind, L. — **yoni**, m. 'wood-born,' fire, L.

कृमि *kṛími* or *krími*, *is*, m. (fr. √*kram*, Uṇ.), a worm, insect, VS.; TS.; AV.; ŚBr.; Mn. &c.; 'a spider' (see *-tantu-jāla*); a silk-worm, L.; a shield-louse, L.; an ant, L.; lac (red dye caused by insects), L.; N. of a son (of Uśīnara, Hariv. 1676 ff.; of Bhajamāna, Hariv. 2002); of an Asura (brother of Rāvaṇa), L.; of a Nāga-rāja, Buddh. L.; (*is*), f., N. of the wife of Uśīnara and mother of Kṛimi, Hariv. 1675 & VP. (v. l. *kṛimī*); N. of a river, MBh. vi, 9, 17; [cf. Lith. *kirminis*, *kirmele*; Russ. *červj*; Hib. *cruimh*; Cambro-Brit. *pryv*; Goth. *vaurms*; Lat. *vermi-s* for *quermi-s.*] — **kaṇṭaka**, n. 'destroying worms,' Ficus glomerata, L.; Embelia Ribes; another plant (= *citrā* or *citrâṅga*), L. — **kara**, m. a kind of venomous insect, Suśr. — **karṇa**, m. worms or lice generated in the external ear, Suśr. — **karṇaka**, m. id., ib. — **kṛit**, mfn. generating worms, L. — **kośa**, m. the cocoon of a silk-worm, L.; *-ja*, mfn. silken, Gal.; °*śóttha*, mfn. id., L. — **granthi**, m. a disease of the eyes (caused by animalculæ generated at the roots of the eye-lashes), Suśr. — **ghātin**, m. (= *-kaṇṭaka*) the plant Embelia Ribes, Suśr. (v. l. *krami-gh*°). — **ghna**, mfn. vermifuge, anthelmintic, Suśr.; (*as*, *am*), m. n. = *-ghātin*, Bhpr.; (*as*), m. the onion, L.; the root of the jujube, L.; the marking-nut plant, L.; (*ā*), f. curcuma, Bhpr.; (*ī*), f. = *-ghātin*, L.; the plant Vernonia anthelminthica, L.; = *dhūmra pattrā*, L. — **caṇḍêśvara**, n., N. of a Liṅga, MatsyaP. — **ja**, mfn produced by worms (as silk), Pañcat.; (*ā*), f. a shield-louse, L.; (*am*), n. = *-jagdha*, L. — **jagdha**, n. 'eaten by worms,' Agallochum, Bhpr. — **jala-ja**, m. an animal living in a shell, shell-fish, L. — **jit**, m. = *-ghātin*, Npr. — **tantu-jāla**, n. a cobweb, Ragh. xvi, 20. — **tā**, f. the state of a worm or insect, Hcat. — **dantaka**, m. toothache with decay of the teeth, Suśr. — **drava**, n. cochineal, Npr. — **parvata**, m. an ant-hill, L. — **purīshakā**, f. a kind of blue fly, Gal. — **pūya-vaha**, m., N. of a hell, VP. — **phala**, m. the tree Ficus glomerata, Npr. — **bhaksha**, m., N. of a hell, VP. — **bhojana**, mfn. feeding on worms, BhP.; MārkP.; (*as*), m., N. of a hell, BhP. v, 26, 7 & 18. — **mat**, mfn. (gaṇa *yavâdi*) affected or covered with worms, Gobh. — **rāga**, mfn. dyed red (with lac produced by an insect), R. iv, 22, 18. — **ripu**, m. = *-ghātin*, Bhpr. — **roga**, m. disease caused by worms, Suśr. — **lohaka**, n. 'lac-coloured metal,' iron, Gal. — **varṇa**, m. or n. (?), red cloth, Buddh. L. — **vāri-ruha**, m. = *-jala-ja*, L. — **vṛiksha**, m. the plant Mangifera sylvatica, Bhpr. — **śaṅkha**, m. = *-jala-ja*, L. — **śatru**, m. = *-ghātin*, Npr.; the plant Erythrina fulgens, L. — **śātrava**, m. 'vermifuge,' Acacia farnesiana, L. — **śukti**, f. a bivalve shell, muscle, L. — **śaila**, m. = *-parvata*, L. — **śailaka**, m. id., L. — **śarārī**, f. a kind of venomous insect, Suśr. — **sū**, f. = *-śukti*, L. — **sūtra**, n., N. of a particular disease. — **sena**, m., N. of a Yaksha, Buddh. — **hantṛi**, mfn. vermifuge, anthelmintic, W. — **hara**, m. = *-ghātin*, Bhpr. — **hā**, f. id., L.

Kṛimika, *as*, m. a small worm, MBh. i, 1800; BhP. iii, 31, 27; (*am*), n. (= *kram*°) betel nut, L.

Kṛimiṇa, mf(*ā*)n. (gaṇa *pāmâdi*) having worms, ĀpŚr. xv, 19, 5.

Kṛimin, *ī*, m. a worm, Hariv. 11327 (for the sake of metre); (mfn.) affected with worms, W.

Kṛimila, mf(*ā*)n. having many worms, wormy, Suśr.; (*ā*), f. a woman bearing many children, L.; N. of a town (called after Kṛimi), Hariv. 1678. **Kṛimilâśva**, m., N. of a son of Bāhyâśva, Hariv. 1779.

Kṛimilikā, f. linen cloth dyed with red colour, Buddh. L.

Kṛimiśa, *as*, m., N. of a hell, VP.; of a Yaksha, Divyâv. xxix.

Kṛimī, f., N. of the wife of Uśīnara, = *kṛimi*, q. v.

Kṛimīlaka, *as*, m. Phaseolus aconitifolius, L.

कृमुक *krimuká*, *as*, m. a kind of tree, Kāṭh. xix, 10; ŚBr. vi, 6, 2, 11; Kauś. 28; Mahīdh. on VS. xi, 70; (cf. *kārmuka*, *krumuká*, and *kramuka.*)

कृव् *kriv* = √1. *kṛi*, Pāṇ. iii, 1, 80; Dhātup. xv, 89: *kṛiṇvati*, see √2. *kṛī.*

कृवि *krivi*, *is*, m., N. of a utensil used by a weaver, loom (?), Uṇ. iv, 57; (cf. *krívi.*)

कृश *kṛiś*, cl. 4. P. *kṛiśyati* (perf. *cakárśa*; ind. p. *kṛiśitvā* or *karś'*, Pāṇ. i, 2, 25), to become lean or thin, become emaciated or feeble, AV. xii, 3, 16; ŚBr. xi; to cause (the moon) to wane, Dhātup. xxvi, 117: Caus. *karśayati*, to make thin or lean, attenuate, emaciate, keep short of food, Āp.; Bhag.; Suśr. &c.; to lessen, diminish, Kāvyâd. ii, 109; [cf. perhaps Lat. *parco*, *parcus.*]

Kṛiśá, mf(*ā*)n. (Pāṇ. viii, 2, 55) lean, emaciated, thin, spare, weak, feeble, RV.; AV. &c.; small, little, minute, insignificant, Mn.; MBh.; R.; Mṛicch. &c.; 'poor,' see *kṛiśī-kṛita*; (*as*), m. a kind of fish, Gal.; a kind of bird, Inscr.; N. of a Ṛishi (author of RV. viii, 55), viii, 54, 2 & 59, 3; x, 40, 8; MBh. i, xiii; N. of Sāṃkṛityāyana, Car. i, 12; of Nāga, MBh. i, 2152; (pl.) the descendants of Kṛiśa, g. *yaskâdi* (Gaṇar. 27); (*ī*), f., g. *gaurâdi* (ib. 45): [cf. κολοσσός, fr. κολοκjός.] — **kūṭa**, m. a kind of bird, Gal. — **gava**, mfn. one who has lean cattle, MBh. xii, 228. — **gu** (°*śá-*), mfn. id., AV. iv, 15, 6. — **cañcu**, m. 'having a thin beak,' a heron, Gal. — **tā**, f. leanness, thinness, MBh.; Suśr.; Sāh. — **tva**, n. id., Suśr.; Pañcat. — **dhana**, mfn. having little property, poor, Bhartṛ. ii, 61. — **nāśa**, for *-nāsa*, MBh. xii, 10365. — **nāsa**, m. 'having a thin nose,' N. of Śiva, MBh. xii, 284, 91. — **paśu** (°*śá-*), mfn. performed with lean victims, ŚBr. xi. — **buddhi**, mfn. weak-minded, Subh. — **bhṛitya**, mfn. one who feeds his servants scantily, MBh. xii, 228. — **vṛitti**, mfn. having little livelihood, MBh. xiii, 3180; R.; MārkP. — **śākha**, m. 'small-twigged,' Hedyotis Burmanniana, L. **Kṛiśâksha**, m. 'small-eyed,' a spider, W. **Kṛiśâṅga**, mf(*ī*)n. 'thin-bodied,' emaciate, spare, thin, MBh.; Pañcat. &c.; (*as*), m., N. of Śiva, MBh. xii, 10365; (*ī*), f. a woman with slender shape; the plant Priyaṅgu, L.; N. of an Apsaras, VP. **Kṛiśâtithi**, mfn. one who keeps his guests short of food, MBh. xii, 228. **Kṛiśârtha**, mfn. = °*śa-dhana*, ib. **Kṛiśâśa**, mfn. having little hope, Naish. vi, 76. **Kṛiśâśva**, mfn. having lean horses, Subh.; (*as*), m. (= Zd. *keresâspa*), N. of several persons, MBh.; Hariv. &c.; of an author of directions to players and dancers, Pāṇ. iv, 3, 111. **Kṛiśâśvin**, *inas*, m. pl. the pupils of Kṛiśâśva, ib. (cf. iv, 2, 66); (*ī*), m. a dancer, actor, L. **Kṛiśôdara**, mf(*ī*)n. thin-waisted, Daś.; Kād.; Viddh.

Kṛiśaka, mfn. thin, slender; (*ikā*), f. the plant Salvinia cucculata, L.; (cf. *kārśakeya.*)

1. **Kṛiśana**, *as*, m. the beating of the pulse, pulsation, Gobh. ii, 10, 30.

Kṛiśāluka, mfn. leanish, Divyâv. xxxvii.

Kṛiśita, mfn. emaciated, AitBr. ii, 3.

Kṛiśī, ind. in comp. for °*śá.* — √**kṛi**, to make lean, Kathās. — **kṛita**, mfn. made lean, ib.; made poor, Mṛicch. — √**bhū**, to become lean or emaciated, Hcat.; to become small, shrink.

कृशन 2. *kṛíśana*, *am*, n. a pearl, mother-of-pearl, RV. i, 35, 4 & x, 68, 11; AV. iv, 10, 7; gold, Naigh. i, 2; form, shape, ib. iii, 7; (mfn.) yielding or containing pearls, AV. iv, 10, 1 & 3 (cf. Kauś.

58); (cf. ūrdhvá-k°.) **Kṛiśaná-vat**, mfn. decorated with pearls, RV. i, 126, 4.

Kṛiśanin, mfn. =°ná-vat, RV. vii, 78, 23.

कृशर *kṛiśara*, for *kṛisara*, q. v.

कृशला *kṛiśalā*, f. the hair of the head, L.

कृशाकु *kṛiśāku*, *us*, m. heating, W.; grieving, W.

कृशानवक *kṛiśānavaka*. See °*nuka*.

Kṛiśánu, *us*, m. (fr. √*kṛiś* for *kṛish*?), 'bending the bow,' N. applied to a good archer (connected with *ástṛi*, 'an archer,' though sometimes used alone; Kṛiśānu, according to some, is a divine being, in character like Rudra or identified with him; armed with the lightning he defends the 'heavenly' Soma from the hawk, who tries to steal and bear it from heaven to earth), RV.; VS. iv, 27; AitBr. iii, 26; N. of Agni or fire, VS. v, 32; Śāṅkh-Śr. vi, 12, 3; (hence) fire, Suśr.; Ragh.; Kum.; Bhartṛ.; N. of Vishṇu, VarBṛS. xliii, 54; of a Gandharva; Plumbago zeylanica, L. **–ga**, m. Naravelia zeylanica, Npr. **–retas**, m. 'whose semen virile is fire,' N. of Śiva, L.

Kṛiśānuka or °**navaka** [Gaṇar. 436, Sch.], mfn. containing the word Kṛiśānu, g. *goshad-ādi*.

कृष 1. *kṛish*, cl. 1. P. *kárshati*, rarely Ā. °*te* (perf. *cakarsha*, 2. sg. °*shitha*, Pāṇ. vii, 2, 62, Kāś.; fut. *karkshyati* or *krakshy*°; *krishishy*°, Divyâv. xvii; *karshṭā* or *krashṭā*, Pāṇ. vii, 2, 10, Kāś.; aor. *akṛikshat* [or *akārkshīt*] or *akrākshīt*, iii, 1, 44, Vārtt. 7; inf. *krashṭum*), to draw, draw to one's self, drag, pull, drag away, tear, RV.; AV.; ŚBr. &c.; to lead or conduct (as an army), MBh.; to bend (a bow), Ragh. v, 50; to draw into one's power, become master of, overpower, Mn. ii, 215; MBh. iv, 20; R.; Pañcat.; to obtain, Mn. iii, 66; to take away anything (acc.) from any one (acc.), Vop. v, 8; to draw or make furrows, plough, RV. viii, 22, 6; Lāṭy. v, 1, 4; Vait. (Ā.); R. iii, 4, 12; BhP. (ind. p. *kṛishṭvā*): cl. 6. P. Ā. *kṛisháti*, °*te* (p. *kṛishát*), to draw or make furrows, plough, RV.; AV.; TS.; ŚBr. &c.; Ā. to obtain by ploughing, AV. xii, 2, 16; to travel over, MBh. iii, 16021: Caus. *karshayati*, to draw, drag, RV. x, 119, 11 (aor. 1. sg. *acikṛisham*); R.; Mṛicch.; to draw or tear out, MBh. iii, 2307; to pull to and fro, cause pain, torture, torment, Mn.; MBh. &c.; 'to plough,' see *karshita*: Intens. (pr. p. & Subj. 3. sg. *cárkṛishat*; impf. 3. pl. *acarkṛishur*) to plough, RV.; AV.; *carīkṛishyate* or Ved. *karīk*°, to plough repeatedly, Pāṇ. vii, 4, 64; [cf. Lith. *karszu*, *pleszau*; Russ. *česhu*; Lat. *verro*, *vello*; Goth. *falh*.]

2. **Kṛish**, mfn. See *kaṅsa-k*°.

Kṛisha, *as*, m. a ploughshare, Gal.

Kṛishaka, *as*, m. a ploughman, husbandman, farmer, Cāṇ.; a ploughshare, L.; an ox, L.; (*ikā*), f. cultivation of the soil, Cāṇ.

Kṛishāṇa, mfn. (pr. p. Ā.) ploughing (ifc.), Yājñ. ii, 150; (*as*), m. a ploughman, farmer, Gal.

Kṛishāyu, mfn. ploughing (as an ox), AV. Paipp. ix, 2, 5.

Kṛishí, *is*, f. (exceptionally pl., VS. iv, 10; Subh.) ploughing, cultivation of the soil, agriculture (one of the Vṛittis of a Vaiśya, Vishṇ.), RV.; VS. &c.; the cultivation of the soil personified, ŚBr. xi; the harvest, Yājñ. i, 275; Dhūrtas.; the earth (= *bhū*), MBh. v, 2563. **–kara**, m. a ploughman, VarBṛS.; VarBṛ. **–karman**, n. agriculture, Pañcat. **–karmânta**, n. id., Kāraṇḍ.; Lalit. **–kṛit**, m. = -*kara*, VarBṛS.; VarBṛ. **–grāma**, m. an agricultural village, Lalit. **–jīvin**, m. = -*kara*, VarBṛS. **–tantra**, *āṇi*, n. pl. the fruits of the field, MBh. ii, 5, 117. **–dvishṭa**, m. 'hated by ploughmen,' a kind of sparrow, L. **–phala**, n. harvest, Megh. 16. **–bhāgin**, m. = -*kara*, Hcat. **–rata**, m. id., VarBṛS. **–loha**, n. 'plough-metal,' iron, L. **–saṁśita** (°*shi*-), mfn. stirred up by ploughing, AV. x, 5, 34. **–saṁgraha**, m., N. of a work (said to be written by Parāśara). **–sevā**, f. agriculture, W.

Kṛishika, *as*, m. (Uṇ. ii, 41) a cultivator of the soil, husbandman, L.; the ploughshare, L.

Kṛishī, f. (= °*shi*) field, MBh. i, 7207. **–bala**, m., N. of a sage, MBh. ii, 295.

Kṛishīvala, *as*, m. (Pāṇ. v, 2, 112; vi, 3, 118) a cultivator of the soil, husbandman, Mn. ix, 38 & x, 90; Yājñ.; MBh. ii, 210 &c.

Kṛishṭa, mfn. drawn &c. (ifc.), Ragh.; Śak. &c.; ploughed or tilled (ifc.), Pañcat. &c.; (*ás* or *ám*), m. or n. cultivated ground, ŚBr. v; (*as*), m. 'lengthened,' N. of a particular note (in music), TPrāt. **–ja**, mfn. grown in cultivated ground, cultivated (as plants), Mn. xi, 144. **–pacyá**, mfn. (Pāṇ. iii, 1, 114) ripening in cultivated ground, sown or ripening after ploughing (as rice &c.), cultivated (as plants), VS. xviii, 14; TāṇḍyaBr.; BhP. vii, 12, 18. **–pākya**, mfn. id., L. **–phala**, n. the product of a harvest, Yājñ. ii, 158. **–bhūmi-jā**, f. (for *kṛishṇa-bh*°?) a kind of grass, L. **–matī-√kṛi** (fr. *matya*), to plough and harrow, HPariś. ii, 357. **–rādhi** (*kṛishṭá*-), mfn. successful in agriculture, AV. viii, 10, 24. **–samī-√kṛi** = -*matī-√kṛi*, Śiś. xii, 21; °*mī-kṛita*, mfn. ploughed and harrowed, Pāṇ. ii, 1, 49, Kāś. **Kṛishṭôpta**, mfn. sown on cultivated ground, MBh. xiii, 4702.

Kṛishṭi, *ayas*, f. pl. (once only sg., RV. iv, 42, 1) men, races of men (sometimes with the epithet *mánushīs* [i, 59, 5 & vi, 18, 2] or *náhushīs* [vi, 46, 7] or *mānavīs* [AV. iii, 24, 3]; cf. *carshaṇi*; originally the word may have meant cultivated ground, then an inhabited land, next its inhabitants, and lastly any race of men; Indra and Agni have the N. *rā́jā* or *pátiḥ kṛishṭīnām*; the term *pañca kṛishṭáyas*, perhaps originally designating the five Āryan tribes of the Yadus, Turvaśas, Druhyus, Anus, & Pūrus, comprehends the whole human race, not only the Āryan tribes), RV.; AV.; (*is*), f. ploughing, cultivating the soil, L.; attracting, drawing, L.; 'harvest,' the consequences (*karma-k*°), Naish. vi, 100; (*is*), m. a teacher, learned man or Paṇḍit, Hariv. 3588; SkandaP. **–prá**, mfn. pervading the human race, RV. iv, 38, 9. **–hán**, mfn. subduing nations, ix, 71, 2. **Kṛishṭy-ojas**, mfn. overpowering men, vii, 82, 9.

Kṛishya, mfn. to be ploughed, Ragh. ix, 80; pulled to and fro, R. (ed. Gorr.) ii, 61, 24.

कृषानु *kṛishānu*, for *kṛiśānu*, q. v., L., Sch.

कृष्कर *kṛishkara*, *as*, m., N. of Śiva, L.

कृष्ण 1. *kṛishṇá*, mf(*ā́*)n. black, dark, dark-blue (opposed to *śvetá*, *śuklá*, *róhita*, and *aruṇá*), RV.; AV. &c.; wicked, evil, Vop. vii, 82; (*as*), m. (with or without *paksha*) the dark half of the lunar month from full to new moon, Mn.; Yājñ.; Bhag.; Suśr.; the fourth or Kali-yuga, L.; (*kṛishṇas*), m. black (the colour) or dark-blue (which is often confounded with black by the Hindūs), L.; the antelope, RV. x, 94, 5; VS.; TS.; ŚBr.; BhP.; a kind of animal feeding on carrion, AV. xi, 2, 2 (*kṛishṇá*); the Indian cuckoo or Kokila (cf. R. ii, 52, 2), L.; a crow, L.; Carissa Carandas, L.; N. of one of the poets of the RV. (descended from Aṅgiras), RV. viii, 85, 3 & 4; ŚāṅkhBr. xxx, 9; (a son of Devakī and pupil of Ghora Āṅgirasa) ChUp. iii, 17, 6; N. of a celebrated Avatār of the god Vishṇu, or sometimes identified with Vishṇu himself [MBh. v, 2563; xiv, 1589 ff.; Hariv. 2359 &c.] as distinct from his ten Avatārs or incarnations (in the earlier legends he appears as a great hero and teacher [MBh.; Bhag.]; in the more recent he is deified, and is often represented as a young and amorous shepherd with flowing hair and a flute in his hand; the following are a few particulars of his birth and history as related in Hariv. 3304 ff. and in the Purāṇas &c.: Vasu-deva, who was a descendant of Yadu and Yayāti, had two wives, Rohiṇī and Devakī; the latter had eight sons of whom the eighth was Kṛishṇa; Kaṅsa, king of Mathurā and cousin of Devakī, was informed by a prediction that one of these sons would kill him; he therefore kept Vasu-deva and his wife in confinement, and slew their first six children; the seventh was Bala-rāma who was saved by being abstracted from the womb of Devakī and transferred to that of Rohiṇī; the eighth was Kṛishṇa who was born with black skin and a peculiar mark on his breast; his father Vasu-deva managed to escape from Mathurā with the child, and favoured by the gods found a herdsman named Nanda whose wife Yaśo-dā had just been delivered of a son which Vasu-deva conveyed to Devakī after substituting his own in its place. Nanda with his wife Yaśo-dā took the infant Kṛishṇa and settled first in Gokula or Vraja, and afterwards in Vṛindāvana, where Kṛishṇa and Bala-rāma grew up together, roaming in the woods and joining in the sports of the herdsmen's sons; Kṛishṇa as a youth contested the sovereignty of Indra, and was victorious over that god, who descended from heaven to praise Kṛishṇa, and made him lord over the cattle [Hariv. 3787 ff.; 7456 ff.; VP.]; Kṛishṇa is described as sporting constantly with the Gopīs or shepherdesses [Hariv. 4078 ff.; 8301 ff.; VP.; Gīt.] of whom a thousand became his wives, though only eight are specified, Rādhā being the favourite [Hariv. 6694 ff.; 9177 ff.; VP.]; Kṛishṇa built and fortified a city called Dvārakā in Gujarāt, and thither transported the inhabitants of Mathurā after killing Kaṅsa; Kṛishṇa had various wives besides the Gopīs, and by Rukmiṇī had a son Pradyumna who is usually identified with Kāma-deva; with Jains, Kṛishṇa is one of the nine black Vasu-devas; with Buddhists he is the chief of the black demons, who are the enemies of Buddha and the white demons); N. of an attendant in Skanda's retinue, MBh. ix, 2559; of an Asura, Hariv. 12936; Sāy. on RV. i, 101, 1; of a king of the Nāgas, MBh. ii, 360; Divyâv. ii; of Arjuna (the most renowned of the Pāṇḍu princes, so named apparently from his colour as a child), MBh. iv, 1389; of Vyāsa, MBh.; Hariv. 11089; of Hārita, see -*hārita*; of a son of Śuka by Pīvarī (teacher of the Yoga), Hariv. 980 ff.; of a pupil of Bharad-vāja, Kathās. vii, 15; of Havir-dhāna, Hariv. 83; VP.; BhP. iv, 24, 8; of a son of Arjuna, Hariv. 1892; of an adopted son of A-samañjas, 2039; of a chief of the Andhras, VP.; of the author of a Comm. on the MBh.; of a poet; of the author of a Comm. on the Dayā-bhāga; of the son of Keśavârka and grandson of Jayâditya; of the father of Tāna-bhaṭṭa and uncle of Raṅga-nātha; of the father of Dāmôdara and uncle of Malhaṇa; of the father of Prabhūjika and uncle of Vidyā-dhara; of the father of Madana; of the grammarian Rāma-candra; of the son of Vāruṇêndra and father of Lakshmaṇa; of the father of Hīra-bhaṭṭa (author of the Comm. called Caraka-bhāshya, and of the work Sāhitya-sudhā-samudra); N. of a hell, VP.; (*au*), m. du. Kṛishṇa and Arjuna, MBh. i, 8287; iii, 8279; (*ās*), m. pl., N. of the Śūdras in Śālmala-dvīpa, VP.; (*ā*), f. a kind of leech, Suśr.; a kind of venomous insect, ib.; N. of several plants (Piper longum, L.; the Indigo plant, L.; a grape, L.; a Punar-navā with dark blossoms, L.; Gmelina arborea, L.; Nigella indica, L.; Sinapis ramosa, L.; Vernonia anthelminthica, L.; = *kākolī*, L.; a sort of Sārivā, L.), Suśr.; a kind of perfume (= *parpaṭī*), Bhpr.; N. of Draupadī, MBh.; of Durgā, MBh. iv, 184; of one of the seven tongues of fire, L., Sch.; of one of the mothers in Skanda's retinue, MBh. ix, 2640; of a Yoginī, Hcat.; (with or without *gaṅgā*) N. of the river Kistna, MBh. xiii, 4888; PadmaP.; NārP.; (*ī*), f. night, RV. vii, 71, 1; (*ám*), n. blackness, darkness, i, 123, 1 & 9; the black part of the eye, ŚBr. x, xii, xiii, xiv; Suśr.; the black spots in the moon, TBr. i, 2, 1, 2; a kind of demon or spirit of darkness, RV. iv, 16, 13; black pepper, L.; black Agallochum, L.; iron, L.; lead, L.; antimony, L.; blue vitriol, L.; [cf. *kā́rshṇa*, &c.; cf. also Russ. *černyi*, 'black.'] **–kaṭukā**, f. black Hellehorus, Gal. **–kanda**, n. the red lotus (Nymphæa rubra), L. **–karavīra**, m. a black variety of Oleander, L. **–karkaṭaka**, m. a kind of black crab, Suśr. **–kárṇa**, mf(*ī*)n. (gaṇa *suvāstv-ādi*) black-eared, AV. v, 17, 15; MaitrS. ii, 5, 7; °*rṇāmṛita*, n. 'nectar for Kṛishṇa's ears,' N. of a poem by Bilvamaṅgala. **–karbura-varṇa**, m. 'of a variegated dark colour,' a kind of bird, Gal. **–karman**, n. 'making black,' a peculiar manner of cauterising, Suśr.; (mfn.) doing wrong, criminal, L. **–kali**, f. = -*keli*, L. **–kavaca**, n. a kind of prayer or Mantra, BrahmavP. **–kāka**, m. a raven, L. **–kāpotī**, f. a kind of plant, Suśr.; (cf. *śveta-k*° and *kṛishṇa-sarpā*.) **–kāshṭha**, n. a black variety of Agallochum, L. **–kiṁkara-prakriyā**, f., N. of a work. **–kīrtana**, n. 'praise of Kṛishṇa,' N. of a work. **–kutūhala**, n., N. of a work. **–keli**, f. Mirabilis Jalapa, L. **–keśa**, m. black-haired, ĀpŚr. v, 1, 1, Sch.; N. of an attendant in Skanda's retinue, MBh. ix, 2563. **–kohala**, m. a gamester, gambler, L. **–krīḍita**, n. 'Kṛishṇa's sports,' N. of a poem by Keśavârka (celebrating the god Kṛishṇa). **–khaṇḍa**, n. 'Kṛishṇa-section,' N. of BrahmavP. iv. **–gaṅgā**, f. the river Kistna (see *kṛishṇā*), L. **–gati**, m. 'whose way is black,' fire, MBh. xiii, 4071; Ragh. vi, 42. **–gandhā**, f. Hyperanthera Moringa, Suśr. **— garbha,** m. the plant Myrica sapida (= *kaṭphala*), L.; (*krishṇá-garbhās*), f. pl. the waters contained in the black cavities of the clouds [Comm. on Nir. iv, 24; 'the pregnant wives of the Asura Kṛishṇa,' Sāy.], RV. i, 101, 1. **— gala,** m. 'having a black throat,' a kind of bird, Gal. **— giri,** m., N. of a mountain, R. vi, 2, 34; Pāṇ. vi, 3, 117, Kāś. **— gupta,** m., N. of a man, Bādar. iv, 3, 5, Sch. **— gulma,** m. (= *-garbha*) the plant Myrica sapida, Gal. **— godhā,** f. a kind of venomous insect, Suśr. **— grīva** (*krishṇá-*), mf(*ī*)n. black-necked, VS.; TS.; Kāṭh.; ŚBr. xiii; Hariv. 9874. **— cañcuka,** m. a kind of pea (= *caṇaka*), L. **— caturdaśī,** f. the fourteenth day in the dark half of the month, Kathās.; Vet. **— candra,** m., N. of a copyist who lived about A. D. 1730 (son of Rāma-candra); N. of a prince of the eighteenth century; *-deva-śarman*, m., N. of a logician who lived about A. D. 1736. **— cara,** mfn. belonging formerly or in a former existence to Kṛishṇa, Vop. vii, 67. **— cūḍā,** f. the plant Cæsalpinia pulcherrima, L. **— cūḍikā,** f. the tree Abrus precatorius, L. **— cūrṇa,** n. rust of iron, iron filings, L. **— caitanya,** m., N. of the famous prophet Caitanya; *-purī*, m., N. of a philosopher. **— cchavi,** f. the skin of the black antelope ['a black cloud,' Comm.], MBh. iv, 6, 9. **— ja,** m. 'Kṛishṇa's son,' N. of Pradyumna, Hariv. 9322. **— janhas** (*krishṇá-*), mfn. black-winged ['having a black path,' Sāy. & Gmn.], RV. i, 141, 7. **— jaṭā,** f. Nardostachys Jaṭā-māṇsī, L. **— janaka,** m. 'father of Kṛishṇa,' N. of Vasudeva, Gal. **— janma-khaṇḍa,** n. 'section on Kṛishṇa's birth,' N. of a section of the BrahmavP. **— janmâshṭamī,** f. 'Kṛishṇa's birth-day,' the eighth day of the second half of the month Śrāvaṇa, PadmaP.; (cf. *kṛishṇâshṭamī* below.) **— jī,** m., N. of a man. **— jīra,** m. Nigella indica (having a small black seed used for medical and culinary purposes), Bhpr. **— jīraka,** m. id., KātyŚr. xix, 1, 20, Sch. **— jīvanī,** f. a species of the Tulasī plant, BrahmavP. **— jyotir-vid,** m., N. of an author. **— taṇḍulā,** f. the plant Gynandropsis pentaphylla, L.; Piper longum, L. **— tarkâlaṃkāra,** m., N. of a scholiast. **— tā,** f. blackness, Suśr.; the state of the waning moon, Hcat. **— tāmra,** mfn. dark red, Sūryas.; (*am*), n. a kind of sandal-wood, L. **— tāra,** m. 'black-eyed,' an antelope, L.; (*ā*), f. the black of the eye, Tarkas. **— tāla,** m. Xanthochymus pictorius, Gal. **— tila,** m. (Pāṇ. vi, 2, 3, Kāś.) black sesamum, Suśr. **— °tilya,** mfn., fr. *-tila*, Pāṇ. v, 1, 20, Vārtt. 1, Pat. **— tīrtha,** m., N. of a teacher of Rāma-tīrtha; (*am*), n., N. of a Tīrtha, SkandaP. **— tuṇḍa,** m. 'black-beaked,' a kind of poisonous insect, Suśr. **— tūsha** (°*shṇá-*), mfn. having a black seam or selvage, TS. **— trivṛitā,** f. a kind of Ipomœa (black Teori), L. **— tva,** n. blackness, Suśr.; the state of Kṛishṇa, MBh. i, 4236. **— datta,** m. 'given by Kṛishṇa,' N. of the author of a work on music. **— danta,** mfn. having black teeth, PārGṛ. i, 12, 4; (*ā*), f. the tree Gmelina arborea, L. **— darśana,** m., N. of a pupil of Śaṃkarâcārya. **— dasa,** mfn. = *-tūsha*, Lāṭy.; KātyŚr. **— dāsa,** m., N. of the author of the poem Camatkāra-candrikā; of the author of the work Caitanya-caritāmṛita; of the author of the poem Prôta-tattva-nirūpaṇa; of a son of Harsha (author of the Vimala-nātha-purāṇa). **— dīkshita,** m., N. of a teacher. **— deva,** m., N. of a son of Nārāyaṇa (author of the Prayoga-sāra); of a copyist (son of Paṇḍyā-purushôttama-deva); of another man, Inscr. **— deha,** m. 'black-bodied,' a large black bee, L. **— daiva-jña,** m., N. of a man. **— drá,** n.?, AV. ix, 7, 4. **— dvādaśī,** f. the twelfth day in the dark half of the month Ashāḍha, VarP. **— dvaipāyana,** m. 'black islander,' N. of Vyāsa (compiler of the MBh. and of the Purāṇas; so named because of his dark complexion and because he was brought forth by Satyavatī on a dvīpa or island in the Ganges), MBh.; Hariv.; Bādar. iii, 3, 32, Sch.; VP. **— dhattūra,** °**raka,** m. a dark species of Datura or thorn-apple (Datura fastuosa), L. **— dhānya,** n. a black variety of barley, Āp. **— dhūrjaṭi-dīkshita,** m., N. of an author. **— nagara,** n., N. of a small district (called after a town situated in it). **— nandana,** m. = *-ja*, Hariv. 9331. **— nayana,** mfn. black-eyed, MBh. **— netra,** m. 'black-eyed,' N. of Śiva, MBh. xiv, 8, 21. **— paksha,** m. the dark half of a month (fifteen days during which the moon is on the wane, time from full to new moon), KātyŚr. xv; ĀśvGṛ. iv, 5; Mn.; Yājñ. &c.; 'standing on the side of Kṛishṇa,' N. of Arjuna, L. **— °pakshika,** m. 'standing on the side of the Nāga king Kṛishṇa,' N. of a king of the Nāgas, Buddh. **— °pakshīya,** mfn. pertaining to the wane of the moon, W. **— paṇḍita,** m. (= *-miśra*) N. of the author of the Prab.; of a scholiast on the Prakriyā-kaumudī. **— padī,** f. a female with black feet, gaṇa *kumbhapady-ādi*. **— parṇī,** f. the plant Ocimum pilosum, L. **— pavi** (°*shṇá-*), mfn. having black tires (said of Agni), RV. vii, 8, 2. **— pāṅsu,** mfn. having black earth, Gobh. iv, 7, 2. **— pāka,** m. Carissa Carandas (bearing a small fruit which, when ripe, is of a black colour; commonly Karinda or Karonda), L.; *-phala*, m. id., L. **— pāṇḍura,** mfn. greyish white, L. **— piṅgala,** mf(*ā*)n. dark-brown in colour, R. ii, 69, 14; (*as*), m., N. of a man, and (*ās*), m. pl. his descendants, gaṇa *upakâdi*; (*ā*), f., N. of the goddess Durgā, MBh. vi, 796. **— piṅgā,** f. (= °*ṅgalā*) N. of Durgā, Gal. **— piṇḍītaka,** m. a dark variety of Māyana (Cyperus rotundus or Vangueria spinosa), L. **— piṇḍīra,** m. id., L. **— pipīlī,** f. a kind of black ant, L. **— pilla,** m., N. of a poet. **— puccha,** m. 'black-tailed,' the fish Rohita, Bhpr. **— pucchaka,** m. a kind of antelope, L. **— purushôttama-siddhântôpanishad,** f., N. of an Up. **— pushpa,** m. 'black-blossomed,' = *-dhattūra*, L.; (*ī*), f. the plant Priyaṅgu, L. **— prút,** mfn. moving in darkness ['taking or imparting a black colour,' Sāy.], RV. i, 140, 3. **— premâmṛita,** n. 'nectar of Kṛishṇa's love,' N. of a poem. **— phala,** m. 'having a black fruit,' = *-pāka*, L.; (*ā*), f. the plant Vernonia anthelminthica, Bhpr.; a variety of Mucuna, Bhpr. **— bandhu,** m. friend of darkness, Lalit. **— barbaraka,** m., N. of a plant, L. **— balaksha,** mfn. black and white, Lāṭy. viii, 6, 15; KātyŚr. xxii. **— bīja,** m. 'having a black seed,' a Moringa with red blossoms, L.; (*am*), n. a watermelon, L. **— bhakta,** m. a worshipper of Kṛishṇa, PadmaP.; N. of a Brāhman, SkandaP. **— bhakti,** f. 'worship of Kṛishṇa,' N. of a work; *-candrikā*, f., N. of a drama. **— bhaksha,** mfn. eating dark food, Gobh. **— bhaginī,** f. 'Kṛishṇa's sister,' N. of Durgā, Gal. **— bhaṭṭa,** m., N. of a grammarian; of a poet; (*ī*), f., N. of a Comm. written by Kṛishṇa-bhaṭṭa. **— °bhaṭṭīya,** n., N. of a work composed by Kṛishṇa-bhaṭṭa. **— bhasman,** n. sulphate of mercury, L. **— bhujaṃga,** m. 'black snake,' Coluber Nāga. **— bhū,** f. = *-bhūma*, Gal. **— bhūma,** m. (Pāṇ. v, 4, 75, Kāś.) soil or ground with black earth, Comm. on Yājñ. ii, 6. **— bhūmika,** m. id., Gal. **— bhūmi-ja,** f. 'growing in a black soil,' a species of grass, L. **— bhedā,** f. the plant Helleborus niger, Bhpr. **— bhogin,** m. = *-bhujaṃga*, Gīt. vi, 12. **— maṇḍala,** n. the black part of the eye, Suśr. **— matsya,** m. 'black-fish,' N. of a fish, Suśr. **— mallikā,** f. the plant Ocimum Sanctum, L. **— masūra,** m. a black kind of lentil, Gal. **— mārga,** mfn. (fr. *mṛiga*), coming from the black antelope, Hcat. **— mārgaṇa,** n. the skin of the black antelope, ib. **— māluka,** m. = *-mallikā*, L. **— mitra,** m. 'Kṛishṇa's friend,' N. of the son of Rāma-sevaka (grandson of Devī-datta, author of the Mañjūshā-kuñcikā). **— miśra,** m. (= *-paṇḍita*) N. of the author of Prab.; of another man. **— mukha,** mf(*ī*)n. having a black mouth, Suśr.; having black nipples, ib.; (*as*), m., N. of an Asura, Hariv. 12936; (*ās*), m. pl., N. of a sect, Buddh.; *-taṇḍula*, m. a kind of rice, Gal. **— mudga,** m. a sort of pulse (Phaseolus Mungo), L. **— mūlī,** f. 'having a black root,' a variety of the Sārivā plant, L. **— mṛiga,** m. the black antelope, MBh. iii, 1961; R.; Śak. **— mṛittika,** mfn. having a dark soil or blue mould (as a country), L.; (*ā*), f. black earth, Bhpr.; N. of a Grāma, W. **— mṛid,** f. black soil or earth, L. **— maunin,** m. 'keeping a vow of Kṛishṇa,' N. of an author. **— yajur-veda,** m. the black Yajur-veda. **— °yajurvedīya,** mfn. belonging to the black Yajur-veda. **— yāma** (°*shṇá-*), mfn. having a black path (said of Agni), RV. vi, 6, 1. **— yāmala,** n., N. of a Tantra. **— yudhishṭhira-dharma-goshṭhī,** f., N. of a work. **— yoni** (°*shṇá-*), mfn. having a black pudendum muliebre, RV. ii, 20, 7. **— rakta,** mfn. of a dark-red colour, L. **— rāja,** m., N. of a man. **— rāma,** m., N. of a prince. **— rāmaya,** Nom. Ā. °*yate*, only p. °*yita*, mfn. representing Kṛishṇa and Rāma, BhP. x, 30, 17. **— ruhā,** f., N. of a plant (= *jatukā*), L. **— rūpya,** mfn. = *-cara*, Vop. vii, 67. **— lalāma,** mfn. having a black spot, Kāṭh. xiii, 5. **— lavaṇa,** n. black salt, L.; a factitious salt (either that prepared by evaporation from saline soil, or the medicinal kind [= *viḍ-lavaṇa*], a muriate of soda with a portion of sulphur and iron), L. **— līlā-taraṃgiṇī,** f. 'description of Kṛishṇa's sports,' N. of a poem by Nārāyaṇa-tīrtha. **— loha,** n. the loadstone, Suśr.; iron, Vishṇ. **— lohita,** mfn. dark-red, of a purple colour, L. **— vaktra,** mfn. having a black mouth (as an ape), L. **— varṇa,** mfn. of a black colour, dark-blue, L.; (*ā*), f., N. of one of the mothers in Skanda's retinue, MBh. ix, 2642. **— vartani** (°*shṇá-*), mfn. having a black path (said of Agni), RV. viii, 23, 19; AV. i, 28, 2. **— vartman,** m. 'whose way is black,' fire, Mn. ii, 94; MBh.; R.; Ragh. xi, 42; the marking-nut plant (Plumbago Zeylanica), L.; N. of Rāhu, L.; a man of evil conduct, low man, outcast, blackguard, L. **— vallikā,** f. = *-ruhā*, L. **— vallī,** f. = *-mallikā*, L.; a black variety of Sārivā, L. **— vastra,** mfn. wearing black clothes, Gobh. iii, 2, 13. **— vānara,** m. a black kind of monkey, L. **— vāla** (°*shṇá-*), mfn. black-tailed, MaitrS. iii, 7, 4 (= Kapishṭh.); MBh. i, 20, 5. **— vāsa,** mfn. wearing black clothes (said of Śiva), MBh. xiii, 14, 289. **— vāsas,** mfn. wearing black clothes. R. ii, 69, 14. **— vinoda,** m. 'divertisement of Kṛishṇa,' N. of a work. **— vinnā,** f., v. l. for *-veṇā*. **— vishāṇa,** n. the horns of a black antelope (whose inner sides are covered with dark hair), Lāṭy. ix, 1, 23; (*ā*), f. id., TS. vi; ŚBr. iii, iv, v; KātyŚr. **— vṛintā,** f. the trumpet flower (Bignonia suaveolens), L.; a leguminous plant (Glycine debilis), L.; Gmelina arborea, L. **— vṛintikā,** f. Gmelina arborea, L. **— veṇā,** f., N. of a river, MBh. &c. (vv. ll. °*vennā*, Hariv. 12825 & Pāṇ. ii, 1, 21, Kāś.; °*venyā*, L.; °*veṇvā*, MBh. ii, 372); (*ī*), f. id., BhP. v, 19, 18. **— veṇṇā, -veṇyā, -veṇvā,** see *-veṇā*. **— vetra,** m. the plant Calamus Rotang, Bhpr. **— vyathis** (°*shṇá-*), mfn. one whose path is black (said of Agni), RV. ii, 4, 7. **— vyāla,** m. Plumbago rosea, Gal. **— vrīhi,** m. a black sort of rice, KātyŚr.; Suśr.; (cf. ŚBr. v, 3, 1, 13.) **— śakuni,** m. a crow, AV. xix, 57, 4; Kauś.; PārGṛ. **— śakti,** m., N. of a man, Kathās. **— śaṃkara-śarman,** m., N. of a man, Viddh. **— śapha** (°*shṇá-*), mfn. having black hoofs, MaitrS. iii, 7, 4 (= Kapishṭh.) **— śabala** (°*shṇá-*), mfn. (Pāṇ. ii, 1, 69, Kāś.) of a dark variegated colour, MaitrS. ii, 5, 7. **— śarman,** m. 'protected by Kṛishṇa,' N. of an author. **— śalkin,** m. 'black-twigged,' Cyprinus Rohita, Gal. **— śāli,** m. a black sort of rice, L. **— śiṅśapā,** f. the tree Dalbergia Sissoo, L. **— śigru,** m. the plant Moringa pterygosperma, L. **— śimbikā,** f. a kind of kidney-bean, L. **— śimbī,** f. id., L. **— śilā,** *ās*, f. pl. 'the black stones,' N. of a place, GopBr. i, 2, 7. **— śṛiṅga,** m. a buffalo with black horns, L. **— śrita,** mfn. worshipping or devoted to Kṛishṇa, W. **— shashṭika,** m. or °**kā,** f. a black sort of rice, SāmavBr. **— sakha,** m. 'friend of Kṛishṇa,' N. of Arjuna, L.; (*ī*), f. cummin seed, L. **— samudbhavā,** f. = *-veṇā*, L. **— saras,** n., N. of a lake, SkandaP. **— sarpa,** m. = *-bhujaṃga*, MBh.; R.; Suśr.; Pañcat. &c.; (*ā*), f. = *-kāpotī*, Suśr. **— sarshapa,** m. black mustard, L. **— sāra,** mf(*ī*)n. chiefly black, black and white (as the eye), spotted black, Nal.; R.; Vikr.; Hcat. &c.; (*as*), m. (with or without *mṛiga*) the spotted antelope, Mn. ii, 23; Śak.; Megh. &c.; Dalbergia Sissoo, L.; Euphorbia antiquorum, L.; Acacia Catechu, L.; (*ā*), f. Dalbergia Sissoo, L.; Euphorbia antiquorum, L.; the eyeball, Nyāyad.; *-mukha*, n., N. of a particular position of the hand, PSarv. **— sāraṅga** (°*shṇá-*), mfn. (Kāś. on Pāṇ. ii, 1, 69 & vi, 2, 3) spotted black, ŚBr. iii, xiii; KātyŚr.; (*as*), m. the spotted antelope, Śak. (v. l.); (*ī*), f. a female black antelope, Kathās. lix, 42. **— sārathi,** m. 'having Kṛishṇa for a charioteer,' N. of Arjuna, MBh. vi, 95, 79 & 117, 19; Terminalia Arjuna, L. **— sārivā,** f. a black variety of Sārivā, L. **— sārvabhauma,** m., N. of a poet. **— siṅha,** m., N. of the author of the work Trepana-kriyā-kathā, Jain. **— sīta** (°*shṇá-*), mfn. drawing black furrows ['having a black path,' Sāy.], RV. i, 140, 4. **— sundara,** m., N. of a man, and (*ās*), m. pl. his descendants, gaṇas *upakâdi* & *tika-kitavâdi*. **— sū,** f. 'Kṛishṇa's mother,' N. of Devakī, Gal. **— sūtra,** m., N. of a hell, VP. **— sūnu,** m. = *-ja*, Hariv. 9324. **— sevâhnika,** n., N. of a work. **— saireyaka,** m. a variety of Barleria, Car. vi, 24. **— skandha,** m. 'having a black stem,' a kind of tree, Comm. on L. **— svasṛi,** f. = *-bhaginī*, L. **— hārita,** m., N. of a Ṛishi, AitĀr. **Kṛishṇâksha,** m. a black die, MBh. iv, 1, 25. **Kṛishṇâgata,** mfn. devoted to Kṛishṇa, W. **Kṛishṇâgaru-kāshṭha,** n. a black variety of Aloe wood, Gal. **Kṛishṇâguru,** n. id.,

Kād.; *-maya*, mfn. made of that Aloe wood, Hcat. **Kṛishṇâgraja**, m. 'elder brother of Kṛishṇa,' N. of Bala-deva, Gal. **Kṛishṇâṅga**, m. 'black-bodied,' a kind of parrot, Gal.; (*ī*), f., N. of an Apsaras, VP. **Kṛishṇâṅghri**, mfn. having black legs, Comm. on TPrāt. **Kṛishṇâcala**, m. 'black mountain,' N. of the mountain Raivata (part of the western portion of the Vindhya chain; also one of the nine principal chains that separate the nine divisions or Varshas of the known world), L. **Kṛishṇâjiná**, n. the skin of the black antelope, AV.; TS.; ŚBr.; AitBr. &c.; (*as*), m. 'covered with a skin of the black antelope,' N. of a man, and (*ās*), m. pl. his descendants, gaṇas *upakâdi* and *tika-kitavâdi;* Kāś. on Pāṇ. (v, 3, 82 and) vi, 2, 165; *-grīvá*, mfn. having a skin of the black antelope round the neck, ŚBr. iii. **Kṛishṇâjinin**, mfn. covered with the skin of a black antelope, MBh. xiv, 2113. **Kṛishṇâñjana-giri**, m., N. of a mountain (cf. *añj°*), R. iii, 55, 5. **Kṛishṇâñjanī**, f. (=*kālâñj°*) a kind of shrub, L. **Kṛishṇâñji**, mfn. having black marks, VS. xxiv, 4. **Kṛishṇâtreya**, m., N. of a sage, Car.; Jyot.; SārṅgS. **Kṛishṇâdhvan**, mfn. having a black path (said of Agni), RV. ii, 4, 6; vi, 10, 4. **Kṛishṇā-nadī**, f. the Kistna river, L. **Kṛishṇânanda**, m., N. of a scholiast; of the author of the Tantra-sāra; *-svāmin*, m., N. of a man. **Kṛishṇântara**, n. the loadstone, Gal. **Kṛishṇâbhā**, f., N. of a shrub, L. **Kṛishṇâbhra**, °**bhraka**, n. dark talc, L. **Kṛishṇâmisha**, n. iron, L. **Kṛishṇâmṛita-taraṃgikā**, f., °*ta-mahârṇava*, m., N. of two works. **Kṛishṇâyas**, n. black or crude iron, iron, VarBṛS.; Suśr.; ChUp. vi, 1, 6, Sch. **Kṛishṇâyasa**, n. id., ChUp.; MBh.; Suśr.; (cf. *kālây°* and *kārshṇây°*.) **Kṛishṇârcana-vidhi**, m. 'rules for praising Kṛishṇa,' N. of a work. **Kṛishṇârcis**, m. 'dark-flamed (through smoke),' fire, L. **Kṛishṇârjaka**, m. =°*shṇa-mallikā*, L. **Kṛishṇâlaṃkāra**, m., N. of a Comm. **Kṛishṇâlu**, m., N. of a bulbous plant, L. **Kṛishṇâlpaka**, m. black Aloe wood, VarBṛS. lxxviii, 1, Sch. **Kṛishṇâvatāra**, m. an Avatār or incarnation of Kṛishṇa, W. **Kṛishṇâvadāta**, mfn. black and white, W. **Kṛishṇâvāsa**, m. 'abode of Kṛishṇa,' N. of the holy fig-tree (Ficus religiosa), L. **Kṛishṇâśraya**, m. 'devotion to Kṛishṇa,' N. of a work. **Kṛishṇâśrita**, mfn. devoted to or a votary of Kṛishṇa, W. **Kṛishṇâshṭami-rata**, m. ('metrically for °*mī-r°*) 'rejoicing at Kṛishṇa's birthday (see *kṛishṇa-janmâshṭamī*),' N. of Śiva, MBh. xiii, 14, 290. **Kṛishṇâshṭamī**, f. =°*shṇa-janmâshṭ°*, BhavP.; MatsyaP.; the eighth day in the dark half of any month, Kulârṇ. **Kṛishṇâhi**, m. =°*shṇa-bhujaṃga*, Kathās. lvi, 127; Pañcad. **Kṛishṇâhvaya**, *ās*, m. pl., N. of a school, Caraṇ. **Kṛishṇêkshu**, m. a sort of sugar-cane, L. **Kṛishṇaitá**, mfn. (Pāṇ. vi, 2, 3, Kāś.) spotted black, TS. v, vii. **Kṛishṇôdara**, m. 'having a black belly,' a kind of snake, Suśr.; *-śiras*, m. 'having a black belly and a black head,' N. of a bird, Gal. **Kṛishṇôdumbarikā**, f. the tree Ficus oppositifolia (cf. *kākôdumbara*), L. **Kṛishṇôpanishad**, f., N. of an Up. (in praise of the god Kṛishṇa, being part of the Gopālôpanishad). **Kṛishṇôraga**, m. =*kṛishṇa-bhujaṃga*, MBh. **Kṛishṇo'sy-ākhareshṭhaka**, mfn. (an Adhyāya or Anuvāka) beginning with the words *kṛishṇo'sy ākhare-shṭhāḥ* (TS. i, 1, 11, 1; VS. ii, 1), gaṇa *goshad-ādi*. **Kṛishṇâñjas**, m., N. of an attendant in Skanda's retinue, MBh. ix, 2577.

2. **Kṛishṇa**, Nom. P. °*shṇati*, to behave or act like Kṛishṇa, Vop. xxi, 7.

Kṛishṇaka, *as*, m. (gaṇa *sthūlâdi*) 'blackish,' a kind of plant (perhaps black Sesamum), Kauś. 80; a shortened N. for Kṛishṇājina, Pāṇ. v, 3, 82, Sch.; (*ikā*), f. black, black substance, Kād.; Hcar.; a kind of bird (=*śyāmā*), L.; black mustard (Sinapis ramosa), L.

Kṛishṇála, *am*, n., rarely [Yājñ. i, 362] *as*, m. (gaṇa *sidhmâdi*) the black berry of the plant Abrus precatorius used as a weight (the average weight being between one and two grains), Kāṭh.; TBr.; Mn.; Yājñ.; Comm. on KātyŚr. &c.; a coin of the same weight, Mn.; Yājñ.; a piece of gold of the same weight, TS.; Kauś.; Nyāyam.; (*ā*), f. Abrus precatorius (a shrub bearing a small black and red berry, =*guñjā, raktikā*), L.

Kṛishṇalaka, *as* or *am*, m. or n. ifc. (=°*la*) the black berry of the plant Abrus precatorius used as a weight, Mn. viii, 134; Hcat.

Kṛishṇasa, mfn. blackish ['extremely black,' Sāy.], AitBr. v, 14; TāṇḍyaBr.; KātyŚr.; Lāṭy.

Kṛishṇāya, Nom. P. °*yati*, to represent Kṛishṇa, BhP. x, 30, 15: Ā. °*yate*, to blacken, Hit.; to behave like Kṛishṇa, Vop. xxi, 7.

Kṛishṇikā. See *kṛishṇaka*.

Kṛishṇiman, *ā*, m. (Pāṇ. vi, 4, 161, Kāś.) black, blackness, Mudr.

Kṛishṇiyá, *as*, m., N. of a man (protected by the Aśvins), RV. i, 116, 23 & 117, 7.

Kṛishṇī, ind. in comp. — **√1. as** (Pot. °*shṇī-syāt*), to become black, Vop. vii, 82. — **karaṇa**, n. blackening, Suśr. — **√kṛi**, to blacken, make black, Vop. vii, 82. — **√bhū**, to become black, ib.

Kṛishṇeya, *as*, m., 'N. of a man,' (*ās*), m. pl. his descendants, Pravar.

कृष्य *kṛishya*. See p. 306, col. 2.

कृसर *kṛisara*, *as*, m. (Pāṇ. viii, 3, 59, Vārtt. 1; often spelt *kṛiśara*) a dish consisting of sesamum and grain (mixture of rice and peas with a few spices), ShaḍvBr. v, 2; Kauś.; ĀśvGṛ.; Gobh.; Mn. &c.; (*ās*), m. pl. id., Suśr.; Kathās.; (*ā*), f. id Suśr.; Bhpr.; (*am*), n. id., MBh.; MārkP.

कॄ 1. *kṛī*, cl. 6. P. *kiráti* (Pāṇ. vii, 1, 100; perf. *-cakāra*, Pāṇ. vii, 4, 11, Kāś.; 2nd fut. *karishyati*; 1st fut. *karitā* or *karītā*, Vop. xiii, 2; aor. *akārīt* [Ved. *sáṃ kārishat*]; ind. p. *-kīrya*; Pass. *kiryate*), to pour out, scatter, throw, cast, disperse, RV. i, 32, 13; MBh. &c.; to throw up in a heap, heap up, Kāṭh. xxviii, 4: Ā. *kirate*, to throw off from one's self, RV. iv, 38, 7: P. to strew, pour over, fill with, cover with, MBh.; R.; (perf. 3. pl. *cakarur*) Bhaṭṭ.: Desid. *cikarishati*, Pāṇ. vii, 2, 75: Intens. *cākarti*, Pāṇ. vii, 4, 92, Kāś.; [cf. Gk. κεράννυμι, κίρνημι.]

कॄ 2. *kṛī* (or v. l. *kṛi*), cl. 5. and 9. P. Ā. *kṛiṇoti*, °*ṇute*, °*ṇāti*, °*ṇīte*, to hurt, injure, kill, Dhātup.; Vop. xvi, 2; *kṛiṇváti*, Naigh. ii, 19.

कॄ 3. *kṛī* (v. l. for *gṛī*), cl. 10. Ā. *kārayate*, to know, Dhātup. xxxiii, 33; to inform, ib.

कॄत् *kṛīt*. See √*kīrt*.

कॢप् *klṛip*, cl. 1. Ā. *kálpate* (Pāṇ. viii, 2, 18; perf. *caklṛipe*, 3. pl. *cāklṛipré*, RV. x, 130, 5 & 6; 2nd fut. *kalpishyate* & *kalpsy°* [3. du. *kalpsyete*, AitBr.; vv. ll. *klṛips°* & *klaps°*], or *kalpsyati*; Cond. *akalpishyata* or °*lpsyat*; 1st fut. *kalpitā* or *kalptā* [see Pāṇ. vii, 2, 60]; aor. *aklṛipta* or °*pat*; pr. & perf. only Ā., Pāṇ. i, 3, 91-93), to be well ordered or regulated, be well managed, succeed, AV.; TS.; ŚBr. &c.; to bear suitable relation to anything, correspond, be adapted to, in accordance with, suitable to (instr.), RV. i, 170, 2; AV. &c.; to be fit for (loc.), R.; to accommodate one's self to, be favourable to, subserve, effect (with dat.), VS.; ŚBr. xiv; AitBr.; Mn. &c.; to partake of (dat.), KaṭhUp.; Mn.; Bhag. &c.; to fall to the share, be shared or partaken by (loc., dat. or gen., e. g. *yajñó devéshu kalpatām*, 'let the sacrifice be shared by the gods,' VS. xix, 45), VS.; AitBr.; ChUp.; MBh.; to become (with nom.), RV. x, 130, 5 & 6; AV.; Bhaṭṭ.; (with dat. [Pāṇ. ii, 3, 13, Vārtt. 2], R.; Pañcat.); to happen, occur, BhP. iii, 16, 12; Bhaṭṭ.; to prepare, arrange, Bhaṭṭ. xiv, 89; to produce, cause, effect, create (with acc.), BhP. iii, 7, 25; Bhaṭṭ.; to declare as, consider as (with double acc.), Pañcat. (perf. p. *klṛiptavat*): Caus. P. Ā. *kalpáyati*, °*te*, (aor. *acīklṛipat* or *cāklṛipat* [AV. vi, 35, 3], Subj. *cīklṛipāti*, RV. x, 157, 2), to set in order, arrange, distribute, dispose, RV.; AV.; AitBr.; to bring into suitable connection with, RV. x, 2, 4; to prepare, arrange, RV.; AV.; ŚBr.; MBh. &c.; to fit out, furnish with (instr.), TS. ii; to help any one in obtaining anything (dat. or loc. or gen.), ŚvetUp.; MBh.; R. ii, 43, 19; to fix, settle, Daś.; to declare as, consider as (with double acc., e. g. *mātaram enām kalpayantu*, 'let them consider her as their mother,' Kum. vi, 80), Mn.; MBh. &c.; to make, execute, bring about, RV.; AV.; ŚBr.; MBh. &c.; to frame, form, invent, compose (as a poem &c.), imagine, Mn. i, 102 &c.; to perform (as a ceremony &c.), Lāṭy.; to trim, cut, VarBṛS.; (in Prākṛit) Śak.; to pronounce a formula or verse which contains the √*klṛip*, ŚBr. ix: Desid. *ciklṛipsati* or *cikalpishate*, Pāṇ. i, 3, 92 & vii, 2, 60; [cf. Goth. *hilpa*; Eng. *help*; Germ. *helfe*; Lith. *gelbmi*.]

Klṛiptá, mfn. arranged, prepared, ready, in order, complete, right, perfect, AitBr.; ŚBr.; ŚāṅkhŚr. &c.; at hand, BhP. vi, 10, 32; made, done; formed, framed; caused, produced, effected, invented, contrived, created, BhP. &c.; fixed, settled, prescribed, Mn. iii, 69; xi, 27; ascertained, determined (as an opinion), Kathās. cxxiii, 147; cut, clipt, pared, shorn, Mn.; Suśr. — **kīlā**, f. title deed (lease of a house &c.), L. — **keśa-nakha-śmaśru**, mfn. having the hair, nails, and beard cut or arranged, Mn. iv, 35 & vi, 52. — **dhūpa**, m. olibanum, L. — **nakha**, mfn. having the nails cut or arranged, Suśr.

Klṛipti, *is*, f. preparation, making or becoming conformable, accomplishment, VS. xviii, 11; TS. v; ŚBr. (*klṛipti*, xiii); ŚāṅkhŚr.; ĀśvGr. i, 23, 15; *diśām kl°*, 'fixing the regions' (N. of the verses AV. xx, 128, 1 ff.), AitBr. vi, 32; ŚāṅkhŚr. iv, 9, 2 & xii, 20, 1; invention, contrivance; obtainment, Rājat. v, 463; description, Lāṭy. vi, 9, 1, Sch.; N. of certain formulas or verses containing the √*klṛip*, ŚBr. v, 2, 1, 3; Nyāyam. iii, 8, 14, Sch.

Klṛiptika, *am*, n. =*prakraya*, L.

केकय *kekaya*, *ās*, m. pl., N. of a warrior-tribe, MBh.; R. &c.; (*as*), m. (Pāṇ. vii, 3, 2 & gaṇa *bhargâdi*) a chief of that tribe (prince of the solar race), MBh. iii, 10284; R. ii; (*ī*), f. a princess of that tribe (wife of Daśa-ratha and mother of Bharata), R. ii, 70, 20; (cf. *kaikeya*.)

केकर *kekara*, mfn. squint-eyed, Mn. iii, 159 (v. l.); VarBṛS. lxx, 19; (cf. *kedara, ṭeraka*.) — **netra**, mfn. id., VarBṛS. lxviii, 65. — **locana**, mfn. id., Kathās. cxxiii, 164. **Kekarâksha**, mfn. id.

Kekaraka, mfn. =°*ra*, Cāṇ.

केकल *kekala*, m. (for *kelaka?*) a dancer, W.

केका *kekā*, f. the cry of a peacock, MBh.; Mṛicch.; Megh. &c. — **rava**, m. id., Kād. **Kekâsura**, m., N. of an Asura.

Kekāya, Nom. Ā. °*yate*, to cry (as a peacock), Vāsant.

Kekāvala, *as*, m. a peacock, L.

Kekika, *as*, m. id., gaṇa *vrīhy-ādi*.

Kekin, *ī*, m. (gaṇa *vrīhy-ādi*), id., Bhartṛ. i, 44; SkandaP. **Keki-śikhā**, f. (=*mayūra-ś°*), N. of a shrub, L.

केकाण *kekāṇa*, N. of a locality.

केकासुर *kekâsura*, °*kika*, &c. See *kekā*.

केकेयी *kekeyī*, for *kaik°*, q. v., L.

केचुक *kecuka*, *as*, *ā*, m. f. a plant with an esculent root (Colocasia antiquorum), Suśr. (vv. ll. *kevuka* & °*vūka*); (*am*), n. the esculent root of that plant, L.; (cf. *kacu, kacvī, kemuka*, & *kevuka*.)

केञ्च *keñca*, *as*, m. a kind of sparrow, Gal.

केणिका *keṇikā*, f. a tent, L.

केत *kéta*, *as*, m. (√4. *cit*) desire, wish, will, intention ['wealth,' 'atmosphere, sky,' Sāy.], RV.; VS.; TS.; ŚāṅkhŚr.; a house, abode, BhP.; mark, sign, BhP. i, 16, 34; apparition, shape, Naigh. iii, 9. — **pū**, mfn. purifying the desire or will, VS. ix, 1 & xi, 7; MaitrS. i, 11, 1. — **vedas** (*kéta-*), mfn. knowing the intention ['knowing the wealth of another,' Sāy.], RV. i, 104, 3. — **sáp**, m (nom. pl. *-sápas*) fn. obeying the will (of another), obedient ['touching the sky,' Sāy.], v, 58, 3.

Ketana, *am*, n. a summons, invitation, Mn. iv, 110; MBh.; MārkP.; a house, abode, MBh.; R.; BhP.; Kathās.; 'abode of the soul,' the body, Git. vii, 5 (ifc. f. *ā*); place, site, Kathās. xxvi, 44; sign, mark, symbol (of a deity), ensign (of a warrior), flag or banner (e g. *vānara-k°*, 'one who has a monkey as his ensign or arms,' MBh.; see also *makara-k°*, &c.), MBh.; R.; Ragh. ix, 38; business, indispensable act, Mālatim.

Ketaya, Nom. P. °*yati*, to summon, call or invite, MBh. xiii, 1596; to fix or appoint a time, L.; to counsel or advise, W.; to hear, Vop.

Ketayitṛi, mf(*trī*)n. one who summons, Sāy. on RV. i, 113, 19.

Ketita, mfn. called, summoned, Mn. iii, 190; MBh. xiii, 1613 & 6233; dwelt, inhabited, W.

केतक *ketaka*, *as*, m. the tree Pandanus

odoratissimus, MBh.; R.; Megh. &c.; (*ī*), f. (g. *gaurâdi*, Gaṇar. 46) id., Gīt.; Vet.; Sāh.; ŚivaP.

Ketaki, metrically for °*kī*, f., Suśr.; Bhartṛ.; Gīt.

केतन *ketana*, °*taya*, &c. See *kéta*.

केतलिकीर्ति *ketali-kirti*, *is*, m., N. of the author of the work Megha-mālā.

केतु *ketú*, *us*, m. (fr. √4. *cit*), bright appearance, clearness, brightness (often pl., 'rays of light'), RV.; VS.; AV.; lamp, flame, torch, ib.; day-time, ŚāṅkhBr.; (Naigh. iii, 9) apparition, form, shape, RV.; PārGṛ.; sign, mark, ensign, flag, banner, RV.; AV.; MBh. &c.; a chief, leader, eminent person, RV.; R. iv, 28, 18; Ragh. ii, 33; BhP.; intellect, judgment, discernment(?), RV. v, 66, 4; AV. x, 2, 12; any unusual or striking phenomenon, comet, meteor, falling star, AdbhBr.; Mn. i, 38; VarBṛS.; BhP. &c.; the dragon's tail or descending node (considered in astron. as the 9th planet, and in mythol. as the body of the demon Saiṃhikeya [son of Siṃhikā] which was severed from the head or Rāhu by Vishṇu at the churning of the ocean, but was rendered immortal by having tasted the Amṛita), Hariv. 4259; R.; VP.; 'a pigmy race,' see -*gaṇa* below; disease, L.; an enemy, L.; N. of a son of Agni (author of RV. x, 156), RAnukr.; (with the patr. Vājya), VBr.; N. of a Dānava, Hariv. 198; of a son (of Ṛishabha, BhP. v, 4, 10; of the 4th Manu, viii, 1, 27); *aruṇáḥ ketávaḥ*, 'red apparitions,' a class of spirits (a kind of sacrificial fire is called after them *āruṇaketuka*, q.v.), AV. xi, 10, 1 f. & 7; TĀr.; MBh. xii, 26, 7. **–gaṇa**, m. the dwarfish inhabitants of Kuśa-dvīpa (children of Jaimini), Tāj. **–graha**, m. the descending node (see above s. v. *ketu*), L.; -*vallabha*, m. = °*tu-ratna*, Npr. **–cakra**, n. a kind of diagram. **–tārā**, f. a comet, W. **–dharman**, m., N. of a man (v.l. -*varman*), MBh. xiv, 2154. **–bha**, m. a cloud, L. **–bhūta**, mfn. being or become a banner, Nal. xii, 28. **–mát**, mfn. endowed with brightness, AV.; (interpolation after RV. viii, 56); clear (as a sound), RV. vi, 47, 31; AV. iii, 19, 6; (*ān*), m. a Yaksha, Gal.; N. of a Muni, VāyuP.; of a Dānava, MBh.; Hariv.; of a regent of the western part of the world (son of Rajas), VP.; of a son of Kshema and father of Suketu, Hariv. 1593; of a son of Kshemya and father of Varsha-ketu, 1750; of a warrior, MBh. ii, 122 & 127; of a son of Dhanvantari, BhP. ix, 17, 5; of Ambarīsha, ix, 6, 1; N. of a mountain, Buddh.; of a palace of Vāsu-deva's wife Sunandā, Hariv. 8989; (*tī*), f. a metre (of 2 × 21 syllables); N. of the wife of Sumālin, R. vii, 5, 37; N. of a locality, W. **–māla**, m., N. of a son of Āgnīdhra, VP.; of a boar, R. v, 9, 66; BhP.; (*ās*), m. pl., N. of a people, Hariv. 8227 & 8654; (*as, am*), m. n. one of the nine great divisions of the known world (the western portion or Varsha of Jambū-dvīpa, called after Ketu-māla), Sūryas.; VP.; BhP.; (*ā*), f., N. of a Tīrtha, MBh. iii, 8368 ff. **–mālaka**, m. or n. the Varsha called Ketu-māla (q.v.), VP. **–māli**, see °*lin*. **–mālin**, m., N. of a Dānava, Hariv. (metrically also °*li*); of a Muni, VāyuP. **–yashṭi**, f. a flag-staff, Ragh. xii, 103. **–ratna**, n. 'Rāhu's favourite,' beryl, L. **–varman**, see -*dharman*. **–vīrya**, m., N. of a Dānava, Hariv. 198. **–śriṅga**, m., N. of a king, MBh. i, 230; of a Muni, VāyuP.

केदर *kedara*, mfn. = *kekara*, L; (*as*), m., N. of a plant, L.

केदार *kedāra*, *as*, m. (*am*, n., L.) a field or meadow, especially one under water, Mn. ix, 38 & 44; MBh.; R. &c.; *Kapilasya k*°, 'Kapila's field,' N. of a Tīrtha, MBh. iii, 6042 ff.; *Mataṅgasya k*°, 'Mataṅga's field,' another Tīrtha, 8159; a basin for water round the root of a tree, L.; a bed in a garden or field, W.; plain, area, KātyŚr. xviii, 5, 4, Sch.; N. of a particular constellation, VarBṛ.; of a Rāga (in music); of a mountain country (the modern Kedār, part of the Himâlaya mountains, W.), MBh. vi, 427; NandiP.; N. of Śiva as worshipped in the Himâlaya; of the author of a work entitled Abdhi; (*ī*), f., N. of a Rāgiṇī; (*am*), n., N. of a Tīrtha, MatsyaP.; of a Liṅga, ib.; (in the Himâlaya) ŚivaP. **–kaṭu**, f.(?) a kind of plant, Gal. **–kaṭukā**, f. a kind of Helleborus, L. **–kalpa**, m., N. of a section of the SkandaP., NandiP. **–khaṇḍa**, n. a small dyke (earth raised to keep out water), W.; a break in the dyke raised round a field (to keep out water), MBh. i, ch. 3. **–ja**, n. the fruit of Cerasus Puddum, L. **–tīrtha**, n., N. of a Tīrtha, ŚivaP. **–deva**, m., N. of a man. **–nātha**, m., N. of Śiva as worshipped in the Himâlaya. **–purāṇa**, n., N. of a Purāṇa. **–bhaṭṭa**, m., N. of an author. **–malla**, m., N. of Mandanapāla. **–māhātmya**, n., N. of a section of the VāyuP. **–liṅga**, n., N. of a Liṅga, Śaṃkar. **–śambhu**, m., N. of a Tīrtha, Rasik. **–setu**, m. a dyke raised round a field, Car. iii, 3. **Kedārêśa**, m., N. of a statue of Śiva in Kāśī, SkandaP.; (*am*), n., N. of a Liṅga, NandiP. **Kedārêśvara**, m. (= °*rêśa*), Śiva's statue in Kāśī, SkandaP.; (*am*), n., N. of a Tīrtha in the Himâlaya; -*liṅga*, n., N. of a Liṅga, SkandaP.; -*sthalī*, f., N. of a locality, KapSaṃh.

Kedāraka, *as*, m. a kind of rice, Suśr.; (*ikā*), f. (in music) N. of a Rāgiṇī.

केन *kéna*, instr. ind. (fr. 2. *ká*), by what? ŚBr. iv; MBh. i, ch. 3; whence? MBh. xiii, 2167; R. vi, 12, 4; how? why? Pañcat.; Bhartṛ. **Keneshitôpanishad**, *t*, f., N. of an Up. (beginning with the word *keneshitam*). **Kenôpanishad**, *t*, f. id. (beginning with *kena*).

केनती *kenatī*, f., N. of the wife of Kāma (the god of love), L.

केनव *kenava*, *as*, m., N. of a teacher (pupil of Śākapūrṇi), VP.

केनार *kenāra*, *as*, m. the head, L.; 'a skull' or 'the temples, upper part of the cheek' (*kapāla* or *kapola*), L.; a joint, L.; a division of hell, hell compared to a potter's kiln, L.

केनिप *kenipá*, *as*, m. a sage, RV. x, 44, 4; (cf. *āke-nipá*.)

केनिपात *kenipāta*, *as*, m. the helm, rudder, large oar used as a rudder, L.

Kenipātaka, *as*, m. id., L.

Kenipātana, *am*, n. id., Gal.

केन्दु *kendu*, *us*, m. a kind of ebony (Diospyros embryopteris), L. **–villa**, v.l. for *kindubilva*, q.v.

Kenduka, *as*, m. another variety of ebony (yielding a species of tar, Diospyros glutinosa), L.; (in music) a kind of measure.

केन्द्र *kendra*, *am*, n. (borrowed fr. Gk. κέντρον), the centre of a circle; the equation of the centre; the argument of a circle; the argument of an equation, W.; the distance of a planet from the first point of its orbit in the fourth, seventh, or tenth degree, Sūryas. &c.; the first, fourth, seventh, and tenth lunar mansion, VarBṛS.; VarBṛ.; (cf. *dvitīya-k*°, *patana-k*°, *manda-k*°, *śīghra-k*°.)

Kendrakā, f. for *kecukā* (q.v.), Suśr.

केप् *kep*, cl. 1. Ā. *kepate*, to shake or tremble, Dhātup. x, 7; to go, ib.; (cf. √*gep*.)

Képi, mfn. trembling, shaking, RV. x, 44, 6; unclean, Nir. v, 24.

केमद्रुम *kema-druma*, *as*, m. in astron. = κενο-δρόμος, VarBṛ. xiii, 3 & 6.

केमुक *kemuka*, *as*, m. (= *kecuka*) Colocasia antiquorum, Bhpr.; Costus speciosus, L.

केम्बुक *kembuka*, *am*, n. cabbage, Car.; the kernel of the Areca nut, Npr.

केयूर *keyūra*, *am*, n. a bracelet worn on the upper arm, MBh.; R.; Ragh. &c.; (*as*), m. id., Bhartṛ. ii, 16; a kind of coitus; N. of a Samādhi, Kāraṇḍ. **–dharā**, f. 'wearing a bracelet on the upper arm,' N. of an Apsaras, Kāraṇḍ. **–bala**, m., N. of a Deva-putra, Lalit.

Keyūraka, *as*, m., N. of a Gandharva, Kād.

Keyūrāya, Nom. Ā. °*yate*, to represent a *keyūra*, Sāh.

Keyūrin, mfn. decorated with a bracelet on the upper arm, Kād.; Hcar.; MārkP. xxiii, 102.

केरक *keraka*, for *kerala*, q.v.

केरल *kerala*, *ās*, m pl., N of the inhabitants of Malabar, MBh. (once *keraka*, ii, 1173); Hariv.; R.; VarBṛS.; (*as*), m. (gaṇa *kambojâdi*) the king of the Keralas, MBh. iii, 15250; N. of a son of Ākrīḍa (from whom the people of Kerala is derived), Hariv. 1836; (*ī*), f. a Kerala woman, Kād.; N. of an astronomical treatise, L.; a Horā or period of time equal to about one hour, L.; (*am*), n., N. of the country inhabited by the Keralas, MBh. vi, 352. **–jātaka**, **-tantra**, n., **-siddhânta**, m., N. of works. **Keralôtpatti**, f., N. of a work.

Keralaka, *ās*, m. pl., N. of the inhabitants of Malabar, VarBṛS. xiv, 12; (*as*), m., N. of a Nāga demon, VāmP.; (*ikā*), f., N. of a woman, Vāsav.

केरु *keru*. See *mahi-k*°.

केल् *kel*, cl. 1. P. *kelati*, to shake, tremble, Dhātup. xv, 30; to go or move, ib.; to be frolicsome, sport (cf. Prākrit √*kīl* = *krīḍ*), W.

Kelaka, *as*, m. a dancer, tumbler, one who walks or dances on the edge of a sword, L.; (cf. *kekala*.)

Kelāya, Nom. Ā. °*yate* (fr. √*krīḍ*), to sport, play, gaṇa *kaṇḍv-ādi*.

Keli, *is*, m. f. play, sport, amorous sport, pastime, amusement, Mn. viii, 357; Mṛicch. &c.; disguise, concealment, Gal.; (*is*), f. the earth, L. **–kadamba**, m. (= -*vṛiksha*) a variety of the Kadamba, L. **–kamala**, n. a lotus flower for playing with, Caurap. **–kala**, mfn. amusing one's self, Hariv. ii, 75, 55 (v.l. -*kila*); (*ā*), f. amorous or sportive accents or address, W.; sportive skill, wantonness, W.; the Viṇā or lute of Sarasvatī, L. **–kalaha**, m. a quarrel in jest or joke, L. **–kānana**, n. a pleasure-grove, L. **–kila**, mfn. sporting, amusing one's self, Hariv. 3380 (v.l. -*kala*); finding pleasure in (in comp.), 7671; wanton, arrogant; litigious, quarrelsome, 3209; (*as*), m. the confidential companion of the hero of a drama (in general a sort of buffoon), L.; N. of one of Śiva's attendants, L.; (*ā*), f. sport, amusement, Comm. on L.; N. of Rati (the wife of Kāma-deva), L.; N. of a town, VP. **–kīrṇa**, m. 'full of amusement,' a camel, L. **–kuñcikā**, f. a wife's younger sister, L.; (cf. *kal*°.) **–kailāsa**, m. a mountain that is to represent the Kailāsa mountain, Viddh. **–kośa**, m. 'receptacle of amusement,' a dancer, actor, L. **–gṛiha**, n. a pleasure-house, private apartment, Comm. on Amar. **–nāgara**, m. a sensualist, enjoyer of worldly pleasures, L. **–niketana**, n. = -*gṛiha*, Amar. **–para**, mfn. wanton, sportive, W. **–palvala**, n. a pleasure-pond, Naish. i, 117. **–maṇḍapa**, **-mandira**, n. = -*gṛiha*, Śāntiś.; Caurap. **–mukha**, m. pastime, sport, L. **–raṅga**, m. a pleasure-ground, Dhūrtas. **–raivataka**, n., N. of a treatise, Sāh. **–vana**, n. = -*kānana*, ŚārṅgP. **–vṛiksha**, m. a species of the Kadamba (commonly Keli-kadamba, Nauclea cordifolia, being abundant in the scene of Kṛishṇa's sports with the Gopīs), L. **–śayana**, n. a pleasure-couch, Gīt. xi, 2. **–śushi**, f. the earth, W. **–śaila**, m. a pleasure-hill, Dhūrtan. **–śveta-sahasra-pattra**, Nom. P. °*ttrati*, to represent a white lotus for playing with, Prasannar. **–saciva**, m. minister of the sports, master of the revels, L. **–sadana**, n. = -*gṛiha*, Gīt. xi, 14. **–sāra**, m., N. of a Vidyā-dhara, Bālar. **–sthalī**, f. a place of pleasure, play-ground, Śāntiś. i, 16.

Kelika, mfn. sporting, sportive, W.; the tree Jonesia Aśoka, L.

Kelita, n, ifc., *kali-* – *kelī-kalita*, Subh.

Kelī, f. rarely for *keli* (play, sport). **–kalita**, n. amusement, jest, play, Bālar. **–pika**, m. a cuckoo kept for pleasure, Sāh. **–vanī**, f. a pleasure-park, Sāh. **–śāla-bhañjikā**, f. a small statue, Daś.

केल *kela*, °*lu*, a particular high number, Buddh. L.

केलटक *kelaṭaka* = *kemuka* (q.v.), Npr.

केलाय *kelāya*, °*li*, &c. See √*kel*.

केलास *kelāsa*, *as*, m. crystal, W.

केलूट *kelūṭa*, *am*, n. a kind of pot-herb, Car. i, 27; = *kemuka* or a kind of Udumbara, Npr.

केव् *kev*, cl. 1. Ā. *kevate*, to serve, attend to, Dhātup. xiv, 39; (cf. √*sev*.)

केवट *kévaṭa*, *as*, m. a cave, hollow, RV. vi, 54, 7; (cf. *avaṭá*.)

केवर्त *kevárta*, *as*, m. (= *kaiv*°) a fisherman, VS. xxx, 16.

केवल *kévala*, m(nom. pl. *e*, RV. x, 51, 9) f(*ī*, RV. x, 73, 6; AV.; ŚBr.; *ā*, Mn. &c., see Pāṇ. iv, 1, 30)n. (in comp., Pāṇ. ii, 1, 49) exclusively one's own (not common to others), RV.; AV.; alone, only, mere, sole, one, excluding others, RV.; AV.; TS. &c.; not connected with anything else, isolated, abstract, absolute; simple, pure, uncompounded, unmingled, ŚBr. &c.; entire, whole, all, Mn.; MBh. &c.; selfish, envious, L.; (*am*), ind. only, merely, solely (*na kevalam—api*, not only—but also, Ragh.; VP.; Rājat.; *kevalam—na tu*, only—but not, Śriṅgār.), Mn.; MBh. &c.; entirely, wholly, absolutely, R. ii, 87, 23; but, Kād.; Hcar.; (=*nirṇītam*) certainly, decidedly, L.; (*as*), m. (=*kelaka*) a dancer, tumbler, Gal.; N. of a prince, BhP. ix, 2, 30; (*ā*), f., N. of a locality, MBh. iii, 254, 10 (v.l. °*lī*); (*ī*), f. 'the whole of a philosophical system,' see *pāśaka-k°*; N. of a locality (v.l. for °*lā*, q.v.); (*am*), n. the doctrine of the absolute unity of spirit; the highest possible knowledge (=*kevala-jñāna*), Jain.; N. of a country (v.l. *kerala*), MBh. vi, 9, 34. — **karmin**, mfn. performing mere works (without intelligence), Bādar. iii, 1, 7, Sch. — **jñāna**, n. the highest possible knowledge, Jain. — **jñānin**, m. 'possessing the *kevala-jñāna*,' an Arhat, Jain. — **tas**, ind. only, Comm. on Yājñ. — **tva**, n. the state of standing by itself or alone, VPrāt., Sch. — **dravya**, n. mere matter or substance, RāmatUp.; black pepper, L. — **naiyāyika**, m. a mere logician (not versed in any other science), Pāṇ. ii, 1, 49, Sch. — **putrā**, f., N. of a Tīrtha, Rasik. — **barhis** (*kév°*), mfn. having its own sacrificial straw, ŚBr. ii. — **brahmôpanishad**, f., N. of an Up. — **mānusha**, m. a mere man (and nothing else), MBh. xii. — **vātika**, mf(*ī*)n. applied for diseases of a simple rheumatic kind, Car. — **vaiyākaraṇa**, m. a mere grammarian (not versed in any other science). — **vyatirekin**, mfn. pertaining only to separateness, Tarkas. — **śas**, ind. completely, AitBr. vi, 9. **Kévalâgha**, mfn. alone guilty, RV. x, 117, 6. **Kevalâtman**, mfn. one whose nature is absolute unity, Kum. ii, 4. **Kevalâdin**, mfn. eating by one's self alone, RV. x, 117, 6. **Kevalâdvaita-vāda-kuliśa**, n., N. of a work. **Kevalânvayin**, mfn. pertaining only to connection, Tarkas.; °*yi-grantha*, m., -*rahasya*, n., -*vāda*, m., N. of works.

Kevalin, mfn. alone, one, only, W.; (*ī*), m. 'devoted to the doctrine of the absolute unity of spirit,' a meditative ascetic, BhP. iv, 25, 39; vi, 5, 40; 'possessing the *kevala*(-*jñāna*),' an Arhat, Jain.

केवाल *kevāla*, f. ī, g. *gaurâdi* (not in Kāś. & Gaṇar.) **Kevālī-√as**, -**√kṛi** [=√*hiṇs*, Gaṇar. 97, Sch.], -**√bhū**, g. *ūry-ādi*.

केवासी *kevāsī*, ind. only in comp. — **√as**, -**√kṛi** [=√*hiṇs*, Gaṇar. 73, Sch.], -**√bhū**, g. *ūry-ādi* (not in Kāś.)

केविका *kevikā*, f., N. of a flower (commonly *kevera*), L.

Kevī, f. id., L.

केवुक *kevuka* or °*vūka* = *kecuka*, q. v., Car.

केश 1. *késa*, *as*, m. (√*kliś*, Uṇ.; ifc. *ā* or *ī*, Pāṇ. iv, 1, 54) the hair of the head, AV.; VS.; ŚBr. &c.; the mane (of a horse or lion), MBh. i, 8008; Śak., Sch.; a kind of perfume (*hrīvera*), L.; N. of a mineral, VarBṛS. lxxvii, 23; N. of Varuṇa, L.; of Vishṇu, L.; of a Daitya, L.; of a locality, Romakas.; (pl.) the tail (of the Bos grunniens), Pāṇ. ii, 3, 36, Kāś. (v. l. *vāla*); (*ī*), f. a lock of hair on the crown of the head, L.; the Indigo plant, L.; Carpopogon pruriens, L.; another plant (*bhūta-keśī*), L.; N. of Durgā, L. — **karman**, n. dressing or arranging the hair of the head, MBh. iv, 78. — **karshaṇa**, n. pulling or tearing by the hair, Veṇis. — **kalâpa**, m. a mass or quantity of hair, head of hair, Kathās. lxx, 13. — **kāra**, m. (for *kośa-k°*) a sort of sugar-cane, Bhpr. — **kārin**, mfn. dressing or arranging the hair of the head, MBh. iv, 412. — **kīṭa**, m. a louse or insect in the hair, Mn.; Yājñ.; MBh. &c.; -*ṭāvapatita*, mfn. that on which a louse has fallen, MBh. xiii, 1577; (cf. *kīṭâvapanna*.) — **garbha**, m. =°*bhaka*, W.; N. of Varuṇa, W. — **garbhaka**, m. a braid of hair, L. — **gṛihīta**, mfn. pulled or seized by the hair. — **granthi**, m. a tie of hair, BhP. x, 39, 14. — **graha**, m. pulling the hair, Mn. iv, 83; Kathās. — **grahaṇa**, n. id., R. iii, 46, 2; Megh. — **grāham**, ind. so as to pull the hair, Pāṇ. iii, 4, 50, Kāś. — **ghna**, n. 'destroying the hair,' morbid baldness, falling of the hair, L. — **caṇa**, mfn. known by his hair, having fine hair, Pāṇ. v, 2, 26. — **cūḍa**, mfn. one who has dressed his hair in a top-knot, Pāṇ. ii, 2, 24, Vārtt. 13, Pat. — **caitya**, n., N. of a Caitya, W. — **cchid**, m. a hair-dresser, barber, L. — **jāha**, n. the root of the hair, g. *karṇâdi*. — **damanī**, f. 'destroying the hair,' Prosopis spicigera, Gal. — **dṛiṇhaṇa**, mf(*ī*)n. serving for fastening the hair, AV. vi, 21, 3. — **dhara**, *ās*, m. pl., N. of a people, VarBṛS. xiv, 26. — **dhāraṇa**, n. keeping, i.e. not cutting the hair, BhP. xii, 2, 6. — **dhāriṇī**, f., N. of a plant (the root of sweet flag), L. — **dhṛit**, m. id., L. — **paksha**, m. side of the hair, temple, ŚāṅkhGṛ. i, 28; ĀśvGṛ. i, 7, 16 & 17, 8; much or ornamented hair, tuft, MBh.; Prasannar. (ifc. f. *ā*). — **paṅkti**, f. a row or line or quantity of hair. — **parṇī**, f. Achyranthes aspera (*apâmârga*), L. — **pāśa**, m. much or ornamented hair, tuft, MBh.; Kum.; Vikr.; Ṛitus. (ifc. f. *ā*), &c.; (*ī*), f. a lock of hair hanging down from the top of the head, L. — **piṅgala**, m., N. of a Brāhman. — **pradharshaṇa**, n. = -*karshaṇa*, MBh. vii, 102, 21. — **prasāra**, m. cleaning the hair, BhP. x, 59, 45 & 61, 6. — **bandha**, m. a hair-band, MBh. iv, 190; BhP.; = -*vesha*, L.; a particular position of the hands in dancing. — **bhū**, f. 'hair-ground,' head, L. — **bhūmi**, f. the skull on which hair grows, Jain.; Suśr. — **maṇḍala**, n. a lock of hair, Kauś. — **mathanī**, f. = -*damanī*, L. — **mardana**, n. cleaning the hair (v. l. -*mārjana*, one of the 64 *kalās*), Comm. on BhP. x, 45, 36. — **mārjaka**, m. n. a comb, L. — **mārjana**, n., v. l. for -*mardana*; a comb, L. — **miśrá**, mf(*ā*)n. 'mingled with hair,' soiled by hair, ŚBr. ii, 2, 4, 5. — **mushṭi**, f. a handful of hair, W.; Melia Bukayun, Bhpr. i, 204; another plant (*visha-mushṭi*), L. — **mushṭika**, m. Melia Bukayun, L. — **yantrī**, f., N. of one of the mothers in Skanda's retinue, MBh. ix, 2635. — **racanā**, f. arranging or dressing the hair, Ṛitus. iv, 15. — **rañjana**, n. colouring the hair, ŚārṅgP.; (*as*), m. the vegetable Eclipta prostrata, L. — **rāja**, m. (= -*rañjana*) Eclipta prostrata, L.; Wedelia calendulacea, L. — **ruhā**, f. a species of the Croton plant (*bhadra-dantikā*), L. — **rūpā**, f. 'hair-shaped,' Vanda Roxburghii, L. — **romā**, f. Mucuna pruritus, Gal. — **luñcaka**, m. 'pulling the hair,' a Jain ascetic, Prab. — **luñcana**, m. id., Hcar.; (*am*), n. pulling the hair, Daś. — **vat** (*kéśa-*), mfn. (= *keśavá*, Pāṇ. v, 2, 109) having long hair, MārkP.; having a mane, RV. viii, 116, 5; (*tī*), f., N. of a river. — **vapana**, n. shaving or cutting the hair, ĀśvGṛ. — °**vapanīya**, m. 'hair-cutting or -shaving,' N. of a festival (belonging to the Rāja-sūya), ŚBr. v; TāṇḍyaBr. xviii; KātyŚr.; Lāṭy.; ŚāṅkhŚr. — **várdhana**, mf(*ī*)n. causing the hair to grow, AV. vi, 21, 3 & 137, 1; (*ī*), f. Sida rhomboides, L. — **vesha**, m. (Pāṇ. iv, 1, 42) a tress of hair, ĀśvGṛ. — **veshṭa**, m. the parting of the hair, APrāt. iii, 43, Sch. — **vyaparopaṇa**, n. pulling the hair, Ragh. iii, 56. — **vyudāharaṇa**, n., N. of a work. — **śūla**, n. disease of the hair, MBh. iii, 12846. — **śmaśrú**, n. (gaṇa *rājadantâdi*) the hair of the head and the beard, AV. viii, 2, 17; ŚBr.; KātyŚr.; (*ūṇi*), n. pl. id., ŚāṅkhŚr. — **stuka**, m. a lock of hair, Kauś. 42. — **hantṛi-phalā**, f. 'having fruits that destroy the hair,' = -*damanī*, Npr. — **hantrī**, f. id., L. — **hasta**, m. much or ornamented hair, tuft, MBh. iii, 1822; Śiś. viii, 27; Veṇīs. (quoted in Sāh.); the hair for a hand, Śiś. viii, 27. — **hṛit-phalā**, f. = -*hantṛi-ph°*, Npr. **Keśā-keśi**, ind. (Kāś. on Pāṇ. ii, 2, 27; v, 4, 127 & vi, 3, 137; Gaṇar. 95, Sch.) hair to hair, head to head, Yājñ. ii, 283; MBh. **Keśâgra**, n. the top of a hair, ŚāṅkhGṛ. **Keśâda**, m. 'eating the hair,' N. of a parasitical insect, Car.; Suśr. **Keśânta**, m. (ifc. f. *ā*) the border of the hair on the forehead, ŚāṅkhGṛ.; TUp.; R.; Suśr.; long hair hanging down, lock of hair, tuft, MBh.; R. &c.; cutting off the hair finally (as a religious ceremony performed upon Brāhmans at 16 years of age, Kshatriyas at 22, and Vaiśyas at 24), PārGṛ.; Gobh.; Mn. ii, 65; Yājñ. i, 36; -*karaṇa*, n. id., Gobh. iii, 1, 2. **Keśântika**, mfn. extending to the end of the hair as far as the forehead, Mn. ii, 46; relating to the ceremony of final tonsure, W. **Keśâpahā**, f. =°*śa-damanī*, Npr. **Keśâmbu**, n. Pavonia odorata, Bhpr. **Keśâri**, m. 'enemy of the hair,' Mesua Ferrea, L. **Keśâruhā**, f. =°*śa-vardhanī*, L. **Keśârhā**, f., N. of a plant (*mahā-nīlī*), L. **Keśâli**, m. 'row of hair,' Eclipta prostrata (*keśa-rañjana*), Npr. **Keśâvamarshaṇa**, n. pulling the hair, especially amorously playing with it or rubbing it &c., W. **Keśôccaya**, m. much or handsome hair, W. **Keśôṇḍuka**, m. a sling or knot of hair, Suśr.; net-like apparitions seen while the eyes are shut, AitĀr. (ed. °*ṇḍraka*). **Keśôṇḍraka**, see °*ṇḍuka*.

Keśaka, mfn. bestowing care upon the hair, Pāṇ. v, 2, 66, Kāś.

Keśara, &c. See *késara*.

Keśavá, mfn. (Pāṇ. v, 2, 109) having long or much or handsome hair, AV. viii, 6, 23; ŚBr.; KātyŚr.; (*as*), m., N. of Vishṇu or Kṛishṇa, MBh.; Hariv.; R. &c.; (hence) of the month Mārgaśīrsha, VarBṛS. cv, 14; Rottleria tinctoria, L.; N. of the author of a lexicon called Kalpa-dru; of the author of the Dvaita-pariśishṭa; of the father of Govinda and Rucikara; of the father of Brāhma and uncle of Maheśvara; of the son of Viśva-dhara and brother of Kari-nātha; of the father of Vopa-deva. — **jātaka-paddhaty-udāharaṇa**, n. a Comm. by Viśva-nātha on the work Jātaka-paddhati. — **jī-nanda-śarman**, m., N. of an author. — **dāsa**, m., N. of several authors. — **dīkshita**, m., N. of a man. — **daivajña**, m., N. of an astronomer. — **prabhu**, m., N. of a man. — **bhakti**, f. devotion to Kṛishṇa, W. — **bhaṭṭa**, m., N. of a man. — **miśra**, m., N. of the author of the Dvaita-pariśishṭa and of the Chandoga-pariśishṭa. — **śikshā**, f., N. of a Śikshā. — **śreshṭhin**, m., N. of a merchant. — **svāmin**, m., N. of a grammarian, Śūdradh. **Keśavâcārya**, m., N. of a teacher. **Keśavâditya**, m. a form of the sun, SkandaP. **Keśavâyudha**, m. 'Kṛishṇa's weapon,' the Mango tree, L. **Keśavârka**, m. =°*vâditya*, SkandaP.; N. of the author of the Kṛishṇa-krīḍita (son of Jayâditya and grandson of Rāṇiga); N. of the author of the Jātaka-paddhati; of the author of the Vivāha-vṛindāvana. **Keśavâlaya**, m. 'Keśava's abode,' the holy fig-tree, L. **Keśavâvāsa**, m. id., L.

1. **Keśi**, *is*, m. (=°*śin*), N. of an Asura, Hariv.

2. **Keśi** (in comp. for *keśin*). — **gṛihapati** (°*śi*-), m. 'whose householder is Keśin (Dārbhya),' belonging to Keśin's family, ŚBr. xi, 8, 4, 1. — **tīrtha**, n., N. of a Tīrtha. — **dhvaja**, m., N. of a prince (son of Kṛita-dhvaja), BhP. ix, 13, 20. — **nishūdana**, m. 'slayer of the Asura Keśin,' Kṛishṇa, Bhag. xviii, 1 (v. l. -*nisūd°*). — **mathana**, m. id., Gīt. ii, 11. — **sūdana**, m. id., MBh. ii, 1214. — **han**, m. id., MBh.; Hariv. — **hantṛi**, m. id., MBh. ii, 1402.

Keśika, mfn. having fine or luxuriant hair, Pāṇ. v, 2, 109; (*as*), m. the plant Asparagus racemosus, L.; (*ī*), f., N. of the mother of Jahnu, VP.

Keśin, mfn. (Pāṇ. v, 2, 109) having fine or long hair (said of Rudra [cf. *kapardin*], of his female attendants, of female demons, and of men), AV. xi, 2, 18 (cf. RV. x, 136, 1 ff.) & 31; xii, 5, 48; xiv, 2, 59; having a mane (as Indra's and Agni's horses), RV.; having tips (as rays or flames), RV. i, 140, 8 & 151, 6; (*ī*), m., 'N. of Rudra' (see before); of Vishṇu, L.; 'a horse' (see before); a lion, L.; N. of an Asura slain by Kṛishṇa, MBh.; Hariv. &c.; of a son of Vasu-deva and Kauśalyā, BhP. ix, 24, 47; (Pāṇ. vi, 4, 165) N. of Dārbhya or Dālbhya; (*inī*), f., N. of Durgā; (gaṇa *kurv-ādi*) N. of an Apsaras, MBh. i, 2558; iii, 14562; of a Rākshasī, Buddh.; of the daughter of the king of Vidarbha (wife of Sagara and mother of A-samañjas), Hariv. 797 ff.; R.; of the wife of Ājamīḍha (Suhotra) and mother of Jahnu, MBh. i, 3722; Hariv. 1416 & 1756; of the wife of Viśravas and mother of Rāvaṇa and Kumbha-karṇa, BhP. vii, 1, 43; of a servant of Damayantī, Nal. xxii, 1; of the daughter of a Brāhman, Buddh.: Chrysopogon aciculatus, L.; Nardostachys Jaṭā-māṇsī, L.; (*inī*), f., see *kaiśinā*; (*inīs*), Ved. f. pl. 'the attendants of Rudra' (see before); 'N. of certain female demons' (see before).

Késya, mfn. being in the hair, AV. xiv, 2, 68; suitable to the hair, Suśr.; (*as*), m. (=°*śa-rañjana*) Eclipta prostrata, L.; (*am*), n. black Aloe wood, L.

केश 2. *késa*, *am*, n. 'whose lord is Prajā-pati (see 3. *ká*),' the lunar mansion Rohiṇī.

केशट *keśaṭa*, mfn. 'richly endowed with,' see *madhu-*; (*as*), m. a goat, L.; a louse, L.; Bignonia Indica, L.; the parching arrow of Kāma (the god of love), L.; a brother (cf. *mātṛi-*), L.; N. of Vishṇu, L.; N. of a man, Kathās. cxxiii, 157.

केशव *keśavá*, °*śi*, &c. See 1. *késa*.

केसर *késara*, *am*, n. the hair (of the brow), VS. xix, 91; (in classical literature usually *kesara*), m. or n. (?), the mane (of a horse or lion), R.; Śak.; Pañcat. &c.; (*ā*), f. id., KātyŚr. (*kes°*); (*am*), n. the tail of the Bos grunniens (used as a fan for driving away flies), L.; (*as*, L.; *am*), m. n. the filament of a lotus or of any vegetable, R.; Suśr.; Śak. &c.; a fibre (as of a Mango fruit), Suśr.; (*as*), m. the plants

Rottleria tinctoria, Mimusops Elengi, and Mesua ferrea, MBh. xiii, 5042; R.; Lalit.; Kum.; Megh.; (*am*), n. the flower of those plants, L.; (*as, ā, am*), m. f. n. Asa fœtida, L.; (*am*), n. gold, L.; sulphate of iron, L.; N. of a metre (of 4 × 18 syllables); (*as*), m., N. of a mountain, MBh. vi, 11, 23; [cf. Lat. *cæsaries;* Angl. Sax. *haer;* Engl. *hair;* Germ. *Haar.*] **–grāma**, m., N. of a village, Kshitîś. **–pura**, n., N. of a town, Vāsant. **–prābandhā** (*kéś°*), f., N. of a woman, AV. v, 18, 11. **–mālā**, f., N. of a work. **–vat** (*kéś°*), mfn. having a mane, ŚBr. vi. **–vara**, n. saffron, L. **Keśarâgra**, n. the tips of a mane, Hit. **Keśarâcala**, *ās*, m. pl. 'the filament mountains,' N. of the mountains situated round Meru (which is called 'the seed-vessel of the earth;' see *karṇikâcala*), BhP. v, 17, 6. **Keśarâpīḍa**, m., N. of an art (*kalā*), Gal. **Keśarâmla**, m. the citron tree, L. **Keśarôccaṭā**, f. a variety of Cyperus, L.

Kesarāla, mfn. rich in filaments, Vām. v, 2, 34.

Keśari, *is*, m. (= °*rin*), N. of the father of Hanumat, R. iv, 33, 14; vi; vii, 40, 7.

Keśarikā, f. = *keśa-vardhanī*, L.; a clout for cleaning vessels, HPariś. i, 249.

Keśarin or **kesarin**, mfn. having a mane, MBh. i, iii; (*ī*), m. a lion, MBh.; Suśr.; Bhartṛ. &c.; a horse, TBr., Sch.; N. of an aquatic bird, Car. i, 27; the plant Rottleria tinctoria, L.; the plant Mesua ferrea, L.; a citron tree, L.; a variety of Moringa with red flowers (= *rakta-śigru*), L.; N. of a monkey (husband of the mother of Hanumat), MBh. iii, 11193; R.; Daś.; N. of a prince, Lalit.; of a mountain, VP.; (*iṇī*), f. a lioness, Kathās. lxx, 102. **Kesari-suta**, m. 'son of Kesarin,' N. of Hanumat, L.

केसारुका *kesārukā* (or *keśār°*), f. for *kaśer°*, the back-bone, L., Sch.

केह्लदेव *kehla-deva, as,* m., N. of a man.

कै *kai*, cl. 1. P. *kāyati*, to sound, Dhātup. xxii, 19.

कैंशुक *kaiṃśuka*, mfn. belonging to or coming from a Kiṃśuka tree (or Butea frondosa), Suśr.

कैकय *kaikaya, as,* m. the king of the Kekayas, BhP. ix, 24, 37; (*ās*), m. pl. the sons of that king, ib.; (= *kek°*) the Kekayas, MBh.; Hariv. &c.; (*ī*), f. the daughter of a king of the Kekayas, R.

Kaikeya, *as*, m. (Pāṇ. vii, 3, 2) 'a descendant of Kekaya,' prince of the Kekayas, ŚBr. x; ChUp.; N. of a son of Śivi (from whom the Kaikeyas are derived), Hariv. 1680; BhP. ix, 23, 3; N. of Dhṛishṭaketu (king of the Kaikeyas and father of the five Kaikeyas), VP.; (*ās*), m. pl. the Kekayas, R.; (*ī*), f. the daughter of a prince of the Kekayas (one of the wives of Daśa-ratha and mother of Bharata, R.; Ragh.), MBh.; Daś.; (*am*), n. the language of the Kekayas.

कैकस *kaikasa, as,* m. patr. fr. *kīkasa*, gaṇa *śārṅgaravâdi*; (*ī*), f., N. of a daughter of the Rikshasa Sumālin, R. vii, 5, 40 & 9, 7.

कैकेय *kaikeya.* See °*kaya.*

कैंकरायण *kaiṃkarayaṇa, as,* m. patr. fr. *kiṃkara*, gaṇa 1. *naḍâdi*.

Kaiṃkarya, *am*, n. the office of a servant, servitude, BhP. iii, 2, 22.

कैंकलायन *kaiṃkalāyana, as,* m. patr. fr. *kiṃkala*, gaṇa 1. *naḍâdi*.

कैंकिरात *kaiṃkirāta*, mfn. coming from the tree *kiṃ-kirāta* (or Jonesia Aśoka), Ratnâv.

कैच्छिकिल *kaicchikila, ās,* m. pl., N. of a people, VP.; (cf. *kailik°*.)

कैजव *kaijava, as,* m., N. of a teacher (for *kaitava*?), VāyuP.

कैट *kaiṭa*, mfn. (fr. *kīṭa*), coming from an insect, Suśr.

कैटभ *kaiṭabha, as,* m., N. of an Asura (slain by Vishṇu), MBh. iii; Hariv.; Suśr.; BhP.; BrahmavP. &c.; (*ā* or *ī*), f., N. of Durgā, L.; (*am*), n., N. of a class of writings, Divyâv. xxxiii (Pāli *keṭubha*); VarYogay. **–jit**, m. 'conqueror of the Asura Kaiṭabha,' N. of Vishṇu, Śiś. ix, 30. **–dvish**, m. 'enemy of Kaiṭabha,' id., i, 23. **–bhid**, m. 'slayer of Kaiṭabha,' id., Ānand. **–han**, m. id., L. **Kaiṭabhâri**, m. = °*bha-dvish*, Kād. **Kaiṭabhârdana**, m. = °*bha-jit*, BhP. iii, 24, 18. **Kaiṭabhêśvara-lakshaṇa**, n. (= *kaiṭabha*, n.), N. of a class of writings, Lalit. **Kaiṭabhêśvarī**, f. = °*bhī*, DevīP.

कैटर्य *kaiṭarya*, m., N. of a medicinal plant (Azadirachta indica, L.; Melia Bukayun, L.; Vangueria spinosa, L.; Myrica sapida, Comm. on Car. i, 4), Suśr.

Kaiḍarya, *as*, m., N. of a plant (Cardiospermum Halicacabum, L.; Myrica sapida, L.), Car. vi, 15.

कैतक *kaitaka*, mfn. (fr. *ket°*), coming from the tree Pandanus odoratissimus, Ragh. iv, 55; (*am*), n. the flower of that tree, L.

कैतव *kaitava*, mf(*ī*)n. (fr. *kit°*), deceitful, Hariv. 7095; (*as*), m. patr. of Ulūka, MBh. i, 7002; (*ī*), f. fraud, deceit, Bālar.; (*am*), n. the stake in a game, MBh. ii, 2163; Nal. xxvi, 10; gambling, L.; deceit, fraud, cheating, roguery, R. v, 86, 19; Kum.; Bhartṛ. &c.; beryl, L. **–prayoga**, m. a trick, device. **–vāda**, m. falsehood, evasion, Gīt. viii, 2. **Kaitavâpahnuti**, f. a kind of rhetorical figure, Comm. on Vāsav.

Kaitavaka, *am*, n. a trick in gambling, MBh. ii, 2060.

Kaitavāyana, m. patr. fr. *kitava*, g. *aśvâdi*.

Kaitavāyani, *is*, m. id., gaṇa *tikâdi*.

Kaitaveya, *as*, m. patr. of Ulūka, Hariv. 5019 & 5500.

Kaitavya, *as*, m. id., MBh. v, 5412; 5535 & 5579.

कैतायन *kaitāyana, as,* m. patr. fr. *kita*, gaṇa *aśvâdi*.

Kaiti-putra, *as*, m., N. of a teacher, VāyuP.

कैदर्भ *kaidarbha, as,* m. a patr. fr. *kid°*, gaṇa *bidâdi* (Kāś.)

कैदार *kaidāra*, mfn. being on or growing in a *kedāra* field, Suśr.; (*as*), m. rice, L.; (*am*), n. a multitude of *kedāra* fields, Comm. on L.

Kaidāraka, *am*, n. a multitude of *kedāra* fields, Pāṇ. iv, 2, 40 f.

Kaidārika, *am*, n. id., ib; Śiś. xii, 42.

Kaidārya, *am*, n. id., Pāṇ. iv, 2, 40 f.

कैंदर्भ *kaiṃdarbha*, v. l. for *kaid°*, q. v.

कैंदास *kaiṃdāsa, as,* m. patr. fr. *kiṃ-dāsa*, gaṇa *bidâdi*.

Kaiṃdāsāyana, *as*, m. patr. fr. °*dāsa*, gaṇa *haritâdi*.

कैंनर *kaiṃnara*, mfn. coming from Kiṃnara, gaṇa *takshaśilâdi*.

कैमर्थक्य *kaimarthakya, am,* n. asking the reason (*kim-artham*, 'why?'), Pat. on Pāṇ. iii, 1, 46, Vārtt. 1 & 2, 127, Vārtt. 1; Bādar. i, 3, 33, Sch.

Kaimarthya, *am*, n. id., Pāṇ. i, 4, 3, Pat. (°*thakya*, ed. K.); Pratāpar.; Kāvyâd. ii, 123, Sch.

Kaimāyani, *is*, m. patr. fr. *kim*, Pat. on Pāṇ. iv, 1, 93, Vārtt. 13.

Kaimutika, mfn. relating to or based on the 'how much more?' or 'how much less? (*kim uta*),' only in comp. **-nyāya**, m. the rule of 'how much more?' or 'how much less?' arguing a fortiori, Kuval.; Saṃskārak.; Comm. on Kir. vii, 27 & BhP. x, 33, 30.

Kaimutya, *am*, n. the relation of 'how much more?' or 'how much less?' Kuval. **–nyāya**, m. = °*tika-ny°* (q. v.), Pratāpar.; Comm. on BhP.

कैयट *kaiyaṭa, as,* m., N. of a son of Jaiyaṭa (author of a Comm. on Pat.)

Kaiyyaṭa, *as*, m. id.

कैरणक *kairaṇaka*, fr. *kiraṇa*, gaṇa *arīhaṇâdi*.

कैरली *kairalī*, f. (fr. *kerala*), the plant Embelia Ribes, L.; (cf. *kairāla*.)

Kairaleya, *as*, m. a king of the Keralas, Hariv. 5501.

कैरव *kairava, as,* m. a gambler, cheat, L.; an enemy, L.; for *kaur°*, Hariv. 5020; (*ī*), f. moonlight, L.; Trigonella fœnum græcum, L.; (*am*), n. (gaṇa *pushkarâdi*) the white lotus-flower (blossoming at night), MBh. i, 86; Bhartṛ.; Kathās. &c. **–korakīya**, Nom. P. °*yati*, to resemble a lotus bud, ŚārṅgP. **–bandhu**, m. 'friend of the lotus-flower,' N. of the moon, L.

Kairavin, *ī*, m. the moon, L.; (*iṇī*), f. the white water-lily or lotus, Bhām.; (gaṇa *pushkarâdi*) a place or pond abounding in water-lilies, assemblage of lotuses, L. **Kairaviṇī-khaṇḍa**, n. a multitude of spots filled with water-lilies, g. *kamalâdi* (Kāś.)

कैराटक *kairāṭaka, as,* m. a species of vegetable poison, L.

कैरात *kairāta*, mfn. relating to or belonging to the Kirātas, MBh.; Kathās.; (*as*), m. a prince of the Kirātas, MBh. ii, 1869; N. of a serpent, AV. v, 13, 5; of a bird (belonging to the class called Pratuda), Car. i, 27; a strong man, L.; (*am*), n. the plant Agathotes Chirayta, L.; a kind of sandal wood, L. **–saras**, n., N. of a lake or pond, SkandaP.

Kairātaka, mfn. belonging to the Kirātas, AV. x, 4, 14 (f. °*tikā*); MBh. ii, 1867 (f. °*takī*).

कैराल *kairāla, am,* n. Embelia Ribes (used as a remedy for worms), L.; (*ī*), f. id.; (cf. *kairalī*.)

कैरिशि *kairiśi, is,* m. (fr. *kiriśa*), patr. of Sutvan, AitBr. viii, 28, 18.

कैर्मेदुर *kairmedura*, v. l. for *kaumed°*.

कैल *kaila, as,* m. patr., Pravar.; (*am*), n. (fr. *keli*), sport, pleasure, W.

कैलकिल *kailakila*, v. l. for *kailik°*.

कैलात *kailāta, as,* m. patr. fr. *kil°*, gaṇa *bidâdi*.

Kailātaka, mfn. (for °*lālaka*?, fr. *kilāla*)?, n. with *madhu*, honey, MBh. vii, 4353.

कैलावत *kailāvata, ās,* m. pl., N. of a people, VarBṛS. xiv, 26.

कैलास *kailāsa, as,* m., N. of a mountain (fabulous residence of Kubera and paradise of Śiva; placed in the Himālaya range and regarded as one of the loftiest peaks to the north of the Mānasa lake), MBh. iii, 503 & 1697; Hariv.; R. iii, iv, 44, 27; VarBṛS. &c.; a particular form of temple, VarBṛS. **–nātha**, m. 'sovereign of the Kailāsa mountain,' N. of Kubera, Vikr.; Ragh. v, 28. **–niketana**, m. 'having his abode on the Kailāsa,' N. of Śiva, L. **–paṇḍita**, m., N. of a copyist. **–pati**, m. 'lord of the Kailāsa,' N. of Śiva, L. **–śikhara-vāsin**, m. 'dwelling on the summit of the Kailāsa,' N. of Śiva. **Kailāsaukas**, m. 'having his abode on the Kailāsa,' N. of Kubera, L.

कैलिकिल *kailikila, ās,* m. pl., N. of a people (perhaps a Yavana tribe; v. l. *kailak°*), VP.

कैलिञ्ज *kailiñja*, mf(*ī*)n. made of a thin plank (*kiliñja*), Suśr.

कैवर्त *kaivarta, as,* m. (cf. *kev°*) a fisherman (born of a prostitute by a Kshatriya or of an Āyogava female by a Nishāda father), Mn. viii, 260; x, 34; MBh.; R. &c.; (*ī*), f. the wife of a fisherman, L.; the grass Cyperus rotundus, L. **–musta**, n. the grass Cyperus rotundus, L.; (*ā*), f. id., Bhpr. **–mustaka**, n. id., Comm. on Car. i, 3. **Kaivarti-mustaka**, n. id., L.

Kaivartaka, *as*, m. a fisherman, R. ii, 83, 15; Kathās. cxii, 113; (*ikā*), f., N. of a plant, L.

Kaivarti-mustaka, *am*, n. = °*rtī-m°* above, L.

Kaivartīya, mfn. relating to a fisherman (as a tale), Kathās. cxii, 111.

कैवल *kaivala, am,* n. = *kairāla*, L.

कैवल्य *kaivalya, am,* n. (fr. *kévala*), isolation, Vām.; absolute unity, Vedāntas.; BhP.; perfect isolation, abstraction, detachment from all other connections, detachment of the soul from matter or further transmigrations, beatitude, MBh.; KapS.; Sāṃkhyak. &c.; for *vaikalya*, Rājat. vii, 1149; (mf(*ā*)n.) leading to eternal happiness or emancipation, MBh. xiii, 1101. **–kalpa-druma**, m., N. of a Comm. **–tantra**, n., N. of a Tantra. **–dīpikā**, f., N. of a Comm. by Hemādri. **Kaivalyânanda**, m., N. of a teacher. **Kaivalyâśrama**, m., N. of a pupil of Govinda (author of a Comm. on Anand.) **Kaivalyêndra**, m., N. of the instructor of Rāyanendra. **Kaivalyôpanishad**, f., N. of an Up.

कैशव *kaiśava*, mf(*ī*)n. (fr. *keś°*), relating or belonging to Kṛishṇa, Hariv. 15377; Ragh. xvii, 29.

Kaiśika, mf(*ī*)n. (fr. *keśa*), hair-like, fine as a hair, Suśr.; (*as*), m. (in music) N. of a Rāga; love, passion, lust, L.; N. of a prince (son of Vidarbha and brother of Kratha); of several men, Hariv.; VP.; (*ās*), m. pl., N. of a subdivision of the Yādavas (descended from Kaiśika), MBh. ii, 585; Ragh.; Mālav.; (*ī*), f. (scil. *vritti*) one of the four varieties of dramatic style (graceful style, suited especially to the passion of love), Bhar. xx, 45 ff.; Daśar. ii, 44; Pratāpar.; Sāh. (v. l. *kauśikī*); N. of a locality or of a river, MBh. iii, 10095; for *kauśikī* (N. of Durgā), L.; (*am*), n. the whole mass of hair, head of hair, Pāṇ. iv, 2, 48.

Kaiśiná, mf(*ī*)n. (Pāṇ. vi, 4, 165) taught by Keśin Dārbhya, ŚāṅkhBr. vii, 4 (°*nī dīkshā*, also *keś*° *d*°, N. of a number of Mantras, ĀpŚr. x, 10, 6); descended from Keśin, Kāṭh. xxvi, 9; ŚBr. xi, 8, 4, 6.

Kaiśinya, *as*, m. metron. fr. *keśinī*, g. *kurv-ādi*.

Kaiśya, *am*, n. (Pāṇ. iv, 2, 48) the whole mass of hair, head of hair, Naish. iv, 114.

कैशोर *kaiśora*, *am*, n. (fr. *kiś*°; Pāṇ. v, 1, 129, Kāś.), youth, boyhood (from the age of ten to that of fifteen), BhP. iii, 28, 17; (ifc.) iv, 25, 24 & x, 45, 3. **–vayas**, mfn. having the age of a youth, ix, 2, 15.

Kaiśoraka, mf(*ikā*)n. youthful, Bhpr. iv, 226; (*am*), n. the youths and girls, Hariv. 4081. **–guggulu**, n. a kind of elixir, ŚārṅgS. ii, 7, 17.

Kaiśori, *is*, m. patr., gaṇa *kurv-ādi*.

Kaiśorikeya, *as*, m. metron. fr. *kiśorikā*, gaṇa *śubhrâdi*.

Kaiśorya, *as*, m. (gaṇa *kurv-ādi*) patr. fr. *kaiśori*, N. of Kāpya, ŚBr. xiv, 5, 5, 22 & 7, 3, 28.

कैश्य *kaiśya*. See above.

कैष्किन्ध *kaishkindha*, mfn. coming from Kishkindhā, gaṇa *sindhv-ādi*.

को *ko*, ind. Oh no! (?), Divyâv. iv; a prefix in *ko-jāgara*, *ko-mala*, *ko-vida*, &c., related to 1. *ku*; (cf. the prefixes *ka*, *kava*, *kā*, *kim*, *ku*.)

कोक *kóka*, *as*, m. (onomat.) a wolf, R. iii, 52, 45; v, 26, 9; 'a cuckoo,' see *-yātu* below; the ruddy goose, MBh. xiii, 1816; VarBṛS. xii, lxxxvi; Git.; Sāh.; a frog, L.; a small house-lizard, L.; a kind of noxious parasitical animal, AV. v, 23, 4; viii, 6, 2; the wild date tree, L.; N. of Vishṇu, L.; of an attendant in Skanda's retinue, MBh. ix, 2562 (?); of a son of Śoṇa, ŚBr. xiii; (*ā*), f., N. of a river (v. l. for *kośā*), VP.; of a locality (= *kokâmukha*), VārP.; (*ī*), f. the female of the ruddy goose, Kuval. **–deva**, m. a pigeon, L.; N. of an author. **–nakha**, *ās*, m. pl., N. of a people (v. l. for *koka-baka*, q. v.) **–nada**, *ās*, m. pl., N. of a people, MBh. ii, 1026; (*as*), m., N. of an attendant in Skanda's retinue, MBh. ix, 2562 f. & 2576; (*am*), n. the flower of the red water-lily, MBh.; Śiś. iv, 46; Git. x, 5; *-cchavi*, m. the colour of the red lotus, L.; (mfn.) of the colour of the red lotus, L. **–nadaya**, Nom. P. °*yati*, to take for a red lotus, Bhām. **–nadinī**, f. the red water-lily, Kathās. xxx, 78. **–pitṛi**, m. 'father of Koka' or 'whose father is named Koka,' N. of a man, ŚBr. xiii, 5, 4, 17. **–baka**, *ās*, m. pl., N. of a people, MBh. vi, 369 (vv. ll. *-nakha* and *kokaraka*). **–bandhu**, m. 'friend of the ruddy goose,' the sun, L. **–mukha**, mf(*ā*)n. wolf-faced (Durgā), MBh. vi, 800. **–yātu** (*kóka-*), m. a ghost in the shape of a cuckoo, RV. vii, 104, 22. **–vāca**, m. = *kokaḍa*, L. **–śāstra**, n., N. of an indecent treatise on the art of love (ascribed to a Paṇḍit named Koka). **Kokâksha**, m. 'wolf-eyed,' see *kaukâksha*. **Kokâgra**, m., N. of a shrub (*samashṭhila*), L. **Kokâmukha**, n., N. of a Tīrtha, MBh. iii, 8136; xiii, 1738; Hariv.; VārP.

Kokaḍa, *as*, m. the Indian fox, L.

Koko-vāca, *as*, m. (= *koka-v*°), id., Npr.

कोकथु *kokathu*, *us*, m. the wood-pigeon, Gal.; (cf. °*ka-deva*.)

कोकनद *koka-nada*, &c. See *kóka*.

कोकरक *kokaraka*. See *koka-baka*.

कोकलिक *kokalika*, *as*, m., N. of a man, Buddh.

Kokalī, f., N. of a woman, ib.

कोकामुख *kokā-mukha*. See *kóka*.

कोकाह *kokāha*, *as*, m. a white horse, L.

कोकिल *kokila*, *as*, m. (onomat.; √*kuk*, Uṇ.) the Kokila or Koïl (black or Indian cuckoo; frequently alluded to in Hindū poetry, its musical cry being supposed to inspire tender emotions), MBh.; R. &c.; a kind of mouse, Suśr.; Ashṭâṅg.; a kind of snake, Gal.; a kind of venomous insect, Suśr.; a kind of sugar-cane (cf. °*lêkshu*), Gal.; a lighted coal, L.; N. of an author, Bhojapr.; Śūdradh.; of a Rāja-putra (considered as a Ṛishi), KāṭhAnukr.; of a mouse, MBh. v, 5444; (*ā*), f. (g. *ajâdi*) the female of a Kokila, Kum.; Ragh.; Bhartṛ. **–nayana**, m. 'having eyes like those of the Koïl,' a plant bearing a dark black flower (Capparis spinosa or Asteracantha longifolia or Barleria longifolia), L. **–priya**, m. 'dear to the Kokila,' (in music) a kind of measure. **–maitrāvaruṇa**, n. 'relating to the duties or office of the Maitrāvaruṇa priest at the Kaukila ceremony,' N. of a treatise. **–smṛiti**, f., N. of a similar treatise. **–hotra**, n. 'relating to the duties or office of the Hotṛi priest at the Kaukila ceremony,' N. of a treatise. **Kokilâksha**, m. = °*lanayana*, Hcar. **Kokilâkshaka**, m. id., L. **Kokilâbhivyāhārin**, mfn. speaking like the Koïl, Pān. vi, 2, 80, Kāś. **Kokilâvāsa**, m. 'abode of the Koïl,' the mango tree, L. **Kokilêkshu**, m. the black variety of sugar-cane (cf. *krishṇêkshu*), L. **Kokilêshṭā**, f. 'dear to the Koïl,' a kind of Jambū tree, L. **Kokilôtsava**, m. 'a festival to the Koïl,' = °*lâvāsa*, L.

Kokilaka, *as*, m. the Indian cuckoo; N. of an attendant in Skanda's retinue, MBh. ix, 2575; (*am*), n. a metre (of 4 × 17 syllables).

Kokilā (f. of *kokila*, q. v.) **–devī**, f., N. of a goddess. **–māhātmya**, n., N. of a section of the SkandaP. **–rahasya**, n., N. of a work. **–vrata**, n., N. of an observance.

कोकोवाच *koko-vāca*. See *kóka*.

कोक्कट *kokkaṭa* = *koṅk*°, q. v.

कोक्कोक *kokkvoka*, *as*, m., N. of the author of the Rati-rahasya, Mallin.

कोङ्क *koṅka*, *ās*, m. pl., N. of a people, BhP. v, 6, 8 & 10; (cf. *kauṅka*.)

कोङ्कट *koṅkaṭa*, *as*, m., N. of a scholiast on the Amara-kośa (v. l. *kokk*°).

कोङ्कण *koṅkaṇa*, *ās*, m. pl., N. of a people on the western shore of the Dekhan, MBh. vi, 9, 60; VarBṛS. xiv, 12; Daś.; Rājat. iv, 159; (*ā*), f. a Koṅkaṇa woman, W.; N. of the mother of Paraśu-Rāma, L.; (*am*), n. a kind of weapon, L.

Koṅkaṇaka, *ās*, m. pl. (= °*ṇa*), N. of a people on the western shore of the Dekhan, Hariv. 784.

Koṅkaṇā (f. of °*ṇa*, q. v.) **–vatī**, f., N. of a river, Hariv. 9510. **–suta**, m. 'son of Koṅkaṇā,' N. of Paraśu-Rāma, L.

Koṅkāṇa, mf(*ī*)n. coming from Koṅkaṇa (as a horse; cf. *kauṅkaṇôdbhūta*), Kathās. cxxi, 278.

कोंकार *koṃ-kāra*, *as*, m. the sound *kom*, Pañcat.

कोङ्गि *koṅgi*, a kind of weapon, Gal.

कोच *koca*, *as*, m. (gaṇa *jvalâdi*) drying up, desiccation, Suśr.; a man of mixed caste (offspring of a fisherman by a female of the butcher tribe), BrahmavP. (v. l. *koñca*.)

कोजागर *ko-jāgara*, *as*, m. a kind of festival (night of full moon in month Āśvina [September–October], celebrated with various games; accord. to some fr. *kaḥ* and *jāgara*, 'who is awake?' the exclamation of Lakshmī, who descending on this night, promised wealth to all that were awake; hence the night is spent in festivity in honour of the goddess), LiṅgaP. **–māhātmya**, n., N. of a work.

कोञ्च *koñca*, v. l. for *koca*, q. v.

कोञ्ज *koñja*, *as*, m. = *kauñca*, q. v., L., Sch.

कोट *koṭa*, *as*, m. (gaṇa *aśmâdi*) a fort, stronghold (cf. *koṭṭa*), Vāstuv. xi, 28; a shed, hut, L. (cf. *kuṭī*); curvature (fr. √*kuṭ*), W.; a beard, L.; a kind of diagram (?); (*ā*), f., Pāṇ. iii, 1, 17, Pat.; cf. *a-*, *amara-*, *devī-*. **–cakra**, n. a kind of diagram. **–pa**, m. 'guarding the fort,' a kind of official man, Gal.; *-rāja*, m., N. of a prince, Vātsyāy. v, 5, 25. **–pāla**, m. 'guarding the fort,' the tutelar deity of a fort, Vāstuv. xi, 23 & 53; see also *koṭṭa-p*°. **–yuddha-nirṇaya**, m. 'disquisition on fighting from strongholds,' N. of a work. **–śiras**, n. the parapet of a wall, Gal. **Koṭâdri**, m., N. of a mountain, Rājat. iv, 5.

Koṭaka, *as*, m. curving, bending, W.; (*as*), m. a builder of sheds or huts, thatcher, carpenter (man of mixed caste, son of a mason and of the daughter of a potter), BrahmavP.

Koṭana, *as*, m. winter, L.

Koṭara [*as*, m., L.], *am*, n. (Pāṇ. vi, 3, 117; viii, 4, 4; gaṇa *aśmâdi*) the hollow of a tree, MBh.; Śak.; Mālav. &c.; cave, cavity, BhP. x; MārkP.; Rājat. v, 439; ŚārṅgP.; Alangium decapetalum, L.; N. of a man; (*ā*), f. Ipomœa Turpethum, Car. vii, 7; N. of one of the mothers in Skanda's retinue, MBh. ix, (2632 &) 2635; of the mother of Bāṇa, BhP. x, 63, 20; (*ī*), f. a naked woman, L.; N. of Durgā, L. **–pushpa**, m., N. of a plant, Gal.; (cf. *koṭhara-pushpī*.) **–vāsinī**, f. 'dwelling in hollow trees,' a white variety of Ipomœa Turpethum, Npr. **–sthā**, f. id., ib. **Koṭarā-vaṇa**, n., N. of a wood in which there are hollow trees, Pān. vi, 3, 117; viii, 4, 4.

Koṭavika, *am*, n. a kind of salt, L.

Koṭavī, f. (for *koṭṭ*°) a naked woman, L.; a form of Durgā and mother of Bāṇa, Hariv. (v. l. *koṭṭ*°); N. of the tutelar deity of the Daityas, VP. (v. l. *koṭṭ*°).

Koṭāya, Ā. °*yate*, fr. *koṭā*, Pāṇ. iii, 1, 17, Pat.

Koṭi, *is*, f. the curved end of a bow or of claws, &c., end or top of anything, edge or point (of a sword), horns or cusps (of the moon), MBh. &c.; the highest point, eminence, excellence, Pañcat.; Ratnâv.; Sarvad.; 'a point or side in an argument or disputation,' (if there are two) 'alternative,' see *-dvaya* below; the highest number in the older system of numbers (viz. a Krore or ten millions), Mn.; Yājñ.; MBh. &c.; the complement of an arc to 90°; the perpendicular side of a right-angled triangle, Sūryas.; Medicago esculenta, L. **–kṛit**, m., N. of Guṇâḍhya, Gal. **–jit**, m. 'conquering ten millions,' N. of Kāli-dāsa, L. **–jīvā**, f. the cosine of an angle in a right-angled triangle. **–jyā**, f. id., Sūryas. **–tīrtha**, n., N. of a Tīrtha, MBh. iii, 4091 & 5087; MatsyaP.; ŚivaP. **–dvaya**, n. 'the two ends,' i. e. two alternatives, Sāh.; Sarvad.; Comm. on KapS. and Prab. **–dhvaja**, m. a millionaire, Siṃhâs. **–pātra**, n. a rudder, L. **–pāla**, for *koṭṭa-p*°. **–pura**, n., N. of a town, Kathârn. **–mat**, mfn. furnished with a point, Śak. **–lakshâkshī**, f. 'having lacs of Krores of eyes,' N. of a goddess. **–liṅga**, n., N. of a Tīrtha, Rasik.; °*ṅgêśvara*, n. id., KapSaṃh. **–varsha**, n., N. of a city (Vāṇa-pura or Devikote on the Coromandel coast), VarBṛS. ix, 11; VāyuP.; (v. l. °*ṭī-v*°, L.); (*ā*), f. Medicago esculenta, L. (v. l. °*ṭī-v*°). **–vedhin**, mfn. 'striking an edge,' i. e. performing most difficult things, Rājat. i, 110; (*ī*), m., N. of a plant, Kālac. v, 225. **–śas**, ind. by ten millions, in innumerable multitudes, MBh.; R.; Ragh.; BhP. **–śrī**, f., N. of Durgā, L. **–sthā**, f., N. of the tutelar deity of the family of Cyāvāna, BrahmaP. **–homa**, m. a kind of sacrificial offering, AV. Pariś.; BhavP.; *-vidhi*, m., N. of a work. **Koṭîśvara**, m. 'the lord of ten millions,' a millionaire, Kathās. lvi, 64; *-tīrtha*, n., N. of a Tīrtha, ŚivaP.

Koṭika, *as*, m. (scil. *maṇḍūka*) a kind of frog, Suśr.; an insect (coccinella of various kinds), L.; N. of the son of a prince, MBh. iii, 15586; (*ā*), f. 'lowest end of anything,' the vilest of (in comp.), Pañcat.; the plant Trigonella corniculata, Bhpr. **Koṭikâsya**, m., N. of a son of king Su-ratha, MBh. iii, 15582 ff.

Koṭira, *as*, m. the hair (collected on the forehead in the shape of a horn), L.; an ichneumon, L.; (= *koṭika*) an insect (coccinella of various kinds), L.; N. of Indra, L.; (*ā*), f., N. of one of the mothers in Skanda's retinue, MBh. ix, 2632 (*koṭarā*, v. l.)

Koṭiśa, *as*, m. 'pointed,' a harrow, L.; N. of a Nāga, MBh. i, 2146.

Koṭī, f. = *koṭi*. **–karṇa**, m., N. of Śroṇa, Divyâv. i. **–dhvaja**, m., v. l. for °*ṭi-dhv*°, q. v. **–varsha**, n., v. l. for °*ṭi-v*°, q. v.; (in Prākrit *koḍī-varisa*, Jain.; cf. *kauṇḍī-vṛisha*.)

Koṭīra, *as*, m. (= °*ṭira*) long entangled hair, Naish. xi, 18; a crest, diadem, Pārśvan. ii, 1 & 54.

Koṭīśa, *as*, *am*, m. n. (= °*ṭiśa*) a harrow, L.

Koṭṭa, *as*, m. [*am*, n., L.] a fort, stronghold (= *koṭa*), Kathās. **–kāraka**, m. 'making a stronghold,' a sort of animal, Car. i, 27. **–pāla**, m. (cf. *koṭa-p*°) the commander of a stronghold, Pañcat.; Vet. xiii, 11 ff. (vv. ll. *koṭa-* & *koṭi-*). **–pura**, n., N.

of a town in Magadha, Bhadrab. **-rāja, °jan,** m. the governor of a castle, Lalit.; Divyâv. iii, xix.

Koṭṭavī, f. (= *koṭavī*) a naked woman, Rājat. v, 439; v. l. for *koṭavī*, q. v. **-pura,** n., N. of the town *koṭi-varsha* (q. v.), L.

Koṭṭāra, *as*, m. a fortified town, stronghold, L.; a pond or well, L.; the stairs of a pond, L.; a libertine (= *nāgara*), L.

Koṭya, *ās*, m. pl. = *koḍya*, R. ii, 82, 7.

कोठ *koṭha, as*, m. (fr. *kushṭha*), a species of leprosy with large round spots (ringworm, impetigo), Suśr.

Koṭhaka, *as*, m. Alangium hexapetalum, Gal.

Koṭhara, *as*, m. id., L.; (cf. *koṭara*.) **-pushpī,** f. Convolvulus argenteus, L.

कोडा *koḍā*, f. (in music) N. of a Rāgiṇī (v. l. *kodrā*).

कोड्य *koḍya, ās*, m. pl., N. of a people, Lalit. (vv. ll. *kauḍya* & *kauta*; cf. *koṭya*).

कोण *koṇa, as*, m. a corner, angle, Pañcat.; Daś.; RāmatUp.; Kathās.; an intermediate point of the compass, VarBṛS.; (hence) the number 'four,' Hcat.; the quill of a lute, fiddle-stick, drum-stick, &c., R. ii, 71, 26 & 81, 2; Kād.; a sort of musical instrument, stringed musical instrument, L.; the sharp edge of a sword, W.; a staff, club, Hcar.; the planet Saturn (fr. Κρόνος), Āryabh.; VarBṛ.; the planet Mars, L. **-kuṇa,** m. a bug, L.; (cf. *kola-k°*.) **-koshṭha,** a corner field, AgP. xl, 15. **-koshṭhaka,** id., ib. 17. **-diś,** f. an intermediate point of the compass, VarBṛS. **-deśa,** m., N. of a locality, Virac. **-nara,** m. = *-śaṅku*, Gaṇit. **-pa,** m. (for *kauṇapa*?) = *nirṛiti*, BhP. x, 12, 29, Sch. **-vādin,** m., N. of Śiva, L. **-vṛitta,** n. a vertical circle extending from north-east to south-west or from north-west to south-east, Gol. **-śaṅku,** m. the sinus of the height of the sun (the sun standing neither in the vertical circle (*-vṛitta*, q. v.) nor in the Unmaṇḍala), Gol. **-spṛig-vṛitta,** n. a circle in contact with the angles of a figure; an exterior circle (one circumscribed). **Koṇā-koṇi,** ind. (cf. Pāṇ. v, 4, 127) from angle to angle, from one corner to the other, cornerwise, diagonally, W. **Koṇâditya,** n. (perhaps) = *koṇârka*. **Koṇârka,** n., N. of a place sacred to Purushôttama.

कोणि *koṇi*, mfn. (= *kuṇi*) having a crooked arm, L.

Koṇeya, koṇeyana. See *kauṇeyá*.

Koṇera-bhaṭṭa, *as*, m., N. of a son of Vishṇu and father of Rudra-bhaṭṭa.

कोण्डभट्ट *koṇḍa-bhaṭṭa, as*, m., N. of the author of the Vṛiddha-vaiyākaraṇa-bhūshaṇa.

कोतना *kótanā*. See *kūtanā*.

कोथ *kotha*, mfn. (√*kuth*) 'afflicted with pain' or 'churned' (*śaṭita* or *mathita*), L.; (*as*), m. putrefaction, corruption, Suśr.; a sore, gangrene, Suśr.; a disease of the eyes (inflammation and ulceration of the angles of the eyelids), L.; churning, L.

कोथरी *kotharī*, f. Cactus opuntia, L.

कोदण्ड *ko-daṇḍa*, [m. n., L.] a bow, Mālav.; Bhartṛ.; BhP.; Kathās. xxii, 92; Rājat. v, 104; Hit.; (*as*), m. an eyebrow (shaped like a bow), L.; a creeping plant, L.; N. of a country, L.

Kodaṇḍin, mfn. armed with a bow (said of Śiva).

कोदार *kodāra, as*, m. a kind of grain, Comm. on KātyŚr. i, 6, 8.

कोद्रव *kodrava, as*, m. a species of grain eaten by the poor (Paspalum scrobiculatum), MBh. xiii, 4363; Suśr.; Bhartṛ.; KātyŚr. Paddh. & Sch.

कोद्रा *kodrā*. See *koḍā*.

कोनालक *konālaka, as*, m. a kind of aquatic bird, Suśr.

Konāli, *is*, m. id. (?), ib.

Konīla, *as*, m. id., Npr.

कोन्तल *kontala*, for *kaunt°*, q. v.

कोन्व *konva, as*, m., N. of a mountain, VP.; (cf. *kola-giri* and *kolla-g°*.)

Konvaśira, *ās*, m. pl., N. of a degraded warrior-tribe, MBh. xiii, 2158; (cf. *kolvagireya*.)

कोप *kopa, as*, m. (√*kup*) morbid irritation or disorder of the humors of the body, Suśr.; fury (of fire, arms, war, &c.), VarBṛS.; VarBṛ.; passion, wrath, anger, rage (with loc., gen., *prati* or *upari*, or ifc.), Mn. iii, 230 & viii, 280; MBh. &c. (rarely pl., Hit.; ifc. f. *ā*, Mālav.; *sa-kopa*, 'enraged,' Pañcat.; *sa-kopam*, 'angrily,' Pañcat.; Hit.); the state of being in contradiction with, incompatibleness with, Bādar. ii, 1, 26. **-kāraṇa,** n. cause of anger. **-krama** (1. *kopa-krama*, for 2. see below), m. one who goes to anger, passionate, W. **-cchada,** m. a kind of incense (*dhūpa*), VarBṛS. **-janman,** mfn. produced by wrath or anger, Kir. ii, 37. **-jvalita,** mfn. inflamed with wrath, enraged. **-tas,** ind. through anger, angrily. **-dīpta,** mfn. incensed or inflamed with anger. **-pada,** n. appearance of anger, pretended wrath, W. **-parīta,** mfn. affected by anger. **-latā,** f. the plant Gynandropsis pentaphylla, L. **-vat,** mfn. angry, passionate, W.; (*tī*), f. a metre of four lines of fourteen syllables each. **-vaśa,** m. subjection to anger. **-vega,** m. impetuosity of anger or passion, W.; N. of a Ṛishi, MBh. ii, 111. **-vairin,** m. 'enemy of (i. e. removing) the morbid irritation of the humors of the body,' the plant Sesbania grandiflora, Npr. **-samanvita,** mfn. affected by anger. **Kopâkula,** mfn. agitated with anger, furious, enraged. **Kopā-kopi,** ind. (cf. Pāṇ. v, 4, 127) in mutual anger, in reciprocal wrath, W. **Kopâvishṭa,** mfn. affected with anger.

Kopaka, mfn. inclined to feel angry, Mcar.

Kopana, mf(*ā*)n. inclined to passion, passionate, wrathful, angry, MBh.; R. &c.; irritating, causing morbid irritation or disorder of the humors, Suśr.; (*as*), m., N. of an Asura, Hariv. 2284; (*am*), n. irritating, MBh. xiv, 466; morbid irritation of the humors of the body, Pāṇ. v, 1, 38, Vārtt. 1; Suśr.; making angry, MBh. xiii, 2426; (*ā*), f. a passionate woman, W.

Kopanaka, *am*, n. a kind of perfume (= *coraka*), L.

Kopanīya, mfn. to be made angry, W.; tending to make angry, Sarvad.

Kopayishṇu, mfn. intending to exasperate, MBh. i, 6836.

Kopāya, Nom. Ā. °*yate*, to rage (as a passion), Hariv. 15567 (v. l.)

Kopita, mfn. enraged, furious, Mn. ix, 315; MBh. i, 1323; R. iv, 33, 32; BhP. i, 7, 48.

Kopin, mfn. angry, passionate (with loc.), R. iii, 16, 29; Gīt. x, 3; (ifc.) irritating, stirring up, Suśr; (*ī*), m. the water-pigeon (*jala-pārāvata*), L.

Kopi-yajña, m., N. of a man, Saṃskārak.

Kopya, mfn. to be made angry, MBh. v, 34.

कोपक्रम 2. *kópakrama, am*, n. (fr. 3. *ká*), Brahmā's creation, L., Sch.

Kôpajña, *am*, n. id., ib.

कोम *koma, am*, n. = *kloma*, Comm. on L.

कोमल *komala*, mf(*ā*)n. (fr. *ko* = *ku*, *mala* fr. √*mlai*, 'easily fading away'?), tender, soft (opposed to *karkaśa*), bland, sweet, pleasing, charming, agreeable, R.; Mṛicch.; Suśr.; Śak. &c. (said of the style, *rīti*, Kpr.); (*ā*), f. a kind of date, L.; (*am*), n. water, L.; silk, Gal.; nutmeg, ib.; (for *kosala*, Hariv. 12832; VāyuP.) **-gīta,** n. a sweet song. **-gītaka,** n. id. **-cchada,** m. 'tender-leaved,' N. of a plant, Gal. **-taṇḍula,** m. a sort of rice, ib. **-tā,** f. softness, tenderness. **-tva,** n. id. **-dala,** m. n. 'tender-leaved,' = *kamala* (Lotus Nelumbium). **-valkalā,** f. 'having tender bark,' the plant Cicca disticha, Bhpr. **-svabhāva,** mfn. tender-natured. **Komalâṅga,** mf(*ī*)n. having a tender body, Daś.

Komalaka, *am*, n. the fibres of the stalk of a lotus, L.

कोमासिका *komāsikā*, f. a budding fruit (= *jālikā*), L.

कोम्य *komyá*, mfn. polished (?; = *kāmya*, 'lovely,' Sāy.). RV. i, 171, 3.

कोयष्टि *ko-yashṭi, is*, m. 'having legs like sticks,' the lapwing (or 'a small white crane, commonly called a paddy-bird'), Mn. v, 13; Yājñ. i, 173; BhP. viii, 2, 15; Vet. vi, 10. **-bha,** m. id. (= *ṭiṭṭibha*, Comm.), R. ii, 54, 41.

Koyashṭika, *as*, m. id., MBh. xiii, 2835; R. iii, 78, 23 & vi, 15, 9; Suśr.; Mālatīm.

कोर *kora*, m. (√*kur*) a movable joint (as of the fingers, the knee, &c.), Suśr.; amphiarthrosis, W.; a bud, W. **-dūsha,** m. = *kodrava* (q. v.), Suśr. **-dūshaka,** m. id., MBh. iii, 13027; Suśr.; KātyŚr. ii, 1, Paddh.

Koraka, *as*, *am*, m. n. (gaṇa *tārakâdi*) a bud, R. ii, 59, 8; Suśr.; Śak.; (ifc., Bhāshāp.; Gīt. xii, 14); the fibres of the stalk of a lotus, L.; a species of perfume (commonly Cor, *cora*), L.; another perfume (a berry containing a resinous and fragrant substance, = *kakkolaka*), L.

Korakita, mfn. (gaṇa *tārakâdi*) covered with buds, Naish. iii, 121; ifc. filled with, Siṇhās.

Korita, mfn. scraped out of the ground, Bhpr. ii, 26; pounded, ground, W.; budded, sprouted, W.

कोरङ्गी *koraṅgī*, f. small cardamoms, L.

कोरली *koralī*, f., N. of a town, ŚivaP.

Korilā, f. id., ib.

कोर्प्य *korpya* = *kaurpya*, q. v.

कोल *kola, as*, m. (*jvalâdi*), a hog (cf. *kroḍa*), Yājñ. iii, 273; Vop.; a raft, Divyâv. iii; the breast, haunch, hip or flank, lap (cf. *kroḍa*), L.; an embrace, embracing, L.; a kind of weapon, L.; N. of a plant (= *citra*, *citraka*), L.; the planet Saturn, L.; N. of Śiva, Gal.; N. of a son of Ākrīḍa, Hariv. 1836; N. of a degraded warrior-tribe (outcast, one degraded by Sagara from the military order), Hariv. (v. l. *koli-sarpa*, q. v.); a man of a mixed caste, BrahmavP.; a barbarian, Kol, of a tribe inhabiting the hills in central India, W.; (*as, am*), m. n. the weight of one Tola (= 2 *ṭaṅka* [or *śāṇa*, Ashṭāṅg.] = ½ *karsha*, ŚārṅgS.); (*ā*), f. Piper longum, L.; Piper Chaba, L.; (*a, ī*), f. the jujube tree, L.; (*am*), n. the fruit of the jujube (cf. *kuvala*), ChUp. vii, 3, 1; Lalit.; Suśr.; black pepper, L.; the grain of Piper Chaba, L. **-kanda,** m. a sort of bulbous plant (used as a remedy for worms), L. **-karkaṭikā,** f. a variety of date (= *madhukharjūrikā*), L. **-karkaṭī,** f. id., Gal. **-kila,** *ās*, m. pl., N. of a people, VP. (v. l. *koli-k°*). **-kuṇa,** m. a bug, L.; (cf *koṇa-k°*.) **-gajinī,** f. Scindapsus officinalis, Npr. **-giri,** m., N. of a mountain, MBh. ii, 1171. **-tā,** f. the state of a hog, Śis. xiv, 86. **-dala,** n. a kind of perfume, L. **-nāsikā,** f. 'resembling the nose of a hog,' N. of a plant (= *vaṅkinī*), L. **-puccha,** m. a heron, L. **-muktā,** f., N. of a plant, Gal. **-mūla,** n. the root of long pepper, L. **-vallī,** f. the plant Pothos officinalis (with a pungent fruit resembling pepper), L.; Piper Chaba, L. **-śimbī,** f. Carpopogon pruriens (commonly Ālukuśī), Bhpr. **Kolā-koli,** ind. (cf. Pāṇ. v, 4, 127) with mutual embraces, W. **Kolâksha,** n. 'a hog's eye,' a particular hole in wood, VarBṛS. lxxix, 32 f. **Kolâkhya,** n. 'named after a hog,' id., Vāstuv. x, 93. **Kolâñca,** m., N. of Kaliṅga (the Coromandel coast from Kuttack to Madras; but, accord. to some, this place is in Hindustān, with Kanouj for its capital), W. **Kolâtmaja,** m. 'produced by the Kolā plant (Zizyphus Jujuba),' the fruit of the jujube, Npr. **Kolā-pura,** n., N. of a town, SkandaP.; Virac. **Kolā-vidhvaṇsin,** *inas*, m. pl., N. of a royal family, MārkP. lxxxi, 4 f. **Kolêkshaṇa,** n. = *kolâksha*, VarBṛS. lxxix, 36.

Kolaka, *as*, m. Alangium hexapetalum, L.; Cordia Myxa, L.; (*am*), n. a kind of perfume, Bhpr.; black pepper, L. **-grāma,** m., N. of a village.

Kolika-gardabha, m. a kind of ass, Divyâv. xii.

कोलम्बक *ko-lambaka, as*, m. the body of a lute (the whole of it except the strings), L.

Ko-lambī, f. Śiva's lute, Gal.

कोलाहल *kolāhala, as, am*, m. n. (onomat.) a loud and confused sound, uproar, great and indistinct noise (of men, animals, &c.), R. iii, vi; Pañcat.; Daś.; MārkP. &c.; (*as, ā*), m. f. (in music) a kind of Rāga; (*as*), m., N. of a prince, VP.; of a personified mountain, MBh. i, 2367 f.

Kolāhalin, mfn. ifc. filled with noise, Kād.

कोलि *koli, is*, m. f. the jujube tree (Zizyphus Jujuba), L. **-kila,** *ās*, m. pl., v. l. for *kola-k°*, q. v. **-sarpa,** *ās*, m. pl., N. of a degraded warrior-tribe, MBh. xiii, 2104; Hariv. 782 (v. l. *-sparśa*). **-sparśa,** see *-sarpa*.

कोलित *kolita, as*, m., N. of Maudgalyāyana, Buddh. (Divyâv. xxvii).

कोलूक *kolūka*, N. of a country, R. iv, 43, 8

(vv. ll. *kolūta* and *śailūta*); (cf. *ulūka, ulūṭa, utūla, kulūṭa, kulūta, kaulūta.*)

कोल्या *kolyā*, f. (=*kolā*) Piper longum, L.

कोल्लक *kollaka*, *as*, m., N. of a mountain, BhP. v, 19, 16; (cf. *konva, konvaśira, kola.*)

Kolla-giri, *is*, m. (=*kola-g°*) id., VarBṛS. xiv.

Kollagireya, *ās*, m. pl. 'dwelling on the Kolla mountain,' N. of a people or tribe, MBh. xiv, 2476 (*kolvag°*, ed. Calc.)

Kolla-pura, n. = *kolā-p°*, Virac. ix.

कोल्वगिरेय *kolvagireya*. See *kollag°*.

कोविद *ko-vida*, mf(*ā*)n. (√*vid*) experienced, skilled, learned in (loc., gen., or ifc., e.g. *aśveshu* or *aśvānām* or *aśva-kovida*, 'skilled in horses'), Mn. vii, 26; MBh.; R. &c.; (*ās*), m. pl., N. of the Kshatriyas in Kuśa-dvīpa, BhP. v, 20, 16. —**tva**, n. skilfulness (ifc.), Daś.

कोविदार *ko-vidāra*, m. 'easily to be split,' or 'to be split with difficulty' (? cf. *kuddala, kuddāla*), Bauhinia variegata, Gobh.; MBh.; R.; Suśr.; Ṛitus.; one of the trees of paradise, Hariv. 7169; Lalit.

कोश *kóśa*, *as*, m. (*am*, n., L.; in class. literature *kośa* or *kosha*; fr. √*kuś* or *kush*?, related to *kukshi* and *koshṭha*?), a cask, vessel for holding liquids, (metaphorically) cloud, RV.; AV.; Suśr.; a pail, bucket, RV.; a drinking-vessel, cup, L.; a box, cupboard, drawer, trunk, RV. vi, 47, 23; AV. xix, 72, 1; ŚBr.; the interior or inner part of a carriage, RV.; (ifc.) MBh. viii, 1733; a sheath, scabbard, &c., MBh.; R.; VarBṛS.; a case, covering, cover, AV.; ChUp.; MuṇḍUp.; TUp.; PārGṛ.; BhP.; store-room, store, provisions, Mn.; MBh. &c.; a treasury, apartment where money or plate is kept, treasure, accumulated wealth (gold or silver, wrought or unwrought, as plate, jewellery, &c.), ib.; (in surg.) a kind of bandage, Suśr.; a dictionary, lexicon or vocabulary; a poetical collection, collection of sentences &c., Kāvyād. i, 13; Sāh.; a bud, flower-cup, seed-vessel (cf. *bīja-*), R.; Ragh.; BhP.; Dhūrtas.; the sheath or integument of a plant, pod, nut-shell, MārkP.; a nutmeg, L.; the inner part of the fruit of Artocarpus integrifolia and of similar fruits, L.; the cocoon of a silk-worm, Yājñ. iii, 147; Vedāntas.; the membrane covering an egg (in the womb), Suśr.; VarBṛ.; MārkP.; the vulva, L.; a testicle or the scrotum, Suśr.; VarBṛS.; the penis, W.; an egg, L.; (in Vedānta phil.) a term for the three sheaths or succession of cases which make up the various frames of the body enveloping the soul (these are, 1. the *ānanda-maya k°* or 'sheath of pleasure,' forming the *kāraṇa-śarīra* or 'causal frame;' 2. the *vijñāna-maya* or *buddhi-m°* or *mano-m°* or *prāṇa-m° k°*, 'the sheath of intellect or will or life,' forming the *sūkshma-śarīra* or 'subtile frame;' 3. the *anna-m° k°*, 'the sheath of nourishment,' forming the *sthūla-śarīra* or 'gross frame'), Vedāntas.; (ifc.) a ball or globe (e.g. *sūtra-*, a ball of thread, L.; *netra-*, the eye-ball, R. iii, 79, 28); the water used at an ordeal or judicial trial (the defendant drinks thrice of it after some idol has been washed in it), Yājñ. ii, 95; an oath, Rājat. v, 325; a cup used in the ratification of a treaty of peace (*°śam* √*pā*, to drink from that cup), Rājat. vii, 8; 75; 460 & 493; viii, 283; N. of a conjunction of planets, VarBṛS.; of the 2nd astrological mansion, VarYogay.; (with Buddh.) of a collection of Gāthā verses, Kāraṇḍ.; Hcar.; (*ā*), f., N. of a river, MBh. vi, 9, 34; of a courtesan, HPariś. viii, 8; (*ī*), f. 'a bud,' see *arka-*; a seed-vessel, L.; the beard of corn, L.; a shoe, sandal, L.; a kind of perfume, Gal.; an iron ploughshare, ib.; [cf. κόκκος.] —**kāra**, m. one who makes scabbards or cases or boxes, &c., R. iv, 40, 26 (*kauśi-k°*, Hariv. 12831); (f. *ī*), VS. xxx, 14; a compiler of a dictionary, lexicographer, RāmatUp.; the silk-worm (or the insect while in its cocoon, W.), KapS.; BhP.; MārkP.; a chrysalis or pupa, W.; (*as, am*), m. n. a kind of sugar-cane, Suśr.; Bhpr.; Bālar.; *-kīṭa*, m. a silk-worm, L.; *-vasana*, n. a silken garment, VarBṛ. xxvii, 31. —**kāraka**, m. a silk-worm, Yājñ. iii, 147; (*ikā*), f. a female bee, Gal.; N. of a collection of Gāthā verses (ascribed to Vasubandhu), Buddh. —**kālin**, m. or °**lī**, f. a kind of aquatic bird, Npr. —**kṛit**, m. a kind of sugar-cane, Suśr. —**gṛiha**, n. a treasury, room in which valuable garments, precious stones &c. are kept, R. ii, 39, 16 f.; Ragh. v, 29. —**grahaṇa**, n. 'drinking the water used at an ordeal,' undergoing an ordeal, W. —**cañcu**, m. the Indian crane, L. —**ja**, n. 'coming from the cocoon,' silk, L. —**jāta**, n. treasure, wealth, Ragh. v, 1. —**dāsa**, m. 'treasure-slave,' N. of a man, Daś. —**dhānya**, n. any leguminous plant, VarBṛS. viii, 8; (cf. *kośī-dh°, kauśī-dh°*.) —**dhāvana**, mf(*ī*)n. slipping out of the frame (a door), TBr. iii, 6, 2, 2 (*á-k°*, neg.) —**nāyaka**, m. a chief over treasure, treasurer, W.; N. of Kubera, W. —**pāla**, m. a treasure-guardian, MBh. xv, 612. —**pīṭhin**, mfn. one who exhausts or has exhausted the wealth of any one, Rājat. v, 422 & vi, 211. —**peṭaka**, m. n. a chest or strong box in which treasure is kept, Vikr. —**phala**, n. the scrotum, VarBṛS. lxvii, 9; a nutmeg, L.; a kind of perfume (a berry containing a waxy and fragrant substance), L.; (*as*), m. Luffa fœtida or a similar plant, L.; (*ā*), f. a cucurbitaceous plant (= *pīta-ghoshā*), L.; the plant Cucumis utilissimus, L.; the plant Ipomœa Turpethum, Npr. —**bhūta**, mfn. treasured, stored, accumulated, W. —**rakshin**, m. = *-pāla*, Kathās. lxx, 33. —**vat**, mfn. forming a receptacle (as a wound), Car. vi, 13; possessing treasures, rich, wealthy, MBh.; Kathās. lxi, 215; (*ān*), m. 'having a sheath,' a sword, Gal.; (*tī*), f. Cucumis acutangulus or sulcatus, Suśr. —**vāri**, n. water used at an ordeal, Kathās. cxix, 35 & 42. —**vāsin**, m. 'living in a shell,' any animal incased in a shell, Suśr.; a chrysalis or pupa, W. —**vāhana**, n. treasure and vehicles, Daś. —**vṛiddhi**, f. swelled testicle, enlargement of the scrotum from hernia &c., L. —**veśman**, n. a treasury, Kathās. xxiv, 133. —**śāyikā**, f. a clasp-knife or one lying in a sheath, L. —**śuddhi**, f. purification by ordeal, W. —**skṛit**, m. a silk-worm, BhP. vii, 6, 13. —**stha**, m. 'incased,' any shelled insect or animal (as a snail &c.), Suśr.; a chrysalis or pupa, silk-worm in its cocoon, W. —**hīna**, mfn. without treasure, deprived of riches, Mn. vii, 148. **Kośâṅśa**, m. part of a treasure, portion of any one's wealth. **Kośâgāra**, m. n. a treasure-house, store-room, treasury, MBh.; R.; Kathās.; *°rādhikārin*, m. a treasurer, Kathās. **Kośâṅga**, m. or n. a kind of reed or grass (commonly Ikāda), L. **Kośâṇḍa**, m. (= *aṇḍa-kośa*) the scrotum, Gal. **Kośâdhipati**, m. a superintendent of the treasury, treasurer, W.; N. of Kubera, W. **Kośâdhīśa**, m. id., W. **Kośâdhyaksha**, m. a treasurer, VarBṛS.; Pañcat.; Kathās.; N. of Kubera, W. **Kośâpaharaṇa**, n. carrying off treasure. **Kośâpahartṛi**, m. one who carries off treasure, Mn. ix, 275. **Kośâmra**, m. Mangifera sylvatica, Bhpr.; (*am*), n. the fruit of that plant, Suśr. **Kośī-dhānya**, n. = *kośa-dh°*, ĀpŚr. iv, 2 f., Sch. **Kośêkshaṇa**, mfn. having projecting or prominent eyes, VarBṛS. lxix, 20. **Kośêśa**, m. a treasurer, Siṇhâs.

Kośaka, *as*, m. an egg, testicle, L.; (*ikā*), f. a drinking-vessel, L.; (*am*), n. case, receptacle of (in comp.), MārkP. xi, 5.

Kóśayī, f. (perhaps) the contents of a cupboard or drawer, RV. vi, 47, 22.

Kośikā, f. of *kośaka*, q.v.

Kośin, *ī*, m. the mango tree, L.

Kośilā, f. a kind of bean (Phaseolus trilobus), L.

Kośyá, *au* or *e* (?), m. or n. (?) du. two lumps of flesh near the heart of a sacrificial horse, VS. xxxix, 8; (cf. *ni-kośyà*.)

कोशल *kośala*, &c. See *kosala*.

कोशातक *kośātaka* (or *koshāt°*), *as*, m. hair, L.; (*ī*), f. (gaṇas *gaurâdi* and *harītaky-ādi*), N. of a plant and of its fruit (Trichosanthes diœca, or Luffa acutangula, or Luffa pentandra, L.), ŚāṅkhGṛ.; Car.; Suśr.; (cf. *mahā-k°*); a moonlight night, L.; (*am*), n. the fruit of the plant Kośātakī, Car.

Kośātakin, *ī*, m. trade, business, L.; a trader, merchant, L.; submarine fire, L.

कोशिका *kośikā*, *°śin*, *°śilā*, &c. See *kóśa*.

कोष 1. *kosha*. See *kośa*.

कोष 2. *koshá*, *ās*, m. pl. (gaṇa *pacâdi*), N. of a family of priests, ŚBr. x, 5, 5, 8; (*ā*), f. 'N. of a river,' v. l. for *kośā*. —**dhāvana**, see *kośa-dh°*.

Koshaṇa, *am*, n. (√*kush*) tearing &c., Comm. on APrāt. iii, 75; (*ī*), f., see *jīva-k°*.

कोष्ठ *koshṭha*, *as*, m. (√*kush*?; probably related to *kukshi* and *kóśa*), any one of the viscera of the body (particularly the stomach, abdomen), MBh.; Suśr. &c.; (*as*, L.; *am*), m. n. a granary, store-room, MBh.; BhP. (ifc. f. *ā*); a treasury, W.; (*as*), m. an inner apartment, L.; the shell of anything, W.; a kind of pan, pot, Kauś.; Pat.; Car.; Bhpr.; property (or mfn. 'own'), L.; night, L.; (*am*), n. a surrounding wall, BhP. iv, 28, 57; any enclosed space or area, chess square, VarBṛS. liii, 42; Hcat.; Tithyād.; KātyŚr., Sch. —**koṭi**, m., N. of an attendant of Śiva, L., Sch. —**tāpa**, m. excessive heat in the abdomen, Gal. —**pāla**, m. a municipal officer, constable, W.; a watch, guard, watch of a city, W.; a store-keeper, treasurer, W. —**bheda**, m. = *-śuddhi*, ŚārṅgS. i, 7, 57. —**roga**, m. a disease of the abdomen, VarBṛS. civ, 5. —**vat**, m., N. of a mountain, MBh. xiv, 1174. —**śuddhi**, f. evacuation of the bowels. —**saṃtāpa**, m. = *-tāpa*, L. **Koshṭhâgāra**, n. a store-room, store, Mn. ix, 280; R. &c.; a treasury, W.; any enclosed space or area; the lunar mansion Maghā, VarBṛS. **Koshṭhâgārika**, m. 'living in store-rooms,' a wasp, Suśr.; Bhpr.; a steward, Divyâv. xx. **Koshṭhâgārin**, m. = *°rika*, a wasp, Suśr. **Koshṭhâgni**, m. 'fire in the stomach,' the digestive faculty, GarbhUp. **Koshṭhânāha**, m. constipation, costiveness, Car. **Koshṭhī-pradīpa**, m., N. of a work on astronomy. **Koshṭhêkshu**, m. a kind of sugar-cane, L.

Koshṭhaka, *as* or *am*, m. or n. a receptacle for (in comp.), Car.; 'a granary, store-room,' see *anna-k°*; (*ikā*), f. a kind of vessel, pan, Bhpr.; (*am*), n. a treasury, W.; a surrounding wall (ifc.), BhP. iv, 28, 56; a surrounded field, quarter, VarBṛS.; AgP.; Hcat. (ifc. f. *ā*); a brick trough for watering cattle, W.; N. of a town, Buddh. (Divyâv. xxix).

Koshṭhakī-kṛitya, ind. p. surrounding, enclosing, MBh. vi, 2463; xiv, 2230.

Koshṭhila, *as*, m., N. of a man, Buddh.; (cf. *kaushṭh°*.)

Koshṭhī-√kṛi, to surround, enclose, MBh. vi, 101, 32.

Koshṭhya, mfn. proceeding from the chest, emitted (as a sound) from the centre of the lungs, RPrāt. xiii, 1.

कोष्ण *kôshṇa*, mfn. (Pāṇ. vi, 3, 107) moderately warm, tepid, Suśr.; Ragh. i, 84; (*am*), n. warmth, W.; (cf. *kavôshṇa, kad-ushṇa*.)

कोसल *kosala*, *ās*, m. pl. (in later texts generally spelt *kośala*), N. of a country and the warrior-tribe inhabiting it (descendants of Māthavya Videgha, ŚBr. i), Pāṇ. iv, 1, 171; MBh. &c. (*kosalānām* [v. l. *kauśal°*, R. vi, 86, 43] *nakshatra*, N. of a lunar mansion, R. (ed. Bomb.) vi, 103, 35); (*ās*), m., N. of the country of Kosala, R. i, 5, 5; N. of the capital of that country or Ayodhyā (the modern Oude), L.; (*ā*), f. id., MBh.; Nal.; Ragh. (ed. Calc.) i, 35, &c. —**videhá**, *ās*, m. pl. the Kosalas and the Videhas, ŚBr. i. —**jā**, f. 'the daughter of a king of the Kosalas,' N. of Daśa-ratha's wife (mother of Rāma), RāmatUp. **Kosalâtma-jā**, f. id., L.

कोसार *kosāra*, *as*, m. (=*karshū*) a furrow, trench, Comm. on KātyŚr. xv, 1, 9 & xxi, 3, 26.

कोसिद *kosida*, for *kaus°*, q.v.

कोहड *kohaḍa*, m., N. of a man, g. *śivâdi*.

Kohara, *as*, m., v. l. for *kohala*, q.v.

Kohala, mfn. speaking indistinctly, L.; (*as*), m. a sort of spirituous liquor (made of barley), Suśr.; a kind of musical instrument (?), L.; N. of a Muni (inventor or first teacher of the drama), MBh. i, xiii; VāyuP.; N. of a Prākrit grammarian (v. l. *kohara*); of a writer on music; (*ī*), f. a kind of spirituous liquor (= *kushmāṇḍa-surā*), Npr. **Kohalêśvara-tīrtha**, n., N. of a Tīrtha, ŚivaP.

Kohalīya, *am*, n., N. of Kohala's work on music.

कोहित *kohita*, m., N. of a man, g. *śivâdi*.

कोहिन् *kohin*, *ī*, m. the tree Wrightia antidysenterica, L.

कोह्लास *kohlāsa*, *as*, m. (in music) N. of a Rāga.

कौकाक्ष *kaukâksha*, v. l. for *gaukaksha*.

कौकिल *kaukila*, *as*, *ī*, m. f., N. of a ceremony, Lāṭy. v, 4, 20 f.; TBr., Sch.; (*as*), m. patr. fr. *kokila*, and metron. fr. *kokilā*, Pāṇ. iv, 1, 120, Pat.

कौकुट्टक *kaukuṭṭaka*, *ās*, m. pl., N. of a people (vv. ll. *°kuntaka* & *°kundaka*), MBh. vi, 367; VP.

कौकुण्डिहि *kaukuṇḍihi, is,* m., N. of a Ṛishi.

कौकुन्तक *kaukuntaka.* See °*kuṭṭaka.*

कौकुर *kaukura, ās,* m. pl. (fr. *kukura*), N. of a people, MBh. ii, 1804 & 1871; xvi, 134.

कौकुरुण्डि *kaukuruṇḍi, is,* m., N. of a teacher, SaṃhUp. v.

कौकुलिका *kaukulikā,* f., N. of one of the mothers in Skanda's retinue, MBh. ix, 2633.

कौकुवादि *kaukuvādi, is,* m. patr. (fr. *ku-ku-vāda* = -*vāc* ?), Pravar.

कौकूस्त *kaukūstá, as,* m., N. of a man, ŚBr. iv.

कौकृत्य *kaukṛitya, am,* n. (fr. *ku-kṛita* or -*kṛitya*), evil doing, wickedness, L.; repentance, L.

कौक्कुट *kaukkuṭa,* mfn. (fr. *kukk*°), relating to a cock or domestic fowl, gallinaceous, R. ii, 91, 65; Suśr.; (*am*), n. (scil. *āsana*) a particular manner of being seated, NārP.

Kaukkuṭika, m. a poulterer, one who sells fowls, L.; a kind of low caste, Kāraṇḍ.; (Pāṇ. iv, 4, 46) a kind of mendicant who walks with his eyes fixed on the ground for fear of treading upon insects &c., L.; a hypocrite, L.; a pigeon, L.

Kaukkuṭi-kandala, *as,* m. a species of snake, L.; (cf. *kukkuṭâbha* and °*ṭâhi.*)

Kaukkuḍīvaha, *am,* n., N. of a village of the Bāhīkas, Pāṇ. iv, 2, 104, Vārtt. 26 (v. l. °*kkuṭīv*°).

Kaukkuḍīvahaka, mfn. coming from that village, ib. (v. l. °*kkuṭīv*°).

कौक्ष *kauksha,* mfn. (fr. *kukshí*), abdominal, ventral, Pāṇ. iv, 2, 96, Kāś.

Kaukshaka, mfn., gaṇa *dhūmâdi.*

Kauksheya, mfn. being in the belly, Pāṇ. iv, 3, 56; (*as*), m. 'sheathed,' a sword, Bhaṭṭ. iv, 31.

Kaukshеyaka, *as,* m. (Pāṇ. iv, 2, 96) 'being in a sheath,' a sword, Daś.; Pratāpar.; a scymitar, knife, Kād.

कौङ्क *kauṅka, as,* m. the country Koṅka (= *koṅkaṇa*), L.

Kauṅkaṇa, *ās,* m. pl. (= *koṅk*°), N. of a people, MBh. vi, 367 (*koṅk*°, ed. Bomb.); VarBṛS. xvi, 11. **Kauṅkaṇôdbhūta,** mfn. coming from Koṅkaṇa (as a horse of good breed), Gal.; (cf. *koṅkāṇa.*)

Kauṅkiṇa, *ās,* m. pl. = °*kaṇa,* L.

कौङ्कुम *kauṅkuma,* mf(ī)n. consisting of saffron (*kuṅkuma*), Hcat.; dyed with saffron, Hariv. 7072; of saffron colour, Viddh.; (*ās*), m. pl., N. of sixty particular Ketus, VarBṛS. xi, 21.

कौचवार *kaucavāra, as,* m. patr. fr. *kūcavāra,* gaṇa *bidâdi.*

Kaucavārya, mfn. coming from Kūcavāra, Pāṇ. iv, 3, 94.

कौचहस्ति *kaucahasti, is,* m. patr. fr. *kucahasta,* Saṃskārak. (pl.)

कौचापाक *kaucā-pāka, as,* m. a kind of decoction.

कौचुमारयोग *kaucumāra-yoga, as,* m. (fr. *kuc*°), a particular art (*kalā*), BhP. x, 45, 36, Sch.

कौज *kauja,* mfn. (fr. *ku-ja*), relating or belonging to the planet Mars, VarBṛ. viii, xviii, xxiv; (said of Tuesday), Vishṇ. lxxviii, 3.

Kaujapa, *as,* m. patr. fr. *kuja-pa,* Pāṇ. vi, 2, 37.

कौञ्च *kauñca, as,* m. (for *krauñca* ?), N. of a mountain (part of the Himālaya range), L.; (*ī*), f., N. of a locality, Romakas. **Kauñcâdri,** m. the Kauñca mountain, Bālar.

Kauñcikī, f. (with Kaulas) one of the eight A-kulas, Kulârṇ.

कौञ्जर *kauñjara,* mf(ī)n. (fr. *kuñj*°), belonging to an elephant, MBh. xii, 8032 (= xiii, 5580); BhP. viii, 4, 12; (*am*), n. a particular method of sitting, NārP.

कौञ्जायन *kauñjāyana, ās,* m. pl. (fr. *kuñja*), N. of a mountain tribe (descended from Kuñja), Pāṇ. iv, 1, 98 & v, 3, 113; (*ī*), f. a princess of that tribe (or the wife of a Brāhman or of any venerable personage belonging to that tribe, L.), ib.

Kauñjāyanya, *as,* m. a prince of the Kauñjāyanas, ib.

Kauñji, m. patr. fr. *kuñja,* Pāṇ. iv, 1, 98, Kāś.

कौट 1. *kauṭa,* mfn. (fr. *kuṭi*), living in one's own house, independent, free, Pāṇ. v, 4, 95; (*as*), m. (= *kuṭa-ja*) Wrightia antidysenterica, Bhpr. i, 206. **—taksha,** m. an independent carpenter (who works at home on his own account and not for a village or corporation), Pāṇ. v, 4, 95. **—phala,** n. a fruit of *kauṭa,* Car. viii, 11.

Kauṭaja, mfn. coming from the plant Wrightia antidysenterica (*kuṭa-ja*), Suśr.; (*as*), m. the plant Wrightia antidysenterica, Bhpr. iii, 159.

Kauṭajabhārika, mfn. (fr. *kuṭaja-bhāra*), carrying or bearing a load of Wrightia antidysenterica, gaṇa *vaṅśâdi.*

Kauṭajika, mfn. id., ib.

Kauṭāyana, *as,* m. patr. fr. *kuṭa,* gaṇa *aśvâdi.*

Kauṭi, *is,* m. id., g. *krauḍy-ādi* (not in Kāś.)

1. **Kauṭya,** *as,* m. id., gaṇa *kurv-ādi;* (*ā*), f. of *kauṭi,* gaṇa *krauḍy-ādi* (not in Kāś.)

कौट 2. *kauṭa,* mfn. (fr. *kūṭa*), fraudulent, dishonest; snared, wired, W.; (*am*), n. fraud, falsehood, W. **—sâkshin,** m. a false witness (= *kūṭa-s*°), Comm. on Yājñ. **—sâkshya,** n. false evidence, Gaut.; Mn. viii, 117 & 122 f.; xi, 56.

Kauṭakika, mfn. one whose occupation is to catch animals in traps or caves &c., L.; (*as*), m. a vendor of the flesh of birds or beasts, hunter, poacher, butcher, &c., L.

Kauṭasthya, *am,* n. the state of being *kūṭastha,* i. e. uniform or unchangeable, Sarvad.; Sch. on Sāṃk. on Bādar. ii, 2, 10.

Kauṭika, mfn. (gaṇa *kumudâdi;* = *kauṭakika*) one whose business is to catch animals in traps &c., L.; relating to a snare or trap, W.; fraudulent, dishonest, W.; (*as*), m. one who kills animals and sells their flesh for his own subsistence, poacher, L.

Kauṭilya, mfn., gaṇa *kṛiśâśvâdi.*

2. **Kauṭya,** mfn., gaṇa *saṃkāśâdi.*

कौटभी *kauṭabhī,* for *kaiṭ*°, q. v.

कौटलि *kauṭali, is,* m. patr., Saṃskārak.

Kauṭalya, *as,* m. (for °*ṭilya*), N. of Cāṇakya, L.

कौटवी *kauṭavī,* f. = *koṭ*°, a naked woman, L.

कौटस्थ्य *kauṭasthya.* See 2. *kauṭa.*

कौटायन *kauṭāyana,* °*ṭi.* See 1. *kauṭa.*

कौटिक *kauṭika.* See 2. *kauṭa.*

कौटिर्या *kauṭiryā,* v. l. for °*ṭiryā.*

कौटिलिक *kauṭilika, as,* m. (fr. *kuṭilikā;* Pāṇ. iv, 4, 18) 'deceiving the hunter [or the deer, Sch.] by particular movements,' a deer ['a hunter,' Sch.], Kāś.; 'using the tool called *kuṭilikā,*' a blacksmith, ib.

Kauṭilya, *as,* m. (fr. *kuṭila*), N. of Cāṇakya, Daś.; Mudr.; N. of a grammarian (?), Hemac.; Mallin. on Kum. vi, 37 & on Ragh. iii f., xv & xvii f.; (*am*), n. crookedness, curvature, curliness of the hair, Pāṇ. iii, 1, 23; Pañcat.; falsehood, dishonesty, Pañcat.; Rājat.; a kind of horse-radish, L. **—śâstra,** n. Cāṇakya's doctrine (diplomacy), Kād.

कौटीगव *kauṭīgava,* mfn. fr. °*vya,* gaṇa *kaṇvâdi.*

Kauṭīgavya, m. patr. fr. *kuṭī-gu,* g. *gargâdi.*

कौटीय *kauṭīya.* See 2. *kauṭa.*

कौटीर *kauṭīra,* mfn. belonging to or made from the plant Kuṭīra, gaṇa *bilvâdi.*

Kauṭīryā, f. 'living in a hut (? *kuṭīra*),' N. of Durgā, Hariv. 10245 (v. l. °*ṭiryā*).

कौटुम्ब *kauṭumba,* mfn. (fr. *kuṭ*°), necessary for the household, ĀśvGṛ. ii, 6, 10; (*am*), n. family relationship, Rājat. v, 395.

Kauṭumbika, mfn. belonging to or constituting a family, BhP. v, 14, 3; (*as*), m. the father or master of a family, BhP. iv, 28, 12 & v, 13, 8.

कौट्टन्य *kauṭṭanya, am,* n. (fr. *kuṭṭanī*), the procuring of women for immoral purposes, Rājat. vii, 289 & 297.

कौट्य 1. & 2. *kauṭya.* See 1. & 2. *kauṭa.*

कौठार *kauṭhāra, as,* m. patr. fr. *kuṭhāra,* gaṇa *śivâdi.*

Kauṭhārikeya, *as,* m. metron. fr. *kuṭhārikā,* gaṇa *śubhrâdi.*

कौठुम *kauṭhuma,* mf(ī)n. fr. *kuṭhumi,* W.; (cf. *kauthuma.*)

कौडविक *kauḍavika,* mf(ī)n. (Kāś. on Pāṇ. v, 1, 52 & vii, 3, 17) sown with a Kuḍava of grain (as a field &c.), containing a Kuḍava, Car. vi, 17.

कौडेयक *kauḍeyaka,* mfn. fr. *kuḍyā,* gaṇa *kattry-ādi.*

कौडोदरि *kauḍodari, is,* m. (for *kauṇḍ*° ? fr. *kuṇḍôdara*), N. of a man, Pravar.

कौड्य *kauḍya,* v. l. for *koḍya,* q. v.

कौणकुत्स्य *kauṇakutsya, as,* m. (cf. *kūṇakuccha*), N. of a Brāhman, MBh. i, 962.

कौणप *kauṇapa,* mfn. (fr. *kuṇ*°), coming from corpses, Bālar.; (*as*), m. 'feeding upon corpses,' a Rākshasa or goblin,' MBh. i, 6450; Śak. (v. l.); BhP. x, 12, 29; N. of a Nāga (these beings are supposed to eat human flesh), MBh. i, 2147. **—danta,** m., N. of Bhīshma (uncle of the Pāṇḍus), L. **Kauṇapâśana,** m., N. of a Nāga, MBh. i, 1559.

कौणिन्द *kauṇinda, ās,* m. pl. (v. l. *kaulinda,* q. v.), N. of a people, VarBṛS. xiv, 30; (*as*), m. a prince of that people, ib. 33.

कौणेय *kauṇeyá, as,* m. (fr. *kuṇi*), patr. of Rajana, TS. ii, 3, 8, 1; TāṇḍyaBr. xiii, 4, 11; (*koneya* & °*yana*), Kāṭh. xi, 1.

कौण्ठरव्य *kaunṭharavya, as,* m. patr. fr. *kuntha-rava,* AitĀr.

Kaunṭhya, *am,* n. (fr. *kunṭha*), bluntness, VarBṛS. l, 26.

कौण्डपायिन *kauṇḍapāyina,* mfn. with *ayana,* N. of a Soma libation (= *kuṇḍa-pāyinām ay*°), Lāṭy.; *kauṇḍapāyinām ay*° for °*nam ay*° or for *kuṇḍa-pāyinām ay*°, ŚāṅkhŚr. xiii, 24, 1; Lāṭy. i, 4, 23, Sch.; KātyŚr. iv, 1, 1, Sch.; Bādar. iii, 3, 40, Sch.

कौण्डल *kauṇḍala,* mfn. (fr. *kuṇḍ*°), furnished with rings, gaṇa *jyotsnâdi.*

Kauṇḍalika, mfn. id., gaṇa *kumudâdi.*

कौण्डाग्नक *kauṇḍāgnaka,* v. l. for *kāṇḍ*°.

Kauṇḍāyana, mfn. fr. *kuṇḍa,* gaṇa *pakshâdi.*

कौण्डिन *kauṇḍina,* mfn. fr. °*nya,* gaṇa *kaṇvâdi;* (*ī*), f. of °*nya,* see *pārāśarī-kauṇḍinī-putra.*

Kauṇḍineyaka, mfn. fr. *kuṇḍina,* gaṇa *kattry-ādi.*

Kaúṇḍinya, *as,* m. patr. fr. *kuṇḍina* (or metron. fr. *kuṇḍinī,* gaṇa *gargâdi*), ŚBr. xiv; ĀśvŚr.; Pravar.; MBh. ii, 111; Lalit.; Divyâv. xxxii; N. of an old grammarian, TPrāt. i, 5 & ii, 5 ff.; (*vyākaraṇa-*) Buddh.; of Jaya-deva; (cf. *vidarbhī-k*° and *ājñāta-k*°); mfn. coming from Kuṇḍina, Prasannar.

Kauṇḍinyaka, *am,* n., N. of a Kalpa-sūtra, Comm. on Jaim. i, 3, 11.

Kaúṇḍinyāyana or °*ná, as,* m. patr. fr. °*nya,* ŚBr. xiv, 5, 5, 20 & 7, 3, 26.

Kauṇḍila, °*lya,* for °*nya,* Lalit.; Hit.

कौण्डिल्यक *kauṇḍilyaka, as,* m. a kind of venomous insect, Suśr.

कौण्डीवृष *kauṇḍī-vṛisha, ās,* m. pl = *kuṇḍīvisha,* MBh. vi, 2410 (*kuṇḍ*°, ed. Bomb.)

Kauṇḍīvṛisi, ?, Pāṇ. vi, 3, 34, Vārtt. 4, Pat.

Kauṇḍīvṛisya, ?, ib.; (cf. *koṭī-varsha.*)

कौण्डोदरि *kauṇḍôdari.* See *kauḍ*°.

Kauṇḍôparatha, *ās,* m. pl., N. of a warrior-tribe, Pāṇ. v, 3, 116.

Kauṇḍôparathīya, a prince of that tribe, ib.

कौण्य *kauṇya, am,* n. (fr. *kuṇi*), paralysis of the hands, Suśr.

कौत *kauta,* v. l. for *koḍya,* q. v.

कौतप *kautapa,* mfn. fr. *ku-tapa,* gaṇa *jyotsnâdi.*

कौतस्कुत *kautaskuta,* mfn. fr. *kutaḥ kutaḥ,* gaṇa *kaskâdi.*

कौतस्त *kautasta, as,* m patr. fr. *kutasta,* TāṇḍyaBr. xxv, 15, 3.

कौतुक *kautuka*, *am*, n. (fr. *kut°*; gaṇa *yuvâdi*), curiosity, interest in anything, vehement desire for (loc. or in comp.), eagerness, vehemence, impatience, Pañcat.; Kathās. (ifc. f. *ā*) &c.; anything causing curiosity or admiration or interest, any singular or surprising object, wonder, Pañcat.; Kathās.; Vet.; festivity, gaiety, festival, show, solemn ceremony (esp. the ceremony with the marriage-thread or necklace preceding a marriage), Kum.; Daś.; Bhartṛ.; BhP. &c.; the marriage-thread or necklace, Kathās. li, 223; pleasure, happiness, prosperity, BhP. i, 17, 26; N. of nine particular substances, Hcat. i, 110, 19; ii, 49, 10; sport, pastime, L.; public diversion, L.; song, dance, show, spectacle, L.; season of enjoyment, L.; kind or friendly greeting, civility, L.; (*āt*), abl. ind. out of curiosity or interest, Kathās.; Hit.; for amusement, as a relaxation, W. **–kriyā**, f. a marriage ceremony, Ragh. xi, 53. **–gṛiha**, n. the house in which a marriage takes place, Hcar.; ŚāṅkhGṛ. i, 12, Sch. **–cintāmaṇi**, m., N. of a work. **–toraṇa**, n. (ifc. f. *ā*) a triumphal arch erected at certain festivals, BhP. i, 11, 14. **–pura**, n., N. of a town, Kathās. liv, 152. **–maṅgala**, n. (ifc. f. *ā*) an auspicious ceremony (esp. the ceremony with the marriage-thread preceding a marriage), MBh. i, 5056; R.; BhP. &c. **–maya**, mfn. being full of curiosity (as youth, *vayas*), Kād. **–rahasya**, n., N. of a comedy. **–līlāvatī**, f., N. of a work. **–vat**, mfn. interesting (as news), Prasannar. **–sarvasva**, n., N. of a comedy. **–Kautukâgāra**, m. n. a room for festivity, room in which a marriage ceremony takes place, Kum. vii, 94; Kathās. li, 221; ciii, 189.

Kautuki (in comp. for *°kin*). **–tā**, f. curiosity, desire, eagerness, Naish. v, 13. **–bhāva**, m. id., 60.

Kautukita, mfn. eagerly interested, eager, Prasannar.

Kautukin, mfn. full of curiosity or admiration or interest in anything, vehemently desirous, eager (ifc.), Kathās. liv, 52; Sāh.; Prasannar.; festive, gay, jocose, W.

कौतूहल *kautūhala*, *am*, n. (fr. *kut°*; gaṇa *yuvâdi*), curiosity, interest in anything, vehement desire for (loc., or acc. with *prati*, or inf.), MBh.; R. &c.; anything causing curiosity, any unusual phenomenon, Megh. 48; a festival, MBh. i, 7918; Divyâv. i. **–tā**, f. curiosity, interest in anything, R. vii, 76, 35. **–para**, mfn. curious, inquisitive. **Kautūhalânvita**, mfn. eager, vehement, curious, MārkP.

Kautūhalya, *am*, n. curiosity, g. *brāhmaṇâdi*.

कौतोमत *kautomata*, *am*, n. (fr. *kuto matam*), an inquiry as to the origin of an opinion (?), MantraBr. ii, 4, 8; (*as*), m. the Mantra beginning with *kautomatam* (?), Gobh. iv, 5, 19.

कौत्स *kaútsa*, mfn. relating to Kutsa, RPrāt.; (*as*), m. patr. of a teacher, ŚBr. x; ĀśvŚr.; Nir. &c.; of Durmitra and Sumitra, RAnukr.; of a pupil of Vara-tantu, Ragh. v, 1; of a son-in-law of Bhagī-ratha, MBh. xiii, 6270; of Jaimini, MBh. i, 2046; N. of a degraded family (see √*kuts*), KātyŚr.; (*ī*), f. 'a female descendant of Kutsa,' see *kaútsī-pútra*; (*am*), n., N. of a Sûkta (composed by Kutsa), Mn. xi, 249; of different Sāmans, ĀrshBr.; Lāṭy. **Kaútsī-pútra**, m. 'the son of Kautsī,' N. of a teacher, ŚBr. xiv, 9, 4, 31.

Kautsāyana, mf(*ī*)n. fr. *kutsa*, gaṇa *pakshâdi*; relating to Kutsāyana, MaitrUp. v, 1.

कौथुम *kauthuma*, *as*, m. patr. fr. Kuthumin, N. of a teacher, Pravar.; BrahmavP.; of Pārāśarya, VāyuP.; (*ī*), f. a female descendant of Kuthumin, Vop. iv, 15; (*ās*), m. pl. the school of Kuthumin, Pāṇ. vi, 4, 144, Vārtt. 1; gaṇa *kārta-kaujapâdi*; (*kaudhuma*) Divyâv. xxxiii.

Kauthumaka, *am*, n. the Brāhmaṇa of the school of Kuthumin, Comm. on Bādar. iii, 3, 1.

कौदालिक *kaudālika*, *as*, m. (fr. *kudāla*), a man of a mixed caste (son of a fisherman by a woman of the washerman caste), W.

Kaudālīka, *as*, m. id., BrahmavP.

Kauddāla, mf(*ī*)n. made of *kuddāla* wood, Baudh. iii, 1, 7 & 2, 5 f.

कौद्रविक *kaudravika*, *am*, n. (fr. *kodrava*), sochal salt, L.

Kaudravīṇa, mfn. sown with Kodrava (as a field &c.), Pāṇ. v, 2, 1, Kāś.

Kaudravīṇaka, mfn. id., Gal.

कौद्रायण *kaudrāyaṇa*, *°ṇaka*, gaṇa *arihaṇâdi* (v. l. *kaundr°*; Gaṇar. 289; not in Kāś.)

कौद्रेय *kaudreya*, *as*, m. (gaṇa *grishṭy-ādi*) patr. fr. Kudri, KātyŚr. x, 2, 21; Pravar.

कौनकीय *kaunakīya*, *ās*, m. pl., N. of a school of the AV. (for *°nakhīya*?), Caraṇ.

कौनख्य *kaunakhya*, *am*, n. (fr. *ku-nakha*), the condition of one who has a disease of the nails, Mn. xi, 49; ugliness of the nails, W.

कौनामि *kaunāmi*, *is*, m. patr. fr. *ku-nāman*, gaṇa *bāhv-ādi*.

Kaunāmika, mf(*ā* or *ī*)n., gaṇa *kāśy-ādi*.

कौन्त *kauntá*?, MaitrS. iv, 2, 6.

कौन्तल *kauntala*, *ās*, m. pl., N. of a people, Hariv. 784 (v. l. *kont°*).

कौन्तायनि *kauntāyani*, mfn. fr. *kuntī*, gaṇa *karṇâdi*.

कौन्ताली *kauntālī*, f.?, Bālar.

कौन्तिक *kauntika*, *as*, m. (fr. *kunta*), a spearman, soldier armed with a spear, L.

Kauntī, f. (fr. *kunta* or *°ti*), a sort of perfume, Car. vi, 17; Bhpr.; N. of a river, BhP. xii, 1, 37.

कौन्तेय *kaunteya*, *as*, m. metron. fr. Kuntī, N. of Yudhishṭhira, Bhīma-sena, and Arjuna, MBh. iii, 19; Nal.; Hit.; the tree Terminalia Arjuna, L.

Kauntya, *as*, m. a king of the Kuntis, Pāṇ. iv, 1, 176, Kāś.

कौन्द *kaunda*, mf(*ī*)n. relating to or coming from jasmine (*kunda*), Vikr.; Amar. 54.

कौन्द्रायण *kaundrāyaṇa*, v. l. for *kaudr°*.

कौप *kaupa*, mf(*ī*)n. (fr. *kūpa*), coming from a well or cistern, Suśr.; Sāh.; (*am*), n. well-water, W.

Kaupīna, n. the pudenda, privities, MBh.; BhP.; Pañcat.; Kathās.; a small piece of cloth worn over the privities by poor persons, Pañcat.; Daś.; Bhartṛ.; (= *a-kārya*, Pāṇ. v, 2, 20) a wrong or improper act, sin, MBh. v, 2684; (xiii, 2491.) **–vat**, mfn. one who has only a piece of cloth over the privities.

Kaupya, mfn. coming from a well, Suśr.

कौपादकी *kaupādakī* = *kaumod°*, L., Sch.

कौपिञ्जल *kaupiñjala*, *as*, m. patr. fr. *ku-p°*, gaṇa *śivâdi*; mfn., Pāṇ. iv, 3, 112.

कौपीन *kaupīna*. See *kaupa*.

कौपुत्रक *kauputraka*, *am*, n., fr. *ku-putra*, gaṇa *manojñâdi*.

कौपोदकी *kaupodakī* = *kaumod°*, L., Sch.

कौप्य *kaupya*. See *kaupa*.

कौबेर *kaubera*, mf(*ī*)n. relating or belonging to Kubera (as *kāshṭhā* or *diś*, the region), MBh.; Hariv.; R. &c.; (*ī*), f. (scil. *diś*) Kubera's region, i.e. the north quarter, R.; Ragh. &c.; the Śakti or female energy of Kubera, L.; the plant Costus speciosus or arabicus, L. **–tīrtha**, n., N. of a Tīrtha, ŚivaP.

Kauberikeya, *as*, m. metron. fr. *kuberikā*, gaṇa *śubhrâdi*.

Kauberiṇī, f. the Śakti of Kubera, Bālar. (pl.)

कौब्ज्य *kaubjya*, *am*, n. (fr. *kubjá*), humpbackedness, Suśr.

कौमार *kaúmāra*, mf(*ī*)n. (fr. *kumārá* or *°rī*, Pāṇ. iv, 2, 13), juvenile, youthful, belonging to a youth or young girl, maiden, maidenly, (*kaúmāra loká*, the youths and girls, AV. xii, 3, 47; *kaumārī bhāryā* [Pat. & Kāś. on Pāṇ. iv, 2, 13], 'a virgin wife, one who has not had a husband previously,' R.; *kaumāra pati* [Kāś.; or *°ra bhartṛi*, Pat. on Pāṇ. iv, 2, 13], 'a man who marries a virgin,' Kathās. cxxvii, 55; *kaumāra vrata*, a vow of abstinence, MBh.); soft, tender, W.; relating to the god of war, belonging or peculiar to him, relating to Sanat-kumāra, MBh.; BhP.; Kathās. ii, 76; Paraś.; Madhus.; (*as*), m. the son of a maiden, L.; N. of a mountain (cf. *-parvata*), MBh. vi, 426; (*ās*), m. pl. the followers of Kumāra's grammar, Prauḍh.; (*ī*), f. one of the seven Mātṛis or personified energies of the gods, Śakti of Kumāra or Kārttikeya (the god of war), BrahmaP.; DevībhP.; a kind of bulbous root (= *vārāhī-kanda*), L.; (in music) N. of a Rāgiṇī; (*am*), n. childhood, youth (from birth to the age of five), maidenhood (to the age of sixteen), Mn. ix, 3; MBh.; R. &c.; (ifc. f. *ā*) Kathās. **–cārin**, mfn. abstinent, chaste (= *brahma-c°*), MBh. xiii, 5853. **–tantra**, n. the section of a medical work treating of the rearing and education of children. **–parvata**, m., N. of a mountain, NarasP. **–brahma-cārin**, mfn. = *-cārin*, MBh. i, 443 & 4733; Kathās. lxvi, 155. **–vrata-cārin**, mfn. id., MBh. xiii, 2039. **–hara**, mfn. devirginating, Sāh.

Kaumāraka, *am*, n. childhood, juvenile age, MārkP.; Sāh.; (*ikā*), f. (in music) N. of a Rāgiṇī.

Kaumāraprabhṛityaka, *am*, n. (fr. *kumāra-prabhṛiti*), the rearing and education of children (a department of medical science), Car. i, 30.

Kaumārabhṛitya, *am*, n. (fr. *kumāra-bhṛityā*), id., Suśr.

Kaumārarājya, *am*, n. (fr. *kumāra-rāja*), the position of an heir-apparent, R. ii, 58, 20 (v. l. *kum°*).

Kaumārahārita, *as*, m. patr. fr. *kumāra-hārita*, Pravar.

Kaumārāyaṇa, *as*, m. (gaṇa 1. *naḍâdi*) patr. fr. *kumāra*, Pravar.

Kaumārika, mfn. liking girls or daughters, MBh. i, 4054; relating to Kumāra (as a Tantra). **–tantra**, n., N. of a Tantra, Ānand., Sch.

Kaumārikeya, *as*, m. metron. fr. *kumārikā*, gaṇa *śubhrâdi*.

Kaumārila, mfn. relating to or composed by Kumārila, Comm. on Prab.

कौमुद *kaumuda*, *as*, m. patr. fr. Kumuda, ĀrshBr.; the month Kārttika (October–November), MBh. xiii; (*ī*), f. moonlight, moonshine (from its causing the Kumudas to blossom; also Moonlight personified as the wife of Candra or the moon), Ragh.; Kum.; Bhartṛ. &c.; elucidation (the word Kaumudī being metaphorically used like other words of similar import [cf. *candrikā*] at the end of grammatical commentaries and other explanatory works to imply that the book so designated throws much light on the subject of which it treats, e.g. *padârtha-k°*, *prakriyā-k°*, *laghu-k°*, *vaishamya-k°*, *siddhânta-k°*); the day of full moon in the month Kārttika (sacred to Kārttikeya), festival in honour of Kārttikeya held on that day, MBh. i, 7648; xiii, 6132; PSarv.; the day of full moon in the month Āśvina, L.; a festival in general, L.; (= *kumud-vatī*) the water-lily (Nymphæa esculenta), BhP. x, 65, 18; a metre (of 2 × 24 syllables); N. of a river, Śaṃkar.; (*am*), n. (with *vrata*) N. of a particular observance, AgP.

Kaumudagandhyā, f. patr., Pāṇ. vi, 1, 13, Vārtt. 2, Pat.

Kaumudika, mfn. relating to water-lilies, abounding with them, Pāṇ. iv, 2, 80; (*ā*), f., N. of a female friend of Umā, L.; of a female servant in Kāli-dāsa's play Mālav.

Kaumudī (f. of *°da*, q.v.) **–cāra**, m. n. the day of full moon in month Āśvina, L. **–jīvana**, m. 'living on the water-lily,' N. of the bird Cakora, L. **–taru**, m. the stick of a lamp, Gal. **–nirṇaya**, m., N. of a work. **–pati**, m. 'husband of the moonlight,' the moon, L. **–pracāra**, m. a kind of game, Vātsyāy. **–prabhā**, f., N. of a Comm. **–rajanī**, f. a moonlight night, Hcar. **–vilāsa**, m., N. of a work. **–vṛiksha**, m. = *-taru*, L.

Kaumudvateya, *as*, m. metron. fr. *kumudvatī*, Ragh. xviii, 2.

कौमेदुर *kaumedura*, N. of a locality, gaṇa *takshaśilâdi* (Kāś.); (mfn.) ib.

कौमोदकी *kaumodakī*, f. (fr. *ku-modaka*?), N. of the club of Vishṇu or Kṛishṇa (given to him by Varuṇa), MBh. i, 8200; Hariv.; BhP. &c.

Kaumodī, f. = *°dakī*, L.

कौम्भ *kaumbha*, mfn. (fr. *kumbhá*, gaṇa *saṃkalâdi*), put into a pot, Suśr.

Kaumbhakarṇa, mfn. belonging to Kumbhakarṇa, Bālar.

Kaumbhakarṇi, *is*, m. patr. fr. Kumbhakarṇa, Bhaṭṭ. xv, 120.

Kaumbhakāraka, *am*, n. 'anything made by a potter,' gaṇa *kulālâdi*.

Kaumbhakāri, *is*, m. the son of a potter, Pāṇ. iv, 1, 153, Kāś.

Kaumbhakāreya, *as*, m. the son of a female potter, Pat. on Pāṇ. iv, 1, 14, Vārtt. 5 & 48, Vārtt. 8.

Kaumbhakārya, *as*, m. = °*kāri*, Pāṇ. iv, 1, 153, Sch. (not in Kāś.)

Kaumbhāyana, mfn. fr. *kumbha*, gaṇa *pakshâdi*.

Kaumbhāyani, mfn. fr. *kumbhī*, gaṇa *karṇâdi*.

Kaumbheyaka, mfn. fr. *kumbhī*, gaṇa *kattry-ādi*.

Kaumbhya, mfn. (gaṇa *saṃkāśâdi*) put into a pot (*ghṛita*), SāmavBr. ii, 2, 3 & 8, 4; (*as*), m. patr. of Babhru, TāṇḍyaBr. xv, 3, 13.

कौरम *kaurama*, *as*, m., N. of a man (v.l. °*ruma*), AV. xx, 127, 1.

कौरयाण *kaúrayāṇa*, *as*, m. (fr. *kur*°?), patr. of Pāka-sthāman, RV. viii, 3, 21 (Nir. v, 25).

कौरव *kaurava*, mf(*ī*)n. (=°*vaka*, Pāṇ. iv, 2, 130; gaṇas *utsâdi* and *kacchâdi*) relating or belonging to the Kurus, MBh.; VarBṛS.; (*kshetra*= *kuru-ksh*°) Megh.; (*as*), m. patr. fr. Kuru, descendant of Kuru (generally used in pl.), MBh.; Hariv. &c. (ifc. f. *ā*, MBh. i, 7961); (*ī*), f. Trigonella fœnum græcum, Gal. **-pāṇḍavīya,** mfn. relating to the Kauravas and Pāṇḍavas, Pracaṇḍ.

Kauravaka, mfn. fr. *kúru*, Pāṇ. iv, 2, 130; gaṇa *kacchâdi*.

Kauravāyaṇi, *is*, m. patr. fr. *kúru*, g. *tikâdi*.

Kauraveya, *ās*, m. the descendants of Kuru, MBh. i, 5689 f.; iii, 313 & 14744; iv, 1136.

Kauravyá, *as*, m. (gaṇas *tikâdi* and *bhargâdi*) patr. fr. Kuru, descendant of Kuru, AV. xx, 127, 8 (*kaúravya*); ŚBr. xii; ŚāṅkhŚr.; MBh. &c.; N. of a Nāga (father of Ulūpi), MBh. i; (*ās*), m. pl. = *pāṇḍavās*, MBh.; N. of a people, MBh. vi, 362.

Kauravyāyaṇa, *as*, m. patr. fr. °*vyá*, descendant of Kauravya, Pravar.; (*ī*), f. of *kauravyá*, Pāṇ. iv, 1, 19. **Kaúravyāyaṇī-pútra,** m. 'son of a female descendant of Kuru,' N. of a teacher, ŚBr. xiv, 8, 1, 1.

Kauravyāyaṇi, *is*, m. patr. fr. °*vyá*, g. *tikâdi*.

Kaurukātya, *as*, m. patr. fr. *kuru-kata*, gaṇa *gargâdi*.

Kaurukullaka, *ās*, m. pl. (fr. *kuru-kullā*), N. of a Buddhist school.

Kaurujaṅgala or °**jāṅgala,** mfn. fr. *kuru-jaṅgala*, Pāṇ. vii, 3, 25, Kāś.

Kaúrupañcāla, for °*pāñc*°, ŚBr. xi, 4, 1, 2.

Kaurupathi, *is*, m. patr. fr. *kuru-patha*, N. of a Ṛishi, Kauś.

Kaúrupāñcāla, mfn. (gaṇa *anuśatikâdi*) belonging to the race of the Kurus and Pañcālas, ŚBr. i, 7, 2, 8.

कौरुम *kauruma*. See *kaurama*.

कौर्पर *kaurpara*, mfn. (fr. *kūrp*°), being at the elbow, Suśr.

कौर्पि *kaurpi*, *is*, m. (borrowed fr. Gk. σκορπίος) the sign Scorpio, VarBṛ. i, 7 (v. l.)

Kaurpya, *as*, m. id., ib.

कौर्म *kaurma*, mfn. (fr. *kūrma*), relating or belonging or peculiar to a tortoise, Pañcat.; (*as*), m. (scil. *avatāra*) the Avatāra of Vishṇu as a tortoise, BhP. xi, 4, 18; N. of a great period or Kalpa (the day of full moon of Brahmā); (*am*), n. (scil. *āsana*) a particular manner of being seated, NārP.; (scil. *purāṇa*) N. of a Purāṇa (on the subject of Vishṇu's descent as a tortoise), Sarvad. **Kaurmôpapurāṇa,** n., N. of an Upa-purāṇa.

कौर्वत *kaurvata*, mfn. fr. *kurvat*, Pāṇ. iii, 2, 124, Vārtt. 3, Pat.

कौल *kaula*, mf(*ī*)n. (fr. *kúla*), relating or belonging to a family, extending over a whole family or race, R. iv, 28, 9; heritable in a family, BhP. xii, 3, 36; sprung from a noble family, L.; belonging or particular to the Kaulas, Kulârṇ.; (*as*), m. a worshipper of Śakti accord. to the left-hand ritual, ib.; a kind of weight (*kola*), Gal.; (*ī*), f. noble descent, VarYogay.; (*am*), n. the doctrine and practices of the left-hand Śāktas, Kulârṇ. **-mārga,** m. (= *kul*°) the doctrine of the Kaulas, Tantr. **-rahasya,** n. 'esoteric doctrine of the Kaulas,' N. of a work. **-vrata,** n. living accord. to the traditional rule of a family. **Kaulârcana-dīpikā,** f., N. of a work. **Kaulâvalīya,** n., N. of a Tantra, Tantras. **Kaulêśa-bhairavī,** f. a form of Durgā, ib. **Kaulêśvara,** m. (with Śāktas) N. of an author of Mantras, Tantr. **Kaulôpanishad,** f., N. of an Up.

Kaulakeya, mfn. sprung from a noble family, L.; (*as*), m. for *kaulaṭeya*, q. v., L.

Kaulattha, mf(*ī*, Pāṇ. iv, 4, 4)n. (fr. *kul*°), made or prepared with Dolichos uniflorus, Suśr.; (*am*), n. a drink prepared with Kulattha, ib.

Kaulatthīna, mfn. sown with Dolichos uniflorus (as a field), Pāṇ. v, 2, 1, Kāś.

Kaulapata, mf(*ī*)n. fr. *kula-pati*, gaṇa *aśvapaty-ādi*.

Kaulapatya, *am*, n. (fr. *kula-pati*), the state of the head of a family, R. vii, 59, 2, 38 f. & 47.

Kaulaputra, *am*, n. (fr. *kula-p*°), the state of a son of a good family, Hcar.

Kaulaputraka, *am*, n. id., gaṇa *manojñâdi*.

Kaulika, mfn. belonging to a family or race, ancestral, customary or heritable in a family, W.; (*as*), m. a weaver, VarBṛS. lxxxvii, 20; Pañcat.; a follower of the left-hand Śākta ritual, Kulârṇ.; Tantras.; (hence) a heretic, L. **-tantra,** n., N. of a Tantra, Tantras.

Kaulīna, mf(*ā*)n. belonging or peculiar to a noble family, R. v, 87, 12; (*as*), m. a follower of the left-hand Śākta ritual, W.; (= *kaulakeya*) the son of a female beggar, W.; (*ās*), m. pl. the pupils of Kaulīni, Pāṇ. iv, 1, 90, Vārtt. 4, Pat.; (*am*), n. rumour, report, evil report, detraction, Śak.; Ragh. xiv, 36 & 84; Megh.; Kathās. (ifc. f. *ā*); family scandal, W.; disgraceful or improper act, Kād.; high birth (fr. *kulīna*), Kathās. lii, 182 (?); combat of animals or birds or snakes &c., cock-fighting &c., gambling by setting animals to fight together, L.; the pudenda, privities (for *kaupīna*?), L.

Kaulīni, *is*, m. patr. fr. *kulīna*, Pāṇ. iv, 1, 90, Vārtt. 4, Pat.

Kaulīnya, *am*, n. high birth, nobility, Pañcat.; family honour, W.; family trouble or scandal, W.

Kauleya, mfn. sprung from a noble family, Comm. on L.; of the left-hand Śākta sect, W.; (*as*), m. 'a domestic animal,' i. e. 'a dog,' see *-kuṭumbinī*. **-kuṭumbinī,** f. 'a dog's wife,' bitch, Kād.

Kauleyaka, mfn. sprung from a noble family, Pāṇ. iv, 1, 140; pertaining to a family, W.; (*as*), m. (Pāṇ. iv, 2, 96) 'domestic animal' (or 'of good breed'?), a dog (esp. a hunting dog), Kād.; Hcar.

Kaulya, mfn. sprung from a noble family, Comm. on L.; of the left-hand Śākta sect, W.; (*am*), n. noble descent, MBh. v, 1240.

कौलक *kaulaka*, mfn. fr. *kúla*, gaṇa *dhūmâdi*. **Kaulakâvatī,** nom. du. m. (fr. *kúla* and *âvat*?), N. of two Ṛishis, MaitrS. ii, 1, 3.

Kaulaki, *is*, m. patr., Pravar.

Kauli, *is*, m. (Pāṇ. Siddh.) patr., Pravar.

कौलकेय *kaulakeya*. See *kaula*.

कौलटिनेय *kaulaṭineya*, *as*, *ī*, m. f. (fr. *kulaṭā*), the son or daughter of a female beggar (or of a disloyal wife, L.), Pāṇ. iv, 1, 127, Kāś.

Kaulaṭeya, *as*, *ī*, m. f. id., ib.

Kaulaṭera, *as*, *ā*, m. f. the son or daughter of a disloyal wife, ib.; of a female beggar, Comm. on L.

कौलत्थ *kaulattha*, &c. See *kaula*.

कौलब *kaulaba*, *as*, m., N. of the third Karaṇa or astronomical period, VarBṛS. ic, 4 & 6.

Kaulava, *as*, m. id., Koshṭhīpr. **Kaulavârṇava,** m., N. of a Tantra.

कौलाल *kaulālá*, *as*, m. (Ved. = *kúl*°, Pāṇ. v, 4, 36, Vārtt. 1) a potter ['the son of a potter,' Comm.], VS. xxx, 7; (*am*), n. (fr. *kúl*°), potter's ware, pottery, ĀśvGṛ. iv, 3, 19. **-cakrá,** n. a potter's wheel, ŚBr. xi, 8, 1, 1.

Kaulālaka, *am*, n. anything made by a potter, earthenware, porcelain, Pāṇ. iv, 3, 118.

कौलास *kaulāsa*, mfn. fr. *kūl*°, gaṇa *saṃkalâdi*.

कौलि *kauli*. See *kaulaka*.

कौलिक *kaulika*. See *kaula*.

कौलितर *kaulitará*, mfn.? (said of the demon Śambara), RV. iv, 30, 14.

कौलिन्द *kaulinda*, *ās*, m. pl., N. of a people, VarBṛS. (v. l. for *kauṇinda*); (*as*), m. a prince of that people, iv, 24.

कौलिशायनि *kauliśāyani*, mfn. fr. *kuliśa*, gaṇa *karṇâdi*.

Kauliśika, mf(*ī*)n. resembling a thunderbolt, gaṇa *aṅguly-ādi*.

कौलीक *kaulīká*, *as*, m. (=*kulīkā*) a kind of bird, VS. xxiv, 24; MaitrS. iii, 14, 5.

कौलीन *kaulīna*, &c. See *kaula*.

कौलीरा *kaulīrā*, f. (fr. *kulīra*), N. of a plant (= *karkaṭa-śriṅgī*), L.

कौलूत *kaulūta*, *ās*, m. pl., N. of a people, VarBṛS. x, 11; (*as*), m. a prince of that people (v. l. °*lūbha*), Mudr.; (mfn.) fr. *kul*°, g. *kacchâdi* (vv. ll. °*lūtara*, °*lūna* [Kāś.] & *ulūpa* [Gaṇar. 327, Sch.]).

Kaulūtara, °**lūna.** See °*lūta*.

कौलेय *kauleya*, °*leyaka*. See *kaula*.

कौल्मलबर्हिष *kaulmalabarhisha*, *am*, n., N. of several Sāmans (called after *kulmala-b*°), Tāṇḍya-Br. xv, 3, 20, Lāṭy. iv, 5, 26 & vii, 2, 1; 13 & 15.

कौल्माषिक *kaulmāshika*, mf(*ī*)n. (fr. *kulmāsha*) = *kulmāshe sādhu*, gaṇa *guḍâdi*.

Kaulmāshī, f. a day of full moon on which Kulmāsha is eaten, Pāṇ. v, 2, 83.

Kaulmāshīṇa, mf(*ā*)n. sown with or fit for Kulmāsha (as a field), Comm. on L.

कौल्य *kaulya*. See *kaula*.

कौवल *kauvala*, *am*, n. (=*kuv*°) the jujube, Pat. on Pāṇ. iv, 3, 140, Vārtt. 1 & 156, Vārtt. 3.

कौविदार्य *kauvidārya*, mfn. fr. *ko-vidāra*, gaṇa *pragady-ādi*.

कौविन्दी *kauvindī*, f. (fr. *kuvinda*), the wife of a weaver, SkandaP.

कौश 1. *kauśá*, mf(*ī*)n. made of Kuśa grass, ŚBr. v; KātyŚr.; ŚāṅkhŚr.; MBh.; (*as*), m. = *kuśa-dvīpa*, VP.; (*am*), n. (scil. *nagara*) 'the town of Kuśa,' N. of Kānyakubja, L. **Kauśâmbhas,** n. water in which Kuśa grass has been boiled, Devīm.

1. **Kauśika,** mfn. (fr. *kuśā* or *kuśi*), 'having paws,' an owl, Suśr.; VarBṛS.; Pañcat. &c.; an ichneumon, L.; (mfn.) coming from an owl, Suśr. **-tā** (°*ká-*), f. the state of being kept together by two pins (and 'the state of being Sūrya [see 3. *kauśiká*]),' TBr. i, 5, 10, 2. **-1. -tvá,** n. id., MaitrS. iv, 5, 7. **Kauśikâṅguli,** m. 'having paws like an owl,' N. of a teacher, Pravar. **Kauśikârāti,** m. 'enemy of owls,' a crow, L. **Kauśikâri,** m. id., L. **Kauśiky-oja,** m. 'abode of owls' (*oja* = *ojas*), N. of a tree (= *śākhoṭa*), L.

Kauśya, mfn. made of Kuśa grass, MBh.; (*as*), m. patr. fr. Kuśa (= *kaúshya*), ŚBr. x, 5, 5, 1, Sch.

कौश 2. *kauśa*, mfn. (fr. *kóśa*), silken, BhP. iii, 4, 7; Buddh. L.

Kauśakī, f. (for °*śikī*?), N. of one of the eight A-kulas, Kulârṇ.

2. **Kauśika,** mfn. forming a receptacle (as a wound; see *kośa-vat*), Bhpr. vi, 35 (v. l. *kaushṭhika*); sheathed (a sword), MBh. iii, 11461; silken, MBh. iii; (*as*), m. one who is versed in dictionaries, L.; a lexicographer, L.; one who catches snakes, L.; the fragrant substance bdellium, L.; marrow, L.; a kind of seed, L.; (*ā*), f. a drinking-vessel (v. l. *kośikā*), L.; (*ī*), f., N. of a goddess sprung from the body of Pārvatī, MārkP. lxxxv, 40; KālP.; DevīP.; (*am*), n. silk, silk cloth, Yājñ. i, 186; MBh. xiii, 5502; a silk garment, BhP. x, 83, 28.

Kauśi-kāra. See *kośa-kāra*.

Kauśī-dhānya, *am*, n. = *kośa-dh*°, q. v., Baudh. (Comm. on KātyŚr. ii, 1, 10).

Kauśeya, mfn. silken, MBh. &c.; (*am*), n. silk, silk cloth, silk petticoat or trowsers, a woman's lower garments of silk, Pāṇ. iv, 3, 42; Mn.; Yājñ.; MBh. &c.; N. of a locality, Romakas.

Kauśeyaka, *am*, n. silk cloth, VarBṛS. xxvii, 27.

कौशल *kauśala*, n. (fr. *kuś*°; g. *yuvâdi*) well-being, welfare, good fortune, prosperity, MBh. iv, 486; BhP.; skilfulness, cleverness, experience (with loc. or ifc.), Suśr.; Mṛicch.; Pañcat. &c.; (*ī*), f. friendly inquiry, greeting, salutation, L.; a respectful present, Nazr, L.; (see also *kausala*.)

Kauśali, *is*, m. metron. fr. *kuśalā*, g. *bāhv-ādi*.

Kauśalikā, f. a present, respectful gift, Kathās.

Kauśalya, *as*, m. a kind of pavilion, Vāstuv.; (*am*), n. (gaṇa *brāhmaṇâdi*) welfare, well-being, prosperity, MBh.; R.; cleverness, skilfulness, experience (ifc.), SaddhP.; Bhpr.; (*ā*), f., see *kausalya*.

कौशाम्ब *kauśāmba*, mfn. (fr. *kuś*°), belonging to Kauśāmbī (as a territory, *maṇḍala*), Inscr.; (*ī*), f. (g. *nady-ādi*), N. of an ancient city (now represented by the village of Kosam, on the Jumnā, near Allahābād; also called *vatsa-pattana*), R. i, 34, 6; Divyâv. xxxvi f.; Pāṇ. iv, 2, 68, Kāś.; Kathās. iv, 18; ix, 5; lxvi, 193; MatsyaP.; Hit.

Kauśāmbi, *is*, f. = °*bī*, VarBṛS. xvi, 3.

Kauśāmbikā, f., N. of a woman, Ratnâv.

Kauśāmbīya, mfn. coming from Kauśāmbī, ib.

Kauśāmbeyá, *as*, m. (gaṇa *śubhrâdi*) patr. fr. *kuśāmba*, ŚBr. xii, 2, 2, 13; GopBr. i, 4, 24; mfn. fr. *kauśāmbī*, gaṇa *nady-ādi*.

Kauśāmbya, *as*, m. a prince of Kauśāmbī, Hariv. 5017 & 5498.

कौशाम्वी *kauśâśvī*, v. l. for °*śāmbī*, R.

कौशिक 3. *kauśiká*, mfn. relating to Kuśika (or to Kauśika), MBh. xiii, 2719; (*as*), m. (gaṇa *bidâdi*) patr. of Viśvā-mitra (who was the son or grandson of Kuśika), interpolation after RV. x, 85; MBh.; R.; of Gādhi, Hariv. 1457; of Bhadra-śarman, VBr.; N. of a teacher (author of the Kauśika-sūtra, brother of Paippalādi), BṛĀrUp.; Kauś.; Pāṇ. iv, 3, 103; Hariv. 11074; N. of a grammarian, Hariv. 5501; of one of Jarāsandha's generals, MBh. ii, 885; N. of Indra (as originally perhaps belonging to the Kuśikas or friendly to them), RV. i, 10, 11; ŚBr. iii, 3, 4, 19; ShaḍvBr.; TĀr.; ĀśvŚr.; MBh. &c.; of Sūrya, TBr. i, 5, 10, 2, Sch.; of a son of Vasu-deva, VP.; of Śiva, L.; of an Asura, Hariv. 2288; Vatika robusta, L.; (in music) N. of a Rāga; (for *kaiśika*) love, passion, L.; (*ās*), m. pl. the descendants of Kuśika, Hariv. 1770 ff.; (of Kuśa) R. i, 35, 20; (*ī*), f. (in music) N. of a Rāgiṇī; N. of Durgā, Hariv. 3260 & 3270; N. of a Śikshā; of a river in Bahar (commonly Kosi or Koosa, created by Viśvā-mitra, or identified with Satyavatī, the sister of Viśvā-mitra), MBh.; Hariv.; R. &c.; N. of a Buddhist female beggar, Mālav.; for *kaiśikī*, q. v., Sāh. **–tā** (°*kâ-*), f., see 1. *kauśika*. **–tvá**, n., see ib.; the state of being a descendant of Kuśika, Hariv. 1774; the state of being Kauśika (i. e. Indra), 12489. **–priya**, m. 'dear to Kauśika,' N. of Rāma, L. **–phala**, m. the cocoa-nut (said to have been created by Viśvā-mitra, i. e. Kauśika, when endeavouring to form a human being in rivalry of Brahmā, the nut being the rudiment of a head, W.), L. **Kauśikâtmaja**, m. 'Indra's son,' N. of Arjuna, L. **Kauśikâditya**, n., N. of a Tīrtha, SkandaP. **Kauśikâyudha**, n. 'Indra's bow,' the rainbow, L. **Kauśikâraṇya**, n. 'Kauśika's wood,' N. of a town, Hariv. iii, 44, 48.

Kauśikāyani, *is*, m. patr. fr. *kauśiká*, N. of a teacher, ŚBr. xiv, 5, 5, 21 & 7, 3, 27.

Kauśikin, *inas*, m. pl. the pupils of Kauśika, Pāṇ. iv, 3, 103; iv, 2, 66, Kāś.

Kauśikī (f. of °*ka*, q. v.) **–putra**, m., N. of a teacher, BṛĀrUp. vi, 5, 1.

Kauśila, *as*, m. a familiar N. for Kauśika, Vām. v, 2, 63.

Kauśilya, *as*, m. patr. of the prince Hiraṇyanābha, VāyuP.

कौशिज *kauśija*, *ās*, m. pl., N. of a people, MBh. vi, 349 (v. l. *kosala*).

कौशिल *kauśila*, °*lya*. See 3. *kauśiká*.

कौशीधान्य *kauśī-dhānya*. See 2. *kauśa*.

कौशीरकेय *kauśīrakeya*, mfn. fr. *kuśīraka*, gaṇa *sakhy-ādi*.

कौशीलव *kauśīlava*, *am*, n. (fr. *kuś*°), the profession of an actor or dancer, Gobh. iii, 1, 19.

Kauśīlavya, *am*, n. id., Mn. xi, 65.

कौशेय *kauśeya*, °*yaka*. See 2. *kauśa*.

कौश्य *kauśya*. See 1. *kauśa*.

कौश्रेय *kauśreya*, *as*, m. patr. fr. *kuśri*, Kāṭh. xx, 8 & xxi, 9.

कौषारव *kaushārava*, *as*, m. patr. fr. Kushāru, AitBr. viii, 28 (N. of Maitreya); BhP. i, 13, 2; iii.

Kaushāravi, m. id., BhP. ii, 10, 49; iii, 10, 3.

कौषीतक *kaushītaka*, *as*, m. patr. fr. *kush*°, N. of Kahoḍa, ĀśvGṛ.; (*ī*), f. patr. of Agastya's wife, L.; N. of a Śākhā of the RV.; (*am*), n., N. of a Brāhmaṇa, ŚāṅkhBr.; ŚāṅkhŚr.; Bādar. iii, 3, 1, Sch.

Kaúshītaki, *is*, m. (Pāṇ. iv, 1, 124, Kāś.) patr. fr. *kushītaka*, ŚBr. ii; TāṇḍyaBr. xvii (pl.); ŚāṅkhŚr.; ChUp.; Pravar. **–brāhmaṇa**, n., N. of a Brāhmaṇa (= ŚāṅkhBr.); = KaushUp., Bādar. i, 4, 16, Sch. & iii, 3, 10, Sch.; °*nôpanishad*, f. id., i, 1, 28, Sch. **–rahasya**, n. id., iii, 3, 26, Sch.; *-brāhmaṇa*, n. id., Comm. on Mn. iv, 23. **Kaushītaky-upanishad**, f., N. of an Up.

Kaushītakin, *inas*, m. 'the pupils of °*ka*,' N. of a school, ĀśvGṛ. i, 23, 5; Bādar., Sch.

Kaúshītakeya, *as*, m. = °*ka*, N. of Kahoḍa, ŚBr. xiv, 6, 4, 1; of a Kāśyapa, Pāṇ. iv, 1, 124.

कौषीद्य *kaushīdya*. See *kausīdya*.

कौषेय *kausheya*, *as*, m. (fr. *koshá*), N. of a Ṛishi, R. vii, 1, 4; also v. l. for *kauśeya* (q. v.), R. iii, iv; MārkP. xv, 27.

Kaúshya, *as*, m. patr. fr. *koshá*, Kāṭh. xxii, 6 f.; ŚBr. x, 5, 5, 1.

कौष्टचित्क *kaushṭacitka*, mfn. fr. *kushṭa-cit*, gaṇa *kathâdi* (Kāś.), v. l. for °*shṭhavitka*.

कौष्ठ *kaushṭhá*, mfn. (fr. *koshṭha*), being in the stomach or abdomen, Sarvad.; being in a store-room, ŚBr. i, 1, 2, 7.

1. **Kaushṭhika**, v. l. for 2. *kauśika*.

Kaushṭhya, mfn. being in the abdomen, Yājñ. iii, 95; extremely rich (?), TĀr. vi, 5, 2.

कौष्ठिक 2. *kaushṭhika*, mfn. (fr. *kushṭha*), treating of leprosy, Car. ii, 5 & vi, 18.

Kaúshṭhavitka, mfn. (fr. *kushṭha-vid*), useful for the knowledge of leprosy [Gaṇar. 337, Sch.], g. *kathâdi*; (cf. *kaushṭacitka*.)

कौष्ठिल *kaushṭhila*, &c. See *mahā-k*°.

कौष्माण्ड *kaushmāṇḍa*, mfn. addressed to the demons called Kūshmāṇḍa (as a Mantra), VarBṛS.

Kaushmāṇḍika, mfn. id., AV. Pariś. xlii, 2.

कौष्य *kaúshya*. See *kausheya*.

कौसल *kausala* (often spelt *kauśala*), mfn. belonging to the Kosalas (a country), Divyâv. vii, xii; (*ās*), m. pl., N. of a people, VarBṛS. x, 14; Romakas.; SSaṃkar.; of a dynasty, BhP. xii, 1, 33; v. l. for *kos*°, q. v.; (*ā*), f., N. of one of Kṛishṇa's wives, x, 83, 6; (*ī*), f., N. of one of Vasu-deva's wives, VP.

Kausalaka, *ās*, m. pl. (spelt *kauśal*°), N. of a people, VarBṛS.; (mfn.) belonging to the Kosalas, ib.

Kausaleya, *as*, m. = °*lyeya*, L.

Kaúsalya, mfn. (often spelt *kauś*°) belonging to the people of the Kosalas; (*as*), m. (Pāṇ. iv, 1, 171) a prince of the Kosalas, ŚBr. xiii; ŚāṅkhŚr.; PraśnUp.; Hariv. &c.; (*ā*), f. 'daughter of a prince of the Kosalas,' N. of the wife of Pūru and mother of Janam-ejaya, MBh. i, 3764; of the wife of Satvat, Hariv. 1999; of Daśa-ratha's wife (mother of Rāma-candra), MBh. iii, 15879; R.; of the mother of Dhṛita-rāshṭra, L.; of the mother of Pāṇḍu, L.

Kausalyā (f. of °*lya*, q. v.) **–nandana**, m. 'son of Kausalyā,' Rāma, L. **–mātṛi**, m. 'having Kausalyā for his mother,' Rāma, MBh. iii, 16572.

Kausalyāyani, *is*, m. patr. fr. °*lya*, Pāṇ. iv, 1, 155; metron. fr. °*lyā* (or patr. fr. *kosala*), N. of Rāma, Bhaṭṭ. vii, 90.

Kausalyeya, *as*, m. metron. fr. °*lyā*, N. of Rāma-candra, Prasannar.

कौसित *kausitá*, *as*, m., N. of a pool (mentioned in connection with *kusitâyī*, q. v.), MaitrS. ii, 1, 11; MānGṛ. i, 6.

Kausida, *as*, m. (spelt *kos*°) id., Kāṭh. x, 5.

Kausīda, mf(*ī*)n. (fr. *kus*°), connected with or relating to a loan, usurious, Mn. viii, 143.

Kausīdya, *am*, n. sloth, indolence, Lalit. (printed ed. *kaush*°); the practice of usury, L.

कौसुम *kausuma*, mf(*ī*)n. (fr. *kus*°), coming from or belonging to flowers (as pollen), Sāh.; made of flowers, Naish. vii, 28; AgP. xliii, 10; Kathās. civ, 13; Bālar.; (*am*), n. (= *kusumâñjana*) the ashes of brass (used as a collyrium), L.

Kausumâyudha, mfn. (fr. *kus*°), relating to the god of love, Vet. xx, 19.

कौसुम्भ *kausumbha*, mf(*ī*)n. prepared with safflower, Suśr.; (Pāṇ. iv, 2, 1, Kāś.) dyed with safflower, orange, Ratnâv.; (*as*), m. wild safflower, L.; (*am*), n. (with *śāka*) safflower prepared as a potherb, VārP.; anything dyed with safflower, Cāṇ.

Kausumbhaka, mfn. dyed with safflower, AgP.

कौसुरुबिन्द *kausurubinda*, *as*, m. patr. fr. *kus*°, GopBr. i, 4, 24; N. of a Daśa-rātra ceremony, KātyŚr. xxiii f.; Drāhy. xxx, 3.

Kaúsurubindi, *is*, m. patr. fr. *kusurubinda*, ŚBr. xii, 2, 2, 13.

कौसृतिक *kausṛitika*, *as*, m. (fr. *ku-sṛiti*), a juggler, conjurer, Pāṇ. v, 2, 75, Kāś.

कौस्तुभ *kaustubha*, *as*, *am*, m. n. (cf. *kust*°), N. of a celebrated jewel (obtained with thirteen other precious things at the churning of the ocean and suspended on the breast of Kṛishṇa or Vishṇu), MBh.; Hariv.; R. &c.; (*as*), m. a manner of joining the fingers, Tantras.; = *kiṃtughna*, AV. Jyot.; (*am*), n. a kind of oil (*sarshapôdbhava*), KātyŚr. i, 8, 37, Sch.; N. of a work. **–dhāman**, m. 'abode of the Kaustubha,' Vishṇu, Prasannar. **–bhṛit**, m. 'wearing the Kaustubha,' id., Kpr. **–lakshaṇa**, m. 'whose mark is the Kaustubha,' id., W. **–vakshas**, m. 'whose breast is decorated with the Kaustubha,' id., L. **Kaustubhôras**, m. id., Gal.

Kaustubhīya, mfn. relating or belonging to the Kaustubha jewel, Bālar.

कौस्त्र *kaustra*, *am*, n. the state of being a bad wife (*ku-strī*), gaṇa *yuvâdi*.

कौहड *kauhaḍa*, *as*, m. patr. fr. *koh*°, gaṇa *śivâdi*; Pāṇ. ii, 4, 58, Kāś.

Kauhaḍi, *is*, m. id., ib.

Kauhala, *as*, m. patr. fr. *koh*°, VBr. **Kauhalīputra**, m. 'son of a female descendant of Kohala,' N. of a grammarian, TPrāt. ii, 5.

Kauhalīya, *ās*, m. pl., N. of a school, Gobh. iii.

कौहित *kauhita*, *as*, m. patr. fr. *koh*°, gaṇa *śivâdi*.

क्नंस् *knaṃs*, cl. 1. 10. P. °*sati*, °*sayati*, Dhātup. xxxiii, 90; (cf. √*kuṇś*, *kuṇs*, *knas*, *kraṇś*.)

क्नथ् *knath*, cl. 1. P. °*thati*, to hurt, Dhātup. xix, 38; (cf. √*krath*, *klath*.)

क्नस् *knas*, cl. 4. P. °*syati*, to be crooked (in mind or body), Dhātup. xxvi, 26; to shine, ib.: Caus. *knasayati*, to shine, Dhātup. xix, 65; Vop.; (cf. √*knaṃs*.)

Knasa, mfn. shining (?), Vop. xxvi, 30; (cf. *caknasa*.)

क्नु *knu* or *knū*, cl. 9. P. Ā. *knunāti*, °*nīte* or *knūnāti*, °*nīte*, to sound, Dhātup. xxxi, 10.

क्नूय् *knūy*, cl. 1. Ā. *knūyate* (ind. p. *knoyitvā*, Vop. xxvi, 207), to be wet, Dhātup. xiv, 14; to make a creaking sound, ib.; to stink, L.: Caus. P. *knopayati* (Pāṇ. vii, 3, 36 & 86), to make wet, Nir. vii, 14 (Sāy. on RV. i, 1, 1).

Knūta, mfn. stinking, W.; noisy, W.; wet, W.

Knūyitṛi, mfn. stinking, Pāṇ. iii, 2, 152, Kāś.

Knopana. See *a-kn*°.

Knopam, ind. ifc. See *cela-k*°, *vastra-k*°.

क्मर् *kmar*, cl. 1. P. *kmarati*, to be crooked (in body or mind), be fraudulent, Dhātup. xv, 47; (cf. √*hvṛi*.)

क्य *kyà*, *am*, n (fr. 3. *ká*), anything agreeable to Prajā-pati, ŚBr. x, 3, 4, 2 & 4; 4, 1, 4 & 15 ff.

क्यत् *kyàt* = *kíyat* (q. v.), how much? TBr. iii, 2, 9, 7.

क्याकु *kyāku*, *u*, n. a fungus, Āp.; Gaut.

क्याम्बू *kyāmbū*, *ūs*, f. = *kiyâmbu*, AV. xviii, 3, 6; TĀr. vi, 4, 1 (*kyāmbú*).

क्रंश् *kraṇś*, cl. 1. P. (?) °*sati*, to illuminate, Nir. ii, 25; (cf. √*knaṃs*, *knas*.)

क्रकच *krakaca*, *as*, *am*, m. n. a saw, MBh. &c.; (*as*), m. a kind of musical instrument, MBh. vii, 1676; ix, 2676; Ardea virgo, Npr.; N. of a plant (Capparis aphylla, L.), Kād.; of a hell, PadmaP.; of a Kāpālika priest, SSaṃkar.; (*ā*), f. **=-cchada**, L. **–cchada**, m. 'saw-leaved,' Pandanus odoratissimus, L. **–tvac**, m. id., Npr. **–pattra**, m. the teak tree, L. **-pad** (nom. *-pād*), m. 'saw-footed,' a lizard, chameleon, L. **-pṛishṭhī**, f. 'saw-backed,' Cojus Cobojus (a fish with numerous small spines in the back), L. **-vyavahāra**, m. a particular method of computing or rating a heap of wood, Līl.

Krākacika, *as*, m. a sawyer, R. ii, 83, 14.

Krākacya, mfn. to be sawed, Līl. **-vyavahṛiti**, f. = *krakaca-vyavahāra*, ib.

क्रकण *krakaṇa, as*, m. (onomat.) a kind of partridge (commonly Kayar, Perdix sylvatica), W.; (cf. *kṛikaṇa.*)

Krakara, *as*, m. id., Suśr.; (see also *-tva*); (= *krakaca*) Ardea virgo, L.; the plant Capparis aphylla, L.; a saw, L.; a poor man, L.; disease, L. **-tva**, n. the state of a partridge, MBh. xiii, 5501 (= MārkP. xv, 27).

क्रकरट *krakaraṭa, as*, m. a lark, Dhanv.

Krakarāṭa, *as*, m. id., ib.

क्रकुच्छन्द *krakucchanda, as*, m., N. of the 1st of the five Buddhas of the present Kalpa, Buddh.

क्रक्ष् *kraksh*, an obs. rt., see *ava-krakshín, vana-krakshá.*

Krákshamāṇa, mfn. (pr. p. Ā.) roaring, raving, RV. viii, 76, 11.

क्रडन *kraḍana, am*, n. (for *kruḍ*°?) submerging, ducking, Comm. on KātyŚr. v, 5, 31.

क्रतु *krátu, us*, m. (√1. *kṛi* or 2. *kṛi*), plan, design, intention, resolution, determination, purpose, RV.; VS.; ŚBr.; BṛĀrUp.; desire, will (instr. *krátvā*, willingly, readily, RV.; *ékena krátunā*, through the mere will, RV. ii, 13, 11); power, ability, RV.; deliberation, consultation, RV.; VS.; intelligence, understanding (e. g. *bhadrá krátu*, right judgment, good understanding; also in conjunction or in comp. or ifc. with *dáksha*, see *krátu-dákshau* and *daksha-kratú*), RV.; VS.; TS.; ŚBr.; inspiration, enlightenment, RV.; a sacrificial rite or ceremony, sacrifice (as the Aśva-medha sacrifice), offering, worship (also personified, R. vii, 90, 9), AitBr.; ŚBr. xi; ĀśvŚr. &c.; Kratu as intelligence personified (as a son of Brahmā and one of the Prajā-patis or the seven or ten principal Ṛishis, Mn. i, 35; MBh. i, 2518 & 2568; Hariv. &c.; [N. of a star] VarBṛS.; married to Kriyā and father of 60,000 Vālikhilyas, BhP. iv, 1, 39; husband of Haya-śirā, vi, 6, 33); N. of one of the Viśve-devās, VP.; of a son of Kṛishṇa, BhP. x, 61, 12; of a son of Ūru and Āgneyī, Hariv. 73; of the author of a Dharma-śāstra, Parāś.; Śūdradh.; (*us*), m. or f. (?), N. of a river in Plaksha-dvīpa (v. l. *kramu*), VP.; [cf. *a-, ádbhuta-, abhí-*, &c.; cf. also κράτος.] **-karaṇa**, n., N. of a sacrificial offering, ĀpŚr. xii, 6, 5 & iv, 1, 5. **-karman**, n. a sacrificial ceremony, L. **-kriyā**, f. id. **-cchada**, m. one skilled in sacrifice (?), W.; for *kraku-cchanda*, W. **-jit**, m., N. of a man, TS. ii; Kāṭh.; (cf. *-víd.*) **-tulya**, mfn. equal to an Aśva-medha in merit, W. **-dakshiṇā**, f. sacrificial reward, ŚāṅkhŚr. **-deva**, m., N. of a man, Kathās. cxiv, 91. **-druh** (nom. *-dhruk*), m. an enemy of sacrifices, Asura, L. **-dvish** (nom. *-dviṭ*), m. id., L. **-dhvaṇsin**, m. 'destroyer of Daksha's sacrifice,' N. of Śiva, L. **-dhvaja**, m., N. of a Rudra, BhP. iii, 12, 13 (v. l. *ṛitu-dh*°). **-pati**, m. 'lord of a sacrifice,' the performer of a sacrifice, iv, 19, 29. **-paśu**, m. a sacrificial animal, ŚāṅkhŚr. xv, 1, 21; a horse (especially one fit for the Aśva-medha), L. **-pā́**, mfn. watching one's sentiments or intentions, TS. iii, 3, 10, 1. **-purusha**, m., N. of Vishṇu, L. **-prā́**, mfn. granting a desire or power, RV. x, 100, 12; becoming inspired or enlightened, iv, 39, 2. **-prā́van**, mfn. granting a desire or power, x, 100, 11. **-phala**, n. the reward of a sacrifice, object for which it is performed. **-bhuj**, m. 'one who eats the sacrificial oblation,' a god, deity, L. **-mat** (*krátu-*), mfn. intelligent, prudent, wise, RV.; having power, vigorous (as Indra), RV.; (*ān*), m., N. of a son of Viśvā-mitra, BhP. ix, 16, 36. **-máya**, mfn. endowed with intelligence, ŚBr. x; ChUp. **-yashṭi**, f. a kind of bird, Gal. **-rāj**, m. the chief of sacrifices, most excellent sacrifice (i. e. the Aśva-medha), Mn. xi, 260; (the Rāja-sūya), BhP. x. **-rāja**, m. the chief of sacrifices (i. e. the Rāja-sūya sacrifice performed by a monarch who has made all the princes of the world tributary to himself), BhP. x, 72, 3. **-rāta**, m., v. l. for *kīrti-r*°, VP. **-vikrayin**, mfn. one who sells the possible benefits of a sacrifice performed by himself, Mn. iv, 214. **-vikrāyaka**, mfn. id., ib., Kull. **-víd**, mfn. granting power or knowledge, RV.; causing inspiration, inspiring, RV.; prudent, wise, RV.; (*t*), m., N. of a man, AitBr. vii, 34; (cf. *-jít.*) **-śesha**, m., N. of a work. **-saṃkhyā**, f., N. of the thirteenth of Kātyāyana's Pariśishṭas. **-saṃgraha**, m., N. of a Pariśishṭa of the SV.; *-pariśishṭa*, n. id. **-siddhi**, f. completion of a sacrifice, attainment of the object for which it is performed. **-sthalā́**, f., N. of an Apsaras (= *kṛita-sth*°, q. v.), VS. xv, 15; (cf. *ṛitu-sth*°, *ghṛita-sth*°.) **-spṛiś**, mfn. causing inspiration, ĀśvŚr. v, 19. **-haya**, m. a sacrificial horse, L. **Kratūttama**, m. = *kratu-rāja*, L.

Krátū-dákshau, nom. du. m. intelligence and ability, VS. vii, 27; ŚBr. iv, 1, 4, 1; xiv, 3, 1, 31.

Kratv-aṅga, n. a sacrificial utensil, VarBṛS. lxix, 24. **Krátvā-magha**, mfn. constituting a reward gained through intelligence (horses), RV. v, 33, 9.

Kratūya, Nom. P. °*yáti*, to exert the intellect, RV. iv, 24, 4; x, 64, 2.

क्रथ् *krath*, cl. 1. P. °*thati*, to hurt, kill, Dhātup. xix, 39: Caus. *krāthayati*, to hurt, injure, destroy (with gen. of the person hurt, Pāṇ. ii, 3, 56), Dhātup. xxxiv, 19; to rejoice, revel, be in high gig, TBr. ii, 3, 9, 9; (cf. √*knath, klath.*)

Kratha, *ās*, m. pl., N. of a race (always named together with the Kaiśikas and belonging to the Yādava people), MBh. ii, 585; Ragh.; Mālav.; Bālar.; SSaṃkar.; N. of a son of Vidarbha and brother of Kaiśika (ancestor of the Krathas), MBh.; Hariv.; BhP.; N. of an attendant in Skanda's retinue, MBh. ix, 2572; (= *krathana*) N. of an Asura, i, 2665 f.; Hariv. 2284; 12940 & 14287.

Krathana, mfn. one who is in danger of suffocation, Car.; (*as*), m., N. of an Asura, MBh. i; Hariv. 12696; of a Nāga (son of Dhṛita-rāshṭra), MBh. i, 4550; of a monkey, R. iv, v, vi; (*am*), n. cutting through (as with an ax), Prab.; slaughter, killing, L.; sudden interruption of breath, Suśr.

Krathanaka, *as*, m., N. of a camel, Pañcat.; (*am*), n. a black sort of Agallochum, L.

क्रद् *krad*. See √*krand.*

क्रधिष्ठ *kradhishṭha*, mfn. superl. of *kṛidhú*, q. v., Kāṭh. xxv, 7 f. & 10; xxix, 8; KāṭhAnukr.

Kradhīyas, mfn. compar. of *kṛidhú*, q. v., ib.

क्रन्द् *krand*, cl. 1. P. Ā. *krándati, krandate* (v. l. *kradate* fr. √*krad*, Dhātup.; Subj. *krándat*; impf. *krandat* & *ákrandat*; aor. 2. sg. *kradas, cakradas*, & *ákrān*, 3. sg. *akrān* & *ákrān*; *akrandīt*, Pāṇ. vii, 4, 65, Kāś.; p. *krándat*), to neigh (as a horse), roar (metaphorically applied to the clouds and to wind and water), RV.; VS.; ŚBr. vi; to creak (as a wheel), ŚBr. xi; to sound, make a noise, Ratnāv.; to cry piteously, weep, lament, grieve, be confused with sorrow, RV. x, 95, 13; MBh. &c.; to call out piteously to any one (acc.), Kathās. (perf. *cakranda*); MārkP.: Caus. *krandayati* (aor. *ácikradat*, 3. pl. °*dan*), to cause to roar, RV.; VS.; AV.; to cause to weep or lament, Suśr.; to roar, rave, RV.; VS.; AV.; to neigh after (acc.), RV. ix, 67, 4 & x, 96, 10: Intens. P. *kánikrantti* (Ā. °*ntte*, AdbhBr.; p. *kánikradat*, once *kánikrat*, RV. ix, 63, 20; p. Ā. *kanikradyámana*, ŚBr. vi), to neigh, roar, rave, cry out, RV.; AV.; to creak, crackle, RV.; [cf. Goth. *grēta*, 'to lament.']

Kránda, *as*, m. neighing, AV. xi, 2, 22; a cry, calling out, AV. xi, 2, 2 & 4, 2.

Krandád-ishṭi, mfn. moving with a great noise or roaring (said of Vāyu), RV. x, 100, 2.

Krandana, *as*, m. 'crier,' a cat, L.; (*am*), n. crying out, calling; mutual daring or defiance, challenging, L.; lamenting, weeping, Pañcat.; Hit. **-dhvani**, m. cry of grief, lamentation, Hit.

Krandanú, *us*, m. roaring, shaking, RV. vii, 42, 1.

Krándas, *as*, n. battle-cry, RV. viii, 38, 1; (*asī*), du. two contending armies shouting defiance ['heaven and earth,' Sāy.], RV. ii, 12, 8; vi, 25, 4; x, 121, 6.

Krandita, mfn. wept, called or cried out, Kathās. cxiv, 120; (*am*), n. weeping, L.; calling, L.; mutual daring, W.

Kranditṛi, mfn. crier, roaring, crying, W.

Krándya, *am*, n. neighing, TBr. ii, 7, 7, 1; (cf. *parjánya-k*°.)

क्रप् *krap*, cl. 1. Ā. *krapate*, to compassionate, Dhātup. xix, 9; to go, ib.; (cf. √*kṛip.*)

क्रम् *kram*, cl. 1. P. Ā. *krā́mati* (Pāṇ. vii, 3, 76; ep. also *kramati*), *kramate* (Pāṇ. i, 3, 43, ep. also *krāmate*; according to Pāṇ. iii, 1, 70 also cl. 4. P. *krāmyati* [*kramyati*, Vop.]; aor. *akramīt*, RV. &c.; Ā. *krámishṭa, kraṇsta* [RV. i, 121, 1], 3. pl. *cákramanta* [RV. ii, 19, 2]; perf. *cakrāma* or *cakrame*; p. *cakramāṇá*, RV. x, 123, 3; fut. *kramishyati* or *kraṇsyate*, ind. p. *krāntvā, krantvā*, or *kramitvā*, Pāṇ. vi, 4, 18 & vii, 2, 36), to step, walk, go, go towards, approach (with *áccha, ádhi*, acc. or loc.), RV.; AV.; TS. &c.; to approach in order to ask for assistance (with loc.), AV. iv, 11, 12 & xix, 17, 1; to go across, go over, MBh.; R. &c.; Ved. to climb (as on a tree's branch), Pāṇ. vii, 1, 40, Kāś.; to cover (in copulation), AV. iv, 4, 7; to stretch over, project over, tower above, (ind. p. *krāntvā*) Ragh. i, 14; to take possession of, Pañcat.; Ā. to undertake, strive after, make effort for (dat.), Pāṇ. i, 3, 38; iii, 1, 14, Kāś.; (loc.) Bhaṭṭ. xv, 20; Ā. (Pāṇ. i. 3, 38) to proceed well, advance, make progress, gain a footing, succeed, have effect, MBh.; R.; Bhaṭṭ.; to be appliable or practicable, Sarvad.; P. to be liable to the peculiar arrangement of a Vedic text called Krama (i. e. to be doubled, as a letter or word), RPrāt. vi, 4; Ā. to read according to the Krama arrangement of a Vedic text, RPrāt.; Lāṭy. (*a-krānta*): Caus. P. *kramayati*, to cause to step, ŚBr. v; xi; *kramayati* or *krām*°, to make liable to the peculiar arrangement called Krama (i. e. to double a letter or word), RPrāt. &c.: Intens. *caṅkramyate* (Pāṇ. iii, 1, 23, Kāś.; p. *caṅkramyámāṇa* [TS. vii, 1, 19, 3; MBh.] or °*kramam*°, MBh. i, 7919 & BhP. v, 6, 7) or *caṅkramīti* (MBh. xiv, 137 & 141; impf. 2. pl. *caṅkramata*, RV. viii, 55, 4; fut. p. *caṅkramishyát*, TS. vii, 1, 19, 3; ind. p. °*mitvā*, Vop. v, 3; cf. °*mitá*), to step to and fro, walk or wander about.

Kráma, *as*, m. a step, AV. x, 5, 25 ff.; TS. iii; MBh. &c.; going, proceeding, course (cf. *kāla-k*°), Mṛicch.; Pañcat.; Mālatīm.; Hit.; the way, R. ii, 25, 2; a position taken (by an animal &c.) before making a spring or attacking, Pañcat.; Bhaṭṭ. ii, 9; the foot, MBh. iii, 14316; uninterrupted or regular progress, order, series, regular arrangement, succession (e. g. *varṇa-krameṇa*, 'in the order of the castes,' Mn. viii, 24 & ix, 85), AV. viii, 9, 10; RPrāt. xv, 5; KātyŚr.; R. &c.; hereditary descent, Yājñ. ii, 119; method, manner (e. g. *yena krameṇa*, in which manner, R. ii, 26, 20; *tad-anusaraṇa-krameṇa*, so as to go on following him, Hit.); diet, Car. vi, 13; custom, rule sanctioned by tradition, MārkP. xxiii, 112; (*kramam* √1. *kṛi*, 'to follow that rule'), Nyāyam.; occasion, cause (with gen. or ifc.), Kathās. xviii, 380; Hit.; 'progressing step by step,' a peculiar manner or method of reading and writing Vedic texts (so called because the reading proceeds from the 1st member, either word or letter, to the 2nd, then the 2nd is repeated and connected with the 3rd, the 3rd repeated and connected with the 4th, and so on; this manner of reading in relation to words is called *pada-* [TPrāt. ii, 12], in relation to conjunct consonants *varṇa-* [ib.]), Prāt.; the words or letters themselves when combined or arranged in the said manner, ib.; (in dram.) attainment of the object desired (or accord. to others 'noticing of any one's affection'), Daśar. i, 36 f.; Sāh.; Pratāpar.; (in rhet.) a kind of simile (in which the comparisons exhibited correspond to each other in regular succession), Vām. iv, 3, 17; power, strength, L.; (*eṇa, āt*), instr. abl. ind. in regular course, gradually, by degrees, R.; Pañcat.; Ragh. &c.; according to order or rank or series, Mn.; Ragh. &c. **-kārikā**, f., N. of a work. **-kāla**, m. = *-pāṭha*, APrāt. iv, 123 f., Sch.; *-yoga*, m. (= *kāla-*) the events as resulting successively in time, MBh. iii, 8733. **-kṛit**, mfn. following traditional rule or custom, Nyāyam. **-ghana**, m. a kind of Krama-pāṭha. **-caṭa**, m. id. (v. l. *-jaṭā*). **-candrikā**, f., N. of a work. **-ja**, mfn. produced by the Krama arrangement, APrāt.; VPrāt. **-jaṭā**, f., see *-caṭa*. **-jit**, m., N. of a prince, MBh. ii, 123. **-jyakā**, f. the sinus, Gol. **-jyā**, f. id., Sūryas. ii, 32 & 60. **-tas**, ind. gradually, successively; in order. **-trairāśika**, a particular method of applying the direct rule of three (opposed to *vyasta-tr*° or *viloma-tr*°). **-daṇḍa**, m. a kind of Krama-pāṭha. **-dīpikā**, f., N. of a work. **-dhvaja**, m. a kind of Krama-pāṭha. **-pada**, n. the conjunction of words in the Krama reading (more usually *pada-krama*), APrāt. iv, 110.

—pāṭha, m. the Krama reading (i. e. a peculiar 'step by step' arrangement of a Vedic text made to secure it from all possible error by, as it were, combining the Saṃhitā-pāṭha and the Pada-pāṭha, i. e. by giving the words both as connected and unconnected with following and preceding words; see also *krama* above), VPrāt. iv, 180, Sch.; Pāṇ. viii, 4, 28, Kaiy. **—pāra**, m. a kind of Krama-pāṭha. **—pūraka**, m., N. of a tree (perhaps Getonia floribunda), L. **—pravaktṛi**, m. a teacher of the Krama(-pāṭha), RPrāt. xi, 33. **—prâpta**, mfn. obtained by hereditary descent, Nal. xii, 36. **—bhaṅga**, m. interruption of order. **—bhāvin**, mfn. successive, Nyāyad. iii, 1, 3, Sch. **—bhrashṭa**, n. interrupted or irregular order of words or meanings, Pratāpar. **—mālā**, f. a kind of Krama-pāṭha. **—yoga**, m. succession, regular order, successive or methodical practice, Mn. i, 42; R. vi, 16, 60; (*ena*), instr. ind. in regular manner, Mn.; MBh. i, 5287. **—yaugapadya**, *e*, n. du. successive order and simultaneousness, Sarvad. **—ratnâvalī**, f., N. of a work. **—ratha**, m. a kind of Krama-pāṭha. **—rājya**, n., N. of a locality, Rājat. v, 87. **—lekhā**, f. a kind of Krama-pāṭha. **—vat**, ind. in the manner of the Krama(-pāṭha), APrāt. iv, 123. **—vattu**, N. of a district in Kaśmīra, Rājat. v, 39; (*-varta*) iii, 227. **—varta**, see *-vattu*. **—vṛiddhi**, f. gradual growth or increase, MBh. xii, 3308. **—śaṭha**, m. a kind of Krama-pāṭha. **—śas**, ind. gradually, by degrees, Mn.; R.; Suśr.; KapS. &c.; regularly, seriatim, Mn.; R.; Sāṃkhyak. &c. **—śāstra**, n. rules relating to the Krama(-pāṭha), RPrāt. **—śikhā**, f. a kind of Krama-pāṭha. **—saṃhitā**, f. a Vedic Saṃhitā written according to the Krama method, Comm. on VPrāt.; °*tôdāharaṇa*, n. an example from a Krama-saṃhitā. **—saṃgraha**, m., N. of a treatise. **—saṃdarbha-prabhāsa**, m., N. of a chapter (*khaṇḍa*) in a particular work. **—saras**, n., N. of a sacred pond, Kathās. lxxiii, 95. **—sāra**, m., N. of a work. **—stuti**, f., N. of a work. **Kramâkrama**, *au*, m. du. = *krama-yaugapadya*, q. v., Sarvad. **Kramâkrānta**, mfn. attacked by any one who has taken up a position of advantage, Kād. **Kramâgata**, mfn. descended or inherited lineally, (anything) coming from one's ancestors in regular succession, Nār.; (a servant) Pañcat. &c.; often ifc., Mn. ii, 18; Yājñ.; Pañcat.; Hit.; successive, in due order, Car. iii, 8; *-tva*, n. hereditary succession or possession, W. **Kramâditya**, m., N. of king Skanda-gupta. **Kramâdhyayana**, n. reciting or reading according to the Krama method, APrāt. iv, 108 f., Sch. **Kramâdhyāyin**, mfn. studying the Krama arrangement of a Vedic text, VPrāt. iv, 179, Sch. **Kramânuyāyin**, mfn. following the methodical order. **Kramânusāra**, m. regular order, due arrangement. **Kramânvaya**, m. id. **Kramâyāta**, mfn. descended or inherited lineally, coming from one's ancestors in regular succession, W.; one who has acceded to the throne by succession, Pañcat.; proceeding in regular order, W. **Kramâvasāna**, n. the end of a word in the Krama-pāṭha. **Kramêtara**, mfn. not arranged according to the Krama-pāṭha, gaṇa *ukthâdi*. **Kramôkta**, mfn. enjoined for the Krama arrangement, W. **Kramôḍhā**, f. married in order (i.e. not before an elder sister), Kāty. **Kramôdvega**, m. an ox, L.

Kramaka, mfn. going, proceeding, W.; orderly, methodical, W.; (*as*), m. succession, Jaim. v, 4, 1; a student who goes through a regular course of study, who proceeds methodically, W.; one who reads or knows the Krama(-pāṭha), Pāṇ. iv, 2, 61.

Krámaṇa, *as*, m. a step, KātySr. iii, 8, 11, Sch.; the foot, L.; a horse, L.; N. of a son of Bhajamāna, Hariv. 2002; (*am*), n. stepping, walking, going, RV. vi, 70, 3; Yājñ. i, 188; Mṛicch.; BhP.; stepping or treading upon (in comp.), ŚāṅkhGṛ.; transgressing (ifc.), MBh. xii, 16254; R. v, 1 (at end); a step, RV. i, 155, 5; approaching or undertaking anything (dat.), Pāṇ. iii, 1, 14; treatment of words or letters according to the Krama arrangement (i.e. doubling letters or words &c.), RPrāt. xiv.

Kramaṇīya, mfn. to be gone to or beyond, W.

Kramad-īśvara, *as*, m., N. of the author of the grammar called Saṃkshipta-sāra.

Kramamāṇa, mfn. (pr. p. Ā.) proceeding.

Kramika, mfn. (anything) that comes from one's ancestors in regular succession, inherited lineally, MBh. ii, 166; successive, Comm. on KapS. i, 38 & 40; Kuval.

Kramitṛi, mfn. walking &c., Vop. xxvi, 28.

Kramya, mfn. to be treated or attended medically, Car. viii, 2; (cf. *saha-k*°.)

Krā. See *udadhi-*; *dadhi-* & *rudhi-krā́*.

Krāntá, mfn. gone, gone over or across; spread, extended; attacking, invading, gone to or against; overcome (as by astonishment), Ragh. xiv, 17; surpassed; (*as*), m. a horse, L.; (in astron.) declination, W.; (*ā*), f., N. of a plant (a kind of Solanum), L.; a species of the Atyashṭi metre; (*am*), n. a step (*Vishṇoḥ krānta*, 'the step of Vishṇu,' N. of a ceremony, ŚBr. xiii; cf. *vishṇu-krama*), ŚBr.; Mn. xii, 121; (in astron.) a certain aspect when the moon is in conjunction with a planet.

Krānti, *is*, f. going, proceeding, step, L.; overcoming, surpassing, W.; attacking, L.; declination of a planet, Sūryas. i, 68; ii, 28 & 58 ff.; the sun's course (ifc.), HPariś. vii, 3; the sun's course on the globe, ecliptic. **—kakshā**, f. the sun's course, ecliptic. **—kshetra**, n. a figure described by the ecliptic. **—jīvā**, f. the sine of the ecliptic, Gaṇit. **—jyakā**, f. id., Gol. vii, 46. **—jyā**, f. id., Sūryas. ii, iii, xi. **—pāta**, m. the intersection of the ecliptic and equinoctial circles (i.e. the equinoctial points or nodes of the ecliptic), Sūryas.; Gol.; *-gati*, f. motion of the nodes of the ecliptic, precession of the equinox. **—bhāga**, m. the declination of a point of the ecliptic. **—bhujā**, f. the cosinus of declination, Āryabh. iv, 24, Sch. **—maṇḍala**, n. 'the circle of the sun's course,' ecliptic, W. **—maurvī**, f. = *-jīvā*, Gol. **—valaya**, m. = *-maṇḍala*, Sūryas.; the space within the tropics, W. **—vṛitta**, n. = *-maṇḍala*, Comm. on Sūryas. v, 1. **—śiñjinī**, f. = *-jīvā*, Gol. viii, 60.

Krāntu, *us*, m. a bird, Uṇ. v, 43.

Krāntvā, ind. p. See s. v. √*kram*.

Krāmaṇa, *am*, n. a particular process applied to mercury, Sarvad.

Krāmat, mfn. (pr. p. P.) walking, going, &c.

Krāmika, mfn. one who studies or knows the Krama(-pāṭha), gaṇa *ukthâdi* (Kāś.)

Krāmêtaraka, mfn. one who studies or knows a *krāmêtara* text, gaṇa *ukthâdi*.

क्रमि *krami*, for *kṛimi* (q. v.), a worm, MBh. xii, 4872 (*kṛimi*, ed. Bomb.); Suśr.; MārkP. xv, 22.

क्रमु *kramu*, *us*, m. the betel-nut tree (Areca Faufel or Catechu), L.; N. of a river in Plaksha-dvīpa (v. l. for *kratu*), VP.

Kramuka, *as*, m. (cf. *kṛim*°) the betel-nut tree (Areca Faufel or Catechu), ShaḍvBr. iv, 4; Suśr.; BhP.; the mulberry tree (Morus indica, *brahmadāru*), L.; a red variety of the Lodhra tree (*paṭṭika-lodhra*), L.; a variety of Cyperus (*bhadramustaka*), L.; the fruit of the cotton tree, L.; (*ās*), m. pl., N. of a people, Rājat. iv, 159; (*ī*), f. the betel-nut tree, L. **—pushpaka**, m., N. of a tree, Gal. **—phala**, n. the Areca nut, L.

क्रमुञ्ज *kramuñja*, *as*, m., N. of a mountain, VP.

क्रमेल *kramela*, *as*, m. (borrowed fr. Gk. κάμηλος) the camel, L.

Kramelaka, m. id., Pañcat.; Naish. vi; ŚārṅgP.

क्रम्य *kramya*. See √*kram*.

क्रय *krayá*, &c. See √*krī*.

क्रवण *kravaṇá*, mfn. timid [NBD.; 'worshipping,' Sāy.], RV. v, 44, 9.

क्रवि *kravi*. See *á-kravi-hasta*.

Kravishṇú, mfn. desirous of raw flesh, x, 87, 5.

Kravís, *is*, n. raw flesh, carrion, i, 162, 9 & 10; x, 87, 16; AV. viii, 6, 23; [cf. Gk. κρέας; Lat. *cruor*, *cruentus*, *crūdus*, *caro*; Lith. *krauja-s*, 'blood;' Russ. *krovj*; Hib. *cru*; Old Germ. *hreo*.]

Kravyá, mfn. = *krūrá*, TS. v; (*as*), m. perhaps = *Agni kravyâd* (q. v.), ŚāṅkhŚr.; (*am*), n. (Nir.) raw flesh, carrion, BhP.; Kathās. **—ghātana**, m. 'killed for its flesh (cf. BhP. v, 26, 12),' a deer, antelope, L. **—bhakshin**, mfn. eating carrion, carnivorous, Kathās. **—bhuj**, mfn. id., Suśr.; (*k*), m. a Rākshasa, W. **—bhojana**, mfn. carnivorous, W. **—mukha**, m. 'one who has flesh in his mouth,' N. of a wolf, Pañcat. **—vâhana**, mfn. carrying corpses (said of Agni) [v. l. *kavya-v*° (q. v.), Sāy.; cf. VS. xix, 65], RV. x, 16, 11. **Kravyâkhya**, see *kravyâda* at end. **Kravyâd**, mfn. (Pāṇ. iii, 2, 69) consuming flesh or corpses (as the fire of the funeral pile or Agni in one of his terrible forms), RV. x, 16, 9 & 10; 87, 5; VS. i, 17; AV.; ŚBr.; Kauś.; (said of a Yātu-dhāna and other evil beings, imps, and goblins) RV. &c.; carnivorous, Mn.; Yājñ.; MBh.; (*t*), m. a carnivorous animal, beast of prey, Kathās.; N. of a Rakshas, W. **Kravyâda**, mf(*ā*)n. (Pāṇ. iii, 2, 69, Kāś.) consuming flesh or corpses (as Agni), MBh. i, 932; Gṛihyas. i, 11; Tithyād.; (*as*), m. a carnivorous animal, beast of prey, MBh. i, 115, 24; a lion, L.; a hawk, L.; a goblin, Rākshasa, W.; the fire of the funeral pile, W.; N. of a metallic substance, Bhpr. iv, 30; (*ā*), f., N. of one of the nine Samidhs, Gṛihyas. i, 27; (*ās*), m. pl., N. of a class of Manes, VP.; of a people, VarBṛS. xiv, 18 (v. l. °*vyâkhya*). **Kravyâdas**, m. a beast of prey, Āp. **Kravyâśin**, mfn. carnivorous, W.; (*ī*), m. a demon, W.; an anthropophagus, W.

क्रशित *krasita*, mfn. (fr. *kraśaya*, Nom. P.; fr. *kṛiśá*), made thin or lean, emaciated, Śiś. ix, 61.

Kraśiman, *ā*, m. (gaṇa *dṛiḍhâdi*) leanness, emaciation, Kād.; shallowness (of a river), ib.

Kraśishṭha, mfn. superl. of *kṛiśá*, Pāṇ. vi, 4, 161, Pat.

Kraśīyas, mfn. (compar. of *kṛiśá*, ib.) extremely lean, Naish. i, 84.

क्रष्टव्य *krashṭavya*, mfn. (√*kṛish*), to be dragged, Pāṇ. ii, 3, 71, Kāś.; to be drawn out (as from the womb), Kathās. xxvi, 164.

क्रा *krā*. See √*kram*.

क्राकचिक *krākacika*, °*cya*. See *krakaca*.

क्राणा *krāṇā́*, ind. willingly, readily, speedily, RV. i, 58, 3 & 139, 1; v, 10, 2; ix, 86, 19 & 102, 1; x, 61, 1; [fr. √1. *kṛi*, '= *kurvāṇa*, *kartṛi*, &c.,' Sāy.]

क्राथ *krātha*, *as*, m. (√*krath*), killing, murder, L.; patr. fr. Kratha, Hariv.; N. of a prince, MBh. i, 2676; iii, 489; of a son of Dhṛita-rāshṭra, i, 3747; of an attendant in Skanda's retinue, ix, 2572; of a Nāga, xvi, 120; of a monkey, iii, 16287.

Krāthêśvara, m., N. of a pupil of Āpastamba, VāmP. (v. l. *krodhêśv*°).

Krāthana, *am*, n. moving, Sarvad.

Krāthin. See *para-k*°.

क्रान्त *krāntá*, *krānti*, &c. See √*kram*.

Krāmaṇa, °*mat*, °*mika*. See ib.

क्रायक *krāyaka*. See √*krī*.

क्रिमि *krími*, for *kṛími*, q. v.

Krimṇa, mfn. (= *kṛimiṇa*) having worms, ĀpŚr. ix, 20, 2.

क्रिय *kriya*, *as*, m. (borrowed fr. Gk. κριός) the sign Aries, VarBṛ. i, iii, x, xvii; Gaṇit.; Horāś.

क्रियमाण *kriyamāṇa*, mfn., Pass. p. √1. *kṛi*, q. v.

Kriyamāṇaka, n. a literary essay, VarBṛS. i, 5.

Kriyā, f. (Pāṇ. iii, 3, 100), doing, performing, performance, occupation with (in comp.), business, act, action, undertaking, activity, work, labour, KātyŚr.; Mn.; Yājñ. &c.; bodily action, exercise of the limbs, L.; (in Gr.) action (as the general idea expressed by any verb), verb, Kāś. on Pāṇ. i, 3, 1 &c. (according to later grammarians a verb is of two kinds, *sakarma-kriyā*, 'active,' and *akarma-k*°, 'intransitive'); a noun of action, W.; a literary work, Vikr.; medical treatment or practice, applying a remedy, cure (see *sama-kriya-tva* and *vishama-k*°), Suśr.; a religious rite or ceremony, sacrificial act, sacrifice, Mn.; Yājñ.; MBh. &c.; with *caramā*, 'the last ceremony,' rites performed immediately after death, obsequies, purificatory rites (as ablution &c.), MBh. iv, 834; R. vi, 96, 10; religious action, worship, BhP. vii, 14, 39; Rāmat-Up.; Religious Action (personified as a daughter of Daksha and wife of Dharma, MBh. i, 2578; Hariv. 12452; BhP.; or as a daughter of Kardama and wife of Kratu, BhP.); judicial investigation (by human means, as by witnesses, documents, &c., or by superhuman means, as by various ordeals), Comm. on Yājñ.; atonement, L.; disquisition, L.; study, L.; means, expedient, L. **—kara**, m. one who performs an action, W.; a student, W. **—kartṛi**, m. a doer of an action, agent, W. **—kalāpa**, m., N. of a work; the great body of ceremonies enjoined in the Hindū law, W.; a number of actions of any kind, W.; all the particulars of any business, W. **-kāṇḍa,** n. the portion of a Śruti text treating of the sacrifices. **-kāra,** m. a beginner, novice, L.; an agreement, Kāraṇḍ. xvii; an arrangement, rule, Divyâv. **-kaumudī,** f., N. of a work by Govindânanda. **-gupta,** n. a phrase the verb of which is hidden, ŚārṅgP. **-guptaka,** n., N. of a work (?), Gaṇar. **-gupti,** f. = °*pta,* Sāh. **-tantra,** n. 'a Tantra of action,' one of the four classes of Tantras, Buddh. **Kriyâtipatti,** f. the non-realization of an action, Pāṇ. iii, 3, 139; (hence) the characteristics and the terminations of the conditional, Kāt. iii, 1, 33. **Kriyâtmaka,** mfn. (anything) the nature of which is action, Vedântas. (*-tva,* n., abstr.) **Kriyā-dīpaka,** n. a simile in which a verb forms the Tertium comparationis, Kāvyâd. ii, 99, Sch. **Kriyā-dveshin,** m. one who is averse to the part of a law-suit called *kriyā,* i. e. to witnesses, documents, ordeals, &c. (one of the five kinds of witnesses whose testimonials are hurtful to the cause), Comm. on Yājñ. ii, 6. **Kriyā-dvaita,** n. efficient cause (as resigning all to God), W. **Kriyā-nibandha,** m., N. of a work. **Kriyā-nirdeśa,** m. evidence. **Kriyânurūpa,** mfn. conformable to the act, according to the action. **Kriyântara,** n. interruption of an action, Pāṇ. iii, 4, 57; another action, Pāṇ. ii, 3, 37, Kāś. **Kriyânvita,** mfn. practising ritual observances. **Kriyā-paṭu,** mfn. clever, dextrous. **Kriyā-patha,** m. manner of medical treatment or application of remedies, Suśr. iv; °*tham atikrānta,* mfn. 'beyond medical treatment,' incurable, Car. v, 11. **Kriyā-pada,** n. 'action-word,' a verb. **Kriyā-paddhati,** f., N. of a work. **Kriyā-para,** mfn. attentive to the performance of one's duties, W. **Kriyâpavarga,** m. end of an affair, W.; liberation from ceremonial acts, W. **Kriyā-pātra,** n. a man praisable for his actions. **Kriyā-pāda,** m. the third division of a suit at law (witnesses, written documents, and other proofs adduced by the complainants, rejoinder of the plaintiff). **Kriyā-prabandha,** m. uninterrupted continuity of an action, Pāṇ. iii, 3, 135. **Kriyā-prasaṅga,** m. course of proceeding, W. **Kriyā-phala,** n. result or consequence of acts. **Kriyâbhyupagama,** m. special compact or agreement, Mn. ix, 53. **Kriyâmbudhi,** m., N. of a work by Prāṇa-kṛishṇa. **Kriyā-yukta,** mfn. active, moving, L. **Kriyā-yoga,** m. the connection with an action or verb, APrāt.; Pāṇ. i, 1, 14, Kār.; the employment of expedients or instruments, MBh. iii, 69; Suśr.; the practical form of the Yoga philosophy (union with the deity by due performance of the duties of every day life, active devotion), Yogas. ii, 1; BhP. iv, 13, 3; N. of a work; *-sāra,* m. a section of the PadmaP. **Kriyā-ratna-samuccaya,** m., N. of a work. **Kriyâroha,** m. = *cakra-vāṭa,* L. **Kriyârtha,** m. an action as object, Jaim. i, 1, 25; mf(*ā*)n. having an action (i. e. another action) as its aim, Pāṇ. ii, 3, 14; *-tva,* n. the state of aiming at or leading to actions, Jaim. i, 2, 1. **Kriyā-lāghava,** n. ease in the functions (of an organ), Bhpr. **Kriyā-lopa,** m. discontinuance or loss of any of the essential ceremonies, Mn. ix, 180; x, 43; BrahmaP. **Kriyā-vat,** mfn. one who performs an action, active, busy, understanding business, fit for it, MuṇḍUp.; Hit.; (ifc.) Dhūrtas. i, 12; performing ceremonies in the right manner, ŚāṅkhGṛ.; MuṇḍUp.; MBh.; R.; consisting of or connected with a religious ceremony (as the rite of initiation). **Kriyā-vaśa,** mfn. subject to the influence of acts, W.; (*as*), m. necessary influence of acts done or to be done, necessity, W. **Kriyâvasanna,** mfn. one who loses a lawsuit through the statements of the witnesses &c. **Kriyā-vācaka,** mfn. expressing an action (as a verbal noun). **Kriyā-vācin,** mfn. id., W. **Kriyā-vādin,** m. one who states the arguments in a law-suit, Comm. on Yājñ.; a plaintiff, ib. **Kriyā-vidhi,** m. a rule of action, Mn. ix, 220; xii, 87; mode of performing any rite, W.; conduct of affairs, W.; *-jña,* mfn. conversant with business, Pañcat.; understanding the ritual, W. **Kriyā-viśāla,** n., N. of the thirteenth of the fourteen Pūrvas or most ancient Jaina writings. **Kriyā-viseshaṇa,** n. 'that which defines an action more closely,' an adverb, Pāṇ. ii, 3, 33, Kāś. **Kriyā-vyavadhāyaka,** mfn. interrupting an action, Pāṇ. iii, 4, 57, Kāś. **Kriyā-śakti,** f. 'capability to act,' = *karmêndriya* (q. v.); a Śakti or supernatural power as appearing in actions (opposed to *dhī-ś°*), Sarvad. vi; *-mat,* mfn. possessing the power of action, Vedântas. **Kriyā-saṃskāra,** m. combining or confounding different methods of medical treatment, Bhpr. **Kriyā-samabhihāra,** m. repetition of any act or intensity of action (as represented by the Intens.), Pāṇ. iii, 1, 22 & 4, 2. **Kriyā-samuccaya,** m., N. of a work. **Kriyā-samūha,** m. the whole of the ceremonies from impregnation (*visheka*) to cremation (*śmaśāna*), Vishṇ. **Kriyā-sāra,** m., N. of a work. **Kriyā-siddhi,** f. accomplishment of an action. **Kriyā-sthānaka-vicāra,** m., N. of a Jain work. **Kriyêndriya,** n. = *karmênd°* (q. v.), L.

क्रिवि *krívi, is,* m., a N. of Rudra (v. l. *krāyin,* q. v.); a leather bag (metaphorically 'a cloud'), RV.; a well, Naigh. iii, 23; N. of an Asura, Sāy.; (*is, ayas*), m. sg. & pl. the original N. of the Pañcālas, ŚBr. xiii, 5, 4, 7; (perhaps also RV. viii, 20, 24 & 22, 12); (cf. *kraivya.*)

क्री 1. *krī,* cl. 9. P. Ā. *krīṇāti, krīṇīte* (fut. p. *kreshyat,* Lāṭy.; ind. p. *krītvā,* AV.; Mn.), to buy, purchase (with instr. of the price, and abl. or gen. of the person from whom anything is bought, e. g. *ká imám I'ndraṃ daśábhir dhenúbhir máma krīṇāti,* who will buy this Indra of me for ten cows? RV. iv, 24, 10; *yam mātā-pitror antikāt* [or *sakāśāt*] *krīṇīyāt,* whom he may buy from his father and mother, Mn. ix, 174; *krīṇīshva tad daśabhiḥ suvarṇaiḥ,* buy that for ten suvarṇas): Caus. P. *krāpayati,* Pāṇ. vi, 1, 48; [cf. Hib. *creanaim,* 'I buy, purchase;' Gk. *πρίαμαι, πέρνημι*; Lith. *prekis, perku* (?); Lat. *pretium*; Eng. *hire.*] **Kry-ādi,** *ayas,* m. pl. the roots beginning with *kṛī,* i. e. those of the ninth class.

Krayá, *as,* m. buying, purchase, VS.; TS.; ŚBr.; KātyŚr.; Mn. &c.; the purchase-price, VarBṛS. lxxxii, 9. **-krīta,** mfn. bought, purchased, Hit. **-dravya,** n. anything for which anything else is bought or exchanged, KātyŚr. i, 8, 21, Sch. **-lekhya,** n. deed of sale, conveyance, Bṛihasp. **-vikraya,** *as, au,* m. sg. & du. buying and selling, trade, Mn.; MBh.; Pañcat. iii; °*yânuśaya,* m. repenting of a purchase, annulling of purchase or sale, Mn. viii, 5. **-°vikrayika,** m. a trader or merchant, dealer, Pāṇ. iv, 4, 13. **-vikrayin,** mfn. one who buys or sells, who strikes a bargain, Mn. v, 51; viii, 400; (ifc.) Yājñ. ii, 262. **-śīrsha,** n. (= *kapi-ś°*) the coping of a wall, L. **Krayâkraya,** 'buying and not buying,' commerce, Car. i, 15. **Krayâkrayikā,** f., g. *śāka-pārthivâdi.* **Krayâroha,** m. 'place where goods are piled up for sale,' a market, fair, L.

Krayaṇa, *am,* n. buying, KātyŚr. x, xiv; Lāṭy.

Krayaṇīya, mfn. to be bought, KātyŚr. xvi.

Krayāṇaka, *am,* n. any purchasable object, ware, Vet. iii; Siṃhâs.; Jain. Comm.

Krayika, mfn. (Pāṇ. iv, 3, 13, Siddh.) buying, MBh. xiii, 5633; (*as*), m. a buyer, trader, dealer, Uṇ. ii, 45.

Kráyin, *ī,* m. a buyer, purchaser, Yājñ., Sch.; N. of Rudra, TS. i, 8, 14, 2; TBr. i; (*krívi,* VS. x, 20.)

Kráyya, mfn. (Pāṇ. vi, 1, 82) exhibited for sale, purchasable, ŚBr. iii, 3, 3, 1; KātyŚr. vii, 8, 2 f.; xix.

Krāyaka, *as,* m. a buyer, trader, L.

Krāyika, *as,* m. id., Divyâv. xxxv.

2. **Krī.** See *yava-krī, sadyaḥ-krī.*

Krītá, mfn. bought, purchased, ŚBr.; Mn. &c.; purchased from his natural parents (as a son; one of the twelve kinds of sons acknowledged by the ancient Hindū law), Mn. ix, 160; won by (instr.), Śak. iii (v. l.); ifc. (with the purchase-price; f. *ī*), Pāṇ. iv, 1, 50; vi, 2, 151; (f. also *ā*) Siddh.; (*ás*), m., N. of a man, MaitrS. iv, 2, 6; (*ās*), m. pl. a sort of despised caste, W.; (*am*), n. a bargain, Comm. on Yājñ. ii, 6. **-tva,** n. the being bought, Jaim. vi, 1, 19. **Krītânuśaya,** m. repenting a purchase, returning a purchase upon the seller (admissible in some cases by law). **Krītā-pati,** m. the husband of a wife acquired by purchase, Nir. vi, 9.

Krītaka, mfn. bought from his natural parents (and adopted as male issue), Mn. ix, 174; Pravar.

Kreṇi, *is,* m. buying, purchasing, L.

Kreṇī, f. id., Comm. on Uṇ. iv, 48.

Kretavya, mfn. purchasable, MBh. xiii, 2450.

Kretṛi, *tā,* m. a buyer, purchaser, Yājñ. ii, 168 & 253; MBh. iii, 13711.

Kreya, mfn. (Pāṇ. vi, 1, 82, Kāś.) purchasable, Rājat. v, 270 (ifc.) **-da,** m. one who exhibits anything for sale, seller, L.

क्रीड् *krīḍ,* cl. 1. P. *krīḍati* (or *krīḷati,* RV.; ep. also Ā.; perf. *cikrīḍa,* MBh.; fut. p. *krīḍishyat,* BhP. iii, 17, 24; aor. *akrīḍīt,* Bhaṭṭ.), to play, sport, amuse one's self, frolic, gambol, dally (used of men, animals, the wind and waves, &c.), RV.; VS.; AV. &c.; to jest, joke with (instr. or instr. with *saha* or *sārdham*; once acc., Mṛicch.), Mn.; Yājñ.; MBh. &c.: Caus. *krīḍayati,* to cause to play, allow to play, MBh. i, 6440; iv, 329; BhP.

Krīḍá, mfn. playing, sporting (said of the winds), RV. i, 37, 1 & 5; 166, 2; (*as*), m. sport, play, L.; (*ā*), f. sport, play, pastime, amusement, amorous sport (often in comp., e. g. *krīḍā-mudaḥ,* f. pl. the pleasures of playing or of amorous sport, Gīt. ix, 9; *Kṛishṇa-k°,* sport with Kṛishṇa, BhP. ii, 3, 15; *jala-k°,* playing about in water, MBh.; Pañcat.; BhP.; *toya-k°,* id., Megh.), VS. xviii, 5; R.; Suśr. &c.; working miracles for one's amusement, Lalit.; disrespect shown by jest or joke, L.; a play-ground, MBh. iii, 12318; (in music) a kind of measure.

Krīḍaka, *as,* m. one who sports, player, L.

Krīḍat, mfn. playing, sportive, RV.; AV. &c.

Krīḍana, *as,* m. 'playing,' N. of the wind, Gal.; (*am*), n. playing, play, sporting, &c., R.; BhP.; Hit.

Krīḍanaka, mf(*ikā*)n. playing, jesting, L.; (*as*), m. a plaything, MBh.; Śak.; BhP. &c.; (*ikā*), f. a nurse who entertains children with plays, Divyâv. **-tā,** f. 'the state of a plaything,' (*ayā*), instr. ind. after the manner of a plaything, BhP. v, 26, 32.

Krīḍanīya, *am,* n. a plaything, toy, MBh. xiii, 4206; Kād.

Krīḍanīyaka, *as,* m. id., Kathās. li, lxxi. **-saṃnibha,** mfn. like a toy or doll, Kathās. xii, 74.

Krīḍamāna, mfn. (ep.) sporting, MBh.; R.

Krīḍā (f. of °*ḍá,* q. v.) **-kapi-tva,** n. imitating an ape for amusement or in jest, Mcar. **-kānana,** n. a pleasure-grove, Bhartṛ. iii, 15. **-kāsāra,** a pleasure-pond, Daś. p. v. **-kumāra,** m., N. of a Gandharva, Bālar. iv, 8. **-°kūṭa** (*krīḍâk°*), n. sportive or wanton purpose or desire, W. **-ketana,** n. a pleasure-house, Kathās. cxiv, 57. **-kopa,** m. anger in sport, assumed anger, Amar. **-kautuka,** n. wanton curiosity, Kathās. xviii, 153; sport, pastime, enjoyment, W.; lasciviousness, W. **-kauśala,** n. the art of joking, Daś. **-khaṇḍa,** n., N. of GaṇP. ii. **-gṛiha,** m. n. a pleasure-house, R.; Sāh. 675, Sch. **-caṅkramaṇa,** N. of a locality, Rājat. vi, 308. **-candra,** a metre of 4 × 18 syllables; (*as*), m., N. of a poet. **-tāla,** m. (in music) a kind of measure. **-nārī,** f. a harlot, courtezan, Hariv. 8309. **-paricchada,** m playthings, toy, BhP. vii, 5, 56. **-parvata,** m. a play-hill or pleasure-hill, pleasure-mound or hillock in a garden, Kād. **-parvataka,** m. id., ib. **-pura,** n. a town visited for amusement. **-pradeśa,** m. a play-ground, MBh. iii, 164, 6. **-maya,** mf(*ī*)n. consisting of play or sport, MBh. xiv, 1486. **-mayūra,** m. a peacock kept for amusement, Ragh. xvi, 14. **-markaṭa-pota,** m. a young monkey serving as a plaything, Kathās. lxxv, 26. **-mahīdhra,** m. = *-parvata,* Ratnâv. iv, 14. **-mṛiga,** m. an animal kept for pleasure, toy-deer, R. v, 20, 12; BhP. vi, 2, 37. **-ratna,** n. 'gem of sports,' copulation, L. **-ratha,** m. a pleasure-chariot, carriage used for amusement (opposed to a war-chariot), MBh. xiii, 2782. **-rasa,** m. enjoying sport, Ratnâv. i; *-maya,* mfn. consisting of pleasure-water, Kathās. xxviii, 99. **-rasātala,** n., N. of a work, Sāh. 550, Sch. **-rājata-sudhā-pātra,** Nom. P. °*trati,* to represent a silver liquor-cup used as an object of amusement, Prasannar. **-rudrāya,** Nom. Ā. °*yate,* to resemble Rudra while playing. **-vat,** mfn. sportive, playful. **-vana,** n. a pleasure-grove, park. **-vāpī,** f. a pleasure-pond (in which turtles, fishes, &c. are kept for pleasure), VarBṛS. **-veśman,** n. a pleasure-house, Vikr. ii, 22. **-śakunta,** m. a bird kept for amusement, Pañcat. i, 155. **-śaila,** m. = *-parvata,* Megh.; Hcat. i, 6. **-saras,** n. a pleasure-pond, Hit. **-sthāna,** n. a play-ground, R. vi, 83, 48; Pañcad. **Krīḍôddeśa,** m. id., R. ii, 94, 12.

Krīḍāpanikā, f. = °*ḍanikā,* Divyâv. xxxii.

Krīḍi or **krīḷi,** mfn. playing, sporting, RV.; MaitrS. i, 10, 6; (said of the winds) RV. i, 87, 3.

Krīḍita, mfn. having played, Pañcat.; (*am*), n. sport, play, MBh. iii, 11067; R. v, 13, 23 & 55.

Krīḍitaka. See *mānavaka-k°.*

Krīḍitṛi, *tā,* m. one who sports, player, BhP. i, 13, 40.

Krīḍin, mfn. playing, sporting (said of the winds), VS.; TS. i, 6, 7, 5; ŚBr. ii, 5, 3, 20; (cf. *sva-k°*); (*ī*), m., N. of a man, Pravar. **Krīḍi-tvá,** n. the state of one who is sporting, TBr. i, 6, 7, 5.

Krīḍú or **krīḷú**, mfn. playing (Soma), RV. ix, 20, 7. **-mát**, mfn. id. (flames), x, 3, 5.

क्रीत *krītá*, &c. See √*krī*.

क्रीब *krība*, mfn. = *klība*, accord. to a gloss on KātyŚr. xv, 10, 18.

क्रु *kru*. See *mitra-krú*.

क्रुक्त *krukta*. See √1. *kruñc*.

क्रुञ्च् 1. *kruñc* (Pāṇ. iii, 2, 59), cl. 1. P. *kruñcati*, 'to curve or make crooked' or 'to be crooked, move crookedly,' Dhātup. vii, 4; 'to become small, shrink,' or 'to make small, lessen,' ib.; to go towards, approach, Vop.

Krukta, mfn. crooked, curved, W.

2. **Krúñc**, *ṅ*, m. (Pāṇ. iii, 2, 59) a kind of snipe, curlew, VS. xix, 73; TāṇḍyaBr. xiii; Bhaṭṭ.; N. of a Ṛishi [Comm.], TāṇḍyaBr. xiii; (cf. *krauñcá*.)

Krúñca, *as*, m. a kind of snipe, curlew, VS. xxiv, 22 & 31; MaitrS.; Āp.; (= *krauñca*) N. of a mountain, L.; (*au*), m. du.?, VS. xxv, 6; (*ā*), f. (Pāṇ. iv, 2, 91, Vārtt. 4, Pat.; g. *ajâdi*; g. *vyāghrâdi*, Gaṇar. 108) a female snipe or curlew, L.; a kind of Vīṇā or lute, L. **Kruñcā-mat**, mfn., g. *yavâdi*.

Kruñcakīya, *ās*, m. pl. [Kāś.] or °*yā*, f. (fr. *kruñcā*, Pāṇ. iv, 2, 91, Vārtt. 2), N. of a locality, gaṇa *bilvakâdi*.

क्रुड् *kruḍ*, cl. 6. P. *kruḍati*, to sink, dive, Dhātup. xxviii, 100; to be or become thick, Comm. on VS. xxv, 8; (cf. *kraḍana*, √*kūḍ*, and *krūḍ*): Caus. or cl. 10. P. fr. √*krūḍ*, *krūḍayati*, to make thick (?), Kāṭh. vi, 3 & 7.

क्रुद *krud*. See *utkrodá*.

क्रुध् 1. *krudh*, cl. 4. P. *krúdhyati* (ep. rarely Ā. °*te*, MBh. i, 59, 21; (see also *krudhyamāna*); perf. *cukrodha*, ŚBr.; MBh. &c.; fut. 2nd *krotsyati*, Pāṇ. viii, 2, 37, Kāś.; fut. 1st *kroddhā*, Pāṇ. vii, 2, 10, Siddh.; aor. Subj. 2. sg. *krudhas*, AV.; MBh.; inf. *kroddhum*, Nal.), to become angry, be wrathful or angry with (dat. [Pāṇ. i, 4, 37] or gen.), on account of (loc.): Caus. *krodháyati* (aor. *ácukrudhat*, RV. v, 34, 7; Subj. 1. sg. *cukrudham*, 1. pl. °*dhāma*), to make angry, provoke, irritate, RV.; AV.; R. (inf. *krodhayitum*); [cf. Lith. *rus-tus*, 'angry;' *rus-tybê*, 'anger;' Gk. κότος; Germ. *groll*; Hib. *corruidhe*, 'anger, wrath, motion;' *corruigh*, 'fury, resentment.']

Kruddhá, mfn. irritated, provoked, angry with (dat., gen., loc., or *upari* or *prati*) on account of (acc. with *anu*, Bhaṭṭ.), RV.; AV.; TS.; ŚBr.; MBh. &c.; fierce, cruel, W.; (*am*), n. anger, W.

2. **Krudh**, *t*, f. anger, wrath, Kathās. lxxvi, 18 (instr. °*dhā*, 'in a passion'); (*dhas*), f. pl. anger, Rājat. iii, 514 (516 ed. Calc.)

Krudhā, f. anger, L., Sch.

Krúdhmi, mfn. irritable, RV. vii, 56, 8.

Krudhyat, mfn. being angry, feeling provoked, Mn. vi, 48; MBh.

Krudhyamāna, mfn. id., BhP. vi, 4, 5.

Krodha, *as*, m. anger, wrath, passion, VS. xxx, 14; AV.; ŚBr. &c.; (ifc. f. *ā*) Amar.; Anger (personified as a child of Lobha and Nikṛiti; or of Death; or of Brahmā), VP.; N. of a Dānava, MBh. i, 2543; Hariv.; of the mystic syllable *hum* or *hrūm*, Rāmat-Up.; (*ā*), f., N. of one of the thirteen daughters of Daksha and wife of Kaśyapa, MBh. i, 2520; Hariv.; (*ī*), f. (in music) N. of a Śruti; (*am*), n., N. of the fifty-ninth year of the sixty years' Bṛihaspati cycle, VarBṛS. **-cakshus**, n. an eye glowing with anger, Hit. **-ja**, mfn. proceeding from or engendered by wrath (as the eight vices, hatred, envy, oppression, violence, &c.), Mn. vii, 45–51. **-bhairava**, m. a form of Bhairava (or Śiva), BrahmavP. **-mantra**, m., N. of a Mantra. **-máya**, mfn. one whose nature is anger, ŚBr. xiv; of angry disposition, passionate, R. vii, 65, 31. **-mukha**, mf(*ī*)n. one who has an angry countenance, Cāṇ.; Subh. **-mūrchita**, mfn. infatuated with anger, passionate, MBh. iii, 1864; R. i, 1, 48; (*as*), m. a kind of perfume, L. **-varjita**, mfn. free from wrath, calm. **-vardhana**, m., N. of a Dānava, MBh. i, 2682; Hariv. **-vaśa**, m. the power of anger, MBh. i, 3949 (cf. Mn. ii, 214); (mfn.) with *gaṇa*, or (*as*, *ās*), m. sg. & pl. 'passionate,' N. of several kinds of evil spirits, MBh.; Hariv.; BhP.; (*as*), m., N. of a Rakshas, MBh. iii, 16365; xiii, 4291; (*ā*), f., N. of a daughter of Daksha and wife of Kaśyapa, MBh. i, 2624; Hariv.; R.; BhP.; *-ga*, mfn. subject to anger, Pañcat. **-śatru**, m., N. of an Asura, MBh. i, 65, 35. **-samanvita**, mfn. filled with anger. **-hantṛi**, m., N. of an Asura, MBh. i, 2543 & 2682; Hariv. **-hāsa**, m. wrathful laughing, Bālar. **Krodhânvita**, mfn. wrathful, angry. **Krodhâmarsha-jihma-bhrū**, mfn. bending the brow with anger and impatience. **Krodhêśvara**, m. = *krāthêśv*°, q. v. **Krodhôjjhita**, mfn. free from wrath, composed, calm. **Krodhôdana**, m., v.l. for *śuddhôd*° (q. v.), VP.

Krodhana, mf(*ā*)n. (Pāṇ. iii, 2, 151) inclined to wrath, passionate, angry (with loc., Yājñ. i, 333), MBh. &c.; m. (= *krodha*) the 59th year in the sixty years' Bṛihaspati cycle, Romakas.; N. of a son of Kauśika and pupil of Garga, Hariv. 1189; of a son of A-yuta and father of Devâtithi, BhP. ix, 22, 11; of a man, Kathās. lviii, 84; of a Śākta author of Mantras; (*ā*), f. a passionate woman, vixen, L.; N. of one of the mothers in Skanda's retinue, MBh. ix, 2624; of a Yoginī, Hcat.; (*am*), n. 'the being angry, anger,' only ifc. *sa-kr*° (q. v.)

Krodhanīya, mfn. anything which may produce anger, provocative, R. ii, 41, 3; (*am*), n. (hence) an injury, W.

Krodhālu, mfn. passionate, violent, Suśr. vi.

Krodhin, mfn. id. iii, 4, 62; m. a buffalo, L.; a dog, L.; a rhinoceros, L.; the 38th year of the sixty years' Bṛihaspati cycle, VarBṛS. viii, 41; Romakas.; (*inī*), f. a mystical N. of the letter *r*. **Krodhi-tva**, n. the state of being passionate, R. vii, 18, 16.

Krodhishṭha, mfn. very irate or wrathful, L.

क्रुन्थ् *krunth*, v.l. for √*kunth*, Dhātup.

क्रुमु *krúmu*, *us*, f., N. of a river (tributary of the Indus), RV. v, 53, 9 & x, 75, 6.

क्रुमुक *krumuká*, *as*, m. (cf. *kṛimuká*, *kram*°) a piece of wood or match used to catch the sacrificial fire when kindled by friction, TS. v, 1, 9, 5; TBr. i, 4, 7, 3; ĀpŚr. xiv, 24.

क्रुश् *kruś*, cl. 1. P. *krośati* (rarely Ā., see *krośamāna*; aor. *ákrukshat*, RV. x, 146, 4; perf. *cukrośa*, R.; fut. 2nd *krokshyati* and 1st *kroshṭā*, Pāṇ. vii, 2, 10, Siddh.), to cry out, shriek, yell, bawl, call out, halloo, RV.; AV.; MBh. &c.; to exclaim, R. i, 9, 59; to lament, weep, Mn.; MBh. &c.; to make a singing noise (as the ear), Kauś. 58: Intens. *cokruśiti*, Pāṇ. vii, 4, 82, Sch.; [cf. Lith. *klykiu*, 'to cry;' *kryksztauju*; Hib. *cruisigh*, 'music, song;' Lat. *crocis*, *crocito*; Gk. κρώζω, κράζω, κραγγή; Goth. *krukja*.]

Kruśvan, *ā*, m. 'crier,' a jackal, Uṇ. iv, 115.

Krushṭa, mfn. calling or crying at (acc.), scolding, MBh. xiii, 2135; called at, abused, Buddh.; cried, wept, W.; cried aloud, bawled, W.; clamorous, loud (said of a particular Svara), SāmavBr. (also superl. *-tama*); TPrāt.; (*am*), n. crying, weeping, sobbing, noise, L.

Krośa, *as*, m. (cf. *klośa*) a cry, yell, shriek, shout, VS. xxx, 19; TS. vii; (cf. *karṇa-k*°); 'the range of the voice in calling or hallooing,' a measure of distance (an Indian league, commonly called a Kos = 1000 Daṇḍas = 4000 Hastas = $\frac{1}{4}$ Yojana; according to others = 2000 Daṇḍas = 8000 Hastas = $\frac{1}{2}$ Gavyūti), KātyŚr.; MBh. &c.; (*ám*), n. (gaṇa *jvalâdi*), N. of different Sāmans, TS. vii; Lāṭy.; ĀrshBr. **-tāla**, m. a large or double drum, L. **-dhvani**, m. id., L. **-mātra-gata**, mfn. gone to the length of a Krośa. **-mātra-sthita**, mfn. standing at the distance of a Krośa. **-yuga**, n. a measure of two Krośas (= 4000 yards or about $2\frac{1}{2}$ miles; this seems to correspond to the modern Krośa [or Kos], but the standard varies).

Krośat, mfn. crying or calling at (acc.), RV. x, 94, 4; lamenting, weeping, R. i, 54, 7; calling out.

Krośaná, mfn. crying, RV. x, 27, 18; (*ā*), f., N. of one of the mothers in Skanda's retinue, MBh. ix, 2635; (*am*), n. crying, Suśr. iii, 9, 10.

Krośamāna, mfn. crying, R. i, 60, 19; iii, 66, 17.

Krośin. See *ushṭra-k*° (also Pāṇ. vi, 2, 80, Kāś.)

Kroshṭu (*must* form strong cases and *may* form weak cases from *kroshṭṛi*, Gramm. 128. c; Pāṇ. vii, 1, 95 & 97), m. 'crier,' a jackal, Yājñ. i, 148; N. of a son of Yadu and father of Vṛijinīvat, Hariv. 1906 & 1969. **-karṇa**, N. of a locality, g. *taksha-śilâdi*. **-pāda**, m., N. of a man, and (*ās*), m. pl. his family, gaṇa *yaskâdi*. **-pucchikā**, f. Hemionitis cordifolia, L. **-pucchī**, f. id., L. **-phala**, m. Terminalia Catappa, L. **-māna**, m., N. of a man, and (*ās*), m. pl. his family, gaṇa *yaskâdi*. **-māya**, m., N. of a man, and (*ās*), m. pl. his family, ib. (Gaṇar. 26). **-vinnā**, f. = *-pucchikā*, L.

Kroshṭuka, *as*, m. a jackal, MBh.; 'N. of a man,' see *kraushṭuki*; (*ī*), f. 'a female jackal,' N. of a daughter of Krodha-vaśā and mother of the yellow apes, R. iii, 20, 22 & 26. **-pucchikā**, f. = *kroshṭu-p*°, L. **-māna**, v. l. for *kroshṭu-m*°. **-mekhalā**, f. = *-pucchikā*, L. **-śiras**, n. a disease of the knee, Suśr. ii, 1, 75; iii, 8, 14; iv, 5, 32.

Kroshṭṛi, mfn. crying, lamenting, BhP. x, 15, 36; (*ṭá*), m. (not used in the weakest cases, see *kroshṭu*; Pāṇ. vii, 1, 95 & 97) 'crier,' a jackal, RV. x, 18, 4; AV.; VS.; MBh.; N. of a son of Yadu and father of Vṛijinīvat, MBh. xiii, 6832; Hariv. 1843; BhP.; (*ṭrī*), f. (gaṇa *gaurâdi*) the female of a jackal, L.; a kind of Convolvulus, L.; another plant (= *lāṅgalī*), L.

Kroshṭrīya, *ās*, m. pl., N. of a school of grammarians, Pat. on Pāṇ. i, 1, 3, Vārtt. 6.

क्रूड् *krūḍ*. See √*kruḍ*.

क्रूर *krūrá*, mf(*ā*)n. (fr. *kravi-s*, cf. *sthūrá* & *sthávira*), wounded, hurt, sore, ŚBr.; 'bloody, raw,' cruel, fierce, ferocious, pitiless, harsh, formidable, AV.; TS. vi; Mn. &c.; inauspicious (as opposed to *saumya* and *a-krūra*, said of the first, third, fifth, seventh, ninth, and eleventh signs of the zodiac, which are supposed to have a malignant influence, Jyot.; said of planets, VarBṛS.); hard, solid, Suśr.; Śak.; Pañcat.; strong (as a bow, opposed to *manda*), Nār.; hot, sharp, disagreeable, L.; (*am*), ind. in a formidable manner, MBh. iii, 15669; (*as*, *am*), m. n. boiled rice (cf. *kūra*), L.; (*as*), m. a hawk, L.; a heron, L.; red oleander (= *rakta-karavīra*), L.; (*ā*), f. a variety of Punarnavā with red blossoms, L.; (*ám*), n. a wound, sore, AV.; VS.; TS.; ŚBr.; blood-shedding, slaughter, cruelty, any horrible deed, harshness, AV.; AitBr. i, 26; Mn. i, 29 &c.; any frightful apparition, AdbhBr.; a kind of house, Gal. **-karmán**, n. a bloody or terrible deed, ŚBr. v; Suśr.; any hard or difficult labour, Śak. (v. l.); (mfn.) performing bloody or terrible deeds, fierce, cruel, unrelenting, MBh. iii, 13253; R.; Pañcat.; Vet.; (*ā*), m., N. of a plant (= *kaṭu-tumbinī*), L.; (*krūra-karma*)-*kṛit*, mfn. perpetrating cruel actions, W.; (*t*), m. a rapacious animal, Mn. xii, 58. **-kṛikara**, m. a heron, Gal. **-kṛít**, mfn. performing bloody or terrible deeds, cruel, TBr. i. **-koshṭha**, m. costive bowels unaffected by strong purgatives; (mfn.) one whose bowels are costive, Suśr. **-gandha**, m. 'smelling formidably,' sulphur, L.; (*ā*), f. a variety of Opuntia (= *kanthārī*), L. **-gandhaka**, m. sulphur, Gal. **-carita**, mfn. addicted to cruel practices, cruel, ferocious. **-ceshṭita**, mfn. id., Pañcat. **-tā**, f. cruelty, Mn. x, 58. **-tva**, n. id. **-dantī**, f. 'having bloody or cruel teeth,' N. of Durgā, L. **-dṛiś**, mfn. evil-eyed (said of an owl), Kathās. lxii, 27; of terrible aspect, mischievous, cruel; (*k*), m., N. of the planet Śani or Saturn; of the planet Mars; (*krūra-dṛik*)-*patha*, 'one whose path gives an inauspicious aspect,' m. the planet Saturn, Gal. **-dṛishṭi**, f. a formidable look or glance, Pañcat. **-dhūrta**, m. a kind of thorn-apple, L.; (cf. *kṛishṇa-dattūraka*.) **-niścaya**, mf(*ā*)n. one who has made a cruel resolution, Ragh. xii, 4. **-prakṛitika**, mfn. of a cruel character, Prab. **-buddhi**, mfn. cruel-minded, MBh. i, 154, 7. **-mānasa**, mfn. id., MBh. i, 209, 3. **-rava**, m. 'having an inauspicious or frightful cry,' a jackal (?), W. **-rāvin**, m. a raven, L. **-locana**, m. 'of an inauspicious aspect,' N. of the planet Saturn,' L.; N. of an owl, Kathās. lxii, 101. **-samācāra**, mf(*ā*)n. behaving cruelly or fiercely, R. vi, 98, 23. **-sarpa-vat**, ind. like an enraged serpent, W. **-svara**, mfn. crying frightfully, R. iii, 64, 2. **Krūrâkṛiti**, m. 'of a formidable appearance,' N. of Rāvaṇa (the ruler of Laṅkā), L. **Krūrâksha**, m. 'evil-eyed,' N. of an owl (minister of the owl-king Ari-mardana), Pañcat. iii. **Krūrâcāra**, mfn. following cruel or savage practices, behaving cruelly, Mn. iv, 246; *-vihāra-vat*, mfn. behaving cruelly and rejoicing in cruelties, Mn. x, 9. **Krūrâtman**, m. 'of a cruel nature,' N. of the planet Saturn, L. **Krūrâlāpin**, m. = °*ra-rāvin* (q. v.), Npr. **Krūrâśaya**, mf(*ā*)n. one whose bowels are torpid or costive, Suśr.; containing fierce animals (as a river), Bhartṛ. i, 80; of a terrible or fierce disposition (as women), ib. **Krūrôpasaṃhata,** mfn. connected with cruelty, W.

Krūrī-√kṛi, to make sore, wound, ŚBr.

क्रूर्च *krūrca*, for *kūrca* (the beard), W.

क्रेङ्कार *kreṅ-kāra, as,* m. the sound *kreṅ*, Kād.; Bālar. iv, 11; x.

Kreṅ-kṛiti, *is,* f. id., Bhojapr.

क्रेङ्कारव *kreṅkā-rava* = *kekā-r°*, Hcar.

क्रेणि *kreṇi, °ṇī, kretavya,* &c. See √1. *krī.*

क्रैडिन *kraiḍiná*, mf(ī)n. (fr. *krīḍín*), belonging to the Maruts or winds, ŚBr. xi, 5, 2, 4; ĀśvŚr. ix, 2; ŚāṅkhŚr. xiv, 10, 7; KātyŚr. ii & iv, Sch.

Kraiḍinīyā, f., scil. *ishṭi*, the Ishṭi or sacrificial oblation sacred to the Maruts, KātyŚr. ii & iv, Sch.

क्रैव्य *kraivya, as,* m. a king of the Krivis, ŚBr. xiii, 5, 4, 7.

क्रोञ्च *krońca, as,* m. (for *krauñca*), N. of a mountain, Gal. **—kumārikā,** f. a kind of Rākshasī, Divyâv. xviii, xxxv. **—dāraṇa** = *krauñca-d°*, q. v., L., Sch. **—padī,** see *krauñca p°*.

क्रोड *kroḍá, as,* m. (*am,* n. in later language, L.) the breast, chest, bosom (of men and animals), AV.; VS.; KātyŚr. &c.; (of a bird) R. vii, 18, 32; (pl.) MBh. xiii, 2660; (named as a place where money is kept) Mṛicch. ii; ifc. f. *ā*, Pāṇ. iv, 1, 56 (e. g. *kalyāṇa-kroḍā*, a woman with a well-formed breast, Kāś.); the flank, hollow above the hip, W.; the lap (= *aṅka*), L.; the interior of anything, cavity, hollow, Bālar. vi, 65; Hit.; m. a hog, Pañcat.; BhP.; VārP.; Kathās.; N. of the planet Saturn, L.; 'anything left in the bosom,' an additional verse or note, Kām., Sch.; N. of a teacher, Kaiy. on Pāṇ. iv, 2, 66, Vārtt. 6, Pat. (cf. *krauḍa*); (*ā*), f. the breast, bosom, L.; N. of a plant, L.; (*ī*), f. a sow, Kathās. liii, 120; the yam root, L.; (*am*), n. id., L. **—kanyā,** f. the yam root, L. **—kaseruka,** m. Cyperus rotundus, Bhpr. **—kāntā,** f. 'dear to Saturn (?),' the earth, L. **—khorā,** f., N. of a plant, Gal. **—cūḍā,** f., N. of a plant (= *mahā-śrāvaṇikā*), L. **—tīrtha,** n., N. of a Tīrtha, KapSaṃh. **—pattra,** n. (cf. *kroḍa*) an additional leaf, postscript, supplement, codicil to a will. **—parṇī,** f. a prickly nightshade (Solanum Jacquini), L. **—pāda,** m. a tortoise, L. **—pālī,** f. the chest, Bālar. **—malla,** °**llaka,** m. a beggar, Buddh. **—loman,** *āni,* n. pl. hairs on the breast, Kauś. **—vallabhā,** f. a variety of Cyperus, Gal. **—vāla,** m. a pig's bristle, Kathās. **Kroḍâṅka,** m. a tortoise, W. **Kroḍâṅghri,** m. id., L. **Kroḍâsya,** mfn. having a snout like a hog, VarYogay. vi, 23. **Kroḍêshṭā,** f. 'dear to hogs,' the grass Cyperus rotundus, L.

Kroḍī, f. and ind. in comp. **—karaṇa,** n. embracing, L. **—√kṛi,** to embrace, Hit.; to become master of, Hcar. **—kṛiti,** f. embracing, L. **—mukha,** m. 'having a snout like a sow,' a rhinoceros, L.

क्रोथ *krotha*, for *krātha* (but cf. √*krunth*), killing, murder, W.

क्रोध *kródha*, &c. See √1. *krudh.*

क्रोश *krósa*, &c. See √*kruś.*

क्रोष्ट *kroshṭa, as,* m., N. of a man, Pravar. **Kroshṭêkshu,** for *koshṭhêkshu*, q. v., L.

क्रोष्टु *kroshṭu, kroshṭuka.* See √*kruś.*

Kroshṭṛi, kroshṭṛiya. See ib.

क्रौञ्च *krauñcá*, mfn. (fr. *krúñca*, g. *prajñâdi*), 'curlew-like,' with *vyūha*, = °*câruṇa*, MBh. vi, 51, 1; (*as*), m. a kind of curlew, TS. v; Āp. i, 17, 36; Mn. &c.; the emblem of the fifth Arhat of the present Avasarpiṇī, L.; an osprey, L.; patr. (or metron. fr. *kruñcā*, Pāṇ. iv, 1, 120, Kār.), N. of a pupil of Śākapūrṇi, VP.; N. of a mountain (part of the Himālaya range, situated in the eastern part of the chain on the north of Assam; said to have been split by Kārttikeya, VP.), TĀr. i, 31, 2; MBh. iii, 14331; vi, 462; ix, 2700 ff.; R. &c.; N. of one of the Dvīpas of the world (surrounded by the sea of curds), VarBṛS.; BhP.; MatsyaP.; BhavP.; VārP.; N. of an Asura or Rakshas, W.; (*ā*), f. the female curlew, Comm. on L.; (*ī*), f. id., R.; N. of a daughter of Tāmrā and mother of the curlews, R.; (*am*), n. a kind of poison, Car. vi, 23; (scil. *astra*) N. of a mythical weapon, R. i, 29, 12 & 56, 9; N. of several Sāmans, TāṇḍyaBr. xi; xiii; Lāṭy.; ĀrshBr.; of a particular kind of recitation, TS. ii, 5, 11, 1; ChUp. ii, 22, 1 (scil. *gāna*); a particular method of sitting, NārP. **—dāraṇa,** m. 'Krauñca-splitter,' Kārttikeya, L. **—dvīpa,** m., N. of a Dvīpa (see *krauñca*), L. **—nishadana,** n. a particular kind of being seated (practised by Yogins), Sarvad. **—nishūdana,** m. = *-dāraṇa*, MBh. iii, 8138 (ed. Bomb.) **—paksha,** mfn. (horses) the flanks of which are similar to the wings of a curlew, R. v, 12, 35. **—padā,** f. a metre of 4 × 25 syllables. **—padī,** f., N. of a locality, MBh. xiii, 1728 (v. l. *krońc°*). **—pura,** n., N. of a town, Hariv. **—bandham,** ind. so as to make a knot called after the wings of a curlew, Pāṇ. iii, 4, 42, Kāś. **—bradhna,** m., N. of a Ṛishi, BrahmaP. (also pl.) **—randhra,** n. the Krauñca pass (split by the deity Kārttikeya and by Paraśu-rāma), Megh. **—ripu,** m. 'enemy of the Krauñca mountain,' = *-dāraṇa*, Pañcat. **—vat,** m., N. of a mountain (= *krauñca*), Hariv. 11447. **—vana,** n., N. of a town, R. vii, 59, 20. **—śatru,** m. = *-ripu*, Mṛicch. **—sūdana,** m. id., Suśr. **Krauñcâcala,** m. the Krauñca mountain; *-dveshin*, m. 'enemy of the Krauñca mountain,' N. of Paraśu-rāma (see *krauñca-randhra*), Bālar. **Krauñcâdana,** n. 'curlew's food,' the fibres of the stalk of the lotus, Car. i, 27; the plant Arum orixense, L.; long pepper, L.; another plant (= *ciñcoṭaka*), L.; (*ī*), f. the seed of a lotus, L. **Krauñcâraṇya,** n., N. of a forest, R. vi, 74, 18 (cf. iii, 74, 7). **Krauñcârāti,** m. = *krauñca-ripu*, L. **Krauñcâri,** m. id., L.; (= °*câcala-dveshin*), N. of Paraśu-rāma, Bālar. iv, 22. **Krauñcâruṇa,** m. a kind of battle array, MBh. vi, 50, 40.

Krauñcâkshi, m. patr. fr. °*ksha*, Saṃskārak.

Kraúñciki-pútra, *as,* m., N. of a teacher, ŚBr. xiv, 9, 4, 32.

क्रौड *krauḍa*, mf(ī)n. (fr. *kroḍá*), belonging to a hog, BhP. ii, 7, 1; coming from a hog, VarBṛS.; (= *vārāha*) relating to Vishṇu's Avatār as a hog, BhP. xi, 4, 18; (*ās*), m. pl. the school of Kroḍa, Pat. on Pāṇ. iv, 2, 66, Vārtt. 6.

Krauḍi, *is,* m. patr. fr. *kroḍá*, Pāṇ. iv, 1, 80.

Krauḍyā, f. of °*ḍi*, ib.

Kraulāyana, *as,* m. patr. fr. *krola* (for °*ḍa*), Pravar. (*krol°*, MS.)

क्रौर्य *kraurya, am,* n. (fr. *krūrá*), cruelty, fierceness, hard-heartedness, Mn. xii, 33; Śak. vii; VarBṛS.; Kathās. cvi, 130 (pl.); terribleness, W.

क्रौलायन *kraulāyana.* See *krauḍa.*

क्रौशशतिक *krauśaśatika*, mfn. (fr. *krośa-śata*), one who goes 100 Krośas or leagues, Pāṇ. v, 1, 74, Vārtt. 1; one who deserves to be approached from a distance of 100 leagues (a teacher), Vārtt. 2.

Kraushṭâyana, v. l. for °*shṭrāy°*.

Kraushṭukarṇa, mfn. coming from Kroshṭukarṇa, gaṇa *takshaśilâdi*.

Kraushṭuki, *is,* m. patr. fr. *kroshṭuka*, N. of a grammarian, Nir. viii, 2; Bṛih.; of an astrologer, AV.Pariś.; VarBṛS. i, 11, Sch.; (*ayas*), m. pl., N. of a warrior-tribe belonging to the Trigarta-shashṭhas, Pāṇ. v, 3, 116, Kār.

Kraushṭukīya, *as,* m. a prince of the warrior-tribe called Kraushṭukis, Pāṇ. v, 3, 116, Kār.

Kraushṭra, mfn., fr. *kroshṭṛi*, Pat. on Pāṇ. vii, 2, 117, Vārtt. 1.

Kraushṭrāyaṇa, *as,* m. patr. fr. *kroshṭṛi*, gaṇa *arīhaṇâdi*.

Kraushṭrāyaṇaka, mfn., fr. °*yaṇa*, ib.

क्र्यादि *kry-ādi.* See √*krī.*

क्लथ् *klath*, cl. 1. P. (p. *kláthat*) to be formed into clots or lumps, VS. xxxix, 5; to hurt, kill, Dhātup. xix, 40.

Klathana, *am,* n. forming into clots or lumps, Mahīdh. on VS. xxxix, 5.

क्लद् *klad.* See √*klana.*

क्लदीवत् *kladívat* (cf. √*klid*), wet, moist (?), AV. vii, 90, 3.

क्लन्द् *kland* (cf. √*krand*), cl. 1. P. *klandati*, to call, Dhātup. iii, 35; to lament, weep, ib.; Ā. *klandate* (v. l. *kladate*, fr. √*klad*), to be confounded or troubled, Dhātup. xix, 12; to sound, ŚiraUp.; [cf. κλάζω.]

Klandá, mf(*ā*)n. crying, noisy, AV. ii, 2, 5.

क्लप् *klap*, v. l. for √*hlap*, q. v.

क्लपुष *klapusha, am,* n. the bladder, Gal.

क्लम् *klam* (= √*śram*, q. v.), cl. 1. 4. *klāmati, klāmyati* (Pāṇ. iii, 1, 70; vii, 3, 74 f.), to be or become fatigued, be weary or exhausted, Bhaṭṭ. v, xii, xiv, xvii, 10 & 102; Kād.: Caus. *klāmayati*, to fatigue, ŚiraUp.

Klama, *as,* m. fatigue, exhaustion, languor, weariness, MBh.; Śak. iii, 18; Suśr.; BhP.; (ifc., Mn. &c.; f. *ā*, MBh.; Nal.)

Klamatha, *as,* m. fatigue, exhaustion, L.

Klamathu, *us,* m. id., L.

Klamin, mfn. becoming tired, languishing, gaṇa *śamâdi*. **Klami-tā,** f., **-tva,** n. exhaustion, W.

Klānta, mfn. tired, fatigued, exhausted, languishing, wearied, MBh.; R.; Śak.; Megh. &c.; depressed in spirits, VarYogay.; dried up, withering, Śak.; Ragh. x, 49; thin, emaciated, Śak. (compar.) **—manas,** mfn. languid, low-spirited, Śak. **—vadana,** mfn. having a weary face.

Klānti, *is,* f. fatigue, weariness, Bhartṛ. i, 36. **—cchid,** mfn. relieving fatigue, refreshing. **—ccheda,** m. removing fatigue, restoring.

क्लव् *klav*, cl. 1. Ā. *klavate*, to fear, be afraid, Dhātup. xix, 13 (Vop.)

Klavita, mfn. uttered hesitatingly, stammered, SaṃhUp. vii, 3.

क्लिद् *klid*, cl. 4. *klidyati* (rarely Ā. °*te*, Vet.), to be or become wet or damp, Suśr.; Bhaṭṭ.; Hit.; to rot, putrefy, Car. vi, 30: Caus. P. *kledayati*, to bedew, wet, moisten, Bhag. ii, 23; Suśr. i, 6, 3; iii, 5, 1; (aor. *aciklidat*) Bhaṭṭ. xv, 48; 'to soil,' see *kledita.*

Klindat, mfn. (√2. *klind*) wet, Mudr. iii, 20.

Klinna, mfn. moistened, wet, MBh.; R. &c.; running (as an eye), Pāṇ. v, 2, 33, Vārtt. 2; rotted, putrefied, Car. i, 11 & 27; Lalit. xii; soft, moved (the heart), BhP. iv, 3, 10 & ix, 11, 5; (*as*), m., N. of a Śākta author of Mantras; (*ā*), f. the plant Solanum diffusum, L. **—tva,** n. the being wet, Suśr. **—netra,** mfn. having running eyes, L.; having moist eyes, pitiful, L. **—vartman,** n. excess of the lachrymal discharge, watering of the eyes, Suśr. **—hṛid,** mfn. tender-hearted. **Klinnâksha,** mfn. having moist eyes, blear-eyed, L.

Klinnaka, mfn. moistened a little, Comm. on Gobh. ii, 1, 10.

Kleda, *as,* m. wetness, dampness, moisture, Yājñ.; MBh.; R.; Suśr. &c.; running, discharge (from a sore), Suśr.; rotting, putrefying, Car. i, 20 & vi, 11. **—vat,** mfn. moist, flowing, Suśr. iv, 1, 64 & 6, 1.

Kledaka, mfn. wetting, moistening, W.: (*as*), m. phlegm in the stomach, excess of saliva, W.

Kledan, *ā,* m. the moon, Uṇ. i, 158.

Kledana, mfn. making wet, moistening, Suśr.; (*as*), m. phlegm, phlegmatic or watery humor (cf. *kapha*), L.; a species of phlegm, L.; (*am*), n. wetting, moistening, Suśr.; BhP.; oozing, trickling, W. **—bhāva,** m. the being moistened or wet, Tattvas.

Kledita, mfn. soiled, Subh.

Kledin, mfn. moistening, wet, Kpr.; (*inī*), f., N. of a plant, Hariv. 3843 (v. l. *ketakī*).

Kledu, *us,* m. the moon, Uṇ. i, 10; a morbid combination (*saṃnipāta*) of the three humors of the body, complication of disorders, L.

Kledya, mfn. See *a-kl°* (Bhag. ii, 24).

क्लिन्द् 1. *klind*, cl. 1. P. Ā. *klindati*, °*te*, to lament, Dhātup. ii, 14; iii, 36; (cf. √*kland.*)

क्लिन्द् 2. *klind*, pr. p. °*dat.* See √*klid.*

Klinna, °**nnaka.** See ib.

क्लिब् *klíb*, *p*, f. (v. l. *klṛib*; √*klṛip*?) accomplishment ['the created world,' Sāy.], VS. xl, 15; ŚBr. xiv, 8, 3, 1.

क्लिश् *kliś*, cl. 9. P. *kliśnāti* (perf. *cikleśa*; ind. p. *kliśitvā* or *klishṭvā*, Pāṇ. i, 2, 7; vii, 2, 50), to torment, trouble, molest, cause pain, afflict, MBh.; R. &c.; to suffer, feel pain, Bhaṭṭ.: cl. 4. P. *kliśyati*, to torment, cause pain (with acc.), MBh. xii, 6621; Ragh. xiii, 73; Ā. *kliśyate* (rarely P. °*ti*, Mn. viii, 169; MBh. iii, 10241; p. *kliśyamāna*), to be tormented or molested, be afflicted, feel pain, MBh.; R. &c.; (P.) to be sinful, Divyâv. xx: Caus. P. *kleśayati* (rarely Ā., Suśr.; aor. Subj. 2. sg. *cikliśas*, Bhaṭṭ.), to torment, molest, R. v, 27, 33; Suśr.; Bhaṭṭ. vi, 17.

Kliśita, mfn. molested, Pāṇ. vii, 2, 50. **-vat**, mfn. suffering pain or distress, W.

Kliśyamāna, mfn. being distressed, MBh.; R.

Klishṭa, mfn. (Pāṇ. vii, 2, 50) molested, tormented, afflicted, distressed, R.; Mālav.; Śak. &c.; wearied, hurt, injured, being in bad condition, worn, R.; Śak.; Megh.; Suśr.; connected with pain or suffering, KapS. ii, 33; Yogas.; Pañcat.; (in rhet.) forced, obscure, not easily intelligible (cf. √*kleś*), Sāh.; Pratāpar.; Vām. ii, 1, 21 ff.; (*am*), ind. in distress, BhP. i, 9, 12. **-tva**, n. obscurity (of a passage), Sāh. **-vartman**, n. a disease of the eyelids (cf. *klinna-v*°), Suśr. vi, 3, 16. **-vṛitti**, mfn. leading a wretched life, Kathās. iii, 14.

Klishṭi, *is*, f. affliction, distress, L.; service, L.

Kleśa, *as*, m. pain, affliction, distress, pain from disease, anguish, ŚvetUp.; Mn.; Yājñ.; MBh. &c.; (in Yoga phil. five Kleśas are named, viz. *a-vidyā*, 'ignorance,' *asmi-tā*, 'egotism,' *rāga*, 'desire,' *dvesha*, 'aversion,' and *abhiniveśa*, 'tenacity of mundane existence,' Yogas.; Prab.; Sarvad.; the Buddhists reckon ten, viz. three of the body [murder, theft, adultery], four of speech [lying, slander, abuse, unprofitable conversation], three of the mind [covetousness, malice, scepticism], Buddh.; Sarvad.); wrath, anger, L.; worldly occupation, care, trouble (= *vyavasāya*), L. **-kārin**, mfn. causing pain, afflicting, Pañcat. **-kshama**, mfn. capable of enduring pain and trouble, Suśr. **-da**, mfn. distressing. **-nāśana**, mfn. destroying or palliating trouble. **-prahāṇa**, n. termination of distress (especially of worldly cares and passions), W. **-bhāgin**, mfn. having trouble. **-bhāj**, mfn. id. **Kleśâpaha**, mfn. (Pāṇ. iii, 2, 50) allaying pain or suffering, consolatory, consoling (said of a son), Kāś.; palliative, W.; (*as*), m. a son, W.

Kleśaka, mfn. giving pain, troublesome, annoying, afflicting, Pāṇ. iii, 2, 146.

Kleśana, *am*, n. disgust (ifc.), Car. ii, 1.

Kleśala, *as*, m. pain, BhP. x, 14, 4.

Kleśita, mfn. pained, distressed, afflicted, MBh. iii, 10872 & 11173; iv, 1296; MārkP. xx; Śṛiṅgār.

Kleśin, mfn. causing pain or suffering (ifc.), Ragh. xii, 76 (ed. Calc.); hurting, injuring, Megh.

Kleshṭṛi, *tā*, m. one who causes pain or suffering, MBh. iii, 1076.

क्लीत *klīta*, *as*, m. a kind of venomous insect, Suśr. v, 8, 9.

Klītaka, mfn. (grains) prepared as dough or paste, Gobh. ii, 1, 10; (*am*), n. dough or paste (ifc.), ĀśvGṛ. iii, 8, 8; (prepared from sweet root) Bhpr.; Glycyrrhiza glabra or echinata (sweet root), Car. i, 1; (*ā*), f. id., ĀpŚr. xv, 3, 16; m. or n., N. of a plant with a poisonous root, Suśr. v, 2, 3.

Klītakikā, f. the Indigo plant (*kāla-klītaka*), L.

Klītanaka, *am*, n. a variety of the sweet root plant, L.

Klītanāyaka, *am*, n. id., L.

Klītanī, f. the Indigo plant, L.

Klaitakika, *am*, n. a fermented liquor prepared from the Klītaka root, wine, spirituous liquor, L.

क्लीब् *klīb*, cl. 1. Ā. *klībate*, to be impotent, behave like a eunuch, Pāṇ. iii, 1, 11, Pat.; to be timorous or modest or unassuming, Dhātup. x, 18; cl. 10. Ā. *klībayate*, to be unmanly or timorous, MBh. vi, 4334 (v.l.); Kathās. civ, 126.

Klībá, mf(*ā*)n. (Pāṇ. iii, 1, 11, Vārtt. 3) impotent, emasculated, a eunuch, AV.; VS.; TS.; ŚBr.; Mn. &c.; unmanly, timorous, weak, idle, a coward, MBh.; Mṛicch.; BhP. &c.; having no water (as a cloud), Daś.; (in lexicography) of the neuter gender; (*am*), n. (in lexicography) the neuter gender. **-tā**, f. impotence, Suśr.; weakness (as of a grass), ŚārṅgP.; (*a-k*°, 'manliness,' Ragh. viii, 83); the being neuter. **-tva**, n. impotence, MBh. ii, 1457. **-yoga**, m., N. of a particular constellation, VarBṛ. **-rūpa** (°*bá-*), mfn. similar to a eunuch, AV. viii, 6, 7. **-liṅga**, n. the neuter gender, W. **-vat**, ind. like a base man, like a weak-minded or effeminate person.

Klībāya, Nom. Ā. °*yate*, to behave like a eunuch, Vop. xxi, 7.

Klaibya, *am*, n. impotence, TS. ii; Suśr.; Hit.; unmanliness, weakness, timidity, cowardice, MBh.; R.; BhP.; Hit.; weakness (as of a lotus leaf), Ragh. xii, 86; the neuter gender, W.

क्लीव् *klīv*, *klīva*, for *klīb*, &c., q.v.

क्लु *klu*, cl. 1. Ā. *klavate*, to move, Dhātup. xxii, 60.

क्लेद *kleda*, &c. See √*klid*.

क्लेश् *kleś*, cl. 1. Ā. *kleśate*, to speak articulately, Dhātup. xvi, 6; to speak inarticulately (cf. *klishṭa*), ib.; to strike, kill, ib.

क्लेश *kleśa*, &c. See √*kliś*.

क्लैतकिक *klaitakika*. See *klīta*.

क्लैब्य *klaibya*. See √*klīb*.

क्लोम *kloma*, *am*, n. = *klóman*, L.

Klóman, *ā*, m. the right lung, AV.; VS.; Kāṭh.; ŚBr. &c.; (*ānas*), m. pl. the lungs, VS. xxv, 8; ŚBr. x, 6, 4, 1; (*a*), n. the right lung, Suśr.; [cf. Gk. πνεύμων and πλεύμων; Lat. *pulmo*.] **-hṛidayá**, n. sg. the right lung and the heart, ŚBr. iv, 5, 4, 6.

क्लोश *klóśa*, *as*, m. (= *króśa*) calling out to ['fear,' Sāy.], RV. vi, 46, 14.

क्व *kvà*, ind. (fr. 1. *ku*, Pāṇ. v, 3, 12; vii, 2, 105), loc. of 2. *ká* = *kasmin* or *katarasmin*, Mn. x, 66 (*kva śreyas-tvam*, in whom is the preference?); Kathās. lxxxiii, 36; where? in what place? whither? RV. (sometimes connected with particles *áha*, *íd*, *iva*, *svid*) &c.; (connected with *nu*) Nal.; Mālav.; (with *nu khalu*) Śak.; (with √*bhū*, √1. *as*) how is it with? what has become of? i.e. it is done with, RV. i, 161, 4; vii, 88, 5; AV. x, 8, 7; ŚBr.; Pāṇ. iii, 1, 12, Vārtt. 1, Pat.; (with *gata*) how is it with? Nal.; Daś. (*kva gatas tava mayy anurāgaḥ*, what has become of your affection for me?); or *kva* alone may have the same meaning (e.g. *kva sukham*, where is happiness? i.e. there is no such thing as happiness, Śāntis.), Pañcat.; Naish. i, 20; (after a negative phrase) how much less? R. i, 67, 10; *kva—kva* or *kutra—kva* (implying excessive incongruity) where is this? where is that? how distant is this from that? how little does this agree with that? (e.g. *kva sūrya-prabhavo vaṇśaḥ kva câlpa-vishayā matiḥ*, how can my limited intellect describe the solar race? Ragh. i, 2), MBh.; R. &c.; *kvâpi*, anywhere, somewhere, to some place, in a certain place, Nal.; Pañcat.; Kathās.; sometimes, Sāh.; Hit.; *na kva ca*, nowhere, never, BhP. iv, 29, 64; *na kva cana*, nowhere, MBh. xiv, 560; *kva cid* = *kasmiṇś-cid*, Pañcat.; anywhere, somewhere, to any place, in a certain place, Mn.; R.; Śak. &c.; in a certain case, at some time, once upon a time, Nal.; Pañcat. &c.; sometimes, Comm.; *kvacid—kvacid*, here—there, here and there, in various places, MBh. i; now—then, now and then, R. iii, 50, 7; Bhartṛ. i, 4; *na kvacid*, nowhere, never, by no means, Mn.; Yājñ.; Nal. &c.; *kvacid api na*, id., Megh.; *yatra kvâpi*, wherever, in whatsoever place, Bhartṛ. iii, 91; *yátra kvà-ca*, id., ŚBr.; ChUp.; Lāṭy.; BhP.; *yatra kva-cana*, in or to whatsoever place; in any case or matter whatever, Mn. ix, 233; whenever, BhP. v, 21, 9; *yatra kva vātha—tatra tatrâpi*, wherever—there, BhP. i, 17, 36. **-janman**, mfn. where born? MBh. i, 7114. **-nivāsa**, mfn. where dwelling? MBh. i, 190, 31. **-stha**, mfn. where being? Pat. on Śivas. 2, Vārtt. 3.

Kvatya, mfn. being where? Pāṇ. iv, 2, 104, Pat.

Kvatyaka, mf(*ikā*)n. id., Vop. iv, 7.

Kvācitka, mf(*ī*)n. (fr. *kva-cid*), met with occasionally or somewhere (as a reading), Nyāyam.; Comm. on TS. & ĀpŚr.

क्वङ्गु *kvaṅgu*, *us*, m. (= *kaṅgu*) a variety of Panic (Panicum italicum), L.

क्वण् *kvaṇ*, cl. 1. P. *kvaṇati* (pr. p. *kvaṇat*), to sound, make any sound, tinkle, Amar.; Kathās. lxxxv, 25; Hit.; to hum (as a bee), Bhaṭṭ. vi, 84; (said of Kiṃnaras and Yātu-dhānas) Kum. i, 55 & Bhaṭṭ. (aor. 3. pl. *akvāṇishur*): Caus. P. *kvaṇayati* (pr. p. f. °*yatī*), to cause to sound, make sound (as a musical instrument), blow (the flute), BhP. iii, 15, 21; x, 44, 13 & 16; to produce a sound with (instr.), iv, 24, 12; x, 60, 8.

Kvaṇa, *as*, m. the sound or tone of any musical instrument, L.; sound in general, L.

Kvaṇana, *am*, n. sounding, sound of any musical instrument, L.; (*as*), m. a small earthen pot, L.

Kvaṇita, mfn. sounded, twanged (as a stringed instrument), W.; humming (as a bee), Vikr.; (*am*), n. sound, twang, Ragh. & Gīt. (ifc.); Bhaṭṭ. **-veṇu**, mfn. one who has breathed the flute, BhP. x, 21, 12.

Kvaṇitêkshaṇa, m. a vulture, Npr.

Kvāṇa, *as*, m. sounding, sound (especially of a musical instrument), Sāh. 732, Sch.; Kathās. cxx, 106.

क्वथ् *kvath*, cl. 1. Ā. *kvathate*, to boil, prepare by heat, Kāṭh.; to digest, W.; to be hot (as the heart), Hcar.: Caus. *kvāthayati*, to cause to boil, decoct, Kauś.; ŚārṅgS.; (Pass. *kvāthyate*) MBh.; Suśr. i, 45, 31; MārkP. xii, 36.

Kvatha, *as*, m. (gaṇa *jvalâdi*) a decoction, extract.

Kvathana, *am*, n. boiling by (in comp., *agni-*), Suśr. i, 45, 4.

Kvathikā, f. a decoction made with milk, Npr.

Kvathita, mfn. boiled, decocted, stewed, Mn. vi, 20; Suśr.; BhP. &c.; being hot, Kathās. xc, 61; digested, W.; (*ā*), f. a decoction prepared with Curcuma, Asa fœtida, and milk, Bhpr.; (*am*), n. a spirituous liquor (prepared with honey), Npr. **-drava**, m. spirituous liquor, Npr.

Kvātha, *as*, m. (g. *jvalâdi*) boiling, Yājñ. iii, 253, Sch.; a decoction, any solution or infusion prepared with a continued or gentle heat, VarBṛS. vli, 49; Suśr.; ŚārṅgS.; the mixture of the materials for a decoction, W.; pain, sorrow, distress, L. **Kvāthôdbhava**, mfn. produced by boiling, L.; (*am*), n. blue vitriol used as a collyrium, W.

Kvāthayitavya, mfn. to be boiled, VarBṛS. lvii, 2.

Kvāthi, *is*, m. (fr. *kvatha*, 'boiling pot,' cf. *kumbha-janman*), N. of Agastya, L.

क्वधःस्थ *kv-adhaḥ-stha*, mfn. (fr. 2. *ku*), 'standing below on the earth,' KaṭhUp. i, 28 (a wrong reading).

क्वयि *kváyi*, *is*, m. a kind of bird, VS. xxiv, 29; TS. v, 5, 17, 1 (= *mṛiga-viśesha*, Sch.)

क्वल *kvàla*, *ās*, m. pl. (= *kúvala*) jujube fruit (used for coagulating substances), TS. ii, 5, 3, 5.

क्वह *kv-aha*. See 2. *ku* at end.

क्वाचित्क *kvācitka*. See *kvà*.

क्वाण *kvāṇa*. See √*kvaṇ*.

क्वाथ *kvātha*, &c. See √*kvath*.

क्वापि *kvâpi*. See *kvà*.

क्वेल् *kvel*, v.l. for √*kshvel*, q.v.

क्शा *kśā* (Pāṇ. ii, 4, 54, Vārtt. 1) = √*khyā*, MaitrS.; Kāṭh. (see *anu-kśāti* &c.; xv, 5: 2. du. Ā. *cakśāthe* for *cakshāthe* of the RV.); accordingly √*kśā* is mentioned as forming some tenses of √*khyā* and √*caksh*, Pāṇ. ii, 4, 54, Kāś. (*ā-kśātā*, *ā-kśātum*, *ā-kśātavya*); Vop. ix, 37 f.

क्ष 1. *ksha* (fr. √1. or 2. *kshi*), see *dyu-kshá*; (*as*), m. a field, L.; the protector or cultivator of a field, peasant, L.

क्ष 2. *ksha*, mfn. (fr. √4. *kshi*), see *tuvi-kshá*; (*as*), m. destruction, loss, L.; destruction of the world, L.; lightning, L.; a demon or Rakshas, L.; the fourth incarnation of Vishṇu (as the man-lion or nara-siṇha), L.

क्षज् *kshaj* or *kshañj*, cl. 1. Ā. *kshajate* or *kshañj*°, to go, approach, Dhātup. xix, 7; to give, ib.: cl. 10. P. *kshañjayati*, to live in pain or want, Dhātup. xxxii, 78.

क्षण् *kshaṇ*. See √*kshan*.

क्षण 1. *kshaṇa*, *as*, m. any instantaneous point of time, instant, twinkling of an eye, moment, Nal.; Śak.; Ragh. &c.; a moment regarded as a measure of time (equal to thirty Kalās or four minutes, L.; or (in astron.) to 48 minutes, VarBṛS. &c.; or to $\frac{4}{5}$ or $\frac{24}{35}$ seconds, BhP. iii, 11, 7 & 8); a leisure moment, vacant time, leisure (e.g. *kshaṇam* √*kṛi*, to have leisure for, wait patiently for, MBh.; cf. *kṛita-kshaṇa*); a fit or suitable moment, opportunity (*kshaṇam* √*kṛi*, to give an opportunity, MBh. iv, 666; cf. *datta-kshaṇa* & *labdha-ksh*°); a festival, Megh.; Daś.; BhP. iii, 3, 21; a certain day of the fortnight (as the full moon, change of the moon, &c.), Sarvad.; dependence, L.; the centre, middle, L.; (*am*), n. an instant, moment, Bhartṛ. (= Subh.); (*am*), acc. ind. for an instant, R. vi, 92, 35; BrahmaP.; Vet. &c.; in a moment, Ragh. xii, 36; Śāntiś.; (cf. *tat-kshaṇam*); (*ena*), instr. ind. in a moment, Nal.; R. &c.; (*āt*), abl. ind. after an instant, immediately, at once, Mn.; R.; Śak. &c.; *tataḥ kshaṇāt* (= *tat-kshaṇāt*, q. v.), immediately upon that, Kathās.; *kshaṇāt—kshaṇāt*, in this moment—in that moment, Rājat. viii, 898; (*eshu*), loc. ind. immediately, at once, R. vi, 55, 19; *kshaṇe kshaṇe*, every instant, every moment, Rājat. v, 165 & 337. **-kleśa**, m. momentary pain, Ragh. xii, 76; Vikr.; Megh. **-kshaṇam**, ind. = *-mātram*, L. **-kshepa**, m. a momentary delay. **-da**, m. an astrologer, L.; (*ā*), f. 'giving leisure,' night (= *kshaṇinī*), Ragh.; BhP.; lightning, L.; turmeric, L.; (*am*), n. (= *kshaṇadāndhya*) night-blindness, Suśr. vi, 17, 15; water, L.; (*kshaṇadā*)-*kara*, m. 'making night,' the moon, Śiś. ix, 70; *-kṛit*, m. id., Vāsav.; *-cara*, m. 'night-walker,' Rakshas, goblin, MBh.; R. iii, 35, 4 & 55, 12; v, 88, 22; Ragh. xiii, 75; *kshaṇadāndhya*, n. night-blindness, nyctalopsis (cf. *kshapāndhya*, *naktāndhya*), Suśr.; *kshaṇadêśa*, m. 'lord of the night,' the moon, Bālar. iv, 5. **-dṛishṭa**, mfn. seen for an instant, momentarily visible; *-nashṭa*, mfn. seen for an instant and immediately lost out of sight, Pañcat.; Mcar. v, 1; Hcar. **-dêśa**, see *kshaṇa-da* at end. **-dyuti**, f. momentary flash, lightning, W.; (cf. *-prabhā* and *a-cira-dy°*.) **-nashṭa-dṛishṭa**, inaccurately for *-dṛishṭa-nashṭa* (q. v.), Mṛicch. v, 4. **-niśvāsa**, m. 'breathing momentarily,' the Gangetic porpoise, L. **-prakāśā**, f. = *-dyuti*, W. **-prabha**, mfn. gleaming or flashing for an instant, W.; (*ā*), f. = *-dyuti*, L. **-bhaṅga**, m. (with Buddh.) continual decay of things (denial of the continued identity of any part of nature, maintainment that the universe perishes and undergoes a new creation every instant), Sarvad.; *-vāda*, m. the doctrine of the continual decay of things, Bādar. ii, 1, 18, Sch.; *-vādin*, mfn. one who asserts that doctrine, Sarvad. **-bhaṅgin**, mfn. perishing in an instant, transient, perishable, Kathās. xxv, 163; Rājat. iv, 388. **-bhaṅgura**, mf(*ā*)n. id., Bhartṛ.; Pañcat.; BhP.; Kām.; Hit. **-bhūta**, mfn. momentary, short-lived, R. i, 45, 3. **-mātra**, n. 'only a moment,' (*am*), ind. only for a moment, Ragh. i, 73; (*eṇa*), instr. ind. in a mere moment, R. iv, 38, 36; *°trânurāgin*, mfn. one whose affection lasts only a moment, L. **-rāmin**, m. 'loving for a moment only,' a pigeon, L. **-vighna**, n. a momentary hindrance. **-vighnita**, mfn. hindered for a moment, Ragh. xii, 53. **-vidhvaṇsin**, mfn. collapsing or perishing in a moment, Hit.; (*ī*), m. 'one who professes the doctrine of the *kshaṇa-vidhvaṇsa* (= *-bhaṅga*, q. v.),' a Buddhist. **-vīrya**, n. an auspicious Kshaṇa or Muhūrta, VarYogay. **-vṛishṭi**, f. rain that is to be expected in a moment, VarBṛS.; (cf. *sadyo-v°*.) **-śas**, ind. for moments only, MBh. v, 2842. **Kshaṇântara**, n. 'the interval of a moment,' (*e*), loc. ind. after a little while, the next moment, thereupon, Pañcat.; Kathās.; *kiṃcit kshaṇântaram*, acc. ind. for a moment, R. ii, 114, 12. **Kshaṇârdha**, n. half the measure of time called Kshaṇa, half a moment, small space of time, W. **Kshaṇe-pāka**, mfn. ripe or done in a moment, gaṇa *nyaṅkv-ādi*.

Kshaṇika, mf(*ī*)n. momentary, transient, Ragh.; Prab.; Bhāshāp. &c.; having leisure, profiting of an opportunity, BhP. xi, 27, 44; Hit.; (*ā*), f. lightning, L. **-tā**, f. momentariness, continual decay and change of everything (cf. *kshaṇa-bhaṅga*), Bādar. ii, 2, 25, Sch. **-tva**, n. id., Sarvad. **-vāda**, m. = *kshaṇa-bhaṅga-v°* (q.v.), Bādar. ii, 1, 18, Sch. (v.l.)

Kshaṇita, mfn. having a leisure moment, gaṇa *tārakâdi*.

Kshaṇin, mfn. id., MBh. ii, 558; momentary, transient, W.; (*inī*), f. (= *kshaṇa-dā*, q.v.) night, L.

क्षण 2. *kshaṇa*, *°ṇatu*, *°ṇana*, &c. See √*kshan*. **Kshata, kshati, kshatin.** See ib.

क्षत्तृ *kshattṛí*. See √*kshad*.

क्षत्र *kshatrá*, *am*, n. (√1. *kshi*?; gaṇa *ardharcâdi*) sg. & pl. dominion, supremacy, power, might (whether human or supernatural, especially applied to the power of Varuṇa-Mitra and Indra), RV.; AV.; VS.; ŚBr. ii; xi; sg. & pl. government, governing body, RV.; AV.; VS. x, 17; TBr. ii; the military or reigning order (the members of which in the earliest times, as represented by the Vedic hymns, were generally called Rājanya, not Kshatriya; afterwards, when the difference between Brahman and Kshatra or the priestly and civil authorities became more distinct, applied to the second or reigning or military caste), VS.; AV.; TS. &c.; a member of the military or second order or caste, warrior, Mn.; MBh. &c. (fancifully derived fr. *kshatāt tra* fr. √*trai*, i. e. 'a preserver from injury,' Ragh. ii, 53); the rank of a member of the reigning or military order, authority of the second caste, AitBr. viii, 5; ŚBr. xiii, 1, 5, 2; BhP. iii, ix; wealth, Naigh. ii, 10; water, i, 12; the body, L.; Tabernæmontana coronaria (v. l. *chattra*), L.; (*ī*), f. a woman of the second caste, L. **-deva**, m., N. of a man (with the patr. Śaikhaṇḍi), MBh. vii, 955. **-dharma**, m. the duty of the second caste or of a Kshatriya, bravery, military conduct, Mn. v, 98; MBh.; R.; N. of a prince (= *°rman*), VP.; *°rmânuga*, mfn. following or observing the duty of a soldier. **-dharman**, mfn. fulfilling the duties of the second caste, MBh. v, 179, 37; N. of a prince, Hariv.; VP.; BhP. ix, 17, 18. **-dhṛiti**, f. 'support of supreme power,' N. of part of the Rāja-sūya ceremony, KātyŚr. xv, 9, 20; Lāṭy. viii, 11, 11. **-pa**, m. a governor, Satrap (a word found on coins and in Inscr.); (cf. *mahā-ksh°*.) **-pati** (*°trá-*), m. the possessor of dominion, VS. x, 17; TBr. ii; ŚBr. xi; KātyŚr. **-bandhu**, mfn. one who belongs to the military order, W.; (*us*), m. a member of the Kshatriya caste, Mn.; MBh. &c.; 'a mere Kshatriya,' i. e. a Kshatriya by birth but not by his actions (a term of abuse), R.; BhP. **-bhṛit**, mfn. one who holds or confers dominion, VS. xxvii, 7; TS. ii (pl.); TBr. ii; ŚāṅkhŚr.; ĀśvŚr.; (*t*), m. a member of the second caste, R. ii, 95, 21. **-bheda**, m., N. of Śata-dhanvan, Gal. **-mātrá**, n. anything included by the term Kshatra, ŚBr. xiv. **-yogá**, m. union of the princely order, AV. x, 5, 2. **-rūpa**, n. the nature of the Kshatra, AitBr. viii, 7. **-vat**, mfn. endowed with princely dignity, ĀśvŚr.; ŚāṅkhŚr. **-váni**, mfn. favourable to the princely order, VS. **-várdhana**, mfn. promoting dominion, AV. x, 6, 29. **-vidyā**, f. (Pāṇ. iv, 2, 60, Pat.; gaṇa *ṛig-ayanâdi*) the knowledge or science possessed by the Kshatriya or military order (= *dhanur-veda*, Comm.), ChUp. vii, 1, 2 ff. **-vṛiksha**, m. Mucukunda (Pterospermum suberifolium), L. **-vṛiddha**, m., N. of a prince, Hariv. 1517; BhP. ix, 17, 1–18; VP. **-vṛiddhi**, f. increase of power, Āp.; (*is*), m., N. of one of the sons of Manu Raucya, Hariv. 489. **-vṛidh**, m. = *-vriddha*, BhP. ix, 17, 2. **-veda**, m. the Veda of the Kshatriya or military order, R. i, 65, 22. **-śrí**, f. having the glory of sovereignty or power, RV. i, 25, 5 & vi, 26, 8. **-saṃgrahītṛi**, m. pl., see *kshāttra-saṃg°*. **-sava**, m., N. of a sacrificial ceremony, ŚāṅkhŚr. xiv; (ifc.) Mn. v, 23. **-sāman**, n., N. of two Sāmans, TāṇḍyaBr. ix. **Kshatrânvaya**, mfn. belonging to the second or military caste, R. i, 1, 96. **Kshatrâyatanīya**, mfn. based on the Kshatra or kingly power, Lāṭy. vi, 6, 8 & 18; 8, 3. **Kshatrâujas**, m., N. of a prince, VP.

Kshatrin, *ī*, m. a man of the second caste, L.

Kshatriya, mfn. (Pāṇ. iv, 1, 38; gaṇa *śreny-ādi*) governing, endowed with sovereignty, RV.; AV. iv, 22, 1; VS.; TBr. ii; (*as*), m. a member of the military or reigning order (which in later times constituted the second caste), AV.; ŚBr.; AitBr.; KātyŚr.; Mn. &c.; (ifc. f. *ā*) MBh.; N. of a Daśa-pūrvin, Jain.; a red horse, Gal.; (*ās*), m., N. of a people, VarBṛS. xiv, 28; (*ā*), f. (Pāṇ. iv, 1, 49, Vārtt. 7) a woman of the military or second caste, Mn.; Yājñ.; MBh. (e. g. *ksh° te*, your wife that belongs to the second caste); N. of Durgā, Hariv. 3290; (*ī*), f. the wife of a man of the second caste, Pāṇ. iv, 1, 49, Siddh.; (*am*), n. the power or rank of the sovereign, RV. iv, 12, 3; v, 69, 1; vii, 104, 13; AV. vi, 76, 3. **-jāti**, f. the military tribe or caste, Mn. x, 43. **-tā**, f. the order or rank of a Kshatriya, AitBr. vii, 24. **-tva**, n. id., MBh. iii, 13957. **-dharma**, m. the duty or occupation of the warrior-tribe, war, government, &c., Mn. x, 81; Nal.; R.; BhP. **-dharman**, mfn. having the duties of a soldier or of the second caste, W. **-prāya**, mfn. mostly consisting of the military tribe. **-bruva**, mfn. pretending to be a Kshatriya, MBh. xii, 3565. **-mardana**, mfn. destroying the Kshatriyas, MBh. vii, 3652 & 5060; (*sarva-ksh°*) i, 5125. **-yajñá**, m. the sacrifice of a Kshatriya, ŚBr. xiii, 4, 1, 2. **-yuvan**, mfn., g. *yuvâdi*. **-rāja**, m. the chief of Kshatriyas, W. **-ṛshabha** (*ṛish°*), m. the best of Kshatriyas: (cf. gaṇa *vyāghrâdi*.) **-varā**, f. a wild variety of Curcumis, L. **-hana**, mfn. one who destroys the military caste, MBh. v, 7116. **Kshatriyânta-kara**, m. id., N. of Paraśu-rāma, Mcar. ii, vishk. **Kshatriyâri**, m. 'enemy of the Kshatriyas,' N. of Paraśu-rāma, Gal.

Kshatriyakā, f. a woman belonging to the military or second caste, Pāṇ. vii, 3, 46, Kāś.

Kshatriyāṇī, f. id., Pāṇ. iv, 1, 49, Vārtt. 7; the wife of a man of the second caste, Vop. iv, 24.

Kshatriyikā, f. = *°yakā*, Pāṇ. vii, 3, 46, Kāś.

Kshātra, mf(*ī*)n. (fr. *kshatrá*), belonging or relating or peculiar to the second caste, Mn. vii, 87; Yājñ.; MBh. &c.; (*am*), n. the dignity of a ruler or governor, MBh. iii, 5097 & xiii, 3026; R. ii f., v.

Kshātravidya, mfn. fr. *kshatra-vidyā*, Pāṇ. iv, 2, 60, Pat.; gaṇa *ṛig-ayanâdi*.

Kshātri, *is*, m. (fr. *kshatrá*) the son of a man of the second caste, Pāṇ. iv, 1, 138, Kāś.

क्षद् 1. *kshad*, cl. 1. Ā. *kshádate* (perf. p. *cakshadānā́*), to cut, dissect, divide, kill, RV. i, 116, 16 & 117, 18; AitBr. i, 15; to carve (meat), distribute (food), AV. x, 6, 5; to take food, consume, eat, RV. i, 25, 17 (2. sg. Ā. or dat. inf. *kshádase*) & x, 79, 7 (perf. *cakshadé*). [As a Sautra rt. *kshad* means 'to cover, shelter.']

Kshattṛi, *ttā*, m. (Pāṇ. iii, 2, 135, Vārtt. 6; vi, 4, 11) one who cuts or carves or distributes anything, RV. vi, 13, 2; AV.; ŚBr. xiii; ŚāṅkhŚr.; an attendant, (especially) door-keeper, porter (cf. *anuksh°*), AV. ix, 6, 49; VS. xxx, 13; TBr. &c.; a chamberlain, Kathās. lii, 106 & 117; a charioteer, coachman, VS. xvi, 26 (ŚatarUp. iv); ŚāṅkhŚr. xvi, 1, 16 (v.l. for *kshatra*); the son of a Śūdra man and a Kshatriya woman (or the son of a Kshatriya man and a Śūdra woman [called Ugra, Mn. x, 12], L.; or the son of a Śūdra man and a Vaiśya woman [called Āyogava, Mn. x, 12], Uṇ. ii, 90), Mn. x, 12–26 & 49; Yājñ. i, 94; the son of a female slave, L.; (hence) N. of Vidura (as the son of the celebrated Vyāsa by a female slave), MBh. i, 7381; iii, 246; BhP. iii, 1, 1–3; N. of Brahmā, L.; a fish, L.

2. **Kshad.** See *bāhu-kshád*.

Kshadana, *am*, n. carving, dividing, W.

Kshádman, *a*, n. a carving knife, RV. i, 130, 4 & x, 106, 17; (pieces of) food (cut off or carved), Naigh. ii, 7; water, i, 11.

Kshāttra, n. (fr. *kshattṛí*), 'a number of charioteers,' in comp. **-saṃgrahītṛi**, m. pl. charioteers and drivers, ŚBr. xiii, 4, 2, 5 & 5, 2, 8; KātyŚr. xx, 1, 16; (*kshatra-s°*, ŚāṅkhŚr. xvi, 1, 16.)

क्षन् 1. *kshan* (or *kshaṇ*), cl. 8. P. *kshaṇóti* (aor. *akshaṇīt*, Pāṇ. vii, 2, 5; cf. *a-kshaṇvat*), to hurt, injure, wound, ŚBr. (inf. *kshaṇitos*, xiv, 8, 14, 4); Kum. v, 54; to break (a bow), Ragh. xi, 72: Ā. *kshaṇuté* (aor. Subj. 2. sg. *kshaṇishṭhās*, Pot. *kshaṇvīta*), to hurt one's self, be injured or wounded, AV. x, 1, 16; ŚBr. iv, 4, 3, 13 & 6, 1, 6; TBr. iii; [cf. κτείνω, καίνω, ξαίνω, σίνομαι for ξίνομαι?]

2. **Kshaṇa**, *as*, m. killing (= *māraṇa*), Gal.

Kshaṇana, *am*, n. hurting, injuring, Suśr. iv, 7, 31 & 34, 17; killing, slaughter, W.

Kshaṇanu, *us*, m. a wound, sore, L.

Kshatá, mfn. wounded, hurt, injured, ŚBr. vi; Yājñ. &c.; broken, torn, rent, destroyed, impaired, MBh. &c.; diminished, trodden or broken down; (*ā*), f. a violated girl, Yājñ.; (*am*), n. a hurt, wound, sore, contusion, MBh.; Suśr. &c.; rupture or ulcer of the respiratory organs; N. of the sixth astrological mansion, VarBṛ. i, 16. **-kāsa**, m. a cough produced by injury, Bhpr. **-kṛit**, m. 'producing sores,' Semecarpus Anacardium, Npr. **-kṛita**, mfn. produced by injury, Bhpr. vi. **-ghna**, mfn. 'removing sores,' the plant Conyza lacera, W.; (*ā*, *ī*), f. lac, the animal dye, L. **-ja**, mfn. produced by a wound or injury (e. g. *kāsa*, a kind of cough; also *visarpa*, Bhpr. vi), Suśr.; (*am*), n. blood, MBh. ii, 403; R.; Suśr.; Ragh. vii, 40; pus, matter, L.; *-pāta*, m. issue of blood, VarBṛS. vc, 48; *-shṭhīvin*, mfn. vomiting blood, Bhpr. iii. **-janman**, n. 'produced by a wound,' blood, Gal. **-tejas**, mfn. dimmed, obscured (as light or power). **-puṇya-leśa**, mfn. one who has his stock of merit exhausted, BhP. iii, 1, 9. **-yoni**, f. having a violated womb. **-rohaṇa**, n. healing or closing of a wound, MBh. xiii, 5189. **-vikshata**, mfn. covered with cuts and wounds, mangled, W. **-vidhvaṇsin**, m. 'removing sores,' the plant Argyreia speciosa or argentea, L. **-vṛitti**, mfn. being without the means of support, R. ii, 32, 28; (*is*), f. destitution, W. **-vraṇa**, m. a sore produced by an injury, Bhpr. **-vrata**, mfn. one who has violated a vow or religious engagement, L. **-sarpaṇa**, n. loss of the faculty of moving, Suśr. **-hara**, n. 'removing sores,' Agallochum or Aloe wood, L. **Kshatâbhyaṅga**, m. 'mutilated portion of a Havis,' i.e. the portion from which anything has been taken away, KātyŚr. iii, 3, Paddh. **Kshatâri**, mfn. 'one whose enemies are destroyed,' victorious, triumphant. **Kshatôttha**, mfn. produced by injury (as cough), Suśr. **Kshatôdara**, n. injury of the bowels by any indigestive substance, flux, dysentery, Bhpr. **Kshatôdbhava**, mfn. produced by injury, Suśr.; (*am*), n. (= *kshata-ja*) blood, MBh. xiii, 2797. **Kshatáujas**, mfn. 'of diminished power,' impaired, weakened, reduced.

Kshati, *is*, f. injury, hurt, wound, MBh. &c.; loss, want (of the means of living, cf. *kshata-vritti*), Hit.; damage, disadvantage, MBh. &c.; defect, fault, mistake, Sāh.; destruction, removal of (in comp.), Kum. ii, 24; Rājat. v, 234; Śāntiś. **-mat**, mfn. wounded, Śiś. xix, 78.

Kshatin, mfn. wounded, injured, Car. vi, 17; (for *kshata-kāsin*) one who has a cough produced by an injury, Bhpr. i.

क्षन् 2. *kshan*, aor. Subj. 3. pl. √*ghas*, q. v.

क्षन्तव्य *kshantavya*, °*ntṛi*. See √*ksham*.

क्षप् 1. *kshap*, cl. 1. P. Ā. *kshapati*, °*te* (pr. p. *kshápamāṇa*; inf. *kshapitum*, BhP. iii, 23, 6), to be abstinent, fast, do penance, SV.; Kauś.; Mn. v, 69; MBh. &c.; (for √*kship*, Ṛitus. v, 9.)

Kshapa, mfn., v. l. for *kshama*, q. v.

Kshapaka, mfn. one who is abstinent, HPariś.

1. **Kshapaṇa**, *as*, m. 'fasting,' a religious mendicant, Jaina (or Buddhist) mendicant, L.; N. of a Samādhi, Kāraṇḍ.; (*ās*), m. pl., N. of a Buddhist school, L.; (*ā*), f., N. of a Yoginī, Hcat.; (*am*), n. abstinence, chastisement of the body ['pause, interruption (of study),' defilement, impurity,' Comm.; cf. 2. *kshapaṇa*], PārGṛ.; Gaut.; Mn. iv, 222; v, 71; MBh. xiii, 5145.

Kshapaṇaka, *as*, m. a religious mendicant, (especially a) Jaina mendicant who wears no garments, MBh. i, 789; Cāṇ.; Pañcat.; Kād. &c.; N. of an author supposed to have lived at the court of king Vikramâditya (perhaps the Jaina astronomer Siddha-sena). **-vihāra**, m. a Jaina monastery, Daś.

Kshapaṇī-bhūta, mfn. one who has adopted the habit or appearance of a religious mendicant, Daś.

1. **Kshapayishṇu**, mfn. one who intends to efface or do penance for (acc.), BhP. x, 82, 6.

क्षप् 2. *kshap*, cl. 10. P. *kshapayati*, to throw, cast, Dhātup. xxxv, 84; (cf. √*kship*.)

Kshapaṇī, f. = *kshep*°, W.

क्षप् 3. *kshap* = Caus. √4. *kshi*, q. v.

2. **Kshapaṇa**, mfn. ifc. (cf. *aksha-ksh*°) one who destroys, destructive, BhP.; (*as*), m., N. of Śiva; (*am*), n. destroying, diminishing, suppressing, expelling, MBh.; Suśr.; BhP.; 'passing (as time), waiting, pause,' = 1. *kshapaṇa*, q. v.

Kshapaṇyu, *us*, m. an offence, L.

2. **Kshapayishṇu**, mfn. destroying, BhP. x, 37, 22.

Kshapita, mfn. destroyed, ruined, diminished, suppressed, Ragh. viii, 46; BhP. i, 31, 6.

Kshapitavya, mfn. to be passed away or finished, Kād.

क्षप् 4. *kshấp*, *p*, f. night, RV.; a measure of time equivalent to a whole day of twenty-four hours, RV.; darkness, RV. i, 64, 8; water, Naigh. i, 12; *kshấpaḥ*, *kshapấḥ*, 1. *kshapấ*, acc. pl., gen. sg., instr. ind. at night, RV.; [cf. Gk. κνέφας; Lat. *crepus-culum*.]

2. **Kshapấ**, f. (Naigh. i, 7; for 1. *ksh*° see 4. *kshấp*) night, RV. iv, 53, 7 (instr. pl. °*pấbhis*); AitBr. i, 13; MBh. &c.; a measure of time equivalent to a whole day of twenty-four hours, Jyot.; turmeric, L. **-kara**, m. 'making the night,' the moon, VarBṛS.; VarBṛ.; Daś.; Kād. **-kṛit**, m. id., Śiś. xiii, 53. **-ghana**, m. a dark cloud or dark nocturnal clouds. **-cara**, m. 'night-walker,' a Rakshas, goblin, MBh.; R.; HYog.; any animal that goes out for prey in the night (as owls, jackals, &c.), VarBṛS. vli, 66. **-jala**, n. night-dew, Kād. **Kshapâṭa**, m. 'night-walker,' a Rakshas, goblin, Bhaṭṭ. ii. 30. **Kshapâtyaya**, m. end of the night, dawn, R.; Ragh.; Daś. **Kshapā-nātha**, m. 'lord of the night,' the moon, VarBṛ. v, 2; Śiś. iii, 22. **Kshapândhya**, n. night-blindness (= *kshaṇadândhya*), Suśr. vi, 17, 23. **Kshapā-pati**, m. = -*nātha*, L.; camphor, L. **Kshapâpaha**, m. 'removing night,' the sun, R. vii, 23, 2, 12. **Kshapā-ramaṇa**, m. 'night-lover,' the moon; -*śekhara*, m. 'wearing the moon on his head,' N. of Śiva, Rājat. iii, 269. **Kshapârdha**, n. midnight, Sūryas. **Kshapâvasāna**, n. end of the night; (*e*), loc. ind. on the following morning, Daś. **Kshapā-vṛitti**, mfn. going out for food in the night, VarBṛS. **Kshapā-vyapâya**, m. = °*pâtyaya*, R. v, 19, 35. **Kshapâśaya**, mfn. lying on anything (in comp.) during night, MBh. iv, 597. **Kshapâha**, n. a day and night, Mn. i, 68. **Kshapêśa**, m. = *kshapā-nātha*, Vāsant.

क्षपण *kshapaṇa*, see √1. & 3. *kshap*; (*ī*), ind., see 1. *kshapaṇa*; f., see √2. *kshap*.

Kshapaṇyu, °**payishṇu**. See √1. & 3. *kshap*.

क्षपा *kshapấ*. See 4. *kshấp*.

क्षपावत् *ksha-pấvat*. See 2. *kshấm*.

क्षपितव्य *kshapitavya*. See √3. *kshap*.

क्षम् 1. *ksham*, cl. 1. Ā. *kshámate* (ep. also P. °*ti*; Ved. cl. 2. P. *kshamiti*, Pāṇ. vii, 2, 34; cl. 4. P. *kshāmyati* [cf. Impv. Ā. 3. sg. *kshamyatām*, BhP. vi, 3, 30], Pāṇ. vii, 3, 74; perf. *cakshame*, MBh. &c., 3. pl. °*mire*, ŚBr.; 1. du. *cakshaṇvahe* & 1. pl. °*ṇmahe*, Pāṇ. viii, 2, 65, Sch.; fut. 2nd *kshaṅsyate*, °*ti*, *kshamishyati*; aor. 2. sg. *akshaṅsthās*, Bhaṭṭ.; inf. *kshantum*, MBh. &c.), to be patient or composed, suppress anger, keep quiet, RV. x, 104, 6; MBh.; R. &c.; to submit to (dat.), ŚBr. iii; iv; to bear patiently, endure, put up with (acc.), suffer, MBh.; R.; Ragh.; to pardon, forgive anything (acc.) to (gen. or dat.), MBh.; R. &c. (e. g. *kshamasva me tad*, forgive me that, Ragh. xiv, 58); to allow, permit, suffer, Sāh. (Kuval.); (with Pot.) Daś.; to bear any one, be indulgent to, MBh. iii, 13051; R. iv, 27, 22; VarBṛS.; Pañcat. (Pass.); Hit.; to resist, Pāṇ. i, 3, 33, Sch.; to be able to do anything (inf.), Śiś. i, 38 & ix, 65; to seem good, Divyâv. iv: Caus. P. Ā. *kshamayati*, *kshāmayate*, to ask any one (acc.) pardon for anything (acc.), MBh.; Bhag.; Pañcat.; (perf. *kshamayām āsa*) to suffer or bear patiently, R. v, 49, 11; (cf. *kshamāpaya*); [cf. Goth. *hramja*(?); Angl. Sax. *hremman*, 'to hinder, disquiet.']

Kshantavya, mfn. to be borne or endured or suffered or submitted to patiently; to be pardoned or forgiven, Mn.; MBh.; R. &c.; (*am*), n. impers. pardon to be given by any one (gen.) for (abl.), MBh. i, 40, 53; Kathās. cxix, 53.

Kshantṛi, mfn. one who pardons or bears patiently, MBh. xiii, 4873.

2. **Kshám**, f. (nom. *kshấs*, acc. *kshấm*, instr. *kshamấ*, once *jmấ* [RV. vi, 52, 15], dat. *kshe* [?RV. iv, 3, 6], gen. abl. *gmás*, *jmás*, once *kshmás* [RV. i, 100, 15], loc. *kshámi*; du. nom. *kshấmā* [RV. ii, 39, 7; x, 12, 1; cf. *dyấvā-kshấmā*]; pl. nom. *kshấmas* [RV. viii, 70, 4; *kshấmīs* fr. °*mi*, SV.], *kshấs* [RV. iv, 28, 5], acc. *kshấs* [RV. x, 2, 6], loc. *kshấsu*, RV. i, 127, 10 & v, 64, 2) the ground, earth, χθών, RV.; AV.; VS.; ŚBr. vi; [cf. *kshmā*; cf. also Gk. χαμαί, χθαμαλός; Lat. *humus*, *homo*.] **Ksha-pấvat** & **kshá-p°**, m. 'earth-protector,' ruler, governor, RV. i, 70, 3 & x, 29, 1; (*kshá-p°*) iii, 55, 17; vii, 10, 5 & viii, 71, 2.

Kshamá, mf(*ấ*)n. (g. *pacâdi*) patient (said of the earth, perhaps with reference to 2. *kshám*), AV. xii, 1, 29; ifc. (Pāṇ. iii, 2, 1, Vārtt. 8) enduring, suffering, bearing, submissive, resisting, MBh.; Śak.; Kum. v, 40; adequate, competent, able, fit for (loc. or inf. or in comp., e. g. *vayam tyaktuṃ kshamāḥ*, 'we are able to quit,' Śāntiś.), Nal.; R.; Ragh. &c.; favourable to (gen.), R. ii, 35, 31; bearable, tolerable, Śak.; Pañcat. (= Subh.); fit, appropriate, becoming suitable, proper for (gen., dat., loc., inf. or in comp.), MBh. (e. g. *kshamam Kauravāṇām*, 'proper for the Kauravas,' iii, 252); R. (e. g. *na sa kshamaḥ kopayitum*, 'he is not a fit object for anger,' iv, 32, 20) &c.; (*as*), m. 'the patient,' N. of Śiva; a kind of sparrow, L.; (*ā*), f. patience, forbearance, indulgence (one of the *sāmānya-dharmās*, i. e. an obligation to all castes, Vishṇ.), Mn.; MBh. &c.; *kshamām* √*kṛi*, to be indulgent to, have patience or bear with (*prati*, MBh. iii, 1027; or gen., Śāntiś.); 'Patience' (personified as a daughter of Daksha and wife of Pulaha, VP.), Hariv. 14035; Prab.; tameness (as of an antelope), R. iii, 49, 25; resistance, Pāṇ. i, 3, 33, Sch.; (= 2. *kshám*) the earth, VarBṛS.; Pañcat. &c.; (hence) the number 'one;' N. of Durgā, DevīP.; the Khadira tree (Acacia Catechu), L.; N. of a species of the Atijagatī metre; N. of a female shepherd, BrahmaP.; of a Śākta authoress of Mantras; of a river (= *vetravatī*), Gal.; for *kshapấ* (night), L.; (*am*), n. propriety, fitness, W. [cf. Hib. *cam*, 'strong, mighty; power;' *cama*, 'brave.'] **-tā**, f. ability, fitness, capability. **-tva**, n. id. (with loc. or ifc.), Sāh.; Sarvad.; Comm. on KapS. & on Mn. ix, 161. **-vat**, mfn. knowing what is proper or right, R. v, 89, 68; for *kshấm*°, q. v.

Kshamaṇīya, mfn. to be suffered or patiently borne, R. v, 79, 9; vii, 13, 36.

1. **Kshamấ** (instr. of 2. *kshấm*, q. v.), ind. on the earth, on the floor, gaṇa *svar-ādi*; [cf. Gk. χαμᾶ-ζε, χαμᾶ-θεν.] **-cará**, mfn. being in the ground or under the earth, VS. xvi, 57.

2. **Kshamấ** (f. of °*má*, q. v.) **-kara**, mfn. 'one who has patience with any one or is indulgent,' N. of a Yaksha, Gal. **-kalyāṇa**, m., N. of a pupil of Jinalābha-sūri (who composed 1794 A.D. a Comm. on the Jiva-vicāra). **Kshamâcārya**, m., N. of a Śākta author of Mantras. **Kshamā-tanaya**, m. 'son of the earth,' the planet Mars, VarBṛS. vi, 11. **Kshamā-tala**, n. the surface of the earth, ground, Bālar. iii, 79. **Kshamā-daṅśa**, m. Moringa pterygosperma, L. **Kshamânvita**, mfn. endowed with patience, patient, forgiving (with loc.), Mn. vii, 32, &c. **Kshamā-pati**, m. 'lord of the earth,' a king, Rājat. v, 126. **Kshamâpanna**, mfn. = °*mânvita*. **Kshamā-para**, mfn. very patient, forbearing. **Kshamā-bhuj**, m. patient, W.; (*k*), m. 'earth-enjoying,' a prince, king, W. **Kshamā-bhṛit**, m. 'earth-supporter,' a mountain, Kād.; a prince, Śiś. xix, 30. **Kshamā-maṇḍala**, n. the orb, whole earth, Prab. **Kshamā-yukta**, mfn. = °*mânvita*. **Kshamā-liṅgâtma-pīḍā-vat**, mfn. (any legal affair) in which testimonies for patience practised and an estimate of one's damage or loss are given, Comm. on Yājñ. ii, 6. **Kshamā-vat**, mfn. patient, enduring, forbearing, MBh.; R. &c.; tame (as elephants), MBh. ii, 1878; (*tī*), f., N. of the wife of Nidhi-pati. **Kshamâvarta**, m. 'whirlpool of patience,' N. of a son of Devala, VP. **Kshamā-śīla**, mfn. practising patience, patient, MBh. **Kshamā-śramaṇa**, m. a Jaina ascetic, HPariś. **Kshamā-shoḍaśī**, f., N. of a work.

Kshamāpaṇa, *am*, n. the begging pardon, Bhām.

Kshamāpaya, Nom. P. Ā. °*yati*, °*yate*, to ask any one's (acc.) pardon, BhP. iv; v, 10, 16; ix, 4, 71.

Kshamita, mfn. pardoned, MBh. ii, 1582.

Kshamitavya, mfn. to be endured or patiently borne or pardoned, R. v, 24, 7.

Kshamitṛi, mfn. enduring, patient, L.

Kshamin, mfn. (Pāṇ. iii, 2, 141) id. (with loc.), Yājñ. i, 133; ii, 200; MBh.; BhP.; Bhartṛ.; Vet.

Kshamī-√bhū, to become able to do anything (dat.), HPariś. i, 229.

Kshámya, mfn. being in the earth, terrestrial, χθόνιος, RV. ii, 14, 11 & vii, 46, 2.

Kshấ, f. (derived fr. some forms of 2. *kshám*) the earth, ground, Naigh. i, 1; Nir. ii, 2; Sāy.

1. **Kshānta**, mfn. (gaṇa *priyâdi*) borne, endured (= *soḍha*), L.; pardoned, MBh.; Pañcat.; (Pāṇ. iii, 2, 188, Kār.) enduring, patient, Mn. v, 158; Yājñ.; R.; Ragh. (compar. -*tara*); (*as*), m. (gaṇa *utkarâdi*) N. of a man, gaṇa *aśvâdi*; of a hunter, Hariv. 1206; of Śiva (cf. *kshama*); (*ā*), f. 'the patient one,' the earth, L.; (*am*), n. patience, indulgence, R. i, 34, 32 & 33.

Kshāntāyana, *as*, m. patr. fr. °*ta*, g. *aśvâdi*.

Kshānti, *is*, f. patient waiting for anything, Vop. xxiii, 3; patience, forbearance, endurance, indulgence, Mn. v, 107; MBh.; R. &c.; the state of saintly abstraction, Divyâv. vi, xii, xviii; (in music) N. of a Śruti; N. of a river, VP. **-pāramitā**, f. the Pāramitā or accomplishment of indulgence, Kāraṇḍ. **-pāla**, m., N. of a prince, Buddh. **-priyā**, f., N. of a Gandharva girl, Kāraṇḍ. i. **-mat**, mfn. patient, enduring, indulgent, Rājat. v, 4. **-vādin**, m., N. of a Ṛishi, Kāraṇḍ. x. **-śīla**, m., N. of a man, Kathās. lxxv, 23.

Kshāntīya, mfn. fr. °*ta*, gaṇa *utkarâdi*.

Kshāntu, mfn. patient, enduring, Uṇ.; (*us*), m. a father, L.

Kshấman, *a*, n. earth, soil, ground, RV.

1. **Kshámi.** See s. v. 2. *kshám.*

Kshāmya, mfn. to be borne patiently or pardoned, MBh. ii, 1517 & 1582.

क्षमस्य *kshamasya*=*kshāmâsya* (q. v.), L.

क्षमा *kshamá*, &c. See √1. *ksham.*

क्षमुद *kshamuda, as* or *am,* m. or n (?) a particular high number, Buddh. L.

क्षम्प् *kshamp,* cl. 1. & 10. P. °*pati,* °*payati,* to suffer, bear, Dhātup. xxxii, 77; to love, like, ib.

क्षम्य *kshámya.* See √1. *kshám.*

क्षय *ksháya.* See √1. 2. & 4. *kshi.*

Kshayaṇa. See √2. & 4. *kshi.*

क्षयथु *kshayathu,* m. for *kshav°,* q. v., L.

क्षयद्वीर *kshayád-vīra.* See √1. *kshi.*

क्षयिक *kshayika,* °*yita,* &c. See √4. *kshi.*

Kshayya. See *a-kshayyá.*

क्षर् *kshar,* cl. 1. P. *kshárati* (ep. also Ā. °*te;* Ved. cl. 2. P. *kshariti,* Pāṇ. vii, 2, 34; Subj. *ksharat;* impf. *áksharat;* aor. 3. sg. *akshār* (cf. Nir. v, 3); *akshārīt,* Pāṇ. vii, 2, 2; p. *ksharat;* inf. *ksharadhyai,* RV. i, 63, 8), to flow, stream, glide, distil, trickle, RV.; AV.; ŚBr.; R. &c.; to melt away, wane, perish, Mn.; MBh. iii, 7001; to fall or slip from, be deprived of (abl.), MBh. xiii, 4716; to cause to flow, pour out, RV.; AV. vii, 18, 2; Mn. ii, 107; MBh. &c. (with *mūtram,* 'to urine,' Car. ii, 4); to give forth a stream, give forth anything richly, MBh.; Hariv. 8898 (pf. *cakshāra*); R.; Ragh.: Caus. *ksharayati,* to cause to flow (as urine), Vait.; to overflow or soil with acrid substances (cf. *kshāra*), MārkP. viii, 142; (cf. *kshārita.*)

Kshara, mf(*ā*)n. (gaṇa *jvalâdi*) melting away, perishable, ŚvetUp.; MBh.; Bhag.; (*as*), m. a cloud, L.; (*am*), n. water, L.; the body, MBh. xiv, 470. **–ja,** mfn. (=*kshare-ja,* Pāṇ. vi, 3, 16) produced by distillation, W. **–pattrā,** f., N. of a small shrub, W. **–bhāva,** mfn. mutable, dissoluble. **Ksharâtmaka,** mfn. of a perishable nature, perishable, MārkP. xxiii, 33. **Kshare-ja,** mfn. =°*ra-ja,* Pāṇ. vi, 3, 16.

Ksharaka, mf(*ikā*)n. pouring forth (ifc.), Devīm.

Ksharaṇa, *am,* n. flowing, trickling, distilling, dropping (e. g. *anguli-,* perspiration of the fingers, Ragh. xix, 19), Suśr.; pouring forth, Vop.; splashing, spattering, ib.

Ksharita, mfn. dropped, liquefied, oozed, W.; flowing, trickling, W.

Ksharin, *ī,* m. 'flowing, dropping, trickling,' the rainy season, L.

Ksharya, mfn. fr. °*ra,* gaṇa *gav-ādi.*

Kshāra, mf(*ā*)n. (gaṇa *jvalâdi*) caustic, biting, corrosive, acrid, pungent, saline, converted to alkali or ashes by distillation (fr. √*kshai?*), R.; Pañcat.; BhP. &c.; sharp, keen (as the wind), Kāvyâd. ii, 104; (*as*), m. any corrosive or acrid or saline substance (esp. an alkali such as soda or potash), caustic alkali (one species of cautery), Kāty.; Yājñ. iii, 36; MBh. &c.; juice, essence, W.; treacle, molasses, L.; glass, L.; (*am*), n. any corrosive or acrid substance, Kathās. xciii, 14; a factitious or medicinal salt (commonly black salt, *viḍ-lavaṇa* and *krishṇa-l°*), W.; water, W. **–kardama,** m. 'a pool of saline or acrid mud,' N. of a hell, BhP. v, 26, 7 & 30. **–karman,** n. applying caustic alkali (Lapis infernalis) to proud flesh &c., applying acrid remedies in general. **–kīṭa,** m. a kind of insect, L. **–kṛitya,** mfn. to be treated with caustic alkali, Suśr. i, 11, 15. **–kshata,** mfn. damaged by factitious salt or saltpetre, Mṛicch. iii, 14. **–kshīṇa,** mfn. id., 12. **–tantra,** n. the method of cauterization, Car. vi, 5. **–taila,** n. oil cooked with alkaline ingredients, GāruḍaP. **–traya,** n. 'a triad of acrid substances,' natron, saltpetre, and borax, L. **–tritaya,** n. id., L. **–dalā,** f. a variety of Chenopodium, L. **–dru,** m. 'a tree that yields abundant potash,' Schreberia Swietenoides, L. **–dvaya,** n. a pair of acrid substances (i. e. *svarjikā* and *yāva-śūka*), Bhpr. **–nadī,** f. 'alkaline river,' N. of a river in one of the hells, R. vii, 21, 15; Divyâv. viii; MārkP. xiv, 68. **–pattra,** m. n. =*-dalā,* L. **–pattraka,** m. id., L.; (*ikā*), f. id., L. **–payas,** m. 'the salt ocean,' in comp. °*yo-bhū,* m. a snake, Viddh. iii, 19. **–pāṇi,** m., N. of a Ṛishi, Hariv. 9575; (v. l. for *kshīra-p°*) Bhpr. **–pāta,** m. applying acrid remedies, Hcar. **–pāla,** m., N. of a Ṛishi (v. l. for *-pāṇi*). **–pūrva-daśaka,** n. a decade of acrid substances, L. **–bhūmi,** f. saline soil, L. **–madhya,** m. Achyranthes aspera, L. **–mṛittikā,** f. saline soil (especially an impure sulphate of soda), KātyŚr. iv, 8, 16, Sch. **–melaka,** m., N. of an alkaline substance, L. **–meha,** m. a morbid state of the urine (in which its smell and taste resemble that of potash), Car. ii, 4; Suśr. **–mehin,** mfn. one whose urine has that smell and taste, ib. **–rasa,** m. a saline or alkaline flavour, W. **–lavaṇa,** *e,* n. du. any alkaline substance and salt, MānGṛ.; *-varjana,* n. keeping off alkaline substances and salt, Hcat.; (cf. *a-ksh°*.) **–vṛiksha,** m. =*-dru,* L. **–śreshṭha,** m. id., L.; the tree Butea frondosa, L.; (*am*), n. alkaline earth (=*vajra-kshāra*), L. **–shaṭ-ka,** n. six kinds of trees distinguished by their sap (Butea frondosa, Grislea tomentosa, Achyranthes aspera, Cowach, Ghaṇṭā-pāṭali, Coraya), W. **–samudra,** m. the salt ocean, BhP. v, 17, 6; Romakas. **–sindhu,** m. id. **–sūtra,** n. caustic thread (applied to fistulas &c.), Suśr. **Kshārâksha,** mfn. having an artificial eye made of glass, Buddh. L. **Kshārâgada,** m. an antidote prepared by extracting the alkaline particles from the ashes of plants, Suśr. v, 7, 3. **Kshārâccha,** n. sea-salt, L. **Kshārâñjana,** n. an alkaline unguent, Suśr. **Kshārâmbu,** n. an alkaline juice or fluid, Śak., Sch. **Kshārâmbudhi,** m. the salt ocean, W. **Kshārôda,** m. id., BhP. v. **Kshārôdaka,** n. =°*râmbu,* Suśr.; (in comp. with *amlôdaka*) Mn. v, 114 & Yājñ. i, 190. **Kshārôdadhi,** m. =°*râmbudhi,* W.

Kshāraka, *as,* m. alkali, Suśr.; a juice, essence, W.; a net for catching birds, MBh. xii, 5473 & 5560; a cage or basket for birds or fish, L.; a multitude of young buds (cf. *-jāta*), Comm. on L.; a washerman, L.; (*ikā*), f. hunger, L. **–jāta,** mfn. blossoming, Lalit. vii.

Kshāraṇa, *am,* n. distilling, W.; converting to alkali or ashes, W.; a particular process applied to mercury, Sarvad. ix; (*ā*), f. accusing of adultery (cf. *ā-kshāraṇā*), L.

Kshārita, mfn. distilled from saline matter, strained through alkaline ashes &c., L.; calumniated, falsely accused (esp. of adultery), accused of a crime (loc.), MBh. ii, 238; (instr.) R. (ed. Gorr.) ii, 109, 55.

Kshārīya, mfn. fr. °*ra,* gaṇa *utkarâdi.*

क्षल् 1. *kshal,* v. l. for √*kshar,* Dhātup. xx.

क्षल् 2. *kshal* (related to √*kshar*), cl. 10. P. *kshālayati,* to wash, wash off, purify, cleanse, clean, Śiś. i, 38; Kathās.; Hit.; [cf. Lith. *skalauju,* 'to wash off;' *skalbju,* 'to wash;' Mod. Germ. *spüle?*]

Kshāla, *as,* m. washing, washing off.

Kshālana, mfn. washing, washing or wiping off, Pañcat. (ifc.); (*am*), n. washing, washing off, cleansing with water, MBh. ii, 1295; Pañcat.; MārkP.; Kathās. lii, 239; sprinkling, W.

Kshālanīya, mfn. to be washed or cleansed.

Kshālita, mfn. washed, cleansed, cleaned, Suśr.; Prab. v, 24; wiped away, removed, Rājat. v, 59.

Kshālitavya, mfn. =°*lanīya.*

क्षव *kshava,* °*vaka,* °*vathu.* See √1. *kshu.*

क्षा *kshā.* See √1. *ksham.*

क्षाति *kshāti.* See √*kshai.*

क्षात्त्र *kshāttra.* See √*kshad.*

क्षात्र *kshātra,* &c. See *kshatrá.*

क्षान्त 1. *kshānta,* mfn. ending with the letter *ksha,* RāmatUp.

क्षान्त 2. *kshānta.* See √1. *ksham.*

Kshāntāyana, °*nti,* °*ntīya,* °*ntu,* see ib.

Kshā-pavitra, N. of a formula, Baudh. iv, 7, 5.

क्षापय *kshāpáya.* See Caus. √*kshai.*

Kshāmá. See ib.

क्षामन् *kshā́man.* See √1. *ksham.*

1. **Kshāmi.** See s. v. 2. *kshám.*

क्षामि 2. *kshāmi,* °*min.* See √*kshai.*

क्षाम्य *kshāmya.* See √1. *ksham.*

क्षायिक *kshāyika.* See √4. *kshi.*

क्षार *kshāra,* °*raka,* °*raṇa,* &c. See √*kshar.*

क्षाल *kshāla,* °*lana,* &c. See √2. *kshal.*

क्षास् *kshās,* nom. sg., nom. & acc. pl. of 2. *kshám,* q. v.

क्षि 1. *kshi,* cl. 1. P. *ksháyati* (2. du. *kshá-yathas* or *kshay°,* 2. pl. *ksháyathā;* Subj. 1. *ksháyat* or *kshayat,* RV. vi, 23, 10 & vii, 20, 6; x, 106, 7; pr. p. *ksháyat*), to possess, have power over, rule, govern, be master of (gen.), RV.; [cf. Gk. κτάομαι.]

1. **Kshaya,** *as,* m. 'dominion,' Sāy. (on RV. vii, 46, 2).

Kshayád-vīra, mfn. ruling or governing men (Indra, Rudra, and Pūshan), RV.; ['possessed of abiding or of going heroes such as sons &c.,' Sāy.]

1. **Kshit,** mfn. ifc. 'ruling,' see *adhi-kshít, kshiti-, pṛithivī-, bhū-, mahī-.*

1. **Kshiti,** *is,* f. dominion (Comm.), MBh. xiii, 76, 10.

क्षि 2. *kshi,* cl. 2. 6. P. *kshéti, kshiyáti* (3. du. *kshitás,* 3. pl. *kshiyanti;* Subj. 2. *kshayat,* 2. sg. *ksháyas,* 3. du. *kshayatas,* 1. pl. *ksháyama;* pr. p. *kshiyát;* aor. Subj. *ksheshat;* fut. p. *ksheshyát*), to abide, stay, dwell, reside (used especially of an undisturbed or secret residence), RV.; to remain, be quiet, AV.; ŚBr.; to inhabit, TBr. iii; to go, move (*kshiyati*), Naigh. ii, 14; Dhātup.: Caus. (Impv. 2. sg. *kshayáyā;* Subj. *kshepayat*) to make a person live quietly, RV. iii, 46, 2 & v, 9, 7; [cf. Gk. κτίζω.]

2. **Ksháya,** mfn. dwelling, residing, RV. iii, 2, 13; viii, 64, 4; (*as*), m. an abode, dwelling-place, seat, house (cf. *uru-* & *su-ksháya, rátha-, divi-kshayá*), RV.; VS. v, 38; TS.; Pāṇ.; MBh.; R.; BhP.; the house of Yama (cf. *yama-ksh°, vaivasvata-ksh°*); abode in Yama's dominion, Comm. on R. (ed. Bomb.) ii, 109, 11; (=*kshiti*) family, race, RV. i, 123, 1. **–taru,** m. the plant Bignonia suaveolens, L.

1. **Kshayaṇá,** mfn. habitable [? (*as*), m. 'a place with tranquil water,' Comm.], VS. xvi, 43; (*ksháyaṇa*) TS. iv; (*kshenā́*) MaitrS.; (*as*), m. a bay, harbour, Comm. on RPrāt.; (*am*), n. a dwelling-place, Nir. vi, 6.

Kshayas. See *aurukshayasa.*

3. **Kshi,** *is,* f. abode, L.; going, moving, L.

2. **Kshit,** mfn. ifc. 'dwelling, inhabitant of (in comp.),' see *acyuta-, apsu-, ā-, upa-, giri-, divi-, dhruva-, pari-, bandhu-, vraja-* & *sa-kshít; antariksha-, pṛithivī-, loka-, sindhu-.*

Kshitā, f. for 2. *kshiti* (q. v.), MBh. xiii, 2017.

2. **Kshití,** *is,* f. an abode, dwelling, habitation, house (cf. also *uru-* & *su-kshiti, dhruvá-*), RV.; (Naigh. i, 1) the earth, soil of the earth, Mn.; MBh.; R. &c.; the number 'one,' Bījag.; (*áyas*), f. settlements, colonies, races of men, nations (of which five are named; cf. *krishṭi*), RV.; (said of the families of the gods) iii, 20, 4; estates, Rājat. v, 109; (cf. *uru-* & *su-kshiti, dhārayát-, dhruvá-, bhava-, raṇa-, samara-.*) **–kaṇa,** m. a particle of earth, dust, L. **–kampa,** m. an earthquake, MBh. vii, 7867; R. vi, 30, 30; VarBṛS. v, xxi, xxxii. **–kampana,** m., N. of an attendant in Skanda's retinue, MBh. ix, 2561; of a Daitya, Hariv. 12932. **–kshama,** m. the tree Acacia Catechu, L. **–kshit,** m. 'ruler of the earth,' a prince, king, Śiś. xiii, 4. **–kshoda,** m. a particle of earth, dust, Kād. **–khaṇḍa,** m. a clod or lump of earth, W. **–garbha,** m., N. of a Bodhi-sattva, Buddh. **–calana,** n. =*-kampa,* VarBṛS. **–ja,** mfn. earth-born, produced of or in the earth, Suśr.; (*as*), m. a tree, MBh. iii, 10248; R. vi, 76, 2; a kind of snail or earth-worm (*bhū-nāga*), L.; 'earth-son,' N. of the planet Mars, VarBṛ.; Gaṇit.; of the demon Naraka, W.; (*ā*), f., N. of Sītā (the wife of Rāma), W.; (*am*), n. the horizon, Āryabh.; Sūryas.; *-tva,* n. the state of the horizon, Gol. **–jantu,** m. a kind of snail or earth-worm (=*bhū-nāga*), L. **–jīvā,** f. the sine of the bow formed by the horizon and the Unmaṇḍala, Gaṇit. **–jyā,** f. id., Sūryas. ii, 61; Gol. **–tanaya,** m. (=*-ja*) N. of the planet Mars, VarBṛS.; (*ā*), f. 'daughter of the earth,' N. of Sītā, Bālar.; *-dina,* n. Tuesday, VarBṛS.; *-divasa-vāra,* m. id., ib. **–tala,** n. the surface of the earth, ground, Pañcat.; Bhartṛ. iii, 5; °*lâpsaras,* f. an Apsaras who walks or lives on the earth, Kathās. xvii, 34. **–trāṇa,** n. protection of the earth (one of the duties of the Kshatriya caste), Vishṇ. **–dina,** n. a common or Sāvana day, Gaṇit. **–deva,** m.

'earth-god,' i. e. a Brāhman, BhP. iii, 1, 12. **-devatā**, f. id., MBh. xiii, 6451. **-dhara**, m. 'earth-supporter,' a mountain, Kum. vii, 94; Bhartṛ. **-dhārin**, mfn. carrying soil or earth, Yājñ. ii, 152; Git. **-dhenu**, f. the earth considered as a milch-cow, Bhartṛ. ii, 38. **-nanda**, m., N. of a king, Rājat. i, 338. **-nandana**, m. (= *-ja*) N. of the planet Mars. **-nāga**, m. (= *-jantu*) a kind of snail or earth-worm, L. **-nātha**, m. 'lord of the earth,' a king, L. **-pa**, m. 'earth-protector,' a king, Suśr.; Pañcat.; Śak.; Ragh. **-pati**, m. 'lord of the earth,' id., Nal.; R.; Ragh.; Kathās. **-pāla**, m. = *-pa*, VarBṛS.; Ragh. ii, vii; Bhaṭṭ.; Caurap.; Prab. **-pīṭha**, n. the surface of the earth, W.; N. of a town, HPariś. **-putra**, m. 'son of the earth,' N. of the demon Naraka, KālP. **-puru-hūta**, m. 'the Indra of the earth,' a king, Inscr. **-pratishṭha**, mfn. dwelling or abiding on the earth, W. **-badarī**, f., N. of a plant (= *bhū-b°*), L. **-bhartṛi**, m. = *-nātha*, Naish. ix, 22. **-bhuj**, m. 'one who possesses the earth,' a king, Bhartṛ.; Śāntiś.; Prab.; Rājat. **-bhū**, f. (= *-tanayā*) N. of Sītā, Bālar. **-bhṛit**, m. 'earth-supporter,' a mountain, Vikr.; Ṛitus.; Kir.; a king, Bhartṛ. (v. l. *-bhuj*); *-tā*, f. the state of a king, reign, Naish. vi, 94. **-maṇḍala**, n. the globe, earth, W. **-rasa**, m. the juice or essence of the earth, VP. **-rāja**, m. a prince, king. **-ruh**, m. 'growing from the earth,' a tree, Bhartṛ.; Prab. **-ruha**, m. id., Śiś. vii, 54; Sāh. **-lava-bhuj**, m. 'possessing only a small tract of the earth,' a petty prince, Bhartṛ. iii, 100. **-vardhana**, m. a corpse, L. **-vṛitti-mat**, mfn. 'of a behaviour similar to that of the earth,' patient like the earth, BhP. iv, 16, 7. **-vyudāsa**, m. a cave within the earth, L. **-śacī-pati**, m. = *-puru-hūta*, Rājat. i, 99. **-śata-kratu**, m. id., iii, 329. **-śiñjinī**, f. = *-jivā*, Gaṇit. **-suta**, m. (= *-ja*) the planet Mars, VarBṛS.; VarBṛ.; N. of the demon Naraka, W. **-sura**, m. = *-deva*. **-spṛiś**, m. an inhabitant of the earth, Ragh. viii, 80. **Kshitī-garbha**, for *°ti-g°*, q. v. **Kshitîndra**, m. 'lord of the earth,' a king, Vcar. **Kshitîśa**, m. 'ruler of the earth,' a king, MBh. iii, 13198; VarBṛS.; Ragh.; Rājat.; N. of a prince of Kānyakubja; *-vaṃśâvalī-carita*, n. 'genealogy and history of Kshitîśa's family,' N. of a work composed in the last century. **Kshitîśvara**, m. 'lord of the earth,' a king, Ragh. iii, 3; xi, 1; BhP. iii, 13, 9.

Kshity (by Sandhi for *kshiti*). **-aditi**, f. 'the Aditi of the earth,' N. of Devakī (mother of Kṛishṇa), L. **-adhipa**, m. 'lord of the earth,' a king, VarBṛ. xi, 1. **-utkara**, m. a heap of mould, ii, 12.

क्षि 4. *kshi*, cl. 1. P. *kshayati* (only once, R. iv, 6, 14), cl. 5. P. *kshiṇóti* (ŚBr.; Mn.; MBh. &c.; 1. sg. *kshiṇómi*, VS. for *°ṇāmi* of AV.), cl. 9. P. *kshiṇāti* (3. pl. *kshiṇánti*; perf. 3. du. *cikshiyatur*, Kāś. on Pāṇ. vi, 4, 77 & vii, 4, 10), to destroy, corrupt, ruin, make an end of (acc.), kill, injure, RV.; AV. &c.: Pass. *kshīyáte* (AV. xii, 5, 45; 3. pl. *kshíyante*, RV. i, 62, 12; aor. Subj. *ksheshṭa* [AV. iv, 34, 8] or *kshāyi*, TBr. i; Cond. *aksheshyata*, ŚBr. viii), to be diminished, decrease, wane (as the moon), waste away, perish, RV.; AV.; ŚBr. &c.; to pass (said of the night), Kathās.: Caus. P. *kshapayati* (fut. *°yishyati*), rarely Ā. *°te* (MBh. i, 1838; Daś.), very rarely *kshayayati* (MBh. v, 2134, ed. Calc.), to destroy, ruin, make an end of (acc.), finish, MBh.; R. &c.; to weaken, Mn. v, 157; MBh. i, 1658; Kum. v, 29; to pass (as the night or time, *kshapām*, *°pās*, *kālam*), Pañcat.; Kād.; ŚārṅgP.; [cf. φθί-νω, φθί-σι-ς, &c.]

3. **Kshaya**, *as*, m. (Pāṇ. vi, 1, 201) loss, waste, wane, diminution, destruction, decay, wasting or wearing away (often ifc.), Mn.; MBh. &c.; fall (as of prices, opposed to *vṛiddhi*, e. g. *kshayo vṛiddhiś ca paṇyānām*, 'the fall and rise in the price of commodities'), Yājñ. ii, 258; removal, W.; end, termination (e. g. *nidrā-ksh°*, the end of sleep, R. vi, 105, 14; *dina-kshaye*, at the end of day, MBh. i, 699; R. iv, 3, 10; *jīvita-kshaye*, at the end of life, Daś.; *āyushaḥ ksh°*, id., Ragh.; *kshayam √gam*, *√yā*, *√i*, or *upa √i*, to become less, be diminished, go to destruction, come to an end, perish, Nal.; R.; Suśr.; VarBṛS.; Daś.; Amar.; Hit.; *kshayam √nī*, to destroy, R. v, 36, 51); consumption, phthisis pulmonalis, Suśr.; Hcat.; sickness in general, L.; the destruction of the universe, Pañcat.; (in alg.) a negative quantity, minus, Āryabh.; = *-māsa*, Jyot.; = *kshayâha*, Gaṇit.; N. of a prince, VP.; (*ā*), f., N. of a Yoginī, Hcat.; (*am*), n., N. of the last year in the sixty years' Bṛihaspati cycle, VarBṛS. **-kara**, mfn. ifc. causing destruction or ruin, destructive, terminating, MBh. ii, 2494; Suśr.; liberating from existence, W.; perhaps for *kshayi-kala* (said of the moon 'the portions of which are waning'), Cāṇ.; (*as*), m., N. of the 49th year of the sixty years' Bṛihaspati cycle, VarBṛS. **-kartṛi**, mfn. ifc. causing destruction or ruin, VP. **-kāla**, m. the period of destruction, end of all things. **-kāsa**, m. a consumptive or phthisical cough, Car. vi, 20. **-kāsin**, mfn. one who has a consumptive cough. **-kṛit**, mfn. causing ruin or loss or destruction, VarYogay.; Bhag. xi; Suśr.; (*t*), m. (= *kshaya*) N. of the last year of the sixty years' Bṛihaspati cycle. **-ṃ-kara**, mf(*ī*)n. causing destruction or ruin (with gen. or ifc.), MBh.; Hcat. **-ja**, mfn. produced by consumption (as cough), Suśr. **-divasa**, m. the day of the destruction of the universe, Hcar. **-nāśinī**, f. 'removing consumption,' Celtis orientalis (= *jīvantī*), L. **-paksha**, m. the fortnight of the moon's wane, dark fortnight, Kir. ii, 37. **-pravṛitta**, mfn. = *-ja*, Suśr. **-māsa**, m. a lunar month that is omitted in the adjustment of the lunar and the solar calendar, Jyot.; Gaṇit. **-yukta**, mfn. ruined (a prince), Kir. ii, 11. **-yukti**, f. ruin, ii, 9; necessity or opportunity of destroying, W. **-yoga**, m. id., W. **-roga**, m. consumption, VarBṛS.; Hcat. **-°rogin**, mfn. consumptive, Yājñ.; Hcat.; *°gi-tā*, f. consumption; *°gi-tva*, n. id., Mn. **-vāyu**, m. the wind that is to blow at the end of the world, W. **-sampad**, f. total loss, ruin, destruction, W. **Kshayâha**, m. a lunar day that is omitted in the adjustment of the lunar and the solar calendar, Gaṇit. **Kshayôpaśama**, m. complete annihilation of the desire of being active, Jain. (Sarvad. iii).

2. **Kshayaṇa**, mfn. ifc. 'destroying, annihilating, driving away, dispersing,' see *arāya-*, *asura-*, *piśāca-*, *bhrātṛivya-*, *yātudhāna-*, *sadānvā-* & *sapatna-kshâyaṇa*.

Kshayathu, for *kshavathu*, q. v.

Kshayayitavya, mfn. to be destroyed, R. vi, 17, 4.

Kshayi (in comp. for *°yin*, q. v.) **-kala**, see *kshaya-kara*. **-tva**, n. perishableness, fragility, Sarvad. iv; KapS. i, 1, Sch.

Kshayika, mfn. consumptive, Nār.

Kshayita, mfn. destroyed, ruined, put an end to, finished, MBh.; R.; Megh.; BhP.; Kathās.; (in math.) divided, Sūryas. i, 51. **-tā**, f. the being destroyed or annihilated, Bādar. iii, 1, 8, Sch.

Kshayin, mfn. (Pāṇ. iii, 2, 157) wasting, decaying, waning, Mn. ix, 314; Ragh.; Daś.; Bhartṛ.; perishable, Śak.; Megh. &c.; consumptive, Mn. iii, 7; MBh. xiii, 5089; VarBṛ. xxiii, 17.

Kshayishṇu, mfn. perishable, BhP. vii, 7, 40; destroying, removing, ib. vi, 16, 41; (ifc.) iii, 13, 25.

Kshayya, mfn. (anything) that can be destroyed or removed, Pāṇ. vi, 1, 81; see also *a-kshayyá*.

Kshāyika, mfn. resulting from the (*kshayôpaśama* or) annihilation of the desire of being active, Jain. (Sarvad. iii).

5. **Kshi**, *is*, f. destruction, waste, loss, L.

Kshitá, mfn. (= φθι-τό-ς) wasted, decayed, exhausted, TS. vi; weakened, miserable (as an ascetic), Pāṇ. vi, 4, 61, Kāś.; (see also *á-*) **Kshitâyus**, mfn. one whose life goes to an end, RV. x, 161, 2; one whose life is forfeited, Pāṇ. vi, 4, 61, Kāś.

3. **Kshiti**, *is*, f. wane, perishing, ruin, destruction, AV.; the period of the destruction of the universe, end of the world, L.; (cf. *á-*, *ásura-*.)

Kshitvan, *ā*, m. the wind, Uṇ. iv, 115.

Kshiyā, f. (g. *bhidâdi*) loss, waste, destruction, L.; offence against the customs, Pāṇ. viii, 1, 60 & ii, 104.

Kshiṇá, mfn. diminished, wasted, expended, lost, destroyed, worn away, waning (as the moon), ŚBr.; MuṇḍUp.; ŚvetUp.; Mn. &c.; weakened, injured, broken, torn, emaciated, feeble, Mn. vii, 166; Suśr.; Kāś. on Pāṇ. vi, 4, 61 & viii, 2, 46 &c.; delicate, slender, Śak.; Git. iv, 21; Naish. vii, 81; poor, miserable, Pañcat. iv, 16 & 32; (*am*), n., N. of a disease of the pudenda muliebria, Gal. **-karman**, m. 'one whose desire of being active is completely annihilated,' a Jina. **-kośa**, mfn. one whose wealth is exhausted, Rājat. v, 165. **-gati**, mfn. with slackened or diminished motion or progress. **-jīvita**, mfn. one who has no means of subsistence, R. **-tamas**, m., N. of a Vihāra, Rājat. i, 147. **-tā**, f. the state of wasting away, diminution, decay, W.; the state of being worn away or injured, Mṛicch.; emaciation, W. **-tva**, n. the wane (of the moon), Subh. **-dhana**, mfn. having diminished wealth, impoverished. **-pāpa**, mfn. one whose sins are destroyed, purified after having suffered the consequences of sin, W. **-puṇya**, mfn. one whose merit is lost, who has enjoyed the fruits of merit and is doomed to labour for more in another birth, W. **-madhya**, mfn. slender-waisted, W. **-mohaka**, n. (scil. *guṇa-sthāna*) N. of the twelfth of the fourteen degrees by which final beatitude is attained, Jain. **-vat**, mfn. wasted, decayed, W. **-vāsin**, mfn. inhabiting a dilapidated house, W.; (*ī*), m. a dove or pigeon, W. **-vikrānta**, mfn. one who has lost courage, destitute of prowess, W. **-vṛitti**, mfn. out of employ, having no means of subsistence or maintenance, Mn. viii, 341. **-śakti**, mfn. one whose strength is wasted, weak, impotent, W. **-śarīra**, mfn. one who has a thin or emaciated body, W. **-sāra**, mfn. (a tree) the sap of which is gone, withered, MBh. xiii, 5, 19. **-sukṛita**, mfn. one whose stock of merit is exhausted, W. **Kshīṇâṅga**, mfn. one who has emaciated limbs, W. **Kshīṇâjya-karman**, mfn. 'one who has done with sacrificial ceremonies,' a Buddhist, W. **Kshīṇâdhi**, mfn. delivered from distress, Daś. **Kshīṇâyus**, mfn. (= *kshitây°*) one whose life goes to an end, MBh.; Kathās. **Kshīṇârtha**, mfn. deprived of property, impoverished, Mṛicch. **Kshīṇâsrava**, mfn. with sin gone, Divyâv. xxxvi. **Kshīṇâshṭa-karman**, m. 'one who has suppressed any of the eight groups of actions,' an Arhat, Jain. **Kshīṇôpâya**, mfn. destitute of anything to rely upon, Amar.; Ṛitus.; Rājat. v, 60; 165 & 287.

Kshīyamāṇa, mfn. (Pass. p.) perishing, wasting away, decaying, BhP. v, 22, 9; Hit.; (cf. *á-*.)

Ksheya, mfn. to be destroyed or removed, Pāṇ. vi, 1, 81, Kāś.

Ksheshṇú, mfn. (Vop. xxvi, 144) perishable, MaitrS. i, 6, 10.

क्षिण् *kshiṇ*, cl. 8. P. Ā. *°ṇoti*, *ṇute*, = √4. *kshi*, q. v., Dhātup. xxx, 4.

क्षित् *kshit*. See √1. & 2. *kshi*.

Kshitá, mfn., see √4. *kshi*; (*ā*), f., see √2. *kshi*.

1. 2. **Kshiti**, 3. **kshiti**, see √1. 2. & 4. *kshi*.

क्षिति 4. *kshiti*, *is*, m., N. of a man, Pravar.; (*is*), f. a sort of yellow pigment, L.; a sort of base metal; = *kshiti-kshama* (s. v. 2. *kshiti*), Gal.

क्षित्वन् *kshitvan*. See √4. *kshi*.

क्षिद्र *kshidra*, *as*, m. disease, L.; the sun, L.; a horn, L.

क्षिप् 1. *kship*, cl. 6. P. *kshipáti*, Ā. *kshipate* (MBh. &c.; cl. 4. P. *kshipyati*, only Bhaṭṭ.; Subj. *kshipát*; perf. *cikshepa*, MBh. &c.; ep. also *cikshipe*; fut. 2nd *kshepsyati*, MBh. &c.; ep. also *°te*; inf. *ksheptum*; cf. Pāṇ. vii, 2, 10, Siddh.), to throw, cast, send, despatch, AV. ix, 1, 10 & 20; Mn.; MBh. (Pass. pr. p. *kshipyat*, i, 1126) &c.; to move hastily (the arms or legs), Mṛicch.; BhP. x, 36, 14; to throw a glance (as the eye), Bhartṛ. i, 94; to strike or hit (with a weapon), RV. i, 182, 1-3; to put or place anything on or in (loc.), pour on, scatter, fix or attach to (loc.), Yājñ. i, 230; Bhag.; Mṛicch. &c.; to direct (the thoughts) upon (loc.), Sarvad.; to throw away, cast away, get rid of, Bhartṛ. ii, 69; Kathās.; to lay (the blame) on (loc.), Hit.; to utter abusive words, insult, revile, abuse, Mn.; MBh. &c.; 'to disdain,' i. e. to excel, beat, outvie, BhP. iv, 8, 24 & 15, 17; to strike down, ruin, destroy, BhP. vi, 1, 14; BrahmaP.; (Ā. 'to destroy one another, go to ruin,' Pot. 3. pl. *kshiperan*, MBh. iii, 1094); to pass or while away (the time or night, *kālam*, *kshapām*), Kathās. lv, 154; xcii, 84; to lose (time, *kālam*; cf. *kāla-kshepa*), R. vii, 80, 14; to skip or pass over (a day, *dinam*), Car. vi, 3; (in math.) to add, Gol.: Caus. P. *kshepayati*, to cause to cast or throw into (*antar*), Kathās. xiii, 160; to throw into, R. ii, 76, 16; to cause to descend into (loc.), Kathās. lxxv, 121; to pass or while away (the night, *kshapām*), ib. lvi, 75; (aor. Subj. 2. sg. *cikshipas*) to hurt, injure, RV. x, 16, 1; (cf. Subj. *kshepayat*, s. v. √2. *kshi*); [cf. Lat. *sipo*, *dissipo*, for *xipo*.]

2. **Kship**, *pas*, f. pl. (only used in nom.; the instr. is formed fr. *kshipā*, RV. ix, 59, 57) 'the movable ones,' the fingers, RV. iii, v, ix (Naigh. ii, 5).

Kshipa, mfn. 'throwing, casting,' see *giri-ksh°*; (*as*), m. a thrower, W.; (*ā*), f. throwing, sending, casting, g. *bhidādi*; (for *kshapā*) night, Comm. on L.; (*kshipā*), f. only instr. pl. *°pābhis*, see 2. *kship*.

Kshipaka, *as*, m. an archer, L.; (*ā*), f.?, Pāṇ. vii, 3, 45, Vārtt. 5; g. *prêkshādi*.

Kshipakin, mfn. fr. *°kā*, g. *prêkshādi*.

Kshipaṇi, *is*, f. 'moving speedily,' gallop [NBD.], RV. iv, 40, 4; a missile weapon, Uṇ.; a kind of net, L.; = *mantra*, L.; = *adhvaryu*, L.; an oar, Comm. on L. (also *°ṇī*, f., ib.)

Kshipaṇú, *us*, m. 'an archer,' or (*ú*), n. 'a missile weapon,' RV. iv, 58, 6; (*us*), m. air, wind, Uṇ. iii, 52.

Kshipaṇyu, mfn. diffusive, what may be sent or scattered, fragrant, L.; (*us*), m. the body, L.; spring, Uṇ. iii, 51, Sch.

Kshipati, *ī*, du. the arms, Naigh. ii, 4, Sch.

Kshípasti, *ī*, du. id., Naigh. ii, 4.

Kshiptá, mfn. thrown, cast, sent, despatched, dismissed, RV. i, 129, 8; MBh. &c.; reviled, despicable (on account of, instr. or *-tas*), Pāṇ. v, 4, 46, Kāś.; (*ā*), f. (for *kshapā*) night, L.; (*ám*), n. a wound caused by shooting or throwing, AV. vi, 109, 3; 'scattered,' distraction or absence of mind, Sarvad. **-citta**, mfn. distracted in mind, absent; *-tā*, f. absence of mind, MBh. ii, 241. **-deha**, mfn. one who prostrates the body, who lies down. **-bheshaja**, mf(*ī*)n. healing wounds caused by missile weapons, AV. vi, 109, 1. **-yoni**, mfn. of despicable descent (one for whom a Brāhman is not allowed to act as Ṛitv-ij), ĀśvGr. i, 23. **-laguḍa**, mfn. one who flings the staff, W. **Kshiptôttara**, n. (scil. *vacas*, speech) 'the answer of which is destroyed or rendered impossible,' unanswerable speech, Kām. v, 26.

Kshipti, *is*, f. sending, throwing, W.; solving a riddle, W.; explaining or understanding a hidden meaning, W.; (in dram.) the becoming known or exposure of a secret, Sāh. 373; (in alg.) = *kshiptikā*.

Kshiptikā, f. (in alg.) the quantity to be added to the square of the least root multiplied by the multiplicator (to render it capable of yielding an exact square root).

Kshipnu, mfn. (Pāṇ. iii, 2, 140) = *nirākarishṇu* ('throwing obstacles in the way,' obstructive, W.; scornful or fond of abusing, BRD.), L.

Kshipyat, mfn. pr. p. Pass., see √1. *kship*; (pr. p. P.) throwing, sending, W.

Kshipyamāṇa, mfn. (pr. p. Pass.) being thrown &c.; (pr. p. Ā.) throwing, tossing, W.; casting aside, throwing off, W.; sending, directing, W.

Kshiprá, mf(*ā*)n. (compar. *kshépīyas*, superl. *kshépishṭha*, qq. vv.) springing, flying back with a spring, elastic (as a bow), RV. ii, 24, 8; quick, speedy, swift, ŚBr. vi; ix; (said of certain lunar mansions) VarBṛS.; (*as*), m., N. of a son of Kṛishṇa, Hariv. 9195; (*ám*), ind. (Naigh. ii, 15) quickly, immediately, directly, AV.; ŚBr. iv; v; xiii; Mn.; MBh. &c.; (*am*), n. a measure of time (= 1/15 Muhūrta or 15 Etarhis), ŚBr. xii, 3, 2, 5; the part of the hand between the thumb and forefinger and the corresponding part of the foot, Suśr.; (*á*), ind. (Ved. acc. pl. n.) with a shot, RV. iv, 8, 8; (*āt*), abl. ind. directly, immediately, Kathās.; (*é*), loc. ind. id., ŚBr. i; iv; v; x; [cf. Gk. κραιπνός.] **-kāma**, mfn. one who wishes to obtain anything speedily, SāmavBr. **-kārin**, mfn. acting or working quickly, skilful, MBh.; R.; Sāh.; *°ri-tā*, f. working quickly, skill, Uttarar. **-gati**, mfn. going quickly, DaivBr. **-garbha**, m. Myrica sapida, Npr. **-dhanvan** (*°prá-*), mfn. armed with an elastic bow which flies back with a spring, RV. ix, 90, 3; AV. xi, 4, 23. **-niścaya**, mfn. one who decides or resolves quickly, Mn. vii, 179. **-pākin**, m. 'ripening quickly,' Hibiscus populneoides, L. **-mūtra-tā**, f., N. of a disease of the bladder, ŚārṅgS. **-śyená**, m. a species of bird, MaitrS. iii, 14, 11; ŚBr. x. **-saṃdhi**, m. a species of Sandhi (cf. *kshaipra*) produced by changing the first of two concurrent vowels to its semivowel, ŚāṅkhŚr. xii, 13, 5; (mfn.) changed by that Sandhi (as a vowel or syllable). **-hasta**, m. 'swift-handed,' N. of Agni, AV.Paipp.; of a Rakshas, R. vi, 18, 41. **-homa**, m. a speedy sacrifice (in which several ceremonies are omitted), Comm. on Gobh. i, 3, 1. **Kshiprârtha**, m. any affair which requires speedy action, MBh. v, 1004. **Kshiprêshu**, mfn. one who has quick arrows (Rudra), RV. vii, 46, 1.

Kshepa, *as*, m. a throw, cast, W.; throwing, casting, tossing, W.; stretching (as of the legs), Suśr.; a clap (of wings), R. iv, 62, 12; a stroke (of an oar &c.), L.; (cf. *apaṭī-ksh°*, *drishṭi-ksh°*, *bhrū-ksh°*, *saṭā-ksh°*); moving to and fro, Megh. 47; sending, dismissing, W.; laying on (as paint &c.), besmearing, L.; transgressing (*laṅghana*), L.; delay, procrastination, dilatoriness, Sarvad.; 'loss,' see *manaḥ-ksh°*; accusation, Yājñ. ii, 210; (Pāṇ. ii, 1, 26 & v, 4, 46) insult, invective, abuse, reviling, MBh. i, 555; iii, 631; Yājñ. ii, 204 & 211; disrespect, contempt, L.; pride, haughtiness, L.; application of a term to something else, Bādar. iv, 1, 6, Sch.; a nosegay, L.; (in arithm.) an additive quantity, addendum; the astronomical latitude, Sūryas.; Gol. **-dina**, n. = *kshayâha* (q. v.), Gol. **-pāta**, m. the point where the planets and the moon pass the ecliptic, Gol. vi, 14 & 20. **-vṛitta**, n. the course of the planets and of the moon, ib. v, 13 ff.

Kshepaka, mfn. ifc. one who throws or sends, Kathās. lxi, 9; destroying, Bādar., Sch.; inserted, interpolated, R. ii, ch. 96, Sch.; Naish. xxii, 48, Sch.; abusive, disrespectful, W.; (*as*), m. a spurious or interpolated passage, W.; (in arithm.) an additive quantity; a pilot, helmsman, Gal.

Kshepaṇa, *am*, n. the act of throwing, casting, letting fly or go (a bow-string), Nir. ii, 28; MBh. iv, 352 & 1400; throwing away (in boxing), VP. v, 20, 54; sending, directing, W.; sending away, MBh. iii, 13272; passing away or spending time (v. l. *kshapaṇa*); 'omitting,' for 1. *kshapaṇa*, Mn. iv, 119; a sling, BhP. iii, 19, 18; x, 11, 38; (*ī*), f. id., R. vi, 7, 24; an oar, L.; a kind of net, L. **-sāra**, m., N. of a work.

Kshepaṇi, *is*, f. = *°ṇī*, an oar, L.

Kshepaṇika, *as*, m. a boatman, navigator, Vāsav.; (mfn.) destroying (*nāśaka*), ib.; = *karkarâdi*, L.

Kshepaṇīya, mfn. to be thrown or cast; (*am*), n. a sling, Ragh. iv, 77.

Kshepan, *ā*, m. 'throw, cast,' only (*°pṇā*), instr. ind. quickly, destroying, TāṇḍyaBr. vii, 6, 4.

Kshepāya, Nom. Ā. *°yate* (p. *°yamāṇa*), to abuse, revile, W.

Kshepiman, *ā*, m. great velocity, speed, Pāṇ. vi, 4, 156; g. *pṛithv-ādi*.

Kshépishṭha, mfn. (see *kshiprá*; Pāṇ. vi, 4, 156) quickest, speediest, TS. iii, 4, 3, 2.

Kshépīyas, mfn. (see ib.; Pāṇ. vi, 4, 156) more quick, speedier, ŚBr. vi, 3, 2, 2; (*as*), ind. as quickly as possible, Śāntiś. iii, 6.

Ksheptavya, mfn. to be cast or thrown into, Kathās. lxxi, 174; to be reviled or abused, MBh. i, 1467.

Ksheptṛi, mfn. (Pāṇ. iii, 1, 94, Sch.) a thrower, caster, R. iv, 9, 84 & 18, 21.

Kshepnú, *us*, m. springing or flying (of a bow-string), RV. x, 51, 6.

Kshepya, mfn. to be thrown or being thrown, Hariv. 7524; to be thrown (into, loc.), Suśr.; to be placed into, Kathās. lxxxix, 26; to be put on (as an ornament), Śak., Sch.; to be destroyed, Bādar. iv, 3, 14, Sch.; (in arithm.) to be added, Gol. vi, 19; Gaṇit.

क्षिया *kshiyā*. See √4. *kshi*.

क्षिल्लिका *kshillikā*, f., N. of the grandmother of king Cakra-varman, Rājat. v, 289.

क्षिव् *kshiv*, cl. 1. 4. P. *kshevati*, *kshivyati*, to eject from the mouth, spit, vomit, Dhātup. xv, 59 (v. l. *kshev*); xxvi, 4; (cf. √*shṭhiv* & *kshīb*.)

क्षी *kshī*, = √4. *kshi* (derived fr. *kshiṇá*, *-kshīya*), Dhātup. xxxi, 35 (v. l.)

क्षीज् *kshīj*, cl. 1. P. *°jati*, to sound inarticulately, sigh or groan (as in distress), Dhātup. vii, 63.

Kshījana, *am*, n. the whistling of hollow reeds or bamboos, L.

क्षीण *kshīṇá*. See √4. *kshi*.

क्षीब् *kshīb* (or *kshīv*), cl. 1. P. *kshībati* (or *kshīvati*), to eject from the mouth, spit, Dhātup. xv, 59; to be drunk or intoxicated, W.: Caus. *kshībayati*, to excite, Bālar. viii, 62; [cf. √*kshiv* &c.; cf. also Hib. *siobhas*, 'rage, madness.']

Kshība (or *kshīva*), mf(*ā*)n. (pf. p. Pass. √*kshīb*, Pāṇ. viii, 2, 55) excited, drunk, intoxicated, MBh.; R.; Bhartṛ.; BhP. &c. **-tā**, f. intoxication, drunkenness, Kathās. xiii, 10; lvii, 8. **-tva**, n. id., ib. xxxvi, 87.

Kshīban (or *kshīvan*), mfn. = *°ba* BhP. v, 17, 20.

Kshībika (or *kshīvika*), mfn. = *kshībeṇa tarati*, Pāṇ. viii, 2, 6, Vārtt. 7, Pat.

क्षीर *kshīrá*, *am*, n. (fr. √*śyai*? ; fr. √*kshar* or √*ghas*, Nir. ii, 5; fr. √*ghas*, Uṇ. iv, 34; g. *ardharcâdi*), milk, thickened milk, RV.; AV.; VS.; TS. &c. (ifc. f. *ā*, MBh. xiii, 3700); the milky juice or sap of plants, R.; Suśr.; Megh. 106; Śak. (v.l.); = *-śīrsha* (q. v.), L.; water, L.; (*as*), m., N. of a grammarian (cf. *-svāmin*), Rājat. iv, 488; (*ā*), f., N. of a plant (= *kakolī*), L.; (*ī*), f. a dish prepared with milk, Bhpr.; N. of several plants containing a milky sap (Asclepia rosea, Mimosa Kauki, gigantic swallow-wort, Euphorbia, &c.), L. **-kañcukin**, m. (= *kshīrīśa*, q. v.) Lipeocercis serrata, L. **-kaṇṭha**, m. 'having milk in his throat,' a youngling, Bālar. iv, 1; vi, 30; Prasannar. **-kaṇṭhaka**, m. id., L. **-kanda**, m. Batatus paniculata, L.; (*ā*), f. id., L. **-kalambha**, m. 'N. of a man,' see *kshairakalambhi*. **-kākolikā**, f., N. of a root from the Himālaya (yielding a milky juice and used by the Hindūs as one of the 8 principal medicaments), L. **-kākolī**, f. id., Suśr. i, iv. **-kāṇḍaka**, m. = *-dāru*, q. v., L.; = *-cchada*, L. **-kāshṭhā**, f. '(a plant) the wood of which yields a milky juice,' a variety of the fig-tree, L. **-kīṭa**, m. an insect or animalcule generated by the fermentation of milk, L. **-kuṇḍa**, n. a milk-pot, Kathās. lxiii, 189. **-kshaya**, m. drying up of the milk (in the udder), Pañcat. ii. **-kshava**, for *-yava*, q. v. **-kharjūra**, m. a variety of date tree, L. **-garbha**, m., N. of a certain Brāhman who was born again as a flamingo, Hariv. **-guccha-phala**, m. Mimusops Kauki, L. **-ghṛita**, n. purified butter mixed with milk, Suśr.; (cf. *-sarpis*.) **-cchada**, m. Calotropis gigantea (the leaves of which yield a milky juice), Gal. **-ja**, n. coagulated milk, L. **-jāla**, m. a kind of fish, Gal. **-taraṃgiṇī**, f., N. of a grammar (by Kshīra-svāmin). **-taru**, m. a tree with a milky juice, VarBṛS.; VarYogay. **-tumbī**, f. the bottle-gourd, L. **-taila**, n. a kind of unguent prepared with milk, oil, &c., Suśr. **-toyadhi**, m. = *kshīra-dhi* (q. v.), R. vi, 26, 6. **-da**, mfn. milk-giving, (anything) that yields milk, W. **-dala**, m. = *-cchada*, L. **-dātrī**, f. (a cow) who yields milk, MBh. xiii, 4919. **-dāru**, m. (= *-kāṇḍaka*) Tithymalus antiquorum, Car. vii, 10. **-druma**, m. the holy fig-tree, L. **-dhara**, m., N. of a prince. **-dhātrī**, f. a wet-nurse, Buddh. L. **-dhi**, m. the ocean of milk. **-dhenu**, f. a milk-cow (symbolically represented by milk &c. offered as a gift to a Brāhman), VārP.; BhavP. **-nadī**, f., N. of a river in the south (Pālār.) **-nāśa**, m. Trophis aspera. **-nidhi**, m. = *-dhi*, Ragh. i, 12; Pāṇ. i, 4, 51, Siddh. **-nīra**, n. (in comp.) milk and water, Vet.; 'union like the mixing of milk and water,' embracing, embrace, L.; *-nidhi*, m. = *kshīra-dhi*. **-pa**, mfn. drinking only milk (said of infants, Suśr. i, 35, 25; of a class of ascetics, MBh. xiii, 646); m. an infant, young child, xiii, 5986. **-parṇin**, m. = *-cchada*, L. **-palāṇḍu**, m. a kind of onion, Suśr. **-pāká**, mfn. cooked in milk, RV. viii, 77, 10; *-vidhi*, m. preparing of medicinal drugs by cooking them in milk, Bhpr. **-pāṇa**, mf(*ī*)n. (any vessel) out of which milk is drunk, L. (also *-pāna*, id.); (*ās*), m. pl. 'milk-drinkers,' N. of the Uśīnaras, Pāṇ. viii, 4, 9, Kāś. **-pāṇi**, m., N. of a physician, Bhpr. **-pāna**, mf(*ī*)n. = *-pāṇa* (q. v.), L. **-pāyin**, mfn. drinking milk, W.; drinking or imbibing water repeatedly, W.; (*iṇas*), m. pl. (= *-pāṇa*) 'milk-drinkers,' N. of the Uśinaras, Pāṇ. iii, 2, 81, Kāś. **-pushpikā**, f. a white variety of Vishṇu-krāntā, Npr. **-pushpī**, f. Andropogon aciculatus, Npr. **-phala**, m. Carissa Carandas, Npr. **-bhaṭṭa**, m. = *-svāmin*. **-bhṛita**, mfn. supported by milk, receiving wages in the form of milk, Mn. viii, 231. **-madhurā**, f. = *-kākolī*, L. **-maya**, mfn. representing milk (as wishes or desires), BhP. iv, 18, 9. **-mahârṇava**, m. = *-dhi*, Kād. **-mṛitsna**, m., N. of a tree, Hcar., Sch. **-mocaka**, m. a variety of Moringa (M. hyperanthera), L. **-moraṭa**, m. a kind of creeping plant, Suśr. **-yava**, m. dolomite, L. **-yashṭika**, m. (for *-shāshṭ°*?) a dish of liquorice and milk, W. **-yājin**, mfn. presenting oblations of milk (to the gods), ŚBr. i, 6, 4, 14. **-latā**, f. = *-kanda*, L. **-leham**, ind. so as to lap milk, Kauś. 30. **-vat** (*°rá-*), mfn. furnished with milk, AV. xviii, 4, 16; (*tī*), f., N. of a river, MBh. iii, 8046. **-vanaspati**, m. = *-taru*, Hcat. **-vallikā**, f. = *-kākolī*, Bhpr. **-vallī**, f. = *-kanda*, L. **-vaha**, mf(*ā*)n. running with milk (as a river),

Hcat. **–vāri**, m. = *-dhi*, L.; °*ri-dhi*, m. id., Kathās. xxii, 188; cxiv, 54. **–vikṛiti**, f. any product made from milk (as cheese &c.), L. **–vidārikā**, f. = *-kanda*, L. **–vidārī**, f. id., L. **–vishāṇikā**, f. = *-śṛiṅgī*, L.; = *-kākolī*, L. **–vṛiksha**, m. = *-taru*, VarBṛS.; a common N. for the 4 trees *nyagrodha, udumbara* (the glomerous fig-tree, Śak. iv; Suśr.), *aśvattha*, and *madhūka*, Suśr.; = *-gucchaphala*, L. **–vrata**, n. living upon milk in consequence of a vow, KātyŚr. **–śara**, m. the surface or skim of milk, cream, curds, L.; (*ā*), f. id., Gal. **–śāka**, n. id., Bhpr. **–śīrsha**, m. the resin of Pinus longifolia, L. **–śīrshaka**, m. id., Gal. **–śukla**, m. Trapa bispinosa, L.; = *-rājādanī*, L.; (*ā*), f. = *-kanda*, Suśr.; = *-kākolī*, Bhpr. **–śṛiṅgī**, f. Tragia involucrata, Gal. **–śrī**, mfn. mixed with milk, VS. viii, 57; TS. iv; ŚBr. xii. **–shāshṭika**, n. Shashṭika rice cooked with milk, Yājñ. i, 303 (°*shṭh*°, ed.) **–saṃtānikā**, f. curds mixed with milk, L. **–samudra**, m. = *-dhi*, Pañcat.; (in Śvetadvīpa), Tantras. **–sambhava**, n. sour milk, Gal. **–sarpis**, n. = *-ghṛita*, Suśr. **–sāgara**, m. = *-dhi*, BhP. viii, 5, 11; *-sutā*, f. 'born from the ocean of milk,' N. of Lakshmī. **–sāra**, m. 'essence of milk,' cream, L.; butter, W. **–sindhu**, m. = *-dhi*, Pañcar. **–sphaṭika**, m. a precious stone (described as a kind of milky crystal, perhaps a species of opal), L. **–srāva**, m. = *-śīrsha*, Npr. **–svāmin**, m., N. of a grammarian and Comm. on the Amara-kosha (according to Kaśmīrian tradition the same with Kshīra, q.v.), Comm. on Kum. vi, 46 &c. **–hotṛi** (°*rá-*), mfn. (g. *yuktârohy-ādi*) = *-yājin*, ŚBr. ii; KātyŚr. **–°homin**, mfn. id., KātyŚr. **–hrada**, m., N. of a man, g. *śivâdi*. **Kshīrâda**, m. 'sucking milk,' an infant at the breast, sucking child, W. **Kshīrânna**, n. rice cooked with milk, Subh.; °*nnâda*, mfn. eating rice cooked with milk (as an infant older than two years; or 'eating milk and food,' as an infant which is both suckled and fed), Suśr. **Kshīrâbdhi**, m. = °*ra-dhi*, VP.; Kathās. xxii, 186; *-ja*, m. the Amṛita or any of the precious objects produced at the churning of the ocean, L.; the moon, L.; Śesha, L.; Tārkshya, L.; (*ā*), f., Lakshmī (cf. °*ra-sāgara-sutā*), L.; (*am*), n. sea-salt, L.; a pearl, L.; *-tanayā*, f. = *-jā*, L.; *-putrī*, f. id., Gal.; *-mānushi*, f. id., L. **Kshīrâmbu-dhi**, m. = °*ra-dhi*, Veṇis.; Bālar.; Kathās. xvii, 8. **Kshīrârṇava**, m. id., Hcat. **Kshīrâhva**, m. = °*ra-śīrsha*, L. **Kshīrâhvaya**, m. id., L. **Kshīrôttarā**, f. inspissated milk, Gal. **Kshīrôttha**, n. 'produced from milk,' fresh butter, Gal. **Kshīrôda**, m. (Pāṇ. vi, 3, 57, Vārtt.) (= °*ra-dhi*) the ocean of milk, MBh.; Hariv. 12834; R.; Suśr.; Kum.; BhP.; Nom. P. °*dati*, to become the ocean of milk, Subh.; *-jā*, f. (= *kshīrâbdhi-jā*) N. of Lakshmī (in comp. *-vasati-janma-bhū*, 'the birth-place of [Lakshmī's abode or] the lotus flowers,' i.e. water), Sāh.; *-tanayā*, f. (= *-jā*) N. of Lakshmī (in comp. *-pati*, 'the husband of Lakshmī,' i.e. Vishṇu); *-nandana*, m. (= *kshīrâbdhi-ja*) the moon, L.; *-mathana*, n. the churning of the ocean of milk (undertaken by the Devas and Asuras to obtain the Amṛita &c.), MBh. i, 366; R. i, 45, 18; VarBṛS.; Devīm.; °*dârṇava*, m. the ocean of milk, NṛisUp.; Hcat. **Kshīrôdaka**, m., N. of a tree, Hcar., Sch. **Kshīrôdadhi**, m. = °*ra-dhi*, MBh. xii, 12778; BhP. **Kshīrôdanvat**, m. id., Prasannar. **Kshīrôdīya**, Nom. P. to behave like the ocean of milk, Sāh. **Kshīrôpasecana**, n. pouring milk upon, BhP. **Kshīrôrmi**, m. f. a wave of the ocean of milk, Ragh. iv, 27. **Kshīraudaná**, m. (Pāṇ. ii, 1, 34, Kāś.) rice boiled with milk, ŚBr. ii, 5, 3, 4; xi, 5, 7, 5; xiv (°*raudana*); Kauś.; Suśr.

Kshīraka, *as*, m., N. of a fragrant plant, L.; (*ikā*), f. a dish prepared with milk, Bhpr.; a variety of the date tree, MBh. iii, 11570 (= iii, 158, 47, ed. Bomb.; v. l. °*ka*); Lalit. xxiv.

Kshīrasa, for *kshīra-rasa*, q. v., L.

Kshīrasya, Nom. P. °*syati*, to long for milk or for the breast, Pāṇ. vii, 1, 51.

Kshīrāya, Nom. P. °*yati*, to be changed into milk, Vet.

Kshīrāvikā, °*vī*, f. a variety of Asclepias, L.

Kshīrika, *as*, m. a kind of serpent, Suśr. v, 4, 35; for °*rikā*, see s. v. °*raka*.

Kshīrin, mfn. milky, yielding milk, having plenty of milk, AV. vii, 50, 9; Yājñ. i, 204; Mṛicch.; containing milky sap (as a tree or plant), ŚBr. vi; KātyŚr.; Gobh.; ĀśvGṛ.; Mn. &c.; (*ī*), m., N. of several plants containing a milky sap (see *kshīrī*), Suśr.; (*iṇī*), f. a dish prepared with milk, Kathās. lxv, 142 f.; N. of several plants (Mimusops Kauki, L.; a variety of acid Asclepias used in medicine, L.; &c.), Suśr. iv, 9, 26. **Kshīrīśa**, m. 'lord of the plants with a milky sap,' = °*ra-kañcukin*, L.

Kshīrī-√bhū, to be changed into milk, Bādar. ii, 2, 5, Sch.

Kshīrīya, Nom. P. °*yati*, to desire milk, Pāṇ. vii, 1, 51, Kāś.

Kshīreyī, for *kshair*° (q. v.), L.

क्षीव् *kshīv, kshīva.* See √*kshīb.*

क्षु 1. *kshu*, cl. 2. P. *kshauti* (Gaut.; pr. p. *kshuvat*, TāṇḍyaBr.; Mn. iv, 43; BhP. ix, 6, 4; perf. *cukshāva*, Bhaṭṭ.; Pass. *cukshuve*, Śiś. ix, 83; fut. 2nd *kshavishyati*, Pāṇ. vii, 2, 10, Siddh.; fut. 1st *kshavitā*, Vop.; ind. p. *kshutvā*, Mn. v, 145; MBh.), to sneeze; to cough, W.: Desid. *cukshūshati*, to try to sneeze, JaimBr.: Caus. Desid. *cukshāvayishati*, Pāṇ., Siddh.; [cf. Lith. *czaudmi*.]

Kshava, *as*, m. sneezing, AV. xix, 8, 5; cough, catarrh, L.; black mustard (Sinapis dichotoma), L. **–kṛit**, m. '(anything) which causes sneezing,' the plant Artemisia sternutatoria, Bhpr.

Kshavaka, *as*, m. the plant Achyranthes aspera (= *apâmārga*), L.; black mustard, L.; another plant (= *bhūtâṅkuśa*), L.; (*ikā*), f. a variety of Solanum, L.; a species of rice, W.; a woman, W.; (*am*), n. a kind of pot-herb, Suśr. i, vi.

Kshavathu, m. (Pāṇ. iii, 3, 89, Kāś.) sneezing, Āp. ii, 3, 2; Suśr.; catarrh, cough, irritation of the throat, sore throat (*kshayathu*, L.), W.

1. **Kshut**, *t*, f. a sneeze, sneezing, MārkP. xxxv, 24. **Kshuj-janikā**, f. 'causing a sneeze,' mustard, Npr. **Kshut-karī**, f. id. (commonly *kaṅkālikā*), L. **Kshud-vibodhana**, m. black mustard, Npr.

Kshuta, mfn. one who has sneezed, MBh. xiii, 7584; (= *ava-ksh*°) sneezed upon, ib. 1577; for *kshṇuta* (sharp), L.; (*as*), m. black mustard, Gal.; (*am*), n. (also *as, ā*, m. f., L.) sneezing, Yājñ. i, 196; Suśr. **–vat**, mfn. (perf. p. P.) one who has sneezed, Caurap. **Kshutâbhijanana**, m. 'causing a sneeze,' black mustard, L.

Kshutaka, *as*, m. black mustard, L.

Kshuti, *is*, f. sneezing, Vop. ix, 53.

Kshuvat, mfn. pr. p., see s. v. √1. *kshu*.

क्षु 2. *kshú*, *u*, n. (√*ghas*; Naigh. ii, 7) food, RV. ix, 97, 22 & x, 61, 12. **–mat**, mfn. abounding in food, nourishing, nutritious, RV.; TBr. ii; strong, powerful, robust, RV.

क्षुज्जनिका *kshuj-janikā.* See 1. *kshut.*

क्षुण *kshuṇa*, *as*, m. the soap-berry plant (Sapindus saponaria, = *arishṭa*), L.

क्षुण्ण *kshuṇṇa*, °*ṇṇaka.* See √*kshud.*

क्षुत् 1. *kshut, kshuta*, &c. See √1. *kshu.*

क्षुत् 2. *kshut*, for 2. *kshúdh*, q. v.

क्षुद् 1. *kshud*, cl. 1. P. *kshódati*, to strike against, shake, RV. vii, 85, 1 (Naigh. ii, 14); Ā. to move, be agitated or shaken, RV. v, 58, 6: cl. 7. P. Ā. *kshuṇatti, kshuntte* (impf. *akshuṇat*; aor. 3. pl. *akshautsur*; fut. *kshotsyati*, Pāṇ. vii, 2, 10, Siddh.), to stamp or trample upon, Bhaṭṭ.: Caus. *kshodayati* (impf. *ákshodayat*), to shake or agitate by stamping, RV. iv, 19, 4; to crush, pound, pulverise, Suśr.; (Nom. P. fr. *kshudrá*) to reduce, diminish, Bhaṭṭ. xviii, 26; [cf. Gk. ξύω, ξέω for ξέϝω, ξυστός, ξεστός; Lith. *skausti*?]

Kshuṇṇa, mfn. stamped or trampled upon, MBh. viii, 4845; VarBṛS. liv; Ragh. i, 17; Pañcat. &c.; pounded, bruised, crushed, pulverised, Suśr.; Pāṇ. iv, 2, 92, Kāś.; broken to pieces, shattered, pierced, MBh. iii, 678; Mṛicch.; BhP.; MārkP.; violated (as a vow), R. i, 8, 9 (*a-ksh*°); practised, exercised (as the body), Suśr.; thought over repeatedly, reflected on again and again, W.; one versed in sacred science but unable to explain or teach it, W.; defeated, overcome, W.; multiplied, Sūryas.; (cf. *a-ksh*°.) **–manas**, mfn. contrite in heart, penitent, W.

Kshuṇṇaka, *as*, m. a kind of drum beaten at a funeral, L.

Kshuda, *as*, m. flour, meal, L.

Kshudrá, mf(*ā*)n. (compar. *kshodīyas*, superl. °*dishṭha*, qq. vv.) minute, diminutive, tiny, very small, little, trifling, AV.; VS. xiv, 30; TBr. iii; ŚBr.; ChUp.; AitUp.; Yājñ. &c.; mean, low, vile, Mn. vii, 27; Yājñ. i, 309; MBh. &c.; wicked (said in joke), Mālav.; niggardly, avaricious, L.; cruel, L.; poor, indigent, L.; (*as*), m. a small particle of rice, L.; = *-roga* (q. v.), Suśr.; = *-panasa* (q. v.), L.; (*ā*), f. (Pāṇ. iv, 3, 119) a kind of bee, Bhpr.; a fly, gnat, L.; a base or despicable woman, Pāṇ. iv, 1, 131; a maimed or crippled woman, ib., Pat.; a whore, harlot, L.; a dancing girl, L.; a quarrelsome woman, L.; N. of several plants (Solanum Jacquini, also another variety of Solanum, Oxalis pusilla, Coix barbata, Nardostachys Jaṭā-māṇsī?), L.; (*ám*), n. a particle of dust, flour, meal, RV. i, 129, 6 & viii, 49, 4; [cf. Lith. *kūdikis*, 'an infant;' Pers. كودك *kūdak*, 'small, a boy.'] **–kaṇṭakārī**, f. a species of small prickly nightshade (Solanum Jacquini), L. **–kaṇṭakī**, f. 'having small thorns,' a variety of Solanum. **–kaṇṭārikā**, f. = °*ṭakārī*, L. **–kaṇṭikā**, f. = °*ṭakī*, L. **–kambu**, m. a small shell, W. **–karman**, mfn. acting in a low or vile manner, R. ii, 53, 18. **–kalpa**, m. 'the smaller ritual,' N. of a class of works. **–kāralikā**, f. a kind of Cucurbitaceous plant, L. **–kāravellī**, f. id., L. **–kuliśa**, m. a precious stone, L. **–kushṭha**, n. a mild form of leprosy (comprising eleven varieties, whereas the *mahā-k*° contains seven severe forms of leprosy), Suśr. **–klṛipti**, f. arrangement of the minor requirements (of a sacrifice), Lāṭy. vi, 9, 1, Sch. **–kshura**, m. a variety of Asteracantha longifolia, L. **–guḍa**, m. lump-sugar, Gal. **–go-kshuraka**, m. = *-kshura*, L. **–ghaṇṭikā**, f. a tinkling ornament, girdle of small bells, L. **–ghaṇṭī**, f. id., L. **–gholī**, f., N. of a small shrub (= *civillikā*), L. **–cañcu**, f. 'having small points,' N. of a plant, L. **–candana**, n. red sandal-wood, L. **–campaka**, m. a variety of the Campaka tree, Bhpr. **–cirbhitā**, f. a variety of Curcumis, L. **–cūḍa**, m. 'having a small tuft,' a kind of small bird (commonly *gośālika*), L. **–jantu**, m. any small animal, Pāṇ. ii, 4, 8; VarBṛS.; Hit.; a kind of worm (Julus, *śata-padī*), L. **–jātī-phala**, n. a kind of Myrobalan, L. **–jīra**, m. small cummin, L. **–jīvā**, f., N. of a plant (= *jīvantī*), L. **–mcara**, mfn. grazing on small or minute herbs (as a deer), BhP. iv, 29, 53. **–taṇḍula**, m. a grain of rice, W. **–tā**, f. minuteness, smallness, W.; inferiority, insignificance, W.; meanness, W. **–tāta**, m. (= *kshulla-t*°) a father's brother, L. **–tulasī**, f. a variety of Ocimum, L. **–tva**, n. = *-tā*, W. **–daṇśikā**, f. a small gad-fly, L. **–daṇśī**, f. id., W. **–durālabhā**, f., N. of a thorny plant (much eaten by camels, a variety of Alhagi), L. **–duḥsparśā**, f. = *-kaṇṭārī*, L. **–dhātrī**, f., N. of a plant (= *karkaṭa*), L. **–dhānya**, n. an inferior kind of grain, VarBṛS.; Bhpr.; shrivelled grain, L. **–nadī**, f. a rivulet, VP. ii, 4, 66. **–nāsika**, mfn. one who has a small nose, L. **–pakshika**, m. a small bird, L. **–pattrā**, f. 'having small leaves,' Oxalis pusilla, L. **–pattrī**, f. another plant (= *vacā*), Bhpr. **–pada**, n. 'a small foot,' a kind of measure of length (equal to 10 Aṅgulas), Śulb. i, 6. **–panasa**, m. the plant Artocarpus Lacucha (*lakuca* or *ḍahu*), Bhpr. **–parṇa**, m. = *-tulasī*, L. **–paśu**, m. small cattle, Gaut. xiii, 14; *-mat*, mfn. possessed of small cattle, Āp. **–pāshāṇa-bhedaka**, m. [Gal.], °*dā*, °*dī*, f., N. of a plant (= *catuḥpattrī, pārvatī, nagna-bhū*, &c.), L. **–pippalī**, f. wild pepper (= *vana-p*°), L. **–pṛishatī** (°*drá-*), f. (a cow) covered with small spots, VS. xxiv, 2; MaitrS. iii, 13, 3. **–potikā**, f., N. of a pot-herb (a variety of Basella), L. **–phalaka**, m., N. of a plant (= *jīvana*, Celtis orientalis), L. **–phalā**, f. 'having small fruits,' N. of several plants (Ardisia solanacea, Solanum Jacquini, &c.), L. **–baka**, v. l. for *kshudraka*, q. v. **–balā**, f. = *-potikā*, L. **–buddhi**, m. 'of little understanding' or 'of a low character,' N. of a jackal, Hit. **–bha**, m. a particular measure of weight (= a Kola), ŚārṅgS. i, 1, 16. **–bhaṇṭākī**, f. = *-kaṇṭakī*, Bhpr. **–bhṛit**, m., N. of a man, BhP. x, 85, 51. **–mahā**, for *-sahā*, q. v. **–mīna**, m. pl., N. of a people, VarBṛS. xiv. **–mustā**, f. the root of Scirpus Kysoor, L. **–rasa**, *ās*, m. pl. base pleasures, BhP. v, 13, 10; (*ā*), f. the plant Pongamia glabra, L. **–ruhā**, f. the Colocynth, Gal. **–roga**, *ās*, m. pl. a class of minor diseases (of which forty-four are enumerated, especially exanthemas of different kinds), Suśr. **–°rogika**, mfn. affected with a disease called *kshudraroga*, Suśr. **–vaṇśā**, f. 'small reed,' the plant Mimosa pudica, L. **–vajra**, m. = *-kuliśa*, Gal. **–varvaṇā**, f. = *-daṇśikā*, L. **–vallī**, f. = *-potikā*, L. (v. l.) **–vārtākinī**, f. = *-kaṇṭakī*, L. **–vārtākī**, f. id., L. **–vāstukī**, f. a variety of Chenopodium, L. **-vaidehī**, f. the plant Scindapsus officinalis, L. **-śaṅkha**, m. a small conch shell, L. **-śaṇa-pushpikā**, f. a variety of Crotolaria, L. **-śarkarā**, f. a kind of sugar (coming from the Yavanāla), L. **-śarkarikā**, f. id., L. **-śārdūla**, m. 'a small tiger,' leopard, L. **-śīrsha**, m. the tree Celosia cristata (=*mayūra-śikhā*), L. **-śīla**, mfn. of a vile character, R. iii, 35, 60. **-śukti**, f. a bivalve shell (=*jala-ś°*), L. **-śuktikā**, f. id., L. **-śyāmā**, f. the tree Kaṭabhī, L. **-śleshmântaka**, m. the plant Cordia Myxa, L. **-śvāsa**, m. short breath, Suśr. **-śvetā**, f. =*-śyāmā*, Suśr. **-samācāra**, mfn. proceeding in a vile manner, Pañcat. **-sahā**, f. Phaseolus trilobus, Car. (v. l. *-mahā*); Suśr.; =*-ruhā*, L. **-suvarṇa**, n. bad gold, prince's metal, L. **-sûkta**, n. a short hymn, ŚāṅkhGṛ. ii, 7; (*as*), m. an author of short hymns, ĀśvGṛ. iii, 4, 2; ŚāṅkhGṛ. iv, 10. **-sphoṭa**, m. a pustule, L. **-svarṇa**, n. =*-suvarṇa*, Gal. **-han**, m. 'killing the wicked,' N. of Śiva. **-hiṅgulikā**, f. =*-kaṇṭakārī*, L. **-hiṅgulī**, f. id., W. **Kshudrâksha**, mfn. having small eyes, i. e. holes (as a net), MBh. v, 1160 & 4340 (v. l. *kshudrôksha*). **Kshudrâgni-mantha**, m. Premna spinosa (used for kindling fire), L. **Kshudrâcarita**, mfn. visited by common people (as a country), Āp. **Kshudrâñjana**, n. a kind of unguent (applied to the eyes in certain diseases), Suśr. **Kshudrâṇḍa**, m. 'born from minute eggs,' in comp. *-matsya-saṃghāta*, m. small fry, L. **Kshudrâtman**, mfn. of a low character, R. iii, 35, 68. **Kshudrântra**, n. the small cavity of the heart, W. **Kshudrâpāmārga**, °rgaka, m. Desmochæta atropurpurea (=*raktâp°*, a biennial plant), L. **Kshudrâmalaka**, n. Myrobalan, L.; *-saṃjña*, m., N. of a tree (=*karkaṭa*), L. **Kshudrâmbu-panasa**, m., v. l. for *kshudrâmla-p°*, L. **Kshudrâmra**, m. Mangifera sylvatica (*kośâmra*), L. **Kshudrâmla-panasa**, m. =*kshudra-panasa*, L. **Kshudrâmlā**, f. wood-sorrel, L.; a species of gourd, L. **Kshudrâmlikā**, f. =*kshudra-pattrā*, L. **Kshudrêksha**, for °*drâksha*, q. v. **Kshudrêṅgudī**, f. Alhagi Maurorum, L. **Kshudrêrvāru**, m. a species of gourd, L. **Kshudrâilā**, f. small cardamoms (different from those called *sûkshmâilā*), Suśr. **Kshudrôdumbarikā**, f. Ficus oppositifolia (=*kākôd°*), L. **Kshudrôpodaka-nāmnī**, f., N. of a pot-herb (a variety of Basella), L. **Kshudrôpodakī**, f., N. of a pot-herb, L. **Kshudrôlūka**, m. a kind of small owl, L.

Kshudraka, mfn. small, minute, Mn. viii, 297; short (as the breath), Suśr.; (*as*), m., N. of a prince (son of Prasenajit), BhP. ix, 12, 14; VP. (v. l. *kshudra-baka*); (*ās*), m. pl., N. of a people living by warfare (the 'Οξυδρακοι), MBh. ii, 1871; vi, 2106; Pāṇ. v, 3, 114, Kāś.; (*ikā*), f. a kind of gad-fly, L.; small bells employed for ornament (cf. *kshudra-ghaṇṭikā*), L.; (*am*), n., N. of a collection of Buddhist works. **-mānasa**, n., N. of a lake (in Kaśmīr), Suśr.

Kshudrala, mfn. minute, small, unimportant (applied to animals and diseases), g. *sidhmâdi*.

Kshudrīya, mfn., fr. °*drá*, g. *utkarâdi*.

Kshottavya, mfn. to be mashed (as a louse &c.), Pat. on Pāṇ. ii, 4, 8.

Kshottṛi, *ttā*, m. a pestle, any implement for grinding, Comm. on Uṇ. ii, 94.

Kshoda, *as*, m. stamping, shattering, crushing into pieces, Bālar.; pounding, grinding, W.; the stone or slab on which anything is ground or powdered, mortar &c., W.; any pounded or ground or pulverized substance, flour, meal, powder, dust, R. ii, 104, 12; Kād.; SkandaP.; Kathās.; a drop, Kād.; a lump, piece, ib.; multiplication, Gaṇit. **-kshama**, mfn. '(anything) that endures stamping or pounding,' solid, valid, Naish. vi, 113; Sāh. **-raja**, mfn. ground to dust, W.

Kshódas, n. (Naigh. i, 12) water in agitation, swell of the sea, rushing or stream of water, RV.

Kshodita, mfn. pounded, ground, W.; (*am*), n. any substance pulverized or ground, powder, dust, flour, meal, L.

Kshodiman, *ā*, m. minuteness, excessive smallness or inferiority, g. *pṛithv-ādi*.

Kshódishṭha, mfn. (see *kshudrá*; Pāṇ. vi, 4, 156) smallest, thinnest, MaitrS. i, 8, 6; GopBr. ii, 1, 9; very small or minute, W.

Kshodīyas, mfn. (see *kshudrá*; Pāṇ. vi. 4, 156) smaller, still inferior, Kāṭh. xv, 5; Hcar.; very fine or minute, Śiś. ii, 100 (Sāh.); Hcat. i, 1, 1.

Kshodya, mfn. to be stamped or trampled on, R. ii, 80, 10; to be pounded, W.

क्षुद् *kshud.* See 1. *kshut* & √1. *kshudh.*

क्षुध् 1. *kshudh*, cl. 4. P. *kshúdhyati* (p. *kshúdhyat*; impf. *ákshudhyat*; aor. Subj. *kshudhat*; fut. 1st *kshoddhā*, Pāṇ. vii, 2, 10, Siddh.; ind. p. *kshudhitvā*, Pāṇ. vii, 2, 52; Bhaṭṭ. ix, 39), to feel hungry, be hungry, RV. i, 104, 7; AV. ii, 29, 4; TS. v, 5, 10, 6; vii, 4, 3, 1; Bhaṭṭ.

2. **Kshut** (in comp. for 2. *kshúdh*). **-kshāma**, mfn. emaciated by hunger, MBh. i, 50, 1; Pañcat.; Bhartṛ.; Rājat.; *-kaṇṭha*, mfn. id., Pañcat. **-tṛit-parîta**, mfn. suffering from hunger and thirst, W. **-tṛiḍ-udbhava**, mfn. beginning to feel hungry and thirsty, W. **-tṛishânvita**, mfn. suffering from hunger and thirst, W. **-tṛishṇôpapīḍita**, mfn. id., Mn. viii, 67. **-para**, mfn. very hungry, MBh. xiii, 4463. **-parîta**, mfn. overcome with hunger, W. **-pipāsā-pariśrānta**, mfn. wearied by hunger and thirst, R. **-pipāsā-paritâṅga**, mfn. one whose body is affected with hunger and thirst, W. **-pipāsârta**, mfn. afflicted with hunger and thirst, W. **-pipāsita**, mfn. hungry and thirsty, Mn. viii, 93. **-pratīkāra**, m. allaying hunger, eating, Mn. x, 105. **-sambādha** (*kshút-*), mfn. suffering from famine, TS. vii, 4, 11, 2.

Kshud (in comp. for 2. *kshúdh*). **-roga**, m. pain of hunger, Pañcat. **-vat**, mfn. hungry, L.

2. **Kshudh**, *t*, f. hunger, RV.; AV. &c.

Kshudhā, f. (g. *ajâdi*, Gaṇar. 40) id., Nal.; Pañcat.; a mystical N. of the letter *y*, RāmatUp. **-kara**, mfn. causing hunger, Vedântas.; Dhūrtas. **-kuśala**, m., N. of a tree, L. **-dhvaṇsa**, m. allaying hunger, W. **-nāśana**, n. 'allaying hunger,' food, Gal. **-°nvita** (°*dhân°*), mfn. afflicted with hunger, W. **-pīḍita**, mfn. id., W. **-°bhijanana** (°*dhâbh°*), for *kshutâbh°* (q. v.), L. **-mārá**, m. death caused by starvation, AV. iv, 17, 6 f. **-°rta** (°*dhâr°*), mfn. =°*dhânvita*, Mn. x, 107; MBh.; Hit. **-°rdita** (°*dhâr°*), mfn. id., MBh. **-vat**, mfn. =*-kara*, W. **-°vishṭa** (°*dhâv°*), mfn. affected by hunger, W. **-śānti**, f. allaying hunger, satiety, satisfaction, Bhartṛ. ii, 23. **-sāgara**, m. a kind of drug (used to stimulate the appetite), L.

Kshudhālu, mfn. hungry, continually hungry, Pañcat. i; VarBṛS. lxviii, 110 & 114; ci, 9.

Kshudhi, *is*, m., N. of a son of Kṛishṇa, BhP. x, 61, 16.

Kshudhita, mfn. hungered, Pāṇ. vii, 2, 52; (g. *tārakâdi*) hungry, ChUp.; MBh.; R.; Suśr.; Ragh.

Kshun (in comp. for 2. *kshúdh*). **-nivṛitti**, f. cessation of hunger, appeasing of appetite, W. **-mat**, mfn. hungry, Veṇīs. vi.

Kshódhuka, mfn. hungry, TS. i, v, vi; ŚBr. xii.

क्षुधुन *kshudhuna*, *ās*, m. pl., N. of a barbarous race, Uṇ. iii, 55.

क्षुप् *kshup*, cl. 6. P. *kshupati*, to be depressed or afraid, R. vii, 76, 34.

क्षुप *kshupa*, *as*, m. a bush, shrub (a small tree with short branches and roots, W.), Yājñ. ii, 229; MBh.; R. ii, 25, 7; VarBṛS.; N. of an old king (son of Prasaṃdhi and father of Ikshvāku), MBh.; N. of a son of Kṛishṇa by Satya-bhāmā, Hariv. 9183 (v. l. *kṛipa*); N. of a mountain westward from Dvārakā, ib. 8950 (v. l. *a-kshaya*); (*ā*), f. a bush, shrub, Suśr. **-doḍa-mushṭi**, m. Hoya viridiflora, L. **Kshupâlu**, for *anūpâlu*.

Kshupaka, *as*, *ā*, m. f. a bush, shrub, Suśr.

Kshúmpa, *as*, m. id., RV. i, 84, 8 (=*ahi-cchattraka*, Nir. v, 16).

क्षुभ् 1. *kshubh*, cl. 1. Ā. *kshobhate* (only once, ChUp.), cl. 4. P. Ā. *kshubhyati* [MBh. &c.], °*te* [Nir. v, 16; MBh. &c.], cl. 5. P. (only Pot. 3. pl. *kshubhnuyur*, JaimBr.), cl. 9. P. *kshubhnāti* (only Bhaṭṭ. according to Pāṇ. viii, 4, 39; perf. P. *cukshobha*, BhP.; *cukshubhe*, MBh.; R.; Ragh. &c.: Cond. Ā. *akshobhishyata*, Bhaṭṭ. xxi, 6), to shake, tremble, be agitated or disturbed, be unsteady, stumble (literally and metaphorically): Caus. P. *kshobhayati*, rarely Ā. °*te*, to agitate, cause to shake, disturb, stir up, excite, Mn. viii; MBh.; R. &c.: Desid. of Caus., see *cukshobhayishu*; [cf. Cambro-Brit. *hwbiau*, 'to make a sudden push;' Gk. κοῦφος; Mod. Germ. *schiebe*.]

Kshubdha, mfn. agitated, shaken, MBh. iii, 12544; expelled (as a king), Pāṇ. vii, 2, 18, Siddh.; agitated (mentally), excited, disturbed (in comp. with *citta* or *manas*), Suśr.; (*as*), m. the churning-stick, Pāṇ. vii, 2, 18; a kind of coitus. **-tā**, f. agitation, Bhartṛ. iii, 94. **Kshubdhârṇava**, m. a stormy ocean, W.

2. **Kshúbh**, f. (only instr. °*bhā́*) a shake, push, RV. v, 41, 13.

Kshubhā, f. a kind of weapon ['the deity that presides over punishment,' Sch.], MBh. iii, 199.

Kshubhita, mfn. agitated, shaken, tossed, set in motion, MBh.; R.; Suśr.; Vikr.; Kathās.; agitated (mentally), disturbed, frightened, alarmed, afraid (mostly in comp.), R.; Pañcat.; Kathās.; angry, enraged, W.

Kshobha, *as*, m. shaking, agitation, disturbance, tossing, trembling, emotion, MBh.; R.; Ragh.; Vikr.; Megh. &c.; (in dram.) an emotion that is the cause of any harsh speeches or reproaches, Sāh. 471 & 480; (cf. *bala-ksh°*.)

Kshobhaka, mfn. shaking, causing agitation, VP. i, 2, 31; (*as*), m., N. of a mountain in Kāmâkhyā (sacred to the goddess Durgā), KālP.

Kshóbhaṇa, mfn. shaking, agitating, disturbing, causing emotion, RV. x, 103, 1; R. iii, 36, 10; (*as*), m., N. of Śiva, MBh. xii, 10384; of Vishṇu, ib. xiii, 6990; N. of one of the five arrows of the god of love, Gīt. viii, 1, Sch.

Kshobhayitṛi, mfn. one who gives the first impulse for anything, Bādar. ii, 2, 8, Sch.

Kshobhiṇī, f. (in music) N. of a Śruti.

Kshobhya, mfn. to be agitated or disturbed (ifc.), Kathās. lv, 120.

क्षुमत् *kshu-mát.* See 2. *kshú.*

क्षुमा *kshumā́*, f., N. of an arrow ('causing to tremble,' for *kshubhā*?, Comm.), VS. x, 8; N. of several plants (linseed, Linum usitatissimum; a sort of flax, Bengal San, *śaṇa*; the Indigo plant; a sort of creeper), L.; (cf. *kshauma*.)

क्षुम्प् *kshump*, cl. 1. P. *kshúmpati*, to go, Naigh. ii, 14.

क्षुम्प *kshúmpa.* See *kshupa.*

क्षुर् *kshur*, cl. 6. P. *kshurati*, to cut, dig, scratch, Dhātup. xxviii, 54; to make lines or furrows, ib.; (cf. √*chur*.)

Kshurá, *as*, m. (fr. √*kshṇu*?; cf. Gk. ξυρόν) a razor, RV. i, 166, 10; viii, 4, 16; x, 28, 9; AV.; ŚBr. &c.; a razor-like barb or sharp blade attached to an arrow, R. iii, 72, 14; (cf. *-pra*) Asteracantha longifolia, L.; =*-pattra*, L.; a thorny variety of Gardenia or Randia, L.; Trilobus lanuginosus, L.; (for *khura*) the hoof of a cow, W.; (for *khura*) a horse's hoof, W.; (for *khura*) the foot of a bedstead, L.; (*ī*), f. a knife, dagger (cf. *churī*), L.; (mfn.) =*kshura-vat*, 'having claws or hoofs,' Sāy. on RV. x, 28, 9. **-karṇī**, f., N. of one of the mothers in Skanda's retinue, MBh. ix, 2643. **-karman**, n. the operation of shaving, VarBṛS. **-kṛitya**, n. id., Gobh. iii, 1, 22. **-klṛipta**, mfn. shaved, Kathās. xii, 168. **-kriyā**, f. the employment of a razor, Pañcat. **-catushṭaya**, n. the four things necessary for shaving (viz. *kshura*, *nava-kuśa-tṛiṇāni*, *try-eṇī śalalī*, *āpaḥ*), Kāty-Śr. v, 1, Paddh. **-dhāná**, n. a razor-case, ŚBr. xiv. **-dhāra**, mfn. razor-edged, sharp as a razor, MBh. iv, 168; xiii, 3259; (*as*), m. a sharp-edged arrow, ib. iv, 2063. **-dhārā**, f. the edge of a razor, MBh. xiii, 2230; (pl.) R. vii, 21, 15; N. of a hell, Buddh. L. **-nakshatra**, n. any lunar mansion that is auspicious for shaving, VarBṛS. iic, 12. **-pattra**, n. Saccharum Sara (*śara*), L. **-pattrika**, f., N. of a pot-herb (Beta bengalensis), L. **-pavi** (°*rá-*), mfn. sharp-angled, sharp-edged, very sharp, AV. xii, 5, 20 & 55; TS.; ŚBr.; Suparṇ.; (*is*), m. a sharp-edged wheel-band, MaitrS. i, 10, 14 (=Kāṭh. xxxvi, 8; =Nir. v, 5); N. of a sacrifice performed in one day (*ekâha*), ŚāṅkhŚr.; (*am*), n., N. of several Sāmans, ĀrshBr. **-pra**, mfn. sharp-edged like a razor, BhP. iii, 13, 30; (*as*), m. a sharp-edged arrow, MBh. iii, 14892; iv, 1732; Ragh. ix, 62; xi, 29; BhP.; Śāntiś.; Devīm.; a sharp-edged knife (*tīkshṇa-śastra*, ed. Bomb.), Pañcat. i; a sharp-edged arrow-head, ŚārṅgP.; a sort of hoe or weeding spade, W.; *-ga*, n. a sharp-edged arrow, L. **-bhaṭṭa**, m., N. of a man, Sāy. (v. l. *pur°*). **-bhāṇḍa**, n. =*-dhāná*, Pañcat. i. **-bhṛishṭi**

(°*rá-*), f. furnished with sharp angles, AV. xii, 5, 66. **-mardin**, m. a barber, L. **Kshurâṅga**, m. Trilobus lanuginosus, L. **Kshurâṅgaka**, m. id., Gal. **Kshurâbhraka**, N. of particular clouds, VarBṛS. xxxiv, 7. **Kshurârpaṇa**, m., N. of a mountain, VarBṛS. xiv, 20.

Kshuraka, *as*, m. = °*râṅga*, Suśr.; Bhpr.; several other plants (Asteracantha longifolia; the tree Tilaka; = *bhūtâṅkuśa*), L.; the hoof of a cow, L.; N. of particular clouds, VarBṛS.; (*ikā*), f. (cf. *churikā*) a knife, dagger, Rājat. v, 437; Kathās. liv, 40; a small razor, W.; a sort of earthen vessel, L.; = *kshura-pattrikā*, L.

Kshurikā (f. of °*raka*, q. v.) **-pattra**, m. = *kshura-p*°, L. **-phala**, n. the blade (of a dagger), L. **Kshurikôpanishad**, f., N. of an Up. belonging to the AV.

Kshurin, *ī*, m. a barber, L.; (*iṇī*), f. the wife of a barber, L.; the plant Mimosa pudica, L.

Kshora, *as*, m. the act of shaving, Vop. (Dhātup. xxviii, 52).

क्षुलिक *kshulika*, for *kshullaká*, q. v.

क्षुल्ल *kshulla*, mfn. (originally a Prākṛit form of *kshudrá*; derived fr. 2. *kshúdh* and √*lā*, Pāṇ. vi, 2, 39, Kāś.) small, little, minute, inferior, BhP. **-tāta**, m. (= *kshudra-t*°) the younger brother of a father, L. **-tātaka**, m. the father's brother, L.

Kshullaká, mf(*ā*)n. (Naigh. iii, 2) little, small, AV. ii, 32, 5; TS.; ŚBr. i; BhP.; low, vile, L.; poor, indigent, L.; wicked, malicious, abandoned, L.; hard, L.; youngest, L.; pained, distressed, L.; (*as*), m. a small shell, L.; N. of a prince, VP. (v. l. *kshulika*); (*am*), n. a sort of play or game (= *mushṭi-dyūta*), L. **-kāleya**, n., N. of a Sāman, ĀrshBr. **-tāpaścitta**, n. the shortest one of the four kinds of Tāpaścitta, ĀśvŚr. xii, 5; KātyŚr.; ŚāṅkhŚr. **-vātsapra**, n., N. of a Sāman, ĀrshBr. **-vaiśvadeva**, n. (cf. *mahā-v*°), Pāṇ. vi, 2, 39. **-vaishṭambha**, n., N. of a Sāman, ĀrshBr.

क्षुवत् *kshuvat*. See √1. *kshu*.

क्षेड *ksheḍa*, °*ḍita*, for *ksheveḍa*, °*ḍita*, q. v.

क्षेण *kshenā́*. See 1. *kshayaṇā́*.

क्षेतिवत् *ksheti-vat*, mfn. containing a form of √2. *kshi* (which forms the 3. sg. *kshéti*), AitBr. v, 20 & 21.

क्षेत्र *kshétra*, *am*, n. (√2. *kshi*) landed property, land, soil (*kshétrasya páti*, 'lord of the soil,' N. of a kind of tutelary deity, RV.; AV. ii, 8, 5; also *kshétrasya pátnī*, 'mistress of the soil,' & *kshétrāṇām páti*, 'the lord of the soil,' N. of tutelary deities, AV. ii, 12, 1; VS. xvi, 18); 'soil of merit,' a Buddha or any holy person, Divyâv.; a field (e. g. °*tram* √*kṛi*, 'to cultivate a field,' Mn.; Yājñ. ii, 158; cf. *sasya-ksh*°), RV. &c.; place, region, country, RV.; AV. iii, 28, 3; TS. vii; Suśr.; Megh.; Vet.; a house, L.; a town, L.; department, sphere of action, MBh. xiv, 126; R. &c.; place of origin, place where anything is found, Yogas. ii, 4; Suśr.; BhP. viii, 12, 33; a sacred spot or district, place of pilgrimage (as Benares &c.; often ifc.), BrahmaP.; an enclosed plot of ground, portion of space, superficies (e. g. *sv-alpa-ksh*°, of a small circuit, Yājñ. ii, 156); (in geom.) a plane figure (as a triangle, circle, &c.) enclosed by lines, any figure considered as having geometrical dimensions, Gol.; a diagram, W.; a planetary orbit, Gaṇit.; a zodiacal sign, Sūryas.; an astrological mansion, VarBṛS.; VarBṛ. i, xi; (in chiromancy) certain portions marked out on the palm, VarBṛS. lxviii, 1; 'fertile soil,' the fertile womb, wife, Mn.; Yājñ. ii, 127; MBh.; R.; Śak.; BhP.; the body (considered as the field of the indwelling soul), Yājñ. iii, 178; Bhag. xiii, 1 & 2; Kum. vi, 77; (in Sāṃkhya phil.) = *a-vyakta* (q. v.), Tattvas.; (*ī*), f. only dat. °*triyai* for °*triyāt* (AV. ii, 10, 1), TBr. ii, 5, 6, 1; [cf. *á-ksh*°, *anya-* & *kuru-kshetrá*, *karma-ksh*°, *deva-ksh*°, *dharma-ksh*°, *raṇa-ksh*°, *siddha-ksh*°, *su-ksh*°, *surêśvarī-ksh*°; cf. also Goth. *haithi*, Them. *haithjo*; Germ. *Heide*.] **-kara**, mfn. cultivating a field, Pāṇ. iii, 2, 21; (*as*), m. a husbandman, ib. **-karkaṭī**, f. a kind of gourd, L. **-karman**, n. 'soil-cultivation,' in comp. °*rma-kṛit*, m. a husbandman, Kathās. xx, 11. **-karshaka**, m. soil-plougher, husbandman, Gaut. xvii, 6. **-gaṇita**, n. 'calculating plane figures,' geometry. **-gata**, mfn. 'relating to plane figures,' geometrical; °*tôpapatti*, f. a geometrical proof. **-cirbhiṭā**, f. a kind of gourd, L. **-ja**, mfn. produced in a field (as corn &c.), L.; (*as*), m. (scil. *putra*) 'born from the womb,' a son who is the offspring of the wife by a kinsman or person duly appointed to raise up issue to the husband (this is one of the twelve kinds of issue allowed by the old Hindū law), Baudh.; Gaut.; Mn. ix, 159 ff.; Yājñ. i, 68 & 69; ii, 128; (*ā*), f., N. of several plants (= *śveta-kaṇṭakārī*, *śaśâṇḍulī*, *go-mūtrikā*, *śilpikā*, *caṇikā*), L. **-jāta**, mfn. begotten on a wife by another, Yājñ. ii, 128. **-jeshá**, m. contest for landed property, acquisition of land, RV. i, 33, 15. **-jñá**, mfn. knowing localities, TBr. iii; AitBr.; TāṇḍyaBr.; ŚBr. xiii; ChUp.; familiar with the cultivation of the soil (as a husbandman), L.; clever, dexterous, skilful (with gen.), MBh. i, 3653; cunning, L.; (*as*), m. 'knowing the body,' i. e. the soul, the conscious principle in the corporeal frame, ŚvetUp.; Mn. viii, 96; xii, 12 & 14; Yājñ.; MBh.; Hariv. 11297, &c.; a form of Bhairava (or Śiva); N. of a prince, BhP. xii, 1, 4 (vv. ll. *kshatrâujas* & *kshemârcis*); (*ā*), f. a girl fifteen years old who personates the goddess Durgā at a festival of this deity. **-m-jayá**, mfn. conquering landed property, Maitr. ii, 2, 11. **-tattva**, n. a part of the work Smṛiti-tattva. **-tara** (*kshétra-*), n. any place or country very fit for being cultivated, ŚBr. i. **-tā**, f. the state of being a seat or residence, seat, place of residence, Kathās. iii, 3. **-da**, m. a form of Bhairava, L. **-dūtikā**, f. Solanum diffusum, Bhpr. **-dūtī**, f. id., L. **-devatā**, f. 'the deity of the fields,' N. of a serpent, Pañcat. **-dharman**, m., N. of a prince, VP. **-pa**, m. a deity protecting the fields, Pañcad.; = *-da*, L. **-pati**, m. (g. *aśva-paty-ādi*) the owner of a field, landowner, landlord, farmer, Hit.; = *kshétrasya páti* (see s. v. *kshétra*), Kāṭh. xxiv, 10. **-pada**, n. a place sacred to a deity (gen.), BhP. ix, 4, 20. **-parpaṭa**, m. Oldenlandia biflora or another species, L.; (*ī*), f. id., L. **-pāla**, m. a man employed to guard fields, Pañcat.; MārkP. &c.; a tutelary deity (their number is given as 49, Prayog.), Pañcat. iii; AgP.; Pañcad.; N. of Śiva; *-rasa*, m. a kind of medicinal drug, L. **-phala**, n. (in geom.) the superficial contents of a figure, Gol.; KātyŚr., Sch. **-bhakti**, f. the division of a field, Pāṇ. v, 1, 46, Kāś. **-bhūmi**, f. cultivated land, W. **-yamānikā**, f., N. of a plant (= *vacā*), L. **-raksha**, m. a man employed to guard fields from depredation, Pañcat. **-rāśi**, m. quantity represented by geometrical figures. **-ruhā**, f. a kind of gourd, L. **-liptā**, f. a minute of the ecliptic; °*ptī-karaṇa*, n. reducing to minutes of the ecliptic. **-vasudhā**, f. cultivated land, R. iii, 4, 17. **-víd**, mfn. (= *-jñá*) familiar with localities, RV. (also compar. *-vit-tara*, x, 25, 8); TS. v, 2, 8, 5; experienced, clever, skilful, Kum. iii, 50; knowing the body (as the soul), Tattvas.; (*t*), m. 'knowing the cultivation of fields,' a husbandman, W.; one who possesses spiritual knowledge, sage, W.; the soul, BhP. iv, 22, 37; (cf. *á-ksh*°.) **-vyavahāra**, m. ascertainment of the dimensions of a plane figure, Līl.; (in geom.) drawing a figure, W.; geometrical demonstration, W. **-saṃhitā**, f. any geometrical work like Euclid, W. **-samāsa**, m., N. of a Jaina work. **-sambhava**, m. 'growing on the fields,' Abelmoschus esculentus, L.; Ricinus communis; (*ā*), f. a kind of gourd (= *śaśâṇḍulī*), L. **-sambhūta**, m. 'growing on the fields,' a kind of grass, L. **-sāti** (*kshétra-*), f. acquisition of fields or land, RV. vii, 19, 3; (cf. i, 112, 22.) **-sādhas**, m. one who divides the fields, who fixes the landmarks, RV. iii, 8, 7 & viii, 31, 14 (Nir. ii, 2). **-sīmā**, f. the boundary of a field or holy place, W. **-stha**, mfn. residing at a sacred place, W. **Kshetrâṅśa**, m. a degree of the ecliptic, Sūryas. **Kshetrâjīva**, mfn. living by agriculture, L.; (*as*), m. a cultivator, L. **Kshetrâdhidevatā**, f. the tutelary deity of any consecrated ground, Prayog. **Kshetrâdhipa**, m. id.; the regent of a sign of the zodiac. **Kshetrâmalakī**, f. (= *bhumy-ām*°) Flacourtia cataphracta L. **Kshetrā-sā́**, mfn. gaining or procuring land, RV. iv, 38, 1. **Kshetrêkshu**, m. Andropogon bicolor (= *yāvanāla*), L. **Kshetrôpêksha**, m., N. of a son of Śva-phalka, BhP. ix, 24, 15.

Kshetrika, mfn. relating to a field, having a field, agrarian, W.; (*as*), m. the owner of a field, Gaut.; Mn. viii, 241 ff.; ix, 53 f.; a farmer, cultivator, W.; a husband, Nār.; Mn. ix, 145.

Kshetrin, mfn. owning a field, cultivating land, agricultural, W.; (*ī*), m. the owner of a field, Mn. ix, 51 f.; Yājñ. ii, 161; (cf. also *a-ksh*°); an agriculturist, husbandman, L.; a husband, Mn. ix, 32; Śak. v; the soul, Bhag. xiii, 33; (*iṇī*), f. Rubia Munjista, L.

Kshetriyá, mfn. 'organic' (as a disease), incurable ('curable in a future body, i. e. incurable in the present life,' Pāṇ. v, 2, 92), Kpr.; (*as*), m. one who seduces other men's wives, adulterer, L.; (*ám*), n. (*as*, m., L.) an organic and incurable disease, AV.; meadow grass, herbage, L.; (*ā́ṇi*), n. pl. the environs of a place, AV. ii, 14, 5. **-nā́śana**, mf(*ī*)n. removing a chronic disease, AV. ii, 8, 2.

Kshetrī- √1. **kṛi**, to occupy, take possession or become master of (acc.), Kād.; AgP. xxx, 22.

Kshetrīya, Nom. P. °*yati*, to desire another man's wife, Śāntiś. i, 26.

क्षेद *ksheda*, *as*, m. sorrowing, moaning, W.

क्षेप *kshepa*, °*paka*, °*pana*, &c. See √*kship*.

क्षेम *kshéma*, mf(*ā*)n. (√2. *kshi*) habitable; giving rest or ease or security, MBh.; R.; at ease, prosperous, safe, W.; (*as*), m. basis, foundation, VS. xviii, 7; AV. iii, 12, 1 & iv, 1, 4; ŚBr. xiii; KapS. i, 46; residing, resting, abiding at ease, RV. x; AV. xiii, 1, 27; TS. iii; viii; (*as*, *am*), m. n. (Ved. only m.; g. *ardharcâdi*), safety, tranquillity, peace, rest, security, any secure or easy or comfortable state, weal, happiness, RV.; AV.; VS.; Mn.; MBh. &c. (*kshéma* & *yóga* [or *pra-yuj*], rest and exertion, enjoying and acquiring, RV.; VS. xxx, 14; PārGṛ.; MBh. xiii, 3081; cf. *kshema-yoga* & *yoga-ksh*°; *kshemaṃ te*, 'peace or security may be to thee' [this is also the polite address to a Vaiśya, asking him whether his property is secure, Mn. ii, 127], Śāntiś. ii, 18); final emancipation, L.; (*as*), m. a kind of perfume (= *caṇḍā*), L.; Ease or Prosperity (personified as a son of Dharma and Śānti, VP.; as a son of Titikshā, BhP. iv, 1, 51); N. of a prince, MBh. i, 2701; Divyâv. xviii; of a son of Śuci and father of Su-vrata, BhP. ix, 22, 46; N. of a kind of college (*maṭha*), Rājat. vi, 186; (*eṇa*), instr. ind. at ease; in security, safely, R.; Mṛicch.; Pañcat.; BhP.; (ifc. with *yathā*, R. ii, 54, 4); (*ais*), instr. pl. ind. id., MBh. xiii, 1519; (*ā*), f. a kind of perfume (= *kāshṭha-guggula* or *coraka*, Comm.), VarBṛS. il; N. of Durgā, L.; of another deity (= *kshemaṃ-karī*), DevīP.; of an Apsaras, MBh. i, 4818; (*am*), n., N. of one of the seven Varshas in Jambū-dvīpa, BhP. v, 20, 3. **-kara**, mfn. conferring peace or security or happiness, MBh. xiv, 973; (*ī*), f. a form of Durgā (cf. *kshemaṃ-k*°), VP. **-karṇa**, m., N. of a son of Maheśa (who composed, A. D. 1570, the work Rāga-mālā). **-karman**, mfn. = *-kara*, BhP. ii, 6, 5; N. of a prince, VāyuP. (v. l. *-dharman*, q. v.) **-kāma** (*kshéma-*), mfn. longing for rest, RV. x, 94, 12. **-kāra**, mfn. (Pāṇ. iii, 2, 44) = *-kara*, L. **-kāraka**, mfn. id., Pañcat. **-kutūhala**, n., N. of a medical work by Kshema-śarman. **-kṛit**, mfn. = *-kara*, Āp.; Cāṇ. **-gupta**, m., N. of a king of Kaśmīr, Rājat. vi, 150 ff. **-m-kara**, mfn. (= *-kāra*, Pāṇ. iii, 2, 44) = *-kara*, Cāṇ. (= ŚārṅgP.); Bhaṭṭ. vi, 105; (*as*), m., N. of a king of the Trigartas, MBh. iii, 15731; of a son of Brahma-datta (Udayana), Buddh.; of the author of a recension of Siṇhās.; of a mythical Buddha, Divyâv. xviii; (*ī*), f. Durgā, VP. v, 1, 83; N. of another goddess, DevīP.; of the sister of Brahma-datta's son Kshemaṃ-kara, Buddh. **-m-karin**, m. the Brāhmaṇī kite or Coromandel eagle (bird of good omen), Falco ponticerianus, Gal. **-jit**, m., N. of a prince, MatsyaP. (vv. ll. *kshatrâujas*, *kshemârcis*). **-tara**, n. a more comfortable state, greater happiness, Bhag. i, 46. **-taru**, m., N. of a tree, VarBṛS. **-darśin**, m., N. of a prince of the Kosalas, MBh. xii, 3060 ff. & 3850 ff. **-°darśīya**, mfn. relating to Kshema-darśin (as a tale, *itihāsa*), ib. 3849. **-dhanvan**, m., N. of a son of the third Manu Sāvarṇa, Hariv. 480; of a prince (son of Puṇḍarīka), Hariv. 824; BhP. ix, 12, 1; Ragh. xviii, 8; (cf. *-dhṛitvan*.) **-dharman**, v.l. for *-karman* (q. v.), BhP. xii, 1, 4. **-dhūrta**, *ās*, m. pl., N. of a people, VarBṛS. **-dhūrti**, m., N. of a warrior, MBh. i, 67, 64 (v. l. *-mūrti*); vii, 4013 ff. **-dhṛitvan**, m. (= *-dhanvan*) N. of a son or descendant of Puṇḍarīka, TāṇḍyaBr. xxii. **-phalā**,

f. Ficus oppositifolia, L. **-bhūmi**, m., N. of a prince, VāyuP. (v. l. *deva-bh°*). **-mūrti**, m., N. of a prince, MBh. i, 2700 (v. l. *-dhūrti*) & 2735; *-tīrtha*, n., N. of a Tirtha, SkandaP. **-yuktam**, ind. in a prosperous way, R. i, 13, 10. **-yoga**, *au*, m. du. rest and exertion, AitBr. **-rāja**, m. (probably = *°mêndra*, q. v.) N. of a Śaiva philosopher (pupil of Abhinava-gupta and author of the Stava-cintāmaṇi-vṛitti, the Sva-cchandôddyota, the Paramêśa-stotrâvalī-vṛitti, the Paramârtha-saṃgraha-vivṛitti, the Pratyabhijñā-hṛidaya, the Sāmba-pañcāśikā-vivaraṇa, and of other works). **-vat**, mfn. attended with tranquillity and security, prosperous, Pāṇ. Siddh.; (*ān*), m., N. of a prince, VP.; (*atī*), f., N. of a woman, Buddh.; of a locality. **-varman**, m., N. of a prince, VP. **-vāha**, m., N. of an attendant of Skanda, MBh. ix, 2568. **-vid**, m., N. of a prince, VP. **-vṛiksha**, m. = *-taru*, VarBṛS., Sch. **-vṛiddhi**, m., N. of a Sālva general, MBh. iii, 669 ff.; (*ayas*), m. pl., N. of a warrior family (the women are called *tanu-keśyas*), Pāṇ. vi, 3, 35, Vārtt. 5, Pat. **-vṛiddhin**, m., N. of a man, g. *bāhv-ādi*. **-śarman**, m., N. of an author. **-śūra**, m. 'a hero in a safe place,' a boaster, BhP. x, 4, 36. **Kshemâditya**, m., N. of a man. **Kshemâdhi**, m., N. of a prince of Mithilā, BhP. ix, 13, 23; (cf. *kshemâri*.) **Kshemânanda**, m., N. of an author. **Kshemā-phalā**, for *°ma-ph°*, L. **Kshemâri**, m. = *kshemâdhi*, VP. **Kshemârcis**, v. l. for *°ma-jit*, q. v. **Kshemā-vatī**, f., N. of a town, Divyâv. xviii. **Kshemêndra**, m., N. of a celebrated poet of Kaśmīr (surnamed Vyāsa-dāsa and flourishing in the middle of the eleventh century, author of the Bṛihat-kathā(-mañjarī), Bhārata-mañjarī, Kalā-vilāsa, Rāmāyaṇa-mañjarī or -kathā-sāra, Daśâvatāra-carita, Samaya-mātṛikā, Vyāsâshṭaka, Suvṛitta-tilaka, Loka-prakāśa, Nīti-kalpa-taru, Rājâvalī); N. of a Śaiva philosopher (who is probably identical with *-rāja*; he is the author of the Spanda-nirṇaya and Spanda-saṃdoha); N. of the author of the Aucityâlaṃkāra and of the Kavi-kaṇṭhâbharaṇa. **Kshemêśvara**, for *°mīśv°*, q. v.

Kshemaka, *as*, m. a kind of perfume (= *caura*), L.; N. of a Nāga, MBh. i, 1556; of a Rakshas, Hariv.; of an attendant of Śiva, L.; of an old king, MBh. ii, 117; of a son of Alarka (also called Sunītha), Hariv. 1749; of a son of Nirāmitra, MatsyaP.; of the last descendant of Parīkshit in the Kali-yuga, VP.; BhP. ix, 22, 42 f.; (*am*), n., N. of a Varsha in Plaksha-dvīpa ruled by Kshemaka, VP. ii, 4, 5.

Kshemayát, mfn. (pr. p. fr. Nom. P. *°ya* fr. *kshéma*) resting, RV. iii, 7, 2; granting rest or an abode, RV. iv, 33, 10 & v, 47, 4.

Kshemin, mfn. enjoying peace or security, safe, secure, MBh. (e. g. Nal. xii, 90); BhP. x, 88, 39; Kām. **Kshemīśvara**, m., N. of the author of the Caṇḍa-kauśika.

Kshemyá, mf(*ā*)n. (= *°ma*, Pāṇ. v, 4, 36, Vārtt. 5, Pat.) resting, at leisure, at ease, RV. x, 28, 5; AV. xii, 2, 49; VS. xvi, 33 (*kshémya*); ŚBr. vi, 7, 4, 7; xiii, 1, 4, 3; PārGṛ.; yielding peace and tranquillity (as a country; 'healthy,' W.), Mn. vii, 212; giving peace and tranquillity, MBh. xiv, 1691; prosperous, auspicious, VarBṛS.; (*as*), m., N. of Śiva, MBh. xiv, 194; N. of several princes [a son of Sunītha and father of Ketumat, Hariv. 1592 f.; 1750; a son of Ugrâyudha and father of Su-vīra, ib. 1084; VP.; BhP. ix, 21, 29; (= *kshema*) a son of Śuci and father of Suvrata, VP.]; (*ā*), f. a form of Durgā, VP. v, 1, 83; (*ám*), n. resting, TS. v, 2, 1, 7.

क्षेय *ksheya*. See √4. *kshi*.

क्षेव् *kshev*, for √*kshiv*, q. v.

क्षेष्णु *ksheshṇú*. See √4. *kshi*.

क्षै *kshai*, cl. 1. P. *kshāyati*, to burn, catch or take fire, KātyŚr. xxv, 8, 21, Sch.; = √4. *kshi*, Dhātup. xxii, 16: Caus. *kshāpayati* (Impv. *kshāpáya*), to singe, burn, AV. xii, 5, 51; TāṇḍyaBr. xvii, 5, 7.

Kshāti, *is*, f. singeing, heat, RV. vi, 6, 5.

Kshāmá, mf(*ā*)n. burning to ashes, charring, MaitrS. i, 8, 9; (Pāṇ. viii, 2, 53) scorched, singed, KātyŚr.; Jaim.; dried up, emaciated, wasted, thin, slim, slender, Yājñ. i, 80; MBh.; R.; Megh. &c.; weak, debilitated, infirm, slight (especially applied to the voice), R. iii, 58, 14; Suśr.; Amar.; Rājat. v, 219. **-karsha-miśrá**, mfn. (= *sá-kshāma-karsha*, ŚBr. iii) mingled with scorched or singed particles that have been scratched off, ŚBr. ii, 5, 2, 46. **-kshāma**, mfn. quite emaciated, Śak. iii, 7. **-tā**, f. emaciation, thinness, W.; debility, W. **-tva**, n. id., W. **-vat** (*kshā́ma-*), mfn. burnt to coal, charred (said of Agni), MaitrS.; TS. ii; AitBr. vii, 6; KātyŚr. xxv; ŚāṅkhŚr.; (*tī*), f. (scil. *ishṭi*) N. of a particular sacrificial ceremony, BhavP. **Kshāmâṅga**, mfn. having a slender body, Bhām. **Kshāmā-prastha**, m., N. of a town, g. *mālâdi*. **Kshāmâśya**, n. any diet or any state of the body (as menstruation) incompatible with a particular medical treatment, L. (v. l. *kshamasya*).

2. **Kshāmi**, *is*, m. patr. fr. *°ma*, Pāṇ. viii, 2, 1, Kāś. **Kshāmin**, mfn. (= *kshāmo 'syâsti*), ib. **Kshāmi-mat**, mfn. ib.

Kshāmī-√kṛi, to shorten, ŚārṅgP.

क्षैण्य *kshaiṇya*, *am*, n. (fr. *kshīṇa*), destruction, wasting away (ifc.), Rāj. v, 262; leanness, slenderness, emaciation, W.

Kshaiti, patr. fr. *kshitá*, Pāṇ. viii, 2, 42, Vārtt. 4.

क्षैत *kshaitá*, *as*, m. (fr. 2. *kshití*), the chief of a race, prince, RV. ix, 97, 3. **-vat** (*kshaitá-*), mfn. princely, RV. vi, 2, 1.

Kshaitra, n. (fr. *kshétra*), landed property, RV. viii, 71, 12; a multitude of fields, g. *bhikshâdi*.

Kshaitrajitya, *am*, n. (fr. *kshetra-jit*), acquisition of land, victorious battle, VS. xxxiii, 60.

Kshaitrajña, *am*, n. (fr. *kshetra-jñá*, g. *yuvâdi*), spirituality, nature of the soul, W.; the knowledge of the soul, W.

Kshaitrajñya, *am*, n. (g. *brāhmaṇâdi*), id., W.

Kshaitrapata, mf(*ī*, g. *aśva-paty-ādi*)n. relating to the owner of a field (*kshetra-pati*), ĀpŚr.

Kshaitrapatya, *am*, n. (fr. *kshetra-pati*), dominion, property, RV. i, 112, 13; (*°tyá*), mfn. belonging to the lord of the soil, TS. i, 8, 20, 1; ii, 2, 1, 5; ŚBr. v, 5, 2, 7; TBr. i, 4, 4, 2; KātyŚr. xv.

क्षैप्र *kshaipra*, mfn. (fr. *kshiprá*), 'produced by speaking quickly,' a term for a kind of Sandhi produced by changing the first of two concurrent vowels to its semivowel, RPrāt.; the Svarita accent on a syllable formed with that Sandhi, RPrāt.; VPrāt.; APrāt.; (*am*), n. quickness, speediness, g. *pṛithv-ādi*. **-yukta**, mfn. joined by the Kshaipra Sandhi, W. **-varṇa**, mfn. containing a semivowel, RPrāt. **Kshaiprī-bhāvya**, mfn. id., RPrāt. vii, 5.

Kshaiprya, n. quickness, Bādar. iv, 3, 1, Sch.

क्षैमवृद्धि *kshaimavṛiddhi*, *is*, m. a patr. fr. *kshema-vṛiddhin*, gaṇas *gahâdi* and *raivatikâdi*.

Kshaimavṛiddhīya, mfn. fr. *°ddhi*, ib.

क्षैरकलम्भि *kshairakalambhi*, *is*, m. a patr. fr. *kshīra-kalambha*, N. of a teacher, Lāṭy. x, 10, 20.

Kshairahrada, *as*, m. patr. fr. *kshīra-hr°*, g. *śivâdi*.

Kshaireya, mf(*ī*)n. prepared with milk, milky, Pāṇ. iv, 2, 20; (*ī*), f. a dish prepared with milk, L.

क्षोट् *kshoṭ*, cl. 10. P. *kshoṭayati*, to throw, cast, Dhātup. xxxv, 23; (cf. √*khoṭ*.)

क्षोड *kshoḍa*, *as*, m. the post to which an elephant is fastened, L.; (cf. *a-kshobha*.)

क्षोण *kshoṇá*, mfn. immovable [or (*as*), m. 'a kind of lute,' Sāy.; = *kshayaṇa*, Nir. v, 6], RV. i, 117, 8; (*ī́*), f. (nom. sg. also *°ṇis*, nom. pl. *°ṇís*, once *°ṇáyas*, RV. x, 22, 9) a multitude of men, people (as opposed to the chief), RV.; the earth, R. i, 42, 23; BhP. v, 18, 28 & viii, 6, 2; (*ī́*), f. Ved. nom. du. 'the two sets of people,' i. e. the inhabitants of heaven and earth ['heaven and earth,' Naigh. iii, 30], RV. ii, 16, 3; viii, 7, 22; 52, 10; 99, 6.

Kshoṇi, *is*, f. (= *°ṇī*) the earth, BhP. iv, 21, 35; (*áyas*), f. pl., see *kshoṇá*. **-pati**, m. 'earth-lord,' a king. **-pāla**, m. 'earth-protector,' id., Prasannar. vii, 65. **Kshoṇîndra**, m. = *°ṇi-pati*.

Kshoṇī (f. of *°ṇá*, q. v.) **-deva**, m. 'earth-god,' a Brāhman. **-dhara-miśra**, m., N. of a commentator. **-pati**, m. = *°ṇi-p°*, Kathās. vc, 92. **-maṇḍala**, n. the orb of the earth, Bālar. **-maya**, mfn. containing or representing the earth (said of Vishṇu in his fish-incarnation), BhP. ii, 7, 12. **-ramaṇa**, m. 'earth-lord,' a king, Vāsant. **-ruh**, m. 'growing from the earth,' a tree, Prasannar. iv, 6.

Kshauṇī, f. the earth, BhP. iii, 14, 3 & 24, 42. **-tala**, n. the surface of the earth, W. **-prācīra**, m. 'surrounding the earth,' the ocean, L. **-bhuj**, m. 'enjoying the earth,' a king, Śāntiś. i, 10. **-bhṛit**, m. 'upholder of the earth,' mountain, Uttarar. ii, 29.

क्षोत्तव्य *kshottavya*, &c. See √*kshud*.

Kshoda, **kshódas**, *°dita*, &c. See ib.

क्षोधुक *kshódhuka*. See √1. *kshudh*.

क्षोभ *kshobha*, *°bhaka*, &c. See √*kshubh*.

क्षोम *kshoma*, *as*, *am*, m. n. (√*kshu*, Uṇ. i, 138) a room on the house-top (*aṭṭa*), Comm. on L.; (*am*), n. (for *kshauma*) linen (*dukūla*), L.

Kshomaka, *as*, m. = *kshaum°*, L.; (cf. *kshema*.)

क्षोर *kshora*. See √*kshur*.

क्षौणी *kshauṇī*. See *kshoṇá* above.

क्षौद्र *kshaudra*, *as*, m. (fr. *kshudra* & *°drā*), Michelia Campaka, MBh. iii, 11569; N. of a mixed caste (son of a Vaideha and a Māgadhī), MBh. xiii, 2584; (*am*), n. smallness, minuteness, g. *pṛithv-ādi*; honey, species of honey, L.; water, L.; N. of a Sūtra of the SV. **-jā**, f. honey-sugar, L. **-dhātu**, m. a kind of mineral substance (= *mākshika*), L. **-priya**, m., N. of a tree (species of Bassia), L. **-meha**, m. the disease diabetes mellitus, Suśr. **-°mehin**, mfn. affected with that disease, ib. **-śarkarā**, f. = *-jā*, L.

Kshaudraka, *as*, m. patr. fr. *kshudr°*, Pāṇ. iv, 1, 168, Vārtt. 1, Pat. (pl.); (*ī*), f. of *kshaudrakya*, Pāṇ. v, 3, 114, Kāś.; (*am*), n. (fr. *kshudrā*), honey, Gal.

Kshaudrakamālava, mf(*ī*)n. formed by Kshudrakas and Mālavas (an army), Pāṇ. iv, 2, 45, Pat.

Kshaudraka-mālavaka, mfn., ib.

Kshaudrakya, *as*, m. patr. fr. (or a servant of) *°ka*, Pāṇ. iv, 1, 168, Vārtt. 1, Pat.; (mfn.) small, L.

Kshaudreya, *am*, n. (fr. *kshudrā*), wax, L.

क्षौम *kshauma*, mf(*ī*)n. (fr. *kshumā*; = *kshoma*, Uṇ. i, 138), made of linen, linen, Lāṭy.; Gobh.; PārGṛ. &c.; covered with linen, W.; prepared from linseed (as oil), Suśr.; (*as*, *am*), m. n. = *aṭṭa* (an airy room on the top of a house, apartment on the roof, back of an edifice, fortified place in front of a building, building of a particular form, W.; cf. *kshoma*), L.; (*ī*), f. flax (Linum usitatissimum), L.; (*am*), n. linen cloth or garment, KātyŚr.; Gaut.; Mn. &c. (also = *dukūla*, L.); linseed, Suśr.; the flower of flax, L. **-maya**, mfn. made of linen, Hcat.

Kshaumaka, *as*, m. (cf. *kshom°*) a kind of perfume, L.

Kshaumika, mf(*ī*)n. made of linen, Kauś. 57.

क्षौर *kshaura*, mfn. (fr. *kshurá*), performed with a razor (with *karman*, 'shaving'), VarBṛS. iic, 12; (*as*), m. = *-mantra*, Sāy. on TS. i; (*ī*), f. a razor, W.; (*am*), n. shaving the head, shaving in general (*°raṃ* √1. *kṛi*, to shave, Hit.; *°raṃ*, Caus. √1. *kṛi*, to have one's self shaved, Hit.), Cāṇ. **-karaṇa**, n. shaving, Hit. **-karman**, n. id., Cāṇ.; (see also s. v. *kshaura*.) **-nakshatra**, n. (= *kshura-n°*) any lunar mansion auspicious for shaving, cf. VarBṛS. iic, 12. **-nirṇaya**, m., N. of a work. **-mantra**, *ās*, m. pl., N. of the formulas TS. i, 2, 1, 1 ff., Sāy. **-rksha** (*-ṛiksha*), n. = *-nakshatra*, VarYogay. ii, 35. **-vidhi**, m. = *-karaṇa*.

Kshaurapavya, mfn. (fr. *kshurá-pavi*), very sharp-edged, very sharp, BhP. vi, 5, 8 ('formed out of razors and thunderbolts,' Burnouf).

Kshaurika, *as*, m. a barber, shaver, L.

क्ष्णु *kshṇu*, cl. 2. P. *kshṇauti* (Dhātup. xxiv, 28; fut. 1st *kshṇavitā*, Pāṇ. vii, 2, 10, Siddh.; pr. p. *kshṇuvāná*), to whet, sharpen, AV. v, 20, 1; [cf. Gk. ξύω, ξυρόν, *kshurá*.]

Kshṇut. See *anyataḥ-* & *ubhayataḥ-kshṇút*.

Kshṇutá, mfn. whetted, sharpened, ŚBr. vi.

Kshṇótra, *am*, n. a whet-stone, RV. ii, 39, 7.

क्ष्मा *kshmā́*, f. (cf. 2. *kshám*; Naigh. i, 1; Nir. x, 7) the earth, R. iii, 35, 63; BhP.; Ragh.; Bhartṛ. &c.; (*ayā́*), instr. ind. (= 1. *kshamā́*) on the earth, RV.; VS. xxxiii, 92. **-°ṇśa** (*°mâṅ°*), m. a district of land, L. **-cakra**, n. the orb, Bālar. iii, 70. **-ja**, m. 'earth-born,' the planet Mars; n. the horizon, Gol. **-tala**, n. the surface of the earth, MārkP. xxiii, 47. **-dhara**, m. 'upholder of the earth,' a mountain, Mālatīm.; Bālar.; (hence) the number 'seven,' Gaṇit. **-dhṛiti**, m. 'one who has to support the earth,' a king, Rājat. v, 476. **-°nta** (*°mân°*), m. 'the ends of the earth,' i. e. the whole earth, Pañcat. **-pa**, m. 'earth-protector,' a king, Rājat. v, 314 & 457. **-pati**, m. 'earth-lord,' id., v, 59;

(ifc.) Gīt. i, 4. **-pāla**, m. = *-pa*, Prasannar.; Rājat. v, 319. **-bhartṛi**, m. = *-pati*, Daś. p. i. **-bhuj**, m. 'enjoying the earth,' a king, Rājat. v, 50. **-bhṛit**, m. (= *-dhara*) a mountain, BhP. x, 67, 7; Kathās.; = *-dhṛiti*, Pañcat.; Kathās. lxxiii, 330; Bālar. iii, 63. **-ruh**, m. 'growing from the earth,' a tree, Rājat. viii, 240. **-valaya**, m. n. = *-cakra*, Siṉhās.; (= *-ja*) the horizon, Gol. **-vṛisha**, m. 'earth-bull,' i. e. a mighty king, Rājat. v, 126. **-śayana**, n. lying or being buried in the earth, MBh. iii, 13456.
Kshmêśa, m. = *kshmā-pati*, VarBṛS. xix, 2.

क्ष्माय् *kshmāy*, cl. 1. Ā. °*yate* (impf. *akshmāyata* & perf. *cakshmāye*, Bhaṭṭ.), to shake, tremble, Dhātup. xiv, 45: Caus. P. *kshmāpayati* (Pāṇ. vii, 3, 36), to cause to shake, Bhaṭṭ. xvii, 85.
Kshmāyita, mfn. shaken, made to tremble, W.; trembling, W.
Kshmāyitṛi, mfn. (Pāṇ. iii, 2, 152, Kāś.) trembling, shaking, W.

क्ष्मील् *kshmīl*, cl. 1. P. °*lati*, to twinkle, close the eyelids, Dhātup. xv, 13; (cf. √*mīl*.)

क्ष्रौम् *kshraum*, ind. a mystic exclamation, BhP. v, 18, 8.

क्ष्विङ्का *kshviṅkā*, f. a kind of animal, RV. x, 87, 7; ('red-mouthed monkey,' Sch.) TS. v, 5, 15, 1.

क्ष्विड् 1. *kshviḍ* (or 1. *kshvid*), cl. 1. P. *kshveḍati* (Suśr.; Pot. °*ḍet*, Mn. iv, 64; pr. p. °*ḍat*, R. iv, 45, 8; *kshvedati*, Kāṭh.), to utter an inarticulate sound, hum, murmur, growl, roar, hiss, whistle, rattle: Caus. P. *kshveḍayati*, id., MBh. iii, 12379.
1. **Kshviṇṇa**, mfn. (fr. √1. *kshvid*, Kāś. on Pāṇ. iii, 2, 187 & vii, 2, 16), sounded inarticulately, Pat. Introd. on Vārtt. 18.
1. **Kshveḍa**, mfn. curved, crooked, bent, L.; wicked, depraved, W.; difficult to be approached, L.; (*as*), m. singing or buzzing in the ear (from hardening of the wax &c.; cf. *karṇa-ksh*°), Suśr.; sound, noise, L.; a Cucurbitaceous plant (Luffa pentandra or acutangula, = *pīta-ghoshā*), Car.; a mystical N. of the letter *m* (also *kshvela*, RāmatUp.; cf. *visha* = 2. *kshveḍa*); (*ā*), f. 'the roaring of a lion' or 'battle-cry,' L.; a bamboo rod or stake, L.; a kind of Cucurbitaceous plant (= *kośātakī*), L.; (*am*), n. the flower of the Luffa or Ghosha plant, L.; the fruit of a red kind of swallow-wort, L.
Kshveḍana, *am*, n. hissing, Mn. iv, 64, Sch.; hissing pronunciation (of sibilants), RPrāt. xiv, 6.
1. **Kshveḍita**, *as*, *am*, m. n. (g. *ardharcâdi*) humming, murmuring, growling, MBh. i, 2820; Hariv. 13238 ff.; 'a lion's roaring' or 'battle-cry,' L.
Kshveḍin. See *gehe-kshv*°.

क्ष्विड् 2. *kshviḍ* (or 2. *kshvid* = √*svid*), cl. 1. Ā. *kshveḍate*, *kshvedate*, to be wet or unctuous, exude, emit sap, Dhātup. xviii, 4: cl. 4. P. *kshvidyati*, id., ib. xxvi, 134.
2. **Kshviṇṇa**, mfn. (fr. √2. *kshvid*), unctuous, W.
2. **Kshveḍa**, *as*, m. venom, poison, MBh. iii, 12389; Kuval.

क्ष्विद् *kshvid*. See √1. & 2. *kshviḍ*.
1. & 2. **Kshveda**, &c. See ib.

क्ष्वेडिका *kshveḍikā* = *kshvelikā*, q. v.
2. **Kshveḍita** = *kshvelita*, q. v.

क्ष्वेल् *kshvel*, cl. 1. P. °*lati* (v. l. *kvel*, Dhātup. xv, 32; probably fr. Prākṛit √*kel* = *krīḍ*), to leap, jump, play, R. v; vi; to shake, tremble, W.; [cf. Old Germ. *suillu*, *sual*, *suall*.]
Kshvelana, *am*, n. play, jest, BhP. xi, 17, 32.
Kshveli, *is*, f. (= *keli*) id., BhP. v, 1, 29; x, xi.
Kshvelikā, f. id., BhP. v, 8, 18; for *kshveḍikā* see *udaka-ksh*°.
Kshvelita, *am*, n. (also *as*, m., Pāṇ., Siddh.) id., BhP. x, 22, 12; (pl.) viii, 9, 11; (*kshveḍita*) MBh. xiv, 1760 (Sch.)

क्ष्वेल *kshvela*, for 1. *kshveḍa*, q. v.

क्ष्वेलन *kshvelana*, &c. See √*kshvel*.

ख KHA.

ख 1. *kha*, the second consonant of the alphabet (being the aspirate of the preceding consonant; often in MSS. & Inscr. confounded with *sha*).
-kāra, m. the letter or sound *kha*.

ख 2. *kha*, *as*, m. the sun, L.

ख 3. *khá*, *am*, n. (√*khan*) a cavity, hollow, cave, cavern, aperture, RV.; an aperture of the human body (of which there are nine, viz. the mouth, the two ears, the two eyes, the two nostrils, and the organs of excretion and generation), AV. xiv, 2, 1 & 6; Prāt.; KaṭhUp.; Gaut.; Mn. &c.; (hence) an organ of sense, BhP. viii, 3, 23; (in anat.) the glottis, W.; 'the hole made by an arrow,' wound, Mn. ix, 43; the hole in the nave of a wheel through which the axis runs, RV.; ŚBr. xiv; vacuity, empty space, air, ether, sky, ŚBr. xiv; PraśnUp.; Mn. xii, 120 &c.; heaven, L.; Brahma (the Supreme Spirit), W.; (in arithm.) a cypher, Sūryas.; Sāh.; the Anusvāra represented by a circle (*bindu*), L.; N. of the tenth astrological mansion, VarBṛ.; talc, L.; a city, L.; a field, L.; happiness (a meaning derived fr. *su-kha*, *duḥ-kha*), L.; action, L.; understanding, L.; (*ā́*), f. a fountain, well, RV. ii, 28, 5 (*khā́m ṛitásya*, cf. Zend *ashahe khāo*) & vi, 36, 4; [cf. Gk. χάος; Lat. *halo*.] **-kāminī**, f. 'liking the sky,' the female of the Falco Cheela (*cillæ*), L.; N. of Durgā (*carcikā*), L. **-kuntala**, m., N. of Śiva, L. **-khôlka**, m. 'sky-meteor,' the sun, SkandaP.; GāruḍaP.; °*lkâditya*, m. a form of the sun, SkandaP. **-ga**, mfn. moving in air, MBh. iii, 12257; (*as*), m. a bird, Mn. xii, 63; MBh. &c.; N. of Garuḍa (cf. *-ga-pati*), Gal.; any air-moving insect (as a bee), R. ii, 56, 11; a grasshopper, L.; the sun, Hcat.; a planet, Gol.; air, wind, MBh. iii, 14616; a deity, L.; an arrow, L.; *-pati*, m. 'chief of birds,' Garuḍa (Vishṇu's vehicle); *-pati-gamanā*, f., N. of a goddess, Kālac.; *-pattra*, mfn. furnished with bird's feathers (as an arrow), MBh. iii, 285, 14; *-rāj*, m. = *-pati*, Gal.; *-vaktra*, m. Artocarpus Lakucha, L.; *-vatī*, f. the earth, L.; *-śatru*, m. 'enemy of birds,' Hemionitis cordifolia, L.; *-sthāna*, n. 'a bird's nest,' the hollow of a tree, L.; °*gâdhipa*, m. = °*ga-pati*, R. i, 42, 16; °*gântaka*, m. 'destroyer of birds,' a hawk, falcon, L.; °*gâbhirāma*, m., N. of Śiva; °*gâsana*, m. 'seat of the sun,' N. of the mountain Udaya (the eastern mountain on which the sun rises), L.; 'sitting on a bird (i. e. on the Garuḍa),' Vishṇu, L.; °*gêndra*, m. the chief of the birds, Pañcat.; a vulture, L.; Garuḍa, L.; N. of a prince, Rājat. i, 89; °*gêndra-dhvaja*, m., N. of Vishṇu, BhP. i, 18, 16; °*gêśvara*, m. 'the chief of the birds,' a vulture, L.; Garuḍa, L. **-gaṅgā**, f. the Gaṅgā (Ganges) of the sky, L. **-gañja**, m., N. of the father of Gokarṇêśvara. **-gaṇa**, m., N. of a prince (son of Vajranābha), VP.; BhP. ix, 12, 3. **-gata**, mfn. moving in the air, R. v, 56, 144; extending far up to the sky, Hariv. 5336. **-gati**, f. 'flight in the air,' a metre of 4 × 16 syllables. **-gama**, mfn. moving in the air, flying (said of Gandharvas and of missile weapons), MBh. iii, 820 & 14983; xiv, 2188; (*as*), m. a bird, Nal. i, 23; N. of a Brāhman, MBh. i, 995. **-garbha**, m., N. of a Bodhi-sattva, Buddh. **-galya**, n., N. of a part of a wheel, ĀpŚr. xvi, 18. **-guṇa**, mfn. (in arithm. or alg.) having a cypher as multiplier. **-gola**, m. the vault or circle of heaven, celestial sphere, Gol.; *-vidyā*, f. knowledge of the celestial sphere, astronomy, W. **-golaka**, m. = *-gola*, Gol. **-m-kara**, m. 'making or filling space(?),' a lock of hair, L. **-camasa**, m. 'the drinking-vessel in the sky,' N. of the moon, L. **-cara**, mfn. moving in the air, flying, MBh.; R.; BhP.; (*as*), m. a bird, R.; a planet, Sūryas.; Gol.; the sun, L.; a cloud, L.; the wind, L.; an aerial spirit, Vidyādhara, Kathās. cx, 139; a Rakshas or demon, L.; (in music) a kind of Rūpaka or measure, L.; (*ās*), m. pl., N. of a fabulous people, VarBṛS.; *-tva*, n. the state of a Rakshas or demon, HYog. **-cārin**, mfn. moving in the air, flying (said of Skanda), MBh. iii, 14635; (*ī*), m. a planet, Sūryas. **-citra**, n. 'a picture in the sky,' anything impossible or not existing, Kathās. il, 142. **-jala**, n. 'air-water,' i. e. dew, rain, fog, L. **-jit**, m. 'conquering heaven,' N. of a Buddha, L. **-jyotis**, m. a shining flying insect, fire-fly &c., L. **-tamāla**, m. a cloud, L.; smoke, L. **-tilaka**, m. 'sky-ornament,' the sun, L. **-dūra**, see *khaḍūra*; *-vāsinī*, f. (with Buddhists) N. of a female deity or Śakti, L. **-°dūraka**, m., N. of a man, g. *śivâdi*. **-dyota**, m. = *-jyotis*, ChUp.; MBh.; R. &c.; (applied fig. to transient happiness) Sarvad. xi; the sun, L.; (*ā*), f. (scil. *dvār*) 'shining-insect-like door,' the left eye, BhP. iv; N. of a deity, Buddh. **-dyotaka**, m., N. of a poisonous plant, Suśr. **-dyotana**, m. 'sky-illuminator,' the sun, L. **-dhūpa**, m. air-pervading perfume, Bhaṭṭ.; a rocket, fire-work, W. **-parāga**, m. darkness, L. **-pura**, n. a city built in the sky (as that of the Kālakeyas, MBh. iii, 12208 & 12258; or as that of Hari-ścandra, L.); the Fata Morgana, VarBṛS.; a water-jar, L.; m. tympany, wind-dropsy, L.; the betel-nut tree, L.; Cyperus pertenuis, L.; a kind of perfume (*vyāla-nakha*), L. **-pushpa**, n. 'sky-flower,' = *-citra*, Hcar. v, 238; *-ṭīkā*, f., N. of a Comm. **-bāshpa**, m. 'tears of the sky,' dew, frost, L. **-bha**, m. 'shining in the air,' a planet, L. **-bhrānti**, m. 'gliding through the air,' a kind of falcon (*cilla*, cf. *-kāminī*), L. **-maṇi**, m. = *-tilaka*, Pañcar. iii, 1, 19. **-milana**, n. sleepiness, lassitude, L. **-mūrti**, f. a celestial body or person; *-mat*, mfn. having a divine or celestial person or form, Mn. ii, 82. **-mūli**, °**likā**, °**lī**, f. an aquatic plant (Pistia Stratiotes), L. **-yoga**, m. (= *nābhasa-y*°) N. of a particular constellation, VarBṛ. xxviii, 2. **-vallī**, f. (= *ākāśa-v*°) Cassyta filiformis, L. **-vāri**, n. rain-water, dew, vapour &c., L. **-śabdâṅkura-ja**, v. l. for *kharâbdâṅkuraka*, q. v. **-śaya**, m. (Pāṇ. vi, 3, 18, Kāś.) 'resting or dwelling in the air,' N. of a Jina, Gal.; (cf. *-sama*.) **-śarīra**, n. a celestial body, W. **-°śarīrin**, mfn. gifted with an ethereal body (cf. *-mūrti-mat*), Mn. iv, 243. **-śvāsa**, m. wind, air, L. **-sama**, m., N. of a Buddha, L.; (cf. *-śaya*.) **-samuttha**, mfn. produced in the sky, ethereal, W. **-sambhava**, mfn. id., W.; (*ā*), f. spikenard (= *ākāśa-māṅsī*), L. **-sarpaṇa**, m., N. of a Buddha, L.; (*am*), n. gliding through the air, W. **-sindhu**, m. (cf. *-camasa*) N. of the moon, L. **-sūci**, f. 'a needle pricking the air,' ifc. one who continually makes mistakes (as a grammarian), Kāś. & Gaṇar. on Pāṇ. ii, 1, 53. **-stanī**, f. 'having the atmosphere for its breast,' N. of the earth, L. **-sphaṭika**, m. 'aerial crystal,' N. for the sun- and moon-gem (*sūrya-kānta* and *candra-k*°; cf. *ākāśa-sph*°), L. **-hara**, mfn. (in arithm.) having a cypher for its denominator (as a fraction). **Khâtman**, mfn. having the air as one's nature, W. **Khâpagā**, f. 'a stream in the air,' N. of the Ganges, L. **Khâpara**, *ās*, m. pl., N. of a people, Romakas. **Khôlka**, m. sky-meteor, W.; a planet, W.; (cf. *kha-kh*°.) **Khôlmuka**, m. the planet Mars, L.; (cf. *gaganôlm*°.)
Khe, loc. of 3. *khá*, in comp. **-gamana**, m. 'moving in the air,' a kind of gallinule (= *kālakanṭha*), L. **-cara**, mf(*ī*)n. moving in the air, flying, MBh.; R. &c.; (*as*), m. a bird, MBh.; Nal.; any aerial being (as a messenger of the gods), MBh. i; a Gandharva, iii; a Vidyā-dhara, BhP. x, 82, 8; Kathās. lii, lxv; a Rakshas, R. iii, 30, 37; a planet; (hence) the number 'nine;' quicksilver, L.; N. of Śiva, L.; (*ā*), f. (in music) a particular Mūrchanā; (*ī*), f. with *siddhi* or *gati*, the magical power of flying, Kathās. xx, 105; Sarvad. ix &c.; Durgā, MBh. iv, 186; a Vidyā-dharī, Rudray.; a particular Mudrā or position of the fingers; an earring or a cylinder of wood passed through the lobe of the ear, W.; (*am*), n. green vitriol; *-tā*, f. the magical power of flying, Sarvad. ix; *-tva*, n. id., Kathās. iii, 49; °*râñjana*, green vitriol, Npr.; °*rânna*, n. a particular dish made of rice. **-1. -ṭa**, m. 'moving in the air,' a planet; the ascending node or Rāhu, W.; *-karman*, n. calculation of the motion &c. of planets; *-pīṭha-mālā*, f., *-bodha*, m., *-bhūshaṇa*, n., N. of astronomical works. **-paribhrama**, mf(*ā*)n. flying about in the air, R. i, 2, 14. **-śaya**, mfn. (cf. *kha-ś*°) lying in the air, Pāṇ. vi, 3, 18, Kāś. **-sara**, for *vesara*, q. v., L.

खक्ख् *khakkh*, v. l. for √*kakh* (to laugh), q. v., Dhātup. v, 6.

खक्खट *khakkhaṭa* = *kakkh*° (q. v.), hard, solid, L., Sch.; harsh (as sound), Divyâv. xxxvi.

खक्खर *khakkhara*, *as*, m. (?), a beggar's staff, Buddh.; (cf. *hikkala*.)

खग *kha-ga*, &c. See 3. *khá*.

खगोड *khagoḍa*, *as*, m. a kind of reed (Saccharum spontaneum), W.
Khaggaḍa, *as*, m. id., L.

खंकर *khaṃ-kara*. See 3. *khá*.
Khaṅkhaṇa, *as*, m. = *khaṃ-kara*, Gal.

खङ्ख *khaṅkha*, *as*, m., N. of a minister of king Bālâditya, Rājat. iii, 483; 497; 522 ff.

खङ्खण *khaṅkhaṇa*, see *khaṃ-kara*; (*ā*), f. the tinkling sound (of a bell &c.), W.

Khaṅkhara = *khaṃ-kara* (q.v.), L.

खङ्ग *khaṅgá*, for *khaḍgá*, q.v.

खङ्गाह *khaṅgāha* = *khoṅg°*, q.v., Gal.

खच् *khac*, cl. 1. P. °*cati* (only p. p. °*cat*), to come forth, project (as teeth), Kathās. xxiii; xxvi: cl. 9. P. *khacñāti*, to be born again, Dhātup. xxxi, 59; to cause prosperity, ib.; to purify, ib: cl. 10. P. *khacayati*, to fasten, bind, ib. xxxv, 84.

Khacita, mfn. prominent (?), Dhūrtas.; (ifc. or with instr.) inlaid, set, studded (e. g. *maṇi-kh°*, inlaid with jewels), MBh. vii; xiii; Hariv.; Megh. &c. (= *karambita*, 'combined with,' L.)

खज् *khaj*, cl. 1. P. °*jati*, to churn or agitate, Dhātup. vii, 57.

Khája, *as*, m. stirring, agitating, churning, Car.; contest, war (cf. -*kṛit*, &c.), Naigh. ii, 17; a churning stick, MBh. xii, 7784; Suśr.; a ladle, spoon, L., Sch.; (*ā*), f. a churning stick ('a poker,' Sch.), MBh. iv, 231; a ladle, L.; the hand with the fingers extended, L.; churning, stirring, W.; killing, L. — **kṛit**, mfn. causing the tumult or din of battle (Indra), RV. vi, 18, 2; vii, 20, 3; viii, 1, 7. — **m-kará**, mfn. id., RV. i, 102, 6; TBr. ii, 7, 15, 6.

Khajaka, *as*, m. a churning stick, L.; (*ikā*), f. a ladle or spoon, L.

Khajapa, *am*, n. ghee or clarified butter, Uṇ.

Khajāka, *as*, m. a bird, Uṇ.; (*ā*), f. a ladle, L.

खञ्ज् 1. *khañj*, cl. 1. P. *khañjati*, to limp, walk lame, Suśr. ii, 1, 76; Naish. xi, 107; [cf. Gk. σκάζω; Germ. *hinke*.]

2. **Khañj**, mfn. (nom. *khan*) limping, Vop. iii, 134.

Khañja, mfn. (g. *kaḍārâdi*) id., Mn.; Suśr.; Bhartṛ.; (with *pādena*, 'limping with one leg') Pāṇ. ii, 3, 20, Kāś.; (*ā*), f., N. of several metres (one consisting of 2 × 28 short syllables + 1 long and 30 short syllables + 1 long; another containing 30 short syllables + 1 long and 28 short syllables + 1 long; another containing 2 × 36 short syllables + 1 Amphimacer). — **kheṭa**, m. the wagtail, L. — **khela**, m. id., L. — **caraṇa**, mfn. limping, lame, VarBṛS. — **tā**, f. limping, lameness, Suśr.; Kād. — **tva**, n. id., Sāh. — **bāhu**, for *kaṃja-b°*. — **lekha**, for -*khela*, L.

Khañjaka, mfn. limping, L.

Khañjana, *as*, m. the wagtail (Montacilla alba), VarBṛS.; Suśr. &c.; N. of a man, g. *śivâdi*; (*ā*), f. a kind of wagtail, L.; (*am*), n. going lamely, L. — **rata**, n. the secret pleasures of the Yatis, cohabitation of saints, L. **Khañjanâkṛiti**, f. a kind of wagtail, L.

Khañjanaka, *as*, m. the wagtail, VarBṛS. vi, 1; (*ikā*), f. a kind of wagtail, L.

Khañjara, mfn. g. *kaḍārâdi* (Kāś.)

Khañjarīṭa, *as*, m. the wagtail, Yājñ. i, 174; Amar.; Caurap.; = *khaḍgār°*, L.; (*ī*), f. (in music) a kind of measure.

Khañjarīṭaka, *as*, m. the wagtail, Mn. v, 14; Divyâv. xxxiii; Suśr. i, 46, 62.

खञ्जार *khañjāra*, m., N. of a man, g. *śivâdi*.

Khañjāla, *as*, m., N. of a man, ib.

खट् 1. *khaṭ*, cl. 1. P. °*ṭati*, to desire, Dhātup.

खट् 2. *khaṭ*, ind. a particle of exclamation, TĀr. iv, 27.

खट *khaṭa*, *as*, m. phlegm, phlegmatic or watery humor (cf. *kapha*), L.; a blind well, VarBṛS., Sch.; an axe, hatchet, chisel (*ṭaṅka*), L.; a plough, L.; a kind of blow ('the closed or doubled fist, as for striking,' W.), L.; grass (used to thatch houses; cf. *kaṭa*, *khaḍa*), L.; a fragrant kind of grass, L.; (*ī*), f. chalk, L. — **kaṭāhaka**, a spitting-box, Buddh. L. — **khādaka**, m. an eater, W.; a glass vessel, W.; a jackal, W.; an animal, W.; a crow, W.

Khaṭaka, *as*, m. a go-between, negotiator of marriages (cf. *ghaṭaka*), L.; the half-closed hand (v. l. °*ṭika*), L.; the doubled fist of wrestlers, W.; (*ā*), f. a slap, Divyâv. xxvi; (*ikā*), f. chalk, Prab.; Gol.; AgP.; the external opening of the ear, L.; Andropogon muricatus, L. **Khaṭakā-mukha**, m. a particular position of the hand, Amar.; PSarv. **Khaṭakā-vardhamāna**, m. id. **Khaṭakâsya**, m. id.

Khaṭika, v. l. for °*ṭaka*, q.v.; (*ikā*), f., see ib.

Khaṭinī, f. chalk, Bhpr. iii.

Khaṭya, mfn. fr. °*ṭa*, g. *gav-ādi* (Kāś.)

खटक्किका *khaṭakkikā*, f. a side door, L.

खटखटाय *khaṭakhaṭāya* (onomat.), Ā. °*ṭāyate*, to crackle, Mṛicch. i, ām.

खटिनी *khaṭinī*. See *khaṭa*.

खटु *khaṭu* = °*ṭa*, the fist, Divyâv. xiii.

खटुकी *khaṭukī*, f. (perhaps = *khaṭṭikī*) one of the eight Kulas (with Śāktas).

खटू *khaṭū*, *ūs*, m. or f. (?), an ornament worn on the wrist or ancle, W.

खट्ट् *khaṭṭ*, cl. 10. P. °*ṭṭayati*, to cover, screen, Dhātup. xxxii, 88.

खट्ट *khaṭṭa*, mfn. sour, Gal.; (*ā*), f. for *khaṭvā*, q.v. **Khaṭṭâṅga**, see ib. **Khaṭṭâsa**, m. 'eating sour food' (?), the civet or zebet cat (Viverra Zibetha), L.; (*ī*), f. id., L.; another animal, L.

Khaṭvara, mfn. sour, Gal.; (*as*), m., N. of a man, g. *śubhrâdi* (Kāś.)

खट्टन *khaṭṭana*, *as*, m. a dwarf, L.

Khaṭṭeraka, mfn. dwarfish, short of stature, L.

खट्टास *khaṭṭāsa*, for °*ṭṭâsa*. See *khaṭṭa*.

खट्टि *khaṭṭi*, *is*, m. a bier (the bed on which the corpse is carried to the pile), L.

खट्टिक *khaṭṭika*, *as*, m. a butcher, hunter, fowler, one who lives by killing and selling game, L.; the cream on buffalo-milk, L.; (*ā*), f. for *khaṭvikā*, q.v.; (*ī*), f. a woman who sells meat, Kālac.

खट्टेरक *khaṭṭeraka*. See *khaṭṭana*.

खट्य *khaṭya*. See *khaṭa*.

खट्वका *khaṭvakā*, f. a small bedstead, Pāṇ. vii, 3, 48, Kāś.

Khaṭvaya, Nom. P. °*yati*, to make into a bed or couch, Śiś. ii, 77.

Khaṭvā, f. a bedstead, couch, cot, Kauś.; Mn. viii, 357 &c. (*khaṭvāṃ samārūḍha*, lying on the sick-bed, MBh. v, 1474 = xii, 10599); a swing, hammock, L.; a kind of bandage, Suśr.; N. of a plant (*kola-śimbī*), L. — °**ṅga** (°*vâṅ°*), m. n. 'a club shaped like the foot of a bedstead,' i.e. a club or staff with a skull at the top (considered as the weapon of Śiva and carried by ascetics and Yogins), Gaut.; VarBṛS.; Mālatīm. v, 4; Kathās.; (*as*), m. the back-bone, Gal.; N. of a plant, ib.; wood from a funeral pile, W.; N. of a king of the solar line, MBh. i, 2109; VP. (v. l. *khaṭvâṅgada*); BhP. ii; xi; (= Dilīpa) Hariv. 808 & BhP. ix; N. of an attendant in the retinue of Devī; (*ī*), f., N. of a plant, Gal.; of a river, Hariv. 5329; -*dhara*, m. 'staff-bearer,' N. of Śiva, BhP. iv, 19, 20; -*dhāra*, m. id., Hariv. 10680; -*nāmikā*, f. 'named after the *khaṭvâṅga*,' N. of a plant (resembling Plectranthus), L.; -*bhṛit*, mfn. one who bears the *khaṭvâṅga* staff, Mn. xi, 105, Sch.; (*t*), m., N. of Śiva, L.; -*vana*, n., N. of a forest, Hariv. 4171; -*śūlin*, mfn. bearing the weapons called *kh°* and *śūla*, Hcat. — °**ṅgaka** (°*vâṅ°*), m. = °*ṅga*, Hcat. — °**ṅgin** (°*vâṅ°*), mfn. one who bears the *khaṭvâṅga* staff, Mn. xi, 105; (*ī*), m. Śiva, Bālar. ii, 34. — **tale**, loc. ind. under the bedstead, Hit. — °**pluta** (°*vâp°*), mfn. 'mounted on a bed,' low, vile, iniquitous ('silly, stupid,' W.), Pāṇ. ii, 1, 26, Kāś. — **bhāra**, m. a load consisting of bedsteads, g. *vaṃśâdi*. — °**rūḍha** (°*vâr°*), mfn. = °*ṭvâpluta*, Pāṇ. ii, 1, 26, Kāś.; g. *pravṛiddhâdi*.

Khaṭvākā, f. ifc. for °*ṭvā*, a bedstead, Pāṇ. vii, 3, 49, Kāś.

Khaṭvikā, f. a small bedstead, ib. 48, Kāś.

Khaṭvīya, Nom. P. to treat as a bedstead, Pat. on Pāṇ. i, 4, 2, Vārtt. 12.

खड् *khaḍ*, cl. 10. P. *khāḍayati*, to divide, break, Dhātup. xxxii, 44; (cf. √*khaṇḍ*.)

Khaḍa, *as*, m. (g. *madhv-ādi*) dividing, breaking, L.; buttermilk boiled with acid vegetables and spices, Car. vi, 9; Suśr. i, vi; N. of a man, g. *aśvâdi*; (*as*, *am*), m. n. (= *khaṭa*) a kind of small grass, straw, L.; (*ī*), f. (= *khaṭī*) chalk, L. — **vat**, mfn. fr. *khaḍa*, g. *madhv-ādi*. **Khaḍônmattā**, f., N. of a woman, g. *śubhrâdi*.

Khaḍaka, *am*, n. a bolt or pin, KātyŚr. xiv, 3, 12, Sch. (= *sthāṇu*); (*ikā*), f. (= *khaṭikā*) chalk, L.

Khaḍika, g. *sutaṃgamâdi*.

खडक्किका *khaḍakkikā* = *khaṭakk°*, L.

खडण्ड *khaḍaṇḍa*, for *shaḍ-aṇḍa*, q. v.

खडतु *khaḍatū*, *ūs*, m. = *khaṭu*, L.

Khaḍukā, f. id. (v. l. for *khaḍḍukā*).

Khaḍū, *ūs*, f. (?) id., Uṇ., Sch.; = *khaṭṭi*, ib.

खडूर *khaḍūra*, ?, AV. xi, 9, 16; m., N. of a man, g. *śubhrâdi* (*kha-dūra*, Gaṇar. 220).

खड्ग *khaḍgá*, *as*, m. (fr. √*khaḍ* for *khaṇḍ*?) a sword, scymitar, MBh.; R. &c. (ifc. f. *ā*, Kathās.); a large sacrificial knife, W.; a rhinoceros, MaitrS. iii, 14, 21 = VS. xxiv, 40 (*khaṅgá*); ŚāṅkhŚr.; Mn.; MBh. &c.; a rhinoceros-horn, L.; a Pratyeka-buddha (so called because he is a solitary being like a rhinoceros; cf. *eka-cara* & -*cārin*), L.; N. of an attendant in Skanda's retinue, MBh. ix, 2569; of the son of a merchant, Kathās. lvi, 151; (*am*), n. iron, L. — **kośa**, m. the sheath of a sword, scabbard, L.; Scirpus maximus, L. — **grāhin**, m. 'a sword-bearer,' a particular dignitary, Hcar. — **carma-dhara**, m. a soldier armed with a sword and shield, W. — **jvalanā**, f., N. of a female Kiṃnara, Kāraṇḍ. i. — **dṛih**, -*dhṛik*, mfn. grasping a scymitar, W. — **dhara**, m. a swordsman, W.; N. of a soldier, Kathās. — **dhārā**, f. a sword-blade, R. ii, 23, 35; -*vrata*, n. (= *asi-dhārā-v°*) any extremely difficult task. — **dhenu**, f. a female rhinoceros, L.; (= *asi-dh°*) a small knife, Rājat. viii, 3315. — **pattra**, m. (cf. *asi-p°*) 'sword-leaved,' Scirpus maximus (= -*kośa*), L.; (*am*), n. the blade of a sword, W.; -*vana*, n. 'a forest having swords for leaves,' N. of a hell, R. (ed. Bomb.) iii, 53, 20. — **pāṇi**, mfn. sword in hand, W. — **pāta**, m. = -*prahāra*, Kathās. — **pātra**, n. a vessel (formed of buffalo's horns) being a large salver or charger on which the sacrificial knife is laid, W. — **pidhāna**, n. the sheath of a sword, scabbard, L. — **pidhānaka**, n. id., L. — **putrikā**, f. (= *asi-p°*) a small sword, knife, L. — **prahāra**, m. a sword-cut, Kathās. — **phala**, n. = -*dhārā*, L. — **bandha**, m. a kind of artificially-formed verse, Sāh. — **maṇi**, m. an excellent sword (one of the royal insignia), Divyâv. xii. — **maya**, mfn. consisting of swords, Kathās. cix, 110. — **māṃsa**, n. = *khaḍgâmisha*, q.v., W. — **mālā-tantra**, n., N. of a work. — **roman**, m. 'sword-haired,' N. of the charioteer of Jālaṃdhara, PadmaP. — **lekhā**, f. a row of swords, W. — **vat**, mfn. armed with a sword, MBh. iii, 10963. — **vidyā**, f. swordmanship, Kathās. — **śimbī**, f. 'sword bean,' French bean, L. — **sakha**, mfn. 'having a sword for one's friend,' armed with a sword, Mudr. — **sadman**, n. = -*pidhāna*, Gal. — **sena**, m., N. of a man, Vāsant. — **hasta**, mfn. = -*pāṇi*, Vet.; (*ā*), f., N. of a female attendant in the retinue of Devī. **Khaḍgâghāta**, m. a sword-cut, W. **Khaḍgâdhāra**, m. 'sword-holder,' scabbard, W. **Khaḍgâbhihata**, mfn. cut or struck with a sword, W. **Khaḍgâmisha**, n. rhinoceros-flesh, Mn. iii, 272; Yājñ. i, 259. **Khaḍgâhva**, m. 'named after a sword,' a rhinoceros, Suśr. i, 6, 10.

Khaḍgaṭa, *as*, m. a large kind of reed (Saccharum spontaneum, *bṛihat-kāśa*), L.

Khaḍgārīṭa, *as*, m. a sword-blade, L.; one who moves the feet backwards and forwards on the edge of a red-hot sword (as a penance), L. (v. l. *khañjar°*).

Khaḍgi (for °*dgin*). — **dhenukā**, f. a female rhinoceros, Kād. — **māra**, m. Scirpus maximus, L.

Khaḍgika, *as*, m. a swordsman, L.; (= *khaṭṭika*) a butcher, vender of flesh-meat, L.; (= *khaṭṭika*) the cream of buffalo's milk, L.

Khaḍgin, mfn. armed with a sword, MBh.; R.; BhP.; (*ī*), m. Śiva, MBh. xiii, 1157; a rhinoceros, R. i, 26, 14; Suśr. i, 46, 88 & 97; Kād.; N. of Mañjuśrī (cf. *khaḍga*, 'a Pratyeka-buddha'), L.

Khaḍgīka, *as*, m. a sickle, small scythe, L.

खड्डुका *khaḍḍukā* = *khaḍukā*, L.

खण *khaṇa*, *as*, m. the backbone, Gal.

खणखणाय *khaṇakhaṇāya* (onomat.), Ā. °*yate*, to utter or give out any peculiar sound, tick, tinkle, crack, &c., BhP. v, 2, 5; VārP. Introd.

Khaṇakhaṇāyita, mfn. tinkling &c., Kād.; Hcar.

Khaṇatkhaṇi-kṛita, mfn. caused to crack or tinkle, Mcar. v, 1.

खण्ड् *khaṇḍ*, cl. 1. Ā. °*ṇḍate*, to break, divide, destroy, Dhātup. viii, 31: cl. 10. P. *khaṇḍayati*, to break, tear, break into pieces, crush, cut, divide, Pañcat.; Bhaṭṭ. (aor. *acakhaṇḍat*); to destroy, remove, annihilate, Rājat. v, 281; Naish. v, 4; to defeat, conquer, Bhaṭṭ. xii, 17; to refute; to interrupt, disturb, R. iii, 14, 14; Kathās.; to disregard (an order), Rājat. vi, 229; Kathās. cxxiv, 79; 'to disappoint, deceive, cheat,' see *khaṇḍita*.

Khaṇḍa, mf(*ā*)n. broken, having chasms or gaps or breaks, Suśr.; VarBṛS.; Pāṇ. ii, 1, 30, Kāś.; deficient, defective, crippled (cf. *shaṇḍa*), Āp.; ŚāṅkhŚr. xvi, 18, 18, Sch.; (in comp. or ifc., Pāṇ. ii, 2, 38, Pat.); not full (as the moon), KātyŚr., Sch.; Subh.; (*as, am*), m. n. (g. *ardharcâdi*) 'a break or gap,' cf. *kedāra-kh°*; a piece, part, fragment, portion, R.; Suśr.; Megh. &c. (*indoh kh°* or *tārâdhipa-kh°* [cf. also *khaṇḍêndu*] 'the crescent,' Prasannar.); treacle or molasses partially dried, candied sugar, Bhpr.; Naish.; Sāh.; a section of a work, part, chapter (e. g. of AitĀr.; KenUp. &c.); a continent, Gaṇit.; (in alg.) a term in an equation, Gaṇit.; a party, number, multitude, assemblage, MBh. (sometimes not to be distinguished from *shaṇḍa*); R. i, 30, 15 &c. (ifc. m. or n., cf. Kāś. on Pāṇ. iv, 2, 38 & 51); (*as*), m. a flaw in a jewel, L.; a calf with horns half grown, Gal.; (in music) a kind of measure; (*ās*), m. pl., N. of a people (v. l. *shaṇḍa*), VarBṛS.; (*am*), n. a variety of sugar-cane, W.; black salt (*viḍ-lavaṇa*), L.; (cf. *uttara-, karka-, kāla-, kāśī-, śrī-, sitā-*.) **–kathā**, f. a particular kind of tale ('a tale or story divided into sections,' W.), L. **–kanda**, n., N. of a bulbous plant, L. **–kāpālika**, m. an inferior Kāpālika ascetic, Kathās. cxxi, 6 & 13; N. of a teacher (?). **–kāra**, m. one who makes candied sugar, R. ii. **–kāvya**, n. a defective or minor poem (i. e. one not on any heroic or sacred subject, and having only one topic, like Megh., Caurap. &c.), Sāh. **–kushmāṇḍaka**, n. a particular electuary, Bhpr. **–khaṇḍā**, f., N. of one of the mothers in Skanda's retinue, MBh. ix, 2638. **–khāṭṭaka, -khāḍaka**, vv. ll. for *-khādyaka* = *-khādya*, q. v., Comm. on VarBṛ. **–khādya**, m. dainty, nice thing, Hariv. 8445; Bhpr.; (*am*), n., N. of an astronomical Karaṇa (vv. ll. *-khāṭṭaka, -khāḍaka*), VarBṛ., Sch.; *-karaṇa*, n. id., ib. **–giri**, m., N. of a mountain, Buddh. **–ja**, m. treacle, candied sugar (= *guḍa, yavāsa-śarkarā*), L. **–tā**, f. the being divided, division. **–tāla**, m. (in music) a kind of measure. **–deva**, m., N. of an author of a Comm. on Jaim. (called Bhaṭṭa-dīpikā) and of another work (called Mīmāṇsā-kaustubha). **–dravya**, m., N. of a man, Buddh. **–dhārā**, f. shears, scissors, L.; a kind of dance or air in music (?), Vikr. **–pattra**, n. a bundle of various leaves, W. **–paraśu**, m. 'cutting (his foes) to pieces with an axe,' Śiva; Vishṇu, Vishṇ. **–parśu**, m. (= *-paraśu*) Śiva, L.; Paraśu-rāma, L.; Rāhu, L.; an elephant with a broken tusk, L.; a spreader of unguents or fragrant powders &c., L.; a drug (commonly *khaṇḍâmalaka*), L. **–pāka**, m. syrup prepared with spices, Bhpr. **–pāṇi**, m., N. of a prince (v. l. *daṇḍ°*). **–pāla**, m. a seller of sweetmeats, confectioner, L. **–pralaya**, m. partial destruction of the universe (all the spheres beneath Svarga or heaven being dissolved), W.; the dissolution of the bonds of friendship, quarrel (for *-praṇaya*?), W. **–praśasti**, f., N. of a poem attributed to Hanūmat (an older N. for the play called after him). **–prastāra**, m. (in music) a kind of measure. **–phaṇa**, m. a kind of serpent, Suśr. **–maṇḍala**, n. 'incomplete sphere,' a segment of a circle, W.; (mfn.) not full or round, gibbous, W. **–maya**, mfn. consisting of pieces, W. **–mātrā**, f. a kind of song, Sāh. **–modaka**, m. = *-ja*, L. **–raksha**, m. superintendent of wards, Jain.; Inscr. **–rasa**, m. (in rhet.) a partial Rasa (= *saṃcāri-r°*), Sāh. **–lavaṇa**, n. black salt, L. **–lekhaka**, m. (= *khañja-lekha*) a wagtail, Gal. **–vaṭaka**, m. n., N. of a village or town, Kathās. cxxiv. **–vikṛiti**, f. candied sugar, W. **–śarkarā**, f. candied sugar, sugar in pieces, Suśr. **–śas**, ind. in pieces, by pieces, bit by bit, piece by piece, MBh.; R.; Suśr.; *°śaḥ* √*kṛi*, to divide or cut into pieces, Pañcat.; *°śo* √*gam* or *bhū* or *yā*, to be divided or cut into pieces, fall into pieces, Pañcat.; VarBṛS.; Kathās. **–śākhā**, f., N. of a creeper (cf. *kāṇḍa-ś°*), L. **–śīlā**, f. 'unsteady in conduct,' an unchaste wife, L. **–sāra**, m. = *-ja*, L. **–sphuṭa-pratisaṃskaraṇa**, n. repairing of dilapidations, Divyâv. i; (Pāli *°ṇḍa-phulla-*.) **Khaṇḍâbhra**, n. scattered clouds, L.; a bite or impression of the teeth in amorous sport, L. **Khaṇḍâmalaka**, n. myrobalan cut up into small pieces (used as a medicine), L. **Khaṇḍâmra**, n. id., L. **Khaṇḍâlī**, f. a measure for oil, W.; a pond, W.; a woman whose husband has been guilty of infidelity, W. **Khaṇḍêndu**, m. 'defective moon,' the crescent, Hcat.; *-maṇḍana*, m. 'having the crescent for his ornament,' Śiva, Rājat. i, 280. **Khaṇḍôdbhava**, **°dbhūta**, m. = *khaṇḍa-ja*, Gal. **Khaṇḍoshṭha**, m. a particular disease of the lips, ŚārṅgS. i, 7, 74.

Khaṇḍaka, mfn. ifc. breaking to pieces, destroying, removing, rendering ineffectual, W.; (*as*), m. (g. *ṛiśyâdi*) a fragment, part, piece, Sūryas.; Kathās. xxiv, 121; treacle or molasses, candied sugar, Hariv. 8445 (v. l.); one who has no nails ('pared or clipped finger nails,' W.), L.; a kind of dance or tune (?), Vikr.; for *skandhaka* (N. of a metre), q. v.; (*ikā*), f. ? ('a piece of wood,' NBD.), Pāṇ. iii, 4, 51, Kāś.; a piece, Divyâv. ii; a section of a work; a kind of air or tune, W.; (*am*), n. (= *khaṇḍa*) a term in an equation, Gaṇit. **Khaṇḍakâlu**, **°luka**, n. an esculent root, sweet potato, L.

Khaṇḍana, mfn. ifc. breaking, dividing, reducing to pieces, destroying, annihilating, removing, Gīt.; (*am*), n. the act of breaking or cutting or dividing or grinding, Hit.; hurting, injuring (esp. with the teeth), Pañcat.; Kathās. ciii; Gīt.; Caurap.; interrupting, disappointing, frustrating, Mālav.; Ragh.; Pañcat. &c.; refuting (in argument), W.; cheating, deceiving, Ragh. xix, 21; Hit.; rebellion, opposition, W.; = *khaṇḍana-khaṇḍa-khādya*, Naish. vi, 113; (*ā*), f. discarding, dismissal, Sāh. **–kāra**, m. 'author of the work called *khaṇḍana* (*-khaṇḍa-khādya*),' N. of Harsha. **–kṛit**, m. id. **–khaṇḍa-khādya**, n., N. of a work on logic by Harsha. **–rata**, n. skilful in cutting or destroying, destructive, W.

Khaṇḍanīya, mfn. to be broken or divided, Pañcat.; destructible, W.; refutable, W.

Khaṇḍara, (g. *aśmâdi*) a sweetmeat, Bhpr. ii; (*khaṇḍava*) Car. vi, 16.

Khaṇḍala, m. n. (g. *ardharcâdi*) a piece, L.

Khaṇḍava, *as, am*, m. n. (cf. *khāṇḍ°*)?, L.; (*as*), m. for *°ṇḍara*, q. v.

Khâṇḍika, *as*, m. 'one who learns section by section of a work,' pupil (? 'a sugar-boiler, sugar-baker,' NBD.), Pāṇ. iv, 2, 45; g. *purohitâdi*; pease, Car. i, 27 (*khaṇḍīka*); the armpit, L.; N. of a man, ŚBr. xi; Pāṇ. iv, 3, 102; (*shâṇḍika*) MaitrS.; m. pl., N. of a people, Pāṇ. iii, 2, 115, Vārtt. 1, Pat.; (*ā*), f., see *°ṇḍaka*. **Khaṇḍikôpâdhyāya**, m. a teacher of *khaṇḍika* pupils, Pāṇ. i, 1, 1, Vārtt. 13, Pat.

Khaṇḍita, mfn. (g. *tārakâdi*) cut, torn, broken in pieces, scattered, dispersed, destroyed, removed, Vikr.; Pañcat.; Kathās.; Prab.; Hit.; injured (esp. by the teeth), Pañcat.; broken as allegiance, disobeyed against, rebelled; refuted, controverted; disappointed, betrayed, abandoned (as a lover), Ragh. v, 67; Megh.; Śāntiś.; (*ā*), f. a woman whose husband or lover has been guilty of infidelity, Sāh. **–vigraha**, mfn. 'one whose body is injured,' maimed, mutilated, Kir. v, 43. **–vṛitta**, mfn. one whose manner of life is dissolute, Mṛicch. ii. **Khaṇḍitâśaṇsa**, mfn. having the hopes disappointed, frustrated, W.

Khaṇḍin, mfn. 'annihilating, removing;' see *yaśaḥ-*; consisting of pieces, W.; divided, comminuted, W.; (*ī*), m. the wild kidney-bean (*vana-mudga*), L.; a N. of Harsha (cf. *khaṇḍana-kāra*), SŚaṃkar.; (*inī*), f. 'having continents,' the earth, L.

Khaṇḍiman, *ā*, m. defectiveness, g. *pṛithv-ādi*.

Khaṇḍīka, *as*, m., see *°ṇḍika*.

Khaṇḍī-√kṛi, to divide or break into small pieces, cut up, tear to pieces, Ragh. xvi, 51; Pañcat.

Khaṇḍīya, mfn. fr. *°ṇḍa*, g. *utkarâdi*.

Khaṇḍīra, *as*, m. a kind of kidney-bean, L.

Khaṇḍu, ? ('a kind of sugar,' W.), g. *arīhaṇâdi*; (cf. *khāṇḍava*.)

Khaṇḍerāya, *as*, m., N. of an author.

Khaṇḍya, mfn. to be broken or divided, fragile, destructible, W.; to be destroyed or removed, Bhaṭṭ. xii, 17 (*a-*, neg.)

खण्वखा *khaṇvakhā*, f. (an onomat. word) 'one who croaks,' a female frog, AV. iv, 15, 15; (cf. *khaimakhā*.)

खतमाल *kha-tamāla*, &c. See 3. *khá*.

खत्त *khatta*, *as*, m., N. of an astronomer. **–khutta**, m. id.

खद् *khad*, cl. 6. P. *khadati* (pr. p. *khadát*), to be steady or firm or solid, ŚBr. i, 4, 7, 10; to strike, hurt, kill, Dhātup. iii, 13; (for √*khād*) to eat, ib.

Khadana, *am*, n. juice, Gal.

Khadā, f. a hut, stable (?, a natural cavern ?), Kauś.

Khadikā, *ās*, f. pl. fried or parched grain, L.; (cf. *khājika*.)

Khadirá, *as*, m. Acacia Catechu (having very hard wood, the resin of which is used in medicine, called Catechu, Khayar, Terra japonica), RV. iii, 53, 19; AV.; TS. &c.; N. of Indra, L.; the moon, L.; N. of a man, g. *aśvâdi*; (*ā*), f. a sensitive plant (Mimosa pudica; 'a kind of vegetable,' NBD.), L.; (*ī*), f. id., L. **–kuṇa**, m. the fruit time of the Khadira tree, g. *pīlv-ādi*. **–cañcu**, m. 'having a beak hard like Khadira wood,' N. of a bird (= *vañjulaka*), VarBṛS. **–ja**, mfn. made from Khadira wood. **–pattrikā, -pattrī**, f. a sensitive plant (kind of Mimosa), L. **–bhū**, mfn. = *-ja*. **–maya**, mfn. id. **–rasa**, m. the resin of the Acacia Catechu, Gal. **–vaṇa**, n. a Khadira forest, Pāṇ. viii, 4, 5. **–°vaṇika**, m., N. of a Buddhist Bhikshu (vv. ll. *°vanika, vanika*, Lalit.) **–vatī**, f. 'overgrown with Khadira,' N. of a locality, g. *ajirâdi*; Pāṇ. vi, 1, 220, Kāś. **–°vanika**, &c., see *°vaṇika*. **–varṇa-paksha, -varṇa-parṇa**, m. 'having wings or feathers of the colour of Khadira wood,' N. of a bird, Gal. **–varman**, m., N. of a king, VS. ix, 40, Sch. **–vāri**, n. = *-rasa*, Suśr. **–sāra**, m. id., ib.; Pāṇ. iii, 3, 17, Kāś. **–svāmin**, m., N. of a scholiast. **Khadirâjira**, ?, AV. viii, 8, 3. **Khadirâshṭaka**, n. a decoction made of Catechu and seven other substances, L. **Khadirôdaka**, n. = *°ra-rasa*, Suśr. iv. **Khadirôpama**, n. a kind of Mimosa (= *kadara*), L.

Khadiraka, *as*, m. (g. *ṛiśyâdi*) N. of a mountain, Divyâv. xvii, xxx; (*ā*), f. lac (*lākshā*), L.

खदूर *kha-dūra*, *°raka*, &c. See 3. *khá*.

Kha-dyota, *°taka*, &c. See ib.

खन् *khan*, cl. 1. P. *khánati* (impf. *ákhanat*; perf. *cakhāna*, 3. pl. *cakhnur*, R. i; Ā. *cakhne*, Pāṇ. vi, 4, 98; pr. p. Ā. *khánamāna*, RV. i, 179, 6; MBh. iii, 1897; Impv. *khanatāt*, AitBr. [Pāṇ. vii, 1, 44, Kāś.]; Pot. *khanyāt* or *khāyāt*, Vop.; Pass. *khāyáte* [TS. vi; ŚBr. iii] or *khanyate*, MBh. xii; R.; Pañcat.; inf. *khanitum*, Pañcat.), to dig, dig up, delve, turn up the soil, excavate, root up, RV.; VS.; AV. &c.; to pierce (said of an arrow), Bhartṛ. (v. l.): Caus. *khānayati* (once *khan°*, R. ii, 80, 12), to cause to dig or dig up, ŚāṅkhŚr.; MBh. &c.: Desid. *cikhanishati*, Pāṇ. vi, 4, 42, Kāś.: Intens. *caṅkhanyate* or *cākhāyate*, Pāṇ. vi, 4, 43; *caṅkhanti* or *cākhāti*, Vop. [cf. χαίνω, χανῶ, χώννυμι; Old Germ. *ginēm, ginōm*; Mod. Germ. *gähne*; Angl. Sax. *cina, cinan*; Lat. *cuniculus, canalis*.]

Khaná, mfn. digging, rooting up, AV. xvi, 1, 3 (cf. *mṛit-kh°*); (*ī*), f. a mine, L. **–pāna**, m., N. of a prince (son of Aṅga and father of Divi-ratha), BhP. ix, 23, 6 (v. l. *an-āp°*).

Khanaka, *as*, m. one who digs, digger, excavator, MBh. iii, 640; R.; a miner, L.; a house-breaker, thief, L.; a rat, L.; N. of a friend of Vidura, MBh. i, 5798 f.; (*ī*), f. a female digger or excavator, Pāṇ. iii, 1, 145, Pat.; iv, 1, 41, Kāś.

Khanati, *is*, m., N. of a man, Daś. iii.

Khanana, *am*, n. the act of digging or excavating, Daś.; Bhartṛ.; PSarv. &c.; digging into the earth, burying, PSarv.; Ragh. viii, 25, Sch.

Khananīya, mfn. to be dug, Bhaṭṭ. vi, 56, Sch.

Khanayitrī, f. a spade, Pañcar.

Khanātaka, mfn. dug up or unearthed with a spade, ĀpŚr. xvii, 26.

Khaní, mfn. (Uṇ.) digging or rooting up, AV. xvi, 1, 7; (*is*), f. a mine (esp. of precious stones), Ragh. xvii, 66; xviii, 21; VarBṛS. lxxx, 10; Vop.; a quarry, cave, W. **–netra**, m., N. of the prince Karaṃdhama, BhP. ix, 2, 25; (cf. *khanī-n°*.)

Khanika, *as*, m. (= *°naka*) a house-breaker, thief. Gal.

Khanitṛí, *tā*, m. a digger, delver, RV. x, 97, 20; AV. iv, 6, 8; VS. xii, 100; Hit.

Khanítra, *am*, n. (Pāṇ. iii, 2, 184) an instrument for digging, spade, shovel, RV. i, 179, 6; TāṇḍyaBr.; Lāṭy.; Mn. &c.; (*ā*), f. id., R. (ed. Bomb.) i, 40, 27; (*as*), m., N. of a prince, VP.; BhP. ix, 2, 24; MārkP. cxviii, 9 & 20.

Khanitraka, *am*, n. a small shovel or scoop, Pañcat.; Kathās. lxi, 109; (*ikā*), f. id., L.

Khanítrima, mf(*ā*)n. produced by digging, RV. vii, 49, 2; *°tríma*, AV. i, 6, 4; v, 13, 9; xix, 2, 2.

Khanitvā, ind. p. having dug, Hit.

Khanī (f. of °*na*, q.v.) — **netra**, m. (= °*ni-n*°) N. of the prince Karaṃdhama, MBh. xiv, 70 f.

Khánya, mf(*ā*)n. (Pāṇ. iii, 1, 123) coming from excavations or ditches, TS. vii, 4, 13, 1.

Khā, mfn. digging (ifc., e. g. *kūpa-; bisa-khá*), Pāṇ. iii, 2, 67.

Khātá, mfn. (Pāṇ. vi, 4, 42) dug, dug up, excavated, RV. iv, 50, 3; AV.; ŚBr. iii &c.; digged into the earth, buried, MBh. xiii, 3089; torn, rent, W.; m. a ditch, Hcat. i, 3, 921; n. (Naigh. iii, 23) a ditch, fosse, moat, well, pond, ŚBr. ix, 4, 3, 9; Śāṅkh-Śr.; Pañcat.; BhP. &c.; an excavation, cavern; digging a hole, W.; (*ā*), f. an artificial pond, L.; (cf. *deva-kh°, vishama-kh°, sama-kh°, sūcī-kh°*.) — **bhū**, f. a moat, ditch, L. — **mūla**, mfn. anything the root of which is dug up, AV.Paipp. xiii, 1, 5. — **rūpa-kāra**, m. a potter, L.

Khātaka, m. a digger, delver, W.; a debtor (cf. *khādaka*), L.; n. a ditch, moat, BhP. vi, 12, 22; Kathās.; Hcat. i, 5, 869; (*ikā*), f. a ditch, L.

Khātana, mfn., see *bhitti-kh°*.

Khāti, *is*, f. digging, Pāṇ. vi, 4, 42, Kāś.

Khātṛi, *tā*, m. a digger, Cāṇ.

Khātra, n. a spade, shovel, Uṇ. iv, 161; a moat, square or oblong pond, ib. (= *khānika*); a wood, L.; a thread, L.; horror, L. — **khanana**, n. digging holes in a wall or breaches, HPariś. ii, 170.

Khānaka, mfn. ifc. one who digs or digs out, Mn. viii, 260; (cf. *kūpa-*); m. a house-breaker, thief, VarBṛS. lxxxix, 9; (*ikā*), f. a ditch, Gal.

Khānam, ind. p. so as to dig, HPariś. ii, 376.

Khāni, *is*, f. a mine, Śatr. x, 112 (ifc.)

Khānika, n. an opening in a wall, breach, L.

Khānina, mfn., v. l. for °*nila*, L.

Khānila, mfn. a house-breaker, L.

Khānya, mfn. (Pāṇ. iii, 1, 123) anything that is being digged out, Lāṭy. viii, 2, 4 f.

Kheya, mfn. (Pāṇ. iii, 1, 111; Bhaṭṭ.) to be digged out, that can be digged, Nār. (Yājñ. ii, 156, Sch.); ĀpŚr. xv, 1, Sch.; n. a ditch, L.

खपराग *kha-parāga*. See 3. *khá*, p. 334.

Kha-pura, -pushpa, &c. See ib.

खम् *kham*, ind., g. *cādi* (v. l.)

खमणि *kha-maṇi*, &c. See 3. *khá*, p. 334.

खम्ब् *khamb*, cl. 1. P. °*bati*, to go or move, Dhātup. xi, 35 (v. l.)

खयोग *kha-yoga*. See 3. *khá*, p. 334, col. 3.

खर *khára*, mf(*ā*)n. hard, harsh, rough, sharp, pungent, acid (opposed to *mṛidú* and *ślakshṇá*), MBh.; R. &c.; solid (opposed to *drava*, fluid), Pāṇ. vii, 3, 69, Pat.; Kāś. on Pāṇ. ii, 1, 35 & iv, 2, 16; dense (clouds), R. vi, 87, 3; sharp, hot (wind), Suśr. i, 20, 22; hurtful, injurious, cutting (as speech or word), MBh.; R. &c.; sharp-edged, L.; cruel, W.; (*as*), m. a donkey (so called from his cry), KātyŚr.; Mn.; MBh. &c.; a mule, L.; an osprey, L.; a heron, L.; a crow, L.; a thorny plant (sort of prickly nightshade or perhaps Alhagi Maurorum), L.; N. of a fragrant substance, Gal.; a quadrangular mound of earth for receiving the sacrificial vessels (cf. ἐσχάρα), ŚBr. v, 1, 2, 15; xiv; ĀśvŚr.; KātyŚr.; a place arranged for building a house upon, N. of the 25th year of the sixty years' Bṛihaspati cycle, VarBṛS.; a Daitya or demon, L.; N. of the Asura Dhenuka, Hariv. 3114; BhP. ii, 7, 34; N. of a Rakshas slain by Rāma (younger brother of Rāvaṇa), MBh. iii, 15896; R.; BhP.; Ragh.; N. of an attendant [of the Sun (= Dharma), L.; of Śiva, L.]; of a Rudra (?), Hariv. (v. l.); (*am*), ind. in a sharp way, R. iii, 29, 9; (*ā*), f. Andropogon serratus, L.; (*ī*), f. (Pāṇ. iii, 2, 30, Siddh.) a she-ass, Kathās. lxiii; 'a she-mule,' see *kharī-vātsalya*; N. of one of the mothers in Skanda's retinue, MBh. ix, 2624. — **kaṇṭha** (*khará-*), m., N. of a mythical being, Suparṇ. xxiii, 4. — **kaṇḍūyana**, n. 'scraping or rubbing with a sharp object,' making worse any evil, MBh. iii, 33, 66. — **kaṇḍūyita**, n. id., ib. (C). — **karṇī**, f. 'ass-eared,' N. of one of the mothers in Skanda's retinue, MBh. ix, 2644. — **kāshṭhikā**, f. 'having hard wood,' Sida cordifolia, L. — **kuṭī**, f. a barber's shop, L.; used also as an epithet of a man, Pāṇ. iv, 1, 3, Kār. (Pat.); v, 3, 98, Vārtt. 1, Pat.; vi, 1, 103, Kār., Pat.; 204, Kāś. — **ketu**, m., N. of a Rakshas, R. vi, 74, 4. — **koṇa**, m. the francoline partridge, L. — **komala**, m. 'bracing yet mild,' the month Jyaishṭha, L. — **kvāṇa**, m. = *-koṇa*, W. — **kshaya**, m. = *-sāda*, Gal. — **gandhanibhā, -gandhā**, f. Uraria Lagopodioides, L. — **gṛiha**, n. = *-geha*, L.; a tent, Gal. — **geha**, n. a stable for asses, L. — **go-yuga**, n. a pair of donkeys, Pāṇ. v, 2, 29, Vārtt. 3, Pat. — **graha**, m. id., L. — **ghātana**, m. 'destroying asses,' Mesua ferrea, L. — **cchada**, m. 'sharp-leaved,' N. of a tree (= *bhūmī-saha*), Bhpr. v, 5, 75; a kind of grass (*ulūka* or *kundara*), L.; a kind of reed (*itkaṭa*, commonly Okera), L.; N. of a small shrub (*kshudra-gholī*), L. — **jaṅghā**, f., N. of one of the mothers in Skanda's retinue, MBh. ix, 2640. — **jru** (°*rá-*), mfn. sharp or quick in motion, RV. x, 106, 7. — **ṇas**, m. 'sharp-nosed,' N. of a man, Pāṇ. v, 4, 118, Pat. — **ṇasa**, m. id., ib., Kāś. & Siddh.; Pāṇ. viii, 4, 3, Kāś. — **tara**, mfn. sharper, very sharp, R. iii, 28, 1; N. of Jineśvara (who in 1024 A.D. overcame the Caitya-vāsins and founded the *gaccha* of the Śvetāmbaras called after him). — **tva**, n. the state of an ass, Hcat. — **tvac**, f. 'having a rough bark,' N. of a plant (= *alambushā*), Bhpr. — **daṇḍa**, n. 'rough-stemmed,' the lotus, BhP. iv, 6, 29. — **dalā**, f. 'sharp-leaved,' the opposite-leaved fig-tree, L. — **dūshaṇa**, m. 'killing asses,' the thorn-apple, L.; m. du. the two demons Khara and Dūshaṇa, R. iii, 23, 39; *-vadha*, m. slaughter of those demons, N. of PadmaP. iv, 17. — **dhāra**, mfn. having a harsh edge or one full of notches (like that of a saw), Suśr. — **dhvaṇsin**, m. 'destroyer of the demon Khara,' N. of Rāma, L. — **nakhara**, m. 'having sharp claws,' N. of a lion, Pañcat. iii. — **nāda**, m. the braying of an ass, W.; N. of a medical author, Bhpr. — **nādin**, mfn. braying like an ass, Pāṇ. vi, 2, 80, Kāś.; m., N. of a man, g. *bāhv-ādi*; of a Ṛishi, Buddh. L.; (*inī*), f. a kind of perfume or drug, L. — **nāla**, n. = *-daṇḍa*, BhP. iii, 8, 19. — **pa**, m., N. of a man, g. 1. *naḍâdi*; (*ās*), m. pl. the descendants of that man, g. *yaskâdi*. — **pattra**, m. 'sharp-leaved,' a kind of Ocimum (*tulasī*); = *maruvaka* (another kind of Ocimum), L.; a kind of cane, L.; a variety of Kuśa grass, L.; Trophis aspera, Gal.; Tectona grandis (v. l. *śara-p°*), L.; (*ā*), f. a variety of the fig-tree, L.; (*ī*), f. = *-parṇinī*, L.; the opposite-leaved fig-tree, L. — **pattraka**, m. a variety of Ocimum, L. — **parṇinī**, f. 'sharp-leaved,' Phlomis esculenta, Bhpr. v, 3, 297. — **pātra**, n. an iron pot, L. — **pādâḍhya**, m. the elephant or wood apple, L. — **pāla**, m. a wooden vessel, W. — **pushpa**, m. a variety of Ocimum, Suśr. i, 46, 4, 11; (*ā*), f. id., L. — **prâṇa**, a particular vessel, Hcar. — **priya**, m. 'the donkey's friend,' a pigeon, L. — **majrá**, mfn. one who cleans very sharply (Sāy.), RV. x, 106, 7. — **mañjari**, °*rī*, f. Achyranthes aspera (*apâmārgá*), Suśr. iv, vi; Pañcar. — **mayūkha**, m. 'hot-rayed,' the sun, Dhūrtan. — **mukhikā**, f. a kind of musical instrument, Jain. Sch. — **yashṭikā**, f. 'rough-stemmed,' N. of a plant, L. — **yāna**, n. vehicle drawn by a donkey, donkey-cart, Mn. xi, 202. — **raśmi**, m. = *-mayūkha*, L. — **roman**, m. 'having rough hair,' N. of one of the Nāga chiefs inhabiting hell, L. — **loman**, v. l. for *-roman*, W. — **vallikā**, f. = *-gandha-nibhā*, L. — **vṛishabha**, m. a jackass, Car. iv, 8. — **śabda**, m. 'harsh-voiced,' an osprey, L.; the braying of an ass, W. — **śāka**, m. Clerodendrum siphonanthus, Bhpr. — **śāla**, m. produced in a donkey-stall, Pāṇ. iv, 3, 35; (*ā*), f. a donkey-stable, L. — **sāda**, m. swooning, fainting-fit, Gal. — **soni**, m. an iron vessel, L. — **sonda**, m. id., L. — **solla**, m. id., W. — **skandha**, m. 'having a rough stem,' Buchanania latifolia, Bhpr.; N. of a demon, SaddhP.; (*ā*), f. Phœnix sylvestris, L. — **sparśa**, mf(*ā*)n. sharp, hot (as wind), MBh. iii, 11396; BhP. i, 14, 16. — **svarā**, f. wild jasmine (*vana-mallikā*), L. **Kharâṅśu**, m. = °*ra-mayūkha*; *-tanaya*, m. 'son of the sun,' the planet Saturn. **Kharâgarī**, f. Andropogon serratus, L. **Kharâṇḍaka**, m., N. of one of Śiva's attendants, L. **Kharâbdâṅkuraka**, n. lapis lazuli, L. (v. l. *kha-śabdâṅkura-ja*.) **Kharâlaka**, v. l. for °*lika*, q. v. **Kharâlika**, m. an iron arrow (v. l. °*laka*, W.), L.; a pillow, L.; a barber (*grāmaṇī*), L.; a razor-case, L. **Kharâśvā**, f. = °*râhvā*, Bhpr. v, 1, 78; Celosia cristata, L.; = *aja-gandhā* or *karavī* (commonly *vanayamānī*), L. **Kharâsyā**, f. 'donkey-faced,' N. of a sorceress, Vīrac. xxii. **Kharâhvā**, f. the plant *aja-modā*, L. **Kharôshṭra**, n. sg. ass and camel, Yājñ. ii, 160.

Kharāyita, n. behaviour of an ass, Kathās. lxiii.

Kharikā, f. powdered musk, L.

Kharita, *as*, m. the brother's son, Gal.

Kharim (in comp. for °*rīm*, acc. of °*rī*, q. v.) — **dhama**, mfn. ?, Pāṇ. iii, 2, 30, Siddh.; (cf. *khārim-dh°*.) — **dhaya**, mfn.? drinking ass's milk, ib.; (cf. *khārim-dh°*.)

Kharī, f. of °*ra*, q. v. — **khan**, m., N. of a man, & (*ānas*), m. pl. his descendants, g. *upakâdi* (Gaṇar. 31). — **jaṅgha**, m., N. of a man, & (*ās*), m. pl. his descendants, g. *upakâdi*. — **vātsalya**, n. 'maternal love of a she-mule,' motherliness not wanted, MBh. v, 4587. — **vishāṇa**, n. 'an ass's horn,' anything not existing, SŚaṃkar. i, 8. — **vṛisha**, m. a jackass (cf. °*ra-vṛishabha*), Pāṇ. vi, 2, 144, Kāś.

Kharī-√bhū, to become acute (as a disease), Car. vi, 18.

Kharya, mfn. fr. °*ra*, g. *gav-ādi*.

खरटखरटा *kharaṭa-kharaṭā*, ind. (onomat.) only in comp. with -√1. **kṛi**, to make the sound *kharaṭa*, Pāṇ. v, 4, 57, Kāś.

खरणस् *khara-ṇas*, &c. See *khára*.

खरनराय *kharana-rāya*, *as*, m., N. of a son of Śatânanda, Śaṃkaracetov. ii.

खरनाद *khara-nāda*, &c. See 1. *khára*.

खरु *kharu*, mfn. white, L.; foolish, idiotic, Uṇ.; harsh, cruel, ib.; desirous of improper or prohibited things, L.; (*us*), m. a tooth, L.; a horse, L.; Uṇ.; pride, L.; love or Kāma (the god of love), Uṇ.; N. of Śiva, L.; (*us*), f. (Pāṇ. iv, 1, 44, Vārtt.) a girl who chooses her own husband, Pāṇ. Siddh.

खरोष्टी *kharoshṭī*, f. a kind of written character or alphabet, Lalit. x, 29; °*roṭṭhi*, Jain.

खर्खोद *kharkhoda*, a kind of magic, Rājat. v, 238; (*khārkhoṭa*) Car. vi, 23.

खर्गल *khargála*, *as*, m., N. of a man, Tāṇḍya Br. xvii, 4, 3, Sch.; (*ā*), f. an owl or any similar night-bird, RV. vii, 104, 17; Kauś.; (cf. *khṛig°*.)

खर्ज् *kharj*, cl. 1. P. °*jati*, to creak (like a carriage-wheel), KātyŚr.; to worship, treat with respect or courtesy, Dhātup. vii, 54; to pain, make uneasy, ib.; to cleanse, ib.

Kharja, mfn., Pāṇ. vii, 3, 59, Kāś.

Kharjikā, f. a relish that provokes drinking, L.

Kharju, *us*, f. scratching, itching, itch, scab, L.; a kind of insect, worm, L.; the wild date tree, L. — **ghna**, m. 'itch-remover,' the thorn-apple, Gal.; Cassia Alata or Tora (*cakra-marda*), Gal.

Kharjura, *as*, m. a kind of date, L.; (*am*), n. silver, L. — **karṇa**, v. l. for °*rjūra-k°*, q. v.

Kharjū, *ūs*, f. (= °*ju*) itching, Uṇ.; a kind of insect, worm, Uṇ. — **ghna**, m. (= °*rju-gh°*) the thorn-apple, L.; Cassia Alata or Tora, L.; Calotropis gigantea, L.

Kharjūra, m. Phœnix sylvestris, TS. ii, 4, 9, 2; Kāṭh.; MBh. &c.; a scorpion, L.; N. of a man, g. *aśvâdi*; (*ī*), f. Phœnix sylvestris, VarBṛS.; Kathās. lxi; the wild date tree, L.; (*am*), n. the fruit of Phœnix sylvestris, Kathās. lxi; (= *kharjura*) silver, L.; yellow orpiment, L.; = *khala*, L.; the interior part of a cocoa-nut, L. — **karṇa**, m., N. of a man, g. *śivâdi* (Kāś.; Gaṇar. 216). — **pura**, n. the town Khajurāho in Bundelkhand, Inscr. — **rasa**, m. the juice or extract of the wild date or Tāḍi (used to leaven bread and as an intoxicating liquor), W.

Kharjūraka, m. a scorpion, Vasantar. xv, 8; (*ikā*), f. a sweetmeat; (cf. *piṇḍa-, muni-*.)

Kharjūrī, f. of °*ra*, q. v. — **rasa-ja**, m. 'made from the juice of the wild date,' a kind of sugar, Gal.

Kharjūla, m., N. of a man, g. *aśvâdi* (Kāś.)

Kharjya, mfn., Pāṇ. vii, 3, 59, Kāś.

खर्द् *khard*, cl. 1. P. °*dati*, to bite, sting, sting venomously, Dhātup. iii, 23.

खर्पर *kharpara*, *as*, m. a thief, L.; a rogue, cheat, L.; the skull, L.; the half of a skull, W.; a beggar's bowl or dish, L.; an umbrella or parasol, L.; N. of a man, Vīrac. xviii; n. & (*ī*), f. a kind of mineral substance (used as a collyrium), Bhpr. v, 7, 145; 26, 118 & 232; (cf. *karpara*.)

Kharparikā, f. an umbrella, Gal.; = °*rī*, L.

Kharparī, f. of °*ra*, q. v. — **tuttha**, n. a kind of collyrium, L. — **rasaka**, n. id., L.

खर्पराल *kharparāla*, *as*, m. (= *kandar°*) N. of a plant, W.

खर्ब् *kharb*, cl. 1. P. °*bati*, to go or move.

Dhātup. xi, 27; [cf. Old Germ. *hwarb, hwarp, hwirbu*, &c.; Goth. *bi-hvairba*, 'to go round.']

खर्बूज *kharbūja, am*, n. (fr. the Pers. خربزه, *kharbūza*), the water-melon, Bhpr. v, 6, 43 f.

खर्म *kharma*, n. harshness, Vāsav. 288; =*paurusha* (virility, for *pārushya*?), L.; wove silk, Vāsav. 288.

खर्य *kharya*. See *khára*.

खर्व् *kharv* (=√*garv*), cl. 1. P. °*vati*, to be proud or haughty, Dhātup. xv, 73.

खर्व *kharvá*, mfn. (cf. *á-, tri-*) mutilated, crippled, injured, imperfect, TS. ii, 5, 1, 7; low, dwarfish, L.; (*as, am*), m. n. a large number (either 10,000,000,000 [L.], or 37 cyphers preceded by 1, R. vi, 4, 59); (*as*), m., N. of one of the nine Nidhis or treasures of Kubera, L.; Rosa moschata, L. **-pattrā**, f. 'having imperfect leaves,' a kind of low shrub, L. **-vāsin**, mfn. being or abiding in a mutilated object, AV. xi, 9, 16. **-śākha**, mfn. 'having small branches,' dwarfish, small, L.

Kharvaka, mf(*khárvikā*)n. mutilated, imperfect, AV. xi, 9, 16; (*ikā*), f. (scil. *paurṇamāsī*) not quite full (as the moon), Sch. on KātyŚr. &c.

Kharvita, mfn. (anything) that has become dwarfish, Kathās. li, 1.

Kharvī-krita, mfn. made low, pressed down, Amar. 36, Sch.

खर्वट *kharvaṭa*, m. (n., L.) a mountain village (=*karv*°), BhP. i, 6, 11; iv, 18, 31; vii, 2, 14.

खर्वुरा *kharvurā*, f., N. of a thorny plant, L.

Kharvūrā, f. id., Gal.

खल् *khal*, cl. 1. P. °*lati* (Nir. iii, 10), to move or shake, Dhātup. xv, 38; to gather, ib.; (cf. √*khall*.)

खल *khála, as*, m. (*am*, n., g. *ardharcâdi*) a threshing-floor, granary, RV. x, 48, 7; AV.; ŚāṅkhŚr. &c.; earth, mould, soil, L.; place, site, L.; (*as*), m. contest, battle, Naigh.; Nir.; sediment or dregs of oil, Pañcat. ii, 53; (=*khaḍa*) butter-milk boiled with acid vegetables and spices, Suśr. i, vi; a mischievous man, Mṛicch.; Cāṇ.; BhP.; Pañcat. &c.; the sun, L.; Xanthochymus pictorius (*tamāla*), L.; the thorn-apple, L.; (*ā*), f. a mischievous woman, Amar.; N. of a daughter of Raudrâśva, Hariv.; VāyuP. ii, 37, 122; (*ī*), f. sediment or deposit of oil, Car.; Bhartṛ. ii, 98. **-kula** (*khalá-*), n. a low or base family, VarBṛ.; m. (=*kulattha*) Dolichos uniflorus, ŚBr. xiv, 9, 3, 22; Kauś. **-já**, mfn. produced on a threshing-floor, AV. viii, 6, 15. **-tā**, f. wickedness, villainy; filthiness, W. **-tula-parṇī**, f. (perhaps) N. of a plant, Kauś. **-tva**, n. =*-tā*, W. **-dhāna**, °*nya*, n. a threshing-floor, L. (v.l. *khalâdhāna*). **-pū**, mfn. (Kāś. on Pāṇ. vi, 1, 175 & viii, 2, 4) 'one who cleans a threshing-floor,' a sweeper, cleaner, Mehter or Ferash, L. **-prīti**, f. the friendship or favour of low or wicked persons, W. **-mālin**, mfn. garlanded with threshing-floors, PārGṛ. **-mūrti**, m. quicksilver, L. **-yajña**, m. a sacrifice performed on a threshing-floor, Gobh. iv. **-samsarga**, m. associating with bad company, W. **Khalâjina**, ?, g. *utkarâdi*. **Khalâjinīya**, mfn., ib. **Khalâdhāna**, v.l. for *khala-dh*°, q.v. **Khalâdhārā**, f. a kind of cockroach, L. **Khale-dhānī**, &c., see s.v. *khale*. **Khalôkti**, f. low or wicked language, abuse, W.

Khalāya, Nom. Ā. °*yate*, to act like a wicked person, Bhartṛ.

Khali, *is*, m. sediment of oil or oil-cake, L.; =*-druma*, Npr. **-druma**, m. (=*khalla*) Pinus longifolia, Npr.

Khalin, mfn. one who possesses threshing-floors (said of Śiva), MBh. xiii, 1172; (*inas*), m. pl., N. of a class of Dānavas, 7282 ff.; (*inī*), f. a multitude of threshing-floors, Pāṇ. iv, 2, 51; Anethum graveolens, L.; Curculigo orchioides, L.

1. **Khalina**, *as*, m., N. of a place (named after the Khalins), MBh. xiii, 7288.

Khalī, ind. fr. °*la*, q.v. **-kāra**, m. ill-treatment, abusing, reviling, Kād.; Śāntiś.; Kathās. **-√kṛi**, 'to reduce to sediment, crush,' to hurt, injure, treat ill, Mṛicch.; Kād.; Hcar.; Kathās.; (sometimes confounded with *khilī-√kṛi*.) **-kṛiti**, f. =*-kāra*, Kathās. xiii, 157.

Khale, loc. of °*la*, q.v. **-dhānī**, f. =*-vālī*, L. **-busam**, ind. at the time when the chaff is on the threshing-floor, at the threshing-time, g. *tishṭhadgv-ādi*. **-yavam**, ind. at the time when barley is on the threshing-floor, at the barley threshing-time, ib. **-vālī**, f. the post of a threshing-floor, TāṇḍyaBr. xvi, 13, 8; ĀśvŚr. ix, 7, 15; KātyŚr.; Nyāyam. x.

Khálya, mfn. being on a threshing-floor, VS. xvi, 33; MaitrS. ii; fit for a threshing-floor ('fit for oil-cake' &c.?), Pāṇ. v, 1, 7; (*ā*), f. a multitude of threshing-floors, Pāṇ. iv, 2, 50; N. of a woman, g. *tikâdi* (v.l.) **Khalyâṅga**, m., N. of a fish, Gal.

Khalyakā, f., N. of a woman, g. *tikâdi*.

खलखलाय *khalakhalāya* (onomat.), Ā. °*yate*, ?, Cāṇ.

खलति *khalati*, mfn. (g. *bhīmâdi*; ifc. or in comp., g. *kaḍārâdi*; √*khal*, Uṇ.) bald-headed, bald, VS.; TS.; ŚBr. xiii; KātyŚr. &c.; (*is*), m. baldness, Sāy. on RV. viii, 102; (cf. *kulva, khalliṭa*, &c.)

Khalatika, *as*, m. the sun, Gal.; N. of a mountain, Pat. on Pāṇ. i, 2, 52, Vārtt. 4; Inscr.; (*am*), n., N. of a forest situated near that mountain, Pat. on Pāṇ. i, 2, 52, Vārtt. 4.

खलिन 2. *khalina, as, am*, m. n. (cf. χαλινός) the bit of a bridle, VarBṛS. xliv, 22; xciii, 9.

Khalīna, *am*, n. (g. *ardharcâdi*), id., MBh. i, 7343; vi, 2293; Pañcat. iv, 6, ½; v, 11, ½.

खलिश *khaliśa, as*, m. a kind of fish (Trichopodus Colisa, W.; or =*kaṅka-troṭa*, Esox Kankila), L.; (v.l. *khalliśa*; cf. *khaśeṭa*.)

Khaleśa, °*śaya, as*, m. id., L.

खलीन *khalīna*. See 2. *khalina*.

खलु *khálu*, ind. (as a particle of asseveration) indeed, verily, certainly, truly, R.; Śak. &c.; (as a continuative particle) now, now then, now further, RV. x, 34, 14; TS. &c.; (as a particle in syllogistic speech) but now, =Lat. *atqui*, TBr.; ŚBr. &c.; [*khalu* is only exceptionally found at the beginning of a phrase; it is frequently combined with other particles, thus *átha kh*°, *u kh*°, *vaí kh*°, *kh*° *vaí*, =now then, now further, TS.; TBr.; ŚBr. &c.; in later Sanskṛit *khalu* frequently does little more than lay stress on the word by which it is preceded, and is sometimes merely expletive; it is also a particle of prohibition (in which case it may be joined with the ind. p. [*khalu kṛitvā*, 'desist from doing that'], Nir. i, 5 [also °*tam*]; Pāṇ. iii, 4, 18; Śiś. ii, 70); or of endearment, conciliation, and inquiry, L.; *na khalu*, by no means, not at all, indeed not, R. &c.] **-tas**, ind. (=*khalu*) certainly, Saṃh-Up. v, 8.

खलुज् *khaluj*, m. (*kha-luk*?) darkness, L.

खलुरेष *khaluresha, as*, m. a kind of wild quadruped, L.

Khalureshaka, *as*, m. id., W.

खलूरिका *khalūrikā*, f. a parade, place for military exercise, L.; (cf. *khuralī*.)

Khalūrī, f. id., Gal.

खलेश *khaleśa*, °*śaya*. See *khaliśa*.

खल्य *khálya*, &c. See *khála*.

खल्ल् *khall* (=√*khal*), cl. 1. Ā. *khallate*, to shake, be loose, Suśr. ii, 15, 5.

Khalla, *as*, m. a little case or cap formed by rolling up paper &c. (used for holding any small articles of grocery), Suśr. i, vi; (=*khalva*) a mill, stone or vessel for grinding drugs, Bhpr.; a kind of cloth or clothes, L.; leather, leather garments, L.; a leather water-bag, L.; a canal, cut, creek, trench, L.; the Cātaka (kind of cuckoo), L.; n. a slender waist, L.; (*ī*), f. shooting pain in the extremities, Car. i, 14, 21 & 28, 16; vi; Bhpr. vii, 36, 160 f.; (=*khali*) Pinus longifolia, Npr.

Khalli, *is*, f. (=*kallī*) shooting pain in the extremities, Car. vi, 26.

Khallita, mfn. slack (as a female breast), Bhpr.

खल्लाटक *khallāṭaka*, m. (for °*lvāṭ*, 'bald') N. of the first minister of king Bindu-sāra, Divyâv. xxvi, 456.

खल्लासर *khallāsara*, the 10th Yoga (in astr.)

खल्लिका *khallikā*, f. a frying-pan, L.

खल्लिट *khalliṭa*, mfn. (=*khalati*) bald, L.

खल्लिश *khalliśa*. See *khaliśa*.

खल्लीट *khallīṭa*=°*lliṭa*, L.

खल्व *khálva*, m. a kind of grain or leguminous plant, AV.; VS.; ŚBr. xiv; Kauś.; Gṛihyas.; (=*khalla*) a mill or stone for grinding drugs, Bhpr.

Khalvakā, f. =°*lyakā*, Gaṇar. 230.

खल्वट *khalvaṭa, as*, m. a severe cough, W.

खल्वल *khalvala, ās*, m. pl., N. of a school of the SV., Caraṇ.

खल्वाट *khalvāṭa*, mfn. (=*khalliṭa*) bald-headed, bald, Bhartṛ.; Kathās. lxi, 53 & 184. **-°bil-vīya**, g. *kākatālâdi* (Gaṇar. 195).

खव् *khav* (cl. 9. P. *khaunāti* or *khunāti*), v.l. for √*khac*, Dhātup. xxxi, 59.

खवल्ली *kha-vallī*, &c. See 3. *khá*, p. 334.

खश *khaśa*, for *khasa*, q.v.

खशय *kha-śaya*, &c. See 3. *khá*, p. 334.

खशीर *khaśīra, ās*, m. pl., N. of a people, MBh. vi, 375 (v.l. *khāś*°).

खशेट *khaśeṭa, as*, m.=*khaliśa*, L.

Khaśera, *as*, m. id., Gal.

खश्वास *kha-śvāsa*. See 3. *khá*, p. 334.

खष् *khash*, cl. 1. P. °*shati*, to hurt, injure, kill, Dhātup. xvii, 35; (cf. √*kash*.)

खष्प *khashpa, as*, m. (√*khan*, Uṇ.) violence, oppression, Uṇ.; anger, passion, ib.

खस *khasa*, m. itch, scab, any irritating disease of the skin, L.; (*ās*), m. pl., N. of a people and of its country (in the north of India), Mn. x, 44; MBh.; Hariv.; AV.Pariś. &c.; (*as*), m. a native of that country (considered as a degraded Kshatriya), Mn. x, 22; (*ā*), f. a kind of perfume (*murā*), L.; N. of a daughter of Daksha (one of the wives of Kaśyapa and mother of the Yakshas and Rākshasas), Hariv. **-kanda**, m., N. of a bulbous plant, Npr. (v.l. °*nna*). **-gandha**, m. id., L. (v.l.) **-tila**, m. poppy (*khaskhasa*), Bhpr. **-phala-kshīra**, n. poppy-juice, opium, ib. **-bīja**, n. =*-tila*, ib. **Khasâtmaja**, m. 'born by Khasā,' a Rakshas, L.

खसम *kha-sama*, &c. See 3. *khá*, p. 334.

खसाक *khasāka*, v.l. for *khaśīra*.

खसात्मज *khasâtmaja*. See *khasa*.

खसिन्धु *kha-sindhu*. See 3. *khá*, p. 334.

खसीक *khasīka*, v.l. for *khaśīra*.

खसूचि *kha-sūci*. See 3. *khá*, p. 334.

खसृम *khasṛima, as*, m., N. of a Daitya (son of Vipracitti and Siṃhikā), Hariv. 2288; N. of a son of Kauśika (or Viśvā-mitra), 1190.

खस्खस *khaskhasa, as*, m. (=*khasa-tila*) poppy, L. **-rasa**, m. poppy-juice, opium, L. **-sāra**, m. id., Npr.

Khākhasa, *as*, m. poppy, Bhpr. **-tila**, m. id., ib.

खस्तनी *kha-stanī*, &c. See 3. *khá*, p. 334.

खा *khā*. See √*khan*, p. 337, col. 1.

खाखस *khākhasa*. See *khaskhasa*.

खागि *khāgi, is*, f., N. of an Agra-hāra, Rājat. i, 90.

Khāgikā, f. id., ib. 342.

खाजिक *khājika, as*, m.=*khadikā*, L.

खाञ्जार *khāñjāra, as*, m. patr. fr. *khañj*°, g. *śivâdi*.

Khāñjārāyana, *as*, m. id., g. *aśvâdi*.

Khāñjāla, *as*, m. patr. fr. *khañj*°, g. *śivâdi*.

खाञ्ज्य *khāñjya, am*, n. (fr. *khañja*), limping, Sāṃkhyak. 49, Sch.

खाट् *khāṭ*, ind. (onomat.) 'the sound made in clearing the throat,' in comp. with **-√kṛi**, to clear the throat, Pāṇ. i, 4, 62, Kāś. & Siddh.

खाट *khāṭa, as*, m. (=*khaṭṭi*) a bier, cot or bedstead on which dead bodies are conveyed to the pyre, L.; (*ā*), f. id., L.; (*ī*), f. id., Gal.

Khāṭi, f. id., L.; a scar, L.; Uṇ., Sch.; caprice, L.

Khāṭikā, f. (=*khaṭṭ*°) a bier, L.

खाट्वरेय *khāṭvareya*, *as*, m. patr. fr. *khaṭvara*, g. *śubhrâdi* (Kāś.)

खाट्वाभारिक *khāṭvābhārika*, mfn. (fr. *khaṭvā-bhāra*), laden with bedsteads, g. *vaṅśâdi*.

Khāṭvika, mfn. (fr. *khaṭvā*), id., ib.

खाडण्डक *khāḍaṇḍaka*, for *shāḍ°*.

खाडव *khāḍava*, for *khāṇḍ°*, q. v.

खाडायन *khāḍāyana*, m. patr. fr. Khaḍa, g. 1. *aśvâdi*; Pāṇ. iv, 3, 104, Vārtt. 2. — **bhakta**, n. a district inhabited by Khāḍāyanas, g. *aishukāry-ādi*.

Khāḍāyanaka, mfn. fr. *°na*, g. *arīhaṇâdi*.

Khāḍāyanin, m. pl. (g. *śaunakâdi*) the school of Khāḍāyana, Anup. iii, 5; vii, 9.

Khāḍāyanīya, mfn. fr. *°na*, g. *gahâdi*.

Khāḍika, *ās*, m. pl., N. of a school of the Yajur-veda, AV.Pariś. il (for *khāṇḍ°*?).

Khāḍiki, mfn. fr. *khaḍika*, g. *sutaṃgamâdi*.

Khāḍī, f., N. of a locality, Kshitîś. vii, 3.

Khāḍônmatteya, *as*, m. metron. fr. *khaḍônmattā*, g. *śubhrâdi*.

खाडूरेय *khāḍūreya*, v.l. for *khāṭvar°*.

खाड्ग *khāḍga*, mfn. (fr. *khaḍgá*), coming from a rhinoceros (as armour made of rhinoceros hide), ŚāṅkhŚr. xiv, 33, 20.

खाण्ड *khāṇḍa*, *am*, n. (fr. *khaṇḍa*), the state of having fractures or fissures or gaps, g. *pṛithv-ādi*.

Khāṇḍaka, mfn. fr. *khaṇḍa*, g. *dhūmâdi* (v. l.) & *arīhaṇâdi* (Kāś.)

Khāṇḍaparaśava, mfn. (fr. *khaṇḍa-paraśu*), belonging to Śiva, Bālar. iii, $\frac{62}{63}$.

Khāṇḍavá, *as*, *am*, m. n. sugar-candy, sugar-plums, sweetmeats, MBh. xiii; R. i, vii; N. of a forest in Kuru-kshetra (sacred to Indra and burnt by the god of fire aided by Arjuna and Kṛishṇa, MBh.; Hariv.; BhP. i, 15, 8; Kathās.): TāṇḍyaBr. xxv, 3; TĀr.; (*ī*), f., N. of a town built by Sudarśana, L. — **prastha**, m. (= *indra-pr°*) N. of a town situated in the Khāṇḍava forest (founded by the Pāṇḍavas), MBh.; BhP. x. — **rāga**, m. (= *rāga-khāṇḍava*) sugar-candy, sweetmeats, MBh. xiv, 2684.

Khāṇḍavaka, mfn. fr. *khaṇḍu*, g. *arīhaṇâdi*.

Khāṇḍavāyana, *ās*, m. pl., N. of a family of Brāhmans, MBh. iii, 10208.

Khāṇḍavika. See *rāga-kh°*.

Khāṇḍa-vīraṇa, g. *arīhaṇâdi* (in Kāś. two separate words *khaṇḍa* & *vīraṇa*; cf. Gaṇar. 286).

Khāṇḍavīraṇaka, mfn. fr. *°ṇa*, ib.

Khāṇḍāyana, pl., N. of a family, Pravar. ii, 3, 1.

Khāṇḍika, *as*, m. (fr. *khaṇḍa*), a seller of sugar-plums, confectioner, L.; (pl.) the whole number of pupils, Gobh. iii, 3, 8; N. of a school of the black Yajur-veda, Caraṇ.; (*am*), n. a multitude of pupils (? cf. *khaṇḍ°*), Pāṇ. iv, 2, 45.

Khāṇḍikīya, *ās*, m. pl. (Pāṇ. iv, 3, 102) 'the followers of Khaṇḍika,' N. of a school of the black Yajur-veda, Caraṇ.

Khāṇḍikeya, m. pl., id., DevīP. (= Caraṇ.)

Khāṇḍikya, *as*, m., N. of Janaka, VP. vi, 6, 5 ff.; of Mita-dhvaja, BhP. ix, 13, 20; n. (fr. *khaṇḍika*), the state of a pupil (?), g. *purohitâdi*. — **janaka**, m., N. of Janaka, VP. vi, 5, 81; 6, 8.

Khāṇḍiti, mfn. fr. *khaṇḍita*, g. *sutaṃgamâdi*.

Khāṇḍitya, mfn. id., g. *pragady-ādi*.

खात् *khāt*, v. l. for *khāṭ*, q. v.

खात *khātá*, *khātaka*, &c. See √*khan*, p. 337.

खात्मन् *khâtman*. See 3. *khá*, p. 334.

खाद् *khād*, cl. 1. P. *khādati* (ep. also Ā. *°te*; aor. *akhādīt*, Bhaṭṭ.; perf. *cakhāda*, ib.), to chew, bite, eat, devour, feed, prey upon, RV. i, 64, 7; AV.; VS. &c.; to hurt, Suśr.; to ruin, Subh.: Caus. P. *khādayati*, to cause to be eaten or devoured by (instr.; cf. Pāṇ. i, 4, 52, Vārtt. 5), Gaut.; Mn.; Hcat.; to eat or devour, MBh. iii, 2435: Desid. *cikhādishati*, to desire to eat, MBh. vii, 205 (v. l.); HYog. iii, 18.

Khādá, mfn. 'eating, devouring,' ifc., see *amitra-* & *vṛitra-khādá*; m. eating, devouring, AitBr. v, 12, 10; food, AV. ix, 6, 12; ŚBr. xiii, 4, 2, 17.

Khādaka, *as*, m. (Pāṇ. iii, 2, 146) an eater, devourer, Gobh.; Mn. v, 51; MBh. xiii; a debtor, borrower (cf. *khātaka*), Comm. on Yājñ.; (*ikā*), f. 'eating,' ifc., e. g. *abhyūsha-*, *bisa-*, qq. vv.

Khādag-dát, mfn. one who has biting teeth (Sch.), TĀr. i, 12, 4.

Khādata (Impv. 2. pl. fr. √*khād*, q. v.) — **modatā**, f. (Impv. 2. pl. fr. √*mud*) 'eat and rejoice,' continual eating and rejoicing, g. *mayūra-vyaṅsakâdi*. — **vamatā**, f. (Impv. 2. pl. fr. √*vam*) continual eating and vomiting, ib. (v. l.) **Khādatâcamatā**, f. (Impv. 2. pl. fr. *ā-*√*cam*) continual eating and rinsing the mouth, ib.

Khādana, m. a tooth, L.; n. chewing, eating, Vop.; food, victuals, R. ii, 50, 25 & 31; (*ā*), f., N. of a wife of king Megha-vāhana, Rājat. iii, 14.

Khādanīya, mfn. eatable, edible, Lalit.; Divyâv.

Khādikā. See *°daka*.

Khādas, m. 'devouring,' only in comp. **Khādo-arṇa** or *°rṇas*, mfn. 'having a devouring flood,' i. e. having a flood that carries away the bank (said of a river), RV. v, 45, 2 (Naigh. i, 13).

Khāditá, mfn. eaten, devoured, ŚBr. iii; Suśr.; Bhaṭṭ.; Hit. — **vat**, mfn. having eaten, iii, 6, $\frac{9}{1}$.

Khāditavya, mfn. to be eaten, iv, 5, $\frac{9}{1}$.

Khāditṛi, m. an eater, devourer, MBh. xii, 846.

1. **Khādin**, mfn. ifc. eating, Mn. iv, 71 (= MBh. xiii, 4968).

Khāduka, mfn. mischievous, injurious, L.

Khādya, *am*, n. 'eatable, edible,' food, victuals, MBh. ii, 98; Pañcat. i; Bhartṛ.; (*as*), m. (= *khadira*) Acacia Catechu, Gal.; (cf. *khaṇḍa-kh°*.)

Khādyâkhādya, mfn. fit or unfit for food, W.

Khādyaka, *as*, m., N. of a particular food, Gal.

खादाक्य *khādākya*, fr. *khadākā*, g. *kurv-ādi* (Hemac.; *shāḍāk°*, Gaṇar., Sch.)

खादि *khādí*, m. (f.?) a brooch, ring (worn on the hands or feet by the Maruts), RV. i, v, vii; (cf. *vṛisha-*, *hiraṇya-*; *su-khādí*.) — **hasta** (*khādí-*), mfn. having the hands ornamented with bracelets or rings (said of the Maruts), v, 38, 2.

2. **Khādín**, mfn. decorated with bracelets or rings (as the Maruts), RV. ii, 34, 2; vi, 16, 40 (perhaps = *khādí*); x, 38, 1.

खादिर *khādirá*, mf(*ī*)n. (g. *palāśâdi*) made of or coming from the Khadira tree (Acacia Catechu), TS. iii; ŚBr.; AitBr.; Kauś.; Mn. &c.; (*as*), m. = *-rasa*, L.; (*ī*), f. (perhaps) N. of a locality, g. *nady-ādi*. — **gṛihya**, n., N. of a work. — **sāra**, m. Catechu (resinous extract of the Khadira tree), L.

Khādiraka, mfn. fr. *khadirá*, gaṇas *arīhaṇâdi* & *varāhâdi*.

Khādirāyaṇa, m. patr. fr. *khadirá*, g. *aśvâdi*.

Khādireya, mfn. fr. *°rī*, g. *nady-ādi*.

खादुक *khāduka*. See √*khād*.

खादूरक *khādūraka*, *as*, m. patr. fr. *kha-d°*, g. *śivâdi* (for *khāṭvar°*?).

खादोअर्ण *khā́do-arṇa*, &c. See √*khād*.

खाधूया *khādhūyā*, f., N. of an Agra-hāra, Rājat. v, 23.

खान 1. *khāna*, *am*, n. (fr. √*khād*?), eating, GaruḍaP. **Khānôdaka**, m. the cocoa-nut tree, L.

खान 2. *khānu*, *us*, m. (= خان) a Khan (or Mogul emperor), Rājat. — **khāna**, m., N. of a Khan (or Mogul emperor), Vaidyajīv., Sch. Concl.

Khānā-rāya, m., N. of a man (A. D. 1500).

खानक *khānaka*, *°ni*, *°nika*, &c. See √*khan*.

खानिष्क *khānishka*, *as*, m. a kind of dish (consisting of small pieces of meat prepared with spices), Suśr. i, 46, 8, 24; Madanav.

Khānishṭa, *am*, n. id., Madanav.

खानुल *khānula*, m., N. of a man (father of Bahula, Virac. vi; of Vopula, xix f., xxii).

खान्य *khānya*. See √*khan*, p. 337, col. 1.

खापगा *khâpagā*, *khâpara*. See 3. *khá*, p. 334.

खार *khāra*, *as*, m. (ifc., Pāṇ. v, 4, 101) a measure of grain (commonly Khāri, = 18 Droṇas or about 3 bushels; it is also reckoned at 1½ Śūrpa or 3 Droṇas; also at 46 Gauṇīs or 4096 Palas, or at 4 Droṇas), Pāṇ. ii, 3, 46, Sch. (*°rī*, Kāś.); (*ī*), f. id., RV. iv, 32, 17; Pāṇ.; Pañcat.; Rājat. — *°śatika*, mfn. containing or sown with a hundred Khāri measures, Pat. on Pāṇ. v, 1, 58, Vārtt. 6. — **sahasrika**, mfn. containing or sown with a thousand Khāra measures, ib.

Khāri, *is*, f. (ifc., Pāṇ. v, 4, 101, Kāś.) = *khāra*, Siddh. stry. 32. — **grīvi**, v. l. for *°ragr°*.

Khārim (in comp. for *°rim*, acc. of *°ri* (q. v.), or shortened acc. of *°rī*). — **dhama**, mfn.?, Pāṇ. iii, 2, 29, Pat.; (cf. *khariṃ-dh°*.) — **dhaya**, mfn.?, ib.; (cf. *khariṃ-dh°*.) — **paca**, mfn. 'cooking a Khāri by measure,' (a vessel) in which a Khāri may be cooked, Pāṇ. iii, 2, 33, Kāś.

Khārika, mfn. = *°rīka*, L., Sch.; (*ā*), f. = *khāra*, Sarvad. v, 38.

Khārī, f. of *°ra*, q. v. — **jaṅgha**, for *khar°*, Kāś. — **vāpa**, mfn. sown with a Khāri of grain, L.

Khārīka, mfn. (Pāṇ. v, 1, 33, Vārtt. 1) sown with a Khāri of grain, v, 1, 45, Kāś.; (ifc.) v, 1, 33.

खारग्रीवि *khāragrīvi*, m. pl. (patr. fr. *kharagrīvan*) N. of a family, Pravar. ii, 2, 1.

Khāranādi, m. pl. (patr. fr. *khara-nādin*, g. *bāhv-ādi*), id., ib. (*°raṇādi*, MSS.)

Khārapāyaṇa, patr. fr. *khara-pa*, g. 1. *naḍâdi*.

Khārīkhaṇa, m. pl. the descendants of Kharīkhan, Gaṇar. 31, Sch.

खार्कार *khār-kāra*, *as*, m. (*khār*, onomat., probably connected with *khára*) the braying of an ass, BhP. iii, 17, 11.

खार्खोट *khārkhota* = *kharkhoda*, q. v.

खार्गलि *khārgali*, *is*, m. patr. fr. *khargála*, Kāṭh. xxx, 2; TāṇḍyaBr. xvii, 4, 3.

खार्जुरकर्ण *khārjurakarṇa*, for *°rjūr°*.

Khārjūra, mfn. (fr. *kharj°*), coming from or made of Phœnix sylvestris, Suśr.; Mn. xi, 96, Sch.

Khārjūrakarṇa, *as*, m. patr. fr. *kharjūrak°*, g. *śivâdi*.

Khārjūrāyaṇa, patr. fr. *kharjūra*, g. *aśvâdi*.

Khārjūlāyana, m. patr. fr. *kharjūla*, ib. (Kāś.)

खार्दभीमुख *khārdabhīmukha*. See *gard°*.

खार्दमायन *khārdamāyana*, m. pl., N. of a family, Pravar. i, 7; cf. *kārd°*.

खार्वा *khārvā*, f. (fr. *kharva*), the second ('third,' NBD.) Yuga of the world.

खालत्य *khā́latya*, *am*, n. (fr *khalatí*), morbid baldness, AV. xi, 8, 19.

Khālitya, *am*, n. id., Car. vi, 9; Suśr. i ff.

खालिक *khālika*, mf(*ī*)n. = *khala iva* (like a threshing-floor), g. *aṅguly-ādi* (not in Kāś.)

खालीय *khālīya*, *as*, m., N. of a teacher, VāyuP. i, 60, 64; (*śālīya*, BhP. & VP.)

खाल्यकायनि *khālyakāyani*, *is*, m. metron. fr. *khalyakā*, g. *tikâdi* (*khālvak°*, Gaṇar. 230).

खाशि *khāśi*, *is*, m., N. of a country to the east of Bengal (the Cossia hills), W.; (cf. *khasa*.)

Khāśika, *as*, m. id., W.

खाशीर *khāśīra*, v. l. for *khaś°*, q. v.

खाश्मरी *khāśmarī*, f. = *kāśm°*, W.

खासता *khāsatā*, f., N. of a place in Kaśmīr, Rājat. i, 344.

खास्यलिपि *khāsya-lipi*, f. (fr. *khasa*?), a kind of written character or alphabet, Lalit. x, 32.

खिक्खिमिन् *khikkhimin*, mfn. speaking indistinctly, VarBṛS. lxxviii, 18.

खिखि *khikhi*, *is*, f. (= *kikhi*) a fox, L.

Khiṅkhira, *as*, m. id., L.; (= *khaṭvāṅga*) the foot of a bedstead (one of Śiva's weapons), L.; a kind of perfume (commonly Hāla), L.; (*ī*), f. a fox, L.

खिचा *khiccā*, f. a kind of dish (made of rice and pease &c.), Npr.

Khicci, *is*, *°ccī*, f. id., Gal.

खिट् *khiṭ*, cl. 1. P. *kheṭati*, to be terrified or frightened, Dhātup. ix, 15; to terrify, alarm, ib.

Kheṭita, mfn. frightened, W.; ploughed, L.

खिड्ग *khiḍga*, for *shiḍga*, Vāsav. 307.

खिद् *khid*, cl. 6. *khindati* (Pāṇ. vii, 1, 59; Ved. *khidati*, ib.; perf. *cikheda* or Ved. *cakhāda*, Pāṇ. vi, 1, 52; fut. *khetsyati*, Pāṇ. vii, 2, 10, Siddh.), to strike, press, press down, Pāṇ. vi, 1, 52, Kāś.; Dhātup.; to be depressed or wearied, BhP. x, 69, 40: cl. 7. Ā. *khintte*, to be pressed down, suffer pain, Bhaṭṭ. vi, 37: cl. 4. Ā. *khidyate* (rarely P., MBh. ii, 2428; BhP.; Bhaṭṭ.), to be pressed down or depressed, be distressed or wearied, feel tired or exhausted, R.; Śak.; Pañcat. &c.: **Caus. P.** *khe-*

dayati (rarely Ā., BhP. ii, 5, 7), to press down, molest, disturb, make tired or exhausted, Mṛicch. ix, 10; Megh. 85 (v.l.); BhP. &c.; [cf. Gk. κῆδος?]

Khidira, *as,* m. an ascetic, penitent, Uṇ. vṛ.; a pauper, ib.; the moon, Uṇ. i, 52; N. of Indra, L.

Khidrá, m. a pauper, ii, 13; disease, sickness, ib.; n. (Nir. xi, 37) an instrument for splitting, RV. v, 84, 3; (cf. *á-khidra-yāman.*)

Khidvas, mfn. (irr. pf. p. P.) pressing upon, oppressing, RV. vi, 22, 4.

Khinna, mfn. depressed, distressed, suffering pain or uneasiness, Mn. vii, 141; MBh. &c.; wearied, exhausted, VarBṛS. xxxii, 1 &c.

Kheda, *as,* m. lassitude, depression, R. &c.; exhaustion, pain, affliction, distress, Pañcat. &c.; sexual passion, Pat. Introd. on Vārtt. 1; (*khédā*), f. an instrument for splitting (belonging to Indra), RV. viii, 72, 8; 77, 3; x, 116, 4; N. of a locality, Rājat. ii, 135. **–vigama,** m. removal of sexual passion, Pat. Introd. on Vārtt. 1. **Khedâṅga-sāra,** m., N. of a Tantra, BrahmavP. i, 16, 19. **Khedânvita,** mfn. distressed, pained.

Khedana, mfn. piercing, Nir. xi, 37; n. lassitude, exhaustion, HaṃsUp.; pain, sorrow, affliction, W.

Khedayitavya, mfn. to be depressed or made distressed, Ratnâv. ii, $\frac{1}{2}$; Prab. vi, $\frac{2}{2}$.

Khedita, mfn. disturbed, annoyed, MBh. xiv, 1825; injured (as by arrows), VarBṛS. xxiv, 32; afflicted, distressed, R. &c.

Kheditavya, n. impers. to be depressed or cast down or troubled, R. iii, 49, 57.

Khedin, mfn. tired, Bālar. vi, 49; (cf. *a-khedi-tva*); (*inī*), f. the creeper Marsilea quadrifolia, L.; another plant (*aśana-parṇī*), L.

खिन्दक *khindaka, as,* m., N. of the Arabic astronomer Alkindi.

Khindhi, *is,* °*ndhika, as,* m. id.

खिमिडी *khimiḍī,* f., N. of a district in the Central Provinces, Inscr.

खिरहिट्टी *khirahiṭṭī,* f., N. of a plant, L.

खिल *khilá, as,* m. (*am,* n., L.) a piece of waste or uncultivated land situated between cultivated fields, desert, bare soil, AV. vii, 115, 4; ŚBr. viii; ŚāṅkhBr.; Kauś.; (*am*), n. 'a space not filled up, gap,' that which serves to fill up a gap, supplement (of a book &c.), additional hymn appended to the regular collection, MBh. iii, 232; MBh. i; VāyuP.; ŚivaP. &c.; a compendium, compilation (esp. of hymns and prayers), L.; n. pl. remainder, BhP. vi, 4, 15; sg. (in alg.) an insolvable problem, Gol.; obduracy, Lalit. xix, xxi; =*vedhas* (Brahmā or Vishṇu, W.), L.; mfn. defective, insufficient, BhP. i, vi. **–kāṇḍa,** n. 'supplementary section,' N. of MaitrS. v and BṛĀrUp. v f. **–kshetra,** n. an uncultivated field, Hcar. **–grantha,** m., N. of a work. **–pāṭha,** m. (opposed to *sūtra-p°*) a collective N. for Dhātup., Gaṇap., and Vārtt., Pāṇ. i, 3, 2, Kāś.

Khilī, ind. fr. °*la,* q.v. **–√1. kṛi,** (ind.p.-*kṛitya*), to make vain or powerless, Śiś. ii, 34; Rājat. **–kṛita,** mfn. turned into a desert, devastated, made impassable, Ragh. xi, 14 & 87; made powerless, Daś. vii; MārkP. **–bhūta,** mfn. (anything) that has become a desert, abandoned, unfrequented (by, gen.), Car. v, 12; Kum. ii, 45; Hcar.; Naish. xvii, 37; frustrated, Śak. vi, 22.

Khilyá, *as,* m. a piece of waste or uncultivated land situated between cultivated fields, RV. x, 142, 3; a piece of rock in the earth, mass, heap, lump, RV. vi, 28, 2; (ifc.) ŚBr. xiv, 5, 4, 12.

खीर *khīra,* N. of a place, Rājat. i, 337.

खील *khīla, as,* m. (=*kīla*) a post, AV. x, 8, 4; TBr. iii, 7, 6, 19.

खु *khu,* cl. 1. Ā. *khavate,* to sound, Dhātup. xxii, 58.

खुङ्खुणी *khuṅkhuṇī,* f. a kind of lute, L.

खुङ्गाह *khuṅgāha, as,* m. a black horse, L

खुज् *khuj,* cl. 1. *khojati,* to steal, vii, 18.

खुज्जाक *khujjāka, as,* m. Lipeocercis serrata, L.

खुड् *khuḍ* (*khoḍayati*) v.l. for √*khuṇḍ.*

खुड *khuḍa, as,* m. (?), rheumatism, Ashṭâṅg. iii, 16, 4; Npr. **–vāta,** m. id., ib.; (mfn.) rheumatic, Car. vi, 26.

खुडक *khuḍaka,* the ankle-joint, Suśr. ii, 1, 78; (cf. *khulaka.*)

खुडुल *khuḍula, as,* m., N. of a lexicographer (mentioned by Śāśvata).

खुड्डक *khuḍḍaka,* mfn. (Prākrit form of *kshudraka*) small, minor, Car. i, 9 (v.l.)

Khuḍḍāka, mf(*īkā*)n. id., i, 9; iv, 4; vi, 29, 102.

खुण्ड् *khuṇḍ,* cl. 1. Ā. °*ḍate,* to break in pieces, Dhātup. viii, 31; to limp, Vop.; cl. 10. P. *khuṇḍayati* (v.l. *khoḍayati,* cf. *kshodayati* fr. *kshudrá*), to break in pieces, Dhātup. xxxii, 47.

खुद् *khud,* cl. 6. P. *khudáti,* to sport wantonly or amorously, RV. x, 101, 12: Intens. (p. *canīkhudat*) id., ĀśvŚr. ii, 10, 14; (*kánīkhunat,* fr. √*khun*) TBr. ii, 4, 6, 5.

खुन् *khun*=√*khud,* q.v.

खुनमुख *khuna-mukha,* for *khon°,* q.v.

खुम् *khum.* ind. a particle of exclamation, g. *câdi.*

खुर् *khur* (=√*kshur, chur*), cl. 6. P. °*rati,* to cut, cut up, break in pieces, Dhātup. xxviii, 52; to scratch, ib.

Khura, *as,* m. a hoof, horse's hoof, KātyŚr.; Mn. &c. (ifc. f. *ā* [g. *kroḍâdi*], MBh. i; Hcat.; once *ī,* i, 7, 38); a particular part of the foot of a bedstead, VarBṛS. lxxix; a sort of perfume (dried shell-fish shaped like a hoof), L.; (for *kshurá*) a razor, L.; (*ī*), f., g. *bahv-ādi* (not in Kāś. & g. *śoṇâdi*). **–kshepa,** m. a kick with a hoof, W. **–ṇas,** mfn. 'having a nose like a horse's hoof,' flat-nosed, Pāṇ. v, 4, 118, Pat. **–ṇasa,** mfn. id., ib., Kāś. & Siddh. **–trāṇa,** n. a horse-shoe, Gal. **–padavī,** f. a horse's footmarks, W. **–pra,** m. (for *kshur°*) a sharp-edged arrow, Bālar. iv, 54; a sickle, Gal. **Khurâghāta,** m. =°*ra-kshepa,* W. **Khurâbhighāta,** m. id., W. **Khurâlaka,** m. an iron arrow, L. **Khurâlika,** m., v.l. for *khur°,* q.v.

Khuraka, mfn.? (said of a kind of tin), Bhpr. v, 7, 30 f. & 26, 71; m. a kind of dance, Vikr. iv, $\frac{2}{2}$ f.; Sesamum indicum, L.

Khurin, *ī,* m. an animal with hoofs, VarBṛS.

खुरखुर *khurakhura,* m. (or °*rā,* f.) rattling (in the throat), Lalit. xiv, 34.

Khurukhurāya, Nom. Ā. °*yate,* to rattle (as the throat), xv, 112; Car. vi, 8.

खुरली *khuralī,* f. military exercise, practising archery &c., Bālar. iv, $\frac{1}{1}$; place for military exercise, Vcar. vi, 46; (cf. *khalūrikā.*)

खुराक *khurāka, as,* m. an animal ('an animal with hoofs'?, fr. °*ra*), Uṇ. k.

खुरालक *khurâlaka,* &c. See *khura.*

खुरासाण *khurāsāṇa,* Khurāsān.

Khurāsāṇa, id.; mf(*ī*)n. coming from Khurāsān, Bhpr. v, 1, 80 $\frac{8}{5}$.

खुरुखुराय *khurukhurāya.* See *khurakhura.*

खुर्द् *khurd* (=√*kurd, gurd*), cl. 1. Ā. *khūrdate,* to play, sport, Dhātup. ii, 21.

खुलक *khulaka*=*khuḍaka,* Suśr. iv, 18, 24.

खुल्ल *khulla,* mfn. (cf. *kshulla;* Prākrit form for *kshudrá*) small, little, W.; (*am*), n. (=*khura*) a kind of perfume, W. **–tāta,** m. (=*kshull°*) a father's younger brother, L.

Khullaka, mfn. =*kshudraka,* L., Sch.

खुल्लम *khullama, as,* m. a road, L.

खूर्द् *khūrd*=√*khurd,* q.v.

खृगल *khṛigala, as,* m. a staff, crutch (?, 'a coat of mail,' Sāy.), RV. ii, 39, 4; AV. iii, 9, 3.

खेखीरक *khekhīraka,* a hollow bamboo, L.

खेगमन *khe-gamana,* &c. See 3. *khá,* p. 334.

खेट् *kheṭ,* cl. 10. *kheṭayati,* to eat, consume, Dhātup. xxxv, 22 (v.l. *kheḍ*).

खेट *kheṭa, as,* m. a village, residence of peasants and farmers, small town (half a Pura, Hcat.), MBh. iii, 13220; Jain.; BhP.; VP.: the phlegmatic or watery humor of the body, phlegm, Car. iv, 4; snot, glanders, L.; a horse, L.; the club of Balarāma, L.; m. n. hunting, chase (cf. *ā-kheṭa*), L.; a shield, Hcat. i, 5, 529 [MārkP.] & 532 [BṛNārP.]; ii, 1; (ifc.) expressing defectiveness or deterioration (Pāṇ. vi, 2, 126; e.g. *nagara-*, 'a miserable town,' ib., Kāś.; *upānat-*, 'a miserable shoe,' ib., Kāś.; *muni-*, 'a miserable sage,' Bālar. ii); n. grass, L.; (mfn.) low, vile, Bhar. xxxiv, 109; armed, W. **–piṇḍa,** 'a ball of phlegm,' i.e. anything useless, Lalit. xvi, 67 (*pakva-*).

Kheṭaka, *as, am,* m. n. a small village, residence of agricultural peasants, VP.; Hcat.; a shield, MBh. iv, 181; vi, 799; VarBṛS.; Hcat. &c.; n. the club of Bala-rāma (?), L. **–pura,** n., N. of a town, W.

Kheṭin, *ī,* m. a lecher, libertine, L. **Kheṭi-tāla,** m. (=*vaitālika*) a minstrel, family bard or piper (?), L. (vv. ll. *kheṭṭi-t°* & *kheḍi-t°*).

खेऽट *khe'ṭa.* See 3. *khá,* p. 334, col. 3.

खेटिक *kheṭika,* m., N. of a man, Pravar. ii, 1, 2 (Kāty.; *kharika,* Viśv.)

खेटित *kheṭita.* See √*khiṭ.*

खेटिताल *kheṭi-tāla,* °*ṭin.* See above.

खेड् *kheḍ,* v.l. for √*kheṭ,* q.v.

खेड *kheḍa,* (g. *aśvâdi,* Kāś.) for *kheṭa,* a village, Jain.; (cf. *gandha-kh°.*)

Kheḍi-tāla, v.l. for *kheṭi-t°.*

खेद *kheda,* °*dana,* &c. See √*khid.*

खेदि *khédi, ayas,* pl. rays, Naigh. i, 5.

खेदित *khedita,* °*tavya,* &c. See √*khid.*

खेपरिभ्रम *khe-paribhrama.* See 3. *khá.*

खेमकर्ण *khema-karṇa,* m. (for *kshem°*?), N. of an ancestor of Bala-bhadra, Hāyan. Introd. 4.

खेय *kheya.* See √*khan.*

खेल् *khel,* cl. 1. P. °*lati,* to shake, move to and fro, swing, tremble, R.; Naish.; Gīt.; Sāh.: Caus. P. *khelayati,* to cause to move to and fro, swing, shake, Pañcat. iv, 5, $\frac{0}{1}$; Kathās. ix, 76.

Khelá, mfn. (in comp. or ifc., g. *kaḍārâdi,* Gaṇar. 90) moving, shaking, trembling, Vikr.; Ragh.; m. N. of a man, RV. i, 116, 15; (*am*), ind. so as to shake or tremble, R. ii; (*ā*), f. sport, play, g. *kaṇḍv-ādi.* **–gati,** mfn. having a stately walk, VarBṛ. xvi, 16. **–gamana,** mf(*ā*)n. id., Vikr. iv, 74. **–gāmin,** mfn. id., MBh. i, 7080; xv, 662; Kum. vii, 49.

Khelana, n. moving to and fro, shaking, W.; quivering motion (of the eyes), Gīt. i, 40; play, pastime, sport, Bālar. iv, $\frac{1}{1}$; (*ā*), f. moving to and fro, Padyasaṃgr. 16; (*ī*), f. a chessman, L.

Khelanaka, n. play, sport, KāśīKh. xii, 72.

Khelāya, Nom. P. °*yati* (g. *kaṇḍv-ādi*), to play, sport, Bhaṭṭ. v, 72.

Kheli, *is,* f. (=*keli*) play, sport, Gīt. xi, 30; (*is*), m. an animal, L.; a bird, L.; the sun, L.; an arrow, L.; a song, L.

खेलुद *kheluda,* a particular high number, Buddh. L.

खेव् *khev* (=√*sev*), to serve, wait upon, Dhātup. xiv, 37.

खेशय *khe-śaya,* &c. See 3. *khá,* p. 334.

खै *khai,* cl. 1. P. *khāyati,* to make firm, Dhātup. xxii, 15; to be firm or steady, ib.; to strike, injure, kill, ib.; (derived fr. *khāyáte,* Pass. of √*khan*) to dig, ib.; to mourn, sorrow, ib.

खैमखा *khaimakhā,* f. (onomat.) 'croaker,' N. of a female frog, AV. iv, 15, 15; cf. *khaṇvakhā.*

खैलायन *khailāyana,* mfn. fr. *khila,* g. *pakshâdi;* m. patr. fr. *kheḍa,* g. *aśvâdi* (Kāś.)

Khailika, mfn. supplementary, additional, added afterwards, RV. AnuvAnukr. 39.

खोङ्गाह *khoṅgāha, as,* m. (=*khuṅg°*) a white and brown horse, L.

खोट् *khoṭ,* cl. 1. P. °*ṭati*=√*khor,* Dhātup. xv, 44: cl. 10. P., v.l. for √*kshoṭ,* q.v.

Khoṭa, mfn. v.l. for *khora,* q.v.

Khoṭana, n. limping, Dhātup. ix, 57; xv, 44.

खोटि khoṭi, is, f. a cunning or scheming woman (v. l. khori), L.

खोटी khoṭī, f. Boswellia thurifera, L.

खोड् khoḍ, cl. 1. P. °ḍati = √khor, q. v., Dhātup. xv, 44: cl. 10. P. = √kshoṭ, q. v.

Khoḍa, mfn. (in comp. or ifc., g. kaḍārâdi, not in Kāś.) limping, lame, L.; (cf. khora.)

Khoḍaka-śīrshaka, am, n. (= kapi-ś°) the arched roof of a house, coping of a wall, L.

खोनमुख khona-mukha, as, m., N. of a village (the modern Khunmoh), Vcar. xviii, 71; Rājat. i, 90 (-musha).

खोर् khor (= √khoṭ, khoḍ, khol), cl. 1. P. °rati, to limp, be lame, Dhātup. xv, 44.

Khora, mfn. limping, lame, KātyŚr. xxii, 3, 19; Lāṭy. viii, 5, 16; Gaut. xxviii, 6; (ī), f., see dīpa-.

Khoraka, as, m. a particular disease of the feet, MBh. xii, 10261; Hariv. 10535 & 10559.

खोरि khori, v. l. for khoṭi, q. v.

खोल् khol = √khor, Dhātup. xv, 44.

Khola, mfn. (cf. χωλός) limping, lame, L.; m. n. a helmet or a kind of hat, Kād. v, 1082; Hcar. vii; cf. mūrdha-kh°. – **śiras**, mfn. furnished with a helmet, Buddh. L.

Kholaka, as, m. a helmet, L.; an ant-hill, L.; a pot, saucepan, L.; the shell of a betel-nut, L.

Kholi, is, f. a quiver, L.

खोल्क khólka, &c. See 3. khá, p. 334, col. 3.

खोषडह khoshaḍaha, N. of a district, Kshitīś. v, 55.

ख्या khyā, cl. 2. P. khyāti (in the non-conjugational tenses also Ā., perf. cakhyau, cakhye, Vop.; impf. akhyat, akhyata, Pāṇ. iii, 1, 52), Dhātup. xxiv, 52; the simple verb occurs only in Pass. and Caus.: Pass. khyāyate, to be named, be known, MBh. iii; (aor. akhyāyi) to be named or announced to (gen.), Bhaṭṭ. xv, 86: Caus. khyāpayati, to make known, promulgate, proclaim, Mn.; Yājñ.; MBh. &c.; to relate, tell, say, declare, betray, denounce, Mn. viii, 171; MBh. iii; Pañcat.; Kathās.; 'to make well known, praise,' see khyāpita; [cf. Lat. in-quam, &c.]

Khyāta, mfn. named, called, denominated, MBh. &c.; known, well known, celebrated, notorious, ib.; told, W. – **garhaṇa**, mfn. having a bad name or evil report, notoriously vile, L. – **garhita**, mfn. id., L. – **viruddha-tā**, for khyāti-v°, q. v.

Khyātavya, mfn. to be styled or called, W.; to be told, W.; to be celebrated, W.

Khyāti, f. 'declaration,' opinion, view, idea, assertion, BhP. xi, 16, 24; Sarvad. xv, 201; perception, knowledge, Yogas.; Tattvas. (= buddhi); Sarvad.; renown, fame, celebrity, Mn. xii, 36; MBh. iii, 8273; R. &c.; a name, denomination, title, MBh. i; xiv; R. iii, 4, 17; Celebrity (personified as daughter of Daksha, VP. i, 7, 23; 8, 14 f.; 9 f.; or of Kardama, BhP. iii, 24, 23), Hariv. 7740; N. of a river in Krauñca-dvīpa, VP. ii, 4, 55; m., N. of a son of Ūru by Āgneyī (v. l. svāti), Hariv. 73; VP. i; of a son of the 4th Manu, BhP. viii, 1, 27. – **kara**, mfn. causing renown, glorious, W. – **janaka**, mfn. id., W. – **ghna**, mfn. destroying reputation, disgraceful, W. – **bodha**, m. sense of honour, W. – **mat**, mfn. renowned, Kathās. – **viruddha-tā**, f. (v. l. khyāta-v°) the state of being contradictory to general opinion (a defect of expression in rhet.), Sāh. vii, 10 & 22.

Khyāna, n. perception, knowledge, KapS. v, 52.

Khyāpaka, mfn. ifc. making known or declaring, indicative, Suśr.; Sāh. vi, 60; one who confesses, W.

Khyāpana, am, n. declaring, divulging, making known, Kathās. lxi, 258; confessing, public confession, Mn. xi, 228; MBh.; MārkP.; making renowned, celebrating, Rājat. v, 160.

Khyāpanīya, mfn. to be declared, Nyāyad., Sch.

Khyāpita, mfn. declared, denounced, MBh. xiii, 4055; praised, R. iii, 27, 19; BhP. iv, 17, 1.

Khyāpin, mfn. ifc. making known, Kathās. lxxvii, 15.

Khyāpya, mfn. to be related, MBh. iii, 12406.

ग GA.

ग 1. ga (3rd consonant of the alphabet), the soft guttural having the sound g in give; m., N. of Gaṇeśa, L. – **kāra**, m. the letter ga.

ग 2. ga, mf(ā)n. (√gam) only ifc. going, moving (e. g. yāna-, going in a carriage, Mn. iv, 120; Yājñ. iii, 291; śīghra-, going quickly, R. iii, 31, 3; cf. antariksha- &c.); having sexual intercourse with (cf. anya-strī-); reaching to (cf. kaṇṭha-); staying, being, abiding in, VarBṛ.; Ragh. iii, 13; Kathās. &c. (e. g. pañcama-, abiding in or keeping the fifth place, Śrut.); relating to or standing in connection with, R. vi, 70, 59; BhP. &c.; (cf. a-, agra-, a-jihma-, atyanta-, &c.; agre-gá, &c.)

ग 3. ga, mf(ī, Pāṇ. iii, 2, 8)n. (√gai) only ifc. singing (cf. chando-, purāṇa-, sāma-); (as), m. a Gandharva or celestial musician, L.; (ā), f. a song, L.; (am), n. id., L.

ग 4. ga, (used in works on prosody as an abbreviation of the word guru to denote) a long syllable, W.; (in music used as an abbreviation of the word gāndhāra to denote) the third note.

गइष्टि ga-ishṭi, for gáv-ishṭi, Kāṭh. vii, 17.

गंह्मन् ganhmán, v. l. for gah°, q. v.

गगण gagaṇa, for gagana, q. v.

गगन gagana, n. the atmosphere, sky, firmament, R.; Suśr.; Ragh.; NārUp. &c.; talc, Bhpr. – **kusuma**, n. 'flower in the sky,' any unreal or fanciful thing, impossibility. – **ga**, m. 'moving in the sky,' a planet, VarBṛ. ii, 1, Sch. – **gañja**, m. a kind of Samādhi, Kāraṇḍ. xxiii, 162; N. of a Bodhisattva, xii, xvi; Lalit. xx, 83. – **gati**, m. 'moving in the air,' a sky-inhabitant, Megh. – **cara**, m. 'moving in the air,' a bird, MBh. i, 1339. – **cārin**, mfn. coming from the sky (voice), Daś. i, 111. – **tala**, n. the vault of the sky, firmament, VarBṛS.; Kād. – **dhvaja**, m. the sun, L.; a cloud, L. – **nagara**, n. 'a town in the sky,' Fata Morgana, Siṇhâs. – **pushpa**, n. = -kusuma, W.; (cf. kha-p°.) – **priya**, m. 'fond of the sky,' N. of a Dānava, Hariv. – **bhramaṇa**, m. = -ga, VarBṛ., Sch. – **mūrdhan**, m., N. of a Dānava, MBh. i; Hariv. – **romantha**, m. 'ruminating on the sky,' nonsense, absurdity, Sarvad. xiii. – **romanthāyita**, n. 'something like ruminating on the sky,' absurdity, iv, 48. – **lih**, mfn. reaching up to heaven, Śiś. xvii, 39. – **vallabha**, n. 'sky-favourite,' N. of a town of the Vidyā-dharas, HPariś. ii, 644. – **vihārin**, mfn. moving or sporting in the sky (the moon), Hit. i, 2, 15, Sch.; m. a heavenly luminary, W.; the sun, W.; a celestial being or divinity, W. – **sad**, m. an inhabitant of the air, celestial being, Śiś. iv, 53; = -ga, Gol. – **sindhu**, f. the heavenly Gaṅgā, Kād. – **stha**, mfn. situated or being in the sky, W. – **sthita**, mfn. id., W. – **sparśana**, m. 'touching the sky,' N. of one of the 8 Maruts, Yājñ. ii, 100 ff., Sch.; air, wind, W. – **spṛiś**, mfn. touching, i. e. inhabiting the air, Śiś. xiii, 63; = -lih, Ragh. iii, 43. **Gaganâgra**, n. summit or highest part of heaven, W. **Gaganâṅganā**, f. a metre of 4 × 25 syllabic instants. **Gaganâdhivāsin**, m. = °na-ga, VarBṛ. vi, 12, Sch. **Gaganâdhvaga**, m. 'wandering in the sky,' the sun, L.; a planet, W.; a celestial spirit, W. **Gaganânanda**, m., N. of a teacher. **Gaganâpagā**, f. = °na-sindhu, Kād. iii. **Gaganâmbu**, n. rain-water, Suśr. i, 45. **Gaganâyas** or °yasa, n. a particular mineral, W. **Gaganâravinda**, n. = °na-kusuma, Saṃkar. xxii, 5; Tarkas. 103. **Gaganecara**, mfn. going in the air, R. iii, 39, 26; BhP. vi, 17, 1; m. a bird, MBh. i, 1317; a planet, Siddhântaś.; a lunar mansion, ib.; a heavenly spirit, W. **Gaganôlmuka**, m. the planet Mars, L.

गगल gagala, n. venom of serpents, Gal.

गग्घ् gaggh, v. l. for √kakh, to laugh, Dhātup. v, 53.

गग्नु gagnu, v. l. for vagnu, Naigh. i, 11.

गङ्ग gaṅga (in comp. for °ṅgā, Pāṇ. vi, 3, 63). – **datta**, m., N. of a king of the frogs, Pañcat. iv, 16. – **dāsa**, m., N. of the author of a Comm. on the poem Khaṇḍa-praśasti; (cf. gaṅgā-a°.)

Gaṅgakā, f. (dimin. fr. °ṅgā), the Ganges, Vop.

Gáṅgā, f. (√gam, Uṇ.) 'swift-goer,' the river Ganges (personified and considered as the eldest daughter of Himavat and Menā, R. i, 36, 15; as the wife of Śāntanu and mother of Bhīshma, MBh. i, 3800; Hariv. 2967 ff.; or as one of the wives of Dharma, PadmaP.; there is also a Gaṅgā in the sky [ākāśa- or vyoma-g°, qq. vv.; cf. khâpagā, gaganâpagā &c.] and one below the earth, Hariv. 12782; Bhagī-ratha is said to have conducted the heavenly Gaṅgā down to the earth, 810 ff.; R. i, ch. 44), RV. x, 75, 5; ŚBr. xiii; TĀr. &c.; N. of the wife of Nīla-kaṇṭha and mother of Śaṃkara; ifc., see dviveda-gaṅga. – **kshetra**, n. 'the sacred district of the Gaṅgā,' i. e. the river Ganges and two Krośas on either of the banks (all dying within such limits go to heaven whatever their crimes), W. – **campū**, f., N. of a work. – **cillī**, f. 'Gangetic kite,' the black-headed gull (Larus ridibundus), L. – **ja**, m. 'the son of Gaṅgā,' N. of the deity Kārttikeya, MBh.; of Bhīshma, L. – **jala**, n. the water of the Ganges, holy water by which it is customary to administer oaths, W. – °**ṭeya** (°gâṭ°), m. 'going in the Ganges,' a shrimp or prawn, L. – **tīra**, n. the bank of the Ganges, W. – **tīrtha**, n., N. of a Tīrtha, Hariv. 9520. – **dāsa**, m., N. of the author of the Chando-govinda, of the Chando-mañjarī and of the Acyuta-carita; N. of a copyist (about 1542 A. D.) – °**ditya** (°gâd°), m., a form of the sun, KāśīKh. vli, 46; li. – **devī**, f., N. of a woman. – **dvāra**, n. 'the door of the Ganges,' N. of a town situated where the Ganges enters the plains (also called Hari-dvāra), MBh. i; iii; xiii; -māhâtmya, n., N. of a part of the SkandaP. – **dhara**, m. 'Ganges-receiver,' the ocean, L.; 'Ganges-supporter,' N. of Śiva (according to the legend the Ganges in its descent from heaven first alighted on the head of Śiva and continued for a long period entangled in his hair, cf. R. i, ch. 44); N. of a man; of a lexicographer; of a commentator on the Śārīraka-sūtras; of a commentator on Bhāskara; -cūrṇa, n. a particular powder; -pura, n., N. of a town; -bhaṭṭa, m., N. of a scholiast; -mādhava, m., N. of the father of Dādābhaī; -rasa, m. (in med.) N. of a drug. – **dhāra**, m. (= -dhara) the ocean, Gal. – **nāga-rāja**, m., N. of a Nāga, Buddh. L. – **nātha**, m., N. of the founder of a sect, Śaṃkar. xlii. – **pattrī**, f., N. of a plant, L. – **pāra**, n. the opposite bank of the Ganges. – **putra**, m. (= -ja) N. of Bhīshma, L.; a man of mixed or vile caste (employed to remove dead bodies), BrahmavP.; a Brāhman who conducts pilgrims to the Ganges (especially at Benares), W. – **purī-bhaṭṭāraka**, m., N. of a man. – **bhṛit**, m. (= -dhara) N. of Śiva, L. – **madhya**, n. the bed or stream of the Ganges, W. – **maha**, m. 'a kind of festival,' cf. gāṅgāmahika. – **mahā-dvāra**, n. = -dvara, MBh. v, 111, 16. – **māhâtmya**, n. a poem or any composition in praise of the Ganges. – °**mbu** (°gâm°), n. Ganges-water, W.; pure rain-water (such as falls in the month Āśvina), W. – °**mbhas** (°gâm°), n. id., W. – **yamune**, f. du. the Ganges and Yamunā rivers, Pāṇ. ii, 4, 7, Kāś. – **yātrā**, f. pilgrimage to the Ganges (especially carrying a sick person to the river side to die there), W. – **rāma**, m., N. of the father of Jaya-rāma and uncle of Rāma-candra. – **laharī**, f. 'wave of the Ganges,' N. of a work; N. of a statue, Kathās. cxxi, 278. – °**vataraṇa** (°gâv°), n. 'Ganges-descent,' N. of a poem, Hariv. 8690; -campū-prabandha, m., N. of a poem by Śaṃkaradikshita. – **vākyâvalī**, f., N. of a work, Śudradh.; Smṛitit. – **vāsin**, mfn. dwelling on the Ganges. – **vāha-tīrtha**, n., N. of a Tīrtha, ŚivaP. – **śoṇa**, n. sg. the Ganges and the Śoṇa rivers, Pāṇ. ii, 4, 7, Kāś. – °**shṭaka** (°gâsh°), 8 verses addressed to Gaṅgā. – **saptamī**, the 7th day in the light half of month Vaiśākha, Vratapr. – **saras**, n., N. of a Tīrtha, Kathās. lii, 17. – **sāgara**, n. the mouth of the Ganges where it enters the ocean (considered as a Tīrtha), Hariv. 9524. – **suta**, m. (= -ja) N. of the deity Kārttikeya, MBh. iii, 14642; of Bhīshma, L. – **sūnu**, m. (= -ja) Bhīshma, Dhanaṃj. 60. – **stuti**, f. 'Ganges-praise,' N. of a work, Kavik. iii. – **stotra**, n. id., KāśīKh. xxvii, 165, Sch. – **snāna**, n. bathing in the Ganges, W. – **hrada**, m. N. of a Tīrtha, MBh. iii, xiii; cf. gāṅga with hrada. **Gaṅgêśa**, m. N. of the author of the Tattva-cintāmaṇi. **Gaṅgêśvara**, m. id.; -liṅga, n. N. of a Liṅga, KāśīKh. xci. **Gaṅgôdaka**, n. Ganges-water, W. **Gaṅgôdbheda**, m. the source of the Ganges (sacred place of pilgrimage), MBh. iii, 8043; Hariv. 9524.

Gaṅgākā, f. (a dimin. fr. °ṅgā), the Ganges, Vop. iv, 8.

Gaṅgikā, f. id., ib.

Gaṅgī (ind. for °ṅgā, q. v.) – **bhūta**, mfn. become (as sacred as) the Ganges, W.

गङ्गुक *gaṅguka*, for *kaṅg°*, Suśr. i, 20, 2.

गङ्गूय *gaṅgūya* (onomat.), P. °*yati*, to shout, give a shout, TāṇḍyaBr. xiv, 3, 19.

गच्छ *gaccha*, *as*, m. (√*gam*) a tree, L.; the period (number of terms) of a progression, Āryabh. ii, 20 & Sch. on 19; family, race, Jain.; (*ās*), m. pl., N. of a people (v.l. for *kaksha*).

Gacchat, mfn. pr. p. P. fr. √*gam*, q.v.

गज् *gaj* (for √*garj*), cl. 1. P. °*jati* (Dhātup. vii, 72), to sound, roar, Bhaṭṭ. xiv, 5; (derived fr. *gaja*) to be drunk or confused, Dhātup. vii, 72: cl. 10. P. *gajayati*, to sound, roar, ib. xxxii, 105.

Gaja, m. an elephant, ShaḍvBr. v, 3; Mn. &c. (ifc. f. *ā*, R. ii, 57, 7); (=*dig-g°*) one of the 8 elephants of the regions, W.; (hence) the number 'eight,' Sūryas.; a measure of length (commonly Gaz, equal to two cubits = $1\frac{3}{4}$ or 2 Hastas), L.; a mound of earth (sloping on both sides) on which a house may be erected, Jyot.; = *-puṭa*, q.v.; (in music) a kind of measure; N. of a man, MBh. vi, 3997; of an Asura (conquered by Śiva), KāśīKh. lxviii; of an attendant on the sun, L.; (*ā*), f. = *-vīthi*, VarBṛS. ix, 1 ff., Sch.; (*ī*), f. a female elephant, BhP. iv, 6, 26; x, 33, 23. **-kanda**, m. (=*hasti-k°*) a kind of bulbous plant, L. **-kanyā**, f. a female elephant, R. ii. **-karṇa**, m. 'elephant-ear,' N. of a Yaksha, MBh. ii, 397; (*ī*), f. a kind of bulbous plant, Bhpr. v, 9, 108. **-kūrmâśin**, m. 'devouring an elephant and a tortoise,' N. of Garuḍa (in allusion to his swallowing both those animals whilst engaged in a contest with each other, cf. MBh. i, 1413), L. **-kṛishṇā**, f. Scindapsus officinalis, Bhpr. **-gati**, f. a stately gait like that of an elephant, W. **-gāminī**, f. a woman of a stately elephant-like walk, W. **-carman**, n. an elephant's skin; a kind of leprosy. **-cirbhaṭā**, f. Cucumis maderaspatanus, L. **-cirbhiṭa**, m. id., L.; (*ā*), f. another kind of gourd, L. **-cchāyā**, f. 'an elephant's shadow,' a particular constellation, Yājñ. i, 218; PSarv.; (cf. Mn. iii, 274.) **-jhampa**, m. (in music) a kind of measure. **-ḍhakkā**, f. a kettle-drum carried on an elephant, L. **-tā**, f. the state of an elephant, Kathās. lxxiv, 22; a multitude of elephants, Pāṇ. iv, 2, 43, Pat. **-turaṃga-vilasita**, n., N. of a metre; (cf. *ṛishabha-gaja-v°*.) **-tva**, n. the state of an elephant, BhP. viii, 4, 12. **-daghna**, mfn. (cf. Pāṇ. v, 2, 37) as high or tall as an elephant, W. **-danta**, m. an elephant's tusk, ivory, VarBṛS. lxxix, 19; a pin projecting from a wall, L.; N. of Gaṇeśa (who is represented with an elephant's head), L.; a particular position of the hands, PSarv.; *-phalā*, f. a kind of pumpkin, L.; *-maya*, mf(*ī*)n. made of ivory, MBh. ii, 1853; R. v, 27, 11. **-dāna**, n. the exudation from an elephant's temples, L. **-daitya-bhid**, m. 'conqueror of the Daitya (or Asura) Gaja,' N. of Śiva, Gal. **-dvayasa**, mfn. (cf. Pāṇ. v, 2, 37) = *-daghna*, W. **-nakra**, m. 'elephant-crocodile,' a rhinoceros, Gal. **-nāsā**, f. the trunk of an elephant, R. ii, 30, 30. **-nimīlikā**, f. (=*ibha-n°*) 'shutting the eyes (at anything) like an elephant,' feigning not to look at anything, Rājat. vi, 73; inattention, carelessness, L. **-nimīlita**, n. (= °*likā*) feigning not to look at anything, Kād. iii, 1080. **-pati**, m. a lord or keeper of elephants, Siṇhâs.; a title given to kings (e.g. to an old king in the south of Jambu-dvīpa), Rasik. vii, 3; a stately elephant, Śiś. vi, 55. **-pādapa**, m. 'elephant-tree,' Bignonia suaveolens, Bhpr. **-pippalī**, f. = *-kṛishṇā*, Suśr. vi, 40, 36. **-puṃgava**, m. a large elephant, Bhartṛ. **-puṭa**, m. a small hole in the ground for a fire (over which to prepare food or medicine), Bhpr. **-pura**, n. the town called after the elephant (i.e. Hāstina-pura), MBh. xiii, 7711. **-pushpamaya**, mf(*ī*)n. made of Gaja-pushpī flowers (as a wreath), R. iv, 12, 45. **-pushpī**, f., N. of a flower, ib. 46. **-priyā**, f. 'dear to elephants,' Boswellia serrata, L. **-bandhana**, n. a post to which an elephant is bound, L.; (*ī*), f. id., L. **-bandhinī**, f. id., L. **-bhakshaka**, m. 'elephant's (favourite) food,' Ficus religiosa, L. **-bhakshā**, f. (= *-priyā*) the gum Olibanum tree, L. **-bhakshyā**, f. id., L. **-bhujaṃgama**, m. du. an elephant and a serpent, W. **-maṇḍana**, n. the ornaments with which an elephant is decorated (especially the coloured lines on his head), L. **-maṇḍalikā**, f. a ring or circle of elephants surrounding a car &c., W. **-mada**, m. = *-dāna*, VarYogay. ix, 18. **-malla**, m., N. of a man. **-mâcala**, m. = *kari-m°*, q.v., L. **-mātra**, mfn. as tall as an elephant, W. **-muktā**, f. pearl supposed to be found in the projections of an elephant's forehead, L. **-mukha**, m. 'elephant-faced,' Gaṇeśa, VarBṛS. lviii, 58. **-mocana**, m. = *-moṭana*, W. **-moṭana**, m. = *-mâcala*, L. **-mauktika**, n. = *-muktā*, Kir. xii, 41. **-yāna-vid**, mfn. expert in managing an elephant, W. **-yūtha**, n. a herd of elephants, Hit. **-yodhin**, mfn. fighting on an elephant, MBh. v, 5959; vi; Hariv. 13514. **-rāja**, m. 'king of elephants,' a noble elephant, W.; *-muktā*, f. = *gaja-m°*. **-reva**, m., N. of an author of Prākṛit verses, Hāl. **-līla**, m. (in music) a kind of measure. **-vat**, mfn. furnished with elephants, Ragh. ix, 10. **-vadana**, m. = *-mukha*, Kathās. c, 44. **-vara**, m. the choicest or best of elephants, Jain. **-vallabhā**, f. = *-priyā*, L.; a kind of Kadalī (growing on mountains), L. **-vāja**, n., g. *rājadantâdi* (Kāś.). **-vikāśī**, f. a variety of nightshade, Gal. **-vilasitā**, f., N. of a metre, W. **-vīthi**, °**thī**, f. 'the course of the elephant' or that division of the moon's course in the heavens which contains the signs Rohiṇī, Mṛiga-śiras, and Ārdrā, or (according to others) Punar-vasu, Tishya, and Āśleshā, AV. Pariś. lii; VarBṛS. ix, 1 f. **-vraja**, mfn. walking like an elephant, W.; n. the pace of an elephant, W.; a troop of elephants, W. **-śāstra**, n. a work treating of elephants or the method of breaking them in, Comm. on Pratāpar. **-śikshā**, f. the knowledge or science of elephants, elephant-lore, MBh. i, 4355. **-śiras**, m. 'elephant-headed,' N. of an attendant in Skanda's retinue, MBh. ix, 2562; N. of a Dānava, Hariv. 12934. **-śīrsha**, m. 'elephant-headed,' N. of a Nāga, Buddh. L. **-sâhvaya**, n. (= *-pura*) 'named after an elephant,' the city Hāstina-pura, MBh. iii, 9 & 1348; Kathās. xv, 6. **-siṇha**, m., N. of an author of Prākṛit verses; of a prince; *-caritra*, n., N. of a work. **-sukumāra-caritra**, n., N. of a work. **-skandha**, m. 'having shoulders like an elephant,' N. of a Dānava, Hariv. 12934; 'having a stem like an elephant's trunk,' Cassia Alata or Tora, L. **-sthāna**, n. a place where elephants are kept, elephant's stall, Yājñ. i, 278; N. of a locality, Romakas. **-snāna**, n. 'ablution of elephants,' unproductive efforts (as elephants, after squirting water over their bodies, end by throwing dust and rubbish), W. **Gajâkhya**, m. 'named after an elephant (cf. *gaja-skandha*),' Cassia Alata or Tora, L. **Gajâgraṇī**, m. 'the most excellent among the elephants,' N. of Indra's elephant Airāvata, L. **Gajâjīva**, m. 'getting his livelihood by elephants,' an elephant-keeper or driver, L. **Gajâṇḍa**, n. 'an elephant's testicle,' a kind of carrot, L. **Gajâdana**, v.l. for °*jâśana*. **Gajâdi-nāmā**, f. 'named by *gaja* and other names of an elephant,' = °*ja-pippalī*, Suśr. iv, 18, 43. **Gajâdhipati**, m. = °*ja-rāja*, W. **Gajâdhyaksha**, m. the master of the elephants, VarBṛS. lxxxvi, 34; Pañcat. iii, $\frac{8}{7}$. **Gajânana**, m. = °*ja-mukha*, GaṇP.; Siṇhâs. **Gajânīka**, m. 'having an army of elephants,' N. of a man, MBh. vii, 7011; Kathās. lviii. **Gajâpasada**, m. a low-born elephant, Pañcat. i, 15, $\frac{3}{4}$. **Gajâyurveda**, m., N. of a medical work on the elephants. **Gajâri**, m. (= °*ja-mâcala*) 'enemy of elephants,' a lion, L.; N. of a tree, L. **Gajârūḍha**, mfn. riding on an elephant, W. **Gajâroha**, m. 'riding on an elephant,' an elephant-driver, R. iii, v. **Gajâśana**, m. = °*ja-bhakshaka*, L. (v.l. °*jâdana*); (*ā*), f. = °*ja-priyā*, Suśr. vi, 40, 150; hemp, L.; a lotus-root, L. **Gajâsura**, m. the Asura Gaja (slain by Śiva), Bālar. ii, 34; *-dveshin*, m. = °*ja-daitya-bhid*, L. **Gajâsuhṛid**, m. 'enemy of Gaja,' id., L. **Gajâsya**, m. = °*ja-mukha*, L. **Gajâhva**, n. = °*ja-sâhvaya*, L.; (*ā*), f. = °*ja-pippalī*, L. **Gajâhvaya**, n. = °*ja-sâhv°*, MBh. iii, 279; BhP. i, 15, 38; m. pl. the inhabitants of Hāstina-pura, VarBṛS. xiv, 4. **Gajī-bhūta**, mfn. one who has become an elephant, Kathās. **Gajêkshaṇa**, m. 'elephant-eyed,' N. of a Dānava, Hariv. 12934. **Gajêndra**, m. = °*ja-rāja*, MBh. i; Nal. xii, 40; *-karṇa*, m. 'having ears like the chief among elephants,' N. of Śiva, MBh. xii, 10351; *-nātha*, m. a very princely elephant, W.; *-mokshaṇa*, n. 'liberation of the elephant (into which a Gandharva had been transformed),' N. of VāmP. lxxxiv (also said to be the N. of a part of MBh.); *-vikrama*, mfn. having the valour of an excellent elephant, W. **Gajêshṭā**, f. 'dear to elephants,' Batatas paniculata, L. **Gajôdara**, m. 'elephant-bellied,' N. of an attendant in Skanda's retinue, MBh. ix, 2562; of a Dānava, Hariv. 12934. **Gajôshaṇā**, f. = °*ja-pippalī*, L.

Gajin, mfn. riding on an elephant, MBh. vi, 3301; BhP. x, 54, 7.

गजनवी *gajanavī* = غزنوى.

गञ्ज् *gañj*, cl. 1. P. °*jati*, to sound, give out a particular sound, Dhātup. vii, 73.

1. **Gañja**, *as*, m. disrespect, L.

Gañjana, mfn. ifc. 'contemning,' excelling, Git. i, 19; x, 7; xii, 19; Sāh. iii, 59, Sch.; m. for *griñj°*.

गञ्ज 2. *gañja*, m. n. = گنج a treasury, jewel room, place where plate &c. is preserved, Rājat. iv f., vii; Kathās. xliii, 30; lxxv, 30; (*as*, *ā*), m. f. a mine, L.; (*as*), m. a cowhouse or station of cowherds, L.; a mart, place where grain &c. is stored for sale, W.; (*ā*), f. a tavern, Rājat. viii, 3028; a drinking-vessel (esp. one for intoxicating liquors), L.; hemp, Bhpr. v, 1, 233; a hut, hovel, abode of low people (*pāmara-sadman*), W.; for *guñjā* (Abrus precatorius), W.; cf. *gagana-*, *dharma-*. **-vara**, m. = گنج ور a treasurer, Rājat. v, 176.

Gañjâjikā, f. hemp, Npr.

Gañjākinī, f. the points of hemp, Dhūrtas. ii, $\frac{1}{2}$.

Gañjikā, f. a tavern, L.

गड् *gaḍ*, cl. 1. P. °*ḍati*, to distil or drop, run as a liquid, Dhātup. xix, 15: cl. 10. P. *gaḍayati*, to cover, hide, xxxv, 84.

Gaḍa, *as*, m. a kind of gold-fish (the young of the Ophiocephalus Lata or another species, Cyprinus Garra), L.; a screen, covering, fence, L.; a moat, ditch, L.; an impediment, L.; N. of a district (part of Malva, commonly Garha or Garha Maṇḍala), L.; (*ā*), f. (in music) a kind of Rāgiṇī; (cf. *tṛiṇa-g°*, *payo-g°*.) **-deśa-ja**, n. 'coming from the district Gaḍa (in the province of Ajmīr),' rock or fossil salt, L. **-lavaṇa**, n. id., L. **Gaḍâkhya**, n. id., Bhpr. v, 1, 242. **Gaḍôttha**, n. id., L.

Gaḍaka, *as*, m. (= *ḍa*) a kind of gold-fish, L.; (cf. *paṅka-g°*.)

Gaḍayanta, *as*, m. (fr. pr. p.) 'covering,' a cloud, Uṇ. iii, 128; (cf. *gaṇḍ°*.)

Gaḍayitnu, *us*, m. id., L.; (cf. *garday°*.)

Gaḍera, m. id., Uṇ.; a torrent, Gaṇar. 34, Sch.

Gaḍeraka, m., N. of a man, Gaṇar. 34.

गडि *gaḍi*, m. = *gali* (a young steer), Kpr.

गडिक *gaḍika*, g. *sutaṃgamâdi*.

गडु *gaḍu*, *us*, m. an excrescence on the neck (goitre or bronchocele), hump on the back, Pāṇ. ii, 2, 35, Vārtt. 3; i, 3, 37, Kāś.; any superfluous addition (to a poem), Kpr. (cf. Sāh. x, 13); a hump-backed man, L.; a javelin, spear, L.; an earth-worm, L.; a water-pot, W.; (cf. *dor-g°*.) **-kaṇṭha**, mfn. having a goitre, Pāṇ. ii, 2, 35, Vārtt. 3, Pat. & Kāś.; Gaṇar. 91, Sch. **-śiras**, mfn. having an excrescence on the head, ib. **Gaḍv-ādi**, a Gaṇa of Pāṇ. ii, 2, 35, Vārtt. 3 (Gaṇar. 91).

Gaḍuka, m. a water-pot, W.; a finger-ring, W.; N. of a man, (pl.) his descendants, g. *upakâdi*.

Gaḍura, mfn. hump-backed, L.

Gaḍula, mf(*ī*, g. *gaurâdi*)n. (gaṇas *sidhmâdi*, *brāhmaṇâdi*, [in comp. or ifc.] *kaḍārâdi*) hump-backed, ShaḍvBr. iv, 4; (cf. *gaṇḍula*.)

Gaḍḍuka, *as*, m. a kind of water-jar, L.; a vessel used for boiled rice, Bhagavatī xvi, 4, 1, Sch.

Gaḍḍūka, *as*, m. a kind of water-jar, L.

गडेर *gaḍera*, °*raka*. See √*gaḍ*.

गडोल *gaḍola*, *as*, m. (= *gaṇḍ°*; √*gaḍ*, Uṇ.) raw sugar, Uṇ. i, 67; a mouthful, L.

गड्डारिका *gaḍḍārikā*, f., N. of a river with a very slow current (of which the source and course are unknown), Kpr., Sch.; a single ewe going in front of a flock of sheep, ib.

Gaḍḍālikā, f. id. (only in comp.) **-pravāheṇa**, instr. ind. 'like the current of the Gaḍḍālikā river,' very slowly, Sāh. vi, 212 $\frac{8}{9}$.

गड्डुक *gaḍḍuka* & °*ḍḍūka*. See *gaḍu*.

गढादेश *gaḍhā-deśa*, *as*, m., N. of a country, Inscr. (A.D. 1668); (cf. *gaḍa*.)

गण् *gaṇ*, cl. 10. P. *gaṇayati* (ep. also Ā. °*te*; aor. *ajīgaṇat* [Kathās. lxxviii] or *ajag°*, Pāṇ. vii, 4, 97; ind. p. *gaṇayya*, BhP. [with *a-*, neg., iv, 7, 15]), to count, number, enumerate, sum up, add up, reckon, take into account, MBh.; R. &c.; to think worth, value (with instr., e.g. *na gaṇayāmi taṃ triṇena*, 'I do not value him at a straw,' MBh. ii, 1552); to consider, regard as (with double acc.), Ragh. viii; xi; Daś.; Pañcat.; Gīt.; Kathās.; to enumerate among (loc.), MBh. i, 2603; Daś.; to ascribe, attribute to (loc.), Bhartṛ. ii, 44; to attend to, take notice of (acc.; often with *na*, not to care about, leave unnoticed), MBh. &c.; to imagine, excogitate, Megh. 107; to count one's number (said of a flock or troop), Pāṇ. i, 3, 67, Kāś.

Gaṇá, *as*, m. a flock, troop, multitude, number, tribe, series, class (of animate or inanimate beings), body of followers or attendants, RV.; AV. &c.; troops or classes of inferior deities (especially certain troops of demi-gods considered as Śiva's attendants and under the special superintendence of the god Gaṇeśa; cf. *-devatā*), Mn.; Yājñ.; Lalit. &c.; a single attendant of Śiva, VarBṛS.; Kathās.; Rājat. iii, 270; N. of Gaṇeśa, W.; a company, any assemblage or association of men formed for the attainment of the same aims, Mn.; Yājñ.; Hit.; the 9 assemblies of Ṛishis under the Arhat Mahā-vīra, Jain.; a sect in philosophy or religion, W.; a small body of troops (= 3 Gulmas or 27 chariots and as many elephants, 81 horses, and 135 foot), MBh. i, 291; a series or group of asterisms or lunar mansions classed under three heads (that of the gods, that of the men, and that of the Rākshasas), W.; (in arithm.) a number, L.; (in metre) a foot or four instants (cf. *-cchandas*); (in Gr.) a series of roots or words following the same rule and called after the first word of the series (e.g. *ad-ādi*, the g. *ad* &c. or the whole series of roots of the 2nd class; *gargâdi*, the g. *garga* &c. or the series of words commencing with *garga*); a particular group of Sāmans, Lāṭy. i, 6, 5; VarYogay. viii, 7; a kind of perfume, L.; = *vāc* (i.e. 'a series of verses'), Naigh. i, 11; N. of an author; (*ā*), f., N. of one of the mothers in Skanda's retinue, MBh. ix, 2645; (cf. *ahar-*, *marúd-*, *vṛisha-*, *sá-*, *saptá-*, *sárva-*; *deva-*, *mahā-*, & *vida-gaṇá*.) **–karṇikā**, f. Cucumis coloquinthida, L. **–karman**, n. a rite common to a whole class or to all, Kauś. **–kāma**, mfn. desirous of a body of attendants, ŚāṅkhGṛ. ii, 2, 13. **–kāra**, m. arranging into classes, classifier, W.; one who collects grammatical Gaṇas, Kāt., Sch.; v.l. for *°ri*. **–kāri** (or *gaṇakâri*, 'enemy of astrologers'?), m., N. of a man, g. *kurv-ādi*; (cf. *gāṇagāri*.) **–kāritā**, f., N. of a work, Sāh., Sch. **–kumāra**, m., N. of the founder of a sect worshipping Haridrā-gaṇapati, Śaṃkar. **–kṛitvas**, ind. for a whole series of times, Vop. vii, 70. **–cakra**, n., N. of a magical circle, Hit. **–cakraka**, n. a guild dinner, L. **–cchandas**, n. a metre measured by feet. **–tā**, f. the forming a class or multitude, L.; the belonging to a party, L.; a cabal, W.; collusion, W.; classification, W.; arithmetic, W. **–tva**, n. the forming a multitude, Kauś. (dat. *-tvāyai*); the office of an attendant of Śiva, Kathās. vii, 110. **–dāsa**, m., N. of a dancing-master, Mālav.; of a physician, Bhpr. **–dīkshā**, f. initiation of a number or class, performance of rites for a number of persons, W.; initiation of a particular kind in which Gaṇeśa is especially worshipped, L.; *-prabhu*, m., N. of an author of Mantras (with Śāktas). **–°dīkshin**, mfn. one who officiates for a number of persons or for a corporation (as a priest), Yājñ. i, 161; one who has been initiated into the worship of Gaṇeśa, W. **–deva**, m., N. of a poet, ŚārṅgP. **–devatā**, *ās*, f. pl. troops of deities who generally appear in classes (Ādityas, Viśvas, Vasus, Tushitas, Ābhāsvaras, Anilas, Mahārājikas, Sādhyas, and Rudras), L. **–dravya**, n. property of a corporation, Yājñ. ii, 187. **–dvīpa**, m. a group of islands (or the N. of a particular island?), R. iv, 40, 33. **–dhara**, m. the head of an assemblage of Ṛishis under the Arhat Mahā-vīra, Jain. **–dhātu-paribhāshā**, f., N. of a grammatical treatise. **–nātha**, m. 'lord of various classes of subordinate gods,' Śiva, L.; Gaṇeśa, BhavP.; Vet. Introd. 1. **–nāyaka**, m. the leader of the attendants of any god, BhP. v, 17, 13; BhavP.; 'chief of Śiva's attendants,' Gaṇeśa, MBh. i, 77; Kathās. c, 41; the head of an assemblage or corporation, VarBṛS. xv, 15; (*ikā*), f. Durgā, L. **–pa**, m. (= *-nātha*) Gaṇeśa, Śaṃkar. xiv, 6; the head of a corporation, VarBṛS. xxxii, 18. **–pati** (*°ṇá-*), m. (g. *aśvapaty-ādi*) the leader of a class or troop or assemblage, VS.; (Bṛihaspati) RV. ii, 23, 1 (cf. RTL. p. 413); (Indra) x, 112, 9; Śiva, L. (cf. RTL. pp. 77 & 211); Gaṇeśa (cf. also *mahā-g°*), Pañcat.; N. of the author of a Comm. on Caurap.; of a poet, ŚārṅgP.; pl., N. of a family, Pravar. iii, 1; *-khaṇḍa*, m. n., N. of BrahmavP. iii; *-nātha*, m., N. of a man; *-pūjana*, n. the worship of Gaṇeśa, W.; *-pūrva-tāpanīyôpanishad*, f., N. of an Up.; *-pūrva-tāpinī*, f. id.; *-bhaṭṭa*, m., N. of the father of Govindânanda; *-stava-rāja*, m., N. of a hymn in praise of Gaṇeśa; *-stotra*, n. prayers addressed to Gaṇeśa; *-hṛidayā*, f., N. of a goddess, Buddh.; *°ty-ārādhana*, m. a hymn in honour of Gaṇeśa (attributed to Kaṅkola); *°ty-upanishad*, f., N. of an Up. **–parvata**, m. 'the mountain frequented by troops of demi-gods,' N. of the Kailāsa (this mountain being the residence of Śiva's attendants as well as of the Kiṃnaras and Yakshas, attendants of Kubera), L. **–pāṭha**, m. a collection of the Gaṇas or series of words following the same grammatical rule (ascribed to Pāṇini). **–pāda**, m., g. *yuktârohy-ādi*. **–pīṭhaka**, n. the breast or bosom, L. **–puṃgava**, m. the head of a corporation, VarBṛS. iv, 24. **–pūjya**, m. id., xvi, 33. **–pūrva**, m. id., MBh. xiii, 1591. **–pramukha**, m. id., Buddh. L. **–bhartṛi**, m. (= *-nātha*) Śiva, Kir. v, 42. **–bhṛit**, m. = *-dhara*, Jain. **–bhojana**, n. eating in common, Buddh. **–mukhya**, m. = *-puṃgava*, VarBṛS. **–yajña**, m. = *-karman*, KātyŚr. xxii, 11, 12; xxv, 13, 29. **–yāga**, m. worship of the troops or classes of deities, VarBṛS. ii. **–ratna**, n. 'pearls of Gaṇas' (only in comp.), *-kāra*, m. 'author of the pearls of Gaṇas,' i.e. Vardhamāna; *-mahôdadhi*, m. 'great ocean in which the Gaṇas form the pearls,' a collection of grammatical Gaṇas by Vardhamāna. **–rājya**, n., N. of an empire in the Deccan, xiv, 14. **–rātra**, m. n. a series of nights, Hcar. i, 353. **–rūpa**, m. the swallow-wort, L. **–rūpaka**, m. id., L. **–rūpin**, m. id., L. **–vat** (*°ṇá-*), mfn. consisting of a series or class, TS. ii; TBr. ii; followed by attendants, ib.; containing the word *gaṇa*, Kāṭh. xi, 4; (*tī*), f., N. of the mother of Divo-dāsa or Dhanvantari, L.; *°tī-suta*, m. 'son of Gaṇavatī,' N. of a sage and physician (also called Divo-dāsa or Dhanvantari or Kāśi-rāja), L. **–vara**, n., N. of a town, Śaṃkar. xiv, 6. **–vṛitta**, n. = *-cchandas*. **–vyākhyāna**, n. 'Gaṇa-explanation,' N. of a grammatical treatise. **–vyūha**, m., N. of a Sūtra, Buddh. **–śás**, ind. (Pāṇ. i, 1, 23) by troops or classes, TS. ii; v; TBr. i; ŚBr. xiv; ĀśvŚr. &c. **–śrí**, mfn. associated in troops, associating, RV.; VS.; Kāṭh. **–hāsa**, m. a species of perfume, L. **–hāsaka**, m. id., Bhpr. **–homa**, m., N. of a work. **Gaṇâgraṇī**, m. (= *°ṇa-nāyaka*) N. of Gaṇeśa, L. **Gaṇâcala**, m. = *°ṇa-parvata*, L. **Gaṇâcārya**, m. 'teacher common to all,' teacher of the people, Buddh. **Gaṇâdhipa**, m. the chief of a troop, VishṇuS. (Hcat. i, 9, 11); N. of Śiva, L.; of Gaṇeśa; = *°ṇa-dhara*, Jain. **Gaṇâdhipati**, m. (= *°pa*) N. of Śiva, Śiś. ix, 27; of Gaṇeśa, L. **Gaṇâdhipatya**, n. the predominance among a troop of gods, ŚiraUp. **Gaṇâdhīśa**, m. (= *°dhipa*) N. of Gaṇeśa, Kathās. lxxiii. **Gaṇâdhyaksha**, m. id., lv, 165. **Gaṇânna**, n. food prepared for a number of persons in common, Mn. iv, 209 & 219. **Gaṇâbhyantara**, m. 'one of a troop or corporation,' a member of any (religious) association, iii, 154. **Gaṇâvarā**, f. 'last or lowest of her class,' N. of an Apsaras, v.l. for *guṇâv°*. **Gaṇêndra**, m., N. of a Buddha, Lalit. xx, 82. **Gaṇêśa**, m. (= *°ṇa-nātha*) N. of the god of wisdom and of obstacles (son of Śiva and Pārvatī, or according to one legend of Pārvatī alone; though Gaṇeśa causes obstacles he also removes them; hence he is invoked at the commencement of all undertakings and at the opening of all compositions with the words *namo Gaṇêśāya vighnêśvarāya*; he is represented as a short fat man with a protuberant belly, frequently riding on a rat or attended by one, and to denote his sagacity has the head of an elephant, which however has only one tusk; the appellation Gaṇeśa, with other similar compounds, alludes to his office as chief of the various classes of subordinate gods, who are regarded as Śiva's attendants; cf. RTL. pp. 48, 62, 79, 392, 440; he is said to have written down the MBh. as dictated by Vyāsa, MBh. i, 74 ff.; persons possessed by Gaṇeśa are referred to, Yājñ. i, 270 ff.); N. of Śiva, MBh. iii, 1629; = *gaṇa-puṃgava*, VarBṛ. xiii, 8; m. pl. (= *vidyêśa* or *°śvara*) a class of Siddhas (with Śaivas), Hcat. i, 11, 857 ff.; N. of a renowned astronomer of the 16th century; of a son of Rāma-deva (author of a Comm. on Nalôd.); of a son of Viśvanātha-dīkshita and grandson of Bhāvarāma-kṛishṇa (author of a Comm. called Ciccandrikā); *-kumbha*, m., N. of a rocky cave in Orissa; *-kusuma*, m. a variety of oleander with red flowers, L.; *-khaṇḍa*, m. n., N. of BrahmavP. iii; of a section of the SkandaP.; *-gītā*, f., N. of a song in praise of Gaṇeśa; *-caturthī*, f. the fourth day of the light half of the month Bhādra (considered as Gaṇeśa's birthday), RTL. p. 431; *-tāpinī*, f., N. of an Up. (cf. *gaṇapati-pūrva-t°*); *-purāṇa*, n., N. of an Upa-purāṇa; *-pūjā*, f. the worship of Gaṇeśa, see RTL. pp. 211–217; *-bhujaṃga-prayāta-stotra*, n., N. of a hymn in praise of Gaṇeśa (attributed to Śaṃkarâcārya); *-bhūshaṇa*, n. red lead; *-miśra*, m., N. of a copyist of the last century; *-yāmala*, n., N. of a work; *-vimarśinī*, f. 'appeasing Gaṇeśa,' N. of a work; *-sahasra-nāman*, n., N. of a part of the GaṇP.; *-stava rāja*, m., N. of a part of the BhavP.; *-stuti*, f. a hymn in honour of Gaṇeśa by Rāghava; *°śôpapurāṇa*, n. = *°śa-pur°*. **Gaṇêśāna**, m. the god Gaṇeśa, MBh. i, 75; Hcat. **Gaṇêśvara**, m. the chief of a troop, leader of a band (gen. or in comp.), MBh. xiii; R. iv; v; N. of a demon causing diseases, Hariv. 9556; 'chief of the animals,' the lion, L. **Gaṇôtsāha**, m. 'avoiding assemblages,' the rhinoceros, L.

Gáṇaka, mfn. bought for a large sum, Pāṇ. v, 1, 22, Kāś.; (*as*), m. one who reckons, arithmetician, MBh. ii, 206; xv, 417; a calculator of nativities, astrologer, VS. xxx, 20; R. i, 12, 7; Kathās.; m. pl., N. of a collection of 8 stars, VarBṛS. xi, 25; (*ī*), f. the wife of an astrologer, Pāṇ. iv, 1, 48, Kāś.; (*ikā*), f. a harlot, courtezan, Mn. iv; Yājñ. i, 161; MBh. xiii; Mṛicch. &c.; a female elephant, L.; Jasminum auriculatum, L.; Æschynomene Sesban, L.; = *gaṇikârikā*, q.v., L.; counting, enumerating, W.; apprehension, W. **Gaṇakâri**, see *gaṇa-kāri*.

Gaṇatitha, mfn. forming a troop or assemblage, Pāṇ. v, 2, 52; (Vop. vii, 42.)

Gaṇatrikā. See *°ṇayitr°*.

Gaṇana, *am*, n. reckoning, counting, calculation, Pāṇ. v, 4, 17; Pañcat.; Hit.; (*ā*), f. id., MBh. iii; Megh.; Ragh. &c.; the being enumerated among (in comp.), Ragh. viii, 94; considering, supposing, Daś. vii, 185; Hit.; regarding, taking notice of (gen.), consideration, Prab. i, $\frac{2}{2}\frac{0}{1}$; Rājat. v, 308.

Gaṇanā, f. of *°na*, q.v. **–gati**, f. a particular high number, Lalit. xii, 161 f. **–pati**, m. an arithmetician, Buddh. L.; 'master of prudent calculation,' Gaṇeśa, Rājat. v, 26. **–pattrikā**, f. reckoning-book, Rājat. vi, 36. **–mahā-mātra**, m. a minister of finance, Buddh. L.

Gaṇanīya, mfn. to be counted or reckoned or classed, calculable, L.; (cf. *gaṇeya*.)

Gaṇayitrikā, f. 'counter,' a rosary, Jain. (only Prākrit *°ṇettiyā*); (irr. *°ṇatr°* & *°ṇitr°*) Hcat. i, 5.

1. **Gaṇi**, m. (for *°ṇin*, only at the end of names) one who is familiar with the sacred writings and the auxiliary sciences, Jain.; pl. N. of a family, Pravar. ii, 1, 2; (*is*), f. counting, L.

Gaṇikā, f. of *°ṇaka*, q.v. **Gaṇikânna**, n. food coming from or presented by a courtezan, Mn. iv, 209 & 219; cf. Yājñ. i, 161. **Gaṇikâ-pāda**, mfn., g. *hasty-ādi*. **Gaṇikârikā**, *°rī*, f. (= *°ṇikā*) Premna spinosa (commonly Gaṇiyārī or also Vada-gaṇ°, a small tree with a very fetid leaf, the wood being used in attrition for the purpose of producing flame), L.

Gaṇita, mfn. counted, numbered, reckoned, calculated, MBh.; BhP.; Vet.; (*am*), n. reckoning, calculating, science of computation (comprising arithmetic, algebra, and geometry, *pāṭī-* or *vyakta-*, *bīja-*, & *rekhā-*), MBh. i, 293; Mṛicch. i, 4; VarBṛS. &c.; the astronomical or astrological part of a Jyotiḥśāstra (with the exception of the portion treating of nativities), VarBṛS.; the sum of a progression; sum (in general). **–kaumudī**, f., N. of a Comm. on Līl. **–tattva-cintāmaṇi**, m., N. of a Comm. on Sūryas. **–nāma-mālā**, f., N. of a mathematical work. **–pañcaviṅśatikā**, f. id. **–pāśa**, m. (in arithm.) a combination, Līl. **–mālatī**, **-latā**, f., **-sāra**, m., N. of three mathematical works. **–śāstra**, n. the book or science of computation, W. **Gaṇitâdhyāya**, m., N. of a chapter in the Brahmasiddhânta. **Gaṇitâmṛita-sāgarī**, f., N. of a Comm. on Līl.

Gaṇitavya, mfn. = *gaṇanīya*, W.

Gaṇitā, f. of *°ta*, q.v. **–devī-tīrtha**, n., N. of a Tīrtha, RevāKh. cccxv.

Gaṇitin, mfn. one who has calculated, g. *ishṭâdi*.

Gaṇitrikā. See °*ṇayitr*°.

Gaṇin, mfn. (Pāṇ. vi, 4, 165) one who has attendants, Kāṭh. xi, 4; surrounded by (instr. or in comp.), MaitrS. ii, 2, 3; Ragh. ix, 53; m. 'having a class of pupils,' a teacher, L. (Jain.)

2. **Gaṇi**, in comp. for °*nin*. **-piṭaka**, n. the twelve sacred writings or Aṅgas of the Jainas collectively, L. **-mat**, m., N. of a Siddha, Gal. **-sthārāja**, m., N. of a tree, L.

Gaṇima, mfn. (anything) that is calculated or counted, Nār. xi, 3.

Gaṇī-bhūta, mfn. included in any class or troop, calculated, W.

Gaṇeya, mfn. calculable, to be counted, Naish. iii, 40; (*a-*, neg.) MBh. viii, 2554; 2838.

Gaṇeyu, m., N. of a son of Raudrâśva, VP. iv, 19, 1 (v. l.)

Gaṇeru, *us*, m. Pterospermum acerifolium, L.; (*us*), f. a harlot, L.; a female elephant, L.; cf. *kaṇ*°.

Gaṇeruka, *as*, m. (= °*ru*) Pterospermum acerifolium, L.; (*ā*), f. a bawd, L.; a female servant, L.

Gaṇêśa, °*śāna*, °*śvara*. See s. v. *gaṇá*.

Gáṇya, mfn. (Pāṇ. iv, 4, 84) 'consisting of series (of words or feet),' i. e. consisting of metrical lines (as a hymn), RV. iii, 7, 5 ['to be worshipped,' Sāy.]; belonging to a multitude or class or troop, gaṇas *dig-ādi* & *vargyâdi* (ifc.); to be counted or calculated, L.; 'to be considered or regarded,' see *agra-g*°; to be taken notice of, Naish. xi, 20 (*a-*, neg.)

गण्ड् *gaṇḍ* (derived fr. *gaṇḍa*), cl. 1. P. °*ḍati*, 'to affect the cheek,' Dhātup. ix, 79; (cf. *gaṇḍā*.)

Gaṇḍa, *as*, m. (cf. *galla*) the cheek, whole side of the face including the temple (also said of animals, e. g. of an ox, VarBṛS.; of a horse, ib.; of an elephant [cf. *-karaṭa*], Pañcat.; BhP. &c.), Yājñ. &c. (ifc. f. *ā*, Ṛitus.; f. *ī*, Kathās. xx); the side, Rāmapūjāśar.; a bubble, boil, pimple, Suśr.; Śak. ii (Prākṛit); Mudr.; Vop.; a goitre or any other excrescence of the neck, AitBr. i, 25; Car. i; Suśr.; a joint, bone, L.; the bladder, L.; a mark, spot, L.; part of a horse's trappings, stud or button fixed as an ornament upon the harness, L.; a rhinoceros (cf. *gaṇḍaka* & °*ḍâṅga*), L.; a hero (cf. *gaṇḍīra*), L.; 'the chief,' best, excellent (only in comp.; cf. *-grāma*, *-mūrkha*, *-śilā*, &c.), L.; N. of the 10th astrological Yoga; an astronomical period (cf. *gaṇḍânta*), W.; m. n. the abrupt interchange of question and answer (one of the characteristics of the dramatic composition called Vīthi), Sāh. vi, 256 & 260; Daśar.; Pratāpar.; (*ā*), f., N. of the female attendant of the seven sages, MBh. xiii, 4417; the verbal rt. *gaṇḍ*, 4499; for *khaṇḍa*, Kathās. xciv, 66; (cf. *gaḍu*.) **-kaṇḍu**, m. 'scratching the cheek,' N. of a Yaksha, MBh. ii, 397 (°*ḍū*, B.) **-karaṭa**, m. an elephant's temple, Bhartṛ. iii, 73. **-kārī**, f. = *-kālī*, L.; Mimosa pudica, L. **-kālī**, f. (= *kārī*) a kind of pot-herb, L. **-kusuma**, n. the juice that exudes from the elephant's temples during rut, L. **-kūpa**, m. the tableland of a mountain, L. **-gātra**, n. the fruit of Anona reticulata or squamosa (commonly Ātā or custard apple), L. **-gopāla**, m., N. of a poet (called so after a verse of his), ŚārṅgP. **-gopālikā**, f. a particular worm, Bhpr. vii, 56, 36. **-grāma**, m. any large village, L. **-dūrvā**, f. a kind of grass, v, 3, 176. **-deśa**, m. the region of the cheeks, cheek, W. **-pāda**, mfn., g. *hasty-ādi*. **-pradeśa**, m. = *-deśa*, W. **-phalaka**, n. the cheek fancifully regarded as a flat piece of wood (cf. *-bhitti*), W. **-bhitti**, f. the cheek fancifully regarded as a flat wall, cheek-bone, Ragh. v, xii; Bhartṛ. i, 49; Caurap. **-māla**, m. inflammation of the glands of the neck, L.; (*ā*), f. id., Car. i, 28; Suśr.; (*ī*), f., N. of a plant, Gal. **-mālaka**, m. (= °*la*) inflammation of the glands of the neck, Hcat. i, 5, 374; (*ikā*), f. Mimosa pudica, L. **-mālin**, mfn. having the glands of the neck inflamed, Mn. iii, 161. **-mūrkha**, mfn. exceedingly foolish, L. **-lavaṇa**, for *gaḍa-l*°, Gal. **-lekhā**, f. = *-deśa*, Ragh. vii; x; Kum. vii; Kir. xvi, 2. **-vyūha**, m., N. of a Buddhist Sūtra work (one of the nine Dharmas). **-śilā**, f. any large rock, BhP. iii, 13, 22. **-śaila**, m. (ifc. f. *ā*) id., Hariv.; Śiś.; Bālar. viii, $\frac{8}{8}$; Rājat.; (= *-bhitti*) the cheek-bone, cheek, Śiś. iv, 40; N. of a pleasure-grove of the Apsaras, Kathās. cix, 41. **-sâhvayā**, f. 'named after the *gaṇḍa*,' (probably = *gaṇḍakī*) N. of a river, MBh. iii, 14230. **-sthala**, n. (ifc. f. *ā* or *ī*) = *-deśa*, Mālav.; Bhartṛ.; Pañcat. &c.; (*ī*), f. id., Ragh. vi. 72; Amar. **Gaṇḍâṅga**, m. (= *gaṇḍa*) a rhinoceros, L. **Gaṇḍânta**, n. the first fourth of an asterism preceded by a node of asterisms, Sūryas. **Gaṇḍâri**, m. 'enemy of the cheek,' Bauhinia variegata, Bhpr. **Gaṇḍâlī**, f. = *gaṇḍa-dūrvā*, L.; white Dūrvā grass, L.; = *sarpâkshī*, Bhpr. **Gaṇḍâśman**, m. = °*ḍa-śilā*, L. **Gaṇḍôpadhāna**, n. a pillow, Suśr.; Pañcat. ii, 3, $\frac{2}{2}\frac{3}{6}$. **Gaṇḍôpadhānīya**, n. id., $\frac{2}{2}\frac{3}{6}$ (v. l. *gal-lôp*°). **Gaṇḍôpala**, m. = °*ḍa-śilā*, Mcar. vi, 24.

Gaṇḍaka, *as*, m. a rhinoceros, L.; an obstacle, L.; disjunction, separation, L.; a mode of reckoning by fours, W.; a coin of the value of four cowries, L.; a kind of science (astrological science or part of it, W.), L.; (ifc.) a mark, spot (?), Buddh.; a metre of 4 × 20 syllables; N. of Kāla (brother of Prasenajit), Buddh.; (*ās*), m. pl., N. of the Videhas living on the river Gaṇḍakī, MBh. ii, 1062; (*ā*), f. a lump, ball, W.; (*ī*), f., N. of a river in the northern part of India, MBh.; Hariv. &c.; (*ikā*), f. a hill [Sch.], MBh. vi, 230 & 282; = *shaṇḍa-viśesha*, Bhagavatī, xvi, 4, Sch.; a little knot in the wood (?), Car. vi, 18, 77; anything advanced beyond the first stage or commencement, L.

Gaṇḍayanta, Pāṇ. vi, 4, 55, Kāś.; (cf. *gaḍ*°.)

Gaṇḍalin, *ī*, m., N. of Śiva, MBh. xiii, 1204.

Gaṇḍi, *is*, m. the trunk of a tree from the root to the beginning of the branches, L.; goitre or bronchocele, W.; (*is*), f. a fox, Gal.

Gaṇḍikā, f. of °*ḍaka*, q.v. **Gaṇḍikâkāra-yoga**, ?, MBh. xiv, 247.

Gaṇḍinī, f., N. of Durgā, L.

Gaṇḍira. See *pāda-g*°.

Gaṇḍilaka, n. a kind of grass, Bhpr. vii, 66, 151.

Gaṇḍīra, *as*, m. a kind of pot-herb (described as growing in watery ground, but according to some a species of cucumber), Suśr. i; iv, 4, 30; a hero, L.; (*ī*), f. Tithymalus antiquorum, L.; (cf. *gāṇḍ*°.)

Gaṇḍu, m. f. (g. *sidhmâdi*) a pillow, Pañcat. ii, 3, $\frac{2}{2}\frac{3}{6}$; oil, Uṇ., Sch.; m. N. of a man, g. 2. *lohitâdi*.

Gaṇḍut, a kind of grass, L.; (cf. *garmut*.)

Gaṇḍula, mfn. (fr. °*ḍu*, g. *sidhmâdi*, not in Kāś. & Gaṇar.) = *gaḍula* (hump-backed), L., Sch.

Gaṇḍū, *ūs*, f. (= °*ḍu*) a pillow, Uṇ. i, 7, Sch.; oil, ib.; a joint, bone, W. **-pada**, m. a kind of worm, earth-worm, AitBr. iii, 26, 3; Suśr. i, ch. 7 f.; vi, ch. 41 & 54; (*ī*), f. a small or female worm, L.; *-bhava*, n. lead, L.; °*dôdbhava*, n. id., Gal.

गण्डूष *gaṇḍūsha*, *as*, m., rarely *am*, n., (*ā*, f., L.) a mouthful of water, water &c. held in the hollowed palm of the hand for rinsing the mouth, draught, nip, MBh. viii, 2051; Suśr.; Kum. iii, 37; SkandaP. &c.; filling or rinsing the mouth, L.; (*as*), m. the tip of an elephant's trunk, L.; N. of a son of Śūra and brother of Vasu-deva, Hariv. 1927 & 1939; VP. iv, 14, 10. **Gaṇḍūshī-√kṛi**, to swallow in one draught, BhP. ix, 15, 3.

Gaṇḍūshaya, Nom. P. °*yati*, to sip, sup, swallow, Bālar. v, $\frac{6}{7}\frac{0}{0}$; Viddh. i, $\frac{1}{1}\frac{6}{7}$.

गण्डोल *gaṇḍola*, m. n. (= *gaḍ*°) raw sugar, L.; m. (= °*ḍūsha*) a mouthful, L.; N. of a Buddh. temple. **-pāda**, mfn., g. *hasty-ādi*; (cf. *kaṇḍ*°.)

Gaṇḍolaka, *as*, m. a worm, Sarvad. iii, 154; a mouthful, Gal. **-pāda**, mfn., g. *hasty-ādi*.

गण्य *gáṇya*. See √*gaṇ*, last col.

गत् *gat*, *gatá*, *gáti*, &c. See √*gam*.

गद् *gad*, cl. 1. P. °*dati* (perf. *jagāda*; aor. *agadīt* [Bhaṭṭ. xv, 102] or *agādīt*, Pāṇ. vii, 2, 7), to speak articulately, speak, say, relate, tell anything (acc.) to any one (acc.), MBh.; R. &c.: cl. 10. P. *gadayati*, to thunder, Dhātup. xxxv, 8: Desid. *jigadishati*, to intend or wish to speak or tell, MBh. xii, 1604; [cf. Lith. *gadijos*, *zadas*, *zodis*, *giedmi*; Pol. *gadać*; Hib. *gadh*.]

Gada, m. a sentence, MBh. i, 1787; disease, sickness, Suśr.; Ragh. &c.; N. of a son of Vasu-deva and younger brother of Kṛishṇa, MBh.; Hariv.; BhP.; of another son of Vasu-deva by a different mother, ix, 24, 51; n. poison, L.; (*ā*), f. a series of sentences, RāmatUp. ii, 5, 4; a mace, club, bludgeon, MBh.; R. &c.; Bignonia suaveolens, L.; N. of a musical instrument; of a constellation, VarBṛ.; Laghuj.; v. l. for *gadhā*, TS., Sch.; (cf. *a-gadá*, *á-vijñāta-g*°.) **-nigraha**, m., N. of a work. **-varman**, m., N. of a man, VP. **-siṅha**, m., N. of an author, Smṛitit. i. **Gadâkhya**, n. 'named after a disease (i. e. after leprosy),' Costus speciosus (*kushṭha*), L. **Gadâgada**, m. du. 'Gada and Agada,' the two Aśvins (physicians of heaven), L.; (cf. *gadântaka*.) **Gadâgraja**, m. 'elder brother of Gada,' N. of Kṛishṇa, MBh. iii, 733; BhP. iv, 23, 12. **Gadâgraṇī**, m. 'chief of all diseases,' consumption, L. -1. **Gadâdhara**, mfn. having a sick lip, Vcar. **Gadântaka**, *au*, m. du. 'removing sickness,' N. of the two Aśvins, L. **Gadâmbara**, m. a cloud, L. **Gadârāti**, m. 'the enemy of diseases,' a drug, medicament, L. **Gadâhva**, n. = °*dâkhya*, L. **Gadâhvaya**, m. id., L.

Gadana, n. telling, relating, AitĀr. v, 3, 3, 5.

Gadayitnu, mfn. loquacious, talkative, Uṇ.; libidinous, lustful, L.; (*us*), m. a sound, Uṇ. iii, 29, Sch.; a bow, L.; a N. of Kāma (the god of love), L.; for *gaḍay*° (a cloud), Gal.

Gadā, f. of °*da*, q. v. **-°gra-pāṇi** (°*dâg*°), mfn. having a mace in the right hand, W. **-2. -dhara**, mfn. bearing a club, VarBṛS. lviii, 34; Siṅhâs.; m. Kṛishṇa (cf. *kaumodakī*), BhP. i, 8, 39; N. of a physician; of the author of the work Vishaya-vicāra; of the father of Mukunda-priya and uncle of Rāmânanda; *-bhaṭṭa*, m., N. of an author. **-parvan**, n., N. of part of MBh. ix. **-bhṛit**, m. (= *-dhara*), N. of Kṛishṇa, BhP. **-yuddha**, n. a fight with clubs; *-parvan*, n. = *gadā-p*°. **-°yudha** (°*dây*°), mfn. armed with a club, W. **-°vasāna** (°*dâv*°), n. 'resting-place of the mace (thrown by Jarāsandha),' N. of a place near Mathurā, MBh. ii, 764. **-hasta**, mfn. armed with a mace, W.; mace-handed, W.

Gadāya, Nom. Ā. °*yáte*, 'to become sick,' to become lazy or idle, ŚBr. xii, 4, 1, 10.

Gadi, *is*, f. speaking, speech, BhP. xi, 12, 19.

Gadita, mfn. spoken; said, related, MBh. &c.; spoken to, Kathās. lx, 63; enumerated, MBh. iii, 13425; Suśr.; named, called; (*am*), n. speaking, speech, Śak. iv, 6 (v. l.)

Gadin, mfn. (fr. °*da*) sick, Bhpr. vii, 14, 96; (fr. °*dā*) armed with a club (said of Kṛishṇa), MBh. vii, 9455; Bhag.; m., N. of Kṛishṇa, L. **Gadi-siṅha**, m., N. of a grammarian.

Gadgada, mf(*ā*)n. stammering, stuttering (said of persons and of utterances), MBh. &c.; n. stammering, indistinct or convulsive utterance (as sobbing &c.), ib. **-gala**, mfn. stammering, Bhartṛ. iii, 22. **-tā**, f. stammering, Ratnâv. **-tva**, n. id., Suśr. **-dhvani**, m. low inarticulate expression of joy or grief, L. **-pada**, n. inarticulate speech, W. **-bhāshaṇa**, n. stammering, Hcat. **-bhāshin**, mfn. stammering (ifc.), R. iv. **-vākya**, mfn. id., Suśr. **-vāc**, mfn. id., ib.; Hcat. **-śabda**, mfn. id., R. ii, 42, 26. **-svara**, mf(*ā*)n. id., Daś. vii, 167; (*as*), m. stammering utterance, Sāh. iii. 113; a buffalo, L.; N. of a Bodhi-sattva, SaddhP. xxiii.

Gadgadaka, mfn. = *gadgade kuśala*, g. *ākarshâdi*; (*ikā*), f. stammering, Kād.; Hcar. v, viii.

Gadgadita, mfn. stammered, PāṇŚ. (RV.) 35.

Gadgadya, Nom. P. °*dyati*, to stammer, g. *kaṇḍv-ādi*.

Gadya, mfn. (Pāṇ. iii, 1, 100) to be spoken or uttered, Bhaṭṭ. vi, 47; (*am*), n. prose, composition not metrical yet framed in accordance with harmony, elaborate prose composition, MBh. iii, 966; Kāvyâd.; Sāh. &c. **-padya-maya**, mf(*ī*)n. consisting of prose and verses, vi, 336. **-rāmāyaṇa-kāvya**, n. a Rāmâyaṇa written in prose, Uṇ. iv, 139, Sch.

गद्याण *gadyāṇa*, m. a weight (= 32 Guñjās or berries of Abrus precatorius, or = 64 such Guñjās with physicians; = 6 Māshas of 7 or 8 Guñjās each, ŚārṅgS.), Yājñ. iii, 258, Sch.

Gadyāṇaka, *as*, m. id., W.

Gadyāna [ŚārṅgS. i, 41], °*naka*, [W.] m. id.

Gadyālaka, *as*, m. id., W.

गध् *gadh*, cl. 4. *gadhyati*, to be mixed, Nir. v, 15.

Gadhā, f. a particular part of a cart, TS. ii, 4, 8, 1, Sch. (v. l. *gadā*).

Gádhita, mfn., Naigh. iv, 2; (cf. *ā́-*, *pári-*.)

Gádhya, mfn. (Naigh. iv, 2; Nir. v, 15) to be seized or gained as booty, RV. iv, 16, 11 & 16; 38, 4; vi, 10, 6 & 26, 2; cf. *vāja-gandhya*.

गन्तवे *gántave*, *gántavaí*, fr. √*gam*, q. v.

Gantavya, **gántu**, **gántṛi**. See ib.

गन्दिका *gandikā*, v. l. for *gabd*°, q. v.

गन्ध् *gandh*, cl. 10. Ā. *gandhayate*, to injure, hurt, Dhātup. xxxiii, 11; to move or go, L.

1. **Gandhana**, *am*, n. hurting, injury, L.; pointing out or alluding to the faults of others, derision,

Hcar. iv; continued effort, perseverance, Pāṇ. i, 2, 15 & 3, 32.

गन्ध *gandhá*, *as*, m. smell, odour (nine kinds are enumerated, viz. *ishṭa*, *anishṭa*, *madhura*, *kaṭu*, *nirhārin*, *saṃhata*, *snigdha*, *rūksha*, *viśada*, MBh. xii, 6848; a tenth kind is called *amla*, L.), RV. i, 162, 10; AV.; VS. &c. (ifc. f. *ā*, MBh.; BhP.); a fragrant substance, fragrance, scent, perfume (generally used in pl.; in comp. = 'fragrant,' cf. *-jala* &c.), Gobh.; Lāṭy.; PārGṛ. &c.; sulphur; pounded sandal-wood, Caurap.; a sectarial mark on the forehead (called so in the south of India), RTL. p. 66; myrrh, L.; Hyperanthera Moringa, L.; (ifc.) the mere smell of anything, small quantity, little, MBh. i, 989; Pāṇ. v, 4, 136; Pat.; Suśr. i, 13; connection, relationship, L.; a neighbour, L.; pride, arrogance, Megh. 9 (for *gardha*?); Śiva, MBh. xii, 10378; (*ā*), f. = *-palāśī*, L.; Desmodium gangeticum, L.; = *-mohinī*, L.; a metre of 17 + 18 + 17 + 18 syllables; (*am*), n. smell, DhyānabUp. 7 & 9; black aloe-wood, L. **-kandaka**, m. the root of Scirpus Kysoor. **-kāraka**, m., N. of a prince (v. l. for *andha-k°*); (*ikā*), f. = *-kārī*, HPariś.; a female artisan living in the house of another woman, L. **-kārī**, f. a female servant whose business is to prepare perfumes, ii, 142. **-kālikā**, f., N. of an Apsaras, R. vi, 82, 160; = *-kālī*, L. **-kālī**, f., N. of the mother of the poet Vyāsa, MBh. i, 3801; Hariv. 1088. **-kāshṭha**, n. a fragrant wood (as sandal, aloe-wood, &c.), L.; a species of sandal-wood, L. **-kuṭī**, f. a kind of perfume, Bhpr. **-kusumā**, f. 'having fragrant blossoms,' N. of a plant, L. **-kūṭī**, f. (for *-kuṭī*?) the hall of fragrances, Buddh. **-kelikā**, for *-celikā*, L. **-kokilā**, f. a kind of perfume, Bhpr. **-kheḍa**, n. Andropogon Schœnanthus, L. **-kheḍaka**, n. = *-tṛiṇa*, L. **-ga**, mfn. taking a scent, smelling, W.; redolent, W. **-gaja**, m. 'scent-elephant,' an elephant during rut, Kād. **-guṇa**, mfn. having the property of odour, W. **-grāhaka**, mfn. perceiving odour (the nose). **-grāhin**, mfn. perfumed, Daś. xi, 170. **-ghrāṇa**, n. the smelling of any odour, W. **-celikā**, f. musk, L. (v. l. *-kel°*); = *-mārjāra*, L. **-ja**, mf(*ā*)n. consisting of fragrant substances, AgP. **-jaṭilā**, f. Acorus Calamus, L. **-jala**, n. fragrant water, BhP. i, 11, 15. **-jāta**, n. the leaf of Laurus Cassia, L. **-jñā**, f. 'knowing odours,' the nose, L. **-taṇḍula**, m. fragrant rice, L. **-tūrya**, n. a musical instrument of a loud sound (used in battle as drum or trumpet), L. **-tṛiṇa**, n. Andropogon Schœnanthus, L. **-taila**, n. a kind of oil prepared with fragrant substances, MBh. vi, 4434; R. iv; Suśr. iv; sulphur-butter, L. **-toya**, n. fragrant water. **-tvac**, f. the fragrant bark of Feronia elephantum, L. **-dalā**, f. 'fragrant-leaved,' N. of a plant (*aja-modā*), L. **-dāru**, n. aloe-wood, L. **-dravya**, n. a fragrant substance, L. **-dvārā**, mf(*ā*)n. perceptible through the odour, TĀr. x. **-dvipa**, m. = *-gaja*, Vikr.; Ragh.; Kir. **-dvirada**, m. id., Inscr. **-dhārin**, m. 'possessing perfumes,' N. of Śiva, MBh. xiii, 1159. **-dhūma-ja**, m. a kind of perfume, L. **-dhūma-bhava**, m. id., Gal. **-dhūli**, f. musk, L. **-nakula**, m. the musk rat of Bengāl (Sorex moschatus), L. **-nākulī**, f., N. of a plant (Piper Chaba, L.; Vanda Roxburghii, L.; Artemisia vulgaris, L.), Suśr. v f. (metrically also *°li*). **-nāḍī**, f. = *-nālī*, Gal. **-nāman**, m. a variety of Ocimum with red blossoms; (*mnī*), f. one of the minor diseases (*kshudra-roga*), Suśr.; Bhpr. **-nālikā**, f. the nose, L. **-nālī**, f. id., L. **-nilayā**, f. a kind of jasmine, L. **-niśā**, f. a variety of Curcuma, L. **-pa**, *ās*, m. pl. 'inhaling the odour,' N. of a class of manes, MBh. xiii, 1372. **-pattra**, m. 'fragrant-leaved,' a kind of Ocimum, L.; Ægle Marmelos, L.; the orange tree, L.; (*ā*), f. = *-niśā*, L.; (*ī*), f. Physalia flexuosa; the plant Ambashṭhā, L.; the plant Aśva-gandhā, L. **-pattrikā**, f. (= *°ttrī*) Physalis flexuosa, L.; = *-niśā*, L.; Apium involucratum, L. **-parṇa**, m. 'fragrant-leaved,' Alstonia scholaris, L. **-palāśikā**, f. turmeric, L. **-palāśī**, f. (= *gandhā*) Curcuma Amhaldi or Zerumbet, L. **-pāna**, n. a fragrant beverage, MānGṛ. **-pālin**, m. 'preserving perfumes,' Śiva, MBh. xiii, 1242. **-pāshāṇa**, m. sulphur, L.; *-vat*, mfn. sulphured, Daś. xi, 107. **-piṅgalā**, f., N. of a woman, g. *śubhrâdi*. **-piśācikā**, f. the smoke of burnt fragrant resin ('imp-like' from its dark colour or cloudy nature), L. **-pītā**, f. = *-niśā*, L. **-pushpa**, n. a fragrant flower, R. i, 73, 19; flowers and sandal (presented together at seasons of worship), W.; (*as*), m. Calamus Rotang, L.; Alangium hexapetalum, L.; Cordia Myxa; (*ā*), f. the Indigo plant, L.; Pandanus odoratissimus; = *gaṇikārī* (Premna spinosa), L. **-pūtanā**, f. a kind of imp or goblin (causing a particular disease), Hariv. 9542. **-phala**, m. 'having a fragrant fruit,' Feronia elephantum, L.; Ægle Marmelos, L.; the plant Tejaḥ-phala, L.; (*ā*), f. the plant Priyaṃgu, L.; Trigonella fœnum græcum, L.; Batatas paniculata, L.; the Olibanum tree, L.; (*ī*), f. the plant Priyaṃgu, ŚārṅgP.; = *-mohinī*, L. **-bandhu**, m. the mango tree, L. **-bahala**, m. a kind of Ocimum, L. **-bahula**, m. = *-taṇḍula*, L.; (*ā*), f. the plant Gorakshī, L. **-bījā**, f. 'having fragrant seeds,' Trigonella fœnum græcum, L. **-bhadrā**, f. the creeper Gandha-bhādāliyā, L. **-bhāṇḍa**, for *gardabhāṇḍa*, q.v. **-mañjarī**, f., N. of a woman, Vīrac. viii. **-madana**, metrically for *-mād°*, q. v. **-maya**, mf(*ī*)n. = *-ja*, Hcat. i, 7, 60. **-māṃsī**, f. a kind of Indian spikenard (Valeriana), VarBṛS. li, 15 (metrically shortened *°si*). **-mātṛi**, f. 'mother of odour,' the earth (the quality of odour residing in earth, cf. Mn. i, 78), L. **-māda**, m., N. of a son of Śvaphalka, BhP. ix, 24, 16; of a monkey (attendant of Rāma), 10, 19. **-mādana**, m. 'intoxicating with fragrance,' = *-modana*, L.; 'delighting in fragrances,' a large black bee, L.; N. of a mountain (forming the division between Ilāvṛita and Bhadrâśva, to the east of Meru, renowned for its fragrant forests), MBh.; Hariv. &c. (once *-mad°*, Hcat. i, 6, 24); N. of Rāvaṇa, MBh. ii, 410; of a monkey (attendant of Rāma), MBh. iii, 16273; R. i, 16, 13; iv; v, 73, 26; vi; (*ī*), f. = *°dhôttamā*, L.; a parasitical plant, L.; a kind of perfume, L.; (*am*), n. the forest on the mountain Gandha-mādana, L.; *-varsha*, m. n. the division of Jambū-dvīpa formed by the mountain Gandha-mādana, VP. ii. **-mādinī**, f. 'strong-scented,' lac, L.; (= *°danī*) a sort of perfume, L.; = *°dhôttamā*, W. **-mārjāra**, m. the civet cat, Bhpr. **-mālatī**, f. a kind of perfume, v, 2, 117. **-mālin**, m. 'having fragrant garlands,' N. of a Nāga, Kathās. lxxii, 33; (*inī*), f. a kind of perfume, L. **-mālya**, n. du. fragrances and garlands, ChUp. viii, 2, 6; n. pl. id., Mn. iii, 209; MBh. &c. (ifc. f. *ā*, Ragh. ii, 1); *-loka*, m. the world of fragrances and garlands, ChUp. **-muṇḍa**, m. = *-bhāṇḍa*. **-mūla**, m. 'having a fragrant (and tuberous) root,' Alpinia Galanga, L.; (*ā*), f. the Olibanum tree, L.; = *-palāśī*, L.; (*ī*), f. id., L. **-mūlaka**, m. id., L.; (*ikā*), f. id., L.; Emblica officinalis, L. **-mūshika**, m. = *-nakula*, L.; (*ā*), f. id., L. **-mūshī**, f. id., L. **-mṛiga**, m. = *-mārjāra*, Bālar. iii, 28; the musk deer, W.; (hence) *°gâṇḍajā*, f. musk, Gal. **-maithuna**, m. a bull, L. **-moksha**, m. (= *-māda*) N. of a son of Śvaphalka, VP. iv, 14, 2. **-moca**, v.l. for *-moksha*. **-modana**, m. (= *-mād°*) sulphur, L. **-mohinī**, f. the bud of Michelia Campaka, L. **-yukti**, f. the blending of fragrant substances, preparation of perfumes (one of the 64 Kalās, see s. v. *kalā*); N. of VarBṛS. lxxvii; *-jña*, mfn. skilled in the preparation of perfumes, xv, 12; *-vid*, mfn. id., xvi, 18. **-yuti**, f. fragrant powder, L. **-ratā**, f., N. of a plant, Gal. **-rasa**, (cf. *rasa-gandha*) in comp., odour and flavour, MBh. v, 777; vi, 5786; perfumes and spices, Gaut. vii, 9; m. myrrh, L.; Gardenia florida, L.; *°sâṅgaka*, m. turpentine, L. **-rāja**, m. a kind of jasmine, L.; a kind of bdellium, L.; N. of an author of Prākrit verses; (*ī*), f. a kind of perfume (commonly Nakhī), L.; (*am*), n. sandal-wood, L.; a kind of perfume, L.; a kind of white flower, L. **-latā**, f. 'fragrant creeper,' the plant Priyaṃgu, Bhpr. **-lubdha**, mfn. desirous of odours (a bee), Kām. **-lolupā**, f. 'desirous of fragrances,' a fly or gnat, L. **-vajrā**, *°jrī*, f., N. of a goddess, Kālac. **-vaṭikā**, f. incense in small round pieces, Lalit. xiii f. **-vaṇij**, m. a seller of perfumes, Parāś., Sch. **-vat**, mfn. endowed with the quality of smell, Tarkas.; (g. *rasâdi*) endowed with fragrance, scented, odoriferous, Gobh.; MBh.; R. &c.; (*tī*), f. = *-mātṛi*, L.; a kind of jasmine, L.; = *°dhôttamā*, L.; a kind of perfume, L.; = *-kālī*, MBh. i, 2411; N. of a city belonging to Vāyu, SkandaP.; of a city belonging to Varuṇa, L.; N. of a river, Megh. 34. **-vadhū**, f. = *-palāśī*, L.; a kind of perfume, L. **-valkala**, n. the cassia bark (Laurus Cassia), L.; Sarsaparilla, W. **-vallarī**, f., N. of a plant, L. **-vallī**, f. id., L. **-vaha**, mfn. bearing fragrances (said of wind), Mn. i, 76; BhP. ii, 10, 20; m. wind, MBh. ii, 390; Śak. v, 4; Kum. &c.; (*ā*), f. the nose, L.; *-śmaśāna*, n. N. of a cemetery, Pañcad. i, 39; v, 12. **-vāha**, m. (= *-vaha*) the wind, Gīt. i, 35; the musk deer, L.; (*ā*), f. the nose, L. **-vihvala**, m. wheat, L. **-vṛikshaka**, m. the Śāl tree (Shorea robusta), L. **-vyākula**, n. a fragrant berry, L. **-śaṭī**, f. = *-palāśī*, L. **-śāka**, n. a kind of vegetable, L. **-śāli**, m. = *-taṇḍula*, Daś. xi, 175. **-śuṇḍinī**, f. the musk rat, L. **-śekhara**, m. musk, L. **-śaila**, m. = *-mādana* (N. of a mountain), Gol. **-sāra**, m. sandal-wood, L.; a kind of jasmine, L. **-sāraṇa**, m. a kind of perfume, L. **-sukhī**, f. = *-śuṇḍinī*, W. **-sūyī**, f. id., W. **-sevaka**, mfn. using fragrances, Bhar. **-soma**, n. the white esculent water-lily, L. **-srag-dāma-vat**, mfn. furnished with fragrant garlands, MānGṛ. **-hastin**, m. = *-gaja*, R. v f.; N. of an antidote (said to be very efficacious), Car.; of the author of a Comm. on Ācārâṅga (i, 1), Śil.; *°sti-mahā-tarka*, m., N. of a work. **-hārikā**, f. a female servant who bears perfumes behind her mistress, L. **Gandhâkhu**, m. the musk rat, L. **Gandhâjīva**, m. 'living by perfumes,' vendor of perfumes, L. **Gandhâḍhya**, mfn. rich in odour, fragrant, Nal. v, 38; Subh.; m. the orange tree, L.; (*ā*), f. = *°dha-niśā*, L.; yellow jasmine, L.; Pæderia fœtida, L.; the plant Rāmataruṇī, L.; the plant Ārāma-śītalā, L.; = *°dha-nakula*, Gal.; (*am*), n. sandal-wood, L.; a kind of perfume, L. **Gandhâdhika**, n. a kind of perfume, L. **Gandhâpakarshaṇa**, n. removing smells, W. **Gandhâmbu**, n. = *°dha-jala*, L. **Gandhâmbhas**, n. id., VarBṛS. **Gandhâmlā**, f. the wild lemon tree, L. **Gandhâlā**, f. Celtis orientalis (commonly Jiyatī), L. **Gandhâlī**, f. a wasp, L.; Pæderia fœtida, L.; *-garbha*, m. small cardamoms, L. **Gandhâśman**, m. = *°dha-pāshāṇa*, L. **Gandhâshṭaka**, n. a mixture of 8 fragrant substances varying according to the deities to whom they are offered (e. g. the eight articles, sandal, agallochum, camphor, saffron, valerian, and some fragrant grasses). **Gandhâhvā**, f. 'called after its odour,' N. of a plant, Suśr. iv. **Gandhêcchā**, f. 'wishing fragrances,' N. of a goddess, Kālac. **Gandhêndriya**, n. the organ of smell, Suśr. iii. **Gandhêbha**, m. = *°dha-gaja*, Rājat. i, 300. **Gandhêśa**, m. 'lord of fragrances,' N. of a Vīta-rāga. **Gandhotu**, for *°dhâutu*, L. **Gandhôtkaṭa**, m. Artemisia Abrotanum, Bhpr. **Gandhôttamā**, f. spirituous or vinous liquor, L. **Gandhôda**, n. = *°dha-jala*, BhP. ix, 11, 26. **Gandhôdaka**, n. id., MānSr. xi, 3 **Gandhôpajīvin**, m. = *°dhâjīva*, R. ii, 83, 14. **Gandhôpala**, m. = *°dha-pāshāṇa*, L. **Gandhôshṇīsha**, m. 'having a fragrant mane,' a lion, Gal. **Gandhâutu**, m. = *°dha-mārjāra*, L.

Gandhaka, mf(*ikā*)n. ifc. 'having the smell of, scenting,' see *aja-*, *avi-*; m. (g. *sthūlâdi*, Gaṇar. 182) 'perfumes,' see *-peshikā*; sulphur; Hyperanthera Moringa, L. **-peshikā**, f. a female servant who grinds or prepares perfumes, Hariv. 8394.

Gandhakīya, mfn. relating to sulphur.

2\. **Gandhana**, *am*, n. the spreading or diffusion of odours, Dhātup. xxiv, 42 (Suśr. i, 21, 3); m. (= *°dha-taṇḍula* &c.) a kind of rice, Car. i, 27, 10.

Gandhālu, mfn. 'fragrant,' see *ati-g°*; (*us*), m. fragrant rice, L.

Gandhi, mfn. only ifc. (Pāṇ. v, 4, 135–137) having the smell of, smelling of, perfumed with, MBh. xiii; R.; Ragh. ii, vii, &c.; (Pāṇ. v, 4, 136) having only the smell of, containing only a very small quantity, bearing only the name of, R. vii, 24, 29.

Gandhika, mfn. ifc. 'having the smell of, smelling of,' see *utpala-*; having only the smell, having a very little of anything (e. g. *bhrātṛi-*, being a brother only by name, MBh. iii, 16111); m. a seller of perfumes, Buddh. L.; sulphur, L.; (*ā*), f. v. l. for *gabdikā* (N. of a country), q. v. **Gandhikâpaṇa**, n. a place where fragrances are sold, Pañcad. ii, 65.

Gandhin, mfn. having a smell, odoriferous, MBh. xiv, 1398; smelling of (in comp.), MBh.; R.; Ragh. xv; BhP.; ifc. having (only the smell, i. e.) a very little of anything, Naish. vi, 38; (*mātṛi-gandhinī*, 'a mother only by name') R. ii, 75, 12; for *gardhin*, Kathās. xii, 48; (*ī*), m. a bug, flying bug, L.; Xanthophyllum virens, L.; (*inī*), f. a kind of perfume, L.; (*i*), n. id., L. **Gandhi-parṇa**, m. = *°dha-p°*, L.

Gandholi, *is*, f. = *°dha-palāśī*, L.

Gandholī, f. id., L.; Pæderia fœtida, L.; Cyperus rotundus, L.; dried ginger, L.; (= *°dhâlī*) a wasp, L.; N. of Indrāṇī, Gal.

Gandhya. See *vāja-g°*.

गन्धर्व *gandharvá, as*, **m.** a Gandharva [though in later times the Gandharvas are regarded as a class, yet in RV. rarely more than one is mentioned; he is designated as the heavenly Gandharva (*divyá g°*, RV. ix, 86, 36 & x, 139, 5), and is also called Viśvā-vasu (RV. x, 85, 21 & 22; 139, 4 & 5) and Vāyu-keśa (in pl., RV. iii, 38, 6); his habitation is the sky, or the region of the air and the heavenly waters (RV. i, 22, 14; viii, 77, 5; ix, 85, 12; 86, 36; x, 10, 4; AV. ii, 2, 3); his especial duty is to guard the heavenly Soma (RV. ix, 83, 4 & 85, 12), which the gods obtain through his intervention (RV.; AV. vii, 73, 3; cf. RV. i, 22, 14); it is obtained for the human race by Indra, who conquers the Gandharva and takes it by force (RV. viii, 1, 11 & 77, 5); the heavenly Gandharva is supposed to be a good physician, because the Soma is considered as the best medicine; possibly, however, the word Soma originally denoted not the beverage so called, but the moon, and the heavenly Gandharva may have been the genius or tutelary deity of the moon; in one passage (RV. ix, 86, 36) the heavenly Gandharva and the Soma are identified; he is also regarded as one of the genii who regulate the course of the Sun's horses (i, 163, 2; x, 177, 2; cf. 135, 5); he knows and makes known the secrets of heaven and divine truths generally (x, 139, 5 & 6; AV. ii, 1, 2; xx, 128, 3; VS. xi, 1; xxxii, 9); he is the parent of the first pair of human beings, Yama and Yamī (RV. x, 10, 4), and has a peculiar mystical power over women and a right to possess them (RV. x, 85, 21 & 22; 40 & 41); for this reason he is invoked in marriage ceremonies (AV. xiv, 2, 35 & 36); ecstatic states of mind and possession by evil spirits are supposed to be derived from the heavenly Gandharva (cf. *-gṛihīta, -graha*); the Gandharvas as a class have the same characteristic features as the one Gandharva; they live in the sky (RV.; AV.; ŚBr. xiv), guard the Soma (RV. ix, 113, 3; ŚBr. iii; AitBr. i, 27), are governed by Varuṇa (just as the Apsarasas are governed by Soma), ŚBr. xiii; ĀśvŚr. x, 7, 3, know the best medicines (AV. viii, 7, 23; VS. xii, 98), regulate the course of the asterisms (AV. xiii, 1, 23; BhP. iv, 29, 21; hence twenty-seven are mentioned, VS. ix, 7), follow after women and are desirous of intercourse with them (AV.; ŚBr. iii); as soon as a girl becomes marriageable, she belongs to Soma, the Gandharvas, and Agni (Gṛihyās. ii, 19 f.; Pañcat.; Suśr.); the wives of the Gandharvas are the Apsarasas (cf. *gandharvâpsarás*), and like them the Gandharvas are invoked in gambling with dice (AV. vii, 109, 5); they are also feared as evil beings together with the Rākshasas, Kimīdins, Piśācas, &c., amulets being worn as a protection against them (AV.; Suśr.); they are said to have revealed the Vedas to Vāc (ŚBr. iii; cf. PārGṛ. ii, 12, 2), and are called the preceptors of the Ṛishis (ŚBr. xi); Purūravas is called among them (ib.); in epic poetry the Gandharvas are the celestial musicians or heavenly singers (cf. RV. x, 177, 2) who form the orchestra at the banquets of the gods, and they belong together with the Apsarasas to Indra's heaven, sharing also in his battles (Yājñ. i, 71; MBh.; Hariv. &c.; cf. RTL. p. 238); in the more systematic mythology the Gandharvas constitute one of the classes into which the higher creation is divided (i. e. gods, manes, Gandharvas, AV. xi, 5, 2; or gods, Asuras, Gandharvas, men, TS. vii, 8, 25, 2; cf. ŚBr. x; or gods, men, Gandharvas, Apsarasas, Sarpas, and manes, AitBr. iii, 31, 5; for other enumerations cf. Nir. iii, 8; Mn. i, 37 [RTL. p. 237] & iii, 196; vii, 23; xii, 47; Nal. &c.); divine and human Gandharvas are distinguished (TUp. ii, 8; the divine or Deva-Gandharvas are enumerated MBh. i, 2550 ff. & 4810 ff.); another passage names 11 classes of Gandharvas (T-Ār. i, 9, 3); the chief or leader of the Gandharvas is named Citra-ratha (Bhag. x, 26); they are called the creatures of Prajāpati (Mn. i, 37) or of Brahmā (Hariv. 11793) or of Kaśyapa (11850) or of the Munis (MBh. i, 2550; Hariv. 11553) or of Prādhā (MBh. i, 2556) or of Arishṭā (Hariv. 234; VP. i, 21) or of Vāc (PadmaP.); with Jainas the Gandharvas constitute one of the eight classes of the Vyantaras]; N. of the attendant of the 17th Arhat of the present Avasarpiṇī, L.; a singer, VarBṛS. lxxxvii, 33; BhP. i, 11, 21; the Koïl or black cuckoo, L.; a sage, pious man, Mahīdh. on VS. xxxii, 9; a horse, MBh. iii, 11762; cf. ii, 1043; the musk deer (derived fr. *gandha*), L.; the soul after death and previous to its being born again (corresponding in some respects to the western notion of a ghost), L.; N. of the 14th Kalpa or period of the world, VāyuP. i, 21, 30; of the 21st Muhūrta, Sūryapr.; of a Svara or tone (for *gāndhāra*?), Hariv. ii, 120, 4; m. pl. the Gandharvas (see above); N. of a people (named together with the Gāndhāras), R. vii, 100, 10 f. & 101, 2 ff. & 11; VarBṛS. xiv, 31; (*ā*), f. Durgā, Hariv. ii, 120, 4 (v. l. *gāndharvī*); (*ī*), f. Gandharvī (daughter of Surabhi and mother of the race of horses, MBh. i, 2631 f.; R. iii, 20, 28 f.; VāyuP.), RV. x, 11, 2; R.; night, BhP. iv, 29, 21; [cf. Gk. κένταυρος fr. κενθαρϝο-ς.] **— kanyā**, f. a Gandharva virgin, Kāraṇḍ. i. **— khaṇḍa**, m. n. one of the 9 divisions of Bhārata-varsha. **— gṛihīta** (*°rvá-*), mfn. possessed by a Gandharva, ŚBr. xiv; AitBr. v, 29, 2. **— graha**, m. the being possessed by a Gandharva, Suśr. vi, 60, 8. **— taila**, n. castor-oil, Bhpr. **— tva**, n. the state of a Gandharva, Kathās. lxxiv, 312. **— dattā**, f., N. of a daughter of the Gandharva prince Sāgara-datta, cvi, 9. **— nagara**, n. 'Gandharva-city,' an imaginary town in the sky, MBh. ii, 1043; Hariv.; R. v &c.; Fata Morgana, Pāṇ. iv, 1, 3, Kār.; VarBṛS. xxx; xxxvi, 4; BhP. v, 14, 5; Kād.; the city of the Gandharva people, R. vii. **— patnī** (*°rvá-*), f. the wife of a Gandharva, an Apsaras, AV. ii, 2, 5. **— pada**, n. the abode of the Gandharvas, AV.Pariś. **— pura**, n. (= *-nagara*) the city of the Gandharvas, Kathās.; Fata Morgana, VarBṛS.; BhP. v. **— rāja**, m. a chief of the Gandharvas, MBh.; N. of Citra-ratha, W. **— rtú** (*rit°*), m. the time or season of the Gandharvas, AV. xiv, 2, 34. **— loká**, m. pl. the worlds of the Gandharvas, ŚBr. xiv, 6, 6, 1 & 7, 1, 37 f. **— vidyā**, f. 'Gandharva-science,' music, MBh.; (pl.) R. i, 79, 21. **— vivāha**, m. 'the form of marriage peculiar to the Gandharvas,' a marriage proceeding entirely from love without ceremonies and without consulting relatives (allowed between persons of the second or military class); cf. Mn. iii, 26. **— veda**, m. = *-vidyā* (considered as a branch of the SV.), Caraṇ. **— hasta**, m. 'Gandharva-handed (the form of the leaves resembling that of a hand),' the castor-oil tree, Suśr.; (*a-manushyasya h°*, Kāvyād. iii, 121.) **— hastaka**, m. id., Suśr. **Gandharvâpsarás**, *asas*, f. pl. the Gandharvas and the Apsarasas, VS. xxx, 8; AV.; ŚBr. &c.; (*asau*), f. du. Gandharva and the Apsarasas, ĀrshBr. **Gandharveshṭhá**, mfn. being with Gandharva, MaitrS. i, 3, 1.

गन्धार *gandhāra, ās*, m. pl. (gaṇas *kacchâdi* & *sindhv-ādi*) N. of a people, ChUp.; AV.Pariś.; MBh. i, 2440; (*as*), m. (= *gāndh°*) the third note, L.; (in music) a particular Rāga, L.; red lead, L.; (*ī*), f. for *gāndh°* (N. of a Vidyā-devī), L.

Gandhāri, *ayas*, m. pl., N. of a people, RV. i, 126, 7; AV. v, 22, 14; (cf. *gāndh°*.)

गन्धाला *gandhâlā*, &c. See *gandhá*.

गन्मुत् *ganmut*. See *garmút*.

गब्दिका *gabdikā*, f., N. of a country, g. *sindhv-ādi*; Pāṇ. ii, 4, 10, Pat.; ii, 1, 6, Kāś.

गभ *gabhá*, *as*, m. (√*gabh* = *gambh* = *jambh*) 'slit,' the vulva, VS. xxiii; ŚBr. xiii, 2, 9, 6.

Gabhas-tala, n. = *gabhasti-mat*, q. v.

Gábhasti, m. 'fork (?),' arm, hand, RV.; ŚBr. iv, 1, 1, 9; (Naigh. i, 5) a ray of light, sunbeam, MBh.; R.; Pañcat. &c.; the sun, L.; N. of an Āditya, Rāmapūjāśar.; of a Ṛishi, BrahmaP. ii, 12; f., N. of Svāhā (the wife of Agni), L.; m. (or f.) du. the two arms or hands, RV. i, iii, v ff.; (*ī*), f., N. of a river, VP. ii, 4, 36; mfn. shining ('fork-like,' double-edged or sharp-edged, pointed?), RV. i, 54, 4; TBr. ii; (cf. *syū́ma-g°*.) **— nemi**, m. 'the felly of whose wheel is sharp-edged (?),' N. of Kṛishṇa, MBh. xii, 1512. **— pāṇi**, m. 'having rays for hands,' the sun, L. **— pūta** (*gábh°*), mfn. purified with the hands, RV. ii, 14, 8; ix, 86, 34; VS. vii, 1. **— mat**, mfn. shining, brilliant, MBh. ii, 443; iii, 146; m. the sun, Ragh. iii, 37; Kād. vi, 1158; a particular hell, VP. ii, 5, 2; (*gabhas-tala*, VāyuP.); m. n., N. of one of the nine divisions of Bhārata-varsha, VP. ii, 3, 6; Gol. iii, 41. **— mālin**, m. 'garlanded with rays,' the sun, Kād. iii, 945; v, 633; Hcar. v, 408; Bālar. ii. **— hasta**, m. = *-pāṇi*, L. **Gabhastîś-vara**, n., N. of a Liṅga, KāśīKh. il.

Gabhi-shák, ind. (√*sañj*, cf. *ānushák*) deeply down, far down or within, AV. vii, 7, 1; (? xix, 56, 2.)

Gabhīkā, v. l. for *gargarikā*, q. v.

Gabhīrá, mf(*ā*)n. deep (opposed to *gādha* and *dīna*), RV. &c.; (Naigh. i, 11) deep in sound, deep-sounding, hollow-toned, RV. v, 85, 1; Ṛitus.; profound, sagacious, grave, serious, solemn, secret, mysterious, RV.; AV. v, 11, 3; (*gambh°*, MBh. &c.); Prab. iv, 15; Sāh.; dense, impervious, BhP. viii, 3, 5; (*gambh°*, R. iii); not to be penetrated or investigated or explored, inscrutable; 'inexhaustible,' uninterrupted (time), BhP. i, 5, 8; (*gambh°*, iv, 12, 38; v, 24, 24); m., N. of a son of Manu Bhautya or of Rambha, VP. iii, 2, 43; BhP. ix, 17, 10. **— vepas** (*°rá-*), mfn. (= *gambh°*) moved deeply or inwardly, deeply excited, RV. i, 35, 7.

Gabhīrikā, f. 'deep-sounding,' a large drum, L.; a gong, W.

Gabhvara, *am*, n. (= *gahv°*) an abyss, depth, Karaṇḍ. x, 7.

Gámbhan, *a*, n. depth, VS. xiii, 30.

Gambhára, *am*, n. id., RV. x, 106, 9 ('water,' Naigh. i, 12).

Gámbhishṭha, mfn. superl. of *gabhīrá*, ŚBr. vii.

Gambhīrá, mfn. = *gabh°*, RV. (only in the beginning of Pādas, six times); AV. &c. (in post-Vedic writings *gambh°* is more used than *gabh°*; the deepness of a man's navel, voice, and character are praised together, VarBṛS. lxviii, 85; hence a person who is said to have a deep navel, voice, and character is called *tri-g°*, mf(*ā*)n., MBh. iv, 254; v, 3939); m. (= *jambh°*) the lemon tree, L.; a lotus, L.; a Mantra of the RV., L.; (= *gabh°*) N. of a son of Bhautya, VP. (v. l.); (*ā*), f. a hiccup, violent singultus (with *hikkā*, Suśr.), W.; N. of a river, Megh. 41; (*am*), n. 'depth,' with *Jamad-agneh*, N. of a Sāman. **— gati**, mfn. extending deeply (as a sore), Suśr. i. **— cetas** (*°rá-*), mfn. of profound mind, RV. viii, 8, 2. **— tā**, f. depth (of water), W.; depth (of a sound), W.; profoundness, earnestness, sagacity, W. **— tva**, n. id., W. **— dhvani**, m. a deep sound, low tone, W. **— nāda**, m. deep or hollow sound, thundering, roaring, W. **— nirghosha**, m. 'deep-sounding,' N. of a Nāga, Buddh. **— paksha**, m., N. of a prince, ib. **— buddhi**, m. 'of profound mind,' N. of a son of Manu Indra-sāvarṇi, BhP. viii, 13, 34. **— vedin**, mfn. 'deeply sensitive,' restive (an elephant), Ragh. iv, 39; Siṇhâs. Introd. 9; inscrutable, ib. **— vedha**, mfn. very penetrating, W. **— vepas** (*°rá-*), mfn. = *gabh°*, RV. x, 62, 5; AV. xix, 2, 3. **— śaṇsa** (*°rá-*), mfn. ruling secretly or in a hidden manner (as Varuṇa), RV. vii, 87, 6 ['whose praise is inexhaustible,' Sāy.] **— śīla**, m. 'of a profound character,' N. of a Brāhman, Buddh. L. **— sattva-svara-nābhi**, mfn. = *tri-g°* (see above), Suśr. **— svāmin**, m. 'the inscrutable lord,' N. of a statue of Nārāyaṇa, Rājat. iv, 80. **Gambhīrârtha**, mfn. having a profound sense or meaning, Subh.

Gambhīraka, mf(*ikā*)n. lying deep (a vein), Suśr. iv, 16, 19; (*ikā*), f. with *dṛishṭi*, a particular disease of the eye (which causes the pupil to contract and the eye to sink in its socket), vi, 1, 28 & 7, 39; (= *°rā*) N. of a river, VarBṛS. xvi, 16.

गभोलिक *gabholika*, *as*, m. a small round pillow, L.

गभ्वर *gabhvara*. See *gabhá*.

गम् 1. *gam*, Ved. cl. 1. P. *gámati* (Naigh.; Subj. *gamam, gámat* [*gamātas, gamātha*, AV.], *gamāma, gaman*, RV.; Pot. *gaméma*, RV.; inf. *gámadhyai*, RV. i, 154, 6): cl. 2. P. *gánti* (Naigh.; Impv. 3. sg. *gantu*, [2. sg. *gadhi*, see *ā-*, or *gahi*, see *adhi-, abhy-ā-, ā-, upá-*], 2. pl. *gántā* or *gantana*, RV.; impf. 2. & 3. sg. *ágan* [RV.; AV.], 1. pl. *águnma* [RV.; AV.; cf. Pāṇ. viii, 2, 65], 3. pl. *ágman*, RV.; Subj. [or aor. Subj., cf. Pāṇ. ii, 4, 80, Kāś.] 1. pl. *ganma*, 3. pl. *gmán*, RV.; Pot. 2. sg. *gamyās*, RV. i, 187, 7; Prec. 3. sg. *gamyās*, RV.; pr. p. *gmát*, x, 22, 6): cl. 3. P. *jaganti* (Naigh. ii, 14; Pot. *jagamyām*, *°yāt*, RV.; impf. 2. & 3. sg. *ajagan*, 2. pl. *ajaganta* or *°tana*, RV.): Ved. & Class. cl. 1. P. (also Ā., MBh. &c.), with substitution of *gacch* [= βάσκ-ω] for *gam*, *gácchati* (cf. Pāṇ. vii, 3, 77; Subj. *gácchāti*, RV. x, 16, 2; 2. sg. *gacchās* [RV. vi, 35, 3] or *gacchāsi* [AV. v, 5, 6]; 2. pl. *gacchāta*, RV. viii, 7, 30; 3. pl. *gácchān*, RV. viii, 79, 5; impf. *ágacchat*; Pot. *gacchet*; pr. p. *gácchat*, RV. &c.; aor. *agamat*, Pāṇ. iii, 1, 55; vi, 4, 98, Kāś.; for Ā. with prepositions, cf. Pāṇ. i, 2, 13; 2nd fut. *gamishyati*, AV. &c.; 1st fut. *gántā* [Pāṇ. vii, 2, 58], RV. &c.; perf. 1. sg. *jagamā* [RV.], 3. sg. *jagāma*, 2. du. *jagmathur*, 3. pl. *jagmúr*, RV. &c.; p. *jaganvás*

[RV. &c.] or *jagmivas*, Pāṇ. vii, 2, 68, f. *jagmushī*, RV. &c.; Ved. inf. *gántave*, *gántavai*; Class. inf. *gantum*; Ved. ind. p. *gatvāya*, *gatvī*; Class. ind. p. *gatvā́* [AV. &c.], with prepositions *-gamya* or *-gatya*, Pāṇ. vi, 4, 38) to go, move, go away, set out, come, RV. &c.; to go to or towards, approach (with acc. or loc. or dat. [MBh.; Ragh. ii, 15; xii, 7; cf. Pāṇ. ii, 3, 12] or *prati* [MBh.; R.]), RV. &c.; to go or pass (as time, e. g. *kāle gacchati*, time going on, in the course of time), R.; Ragh.; Megh.; Naish.; Hit.; to fall to the share of (acc.), Mn. &c.; to go against with hostile intentions, attack, L.; to decease, die, Cāṇ.; to approach carnally, have sexual intercourse with (acc.), ĀśvGṛ. iii, 6; Mn. &c.; to go to any state or condition, undergo, partake of, participate in, receive, obtain (e. g. *mitratām gacchati*, 'he goes to friendship,' i. e. he becomes friendly), RV.; AV. &c.; *jānubhyām avanīm √gam*, 'to go to the earth with the knees,' kneel down, MBh. xiii, 935; Pañcat. v, 1, 14/15; *dharanīm mūrdhnā √gam*, 'to go to the earth with the head,' make a bow, R. iii, 11, 6; *mánasā √gam*, to go with the mind, observe, perceive, RV. iii, 38, 6; VS.; Nal.; R.; (without *mánasā*) to observe, understand, guess, MBh. iii, 2108; (especially Pass. *gamyate*, 'to be understood or meant') Pāṇ. Kāś. & L., Sch.; *doshena* or *doshato √gam*, to approach with an accusation, ascribe guilt to a person (acc.), MBh. i, 4322 & 7455; R. iv, 21, 3: Caus. *gamayati* (Pāṇ. ii, 4, 46; Impv. 2. sg. Ved. *gamayā* or *gāmaya* [RV. v, 5, 10], 3. sg. *gamayatāt*, AitBr. ii, 6; perf. *gamayām cakāra*, AV. &c.) to cause to go (Pāṇ. viii, 1, 60, Kāś.) or come, lead or conduct towards, send to (dat., AV.), bring to a place (acc. [Pāṇ. i, 4, 52] or loc.), RV. &c.; to cause to go to any condition, cause to become, TS.; ŚBr. &c.; to impart, grant, MBh. xiv, 179; to send away, Pāṇ. i, 4, 52, Kāś.; 'to let go,' not care about, Bālar. v, 10; to excel, Prasannar. i, 14; to spend time, Śak.; Megh.; Ragh. &c.; to cause to understand, make clear or intelligible, explain, MBh. iii, 11290; VarBṛS.; L., Sch.; to convey an idea or meaning, denote, Pāṇ. iii, 2, 10, Kāś.; (causal of the causal) to cause a person (acc.) to go by means of another, Pāṇ. i, 4, 52, Kāś.: Desid. *jigamishati* (Pāṇ., or *jigāṇsate*, Pāṇ. vi, 4, 16, Siddh.; impf. *ajigāṇsat*, ŚBr. x) to wish to go, be going, Lāṭy.; MBh. xvi, 63; to strive to obtain, ŚBr. x; ChUp.; to wish to bring (to light, *prakāśam*), TS. i: Intens. *jánganti* (Naigh.), *jangamīti* or *jangamyate* (Pāṇ. vii, 4, 85, Kāś.), to visit, RV. x, 41, 1 (p. *gánigmat*); VS. xxiii, 7 (impf. *aganīgan*); [cf. βαίνω; Goth. *qvam*; Eng. *come*; Lat. *venio* for *gvemio*.]

Gat, mfn. ifc. (Pāṇ. vi, 4, 40), see *adhva-*, *jana-*, *dvi-*.

Gatá, mfn. gone, gone away, departed, departed from the world, deceased, dead, RV. i, 119, 4; AV. &c.; past (as time), gone by, Mn. viii, 402; MBh. &c.; disappeared (often in comp.), Mn. vii, 225; MBh. &c.; come, come forth from (in comp. or abl.), R. iv, 56, 10; Kathās. ii, 11; come to, approached, arrived at, being in, situated in, contained in (acc. or loc. or in comp., e.g. *sabhām g°*, 'come to an assembly,' Mn. viii, 95; *Kānyakubje g°*, gone to Kānyakubja, Pañcat. v; *ratha-g°*, sitting or standing in a carriage, R. iii; *ādya-g°*, *turya-g°*, *antya-g°*, taking the first, fourth, last place; *sarva-g°*, spread everywhere, Nal. ii, 14), RV. i, 105, 4; AV. x, 10, 32; ŚBr. &c.; having walked (a path, acc.); gone to any state or condition, fallen into (acc. or loc. or in comp., e.g. *kshayam* or *°ye g°*, gone to destruction; *āpad-g°*, fallen into misfortune, Mn. ix, 283), TUp.; Mn. &c.; relating to, referring to, connected with (e. g. *putra-g° sneha*, love directed towards the son, R. i; *tvad-g°*, belonging to thee); walked (a path), frequented, visited, RV. vii, 57, 3; R.; Kum.; spread abroad, celebrated, MBh. iii; 'known, understood,' having the meaning of (loc.), L.; n. going, motion, manner of going, MBh. iv, 297; R.; Śak. vii, 7; Vikr. &c.; the being gone or having disappeared, Cāṇ.; the place where any one has gone, Pāṇ. Kāś.; anything past or done, event, W.; diffusion, extension, celebration, ChUp. vii, 1, 5; manner, Pāṇ. i, 3, 21, Vārtt. 5. **-kalmasha**, mfn. freed from crime, W. **-kāla**, m. past time, W. **-kīrti**, mfn. deprived of reputation, W. **-klama**, mf(*ā*)n. 'one whose lassitude is gone,' rested, refreshed, Mn. vii, 225; Nal. &c. **-cetana**, mfn. deprived of sense or consciousness, senseless, void of understanding, fainted away, Nal.; R. ii; iv, 22, 30. **-cetas**, mfn. bereft of sense, W. **-jīva**, mf(*ā*)n. exanimate, dead, Kathās. **-jīvita**, mfn. id., Daś. **-jvara**, mfn. freed from fever or sickness, convalescent, recovered, W.; free from trouble or grief, Nal.; R. vi, 98, 7. **-toyada**, mfn. cloudless, cleared up, fair, i, 44, 22. **-trapa**, mfn. free from fear or shame, bold, BhP. viii, 8, 29. **-dina**, n. the past day, yesterday, W.; (*am*), ind. yesterday, W. **-divasa**, m. the past day, yesterday, W.; (*am*), ind. yesterday, W. **-nāsika**, mfn. noseless, L. **-nidhana**, n., N. of a Sāman, TāṇḍyaBr. xv. **-pāpa**, mfn. free from sin or guilt, W. **-pāra**, mfn. one who has reached the highest limit (of knowledge or of a vow), MBh. v, 1251. **-puṇya**, mfn. devoid of holiness or religious merit, W. **-pratyāgata**, mfn. (Pāṇ. ii, 1, 60, Vārtt. 5) gone away and returned, come back again after having gone away, Mn. vii, 186; ix, 176. **-prâṇa**, mfn. = *-jīva*, R. **-prāya**, mfn. almost gone or vanished, MBh. iv, 376; Śāntiś.; Kathās. ii, 27. **-bhartṛikā**, f. ('a wife) whose husband is dead,' a widow, W. **-bhī**, mfn. free from fear, W. **-manas** (*°tá-*), mfn. = *-jīva*, TS. vi. **-manas-ka**, mfn. thinking of (loc.), Ragh. ix, 67. **-mātra**, mfn. just gone, MBh. **-māya**, mfn. without deceit, W.; without compassion, W. **-rasa**, mfn. (anything) which has lost its flavour or sap, dried, withered, W. **-rātri**, f. the past night, last night, W. **-roga**, mfn. freed from disease, recovered. **-lakshmīka**, mfn. unfortunate, suffering losses, R. i, 60, 17. **-lajja**, m. 'shameless,' N. of an author of Prākrit verses. **-vat**, mfn. going, passing, W.; obtaining, W.; falling into, feeling, entertaining, W. **-vayas**, mfn. 'one whose youth is gone,' advanced in life, Pañcat. **-vayaska**, mfn. id., W. **-varsha**, m. n. the past year, W. **-vitta**, mfn. bereft of wealth, impoverished, W. **-vibhava**, mfn. id., W. **-vaira**, mfn. reconciled, W. **-vyatha**, mfn. freed from pain, unanxious, MBh. i, iii; BhP. iii, 22, 24. **-śaiśava**, mfn. past infancy, above eight years of age, W. **-śrī** (*°tá-*), mfn. (gen. *-śres*, ŚBr. i) one who has obtained fortune or happiness, TS. ii, vii; TBr. ii, 1, 8, 1; AitBr. &c. **-śrī-ka**, mfn. one who has lost fortune or high rank, MBh. iii, 267, 17; bereft of beauty, disfigured, Hariv. 3722. **-saṃkalpa**, mfn. bereft of sense, foolish, W.; free from wishes, MBh. iii, 2187. **-saṅga**, mfn. free from attachment, detached from, dissevered, W.; adverse or indifferent to, W. **-sattva**, mfn. annihilated, lifeless, dead, W.; 'without good qualities,' base, W. **-saṃdeha**, mfn. free from doubt, W. **-sanna-ka**, m. an elephant out of rut, L. **-sādhvasa**, mfn. afraid, W. **-sāra**, mfn. worthless, idle, Subh. (?) **-sauhṛida**, mfn. bereft of friendship or friendly feeling, MBh. iii, 2776; BhP. iv; unkind, indifferent, W.; bereft of friends, W. **-spṛiha**, mfn. having no desire, not finding any pleasure in (loc. or gen.), R. ii; BhP. vii; Kathās. xxxiv, 181; disinterested; pitiless, Kām. **-svârtha**, mfn. useless, BhP. i. **Gatâksha**, mfn. 'sightless,' blind, L. **Gatâgata**, mfn. (g. *akshadyūtâdi*) going and coming, BhP. xi, 28, 26; n. going and coming, going to and fro, reiterated motion in general, Bhag. ix, 21; Kathās. iii, (pl.) iic, cxviii, 119; the flight of a bird backward and forward, MBh. viii, 1902; (in astron.) irregular course of the asterisms, VarBṛ.; appearance and disappearance, growth and decline, R. vii, 51, 24; n. pl. with *√kṛi*, to enter into a negotiation or treaty, Rājat. viii; cf. *gamâgama*. **Gatâgati**, f. 'going and coming,' dying and being born again, R. **Gatâdhi**, mfn. free from anxiety, happy, Daś. i, 103. **Gatâdhvan**, mfn. one who has walked a path, Mālav. v, 9/10; 'who has accomplished a journey,' familiar with (loc.), MBh. xii; 'one whose time of life is (nearly) gone,' old, iii, 123, 5; (*ā*), f. (scil. *tithi*) the time immediately preceding new moon (when a small streak of the moon is still visible), Gobh.; Kāty. **Gatânugata**, n. the following what precedes, following custom, g. *akshadyūtâdi*. **Gatânugatika**, mfn. following what precedes, following custom or the conduct of others, imitative, Hcar. ii, 98; Pañcat.; Naish.; Hit. **Gatânta**, mfn. one whose end has arrived, R. ii, 12, 31. **Gatâyāta**, mfn. coming and going, W. **Gatâyus**, mfn. one whose vital power has vanished, decayed, very old, R.; Suśr.; Hit.; dead, R. vi; Pañcat. i, 21, 8/9. **Gatârtavā**, f. a woman past her courses or past child-bearing, L.; a barren woman, W. **Gatârtha**, mfn. (= *artha-gata*, g. *āhitâgny-ādi*) unmeaning, nonsensical, Sāh. iii; understood, (*a-*, neg.) vi, 34; void of an object, poor, W. **Gatâlīka**, mfn. 'void of untruth,' real, true, W. **Gatâsu**, mfn. one whose breath has gone, expired, dead, RV. x, 18, 8; AV.; ŚBr. &c. **Gatôtsāha**, mfn. dispirited, W. **Gatôdvega**, mfn. freed from sorrow, comforted, MBh. **Gataûjas**, mfn. bereft of strength, W.

Gataka, mfn. ifc. relating to (?), MBh. viii, 4669.

Gáti, *is*, f. going, moving, gait, deportment, motion in general, RV. v, 64, 3; VS.; TS. &c.; manner or power of going; going away; Yājñ. iii, 170; procession, march, passage, procedure, progress, movement (e. g. *astra-g°*, the going or flying of missile weapons, R. v; *param gatim √gam*, 'to go the last way,' to die; *daiva-g°*, the course of fate, R. vi; Megh. 93; *kāvyasya g°*, the progress or course of a poem, R. i, 3, 2); arriving at, obtaining (with gen., loc., or ifc.), ŚBr. ix; MBh. &c.; acting accordingly, obeisance towards (loc.), Āp. i, 13 f.; path, way, course (e. g. *anyatarām gatim √gam*, 'to go either way,' to recover or die, ĀśvŚr.), R.; Bhag. &c.; a certain division of the moon's path and the position of the planet in it (the diurnal motion of a planet in its orbit?), VarBṛS.; issue, Bhag. iv, 29; running wound or sore, Suśr.; place of issue, origin, reason, ChUp. i, 8, 4 f.; Mn. i, 110; R.; Mudr.; possibility, expedient, means, Yājñ. i, 345; R. i; Mālav. &c.; a means of success, way or art, method of acting, stratagem, R. iii, vi; refuge, resource, Mn. viii, 84; R.; Kathās., Vet. iv, 20; cf. RTL. p. 260; the position (of a child at birth), Suśr.; state, condition, situation, proportion, mode of existence, KaṭhUp. iii, 11; Bhag.; Pañcat. &c.; a happy issue; happiness, MBh. iii, 17398; the course of the soul through numerous forms of life, metempsychosis, condition of a person undergoing this migration, Mn.; Yājñ.; MBh. &c.; manner, ĀśvGṛ. i, Sch.; the being understood or meant, Pat.; (in gram.) a term for prepositions and some other adverbial prefixes (such as *alam* &c.) when immediately connected with the tenses of a verb or with verbal derivatives (cf. *karmapravacanīya*), Pāṇ. i, 4, 60 ff.; vi, 2, 49 ff. & 139; viii, 1, 70 f.; a kind of rhetorical figure, Sarasv. ii, 2; a particular high number, Buddh.; 'Motion' (personified as a daughter of Kardama and wife of Pulaha), BhP. iv, 1; m., N. of a son of Anala, Hariv. i, 3, 43. **-tālin**, m., N. of an attendant in Skanda's retinue, MBh. ix, 2569. **-bhaṅga**, m. impediment to progress, stoppage, Śak. iv, 11/12. **-bheda**, m. id., vi, 22/23. **-mat**, mfn. possessed of motion, moving, MBh. xiii, &c.; having issues or sores, Suśr.; connected with a preposition or some other adverbial prefix, Pāṇ. ii, 2, 18, Vārtt. 4, Pat. **-śakti**, f. the power of motion, W. **-hīna**, mfn. without refuge, forlorn, W.

Gatika, *am*, n. going, motion, W.; course, W.; condition, W.; refuge, asylum, W.

Gatilā, f. the not being different from one another (?), L.; N. of a plant, Uṇ. i, 58, Sch.; of a river, L.

Gatī, f. (metrically) for *°ti*, going, R. vii, 31, 41.

Gatīka. See *a-g°*.

Gaty (by Sandhi for *°ti*). **-anusāra**, m. following the way of another, W. **-āgati**, f. (in comp.) coming and going, appearance and disappearance, Siṇhâs. iii, 3/4. **-ūna**, mfn. difficult of access, impassable, W.; desert, helpless, W.

Gatvan. See *pūrva-*.

Gatvara, mf(*ī*)n. going to a place (in comp.), Hcar.; beginning or undertaking (with dat.), Naish. xvii, 71; transient, perishable, Pāṇ. iii, 2, 164; Śāntiś. i, 20; Rājat. viii, 858.

Gatvā́, *gatvāya*, *gatví*. See 1. *gam*.

Gántave, *gántavaí*. See ib.

Gantavya, mfn. to be gone, Nal.; R. &c.; to be accomplished (a way), PraśnUp. iv; Kathās. xxv; to be gone to or attained, MBh.; R.; Megh. &c.; to be approached for sexual intercourse, MBh. xiii, 4973; to be undergone, iii, 14825; R. iii, 1, 32; to be approached with an accusation or accused of (instr.), MBh. xiii, 65 & 68; to be understood, Pat.; approaching, imminent, Āryabh. ii, 11/12, 9.

1. **Gántu**, *us*, m. a way, course, RV. i, 89, 9 & iii, 54, 18; a traveller, wayfarer, Uṇ. i, 70.

2. **Gantu** (in comp. for *°tum*, inf. *√gam*). **-kāma**, mfn. wishing to go, on the point of departure, W.; about to die, W.

Gántṛi, mfn. one who or anything that goes or moves, going, coming, approaching, arriving at (acc. or loc. or [Pāṇ. ii, 3, 12, Siddh.] dat.), RV. &c. (f. *trī*, Yājñ. iii, 10); (Pāṇ. vi, 2, 18, Sch.) going to a woman (loc.) for sexual intercourse, BhP. xi, 18, 43; (*trī*), f. a cart or car (drawn by horses, Hcar. vii; Hcat. i, 9, 82; or by oxen, L.)

Gantrikā, f. a small cart, Uṇ. iv, 158, Sch.

Gantrī, f. of *°tṛi*, q. v. **-ratha**, m. = *gantrī*, L.

Gantva. See *su-g°*.

Gama, mf(*ā*)n. (Pāṇ. iii, 3, 58) ifc. going (e.g. *aram-, kāma-, kha-, tiryag-*, &c.); riding on (in comp.), Hcat. i, 11, 718; m. going, course, Pāṇ. v, 2, 19; march, decampment, VarYogay. iv, 58; intercourse with a woman (in comp.), Mn. xi, 55; Yājñ. ii, 293; going away from (abl.), Caurap.; (in math.) removal (as of fractions), Bījag.; a road, L.; flightiness, superficiality, L.; hasty perusal, W.; a game played with dice and men (as backgammon &c.), L.; a similar reading in two texts, Jain. **-kāri-tva**, n. inconsiderateness, rashness, L. **Gamâgama**, m. going and coming, going to and fro, Kathās. lxxvii; m. sg. & pl. negotiation, Kād.; Rājat. vii, 1274; (cf. *gatâgata*); *-kārin*, m. a negotiator, messenger, VarBṛS. x, 10, Sch.

Gamaka, mfn. causing to understand, making clear or intelligible, explanatory, leading to clearness or conviction (e.g. *hetu*, 'a convincing reason'), Sarvad. i, 35; indicative of (gen.), Mālat. i, 7; n. (in music) a deep natural tone, PSarv. **-tā**, f. convincingness, Dāyabh. **-tva**, n. id., ib.; Sāh. v, 4/8, 12.

Gamatha, m. a traveller, Uṇ. iii, 113; a road, ib.

Gámadhyai, Ved. inf. See s. v. 1. *gam*.

Gamana, *am*, n. going, moving, manner of going, Ragh.; Megh. &c. (ifc. f. *ā*); going to or approaching (with acc. or gen. [R. i, 3, 22] or *prati* or a local adverb or ifc.), KātyŚr.; MBh. &c.; going away, departure, decampment, setting out (for war or for an attack); ifc. sexual intercourse (with a woman), PārGṛ. ii; R.; Suśr.; (with a man) Gaut.; ifc. undergoing, attaining, iv, 22; Mn. i, 117; R. v, 15, 48; footmarks (?), iii, 68, 50. **-vat**, mfn. furnished with motion, Vedântas. (ifc.); passing away, Sāy. on RV. i, 113, 15. **Gamanâbādha**, n. hindrance in travelling, Pāṇ. vi, 2, 21, Kāś. **Gamanârha**, mfn. to be sought, fit, desirable, W.

Gamanikā, f. explanatory paraphrase, TPrāt., Sch.; Jain. Sch.

Gamanīya, mfn. accessible, approachable, that may be gone to or reached (by, gen.), Mn. vii, 174 (superl. *-tama*); MBh. iii; Śak. i, 24/25 (Prākrit); to be understood, intelligible, W.; to be followed or practised or observed, W.; ifc. relating to going &c. (e.g. *guru-strī-*, 'relating to or consisting in the intercourse with the wife of a teacher,' as a sin, Mn. xi).

Gamayitavya, mfn. to be spent (time), Vikr. iii, 4.

Gamayitṛi, mfn. causing to arrive at, leading to (in comp.), Bādar. iv, 3, 5, Sch.

Gami, m. the √*gam*, Pat. Introd. on Vārtt. 5.

Gamita, mfn. caused to go, sent, brought, Mālav. iv, 2 &c.; reduced, driven to, W.; made to decease or die, MBh. xii, 1042.

Gamin, mfn. intending to go (with acc. or ifc.), Pāṇ. iii, 3, 3; Vārtt. on ii, 1, 24; Kāś. on ii, 3, 70.

Gamy-ādi, a Gaṇa of Pāṇ. (iii, 3, 3).

Gámishṭha, mfn. (superl. fr. *gántṛi*) most ready to go, most willing to come, RV.; AV. v, 20, 12.

Gamishṇú, mfn. going, TBr.; intending to go to (acc.), Daś. ii, 75.

Gamya, mfn. to be gone or gone to, approachable, accessible, passable, attainable (often *a-*, neg.), MBh. &c.; to be fixed (as to the number, *saṃkhyayā*), countable, RPrāt. xiv, 28; accessible to men (a woman), fit for cohabitation, Yājñ. ii, 290; MBh. i; BhP. i, &c.; (a man) with whom a woman may have intercourse, v; libidinous, dissolute, Daś. vii, 32; 'easily brought under the influence of (a drug),' curable by (gen.), Bhartṛ. i, 88; approaching, impending, Gaṇit.; Gol.; to be perceived or understood, intelligible, perceptible, Mn. xii, 122; Megh. &c.; intended, meant, L.; desirable, suitable, fit, Yājñ. i, 64. **-tā**, f. accessibility, W.; perceptibility, intelligibleness, clearness; the being intended or meant, Sāh. x, 25. **-tva**, n. id., 61.

Gamyamāna, mfn. (Pass. p.) being gone or gone to, W.; being understood, W.

गम् 2. *gam*, gen. abl. *gmás*, see 2. *kshám*.

गमात्र *ga-mātra*, a particular high number, Buddh. L.

गम्ब् *gamb*, cl. 1. P. *°bati*, to go or move, L.

गम्भन् *gámbhan*, *°bhára*. See *gabhá*.

गम्भारिका *gambhārikā*, f. = *°bhārī*, L.

Gambhārī, f. the tree Gmelina arborea (also its flower, fruit, and root), L.

गम्भिष्ठ *gámbhishṭha*. See *gabhá*.

Gambhīrá, *°raka*. See ib.

गम्य *gamya*, &c. See √*gam*.

गय *gáya*, *as*, m. (g. *vṛishâdi*; √*ji*, cf. *śamgayá*) 'what has been conquered or acquired,' a house, household, family, goods and chattels, contents of a house, property, wealth, RV.; AV.; a species of ox (the Gayal or Bos gavæus), L.; N. of a Ṛishi (son of Plati), RV. x, 63, 17 & 64, 16; Ait-Br. v, 2, 12; (said to know charms) AV. i, 14, 4; (descendant of Atri and author of RV. v, 9 & 10) R-Anukr.; N. of a Rājarshi (performer of a celebrated sacrifice, MBh. i, iii, iv, ix, xiii; R. ii; he was conquered by Māndhātṛi, MBh. vii, 2281); of a son (of Amūrta-rajas, iii, vii, xii; of Āyus, i, 3150; of a Manu, Hariv. 870; BhP. ii; of Havir-dhāna by Dhishaṇā, Hariv. 83; BhP. iv; of Ūru by Āgneyī, Hariv. 73; of Vitatha, 1732; of Sudyumna, 631; BhP. ix, 1, 41; of Nakta by Druti, v, 15, 5); N. of an Asura (slain by Śiva [cf. RTL. p. 87], and who like the Rājarshi Gaya is connected with the town Gayā), VāyuP. ii, 44; of one of Rāma's monkey followers, MBh. iii, 16271; R. iv, vi; (= *-śiras*) of a mountain near Gayā, MBh. iii, 8304; m. pl. the vital airs (used only for the etym. of *gāyatrī*), ŚBr. xiv, 8, 15, 7; N. of a people living round Gayā and of the district inhabited by them, MBh. ii, ix; R. ii; (*ā*), f. (g. *varaṇâdi*) the city Gayā (famous place of pilgrimage in Behar and residence of the saint Gaya; cf. RTL. p. 309; sanctified by Vishṇu as a tribute to the piety of Gaya, the Rājarshi, or (according to another legend) to Gaya, the Asura, who was overwhelmed here with rocks by the gods; the Śrāddha should be performed once at least in the life of every Hindū to his progenitors at Gayā), Yājñ. i, 260; MBh. &c.; cf. *buddha-g°*; N. of a river, i, 7818. **-dāsa**, m., N. of a physician, Bhpr. ii, 171/172; Nid., Sch. **-śiras**, n., N. of a mountain near Gayā (renowned place of pilgrimage), MBh. iii, xiii; BhP. vii; the western horizon, Nir. xii, 19. **-sâdhana**, mfn. promoting domestic wealth (Soma), RV. ix, 104, 2. **-siṇha**, for *gaja-s°* (N. of a prince); *-rāja-caritra*, n. = *gajasiṇha-c°*. **-sphāti** (*gáya-*), f. for *páya-sph°* (= *páyaḥ-sph°*), AV. xix, 31, 10. **-sphāna**, mfn. = *-sâdhana*, RV. i, 91, 12 & 19; vii, 54, 2; (AV. xix, 15, 3?) **-sphāyana**, mfn. id., Pāṇ. vi, 1, 66, Vārtt. 7, Pat.

Gayā, f. of *°ya*, q. v. **-kāśyapa**, m., N. of a pupil of Śākya-muni, Buddh. **-kūpa**, m., N. of a well near Gayā, Kathās. xciii. **-tīrtha**, n. Gayā as a renowned place of pilgrimage, SkandaP.; VāyuP. **-dāsa**, m., N. of an author. **-māhātmya**, n., N. of VāyuP. ii, 43 ff. **-śikhara**, n. the mountain Gaya (-śiras) near Gayā, Buddh. **-śiras**, n. id., VāyuP. **-śīrsha**, n. id.; *-parvata*, m. id., Lalit. xvii, 43; 75.

Gayin, m., N. of the author of a Comm. on Suśr.

गर *gará*, mfn. (√2. *gṛī*) 'swallowing' (g. *pacâdi*), see *aja-*; m. (g. *uñchâdi*; Kāś. on Pāṇ. iii, 3, 29 & 57) any drink, beverage, fluid, ŚBr. xi, 5, 8, 6; a noxious or poisonous beverage, Tāṇḍya-Br. xix; TĀr.; R.; Suśr.; BhP.; a factitious poison ('an antidote,' W.), L.; a kind of disease (perhaps one attended with difficulty of swallowing?; 'disease in general,' L.), Suśr. i, iv; vi, 39, 208; N. of a man, TāṇḍyaBr. ix, 2, 16; (*ā*), f. swallowing, L.; (*ā, ī*), f. Andropogon serratus, L.; (*ī*), f., N. of a district, g. *gaurâdi* (Gaṇar. 48); (*am*), n. a poisonous beverage ('a kind of poison,' L.), MBh. i, 5582; BhP. viii; the fifth of the eleven Karaṇas (in astron.), VarBṛS.; sprinkling, wetting (? *karaṇa*), W. **-gir**, mfn. (√2. *gṛī*) one who has swallowed a noxious draught, poisoned, TāṇḍyaBr. xvii, xix; TĀr.; KātyŚr. **-gīrṇá**, mfn. id., AV. v, 18, 13; ĀśvŚr. **-gīrṇin**, m., N. of a Ṛishi, Kāṭh. xl, 8. **-ghna**, mfn. removing poison or the disease called Gara, Suśr. i, 45, 11, 11; sanative, W.; m. = *-han*, L.; another variety of Ocimum, L.; (*ī*), f. a kind of fish (commonly Garaī; 'the young of the Ophiocephalus Lata,' W.), Bhpr. **-da**, mfn. occasioning sickness, unwholesome, W.; m. 'giving poison,' a poisoner, Gaut. xv, 18; Mn. iii, 158; MBh. v, xiii &c.; n. poison, L. **-dāna**, n. giving poison, BhP. vii, 5, 43. **-druma**, m. Strychnos nux vomica, L. **-vrata**, m. (= *gala-vr°*) a peacock, L. **-han**, m. (= *-ghna*) a kind of basil, L. **Garâgarī**, f. (= *agarī*) Lipeocercis serrata, Car. vii, 2, 1; viii, 11, 10. **Garâtmaka**, n. the seed of Hyperanthera Moringa, L. **Garâdhikā**, f. the insect called Lākshā or the red dye obtained from it, L. (v. l. *garāshikā*).

Garaṇa, *am*, n. the act of swallowing, L.; wetting, sprinkling, W. **-vat**, mfn. occupied in swallowing (used for the etym. of *garútmat*), Nir. vii, 18.

Garala, n. (m., L.) poison, MBh. viii, 3387; Pañcat.; Gīt. &c.; the venom of a snake, L.; Aconitum ferox, L.; a bundle of grass or hay, L.; a measure (in general), L. **-vrata**, m. = *gara-vr°*, Gal. **Garalâri**, m. (= *garuḍâśman*) an emerald, L.

Garalin, mfn. poisonous, venomous, W.

Garikā, f. the kernel of a cocoa-nut, Gal.

Garita, mfn. poisoned, g. *tārakâdi*.

गरभ *garabha*, for *garbha* (embryo), L.

गराषिका *garāshikā*, for *°rādhikā*, q. v.

गरिका *garikā*, *garita*. See *gará*.

गरिमन् *gariman*, *ā*, m. (fr. *gurú*, Pāṇ. vi, 4, 157) heaviness, weight, BhP. viii, x; Śiś. ix, 49; one of the 8 Siddhis of Śiva (making himself heavy at will), Vet. Introd. 15; Yogas. iii, 46, Sch.; importance, dignity, venerableness, Pañcat.; Kathās.; Sāh.; a venerable person (as Rudra), BhP. iv, 5, 21.

Garishṭha, mfn. (superl. fr. *gurú*, Pāṇ. vi, 4, 157) heaviest, excessively heavy, W.; most venerable, BhP. vii, xii; Sāh. iii, 4/8; thickened excessively, Gīt. i, 6; worst, W.; m., N. of a man, MBh. ii, 294; of an Asura, Hariv. 14289 (cf. *gavishṭha*).

Gárīyas, mfn. (TBr. i; compar. fr. *gurú*, Pāṇ. vi, 4, 157) heavier, W.; extremely heavy, R. vi; greater than (abl.), MBh. xiv, 255; more precious or valuable, dearer than (abl.), Gaut.; Mn.; MBh. &c.; extremely important, i, 8426; very honourable, Pañcat.; highly venerable, more venerable than (abl.), Mn.; Yājñ.; MBh. &c.; dearer than (abl.), dearer, MBh. &c.; worse, i, 1886; Cāṇ. **-tara**, mfn. greater, MBh. vii, 5324. **-tva**, n. great weight, Kathās. lxxiv, 192; importance, MBh.; R.; Kām.

Garīyasa, mfn. dearer than (instr.), MBh. i, 67, 114.

Garu, for *guru* in *agaru*, q. v.

गरुड *garuḍá*, m. (√2. *gṛī*, Uṇ. iv, 155, 'devourer,' because Garuḍa was perhaps originally identified with the all-consuming fire of the sun's rays), N. of a mythical bird (chief of the feathered race, enemy of the serpent-race [cf. RTL. p. 321], vehicle of Vishṇu [cf. RTL. pp. 65; 104; 288], son of Kaśyapa and Vinatā; shortly after his birth he frightened the gods by his brilliant lustre; they supposed him to be Agni, and requested his protection; when they discovered that he was Garuḍa, they praised him as the highest being, and called him fire and sun, MBh. i, 1239 ff.; Aruṇa, the charioteer of the sun or the personified dawn, is said to be the elder [or younger, cf. RTL. p. 104] brother of Garuḍa; Svāhā, the wife of Agni, takes the shape of a female Garuḍī = *suparṇī*, MBh. iii, 14307 & 14343), Suparṇ.; TĀr. x, 1, 6; MBh. &c.; a building shaped like Garuḍa, R.; VarBṛS.; N. of a peculiar military array, Mn. vii, 187; N. of the attendant of the 16th Arhat of the present Avasarpiṇī, L.; N. of the 14th Kalpa period; N. of a son of Kṛishṇa, Hariv. 9196; (*ī*), f. of *°ḍá*, q. v. **-ketu**, m. 'having Garuḍa for his symbol,' Vishṇu or Kṛishṇa. **-dhvaja**, mfn. (cf. g. *arcâdi*, Gaṇar. 185, Sch.) having Garuḍa in its banner (Kṛishṇa's chariot), BhP. x; m. = *-ketu*, MBh.; BhP.; Prasannar. iv, 41. **-paksha**, m. a particular position of the hands **-purāṇa**, n., N. of the seventeenth Purāṇa; cf. RTL. pp. 288; 293; 298; 301. **-māṇikya**, n. (= *tārkshya-ratna*) 'an emerald,' *-maya*, mfn. consisting of emeralds, Kathās. xxiii. **-ruta**, n. a metre of 4 × 16 syllables. **-vega**, m. 'having the swiftness of Garuḍa,' N. of a horse, cxxi, 277; (*ā*), f., N. of a plant, VarBṛS. liv, 87. **Garuḍâgraja**, m. 'elder brother of Garuḍa,' N. of Aruṇa (charioteer of the sun), Kuval. 393. **Garuḍâṅka**, m. = *°ḍa-ketu*, L. **Garuḍâṅkita**, m. = *°ḍa-māṇikya*, L. **Garuḍâditya**, m. a form of the sun, KāśīKh. l. **Garuḍârdha**, a kind of arrow, L. **Garuḍâśman**, m. = *°ḍa-māṇikya*, L. **Garuḍeśa**, m. = *°ḍâditya*, KāśīKh. l. **Garuḍeśāna**, m. Garuḍa as the lord of birds, R. vii, 7, 38. **Garuḍottīrṇa**, n. = *°ḍa-māṇikya*, L. **Garuḍodgīrṇa**, m. id., Gal. **Garuḍodbhava**, m. a particular precious stone, Gal. **Garuḍopanishad**, f., N. of an Up.

Garut, m. n. (g. *yavâdi*) the wing of a bird, Prasannar. v, 53. **-mat** (*garút-*), mfn. (in Veda only found in connection with *su-parṇá*, and apparently applied to a heavenly bird or to the sun) winged (?), RV. i, 164, 46; x, 149, 3; AV. iv, 6, 3; VS. xii;

xvii, 72; winged, Ragh. iii, 57; m. the bird Garuḍa, Suparṇ.; MBh. &c.; a bird (in general), Nal. i, 22.

Garud (in comp. for °*rut*, q. v.) **-yodhin**, m. 'fighting with the wings,' a quail, L.

Garula, for °*ruḍa*, L.

गर्ग *garga*, m., N. of an old sage (descendant of Bharad-vāja and Aṅgiras, author of the hymn RV. vi, 47); of an astronomer, AV.Pariś. (called 'the old one,' *vṛiddha-*); MBh. ix, 2132 ff.; VarBṛS.; of a physician; of a teacher of law; of a son [Hariv. 1732; BrahmaP.; or of a grandson, VP.; MatsyaP.; BhP. ix, 21, 1 & 19] of king Vitatha; a bull, L.; an earth-worm, L.; (in music) a kind of measure; = *-try-aha*, Vait. xli, 2; m. pl. (Pāṇ. ii, 4, 64) the descendants of Garga, Kāṭh. xiii, 12; ĀśvŚr. &c.; (*ā*), f., N. of a woman, Rājat. v, 250; (*ī*), f. (for *gārgī*), N. of the learned woman Vācaknavī, ĀśvGṛ. **-kula**, n. = *gārgyasya* or *gārgyayoḥ* or *gargāṇām k°*, Pāṇ. ii, 4, 64, Pat. **-tara**, m. an excellent representative of the Garga family, v, 3, 55, Pat. **-tri-rātra**, m. (g. *yuktârohy-ādi*) N. of a ceremony lasting 3 days, ŚāṅkhŚr. xvi. **-try-aha**, m. id., ĀśvŚr.; KātyŚr.; ŚāṅkhŚr. **-bhaginī**, f. *garga-bhago 'syā astîti*, Pāṇ. viii, 4. 11, Pat. **-bhaginī**, f. a sister of the Gargas, ib., Vārtt. **-bhārgavikā**, f. a marriage between descendants of Garga and Bhṛigu, iv, 1, 89, Vārtt. 5 (cf. ii, 4, 62, Vārtt. 8, Pat.) **-bhūmi**, m., N. of a prince (v. l. *bhārgabh°*), VāyuP. **-maya**, mfn. coming from the Gargas, Pāṇ. ii, 4, 62, Vārtt. 3, Pat. **-rūpya**, mfn. id., ib. **-vāhaṇa**, n. a carriage used by the Gargas, viii, 4, 8, Pat. **-vāhana**, n. a carriage belonging to the Gargas but out of use, ib. **-śiras**, m., N. of a Dānava, Hariv. 198. **-saṃhitā**, f., N. of a work. **-srotas**, n., N. of a Tīrtha, MBh. ix, 2132 ff.

Gargâdi, a Gaṇa of Pāṇ. (iv, 1, 105; Gaṇar. 246 ff.)

गर्गर *gárgara*, m. (onomat.) a whirlpool, eddy, AV. iv, 15, 12; ix, 4, 4; a kind of musical instrument, RV. viii, 69, 9; a churn, MBh. xii; Hariv.; the fish Pimelodus Gagora, L.; N. of a man, g. *kurv-ādi*; (*ā*), f. a churn, Lalit. xvii, 137; (*ī*), f. id., Hariv.; a water-jar (*kalaśī*); [cf. Lat. *gurges*.]

Gargaraka, m. the fish Pimelodus Gagora, Suśr.; N. of a plant with a poisonous root, ib.; (*ikā*), f., N. of a plant and its fruit, g. *harītaky-ādi* (Kāś.)

Gargāṭa, *as*, m. the fish Pimelodus Gagora, L.

गर्ज् *garj*, cl. 1. P. *garjati* (perf. *jagarja*, R.; aor. *agarjīt*, Bhaṭṭ.; p. *garjat* or °*jamāna*, MBh.; Pañcat. i, $\frac{2}{3}\frac{8}{2}$), to emit a deep or full sound, sound as distant thunder, roar, thunder, growl, MBh. &c.; [cf. Lat. *garrio*; Old Germ. *kurran, krago, kragil, krachōn, gellan, kallōn, kallari*; Mod. Germ. *quarren, girren*.]

Garja, *as*, m. (Pāṇ. vii, 3, 59, Kāś.) a (roaring) elephant, L.; the roaring (of elephants), rumbling (of clouds), &c., ŚārṅgP. (v. l.); (*ā*), f. id., L.

Garjaka, *as*, m. a kind of fish, L.

Garjana, *am*, n. crying, roaring, rumbling (of clouds), growl, grunt, R.; Hit.; passion, L.; battle (*yudh*), L.; excessive indignation, reproach, L.

Garjanīya, mfn. to be sounded or roared, W.

Garjara, *am*, n. a kind of grass, L.

Gárjā, f. of °*ja*, q. v. **-phala**, m. Asteracantha longifolia.

Garji, m. the rumbling (of clouds), Vcar. ix, 71; ŚārṅgP.

Garjita, mfn. sounded, roared, bellowed; boasted, swaggered, vaunted, Ratnâv. iv, $\frac{8}{10}$; (*as*), m. (g. *tārakâdi*) a (roaring) elephant in rut, L.; (*am*), n. = *garji*, Yājñ. i, 145; R.; Kum.; Megh. &c.; crying, roaring (as of elephants or Daityas), MBh.; R. &c. **-rava**, m. id., ŚārṅgP. **Garjitâsaha**, m. 'not bearing (an elephant's) roaring,' a lion, Gal.

Garjya, mfn. = °*janīya*, Pāṇ. vii, 3, 59, Kāś. & 52, Siddh.

गर्त 1. *gárta*, *as*, m. a high seat, throne (of Mitra and Varuṇa), RV. ('a house,' Naigh.); the seat of a war-chariot, vi, 20, 9; (Nir. iii, 5) a chariot, Gaut. xvi, 7; a table for playing at dice, Nir. iii, 5. **-sád**, mfn. sitting on the seat of a war-chariot, RV. ii, 33, 11. **Gartā-rúh**, mfn. (nom. *-rúk*, the final vowel of *garta* being lengthened before *r*) ascending the seat of a war-chariot, i, 124, 7.

गर्त 2. *gárta*, *as*, m. (= *kartá*, q. v.) a hollow, hole, cave, grave, ŚBr. xiv; ŚāṅkhBr.; ĀśvGṛ.; ŚāṅkhGṛ.; Kauś.; MBh. &c.; a canal, Mn. iv, 203; the hollow of the loins, L.; a kind of disease, L.; N. of a country (part of Tri-garta, in the north-west of India), L. (cf. Pāṇ. iv, 2, 137); n. a hole, cave, MBh. vii, 4953; (*ā*), f. a hole, cave, Pañcat. i; ii, 6, $\frac{2}{3}\frac{3}{8}$; N. of a river, ŚivaP. **-patya**, n. the falling into a hole, ŚāṅkhBr. xvi. **-mit**, f. a post entered into a hole, TS. vi; Kāṭh. **Gartâśraya**, m. any animal living in holes (a mouse, rat, &c.), Mn. vii, 72. **Gartêśa**, m. 'master of a cave,' N. of Mañju-śrī, Buddh. **Garte-shṭhá**, mfn. being in a hole, MaitrS. iii, 9, 4 (Nir. iii, 5). **Gartôdaka**, n. hole-water, ĀśvGṛ. iv, 2 (v. l.); cf. Sāy. on RV. x, 14, 9.

Gartaki, f. = °*tikā*, Gal.

Gartan-vát, mfn. (a post) having a hole (into which it is entered), ŚBr. v, 2, 1, 7.

Gartā, f. of °*ta*, q. v. **-kukkuṭa**, m. (= *kulāla-k°*) a kind of bird, VarBṛS. **-rúh**, see s. v. 2. *gárta*.

Gartikā, f. (g. *kumudâdi*) a weaver's workshop (so called because a weaver sits at his loom with his feet in a hole below the level of the floor), L.

Gartin, mfn., g. *prekshâdi*.

Gartīya, mfn., g. *utkarâdi*.

Gartya, mfn. (Pāṇ. v, 1, 67, Kāś.) deserving to be thrown into a hole, ŚāṅkhBr. x, 2.

गर्द् *gard*, cl. 1. P. °*dati*, to shout, give shouts of joy, TāṇḍyaBr. xiv, 3, 19; to emit any sound, Dhātup.: cl. 10. *gardayati*, id., ib.

Gárda, mf(*ā*)n. crying (?, cf. *galda*; 'hungry,' Sch.), TS. iii, 1, 11, 8.

Gardabh, mfn. (fr. °*bhaya*; nom. °*rdhab*), Pāṇ. viii, 2, 32, Pat.

1. **Gardabhá**, m. 'crier, brayer (?),' an ass, RV.; AV. &c. (ifc. f. *ā*, Kathās. lxx); a kind of perfume, L.; pl. N. of a family, Pravar. ii, 3, 3; v, 4; n. the white esculent water-lily, L.; Embelia Ribes, L.; (*ī*), f. a she-ass, AV. x; ŚBr. xiv; Kauś.; MBh. &c.; a kind of beetle (generated in cow-dung), Suśr. v; N. of several plants (*aparājitā, kaṭabhī, śveta-kaṇṭakārī*), L.; = *gardabhikā*, L. **-gada**, m. = *gardabhikā*, L. **-nādin**, mfn. braying like an ass, AV. viii, 6, 10. **-pushpa**, m. = *khara-p°*, Suśr. i, Sch. **-ratha**, m. a donkey-cart, AitBr. iv, 9, 4. **-rūpa**, m. 'ass-shaped,' N. of Vikramâditya. **-vallī**, f. Clerodendrum Siphonanthus, Gal. **-śāka**, m. id., L. **-śākhī**, f. id., L. **Gardabhâksha**, m. 'ass-eyed,' N. of a Daitya (descendant of Hiraṇya-kaśipu and son of Bali), Hariv. 191. **Gardabhâṇḍa**, m. 'donkey's testicle,' = °*ṇḍaka*, L.; Ficus infectoria, L.; mfn. = °*ṇḍīya*, Pāṇ. v, 2, 60, Kāś. **Gardabhâṇḍaka**, m. (= °*ṇḍa*) Thespesia populneoides (commonly Pārspīpal), L. **Gardabhâṇḍīya**, mfn. containing the word *gardabhâṇḍa* (as an Adhyāya or Anuvāka), Pāṇ. v, 2, 60, Pat. & Kāś. **Gardabhêjyā**, f. an ass-sacrifice, KātyŚr. i, 1, 13 (cf. 17).

2. **Gardabha**, Nom. P. °*bhati*, to represent an ass, Sāh. x, $21\frac{8}{9}$.

Gardabhaka, *as*, m. anybody or anything resembling an ass, Pāṇ. v, 3, 96, Kāś.; a cutaneous disease (eruption of round, red, and painful spots), AgP. xxxi, 36; (*ikā*), f. id.; (cf. *kīṭa-*.)

Gardabhaya, Nom. °*yati*, Pāṇ. viii, 2, 32, Pat.

Gardabhi, for *gārd°*; (cf. *haya-g°*.)

Gardabhikā. See °*bhaka*.

Gardabhila, m., N. of the father of Vikramâditya; m. pl., N. of a dynasty, VP. iv, 24, 14.

Gardabhilla, *as*, m. = °*bhila*, Jain.

Gardabhí, f. of °*bhá*, q. v. **-mukha**, m., N. of a teacher, VBr. ii, 6; Pravar. v, 4 (v. l. *khārd°*). **-vidyā**, f., N. of a charm, Kālakâc. **-vipīta** (°*bhí-*), m., N. of a man, ŚBr. xiv, 6, 10, 11.

Gardayitnu, *us*, m. (= *gaday°*) 'rumbler,' a cloud, L.

गर्ध *gardha*, *as*, m. (√*gridh*) desire, greediness, eagerness (ifc.), Pāṇ. vii, 4, 34; Kathās.; Sarvad. xv, 213; Naish. vii, 71; = *gardabhâṇḍaka*, L.

Gardhana, mf(*ā*)n. greedy, covetous, Pāṇ. iii, 2, 150; Bhaṭṭ. vii, 16; (*ā*), f. greediness, L.

Gardhita, mfn. greedy, g. *tārakâdi*.

Gardhin, mfn. ifc. desirous, greedy, eager after, longing for, Mn. iv, 28; MBh. iii, 16448; R. ii f., vii; Kathās. cxxi, 29.

गर्ब् *garb*, cl. 1. P. °*bati*, to go or move, Dhātup. xi, 28.

गर्भ *gárbha*, m. (√*grabh* = *grah*, 'to conceive;' √2. *grī*, Uṇ. iii, 152) the womb, RV.; AV. &c.; the inside, middle, interior of anything, calyx (as of a lotus), MBh.; VarBṛS. &c. (ifc. f. *ā*, 'having in the interior, containing, filled with,' ŚāṅkhŚr.; RPrāt.; MBh. &c.); an inner apartment, sleeping-room, L.; any interior chamber, adytum or sanctuary of a temple &c., VarBṛS.; RTL. p. 445; a fœtus or embryo, child, brood or offspring (of birds), RV.; AV. &c.; a woman's courses, Vishṇ.; 'offspring of the sky,' i. e. the fogs and vapour drawn upwards by the rays of the sun during eight months and sent down again in the rainy season (cf. Mn. ix, 305), R. iv, 27, 3; VarBṛS.; Bālar. viii, 50; the bed of a river (esp. of the Ganges) when fullest, i. e. on the fourteenth day of the dark half of the month Bhādra or in the height of the rains (the Garbha extends to this point, after which the Tīra or proper bank begins, and extends for 150 cubits, this space being holy ground); the situation in a drama when the complication of the plot has reached its height, Daśar. i, 36; Sāh. vi, 68 & 79; the rough coat of the Jaka fruit, L.; fire, L.; joining, union, L.; N. of a Ṛishi (called Prājāpatya), Kāṭh.; [cf. *amṛita-, ardha-, kṛishṇa-, mūḍha-, viśva-, hiraṇya-*; cf. also δελφός; Hib. *cilfin*, 'the belly;' Angl. Sax. *hrif*; Germ. *kalb*; Engl. *calf*.] **-kara**, m. 'producing impregnation,' Nageia Putramjiva, Bhpr. **-káraṇa**, n. anything which causes impregnation, AV. v, 25, 6. **-kartṛi**, m. 'composer of the Garbha-hymn,' N. of Tvashṭri (author of RV. x, 184), RAnukr. **-kāma**, mf(*ā*)n. desirous of impregnation, PārGṛ. **-kāra**, m. 'impregnating,' N. of a Śastra (or recitation), ĀśvŚr.; Vait. **-kārin**, mfn. producing impregnation, Bhpr. **-kāla**, m. the time of impregnation, Hariv.; = *-divasa*, VarBṛS. **-kośa** or **-kosha**, m. 'embryo-receptacle,' the uterus, Suśr. i. **-kleśa**, m. pains of childbirth, MārkP. xxii, 45. **-kshaya**, m. 'loss of the embryo,' miscarriage, Suśr. i. **-gurvī**, f. 'great with child,' pregnant, Sāh. **-gṛiha**, n. an inner apartment, sleeping-room, MBh. v, 3998; Suśr.; Daś. &c.; the sanctuary or adytum of a temple (where the image of a deity is placed), Kād.; Kathās. (once *-geha*, lv, 173); RTL. p. 440; ifc. a house containing anything (e. g. *śara-g°*, a house containing arrows, MBh. vii, 3738). **-geha**, n. = *-gṛiha*, q. v. **-graha**, m. conception; °*hârtava*, n. time fit for conception, Bādar. **-grahaṇa**, n. = °*ha*, Pāṇ. Kāś.; VarBṛ., Sch. **-grāhikā**, f. a midwife, Kathās. xxxiv. **-ghātinī**, f. 'embryo-killer, producing abortion,' the poisonous plant Methonica superba, L. **-calana**, n. the motion of the fœtus in the uterus, W. **-ceṭa**, m. a servant by birth, Rājat. iii, 153. **-cchidra**, m. the mouth of the womb, Bhpr. ii, $\frac{1}{1}\frac{7}{7}\frac{7}{4}$. **-cyuta**, mfn. fallen from the womb (child), W.; miscarrying, W. **-cyuti**, f. falling from the womb, delivery, Hit.; miscarriage, W. **-tā**, f. the sky's state of having offspring (see *gárbha*), VarBṛS. **-tvá**, n. impregnation, RV. i, 6, 4. **-da**, mfn. 'granting impregnation,' procreative, Suśr. vi, 39, 210; m. = *-kara*, L.; (*ā*), f., N. of a shrub, L. **-dātrī**, f. = *-dā*, L. **-dāsa**, m. a slave by birth, KātyŚr.; KapS.; VarBṛS.; (f. *ī*, Ratnâv. ii, $1\frac{3}{4}$, Prākṛit.) **-divasa**, *ās*, m. pl. (= *-kāla* or *-samaya*, the time or) the days on which the offspring of the sky (see *gárbha*) shows the first signs of life (195 days or 7 lunar months after its first conception), VarBṛS. xxi, 5. **-drāvaṇa**, n. a particular process applied to minerals (esp. to mercury). **-druti**, f. id., Sarvad. ix, 33. **-druh**, mfn., see *-bhartṛi-dr°*. **-dvādaśa**, m. pl. the 12th year reckoning from conception, Āp. i, 1, 18; (cf. Mn. ii, 36.) **-dhá**, mfn. impregnatory, VS. xxiii, 19. **-dharā**, f. bearing a fœtus, pregnant, MBh. iii, 12864. **-dhāna**, for °*rbhâdhāna*, xii, 9648. **-dhāraṇa**, n. gestation, pregnancy, iii, 10449; (*ā*), f. 'pregnancy (of the sky),' N. of VarBṛS. xxii. **-dhārita**, mfn. contained in the womb, conceived, W.; borne, W. **-dhi**, m. 'breeding-place,' nest, RV. i, 30, 4. **-dhṛita**, mfn. contained in the womb, MBh. iv, 13, 12. **-dhṛiti**, f. = *-druti*. **-dhvaṃsa**, m. = *-kshaya*, W. **-nāḍī**, f. 'embryo-artery,' the umbilical cord, Suśr. iii, 10, 6. **-nābhi-nāḍī**, f. id., 3, 28. **-nidhāna**, mf(*ī*)n. receiving or sheltering an embryo, Nir. iii, 6. **-nirharaṇa**, n. drawing out a child (from the womb), Suśr. iv, 15, 2. **-nishkṛiti**, f. a fœtus completely developed, Hcat. **-nud**, m. = *-ghātinī*, Bhpr. **-parisrava**, m. secundines, W. **-pākin**, m. rice ripening (during the latter period of the sky's pregnancy, i. e.) in sixty days, L. **-pāta**, m. miscarriage (after the fourth month of pregnancy), W. **-pātaka**, m. 'causing miscarriage,' a red kind of Moringa, L. **-pātana**, m. (= °*taka*) a variety of Karañja, Bhpr.; = *-nud*, L.; n. causing miscarriage, Kathās. lxxii; Sāh. x, 43, Sch. **-pātinī**, f. 'causing miscarriage,' the plant *viśalyā*, L. — **puroḍāśa**, m. an embryo-Puroḍāśa (offered after a Paśu-puroḍāśa, if the sacrificial animal is pregnant), ĀpŚr. — **poshaṇa**, n. 'nourishing a fœtus,' gestation, W. — **bhartṛi-druh**, mfn. (nom. *-dhruk*) doing harm to the embryo and to the husband, Mn. v, 90. — **bharman**, n. 'supporting a fœtus, gestation, Ragh. iii, 12. — **bhavana**, n. (= *-gṛiha*) the sanctuary of a temple, Mālatīm. i, $\frac{2}{3}$; Kathās. lv, 175. — **bhāra**, m. the weight of the fœtus, xxvi, 216. — **maṇḍapa**, m. an inner apartment, sleeping-room, 77. — **mās**, m. month of pregnancy, SāmavBr. ii, 2, 1. — **māsa**, m. id., ĀśvGṛ.; Gaut.; Kathās. — **moksha**, m. delivery, VarBṛ. — **mocana**, n. id., L. — **yamaka**, n. (in rhet.) a Yamaka (q. v.) exhibited in an inserted phrase (e. g. Bhaṭṭ. x, 18). — **yutā**, f. = *-gurvī*, VarBṛ. — **yoshā**, f. a woman pregnant with (gen.; said of the Ganges), MBh. xiii, 1846. — **rakshaṇa**, n. 'protecting the fœtus,' N. of a ceremony performed in the fourth month of gestation, ŚāṅkhGṛ. — **rakshā**, f. protecting the fœtus, Kathās. xxiii. — **randhi**, f. complete cooking, BhP. v, 10, 23. — **rasa** (*gárbha-*), mf(*ā*)n. desirous of impregnation, RV. i, 164, 8. — **rūpa**, m. 'fœtus-like,' a youth, young man (pl. 'young people'), Bālar. vi, $\frac{3}{4}$; Naish. xi, 78, Sch.; n. pl. the children, young family, Divyâv. xviii, 195. — **rūpaka**, m. id., Mcar. i, $\frac{9}{10}$. — **lakshaṇa**, n. symptom of pregnancy, Suśr.; 'symptom of the sky's pregnancy (see °*rbha-divasa*),' N. of VarBṛS. xxi. — **lambhana**, n. 'facilitation of conception,' N. of a ceremony, ĀśvGṛ. (cf. Mn. ii, 27). — **vatī**, f. pregnant, MBh. iii; Hit. — **vadha**, m. killing of the embryo; *-prāyaścitta*, n. penance for killing an embryo. — **vartman**, n. 'embryo-path,' passage leading from the womb, Bhpr. ii, 307. — **vasati**, f. 'embryo-abode,' the womb, Hariv. 3312. — **vāsa**, m. id., Mn. xii, 78; Yājñ.; MBh.; Bhartṛ.; *-kleśa*, m. puerperal fever, Hcat. i. — **vicyuti**, f. abortion in the beginning of pregnancy, Suśr. — **vipatti**, f. the death of the fœtus. — **vedana**, a Mantra producing impregnation, Vait.; (*ā*), f. = *-kleśa*, W. — **vedinī**, f. = °*dana*, MānGṛ. — **veśman**, n. an inner apartment, Ragh. xix, 42; a lying-in chamber, iii, 12 (C); = *-vasati*, ib. — **vyākaraṇa**, n. careful description of the embryo (part of the Śārīra section in medical works), Suśr. iii, 4. — **vyāpad**, f. = *-vipatti*. — **vyūha**, m. a kind of battle array, MBh. vii, 3110. — **śaṅku**, m. an instrument for extracting the dead fœtus. — **śayyā**, f. = *-vasati*, xii; Sāh. vi, 97$\frac{a}{b}$; Bhpr. — **śātana**, n. the procuring abortion, Āp.; a drug procuring abortion, Suśr. — **śrī-kānta-miśra**, m., N. of an author, Sarvad. ix, 58. — **saṃsravaṇa**, n. abortion, Mn. v, 66, Sch. — **saṃkarita**, m. a mongrel, Hariv. 1165. — **saṃkramaṇa**, n. entering the womb, MBh. xiv, 472. — **samaya**, m. = *-divasa*, VarBṛS. — **samplava**, m. abortion, MBh. ii, 17, 38. — **sambhava**, m. the production of a fœtus, becoming pregnant, Yājñ. i, 69; (*ā*), f. a kind of cardamoms, Gal. — **sambhūti**, f. = °*bhava*, Kathās. v, 61. — **subhaga**, mf(*ā*)n. blessing the fœtus. — **sūtra**, n., N. of Buddhist Sūtra work. — **stha**, mfn. situated in the womb, MBh.; Suśr.; Pañcat.; Kathās.; being in the interior of (gen.), MBh. vii, 3110. — **sthāna**, n. = *-vasati*, Gal. — **srāva**, m. = *-saṃsravaṇa*, Mn. v, 66; Yājñ. iii, 20; AgP. &c. — **srāvin**, mfn. producing abortion, Pañcar.; m. Phœnix paludosa, L. — **hantṛi**, m. 'embryo-killer,' N. of a demon, MārkP. li, 76. **Garbhâgāra**, n. = °*rbha-vasati*, L.; an inner apartment, bed-room, L.; a lying-in room, L.; = °*rbha-gṛiha*, the sanctuary of a temple, Kathās. vii, 71; *-jvara*, m. = °*rbha-vāsa-kleśa*, Hcat. **Garbhâṅka**, m. interlude during an act, Bālar. iii; Sāh. vi, 20. **Garbhâdá**, mfn. consuming the fœtus, AV. i, 25, 3. **Garbhâdi**, mfn. beginning with conception, Gaut. i, 7. **Garbhâdhāna**, n. impregnation (of, loc.), MBh. xii, 9648; Megh. 9; Pāṇ. iii, 3, 71, Kāś.; 'impregnation-rite,' a ceremony performed before conception or after menstruation to ensure conception, Yājñ. i, 11; Gṛihyās.; MBh. iii; KapS.; cf. RTL. p. 353 f. **Garbhâri**, m. 'fœtus-enemy,' small cardamoms, L. **Garbhâvakrānti**, f. 'descent of the fœtus into a womb,' conception, Car. iv, 4, 1. **Garbhâvataraṇa**, °*tāraṇa*, n. id., Bhpr. **Garbhâśaṅkā**, f. suspicion of pregnancy, W. **Garbhâśaya**, m. = °*rbha-vasati*, MBh. xiv; Suśr. **Garbhâshṭama**, m. the eighth month of uterine gestation, W.; the eighth year reckoning from conception, ĀśvŚr.: ŚāṅkhŚr. &c.: (pl.) Āp. i, 1, 18 & Gobh.; mfn. with *abda*, id., Mn. ii, 36; Yājñ. **Garbhâspandana**, n. non-quickening of the fœtus, Suśr. **Garbhâsrāva**, m. = °*bha-sr*°, Suśr. i, 45, 2, 3. **Garbhetṛipta**, mfn. 'contented already in the womb (or from the first origin),' indolent, gaṇas *pātre-samitâdi* & *yuktârohy-ādi*. **Garbhêśvara**, m. 'sovereign by birth,' (*ī*), f. a princess by birth, Bālar. vi, $\frac{18}{19}$; *-tā*, f. sovereignty attained by inheritance, Rājat. v, 198; *-tva*, n. id., Kād. **Garbhâikādaśa**, m. pl. the 11th year reckoning from conception, Āp. i, 1, 18; (cf. Mn. ii, 36.) **Garbhôtpatti**, f. the formation of the embryo. **Garbhôtpāda**, m. id. **Garbhôpaghāta**, m. miscarriage of the sky's offspring (see *gárbha*), VarBṛS. xxi, 25. **Garbhôpaghātinī**, f. miscarrying (as a cow or female), L. **Garbhôpanishad**, f., N. of an Up.

Garbhaka, *as*, m. a chaplet of flowers worn in the hair, L.; a period of two nights with the intermediate day, L.

Garbhiṇī, f. of °*rbhin*, q. v. — **tva**, n. the being pregnant or filled with, TāṇḍyaBr., Sch. — **vyākaraṇa**, n. (or *garbhinyā vyākṛiti*) careful description of a pregnant woman (particular heading or subject in med.), Suśr. iii, 10, 1. **Garbhiṇy-avêkshaṇa**, n. attendance and care of pregnant women, midwifery, L.

Garbhita, mfn. (g. *tārakâdi*) contained in anything, Sāh. vi, 142; (in rhet.) inserted (as a phrase), Kpr. vii, 6; ifc. pregnant or filled with, containing inside, Siṇhâs. xxiii. — **tā**, f. (in rhet.) insertion of one phrase within another, Sāh. — **tva**, n. id., ib.

Garbhín, mfn. pregnant, impregnated or filled with (acc., ŚBr. vi, viii f., xi; or instr., xiv, 9, 4, 21), RV. iii, 29, 2; TS. (f. pl. *garbhíṇayas*, ii, 1, 2, 6; cf. Pāṇ. vii, 3, 107, Pat.) &c.; (*iṇī*), a pregnant woman, Mn.; Yājñ. i, 105; MBh. &c.; pregnant (as an animal), VarBṛS. lxvii, 10 (cf. Uṇ. iii, 152); ifc. with words denoting animals (e. g. *go-garbhiṇī*, a pregnant cow), Pāṇ. ii, 1, 71.

Garbhī-karaṇa, n. 'making anything an embryo or product,' producing, Sāh. vi, 79$\frac{a}{b}$.

Garbhya, mfn. ?, Kāṭh. xxvi, 3; (cf. *sa-g*°.)

गर्भण्ड *garbhaṇḍa*, *as*, m. (fr. *garbha* + *aṇḍa*?), enlargement of the navel, L.

गर्मुटिका *garmuṭikā*, for °*rmūṭ*°, W.

Garmút, f. (√2. *gṛī*, Uṇ.) a kind of wild bean, TS. ii, 4, 4, 1 f.; (*ganm*°) Kāṭh. x, 11; a kind of grass or reed ('a creeper,' L.; cf. *gandut*), Hcar. ii, 33; gold, Uṇ. i, 97; (cf. *gārmutá*.)

Garmud, v. l. for °*rmut* (Hcar. ii, 33).

Garmūc-chada, *as*, m. (fr. °*mūt* for °*mut* or °*mud*) a kind of rice (commonly Māḍuyā), L.

Garmūṭikā, f. id., L.

Garmūṭī, f. id., Car. i, 27, 14 (v. l. *gharm*°).

Garmoṭikā, f. a kind of grass, L.

गर्व् *garv*, cl. 1. P., 10. Ā. °*rvati*, °*rvayate*, to be or become proud or haughty, Dhātup.; [cf. Lith. *garbė*, 'honour, glory;' Old Germ. *gelban*, *gelf*.]

Garva, *as*, m. pride, arrogance, R. ii, 31, 20; Ragh. (C) iii, 51; VarBṛS. &c.; (in dram.) proud speech, Sāh. vi, 200.

Garvaya, Nom. P. °*yati*, to make any one (acc.) proud, R. ii, 8, 49 (G).

Garvara, mfn. haughty, Uṇ. ii, 123; m. haughtiness, ib.; (*ī*), f., N. of Durgā, L.

Garvāya, Nom. °*yate*, to show pride or arrogance, MBh. xii, 10300; Prab. ii, $\frac{1}{2}$; ŚārṅgP.

Garvita, mfn. (g. *tārakâdi*) haughty, conceited, proud of (in comp.), R.; Pat. (with instr.); Ragh. ix, 55; Śak. vi, $\frac{2}{3}$ & $\frac{3}{4}$; BrahmaP. &c.

Garvishṭha, mfn. extremely proud, L.

गर्वाट *garvāṭa*, *as*, m. a doorkeeper, watchman (sort of village constable, = *darvaṭa*), L.

गर्ह् *garh*, cl. 1. 10. P. Ā. °*hati*, °*hate*, °*hayati*, °*hayate* (the Ā. is more common than P.; perf. *jagarha*, °*rhe*); to lodge a complaint (acc.) before any one (dat.), RV. iv, 3, 5; to accuse, charge with, reproach, blame, censure any one or anything (acc.), Mn. iv, 199; MBh.; R. &c.; to be sorry for, repent of (acc.), Mn. xi, 230; Jain.

Garhaṇa, mfn. containing a blame (as a question), Kathās. lxxxiii; n. censuring, censure, blame, reproach, MBh. xii, 9153; R.; Sarvad. iv, 1; (in rhet.) Sāh. vi, 174 & 190; (*ā*), f. id., MBh. iii, 1283; °*ṇāṃ* √*yā*, to meet with reproach, Mn. ii, 80.

Garhaṇīya, mfn. to be blamed, blamable, Yājñ. i, 86; MBh. i, 3604; iii, 3888.

Garhā, f. censure, abuse, MBh.; Pāṇ.; Pañcat.; disgust exhibited in speech, Sāh. iii, 180.

Garhita, mfn. blamed, censured by (instr. [MBh.; R.; cf. Mn. ix, 109] or gen. [Mn. x, 39; R.] or loc. [Mn. xi, 42] or in comp.); contemned, despised, contemptible, forbidden, vile, ĀśvGṛ. ii, 8, 3 & 5; Mn. &c.; worse than (abl.), MBh. iii, 1040; (*am*), ind. badly, Vop. xx, 5.

Garhitavya, mfn. = °*haṇīya*, MBh. v; R. iii.

Garhin, mfn. ifc. abusing, BhP. iv, 4, 18.

Garhya, mfn. deserving reproach, contemptible, vile, Mn. v, 149; R.; BhP. &c.; (*as*), m., N. of a tree (?), Kauś. 8. — **vādin**, mfn. speaking ill or vilely or inaccurately, L.

Garhyāṇaka, mfn. vile, Gal.

गल् 1. *gal*, cl. 1. P. °*lati*, to drip, drop, ooze, trickle, distil, Pañcat. v; BrahmaP.; Kathās. &c.; to fall down or off, Ragh. vii, 10; Bhaṭṭ.; Git.; Prab. ii; to vanish, perish, pass away, Daś.; Kathās.; Kuval.: Caus. *gālayati*, to cause to drop, filter, strain, Suśr.; Daś.; to cause (the water of a dropsical person) to go off, Car. vi, 18; to fuse, liquefy, dissolve, melt, Suśr.: Ā. °*te*, to flow, Dhātup. xxxiii, 26: Intens. p. *jalgalyamāna*, causing to drop from one's body, Nir. vii, 13; [cf. Old Germ. *qvall*, *quillu*, *qual*, and *quella*, 'a well.']

1. **Gala**, *as*, m. 'oozing,' resin (especially that of the plant Shorea robusta), L.; = *galaka*, L.; a kind of musical instrument, L.; a reed (large kind of Saccharum cylindricum), L.; a rope (made of that reed), L.; (*ā*), f. (for *medo-g*°) a plant akin to the Mimosa pudica, L. — **mocikā**, f. 'dropping resin,' N. of a plant, Gal.

1. **Galaka**, *as*, m. a kind of fish (small kind of Cyprinus, perhaps Cyprinus Garra), L.

Galat-kushṭha, n. = *galita-k*°, Bhartṛ. i, 89.

Galana, mfn. dropping, flowing, Nir. i, 24; n. dropping, trickling, VS. i, 2, Sch.; melting, fusing, VarBṛS. xciv, 7; falling down or off, W.; leaking, W.

Galanīya, mfn. fusible, soluble, W.

Galantikā, f. a water-jar (with a hole in the bottom from which water drops upon a Liṅga or a Tulasi plant), KāśīKh. xii, 55; Hcat. i, 5, $\frac{735}{6}$.

Galantī, f. id., L.

Galāvala, *as*, m., N. of a tree, Kauś. 8.

1. **Galita**, mfn. dropped, oozed, trickling, Hariv. 2; Ragh.; Amar.; fallen down or off, loosed, Megh. 45; Śiś. ix, 75; BhP. i, 1, 3 &c.; lost, perished, decayed, Ragh. iii, 70; Bhartṛ. &c.; waning (as the moon), VarBṛ. xiii, 8; xxiii, 8; 'dropped' (said of the verses omitted in the Pada-pāṭha of the RV. because of their occurrence in a previous passage), VPrāt., Sch.; for *gālita* (liquefied, melted), W. — **kushṭha**, n. advanced and incurable leprosy (when the fingers and toes fall off), W. — **danta**, mfn. having the teeth decayed, toothless, W. — **nakha**, mfn. having the claws or nails fallen off, W.; *-danta*, mfn. one who has lost his claws and teeth, Hit. i, 2, $\frac{4}{5}$. — **nayana**, mfn. one who has lost his eyes, blind, 4, $\frac{4}{5}$. — **pradīpa**, m. 'light of dropped verses,' N. of a treatise giving in full the verses omitted in the Pada-pāṭha of the RV. — **pradīpikā**, f. id.

Galitaka, *as*, m. a kind of dance, gesticulation, Vikr. iv, $\frac{64}{65}$; N. of a metre, Sāh. vi, 326.

1. **Galyā**, f. (g. *pāśâdi*) a quantity of *gala* reeds, L.; a quantity of ropes (made of the *gala* reed), L.

1. **Gāla**, *as*, m. flowing, liquefying, W.; dropping, W.; a flux, W.

1. **Gālana**, *am*, n. straining fluids, Nir. vi, 24.

Gālita, mfn. strained, Suśr. i; melted, iv, 7, 18.

1. **Gālin**, mfn. distilling, fusing, W.

गल् 2. *gal* (= √2. *gṛī*), cl. 1. P. °*lati*, to eat, swallow, Dhātup. xv, 39.

2. **Gala**, m. (Pāṇ. viii, 2, 21, Kāś.) 'swallower,' the throat, neck, MBh.; Mṛicch. &c. (ifc. f. *ā* [g. *kroḍâdi*], Hcat. i, 7, 334; f. *ī*, g. *bahv-adi*); [cf. Lat. *gula*.] — **kambala**, m. a bull's dewlap, L.; (*go-g*°) Uṇ. — **gaṇḍa**, in comp. neck and cheek, MBh. ii, 902; m. goitre, Suśr. i ff.; Dhūrtas. ii, 11; = *gaṇḍa-mālā*, L. — °**gaṇḍin**, mfn. having a goitre, Suśr. — **godikā**, °**dī**, f. a kind of snake, Car. vi, 23. — **golī**, f. id., Suśr. — **graha**, m. seizing by the throat, throttling, W.; compression of the throat (a kind of disease), MBh. xii, 11267; Suśr.; VarBṛS.; a fish-sauce (prepared with salt, pepper, ghee &c.), L.; N. of certain days in the dark fortnight (viz. the 4th, 7th, 8th, 9th, 13th, and 3 following days), Nār.; begun but immediately inter-

rupted study, Rājamārt. **-carman**, n. the gullet, throat, Suśr. **-dvāra**, n. 'throat-door,' the mouth, MBh. vii, 6793. **-mekhalā**, f. a necklace, L. **-vārtta**, mfn. living only for one's throat, Pañcat. iii, 2, 6. **-vidradhi**, m. abscess in the throat, Suśr. **-vrata**, m. (=*gara-v°*) a peacock, L. **-śālūka**, n. tumor in the throat, Car. i, 28, 8. **-śuṇḍikā**, f. the uvula, iv, 7; Suśr. iv; swelling of the uvula, 1 f., iv; f. du. the soft palate, Yājñ. iii, 98. **-śuṇḍī**, f. swelling of the uvula, Car.; Suśr. **-stanī**, f. (=*°le-st°*) 'having (small fleshy protuberances, resembling) nipples depending from the throat,' a she-goat, L. **-hasta**, m. 'the hand at the throat,' seizing by the throat, throttling, Kathās. iv, 68; Naish., Sch. **-°hastaya**, Nom. P. *°yati*, to seize by the throat, throttle, strangle, Hit. **-°hastita**, mfn. seized by the throat, Naish. vi, 25. **Galâñkura**, m. a particular disease of the throat (inflammation of the throat and enlargement of the tonsils). **Galânika**, v. l. for *°nila*. **Galânila**, m. (=*gaṅgâteya*) a prawn or shrimp, L. **Galâvila**, v. l. for *°lânila*. **Galôdbhava**, m. the tuft of hair on the neck of a horse, L. **Galâugha**, m. tumor in the throat, Suśr. ii, 16, 44 & 58.

2. **Galaka**, m. the throat, neck, VarBṛS. lxv (v. l.)

2. **Galita**, mfn. swallowed, Pañcat. ii, 3, 10 (not in B C).

Gale, loc. of 2. *gala*. **-gaṇḍa**, m. 'having a pendulous fleshy purse hanging from the throat,' the bird called Adjutant or Ardea Argala. **-copaka**, mfn. moving the neck, Kāś. on Pāṇ. ii, 1, 32 & iii, 3, 113. **-stanī**, f. = *gala-st°*, L.; (cf. *ajā-gala-stana*.)

2. **Galyā**, f. (g. *pāśâdi*) a multitude of throats, L.

2. **Gāla**, mfn. produced with the throat, L.

गलडा *galaḍā*, f., g. *bāhv-ādi* (Gaṇar. 206); cf. *jal°*, *lagahā*.

गलि *gali*, *is*, m. (=*gaḍi*) a young steer, L.; Uṇ. iv, 117, Sch.

गलित *galita*. See √1. & 2. *gal*.

गलुन्त *galuntá*, *as*, m.?, AV. vi, 83, 3.

गलू *galū*, *ūs*, m. a sort of gem, L.

Gallaka, = *galv-arka*, q. v.

Galv (in comp. for *°lū*). **-arka**, m. crystal, Hcar. v, 115; see *masāra-g°*; a small crystalline vessel for drinking spirituous liquor (in Prākrit *gallakka*, Mṛicch. v, $\frac{4}{7}$; viii, $\frac{28}{29}$), L.; (*gallaka*) Hcar. vii.

Galva. See *musāra-g°*.

गलून *galūna*, *as*, m., N. of a minister, Rājat. iii, 475 f.

गलेगण्ड *gale-gaṇḍa*, &c. See above.

गलोड्य *galoḍya*, *as*, m., N. of a plant, Car. i, 27, 103; Suśr. iv, 5, 9; (cf. *gāl°*, *gil°*.)

गल्द *galda*, *as*, m. speech (cf. *gárda*), Naigh. i, 11 (v. l.); (*á*), f. id., ib.; (*gáldā*), f. (√1. *gal*) straining (?), RV. viii, 1, 20 (Nir. vi, 24).

गल्भ् *galbh*, cl. 1. Ā. *°lbhate*, to be bold or confident, Dhātup. x, 32; [see *ava-* & *pra-√galbh*; cf. √*garv*; cf. also Hib. *galbha*, 'rigour, hardness.']

Galbha, mfn. bold, Vop. xxi, 7. See *apa-g°*.

Galbhāya, Nom. Ā. *°yate*, to be bold, ib.

गल्या *galyā*. See √1. & 2. *gal*.

गल्ल *galla*, m. (fr. *gaṇḍa*) the cheek, Kāśī-Kh. viii, 59; Vīrac. viii, 67; ŚārṅgP.; cf. *aja-gallikā*. **-cāturī**, f. a small round pillow to put underneath the cheek, L. **-masūrī**, f. id., Pañcad. ii, 84. **-vādya**, n. sounding or music produced with the cheek, Gal. **Gallôpadhānīya**, n. = *°lla-cāturī*, v. l. (Pañcat. ii, 3, $\frac{22}{23}$) for *gaṇḍôp°*, q. v.

गल्लक *gallaka*. See *galū*.

गल्लकी *gallakī*, f. N. of a river, Rasik. xi, 80.

गल्लिका *gallikā*. See *aja-g°*.

गल्वर्क *galv-arka*. See *galū*.

गल्ह् *galh* = √*garh*, to blame, Dhātup. xvi.

गव् *gav*, in Ved. comp. for *gó*. **-acī**, f. = *ga-vâcī*, L. **-ādi**, a Gaṇa of Pāṇ. (v, 1, 2). **-āśir** (*gáv-*), mfn. mixed with milk (as Soma), RV. **-ísh**, mfn. wishing for cows, desirous (in general), eager, fervent, iv, 41, 7; viii, x. **-ishá**, mfn. id., iv, 13, 2 & 40, 2. **-ishṭi** (*gáv-*), mfn. id., RV.; f. desire, eagerness, ardour, fervour, RV.; desire for fighting, ardour of battle, battle, RV. **-īśa**, m. an owner of kine, Vop. ii, 15. **-īśvara**, m. id., L. **-esh**, cl. 1. Ā. *°shate*, to seek, search or inquire for (acc.), SaddhP.; Ṛitus. i, 21: cl. 10. *°shayati*, *°te*, id., MBh. iii, xii; Kathās.; Vīrac. viii, 6. **-esha**, mfn. (g. *saṃkalâdi*), see *dharma-*. **-éshaṇa**, mfn. desiring ardently or fervently, RV.; desirous of combat, RV.; AV. v, 20, 11; m., N. of a Vṛishṇi, MBh. i, 6999; Hariv.; n. seeking after, searching for, R. vi, 109, 40; Kathās. xxi, lxxxvi; (*ā*), f. id., L. **-eshaṇīya**, mfn. deserving to be sought for, Sāy. **-eshita**, mfn. sought, sought for, Kathās. cxviii. **-eshin**, mfn. ifc. seeking, searching, MBh. iii; Lalit. xvii f.; Kathās.; m., N. of a son of Citraka and brother of Pṛithu, Hariv. **-yūta**, n. (=*go-yuta*) the measure commonly called Gav-yūti (also half its length, L.), Pañcad. ii, 105. **-yūti** (*gáv-*), f. (Pāṇ. vi, 1, 79, Vārtt. 2 f.) a pasture, piece of pasture land, district, place of residence, RV.; AV.; TS. ii; (cf. *a-*, *urú-*, *dūré-*, *paro-*, *svastí-*); a measure of length (=4000 Daṇḍas or 2 Krośas), TāṇḍyaBr. xvi, 13, 12; MBh.; R.; BhP.; Rājat.

1. **Gava**, in comp. before a word beginning with a vowel [Pāṇ. vi, 1, 123 f.] and ifc. [v, 4, 92 & vi, 2, 72; f. *ī*, cf. *guru-gavī*, *brahma-gavī*, *brāhmaṇa-*, *bhilla-*, *strī-*] for *gó*, a cow, cattle (cf. *shaḍ-gavá*, *dvādaśa-gavá* &c.); (*ī*), f. ifc. for *gó*, a cow (see before); speech, Śiś. ii, 68. **-rāja**, m. a bull, W. **Gavâkṛiti**, mfn. cow-shaped, W. **Gavâksha**, m. (Kāś. on Pāṇ. v, 4, 76 & vi, 1, 123) 'a bull's eye,' an air-hole, loop-hole, round window, R.; Ragh. (ifc. f. *ā*, Ragh. xi, 93); Kum. &c.; the mesh of a shirt of mail, Hariv. 2439; N. of a warrior (brother of Śakuni), MBh. vi, 3997; vii, 6944 (B.); of a monkey-chief attached to Rāma (son of Vaivasvata and leader of the Golāṅgūlas), iii, 16272; R. iv, 25, 33 & 39, 27; vi, 3, 36 & 22, 2; m. or n., N. of a lake, Rājat. v, 423; N. of a plant (Cucumis maderaspatanus, L.; Cucumis coloquintida, L.; Clitoria Ternatea, L.), Car. vi, 4, 53; Suśr. i, iv ff.; *-jāla*, n. (cf. *jāla-g°*) a lattice, trellis-work, W. **Gavâkshaka**, m. (=*°ksha*) an air-hole, loop-hole, round window, MBh. i, 5003; Mṛicch.; VarBṛS.; ifc. MBh. xiii, 976; Kathās. **Gavâkshita**, mfn. furnished with windows or air-holes, Suśr.; forming a lattice, lattice-like, R. (B) iii, 15, 15; Suśr.; (with instr.) Kād. v, 1043; ifc. Car. vi, 18, 51. **Gavâkshin**, m. Trophis aspera, L. **Gavâgra**, n. = *gó-agra*, Vop. ii, 18. **Gavâcī**, f. (of *gavâñc*) a kind of fish (Ophidium punctatum or Macrognathus Pankalus), L. **Gavâñc**, mf(*gocī*)n., iii, 165. **Gavâdana**, n. 'cattle-food,' pasture or meadow grass, L.; (*ī*), f. (g. *gaurâdi*) a trough for holding grass to feed cattle, L.; a species of cucumber (Cucumis coloquintida), L.; Clitoria Ternatea, L. **Gavânṛita**, n. a lie told with respect to a cow, Mn. viii, 98. **Gavâmṛita**, n. 'cow-nectar,' cow-milk, MBh. iii, 17351. **Gavâyuta**, n. N. of a Tīrtha, BhP. x, 79, 18. **Gavâyus**, n. sg. & du. the Ekâha ceremonies called Go and Āyus, Vait. xxxi, 14; xl. **Gavârtham**, ind. for the sake of a cow, W. **Gavârthe**, ind. loc. id., Mn. x, 62; xi, 80; MBh. xiii; Pañcat. ii, 3, 35. **Gavârha**, mfn. of the value of a cow, MBh. ii, 828. **Gavâvika**, n. sg. cattle and sheep, g. *gavâśvâdi*. **Gavâśana**, m. (=*go-bhakshaka*) a worker in leather, shoemaker, Subh. **Gavâśva**, n. sg. (cf. *go-aśvá* & *go-'śvá*) cattle and horses, MBh. i, iii; R. i, 6, 7; *°śvâdi*, a Gaṇa of Pāṇ. (ii, 4, 11). **Gavâhnika**, n. the daily amount of food given to a cow, MBh. xiii, 6175 ff. **Gavêndra**, m. (Pāṇ. vi, 1, 124)?, Kāś.; = *gav-īśa*, Vop. ii, 15; a bull, Hcat. **Gavêśa**, m. = *gav-īśa*, Vop. ii, 15; v. l. for *gav-esha*. **Gavêśakā**, f. (=*gavedhukā*) Hedysarum lagopodioides, L. **Gavêśvara**, m. = *gav-īś°*, L. **Gavâiḍaka**, n. sg. (g. *gavâśvâdi*) kine and sheep, MānGṛ. ii, 13; *gavelaga*, Jain. **Gavôdgha**, m. an excellent cow, Pāṇ. ii, 1, 66, Sch.

1. **Gavaya**, Nom. P. (fr. *gó*) *°yati* (aor. *ajūgavat*), Pāṇ. iii, 1, 21, Siddh. 40.

2. **Gavayá**, *as*, m. the Gayal (a species of ox, Bos gavæus, erroneously classed by Hindū writers as a species of deer; cf. *go-mṛigá*), RV. iv, 21, 8; VS.; ŚBr.; AitBr. &c.; N. of a monkey-chief attached to Rāma (a son of Vaivasvata), MBh. iii, 16271; R. iv, 25, 33; vi; (*ī*), f. (Pāṇ. iv, 1, 63, Vārtt.; g. *gaurâdi*) the female Gayal, VS. xxiv, 30.

Gavala, m. the wild buffalo, VarYogay. vi, 25; n. buffalo's horn, VarBṛS. xxxii, 17.

Gavām (gen. pl. of *gó*; in comp.) **-aya**, m. 'going of cows,' N. of a ceremony, MBh. iii, 8176; xiii, 5177 & 7128. **-ayana**, n. id., AitBr. iv, 17; ĀśvŚr.; KātyŚr.; MBh. iii, 8080. **-pati**, m. (*gávām páti*, TBr. iii) 'cow-lord,' a bull, MBh. iii, 11737; iv, 588; 'lord of rays,' N. of the sun, iii, 192; of Agni, 14182; of a snake demon, Kāraṇḍ. i, 18; of a Buddh. mendicant, Lalit. i, 6 f.; SaddhP. i. **-medha**, m. sacrifice of cows, MBh. iii, 8040; xiii, 5231 & 5378.

Gavālūka, *as*, m. (=*°vayá*) the Gayal, L.

Gavi (loc. sg. of *gó*; in comp.) **-jāta**, m. 'cow-born,' N. of a muni, MBh. xiii, 2682 ff. **-putra**, m. 'cow-son,' N. of Vaiśravaṇa, iii, 15883. **-shṭhira** (*gávi-*), m. (Pāṇ. viii, 3, 95; g. *haritâdi*), N. of a Ṛishi of Atri's family, RV. v, 1, 12; x, 150, 5; AV. iv, 29, 5 (*gaví-*); ĀśvŚr. xii, 14, 1; Pravar. **-shṭhila**, for *-shṭhira*, g. *haritâdi* (Śākaṭ. & Gaṇar.) **Gaviḍā**, f. the cow from which the milk is taken for a libation, Vait. vii, 2; xliii, 6.

Gavinī, f. a herd of cows, g. *khalâdi*.

Gavishṭha, *as*, m. (superl. of *gó*, 'a ray;' or fr. *gavi* + *stha*, 'standing in water') the sun, BhP. i, 10, 36; N. of a Dānava, MBh. i, 2538 & 2670; Hariv. 2285 ff.; 12695; 12942; 14288.

Gavī, f. of *°va*, q. v.

Gaveshṭhin, *ī*, m., N. of a Dānava, Hariv. 197.

1. **Gavya**, Nom. P. *°vyati*, to desire cattle or cows, Vop. xxi, 2; see *gavyát*.

2. **Gávya** (or less common *gavyá*, RV. six times; TS. v; ŚBr. xiii), mfn. (Pāṇ. v, 1, 2 & 39; iv, 3, 160) consisting of cattle or cows, coming from or belonging to a cow (as milk, curds, &c.; cf. *pañca-g°*), RV.; VS. &c.; proper or fit for cattle, L.; sacred to the cow, worshipping the cow, Pāṇ. iv, 1, 85, Vārtt. 9, Pat.; m. pl., N. of a people (living to the north of Madhya-deśa), VarBṛS.; 1. (*ā*), f. a cow-herd, Pāṇ. iv, 2, 50; the measure commonly called Gav-yūti (q. v.), L.; see also *gavyā́*; (*ā*, *am*), f. n. a bow-string, L.; = *gavya-dṛiḍha*, L.; (*am*), n. cattle, cow-herd, RV. i, 140, 13; v, 34, 8; vii, 18, 7 (*gavyá*); ix, 62, 23; pasture land, AitBr. iv, 27, 9; Lāṭy. x, 17, 4; cow-milk, Kum. vii, 72. **-dṛiḍha**, the bile-stone of cattle (used as a colouring substance; cf. *go-rocanā*), L.

Gavyát, mfn. (pr. p. fr. 1. *gavya*) wishing for or desirous of cattle, RV.; ardently or fervently desiring, fervent, RV.; desirous of battle, RV.

Gavyáya, mf(*ī*)n. belonging to or coming from cattle, ix, 70, 7 & x, 48, 4.

Gavyayú, mfn. desirous of cattle, ix, 36 & 98.

2. **Gavyā́**, f. (fr. 1. *gavya*) desire for or delight in cows, viii, 46, 10 & ix, 64, 4 (instr. *°vyā́*); desire for (what comes from a cow, i. e. for) milk, viii, 93, 17 (instr. *°vyayā́*).

Gavyú, mfn. desirous of or delighting in cows, RV.; desirous of milk, ix, 97, 15; fervent, 27, 4; desirous of battle, RV.

गवदिक *gavadika*, m. pl., see *gabd°*.

गवल्गण *gavalgaṇa*, *as*, m., N. of Saṃjaya's father, MBh. i, 2426; (cf. *gāvalgaṇi*.)

गवीधु *gavīdhu*—*°dhuka* in comp. **-mat**, n., N. of a town, Pāṇ. ii, 3, 28, Vārtt. 4, Pat.

Gavīdhuka, m. Coix barbata, TS. v, 4, 3, 2; (*ā*), f. id., ĀpŚr. xv, 3, 16; xvi f. **-yavāgū**, f. rice-gruel boiled with Coix barbata, TS. v, 4, 3, 2.

Gaveḍu, *us*, f. = *°vīdhu*, L.; (*us*), m. a cloud, W.

Gaveḍukā, f. = *°vīdhu*, L., Sch.

Gavedhu, *us*, f. id., Bhpr. vii, 72, 49.

Gavédhuka, m. id., Hariv. 11164; Suśr. i, 46, 1, 18; a kind of serpent, v, 4, 32; n. = *gaveruka*, L.; (*ā*), f. = *°vī́dh°*, ŚBr. v, xiv; Sida alba, Bhpr.; = *gavêśakā*, L. **Gavedhukā-saktú**, m. pl. barley-meal prepared with Coix barbata, ŚBr. ix, 1, 1, 8; KātyŚr.

गवीनिका *gavīnikā*, f. du. the groins (or another part of the body near the pudenda), AV. i, 11, 5 & ix, 8, 7.

Gavīní, f. du. id., i, 3, 6; v, 25, 10-13; TS. iii.

गवीश *gav-īśa*, &c. See *gav*.

गवेडु *gaveḍu*, &c., *°védhuka*. See *°vīdhu*.

गवेरणि *gaveraṇi*, pl. N. of a family, Pravar. ii, 3, 1; (i, 1 *garevaṇi*, v. l. *vir°*.)

गवेरुक *gaveruka*, *am*, n. (=*°vedhuka*) red chalk, L.

गवेश *gavêśa*, &c. See *gava*.

Gav-esh, -esha, -éshaṇa, &c. See *gav*.

Gavya &c., **gáv-yūti.** See ib.

गह् *gah* (cf. *gabhá* & √*gāh*), cl. 10. P. *gahayati*, to enter deeply into (acc.), Dhātup. xxxv, 84; (cf. √*jaṅh*.)

Gaha?, see *dur-g°*. **Gahâdi**, a Gaṇa of Pāṇ. (iv, 2, 138; Gaṇar. 317–321.)

Gáhana, mf(*ā*)n. (g. *kshubhnâdi*) deep, dense, thick, impervious, impenetrable, inexplicable, hard to be understood, MBh.; R. &c.; (*ā*), f. ornament, DevīP.; (*am*), n. an abyss, depth ('water,' Naigh.; Nir.), RV. x, 129, 1; an inaccessible place, hiding-place, thicket, cave, wood, impenetrable darkness, i, 132, 6; ŚBr. xiv, 7, 2, 17; MBh. &c.; pain, distress, L.; a metre consisting of thirty-two syllables. **-tva**, n. density, Sāh. ii, ½ (*ati-*); impenetrability, MBh. ii, 2355. **-vat**, mfn. having hiding-places or thickets, W. **Gahanī-krita**, mfn. made inaccessible, Kād. v, 1018.

Gahanāya, Nom. Ā. *°yate*, 'to lie in wait for any one in a secret place,' to have treacherous intentions towards another, Pāṇ. iii, 1, 14, Vārtt.

Gahi, m. pl. N. of a family, Pravar. ii, 4, 1.

Gahīya, mfn. fr. *°ha*, Pāṇ. iv, 2, 138.

Gahmán, m. (= *gámbhan*) depth, TBr. ii, 7, 7, 6 (v. l. *gaṅh°*).

Gáhvara, mf(*ā*, *ī*)n. (g. *aśmâdi*) deep, impervious, impenetrable, TS. v; Hariv.; BhP.; confused (in mind), Kathās. lxi, 39 & 41; m. an arbour, bower, L.; a cave, cavern, L.; (*ā*), f. the plant Embelia Ribes, L.; (*ī*), f. a cave, cavern, L.; the earth, Gal.; (*am*), n. 'an abyss, depth' ('water,' Naigh.; Nir.), see *°re-shṭhá*; a hiding-place, thicket, wood, AV. xii, 2, 53; MBh.; R. &c.; an impenetrable secret, riddle, MBh. xiii, 1388; a deep sigh, L.; hypocrisy, L.; Abrus precatorius (?), L. **Gahvarī-bhūta**, mfn. having become a desert or vacuity, Hariv. 11285. **Gahvare-shṭhá**, mfn. being at the bottom or lowest depths, VS. v, 8; xvi, 44; KaṭhUp. ii.

Gahvarita, mfn. absorbed (in one's thoughts), MBh. ii, 2294.

गा 1. *gā*, cl. 3. P. *jígāti* (RV.; *jagāti*, Naigh. ii, 14 (v. l.); Subj. *jigāt*; Impv. *jigātu*; aor. *agāt*; 3. pl. *agan*, BhP. i, 9, 40; Subj. [1. sg. *gesham*, see *anu-* & *upa-*], 2. sg. *gās*, 3. sg. *gāt*, 2. pl. *gātá*, 3. pl. *gur*; [perf. *jigāya*, see *ud-*], perf. Pot. *jagāyāt* [Naigh. ii, 14], RV. x, 28, 1; inf. *gátave*, RV. iii, 31, 1; in Class. Sanskrit only the aor. P. *agāt* occurs, for Ā. see *adhi-*; aor. Pass. *agāyi*, *agāsātām*, Kāś. on Pāṇ. ii, 4, 45 & 77; cl. 2. P. *gāti*, Naigh. ii, 14; Ā. *gāte*, Dhātup. xx, 53) to go, go towards, come, approach (with acc. or loc.), RV.; AV. &c.; to go after, pursue, RV. iv, 3, 13; x, 18, 4; to fall to one's (dat.) share, be one's (acc.) due, viii, 45, 32; Ragh. xi, 73; to come into any state or condition (acc.), undergo, obtain, MBh. iii, 10697; R. &c.; to go away (from, abl.; to any place, loc.), RV. x, 108, 9; to come to an end, Naish. viii, 109; to walk (on a path, acc. or instr.), RV. viii, 2, 39 & 5, 39; (*jigāti*) to be born, Vop. on Dhātup. xxv, 25: Desid. *jigīshati*, to desire to go, BhP. ii, 10, 25; [cf. βίβημι, ἔβην; Old Germ. *gām*, *gās*, &c.; Goth. *ga-tvo*; Eng. *to go*.]

2. **Gā**, mfn. Ved. ifc. 'going' (cf. *a-gā*; *agre-*, *tamo-*, *puro-*, *samana-* & *svasti-gā*), Pāṇ. iii, 2, 67.

1. **Gātú**, *us*, m. going, motion, unimpeded motion, RV.; AV. x, 2, 12; way, course, egress, access, RV. (rarely f., i, 136, 2 & v, 32, 10); AV. xiii; VS. ii, 21; progress, increase, welfare, RV.; AV. ii; ŚBr. i; free space for moving, place or abode ('earth,' Naigh.), RV.; AV. x, xiii; (for *gátave* see s. v. √1. *gā*; cf. *árishṭa-g°*, *turá-g°*, *su-g°*.) **-mát**, mfn. spacious, commodious ('having good moving-space,' Gmn.), RV. vii, 54, 3. **-vid**, mfn. clearing the way for unimpeded motion or progress, finding or opening a way, promoting welfare, RV. i; iii, 62, 13; viii f.; AV. vii, xi; xiii, 2, 43.

Gātuya, Nom. P. (Impv. 2. sg. *°yā*; pr. p. *°yát*; 3. pl. *gātūyánti*, Pada-p. *gātuy°*) to wish to obtain or to procure free progress, RV. i, 52, 8 & 169, 5; viii, 16, 12.

Gátra, n. 'instrument of moving,' a limb or member of the body, RV.; AV. &c. (ifc. *ā* [MBh. ix; Pañcat. ii, 4, ¾] or *ī* [Mṛicch. i, 21; Śak.; Kum. &c.], cf. Pāṇ. iv, 1, 54, Kāś.); the body, Mn. iv, 122; 169; Nal. &c.; the forequarter of an elephant (cf. *gātrâvara*), L.; (*ā*), f. id., L.; the earth, Naigh. i, 1; (*as*), m., N. of a son of Vasishṭha, VP. i, 10, 13; VāyuP.; mfn. = *-yuta*, L. **-kampa**, m. trembling of the body, YogaśUp. 1. **-karśana**, mfn. emaciating the body, W. **-gupta**, m., N. of a son of Kṛishṇa and Lakshmaṇā, Hariv. 9189. **-bhaṅga**, m. = *-bhañjana*, Kām. v, 23; Sāh. iii, 158; (*ā*), f. a kind of cowach, L. **-bhañjana**, n. stretching one's limbs (as in sleepiness), HaṇsUp. **-mārjanī**, f. 'limb-rubber,' a towel, W. **-yashṭi**, f. (in Prākṛit *gāya-laṭṭhi*, Jain.) a thin or slender body, Ragh. vi, 81; Kād. iv, 119; ifc. *i* [v, 799; Ṛitus. iii, 1] or *ī* [iv, vi]. **-yuta**, mfn. large, L. **-ruha**, n. 'growing on the body,' the hairs on the body, BhP. ii, 3, 24 (cf. *aṅga-r°*). **-latā**, f. = *-yashṭi*, BrahmaP. **-vat**, mfn. having a handsome body, R. (B) ii, 98, 24 (v. l.); m., N. of a son of Kṛishṇa and Lakshmaṇā, Hariv. 9189; VP. v, 32, 4; BhP. x, 61, 15; (*tī*), f., N. of a daughter of Kṛishṇa and Lakshmaṇā, Hariv. 9190. **-vinda**, m., N. of a son of Kṛishṇa and Lakshmaṇā, 9189. **-veshṭana**, n. spasmodic sensation, Car. vi, 27. **-vairūpya-tā**, f. deformity of the limbs, MBh. iii, 2803. **-śoshaṇa**, mfn. consuming the body (as grief), MBh. xii, 900. **-saṃkocanī**, f. 'contracting its body,' a hedgehog, VS. xxiv, 36, Sch. **-saṃkocin**, m. id., L. **-saṃplava**, m. 'body-diver,' the bird Pelicanus fusicollis, L.; (cf. *plava*.) **-sparśa**, m. contact of the limbs, W. **Gātrânulepanī**, f. fragrant unguents &c. smeared upon the body, perfume for the person, L. **Gātrâvara**, in comp., the fore and hindquarter of an elephant, MBh. vi, 54, 57. **Gātrâvaraṇa**, n. 'body-covering,' a shield, vii, 79. **Gātrôtsādana**, n. cleaning the person with perfumes, Mn. ii, 211.

Gātraka, *am*, n. the body, Vikr.; (*ikā*), f. 'a girdle (?),' see s. v.

Gātraya, Nom. Ā. *°yate*, 'to be loosened' or 'to loosen,' Dhātup. xxxv, 82 (Vop.)

Gātrikā, f. of *°traka*. **-granthi**, m. a particular knot, Hcar. i, 59. **-bandha**, m. a girdle (?), L.

1. **Gāya**. See *uru-g°*.

गा 3. *gā*, mfn. (√*gai*) ifc. 'singing,' see *sāma-gā*; (*ā*), f., see s. v. 3. *ga*.

Gātavya, mfn. to be sung, Nyāyam. (i, ix), Sch.

2. **Gātú**, m. a song, RV.; a singer (i, 100, 4?), Uṇ. i, 73; a Gandharva or celestial chorister, ib.; the male Koïl or Indian cuckoo, ib.; a bee, ib.; N. of a descendant of Atri (author of RV. v, 32), R-Anukr.; mfn. angry, wrathful, L.

Gātṛi, m. a singer, ChUp. i, 6, 8; Hariv. 3051; R. vii, 94, 9; (= *gātú*) a Gandharva, L.; the male Koïl, L.; a bee, L.; an angry man, L.; N. of a man with the patr. Gautama, VBr. ii, 2.

Gāthá, *as*, m. a song, RV. i, 167, 6 & ix, 11, 4; SV.; (*gāthā*), f. id., RV.; a verse, stanza (especially one which is neither Ṛic, nor Sāman, nor Yajus, a verse not belonging to the Vedas, but to the epic poetry of legends or Ākhyānas, such as the Śunaḥśepa-Ākhyāna or the Suparṇ.), AV.; TS.; TBr.; ŚBr. &c.; the metrical part of a Sūtra, Buddh.; N. of the Āryā metre; any metre not enumerated in the regular treatises on prosody; (cf. *ṛig-gāthā*, *ṛiju-gātha*, *yajña-gāthā*.) **-pati** (*°thá-*), m. lord of songs, RV. i, 43, 4. **-śravas** (*°thá-*), mfn. famous through (epic) songs (Indra), viii, 2, 38.

Gāthaka, *as*, m. (Pāṇ. iii, 1, 146) a singer (chanter of the Purāṇas), Pāṇ. i, 1, 34, Kāś.; Rājat. vii, 934; (*ikā*), f. an epic song, Yājñ. i, 45; MBh. iii, 85, 30; Ratnâv. ii, ⅛.

Gāthā, f. of *°thá*, q. v. **-kāra**, m. author of (epic) songs or verses, Pāṇ. iii, 2, 23; a singer, reciter, W. **-nārāśaṇsī**, f. du. epic songs and particularly those in praise of men or heroes, MaitrS. i, 11, 5; f. pl., id., ŚBr. xi, 5, 6, 8; (cf. *nārāśaṇsī*.) **-nī**, mfn. leading a song or a choir, RV. i, 190, 1 & viii, 92, 2. **Gāthântara**, m., N. of the fourth Kalpa or period of the world.

Gāthi (in comp. for *°thin*, q. v.) **-ja**, m. 'Gāthin's son,' N. of Viśvā-mitra, Bṛih., Sch.

Gāthikā, f. of *°thaka*, q. v.

Gāthin, mfn. familiar with songs, singer, RV. i, 7, 1; MBh. ii, 1450; (*ī*), m. (Pāṇ. vi, 4, 165) N. of Viśvā-mitra's father (son of Kuśika), RAnukr.; (*inas*), m. pl. the descendants of Gāthin, AitBr. vii, 18 (v. l.); (*inī*), f., N. of a metre (containing 12 + 18 + 12 + 20 or 32 + 29 syllabic instants.

Gāthina, m. (Pāṇ. vi, 4, 165) patr. fr. Gāthin, RAnukr.; AitBr. vii, 18; ĀśvŚr. xii, 14, 6; Pravar.

Gādhi, m. for *°dhin*, MBh. iii, ix, xii f.; Hariv.; Pāṇ. iv, 1, 104, Pat.; R.; BhP.; m. pl. the descendants of Gādhi, ix, 16, 32. **-ja**, m. = *gāthi-ja*, Mn. vii, 42; R. i. **-nagara**, n. 'Gādhi's city,' N. of Kānyakubja. **-nandana**, m. = *-ja*, R. i. **-putra**, m. id., i, iii. **-pura**, n. = *-nagara*, Bālar. x, 88; Rājat. iv. **-bhū**, m. = *-ja*, L. **-sūnu**, m. id., Bṛih.

Gādhin, m. (= *gāthin*) N. of Viśvā-mitra's father (king of Kānyakubja), MBh. i, iii; R. i, 20, 5.

Gādheya, m. patr. of Viśvā-mitra, Hariv. 1766; R. i; (*ī*), f. patr. of Satyavatī, MBh. xiii, 242.

Gāna, n. singing, song, KātyŚr.; Lāṭy. i, vii; Hariv. 11793; Śiś. ix, 54; a sound, L.; (cf. *araṇya-*, *ūha-*, *ūhya-*.) **-cchalā**, f., N. of a section of the Sāmaveda-cchalā. **-bandhu**, m. 'friend of songs,' N. of an interlocutor in a work imitative of the R. **-vidyā**, f. the science of vocal music, W.

Gāninī, f. Orris root (*vacā*, a medicinal plant, supposed to be of use in clearing the voice), L.

Gānīya, mfn. musical, W.; n. a song, R. i, 3, 70.

1. **Gāntu**, m. for *gātu*, a singer, Uṇ. vṛ.

Gāman. See *dyumad-g°*.

2. **Gāya**, n. 'a song,' see *uttama-*, *sāma-*.

Gāyaka, mfn. one who sings, W.; m. a singer, MBh. xii, xiv; R.; BhP. iii, x; Bhartṛ.; (*ī*), f. a female singer (one of the 8 Akulas with Śāktas).

Gáyat, mfn. pr. p. √*gai*, q. v.; (*antī*), f., N. of Gaya's wife, BhP. v, 15, 2.

Gāyatrá, m. n. a song, hymn, RV.; VS. xi, 8; ChUp. ii, 11, 1; n. a hymn composed in the Gāyatrī metre, RV.; the Gāyatrī metre, VP. i, 5, 52; N. of a Sāman, ŚBr ix; KātyŚr.; mf(*ī*)n. consisting in or connected with the Gāyatrī, formed in accordance with the Gāyatrī (e. g. in accordance with the number of syllables of a Gāyatrī verse), VS.; TS. &c.; with *vrata*, = *brahma-carya*, BhP. x, 45, 29; (*ī*), f. an ancient metre of twenty-four syllables (variously arranged, but generally as a triplet of eight syllables each), any hymn composed in the Gāyatrī metre, RV. x, 14, 16 & 130, 4; VS.; AV. &c.; the Gāyatrī (i. e. RV. iii, 62, 10: *tát savitúr váreṇyam bhárgo devásya dhīmahi dhíyo yó naḥ pracodáyāt*, ŚBr. xiv; ŚāṅkhGṛ.; MBh. &c.; this is a very sacred verse repeated by every Brāhman at his morning and evening devotions; from being addressed to Savitṛi or the Sun as generator, it is also called Sāvitrī; cf. RTL. pp. 19; 342; 361; 403; the Gāyatrī verse is personified as a goddess, the wife of Brahmā and mother of the four Vedas, Hariv. 11666 ff.; it is often mentioned in connection with the Amṛita, both together constituting as it were the essence and type of sacred hymns in general, AV.; the Gāyatrī personified is also considered as the mother of the first three classes in their capacity of twice-born, W.; cf. RTL. pp. 200 f.; some other verse [perhaps RV. x, 9, 1] is denoted by Gāyatrī, Suśr. vi, 28, 7; with Tāntrikas a number of mystical verses are called Gāyatrīs, and each deity has one in particular); N. of Durgā, MatsyaP.; Kathās. liii, 172; Acacia Catechu, L. **-kakubha**, mfn. consisting of metres Gāyatrī and Kakubh (as a Pragātha), RPrāt. xviii, 5. **-cchandas** (*°trá-*), mfn. one to whom the Gāyatrī metre belongs or to whom it is sacred, relating to it, AV. vi, 48, 1; MaitrS. ii, 3, 3; VS. &c.; n. a Gāyatrī metre, Lāṭy. iii, 1, 28; (cf. Vait. xix, 16.) **-pārśva**, n. 'Gāyatrī-sided,' N. of a Sāman, TāṇḍyaBr.; Lāṭy. **-bārhata**, mfn. consisting of the metres Gāyatrī and Bṛihatī (as a Pragātha), RPrāt. xviii. **-vartani** (*°trá-*), mfn. moving in Gāyatrī measures, RV. viii, 38, 6; VS. xi, 8. **-vepas** (*°trá-*), mfn. (cf. *gāthá-śravas*) inspired by (epic) songs (Indra), RV. i, 142, 12 & viii, 1, 10.

1. **Gāyatri**, metrically for *°trī*, Hariv. 11516.

2. **Gāyatri**, in comp. for *°trin*, q. v. **-sāra**, m. Catechu (Terra japonica), Suśr. vi, 41, 50 & 52, 22.

Gāyatrin, m. one who sings hymns, RV. i, 10, 1 (MBh. xii, 10352); (= *°trī*) Acacia Catechu, L.

Gāyatrī, f. of *°trá*, q. v. **-kāram**, ind. p. so as to change into Gāyatrī verses, ĀśvŚr. **-pañcâṅga**, **-pañjara**, **-puraścaraṇa**, **-bhāshya**, n., N. of works on the Gāyatrī. **-mantra**, m. prayers connected with the Gāyatrī. **-yāman**, mf(*mnī*)n. approaching with Gāyatrī verses, ĀpŚr. **-rahasya**, n., N. of a work on the Gāyatrī. **-vallabha**, m. 'friend of Gāyatrī,' N. of Śiva. **-sāman**, n., N. of several Sāmans (recited in the Gāyatrī metre), Lāṭy. vi f. **Gāyatry-āsita**, n., N. of a Sāman.

Gāyatrya, mfn. said of a kind of Soma, Suśr. iv.

Gāyana, *as*, m. (Pāṇ. iii, 1, 147) a singer, praiser, MBh. i, iii, v, xiii; R. i; Rājat.; a talker, L.; N. of an attendant in Skanda's retinue, MBh. ix, 2569; (*ī*), f. a female singer, Pāṇ. iii, 1, 147;

(*am*), n. singing, song, Cāṇ.; BhP. iii, vii; PSarv.; professing or practising singing as a livelihood, W.

Gāyantikā, f. (fr. °*nti*, f. of *gāyat*), 'singing,' N. of a cave in the Himālaya, MBh. v, 2836.

Gāyas. See *ánu-g°*.

गां *gām* (acc. of *gó*, q. v.) **-gaucyá**, m. (cf. *gavâñc?*) N. of a divine being, MaitrS. ii, 9, 1. **-dama**, m. 'cow-tamer,' = *kāṃdama*, TāṇḍyaBr. xxi. **-doha-samnéjana**, n. water to clean a milk-pail, MaitrS. i, 8, 3. **-manya**, mfn. thinking one's self a cow, Pāṇ. vi, 3, 68, Kāś.

गागनायस *gāganâyasa*, mfn. fr. *gag°*.

गाङ्ग *gāṅga*, mf(ī)n. (fr. *gáṅgā*), being in or on the Ganges, coming from or belonging or relating to the Ganges, MBh. (*hrada*, v, 996); R.; Kum. v, 37 &c.; m. (g. *śivâdi*) metron. of Bhīshma (cf. *gāṅgāyani*), Hariv. 1824; of Skanda or Kārttikeya, L.; n. (scil. *ambu*) rain-water of a peculiar kind (supposed to be from the heavenly Ganges), Suśr. i, 45, 1, 1; (*ī*), f., N. of Durgā (vv. ll. *gārgī* & *gaṅgā*), Hariv. 10243. **-deva**, m., N. of a poet.

Gāṅgâṅgha, m. the current of the Ganges, W.

Gāṅgaṭa, °*ṭaka*, °*ṭeya*, m. = *gaṅgaṭeya*, L.

Gāṅgāmahika, mfn. fr. *gaṅgā-maha*, Pāṇ. v, 1, 12, Vārtt. 1, Pat.

Gāṅgāyana, m. patr., Pravar. i, 7; v, 4.

Gāṅgāyani, m. (g. *tikâdi*) metron. fr. *gáṅgā*, Pravar. ii, 4, 1; iv, 8; Bhīshma (son of Śāntanu's first wife Gaṅgā), L.; Skanda (generated from Śiva's vivifying principle first cast into Agni and afterwards received by Gaṅgā), L.; for °*gyāy°*, W.

Gāṅgi, v. l. for °*gāyani* (Pravar. ii, 4, 1).

Gāṅgika, v. l. for *bhāṅgika*, q. v.

Gāṅgilā, f., N. of a woman, HPariś. ii, 320.

Gāṅgū, m., N. of a thief, Kathārṇ. xi.

Gāṅgeya, mfn. being in or on the Ganges, coming from or belonging or relating to the Ganges, MBh.; R. vi; m. (g. *śubhrâdi*, Kāś. & Gaṇar.; = *gāṅgāyani*) Bhīshma, MBh.; N. of Skanda, ix, 2465; xiii, 4096; the Hilsa or Illias fish (*illiśa*), L.; the root of a kind of grass, L.; m. pl., N. of a family, Saṃskārak.; n. the root of Scirpus Kysoor or of a Cyperus (*kaśeru*), Suśr. vi, 17, 15 & 39, 94; gold, L.

Gāṅgeruka, n. the grain of °*kī*, Suśr. i, 46, 3, 32; (*ī*), f. the plant Uraria lagopodioides, 25.

Gāṅgeshṭhī, f. Guilandina Bonducella, L.

Gāṅgôdaki, m. patr., Pravar. ii, 2, 1.

Gāṅgyá, mfn. being on the Ganges, RV. vi, 45, 31; belonging to the Ganges (v. l. *gāṅga*), Kām. v, 8; m. metron. fr. *gáṅgā*, KaushUp. i, 1, Sch.

Gāṅgyāyani, m. patr. fr. Gāṅgya, KaushUp. i, 1 (v.l. *gārgyāyaṇi*, Parāś. i, 8/8, 4, 22).

गांगौच्य *gām-gaucyá.* See *gām*.

गाज *gāja*, n. a multitude of elephants, Gaṇar. 83, Sch. **-vāja**, for *gaj°*, 83.

गाञ्जिकाय *gāñji-kāya*, m. a quail, L.

Gāñjī-kāya, *as*, m. id., Npr.

Gāñjīvin, *ī*, m. id., L.

गाडव *gāḍava*, *as*, m. (=*gaveḍu*) a cloud, L.

गाडिवि *gāḍivi*, mfn. fr. *gaḍiva*, g. *sutaṃgamâdi*.

गाडुल्य *gāḍulya*, *am*, n. (fr. *gaḍula*), hump-backedness, g. *brāhmaṇâdi*.

गाडेरकि *gāḍeraki*, m. pl. the descendants of Gaḍeraka, Gaṇar. 34, Sch.

गाढ *gāḍha*. See √*gāh*.

गाणकार्य *gāṇakārya*, *as*, m. patr. fr. *gaṇa-kāra* (or °*ri* or °*rin*), g. *kurv-ādi*.

Gāṇagāri, m., N. of a teacher, ĀśvŚr. iii, 11; v, 6 & 12; vi, 7; vii-ix; *gaṇ°*, Pravar. ii, 3, 1.

Gāṇapata, mfn. relating to Gaṇa-pati or Gaṇêśa, g. *aśvapaty-ādi*.

Gāṇapatya, mfn. relating to Gaṇêśa; m. a worshipper of Gaṇêśa, Kulârṇ.; (with Śāktas) N. of an author of Mantras; n. the leading of troops, chieftainship, VS. xi, 15; TS. v, 1, 2, 3; MBh. iii; Hcat. **-pūrva-tāpanīyôpanishad**, f. = *gaṇapati-p°*.

Gāṇāyana, pl. Gaṇa's descendants, g. *kuñjâdi*.

Gāṇāyanya, *as*, m. a descendant of Gaṇa, ib.

Gāṇika, mfn. familiar with the Gaṇas (in Gr.), gaṇas *ukthâdi* & *kathâdi*.

Gāṇikya, *am*, n. (fr. *gaṇikā*), an assemblage of courtezans, Pāṇ. iv, 2, 40, Pat.

Gāṇitika, m. (fr. *gaṇita*), an arithmetician, Līl.

Gāṇina, *as*, m. patr. fr. *gaṇin*, Pāṇ. vi, 4, 165.

Gāṇêśa, mfn. relating to Gaṇêśa, LiṅgaP.; GaṇP.; m. a worshipper of Gaṇêśa, PadmaP. v, 133, 26.

Gāṇêśôpapurāṇa, n. = *gaṇ°*, W.

गाण्डव्य *gāṇḍavya*, m. patr. fr. *gaṇḍu*, g. *gargâdi*; f. °*vyāyanī*, g. 2. *lohitâdi* (not in Kāś.)

गाण्डाली *gāṇḍālī*, f. a kind of grass, Gal.

गाण्डिव *gāṇḍiva*, *as*, *am*, m. n. (Pāṇ. v, 2, 110, Kāś.) the bow of Arjuna (presented by Soma to Varuṇa, by him to Agni, and by Agni to Arjuna; also said to have belonged to Prajā-pati, Brahmā, and Śiva), MBh. iii, v; BhP. i, 9, 15; a bow (in general), L. **-dhara**, m. 'holding the Gāṇḍiva bow,' N. of Arjuna, Veṇīs. ii, 24.

Gāṇḍi, f. (Pāṇ. v, 2, 110) 'a rhinoceros' or = '*vajra-granthi*,' MBh. v, 3540, Sch. **-maya**, mfn. made of *gāṇḍi* (Arjuna's bow Gāṇḍīva), 3540.

Gāṇḍīva, m. n. (g. *ardharcâdi*, Pāṇ. v, 2, 110) = °*diva* (Arjuna's bow), MBh.; Hariv. 9798; BhP. i, 7, 16; Pañcat. iii, 14, 11; a bow (in general), L. **-dhanvan**, m. 'having Gāṇḍīva for his bow,' Arjuna, MBh.; Megh. 48; Prab. iv, 14. **-mukta**, mfn. discharged from the bow Gāṇḍīva, W.

Gāṇḍīvin, m. = °*va-dhanvan*, MBh. xiii, 6898; BhP. x, 58, 54; Terminalia Arjuna, L.

गाण्डीर *gāṇḍīra*, mfn. coming from the plant Gaṇḍīra, Suśr. i, 46, 4, 28.

गातवे *gâtave.* See √1. *gā*.

गातव्य *gātavya.* See 3. *gā*.

गातागतिक *gātâgatika*, mf(ī)n. (fr. *gatâgata*), caused by going and coming, g. *akshadyūtâdi*.

Gātânugatika, mf(ī)n. (fr. *gatânugata*), caused by following or imitating what precedes, ib.

गातु *gātú*, &c. See √1. *gā* & 3. *gā*.

Gátra, °*traka*, °*trikā*. See √1. *gā*.

Gāthá, **gāthā**, **gāthín**. See 3. *gā*.

गादाधरी *gādādharī*, f., N. of a Comm. by Gadā-dhara.

Gādāyana. See *vād°*.

Gādi, m. patr. fr. *gada*, g. *bāhv-ādi*.

Gāditya, fr. *gadita*, g. *pragady-ādi*.

Gādgadya, n. (fr. *gadgada*), stammering, Suśr.

गाध् *gādh* (cf. √*gāh*), cl. 1. Ā. °*dhate*, to stand firmly, stay, remain, Dhātup. ii, 3; to set out for (acc.), Bhaṭṭ. viii, 1; xxii, 2; to desire (cf. √*gardh*), Dhātup.; to compile, string together, ib.

Gādha, mf(*ā*)n. (ifc., Pāṇ. vi, 2, 4) offering firm standing-ground, fordable (as a river), not very deep, shallow, KaushBr. ii, 9; Nir.; MBh. &c.; (*ám*), n. ground for standing on in water, shallow place, ford, RV.; TS. iv; ŚBr. xii; TāṇḍyaBr. &c. (with *Bhāradvājasya*, N. of a Sāman, ĀrshBr.); (*as*), m. id., R. v, 94, 12; = *sthāna*, L.; desire, cupidity, L.; m. pl., N. of a people, AV.Pariś. li, 22. **-pratishṭhā́**, f. 'standing on a ford,' N. of particular divisions of the ritual, ŚBr. xii, 2, 1, 9; GopBr. i, 5, 2.

Gādhana, a kind of arrow, Hariv. 8865; (*ī*), f. the calf, Gal.

Gādhera, g. *vākinâdi* (*gaudh°*, Gaṇap.; Gaṇaratnâv.; *gāredha*, Kāś.; *gāreṭa*, Hemac. & Bhoj.)

Gādherakāyani, °*dheri*, m. patr. fr. °*dhera*, ib.

गाधि *gādhi*, °*dhin*, °*dheya*. See 3. *gā*.

Gāna, °*ninī*, °*nīya*, 1. °*ntu*. See ib.

गान्तु 2. *gāntu*, m. (√*gam*) a traveller, Uṇ.

Gāntra, n. & (*ī*), f. = *gantrī*, Uṇ. iv, 159.

गांदम *gām-dama.* See *gām*, col. 1.

गान्दिक *gāndika*, v. l. for *gābd°*.

गान्दिनी *gāndinī*, f., N. of a princess of Kāśi (wife of Śvaphalka and mother of A-krūra), Hariv. 1912 & 2082; (*gāndī*) 2115; BhP. ix, 24, 14; N. of Gaṅgā (v. l. °*ndhinī*), L. **-suta**, m. 'son of Gāndinī,' A-krūra, BhP.; (= *gāṅgāyani*) Bhīshma, L.

Gāndī, f. = °*dinī*, q. v.

गांदोहसंनेजन *gām-doha-saṃnéjana.* See *gām*, col. 1.

गान्धपिङ्गलेय *gāndhapiṅgaleya*, m. metron. fr. *gandha-piṅgalā*, g. *śubhrâdi* (*śauddhap°*, Kāś.)

गान्धर्व *gāndharvá*, mf(*gāndharvī*)n. belonging or relating to the Gandharvas (especially *vivāha* or *vidhi*, the form of marriage called after the Gandharvas which requires only mutual agreement, ĀśvGṛ. i, 6, 5; Mn.; Yājñ.; MBh. i, &c.; cf. *gandharva-vivāha*), RV. x, 80, 6; ŚBr. xiv &c.; relating to the Gandharvas as heavenly choristers (cf. *-kalā*, *-veda*, &c.), MBh.; Hariv. &c.; m. (= *gandh°*, g. *prajñâdi*, Gaṇar. 175) a singer, R. vii, 94, 6; VarBṛS. xv, xxxii; N. of a musical note, Hariv. 16291; VāyuP. i, 21, 30; of one of the 9 divisions of Bhārata-varsha, VP. ii, 3, 7; n. the art of the Gandharvas, song, music, concert, MBh.; Hariv. &c.; N. of a Tantra; (*ī*), f. speech (according to the legend that the gods gave speech to the Gandharvas and received from them the Soma in return, AitBr. i, 27 &c.), Naigh. i, 11; N. of Durgā, Hariv. 10243 (v. l. *gandharvā*); N. of an Apsaras, VP. **-kalā**, f. pl. the art of the Gandharvas, song, music, Gīt. xii, 28. **-citta**, mfn. one whose mind is possessed by the Gandharvas, Suśr. **-vidyā**, f. = *-kalā*, ĀpŚr., Sch. **-veda**, m. the Veda of music (considered as an appendix of the SV. and ascribed to Bharata), MBh. iii, 8421; Hariv.; BhP. iii. **-śālā**, f. music-hall, concert-room, Kathās. xii, 31. **-śāstra**, n. = *-kalā*, MBh. xiii, 5103.

Gāndharvaka = °*vika*, VarBṛS. vc, Sch. (v. l.)

Gāndharvika, m. a singer, vc, 21; Kathās. lxiii.

गान्धार *gāndhāra*, mfn. fr. *gandh°*, gaṇas *kacchâdi* & *sindhv-ādi*; (*gā́ndh°*), m. (Pāṇ. iv, 1, 169) a prince of the Gāndhāris, ŚBr. viii, 1, 4, 10; AitBr. vii, 34; Hariv. 8395 (*-kanyā*); N. of a prince (from whom the Gāndhāras derive their origin), 1839; BhP. ix, 23, 14; the third of the 7 primary notes of music, MBh. iv, xii, xiv; VarBṛS. lxxxvi, 40; (also personified as a son of Rāga Bhairava); minium or red lead, L.; m. pl., N. of a people and of their country (north-east of Peshawar and giving its N. to Kandahar; Pāṇini is said to have been a Gāndhāra; cf. *gandh°*, *gandhāri*, *gāndhāri*), MBh.; Hariv.; R. iv, vii; VarBṛS. &c.; n. gum myrrh, L.; (= *gañjâkinī*) the points of hemp; (*ī*), f. (Pāṇ. iv, 1, 14, Vārtt. 4, Pat.) a princess of the Gāndhāris (esp. the wife of Dhṛita-rāshṭra), MBh.; Hariv.; BhP. i, ix; N. of a Vidyā-devī, MBh. iii, 14562; (fulfilling the commands of the twenty-first Arhat of the present Avasarpiṇī, Jain.); (in music) N. of a Rāgiṇī; Alhagi Maurorum, L.; a particular vein in the left eye, Goraksh. 26; a kind of fly, Gal. **-grāma**, m. a kind of musical scale. **-rāja**, m. the king of Gāndhāra named Su-bala, MBh. iii; Hariv. (6585) 8982.

Gāndhāraka, *ās*, m. pl. (g. *kacchâdi*) N. of the people called Gāndhāra, MBh. vii, 180 & 3532; (*ikā*), f. (= °*rī*) Alhagi Maurorum, Nirṇayas.

Gāndhāri, m. = °*reya*, MBh. ii f., v, vii, 3457; m. pl. (Pāṇ. iv, 1, 169; 2, 52, Vārtt. 2) N. of a people (also called Gandhāras or Gāndhāras), MBh. viii, 2135. **-sapta-sama**, m., Pāṇ. vi, 2, 12, Kāś.

Gāndhāreya, m. metron. fr. °*rī*, N. of Duryodhana (son of Dhṛita-rāshṭra), L.

गान्धिक *gāndhika*, *as*, m. (fr. *gandhá*), a vender of perfumes, perfumer (kind of mixed caste, Parāś.), Kād.; Sāh. iii, 15/16 & 17/18; a clerk, L.; a kind of worm having a strong fetid smell (*gāndhipokā*, a tree-bug), L.; n. fragrant wares, perfumes, Pañcat. i, 17; (*ī*), f. a female vender of perfumes, Parāś.

गान्धिनी *gandhinī*, v. l. for °*ndinī*, q. v.

गान्मुत *gānmuta.* See *gārm°*.

गाब्दिक *gābdika*, mfn. fr. *gabdikā*, g. *sindhv-ādi* (Kāś.)

गामन् *gāman.* See *dyumad-g°*.

गामिक *gāmika*, mfn. ifc. going, leading to (as a way), R. vi, 106, 7.

Gāmin, mfn. going anywhere (local adv. [MBh. i] or acc. [Pāṇ. ii, 3, 70, Kāś.] or *prati*, MBh. iv); (in the following meanings only) ifc. (Pāṇ. ii, 1, 24, Vārtt. 1) going or moving on or in or towards or in any peculiar manner, Mn. iii, 10; MBh. &c.; having sexual intercourse with, Yājñ. ii, 234; (cf. *mātṛi-g°*); reaching or extending to, R. v; VarBṛS.; coming to one's share, due, Yājñ. ii; MBh. xiii; Hariv.; Śak. &c.; attaining, obtaining, Mālav. v, 1/2; directed towards, Mn. xi, 56; Bhag. viii, 8; relating to, MBh. ii, 26; Sāh. vi, 180; (cf. *agra-*, *anta-*, *anya-*, *āśu-*, *ṛitu-*, *kāma-*.)

Gāmuka, mf(*ā*)n. going, Pāṇ. iii, 2, 154.

गाम्भीर *gāmbhīra*, fr. *gambh°*, g. *saṃkalâdi*.

Gāmbhīrya, mfn. being in the depths, Pāṇ. iv, 3, 58; n. deepness, depth (of water, sound, &c.), MBh. xiii, 4637; R.; (of the voice of a Jaina saint) W.; depth or profundity of character, earnestness, R. &c.; depth of meaning, deep recondite sense, W.; dignity, Kathās. lxxxvi, 32; generosity, cxxiv, 83; calmness, composure, Daśar. ii, 12; Sāh. iii, 50 & 53; (in rhet.) a hidden allusion, Pratāpar.

गांमन्य *gām-manya.* See *gām*, p. 353, col. 1.

गाय 1. & 2. *gāya.* See √1. *gā* & 3. *gā*.

गाय 3. *gāya*, mfn. relating to Gaya, AitBr. v, 2, 12.

गायक *gāyaka*, *gāyat.* See 3. *gā*.

Gāyatrá, °**trin**, °**trí**, &c. See ib.

गार *gāra*, n., N. of a Sāman (composed by Gara), TāṇḍyaBr. ix, 2, 16; (cf. *madra-g°*.)

Gāraka, m. Eclipta prostrata, Gal.

Gāritra, n. rice, corn, grain, Uṇ. iv, 170.

गारुगि *gārugi*, *is*, m. (in music) a kind of measure.

गारुड *gāruḍa*, mfn. (fr. *gar°*), shaped like the bird Garuḍa, coming from or relating to Garuḍa, MBh. vi; R. vi, vii &c.; N. of a Kalpa period, MatsyaP. liii, 52; a kind of rice, Gal.; (*ī*), f., N. of a creeper, L.; (*am*), n. (= *garuḍa-māṇikya*) an emerald, Ragh. xiii, 53 (?); (used as an antidote) Kād. iii, 29; gold, L.; a Mantra against poison, L.; N. of a Tantra work. **-purāṇa**, n. = *gar°*.

Gāruḍôpanishad, f. = *gar°*.

Gāruḍika, *as*, m. a charmer, dealer in antidotes, Siṇhâs.

Gārutmata, mfn. (fr. *garút-mat*), coming from or sacred or relating to the bird Garuḍa, Ragh. xvi, 77; (*aśman* = *garuḍâśman*, q.v.) Rājat. iv, 331; (m., Gal.) n. an emerald, Hcat. i, 5; 6, 16; Bhpr. **-pattrikā**, f. 'emerald-leaved,' N. of a plant, L.

गारेध *gāredha.* See *gādhera*.

गार्ग *gārga*, mfn. fr. *gārgya* (with *saṅgha*, *aṅka*, and *lakshaṇa*), Pāṇ. iv, 3, 127; (with *ghosha*) Vārtt. 1; m. contemptuous metron. fr. *gārgī*, 1, 147, Sch. (*gārgya*, Kāś.); mf(*ī*)n. composed by Garga (the astronomical Saṃhitā); m. (in music) a kind of measure; (*gā́rgī*), f. of the patr. *gārgya* (Pāṇ. iv, 1, 16 & vi, 4, 150), N. of Vācaknavī (cf. *gargī*), ŚBr. xiv; ŚāṅkhGṛ.; Durgā, Hariv. 10243; f. du. Gārgī and Gārgyāyaṇa, Pāṇ. i, 2, 66, Kāś.

Gārgaka, mfn. (fr. *gārgya*, vi, 4, 151, Kāś.), belonging to Gārgya, iv, 2, 104, Vārtt. 22; worshipping Gārgya, Vārtt. 18; (*ikā*), f. descent from Garga, v, 1, 134, Kāś.; (*am*), n. an assemblage of the descendants of Garga, L., Sch.

Gārgā, f. of °*ga*, iv, 1, 147, Vārtt. 6 f., Pat. **-bhārya**, mfn. having a wife from Garga's family, Vārtt. 5, Pat.

Gārgi, m., N. of an astronomer, VarBṛ., Sch.

Gārgika, *as*, m. contemptuous metron. fr. *gārgī*, Pāṇ. iv, 1, 147, Kāś.

1. **Gārgī**, f. of °*gya*, see *gārga*. **-pútra** (*gā́rgī-*), m. (159, Kāś.) 'son of Gārgī,' N. of a teacher, ŚBr. xiv, 9, 4, 30. **-brāhmaṇa**, n., N. of a section of the ŚBr. (xiv, 6, 6) called after Gārgī (Vācaknavī). **-māta**, = °*tri*, Pāṇ. vii, 3, 107, Pat.

2. **Gārgī**, ind. fr. °*gya*. **-bhūta**, mfn. one who has become a Gārgya, vi, 4, 152, Kāś.

Gārgīputrakâyaṇi, *is*, m. a descendant of Gārgī-putra, iv, 1, 159, Kāś.

Gārgīputrâyaṇi, °**putri**, *is*, m. id., ib.

1. **Gārgīya**, Nom. P. °*yati*, to treat any one as a Gārgya, vi, 4, 152, Kāś.: Ā. °*yate*, to behave like a Gārgya, ib.

2. **Gārgīya**, mfn. coming from or composed by Garga, VarBṛS. xi, 1; coming from Gārgya, Kāś. on Pāṇ. iv, 2, 114 & vii, 1, 2; m. pl. (i, 1, 73, Pat. & Vārtt. 1, Pat.) the pupils of the descendants of Garga, iv, 1, 89, Vārtt. 2, Pat. & Kāś.; the pupils of Gārgyāyaṇa, 91, Kāś.

Gārgeya, m. metron. fr. *gārgī*, 1, Vārtt. 9, Pat.; 147, Kāś.; mfn. composed by Garga (Śruti), Parāś. i.

Gārgya, mfn. fr. *garga*, AV. Pariś. lxxi, 23; ifc. (after numerals) for °*rgī*, cf. *daśa-*, *pañca-*; m. (Pāṇ. iv, 1, 105) patr. fr. *garga*, N. of several teachers of Gr., of the ritual &c. (one is said to be the author of the Pada-p. of the SV., Nir. iv, 4, Sch.), ŚBr. xiv, 5, 1, 1; BṛĀrUp.; Lāṭy.; ĀśvGṛ.; ŚāṅkhGṛ.; Prāt.; Kauś. &c. (*vriddha-g°*, 'the old Gārgya,' MBh. xiii &c.); N. of a king of the Gandharvas, R. vi, 92, 70; (°*gī*), f., see s. v. *gārga*; (*ās*), m. pl., N. of a people, MBh. vii, 396. **-tara**, m. a Garga superior to a Gārgya or a superior Gārgya, Pāṇ. v, 3, 55, Pat. 39 f. & 42. **-tva**, n. the state of a descendant of Garga, i, 2, 58, Vārtt. 1, Pat. **-pariśishṭa**, n., N. of a section of the AV. Pariś., Nirṇayas.

Gārgyāyaṇa, m. (Pat.; Kāś. on Pāṇ. iv, 1, 101 & i, 2, 66) patr. fr. *gārgya*, N. of a teacher, BṛĀrUp.; pl., Pravar. i, 1; (*ī*), f. = *gārgī*, Pāṇ. iv, 1, 17, Kāś.; Pat. on vi, 3, 34, Vārtt. 4 & on 35, Vārtt. 11.

Gārgyāyaṇaka, mfn. (cf. *gārgaka*) belonging to the Gārgyāyaṇas, Pāṇ. iv, 1, 90, Vārtt. 5, Pat.; worshipping Gārgyāyaṇa, ib.; n. an assemblage of Gārgyāyaṇas, ib.

Gārgyāyaṇi, patr. fr. °*ṇa*. See *gāṅgyāyani*.

Gārgyāyaṇīya, pl. the pupils of °*yaṇa*, 91, Kāś.

गार्गर्य *gārgarya*, *as*, m. patr. fr. *gargara*, g. *kurv-ādi* (*gārgya*, Kāś.)

गार्गि *gārgi*, &c. See *gārga*.

गार्जर *gārjara*, *as*, m. a carrot, L.

गार्तक *gārtaka*, mfn. fr. *garta*, g. *dhūmâdi*.

गार्त्समद *gārtsamada*, mfn. relating to Gṛitsamada, AitBr. v, 2, 4; ŚāṅkhŚr.; MBh. xiii, 2006; m. a descendant of Gṛitsamada, ĀśvŚr.; (pl.) Pravar. i, 7; n., N. of a Sāman.

गार्दभ *gā́rdabha*, mfn. (fr. *gard°*), belonging to or coming from an ass, AV. vi, 72, 3; MBh. viii, xii; Suśr.; drawn by asses (a cart), Āp. i, 32, 25.

Gārdabharathika, mfn. fit for a donkey-cart, Pāṇ. vi, 2, 155, Kāś. (also *a-*, *vi-*, neg.)

Gārdabhi, *is*, m., N. of a man, Pravar. i, 2 (v. l. *gardabha*); MBh. xiii, 258.

Gārdabhin, *inas*, m. pl., N. of a dynasty, BhP. xii, 1, 27; (cf. *gardabhila*.)

गार्द्ध्य *gārddhya*, *am*, n. (fr. *griddha*), desire, greediness, Śiś. (? *ati-*); HYog. i, 31; Vop. xi, xxvi.

Gārdhra (often wrongly spelt *gārdha*), mfn. (fr. *gridhra*, Pāṇ. iv, 3, 156, Vārtt. 4, Pat.) 'vulturine,' in comp.; rapacious, greedy (?), W.; m. = *-paksha*, W.; (for *gārddhya*) desire, greediness, W. **-paksha**, m. an arrow decorated with vulture's feathers, L. **-pattra**, mfn. decorated with vulture's feathers (as an arrow), MBh. iv, v, vi, viii. **-prishṭa** (for *-spṛ°*; in Prākrit *geddha-paṭṭhaga*), 'touched (i. e. seized) by vultures,' a kind of death not sanctioned by the Jainas (probably with reference to the Pārsī custom of exposing corpses to vultures). **-rājita**, mfn. = *-pattra*, iii, 12230. **-vājita**, mfn. id., iv, 1515. **-vāsas**, mfn. id., iii, 1350.

गार्भ *gārbha*, mfn. (fr. *gárbha*), born from a womb, BhP. iii, 7, 27; relating to a fœtus or to gestation, Mn. ii, 27.

Gārbhâyaṇa, m. pl. patr., Pravar. i, 7.

Gārbhika, mfn. relating to the womb, ib.

Gārbhiṇa, *am*, n. (fr. *garbhiṇī*), a number of pregnant women, g. *bhikshâdi*.

Gārbhiṇya, *am*, n. id., L.

गार्मुत *gārmutá*, mfn. made from the bean called *garmút*, MaitrS. ii, 2, 4; TS. ii; (*gānm°*) Kāṭh. x, 11; m. the bean called *garmút*, ĀpŚr. xvi, 19; n. a kind of honey, Pāṇ. iv, 3, 116, Vārtt. 2, Pat. (vv. ll. *kārm°* & *kārmuka*, 117, Kāś.)

गार्ष्टेय *gārshṭeyá*, mfn. (proparox., Pāṇ. iv, 1, 136) born from a heifer (*grishṭí*), RV. x, 111, 2.

गार्ह *gārha*, mfn. (fr. *grihá*), 'domestic,' in comp. **-medha**, m. (= *griha-m°*) a domestic sacrifice, BhP. v, 11, 2.

Gārhakamedhika, *ās*, m. pl. (scil. *dharmās*) the duties of a householder (*griha[ka]-medhin*), x, 59, 43.

Gārhapatá, *am*, n. (fr. *grihá-pati*, g. *aśva-paty-ādi*) the position and dignity of a householder, ŚBr. v; TāṇḍyaBr. x; KātyŚr.; Lāṭy.; (cf. *kuru-g°*.)

Gārhapatya, mfn. with *agni*, or m. (Pāṇ. iv, 4, 90) the householder's fire (received from his father and transmitted to his descendants, one of the three sacred fires, being that from which sacrificial fires are lighted, RTL. 364), AV.; VS.; ŚBr. &c.; m. or n. = *-sthāna*, ŚBr. vii, 1, 2, 12; KātyŚr. xvii, 1, 3; m. pl., N. of a class of manes, MBh. ii, 462; n. the government of a family, position of a householder, household, RV. i, 15, 12; vi, 15, 19; x, 85, 27 & 36. **-sthāna**, n. the place where the Gārhapatya fire is kept, KātyŚr. **Gārhapatyâgārá**, m. id., ŚBr. i; KātyŚr. iv, 7, 15. **Gārhapatyâyatana**, n. id., 8, 24. **Gārhapatyêshṭakā**, f. a kind of sacrificial brick, Vait. xxviii, 25.

Gārhasthya (sometimes wrongly spelt °*stha*), mfn. (fr. *griha-stha*), fit for or incumbent on a householder, MBh. ix, xiii; n. the order or estate of a householder, of the father or mother of a family, Gaut. iii, 36; MBh. i, iii; R. ii, &c.; household, domestic affairs, MBh. xiv, 162; BhP. iii; ix, 6, 47.

Gārhya, mfn. (fr. *grihá*), domestic.

गाल 1. & 2. *gāla.* See √1. & 2. *gal*.

Gālakya-ja, *am*, n. a kind of salt, Gal.

1. **Gālana.** See √1. *gal*.

गालडि *gālaḍi*, m. metron. fr. *galaḍā*, g. *bāhv-ādi* (Gaṇar. 206); cf. *jāl°*, *lāgahi*.

गालन 2. *gālana*, *am*, n. reviling, MBh. xii, 68, 31, Sch.; ?, HYog. iii, 110.

Gāli, *ayas*, f. pl. reviling speech, invectives, execrations, Bhartṛ.; Rājat. vi, 157. **-dāna**, n. reviling, vii, 305. **-pradāna**, n. id., Prab. ii, 8/7, Sch. **-mat**, mfn. uttering execrations, Bhartṛ. iii, 99.

2. **Gālin**, mfn. reviling, abusive, W.; (*inī*), f. a particular position of the fingers, Tantras.

Gālī, *yas*, f. pl. = °*li*, Rājat. vii, 1172.

गालव *gālava*, *as*, m. Symplocos racemosa (the bark of which is used in dyeing) or a pale species of the same, L.; a kind of ebony, L.; N. of an old sage and preceptor (son [Hariv.] or pupil [MBh.] of Viśvā-mitra), BṛĀrUp.; VāyuP. (v. l. *gol°*); (a grammarian) Nir. iv, 3 & Pāṇ.; (author of a Dharma-śāstra, W.); m. pl. (i, 1, 44, Vārtt. 17, Pat.) the descendants of Gālava, Pravar. i, 1; iv, 1; Hariv. 1467; N. of a school of the SV. **-gaḍula**, m. = *gaḍula-gālava*, Gaṇar. 89, Sch.

Gālavi, m. patr. fr. °*va*, MBh. ix, 2995; VāyuP.

गालि *gāli*, &c. See 2. *gālana*.

गालोडय *gāloḍaya*, P. °*ḍayati* = *ḍitam ā-cashṭe*, Vop. xxi, 15: Ā. °*ḍayate*, to examine, investigate, Dhātup. xxxv, 86.

Gāloḍita, mfn. = *unmāda-śīla*, L.; *rogârtta*, L.; *mūrkha*, L.; n. examination, investigation, Vop.

Gāloḍya, *am*, n. (cf. *gal°*, *gil°*) the seed of the lotus, Bhpr. v, 6, 88; (cf. *aṅka-lodya*, *aṅga-l°*.)

गावय *gāvaya*, mfn. coming from the Gayal (*gavayá*, as beef), Vishṇ. lxxx, 9.

गावल्गणि *gāvalgaṇi*, *is*, m. (fr. *gavalgaṇa*), patr. of Saṃjaya, MBh. i, ii, v, xv; BhP. i, 13, 30.

गावामयनिक *gāvāmayanika*, mfn. belonging to the ceremony called *gavām-ayana*, Nyāyam.

Gāvishṭhira, m. (g. *haritâdi*) patr. fr. *gav°*, ĀśvŚr. xii, 14, 1 (Pravar. iii, 1).

Gāvishṭhirāyaṇa, *as*, m. id., g. *haritâdi*.

Gāvishṭhila, °**lāyana**, ib. (Śākaṭ.; Gaṇar.)

Gāvī, f. (in dialect) for *gó*, a cow, Pat. Introd. 35; 94; 97, & on Vārtt. 6.

गावीधुक *gāvīdhuká*, mfn. made from the Gavīdhuka grass, MaitrS. ii, 6, 3; TS.; TBr.; ĀpŚr.

Gāvedhuká, mf(*ī*, g. *bilvâdi*)n. id., ŚBr. v; KātyŚr. i, 1, 12; xv, 1, 27; ŚāṅkhGṛ. v, 6, 2.

गावेश *gāvêsa*, v. l. for °*vesha*.

Gāvesha, fr. *gav-esha*, g. *saṃkalâdi*.

गाह *gāh* (cf. √*gādh*), cl. 1. Ā. *gā́hate* (ep. also P. °*hati*; perf. *jagāhe*, fut. 2nd *gāhishyate* [fut. 1st *-gāhitā* or *-gāḍhā*, Kāś. on Pāṇ. vii, 2, 44]; aor. *agāhishṭa* [Bhaṭṭ. xv, 59] or *agāḍha*, Pāṇ. viii, 3, 13, Sch. [not in Kāś.]; inf. *gāhitum*) to dive into, bathe in, plunge into (acc.), penetrate, enter deeply into (acc.), AitBr. iii, 48, 9; TāṇḍyaBr. xiv f.; Kauś.; MBh. &c. (with *kaksham*, 'to be a match for (gen.),' Vcar. ii, 11); to roam, range, rove, Megh. 49; Pāṇ. ii, 4, 30, Kāś.; Bhaṭṭ.; to be absorbed in (acc.), Kum. v, 46.

Gāḍha, mfn. dived into, bathed in, Ragh. ix, 72; 'deeply entered,' pressed together, tightly drawn, closely fastened, close, fast (opposed to *śithila*), MBh. iv, 152 (said of a bow); R.; Ragh. &c.; thick, dense, L.; strong, vehement, firm, MBh. &c.; (*am*, in comp. *a-*), ind. tightly, closely, firmly, Mṛicch.; Megh.; Suśr. &c.; strongly, much, very much, excessively, heavily, MBh. &c. **-karṇa**, m. an ear penetrated by sound, an attentive ear, BhP. iv, 29, 40. **-tara-** in comp. or °**ram**, ind. more tightly or closely or firmly,

Pañcat.; Amar.; more intensely, Suśr. **-tā**, f. closeness, firmness, hardness, intensity, Kathās. xc. **-tva**, n. intensity, Daś. viii, 78. **-nidra**, mfn. deeply sleeping, x, 70. **-mushṭi**, mfn. 'close-fisted,' avaricious, niggardly, L.; m. a scymitar, L. **-vacas**, m. 'making a penetrating sound,' a frog, Gal. **-varcas**, mfn. costive, constipated, Car.; *-tva*, n. costiveness, Suśr. **-śoka-prahāra**, mfn. inflicting the keenest anguish, W. **Gāḍhâṅgada**, mfn. having closely-fitting bracelets, Ragh. xvi, 60. **Gāḍhâliṅgana**, n. a close embrace, Amar.; Hit.; Vet. i, 15. **Gāḍhī-karaṇa**, n. making stiff.

Gāha, mfn. (g. *pacâdi*) ifc. 'diving into,' see *uda-*, *udaka-*; (*ás*), m. depth, interior, innermost recess, RV. ix, 110, 8; (*ī*), f., g. *gaurâdi* (Gaṇar.)

Gāhana, n. diving into, bathing, Daś. xii, 111.

Gāhanīya, mfn. to be dived into, 98 & 111.

Gāhita, mfn. plunged into, bathed in, W.; shaken, agitated, W.; destroyed, W.; (*am*), n. depth, interior, MBh. iii, 8772.

Gāhitṛi, mfn. (cf. Pāṇ. vii, 2, 44, Kāś.) one who plunges into or bathes, W.; one who penetrates, W.; shaking, agitating, W.; destroying, W.

Gāhya, mfn., see *dur-g°*.

गिद् gida, *as*, m., N. of a divine being (Sch.), TāṇḍyaBr. i, 7, 7; Lāṭy. ii, 8, 11.

गिध्र gidhra, g. *mūla-vibhujâdi* (not in Pat. & Kāś.)

गिन्दुक ginduka=*gend°*, L., Sch.

गिर् 1. gir, mfn. (√1. *gṝ*) addressing, invoking, praising, RV.; (*ír*), f. invocation, addressing with praise, praise, verse, song, RV. (the Maruts are called 'sons of praise,' *sūnávo giráḥ*, i, 37, 10); AV.; speech, speaking, language, voice, words (e.g. *mānushīm giram* √1. *kṛi*, to assume a human voice, Nal. i, 25; *girām prabhavishṇuḥ* [VarBṛS.] or *pati* [VarYogay.] = *gir-īśa*, q. v.; *tad-girā*, on his advice, Kathās. lxxv), ChUp.; Mn.; Yājñ.; MBh. &c.; = *gīr-devī*, fame, celebrity, W.; a kind of mystical syllable, RāmatUp.; [cf. Hib. *gair*, 'an outcry, shout;' Gk. γῆρυς.] **-1. -īśa**, m. 'lord of speech,' N. of Bṛihaspati (regent of the planet Jupiter), L. **-vaṇas** (*gír-*), mfn. (fr. *vanas*), 'delighting in invocations,' fond of praise (Indra, Agni), RV. (once said of Soma, ix, 64, 14). **-vaṇasyú**, mfn. id., x, 111, 1 (Indra). **-van** (*gír-*), mfn. id., ŚBr. iii (Indra); (*girva*)-*vāh*, m(nom. pl. *-vāhas*)fn. bearing one who is fond of hymns, SV. (*gir-vāhas*, RV. vi, 24, 6). **-vāhas** (*gír-*), mfn. one to whom invocations are addressed, praised in song (Indra), RV.

1. Gira, ifc. = 1. *gir*, speech, voice, VarBṛS. xxxii, 5; 1. (*ā*), f. (g. *ajâdi*, Gaṇar. 41, Sch.) id., L.

2. Girā, instr. of 1. *gír*. **-vṛídh**, mfn. delighting in or thriving by praise (Soma), RV. ix, 26, 6.

Girâṅkas, see *ā-g°*.

1. Giri, loc. of 1. *gír*. **-jā́**, see s. v. 3. *girí*.

Gī (in comp. for 1. *gír*). **-ratha**, m. 'the vehicle of speech,' = *gir-īśa*, L.

Gīḥ (in comp. for 1. *gír*). **-kāmya**, Nom. P. *°yati*, to like speech, Pāṇ. viii, 3, 38, Vārtt. 2, Pat. **-pati**, m. = *gīsh-p°*, g. *ahar-ādi*.

Gīr (in comp. for 1. *gír*). **-devī**, f. the goddess of speech, Sarasvatī, L. **-pati**, m. = *gīsh-p°*, g. *ahar-ādi*. **-bāṇa**, see *-vāṇa*. **-latā**, f. Cardiospermum Halicacabum, L. **-vat**, mfn. Ved. 'possessed of speech,' Pāṇ. viii, 2, 15, Kāś.; (cf. *gír-van*.) **-vāṇa** (or *-bāṇa*), 'whose arrow is speech' (a corruption fr. *gír-vaṇas*), a god, deity, BhP. iii, viii f.; Kathās. cxvi f.; *-kusuma*, n. 'flower of the gods,' cloves, L.; *-pada-mañjari*, f., N. of a work; *-vartman*, n. 'path of gods,' the sky, Kād.; *-senā-pati*, m. 'army-chief of the gods,' N. of Skanda, Bālar. iv, 17; *°ṇêndra-sarasvatī*, m., N. of a teacher.

Gīsh (in comp. for 1. *gír*). **-pati**, m. (Pāṇ. viii, 2, 70, Kāś.) = *gir-īśa*, L.; a learned man, Paṇḍit, L.

Gīs (in comp. for 1. *gír*). **-tarā**, f. (compar.) excellent speech or voice, Pāṇ. viii, 3, 101, Kāś. **-tva**, n. the state of speech or voice, Vop. vii, 25.

गिर् 2. gir, mfn (√2. *gṝ*) ifc. 'swallowing,' see *gara-* & *muhur-gir*.

2. Gira, mfn. id., Vop. xxvi, 32.

Giraṇa, *am*, n. (= *gilana*) swallowing, W.

2. Giri, *is*, f. id., g. *krishy-ādi*.

Girita, mfn. swallowed, L., Sch.

गिर् 3. gir, m. = *giri*, a mountain, RV. v, 41, 14 & vii, 39, 5; Śiś. iv, 59.

3. Gira, ifc. = *°ri* (e.g. *anu-giram*), Pāṇ. v, 4, 112. **-pura**, n., N. of a town, MS. (A.D. 1511).

3. Girí, *is*, m. (for *gari*, Zd. *gairi*, cf. *gurú*, *gárīyas*; ifc., Pāṇ. vi, 2, 94) a mountain, hill, rock, elevation, rising-ground (often connected with *párvata*, 'a mountain having many parts' [cf. *párvan*], RV.; AV.), RV. &c.; the number 'eight' (there being 8 mountains which surround mount Meru), Śrut.; a cloud, Naigh. i, 10; Nir.; Sāy.; a particular disease of the eyes, Pāṇ. vi, 2, 2, Sch. (*kiri*, Kāś.); Uṇ.; = *-guḍa*, L.; a peculiar defect in mercury, L.; = *gairīyaka*, L.; a honorific N. given to one of the ten orders of the Daś-nāmī Gosains (founded by ten pupils of Śaṃkarâcārya; the word *giri* is added to the name of each member; cf. *gairika*); N. of a son of Śvaphalka, VP.; f. (= *girikā*) a mouse, L., Sch.; mfn. coming from the mountains, RV. vi, 66, 11; venerable, L. (R. iv, 37, 2, Sch.); [cf. Slav. *gora*; Afghan. *ghur*.] **-kacchapa**, m. a mountain tortoise, MBh. xiii, 6151. **-kaṇṭaka**, m. Indra's thunderbolt, L. **-kadamba**, m. a mountain Kadamba tree, L. **-kadambaka**, m. id., Suśr. vi. **-kadalī**, f. the mountain or wild Kadalī, L. **-kandara**, m. a mountain cave or cavern, W. **-karṇā**, f. Clitoria Ternatea, L. **-karṇikā**, f. id., i, iv; 'having mountains for seed-vessels,' the earth, L.; a variety of Achyranthes with white blossoms, L. **-karṇī**, f. = *°ṇā*, L.; Alhagi Maurorum, L. **-kāṇa**, mfn. one-eyed from the disease called *giri*, Pāṇ. vi, 2, 2, Sch. (*kiri-k°*, Kāś.). **-kānana**, n. a mountain-grove, W. **-kuhara**, n. = *-kandara*. **-kūṭa**, n. the summit of a mountain, BhP. v. **-kshít**, mfn. living in mountains or on high (Vishṇu), RV. i, 154, 3; N. of an Auccāmanyava, TāṇḍyaBr. x, 5, 7 (cf. *gairikshitá*). **-kshipa**, m., N. of a son of Śvaphalka, Hariv. 2084 (v. l. *-raksha*). **-gaṅgā**, f. 'the mountain Gaṅgā,' N. of a river. **-guḍa**, m. a ball for playing with, L. **-guhā**, f. = *-kandara*, W. **-gairika-dhātu**, for *girer gair°*, MBh. v, 7273. **-cakravartin**, m. 'the mountain-king,' N. of the Himavat, Kum. vii, 52. **-cará**, mfn. living in mountains, VS. xvi, 22; (as elephants) Śak. ii, 4; m. a wild elephant, Kād. **-cārin**, mfn. living in mountains (as elephants), VarBṛS. **-ja**, m. 'mountain-born,' the Mahwa tree (Bassia), L.; Bauhinia variegata, L.; N. of a Bābhravya, AitBr. vii, 1, 7; (*ā*), f., N. of several plants (a kind of lemon tree; *kārī*; *kshudra-pāshāṇa-bhedā*; *giri-kadalī*; *trāyamāṇā*; *śveta-buhvā*), L.; N. of the goddess Pārvatī (as the daughter of the personified Himâlaya mountain), BhP. i, x; Kathās.; Ānand.; n. talc, L.; red chalk, ruddle, L.; iron, L.; benzoin or gum benjamin, W.; (*girijā*)-*kumāra*, v. l. for *giri-rāja-k°*; *-dhava*, m. 'lord of Girijā or Pārvatī,' N. of a Śiva, Kathās. lii, 403; *-pati*, m. id., vii, lix, cvii; *-putra*, m., N. of a chief of the Gāṇapatyas, Śaṃkar. xv, 25 ff. & 50 (*-suta*, 51); *-priya*, m. = *-dhava*, SŚaṃkar. i, 40; *girijâmala*, n. talc, L., Sch.; (*girijā*)-*māhātmya*, n. 'the glory of Girijā,' N. of a work. **-jā́**, mfn. proceeding from the mountains [NBD.; 'proceeding from the voice' (*giri*, loc. fr. 1. *gir*), Sāy.], RV. v, 87, 1. **-jāla**, n. a range of mountains, R. iv, 43, 11 & 25. **-jvara**, m. = *-kaṇṭaka*, L.; *-samudbhava* (= *giri-ja*), red chalk, ruddle, Gal. **-ṇakha**, g. *girinady-ādi*. **-ṇadī**, f. (g. *girinady-ādi*) a mountain-torrent, Śāntiś. **-ṇaddha**, mfn. enclosed by mountains, g. *girinady-ādi*. **-ṇitamba**, m. the declivity of a mountain, ib. **-trá**, mfn. protecting mountains (Rudra-Śiva), VS. xvi, 3; BhP. ii, iv, viii. **-durga**, n. 'of difficult access as being surrounded by mountains,' a hill-fort, Mn. vii, 70 f.; MBh.; N. of a locality, Romakas. **-duhitṛi**, f. (= *-jā*) N. of Pārvatī, Bālar. iv, 26. **-dvāra**, n. a mountain-pass, MBh. vii, 349. **-dhara**, m., N. of a copyist of the 17th century. **-dhātu**, m. (= *-ja*) red chalk, R. ii, 96, 19; m. pl. mountain-minerals, 63, 18. **-dhvaja**, m. = *-jvara*, W. **-nakha**, g. *girinady-ādi*. **-nagara**, n. (g. 1. *kshubhnâdi*) 'mountain-city,' N. of a town in Dakshiṇā-patha (the modern Girnār, RTL. p. 349), VarBṛS. xiv, 11. **-nadikā**, f. a small mountain-torrent, Kād. **-nadī**, f. = *-ṇadī*, MBh. i, 6066; Nal.; Pañcat.; Hit.; N. of a torrent, g. 2. *kshubhnâdi*; *°dy-ādi*, a Gaṇa of Kāty. (Pāṇ. viii, 4, 10, Vārtt.) **-naddha** = *-ṇaddha*, g. *girinady-ādi*. **-nandinī**, f. 'mountain-daughter,' a mountain-torrent, Hariv. 7738; = *-duhitṛi*, Prasannar. i, ½. **-nitamba**, m. = *-ṇit°*, g. *girinady-ādi*. **-nimnagā**, f. = *-nadī*, R. ii, 97, 1. **-nimba**, m. the mountain Nimba tree, L. **-pati**, m. 'mountain-chief,' a great rock, Bālar. vii, 29. **-pára**, mfn. following after *giri* (as a N. of Rudra), MaitrS. i, iv. **-pīlu**, m. the mountain Pīlu tree (Grewia asiatica), L. **-pura**, n. mountain-town (perhaps N. of a town), Hariv. 5161. **-pushpaka**, n. a fragrant resin (benzoin), L. **-pṛishṭha**, n. the top of a hill, Mn. vii, 147. **-prapāta**, m. = *-nitamba*, MBh. xiii, 4729. **-prastha**, m. the table-land of a mountain, R. ii, 97, 1. **-priyā**, f. 'fond of mountains,' the female of Bos grunniens, L. **-bāndhava**, m. 'friend of mountains,' N. of Śiva; cf. *-tra*. **-budhna** (*°rí-*), mf(*ā*)n. = *ádri-b°*, ŚBr. vii, 5, 2, 18. **-bhid**, mfn. breaking through mountains (a river), KātyŚr.; ĀpŚr.; f. Plectranthus scutellarioides, Bhpr. **-bhū**, f. (= *-jā*) the plant *kshudra-pāshāṇa-bhedā*, L.; N. of Pārvatī, W. **-bhráj**, mfn. breaking forth from mountains, RV. x, 68, 1. **-mallikā**, f. Wrightia antidysenterica, Car. vii, 5. **-mātrá**, mfn. having the size or dimensions of a mountain, ŚBr. i. **-māna**, m. '= *-mātrá*,' a large elephant, L. **-māla**, *°laka*, m., N. of a tree, KātyŚr. xxii, 3, 9, Sch. **-mṛid**, f. (= *-ja*) 'mountain-soil,' red chalk, L.; *-bhava*, m. id., L. **-meda**, m. Vachellia farnesiana, L. **-raksha**, m., v. l. for *-kshipa*, q. v. **-rakshas**, m. id., VP. **-rāj**, m. 'mountain-king,' N. of the Himavat, MBh. vi, 3419; BhP. vi, viii. **-rāja-kumāra**, m., N. of a pupil of Śaṃkarâcārya, Śaṃkar. lxxi. **-rūpa** (*°rí-*), mfn. mountain-shaped, TBr. iii. **-vartikā**, f. the mountain quail, Car. i, 27. **-vāsin**, m. 'living or growing on or in mountains,' a kind of bulbous plant (*hasti-kanda*), L. **-vraja**, m. 'mountain-fenced,' N. of the capital of Magadha, MBh.; Hariv. 6598; R. i, ii; VarBṛS. **-śa**, m. (g. *lomâdi*) 'inhabiting mountains,' N. of Rudra-Śiva, VS. xvi, 4 (voc.); MBh.; Ragh.; Kum. &c.; N. of a Rudra, RāmatUp.; (*ā*), f. = *-śāyikā*, Suśr. i, 46, 2, 14; N. of Durgā, Hariv. 9423 (v. l. *guhasya jananī*). **-śanta**, mfn. (= *-śa*) inhabiting mountains (Rudra-Śiva), VS. xvi, 2 f. **-śayá**, mfn. id., 29. **-śarman**, m., N. of a teacher, VBr. **-śāyikā**, f. (= *-śā*) a kind of bird, Gal. **-śālinī**, f. = *-karṇā*, VāmP. **-śikhara**, m. n. = *-kūṭa*, BhP. v; Nāg. iv, ⅞. **-śṛiṅga**, n. the peak of a mountain, W.; N. of a place, AV.-Pariś. li, 4; of a Gaṇeśa, L. **-shad**, mfn. sitting on mountains (Rudra), PārGṛ. **-shṭhá**, mfn. (Nir. i, 20) inhabiting mountains (said of deer and the Maruts), RV.; coming from the mountains (Soma), RV. **-sambhava**, m. a kind of hill-mouse, Gal.; n. bitumen, Gal. **-sarpa**, m. a kind of snake, Suśr. v, 4, 32. **-sānu**, n. = *-prastha*, L. **-sāra**, m. iron, L.; tin, L.; N. of the Malaya mountains (in the south of India), L.; *-maya*, mf(*ī*)n. made of iron, MBh. vi; R. vi. **-sutá**, m. 'mountain-son,' N. of a divine being, MaitrS. ii, 9, 1; (*ā*), f. (= *-jā*) N. of Pārvatī, VarBṛS.; Pañcat.; (*gireḥ sutā*, VāmP.); *°tā-kānta*, m. 'Pārvatī's lover,' N. of Śiva, Kathās. cxxiv. **-sena**, m., N. of a man, Buddh. **-sravā**, f. = *-ṇadī*, MBh. xiii, 6362. **-hvā**, f. 'called after a mountain,' = *-karṇā*, Suśr. iv f. **Girī-√kṛi**, to heap up so as to form a mountain, HPariś. **Girîndra**, m. 'prince among mountains,' a high mountain, Kām. i, 42; (= *°rî*) the number 'eight.' 2. **Girîśa**, m. (= *°rîndra*) a high mountain; N. of the Himavat, L.; 'mountain-lord,' Śiva, MBh. xiii, 6348; Kum.; one of the 11 Rudras, Yājñ. ii, 1⅔, 34; (*ā*), f., N. of Durgā, Hariv. 9424 (cf. *giri-śā*). **Giry-āhvā**, f. = *°ri-hvā*, Suśr. v, 2, 50.

Giriká, mfn.? (said of the hearts of the gods), MaitrS. ii, 9, 9; (*kir°*, VS.); m. Śiva, MBh. xii, 10414; (g. *yāvâdi*, Gaṇar. 189, Sch.) = *giri-guḍa*, L.; N. of a chief of the Nāgas, Buddh.; of an attendant of Śiva; (*ā*), f. 'making hills (?),' a mouse, L.; N. of the wife of Vasu (daughter of the mountain Kolāhala and of the river Śaktimatī), MBh. i 2371; Hariv. 1805; (cf. *caṇḍa-g°*.)

Giriyaka, *°yāka*, *as*, m. = *giri-guḍa*, L.

गिरित girita. See 2. *gir*.

गिरिश giri-śa, &c. See s. v. 3. *girí*.

1. Gir-īśa & **2. girîśa**. See 1. *gir* & 3. *girí*.

Gír-vaṇas, &c. See 1. *gír*.

गिल gila, mfn. (= 2. *gira*) ifc. 'swallowing,' see *a-saṃsūkta-gilá*, *timiṃ-*; m. the citron tree, L. **-gila**, mfn. swallowing, Pāṇ. vi, 3, 70, Vārtt. 7; cf. *timiṃ-*. **-grāha**, m. a crocodile, L.

Gilat, mfn. (pr. p. √2. *gṝ*) swallowing, BhP. x, 13, 31.

Gilana, *am*, n. swallowing, Bhpr.
Gilāyu, *us*, m. hard tumor in the throat, Suśr.
Gili, *is*, f. = 2. *giri*, L., Sch.
Gilita, mfn. (= *girita*) swallowed, Vet. xi, $\frac{8}{9}$.

गिलोड्य *giloḍya*, (cf. *gal°*, *gāl°*) the bulb of a small variety of the Nymphæa, Car. i, 27; Suśr.

गिष्णु *gishṇu* (= *gesh°*), a professional singer, Uṇ. k.; a chanter of the SV., ib.; an actor, W.

गीःकाम्य *gīḥ-kāmya*, *-pati*. See 1. *gír*.

गीत *gītá*, mfn. (√*gai*) sung, chanted, praised in songs, Mn. ix, 42; MBh. &c.; n. singing, song, VS. xxx; TBr. iii; ŚBr. iii, vi; Āp. &c.; N. of four hymns addressed to Kṛishṇa; (*ā*), f. a song, sacred song or poem, religious doctrines declared in metrical form by an inspired sage (cf. Agastya-g°, Bhagavad-g° [often called Gītā, Prab. vi, $\frac{1}{16}$ &c.], Rāma-g°, Śiva-g°); N. of a metre. **–kaṇḍikā**, f., N. of a SV.Pariś. **–krama**, m. the arrangement of a song, W.; = *varṇa*, L. **–kshama**, mfn. (anything) that may be sung, Śak. vii, 5. **–gaṅgā-dhara**, n. 'the ocean of songs,' N. of a poem by Kalyāṇa. **–girīśa**, n., N. of a poem by Rāma. **–govinda**, n. 'Govinda (i. e. Kṛishṇa) celebrated in song,' N. of a lyrical drama by Jayadeva (probably written in the beginning of the twelfth century; it is a mystical erotic poem describing the loves of Kṛishṇa and the Gopīs, especially of Kṛishṇa and Rādhā, who is supposed to typify the human soul). **–jña**, mfn. versed in the art of singing, acquainted with songs, Yājñ iii, 116. **–nṛitya**, n. sg. song and dance, R. i, 24, 5; a particular dance. **–pustaka**, n., N. of a collection of songs, Buddh.; *-saṃgraha*, m. id., ib. **–priyā**, f. 'fond of songs,' N. of one of the mothers attending on Skanda, MBh. ix, 2625. **–bandhana**, n. an epic poem to be sung, R. vii, 71, 21. **–mārga**, m. = *daśa-pada-caṃkramaṇa*, Daś. xi, 43. **–modin**, m. 'gladdening with songs,' a Kiṃnara or celestial chorister, L. **–vādana**, n. sg. singing and music, Mn. ii, 178. **–śāstra**, n. the science of song, W. **Gītâcārya**, m. a singing-master, Kathās. lxxi, 73. **Gītâyana**, mfn. accompanied with songs, BhP. iv, 4, 5. **Gītârtha**, m. an ascetic who has (sung, i. e.) finished his studies, HPariś. viii, 385; xiii, 82.

Gītaka, n. a song, hymn, Yājñ. iii, 113; BhP. viii; VP. (Sāh. i, $\frac{2}{3}$, 14); Kathās.; a kind of metre (*narkuṭaka*), VarBṛS. civ, 52; melody (seven in number), MārkP. xxiii, 51 & 59; (*ikā*), f. a short song or hymn, MBh. iii, 8173 (*gāthikā*, ed. Bomb.); a metre of 4 × 20 syllables; a stanza composed in the Gīti metre, Kathās. cxvii, 109 (with reference to 65 f.); (cf. *daśa-gītikā*.)

Gīti, *is*, f. song, singing, Nir. x; Lāṭy.; Jaim.; Śak.; a metre consisting of 4 lines of 12 and 18 syllabic instants alternately. **–viśesha**, m. a kind of song, W. **–sūtra**, n. a Sūtra composed in the Gīti metre, Sūryad. (on Āryabh.) Introd. 43. **Gītyāryā**, f. a metre of 4 × 16 short syllables.

Gītin, mfn. one who recites in a singing manner, PāṇŚ. (RV.) 32.

Gíthā, f. (only for the etym. of *ud-gīthá*) a song, ŚBr. xiv, 4, 1, 25.

गीरथ *gī-ratha*. See 1. *gír*.

गीर्ण 1. *gīrṇa*, mfn. (√1. *gṛī*) praised, L.
1. **Gīrṇi**, *is*, f. praise, applause, W.; celebrity, W.

गीर्ण 2. *gīrṇá*, mfn. (√2. *gṛī*) swallowed, RV. x, 88, 2; AitBr. iii, 46; 'swallowed (voice),' i. e. not uttered, BhP. ix, 10, 13; (cf. *gara-gīrṇá*.)
2. **Gīrṇi**, *is*, f. swallowing, L.
Gīrvi, mfn. swallowing, Vop. xxvi, 167.

गीर्देवी *gīr-devī*, *-pati*, &c. See 1. *gír*.
Gīsh-pati, **gīs-tarā**, &c. See ib.

गु 1. *gu* (cf. √1. *gā*), cl. 1. Ā. *gávate*, to go, Naigh. ii, 14.
2. **Gu**, ifc. 'going,' see *ádhri-gu*, *vanar-gú* (cf. also *priyáṃgu*, *śāci-gu*); 'fit for,' see *tāta-gu*, *ni-gu*; (cf. *agre-gū*.)

गु 3. *gu*, cl. 1. Ā. *gavate*, to sound, Dhātup. xxii, 52: Intens. Ā. (1. & 3. sg. *jóguve*, p. *jóguvāna*) 'to cause to sound,' proclaim, RV. i, 61, 14; v, 64, 2; TBr. ii; Kāṭh. xiii, 11 f.: P. (impf. *agaṅgūyat* for *aguṅg°*) to shout with joy, Tāṇḍya-Br. xiv, 3, 19; (cf. *prati*-√3. *gu* & *jógū*.)

गु 4. *gu* (= √1. *gū*, q. v.), cl. 6. P. *guvati*, to void by stool, Dhātup. xxviii, 106; (cf. *vi-gūna*.)

गु 5. *gu*, ifc. = *gó*, 'cow; earth; ray' (Pāṇ. i, 2, 48), see *á-gu*, *anu-gu*, *anushṇa-gu*, *ádrishṭa-gu*, *upa-gu*, *ushṇa-gu*, *kṛiśá-gu*, *tamo-gu*, &c.; (*u*), n. water, L.; the hair on the body, L.

गुग्गुल *guggula*, *as*, m. (= *°lu*) bdellium, Hariv. 6283; VarBṛS. lvii, 3 & 5 (v. l. *°lu*); lxxvii, 9 (15). **Guggulâksha**, m., N. of a plant, Gal.
Gugguli, pl. N. of a family, Pravar. vi, 4.
Gúggulu, n. (= *gúlg°*) bdellium or the exudation of Amyris Agallochum (a fragrant gum resin, used as a perfume and medicament), AV. (called *saindhavá* or *samudríya*, 'obtained near rivers or the sea,' xix, 38, 2); Kauś.; ĀśvŚr. xi, 6, 3; m. id., Yājñ. i, 278; MBh. xiii; Suśr.; Bhpr.; = *-dru*, L.; (*ūs*), f. (Pāṇ. iv, 1, 71, Pat.) N. of an Apsaras, AV. iv, 37, 3; (cf. *kaṇa-*, *gaugguḷava* & *gaulg°*.) **–dru**, m. a variety of Moringa with red flowers, L.
Gugguluka, *as*, *ī*, m. f. a man or woman who deals in bdellium, g. *kisarâdi*.

गुंकार *guṃ-kāra*, *-karaṇa*. See *gum*.

गुङ्गु *guṅgú*, m. (Intens. √3. *gu*) 'N. of a man,' m. pl. his descendants, RV. x, 48, 8; (*ūs*), f. (= 1. *kuhū*) the new moon personified, ii, 32, 8.

गुच्छ *guccha*, *as*, m. (= *gutsa*) a bush, shrub, Mn. i, 48; Yājñ. ii, 229; Jain.; a bundle, bunch of flowers, cluster of blossoms, clump (of grass &c.), bunch (of peacock's feathers), Gīt. xi, 11; a pearl necklace of 32 (or of 70) strings (cf. *ardha-*), VarBṛS. lxxxi, 33; a section in a tale, Gal. **–kaṇiśa**, m. a kind of corn (*rāgin*), L.; (cf. *bahuta-ra-kaṇ°*.) **–karañja**, m. a variety of Karañja, L. **–dantikā**, f. Musa sapientum, L. **–pattra**, m. 'having bunches of leaves,' the palm tree, L. **–pushpa**, m. Alstonia scholaris, L.; (*ī*), f. Grislea tomentosa, L.; N. of a shrub (*śimṛiḍī*), L. **–pushpaka**, m. two varieties of Karañja (*rīṭhā-k°* & *guccha-k°*), L. **–phala**, m. 'bunch-fruited,' a kind of Karañja (*rīṭhā-karañja*), L.; Strychnos potatorum, L.; Mimusops hexandra, L.; (*ā*), f. = *-dantikā*, L.; the vine, L.; Solanum indicum, L.; Solanum Jacquini, L.; a kind of leguminous plant (*nishpāvī*), L. **–budhnā**, v. l. for *-vadhrā*. **–mūlikā**, f. Scirpus Kysoor, L. **–vadhrā**, f., N. of a plant (*gundālā*), L. **Gucchârka**, v. l. for *galv-arka*, L. **Gucchârdha**, m. a pearl necklace of twenty-four strings, L. **Gucchâhva-kanda**, m. a kind of esculent root (*gulañca-k°*), L.
Gucchaka, *as*, m. a bunch, bundle, cluster (of blossoms), bunch (of peacock's feathers), clump (of grass), L.; a pearl necklace of 32 strings, L.; = *gucchin*, L.; n. N. of a fragrant plant, Bhpr. v, 2, 107.
Gucchala, *as*, m. a kind of grass, Gal.
Gucchāla, m. Andropogon Schœnanthus, L.
Gucchin, *ī*, m. = *guccha-karañja*, L.

गुज् *guj* (= √*guñj*), cl. 1. 6. P. *gojati*, *gujati*, to buzz, hum, Dhātup. vii, 23; xxviii, 76.

गुज्जरी *gujjarī*, for *gurj°*.

गुञ्ज् *guñj* (= √*guj*), cl. 1. P. *°jati* (pr. p. *°jat*; perf. *juguñja*, Bhaṭṭ.), to buzz, hum, Ṛitus.; Kathās.; Gīt. &c.; (cf. *sam-ud*-√*guñj*.)
Guñja, m. humming, ŚārṅgP.; (= *guccha*) a bunch, bush, cluster of blossoms, nosegay, L.; (*ā*), f. humming, L.; a kettle-drum, Bhaṭṭ. xiv, 2; Abrus precatorius (bearing a red and black berry which forms the smallest of the jeweller's weights), Suśr.; VarBṛS.; Pañcat.; the berry of Abrus precatorius (averaging about $1\frac{5}{16}$ grains troy) or the artificial weight called after it (weighing about $2\frac{3}{16}$ grains, = $\frac{1}{4}$ Ādya-māshaka or Māshaka, = 3 or 2 barley-corns, = 4 grains of rice, = 2 grains of wheat, L.; with physicians 7 Guñjās = 1 Mātha, with lawyers $7\frac{1}{2}$ Guñjās), Yājñ. iii, 273; Cāṇ.; VarBṛS.; a kind of plant with a poisonous root, Suśr. v, 2, 3; (= *gañjā*) a tavern, L.; reflection, meditation, L. **–kṛit**, m. 'humming-maker,' a bee, L.
Guñjaka, m., N. of a plant, Gal.; (*ikā*), f. the berry of Abrus precatorius, L.
Guñjana, n. buzzing, W.; cf. *madhu-*.
Guñjita, mfn. uttered in a low tone, murmured, W.; humming, Kād.; Bhaṭṭ. ii, 19; Kathās. xviii, 353; song (of the Koil), ŚārṅgP.
Guñjin, mfn. murmuring, Bālar. vi, 12 (*a-*, neg.)

गुटिका *guṭikā*, f. a small globe or ball, Mṛicch. v, $\frac{11}{12}$, 5; a pill, Suśr.; a pearl, Ragh. v, 70 (v. l. *gulikā*); a small pustule, W.; the cocoon of the silk-worm, W.; a goblet, Ānand.; (cf. *guḍa*.) **–°ñjana** (*°kâñ°*), n. collyrium formed like a globe or ball, Suśr. **–pāta**, m. falling of the ball, i. e. drawing lots. **–mukha**, mfn. having a rounded orifice, iv, 35, 6. **–°stra** (*°kâs°*), n. a bow from which balls of clay are thrown, Vāsav. 461.
Guṭiki-kṛita, mfn. formed into a pill, Suśr. i, 44.

गुड् *guḍ*, cl. 6. P. *°ḍati*, to guard, preserve, Dhātup. xxviii, 77; (cf. √*guṇḍ*, *ghuḍ*.)

गुड *guḍa*, m. (cf. *guṭikā*, *gula*; √*guḍ*, Uṇ. 1) a globe or ball, MBh. iii, vii; a ball to play with (cf. *giri-*), L.; a pill, ŚārṅgS. xiii, 1; a bit, mouthful, L.; sugar which forms itself into lumps, dry sugar, treacle, molasses, first thickening of the juice of the sugar-cane by boiling, Kāty.; Mn.; Yājñ.; MBh. &c.; an elephant's trappings or armour, L.; the cotton tree, L.; Euphorbia antiquorum, L.; (pl.) N. of a people (in Madhya-deśa), VarBṛS. xiv, 3; (*ā*), f. a small ball, pill, L.; the reed *uśīrī*, L.; Euphorbia antiquorum, Car. vii, 10; (*ī*), f. id., L.; (cf. *gauḍa*, *bahu-guḍā*.) **–karī**, for *gurjarī*. **–kshīra-maya**, mfn. consisting of molasses and milk, Hcat. i, 7. **–kshoda**, m. sugar in the form of powder, L. **–jihvikā**, f. shortened for *-nyāya*, Abhinav.; *-nyāya*, m. 'rule of the sugar and the tongue,' transitory impression soon lost, momentary opinion, TPrāt. viii, 16, Sch. **–tṛiṇa**, n. sugar-cane, L. **–tvac**, n. the aromatic bark of Laurus Cassia, Bhpr. **–tvaca**, n. id., L.; mace, L. **–dāru**, m. n. = *-tṛiṇa*, L. **–dhānā**, f. pl. grains with sugar, Pāṇ. ii, 1, 35, Vārtt. 4, Pat. & Kāś. **–dhenu**, f. a sugar-cow (presented to Brāhmans), PadmaP. **–nakha**, n. the perfume Nakha formed into pills, VarBṛS. lxxvii. **–parpaṭaka**, m. a kind of sweet-meat, Gal. **–pishṭa**, n. 'flour and sugar ground and boiled together,' a sort of sweetmeat, Yājñ. i, 288; (cf. Kathās. ii, 56.) **–pushpa**, m. 'sugar-flowered,' Bassia latifolia or another kind of Bassia (the flowers being full of saccharine matter), L. **–pṛithukā**, f., Pāṇ. ii, 1, 35, Kāś. **–phala**, m. Careya arborea or Salvadora persica, L.; (= *gūḍha-ph°*) jujube, L. **–bīja**, m. a kind of pease, L. **–bhā**, f. sugar prepared from Yava-nāla, L. **–maya**, mf(*ī*)n. consisting of sugar, Hcat. i, 6 f. **–miśra**, n. = *-pishṭa*, W. **–mūla**, m. Amaranthus polygamus, L. **–lih**, mfn. sugar-licking, Pāṇ. viii, 2, 1, Kāś.; (*-lin*)*-mat*, mfn. having sugar-lickers, ib. **–śarkarā**, f. sugar, refined sugar, Suśr. **–śigru**, m. a Moringa with red blossoms, L. **–śṛiṅgikā**, f. an apparatus for throwing balls (from a wall), MBh. iii, 643. **–harītakī**, f. myrobalan preserved in molasses, Suśr. iv, 5, 10 (cf. 14, 8). **Guḍā-keśa**, m. 'thick-haired,' the hero Arjuna, MBh. iii, iv, xii; Bhag.; BhP. i; Śiva, L. **Guḍâdi**, a Gaṇa of Pāṇ. (iv, 4, 103). **Guḍâpūpa**, m. = *°ḍa-pishṭa*, Pāṇ. v, 2, 82, Kāś. **Guḍâpūpikā**, f. (scil. *paurṇamāsī*) N. of a full-moon day on which sweetmeats are eaten, ib. **Guḍâlaka**, m. n. a lock of hair, BhP. x, 38, 9. **Guḍâśaya**, m. a species of Pīlu growing on mountains, L. **Guḍâshṭaka**, n. 'consisting of 8 sweet substances,' a kind of mixture, Bhpr. **Guḍôdaka**, n. (Pāṇ. vi, 2, 96, Kāś.) water mixed with molasses, Suśr.; mfn. containing water instead of molasses, MBh. vii, 2286. **Guḍôdana** = *guḍâud°*, xiii, 6162. **Guḍôdbhavā**, f. sugar, L. **Guḍâudana**, n. boiled rice and coarse sugar, Yājñ. i, 303.
Guḍaka, m. a ball (cf. *nābhi-g°*), MBh. iii, 643 (ifc. f. *ā*); a bit, mouthful, Uṇ., Sch.; a kind of drug prepared with treacle; n. molasses, W.; (*ikā*), f. a pill; a kernel, VarBṛS. lxxxi, 8 (v. l. *gulikā*).
Guḍara, mfn. fr. *°ḍa*, g. *aśmâdi* (not in Kāś.)
Guḍala, n. a sort of rum (distilled from molasses), Svapnac.
Guḍera, **°raka**, m. a bit, mouthful, L.

गुडची *guḍacī* = *°ḍūcī*, L., Sch.

गुडाका *guḍākā*, f. (a word formed for the etym. of *guḍā-keśa*) 'sloth,' L.

गुडाला *guḍālā*, for *guṇḍ°*, q. v.

गुडुगुडायन *guḍuguḍāyana*, n. (onomat.) grumbling (of the belly), Suśr. vi, 42, 116; (cf. Car. vi, 18.)

गुडूची *guḍūcī* = *°ḍūci*, L.

गुडुह *guḍuha*, m. pl., N. of a people in

Madhya-deśa (vv. ll. *guru-ha*, *guluha*, *gulaha*), VarBṛS. xiv, 23.

गुडूचिका *guḍūcikā*, f. = °*cī*, Car. vi, 17.

Guḍūcī, f. Cocculus cordifolius, Suśr. i, 12; 25; 38; ii, 1, 126; (cf. *kanda-*; °*ḍacī*, °*ḍucī*.)

गुण *guṇá*, m. (√*grah*, Uṇ.) a single thread or strand of a cord or twine (e.g. *tri-g*°, q.v.), string or thread, rope, TS. vii; Mṛicch.; Kum.; Ragh.; a garland, W.; a bow-string, R. iii, 33, 16 (*cāpa-*); Ragh. ix, 54; Ṛitus.; Hit.; (in geom.) a sinew; the string of a musical instrument, chord, Śiś. iv, 57; ifc. (f. *ā*) with numerals 'fold, times' (see *catur-*, *tri-*, *daśa-*, *dvi-*, *pañca-*; rarely the numeral stands by itself along with *guṇá* [e.g. *viśishṭo daśabhir guṇaiḥ*, 'of ten times higher value,' Mn. ii, 85], AV. x, 8, 43; MBh. iii, 15649; Hariv. 509; [*guṇa* = *bhāga*] Pāṇ. v, 2, 47, Kāś.); a multiplier, co-efficient (in alg.); subdivision, species, kind (e.g. *gandhasya guṇāḥ*, the different kinds of smell, MBh. xii, 6847); the 6 subdivisions of action for a king in foreign politics (viz. peace, war, march, halt, stratagem, and recourse to the protection of a mightier king), Mn. vii, 160; Yājñ. i, 346; MBh. ii, 155; = *upâya* (q.v., denoting the 4 ways of conquering an enemy), R. v, 81, 41; 'requisite,' see °*nôpêta*; a secondary element, subordinate or unessential part of any action (e.g. *sarva-g*°, mfn. 'reaching to all subordinate parts,' hence 'valid throughout,' KātyŚr.), ŚāṅkhŚr.; ĀśvŚr.; Kāty-Śr.; R. v, 1, 71; an auxiliary act, ŚāṅkhBr. xxvi, 4; a secondary dish (opposed to *anna*, i.e. rice or the chief dish), side-dish, Mn. iii, 224 ff.; (= *-karman*, in Gr.) the secondary or less immediate object of an action, Pāṇ. i, 4, 51, Sch.; a quality, peculiarity, attribute or property, Lāṭy.; ŚāṅkhGṛ.; Mn. iii, ix, &c.; an attribute of the 5 elements (each of which has its own peculiar quality or qualities as well as organ of sense; thus 1. ether has *śabda* or sound for its Guṇa and the ear for its organ; 2. the air has tangibility and sound for its Guṇas and the skin for its organ; 3. fire or light has shape or colour, tangibility, and sound for its Guṇas, and the eye for its organs; 4. water has flavour, shape, tangibility, and sound for its Guṇas, and the tongue for its organ; 5. earth has the preceding Guṇas, with the addition of its own peculiar Guṇa of smell, and the nose for its organ), Mn. i, 20 & 76–78; MBh. xii, 6846 ff.; Śak. i, 1; BhP. iii, 5, 35; (in Sāṃkhya phil.) an ingredient or constituent of Prakṛiti, chief quality of all existing beings (viz. *sattva*, *rajas*, & *tamas*, i.e. goodness, passion, and darkness, or virtue, foulness, and ignorance; cf. RTL. pp. 31; 36; 163), Mn. i; iii, 40; xii, 24 ff.; Sāṃkhyak.; Bhag. xiii f.; (hence) the number 'three,' VarBṛS. iic, 1; a property or characteristic of all created things (in Nyāya phil. twenty-four Guṇas are enumerated, viz. 1. *rūpa*, shape, colour; 2. *rasa*, savour; 3. *gandha*, odour; 4. *sparśa*, tangibility; 5. *saṃkhyā*, number; 6. *parimāṇa*, dimension; 7. *pṛithaktva*, severalty; 8. *saṃyoga*, conjunction; 9. *vibhāga*, disjunction; 10. *paratva*, remoteness; 11. *aparatva*, proximity; 12. *gurutva*, weight; 13. *dravatva*, fluidity; 14. *sneha*, viscidity; 15. *śabda*, sound; 16. *buddhi* or *jñāna*, understanding or knowledge; 17. *sukha*, pleasure; 18. *duḥkha*, pain; 19. *icchā*, desire; 20. *dvesha*, aversion; 21. *prayatna*, effort; 22. *dharma*, merit or virtue; 23. *adharma*, demerit; 24. *saṃskāra*, the self-reproductive quality); an epithet, KātyŚr.; good quality, virtue, merit, excellence, Mn.; MBh. &c.; the merit of composition (consistency, elegance of expression, &c.), Kāvyâd. i, 41 f.; Kpr. viii; Sāh. viii; the peculiar properties of the letters (11 in number, viz. the 8 *bāhya-prayatnās* [q.v.] and the 3 accents), Kāś. on Pāṇ. i, 1, 9 & 50; (cf. *-mātra*); the first gradation of a vowel, the vowels *a* (with *ar*, *al*, Pāṇ. i, 1, 51), *e*, *o*, Nir. x, 17; RPrāt. xi, 6; Pāṇ.; an organ of sense, L.; a cook (cf. *-kāra*), L.; Bhīma-sena (cf. *-kāra*), L.; (*ā*), f. Sanseviera Roxburghiana, L.; the plant *māṃsa-rohiṇī*, L.; N. of a princess, Rājat. iv, 695; (cf. *nir-*, *vi-*, *sa-*; *gauṇa*.) **—karaṇḍa-vyūha**, m., N. of a Buddh. work; (cf. *kar*°.) **—karī**, f. (in music) N. of a Rāgiṇī; (cf. *-kirī* & *guḍa-karī*.) **—karman**, n. an unessential secondary action, Madhus.; Nyāyam., Sch. (°*ma-tva*); (in Gr.) the secondary or less immediate object of an action, Pāṇ. ii, 3, 65, Sch.; °*rma-vibhāga*, mfn. distinguishing an action and an attribute, W.; m. separation of an action and an attribute, W. **—kāra**, mfn. productive of good qualities, profitable, W.; m. (in math.) the multiplier, Āryabh. ii, 23; VarBṛ. viii, 4, Sch.; 'preparing side-dishes or any secondary article of food,' Bhīma-sena (who performed the duties of a cook while the Pāṇḍava princes were servants to Virāṭa, MBh. iv, 28 ff.; 231 ff.), L. **—kāraka**, m. (= °*ra*) Bhīma-sena, Gal. **—kiraṇâvalī**, f., N. of a literary work. **—kirī**, f. = *-karī*. **—kīrtana**, n. telling the merits, Sāh. **—kṛitya**, n. the function of a bow-string, Kum. iv, 15. **—ketu**, m., N. of a Buddha, Lalit. i, 68. **—keśī**, f., N. of a daughter of Indra's charioteer Mātali, MBh. v, 3513 & 3647. **—krī**, f. = *-kirī*. **—gaṇa**, m. a number or series of good qualities, BhP. v, 3, 11; *-vat*, mfn. endowed with a number of good qualities, Bhām. i, 19. **—gāna**, n. praising the virtues of another, panegyric, W. **—gṛidhnu**, mfn. desiring good qualities, BhP. iii, 14, 20. **—gṛihya**, mf(*ā*)n. admiring virtue, attached to merit, Kir. ii, 4; Siṇhâs. **—grahaṇa**, n. acknowledging or appreciating merit or good qualities, Hcar. vi; Siṇhâs. **—grahītṛi**, mfn. 'receiving ropes' and 'acknowledging merit,' Bhām. i, 8. **—grāma**, m. an assemblage of virtues or merits, Bhartṛ. iii, 23; Gīt. ii, 10. **—grāhaka**, mfn. appreciating merit, W. **—grāhin**, mfn. id., Ratnâv. i, 5; Priy. i, 3. **—ghātin**, mfn. 'destroying merit,' detractor, envious, Hit. **—candra**, m., N. of a man, Śukas.; N. of a disciple of Deva-sūri (author of a Comm. called Tattva-prakāśaka-vṛitti). **—ccheda**, m. 'the breaking of a cord' and 'the cessation of good qualities,' Subh. **—jña**, mfn. = *-grahaṇa*, Bhartṛ. ii, 33; Kathās. iv, 10; Hit. (Udbh.); *-tā*, f. appreciation of good qualities, Mālatim. iii, 12. **—tantra**, mfn. judging according to the merits, laying stress on merits, Kum. iii, 1, Sch. **—tas**, ind. according to the three chief qualities of all existing beings, Bhag. xviii; from the side of the good qualities or virtues, Mn. xi, 186; R. iii, v; according to property or quality, W.; according to desert, W.; according to the properties of the letters, Pāṇ. i, 1, 50, Kāś. **—tā**, f. subordination, dependance, MBh. iii, 11236; BhP. iii; Nyāyam. ii; the being a merit, Sāh. vii, 32; the possession of attributes or qualities, W.; multiplication, W. **—tyāgin**, mfn. giving up what is excellent, Subh. **—traya**, n. the three constituent properties of Prakṛiti (see *guṇa*), W.; °*yâbhāsa*, m. 'appearance of the *guṇa-traya*,' life, W. **—tritaya**, n. = *-traya*, W. **—tva**, n. the condition of a string, Hit.; subordination, KātyŚr.; the possession of qualities, Sarvad. x, 35 & 52; excellence, Suśr. i, 45, 7, 19; multiplication, W. **—dīdhiti-ṭippanī** and °*ti-ṭīkā*, f., N. of two Comm. on *-prakāśa-vivṛiti*. **—dīpaka**, n. a simile in which a word denoting a quality forms the tertium comparationis, Kāvyâd. ii, 100, Sch. **—deva**, m., N. of a pupil of Guṇâḍhya, Kathās. viii, 36. **—dosha**, m. du. virtue and vice, Mn.; n. sg. id., R. iii, 44, 8; *-parīkshaṇa*, n. test or investigation of merits and defects, W.; °*shī-karaṇa*, n. making a defect out of a merit, Kuval. **—dhara**, mfn. possessing good qualities, W. **—dharma**, m. the virtue or duty incident to the possession of certain qualities (as clemency is the virtue and duty of royalty &c.), W. **—nidhi**, m. 'treasury of good qualities,' an excellent man; N. of a man, SkandaP. **—padī**, f. (a woman) having feet thin as cords, g. *kumbha-padyādi*. **—pālita**, m. 'protected by one's merits,' N. of a man, Kathās. ci. **—pūga**, n. great merit, excellence, Śiś. ix, 64. **—prakarsha**, m. id., Mṛicch. iv, 22; Kpr. vii, $\frac{1}{1}\frac{1}{1}$. **—prakāśa-dīdhiti-māthurī**, f., N. of a Comm. on °*śa-vivṛiti*. **—prakāśa-vivṛiti**, f., N. of a Comm. **—prabha**, m., N. of a Buddh. teacher. **—priya**, mfn. fond of merit or excellence, W. **—baddha**, mfn. 'bound with ropes' and 'won by merits,' Kathās. xviii. **—bhadra**, m., N. of the author of the Atmânuśāsana. **—bhāj**, mfn. = *-dhara*. **—bhinna**, mfn. separated according to the 3 Guṇas *sattva*, *rajas*, and *tamas*, NṛisUp. **—bhuj**, mfn. = *-bhāj*, W. **—bhūta**, mfn. unessential, secondary, Sarvad. vi, 55 & 69; dependent, Pāṇ. v, 1, 119, Vārtt. 5, Pat. **—bheda-tas**, ind. according to the difference of quality, W. **—bhoktṛi**, mfn. perceiving the properties of things, Bhag. xiii, 14. **—bhraṇśa**, m. the loss of all good qualities, L. **—mata**, n. the doctrine of those who worship the qualities, Śaṃkar. **—mati**, m., N. of a Buddh. teacher, Lalit. **—maya**, mfn. 'consisting of single threads' and 'formed by or possessing merits,' MBh. i, 6546; SārṅgP.; produced by or consisting of the three constituent properties of Prakṛiti, ·sting on them or containing them, MBh. xiv, 1327; Bhag. vii; BhP. i, iii. **—mahat**, n. = *-pūga*, W. **—mātra**, n. only (one of the Guṇas in Gr., viz.) the accent, Pāṇ. viii, 2, 101, Kāś. **—mukhyā**, f. 'superior by good qualities,' N. of an Apsaras, VP. **—yukta**, mfn. 'bound with a cord' and 'possessed with virtues.' **—yoga**, m. 'contact with a cord' and 'contact with any one's peculiarities,' KapS. iv, 26; the application of the secondary sense of a word, W. **—ratna**, n. 'pearl of good qualities,' N. of a short collection of sentences by Bhava-bhūti; 'pearl of qualities,' N. of a work on Nyāya phil.; *-kośa-stotra*, n., N. of a hymn by Parāśara-bhaṭṭa; *-maya*, mfn. possessed of pearl-like virtues, HPariś. ii; *-mālā*, f., N. of a medical work, Bhpr. **—rāga**, m. delighting in the good qualities of others, Kathās. ii, 51. **—rāja-prabhāsa**, m., N. of a Buddha, Lalit. xx. **—rāśi**, m. 'having a great number of qualities,' Śiva; N. of a Buddha, Lalit. i, 76. **—rddha** (*-ṛid*°), mfn. powerful through peculiar qualities, NṛisUp. **—lakshaṇa**, n. mark or indication of internal property, W. **—layanikā**, °*nī*, f. a tent, L. **—leśa-sukha-da**, 'giving pleasure to people of little understanding,' N. of a work. **—lubdha**, mfn. = *gṛidhnu* (as wealth or luck), Siṇhâs. (Hit.; Sāh. vii, 12$\frac{5}{8}$, 25). **—vacana**, n. 'word denoting a quality,' an attributive, adjective, Pāṇ.; mfn. denoting a quality, used as an adjective, iv, 1, 42, Kāś. **—vat**, mfn. 'furnished with a thread or string' and 'endowed with good qualities,' Pañcat.; SārṅgP.; Subh.; endowed with the five qualities or attributes of elements, Sāṃkhyak. 60; endowed with good qualities or virtues or merits or excellences, excellent, perfect, MBh.; R. &c.; m., N. of a son of Guṇavatī, Hariv. 8840; (*tī*), f., N. of a combination of three Ślokas forming all one phrase, Kāvyâd. i, 13, Sch.; of a daughter (of Sunābha and wife of Sāmba, Hariv. 8762; 8779; 8840; of the prince Guṇa-sāgara, Kathās. cxxiii); *-tama*, mfn. (superl.) most excellent, Yājñ. ii, 78; *-tara*, mfn. (compar.) more excellent, Mn. v, 113; R. iii; Pañcat.; *-tā*, f. the state of possessing qualities, W.; possession of good qualities or virtues, excellence, MBh. xiv, 86; R. ii; Ragh. viii; *-tva*, n. the state of possessing qualities, Sāh. i, $\frac{2}{3}$, 37 f. **—varṇana**, n. describing the merits of any one, W. **—vartin**, mfn. being on the path of virtue, R. ii. **—varman**, m., N. of a man, Kathās. xviii, 74. **—vācaka**, mfn. denoting a quality (an adjective), Vop. iv, 17; Pāṇ. viii, 1, 12, Sch. (*-vacana*, Kāś.) **—vāda**, m. a statement meant figuratively, Jaim. i, 2, 10; a statement contradictory to other arguments, Madhus. **—vādin**, mfn. pointing out any one's merits, MBh. xii, 4221. **—vidha**, for °*dhi*, 11466. **—vivecana**, mfn. examining the good qualities (of speech; N. of Sāh. viii); (*ā*), f. discernment in appreciating any one's merits, just sense of merit, W. **—viśesha**, m. a different property, W. **—vishṇu**, m., N. of a scholiast. **—vistara**, mfn. abounding in excellent qualities, Hit. **—vṛiksha**, °**kshaka**, m. a post to which a boat is fastened, L. **—vṛitti**, f. a secondary or unessential condition or relation (opposed to *mukhya vṛ*°), KātyŚr.; the secondary force of a word, W.; character or style of qualities or merits, W. **—vṛiddhi**, f. du. (= *vṛiddhi-guṇau*) the gradations of vowels called Guṇa and Vṛiddhi, g. *rājadantâdi*. **—vedin**, mfn. knowing the properties or qualities, Bhpr.; knowing the merits of (in comp.), Mn. vii, 167. **—vaicitrya**, n. a variety of qualities, W. **—vaiśeshya**, n. pre-eminence of merit or of any property, ix, 296 (ifc.) **—vrata**, n. 'vow or duty of secondary importance,' a term for 3 particular duties (forming with the 5 *aṇu-vratāni* and the 4 *śikshā-padāni* the 12 duties of the laymen adhering to the Jaina faith), HYog. **—śata**, n. a hundred excellent qualities, W.; *-śālin*, mfn. possessed of a hundred excellent qualities. **—śabda**, m. the twang of a bow-string, Divyâv.; (= *-vacana*) an adjective, L. **—śaila**, m. 'excellent rock,' N. of a Caitya, HPariś. **—śīla**, see *a-g*°; *-tas*, ind. according to virtues and character, BhP. iv, 1, 64. **—ślāghā**, f. encomium, praise, Hit. **—saṃyukta**, mfn. endowed with good qualities, MBh. i. **—saṃskāra**, in comp. quality and preparation, Gaut. xv, 6; m. the highest limit of excellence, R. v, 85, 5. **—saṃkīrtana**, n. celebration of qualities, MBh. i, 1521; R. (ed. Gorr.) ii. **—saṃkhyāna**, n. the (enumeration, i.e. the) theory of the 3 essential properties, Bhag. xviii, 19; the appearance of a quality, BhP. v, 17, 17 (ifc. with *sarva-*). **—saṅga**, m. association with properties or qualities, W.; m. pl. the good qualities peculiar to a person, R. v, 27, 32. **-saṃgraha,** m. a collection of merits or properties, BhP. iv, 20, 26; =*-grahaṇa*, W. **-samudra,** n. an ocean of virtues, one endowed with all virtues, Bhaktâm. 4. **-sampad,** f. great merit, perfection, R. i; VarBṛS.; Kir. v, 24. **-sampanna,** mfn. endowed with good qualities or virtues, Gaut. xxviii. **-sāgara,** m. =*-samudra*, MBh. iii, 16762; R. ii; Śukas.; Brahmā, L.; N. of a Buddha, L.; of a prince, Kathās. cxxiii; mfn. endowed with all good qualities, W. **-sundara,** m., N. of a Daśa-pūrvin, Jain. **-stuti,** f. = *-ślāghā*, Hit. **-sthāna-prakaraṇa,** n., N. of a Jaina work. **-hāni,** f. want of merits, Āp. ii, 17, 5. **-hīna,** mfn. void of merit, Mn. ix, 89; free from properties, W.; poor (as food), W. **Guṇâkara,** m. a mine or multitude of merits, one endowed with all virtues, MārkP. xx, 20; (= °*ṇa-rāśi*) Śiva; N. of Śākya-muni, L.; of a poet; ŚārṅgP.; of a minister, Kathās. lxix; of a Buddhist, mf(*ā*)n. possessing all excellences, Lalit. xx, 43; *-sūri*, m., N. of the author of a Comm. on Bhaktâm. **Guṇâkshara,** for *ghuṇ*°. **Guṇâguṇa,** m. pl. merits and defects, Mn. iii, 22; ix, 331; *-jña*, mf(*ā*)n. a judge of merit and demerit, MBh. xiii, 24; ŚārṅgP. **Guṇâgra-dhārin,** m. 'endowed with the best qualities,' N. of a man, Lalit. xiii, 163. **Guṇâgrya,** n. the best of the 3 chief qualities, i. e. *sattva* (q.v.), Ragh. iii, 27. **Guṇâṅga,** n. pl. actions resulting from good qualities, R. ii, 77, 12. **Guṇâḍhya,** mfn. rich in virtues or excellences, R. i, 7, 6; m., N. of the famous author of the Bṛihat-kathā, Vāsav. 346; Kshem.; Kathās. i, vi; =°*ḍhyaka*, Gal. **Guṇâḍhyaka,** m. Alangium decapetalum, L. **Guṇâtipāta,** m. detraction of acknowledged merits, Sāh. vi, 173; 184. **Guṇâtiśaya,** m. (in dram.) heightening acknowledged merits, ib. **Guṇâtīta,** mfn. freed from or beyond all properties, Bhag. xiv, 25. **Guṇâtman,** mfn. having qualities, W. **Guṇâdi,** a Gaṇa of Pāṇ. (vi, 2, 176). **Guṇâdhāna,** n. 'addition of accessory qualities,' rendering more fit for any purpose, Car. iii, 1; Bādar., Sch.; (=*pratiyatna*) Pāṇ. i, 3, 32, Sch. **Guṇâdhāra,** m. 'receptacle of virtues,' a virtuous person, L. **Guṇâdhipa,** m. 'lord of virtues,' N. of a king, Vet. ii, ½. **Guṇâdhishṭhāna,** °**naka,** n. the region of the breast where the girdle is fastened, L. **Guṇânanda,** m., N. of an author; (*ī*), f., N. of a Comm. by °*da*. **Guṇânurāga,** m. delight in good qualities, approbation, L. **Guṇânurodha,** m. conformity to good qualities, W. **Guṇântara,** n. a different quality or kind of merit, Pāṇ. v, 3, 55, Pat. 20 & 33; °*raṃ* √*vraj*, to obtain a better quality, become superior, Mālav. i, 6; °*râdhāna*, n. 'addition of another or better quality,' being active or caring for (gen.), Kāś. on Pāṇ. i, 3, 32 & ii, 3, 53; Bhaṭṭ. viii, Sch.; °*râpatti*, f. attainment of another quality, Nyāyad. ii, 2, 59. **Guṇânvaya,** mfn. having qualities, ŚvetUp. v, 7. **Guṇânvita,** mfn. id., vi, 4; endowed with virtues, excellent, Mn. ii, vii (ifc. with *rūpa*); Vedântas.; auspicious (a Nakshatra), Mn. ii. 30. **Guṇâpavāda,** m. detracting from merit, W. **Guṇâbdhi,** m. (= °*ṇa-sāgara*) N. of a Buddha, L. **Guṇâbhāsa,** m. (ifc.) semblance of qualities, ŚvetUp. iii, 17 (= Bhag. xiii, 14). **Guṇâbhilāshin,** mfn. =°*ṇa-gridhnu*, Ragh. iii, 36. **Guṇâyana,** mfn. =°*ṇa-vartin*, BhP. iv, 21, 43. **Guṇârāma,** m. 'pleasure-grove of good qualities,' N. of an actor. **Guṇâlaṃkṛita,** mfn. adorned with virtues or good qualities, W. **Guṇâlaya,** m. 'abode of good qualities,' one endowed with all virtues, Pañcat. i, 16, 16; (*sarva-*) Subh. **Guṇâlābha,** m. inefficiency, Suśr. i, 35, 40 f. **Guṇâvarā,** f. 'lowest as to virtues,' N. of an Apsaras, MBh. i, 4817. **Guṇâvaha,** mfn. having the proper qualities, Bhpr. **Guṇâśraya,** m. 'abode of qualities,' substance, matter, L.; one endowed with virtues, a very virtuous man, Hit. **Guṇêśa,** m the lord of the 3 qualities, ŚvetUp. vi, 16; N. of a mountain, W. **Guṇêśvara,** m. (= °*śa*) N. of the mountain Citrakūṭa (or Chatarkot in Bundelcund), L. **Guṇôtkarsha,** m. superiority in merit or in good qualities, R. i, 24, 19; Kāvyâd. ii, 95, extraordinary merits; a present consisting in a sword, Gal. **Guṇôtkīrtana,** n. =°*ṇa-kīrt*°, Siṃhâs. **Guṇôtkṛishṭa,** mfn. superior in merit or in good qualities, Mn. viii, 73. **Guṇôttara,** mfn. id., Suśr. i, 45, 64. **Guṇôpapanna,** mfn. endowed with good qualities, VarYogay.; (cf. Mn. ix, 141; Nal.) **Guṇôpâsaka,** m. a worshipper of the qualities (belonging to a particular philosophical school), Śaṃkar. xxxix f. **Guṇôpêta,** mfn. endowed with good qualities, Mn. iii, 40; Nal.; R. i; Śak.; Hit.; endowed with any requisites, Yājñ. i, 347. **Guṇâugha,** m. =°*ṇa-pūga*, MBh.

Guṇaka, m. a calculator, reckoner (for *gaṇ*°), W.; (in arithm.) the multiplier, VarBṛ. viii, 4; ifc. quality, Vedântas. 43; N. of a maker of garlands, Hariv. 4479; (*ikā*), f. a tumor (or 'a cipher'?), L.

Guṇana, n. multiplication; enumeration, W.; pointing out merits or virtues, Gīt. vii, 29; reiterated study, repetition, Gal.; (*ī*), f. id., L.

Guṇanikā, f. (=°*nī*) reiterated study, repetition (or 'reiteration, tautology'?), Śiś. ii, 75; determining of the various readings of a MS. (*pāṭha-niścaya* or °*ścita*), L.; a jewel, gem ('a garland, necklace,' Sch.), Ānand. 3; Bālar. vi, 29; dancing, L.; the prologue to a drama, L.; (in arithm.) a cipher, L.

Guṇanīya, mfn. to be multiplied, VarBṛ. xxiv, 11, Sch.; to be advised, W.; m. (=°*nikā*) reiterated study, W.; n. the multiplicand, W.

Guṇaya, Nom. P. °*yati*, to multiply, VarBṛS. viii, 20; to advise, invite, Dhātup. xxxv, 41; (cf. *saṃ-*.)

Guṇala, m., N. of a son of Bhoja.

Guṇāya, Nom. Ā. °*yate*, to become or appear as a merit, Cāṇ.

Guṇi, in comp. for °*ṇin*. **-gaṇa,** m. a number of virtuous persons, Pañcat. Introd. 7. **-tā,** f. the state of possessing good qualities, virtuousness, W. **-dvaidha,** n. equality of merit on both sides, W. **-liṅga,** mfn. taking the same gender as a substantive, L. **-sarvasva,** n., N. of a work.

Guṇita, mfn. multiplied (with, instr. or in comp.), MBh. iii, 7030; Vikr. iii, 22; VarBṛS. liii; Pañcat.; augmented, intensified, Megh. 107; often practised, Bālar. viii, 26; connected or filled with (in comp.), BhP. xi, 7, 66; (cf. *anu-*, *pari-*, *pra-*.)

Guṇitavya, mfn. to be multiplied.

Guṇin, mfn. 'furnished with a string or rope (as a hunter)' and endowed with good qualities,' ŚārṅgP.; Subh.; containing parts, consisting of parts, Pāṇ. v, 2, 47, Vārtt. 1; endowed with good qualities or merits, ŚvetUp. vi; Mn. viii, 73; Yājñ. &c.; auspicious (a day), Daś. vii, 296 f.; endowed with the good qualities of or contained in (in comp.), MārkP. xxvii, 9; requiring the first gradation (a vowel), Kāt. iii f.; 'possessing qualities' or (m.) 'quality-possessor,' object, thing, noun, substantive, Yājñ. iii, 69; BhP. ii, 8, 14; m. 'furnished with a string,' a bow, L.

Guṇī, in comp. for °*ṇá*. **-√as,** to make one's self subordinate to (gen.), SāmavBr. ii, 6, 7. **-karaṇa,** n. making a merit out of (a defect, *dosha-*), Kuval. **-bhāva,** m. the becoming subordinate, Sāh. iv, 14, 32; vii, 4, 18 & 25. **-√bhū** = -√1. *as*, SāmavBr. **-bhūta,** mfn. subordinate to (gen.), made secondary or unimportant, MBh. ii, xiv; Kpr. v, 2; Sāh. iv, 1 & 13; invested with attributes, W.; varied according to qualities, W.; having a certain force or application (as a word), W.

Guṇya, mfn. endowed with good qualities or virtues, Pāṇ. v, 2, 120, Vārtt., Pat.; to be enumerated, W.; to be described or praised, W.; to be multiplied, multiplicand, Āryabh. ii, 23, Sch. (*-tva*, n.)

गुण्ठ् **gunṭh** (cf. √*guṇḍ*, *gudh*), cl. 10. P. °*ṭhayati*, to enclose or envelop, surround, cover, Dhātup. xxxii, 46 (v. l.); (cf. *ava-*.)

Guṇṭhana, n. concealing, covering with (in comp.), Prab. ii, 26 (v. l. *guṇḍana*); (*ā*), f. id., Bālar. ii, 3.

Guṇṭhita, mfn. enveloped, covered with (instr. or in comp.), MBh.; R. ii f., vi; Kathās. lxiv, 122; for *guṇḍita*, pounded, ground, L., Sch.; (cf. *ava-*, *ā-*, *pari-*, *sam-ava-*.)

गुण्ड् **guṇḍ** (cf. √*guṇṭh*), cl. 10. °*ḍayati*, to cover, conceal, protect, Dhātup. xxxii, 46; to pound, comminute, ib.

Guṇḍa, m. Scirpus Kysoor, L.; (*ā*), f. a kind of reed, L. (v. l.) **-kanda,** m. the root of Scirpus Kysoor, L. **Guṇḍârocanikā,** f. the plant *kāmpilya*, L. **Guṇḍârocanī,** f. id., Car. i, 1, 82, Sch. **Guṇḍâsinī,** f. a kind of grass, L. (v. l. °*ḍâsinī*).

Guṇḍaka, m. dust, powder, Kṛishis. xxi, 2; an oil vessel, L.; a low pleasing tone, L.; = *malina*, L.; (*ikā*), f.? (mentioned in connection with *lipi*), Varāhit.; the lower part of the hilt of a sword, Gal.

Guṇḍana. See *gunṭhana*.

Guṇḍālā, f., N. of a plant (*jalôdbhūtā*, *guccha-vadhrā*), L.; a kind of grass (v. l. *guḍ*°), L.

Guṇḍika, m. pl. flour, meal; (*ā*), see °*ḍaka*.

Guṇḍita, mfn. pounded, ground (*rūshita*), L.; covered with dust, L.; = *karambita*, *khacita*, L.

गुण्डिचा *guṇḍicā*, f., N. of the place where the image of Purushôttama or Jagan-nātha is placed after being carried about at the Ratha-yātrā, Utkalakh.

गुण्ड्र *guṇḍra*, m. or °*ḍrā*, f. a kind of Cyperus, VarBṛS. liv, 100 (ifc. *sa-guṇḍra*, v. l. *-gundra*).

गुण्य *guṇya*. See *guṇá*.

गुत्स *gutsa*, m. (= *guccha*; √*gudh*, Uṇ. iii) a bunch, bundle, clump (of grass), cluster (of blossoms), nosegay, L.; a pearl necklace consisting of thirty-two strings, L.; the plant or perfume *granthi-parṇa*, L. **Gutsârdha,** m. = *gucchâr*°, L.

Gutsaka, m. a bundle, bunch, cluster of blossoms, L.; a chowri, L.; a section of a work, L. **-pushpa,** m. (= *guccha-p*°) Alstonia scholaris, L.

गुड् *guḍ*, cl. 1. Ā. *godate*, to play, sport, Dhātup. ii, 23; (cf. √*gūrd*, *gudh*.)

गुद *gudá*, m. an intestine, entrail, rectum, anus, VS.; TS. vi; ŚBr. iii, viii; Kauś. &c.; (ifc. f. *ā*, g. *kroḍâdi* [or *ī*, g. *bahv-ādi*, not in Kāś. & in g. *śoṇâdi*]); n. id.; m. du. with *kaushṭhyau*, the two intestines, Yājñ. iii, 95; (*gúdās*), f. pl. the bowels, RV. x, 163, 3; VS.; AV. ix-xi; ŚBr. x, xii. **-kīla,** m. piles, Suśr. i, 46, 1, 34 & 6, 10. **-kīlaka,** m. id., L. **-graha,** m. spasm of the rectum, Car. v, 10, 13. **-ja,** m. n. pl. = *-kīla*, vi, 9 & 18; Bhpr. vii, 17, 55. **-nirgama,** m. prolapsus ani, 14, 74. **-niḥsaraṇa,** n. id., Car. vi, 10; Bhpr. **-pariṇaddha,** see *śva-g*°. **-pāka,** m. inflammation of the anus, Car. vi, 10; Suśr. **-bhraṇśa,** m. = *-nirgama*, Car. vi, 10; Suśr. **-yoni,** mfn. pathic, Bhpr. **-roga,** m. a disease of the last of the large intestines, MārkP. xv. **-vadana,** n. the anus, Siṃhâs. xx, 7; (*ā*), f., N. of a goddess, Kālac. **-vartman,** n. the anus, L. **Gudâṅkura,** m. piles, Bhpr. vii, 17, 15. **Gudâvarta,** m. constipation, Sāṃkhyak. 49, Sch. **Gudôdbhava,** m. piles, Suśr. iv, 6, 17. **Gudâushṭha,** n. the aperture of the anus, ii, 2, 3 f.

गुध् *gudh*, cl. 4. P. °*dhyati* (ind. p. *gudhitvā*, Pāṇ. i, 2, 7; see *upa-gudha*), to wrap up, envelop, cover, clothe (cf. √*gunṭh*), Dhātup. xxvi, 13: cl. 9. P. °*dhnāti*, to be angry, xxxi, 45: cl. 1. Ā. *godhate*, to play, sport (cf. √*gūrd*, *guḍ*), ii, 23; [cf. Gk. κεύθω; Old Germ. *hût*; Germ. *haut*; Angl. Sax. *hyde*, *hyd*; Lat. *cutis*?]

Gudhita, mfn. surrounded, enclosed, W.

Gudhera, mfn. protecting, Uṇ. i, 62.

गुन्दल *gundala*, m. the sound of a small oblong drum, L.

गुन्दाल *gundāla*, for °*drāla*, W.

गुन्द्र् *gundr*, v. l. for √*kundr*, q. v.

गुन्द्र *gundra*, m. Saccharum Sara (*śara*), L.; the plant Paṭaraka, Bhpr.; m. n. the root of Cyperus pertenuis, L.; (*ā*), f. id., Suśr.; (cf. *guṇḍra*) Typha angustifolia, Bhpr.; Cyperus rotundus, L.; Coix barbata (*gavedhukā*), L.; = *priyaṃgu*, L. **-phalā,** f. Aglaia Roxburghiana, Bhpr.

Gundrāla, m. a sort of pheasant, L.

गुप् 1. *gup*, cl. 4. P. °*pyati* (p. Ā. *gupyamāna*, in Prākrit *guppam*°, Jain.), to become perplexed or confused, Dhātup. xxvi, 123.

गुप् 2. *gup* (for pr. &c. see *gopaya* & °*pāya*, from which the root is derived [cf. Pāṇ. iii, 1, 28 & 31]; perf. *jugopa*, MBh. &c.; 3. pl. *jugupur*, RV. vii, 103, 9; AV. &c.; fut. 2nd *gopsyati*, AV.; ŚBr. vi &c.; fut. 1st *goptā* or *gopitā*, Pāṇ. vii, 2, 44; aor. *agaupsīt* or *agopīt*, Pāṇ. iii, 1, 50, Kāś.) to guard, defend, protect, preserve (from, abl.), RV. vii, 103, 9; AV. &c.; to hide, conceal, Śiś. xvi, 30 (inf. *gopitum*): Caus *gopayati* &c., see ss. vv. *gopaya* & °*pāya*: Desid. Ā. *jugupsate* (Pāṇ. iii, 1, 5; ep. also P. °*ti*) to seek to defend one's self from (abl.), be on one's guard (cf. i, 4, 24, Vārtt. 1), ŚāṅkhGṛ. iv, 12; Gobh.; ChUp. v, 10, 8; to beware of, shun, avoid, detest, spurn, despise (with acc.), Mn.; Yājñ.; MBh. &c.; to feel offended or hurt, MBh. i, 6375; iii, 1934: Desid. of Desid. *jugupsishate*, Pāṇ. iii, 1, 7, Vārtt. 15, Pat.; vi, 1, 9, Kāś.

3. **Gup,** mfn. ifc. 'defending, protecting,' see *dharma-*; being on one's guard or preserving one's self from, Naish. vi, 66.

Gupitá, mfn. protected, guarded, RV. x, 85, 4 & 109, 3; AV. ii, 28, 4; x, 10, 4; xviii, 4, 70.

Gupila, m. 'a protector,' king, Uṇ. i, 57.

Guptá, mfn. protected, guarded, preserved, AV. &c.; hidden, concealed, kept secret, secret, Bhartṛ.; Pañcat.; Kathās. &c. (with *daṇḍa*, a secret fine, fine secretly imposed or exacted, Hit.; cf. *gūḍha-d°*); = *saṃgata* (?joined, combined), W.; (*am*; in comp. *a-*, Hcat.), ind. secretly, privately, Kathās.; (*su-*) Pañcat. iv; (*e*), loc. ind. in a hidden place, Kathās. lxxv; (*as*), m. (Pāṇ. vi, 1, 205, Kāś.) N. of several men belonging to the Vaiśya caste (PārGṛ. i, 17; cf. RTL. p. 358), especially of the founder of the renowned Gupta dynasty in which the names of the sovereigns generally end in *gupta* (cf. *candra-*, *samudra-*, *skanda-*; *gupta* is also often found ifc. in names of the Vaiśya class); (*ā*), f. a married woman who withdraws from her lover's endearments, L.; Mucuna pruritus, Suśr. iv, 26, 33; vi, 46, 21 (°*ptā*); N. of a woman, Pāṇ. iv, 1, 121, Sch. (*gopā*, Kāś.); of a Śākya princess, Buddh. **–kathā**, f. a confidential communication, W. **–gati**, m. 'going secretly,' a spy, L. **–gṛiha**, n. 'secret room,' bed-room, Gal.; Pañcad. **–cara**, m. 'going secretly,' Bala-rāma, L. **–tama**, mfn. carefully guarded (as the senses), Ragh. i, 55. **–tīrtha**, n., N. of a Tīrtha, SkandaP. **–dāna**, n. a hidden gift, W. **–dīkshā-tantra**, n., N. of a Tantra. **–dūta**, m. a secret messenger, W. **–dhana**, n. money kept secret, Pañcat. ii, 6, 1/2; mfn. guarding one's money, ib. **–prayāga**, m., N. of a locality, Rasik. xi, 41. **–maṇi**, m. a hidden place, Gal. **–mati**, m. 'hidden-minded,' N. of a merchant, HPariś. i, 269. **–rajasvalā**, f. a girl who has begun to have her courses, Gal. **–vatī**, f., N. of a Tantra. **–vesha**, m. dress used for concealment, disguise, W.; (*e*), loc. ind. in disguise, W. **–śīla**, mf(*ā*)n. 'of a hidden character,' cunning; (cf. *śīla-g°*.) **–sarasvatī**, f., N. of a river (also called eastern Sarasvatī), KapSaṃh. xx. **–sādhana-tantra**, n., N. of a Tantra. **–sneha**, mf(*ā*)n. having a secret affection; (*ā*), f. 'having the oil hidden,' Alangium hexapetalum, L. **–sveda**, m. = *-snehā*, Gal. **Guptârma**, n., N. of a locality, Pāṇ. vi, 2, 90, Kāś.; (cf. *árman*.) **Guptâryaka**, m. the prince Āryaka (who in youth was kept hidden), Mṛicch. vii, 5/8. **Guptâvadhūta**, mfn. one who has secretly shaken off from himself worldly obligation (opposed to *vyaktâv°*). **Guptâsana**, n. a particular method of sitting (= *siddhâs°*).

Guptaka, m. a preserver, W.; N. of a Sauvīraka prince, MBh. iii, 15597.

Gúpti, f. preserving, protecting, protection, AV. vi, 122, 3; xii, 3, 7; TS. v f.; TBr. &c.; restraint (of body, mind, and speech), HYog.; Sarvad. iii, 191 & 210 f.; concealing, hiding, keeping secret (ifc.), Kām. (Hit.); Sāh.; Sarvad. xv; a means of protection, fortification, rampart, R. v f.; Kum. v, 38; a prison, VarBṛ. v, 10; 'place of concealment,' a hole in the ground, sink, cellar, L.; digging a hole in the ground, L., Sch.; 'a leak in a ship' or 'the well or lower deck of a boat,' L. **–bandham**, ind. p., Pāṇ. iii, 4, 41, Sch. (not in Kāś.) **–vāda**, m. a secret conversation, L. **Gupty-adhikṛita**, m. a jail-superintendent, VarBṛ. xii, 15.

Guptika, m., N. of a man, Avadānaś.; (*ā*), f. (cf. *svara-gupti*) depth (of voice), Divyâv. i, 372.

Gupti-√kṛi, to hide, conceal, Uttamac. 231.

गुफ् *guph* (= √*gumph*), cl. 6. °*phati* (Pāṇ. vii, 1, 59, Kāś.; ind. p. *guphitvā*, i, 2, 23), to string together, tie or string as a garland, Dhātup. xxviii, 31.

Guphita, mfn. (fr. *gushpita*), arranged, placed in order, W.

गुम् *gum*, onomat. imitation of the humming of bees, only in comp.

Gum (in comp. for *gum*). **–kāra**, m. humming (of bees), Alaṃkārat. **–kvaṇa**, mfn. speaking through the nose, Gal.

Gumagumāyita, n. = *gum-kāra*, Vāsav. 334.

गुम्फ् *gumph* (= √*guph*), cl. 6. P. °*phati* (Pāṇ. vii, 1, 59, Kāś.; ind. p. *gumphitvā* [Pāṇ. i, 2, 23], Bhaṭṭ. vii), to string together, tie or string as a garland, Naish. viii, 82: Caus. °*phayati*, id., Kathās. lxxii, 79.

Gumpha, m. tying or stringing as a garland, L.; stringing, filing, combining with each other, Bālar. i, 1; Kuval. 289; 319; a bracelet, L.; a whisker, L.

Gumphaka, mf(*ikā*)n. See *mauktika-*.

Gumphana, n. winding (a garland), L.; stringing, filing (as words), Bālar. x, 86; (*ā*), f. id. (among the *śabdâlaṃkārāḥ*), Sarasv. ii; see *mauktika-*.

Gumphita, mfn. tied, strung together, Kathās. lvi, lxxiii; Prab. i, 2; arranged, placed in order, W.

गुर् *gur* (cf. √1. *gṛī*), cl. 6. *gurate*, to raise, lift up (or 'to make effort'), Dhātup. xxviii, 103; (cf. *ati-*, *apa-*, *abhi-*, *ava-*, *ā-*, *ud-*, *pra-*): *gur* or *gūr*, cl. 4. *gūryate*, to hurt, xxvi, 45; to go, ib.: Caus. *gorayate* or *gūray°*, to raise, lift up (or 'to make effort'), xxxiii, 21; to eat, ib.; (cf. √*gūr*.)

Guraṇa, n. = *udyama*, L.

Gūrtá, mfn. (Pāṇ. viii, 2, 61) approved, welcome, agreeable, (= Lat.) *gratus*, RV. i, 167, 1; iv, 19, 8; (cf. *abhí-*, *rā́dho-*, *viśvá-*, *svá-*; *ari-* & *puru-gūrtá*.) **–manas** (°*tá-*), mfn. with grateful mind ('with prepared mind,' Sāy.), vi, 63, 4. **–vacas** (°*tá-*), mfn. speaking agreeably, x, 61, 1 f. **–śravas** (°*tá-*), mfn. one whose praise one likes to hear (Indra), i, 61, 5 & 122, 10. **Gūrtá-vasu**, mfn. one whose treasures are welcome, ix, 132, 1.

Gūrtí, f. approval, praise, i, 56, 2; viii ff.

गुरु *gurú*, mf(*vī*)n. (cf. *girí*; comp. *gárīyas*, once °*yas-tara*, *guru-tara*, superl. *garishṭha*, *guru-tama*, see ss. vv.) heavy, weighty (opposed to *laghu*), RV. i, 39, 3 & iv, 5, 6; AV. &c. (g. *śauṇḍâdi*, Gaṇar. 101); heavy in the stomach (food), difficult to digest, MBh. i, 3334; Suśr.; great, large, extended, long, Yājñ. (see *-kratu*); Bhartṛ. &c.; (in prosody) long by nature or position (a vowel), Prāt. (a vowel long both by nature and by position is called *garīyas*, RPrāt. xviii, 20); Pāṇ. i, 4, 11 & 12; high in degree, vehement, violent, excessive, difficult, hard, RV.; MBh. &c.; grievous, Megh. 80; important, serious, momentous, MBh. &c.; valuable, highly prized, Yājñ. ii, 30 (*guru* = *garīyas*) &c.; haughty, proud (speech), Pañcat.; venerable, respectable; m. any venerable or respectable person (father, mother, or any relative older than one's self), Gobh.; ŚāṅkhGṛ.; Mn. &c.; a spiritual parent or preceptor (from whom a youth receives the initiatory Mantra or prayer, who instructs him in the Śāstras and conducts the necessary ceremonies up to that of investiture which is performed by the Ācārya, Yājñ. i, 34), RPrāt.; ĀśvGṛ.; PārGṛ.; Mn. &c.; the chief of (gen. or in comp.), Cāṇ.; Ragh. ii, 68; (with Śāktas) author of a Mantra; 'preceptor of the gods,' Bṛihaspati, Mn. xi; (hence) the planet Jupiter, Jyot.; VarBṛS.; Bhartṛ. &c.; 'Pāṇḍu-teacher,' Droṇa, L.; Prabhā-kara (celebrated teacher of the Mīmāṅsā, usually mentioned with Kumārila), SŚaṃkar. vi, 50; xv, 157; (= *dharma*) 'venerable,' the 9th astrological mansion, VarBṛS. i, 16; Mucuna pruritus, L.; N. of a son of Saṃkṛiti, BhP. ix, 21, 2; m. du. parents, MBh.; m. pl. parents and other venerable persons, Mn. iv; Vikr. v, 10; Kathās.; a honorific appellation of a preceptor (whose N. is also put in the pl.), Jain.; Hit.; (*vī*), f. 'venerable woman,' a mother, Āp. i, 21, 9; 'great (with child),' pregnant, a pregnant woman, L.; the wife of a teacher, W.; [cf. βαρύς; Lat. *gravis*; Goth. *kauriths*; Lith. *giëras*.] **–kaṇṭha**, m. a peacock, Gal.; (cf. *guruṇṭaka*.) **–karman**, n. any affair of a spiritual teacher, Āp. i, 5, 25. **–kāra**, m. worship, adoration, L. **–kārya**, n. a serious or momentous affair, Yājñ. ii, 5/8, 31; = *-kárman*, W. **–kula**, n. the house of a Guru, MBh. i, ch. 3; Pāṇ. ii, 1, 42, Vārtt., Pat.; *-vāsa*, m. residence in the house of a Guru, a pupil's life, MBh. i, 743; °*lâvāsin*, m. 'abiding in °*la*,' a pupil, Gal. **–kṛita**, mfn. highly prized or praised, Bhartṛ. (ŚārṅgP.); worshipped, W. **–kopa**, m. violent wrath, W. **–kratu**, m. a great sacrifice, Yājñ. iii, 328. **–krama**, m. succession of teachers or (with Śāktas) of authors of Mantras. **–kshepa**, m., N. of a prince, VP. **–gata**, mfn. being with or belonging to a spiritual teacher, W. **–gavī**, f. the cow of a spiritual teacher, ĀśvGṛ. ii, 10, 8 (*a-*, neg.) **–gītā**, f., N. of a section of SkandaP. (relating to a spiritual teacher); *-stotra*, n. id. **–gṛiha**, n. = *-kula*, MBh. i, ch. 3; 'Bṛihaspati's house,' the signs Sagittarius and Pisces, VarBṛ. viii, 11. **–ghna**, m. 'killing a spiritual teacher,' white mustard, L. **–jana**, m. any venerable or elderly person (father, mother, the elders of a family &c.) **–tama**, mfn. (superl.) most important, W.; m. the best teacher, W. **–tara**, mfn. heavier, very heavy, MBh. iii, 13293; heavy, xii, 6856; greater, worse, very hard or bad, Mn. vii, ix, xi; MBh. &c.; more important, very important or valuable, Vikr. iv, 31; Bhartṛ.; Pañcat.; more venerable, MBh.; very venerable, R. ii, 79, 2. **–talpa**, m. 'a teacher's bed,' in comp.; the violation of a teacher's bed (intercourse with his wife), Gaut. xxiv, 10; Mn. ix, xi; Yājñ. iii, 231; a violator of his teacher's bed, MBh. iii, 1761; *-ga*, mfn. one who violates his teacher's bed, TĀr. x, 64; Gaut.; Mn. ix, xi, xii; Yājñ. &c.; *-gāmin*, mfn. id., Āp. i, 25, 1 & 28, 15; *-rata*, mfn. id., VarBṛ. xxi, 6; *-vrata*, n. penance for violating a teacher's bed, Mn. xi, 171; °*lpâpanutti*, f. the violation of a teacher's bed, 107; °*lpâbhigamana*, n. id., Kathās. xx, 154; (cf. *gaurutalpika*.) **–°talpin**, mfn. = °*lpa-ga*, Mn. xi, 104 (v. l.); MBh. v, xiii. **–tā**, f. weight, heaviness, Śak. ii, 2; Suśr.; 'heaviness' and 'dignity,' Sāh. iii, 52 [?]; burden, trouble, R. ii, 27, 22; importance, Śiś. ix, 22; the office of a teacher, Kathās. xix. **–tāpa**, m. excessive heat, W. **–tāla**, m. (in music) a kind of measure. **–tīrtha**, n., N. of a Tīrtha, PadmaP. **–tva**, n. weight, heaviness, Suśr.; Ragh.; Pañcat.; (in prosody) length (of a vowel), TPrāt. xxiv, 5; burden, trouble, W.; severity, violence (of medical treatment), Suśr.; dulness, Sarvad. xv, 158; greatness, magnitude, W.; respectability, dignity, venerableness, Ragh. x, 65; the office of a teacher, MBh. v, 178, 44. **–tvaka**, n. heaviness, Bhāchāp. **–dakshiṇā**, f. a fee given to a spiritual preceptor, W. **–darśana**, n. seeing the teacher, Gaut. ii. **–dāna**, n. a present to a religious teacher, W. **–dāra**, m. sg. the teacher's wife, Āp. i, 25, 10. **–dāsa**, m., N. of a teacher (mentioned in the introduction to the Guru-gītā). **–divasa**, m. 'Bṛihaspati's day,' Thursday (?), Āryabh. i, 3. **–dīkshā**, f. initiation into the office of a spiritual preceptor, SkandaP.; *-tantra*, n., N. of a Tantra. **–devata**, n. 'having Bṛihaspati for its deity,' the 8th lunar mansion Pushya, Gal. **–deva-svāmin**, m., N. of a scholiast. **–daivata**, n. = *-dev°*, L. **–dhī**, v. l. for *rucira-dhī*, q.v. **–dhur**, f. pl. hard labour, MBh. i, 741. **–pattra**, n. tin, L.; (*ā*), f. the tamarind tree, L. **–pattraka**, n. tin, Gal. **–patnī**, f. = *-dāra*, Mn. ix, 57. **–paripāṭī**, f. 'succession of teachers,' N. of a work, Jain. **–pāka**, mfn. difficult of digestion, W. **–pādâśraya**, m. the worship of (the feet of) a teacher, W. **–putra**, m. a teacher's son, Pāṇ. i, 1, 56, Vārtt. 1, Pat. **–pūjā**, f. the worship of one's spiritual teacher, VarYogay. iv, 40; the ceremonies in propitiation of Bṛihaspati when a work is to be performed or undertaken, W. **–pramoda**, m. happiness, delight, W. **–prasāda**, m. propitiousness or the favour of one's Guru, W.; 'product of a Guru's favour,' i. e. learning, W. **–prasādanīya**, mfn. fit for propitiating one's Guru, Āp. i, 5, 9. **–prasūta**, mfn. allowed by one's elder relations, Gaut. xviii, 5. **–priya**, mfn. dear to a preceptor, W. **–bha**, m. 'Bṛihaspati's constellation,' = *-devata*, VarBṛS. lv, 31; lic, 12; VarYogay. v, 1. **–bhāra**, m. 'of heavy weight,' N. of a son of Garuḍa, MBh. v, 3598. **–°bhārika**, mfn. heavy (in the stomach; food), Bhpr. v, 21, 23. **–bhāryā**, f. = *-dāra*, Gaut. ii, 33. **–bhāva**, m. the condition of a Guru, W.; importance, weight, W. **–bhṛit**, mfn. bearing heavy things (the earth), AV. xii, 1, 48. **–mat**, mfn. containing a vowel which is long by nature or position, Pāṇ. iii, 1, 36; (*tī*), f. pregnant, BhP. x, 2, 21; *-tā*, f. heaviness, 7, 27. **–madhya**, mfn. = *madhye-guru*, heavy in the middle part, Gaṇar. 91, Sch. **–mardala**, m. a kind of drum, L. **–mushṭi**, m. a great handful, Kāṭh. xxi, 7; (of sacrificial grass, *darbha-gurumushṭī*) MaitrS. iii, 3, 6; (cf. *gru-m°*.) **–meru**, m. (in music) a kind of measure. **–ratna**, n. 'Bṛihaspati's jewel,' topaz, L. **–laghu-tā**, f. heaviness and lightness, W.; great and little value, Bhartṛ. ii, 37 (Subh.) **–lāghava**, n. great and small importance, relative importance or value, Mn. ix, 299; MBh. iii, xiii; R.; Śak. v, 2/3 [?]; length and shortness of vowels, Śrut. **–vaṅśa**, m., N. of a work. **–vat**, ind. like a Guru, Mn. ii, 208; 210; as if to a Guru, Pāṇ. i, 1, 56, Vārtt. 1; (*-vad*)*-vritti*, f. behaving to any one with as much respect as to a sacred teacher, Mn. ii, 205; 207; 247. **–varco-ghna**, m. 'removing constipation,' the lime or citron (*limpāka*), L. **–varṇa**, m. a vowel long by nature or by position, W. **–vartaka**, mfn. behaving respectfully towards parents or venerable persons, R. (G) ii, 107, 19. **–vartin**, mfn. id., MBh. x, 696; xiii, 3563; R. iv; °*ti-tā*, f. respectful behaviour towards venerable persons, ii, 115, 19. **–vāra**, m. = *-divasa*, Hcat. i, 3, 389 (MBh.) **–vāsa**, m. = *-kula-vāsa*, MBh. xiv, 26, 4 & (pl.) 33, 5. **–vṛitta**, mfn. = *-vartaka*, R. iv, 17, 36. **–vṛitti**, mfn. long by nature (vowel), W.; f. behaviour towards one's Guru, MBh. i, 706; *-para*, mfn. trying to behave respectfully towards a Guru, VP. iii, 5, 3. **-vyatha**, mfn. heavily distressed, Vikr. iii, 9. **-śiṇśapā**, f. = *śiṇśapā*, W. **-śikharin**, m. 'venerable mountain,' the Himâlaya, W. **-śishya-saṃvāda**, m. 'dialogue between teacher and pupil,' N. of a philosophical dialogue by Carana-dāsa. **-śuśrūshā**, f. obedience to one's Guru or Gurus, ŚāṅkhGṛ.; PārGṛ. ii; Vishṇ.; Mn. ii; MBh. &c. **-śuśrūshu**, mfn. obedient to one's Guru, Pāṇ. iii, 1, 26, Vārtt. 14, Pat. **-śokânala**, m. the fire of heavy sorrow, W. **-śrī-pādukā-pūjā**, f. = *-pādâśraya*, Kulârn. **-sakhī**, f. the female friend of an elder relation, Āp. i, 21, 9 (v. l. °*khi*). **-saṃnidhi**, m. presence of one's Guru, 10, 14; Mn. &c. **-samavâya**, m. a number of Gurus, Āp. i, 7, 14. **-sārā**, f. = *-śiṇśapā*, W. **-sevā**, f. obsequiousness to a Guru, Mn. xii, 83. **-skandha**, m. 'large-trunked,' the tree *śleshmaṇā*, L.; N. of a mountain, MBh. xiv, 1175. **-strī-gamanīya**, mfn., see *gam°*. **-sthira**, mfn. very firm, W. **-ha**, v. l. for *guḍuha*, q. v. **-han**, m. the murderer of a Guru, L. **Gurûdara-tva**, n. dyspepsia, Suśr. vi, 39, 102.

Guruka, mfn. a little heavy, MBh. iii, 11477; (said of limbs slightly affected with sickness) Suśr. i, 31, 22; iv, 5, 41; (in prosody) long, Śrut. 12 f.

Gurū, in comp. **-karaṇa**, n. the making heavy or venerable, Kād. iii, 1076. **-√kṛi**, to make any one (acc.) one's Guru, HYog. iii, 25.

Gurv, in comp. for °*rú*, q. v. **-akshara**, n. a long syllable, W. **-aṅganā**, f. = °*ru-dāra*, W.; any woman entitled to great respect, W. **-anta**, mfn. = *ante-guru*, heavy at the end, Gaṇar. 91, Sch. **-artha**, mfn. one who seeks to provide a maintenance for his Guru, Gaut. v, 21; Mn. xi, 1; important, W.; m. anything of importance, MBh. vi, 120, 1; a Guru's fee for instructing a pupil, i, iii, xiv; Ragh. v, 17; AgP. iv, 9; anything relating to one's Guru, Gaut. xxiii, 30; MBh. i, ch. 3; deep meaning, BhP. iii, 16, 14; (*am*), acc. ind. for one's parents, R. ii, 63, 36; for or on account of one's Guru, MBh. i, ch. 3; Pāṇ. ii, 1, 36, Vārtt. 5, Pat.; Ragh. v, 24; Hcat. **-āvali**, f. 'succession of teachers,' N. of several works, Jain.

Gurviṇī, f. (for °*rvī* formed after *garbhiṇī*) pregnant, a pregnant woman, MBh. xiv, 1843; MārkP. xxvii, 20; an irr. species of Āryā metre.

Gurvī, f. of °*rú*. **-sakhī**, f. the female friend of an elder female relation, Āp. i, 21, 9 (v. l. °*khi*).

गुरुण्टक *guruṇṭaka*, m. (cf. *guru-kaṇṭha*) a kind of peacock, L.

गुरेटक *gureṭaka*, a kind of grass, L.

गुर्गण *gurgaṇa*, m. pl., N. of a people, MārkP. lvii, 56.

गुर्जर *gurjará*, m. (cf. *gūrj°*) the district Gurjara or Gujarat, Pañcat. iv, 9 (14), ♀; Rājat. &c. (pl. the people of Gujarat, W.); (*ī*), f. id., Siṇhâs.; (in music) N. of a Rāgiṇī (v. l. *gujj°* & *guḍa-karī*).

गुर्द *gurd* or *gūrd* (q. v.), cl. 1. *gurdate* or *gūrd°*, to play, sport, jump, Dhātup. ii, 22; cl. 10. *gurdayati* or *gūrd°*, to dwell, inhabit, xxxii, 125.

गुर्व् 2. *gurv* (= √*gur*), cl. 1. P. *gūrvati*, to raise, lift up (or 'to make effort'), Dhātup. xv, 65.

गुल *gula*, m. (= *guḍa*) raw or unrefined sugar, molasses, L.; the glans penis, L.; the clitoris, L.; (*ā*), f. Tithymalus antiquorum, L.; (*ī*), f. any small globular substance, pill, L.; small pox, L.; (cf. *gola*.)

Gulikā, f. (= *guḍikā*) a ball (as a missile), Naish. iii, 127; a small ball or globule, Kād. (ifc.); a ball for playing with, Kathās. lxv; a pearl (v. l. for *guṭikā*); a pill, Kathās. lxxxix; Kālac.; 'a kernel,' see *guḍikā*; a head (of cattle), Āryabh. **-krīḍā**, f. playing with a ball (bat and ball, golf, &c.), W.

Gulya, n. a sweet or saccharine taste, L.

गुलञ्चकन्द *gulañca-kanda* = °*luccha-k°*, L.

गुलह *gulaha*, v. l. for *guḍuha*, q. v.

गुलिक *gulika*, m., N. of a hunter, BṛNārP. xxxv; (*ā*), f., see *gula*.

गुलिङ्क *guliṅka*, m. (= *kul°*) a sparrow, L.

गुलुगुधा *gulugudhā*, ind. (v. l. *gulūg°*) only in comp. **-√kṛi** (g. *ūry-ādi*) 'to torment' or 'to play, sport,' Gaṇar. 96, Sch.

गुलुगुला *gulugulā*, g. *ūry-ādi*, Gaṇar. 96.

Gulugulita, n. the roaring (of an elephant), Bālar. ii, 58.

गुलुच्छ *guluccha*, m. (= *guccha*) a bunch, nosegay, cluster of blossoms, L. **-kanda**, m., N. of a bulbous root, L. (v. l. °*lañca-k°*).

Guluñca, °**ñcha**, °**ñchaka**, = °*luccha*, L.

गुलुह *guluha*, v. l. for *guḍuha*, q. v.

गुलूगुधा *gulūgudhā*, for °*lug°*.

गुल्गुलु *gúlgulu*, n. (= *gúgg°*) bdellium, TS. vi, 2, 8, 6; ŚBr. iii; AitBr. i, 28; TāṇḍyaBr.; KātyŚr.

गुल्फ *gulphá*, m. (= *kulphá*; √*gal*, Uṇ. v) the ancle, AV. x, 2, 1 f.; Kauś.; Yājñ. iii, 86; MBh. &c. (ifc. f. *ā* [Pāṇ. iv, 1, 54, Kāś.], MBh. iv, 253). **-jāha**, n. the root of the ancle, g. *karṇâdi*. **-daghna**, mfn. reaching down to the ancle, Kāṭh. xxvi, 3; Mālatīm. iii, 16. **-dvayasa**, mfn. id., Kād.

गुल्फित *gulphita*, n. (= *gushpitá*) accumulation, ĀpŚr. x, 10, 3 (= xiii, 7, 16); (cf. *vi-gulpha*.)

Gulphinī, f. (for °*lminī*?) an army, Gal.

गुल्म *gúlma*, m. (rarely n., MBh. x; BhP. viii, x) a cluster or clump of trees, thicket, bush, shrub, VS. xxv, 8; Mn.; Yājñ. &c.; a troop or guard of soldiers, body of troops, division of an army (consisting of 45 foot, 27 horse, 9 chariots, and 9 elephants, MBh. i, 290; or of 135 foot, 81 horse, 27 chariots, and 27 elephants, L.; cf. MBh. v, 5270), Mn. vii, ix; MBh. &c.; a fort, entrenchment, W.; disciplining an army, W.; m. a chronic enlargement of the spleen or any glandular enlargement in the abdomen (as that of the mesenteric gland &c.), Suśr.; VarBṛ. xxi, 8; Kathās. xv; the spleen, L.; 'a wharf or stairs, Ghaṭ,' see *-tara-paṇya*; (*ī*), f. a cluster or clump of trees, L.; the Myrobalan tree, L.; jujube, L.; small cardamoms, L.; a tent, L. **-kālânanarasa**, m. (in med.) a kind of mixture. **-kushṭha**, n. a kind of leprosy. **-ketu**, m. sorrel, L. **-keśa**, mfn. bushy-haired, L. **-tara-paṇya**, in comp. wharf- and ferry-dues, Divyâv. viii, 30. **-mūla**, n. fresh ginger, L. **-vat**, mfn. affected with the Gulma disease, Baudh. (Hcat. i, 11, 5). **-vallī**, f. Sarcostemma viminale, L. **-vāta**, m. a disease of the spleen, W. **Gulmôdara**, n. a disease of the spleen, W.

Gulmaka, m. a cluster or clump of trees, Kathāṣ. vc; N. of a son of the Brāhman Soma-śarman, vi, 9.

Gulmin, mfn. = °*lma-vat*, Car. v, 9; Suśr. vi, 42, 7; composed of different divisions (as force &c.), W.; growing in a clump or cluster, bushy, R. vii, 54, 11; (*inī*), f. a spreading creeper, L.

Gulmī-bhūta, mfn. 'become a bush,' become worthless, SaṃhUp. i, 14.

गुल्य *gulya*. See *gula*.

गुवाक *guvāka*, m. (Uṇ. iv, 15; = *gūv°*) the betel-nut tree, PSarv.

गुश्रि *guśri*, m. (= *kuśri*) 'N. of a man,' see *gauśra*.

गुष्पित *gushpitá*, n. (= *guphita*, *gulph°*) accumulation, RV. viii, 40, 6; AV. iii, 7, 2; ŚBr. iii, 2, 2, 20 (°*shṭitá*); AV.Prāy. i, 4.

गुसायिन् *gusāyin*, m. Hussein.

गुह् 1. *guh*, cl. 1. P. Ā. *gūhati*, °*te* (cf. Pāṇ. vi, 4, 89; impf. *ágūhat*, RV. ii, 24, 3; perf. *jugūha*, Ragh. xiv; fut. *gūhishyati*, Bhaṭṭ. xvi, 41; aor. *agūhīt*, xv; Subj. 2. sg. *ghukshas* [vi] or Ved. *guhas* [RV. viii, 6, 17]; pr. p. P. *gúhat*, iv, 51, 9; Ā. *gūhamāna*, MBh. &c.; Pass. *guhyámāna*, RV. iv, 58, 4; VS. ii, 17; aor. *guhámāna*, RV. iv, 1, 11; Ved. ind. p. *gūḍhvi*, vii, 80, 2) to cover, conceal, hide, keep secret, RV. &c.: Desid. *jughukshati* (Pāṇ. vii, 2, 12; 3. du. *jugukshatas*, Pada-p. *jughuksh°*) to wish to conceal or hide away, RV. viii, 31, 7.

2. **Gúh** (only acc. *gúham* & instr. 1. *guhā́*), f. a hiding-place, RV. i, 67, 6.

Guha, m. (g. *aśmâdi*) 'reared in a secret place,' N. of Skanda (the god; cf. Kārttikeya), MBh. iii, ix, xiii; Hariv. 10478; Suśr.; Kum. &c.; N. of Śiva, MBh. xiii, 1263; of Vishṇu, W.; of a king of the Nishādas (friend of Rāma), R. i f., vi; Mcar. iv, ६०; N. belonging to persons of the writer caste, W.; a horse ('a swift horse,' W.), L.; m. pl., N. of a people in the south of India, MBh. xii, 7559; (2. *gúhā*), f. (gaṇas *vrishâdi* & *bhidâdi*) a hiding-place, cave, cavern, VS. xxx, 16; TBr. i; MBh. &c. (ifc. f. *ā*, Hcat. i, 7 & 10); (fig.) the heart, ŚvetUp. iii, 20; MBh. xii; BhP. ii, 9, 24; Hemionitis cordifolia, Suśr. i, 19, 27; v, 7, 1; (cf. *prati-g°*); Desmodium gangeticum, L.; (3. *gúhā*), Ved. instr. ind. in a hiding-place, in secret, secretly (opposed to *āvís*, and especially with √*dhā*, *ni-*√*dhā*, √*kṛi*, 'to conceal, remove'), RV.; AV.; ŚBr. xi, xiii. **-ka**, n. pl. 'Skanda's heads,' the number 'six.' **-gupta**, m. 'protected by Guha,' N. of a Bodhi-sattva, Kāraṇḍ. i, 4. **-candra**, m., N. of a merchant, Kathās. xvii, 72. **-deva**, m., N. of a teacher, VBr. **-priyā**, f., N. of Indra's daughter, Gal. **-rāja**, m. a peculiar form or construction of a temple, VarBṛS. **-vaktra**, n. pl. 'Skanda's faces,' the number 'six.' **-vāhana**, n. 'Skanda's vehicle,' i. e. his peacock, Bālar. ii, 43. **-śiva**, m., N. of a king of Kaliṅga. **-shashṭhī**, f. the 6th day in the light half of Mārgaśirsha. **-sena**, m., N. of a prince; of a merchant, Kathās. xiii, xvii. **-hata**, mfn. 'struck by Skanda,' the Krauñca mountain, Gal. **Guhâgarī**, f. a kind of betel, Gal.

Guhati, m. the root *guh*, TUp. ii, 1, Sch.

Guhād-avadya, mfn. concealing deficiencies, RV. ii, 19, 5.

Guhara, mfn. fr. °*ha*, g. *aśmâdi*.

Guhalu, *us*, m., N. of a man, g. 2. *lohitâdi* (*gūh°*, Hemac.; *gulu* & *guggulu*, Kāś.)

2. & 3. **Guhā**, see s. v. *guha*. **-kāram**, ind. so as to conceal one's self, TBr. i. **-gahana-vat**, mfn. furnished with caverns and thickets, R. iv, 48, 6. **-gṛiha**, n. a cavern, W. **-cara**, mfn. moving in secret i. e. in the heart, MuṇḍUp. **-mukha**, mfn. wide-mouthed, open-mouthed, MBh. iii, 16118; Kathās. lv. **-vāsin**, m. 'dwelling in secret,' N. of a Muni, VāyuP. xxiii, 164; °*si-tīrtha*, n., N. of a Tīrtha, ŚivaP. **-śaya**, mfn. dwelling in hiding-places or in caverns, Ragh. iv, 72; Suśr.; being in the heart, Āp.; MuṇḍUp.; ŚvetUp.; MBh. xiv; BhP. ('N. of Vishṇu,' L.); m. a tiger, L. **-hita**, mfn. being in a secret place i. e. in the heart, KaṭhUp.

Guhêśvara, m. 'lord of caverns,' N. of an attendant in Śiva's retinue, Kathās. cxiv, 61.

Guhina, n. a wood, thicket, L.

Guhila, m., N. of a prince (descendant of Bappa), Ratnak.; n. (g. *kāśâdi*) = °*hina*, Uṇ. i, 57.

Guhera, m. a smith, 62; a guardian, Uṇ. vr.

Gúhya, mfn. (Pāṇ. iii, 1, 109, Kāś., g. *daṇḍâdi*) to be covered or concealed or hidden or kept secret, concealable, private, secret, mysterious, mystical, RV.; AV. &c.; m. hypocrisy, L.; a tortoise, L.; N. of Vishṇu (RTL. p. 106), W.; (*am*), ind. secretly, privately, MBh. xii, 902; (*am*), n. a secret, mystery, MBh. (ifc. f. *ā*, xiii, 5876); Mn. xii, 117; Bhag. &c.; the pudenda, Suśr.; VarBṛS.; Kathās. ii, 56; (cf. 1. *gṛihya*) the anus, W. **-kāli**, f. 'mysterious Durgā,' a form of Durgā, Tantras. ii. **-guru**, m. (cf. *grihya-g°*) 'the mystic Guru,' Śiva (considered as the especial teacher of the Tantras), L. **-tantra**, n., N. of a Tantra, Ānand. 31, Sch. **-dīpaka**, m. a flying insect which gives out light, fire-fly, L. **-devī**, f., N. of a goddess, Buddh. **-nishyanda**, m. urine, L. **-pati**, m. 'lord of the mysteries,' N. of Vajra-dhara, Buddh.; *-vidyā*, f., N. of a prayer, ib. **-pattra**, m. 'having concealed leaves or blossoms,' Ficus religiosa, Npr. **-pattraka**, m. id., Gal. **-pidhāna**, n. a covering for the privities, L. **-pushpa**, m. = *-pattra*, L. **-bīja**, m. 'having concealed seeds,' Andropogon Schœnanthus, L. **-bhāshita**, n. secret speech, mystical prayer or incantation, L. **-ruj**, f. a disease of the pudenda, VarBṛS. v, 86. **-roga**, m. id., Ashṭâṅg. vi, ch. 33. **-vidyā**, f. knowledge of Mantras or mystical incantations, VP. i, 9, 117. **Guhyêśvarī**, f. 'mystic deity,' i. e. Prajñā (female energy of the Ādi-buddha), SvayambhūP.

Guhyaka, m., N. of a class of demi-gods who like the Yakshas are attendants of Kubera (the god of wealth) and guardians of his treasures (they may have received their N. from living in mountain caverns), Mn. xii, 47; MBh.; Hariv. &c. (identified with Yakshas, MBh. v, 7480; Megh. 5 &c.); the number 'eleven,' Sūryas.; N. of Kubera, L.; m. 'mystery,' see *tathāgata-g°*. **-pūjana**, n. worship of the Guhyakas, VarBṛ. **Guhyakâdhipati**, m. 'lord of the Guhyakas,' N. of Kubera, MBh. ii, 1760. **Guhyakêśvara**, m. id., L.

Gūḍhá (*gūḷhá*, RV.), mfn. covered, hidden, concealed, invisible, secret, private, RV. &c.; disguised,

Mn. ix, 261; MBh. iii, 17311; n. a secret place or mystery, KaṭhUp. i, 1, 29; one of the Śabdâlaṃkāras, Sarasv. ii, 19; (*am*), ind. secretly, Daś. vii, 248; Rājat. v, 268; (*ā*), f., N. of a Śruti, Gal.; (*e*), loc. ind. secretly, Mn. vii, 186; ix, 170. **–caturtha-pāda-prahelikā**, f. a riddle in which the fourth Pāda (of a stanza) is hidden, Kād. i, 74 f. **–cāra**, m. (= *-cārin*) a spy, Daś. i, 51. **–cārin**, mfn. going about secretly, Yājñ. ii, 268; m. a spy, W. **–ja**, mfn. (= *gūḍhôtpanna*) born privately (a son born during the absence of the husband, the real father being unknown; one of the 12 forms particularised in Hindū law, the child belonging to the husband of the disloyal wife), ii, 129. **–tā**, f. 'concealment, secresy,' (*ayā*), instr. ind. privately, secretly, Vyavahārat. vii, 7. **–tva**, n. obscurity (of sense), MBh. i, 82. **–daṇḍa**, m. a fine secretly imposed or exacted (cf. *guptá* with *daṇḍa*), Rājat. vii, 1070. **–nīḍa**, m. 'having its nest concealed,' the wagtail, L. **–pattra**, m. 'hidden-leaved,' Capparis aphylla, L.; = *-mallikā*, L. **–patha**, m. 'having a hidden path,' the mind, intellect, L.; = *-mārga*, W. **–pad**, nom. *-pād*, m. 'hidden-footed,' a snake, L. **–pāda**, mfn. having the feet hidden in (in comp.), ŚārṅgP. (Hit.); m. = *-pad*, MBh. vii, 5407. **–purusha**, m. a spy, disguised agent, L. **–pushpaka**, m. 'hidden-blossomed,' Mimusops Elengi, L. **–phala**, m. 'hidden-fruited,' for *guḍaph°*, L. **–bhāshita**, n. secret intelligence, private communication, W. **–mallikā**, f. Alangium hexapetalum, L. **–māya**, mf(*ā*)n. keeping secret one's artifices or tricks, MBh. iii, 31, 37. **–mārga**, m. a bye-path, private way, L. **–maithuna**, n. secret copulation, Cāṇ.; m. 'copulating in secret,' a crow, L. **–varcas**, mfn. = *°ḍhârcis*, BhP. i, 19, 28; m. 'concealing its feces,' a frog, L. **–vallikā**, v. l. for *-mall°*, L. **–vasati**, f. abode in a secret place, Daś. iv, 45. **–sâkshin**, m. a concealed witness (placed by the plaintiff so as to hear the defendant without being noticed by him), Nār. (Smṛitit. x). **Gūḍhâgāra**, n. a dungeon, W. **Gūḍhâgūḍha-tā**, f., **-tva**, n. obscurity and perspicuity, Sāh. ii, 10 & 11. **Gūḍhâṅga**, m. 'hidden-bodied,' a tortoise, L. **Gūḍhâṅghri**, m. = *°ḍha-pad*, L. **Gūḍhârcis**, mfn. of concealed glory, W. **Gūḍhârtha**, m. the hidden or mystic sense, Ānand., Sch.; having a hidden meaning, Vām. ii, 1, 11 & 14; *-candrikā*, *-tattva-dīpikā*, *-dīpikā*, *-ratna-mālā*, f., N. of different commentaries. **Gūḍhâśaya**, mfn. concealing one's intentions. **Gūḍhôtpanna**, mfn. = *°ḍha-ja*, Mn. ix, 159 & 170. **Gūḍho'tman** (for *°ḍhâtman*), m., Pāṇ. vi, 3, 109, Siddh.

Gūha, mf(*ā*)n., see *jñāna-*.

Gūhana, n. concealing, hiding, MBh. xi, xii.

Gūhitavya, mfn. to be hidden or concealed or kept secret, MBh. iii, 10613.

गू 1. *gū* = √4. *gu*, q. v.

Gūtha, m. (also n., g. *ardharcâdi*) 'feces, ordure' (in the Pāyāsi-sutta in Pāli), see *karṇa-*. **–lakta**, m. the bird Turdus Salica, L.

Gūthaka, m., see *karṇa-*; the plant Granthiparṇa, L.

Gūna, mfn. voided (as ordure), Pāṇ. viii, 2, 44, Vārtt. 2.

गू 2. *gū*, mfn. 'going.' See *agre-gū*.

गूक *gūka*, m. a fish, Gal.

गूढ *gūḍha*. See √1. *guh*.

गूथ *gūtha*, *°thaka*, *gūna*. See √1. *gū*.

गूर् *gūr*. See √*gur*.

Gūraṇa, n. reproach, Rājat. vii, 1605; = *gur°* (*udyama*), L.

Gūrṇa, mfn., Pāṇ. viii, 2, 61, Kāś.

Gūrtá, **gūrti**. See √*gur*.

गूर्द् *gūrd* (= √*gurd*, q. v.), cl. 1. P. *°dati*, to leap after (loc.)

Gūrda, m. a jump, Kāṭh. xxxix, 5; ĀpŚr. xvi; ('a particular food of the Asuras,' Sch.) N. of a Sāman, TāṇḍyaBr. xiii, 12, 8; Lāṭy. vii, 1, 1 f.; *Prajāpater g°* or *°teḥ kūrda*, 'jump of Prajāpati,' N. of two Sāmans, ĀrshBr.; (*ī*), f., g. *gaurâdi*.

गूर्ध् *gūrdh*, cl. 10. P. *°dhayati* (Naigh. iii, 14) to praise, RV. viii, 19, 1.

गूला *gūlā*. See *uru-gūlā*.

गूवाक *gūvāka* = *guv°*, L.

गूषणा *gūshaṇā*, f. the eye in a peacock's tail, L.

गूह *gūha*, *°hana*, &c. See √1. *guh*.

गृ *gṛi*, cl. 1. P. *garati*, to sprinkle, moisten, Dhātup. xxii, 39; (cf. √*ghṛi*.)

गृज् *gṛij* or *gṛiñj* (= √*garj*), cl. 1. *garjati* (see √*garj*) or *gṛiñjati*, to sound, roar, vii, 74 f.

Gṛiñja, m., N. of a plant, Car. vi, 21; Suśr. vi.

Gṛiñjana, m. (n., L.) a kind of onion or garlic or a small red variety of it (prohibited as food), Mn. v, 5; Yājñ. i, 176; Bhpr.; Nyāyam &c.; a turnip, W.; the tops of hemp chewed to produce an inebriating effect (the Gāñja), W.; n. poisoned flesh (meat of an animal destroyed by a poisoned arrow), L.

Gṛiñjanaka, m. (= *°na*) a kind of onion or garlic, Car. i, 27; vi, 9; n. the two side-pieces of the hilt of a sword, Gal.

Gṛiñjina (v. l. *°jima*), m., N. of a son of Śūra and brother of Vasu-deva, Hariv. 1926.

गृणत् *gṛiṇát*, *°ṇānā*, &c. See √1. *gṛī*.

गृण्डिव *gṛiṇḍiva*, m. a kind of jackal, L. (v. l. *°ḍīva*).

गृत्स *gṛitsa*, mfn. (Naigh. iii, 15; √*gṛidh*?) clever, dexterous, judicious, wise, RV.; m. a sharp fellow, VS. xvi, 25; the god of love, Uṇ.; (cf. *ratha-gṛitsá*.) **–tama**, v. l. for *dīrgha-t°*, VP. **–pati** (*gṛít°*), m. the chief of a number of sharpers, VS. xvi, 25. **–mati**, m. 'clever-minded,' N. of a son of Su-hotra, Hariv. 1733 f. **–madá**, m., N. of a son of Śaunaka of Bhṛigu's family (formerly a son of Śuna-hotra [Su-hotra, VP.; BhP.] of the family of Aṅgiras, but by Indra's will transferred to the Bhṛigu family; author of most of the hymns of RV. ii), RAnukr.; ĀśvŚr. xii, 10, 13; ĀśvGṛ. iii, 4, 2; ŚāṅkhGṛ.; MBh. xiii; Hariv. &c.; m. pl. Gṛitsamada's family, RV. ii, 4, 9; 19, 8; 39, 8; 41, 18.

गृद *gṛidá* (= *gudá*?), a part of a horse's hind quarter near the anus, TS. vii, 4, 19, 1.

गृध् *gṛidh*, cl. 4. P. *gṛídhyati* (perf. 3. pl. *jagṛidhur*, BhP. v, 4, 1; *jāgṛidhúr*, RV. ii, 23, 16; aor. *ágṛidhat*, RV. x, 34, 4; fut. *gardhishyati*, ŚBr. iii; pr. p. *gṛídhyat*, RV. iv, 38, 3; ind. p. *gṛiddhvā*, BhP. x, 64, 40), to endeavour to gain, RV. iv, 38, 3; AV. viii, 6, 1; to covet, desire, strive after greedily, be desirous of or eager for (loc. [RV.; AV. &c.] or acc., ĪśUp.; MBh. iv, 276; BhP. v, vi, x): Caus. P. *gardhayati*, to be greedy, Dhātup. xxxii, 124; to make desirous or greedy, Pāṇ. i, 3, 69, Kāś.; Ā. *°yate*, to deceive, cheat, ib.; Bhaṭṭ. viii, 43: Intens. 2. sg. impf. *ajarghāḥ*, Pāṇ. viii, 3, 14, Kāś.: [cf. *anu-*, *prati-*; *abhi-ghṛidhna*, *pra-gardhin*; cf. also Old Germ. *gir*: Mod. Germ. *gier*: Engl. *greedy* (?); Goth. *gredags*, *gaurs*: Hib. *greadaim*, 'I burn'; *greadhnach*, 'joyful, glad;' *gradh*, 'love, charity; dear;' *graidhneog*, 'a beloved female,' &c.: Lith. *godus*, *gedu*: Slav. *glad*, 'hunger.']

Gṛiddha, mfn. desirous of, eagerly longing for (loc.), MBh.

Gṛiddhin, mfn. ifc. eagerly longing for, MBh.; being very busy with (in comp.), Hariv. 3406.

Gṛiddhi-tva, n. eagerly longing for (in comp.), MBh. v, 2591.

Gṛidhu, mfn. libidinous, Uṇ. vṛ.; m. (= *gṛitsa*) the god of love, Uṇ. i, 24.

Gṛidhū, m. air voided downwards (*apâna*), Uṇ. vṛ.; intellect (cf. MBh. v, 932), ib.; = *kutsita*, ib.

Gṛidhnin, mfn. eagerly longing for, R. ii, 79, 12.

Gṛidhnú, mfn. (Pāṇ. iii, 2, 140) hasty, swift, RV. i, 70, 11 & 162, 20; TBr. ii; greedily desirous of (loc. [R. ii] or in comp., Megh. 9 [v. l.]; BhP. iii, 14, 20); (*a-*, 'not greedy,' Ragh. i, 21); [cf. Goth. *gairns*, *gairnja*; Lith. *godùs*.] **–tā**, f. greediness, L.; great desire for (in comp.), Kathās.

Gṛidhya, mfn. longed for greedily, Bhaṭṭ. vi, 55; m.?, AV. xii, 2, 38; (*ā*), f. greediness after, desire for (in comp.), MBh. xii, 11274; xiii, 5590.

Gṛidhra, mfn. desiring greedily or fervently, RV.; eager for, desirous of (in comp.), MBh. vii, 210; Pañcat.; BhP. xi; m. a vulture, RV.; AV.; TS. v; AdbhBr.; Mn. &c.; N. of a son of Kṛishṇa, Bhp. x, 61, 16; of a Ṛishi in the 14th Manv-antara, VP.; of a Rakshas, GaṇP.; (*ī*), f. a female vulture, Yājñ. iii, 256; Prab. iv, 3; = *°dhrikā*, Hariv. 223; [cf. Old Germ. *gīr*; Mod. Germ. *geier*.] **–kūṭa**, m. 'vulture-peak,' N. of a mountain near Rājagṛiha, MBh. xii, 1797; Lalit. &c.; Hit. **–cakra**, m. du. the vulture and the Cakra-vāka, W. **–jambūka**, m., N. of an attendant of Śiva, L. (*°mbhūka*, MS.) **–dṛishṭi**, mfn. vulture-eyed, MBh. xii, 5309. **–nakhī**, f. 'vulture-clawed,' Asteracantha longifolia, Suśr. i; the jujube, L. **–pati**, m. 'lord of vultures,' Jaṭāyu, R. iii, 56, 41. **–pattra**, m. 'vulture-feathered,' N. of an attendant of Skanda, MBh. ix, 2576; (*ā*), f. the plant Dhūmra-pattrā, L. **–putrikā**, f. id., Gal. **–mojântaka**, m., N. of a son of Śvaphalka, Hariv. 1918; 2084; v. l. *gandha-moksha*. **–yātu** (*gṛidh°*), m. a vulture-shaped demon, RV. vii, 104, 22. **–rāj**, m. = *-pati*, BhP. iv, 19, 16. **–rāja**, m. id., R. iii, vi. **–vaktrā**, f. 'vulture-faced,' N. of a goddess, Kālac. **–vaṭa**, N. of a Tīrtha, VarP. clvi. **–vāja**, mfn. = *-vājita*, MBh. ix, 1413. **–vājita**, mfn. (= *gārdhra-v°*) furnished with vulture-feathers (an arrow), xiv, 2454. **–śīrshan** (*gṛidh°*), mf(*shṇī*)n. vulture-headed, TĀr. i, 28, 1. **–sád**, mfn. sitting on a vulture, TS. iv, 4, 7, 1. **–sī**, f. (metrically also *-si*) rheumatism affecting the loins, Car. i, 5 & 20; vi, 5 & 24; Suśr. **Gṛidhrêśvara**, m., N. of a mountain, ĀdityaP.

Gṛidhrāṇa, mfn. 'greedy as a vulture,' eagerly desiring, BhP. v, 7, 13; (*ā*), f. = *gṛidhra-pattrā*, L.

Gṛidhrikā, f. (= *°dhrī*) N. of a daughter of Kaśyapa by Tāmrā (mother of vultures), Hariv. 222.

गृभ् *gṛibh*, f. (only acc. *gṛibham*, instr. *gṛibhā*, abl. *°bhás*; for dat. *°bhé*, see √*grah*) grasping, seizing, RV. vii, 4, 3; viii, 17, 15; VS. xxi, 43; mfn. 'grasping,' ifc., see *jīva-*, *sute-*, *syūma-gṛibh*.

Gṛibhá, m. (= *gṛihá*) dwelling-place, RV. vii, 21, 2.

Gṛibháyat, mfn. (irr. pr. p.) seizing, i, 148, 3.

Gṛibhāya, Nom. P. *°yáti* (cf. Pāṇ. iii, 1, 84 & Vārtt.; only Impv. *°yá* & *°yáta*; cf. *anu-*, *ā-sam-*, *ud-*, *prati-*, *saṃ-*, *sam-ā-√grah*; fr. *gṛibhāya* are to be derived the forms of √*grah* (q. v.) beginning with *gṛibhī*, *grabhī*, *gṛihī*, *grahī*), to grasp, seize, RV. vii, 104, 18; viii, 17, 5 & 69, 10; AV. ii.

Gṛíbhi, mfn. (cf. *gárbha*) holding, containing (with gen.), AV. xii, 1, 57; (cf. *pád-*; *dur-gṛibhi*.)

Gṛibhita, mfn. grasped, seized, BhP. iii, 21, 24.

Gṛibhītá, mfn. (= *gṛihītá*) id., RV.; VS. xvii, 55; BhP. x, 87, 14; (cf. *gṛíbhi*) impregnated, bearing fruit, AitBr. ii, 1, 6. **–tāti** (*°tá-*), f. the being seized, RV. v, 74, 4.

Gṛibhītvā́, ind. p. √*grah*, q. v.

Gṛih, mfn. only ifc. 'seizing' (the mind), moving, Śiś. ix, 55.

Gṛihá, m. an assistant, servant, RV. x, 119, 13; (m. sg. & pl., in later language m. pl. & n. sg.) a house, habitation, home, RV. (*mṛin-máya g°*, 'house of earth,' grave, vii, 89, 1); AV. (*adharâd g°*, 'the lower world,' ii, 14, 3) &c.; (ifc. f. *ā*, R. i, 5, 9; *ī*, Pañcat. i, 17, 5); ifc. with names of gods 'a temple' (cf. *caṇḍikā-*, *devatā-*), of plants 'a bower;' m. pl. a house as containing several rooms, RV.; AV. &c.; the inhabitants of a house, family, ŚBr. i; BhP. iii, 2, 7; Kathās. xx, 21; a wife, Pāṇ. iii, 1, 144, Kāś.; m. a householder, BhP. xi, 8, 9; n. a wife, Pañcat. iii, 7, 13; a sign of the zodiac, VarBṛS. vci, civ; an astrological mansion, VarBṛ. i, iv f.; N. of the 4th astrological mansion, i, 16; a square (in chess or in any similar game), Kād. i, 48; Pāṇ. v, 2, 9, Kaiy.; a name, appellation, L.; (cf. *anti-*, *bhumi-*, *śayyā-*, *su*); [cf. Zd. *geredha*; Got. *gards*; Lat. *hortus*.] **–kacchapa**, m. 'house-tortoise,' a small flat oblong stone (shaped like the shell of a tortoise) used for grinding condiments &c., L. **–kanyā**, f. Aloe perfoliata (*ghṛita-kumārī*), Bhpr.; (cf. *kanyakā*.) **–kapota**, m. a domestic pigeon, Śiś. iv, 52; Sāh. iii, 88. **–kapotaka**, m. id., L. **–karaṇa**, n. house-building, W.; household affairs, W. **–kartṛi**, m. a house-builder, carpenter, R. vii, 5, 19; a kind of sparrow, L. **–karman**, n. = *-kārya*, Pañcat. ii, 3, 8; BhP. x; Sāh. x, 88, 3; a domestic rite (performed at the solemn entrance into a house); *°rma-kara*, m. a domestic servant, Pañcat.; *°rma-dāsa*, m. id., Bhartṛ. i, 1. **–kalaha**, m. domestic dissension, W. **–kāraka**, m. a house-builder, mason, carpenter (kind of mixed caste), Yājñ. iii, 146; Parāś. Paddh. **–kārin**, m. 'house-builder,' a kind of wasp, Mn. xi, 66; Yājñ. iii, 214. **–kārya**, n. a domestic affair, Mn. v, 150; Daś. xi, 207. **–kukkuṭa**, m. a domestic cock, Suśr. iv, 9, 18; Prab. v, 20. **–kumārī**, f. = *-kanyā*, L.

— kuliṅga, m. a kind of bird, Suśr. i, 46, 2, 14. **— kūlaka**, m. Trichosanthes anguina, Bhpr. **— kṛitya**, n. household matters or affairs, BhP. x, 8, 30; 9, 22; RV. i, 48, 5, Sāy.; 'affairs of a royal house,' a kind of tax or duty, Rājat. v, 166 (see *aṭṭa-pati-bhāgâkhya-g°*); 175; 300. **— kshata**, m. a kind of divine being, Vāstuv.; Hcat. **— kshetrin**, mfn. possessing a house and fields, Hariv. 3493. **— gupta**, N. of a man, Daś. xi, 211. **— godhā**, f. the small house-lizard, Kathârṇ. x. **— godhikā**, f. (= *āgāra-g°*) id., VarBṛS.; Suśr. (said to be venomous). **— gopikā**, f. a kind of demon (v. l. *-golikā*), vi, 49, 28. **— golaka**, m. = *-godhā*, MārkP. xv, 24; (*ikā*), f. id., L.; v. l. for *-gopikā*. **— ghnī**, f. pernicious to a house (a woman), PārGṛ. i, 11, 2 ff. **— caṭaka**, m. a house-sparrow, W. **— cullī**, f. two rooms contiguous to each other (one facing west, the other east), VarBṛS. liii, 40. **— cetas**, mfn. thinking only of one's house, BhP. ix, 11, 17. **— cchidra**, n. 'a breach in a house,' family dissensions, Vet. Introd. 12; Hit. **— ja**, mfn. born in the house (a slave), Mn. viii, 415; Yājñ. ii, 181/4 (Nār.) **— jana**, m. the family, Mudr. i, 2/5. **— jāta**, mfn. = *-ja*, Yājñ. ii, 181/4; (said of animals) VarBṛS. lxi, 7; Pañcat. i, 1, 83; Kathās. lx. **— jālikā**, f. disguise, L. **— jñānin**, v. l. for *grihe-jñ°*. **— taṭī**, f. a terrace in front of a house, threshold, L. **— dāru**, n. a house-post, Mṛicch. iv, 3. **— dāsa**, m. a domestic slave, W.; (*ī*), f. a female domestic slave, BhP. x, 9, 1. **— dāsikā**, f. = *°sī*, 83, 39. **— dāha**, m. a fire, conflagration, ĀpŚr. ix, 3, 17; ŚāṅkhŚr. iii, 4. **— dīpti**, f. the splendour or ornament of a house (a virtuous woman), Mn. ix, 26; MBh. v, 1408. **— devatā**, f. the deity of a house, Bhām. iii, 12; (pl.) ĀśvGṛ.; Gaut.; Mṛicch. i, 1/4; Kathās. iv, 74. **— devī**, f., N. of a Rākshasī who protects the house, MBh. ii, 730. **— druma**, m. Odina pennata, L.; Tectona grandis, L. **— dvāra**, n. a house-door, Gobh. iv, 7, 20. **— dhūma**, m. (= *āgāra-dh°*), N. of a plant (= *dhundhu-māra*, L.), Suśr. iv f. **— nadikā**, f. a ditch in a house, Kād. **— namana**, g. 2. *kshubhnâdi*. **— naraka**, m. a hell of a house, W. **— nāśana**, m. (= *graha-n°*) 'destroying (walls of) a house (by building in and about it),' a pigeon, L. **— nīḍa**, m. 'having its nest in houses,' a sparrow, L. **— pá**, m. the guardian of a house, VS. xxx, 11. **— pati** (*°há-*), m. (Pāṇ. vi, 2, 18) the master of a house, householder, RV. vi, 53, 2; AV.; ŚBr. iv, viii; Kauś. &c.; N. of Agni, RV.; VS.; AV.; ŚBr. i, v; MBh. iii, 14211; xii, 8883 (gen. pl. *°tinām* metrically for *°tīnām*); for *graha-p°* (q. v.); a householder of peculiar merit (giving alms and performing all the prescribed ceremonies), esp. one who has the precedence at a grand sacrifice (*sattrá*), AitBr. v, viii; ŚBr. viii, xi f.; TāṇḍyaBr. &c.; the head or judge of a village, Daś. viii, 207; Mṛicch. ii, 1/4, 8, Sch.; a Brāhman of the 2nd order who after having finished his studies marries, W.; = *dharma* (the maintenance of a sacred and perpetual fire, the duty of a householder, hospitality &c.), L.; = *-vitta*, L. **— patin**, only gen. pl. *°tinām*, see *-pati*. **— patnī** (*°há-*), f. the mistress of a house, a householder's wife, RV. x, 85, 26; AV.; Kauś. 23 f. **— pāta**, m. the falling in (of a house), Kathās. xxviii. **— pāla**, m. a house-guardian, MBh. iii, 10774; a house-dog, BhP. i; iii, 30, 16; *°lāya*, Nom. Ā. *°lāyate*, to resemble a house-dog, vii, 15, 18. **— potaka**, m. the site of a habitation, L. **— poshaṇa**, n. maintenance of a household, Kathās. ii, 55. **— prakaraṇa**, n., N. of a work. **— praveśa**, m. solemn entrance into a house. **— babhru**, m. the musk rat, L.; (cf. *geha-nakula*.) **— bali**, m. a domestic oblation (offering of the remnants of a meal to all creatures, such as animals and certain deities; see RTL. p. 422), Mn. iii, 265; MārkP. xxix; *-devatā*, f. pl. certain deities to whom domestic oblations are offered, ĀśvGṛ. Pariś.; *-priya*, m. 'fond of domestic oblations,' the crane Ardea nivea, L.; *-bhuj*, m. 'enjoying domestic oblations,' a sparrow, L.; a crow, L.; the crane Ardea nivea, Megh. 24. **— bhaṅga**, m. 'driven from his house,' an exile, W.; destroying a house, breaking into a house, W.; family decay, failure or ruin (of a family, firm or association), W. **— bhañjana**, n. the breaking down or destroying a house, W.; causing the ruin of a family, W. **— bhadraka**, n. an audience-hall, Gal. **— bhartṛi**, m. the master of a house, VarBṛS. liii, 58. **— bhitti**, f. a house-wall, L. **— bhūmi**, f. = *-potaka*, L. **— bhedin**, mfn. prying into domestic affairs, causing family quarrels, W. **— bhojin**, m. an inmate of the same house, Rājat. v, 402. **— maṇi**, m. 'house-jewel,' a lamp, L. **— mācikā**, f. (= *-moc°*) a bat, L. **— mārjanī**, f. 'cleaning the house,' a female servant of the house, BhP. x, 83, 11. **— mukha**, m. = *upakuı vāṇa*, Gal. **— mūḍhadhī**, mfn. bewildered with domestic cares, W. **— mṛiga**, m. a dog, L. **— megha**, m. a multitude of houses, R. v, 10, 5. **— medhá**, m. a domestic sacrifice, MaitrS. i, 10, 15; ŚBr. x; Pāṇ. iv, 2, 32; mfn. one who performs the domestic sacrifices or is the object of them (as the Maruts), RV. vii, 59, 10; MaitrS. i, 10, 1 & 15, ŚāṅkhŚr. iii; connected with domestic rites or a householder's duties, BhP. ii f.; m. a householder's duties, Āp.; m. pl., N. of particular winds causing rain, TĀr. i, 9, 5; RV. ii, 12, 12, Sāy. **— °medhín**, mfn. one who performs the domestic sacrifices, religious man, AV.; TS. iii; ŚBr. xiii &c.; being the object of domestic rites (as the Maruts), VS. xvii, xxiv; TS. i; TBr. i; ŚBr. ii; KātyŚr.; m. the householder who performs the domestic rites, a married Brāhman who has a household, a Brāhman in the 2nd period of his life, Mn. iii f., vi; MBh. &c.; (*inī*), f. the wife of a householder, BhP. iv, 26, 13 ('natural intelligence,' Sch.); *°dhi-tā*, f. the state of a householder, Bālar. vi, 30; *°dhi-vrata*, n. a rite observed by a householder along with his wife, Gobh. i, 4, 18. **— °medhíya**, mfn. (Pāṇ. iv, 2, 32) relating to the *°dhá* or domestic sacrifice, RV. vii, 56, 14; TBr. i; ŚBr. xi; ŚāṅkhŚr. xiv; BhP.; n. a domestic sacrifice, Lāṭy. x, 12, 8. **— °medhya**, mfn (Pāṇ. iv, 2, 32) relating to the *°dhá* or domestic sacrifice, Kāṭh. xxxvi, 9. **— mocikā**, f. = *-māc°*, Gal. **— yantra**, n. an apparatus to which on festive occasions the flags of a house are fastened, Kum. vi, 41. **— raksha**, f. the guarding of a house, Hit. ii, 3, 2/9. **— randhra**, n. = *-cchidra*, W. **— rājá**, m. the lord of the house (Agni), AV. xi, 1, 29. **— vat**, m. the possessor of a house, householder, Pañcat. ii; BhP. x, 60, 59. **— varman**, m., N. of a prince, Hcar. iv, vi. **— vāṭikā**, *°ṭī*, f. a garden or grove near a house, L. **— vāsa**, m. living in one's own house, office of a householder, MBh. xiii. **— vāsin**, mfn. living in one's own house, MBh. xiii, 94, 28, Sch. **— viccheda**, m. the extinction or destruction of a family, W. **— vitta**, m. = *-pati*, L. **— vṛikshavāṭikā**, f., N. of a literary work, Sāh. vi, 194 8/9. **— vyāpāra**, m. household affairs, domestic economy, Pañcat.; Subh. **— vrata**, mfn. devoted to home, BhP. vii, 5, 30. **— śāyin**, m. 'dwelling in the house,' a pigeon, Npr. **— śikhaṇḍin**, m. a peacock kept in a house, Mṛicch. v, 1; Kāvyâd. ii, 105. **— śuka**, m. a parrot kept in a house, Amar.; a domestic poet, Rājat. v, 31. **— śuddhi**, f. ceremonies for the purification of a house, W. **— saṃrodha**, m. besetting a house (for recovering a debt). **— saṃveśaka**, m. a house-builder, Mn. iii, 163. **— saṃstha**, mfn. = *-vāsin*, MBh. xiii, 94, 28. **— sāra**, property, Mudr. i, 2/5, 5. **— sārasa**, m. the crane Ardea sibirica, Kād. **— stha**, mfn. ifc. living or staying in any one's house, MBh.; m. a householder, Brāhman in the 2nd period of his religious life (performing the duties of the master of a house and father of a family after having finished his studies and after investiture with the sacred thread; cf. RTL. pp. 138; 150; 362 & 386), Gaut.; Āp.; Mn.; BhP. vii, &c.; (*ā*), f. a housewife, Vet. ii, 1/10; *-tā*, f. the office of a householder, Mcar. iv, 33; *-dharma*, m. a householder's duty, Hit.; *°sthâśrama*, m. the order of a householder, Mn. iii, 2; *°sthôpanishad*, f. religious knowledge of a householder, MBh. i, 3629. **— sthāna**, n. a royal tent, L. **— sthiti**, f. the state of a householder, Kathās. lxxiii. **— sthūṇa**, n. the pillar of a house, Siddh. stry. 22, Sch. **— svāminī**, f. a housewife, Pañcad. i, 10. **— han**, mf(*ghnī*)n., see *-ghnī*. **Gṛihâksha**, m. 'house-eye,' a loop-hole, round or oblong window, L.; (cf. *gavâksha*.) **Gṛihâgata**, mfn. coming to a house, Ragh. iii, 11; m. a guest, L. **Gṛihâcāra**, m. 'house-custom,' the duties of a householder or housewife towards a guest, Kathās. lvii. **Gṛihâjira**, n. a house-yard, Pañcat. ii, 6, 1/3, 8. **Gṛihâdhipa**, m. 'house-lord,' a householder, L. **Gṛihânubaddha**, mfn. confined to the house, W. **Gṛihâpaṇa**, m. a bazaar, Sūryapr., Sch. **Gṛihâbhipālin**, mfn. watching or taking care of the house, W.; m. a watchman, W. **Gṛihâmbu**, n. sour gruel made from the fermentation of rice-water, L. **Gṛihâmla**, n. id., L. **Gṛihâyaṇika**, m. a householder, W. **Gṛihâyanika**, m. id., L. **Gṛihârambha**, m. building a house, MBh. xii, 6649 (= BhP. xi, 9, 15). **Gṛihârāma**, m. = *°ha-vāṭikā*, L. **Gṛihârūḍha-cetas**, mfn. devoted to home, W. **Gṛihârtha**, m. household affairs, any household care, Mn. ii, 67. **Gṛihâlikā**, m., *°likī*, *°lī*, f. = *griha-golaka*, L. **Gṛihâvagrahaṇī**, f. = *°ha-taṭī*, Hcar. v, 94. **Gṛihâvagrahiṇī**, f. id., L. **Gṛihâvasthita**, mfn. dwelling or living in a house, W.; situated or abiding in any dwelling-place, W. **Gṛihâśayā**, v. l. for *°śrayā*. **Gṛihâśman**, m. = *°ha-kacchapa*, L. **Gṛihâśrama**, m. the order of a householder or Gṛiha-stha (q. v.), Mn. vi, 1; MBh. i, xii; BhP. v; *-vat*, m. the Brāhman as a householder. **Gṛihâśramin**, m. = *°ma-vat*, x, 86, 14; MārkP. xxix. **Gṛihâśrayā**, f. the betel tree, L. **Gṛihe-jñānin**, mfn. 'wise only inside a house,' inexperienced, stupid, MBh. xiii, 4576 (*°ha-jñ°*, ed. Bomb.) **Gṛihe-ruha**, mfn. growing in a house (a tree), 6070. **Gṛihe-vāsin**, mfn. living in a house, TBr. i. **Gṛihêśa**, m. the regent of zodiacal sign. **Gṛihêśvara**, m. = *°hâdhipa*, VarBṛS. liii; (*ī*), f. a housewife, BhP. x, 60, 54. **Gṛihôtpāta**, m. any domestic nuisance (vermin &c.), W. **Gṛihôdyāna**, n. = *°ha-vāṭikā*, Kathās. lxxv, 120. **Gṛihôpakaraṇa**, n. any domestic utensil, xx, 150.

Gṛihaṇī, f. = *grihâmbu*, L.

Gṛihaya, Nom. Ā. *°yate*, to grasp, Dhātup. xxxv, 45; (cf. *gribhâyat*.)

Gṛihayāyya, m. a householder, Uṇ. iii, 96.

Gṛihayālu, disposed to grasp, Pāṇ. iii, 2, 158.

Gṛihala, m., N. of a man, Pravar. v, 4.

1. **Gṛihāya**, irr. ind. p. (√*grah*) grasping, Hariv. ii, 84, 57 (v. l. *grah°*).

2. **Gṛihāya**, Nom. Ā. *°yate*, to become a house, Kulârṇ. ix, 59.

Gṛihi, only gen. pl. *°hīṇām*, see *°hin*; for *°haye* (Ved. inf.), see √*grah*.

Gṛihin, mfn. possessing a house, TS. v, 5, 2, 2; m. the master of a house, householder, Gṛiha-stha, Mn.; Yājñ.; VarBṛS.; BhP. (gen. pl. *°hiṇām* for *°hinām*, x, 8, 4) &c.; (*iṇī*), f. the mistress of a house, wife (RTL. p. 397), Śak. iv, 18 f.; Ragh.; Kum.; Pañcat. &c.

Gṛihi-√bhū, to become a house or habitation, Śak. vii, 20.

Gṛihītá, mfn. (√*grah*, but see *gribhâya*) grasped, taken, seized, caught, held, laid hold of, ChUp.; ĀśvGṛ. &c.; received, accepted; received hospitably (as a guest), BhP. iii, 5, 19; obtained, gained; 'taken on one's self,' see *-mauna*; mentioned, Pañcat.; perceived, understood, Śak. (v. l.); Mudr.; received completely into one's mind (opposed to *adhīta*, 'studied,' but not successfully), Pāṇ. ii, 3, 6, Kāś.; BhP. i, 2, 12. **— khaḍga-carman**, mfn. grasping sword and shield, W. **— garbhā**, f. (a wife) who has conceived an embryo, pregnant, Suśr. iii, 3, 10 & 4, 21. **— cetas**, mfn. one whose mind or heart is captivated, BhP. vi, 18, 38. **— dik-ka**, mfn. = *-diś*, Śiś. i, 64. **— diś**, mfn. running away, flying, escaped, L. **— deha**, mfn. incarnate, W. **— nāman**, mfn. one who has received a name, named, Nal. xii, 35; *su-g°*, mfn. one who has received a good name, named according to the ordinances, Mudr. i, 1/8. **— pāṇi**, mfn. grasped by the hand, Gaṇar. 91, Sch. **— prishṭha**, mfn. seized from behind, R. (ed. Gorr.) ii, 109, 56. **— mauna**, mfn. one who has taken upon himself the vow of silence, Kathās. vii, 1; *-vrata*, mfn. id., BhP. v, 5, 29 **— vasatīvarīka**, mfn. one who has taken up the waters called *vasatī-varī*, ĀpŚr. xi, 20, 12, Sch. **— vidya**, mfn. one who has acquired knowledge, learned, W. **— vetana**, mfn. one who has received his wages, paid, Yājñ. ii, 292. **— śara-kārmuka**, mfn. handling arrows and bows, W. **— śarâvāpa**, mfn. taking a bow, W. **— sāra**, mfn. deprived of one's strength, BhP. v, 14, 19. **— hṛidaya**, mfn. = *-cetas*, W.; captivating the heart, 3, 2. **Gṛihītâkshara**, mf(*ā*)n. one who has received into his mind the syllables or the sounds (of speech, gen.), Ratnâv. ii, 2/9, 43 (in Prākṛit). **Gṛihītâmisha**, mfn. seizing prey, W. **Gṛihītârtha**, mfn. comprehending the sense or meaning, Cāṇ. **Gṛihītâstra**, mfn. one who has taken up arms, W.

Gṛihītavya, mfn. (for *grah°*) to be seized or taken or accepted from (abl.), MBh. iv, 1481 f.; to be understood, meant, Pāṇ. i, 1, 20, Sch.

Gṛihīti, f. 'seizing, taking' (the hand, 1. *kara-*), and 'levying' (taxes, 2. *kara-*), Hcar. iv, 23; perception, Bādar. iii, 3, 16; taking anything to mean or understanding by anything, 4, 23, Sch.

Gṛihītin, mfn. one who has grasped &c. anything (loc.), g. *ishṭâdi*.

Gṛihītṛi, mfn. (for *grah°*) one who seizes, L.

Gṛihītvā, ind. p. √*grah*, q. v.

Gṛihú, *ús*, m. one who receives alms, beggar, RV. x, 117, 3.

Gṛiholikā, f. = °*hâlika*, L.

Gṛihṇát, °**hṇānā**, mfn. pr. p. √*grah*, q. v.

1. **Gṛihya**, ind. p. Ved. ifc., 'seizing by,' see *karṇa-*, *pāda-*, & *hasta-gṛihya*; *haste-*.

2. **Gṛíhya**, mfn. (fr. √*grah*) to be grasped or taken, AV. v, 20, 4; ŚāṅkhGṛ. v, 2, 5; perceptible, ŚvetUp. i, 13; (*á-*, neg.) ŚBr. xiv; (Pāṇ. iii, 1, 119) 'to be taken together with' (in comp.), adhering to the party of (Kāś.), being in close relation to (as the lotus to the moon), Kāvyâd. ii, 179; Daś. vi; vii, 254, Kir. ii, 5; Bhaṭṭ. vi, 61; to be acknowledged or admitted, W.; to be adopted or trusted or relied on, W.; = *ava-*, Vop. xxvi, 20; n. for *guhya* (anus), L.; (*ā*), f. (Pāṇ. iii, 1, 119) ifc. being outside (of a town or village, as *senā*, an army), Kāś.; a suburb, L.

3. **Gṛíhya**, mfn. (fr. *gṛihá*) belonging to a house, domestic (said of an Agni), TS. v; MaitrS.; AitBr. viii, 10, 9; Gobh. &c. (said of a series of ceremonies relating to family or domestic affairs, such as marriages, births &c., and treated of in the Gṛihya-sūtras, q. v.), living in houses, domesticated (as animals), L.; not free, dependent, (*a-*, neg.) Bhaṭṭ. vi, 61; m. the domestic Agni, ŚāṅkhGṛ. v, 2, 5; a domesticated animal, L.; m. pl. the inmates of a house, domestics, ŚBr. ii f., xii; KātyŚr.; PārGṛ. ii; n. a domestic rite, Gaut.; a domestic rule or affair, BhP. x, 8, 25; Hcat.; = *-sūtra*; (*ā*), f. domestic rites and the rules relating to them, Gṛihyās. **–karman**, n. a domestic rite. **–kārikā**, f. the ĀśvGṛ. in metrical form, W. **–guru**, for *guhya-g°*, W. **–grantha**, m., **-tāt-parya-darśana**, n., **-paddhati**, f., **-pariśishṭa**, n., N. of works on domestic rites. **–vat**, mfn. having many adherents or partisans, TāṇḍyaBr. xiii, 11, 13, Sch. **–vivaraṇa**, n., N. of a Comm. **–saṃgraha**, m., N. of a work on domestic rites (by the son of Gobhila). **–sūtra**, n. a ritual work containing directions for domestic rites and ceremonies (as ĀśvGṛ.; ŚāṅkhGṛ. &c.; cf. RTL. p. 281). **Gṛihyâgni**, m. 'domestic Agni,' a sacred fire which it is incumbent on every Brāhman to keep up, W. (RTL. p. 365).

Gṛihyaka, mfn. domesticated (as animals), Pāṇ. iii, 1, 119, Kāś.

Gṛihyā, f. of 2. & 3. °*hya*, q. v. **–karman**, n. = °*hya-k°*, Gobh. i, 1, 1; Gṛihyās. i, 33. **–saṃgraha**, m. = °*hya-s°*.

गृष्टि *gṛishṭí*, f. a cow which has had only one calf, young cow, RV. iv, 18, 10; AV.; Kauś.; MBh. &c.; (ifc. with names of other animals, Pāṇ. ii, 1, 65) any young female animal (e. g. *vāsitā-g°*, a young female elephant, MBh. xi, 642); Gmelina arborea, L.; a variety of Dioscorea, L.; m. for *ghṛishṭi*, a boar, L.; N. of a man, Uttarar. iv, $\frac{6}{8}$ & $\frac{16}{17}$.

Gṛishṭy-ādi, a Gaṇa of Pāṇ. (iv, 1, 136).

Gṛishṭikā, f. = °*ṭi*, a young cow, Hcat. i, 10, 89; N. of a plant, Suśr. iv, 9, 8.

गृह् *gṛih*, *gṛihá*, &c. See *gṛíbh*, p. 361, col. 3.

गॄ 1. *gṝ*, cl. 9. P. Ā. *gṛiṇā́ti*, °*ṇīté* (1. sg. Ā. & 3. sg. Pass. *gṛiṇé*, RV.; 1. sg. Ā. *gṛiṇishé*, RV.; 2. pl. *gṛiṇātá*, AV. v, 27, 9; p. P. *gṛiṇát*, RV. &c.; Ā. & Pass. *gṛiṇāná*, RV.; Ved. inf. Impv. *gṛiṇīshá́ṇi*, RV. vi, 15, 6 & viii, 12, 19), to call, call out to, invoke, RV.; AV.; ŚBr. iv; Bhag. xi, 21; to announce, proclaim, RV.; to mention with praise, praise, extol, RV.; BhP. xi, 13, 41; Bhaṭṭ. viii, 77; to pronounce, recite, MBh. vii, 1754; Ragh.; BhP. i, 1, 14; to relate, teach in verses, 4, 9; Gaṇit. i, 4, 5; [cf. γηρύω, γλῶσσα; Hib. *goirim*; Old Germ. *quar*, *quir*, &c.; Old Pruss. *gerbu*, 'to speak;' Angl. Sax. *gale*; Germ. *Nachtigal*; Lat. *gallus*?]

गॄ 2. *gṝ*, cl. 6. P. *girati* or (cf. P. viii, 2, 21) *gilati* (ŚBr. i; MBh.; Suśr.), ep. also Ā. *girate* (1. sg. *girāmi*, AV. vi, 135, 3; perf. *jagāra*, RV.; aor. Subj. 3. pl. *garan*, RV. i, 158, 5), to swallow, devour, eat, RV. &c.; to emit or eject from the mouth, MBh. xii, 12872: Caus. (aor. 2. sg. *ajīgar*) to swallow, RV. i, 163, 7: Intens. *jegilyate*, Pāṇ. viii, 2, 20: Desid. *jigarishati*, vii, 2, 75; [cf. √2. *gal*, 2 *gir*, *gila*, 2. *gīrṇá*; Lith. *gerru*, 'to drink;' Lat. *glu-tio*, *gula*; Slav. *gr-lo*; Russ. *žora*.]

गॄ 3. *gṝ* (= √3. *kṝ*), cl. 10. Ā. *gārayate*, to know, Dhātup. xxxiii, 33; to make known, teach, ib.

गेण्डु *geṇḍu*, m. a ball to play with, L.

Geṇḍuka, m. id., L.; a cushion, Śiś. ii, 77, Sch.

Geṇḍūka, m. a ball to play with, L.

Genduka, m. id., L.; a cushion, Śiś. ii, 77, Sch.

गेप् *gep* (= √*kep*), cl. 1. Ā. °*pate*, to go, move, Dhātup. x, 8; to shake, tremble, ib.

गेय *geya*, &c. See √*gai*.

गेल *gela*, °*lu*, a particular number, Buddh.

गेव् *gev* (= √*kev*, *khev*, *sev*), cl. 1. Ā. °*vate*, to serve, Dhātup. xiv, 31.

गेष् *gesh* (cf. *gav-esh*), cl. 1. Ā. °*shate*, to seek, search, Dhātup. xvi, 13.

Gesha, m., N. of a Nāga, BhavP.

गेष्ण *geshṇa*, &c. See √*gai*.

गेह *gehá*, n. (corrupted fr. *gṛihá*), a house, dwelling, habitation, VS. xxx, 9; Mn.; MBh. &c.; n. du. 'the two habitations,' the house and the body, BhP. x, 60, 20; (*ī*), f. = *ud-g°*, a kind of ant, Gal. **–dāha**, m. a conflagration, KātyŚr. xxv. **–nakula**, m. (= *gṛiha-babhru*) the musk rat, L. **–pati**, m. the master of a house, householder, husband, BhP. vii, 9, 40. **–bhū**, f. = *gṛiha bhūmi*, q. v., L. **Gehânuprapātam**, ind. so as to rush into one house after the other, Pāṇ. iii, 4, 56, Kāś. **Gehânuprapādam**, ind. so as to go into one house after the other, ib. **Gehânupraveśam**, ind. id., ib.; °*veśanīya*, Pāṇ. v, 1, 111, Pat. **Gehâvaskandam**, ind. = °*hânuprapātam*, Pāṇ. iii, 4, 56, Kāś. **Gehekshvedin**, &c., see s. v. *gehe*. **Gehôpavana**, n. a small forest near a house, L.

Gehinī, f. = *gṛih°*, a housewife, L.

Gehinī, f. id., Megh.; Ragh. viii, 72; Pañcat. ii.

Gehīya, Nom. P. °*yati*, to take anything (acc.) for a house, VarYogay. ii, 5.

Gehe (loc. of °*há*, q. v.) **–kshvedin**, mfn. 'blustering at home,' a house-hero, coward, gaṇas *pātre-samitâdi* & *yuktârohy-ādi*. **–dāhin**, mfn. 'scorching and burning at home,' id., ib. **–dṛipta**, mfn. 'overbearing at home,' id., ib. **–dhṛishṭa**, mfn. 'insolent at home,' id., ib. **–nardin**, mfn. 'shouting defiance at home,' id., ib.; Bhaṭṭ. v, 41. **–mehin**, mfn. 'making water at home,' a lazy or indolent man, gaṇas *pātre-samitâdi* & *yuktârohy-ādi*. **–vijitin**, mfn. 'victorious at home,' a house-hero, boaster, ib. **–vyāḍa**, m. 'fierce at home,' id., ib. **–śūra**, m. a house-hero, carpet-knight, ib.

Géhya, mfn. being in a house, domestic, VS. xvi, 44; TS.; (*àm*), n. domestic wealth, RV. iii, 30, 7.

गै *gai*, cl. 1. P. *gā́yati*, rarely Ā. °*te* (1. sg *gā́ye* [RV. viii, 46, 17] & *gāyishe* [RV. vii, 96, 1]; Lāṭy.; MBh. &c.), exceptionally cl. 2. *gāti* (MBh. iii, 15850; xii, 10299: cl. 3. P. *jigāti*, Dhātup. xxv, 25; perf. *jagau*, AitBr. &c.; aor. *agāsīt*; Prec. *geyāt*, Pāṇ. vi, 4, 67; pr. p. P. *gā́yat*, RV. &c.; ind. p. *gītvā* [with prep. *-gāya* (Pāṇ. vi, 4, 69), AitBr., or *-gīya*, ŚBr. &c.]; inf. *gātum*), to sing, speak or recite in a singing manner, sing to (dat., RV.), praise in song (with acc.), relate in metrical language, RV.; AV. &c.; to sing before (acc.), Kathās. i, 53: Pass. *gīyáte* (p. °*yámāna*), to be sung or praised in song, RV. &c.; to be called, MBh. i, 4329; Kum. ii, 5; Kathās. xci (perf. *jage*), &c.: Caus. *gāpayati* (Pot. 3. pl. *gāyayeyur*, JaimUp.), to cause to sing or praise in song, Lāṭy.; ŚāṅkhGṛ.; Ragh.; BhP. &c.: Intens. *jegīyate* (Pāṇ. vi, 4, 66), to sing, MBh. xii, 12200; to be sung or praised in song, VarBṛS. xix, 18; Daś. i, 6; to be asserted obstinately, Sarvad. iii, 224; xii, 1; [cf. 3. *gā*; cf. also Lith. *zaidziu*.]

Geya, mfn. (Pāṇ. iii, 1, 97, Kāś.) to be sung, being sung or praised in song, Lāṭy.; Hariv.; Pāṇ. iii, 4, 68; BhP. x; singing, singer of (gen.), Pāṇ. iii, 4, 68; n. a song, singing, MBh.; R.; Megh. &c. (said of the flies' humming, Pañcat. i, 15, $\frac{1}{8}$); cf. *āśīr-*, *prātar-*. **–jña**, mfn. skilful in song, VarBṛS. **–pada**, n. a song sung before any one with the lute, Sāh. vi, 212. **–rājan**, m. 'king of songs,' N. of a Cakra-vartin, Buddh. L.

Geshṇa, m. a singer ('a joint,' Sch.), ChUp. i, 6 f.; = *udgīthá*, chanting of the SV., AitĀr. ii, 3, 6. 8; Pushpas. x, 5, 3; = *geshṇu*, L.; a chanter of the SV., L.; (cf. *abhi-*.)

Geshṇu, m. a professional singer, actor, mime, L.

गैर *gaira*, mfn. (fr. 3. *giri*) coming from or growing on mountains, W.; (*ī*), f. Methonica superba, L.

Gairāyaṇa, m. patr. fr. *giri*, g. *aśvâdi*.

Gairika, mfn. = °*ra*, W.; n. gold, L.; red chalk (sometimes used as a red ornament), MBh. vii, ix, xiv; R.; Suśr.; VarBṛS.; m. pl. a class of ascetics, Śīl. (in Prākṛit *geruya*); (*ā*), f. red chalk, Suśr. iv, 25, 36. **–dhātu**, m. id., MBh. iii, vii; R. v. **Gairikâksha** or °**kâkhya**, m. the plant Jala-madhūka, L. **Gairikâcala**, m. a mountain containing red chalk, MBh. vii, 7919. **Gairikâñjana**, n. an unguent prepared from red chalk, R. v, 5, 12; Suśr.

Gairikshitá, m. patr. fr. *giri-kshit*, N. of Trasadasyu, RV. v, 33, 8; m. pl., N. of (a family of) the Yaskas, Kāṭh. xiii, 12; Pravar. i, 4.

Gairīyaka, (perhaps) = °*reya*, L.

Gaireya, n. 'mountain-born,' bitumen, L.; red chalk, W.

गैरकंबूल *gaira-kaṃvūla*, or °*ri-k°* (fr. غير & قبول), the 9th Yoga (in astron.)

गो *gó*, *gaús* (acc. *gā́m*, instr. *gávā*, dat. *gáve*, gen. abl. *gós*, loc. *gávi*; du. *gā́vā* [Ved.], *gā́vau*; pl. nom. *gā́vas*, acc. *gā́s* [rarely *gā́vas*, TBr. iii; TUp.; MBh. iv, 1506; R. ii], instr. *góbhis*, dat. abl. *góbhyas*, gen. *gávām* [once at the end of a Pāda, RV. iv, 1, 19] and [in RV. at the end of Pādas only, cf. Pāṇ. vii, 1, 57] *gónām*, loc. *góshu*), m. an ox, f. a cow, (pl.) cattle, kine, herd of cattle, RV. &c. (in comp. before vowels [cf. Pāṇ. vi, 1, 122 ff.] *gav*, *gava*, qq. vv.; cf. also *gavām*, *gavi*, *gām*, ss. vv.; *gavām vrata*, N. of a Sāman; *gavām tīrtha*, see *go t°*; *góshu* √*gam*, to set out for a battle [to conquer cows], RV. ii, 25, 4; v, 45, 9; viii, 71, 5); 'anything coming from or belonging to an ox or cow,' milk (generally pl.), flesh (only pl., RV. x, 16, 7; 'fat,' Gmn.), skin, hide, leather, strap of leather, bow-string, sinew (RV. x, 27, 22; AV. i, 2, 3), RV.; = *gó-shṭoma* (q. v.), AitBr. iv, 15; ŚBr. xiii (see also *go-āyus*); (pl.) 'the herds of the sky,' the stars, RV. i, 154, 6 & vii, 36, 1; (m. [also f., Uṇ., Sch.]) rays of light (regarded as the herds of the sky, for which Indra fights with Vṛitra), MBh. i, iii; Hariv. 2943; R. &c.; m. the sign Taurus, VarBṛS. xl f.; VarBṛ.; Laghuj.; the sun (cf. *-putra*), Nir. ii, 6 & 14; the moon, L.; a kind of medicinal plant (*ṛishabha*), L.; a singer, praiser (fr. √*gai*), Naigh. iii, 16; 'a goer,' horse (fr. √1. *gā*), Sāy. on RV. i, 121, 9 & iv, 22, 8; N. of two Ṛishis of the SV. (with the patr. Āṅgirasa [TāṇḍyaBr. xvi] and Māyūka); N. of a man (who with Pushkara is said to be the *balâdhyaksha* of the sons and grandsons of Varuṇa), MBh. ii, 381 (cf. R. vii, 23, 28); m. or f. (?) the sun's ray called Sushumṇa, Nir. ii, 6; water, BhP. i, 10, 36 (also f. pl., xi, 7, 50); an organ of sense, BhP. vii, 5, 30; the eye, Kuval. 70; a billion, TāṇḍyaBr. xvii, 14, 2; m. f. the sky, Naigh. i, 4 (perhaps VS. xxiii, 48); the thunderbolt, Sāy. on RV. v, 30, 7; the hairs of the body, L.; f. an offering in the shape of a cow (= *dhenu*, q. v.), W.; a region of the sky, L.; (Naigh. i, 1) the earth (as the milk-cow of kings), Mn. iv, xii; MBh.; R. &c.; (hence) the number 'nine,' Jyot.; Sūryas.; = *go-vīthi*, Sch. on VarBṛS. ix, 1 ff.; a mother, L. (cf. VarBṛS. iii, 68); (Naigh. i, 11) speech, Sarasvatī (goddess of speech), MBh. i, iii, v; Ragh. ii, v; Cāṇ.; voice, note (fr. √*gai*), Śiś. iv, 36; N. of Gaurī, Gal.; of the wife [or of a daughter-in-law, BhP. ix, 21, 25] of Śuka (a daughter of the manes called Sukālas), Hariv. 986; MatsyaP.; N. of a daughter of Kakut-stha and wife of Yayāti, Hariv. 1601; [cf. βοῦς; Lat. *bos*; Old Germ. *chuo*; Mod. Germ. *Kuh*; Eng. *cow*; Lett. *gohw*; cf. also γαῖα, γῆ; Goth. *gavi* and Mod. Germ. *Gau*.] **–agra** (*gó-*), mf(*ā*)n. (Pāṇ. vi, 1, 122, Kāś.) headed by cows, having cows or milk as the chief or most excellent part, RV. **–ájana**, mfn. serving to drive cattle (a stick, goad), vii, 33, 6. **–arghá**, mfn. of the value of a cow, TS. vi, 1, 10, 1 (also *á-g°*, neg.) **–arṇas** (*gó-*), mfn. (flowing with, i. e.) abounding in cattle, RV. i, 112, 18; x, 38, 2 & 76, 3; abounding in stars or rays, ii, 34, 12. **–aśvá**, n. sg. cattle and horses, ChUp. vii, 24, 2; m. pl. id., ŚBr. xiv, 9, 1, 10; (cf. *gavâśva*.) **–āśvīya**, n., N. of a Sāman. **–āyus**, *ushī*, n. du. the two Ekāhas *gó* (= *gó-shṭoma*) & *āyus*, xii, 1, 2, 2; Lāṭy. **–ṛijīka** (*gó-*), mfn. prepared or mixed with milk, RV. iii, 58, 4; vi, 23, 7; vii, 21, 1. **–opaśa** (*gó-*), mfn. furnished with a twist or tuft of leather straps, RV. vi, 53, 9. **–kaksha**, m., N. of a man, g. *kaṇvâdi*. **–kaṇṭa**, m. 'cattle-thorn,' Asteracantha longifolia, L. **–kaṇṭaka**, mfn. 'thorny through cattle,' trodden down (as a road) by cattle and so made difficult to pass, Divyâv. i, 351; m. the print of a cow's hoof or a spot so marked, W.; a cow's hoof, L.; =

-kaṇṭa, L. — **karṇa**, mfn. cow-eared (as men or demons), L.; m. 'cow-eared,' Śiva, MBh. xii, 10351; a cow's ear, Kathās. vi, 57; the deer Antilope picta, R. ii, 103, 41; Car. i, 27; Suśr.; a mule, L.; a serpent, MBh. viii, 90, 42 (perhaps a kind of arrow); the span from the tip of the thumb to that of the ring finger, MBh. ii, 2324; Hcat.; a place of pilgrimage on the Malabar coast (sacred to Śiva), MBh.; Hariv.; R. &c.; Śiva as worshipped in Gokarṇa, Kathās. xxii, xc; N. of one of Śiva's attendants, L.; of a Muni, VāyuP. i, 23, 161; of a king of Kaśmīr (who erected a statue of Śiva called after him Gokarṇêśvara), Rājat. i, 348; (*ā*), f. a female serpent, MBh. viii, 90, 42; N. of one of the mothers attending on Skanda, ix, 2643; (*ī*), f. Sanseviera zeylanica, L.; *-liṅga*, n., N. of a Liṅga, Rasik. xi, 37; *-śithila*, mfn. 'swinging like a cow-ear,' trimming between parties (as a witness), MBh. ii, 68, 75; °*rṇêśa* & °*rṇêśa-liṅga*, n., N. of a Liṅga, SkandaP.; °*rṇêśvara*, m., N. of a statue of Śiva (see before); N. of a holy man, Buddh. — **karman**, n. taking care of cows, Pañcat. iii, 14, 13. — **kāma** (*gó-*), mfn. desirous of cattle, RV. x, 108, 10; ŚBr. xi, xiv. — **kāmyā**, f. desire for cows, Mṛicch. iii, 1/8. — **kirāṭikā**, °*ṭī*, f. the bird Turdus Salica, L. — **kila**, **-kīla**, m. a plough, L.; a pestle, L. — **kuñjara**, m. an excellent ox, Pāṇ. ii, 1, 62, Kāś. — **kuṇika**, m., v. l. for *-kaṇṭaka*, L. — **kula**, n. a herd of kine, MBh.; R. &c.; a cow-house or station, ib.; a village or tract on the Yamunā (residence of Nanda and of Kṛishṇa during his youth, BhP.; [RTL. p. 113] the inhabitants of that place), BhP. ii, 7, 31; N. of a certain sanctuary or holy place, Rājat. v, 23; *-jit*, m., N. of an author of the 17th century; *-nātha*, m., N. of the author of the Padavākya-ratnâkara; of the author of the Rasa-mahârṇava; *-stha*, m. pl., N. of a Vaishṇava sect; °*lâshṭaka*, n., N. of a poem; °*lêśa*, m. 'lord of the Gokula,' N. of Kṛishṇa, Gal.; °*lôdbhavā*, f., N. of Durgā, L. — °**kulika**, mfn. one who gives help (or gives no help, NBD.) to a cow in the mud, L.; squint-eyed, L.; (*ās*), m. pl., N. of a Buddh. sect. — √1. **kṛi**, to transform into a cow, Uṇ. ii, 67, Sch. — **kṛita**, n. cow-dung, L. — **kshīrá**, n. cow's milk, ŚBr. xiv; Suśr.; MBh. xii, 174, 32, Sch. — **kshura**, m. = *-kaṇṭa* or Tribulus lanuginosus, Suśr.; a cow's hoof, W.; v. l. for *-khura*, q. v.; *-dugdhā*, f., N. of a plant, L. — **kshuraka**, m. the plant *-kshura*, Suśr.; VarBṛS. lxxvi; a cow's hoof, W. — **kshoḍaka**, m. a kind of bird, Suśr. i, 46, 2, 14. — **kshveḍa**, m. id., Gal. — **kha**, 'cow-aperture,' a particular part of the body, g. *kroḍâdi* (not in Kāś. & Gaṇar., but mentioned by Śākaṭ., Gaṇar. 43, Sch.); *-piṅgali*, m. pl. N. of a family, Pravar. ii, 2, 1; cf. *gocchā*. — **khala**, m., N. of a teacher, VP. iii, 4, 22 (v. l. °*lu*); (°*lya*) BhP. xii, 6, 57. — **khalu**, °**lya**, see °*la*. — **khura**, m. = *-kaṇṭa*; Tribulus lanuginosus, L.; N. of a Dānava, Hariv. 12937 (v. l. *-kshura*). — **khuri**, m. = *-kaṇṭa*, L. — **gaṇa**, m. pl. a multitude of rays of light, BhP. iv, 16, 14. — **gati** (*gó-*), f. the way or path of cows, AV. xx, 129, 13. — **gamana**, n. intercourse with a cow, Prāyaśc. — **gṛishṭi**, f. (= *grishṭi*) a young cow which has had only one calf, Pāṇ. ii, 1, 65, Kāś. — **goshṭha**, n. a station for cattle, cow-stable, Pāṇ. v, 2, 29, Vārtt. 3, Pat.; (cf. *gavāṃ g°*, Mn. iv, 58.) — **granthi**, m. dried cow-dung, L.; = *-goshṭha*, L.; = *-jihvā*, L. — **graha**, m. capture of cattle, booty, MBh. vi, 4458; *-tīrtha*, n., N. of a Tīrtha, KapSaṃh. — **grāsa**, m. = *-ghāsa*, ŚāṅkhGṛ. iii, 14, 4; the ceremony of presenting a mouthful of grass to a cow when performing an expiatory rite, W.; the feeding like a cow, L. — **ghātá**, m. a cow-killer, VS. xxx, 18. — **ghātaka**, m. id., L. — **ghātin**, m. id. — **ghāsa**, m. grass for a cow, W. — **ghṛita**, n. melted butter coming from a cow, KātySr. i, 8, 37, Sch.; 'Ghṛita of the sky or earth,' rain, L. — **ghná**, mfn. noxious to kine, RV. i, 114, 10; m. = *-ghātá*, Mn. xi, 109 & 116; Yājñ.; R.; BhP. vi; Hit.; one for whom a cow is killed, guest, Pāṇ. iii, 4, 73. — **candana**, n. (= *-śīrsha*) a kind of sandal-wood, Suśr.; (*ā*), f. a sort of venomous leech, ib. — **capalā**, f., N. of the daughter of Raudrâśva and Ghṛitâcī, Hariv. 1662. — **cara**, m. pasture ground for cattle, ĀpŚr. i, 2, 4; (R. iv, 44, 80); range, field for action, abode, dwelling-place, district (esp. ifc. 'abiding in, relating to;' 'offering range or field or scope for action, within the range of, accessible, attainable, within the power'), KaṭhUp. iii, 4; Mn. x, 39; MBh. &c.; the range of the organs of sense, object of sense, anything perceptible by the senses, esp. the range of the eye (e. g. *locana-gocaram √yā*, to come within range of the eye, become visible, Pañcat.), MBh. vii, 5616; Suśr.; Vikr. iv, 9 &c.; the distance of the planets from the Lagna and from each other, VarBṛS. civ, 2; Romakas.; mf(*ā*)n. being within the range of, attainable for (gen.), BhP. iii, 25, 28; perceptible (esp. to the eye), MBh. xiii, 71, 33 & 91, 24; having (or used in) the meaning of (loc.), L., Sch.; *-gata*, mfn. one who has come within the range of or in connection with (gen.), Bhartṛ.; *-tā*, f. the state of being liable to (in comp.), Sarvad. iv, 253; *-tva*, n. id., 42; *-prakaraṇa*, N. of a work; *-phala*, N. of VarBṛS. civ; *-pīḍā*, f. inauspicious position of stars within the ecliptic, VarBṛS. xli, 13; °*râdhyāya*, m. = °*ra-phala*; °*rântara-gata*, mfn. being within the power of (gen.), Pañcat.; °*rī-kṛita*, mfn. within the range of observation, Sāh. iii, 28/8; overcome (by fatigue, *glānyā*), Hcar. v, 139. — °**caraya**, Nom. P. °*yati*, to be current, Yājñ. ii, 96/8. — °**carika**, mfn. 'accessible to,' a friend of (in comp.), Divyâv. — **carman**, n. an ox-hide, cow's hide, MBh. xiii, 1228; a particular measure of surface (a place large enough for the range of 100 cows, one bull, and their calves, Gṛihyās.; or a place ten times as large, Parāś. xii; a place 300 feet long by 10 broad, W.; or a place 30 Daṇḍas long by 1 Daṇḍa and 7 Hastas broad, Bṛihasp. [MBh. xiii, 3121, Sch.]; it is also defined as an extent of land sufficient to support a man for a year, Vishṇ. v, 181 ff.; originally probably a piece of land large enough to be encompassed by straps of leather from a cow's hide, cf. ŚBr. i, 2, 5, 2), MBh. xiii, 3121; Hcat. i, 3, 864 ff.; ii, 1; BṛNārP. xxxiv, 43. — **caryā**, f. seeking food like a cow, BhP. xi, 18, 29. — **cāraka**, m. a cowherd, W. — **cāraṇa**, n. the tending of cows, x, 38, 8. — **cārin**, mfn. one who seeks his nourishment like a cow, seeking food with the mouth (said of certain Yatis, cf. *mṛiga-c°*), MBh. xiii, 647; (cf. i, 3644.) — **citi**, f. a particular way of piling up sacrificial bricks, ĀpŚr. xvii, 4. — **jara**, m. an old ox or bull, BhP. iii, 30, 14. — **jala**, n. cow's urine, L. — '**javāja**, v. l. for *gaja-v°*, q. v. — **jā́**, mfn. (Pāṇ. iii, 2, 67, Kāś.) produced by milk ('born amidst rays,' Sāy.; 'born in the earth,' Mahīdh.), RV. iv, 40, 5 (KaṭhUp. v, 2). — **jāgarika**, m. a kind of prickly nightshade, L.; n. happiness, fortune, L.; = *bhakshya-kāraka* (preparer of food, baker?), L. — **jāta** (*gó-*), mfn. born in the starry sky (said of the gods; 'born in the middle region,' Sāy.), RV. vi, 50, 11; vii, 35, 14 & x, 53, 5. — **jā-parṇī**, f. the shrub Dugdha-phenī, L. — **jit**, mfn. conquering or gaining cattle, RV.; AV. — **jihvā**, f., N. of a plant (Phlomis or Premna esculenta, L.; Elephantopus scaber, L.; Coix barbata or a kind of Hieracium, L.), Car. i, 27, 86; Suśr. i, 46, 4, 51. — **jihvikā**, f. the uvula, Car. iv, 7; = °*hvā*, Suśr.; Mn. vi, 14, Sch. — **jīra** (*gó-*), mf(*ā*)n. stimulated by milk added (Soma), RV. ix, 110, 3. — **jīva**, mfn. living on (trade with) cattle, Hcat. i, 7. — **ḍimba**, m. (= *-ḍumba*) the water-melon, L. — **ḍumba**, m. = *-ḍimba*, L.; (*ā*), f. = *-ḍumbikā*, Car. i, 1, 76, Sch.; a coloquintida, L. — **ḍumbikā**, f. Cucumis maderaspatanus, L. — **tama** (*gó-*), m. (superl.) N. of a Ṛishi belonging to the family of Aṅgiras with the patr. Rāhū-gaṇa (author of RV. i, 74-93), RV.; AV.; ŚBr. i, xi, xiv; ShaḍvBr. &c.; (for *gaut°*) N. of the chief disciple of Mahā-vīra; of a lawyer (cf. *gautamá*); of the founder of the Nyāya phil.; 'the largest ox' and 'N. of the founder of Nyāya phil.,' Naish. xvii, 75; N. of a son of Karṇika, Buddh.; ?, MBh. xiii, 4490 (cf. *-dama*); m. pl. (Pāṇ. ii, 4, 65) the descendants of the Ṛishi Gotama, RV.; ĀśvŚr. xii, 10; Lāṭy.; n. a kind of poison, Gal.; (*ī*), f., v. l. for *gaut°* in g. *gaurâdi*; *-gaura*, m. = *gaura-gotama*, the white Gotama, Gaṇar. 89, Sch.; *-pricchā*, f. 'questions of (Mahā-vīra's pupil) Gotama (put forth in a discussion with Pārśva's pupil Keśin),' N. of a Jain work; *-stoma*, m., N. of an Ekâha sacrifice, ĀśvŚr.; ŚāṅkhŚr.; (cf. ŚBr. xiii, 5, 1, 1); *-svāmin*, m. Mahā-vīra's pupil Gotama; °*mânvaya*, m. N. of Śākya-muni, L.; °*mī-putra*, m. 'son of Gotamī,' N. of a king (50 B. C. or A. D.), Inscr.; VāyuP.; MatsyaP.; °*mêśvara-tīrtha*, n. N. of a Tīrtha, ŚivaP. — **tara**, m. (compar.) a better ox, Pāṇ. v, 3, 55, Pat.; (*ā*), f. a better cow, ib. — **taraṇi**, a kind of flower, Buddh. L. — **tarpaṇa**, n. anything arranged for the pleasure of cows, AV.Pariś. lxix, 7. — **tallaja**, m. an excellent cow, Pāṇ. ii, 1, 66, Sch. — **tā**, f. 'cowship,' (in dialect) a cow, Pat. Introd. 35; 97, & on Vārtt. 6. — **tīrtha**, n., N. of a Tīrtha, Suśr. vi, 31, 6; (*gavāṃ t°*) BhP. iii, 1, 22. — **tīrthaka**, m. with *ccheda*, an oblique cut applied to fistula of the rectum, Suśr. iv, 8, 11. — **tulya**, m. 'resembling an ox,' the Gayal, Gal. — **trá**, n. (√*trai*) protection or shelter for cows, cow-pen, cow-shed, stable for cattle, stable (in general), hurdle, enclosure, RV. (once m., viii, 50, 10); 'family enclosed by the hurdle,' family, race, lineage, kin, ChUp.; ŚāṅkhŚr.; Kauś. &c. (a polysyllabic fem. in *ī* shortens this vowel before *gotra* in comp. [e. g. *brāhmaṇi-gotrā*, 'a Brāhman woman only by descent or name,' Kāś.], Pāṇ. vi, 3, 43 ff.); the family name, ĀśvGṛ.; MBh. xiii, 548; VarBṛS.; name (in general), Śak. vi, 5; Ragh. &c.; (in Gr.) the grandson and his descendants if no older offspring of the same ancestor than this grandson lives (if the son lives the grandson is called *yuvan*), Pāṇ. ii, 4, 63; iv, 1, 89 ff. & 162 ff.; 2, 111 & 3, 80 & 126; an affix used for forming a patr., L.; a tribe, subdivision (in the Brāhman caste 49 Gotras are reckoned and supposed to be sprung from and named after celebrated teachers, as Śāṇḍilya, Kaśyapa, Gautama, Bharad-vāja, &c.), W.; a genus, class, species, W.; a multitude, L.; increase, L.; possession, L.; a forest, L.; a field, L.; an umbrella or parasol, L.; knowledge of probabilities, L.; (*am*), ind. after a verb denoting repetition and implying a blame, Pāṇ. viii, 1, 27 & 57; (*eṇa*), instr. ind. with regard to one's family name, g. *prakṛity-ādi*; (*as*), m. a mountain (a meaning probably derived fr. *-bhid*), BhP. ii, iii, vi; a cloud (cf. *-bhid*), Naigh. i, 10; a road, L.; (*ā*), f. a herd of kine, Pāṇ. iv, 2, 51; the earth, L. (cf. *gotrêśa*); *-kartṛi*, m. the founder of a family, MBh. xiii, 248; *-kārin*, mfn. founding a family, Pravar.; *-kīlā*, f. (= *acala-k°*) the earth, L.; *-kshānti*, f., N. of a Kiṃnara virgin, Kāraṇḍ. i; *-ja*, mfn. born in the same family, relation (in law, nearly = 'Gentile' of Roman law, and applied to kindred of the same general family, who are connected by offerings of food and water; hence opposed to *bandhu* or cognate kindred not partaking in the offerings to common ancestors), Yājñ. ii, 135; BhP. iii, 7, 24; Kathās. vi, xxii, iic; *-devatā*, f. family deity, Siṇhās. iv; *-nāman*, n. the family name, ŚāṅkhGṛ. i, 6, 4; *-paṭa*, m. a genealogical table, pedigree, Lāṭy. i, 2, 24, Sch.; *-pravara-dīpa*, °*ra-nirṇaya*, m., °*ra-mañjarī*, f., N. of works; *-bhāj*, mfn. belonging to the family, Gaut. xxviii, 33; *-bhíd*, mfn. opening the cow-pens of the sky ('splitting the clouds or mountains,' Sāy.; said of Indra and Bṛihaspati's vehicle), RV. ii, 23, 3; vi, 17, 2 & x, 103, 6; VS. xx, 38; m. 'splitting the mountains (with his thunderbolt, cf. *adri-bhid*),' Indra, Ragh.; Kum. ii, 52; 'Indra' and 'destroyer of families,' Rājat. i, 92; 'Indra' and 'destroyer of names,' Śiś. ix, 80; *-bhūmi*, f. 'family-range,' one of the periods in a Śrāvaka's life, Buddh. L.; *-maya*, mfn. forming a family (with *kshātra*, 'a Kshatriya family'), Bālar. iii, 60; *-rik-tha*, n. du. the family name and the inheritance, Mn. ix, 142; *-rikthâṅśa*, in comp. the family name and part of the inheritance, 165; *-vat*, mfn. belonging to a noble family, R. ii, 98, 24; *-vardhana*, m., N. of a prince, Kathās. lxv; *-vriksha*, m., N. of a tree, Bhpr.; *-vrata*, n. a family rule, Bhartṛ. (Mudr. ii, 18; Subh.); *-sthiti*, f. 'id.' and 'standing like a mountain;' °*trâkhyā*, f. family name, patronymic, L.; °*trâdi*, a Gaṇa of Pāṇ. (viii, 1, 27); °*trânta*, m. 'destruction of families' and 'destruction of mountains,' Rājat. v, 377; (scil. *śabda*) 'ending with a Gotra affix,' a patronymic, L.; °*trâbhidhāyam*, ind. so as to name one's name, Bhaṭṭ. iii, 50; °*trêśa*, m. 'earth-lord,' a king; °*trôccāra*, m. 'recitation of the family pedigree,' N. of a ceremony, RTL. p. 407. — °**traka**, n. family, Yājñ. ii, 85. — °**trika**, mfn. relating to a family (with *karman*, 'the consciousness of family descent,' one of the 4 pure Karmans), Jain. — °**trin**, mfn. belonging to the same family, relation, Vet. xv, 8/8; °(*tri*)*-tva*, n. relationship. — **tvá**, n. the being a cow, state of a cow, MaitrS.; TāṇḍyaBr. xvi; MārkP.; RāmatUp.; Sarvad.; the nature of an ox, Kāvyâd. i, 6. — **tvac**, f. 'an ox-hide or cow's hide,' *-(tvag)-ja*, mfn. made of leather, VarYogay. vi, 18. — 1. **-da**, mfn. (Pāṇ. iii, 2, 3, Kāś.) giving cattle or cows, Mn. iv, 231; m. du., N. of a village, Pāṇ. i, 2, 52, Kāś.; g. *varaṇâdi*; m. pl., N. of a tribe, Inscr.; (*ā*), f. the river commonly called *go-dāvarī*, Kathârṇ. (cf. *anu-godam*). — **dattra**, mfn. granting cattle (Indra), RV. viii, 21, 16. — **danta**, m. a cow's tooth, Suśr.;

yellow orpiment, L.; a white mineral substance (apparently an earthy salt), W.; mfn. having cow's teeth, Buddh. L.; armed, armed with a coat of mail, L.; m., N. of a man, g. *śubhrâdi;* of a Dānava, Hariv. 12937; *-maṇi,* m. a particular precious stone, Hcat. viii, 15. **—dama,** mfn. (conquering, i. e.) attaining heaven and earth (Sch.), MBh. xiii, 4490 (ed. Bomb.) **—dari,** mfn. opening the stables of the sky (Indra, cf. *gotra-bhid;* 'splitting the clouds or mountains,' Sāy.), RV. viii, 92, 11. **—dā́,** mfn. presenting with cattle or kine, RV. **—1. -dāna,** n. gift of a cow, MBh. xiii, 3345; R. vii; PSarv. **—2. -dā́na,** &c., see s. v. **—°dānīya,** m., N. of a Dvīpa, Lalit. xii, 186; (cf. *apara-godāna.*) **—dāya,** mfn. intending to present with cattle or cows, Pāṇ. iii, 3, 12, Kāś. **—dāraṇa,** n. 'opening the earth,' a plough, L.; a spade or hoe, L. **—dāvarī,** f. (= *-dā,* s. v. 1. *-da*) 'granting water or kine,' N. of a river in the Dekhan, MBh. iii; Hariv. 12826; R. iii, vi; Ragh. &c.; *-tīrtha,* n., N. of a Tīrtha, SkandaP.; *-māhātmya,* n. 'glory of the Godāvarī,' N. of a work; *-saṃgama,* m., N. of a place. **—dugdha,** n. = *-kshīrá,* W.; (*ā*), f. the Caṇikā grass, L.; *-dā,* f. id., L. **—dúh,** m(nom. *-dhuk*)fn. (Pāṇ. iii, 2, 61) a milkman or milkmaid, cowherd, RV. i, 4, 1 & 164, 26; viii, 52, 4; AV. vii, 73, 6; Pāṇ. v, 1, 5, Kāś. **—duha,** mfn. id., L., Sch. **—doha,** m. (cf. *gām-doha-saṃnéjana*) the milking of cows, VarBṛS. vii, 6; (*am*), ind. as long as the cows are being milked, Pāṇ. i, 4, 51, Pat. on Kār. 7. **—dohaka,** m. = *-dúh,* Kathās. lxi; (*ikā*), f. 'a milkman's sitting,' a particular kind of being seated, HYog. **—dohana,** n. = °*ha,* Jain., Sch.; the time necessary for milking a cow, BhP. i, 19, 39; (*ī*), f. a milk-pail, Pāṇ. iii, 3, 117, Kāś. **—drava,** m = *-jala,* L. **—dhana,** n. possession of cows, herd of cows, multitude of cattle (esp. considered as property), MBh. iv, xiii; Hariv. 3515; R. i; Kād. vi, 611; a station of cows, R. (G) ii, 32, 42; m. a broad-pointed arrow, Hariv. 8865 (v. l. *gādh*°); N. of a son of Śvaphalka, LiṅgaP. i, 69, 27 (Gandhamoca, VP.) **—dhara,** m., N. of a king of Kaśmīr, Rājat. i, 95 f. **—dharma,** m. 'rule of cattle,' i. e. open and unconcealed intercourse of the sexes, MBh. i, 4195. **—dhā́,** see s. v. **—dhāyas** (*gó-*), mfn. supporting or fostering cows, RV. vi, 67, 7. **—1. -dhi,** m. 'hair-receptacle,' the forehead, L. **—dhuma,** for *-dhūma,* wheat, L. **—dhū́ma,** m. (√*gudh,* Uṇ.) 'earth-smoke,' wheat (generally pl.), VS.; TBr. i; ŚBr. v (sg.), xii, xiv; ŚāṅkhŚr.; Mn. &c.; the orange tree, L.; N. of a medicinal plant, L.; (*ī*), f. = *-lomikā,* L.; *-cūrṇa,* n. wheat-flour, L.; *-ja,* n. a particular concrement in wheat, L.; *-saṃcaya-maya,* mfn. consisting of a heap of wheat, Hcat.; *-sambhava,* n. sour gruel made from wheat-flour, sour paste, L. **—°dhūmaka,** m. a kind of serpent, Suśr. v, 4, 34. **—dhūli,** f. 'earth-dust,' i. e. 'a time at which mist seems to rise from the earth,' a period of the day (in the hot season) when the sun is half risen, (in the cold and dewy seasons) when the sun is full but mild, (and in the 3 other seasons) sunset, Dīp. **—dhūlikā,** f. id., Romakas. **—dhenu,** f. a milk-cow, L.; (cf. *gaudhenuka.*) **—nanda,** m., N. of an attendant in Skanda's retinue, MBh. ix, 2567; of a Muni; of 3 old kings of Kaśmīr, Rājat. (cf. *-narda*); m. pl., see *-narda;* (*ā*), f., N. of a goddess, Hariv. 9534; (*ī*), f. the female of Ardea sibirica (cf. *-narda*), L. **—narda,** m. 'bellowing like a bull,' Śiva, MBh. xii, 10430; the bird Ardea sibirica (cf. *-nandī*), Car. i, 27, 54; N. of a king of Kaśmīr, Hariv. (cf. *-nanda*); of an author, Kum. vii, 95, Sch.; of a mountain (v. l. *go-manta*), VarBṛS. v, 68, Sch.; m. pl., N. of a people in the Dekhan (or in the east, Pāṇ. i, 1, 75, Kāś.), VarBṛS. (v. l. *-nana*°); n. Cyperus rotundus, L. **—°nardīya,** m. 'belonging to the people called Gonardas (Pāṇ. i, 1, 75, Kāś.),' Patañjali (founder of the Yoga phil.), L.; N. of a grammarian (apparently identified with Pat. by Kaiy.), Pat. on Pāṇ. i, 1, 21 & 29; iii, 1, 92; vii, 2, 101; of the author of a work on the treatment of a wife (perhaps the same with the grammarian), Vātsyāy. i, iv; Ragh. xix, 29 ff., Sch. **—nasa,** m. (Pāṇ. v, 4, 118, Kāś.) 'cow-nosed,' a kind of large snake, Suśr. v, 4, 33; a kind of gem, L.; (*ā*), f. the projecting snout of a cow, Suśr. iv, 30, 12; (*ī*), f. a kind of plant, 3 & 12; (cf. *-nāsa.*) **—nāga,** m. an excellent ox, Pāṇ. ii, 1, 62, Kāś.; °*gônîśvara-tīrtha,* n., N. of a Tīrtha, ŚivaP. **—nādika** or °**dīca,** m., N. of a plant, L. **—nātha,** m. a bull, L.; a cowherd, W. **—nāda,** m. 'bellowing like a bull,' the bird Anas Casarca, L. **—nāmá,** pl., N. of particular sacrificial formulas, MaitrS. iv, 2, 1 & 10. **—nāman,** n. a name for a cow, Lāṭy.; Gobh. **—°nāmika,** mfn. 'called after the *go-nāmá* formulas,' N. of MaitrS. iv, 2. **—nāya,** m. a cowherd, ChUp. vi, 8, 3. **—nāśana,** m. 'cattle-destroyer,' a wolf, Gal. **—nāsa,** mfn. cow-nosed, Buddh. L.; m. a kind of snake (cf. *-nasa*), L.; N. of a mountain, Viddh. i, 3; n. a kind of gem (*vaikrānta-maṇi*), L.; (*ā*), f. = *-nasā,* MBh. ix, 2589. **—nishkramaṇa,** n. 'the going out of cows on the pasture-ground,' PSarv.; *-tīrtha,* n., N. of a Tīrtha, VarP. **—nishyanda,** m. = *-jala,* L. **—nihāra,** m. cow-dung, Vishṇ. iii, 16. **—nṛi,** m. a bull, Gal. **—nyoghas** (*gó-*), mfn. streaming or flowing among milk ('having quantities of fluid streaming down,' Sāy.), RV. ix, 97, 10. **—pá,** &c., see s. v. **—pati** (*gó-*), m. the lord of cowherds, leader, chief (a N. often applied to Indra), RV.; AV.; VS. i, 1; a bull, MBh. xii, 4877; R. iii, iv; VarBṛS.; (hence) the medicinal plant Ṛishabha, L.; 'lord of rays,' the sun, MBh. i, ii, iii; Hariv.; BhP.; 'lord of stars,' the moon, Subh.; 'earth lord,' a king, L.; 'the chief of herdsmen,' Kṛishṇa or Vishṇu, MBh. xiii, 7002 & 7012; Hariv. 4067; 'lord of waters,' Varuṇa, MBh. v, 3532 & 3801; Śiva, xiii, 1228; R. vii, 16, 23; Indra, L.; N. of a Deva-gandharva (cf. *go-pá*), MBh. i, 2550 & 4811; of a demon slain by Kṛishṇa, MBh. iii, 492; Hariv. 9141; of a son of Śibi, MBh. xii, 1794; *-cāpa,* m. 'Indra's bow,' the rainbow, W.; *-dhvaja,* m., N. of Śiva, R. vii, 87, 12. **—patha,** m. a way or ground for cows, Nyāyam., Sch.; N. of a Brāhmaṇa of the AV.; *-brāhmaṇa,* n. id. **—pada,** n. the mark or impression of a cow's hoof in the soil, Pāṇ. vi, 1, 145, Kāś.; (cf. *gósh-p*°.) **—parīṇas** (*gó-*), mfn. abundantly furnished with cattle or milk, RV. viii, 45, 24 & x, 62, 10. **—parvata,** n., N. of a Tīrtha. **—pávana,** m., N. of a Ṛishi of Atri's family, RV. viii, 74, 11; KātyŚr. x, 2, 21; °*nâdi,* a Gaṇa of Pāṇ. (ii, 4, 67). **—paśu,** m. a sacrificial ox or cow, ŚāṅkhBr. xviii; ŚāṅkhGṛ. ii, iii. **—pā́,** m. (nom. *ā́s,* acc. *ā́m,* du. *ā́* or *aú,* pl. nom. *ā́s,* instr. *ā́bhis*) a herdsman, guardian, RV.; AV.; VS.; TBr. iii; ChUp.; ŚvetUp.; (*ās*), f. a female guardian, AV. xii, 1, 57; TBr. iii; (cf. *go-pá* s. v., *á-, devá-, vāyú-, saná-, sóma-, su-gopā́*); *gopā́-jihva,* mfn. 'having (the tongue, i. e.) the voice of a cowherd,' RV. iii, 38, 9 [the NBD. proposes to read *gopā́jihmásya* instead of *gopā́-jihvasya*]; *gopā-putra,* m. a bird belonging to the Pratudas, Car. i, 27, 55; *gopā́-vat,* mfn. furnished with guardians, RV. vii, 60, 8. **—pārêśvara-tīrtha,** n., N. of a Tīrtha, ŚivaP. **—pālá,** m. (proparox., Pāṇ. vi, 2, 78) a cowherd, VS. xxx, 11; ŚBr. iv; Mn. iv, 253; Yājñ. &c. (ifc. f. *ā,* R. ii, 67, 25); 'earth-protector,' a king (and 'cowherd'), Pañcat.; (= *-pati*) Kṛishṇa, MBh. iii, 15530; Śiva, L.; N. of a demon causing fever, Hariv. 9556; of a Nāga, Buddh.; of a minister of king Bimbi-sāra, ib.; of a king, ib.; of a general of king Kīrti-varman, Prab. i, 4; of a scholar, Pratāpar., Sch.; = *-pālaka,* q. v.; (*ī*), f. = °*la-karkaṭī,* L.; another plant (*go-rakshī*), L.; N. of one of the mothers attending on Skanda, MBh. ix, 2622; of a Cāṇḍālī, Buddh.; *-kaksha,* m., N. of a country, MBh. ii, 1077; vi, 364; m. pl. the inhabitants of that country, ib. (v. l. *-kaccha*); *-karkaṭī,* f. a kind of cucumber (*gopa-karkaṭikā, gopālī, kshudra-cirbhiṭā, kshudra-phalā, kshudrêrvāru*), L.; *-kalpa,* m., N. of a work; *-keli-candrikā,* f., N. of a drama; *-keśava,* m., N. of a statue of Kṛishṇa (called after *-varman*), Rājat. v, 243; *-giri,* m., N. of a mountain, Uttamac. 250; *-cakravartin,* m., N. of a scholiast; *-campū,* f., N. of a work; *-tāpanīyôpanishad* or *-tāpinī,* f., N. of an Up.; *-tīrtha,* m., N. of a man; *-dāsa,* m., N. of the author of a work on elephants; of a copyist (1736 A. D.); *-deva,* m., N. of a poet, ŚārṅgP.; Bhojapr. 212/13 ff. (also °*la*); *dhānī-pūlāsa,* n. g. *rājadantâdi; -pura,* n., N. of a town (called after *-varman*), Rājat. v, 243; *-prasāda,* m., N. of a teacher of Rāma-candra; *-bhaṭṭa,* m., N. of a man; *-maṭha,* m., N. of a college (called after *-varman*), Rājat. v, 243; *-miśra,* m., N. of a man; *-yogin,* m., N. of the author of a Comm. on Kaṭhavallī-bhāshya; *-rahasya,* n., N. of a work; *-varman,* m., N. of a king of Kaśmīr, Rājat. v; *-sarasvatī,* f., N. of a pupil of Śiva-rāma and teacher of Govindânanda; *-sahasra-nāma-bhūshaṇā,* f. 'decorated with the thousand names of Kṛishṇa,' N. of a work; *-sāhi,* m., N. of a prince, Inscr.; °*lâcārya,* m., N. of a teacher; °*lârcana-candrikā,* f., N. of a work (in honour of Kṛishṇa); °*lôttara-tāpinī,* f., N. of an Up. **—pālaka,** m. a cowherd, MBh. iii, 14854; Kathās. xviii; N. of Kṛishṇa, Kramadīp.; of Śiva, L.; of a son of king Caṇḍa-mahā-sena, Kathās. (°*la,* xvi, 103); (*ikā*), f. (Pāṇ. iv, 1, 48, Pat.) a cowherd's wife, MBh. i, 7980; a kind of worm or fly found on dung-heaps, L. **—pāli,** m., N. of Śiva, MBh. xiii, 1228; of a man, Pravar. vi, 3. **—pālita,** m., N. of a lexicographer, Sch. on Uṇ. iii, 22 and iv, 1. **—pā́-vat,** see s. v. *-pā́.* **—piṭaka,** n. a kind of round basket, Divyâv. iv, 68. **—pitta,** n. ox-bile or the bile of cows (from which the yellow orpiment Go-rocanā, Rocanā or Rocanī, is supposed to be prepared), Pañcat. i, 1, 81; orpiment, L. **—pīta,** m., N. of one of the 4 water-wagtails (regarded as birds of augury), VarBṛS. vi, 3. **—1. -pīthá,** m. (√1. *pā*) a draught of milk, RV. i, 19, 1; ŚBr. iii. **—2. -pīthá,** m. (√3. *pā*) protection, RV. v, 65, 6; x, 35, 14 & 77, 7; AV.; TS. ii; TBr. i; BhP. i, iv, v; n. a place of pilgrimage, Uṇ. ii, 9, Sch. **—°pīthya,** n. granting protection, RV. x, 95, 11 ('protection of the earth,' Sāy.) **—puccha,** n. (g. *śarkarâdi*) a cow's tail, Pāṇ. iv, v; VarBṛS.; Sāh. vi, 11; a particular point of an arrow, ŚārṅgP.; m. (= *-lāṅgūla*) a sort of monkey, MBh. iii; R. i, iv, vi; BhP. iii, viii; a sort of necklace (of 2 [or of 4 or of 34, W.] strings), L.; a kind of drum, L.; °*cchâkṛiti,* m. 'resembling a cow's tail,' id., Gal. **—pucchaka,** mfn. having a tail like that of a cow, Kām. vii, 11, Sch. **—puṭā,** f. large cardamoms, L. **—puṭika,** m. a temple consecrated to Śiva's bull, L. **—putra,** m. a young bull, MBh. xiii, 5733; a kind of gallinule (cf. *go-pā-p*°), Gal.; 'son of the sun,' Karṇa, viii, 4668. **—pura,** n. a town-gate, MBh.; R.; BhP.; (ifc. f. *ā,* MBh. iii; R. v); a gate, VarBṛS. lxxxix, 19; the ornamented gateway of a temple, W.; (= *-narda*) Cyperus rotundus, Bhpr. v, 2, 123; m. N. of a physician, Suśr. i, 1, 1; Ṭoḍar.; (*ā*), f. = *-puṭā,* Gal. **—puraka,** m. the resin of Boswellia thurifera, L. (°*raga,* Gal.) **—purīsha,** n. cow-dung, L. **—puro-gava** (*gó-*), mfn. having a cow as a leader, AV. viii, 7, 12. **—potalikā,** f. a cow, Pat. Introd. 35; 97, & on Vārtt. 6. **—poshá,** m. increase of cowherds, AV. xiii, 1, 12. **—prakāṇḍa,** n. an excellent cow, Pāṇ. ii, 1, 66, Kāś. **—pracāra,** m. pasturage for cattle, Yājñ. ii, 166. **—pratāra,** m. 'ox-ford,' N. of a place of pilgrimage on the Sarayū, MBh. iii, 8048 ff.; R. vii, 110, 23; Ragh. xv, 101; 'leading cattle across the water,' N. of Śiva, MBh. xii, 10430. **—pradāna,** n. = 1. *-dāna,* Pañcat. i, 11, 2 (Hit.) **—°pradānika,** mfn. relating to the gift of cows (as an Adhyāya, like MBh. xiii, ch. 79 ff.) **—prapadanīya,** n., Pāṇ. v, 1, 111, Vārtt. 1, Pat. **—praveśa-samaya,** m. the time when the cows come home, evening twilight, VarBṛS. xxiv, 35. **—prêkshaka,** N. of a Liṅga, LiṅgaP. i, 1, 3. **—prêraka,** m. 'cow-inciter,' the bird Bhṛiṅga-rāja, Gal. **—phaṇā,** f. a bandage hollowed out to fit the chin or nose &c., Suśr. **—phaṇikā,** f. id., i, 25, 20. **—baka,** m. the bird Ardea Govina, W. **—bandhu** (*gó-*), mfn. (= *-mātṛi*) having a cow as a relative (the Maruts), RV. viii, 20, 8. **—balá,** m., N. of a man, TBr. iii, 11, 9, 3. **—balivarda-nyāyena,** instr. ind. after the manner of 'a bull of cattle,' an expression to denote when a pleonasm is allowed, Nāg. on Pat. Introd.; Mn. viii, 28, Sch. **—ballava,** m. a cowherd, Pāṇ. vi, 2, 66, Kāś. **—brāhmaṇa,** n. sg. a cow and (or) a Brāhman, Mn. v, 95 & xi, 80; MBh. xiii; Hariv. 3157 f.; *-manushya,* m. pl. cows, Brāhmans, and men, W. **—bhaṭṭa,** m., N. of a poet, ŚārṅgP. **—bhaṇḍīra,** m. a kind of aquatic bird, L. **—bhartṛi,** m. a bull, Gal. **—bhāj,** mfn. used for the benefit of cows, RV. x, 97, 5. **—bhānu,** m., N. of a son of Vahni, Hariv. 1830; VP. **—bhuj,** m. 'enjoying the earth,' a king, Rājat. v, 6. **—bhṛit,** m. (g. *saṃkalâdi*) 'earth-supporter,' a mountain, W.; a king, Rājat. vii, 1072. **—makshikā,** f. a gad-fly (*daṇśa*), L. **—magha** (*gó-*), mfn. granting cattle or cows, RV. vi, 35, 3 & 4; vii, 71, 1. **—macarcikā,** f. = *-prakāṇḍa,* Pāṇ. ii, 1, 66, Kāś. **—maṇimda,** m. a cowherd, vi, 2, 66, Kāś. **—maṇḍala,** n. a herd of cows, Pat. on Pāṇ. i, 3, 62, Vārtt. 5 & iii, 1, 5, Vārtt. 1; 'earth-orb,' the globe, W. **—mat** (*gó-*), mfn. possessing or containing cattle or cows or herds, rich in cattle, consisting of cattle, RV.; AV.; VS.; MBh.

ii, v; containing or mixed with milk, RV.; n. possession of cattle, RV.; PārGṛ. iii, 4, 4; (*gó-matī*), f. a place abounding in herds of cattle, RV. iv, 21, 4 & v, 61 19; N. of a village in the north, g. *palady-ādi; (go-matí)*, f., N. of a river falling into the Indus, RV. viii, 24, 30 & x, 75, 10; another river falling into the Ganges, MBh. iii, iv (metrically °*ti*, 513), vi, xii, xiii; Hariv.; R. &c.; (with or without *vidyā*) N. of a Vedic hymn or formula to be repeated during expiation for killing a cow, MBh. xiii; Hcat. i, 7; N. of Dākshāyaṇī in the Go-manta mountain, MatsyaP. xiii, 28. – °**mata**, Nom. °*tati*, to behave like a cattle-owner, Pāṇ. vi, 4, 14, Siddh. – **matallikā**, f. (ii, 1, 66, Kāś.) an excellent cow, Śiś. xii, 41. – **mati**, for °*tī*, see s. v. *-mat*. – **matī**, f. of *-mat*, q. v.; *-tīrtha*, n., N. of a Tīrtha, SkandaP.; *-putra*, m., N. of a prince, VP. iv, 24, 13; *-sāra*, N. of a work. – °**matya**, Nom. P. °*tyati* = *gomantam icchati*, Pāṇ. vii, 1, 70, Pat. & Kāś.; vi, 4, 14, Siddh.: Ā. °*tyate*, to behave like a cattle-owner, Pāṇ. i, 4, 2, Vārtt. 25, Pat. – **matsya**, m. a kind of fish living in rivers, Suśr. i, 46, 2, 57. – **matha**, g. *kumudādi*. – **madhya-madhya**, mfn. slender in the waist, W. – **manta**, m., N. of a mountain, MBh. ii, 618; vi, 449 (v. l. °*nda*); Hariv.; VarBṛS. &c.; an owner of cattle, W.; a herd of cattle, W.; a multitude of cattle-owners, W.; m. pl., N. of a people, MBh. vi, 351 (v. l. *goghnata*). – **manda**, see *-manta*. – 1. **-máya**, mfn. consisting of cattle, RV. x, 62, 2; defiled with cow-dung, R. ii, v; n. often pl., rarely m. (g. *ardharcādi*) cow-dung, ŚBr. xii; ĀśvGṛ.; Kauś.; Gobh.; Mn. &c.; dung, VarBṛS. lv, 30; *-kārshī*, f. a piece of dried cow-dung, Divyâv.; *-cchattra*, n., *-cchattrikā*, f. a fungus, L.; *-pāyasīya-nyāya-vat*, ind. 'in the manner of cow-dung and of milky food,' i. e. very different in nature though having the same origin, Sarvad. ii, 169; *-priya*, m. 'fond of cow-dung,' Andropogon Schœnanthus, L.; *-maya*, mf(*ī*)n. made of cow-dung, Kād.; °*yâmbhas*, n. water with cow-dung, Prab. ii, 10; °*yôtthā*, f. 'originating in cow-dung,' a gad-fly or a kind of beetle found in cow-dung, L.; °*yôdbhava*, m. 'originating in cow-dung,' Cathartocarpus fistula, L. – 2. **-maya** (for the sake of euphony shortened for °*yaya*), Nom. P. °*yati*, to smear with (cow-dung), Dhātup. xxxv, 24. – °**mayāya**, Nom. °*yate*, to resemble cow-dung (in taste), Hit. iii, 6, 33. – **mahisha-dā**, f. 'granting cattle and buffaloes,' N. of one of the mothers attending on Skanda, MBh. ix, 2646. – **mātṛi** (*gó-*), mfn. having a cow for mother (the Maruts; cf. *pṛiśni-m°* & *gó-bandhu*), RV. i, 85, 3; f. 'mother of cows,' cow of plenty, W. – **māyu** (*gó-*), mfn. making sounds like cattle (a frog), RV. vii, 103, 6 & 10; m. a kind of frog, Kauś. 93 & 96; a jackal, ShaḍvBr. v, 8; Mn.; MBh. &c.; N. of a jackal, Pañcat. i; the bile of a cow, W.; N. of a Gandharva or celestial musician, Hariv. 14157; *-bhaksha*, m. pl. 'jackal-eaters,' N. of a people, VarBṛS. xvi, 35. – **māyukêśvara**, N. of a Liṅga, LiṅgaP. i, 1, 3. – **mitra**, m. for *-mūt°*, BrahmaP. ii, 12 & 18, 16. – **mithuna**, n. sg. a bull and a cow, ĀśvGṛ.; Gobh.; Mn. iii; m. du. id., ŚāṅkhŚr. iii, 14, 17. – **min**, m. (Pāṇ. v, 2, 114; g. *aśvādi*) the owner of cattle or cows, Mn. ix, 50; Yājñ. ii, 161; MBh. xii; VarBṛS.; a jackal, L.; a layman adhering to Buddha's faith, L.; = *nindya* & = *praśasta*, L. – **mīna**, m. = *-matsya*, L. – **mukha**, m. (Pāṇ. vi, 2, 168) 'cow-faced,' a crocodile, L.; a hole in a wall of a peculiar shape made by thieves, L.; N. of one of Śiva's attendants, L.; of a son of Mātali, MBh. v, 3574; R. vii, 28, 10; of a king of Kauśāmbī, Kathārṇ.; of a son of the treasurer of king Vatsa, Kathās. xxiii; of an attendant of the 1st Arhat of the present Avasarpiṇī, L.; v. l. for *-khala;* m. (n., L.) a kind of musical instrument (sort of horn or trumpet?), MBh. iv, vii, ix; Bhag. i, 13; R. (ifc. f. *ā*); BhP.; n. (= *-mukhī*) a cloth-bag for containing a rosary, L.; a house built unevenly (viz. with angles or projections), L.; a particular method of sitting, Haṭhapr.; plastering, smearing with (in comp.), Śiś. iii, 48 (pl.); (*ī*), f. a cloth-bag for containing a rosary (the beads of which are counted by the hand thrust inside), W. (RTL. pp. 92 & 406); a chasm in the Himâlaya mountains (through which the Ganges flows, erroneously conceived to be shaped like a cow's mouth), W.; N. of a river in Rādha, W.; *-vyāghra*, m. 'cow-faced tiger,' a wolf in sheep's clothing, W. – **mukhyā**, f. a particular way of beating a drum. – **muṇḍa**, m. anything put up for measuring or protecting a field, Vāsav. 494. – **mūḍha**, mfn. stupid as an ox, W. – **mūtra**, n. cow's urine, Kāṭh.; KātyŚr. xxv; Kauś.; Mn. &c.; m. pl. N. of a family, Pravar. v, 4; *-jāti*. f. a verse called *gomūtrikā*, q. v. – °**mūtraka**, mfn. 'similar to the course of cow's urine,' going alternately to the one and to the other side, zigzagging, MBh. ix, 3268; ? g. *sthūlādi*; (*ikā*), f. zigzag, Daś. xi, 51; an artificial verse to be read in zigzag, Kāvyâd. iii, 78 f.; Sarasv.; Sāh. x, 13$\frac{8}{9}$; a form of calculation, W.; the reddish grass Tāmbaḍu, L.; °*trikā-bandha*, m. = °*tra-jāti*. – **mūtrin**, m. a kind of Terminalia, L. – **mṛigá**, m. (= 2. *gavayá*, q. v.) the Gayal, VS. xxiv; TS. ii; ŚBr. xiii; KātyŚr.; *-kāka-caryā*, f. the manner of cows (when going), of deer (when standing), and of crows (when sitting), BhP. v, 5, 34; °*gêndra*, m. = °*gá*, Gal. – **meda**, m. 'cow-fat,' a gem brought from the Himālaya and the Indus (being of 4 sorts, white, pale yellow, red, and dark blue), RTL. p. 468; the tree *kakkola*, L.; a kind of fish, Gal.; N. of a mountain, VP. ii, 4, 7; of a Dvīpa, Romakas.; MatsyaP. cxxii; *saṃnibha*, m. 'resembling the Gomeda,' dolomite, L.; the plant Dugdha-pāshāṇa, L. – **medaka**, m. n., N. of a gem (= °*da*), Hcat. i, 5 & 7; a kind of poison (?, *kākola*, for *kakk°*?), L.; = *pattraka* (smearing the body with unguents, W.), L.; the Dvīpa °*da*, Gol. iii, 25; MatsyaP. cxxii. – **medha**, m. (cf. *gavām-m°*) a cow-sacrifice, R. vii, 25, 8; VarP. xvi; N. of the attendant of the 22nd Arhat of the present Avasarpiṇī, L. – **'mbu**, n. = *-jala*, Bhpr. vii, 57, 15. – **'mbhas**, n. id., L. – **yajña**, m. sacrifice of cattle, Gobh.; PārGṛ.; a sacrifice in honour of cows, Hariv. 3851. – **yāna**, n. a carriage drawn by oxen or cows, cart (in general), Mn. xi, 175; Suśr. – **yukta**, mfn. drawn by oxen or cows, ĀśvGṛ.; Gobh. – **yuga**, n. (Pāṇ. v, 2, 29, Vārtt. 3, Pat.) a yoke or pair of cattle, pair of animals (in general), MBh. xii, xiii; Pañcat. – **yuta**, mfn. frequented by cattle, R. ii, 49, 10; n. = *gav-yūta* (q. v.), MBh. xiv, 1934. – **yūti**, f. (= *gáv-y°*) id., Pāṇ. vi, 1, 79, Vārtt. – **raksh**, mfn. tending or guarding cattle, Vop. iii, 151. – **raksha**, mfn. id., W.; m. a cowherd, L.; a Gorkha or inhabitant of Nepāl, W.; Śiva, L.; N. of an author (= °*ksha-nātha*); the orange tree, L.; the medicinal plant Ṛishabha, L.; n. = °*kshā*, for °*kshya*, q. v., Mn. x, 82; MBh. ii, iii, xiii; R. ii; (*ā*), f. tending or breeding cattle, business of a herdsman, MBh. i (ifc. f. *ā*), ii; Hariv. 363; (*ī*), f., N. of several plants used for forming fences (*gandha-bahulā, go-pālī, citralā, dīrgha-daṇḍī, pañca-parṇikā, sarpa-daṇḍī, su-daṇḍikā*), L.; = °*ksha-tumbī*, L.; = °*ksha-dugdhā*, L.; *-karkaṭī*, f. the cucumber *cirbhiṭā*, Bhpr. v, 6, 36; *-kalpa*, m., N. of a work; *-jambū*, f. wheat, L.; = °*ksha-taṇḍula*, L.; = *ghoṇḍā-phala* (the jujube fruit, W.), L.; *-taṇḍula*, n., °*lā*, f. Uraria lagopodioides, L.; *-tumbī*, f. a kind of cucumber (*kumbha-t°*), L.; *-dāsa*, m., N. of a prince, Inscr.; *-dugdhā*, f. a small kind of shrub, L.; *-nātha*, m., N. of the author of *-śataka;* *-pura*, n., N. of a town (the modern Gorakhpur), RTL. p. 158; *-śataka*, n., N. of a work; *-sahasranāman*, n. 'the thousand names of Śiva,' N. of a work; °*kshâsana*, n. a particular method of sitting, Haṭhapr. – **rakshaka**, mfn. tending or keeping or breeding cattle (one of the Vṛittis of a Vaiśya, Vishṇ. ii, 13), Mn. viii, 102; MBh. xiii; m. a cowherd, Hit.; N. of a man, Tantr. – **rakshaṇa**, n. tending cattle, W. – **rakshya**, n. = °*kshā*, Āp.; Mn. x, 116; MBh.; Bhag.; °*kshyâṭṭa*, m., N. of a locality, Rasik. – **raṅku**, m. a waterfowl, L.; a chanter, bard (*lagna*), L.; a bailsman, guarantee, L.; a naked man (*nagna* for *lagna*?), W. – **rajas**, n. a particle of dust on a cow-hair (named as a very small measure), Lalit. xii; 'sun-dust,' an atom. – **ratha**, m. 'cow-cart,' N. of a mountain, MBh. ii, 797; Śiva, W. – **rathaka**, m. a carriage drawn by cattle, SaddhP. iii. – **rabhasa** (*gó-*), mfn. strengthened with milk (Soma), RV. i, 121, 8. – **rambha**, m., N. of a man, Pañcat. i. – **rava**, m. saffron, L. – **rasa**, m. cow-milk, MBh.; R.; Yājñ. i; Suśr.; VarBṛS.; milk, Car. i, 27; buttermilk, L.; curdled milk, L.; *-ja*, n. buttermilk, L. – **rāja**, m. (= *-pati*) a bull, L. – **rāṭikā**, °**ṭī**, f. = *-kirāṭ°*, L. – **rāsya**, m. 'playing with cows,' Kṛishṇa, Pañcar. iv, 8, 16. – **ruta**, n. 'as far as a cow's lowing may be heard,' = *-yuta*, Daś. x, 138. – **rudha**, see *á-g°*. – **rūpá**, mfn. cow-shaped, AV. ix, 7, 25; MBh. xiii, 737; n. the shape of a cow, Siṇhâs. Introd. $\frac{42}{1}$. – **roca**, n. = °*canā*, L. – **rocanā**, f. a bright yellow orpiment prepared from the bile of cattle (employed in painting, dyeing, and in marking the Tilaka on the forehead; in med. used as a sedative, tonic, and anthelmintic remedy), MBh. xiii, 6149; Vikr. v, 19; Kum.; VarBṛS. &c. – **lakshaṇa**, n. 'marks of a cow,' see *gaulakshaṇika*. – **láttikā**, f. a kind of animal, VS. xxiv, 37; TS. v. – **lava**, m., N. of a teacher, VāyuP. (v. l. for *gālava*). – **lavaṇa**, n. the quantity of salt given to a cow, Pāṇ. vi, 2, 4, Kāś. – **lāṅgula**, m. for °*gūla* (q. v.) a kind of monkey, MBh. iii, 16272; R.; (*ī*) f. the female of that monkey, R. i, 16, 21; *-parivartana*, m., N. of a mountain near Rāja-gṛiha, Buddh. (v. l. *golī-gula-p°*). – **lāṅgūla**, m. (= *-puccha*) 'cow-tailed,' a black kind of monkey, MBh. i, 2628; R. – **liha**, m. 'cow-licked,' Bignonia suaveolens, Bhpr. v, 5, 67. – **līḍha**, m. id., ib. – **loka**, m. (n., Tantr.) 'cow-world,' a part of heaven, or (in later mythol., RTL. 118 & 291) Kṛishṇa's heaven, MBh. xiii, 3195 (cf. 3347); Hariv. 3994 (cf. 3899); R. ii; BrahmaP.; *-varṇana*, n., N. of BrahmavP. iv, 4; of part of the Sadā-śiva-saṃhitā; of part of SkandaP. – **loman**, n. a cow's hair (from which Dūrvā grass is said to spring), Pāṇ. i, 4, 30, Pat.; Pañcat. i, 1, 81. – **lomikā**, f. Hemionitis cordifolia, L. – **lomī**, f., N. of a plant (white Dūrvā grass, L.; *bhūta-keśa* or °*śī*, L.; *vacā*, L.), Car. i, 4, 16, 3; Suśr. iv, vi; = *vara-yoshā* ('an excellent woman' or 'a harlot'), L. – **vatsa**, m. 'a calf,' in comp.; *-dvādaśī-vrata*, n. a kind of observance, BhavP.; °*tsâdin*, m. 'calf-eater,' a wolf, L.; °*tsâri*, m. 'calf-enemy,' id., L. – **vatsaka**, m. a kind of bird, Vasantar. viii, 48. – **vatsalatīrtha**, n., N. of a Tīrtha, SkandaP. – **vadha**, m. the killing of a cow, Mn. xi, 60. – **vandanī**, f. the Priyaṃgu plant, L.; the plant Gandha-vallī, L. – **vapus** (*gó-*), mfn. shaped like a cow, RV. x, 68, 9. – **vara**, m., N. of a village; n. cow-dung pulverized, Bhpr. (v. l. *gor-v°*). – **vardhana**, m. a celebrated hill in Vṛindāvana near Mathurā (lifted up and supported by Kṛishṇa upon one finger for 7 days to shelter the cowherds from a storm of rain sent by Indra to test Kṛishṇa's divinity, cf. RTL. p. 113), Inscr.; MBh. ii, 1441; v, 4410; Hariv.; Ragh. &c.; N. of a holy fig-tree in the country of the Bāhikas, MBh. viii, 2031; N. of the author of °*nasaptaśatī* (of the 12th or 13th century A. D.), Git. i, 4; ŚārṅgP.; Sch. on Uṇ. &c.; N. of one of the 5 Śruta-kevalins, Jain.; = °*na-dhara*, Cāṇ.; *-dhara*, m. 'Govardhana-supporter,' Kṛishṇa, Hariv. 10406; Rājat. iv, 198; *-māhātmya*, n. 'the glory of the Govardhana hill,' N. of a part of VarP.; *-saptaśatī*, f. 700 stanzas in the Āryā metre on chiefly erotic subjects by Govardhanâcārya; °*nâcārya*, °*nânanda*, m. the renowned author Govardhana. – °**vardhanīya**, mfn. composed by Govardhana. – **vaśā**, f. a barren cow, Kāt. – **vāṭa**, m. a hurdle for cattle, Hariv. 3397 & 3485; Kathās. xx (ifc. f. *ā*). – **vāla**, mf(*ī*)n. having hair like a cow, Pāṇ. iv, 1, 64, Kāś.; m. a cow's hair, Mn. viii, 250 (pl.); N. of the father of the astronomer Viśva-nātha. – °**vālin**, mfn. 'cow-haired' (a kind of *gaja*), Buddh. L. – 1. **-vāsa**, m. the abode of cows, cow-house, MBh. ii, 825. – 2. **-vāsa**, m. pl. 'covered with ox-hides,' N. of a people, viii, 3650. – **vāsana**, m. pl. id., ii, 1825; m. sg. (g. *kāśy-ādi*) N. of a king of the Śibis, i, vi f. – **vikartá**, m. a cow-slaughterer, MaitrS. ii; ŚBr. v, 3, 1, 10; KātyŚr. – **vikarttṛi**, m. id., MBh. iv, 36. – **vitata**, for *-vinata*, i, 3121. – **víd**, mfn. acquiring or procuring cows or cattle, RV.; m., N. of Saha-deva (cf. MBh. iv, 19, 32), Gal. – **vinata** (*gó-*), m. a form of the Aśva-medha sacrifice, ŚBr. xiii; (cf. *-vitata*.) – **vinda**, m. (Pāṇ. iii, 1, 138, Vārtt. 2) '= *-vid* (or fr. Prākrit *gov'-inda* = *gopêndra*?),' Kṛishṇa (or Vishṇu), MBh.; Hariv.; Bhag.; BhP.; (cf. RTL. p. 405); Bṛihaspati (cf. *gotra-bhid*), L.; (= Vishṇu) N. of the 4th month, VarBṛS. cv, 14; (fr. Prākrit *gov'-inda* = *gopêndra*) a chief herdsman, L.; N. of a prince; of several teachers and authors; of a mountain, MBh. vi, 460; *-kūṭa*, m. id., Kathās. xxv, 293; cviii; *-gira*, N. of a copyist (1770 A. D.); *-canda*, for *-candra;* *-candra*, m., N. of a prince; *-datta*, m., N. of a Brāhman, vii, 42; *-dīkshita*, m., N. of a man; *-deva*, m., N. of the father of Sundara-deva; *-dvādaśī*, f. the 12th day in the light half of month Phālguna; *-nātha*, m., N. of one of Śaṃkara's teachers; *-nāyaka*, m., N. of a sage, Sarvad. ix, 21; *-pāla*, m., N. of a prince; *-prakāśa*, m., N. of a work; *-bhagavat-pādâcārya*, m., N. of a teacher, 9; 20; 35; *-bhaṭṭa*, m., N. of an author; *-mānasôllāsa*, m., N. of a work; *-rāja*, m., N. of a commentator on Mn. (mentioned by Kull. on ix, 125; 136 & 141); N. of a poet, ŚārṅgP.; *-rāma*, m., N. of a prince, Kshitîś. v, 48; of a scholiast; *-rāya*, m., N. of a prince, Kshitîś. vi, 1; *-vrindā-vana*, N. of a work; *-siṇha*, m., N. of a prince, Inscr.; N. of one of the ten chief Gurus of the Sikhs, RTL. pp. 164; 166 & 167; *-sūri*, m., N. of a commentator on the MBh. (father of Nīla-kaṇṭha); *-svāmin*, m., N. of a Brāhman, Kathās. xxv, 74; °*ndânanda*, m., N. of a scholiast; °*ndârcana-sudhā*, f. 'nectar of Kṛishṇa's praise,' N. of a work; °*ndârṇava*, m., N. of a work; °*ndâshṭaka*, n. 'the 8 verses of Govinda,' N. of a work. — °**vindinī**, f., N. of a fragrant plant, Gal. — **vindú**, mfn. searching for milk, RV. ix, 96, 19. — **vish**, f. cow-dung, L. — **vishāṇa**, n. cow-horn, MBh. xii, 5303; Suśr. — °**vishāṇika**, m. (cf. *mukha*) a kind of musical instrument, trumpet, MBh. vi, ix. — **vishṭhā**, f. = *-vish*, Bhpr. v, 26, 23. — **visarga**, m. (= *-sarga*) 'time at which cows are let loose,' day-break, R. vii, 111, 9; AV.Pariś. — **vīthī**, f. 'cow-path,' that portion of the moon's path which contains the asterisms Bhadra-padā, Revatī, and Aśvinī (or according to others, Hasta, Citrā, and Svātī), lii, 19; VarBṛS. ix, 1 f. — **vīrya**, n. the value or price received for milk, Nār. — **vṛinda**, n. a drove of cattle, L. — **vṛindāraka**, m. an excellent ox, Pāṇ. ii, 1, 62, Kāś. — **vṛisha**, m. (Pāṇ. vi, 2, 144, Kāś.) a bull, Mn. ix, 150; MBh.; Hariv. &c.; Śiva, MBh. xii, 10372 (cf. xiii, 914); *-dhvaja*, m. id., xiii, 4002. — **vṛishaṇa**, n. the scrotum of a bull, Suśr. i, 13, 6. — **vṛishabha**, m. a bull, MBh.; °*bhâṅka*, m., N. of Śiva, xiii, 6296. — **vesha**, mfn. having the appearance of a bull, iv, 588. — **vaidya**, m. a cow-doctor, W. — **vaidyaka**, n., N. of a medical work, Uṇ. ii, 109, Sch. — **vyacchá**, mfn. one who torments a cow, VS. xxx, 18; Kāṭh. xv, 4. — **vyāghra**, n. sg. a cow and a tiger, Pāṇ. ii, 4, 9, Sch. (not in Kāś.) — **vyādhi**, m. N. of a man, Pravar. vii. — **vraja**, m. a cow-pen, Mn. iv, xi; MBh. i; Hariv.; R. ii; N. of an attendant of Skanda, MBh. ix, 2568; of a Dānava, Hariv. 12937. — **vrata**, mfn. one who imitates a cow in frugality, MBh. v, 3560. — °**vratin**, mfn. id., 3559; xiii, 3583; Hcat. i, 7. — **śakaṭa**, m. n. = *-rathaka*, L. — **śakṛit**, n. = *-vish*, Mn. ii, 182; Suśr.; °*kṛid-rasa*, m. dung-water, Mn. xi, 92. — **śata**, n. a present of 100 cows sent to a Brāhman, W. — °**śatin**, mfn. possessing 100 cows, MBh. xiii, 3742; (*gavāṃ ś*°, 4885.) — **śaphá**, m. a cow's hoof, VS. xxiii; ŚāṅkhŚr.; Lāṭy. — **śarya** (*gó-*), m., N. of a man, RV. viii, 8, 20; 49, 10 & 50, 10. — **śāla**, n. a cow-stall, Pāṇ. iv, 3, 35; m. (Pāṇ. iv, 3, 35) 'born in a cow-stall' (cf. Bhagavatī xv), N. of a pupil and rival of Mahā-vīra (who founded or became the head of the Ājīvika sect), Buddh. (v. l. °*li*); Jain.; N. of a Gauḍa prince; (*ā*), f. a cow-stall, Kauś. — **śāli**, v. l. for °*la*, q. v. — **śila**, m. pl. 'cow-stone,' N. of a family, Pravar. v, 4. — **śīrsha**, m. 'cow-headed,' N. of a Nāga, Kāraṇḍ. i, 19; n. a kind of arrow, MBh. vii, 8097 (°*sha* or °*shan*); the head of a cow, W.; (also m., L.) a kind of sandal-wood (brass-coloured and very fragrant), R. iv, 41, 59; Buddh.; Jain.; camphor, Gal.; *-candana*, n. id., Kāraṇḍ. xii; Kād. iv, 663. — **śīrshaka**, m. the shrub Droṇa-pushpī, L.; a kind of sandal-wood, Kād. (v. l.) — **śṛiṅga**, n. a cow's horn, Kauś.; Kathās. lix; for *gauśṛ*°, q. v.; m. 'cow-horned,' Acacia arabica, L.; N. of a mountain, MBh. ii, 1109; R. iv; Buddh.; *-vratin*, m. pl., N. of a Buddh. sect, Buddh. L. — **śe**, for *-se*, see s. v. *-sa*. — **śrīta** (*gó-*), mfn. mixed with milk (Soma), RV. i, 137, 1; viii, 21, 5. — **śruti**, m. N. of a man with the patr. Vaiyāghrapadya, ChUp. v, 2, 3. — **'śvá**, n. sg. (Pāṇ. ii, 4, 11, Kāś.) cattle and horses, ŚBr. xii; KātyŚr.; m. du. an ox or a cow and a horse, Pāṇ. ii, 4, 11, Kāś. — °**shaka**, m. (fr. *-shán*), N. of a Buddh. author. — **shakhi** (*gó-*), *ā*, m. 'having cattle as friends (*sákhi*),' possessing cattle, RV. viii, 14, 1; (cf. *-sakhi.*) — **shaḍ-gava**, n. 3 pairs of cattle, Vop. vii, 76. — **sháṇi**, mfn. acquiring or procuring cattle, RV. vi, 53, 10; (cf. *-sáni.*) — **shá-tama**, see *-shán*. — **shád**, mfn. sitting among cattle, MaitrS. i, 1, 2; Kāṭh. i, xxxi; (*ghoshád*, TS. i, 1, 2, 1); *-ādi*, a Gaṇa of Pāṇ. (v, 2, 62; Gaṇar. 435 f.) — **shada**, for *-shad*, ib., Kāś. — °**shadaka**, mfn. containing the word *go-shád* (an Adhyāya or Anuvāka), g. *goshad-ādi*. — **shán**, mfn. (√*san*) = *-sháṇi*, RV. iv, 32, 22; *-(shá)-tama*, mfn. (superl.), vi, 33, 5. — **shā́**, mfn. (√*sā* = *san*, Kāś. on Pāṇ. iii, 2, 67 & viii, 3, 108) = *-sháṇi*, RV. ix, 2, 10; 16, 2; 61, 20; x, 95, 3. — **shā́ti** (*gó-*), f. acquiring or fighting for the sake of cattle, viii, 84, 7; x, 38, 1. — **shādī**, f. (√*sad*) 'settling on cows,' a kind of bird, VS. xxiv, 24; (*ghosh*°) MaitrS.; (cf. *-sāda.*) — **shûkta**, m. (*sûkta*), N. of the father or ancestor of Gaushûkti, TāṇḍyaBr. xix, Sch. — °**shûktin**, m. (*sûkt*°), N. of the author of RV. viii, 14 f. — **shedhā́**, f. (√*sidh*) a kind of evil being, AV. i, 18, 4. — **shṭa**, for 2. *-shṭha*, q. v. — **shṭoma** (*gó-*), m. (*stóma*, Pāṇ. viii, 3, 105, Kāś.) an Ekâha ceremony forming part of the Abhiplava which lasts 6 days (also called *gó*, q. v.), TS. vii; Lāṭy. x; (cf. AitBr. iv, 15 & *-stoma.*) — 1. **-shṭhá**, m. (n., L.; fr. *stha*, Pāṇ. viii, 3, 97) an abode for cattle, cow-house, cow-pen, fold for cattle, RV.; VS.; AV. &c.; stable or station of animals (in general, Pāṇ. v, 2, 29, Vārtt. 3), MBh.; meeting-place, xii, 6547 (= 9953); with *aṅgirasām*, N. of a Sāman, TāṇḍyaBr. xiii; *apāṃ g*°, a water-vessel, AV. xi, 1, 13; 'refuge (of men),' Śiva, MBh. xiv, 198; N. of an author, Buddh.; n. = °*shṭhī-śrāddha*, Kull. on Mn. iii, 254; (*ā*), f. a place where cows are kept, Gaṇar. 56, Sch.; (*ī*), f. an assembly, meeting, society, association, family connections (esp. the dependent or junior branches), partnership, fellowship, MBh. (metrically °*shṭhi*, v, 1536) &c.; conversation, discourse, dialogue, Pañcat.; Kād.; a kind of dramatic entertainment in one act, Sāh. vi, 274; N. of a village, g. *palady-ādi* (Kāś.; Gaṇar. 325); *-karman*, n. a rite relating to the cow-stable, Kauś. 19; *-kukkuṭa*, m. a kind of crow, Npr.; *-gocara*, m. id., ib.; *-cara*, m. a kind of hawk, Gal.; *-ja*, m. 'born in a cow-pen,' N. of a Brāhman, PhiṭS.; *-pati*, m. a chief herdsman, L.; *-śva*, m. (fr. *śvân*) 'a dog in a cow-pen (which barks at every one),' one who stays at home and slanders his neighbours, malicious or censorious person, L.; °*shṭhâgāra*, m. n. a house in a cow-pen, L.; °*shṭhâdhyaksha*, m. = °*shṭha-pati*, L.; °*shṭhâshṭamī*, f., N. of a festive day (cf. *gopâshṭ*°); °*shṭhe-kshvedin* &c., see s. v. *-shṭhe*. — 2. **-shṭha**, Nom. Ā. (fr. 1. *-shṭha*) °*shṭhate*, to assemble, collect, Dhātup. viii, 4. — **shṭhā́na**, mfn. (*sth*°) serving as an abode for cows, VS. i, 25. — **shṭhi**, see s. v. *-shṭha*. — °**shṭhika**, mfn. relating to an assemblage or society, Pañcat. i, 14. — **shṭhī**, f. of *-shṭhá*, q. v.; *-pati*, m. the chief person or president of an assembly, W.; *-bandha*, m. meeting for conversation, Kād. v, 825; *-yāna*, m. a society-carriage, Mṛicch. vi, 4; *-śālā*, f. a meeting-room; *-śrāddha*, n. a kind of Śrāddha ceremony, Kull. on Mn. iii, 254 (RTL. p. 305). — °**shṭhīna**, v. l. for *gaushṭh*°, q. v. — **shṭhe**, loc. of *-shṭhá*, q. v.; *-kshveḍin*, mfn. 'bellowing in a cow-pen,' a boasting coward, gaṇas *pātre-samitâdi* & *yuktârohy-ādi*; *-paṭu*, mfn. 'clever in a cow-pen,' a vain boaster, ib.; *-paṇḍita*, mfn. id., ib.; *-pragalbha*, mfn. 'courageous in a cow-pen,' a boasting coward, ib.; *-vijitin*, mfn. 'victorious in a cow-pen,' id., ib.; *-śaya*, mfn. sleeping in a cow-stable, Yājñ. iii, 263; *-śūra*, m. a hero in a cow-pen, boasting coward, gaṇas *pātre-samitâdi* & *yuktârohy-ādi*. — °**shṭhya** (*gó-*), mfn. being in a cow-stable, VS. xvi, 44. — 1. **-sa**, m. (√*so*) = *-visarga*, L.; (*e*), loc. ind. (v. l. *go-śe*) at day-break, L., Sch.; (in Prākṛit, Hāl.) — **sakhi** (*gó-*), mfn. (m. acc. °*khāyam*) 'having milk as its friend,' mixed with milk (Soma), RV. v, 37, 4; (cf. *-shakhi.*) — **saṃkhya**, m. (Pāṇ. vi, 2, 66, Kāś.) 'counting the cows,' a cowherd, MBh. iv, 284 & 289. — **saṃkhyātṛi**, m. id., 67. — **saṅga**, for *-sarga*, L. — **sattrá**, n. a particular sacrifice, TS. vii, 5, 1, 1. — **sadṛiksha**, m. = *-tulya*, L. — **sáni**, mfn. (Kāś. on Pāṇ. iii, 2, 27 & viii, 3, 108) = *-sháṇi*, AV. iii, 20, 10; VS. viii, 12 (TS.); (*im*), g. *savanâdi*. — **saṃdāya**, mfn. presenting with a cow, Pāṇ. iii, 2, 3, Kāś. — **samādhi**, N. of a locality, Rasik. xi, 17. — **sambhava**, mfn. produced from or by a cow, L.; (*ā*), f. = (*-lomī*) white Dūrvā grass, L. — **sarga**, m. = *-visarga*, Suśr. — **sarpa**, m. Lacerta Godica (*godhikā*), W. — **savá**, m., N. of an Ekâha ceremony, TBr. ii; Lāṭy.; KātyŚr. &c.; a cow-sacrifice, W. — **sahasra**, n. a thousand kine, W.; mfn. possessing a thousand kine, MBh. xiii, 102, 43; (*ī*), f., N. of two festive days (the 15th day in the dark half of month Kārttika and of month Jyaishṭha). — **sāda**, °*di*, Pāṇ. vi, 2, 41; (cf. *-shādī.*) — **sārathi**, ib. — **sāvitrī**, f., N. of a hymn (cf. *gāyatrī*), Hcat. i, 5. — **sûkta**, n., N. of a hymn, ĀśvMantraS. — **sūtrikā**, f. a rope fastened at both ends having separate halters for each ox or cow, W. — **sevā**, f. attendance on a cow, W. — **stana**, m. a cow's dug MBh. iii, 32, 4; a cluster of blossoms, nosegay, W.; a pearl necklace consisting of 4 (or of 34, W.) strings, L; a kind of fort; (*ī*), f. a kind of red grape, Bhpr. v, 6, 108; N. of one of the mothers attending on Skanda, MBh. ix, 2621; °*nâkāra*, mfn. shaped like a cow's dug, Suśr. ii, vi; Bhpr. v; °*nī-sava*, m. a kind of wine, Npr. — **stoma**, m. (Pāṇ. viii, 3, 105, Kāś.) = *-shṭoma*, ĀśvŚr. ix, 5, 2. — **sthāna**, n. a station for cattle, cow-pen, Hariv. 3397; (cf. *-shṭhāna.*) — **sthānaka**, n. id., L. — **sphuraṇa**, n. a twitching of any particular part of the hide of a cow (as on being touched &c.), W. — **svāmin**, m. the master or possessor of a cow or of cows, KātyŚr.; Mn. viii, 231; VarBṛS.; a religious mendicant (commonly *gosāin*, cf. RTL. pp. 87; 135; 142; also affixed as a honorary title to proper names, e. g. *Vopadeva-g*°); 'lord of cows,' Kṛishṇa, W.; °*mi-sthāna*, n., N. of a mountain peak in the middle of the Himālaya, W. — **hatyā**, f. = *-vadha*, Mn. xi, 116. — **hán**, mfn. killing cattle, RV. vii, 56, 17. — **hantṛi**, m. a cow-killer, Gaut. xxi, 11. — **hara**, m. stealing of cows, VarBṛS. lxxxix, 9 (v. l. *-graha*). — **haraṇa**, n. id., 5; Pañcat. i, 8, 36; N. of MBh. iv, ch. 25–69. — **harītakī**, f. Ægle Marmelos, L. — **hiṇsā**, f. hurting a cow, W. — **hita**, m. 'proper for cattle,' = *-harītakī*, L.; Luffa fœtida or a similar plant, L. — **hiraṇya**, n. sg. cattle and gold, MBh. ii, 1833.

Gokā, f. (a dimin. of *gó*) a small cow, Pāṇ. vii, 4, 13, Kāś. — **mukha**, m. 'cow-faced,' N. of a mountain, BhP. v, 19, 16.

Gor (for *gos*, gen. sg. of *gó*). — **vara**, see *go-v*°.

Gosh (id.) — **pada** (*gósh-*), mfn. (Pāṇ. vi, 1, 145) 'showing marks of cow's hoofs,' frequented by kine, Kāś.; n. 'mark of a cow's foot in the soil,' water filling up such a mark, any small puddle, Suparṇ.; MBh. i, vii, ix; R. vi; BhP. x; *-tṛitīyā-vrata*, n. a kind of religious observance, BhavP.; *-trirātra-vrata*, n. id., ib.; *-pūram* or *-pram*, ind. so as to fill only the impression of a cow's hoof, Kāś. on Pāṇ. iii, 4, 32 & vi, 1, 145; Bhaṭṭ. xiv, 20; *-mātra*, mfn. as large as the impression of a cow's hoof, Pāṇ. vi, 1, 145, Kāś.; (cf. *go-pada.*)

Goshu (loc. pl. of *gó*). — **cara**, mfn. walking among cattle, Pāṇ. vi, 3, 1, Vārtt. 5. — **yúdh**, mfn. fighting for the sake of cattle (or booty), RV. i, 112, 22; vi, 6, 5; x, 30, 10.

गोघ्नत *goghnata*, for *go-manta*, q. v.

गोच्छा *gocchā*, f. the furrow of the upper lip, VarBṛS. lviii, 9; (cf. *go-kha*, p. 364, col. 1.)

गोच्छाल *gocchāla*, m. the plant Kulāhala (or *alambusha*; 'the palm of the hand with the fingers extended,' W.), L.

गोजि *goji*, for °*jī*, q. v. — **kāya**, m. for *gāñjik*°, Gal.

Gojika, m. for *gauñj*°, q. v., Gal.; (*ā*), f. = *go-jihvā*, Bhpr. v, 3, 297.

Gojī, f., N. of a plant with sharp leaves, Suśr. i, 8, 11; iv, 9 & 18 f.; v, 7, 1; vi, 24, 26.

गोड *goḍa*, m. (= *goṇḍa*) a fleshy navel, L.

Goḍaka-grāma, m., N. of a village, Bharaṭ. v.

Goḍu, v. l. for °*ḍa*, W.

गोण *goṇa*, m. (fr. Pāli & Prākṛit) an ox, SaddhP. iii; Hemac.; (*ā*), f. (Pāṇ. iv, 1, 42) a kind of grass, Gaṇar. 54; (*ī*), f. (in Prākṛit) a cow, Pat. Introd. 35; 97; & on Vārtt. 6; a sack, Pāṇ. iv, 1, 42; Suśr.; Daś.; Śiś. xii, 10; ŚārṅgP.; a measure of 4 Droṇas, ŚārṅgS. i, 29; (ifc. after numerals °*ṇi*) Pāṇ. i, 2, 50, Kāś.; torn or ragged clothes, L.; (cf. *gauṇika.*) **Goṇâśman**, m. a kind of gem, L.

Goṇikā, f. (in Pāli *goṇaka*) a kind of woollen cloth, SaddhP. iii. — **putra**, m., N. of the author of a work on the relations towards the wives of others, Vātsyāy. i, 5, 5 & 35; v, 1, 8; 4, 26 & 33; 6, 48.

Goṇī, f. of °*ṇa*, q. v. — **tarī**, f. a small sack, Pāṇ. v, 3, 90. — **patha**, N. of a man, Pravar. iii, 1.

गोण्ड *goṇḍa*, m. a fleshy navel, L.; a person with a fleshy or prominent navel, L.; a man of a low tribe, mountaineer, esp. inhabiting the eastern portion of the Vindhya range between the Narmadā and Kṛishṇā. — **kirī**, f. (in music) N. of a Rāginī; (cf. *gauṇḍa-k*°.) — **vana**, n. 'Goṇḍa forest,' N. of a country. — **vāra**, id. **Goṇḍâ-krī**, f. = °*ḍa-kiri*.

गोतम *gó-tama*, &c. See *gó*, p. 364, col. 2.

Go-trá, gotrika, gotrin, &c. See ib., col. 3.

गोद 2. *goda*, m. n. the brain, L.

गोदान 2. *godāna*, n. (*dāna*, fr. √*do*? 'place where the hair (*go*) is cut,' Ragh. iii, 33, Sch.) the side-hair, ŚBr. iii; KātyŚr.; PārGṛ.; = -*maṅgala*, ĀśvGṛ.; Kauś.; ŚāṅkhGṛ.; Gobh.; Gaut.; R. **-maṅgala**, n. a ceremony performed with the side-hair of a youth of 16 or 18 years (when he has attained puberty and shortly before marriage), R. (G) i, 73, 22. **-vidhi**, m. id., Ragh. iii, 33.

Godānika, mfn. = *gaud*°, Gobh. iii, 1, 28.

गोदानीय *godānīya*, &c. See *gó*, p. 365, col. 1.

Go-dāvarī, go-dúh, &c. See ib.

गोध *godha*, m. pl., N. of a people, MBh. vi, 9, 42 (*sodha*, C).

गोधन *go-dhana*, *-dhara*, &c. See *gó*, p. 365.

गोधा *godhā́*, f. (g. *bhidâdi*) a sinew (cf. *gó*), RV. x, 28, 10 & 11; AV. iv, 3, 6; a chord, RV. viii, 69, 9; a leathern fence wound round the left arm to prevent injury from a bow-string, MBh. iii, iv, vii; R. i, ii; an Iguana (either the Gosamp or the alligator, commonly *gosāpa*), VS. xxiv, 35; Bṛih.; Mn. &c.; = -*vatī*, Gal.; N. of the authoress of a Sāman. **-padikā**, f. Cissus pedata, L. **-padī**, f. (g. *kumbhapady-ādi*) id., L. **-vatī**, f. the plant Irāvatī, L. **-viṇākā**, f. a kind of stringed instrument, KātyŚr. xiii, 3, 17. **-°sana** (°*dhâś*°), m. 'Iguana-eater,' N. of a man, v. l. for *go-vāsana*. **-sāman**, n. the Sāman of Godhā, ĀrshBr. **-skandha**, m. Vachellia farnesiana (*viṭ-khadira*), L.

Godhāya, Nom. P. °*yati*, to move curvedly like an Iguana, g. *kaṇḍv-ādi* (Gaṇar. 439).

Godhāra, m. = *gaudh*°, Kād. v, 1042 (v. l.)

2. **Godhi**, m. id., L.

Godhikā, f. a kind of lizard or alligator (Lacerta Godica), Kād. v, 1042 (v. l. *golikā*). **Godhikât-maja**, m. a kind of lizard, L.

Godhinī, f. a variety of Solanum, L.

Godheraka, m. = *gaudh*°, Suśr. v, 8, 36.

गोधूम *go-dhūma*, &c. See *gó*, p. 365, col. 1.

गोधेर *godhera*, m. (= *guh*°) a guardian, L.

गोधेरक *godheraka*. See *godhā́*.

गोनन्द *go-nanda*, *-narda*, &c. See *gó*, p. 365.

गोप *go-pá*, m. (= -*pá* s. v. *gó*) a cowherd, herdsman, milkman (considered as a man of mixed caste, Parāś.), Mn. viii; MBh. (ifc. f. *ā*, i, 3213); Hariv. &c.; a protector, guardian, RV. x, 61, 10; TāṇḍyaBr.; KātyŚr.; MBh.; the superintendent of several villages, head of a district, L.; a king, L.; 'chief herdsman,' Kṛishṇa, MBh. ii, 1438; a particular class of plants, BhP. xii, 8, 21; = -*rasa*, L.; N. of a Gandharva (cf. *go-pati*), R. ii, 91, 44; of a Buddh. Arhat, W.; (*ā*), f., N. of one of the wives of Śākya-muni, Lalit. xii &c.; cf. *gaupeya*; Ichnocarpus frutescens, L.; (*ī*), f. id., L.; (Vop. iv, 22; cf. Pāṇ. iv, 1, 48) a cowherd's wife, Hit. ii, 7, $\frac{1}{2}$; a cowherdess, milkmaid (esp. the cowherdesses of Vṛindāvana, companions of Kṛishṇa's juvenile sports, considered sometimes as holy or celestial personages; cf. RTL. pp. 113 & 136), MBh. ii, 2291; Hariv. 4098; BhP.; Gīt.; a protectress, female guardian, Ragh. iv, 20 (ifc.); = *prakṛiti*, nature, Kramadīp.; Abrus precatorius, L.; (cf. *ahi-*, *indra-*, *kula-*, *tridaśā-*, *vāta-*, *surêndra-*.) **-kanyakā**, f. a cowherdess, Hariv. 4095. **-kanyā**, f. id., 4081 & 4085; the *gopā* plant, Bhpr. v. **-karkaṭikā**, f. = *gopāla-karkaṭī*, L. **-ghaṇṭa**, m. Flacourtia sapida, Gal. **-ghaṇḍā**, f. id., Suśr. v, 7, 1. **-ghoṇṭā**, f. id., i, iv. **-jalā**, f. = *go-capalā*, VāyuP. ii, 37, 122. **-jīvin**, m., N. of a mixed caste. **-tā**, f. a herdsman's office, Hariv. 3302. **-tva**, n. id., 3160 ff. **-datta**, m., N. of a Buddh. author. **-danta**, m., N. of an author, Uṇ. iv, 16, Sch. **-dala**, m. the betel-nut tree, L. **-nagara**, n., N. of a town. **-bhaṭṭa**, v. l. for *go-bh*°. **-bhadra**, n. the fibrous esculent root of a water-lily, L.; (*ā*), f. = -*bhadrikā*, L. **-bhadrikā**, f. Gmelina arborea, L. **-rasa**, m. myrrh, L. **-rāshṭra**, m. pl., N. of a people, MBh. vi, 351. **-vadhū**, f. a cowherd's wife, BhP. i, 9, 40; the *gopā* plant, Bhpr. **-vadhūṭī**, f. the youthful wife of a cowherd, Bhāshāp. 1. **-vallī**, f. the *gopā* plant, Suśr. vi, 51, 24; Sanseviera Roxburghiana, L. **-vesha**, mfn. dressed as a herdsman, Megh. **Gopâgrahāra**, m. pl., N. of several Agrahāras, Rājat. i, 343. **Gopâcala**, m. 'cowherd-mountain,' = *gopāla-giri*, Uttamac.[2] 602. **Gopâditya**, m., N. of a king of Kaśmīr, Rājat. i, 341; N. of a poet. **Gopâdri**, m. = °*pâcala*, 343. **Gopâdhyaksha**, m. an overseer of herdsmen, chief herdsman, MBh. iv, 1155. **Gopânasī**, f. the wood or bamboo frame-work of a thatch, Lalit. xiv, 34; xvii; Kāraṇḍ.; Car. i, 30, 3; Śiś. iii, 49. **Gopā-putra**, see *go-pā*, s. v. *gó*. **Gopâshṭamī**, f. the 8th day in the light half of month Kārttika (on which Kṛishṇa who had formerly been a keeper of calves became a cowherd; cows are esp. to be worshipped on this day), KūrmaP. **Gopêndra**, m. 'chief herdsman,' Kṛishṇa, MBh. vi, 799; N. of the author of Kāvyâlaṃkāra-dhenu. **Gopêśa**, m. (= °*pêndra*) Kṛishṇa, W.; N. of Nanda (Kṛishṇa's foster-father), Vop. v, 7; of Śākya-muni, L. **Gopêśvara**, m. a form of Śiva; N. of a man; -*tīrtha*, n., N. of a Tīrtha, RevāKh. ccxliv, ccl.

Gopaka, m. (g. *yājakâdi*, Gaṇar. 99, Sch.) a cowherd, Dhūrtan.; (fr. *gopaya*) guardian (ifc.), see *cīvara-*; the superintendent of a district, L.; myrrh, L.; (*ikā*), f. (g. *śivâdi*) a cowherd's wife, cowherdess, BhP. x, 9, 14 f.; a protectress, W.

Gopat, mfn. = °*payat*, Gīt. vi, 12.

Gópana, n. (√*gup*) guarding, protection, preservation, AV. xii, 4, 10; MBh. vi, xiii; hiding, concealment, Sāh.; Sarvad.; Kull. on Mn. ix, 72; reviling, abuse, W.; flurry, hurry, alarm, W.; light, lustre, W.; the leaf of Laurus Cassia, L.; (*ā́*), f. protection, ŚBr. iii, 6, 2, 12 & 15; MBh. xii, 11907.

Gopanīya, mfn. to be preserved or protected, Nāḍīpr.; to be prevented, MBh. xii, 5399; to be concealed or hidden (with abl.), Sāh. vi, $\frac{149}{151}$; secret, mysterious, W. **-tā**, f. concealableness, W. **-tva**, n. id., W.

Gopaya, caus. fr. √*gup* or Nom. P. Ā. (fr. *go-pá*; cf. √*gup*) °*yati*, °*yate* (aor. Ved. 2. du. *ajūgupatam*, Pāṇ. iii, 1, 50, Kāś.), to guard, protect, preserve, ŚāṅkhŚr.; MBh. (Pass. *gopyate*, ii, iii); BhP.; to keep, VarBṛS. lxxxix, 13; to hide, conceal, keep secret, Pañcat.; RV. i, 11, 5, Sāy.; Mn. x, 59, Kull.; 'to speak' or 'to shine,' Dhātup. xxxiii, 98; (cf. *abhi-*, *pra-*, *saṃ-*.)

Gopayátya, mfn. (Nir. v, 1) to be protected, RV. viii, 25, 13.

Gopayitavya, mfn. v. l. for °*pāy*°.

1. **Gopāya**, Nom. P. (fr. *go-pā́*; cf. √*gup*) °*yáti* (cf. Pāṇ. iii, 1, 28 & 31; aor. *agopāyīt*, Vop. viii, 65), to represent a cowherd, act like a herdsman, BhP. x, 30, 17; to guard, protect, preserve, RV. vi, 74, 4 & x, 154, 4; VS.; AV. &c.; to hide, conceal, Amar. (Pass. *gopāyyate*); Rājat. v, 222; Dhūrtas. i, 30: Caus. *gopāyayati*, to preserve, protect, MBh. iii, 10835; (cf. *abhi-*, *pari-*.)

2. **Gopāya**, mfn. ifc. preserving, Āp. i, 4, 24.

Gopāyaka, mfn. id., W.

Gopāyana, mfn. id., MBh. vi, 3131; m. N. of a teacher, VāmP. vi (v. l. *go-māyu*), cf. Smṛitik. ii, 4, 3; n. protecting, preserving, protection, ŚāṅkhGṛ. iii, 10, 2; Hariv. 2142; R. vii, 4, 9.

Gopāyita, mfn. preserved, protected, L.

Gopāyitavya, mfn. to be hidden, Kād. vi, 400.

Gopāyitṛi, m. a protector, MBh. xii, 2726.

Gopika, m. the Mokshaka tree, Gal.

Gopikā, f. of °*paka*, q. v. **-saras**, n., N. of a lake, SkandaP.

Gopita, mfn. preserved, guarded, MBh. i, iii; guarded (as the senses), kept in subjection, Divyâv.; concealed, kept secret, Kathās. xiv; Rājat. v, 124.

Gopinī, f. the *gopā* plant, L.

Gopila, mfn. (g. *sakhy-ādi*, v. l.) one who preserves or protects, L.

Gópishṭha, mfn. superl. of *goptṛi*, q. v.

Gopī, f. of °*pa*, q. v. **-candana**, n. a species of white clay (said to be brought from Dvārakā and used by Vishṇu's worshippers for marking the face, RTL. pp. 67 & 400; 'a kind of sandal-wood,' W.); °*nôpanishad*, f., N. of an Up. **-nātha**, m. 'lord of the cowherdesses,' Kṛishṇa; N. of several men; -*sapta-śatī*, f., N. of a work (perhaps = *govardhana-s*°). **-premâmṛita**, n. 'nectar of (Kṛishṇa's) love for the cowherdesses,' N. of a work. **-ramaṇa**, m. 'lover of cowherdesses,' N. of a man, Kshitîś. v, 3 ff. **-rasa-vivaraṇa**, n., N. of a work.

Goptavya, mfn. to be preserved, MBh. xii, 3449.

Goptṛi, mf(*trī́*, ŚBr.; Gobh.; MBh. xiii)n. (g. *yājakâdi*, Gaṇar. 99) one who preserves or protects or defends or cherishes, AV.; TS. vi; TBr.; ŚBr. (superl. *gópishṭha*, ii); ĀśvGṛ. &c. (n. °*ptṛi*, BhP. vii, 10, 28); one who conceals anything (in comp.), Yājñ. i, 310. **-mat**, mfn. having a protector, Kaush-Up. ii, 1.

Gopya, mfn. (Pāṇ. iii, 1, 114, Kāś.) to be preserved or protected, MBh. xii, 1481; to be kept or taken care of (a pledge, *ādhi*), Yājñ. ii, 59; to be kept secret or hidden, Daś. viii, 80 (superl.); Pañcat.; Kathās.; Hit.; m. a servant, slave, L.; the son of a female slave, L.

Gopyaka, m. a slave, servant, L.

गोपालव *gopālava*, m. pl., N. of a family of Brāhmans, Pāṇ. v, 3, 114, Kāś.

गोफिल *gophila*, g. *sakhy-ādi* (*gobh*°, Bhoj.; *gop*° & *goh*°, vv. ll.)

Gobhila, m., N. of the author of Pushpas. and of the Gṛihya-sūtra of the SV. (said to have also composed a Śrauta-sūtra and a Naigeya-sūtra); pl. N. of a family, Pravar. v, 4 (v. l. *go-bida*).

Gobhilīya, mfn. relating to or proceeding from Gobhila.

गोरट *goraṭa*, m. a kind of Acacia, L.

गोरण *goraṇa* = *gur*°, L., Sch.

गोरिका *gorikā*, f. = *go-rāṭikā*, L.

गोर्द *gorda*, n. = *goda*, W.

Gordha, n. id., L.

गोर्वर *gor-vara*. See *gó*, p. 367, col. 3.

गोल *gola*, m. (= *guḍa*) 'a ball,' see -*krīḍā*; globe (as the celestial globe or as the globe of the sun or of the earth), Sūryas.; Sūryapr.; BhP. &c.; a hemisphere (of the earth), Sūryas.; = -*yantra*, Gol. xi, 2; Vangueria spinosa, L.; myrrh, L.; a widow's bastard, Yājñ. i, 222; VarP.; Śūdradh.; the conjunction of all the planets in one sign, Laghuj. x, 11; N. of a country, Romakas. (cf. *golla*); of a son of Ākrīḍa, Hariv. (*kola*, ed. Calc.); n. & (*ā*), f. a circle, sphere (*maṇḍala*), L.; a large globular water-jar, L.; (*ā*), f. a ball to play with, L.; red arsenic, L.; ink, L.; a woman's female friend, L.; N. of Durgā, L.; of a river (= *go-dā* or *go-dāvarī*), L.; (cf. *gala-golin*.) **-krīḍā**, f. playing with balls, Hariv. 15542 ff. **-gola**, m. a globe consisting of several globes, Sūryapr. **-grāma**, m., N. of a village (situated on the Godâvarī). **-puñja**, m. a number of globes, Sūryapr. **-yantra**, n. a kind of astronomical instrument, Gol. xi, 3. **Golâṅka**, m., N. of a man, g. *aśvâdi* (°*ṅkya*, Kāś.) **Golâdhyāya**, m. N. of ch. i of Bhāskara's Siddhânta-śiromaṇi treating of the terrestrial and celestial globes. **Golâvalī**, f. a series of globes, Sūryapr. **Golâsana**, n. 'ball-thrower,' a kind of gun, Gal.

Golaka, m. a ball or globe, BhP. v, 16, 4; VS. xxxi, 22, Sch. &c.; a ball for playing with, Hariv. 15549; glans penis, Sāy. on AitBr. i, 20; a kind of pease (= *palāśa*), Gobh. iv, 4, 26; ŚāṅkhGṛ. iv, 19, 4; myrrh, L.; a globular water-jar, L.; a kind of dish, Gal.; a widow's bastard, Mn. iii, 156 & 174; MBh. iii, 13366; the conjunction of all the planets in one sign, VarBṛ. xii, 3 & 19; N. of a pupil of Deva-mitra, VāyuP. i, 60, 64; n. a ball or globe, Nyāyam., Sch.; = *go-loka*, Tantr.; (*ikā*), f. a small ball or globule, SāmavBr. iii, 4, 3; (used for playing) HPariś.; the jujube, Gal.; for *godhikā*, q. v.

Golī-gula-parivartana, for *go-lāṅg*°, Lalit. iii, 88 f.

गोलत्तिका *go-láttikā*, &c. See *gó*, p. 366, col. 3.

Go-lava, °*vaṇa*, **-lāṅgula**, &c. See ib.

गोलाममामुद *golāma-māmuda*, غلام محمود.

गोलास *golāsa*, m. a fungus, L.

गोलिह *go-liha*, *-līḍha*. See *gó*, p. 366.

गोलुन्द *golunda*, N. of a man, g. *gargâdi*.

गोलोक *go-loka*, *-loman*, &c. See *gó*, p. 366.

गोल्ल *golla*, N. of a country, H aris. viii, 194; (cf. *gola*.)

गोल्हाट *golhāṭa*, a kind of mystical diagram, Rasik. xiv, 34.

गोवत्स *go-vatsa*, &c. See *gó*, p. 366, col. 3.

गोवय *govaya*, Nom. P. (for *gopaya*) °*yati*, to keep off from (abl.), TāṇḍyaBr. xvi, 2, 3 f.

गोवर *go-vara*, °*rdhana*, &c. See *gó*, p. 366.

Go-víd, go-vinda, &c. See ib.

Go-śīrsha, &c., **go-shaka**, &c. See ib.
Go-shṭhá, &c., **gósh-pada**, &c. See ib.

गोस 2. *gosa*, m. myrrh, L. **–gṛiha**, n. an inner apartment, W. **–śasa**, m. myrrh, L., Sch.

गोसखि *gó-sakhi*, &c. See *gó*, p. 367, col. 2.

गोह *góha*, m. (√*guh*) a hiding-place, lair, RV. iv, 21, 6–8; 'a secret place for hiding refuse or filth,' see *ūbadhya-*.

Gohana, mfn., see *avadya-*.
Gohi, g. *suvāstv-ādi*, v. l.
Gohira, n. 'hidden part (?),' the heel, L.
Gohila, m., g. *sakhy-ādi* (Kāś.)
Gohilla, m., N. of a man, Jyotirv. x, 112, Sch.
Gohya, mfn. (Pāṇ. iii, 1, 109; g. *suvāstv-ādi*, Kāś.) 'to be concealed,' see *á-*; m., N. of an Agni in the water, MantraBr. i, 7, 1.

गोहत्या *go-hatyā*, *-hán*, &c. See *gó*, p. 367.

गोहालिया *gohāliyā*, f., N. of a plant, GarP.

गोहिर *gohira*, &c. See *góha*.

गौकक्ष *gaukaksha*, m. pl. of °*kshya*, g. *kaṇvâdi*; Pāṇ. iv, 3, 130, Kāś.; (*ī*), f. of °*kshya*, only in comp.

Gaukakshī, f., see °*ksha*. **–pati**, m. the husband of Gaukakshī, Gaṇar. 37, Sch. **–putra**, m. the son of Gaukakshī, Pāṇ. iv, 1, 74, Pat.

Gaukakshya, m. a patr. fr. *go-kaksha*, g. *gargâdi*; (*ā*), f., g. *krauḍy-ādi*.

Gaukakshyā, f. of °*kshya*, q. v. **–pati**, n. = °*kshī-p°*, Gaṇar. 37, Sch. **–putra**, m. = °*kshī-p°*, Pāṇ. iv, 1, 74, Pat.

Gaukakshyāyaṇa, m. patr. fr. °*kshya*, f. *ī*, a female descendant of °*kshya*, 75, Pat.

Gaukakshyāyaṇi, m. = °*ṇa*, g. *tikâdi*.

गौग्गुलव *gauggulava*, mfn. (fr. *gúggulu*), made from bdellium (an unguent), TāṇḍyaBr. xxiv, 13, 4 (v. l. *gaulg°*); m. patr., f. *ī*, g. *śārṅgaravâdi*.

गौङ्गव *gauṅgava*, n. (fr. *guṅgú*), N. of several Sāmans, xiv, 3, 18 f.

गौञ्जिक *gauñjika*, m. (fr. *guñjā*), a jeweller, L.

गौड *gauḍa*, mf(*ī*)n. (fr. *guḍa*), prepared from sugar or molasses, MBh. viii, 2050; Suśr.; Hcat.; relating or belonging to the Gauḍas, Vātsyāy.; Kāvyâd. i, 35; Sarvad. xv; (esp. f. *ī* with *rīti*, the Gauḍian style of poetry, viz. the bold and spirited style, Kāvyâd. i, 40; Vām.; Pratāpar. &c.); m. (scil. *deśa*) or n. (scil. *rāshṭra*) 'sugar country,' N. of a country (district of Gaur, central part of Bengal, extending from Vaṅga to the borders of Orissa; the ruins of its capital called by the same N. are still extensive), Rājat.; Prab. ii, 7; Hit.; m. pl. the inhabitants of that country, Vātsyāy.; Rājat.; Śūdradh.; m. sg. a prince of the Gauḍas, Kathās. cxxii, 3; N. of a lexicographer; n. sweetmeats, R. i, 53, 4; vii, 92, 12; (*ī*), f. with *rīti*, see before; rum or spirit distilled from molasses (RTL. p. 193), Mn. xi, 95; MBh. viii, 2034; Gṛihyās. ii, 16; (in music) N. of a Rāgiṇī. **–grantha**, m., N. of a work. **–tithi-tattva**, n., N. of a work. **–deśa**, m. the Gauḍa country, SkandaP. **–°deśīya**, mfn. coming from the Gauḍa country, Pañcad. **–nibandha**, m., N. of a work. **–pāda**, m., N. of a commentator on several Upanishads and on Sāṃkhyak. **–pura**, n., N. of a town, Pāṇ. vi, 2, 100. **–bhṛitya-pura**, n., N. of a town, ib., Siddh.; (cf. *andhrá-bhṛitya*.) **–mālava**, m. (in music) N. of a Rāga. **–vyavahāra-nirṇaya**, m., N. of a work. **–śuddhi-tattva**, n., N. of a work. **–sāraṅgī**, f. (in music) N. of a Rāgiṇī. **Gauḍâbhinanda** or °**dana**, m. N. of a poet, ŚārṅgP. **Gauḍêśvarâcārya**, m. N. of a teacher. **Gauḍôrvī-kula-praśasti**, f. N. of a work.

Gauḍaka, m. pl., N. of a people living to the east of Madhya-deśa, VarBṛS. xiv, 7. **–mṛiga**, m. a wild horse, L.; (cf. *gaura-khara*.)

Gauḍika, mfn. prepared with sugar or molasses, Suśr. i, 46, 9, 3; fit for the preparation of sugar, Pāṇ. iv, 4, 103; n. rum (prepared with sugar), Suśr. vi, 58, 28.

Gauḍīya, mfn. relating to Gauḍa or Bengāl (as *mārga* [Kāvyâd. i, 40] or *rīti* [Vām.; Pratāpar. &c.], 'the Gauḍian style').

गौण *gauṇa*, mf(*ī*)n. (fr. *guṇá*), relating to a quality, MBh. xii, 13138 f.; having qualities, attributive, W.; subordinate, secondary, unessential, MBh. xii, xiii; Pat.; KapS. &c. (with *karman*, [in Gr.] the less immediate object of an action, Vop. xxiv, 13); metaphorical, figurative, W.; secondary (applied to the month reckoned from full moon to full moon), W.; relating to multiplication or enumeration, W. **–tva**, n. the state of being subordinate or secondary, Vop.; KātyŚr., Sch. **–paksha**, m. the minor or weaker side of an argument, W. **–sādhy-avasānā**, f. (scil. *lakshaṇā*) a kind of ellipse, Sarvad. xv, 289. **–sāropā**, f. (scil. *lakshaṇā*) a kind of ellipse, ib.

1. **Gauṇika**, mf(*ī*)n. relating to the three qualities (of *sattva*, *rajas* & *tamas*), Mn. xii, 41; = *guṇe sādhu*, g. *kathâdi*; = *guṇam adhīte veda vā*, gaṇas *ukthâdi* & *vasantâdi*; relating to or connected with qualities, W.; subordinate, W.

Gauṇya, m. merit, Hariv. 5907; n. subordination, secondariness, Vop.; the being a merit, Hariv. 14240.

गौणिक 2. *gauṇika*, mf(*ī*)n. (fr. *goṇī*), resembling a sack, g. *aṅguly-ādi*.

गौण्डकिरी *gauṇḍa-kirī*, f. (in music) N. of a Rāgiṇī (cf. *goṇḍ°*).

गौतम *gautamá*, mf(*ī*)n. relating to Gotama (with *pada-stobha*, m. pl., N. of a Sāman); m. patr. fr. Gotama (N. of Kuśri, Uddālaka, Aruṇa, ŚBr.; of Śaradvat, Hariv.; Mṛicch. v, 30; VP.; of Śatānanda, L.; of Śākya-muni; of Nodhas & Vāma-deva, RAnukr.; of a teacher of ritual, Lāṭy.; ĀśvŚr.; ĀśvGṛ.; of a grammarian, TPrāt.; Lāṭy. [with the epithet *sthavira*]; of a legislator, Yājñ. i, 5; the father of Ekata, Dvita, and Trita, MBh. ix, 2073); (= *got°*) N. of the first pupil of the last Jina (one of the three Kevalins); N. of a Nāga (also °*maka*), Divyâv. ii; m. pl. Gautama's family, Hariv. 1788; Pravar.; a kind of poison, L.; n., N. of several Sāmans, ĀrshBr.; Lāṭy. iv, 6, 16; fat (cf. *bhāradvāja*, 'bone'), L.; (*gaútamī*), f. (gaṇas *gaurâdi* & *śārṅgaravâdi*) a female descendant of Gotama (N. of Kṛipī, Hariv.; BhP.; of Mahā-prajāpatī, Lalit. vii, xv), MBh. xiii, 17 ff.; Śak.; N. of Durgā, Hariv. 10236; of a Rākshasī, L.; of a river (= *go-dāvarī* or *go-matī*), MBh. xiii, 7647; R. vi, 2, 27; the bile-stone of cattle (*go-rocanā*), L.; = *rājanī*, L. **–nyagrodha**, m. 'Gautama's Nyagrodha,' N. of a fig-tree near Vaiśālī, Divyâv. xvii, 6 & 12. **–pṛicchā**, f. = *got°*. **–vana**, n. 'Gautama's grove,' N. of a locality, TBr. iii, 8, 1, 2, Sāy. **–sa**, mfn. with *arka*, N. of two Sāmans. **–sambhavā**, f. the Gautamī river, L. **–saras**, n. 'Gautama's pond,' N. of a lake, SkandaP. **–svāmin**, m. = *got°*, HPariś. **Gautamâraṇya**, n., N. of a forest, Hit. iv. **Gautamârdhika**, mfn. belonging half to the Gautama family, Pāṇ. iv, 3, 4, Vārtt. 1, Pat. & Kāś. **Gautamâśrama**, m. N. of a hermitage, GaṇP. ii, 95. **Gautamêśa**, m. N. of a Liṅga. **Gautamêśvara-tīrtha**, n., N. of a Tīrtha, RevāKh. ciic, cclvi.

Gautamaka, m. N. of a Nāga king, Divyâv. ii.

Gautami, m. patr. fr. °*má*, ŚāṅkhGṛ. iv, 10, 3; Parāś. Introd. 4.

Gautami-nandana, m. (metrically for °*mī-n°*) metron. of Aśvatthāman, MBh. vii, 6847.

Gaútamī, f. of °*má*, q. v. **–tantra**, n., N. of a Tantra. **–pútra** (*gaút°*), m. 'son of Gautamī,' N. of a teacher, ŚBr. xiv, 9, 4, 31. **–suta**, m. = °*mīnandana*, MBh. vii, 6857.

Gautamīya, mfn. belonging to or coming from Gautama, Lāṭy. &c. (f. °*yā* with *mitâksharā*, N. of Hara-datta's Comm. on Gaut.)

गौतमस *gautamasa* = °*ma-sa* (q. v.) or fr. *go-tamas*?

गौदन्तेय *gaudanteya*, m. patr. fr. *go-danta*, g. *śubhrâdi* (not in Kāś., but in Gaṇar. 223).

गौदपरिणद्धि *gaudapariṇaddhi*, m. patr. fr. *guda-pariṇaddha*, Gaṇar. 33, Sch. (*svāgudap°*, Kāś.)

Gaudāyana, m. patr. fr. *guda*, Pravar. i, 4 (v. l. *god°*); also *godāyani*, pl. iv, 8.

Gaudeya, m. metron. fr. *gudā*, g. *śubhrâdi* (Kāś.)

गौदानिक *gaudānika*, mfn. (g. *mahānāmny-ādi*) relating to the Godāna ceremony, ĀśvGṛ. iii, 8, 6; (*god°*, Gobh.)

गौधार *gaudhāra*, m. (metron. fr. *godhā*, Pāṇ. iv, 1, 130) = *godh°*, an Iguana, L.

Gaudhâsanika, v. l. for *gauvāsan°*.

Gaudheya, m. (g. *śubhrâdi*) = °*dhāra*, L.; pl. N. of a school of the black Yajur-veda (v. l. *baudh°*).

Gaudhera, m. (Pāṇ. iv, 1, 129) = °*dhāra*, L.

Gaúdheraka, m. a kind of small venomous animal, Suśr. v, 8, 26; cf. *godh°*.

Gaudherakāyaṇi, m. patr. fr. °*ra*, g. *vākinâdi*.

गौधिलि *gaudhili*, pl. patr., Pravar. vi, 1.

गौधूम *gaudhūmá*, mf(*ī*, g. *bilvâdi*)n. made of wheat, MaitrS. i; Hcat. i, 7 (f. *ā*); made of wheat straw, ŚBr. v, 2, 1, 6; KātyŚr. xiv, 1, 22 & 5, 7.

Gaudhūmra, N. of the author of part of ŚatarUp.

Gaudhenuka, n. (fr. *go-dhenu*), a herd of milch-cows, L.

गौधेय *gaudheya*, &c. See °*dhāra*.

गौनर्द *gaunarda*, mfn. fr. *go-n°*, Pāṇ. i, 1, 75, Siddh.

गौप *gaupa*, m. patr. fr. *go-pá*, TāṇḍyaBr. xiii, 12, 5, Sch. (for *go-pa*?).

Gaupatyá, n. (fr. *gó-pati*), the possession of cattle, VS. iii, xi; TS. i, iii; Gobh. iv, 5, 18.

Gaupanya, m. pl. patr., Pravar. iii, 1 (*gopana*, MatsyaP. cvci, 3).

Gaupavana, m. (g. *bidâdi*) patr. fr. *go-p°*, BṛĀrUp.; Pravar. iii, 1 & 5; (pl.) Pāṇ. ii, 4, 67; n., N. of a Sāman.

Gaupāyana, m. pl. the descendants of *go-pá* (or *gaupa*, TāṇḍyaBr., Sch.), TāṇḍyaBr. xiii; Pravar. vi, 1 (*gop°*); (authors of RV. x, 57–60) RAnukr.

Gaupālapaśupālikā, f. the state or office of Gopālas (cowherds) and Paśupālas (herdsmen), Pāṇ. v, 1, 133, Kāś.

Gaúpālāyana, m. patr. fr. *go-pālá*, MaitrS. iii, 10, 4; AitBr. iii, 48, 9.

Gaupāli, m. id., Pāṇ. ii, 4, 9, Kāś. (mentioned as having had a quarrel with the Sālaṅkāyanas); cf. *gop°*.

Gaupālika, m. (fr. *go-pālikā*) = °*pika*, g. *śivâdi* (Gaṇar. 217).

Gaupāleya, m. id., TāṇḍyaBr. xii, 13, 11.

Gaupika, m. (fr. *gopikā*), the son of a herdsman's wife, g. *śivâdi* (not in Kāś.)

Gaupuccha, mf(*ī*)n. (fr. *go-p°*), resembling a cow's tail, g. *śarkarâdi*.

Gaupucchika, mfn. = *go-pucchena tarat*, Pāṇ. iv, 4, 6; v, 1, 19.

Gaupeya. See *gaupteya*.

Gaubhṛita, mfn. fr. *go-bhṛit*, g. *saṃkalâdi*.

Gaumaṭhika. See °*mathika*.

Gaumata, mfn. coming from the Gomatī village, g. *palady-ādi*; being in the Gomatī river (as fishes), Pāṇ. i, 1, 75, Kāś.; (*ī*), f. for *gautamī* (N. of a river).

Gaumatāyana, mfn. fr. *go-mat*, g. *arīhaṇâdi*.

Gaumatāyanaka, mfn. fr. °*na*, ib.

Gaumathika, mfn. fr. *go-matha* (= *parvata* or *hrada* or *go-medha*, Gaṇar., Sch.), g. 2. *kumudâdi* (°*maṭhika*, Hemac. & Gaṇar.)

Gaumaya, mfn. (fr. *go-m°*) coming from cow-dung (as ashes), Pāṇ. iv, 3, 155, Vārtt. 5, Pat.

Gaumāyana, m. (g. *aśvâdi*), patr. fr. *go-min*, Pravar. v, 1 (v. l. °*mayāna*; °*majāta*, Kāty.)

गौप्तेय *gaupteya*, m. metron. fr. *guptā*, Pāṇ. iv, 1, 114, Vārtt. 2, Pat.; 121, Sch. (*gaupeya*, Kāś.)

गौफिल *gauphila*. See °*laka*.

Gauphilaka, m. patr., g. *śivâdi* (Gaṇar.; °*la* & *gauhila*, Hemac.; °*lika*, Kāś., v. l. *gaubhilika*).

Gauphileya, mfn. fr. *gophila*, g. *sakhy-ādi* (*gaubhil°*, Bhoj.)

Gaubhila, n. Gobhila's Gṛihya-sūtra, Gṛihyās. ii, 94 (v. l. *gobh°*).

Gaubhileya. See *gauphil°*.

गौभृत *gaubhṛita*, &c. See before.

गौर *gaurá*, mf(*ī*)n. (in comp. or ifc., g. *kaḍārâdi*) white, yellowish, reddish, pale red, RV. x, 100, 2; TS. v &c.; shining, brilliant, clean, beautiful, Caurap.; m. white, yellowish (the colour), W.; a kind of buffalo (Bos Gaurus, often classed with the Gavaya), RV.; VS. &c.; white mustard (the seed of which is used as a weight, = 3 Rāja-sarshapas), Yājñ. i, 362; Grislea tomentosa (*dhava*), L.; a species of rice, Gal.; the moon, L.; the planet Jupiter, L.; N. of the Nāga Śesha, Gal.; of Caitanya (cf. *-candra*); of a Yoga teacher (son of Śuka and Pivarī), Hariv. 981; pl. N. of a family (cf. °*râtreya*), Pravar. iv, 1; n. white mustard, L.; N. of a pot-herb, Gal.; saffron (cf. *kanaka-*), L.; the filament of a lotus, L.; gold, L.; orpiment, Gal.; (*ā*), f. = *rī*, L. (cf. *gaulā*); (*ī*), f. the female of the Bos Gaurus, RV. ('Vāc or voice of the middle region of the air,' i, 164, 41 according to Naigh. i, 11 & Nir. xi, 40); = *gaurikā*, Gṛihyās. ii, 18; Pañcat.; the earth, L.; red chalk, Kālac.; a yellow pigment or dye (*go-rocanā*, 'orpiment,' Gal.), L.; turmeric (*rajanī*), Suśr.; N. of several other plants (*priyaṃgu, mañjishṭhā, śveta-dūrvā, mallikā, tulasī, suvarṇa-kadalī, ākāśa-māṇsī*), L.; N. of several metres (one of 4 × 12 syllables; another of 4 × 13 syllables; another of 4 × 26 long syllables); (in music) a kind of measure; (ib.) N. of a Rāgiṇī; 'brilliant Goddess,' Śiva's wife Pārvatī, AV.Pariś.; NṛisUp. i, 4, 3, 10 &c.; N. of Varuṇa's wife, MBh. v, xiii; of a Vidyā-devī, iii, 231, 48; Hariv.; of Śākya-muni's mother, L.; of the wife of Vi-rajas and mother of Su-dhāman, VāyuP. i, 28, 11; of several other women; of several rivers (one originally the wife of Prasena-jit or Yuvanâśva, changed by his curse into the river Bāhu-dā, Hariv.; VP.), MBh. vi, 333; VP. ii, 4, 55; [cf. Lat. *gilvus*?] **–kṛishṇa**, m., N. of a prince, MatsyaP. **–khara**, m. a wild donkey, L.; (cf. *gauḍaka-mṛiga*.) **–gaṇôddeśa**, m., N. of a work. **–gotama**, m. = *gotama-gaura*, Gaṇar. 89, Sch. **–grīva**, m. pl. 'white-necked,' N. of a people, VarBṛS. xiv, 3. **–°grīvi**, m. patr. fr. °*va*, Pravar. iii, 1. **–°grīviya**, mfn. belonging to °*vi*, g. *raivatikâdi*. **–candra**, m., N. of Caitanya, AnSaṃh. **–jīraka**, m. white cumin, L. **–tittiri**, m. a kind of partridge, Suśr.; Bhpr. v, 10, 22 & 61. **–tva**, n. the being white, Naish. viii, 99, Sch. **–tvac**, m. 'white-barked,' Terminalia Catappa, L. **–pṛishṭha**, m. 'white-backed,' N. of a prince, MBh. ii, 332. **–mantra**, m., N. of a Mantra (?); (cf. °*rī-m*°.) **–mukha**, m. 'white-faced,' N. of a pupil of Śamīka, i, 1738 ff.; of the Purohita of king Ugra-sena, BhavP.; of a sage, VarP. xi ff.; (*ā*), f., N. of a woman, Pāṇ. iv, 1, 58, Kāś. **–mṛigá**, m. the Bos Gaurus, VS. xxiv, 32; AitBr.; BhP. viii; Sāy. **–lalāma** (°*rá-*), mfn. having a white spot on the forehead, TS. v. **–vallī**, f. (= *gaurī*) panic (*priyáṃgu*), Npr. **–vāhana**, m. 'having white vehicles or draught-cattle,' N. of a prince, MBh. ii, 1271. **–śāka**, m. a variety of the Bassia plant, L. **–śāli**, m. a species of rice, VarYogay. vii, 4. **–śiras**, m. 'white-headed,' N. of a Muni, MBh. ii, 292; xii, 2094. **–saktha**, mf(*ī*)n. having reddish legs, Pāṇ. v, 4, 113, Vārtt., Sch. **–sarshapa**, m. white mustard (Sinapis glauca; the seed used as a weight, Mn. viii, 133 f.), PārGṛ.; Āp.; Mn.; Yājñ.; Suśr. **–suvarṇa**, n. a kind of vegetable, L. **Gaurâṅga**, mf(*ī*)n. having a white or yellowish body; m., N. of Caitanya; (*ī*), f. cardamoms, L.; *-mallikā*, m., N. of a man. **Gaurâjājī**, f. = °*ra-jīraka*, L. **Gaurâtikā**, f. a kind of crow, L. **Gaurâtreya**, m. pl., N. of a family, Pravar. iii, 1. **Gaurâdi**, N. of two Gaṇas of Pāṇ. (iv, 1, 41 & vi, 2, 194). **Gaurârdraka**, m. a kind of poison, L. **Gaurâśva**, m. 'having white horses,' N. of a prince, MBh. ii, 329. **Gaurâsya**, m. 'white-faced,' a kind of black monkey with a white face, L. **Gaurâhika**, m. a kind of serpent, Suśr. v, 4, 35.

Gauraka, m. (= °*ra*) a kind of rice, Gal.; (*ikā*), f. = °*rī*, a girl 8 years old prior to menstruation, L.

Gauraki, m. patr., Pravar. iii, 4 (vv. ll. °*ragi*, °*raṅgi*, °*riki*).

Gauri, in comp. for °*rī*, q. v. **–mat**, m., N. of a man, g. *śārṅgaravâdi*; (*tī*), f., N. of a woman, ib. **–vīta**, mfn. (= *gaurīvita*) fr. °*ti*, AitBr. iii, 19; viii, 2. **–vīti** (*gaúri-*), m. (= *gaurī-viti*) N. of a Ṛishi (descendant of Śakti), RV. v, 29, 11; AitBr. iii, 19. **–śravas**, m. pl., N. of a family, Pravar. vi, 1 (v. l. °*ra-ś*°). **–shaktha**, mfn. 'white-legged,' N. of a Muni, g. *sushāmâdi*.

Gaurika, m. white mustard, Suśr. iv, 20, 18; metron. of Māndhātṛi, VāyuP. ii, 26, 66; (*ā*), see °*raka*.

Gaurijeya, n. (for *gair*°?) talc, L.

Gaurita, m. pl., N. of a family, Pravar. iii, 4.

Gauriman, m. the being white, Naish. viii, 99.

Gaurila, m. white mustard, L.; iron filings, L.

Gauriva, m. pl., N. of a family, Pravar. ii, 2, 1.

Gaurivāyana, m. patr. fr. °*va*, ii, 2, 1; v, 1.

Gaurī́, f. of °*rá*, q. v. **–kalpa**, m., N. of a period of the world or Kalpa. **–kānta**, m., N. of the author of a Comm. on the Tarka-bhāshā; *-sārva-bhauma*, m., N. of the author of a Comm. called Ānanda-laharītarī. **–gāyatrikā**, °*trī*, f., N. of a verse (in honour of Gaurī), Hcat. i, 5. **–guru**, m. 'father of Gaurī,' the Himâlaya, Śak. vi, 17; Ragh.; Kir.; Rājat. **–caturthī**, f. the 4th day in the bright half of month Māgha, Vratapr. **–carita**, n. 'life of Gaurī,' N. of a work. **–ja**, m. metron. of Kārttikeya, W.; n. = °*rijeya*, L. **–jātaka**, n., N. of a work. **–tīrtha**, n., N. of a Tīrtha, Kathās. lxxx, 5. **–nātha**, m. 'lord of Gaurī,' Śiva, Bhartṛ. iii, 87. **–paṭṭa**, m. Gaurī's plate (on which is placed the Liṅga of Śiva). **–pati**, m. = *-nātha*, Kathās.; N. of the father of the scholiast Vaṭêśvara. **–pāshāṇa**, m. white arsenic, Npr. **–putra**, m. = *-ja*, Kārttikeya, L. **–pushpa**, m. 'white-flowered,' panic (*priyáṃgu*), L.; Nerium odorum, L. **–pūjā**, f. 'adoration of Gaurī,' N. of a festival on the 4th day in the bright half of month Māgha; (cf. *-caturthī*.) **–bhartṛi**, m. = *-nātha*. **–mantra**, m. a prayer to Gaurī, W.; (cf. °*ra-m*°.) **–muṇḍa**, m., N. of a Vidyā-dhara prince, Kathās. cvii, cxii. **–lalita**, n. orpiment, L. **–vara**, m. 'lover of Gaurī,' Śiva; a favour of Gaurī, lix. **–vita**, mfn. = °*ri-vīta*, TāṇḍyaBr. xiii, 5, 16; xviii, 6, 18; Lāṭy.; KātyŚr.; n. N. of several Sāmans, ĀrshBr. **–viti** (*gaúrī-*), m. = °*ri-vīti*, ŚBr. xii; TāṇḍyaBr. xi f. **–vivāha**, m. the marriage of Gaurī, W. **–vrata**, n. 'vow of Gaurī,' a kind of rite in honour of Gaurī, PadmaP. i, 22; BhavP.; Hit. i, 9. $\frac{2}{8}$. **Gaurîśa**, m. = °*rī-nātha*, MBh. xiv, 210; Rājat. v, 158. **Gaury-aśman**, m. = °*rī-pāshāṇa*, Npr.

Gaurī-kṛita, mfn. made white or brilliant, Siṇhâs.

गौरक्ष्य *gaurakshya*, n. for *go-r*°, Bhag. xviii, 44, Sch.

Gauratha, m. patr. fr. *go-r*°, Pravar. vi, 2 (v. l. *gor*°).

गौरव *gaurava*, mfn. relating or belonging to a Guru or teacher, BhP. i, 7, 46; m. N. of a poisonous plant, Gal.; n. (g. *pṛithv-ādi*) weight, heaviness, MBh.; R. &c.; difficulty, Car. iii, 4; heaviness in argumentation, cumbrousness, needless multiplication of causes, Sarvad. ii, xi f.; KapS. i, 89, Sch.; length (in prosody), Śrut. &c.; importance, high value or estimation, R. &c.; gravity, respectability, venerableness, Āp.; Mn. ii, 145; MBh. &c.; respect shown to a person (e. g. *mātṛi-gauravāt*, 'out of respect for one's mother,' Pañcat.), R.; Śak. &c. **–jāta**, mfn. filled with respect, Lalit. xv. **–lāghava-vicāra**, m. N. of a work. **–vat**, mfn. important, W. **Gauravâsana**, n. a seat of honour, W. **Gauravêrita**, mfn. praised, celebrated, W.

Gauravita, mfn. highly esteemed, g. *tārakâdi*.

Gauravya, m. patr., Pravar. vi, 1.

Gaurutalpika, m. = *gurutalpa-ga*, g. *paradārâdi*.

गौर्जर *gaurjara*, n. 'coming from Gurjara,' pottern-ore, Npr.; = *gurj*°, Guzerat, Uttamac.[2] 601.

गौलक्षणिक *gaulakshaṇika*, m. (fr. *golakshaṇa*), one who knows the good marks of a cow, Pāṇ. iv, 2, 60, Pat.

गौलन्द *gaulanda*, &c. See °*lunda*.

गौला *gaulā*, f. for *gaurā* = °*rī*, Śiva's wife Pārvatī, L.

गौलाङ्कायन *gaulâṅkāyana*, m. patr. fr. *golâṅka*, g. *aśvâdi*.

गौलिक *gaulika*, m. Bignonia suaveolens (= *go-liha*, *-līḍha*), L.

गौलुन्द *gaulunda*, mf(*ī*)n. of °*ndya*, g. *kaṇvâdi* (v. l. °*landa*).

Gaulundya, m. patr. fr. *golunda*, g. *gargâdi* (v. l. °*landya*).

गौलोमन *gaulomana*, mfn. resembling cow's hair (*go-loman*), g. *śarkarâdi* (°*ma*, Bhoj.)

गौल्गुलव *gaulgulava*, mfn. = *gaugg*°, made of bdellium, Lāṭy. x, 4, 10 & 14, Sch.; (*ī*), f. patr. fr. *gúlgulu*, only in comp.

Gaulgulavī, f. of °*va*, q. v. **–putra**, m. metron. of Gobhila, VBr. iii, 10.

गौल्मिक *gaulmika*, mfn. (Pāṇ. iv, 2, 104, Vārtt. 13, Pat.) treating on the glandular swellings called *gulma*, Car. vi, 11; m. a single soldier of a troop, MBh. x, 359 & 419; the chief of a troop, Inscr. (10th century).

गौल्य *gaulya*, mfn. (fr. *gula*), having a sweet taste, L.; n. sweetness, L.; syrup, L.; spirituous liquor, W.

गौवासनिक *gauvāsanika*, mf(*ā* or *ī*)n. of *go-vāsana*, g. *kāśy-ādi* (*gaudhâsan*°, Kāś.)

Gauśakaṭika, mf(*ī*)n. possessing a carriage drawn by oxen (*go-śakaṭa*), Pāṇ. v, 2, 118, Kāś.

Gauśatika, mf(*ī*)n. possessing 100 oxen or cows (*go-śata*), ib.

Gauśṛiṅga, n. (fr. *go-ś*°) N. of a Sāman, Lāṭy. vi f.

Gaushûkta, n. (fr. *go-shûktin*) N. of a Sāman, TāṇḍyaBr. xix, 4, 9; Lāṭy. vii, 2, 1.

Gaushûkti, m. patr. fr. *go-shûktin*, TāṇḍyaBr.

Gaushṭha, mf(*ī*)n. coming from a village *goshṭhī* (or *gaushṭhī*, v. l.), g. *palady-ādi*.

Gaushṭhika, mfn. relating to an assembly (*goshṭhī*), Pañcat. i, 14, Sch.

Gaushṭhīna, mfn. (any place) where a cow-pen has been before, Pāṇ. v, 2, 18 (*goshṭh*°, Kāś.); n. the site of an old and abandoned cow-pen, Hcar. ii, 478 (v. l. *goshṭh*°).

Gausahasrika, mf(*ī*)n. possessing 1000 cows, Pāṇ. v, 2, 118, Kāś.

गौश्र *gauśra*, m. patr. fr. *guśri*, ŚāṅkhBr.

Gauśrāyaṇi, m. patr. fr. °*śra*, xxiii, 5.

Gauśla, m. = °*śra* (fr. *guśli*), AitBr. vi, 30, 8.

गौषूक्त *gaushûkta*, &c. See above.

गौहलव्य *gauhalavya*, m. patr. fr. *guhalu*, g. 2. *lohitâdi*.

Gauhalavyāyanī, f. of °*vya*, ib.

गौह्य *gauhya*, mf(*ī*)n. of *gohi* or °*hya*, g. *suvāstv-ādi*.

Gauhileya, for *gauphil*°, Kāś.

Gauhyaka, mfn. relating to the Guhyakas, BhP. x, 55, 23.

ग्ध 1. *gdha*, aor. Ā. √*ghas*. See *api-√ghas*.

2. Gdha, mfn. p. p. √*ghas*. See *a-gdhâd*.

Gdhi, f. See *sá-*.

ग्ना *gnā́*, f. (nom. sg.? *gnā́s*, RV. iv, 9, 4) 'wife' (= γυνή, √*jan*), a divine female, kind of goddess, RV.; ŚāṅkhŚr. viii; = *vāc* (speech, voice), Naigh. i, 11. **–vat** (*gnā́-*), mfn. accompanied by divine females, RV. i, 15, 3 & ii, 1, 5 (voc. & nom. [!?] *-vas*; *gnāvas* = *stuti-vācas*, 'words of praise,' Sāy.); KātyŚr. ix, 8, 13.

Gnās (gen. & nom. of *gnā́* in comp.) **–páti**, m. the husband of a divine wife, RV. ii, 38, 10. **–pátnī**, f. a divine wife, iv, 34, 7.

ग्मन् *gman*. See *prithu-gmán*.

Gmā́, f. 'the earth' (a form drawn fr. *gmás*, abl. gen. of 2. *kshám*, q. v.), Naigh. i, 1.

ग्र *gra*. See *tuvi-grá*.

ग्रथ् 1. *grath* or *granth*, cl. 9. P. *grathnā́ti* (fut. p. *granthishyat*, Kāṭh. xxv, 8; perf. 3. pl. *jagranthur* or *grethur*, Pāṇ. i, 2, 6, Siddh.; ind. p. *granthitvā* or *grath*°, 23, Kāś.), to fasten, tie or string together, arrange, connect in a regular series, TS. vi f.; Kāṭh. xxv, 8; Bhaṭṭ.; to string words together, compose (a literary work), Prab. vi, 5: cl. 1. P. Ā. *grathati*, °*te*, Dhātup. (v. l.); P. *granthati*, xxxiv, 31; Ā. *granthate* (aor. *agranthishṭa*), to be strung together or composed (a literary work), Bhāradv. on Pāṇ. iii, 1, 89: Caus. P. Ā. *granthayati*, °*te*, to string together, MBh. iv, 262; [cf. κλώθω; Lat. *glut-en*?]

Grathana, n. tying, binding, stringing together, Nyāyam., Sch.; thickening, becoming obstructed or clogged with knotty lumps, Suśr. ii, 11, 19; (in dram.) intimation of the issue of a plot, Daśar. i, 51; Sāh. vi, 110; Pratāpar.; (*ā*), f. tying, binding, ensnaring, Bālar. vi, $\frac{1}{2}\frac{1}{8}$.

Grathanīya, mfn. to be tied or strung or bound, Nyāyam. ix, 2, 8, Sch.

Grathitá, mfn. strung, tied, bound, connected, tied together or in order, wound, arranged, classed, RV. ix, 97, 18; ŚBr. xi; MBh. &c.; set with, strewn with, MBh. &c.; artificially composed or put together (the plot of a play), Śak. i, $\frac{1}{2}$; Mālav. i, $\frac{1}{2}$; Vikr.; closely connected with each other, difficult to be distinguished from each other, MBh. i, v, xii; BhP. iv f.; having knots, knotty, Suśr. i f., iv; coagulated, thickened, hardened, vi; hurt, injured, L.; seized, overcome, L.; n. the being strung, Sch.; a tumor with hard lumps or knots, Suśr. ii, 14, 1 & 4; iv, 21, 3.

Grathitavya, mfn. = °*thanīya*, Bādar. iv, Sch.

Grathin. See √2. *grath*.

Grathila, mfn. possessed by an evil spirit, Siṅhâs. i, $\frac{9}{10}$; (cf. *grahila.*)

Grathna, m. a bunch, tuft, Gobh. ii, 7, 4; (*grapsa*, PārGṛ. i, 15, 4; *glapsa*, ĀśvGṛ. i, 14, 4.)

Grathya, mfn. = °*thanīya*, Nyāyam. ix, 2, 8.

Grantha, m. tying, binding, stringing together, L.; = °*thi*, a knot, TS. vi, 2, 9, 4 (v. l.); honeycomb, Pāṇ. iv, 3, 116, Vārtt.; an artificial arrangement of words (esp. of 32 syllables, = *śloka*, Jain.), verse, composition, treatise, literary production, book in prose or verse, text (opposed to *artha* 'meaning,' VarBṛS.; Vākyap.; Sarvad.), Nir. i, 20; Pāṇ.; MBh.; Up. &c.; a section (of Kāṭh.); the book or sacred scriptures of the Sikhs containing short moral poems by Nānak Shāh and others (cf. RTL. pp. 158–177); wealth, property, Jain. Sch.; (cf. *uttara-, nir-, shaḍ-.*) **— karaṇa,** n. composition of books or treatises, W. **— kartṛi,** m. a book-maker, author, W. **— kāra,** m. id., MBh. xiii, 690; Vedāntas. 1, Sch. **— kuṭī,** f. a library, L.; a study, W. **— kūṭī,** for *-kuṭī*. **— kṛit,** m. = *-kartṛi*, MBh. xiii, 694. **— parṇī,** f. 'knot-leaved,' a kind of Dūrvā grass, L. **— vistara,** m. a voluminous text, VarBṛS. i, 2; a multitude of Granthas (of 32 syllables each), BrahmabUp.; AmṛitabUp. **— vistāra,** m. diffuseness of style, voluminousness, W. **— saṃdhi,** m. a section of a work, chapter, L. **Granthâvṛitti,** f. a quotation (?), L.

Granthana, n. (ifc.) stringing, tying or connecting together (as a chapter or book), arranging, composing, Pāṇ. iii, 1, 26, Vārtt. 15, Pat. (v. l. *gaḍu* or *gaḍuka*); Vet. i, $\frac{9}{10}$; (*ā*), f. id., L.

1. **Granthi,** m. a knot, tie, knot of a cord, knot tied in the end of a garment for keeping money (Pañcat.), bunch or protuberance of any kind (esp. if produced by tying several things together), RV. ix, 97, 18 & x, 143, 2; AV.; TS. &c.; the joint of a reed or cane, Prab. vi, 8; joint of the body, Mṛicch. i, 1; Dhūrtas.; Sāh.; a complaint, (knotting, i. e.) swelling and hardening of the vessels (as in varicocele), R.; Suśr.; 'a knot tied closely and therefore difficult to be undone,' difficulty, doubt, ChUp.; KaṭhUp.; MuṇḍUp.; MBh. &c.; a bell, Kathās. lxv, 135 f.; N. of several plants and bulbous roots (*granthi-parṇa, hitâvalī, bhadra-mustā, piṇḍâlu*), L.; (cf. *udara-, kaṭu-, kāla-, kṛimi-, keśa-, go-, dāma-,* &c.) **— cchedaka,** m. (= *-bheda*) a purse-cutter, pickpocket, Śak. vi, $\frac{1}{2}$ (in Prākṛit) **— tva,** n. the becoming knotty, hardening, Suśr. **— dala,** m. 'knotty-leaved,' a kind of perfume (*coraka*), L.; (*ā*), f. a kind of bulbous root, L. **— dūrvā,** f. a kind of Dūrvā grass, L. **— pattra,** m. = *-dala* (*coraka*), L. **— parṇa,** m. id., L.; n. = *-parṇaka*, L.; (*ā*), f. the plant Jatukā, L.; (*ī*), f. = °*nthap°*, L.; *-maya*, mfn. made of the perfume °*thiparṇa*, Hcat. i, 7. **— parṇaka,** a kind of fragrant plant, Kād. iii, 1538. **— phala,** m. 'knotty-fruited,' Feronia elephantum, L.; Vanguiera spinosa, L.; the plant Sākuruṇḍa, L. **— bandhana,** n. tying a knot, W.; tying together the garments of the bride and bridegroom at the marriage ceremony, W. **— bandham,** ind. (with √*grath*) so as to form a knot (in tying), Bālar. **— barhin,** m. = *-parṇaka*, L. **— bheda,** m. = *-cchedaka*, Mn. ix, 277; Yājñ. ii, 274. **— bhedaka,** m. id., Jain. (in Prākṛit *ganṭhi-bheyaga*); Śak. vi (v. l. for *-cched°*). **— mat,** mfn. tied, bound, Kum. iii, 46; m. 'knotty,' Heliotropium indicum, Bhpr. v, 3, 225; *-phala*, m. 'bulb-fruited,' Artocarpus Lacucha, L. **— mūla,** n. 'bulb-rooted,' garlic, L.; (*ā*), f. = *-dūrvā*, L. **— mocaka,** m. = *-cchedaka*, W. **— vajraka,** m. a kind of steel, L. **— vīsarpa,** m. a kind of erysipelas, Car. vi, 11. **— vīsarpin,** mfn. having the °*rpa* disease, ib. **— hara,** m. removing difficulties, L.

Granthika, m. a relater, narrator (?, 'one who understands the joints or divisions of time, of the year, &c.' [fr. *granthi*, cf. *kāla-granthi*], an astrologer, fortune-teller, L.), MBh. xiv, 2039; Pat. on Pāṇ. i, 4, 29 & iii, 1, 26, Vārtt. 15; a kind of disease of the outer ear, Suśr.; a kind of plant or substance, Car. vi, 18; a N. assumed by Nakula (when master of the horse to king Virāṭa), MBh. iv, 63 & 319; = *saha-deva*, L.; m. n. Capparis aphylla, L.; a kind of resin, bdellium, L.; n. = °*nthika*, pepper, Suśr. iv, 37, 35; vi, 42, 23; = °*nthiparṇaka*, L.; a kind of disease of women, Gal.

Granthita, mfn. for *grath°*, L.

Granthin, mfn. strung together (?), RV. x, 95, 6; one who reads books, well-read, Mn. xii, 103.

Granthinikā, f. a kind of bulbous plant, Gal.; (cf. *chinna-g°*.)

Granthila, mfn. knotted, knotty, g. *sidhmâdi*; m. N. of several plants and roots (Flacourtia sapida, Capparis aphylla, Amaranthus polygonoides, Asteracantha longifolia, Cocculus cordifolius, *hitâvalī*), L.; a kind of perfume, L.; n. = °*nthika*, L.; green or undried ginger, L.; (*ā*), f. N. of two kinds of Dūrvā grass and of a kind of Cyperus, L.

Granthilī-√bhū, to become bulbous, Car. i, 1, Sch.

Granthīka, n. the root of long pepper, L.

Granthī-√bhū, to become bulbous, Bālar. ii, $\frac{3}{8}\frac{4}{8}$.

ग्रथ् 2. *grath* or *granth*, cl. 1. Ā. *grathate* or *granth°*, to be crooked (lit. and fig.), Dhātup. ii, 35.

Grathin, mfn. false, RV. vii, 6, 3.

2. **Granthi,** m. crookedness (lit. and fig.), L.

ग्रप्स *grapsa.* See *grathna.*

ग्रभ् *grabh, grábha,* &c. See √*grah.*

ग्रस 1. *gras*, cl. 1. P. Ā. *grásati*, °*te* (perf. Pot. Ā. *jagrasīta*, RV. v, 41, 17; p. Ā. & Pass. *jagrasānā*, RV.), to seize with the mouth, take into the mouth, swallow, devour, eat, consume, RV.; TS. &c.; to swallow up, cause to disappear, MBh. iii, 1597; R. i, 56, 13–17; to eclipse, MBh. i, 1166; R. &c.; to swallow or slur over words, pronounce indistinctly, PāṇŚ. (RV.) 27; to suppress, stop or neglect (a lawsuit), Mn. viii, 43: Caus. P. *grāsayati*, to cause to swallow or devour, ŚBr. xii; KātyŚr.; to consume, swallow, Dhātup. xxxiii, 76; [cf. γράω; Lat. *grā-men*; Germ. *gras*; Engl. *grass.*]

2. **Gras,** mfn. ifc. 'swallowing' (e. g. *piṇḍa-*, q. v.)

Grasatī, f. (irreg. pr. p. f.), N. of a Nāga virgin, Kāraṇḍ. i, 45.

Grasana, n. swallowing, Suśr.; a kind of partial eclipse of the sun or moon, VarBṛS. v, 43 & 46; seizing, W.; the mouth, jaws, BhP. iii, 13, 35.

Grásishṭha, mfn. (superl.) swallowing most, RV. i, 163, 7.

Grasishṇu, mfn. accustomed to swallow or absorb, Bhag. xiii, 16.

Grasta, mfn. swallowed, eaten, Pañcat.; taken, seized, W.; surrounded or absorbed, Suśr.; possessed (by a demon), Daś. iv; Hit.; involved in, MBh. xiii, 7292; R. iv, 50, 11; tormented, affected by, Yājñ. iii, 245; Pañcat. &c.; eclipsed, MBh. iii, 2667; R. &c.; inarticulately pronounced, slurred, RPrāt.; Lāṭy.; PāṇŚ. (RV.) 35; Pat.; (*a-*, neg.) ChUp.; n. inarticulate pronunciation of the vowels, Pat. Introd. on Vārtt. 18. **— tva,** n. the being refuted (by arguments), Sarvad. ii, xii. **Grastâsta,** m. the setting of the sun or moon while eclipsed, W. **Grastôdaya,** m. the rising of the sun or moon while eclipsed, W.

Grasti, f. the act of swallowing, Prab. vi, 8.

Grastri, m. an eclipser, Hariv. 12465.

Grasya, mfn. devourable, MBh. v, 1107.

Grāsa, mfn. ifc. swallowing, NṛisUp. ii, 5, 10; m. a mouthful, lump (of rice &c. of the size of a peacock's egg), Mn.; Yājñ. &c.; food, nourishment, Gobh.; ŚāṅkhGṛ.; Pāṇ. viii, 2, 44, Vārtt. 4; Mn. viii &c.; the quantity eclipsed, amount of obscuration, Sūryas.; (in geom.) a piece cut out by the intersection of 2 circles, W.; the erosion, morsel bitten, W.; = *grasti*, Bhartṛ. ii, 22; Subh.; the act of eclipsing, VarBṛS. v; an eclipse, Sūryas.; the first contact with an eclipsed disk, ib.; slurring, inarticulate pronunciation of the gutturals, RPrāt. xiv, 4. **— pramāṇa,** n. the size of a morsel, Gaut. xxvii, 10; a kind of process applied to mercury, Sarvad. ix, 33. **— śalya,** n. any extraneous substance lodged in the throat, Suśr. **Grāsâcchādana,** n. sg. food and clothing, bare subsistence, Mn. ix, 202; MBh. xiv, 1291. **Grāsâmbu,** n. sg. food and drink, ŚvetUp. v, 11.

Grāsikā, f. See *agra-*.

Grāsī, ind. **— √kṛi,** to swallow, Kathās. ix, 57. **— kṛita,** mfn. swallowed, Hcar. v, 141; Bālar. vii, 52.

ग्रह् *grah* [RV. in a few passages only; AV. &c.] or *grabh* [RV.; rarely AV.], cl. 9. P. *gṛibhṇāti, gṛihṇāti* (also Ā. *gṛihṇīte*, irreg. *gṛihṇate*, MuṇḍUp.; 3. pl. *gṛibhṇate*, RV.; Impv. 2. sg. *gṛihāṇá*, [°*ṇā*, Saṃhitā-p., p. Pass. nom. pl. n., Gmn.] x, 103, 12; AV. xi, 1, 10; ŚBr. &c.; *gṛibhṇāṇá* & *gṛihṇ°* (Ved.); *gṛihṇa*, Hcat.; *prati-gṛihṇāhi, -gṛibhṇihi*, see *prati-√grabh*; Ā. *gṛibhṇishva* [VS. i, 18] or *gṛihṇ°*; 3. sg. P. *gṛihṇītāt*; Ved. Impv. *gṛibhāyá* &c., see s. v. °*ya*, cf. *gṛihaya*; perf. *jagrāha*, RV. x, 161, 1; AV. &c.; 1. sg. °*grabhá*, RV.; °*gṛibhmá*, RV.; Ā. °*gṛihe*, x, 12, 5 &c.; 3. pl. °*gṛibhré* & °*gṛibhriré*, RV.; P. Pot. °*gṛibhyāt*, x, 31, 2; p. °*gṛibhvás*, iv, 23, 4; fut. 2nd *grahīshyati*, °*te*, MBh. &c. [cf. Pāṇ. vii, 2, 37]; sometimes wrongly spelt *gṛih°*, MBh. iv, 1650; xii, 7311; *grahishy°*, R. vi, 82, 74; Cond. *agrahaishyat*, AitUp. iii, 3 ff.; fut. 1st *grahītā*, Pāṇ. vii. 2, 37; aor. *agrabham*, RV. i, 191, 13; AV.; °*bhīt*, RV. i, 145, 2; AV. &c.; °*hīt* (Pāṇ. vii, 2, 5), AV. &c.; *-ájagrabhīt* &c., see *sam-√grah*; Subj. 2. pl. *grabhīshṭa*, RV. ii, 29, 5; Ā. *agrahīshṭa*, BhP. iv, 30, 11; *aghṛikshata*, Pāṇ. vii, 3, 73, Sch. (not in Kāś.); Ved. 3. pl. *agṛibhran* [RV. v, 2, 4] & *agṛibhīshata*; ind. p. *gṛibhītvā́*, AV. xii, 3, 20; *gṛihītvā́*, xii, 58, 3 &c.; *grahāya*, Hariv.; Divyâv.; inf. *grahītum* [MBh. &c.; cf. Pāṇ. vii, 2, 37; wrongly spelt *gṛih°*, R. v, 2, 25; Hit.]; Pass. *gṛihyate* [fut. 1st *grahītā* or *grāhitā*, fut. 2nd *grahīshyate* or *grāhishy°*, aor. *agrāhi*, 3. du. *agrahīshātām* or *agrāhish°*, Pāṇ. vi, 4, 62 & vii, 2, 37]; Ved. Subj. 3. pl. *gṛihyāntai*, Kāś. on iii, 4, 8 & 96; Ved. Pass. 3. sg. *gṛihate* [RV. v, 32, 12] or *gṛihe* [MaitrS. i, 9, 5] or *gṛihaye* [Kāṭh. ix, 13; cf. *gṛihaya*]; Subj. 1. pl. *gṛihāmahi*, RV. viii, 2, 16; Pot. *gṛihīta*, MaitrS. ii, 5, 2) to seize, take (by the hand, *pāṇau* or *kare*, exceptionally *pāṇim* (double acc.), RV. i, 125, 1, Sāy.; cf. Vop. v, 6), grasp, lay hold of (e. g. *paksham*, to take a side, adopt a party, Prab.; *pāṇim*, 'to take by the hand in the marriage ceremony,' marry, AV. xiv, 1, 48 ff.; Gobh. ii, 1, 11; MBh. &c.), RV. &c.; to arrest, stop, RV. ix, 78, 1; Kathās. iv, 32; to catch, take captive, take prisoner, capture, imprison, RV. &c.; to take possession of, gain over, captivate, MBh. xiii, 2239; R. ii, 12, 25; Ragh.; Cāṇ.; to seize, overpower (esp. said of diseases and demons and the punishments of Varuṇa), RV.; AV.; MaitrS. &c.; to eclipse, VarBṛS. v; to abstract, take away (by robbery), R. iv, 53, 25; Śak. iii, 21; Bhaṭṭ.; to lay the hand on, claim, Mn.; Yājñ.; Ragh. i, 18; Pañcat.; to gain, win, obtain, receive, accept (from, abl., rarely gen.), keep, RV. &c. (with double acc., Vop. v, 6); to acquire by purchase (with instr. of the price), Mn. viii, 201; Yājñ. ii, 169; R. &c.; to choose, MBh. xiii; R. i, 39, 13 f.; Kathās. liii; to choose any one (acc.) as a wife; to take up (a fluid with any small vessel), draw water, RV. viii, 69, 10; VS. x, 1; TS. vi &c.; to pluck, pick, gather, Hariv. 5238; Śak. iv, vi; to collect a store of anything, VarBṛS. xlii, 10 f.; to use, put on (clothes), Mn. ii, 64; MBh. iii, 16708; Bhag.; Ratnâv. i &c.; to assume (a shape), BhP. i f.; to place upon (instr. or loc.), Mn. viii, 256; Kathās.; to include, Pāṇ. viii, 4, 68, Sch.; Vop. i, 5; to take on one's self, undertake, undergo, begin, RV. x, 31, 2; MBh. iii, xiii; BhP. &c.; to receive hospitably (a guest), take back (a divorced wife), MBh. v, 7068; R. i; Śak. v, 25; BhP. iii, 5, 19; 'to take into the mouth,' mention, name, RV. i, 191, 13 & x, 145, 4; AV.; TS. &c.; to perceive (with the organs of sense or with *mánas*), observe, recognise, RV. i, 139, 10 & 145, 2; VS. i, 18; ŚBr. xiv; MuṇḍUp.; ŚvetUp. &c.; (in astron.) to observe, VarBṛS. xliii, 30; to receive into the mind, apprehend, understand, learn, Nal.; R.; Ragh. v, 59; Pañcat. i, 1, 23; (in astron.) to calculate, Sūryas.; to accept, admit, approve, MBh. i, 6299; R. ii; Mṛicch. ix, 18; Kād.; BhP. i, 2, 12; Kathās.; to obey, follow, MBh.; R.; Mṛicch. ix, $\frac{3}{3}\frac{2}{1}$; BhP. iii f.; to take for, consider as, Mn. i, 110; Mālav. v &c.; (Pass.) to be meant by (instr.), Yājñ., Sch.; Pāṇ. Siddh. & Sch.: Caus. *grāhayati*, to cause to take or seize or lay hold of, R. vii; Suśr.; Ragh. xv, 88; Daś.; to cause to take (by the hand [*pāṇim*] in the marriage ceremony), Ragh. xvii, 3; to cause to marry, give away a girl (acc.) in marriage to any one (acc.), Kum. i, 53; to cause any one to be captured, Yājñ. ii, 169; R. vi, 1, 21; Daś.; to cause any one to be seized or overpowered (as by Varuṇa's punishments or death &c.), TS. ii, vi f.; TBr. i; MBh. viii, 3281; to cause to be taken away, Hit.; to make any one take, deliver anything (acc.) over to any one (acc.; e. g. *āsanam* with acc. 'to cause to take a seat, bid any one to sit down,' Rājat. v, 306), Mṛicch.; Vop. xviii, 7; to make any one choose, Rājat. v, 102 (aor. *ajigrahat*); to make any one learn, make acquainted or familiar with (acc.), Nir. i, 4; Āp. i, 8, 25; Mn. i, 58; MBh. &c.: Desid. *jighṛikshati* (cf. Pāṇ. i, 2, 8 & vii, 2, 12), also °*te*, to be about to seize or take, Gobh. i, 1, 8 & 20; MBh.; R.; Kathās.; to be about to eclipse, R. vii, 35, 31; to be about to take away, BhP. i, 17, 25; to desire to perceive (with the organs of sense), strive to apprehend or recognise, AitUp. iii, 3 ff.; BhP. ii, iv: Intens. *jarīgrihyate*, Pāṇ. vi, 1, 16, Kāś.; [cf. Zd. *gerep, geurv*; Goth. *greipa*; Germ. *greife*; Lith. *grēbju*; Slav. *grabljū*; Hib. *grabaim*, 'I devour, stop.']

Grábha, m. the taking possession of, RV. vii, 4, 8.

Grabhaṇa, see *a-grabhaṇá*. **-vat** (*grábh°*), mfn. yielding any hold or support, RV. i, 127, 5.

Grábhītṛi, mfn. one who seizes, AV. i, 12, 2.

Gráha (Pāṇ. iii, 3, 58; g. *vrishâdi*), mfn. ifc. (iii, 2, 9, Vārtt. 1) seizing, laying hold of, holding, BhP. iii, 15, 35; (cf. *aṅkuśa-*, *dhanur-*, &c.); obtaining, v, viii; perceiving, recognising, iv, 7, 31; m. 'seizer (eclipser),' Rāhu or the dragon's head, MBh. &c.; a planet (as seizing or influencing the destinies of men in a supernatural manner; sometimes 5 are enumerated, viz. Mars, Mercury, Jupiter, Venus, and Saturn, MBh. vi, 4566 f.; R. i, 19, 2; Ragh. iii. 13 &c.; also 7, i. e. the preceding with Rāhu and Ketu, MBh. vii, 5636; also 9, i. e. the sun [cf. ŚBr. iv, 6, 5, 1 & 5; MBh. xiii, 913; xiv, 1175] and moon with the 7 preceding, Yājñ. i, 295; MBh. iv, 48; VarBṛS.; also the polar star is called a Graha, Garg. (Jyot. 5, Sch.); the planets are either auspicious *śubha-*, *sad-*, or inauspicious *krūra-*, *pāpa-*, VarBṛS.; with Jainas they constitute one of the 5 classes of the Jyotishkas); the place of a planet in the fixed zodiac, W.; the number 'nine;' N. of particular evil demons or spirits who seize or exercise a bad influence on the body and mind of man (causing insanity &c.; it falls within the province of medical science to expel these demons; those who esp. seize children and cause convulsions &c. are divided into 9 classes according to the number of planets, Suśr.), MBh. &c.; any state which proceeds from magical influences and takes possession of the whole man, BhP. vii, ix; BrahmaP.; Hit. ii, 1, 20; a crocodile, MBh. xvi, 142 (ifc. f. *ā*); R. iv f.; BhP. viii; any ladle or vessel employed for taking up a portion of fluid (esp. of Soma) out of a larger vessel, Mn. v, 116; Yājñ. i, 182; N. of the 8 organs of perception (viz. the 5 organs of sense with Manas, the hands and the voice), ŚBr. xiv; NṛisUp. i, 4, 3, 22; (= *griha*) a house, R. vii, 40, 30; (cf. *a-*, *khara-*, *-druma* & *-pati*); 'anything seized,' spoil, booty, MBh. iii, 11461; (cf. °*hâluñcana*); as much as can be taken with a ladle or spoon out of a larger vessel, ladleful, spoonful (esp. of Soma), RV. x, 114, 5; VS.; TS.; AitBr.; ŚBr. &c.; the middle of a bow or that part which is grasped when the bow is used, MBh. iv, 1351 (*su-*, 1326); the beginning of any piece of music; grasp, seizing, laying hold of (often ifc.), Kauś. 10; MBh. &c.; keeping back, obstructing, Suśr.; imprisoning, imprisonment (°*haṃ* √*gam*, 'to become a prisoner,' Kām.), R. ii, 58, 2; seizure (by demons causing diseases, e. g. *aṅga-*, spasm of the limbs), Suśr.; seizure of the sun and moon, eclipse, AV. xix, 9, 7 & 10; VarBṛS.; stealing, robbing, Mn. ix, 277; MBh. vi, 4458; effort, Hit.; insisting upon, tenacity, perseverance in (loc. or in comp.), BhP. vii, 14, 11; Naish. ix, 12; Kathās.; Rājat. viii, 226; taking, receiving, reception, Mn. viii, 180; Śṛiṅgār.; taking up (any fluid); choosing, MBh. xii, 83, 12; Sāh. vi, 136; 'favour,' see *-nigraha*; mentioning, employing (a word), Mn. viii, 271; Pāṇ. vii, 1, 21, Kār. 2; Amar.; Rājat.; apprehension, perception, understanding, Bhāshāp.; BhP.; Sarvad.; Sch. on Jaim. & KapS.; (*āya*), dat. ind. = *grihītvā*, see √*grah*; (cf. *guda-*, *śiro-*, *hanu-*, *hṛid-*.) **-kallola**, m. 'wave (? or enemy) of the planets,' Rāhu, L. **-kāṇḍa**, n. 'section treating of Grahas of Soma which are taken up by a ladle,' N. of ŚBr. iv. **-kuṇḍalikā**, f. the mutual relation of planets and prophecy derived from it, VarBṛ. xviii, 10 f., Sch. **-koshṭhaka**, n. N. of a work. **-kautuka**, n. N. of a work. **-kshetrin**, for *griha-ksh°*, Hariv. ii, 8, 19. **-gaṇa**, m. a whole number of demons causing diseases, Suśr. vi, 60, 4; a whole number of planets taken collectively, W. **-gaṇita**, n. 'calculation of the planets,' the astronomical part of a Jyotiḥ-śāstra, VarBṛS. ii. **-gocara**, n., N. of a work. **-grasta**, mfn. possessed by a demon, Hcat. iv. **-grāmaṇī**, m. 'planet-chief,' the sun, Bālar. iii. **-carita-vid**, m. 'knowing the course of planets,' an astrologer, viii. **-cintaka**, m. id., VarBṛS. xxiv, 4. **-tā**, f. the state of being a planet, v, 1. **-tilaka**, m., N. of a work. **-tva**, n. = *-tā*, Hariv.; BhP. v f.; the state of a ladleful or spoonful, Kāṭh. ix, 16. **-daśā**, f. the aspect of the planets, W. **-dāya**, m. the length of life as granted by the planets, VarBṛ. vii, 9. **-dīpikā**, f., N. of a work. **-druma**, for *griha-d°*, L. **-dhāra**, m. = *grahâdh°*, Gal. **-nāyaka**, m. = *-grāmaṇī*, Hcat. i, 8, 435; the planet Saturn, L. **-nāśa**, m. 'destroying (the influence of) planets,' Alstonia scholaris, L. **-nāśana**, m. id., L.; for *griha-n°* (a pigeon), L. **-nigraha**, m. du. favour and punishment, Hit. **-nemi**, m. the moon, L.; the section of the moon's course between the asterisms Mūla and Mṛiga-śiras, Gal. **-pati**, m. = *-grāmaṇī*, L.; the moon, MBh. xii, 6288 (*griha-p°*, B); for *griha-p°*, xiii, 4133; Calotropis gigantea, L. **-pīḍana**, n. 'pain by Rāhu,' an eclipse, R. v, 73, 58; Hit. i, 2, 48. **-pīḍā**, f. id., MārkP. lviii; Devīm. **-pusha**, m. 'cherishing the planets (with light),' the sun, L. **-pūjā**, f. worship of the planets. **-bhakti**, f. division (of countries) with respect to the presiding planets, VarBṛS.; pl. N. of VarBṛS. xvi. **-bhīti-jit**, m. 'conquering the fear of the demons,' N. of a perfume, L. **-bhojana**, m. a horse, L. **-maya**, mfn. consisting of planets, Bhartṛ. i, 16. **-marda**, m. (friction i. e.) opposition between certain planets. **-mardana**, n. id., VarBṛS. xvi, 40. **-mātṛikā**, f., N. of a Buddh. goddess. **-mush**, m. (? for *-push* = *-pusha*) the sun, Gal. **-yajña**, m. a sacrifice offered to the planets, Yājñ. i, 294; VarBṛS.; MatsyaP. ccxxxviii; *-tattva*, n., N. of part of Smṛitit. **-yāga**, m. = *-yajña*; *-tattva*, n., N. of a work. **-yāmala-tantra**, n., N. of a Tantra. **-yuti**, f. conjunction of planets. **-yuddha**, n. = *-marda*, AV. Pariś.; VarBṛS.; N. of VarBṛS. xvii. **-yoga**, m. = *-yuti*, Romakas. **-rāja**, m. = *-grāmaṇī*, L.; the moon, L.; the planet Jupiter, L. **-lāghava**, n., N. of an astronomical work of the 16th century. **-varman**, v. l. for *guha-v°*. **-varsha**, m. a planetary year, VarBṛS.; *-phala*, n. N. of VarBṛS. xix (describing the good and evil fortune belonging to certain days, months, or years ruled over by particular planets). **-vicārin**, m. = *-cintaka*, Sāh. **-vinoda**, m. N. of a work. **-vipra**, m. = *-cintaka*, W. **-vimarda**, m. = *-marda*, VarBṛS. cvii, 2. **-śānti**, f. propitiation of the planets (by sacrifices &c.), xliii. **-śṛiṅgāṭaka**, n. triangular position of the planets with reference to each other, xx; N. of VarBṛS. xx (treating also of many other positions of the planets). **-samāgama**, m. = *-yuti*, xx, 5. **-sāraṇī**, f., N. of a work. **-sthiti-varṇana**, n., N. of a work. **-svara**, m. the 1st note of a musical piece. **Grahâgama**, m. demoniacal possession, L.; *-kutūhala*, n., N. of a work. **Grahâgresara**, m. 'planet-chief,' the moon, Daś. viii, 100. **Grahâdi**, a Gaṇa of Pāṇ. (iii, 1, 134; Gaṇar. 457–459); another Gaṇa, 445; Hemac. **Grahâdhāra**, m. 'planet-support,' the polar star, L. **Grahâdhipati**, m. the chief of the demons causing diseases, Suśr. **Grahâdhishṭhāpana**, n., N. of a work. **Grahâdhīna**, mfn. subject to planetary influence, W. **Grahâdhyāya**, m., N. of a work. **Grahâpaha**, n. 'removing (the influence) of planets,' the bile-stone of cattle, Npr. **Grahâmaya**, m. = °*hâgama*, L. **Grahârāma-kutūhala**, n., N. of an astronomical work by Bhāskara. **Grahâluñcana**, n. pouncing on prey, Mṛicch. iii, 20. **Grahâvamardana**, n. = °*ha-marda*, VarBṛS. iii, 83. **Grahâvarta**, m. = *lagna*, horoscope &c., Gal. **Grahâśin**, m. = °*ha-nāśa*, L. **Grahâśraya**, m. = °*hâdhāra*, L. **Grahâhvaya**, m. 'called after the demons,' the plant Bhūtâṅkuśa (*bhūta* = *graha*?), L. **Grahêśa**, m. = °*ha-grāmaṇī*, L. **Grahêshṭaka**, n. sg. a ladleful (of any fluid) and the bricks, Jaim. v, 3, 15. **Grahôktha**, n. a hymn sung while a ladleful (of Soma) is being taken up, AitBr. iii, viii.

Grahaka, m. a prisoner, L.; (*ikā*), see *grāh°*.

Grahaṇa, mfn. ifc. seizing, holding, Hariv. 7324; resounding in (?), Śak. ii, $\frac{8}{9}$, 6; n. the hand, L.; an organ of sense, Yogas. i, 41; a prisoner, MBh. xiii, 2051; a word mentioned or employed (e. g. *vacana-*, 'the word *vacana*'), Pat. & Kāś.; seizing, holding, taking, ŚBr. xiv; Mn. ii, 317; MBh. &c.; taking by the hand, marrying, i, 1044; catching, seizure, taking captive; Mn. v, 130; MBh. &c.; seizure (as by a demon causing diseases), demoniacal possession, Hcat.; seizure of the sun or moon, eclipse, Āp. i, 11; Yājñ. i, 218; VarBṛS. &c.; gaining, obtaining, receiving, acceptance, R. i, 3, 18; Pañcat.; Kathās. xci, 37; choosing, Sāṃkhyak.; Prab.; Sāh. vi, 201; purchasing, Pañcat.; taking or drawing up (any fluid), ŚBr. iv; KātyŚr.; the taking up of sound, echo, W.; attraction, Megh.; Ragh. vii, 24; Pañcat. v, 13, $\frac{8}{9}$; putting on (clothes), MBh. ii, 840; Ragh. xvii, 21; assuming (a shape), Yājñ. iii, 69; MBh. xiv; Devīm.; undertaking, devoting one's self to (in comp.), R. v, 76, 22; Pañcat.; service, BhP. iii, 1, 44; including, Pāṇ. Kāś.; mentioning, employing (a word or expression), KātyŚr.; Lāṭy.; VPrāt.; Pāṇ. Vārtt., Pat. & Kāś.; Sāh. vi, 205; mentioning with praise, acknowledgment, Suśr.; assent, agreement, W.; perceiving, understanding, comprehension, receiving instruction, acquirement of any science, Mn. ii, 173; MBh. iii, xiv; Ragh. &c.; acceptation, meaning, Pāṇ. i, 1, 68, Vārtt. 5, Pat.; Kāś. & Siddh. on Pāṇ.; (*ī*), f. an imaginary organ supposed to lie between the stomach and the intestines (the small intestines or that part of the alimentary canal where the bile assists digestion and from which vital warmth is said to be diffused), Suśr.; = °*ṇī-gada*, Ashṭâṅg. iii, 8; Hcat. i, 7; (cf. *kara-*, *keśa-*, *garbha-*, *cakshur-*, *nāma-*, *pāṇi-*, *punar-*.) **-gata**, mfn. eclipsed, VarBṛS. xv, 31. **-pañcâṅga**, **-phala**, n., N. of two astronomical works. **-vat**, mfn. meant in reality, not to be taken in a different way, Pat. on Pāṇ. iv, 1, 1 & Vārtt. 1 & iv, 1, 4, Vārtt. 2. **-sambhavâdhikāra**, m., N. of an astronomical work. **Grahaṇânta**, mfn. being at the close of study, ĀśvGṛ. i, 22, 3; Gaut. ii, 47. **Grahaṇântika**, mfn. id., Mn. iii, 1; Yājñ. i, 36.

Grahaṇi, f. = °*ṇī*, Uṇ. **-roga**, see °*ṇī-r°*.

Grahaṇī, f. of °*ṇa*, q. v. **-kapāṭa**, m. a kind of mixture (for curing diarrhœa &c.) **-gada**, m. a morbid affection of the Grahaṇī, dysentery, Bhpr. **-dosha**, m. id., MBh. iii, 13857 ('constipation,' Sch.); Suśr. **-pradosha**, m. id., Suśr. **-ruj**, f. id., L. **-roga**, m. id., Suśr. (metrically also °*ṇi-r°*). **-°rogin**, mfn. affected with dysentery, Suśr.; Hcat. i, 7. **-hara**, n. 'removing dysentery,' cloves, L.

Grahaṇīya, mfn. to be accepted as a rule or law, to be taken to heart, MBh. v, xii. **-tā**, f. acceptableness, W. **-tva**, n. id., W.

Grahayāyya, v. l. for *grih°*, Vop. xxvi, 164.

Grahayālu, v. l. for *grih°*, 148.

Grahi, m. anything that holds or supports, Gṛihyās. ii, 29; (cf. *phala-*, °*le-*.)

Grahila, mf(*ā*)n. (g. *kāśâdi*) taking interest in, inclined to (in comp.), Sāh. iii, 4, $\frac{8}{9}$; (= *grathika*) possessed by a demon, HPariś. ii, 539; Śuk.

Grahishṇu, mfn. See *phala-*.

Grahītavyà, mfn. to be taken or received, ŚBr. iv; Mn. vii f.; Hit.; to be taken up or down (a fluid), TS. vi; to be perceived, W.; to be learned, W.; n. obligation to take or receive, MBh. xii, 7313.

Grahītṛi, mfn. one who takes or seizes, ŚvetUp. iii, 19; one who receives, Mn. viii, 166; a purchaser, Pañcat.; one who perceives or observes, Mn. i, 15; Yogas. i, 41; one who notices or hears, Bālar. ii, $\frac{48}{49}$; (cf. *pāṇi-*.)

Gráhya, mfn. belonging to or fit for a Graha (ladleful of any fluid), VS. iv, 24.

Grābhá, m. 'one who seizes,' a demon causing diseases, AV. xiv, 1, 38; what is seized, grasp, RV. viii, 81, 1; ix, 106, 3; (cf. **uda-**, *grāva-*, *tuvi-*, & *hasta-grābhá*.)

Grāhá (Pāṇ. iii, 1, 143), mf(*ī*)n. ifc. seizing, holding, catching, receiving, Yājñ. ii, 51; R. iv, 41, 38; taking (a wife), Yājñ. ii, 51; (cf. *karṇa-*, *gila-*, *dhanur-*, *pāṇi-*, *pārshṇi-*, *vandi-*, *vyāla-*, *hasta-*); m. a rapacious animal living in fresh or sea water, any large fish or marine animal (crocodile, shark, serpent, Gangetic alligator, water elephant, or hippopotamus), Mn. vi, 78; MBh. &c. (ifc. f. *ā*, iv, 2017; xvi; R. ii); a prisoner, L.; the handle (of a sword &c.), Gal.; seizure, grasping, laying hold of, Pañcat. i, 10, 1 (v. l. for *graha*); morbid affection, disease, ŚBr. iii; paralysis (of the thigh, *ūru-grāhá*, AV. xi, 9, 12 [*ur°*, MSS.]; MBh. v, 2024 & vi, 5680); 'mentioning,' see *nāma-*; fiction, whim, Bhag. xvii, 19; conception, notion of (in comp.), Vajracch. 6 & 9; (*am*), ind., see s. v.; (*ī*), f. a female marine animal or crocodile, R. vi, 82, 73 ff. **-vat**, mfn. containing or abounding with large marine animals, W.

Grāhaka, mf(*ikā*)n. one who seizes or takes captive, Yājñ. ii, 266; one who seizes (the sun or moon), who eclipses, Sūryas. iv, vi; one who receives or accepts, Hcat. i, 7; a purchaser, Pañcat.; Kathās. lxi; Tantras.; containing, including, Sāh.; Sch. on RPrāt. & KapS. i, 40; perceiving, perceiver, (in phil.) subject, MBh. iii, 13932; KapS. v, 98 & vi, 4; Sāṃkhyak. 27, Sch.; Sarvad.; captivating, persuading, MBh. xii, 4202; R.; m. a hawk, falcon (catching snakes), L.; Marsilea quadrifolia, L.; N. of a demon causing diseases, Hariv. 9561; (*ikā*), f. with *vali*, one of the 3 folds which lead off the feces from the body, ŚarṅgS. vi, 8; ifc. the taking hold of, Daś. vii, 193 (v. l. *grah°*). **-kṛikara**, m. a partridge used as call-bird, Hcar. vii. **-vihaṃga**, m. a call-bird, Kād. vii, 186.

Grāham, ind. so as to seize, (ifc.) Pāṇ. iii, 4, 39; (with loc. or instr. or ifc.) 50, Kāś.; (with acc. or ifc.) 53, Kāś.; (cf. *nāma-grāh°*.)

Grāhayitavya, mfn. to be urged to undertake anything (acc.), Daś. viii, 218.

1. **Grā́hi**, f. a female spirit seizing men (and causing death and diseases, swoon, fainting fit), RV. x, 161, 1; AV. (Sleep is described as her son, xvi, 5, 1).

2. **Grāhi**, in comp. for *°hin*. **-phala**, m. 'having astringent fruits,' Feronica elephantum, L.

Grāhika, mfn. insisting upon with tenacity, Kathās. il, 16.

Grāhita, mfn. made to take or seize, W.; made to accept or take (a seat &c.), Vikr. iii, $\frac{6}{7}$; Daś. vii, 266; Kathās. li, 71; made to undertake or to be occupied with (instr.), R. (G) i, 7, 14; taught, MBh. iii, 12195.

Grāhin (Pāṇ. iii, 1, 134), mfn. ifc. seizing, taking, holding, laying hold of, R.; Śak. ii, $\frac{6}{7}$ (v. l.); Bhartṛ.; Kathās.; catching, engaged in catching, xxv, 49; picking, gathering, Sāh. ii, $\frac{5}{6}$; containing, holding, Daś. vii, 207; gaining, obtaining, acquiring, R. iii, 72, 1; keeping, Cāṇ. (Subh.); purchasing, Kathās. lvii, 20; drawing, attracting, fascinating, alluring, MBh. xiii, 1403; R. i, v; choosing, MārkP. xxvii, 28; searching, scrutinizing, Śak. ii, $\frac{6}{7}$; 'perceiving, acknowledging,' see *guṇa-*; astringent, obstructing, constipating, Car. vi, 8; Suśr.; m. = *°hi-phala*, L.; (*iṇī*), f. a variety of the Alhagi plant, L.; a variety of Mimosa, Npr.; a great kind of lizard, Npr.

Grā́huka, mfn. seizing (with acc.), TS. vi, 4, 1, 1.

Grāhyà, mfn. to be seized or taken or held, RV. x, 109, 3; Mn.; Yājñ.; MBh. &c.; to be clasped or spanned, Kathās. lxxiv, 217; to be captured or imprisoned, Yājñ. ii, 267 & 283; MBh. &c.; to be overpowered, Prab. ii, $\frac{5}{6}$; (*a-*, neg.) R. (B) iii, 33, 16; to be picked or gathered, R. iv, 43, 29; to be received or accepted or gained, Mn.; Yājñ.; MBh. &c.; to be taken in marriage, xiii, 5091; to be received in a friendly or hospitable manner, xii, 6282; to be insisted upon, Kathās. xvii, 83; to be chosen or taken account of, Rājat. iv, 612; to be perceived or recognised or understood, Mn. i, 7; MBh. &c.; (cf. *a-*); (in astron.) to be observed, VarBṛS.; to be considered, R. v, vii; VarBṛS. lxi, 19; to be understood in a particular sense, meant, Vop. vi, 15; Pāṇ., Sch.; to be accepted as a rule or law, to be acknowledged or assented to, to be attended to or obeyed, to be admitted in evidence, Mn. viii, 78; Yājñ.; MBh. &c.; to be undertaken or followed (a vow), Kathās. vcii, 38; to be put (as confidence) in (loc.), lviii, 36; m. an eclipsed globe (sun or moon), Sūryas.; n. poison (NBD.; 'a present,' BR.), L.; the objects of sensual perception, Yogas. i, 41; (*ā*), f. archery exercise, Gal.; (cf. *dur-*, *sukha-*, *svayam-*.) **-gir**, mfn. one whose words are to be accepted or followed, Hcar. v, 485. **-tva**, n. perceptibleness, Sarvad. iii, x, xii, xiv. **-rūpa**, mfn. to be taken to heart, MBh. i, 220, 23. **-vat**, mfn. = *-gir*, TāṇḍyaBr. xiii, 11, 13. **-vāc**, mfn. id., W.

Grāhyaka. See *a-*.

ग्राम *grā́ma*, m. an inhabited place, village, hamlet, RV. i, x; AV.; VS. &c.; the collective inhabitants of a place, community, race, RV. x, 146, 1; AV. &c.; any number of men associated together, multitude, troop (esp. of soldiers), RV. i, iii, x; AV. iv, 7, 5; ŚBr. vi, xii; the old women of a family, PārGṛ. i, 9, 3, Sch.; ifc. (cf. Pāṇ. vi, 2, 84) a multitude, class, collection or number (in general), cf. *indriya-*, *guṇa-*, *bhūta-*, &c.; a number of tones, scale, gamut, Pañcat. v, 43; MārkP. xxiii, 52; = *indriya-*, Jain.; m. pl. inhabitants, people, RV. ii, 12, 7; x, 127, 5; n. a village, R. ii, 57, 4; Hcat. i, 7, $\frac{7}{8}\frac{3}{8}\frac{4}{5}$; [cf. *arishṭa-*, *mahā-*, *śūra-*, *saṃ-*; cf. Hib. *gramaisg*, 'the mob;' *gramasgar*, 'a flock.'] **-kaṇṭaka**, m. 'village-thorn,' a boor (?), Jain.; Cāṇ. **-kanda**, m. a kind of bulbous plant, L. **-kāma** (*grā́ma-*), mfn. one who wishes to possess a village, TS. ii; Kauś.; KātyŚr.; desirous of villages, fond of living in villages, ĀśvGṛ. iv; ŚāṅkhGṛ. **-kukkuṭa**, m. a domestic cock, Mn. v, 12 & 19; Yājñ. i, 176. **-kumāra**, m. a village boy, g. *manojñâdi*. **-kumārikā**, f. the state or life of a village boy, ib. **-kulāla**, m. a village potter, Pāṇ. vi, 2, 62, Kāś. **-°kulālikā**, f. the state or business of a village potter, g. *manojñâdi* (not in Kāś.) **-kūṭa**, m. = *-kūṭaka*, L.; N. of an author of Prākṛit verses, Hāl. **-kūṭaka**, m. the chief of a village (belonging to the Śūdra caste), Subh. (v. l. for *-kaṇṭaka*). **-kola**, m. a domestic pig, L. **-kroḍa**, m. id., L. **-khaṇḍa**, v. l. for *-shaṇḍa*. **-ga**, mfn. going to a village, W. **-gata**, mfn. gone to a village, Pāṇ. ii, i, 24, Kāś. **-gamin**, mfn. = *-ga*, ib., Vārtt. 1, Pat. **-gāmin**, mfn. id., ib. **-gṛihya**, mfn. 'adjoining the houses of a village,' being outside a village (an army), iii, 1, 119, Kāś. **-gṛihyaka**, m. a village carpenter, Gal. **-geya**, n. 'to be sung in a village,' N. of one of the 4 hymn-books of the SV.; *-gāna*, n. id. **-go-duh**, *-dhuk*, m. a village herdsman, g. *yuktârohy-ādi*. **-ghāta**, m. plundering a village, Mn. ix, 274; VarBṛS. **-ghātaka**, m. plunderer of a village, Buddh. **-ghātin**, mfn. plundering a village, MBh. xii, 1213; m. a village slaughterer, Buddh. **-ghoshín**, mfn. sounding among men or armies (as a drum), AV. v, 20, 9. **-caṭaka**, m. a domestic sparrow, Gal. **-cara**, m. inhabitant of a village, husbandman, Gal. **-caryā**, f. 'village custom,' sexual intercourse, ĀśvŚr. xii, 8. **-caitya**, n. the sacred tree of a village, Megh. 24. **-ja-nishpāvī**, f. 'pulse grown in cultivated ground,' Phaseolus radiatus, L. **-jā**, f. 'growing in villages (i. e. in cultivated ground),' a kind of bean, Npr. **-jāta**, mfn. village-born, rustic, W.; grown in cultivated ground, Mn. vi, 16. **-jāla**, n. a number of villages, district, L. **-°jālin**, m. the governor of a district, L. **-jít**, mfn. conquering troops, RV. v, 54, 8; AV. vi, 97, 3. **-ṇi**, m. metrically for *-ṇī*, MBh. vii, 1125 & 4099; n. of *ṇī*, q. v.; *°bhogīna*, mfn., Pāṇ. v, 1, 7, Vārtt. 3, Pat. **-ṇī́**, m. (fr. *-nī*, Pāṇ. viii, 4, 14, Siddh.; vi, 4, 82; gen. pl. *-nyām* or Ved. *-ṇīnām*, vii, 1, 56; 3, 116, Sch., not in Kāś.; *i*, n. 'leading, chief,' vii, 1, 74, Kāś.) the leader or chief of a village or community, lord of the manor, squire, leader of a troop or army, chief, superintendent, RV. x, 62, 11 & 107, 5; VS.; AV. &c.; (mfn., see before *-ṇi*, n.) chief, pre-eminent, W.; a village barber (chief person of a village), L.; a groom (*bhogika*), L.; a Yaksha, VP. ii, 10, 2 f.; BhP. v, 21, 18; N. of a Gandharva chief, R. iv, 41, 61; of a demon causing diseases, Hariv. 9556; of one of Śiva's attendants, L.; of a locality, g. *takshaśilâdi*; f. a female peasant or villager, L.; a harlot, L.; (for *°miṇī*) the Indigo plant, L.; *-tva*, n. the condition or office of a chief or leader, MBh. xii, 4861; *-putra*, m. the son of a harlot, W.; *-sava*, m., N. of an Ekâha rite, ŚāṅkhŚr. xiv, 22, 3. **-ṇīthya** (*grā́ma-*), n. (fr. *-nīthya*) the station of the chief of a village or community, MaitrS. i, 6, 5; ŚBr. viii, 6, 2, 1. **-taksha**, m. = *-gṛihyaka*, Pāṇ. v, 4, 95. **-tas**, ind. from a village, W. **-tā**, f. pl. (Pāṇ. iv, 2, 43) a multitude of villages, AitBr. iii, 44. **-tva**, n. id., W. **-daśêśa**, m. the head of 10 villages, Mn. vii, 116. **-devatā**, f. the tutelar deity of a village, Cāṇ.; (RTL. p. 209.) **-druma**, m. a single tree in a village held sacred by the inhabitants, MBh. **-dharā**, f. 'village-supporter,' N. of a rock, Rājat. i, 265. **-dharma**, m. the observances or customs of a village, ĀśvGṛ. i, 7, 1. **-nāpita**, m. the village barber, Pāṇ. vi, 2, 62, Kāś. **-nivāsin**, mfn. living in villages (birds), Mn. v, 11. **-pati**, m. the chief of a village, Inscr. (10th century). **-pātra**, n. id., L. **-pāla**, m. a village guardian, MārkP. xix, 24. **-pālaka**, m. id., Vet. **-pishṭa**, mfn. ground at home, KātyŚr. **-putra**, m. = *-kumāra*, g. *manojñâdi*. **-°putrikā**, f. = *-°kumārikā*, ib. **-purusha**, m. the chief of a village or town, VarBṛ. xviii, 9. **-prêshya**, m. the messenger or servant of a village or community, MBh. xii, 2359; (*prêshya grāmasya*, Mn. iii, 153.) **-bāla-jana**, m. a young peasant, Vet. i. **-bhṛita**, m. = *-prêshya*. **-madgurikā**, f. = *°mya-m°*, L.; = *-yuddha*, L. **-mahishī**, f. a tame buffalo-cow, ShaḍvBr. **-mukha**, m. n. a market place, L. **-mṛiga**, m. 'village animal,' a dog, L. **-maukhya**, ('head of a village'?), Hit. **-yājaka**, mfn. offering sacrifices or conducting the ceremonies for every member of a community including unworthy persons (doing it out of avarice), Gaut. xv, 16; MBh. iii, 13355 & xii, 2874. **-yājin**, mfn. id., Mn. iv, 205; Sāy. on AitBr. i, 16, 40. **-yuddha**, n. a riot, village tumult, L. **-rajaka**, m. a village dyer, Buddh. **-rathyā**, f. a village street, Pāṇ. vi, 2, 62, Kāś. **-luṇṭhana**, n. = *-ghāta*, Mn. ix, 274, Sch. **-lekhaka**, m. a village copyist, Buddh. **-vat**, mfn. furnished with villages, MBh. viii, 4570. **-vāsa**, m. living in a village, Pāṇ. vi, 3, 18, Kāś. **-vāsin**, mfn. (ib.) living in villages, tame, Yājñ. i, 172; MBh. vi, 166 ff.; m. = *-vāstavya*, Mn. vii, 118; Kathās. lxi, 39. **-vāstavya**, m. the inhabitant of a village, villager, MBh. xii, 4803. **-viśesha**, m. variety of the scales in music, W. **-vṛiddha**, m. an old villager, Megh. 30. **-śata**, n. 100 villages, province, Mn. vii, 114 (pl. = sg.); *°tâdhyaksha*, m. the governor of a province, 119; *°têśa*, m. id., 117. **-shaṇḍa**, m. g. *manojñâdi* (*-khaṇḍa*, Kāś.; *-sanḍa*, Gaṇar. 410; *-sāṇḍa*, ib., Sch.) **-°shaṇḍikā**, f. the state of a *grāma-shaṇḍa*, ib. **-saṃkara**, m. the common sewer or drain of a village, W. **-saṃgha**, m. a village corporation, municipality, W. **-sad**, mfn. abiding or residing in villages, MānGṛ. **-siṇha**, m. 'village-lion,' = *mṛiga*, BhP. iii, x. **-sīmā**, f. village boundary or village field, Kād. **-sukha**, n. = *grāmya-s°*, MBh. iii, 3225. **-śūkara**, m. = *-kola*, Āp. i, 17, 29. **-stha**, mfn. = *-sad*, W.; belonging to a village, rustic, W.; m. a village, W. **-hāsaka**, m. a sister's husband, L. **Grāmâkshapaṭalika**, m. a village archivist, Hcar. vii, 23. **Grāmâgni**, m. 'village fire,' the common fire, PārGṛ. iii, 10, 12. **Grāmâcāra**, m. = *°ma-dharma*, W. **Grāmâdhāna**, n. a small village, L. **Grāmâdhikṛita**, m. superintendent or chief of a village, W. **Grāmâdhipa**, m. id., Kathās. lxiv, 115. **Grāmâdhipati**, m. id., W.; (*grāmasyâdh°*, Mn. vii, 115.) **Grāmâdhyaksha**, m. id., W. **Grāmâdhyayana**, n. study in a village, ŚāṅkhGṛ. vi, 1, 8. **Grāmântá**, m. the border of a village, ŚBr. xiii; PārGṛ. ii, 11; (*e*), loc. ind. in the neighbourhood of a village, Mn. iv, 116; xi, 78. **Grāmântara**, n. another village, W. **Grāmântika**, n. the neighbourhood of a village, W. **Grāmântīya**, n. place near a village, Mn. viii, 240. **Grāmâraṇya**, n. a forest belonging to a village, ŚāṅkhGṛ. iv, 7; n. du. village and forest, Āp. i, 11, 9. **Grāme-geya**, &c., see s. v. *grāme*. **Grāmêśa**, m. the head man of a village, W. **Grāmêśvara**, m. id., W. **Grāmôpâdhyāya**, m. the religious instructor of a village, W.

Grāmaka, m. a small village, Hcar. viii, 3; a village, MBh. v, 1466; N. of a town, Buddh.; n. = *°ma-caryā*, BhP. iv, 25, 52.

Grāmaṭikā, f. a miserable village, Prasannar. i, $\frac{3}{3}\frac{4}{5}$; iii, $\frac{1}{1}\frac{2}{3}$; Sāh. i, $\frac{3}{4}$ (= vii, $\frac{1}{2}$); iv, $\frac{1}{1}\frac{1}{2}$.

Grāmaṇa, mf(*ī*)n. coming from Grāma ṇī, g. *takshaśilâdi*.

Grā́maṇīya, n. (fr. *°ma-ṇī́*) = *°ma-ṇīthya*, TS. vii; m. pl., N. of a people, MBh. ii, 1191; iv, 1038.

Grāmaya, Nom. P. *°yati*, to invite, Dhātup.

Grāmi, in comp. for *°min*, q. v. **-putra**, m. a rustic boy, Nal. xiii, 23.

Grāmika, m. rustic, W.; (in music) chromatic, W.; m. a villager, W.; = *°mêśa*, Mn. vii, 116 & 118; MBh. xii, 3264 ff.

Grāmikya, n. the condition or life of a *grāmika*, g. *purohitâdi*.

Grāmin, mfn. surrounded by a village or community or race, TS. ii; pertaining to a village, rustic, W.; m. a villager, peasant (*°miṇām rati* = *°ma-caryā*, BhP. iv, 29, 14); = *°mêśa*; (*iṇī*), f. (cf. *°ma-ṇī*) the Indigo plant, L.

Grāmīṇa, mfn. (Pāṇ. iv, 2, 94; 3, 25, Kāś.) produced in or peculiar to a village, W.; rustic, vulgar, rude, Bhpr.; ifc., see *eka-*; = *grāmaiḥ sambhṛita*, L. (*°mīna*); (in music) chromatic, W.; m. a villager, peasant, Kauś. 11; Bhartṛ. &c.; a dog, L.; = *°ma-kola*, L.; a crow, L.; (*ā*), f. = *°miṇī*, L.; = *°mya-vallabhā*, L.

Grāmīna, for *°miṇa*, q. v.

Grāmīya. See *samāna-*.

Grāmīyaka, m. the member of a community, Mn. viii, 254.

Grāme, loc. of *°ma*, q. v. **-geya**, mfn. to be sung in the village, SaṃhUp. iii, 7; (cf. *°ma-g°*.) **-cara**, m. a villager, householder, BhP. xi, 12, 23. **-vāsa**, m. = *°ma-v°*, Pāṇ. vi, 3, 18, Kāś. **-vāsin**, mfn. = *ma-v°*, ib.

Grāmeya, m. a villager, MBh. xii, 3264; (*ā*), f. a female villager, L.

Grāmeyaka, m. (Pāṇ. iv, 2, 95, Vārtt.) = *°ya*, Inscr. (5th century?); (*ā*), f. = *°yā*, Hcar. vii.

Grāmyá, mfn. (Pāṇ. iv, 2, 94) used or produced in a village, TS. v; AitBr. vii, 7, 1; Kauś.; relating to villages, Mn. vii, 120; prepared in a village (as food), ŚBr. ix, xii; Mn. vi, 3; living (in villages, i. e.) among men, domesticated, tame (an animal), cultivated (a plant; opposed to *vanya* or *aranya*, 'wild'), RV. x, 90, 8; AV.; VS. &c.;

allowed in a village, relating to the sensual pleasures of a village, MBh. xii, 4069; R. iii f.; BhP. iv, vi; rustic, vulgar (speech), Vām. ii, 1, 4; (see *-tā* & *-tva*); relating to a musical scale, W.; m. a villager, Yājñ. ii, 166; MBh. xiii; BhP. &c.; a domesticated animal, see *-māṅsa; = °ma-kola*, W.; n. rustic or homely speech, W.; the Prākṛit and the other dialects of India as contra-distinguished from the Sanskṛit, W.; food prepared in a village, MBh. i, 3637; KātyŚr. xxii, Sch.; sensual pleasure, sexual intercourse, MBh. ii, 2270; BhP. iv; (*ā*), f. = °*miṇī*, L.; = °*ma-ja-nishpāvī*, L. **–kanda**, m. (or *a-gr°*?) a kind of bulbous plant, L. **–karkaṭī**, f. Benincasa cerifera, L. **–karman**, n. = °*ma-caryā*, BhP. v, 14, 31. **–kāma**, m. pl. id., Up. **–kukkuṭa**, m. = °*ma-k°*, Gaut. xvii, 29. **–kuṅkuma**, n. safflower, L. **–kola**, m. = °*ma-k°*, L. **–kośātakī**, f., N. of a cucurbitaceous plant, L. **–kroḍa**, m. = °*ma-k°*, L. **–gaja**, m. a village-born or tame elephant, MBh. iii, 65, 8. **–tā**, f. rustic or vulgar speech, Sāh. **–tva**, n. id., Sāh.; (*a-* neg., 'urbanity') Vām. iii, 2, 12. **–dharma**, m. a villager's duty, Pañcat. i, 3, $\frac{24}{25}$; 'a villager's right (opposed to the right of a recluse),' sexual intercourse, MBh. iii; Hariv. 1259; Suśr.; BhP. iii; BrahmaP. **–°dharmin**, mfn. addicted to sexual intercourse, MBh. xiii, 2574. **–paśu**, m. a domestic animal, Pāṇ. i, 2, 73; (applied contemptuously to a man) BhP. vi, 15, 16. **–buddhi**, mfn. clownish, ignorant, W. **–madgurikā**, f. (= °*ma-m°*) the fish Silurus Singio, L. **–māṅsa**, n. the flesh of domesticated animals, Suśr. **–mṛiga**, m. = °*ma-m°*, Śiś. xv, 15. **–rāśi**, m., N. of several signs of the zodiac, Jyot. **–vallabhā**, f. Beta bengalensis, L. **–vādin**, m. a village bailiff, TS. ii, 3, 1, 3. **–vārttā**, f. local gossip, W. **–sukha**, n. 'a villager's pleasure,' sleep, sexual intercourse, MBh. i, v; R. iv, vi; BhP. (*grāmya sukha*, ix, 18, 40). **–sūkara**, m. = *-kola*, Gaut. xvii, 29. **Grāmyâśva**, m. 'village-horse,' an ass, L. **Grāmyêhôparama**, m. ceasing from sexual desires, BhP. vii, 11, 9.

Grāmyāyaṇi, m. (g. *tikâdi*) patr. fr. °*mya*, Pravar. i, 2 (v. l. °*ṇa*).

ग्राव *grāva*, in comp. for °*van*. **–grābhá**, m. one who handles the Soma stones, RV. i, 162, 5. **–rohaka**, m. 'growing on stones,' Physalis flexuosa, L. **–stút**, m. (Pāṇ. iii, 2, 177) 'praising the Soma stones,' one of the 16 priests (called after the hymn [RV. x, 94, 1 ff.] addressed to the Soma stones), AitBr. vi, 1; vii, 1; ŚBr. iv, 3, 4; xii; TāṇḍyaBr.; ĀśvŚr.; ŚāṅkhŚr. **–°stotriyā**, f. (scil. *hotrā*) the praise addressed to the Soma stones, ŚāṅkhBr. xxix, 1. **–°stotrīya**, mfn. relating to the praise of the Soma stones (*hotrā*), AitBr. vi, 2; n. the duties of the Grāva-stut, KātyŚr. xxiv; (*ā*), f. = °*triyā*, ĀpŚr. xiii, 1, 6. **–hasta** (*grā́v°*), mfn. = *-grābhá*, RV. i, 15, 7.

Grávan, m. a stone for pressing out the Soma (originally 2 were used, RV. ii, 39, 1; later on 4 [ŚāṅkhBr. xxix, 1] or 5 [Sch. on ŚBr. &c.]), RV.; AV.; VS.; ŚBr.; a stone or rock, MBh. iii, 16435; Bhartṛ.; Śiś.; BhP. &c.; a mountain, L.; a cloud, Naigh. i, 10; = *grāva-stút*, Hariv. 11363; mfn. hard, solid, L.

Grāvāyaṇa, m. patr. fr. °*van*, Pravar. v, 1.

ग्रास *grāsa*, &c. See √*gras*.

ग्राह *grāhá*, °*haka*, &c. See √*grah*.

ग्रि *gri*. See *tuvi-grí*.

ग्रीव *grīva*, m. the neck, ĀrshBr.; a corridor (?), Bālar. x, $\frac{100}{101}$; (*ā́*), f. the back part of the neck, nape, neck (in the earlier literature generally pl.; cf. also Pāṇ. iv, 3, 57), RV.; VS.; AV. &c. (ifc. [cf. Pāṇ. vi, 2, 114] f. *ā*, MBh. i, 6662); the tendon of the trapezium muscle, L.; the neck part of the hide of an animal, ŚBr. iii; the neck of a bottle, VarBṛS. iii, 37; [cf. *ásita-, ṛíksha-, kambu-, kalmā́sha-, kṛishṇá-, tuvi-, nishká-*, &c.; cf. also Lith. *galwà*; Russ. *glava* & *golova*.] **–cchinná**, mf(*ā́*)n. one whose neck is cut, Suparṇ. xxv, 6. **–daghná**, mfn. reaching up to the neck, TS. v, 6, 8, 3. **Grīvâksha**, m. 'having (eyes i.e.) spots in the neck,' g. *śivâdi* (v. l.)

Grīvā, f. of °*va*, q. v. **–ghaṇṭā**, f. a bell hanging down from the neck of a horse, L. **–bila**, n. the hollow in the nape of the neck, L.

Grīvālikā, f. the neck, W.

Grīvin, m. 'long-necked,' a camel, L.

ग्रीष्म *grīshmá*, m. (√*gras*, Uṇ.) the summer, hot season (the months Śuci and Śukra, VS. xiv, 6; Suśr.; or Jyeshṭha and Āshāḍha, from the middle of May to the middle of July), RV. x, 90, 6; AV. &c.; summer heat, heat, Pañcat.; N. of a man, g. *aśvâdi*; (*ā*), f. Symplocos racemosa, L.; (*ī*), f. = °*shma-bhavā*, L.; [cf. Hib. *gris*, 'fire;' *griosgaim*, 'I fry, boil;' *griosach*, 'burning embers.'] **–kāla**, m. the hot season, W. **–jā**, f. 'growing in summer,' Anona reticulata, L. **–dhānya**, n. summer corn, VarBṛS. viii, 47. **–pushpī**, f. 'blossoming in summer,' the plant Karuṇī, L. **–bhavā**, f. 'growing in summer,' Jasminum Sambac, L. **–vana**, n. a grove frequented in summer, Kathās. cxxii, 65. **–samaya**, m. = *-kāla*, Śak. i, $\frac{3}{4}$; Hit. iii. **–sundaraka**, m. Erythraea centaureoides (or Mollugo spergula), L. **–hāsa**, n. 'summer-smiles,' the flocculent seeds, down, &c. blown about in the air in summer, L. **–hemantá**, m. du. summer and winter, ŚBr. i. **Grīshmôdbhavā**, f. = °*shma-bh°*, L.

ग्रुच् *gruc* (= √*gluc*), cl. 1. P. *grocati* (aor. *agrucat* or *agrocīt*, Pāṇ. iii, 1, 58; in derivatives *k* for *c*, vii, 3, 59, Siddh.) to steal, Dhātup. vii, 17; to go, ib.

ग्रुमुष्टि *gru-mushṭí*, m. = *guru-m°*, TS. v, 4, 5, 2 & 3.

ग्रैव *graiva*, mfn. (fr. *grīvā́*, Pāṇ. iv, 3, 57) representing the neck, ŚāṅkhŚr. xviii, 3, 1; n. a necklace, L.; a chain worn round the neck of an elephant, Ragh. iv, 48.

Graivâksha, m. patr. fr. *grīv°*, g. *śivâdi* (v. l.)

Graiveya, n. (Pāṇ. iv, 3, 57) a necklace, L.; m. n. a chain worn round the neck of an elephant, MBh. vi f.; R. i; Ragh. iv, 75; Daś. vii, 191.

Graiveyaka, n. (m., Pāṇ. iv, 2, 96, Kāś.) a necklace, Devīm.; Sāh.; a chain worn round the neck of an elephant, Daś. vii, 191; m. pl. a class of deities (9 in number) who have their seat on the neck of the Loka-purusha or who form his necklace, Jain.

Graívya, mfn. relating to the neck, AV. vi f.

ग्रैष्म *graíshma*, mf(*ī*, g. *utsâdi*)n. (fr. *grīshmá*) relating to or belonging to the summer, AV. xv, 4, 2; VS.; TS. v; ŚBr. iv &c.; produced by the hot season (as a disease), AV. v, 22, 13; sown in summer, Pāṇ. iv, 3, 46; (*ī*), f. = *grīshmī*, L.

Graishmaka, mfn. sown in summer, Pāṇ. iv, 3, 46; to be paid in summer (a debt), 49.

Graishmāyaṇa, m. patr. fr. *grīshma*, g. *aśvâdi*.

Graishmika, mfn. = *grīshmam adhīte veda vā*, g. *vasantâdi*; n. anything that grows in summer, VarBṛS. ix, 43; xl, 2. **–dhānya**, n. = *grīshma-dh°*, xl, 13.

ग्ल *gla*. See √*glai*.

Glap. See Caus. √*glai*, q. v.

Glapana, mfn. wearying, making tired, Bhpr.; n. relaxation, Suśr. i, 41, 4; fading, Ratnâv. iv, 14.

Glapita, mfn. exhausted, dissipated, heated, MBh. i, 7795; Ragh. xvi, 38; Kir. xiv, 65; Bhaṭṭ.; = *hṛita*, R. vii, 7, 47.

ग्लप्स *glapsa*. See *grathna*.

ग्लस् *glas* (= √*gras*), cl. 1. Ā. °*sate*, to eat, Dhātup. xvi, 30.

Glasta, mfn. = *grasta*, eaten, L.

ग्लह् *glah*, cl. 1. Ā. °*hate* (Cond. P. *aglahishyat*, MBh. ii, 2397), to gamble, play with any one (instr.) at dice for (acc.), win by gambling, MBh. ii, vii f.; = √*grah*, to take, receive, Dhātup. xvi, 49.

Gláha, m. (√*grah*, Pāṇ. iii, 3, 70) cast of the dice, game at dice, AV. iv, 38, 1 f.; Yājñ. ii, 199; MBh. ii (*glahaṃ* √*div*, to play at dice for [instr.], 2179), v; the stake in playing at dice, MBh. ii f.; Hariv. 6735 ff.; BhP. vi, x; a die, MBh. viii, 3763; a dice-box, ii, 1968; contention, bet, iii, 10652; Daś. vii, 135; the prize or object fought for in a contest, person aimed at, MBh. vi, vii f.; Bālar. v, 1; a chess-man, W.; (*ā*), f.?, AV. vi, 22, 3; (cf. *aksha-*).

Gláhana, n. playing at dice, AV. vii, 109, 5.

ग्ला *glā*. See √*glai*.

Glātṛi, *glāná*, °*ni*, &c. See ib.

ग्लुच् *gluc* (= √*gruc*), cl. 1. P. *glocati* (aor. *aglucat* or *aglocīt*, Pāṇ. iii, 1, 58), to steal, rob, Bhaṭṭ. xv, 30; to go, move, Dhātup. (v. l.); (cf. √*gluñc*.)

Glucuka, m., 'N. of a man,' see °*kāyani*.

Glucukāyani, m. patr. fr. °*ka*, Kāś. on Pāṇ. iv, 1, 160 & 3, 99; cf. *glaucukāyana*.

ग्लुञ्च् *gluñc*, cl. 1. P. °*cati* (aor. *aglucat* or *agluñcīt*, iii, 1, 58; in derivatives *k* for *c*, vii, 3, 59, Siddh.), to go, move, Dhātup. vii, 21; (cf. √*gluc*.)

ग्लुन्थ *gluntha*, m. See *madhu-*.

ग्लेप् *glep*, cl. 1. Ā. °*pate*, to be poor or miserable, x, 5 & 8; to shake, tremble, ib.; to move, ib.

Glepana, n. a meaning of √*mad*, xix, 54.

ग्लेय *gleya*. See √*glai*.

ग्लेव् *glev*, cl. 1. Ā. °*vate*, to serve, worship, xiv, 32; (cf. √*gev, khev, sev*.)

ग्लेष् *glesh*, cl. 1. Ā. °*shate*, to seek, investigate, xvi, 13 (v. l.); (cf. √*gesh, gav-esh*.)

ग्लै *glai*, cl. 1. P. *glāyati* (ep. also Ā. °*te*; cl. 2. P. *glāti*, MBh. iii, 13730; xiii, 7365; perf. *jaglau*, Pāṇ. vii, 4, 60, Kāś.; 2. *jaglitha* & °*glātha*, Vop. viii, 83; Ā. *jagle*, Pāṇ. vi, 1, 45, Pat. & Kāś.; aor. *aglāsīt*, Bhaṭṭ.; Subj. 2. sg. *glāsis*, MBh. iii, 1210; Prec. *glāyāt*, *gley°*, *glāsīshta*, Pāṇ. vi, 4, 68, Kāś.), to feel aversion or dislike, be averse or reluctant or unwilling or disinclined to do anything (dat. [ŚBr. ii, iii, ix; KātyŚr.; Lāṭy.] or instr. [MBh. iii, 1210] or abl. [14541] or inf. [Pāṇ. iii, 4, 65]); to be languid or weary, feel tired, be exhausted, fade away, faint, MBh.; Śāntiś.; Bhaṭṭ.; to be hard upon any one (acc.), MBh. iii, 13730: Caus. *glapayati* (*-glāp°*, see *ava-, pra-, vi-*; ep. also Ā. °*te*, xiii, 4694; aor. 2. sg. *ajiglapas*, Bhaṭṭ. xv, 18), to exhaust, tire, be hard upon, injure, cause to faint or perish, MBh.; Śak. iii, 14; Vikr.; VarBṛS.; Sāh.; (with *manas*) to make desponding, MBh. iii, v; (irreg. Pot. *glapet*) to become cast down or desponding, 1650.

Gla, mfn. ifc. See *su-gla*.

Glā, *ās*, f. = *glāni*, Gal.

Glātṛi, mfn. one who feels tired, W.

Glāná, mfn. feeling aversion or dislike, ŚBr. i, 2, 5, 8; wearied, languid, exhausted, emaciated, MBh.; R. iii, 39, 30; Śak. iii, 7 (v. l.); torpid, Bādar. ii, 2, 29, Sch.; sick, L.; n. exhaustion, MBh. xiii, 3519; VarBṛS. lxxviii, 12; sickness, Buddh. **–pratyaya**, m. a requisite for sick persons, Divyâv. xii. **–manas**, mfn. one whose mind feels aversion or dislike, MBh. xv, 132.

Glāni, f. (Pāṇ. iii, 3, 95, Vārtt. 4) exhaustion, fatigue of the body, lassitude, languor, depression of mind, debility, Mn. i, 53; MBh. &c.; sickness, Suśr.; decrease, MBh. xii, 4750; Bhag. iv, 7.

Glānīya, mfn. to be felt tired, Pāṇ. vi, 1, 45, Pat.

Glānya, n. decrease of strength, SaddhP. iv.

Glāpita, mfn. emaciated, Ratnâv. ii, 12.

Glāyaka, mfn. ifc., *anna-*, diminishing one's food successively (a particular form of austerity), Jain.

Glāva, m. 'displeased,' N. of a man with the metron. Maitreya, TāṇḍyaBr. xxv, 15, 3; ShaḍvBr. i, 4; GopBr. i, 1, 31; ChUp. iii, 12.

Glāvín, mfn. displeased, inactive, VS. xxx, 17.

Glāsnu, mfn. exhausted by fatigue or disease, languid, Pāṇ. iii, 2, 139; Car. iii, 1, 3; v, 8, 16.

Gleya, mfn. to be wearied or exhausted, W.

ग्लौ *glau*, *aus*, m. (√*glai*, Uṇ.) a round lump, wen-like excrescence, AV. vi, 83, 3; the moon, L.; camphor, W.; the earth, L.; (*āvas*), m. pl. lumps or parts of flesh of the sacrificial victim (certain arteries or vessels of the heart, Sch.), VS. xxv, 8 = MaitrS. iii, 15, 7; AitBr. i, 25. **–√as**, to become (like) the moon, Uṇ. ii, 65, Sch. **–√kṛi**, to transform into the moon, ib. **–√bhū**, = *-√as*, ib.

ग्लौचुकायन *glaucukāyana*, m. patr. fr. *glucukāyani*, Pāṇ. iv, 1, 90, Vārtt. 4, Pat.; m. pl. the pupils of Glaucukāyana, ib.

Glaucukāyanaka, mfn. belonging to Glucukāyani, 3, 126, Kāś.; worshipping Gluc°, 99, Kāś.

ग्व *gva*, ifc. See *atithi-gvá, éta-, dáśa-, náva-*.

Gvin, ifc. See *śata-gvin*.

घ GHA.

घ 1. *gha*, the 4th consonant of the Sanskrit alphabet (aspirate of the preceding). **—kāra**, m. the letter or sound *gha*.

घ 2. *gha*, ind. (used to lay stress on a word) at least, surely, verily, indeed, especially (= Gk. γε), RV.; AV. v, 13, 10 & 11; vi, 1, 3. In the Saṃhitā the final vowel is generally lengthened (*ghā*, cf. Pāṇ. vi, 3, 133); as a rule it is preceded by other particles (*utá, utó, utá vā, cid, ná, vā*) or by a pronoun or a preposition; it is also found between *iva* and *íd*, or between *iva* and *íd aha*, or between *vā* and *íd*; sometimes it occurs in the clause which depends on a conditional or relative sentence (e. g. *ā́ ghā gamad yádi śrávat*, 'he will surely come when he hears,' RV. i, 30, 8), i, 161, 8; viii, 46, 4.

घ 3. *gha*, mfn. (√*han*) ifc. 'striking, killing,' cf. *jīva-, tāḍa-, pāṇi-, rāja-*, &c. (cf. also *parigha*); (*ā*), f. a stroke, L.

घ 4. *gha*, m. a rattling or gurgling or tinkling sound, L.; a bell, L.; (*ā*), f. a tinkling ornament worn by women round the waist.

घंष् *ghaṇsh* (& *ghaṇs*), cl. 1. Ā. °*shate* (& °*sate*), to diffuse lustre or splendour, Dhātup. xvi, 50; to flow, stream, ib.

घंस् *ghaṇs*. See *ghaṇsh*.

घग्घ् *ghaggh* (& *ghagh*), cl. 1. P. °*gghati* (& °*ghati*), to laugh, v, 53; (cf. √*kakh*.)

घघ् *ghagh*. See √*ghaggh*.

घट् *ghaṭ*, cl. 1. Ā. °*ṭate* (exceptionally P. °*ti*, MBh. iii, 14703; Vet. ii, $\frac{8}{10}$; *jaghaṭe*, *ghaṭishyate* [Naish.], *aghaṭishṭa*, Bhaṭṭ.), to be intently occupied about, be busy with, strive or endeavour after, exert one's self for (loc., dat., acc. [MBh. iii, 14703], *prati, -artham* & *arthe*; inf., Pāṇ. iii, 4, 65; Bhaṭṭ.); to reach, come to (loc.), Vet. ii, $\frac{8}{10}$; to fall to the share of (loc.), Naish. x, 47; to take effect, answer, Kathās. cxxiv; Rājat. vi, 361; to happen, take place, be possible, suit, BhP.; Hcar.; Śiś. ix, 4; Ratnâv.; Naish.; Sarvad. &c.; to be in connection or united with (instr.), Mālatīm. ii, 8; Daś. viii, 34; Rājat. iv, 617; (for √*ghaṭṭ*) to hurt with words, speak of malignantly, Hariv. ii, 1, 31: Caus. P. *ghaṭayati* (Pāṇ. vi, 4, 92; exceptionally Ā. °*te*, Rājat. iv, 543), to join together, connect, bring together, unite, Suśr.; Śiś. ix, 87; Naish. i, 46; Ratnâv.; to shut, Hcar. v, 253 (v. l.); to put or place or lay on (loc.), Gīt. v, vii, xii; to bring near, procure, Bhartṛ. iii, 18; Amar.; Kathās. xviii; Vet.; to effect, accomplish, produce, make, form, fashion, Mṛicch.; VarBṛ.; Pañcat. &c.; to do a service (acc.) to any one (gen.), Rājat. v, 543; to impel, Bhaṭṭ. x, 73; to exert one's self, MBh. iii, 14702, (for √*ghaṭṭ*, Caus.) to rub, graze, touch, move, agitate, iv, vi (C), vii, xii (5363, C): Caus. *ghāṭayati*, to hurt, injure, Dhātup. xxxiii, 49; to unite or put together, ib.; 'to speak' or 'to shine,' 93.

Ghaṭa, mfn. intently occupied or busy with (loc.), Pāṇ. v, 2, 35; = *ghaṭā yasyâsti*, g. *arśa-ādi*; m. a jar, pitcher, jug, large earthen water-jar, watering-pot, Mn. viii, xi; Yājñ. iii, 144; AmṛitUp.; MBh. &c.; the sign Aquarius, VarBṛS.; a measure = 1 Droṇa (or = 20 Droṇas, W.), Ashṭâṅg. v, 6, 28; ŚārṅgS. i, 28; the head, MBh. i, 155, 38, Sch.; a part of a column, VarBṛS. liii, 29; a peculiar form of a temple, lvi, 18 & 26; an elephant's frontal sinus, L.; a border, L.; (= *kumbhá*) suspending the breath as a religious exercise, L.; (along with *karpara*, cf. *-karpara*) N. of a thief, Kathās. lxiv, 43; (*ā*), f. (gaṇas *arśa-ādi, sidhmâdi* & *picchâdi*) effort, endeavour, L.; an assembly, L.; a number, collection, assemblage, BhP. iii, 17, 6; Kpr. vii, $\frac{11}{12}$; a troop (of elephants) assembled for martial purposes, Mālatīm. v, 19; VarBṛS. xliii; Śiś. i, 64; Kathās.; Rājat.; justification (°*ṭām* √*aṭ*, 'to have one's self justified by another'), Bhadrab. iv; (perhaps °*ṭa*, m.) a kind of drum; a sweet citron, L.; (*ī*), f. a water-jar, Prab. ii, $\frac{7}{8}$; (also °*ṭi*, q. v.; cf. °*ṭī-ghaṭa*) a period of time (= 24 minutes), Sch. on Yājñ. ii, 100-102 & on Sūryas. i, 25; the Gharī or Indian clock (plate of iron or mixed metal on which the hours are struck), L.; a particular procession, PSarv.; (cf. *dur-, bhadra-*.) **—kañcuki**, n. an immoral rite practised by Tāntrikas and Śāktas (in which the bodices of different women are placed in a receptacle and the men present at the ceremony are allowed to take them out one by one and then cohabit with the woman to whom each bodice belongs), Āgamapr. **—karkaṭa-tāla**, m. (in music) a kind of measure. **—karpara**, m., N. of the author of a highly artificial poem called after him (also author of the Nītisāra and mentioned as one of the 9 gems of king Vikramâditya's court); n. the fragments of a pot, Ghaṭ.; Pañcat.; N. of Ghaṭa-karpara's poem; *-kulaka-vṛitti*, f., N. of a Comm. on the preceding. **—kāra**, m. a potter, VarBṛS. xv, 1; Laghuj. ix, 7. **—kṛit**, m. id., VarBṛS. xvi, 29. **—graha**, m. a water-bearer, Pāṇ. iii, 2, 9, Vārtt. 1. **—ghātinī**, f. 'jar-destroyer,' a kind of bird, Gal. **—janman**, m. 'jar-born,' Droṇa, Gal. **—jānuka**, m. 'having pot-shaped knees,' N. of a Ṛishi, MBh. ii, 4, 13 (*vara-j*°, C). **—tantra**, n., N. of a Tantra. **—dāsī**, f. a bawd, L. **—puccha**, m. 'pot-tailed,' a kind of rice, Gal. **—prakshayaṇa**, m. 'jar-destroyer,' N. of a man, Kāṭh. xvii, 17. **—bhava**, m. 'jar-born,' Agastya, ŚāṅkhGṛ., Sch. **—bhedanaka**, an instrument used in making pots, Buddh. L. **—yoni**, m. = *-bhava*, BrahmaP. ii, 17. **—rāja**, m. a large water-jar, L. **—śodhana-kāraka**, n. 'cleaning the water-jar,' a collective N. for 6 actions of an ascetic (*dhautī, vastī, netī, trāṭaka, naulika* & *kapāla-bhātī*), Haṭhapr. ii, 23 f. **—śrotra**, m. 'pot-eared,' Kumbha-karṇa, RāmatUp. **—sṛiñjaya**, m. pl., N. of a people, MBh. vi, 371. **—sthāpana**, n. placing a water-pot as a type of Durgā (essential part of various Tāntrika ceremonies), Vratapr. **Ghaṭâṭopa**, m. a covering for a carriage or any article of furniture, W. **Ghaṭâbha**, m. 'resembling a pot,' N. of a Daitya, Hariv. 12698 (vv. ll. *kaṭ*° & *ghaṇṭ*°). **Ghaṭâbhidhā**, f. 'named after (i. e. resembling) a jar,' a round kind of gourd, L. **Ghaṭârgala-yantra**, n. a kind of diagram, Tantr. **Ghaṭâlābu**, f. = °*ṭâbhidhā*, L. **Ghaṭâvasthā**, f. (probably) = *ghaṭa*, suspending the breath as a religious austerity, Haṭhapr. iv, 35 f. **Ghaṭâhvayā**, f. = °*ṭâbhidhā*, Gal. **Ghaṭêśvara**, n., N. of a Liṅga. **Ghaṭôtkaca**, m., N. of a son of Bhīma-sena by the Rākshasī Hiḍimbā, MBh. i, iii; BhP. ix, 22, 29; N. of a Gupta king, Inscr.; °*cântaka*, 'slayer of Ghaṭôtkaca,' Karṇa, L. **Ghaṭôdara**, m. 'pot-bellied,' Gaṇeśa, Kathās. lv, 165; N. of one of Varuṇa's attendants, MBh. ii, 366; of a Rākshasa, R. vi, 84, 12; of a Daitya, Hariv. 12696. **Ghaṭôdbhava**, m. = °*ṭa-bh*°, L. **Ghaṭôdhnī**, (Uṇ. iv, 192) f. (a cow) having a full udder, Ragh. ii, 49.

Ghaṭaka, mfn. accomplishing, Bhartṛ. ii, 66; procuring, iii, 57, Sch.; ready, skilful, Divyâv. xxx, 143; forming a constituent part, Jaim. i, 1, 5, Sch.; m. a pot, jar, Kathās. lvii, 45; a genealogist, Kulad.; a match-maker, negotiator of matrimonial alliances, RTL. p. 377 (cf. *ghaṭa-dāsī*); a tree that produces fruits without apparent flowers, L.; (*ikā*), f. a water-jar, Mṛicch. x, 55 (59); Sāh. iii, $\frac{111}{112}$; (*ghāṭ*°) Pañcat.; a period of time (= 24 [or 48, W.] minutes), Sūryas.; BhP. v, 21, 4 & 10; HYog. iii, 63; Sch. on Jyot. (YV) 25 & 40 f.; Tantr.; (= *kalā*, KātyŚr. ii, 1, 1 & 17, Sch.); the Gharī or Indian clock (see °*ṭī*), Gol. xi, 8; (= *ghuṭ*°) the ancle, L.

Ghaṭana, n. (= °*ṭā*, L.) connection or union with (instr. or in comp.), Vikr. ii, 15 (v. l.); Kathās. xxiv, 231; (*ā*), f. exertion, motion, acting, manner of acting, VarBṛS. l, 1; Pañcat.; Kathās. cxxii, 33; striving after, being occupied or busy with (loc. or in comp.), Śāntiś. ii, 20 (= Nāg. iv, 2); Sāh. iv, $\frac{14}{v}$ (*ishu-*, 'shooting an arrow'); taking effect, answering, accomplishment, (°*nām* √*yā*, 'to take effect, succeed,' Rājat. iv, 365; °*nām* √*nī*, to effect, accomplish, Siṇhâs.); connection, union with (in comp.), Sāh. iii, $\frac{222}{223}$; (= °*ṭa*) a troop (of elephants), L.; a literary composition, viii, 7; a work consisting of (in comp.), Vcar. vi, 33; (*am*), n. or (*ā*), f. procuring, finding, Kathās. cxviii, 197; making, effecting, forming, fashioning, bringing about, Dhūrtas. i, 7; Kathās. cxxiii, 140; HYog. iii, 102.

Ghaṭayitavya, mfn. to be shut (a hole), Pañcat.

Ghaṭāla, mfn. fr. °*ṭā*, g. *sidhmâdi*; (cf. *ghāṭ*°.)

1. Ghaṭi, f. = °*ṭī*, q. v., Uṇ. iv, 117, Sch. **—ṃ-dhama**, m. 'pot-blower,' a potter, Pāṇ. iii, 2, 29, Pat. **—ṃ-dhaya**, mfn. one who drinks a pitcherful, ib. **—yantra**, see °*ṭī-y*°.

2. Ghaṭi, in comp. for °*ṭin*. **—ghaṭa**, m., N. of Śiva, Hariv. 14884; (cf. *ghaṭin*.)

Ghaṭika, mfn. = *ghaṭena tarat*, Pāṇ. iv, 4, 7, Kāś.; m. a waterman, W.; n. the hip, posteriors, L.; (*ā*), f., see °*ṭaka*. **—lagna**, n. ?, Tantr.

Ghaṭikā, f. of °*ṭaka*, q. v. **—maṇḍala**, n. the equatorial circle, Āryabh. iv, 19, Sch. **—yantra**, n. = °*ṭī-y*°, Pañcat. iv, 1, $\frac{8}{9}$ (v. l. *ghāṭ*°). **—lavaṇa**, n. a kind of salt, Npr.

Ghaṭita, mfn. planned, devised, attempted, W.; happened, occurred, W.; connected with, involving (ifc.), Jaim. i, 1, 5, Sch.; shut, Hcar. v, 96; produced, effected by, made, made of (in comp.), Pañcat. &c. **—tva**, n. connection with, involving (ifc.), Jaim. i, 3, 32, Sch.

Ghaṭin, m. 'having a water-jar,' the sign Aquarius, Horāś.; N. of Śiva, MBh. xii, 10419.

Ghaṭila, mfn. fr. °*ṭā*, g. *picchâdi*.

Ghaṭī, f. of °*ṭa*, q. v. **—kara**, m. = *-kāra*, Divyâv. **—kāra**, m. = °*ṭa-k*°, Vop. xxv, 45; (*ī*), f. a potter's wife, ib. **—graha**, m. = °*ṭa-gr*°, Pāṇ. iii, 2, 9, Vārtt. 1. **—ghaṭa**, in comp. & ifc. smaller and larger pots, Hariv. 3415; MārkP. viii, 205. **—māla**, m. 'series of Ghaṭīs,' a period of about 3 hours, Gal. **—yantra**, n. the buckets of a well or any machine for raising water, MārkP. (once metrically °*ṭi-y*°); Vcar. viii, 33; Kuval. 46; (cf. *ara-ghaṭṭa*); a kind of machine to indicate the time with the help of water, Sarvad. xv, 314; Gol. xi, 8, Sch.; diarrhœa, Bhpr. vii, 16, 24. **—yantraka**, n. a small machine for raising water, Kād. v, 841.

Ghaṭīkā, f. = °*ṭikā* (24 minutes), Kālanirṇ.

घट्ट् *ghaṭṭ*, cl. 1. Ā. °*ṭṭate*, see *vi-, sam-*: cl. 10. P. °*ṭṭayati*, to rub (the hands) over, touch, shake, cause to move, Hariv. 6473; Suśr.; Kāvyâd. iii, 110; to stir round, Suśr. iv, 14, 8; to have a bad effect or influence on (acc.), Car. viii, 7, 28; (cf. √*ghaṭ*) to hurt with words, speak of malignantly, MBh. vi, 2894 (B); xii, 5363 (B); Hariv. 3210 (pr. p. °*ṭṭayāna*).

Ghaṭṭa, m. a Ghaṭ, quay or landing-place, bathing-place, steps by a river-side &c., ferry, L. (cf. RTL. p. 435 & 518 f.); (*ā*), f. a kind of metre; (*ī*), f. a small or inferior landing-place, W.; (cf. *ara-*.) **—kuṭī-prabhātāyita**, n. 'acting like the dawn in a hut near a landing-place,' forcing an entrance, Sarvad. xiii, 123. **—gā**, f., N. of a river, L. **—jīvin**, m. 'living on a landing-place,' a ferryman (commonly Pāṭuni, son of a washerman by a Vaiśya woman; 'an attendant at a landing-place, taking care of the clothes of the bathers &c.,' W.)

Ghaṭṭânanda, m., N. of a metre.

Ghaṭṭana, n. pushing, touching, rubbing or striking together, Hariv. 14581; Ragh. xi, 71; Kathās. lxxii, 42; stirring round, MārkP. xii, 38; (*ā*), f. (? for *ghaṭanā*) going, moving, practice, business, means of living, Pāṇ. iii, 3, 107, Vārtt. 1.

Ghaṭṭita, mfn. rubbed, touched, shaken, MBh. vii; Hariv.; R. &c.; pressed down, smoothed, MBh. xiv, 2521; (for *ghaṭita*) shut, Divyâv. ii, 92 & 95; (*ā*), f. a particular way of beating a drum.

Ghaṭṭitṛi, mfn. (for *ghaṭitṛi*) fut. p. one who is about to exert himself or to take great pains, MBh. v, 5890.

घण् *ghaṇ*, cl. 8. P. Ā., v. l. for √*ghṛiṇ*.

घण्ट् *ghaṇṭ*, cl. 1. & 10. P. °*ṭati* & °*ṭayati*, 'to speak' or 'to shine,' Dhātup. xxxiii, 94.

घण्ट *ghaṇṭa*, m. (for *hantra*?) N. of Śiva, MBh. xii, 10377 & 10419; Hariv. 14884; (cf. *ghaṭin*); a kind of dish (sort of sauce, vegetables made into a pulp and mixed with turmeric and mustard seeds and capsicums; cf. *matsya-*), W.; N. of a Dānava, Kathās. cxxi, 229; (*ā*), f. a bell, MBh.; R. &c. (ifc. f. *ā*, MBh. xiv; R. vi); a plate of iron or mixed metal struck as a clock, W. (cf. *ghaṭī*); Bignonia suaveolens, L.; Lida cordifolia or rhombifolia, L.; Uraria lagopodioides, L.; Achyranthes aspera, L.; (*ī*), f., see *kshudra-, mahā-*; N. of Durgā, MBh. iv, 188.

Ghaṇṭā, f. of °*ṭa*, q. v. **—karṇa**, m. 'bell-eared,' N. of an attendant of Skanda, ix, 2526; of an attendant of Śiva (supposed to preside over cutaneous complaints, and worshipped for exemption from them in the month Caitra, Tithyâd.), Hariv. 14849; ŚivaP.; of a Piśāca attendant on Kubera, Hariv. 14630; of a Rākshasa, Hit. ii, 5, $\frac{8}{9}$; (*ī*), f., N. of a goddess, Hcat.; °*rṇêśvara*, n., N. of a Liṅga, SkandaP. **—tāḍa**, mfn. one who strikes a bell, Mn. x, 33. **—tāḍana**, n. striking a bell, W. **—nāda**, m. the sound of a bell, W. **—patha**, m. 'bell-road,' the chief road through a village highway, L.; N. of Malli-nātha's Comm. on Kir.; *-tva*, n. the being known to all the world, Sarvad. xi. **—pāṭali**, m. Bignonia suaveolens, L.; Schreberia Swietenoides, L. **—bīja**, n. the seed of Croton Jamalgota, L. **—°bha** (°*ṭābh*°), v.l. for *ghaṭābha*. **—maṇḍapa**, m. 'bell-vestibule,' N. of one of the 3 vestibules in the Tinnevelly Śaiva temple, RTL. p. 447. **—mukha**, m. 'bell-faced,' N. of a mythical being, Bālar. iv, 19. **—mudrā**, f. a particular way of intertwining fingers (practised in the Pañcāyatana ceremony before ringing a bell), RTL. p. 414. **—rava**, m. the sound of a bell, Pañcat.; (in music) N. of a Rāga; (*ā*), f. Crotolaria of various species, Car. i, 1,77, Sch. **—rāva**, m. = *-rava*, Hit. **—°li** (°*ṭāl*°), f. a series of bells, Kathās. ci, 301; N. of several cucurbitaceous plants, L. **—vat**, mfn. furnished with a bell or with bells, MBh. iv, 2185; BhP. viii, 11, 30. **—vādya**, n. the sound of a clock, W. **—śabda**, m. = *-rava*, W.; 'sounding like a bell,' bell-metal, brass, L.; *-pāṇi*, mfn. having a bell in his hand (an executioner), Divyâv. xxviii, 29. **—svana**, m. = *-rava*, W. **Ghaṇṭêśvara**, m., N. of a son of Maṅgala or Mars by Medhā, BrahmavP. **Ghaṇṭôdara**, v.l. for *ghaṭôd*°.

Ghaṇṭaka, m. Bignonia suaveolens, L.; (*ikā*), f. a small bell, Uṇ. iv, 18, Sch.; (cf. *kshudra-*); the uvula, L.

Ghaṇṭāka, m. = °*ṇṭaka*, L.

Ghaṇṭi, in comp. for °*ṭin*. **—koṇa**, m. a kind of weapon, Gal.

Ghaṇṭika, m. the alligator, Bhpr. v, 10, 39; (*ā*), f., see °*ṭaka*.

Ghaṇṭin, mfn. furnished with a bell, MBh. iv, 6, 10; (said of Śiva) xii, 10377 & 10419.

Ghaṇṭinī-bīja, n. = °*ṇṭā-b*°, L.

Ghaṇṭu, m. a string of bells tied on an elephant's chest as an ornament, L.; heat, L.; (cf. *ni-gh*°.)

घण्ड *ghaṇḍa*, m. a bee (cf. *ghuṇḍa*), L.

घतन *ghatana*. See *ghāt*°.

घन *ghaná*, mf(*ā́*)n. (√*han*) a striker, killer, destroyer, RV. i, 4, 8; iii, 49, 1; iv, 38, 1; viii, 96, 18; compact, solid, material, hard, firm, dense, i, 8, 3 (*ghanā́* for °*nám ā́*); Suśr. &c.; coarse, gross; viscid, thick, inspissated, Suś.; Bhartṛ.; Kathās. xxiv, 93; full of (in comp.), densely filled with (in comp.), MBh. i, xiii; Ragh. viii, 90; Ratnâv. iv, 2; uninterrupted, Pañcat. iii, 14, 11; dark (cf. *-śyāma*), BhP. iv, 5, 3; deep (as sound; colour), MBh. i, 6680; VarBṛS. xliii, 19; complete, all, Kathās. iv, 53; auspicious, fortunate, W.; m. (= φόνος) slaying, RV. vi, 26, 8; an iron club, mace, weapon shaped like a hammer, i, 33, 4; 36, 16; 63, 5; ix, 97, 16; AV. x, 4, 9; any compact mass or substance (generally ifc.), ŚBr. xiv &c. (said of the fœtus in the 2nd month, Nir. xiv, 6; Laghuj. iii, 4); ifc. mere, nothing but (e.g. *vijñāna-ghaná*, 'nothing but intuition,' ŚBr. xiv), MāṇḍUp. 5; PraśnUp. v, 5; BhP. viii f.; (cf. *ambu-*, *ayo-*); a collection, multitude, mass, quantity, W.; vulgar people, Subh.; a cloud, MBh. &c. (ifc. f. *ā*, Hariv. 2660); talc, L.; the bulbous root of Cyperus Hexastachys communis, Suśr. vi; a peculiar form of a temple, Hcat. ii, 1, 389; a particular method of reciting the RV. and Yajur-veda (cf. RTL. p. 409); the cube (of a number), solid body (in geom.), Laghuj.; Sūryas.; phlegm (*kapha*), L.; the body, L.; extension, diffusion, W.; n. any brazen or metallic instrument or plate which is struck (cymbal, bell, gong, &c.), Hariv. 8688; iron, L.; tin, L.; a mode of dancing (neither quick nor slow), L.; darkness, L.; (*am*), ind. closely, Ratnâv. iii, 9; (√*dhvan*, to sound) deep, Rājat. v, 377; very much, W.; (*ā*), f., N. of a stringed instrument; Glycine debilis, L.; a kind of creeper, L. **—kapīvat**, v.l. for *vana-k*°. **—kapha**, m. 'cloud-phlegm,' hail, L. **—kāla**, m. 'cloud-season,' rainy season, Sāh. iv, 2/17. **—kshama**, mfn. what may be hammered, Bhpr. v, 26, 53. **—garjita**, n. the roar of thunder, deep loud roar, W. **—golaka**, m. an alloy of gold and silver, L. **—ghana**, m. the cube of a cube, W.; °*ndugha*, m. a gathering of dark clouds, W. **—caya**, m. a collection of clouds, W. **—cchada**, mfn. involved in clouds, W.; m. 'thick-leaved,' Flacourtia cataphracta, L.; Pinus Webbiana, L.; a kind of Moringa, Npr. **—ja**, 'cloud-born,' talc, Kālac. **—jambāla**, m. a quantity of mire, slough, L. **—jvālā**, f. 'cloud-light,' lightning, L. **—tā**, f. compactness, Śiś. ix, 64; the condition of a cloud, Kuval. 262. **—tāla**, for *-tola*, q.v. **—timira**, n. the darkness of clouds, W.; great darkness, W. **—toya**, n. a particular sea having thick water (enveloping the earth with its atmosphere), BṛĀrUp., Sch. **—tola**, m. 'friend (?) of clouds,' the bird Cātaka, L. **—tva**, n. compactness, firmness, thickness, solidity, VarBṛS. lv, 25. **—tvac**, m. 'thick-barked,' a kind of Lodhra tree, L. **—druma**, m. Asteracantha longifolia, L. **—dhātu**, m. 'inspissated element of the body,' lymph, L. **—dhvani**, mfn. deep-sounding, roaring, W.; m. a deep sound, W.; the muttering of thunder clouds, W. **—nābhi**, m. 'being in the interior of clouds,' smoke (supposed to be a principal ingredient of clouds), L. **—nīhāra**, m. thick hoar-frost or mist, W. **—pattra**, m. 'thick-leaved,' Bœrhavia procumbens, L. **—pada**, n. the cube root, W. **—padavī**, f. 'cloud-path,' the sky, Kir. v, 34. **—payodhara**, m. a firm breast, W. **—pallava**, m. 'thick-twigged,' Guilandina Moringa. **—pāshaṇḍa**, m. 'cloud-heretic,' a peacock (delighting in cloudy weather), L. **—priyā**, f. 'fond of clouds or rain,' N. of a plant, L. **—phala**, m. 'thick-fruited,' Asteracantha longifolia, L.; n. the solid or cubical contents of a body. **—bhitti**, mfn. furnished with thick walls, Car. i, 17. **—mud**, mfn. highly pleased, Caurap. **—mūla**, m. 'thick-rooted,' the plant Moraṭa, L.; n. (in arithm.) cube root. **—rava**, m. 'the roaring of clouds,' W.; 'crying after the clouds,' = *-tola*, L. **—rasa**, m. n. 'thick juice,' extract, decoction, L.; camphor, L.; 'thick-sapped,' the plant Moraṭa, L.; the plant Pīlu-parṇī, L.; m. n. 'cloud-fluid,' water, L. **—ruc**, mfn. shining like a cloud, cloud-like, BhP. iv, 5, 3. **—rucira-kalāpa**, mfn. having a tail glistening like a cloud (a peacock), W. **—rūpā**, f. 'compact in shape,' candied sugar, Npr. **—vara**, n. 'best part of the body,' the face, L. **—vartman**, n. = *-padavī*, Kir. v, 17. **—vallikā**, f. 'cloud-creeper,' lightning, L. **—vallī**, f. id., L.; the plant Amṛitasavā, L. **—vāc**, m. 'coarse-voiced,' a raven, Gal. **—vāta**, m. a thick oppressive atmosphere (enveloping the hells), Jain. **—vāri**, n. rain-water. **—vāsa**, m. 'having a thick (garment, i.e.) shell,' a kind of pumpkin-gourd, L. **—vāhana**, m. 'riding on clouds,' Śiva, L.; Indra (cf. *megha-v*°), W. **—vīthi**, f. = *-padavī*, Śiś. ix, 32; a line of clouds, W. **—vyapâya**, m. 'disappearance of the clouds,' autumn, Ragh. iii, 37. **—vyūha**, m., N. of a Buddh. Sūtra. **—śabda**, m. 'cloud-noise,' thunder, W. **—śṛiṅgī**, f. Odina pinnata, Npr. **—śyāma**, m. 'dark like a cloud (cf. Pāṇ. ii, 1, 55, Kāś.),' Kṛishṇa, VP. v, 18, 39; Rāma, Mahān.; N. of a copyist (of the last century). **—saṃvṛitti**, f. profound secresy, W. **—samaya**, m. = *-kāla*, Bhartṛ. iii, 37. **—sāra**, mfn. 'firm,' see °*ra-bhāva*; m. camphor, Suśr.; Dhūrtas. ii, 9; Kpr. viii, 2/3; (= *-rasa*) water, L.; 'thick-sapped,' a kind of tree, L.; = *dakshiṇâvarta-pārada* ('mercury or some peculiar form of it,' W.), L.; *-bhāva*, m. firmness, Naish. vii, 25. **—siktha**, a kind of gruel, Gal. **—skandha**, m. 'having a solid trunk,' Mangifera sylvatica, L. **—svana**, m. = *-śabda*, W.; Amaranthus polygamus, L. **—hasta-saṃkhyā**, f. (in geom.) the contents of an excavation or of a solid alike in figure, W. **Ghanâkara**, m. 'multitude of clouds,' the rainy season, L. **Ghanâgama**, m. the approach of clouds, rainy season, Ṛitus. ii, 1; Kathās. **Ghanâjñāna**, n. gross ignorance, W. **Ghanâñjanī**, f. 'cloud-unguent (?),' N. of Durgā, L. **Ghanâtyaya**, m. = *-vyapâya*, Car. i, 6, 42; Suśr.; Bālar. v, 29. **Ghanânta**, m. id., 41. **Ghanâmaya**, m. the date tree, L. **Ghanâmala**, m. Chenopodium album, L. **Ghanâmbu**, n. = °*na-vāri*, W. **Ghanârava**, m. (= °*na-r*°) the bird Cātaka, Gal. **Ghanârāva**, m. id., L. **Ghanâruṇa**, mfn. deep red, W. **Ghanâruddha**, mfn. overspread with clouds, W. **Ghanâvaruddha**, mfn. id., W. **Ghanâśraya**, m. 'cloud-abode,' the atmosphere, L. **Ghanâsaha**, mfn. what may not be hammered, Bhpr. v, 26, 54. **Ghanâsthika**, mf(*ā*)n. having a thick bone (a nose particularly formed), Vishṇ.; Yājñ. iii, 89. **Ghanêtara**, mfn. 'opposed to solid,' liquid, L. **Ghanêśvarī**, f., N. of a creeper, Gal. **Ghanôttama**, n. = °*na-vara*, L. **Ghanôttara**, n. id., Gal. **Ghanôda**, n. = °*na-toya*, BṛĀrUp. iii, 3, 2, Sch.; TĀr. i, 22, 8, Sāy. **Ghanôdadhi**, m. a particular sea formed of dense water (enveloping the Ghana-vāta), Jain. **Ghanôdaya**, m. 'approach of clouds,' the beginning of the rainy season, Subh. **Ghanôparuddha**, mfn. = °*nâvar*°, W. **Ghanôpala**, m. 'cloud-stones,' hail, L. **Ghanôru**, f. (a woman) having thick thighs, Veṇis. ii, 20. **Ghanâugha**, m. a gathering of clouds, Kalyāṇam. 32.

Ghanāghaná, mfn. (Pāṇ. vi, 1, 12, Vārtt. 7) fond of slaughter, easily striking down, fond of strife, RV. x, 103, 1 (Indra); MBh. viii, 697 (said of an elephant); compact, thick (a cloud), Mālatīm. ix, 39; m. an elephant in rut, L.; N. of Indra, L.; a thick or rainy cloud, MBh. xii, 12405; Hariv. 4759; BhP.; Kathās.; Rājat.; mutual collision or contact, L.; (*ā*), f. Solanum indicum, L.

Ghanāya, Nom. Ā. °*yate*, to be found in great numbers, Uṇ. i, 108, Sch.

Ghanī, ind. in comp. **—**√**kṛi**, to harden, thicken, solidify, W.; to intensify, Daśar., Sch. **—kṛita**, mfn. hardened, compacted, made solid or firm, W.; thickened, Bhpr. **—bhāva**, m. the becoming hardened or compact or thick, W. **—bhūta**, mfn. become thick, thickened, condensed, thick, inspissated, compact, Hariv. 3484; R. iii, 5, 8; Suśr.

Ghanīya, Nom. P. °*yati*, to long for solid food, Āp. (KātyŚr. vii, 4, 28, Sch.)

घमघमारव *ghamaghamā-rava*, m. a rattling noise, Vāgbh. Alaṃkārat. ii.

घम्ब् *ghamb*, cl. 1. Ā. °*bate*, to go, move, Dhātup. xi, 35 (Vop.); (cf. √*gharb*.)

घर् *ghar*, cl. 10. P. See √2. *ghṛi*, Caus.

घरट्ट *gharaṭṭa*, m. a grindstone, Rājat. vii, 1244; 1303 & 1589; Subh.

Gharaṭṭaka, m. id., HPariś. ii; (*ikā*), f. id., L.

घरणी *gharaṇī*, f., v. l. for °*riṇī*.

Ghariṇī, f. (for *gṛihiṇī*?, Pāli °*raṇī*) a woman possessing a house (?, widow?), Divyâv. ii, 428. **—stūpa**, m., N. of a Buddh. tope, 446.

घर्घट *gharghaṭa*, m. the fish Pimelodus Gagora (*gargara*), L.

घर्घर *gharghara*, mfn. (onomat.) uttered with an indistinct gurgling or purring sound, Kathās. xxv, 66; sounding like gurgling, Rājat. ii, 99; (in music applied to a particular note); m. an indistinct murmur, crackling (of fire), rattling (of a carriage), creaking, L.; laughter, mirth, L.; a duck ('an owl,' BR.), L.; a fire of chaff, L.; a curtain, L.; a door, L.; the post round which the rope of a churning stick is wound, Gal.; a particular form of a temple, Hcat. ii, 1, 390; the river Gogra, L.; (*ā*), f. a bell hanging on the neck of a horse, L.; (*ī*), f. a girdle of small bells or tinkling ornaments worn by women, Bhojapr. 215; (*ā* or *ī*), f. a kind of lute or cymbal. **—dhvani**, m. panting, puffing, Kād. ii, 205; iii, 624.

Ghargharaka, m. the river Gogra, L.; (*ikā*), f. id., L.; a bell used as an ornament, Kād. i, 69; an ornament of small bells, W.; a short stick for striking several kinds of musical instruments, L.; a kind of musical instrument, iii, 744; fried grain, L.

Ghargharā, f. of °*ra*, q.v. **—rava**, m. the sound of small bells, W.

Ghargharita, n. grunting, BhP. iii, 13, 25.

Gharghārya, n. a small bell, Gal.

घर्घुर्घा *gharghurghā*, f. = *ghurghura*, L.

घर्ब् *gharb*, cl. 1. P. °*bati*, to go, Dhātup. xi, 32 (Vop.); (cf. √*ghamb*.)

घर्म *gharmá*, m. (√2. *ghṛi*) heat, warmth (of the sun or of fire), sunshine, RV.; AV. &c.; the hot season, R. i, 63, 24; Ragh. xvi, 43; VarBṛS.; internal heat, R. ii, 75, 45 (v.l.); perspiration, L.; day (opposed to night), Jyot. (YV) 9; a cauldron, boiler, esp. the vessel in which the milk-offering to the Aśvins is boiled, RV.; AV. vii; VS. viii, 61; AitBr. i; ŚBr. xiv; Lāṭy.; a cavity in the earth shaped like a cauldron (from which Atri was rescued by the Aśvins; 'heat,' Gmn.), RV.; hot milk or any other hot beverage offered as an oblation (esp. to the Aśvins), RV.; AV. iv, 1, 2; VS. xxxviii; ŚBr. iv, xiv; KātyŚr.; ĀśvŚr.; N. of Tāpasa (author of RV. x, 114); of Saurya (author of 181, 3); of a son of Anu (father of Ghṛita), Hariv. 1840 (v.l.); [cf. θερμός, θέρμη; Lat. *formus*; Zd. *garĕma*; Goth. *varmya*; Germ. *warm*.] **—kāla**, m. the hot season, Kathās. vc, 12. **—ga**, m. id., R. vi, 54, 20; (cf. *ushṇa-ga*.) **—carcikā**, f. eruptions caused by heat and suppressed perspiration, Prayog. **—ccheda**, m. cessation of the heat, Vikr. iv, 13. **—jala**, n. 'heat-water,' perspiration, Kāvyâd. ii, 73. **—tanu**, °**nū**, f., N. of 2 Sāmans, AitBr. i, 21, 2; ĀrshBr.;

(°*rmasya tanvau*) KātyŚr. & Lāṭy. **— tapta,** mfn. perspiring, W. **— toya,** n. = *-jala,* Śiś. xvii, 2 (ifc. f. *ā*). **— tvá,** n. the condition of a cauldron, TĀr. v, 1, 5. **— da,** mf(*ā*)n. causing heat. **— dīdhiti,** m. 'having warm rays,' the sun, Ragh. xi, 64. **— dú-gha,** mf(*ā*)n. giving warm milk or the substance used for the Gharma offering, AV. iv, 22, 4; ŚBr. iv, xiv; ĀśvŚr.; KātyŚr. **— dúh,** *-dhúk,* mfn. id., TBr. ii; Nir. xi; KātyŚr. **— dyuti,** m. = *-dīdhiti,* Kir. v, 41. **— payas,** n. = *-jala,* Śiś. ix, 35; warm water, W. **— pāvan,** mfn. drinking hot milk, VS. xxxviii, 15. **— bindu,** m. a drop of perspiration. **— bhānu,** m. = *-dīdhiti,* Śiś. xi f. **— māsa,** m. a month of the hot season, Hariv. 3545. **— raśmi,** m. = *-dīdhiti,* heat, radiance, W. **— rocana,** n. with *sarpasya,* N. of a Sāman, ĀrshBr. **— vat** (°*rmá-*), mfn. possessed of heat (Indra), TS. ii, 2, 7, 2. **— vā-ri,** n. = *-jala,* Śiś. xiii, 45. **— vicarcikā,** f. = *-carc°,* Prayog. **— śiras,** n. 'head of the Gharma oblation,' N. of some initial verses of TBr. i, 1, 7, ĀśvŚr. v, 11 f. **— sád,** mfn. (said of the manes) sitting near the fire or living in the heat (of the sky), RV. x, 15, 9 f. **— sûkta,** n. 'cauldron-hymn,' N. of AV. vii, 73, Vait. **— stúbh,** mfn. shouting in the heat (the Maruts), RV. v, 54, 1. **— svaras** (°*rmá-*), mfn. sounding like the contents of a boiler (said of rivers), iv, 55, 6. **— sveda** (°*rmá-*), mfn. perspiring with heat, x, 67, 7. **Gharmâṅśu,** m. = °*rma-dīdhiti,* MBh. vii; Suśr.; Śak. v, 14; Mālatīm. i, $\frac{18}{1}$. **Ghar-mânta,** m. the end of the hot season, beginning of the rainy season, Hariv. 10130; R. iii; Megh.*; *-kāmukī,* f. 'desirous of the beginning of the rainy season,' a kind of crane, L. **Gharmâmbu,** n. = °*rma-jala,* Suśr. vi, 17, 53. **Gharmâmbhas,** n. id., Śak. i, 29; Kāvyâd.; Mālatīm. **Gharmârta,** mfn. suffering from heat, W. **Gharmêtarâṅśu,** m. 'having other than warm (i. e. cold) rays,' the moon, Prasannar. i, 7. **Gharmêshṭakā,** f. a kind of sacrificial brick, ĀpŚr. **Gharmôcchishṭa,** n. N. of a sacrificial ceremony, Baudh. i, 13, 30. **Ghar-môdaka,** n. = °*rma-jala,* Śak. i, 29, Sch.

Gharmita, mfn. suffering from heat, Bālar. i, 62.

Gharmín, mfn. engaged in preparing the Gharma offering, RV. vii, 103, 8.

Gharmya, n. a vessel in which the Gharma offering is prepared, KātyŚr. xxv f. **Gharmye-shṭhā́,** mfn. = *harm°,* q. v., RV. x, 106, 5.

घर्मूटी *gharmūṭī,* v. l. for *garm°.*

घर्ष *gharsha,* °*rshaṇa,* &c. See √2. *ghṛish.*

घल *ghala,* n. = *ghola,* L.

घस *ghas,* not used in pr. (cl. 1. *ghasati,* Dhātup. xvii, 65), but supplies certain tenses (esp. aor. & Desid., Pāṇ. ii, 4, 37) of √*ad* (aor. 2. & 3. sg. *ághas,* RV.; *aghās* (?), AV. xx, 129, 16; 3. sg. *aghat, aghasat* [?, JaimBr.; Pāṇ. ii, 4, 37], *aji-ghasat* [MaitrS.]; 3. pl. *ákshan,* RV.; AV.; *aghasan,* Bhaṭṭ. [Pāṇ. ii, 4, 37]; 2. du. *ághastām;* 2. pl. *aghasta;* Subj. 2. sg. *ghásas,* 3. sg. °*sat,* RV.; 3. pl. *kshan,* x, 95, 15; Impv. 3. du. *ghástām;* pf. *jaghā́sa,* RV.; AV. &c.; 3. pl. *jakshur,* ŚBr. ii; Pot. *jakshīyā́t,* RV. x, 28, 1; p. *jakshivás,* AV.; VS.; f. °*kshúshī,* ŚBr. ii), to consume or devour, eat: Desid. *jíghatsati* (cf. Pāṇ. ii, 4, 37; vii, 4, 49, Kāś.), to wish to consume or devour, wish to eat, AV. v, 18, 1 & 19, 6; vi, 140, 1; ŚBr. i, 9, 2, 12; MBh. ii, 1485; (cf. √*jaksh.*)

Ghasa, m. 'devourer,' N. of a demon causing diseases, Hariv. 9558; of a Rākshasa, R. v, 12, 12; flesh, meat, Gal.; (cf. *ud-.*)

Ghasana, n. devouring, Dhātup. xxviii, 88.

Ghasi, m. food, VS. (Kāṇv.) ii, 24; (cf. *ghāsí.*)

Ghasmara, mf(*ā*)n. (Pāṇ. iii, 2, 160) voracious, MBh. viii, 1856; Car. i, 13, 48; Bhaṭṭ.; Bhām. (said of fire); ifc. desirous of, eager for, Daś. i, 32; Hcar. i; in the habit to forget (with gen.), HPariś. i, 221; m., N. of (a Brâhman changed into) an antelope, Hariv. 1210.

Ghasra, mfn. hurtful, L.; m., N. of Śiva, Gal.; a day (cf. *ghraṅsá*), Pārśvan. iv, 12; n. saffron, L.

Ghasvara, mfn. voracious, MantraBr. ii, 5, 1.

Ghāsá, m. (Pāṇ. ii, 4, 38; vi, 2, 144) food, meadow or pasture grass, AV. (*ghāsád ghāsám,* 'one bit after the other,' gradually, xviii, 2, 26); VS.; TS. vi; TBr. i; MBh. &c. **— kunda,** g. 2. *kumudâdi* (not in Kāś. & Gaṇar.) **— °kundika,** mfn. fr. °*nda,* ib. **— kūṭa,** n. a hay-rick, Rājat. iv, 312. **— sthāna,** n. pasture ground, L. **Ghāsé-ajra,** mfn. 'impelling to consume,' exciting appetite, VS. xxi, 43.

Ghāsaka. See *a-.*

Ghāsi, m. food, RV. i, 162, 14; 'voracious,' fire, L.

घाट *ghāṭa,* mfn. (√*ghaṭ*) 'working on,' see *danta-;* = *ghāṭā* (or °*ṭe*) *yasyâsti* (or °*sya stas*), g. *arśa-ādi* (not in Kāś.); n. management of an elephant, Gal.; m. for *ghaṭa* (a pot), Hariv. 16117 (C); the nape or back of the neck, cervical ligament, L.; (*ā*), f. id., Car. i, 17, 17; Suśr. vi, 25, 11; (cf. g. *arśa-ādi*); (cf. *kara-.*) **— karkarī,** f. = *ghāṭarī,* ŚāṅkhŚr. xvii, 3, 12.

Ghāṭaka, mfn. = °*ṭa,* see *danta-;* (*ikā*), f. for *ghaṭ°,* q. v.

Ghāṭarī, f. a kind of lute, 15 f.; (cf. *apaghāṭilā, avaghaṭarikā, āghāṭa.*) **Ghāṭala.** See °*ṭala.*

Ghāṭalikā, f. id., Sāy. on RV. x, 146, 2.

Ghāṭāla, mfn. having a neck or a part thinner than the rest, Suśr. ii, 9, 8 (°*ṭala,* Bhpr. vii, 58, 7); (cf. *ghaṭ°.*)

Ghāṭika, m. = *ghāṇṭ°,* q. v.; (*ikā*), f., see °*ṭaka.*

घाण्टिक *ghāṇṭika,* m. (fr. *ghaṇṭā*) a bell-ringer, strolling ballad-singer who carries a bell, bard who sings in chorus (esp. in honour of the gods) ringing a bell in presence of the images, MBh. xiii, 6028; VarBṛS. x, 6 & 12; (also *ghāṭika,* L., Sch.)

घात *ghāta,* mfn. (√*han,* Pāṇ. vii, 3, 32 & 54) ifc. 'killing,' see *amitra-, go-;* m. a blow, bruise, MBh.; R. &c.; slaying, killing, Mn. x, 48; Yājñ.; MBh. &c.; injuring, hurting, devastation, destruction, Yājñ. ii, 159; MBh. &c.; (see *grāma-* & *karma-*); (in astron.) entrance, Sūryapr.; AV. Pariś.; the product (of a sum in multiplication), Gaṇit. **— kara,** mf(*ī*)n. destructive, VarBṛS. **— kṛi-cchra,** n. a kind of urinary disease, ŚārṅgS. vii, 57. **— candra,** m. the moon when in an inauspicious mansion, W. **— tithi,** f. an inauspicious lunar day, W. **— nakshatra,** n. an inauspicious Nakshatra, W. **— vāra,** m. an inauspicious day of the week, W. **— sthāna,** n. a place of execution, Nāg. iv, $\frac{16}{17}$; a slaughter-house, W.

Ghātaka, mf(*ī,* Vet. i, $\frac{18}{19}$; *ikā*)n. killing, killer, murderer, Mn. v, 51; MBh. &c.; destroying, ruining, iii, 1277; (see *viśvāsa-*); mf(*ī*)n. made of the Ghātaka (= Vadhaka) wood, ĀśvŚr. ix, 7, 8.

Ghātana, mfn. killing, Uṇ. v, 42 (also *ghaṭ°*); m., N. of an inhabitant of a hell, L.; n. slaying, killing, slaughter, immolating, MBh. ii, 1558; Kathās. xx, 214; Devīm.; (*ī*), f. a kind of club, Hariv. 2655 & 12537; R. vi, 37, 54; (cf. °*tinī*); (cf. *kravya-*). **— sthāna,** n. a slaughter-house, L.

Ghātaya, Nom. P. °*yati* (rarely Ā. °*yate*), = Caus. √*han,* q. v.

1. **Ghāti,** f. a blow, wound, L.; catching or killing birds, fowling, L.; a bird-net, Uṇ. iv, 124.

2. **Ghāti,** in comp. for °*tin.* **— tva,** n. ifc. execution, Vishṇ. xvi, 11. **— pakshin,** m. 'murderous bird,' an owl or a hawk, L. **— vihaga,** m. id., L.

Ghātin, mfn. (Pāṇ. iii, 2, 51 & 86) ifc. killing, murderous, murderer, Mn. viii, 89; Yājñ.; MBh. &c.; destroying, ruining, destructive, iii, 63; R. iii, v; (*ī*), f. = °*tanī,* Uṇ. iv, 124, Sch.; (cf. *andha-ka-, amitra-, ardhaka-, ātma-,* &c.)

Ghā́tuka, mfn. (Pāṇ. iii, 2, 154) slaying, killing, AV. xii, 4, 7; TBr. ii, 1, 1, 3; ŚBr. xiii, 2, 9, 6; TāṇḍyaBr.; hurtful, mischievous, cruel, L.

Ghātya, mfn. (Pāṇ. iii, 1, 97, Vārtt. 2) to be killed, Pañcat. iii, 14, $\frac{2}{3}$; to be destroyed, Kathās. lxxii, 273.

घान्य *ghānya,* n. (fr. *ghaná*) compactness, Dhātup. xxviii, 88 (Vop.)

घार *ghāra,* m. (√1. *ghṛi*) sprinkling, besprinkling, L.; (*ī*), f. a metre of 4 × 4 syllables.

Ghārtika, m. (fr. *ghṛitá*) pulse ground and fried with clarified butter, Pañcat. v, 5, $\frac{1}{2}$.

Ghārteya, v. l. for *vārt°.*

घास *ghāsá,* °*saka,* °*sí.* See √*ghas.*

घिण्ण *ghiṇṇ* (fr. Prākrit √*geṇh, giṇh* = *grah*), cl. 1. Ā. °*ṇṇate,* to take, grasp, Dhātup. xii, 1; (cf. √*ghuṇṇ, ghṛiṇṇ.*)

घु 1. *ghu,* cl. 1. Ā. *ghavate,* to utter or produce a peculiar sound, xxii, 55.

2. **Ghu,** m. a kind of sound, L. **— ghu,** id., only in comp.; *-krit,* m. 'making the sound *ghu-ghu,*' a pigeon, Npr.

Ghuka, m. fire, Gal.

Ghughulā-rava, m. = *ghu-ghu-krit,* L.

Ghuṭ-kāra, m. (= *ghūt-k°*) shrieking (of owls), Uttarar. ii, 28.

घुट् *ghuṭ,* cl. 6. P. °*ṭati,* to strike again, resist, oppose, Dhātup. xxviii, 91; to protect, 77 (v. l.): cl. 1. Ā. *ghoṭate,* to turn ('to barter, exchange,' W.), xviii, 6; (cf. *ava-ghoṭita* & *vy-ā-* √*ghuṭ.*)

घुट *ghuṭa,* m. the ancle, L.; (*ī*), f. id., L.

Ghuṭi, f. id., L.

Ghuṭika, m. id., L.; (*ā*), f. id., L.; (= *khaṭ°*) chalk, Siṇhâs. xx, $\frac{8}{3}$.

Ghuṇṭa, m. = *ghuṭa,* L.

Ghuṇṭaka, m. id., L.; (*ikā*), f. id., Bhpr. ii, 99.

घुट्टि *ghuṭṭi,* ?, Vīrac. iii.

घुड् *ghuḍ* (= √*ghuṭ*), cl. 6. P. °*ḍati,* to prevent, defend, protect, Dhātup. xxviii, 77 & 91 (v. l.)

घुण् *ghuṇ,* cl. 6. P. °*ṇati,* to go or move about, 48: cl. 1. Ā. *ghoṇate,* id., xii, 4; (cf. √*ghūrṇ, ghol.*)

Ghuṇa, m. a kind of insect found in timber (= *vajra-kīṭa*), ShaḍvBr.; Suśr.; Pañcat. **— kīṭaka,** m. id., MārkP. xv, 31. **— kshata,** mfn. worm-eaten (as wood) so as to exhibit the form of a letter, Śiś. iii, 58. **— jarjara,** mfn. worm-eaten, Bālar. i, 51. **— pri-yā,** f. 'dear to the Ghuṇa insect,' a kind of Ipomœa, Bhpr. v, 3, 197. **— vallabhā,** f. 'dear to the Ghuṇa insect,' Aconitum heterophyllum, 1, 213. **Ghu-ṇâkshara,** n. an incision in wood (or in the leaf of a book) caused by an insect and resembling somewhat the form of a letter, Ratnâv. ii, $\frac{1}{1}\frac{1}{2}$ (Prākṛit *ghuṇ'akkhara*); Rājat. iv, 167; *-nyāya,* m. fortuitous and unexpected manner, happy chance, Pañcat. i, 4, $\frac{4}{4}\frac{1}{2}$; Daś. v, 36; Prasannar. i, $\frac{2}{2}\frac{8}{9}$; *-vat,* ind. by a happy chance, Ratnâv.; Śiś. iii, 58, Sch.

Ghúṇi, mfn. worm-eaten (?; = *bhrānta,* Sāy.), ŚBr. xi, 4, 2, 14.

घुण्ट *ghuṇṭa,* °*ṭaka.* See *ghuṭa.*

घुण्टिक *ghuṇṭika,* n. cow-dung found in thickets, L.; (*ā*), f., see °*ṭaka.*

घुण्ड *ghuṇḍa,* m. = *ghaṇḍa,* Uṇ. i, 114.

घुण्ण् *ghuṇṇ,* cl. 1. Ā. °*ṇṇate,* = √*ghiṇṇ,* Dhātup. xii, 2.

घुत्कार *ghut-kāra.* See *ghu.*

घुम् *ghum,* ind., g. *câdi.*

घुमघुमा *ghumaghumā,* ind. (onomat.) only in comp. **— kāra,** m. 'uttering a particular sound,' a kind of cricket, Npr. **— rava,** m. id., ib.

Ghumaghumāya, Nom. Ā. °*yate,* to hum, Kir. vi, 4, Sch.; (cf. *gumagumāyita.*)

घुर् *ghur,* cl. 6. P. °*rati* (aor. *aghorīt;* pf. 3. pl. *jughurur;* Ā. *jughure*), to cry frightfully, frighten with cries, Bhaṭṭ. xiv f.; (cf. *ghorá.*)

Ghuraghurā, ind. (onomat.) only in comp. **— ghosha,** v. l. for °*rughur°.* **— rāva,** m. cries (of monkeys), HPariś. ii, 732.

Ghuraghurāya, Nom. Ā. °*yate,* to utter gurgling sounds, wheeze, puff, snort, Car.; Suśr. i, 28, 14; Kād. iii, 571; BhP. iii, 30, 17.

Ghuraṇa, m. a particular sound, Uṇ. ii, 83.

Ghurikā, f. snorting, Gal.

Ghurughurā, ind. = *ghuragh°.* **— ghora-nir-ghosha,** m. great noise (produced by panting or puffing), Bālar. ii, 59. **— ghosha,** m. id., $\frac{5}{6}\frac{8}{0}$ (in Prākṛit); viii, 27.

Ghurghura, m. a kind of worm burrowing in the skin (Dracunculus), L.; (*ā*), f. growling (of a dog or cat), W.; (*ī*), f. = *ghumaghumā-kāra,* L. **— tā,** f. = °*raka,* Bhpr. vii, 40, 3.

Ghurghuraka, m. a gurgling or murmuring sound, Suśr. v, 4; (*ikā*), f. id., vi, 51, 6; = °*rī,* L.

Ghurghurāya, Nom. Ā. °*yate,* to whistle (said of a wound), i, 28, 14.

Ghurghuruka, m. = °*raka,* Car. v, 10, 14.

घुलघुलारव *ghulaghulā-rava* = *ghugh°,* L.

घुलञ्च *ghulañca,* m. Coix barbata, L.

घुस्मेश *ghusmêśa,* N. of a Liṅga, ŚivaP.

घुष् 1. ghush, cl. 1. P. ghoshati (rarely Ā. °te, R. v, 56, 139; Subj. ghóshāt; pf. jughosha, JaimBr.; 3. pl. jughushur, Pāṇ. vii, 2, 23, Kāś.; aor. Ā. ghóshi), Ā. to sound, RV. iv, 4, 8; P. to cry or proclaim aloud, call out, announce publicly, declare, i, 139, 8; MBh. xiii, xiv; R. &c.: Caus. ghoshayati (subj. 2. sg. °sháyas), to call to, invite, RV. ix, 108, 3; to cause to proclaim aloud, MBh. i, iii; to proclaim aloud, MBh.; R. &c.

Ghusha, mfn. 'sounding;' see araṃ-ghushá.

Ghushita, mfn. sounded, declared, proclaimed, W.; (cf. Pāṇ. vii, 2, 23, Kāś.)

1. **Ghushṭa**, mfn. sounded, proclaimed, L.; filled with cries, Hariv. 1125. **Ghushṭânna**, n. food given away by proclamation, Mn. iv, 209; (cf. ava- & saṃ-gushṭa.)

Ghushṭra, n. 'creaker (?),' a carriage, W.

Ghushya, mfn. to be proclaimed aloud (Śiva), MBh. xii, 10386; (cf. ghora-).

Ghósha, m. indistinct noise, tumult, confused cries of a multitude, battle-cry, cries of victory, cries of woe or distress, any cry or sound, roar of animals, RV.; AV. &c.; the sound of a drum, of a conch-shell, of the Soma stones, of a carriage, &c., RV.; AV. &c.; the whizzing or whir of a bow-string [TBr. ii], crackling of fire [MBh. ix, 1334], singing in the ear [ŚBr. xiv]; the roaring of a storm, of thunder, of water, &c., RV.; AV.; Suśr.; Megh.; the sound of the recital of prayers, MBh.; R.; Mṛicch. x, 12; the sound of words spoken at a distance, ŚBr. ix; rumour, report (also personified, KātyŚr., Sch.), RV. x, 33, 1; a proclamation, SaddhP. iv; a sound (of speech), ChUp.; Suśr.; the soft sound heard in the articulation of the sonant consonants (g, gh, j, jh, ḍ, ḍh, d, dh, b, bh, ṅ, ñ, ṇ, n, m, y, r, l, v, h), the vowels, and Anusvāra which with the Yamas of the first 10 of the soft consonants make up altogether 40 sounds (cf. a-gh°), RPrāt. xiii, 5 f.; APrāt., Sch.; Pāṇ. i, 1, 9, Sch.; an ornament that makes a tinkling sound, BhP. x, 8, 22; a station of herdsmen, MBh.; Hariv.; R. &c. (ifc., cf. Pāṇ vi, 2, 85); (pl.) the inhabitants of a station of herdsmen, MBh. iv, 1152; a particular form of a temple, Hcat. ii, 1, 389; a musquito, L.; Luffa fœtida or a similar plant, L.; N. of Śiva, MBh. xii, 10386; N. of a man (Sāy.), RV. i, 120, 5; of an Asura, Kāṭh. xxv, 8; of a prince of the Kāṇva dynasty, BhP. xii, 1, 16; of a son of Daksha's daughter Lambā, Hariv. 148 & 12480; of an Arhat, Buddh.; a common N. for a Kāya-stha or one of the writer caste, W.; m. pl. (g. dhūmâdi) N. of a people or country, VarBṛS. xiv, 2; m. n. brass, bell-metal, L.; (ā), f. Anethum Sowa, L.; = karkaṭa-śṛiṅgī, L.; N. of a daughter of Kakshīvat, RV. i, 117, 7; 122, 5 (? Impv. √ghush); x, 40, 5; (cf. ātma-, indra-, uccair-, &c.) **–kṛit**, m. any one making a noise, ŚāṅkhŚr. xvii. **–koṭi**, f. N. of the peak of a mountain (?). **–buddha** (ghósh°), mfn. made attentive by the sound, AV. v, 20, 5. **–mati**, m. N. of a man, SaddhP. i. **–yātrā**, f. walk or procession to the stations of the herdsmen, MBh.; -parvan, n. N. of iii, chapters 235–257. **–vat**, mfn. sounding, making a noise, Āp. i, 11, 8; MBh.; R. v; BhP. ii; sonant, uttered with the soft articulation called Ghosha, RPrāt.; ChUp.; ĀśvGṛ.; Gobh.; PārGṛ. i, 17, 2; Pāṇ. Sch.; m. N. of a man, Buddh.; (atī), f. a peculiar kind of lute, Kathās. xi f., cxi. **–varṇa**, m. a sonant letter, W. **–vasu**, m. N. of a prince of the Kāṇva dynasty, VP. iv, 24, 10. **–vṛiddha**, m. an elder at a station of herdsmen, Ragh. i, 45. **–sthalī**, f. N. of a locality, g. dhūmâdi (not in Gaṇap.) **Ghoshâdi**, a Gaṇa of Pāṇ. (vi, 2, 85). **Ghoshâdí**, see go-shādí.

Ghoshaka, m. ifc. a crier, proclaimer (e. g. paṭaha-, q. v.); the creeping plant Luffa fœtida or a similar plant, L. **Ghoshakâkṛiti**, m. 'resembling the Ghoshaka plant,' N. of a plant (with white blossoms), L.

Ghoshaṇa, mfn. sounding, BhP. iv, 5, 6; n. proclaiming aloud, public announcement, R. v, 58, 18; Hit. (v. l.); (ifc., Ragh. xii, 72); (ā), f. id., Mṛicch. x, 12 & 25; Pañcat.; Daś.; Kathās.

Ghoshaṇīya, mfn. to be proclaimed aloud, RV. vi, 5, 6, Sāy.

Ghoshayitnu, m. a crier, proclaimer, herald, L.; a Brāhman, L.; the Koïl or Indian cuckoo, L.

Ghoshātakī, f. the plant Śveta-ghoshā, L.

Ghóshi, mfn. sounding aloud, RV. vi, 5, 6; (see also s. v. √1. ghush.)

Ghoshín, mfn. sounding, noisy, AV.; ĀśvGṛ.; MBh.; Hariv.; (in Gr.) sonant, having the soft sound called Ghosha, RPrāt.; (iṇyas), f. pl. N. of certain evil spirits (cf. AV. xi, 2, 31), ĀśvGṛ. iv, 8, 27 f.; ŚāṅkhGṛ. iii, 9, 1; (cf. grāma-ghoshín.)

Ghoshila, m. a hog, Npr.; N. of one of king Udayana's 3 ministers, Divyâv. xxxvi; xxxvii, 577 f.

Ghoshṭṛi, mfn. a proclaimer, AitĀr. iii, 2, 4, 19. **–tva**, n. the state of a proclaimer, ib., Sch.

घुष् 2. ghush, cl. 1. P. ghoshati, to kill, L.

2. **Ghushṭa**, mfn. (= ghṛishṭa) rubbed, Bhaṭṭ. v, 57.

घुसृण ghusṛiṇa, n. saffron, Naish. viii, 80; Vcar. xi, 1.

घूक ghūka, m. an owl, Pañcad. i, 42; Subh.

Ghūkâri, m. 'owl-enemy,' a crow, L. **Ghūkâvāsa**, m. 'abode of owls,' Trophis aspera, L.

घूत्कार ghūt-kāra, m. = ghut-k°, Mālatīm. v, 19; Pañcad. i; panting or puffing, Bālar. viii, 27.

घूर् ghūr, cl. 4. Ā. °ryate, to hurt, injure, kill, Dhātup. xxvii, 46; to become old, decay, ib.

घूर्ण् ghūrṇ, cl. 1. P. Ā. °rṇati, °te (perf. jughūrṇe, Kathās. ciii), to move to and fro, shake, be agitated, roll about, MBh.; R. iv; Kathās.; Caurap.: Caus. °rṇayati, to cause to move to and fro or shake, Kum. iv, 12; Bhartṛ. i, 88; Mahān. (Pass. p. ghūrṇyamāna).

Ghūrṇa, mf(ā)n. moving to and fro, shaking, MBh. viii, 4712; BhP. vii, ix; Caurap.; turning round, whirling, rolling, W.; m. Erythraea centauroides, L. **–vāyu**, m. a whirlwind, W.

Ghūrṇana, n. moving to and fro, shaking, Naish. v, 126; Gīt. ix, 11; (ā), f. id., Sāh. iii, 151.

Ghūrṇāyamāna, mfn. moving to and fro, shaking, whirling, revolving, W.

Ghūrṇi, f. = °ṇana, Uṇ. iv, 52, Sch.

Ghūrṇikā, f., N. of a woman, MBh. i, 3302 ff.

घृ 1. ghṛi, cl. 3. P. jígharti (cl. 1. gharati, Dhātup. xxii, 40), to besprinkle, wet, moisten, RV. ii, 10, 4; Pāṇ. vii, 4, 78, Kāś.: Caus. (or cl. 10. P.) ghārayati, id., Dhātup. xxxii, 107.

1. **Ghṛitá**, mfn. sprinkled, L.; n. (g. ardharcâdi) ghee, i.e. clarified butter or butter which has been boiled gently and allowed to cool (it is used for culinary and religious purposes and is highly esteemed by the Hindūs), fat (as an emblem of fertility), fluid grease, cream, RV.; VS.; AV. &c.; (= udaka) fertilizing rain (considered as the fat which drops from heaven), water, Naigh. i, 12; Nir. vii, 24; m., N. of a son of Dharma (grandson of Anu and father of Duduha), Hariv. 1840; (ā), f. a kind of medicinal plant, L. **–kambala**, n. 'ghee and a mantle,' consecration of a king, VarBṛS. ii, 5/8. **–karañja**, m. a kind of Karañja tree, L. **–kīrti**, f. the mentioning of ghee, ŚBr. i, 4. **–kumārikā**, f. 'ghee-virgin,' Aloe indica (supposed to resemble a virgin in delicacy), Bhpr. v, 3, 282. **–kumārī**, f. id., L. **–kumbhá**, m. a jar of ghee, ŚBr. v; Mn. xi, 135; Cāṇ.; Subh.; Hit. **–kulyá**, f. a rivulet of ghee, ŚBr. xi. **–keśa** (°tá-), mfn. one whose hair is dripping with butter (Agni), RV. viii, 60, 2. **–kauśiká**, m. 'ghee-Kauśika (the Kauśika desirous of ghee),' N. of a religious teacher, ŚBr. xiv; m. pl. his family, Pravar. iv, 20. **–kshaudra-vat**, mfn. containing ghee and honey, Hcat. **–ghaṭa**, m. = -kumbha, Gaut. **–cyutā**, f. (cf. -ścút) N. of a river, BhP. v, 20, 16. **–tva**, n. the state or condition of ghee, Kapishṭh. **–dāna-paddhati**, f. N. of a work. **–dīdhiti**, m. 'having rays flowing with ghee,' fire, the deity of fire, L. **–dúh**, mfn. giving ghee, RV. ix, 89, 5. **–dhārā**, f. a stream of ghee, MBh. xiii, 26, 90; N. of a river, Hariv. 12411. **–dhenu**, f. ghee in the shape of a milch-cow, BhavP.; Hcat. **–nidhāyam**, ind. with ni-hita preserved like ghee, Pāṇ. iii, 4, 45, Kāś. **–nirṇij** (°tá-), mfn. having a garment of fat, covered with fat (Agni, the sacrifice), RV. **–pa**, mfn. drinking only ghee (a class of Ṛishis), MBh. xii, 6143. **–pakva**, mfn. boiled with ghee, Bhpr. v; (ā), f. a kind of cake, Gal. **–padī** (°tá-), f. (Iḍā) whose path (pada) is ghee or whose foot (pād) drops with ghee, RV. x, 70, 8; AV. vii, 27, 1; TS. ii; ŚBr. i; ĀśvŚr. i, 7. **–parṇa**, 'ghee-leaved,' = -karañja, Gal. **–parṇaka**, m. id., L. **–paśu**, m. ghee in the shape of a sacrificial animal, Mn. v, 37. **–pāka**, m. a kind of medicinal preparation made of ghee. **–pātra-stana-vatī**, f. (a cow) whose nipples are represented by vessels filled with ghee, Hcat. **–pávan**, mfn. (Pāṇ. vi, 4, 66, Vārtt. 1; iii, 2, 74, Kāś.) drinking ghee, AV. xiii, 1, 24; VS. vi, 19. **–pīta**, mfn. = pīta-ghṛita, one who has drunk ghee, g. āhitâgny-ādi. **–pū́**, mfn. clarifying ghee, RV. x, 17, 10. **–pūra**, m. a sweet-meat (composed of flour, milk, cocoa-nut, and ghee), Suśr.; Pañcat. iii. **–pūrṇa**, m. 'full of ghee(-like sap),' Guilandina Bonducella, Bhpr. **–pūrṇaka**, m. id., L.; = -pūra, Hariv. 8445. **–prúc**, mfn. sprinkling unctuous and fertilizing fluid (heaven and earth), RV. vi, 70, 4. **–pṛishṭha** (°tá-), mf(ā)n. one whose back is brilliant with ghee (esp. Agni and his horses), RV.; AV.; m. (hence) the fire (agni), BhP. v; N. of a son of Priya-vrata by Barhishmatī (sovereign of Krauñca-dvīpa), ib. **–pratīka** (°tá-), mf(ā)n. one whose face is brilliant with ghee (Agni, Ushas), RV.; VS. xxxv, 17; AV. ii, 13, 1. **–prayas** (°tá-), mfn. relishing ghee, RV. iii, 43, 3. **–prasatta** (°tá-), mfn. propitiated with ghee (Agni), v, 15, 1. **–prâśa**, m. swallowing ghee, Mn. xi, 144. **–prâśana**, n. id., Gaut.; Mn. v, 144. **–prí**, mfn. enjoying ghee (as Agni), AV. xii, 1, 20; xviii, 4, 41. **–prush**, mfn. 'sprinkling ghee or fat,' bedewing with welfare and gifts, RV.; VS. xx, 46. **–pluta**, mfn. sprinkled with ghee, Yājñ. i, 235; MBh. xii, f.; BhP. iii, 16, 8. **–bhājana** (°tá-), mfn. fit for receiving ghee, ŚBr. vi, 6. **–bhṛishṭa**, mfn. fried in ghee, W. **–maṇḍa**, m. the scum of melted butter, fattiest part of grease, Car. viii, 6, 79; Suśr.; (ā), f. a Mimosa (the scum of its infusion resembling ghee), L.; °ṇḍôda, m. 'having water resembling the scum of melted butter,' N. of a lake on the Mandara mountain, R. iv, 44, 60. **–maṇḍalikā**, f. = -maṇḍā, L. **–madhu-maya**, mfn. consisting of ghee and honey, Sāh. **–maya**, mf(ī)n. made of ghee, Hcat. i, 7. **–m-inva**, mf(ā)n. melting ghee, MaitrS. ii, 13, 1, 12. **–yājyā**, f. the verse recited with the ghee oblation, AitBr. iii, 32. **–yoni** (°tá-), mfn. abiding or living in ghee (Agni, the sacrifice), RV. iii, 4, 2; v, 8, 6; VS. xxxv, 17; producing fertilizing rain or welfare (Mitra & Varuṇa, Vishṇu), RV. v, 68, 2; VS. v, 38. **–rauḍhīya**, m. pl. the Rauḍhīyas who are desirous of ghee (nickname of a school), Pāṇ. i, 1, 73, Vārtt. 6, Pat. **–lekhanī**, f. a ladle for ghee, L. **–lekhinī**, f. id., L., Sch. **–loli-kṛita**, mfn. mixed with or steeped in ghee, W. **–vat** (°tá-), mfn. abounding in fat, greasy, mixed or smeared with ghee, RV.; AV.; VS.; ŚBr. iii, xii; containing the word ghṛitá (a verse), i f.; (tī), f. N. of a river, MBh. vi, 9, 23; ind. like ghee, W. **–vatsa**, m. ghee in the shape of a calf, Hcat. i, 7, 134. **–vara**, m. = -pūra, L.; -dvīpa, m., N. of a Dvīpa (see ghṛitôda), Jain. **–vartani** (°tá-), mfn. (the chariot of the Aśvins) the tracks of whom are brilliant with ghee, RV. vii, 69, 1. **–varti**, f. a wick fed with grease, BhP. v, 11, 8. **–vikrayin**, m. a vendor of ghee, W. **–vṛiddha** (°tá-), mfn. delighted or nourished with ghee (Agni), AV. xiii, 1, 28. **–vrata**, mfn. living on ghee only, TāṇḍyaBr. xviii, 2, 5; Lāṭy. viii, 9. **–ścút**, mfn. sprinkling or distilling ghee, RV.; AV.; -(ścun)-nidhana, n. = -(ścyun)-n°. **–ścyút**, mfn. = -ścút, VS. xvii, 3; AV. (v. l.); TāṇḍyaBr. ix, 1; -(ścyun)-nidhana, n., N. of a Sāman, xiii. **–śrí**, mfn. mixed with ghee, brilliant with ghee, RV., mixing ghee, VS. xxviii, 9. **–sád**, mfn. abiding in ghee, ix, 2; TBr. i, 3. **–stuti**, f. 'praise of ghee,' N. of the hymn RV. iv, 58, RAnukr. **–stū́** or **–stó**, m. (only acc. pl. -stāvas) a drop of ghee, AV. xii, 2, 17. **–stoká**, m. id., ŚBr. i. **–°stomīya**, mfn. relating to °ma, i. e. to the praise of ghee, ŚāṅkhŚr. xv, 1, 32. **–°stomyá**, mfn. id. (said of certain verses), MaitrS. i, 6, 7. **–sthalā**, f. 'abiding in ghee,' N. of an Apsaras, Hariv. 12475; (cf. ṛitu-sth°, kratu-sth°.) **–sná**, mfn. dropping or sprinkling ghee, RV. iv, 6, 9; viii, 46, 28. **–1. -snú**, mfn. (√1. snu) id., i, 16, 2; iii, 6, 6. **–2. -snu** (°tá-), mfn. (fr. 2. snu) = -pṛishṭha (Nir. xii, 36), one whose surface is brilliant with ghee, RV. **–spriś**, mfn. touching ghee, Pāṇ. i, iii, vi, Kāś. **–hasta** (°tá-), mf(ā)n. having ghee in one's hand, RV. vii, 16, 8. **–hetu**, m. 'cause of ghee,' butter, Npr. **–homa**, m. a sacrificial offering of ghee, Gaut. xxii, 36. **–hrada** (°tá-), mf(ā)n. (a lake) having a basin consisting of ghee, AV. iv, 34, 6. **Ghṛitâkta**, mfn. anointed with ghee, Mn. ix, 60. **Ghṛitâcala**, m. ghee in the shape of a mountain, BhavP. **Ghṛitâci**, m. (derived fr. °cī) N. of a Ṛishi, ĀrshBr. **Ghṛitâcī**, f. (fr.

2. *añc*, Pāṇ. vi, 3, 95, Vārtt. 2, Pat.) abounding in ghee, filled with ghee, sprinkling ghee, shining with ghee, RV.; AV. ix, 1, 4; ĀśvGṛ. ii, 10, 6; (scil. *juhū́*) the sacrificial ladle (with which the ghee is taken up, poured out, &c.), RV; AV. xiii, 1, 27; 'dewy,' the night, AV. xix, 48, 6; Naigh. i, 7; 'shining like grease,' a kind of serpent, AV. x, 4, 24; N. of an Apsaras (loved by Bharad-vāja [MBh. i, 5103 ff.] or Vyāsa [xii, 12188 ff.] or by Viśvā-mitra [R. iv, 35, 7]; wife of Pramati and mother of Ruru [MBh. i, 871; xiii, 2004] or wife of Raudrâśva [Hariv. 1658; BhP. ix, 20, 5] or of Kuśa-nābha [R. i, 34, 11]); *-garbha-sambhavā*, f. large cardamoms, L. **Ghṛitâdi**, N. of a Gaṇa (Pāṇ. vi, 2, 42, Kāś.) **Ghṛitânushiktá**, mf(*ā*)n. sprinkled with ghee, TS. v. **Ghṛitânna**, mfn. one whose food is ghee (Mitra & Varuṇa, Agni), RV. vi, 67, 8 & vii, 3, 1. **Ghṛitânvakta**, mfn. = °*tákta*, MaitrS. i, 6, 7. **Ghṛitâbdhi**, m. a sea of ghee. **Ghṛitârcis**, m. 'brilliant with ghee,' fire, MBh. xiv, 1737; a form of the sun, Hcat. i, 7. **Ghṛitâvani**, f. 'the spot (on the sacrificial post) which is smeared with ghee,' L. **Ghṛitâ-vṛidh**, mfn. °*tá-vṛiddha* ('increasing the ghee,' Sāy.), RV. vi, 70, 4. **Ghṛitâsuti**, mfn. one to whom the ghee oblation belongs (Mitra & Varuṇa, Vishṇu, Indra & Vishṇu), i, 136, 1 & 156, 1; ii, 41, 6; vi, 69, 6. **Ghṛitâhavana**, mfn. id. (Agni), i, 12, 5 & 45, 5; viii, 74, 5. **Ghṛitâhuta**, mfn. one to whom ghee is offered (Agni), AV. iv, 23, 3; xiii, 1, 12 & 28. **Ghṛitâhuti**, f. the ghee oblation, ŚBr. ii, 2, 4, 4; ĀśvGṛ. iii, 3. **Ghṛitâhva**, m. 'called after (the sap resembling) ghee,' the resin of Pinus longifolia, L. **Ghṛitâhvaya**, m. id., L. **Ghṛitêshṭakā**, f. a kind of sacrificial brick, ĀpŚr. xvii, 5. **Ghṛitôda**, m. 'having ghee for water,' N. of the sea surrounding Kuśa-dvīpa (or Ghṛita-vara-dvīpa, Jain.), R. iv, 40, 49 ff.; BhP. v; VP. ii, 4, 45. **Ghṛitôdaṅka**, m. a leather vessel for holding ghee, W. **Ghṛitâudana**, n. (Pāṇ. ii, 1, 34, Sch.) rice sprinkled with ghee, ĀśvGṛ. i; ŚāṅkhGṛ. i, 27.

Ghṛitin, mfn. containing ghee, MBh. xiii, 1840.

Ghṛiteyu, m., N. of a son of Raudrâśva (cf. *ghṛitâcī*), VP. iv, 19 (vv. ll. *kṛiteyu*, *kṛikaṇeyu*.)

Ghṛitelī, f. a cock-roach, L.; (cf. *taila-pāyikā*.)

Ghṛitya, mfn. = °*tin*, TS. ii, 4, 5, 2; ŚBr. iii f.

घृ 2. *ghṛi*, cl. 3. P. *jigharti*, to shine, burn, Dhātup. xxv, 14: cl. 5. (or cl. 8. fr. √*ghṛiṇ*) P. Ā. *ghṛiṇoti*, °*ṇute* or *gharṇoti*, °*ṇute*, id., xxx, 7.

2. **Ghṛita**, mfn. (Pāṇ. vi, 4, 37, Kāś.) illumined, L.

घृङ् *ghṛiń*, ind. (onomat.) tinkle, Kāṭh. xxiv, 7; ŚBr. xiv; (*ghrā̆m*, TĀr. v, 1, 4.) **— karikra**, mfn. (√*kṛi*, Intens.) bleating, Kāṭh. xxiv, 7.

घृण् *ghṛiṇ*. See √2. *ghṛi*.

Ghṛiṇá, m. heat, ardour, sunshine, RV. i, 133, 6; vi, 15, 5; x, 37, 10; (*ā́*), Ved. instr. ind. through heat or sunshine, RV.; (*ā*), f. a warm feeling towards others, compassion, tenderness, MBh. iii, v; R.; Ragh.; BhP.; aversion, contempt (with loc.), Naish. i, 20; iii, 60; horror, disgust, Kād. vii, 199 & 236; Hcar. v, 186; a kind of cucumber, Gal.; (cf. *nir-*, *hriṇīyā*.) **Ghṛiṇârcis**, m. 'having hot rays,' fire, L.; (cf. *ghṛitârc*°.)

Ghṛiṇā, f. of °*ṇá*, q. v. **— cakshus**, mfn. looking with compassion, R. ii, 45, 19. **— vat**, mfn. disgusting, Sarasv. **— vāsa**, for *ghana-v*°, L.

Ghṛiṇālu, mfn. compassionate, BhP. iv, 22, 43.

1. **Ghṛiṇi**, m. = °*ṇá*, RV. ii, 33, 6 (*ghṛiṇīva* for °*ṇer-iva*); vi, 3, 7 (Ved. loc. °*ṇā*) & 16, 38; (?, AV. vii, 3, 1); ŚBr. iii; a ray of light, Ānand.; (Naigh. i, 9) day (opposed to night), Hariv. 3588; a flame, L.; the sun, W.; a wave, W.; water, W.; anger, passion (cf. *hriṇīyamāna*), Naigh. ii, 13; mfn. glowing, shining, i, 17; BhP. vii, 2, 7 (*śuddha-tejo-maya*); (cf. *ā́-*.) **Ghṛiṇi-vat**, mfn. glowing, shining, RV. x, 176, 3; m. a kind of animal, VS. xxiv, 39.

2. **Ghṛiṇi**, in comp. for °*ṇin*. **— tva**, n. compassion, MBh. iii, 1119; vi, 5690; contempt, disregard, censoriousness, Car.

Ghṛiṇita, mfn. pitied, W.; reproached, abused, L.

Ghṛiṇin, mfn. passionate, violent, Gaut.; tender-hearted, compassionate, MBh. iii-v; Suśr.; Pañcat.; Laghuj.; BhP.; censorious, abusive, MBh. v, 5813; Car. vi, 20; m., N. of a son of Devakī, BhP. x, 85, 51.

घृण्ण *ghṛiṇṇ*, cl. 1. Ā. °*ṇṇate*, = √*ghiṇṇ*, Dhātup. xii, 3.

घृत *ghṛitá*. See √1. & 2. *ghṛi*.

Ghṛitin, °**teyu**, °**telī**, **ghṛitya**. See √1. *ghṛi*.

घृष् 1. *ghṛish* = √*hṛish*, L.

Ghṛishu, mfn. lively, agile, mirthful, RV.

1. **Ghṛishvi**, mfn. id., RV. **— rādhas**, mfn. granting with joy, vii, 59, 5 (voc.)

घृष् 2. *ghṛish*, cl. 1. P. *gharshati* (ind. p. *ghṛishṭvā*; Pass. *ghṛishyate*), to rub, brush, polish, Suśr.; Pañcat.; Cāṇ.; Subh.; to grind, crush, pound, Pañcat.; Ā. to rub one's self, MBh. iii, 17228: Caus. *gharshayati*, to rub, grind, Daś. xi, 176.

Gharsha, m. rubbing, friction, R. ii, 54, 6; (cf. *danta-*.)

Gharshaka, mfn. one who rubs, polisher, W.

Gharshaṇa, n. rubbing, polishing, Subh.; grinding, pounding, Gīt. i, 6, Sch.; rubbing, embrocation, Suśr.; (*ī*), f. turmeric, L.; (cf. *kara-*.) **Gharshaṇâla**, m. (for °*laya*) a wooden roller for grinding, L.

Gharshaṇīya, mfn. to be rubbed or cleaned, W.

Gharshita, mfn. rubbed, brushed, ground, R. iii.

Gharshin, mfn. 'rubbing,' see *kara-*.

Ghṛishṭa, mfn. rubbed, ground, pounded, Suśr.; Pañcat.; rubbed so as to be sore, frayed, grazed, MBh. i, iii; Hariv. 12175; Mṛicch. i, 23; iii, 9; Suśr.; rubbed, embrocated, MBh. xiii; Suśr.; VarBṛS. lv, 30.

Ghṛishṭi, m. a hog (cf. *gṛishṭi*), L.; f. rubbing, grinding, pounding, L.; emulation, contest, L.; (= *gṛishṭi*) a variety of Dioscorea, L.; Clitoria ternatea, L. **— netra**, n. 'hog's eye (cf. *gavâksha*),' a hole in timber, Vāstuv.

Ghṛishṭhilā, f., N. of a plant akin to Hemionitis cordifolia, L.

2. **Ghṛishvi**, m. = °*shṭi*, a hog, Uṇ. iv, 56.

घेञ्चुलिका *gheñculikā*, f. Arum orixense (*krauñcâdana*), L.

Gheñculī, f. id., L.

घोङ्घ *ghoṅgha*, m. a kind of animal, Vāsav. 687, Sch.; intermediate space, W.

घोट *ghoṭa*, m. (cf. √*ghuṭ*) a horse, ĀpŚr. xv, 3, 12; the beard, Gal. **— gala**, m. 'horse-throat,' a kind of reed, Npr.

Ghoṭaka, m. a horse, Pañcat. v, 10, ⅛; Siṅhâs.; Uṇ., Sch.; (*ikā*), f. a mare, L.; Portulaca oleracea, Bhpr.; a shrub resembling the jujube, L. **— mukha**, m. 'horse-faced,' N. of a man, Pravar. iv, 15 (v. l. °*ṭam*°); (author of the Kanyā-samprayuktakâdhikaraṇa) Vātsyāy. i, iii; (*ī*), f., N. of a woman, Virac. x f.

Ghoṭakâri, m. 'enemy of horses,' a buffalo, Bhpr.

Ghoḍa (= *ghoṭa*?) only in comp. **Ghoḍâcolin**, m., N. of a man, Haṭhapr. i, 8. **Ghoḍêśvara-tīrtha**, n., N. of a Tīrtha, RevāKh. cclii.

घोणक *ghoṇaka*, m. = °*ṇasa*, Npr.

Ghoṇasa, m. a kind of serpent, L.

Ghonasa, m. id., W.; (cf. *go-n*°.)

घोणा *ghoṇā*, f. (= *ghrāṇā*; ifc. f. *ā*, g. *kroḍâdi*) the nose (also of a horse, MBh. vi, 3390), MBh.; Hariv. 12363; Mṛicch. ii, 1½; Suśr.; the beak (of an owl), MBh. x, 38; a kind of plant causing sneezing, Npr. **Ghoṇânta-bhedana**, m. 'having a snout that is divided at the end,' a hog, L.

Ghoṇikā, m. (scil. *hasta*) 'resembling a nose,' a particular position of the hand, PSarv.

Ghoṇin, m. 'large-snouted,' a hog, L.

घोण्टा *ghoṇṭā*, f. a kind of jujube, L.; the betel-nut tree, L. **— phala**, n. the betel-nut, Suśr. iv, 17, 32; Npr.; m. Uraria lagopodioides, L.

Ghoṇṭi, f. = °*ṇṭā*, L.

घोत्कार *ghot-kāra*, m. (= *ghūt-k*°) panting, puffing, NarasP.

घोनस *ghonasa*. See *ghoṇaka*.

घोर *ghorá*, mf(*ā́*)n. (cf. √*ghur*) venerable, awful, sublime (gods, the Aṅgiras, the Ṛishis), RV.; AV. ii, 34, 4; terrific, frightful, terrible, dreadful, violent, vehement (as pains, diseases, &c.), VS.; AV.; TS. ii; ŚBr. xii &c. (in comp., g. *kāshṭhâdi*); (*am*), ind. 'dreadfully,' very much, g. *kāshṭhâdi*; (*as*), m. 'the terrible,' Śiva, L. (cf. *-ghoratara*); N. of a son of Aṅgiras, ŚāṅkhBr. xxx, 6; ĀśvŚr. xii, 13, 1; ChUp.; MBh. xiii, 4148; (*ā*), f. the night, L.; N. of a cucurbitaceous plant, L.; (scil. *gati*) N. of one of the 7 stations of the planet Mercury, VarBṛS. vii, 8 & 11; (*ī*), f., N. of a female attendant of Durgā, W.; (*ám*), n. venerableness, VS. ii, 32; awfulness, horror, AV.; ŚBr. ix; Kauś.; BhP. iv, 8, 36; Gobh. ii, 3, Sch.; 'horrible action,' magic formulas or charms, RV. x, 34, 14; ĀśvŚr.; ŚāṅkhŚr.; R. i, 58, 8; a kind of mythical weapon, MBh. v, 3491; poison, L.; saffron, L. (cf. *dhīra* & *gaura*). **— ghushya**, n. 'sounding dreadfully,' brass, bell-metal, L. **— ghoratara**, mfn. (compar.) extremely terrific (Śiva), MBh. xii, 10375; Hcat. i, 11, 322. **— cakshas** (°*rá-*), mfn. of frightful appearance, RV. vii, 104, 2. **— °tara**, mfn. more terrible, very awful, W.; (cf. *-ghoratara*.) **— tā**, f. horribleness. **— tva**, n. id., MBh. iii, 13781. **— darśana**, mfn. = *-cakshas*, MBh.; R. i; m. an owl (cf. MBh. x, 38), L.; a hyena, L. **— pushpa**, v. l. for *-ghushya*. **— rāsana**, for *-vāśana*. **— rāsin**, for *-vāśin*. **— rūpa**, mfn. of a frightful appearance, Mn. viii, 121; n. a hideous appearance, W.; (*ā*), f., N. of a female attendant of Durgā, W. **— rūpin**, mfn. of a frightful appearance, hideous, W. **— varpas** (°*rá-*), mfn. id. (the Maruts), RV. i, 19, 5 & 64, 2. **— vāluka**, N. of a hell, MBh. xiii, 111, 93. **— vāśana**, m. 'crying hideously,' a jackal, L. **— vāśin**, m. id., L.; (*inī*), f. a female jackal, Gal. **— saṃsparśa**, mfn. terrible to the touch, AitBr. iii, 4, 6; (superl. °*tama*) ŚāṅkhBr. i, 1. **— saṃkāśa**, mfn. = *-rūpa*, R. i. **— svara**, mfn. of dreadful sound, W. **— hṛidaya**, m. 'of a pitiless heart,' a form of Īśvara, Sarvad. vii, 41. **Ghorâkāra**, mfn. = °*ra-rūpa*, Daś. iv, 106. **Ghorâkṛiti**, mfn. id., Hit. i, 7, ⅛. **Ghorâtighora**, mfn. = °*ra-ghoratara* (said of a hell), Subh. **Ghorâdhyāpaka**, m. a venerable or excellent teacher, Pāṇ. viii, 1, 67, Kāś. **Ghorâśaya**, mfn. having a cruel feeling towards (loc.), Mcar. iii, 43.

Ghoraka, m. pl., N. of a people, MBh. ii, 1870 (*ikā*), f. = *ghurikā*, Gal.

घोल् *ghol* (in Prākṛit for Caus. of √*ghuṇ* = *ghūrṇ*), cl. 10. P. °*layati*, to mix, stir together into a semi-fluid substance, Bhpr. v, 11, 124 & 143.

Ghola, n. buttermilk, Suśr. i, 45, 4, 3; (*ī*), f. purslain, L.; (cf. *araṇya-*, *kshudra-*, & *vana-gholī*.)

Gholi, °**likā**, f. = °*lī*, L.

घोष *ghósha*, °*shaka*, &c. See √1. *ghush*.

घोषद् *ghoshád*, 'money' or 'substance' (Sch.), v. l. for *go-shád*, q. v.

घोषयित्नु *ghoshayitnu*. See √1. *ghush*.

Ghoshātakī, °**shâdí**, **ghóshi**, °**shin**, &c. See ib.

घौर *ghaura*, m. patr. fr. Ghora, ĀśvŚr. xii, 13, 1; n. horribleness, W.

घौषक *ghaushaka*, mfn. relating to the Ghosha people or country, g. *dhūmâdi*.

Ghaushasthalaka, mfn. coming from Ghoshasthalī, ib. (not in Gaṇap.)

Ghausheya, m. metron. fr. *ghóshā* (N. of Suhastya), RAnukr.

घ्न *ghna*, mf(*ā*, MBh. xiii, 2397; Hariv. 9426; *ī*, f. of 2. *han*, q. v.)n. ifc. striking with, Mn. viii, 386; killing, killer, murderer, ix, 232; MBh.; R. iii; destroying, Mn. viii, 127; Yājñ. i, 138; R. i; BhP. iv; removing, Mn. vii, 218; Hariv. 9426; Suśr.; multiplied by, VarBṛS. li, 39; Sūryas. (f. *ī*); n. ifc. 'killing,' see *áhi-*, *parṇaya-ghná*; (cf. *artha-*, *arśo-*, *kāsa-*, *kula-*, *kushṭha-*, *kṛita-*, *kṛimi-*, *gara-*, *guru-*, *go-*, *jvara-*, *purusha-*, &c.)

Ghnát, mfn. pr. p. √*han*, q. v.

Ghnī, ifc. f. of 2. *han*; m. (?, *ahi-*), AV. x, 4, 7.

Ghnya. See *á-*; *ati-ghnyà*.

घ्रंस *ghráṇs*, m. the sun's heat, AV. vii, 18.

Ghraṇsá, m. id., RV. i, 116, 8; vii, 69, 4; Kauś. 48; sunshine, brightness, RV. v, 34, 3 & 44, 7.

घ्रा *ghrā*, irr. cl. 1. or 3. P. *jíghrati* (Pāṇ. vii, 3, 78; ep. also Ā. °*te* & cl. 2. P. *ghrāti*; aor. *aghrāt* or *aghrāsīt*, ii, 4, 78; Prec. *ghrāyāt* or *ghrey*°, vi, 4, 68; aor. Pass. 3. du. *aghrāsātām*, ii, 4, 78, Kāś.; irr. ind. p. *jighritvā*, Hariv. 7059), to smell, perceive odour, ŚBr. xiv; Mn. ii, 98; MBh.; Hariv.; R.; to perceive, BhP. i, 3, 36; to smell at, snuffle at, R.; VarBṛS. lxii, 1; Hit.; to kill, MBh. ix, 2940: Caus. P. *ghrāpayati* (aor. *ajighrapat* or °*ghrip*°, Pāṇ. vii, 4, 6), to cause any one (acc.) to smell at (acc.), Bhaṭṭ. xv, 109: Intens. *jeghrīyate*, Pāṇ. vii, 4, 31.

Ghrāṇa, mfn. (viii, 2, 56) smelled, L.; smelling (*ghrātṛi*), L.; m. n. smelling, perception of odour, ŚBr. xiv; Mn.; BhP.; smell, odour, ŚāṅkhGṛ. iv, 7; MBh. iii, 12844; n. the nose, ChUp. viii, 12, 4; MBh. &c. (ifc. f. *ā*, Kathās. lxi; Hcat.); (*ā*), f. the nose, VarBṛS. (of a bull, lxi, 15). **—cakshuś,** mfn. 'using the nose for eyes,' blind, MBh. viii, 3443. **—ja,** mfn. caused or produced by the nose, W. **—tarpaṇa,** mfn. pleasant to the nose, fragrant, Hariv. 3710; n. odour, perfume, R. ii, 94, 14; Rājat. v, 356. **—duḥkha-dā,** f. 'giving pain to the nose,' Artemisia sternutatoria, Bhpr. v, 3, 304. **—pāka,** m. the disease of the nose called *nāsā-p°*, Sāṃkhyak. 49, Sch. **—puṭaka,** (ifc. f. *ā*) nostril, MārkP. lxv, 22. **—bila,** n. the cavity of the nose, TPrāt. ii, 52, Sch. **—śravas,** m. 'renowned for his nose,' N. of one of Skanda's attendants, MBh. ix, 2559. **—skanda,** m. blowing one's nose, Rājat. v, 417. **Ghrāṇêndriya,** n. the organ or sense of smell, Jain.; Suśr.

Ghrātá, mfn. (Pāṇ. viii, 2, 56) smelled, VS. xx, 7; having smelled, MBh. vii, 5228 (ifc.); perceiving, witnessing, feeling, Rājat. ii, 22 (ifc.)

Ghrātavyà, n. 'to be smelled,' odour, ŚBr. xiv, 7, 1, 24 & 3, 17; PraśnUp. iv, 8; Bhartṛ. i, 7.

Ghrāti, f. smelling, perception of odour, BṛĀrUp. iv, 3; snuffling at, Mn. xi, 68; the nose, L.

Ghrātṛi, mfn. one who smells, ŚBr. xiv; MBh.

Ghreya, n. 'to be smelled,' what may be smelled, smell, odour, ii, xii, xiv; Suśr.; BhP. vii, 12, 28.

घ्राँ *ghrā̃m̐*, ind. See *ghrín*.

घ्राण *ghrāṇa, ghrātá*, &c. See √*ghrā*.

ङ ṄA.

ङ 1. *ṅa*, the 5th consonant of the Sanskṛit alphabet, nasal of the 1st class. No word in use begins with this letter; it is usually found as the 1st member of a conjunct consonant preceded by a vowel. **—kāra,** m. the letter or sound *ṅa*.

ङ 2. *ṅa*, m. an object of sense, L.; desire for any sensual object, L.; Śiva (*bhairava*), L.

ङु *ṅu*, cl. 1. Ā. *ṅavate*, to sound, Dhātup. xxii, 57: Desid. *ñuṇūshate*, Pāṇ. vii, 4, 62, Sch.

च CA.

च 1. *ca*, the 20th letter of the alphabet, 1st of the 2nd (or palatal) class of consonants, having the sound of *ch* in *church*. **—1.-kāra,** m. the letter or sound *ca*.

च 2. *ca*, ind. and, both, also, moreover, as well as (= τε, Lat. *que*, placed like these particles as an enclitic after the word which it connects with what precedes; when used with a personal pronoun this must appear in its fuller accented form (e. g. *tâva ca mâma ca* [not *te ca me ca*], 'both of thee and me'), when used after verbs the first of them is accented, Pāṇ. viii, 1, 58 f.; it connects whole sentences as well as parts of sentences; in RV. the double *ca* occurs more frequently than the single (e. g. *ahâm ca tvâm ca*, 'I and thou,' viii, 62, 11); the double *ca* may also be used somewhat redundantly in class. Sanskṛit (e. g. *kva hariṇakānāṃ jīvitaṃ câtilolaṃ kva ca vajra-sārāḥ śarās te*, 'where is the frail existence of fawns and where are thy adamantine arrows?' Śak. i, 10); in later literature, however, the first *ca* is more usually omitted (e. g. *ahaṃ tvaṃ ca*), and when more than two things are enumerated only one *ca* is often found (e. g. *tejasā yaśasā lakshmyā sthityā ca parayā*, 'in glory, in fame, in beauty, and in high position,' Nal. xii, 6); elsewhere, when more than two things are enumerated, *ca* is placed after some and omitted after others (e. g. *ṛiṇa-dātā ca vaidyaś ca śrotriyo nadī*, 'the payer of a debt and a physician [and] a Brāhman [and] a river,' Hit. i, 4, 55); in Ved. and even in class. Sanskṛit [Mn. iii, 20; ix, 322; Hit.], when the double *ca* would generally be used, the second may occasionally be omitted (e. g. *I'ndraś ca Soma*, 'both Indra [and thou] Soma,' RV. vii, 104, 25; *durbhedyaś câśu-saṃdheyaḥ*, 'both difficult to be divided [and] quickly united,' Hit. i); with lexicographers *ca* may imply a reference to certain other words which are not expressed (e. g. *kamaṇḍalau ca karakaḥ*, 'the word *karaka* has the meaning "pitcher" and other meanings'); sometimes *ca* is = *eva*, even, indeed, certainly, just (e. g. *su-cintitam câushadhaṃ na nāma-mātreṇa karoty arogam*, 'even a well-devised remedy does not cure a disease by its mere name,' Hit.; *yāvanta eva te tāvāṅś ca saḥ*, 'as great as they [were] just so great was he,' Ragh. xii, 45); occasionally *ca* is disjunctive, 'but,' 'on the contrary,' 'on the other hand,' 'yet,' 'nevertheless' (*varam ādyau na cẫntimaḥ*, 'better the two first but not the last,' Hit.; *śāntam idam āśrama-padaṃ sphurati ca bāhuḥ*, 'this hermitage is tranquil yet my arm throbs,' Śak. i, 15); *ca—ca*, though—yet, Vikr. ii, 9; *ca—na ca*, though—yet not, Pat.; *ca—na tu* (v. l. *nanu*), id., Mālav. iv, 8; *na ca—ca*, though not—yet, Pat.; *ca* may be used for *vā*, 'either,' 'or' (e. g. *iha câmutra vā*, 'either here or hereafter,' Mn. xii, 89; *strī vā pumān vā yac cânyat sattvam*, 'either a woman or a man or any other being,' R.), and when a neg. particle is joined with *ca* the two may then be translated by 'neither,' 'nor;' occasionally one *ca* or one *na* is omitted (e. g. *na ca paribhoktuṃ nâiva śaknomi hātum*, 'I am able neither to enjoy nor to abandon,' Śak. v, 18; *na pūrvâhṇe nā ca parâhṇe*, 'neither in the forenoon nor in the afternoon'); *ca—ca* may express immediate connection between two acts or their simultaneous occurrence (e. g. *mama ca muktaṃ tamasā mano manasijena dhanushi śaraś ca niveśitaḥ*, 'no sooner is my mind freed from darkness than a shaft is fixed on his bow by the heart-born god,' vi, 8); *ca* is sometimes = *cẫd*, 'if' (cf. Pāṇ. viii, 1, 30; the verb is accented), RV.; AV.; MBh.; Vikr. ii, 20; Bhartṛ. ii, 45; *ca* may be used as an expletive (e. g. *anyaiś ca kratubhiś ca*, 'and with other sacrifices'); *ca* is often joined to an adv. like *eva, api, tathā, tathâiva*, &c., either with or without a neg. particle (e. g. *vairiṇaṃ nôpaseveta sahâyaṃ caiva vairiṇaḥ*, 'one ought not to serve either an enemy or the ally of an enemy,' Mn. iv, 133); (see *eva, api*, &c.) For the meaning of *ca* after an interrogative see 2. *kâ*, 2. *kathâ*, *kìm*, *kvà*); [cf. τε, Lat. *que*, *pe* (in *nempe* &c.); Goth. *uh*; Zd. *ca*; Old Pers. *cā*.] **—2.-kāra,** m. the particle *ca*, Pāṇ. ii, 3, 72, Kāś. **—samāsa,** m. a Dvandva compound, Vop., Sch. **Cādi,** a Gaṇa of Pāṇ. (including the indeclinable particles, i, 4, 57).

च 3. *ca*, mfn. pure, L.; moving to and fro, L.; mischievous, L.; seedless, L.; m. a thief, L.; the moon, L.; a tortoise, L.; Śiva, L.

चक् *cak*, cl. 1. P. Ā. *°kati*, *°kate*, to be satiated or contented or satisfied, Dhātup. iv, 19; to repel, resist, ib.; to shine, xix, 21; (cf. √*kan* & *kam*.)

Caka, m. (√*kan?*) N. of a Nāga priest, TāṇḍyaBr. xxv, 15, 3 (v. l. *cakka*); (cf. *kuṭi-*.)

Cakana, g. *cūrṇâdi* (vv. ll. *cakkana* & *cakvana*).

Cakita, mfn. trembling, timid, frightened, Mṛicch. i, 16; Ragh.; Megh. &c. (*a-*, neg. 'not staggering,' as the gait, Daś.); n. trembling, timidity, alarm, Mṛicch. &c.; (*am*), ind. tremblingly, with great alarm, Mālav. i, 10; Gīt.; Sāh.; (*ā*), f. a metre of 4 × 16 syllables; (cf. *uc-*, *pra-*.) **—cakita,** mfn. greatly alarmed, BhP.; (*am*), ind. with great alarm, Megh. 14. **—hṛidaya,** mfn. faint-hearted, W.

चकट्योदन *cakaṭy-odana*, n. bad rice, Divyâv. xxxv, 231 ff.

चकास् 1. *cakās* (cf. √*kāś*), cl. 2. P. *cakāsti* (3. pl. *°sati*, Pāṇ. vi, 1, 6; BhP. v; Bhaṭṭ.; p. *°sat*, Śiś. i, 8; BhP. iii, 19, 14; impf. *acakāt*, 2. sg. *°kās* or *°kāt*, Pāṇ. viii, 2, 73 f., Kāś.; Impv. *cakāddhi*, 25, Kār. 1 [Pat.]; *°kādhi*, Pat. [on Kār. 3]; pf. *°kāsām cakāra* [vi, 4, 112, Siddh.], Bhaṭṭ.; cl. 1. Ā.? 3. du. *cakāśete*, MBh. iii, 438; viii, 2328), to shine, be bright: Caus. *cakāsayati* (aor. *acacakāsat* or *acîc°*, Pāṇ. vii, 4, 81, Siddh.), to cause to shine, make bright, Śiś. iii, 6.

2. **Cakās,** mfn. shining, Pāṇ. viii, 2, 73, Kāś.

Cakāsita, mfn. illuminated, splendid, W.

चकित *cakita*. See √*cak*.

चकृवत् *cakṛivat*, n. (for *°vas*, pf. P. p.) a perfect form (of any verb), ŚāṅkhBr. xxii, 3.

चकोर *cakora*, m. (√*cak*, Uṇ.) the Greek partridge (Perdix rufa; fabled to subsist on moonbeams [ŚārṅgP.; cf. Gīt. i, 23], hence 'an eye drinking the nectar of a moon-like face' is poetically called *c°*, BrahmaP.; Kathās. lxxvii, 50; the eyes of the Cakora are said to turn red when they look on poisoned food, Kām.; Naish.; Kull. on Mn. vii, 217), MBh.; Lalit.; Suśr. &c.; (pl.) N. of a people, AV.Pariś. lvi; (sg.) of a prince, BhP. xii, 1, 24; of a town (?), Hcar. vi; (*ī*), f. a female Cakora bird, Kathās. il, 213. **—dṛiś,** mfn. having (eyes like those of the Cakora bird, i. e. having) beautiful eyes, Śiś. vi, 48. **—netra,** mf(*ā*)n. id., MBh. vii; Mṛicch. i, 3; Ragh. **—vrata,** n. 'habit of a Cakora bird,' enjoying the nectar of a moon-like face, Kathās. lxxvi, 11. **Cakshorâksha,** mf(*ī*)n. = *°ra-dṛiś*, Vcar. viii, 42; Bharaṭ. iii, 2.

Cakoraka, m. ifc. = *°ra* (Perdix rufa).

Cakorāya, Nom. Ā. to act like the Cakora bird, Kathās. lxxxix, 41.

चक्क् *cakk*, cl. 10. P. *°kkayati*, to suffer, Dhātup. xxxii, 56; to give or inflict pain (?), ib.

Cakka, v. l. for *caka*.

Cakkana, v. l. for *cakana*.

चक्कल *cakkala*, mfn. (for *cakrala*) round, circular (?), Uṇ. i, 108, Sch.

Cakkalaka, n. a series of 4 Ślokas (= *catur-bhiḥ kulaka*), Rājat. vii, 193; Śiś. xix, 29, Sch.; Śrīkaṇṭh. iii, 50, Sch.; (cf. *cakra-bandha*.)

चक्नस *caknasa*, m. (√*knas*), Vop. xxvi, 30.

चक्र *cakrá*, n. (Ved. rarely m.; g. *ardharcâdi*; fr. √*car?*; √1. *kṛi*, Pāṇ. vi, 1, 12, Kāś.) the wheel (of a carriage, of the Sun's chariot [RV.], of Time [i, 164, 2–48]; *°krâm-√car*, to drive in a carriage, ŚBr. vi), RV. &c.; a potter's wheel, ŚBr. xi; Yājñ. iii, 146; (cf. *-bhrama* &c.); a discus or sharp circular missile weapon (esp. that of Vishṇu), MBh.; R.; Suśr.; Pañcat.; BhP.; an oil-mill, Mn. iv. 85; MBh. xii, 6481 & 7697; a circle, R.; BhP. &c. (*kalâpa-*, 'the circle of a peacock's tail,' Ṛitus. ii, 14); an astronomical circle (e. g. *rāśi-*, the zodiac), VarBṛS.; Sūryas.; a mystical circle or diagram, Tantr.; = *-bandha*, q. v., Sāh. x, 13 f.; a cycle, cycle of years or of seasons, Hariv. 652; 'a form of military array (in a circle),' see *-vyūha*; circular flight (of a bird), Pañcat. ii, 57; a particular constellation in the form of a hexagon, VarBṛS. xx; VarBṛ.; Laghuj.; a circle or depression of the body (for mystical or chiromantic purposes; 6 in number, one above the other, viz. 1. *mūlâdhāra*, the parts about the pubis; 2. *svâdhishṭhāna*, the umbilical region; 3. *maṇi-pūra*, the pit of the stomach or epigastrium; 4. *anāhata*, the root of the nose; 5. *viśuddha*, the hollow between the frontal sinuses; 6. *ājñâkhya*, the fontenelle or union of the coronal and sagittal sutures; various faculties and divinities are supposed to be present in these hollows); N. of a metre (= *-pāta*); a circle or a similar instrument (used in astron.), Laghuj.; Sūryas. xiii, 20; Gol. xi, 10 ff.; (also m., L.) a troop, multitude, MBh. v, ix (*°krâvalī*, q. v.); Hariv.; R. &c.; the whole number of (in comp.), Sarvad. xi, 127; a troop of soldiers, army, host, MBh. (ifc. f. *ā*, iii, 640); BhP. i, ix; Cāṇ.; a number of villages, province, district, L.; (fig.) range, department, VarBṛS. xxx, 33; the wheel of a monarch's chariot rolling over his dominions, sovereignty, realm, Yājñ. i, 265; MBh. i, xiii; BhP. ix, 20, 32; VP.; (pl.) the winding of a river, L.; a whirlpool, L.; a crooked or fraudulent device (cf. *cakrikā*), L.; the convolutions or spiral marks of the Śāla-grāma or ammonite, W.; N. of a medicinal plant or drug, Suśr. v f.; of a Tīrtha, BhP. x, 78, 19; m. the ruddy goose or Brāhmany duck (Anas Casarca, called after its cries; cf. *-vāká*), MBh. ix, 443; Bālar. viii, 58; Kathās. lxxii, 40; ŚārṅgP.; (pl.) N. of a people, MBh. vi, 352; (g. *aśvâdi*) N. of a man, BṛĀrUp. iii, 4, 1, Sch.; of another man, Kathās. lvi, 144; of a Nāga, MBh. i, 2147; of one of Skanda's attendants, MBh. ix, 2539 & 2542; of a mountain, BhP. v, 20, 15; Kathās. liv. 16; (*ā*), f. a kind of Cyperus or another plant, L.; (*ī*), f. a wheel (instr. sg. *°kriyā*; gen. du. *°kryòs*), RV.; (du. *°kriyau*) Kaṭh. xxix, 7; [cf. *a-*, *ashṭā-*, *uccā-*, *éka-*, *kāla-*, *kū-*, *daṇḍa-*, *dik-*, *dharma-*, *mahā-*, *mātṛi-*, *ródha-*, *vishṇu-*, *sa-*, *saptá-*, *hiraṇya-*; *tri-* & *sucakrá*; cf. also κύκλος, Lat. *circus*; Angl. Sax. *hveohl*, Engl. *wheel*.] **—kāraka,** n. the perfume unguis odoratus, Bhpr. v, 2, 80. **—kulyā,** f. a kind of fern (*citra-parṇī*), L. **—gaja,** m. Cassia Tora, L. **—gaṇḍu,** m. a round pillow, L. **—gati,** f. rotation, revolution, W. **—guccha,** m. 'having circular clusters,' Jonesia Aśoka, L. **—gulma,** m. 'having a circular excretion,' a camel, Npr. **—goptṛi,** m. du. 'wheel-protectors,' two men whose business is to preserve the wheels of a carriage from damage, MBh. vii, 1627; (cf. *-raksha*.) **—grahaṇī,** f. 'army-keeper,' a rampart (Sch.) iii, 641. **—cara,** m. pl. 'going in a circle,' N. of a class of superhuman beings, iii, 8214; xiii, 6493 ff.; 'a juggler' (cf. *cakrâta*) or 'a potter' (Sch.), VarBṛS. x, 12. **—cārin,** mfn. flying in a circle (a bird), Hariv. 3494. **—cūḍā-**

maṇi, m. 'round jewel (in a coronet),' a honorific N. of Vop.; N. of the elder brother of the astronomer Bala-bhadra (17th century); N. of a treatise. **–jāti,** f. = *-bandha.* **–jīvaka,** m. 'living by his wheel,' a potter, L. **–jīvin,** m. id., W. **–nadī,** f. = *-nadī*, g. *girinady-ādi*. **–nitamba,** m. = *-nit°*, ib. **–talâmra,** m. a kind of mango tree, L. **–tīrtha,** n., N. of a Tīrtha (cf. *cakra*), VarP.; ŚivaP.; Prab. iv f. &c. **–tuṇḍa,** (°*krá-*), m. 'circular-beaked,' a kind of mythical being, Suparṇ. xxiii, 4; a kind of fish, R. (B) iii, 73, 14. **–taila,** n. oil prepared from the Cakra(-gaja?) plant, Suśr. **–daṇshṭra,** m. 'having curved tusks,' a hog, L. (v. l. *vakr°*). **–datta,** m. (= *-pāṇi-datta*), N. of an author; *-nāmaka-grantha*, m., N. of a work. **–dantī,** f., N. of a plant, L.; *-bīja*, m. 'having seeds resembling those of the plant Cakra-dantī,' N. of a plant, L. **–dīpikā,** f. 'diagram-illuminator,' N. of a work, Tantras. ii. **–°dundubhya,** mfn. relating to a wheel and to a drum, KātyŚr. iv, 3, 13. **–driś,** mfn. 'circular-eyed,' N. of an Asura, BhP. viii, 10, 21. **–deva,** m. 'having the wheel (of a war-chariot) for his deity,' N. of a warrior, MBh. ii, 621; Hariv. 6626 & 6642 f. **–dvāra,** m., N. of a mountain, MBh. xii, 12035. **–dhanus,** m., N. of a Ṛishi, v, 3795. **–dhara,** mfn. or m. bearing a wheel, wheel-bearer, Pañcat. v, 3, $\frac{10}{11}$ ff. (once *-dhāra*); = *-bhṛit*, MBh. i, 6257; Mṛicch. v, 3; Ragh. xvi, 55; driving in a carriage (?, 'a snake' or 'a governor,' Sch.; cf. Mn. ii, 138 & Yājñ. i, 117), MBh. xiii, 7570; m. a sovereign, emperor, iii, xii; Hariv. 10999; governor of a province, L.; = *caraka*, VarBṛ. xv, 1, Sch.; a snake, Rājat. i, 261; a village tumbler (cf. *cakrâṭa*), W.; N. of a man, Karmapr., Sch.; of other men, Kathās. &c.; of a locality, Rājat. iv, 191. **–dharman,** m., N. of a Vidyā-dhara prince, MBh. ii, 408. **–dhāra,** for *-dhara*, q. v.; (*ā*), f. the periphery of a wheel, W. **–nakha,** m. = *-kāraka*, L. **–nadī,** f. (g. *girinady-ādi*) N. of a river, BhP. v, 7, 9. **–nābhi,** f. the nave of a wheel, Suśr. **–nāman,** m. = *-sâhvaya*, Kād.; a pyritic ore of iron (*mākshika*), L. **–nāyaka,** m. the leader of a troop, Rājat. ii, 106; = *-kāraka*, L. **–nārāyaṇī-saṃhitā,** f. N. of a work, Smṛitit. ix. **–nitamba,** m. = *-nit°*, g. *girinady-ādi*. **–nemi,** f. 'wheel-felly,' N. of one of the mothers attending on Skanda, MBh. ix, 2623. **–padmâṭa,** m. = *-gaja*, L. **–parivyādha,** m. Cathartocarpus fistula, L. **–parṇī,** f. = *-kulyā*, Npr. **–pāṇi,** m. 'discus-handed,' Vishṇu, ShaḍvBr. v, 10; MBh. vi, 1900; (°*ṇin*) Hariv. 8193 & 8376; N. of a medical author; *-datta*, m. id. **–pāṇin,** for °*ṇi*, q. v. **–pāta,** m. a metre of 4 × 14 syllables. **–pāda,** m. 'wheel-footed,' a carriage, L.; 'circular-footed,' an elephant, L. **–pāla,** m. the superintendent of a province, W.; one who carries a discus, W.; a circle, W.; the horizon, W.; N. of a poet, Kshem. **–pālita,** m., N. of a man. **–pura,** n., N. of a town (built by Cakra-mardikā, Rājat. iv, 213), Kathās. cxxiii, 213. **–pushkariṇī,** f., N. of a sacred tank at Benares, KāśīKh. **–phala,** n. a missile weapon (kind of discus), L. **–bandha,** m. a stanza artificially arranged in a diagram, Pratāpar.; (*am*), ind. so as to fasten or bind in a particular way, Pāṇ. iii, 4, 41, Kāś. **–bandhanā,** f. a kind of jasmine, Npr. **–bāndhava,** m. 'friend of Cakra(-vāka) birds (supposed to couple only in day-time),' the sun, L. **–bālā,** f. Hibiscus cannabinus, Npr. **–bhaṅga,** m. break of a wheel, Mn. viii, 291. **–bhānu,** m., N. of a Brāhman, Rājat. vi, 108. **–bhṛit,** m. 'discus-bearer,' Vishṇu, Rājat. i, 38. **–bhedinī,** f. 'dividing the Cakra(-vāka) couples (cf. *-bāndhava*),' night, L. **–bhrama,** mfn. turning like a wheel, Mcar. vi, 12; m. = °*mi*, Ragh. vi, 32; Sāṃkhyak. 67 (v. l.) **–bhramaṇa,** m., N. of a mountain, Vīrac. xii. **–bhrami,** f. rotation of a wheel, Sāṃkhyak. 67; Ragh. (C) vi, 32. **–bhrānti,** f. rotation of the wheels (of a chariot), W. **–maṭha,** m., N. of a college (built in a circular form by Cakra-varman), Rājat. v, 403. **–maṇḍalin,** m. the Boa constrictor, L. **–maṇḍa,** m., N. of a Nāga, MBh. xvi, 120. **–marda,** m. = *-gaja*, Suśr. iv, 9, 11. **–mardaka,** m. id., L.; (*ikā*), f., N. of a wife of Lilâditya, Rājat. iv, 213 & 393. **–m-āsajá,** mfn. stopping the wheels (of a chariot), RV. v, 34, 6. **–mīmāṇsā,** f., N. of a work. **–mukha,** m. = *-daṇshṭra*, L. **–musala,** mfn. (a battle) carried on with the discus and club, Hariv. 5346 (cf. 5648). **–medinī,** for *-bhed°*, Gal. **–melaka,** N. of a locality in Kaśmīr, Kathās. cxxiii, 213 & 221; Rājat. vi, 108. **–mauli,** 'having a circular diadem,' N. of a Rākshasa, R. vi, 69, 14. **–maulin,** mfn. having the wheels turned upwards, Hariv. 3415. **–yāna,** n. any wheel-carriage, L. **–yoga,** m. applying a splint or similar instrument by means of pulleys (in case of dislocation of the thigh), Suśr. iv, 3, 25. **–yodhin,** m. 'discus-fighter,' N. of a Dānava, VP. i, 21, 12. **–raksha,** m. du. = *-goptṛi*, MBh. i, iv, vi. **–rada,** m. = *-daṇshṭra*, L. **–rāja,** m. N. of a mystical diagram, Rudray. **–lakshaṇā,** f. Cocculus cordifolius, L. **–lakshaṇikā,** f. id., Bhpr. **–latâmra,** for *-talâmra*, W. **–vat,** mfn. furnished with wheels, wheeled, Pāṇ. viii, 2, 12, Kāś.; armed with a discus, W.; circular, W.; m. an oil-grinder, Mn. iv, 84; N. of Vishṇu, W.; a sovereign, emperor, W.; N. of a mountain, Hariv. 12408 & 12847; R. iv, 43, 32; n. a chariot, Baudh. i, 3, 34; ind. like a wheel, in rotation, W.; *-(vad)-gati*, mfn. turning like a wheel, MBh. xii, 873. **–varta,** see *-vritta*. **–vartin,** mfn. rolling everywhere without obstruction, Kathās. cvii, 133; m. a ruler the wheels of whose chariot roll everywhere without obstruction, emperor, sovereign of the world, ruler of a Cakra (or country described as extending from sea to sea; 12 princes beginning with Bharata are esp. considered as Cakravartins), MaitrUp.; MBh.; Buddh.; Jain. &c.; mfn. supreme, holding the highest rank among (gen. or in comp.), Kum. vii, 52; Gīt. i, 2; Kathās. i, xx; m. Chenopodium album, L.; N. of the author of a Comm. on Alaṃkāras., Pratāpar., Sch.; (*inī*), f. the fragrant plant Jantukā, L.; Nardostachys Jaṭāmāṇsī, L.; = *alaktaka*, L.; °*ti-tā*, f. the state of a universal emperor, Daś. xiii, 79; °*ti-tva*, n. id., Hariv. 8815. **–varman,** m., N. of a king of Kaśmīr, Rājat. v, 287 ff. **–vāká,** m. the Cakra bird (Anas Casarca; the couples are supposed to be separated and to mourn during night), RV. ii, 39, 3; VS. xxiv f.; AV. xiv; MBh. &c.; (*ī*). f. the female of the Cakra (-vāka) bird, Megh. 80; Kathās.; Sāh.; *-bandhu*, m. = °*kra-bāndhava*, L.; *-maya*, mfn. consisting of Cakra birds, Kād. vi, 272; Hcar. iv, 36; *-vatī*, f. 'abounding in Cakra-vākas,' (probably) N. of a river, g. *ajirâdi*; °*kôpakūjita*, mfn. made resonant with the cooing or cry of the Cakra-vāka, MBh. iii, 2512. **–°vākin,** mfn. filled with Cakra-vākas, Ragh. xv, 30. **–vāṭa,** m. a limit, boundary, L.; a lamp-stand, L.; engaging in an action (?, *kriyâroha*), L. **–vāda,** m. fire, Gal.; the mountain-range Cakra-vāla, Kāraṇḍ. xxiii; n. 'a circle,' or 'a troop, multitude,' L. **–vāta,** m. a whirlwind, BhP. x. **–vāla,** n. (fr. *-vāḍa*) a circle, MBh. i, 7021 ff.; Sūryapr.; = °*la-yamaka*, Bhaṭṭ. x, 6, Sch.; m. n. a mass, multitude, number, assemblage, MBh. i; Hariv. 4098; VarBṛS. &c.; m., N. of a mythical range of mountains (encircling the orb of the earth and being the limit of light and darkness), Buddh.; Kāvyâd. ii, 99 (°*lâdri*); *-yamaka*, n. a kind of artificial stanza (as Bhaṭṭ. x, 6); °*lâtman*, f., N. of a goddess, BrahmaP. ii, 18, 12. **–°vālaka,** n. a kind of rhetorical figure, Pratāpar. **–vāladhi,** m. 'curved-tail,' a dog, L.; (cf. *vakr°*.) **–vimala,** N. of a plant, Buddh. L. **–vṛitta** (°*krá-*), mfn. turned on a potter's wheel, MaitrS. i, 8, 3; (*a-cakravarta*, for °*vritta*, neg.) ĀpŚr. vi, 3, 7; (cf. °*kru-v°*.) **–vṛiddhi,** f. interest upon interest, Gaut.; Nār.; Bṛihasp.; Mn. viii, 153; wages for transporting goods in a carriage, 156. **–vyūha,** m. any circular array of troops, MBh. i, 2754; vii, 1471 (cf. also 3108); N. of a Kiṃnara prince, Kāraṇḍ. i, 29. **–śata-pattra,** N. of a plant, Buddh. L. **–śreṇī,** f. Odina pinnata (bearing a curved fruit), L. **–saṃvara,** m., N. of a Buddha (*vajra-ṭīka*), L. **–saktha,** mfn. bow-legged, Pāṇ. vi, 2, 198, Kāś. **–saṃjña,** n. tin, L. **–sâhvaya,** m. the Cakra (-vāka) bird, MBh. xiii, 2836; R. iv, 51, 38. **–sena,** m., N. of a son of Tārā-candra and father of Siṇha; (*ā*), f., N. of a princess, Kathās. liv, 111. **–svastika-nandy-āvarta,** m. 'having the wheel, the Svastika and the Nandy-āvarta emblems,' N. of Buddha, Divyâv. **–svāmin,** m. (cf. *-bhṛit*) Vishṇu. **–hasta,** m. (= *-pāṇi*) id., W. **–hrada,** m., N. of a lake, SkandaP. **Cakrâkāra,** mf(*ā*)n. disc-shaped (the earth), Sūryas. xii, 54. **Cakrâkī,** v. l. for *krâṅkī*, W. **Cakrâkṛiti,** mfn. = °*kāra*, W. **Cakrâṅkā,** f. Cocculus tomentosus, Bhpr. v, 3, 307 (v. l. °*krâhvā*); Cyperus pertenuis, L. **Cakrâṅkitā,** f. a kind of plant, Pañcat. iii, $\frac{7}{4}$. **Cakrâṅkī,** f. = °*ṅgī*, a goose, L. **Cakrâṅga,** m. 'curved-neck,' a gander, MBh. viii, xii f.; R. v, 16, 11; the Cakra(-vāka) bird, Mn. v, 12; 'wheel-limbed (cf. °*kra-pāda*),' a carriage, L.; n. 'disc-shaped,' a parasol, L.; (*ā*), f. = °*ṅkā*, Cocculus tomentosus, W.; (*ī*), f. = °*ṅkī*, a goose, L.; Helleborus niger, L.; Cocculus tomentosus, L; Rubia munjista, L.; Enhydra Heloncha, L.; the plant *karkaṭa-śṛiṅgī*, L. **Cakrâṅganā,** f. the female of the Cakra(-vāka) bird, Kathās. lxxii, 58. **Cakrâṭa,** m. (= °*kra-cara*) a juggler, snake-catcher, snake-charmer, L.; a knave, cheat, L.; a gold coin, Dīnār, L. **Cakrâti,** m. pl., N. of a people, MBh. vi, 352 (*vakrâtapa*, ed. Calc.) **Cakrâdhivāsin,** m. 'abode for Cakra(-vāka) birds,' the orange-tree, L. **Cakrâyudha,** m. 'whose weapon is the discus,' Vishṇu or Kṛishṇa, MBh. i, 1163; Hariv.; R.; Kathās. lxxxi. **Cakrâyodhya,** m. 'not to be conquered by a discus,' N. of a prince, Buddh. **Cakrârdhacakravāla,** a semicircle, Sūryapr. **Cakrâlu,** m. = °*kra-talâmra*, Npr. **Cakrâvarta,** m. whirling or rotatory motion, L. **Cakrâvalī,** f. a number, multitude, MBh. ix, 443. **Cakrâśman,** m. a sling for throwing stones, i, 8257. **Cakrâhva,** m. = °*hvaya*, PāṇŚ. (RV.) 36; Yājñ. i, 173; Suśr.; BhP.; Kathās.; = °*kra-gaja*, L.; (*ā*), f., see °*krâṅkā*. **Cakrâhvaya,** m. = °*kra-sâhvaya*, VarBṛS.; Kād. iii. **Cakrêndraka,** m. a kind of mustard, Npr. **Cakrêśa,** m. (= °*kra-vartin*) sovereign of the world, Padyas. 12. **Cakrêśvara,** m. 'lord of the discus,' Vishṇu, Rājat. iv, 276; 'lord of the troops,' Bhairava, Kathās. lvi, 106; = °*śa*, Padyas. 12; (*ī*), f. one of the Vidyā-devīs (executing the orders of the 1st Arhat), L. **Cakrôttha,** m. a kind of mustard, Npr. **Cakrôllāsa,** m., N. of a work.

Cakraka, mfn. resembling a wheel or circle, circular, W.; m. a kind of serpent (cf. *cakra-maṇḍalin*), Suśr. v, 4, 34; Dolichos biflorus, L.; N. of a Ṛishi, MBh. xiii, 253; n. a particular way of fighting, Hariv. iii, 124, 19 (v. l. *citraka*); arguing in a circle, Pat.; (*ā*), f. a kind of plant having great curative properties (white Abrus, L.), Suśr. vi, 30, 3 & 19; (*ikā*), f. a troop, multitude, Rājat. iv, viii; a crooked or fraudulent device, v. **Cakrakâśraya,** m. arguing in a circle, Sarvad. xi, 27.

Cakrala, mfn. (cf. *cakkala*) crisp, curled (*barbara*), L.; (*ā*), f. a kind of Cyperus, L.

Cakrika, m. a discus-bearer, Buddh. L.; (= °*kraka*) Dolichos biflorus, Npr.; (*ā*), f., see °*kraka*.

Cakrin, mfn. having wheels, L.; driving in a carriage, Gaut.; Mn. ii, 138; Yājñ. i, 117; bearing a discus, or (m.) 'discus-bearer,' Kṛishṇa, Bhag. xi, 17; BhP. i, 9, 4; Rājat. i, 262; m. a potter, L.; an oil-grinder, Yājñ. i, 141; N. of Śiva, MBh. xiii, 745; a sovereign of the world, king, HPariś.; the governor of a province (*grāma-jālika*; *grāma-yājin*, 'one who offers sacrifices for a whole village,' L.), W.; a kind of juggler or tumbler who exhibits tricks with a discus or a wheel (*jālika-bhid*), L.; an informer (*sūcaka*), L.; a cheat, rogue, L.; a snake; the Cakra(-vāka) bird, L.; an ass, L.; a crow, L.; = °*kra-gaja*, L.; 'N. of a man' (?), see *cákri*; Dalbergia ujjeinensis, L.; = °*kra-kāraka*, L.; m. pl., N. of a Vaishṇava sect; (cf. *sa-*.)

Cakriya, mfn. belonging to a wheel or carriage, RV. x, 89, 4; going on a carriage, being on a journey, AitBr. i, 14, 4 (gen. pl. °*yāṇām*; fr. *cakrin* & √*yā*, Sāy.)

1. **Cakrī,** ind. in comp. **–√kri,** to make round or circular, curve or bend (a bow), Kum. iii, 70; Bālar. v, 3; Kuval. 475. **–√bhū,** to be made circular or bent (a bow), Prasannar. vii, 41.

2. **Cakrī,** f. of °*krá*, q. v. **–vat,** mfn. (Pāṇ. viii, 2, 12) furnished with wheels, wheeled, TāṇḍyaBr.; ĀśvŚr.; ŚāṅkhŚr.; KātyŚr.; Lāṭy.; driving in a carriage, Gaut.; m. an ass, L.; N. of a prince, Pāṇ. viii, 2, 12, Kāś.; n. a carriage, ĀpŚr. xv, 20, 18.

1. **Cakru** = °*krá*, 'a wheel,' only in comp. **–vṛitta,** mfn. circular, (*a-*, neg.) Kāṭh. vi, 3.

चक्राण *cakrāṇa*, pf. Ā. p. √1. *kṛi*, q. v.

Cákri, mfn. (Pāṇ. iii, 2, 171, Vārtt. 3) doing, effecting (with acc.), active, RV.; (or *cakrin*?) N. of a man, Pravar. vii, 9; (cf. *uru-cákri*.)

2. **Cakru,** mfn. doing, effecting, Uṇ. i, 23.

चक्वन *cakvana*, v. l. for *cakana*.

चक्ष् *caksh* (a reduplicated form of √*kāś* = *kśā*; in the non-conjugational tenses √*khyā* is substituted, Pāṇ. ii, 4, 54 f.; some pf. forms, however, are found), cl. 2. Ā. *cáshṭe* (2. du. *cakshâthe*, RV.; pf. p. *cákshāṇa*, RV.; BhP. i, 18, 25 [*a-*, neg.]; rarely P., impf. 2. sg. *acakshas*, MBh. viii, 3384, 1. pl. *acakshma*, Naigh. iii, 11; Ved. inf.

cákshase, RV.; AV. vi, 68, 2), to appear, become visible, RV. viii, 19, 16; x, 74, 2 & 92, 6; to see, look at, observe, notice, RV.; BhP.; to tell, inform, MBh. viii, 3384; to take any one (acc.) for (acc.), BhP. x, 73, 11.

Caksha, m. a false friend, VarYogay. iv, 50.

Cákshaṇa, n. appearing, appearance, aspect, RV.; AV.; speaking, saying, W.; (for *jaksh°*?) eating a relish to promote drinking, L.; (cf. *viśvá-; abhi-* & *prati-cáksh°; vi-cakshaṇá*.)

Cakshaṇi, m. an illuminator, RV. vi, 4, 2.

Cákshan, n. du. the eyes, AV. x, 2, 6.

Cákshas, n. radiance, clearness, RV.; AV. vi, 76, 1; (of the sea) Lāṭy. i, 7, 5; look, sight, eye, RV.; (*ase*), dat. inf. √*caksh*, q. v.; m. a teacher, spiritual instructor, L.; 'teacher of the gods,' Bṛihaspati, L.; (cf. *ápāka-, īya-, upāká-, ghorá-, viśvá-, sūra-, svàr-; uru-, duś-, nṛi-* & *su-cáksh°*.)

Cákshu, m. the eye, RV. x, 90, 13; (ifc., AV. iv, 20, 5); N. of a prince, BhP.; (for *vakshu*?) the Oxus river, VP. ii, 2, 32 & 35; 8, 114; Gol. iii, 38. **-nirodha**, m. = °*kshur-n°*, Āp. ii, 27, 17. **-pīḍana**, mfn. causing pain to the eye, ŚvetUp. ii, 10.

Cakshuḥ, in comp. for °*kshus*. **-patha**, see °*kshush-p°*. **-pīḍā**, f. pain of the eyes, W. **-śravas**, m. 'using the eyes for ears,' a snake, MBh. xii, 13803; Kir. xvi, 42; Naish.; KāśīKh. lviii, 161. **-śruti**, m. id., Rājat. v, 1; (cf. *dṛik-ś°*.)

Cakshur, in comp. for °*kshus*. **-apêta**, mfn. one who has lost his eyes, blind, KaushUp. **-indriya**, n. the organ of sight, Suśr. **-gocara**, mfn. coming within the range of the eye, W. **-grahaṇa**, n. morbid affection of the eyes, v, 4. **-dá**, mfn. giving sight, VS. iv, 3. **-dāna**, n. 'gift of sight,' the ceremony of anointing the eyes of an image at the time of consecration, W. **-nimita** (*cáksh°*), mfn. fixed by (a measure taken by) the eye, TBr. i, 1, 4, 1. **-nirodha**, m. (= °*kshu-n°*) a cover or a hindrance for the eyesight, Āp. (v.l.); Yājñ. ii, 26, Sch. **-bahala**, m. Odina pinnata, L. **-bhṛít**, mfn. promoting sight, ŚBr. viii. **-mantra** (*cáksh°*), mfn. bewitching with the eye, AV. ii, 7, 5; xix, 45, 1. **-máya**, mfn. resembling the eye, ŚBr. x, xiv. **-mala**, n. the excretion of the eyes, Buddh. L. **-mukha** (*cáksh°*), mfn. having eyes in the mouth (?), Suparṇ. xxiv, 2. **-mush**, mfn. 'robbing the sight,' blinding the eyes, MBh. xii, 12705. **-loka** (*cáksh°*), mfn. seeing with the eyes, ŚBr. xiv, 6, 9. **-ványa**, mfn. suffering from disease of the eyes, TS. ii, 3, 8, 1. **-vardhanikā**, f. 'refreshing the eyes,' N. of a river, MBh. vi, 433. **-vahana**, m. = *-bahala*, L. **-vishaya**, m. the range of sight, ŚāṅkhŚr.; Mn. ii, 198 (loc. *e*, 'in the presence of'); a visible object, W. **-han**, m(acc. *-hanam*; nom. pl. *-hanas*)fn. killing with a look, MBh. vi f., xiii.

Cakshuś, in comp. for °*kshus*. **-cit**, mfn. collecting the faculty of sight, ŚBr. x, 5, 3, 6.

Cakshush, in comp. for °*kshus*. **-karṇa**, m. = °*kshuḥ-śravas*, Gal. **-kāma** (*cáksh°*), mfn. wishing for the faculty of seeing, TS. ii. **-ṭás**, ind. away from the eye, ŚBr. xii. **-ṭva**, n. the state or condition of the eye, Āryabh., Sch., Introd. **-pati**, m. the lord of the eyes, TUp. i, 6, 2. **-patha**, m. the range of sight, R. iii, 59, 11; Bhartṛ. i, 74. **-pá**, mfn. protecting the eyesight, VS. ii, 6; xx, 34. **-prīti**, f. delight of the eyes. **-mat** (*cáksh°*), mfn. endowed with the faculty of sight, furnished with eyes, seeing, RV. x, 18, 1; AV. xix, 49, 8; TS. i f.; ŚBr. i; MBh. &c.; representing the eye, AitBr. ii, 32, 2; *-tā*, f. the faculty of sight, Ragh. iv, 13; *-tva*, n. id., Kathās. lxxiv, 322.

Cakshusha, ifc. 'the eye,' see *sa-*; m., N. of a son of Ripu (v.l. *cāksh°*), VP. i, 13, 2.

Cakshushya, mfn. pleasing to the eyes, wholesome for the eyes or the eyesight, MBh. xiii, 3423; Suśr.; Hcat.; agreeable to the eyes, pleasing, good-looking, beautiful, ChUp. iii, 13, 8; Car. i, 5, 89; Rājat. iii, 493; 'being in any one's (instr.) range of sight' and 'dear to any one (instr.),' Śiś. viii, 57; m. a kind of collyrium (extracted from Amomum antorhiza), L.; Pandanus odoratissimus, L.; Hyperanthera Moringa, L.; also N. of other plants (*puṇḍarīka, kanaka*), L.; n. two kinds of collyrium (*kharparī-tuttha* & *sauvīrāñjana*), L.; the small shrub *prapauṇḍarīka*, L.; (*ā*), f. a kind of collyrium (calx of brass or a blue stone), L.; Pandanus odoratissimus, L.; Glycine labialis, L.; = °*kshur-bahala*, L.

Cákshus, mfn. seeing, RV. ii, 39, 5; x; AV. v, 24, 9; x, 10, 15; m., N. of a Marut, Hariv. 11545; of a Ṛishi (with the patr. Mānava, author of RV. ix, 106, 4-6), RAnukr.; of another Ṛishi (with the patr. Saurya, author of RV. x, 158), ib.; of a son of Anu, BhP. ix, 23, 1; f., N. of a river, BhP. v, 17, 6 f.; n. light, clearness, RV.; SV.; the act of seeing (dat. inf. = °*kshase*), AV. xviii, 3, 10; aspect, RV. x, 87, 8; faculty of seeing, sight, RV.; AV.; TS. ii, v; AitBr. ii, 6; ŚBr. x, xiv; Mn. &c.; a look, RV.; AV. iv, 9, 6; the eye, RV. &c. (often ifc., cf. *a-, á-ghora-, á-dabdha-*, &c.); *Prajāpates trīṇi cakshūṃshi*, 'the 3 eyes of Prajā-pati,' N. of a Sāman, ĀrshBr.; *Mitrā-Varuṇayoś cakshuḥ*, 'the eye of Mitra and Varuṇa' (cf. RV. vii, 61, 1), another Sāman, ĀrshBr.; = °*kshur-bahala*, L.

Cakshū, in comp. for °*kshus*. **-√kṛi**, Vop. vii, 84. **-rāga**, m. = °*kshush-prīti*, Rājat. v, 382. **-roga**, m. disease of the eye (v. l. °*kshu-r°*).

चखुस् *cakhvás*, mfn. (pf. P. p. √*khan*? [√*caksh*, Sāy.], cf. *khá*) displaying (?), RV. ii, 14, 4.

चघ् *cagh*, cl. 5. °*ghnoti*, to smite or slay, kill, Dhātup. xxvii, 26.

चङ्कुण *caṅkuṇa*, m., N. of a man, Rājat. iv.

चङ्कुर *caṅkura*, m. (√*cak*, Uṇ.) a carriage, L.; a tree, L.; n. any vehicle, L.

चङ्क्रम *caṅkrama*, m. (fr. Intens. √*kram*) going about, a walk, Lalit. xxiv; Divyâv. xxvi; a place for walking about, xxxii; Kāraṇḍ. xviii, xxiii; (*ā*), f. going about, a walk, Kauś. 31. **Caṅkramā-vat**, mfn. moving slowly or crookedly, W.

Caṅkramaṇa, mfn. going about, walking, Pāṇ. iii, 2, 150; going slowly or crookedly, W.; n. going about, walking, Āp.; Suśr.; Pañcat.; Cāṇ.; BhP.; MārkP.; going tortuously or slowly, W.; rotation (of a wheel), Siṅhâs. xvii, 2; a place for walking about, Kāraṇḍ. xii, 79; xviii, 91 & 112.

Caṅkramamāṇa, mfn. irr. pr. p. Intens. √*kram*.

Caṅkramitá, mfn. one who has wandered about, TS. vii, 1, 19, 3; n. walking about, Bālar. v, 66.

चङ्ग *caṅga*, mfn. ifc. understanding, being a judge of, particular in the choice of, Kathās. lxxxii; handsome, L.; m., N. of a man, Rājat. vii, 87. **-dāsa**, m., N. of a grammarian.

चङ्गेरिक *caṅgerika*, n. a basket, Pañcad. ii, 64; (*ā*), f. id., v, 13 & 17 ff.

Caṅgerī, f. id., iv, 12; v, 16.

चचर *cacará*, mfn. (√*car*?) movable (?), RV. x, 106, 8.

चचेण्डा *caceṇḍā*, f., N. of a creeper, L.

चच्चपुट *cacca-puṭa*, m. (in music) a kind of measure, L.; (cf. *cāca-p°*.)

Caccat-puṭa, m. id., W. (v. l. *cañc°*).

Caccarī, f. id.

चञ्च् *cañc*, cl. 1. P. °*cati*, to leap, jump, move, dangle, be unsteady, shake, Bhartṛ.; Veṇīs. (Sāh. vi, 84, Sch.); Ṛitus.; Gīt.; Kathās. &c.

Cañca, m. a basket, Buddh. L.; (*ā*), f. anything made of cane or reeds, basket-work, L.; = °*ñcā-purusha*, Pāṇ. i, 2, 52, Vārtt. 5, Pat.; iv f., Pat. & Kāś.

Cañcatka, mfn. (fr. pr. p. °*cat*) leaping, jumping, dangling, v, 4, 3, Vārtt.

Cañcat-puṭa, m. = *cacc°*, W.

Cañcā, f. of °*ca*, q. v. **-purusha**, m. a straw-man, doll (said contemptuously of a man), Siṅhâs. (ŚārṅgP. xxiii).

चञ्चरिन् *cañcarin*, m. or °*rī*, f. (fr. Intens. √*car*) a bee, Udbh.

Cañcarīka, m. id., Bālar. v, 30; Prasannar.; Dhūrtan. &c. **Cañcarīkâvalī**, f. 'row of bees,' a metre of 4 × 13 syllables.

चञ्चल *cañcala*, mf(*ā*)n. (fr. Intens. √*cal*) moving to and fro, movable, unsteady, shaking, quivering, flickering, MBh. &c.; unsteady, inconstant, inconsiderate, ib.; m. the wind, L.; a lover, libertine, L.; N. of an Asura, GaṇP.; (*ā*), f. lightning, Rājat. iv, 354; a river, Gal.; long pepper, L.; fortune, goddess of fortune (Lakshmī), Gal. (cf. MBh. xii, 8258; R. &c.); a metre of 4 × 16 syllables; (*ī*), f. a kind of cricket, Npr. **-tara**, mfn. (compar.) extremely unsteady, Bhartṛ. iii, 50. **-tā**, f. unsteadiness, fickleness, W. **-taila**, n. Liquidambar orientale, Npr. **-tva**, n. = *-tā*, Bhag. vi, 33. **-hṛidaya**, mfn. 'unsteady-hearted,' capricious, fickle, W. **Cañcalâkshikā**, f. 'unsteady-eyed' (so called as not having a fixed caesura), a metre of 4 × 12 syllables. **Cañcalâkhya**, m. incense, L.

Cañcalita, mfn. caused to shake or quiver, Kād.

चञ्चु *cañcu*, mfn. ifc. (= *caṇa, cuñcu*) renowned or famous for, MBh. xiii, 17, 107; Bhartṛ. iii, 57; m. a deer, L.; the castor-oil plant, L. (cf. *-taila*); a red kind of the same plant, L.; the plant Go-nāḍīka (or Nāḍīca), L.; the plant Kshudra-cañcu, L.; N. of a son of Harita, Hariv. 758; VP. iv, 3, 15; f. a beak, bill, VarBṛS.; Pañcat.; Hit.; = *-pattra*, Bhpr.; (n.?) a box (applied as a N. to one of the 3 kinds of famine), Divyâv. **-tā**, f. = *-tva*, Rājat. v, 304; the state of a beak, W. **-taila**, n. castor-oil, Bhpr. **-tva**, n. the being famous for (in comp.), Daś. i. 223. **-pattra**, m. 'beak-leaved,' a kind of vegetable, L. **-parṇikā**, f. id., Car. i, 27. **-puṭa**, m. or n. the cavity of a beak, a bird's bill when shut, Caurap.; (*ī*), f. id.; N. of a plant, Car. vi, 9. **-puṭaka**, = °*ṭa*, ŚārṅgP. **-prahāra**, m. a peck with a beak, W. **-bhṛit**, 'having a beak,' a bird, L. **-mat**, m. id., L. **-sūci**, °**cika**, m. 'using the beak as a needle,' the tailor-bird (Sylvia sutoria), L.

Cañcukā, f. a beak, bill, L.

1. **Cañcura**, m. = °*cu-pattra*, L.

Cañcū, f. a beak, bill, Vop. iv, 31; = °*ñcu-pattra*, L. **-puṭa**, = °*ñcu-p°*, Amar. 13.

Cañcūka, = °*ñcu-pattra*, Bhpr.; pl., N. of a people (south-west of Madhya-deśa), VarBṛS. xiv, 18.

Cañcūḍa, m. = °*ñcu-pattra*, L.

चञ्चुर 2. *cañcura*, ?. See *puṇya-*.

Cañcūryamāṇa, mfn. fr. Intens. √*car*, q. v.

चञ्चुल *cañcula*, v. l. for *cuñc°*.

चट् *caṭ*, cl. 1. P. °*ṭati*, to fall in (as the flood), Pañcat. i, 12, $\frac{8}{9}$; to reach (with loc.), fall to the share of or into (loc.), Siṅhâs.; Pañcad.; to hang down from (loc.), Subh.; to rain, Dhātup. ix, 6; to cover (v. l. for √*kaṭ*), ib.: Caus. *cāṭayati*, to break, xxx, 47; to kill, ib.; (cf. *uc-, vi-*.)

Caṭa. See *krama-*.

Caṭaka, m. a sparrow, MBh. xii; Hariv.; Suśr.; VarBṛS.; Pañcat.; N. of a poet, Rājat. iv, 496; m. pl. 'sparrows,' a nickname of Vaiśampāyana's school (v. l. for *caraka*), VāyuP.; (*ā*), f. (gaṇas *ajâdi* & *kshipakâdi*) a hen-sparrow, Pañcat. i, 15, $\frac{8}{9}$; 18, $\frac{8}{9}$; a young hen-sparrow, Pāṇ. iv, 1, 128, Vārtt. 2; Turdus macrourus (*śyāmā*), L.; = °*kā-śiras*, L., Sch.; (*ikā*), f. id., L.; a hen-sparrow, L.

Caṭakakā, f. dimin. fr. °*ṭakā*, Pāṇ. vii, 3, 46.

Caṭakā, f. of °*ka*, q. v. **-śiras**, n. the root of long pepper, Bhpr. v, 1, 64.

Caṭakikā, f. = °*kakā*, Pāṇ. vii, 3, 46, Kāś.

Caṭana, n. cracking, splitting, W.; falling off in small pieces, W.

Caṭikā, f. of °*ṭaka*, q. v. **-śira**, m. = °*ras*, L., Sch. **-śiras**, n. = °*ṭakā-ś°*, L.

Caṭita, mfn. gone or driven anywhere (loc.), Siṅhâs.; hanging down from (in comp.), Pañcat. ii, 3, $\frac{3}{4}$; broken, Car. ii, 1; fallen in (a house), Kāraṇḍ. iii, 20 f.; n. = °*taka*, Divyâv. i, 413 & 418 (in comp.)

Caṭitaka, m. a crack, rent, 411.

चटचट *caṭacaṭa* (onomat.), P. °*ṭati*, to crackle (as fire), Vāsav. 607.

Caṭacaṭā, ind. (onomat.) only in comp. **-śabda**, m. crackling (of fire), clashing (of weapons), rattling (of violent rain), &c., MBh. i, iii f., vii, ix; BhP. x, 72, 36; MārkP. viii, 114.

Caṭacaṭâya, °*yate*, = °*ṭa*, Suśr. v, 1, 27; Bhoj.

Caṭacaṭâyana, n. crackling (of fire), Suśr. iv, 1.

Caṭacaṭâyita, mfn. crackling, Daś. xii, 13.

Caṭaccaṭ-iti, ind. so as to crackle, HPariś.

Caṭat, ind. = °*ṭacaṭā*. **-kāra**, m. crackling (of fire), L. **-kriti**, f. id., L.

Caṭad-iti, ind. so as to make a crackling noise, Bālar. v, 77.

चटन *caṭana*, °*ṭikā*, &c. See √*caṭ*.

चटु *caṭu* (m. n., L.; √*caṭ*, Uṇ.; g. *sidhmâdi*), kind or flattering words, amorous chattering (of birds), Śiś. iv, 6; Bālar.; the belly, L.; a devotional posture among ascetics, L.; m. a scream, screech, W.; cf. *cāṭu, cāru*. **-kāra**, mfn. speaking to please or flatter any one, L. **-grāma**, m., N. of a village (dwelling-place of the lexicographer Jaṭādhara). **-lālasa**, mfn. desirous of flattery, W. **Caṭûpamā**, f. a flattery said in a simile, Kāvyâd. ii, 35.

Caṭuka, a wooden vessel for taking up any fluid, Hāl., Sch.

Caṭula, mfn. (g. *sidhmâdi*) trembling, movable, shaking, unsteady, Ragh.; Megh.; Kād.; Bhartṛ. &c.; kind, fine, sweet, Śāntiś. i, 21; Gīt. x, 9; n. pl. sweet or flattering words, VarBṛS. lxxiv, 16; (*ā*), f. (=*cañcalā*) lightning, L.

Caṭulaya, Nom. P. °*yati*, to move to and fro, Bhām. ii, 87 & 97.

Caṭulāya, Nom. Ā. °*yate*, to have a graceful gait, Hcar. vii.

Caṭulita, mfn. shaken, Vāgbh. i, 24.

Caṭullola, mfn. moving gracefully, L.

चट्ट *caṭṭa*, m., N. of a man, HPariś. iii, 197.

चण् *caṇ* (cf. √*can*), cl. 1. P. °*ṇati*, to give, Dhātup. xix, 34; to go, ib.; to injure, ib.; to sound (v.l. for √*van*), xiii, 3: Caus. aor. *acīcaṇat* or *acacāṇat*, Pāṇ. vii, 4, 3, Siddh.

चण *caṇa*, mfn. ifc. (Pāṇ. v, 2, 26; =*cañcu*) renowned or famous for, HPariś. viii, 195; m. the chick-pea, MBh. xiii, 5468; (cf. *akshara-*, *kathā-*, *cāra-*, *māyā-*.) **-tva**, n. the being famous for (in comp.), Daś. i, 223. **-druma**, m. a kind of Tribulus, L. **-pattrī**, f. the shrub Rudantī, L. **-bhojin**, m. 'eating chick-pease,' a horse, Npr. **Caṇêśvarī**, f., N. of Caṇin's wife, HPariś. viii, 194.

Caṇaka, m. the chick-pea, Suśr.; VarBṛS. xv f.; Pañcat.; Kathās.; N. of Cāṇakya's father, L.; of a village, HPariś. viii, 194; (*ā*), f. linseed, L.; (*ikā*), f. a kind of grass (*kshetra-jā*, *go-dugdhā*, *su-nīlā*, *himā*), L. **-lavaṇa**, n. pease with salt, sour pease, Bhpr. **-loṇī**, f. (for *-lavaṇī*) id., Npr. **Caṇakâtmaja**, m. 'Caṇaka's son,' Cāṇakya, L. **Caṇakâmlaka**, n. = °*ka-lavaṇa*, Bhpr. **Caṇakâmla-vār**, n. acid water drops on cicer leaves, W.

Caṇāra-rūpya, n., N. of a village, Pāṇ. iv, 2, 104, Vārtt. 3, Pat.

Caṇin, m., N. of a Brāhman, HPariś. viii, 194.

Caṇī-druma, v.l. for °*ṇa-dr*°.

चण्ड् *caṇḍ* (derived fr. *cáṇḍa*), cl. 1 & 10. Ā. °*ṇḍate*, °*ṇḍayate*, to be angry or wrathful, Dhātup. viii, 26.

Cáṇḍa, mf(*ā*, VarBṛS. lxviii, 92; *ī*, R. ii; Vikr.; Ragh. &c.)n. (probably fr. *candrá*, 'glowing' with passion) fierce, violent, cruel, impetuous, hot, ardent with passion, passionate, angry, MBh.; R. &c.; circumcised, L.; m., N. of a mythical being (*Cáṇḍasya naptyàs*, 'daughters of Caṇḍa,' a class of female demons, AV. ii, 14, 1), AgP. xlii, 20; Śiva or Bhairava, MBh. xii, 10358; Śaṃkar. xxiii (=*sūrya*); Skanda, MBh. iii, 14631; N. of a demon causing diseases, Hariv. 9563; of a Daitya, 12937; of an attendant of Yama or of Śiva, L.; of one of the 7 clouds enveloping the earth at the deluge, MatsyaP.; =*-cukrā*, L.; n. heat, L.; passion, wrath, L.; (*am*), ind. violently, in anger, Mālav. iii, 21; (*ā*), f. (g. *bahv-ādi*), N. of Durgā (esp. as incarnation for the purpose of destroying the Asura Mahisha, this exploit forming the subject of the Devīm. and being particularly celebrated in Bengal at the Durgā-pūjā about Oct. Nov.), MBh. vi, 797; Hariv. 10245; N. of one of the 8 Nāyikās or Śaktis of Durgā, BrahmavP.; DevīP.; N. of an attendant of the 12th Arhat of the present Avasarpiṇī, L.; of a river, L.; of a plant (Andropogon aciculatus, L.; Mucuna pruritus, L.; Salvinia cucullata, L.; white Dūrvā grass, L.; *liṅginī*, L.), Suśr. i, iv; vi, 51; a kind of perfume (commonly Chor), L.; (*ī*), f. (g. *bahv-ādi*) a passionate woman, vixen, W.; a term of endearment applied to a mistress, W.; N. of Durgā, MBh. vi, 797; Hariv. 10233; Kathās. xi; of a female attendant of Durgā; of Uddālaka's wife, JaimBhār. xxiv, 1; a short N. of the Devīm.; a metre of 4×13 syllables; (cf. *uc-*, *pra-*; *a-caṇḍī*, *cāṇḍa*.) **-kara**, m. 'hot-rayed,' the sun; °*rāya*, Nom. °*rāyate*, to resemble the sun, Śukas. **-karman**, m., N. of a Rākshasa, Pañcat. v, 13, $\frac{1}{2}$. **-kāpālika**, m., N. of a teacher, Hathapr. i, 8; (cf. *shaṇḍ*°) **-kiraṇa**, m. =*-kara*, Vcar. xi, 7. **-ketu**, m., N. of a man, Kathās. lxxi, 16. **-kolāhalā**, f. a kind of musical instrument, L. **-kauśika**, m., N. of a son of Kakshīvat, MBh. ii, 698; n., N. of a drama, Sāh. vi, 92 & 96, Sch. **-girika**, m., N. of a man, Divyâv. xxvi. **-grāha-vat**, mfn. filled with fierce crocodiles (a river), MBh. i, 6752. **-ghaṇṭā**, f. 'having hot bells,' N. of Durgā, Tantr.; (cf. *caṇḍika-ghaṇṭa*.) **-ghosha**, m., N. of a man, Daś. ix, 71. **-cukrā**, f. the tamarind tree, Npr. **-tā**, f. warmth, pungency, W.; =*-tva*, Mālav. iii, 20. **-tāla**, m. (in music) a kind of measure. **-tuṇḍaka**, m. 'powerful-beaked,' N. of a son of the bird Garuḍa, MBh. v, 3594. **-tva**, n. warmth of temper, passionateness, Pratāpar.; Sāh. iii, 150. **-dīdhiti**, m. = *-kara*, Kathās. iic, 45. **-dhāman**, m. id., Prasannar. iv, $\frac{38}{40}$. **-nāyikā**, f., N. of one of the 8 Nāyikās of Durgā, BrahmavP. ii, 61, 79; DevīP.; N. of Durgā, L. **-potaka**, m., N. of an elephant, Daś. vi, 55 & 59. **-pradyota**, m., N. of a prince, Jain. **-prabha**, m., N. of a man, Kathās. ci, 48. **-bala**, m., N. of one of Rāma's monkey followers, MBh. iii, 16414. **-bhānu**, m., N. of a man, Ṭoḍar. **-bhārgava**, m., N. of a Brāhman of Cyavana's family, MBh. i, 2045. **-bhujaṃga**, m., N. of a man, Kathās. lxxiv, 178. **-marīci**, m. = *-kara*, Prasannar. vii, $\frac{81}{82}$. **-mahā-roshaṇa-tantra**, n., N. of a Buddhist work. **-mahā-sena**, m., N. of a king of Ujjayinī, Viddh. ii, $\frac{1}{2}$; Kathās. xi, 7 & 40. **-māruta**, N. of a work. **-muṇḍā**, f. a form of Durgā, L.; (cf. *carma-m*°, *cāmuṇḍā*.) **-mṛiga**, m. a wild animal (applied to a passionate man), Buddh. L. **-rava**, m. 'crying harshly,' N. of a jackal, Pañcat. i, 10, $\frac{1}{2}$. **-raśmi**, m. = *-kara*, Hāsy. 1, 49. **-rudrikā**, f. knowledge of mystical nature (acquired by worship of the Nāyikās), L. **-rūpā**, f. 'terribly formed,' N. of a goddess, BrahmaP. **-rocis**, m. = *-kara*, HYog. iii, 60. **-vat**, mfn. violent, warm, passionate, W.; (*tī*), f., N. of one of the 8 Nāyikās of Durgā, BrahmavP. ii, 61, 80; DevīP.; N. of Durgā, L. **-varman**, m., N. of a prince, Daś. vii, 437. **-vikrama**, mfn. of impetuous valour, R. v, 39, 24; N. of a prince, Kathās. xxvi, 177. **-vīra**, m., N. of a Buddh. deity. **-vṛitti**, mfn. 'of an impetuous character,' obstinate, rebellious, Viddh. iv, $\frac{13}{14}$. **-vṛishṭi-prapāta**, m. (or ?*-prayāta*, n.) 'impetuous rainfall,' a metre of 4 lines of 27 syllables each (the first 6 being short and the rest forming 7 Amphimacers). **-vega**, mfn. having an impetuous course or current (said of the sea, of the battle, and of time), R. iv f.; BhP. iv, 29, 20; m., N. of a metre; of a Gandharva chief, 27, 13; (*ā*), f., 'N. of a river;' °*gā-saṃgama-tīrtha*, n. N. of a Tīrtha, RevāKh. xviii. **-śakti**, m. 'of impetuous valour,' N. of a Daitya, Hariv. 12944. **-śīla**, mfn. 'of an impetuous character,' passionate, Daś. vi, 34. **-siṅha**, m. N. of a prince, Kathās. **Caṇḍâṅśu**, m. = °*ṇḍa-kara*, Mahān.; BhP.; Kathās.; Rājat. iv, 401. **Caṇḍâditya-tīrtha**, n. N. of a Tīrtha, RevāKh. cxliii. **Caṇḍântika**, n. for *cáṇḍātaka*, GobhŚrāddh. ii, 19. **Caṇḍâśoka**, m. 'impetuous Aśoka,' N. of a prince (also called Kāmâśoka, and as protector of Buddhism Dharmâśoka), Divyâv. xxvi; Hcar. vii. **Caṇḍêśa**, N. of a Liṅga, LiṅgaP. **Caṇḍêśvara**, m. 'Caṇḍa's lord,' Śiva, Megh. 34; N. of one of Śiva's attendants, W.; N. of a writer on jurisprudence, Śūdradh.; Smṛitit. i; of an astronomer; of an ancestor of Jagaddhara (mentioned in his Comm. on Mālatim.); n., N. of a Tīrtha, KapSaṃh.; *-praśna-vidyā*, f. 'knowledge of Caṇḍêśvara's questions,' N. of a work; *-rasa*, m., N. of a medical preparation (made of mercury, arsenic, &c.) **Caṇḍôgra-śūla-pāṇi**, m. 'holding a powerful and formidable trident,' a form of Śiva, Tantras. ii. **Caṇḍôgrā**, f., N. of one of the 8 Nāyikās or Śaktis of Durgā, BrahmavP. ii, 61, 79.

Caṇḍi, f. = °*ḍī*, N. of Durgā, L., Sch. **-dāsa**, m. = °*ṇḍī-d*°.

Caṇḍika, mfn. (= °*ḍa*) circumcised, Gal. **-ghaṇṭa**, m., N. of Śiva (cf. *caṇḍa-ghaṇṭā*), MBh. xii, 10377.

Caṇḍikā, f., N. of Durgā, ĀtrAnukr., Sch.; Pañcat.; BhP.; Kathās. &c.; a short N. of Devīm.; =*-gṛiha*, Kād.; N. of a Surâṅganā, Siṅhâs.; Linum usitatissimum, L. **-gṛiha**, n. a temple of Durgā, Kād.; Kathās. xxv, 86. **-mahā-navamī**, f. a particular 9th day on which Durgā is worshipped, BhavP. **-māhātmya**, n. 'glory of Caṇḍikā,' another N. of Devīm. **Caṇḍikâlaya**, m. = °*kā-gṛiha*, Siṅhās. **Caṇḍikā-śataka**, n. '100 stanzas in praise of Caṇḍikā,' N. of a poem (ascribed to Bāṇa).

Caṇḍiman, m. (g. *pṛithv-ādi*) passion, violence, cruelty, Bālar. iii, $\frac{8}{9}$; 'passion' and 'heat,' Rājat. vi, 298; intensity, Sāh. iii, 246$\frac{a}{b}$.

Caṇḍila, m., N. of Rudra, L.; a barber, L.; Chenopodium, L.; (*ā*), f., N. of a river, L.

1. **Caṇḍī**, ind. **-kṛita**, mfn. made angry, Mālav.

2. **Caṇḍī**, f. of °*ḍa*, q.v. **-kuca-pañcaśatī**, f. '500 stanzas in praise of the breast of a passionate woman,' N. of a poem. **-kusuma**, n. 'flower of passionate women,' red oleander, L. **-gṛiha**, n. = °*ḍikā-g*°, Kathās. xxv, 111. **-carita**, n., N. of a drama. **-ḍāmara**, m., N. of a work. **-dāsa**, m., N. of the author of a Comm. on Kpr., Sāh. iv, $\frac{14c}{v}$ (°*ṇḍi-d*°) & vii, 31$\frac{a}{b}$. **-devī-śarman**, m., N. of a scholiast. **-pati**, m. 'Caṇḍī's lord,' Śiva, Mcar. ii, 35. **-pāṭha**, m. another N. of Devīm. **-purāṇa**, n. another N. of KālP., Tantr. **-māhātmya**, n. = °*ḍikā-m*°. **-rahasya**, n., N. of a work. **-vidhāna**, n., °*dhi*, m. two names of works. **-vilāsa**, m., N. of a drama. **-°śa** (°*ḍīś*°), m. = *-pati*, BhP. iv, 5, 17; Bālar. iii, 79; Naish.; *-tīrtha*, n., N. of a Tīrtha, SkandaP.; *-paryākrama*, m., N. of a work; *-purāṇa*, n. another N. of ŚivaP. **-°śvara** (°*ḍīś*°), m. = °*śa*, Megh. 33; N. of an author. **-stotra**, n. 'praise of Caṇḍī,' N. of a poem.

चण्डात *caṇḍāta*, m. Nerium odorum (cf. *caṇḍī-kusuma*), L.

Cáṇḍātaka, n. a short petticoat, ŚBr. v, 2, 1, 8; KātyŚr. xiv, 5, 3; cf. *caṇḍântika*.

चण्डाल *caṇḍāla*, m. (=*cāṇḍālá*) an outcast, man of the lowest and most despised of the mixed tribes (born from a Śūdra father and a Brāhman mother), ŚāṅkhGṛ. ii, vi; ChUp.; Mn. &c. (ifc. 'a very low representative of,' Kād.); (*ā*), f. a Caṇḍāla woman, Mn. xi, 176; (*ī*), f. (g. *śārṅgaravâdi*) id. (one of the 8 kinds of women attending on Kaula worship), Kulārṇ. vii; N. of a plant, L. **-kanda**, m., N. of a bulbous plant, L. **-tā**, f. the condition of a Caṇḍāla, R. i, 58, 9. **-tva**, n. id., 8. **-vallakī**, f. the Caṇḍāla or common lute, L.

Caṇḍālikā, f. = °*la-vallakī*, L.; N. of a plant, L.; of Durgā, L. **-bandham**, ind. so as to form a particular knot, Pāṇ. iii, 4, 42, Sch. (not in Kāś.)

चण्डि *caṇḍi*, °*ḍika*, &c. See *cáṇḍa*.

चण्डु *caṇḍu*, m. a rat, L.; a small monkey (Simia erythraea), W.

चत् *cat*, cl. 1. *cátati*, 'to hide one's self.' see *cátat* & *cáttá*; to go, Naigh. ii, 14; P. & Ā. to ask, beg (= √*cad*), Dhātup. xxi, 5: Caus. *cātáyati*, °*te* (aor. *acīcattam*, *acīcate*, TĀr. ii, 4, 5 f.), 'to cause to hide,' scare, frighten away, RV. iv, 17, 9; x, 155, 1; AV. iv, xix; (cf. *niś-*, *pra-*, *vi-*; cf. also *cātaka*, *cātana*, *cāttra*.)

Cátat, mfn. (pr. p.) hiding one's self, RV. i, 65, 1; x, 46, 2.

Catita, mfn. class. = *cattá*, Pāṇ. vii, 2, 34, Kāś.

Catín, mfn. = *cátat*, RV. vi, 19, 4.

Cattá, mfn. (Ved., Pāṇ. vii, 2, 34) hidden, RV. i, 132, 6; AV. ix, 5, 9; (quotation in) Pāṇ. vii, 2, 34, Kāś.; disappeared, RV. x, 155, 2. **-rātra**, m. 'N. of a man,' see *cāttarātra*.

Cattra, n. v.l. for *cāttra*.

Catya, mfn. to be hidden, Pāṇ. iii, 1, 97, Vārtt. 1, Pat.

चतस् *cátasṛi*, pl. f. of *catúr*, 4 (nom. & acc. *cátasras* [cf. Pāṇ. vii, 2, 99, Vārtt. 2]; instr. *catasṛíbhis* [cf. vi, 1, 180 f.], RV. viii, 60, 9; gen. °*sṛiṇâm*, ŚBr. iii, 3, 2, 13; or °*sṛiṇām* [Ved., Pāṇ. vi, 4, 5], R. i, 72, 12 & 73, 32; loc. °*sṛishu*, ŚBr. iii, 5, 1, 1); [see *priya-*; cf. Hib. *ceteora*.]

Catasṛikā, f. pl. id., Hcat. i, 11, 672.

1. **Catu**, mfn. = °*turthá*, TĀr. i, 8, 4.

2. **Catu**, in comp. for °*túr* (before *s* followed by a surd dental and *sh* followed by a surd lingual). **-shṭomá**, m. a Stoma consisting of 4 parts (the 2nd, 3rd, and 4th having 4 verses more than the preceding), VS. xiv; TS. v; ŚBr. xiii; R. i, 13, 43; mfn. connected with a Catushṭoma (an Ekâha), AitBr. iii, 43; TāṇḍyaBr. xxi; KātyŚr.; ŚāṅkhŚr.; Lāṭy. **-staná** or *cát*°, f. (a cow) having 4 nipples, MaitrS. iii, 1, 7; Kāṭh. xxx, 4; ŚBr. vi. **-stotra**, mfn. consisting of 4 Stotras, KātyŚr. xii, 6, 4. **-sthāna**, mfn. having a fourfold basis, Nār. i, 8.

Catuḥ, in comp. for °*túr* & °*tús*. **-pañca**, °*cāśa*, &c., see *catush-p*°, cf. Pāṇ. viii, 3, 43. **-śata** (*cát*°), n. 104, RV. viii, 55, 3; ŚāṅkhŚr.; Lāṭy.; 400, R. vii, 23, 19; BhP. x, 1, 31; mf(*ā*)n. 400, ChUp. iv, 4, 5; (*ī*), f. '400 stanzas,' N. of a Tantric poem, Anand., Sch.; *-tama*, mfn. the 104th (ch. of R. ii & vi). **-śapha** (*cát*°), mfn. four-hoofed, TBr. iii, 8, 2, 1. **-śamī**, f. 4 Śamīs long, Kauś. 137. **-śarāva** (*cát*°), mfn. measuring 4 Śarāvas, MaitrS. i; TS. iii &c. **-śākha**, n. 'having

4 extremities,' the body, L. — **śāla**, mfn. having 4 halls, MBh. i, iii; Pañcat.; MatsyaP.; Rājat.; m. a building with 4 halls, R. ii f.; Mṛicch. iii, 7; Rājat. iii, 13. — **śālaka**, n. id., L.; (*ikā*), f. id., Pañcad. ii, 74. — **śikha**, m. 'four-tufted,' N. of an author. — **śikhaṇḍa** (*cát*°), mf(*ā*)n. four-tufted, TBr. i, iii (°*tush-kaparda*, RV.) — **śila**, n. 4 stones, Kauś. 36. — **śṛiṅga** (*cát*°), mfn. four-horned, RV. iv, 58, 2; m. 'four-peaked,' N. of a mountain, BhP. v, 20, 15. — **śruti**, mfn. (in music) having 4 intervals. — **śrotra** (*cát*°), mf(*ā*)n. four-eared, AV. v, 19, 7. — **shashṭa**, mfn. the 64th (ch. of MBh.); (with *śata*, 100) + 64, KātyŚr.; Lāṭy. — **shashṭi**, f. 64, AitBr. i, 5, 8; Mn. viii, 338; Hariv.; R.; the 64 Kalās, MBh. ii, 2068; N. of RV. (consisting of 64 Adhyāyas), L.; -*kalâgama*, m. a treatise on the 64 Kalās, Daś. x, 147; -*kalā-śāstra*, n. id., Madhus.; -*tama*, mfn. the 64th, AitBr. i, 5, 8; (also applied to chapters of R.); °*shṭy-aṅga*, mfn. having 64 subdivisions (the Jyotiḥ-śāstra), Mudr. i, ⅞. — **shṭomá**, see °*tu-shṭ*°. — **saṃstha**, mfn. consisting of 4 Saṃsthās or kinds of Soma oblation, Vait. — **saṃkara**, mfn. (a lawsuit) in which 4 matters are mingled, Yājñ. ii, 7⅞, 49. — **sana**, mfn. containing the 4 sons of Brahmā (whose names begin with *sana*, viz. Sanaka, Sananda, Sanātana, Sanat-kumāra), BhP. ii, 7, 5. — **saṃdhi**, mfn. composed of 4 parts, AitBr. i, 25, 4. — **saptata**, mfn. the 74th (ch. of MBh.) — **saptati**, f. 74, Caraṇ.; -*tama*, mfn. = °*ptata* (ch. of R.) — **saptâtman**, mfn. having 4 × 7 (i.e. 28) shapes, NṛisUp. ii, 3. — **sama**, mfn. having 4 symmetric parts of the body (viz. arms, knees, legs, and cheeks, Sch.; but cf. -*śākha* & *cátur-aṅga*), R. v, 32, 13 (cf. Hariv. 14779); n. an unguent of 4 ingredients (sandal, agallochum, saffron, and musk, Bhpr. vii). — **samudra** (*cát*°), mf(*ī*)n. having 4 seas, RV. x, 47, 2; surrounded by 4 seas (the earth), Bālar. x, 66; Kathās. lxix, 181. — **sahasra** (*cát*°), n. 4000, RV. v, 30, 15; 1004, W. — **sādhana**, mfn. yielding 4 ways of attaining an object, Nār. i, 8 & 12. — **sāhasraka**, mf(*ikā*)n. consisting of 4000, VāyuP. — **sīta** (*cát*°), mfn. having 4 furrows, TS. v. — **stanā, -stotra, -sthāna**, see *catu-s*°. — **srakti** (*cát*°), mfn. quadrangular, VS. xxxviii, 20; TS. i, vi; ŚBr. i (said of the Vedi), vi f.; f. (scil. *vedi*) = *uttara-vedi*, TĀr. iv f.

Catur, °*tváras*, m. pl., °*tvā́ri*, n. pl., 4 (acc. m. °*túras*, instr. °*túrbhis* [for f., R. iv, 39, 33], gen. °*turṇā́m*, abl. °*túrbhyas*; class. instr., dat., abl., and loc. also oxyt., Pāṇ. vi, 1, 180 f.; ifc., Kāś. & Siddh. on Pāṇ. vii, 1, 55 & 98 ff.; for f. see *cátasri*); [cf. τέσσαρες, τέτταρες, Aeol. πίσυρες; Goth. *fidvor*; Lat. *quatuor*; Cambro-Brit. *pedwar, pedair*; Hib. *ceathair*; Lith. *keturi*; Slav. *cetyrje*.] — **aṃśa-vat**, mfn. consisting of 4 parts, Jyot. — **akshá**, mf(*ī*)n. four-eyed, RV. i, 31, 13; x, 14, 10 f.; AV.; TS. v; ŚBr. xiii; ŚāṅkhBr. iii, 5; KātyŚr. — **akshara** (*cát*°), mfn. consisting of 4 syllables, VS. ix, 31; ŚBr. iv, 1 & 3; n. a combination of 4 syllables, ŚāṅkhŚr.; Lāṭy.; RPrāt.; BhP. vi, 2, 8; -*śas*, ind. in numbers of 4 syllables, Lāṭy. — **agni-vat**, mfn. having 4 fires, Pāṇ. viii, 2, 15, Pat. — **aṅga** (*cát*°), mfn. having 4 limbs (or extremities), RV. x, 92, 11; ŚBr. xii; (with *bala*, an army) comprising (4 parts, viz.) elephants, chariots, cavalry, and infantry, MBh. iii, 790; R. ii, 51, 7; m. Cucumis utilissimus (?), L.; N. of a son of Roma- or Loma-pāda, Hariv. 1697 f.; BhP. ix, 23, 10; n. (scil. *bala*) = °*ṅga-bala*, AV. Pariś.; MBh. ix, 446; a kind of chess (played by 4 parties), Tithyād.; (*ā*), f. (scil. *senā*) = °*ṅga-bala*, AV. Pariś.; -*krīḍā*, f. playing at chess; -*bala*, n. an entire army (comprising elephants, chariots, cavalry, and infantry), MBh. iii, 660; R.; Kathās. iii, 76; -*balâdhipatya*, n. command of a complete army, Śṛiṅgār.; -*balâdhyaksha*, m. the commander-in-chief of a complete army, L.; -*vinoda*, m., N. of a work; -*sainya*, n. = -*bala*, W. — °**aṅgin**, mfn. (= °*ṅga*; with *bala* or *vāhinī*, an army) comprising elephants, chariots, cavalry, and infantry, MBh. i, iv f.; R. i, iii; (*iṇī*), f. (scil. *vāhinī*) = °*ṅga-bala*, BhP. i, 10, 32. — **aṅgulá**, n. 4 fingers of the hand (without the thumb), ŚāṅkhŚr. xvii, 10, 6 f.; 4 fingers broad, 4 inches, ŚBr. x, 2, 2, 4; KātyŚr.; Kauś. 26; m. Cathartocarpus fistula, Car. vii, 8; Suśr. i, iv; -*paryavanaddha*, mfn. overgrown with that plant, Divyâv. viii. — **aṇuka**, n. an aggregate of 4 atoms, Bādar. ii, 2, 11, Sch. — **adhyāyika**, n., °**yikā**, f., °**yī**, f. 'consisting of 4 Adhyāyas,' N. of Śaunaka's APrāt. — **anīka** (*cát*°), mfn. four-faced (Varuṇa), RV. v, 48, 5. — **anugāna**, n., N. of a Sāman. — **anta**, mf(*ā*)n. bordered on all 4 sides (the earth), MBh. i, 2801 & 3100; R. ii, v; Śak. iv, 20; (*ā*), f. 'the earth,' in comp. °*tēśa*, m. 'earth-lord,' a king, Ragh. x, 86 (or *catur-antēśa* = -*dig-īśa*, q. v., Sch.) — **amla**, n. 4 sour substances (viz. *amla-vetasa*, *vṛikshâmla*, *bṛihaj-jambīra*, & *nimbaka*), Bhpr. — **artha**, mf(*ā*)n. having 4 meanings, L. — **avattá**, n. (*ava* √*do*) '4 times cut off or taken up, consisting of 4 Avadānas,' 4 Avadānas, TS. ii; ŚBr. i; KātySr. iii. — °**avattin**, mfn. one who offers oblations consisting of 4 Avadānas, AitBr. ii, 14, 3; Gobh.; KātyŚr., Sch. — **avarârdhya**, mfn. at least 4, Gobh. iv, 2, 6. — **aśīta**, mfn. the 84th (ch. of MBh.) — **aśīti**, f. 84, VarBṛS. lxxvii, 30; -*tama*, mfn. the 84th (ch. of R.); -*yogâdhyāya*, m. 'containing 84 chapters on the Yoga,' N. of a work; -*sāhasra*, mfn. numbering 84000, MārkP. liv, 15. — **aśra**, mf(*ā*)n. four-cornered, quadrangular, KātyŚr.; Kauś.; Pāṇ. v, 4, 120; Hariv. 12378 &c.; regular, Jain.; Kum. i, 32 (Vām. v, 2, 60); m. a quadrangular figure; a square, W.; (in astron.) N. of the 4th and 8th lunar mansions, Laghuj.; (in music) a kind of measure; (scil. *hasta*) a particular position of the hands (in dancing); (pl.) N. of various Ketus, VarBṛS. xi, 25; n. a particular posture (in dancing), Vikr. iv, 4½, Sch.; -*tā*, f. regularity, harmony, Kām.; °*śrī*-√*kṛi*, to make quadrangular, Hcat.; AgP.; KātyŚr., Sch. — °**aśraka**, mf(*ā*)n. four-cornered, forming a quadrangular figure, Hcat.; AgP. xliii, 27; m. a particular posture (in dancing), Vikr. iv, 4½. — **aśri** (*cát*°), mfn. quadrangular, RV. i, 152, 2; iv, 22, 2. — **áshṭaka**, mfn. having 4 days called Ashṭakās, Gobh. iii, 10, 4. — **asra, -asraka**, for -*aśr*°. — **ahá**, m. a period of 4 days, ŚBr. iii, 4, 4, 27; KātyŚr. xiii; a Soma sacrifice lasting 4 days, ŚBr. xii, 2, 2, 12; KātyŚr. xxiii f.; Vait. xl f.; (cf. *atri-c*°.) — **ātman**, mfn. representing 4 persons, having 4 faces or shapes, Hariv. 12884 (Vishṇu); NṛisUp.; Rājat. iv, 507 & v, 25 (Keśava). — **ādhyāyika**, °**yikā**, °**yī**, for -*adh*°. — **ānana**, m. 'four-faced,' Brahmā, VarBṛS. vci, 16; BhP. v, 1, 30; Kathās. xxiv. — **āśramin**, mfn. passing the 4 stages of a Brāhman's life, MBh. vii, 78, 27. — **āśramya**, for *cāt*°. — **iḍas-pada-stobha**, m. (cf. *iḍas-padê*) N. of a Sāman. — **indriya**, mfn. having 4 senses (a class of animals), Jain. — **uttará**, mfn. increasing by 4, AitBr. viii, 6; ŚBr. x, xii f.; RPrāt.; -*stoma*, m. with *Gotamasya*, N. of an Ekāha, ŚāṅkhŚr. xiv. — **ushṭra**, n. the 4 substances taken from a camel, Suśr. vi. — **ūdhnī**, f. (Aditi) having 4 udders, Kāṭh. xxx, 4. — **ūrdhva-pad**, m. (nom. -*pād*) 'having 4 feet more (than other animals),' the fabulous animal Śarabha (with 8 legs), Gal. — **ūshaṇa**, n. the 4 hot spices (black and long pepper, dry ginger, and the root of long pepper; cf. -*jāta* & *try-ūsh*°), Bhpr. v. — **ṛicá**, mfn. possessing 4 Ṛic verses, i. e. obtaining the merit suggested by them, SaṃhUp.; n. a hymn consisting of 4 verses, AV. xix, 23, 1. — **ṛiddhi-pāda-caraṇa-tala-supratishṭhita**, mfn. well-established on the soles of the feet of the supernatural power (Buddha), Divyâv. viii f. — **oghôttīrṇa**, mfn. one who has passed across the 4 floods (Buddha), ib. & xix, 51. — **gaṇa**, m. a series of 4. — **gati**, mfn. having 4 kinds of going, R. (B) v, 35, 19; 'going on 4 feet,' a tortoise, L. — **gandha**, mfn. fragrant on 4 sides, R. v, 32, 12 (v. l. -*vyaṅga*). — **gava**, n. a carriage drawn by 4 oxen, KātyŚr. xxii. — **guṇa** (*cát*°), mf(*ā*)n. fourfold, ŚBr. iii, 3, 2, 9; Hit.; tied with 4 strings (the upper garment), Divyâv. vi, 46. — **gṛihītá**, n. taken up or ladled out (as a fluid) 4 times, taking up (any fluid) 4 times, ŚBr. iii f.; KātyŚr. — **gṛihītin**, mfn. one who has taken up (any fluid) 4 times, Lāṭy. iii, 2, 6, Sch. — **grāma**, 'containing 4 villages,' N. of a country. — **jāta**, n. = *cát*°, L. — **jātaka**, n. id., Suśr.; KātyŚr. xix, Sch. — **ṇavata**, mfn. (= °*nav*°) the 94th, W.; (with *śata*, 100) + 94, KātyŚr. xvi. — **daṇshṭra** (*cát*°), mfn. having 4 tusks, AV. xi, 9, 17; MBh.; R. v; m. a beast of prey, Gal.; Vishṇu, L.; N. of an attendant of Skanda, MBh. ix, 2564; of a Dānava, Hariv. 12935. — **dat**, m(nom. -*dan*)fn. four-toothed, Pāṇ. v, 4, 141, Kāś. — **danta**, mfn. 'having 4 tusks,' Indra's elephant Airāvata, L.; N. of an elephant, Pañcat. iii, 1, ⅛; Kathās. lxii, 30. — **dala**, m. 'four-leaved,' Marsilea quadrifolia, Npr. — **daśá**, mf(*ī*)n. the 14th, Yājñ. ii, 113; R. ii; BhP. i, 3, 18; consisting of 14, VS. ix, 34; ŚāṅkhŚr. ix, xiv; RPrāt. xvii, 19; (*ī*), f. (scil. *rātri*) the 14th day in a lunar fortnight, ŚāṅkhGṛ. ii; iv, 7; ĀśvGṛ. ii, 3; Mn.; MBh.; Kathās.; °*śī-śānti*, f., N. of a work. — °**daśaka**, mfn. the 14th, MBh. i, 4334. — **daśan** (*cát*°), *a*, pl. (loc. °*śásu*, ŚBr. ix, 3, 2, 8) 14, RV. x, 114, 7; ŚBr.; KātyŚr.; [cf. Lat. *quatuordecim*; Lith. *keturōlika*]; °*śa-guṇa*, mfn. having 14 merits, cf. Sch. on R. (B) iv, 54, 2 & MBh. ii, 5, 21; °*śa-guṇa-nāman*, n. pl. N. of a work; °*śa-guṇa-sthāna*, n. N. of a work; °*śa-dhā́*, ind. fourteenfold, ŚBr. x, 4, 2, 11; BhP. v, 26, 38; °*śa-mata-viveka*, m. 'disquisition on the 14 philos. systems,' N. of a work by Śaṃkara; °*śa-rātra*, m. a Soma sacrifice lasting 14 days, ĀśvŚr. xi, 2, 6; °*śa-rcá*, n. a hymn consisting of 14 verses, AV. xix, 23, 11; °*śa-vidha*, mfn. fourteenfold, KapS. vi, 19, Sch.; °*śa-sama-dvandva*, mfn. having the 14 paired parts of the body symmetric, R. (B) v, 35, 19; °*śa-svapana-vicāra*, m. 'disquisition on the 14 kinds of sleep,' N. of a work; °*śâkshara* (*cát*°), mfn. having 14 syllables, VS. ix, 34. — **daśama**, mfn. = °*śaka*, BhP. viii, 13, 34. — °**daśika** (fr. °*śī*), a feast on the 14th day of a lunar fortnight, Buddh. L. — **daśī**, see °*śá*. — **dārikā**, f. N. of Kathās. xxiv–xxvi. — **dik-kam**, ind. towards the 4 quarters, on all sides, all around, cvii, 23; cxviii, 86. — **dikshu**, (loc. pl.) ind. id., W. — **diśam**, ind. id., MBh. ii, 570; BhP. v. — **daiva**, mfn. for *cát*°, Hariv. ii, 58, 17, Sch. — **dola**, m. n. a royal litter, Bhoj. — **dos**, mfn. four-armed, Naish. vii, 65. — **dvāra**, mf(*ā*)n. having 4 doors or openings, MBh. xii, 269, 23 (said of the *purusha*); Pañcad.; -*mukha*, mf(*ī*)n. having 4 doors as mouths, Ragh. xv, 60. — **dvīpa-cakravartin**, m. the sovereign of the 4 Dvīpas, SaddhP. i. — **dhara**, m., N. of a family or race. — **dhā́**, ind. in 4 parts, fourfold, RV. iv, 35, 2 f.; AV.; TS. ii; ŚBr.; MBh.; BhP.; [cf. τέτραχα; Hib. *ceathardha*]; -*karaṇa*, n. dividing into 4 parts, Nyāyam., Sch.; -√*kṛi*, to divide into 4 parts, ib.; -√*bhū*, to be divided into 4 parts, AV. x, 10, 29; -*vihitá*, mfn. divided into 4 parts, ŚBr. i; -*śānti*, f. a religious ceremony performed at the time of making the stated offerings to deceased ancestors, W. — **dhātu**, mfn. fourfold (a term in music). — **dhārin**, m. Cissus quadrangularis, Npr. — **navata**, mfn. (= -*ṇav*°) the 94th (a ch. of MBh.) — **navati**, f. 94, in comp. -*tama*, mfn. the 94th (a ch. of R.) — **nidhana** (*cát*°), mfn. consisting of 4 concluding passages, ŚBr. xii, 8, 3, 26. — **netṛi**, mfn. bringing near the 4 objects desired for by men, Hariv. ii, 121, 16. — **bāhu**, mfn. four-armed, Pañcat. v, 8, ⅛; (Vishṇu) BhP. viii, 17, 4; m., N. of Śiva. — **bila** (*cát*°), mfn. having 4 openings, AV. xviii, 4, 30; (said of an udder) ŚāṅkhGṛ. & ĀśvGṛ. ii, 10. — **bīja**, n. the 4 kinds of seed (viz. of Kālājājī, Candra-śūra, Methikā, and Yavānikā), Bhpr. — **bhadra**, mfn. (4 times, i. e.) extremely auspicious, Hcat.; n. 4 objects of human wishes (viz. *dharma*, *kāma*, *artha*, *bala*, L.; or the first 3 with *moksha*, W.; or *kīrti*, *āyus*, *yaśas*, *bala*, MBh. xiii, 5657; or *dharma*, *jñāna*, *vairāgya*, *aiśvarya*, vii, 2182, Sch.; or *dāna*, *jñāna*, *śaurya*, *bhoga* or *vitta*, ib.; Hit. i, 6, 58); -*tara*, mfn. (compar.) 4 times happier than (instr.), MBh. vii, 2182; 2194; 2207; 2449. — **bhadrikā**, f. a kind of medical preparation for curing fever, Bhpr. vii, 4, 12. — **bhāgá**, m. the 4th part, quarter, ŚBr. iii; KātyŚr. xxiv; Mn. &c.; mf(*ā*)n. forming the 4th part of (gen.), Hcat. — °**bhāgīyā**, f. (scil. *ishṭakā*) a brick of the 4th part of a man's length, Śulbas. — **bhuja**, (in comp.) 4 arms, BhP. iv, vi; mf(*ā*)n. four-armed, MBh. iii, 16424; R. i; BhP. iv; quadrangular; m. Vishṇu or Kṛishṇa (cf. Bhag. xi, 46), R. vi; Ragh.; Pañcat.; BhP. i; N. of Gaṇêśa, Gal.; a quadrangular figure; N. of a Dānava, Hariv. 12934; of the instructor of (the author of a Comm. on SkandaP.) Rāmânanda; of the father of Śiva-datta; -*bhaṭṭâcārya*, m., N. of an author, Smṛitit. iv; -*miśra*, m., N. of the author of a Comm. on MBh. iii f. & vii. — **bhūmika**, mfn. having 4 floors (a house), Pañcat. iv, 9, ⅛. — **bhūyas**, mfn. containing 4 (syllables) more, RPrāt. xvi, 2. — **bhṛishṭi** (*cát*°), mfn. four-cornered, quadrangular, RV. x, 57, 9; four-pointed, AV. x, 5, 50. — **mahā-patha**, n. meeting of 4 great roads, Divyâv. xxxv, 11. — **mahā-rāja**, m. pl. the 4 great kings or guardians of the lowest of the 6 sensuous heavens, W.; -*kāyika*, m. pl. (= *cāt*°) 'belonging to the attendance of those 4 great kings,' N. of a class of deities, Buddh. L. — °**mahārājika**, m., N. of Vishṇu, Vishṇ.; m. pl. = °*ja-kāyika*, Buddh.; (cf. *cāt*°.) — **māsa**, n. a period of 4 months, W.; (*ī*), f. id., Kathās. cxxiv, 154. — **māsya**, n. (= *cāt*°) a Cāturmāsya sacrifice, Kāṭh. xxxv, 20. — **mukha**, (in comp.) 4 faces, Kum. ii, 17; mfn. 'four-faced,' in comp.; four-pointed (an arrow), Hariv. 10630; m., N. of Brahmā, MBh. iii; R. i; BhP. iii, 8, 16; Kathās. xx; of Vishṇu, Hariv. 12344; Ragh. x, 23; of Śiva (cf. *-tva*), MBh. xiii, 6393; of a Dānava, Hariv. 12934; (in music) a kind of measure; *-tva*, n. (Śiva's) state of having 4 faces, VarBṛS. lxxiv, 20; *-tīrtha*, n. N. of a Tīrtha, SkandaP.; *-rasa*, m. a preparation of great curative power, Prayog. — **mushṭi,** m. 4 hands full, Gṛihyās. i, 43. — **mushṭika,** n. pl. id., KātySr. (?) — **muhūrtam,** ind. during 4 Muhūrtas, Gaut. xvi, 44. — **mūrti,** mfn. 'having 4 forms of appearance, four-faced,' in comp.; m., N. of Brahmā, MBh. iii, 13560; of Skanda, ix, 2486; of Vishṇu, Ragh. x, 74; BhP. v, 17, 16; *-tva*, n. the state of being four-faced, MBh. xiii, 6393. — **medha,** m. one who has offered 4 sacrifices (Aśva-, Purusha-, Sarva-, and Pitṛi-medha) or one who knows the Mantras required for them, Āp. ii, 17, 22. — **yama,** n. the having 4 tones of utterance, TPrāt. — **yukta,** mfn. drawn by 4 (horses or oxen), MBh. v, 86, 6. — **yuga,** n. (g. *pātrâdi*) the 4 Yugas (or ages of the world) combined (= a Mahā-yuga, q.v.), Mn. i, 71; MBh. xii, 11227; Hariv. 516 &c.; mf(*ā*)n. (*cát°*) = *-yukta*, RV. ii, 18, 1; comprising the 4 Yugas, Ragh. x, 23. — **yúj,** mfn. put to (as oxen) in a yoke of 4, RV. viii, 6, 48; = *-yukta*, ŚBr. v; KātySr.; MBh. i, vii; R. i. — **lekha,** mfn. having 4 lines on the forehead, R. v, 32, 13. — **vaktra,** mf(*ā*)n. four-faced, Vas.; m., N. of Brahmā, L.; of a Dānava, Hariv. iii, 47, 6; of an attendant of Durgā, Kathās. lii, 246. — **vaya** (*cát°*), mfn. fourfold, RV. i, 110, 3; iv, 36, 4. — **varga,** m. a collection of 4 things (e. g. = *-bhadra*), Ragh. x, 23; HYog. i, 15; Hit.; *-cintāmaṇi*, m., N. of a work by Hemādri. — **varṇa,** (in comp.) the 4 castes; 4 principal colours, W.; four letters, W.; *-maya*, mfn. consisting of the 4 castes, Ragh. x, 23; *°rṇâdi*, a Gaṇa of Kāty. (Pāṇ. v, 1, 124, Vārtt. 1; = *anantâdi* of Gaṇar. 178–180). — **varsha-śatâyus,** mfn. reaching an age of 400 years, Mn. i, 83. — **varshikā,** f. (scil. *go*) a cow 4 years old, L. — **vāhin,** m. (scil. *ratha*) a carriage drawn by 4 (horses or oxen), TāṇḍyaBr. xvi, 13, 12. — **vinśá,** mf(*ī*)n. the 24th, ŚāṅkhŚr.; Gobh.; Yājñ. i, 37; (with *śata*, 100) + 24, KātySr.; MBh. i, 3790; consisting of 24, VS. xiv, 25; TS. vii; ŚBr. vi, ix, xiii; AitBr. v, 29, 5; MBh. iii, 14271; m. (scil. *stóma*) N. of a Stoma having 24 parts, VS. xiv, 23; Lāṭy.; n. (with or without *ahan*) N. of an Ekâha (2nd day of the Gavām-ayana sacrifice), ŚBr. xii; TāṇḍyaBr. iv, 2, 4; KātySr.; Lāṭy.; (*°śika* with *ahan*, Sāy. on RV. iii, 35, 4; *cāturvinśaka*, on RV. i, 165, Introd.); *-stoma*, mfn. connected with the Caturvinśa Stoma, ŚāṅkhŚr. x; *°śâkshara*, mf(*ā*)n. having 24 syllables, Hariv. 12435. — **°vinśaka,** mfn. consisting of 24, MBh. iii, 13918. — **vinśat,** f. 24, only in comp. *°śac-chata*, n. 124, Jyot., Sch. — **vinśati** (*cát°*), f. sg. (once pl.; also once n. sg., BhP. xii, 13, 4 & 7) 24, VS. xviii, 25; ŚBr. &c. (*ā caturvinśates*, 'to the 24th year,' Mn. ii, 38); *-kṛitvas*, ind. 24 times, ĀpŚr.; (*°tim kṛitvas*, ŚBr. iv); *-gavá*, n. sg. a set of 24 oxen, ŚBr. vii, 2, 2, 6; *-tama*, mfn. the 24th (ch. of R.); *-tīrthaṃkara-pūjā*, f. 'worship of the 24 Tīrthaṃkaras (of the Jainas),' N. of a work; *-daṇḍaka-stava*, m., N. of a work; *-dhā*, ind. twenty-fourfold, Hcat.; *-purāṇa*, n. N. of a work; *-mata*, n. 'views of the 24 chief legislators,' N. of a work, Yājñ. iii, $\frac{327}{328}$, 9; 33 & 48; *-māna*, n. a sum of 24 (paid in gold), TāṇḍyaBr. xviii, 3, 2; *-vikrama*, mf(*ā*)n. (*cát°*) measuring 24 paces, ŚBr. iii, 5, 1, 10; *-sāhasra*, mf(*ī*)n. consisting of 24000, MBh. i, 1, 102; R. (G) i, 4, 147; *-smṛiti*, f. = *-mata*; *°ty-akshara*, mf(*ā*)n. (*cát°*) having 24 syllables, ŚBr.; RPrāt.; *°ty-avatāra-caritra*, n. 'history of the 24 incarnations,' N. of a work by Narahara-dāsa; *°ty-ahá*, m. sg. 24 days, ŚBr. xi; Gaut.; PārGṛ. ii, 3. — **°vinśatika,** mfn. consisting of 24, BhP. iii, 26, 11. — **°vinśatima,** mfn. for *°ti-tama*, Hcat. — **°vinśika,** mfn. measuring 24, Śulbas.; with *ahan*, see *°śá*. — **vidya,** mfn. (Pāṇ. v, 1, 124, Siddh.) familiar with the 4 Vedas, MBh. iii, 85, 85 (v.l. *cāt°*); (*ā*), f., g. *anuśatikâdi*. — **vidha** (*cát°*), mfn. fourfold, of 4 sorts or kinds, ŚBr. vii; ŚāṅkŚr.; Mn. &c.; (*am*), ind. in 4 ways, MBh. v, 1118 (ŚārṅgP.); *-saṃśayôdbheda*, m. 'removal of doubts of 4 kinds,' N. of a work; *°dhâhāra-maya*, mfn. made of 4 kinds of food (viz. *bhakshya, bhojya, lehya*, & *peya*), GarbhUp. — **vibhakta,** mfn. divided into 4 parts, Hariv. 12883. — **vīra** (*cát°*), mfn. (said of an unguent), AV. xix, 45, 3–5; m., N. of a Soma sacrifice lasting 4 days, KātySr.; ŚāṅkhŚr.; Vait.; Maś. — **vṛisha,** mfn. having 4 bulls, AV. v, 16, 4. — **veda,** mfn. (g. *brāhmaṇâdi*) containing the 4 Vedas, MBh. iii, 13560 (Brahmā); Hariv. 12884 (Vishṇu); (Pāṇ. v, 1, 124, Siddh.) = *-vidya*, Hariv. 7993; Subh.; m. pl. the 4 Vedas, Hariv. 14074; a class of manes, MBh. ii, 463. — **°vedin,** mfn. = *-vidya*, Ratnâv. ii, $\frac{5}{8}$ (in Prākṛit). — **vaiśāradya-viśārada,** mfn. wise through fourfold knowledge (Buddha), Divyâv. viii, 91; xix, 52. — **vyaṅga,** mfn. = *-hrasva*, R. (B) v, 35, 18 (v. l. *-gandha*). — **vyāpin,** mfn. relating to 4 (persons), Nār. i, 8 & 13. — **vyūha,** mfn. having 4 kinds of appearance, MBh. xii, 13603 (Hari); VāyuP. i, 1, 42 (Mahêsvara); containing 4 chapters, Sarvad. xv, 390; *-vādin*, m. 'asserting the 4 forms (of Purushôttama, viz. Vāsudeva, Saṃkarshaṇa, Pradyumna, Aniruddha),' a Vaishṇava, Bādar, ii, 2, 42, Gov. — **hanu** (*cát°*), mfn. having 4 jaws, AV. v, 19, 7; m., N. of a Dānava, Hariv. 12939 (v.l. *candra-h°*). — **hasta,** mfn. four-handed, W. — **hāyana,** mf(*ī*)n. 4 years old (said of living beings), Pāṇ. iv, 1, 27 (also Pat.); (*ī*), f. a cow of 4 years, L. — **hāyana,** mf(*ā*)n. (g. *kshubhnâdi*) = *°yaṇa* (said of lifeless objects), Pāṇ. iv, 1, 27, Pat. — **hita,** mfn. useful for 4 (persons), Nār. i, 8 & 12. — **hotṛi** (*cát°*), m. sg. or pl., N. of a litany (recited at the new-moon and full-moon sacrifice), AV. xi, 7, 19; AitBr. v; TBr. ii; ŚBr. iv; ŚāṅkhŚr. x; Lāṭy.; m. (cf. *-hotra*) N. of Kṛishṇa, Hariv. 10404 (v.l. for *-netṛi*); *-tvá*, n. the condition of the Caturhotṛi litany, MaitrS. i, 9, 7. — **hotra,** m. (cf. *°tṛi*) Vishṇu, Hariv. 12884; v. l. for *anuha*, VP.; for *cāt°*, q. v. — **°hotraka,** for *cāturhotra*, q.v. — **hrasva,** mfn. having the 4 extremities too short, R. (B) v, 35, 18, Sch.

1. **Catura,** mfn. ifc. = *°túr* (cf. *upa-* & *tri-*, Pāṇ. v, 4, 77, Vārtt.; *a-, vi-, su-*, Vop. vi, 29); (*am*), ifc. ind. (g. *śarad-ādi*), cf. *ā-, upa-*.

1. **Caturikā,** f. (= *°tushka*) a quadrangular courtyard (used for guests), Pañcad. iv, 76; v, 45.

Caturthá, mf(*ī*)n. (g. *yājakâdi*, Gaṇar. 100) the 4th, AV.; VS.; TS. &c.; m. the 4th letter in the first 5 classes of consonants (*gh, jh, ḍh, dh, bh*), RPrāt.; VPrāt.; Kāś.; '4th caste,' a Śūdra, L.; n. 'constituting the 4th part,' a quarter, Gaut. x, 38; (for *°tushṭaya*; ifc.) a collection of 4, Divyâv. xxxiii; (*ī*), f. (scil. *rātri*) the 4th day in a lunar fortnight, KātySr.; (metrically *°thi*) VarYogay. v, 8; 'the 4th day of a marriage,' see *°rthī-karman*; (scil. *vibhakti*) the termination of the 4th case, dative case, Pāṇ.; = *°tur-bhāgīyā*, Śulbas. iii, 26; (*am*), ind. the 4th time, ĀśvGṛ.; ŚāṅkhGṛ. [cf. τέταρτος; Lat. *quartus*; Lith. *ketwirtas*; Slav. *cetvertyi*; Germ. *vierter*.] — **kāla,** mfn. = *°lika*, Āp. i, 25, 10; m. '4th meal,' (*am*), ind. at the 4th meal-time, i.e. at the evening of every 2nd day (of any one's fasting), Mn. xi, 110; (*e*), loc. ind. id., Āp. i, 27, 11. — **°kālika,** mfn. one who takes only every 4th meal, Mn. vi, 19. — **phala,** n. the 2nd inequality or equation of a planet, W. — **bhakta-kshapaṇa,** n. fasting so as to take only every 4th meal, MBh. xiii, 5145. — **bhāj,** mfn. receiving the 4th part (as a tax from one's subjects), ii, 585; (cf. Mn. x, 118.) — **mandrâtisvārya,** mfn. 'to be lengthened in a particular way,' said of a kind of recitation of the SV., SaṃhUp. ii, 5. — **svara,** m. having the 4th tone or accent, ib.; n., N. of a Sāman. **Caturthânśa,** m. a 4th part, Hariv. 9690; mfn. = *°śin*, Mn. viii, 210. **Caturthânśin,** mfn. receiving a quarter, Gaut. xxviii, 34. **Caturthâśrama,** m. the 4th stage of a Brāhman's life, W. **Caturthôdāttatama,** mfn. 'reciting the 4th as the highest tone (or accent),' said of a particular way of reciting the SV., SaṃhUp. iii, 3.

Caturthaka, mfn. the 4th, Śrut.; returning every 4th day (a fever), quartan, τεταρταῖκός, Pāṇ. v, 2, 81; Hariv. 10555; Car.; Suśr.; m. (in music) a kind of measure; (*ikā*), f. a weight of 4 Karshas, ŚārṅgS. i, 24; Ashṭâṅg. v, 6, 27.

Caturthi, for *°thī*, q. v.

Caturthī, f. of *°thá*, q.v. — **karman,** n. the ceremonies performed on the 4th day of a marriage, Gobh. ii, 5, 1; ŚāṅkhGṛ. i, 18, 1.

Caturya, Nom. P. *°ryati* (1st fut. *°ryitā*, inf. *°ryitum*), to wish for 4, Pāṇ. viii, 2, 78, Vārtt. 1.

Catuś, in comp. for *°túr.* — **cakra,** m., N. of a sacrifice, Baudh. i, 13, 30; of a phenomenon in the sky, MBh. vii, 199, 19; n., N. of a mystical diagram, Tantr. — **catvārinśá,** mf(*ī*)n. the 44th (ch. of MBh. or R.); (with *śatá*, 100) + 44, ŚBr. x, 4, 2, 7; containing 44, VS. & TS. v (said of a Stoma); ŚBr. viii, xiii; m. (scil. *stoma*) a Stoma consisting of 44 parts, Lāṭy. — **catvārinśat** (*cát°*), f. 44, VS. xviii, 25; ŚBr. viii; ŚāṅkhŚr.; RPrāt. — **°catvārinśin,** mfn. containing 44 parts, MaitrS. ii, 8, 7. — **caraṇa,** mfn. consisting of 4 parts, Sarvad. vii, 6; m. 'having 4 feet,' a quadruped, VarBṛ. xxi, 6. — **calita,** n. a kind of play or sport, Siṇhâs. — **citya,** mfn. supported by 4 stratums, MBh. xiv, 88, 32.

Catush, in comp. for *°túr.* — **kaparda** (*cát°*), mf(*ā*)n. having 4 tufts, RV. x, 114, 3. — **karṇa,** mfn. four-eared, W.; heard by 4 ears only, Pañcat. i, 1, 86; (*ī*), f., N. of one of the mothers attending on Skanda, MBh. ix, 2643; *-tā*, f. instr. (*ayā*), ind. so that only 4 ears are present, Pañcat. i, 10, $\frac{1}{1}\frac{2}{7}$. — **kala,** mfn. having 4 marks (on the thumb denoting the proficiency in the 4 Vedas), R. (B) v, 35, 18 (v.l. *-kṛishṇa*). — **kārin,** mfn. causing or effecting 4 things, Nār. i, 8 & 14. — **kishku,** mfn. 4 Kishkus long, MBh. v, vii; R. (B) v, 35, 18. — **kṛishṇa,** mfn. having 4 black parts of the body, R. ii, 32, 13 (v.l. for *-kala*). — **koṇa,** mfn. quadrangular, Sūryapr.; Hcat. i, 8, 498$\frac{3}{5}$; m.n. a tetragon, 11, 617. — **krama,** m. a Krama (or method of reading and writing the Veda) consisting of 4 parts, R-Prāt. xi, 10. — **khaṇḍa,** mf(*ā*)n. consisting of 4 parts, CūlUp., Sch. Introd. — **paksha** (*cát°*), mf(*ā*)n. furnished with 4 posts, AV. ix, 3, 21. — **pañca,** mfn. pl. 4 or 5, Rājat. vi, 326; viii, 555; *°can*, BhP. i, 15, 23 & x, 37, 30. — **pañcāśa,** mfn. the 54th (ch. of MBh. or R.) — **pañcāśat** (*cát°*), f. (sg. or pl., Pāṇ. viii, 3, 5, Sch.) 54, ŚBr. vi; *-tama*, mfn. the 54th (ch. of MBh. ed. Bomb.); *°śad-adhika-śata*, mfn. the 154th (ch. of MBh.) — **pattrī,** f. = *°tur-dala*, Bhpr. — **pathá,** m. n. a place where 4 roads meet, cross-way, TBr. i; ŚBr. ii; Kauś. &c.; m. 'walking the 4 paths (i. e. Āśramas, cf. *catur-āśramin*),' a Brāhman, L.; n. one of the 18 ceremonies performed with Kuṇḍas, Tantr.; *-kṛitâśaya*, m. 'having made its abode on a cross-way,' a kind of ghost, Gal.; *-niketā*, f. 'abiding on a cross-way,' N. of one of the mothers attending on Skanda, MBh. ix, 2643; *-ratā*, f. id., 2645; *-sad*, mfn. dwelling at cross-ways, MānGṛ. i, 13; PārGṛ. iii, 15, 8. — **pad** (*cát°*), m(nom. sg *-pād*; pl. *-pādas*, irreg. *-padas*, BhP. v, 1, 14; vi 4, 9; loc. *-pātsu*, AitBr. vi, 2, 7; abl. *-pādbhyas* Pāṇ. iv, 1, 135) f(*-padī*) n(nom. *-pad*, RV. 4 times or *-pād*, RV. twice). (Pāṇ. v, 4, 140) quadruped, (m.) a quadruped, (n.) quadrupeds (collectively), animals, RV.; AV. &c.; having made 4 steps, ĀśvGṛ. i, 7, 19; ŚāṅkhGṛ. i, 14, 6; divided into 4 parts, MāṇḍUp. 2; MBh. v; (in prosody) consisting of 4 Pādas, RV. i, 164, 24; x, 27, 10; having 4 staffs (a ladder), MBh. xii, 8838; (a judicial procedure) consisting of 4 processes (viz. plea, defence, rejoinder, and sentence), Yājñ. ii, 8; (*-padī*). f. 'a female quadruped,' in comp., *°dī-gamana*, n. intercourse with a female quadruped, Suśr. ii, 12, 3. — **pada,** (in comp.) 4 Pādas, Mālav. i, $\frac{1}{1}\frac{2}{6}$; n. sg. or pl., 4 partitions or divisions, AgP. xl, 16 & 18; mf(*ā*)n. (*cát°*), quadruped, MBh.; VarBṛS. xxi; consisting of 4 Pādas, TS. iii, 2, 9, 1; ŚBr. xi; AitBr. i, 7; ChUp.; RPrāt.; Mālav. ii; consisting of 4 words, VPrāt.; comprising 4 partitions or divisions, VarBṛS. liii, 55; (in alg.) tetranomial; m. a quadruped, W.; (= *pāśava?*) a kind of coitus, L.; (pl.) certain zodiacal signs (viz. *mesha, vṛisha, sinha, makara-pūrvârdha, dhanuḥ-parârdha*), Laghuj. i, 11 ff.; N. of a shrub, W.; n. N. of a particular Karaṇa, VarBṛS. ic, 5 & 8; Sūryas. ii, 67; (*ā*), f. a metre of 30 + 4 + 4 syllabic instants. — **°padikā,** f. = *°dā*. — **padī,** f. of *-pad*, q.v. — **parṇī,** f. (cf. *-pattrī*) 'four-leaved,' Oxalis pusilla, L. — **paryāya,** mfn. having 4 reiterations (a Stoma), Vait. xl. — **parva,** mf(*ā*)n. consisting of 4 parts, AitĀr. i, 2, 2, 20. — **pāṭī,** f. 'winding 4 ways (?),' a river, L. — **pāṭhī,** f. a school in which the 4 Vedas are studied, W. — **pāṇi,** m. 'four-handed,' Vishṇu, L. — **pād,** see *-pad*; once in comp., MBh. xii, 5697. — **pāda** (*cát°*), mf(*ī*)n. quadruped, ŚBr. iii, vi; AitBr.; Suśr.; mf(*ā*)n. consisting of 4 parts, MBh. iii, 1459; VāyuP.; Sarvad. xv, 207; m. a quadruped, MBh. iii, 11246; Yājñ. ii, 298; R. v; (scil. *adhyāya*) the chapter treating of the 4 parts of medical science, Car. i, 9 f.; (*ī*), f. a number of 4 feet, Jyot. (YV) 31; *-samanvaya*, m. conjunction of the 4 parts of medical science, Bhpr.; *-siddhi*, f. complete knowledge of the 4 parts of medical science, Car. iii, 8. — °**pādaka**, mf(*ikā*)n. consisting of 4 Pādas, Kāraṇḍ. xii, 33 & 39. — **pārśva**, n. the 4 sides (of a square &c.), W. — **puṭa**, mfn. having 4 folds, ĀpŚr. xii, 2, 14. — **puṇḍrā**, f. Abelmoschus esculentus, L. — **prasthānika**, mfn. pl. divided into 4 sects, Sarvad. ii, 255. — **phalā**, f. 'four-fruited,' Uraria lagopodioides, L.

Catushka, mfn. consisting of 4, Lāṭy.; RPrāt.; Śulbas.; Suśr.; (with *śata*, 100) + 4 (i.e. 4 per cent.), Mn. viii, 142; Bījag.; m. any sign (as the Svastika) having 4 marks, L.; N. of a man, Rājat. viii, 2849; 2859; 2911; 2931; n. a set of 4, collection of 4, Mn. vii, 50; Yājñ. iii, 99; MBh. xii, 12706 (or = *aṅśayoḥ katyoś cântarāla*, Sch.); Mṛicch. ix, 12; Srut.; = *-veśman*, Kum. v, 68; vii, 9; a quadrangular courtyard (used for receiving guests), Pañcat. (ifc. f. *ā*); Prasannar. iii, 6; Pañcad.; a cross-way, L.; a necklace of 4 strings, L.; (*ī*), f. a (large) four-sided pond, L.; a bed- or musquito-curtain, L.; a necklace of 4 strings, W. — **veśman**, n. a hall resting on 4 columns, Vcar. xv, 15.

Catushkikā, f. a set of 4, Rājat. v, 369; = *shka-veśman*, Viddh. i, $\frac{13}{14}$; Rājat. viii, 23; (in Prākṛit) Bālar. v, $\frac{41}{42}$ & $\frac{42}{43}$.

Catushkin, mfn. ifc. having a set of 4 (of anything), MBh. xii, 13340 (cf. 12706).

Cátushṭaya, m(nom. pl. °*ye*, Pāṇ. viii, 3, 101, Kāś.)f(*ī*)n. fourfold, consisting of 4, AV. x, 2, 3; ŚBr. xiii; AitBr. iii, viii; ŚāṅkhŚr.; MBh. &c.; 4, BhP. iii, 15, 28; n. a set of 4, quaternion, KātyŚr. viii; Gṛihyās.; Mn. &c. (ifc. f. *ā*, Hcat.); a square, W.; the 1st, 4th, 7th, and 10th signs of the zodiac, VarYogay. iv, 48; 'a collection of Sūtras consisting of 4 sections,' see *cāt°*.

1. **Catús**, ind. (Pāṇ. v, 4, 18; in comp. before hard gutturals and labials °*tuḥ* or °*tush*, viii, 3, 43) 4 times, AV. xi, 2, 9; TS. ii; ŚBr.; ĀśvGṛ. &c.

2. **Catus**, in comp. for °*túr*. — **tāla**, m. (in music) a kind of measure. — **triṅśá**, mf(*ī*)n. the 34th (Prajā-pati, so called with regard to the other 33 gods), ŚBr. iv f.; TBr. ii; (with *śatá*, 100) + 34, ŚBr. xii; containing 34, Lāṭy.; m. (scil. *stóma*) a Stoma consisting of 34 parts, VS. xiv, 23; AitBr. iv, 18. — **triṅśat** (*cát°*), f. 34, RV. i, 162, 18; x, 55, 3; VS.; °*śaj-jātaka-jña*, m. 'knowing 34 Jātakas,' N. of a Buddha, L.; °*śat-sammita*, n. with *Prajā-pateś* (see s. v. °*śá*), N. of a Sāman, ĀrshBr.; °*śad-akshara*, mf(*ā*)n. (*cát°*) containing 34 syllables, ŚBr. x; °*śad-rātram*, ind. during 34 days, KātyŚr. xxiv. — **tri-dvy-eka-bhāga**, mfn. pl. receiving 4, 3, 2, and 1 part respectively, Yājñ. ii, 125.

Catū, in comp. for °*túr* before *r*. — **rājī**, f. (*rājan*) 'the 4 kings,' N. of the luckiest termination of the Catur-aṅga game (by which one king gains the 4 thrones), Tithyād. — **rātrá**, m. n. 'lasting 4 days,' N. of a ceremony, AV. xi, 7, 11; ŚāṅkhŚr.; KātyŚr.; Lāṭy.; (*am*), ind. during 4 days, KātyŚr.

Catvara, n. rarely m. [Hariv. 6499 ff.; R. v, 49, 15] a quadrangular place, place in which many ways meet, cross-way, MBh. &c.; a levelled spot of ground prepared for a sacrifice, L. — **taru**, m. a tree growing on a cross-way, Svapnac. — **vāsinī**, f. (cf. *catushpatha-niketā*) N. of one of the mothers attending on Skanda, MBh. ix, 2630.

Catvāriṅśá, mf(*ī*)n. (fr. °*śát*) the 40th, RV. ii, 12, 11; (with *śatá*, 100) + 40, ŚBr. xii; Pāṇ. v, 2, 46; m. 'consisting of 40 (parts),' N. of a Stoma, Lāṭy.

Catvāriṅśát, f. (Pāṇ. v, 1, 59; fr. *catvā́ri* [n. pl.] + *daśát*, a decad) 40, RV. i, 126, 4; ii, 18, 5; VS. &c.; [cf. τεσσαράκοντα; Lat. *quadraginta*.] — **pada** (°*śát-*), mf(*ā*)n. having 40 feet, ŚBr. vii, 3, 1, 27. **Catvāriṅśád-akshara**, mf(*ā*)n. consisting of 40 syllables, xiii, 6, 1, 2. **Catvāriṅśad-rātrá**, m. a period of 40 days, ib.; KātyŚr.; ŚāṅkhŚr. **Catvāriṅsan-māna**, mfn. having the weight of 40, ĀpŚr.

Catvāriṅśati, f. = °*śát*. See *dvā-*.

चतुर 2. *catura*, mf(*ā*. cf. g. *arśa-ādi*)n. (√*cat*, Uṇ.) swift, quick, Kathās. x, 108; Rājat. iii, 176; dexterous, clever, ingenious, shrewd, Ragh.; Vikr.; Kum.; Pañcat. &c.; charming, agreeable, Ragh.; Bhartṛ.; visible, L.; m. a round pillow (cf. *cāt°*), L.; the fish Cyprinus Rohita, Gal.; (scil. *hasta*) a particular position of the hand, PSarv.; n. = *-tā*, g. *arśa-ādi*; an elephant's stable, L.; (*am*), ind. quickly, Kathās. ci, 96; Rājat. iii, 188. — **krama**, m. (in music) a kind of measure. — **ga**, mfn. going quickly, W. — **tā**, f. cleverness, skilfulness, Bhartṛ. i, 71. — **tva**, n. id., Daś. i, 223 (v. l. for *caṇa-*).

Caturaka, mf(*ikā*)n. clever, skilful, Kathās. ciii; m., N. of a jackal, Pañcat. i, 15, 35 & 16, $\frac{0}{1}$ (cf. *mahā-*); 2. (*ikā*), f., N. of a woman, Śak. vi, $\frac{8}{9}$ (in Prākṛit) & $\frac{13}{14}$; Kathās. vi, 53; ciii, 20.

चतुर्थ *caturthá*, °*rthaka*, °*rya*. See p. 385.

चतुल *catula*, mfn. = *sthāpayitṛi*, L.

चतुष्क *catushka*, &c. See col. 1.

चत्त *cattá*, *cattra*, *catya*. See √*cat*.

चत्वर *catvara*, °*tvāriṅśá*, &c. See col. 1.

चत्वाल *catvāla*, m. = *cā́tv°*, q. v., L.; = *garbha* or *darbha*, L.

चद् *cad*, cl. 1. °*dati*, °*date*, to ask or beg (cf. √*cat*), Dhātup. xxi, 5.

चदिर *cadira*, m. (= *cand°*) the moon, L.; camphor, L.; an elephant, L.; a snake, L.

चन् 1. *can*, cl. 1. °*nati*, to sound, utter a sound, L.; to hurt, injure, Dhātup. xix, 41.

चन् 2. *can* (cf. √*kan*), only aor. Subj. 2. du. *canishṭám*, 'to delight in, be satisfied with (loc.),' RV. vii, 70, 4; & 3. sg. *cánishṭhat* [*jan°*, SV.], 'to satisfy, please,' RV. viii, 74, 11.

Cánas, n. 'delight, satisfaction,' only with √*dhā*, P. & Ā. to delight in, be satisfied with (acc. or loc.), enjoy, RV.; VS. viii, 7; (cf. *sá-* & *sa-cánas*.)

Canasaya, Nom. °*yati*, to address with the word *canasita*, GopBr. i, 3, 19; ii, 2, 23.

Canasita, mfn. (Pass. p. fr. °*sya*) 'satisfied, gracious' (only the voc. is used in the address to a Brāhman, added after his N.), AitBr. i, 6, 8, Sāy. (Āp.) — **vat**, mfn. (speech or address) containing the word *canasita*, Gop. ii, 2, 23; KātyŚr. vii, 5, 7. **Canasitôttara**, mfn. followed by *canasita* (a N.), Vait.

Canasya, Nom. (Impv. 2. du. °*syátam*) to delight in (acc.), enjoy, RV. i, 3, 1.

Cánishṭha, mfn. (superl. fr. *cánas*) very acceptable, RV.; very favourable, very gracious, vii, 57, 4; 70, 2 & 5.

Cano, in comp. for *cánas*. — **dhā́**, mfn. satisfied, gracious, VS. viii, 7. — **hita**, mfn. made favourable, inclined or willing to do anything, RV. iii, 2, 2 & 7; 11, 2 (Pāṇ. i, 4, 60, Vārtt. 2, Pat.); ix, 75, 1 & 4; VS.

चन *caná* (*ca ná*, SV.), ind. and not, also not, even not, not even (this particle is placed after the word to which it gives force; a preceding verb is accentuated [Pāṇ. viii, 1, 57]; in Vedic language it is generally, but not always, found without any other neg. particle, whereas in the later language another neg. is usually added, e. g. *ā́paś caná prá minanti vratám vām*, 'not even the waters violate your ordinance,' RV. ii, 24, 12; *nā́ha vivyāca pṛithivī́ canâinam*, 'the earth even does not contain him,' iii, 36, 4; in class. Sanskṛit it is only used after the interrogatives *ká*, *katará*, *katamá*, *katham*, *kád*, *kadā́*, *kim*, *kútas*, *kva*, making them indefinite), RV.; AV. &c.; also, RV. i, 139, 2; vi, 26, 7; viii, 78, 10.

चनस् *cánas*, &c. See √2. *can*.

चन्द् *cand* (fr. *ścand*, q. v.), cl. 1. °*dati* (Nir. xi, 5), to shine, be bright, Dhātup. iii, 31; to gladden, ib.; [cf. Lat. *candeo*, *candela*.]

Canda, m. (for °*drá*) the moon, L.; N. of the author of the work Pṛithivī-rāja-rāsaka.

Candaka, mfn. pleasing, W.; m. the moon, W.; moonlight, W.; v. l. for °*draka*, q. v. — **pushpa**, for *candana-p°*, W.

Candana, m. n. sandal (Sirium myrtifolium, either the tree, wood, or the unctuous preparation of the wood held in high estimation as perfumes; hence ifc. a term for anything which is the most excellent of its kind, g. *vyāghrâdi*), Nir. xi. 5; MBh.; R. &c. (ifc. f. *ā*, Ragh. vi, 61); m., N. of a divine being, Lalit. i, 93; of a prince; = °*naka*, Mṛicch. vi, 25; N. of an ape, R. iv, 41, 3; n. the grass Bhadra-kālī, L.; (*ā*), f. a kind of creeper, L.; N. of a river, VP. (v. l. for °*ndrā*); (*ī*), f., N. of a river, R. iv, 40, 20; (cf. *ku-*, *pīta-*, *rakta-*, *śveta-*, *hari-*.) — **giri**, m. 'sandal-mountain,' the Malaya, L. — **gopā**, f. a kind of Ichnocarpus, L. — **dāsa**, m., N. of a man, Mudr. i, $\frac{19}{20}$; of a merchant, Hit. i, 6, $\frac{0}{1}$. — **paṅka**, m. sandal-unguent, Ṛitus. i, 6; Caurap. — **pāta**, m. laying on of sandal-unguent, Kāvyâd. ii, 104. — **pāla**, m., N. of a prince, Buddh. — **putrikā**, °**trī**, f., N. of a mythical doll, Vīrac. xi, xxiv. — **pura**, n., N. of a town, Kathās. lxxvii, 20. — **pushpa**, °**shpaka**, n. cloves, L. — **maya**, mfn. made or consisting of sandal-wood, VarBṛS.; Kād. — **rasa**, m. sandal-water, Ratnâv. iii, 1; Ṛitus. iii, 20. — **vāri**, n. id., MBh. v, 1794; R. iii. — **sāra**, m. id., ii, 23, 39; a kind of alkali, L. — **sārivā**, f. = *-gopā*, L. **Candanâgrya**, m., N. of a man, Lalit. xiii, 160. **Candanâcala**, m. = °*na-giri*, L. **Candanâdri**, m. id., Rājat. iv, 156. **Candanâmbhas**, n. = °*na-rasa*, Kāvyâd. ii, 245. **Candanā-vatī**, f., N. of a river (?), JaimBhār. lxxi. **Candanôdaka**, n. = °*na-rasa*, Kāvyâd. ii, 40; *-dundubhi*, m., N. of Bhava, VP. iv, 14, 4; VāyuP.

Candanaka, m., N. of a man, Mṛicch. vi.

Candanāya, Nom. °*yate*, to become a sandal-tree, Cāṇ.; Subh.

Candanin, mfn. anointed with sandal (Śiva), MBh. xiii, 1249.

Candanīyā, f. a kind of yellow pigment, L.

Candala-devī, f., N. of the princess Candralekhā, Vcar. xi, 68.

Candalā, f., N. of a woman (cf. °*dralā*), Rājat. vii, 1122.

Candira, m. (fr. °*ndrá*) the moon, Bhām. ii, 126; an elephant, L.; = °*dra-ja*, Gal.

Candila, m. a barber, L.

Candrá, mf(*ā*)n. (fr. *ścandrá*, q.v.) glittering, shining (as gold), having the brilliancy or hue of light (said of gods, of water [RV. x, 121, 9; TS. vi] & of Soma), RV.; VS.; TS. vi; TBr. i; m. the moon (also personified as a deity, Mn. &c.), VS.; ŚBr. &c. (ifc. f. *ā*, MBh. ix; R. &c.); ifc. 'the moon of,' i. e. the most excellent among (e. g. *pārthiva-* [g. *vyāghrâdi*, Kāś.] or *narêndra-* [Ratnâv. i, 4], 'a most excellent king'); the number 'one,' Sūryas.; a lovely or agreeable phenomenon of any kind, L.; a spot similar to the moon, BhP. iv, 15, 17; the eye in a peacock's tail, L.; the mark of the Visarga, Tantr.; a kind of reddish pearl, L.; camphor, AgP. xxxv, 15; water, L.; the Kāmpilla plant, L.; a metre of 4 × 19 syllables; N. of a Daitya (= *-varman*, king of the Kāmbojas), MBh. i, 2667; of a son of Kṛishṇa, BhP. x, 61, 13; of a son of Viśva-gandhi and father of Yuvanâśva, ix, 6, 20; of a grammarian (= *-gomin*), Rājat. i, 176; of a king, Pañcat. v, 9, 2 & 10, $\frac{0}{1}$; of one of the ancestors of the Gauḍa Brāhmans; of several other men, Rājat. vi f.; one of the 18 minor Dvīpas, L.; = *-parvata*, R. vi, 26, 6; n. (Naigh. i, 2; also m., L.) gold, RV. ii, 2, 4; AV. xii, 2, 53; VS. iv, xix; ŚBr.; TāṇḍyaBr. vi, 6; KātySr.; n. a kind of sour rice-gruel, L.; N. of a Sāman, KātyŚr. xxvi; Lāṭy.; (*ā*), f. a hall covered only at the top, awning, canopy, L.; cardamoms, L.; Cocculus cordifolius (*guḍūcī*); = °*drâspadā*, L.; N. of a river, VP. ii, 4, 28; (*ī*), f. Serratula anthelminthica, L.; (cf. *ardha-*.) — **kamalâkara**, m., N. of a work. — **kalā**, f. a digit or $\frac{1}{16}$ of the moon's disc (each digit is personified as a female divinity, Tantr.), the crescent on the day before or after the new moon, Kathās. i, 39; the mark of a finger-nail resembling the crescent before or after new moon; the fish Pimelodus Vacha, L.; a kind of drum, L.; (in music) a kind of measure; N. of a drama, Sāh. iii, $\frac{96}{97}$; *-tantra*, n., N. of a work. — **kavi**, m., N. of a poet, ŚārṅgP. — **kāṭuki**, m., N. of a man, Pravar. iii, 3. — **kānta**, mfn. lovely as the moon, Śrut.; m. 'moon-loved,' the moon-stone (a gem supposed to be formed from the congelation of the moon's rays and to dissolve under the influence of its light), Suśr.; Megh.; Bhartṛ. &c.; m. n. the white eatable water-lily (blossoming during night), L.; n. sandal-wood, L.; (*ā*), f. the wife of the moon, W.; night, L.; N. of a Surâṅganā, Siṉhâs.; (*ā*, *am*), f. n. N. of a town, R. vii, 102, 6 & 9; *-maṇi-maya*, mfn. made of the gem Candra-kānta, Siṉhâs.; *-maya*, mfn. id., Kād. v, 796; vi, 271; *-ratna-maya*, mfn. id., Siṉhâs. — **kānti**, f. the brilliancy or lustre of the moon, moonlight, W.; N. of the moon's disc on the ninth day, BrahmaP.; m., N. of a hero of Kālikā, Vīrac. xxx. — °**kāntīya**, Nom. °*yati*, to resemble the moon-stone (*candra-kānta*), ŚārṅgP. cvii, 8. — **kālânala**, n. a kind of diagram; *-cakra*, n. id. — **kīrti**, m., N. of a prince of Ujjayinī, Bhadrab.; of a Sūri of the Jainas. — **kuṇḍa**, m., N. of a pond in Kāma-rūpa, KālP. — **kumāra-śikhara**, n., N. of a place, Rasik. xi, 23. — **kula**, n., N. of a town, Śukas. — **kulyā**, f., N. of a river in Kaśmīr, Rājat. i, 320. — **kūṭa**, m., N. of a mountain in Kāma-rūpa, KālP. — **ketu**, m., N. of a son of Lakshmaṇa, R. vii, 102, 2; Ragh. xv, 90; of several other men, MBh. vii, 1899; VP.; of a Vidyādhara, Kathās. cxv, 24; of a prince of Cakora (slain by an emissary of king Śūdraka), Hcar. vi; of a prince (emissary of king

Śūdrika), Vīrac. xviii, 41 f.; of a hero of Kālikā, xxx. **– keśa,** m., N. of a hero of Kālikā, xxx. **– kesarin,** m. id., ib. **– kośa,** m., N. of a lexicon, Prauḍh. **– krīḍa,** m. (in music) a kind of measure. **– kshaya,** m. 'waning of the moon,' new moon, Mn. iii, 122. **– kshānta,** m., N. of a man. **– garbha,** m., N. of a Buddh. Sūtra. **– giri,** m. = *-parvata;* N. of a prince, LiṅgaP. i, 66, 41; MatsyaP. xii, 53; KūrmaP. i, 21, 59. **– gupta,** m. 'moon-protected,' N. of a renowned king (Σανδρο-κυπτος or Σανδρο-κοττος, reigning at Pāṭali-putra about 315 B.C. as the founder of a new dynasty; installed by the Brāhman Cāṇakya after causing the death of Nanda), Inscr.; Pāṇ. i, 1, 68, Vārtt. 7, Pat.; BhP. xii, 1, 12; Kathās.; Mudr.; N. of two kings of the Gupta dynasty; for *citra-g°,* q.v. **– °guptaka,** m. the king Candra-gupta (of Pāṭali-putra), ŚārṅgP. lxxv, 72. **– gupti,** m., N. of a prince of Avanti, Bhadrab. ii, 7; iii, 96. **– gūtī-giri,** m., N. of a locality, Rasik. xi, 37. **– gomin,** m., N. of a grammarian (also called Candra), Gaṇar. 2. **– gola-stha,** m. pl. 'dwelling in the lunar sphere,' the manes, L. **– golikā,** f. moonlight, L. **– graha,** m. an eclipse of the moon, Hcat. **– grahaṇa,** n. id.; *°ṇôdāhuraṇa,* n., N. of a work. **– cañcala,** m., *°lā,* f. the fish Candraka, L. **– citra,** m. pl. N. of a people, R. (B) iv, 42, 6. **– cūḍa,** m. = *-mukuṭa,* Bhartṛ.; Bālar. ix, $\frac{47}{48}$; Kathās.; a form of Bhairava, BrahmavP. ii, 61, 83; N. of a hero of Kālikā, Vīrac. xxx; of an author (son of Śrī-bhaṭṭa-Purushôttama); of a prince, xv; *°ḍâshṭaka,* n., N. of a hymn. **– cūḍāmaṇi,** m., N. of a work, Tantras. ii. **– ja,** m. 'moon-born,' the planet Mercury, VarBṛS.; *-siṇha,* m., N. of a man. **– janaka,** m. 'moon-progenitor,' the sea, Gal. **– jñāna,** n., N. of a work, Ānand. 31, Sch.; *-tantra,* n. id., ib. **– taram,** ind. (compar.) more lovely, Kāṭh. xxx, 1. **– tāpana,** m., N. of a Dānava, Hariv. 12698 (v. l. *indra-t°*) & 12939. **– tāraká,** n. sg. the moon and the stars, ŚBr. xiv, 6, 7, 13. **– tāla,** m. (in music) a kind of measure. **– tva,** n. the condition of the moon, Kāvyâd. ii, 91. **– dakshiṇa** (*°drá-*), mfn. offering anything bright or gold in sacrifice, VS. vii, 45. **– datta,** m. 'moon-given,' N. of an author. **– dāra,** m. pl. 'moon-wives,' the 27 lunar mansions, L. **– dīpikā,** f., N. of an astrological work, VarBṛ. vi, 6, Sch. **– dūta,** m. 'moon-messenger,' N. of a poem. **– deva,** m., N. of a warrior, MBh. viii, 1078 & 1086; of a Brāhman (of Kāśyapa's family), Rājat. i, 182 ff.; of a poet, ŚārṅgP. **– dyuti,** m. 'moon-bright,' sandal-wood, Bhpr. **– dvīpa,** m., N. of a Dvīpa, Romakas. **– dhvaja-ketu,** m., N. of a Samādhi, Buddh. L. **– nābha,** m. 'moon-navelled,' N. of a Dānava, Hariv. 16254. **– nibha,** mfn. 'moon-like,' bright, handsome, W. **– nirṇij** (*°drá-*), having a brilliant garment, RV. x, 106, 8. **– pañcāṅga,** n. the luni-solar calendar. **– pati,** m., N. of a man. **– parvata,** m. 'moon-mountain,' N. of a mountain, R. vi, 2, 37. **– pāda,** m. a moon-beam, Megh. 71. **– pāla,** m., N. of a hero of Kālikā, Vīrac. xxx. **– putra,** m. = *-ja,* VarBṛS. **– pura,** n. 'moon-town,' N. of a town, Kathās. cxvii, cxxiii; (cf. *cāndr°*). **– pushpā,** f. a kind of Solanum, Bhpr. **– pṛishṭha,** m., N. of a man, Vīrac. **– prakāśa,** m., N. of a work. **– prajñapti,** f., N. of the 6th Upâṅga of the Jainas. **– prabha,** m., N. of an Arhat of the present Avasarpiṇī, Jain.; of a Yaksha, Divyâv.; of a king, ib.; of several other persons, Hariv.; Kathās. &c.; (*ā*), f. moonlight, W.; Serratula anthelminthica, L.; a compound of various drugs (used in jaundice, piles, &c.), Bhpr.; N. of several women, Divyâv. xxxvii; Kathās. xvii, 65; *-svāmi-caritra,* n. 'Candra-prabha's life,' N. of a Jain work. **– prabhāva,** mfn. splendid as the moon, W. **– prabhāsa-tīrtha,** n., N. of a Tīrtha, RevāKh. **– prabhāsvara-rāja,** m., N. of several Buddhas. **– pramardana,** n. 'moon-enemy,' N. of a brother of Rāhu, MBh. i, 2539. **– pramāṇa,** mfn. 'moon-measured,' lunar, Lāṭy. x, 16, 13. **– prāsāda,** m. an apartment on the housetop, Kathās. lxxxv, cxiv. **– priya,** m., N. of a prince. **– bālā,** f. large cardamoms, L. **– bāhu,** m., N. of an Asura, Hariv. (v. l.); of a hero of Kālikā, Vīrac. xxx. **– bindu,** m. 'moon-like spot,' the sign for the nasal ँ; = *candrakita,* Bhpr. **– bimba,** n. the moon-disc, Kāvyâd. ii, 39 & 41; *-prabhā,* f., N. of a Gandharva virgin, Kāraṇḍ. i, 70; *-maya,* mfn. consisting of moon-discs, Kād. **– budhna** (*°drá-*), mfn. having a bright standing-ground, RV. i, 52, 3. **– bha,** m., N. of an attendant of Skanda, MBh. ix, 2577; (*ā*), f. = *-pushpā,* Bhpr. v, 3, 40. **– bhāga,** m., 'N. of a man,' see *cāndrabhāgi;* of a mountain, KālP.; (*ā*), f. (g. *bahv-ādi*) the river Chenab (in the Pañjāb), MBh.; BhP. v, 19, 18; Rājat.; Hit.; (cf. *cāndr°*); (*ī*), f. id., g. *bahv-ādi* (cf. Gaṇar. 52, Sch.); *°gasarit,* f. id., VarBṛS. xvi, 27. **– bhānu,** m., N. of a son of Kṛishṇa, BhP. x, 61, 10. **– bhāsa,** m. (= *-hāsa*) 'moon-brilliant,' a sword, L.; N. of a hero of Kālikā, Vīrac. xxx. **– bhūti,** n. silver, L. **– maṇi,** m. the moon-gem (Candra-kānta), L. **– maṇḍala,** n. = *-bimba,* R.; Suśr.; VarBṛS.; a halo round the moon, W. **– mata,** n. the doctrine of the moon(-worshippers), Śaṃkar. xliv. **– manas,** m. one of the ten horses of the moon, L. **– maya,** mf(*ī*)n. representing the moon, Kād. v, 866; Hcar. iv. **– mas** (*°drá-*), m. (*mas = mā́s;* g. *dāsī-bhārâdi*) the moon, deity of the moon (considered as a Dānava, MBh. i, 2534; Hariv. 190; named among the 8 Vasus, MBh. i, 2583), RV. i; viii, 82, 8; x; VS.; AV. &c.; N. of a hero of Kālikā, Vīrac. xxx. **– °masa,** see *ava-;* (*ā*), f., N. of a river, BhP. (B) iv, 28, 35; (cf. *-vasā.*) **– maha,** m. a dog, L. **– mā,** f., N. of a river, MBh. vi, 337; (cf. *-masā.*) **– mārga,** m. 'moon-path,' the atmosphere, Gal. **– mālā,** f. the metre also called Candra (q.v.); v. l. for *indu-m°.* **– māsa,** m. a lunar month, Jyot. (YV) 31, Sch. **– mukuṭa,** m. 'moon-crested,' Śiva, Prasannar. vii, 92. **– mukha,** m. 'moon-faced,' N. of a man, Rājat. vii, 111; (*ī*), f. = *-vadanā,* W.; a particular blood-vessel in the vulva, Bhpr.; a metre of 4 × 10 syllables; N. of a Surâṅganā, Siṇhâs.; *-varman,* m., N. of a prince, Hcar. **– mauli,** mfn. moon-crested (a Daitya), R. vii; m. = *-mukuṭa,* Ragh.; Kum.; BhP.; Kathās.; N. of a man, Siṇhâs. ix, $\frac{4}{5}$; f. a particular blood-vessel in the vulva, Bhpr. **– maulin,** m. = *-mukuṭa,* Hcat. **– yoga,** m. a conjunction of the moon with any asterism. **– ratna,** n. a pearl, Gal. **– ratha** (*°drá-*), mfn. having a brilliant carriage, RV. **– rāja,** m., N. of a minister of king Harsha, Rājat. vii, 1376; 1382; 1512 ff.; of a man, Siṇhâs. **– rekhā,** f. a digit of the moon, R. v, 20, 3; Serratula anthelminthica, L.; N. of a Surâṅganā, Siṇhâs. **– reṇu,** m. 'having only the dust of the moon,' a plagiarist, L. **– rtu** (*-ṛitu*), m. a lunar season, Sūryapr. **– lalāṭa,** mfn. moon-crested (Śiva), Gaut. xxvi, 12. **– lalāma,** m. = *-mukuṭa,* BhP. xii, 10, 25. **– lekha,** m., N. of a Rakshas, R. vi, 84, 12; (*ā*), f. = *-rekhā,* a digit of the moon, Nal.; R.; BhP.; Serratula anthelminthica, L.; a metre of 4 × 13 syllables; another of 4 × 15 syllables; N. of a daughter of the Nāga Su-śravas, Rājat. i, 218; of Kshema-gupta's wife, vi, 179; of a princess (whose teacher was Bilhaṇa; also called Śaśi-kalā), Vcar. viii, 4; Caurap., Sch.; of two other women, Kathās. cxiii f. **– loká,** m. pl. the worlds or spheres of the moon, ŚBr. xiv; (cf. *candrâdi-l°.*) **– locana,** m. 'moon-eyed,' N. of Dānava, Hariv. 14285. **– lohaka,** n. silver, L. **– lauha,** *°haka,* n. id., L. **– vaṇśa,** m. the lunar race of kings (2nd great line of royal dynasties, the progenitor of which was Soma the Moon, child of the Ṛishi Atri and father of Budha [Mercury, cf. *candra-ja*]; the latter married Iḷā, daughter of the solar king Ikshvāku, and had by her a son, Aila or Purūravas; this last had a son by Urvaśī, named Āyus, from whom came Nahusha, father of Yayāti; the latter had two sons, Puru and Yadu, from whom proceeded the two branches of the lunar line; in that of Yadu was born Kṛishṇa and Bala-rāma; in that of Puru came Dushyanta, hero of the Śakuntalā and father of the great Bharata; 9th from Bharata came Kuru, and 14th from him Śāntanu, who had a son Vicitra-vīrya and a step-son Vyāsa; the latter married the two widows of his half-brother, and had by them Dhṛitarāshṭra and Pāṇḍu, the wars of whose sons form the subject of the MBh.); (cf. *sūrya-v°.*) **– °vaṇśin,** m. one of the lunar dynasty, W. **– vaktrā,** f., N. of a town. **– vat** (*°drá-*), mfn. illuminated by the moon, Ghaṭ. 2; Kathās.; abounding in gold, RV. iii, 30, 20; v, 57, 7; TBr. ii; (*tī*), f., N. of a daughter of Su-nābha and wife of Gada, Hariv. 8762 & 8779; of a princess, BhavP.; Pañcat. ii, 4, $\frac{1}{2}$; of the wife of a potter, Rājat. i, 323; of several other women, Kathās.; of a town, Sukas. (cf. *°drā-v°*). **– vatsa,** m. pl., N. of a people, MBh. v, 2732. **– vadanā,** f. a moon-faced woman, Dhūrtan. **– vandya,** m., N. of a man. **– vapus,** mfn. 'moon-formed,' handsome, Ratnâv. i, 4. **– vara-locana,** m., N. of a Samādhi, Kāraṇḍ. xvii, 12; xxiii, 145. **– varṇa** (*°drá-*), mfn. of brilliant colour, RV. i, 165, 12. **– vartman,** n. 'having a path resembling that of the moon (because of not having any cæsura),' a metre of 4 × 12 syllables. **– varman,** m., N. of a Kāmboja king, MBh. i, 2668; vii, 1437; of a prince conquered by Samudra-gupta, Inscr. **– vallarī,** f. Ruta graveolens or a kind of pot-herb, L. **– vallī,** f. id., L.; Pæderia fœtida, L.; Gærtnera racemosa (?, *mādhavī*), L. **– vaśā,** f., N. of a river, BhP. v, 19, 18 (v. l. *-vasā*). **– vasā,** f. id., iv, 28, 35; (cf. *-masā.*) **– vāhana,** m., N. of a prince of Pratishṭhāna, Vīrac. ii. **– vikrama,** m., N. of a hero of Kālikā, xxx. **– vijña,** m., N. of a prince, BhP. xii, 1, 25. **– vimala,** m. 'pure as the moon,' N. of a Samādhi, Buddh.; *-sūrya-prabhāsa-śrī,* m. 'whose beauty is spotless like the moon and brilliant as the sun,' N. of a Buddha. **– vihaṃgama,** m. 'moon-bird,' the crane Ardea nivea, L. **– vrata,** n. = *cāndrâyaṇa-v°.* **– śarman,** m., N. of a Brāhman. **– śālā,** f. = *-prāsāda,* Ragh.; VarBṛS. lvi (ifc. f. *ā*), moon-light, L. **– śālikā,** f. = *-prāsāda,* L. **– śilā,** f. the moon-stone (Candra-kānta), Bhaṭṭ. xi, 15; v. l. for *-śītā.* **– śītā,** f., N. of one of the mothers attending on Skanda, MBh. ix, 46, 11 (*-śilā,* C). **– śukla,** m. one of the 8 Upa-dvīpas (in Jambu-dvīpa), BhP. v, 19, 30. **– śubhra,** mf(*ā*)n. illuminated by the moon, Kathās. lxx, 26. **– śūra,** m. Lepidium sativum, Bhpr.; n. the seed of that plant, ib. **– śekhara,** m. = *-mukuṭa,* Hariv. 14838; Kum. v, 58; N. of a minister (father of the author of Sāh.); of the author of a Comm. on Śak.; of the author of the play Madhurā-niruddha; of a prince, Kathās. cxxiii, 114; of a mountain (cf. *-parvata*), W.; *-campū-prabandha,* m., N. of a work. **– śrī,** m., N. of a prince, VP.; f., N. of a woman, Kathās. lviii, 58. **– saciva,** m. 'moon-friend,' the god of love, Gal. **– saṃjña,** m. 'having any N. of the moon,' camphor, L. **– sambhava,** m. = *-ja,* W.; (*ā*), f. small cardamoms, L. **– saras,** n. 'moon-lake,' N. of a mythical lake, Pañcat. iii, 1, $\frac{8}{9}$; Kathās. cxii, 29. **– sāman,** n., N. of a Sāman, Vishṇ. **– sāra,** m., N. of a man, Kathās. lxvii, 37. **– sālokya,** n. attainment of the lunar heaven, Mn. iv, 231. **– sāhi,** m., N. of a prince, Inscr. **– siṇha,** m., N. of a king (son of Darpa-nārāyaṇa); of a hero of Kālikā, Vīrac. xxx. **– suta,** m. = *-ja,* VarBṛS.; Laghuj.; VarYogay. **– surasa,** m. Vitex Negundo, L. **– sûkta,** n., N. of two Sāmans, Vishṇ. **– sūtra,** n. pl. the (grammatical) Sūtras of Candra. **– sūri,** m., N. of Sūri of the Jainas. **– sūrya,** m. du. moon and sun, W.; *-jihmī-karaṇa-prabha,* m. 'whose splendour obscures moon and sun,' N. of a Buddha, Lalit. xx, 34 f.; *-pradīpa,* m. 'illuminating moon and sun,' N. of a Buddha; *°ryâksha,* mfn. having moon and sun as his eyes (Vishṇu), Hariv. 14189. **– sena,** m., N. of a prince (son of Samudra-sena), MBh. i f., vii; = *-vāhana,* Virac. ii; N. of a hero of Kālikā, xxx. **– soma,** m., N. of a hero of Kālikā, ib. **– sthala-nagara,** n., N. of a town, Campak. **– svāmin,** m., N. of several men, Kathās. **– han,** m. 'moon-slayer,' N. of a Dānava, Hariv. 2289 & 12939. **– hanu,** m., N. of a Dānava, 12939. **– hantṛi,** m. (= *-han*) N. of a Dānava, MBh. i, 2673; Hariv. **– hāsa,** m. (= *-bhāsa*) 'moon-derider,' a glittering scimitar, Sāh. vi, $\frac{24}{25}$; Rāvaṇa's sword, R. vii, 16, 43; N. of a prince, JaimBhār. lxv–lxxv; of a hero of Kālikā, Vīrac. xxx; n. silver, L.; (*ā*), f. = *-pushpā,* Bhpr.; Cocculus cordifolius, L.; N. of a Yoginī, Hcat.; *-tīrtha,* n., N. of a Tīrtha, RevāKh. **Candrâṇśu,** m. = *°dra-pāda,* Kāvyâd. ii, 40. **Candrâkara,** m., N. of a man, Rājat. vii, 5. **Candrâkṛiti,** mfn. moon-shaped, like the moon (in roundness &c.), W. **Candrâgra,** mf(*ā*)n. brilliant-peaked, RV. v, 41, 14; brilliant-surfaced (a liquid), vi, 49, 8. **Candrâṅgada,** m., N. of a son of king Indra-sena, BrahmôttKh. xviii ff. (v. l. *citrâṅg°*). **Candrâcārya,** m., N. of a Jain teacher. **Candrâtapa,** m. moon-light, Daś.; an open hall, awning, L. **Candrâtmaja,** m. = *°dra-ja,* VarBṛS.; VarYogay. **Candrâtreya,** m. pl. N. of a family, Pravar. iii, 3. **Candrâditya,** m., N. of a prince, Kathās. lxxiv, 215. **Candrâdi-loka,** m. = *°dra-loká,* KapS. vi, 56. **Candrânana,** m. 'moon-faced,' Skanda, MBh. iii, 14632; N. of a Jina; of a hero of Kālikā, Vīrac. xxx. **Candrâpīḍa,** m. = *°dra-mukuṭa,* Bālar. x, 28; N. of a son of Janamejaya, Hariv. 11065 f.; of a king of Kaśmīr (brother of Tārāpīḍa), Rājat. iv, 45; v, 277; of a prince of Kanyakubja, Kathās. lxi, 219; of a hero of Kālikā, Vīrac. xxx. **Candrā-pura,** n., N. of a town, L. **Candrâbha-vaktra,** mfn. moon-faced, W. **Candrâbhāsa,**

m. an appearance in the sky like the moon, false moon, W. **Candrâmṛita-rasa,** m. 'essence of the moon's nectar,' a particular medicine. **Candrâri,** m. 'moon-enemy,' Rāhu, Gal. **Candrârka,** m. du. =°*dra-sūrya,* W.; (*ī*), f., N. of an astron. work by Dina-kara; *-dīpa,* m. = *candra-sūrya-pradīpa.* **Candrârdha,** m. a half-moon, Hariv.; R.; Suśr.; *-kṛita-śekhara,* mfn. one who has adorned his forehead with a crescent mark, Vet. i, 25; *-cūḍāmaṇi,* m. = *candra-mukuṭa,* Bhartṛ. iii, 65; Hit.; *-mauli,* m. id., Prab. i, 2; Caṇḍ. ii, 21. **Candrâloka,** m. N. of a work on rhetoric by Jaya-deva. **Candrâvataṇsaka,** m. N. of a man, HYog. iii, 82. **Candrā-vatī,** f. N. of a place of pilgrimage; of the wife of king Dharma-sena, Vet. xxv. **Candrâvartā,** f. a metre of 4 × 15 syllables. **Candrâvalī,** f., N. of a Yoginī, Hcat. ii, 1, 725; of one of Kṛishṇa's female companions. **Candrâvaloka,** m., N. of a prince. **Candrâśma** [L.], °**śman** [Dharmaśarm. i, 8], m. the moon-stone (Candra-kānta). **Candrâśva,** m., N. of a son of Dhundhu-māra, Hariv. 706. **Candrâspadā,** f. oak-apples on Rhus, L. **Candrâhvaya,** m. =°*dra-saṃjña,* L. **Candrêśa-liṅga,** n. N. of a Liṅga, SkandaP. **Candrêśvara-tīrtha,** n. N. of a Tīrtha, RevāKh. cxx. **Candrêshṭā,** f. 'moon-loved,' a night lotus, L. **Candrôttarya,** m., N. of a Samādhi, Kāraṇḍ. xvii, 19. **Candrôdaya,** m. moon-rise, Suśr.; Kum. iii, 67; (=°*drâtapa*) an open hall, L.; N. of a mercurial preparation; N. of a Pāṇḍava warrior, MBh. vii, 7012; (*ā*), f. a medicine for the eyes; *-makara-dhvaja,* m. N. of a medicinal preparation; *-varṇana,* n. description of moon-rise, SārṅgP. **Candrônmīlana,** n., N. of a work. **Candrôparāga,** m. eclipse of the moon, MatsyaP. **Candrôpala,** m. the moon-stone (Candra-kānta), Prasannar. vii, 53; Siṇhâs.

Candraka, m. the moon, Mālav. v, 7 (ifc. f. *ikā*); a circle or ring shaped like the moon, Śiś. v, 40; a spot similar to the moon, R. v, 42, 3 & 5; Suśr. (ifc. f. *ikā*); Rājat. iii, 382 (?); the eye in a peacock's tail, Gīt. ii, 3; Rājat. i, 260; a finger-nail, L.; N. of a fish (v.l. °*daka,* L.), Suśr. i, 46, 2, 62; N. of a poet, Kshem.; Rājat. ii, 16; of an owl, MBh. xii, 4944; n. black pepper, L.; (*ikā*), f. moonlight, Megh.; Ragh.; Bhartṛ. &c.; ifc. splendour, Vcar. v, 37; ifc. illumination, elucidation (of a work or subject, e. g. *alaṃkāra-, kātantra-,* &c.); N. of a Comm. on Kāvyâd.; 'moonshine,' baldness, Gal.; the Chanda fish, L.; cardamoms, L.; =*candra-śūra,* Bhpr.; Gynandropsis pentaphylla, L.; Jasminum Zambac, L.; Trigonella fœnum græcum; a kind of white-blossoming Kaṇṭakārī, L.; the Utpalinī metre; (in music) a kind of measure; N. of Dākshāyaṇī, MatsyaP. xiii; of a woman, Mālav. iv, 6/7; of a Surâṅganā, Siṇhâs.; of the Candra-bhāgā river, L. **-vat,** m. 'having eyes in the tail,' a peacock, W.

Candrakita, mfn. (g. *tārakâdi*) furnished with brilliant moon-like spots, Kād. iii. 160 (ifc.)

Candrakin, m. =°*ka-vat,* Śiś. iii; Dhanaṃj. 55.

Candraṭa, m., N. of an ancient physician, Suśr. Introd. (not in ed.)

Candrá-mas. See s.v. *candrá.*

Candralā, f., N. of a woman, Rājat. viii, 3421.

Candrāya, Nom. °*yati,* °*yate,* to represent or resemble the moon, R. vii, 31, 28; Sāh. x, 26 a/b; (pf. Pass. p. °*yita,* n. impers.) Prasannar. vii, 47/48.

Candrikā, f. of °*draka,* q. v. **-tulya,** m. 'resembling moonlight,' the Chanda fish (*candraka*), Gal. **-drāva,** m. 'melting in moonlight,' the moonstone (Candra-kānta), L. **-pāyin,** m. 'moonlight-drinker,' the Cakora bird, L. **-°mbuja** (°*kâm*°), n. 'moonshine-lotus,' a lotus blossoming during night, L. **-°śana** (°*kâś*°), m. =°*kā-pāyin,* Gal.

Candrikāya, Ā. to represent the moonlight.

Candrin, mfn. golden, VS. xxi, 31; possessing gold, xx, 37; m. =°*dra-ja,* VarBṛS. ciii, 12 (v.l.)

Candrimā, f. (fr. *candrá-mas*; cf. *pūrṇimā*) moonlight, L., Sch.

Candrila, m. a barber, L.; Śiva, L.; Chenopodium album, L.

चन्धन **candhana.** See *cāndhanāyana.*

चप् **cap,** cl. 1. °*pati,* to caress, soothe, console, Dhātup. xi, 5: cl. 10. *capayati,* 'to pound, knead,' or 'to cheat,' xxxii, 82.

चप **capa,** ? See *cāpa.*

चपट **capaṭa,** for °*peṭa,* L., Sch.

चपल **capala,** mf(*ā*)n. (√*kamp*; gaṇas *śauṇḍâdi, śreṇy-ādi* & *vispashṭâdi*) moving to and fro, shaking, trembling, unsteady, wavering, MBh. &c.; wanton, fickle, inconstant, ib.; inconsiderate, thoughtless, ill-mannered, Mn. iv, 177; MBh. xiv, 1251; quick, swift, expeditious, Hariv. 4104; momentary, instantaneous, Subh.; m. a kind of mouse, Suśr. v, 6, 3; Ashṭâṅg. vi, 38, 1; a fish, L.; the wind, Gal.; quicksilver, L.; black mustard, L.; a kind of perfume (*coraka*), L.; a kind of stone, L.; N. of a demon causing diseases, Hariv. 9562; of a prince, MBh. i, 231; n. a kind of metal (mentioned with quicksilver); (*am*), ind. quickly, Daś. vii, 420 f.; (*ā*), f. lightning, Gīt. vii, 23; long pepper, L.; the tongue, L.; (g. *priyâdi*) a disloyal wife, whore, L.; spirituous liquor (esp. that made from hemp), L.; the goddess Lakshmī or fortune (cf. MBh. xiii, 3861), L.; N. of two metres (cf. *mahā-*); (in music) the 5th note personified. **-gaṇa,** m. a troop of ill-mannered boys, Ratnâv. i, 3. **-tā,** f. trembling, W.; fickleness, inconstancy, Sāh.; Hit.; rudeness, W.; °*tâśaya,* m. indigestion, flatulence, L. **Capalâksha,** mf(*ī*)n. one whose eyes move to and fro, Vcar. ix, 128; (Caurap.) **Capalâṅga,** m. 'swift-bodied,' the gangetic Delphinus, L. **Capalā-jana,** m. 'a fickle or unsteady woman,' and 'the goddess of fortune,' Śiś. ix, 16. **Capalâtmaka,** mfn. of a fickle nature, W.

Capalaka, mfn. fickle, inconsiderate, Hariv. 4546.

Capalaya, Nom. °*yati,* to cause any one to act inconsiderately, Kull. on Mn. iii, 191 & 250.

Capalāya, Nom. °*yate* (g. *bhṛiśâdi*), to move to and fro, jump to and fro (as apes), Hcar. ii, 470.

चपेट **capeṭa,** m. a slap with the open hand, Divyâv. xiii, 125; Kathās. lxvi, 139; Gīt. i, 43, Sch.; (*ā*), f. id., Pāṇ. i, 1, 1, Vārtt. 13, Pat.; (*ī*), f. id., Bālar. ix, 20; the 6th day in the bright half of month Bhādrapada, SkandaP.

Capeṭā, f. of °*ṭa.* **-ghāta,** m. a slap with the open hand, L. **-pātana,** n. 'id.,' in comp. °*nâtithi,* mfn. blown with the open hand, Kpr. vii, 3/4.

Capeṭikā, f. =°*ṭa,* L.

चप्पट्टक **cappaṭṭaka,** m., N. of a Rishi, g. *kurv-ādi* (Gaṇar.)

चप्य **cápya,** n. a kind of sacrificial vessel, VS. xix, 88; ŚBr. xii, 7, 2, 13 & 9, 1, 3.

चफट्टक **caphaṭṭaka** (onomat., Gaṇar. 173, Sch.), m., N. of a king, g. *kurv-ādi* (Gaṇar. & Hemac.); see *cāphaṭṭaki.*

चम् **cam,** cl. 1. °*mati* (perf. *cacāma*; aor. *acamīt,* Vop.; Pass. *acāmi,* ib.), to sip, drink, Nir. x, 12; Bhaṭṭ.; Jaim. iii, 5, 22, Sch.; to eat, Bhaṭṭ. xiv, 53: Ved. cl. 5. *camnoti,* Dhātup. xxvii, 27: Caus. *cāmayati,* xix, 69; (cf. *ā-, anv-ā-*; *pary-ā-cānta, sam-ā-camya.*)

Camana, n. sipping, Jaim. iii, 5, 22, Sch.

चम **cama,** m. pl. = *camaka-sûkta,* Pāṇ. v, 2, 4, Vārtt. 2, Pat. **Camī-kāra,** m. reciting the Camaka-sûkta, Kāṭh. xviii, 7. **Camī-√kṛi,** to recite the Camaka-sûkta over anything, TS. v, 7, 3, 3.

Camaka-sûkta, n. 'the hymn containing *ca me*,' N. of VS. xviii, 1-27, Sāy. on ŚBr. x, 1, 5, 3; cf. *nam*°.

चमक **camaka,** m., N. of a man, Rājat. vii, 289. **-sûkta,** see *cama.*

चमत् **camat,** ind. 'an interjection of surprise,' only in comp. **-karaṇa,** n. astonishment, Sāh. iii, 4 a/b; producing wonder, causing surprise, W.; spectacle, festival, W.; high poetical composition, W. **-kāra,** m. astonishment, surprise, Kathās. xxii, 257; Prab. &c.; show, spectacle, W.; riot, festive turbulence, W.; high poetical composition, W.; Achyranthes aspera, L.; *-candrikā,* f., N. of a grammar; *-cintāmaṇi,* m., N. of a work, Nirṇayas. i, 270 (= ii, 5, 24); *-nagara,* n., N. of a town (= *vṛiddha-n*°), Gal.; *-nṛitya,* n. a kind of dance. **-kārita,** mfn. astonished, Kathās. xxv, 225. **-kārin,** mfn. astonishing, Bijag.; Sāh.; °*ri-tā,* f. the producing of astonishment, iii, 252. **-√kṛi,** to express astonishment, Naish. vi, 13; to produce astonishment, Prasannar. vii, 53. **-kṛita,** mfn. =*-kārita,* Siṇhâs. xiv; xix, 1; Śatr. ii, 476; become proud, Bālar. iii, 30. **-kṛiti,** f. astonishment, surprise.

चमर **camara,** m. a kind of ox called the Yak (Bos grunniens), MBh.; R. &c.; m. n. the bushy tail of the Yak (employed as chowrie or long brush for whisking off insects, flies, &c.; one of the insignia of royalty; cf. *cām*°), MBh. ii, xii; Bhartṛ.; Kathās. lix, 42; a particular high number, Buddh.; m., N. of a Daitya, L.; (*ī*), f. the Bos grunniens, MBh. &c.; a compound pedicle, L. **-puccha,** n. a Yak's tail, W.; m. 'having a bushy tail,' the Indian fox, L. **-vāla,** m. 'having hair as fine as that of a Camara tail,' N. of a prince, Kathās. liv, 144 ff. **Camarâkṛiti,** m. 'resembling the Yak,' a kind of animal (= *sṛimara*), Gal.

Camaraka, m. a bee, Gal.

Camarika, m. 'growing in clusters resembling a chowrie,' Bauhinia variegata, Bhpr. v, 3, 102.

चमस **camasá,** m. (n., g. *ardharcâdi*; *ī,* f., L., Sch.; fr. √*cam*) a vessel used at sacrifices for drinking the Soma, kind of flat dish or cup or ladle (generally of a square shape, made of wood and furnished with a handle), RV.; AV.; VS. &c.; m. a cake (made of barley, rice, or lentils, ground to meal), sweetmeat, flour, L., Sch.; (g. *gargâdi*) N. of a son of Ṛishabha, BhP. v, xi; = *camasôdbheda,* MBh. iii, 5053; (*ī*), f. (g. *gaurâdi,* Gaṇar.; ifc. g. *cūrṇâdi*) a cake, Bhpr. **Camasâdhvaryu,** m. the priest who manages the drinking-vessels, AV. ix, 6, 51; TS. vi; MaitrS.; ŚBr. iii f. &c. **Camasôdbheda,** m., °**dana,** n., N. of a place of pilgrimage (spot of bursting forth of the river Sarasvatī), MBh. iii, ix.

Camasi, f. =°*sī,* a kind of cake, L.

Camasin, mfn. entitled to receive a Camasa (filled with Soma), Jaim. iii, 5, 29 f.; Nyāyam. iii, 5, 14; m., N. of a man, g. 1. *naḍâdi.*

चमीकार **camī-kāra,** &c. See *cama.*

चमुपति **camu-pati.** See °*mū-p*°.

चमू **camū́,** f. (Ved. loc. °*mū́,* RV. six times; once °*mvì,* x, 91, 15; nom. du. °*mvā̀,* iii, 55, 20; gen. loc. °*mvòs*; nom. pl. °*mvàs,* viii, 2, 8; loc. pl. °*mū́shu*) a vessel or part (two or more in number) of the reservoir into which the Soma is poured, RV.; (°*mvaù*), f. du. 'the two great receptacles of all living beings,' heaven and earth, Naigh. iii, 30 (cf. RV. iii, 55, 20); sg. a coffin (?), ŚBr. xiii, 8, 2, 1; ŚāṅkhŚr. xiv, 22, 19; an army or division of an army (129 elephants, as many cars, 2187 horse, and 3645 foot, MBh. i, 292), MBh.; R.; Megh.; BhP. **-cara,** m. a warrior, Prasannar. vii, 13. **-nātha,** m. leader of a division, general, VarBṛS.; (ifc.) BhP. iv. **-nāyaka,** m. id., Vcar. x, 10. **-pa,** m. id., VarBṛS.; Kathās. ci. **-pati,** m. id., MBh. iii, vi; R. &c.; (*camu-p*°, Uṇ., Sch.) **-pāla,** m. id., AV. Pariś. **-shád,** mfn. lying on the Camū vessel, RV. i, 14, 4 & 54, 9; ix; x, 43, 4. **-hara,** m. N. of one of the Viśve Devās, MBh. xiii, 4360.

चमूरु **camūru,** m. a kind of deer (cf. *sam*°), Śiś. i, 8; Caurap. **-dṛiś,** f. an antelope-eyed woman, Prasannar. i, 37 (Sāh. iv, 2/3). **-netrā,** f. id. Prasannar. v, 42.

चम्प् **camp** (cf. √*kamp, capala*), cl. 10. °*payati,* v. l. for √*champ,* Dhātup. xxxii, 76.

Campana, n. a jump (?), Pañcad. i, 71.

चम्प **campa,** m. Bauhinia variegata, L.; N. of the founder of Campā (son of Pṛithulâksha or of Harita), Hariv. 1699; BhP. ix, 8, 1; (*ā*), f. N. of a town in Aṅga (the modern Bhāgalpur or a place in its vicinity; residence of Karṇa, MBh. xii, 134 ff.; of Brahma-datta, Buddh.), MBh. &c. **-karambhā,** f. a kind of plantain, L. **-kunda,** m. a kind of fish, L. **-kośa,** for °*kôlba,* W. **Campâlu,** m. for °*pakâlu,* L.

Campaka, m. Michelia Campaka (bearing a yellow fragrant flower), MBh.; R. &c.; a kind of perfume, VarBṛS. lxxvii, 7; a particular part of the bread-fruit, W.; N. of a man, Rājat. vii; of a relation of the Jaina Meru-tuṅga; of a country, Buddh.; n. the flower of the Campaka tree, MBh.; Suśr. &c.; the fruit of a variety of the plantain, L.; (*ā*), f. N. of a town, JaimBhār.; Hit. **-gandha,** m. 'Campaka-fragrance,' a kind of incense (v. l. °*dhi* or °*dhin*), VarBṛS. lxxvii, 6 (12). **-caturdaśī,** f. 'the 14th day in the light half of Jyaishṭha,' N. of a festival. **-deśa,** m. the Campaka country. **-nātha,** m N. of an author. **-pura,** n. N. of a town, Kathârṇ. xiv. **-prabhu,** m. N. of Kalhaṇa's father. **-mālā,** f. a metre of 4 × 10 syllables; N. of a woman, Vāsant. **-latā,** f. N. of a woman, Vṛishabh. **-vatī,** f. N. of a wood in Magadha, Hit. i, 3, 7/8 (vv. ll. °*kā-v*° & °*kâvalī*); of a town, 5, 1/2 (v. l.)

-vyavahāri-kathā, f. N. of a tale (about the merchant Campaka). **Campakâraṇya**, n. 'Campaka forest,' N. of a place of pilgrimage, MBh. iii, 8111; Romakas. **Campakâlu**, m. the bread-fruit tree, L. **Campakā-vatī**, v. l. for °*ka-v*°; (cf. Pāṇ. vi, 3, 119.) **Campakôlba**, m. = °*kâlu*, L.

Campā, f. of °*pa*, q. v. **-dhipa** (°*pâdh*°), m. a prince of Campā; = °*pêśa*, L. **-purī**, f. the town Campā, BhP. **-vatī**, f. id., VāyuP. ii, 37, 376; BrahmôttKh. xvi; N. of Nidhi-pati's wife, Vet. **-shashṭhī**, f. the 6th day in the bright half of Mārgaśīrsha or Bhādrapada, Vratapr. **Campêśa**, m. 'lord of Campā,' Karṇa, L. **Campôpalakshita**, mfn. 'marked by Campā,' dwelling in Campā and its vicinity, L.

चम्पू *campū*, f. a kind of elaborate composition in which the same subject is continued through alternations in prose and verse (*gadya* & *padya*), Kāvyâd. i, 31; Sāh. vi, 336; Pratāpar.; (cf. *gaṅgā-*, *nala-*.) **-kathā-sūtra**, n. N. of a work. **-bhārata**, n. N. of a reproduction in prose and verse of the contents of MBh. (by Ananta-bhaṭṭa). **-rāmāyaṇa**, n. N. of a reproduction in prose and verse of the contents of R. (by Lakshmaṇakavi).

चम्ब् *camb*, cl. 1. °*bati*, to go, Dhātup. xi.

चम्रिष *camrīsh*, f. 'libations (contained) in sacrificial ladles' (Sāy., fr. *camasá*), RV. i, 56, 1.

Camrīshá, mfn. 'contained in the *camū*' (Sāy.), i, 100, 12.

चय् *cay*, cl. 1. °*yate*, to go, Dhātup. xiv, 5; [cf. κίω, κινέω; Lat. *cieo*; Lith. *koja*, 'foot.']

चय 1. & 2. *caya*, &c. See √1. & 3. *ci*.

चर् *car*, cl. 1. *cárati*, rarely °*te* (Subj. *cárat*, 3 pl. *cárān*, RV.; perf. *cacā́ra* [AV. &c.], 2 sg. *cacartha*, BhP. iv, 28, 52; pl. *cerur*, &c.; °*ratur*, ŚBr. &c.; Ā. *cere*, BhP. iii, 1, 19; fut. *carishyati*, °*te*; aor. *acārīt* [ŚBr. xiv &c.]; inf. *cáritum* [ii; MBh. i, iii; R.] or *cartum* [MBh. iii, xiii; R. iii; BhP. v], Ved. *carádhyai* [RV. i, 61, 12], *cáritave* [113, 5], *caráse* [92, 9 & v, 47, 4], *carā́yai* [vii, 77, 1], *caritos* [AitĀr. i, 1, 1, 7]; ind. p. *caritvā́*, ŚBr. xiv; BhP. x, 75, 19; *cartvā*, MBh. v, 3790; *cīrtvā*, xiii, 495; p. *cárat*) to move one's self, go, walk, move, stir, roam about, wander (said of men, animals, water, ships, stars, &c.), RV.; AV. &c.; to spread, be diffused (as fire), VarBṛS. xix, 7; to move or travel through, pervade, go along, follow, Mn.; MBh. &c.; to behave, conduct one's self, act, live, treat (with instr. or loc.), RV.; AV. &c.; to be engaged in, occupied or busy with (instr., e.g. *yajñéna c*°, 'to be engaged in a sacrifice,' ŚBr.), RV. x, 71, 5; AV. vi, 117, 1; AitBr. &c.; (with [ŚBr. iv; ChUp.; Kauś.; ŚāṅkhŚr.] or without [ŚBr. ii, xiv] *mithunám*) to have intercourse with, have to do with (instr.); (with a p. or adj. or ind. p. or adv.) to continue performing or being (e. g. *arcantaś cerur*, 'they continued worshipping,' ŚBr. i; *svāminam avajñāya caret*, 'he may go on despising his master,' Hit.), RV.; AV.; VS. &c.; (in astron.) to be in any asterism or conjunction, VarBṛS.; to undertake, set about, undergo, observe, practise, do or act in general, effect, make (e. g. *vratāni c*°, 'to observe vows,' AV. &c.; *vighnam c*°, 'to put a hindrance,' MBh.; *bhaikshaṃ c*°, 'to beg,' Mn. ii; *vivādaṃ c*°, 'to be engaged in a lawsuit,' Mn. viii, 8; *mṛigayāṃ c*°, 'to hunt,' MBh.; R.; *sambandhāṇś c*°, 'to enter into connections,' Mn. ii, 40; *mārgaṃ cacāra bāṇaiḥ*, 'he made a way with arrows,' R. iii, 34, 4; *tapasā indriyāṇi c*°, to exercise one's organs with penance, MBh. xiv, 544), RV.; AV. &c.; to consume, eat (with acc.), graze, Yājñ. iii, 324; Pañcat.; BhP. v, x; Subh.; Hit.; to make or render (with double acc., e. g. *narêndraṃ satya-sthaṃ carāma*, 'let us make the king keep his word,' R. ii, 107, 19: Caus. *cārayati*, to cause to move or walk about, AV. xii, 4, 28 (aor. *ácīcarat*); ŚāṅkhBr. xxx, 8; Lāṭy.; to pasture, MBh. xiv; R.; BhP. iii, x; to send, direct, turn, move, MBh. &c.; to cause any one (acc.) to walk through (acc.), MBh. xii; R. v, 49, 14; to drive away from (abl.), MBh. xii, 12944; to cause any one (acc.) to practise or perform (with acc.), Mn. xi, 177 & 192; to cause (any animal, acc.) to eat, Bādar. ii, 2, 5, Sch.; to cause to copulate, Mn. viii, 362; to ascertain (as through a spy, instr.), MBh. iii, xv; R. i, vi; to doubt (cf. *vi-*), Dhātup. xxxiii, 71: Desid. *cicarishati*, to try to go, ŚāṅkhBr. xxx, 8 (p. *cicarshat*); to wish to act or conduct one's self, ŚBr. xi; to try to have intercourse with (instr.), vi: Intens. *carcarīti*, Ā. or rarely [MBh. iii, 12850] Pass. *cañcūryate* (°*curīti* & °*cūrti*, Pāṇ. vii, 4, 87 f.; ind. p. °*cūrya*, R. iv, 29, 22; p. once P. °*cūryat*, Hariv. 3602) to move quickly or repeatedly, walk about, roam about (in, loc.), AV. xx, 127, 4; MBh. &c.; to act wantonly or coquettishly, Bhaṭṭ. iv, 19 (cf. Pāṇ. iii, 1, 24); [cf. πέλομαι, ἀμφί-πολο-ς, ἀνα-τολή &c.]

Cara, mfn. (g. *pacâdi*) moving, locomotive (as animals opposed to plants, or as the Karaṇas in astrol.), VPrāt.; ŚvetUp. iii, 18; Mn. vii, 15; MBh. &c.; (= *saṃcārin*) forming the retinue of any one, BhP. iv, 29, 23; movable, shaking, unsteady, W.; ifc. going, walking, wandering, being, living, practising (e.g. *adhaś-*, *anta-*, *antariksha-*, *ap-*, *ādāya-*, *udake-*, &c.; cf. Pāṇ. iii, 2, 16); ifc. (Pāṇ. v, 3, 53 f.; vi, 3, 35; f. *ī*) having been formerly (e. g. *ādhya-*, *devadatta-*, qq. vv.; *a-drishṭa-* or *na drishṭa-*, 'not seen before,' Kathās. [once f. irr. *ā*, lx, 58]; Sarvad. iii, 16; vii, 19; *an-ālokita-*, id., Bālar. iv, $\frac{8}{9}$); m. a spy, secret emissary or agent, Mn. vii, 122; Hariv. 10316; R. &c.; = *caraṭa*, L.; the small shell Cypræa moneta, L.; the wind, air, BhP. x, 14, 11; the planet Mars, L.; a game played with dice (similar to backgammon), L.; a cowrie, W.; 'passage,' see *a-*, *dus-*; n. (in astron.) ascensional difference, Gol. vii; (*ā*), f. dat. °*rāyai*, inf. √*car*, q.v.; (in music) N. of a Mūrchanā; (*ī*), f. a young woman (cf. *caratī*), L.; = *digambara-prasiddhā*, g. *gaurâdi*; also ifc., see *anu-* & *saha-carī*. **-khaṇḍa**, n. (in astron.) the amount of the ascensional difference, Sūryas. iii, 43; Gol. vii, 1. **-gṛiha**, n. a moving or varying sign of the zodiac, i. e. the 1st, 4th, 7th, and 10th, VarBṛS. vci, 3 & 14; Laghuj. **-jā**, f. (scil. *jyā*) the sign of *-khaṇḍa*, Sūryas. ii, 61; iii, 33. **-jyā**, f. id., 34, Sch.; Gol. vii, 1, Sch. **-dala**, n. = *-khaṇḍa*, VarBṛS. ii, $\frac{9}{1}$; Sūryas. iii, 10; *-jā*, f. = *cara-jā*, xiii, 15. **-deva**, m. N. of a man, Rājat. vii, 1554. **-dravya**, n. pl. 'movables,' goods and chattels, W. **-pushṭa**, m. 'spy-nourished,' a mediator, W. **-bha**, n. = *-griha*, Laghuj. **-bhavana**, n. id., ib. **-mūrti**, f. an idol which is carried about in procession, W. **-śiñjinī**, f. = *-jā*, Gol. vii, 1. 1. **Carâcara**, mfn. movable and immovable, locomotive and stationary, moving and fixed (as animals and plants), Mn. i, iii; Bhag. x f.; R.; BhP.; n. the aggregate of all created things whether animate or inanimate, world, Mn.; Yājñ.; Bhag.; R.; BhP.; *-guru*, m. the lord of the world (Brahmā), MBh. iii, 497; N. of Śiva, Kautuk.

Cáraka, m. a wanderer, wandering religious student, ŚBr. xiv; Pāṇ. v, 1, 11; Lalit. i, 28; a spy, Naish. iv, 116; a kind of ascetic, VarBṛ. xv, 1; a kind of medicinal plant, L.; N. of a Muni and physician (the Serpent-king Śesha, who was the recipient of the Āyur-veda; once on visiting the earth and finding it full of sickness he became moved with pity and determined to become incarnate as the son of a Muni for alleviating disease; he was called Caraka because he had visited the earth as a kind of spy or *cara*; he then composed a new book on medicine, based on older works of Agni-veśa and other pupils of Ātreya, Bhpr.); N. of a lexicographer; m. pl. (cf. Pāṇ. iv, 3, 107) N. of a branch of the black Yajur-veda (the practises and rites enjoined by which are different in some respects from those in ŚBr.), ŚBr. iv; Lāṭy. v, 4, 20; Sch. on VS. & ŚBr.; VāyuP. i, 61, 10; (*ī*), f. a kind of venomous fish, Suśr. v, 3, 8; N. of an evil spirit, VarBṛS. liii, 83; AgP. xl, 18. **-grantha**, m. Caraka's book (on med.) **-tantra**, n. id.; *-vyākhyā*, f. N. of a Comm. on Car. by Hari-candra. **-bhāshya**, n. N. of another Comm. on Car. by Kṛishṇa. **Cárakâcārya**, m. a teacher of the Carakas, VS. xxx, 18. **Cárakâdhvaryu**, m. id. (generally pl.), ŚBr. iii f., viii; BhP. &c.

Caraṭa, m. (= *cara*) a wagtail, L.; (*ī*), f. (= °*raṇṭī*, *ciratī*, *cirantī*) a woman married or single who after maturity resides in her father's house, L., Sch.

Cáraṇa, m. n. (g. *ardharcâdi*) a foot, Gobh.; Mn. ix, 277; Bādar.; MBh. &c. (ifc. f. *ā*, Hariv. 3914; Mālav.); (ifc. pl.) 'the feet of,' the venerable (N. N.), MBh. xii, 174, 24, Sch.; a pillar, support, Hariv. 4643; the root (of a tree), L.; a Pāda or line of a stanza, Śrut.; a dactyl; a 4th part (pāda), VarBṛ.; Līl.; a section, subdivision, Bhpr.; Sarvad. (*catuś-*, q. v.); a school or branch of the Veda, Nir. i, 17; Pāṇ.; MBh. xii, xiii; Pañcat. iv, 3; n. going round or about, motion, course, RV. iii, 5, 5; ix, 113, 9; x, 136, 6 & 139, 6; ŚBr. ii, x; Sāh.; acting, dealing, managing, (liturgical) performance, observance, AV. vii, 106, 1; ŚBr.; ŚāṅkhŚr.; KātyŚr.; VP. iii, 5, 13; behaviour, conduct of life, KātyŚr.; ChUp. v, 10; good or moral conduct, Kauś. 67; MBh. xiii, 3044; Lalit.; practising (generally ifc., cf. *tapaś-* [*tapasaś c*°, Mn. vi, 75], *bhikshā-*, *bhaiksha-*), Gobh. iii, 1, 12; Nal.; grazing, W.; consuming, eating, L.; a particular high number, Buddh. L.; (cf. *dvi-*, *puraś-*, *ratha-*). **-kamala**, n. 'foot-lotus,' a beautiful foot, W. **-kisalaya**, n. id., W. **-gata**, mfn. fallen at one's feet, W. **-granthi**, m. 'foot-joint,' the ancle, ĀpŚr. vii, 2, 6, Sch. **-tra**, 'foot-saver,' a shoe, Kuṭṭanīm. **-dāsa**, m. N. of the author of the Guru-śishya-saṃvāda and of the philos. poem Nāciketûpâkhyāna. **-nyāsa**, m. footstep, Ratnâv. i, 11; foot-mark, Megh. 56. **-pa**, m. 'root-drinker,' a tree, L. **-patana**, n. a foot-fall, Amar. **-patita**, mfn. = *-ga*, W. **-padma**, m. n. = *-kamala*, W. **-parvan**, n. = *-granthi*, L. **-pāta**, m. = *-patana*, Pañcat. iv, 9; tread, kick, Hariv. 13607; Pañcat. ii, $\frac{4}{5}$. **-pṛishṭha**, m. the back of the foot, Daś. viii, 192. **-prasāra**, m. stretching the legs, Mn. ii, 198, Kull. **-bhaṅga**, m. fracture of the foot, Pañcat. i, $\frac{2}{3}\frac{2}{3}$. **-yuga**, n. both feet, W.; two lines of a stanza, W. **-yodhin**, m. 'foot-fighter,' a cock, R. (B) iv, 58, 31. **-lagna**, mfn. = *-gata*, Dhūrtas. **-vat**, mfn. of good conduct, GopBr. i, 2, 5. **-vyūha**, m. N. of a treatise on the schools of the Veda. **-śuśrūshā**, f. = *-patana*, R. iii, 14, 8. **-sevā**, f. 'service on one's feet,' devotion, W. **Caraṇâksha**, m. (= *aksha-pāda*) Gautama, SŚaṃkar. **Caraṇânati**, f. = °*ṇa-patana*, Amar. (Kpr. iv, $\frac{1}{1}\frac{1}{2}$). **Caraṇânamita**, mfn. bent under the feet, trodden down, W. **Caraṇâbharaṇa**, n. a foot-ornament, L. **Caraṇâmṛita**, n. 'foot-nectar,' the water in which the feet of a Brāhman or spiritual guide have been washed, W. **Caraṇâyudha**, mfn. having the feet for weapons, MBh. ix, 2669; R. iii, 56, 35; m. a cock, Car. vi, 2 & 5; Sāh. iii, $\frac{1}{1}\frac{9}{8}\frac{8}{8}$. **Caraṇâravinda**, n. = °*ṇa-kamala*, W. **Caraṇârdha**, n. the half of the foot, W.; half of the fourth of a stanza, W. **Caraṇâskandana**, n. treading down with the feet, W. **Caraṇôdaka**, n. = °*ṇâmṛita*, W. **Caraṇôpaga**, mfn. in contact with the feet, at the feet, W. **Caraṇôpadhāna**, n. a foot-rest, MBh. i, 193, 10.

Caraṇasa, mfn. fr. °*ṇa*, g. *triṇâdi*.

Caráṇi (only gen. pl. °*ṇīnām*) mfn. 'movable,' active (Gmn.), RV. viii, 24, 23.

Caraṇila, mfn. fr. °*ṇa*, g. *kāśâdi*.

Caraṇīyámāna, mf(*ā*)n. engaged in, carrying on (with acc.), RV. iii, 61, 3.

Caraṇṭī, f. = °*raṭī*, L., Sch.

1. **Caraṇya**, Nom. °*ṇyati*, to move, g. *kaṇḍv-âdi*; (cf. *ā-*, *uc-*).

2. **Caraṇya**, mfn. foot-like, g. *śākhâdi*.

Caraṇyu, mfn. movable, RV. x, 95, 6; AV. xx, 48.

Carátha, mfn. moving, living, RV. i, 58, 5; 68, 1; 70, 2 & 4 (*ca rátha*, MSS.); 72, 6; n. going, wandering, course, RV. (i, 66, 9 *carā́tha*); iii, 31, 15; viii, 33, 8; x, 92, 13; (*āya*), dat. inf. = *carayai*, RV.

Caranta, m. N. of a man, VāyuP. ii, 30, 5.

2. **Carācará**, mfn. (√*car* redupl., Pāṇ. vi, 1, 12, Vārtt. 6; vii, 4, 58, Pat.) moving, locomotive, running, RV. x, 85, 11; VS. xxii; ŚBr.; n. Cypræa moneta, L.

Carā́tha, n. See °*rátha*.

Cari, m. an animal, L.; N. of a man, Pravar. i, 1.

Carita, mfn. gone, gone to, attained, W.; 'practised,' in comp.; espied, ascertained (by a spy, *cara*), R. vi, 6, 16 & 7, 21; (*ám*), n. going, moving, course, AV. iii, 15, 4; ix, 1, 3; Gobh. iii; Suśr.; motion (of asterisms), Sūryas.; acting, doing, practice, behaviour, acts, deeds, adventures, RV. i, 90, 2; MBh.; R.; VarBṛS. &c. (ifc. f. *ā*, Gīt. ix, 1); fixed institute, proper or peculiar observance, W.; (cf. *uttara-rāma-*, *duś-*, *sac-*, *saha-*, *su-*). **-guṇa-tva**, n. attainment of peculiar property or use (*sârthaka-tva*, Sch.), Kir. vii, 2. **-pūrva**, mfn. performed formerly, Śak. iv, 21. **-maya**, mf(*ī*)n. ifc. containing or relating deeds or adventures of, Kathās. viii, 35. **-vrata**, mfn. one who has observed a vow, ĀśvGṛ. i, 8, 12; R. i, 3, 1. **Caritârtha**, mf(*ā*)n. attaining one's object, successful in any undertaking, Śak. vii, $\frac{3}{3}\frac{1}{2}$; Mālav. v, $\frac{1}{1}\frac{9}{0}$; Ragh.; Kum.; Pāṇ. Kāś. & Siddh.; *-tā*, f. successfulness, Śak. v, $\frac{8}{9}$; *-tva*, n. id., Sāṃkhyak.; Bhāshāp.; (cf. *cāritârthya*.) **Caritârthaya**, Nom. °*yati*, to cause any one (acc.) to attain his aim, satisfy, Naish. ix, 49. **Caritârthita**, mfn. satisfied, Sarvad. Introd. 2. **Caritârthin**, mfn. desirous of success, W.

Caritavya, mfn. (=*cart°*) to be practised or performed, Mn. xi, 54; MBh. i, 7259; Kathās. lxxii, 101; n. impers. with *upâṅśu vācā*, 'he is to continue speaking low,' AitBr. i, 27, 4.

Caritra, n. (Pāṇ. iii, 2, 184; rarely m., VS. vi, 14; MaitrS. i, 2, 16) a foot, leg, RV.; AV. x, 2, 12; Kauś. 44; n. going, VS. xiii, 19; acting, behaving, behaviour, habit, practice, acts, adventures, deeds, exploits, Mn. ii, 20; ix, 7; R. &c. (ifc. f. *ā*, Pañcat. iv, 7, 5); nature, disposition, W.; custom, law as based on custom, Nār. i, 10 f.; xx, 24; (*ā*), f. the tamarind tree, L.; (cf. *cār°*). **-bandhaka,** m.n. a friendly pledge, Yājñ. ii, 61. **-vat,** mfn. one who has already performed (a sacrifice), ĀśvGṛ. iv, 8, 15.

Carishṇú, mfn. (Nir. vii, 29; Pāṇ. iii, 2, 136) moving, locomotive, unsteady, wandering about, RV.; ŚāṅkhŚr.; ŚāṅkhGṛ.; MBh. xii; BhP. ii; (with *bīja*, the semen of [moving beings, i.e. of] animals) Mn. i, 56; m. N. of a son of Manu Sāvarṇa, Hariv. 465; of a son of Kīrtimat by Dhenukā, VāyuP. i, 28, 16 (*varishṭa* ed.) **-dhūma** (°*shṇú-*), mfn. having moving smoke, RV. viii, 23, 1.

Carītra, n. =°*ritra*, behaviour, conduct, L.

Cárcara, mfn. (√*car* redupl.) = *caraṇa-śīla* (Sāy.), RV. x, 106, 7; (*ī*), f. a kind of song, Vikr. iv; Ratnâv. i, 7/8; musical symphony, Kathās. liv; the recitation of scholars, W.; festive cries or merriment, festive sport, W.; flattery, W.; a metre of 4 × 18 syllables; (for *barbarī*) curled or woolly hair, L.

Carcarikā, f. a kind of gesture, Vikr. iv.

Carcarīka, ifc. =°*rī*, musical symphony, Kathās. ciii, 200; m. a pot-herb, L.; (for *barbar°*) decoration or curling of the hair, L.; a form of Śiva, L.

Cartavya, mfn. to be practised, MBh. xiii.

Carya, mfn. (Pāṇ. iii, 1, 100) to be practised or performed, Mn. iii, 1; m. (=*cara*) the small shell Cypræa moneta, L.; n. ifc. driving (in a carriage), MBh. viii, 4215; (*ā*), f. going about, wandering, walking or roaming about, visiting, driving (in a carriage, *ratha-*, MBh. ix, xiii; R. i, 19, 19), MBh.; R.; BhP. ix, 16, 1; (often ifc.) proceeding, behaviour, conduct, ŚBr. xi, 5, 7, 1; Lāṭy. viii; ĀśvŚr. xii, 4; Mn. vi, 32 &c.; due observance of all rites and customs, Sarvad. vi ff.; a religious mendicant's life, L.; practising, performing, occupation with, engaging in (instr. [Gaut.] or generally in comp.), ŚBr. xiv; ĀśvGṛ. iii, 7; Mn. i, 111; MBh. &c.; deportment, usage, W.; (in music) a kind of composition; N. of Durgā, Gal.; (cf. *brahma-*, *bhikshā-*, *bhaikshya-*).

Caryā, f. of °*rya*, q. v. **-nātha,** m. N. of a sage, Sarvad. **Caryâvatāra,** m. N. of a Buddh. work.

चरम *caramá*, m(nom. pl. °*me* or °*mās*, Pāṇ. i, 1, 33)f(*ā*)n. (in comp., Pāṇ. ii, 1, 58) last, ultimate, final, RV. vii, 59, 3; viii, 20, 14; TS. i, v; BhP. &c. (°*mā kriyā*, 'the [final i. e.] funeral ceremony,' MBh. iv, 834); the outermost (first or last, opposed to the middle one), RV. viii, 61, 15; later, KapS. i, 72; (°*mam kim*, 'what more?' Prasannar. v, 3/4); 'western,' in comp.; lowest, least, L.; a particular high number, Buddh. L.; (*am*), ind. last, MBh. i, iii; at last, at the end, Rājat. v, 7; after any one (gen.), Mn. ii, 194; Kir. **-kāla,** m. the last moments, hour of death, W. **-kshmā-bhṛit,** m. the western ('earth-supporter' or) mountain, L. **-giri,** m. id., Bhojapr. 319. **-tás,** ind. at the outermost end, AV. xix, 15, 3; MaitrS. iii, 10, 1. **-bhavika,** mfn. being in the last earthly state, Buddh. **-vayas,** mfn. (cf. Pāṇ. iv, 1, 20, Pat.) being in the last stage of life, old, Mālatīm. vi, 2; *a-c°*, n. youth, Uttarar. v, 12. **-vaiyākaraṇa,** m. (the last, i. e.) an ignorant grammarian, W. **-śairshika,** mf(*ī*)n. having the points turned towards the west, MBh. xiii, 462. **Caramâcala,** m. =°*ma-giri*, Prasannar. vii, 5/1/2; Hit. **Caramâjā,** f. the last or smallest she-goat, AV. v, 18, 11. **Caramâdri,** m. =°*ma-giri*, L. **Caramâvasthā,** f. the last state, W.

Caramya, Nom. °*myati*, to be the last, g. *kaṇḍv-ādi*.

चरव्य *caravya*. See *carú*.

चराचर *carâcara* & *carâc°*. See √*car*.

Carâtha, cari, carita, °*ritra*, &c., see ib.

चरु *carú*, m. (g. *bhīmâdi*) a kind of vessel (in which a particular oblation is prepared), saucepan, pot, RV.; AV.; ŚBr. xiii; KātyŚr.; Kauś.; Mn.; Yājñ.; a cloud (cf. RV. i, 7, 6), Naigh. i, 10; an oblation (of rice, barley and pulse) boiled with butter and milk for presentation to the gods or manes, VS. xxix, 6; TS. i; ŚBr.; AitBr. i, 1 & 7; KātyŚr. &c. (pl., Yājñ. i, 298). **-celin,** mfn. (for *cār°*?) having portions of offerings on the clothes (Śiva), MBh. xii, 10419. **-vraṇa,** m. a kind of cake, L. **-śrapaṇa,** n. sprinkling an oblation of milk and ghee, W. **-sthālī,** f. the vessel in which the Caru oblation is prepared (made either of clay or udumbara-wood, Karmapr.), Gobh. i; iv, 2, 28; Kauś. **-homa,** m. offering the Caru oblation, W.

Caravya, mfn. (Pāṇ. v, 1, 2, Vārtt. 3, Pat.) destined for the Caru oblation, ĀpŚr. viii, 2, 4, Sch.

चर्करीत *carkarīta*, n. a term for any Intens. formed without the syllable *ya* (like *carkarīti*, √1. *kṛi*), Dhātup. xxiv, 72; Pāṇ. ii, 4, 74, Siddh.

चर्कृति *carkṛiti*, f. (√2. *kṛi*) praising, mention, glory, RV. v, 74, 9; vi, 48, 21.

Carkṛitya, mfn. to be mentioned with praise, renowned, i, 64, 14 & 119, 21; iv, viii, x; AV. vi, 98, 1.

चर्घ् *cargh*, cl. 1. °*ghati*, to go, W.

चर्च् *carc*, cl. 1. °*cati*, to abuse, censure, menace, Dhātup. xvii, 67; to injure, xxviii, 17: cl. 10. °*cayati*, to repeat a word (in reciting the Veda, esp. while adding *iti*), RPrāt. xv, 10 & 12; to talk over, discuss, Hcar. vii; (also Ā., Vop.) to study, Dhātup. xxxiii, 38.

Carca, m. 'repeating over in thought,' considering, deliberation, L., Sch.; (*ā*), f. (Pāṇ. iii, 3, 105; g. *ukthâdi*) repetition of a word (in reciting the Veda, esp. while adding *iti*), VPrāt.; APrāt.; Hcat.; =°*rca* (with gen. or itc.), Naish. v, 38; Siṅhâs.; Hit.; talking about (in comp.), Rājat. v, 303; discussion, vii, 1476; viii, 3342; Bhojapr. 2 1/2 1/3; alternate recitation of a poem by two persons, W.; inquiry, W.; unguent laid on, Kāvyâd. ii, 104; Gīt. ix, 10; Durgā, L.

Carcaka, m. repetition of a word (in reciting the Veda), Hcat. i. 7, 1064 (pl.); Caraṇ.; (*ikā*), f. = *carcā*, L.; N. of Durgā, BrahmaP. ii, 18, 15; Hcat. i, 7, 153; Tantr.; (cf. *gharma-*, *vi-*). **-mālā,** f. a rosary, Kuṭṭanim. 66.

Carcana, n. =°*rcaka*; laying on (unguent), L.

Carcā, f. of °*rca*, q. v. **-pada,** n. pl. the words repeated (in reciting the Veda while *iti* is added), RAnukr.; Pat. Introd. on Vārtt. 11 & 14. **-pāra,** m. = *carcaka*, g. *vedâdhyāyâdi*.

Carcāya, Nom. °*yate*, to be repeated (in reciting the Veda while *iti* is added), RAnukr.

Carci, m. N. of a man, Pravar. vii, 10; cf. *haimac°*.

Carcikā, f. of °*rcaka*, q. v.

Carcikya, n. = *cārc°*, L.

Carcita, mfn. repeated (in reciting the Veda while *iti* is added), RAnukr.; ifc. smeared with, covered with, MBh. ii, 2371; Hariv. 15694, &c.; rubbed off, R. vii; 'thought over,' determined on, BhP. x, 44, 1; investigated, W.; n. unguent laid on, Śṛiṅgār.

चर्चर *cárcara*, °*rikā*, &c. See √*car*.

चर्चस् *carcas*, m. one of the 9 treasures of Kubera, L.

चर्चा *carcā*, °*rcāya*, °*rci*, &c. See √*carc*.

चर्तव्य *cartavya*. See √*car*.

चर्त्य *cartya*, mfn. √*crit*, Pāṇ. iii, 1, 110.

चर्पट *carpaṭa*, mfn. lying flat to the head (ears), VarBṛS. lxviii, 58 (v. l. *cipiṭa*); VarBṛ. xxv, 12, Sch.; m. the open palm of the hand, L.; =°*ṭī*, L.; (*ā*), f. the 6th day in the light half of Bhādrapada, L.; (*ī*), f. a thin biscuit of flour (cf. *parp°*), L.

Carpaṭin, m. N. of the author of the Rasacandrôdaya, Haṭhapr. i, 6; Toḍar.

चर्ब् *carb*, cl. 1. °*bati*, to go, Dhātup. xi, 31.

चर्भट *carbhaṭa*, m. = *cirbh°*, L.; (*ī*), f. = °*rcarī*, cries of joy, L.

चर्म *carma*, in comp. (and twice ifc. see *ṛishabha-* & *sa-*) for *cárman*; n. a shield, L., Sch. **-karaṇa,** n. working in skins or leather, W. **-karta,** m. a piece of skin or leather, TBr. i, 2, 6, 7. **-kaśā** (or *-kashā*), f. N. of a plant (Mimosa abstergens, Bhpr.; a kind of perfume, ib.), Car. i, 1, 76, Sch. (=*saptalā*). **-kāra,** m. a worker in leather, shoemaker (offspring of a Caṇḍāla woman by a fisherman, Parāś.; or of a Vaideha female by a Nishāda, Mn. x, 36; or of a Nishāda woman, MBh. xiii, 2588), VarBṛS. lxxxvii, 35; Rājat. iv; (*ī*), f. a shoemaker's wife, Kulārṇ. vii; Mimosa abstergens, L.; °*râluka*, m. a kind of bulbous plant, Bhpr. **-kāraka,** m. a shoemaker, W. **-kārin,** m. id., W.; (*iṇī*), f. a woman on the second day of her courses. **-kārya,** n. working in leather or skins, Mn. x, 49. **-kāshṭha-maya,** mfn. made of leather and wood, Hcat. **-kāshṭhikā,** f. 'made of leather and wood,' a whip, Mṛicch. i, 22, Sch. **-kīla,** m. n. 'skin-excrescence,' a wart, Suśr. i f.; excrescences considered as a kind of hemorrhoids, ii, 2, 11 & 13. **-kūpa,** m. a leathern bottle, L. **-kṛit,** m. = *-kāraka*, Rājat. iv, 55. **-khaṇḍa,** n. = *-karta*, Bhartṛ. **-khaṇḍika,** m. pl. N. of a people, VāyuP. i, 45, 115. **-goṇī,** f. = *-kūpa*, Suśr. iv, 4, 15. **-grīva,** m. N. of one of Śiva's attendants, L., Sch. **-ghaṭikā,** f. 'sticking to the skin,' a leach, Npr. **-caṭaka,** m. a bat, Buddh. L.; (*ā*), f. id., L. **-caṭikā,** f. id., L. **-caṭī,** f. id., L.; a cricket, Gal. **-citraka,** n. white leprosy, L. **-cela,** a garment with the hide turned outwards, Buddh. L. **-ja,** mfn. made of leather, BhP. x, 64, 4; n. 'skin-born,' the hairs of the body, L.; blood, L. **-taraṁga,** m. a fold of skin, L. **-tila,** mfn. having the skin covered with pimples resembling the seeds of sesamum, Pāṇ. viii, 2, 8, Vārtt. 1, Pat. **-daṇḍa,** m. 'leather-stick,' a whip, L. **-dala,** n. a slight form of leprosy, Car. vi, 7, 11 & 22; Suśr. **-dūshikā,** f. a kind of leprosy with red spots, L. **-druma,** m. 'parchment-tree,' N. of a tree (the bark of which is used for writing upon), L. **-nāsikā,** f. 'leather-thong,' a whip, W. **-paṭṭa,** m. a flat thong, MBh. xiii, 3456; N. of a place, MārkP. lviii, 25. **-paṭṭikā,** f. a flat piece of leather for playing upon with dice, leather backgammon board, W. **-pattrā,** f. = *-caṭaka*, L. **-pādukā,** f. a leather shoe. **-puṭa,** m. a leathern bag or pair of bellows, Hcar. **-puṭaka,** m. a leathern pipe, Car. i, 1, Sch. **-pūram,** ind. so as to cover the hide, Pāṇ. iii, 4, 31. **-prabhedikā,** f. a shoemaker's awl, L. **-prasevaka,** m. = *-puṭa*, L., Sch. **-prasevikā,** f. id., HYog. iii, 131. **-bandha,** m. a leather band or strap, Hit. iv, 12, 18. **-bandhana,** n. pepper, Npr. **-bhastrikā,** f. a leathern bag, Daś. vii, 213. **-maṇḍala,** m. pl. N. of a people, MBh. vi, 355. **-maya,** mf(*ī*)n. made of skin, leathern, Mn. ii, 157; MBh. ii, xii; VarBṛS.; ifc. encased in the skin of, MBh. vi, 1787. **-muṇḍā,** f. a form of Durgā, L. (cf. *caṇḍa-*, *cāmuṇḍā*). **-mná,** m. (for *mla*, √*mlā*) a tanner, RV. viii, 5, 38; VS. xxx, 15. **-yashṭi,** f. = *-daṇḍa*, W. **-raṅga,** m. pl. N. of a people in the north-west of Madhya-deśa, VarBṛS. xiv, 23; (*ā*), f. the plant Āvartakī, L. **-ratna,** n. a leathern lucky-bag, Daś. vii, 253 & 262; *-bhastrikā*, f. id., 199. **-vaṅśa,** m. a kind of flute. **-vat,** mfn. covered with hides, Pāṇ. viii, 2, 12, Kāś.; ind. like a skin, ŚvetUp. vi, 20; (cf. *loha-c°*); m. N. of a warrior, MBh. vi, 3997. **-vasana,** m. (=*kṛitti-vāsas*) Śiva, L. **-vādya,** n. 'skin-instrument,' a drum, tabour, &c., W. **-vṛiksha,** m. = *-druma*, Hariv. 12681. **-vraṇa,** m. 'skin-disease,' herpes, L. **-śilpin,** m. = *-kāraka*, VarBṛS. lxxxvii, 8. **-samudbhava,** n. (= *-ja*) blood, Gal. **-sambhavā,** f. cardamoms, L. **-sāra,** m. 'skin-essence,' lymph, serum, L. **-sâhvā,** f. = *-kaśā*, Car. vii, 11, 1. **-hantrī,** f. 'skin-destroying,' Trigonella fœnum græcum or a similar plant, Bhpr. **Carmâkhya,** n. a form of leprosy, Car. vi, 7, 19. **Carmâcchādita,** mfn. covered with skin, W. **Carmânurañjana,** n. 'skin-colouring,' white cinnabar, Npr. **Carmânta,** m. =°*ma-khaṇḍa*, Suśr. i, 7, 10; v, 5, 2. **Carmâmbhas,** n. =°*ma-sāra*, L. **Carmâvakartana,** n. 'act of cutting leather,' =°*ma-karaṇa*, W. **Carmâvakartin,** m. 'leather-cutter,' =°*ma-kṛit*, Mn. iv, 218. **Carmâvakarttṛi,** m. id., MBh. xii, 1321. **Carmâvanaddha,** mfn. covered with skin, Mn. vi, 76 (= MBh. xii, 12463); bound with leather, W. **Carmâvṛita,** mfn. covered with skin, ŚārṅgP. xix, 10 (Hit.); ifc. covered with the hide of, L. **Carmâsi-mat,** mfn. having shield and sword, W.

Carmaṇā, f. a kind of fly, L. (v. l. °*rvaṇā*).

Carmaṇya, n. leather-work, AitBr. v, 32; Lāṭy.

Cárman-vat, mfn. furnished with skin, TS. vii, 5, 12, 2; (*tī*), f. Musa sapientum, L.; (Pāṇ. viii, 2, 12) N. of a river (flowing through Bundelkhand into the Ganges, the modern Chambal), MBh. (on the origin of the N., vii, 2360; xii, 1016; xiii, 3351); BhP. v, 19.

Cárman, n. hide, skin, RV.; AV. iv f., x ff.; TS. &c.; bark, W.; parchment, W.; a shield, MBh.; R.; BhP.; Kathās.; =°*rmâkhya*, Car. vi, 7, 11; [cf. *gala-*, *duś-*; πέλμα; Lat. *corium;* Hib. *croicionn.*]

Carmaru, m. =°*rma-kṛit*, L.

Carmāra, m. id., L.; =°*raka*, Bhpr. v, 7, 101.

Carmāraka, m. =°*rmânurañjana*, L.

Carmika, mfn. armed with a shield, shield-bearer, gaṇas *vrīhy-ādi* & *purohitâdi*.

Carmin, mfn. (g. *vrīhy-ādi*) id., MBh.; Hariv. 1863; covered with a hide, Caraṇ.; made of leather, W.; m. = °*rma-druma*, L.; (= °*rmaṇ-vatī*) Musa sapientum, L.; N. of an attendant of Śiva, L.; of a man, Pāṇ. iv, 1, 158, Vārtt. 2, Pat. **Carmi-vṛiksha**, m. = °*ma-v*°, Suśr. iv, 11, 7.

चर्मरी *carmarī*, f. N. of a plant, v. 2, 5.

चर्य *carya*, *caryā*. See √*car*.

चर्व् *carv* (cf. √*cūrṇ*), cl. 10. *carvayati* (inf. °*vitum*; Pass. °*vyate*, cl. 1. °*vati*, Dhātup. xv, 70) to grind with the teeth, masticate, chew, Mṛicch. ii, 12; Pañcat. v, 11, $\frac{0}{1}$; Devīm.; Bhpr.; Sch. on KātyŚr. & PārGṛ.; to taste, Sāh. iii, 16.

Carvaṇa, n. 'chewing,' see *carvita-*; tasting, Sāh. iii, 26; 'to be chewed,' solid food, BhP. iii, 13, 35; (*ā*), f. tasting, Sāh. iii, 26; a molar tooth, Gal.; v. l. for °*rmaṇā*, L.

Carvaṇīya, mfn. proper to be chewed, W.

Carvita, mfn. chewed, ŚārṅgP. lxiii, 9. **-carvaṇa**, n. 'chewing the chewed,' tedious reiteration, BhP. vii, 5, 30; Pāṇ. iii, 1, 15, Siddh. **-pātra**, n. a spitting-pot, W. **-pātraka**, n. id., Rāśal.

Carvya, mfn. chewable, BrahmavP.

चर्वन् *carvan*, m. = *capeṭa*, L.

चर्षण *carshaṇa*. See *ratha-*.

Carshaṇi, mfn. (√*kṛish*) 'cultivating,' active, agile, swift, RV.; (AV. vii, 110, 2); MBh. i, 726; seeing (fr. √*caksh?*), Naigh. iii, 11; Nir. v, 24; f. pl. 'cultivators (opposed to nomads),' men, people, race, RV. (*pañca c*° = *p*° *kṛishṭayas* [q. v.], v, 86, 2; vii, 15, 2; ix, 101, 9); AV. xiii, 1, 38; BhP. x, 29, 2; N. of Aryaman's children by Mātṛikā (progenitors of the human race), BhP. vi, 6, 40; (cf. *prá-ratha-*, *vi-*, *viśvá-*). **-prā́**, mfn. satisfying men, RV.

Carshaṇī, in comp. for °*ṇi*; f. a disloyal wife, Rājat. vii, 102; N. of Varuṇa's wife (mother of Bhṛigu), BhP. vi, 18, 4. **-dhṛít**, mfn. supporting or protecting men, RV. **-dhṛiti**, f. support or protection of men, viii, 90, 5 (loc. °*tā*, = instr. of *-dhṛit*, scil. *vájreṇa*, Gmn., but SV. has the nom. °*tiḥ*); SV. (see *-sáh*). **-sáh**, mfn. ruling over or overpowering men, RV. (ix, 24, 4 dat. *-sáhe*, SV. *-dhṛitiḥ*).

चल् *cal* (cf. √*car* & also √*caṭ*), cl. 1. °*lati* (metrically also Ā. °*te*; perf. *cacāla*, pl. *celur*; fut. *calishyati*; aor. *acālīt*), to be moved, stir, tremble, shake, quiver, be agitated, palpitate, MBh. &c.; to move on or forward, proceed, go away, start off, depart, MBh. (*āsanebhyo 'calan*, 'they rose from their seat,' v, 3114) &c.; to set (said of the day), Kathās. lxxii, 406; to be moved from one's usual course, be disturbed, become confused or disordered, go astray, MBh. &c.; to turn away from, swerve, deviate from (abl., e.g. *dharmāt*, to swerve from virtue, Mn. vii, 15; MBh. ii, 2629), fall off (with abl.), MBh. &c.; to sport about, frolic, play (Dhātup. xxviii, 64), Kuval. 320: Caus. *calayati* (Pāṇ. i, 3, 87), to cause to move, move, shake, jog, push, agitate, disturb, Ragh. viii, 52; Ṛitus.; BhP.; Bhaṭṭ.; to cause to deviate, turn off from (abl.), Mṛicch. ix, 21: Caus. *cālay*° (Pass. *cālyate*) to cause to move, shake, jog, push, agitate, MBh. &c.; to drive, drive away, remove or expel from (abl.), MBh. i, 5743; xiii, 3336; Hariv. 2697; to disturb, make confused or disordered, MBh. xii; Vedântas.; BhP. iii, 1, 42; to cause to deviate from (abl.), MBh. iii, 1504; R. iii; to cherish, foster, Dhātup. xxxii, 68 (v. l. for √*bal*): Intens. *cañcalyate* (cf. *cañcala*) or *cāc*° (cf. *á-vicācala* ff.), Vop. xx, 8 f.; [cf. κέλω, κέλλω, ὀκέλλω, κέλης; Lat. *celer*, *pro-cello*, *ex-*.]

Cala, mf(*ā*)n. (g. *pacâdi*) moving, trembling, shaking, loose, MBh. &c.; unsteady, fluctuating, perishable, ib.; disturbed, confused, ib.; m. 'agitation, shaking,' see *bhūmi-*; wind, L.; wind (in med.), Ashṭâṅg. i, 11, 1; quicksilver, L.; a sprout, shoot, Gal.; n. water, Gal.; (*ā*), f. lightning, L.; incense, L.; the goddess of fortune, Kathās. lx, 119; a metre of 4 × 18 syllables; (cf. *a-*, *niś-*, *puṇś-calī*, *cāla*.) **-karṇa**, m. (in astron.) the changeable hypothenuse ('the true distance of a planet from the earth,' W.), Sūryas. ii, 41 & 51. **-kuṇḍala**, m. N. of a man, Pravar. i, 1 (MatsyaP.) **-ketu**, m. (in astron.) N. of a moving Ketu, VarBṛS. xi, 33. **-ghnī**, f. Trigonella corniculata, L. **-cañcu**, m. 'moving its beak,' the Greek partridge, L. **-citta**, mf(*ā*)n. fickle-minded, MBh. xiii; R. iii, v; (ifc.) Bhartṛ. iii, 78; m. N. of a man, Tantr.; n. fickleness of mind, Mn. ix, 15; *-tā*, f. id., Hit. i, 4, 43; frivolity, R. vi, 111, 19. **-tā**, f. shaking, tremulous motion, Suśr. i, 32, 1. **-tva**, n. id., Hariv. 2893; Megh. 94. **-danta**, m. a loose tooth, W. **-dala**, m. 'tremulous-leaved,' Ficus religiosa, L. **-druma**, m. Tribulus lanuginosus, L. **-niketa**, mfn. having a perishable abode, Āp. i, 22, 4. **-pattra**, m. = *-dala*, L. **-puccha**, m. Coracias indica, Npr. **-prakṛiti**, mfn. of unsteady or wanton nature, Pañcat. ii, $\frac{26}{27}$. **-saṃdhi**, m. loose articulation of the bones, diarthrosis, Suśr. **-svabhāva**, mf(*ā*)n. = *-prakṛiti*, MBh. xiii, 2225. 1. **Calâcala**, mfn. movable and immovable, locomotive and stationary, W. **Calâtaṅka**, m. 'fluctuating disease,' rheumatism, L. **Calâtman**, mfn. fickle-minded, R. iv, 55, 7. **Calêndriya**, mfn. having unsteady organs, W. **Calêshu**, for *calâcal*°, Pāṇ. vi, 2, 108, Sch. **Calôrmi**, mfn. having agitated waves, R. i, 14, 18; Megh. 25.

Calat, pr. p. √*cal*, q. v. **-padam**, ind. so as to move, W. **-pūrṇimā**, f. the fish Candraka, L.

Calad, in comp. for °*lat*. **-aṅga**, °*gaka*, m. 'of a palpitating body,' the fish Ophiocephalus aurantiacus, L. **-gu**, mfn. one under whom the earth trembles, BhP. i, 9, 37.

Calana, mf(*ā*)n. moving, movable, tremulous, shaking, Pāṇ. iii, 2, 148; KapS. i, 129, Sch.; moving on feet, Gaut. viii, 2; wanton (a woman), xxii, 26; m. a foot, L.; an antelope, L.; n. shaking motion, shaking, trembling, Pāṇ. i, 3, 87; iii, 2, 148; R. v, 36, 21; Pañcat. &c.; 'motion,' action, function, Vedântas.; Tarkas.; walking about, wandering, roaming, MBh. xii, 3708; turning off from (abl.), iii, 1319; (*a-*, neg.) Kathās. ic, 8 & Sāh. iii, 53; the being disturbed, Sarvad. iii, 174; (*ī*), f. = °*naka*, HPariś. viii, 267; the rope for tying an elephant, L.

Calanaka, m. n. a short petticoat (worn by dancing girls, &c.), ŚBr. v, 2, 1, 8, Sāy.; KātyŚr. xiv, 5, 3, Sch.; (*ikā*), f. silken fringes, Buddh. L.

Calanīya, mfn. to be moved or shaken, W.

2. **Calācalá**, mfn. (√*cal* redupl. Pāṇ. vi, 1, 12, Vārtt. 6; vii, 4, 58, Pat.) ever-moving (the wheel of Saṃsāra), Divyâv. xiii, 267; xix; moving to and fro, movable, tremulous, unfixed, loose, RV. i, 164, 48; R. v, 42, 11; Nīt.; unsteady, changeable, MBh. v, 2758; xii, 4169; m. a crow, L.; N. of a man, Tantr. **Calācalêshu**, mfn. one whose arrow wavers or flies unsteadily, Pāṇ. vi, 2, 108, Kāś.

Calita, mfn. shaking, tremulous, unfixed, MBh. &c.; one who has moved on, MBh.; Sūryas. iii, 11; gone, departed (e.g. *sa calitaḥ*, 'he started off,' Pañcat.; Gīt. iii, 3; Hit.); walked, Vet. iii, ½ (v. l.); being on the march (an army), L.; moved from one's usual course, disturbed, disordered (the mind, senses, fortune, &c.), Hariv. 5669; R. &c.; caused to deviate, turned off from (abl.), Yājñ. i, 360; Bhag. vi, 37; n. unsteady motion (of eyes), Bhartṛ. i, 4. **-sthāna**, mfn. changing its place, R (B) iv, 1, 14.

Calitavya, n. impers. to be gone away, R. iii.

Calī-√kṛi, to cause to move, Naish. i, 114.

चलस् *calas*, n. wood-sorrel, L.

चलि *cali*, m. a cover, W.; a surtout, W.

चलित *calita*, &c. See √*cal*.

चलु *calu*, m. a mouthful of water, L.

Caluka, m. (= *cul*°) id., Pañcat. i; a small pot, gallipot, L.; N. of a man, W.

चवन *cavana*, n. Piper Chaba, L.

Cavi, f. id., L.

Cavika, n. id.; (*ā*), f. id., Suśr. vi, 39, 225; 42, 93.

Cavī, f. id., Kathās. vi, 151.

Cavya, n. id., Suśr. i, iv, vi; (*ā*), f. id., 41, 39; the cotton plant, L.; = *vacā*, L. **-jā**, f. Scindapsus officinalis, L. **-phala**, m. id., L.

चष् *cash*, cl. 1. °*shati*, to hurt, Vop. (Dhātup. xvii, 43); P. & Ā. to eat, Dhātup. xxi, 24.

Cashaka, m. n. (g. *ardharcâdi*) a cup, wine-glass, Ragh. vii, 46; Hcar. viii; Śiś. x &c. (ifc. f. *ā*, Kathās. xxi, 10); spirituous liquor ('honey,' W.), L.; m. a second, Sch. on VarBṛ. vii, 1 & 12 & xxiv.

चषाल *cashā́la*, m. n. (g. *ardharcâdi*) a wooden ring on the top of a sacrificial post, RV. i, 162, 6; TS. vi; Kāṭh. xxvi, 4 (*casāla*); ŚBr. &c.; m. a hive, L.; n. the snout of a hog, MaitrS. i, 6, 3. **-mukha**, m. N. of an Ekâha, ŚāṅkhŚr. xiv, 73, 3. **-yūpa**, m. a sacrificial post furnished with a wooden ring at the top, BhP. iv, 19, 19. **-vat** (°*shā́la-*), mfn. furnished with a wooden ring at the top, RV. iii, 8, 10.

चष्ट *cashṭa*, mfn. (√*caksh*) spoken, W.

चह् *cah*, cl. 1. 10. °*hati*, °*hayati* (aor. *acahīt*, Vop. viii, 80), to cheat, Dhātup. xvii, xxxv.

चाकचक्य *cākacakya*, n. = *ujjvala-tā*, Vedântaparibh.

Cākacikya, n. illusion, Nyāyak.

Cākaciccā, f. N. of a plant, L.

चाक्र *cākrá*, mfn. (fr. *cakrá*) carried on (a battle) with the discus, Hariv. 5648; belonging to a wheel, W.; circular, W.; m. N. of a man, ŚBr. xii.

Cākragartaka, mfn. fr. *cakra-garta*, Pāṇ. iv, 2, 126, Kāś.

Cākrapāleya, fr. *cakra-pāla*, g. *sakhy-ādi*.

Cākravarmaṇa, m. (patr. fr. *cakra-varman*, vi, 4, 170, Kāś.) N. of a grammarian, i, 1, 30; Uṇ. Sch.

Cākravāka, mfn. proper for the Cakra(-vāka) bird, MānGṛ. i, 14.

Cākravākeya, fr. *cakra-vāka*, g. *sakhy-ādi* (°*vāleya* [fr. *cakra-vāla*], Kāś.)

Cākravāleya, see °*vākeya*.

Cā́krāyaṇa, m. (fr. *cakrá*, g. *aśvâdi*; Pravar. v, 1) patr. of Ushasta, ŚBr. xiv, 6; ChUp. i, 10, 1.

Cākrika, mfn. circular, W.; belonging to a wheel or discus, W.; relating to a company or circle, W.; m. a coachman, driver, MBh. xii, 2646; a potter, VarBṛS. x, 9; 'an oil-maker' and 'a companion,' Rājat. vi, 272; a companion, v, 267; a proclaimer, Yājñ. i, 165; Hariv. 9047; a bard, W. **-tā**, f. companionship, Rājat. iv, 688.

Cākriṇa, m. patr. fr. *cakrin*, Pāṇ. vi, 4, 166, Sch.

Cākreya, fr. *cakrá*, g. *sakhy-ādi* (not in Kāś.)

चाक्षुष *cākshushá*, mf(*ī*)n. (fr. *cákshus*) consisting in sight, depending on or produced from sight, proper or belonging or relating to the sight, VS. xiii, 56; ŚBr. xiv; KaṭhUp.; Mālav. i, 4; (*a-*, neg.) Sarvad. x, 112; (with *vidyā*, a magical science) conferring the power of seeing anything, MBh. i, 6478; perceptible by the eye, KaushUp.; Suśr.; Pāṇ. iv, 2, 92, Kāś.; (*a-*, neg.) KapS. i, 61; relating to Manu Cākshusha, Hariv. 279; BhP. iv, 30, 49; m. patr., AV. xvi, 7, 7; N. of Agni (author of several Sāmans); of an author, Ragh. v, 50, Mall.; of the 6th Manu (with 5 others descending from Manu Svāyambhuva, Mn. i, 62; son of Viśvakarman by Ākṛiti, BhP. vi, 6, 15; son of Cakshus, viii, 5, 17), MBh. xiii, 1315; Hariv.; BhP.; N. of a son of Ripu by Bṛihatī (father of a Manu), Hariv. 69; of a son of Kaksheyu (or Anu, VP. iv, 18, 1) and brother of Sabhā-nara, Hariv. 1669; of a son of Khanitra, BhP. ix, 2, 24; m. pl. a class of deities in the 14th Manv-antara, viii, 13, 35; n. = *-jñāna*, W. **-jñāna**, n. knowledge which depends on vision, W. **-tva**, n. perceptibility of sight, Tarkas. 105.

चाक्ष्म *cākshmá*, mfn. (√*ksham*) forbearing, gracious (Brahmaṇaspati), RV. ii, 24, 9.

चाखायितृ *cākhāyitṛi*, mfn. (Intens. √*khan*), Pāṇ. vi, 4, 22, Vārtt. 11.

चाङ्ग *cāṅga*, m. = °*geri*, L., Sch.; n. (fr. *caṅga*) whiteness or beauty of the teeth, W.

Cāṅgerī, f. wood-sorrel, Hariv. 4652; Suśr. vi.

चाचपुट *cāca-puṭa*, = *caccat-p*°.

चाचरि *cācari*, m. (Intens. √*car*) 'moving quickly,' N. of a wrestler, Rājat. vii, 1514.

चाचलि *cācali*, mfn. (Intens. √*cal*) moving much or repeatedly, Vop. xxvi, 154; (cf. *á-vi-*).

Cāñcalya, n. (fr. *cañcala*) unsteadiness, transitoriness, Rājat. vii, 162.

चाञ्चव *cāñcava*, n. (fr. *cañcu*) celebrity for (in comp.), Daś. i, 223 (v. l.)

चाट *cāṭa*, m. a cheat, rogue, Yājñ. i, 335 (Pañcat.); Mṛicch. (Prākrit); VarYogay.; Hcat.; BhavP. **-bhaṭa**, m. for *cāra-bh*° (?), Inscr. (? 940 A. D.)

Cāṭaka-deśa, m. N. of a country, Kālakâc.

Cāṭakāyana, m. patr. fr. *caṭaka*, g. 1. *naḍâdi*.

Cāṭakaira, m. (fr. *caṭakā*, Pāṇ. iv, 1, 128) a young sparrow, Hcar. viii.

चाटलिका *cāṭalikā*, f. N. of a locality, Rājat. viii, 766.

चाटिग्राम *cāṭi-grāma*, m. N. of a place.

चाटु *cāṭu*, m. n. sg. & pl. (cf. *caṭu*) pleasing or graceful words or discourse, flattery, Hariv. 1144; Pañcat.; Kād.; Hcar. &c.; =*piciṇḍa*, L.; mfn. pleasing (?), Rājat. i, 213; speaking distinctly, L. **–kāra**, mfn. speaking agreeably or kindly, flattering, flatterer, Pāṇ. iii, 2, 23; Megh. 32; Rājat. v, 351; Sāh. iii, 82. **–kārin**, m. id., L. **–paṭu**, m. a jester (*bhaṇḍa*), L. **–lola**, mfn. (=*caṭul-l°*) elegantly tremulous, L. **–vacana**, n. a pleasing word, flattery, Gīt. xi, 2. **–vaṭu**, m. =*-paṭu*, L. **–śata**, n. a hundred entreaties, Bhartṛ. ii, 26. **Cāṭûkti**, f. =°*ṭu-vacana*, Śuk.

Cāṭuka, m. pl. pleasing words, BhP. xi, 5. **–śata**, n. =°*ṭu-ś°*, Sarasv. (Kpr. iv, 13ª, Sch.); Sāh. iii, $\frac{60}{61}$.

चाणक *cāṇaka*, m. pl. of °*kya*, g. *kaṇvâdi*.

Cāṇakīna, mfn. fit for (being sown) with the chick-pea (*caṇaka*), L., Sch.

Cāṇakya, mfn. made of chick-peas, Bhpr. v, 11, 37; composed by Cāṇakya, Cāṇ.; m. (g. *gargâdi*) patr. fr. Caṇaka (son of Caṇin, HPariś. viii, 200), N. of a minister of Candra-gupta (said to have destroyed the Nanda dynasty; reputed author of *-śloka* [q. v.], 'the Machiavelli of India'), Pañcat.; Mudr.; Kathās. v, 109 ff. **–mūlaka**, n. a kind of radish (*kauṭilya*), L. **–śloka**, m. pl. Cāṇakya's Ślokas on morals and principles of government, W.

चाणाररूप्य *cāṇārarūpya*, mfn. fr. *caṇ°*, Pāṇ. iv, 2, 104, Vārtt. 2 f., Pat.

चाणूर *cāṇūra*, m. N. of a prince, MBh. ii, 121; v, 4410; Hariv. 6726; of a wrestler in Kaṅsa's service (slain by Kṛishṇa; identified with the Daitya Varāha), Hariv. (*cānūra*, 2361 & 10407); Vop. xxiii, 24. **–mardana**, m. 'Cāṇūra-conqueror,' Kṛishṇa, Gal. **–sūdana**, m. id., L., Sch.

चाण्ड *cāṇḍa*, m. patr. fr. *cáṇḍa*, g. *śivâdi*; n. violence &c., g. *pṛithv-ādi*.

चाण्डाल *cāṇḍālá*, m. =*caṇḍ°* (Ved., Pāṇ. v, 4, 36, Vārtt. 1), VS. xxx, 21; ŚBr. xiv; Kauś.; Mn. &c.; the worst among (in comp., Mn. ix, 87; MBh. xii f.; gen., Cāṇ.); (*ī*), f. a Caṇḍāla woman, Mn. viii, 373; BhP. vi, 3, 12; (said of a woman on the first day of her courses) Vet. i, 10; the plant Liṅginī, L.; (with *bhāshā*) the language of the Caṇḍālas, Sāh. vi, 163. **–veśa**, mfn. clothed like a Caṇḍāla, Prab. iii, $\frac{1}{2}$.

Cāṇḍālaka, n. anything made by a Caṇḍāla, g. *kulâlâdi*; m. N. of a man, Pravar. ii, 1, 2; (*ikā*), f. =*caṇḍ°* (the Caṇḍāla lute; a kind of plant; Durgā), L.

Cāṇḍālaki, patr. fr. *caṇḍāla*, Pāṇ. iv, 1, 97, Pat.

Cāṇḍāli, m. pl. N. of a family, Pravar. vi, 1.

Cāṇḍālikâśrama, m. the hermitage of Cāṇḍālikā, MBh. xiii, 1738 (*cāñjal°*, B).

Cāṇḍālinī, f. N. of a goddess, Tantras.

चातक *cātaka*, m. the bird Cucculus melanoleucus (said to subsist on rain-drops), Śak. vii, 7; Ragh. xvii, 15; Megh. &c.; (*ī*), f. the female of the Cātaka bird, Kathās. cxxiii. **Cātakânandana**, m. 'Cātaka's delight,' the rainy season, L. **Cātakâshṭaka**, n. the 8 verses on the Cātaka bird.

Cātaki, m. N. of a man, MatsyaP. cxciv, 23.

चातन *cātana*, mfn. (√*cat*, Caus.) ifc. 'driving away,' see *abhiśasti-*, *amīva-*, *arāya-*, *durṇāma-*, *piśāca-*, *bhrātṛivya-*, *yātu-*, *sadānvā-*, & *sapatna-cātana*; m. N. of the Ṛishi of the Cātana verses, AV. Anukr.; n. certain verses of the AV. (for exorcising demons), Kauś. 8; 25; 80; 136.

चातुर 1. *cātura*, mfn. (fr. *catúr*) drawn by 4 (a carriage), Pāṇ. iv, 2, 92, Kāś.

Cāturaksha, (fr. *cat°*) a cast of dice with 4 dots, Hariv. 6746.

Cāturarthika, mfn. used in the 4 (*artha* or) senses (taught, Pāṇ. iv, 2, 67–70), iv, 2, 81 ff., Kāś.

Cāturāśramika, mfn. being in one of the 4 periods (*āśrama*) of life, MBh. xiv, 972.

Cāturāśramin, (ed. Calc.) for *cat°*, q. v.

Cāturāśramya, n. (g. *caturvarṇâdi*) the 4 periods of a Brāhman's life, MBh. iii, 11244; xii f.

Cāturika, m. (fr. 1. °*ra*) a charioteer, L.

Cāturjāta, n. an aggregate of 4 substances, Bhpr.

Cāturjātaka, n. id., Suśr. v; Bhpr. v; (cf. *kaṭu-*).

Cāturtha, mfn. (fr. *cat°*) treated of in the 4th (Adhyāya), Mn. ii, 56, Kull.

Cāturthaka, mfn. appearing every 4th day, quartan (fever), Suśr.; Kathās.; AgP. **Cāturthakâri-rasa**, m. a medicine for keeping off quartan ague.

Cāturthâhnika, mfn. (fr. *caturthâhan*) belonging to the 4th day, ŚāṅkhŚr. xv, 7, 1 & 8, 1.

Cāturthika, mfn. (fr. *caturthá*) id., Lāṭy. vii, 7, 29; TāṇḍyaBr., Sch.; m. a quartan ague, W.

Cāturdaśa, mfn. (g. *saṃdhivelâdi*) appearing on the *caturdaśī* (14th day), Pāṇ. iv, 2, 92, Kāś.

Cāturdaśika, mfn. reading sacred texts on the *caturdaśī*, Pāṇ. iv, 4, 71, Kāś.

Cāturdaiva, mfn. sacred to 4 deities (*deva*), Hariv. 6509.

Cāturdhākāraṇika, mfn. (fr. *caturdhā-karaṇa*) connected with a division into 4 parts, ĀpŚr. ii.

Cāturbīja, n. (fr. *cat°*) an aggregate of 4 kinds of aromatic seed, Npr.

Cāturbhadra, n. (fr. *cat°*) a collection of 4 medicinal plants, L.

Cāturbhadraka, n. id., Bhpr. vii, 8, 146 & 206.

Cāturbhuji, a son of Catur-bhuja, Śivak. 541.

Cāturbhautika, mfn. consisting of 4 elements (*catur-bhūta*), KapS. iii, 18; Nyāyas. iii, 1, Sch.

Cāturmahārājakāyika, (pl.) = *cat°*, Buddh.

Cāturmahārājika, m. (= *cat°*) Vishṇu, MBh. xii, 12864; m. pl. = °*jakāyika*, Buddh.

Cāturmāsa, mfn. produced in 4 months, W.

Cāturmāsaka, mfn. one who performs the Cāturmāsya sacrifices, Pāṇ. v, 1, 94, Vārtt. 5.

Cāturmāsika, mfn. occurring every 4 months (the fourth kind of *pratikramaṇa*), Jain. Sch.

Cāturmāsin, mfn. = °*saka*, Pāṇ. v, 1, 94, Vārtt. 5.

Cāturmāsī, f. (of °*syá*; scil. *paurṇamāsī*) full-moon day at the Cāturmāsya sacrifices, Vārtt. 5 & 7.

Cāturmāsyá, n. beginning of a season of 4 months, MBh. xii, 1007; pl. N. of the 3 sacrifices performed at the beginning of the 3 seasons of 4 months (viz. *vaiśvadevám*, *varuṇa-praghāsā́ḥ*, *sākam-edhā́ḥ*), TS. i, 6, 10; TBr. i f.; ŚBr.; ĀśvŚr.; KātyŚr.; Mn. &c.; mfn. belonging to such sacrifices, ŚBr. xiii, 2, 5; KātyŚr. xxii; MuṇḍUp. i, 2, 3. **–kārikā**, f. N. of a work. **–tva**, n. the state of a C° sacrifice, Kāṭh. xxxvi, 2. **–devatā́**, f. the deity of a C° sacrifice, ŚBr. xiii. **–yājín**, mfn. = °*saka*, ii, x.

Cāturvarṇya, n. (g. *caturvarṇâdi*) the four castes, Mn. x; xii, 1 & 97; MBh.; R. i, 1, 92 & 27, 16.

Cāturviṅśaka, fr. *caturviṅśá*, q. v.

Cāturviṅśika, mfn. belonging to the 24th day, ŚāṅkhŚr. xii, 27, 4.

Cāturvidya, mfn. (Pāṇ. v, 1, 124, Siddh.) = *cat°*, MBh. iii, 8227; Rājat. v, 158; n. the 4 Vedas; fourfold knowledge (viz. of *dharma, artha, kāma, moksha*, Nīlak.), MBh. xii, 1574 & 1837; Hariv. 9769.

Cāturvidhya, n. (fr. *cátur-vidha*) the being fourfold, Hariv. ii, 114, 16; Sarvad. ii, x; xiii, 78.

Cāturvedya, n. (fr. *catur-veda*) a number of men versed in the 4 Vedas, Vas. iii, 20.

Cāturvaidya, mfn. (fr. *catur-vidyā*, g. *anuśatikâdi*; fr. *-veda*, Pāṇ. v, 1, 124, Siddh.) versed in the 4 Vedas, MBh. v, 4741; m. = °*rvedya*, Baudh.; knowledge of the 4 Vedas, g. *brāhmaṇâdi*.

Cāturhotrika, mf(*ī*)n. (Pāṇ. iv, 3, 72, Kāś.) relating to the Catur-hotṛi service, MānGṛ. i, 23; MaitrS. i, 9, colophon.

Cāturhotra, mfn. performed by the 4 chief priests (Hotṛi, Adhvaryu, Udgātṛi, and Brahman), ĀtrAnukr.; BhP. i, 4, 19; TĀr. iii, Sāy. Introd.; n. a sacrifice performed by 4 priests, MBh. xii, xiv; Hariv. 3772; 10404 (v. l. *cat°*); BhP. v, 7, 5; vii, 3, 30 (v. l. *catur-hotraka*); the duties of the 4 chief priests, MBh. xii; BhP. ii f.; the 4 chief priests (collectively), MBh. v, xiv; R. i; BhP. iv, 24, 37.

Cāturhotriyá, mfn. attended by 4 chief priests (Agni), TĀr. i, 22, 11.

Cāturhotrīya-brāhmaṇa, n. N. of a particular chapter (called Brāhmaṇa), TĀr. iii, 8, 1, Sāy.

Cātuścaraṇika, mfn. versed in a branch (*caraṇa*) of each of the 4 Vedas, Hcat.; (*ā*), f. the 4 Vedas, ib.

Cātuḥśabdya, n. 4 moods of expression (*śabda*), Pat. on Pāṇ. ii, 3, 69, Vārtt. 2, & iii, 1, 43.

Cātushkoṭika, mfn. divided into 4 parts (*koṭi*), Buddh. L.

Cātushṭaya, mfn. (fr. *cát°*) versed in the Sūtras consisting of 4 sections, Pāṇ. iv, 2, 65, Kāś.

Cātushpatha, mfn. being on a cross-way (*cat°*), ĀpŚr. viii, 18, 1.

Cātushprâśyá, mfn. (fr. *catush-prâśa*, Pāṇ. v, 4, 36, Vārtt. 4) enough for 4 persons to eat, ŚBr. ii, xi; m. (scil. *odana*) id., KātyŚr.; Lāṭy.; n. id., TS. vi.

Cātushprāharika, mfn. presented (as gifts) on 4 occasions, Siṅhâs.[3] i, 59.

Cātuḥshashṭika, mfn. relating to the 64 (*catuḥshashṭi*) Kalās, Vātsyāy. i, 3, 14.

Cātuḥsāgarika, mf(*ī*)n. relating to the 4 oceans (*sāgara*), R. iv, 16, 43.

Cātuḥsvarya, n. the use of 4 (*svara*) accents, (viz. *traisvarya* and *eka-śruti*), Bhāshik. ii, 36; Nyāyam. ix, 2, 15, Sch.; ĀpGṛ. iv, 17, Sch.

चातुर 2. *cātura*, mfn. (fr. 2. *cat°*) clever, shrewd, L.; speaking kindly, flattering, L.; visible, L.; governing, L.; m. a small round pillow, L. (cf. *galla-cāturī*); (*ī*), f. (=°*rya*, Siddh. napuṅs. 4; Vop. iv, 12) dexterity, cleverness, Prasannar. ii, $\frac{8}{9}$; iii, $\frac{13}{14}$; Vcar. vi, 12; amiableness, Sāh. x, 84.

Cāturaka, mfn. flattering, L.; visible, L.; governing, L.; m. a small round pillow, L.

Cāturya, n. (=°*rī*, Siddh. napuṅs. 4; Vop. iv) dexterity, Sarvad. xiii, 134; Subh.; amiableness, MBh. i, 3905; R. i, 6, 3; Bhartṛ. i, 3; Sāh. iii, $\frac{59}{60}$. **–cintāmaṇi**, m. N. of Vop., Vop.

चात्तरात्र *cāttarātra*, m. patr. fr. *catta-r°*, N. of Jamad-agni, Nidān. viii, 4.

Cāttra, m. a spindle, PārGṛ. i, 15, 4; Gobh. ii, 7; the peg (used with the *araṇi*), KātyŚr. iv, Sch.

चात्वारिंश *cātvāriṅśa*, n. 'consisting of 40 (*catvāriṅśát*) Adhyāyas,' the AitBr., Pāṇ. v, 1, 62.

Cātvāriṅśatka, mfn. bought for 40, 22, Kāś.

चात्वाल *cātvāla*, m. n. (=*catv°*) a hole in the ground for constructing the Uttara-vedi, TS. vi f.; TBr. i; ŚBr. iii; KātyŚr.; ĀśvŚr.; Lāṭy.; Kuśa grass (*darbha*), Uṇ. i, 115, Sch. **–vat**, mfn. (a sacrifice) for which this hole is excavated, ĀśvŚr. i, 1, 6.

चानराट *cānarāṭa*, N. of a place, Pāṇ. vi, 2.

चानूर *cānūra*, for *cāṇūra*, q. v.

चान्दन *cāndana*, mf(*ī*)n. consisting of sandal-wood (*cand°*), Bhartṛ. ii, 98; Prasannar. vi, 32.

Cāndanagandhika, mfn. (fr. *candana-gandha*) smelling of sandal, Pāṇ. iv, 2, 65 (not all MSS.)

चान्द्र *cāndra*, mf(*ī*)n. (fr. *candrá*) lunar, Jyot.; VarBṛS.; Sūryas.; Kathās. &c.; composed by Candra, Prauḍh.; m. a lunar month (cf. *gauṇa*, *mukhya*), L.; the light half of a month, W.; the moon-stone, L.; a pupil of the grammarian Candra, Siddh. on Pāṇ. iii, 2, 26 & vii, 2, 10; Prauḍh.; Vop., Sch.; n. (scil. *vrata*) the penance Cāndrāyaṇa (q. v.), Prāyaśc.; (scil. *ahan*) Monday, Vishṇ. lxxviii, 2; (*ī*), f. moonlight, L.; a kind of Solanum, L.; Serratula anthelminthica, L.; N. of a princess, Rājat. vii, 1503. **–māsa**, m. a lunar month. **–vatsara**, m. the lunar year. **Cāndrâkhya**, n. fresh ginger, L.

Cāndraka, mfn. lunar, Kālam.; n. dried ginger, L.

Cāndragupta, mfn. belonging to Candra-gupta, HPariś. viii, 322.

Cāndrapura, m. pl. the inhabitants of Candrapura, VarBṛS. xiv, 5.

Cāndrabhāgā, f. = *candr°*, g. *śoṇâdi*.

Cāndrabhāgi, m. (fr. *candra-bhāga*) a patr. of Agni-veśa, Car. i, 13, 98.

Cāndrabhāgī, f. = *vana-rāji*, Gaṇar. 52, Sch.

Cāndrabhāgeya, m. metron. fr. *candra-bhāgā*, Pāṇ. iv, 1, 113, Kāś.

Cāndrabhāgyā, f. = °*gā*, ib.

Cāndrama, mfn. for °*masá*, lunar, Nidānas. v.

Cāndramasá, mf(*ī*)n. (fr. *candrá-mas*) lunar, relating to the moon, AV. xix, 9, 10; ŚBr. xi, 1, 5, 3; ĀśvŚr. &c.; m. pl. N. of a family, Pravar. i, 1 (°*si*, MatsyaP.); n. the constellation Mṛiga-śiras, L.; (*ī*), f. N. of Bṛihaspati's wife, MBh. iii, 14130.

Cāndramasâyana, m. = *candra-ja*, L.

Cāndramasâyani, m. id., g. *tikâdi*.

Cāndravratika, mfn. acting in the manner (*vrata*) of the moon, Mn. ix, 309.

Cāndrâyaṇa, m. an observer of the moon's course (*candr°*), TāṇḍyaBr. xvii, 13, 17, Sch.; pl. N. of a family, Pravar. i, 2 & ii, 4, 1; n. (Pāṇ. v, 1, 72; scil. *vrata*) a fast regulated by the moon, the food being diminished every day by one mouthful for the dark fortnight, and increased in like manner during the light fortnight (cf. *pipilikā-madhya*, *yava-madhya* or °*dhyama*), Mn. vi, 20; xi, 41 & 106–217; Yājñ. iii, 324 ff.; Pañcat. i, 11, 27; iii, 3, 2. **–bhakta**, mfn. inhabited by Cāndrâyaṇas, g. *aishukāry-ādi*. **–vidhāna**, n. the Cāndrâyaṇa fast, W. **–vrata**, n. id., Hit. i, 4, $\frac{2}{3}$.

Cāndrâyaṇika, mfn. performing the Cāndrâyaṇa fast, Pāṇ. v, 1, 72.

Cāndri, m. = *candra-ja*, VarYogay. iv, 19.

चान्धनायन *cāndhanāyana*, m. patr. of Ānanda-ja, VBr. i, 16; (cf. *aupacandhani*.)

चाप *cāpa*, m.n. (fr. *capa*, g. *tālâdi*) a bow, Mn. vii, 192; MBh. &c.; (in geom.) an arc, Sūryas. ii f., vi, xi; Sagittarius, VarBṛS.; a rainbow (cf. *indra-śakra-*), BhP. i, 11, 28; a kind of astron. instrument, Gol. xi, 2 & 5; a particular constellation (= *dhanus*), VarBṛ. xii, 18; m. N. of a family. **-guṇa**, m. a bow-string, R. iii, 33, 16 &c. **-dāsī**, f. N. of a river, Hariv. 9515. **-dhara**, mfn. bow-armed, R. ii, 86, 22; m. Sagittarius, VarBṛ., Sch. **-paṭa**, m. Buchanania latifolia, L. **-yashṭi**, f. a bow, Kathās. lxxxv, 7. **-latā**, f. id., cviii, 134. **-lekhā**, f. N. of a woman, lii, 248. **-vaṭa**, m. = *-paṭa*, L.; (cf. *upa-v°*). **-veda**, m. = *dhanur-v°*, L. **Cāpâcārya**, m. an instructor in archery, Bālar. ii, 37. **Cāpâdhiropa**, m. stringing and bending a bow, Prasannar. i, 45. **Cāpâropaṇa**, n. id., $\frac{3}{3}$. **Cāpôtkaṭa**, m. N. of a family, Ratnak.

Cāpaya, Nom. °*yati*, (in geom.) to reduce to a bow-form, Āryabh. iv, 25, Sch.

Cāpin, mfn. bow-armed, MBh. xii, 10406; m. Sagittarius, Horāś.

चापड *cāpaḍa*, N. of a village, Kshitîś. iv.

चापल *cāpala*, n. (fr. *cap°*, g. *yuvâdi*) mobility, swiftness, Ragh. iii, 42; BhP. vii, 12, 20; agitation, unsteadiness, fickleness, inconsiderateness, insolence, Gaut. ix, 50; Pāṇ. viii, 1, 12, Vārtt. 5; MBh. &c. **Cāpalâśraya**, m. unsteadiness, W.

Cāpalāyana, m. patr. fr. *capala*, g. *aśvâdi*.

Cāpalya, n. (g. *brāhmaṇâdi*) mobility, Cāṇ.; agitation, unsteadiness, fickleness, flurry, Yājñ. i, 112; iii, 279; R. iii, v; Pañcat. i, 1, $\frac{9}{1}$; Sāh. iii, 170.

चापाल *cāpāla*, N. of a Caitya, Divyâv.

चाप्पट्टक्य *cāppaṭṭakya*, m. patr. fr. *cappaṭṭaka*, g. *kurv-ādi* (Gaṇar. 209).

Cāphaṭṭaki, m. patr. fr. *caphaṭṭaka*, g. *taulvaly-ādi*.

Cāphaṭṭakya, m. id., g. *kurv-ādi* (Gaṇar.)

चाबुका *cābukā*, f. a small pillow, W.

चामर *cāmara*, mfn. coming from the Yak (*cam°*), BhP. viii, 10, 13; belonging to a chowrie, L.; m. = *cam°* (q.v.), a chowrie, Bhoj.; n. id. (a kind of plume on the heads of horses &c., Śak.; Vikr.; Kād.), MBh. &c. (ifc. f. *ā*, Kum. vii, 42); a metre of 4 × 15 syllables; = *daṇḍa* (a stick), L.; (*ā*), f. id., L.; (*ā, ī*), f. a chowrie, L., Sch. **-grāha**, m. a chowrie-bearer, g. *revaty-ādi*. **-°grāhika**, m. patr. fr. °*ha*, ib. **-grāhiṇī**, f. a female chowrie-bearer, Kād.; Bhartṛ. iii, 67; Hcat. **-dhāri**, f. id., Śak. ii, $\frac{9}{1}$, 12, Sch. **-dhāriṇī**, f. id., Bālar. iv, $\frac{3}{8}$. **-pushpa**, m. 'chowrie-blossomed,' Mangifera indica, L.; the betel-nut tree, L.; Pandanus odoratissimus, L.; = °*shpaka*, L. **-pushpaka**, m. Saccharum spontaneum, L. **-vyajana**, n. a chowrie, MBh. i, v; Hariv. 1290; R. iii, 9, 7. **-sâhvaya**, m. = *-pushpaka*, Suśr. iv, 17, 36.

Cāmarika, m. = °*ra-grāha*, Buddh. L.

Cāmarikā, f. a cluster, Hcar. v, 416 (v.l.)

Cāmarin, m. 'plume-adorned,' a horse, L.

चामसायन *cāmasāyana*, m. patr. fr. *camasin*, g. 1. *naḍâdi*.

Cāmasya, m. patr. fr. *camasá*, g. *gargâdi*.

चामीकर *cāmīkara*, n. gold, MBh.; R.; Kum.; Vikr.; VarBṛS.; BhP.; m. the thorn-apple, W. **-prakhya**, mfn. gold-like, Nal. xxi, 11. **-maya**, mf(*ī*)n. = °*rīya*, Hcat. i, 5, 1235 & 7, 520. **Cāmīkarâcala**, m. 'gold-mountain,' Meru, Kād. **Cāmīkarâdri**, m. id., Kalyāṇam. 23.

Cāmīkarīya, mfn. golden, Kum. xiii, 22 & 28.

चामुण्ड *cāmuṇḍa*, m. N. of an author, L., Sch.; (*ā*), f. a form of Durgā (cf. *carma-muṇḍā*), Mālatīm.; Kathās.; Rājat.; MārkP. lxxxvii, 25 (fr. *caṇḍa* & *muṇḍa*); one of the 7 mothers, L., Sch.; one of the 8 Nāyikās of Durgā, BrahmavP. ii, 61, 80; (*ī*), f. N. of a town, Hcar. vi.

Cāmuṇḍā, f. of °*ḍa*, q. v. **-tantra**, n. N. of a work, Ānand. 31, Sch. **-mantra**, m. pl. prayers addressed to Cāmuṇḍā, Tantras. ii.

चाम्पिला *cāmpilā*, f. a river, L.

चाम्पेय *cāmpeya*, m. (fr. *campā*) Michelia Campaka, ŚārṅgP.; Mesua ferrea, L.; = °*yaka*, L.; a prince of Campā, Rājat. viii, 540; N. of a son of Viśvā-mitra, MBh. xiii, 257; m. n. gold, L.

Cāmpeyaka, n. a filament (esp. of a lotus), L.

चाम्य *cāmya*, n. (√*cam*; cf. Pāṇ. iii, 1, 126) food, W.

चाय् *cāy* (cf. √2. & 3. *ci*), cl. 1. *cáyati* (impf. *acāyat*, TS. &c.; aor. *acāyīt* or *acāsīt*, Vop. viii, 128; 1. sg. *acāyisham*, AV. vii, 89, 1; ind. p. *cāyitvā́*), to observe, perceive, notice (cf. Nir. xi, 5), MaitrS. i, 9, 3 f.; Kāṭh.; TāṇḍyaBr. v, xv; to fear, be afraid of (acc.), AV. vii; ix, 1, 1; TS. ii, vi: Ā. (pr. p. 1. *cáyamāna*) to behave respectfully, RV. vii, 18, 8; x, 94, 14: Intens. *cekīyate*, Pāṇ. vi, 1, 21; [cf. *céru*, τίω, τιμή.]

Cāyaka, mfn., Pāṇ. vi, 1, 78, Kāś.

Cāyanīya, mfn. 'perceptible,' Nir. xii, 6 & 16.

2. **Cāyamāná**, m. patr. of Abhyāvartin, RV. vi, 27, 5 & 8; (for 1. *cáy°* see s. v. √*cāy*.)

Cāyitṛi, mfn. one who observes, Nir. v, 25.

Cāyú, mfn. showing respect, RV. iii, 24, 4.

चार *cāra*, m. (√*car*) = *cara*, a spy, Mn. vii, ix; MBh. i, 5604; R.; Mṛicch.; Kathās.; going, motion, progression, course (of asterisms, VarBṛS.; BhP. v, 22, 12), ChUp. vii, 1, 5; R. &c.; wandering about, travelling, W.; 'proceeding,' see *kāma-*; practising, MBh. v, 1410; a bond, fetter, L.; a prison, L.; Buchanania latifolia, Bhpr.; n. a factitious poison, L. (v.l. for *vāra*); (*ī*), f. a particular step (in dancing); a trap, snare, HPariś. i, 353. **-cakshus**, mfn. = *-driś*, Mn. ix, 256; R. iii, 37, 9; n. a spy employed like an eye, Yājñ. ii, $\frac{3}{4}$. **-caṇa**, mfn. graceful in gait, W. **-cuñcu**, mfn. id., W. **-jyā**, for *cara-*. **-tūla**, n. (= *cāmara*) a chowrie, Gal. **-driś**, mfn. 'spy-eyed,' employing spies like eyes, Naish. i, 13. **-patha**, m. a cross-way, L. **-pāla**, m. a secret agent, Divyâv. xxxvii. **-purusha**, m. a spy, Hariv. 10102; Kād. **-bhaṭa**, m. a (valorous) soldier, Bhartṛ.; Hcar. vii; (*ī*), f. heroism, L. **-vāyu**, m. summer-air, L. **Cārâdhikāra**, m. a spy's office or duty, Bālar. iv, $\frac{1}{1}\frac{1}{4}$. **Cārâdhikārin**, m. = °*rapāla*, Kathās. ciii, 79. **Cārântarita**, m. id., W. **Cārêkshaṇa**, mfn. = °*ra-driś*, Śiś. ii, 82.

Cāraka, mfn. ifc. proceeding, R. iii, 66, 18; (√*car*, Caus.) setting in motion, MBh. xiv, 42, 29; composed by Caraka, Pāṇ. iv, 3, 107, Kāś.; m. a spy, MBh. ii, 172 (Pañcat. ii) & iv, 911; (√*car*, Caus., Pāṇ. vii, 3, 34, Kāś.) a driver, herdsman (cf. *go-*), L.; = *bhojaka*, L.; an associate, companion (*saṃcāraka*), L.; a fetter, L.; a prison, Lalit. xv; Daś. vii; Buchanania latifolia, L.; (*ikā*), f. 'a female attendant,' see *antaḥpura-*; journey (of Buddha), Lalit.; Divyâv.; a cock-roach, Npr. **-tri-rātra**, m. a particular ceremony lasting three days (prescribed by Caraka or by the Carakas?), Pāṇ. vi, 2, 97, Kāś.

Cārakīṇa, mfn. fit for a wandering religious student (*cáraka*), Pāṇ. v, 1, 11.

Cāraṭikā, f. the indigo plant, L.

Cāraṭi, f. Flacourtia cataphracta, Car. vi, 14, 36; Bhpr. vii, 64, 6; Hibiscus mutabilis, L. (°*riṭi*, Gal.)

Cāraṇa, mfn. depending on a Vedic school (*caraṇa*), Āp.; belonging to the same Vedic school ('reading the scripture,' W.), Gaut.; m. a wandering actor or singer, Mn. xii, 44; MBh. v, 1039 & 1442; VarBṛS.; Pañcat. &c.; a celestial singer, MBh.; R.; Śak.; BhP.; Gīt. i, 2; a spy, BhP. iv, 16, 12; Bālar.; n. (√*car*, Caus.) 'pasturing, tending,' see *go-*; a kind of process applied to mercury; (*ī*), f. a female celestial singer, Bālar. ix, $\frac{2}{2}\frac{1}{2}$ ff.; Hibiscus mutabilis, Npr. **-tva**, n. a wandering actor's profession, dancing, Rājat. v, 418. **-dāra**, m. pl. wandering actors' wives, female dancers, Mn. viii, 362. **Cāraṇâika-maya**, mf(*ī*)n. inhabited only by wandering actors, Kathās. xxiii, 85.

Cāraṇavidya or °**vaidya**, m. pl. (fr. *caraṇa-vidyā*) N. of a school of AV., Caraṇ.

Cāratha, mfn. wandering, RV. viii, 46, 31.

Cārāyaṇa, m. patr. (fr. *cara*, g. 1. *naḍâdi*) N. of an author, Vātsyāy. Introd. & i, 4, 25; 5, 22 & 37; (*ī*), f., Pāṇ. iv, 1, 63, Kāś.

Cārāyaṇaka, mfn. derived from the Cārāyaṇas, Pāṇ. iv, 3, 80, Kāś.

Cārāyaṇīya, mfn. composed by Cārāyaṇa (a Śikshā); m. pl. (Pāṇ. iv, 1, 89, Sch., not in Kāś.) Cārāyaṇa's school (of the black Yajur-veda), Caraṇ.

Cārika, see *brahma-*, *māsa-*; (*ā*), f., see °*raka*.

Cāriṭi, f. See °*raṭī*.

Cārita, mfn. set in motion, Rājat. iv, 653; caused to be done by (instr.), MBh. xii, 11584.

Cāritârthya, n. (fr. *caritârtha*) attainment of an object, KapS. iii, 69; fitness, R. (B) i, 2, 38, Sch.

Cāritra, m. (√*car*, cf. *śāmitra*) 'moving,' N. of a Marut, Hariv. 11547; n. (= *car°*) proceeding, manner of acting, conduct, R. iii, iv; Pañcat. (ifc. f. *ā*); good conduct, good character, reputation, Hariv. 10204; Nal.; R. &c. ('life in accordance with the 5 great vows,' Jain.); peculiar observance, peculiarity of customs or conditions, W.; a ceremony, Buddh. L.; (*ā*), f. the tamarind tree, L. **-kavaca**, mfn. cased in the armour of good conduct, W. **-vatī**, f. N. of a Samādhi, Buddh. L. **-siṅha-gaṇi**, m. N. of an author.

Cāritrin, mfn. of good conduct, Subh.

Cāritrya, n. good conduct, MBh.; R. &c.

Cārin, mfn. moving, MBh. vii, 372; ifc. moving, walking or wandering about, living, being (e.g. *ambu-*, *eka-*, *kha-*, *giri-*, &c., qq. vv.; *nimeshântara-*, 'going in an instant,' MBh.; Hariv. 9139); acting, proceeding, doing, practising (e.g. *dharma-*, *bahu-*, *brahma-*, &c., qq. vv.), MBh. xiv, 759; R. &c.; living on, Suśr.; 'coming near,' resembling, see *padma-cāriṇī*; m. a foot-soldier, MBh. vi, 3545; a spy, Āp.; (*iṇī*), f. the plant Karuṇī, L.

Cāri-vāc, f. Karkaṭa-śṛiṅgī, W.

Cārya, n. espionage, Kathârṇ.

चारमिक *cāramika*, mfn. = *caramam adhîte veda vā*, g. *vasantâdi*.

चारायण *cārāyaṇa*, °*rita*, &c. See *cāra*.

चारु *cāru*, mf(*us*)n. (√2. *can*) agreeable, approved, esteemed, beloved, endeared, (Lat.) *carus*, dear (with dat. or loc. of the person), RV.; VS. xxxv, 17; TS. iii; TBr. iii, 1, 1, 9; SāṅkhSr. i, 5, 9; pleasing, lovely, beautiful, pretty, RV.; AV.; MBh. &c.; ind. so as to please, agreeably (with dat.), RV. ix, 72, 7 & 86, 21; AV. vii, xii, xiv; beautifully, Hariv.; Caurap.; m. (in music) a particular *vāsaka*; N. of Bṛihaspati, L.; of a son of Kṛishṇa, Hariv. 6699; BhP. x, 61, 9; of a Cakra-vartin, Buddh.; n. (v.l. for *vara*) saffron, L., Sch.; (*vī*), f. a beautiful woman, L.; splendour, L.; moonlight, L.; intelligence, L.; N. of Kubera's wife, L. **-karṇa**, mfn. beautiful-eared, W. **-kesarā**, f. 'beautiful-filamented,' a kind of Cyperus, L.; another plant (*taruṇī*), L. **-garbha**, m. N. of a son of Kṛishṇa, Hariv. 6698 & 9182. **-giri**, m. N. of a mountain. **-gīti**, f. 'pretty Gīti,' a kind of metre. **-gucchā**, f. 'beautiful-graped,' a vine, Gal. **-gupta**, m. N. of a son of Kṛishṇa, Hariv. 6698 & 9182. **-ghoṇa**, mfn. handsome-nosed, W. **-candra**, m. N. of a son of Kṛishṇa, BhP. x, 61, 9. **-caryā**, f. N. of a work; *-śataka*, n. N. of a work. **-citra**, m. N. of a son of Dhṛita-rāshṭra, MBh. i, 4543; vii, 5594; °*trâṅgada*, m. id., i, 2730. **-tama**, mfn. most beloved (with dat.), RV. v, 1, 9; most beautiful, i, 62, 6. **-tā**, f. = *-tvá*, AitBr. iv, 17; loveliness, beauty, Kum.; Mālav. ii, $\frac{2}{1}\frac{6}{7}$; Śāntiś.; VP. **-tvá**, n. endearedness, RV. x, 70, 9. **-datta**, m. N. of a Brāhman, Mṛicch.; of a merchant's son, Hit. i, 9, $\frac{8}{9}$ (v.l. *-danta*). **-darśanā**, f. a good-looking woman, Nal. xvii, 13; R. i, 2, 12. **-dāru**, m. Hibiscus populneoides, Npr. **-deva**, m. N. of the father of the author of Hcat. **-deshṇa**, m. N. of a son of Gaṇḍūsha, Hariv. 1940; of a son of Kṛishṇa, MBh. i, iii, xiii; Hariv.; LiṅgaP. i, 69, 68; BhP. i, 11, 18. **-deha**, m. N. of a son of Kṛishṇa, x, 61, 8. **-dharman**, v. l. for *-varman*. **-dhāman**, m. N. of a plant (?), W. **-dhāmā** or **-dhārā**, f. N. of Indra's wife Śacī, L. **-dhishṇya**, m. N. of one of the 7 Ṛishis in the 11th Manv-antara, Hariv. (v. l. for *uru-*). **-nālaka**, n. red lotus. **-netra**, mf(*ā*)n. beautiful-eyed, Hariv. 11789; R. v, 22, 29; m. a kind of antelope, Gal.; (*ā*), f. N. of an Apsaras, MBh. ii, 392. **-pattra-maya**, mfn. made of beautiful leaves, Hcat. **-pada**, m. N. of a son of Namasyu, BhP. ix, 20, 2. **-parṇī**, f. 'handsome-leaved,' Pæderia fœtida, L. **-puṭa**, m. (in music) a kind of measure. **-pratīka** (*cā́ru-*), mfn. lovely appearance, RV. ii, 8, 2. **-phalā**, f. = *-gucchā*, L. **-bāhu**, m. 'handsome-armed,' N. of a son of Kṛishṇa, Hariv. 6698 & 9183. **-bhadra**, m. N. of a son of Kṛishṇa, ib. **-mat**, mfn. lovely, W.; m. N. of a Cakra-vartin, Buddh.; (*tī*), f. N. of a daughter of Kṛishṇa, Hariv. 6699 & 9183; of a female attendant, Caṇḍ. **-mati**, m. N. of a parrot, Kathās. lxxii, 238. **-mukha**, mfn. handsome-faced, W.; (*ī*), f. a metre of 4 × 10 syllables. **-yaśas**, m. N. of a son of Kṛishṇa, MBh. xiii; LiṅgaP. i, 69, 69.

-ratha, N. of a forest, BrahmaP. ii, 11. **-rava,** mfn. having an agreeable voice (the Krauñca bird), R. i, 2, 32. **-rāvā,** f. = *-dhāmā,* L. **-rūpa,** mfn. = *-pratīka,* MBh. i, 197, 39; m. N. of an adopted son of Asamaujas, Hariv. i, 38, 8. **-locana,** mf(*ā*)n. = *-netra,* Hariv.; R.; m. an antelope, L.; (*ā*), f. a fine-eyed woman, W. **-vaktra,** mfn. = *-mukha,* R. v, 22, 29; m. N. of one of Skanda's attendants, MBh. ix, 2575. **-vadana,** see *cārv-ad°*. **-vardhanā,** f. a woman, L. **-varman,** m. N. of a man, VP. v, 37, 42. **-vaha,** mfn., Pāṇ. vi, 3, 121, Pat. **-vāc,** see *cārvāc.* **-vādin,** mfn. sounding beautifully. **-vinda,** m. N. of a son of Kṛishṇa, Hariv. 6698; 9182. **-vṛiksha,** m. = *-dāru,* Npr. **-veṇī,** f. 'a handsome braid'; N. of a river. **-veśa,** m. 'well-dressed,' MBh. xiii, 621. **-vesha,** m. id., N. of a son of Kṛishṇa, LiṅgaP. i, 69, 68. **-vratā,** f. a female who fasts for a whole month, L. **-śilā,** f. 'beautiful stone,' a jewel, L. **-śīrsha,** m. N. of a man, MBh. xiii, 1300. **-śravas,** m. (= *-yaśas*) N. of a son of Kṛishṇa, MBh. xiii, 621; LiṅgaP. i, 69, 69. **-saṃkāśin,** mfn. = *-pratīka,* AV. Paipp. xx, 5, 5. **-sarvâṅga,** mf(*ī*)n. one whose limbs are all beautiful, R. i; *-darśana,* mfn. id., Nal. xii, 18. **-sāra,** n. 'essence of what is lovely,' gold, Gal. **-hāsin,** mfn. smiling sweetly, Nal. iii, x; R. iii; VP.; (*inī*), f. a metre of 4 × 14 syllabic instants.

Cāruka, m. the seed of Saccharum Śara, Bhpr. v, 8, 82; N. of a man, VP. v, 37, 42.

Cārv, in comp. for *°ru.* **-adana,** mfn. having beautiful teeth, AV. Paipp. xx, 5, 5 (? or for *°ru-vad°* = *-mukha*). **-āghāṭa, -āghāta,** mfn. playing well on an instrument (?), Pāṇ. iii, 2, 49, Vārtt. 2. **-āṭa,** mfn. (said of a Muhūrta), Tantr. **-ādi,** a Gaṇa of Pāṇ. (vi, 2, 160).

Cārvāc, mfn. (for *°ru-v°*) speaking nicely, AV. Paipp. xx, 5, 5.

चार्चिक *cārcika,* mfn. conversant with the repetition of words (*carcā*), g. *ukthâdi.*

Cārcikya, *am,* n. (= *carc°*) smearing the body with unguents, L.

चार्म *cārma,* mfn. made of hide or leather (*carman*), Pāṇ. vi, 4, 144, Vārtt. 2; covered with leather (a car), L., Sch.; defended by a hide, W.

Cārmaṇa, mfn. covered with leather (a car), Pāṇ. vi, 4, 170, Kāś.; n. a multitude of hides or shields, g. *bhikshâdi.* **Cārmika,** mfn. leathern, Mn. viii, 289. **Cārmikāyaṇi,** m. patr. fr. *carmin,* Pāṇ. iv, 1, 158, Vārtt. 2. **Cārmikya,** n. the duty of a shield-bearer (*carmika*), g. *purohitâdi.* **Cārmiṇa,** n. a number of men armed with shields, g. *bhikshâdi.* **Cārmīya,** mfn. fr. *cárman,* g. *utkarâdi.*

चार्य *cārya.* See *cāra.*

चार्वाक *cārvāka,* m. (for *°ru-v°*, = *cārvāc* s.v. *cā́ru*) N. of a Rākshasa (friend of Duryodhana, who took the shape of a mendicant Brāhman, when Yudhishṭhira entered Hāstina-pura in triumph, and reviled him, but was soon detected and killed by the real Brāhmans), MBh. i, 349; ix, 3619; xii, 1414; N. of a materialistic philosopher (whose doctrines are embodied in the Bārhaspatya-sūtras), Vedântas.; Śil.; Rājat. iv, 345; Prab.; Madhus.; a follower of Cārvāka, Sarvad.; mfn. composed by Cārvāka, Prab. ii, $\frac{1}{8}$, Sch. **-darśana,** n. the doctrine of Cārvāka, W. **-mata,** n. id.; *-nibarhaṇa,* n. 'refutation of Cārvāka's doctrine,' N. of Śaṃkar. xxv.

चाल *cāla,* m. (√*cal,* g. *jvalâdi*) 'moving,' see *danta-;* looseness of the teeth, VarBṛS. lxvi, 5, Sch.; a thatch, roof, L.; (for *cā́sha*) the blue jay, L.

Cālaka, m. a restive elephant (said of a person, Rājat. viii, 1644), L.; 'id.' and '= *cākrika,*' Śiś. v.

Cālana, n. causing to move, shaking, wagging (the tail), making loose, MBh. v, 2651; xvi, 267; R. vii, 16, 26; Suśr.; Pañcat.; Bhartṛ.; moving action (of the wind), BhP. iii, 26, 37; throwing off (*niḥsāraṇa;* 'muscular action,' W.), x, 44, 5; a term in astr.; causing to pass through a strainer, W.; a strainer, L., Sch.; (*ī*), f. id., Cāṇ. (Subh.); VS. xix, 16, Sch.

Cālanikā, f. = *°nī,* KātyŚr. xix, 2, 8, Sch.

Cālanīya, mfn. to be moved or shaken, W.

Cālya, mfn. id., Gol. xi, 4, Sch.; (*a-,* neg.) MBh. xiii, 2161; to be loosened, Suśr. vi, 15, 15; to be caused to deviate, BhP. ii, 7, 17.

चालिक्य *cālikya,* = *°lukya,* Inscr. (489 A.D.)

Cāluki, m. N. of a prince.

Cālukya, m. N. of a dynasty, Inscr.

चाल्य *cālya.* See *cāla.*

चाष *cā́sha,* m. the blue jay, RV. x, 97, 13; RPrāt.; Mn. xi, 132; Yājñ. i, 175; MBh. &c.; sugar-cane, L.; mfn. relating to a blue jay, Pāṇ. iv, 3, 156, Vārtt. 4, Pat. **-maya,** mfn. consisting of blue jays, Hcar. **-vaktra,** m. 'jay-faced,' N. of one of Skanda's attendants, MBh. ix, 2578; m. pl. a class of spirits, x, 268.

Cāsa, wrong spelling for *cāsha.*

चाहव *cāhava,* N. of a dynasty, Ratnak.

Cāhuvāṇa, °hūāṇa, N. of a prince of Hammīra's family, ŚārṅgP. Introd.; of a dynasty, Ratnak.

चि 1. *ci,* cl. 5. *cinóti, °nute* (1. pl. *cinumas* & *°nmas,* Pāṇ. vi, 4, 107; perf. *cikāya* & *cicāya,* vii, 3, 58; 2. *cicetha,* 2, 61, Kāś.; 3. pl. *cikyúr,* AV. x, 2, 4; p. *cikivas,* Kāṭh. xxii, 6; Ā. *cikye* & *cicye,* Vop. xii, 2; p. *cikyāná,* TS. v; 2nd fut. p. *ceshyat,* Lāṭy.; 1st fut. *cetā,* Pāṇ. vii, 2, 61, Kāś.; aor. *acaishīt,* Kāś. on iii, 1, 42 & vii, 2, 1; Ved. *cikayām akar,* iii, 1, 42, Kāś.; 1. sg. *acaisham,* 2. sg. *acais,* Kāṭh. xxii, 6; 3. pl. *acaishur,* Bhaṭṭ.; Ā. *aceshṭa,* Pāṇ. i, 2, 11, Kāś.; Prec. *ceshīshṭa,* ib., or *cīyāt,* vii, 4, 25, Kāś.; ind. p. *citvā́,* AV. &c.; Pass. *cīyate,* MuṇḍUp. &c.; fut. *cāyishyate* & *ceshy°,* Cond. *acāyishyata* & *aceshy°,* Pāṇ. vi, 4, 62, Kāś.) to arrange in order, heap up, pile up, construct (a sacrificial altar; P., if the priests construct the altar for another; Ā., if the sacrificer builds it for himself), AV.; VS.; TS. v; Kāṭh.; ŚBr.; to collect, gather together, accumulate, acquire for one's self, MuṇḍUp.; MBh. i, v; to search through (for collecting; cf. √2. *ci*), MBh. v, 1255; Kām. (Pañcat.); to cover, inlay, set with, MBh.; Pass. *cīyate,* to become covered with, Suśr. v, 8, 31; to increase, thrive, Mudr. i, 3; Kpr. x, 52$\frac{a}{b}$ (Sāh.): Caus. *cayayati* & *capay°,* to heap up, gather, Dhātup. xxxii, 85; *cāyayati* & *cāpay°,* Pāṇ. vi, 1, 54: Desid. *cikīshate* (also *°ti,* vii, 3, 58, Kāś.) to wish to pile up, ŚBr. ix; KātyŚr. xvi; *cicīshati* (Pāṇ. vii, 3, 58, Kāś.; vi, 4, 16, [ed. *vivīsh°*] Kāś.) to wish to accumulate or collect, Kir. ii, 19; iii, 11: Desid. Caus. (p. *cicīshayat*) to cause any one to wish to arrange in order, Bhaṭṭ. iii, 33: Intens. *cecīyate,* Kāś. on Pāṇ. vii, 3, 58; 4, 25 & 82.

1. **Caya,** mfn. 'collecting,' see *vṛitaṃ-;* m. (iii, 3, 56, Kāś.; g. *vṛishâdi*) a mound of earth (raised to form the foundation of a building or raised as a rampart), MBh. iii, 11699; Hariv.; R.; Pañcat.; a cover, covering, W.; a heap, pile, collection, multitude, assemblage, MBh.; Hariv. &c.; (in med.) accumulation of the humors (cf. *sam-*), Suśr.; the amount by which each term increases, common increase or difference of the terms, Bījag.; (cf. *agni-*).

Cayaka, mfn. = *caye kuśala,* g. *ākarshâdi.*

Cáyana, n. piling up (wood &c.), AV. xviii, 4, 37; ŚBr. ix f.; KātyŚr. xvi; Hariv. 2161, Sch.; stacked wood, MBh. iii, vii, xiv; collecting, W.

Cayanīya, mfn. to be heaped or collected (*puṇya*), Vop. xxvi, 3.

1. **Cit,** mfn. ifc. 'piling up,' see *agni-, ūrdhva-,* & *pūrva-cít;* (Pāṇ. iii, 2, 92) forming a layer or stratum, piled up, VS. i, xii; TS. i; (cf. *kaṅka-, karma-, cakshuś-, droṇa-, prāṇa-, manaś-, ratha-cakra-, vāk-, śyena-,* & *śrotra-cit.*)

Citá, mfn. piled up, heaped, RV. i, 112, 17; 158, 4; AV. &c.; placed in a line, RV. vii, 18, 10; collected, gained, MuṇḍUp.; forming a mass (hair), Buddh. L.; covered, inlaid, set with, MBh.; R. &c.; n. 'a building,' see *pakvêshṭaka-;* (*ā*), f. a layer, pile of wood, funeral pile, Lāṭy. viii; MBh. &c.; a heap, multitude, L. **-vistara,** m. a kind of ornament, Buddh. L. **Citâgni,** see *°tâgni.* **Citâdha,** mfn. relating to a pile of wood, AitBr. iv, 10, 15.

Citā, f. of *°tá.* **-°gni** (*°tâg°*), m. a funeral pile, MBh. iii, xiii; Kathās. iic, 1; Vet. **-cūḍaka,** n. 'funeral pile mark,' a sepulchre, L. **-caitya-cihna,** n. id., Hcar. vi. **-°dhirohaṇa** (*°tâdh°*), n. ascending the funeral pile, Ragh. viii, 56. **-dhūma,** m. smoke rising from a funeral pile, Kathās. **-°nala** (*°tân°*), m. = *°tâgni,* xviii, 147. **-praveśa,** m. = *°tâdhirohaṇa,* Siṇhâs. **-bhūmi,** f. 'pile place,' N. of a locality, ŚivaP. i, 38, 19.

1. **Citi,** f. a layer (of wood or bricks &c.), pile, stack, funeral pile, TS. v; ŚBr. vi, viii; Pāṇ. iii, 3, 41; Mn. iv, 46; MBh. &c. (metrically *°tī,* Hariv. 2227 & 12360); N. of ŚBr. xiii; collecting, gathering, W.; a heap, multitude, Prab. ii, 17; an oblong with quadrangular sides, W.; (cf. *idhma-;* *amṛita-* & *ṛishi-citi.*) **-klṛipti,** f. the arrangement of a sacrificial altar, Śulbas. ii, 80. **-ghana,** m. the total amount of all the members of an arithmetical progression, Āryabh. ii, 21. **-purīshá,** n. pl. the layer (of wood &c.) and the rubble-stones, ŚBr. viii; n. du. id, KātyŚr. xvii. **-vat,** ind. like a pile, xxi. **-vyavahāra,** m. calculation of the cubic measure of a pile. **City-agni,** m. pl. the bricks used for the sacrificial fire, ĀpŚr. xiv, 8, 6.

Citikā, f. a pile, funeral pile, Pañcat. iii, 4, 12; ifc. 'a layer,' see *páñca-* & *sápta-citika;* a small chain worn round the loins, L.

Citī, f. for *°ti,* q. v.

Citīka (ifc. after numerals, Pāṇ. vi, 3, 127), 'a layer,' see *éka-, tri-, páñca-.*

Cítya, mfn. (iii, 1, 132) to be arranged in order, AV. x, 2, 8; to be piled up, ŚBr. vi; (with or without *agni,* the fire) constructed upon a foundation (of bricks &c.), TS. v; AitBr. v, 28; ŚBr. ii, vi, KātyŚr.; ŚāṅkhŚr.; (fr. 1. *-citi*) coming from the funeral pile or from the place of cremation, R. i, 58, 10; n. = *°tā-cūḍaka,* L. (cf. R. i, 58, 10); (*ā*), f. 'piling up,' building (an altar &c.), see *agni-cityā, maṭha-;* 'a layer, stratum,' see *catuś-citya;* a funeral pile, L. **-yūpa,** m. a post on the place of cremation, Gobh. iii, 3, 34.

Citi, f. collecting, AV. ii, 9, 4.

Cetavyà, mfn. to be piled up, TS. v; ŚBr. vi; ix, 5, 1, 64; Bhaṭṭ. ix, 13; = *cayanīya,* Vop. xxvi, 3.

Ceya, mfn. (Kāś. on Pāṇ. iii, 1, 97 & 132; on vi, 1, 213) to be piled, MBh. xii, 10745; = *cayanīya,* Vop. xxvi, 3.

चि 2. *ci,* Ved. cl. 3. (*ciketi,* fr. √*ki,* Dhātup. xv, 19; Impv. *ciketu,* TS.; Subj. Ā. *cíketa;* impf. *aciket,* RV. x, 51, 3; aor. 2. pl. Ā. *ácidhvam,* RV.; 3. sg. *acait* [fr. √4. *cit,* Gmn.], vi, 44, 7) to observe, perceive (with acc. or gen.), RV.; Kāṭh. viii, 10; to fix the gaze upon, be intent upon, RV. v, 55, 7; TS. iii; to seek for, RV. vi, 44, 7: Class. cl. 5. *cinoti* (p. *°nvat,* Ā. *°nvāna*) to seek for, investigate, search through, make inquiries (cf. √1. *ci*), MBh. iii, 2659; Bhartṛ.; Kathās. xxvi, 136: Intens. *cekite,* see √4. *cit;* [cf. Lat. *scio.*]

2. **Cit,** mfn. ifc. 'knowing,' see *ṛita-cít;* 'giving heed to' or 'revenging [guilt, *ṛiṇa-*],' see *ṛiṇa-.*

1. **Cetṛi,** m. an observer, ŚvetUp. vi, 11.

चि 3. *ci,* cl. 1. *cáyate* (p. *cáyamāna*) to detest, hate (Nir. iv, 25), RV. i, 167, 8 & 190, 5; vii, 52, 2; to revenge, punish, take vengeance on (acc.), ii, 27, 4; ix, 47, 2; AitBr. ii, 7; [cf. *ápaciti, kāti;* τίνομαι τινά, τίω, τίσις, ποινή.]

2. **Caya,** mfn. ifc. 'revenging,' see *ṛiṇaṃ-.*

3. **Cit,** mfn. ifc. 'id.,' see 2. *cit.*

2. **Cetṛí,** m. a revenger, RV. vii, 60, 5.

चिकरिषु *cikarishu,* mfn. (√1. *kṛi,* Desid.) desirous to cast or throw or pour out, W.

चिकर्तिषा *cikartishā,* f. (√2. *kṛit,* Desid.) desire to cut off, Daś. xii, 19.

Cikartishu, mfn. desirous to cut off, Śiś. i, 49; desirous to disembowel, Siṇhâs. xxix, 2.

चिकश *cikaśa,* = *cikkasa* ?, Kauś. 21.

चिकारिषु *cikārishu,* mfn. (√1. *kṛi,* Caus. Desid.) intending to have made (or built), Siṇhâs.

चिकित् *cikít, °kita, °kitāná,* &c. See p. 395.

चिकिन *cikina,* mfn. flat-nosed, Pāṇ. v, 2, 33; flat (the chin), Hcar.; n. flat-nosedness, Pāṇ. v, 2, 33; (cf. *cikka, cipiṭa.*)

चिकिल *cikila,* = *°khalla,* W.

चिकीरषा *cikīrashā.* See *°rshā.*

Cikīrsh, mfn. (√*kṛi,* Desid.) wishing to do, Vop.

Cikīrshaka, mfn. id., Kāś. on Pāṇ. i, 1, 58 & vi, 1, 193. **Cikīrshā,** f. (Pāṇ. iii, 3, 102, Kāś.) intention or desire to make or do or perform (generally ifc.), MBh. i; R. i, v; Pāṇ. ii, 3, 66, Kāś. (with gen.) BhP. ii f.; (*°rashā*) xi, 9, 26; desire for (gen. or in comp.), MBh. i, 1860 & 5172; Hariv. 4907.

Cikīrshita, n. 'intended to be done, designed,' purpose, design, intention, Mn. iv, vii; MBh.; R. &c.

Cikīrshu, mfn. (Pāṇ. iii, 2, 168, Kāś.) intending to make or do or perform (with acc. or ifc.), MBh.; R.; Pāṇ. ii, 3, 69, Kāś.; BhP.; Kathās.; wishing to exercise one's self in the use of (acc.), MBh. viii, 1965; cf. *upahāri-.* **Cikīrshuka,** mfn. = *°rsh* (with acc.), vi, 48, 83. **Cikīrshya,** mfn. to be wished to be done, to be intended, Pāṇ. vi, 1, 185, Kāś.

चिकुर *cikura,* mfn. inconsiderate, rash, L.; m. the hair of the head (also *cihura,* m. pl., L., Sch.) Gīt. vii, xii; Rājat. viii, 367; Naish. vii, 108; hair (of a chowrie), Bālar. iv, $\frac{16}{17}$; a mountain, L.; N. of a plant, L.; a snake, L.; N. of a Nāga, MBh. v, 3640; a kind of bird, L.; a musk-rat (cf. *cikka, cikkira*), L. **–kalâpa,** m. a mass of hair, tuft of hair, L. **–nikara,** m. id. **–paksha,** m. id. **–pāśa,** m. id., L. **–bhāra,** m. id., L. **–racanā,** f. id., L. **–hasta,** m. id., L. **Cikurôccaya,** m. id., L. **Cikurita,** mfn.?, Daś. viii, 146.
Cikūra, for °*kura,* the hair, L.

चिकेतस् *ciketas.* See *na-.*

चिक्क् *cikk,* cl. 10. P. = √*cakk,* Dhātup.

चिक्क *cikka,* mfn. flat-nosed, Pāṇ. v, 2, 33, Vārtt. 1; n. flat-nosedness, ib.; m. (= *cikura*) a musk-rat, L.; (*ā*), f. a mouse, L.; (= *cikkaṇa*) a betel-nut, L.; for *chikkā?*, PSarv.

चिक्कण *cikkaṇa,* mf(*ā*)n. smooth, slippery, unctuous, MBh. xii, 6854; xiv, 1416; Suśr.; Śak.; (*ati-,* 'very smooth') KātyŚr. xxvi, 1, 4, Sch.; m. the betel-nut tree, L.; n. any smooth liquid, gum, VarBṛ. iii, 7, Sch.; the betel-nut, L.; (*ā, ī*), f. id., L.; (*ā*), f. an excellent cow (°*kkiṇā,* W.), L. **–kantha,** n. N. of a town, g. *cihaṇâdi* (v. l. *citk*°). **–tā,** f. smoothness, Suśr. iv, 9, 20. **–tva,** n. id., W. **Cikkiṇa,** mfn. smooth, L.; (*ā*), f., see °*kkaṇā.*

चिक्कस *cikkasa,* m. n. barley-meal, L.

चिक्किण *cikkiṇa.* See °*kkaṇa.*

चिक्किर *cikkira,* m. a kind of mouse (cf. *cikura, chikkara*), Suśr. v, 6, 2; Ashṭâṅg. vi, 38, 1.

चिक्रंसा *cikraṇsā,* f. (√*kram,* Desid.) desire of attacking or springing upon, W.

चिक्रीडिषा *cikrīḍishā,* f. (√*krīḍ,* Desid.) desire to play, BhP. iii, 7, 3. **Cikrīḍishu,** mfn. desiring to play, HPariś. ii, 454.

चिक्लिद *ciklida,* m. (√*klid*) = *kledan,* L.; n. (Pāṇ. vi, 1, 12, Kāś.) moisture, W.

चिखल्ल *cikhalla,* m. (g. *pṛishodarâdi,* Gaṇar. 149, Sch.) mud mire, L. Sch.; (used in Prâkṛit.)

चिखल्लि *cikhalli,* m. pl. N. of a people, Pāṇ. iii, 3, 41, Kāś.

चिखादिषु *cikhādishu,* mfn. (√*khād,* Desid.) desiring to eat, MBh. x, 483; Hariv. 16004.

चिख्यापयिषा *cikhyāpayishā,* f. (√*khyā,* Caus. Desid.) the intention to communicate, Nyāyas. i, 1, 7, Sch.

चिङ्गट *ciṅgaṭa,* m., °*ṭī,* f. a shrimp, L.
Ciṅgaḍa, m. id., L.; (cf. *uc-ciṅgaṭa.*)

चिचरिषु *cicarishu,* mfn. (√*car,* Desid.) trying to go, ŚāṅkhBr. xxv, 13.

चिचलिषु *cicalishu,* mfn. (√*cal,* Desid.) being about to set out, Rājat. viii, 812.

चिचिण्ड *ciciṇḍa,* m., °*ḍā,* f. the gourd Trichosanthes anguina, Bhpr. v, 9, 63 f.

चिचीकुची *cicīkucī* & °*kūcī.* See *cic*°.

चिचीषत् *cicīshat,* p. Desid. √1. *ci,* q. v.

चिच्चन्द्रिका *cic-candrikā.* See √4. *cit.*

चिच्चिक *ciccikā,* m. a kind of bird, RV. x, 146, 2; TBr. ii, 5, 5, 6.

चिच्चिटिङ्ग *cic-citiṅga, -chakti.* See √4. *cit.*

चिच्छित्सु *cicchitsu,* mfn. (√*chid,* Desid.) intending to cut off, MBh. vii, 6001.

चिच्छिल *cic-chila.* See √4. *cit.*
Cic-chuka & °**kī,** for *cit-sukha* & °*khī.*

चिञ्चा *ciñcā,* f. the tamarind tree, Bhpr. v, 9, 27 & 26, 75; vii, 18, 95; (g. *harītaky-ādi*), its fruit, ib.; (cf. *kāka-*). **–°mla** (°*câm*°), n. Rumex vesicatorius (or = *sāra,* Npr.), L. **–sāra,** m. id., L.
Ciñcāṭaka, v. l. for °*ñcoṭ*°, W. **Ciñcikā,** f. = °*ñcā,* Bhpr. v, 26, 167. **Ciñcinī,** f. the tamarind tree, ŚārṅgP.; (onomat.) ind., HaṇsUp. (also *ciṇī*).
Ciñcinī, f. 'rich in tamarind trees,' N. of a town, Kathās. iii, 9. **Ciñcī,** f. Abrus precatorius, W.
Ciñcoṭaka, m. the plant Krauñcâdana, L.

चिट् *ciṭ* (derived from *ceṭa*), cl. 1. P. *ceṭati,* to send out, Dhātup. ix, 28.

चिटिङ्ग *ciṭiṅga.* See *uc-* & *cic-.*

चिटिचिटाय *ciṭiciṭāya,* (onomat.) °*yate,* to make a hissing noise, Divyâv. xxxviii.

चिणी *ciṇī* (onomat.) See *ciñciṇī.*

चित् 1. 2. 3. *cit.* See √1. 2. 3. *ci.*

चित् 4. *cit,* cl. 1. *cétati* (impf. *acetat,* RV. vii, 95, 2; p. *cétat,* RV.), cl. 2. (Ā. Pass. 3. sg. *cité,* x, 143, 4; p. f. instr. *citántyā,* i, 129, 7; Ā. *citāna,* ix, 101, 11; VS. x, 1), cl. 3. irreg. *ciketati* (RV.; Subj. *cíketat,* RV.; Impv. 2. sg. *cikiddhi,* RV.; p. *cikitāná,* RV.; perf. *cikéta,* RV. &c.; *ciceta,* Vop. viii, 37; 3. du. *cetatur,* AV. iii, 22, 2; Ā. & Pass. *cikité,* RV. &c.; 3. pl. °*tre,* RV.; for p. *cikitvás,* see s. v.; Ā. Pass. *cicite,* Bhaṭṭ. ii, 29; aor. *acetīt,* Vop. viii, 35; Ā. Pass. *áceti* & *céti,* RV.; for *acait* see √2. *ci;* fut. 1st *céttā,* i, 22, 5) to perceive, fix the mind upon, attend to, be attentive, observe, take notice of (acc. or gen.), RV.; SV.; AV.; Bhaṭṭ.; to aim at, intend, design (with dat.), RV. i, 131, 6; x, 38, 3; to be anxious about, care for (acc. or gen.), i, ix f.; to resolve, iii, 53, 24; x, 55, 6; to understand, comprehend, know (perf. often in the sense of pr.), RV.; AV. vii, 2, 1 & 5, 5; P. Ā. to become perceptible, appear, be regarded as, be known, RV.; VS. x, xv: Caus. *cetáyati,* °*te* (2. pl. *cetáyadhvam,* Subj. *cetayat,* Impv. 2. du. *cetayethām,* impf. *ácetayat,* RV.; 3. pl. *citáyante,* RV.; p. *citáyat,* RV. (eleven times); *cetáyat,* x, 110, 8, &c.; Ā. *cetayāna* see s. v.) to cause to attend, make attentive, remind of, i, 131, 2 & iv, 51, 3; to cause to comprehend, instruct, teach, RV.; to observe, perceive, be intent upon, RV.; MBh. xii, 9890; Kathās. xiii, 10; Ā. (once P., MBh. xviii, 74) to form an idea in the mind, be conscious of, understand, comprehend, think, reflect upon, TS. vi; ŚBr.; ChUp. vii, 5, 1; MBh.; BhP. viii, 1, 9; Prab.; P. to have a right notion of, know, MBh. iii, 14877; P. 'to recover consciousness,' awake, Bhaṭṭ. viii, 123; Ā. to remember, have consciousness of (acc.), Pāṇ. iii, 2, 112, Kāś.; Bādar. ii, 3, 18, Sch.; to appear, be conspicuous, shine, RV.; TS. iii: Desid. *cikitsati* (fr. √*kit,* Pāṇ. iii, 1, 5; Dhātup. xxiii, 24; exceptionally Ā., MBh. xii, 12544; Impv. °*tsatu,* Subj. °*tsāt,* aor. 2. sg. *ácikitsīs,* AV.; Pass. p. *cikitsyamāna,* Suśr.; Pañcat.) to have in view, aim at, be desirous, AV. v, 11, 1; ix, 2, 3; to care for, be anxious about, vi, x; (Pāṇ. iii, 1, 5, Siddh.) to treat medically, cure, KātyŚr. xxv; MBh. i, xii; Suśr.; Pañcat.; Bhartṛ.; to wish to appear, RV. i, 123, 1: Caus. of Desid. (fut. *cikitsayishyati*) to cure, Mālav. iv, $\frac{1}{4}$, 6 f.: Intens. *cekite* (fr. √2. *ci?*, or for °*tte,* RV. i, 53, 3 & 119, 3; ii, 34, 10; p. *cékitat,* ix, 111, 3; Ā. *cékitāna* RV. eight times) to appear, be conspicuous, shine, RV.
Cikit, mfn. knowing, experienced, RV viii, 51, 3; 97, 14 & 102, 2; shining, x, 3, 1.
Cikita, m. (g. *gargâdi*) N. of a man, ĀśvŚr. xii.
Cikitāná, mfn. pr. or perf. p. √*cit,* q. v.; m. N. of a man, BṛĀrUp. i, 3, 24, Sch.
Cikitāyana, m. (cf. *caik*°) N. of a man, ChUp. i, 8, 1, Sch. **Cíkiti,** mfn. shining, see *cikitú.*
Cikitú, mfn. id., RV. viii, 55, 5 (*cíkiti,* SV.); f. (instr. °*tvā́*) understanding (?), AV. vii, 52, 2.
Cikitván, mfn. attentive, RV. viii, 60, 18.
Cikitvás, mf(°*tushī*)n. having observed or noticed, i, 71, 5; 125, 1 & 169, 1; observing, attending to, attentive, RV.; TS. iii; knowing, understanding, experienced, RV.; 'shining' (?, Agni), RV.; cf. *á-.*
Cikitvít, ind. with deliberation, iv, 52, 4. **Cikitvín-manas,** mfn. attentive, v, 22, 3 ['knowing all hearts,' Sāy.]; well-considered, viii, 95, 5.
Cikitsaka, mfn. (fr. Desid.) a physician, ŚBr. xi (ifc.); Mn. iii f., ix; Yājñ. i, 162; MBh.; Suśr. &c.
Cikitsana, n. ifc. curing of, MBh. iv, 63.
Cikitsā, f. medical attendance, practice or science of medicine (esp. therapeutics, one of the six sections of med.), i, 67; ii, 224; R. vi, 71, 26; Mṛicch.; Suśr.; BhP. **–kalikā,** f. N. of two med. treatises (of about 400 verses each) by Tīsaṭa; *-ṭīkā,* f. a Comm. on one of the two treatises by Candraṭa. **–kaumudī,** f. N. of a med. work by Kāśī-rāja, BrahmavP. i, 16, 15. **–jñāna,** n. a med. work. **–tattva-jñāna,** n. a med. work by Dhanvantari, 13. **–darpaṇa,** n. a med. work by Divo-dāsa, 14. **–paratantra,** n. a med. work, 15. **–śāstra,** n. a manual of med., Sarvad. xv, 390.
Cikitsita, mfn. treated medically, cured, W.; m. N. of a man, g. *gargâdi* (not in Kāś.); n. = °*tsā,* Mn. x, 47; MBh. iii, 1460; iv, 318; Suśr. &c.; (pl.) the chapters of the therapeutical section (of med.), Suśr. (ifc. f. *ā,* i, 13, 6). **Cikitsú,** mfn. wise, cunning, AV. x, 1, 1; treating medically, Naish. iii, 111.
Cikitsya, mfn. to be treated medically, curable, Pāṇ. v, 2, 92; Yājñ. ii, 140; MBh. xii, 418.
Cic, in comp. for *cit.* **–candrikā,** f. a Comm. on Prab. by Gaṇeśa. **–citiṅga,** m. a kind of venomous insect, Suśr. v, 8, 3. **–chakti** (*-śak*°), f. mental power, Sarvad. xv. **–chuka,** see *cit-sukha.*
5. **Cit,** mfn. ifc. 'thinking,' see *a-, duś-, manaś-, vipaś-,* & *huraś-cit;* cf. also *apa-cit;* f. thought, intellect, spirit, soul, VS. iv, 19; KapS.; Bhartṛ.; BhP.; cf. *sa-* & *ā cit;* pure Thought (Brahma, cf. RTL. p. 34), Vedântas.; Prab. **–páti** [VS. iv, 4] or **-patí** [MaitrS. i, 2, 1; iii, 6, 3; Pāṇ. vi, 2, 19, Kāś.], m. the lord of thought. **–para,** n. the Supreme Spirit, LiṅgaP. i, 70, 26 (v. l.) **–prabhā,** f. N. of a work. **–pravṛitti,** f. thinking, reflection, L. **–sabhêśânanda-tīrtha,** m. N. of an author. **–sukha,** m. N. of a scholiast on BhP. (pupil of Śaṃkarâcārya, SŚaṃkar. iii); (*ī*), f. N. of Cit-sukha's Comm. on BhP. **–svarūpa,** n. pure thought, W.
2. **Citi,** f. (only dat. °*táye,* Ved. inf.) understanding, VS.; m. the thinking mind, Devīm. v, 36; Prab. **–mat,** mfn. having the faculty of thought, Bādar. ii, 3, 40, Sch. **–śakti,** f. = *cic-chakti,* Sarvad. xv. **City-upanishad,** f. N. of an Up.
Cittá, mfn. 'noticed,' see *a-citta;* 'aimed at,' longed for, ChUp. vii, 5, 3; 'appeared,' visible, RV. ix, 65, 12; n. attending, observing (*tirás cittāni,* 'so as to remain unnoticed'), vii, 59, 8; thinking, reflecting, imagining, thought, RV.; VS.; ŚBr. &c.; intention, aim, wish, RV.; VS.; AV.; TBr. &c.; (Naigh. iii, 9) the heart, mind, TS. i; ŚvetUp. vi, 5; MBh. &c. (ifc. f. *ā,* Pañcat.); memory, W.; intelligence, reason, KapS. i, 59; Yogas. i, 37; ii, 54; Vedântas.; (in astrol.) the 9th mansion, VarYogay. iv, 1; cf. *iha-, cala-, pūrva-, prâyaś-, laghu-, su-, sthira-.* **–kalita,** mfn. 'calculated in one's mind,' anticipated, W. **–kheda,** m. grief, Ratnâv. iv, $\frac{20}{21}$; Mn. vii, 151, Sch. **–garbhā** (°*ttá-*), f. visibly pregnant, RV. v, 44, 5. **–cārin,** mfn. acting according to any one's (gen.) wish, MBh. iii, 14668. **–cetasika,** m. thought, Divyâv. xxvi, 81 ff. **–caura,** m. 'heart-thief,' a lover, Vāsav. 376. **–ja,** m. 'heart-born,' love, god of love, Daś. xii, 50. **–janman,** m. id., viii, 136; Mālatim. i, 20. **–jña,** mfn. knowing the heart or the intentions of (gen.), knowing human nature, Ragh. x, 57; Sāh. iii, 130 (*-tā,* f., abstr.); Subh. **–tāpa,** m. = *-kheda,* Siṇhās. **–dravī-bhāva,** m. '(melting i. e.) emotion of the heart,' *-maya,* mfn. consisting of emotion, Sāh. viii, 2. **–dhārā,** f. flow of thoughts, Vajr. **–nātha,** m. 'heart-lord,' a lover, Śiś. x, 28. **–nāśa,** m. loss of conscience, R. ii, 64, 68. **–nirvṛiti,** f. contentment of mind, happiness, Pañcat. i, 6, 1 (v. l.) **–pramāthin,** mfn. confusing the mind, exciting any one's (gen. or in comp.) passion or love, Nal. i, 14; R. i, 9, 4. **–praśama,** mfn. satisfied in mind, composed, W. **–prasanna-tā,** f. happiness of mind, gaiety, L. **–prasāda,** m. id., KapS. vi, 31. **–prasādana,** n. gladdening of mind, MBh. iii, 1786; Yogas. i, 33. **–bhava,** mfn. being in the thoughts, felt, W. **–bhū,** m. = *-ja,* W. **–bheda,** m. contrariety of purpose or will, Mcar. iii, 31. **–bhrama,** m. = *-bhrānti,* Sāh. x, 37 $\frac{8}{9}$; mfn. connected with mental derangement (fever), Bhpr. vii, 8, 71; *-cikitsā,* f. 'treatment of mental derangement,' a ch. of the Vaidya-vallabha. **–bhrānti,** f. confusion of mind, Pāṇ. ii, 3, 51, Kāś. **–moha,** m. id., R. ii, 64, 67. **–yoni,** m. = *-ja,* Ragh. xix, 46. **–rakshin,** mfn. = *-cārin,* MBh. iii, 233, 20. **–rāga,** m. affection, desire, W. **–rāja,** m. N. of a Roma-vivara, Kāraṇḍ. xxiii, 36. **–vat,** mfn. 'endowed with understanding,' in comp.; experienced, ChUp. vii, 5, 2; kind-hearted, W.; *-kartṛika,* mfn. (a rt.) employing an intelligent agent, Pāṇ. i, 3, 88. **–vikāra,** m. disturbance of mind, MBh. xviii, 74. **–vikārin,** mfn. changing any one's character or feeling, Hit. ii, 5, 13. **–vikshepa,** m. absence of mind, Vajr. **–vināśana,** mfn. destroying consciousness, g. *nandy-ādi.* **–viplava,** m. disturbance of mind, insanity, HYog. i, 24. **–vibhraṇśa,** m id., MBh.

xiii, 54, 15. **-vibhrama**, m. id., xviii, 74; (scil. *jvara*, cf. *-bhrama*) a fever connected with mental derangement. **-viślesha**, m. 'parting of hearts,' breach of friendship, Pañcat. iv, 7, $\frac{4}{11}$. **-vṛitti**, f. state of mind, feeling, emotion, Śak.; Pañcat.; Ṛitus.; Kathās.; continuous course of thoughts (opposed to concentration), thinking, imagining, Yogas. i, 2; Bhar.; Naish. viii, 47; Sarvad.; Hit.; disposition of soul, Vedāntas. **-vedanā**, f. = *-kheda*, W. **-vaikalya**, n. bewilderment of mind, perplexity, MBh. x, 112 (°*klavya*, ed. Bomb.) **-vaiklavya**, see °*kalya*. **-śānti**, m. composedness of mind, Siṇhâs. x, 4. **-saṃhati**, f. a multitude of thoughts or emotions, many minds, W. **-saṃkhya**, mfn. knowing the thoughts, W. **-samunnati**, f. pride of heart, haughtiness, L. **-stha**, mfn. being in the heart, W. **-sthita**, mfn. id., W.; m. N. of a Samādhi, Buddh. L. **-hārin**, mfn. captivating the heart, Daś. v, 183. **-hṛit**, mfn. id., W. **Cittâkarshaṇa**, n. captivating the heart. **Cittâkarshin**, mfn. = °*tta-hārin*, Mālatim. v, 20. **Cittâkūtá**, n. sg. thought and intention, AV. xi, 9, 1. **Cittânubodha**, m. 'instruction of mind,' N. of a work. **Cittânuvartin**, mfn. = °*tta-cārin*, R. (G) ii, 24, 17; Pañcat. (°*rti-tva*, n. abstr.); Vet. iv, 5 (ifc.) **Cittânuvṛitti**, mfn. id., Kām. v, 54 (°*tti-tva*, n. abstr.); f. gratification of wishes, Ratnâv. iv, 1. **Cittâpahāraka**, °**hārin**, mfn. = °*tta-hārin*, W. **Cittâbhijvalana**, n. illumination by intellect, Bādar. ii, 2, 18, Sch. **Cittâbhoga**, m. full consciousness, L. **Cittârpita**, mfn. preserved in the heart, Naish. ix, 31. **Cittâsaṅga**, m. affection, W. **Cittâsukha**, n. uneasiness of mind, VarYogay. ix, 10. **Cittâikya**, n. unanimity, W. **Cittôttha**, m. '= °*tta-ja*,' the 7th mansion (in astrol.), VarBṛ. i, 20, Sch. **Cittônnatti**, f. = °*tta-samunn*°, L.

1. **Cítti**, f. thinking, thought, understanding, wisdom, RV. ii, 21, 6; x, 85, 7; VS.; TBr. ii; ŚāṅkhŚr.; Kauś. 42; intention (along with *ā́kūti*), AV.; BhP. v, 18, 18; (pl.) thoughts, devotion, [hence = *karman*, 'an act of worship,' Sāy.], RV.; a wise person, i, 67, 5; iv, 2, 11; 'Thought,' N. of the wife of Atharvan and mother of Dadhyac, BhP. iv, 1, 42; cf. *á-*, *pūrvá-*, *prāyaś-*.

Cittín, mfn. intelligent, AV. iii, 30, 5.

Cittī-kṛita, mfn. made an object of thought, BhP. iv, 1, 28.

Citrá, mf(*ā́*)n. conspicuous, excellent, distinguished, RV.; bright, clear, bright-coloured, RV.; clear (a sound), RV.; variegated, spotted, speckled (with, instr. or in comp.), Nal. iv, 8; R.; Mṛicch.; VarBṛS.; agitated (as the sea, opposed to *sama*), R. iii, 39, 12; various, different, manifold, Mn. ix, 248; Yājñ. i, 287; MBh. &c.; (execution) having different varieties (of tortures), Mn. ix, 248; Daś. vii, 281; strange, wonderful, Rājat. vi, 227; containing the word *citrá*, ŚBr. vii, 4, 1, 24; KātyŚr. xvii; (*ám*), ind. so as to be bright, RV. i, 71, 1; vi, 65, 2; in different ways, R. i, 9, 14; (to execute) with different tortures, Daś. vii, 380; (*ás*), m. variety of colour, L., Sch.; Plumbago zeylanica, L.; Ricinus communis, L.; Jonesia Aśoka, L.; a form of Yama, Tithyād.; N. of a king, RV. viii, 21, 18 (*citra*); of a Jābāla-gṛihapati (with the patr. Gauśrāyaṇi), KaushBr. xxiii, 5; of a king (with the patr. Gāṅgyāyani), KaushUp. i; of a son of Dhṛita-rāshṭra, MBh. i, vii; of a Draviḍa king, PadmaP. v, 20, 1 (v.l. °*trâksha*); of a Gandharva, Gal.; (*ā́*), f. Spica virginis, the 12th (in later reckoning the 14th) lunar mansion, AV. xix, 7, 3; TS. ii, iv, vii; TBr. i; ŚBr. ii, &c.; a kind of snake, L.; N. of a plant (Salvinia cucullata, L.; Cucumis maderaspatanus, L.; a kind of cucumber, L.; Ricinus communis, L.; Croton polyandrum or Tiglium, L.; the Myrobalan tree, L.; Rubia Munjista, L.; the grass Gaṇḍa-dūrvā, L.), Car. vii, 12 (= *dravantī*); Suśr.; a metre of 4 × 16 syllabic instants; another of 4 × 15 syllables; another of 4 × 16 syllables; a kind of stringed instrument; a kind of Mūrchanā (in music); illusion, unreality, L.; 'born under the asterism Citrā (Pāṇ. iv, 3, 34, Vārtt. 1),' N. of Arjuna's wife (sister of Kṛishṇa, = *subhadrā*, L.), Hariv. 1952; of a daughter of Gada (or Kṛishṇa, v.l.), 9194; of an Apsaras, L.; of a river, Divyâv. xxx; of a rock, BhP. xii, 8, 17; f. pl. the asterism Citrā, VarBṛS. xi, 57; (*ám*), n. anything bright or coloured which strikes the eyes, RV.; VS.; TS.; ŚBr.; TāṇḍyaBr. xviii, 9; a brilliant ornament, ornament, RV. i, 92, 13; ŚBr. ii, xiii; a bright or extraordinary appearance, wonder, ii; Śak.; Pañcat.; Bhartṛ. &c.; (with *yadi* [Śak. iii, $\frac{9}{10}$] or *yad* [Hariv. 9062; Śak.; Kathās. xviii, 359] or fut. [Pāṇ. iii, 3, 150 f.]) strange, curious (e.g. *citraṃ badhiro vyākaraṇam adhyeshyate*, 'it would be strange if a deaf man should learn grammar,' Kāś.); strange! Hariv. 15652; Kathās. v, vii; Rājat. i, iv; the ether, sky, L.; a spot, MBh. xiii, 2605; a sectarial mark on the forehead, L.; = *kushṭha*, L.; a picture, sketch, delineation, MBh.; Hariv. 4532 (*sa-*, mfn. = *-ga*); R.; Śak. &c. (ifc. f. *ā*, Megh. 64); variety of colour, L.; a forest (*vana* for *dhana*?) of variegated appearance, Sch. on KātyŚr. xxi, 3, 23 & ShaḍvBr. ii, 10; various modes of writing or arranging verses in the shape of mathematical or other fanciful figures (syllables which occur repeatedly being left out or words being represented in a shortened form), Sarasv. ii, 16; Kpr. ix, 8; Sāh.; punning in the form of question and answer, facetious conversation, riddle, iv, $\frac{14}{?}$; Pratāpar.; Kuval.; cf. *a-* & *su-citrá*, *dā́nu-*, *vi-*; *caitra*. **-kaṇṭaka**, m. 'having variegated thorns,' Asteracantha longifolia or Tribulus lanuginosus, Npr. **-kaṇṭha**, m. 'speckled-throat,' a pigeon, L. **-kathâlāpa-sukha**, mfn. happy in telling charming stories, W. **-kambala**, m. a variegated carpet or cloth (used as an elephant's housing), L. **-kara**, m. (Pāṇ. iii, 2, 21) a painter (son of an architect by a Śūdra woman, BrahmavP. i; or by a *gāndhikī*, Parāś. Paddh.), VarBṛS.; Kathās. v, 30. **-karṇa**, m. 'speckled-ear,' N. of a camel, W. **-karman**, n. any extraordinary act, wonderful deed, W.; magic, W.; painting, Śak. (in Prākrit) vi, $\frac{4}{?}$ (v.l.); Kathās. lv, 36; a painting, picture, R. vii, 28, 41; VarBṛS.; Kathās. vi, 50; Mn. iii, 64, Sch.; mfn. devoted to various occupations, BhP. x, 5, 25, m. = *-kara*, W.; 'working wonders,' a magician, W.; Dalbergia oujeinensis, L.; °*rma-vid*, mfn. skilled in the art of painting, W.; skilled in magic, W. **-kavi-tva**, n. the art of composing verses called *citra* (q.v.), PSarv. **-kāṇḍâlī**, f. Cissus quadrangularis, Npr. **-kāya**, m. 'striped-body,' a tiger or panther, L. **-kāra**, m. = *-kara*, MBh. v, 5025; R. (G) ii, 90, 18; Sāh.; 'wonder,' astonishment, Lalit. xviii, 134. **-kuṇḍala**, m. N. of a son of Dhṛita-rāshṭra, MBh. i, 4545 ff. **-kushṭha**, n. white or spotted leprosy. **-kūṭa**, m. 'wonderful peak,' N. of a hill and district (the modern Citrakote or Catarkot near Kāmtā, situated on the river Paisuni about 50 miles S.E. of the Bandah in Bundelkhund; first habitation of the exiled Rāma and Lakshmaṇa, crowded with temples as the holiest spot of Rāma's worshippers), MBh. iii, 8200; R. i-iii; Ragh. xii f.; VarBṛS.; BhP.; a pleasure-hill, Daś. viii, 90; n. N. of a town, Kathās.; (*ā*), f. N. of a river, VP.; *-māhātmya*, n. 'glory of Citrakote,' N. of a work. **-kūlā**, f. a kind of Croton, Npr. **-kṛit**, mfn. astonishing, Śatr.; m. = *-kara*, VarBṛS.; Kathās. v, 28; Subh.; Dalbergia oujeinensis, L. **-kṛitya**, n. painting, Kathās. lxxi, 82. **-ketu**, m. N. of a son (of Garuḍa, MBh. v, 3597; of Vasishṭha, BhP. iv, 1, 40 f.; of Kṛishṇa, x, 61, 12; of Lakshmaṇa, ix, 11, 12; of Devabhāga, 24, 39); of a Sūrasena king, vi, 14, 10 ff. **-kola**, m. 'spotted-breast,' a kind of lizard, L. **-kriyā**, f. = *-kṛitya*, MBh. iv, 1360. **-kshatra**, mfn. whose dominion is brilliant (Agni), RV. vi, 6, 7 (voc.) **-ga**, mf(*ā*)n. represented in a picture, Kathās. v, 31. **-gata**, mfn. id., MBh. vi, 1662; Śak. &c. **-gandha**, n. 'of various fragrances,' yellow orpiment, L. **-gu**, m. 'possessing brindled cows,' N. of a son of Kṛishṇa, BhP. x, 61, 13. **-gupta**, m. N. of one of Yama's attendants (recorder of every man's good & evil deeds), MBh. xiii; SkandaP.; NārP.; VārP; Bādar. iii, 1, 15, Sch.; Kathās. lxxii; (also *candra-g*°, W.); a secretary of a man of rank (kind of mixed caste); a form of Yama, Tithyād.; N. of the 16th Arhat of the future Utsarpiṇī, Jain. L.; of an author (?). **-gṛiha**, n. a painted room or one ornamented with pictures, RV. **-grāvan**, mfn. stony, Daś. xi, 114. **-grīva**, m. (= *-kaṇṭha*) N. of a pigeon-king, Pañcat. ii, $\frac{3}{?}$; Kathās. lxi; Hit. **-ghnī**, f. 'removing spotted leprosy,' N. of a river, Hariv. 9516 (v.l. *mitra-ghnā*). **-cāpa**, m. 'having a variegated bow,' N. of a son of Dhṛita-rāshṭra, MBh. i, 2733. **-ja**, mf(*ā*)n. prepared with various substances, Hcat. **-jalpa**, m. talking on various things. **-jña**, mfn. skilled in composing verses called *citra* (Sch.; or 'skilled in painting?'), R. vii, 94, 9. **-taṇḍula**, m. Embelia Ribes, L.; (*ā*), f. id., Bhpr. v, 1, 112. **-tanu**, m. 'having a speckled body,' the partridge, Npr. **-tala**, mfn. painted or variegated on the surface, W. **-tāla**, m. (in music) a kind of measure. **-tūlikā**, f. a painter's brush, Kād. **-tvac**, m. 'having variegated bark,' the birch, L. **-daṇḍaka**, m. the cotton plant, L. **-darśana**, m. 'variegated-eyed,' N. of a Brāhman changed into a bird, Hariv. (v.l. *chidra-d*°). **-dīpa**, m. N. of a chapter (*prakaraṇa*) of the Pañcadaśī. **-dṛiśīka**, mfn. looking brilliant, RV. vi, 47, 5. **-deva**, m. N. of one of Skanda's attendants, MBh. ix, 2573; (*ī*), f. Mahendra-vāruṇī, L. **-dhara**, m. N. of an author. **-dharman**, m. N. of a prince (identified with the Asura Virūpâksha), i, 2659. **-dhā**, ind. in a manifold way, BhP. iii, vi, x. **-dhrajati** (°*trá-*), mfn. having a bright course (Agni), RV. vi, 3, 5. **-dhvaja**, m. (= *-ketu*) N. of a man, SaddhP. xxiv. **-nātha**, m. N. of a son of Dhṛishṭa, MatsyaP. xii, 21. **-netrā**, f. 'variegated-eyed,' the bird Sārikā, L. **-nyasta**, mfn. = *-ga*, MBh. ix, 43; Kum. ii, 24; Vikr. (v.l.) **-paksha**, m. 'speckled-wing,' = *-tanu*, L.; a kind of pigeon (cf. *-kaṇṭha*), Bhpr. v, 10, 69; N. of a demon causing head-ache, PārGṛ. iii, 6, 3. **-paṭa**, m. a painting, picture, Hariv. 16001; Daś.; Kathās. **-paṭṭa**, m. id., Hariv. 10069; *-gata*, mfn. = *citra-ga*, 9987. **-paṭṭikā**, f. = °*ṭṭa*, W. **-pattra**, m. 'speckled-leaved,' Betula Bhojpatra, Npr.; (*ī*), f. Commelina salicifolia, L. **-pattraka**, m. 'having variegated feathers,' a peacock, Npr.; (*ikā*), f. the plant Kapittha-parṇī, L.; Droṇa-pushpī, L. **-pada**, mfn. full of various (or graceful) words and expressions, MBh. iii, 1160; BhP. i, 5, 10; n. a metre of 4 × 23 syllables; (*ā*), f. Cissus pedata, L.; a metre of 4 × 8 syllables; *-kramam*, ind. at a good or brisk pace, W. **-parṇikā**, f. 'speckled-leaved,' Hemionitis cordifolia, L. **-parṇī**, f. id., L.; Rubia Munjista, L.; Gynandropsis pentaphylla (v.l. *-varṇī*), L.; = *-pattrī*, L.; the plant Droṇa-pushpī, L. **-pāṭala**, N. of a plant, Buddh. L. **-pādā**, f. 'speckled-footed,' = *-netrā*, L. **-piccha**, m. = *-pattraka*, Gal. **-picchaka**, m. id., L. **-puṅkha**, m. 'having variegated-feathers,' an arrow, L. **-putrikā**, f. a female portrait, Kathās. lxxii, cxxii; °*kāyita*, mfn. resembling a female portrait, Siṇhâs. **-pura**, n. N. of a town, Durgāv. xii. **-pushpī**, f. 'variegated-blossomed,' Hibiscus cannabinus, L. **-pṛishṭha**, mfn. having a speckled back, Car. i, 27; m. a sparrow, L. **-pratikṛiti**, f. 'representation in colours,' a painting, Hariv. 7812. **-priya-katha**, mfn. speaking various kind words, W. **-phala**, m. the fish Mystus Citala, L.; Cucumis sativus, L.; (*ā*, *ī*), f. the fish Mystus Karpirat, L.; (*ā*), f. N. of several plants (*cirbhiṭā*, *mṛigêrvāru*, *citra-devī*, *vārtākī*, *kaṇṭakārī*), L. **-phalaka**, m. a tablet for painting, Kathās. cxvii, 24; a painting, Śak., Vikr. & Ratnâv. (in Prākrit); Ratnâv. & Kathās. (ifc. f. *ā*); Sāh. **-barha**, m. = *-piccha*, MBh. ii, 2103; N. of a son of Garuḍa, v, 3597; (cf. °*hin*.) **-barhin**, mfn. having a variegated tail (a peacock, son of Garuḍa), xiii, 4306. **-barhis** (°*trá-*), mfn. having a brilliant bed (of stars; the moon), RV. i, 23, 13 f. **-bala-gaccha**, m. N. of a Jain Gaccha. **-bāṇa**, m. 'having variegated arrows,' N. of a son of Dhṛita-rāshṭra, MBh. i, 4545. **-bāhu**, m. 'speckled-arm,' N. of a son of Dhṛita-rāshṭra, 2732; of a Gandharva, Bālar. iv, 8; of a man, BhP. x, 90, 34. **-bīja**, m. 'having variegated seeds,' red Ricinus, L.; (*ā*), f. = *-taṇḍula*, L. **-bhānu** (°*trá-*), mfn. of variegated lustre, shining with light, RV; AV. iv, 25, 3; xiii, 3, 10; TBr. ii f.; Kauś.; MBh. i, 722; N. of fire, MBh.; Hariv.; R.; BhP.; Sāh.; = °*trârcis*, L.; Plumbago zeylanica, L.; Calotropis gigantea, L.; the 16th year in the 60 years' cycle of Jupiter, VarBṛS. viii, 35; Romakas.; N. of Bhairava, L.; of a prince, VP. iv, 16, 2 (v.l.); of Bāṇa (-bhaṭṭa)'s father. **-bhārata**, n. N. of a work. **-bhāshya**, n. eloquence, MBh. v, 1240. **-bhitti**, f. a painted wall, picture on a wall, MaitrUp.; Mṛicch.; Kathās. **-bhūta**, mfn. painted or decorated, MBh. xiv, 281. **-bheshajā**, f. 'yielding various remedies,' Ficus oppositifolia, L. **-mañca**, m. (in music) a kind of measure. **-maṇḍala**, m. 'forming a variegated circle,' a kind of snake, Suśr. v, 4, 33. **-manas**, m. N. of a horse of the moon, VāyuP. **-mahas** (°*trá-*), mfn. = °*trá-magha*, RV. x, 122, 1; m. N. of the author of x, 122, RAnukr. **-mīmāṇsā**, f. N. of a work on rhet.; *-khaṇḍana*, n. 'refutation of the Citra-mīmāṇsā,' N. of a work. **-mṛiga**, m. the spotted antelope, R. v, 20, 11; Mn. iii, 269, Sch. **-mekhala**, °**laka**, m. = *-piccha*, L. **-yajña**, m. N.

of a comedy by Vaidya-nātha. **-yāna**, m. N. of a prince, Daṭhādh. ii. **-yāma** (°*trá-*), mfn. = *dhra-jati*, RV. iii, 2, 13. **-yodhin**, mfn. fighting in various ways, MBh.; Hariv. 6867; m. Arjuna, L.; Terminalia Arjuna, L.; a quail, Npr. **-rañjaka**, n. tin, Npr. **-ratha** (°*trá-*), mfn. having a bright chariot (Agni), RV. x, 1, 5; m. the sun, L.; the polar star (Dhruva), BhP. iv, 10, 22; N. of a man, RV. iv, 30, 18; the king of the Gandharvas, AV. viii, 10, 27; MBh.; Hariv.; Vikr.; Kād.; BhP.; N. of a king, TāṇḍyaBr. xx, 12; Pañcat.; of a king of the Aṅgas, MBh. xiii, 2351; of a descendant of Aṅga and son of Dharma-ratha, Hariv. 1695 ff.; BhP. ix, 23, 6; of a snake-demon, Kauś. 74; of a son (of Gada or Kṛishṇa, Hariv. 9193; of Ushadgu or Ruśeku, MBh. xiii, 6834; Hariv. 1971; BhP. ix, 23, 30; of Vṛishṇi, 24, 14 & 17; of Gaja, v, 15, 2; of Supārśvaka, ix, 13, 23; of Ukta or Ushṇa, 22, 39); of a prince of Mṛittikāvatī, MBh. iii, 11076 (cf. BhP. ix, 16, 3); of a Sūta, R. ii, 32, 17; of an officer, Rājat. viii, 1438; of a Vidyā-dhara, L.; (*ā*), f. N. of a river, MBh. vi, 341; (*ī*), f. a form of Durgā, Hariv. ii, 109, 48; cf. *caitraratha; -bā-hlīka*, n. sg., g. *rājadantâdi*. **-raśmi**, m. 'having variegated rays,' N. of a Marut, 11546. **-rāti** (°*trá-*), mfn. granting excellent gifts, RV. vi, 62, 5 & 11. **-rādhas** (°*trá-*), mfn. id., RV. viii, 11, 9; x, 65, 3; AV. i, 26, 2. **-rekhā**, f. N. of a Surāṅganā, Siṇhâs. **-repha**, m. N. of a son of Medhātithi (king of Śāka-dvīpa), BhP. v, 20, 25. **-latā**, f. Rubia Munjista, L.; N. of an Apsaras, Bālar. iv, 6. **-likhana**, n. painting, Mn. ii, 240, Sch. **-likhita**, mfn. painted, Kathās. cxxii, 44. **-lekhaka**, m. = *-kara*, Pāṇ. iv, 2, 128, Sch. (not in Kāś.) **-lekhanikā**, f. = *-tūlikā*, Uṇ. iv, 93, Sch. **-lekhā**, f. a picture, portrait, Gīt. x, 15; two metres of 4 × 17 syllables; another of 4 × 18 syllables; N. of an Apsaras (skilful in painting), MBh.; Hariv.; of a daughter of Kumbhâṇḍa, 9930; BhP. x, 62, 14. **-locanā**, f. = *-netrā*, L. **-vat**, mfn. decorated with paintings, Ragh. xiv, 25; Hcar. v, 71; containing the word *citra*, TāṇḍyaBr. xviii, 6; ŚāṅkhŚr. xv; (*tī*), f. a metre of 4 × 13 syllables; N. of a daughter of Kṛishṇa or Gada, Hariv. 9194. **-vadāla**, m. the fish Silurus pelorius, L. **-vana**, n. 'of variegated appearance (see s. v. *citrá*),' N. of a wood near the Gaṇḍakī, Hit. i, 2, $\frac{3}{4}$; cf. *citraka*. **-varṇī**, see *-parṇī*. **-vartikā**, f. = *-tūlikā*, Kād.; Mālatīm. i, $\frac{3}{4}$. **-vartinī**, f. a kind of medicament (*reṇukā*), Npr. **-varman**, m. 'having a variegated cuirass,' N. of a son of Dhṛita-rāshṭra, MBh. i, v, vii; of a king (of the Kulūtas), Mudr. i, 20; v, $\frac{9}{10}$; of Campāvatī and Mathurā, BrahmôttKh. xvi. **-varshin**, mfn. raining in an unusual manner, Hariv. 11145. **-valayā**, f. 'having a variegated bracelet,' N. of a goddess, BrahmaP. ii, 18, 15. **-vallika**, m. the fish Silurus boalis, L. **-vallī**, f. = *-devī*, L.; Cucumis coloquintha, L. **-vahā**, f. 'having a wonderful current,' N. of a river, MBh. vi, 325; xiii, 7652. **-vāja** (°*trá-*), mfn. having wonderful riches (the Maruts), RV. viii, 7, 33; decorated with variegated feathers (an arrow), BhP. iv; m. a cock, L. **-vāhana**, m. 'having decorated vehicles,' N. of a king of Maṇi-pura, MBh. i, 7826; (cf. *caitra-vāhanī*.) **-vicitra**, mfn. variously coloured, W.; multiform, W. **-vidyā**, f. the art of painting, W. **-vīrya**, m. = *-bīja* (v.l.?), L. **-vṛitti**, f. any astonishing act or practice, W. **-vegika**, m. 'having a wonderful velocity,' N. of a Nāga, MBh. i, 2159. **-vesha**, m. 'having a variegated dress,' Śiva. **-vyāghra**, m. 'striped tiger,' a leopard, L. **-śākâpūpa-bhakshya-vikāra-kriyā**, f. the art of preparing various kinds of pot-herbs, sweetmeats and other eatables (one of the 64 Kalās). **-śālā**, f. = *-gṛiha*, R. iii, v; Kād.; a metre of 4 × 18 syllables. **-śālikā**, f. = *-gṛiha*, Ratnâv. iii, $\frac{1}{2}$ (in Prākṛit). **-śikhaṇḍa-dhara**, m. wearing various tufts of hair (Vishṇu), Vishṇ. iic, 65. **-śikhaṇḍin**, m. pl. 'bright-crested,' the 7 Ṛishis (Marīci, Atri, Aṅgiras, Pulastya, Pulaha, Kratu, Vasishṭha [MBh. xii; Bālar. x, 98; Viśvā-mitra, i, 27]), Rājat. i, 55; °*ṇḍi-ja*, m. 'son of Aṅgiras,' the planet Jupiter, L.; °*ṇḍi-prasūta*, m. id., L. **-śiras**, m. = *-śīrshaka*, Suśr. v, 3, 7; N. of a Gandharva, Hariv. 14156. **-śilā**, f. 'stony,' N. of a river, MBh. vi, 9, 30. **-śīrshaka**, m. 'speckled-head,' a kind of venomous insect, Suśr. v, 8, 4. **-śoka**, m. Jonesia Asoka, Npr. **-śocis** (°*trá-*), mfn. shining brilliantly, RV. v, 17, 2; vi, 10, 3; viii, 19, 2. **-śravas-tama** (°*trá-*), mfn. (superl.) having most wonderful fame, i, iii, viii. **-saṃstha**, mfn. = *-ga*, W. **-saṅga**, n. a metre of 4 × 16 syllables. **-sarpa**, m. the large speckled snake (*mālu-dhāna*), L. **-sena** (°*trá-*), mfn. having a bright spear, vi, 75, 9; m. N. of a snake-demon, Kauś. 74; of a leader of the Gandharvas (son of Viśvā-vasu), MBh.; Hariv. 7224; of a son (of Dhṛita-rāshṭra, MBh. i, v, viii; of Parikshit, i, 3743; of Śambara, Hariv. 9251 & 9280; of Narishyanta, BhP. ix, 2, 19; of the 13th Manu, Hariv. 889; BhP. viii, 13, 31; of Gada or Kṛishṇa, Hariv. 9194); of an adversary of Kṛishṇa, 5059; of Tarā-sandha's general (Ḍimbhaka), MBh. ii, 885 f.; of a divine recorder of the deeds of men, Ācāranirṇ.; (= *-gupta*) the secretary of a man of rank, W.; N. of a scholiast on Piṅgala's work on metres; (*ā*), f. N. of an Apsaras, MBh.; Hariv. 12691; of one of the mothers in Skanda's retinue, MBh. ix, 2632; of a courtesan, Vātsyāy. ii, 7, 30; of a river, MBh. vi, 325; (cf. *caitraseni*.) **-stha**, mfn. = *-ga*, Hariv. 7919; Kathās. **-sthala**, n. N. of a garden, Kathās. lxxiii, 39. **-svana**, m. 'clear-voice,' N. of a Rākshasa, BhP. xii, 11, 36. **-hasta**, m. pl. particular movements of the hands in fighting, MBh. ii, 902. **Citrâkṛiti**, f. a painted resemblance, portrait, picture, W. **Citrâksha**, m. 'speckled-eye,' N. of a son of Dhṛita-rāshṭra, i, vii; of a king, VāyuP. ii, 37, 268 (v.l.); of a Draviḍa king, v.l. for *citra*, q.v.; of a Nāga-rāja, Buddh. L.; (*ī*), f. = *-netrā*, L. **Citrā-kshupa**, m. (= °*tra-pattrikā*) the plant Droṇa-pushpī, L. **Citrâṅga**, mfn. having a variegated body, Buddh. L.; m. a kind of snake, L.; Plumbago rosea, L.; N. of a son of Dhṛita-rāshṭra, MBh. i, 4545; PadmaP. iv, 55; of an antelope, Pañcat.; Hit.; of a dog, Pañcat.; n. vermilion, L.; yellow orpiment, L.; (*ī*), f. an ear-wig (Julus cornifex), L.; Rubia munjista, L.; N. of a courtesan, Kathās. cxxii, 68; *-sādana*, m. 'Citrâṅga-killer,' Arjuna, L. **Citrâṅgada**, mfn. decorated with variegated bracelets, MBh. ii, 348; m. N. of a king of Daśârṇa, MBh. xiv, 2471; of a son (of Śāntanu, i; Hariv. ix, 22, 20; of Indra-sena, v. l., see *candrâṅg°*); of a Gandharva (person of the play Dūtâṅgada); of a Vidyā-dhara, Kathās. xxii, 136; of a divine recorder of men's deeds, Ācāranirṇ.; (= *-gupta*) the secretary of a man of rank, W.; (*ā*), f. N. of an Apsaras, MBh. xiii, 1424; of a wife of Arjuna (daughter of Citra-vāhana and mother of Babhru-vāhana), i, xiv; *-sū*, f. 'Citrâṅgada's mother,' Satyavatī (mother of Vyāsa), L. **Citrâṭīra**, m. (= °*trêśa*) the moon, L.; the forehead spotted with the blood of a goat offered to the demon Ghaṇṭā-karṇa, L. **Citrâṇḍaja**, m. a variegated bird, VarYogay. vi, 18. **Citrânna**, n. rice dressed with coloured condiments, Yājñ. i, 303. **Citrâpūpa**, m. speckled cake, L. **Citrā-pūrṇa-māsá**, m. the full moon standing in the asterism Citrā, TS. vii, 4. **Citrā́-magha**, mf(*ā*)n. granting wonderful gifts, RV. (Naigh. i, 8). **Citrâyasa**, n. steel, L. **Citrâyudha**, m. 'having variegated weapons,' N. of a son of Dhṛita-rāshṭra, MBh. i f., vii. **Citrâyus**, mfn. possessed of wonderful vitality, RV. vi, 49, 7. **Citrârambha**, mfn. = °*tra-ga*, Vikr. i, 4. **Citrârcis**, m. the sun, Gal. **Citrârpita**, mfn. = °*tra-ga*, Śak.; Mālav.; Rājat. v, 359; (*citrair arp°*, MBh. xiii, 2660); °*târambha*, mfn. id., Ragh. ii, 31; Kum. iii, 42. **Citrā́-vasu**, mfn. rich in (brilliant ornaments i.e.) shining stars, VS. iii, 18 (TS. i; Kāṭh. vii, 6); ŚBr. ii; n. (scil. *yajus*) the verse VS. iii, 18, ĀpŚr. vi, 16, 10. **Citrâśva**, m. 'having painted horses,' Satyavat (as fond of painting horses), MBh. **Citrâsaṅga**, mfn. having a variegated cloak, Baudh. **Citrâstaraṇa-vat**, mfn. covered with various or variegated carpets, R. iv, 44, 99. **Citrā-svātī**, g. *rājadantâdi*. **Citrêśa**, m. 'lord of Citrā,' the moon, L. **Citrôkti**, f. a marvellous or heavenly voice, L.; a surprising tale, W.; eloquent discourse, W. **Citrôti**, mfn. = °*trá-magha*, RV. x, 140, 3. **Citrôtpalā**, f. 'having various lotus-flowers,' N. of a river, Purushôtt. **Citrôpalā**, f. 'stony,' N. of a river, MBh. vi, 341. **Citrâudana**, m. n. °*trânna*, Grahay.

Citraka, m. a painter, L.; = °*tra-kāya*, MBh. vii, 1320 (*cillaka*, C); Pañcat.; a kind of snake, Suśr. v, 4, 33; (in alg.) the 8th unknown quantity; Plumbago zeylanica, i, 38; iv; Ricinus communis, L.; N. of a son (of Vṛishṇi or Pṛiśni, Hariv.; of Dhṛita-rāshṭra, MBh. i, 2740); of a Nāga, L., Sch.; (pl.) of a people, ii, 1804; n. a mark (only ifc. 'marked or characterised by,' TBr. i, 1, 9, 5, Sch.); a sectarial mark on the forehead, L.; a painting, Hariv. 7074; a particular manner of fighting (cf. °*tra-hasta*), 15979 (v.l. *cakraka*); N. of a wood near the mountain Raivataka, 8952.

Citraṭa, = °*tra-rañjaka*, Npr.

Citraya, Nom. °*yati*, 'to make variegated,' decorate, MBh. xii, 988; to regard as a wonder, Dhātup. xxxv, 63 (Vop.); to throw a momentary glance, ib.; to look, ib.; to be a wonder, ib.

Citrala, mfn. variegated, L.; m. = °*tra-mṛiga*, L.; (*ā*), f. the plant Go-rakshī, L.

Citrika, m. (fr. *citrā́*) the month Caitra, L.

Citrita, mfn. made variegated, decorated, painted, MBh. ii, vi; Hariv. 8945; Suśr. &c.; cf. *vi-*.

Citrin, mfn. having variegated (black and grey) hair, VarBṛS. lxxvii, $\frac{1}{8}$, 6; (*iṇyas*), f. pl. (the dawns) wearing bright ornaments, RV. iv, 32, 2; (*iṇī*), f. a woman endowed with various talents (one of the four divisions into which women are classed), Siṇhâs. vi, $\frac{1}{2}$; (pl.) N. of certain bricks, Nyāyam.

Citriya, mfn. visible at a distance (a species of Aśvattha), TBr. i; m. N. of a man, Rājat. viii, 2181.

Citrī, ind. for °*tra*. **-karaṇa**, n. making variegated, decorating, painting, Dhātup. xxxv, 63; surprise, Pāṇ. iii, 3, 150. **-kāra**, m. id., Lalit. xix, 102. **-kṛita**, mfn. changed into a picture, Śak. vi, 21.

Citrīya, Nom. °*yate* (Pāṇ. iii, 1, 19) to be surprised, Hcar. vii; Mcar.; Bālar.; Prasannar.; Kathās.; (Vop. xxi, 23) to cause surprise, Bhaṭṭ.; (cf. *ati-*).

Citrīyā, f. surprise, Daś. xi, 32.

Citrya, mfn. brilliant, RV. v, 63, 7; vii, 20, 7.

1. **Cid**, in comp. for *cit*. **-acit**, 'thought and non-thought, mind and matter,' in comp.; °*cic-chakti-yukta*, mfn. having power (*śakti*) over mind and matter, W.; °*cin-maya*, mfn. consisting of mind and matter, BhP. xi, 24, 7. **-ambara**, m. N. of the author of a law-book; n. N. of a town, W.; *-pura*, n. id.; *-rahasya*, n. N. of a work; *-sthala*, n. = *-pura*, Śaṃkar. iv, 7. **-asthi-mālā**, f. N. of a Comm. on a grammatical work. **-ātmaka**, mfn. consisting of pure thought, BhP. viii, 3, 2. **-ātman**, m. pure thought or intelligence, i, 3, 30; RāmatUp.; Prab. **-ānanda**, 'thought and joy,' in comp.; *-daśa-ślokī*, f. ten verses in praise of thought and joy; *-maya*, mfn. consisting of thought and joy, RāmatUp.; *-stava-rāja*, m. = *-daśa-ślokī*; °*ndâśrama*, m. N. of a teacher (= *paramânand°*). **-ullāsa**, mfn. shining like thoughts, BhP. ix, 11, 33. **-gagana-candrikā**, f. N. of a work, Ānand. i, Sch. **-ghana**, m. = *-ātman*, Sarvad. viii, 78. **-ratna-cashaka**, N. of a work. **-ratha**, m. N. of a Sāman, ĀrshBr.; (*ī*), f. N. of a Comm. **-rūpa**, mfn. (Vop. ii, 37) = *cin-maya*, KapS. vi, 50; NṛisUp. (*-tva*, n. abstr.); Sarvad.; wise, L.; n. the Universal Spirit as identified with pure thought, W. **-vilāsa**, m. N. of a pupil of Śaṃkarâcārya, Śaṃkar. iv, 5. **-vṛitti**, f. spiritual action, Daśar. ii, 37.

Cin, in comp. for *cit*. **-maya**, mfn. consisting of pure thought, RāmatUp.; Sarvad. ix, 71 f.; Sāh. iii, 2. **-mātra**, mfn. id., KaivUp. 17; Vedântas. 168.

Cékitāna, mfn., see √4. *cit*, Intens.; intelligent (Śiva), MBh. vii, xiii; m. N. of a prince (ally of the Pāṇḍus), i f., v; Bhag. i, 5; Hariv. 5013 & 5494.

Cet, Nom. (fr. *cétas*) °*tati* (Vop. xxi, 8; aor. 3. pl. *acetishur*) to recover consciousness, Bhaṭṭ. xv, 109.

Cetaḥ, in comp. = °*tas*. **-pīḍā**, f. grief, L.

Cetaka, mfn. causing to think, W.; sentient, W.; (*ī*), f. = °*tanikā*, L.; Jasminum grandiflorum, L.

Cétana, mf(*ī*)n. visible, conspicuous, distinguished, excellent, RV.; AV. ix, 4, 21; percipient, conscious, sentient, intelligent, KaṭhUp. v, 13; ŚvetUp. vi, 13; Hariv. 3587; KapS.; Tattvas. &c.; m. an intelligent being, man, Sarvad. ii, 221; soul, mind, L.; n. conspicuousness, RV. i, 13, 11 & 170, 4; iii, 3, 8; iv, 7, 2; soul, mind, R. vii, 55, 17 & 20; (*ā*), f. consciousness, understanding, sense, intelligence, Yājñ. iii, 175; MBh. &c. (often ifc. [f. *ā*], Mn. ix, 67; MBh. &c.); (cf. *a-, niś-, puru-cét°, vi-, sa-, sú-*). **-tā**, f. the state of a sentient or conscious being, intelligence. **-tva**, n. id., Sarvad. vii, 8, Kum. iii, 39, Sch.; KapS. i, 100, Sch. **-bhāva**, m. id., Bādar. ii, 1, 6, Sch. **Cetanâcetana**, pl. sentient and unsentient beings, Megh. 5. **Cetanā-vat**, mfn. having consciousness, knowing, understanding, reasonable, Nir.; MBh. xii, xiv; Sāṃkhyak.; Suśr. **Cetanâshṭaka**, n. N. of a work.

Cetanakā, °*nakī*, f. = °*nikā*, L.

Cetanikā, f. Terminalia Chebula, L.

Cetanī, ind. for °*na*. **-√kṛi**, to cause to perceive or become conscious, BhP. viii, 1, 9, Sch. **-√bhū**, to become conscious, ib.

Cetanīyā, f. the medicinal herb *ṛiddhi*, L.

Cetaya, mfn. sentient, Pāṇ. iii, 1, 138.

Cetayāna, mfn. (irreg. pr. p.) having sense, reasonable, MBh. iii, v, viii; R. ii, 109, 7.

Cetayitavya, mfn. to be perceived, PraśnUp.

Cetayitṛi, mfn. = °*ya*, MBh. xii; ŚvetUp., Sch.

Cétas, n. splendour, RV.; (Naigh. iii, 9) consciousness, intelligence, thinking soul, heart, mind, VS. xxxiv, 3; AV.; Mn. ix, xii; MBh. &c. (ifc. KaṭhUp.; Mn. &c.); will, AV. vi, 116, 3; TBr. iii, 1, 1, 7; cf. *a-cetás, dabhrá-, prá-, laghu-, ví-, sá-, su-cétas*.

Cetasaka, m. pl. N. of a people, MBh. vii, 2095.

Cetasam, ind. ifc. fr. °*tas*, Vop. vi, 62.

Cetāya, Nom. (fr. °*tas*), °*yate*, xxi, 8.

Cétishṭha, mfn. (fr. *céttṛi*) most attentive (with gen.), RV. i, 65, 9 & 128, 8; v, vii; x, 21, 7; (fr. *citrá*) most conspicuous, viii, 46, 20; VS. xxvii, 15.

Cetī, ind. in comp. for °*tas*. — √**kṛi**, Vop. vii, 84.

Cetú, m. heedfulness, RV. ix, 81, 3.

Ceto, in comp. for °*tas*. — **bhava**, m. = *citta-ja*, L., Sch. — **bhū**, m. id., Mālatīm.; Bālar.; Vcar. xi, 94. — **mat**, mfn. endowed with consciousness, living, MBh. iii, 8676. — **mukha**, mfn. one whose mouth is intelligence, MāṇḍUp. — **vikāra**, m. disturbance of mind, Suśr.; Mn. i, 25, Sch. — **vikārin**, mfn. disturbed in mind, Suśr. i, 46, 4, 4. — **hara**, mf(*ā*)n. captivating the heart, Bhām. iii, 10.

Céttṛi, mfn. attentive, guardian, RV. x, 128, 9 (see also s.v. √4. *cit*); AV. iv & vi (*cettṛ́*); TS. i f.

Cétya, mfn. perceivable, RV. vi, 1, 5; (*ā́*), f. = *tú* (?), x, 89, 14.

चित् 6. *cit*, ind. only in comp. — **kāra**, for *cīt-k°*; *-vat*, for *cīt-k°*; *-śabda*, m. = *cītkāra*, W.

2. **Citti**, f. crackling, i, 164, 29.

चित *citá*, 1. *cití*. See √1. *ci*.

चिति 2. *cití*. See √4. *cit*.

चितिका *citikā*, °*ti*, °*tika*. See √1. *ci*.

चित्कणकन्थ *citkaṇa-kantha*. See *cikk°*.

चित्कार *cit-kāra*. See 6. *cit*.

चित्त *cittá*. See √4. *cit*.

चित्तल *cittala*, mf(*ā*)n. (fr. *citrala*) moderate, Kṛishis. ii, 1; vii, 10.

चित्ति 1. *citti*, 2. *cittí*. See √4. *cit* & 6. *cit*.

Cittín, °**ttī**. See √4. *cit*.

चित्य *cítya*. See √1. *ci*.

चित्र *citrá*, °*traka*, °*traṭa*, &c. See √4. *cit*.

चिद् 2. *cid*, ind. even, indeed, also (often merely laying stress on a preceding word; requiring a preceding simple verb to be accentuated [Pāṇ. viii, 1, 57] as well as a verb following, if *cid* is preceded by an interrogative pron. [48]; in Class. only used after interrogative pronouns and adverbs to render them indefinite, and after *jātu*, q. v.), RV.; VS.; AV.; like (added to the stem of a subst., e.g. *agni-, rāja-*), Nir. i, 4; Pāṇ. viii, 2, 101; *cid—cid* or *cid—ca* or *cid—u*, as well as, both—and, RV.

चिन्त् *cint* (cf. √4. *cit*), cl. 10. °*tayati* (cl. 1. °*tati*, Dhātup. xxxii, 2; metrically also °*tayate*, see also °*tayāna*) to think, have a thought or idea, reflect, consider, MBh.; R. &c.; to think about, reflect upon, direct the thoughts towards, care for (acc.; exceptionally dat. or loc. or *prati*), Mn. iv, vii f.; Yājñ. i; MBh. &c.; to find out, R. i, 63, 27; Hit.; to take into consideration, treat of, Sāṃkhyak. 69; to consider as or that, tax (with double acc. or acc. and *iti*), Hariv. 14675; R. v, 67, 7; Mālav.; Pāṇ. ii, 3, 17, Kāś.

Cintaka, mfn. ifc. one who thinks or reflects upon, familiar with (e.g. *daiva-, vaṇśa-*, &c., qq. vv.), Gaut.; Mn. vii, 121; MBh.; Hariv.; R.; Pañcat.; m. an overseer, Divyâv.; N. of the 23rd Kalpa period, VāyuP. i, 21, 48 f.; cf. *kārya-, graha-, megha-*.

Cintana, n. thinking, thinking of, reflecting upon; anxious thought, Mn. xii, 5; MBh.; Kathās.; Rājat. v, 205; Sāh.; consideration, Sarvad. x; xii, 6 ff.

Cintanīya, mfn. to be thought of or investigated, VarBṛS. xliii, 37; Pañcat. 1, $\frac{1}{2}$; iii; BhP. viii, 11, 38.

Cintayāna, mfn. (irr. pr. p.) reflecting, considering, MBh. ii, 1748; iii, 12929; Pañcat. iv, $\frac{14}{15}$. **Cintayitavya**, mfn. to be thought of, Mālav. ii, $\frac{13}{14}$.

Cintā, f. (Pāṇ. iii, 3, 105), thought, care, anxiety, anxious thought about (gen., loc., *upari*, or in comp.), Mn. xii, 31; Yājñ. i, 98; MBh. &c. (°*tayā*, instr. 'by mere thinking of,' VP. i, 13, 50); consideration, Sarvad. xii f.; N. of a woman, Rājat. viii, 3453. — **karman**, n. troubled thoughts, L. — **kārin**, mfn. considering, regarding, L. — °**kula** (°*tâk°*), mfn. disturbed in thought, W. — **kṛitya**, ind. p., g. *sākshād-ādi* (v.l. *cittā-*, Gaṇar. 98, Sch.) — **para**, mfn. lost in thought, Nal. ii, 2; xii, 86. — **bhara**, m. a heap of cares, Siṇhâs. — **maṇi**, m. 'thought-gem,' a fabulous gem supposed to yield its possessor all desires, Hariv. 8702; Śāntiś.; Bhartṛ. &c.; Brahmā, L.; N. of various treatises (e. g. one on astrol. by Daśa-bala) and commentaries (esp. also ifc.); of a Buddha, L.; of an author; f. N. of a courtesan, Kṛishṇakarṇ., Sch.; *-catur-mukha*, m. N. of a medicine prepared with mercury, L.; *-tīrtha*, n. N. of a Tīrtha, W.; *-vara-locana*, m. N. of a Samādhi, Kāraṇḍ. xvii, 9. — **maya**, mfn. 'consisting of mere idea,' imagined, BhP. ii, 2, 12; AgP. xxx, 28; ifc. produced by thinking of, R. ii, 85, 16. — **yajña**, m. a thought-sacrifice, MBh. xiv, 2863. — **ratna**, n. = *-maṇi*, only in °*tnāyita*, n. impers. represented as a gem yielding all desires, Siṇhâs. — **vat**, mfn. = *-para*, W. — **veśman**, n. a council room, L. **Cintôkti**, f. midnight cry, W.

Cintita, mfn. thought, considered, W.; thought of, imagined, Pañcat.; Vet.; found out, investigated, Nal. xix, 4; Hit. (*su-*); treated of, Madhus.; reflecting, considering, W.; n. thought, reflection, care, trouble, VarBṛS. li, 24; Dhūrtas.; intention, R. i; (*ā*), f., see *caintita*. **Cintitôpanata**, mfn. thought of and immediately present, Kathās. xviii, 329. **Cintitôpasthita**, mfn. id., 116 & 146.

Cintiti, f. = *cintā*, thought, care, L. **Cintin**, mfn. ifc. thinking of, Naish. viii, 17. **Cintiyā**, f. = °*titi*, L.

Cintya, mfn. to be thought about or imagined, ŚvetUp. vi, 2; Bhag. x, 17; = °*tayitavya*, R. iv, 17, 56 & 23, 4; 'to be conceived,' see *á-*; to be considered or reflected or meditated upon, ŚvetUp. i, 2; Yājñ. i, 344; MBh. &c.; 'to be deliberated about,' questionable, Siddh. on Pāṇ. vii, 2, 19 & 3, 66; Sāh. i, $\frac{2}{3}$, 17 & 50; n. the necessity of thinking about (gen.), BhP. vii, 5, 49. — **dyota**, m. pl. 'of brightness conceivable only by imagination,' a class of deities, MBh. xiii, 1373. — **saṃgraha**, m. N. of a work.

चिन्ति *cinti*, m. pl. 'N. of a people,' in comp. — **surāshṭra**, m. pl. the Cintis and the inhabitants of Su-rāshṭra, g. *kārta-kaujapâdi*.

चिन्तिडी *cintiḍī*, for *tint°*, L.

चिन्न *cinna*, m. for *cina*, q. v., L.

चिपट *cipaṭa*, mfn. flat-nosed, L.

Cipiṭa, mf(*ā*)n. blunted, flattened, flat, VarBṛS.; Naish. vii, 65; pressed close to the head (the ears), v.l. for *carpaṭa*, q.v.; = °*paṭa*, Pāṇ. v, 2, 33; m. a kind of venomous insect, Suśr. v f.; = °*ṭaka*, L.; (*ā*), f. a kind of grass, L.; cf. *piccita*. — **grīva**, mfn. short-necked, VarBṛS. lxviii, 31. — **ghrāṇa**, mfn. flat-nosed, Kathās. lxi, 15; cxxiii. — **nāsa**, mfn. id., VarBṛS. lxviii, 61. — **nāsika**, mf(*ā*)n. id., Kathās. xx, 108; m. pl. N. of a people (in the north of Madhyadeśa), VarBṛS. xiv, 26. — **vishāṇa**, mfn. blunt-horned, lxi, 2. **Cipiṭâsya**, mfn. flat-faced, VarBṛ.

Cipiṭaka, m. flattened rice, L.; (*ikā*), f. scurf (on a healed wound), Suśr. i, 23, 14, Sch. **Cipiṭikāvat**, mfn. furnished with scurf (a healed wound), 14.

Cipiṭī, ind. for °*ṭa*. — **kṛita**, mfn. flattened, Kād. v, 1059; Bālar. ix, 20.

Cipuṭa, m. = °*piṭaka*, L., Sch.

चिप्प *cippa*. See *cipya*.

चिप्पट *cippaṭa*, n. = *citraṭa*, L. — **jayâpīḍa**, m. N. of a king of Kaśmīr, Rājat. iv, 675.

चिप्य *cipya*, m. a kind of worm (cf. *kipya*), Suśr. vi, 54, 6; n. a disease of the finger-nail, whitlow (also *cippa*), ii, 13, 1 & 17; iii f.; cf. *chippikā*.

चिबि *cibi*, चिबु *cibu*, m. the chin, L.

Cibuka, n. (= *cub°*), id., Yājñ. iii, 98; Suśr.; VarBṛS.; Kathās.; Rājat.; Prab.; (m. or n.?) tongs (*saṃdaṇśa*), Gṛihyās. i, 85; m. Pterospermum rubrifolium, L.; m. pl. N. of a people, MBh. i, 6685.

चिमि *cimi*, m. = 1. *ciri*, L.; N. of a plant (from the fibres of which cloth is made), L.

Cimika, m. = 1. *ciri*, L.

चिमिचिमा *cimicimā*, f. pricking, Ashṭâṅg. i.

Cimicimāya, °*yate*, to prick, Car. i, 18.

चिर *cirá*, mfn. (√1. *ci*?) long, lasting a long time, existing from ancient times, MBh. xii, 9538; Śak.; Megh.; Kathās.; °*raṃ kālam*, during a long time, Hariv. 9942; °*rāt kālāt*, after a long time, R. iii, 49, 50; (*ám*), n. (Pāṇ. vi, 2, 6) delay (e.g. *gamana-*, 'delay in going,' Kāś.; *kiṃ cireṇa*, 'wherefore delay?' R. iv f.; MārkP. xvi, 80; *purā cirāt*, 'to avoid delay,' ŚBr. ix); (*ám*), acc. ind. (g. *svar-ādi*, not in Kāś.) for a long time, TS. vf.; Mn.; MBh. &c.; after a long time, slowly, RV. v, 56, 7 & 79, 9; AitBr. i, 16; Kathās. iv, 31; (*eṇa*), instr. ind. after a long time, late, not immediately, slowly, MBh.; R.; Pāṇ. i, 1, 70, Vārtt. 4, Pat.; Ragh. v, 64; for a long time (see also *kíyat*), MBh. xii, 9484; ever, at all times, Prab. ii, $\frac{23}{24}$; (*āya*), dat. ind. for a long time, MBh.; Śak.; Kum. v, 47; Ragh. xiv, 59 &c.; after a long time, at last, finally, too late, MBh.; R.; Pañcat.; (*āt*), abl. ind. after a long time, late, at last, ŚāṅkhŚr. xiv; R.; Pañcat.; Ragh.; Kathās.; Amar.; for a long time (also °*rāt-prabhṛiti*, Hariv. 9860; Mālav. iii, 19; iv, 13), BhP. v, 6, 3; Kathās.; Hit.; (*asya*), gen. ind. after a long time, late, at last, MBh.; Hariv.; R.; Śak. (v.l.); for a long time, Bhartṛ. iii, 51; (*é*), loc. ind. with some delay, not immediately, ŚBr. xiii, 8, 1, 2. — **kāra**, mfn. working slowly, MBh. xii, 9482. — **kāri**, mfn. id., 9539. — **kārika**, mfn. id., 9483; 9534 ff.; 9547. — **kārin**, mfn. id., xii (also °*ri-tā* & *-tva*, abstr.); making slow progress, Car. vi. — **kāla**, mfn. belonging to a remote time, Pāṇ. iv, 3, 105, Kāś. (*a-*, neg.); (*am*), acc. ind. for a long time, Pañcat.; BrahmaP.; RV. i, 125, 1, Sāy.; (*āt*), abl. ind. on account of the long time passed since, Pañcat. ii, $\frac{59}{60}$; (*āya*), dat. ind. for a long time to come, MBh. vii, 8113; *-pālita*, mfn. protected for a long time, W.; °*lôpârjita*, mfn. = *cira-saṃcita*, Hit. i, 4, $\frac{50}{51}$ & 6, $\frac{15}{16}$. — °**kālika**, mfn. of long standing, old, long-continued, chronic, W. — °**kālīna**, mfn. id., W. — **kīrti**, m. N. of the founder of a religious sect, Śaṃkar. ii. — **kṛita**, mfn. long practised, Daś. vii, 322. — **kriya**, mfn. = *-kāra*, L. — **gata**, mfn. long gone, long absent, MBh. iii, 17261; R. i, 42, 1. — **ceshṭita**, mfn. long sought for, of rare occurrence, W. — **ja**, mfn. born long ago, old. — **jāta**, mfn. 'id.,' (with abl.) older than, MBh. iii, 13334; *-tara*, mfn. id. 13331. — **jīvaka**, m. 'long-lived,' the Jīvaka tree, L.; (*ikā*), f. a long life, KaṭhUp. i, 24. — **jīvin**, mfn. long-lived, MBh. iii, 13262 & 13231; R. ii; VarBṛS.; (said of Mārkaṇḍeya, Aśvatthāman, Bali, Vyāsa, Hanumat, Vibhīshaṇa, Kṛipa, Paraśu-Rāma) Tithyād.; m. Vishṇu, L.; a crow, L.; Salmalia malabarica, L.; = °*vaka*, L.; N. of a crow, Kathās. lxii, 8; °*vi-tā*, f. = °*vikā*, Priy. i, 4; Daśar., Sch. — **m-jīva**, m. long-lived (said of several authors, e.g. of Rāma-deva); (*ā*), f. Trigonella corniculata, L. — **m-jīvin**, m. (= °*ra-j°*) Vishṇu, L.; a crow, L.; Salmalia malabarica, L.; = °*ra-jīvaka*, L.; N. of a kind of bird, Siṇhâs. — **tama**, mfn. superl., (*ena*) instr. ind. extremely slowly, Pāṇ. i, 1, 70, Vārtt. 4, Pat. — **tara**, mfn. compar., (*am*), ind. for a very long time, Bhartṛ. iii, 13; Amar.; (*eṇa*), instr. ind. more slowly, Pāṇ. i, 1, 70, Vārtt. 4, Pat. — **tā**, f. long duration, W. — **tikta**, m. (= *kirāta-t°*) Agathotes Chirayta, L.; (*ā*), f. a species of wild cucumber, Npr. — **dātṛi**, m. N. of a prince of *-pura*, Kathās. lv, 12 f. — **divasam**, ind. for a long time, W. — **nirgata**, mfn. long appeared (a bud), Śak. vi, 4. — **nivishṭa**, mfn. abiding long, having rested for a long time, W. — **paricita**, mfn. long accustomed or familiar, Megh. 93. — **parṇa**, m. N. of a plant (having curative properties), L. — **pākin**, m. 'ripening late,' Feronia elephantum, L. — **pura**, n. N. of a town, Kathās. lv, 13. — **pushpa**, m. 'blossoming late,' Mimusops Elengi, L. — **praṇashṭa**, mfn. long disappeared, R. v, 19, 20. — **pravāsin**, mfn. long absent, Hit. i, 6, 33. — **pravṛitta**, mfn. long or ever existent, Kād. — **prasūtā**, f. (a cow) which has calved a long time ago, L. — **bilva**, m. Pongamia glabra, MBh. ix, 3036; R. iii, 79, 34; Suśr.; VarBṛS.; Sāṃkhyak., Sch. — **bhāvin**, mfn. remote (in future), Kathās. ci, 125. — **mitra**, n. an old friend, Hit. i, 3, $\frac{6}{7}$. — **mehin**, m. 'urining for a long time,' an ass, L. — **mocana**, for *cīr°*, q. v. — **m-bhaṇa**, m. 'crying long,' a kind of falcon (*cilla*), L. — **yāta**, mfn. = *-gata*, MBh. iii, 17256. — **rātra**, [m., L.] a long time, Mn. iii, 266; MBh. xiii, 4240; (*am*), ind. for a long time, Car. vi, 1; (*āya*), dat. ind., id., MBh. iii, 10568; after a long time, at last, MBh.; R. ii, 40, 18; °*trêpsita*, mfn. = *cirâbhilashita*, MBh. v, 169; °*trôshita*, mfn. having lodged for a long time, i, 6412. — **roga**, m. a chronic disease, W. — **labdha**, mfn. obtained after a long time (a son in old age), W. — **loka-loka**, mfn. one whose world is a long-existing world (the manes), TUp. ii, 8. — **viprôshita**, mfn. long-banished, Nal.

xvii, 18. **-vṛitta,** mfn. happened long since, R. i, 4, 16. **-velā,** f., (*ayā*) instr. ind. at so late a time, Pañcat. iv, $\frac{10}{11}$. **-saṃvṛiddha,** mfn. long grown or augmented, R. i, 55, 27. **-saṃcita,** mfn. acquired long ago, Hit. i, 6, $\frac{15}{16}$ (v.l.) **-sambhṛita,** mfn. id., Kathās. **-supta-buddhi,** mfn. one whose mind has been long asleep, long senseless, W. **-sūtā,** f. = *-pras°*, L. **-sūtikā,** f. id., L. **-sevaka,** m. an old servant, W. **-stha,** mfn. long continuing, W.; = *-sthāyin*, W.; = *nāyaka*, L. **-sthāyin,** mfn. long left or preserved (food), Bhpr. v, 27, 3; *°yi-tā*, f. long continuance, durability, W. **-sthita,** mfn. = *-sthāyin*, Mn. v, 25; Suśr. **-sthitika,** mfn. long existing (ifc., *evaṃ-*, 'existing so long'), Lalit. xxii, 33. **Cirâṭikā,** f. a white-blossoming Boerhavia erecta, L. **Cirâtikta,** m. = *°ra-t°*, L. **Cirâd,** m. 'long-eating,' Garuḍa, L. **Cirântaka,** m. N. of a son of Garuḍa, MBh. v, 3598. **Cirâbhilashita,** mfn. long desired, iii, 1851. **Cirâyāt,** mfn. coming late, Pañcat. iv, $\frac{10}{11}$. **Cirâyu,** m. 'long-lived,' the vine-palm, L. **Cirâyuka,** m. id., Gal. **Cirâyusha,** mfn. bestowing long life, Pañcat. v, 5, $\frac{1}{2}$ ($\frac{2}{3}$, BC). **Cirâyushya,** mfn. favoured with long life, Daś. i, 178 (*-tā*, abstr.) **Cirâyus,** mfn. long-lived, Suśr.; m. a deity, L.; a crow, Gal. **Cirârodha,** m. a long or protracted siege, W. **Cirâśrita,** mfn. long maintained or protected, an old dependant, W. **Cirôjjhita,** mfn. long since abandoned, W. **Cirôttha,** mfn. existing a long time, Suśr. **Cirôtsuka,** mfn. desirous for a long time, Kathās. **Cirôshita,** mfn. one who has been long absent, MBh. xiii; Hariv. 1151; BhP. i; = *-sthāyin*, MārkP. xxxiv, 57.

Ciratna, mfn. ancient, Pāṇ. iv, 3, 23, Pat.

Cirantana, mfn. (fr. *°raṃ-t°*, iv, 3, 23; vii, 1, 1) id., Pañcat.; VarBṛS.; Pāṇ. iv, 3, 105, Kāś.; Sāh.; existing from ancient times, Mn. iv, 46, Sch.; m. Brahmā, Gal.; Śiva; m. pl. the ancients, Sāh. viii, 10.

Ciraya, Nom. *°yati*, to act slowly, delay, be absent a long while, Mṛicch. (once Ā.); Mālav. &c.

Cirāya, Nom. P. Ā. (p. *°yamāna*) id., MBh. &c.

Cirāyita, mfn. = *°yamāna*, MBh. i; BhP. x, 82, 41.

चिरण्टी *ciraṇṭī*, f. = *car°*, Pāṇ. iv, 1, 20, Pat.

Ciranṭhī [L.], *°ṇḍhī* [Kathās. lviii, 56], f. id.

चिरि 1. *ciri*, in comp. **-kāka,** m. a kind of crow, MBh. xiii, 111, 123 (*cauri-k°*, 'a thief of a crow,' C). **-bilva,** m. = *°ra-b°*, Bhpr. vii, 59, 49.

चिरि 2. *ciri*, cl. 5. *°riṇoti*, to hurt, kill, Dhātup. xxvii, 30; Pāṇ. viii, 2, 78, Kāś.; cf. *jiri*.

Cirikā, f. a kind of weapon (*cilikā*), L., Sch.

चिरिटीक *ciriṭīka*, m. a kind of bird, Car. i, 27, 46 (v. l. *°rīṭ°*).

चिरिण्टी *cirinṭī*, f. = *°ranṭī*, L.

चिरिल्ल *cirilla*, m. = *cīralli*, L.; (*ī*), f. a kind of bird, VarBṛS. lxxxvi, 44 (v. l.)

चिरीटीक *cirīṭīka*. See *°riṭ°*.

चिरु *ciru*, m. the shoulder-joint, L.

चिर्भट *cirbhaṭa*, m. (cf. *carbh°*) Cucumis utilissimus (also its fruit), Car. vi, 10; (*ī*) f. id., Pañcat. i, 3, $\frac{20}{21}$; v, 7, $\frac{1}{2}$; (cf. *gaja-cirbhaṭā*.)

Cirbhaṭikā, f. id., i, 3, $\frac{20}{21}$.

Cirbhiṭa, n., *°ṭā*, f. another kind of gourd, Car. i, 27, 101 (v. l. *°bhaṭa*); Bhpr. v, 6, 36; (cf. *indra-cirbhiṭī*; *kshudra-*, *kshetra-* & *gaja-cirbhiṭā*.)

Cirbhiṭikā, f. id., L.

चिल् *cil*, cl. 6. *°lati*, to put on clothes, Dhātup. xxviii, 63; (cf. *cela*.)

चिलमीलिका *cilamīlikā*, f. a kind of necklace (*ciliminikā*, Buddh. L.), L.; a firefly, L.; lightning (*cilicīmi* & *°mī*, Gal.), L.; (cf. *cilim°*.)

चिलाति *cilāti*, = *kirātī*, in comp. **-putra,** m. 'son of a Kirāta woman,' a metron., HYog. i, 13.

चिलि *cili*, N. of a man, Pravar. vii, 10.

चिलिका *cilikā*, = *cirikā*, L.

चिलिचिम *cilicima*, m. a kind of fish, Car. i, 25; Suśr. i, 20, 3 & 8.

Cilicima, *°mi*, m. id., L., Sch. See also *cilamīlikā*.

चिलिमिनिका *ciliminikā*. See ib.

चिलिमीनक *cili-mīnaka*, m. = *°licima*, L.

चिलिमीलिका *cilimīlikā*, f. = *°lam°*, L.

चिल्ल *cill*, cl. 1. to become loose, Dhātup.; to exhibit a *bhāva* or *hāva* (derived fr. *cilla*), ib.

Cilla, mfn. blear-eyed (cf. *culla*, *pilla*), Pāṇ. v, 2, 33, Vārtt. 2; m. n. a bleared or sore eye, L.; m. the Bengal kite, L.; (*ī*), f. = *°llakā*, L.; for *bhillī* (Symplocos racemosa), L.; = *°llī*, q. v. **-devī,** f. N. of a goddess. **-bhakshyā,** f. a kind of vegetable perfume, L. **Cillâbha,** m. 'resembling a kite,' a petty thief, pickpocket, L.

Cillaka, m. = *citraka*, q. v.; (*ā*), f. a cricket, L.; (*ikā*), f. a kind of pot-herb (*cilli*), Pañcar. (ifc.)

Cillaṭa or *°***llaḍa,** m. an animal of the *bhūmi-śaya* class, Car. i, 27, 32.

Cilli, m. a kind of bird of prey (cf. *cilla* & *gaṅgā-cillī*), Suśr. i, 7, 4 & 46, 2, 21; f. a kind of pot-herb (*°llī*, Car. i, 27, 88; Suśr. i, iv, vi), i, 20, 2.

Cillikā, f. of *°llaka*, q. v. **-latā,** f. 'Cillikā creeper,' the eye-brow, Daś. xii, 29 f.

Cilvaṭi, m. probably = *°llaṭa*, GopBr. i, 2, 7.

चिविट *civiṭa*, m. = *cipiṭaka*, L., Sch.

चिविल्लिका *civillikā*, f. N. of a shrub, L.

चिश्चा *ciścā́*, ind. onomat. (for a rattling sound), RV. vi, 75, 5 (Nir. ix, 14).

Ciścishā-kāram, = *cuścush°*, ĀpŚr. xiii, 17, 6.

चिहण *cihaṇa*, beginning a Gaṇa of Pāṇ. (vi, 2, 125). **-kantha,** m. N. of a town, ib.

चिहुर *cihura*. See *cikura*.

चिह्न *cihna*, n. a mark, spot, stamp, sign, characteristic, symptom, MBh.; R. &c. (ifc. f. *ā*, Ragh. ii, 7; Ratnâv. i, $\frac{5}{6}$); a banner, insignia, L.; a zodiacal sign, VarBṛS. iii, 3; (in Gr.) aim, direction towards, Vop. v, 7. **-kārin,** mfn. marking, W.; wounding, L.; frightful, L. **-dhara,** mfn. bearing the signs or insignia (of office), Buddh. L. **-dhāriṇī,** f. Hemidesmus indicus, L.; Ichnocarpus frutescens, L. **-bhūta,** mfn. become a mark, Nal. xvii.

Cihnaka, n. a small mark, Kād. vi, 1731.

Cihnana, n. a characteristic, Naish. i, 62.

Cihnaya, Nom. P. (ind. p. *°yitvā*) to stamp, Mn.

Cihnayitavya, mfn. to be marked, VarBṛS. lix.

Cihnita, mfn. marked, stamped, distinguished, Mn. ii, viii, x; Yājñ. i, 318; ii, 6 & 85; Pañcat. &c.

Cihnī-kṛita, mfn. marked, MBh. xiii, 826.

चीआक *cīāka*, N. of a poet, Vallabh.

चीक् *cīk* (= √*śīk*), cl. 1. 10. to endure (√*mṛish*, vv. ll. *ā-* √*mṛish* & *-* √*mṛiś*), Dhātup.

चीचीकूची *cīcīkūcī*, onomat. for the warbling of birds, MBh. xvi, 38; Hariv. 1146; 9297 (v.l. *cic°*); (*cicīkucī*) R. vi, 11, 42 & MārkP. ii, 44.

चीठिका *cīṭhikā*, for *cīrikā*, q. v.

चीडा *cīḍā*, f. a kind of perfume, Jain. Sch.

चीण *cīṇa*, *°ṇaka*, for *cīna* &c., q. v.

चीत् *cīt*, ind. (cf. 6. *cit*) only in comp. **-kāra,** m. cries, noise, MBh. vii, 6666; Kathās. lxxiii, 240; Hit.; *-vat*, mfn. accompanied with cries, Mālatīm. i, 1. **-kṛita,** n. = *-kāra*, Kād.; Bālar.; HPariś. i, 45. **-kṛiti,** f. rattling, Bālar. viii, 38.

चीति *cīti*. See √1. *ci*.

चीन *cīna*, m. pl. the Chinese, Mn. x, 44; MBh. ii f., v f.; R. iv, 44, 14; Lalit.; Jain.; Car.; VarBṛS. (also *cīṇa*); m. sg. a kind of deer, L.; Panicum miliaceum (also *cinna*, L.); a thread, L.; n. a banner, L.; a bandage for the corners of the eyes, Suśr. i, 18, 11; lead, L. **-karkaṭikā,** f. a kind of gourd (also *cīṇa-*, L.), Npr. **-karpūra,** m. a kind of camphor, L. **-ja,** n. steel, L. **-paṭṭa,** a sort of cloth, 10; n. lead, L. **-pati,** m. N. of a kingdom, Buddh. **-pishṭa,** n. minium or red lead, Vcar. xiv, 68; lead, L.; *-maya*, mfn. consisting of minium, Kathās. xxiii, 85. **-rāja-putra,** m. a pear tree, Buddh. **-vaṅga,** n. lead (or tutenag?), L. **-sicaya,** m. a China or silken cloth, Pañcar. **Cīnâṅśuka,** n. id., Hariv. 12745; Śak. i; Kum.; Daś.; Amar. **Cīnā-karkaṭī,** f. = *°na-karkaṭikā*, L. **Cīnâcāra-prayoga-vidhi,** m. N. of a work.

Cīnaka, m. pl. the Chinese, MBh. viii, 236; sg. Panicum miliaceum, Hcat. i, 3; (*cīṇaka*) KātyŚr. Paddh.; fennel, L.; a kind of camphor, Bhpr.

Cīnāka, m. fennel, v, 8, 79.

चीपुद्रु *cīpú-dru*, m. N. of a tree, AV. vi, 127.

चीब् *cīb*. See √*cīv*.

चीभ् *cībh*, v. l. for √*bībh*, q.v.

चीय् *cīy*, v. l. for √*cīv*, q. v.

चीर *cī́ra*, n. (√*ci*, Uṇ.) a strip, long narrow piece of bark or of cloth, rag, tatter, clothes, TĀr. vii, 4, 12; Gaut.; Mn. vi, 6; MBh. &c. (ifc. parox., Pāṇ. vi, 2, 127 & 135); the dress of a Buddhist monk (cf. *cīvara*), W.; a necklace of 4 pearl strings, L.; a crest (*cūḍā*), L.; a stripe, stroke, line, L; = *°raka*, L.; lead, L.; m. for *°rī* (a cricket), Kathās. lxxiii, 240; (*ā*), f. a piece of cloth, rag, VarBṛS. lxxxix, 1; Rājat. iv, 573; (*ī*), f. = *°rī-vāka*, Yājñ. iii, 215; the hem of an under garment, L.; cf. *kuśa-*; *mukha-cīrī*. **-khaṇḍa,** m. a piece of cloth, Kathās. iv. **-nivasana,** m. pl. '= *-bhṛit*,' N. of a people, VarBṛS. xiv, 31. **-pattrikā,** f. a kind of vegetable, L. (v. l. *kshāra-p°*). **-parṇa,** m. Shorea robusta, L. **-prâvaraṇa,** m. pl. '= *-bhṛit*,' N. of a people, MārkP. lviii, 52. **-bhavantī,** f. the elder sister of a wife, L. **-bhṛit,** mfn. clothed in bark or rags, Ragh. iii, 22. **-mocana,** n. N. of a Tīrtha, Rājat. i, 149 & 152. **-vasana,** mfn. = *-bhṛit*, R. ii, vi. **-vāsas,** mfn. id., Mn. xi, 102 & 106; MBh. xiii &c.; m. N. of Śiva, xiii f.; of a Yaksha, ii, 399; of a prince, i, 2697.

Cīraka, f. a public announcement on a slip of paper, L.; (*ikā*), f. id., Kathās. li, lv, lxxi; Lokapr.; (*cīṭhikā*, 'a small slip of paper') Bhojapr. $\frac{331}{332}$; = *°rī-vāka*, L. (v. l. for *°rukā*).

Cīri, f. a veil for the eyes, L.

Cīrita, mfn. 'ragged,' only in comp. **-cchadā,** f. Beta bengalensis, L. **-pattrikā,** f. = *°ra-p°*, Npr.

Cīrin, mfn. = *°ra-bhṛit*, MBh. iii, xiii; Hariv. 10594; BhP. iii, 33, 14; (*iṇī*), f. N. of a river, MBh. iii, 12751 (v. l. *vīr°*; cf. *kuśa-cīrā*).

Cīrī, f. of *°ra*. **-vāka,** m. a cricket, Mn. xii, 63; (*cīvi-vāc*, Vishṇ. xliv, 24); cf. *cīrukā*, *cīlikā*.

चीरल्लि *cīralli*, a kind of large fish, Suśr. vi, 35, 4; cf. *cirilla*.

चीरी *cīrī*. See *cī́ra*.

चीरुक *cīruka*, n. a kind of fruit, L.; (*ā*), f. = *°rī-vāka*, L.

चीर्ण *cīrṇa*, mfn. (√*car*) practised, observed (as a vow, austerity), MuṇḍUp. iii, 2, 10; MBh. xv, 91; Divyâv.; BhP. v, 6, 3; n. conduct, W. **-karkaṭi,** for *cīna-k°*, = *°ṭikā*, Gal. **-parṇa,** m. Azadirachta indica, L.; m. Phœnix sylvestris, L. **-vrata,** mfn. = *carita-v°*, Yājñ. iii, 299; MBh.

चीलिका *cīlikā*, *°llakā*, f. = *cīrī-vāka*, L.

चीव् *cīv* (or *cīb*), cl. 1. *°vati*, *°vate*, to take, Dhātup. xxi, 15; to cover (derived fr. *cīvara*), ib.: cl. 10. *cīvayati*, xxxiii, 101.

चीवर *cīvara*, m. iron filings, Gobh. iv, 9, 7; n. the dress or rags of a religious (esp. Buddhist or Jain) monk, ŚāṅkhŚr. ii, 16, 2; Pāṇ. iii, 1, 20; MBh. i, 36, 38; Mṛicch. &c. **-karṇika,** m. n. lappet of a monk's robe, Divyâv. **-karman,** n. arranging a monk's dress (before a journey), viii, 40 f. (cf. xii, 92). **-gopaka,** m. the keeper of monks' dresses, Buddh. L. **-nivasana,** v. l. for *cīra-n°*. **-bhajaka,** m. distributor of monks' dresses, Buddh. L.

Cīvaraya, Nom. *°yate*, to put on rags, W.

Cīvarin, m. a Buddhist or Jain monk, L.

चीविल्लिका *cīvillikā*, v. l. for *civ°*, L.

चीविवाच् *cīvi-vāc*. See *cīrī-vāka*.

चुकोपयिषु *cukopayishu*, mfn. (√*kup*, Caus. Desid.) wishing to make angry, MBh. viii, 1793.

चुक्क् *cukk*, cl. 10. to suffer pain, Dhātup.

चुक्कस *cukkasa*, m. = *bukk°*, L., Sch.

चुक्कार *cuk-kāra*, v. l. for *buk-k°*, L.

चुक्नत् *cuknat*, mfn., KātyŚr. xxv, 12, 3.

चुक्र *cukra*, [m. n., L.] vinegar made by acetous fermentation (of grain or of *-phala*), Hariv. 8439 ff.; Suśr.; sorrel; n. = *-vedhaka*, L.; (*ā*, *ī*), f. = *-caṇḍikā*, L.; (*ā*), f. Oxalis pusilla, Bhpr. v, 9, 26; (*ī*), f. id., L. **-caṇḍikā,** f. the tamarind tree, Npr. **-phala,** n. the tamarind fruit, L. **-vāstūka,** n. sorrel, L. **-vedhaka,** n. a kind of sour rice-gruel, L. **Cukrâmla,** n. vinegar made of the

Garcinia fruit, L.; (*ā*), f. Oxalis corniculata, L.; = °*kra-caṇḍikā*, L.; = °*kra-vedhaka*, L.

Cukraka, n. sorrel, L.; (*ikā*), f. Oxalis corniculata, Car. vi, 9; Bhpr. v; = °*kra-vedhaka*, L.

Cukriman, m. sourness, g. *dṛiḍhâdi*.

चुक्षा *cukshā*, f. = *śauca*, g. *chattrâdi*.

चुक्षोभयिषु *cukshobhayishu*, mfn. (√*kshubh*, Caus. Desid.) intending to shake or disturb, MBh. vii, 1142; viii, 697.

चुचि *cuci*, m. the female breast, W.

चुचु *cucu*, for *cuccu*, q. v., L.

चुचुक *cucuka*. See *cūc*°.

चुचुन्दरी *cucundarī*, = *chucchun*°, L.

चुचुप *cucupa*. See *cūc*°.

चुचूक *cucūka*. See *cūcuka*.

चुच्चु *cuccu*, a kind of vegetable, Car. i, 27; vi, 23. — **parṇikā**, f. a kind of vegetable, i, 27.

Cuccū, m. f. = °*ccu*, Suśr. i, 46; iv, vi.

चुच्य् *cucy*, v.l. for √*śucy*, q.v.

चुञ्चु *cuñcu*, mfn. ifc. = *cañcu*, renowned for (cf. *akshara-*, *cāra-*), Pāṇ. v, 2, 26; accustomed to, Śiś. ii, 14; m. the musk-rat (cf. *cucundarī*), L.; a mixed caste whose business is hunting (born of a Brāhman father by a Vaideha female, Sch.), Mn. x, 48; N. of a man, VP. iv, 3, 15 (v.l. *cañcu*).

चुञ्चुरी *cuñcurī*, f. a kind of game played with tamarind seeds instead of dice, L.

Cuñculi, °**lī**, f. id., L.

चुञ्चुल *cuñcula*, m. N. of a man, (pl.) his descendants, Hariv. 1466; (*ī*), f., see °*curī*.

चुट् *cuṭ* (& *cuṇṭ*, *cuṇḍ*), cl. 6. 10. *cuṭati* (*cuṇṭ*°), *coṭayati* (*cuṇṭ*°, *cuṇḍ*°), to split, cut off, Dhātup.: cl. 1. *coṭati* (*cuṇṭ*°, *cuṇḍ*°), to become small, ib. (cf. √*cuṭṭ* & *buṭ*).

चुट्ट् *cuṭṭ*, cl. 10. °*ṭṭayati*, to become small, xxxii, 24; cf. √*puṭṭ*.

चुड् *cuḍ*, cl. 6. °*ḍati*, to conceal, xxviii.

चुड्ड् *cuḍḍ*, cl. 1. °*ḍḍati*, = √*cull*, ix, 63.

चुण् *cuṇ*, cl. 6. to split, cut off, xxviii, 84.

चुण्ट् *cuṇṭ*, = √*cuṭ*, q. v.

Cuṇṭā, f. a small well or reservoir near a well, L.

Cuṇṭī, f. id., Suśr. i, 45; cf. *cauṇṭya*, *cūḍaka*.

चुण्ठ् *cuṇṭh*, cl. 10. °*ṭhayati*, to hurt, Dhātup.

चुण्ड् *cuṇḍ*, = √*cuṭ*, q. v.

Cuṇḍya, = °*ṇṭī*, Bhpr.

चुण्ढी *cuṇḍhi*, v. l. for °*ṇṭī*, L.

चुत् *cut*, v.l. for *cyut*, Dhātup. iii, 3.

चुत *cuta*, m., °*ti*, f. = *cūta*, the anus, L.

चुद् *cud*, cl. 1. *códati*, °*te* (Subj. *códat*; Impv. °*da*, °*data*, °*dasva*, (2. du.) °*dethām*; aor. 2. sg. *codīs*; pr. p., see *a-codát*), to impel, incite, animate, RV.; to bring or offer quickly (as the Soma), RV.; Ā. to hasten, RV.: Caus. *codáyati*, rarely °*te* (Subj. 2. sg. °*yāsi*, °*yāse*; aor. *acūcudat*, MBh. xiii, 35; p. *codáyat*; Pan. *codyamāna*), to sharpen, whet, RV. vi, 47, 10 (cf. 3, 5); ix, 50, 1; x, 120, 5; to impel, incite, cause to move quickly, accelerate, RV.; AV. iii, 15, 1; MBh. &c.; (with *cakshus*) to direct (the eye) towards (loc.), Mṛicch. ix, 11; to inspire, excite, animate, RV.; AV. vii, 46, 3; to request, petition, ask, urge on, press or importune with a request, Lāṭy. ii, 9, 15; Mn.; MBh. &c.; help on, assist in the attainment of (dat.), RV.; to bring or offer quickly, vi, 48, 9; vii, 77, 4; to ask for, MBh. xiii; R. vii; BhP. x; to inquire after, MBh. i, 5445; to enjoin, fix, settle, ŚāṅkhŚr.; Lāṭy.; to object, criticise, Bādar., Sch.; to be quick, RV. i, 117, 3; x, 101, 12 & 102, 12; [cf. σπεύδω, σπουδάζω; Lat. *cudo*.]

Códa, m. an implement for driving horses, goad or whip, v, 61, 3; (°*dá*), mfn. animating, inspiring, promoting, i, 143, 6; ii, 13, 9 & 30, 6; (cf. *radhra-codá*.) — **pravṛiddha** (°*dá-*), mfn. exalted by the inspiring (draught of Soma), i, 174, 6.

Codaka, mfn. impelling, MBh. xiii, 71; m. direction, invitation, KātyŚr. i, 10, 1; Nyāyam. x; (in Gr.) = *pari-graha*, q. v., RPrāt. x, 10; xi, 14; asker, objectioner, pupil, Jain.

Códana, mfn. impelling, AV. vii, 116, 1; (cf. *ṛishi-*, *eka-*, *kīri-*, *brahma-*, *radhra-cód*°); (*ā*, *am*), f. n. impelling, invitation, direction, rule, precept, VS. xxix, 7; RPrāt.; ŚāṅkhŚr.; KātyŚr.; Lāṭy.; Mn. ii, &c.; (*ā*), f. reproof (as in Pāli), Divyâv. i, 54; (*ī*), f. N. of a plant (v.l. for *rodanī*), L., Sch. **Codanā-guḍa**, m. a ball to play with, L.

Codayán-mati, mfn. (fr. °*dáyat*, p. √*cud*, Caus.) promoting devotion, RV. v, 8, 6; viii, 46, 19.

Codayitavya, mfn. to be criticised, Bādar., Sch.

Codayitṛi, mf(*trī́*)n. one who impels or animates or promotes, RV. i, 3, 11; vii, 81, 6; Kum. iii, 21.

Codas. See *a-codás*.

Codāyani, m. pl. N. of a family, Pravar. iv, 8.

Coditá, mfn. caused to move quickly, RV. ix, 72, 5; driven, impelled, incited, MBh.; R.; carried on (a business), iv, 28, 21 (*a-*, neg.); invited, directed, ordered, MBh.; Ragh. xii, 59; informed, apprised, W.; inquired after, BP. vii, 15, 13; enjoined, fixed, appointed, ŚāṅkhŚr.; KātyŚr.; Mn. ii f., viii; MBh. xiii, 2439; R. (B) iii, 56, 16. — **tva**, n. the being enjoined, Jaim. vi, 1, 9; (*a-*, neg.) KātyŚr. i, 6.

Coditṛi, mfn. = °*dayitṛi*, RV. (7 times).

Códishṭha, mfn. most animating, viii, 100, 3.

Codya, mfn. to be impelled or incited, MBh. v, 1404 & 4600; (*a-*, neg.) xiii, 4875; to be criticised, Sarvad. xiii, 111; to be thrown, W.; n. raising questions, consideration, MBh. v, 1653; 'to be urged or objected,' a difficult question raised to invite for controversy (*pūrva-paksha*, *praśna*, L.), Sarvad. xiii, 2 & 22; astonishment, wonder, Śiś. ix, 16.

चुनन्द *cunanda*, m. N. of a Buddhist mendicant, Lalit. i, 10.

चुन्द् *cund*, v.l. for √*bund*, q. v.

चुन्द *cunda*, m. N. of a pupil of Śākyamuni, Buddh.; (cf. *mahā-*); (*ī*), f. a bawd, L.

चुप् 1. *cup*, cl. 1. *copati*, to move, MBh. iii, 10648 f. & 17346 f.; cf. *gale-copaka*.

Copana, mfn. moving, Pāṇ. iii, 2, 148, Kāś.

चुप् 2. *cup*, cl. 6., v.l. for √*chup*.

Cupa, m. N. of a man, g. 1. *aśvâdi* (*cumpa*, Kāś.; *-dāsaka*, Hemac.) — **dāsaka**, see *cupa*.

चुपुणीका *cupuṇīkā*, f. N. of one of the 7 Kṛittikās, TS. iv, 4, 5, 1; Kāṭh. xl, 4.

चुबुक *cubuka*, n. (= *cib*°, *chúb*°) the chin, BhP. x, 42, 7; the top of an altar, Śulbas. iii, 164 & 168. — **daghná**, mfn. reaching to the chin, MaitrS. iii, 3, 4; ĀpŚr. vii, 8, 3.

चुब्र *cubra*, n. (√2. *cumb*) the face, Uṇ. ii.

चुमुचुमायन *cumucumāyana*, n. itching (of a wound), Suśr. i, 42, 11.

चुमुरि *cúmuri*, m. N. of a demon (whom Indra sent to sleep to favour Dabhīti), RV. ii, vi f., x.

चुम्ब् 1. *cumb*, cl. 10. to hurt, Dhātup.

चुम्ब् 2. *cumb*, cl. 1. °*bati* (exceptionally Ā., Pañcat. iv, 7; pf. *cucumba*; Pass. p. °*byamāna*, Dhūrtas.), to kiss, MBh.; Hariv. &c.; to touch with the mouth, MBh. viii, 5954; to touch closely or softly: Caus. *cumbayati*, to cause to kiss, Daś. vi, 6; to kiss, Dhātup. xxxii, 91 (v. l.)

Cumba, m. kissing, kiss, L.; (*ā*), f. id., VarBṛS.

Cumbaka, mfn. one who kisses much, L.; 'one who has read much,' superficial, L.; knavish, roguish, L.; m. = *-maṇi*, Prab. vi, 16; AdhyR. i, 1, 18; the upper part of a balance, L.; n. a parallel passage, Setub. xi, 99, Sch. — **maṇi**, m. a loadstone, Mcar.

Cumbana, n. = °*ba*, VarBṛS.; Pañcat.; Amar.; Gīt. (ifc. f. *ā*, ii, 13) &c. — **dāna**, n. giving a kiss, 16.

Cumbita, mfn. kissed, Śak. iii; Sāh. i; touched closely or softly, Mālatīm.; Vcar. xiv, 7; Sarvad.

Cumbin, mfn. ifc. kissing, W.; touching closely, Caurap.; Vcar. viii, 42; affected with, Naish. vi, 66; relating to, viii, 87; busy with, iii, 95.

चुर् *cur*, cl. 10. *corayati* (rarely °*te*, MBh. xiii, 5508; MārkP. xv, 23; aor. *acūcurat*, Śiś. i, 16; cl. 1. *corati*, Vop. xvii, 1), to steal, Mn. viii, 333; MBh. &c.; to rob any one (acc.), Hariv. 11146; to cause to disappear, Siṅhâs. Introd. ⅔ (1. sg. *cūrayāmi*). — **ādi**, the class of rts. beginning with √*cur*, Kāś. on Pāṇ. i, 4, 36 & ii, 3, 56.

Curaṇya, Nom. °*yati*, to steal, g. *kaṇḍv-ādi*.

Curā, f. theft, g. *chattrâdi*.

Corá, m. (gaṇas *pacâdi*, *brāhmaṇâdi*, *manojñâdi*, *pāraskarâdi*) = *caura*, a thief, TĀr. x, 64; MBh. v, 7834; a plagiarist; the plant Kṛishṇa-śaṭī, L.; a kind of perfume, L.; N. of a poet, Prasannar. i, 22; (*ā*), f. = *-pushpī*, L.; (*ī*), f. a female thief, g. *pacâdi* (g. *gaurâdi*, Gaṇar. 46); theft, Gal. — **kaṇṭaka**, m. a kind of grass (the seeds of which stick in the clothes), W. — **karaṇa**, n. calling any-one a thief, Pāṇ. iii, 4, 25, Kāś. — **m-kāram**, ind. with *ā-*√*kruś*, to call any one a thief, ib. — **pushpikā**, °**shpī**, f. Chrysopogon aciculatus, L. — **snāyu**, m. Leea hirta, W.

Coraka, m. a thief, VarBṛS. xvi, 25; Trigonella corniculata, L.; a kind of perfume, L.; (*ikā*), f. theft, L., Sch. — **bandham**, ind. so as to tie in a particular way, Pāṇ. iii, 4, 41, Kāś.

Corāyita, mfn. representing a thief, BhP. x, 37.

Corita, mfn. stolen, Pañcat.; Daś.; n. theft, W.

Coritaka, n. anything stolen, vii; petty theft, W.

चुरी *curī*, f. = *cuṇṭī*, L.

चुरु *curu*, m. a particular worm in the bowels, Car. i, 19, 1, 40; iii, 7; Bhpr. vii, 19, 9.

Cūru, m. a kind of worm, Suśr. vi, 54, 6.

चुरुचुरा *curucurā*, f. (onomat.) See *karṇe-*.

Curcura, ind., in comp. — **dhvani**, m. gnashing (the teeth), Śiś. v, 58, Sch. — **śabda**, m. id., 58.

चुल् *cul*, cl. 10. *colayati*, to raise, Dhātup. xxxii, 62; (for √*bul*) to dive into, ib.

Cula, g. 1. *balâdi* (*vula*, Kāś.)

Culaka, for °*luka*, q. v.; (*ā*), see °*lukā*.

Culya, mfn. fr. °*la*, g. 1. *balâdi*.

चुलु *culu*, m. a handful of water, Gal.

Culuka, m. n. (= *cal*°) the hand hollowed to hold water, handful or mouthful of water, draught, Bālar.; Naish. (v.l. °*laka*, xxii, 41); Viddh. i, 15; Kuval. 462 & Pañcad. (°*laka*) &c.; m. deep mud or mire, L.; a small vessel (gallipot, &c.), L.; N. of a man, g. *kaṇvâdi* (°*laka*, Gaṇaratnâv.); (*ā*), f. N. of a river, MBh. vi, 9, 20 (°*lakā*, C).

Culukin, m. a porpoise, sea-hog (also *ulupin*, *culumpin*, *cullakī*), L. **Culuki-**√*kṛi*, to swallow in one draught, cause to disappear, Bhām. i, 120.

Culukya, m. N. of a race.

चुलुम्प् *culump*, cl. 1. °*pati*, (pf. °*pām cakāra*, Pāṇ. iii, 1, 35, Vārtt., Pat.) = √*lul* or *lup*, L.

Culumpa, m. fondling children, L.; (*ā*), f. a she-goat, L. **Culumpin**, m. = °*lukin*, L.

चुल्य *culya*. See √*cul*.

चुल्ल् *cull* (= √*cuḍḍ*), to exhibit any *hāva* or *bhāva* (derived fr. *culla*), Dhātup. xv, 24.

Culla, mfn. = *cilla*, blear-eyed, Pāṇ. v, 2, 33, Vārtt. 2, Pat.; m. a blear eye, ib.; (*ī*), f. a fire-place, chimney, Mn. iii, 68; Lalit. xviii, 99; Pañcat.; Suśr.; Hcat.; (*cūlhi*) Śil.; a funeral pile, L.; a large hall composed of 3 divisions (one looking north, another east, the third west), VarBṛS. liii, 38; = *gṛiha-cullī*, 42. **Cullâksha**, mfn. blear-eyed, L.

Cullakī, f. a kind of waterpot, L.; = °*lukin*, L.; N. of a race, L. **Culli**, f. = °*llī*, a fire-place, L.

Culhi, f. = °*llī*, Pāpabuddhidharm. 26.

चुश्चुषा *cuścushā*, f. (onomat.) a smacking sound (in eating), Nyāyam. x, 2, 3, Sch. — **kāra**, m. id., x, 2, 3; (*am*), ind. (= *ciścishā-*; to eat) so as to smack, MānŚr. ii, 5, 4; MaitrS.Paddh.

चुस्त *custa*, m. n. v.l. for *busta*, L.

चूंकृत *cūṃ-kṛita*, n. the call 'hallo!' Naish. i, 142.

चूचुक *cūcuka*, mfn. stammering, MBh. xiv, 1016; m. pl. N. of a people, xiii, 207, 42 (*cuc*°, C); n. = °*kâgra* (also *cuc*°, m. n. & *cucūka*, n., L.), R. vi, 23, 13; Suśr.; VarBṛS. lxviii, 27; Kathās. cxx. — **tā**, f. the condition of a nipple, Kautuk. **Cūcukâgra**, n. a nipple (of the breast), Vikr. v, 8; Caurap.

चूचुप *cūcupa*, m. pl. N. of a people, MBh. v, 140, 26 (*cuc*°, C); vi, 75, 21 (*cūlika*, C).

चूड *cūḍa*, mfn. stupid (?), Divyâv. xxxv, 99 f.; m. (cf. *kūṭa*) a sort of protuberance on a sacrificial brick, ŚBr. viii & KātyŚr. (also ifc. f. *ā*); m. or n. = °*ḍā-karaṇa*, Yājñ. iii, 23; m. N. of a man (with the patr. Bhāgavitti), ŚBr. xiv, 9, 3, 17 f.; (*ā*), f. (beginning a Gaṇa of Gaṇar. 365; g. *bhidâdi*) the hair on the top of the head, single lock or tuft left on the crown of the head after tonsure, Ragh. xviii, 50 (ifc.); Parāś.; = °ḍā-karaṇa (cf. °ḍôpanayana), Ragh. iii, 28; Smṛitit. i; the crest of a cock or peacock, L.; any crest, plume, diadem, W.; the head, L.; the top (of a column), Hcat. i, 3; the summit, Hit. i, 1, 1/2; a top-room (of a house), L.; a kind of bracelet, L.; a small well, L.; N. of a metre; of a woman, g. bāhv-ādi (°ḍālā, Kāś.); cf. cūla, coḍa, caula; uc-, candra-, tāmra-, svarṇa-; pañca- & mahā-cūḍā.

Cūḍaka, ifc. = °ḍā(-karaṇa), Mn. v, 67; a well, L.; (ā), f. N. of an Apsaras, Kāraṇḍ. i, 36; (ikā), f. = cūlikā, q.v.; ?, Divyâv. xxxvii, 598.

Cūḍaya, Nom. °yati, to fasten like a crest on any one's (acc.) head, BhP. x, 30, 33.

Cūḍā, f. of °ḍa. — **karaṇa**, n. 'forming the crest,' the ceremony of tonsure (= caula, one of the 12 purificatory rites [RTL. p. 353 & 359] performed on a child in the 1st or 3rd year), Kauś.; Gobh.; PārGṛ.; Gṛihyās.; BhavP.; PSarv.; Smṛitit. iii. — **karṇa**, m. N. of a mendicant, Hit. i, 5, 1/2. — **karman**, n. = -karaṇa, Gobh.; ŚāṅkhGṛ.; Mn. ii, 35. — **danta**, m. a piece of wood projecting from a wall, Gal. — **pakshâvadāna**, n. N. of Divyâv. xxxv. — **pāśa**, n. a mass of hair on the top of the head, Megh. 65. — **pratigrahaṇa**, n. N. of a Caitya, Lalit. xv, 381. — **bhikshuṇī**, f. N. of a Buddh. goddess, W. — **maṇi**, m. a jewel worn by men and women on the top of the head, MBh. i, 4628; vii, 826; R. &c.; ifc. the (gem, i. e. the) best or most excellent of, Kathās. cxxiii, 235; Dhūrtas. i, 3; Vop.; the seed of Abrus precatorius, L.; a metre of 4 × 7 syllables; an eclipse of the sun on a Sunday or an eclipse of the moon on a Monday, Hcat. i, 3; GarP.; a particular way of foretelling the future, ccv; N. of a work on astron.; of another on music; of a Kshatriya, Hit. iii, 9, 1/2; -tā, f. the being a jewel worn on the head, Hariv. 8789; Hcar. vii; -dhara, m. 'Cūḍāmaṇi-wearer,' N. of a Nāga, Buddh. L.; -bhaṭṭâcārya, m. N. of a teacher. — **maha**, m. N. of a festival, Lalit. xv, 380. — °**mla** (°ḍâm°), n. = cukrâmla, L. — **ratna**, n. = -maṇi, a jewel worn on the head, Kathās. cxix. — °**rha** (°ḍâr°), m. Gomphrena globosa, Npr. — **lakshaṇa**, n. tonsure, W. — **vat**, mfn. (g. balâdi) = cūḍāla, being in boyhood, Bālar. iv, 51. — **vana**, m. 'wood-crested,' N. of a mountain, Rājat. viii, 597. — °**valambin** (°ḍâv°), mfn. reclining on the crest or summit, W. **Cūḍôpanayana**, n. pl. tonsure and initiation, MBh. i, 8047.

Cūḍāra, mfn. = °ḍāla (?), g. pragady-ādi.

Cūḍāraka, m. N. of a man, (pl.) his descendants, g. upakâdi (paṇḍ°, Kāś.)

Cūḍāla, mfn. (Pāṇ. v, 2, 96, Kāś.) having a lock of hair on the crown of the head, MBh. x, 288; Rājat. i, 233; n. the head, L.; (ā), f. N. of a woman, g. bāhv-ādi (Kāś.); white Abrus, L.; (ā, ī), f. a kind of Cyperus, L. — **veśa**, mfn. v. l. for cāṇḍ°.

Cūḍika, mfn. = °ḍāla (?), g. purohitâdi (°ḍitika, Kāś.); (ā), f., see °ḍaka.

Cūḍitaka, see cūlit°. **Cūḍitika**, mfn., see °ḍika.

Cūḍin, mfn. = °ḍāla, g. balâdi. **Cūḍi-kalā**, f. N. of a metre.

Cūḍīya, mfn. worn on the crest, Pañcad. ii, 69.

चूण् cūṇ, cl. 10. °ṇayati, to contract, shrink, Dhātup. xxxii, 99.

चूत cūta, m. the mango tree, MBh.; R.; Śak. &c.; (cf. kapi-); = cuta, L. — **mañjarī**, f. N. of a Vidyā-dharī, Kathās. cxii, 9. — **latikā**, f. a kind of sport, Vātsyāy. i, 4; N. of a woman, Ratnâv. i, 1/2.

Cūtaka, m. the mango tree, L.; a small well (= cūḍaka), L. **Cūti**, f. = cuta, W.

चूर् cūr, cl. 4. °ryate, to burn, Dhātup. xxvi, 49; for cl. 10. °rayati, see √cur.

चूरी cūrī, v. l. for curī, L.

चूरु cūru. See curu.

चूर्ण् cūrṇ, cl. 10. (or more properly Nom. fr. cūrṇa) °ṇayati (Pass. °ṇyate) to reduce to powder or flour, pulverise, grind, pound, crush, bruise, MBh.; R.; Pañcat.; BhP.; Kathās. &c.

Cūrṇa, mfn. (√carv) minute, VarBṛS. lxxxi, 6; m. [MBh.; VarBṛS.] n. powder, flour, aromatic powder, pounded sandal, ŚāṅkhŚr.; KātyŚr.; Kauś.; MBh. &c. (ifc., Pāṇ. vi; 2, 134); m. chalk, lime, VarBṛS. lxxvii, 36; Prab. ii, 17, Sch.; N. of a man, Vīrac. xv, xxviii; n. rice mixed with sesam, Yājñ. i, 303; a kind of easy prose, Vām. i, 3, 25; dividing a word by separating a double consonant for obtaining a different sense (in a riddle, &c.), iv, 1, 7. — **kāra**, m. a lime-burner (kind of mixed caste), Parāś. Paddh. — **kuntala**, m. a lock of hair, Vcar. iv, 2. — **kṛit**, m. (for °ṇi-k° ?) N. of Śaṃkarâcārya, Gal. — **keśa**, m. = -kuntala, L. — **khaṇḍa**, m. n. a pebble, gravel, L. — **tā**, f. the state of dust or powder, Rājat. v, 16. — **tva**, n. id., W. — **pada**, n. a peculiar movement (walking backwards and forwards), Daś. xi, 41; a kind of easy prose, Bālar. x, 78. — **pārada**, m. vermilion, L. — **pesham**, ind. (with √pish, to grind) so as to pulverise, Pāṇ. iii, 4, 35. — **mushṭi**, f. a handful of powder or perfume, W. — **yoga**, m. pl. a fragrant compound, perfumed powder, MBh. xii, 2163; (cf. vāsa-). — **śas**, ind. (with √kṛi, to reduce) to powder, i, 3225. — **śākâṅka**, m. a kind of vegetable, L. **Cūrṇâdi**, a Gaṇa of Pāṇ. (iv, 2, 134).

Cūrṇaka, m. a kind of Shashṭika grain, Suśr. i, 46, 1, 5; chalklike paleness, Car. v, 1 & 12; grain fried and pounded, L.; n. fragrant powder, Suśr. vi, 35, 5; a kind of easy prose (expounding the purport of a foregoing verse, W.), Chandom.; (ikā), f. id., W.; grain fried and pounded, L.; a kind of cake, Vet. i, 1/8. **Cūrṇana**, n. pounding, Bālar. viii, 82.

Cūrṇi, °**ṇī**, f. the shell Cypræa moneta (one Kaparda), L., Sch.; 100 Kapardas, Uṇ. iv, 52, Sch.; 'noticing every minute point of difficulty,' N. of Pat.'s Comm. (Mahā-bhāshya), L., Sch.; of the old Prākṛit commentaries on Jain texts; selection of an unanswerable argument, W.; cf. eka-. — **kāra**, m. the author of a Cūrṇi (or Prākṛit Comm. on a Jain text). — **kṛit**, m. 'Cūrṇi-author,' N. of Pat., L.; = -kāra.

Cūrṇita, mfn. = °ṇī-kṛita, MBh.; R. &c.

Cūrṇin, mfn. made or mixed up with anything powdered or pounded, Pāṇ. iv, 4, 23.

Cūrṇī, ind. in comp. for °ṇa; f. = °ṇi, q. v.; N. of a river, W. — **karaṇa**, n. = cūrṇana, Dhātup. xxxii, 46. — √**kṛi**, to reduce to powder or dust, pulverise, grind, bruise, smash, KātyŚr. xv, 9, 29; Suśr. — **kṛita**, mfn. pulverised, smashed, MBh. vi, 5424; R.; VarBṛS. &c. — **cikīrshu**, mfn. intending to pulverise, BhP. x, 12, 30. — √**bhū** (p. -bhavat), to become dust, become smashed, 72, 37; Vikr. i, 4.

चूर्ति cūrti, f. (√car) going, Pāṇ. vii, 4, 89.

चूल cūla, m. (= cūḍa), N. of a man, BṛĀr-Up. vi, 3, 9; (ā), f. the nucleus of a comet, VarBṛS. xi, 9 & 21 (ifc.); the tonsure ceremony, Ragh. iii, 28 (ifc.; caula, S); a top-room of a house, L.; cf. uc-.

Cūlaka, ifc. a crest (cūḍā), Matsyas.; (ikā), f. a cock's comb, VarBṛS. lxiii, 1 (ifc.); the root of an elephant's ear (cūḍikā, Gal.); the top of a column, CūlUp. (cūḍikā, Sch.); summit, Siṇhâs.; N. of a metre (also cūḍikā); of several additional parts of Jain texts; the hinting of a matter or event by those behind the curtain, Daśar. i, 58 & 61; Sāh.; Pratāpar.

Cūlika, m. pl. see cūcupa; n. cake of flour fried with ghee, L.; (ā), f. see °laka.

Cūlikā, f. of °laka. — **paiśācika**, n. °cī, f. N. of a dialect in dramas. **Cūlikôpanishad**, f. N. of an Up.

Cūlitaka, m. N. of a poet, Vallabh.

Cūlin, mfn. = cūḍin, LiṅgaP.; having an ornament on the crown, Hariv. 4440; having a crest (a bird), 2495; m. N. of a Ṛishi, R. i, 34, 38; cf. vi-.

चूष् cūsh, cl. 1. °shati, to suck, suck out, Dhātup. xvii, 22: Pass. °shyate, to be sucked up or dried up (by internal inflammation), Suśr. i f.: Caus. °shayati, to suck up, iv; cf. sam-.

Cūshaṇa, n. sucking (of a leech), i, 13; cf. ā-.

Cūshaṇīya, mfn. what may be sucked, W.

Cūshā, f. an elephant's girdle, L. (°shyā, Gal.)

Cūshiṇī, f. N. of a female attendant of Durgā.

Cūshita, mfn. sucked, sucked up, W.

Cūshya, mfn. see coshya; (ā), f. see °shā.

Cosha, mf(ā)n. ifc. sucking, Hcat. i, 7, 466 (BrahmaP.); m. = shaṇa, W.; drying up or burning (of the skin), heat, dryness (as a disease), Suśr.

Coshaṇa, n. sucking, Bādar. ii, 2, 3, Sch.

Coshya, mfn. = cūshaṇīya, MBh. i f., xii, 191, 16 (cūsh°, C); Hariv. 8255; R. i, 52, 24; Pañcat. &c.

चृत् cṛit, cl. 6. °tati (fut. cartsyati & cartishy°, Pāṇ. vii, 2, 57) to tie, Dhātup. xxviii, 35; to hurt, kill, Bhaṭṭ. xvi, 20: cl. 1. cartati, to shine, VS. xxii, 7, Sch.; to light, Dhātup. xxxiv, 14 (v. l. for √chṛid): Caus. (or cl. 10) cartayati, id., ib.: Desid. cicṛitsati or °cartishati, Pāṇ. vii, 2, 57; see ati-, ava-, ā-, upa-, &c.; cf. √2. & 3. kṛit.

चृप् cṛip, cl. 1. 10, v. l. for √chṛid, Dhātup.

चेकितान cékitāna. See √cit.

चेक्रिय cekriya, mfn. (√1. kṛi, Intens.) active, industrious, W. **Cekrīyita**, n. the characteristic of the Intens. verb, Kāt. iii, 2, 14 & 43; 3, 7.

चेच्चेद् cec-ced, ind. 'if—if!' be quiet! (address to a dog), PārGṛ. i, 16, 24.

चेट ceṭa, m. a servant, slave, Mṛicch.; Kathās. vi, 127 (ifc.); Sāh.; a kind of fish, Āp. i, 17, 38; (ī), f. a female servant, R. ii, 91, 62; Śak. &c.

Ceṭaka, m. a servant, slave, Bhartṛ. i, 91; Kathās. vi & lxxi (ifc.); Hit.; a paramour, L.; (ikā), f. = °ṭī, Kathās. iv, xii, liii. **Ceḍa**, m. a servant, L., Sch.; (ī), f. = ceṭī, ib. **Ceḍaka**, m. = °ḍa, ib.; (ikā), f. = °ḍī, L.

चेत् 1. cet, Nom. °tati. See √cit.

Cetaḥ, °**taka**, °**tana**, &c. See ib.

चेत् 2. cet. See céd.

चेतव्य cetavyà. See √1. ci.

चेतस् cétas &c., °tāya &c. See √cit.

चेतुया cetuyā, N. of a place, Kshitîś. vii.

चेत्तृ céttṛi, cétya. See √cit.

चेद् céd (Padap. ca íd), ind. (never found at the beginning of a sentence or verse) = ca, 'and,' AV. ii, 30, 2 (céd—ca, 'as well as'); xviii, 2, 37; 'when' (the verb being accentuated, cf. Pāṇ. viii, 1, 30), RV. vii, 74, 4; viii, 79, 5; x, 109, 3; AV. v, 17, 8; 'if' (the verb being accentuated, cf. Pāṇ. viii, 1, 30; with pr. [AV. xii, 4, 21; ŚBr. &c.; cf. Pāṇ. iii, 3, 8 f. & 132, Kāś.], Subj. [AV. vi, 122, 2], Pot. [xii, 4, 48; ŚBr. xiv; Mn. &c. (for Cond., MBh. v. 960 & Rājat. v, 478)]; cf. Pāṇ. iii, 3, 9 & 156 Kāś.], perf. [AV. vi, 51, 3; MBh. xii, 986 ff.; perf. p., Pāṇ. iii, 3, 132, Kāś.], aor. [AV. iv, 28, 4; xii, 4, 18; cf. Pāṇ. iii, 3, 132, Kāś.], fut. [ŚBr. i, xiv; MBh.; R.; Śak.; cf. Pāṇ. iii, 3, 8 f.; 132 f. & 156, Kāś.], Cond. [MBh. vii, 3423; Śak.; cf. Pāṇ. iii, 3, 139, Kāś.], perf. or fut. Pass. p. or with an auxiliar verb to be supplied, AV. ix, 5, 6; xii, 2, 36; KātyŚr.; Mn. &c.); **atha ced**, 'but if,' MBh. v, 2775; Bhag. ii, 33; xviii, 58; **api ced**, 'even,' Hariv. 11308; **iti cen** (often placed at the end of an objector's statement) 'if it be argued that ....,' **na**, 'no, it is not so,' Bādar. ii, 1, 35; Sarvad. ii, 158; **na ced** (g. câdi; also separated by the verb [MBh.] or the verb preceded by na placed at the end of the sentence [ŚBr. xiv, 6, 8, 1; Bhag. ii, 33; xviii, 58; Hit.], rarely cen na in reversed order beginning the apodosis, Sāṃkhyak. 1; Sāh.; Śrut.; Hit.) 'if not' (= no ced forming a sentence by itself, ŚBr. xiv, 7, 2, 15), ŚBr. xiv; ŚāṅkhŚr. i, 17, 1; Mn. &c.; **no ced** (g. câdi) id. (forming a sentence by itself, e.g. dūram apasara no ced dhantavyo 'si mayā, 'depart to a distance, if not, i. e. if thou departest not, thou art to be killed by me'), MBh. xii, 7, 21 & 29, 145; Pañcat.; Kathās.; Vet.; Hit.; exceptionally = na ced (beginning a sentence), MBh. xiii, 5809; **na ced** or **no ced** (with Pot.) 'would that not!' (e.g. no cet pradahet, 'would that he did not burn down!'), v, 676 ff. & 966; (with pr. or Pot., the apodosis containing an Impv.) 'if not,' i. e. 'in order that not,' 2714; R.v, 80, 24; **yadi ced** (also separated by the verb) = ced, 'if' (with pr., Pot., fut.), MBh. i, 2403; Hariv. 11895; R. ii, 8, 34 & 48, 19; (cf. néd.)

चेदि cedí, m. pl. N. of a people (who lived in Bundelkhand; renowned for their attachment to ancient laws and institutions, MBh.; their capital was Śuktimatī; some of their kings were Vasu Uparicara, Subāhu, Dhṛishṭa-ketu, Dama-ghosha, Śiśu-pāla &c.), RV. viii, 5, 39; MBh.; R. &c.; m. sg. N. of the supposed ancestor of the Cedis (son of Kaiśika or Uśika), BhP. ix, 24, 2. — **nagarī**, f. = tri-purī, L. — **pa**, m. = -pati, MBh. i, 2342; iii, 462; VarBṛS. xliii, 8; N. of a son of Vasu Uparicara, BhP. ix, 22, 6. — **pati**, m. a prince of the Cedis, MBh. iii (Nal. xvi, 31), xiii. — **purī**, f. the city of the Cedis, ii, 1508; Nal. xvi, 6. — **bhū-bhuj**, m. 'earth-enjoyer of the Cedis,' = -pati, BhP. vii, 1, 13. — **bhūbhṛit**, m. 'protector of the country of the Cedis,' Śiśu-pāla, W. — **rāj**, m. 'king of the Cedis,' id., L.; = -pati, MBh. iii, 898. — **rāja**, m. = -pati, Nal. xii f.; Hariv. 4964; BhP. ix, 24, 38; Śiśu-pāla, W. — **vishaya**, m. the country of the Cedis, MBh. i, 2335. — **hūṇa**, m. pl. the Cedis and the Hūṇas, Mudr.

Cedika, m. pl. the Cedis, VarBṛS. xiv, 8.

चेय ceya. See √1. ci.

चेर *cera*, N. of a southern kingdom, Inscr. **– pāda**, m. pl. N. of a people (?, cf. *īra-p°*), AitĀr.
Ceraka, m. (= *mīmāṅsaka ?*), Lalit. xxiv, 151.
Cerala, m. pl. N. of a family, Pravar. v, 4.

चेरु *céru*, mfn. (√*cāy*) behaving respectfully, worshipping, RV. viii, 61, 7.

चेल् *cel*, cl. 1. = √*cal*, Dhātup. xv, 29.

चेल *cela*, n. (√*cil*) clothes, garment, Gaut.; Mn.; MBh. &c. (ifc. f. *ā*, Hariv. 7946; Naish. xxii, 42); ifc. 'the mere outward appearance of,' a bad representative of (e.g. *bhāryā-cela*, n. 'a bad wife,' Pat. & Kāś.; also mf(*ī*)n., e.g. *brāhmaṇi-celī*, f. 'a bad wife of a Brahman,' *°ṇa-cela*, m. 'a bad Brahman,' Pāṇ. vi, 3, 43, Kāś.; Gaṇar. 114), Pāṇ. vi, 2, 126; m. = *ceṭa*, a servant, slave, MBh. ii, 70, 7, Sch.; cf. *ku-*, *āhara-celā*; *pāpa-celī* & *°likā*. **– kaṇṭhin**, mfn. for *śveta-k°*, Hariv. 6046. **– knopam**, ind. so as to wet the clothes (rain), Pāṇ. iii, 4, 33. **– gaṅgā**, f. N. of a river, Hariv. 7736 & 8493. **– cīrā**, f. a piece torn off from a garment, Rājat. iv, 573. **– nirṇejaka**, m. a washerman, Mn. iv, 216. **– prakshālaka**, m. id., R. (G) ii, 32, 21. **– rucikā**, f. a mourning band (?), Hcar. v, 23 (v.l.) **Celâpahāra**, m. theft of garments, MBh. viii, 2045; (cf. Mn. x, 167.) **Celâśaka**, m. 'clothes-eater,' a moth, Mn. xii, 72, Sch.

Célaka, m. for *chel°*, Npr.; N. of a man, ŚBr. x, 4, 5, 3; (cf. *cailaki*); (m. or n.) = *cela*, ifc. a bad representative of, Rājat. vii, 299; (*ikā*), f. a corset, bodice, PadmaP. iv.

चेलान *celāna*, m. a kind of cucumber, L.
Celāla, m. Cucumis sativus, L.

चेलिचीम *celicīma*, m. = *cilic°*, L., Sch.
Celīma, m. id., W.

चेलुक *celuka*, m. a Buddhist novice, L.

चेल्ल् *cell*, v.l. for √*cel*.

चेवी *cevī*, f. N. of a Rāgiṇī (in music), L.

चेष्ट् *cesht*, cl. 1. *céshṭati*, *°te* (inf. *°ṭitum*) to move the limbs, move, stir, MBh.; R.; BhP.; Śak.; to make effort, exert one's self, struggle, strive, be active, AV. xi, 4, 23 f.; ŚBr. iii; Lāṭy.; Kauś.; Mn.; MBh.; to be busy or occupied with (acc.); to act, do, perform, care for, Gobh. i, 6, 19; MBh.; R.; Śak.; Rājat. iii, 493; to prepare, ŚBr. xiv, 9, 4, 18 (ind. p. *ceshṭitvā*): Caus. *°ṭayati*, *°te* (aor. *aciceshṭat* [Bhaṭṭ. xv, 60] or *acac°*, Pāṇ. vii, 4, 96) to cause to move, set in motion, impel, drive, ŚāṅkhŚr. viii, 9, 3; Mn. xii, 15; MBh.; R.; Suśr. iv, 32, 17.

Ceshṭa, m. 'moving,' a kind of fish (*tapasvin*), L.; n. moving the limbs, gesture, Mn. vii, 63; behaviour, manner of life, Hariv. 5939; (*ā*), f. (Pāṇ. ii, 3, 12) moving any limb, gesture, Mn. vii f.; Yājñ.; MBh. &c. (ifc., Ragh. ii, 43); action, activity, effort, endeavour, exertion, ĀśvŚr. i; ŚvetUp. ii, 9 (ifc.); Mn. iv, 63; Bhag. &c.; doing, performing, Mn. i, 65; behaving, manner of life, Mn. vii, 194; KapS. iii, 51; VarBṛS. (ifc.) &c.; cf. *a-*, *nashṭa-*, *niś-*.
Ceshṭaka, mfn. making effort or exertion, W.; m. a kind of fish (= *°ṭa*), L.; a kind of coitus.
Ceshṭana, n. making effort, W.; motion, Mn. xii, 120; MBh. xii, 6363; R.; BhP.; ifc. performing, KapS. i, 3; effort, exertion, W. **Ceshṭayitṛi**, mfn. one who sets in motion, MBh. xii, 1181.
Ceshṭā, f., see *°ṭa*. **– nāśa**, m. ceasing of every motion, L.; destruction of the world, L. **– nirūpaṇa**, n. observing any one's actions, W. **– °rha** (*°ṭâr°*), mfn. worthy of effort, W. **– vat**, mfn. moveable, Suśr. iii, 5, 23; full of activity, active, W.
Ceshṭita, mfn. set in motion, W.; done with effort, exerted, W.; done, Śak. iii, $\frac{22}{23}$ (v.l.); v, 9; frequented, Ragh. xi, 51; n. moving any limb, gesture, Mn.; Suśr.; VarBṛS.; doing, action, behaviour, manner of life, Mn.; MBh.; R.; KapS. iii, 59 ff.; Śak. &c. (ifc. f. *ā*, Bhar. xxxiv, 118). **Ceshṭitavya**, n. impers. to be done or managed, MBh. xii, 4919.

चैकयत *caikayata*, m. patr., f. *°tyā*, g. *kraudy-ādi* (Gaṇar. 36; *caitay°* [Pāṇ.], Sch.)

चैकित *caikita*, mfn. fr. *°tya*, g. *kaṇvâdi*, m. patr., Pravar. iv, 1 (Kāty.; *vaikṛiti*, MatsyaP.)
Caikitāna, m. patr. fr. *cik°*, BṛĀrUp. i, 3, Sch.
Caikitāneyá, m. patr. fr. (*°na*, BṛĀrUp., Sch.) *cékitāna*, ŚBr. xiv, 4, 1, 26; ShaḍvBr. iv, 1; VBr.
Caikitāyana, m. patr. of Dālbhya (fr. *cik°*, Sch.; or fr. *cikita*), ChUp. i, 8, 1; MatsyaP. lxix, 19.
Caikitya, m. patr. fr. *cikita*, g. *gargâdi*.
Caikitsita, mfn. fr. *°tsitya*, g. *kaṇvâdi*.
Caikitsitya, m. patr. fr. *cikitsita*, g. *gargâdi*.

चैकीर्षत *caikīrshata*, mfn. = *cikīrshat* (p. √1. *kṛi*, Intens.), g. *prajñâdi*.
Caikīrshita, mfn. (fr. *cik°*) for *°shata*, Gaṇar.

चैटयत *caiṭayata*, m. patr. **– vidha**, mfn. inhabited by the Caiṭayatas, g. *bhauriky-ādi*.
Caiṭayatāyani, m. patr. fr. *°ta*, g. *tikâdi*.
Caiṭayatyā, f. of *°ta*, g. *kraudy-ādi*.

चैतकि *caitaki*, m. pl. (fr. *cetaka*) N. of a family, Pravar. ii, 2, 2.

Caitanya, n. (fr. *cétana*) consciousness, MBh. xiv, 529; Suśr. i, 21, 24, &c.; intelligence, sensation, soul, spirit, KapS. iii, 20; Sāṃkhyak. &c.; the Universal Soul or Spirit; m. N. of a reformer of the Vaishṇava faith (born about 1485 A.D., RTL. 138). **– candrôdaya**, m. 'moon-rise of the reformer Caitanya,' N. of a drama. **– caraṇâmṛita**, n. 'nectar of Caitanya's life,' N. of a work by Kṛishṇa-dāsa (abridgement of the Caitanya-caritra, W.) **– caritâmṛita**, n. = *°raṇâm°*. **– caritra**, m. N. of a work (see before). **– deva**, m. N. of a man, Kathârṇ. (colophon). **– bhairavī**, f. a form of Durgā, Tantras. ii. **– maṅgala**, n. N. of a work. **– yukta**, mfn. endowed with consciousness, Yājñ. iii, 81 (ifc.) **Caitanyâmṛita**, n. N. of a grammar.

Caitayata (fr. *cetayat*), see *caikay°*. **Caitasika**, mfn. relating to the mind (*cétas*, as duties), Buddh. L. **Caitika**, m. pl. (fr. 2. *caitya* ?, cf. *caitya-śaila*) N. of a Buddh. school. **Caitta**, mfn. belonging to thought (*cittá*), imagined, Vedântas.; mental, Bādar. ii, 2, 18, Sch.; Prab., Sch. **Caittika**, mfn. belonging to thought, W.

1. **Caitya**, m. (fr. 5. *cit* or 2. *citi*) the individual soul, BhP. iii, 26; 28, 28; 31, 19; Sarvad. ii, 198 f.

चैत्य 2. *caitya*, mfn. relating to a funeral pile or mound (*citā*), ĀśvGṛ. iii, 6; Gṛihyās. ii, 4; m. n. a funeral monument or Stūpa (q. v.) or pyramidal column containing the ashes of deceased persons, sacred tree (esp. a religious fig-tree) growing on a mound, hall or temple or place of worship (esp. with Buddh. & Jain. and generally containing a monument), a sanctuary near a village, ĀśvGṛ. i, 12; Parās.; Yājñ. ii, 151 & 228; MBh. &c.; a Jain or Buddh. image, L.; m. = *°tyaka*, ii, 814. **– taru**, m. a tree (esp. religious fig-tree) standing on a sacred spot, VarBṛS. **– dru**, m. a religious fig-tree, L.; a large tree in a village, W. **– druma**, m. = *-taru*, Mn. x, 50. **– pāla**, m. the guardian of a caitya, R. v, 38, 29. **– mukha**, m. 'having an opening like that of a Buddh. sanctuary,' a hermit's water-pot, L. **– yajña**, m. a sacrificial ceremony performed at a monument, ĀśvGṛ. i, 12. **– vṛiksha**, m. = *-taru*, AV. Pariś. lxxi; Mn. ix, 264; MBh.; R.; a religious fig-tree, L. **– śaila**, m. pl. N. of a Buddh. school; cf. *caitika*. **– sthāna**, n. a place made sacred by a monument or a sanctuary, MBh. xiii, 4729 & 7701.

Caityaka, m. one of the 5 mountains surrounding the town Giri-vraja, ii, 799; 811 ff.; 843.

चैत्र *caitra*, m. N. of the 2nd spring month (its full moon standing in the constellation Citrā, cf. Pāṇ. iv, 2, 23), ŚāṅkhBr. xix, 3; KātyŚr.; Lāṭy.; Mn. vii, 182; MBh. &c.; the 6th year in the cycle of Jupiter, VarBṛS. viii, 8; a Buddh. or Jain religious mendicant, L.; a common N. for any man (like Deva-datta), Gauḍap. on Sāṃkhyak. 5 & 7; Prab. iii, $\frac{1}{2}$, Sch.; Pāṇ. ii, 3, 29, Sch. (not in Kāś.); 'son of Citrā,' N. of a son of Budha and grandfather of Su-ratha, BrahmavP.; = *caitriyāyaṇá*, Anukr. on Kāṭh. xxxix, 14; N. of two Ṛishis, VP. iii, 1, 12 & 18; one of the seven ranges of mountains (dividing the continent into Varshas), L.; n. = *caitya*, a sepulchre, L.; a sanctuary, L.; mfn. for *citra* (B) or *jaitra* (Sch.), MBh. vii, 76; (*ī*), f. (with or without *paurṇamāsī*) the day of full moon in month Caitra, sacrifice offered on that day, ŚāṅkhŚr. iii, 13, 2; KātyŚr. xiii; Lāṭy. x; Pāṇ. iv, 2, 23; MBh. xii, xiv. **– vatī**, for *vetr°*. **– sakha**, m. 'friend of month Caitra,' the god of love, L., Sch. **Caitrâvalī**, f. the day of full moon in month Caitra, L.

Caitraka, m. = *°trika*, L.; m. pl. N. of a warrior tribe, Pāṇ. vi, 2, 34, Kāś. **Caitrakūṭī**, f. (fr. *citra-kūṭa*) N. of a Comm. on a grammatical work.
Caitraga, m. pl. N. of a family, Pravar. v, 1.
Caitrabhānava, mfn. belonging to Agni (*citra-bhānu*), Bālar. vii, $\frac{33}{34}$; viii, $\frac{33}{34}$, 1.
Caitraratha, mfn. treating of the Gandharva Citra-ratha, MBh. i, 313; m. patr. fr. Citra-ratha, i, 3740; (N. of Śaśa-bindu) xii, 998; of a Dvy-aha ceremony, KātyŚr. xxiii, 2, 3; Maś.; n. (with or without *vana*) the grove of Kubera cultivated by the Gandharva Citra-ratha, MBh. iii, v; Hariv.; R.; Divyâv. xiv; BhP.; Ragh. v, 60; Kād.; (*ī*), f. patr. of a daughter of Śaśa-bindu, Hariv. 712.
Caitrarathi, m. patr. fr. Citra-ratha, TāṇḍyaBr. xx, 12; (Śaśa-bindu) Hariv. 1972.
Caitrarathya, n. = *°tha*, Kubera's grove, BhP. iii.
Caitravāhanī, f. patr. of Citrâṅgadā (fr. *citra-vāhana*), MBh. i, 7827; xiv, 2358 & 2405. **Caitraseni**, m. patr. fr. *citra-sena*, vii, 916 & 1091.
Caitrāyaṇa, m. (g. 1. *naḍâdi*) patr. fr. Citra, Pravar. iii, 1; cf. *jait°*; N. of a place, g. *pakshâdi*.
Caitri, v. l. for *°trin*, W. **Caitrika**, m. the month Caitra, Pāṇ. iv, 2, 23. **Caitrin**, m. id., L.
Caitriyāyaṇá, m. (for *°tryāy°*, see *caitra*) patr. of Yajña-sena, TS. v, 3, 8, 1. **Caitrī**, f., see *°tra*. **– paksha**, m. the dark half in Caitra, Lāṭy. x, 5 & 20.
Caitreyá, mfn. coming from a speckled cow (*citrā*), MaitrS. ii, 5, 9; m. metron. fr. Citrā, Pravar.

चैदिक *caidika*, mf(*ā*, *ī*)n. g. *kāśy-ādi*.
Caidyá, m. patr. fr. *cedi*, VP. iv, 12, 15 (pl.); a prince of the Cedis (esp. Śiśu-pāla, MBh. i, 129; ii, 1523; Hariv. 1804 f.; BhP. vii, 1, 15 & 30; ix, 24, 2), RV. viii, 5, 37 f.; (pl.) the Cedi people, L.; (*ā*), f. a princess of the Cedis, MBh. i, 3831.

चैन्तित *caintita*, m. metron. fr. Cintitā, Pāṇ. iv, 1, 113, Kāś.

चैल *caila*, mfn. made of cloth (*cela*), W.; bred in clothes (as insects; m. = *celâśaka*), Mn. xii, 72, Kull.; m. N. of a man (cf. *célaka*), VāyuP. i, 61, 40; pl. N. of a family, Pravar. ii, 2, 1 (v. l. *cela*, *°laka*); n. = *celā*, clothes, garment, Kauś.; Yājñ. ii, 97 (ifc.), MBh. (ifc. f. *ā*, iii, 12725); Pañcat.; BhP. x, 42, 33; Kuval.; a piece of cloth, Car. **– dhāva**, m. = *cela-nirṇejaka*, Yājñ. i, 164. **Cailâśaka**, m. a kind of goblin feeding on moths, Mn. xii, 72.
Cailaka, m. 'clothed with a *cela* (?),' a Buddh. mendicant, Buddh.; (cf. *celuka*.) **Cailaki**, m. patr. fr. *célaka*, N. of Jīvala, ŚBr. ii, 3, 1, 34.
Cailika, a piece of cloth, Suśr. vi, 18, 41 (v. l.)
Caileya, mfn. made of cloth, BhP. x, 41, 40.

चोक *coka*, n. the root of Cleome felina, Bhpr. v, 1, 177.

चोक्ष *coksha*, mf(*ā*)n. (cf. *cukshā*), pure, clean (persons), Mn. iii, 207; MBh. xii f.; (often in Prākṛit *cokkha*, Jain.); dexterous, L.; agreeable, pleasant, L.; sung, L.; *abhīkshṇa* (*tīkshṇa*, W.), L.

चोच *coca*, n. the bark of cinnamon, Suśr.; Pañcar. iii, 13, 11; bark, L.; skin, L.; the cocoa-nut, VarBṛS. xli, 4; the fruit of the fan-palm, L., Sch.; the uneatable part of a fruit, L.; a banana, L., Sch.
Cocaka, n. the bark of cinnamon, Suśr.; bark, L.

चोटिका *coṭikā*, *°ṭī*, f. a petticoat, L.

चोड *coḍa*, m. = *cūḍa*, a sort of protuberance on a brick, TS. v, 3, 7, 1 (ifc.); = *°ḍaka*, SaddhP.; pl. N. of a people, L.; sg. a prince of that people, Pāṇ. iv, 1, 175, Vārtt. (v. l. *cola*); (*ā*), f. N. of a plant, L. **– karṇa**, m. 'projecting-ear,' N. of a man, Kathās. lxix, 164.
Coḍaka, = *colaka*, a jacket, Divyâv. xxvii, 541.

चोद *coda*, *°daka*, *°dana*, &c. See √*cud*.

चोपक *copaka*. See *gale-*.

चोपड *copaḍa*, m. cream, L.

चोपन *copana*. See √1. *cup*.

चोर *corá*, *°raka*, *°rāyita*, &c. See √*cur*.

चोल *cola*, m. (= *coḍa*) a jacket, bodice, Naish. xxii, 42 (ifc. f. *ā*; v. l.); pl. N. of a people in southern India on the Coromandel (= *cola-maṇḍala*) coast, MBh. iii, vi ff.; Hariv. 782 & 9600; R. iv, 41, 18; VarBṛS. &c.; sg. the ancestor of the Colas, Hariv. 1836; a prince of the Colas, MBh. ii, 1893; PadmaP. v, 153 f.; Rājat. i, 300; n. (= *cela*) garment, L.; (*ī*), f. a jacket, L., Sch.; a Cola woman, Vcar. v, 89. **– paṭṭaka**, m. a piece of cloth worn (by Jainas) round the middle of the body, Śil. — **maṇḍala,** n. 'Cola territory,' the Coromandel coast. **Colôṇḍuka,** m. a turban, L.

Colaka, m. (= *coḍaka*) a jacket, HPariś. ii, 38; a cuirass, L.; pl. the Colas, Kathās. xix; n. bark, L.

Colakin, m. a cuirassier, W.; 'sheathed,' a bamboo shoot, L.; the orange tree, L.; the wrist, L.

चोष *cosha,* °*shaṇa,* °*shya.* See √*cūsh.*

चोस्क *coska,* m. an Indus horse, L.

चौक्र्य *caukrya,* n. (fr. *cukra*) sourness, acidity, g. *dṛiḍhâdi.*

चौक्ष *cauksha,* mfn. (fr. *cukshā,* g. *chattrâdi*) = *coksha,* pure, clean (persons), MBh. xii, 4315; m. pl. N. of a family, Pravar. i, (1 &) 7.

Caukshya, mfn. clean, MBh. xii; Suśr. ii, 12, 3.

चौड *cauḍa,* mfn. fr. *coḍa,* see *-deśa;* relating to a crest (*cūḍā*), W.; relating to tonsure, W.; n. = *caula,* Mn. ii, 27; MBh. iii, 12240; Pāṇ. v, 1, 110, Kāś. — **karman,** n. = *caula-k*°, W. — **deśa,** m. the Coḍa (Cola) country, Ratnak.

Cauḍārya, mfn. fr. *cūḍāra,* g. *pragady-ādi.*

Cauḍāli, m. metron. fr. *cūḍālā,* g. *bāhv-ādi.*

Cauḍi, m. metron. fr. *cūḍā,* g. *bāhv-ādi;* cf. *cauli.*

Cauḍikya, n. the state of being *cūḍika,* g. *purohitâdi.* **Cauḍitikya,** n. id., ib. (Kāś.)

चौण्ट्य *cauṇṭya,* mfn. coming from a well (*cuṇṭī*), Suśr. i, 45, 1, 1 & 24; 46, 2, 64.

Cauṇḍa, mfn. (fr. *cuṇḍa* for °*ḍya*) id., L. — **pa,** m. 'well-water-drinker,' N. of the author of Prayoga-ratna-mālā. — **rāja,** m. N. of a king, Inscr.

Cauṇḍya, mfn. = °*ḍa,* Bhpr. v, 10, 129 f. & 12, 48 f.

चौतपल्लव *cautapallava,* mf(*ī*)n. relating to a Cūta shoot (*pallava*), Śiś. ii, 19.

चौदायनि *caudāyani,* m. patr., see *cod*°.

चौद्रायण *caudrāyaṇa,* m. N. of a prince of Daśa-pura, HPariś. xiii, 1.

चौपयत *caupayata,* m. patr. fr. *copayat* (√*cup,* Caus. p.) — **vidha,** mfn. inhabited by Caupayatas, g. *bhauriky-ādi.*

Caupayatāyani, m. patr. fr. °*ta,* g. *tikâdi.*

Caupayatyā, f. of °*ta,* g. *krauḍy-ādi.*

Caupāyana, m. patr. fr. *cupa,* g. 1. *aśvâdi.*

चौर *caura,* mfn. (√*cur*) thievish, HPariś. ii, 170; (= *corá,* g. *prajñâdi;* g. *chattrâdi*) a thief, robber, Mn. iv, viii, xi (ifc.); Hariv. &c.; a dishonest or unfair dealer, usurper, Pañcat. i, 8, $\frac{11}{12}$ & $\frac{18}{19}$ (also in comp. translatable as adj.); (ifc. e. g. *kavi-,* 'a plagiarist') Gaṇar. 114; a (heart-)captivator, Hariv. 7125; 9981 & 9994; the perfume Coraka, L.; 'plagiarist,' N. of a poet (cf. *cora*), ŚārṅgP.; pl. N. of a family, Pravar. i, 7 (Kāty. & Viśvan.); (*ī*), f. a female thief, (heart-)captivator, Kathās. vc, 54; civ, 168; = °*ra-karman,* L. — **karman,** n. thievery, theft, Pañcat. i, 19, $\frac{5}{6}$; v, 7, $\frac{9}{10}$. — **gata,** mfn. stolen, W. — **m-kāram,** ind. for *cor*°. — **tara,** m. (compar.) a great thief, Naish. viii, 59. — **tas,** ind. from theft, W.; from robbers, W. — **dhvaja-baddhaka,** m. a notorious thief, Buddh. L. — **pañcāśikā,** f. irr. abbreviation for *caurī-surata-p*° (for *cauḍi-,* Prākṛit fr. *cāpotkaṭī-*?) '50 stanzas on secret love (or on the love of the Cāpotkaṭa princess),' a famous poem by Bilhaṇa. — **pushpâushadhi,** f. = *cora-pushpī,* L. — **bhavānī,** f. N. of a Tīrtha, Rasik. xi, 33. — **rūpa,** m. a clever thief, W. — **rūpin,** mfn. thief-natured, W. — **hṛita,** mfn. taken by robbery, W. **Caurâṅśā,** f. a metre of 4 × 6 syllables. **Caurâṭavī,** f. a forest inhabited by robbers, Kathās. iic, 12. **Caurâpahṛita,** mfn. = °*ra-h*°. **Caurôddharaṇa,** n. extirpation of robbers. **Caurôddharaṇika,** m. 'thief-extirpator,' a thief-catcher. **Caurôddhartṛi,** m. id., Yājñ. ii, 271.

Cauraka, m. the perfume Coraka, L.; (*ikā*), f. 'a female thief,' see *taila-;* (g. *manojñâdi*) = °*ra-karman,* Mn. i, 82; Pañcat. v, 7, 1; [instr. *ayā,* ind. clandestinely, in the back of (gen.)] iii, 16, $\frac{9}{10}$.

Caurasya-kula, n. a gang of thieves, Pāṇ. vi, 3, 21, Kāś. **Caurâdika,** mfn. belonging to the *cur-ādi* roots. **Cauri-kāka** (fr. °*rin*?), see *ciri-k*°.

Caurī, ind. and f. (see °*ra*) in comp. — **bhūta,** mfn. set on by thieves, BhP. iv, 18, 7. — **surata,** n. = '°*rya-surata,*' *-pañcāśikā,* see *caura-p*°.

Caurya, n. (g. *brāhmaṇâdi*) = °*ra-karman,* Mn. ix, xi; Yājñ. ii, 72; Mṛicch. &c.; trickery, Hariv. 15163 f.; (ifc. with *śulka*) defraudation, Pañcat. iv, 5, $\frac{9}{10}$. — **rata,** n. secret sexual enjoyment, i, 4, 12. — **vidyā,** f. 'thieving science,' a treatise ascribed to Yogâcārya (imparted to him by Kārttikeya), Mṛicch. iii, $\frac{14}{15}$, Sch. — **vṛitti,** mfn. living on thievery, Daś. ix, 11 (v. l. °*ra-v*°); f. practice of theft or robbery, W. — **surata,** n. = *-rata,* Alaṃkāras. **Cauryârjita,** mfn. acquired by robbery, W.

Cauryaka, n. = °*ra-karman,* MBh. xii, 8501.

चौरङ्गिन् *caurangin,* m. N. of a teacher, Haṭhapr. i, 5.

चौरोल *caurola,* N. of a metre, W.

चौर्य *caurya,* °*yaka.* See *caura.*

चौल *caula,* n. (fr. *cūlā* = *cūḍā*) the tonsure ceremony (see *cūḍā-karaṇa*), ĀśvGṛ. i, 17, 1; NārS. i, 13; xxii; Śūdradh.; ifc. (g. *cūrṇâdi*), see *cūlā.* — **karman,** n. id., ĀśvGṛ. i, 4, 1. — **śrī-pati-tīrtha,** n. N. of a Tīrtha, RevāKh. cclxxv.

Caulakāyana, patr. fr. *cūlaka,* Pravar. iv, 1 (B).

Cauli, m. = *cauḍi,* vi, 1 (°*lakāyana* B, °*lika* V).

चौलुक्य *caulukya,* m. (g. *kaṇvâdi*) patr. fr. Culuka, N. of king Kumāra-pāla, Hemac.

चौहाण *cauhāṇa,* or °*hāna,* N. of king Vaijana's dynasty (16th century).

चौहार *cauhāra,* m. a kind of dill, L.

चौहित्थ *cauhittha,* N. of a man, Bhojapr.

च्यव *cyava,* °*va-tāna.* See √2. *cyu.*

Cyávana, cyávāna, cyāva, &c. See ib.

च्यु 1. *cyu* (& *cyus*), cl. 10. *cyāvayati* (*cyosayati*) = √*sah* or *has,* Dhātup. xxxiii, 72.

च्यु 2. *cyu,* cl. 1. *cyávate* (ep. also °*ti;* Subj. 1. sg. *cyávam,* RV. i, 165, 10; 3. pl. *cyavanta,* 48, 2; fut. *cyoshyate,* AitBr. ii, 22; aor. 2. pl. *acyoḍhvam* [Subj. *cy*°, MahānārUp.] & Prec. *cyoshīḍhvam,* Pāṇ. viii, 3, 78, Kāś.) to move to and fro, shake about, RV. i, 167, 8; to stir, move from one's place, go away, retire from (abl.), turn off, vi, 62, 7; x; BhP. ix, 14, 20; to deviate from (abl.), abandon (duty &c., abl.; exceptionally gen., MBh. xv, 463 [C] inf. *cyavitum*), Mn. vii, 98; MBh. iii; to come forth from, come out of, drop from, trickle, stream forth from (abl.; cf. √2. *cyut*), 14598; R. ii, 39, 15; to fall down, fall, slide from (abl.), v, 13, 31; to fall from any divine existence (so as to be re-born as a man), Jain.; to die, Buddh.; 'to fall from,' be deprived of, lose (with abl.), Mn. iii, 140; viii, 103; Bhaṭṭ. iii, 20 (aor. *acyoshṭa*); to fall away, fade away, disappear, vanish, perish, Mn. xii, 96; MBh.; BhP. iii, 28, 18; to fail, MBh. v, 1089; to sink down, sink (lit. and fig.), MuṇḍUp. i, 2, 9; (in the series of re-births) Bhag. ix, 24; to decrease (with instr.), MBh. iii, 14141; to bring about, create, make, RV. i, 48, 2; iv, 30, 22 (pf. 2. sg. *cicyushé,* cf. Pāṇ. vi, 1, 36); viii, 45, 25 (pf. *cucyuvé*); to cause to go away, make forget, MahānārUp.: Caus. *cyāvâyati* (once *cyav*°, ŚāṅkhBr. xii, 5; Pada-p. always *cyav*°; p. *cyāvâyat;* RV. iii, 30, 4; impf. *acucyavur,* i, 166, 5 & 168, 4; pf. *cyāvayām āsa,* MBh. iii, 15920) P. to cause to move, shake, agitate, RV. i; iii, 30, 4; AV. x, xii; Ā. to be moved or shaken, RV. vi, 31, 2; P. to loosen, i, 168, 6; to remove from a place, drive away from (abl.), TS. ii, 2, 7, 5; ŚBr. i, x; MBh.; R.; to cause (rain, *vṛishṭim*) to fall, TS. iii, 3, 4, 1; TāṇḍyaBr. xiii, 5, 13; ŚāṅkhBr. xii, 5; to deprive any one (acc.) of (acc.), R. ii, 53, 7; Intens. (impf. 2. pl. *acucyavītana*) to shake, RV. i, 37, 12: Caus. Desid. *cicyāvayishati* or *cucy*°, Pāṇ. vii, 4, 81.

Cyava, mfn., see *bhuvana-cyavá.* — **tāna** (*cyáv*°), m. N. of a man, RV. v, 33, 9.

Cyávana, mfn. moving, moved, ii, 12, 4; causing to move, shaking, 21, 3; vi, viii, x; AV. vii, 116, 1; promoting delivery (a *mantra*), Suśr. iv, 15, 2; m. one who causes to move, shaker, RV. viii, 96, 4; N. of a demon causing diseases, PārGṛ. i, 16, 23; (later form for *cyávāna*) N. of a Ṛishi (son of Bhṛigu, author of RV. x, 19), AitBr. viii, 21; ŚBr. iv, 1, 5, 1; Nir.; MBh. (father of Ṛicīka, xiii, 207) &c.; of an astronomer, NārS. i, 3; Nirṇayas. i, 563; of a physician, BrahmavP. i, 16, 17; of the author of a law-book (see *-smṛiti*), PārGṛ., Sch. Introd.; of a Saptarshi in the 2nd Manv-antara, Hariv. (v. l. for *niś-cy*°); of a son (of Su-hotra, 1803; BhP. ix, 22, 5; of Mitrâyu, 1); n. motion, Suśr. i, 15, 1; the being deprived of (in comp.), BhP. viii, 20, 5; falling from any divine existence for being re-born as a man, Jain.; dying, Buddh.; trickling, flowing, W.; cf. *duś-cyavaná.* — **dharma,** mfn. destined to sink down in the series of re-births, MBh. xii, 13163. — **dharman,** °**min,** mfn. destined to fall from any divine existence (so as to be re-born as a man), Divyâv. iii, 33 f.; xiv, 1 ff. — **nahusha-saṃvāda,** m. 'discussion between Cyavana and Nahusha,' N. of MBh. xiii, chs. 50–52. — **prâśa,** m. N. of an electuary (cf. *cyāvana*), Mallapr. — **samāgama,** m. N. of PadmaP. iv, 44. — **smṛiti,** f. N. of a work, v, 43; Parāś. iv, Sch. **Cyavanôpâkhyāna,** n. 'tale of Cyavana,' N. of MBh. xiii, chs. 50–52 (2641–2754) & of PadmaP. ii, 80 & iv, 42.

Cyavas, n. 'motion.' See *trishu-cyáv*°.

Cyávāna, mfn. (pr. p. √*cyu*) 'moving,' active, RV. vi, 62, 7; x, 59, 1; (61, 2); 115, 6 (with *trishṭí*); m. (= *cyávana*) N. of a Ṛishi (restored to youth by the Aśvins), RV. i, v, vii, x; BrahmaP. ii, 18, 8; m. du. 'active,' the arms, Naigh. ii, 4.

Cyāva. See *duś-.*

1. **Cyāvana,** mfn. (√*cyu,* Caus.) causing to fall (ifc.), MBh. viii, 1506; n. expulsion, Hariv. 1512.

2. **Cyāvana,** mfn. relating to *Cyavana* (with *prâśa* = *cyavana-pr*°, Car. vi, 1 & 31); m. patr. fr. Cyavana, TāṇḍyaBr. xiii, xix; Pravar. i; ŚāṅkhBr. iii, 2, Sch.; n. N. of several Sāmans, ĀrshBr.

Cyāvayitṛi, m. a causer of motion, Nir. iv, 19.

Cyāvita, mfn. expelled from (abl.), BhP. viii, 17, 12; caused to fall, Hariv. 1326.

1. **Cyut,** mfn. ifc. 'moving,' see *trishu-cyút;* 'shaking, causing to fall, removing, destroying,' see *acyuta-, dhruva-, parvata-, bāhu-, mada-cyút.*

1. **Cyutá,** mfn. moved, shaken, AV. ix, 2, 15; gone away from (abl.), R. ii, 52, 27 & 72, 5; (with abl. or ifc.) deviated from (lit. [Pañcat. v, 3, $\frac{10}{11}$] and fig. [Mn. viii, 418; xii, 70 ff.; Hariv. 11105 & 11188]); (said of arrows) failing an aim (abl.), L.; flying away from (abl. or in comp.; said of missile weapons), MBh. xiii, 4610; Hariv. 8088; R. iii; BhP. iii, 18, 5; expelled from, deprived of (abl.), MBh. iii; Bhaṭṭ. vii, 92; destitute of, free of (in comp.), Pañcat. i, 10, 26; Kathās. lx, 178; abandoned by (in comp.), VarBṛS. li, 2; disappeared, vanished, Hariv. 11173; Ragh. iii, 45; viii, 65; Bhaṭṭ. iii; come forth from, dropped from, streaming forth from (lit. and fig., as speech from the mouth), Mn. vi, 132; MBh. xiii, 2183; R. i–iii; BhP.; Bhaṭṭ. ix, 71; fallen from, fallen, MBh. &c.; fallen from any divine existence for being re-born as a man, Buddh.; Jain.; (in astrol.) standing in the ἀποκλίματα, Laghuj. x, 5; sunk (morally), Kum. v, 81; (in math.) divided, Bījag.; cf. *á-, hásta-.* — **dattâkshara,** mf(*ā*)n. where a syllable has been dropped or added, Sāh. x, 14. — **pathaka,** m. 'deviated from the path,' N. of a pupil of Śākyamuni, Buddh. L. — **saṃskāra,** mfn. offending against grammar, Pratāpar. — **saṃskṛiti,** mfn. id., ib.; Kpr. vii, 2. **Cyutâkshara,** mf(*ā*)n. where a syllable has been dropped, Sāh. x, $\frac{14}{15}$. **Cyutâcāra,** mfn. deviated from duty, PadmaP. v, 20, 9. **Cyutâdhikāra,** mfn. dismissed from an office, W. **Cyutôtsāha,** mfn. having spent one's energies, exhausted.

Cyutaka. See *akshara-mātrā-.*

Cyuti, f. 'banishment,' see *deśa-,* 'coming forth,' see *garbha-;* 'oozing,' see *jaghána-;* falling, falling down, gliding, Gaut.; Suśr.; (with *garbhasya,* 'abortion') VarBṛ. iv, 9, Sch.; fall, degeneration, Bhartṛ. iii, 32; fall from any divine existence (so as to be re-born as a man), Lalit. iv, 4 & 31; HPariś.; deviation from (abl.), MBh. i, 4169; Bhartṛ.; vanishment, loss (ifc.), Suśr.; Kum. iii, 10; Śāntiś.; BhP. x, 22, 20; perishing, dying, W.; the vulva, L.; (= *cuti*) the anus, L.; cf. *sá-, hásta-.*

Cyautná, mfn. animating, promoting (with acc.), RV. x, 50, 4; n. shaking, concussion, vi, 18, 8; enterprise, contrivance, strength (Naigh. ii, 9), RV.

च्युत् 2. *cyut* (= √*ścut, ścyut*), cl. 1. *cyotati* (aor. *acyutat* & *acyotīt; acyutīt,* Vop. viii, 38) to flow, trickle, ooze, Bhaṭṭ. vi, 28; to fall down, 29; to cause to stream forth, Uttarar. iii, 35; Bhaṭṭ. xv, 114: Caus. *cyotayati,* to lixiviate, Car. vi, 24.

3. **Cyut,** mfn. 'distilling.' See *mada-, madhu-.*

2. **Cyuta,** mfn. ifc. id. See *ghṛita-, madhu-.*

Cyota, m. = *ścy*°, L., Sch.

च्युप *cyupa,* m. the mouth, Uṇ. iii, 24.

च्युस् *cyus,* see √1. *cyu;* cl. 10. *cyosayati,* to leave, Dhātup. xxxiii, 72.

च्यूत *cyūta*, v.l. for *cūta*, the anus, W.

च्यौत्न *cyautná*. See √2. *cyu*.

छ CHA.

छ 1. *cha*, the 7th consonant (aspirate of the preceding). **–kāra**, m. the letter or sound *cha*.

छ 2. *cha*, m. (√*cho*) dividing, L.; a fragment, L. **–maṇḍala**, n.=*pradeśa-viśesha*, L.

छ 3. *cha*, mfn. pure, clean, L.; tremulous, unsteady, L.; (*ā*), f. covering, concealing (cf. √*chad*), L.; a mark, sign, L.; cf. *chā*.

छग *chaga*, m.=*chā́ga*, a he-goat, L.

Chagalá, m. id., TS. v, 6, 22, 1; Suśr.; (Pāṇ. iv, 1, 117) N. of a muni, VāyuP. i, 23, 198; of a locality, g. *takshaśilâdi*; pl. N. of a family, Pravar. iii, 1; n. blue cloth, L.; (*ā*), f. N. of a woman, g. *bāhv-ādi*; =°*lântrikā*, L.; (*ī*), f. id., L.; a she-goat, Car. i, 3, 21 (*-payas*, n.) **Chagalâṅghrī**, v.l. for °*lântrī*, L., Sch. **Chagalâṇḍa**, n. 'goat-testicle,' N. of a Tīrtha, MatsyaP. xiii (v.l. *chāg*°); (*ī*), v.l. for °*lântrī*, L., Sch. **Chagalântrikā**, f. Argyreia speciosa or argentea (*ajântrī*), L. **Chagalântrin**, m. 'having goats in the bowels,' a wolf, L. **Chagalântrī**, f. =°*trikā*, Suśr. i, 38, 26 & 39, 2; 46, 4, 39.

Chagalaka, m. a he-goat, L.; (*ikā*), f. a she-goat, Divyâv. xviii, 136. **Chagalin**, m. N. of a teacher (pupil of Kalāpin, Pāṇ. iv, 3, 104, Kāś.), 109.

छगण *chagaṇa* (fr. *śakn-* of *śakṛit*), m. [n., L.] dried cow-dung, Pañcad. iv, 9; cf. *chāg*°.

छगल *chagalá*, &c. See *chaga*.

छच्छिका *chacchikā*, butter-milk, Bhpr. v.

छज्जू *chajjū*, m. N. of a man, Kathārṇ. xxx.

छटा *chaṭā*, f. a mass, lump, assemblage, number, Śiś. i, 47; Kathās.; Rājat. v, 332; Prasannar.; Sāh.; a collection of rays, lustre, Pañcar.; Dhūrtas.; Rājat. iv, 127; Prab.; Sāh.; =*chaḍī*, L.; N. of a Comm. on Vop. (also *chāṭā*). **–phala**, m. the betel-nut tree, L. **Chaṭâbhā**, f. lightning, L.

Chaḍī, f. a kind of palm, L.

छड्डलिका *chaḍḍalikā*, N. of a metre, Sāh.

छत्त्र *chattra*, &c. See √1. *chad*.

छद् 1. *chad*, cl. 1. °*dati*, to cover, Dhātup. xxxii, 41 (v.l.): Caus. (or cl. 10) *chādáyati* (once *chad*°, AitBr. i, 30; *chand*° [fr. √1. *chand*], Dhātup. xxxii, 41; ep. also Ā., pf. *chādayām cakre*, R. iv, 58, 7; p. °*yāna*, MBh. vi, 2430), to cover, cover over, clothe, veil, RV. vi, 75, 18; AV. ix, 3, 14; TS. ii, v; ŚBr. &c.; to spread as a cover, AitBr. i, 30; to cover one's self, ChUp. i, 4, 2; to hide, conceal, keep secret, MBh.; R. v, 90, 16; to protect, ŚāṅkhGṛ. iii, 11; PārGṛ. iii, 9, 6 (KāṭhGṛ. 47): Caus. Desid. *cicchādayishati*, Pāṇ. vii, 4, 83, Vārtt. 2, Pat.; [cf. Goth. *scadus*.]

Chattra, m. (Pāṇ. vi, 4, 97; often spelt *chatra*) a mushroom, L.; Andropogon Schœnanthus, L.; a parasol-shaped bee-hive, W.; n. a parasol, Chattar (ensign of royal or delegated power, Jain.; Rājat. v, 18; PSarv.), KātyŚr. xxi, 3, 6; Gobh.; Kauś.; ĀśvGṛ. iii, 8; AdbhBr.; Mn. &c. (ifc. f. *ā*, MBh. xii, 933); an umbrella, Cāṇ.; a particular constellation, VarBṛ. xii, 8; Laghuj. x, 8; 'shelter (of pupils),' a teacher (a meaning derived fr. *chāttra*), Pāṇ. iv, 4, 62, Pat.; (*ā*), f. N. of a plant growing in Kaśmīr, Suśr. i, 19, 27; iv, 30; Anethum Sowa, L.; Asteracantha longifolia, L.; Rubia Munjista, L.; a mushroom, L.; cf. *ati-*, *ahi-*, *eka-*, *gomaya-*, *sita-*; *ākṛiti-cchattrā*. **–guccha**, m. 'umbrella-clustered,' Scirpus Kysoor, L. **–gṛiha**, n. the room in which the parasol (or badge of royalty) is kept, MBh. v, 3544. **–grāhiṇī**, f. a female parasol-bearer, Kād. **–cakra**, n. (in astrol.) a kind of diagram. **–dhānya**, n. coriander, L. **–dhāra**, m. (Pāṇ. vi, 2, 75, Kāś.) a parasol-bearer, R. iii, 58, 3; Pañcat. (*-tva*, n. abstr., i, 10, $\frac{3}{8}$). **–dhāraṇa**, n. carrying or using a parasol, Mn. ii, 178 (ifc.); Pāṇ. iv, 4, 62, Pat. **–dhārin**, mfn. bearing a parasol, Mṛicch. v, $\frac{1}{1}\frac{1}{2}$; m. N. of a son of Horila-siṇha. **–pa**, m. = *-pati*, W. **–pati**, m. the officer watching over the royal parasol, Siṇhās. xxiii, $\frac{1}{2}$. **–pattra**, m. 'parasol-leaved,' Hibiscus mutabilis, L.; Betula Bhojpatra, Npr. **–parṇa**, m. 'parasol-leaved,' Alstonia scholaris, L. **–pushpaka**, m. 'parasol-flowered,' the Tilaka tree, Bhpr. **–bhaṅga**, m. destruction of the royal parasol,' loss of dominion, L.; anarchy (*svātantrya*), L.; widowhood, L. **–mukhā**, f. 'parasol-faced,' N. of a Nāga virgin, Kāraṇḍ. i, 48. **–yukti**, f. 'use of the parasol,' N. of a chapter of Bhoja's Yukti-kalpa-taru. **–vat**, mfn. furnished with a parasol, Suśr. i, 10, 1; (*tī*), f. N. of a town (*Ahi-cchattra*, Sch.), MBh. i, 6348. **–vṛiksha**, m. Pterospermum suberifolium, Bhpr. **–śāla**, m. N. of prince Sabhā-siṇha's father. **–siṇha**, n. N. of a Tīrtha, Rasik. xi, 38. **–haya**, m. pl. N. of a family, Pravar. ii, 3, 6; v, 1. **Chattrâkāra-śiras**, mfn. having a parasol-shaped head, Divyâv. **Chattrâticchattra**, m. a fragrant grass, L.; (*ā*), f. id., L. **Chattrâdi**, a Gaṇa of Pāṇ. (iv, 4, 62). **Chattrôpânaha**, n. sg. (Pāṇ. v, 4, 106, Kāś.) the parasol and the shoes, Mn. ii, 246; MBh. xiii, 4641.

Chattraka, m. a parasol-shaped temple in honour of Śiva, L.; a parasol-shaped bee-hive (cf. *chāttr*°), W.; Asteracantha longifolia, L.; a mushroom, L.; a kingfisher, L.; n. a parasol, Hcat. i, 7, 268; (*ikā*), f. a parasol, 323 & 1446; a small parasol, Kād. vi, 177; a mushroom, L.; candied sugar, Npr.

Chattrāka, m. a plant akin to Acacia arabica, L., n. a mushroom, ShaḍvBr. v, 6; Mn. v, 19; Yājñ. i, 176; BhP. x, 25, 19; (*ī*), f. the ichneumon plant, L.

Chattrika, m. =°*ttra-dhara*, g. *purohitâdi*.

Chattriṇa, m. N. of a man, Pravar. ii, 3, 5.

Chattrin, mfn. furnished with a parasol, MBh. xiii, 739; Hariv. 14205; R. i, iii; m. a barber, L. **Chattri-nyāya**, m. 'the manner of applying the term *chattrin* to a king,' permitted synonym, MBh. iii, 19, Sch.; TāṇḍyaBr. xiv, 11, 3, Sch.

Chattrī, ind. in comp. for °*ttra*. **–√kṛi**, to use as a parasol, Kād. iii, 983; Kathās. lxix, 150.

Chattvara, m. a house, Uṇ. iii, 1; a bower, ib.

2. **Chad**, mfn. ifc. (Pāṇ. vi, 4, 97) 'covering,' see *dhāma-* & (?) *bhūte-cchád*, *mallikā-*; cf. *ā-*.

Chada, mfn. ifc. covering, BhP. x, 83, 36; m. a cover, covering (ifc.), R. vii, 23, 4, 32; cf. *alpa-*, *uttara-*, *uraś-*, *ghana-*, *tanu-*, *danta-*, *daśana-*, *vadana-*; (ifc. f. *ā*) a wing, Naḷ. ix, 12; a leaf, MBh.; R.; Pañcat.; BhP.; Prab. iv, $\frac{27}{28}$; cf. *a-yuk-*, *kara-*, *karkaśa-*, &c.; *asra-bindu-* & *āyata-cchadā*; the lip, L.; Xanthochymus pictorius, L.; the plant *granthi-parṇa*, L.; n. feathers, Bālar. v, 13. **–pattra**, m. a kind of birch, L.

Chadana, n. a cover, covering, Hariv. 12671; R. ii, 56, 32 (ifc. f. *ā*); cf. *mallikā-*; a sheath, W.; a wing, MBh. iii, 11595; a leaf, Suśr.; the leaf of Laurus Cassia, L. **Chadi**, mfn. ifc. covering, BhP. vii, 14, 13; 'a roof,' see *náva-*. **Chadin**, mfn. ifc. covering, xii, 8, 44; 'having leaves,' see *daśa-*; having wheels (*pattra*=*dhārā*, Sch.), iii, 21, 18.

Chadís, n. (Pāṇ. vi, 4, 97) a cover, roof of a carriage, roof (*gṛiha*, Naigh. iii, 4), RV. x, 85, 10; AV. iii, 7, 3; VS. v, 28; TS. vi; AitBr. i, 29; ŚBr. iii; Lāṭy. i, 2, 22; iii; Kathās. ii, 49; cf. *chādisheya*. **Chádir-darśá**, m. appearance of roofs, MaitrS. ii, 2, 3; ĀpŚr. vi, 25, 6; (*a-cch*°, neg.) xv, 20, 2 & 8; 21, 3 & 10; cf. ĀśvGṛ. iv, 8, 12. **Chadish-mat**, mfn. having a cover or roof (a carriage), ĀpŚr. x, 24, 2. **Chadíḥ-sammita**, mfn. corresponding to a cover, ŚBr. iii, 5, 3, 9.

Chadma, in comp. for °*dman*. **–gati**, f. approaching clandestinely, Nyāyam. ix, 1, 9, Sch. **–ghātin**, mfn. killing deceitfully, Kathās. lxiv, 87. **–tāpasa**, m. a pretended ascetic, L. **–dyūta**, n. deceitful playing at dice, MBh. i, 146. **–rūpin**, mfn. disguised as (in comp.), 1792; R. vi, 11, 32. **–rūpeṇa**, instr. ind. in disguise, W. **–vallabha**, m. the perfume *coraka*, Npr. **–vesha**, m. a deceptive dress, disguise, W. **–veshin**, mfn. of a pretended appearance, BhP. vii, 5, 27; a cheat, W. **–stha**, m. (Prākṛit *chauma-ttha*) 'remaining in error,' a common man or ascetic (not possessing the knowledge of a *kevalin*), Jain. **–sthita**, mfn. ifc. pretending to practise (austerity, *tapaś-*), Pañcat. iii.

Chadman, n. (Pāṇ. vi, 4, 97) a roof, ĀśvGṛ. iii, 8; Lāṭy. i, 7, 15; external covering, deceptive dress, disguise, pretext, pretence, deceit, fraud, Mn.; MBh.; R.; Pañcat. iii, 15, $\frac{1}{2}$; Ragh. xii, 2; (in dram.) deceitful intelligence or tidings, Daśar. i, 38; cf. *kūṭa-*.

Chadmikā, f. Cocculus cordifolius, L.

Chadmin, mfn. ifc. disguised as, MBh. iii.

Chadvara, m. a tooth, W.; a bower, W.

1. **Chanda**, mfn.=°*nna*, L., Sch.

1. **Chandas**, n. 'roof,' see *bṛihác-*; deceit, Uṇ.

Channa, mfn. covered, covered over, MBh. iii, 800; R. i f.; Megh.; BhP. &c. (ifc., cf. Pāṇ. vi, 2, 170); obscured (the moon), MBh. i, 2699; Sūryas. iv, 10 & 22; hidden, unnoticed by (dat.), secret, clandestine, disguised, MBh. iii f.; R. ii, v; BhP.; Kathās.; Rājat.; (*am*), ind. secretly, Mn. ix, 98 & 100; Mṛicch.; Daś.; (in comp. °*nna-*) Rājat. v, 467; (with √*gai*, to sing) privately, in a low voice, Lāṭy. iii, 1, 12 ff.; (*e*), loc. ind. secretly, Hariv. 8686.

Chāttra, m. (fr. *chattra* [q.v.], Pāṇ. iv, 4, 62) 'sheltered,' a pupil, scholar, Pañcat.; Rājat. vi, 87; Vop.; n. a kind of honey, Suśr. i, 45, 8, 2 & 6; Bhpr. v, 21, 14. **–gaṇḍa**, m. a bad scholar (knowing only the beginnings of verses), L. **–gomin**, mfn. any one attendant on pupils, W. **–tā**, f. pupilage, Pañcat. i, 4, $\frac{1}{2}$. **–darśana**, n. 'looked at by pupils,' fresh butter, L. **–nilaya**, n. 'pupils' abode,' a college, Gal. **–priya**, mfn. dear to pupils, Pāṇ. vi, 2, 16, Kāś. **–mitra**, m. 'pupils' friend,' N. of a grammarian, Uṇ. iii, 70, Sch. **–vyaṇsaka**, m. a knavish pupil, g. *mayūra-vyaṇsakâdi*.

Chāttraka, n. =°*ra-tā*, g. *manojñâdi*; =°*ra*, a kind of honey, L.

Chāttri, Pāṇ. vi, 2, 86. **–śāla**, n., ib. (Kāś.); (*ā*), f., ib. **Chāttry-ādi**, a Gaṇa of Pāṇ., ib.

Chāttrikya, n. the office of a parasol-bearer (*chattrika*), g. *purohitâdi*.

Chāda, n. (irr., Pāṇ. vi, 4, 96) a roof, L.

Chādaka, mfn. covering, Priy. i, 7; any obscuring object (as a cloud), Sūryas. iv, 9 f.

Chādana, m. 'coverer,' Barleria cærulea, L.; the skin, L.; covering, cover, MBh. i, 3685; Hariv. 3537; VarBṛS. civ, 8; Pañcat.; Bhartṛ.; concealing, W.; darkening, VarBṛS. xxiv, 34; (in dram.) ignoring or tolerating offences if useful for one's aims, Sāh. vi, 107; a leaf, L., Sch.

Chādita, mfn. covered, covered over, VarBṛS. lxxxiii, 1; Ghaṭ.; Rājat. i, 116; obscured (the moon), Mṛicch. i, 53; concealed, disguised, Kathās. xvii, 44.

Chādin, mfn. ifc. hiding, obscuring, VarBṛS. xxx, 18; (*inī*), f. the skin, Gal.

Chādisheya, mfn. suitable for the roof of a carriage or house (*chadis*), Pāṇ. v, 1, 13; 2, Vārtt. 2, Pat.

Chādmika, mfn. (fr. *chadman*) fraudulent, Mn.

Chādya, mfn. to be sheltered, Pāṇ. iv, 4, 62, Pat.; m. the object obscured, Sūryas. iv, 10.

छद् 3. *chad* or 2. *chand*, cl. 10. *chadáyati* (also °*te* = √*arc*, Naigh. iii, 14 [v.l. °*ti*]: Subj. °*yat*, RV.; 2. pl. °*yátha*, i, 165, 12), *chandayati* (twice cl. 1. *chándati* [= *arcati*, Naigh. iii, 14]), MBh. xii; Ā. [Subj. °*yāte*], RV.; aor. *acacchadat*, Nir. ix, 8; *acchān*, RV.; 2. pl. °*nta*, i, 165, 12; 3. pl. °*ntsur*, x, 119, 3; Subj. *chantsat* [Naigh. ii, 6], RV.; 2. sg. °*tsi*, i, 163, 4; perf. *cacchanda*, vii, 73, 3; Pot. *cacchadyāt*, x, 73, 9) to seem, appear, be considered as, RV.; TāṇḍyaBr. xiv, 5; to seem good, please (with dat.), RV.; ŚBr. viii; (with acc.) MBh. xii, 7379 (cf. 7376); Ā. to be pleased with, delight in (acc. or loc.), RV. viii, 50, 5; x, 27, 8; *chandayati*, to gratify any one (acc.; exceptionally gen., MBh. xii, 7275; R. iii, 3, 15) with anything (instr., esp. *vareṇa*, 'with a boon,' MBh.; Hariv.; R.; BhP.); to try to seduce any one (acc.), BhP. x, 45, 36.

4. **Chad**, mfn. ifc. 'appearing as,' see *prathama-cchád*; 'pleased with,' see *kavi-* & (?) *bhūte-cchád*.

2. **Chánda**, mfn. pleasing, alluring, inviting, RV. i, 92, 6; viii, 7, 36; °*ndá*, praising (*chánda*, Naigh. iii, 16), RV. vi, 11, 3; cf. *madhu-cch*°; m. appearance, look, shape, Hariv. 8359 ff.; cf. *prati-* & *vi-cch*°; pleasure, delight, appetite, liking, predilection, desire, will, Yājñ. ii, 195; MBh. &c.; (*ena*), instr. ind. [also with *svena*, viii, 1249; R. ii, 83, 25; or ifc. with *sva-* (Hariv. 7017) or *ātma-*, MBh. v, xiii; R. v, 26, 18] according to one's own wish, Mn. viii, 176; Nal. xxiii, 15; R. v; according to the wish of (gen.), MBh. iii, 7096; Hariv. 7097; (*a-cch*°, neg. 'against the wish of') 7098 & 8557; (*āt*), abl. ind. according to the wish of (in comp.), MBh. viii, 3542; (*a-cch*°, neg. 'involuntarily,' R. iii, 5, 2); poison, L.; N. of Śākya-muni's charioteer (*chandaka*), Lalit. xv; Divyâv. xxvii, 159; of a prince, W.; cf. *sva-*; *indra-*, *kalāpa-*, *deva-* & *vijaya-*, various kinds of pearl-ornaments. **–gati**, f. interpretation of the Veda (°*nda* for °*ndas*), R. vii, 36, 45. **–cārin**, mfn. complying with the wishes of (gen.), MBh. xiii, 2789. **–ja**, mfn. 'originating from one's own wish,' self-produced (gods), Hariv. 12296. **–tas**, ind. at will, at pleasure, KaṭhUp. i, 25; Yājñ. iii, 203; MBh.; Hariv.;

according to the wish of (gen.), Suśr. **-pātana,** m. = °*ndaka-p*°, W. **-praśasti,** f. N. of a work by Harsha. **-mṛityu,** mfn. having death in one's power, MBh. xii, 1820; BhP. i, 9, 29. **-hānis,** mfn. giving up one's desires (?), Divyâv. xxxv, 173. **Chandânugāmin,** mfn. complying with the wishes (of others), submissive, Cāṇ. **Chandânuvartin,** mfn. id., MBh. iii, 296; R. ii, 53, 10; Pañcat.; Kām.; following one's own will, Rājat. iii, 141. **Chandânuvṛitta,** v. l. for °*do-'nuv*°.

Chandaka, mfn. ifc. 'charming,' see *sarva-;* m. N. of Śākya-muni's charioteer, Divyâv. xxvii, 158; Lalit. **-nivartana,** n. 'Candaka's return,' N. of a Caitya, xv, 378. **-pātana,** m. a hypocrite, L.

Candaḥ, in comp. for °*das.* **-kalpa,** m. collection of ritualistic rules, Āp. ii, 8, 11; *-latā,* f. N. of a work. **-purusha,** m. metre personified, AitĀr. iii, 2, 3, 2 & 4. **-prakaraṇa,** n. a ch. on metre, PSarv. **-prakāśa,** m. N. of a work. **-praśasti,** f. = °*nda-pr*°. **-śāstra,** n. metrical science, Vām. i, 3, 7; = *-sāra.* **-saṃgraha,** m. 'summary of metres,' N. of a work, Tantras. ii. **-sāra,** m. Piṅgala's work on metre, AgP. cccxxvii ff. **-siddhi,** f. a ch. of the Kāvya-kalpa-latā-vṛitti-parimala. **-sudhâkara,** m. N. of a work. **-sūtra,** n. = *-sāra.* **-stut,** mfn. praising in hymns, BhP. v, 20, 8. **-stúbh,** mfn. id., RV. v, 52, 12.

Chandana, mfn. charming, VarBṛS. civ, 61.

Chandaś, = °*das.* **-cit,** mfn. piled with metres, Śulbas. ii, 81. **-cūḍāmaṇi,** m. a work by Hemac.

2. **Chándas,** n. desire, longing for, will, MBh. xii, 7376; Pāṇ. iv, 4, 93, Kāś.; intention, purport, W.; a sacred hymn (of AV.; as distinguished from those of RV., SV. and YajurV.), incantation-hymn, RV. x; AV.; ŚBr. viii; MBh. v, 1224; Ragh. i, 11; the sacred text of the Vedic hymns, ŚBr. xi, 5, 7, 3; ĀśvGṛ.; Kauś.; Gobh.; VPrāt.; Pāṇ.; Mn. &c.; metre (in general, supposed to consist of 3 or 7 typical forms [AV.; VS. &c.] to which Virāj is added as the 8th [ŚBr. viii, 3, 3, 6]; *chándas* opposed to *gāyatrī́* & *trishṭúbh,* RV. x, 14, 16); metrical science, MuṇḍUp. i, 1, 5; MBh. i, 2887; Pañcat.; Śrut.; = °*do-grantha,* Nyāyam. ix, 2, 6, Sch.; [cf. Lat. *scando,* 'to step, scan.'] **-kṛita,** mfn. composed in metre, Mn. iv, 100; (*a-cch*°, neg.) ŚāṅkhBr. iii, 2. **-tva,** n. the state of a sacred hymn or of its metre, ChUp. i, 4, 2. **-paksha** (*chánd*°), mf(*ā*)n. borne aloft on the wings of desire, AV. viii, 9, 12. **-vat** (*chánd*°), mfn. desiring, TS. iv, 3, 11, 1 (*-paksha,* AV.)

Chandasikā, f. = °*ndo-grantha.* **Chandaska,** ifc. (f. *ā*) = °*das,* metre, Nyāyam. ix, 2, 5 & 8, Sch.

Chandasyà, mfn. (Pāṇ. iv, 3, 71 & 4, 93; 140, Vārtt. 1) taking the form of hymns, metrical, relating to or fit for hymns, RV. ix, 113, 6; TS. i, 6, 11, 4; made or done according to one's wish, Pāṇ. iv, 4, 93, Kāś.; (*ā*), f. (with *íshṭakā*) N. of a sacrificial brick, ŚBr. vii, 5, 2, 42; viii, 2 f.

Chandita, mfn. gratified, MBh. xiii; Hariv.

Chándu, mfn. pleasing, RV. i, 55, 4.

Chando, in comp. for °*das.* **-gá,** m. (√*gai*) 'singer in metre,' chanter of the SV., Udgātṛi priest, AitBr. iii, 32; ŚBr. x; ŚāṅkhŚr. &c.; *-paddhati,* f. N. of the work Yajña-pārśva (YajurV. Pariś. xv, Caraṇ.); *-pariśishṭa,* n. Kāty.'s supplement on Gobh., Mn. ii, 44, Kull.; *-brāhmaṇa,* n. = *chāndogya-br*°, AitBr. iv, 18, Sāy.; *-māhaki,* m. N. of a teacher, VBr.; *-vṛishôtsarga-tattva,* n. N. of a work; *-śākhā,* f. a branch of the SV. (quoted in a work on Śrāddhas); *-śrāddha-tattva-pramāṇa,* n. N. of a work by Raghu-nandana; *-śruti,* f. 'tradition of the Chandogas,' the SV., Parāś. ii, $\frac{15}{m}$, 3, 6; *-sopāna,* n. N. of a work; °*gâhnika-paddhati,* f. N of a work by Rāma-kṛishṇa. **-govinda,** n. Gaṅgā-dāsa's work on metre. **-grantha,** m. 'metre-book,' SV. i, Nyāyam. ix, 2, 6, Sch. **-dīpikā,** f. N. of a work. **-deva,** m. N. of Mataṅga, MBh. xiii, 1937; (*ī*), f. 'metre-goddess,' Gāyatrī, Hcat. **-nāmá,** mfn. 'named metre,' metrical, VS. iv, 24. **-nāman,** mfn. id., ib., Sch. **-'nuvṛitta,** n. compliance with any one's wishes, Cāṇ. (Hit.; v. l. °*dânuv*°). **-'nuśāsana-vṛitti,** f. N. of a work. **-'pahārâvali,** f. N. of a work. **-baddha,** mfn. = °*das-kṛita,* Sarvad. xv, 246. **-bhaṅga-vat,** mfn. offending against metre, Sarasv. **-bhāga,** mf(*ā*)n. one whose share is a metre, AitBr. ii, 18. **-bhāshā,** f. (g. *ṛig-ayanâdi*) the language of the Veda, TPrāt.; Caraṇ. (DevīP.) **-bhāshya,** n. N. of a work. **-mañjari,** °*rī,* f. Gaṅgā-dāsa's work on metre. **-máya,** mfn. consisting of or containing or representing sacred hymns, ŚBr. vi, x; AitBr. vi, 27; BhP. **-māna,** n. (g. *ṛig-ayanâdi*) 'measure of a metre,' a syllable regarded as the metrical unit, ŚāṅkhŚr. i, xiii; (ifc.) Pāṇ. vi, 2, 176, Kāś. **-mārtaṇḍa,** m. N. of a work on metre. **-mālā,** f. a similar work. **-ratnâkara,** m. a similar work by Sarvajña-ratnâkara-śānti. **-ruṭ-stoma,** m. (fr. *-ruh-st*°) N. of a Shaḍ-aha rite, ŚāṅkhŚr. x, 8, 33. **-rūpa,** n. a form of metre, ŚāṅkhBr. xx. **-vatī,** f. (in music) a kind of Śruti. **-viciti,** f. (g. *ṛig-ayanâdi*) 'examination of metres,' metrical science, Vām. i, 3, 7; N. of a work (called Vedâṅga), Āp. ii, 8, 11; VarBṛS. civ, 64; Bhar.; Kāvyâd. i, 12. **-vivṛiti,** f. explanation of metres, W.; = °*dah-sāra,* Madhus. **-vṛitta,** n. any metre, MBh. i, 28.

Chandomá, m. (fr. °*do-'ma,* 'hymn's or metre's home'?) the 8th, 9th, & 10th day in the Dvādaśâha rite (but cf. ĀśvŚr. viii, 7, 18), TS. vii; ŚBr. xii; KātyŚr.; ŚāṅkhŚr.; Lāṭy.; N. of the 3 Stomas sung in that rite, TāṇḍyaBr. x, xix. **-tri-kakud,** m. N. of a Try-aha rite, ŚāṅkhŚr. xvi, 29, 16. **-daśarātra,** m. N. of a Daśa-rātra rite, Maś. **-daśâha,** m. id., KātyŚr. xxiii f.; ŚāṅkhŚr. xiii; Vait. **-pavamāna-trirātra,** m. = *-tri-kakud,* Maś. **-vat,** mfn. accompanied by a Chandoma, Maś.; *-parāka,* m. = *-tri-kakud,* Vait. xli, 2.

Chándya, mfn. = °*ndu,* RV. viii, 101, 5.

छद् 5. *chad,* cl. 1. to nourish, Dhātup. xix.

छद्मट् *chadmaṭ.* See *chambaṭ-kara.*

छद्मन् *chadman,* &c. See √1. *chad.*

छनच्छनिति *chanacchan-iti,* ind. (fr. °*naṭ-chanad-iti,* Pāṇ. vi, 1, 99) onomat. (imitative of the noise of drops falling on anything hot), Amar. 89 (v. l. *chamaccham-iti,* ŚārṅgP. cvi, 11, whence the author of the verse is called °*cchamikā-ratna*).

छन्द् 1. & 2. *chand.* See √1. & 3. *chad.*

छन्द् 3. *chand,* v. l. for √*chṛid,* q. v.

छन्द 1. & 2. *chanda.* See √1. & 3. *chad.*

Chandaka, °**dana,** 1. & 2. °**das,** &c. See ib.

Channa. See √1. *chad.*

छम् *cham,* cl. 1. °*mati,* to eat, Dhātup. xiii.

छमच्छमिकारत्न *chamacchamikā-ratna,* m. See *chanacchan-iti* at end.

Chamacchamita, n. crackling, MārkP. viii, 112.

छमण्ड *chamaṇḍa,* m. = *chem*°, L.; a single man (who has no kinsmen), L.

छमण्डल *cha-maṇḍala.* See 2. *cha.*

छम्प् *champ,* cl. 10. to go, Dhātup. xxxii.

छम्पण *champaṇa,* v. l. for *śaṅkhana.*

छम्बंकारम् *chambaṃ-kāram,* ind. (= °*baṭ-k*°) so as to fail, Kathās. xii, 4; xxiii, 1.

Chambáṭ, ind. (g. *câdi*) in comp. **-√kṛi,** to make a failure, TS. ii, 5, 5, 3; TāṇḍyaBr. iv, 10; v, 9. **-kara,** mf(*ī*)n. ruining, BhP. iii, 18, 26 (v. l. *chadmaṭ-k*°). **-kāra,** m. only neg. dat. *á-cchambaṭkārāya,* ind. for not making a failure, ŚBr. xi, xiii. **-kāram,** ind. only neg. *á-cch*°, so as not to make a failure, TS. ii; v, 4, 7, 4; TBr. i, 2, 1, 3.

छर्द *charda,* °*dana,* &c. See √*chṛid.*

छर्दिस् 1. *chardís,* n. (= *chadís*) a fence, secure place or residence (*gṛiha,* Naigh. iii, 4), RV. i, 48, 15 & 114, 5; vi–viii, x; VS. xiii f. **Chardish-pā́,** mfn. protecting a house, RV. viii, 9, 11.

छल् *chal,* cl. 10. (or Nom. fr. *chala*) P. *chalayati* (inf. °*litum,* R. vi, 86, 13) to deceive, cheat, delude, outwit, MBh. iii, ix; Bhag. x, 36; Ragh. xvi, 61; Gīt. i, 9 & 16; to feign, W.

Chala, (√*skhal*) n. (exceptionally m., BhP. vii, 15, 12; g. *ardharcâdi*) fraud, deceit, sham, guise, pretence, delusion, semblance, fiction, feint, trick, fallacy (often ifc., e. g. *upadā-chalena,* 'under pretence of gifts of honour,' i. e. with feigned gifts, Ragh. vii, 27; *rajaś-chalena,* 'under the semblance of dust,' xvi, 28; see *kanyakā-, dharma-, vāk-*), Mn. viii, 49 & (*a-cch*°, neg.) 187; MBh. &c. (ifc. f. *ā,* Kathās. lxii, 164); deceitful disputation, perverting the sense of words, Nyāyas. i, 51 ff.; Sarvad.; wickedness, W.; for *sthala,* MBh. xiii, 7257; m. N. of a son of Dala, VP. iv, 4, 47; (*ā*), f. ifc. in names of several treatises or chapters belonging to SV. (e. g. *ūha-, ūhya-,* &c., qq. vv.) **-kāraka,** mfn. practising fraud, W. **-kārin,** mfn. id., W. **-tā,** f. deception, W. **-dyūta,** n. = *chadma-dy*°, Pañcad. i, 28. **Chalâkshara-sūtra,** n. N. of a work. **Chalôkti,** f. = *vāk-chala,* ĀśvŚr. viii, 12, 13, Sch.

Chalaka, mfn. delusive, Hariv. 11476.

Chalana, n. deceiving, deluding, tricking, outwitting, MBh. vi, 28; (in dram.) contempt (*avamānana*), Pratāpar.; Daśar. i, 46; (*ā*), f. deceiving, iii, 17 (Sāh.) **Chalanā-para,** mfn. deceitful, Śiś. i, 69.

Chalika, n. a song consisting of 4 parts (recited with gesticulation; subdivision of *nāṭya,* Bhar.), Mālav. i, $\frac{3}{4}$ (in Prākṛit) & $\frac{1}{18}$ (v. l. °*litaka*).

Chalita, mfn. deceived, R. ii, 34, 36; Hcar.; Amar. 41; n. a kind of dance performed by men, Kāvyâd. i, 39. **-rāma,** n. 'the outwitted Rāma,' N. of a drama, Sāh. vi, 261$\frac{1}{2}$. **-svāmin,** m. N. of a sanctuary (called after Chalitaka), Rājat. iv, 81.

Chalitaka, m. N. of a man, ib.; n., see °*lika.* **-yoga,** m. pl. N. of a Kalā (q. v.), Vātsyāy. i, 3, 17; BhP. x, 45, 36, Sch.

Chalin, m. a cheat, W.; a swindler, W.

छल्लि *challi,* f. (Prākṛit fr. 1. *chardís*) bark [°*llī,* Kalpabh. i, 165 f.; iv, 324], L.; a cloak, Hāl.

Challita, see *asthi-.* **Challī,** f. bark, L.; a creeper, L.; a kind of flower, L.; offspring (*saṃtāna*), L.

छवि *chavi,* f. skin, cuticle, PārGṛ. iii, 12; Hariv. 15709; Suśr.; VarBṛS. lxix, 28 ff.; colour of the skin, colour, MBh. iii, 12387; Mṛicch.; Megh. &c.; beauty, splendour, Ragh. ix, 34; Śiś. ix, 3; Naish. xxii, 55; a ray of light, L.; cf. *kṛishṇa-cch*°.

Chaví, f. skin, hide, TBr. i f.; TāṇḍyaBr. xvi, 6, 2; ŚāṅkhBr. xxv, 15; KātyŚr. xxii; Lāṭy. viii, 2, 1.

छविल्लाकर *chavillâkara,* m. N. of a historian of Kaśmīr, Rājat. i, 19.

छष् *chash,* cl. 1. P. Ā. to hurt, Dhātup.

छा *chā, ās,* m. a young animal, L.

छाग *chāga,* m. = *chaga* ('limping'?, cf. σκάζω &c.) a he-goat, RV. i, 162, 3; VS. xix, xxi; ŚBr. v; KātyŚr.; Mn. &c.; the sign Aries, VarBṛ. v, 5; N. of one of Śiva's attendants, L., Sch.; mfn. coming from a goat or she-goat, Yājñ. i, 257; Car.; Suśr.; (*ā*), f. a she-goat, ŚBr. iii; ŚāṅkhŚr. vii, 10; (*ī*), f. id., Kathās. lxxi, 273. **-karṇa,** m. 'goat-ear,' Tectona grandis, Npr. **-nāśana,** m. 'goat-destroyer,' a wolf, L. **-maya,** mfn. like a goat, W. **-mitra,** m. 'goat-friend,' N. of a man, g. *kāśy-ādi* (not in Kāś.) **-°mitrika,** mf(*ā, ī*)n. fr. °*tra,* ib. **-mukha,** m. 'goat-faced,' N. of a Kimpuusha, Gal. **-ratha,** m. 'whose vehicle is a goat,' Agni, L. **-roma-maya,** mfn. consisting of goat-hair, L. **-lakshaṇa,** n. N. of Śukla-Yajurveda-Pariś. ii. **-vāhana,** m. = *-ratha,* L. **-śatru,** m. = *-nāśana,* Npr. **Chāgī-kshīra-nāśa,** m. 'goat-milk-destroyer,' Trophis aspera, ib.

Chāgaka, n. herd of goats, Gal.; (*ikā*), f. = °*gī,* L.

Chāgala, mfn. coming from a goat (*chagalá*) or she-goat, Suśr.; Kathās. lxxxii; born in Chagala, g. *takshaśilâdi* (not in Kāś.); m. a goat, Hariv. 3275; R. vi; Pañcat.; Kathās. cxxi; = °*laka,* W.; patr. fr. Chagala (if of Atri's family), Pāṇ. iv, 1, 117; N. of a mountain, VāyuP. i, 23, 108. **Chāgalâṇḍa,** v. l. for *chag*°. **Chāgalânta,** m. = °*ga-nāśana,* L. **Chāgalântrikā,** f. = *chag*°, L. **Chāgalântrin,** m. = *chag*°, L. **Chāgalântrī,** f. = *chag*°, L.

Chāgalaka, m. a kind of fish, L.

Chāgali, m. patr. fr. Chagala (if not of Atri's family, Pāṇ. iv, 1, 117, Kāś.; one of Atri's family, Pravar. iii, 1, v. l. °*la,* °*gava*) or metron. fr. Chagalā (g. *bāhv-ādi*), N. of a prince, Hariv. 5017 & 5498.

Chāgaleya, mfn. fr. *chagalá,* g. *sakhy-ādi;* m. N. of the author of a law-book, PārGṛ., Sch. Introd.; Nirṇayas. ii, 7; v; (pl.) = °*geya,* Caraṇ.

Chāgaleyin, m. pl. (Pāṇ. iv, 3, 109) the pupils of Chagalin, ŚāṅkhŚr. vi, 1, 7, Sch.

Chāgeya, m. pl. N. of a school of the black Yajur-veda, DevīP.; Hcat. i, 7, 1071. **Chāgyāyani,** m. patr. fr. Chāga, Pāṇ. iv, 1, 155, Vārtt.

छागण *chāgaṇa,* m. a fire of dried cow-dung (*chag*°), L.

छागल *chāgala,* &c. See *chāga.*

छागव्य *chāgavya,* m. pl. N. of a family, Pravar. v, 1 (v. l. *sthāg*°); cf. °*va* s. v. °*gali.*

छाछिका *chāchikā,* N. of a Tīrtha, Rasik.

छाटा *chāṭā.* See *chaṭā* at end.

छात *chāta.* See √*cho.*

छात्त्र *chāttra*, °*ttraka*, &c. See √1. *chad.*

Chāda, °daka, °dana, &c. See ib.

छान्द *chānda.* See °*ndasa.*

छान्दड *chāndaḍa*, m. N. of a Brāhman, Kshitīś. i, 13.

छान्दस *chāndasa.* mf(ī)n. having the sacred text of the Veda (*chándas*) as (its) subject, peculiar or relating or belonging to the Veda, Vedic, Kauś.; Pāṇ. iv, 3, 71; Pat.; Hariv. 12284; BhP.; (once °*nda*, BhavP. i); archaistic, Sarvad. vi, 11; (g. *manojñâdi*, Pāṇ. v, 2, 84, Kāś.) studying the holy text of the Vedic hymns, familiar with it, Kathās. lxii, cxviii; (ifc., g. *khasūcy-ādi*, Gaṇar. 114, Sch.); relating to metre, RAnukr., Sch. **–tā**, f. the being Vedic, Nyāyam. ix, 3, 9. **–tva**, n. id., ib.; Pāṇ. vii, 1, 39, Kāś.; APrāt., Sch. &c.; the being archaistic, W.; the being metrical, W. **–baṭhara**, m. the deceitful Chāndasa, Gaṇar. 89, Sch.

Chāndasaka, n. the being familiar with the Vedic hymns, g. *manojñâdi.* **Chāndasīya**, m. one familiar with metrical science, Śrutab. 19.

Chāndoga, mfn. 'relating to the Chando-gas,' in comp. **–brāhmaṇa**, n. = °*gya-br*°, Parāś. i, $\frac{33}{35}$, 4, 28 (v.l. *chand*°). **–sūtra**, n. N. of a work, Nirṇayas, i, $\frac{120}{130}$ (v.l. *chand*°).

Chāndogi. See °*geya.*

Chāndogika, n. = °*gya*, Bṛih. vi, 22. **Chāndogeya**, m. pl. N. of a family, Pravar. iii, 1 (v.l. °*gi*).

Chāndogya, n. 'doctrine of the Chando-gas,' a Brāhmaṇa of the SV. (including the ChUp.), KātyŚr. xxii; Pāṇ. iv, 3, 129; Vedântas. **–brāhmaṇa**, n. id., W. **–bhāshya**, n. = *-mantra-bh*°. **–mantra-bhāshya**, n. Guṇa-vishṇu's Comm. on the prayers and texts in Gobh. **–veda**, m. = °*gya*, KātyŚr. xxii, 1, 1, Sch. **Chāndogyôpanishad**, f. N. of an Up. (part of the *chāndogya*); *-bhāshya*, n. Śaṃkara's Comm. on ChUp.

Chāndobhāsha, mfn. fr. *chando-bhāshā*, g. *ṛig-ayanâdi.* **Chāndoma**, mfn. taken from the Chandomas, ŚāṅkhŚr. xv, 6, 1. **Chāndomāna**, mfn. fr. *chando-m*°, g. *ṛig-ayanâdi.* **Chāndomika**, mfn. belonging to the Chandomas, x, 9, 13; KātyŚr. xxii; Nir. vii, 24. **Chāndovicita**, mfn. fr. *chando-viciti*, g. *ṛig-ayanâdi.*

छाय *chāya*, m. granting shade (Śiva), MBh. xii, 10374; n. (Pāṇ. ii, 4, 22 & 25; vi, 2, 14) ifc. (especially after a word to be taken in the gen.) shadow, Mn. iii, 274; Ragh. iv, 20; vii, 4; xii, 50; reflection, Naish. vi, 34; colour, complexion, beauty, Megh. 102; (*ā́*), f. = σκιά, shade, shadow, a shady place ('a covered place, house,' Naigh. iii, 4), RV. i, 73, 8; ii, 33, 6; vi, 16, 38; AV.; VS. v, xv; AitBr. vii, 12; ŚBr. &c.; the shadow of a gnomon, Sūryas.; shelter, protection, Hit. iii, 8, ½; a reflected image, reflection, RV. v, 44, 6; x, 121, 2; VS. ii, 8; AV. v, 21, 8; PraśnUp.; Mn. &c.; shading or blending of colours, play of light or colours, lustre, light, colour, colour of the face, complexion, features, Suśr.; VarBṛS. lxviii, 89 ff.; Ragh. iv, 5; Megh. (ifc. f. *ā*) &c.; gracefulness, beauty, 77 & 101; VP. iv, 4, 31; Kathās. iic; a series, multitude (*paṅkti*), Pañcat. i, 16, 8; a Sanskṛit gloss on a Prākṛit text; a copy (of a MS.); a little (ifc.), Veṇīs. vi, $\frac{13}{14}$, 1; nightmare, Buddh. L.; a bribe, L.; 'Shadow,' (like Saṃjñā) wife of the sun and mother of the planet Saturn, Hariv. 545 ff.; VP. iii, 2; BhP. vi, viii; MatsyaP.; Kathās. cv; (N. of a Śakti) Hcat. i, 5, 197; the sun, L.; a metre of 4 × 19 syllables; a kind of rhetorical figure, Sarasv. ii, 5; (in music) N. of a Rāga; N. of Kātyāyanī (or Durgā, W.), L.

Chāyaka, mfn. (said of demons) causing nightmare (?), AV. viii, 6, 21.

Chāyā́, see °*ya.* **–kara**, m. 'shading,' a parasol-bearer, L.; a kind of metre, W. **–graha**, m. 'receiving the image or the gnomon's shadow,' a mirror or = *-yantra*, Rājat. iii, 154. **–grāha**, mf(*ī*)n. depriving of the shadow, R. iv, 41, 38. **–°ṅka** (°*yâṅ*°), m. 'marked by a (hare's) image,' the moon, L., Sch. **–tanaya**, m. 'son of Chāyā,' the planet Saturn, L. **–taru**, m. an umbrageous tree, Megh. 1; Śak. iv, 11, Sch. **–toḍī**, f. (in music) N. of a Rāga. **–°tmaja** (°*yât*°), m. = *-tanaya*, L. **–°tman** (°*yât*°), m. 'shadow-self,' one's shadow or reflected image, Megh. 40. **–druma**, m. = *-taru*, Śak. iv, 11. **–dvitīya**, mfn. accompanied by one's shadow, casting a shadow, MBh. iii, 57, 25. **–naṭṭa**, m. (in music) N. of a Rāga. **–nāṭaka**, n. a small drama or one imitative of another (as the Dhūtâṅgada). **–patha**, m. the milky way, L. **–piṅga**, m. = °*yâṅka*, Gal. **–purusha**, m. Purusha in the form of a shadow, Tantr. **–bhartṛi**, m. 'husband of Chāyā,' the sun, Gal. **–bhinna**, mfn. divided in radiance, reflecting light from various surfaces, Megh. 62. **–bhṛit**, m. 'bearing a (hare's) image,' the moon, L. **–máya**, mfn. shadow-like, ŚBr. xiv, 5, 1, 12 & 6, 9, 16; casting a shadow, W.; reflected, Naish. vi, 30. **–māna**, n. an instrument measuring a shadow, L., Sch. **–mitra**, n. 'shade-friend,' a parasol, L. **–mṛiga-dhara**, m. = *-bhṛit*, L. **–yantra**, n. 'shadow-instrument,' a sun-dial, VarBṛS.; Sūryas. xiii, 20; Sūryapr. **–vat**, mfn. umbrageous, R. ii, 94, 10; vii, 54, 11. **–vṛiksha**, m. '= *-taru*,' Hibiscus populneoides, Npr. **–vyavahāra**, m. measuring the shadow cast by the sun on the dial. **–saṃjñā**, f. Chāyā as Saṃjñā, VP. iii, 2, 5. **–suta**, m. = *-tanaya*, VarBṛ. ii, 3, Sch.

छाल *chāla*, m. (g. *ardharcâdi*, not in Kāś. & Gaṇar.) Cyprinus Rohita, Gal.

Chālikya, n. = *chalika*, Hariv.

छि *chi*, m. abuse, L.

छिक्कन *chikkana*, n. sneezing, W.; (*ī*), f. 'causing sneezing,' Artemisia sternutatoria, Bhpr.

Chikkā, f. sneezing, L.; see *cikkā.* **–kāraka**, mfn. causing sneezing, Car. i, 4, Sch.

Chikkika, mfn. sneezing, W.; (*ā*), f. = °*kkanī*, Bhpr. v, 3, 304.

छिक्कर *chikkara*, m. a kind of animal, VarBṛS. lxxxvi, 20; 38 & 44.

Chikkāra, m. a kind of antelope, Dhanv. vi, 69.

छिक्किक *chikkika.* See °*kkana.*

छिटि *chiṭi*, only ifc. with *kāñcika-*, = *kāñcika*, Divyâv. xxxv, 231.

छित *chita.* See √*cho.*

छित्ति *chitti*, °*ttvara.* See √1. *chid.*

छिद् 1. *chid*, cl. 7. *chinátti*, *chintte* (Impv. °*náttu*; 2. sg. °*ndhí* [cf. Pāṇ. vi, 4, 101]; 2. du. °*ntám*; Subj. 1. sg. °*nádai*; Pot. °*ndet*, KshurUp.; cl. 9. 1. sg. *chinnāmi*, Divyâv. xxvii; impf. 2. sg. *achinad* or °*nas*, Pāṇ. viii, 2, 75; pf. *ciccheda*, °*cchide*; p. °*cchidvas*, vii, 2, 67, Kāś.; aor. *acchidat* or *acchaitsīt* [Subj. *ch*°, ŚBr. &c.], Pāṇ. iii, 1, 57; 2. sg. *chitsi*, ŚāṅkhŚr. i, 5, 9; 1. pl. *chedma*, RV. i, 109, 3; Ā. *acchitta* & 2. sg. °*tthās* [Subj. *ch*°, AV. viii, 1, 4], Kāś. on Pāṇ. iii, 1, 57 & viii, 2, 26; fut. *chetsyati*, vii, 2, 10, Kār.; ind. p. *chittvā*, inf. *chettum*; Pass. *chidyate*; p. see *á-cchidyamāna*; aor. *ácchedi* & *chedi*, RV.) to cut off, amputate, cut through, hew, chop, split, pierce, RV.; AV.; VS. &c.; to divide, separate from (abl.; exceptionally instr., ŚBr. xiv, 9, 4, 23); AV.; ŚBr. xiv; ŚāṅkhŚr.; to destroy, annihilate, efface, blot out, ŚBr. x, 5, 2, 5; MuṇḍUp.; MBh. &c.; (in math.) to divide, Sūryas. iv, 26: Pass. to be split or cut, break, ŚāṅkhGṛ. i, 15: Caus. *chedayati* (aor. *acicchidat*) to cut off, ŚāṅkhŚr. xvii; Gobh. iv, 2, 9; MBh. vii, 5954; Suśr.; to cause to cut off or through, Mn. viii, 277; 282 f. & 292; Cāṇ.: Desid., see *cicchitsu*: Intens. *cecchidīti* (Pāṇ. vii, 4, 65, Sch.), °*dyate* (83, Vārtt. 2, Pat.); fut. 1st °*ditā*, 2, 10, Vārtt. 2, Pat.; [cf. σχίζω, σχίδη &c.; Lat. *scindo*; Goth. *skeida.*]

Chitti, f. division, W.; Pongamia glabra, L.

Chittvara, mfn. (Uṇ. iii, 1) fit for cutting off, L.; hostile, L.; (cf. *chatt*°) roguish, L.

2. **Chid**, mfn. ifc. (Pāṇ. iii, 2, 61) cutting, cutting off, cutting through, splitting, piercing, MBh. vii, 4656; (cf. *ukha-cchid*, *keśa-*, *paksha-*, *marma-*, *vana-*, *hṛidaya-*); destroying, annihilating, removing, MBh. v, 1809; Hariv. 4774; Bhartṛ.; BhP.; (cf. *darpa-*, *duḥkha-*, *paṅka-*, *bhava-*); m. the divisor, denominator; f. the cutting off (with gen.), Bālar. viii, 75; 'annihilation of (in comp.),' see *bhava-.*

Chida, mfn. ifc. 'cutting off,' see *mātṛika-*; (*ā*), f. (g. *bhidâdi*) the cutting off (ifc.), HYog. ii, 96.

Chidaka, m. 'thunderbolt' or 'diamond' (cf. Rājat. iv, 51), L. **Chidi**, an axe, Uṇ. iv, 120. **Chidira**, m. id., i, 52; a sword, ib.; fire, L.; a rope, cord, L.

Chidura, mf(*ā*, Pāṇ. iii, 2, 162)n. cutting, dividing, W., easily breaking, Ragh. xvi, 62; Hcar. vi; extinguishing, Śiś. vi, 8; decreasing, Vām. v, 2, 40; annihilating (ifc.), ib.; hostile, L.; roguish, L. **Chidurêtara**, mfn. not breaking, strong, Naish. vii, 64.

Chidrá, mf(*ā*)n. torn asunder, RV. i, 162, 20; containing holes, pierced, KātyŚr. xv ff.; R. i, 73, 20; Suśr. v, 1, 43; leaky, MBh. v, 1307; 1047 (= xii, 8782); n. a hole, slit, cleft, opening, VS.; TS. i, vi; KātyŚr.; Lāṭy.; Kauś.; Mn. &c. (*daiva-kṛita*, 'opening or hole made by nature,' the cartilage of the ear, pupil of the eye, Suśr.; °*draṃ* √*dā*, 'to yield an opening or free access,' BhP. v, 6, 4); defect, fault, blemish, imperfection, infirmity, weak point, foible, MBh. &c.; (in astrol.) the 8th lunar mansion, VarBṛ.; Laghuj. i, 17; the number 'nine' (there being 9 openings in the body), Sūryas. ii, 18; the lower regions, Gal.; (cf. *á-*, *karṇa-*, *kṛita-*, *gṛiha-*, *niś-*, *mahā-*). **–karṇa**, mfn. having the ears bored, Pāṇ. vi, 3, 115. **–tā**, f. 'perforatedness,' the (air's, *ākāśasya*) being pervaded by everything, MBh. xii, 9137. **–darśana**, mfn. 'exhibiting deficiencies,' only *a-cch*°, faultless, MBh. vi, 384 & 402; m. '= °*rśin*,' N. of a (Brāhman changed into a) Cakra-vāka, Hariv. 1216; (°*rśin*, 1255). **–darśin**, mfn. observing deficiencies, 1265; m. = °*rśana*, (q. v. at end). **–dātṛi-tva**, n. the (air's, *ākāśasya*) yielding openings or access to everything, BhP. iii, 26, 34. **–pippalī**, f. Scindapsus officinalis, Gal. **–vaidehī**, f. id., L. **Chidrâṅśa**, m. 'having perforated parts,' reed, Gal. **Chidrâtman**, mfn. one who exposes his weak points, MBh. xii, 11345. **Chidrânusaṃdhānin**, mfn. looking out for faults or flaws, W. **Chidrânusārin**, mfn. id., W. **Chidrântar**, m. 'internally hollow,' reed, L. **Chidrânvita**, mfn. having weak points, Pañcat. iii, 37. **Chidrânveshaṇa**, n. searching for faults, W. **Chidrânveshin**, m. = °*nusaṃdhānin*, W. **Chidrā-phala**, n. a thorn-apple, L. **Chidrôdara**, n. N. of a disease of the abdomen, Car. vi, 18. **Chidrôdarin**, mfn. affected with °*ra*, ib.

Chidraya, Nom. °*yati*, to perforate, Kād. vi, 550.

Chidrāpaya, Nom. °*yati*, id., Vop.

Chidrita, mfn. perforated, Kād. v, 1071; Prab. v, 30, Sch. **Chidrin**, mfn. having holes (a tooth), Suśr. ii, 16, 27. **Chidvara**, mfn. = *chittv*°, W.

Chindaka, m. N. of a race, Ratnak.

Chindat-prâṇi, n. an animal cutting (i.e. living on) grass, ĀpŚr. ix, 13, 1 & 16, 8.

Chinná, mfn. cut off, cut, divided, torn, cut through, perforated, AV. &c.; opened (a wound), Suśr.; interrupted, not contiguous, Bhag. vi, 36; R. iii, 50, 12; VarBṛS.; disturbed (*kiṃ naś chinnam*, 'what is there in this to disturb us?' there is nothing to care about, Amar.), Hariv. 16258; Mṛicch.; ? (said of the belly of a leach), Suśr.; limited by (in comp.), Bhartṛ. iii, 20; taken away or out of, R. ii, 56, 23; Ragh. xii, 80; disappeared, Kathās. lxi, 47; ifc. decaying or exhausted by, Buddh. L.; (*ā*), f. a harlot, L.; = °*nnôdbhavā*, Bhpr. v, 3, 6; (cf. *á-*, *reshmá-*). **–karṇa**, mfn. having the ears shortened (as animals), Pāṇ. vi, 1, 115. **–keśa**, mfn. having the hair cut, W. **–granthinikā**, f. a kind of bulbous plant, L. **–taraka**, mfn. (compar.) = *chinnaka-tara*, v, 4, 4, Vārtt. 1 & 2, Pat. **–druma**, m. a riven tree, W. **–dhanvan**, mfn. (a warrior) whose bow has been broken by his enemy's arrow, W. **–nāsa**, m. 'cut-nose,' N. of a man, Vīrac. xxi. **–nāsya**, mfn. having the nose-rein broken, Mn. viii, 291. **–paksha** (°*nná-*), mfn. having the wings torn off, AV. xx, 135, 12. **–pattrī**, f. 'having divided leaves,' Hibiscus cannabinus, L. **–bandhana**, mfn. having the bands broken, liberated, W. **–bhakta**, mfn. 'having one's meals interrupted,' starving, Divyâv. xxxi. **–bhinna**, mfn. pierced through and through, cut up, destroyed, W. **–bhūyishṭha-dhūma**, mfn. bursting through the thick smoke, W. **–mastakā**, f. 'decapitated,' a headless form of Durgā, W.; °*kī-*√*kṛi*, to decapitate, Naish. iv, 68, Sch. **–mastā**, f. = °*stakā*, Tantras. iv; Mantram. vi. **–mūla**, mfn. cut up by the root, W. **–ruha**, m. Clerodendrum phlomoides, L.; (*ā*), f. = °*nnôdbhavā*, Suśr. i, iv; Bhpr. v, 3, 6; Boswellia thurifera, L.; Pandanus odoratissimus, L. **–vat**, mfn. (pf. p. P.) having cut or cut off, W. **–veshikā**, f. Clypea hernandifolia, L. **–śvāsa**, mfn. breathing at irregular intervals, Suśr. i; m. interrupted or irregular breathing, vi. **–saṃśaya**, mfn. one whose doubts are dispelled, confident, W. **–hasta**, mfn. 'cut-hand,' N. of a man, Vīrac. xvi, xxi. **Chinnântra**, mfn. affected with a *koshṭha-bheda* disease, ŚārṅgS. vii, 76. **Chinnôdbhavā**, f. Cocculus cordifolius, Bhpr. v, 3, 6.

Chinnaka, mfn. 'having a little cut off.' **-tara**, mfn. (compar.), Pāṇ. v, 3, 72, Vārtt. 5.

Chettavya, mfn. to be cut off, Mn. viii, 279; R. vi, 92, 41; to be cut, Nyāyam. ix, 3, 13, Sch.

Chettṛi, mfn. one who cuts off, cutter, wood-cutter, Mn. iv, 71, Sch. (ifc.); Hit. i, 4, 3; a remover (of doubts, *saṃśayānām*, 2, 21), MBh. xiii; Bhag.

Cheda, mfn. ifc. 'cutting off,' see *sthāṇu-*; m. divisor, denominator, VarBṛ. viii, 4; Laghuj. vii, 6; a cut, section, piece, portion, R. ii, 61, 14; Ragh.; VarBṛS. &c.; an incision, cleft, slit, liii, 122; lxxi, 4 f.; cutting off, tearing off, dividing (often ifc.), Mn. viii; Yājñ. &c.; separation (of syllables or words), Sarvad. v, 109; MBh. xii, 101, 5, Sch.; dissipating (doubt, &c.), W.; interruption, vanishing, cessation, deprivation, want, xiii, 1637; Śak.; Vikr.; VarBṛS. &c.; limit of (in comp.), Yājñ. i, 319; smoothing (a conflict, by an ordeal, *divya-*), Kathās. lx, 222; (*ī*), f., g. *gaurâdi* (not in Gaṇar.); cf. *ṛiṇa-*. **-kara**, mfn. making incisions, Jain.; m. a wood-cutter, W. **-gama**, m. disappearance of the denominator. **Chedâdi**, a Gaṇa of Pāṇ. (v, 1, 64; Gaṇar. 370). **Chedôpasthāpanīya**, n. taking the (Jain) vows after having broken with doctrines or practices adhered to formerly, Jain.

Chedaka, mfn. ifc. cutting off, Kathās. lxi, 31; m. the denominator of a fraction; cf. *granthi-*.

Chedana, mfn. cutting asunder, splitting, MBh. i, 1498; ii, 1953; destroying, removing (ifc.), xiv, 423; n. an instrument for cutting, Hcat. i, 9, 204; section, part, L.; (chiefly ifc.) cutting, removal (of doubts, *saṃśaya-*), MBh. iii, xv; Hariv. 913; a medicine for removing the humors of the body, Bhpr.

Chedanīya, mfn. to be cut up or divided, Suśr. i; Nyāyam. i, 4, 56, Sch.; m. Strychnos potatorum, L.

Chedi, mfn. one who cuts or breaks, Uṇ. iv, 118, Sch.; m. a carpenter, ib. **Chedita**, mfn. cut, divided, L. **Cheditavya**, mfn. to be cut, divisable, W.

Chedin, mfn. ifc. cutting off, tearing asunder, Mn. iv, 71; Ragh.; removing, Hariv. 15880; Śak.

Chedya, mfn. to be cut or divided or split or cut off or mutilated, Yājñ. ii, 215; MBh. i, 93; xii, &c.; n. cutting off, cutting, tearing (with teeth or nails), v, 5733 (C); Suśr. i, 5, 1; vi; Sāh. vi, 17; cf. *kuḍya-*, *duḥkha-*, *pattra-*, *laghu-*, *saṃśaya-*.

Chedyaka, n. drawing, projection, Sūryas. vi, 1 & 12. **Chedyakâdhyāya**, m. N. of Sūryas. vi.

छिन्नम *chinnama*, m. N. of a poet, Sarasv.; Gaṇar. 46 & 98, Sch. (vv. ll. °*nnapa*, *chittapa*); ŚārṅgP. iv, 12 (*chitrama* ed.)

छिप्पिका *chippikā*, f. a kind of bird, VarBṛS. lxxxviii, 2 & 35; cf. *cipya*.

छिलिहिण्ड *chilihiṇḍa*, m. N. of a creeper, Bhpr. v, 3, 260 f.

छिस्मक *chismaka*, m. N. of a prince, BrahmâṇḍaP. (v. l. for *śiśuka*).

छुच्छु *chucchu*, m. a kind of animal, VarBṛS. lxxxvi, 37. **Chucchuka-bhaṭṭa**, m. N. of the author of a *laghu-vṛitti* on Kāt.

Chucchundara, m. the musk-rat, Suśr. v, 6, 3 (°*cchūnd*°) & 14; Ashṭâṅg. vi, 38, 2; (*ī*), f. id., VarBṛS. lxxxviii, 5 & 47. **Chucchundari**, m. id., Mn. xii, 65; Yājñ. iii, 213; MBh. xiii, &c.

छुट् *chuṭ*, cl. 6. °*ṭati*, to bind, Dhātup.: cl. 10. *choṭayati*, to cut, split, ib. (v. l. for √*cuṭ*).

Choṭana, n. cutting off, Uttamac. 206.

Choṭi, v. l. for °*ṭin*, L. **Choṭikā**, f. snapping the thumb and forefinger, Ratnâv. iii, $\frac{9}{10}$; Kathās. lxv, 211; Bhpr. v, 28, 111; Tantras.

Choṭita, mfn. cut off, Uttamac. 217; cf. *ā-cch*°.

Choṭin, m. a fisherman, L. (v. l. °*ṭi*).

छुड् *chuḍ*, cl. 6, v. l. for √*thuḍ*; cf. *pra-*.

छुड्ड *chuḍḍa*, m. N. of several men, Rājat. viii; (*ā*), f. N. of a woman, 461; 1124; 1132.

छुद्र *chudra*, n. retaliation, L.; a ray, L.

छुप् *chup*, cl. 6. °*pati* (cf. Pāṇ. vii, 2, 10, Kār.) to touch, Dhātup. xxviii, 125: Intens. *cocchupyate*, Pāṇ. vii, 4, 83, Vārtt. 2, Pat.; cf. *a-cchuptā*.

Chupa, m. touch, L.; a shrub, bush, L.; air, wind, L.; combat, L.

छुबुक *chúbuka*, n. = *cub*°, the chin, RV. x, 163, 1; ŚBr. x, 6, 1, 11; PārGṛ. iii, 6, 2.

छुर् *chur*, cl. 6. °*rati* (cf. Pāṇ. viii, 2, 79) to cut off, cut, incise, etch, Dhātup. xxviii, 79: Caus. *churayati*; to strew or sprinkle with (instr.), Kād. v, 221; Mālatīm. ix, 30; Kathās. xxiv, 1: Caus. *chor*°, to abandon, throw away, Lalit. xv, 447; Divyâv.; Kāraṇḍ. xi, 100.

Churaṇa, n. ifc. strewing with, Viddh. i, 29; Kuval. 129. **Churā**, f. lime, L.

Churita, mfn. strewed, set, inlaid with (instr. or in comp.), blended, MBh. xii, 5487; VarBṛS.; Daś.; BhP. &c.; n. flashing (of lightning), MBh. iii, 695.

Choraṇa, n. abandoning, L.

Chorita, mfn. abandoned, thrown away, Divyâv. i, 94; vii; drawn (a sigh), Kāraṇḍ. xvii, 110.

छुरिका *churikā*, f. (fr. *kshur*°) a knife, Kathās. xii, xxv; Vet. Introd. $\frac{19}{20}$; iv, $\frac{2}{2}\frac{3}{4}$ f.; Beta bengalensis, Bhpr. v, 9, 16. **-phala**, n. = *kshur*°, L.

Churī, f. = *kshurī*, a knife, dagger, L.

Chūrikā, f. a knife, Hcat. i, 9, 97; a cow's nostril, Mn. viii, 325. **-pattrī**, f. 'knife-leaved,' Andropogon aciculatus, L.

Chūrī, f. = *churī*, L.; cf. BhP. v, 3, 3.

छृद् *chṛid*, cl. 7. (Impv. *chṛiṇattu*, 2. sg. *chṛindhi*; fut. *chardishyati* & *chartsy*°, Pāṇ. vii, 2, 57; pf. *caccharda*, 3. pl. °*cchṛidur*, 4, 83, Vārtt. 3, Pat.) to vomit, BhP. x, 11, 49; to utter, leave, TĀr. iv, 3, 3; P. Ā. (*chṛintte*) to shine, Dhātup. xxix, 8; to play, ib.: cl. 1. *chardati* (v. l. °*rpati*) to kindle, xxxiv, 14: Caus. *chardayati*, id., ib. (v. l. °*rpay*°); to cause to flow over, ŚBr. xii, 4, 2, 9; to vomit, eject (with or without acc.), MBh. v, 3493; vi, 93; Suśr.; VarBṛS.; to cause to spit or vomit, Car. i, 13, 88; Suśr.; Ā. to vomit, KātyŚr. xxv; Lāṭy.; Kauś.: Desid. *ciccharдishati* & °*cchṛitsati*, Pāṇ. vii, 2, 57: Caus. Desid. *cicchardayishati*, 4, 83, Vārtt. 2, Pat.; cf. *ā-*, *pra-*.

Charda, v. l. for °*di*, vomiting, L.

Chardana, mfn. causing vomition, Car. vi, 32; m. Vangueria spinosa, Bhpr. v, 1, 161; = °*di-ghna*, L.; = *alambushā*, L.; n. vomition, Kauś.; Gaut.; Suśr.; retching, W. **Chardanīya**, mfn. to be caused to vomit, Car. vi, 32. **Chardayitavya**, mfn. id., ib.

Chardāpanikā, f. (fr. Prākṛit Caus. √*chṛid*) 'emetic,' a kind of cucumber, L.

Chardi, f. vomiting, sickness, KātyŚr. xxv, 11; Gaut.; Suśr.; VarBṛS. xxxii, 18; expulsion (of the breath), KapS. iii, 33. **-ghna**, m. 'anti-emetic,' Azadirachta indica, L.

Chardikā, f. vomition, W.; Clitoria ternatea, L. **-ripu**, m. 'anti-emetic,' cardamoms, L.

Chardita, mfn. got rid of (demerit), Divyâv. xix. 2. **Chardis**, n. (f., L.) vomition, Car. i, vi, viii.

Chardyāyanikā, °*nī*, f. = °*dāpan*°, Npr.

छृप् *chṛip*, cl. 1. 10, v. l. for √*chṛid*, q. v.

छेक *cheka*, mf(*ā*)n. clever, shrewd, Jain. (HPariś. ii, 447); domesticated, L.; m. a bee, L.; = °*kânuprâsa*, Kpr. ix, 2; Sāh. x, 3. **Chekânuprâsa**, m. a kind of alliteration (with single repetitions of several consonants as in Ragh. vii, 22; opposed to *lāṭân*°), Pratāpar.; Alaṃkāraś. x, $\frac{3}{4}$. **Chekôkti**, f. indirect speech, hint, double entendre, Viddh. ii, 5; Siṃhās. Introd. $\frac{3}{4}$; vi, $\frac{1}{2}$; Kuval.

Chekala [Gal.], °**kāla** [L.], mfn. clever.

Chekila, mfn. id., L.

छेत्तव्य *chettavya*, °*ttṛi*, &c. See √1. *chid*.

छेप्प *cheppa*, (fr. *śépa*) tail, Hāl. 62; 240.

छेमण्ड *chemaṇḍa*, m = *cham*°, an orphan, Uṇ. k. **Chemuṇḍā**, f. id., Gal.; cf. *chā*.

छेलक *chelaka*, m. (fr. *chagal*°) a he-goat, Bhpr. v, 10, 75; (*ikā*), f. a she-goat, 76.

छेलु *chelu*, Vernonia anthelminthica, L.

छैदिक *chaidika*, mfn. deserving mutilation (*cheda*), Pāṇ. v, 1, 64; = *chidrâṃsa*, W.

छो *cho*, cl. 4. *chyati* (vii, 3, 71; perf. 3. pl. *cacchur*, cf. 4, 83, Vārtt. 2, Pat.; aor. *acchāt* & *acchāsīt*, ii, 4, 78) to cut off, cut, Bhaṭṭ. xiv f.: Caus. *chāyayati*, Pāṇ. vii, 3, 37; cf. *anu-*, *ava-*, *ā-*.

Chāta, mfn. = *chita*, L.; emaciated, L.

Chita, mfn. cut off, cut, divided, L.

छोज *choja*, N. of a man, Rājat. v, 422.

छोटन *choṭana*, °*ṭi*, &c. See √*chuṭ*.

छोरण *choraṇa*, °*rita*. See √*chur*.

छोलङ्ग *cholaṅga*, m. the citron tree, L.; n. a citron, Alaṃkāraś. xiv, 2; 35; 47.

छौतु *chautu*, m. N. of a man, Nid., Sch.

छ्यु *chyu*, cl. 1. Ā. to go, Dhātup. xxii, 60.

ज JA.

ज 1. *ja*, the 3rd palatal letter (having the sound of *j* in *jump*). **-kāra**, m. the letter *ja*.

ज 2. *ja*, mf(*ā*)n. (√*jan*) ifc. born or descended from, produced or caused by, born or produced in or at or upon, growing in, living at, Mn.; MBh. &c.; (after an adv. or adverbial word) born or produced (e.g. *agra-*, *avara-*; *eka-*, *dvi-*, *ni-*, *pūrva-*, *prathama-*, *saha-* & *sākam-já*), Mn. x, 25; prepared from, made of or with, v, 25; Suśr.; Hcat.; 'belonging to, connected with, peculiar to,' see *anūpa-*, *anna-*, *śakra-*, *sârtha-*; m. a son of (in comp.), Mn. &c.; a father, L.; birth, L.; (*â*), f. a race, tribe, AV. v, 11, 10; ifc. a daughter, MBh. &c.; cf. *jā*.

ज 3. *ja*, mfn. speedy, swift, L.; victorious, L.; eaten, W.; m. speed, L.; enjoyment, L.; light, lustre, L.; poison, L.; a Piśāca, L.; Vishṇu, L.; Śiva, L.; a husband's brother's wife, L.

जंस् *jaṃs*, cl. 1. 10. °*sati*, °*sayati*, to protect, Dhātup. xxxii, 127; to liberate, ib.

जंह् *jaṃh*, Intens. 3. sg. *jáṅgahe*, to move quickly, sprawl, kick, RV. i, 126, 6; [cf. *abhi-vi-*; *jaghána*, *jaṅghā́*; Goth. *gagg-an*; Lith. *zeng-ti*.]

Jáṃhas, n. moving, going, course, vi, 12, 2; cf. *krishṇá-*, *raghu-pátma-*.

जक *jaka*, N. of a Brāhman, Rājat. viii, 474.

जकुट *jakuṭa*, m. n. (= *juk*°) the flower of the egg-plant, L.; m. a dog, L.; the Malaya mountains, L.; n. a pair, L., Sch.

जक्करी *jakkarī*, f. a kind of dance.

जक्ष् 1. *jaksh* (√*has*, redupl.), p. *jákshat*, laughing, RV. i, 33, 7; ŚBr. xiv; ChUp. viii, 12, 3.

जक्ष् 2. *jaksh* (√*ghas*, redupl.), cl. 2. °*kshiti* (cf. Pāṇ. vii, 2, 76; 3. pl. °*kshati*, vi, 1, 6 & 189; vii, 1, 4; Impv. 2. sg. *jagdhi*, BhP. iv, 17, 23; impf. (or aor.; cf. iii, 20, 21) *ajakshīt* & °*kshat*, cf. Pāṇ. vii, 3, 98 f.; 3. pl. °*kshur*, Vop. ix, 28; pf. 3. pl. *jajakshur*, Bhaṭṭ. xiii, 28; ind. p. *jagdhvā́* & °*dhvāya*, see s. v.; inf. °*gdhum*) to wish to eat, BhP. ii, 10, 17; to eat, consume, BhP. (once Ā. iii, 20, 20); Bhaṭṭ.; cf. *pra-*.

Jakshaṇa, n. eating, consuming, L.

Jakshi, f. id., W.

Jakshivás, mf(*kshúshī*)n. pf. p. √*ghas*, q. v.

Jagdhá, mfn. (Pāṇ. ii, 4, 36) eaten, RV. i, 140, 2; AV. v, 29, 5; ŚBr. vi; Mn. v, 125; MBh. vii, 4346; exhausted by (instr.), Hcar. v, 140; n. a place where any one has eaten, Pāṇ. i, 4, 52, Vārtt. 5, Pat.; cf. *apa-*, *nṛi-*, *pari-*, *práti-*, *vi-*, *sāraṃga-*. **-pāpman** (°*gdhá-*), mfn. one whose sin is consumed or blotted out, AV. ix, 6, 25 (also *á-j*°, neg.) **-sāraṃga**, mfn. = *sāraṃga-jagdhin*, Gaṇar. 91, Sch.

Jágdhi, f. eating, consuming, ŚBr. ix, 2, 3, 37 (dat. °*gdhyai*, Ved. inf.); Mn.; Hcar. v, 302 (v. l.); the being eaten by (instr.), Mn. iii, 115; cf. *kalya-*.

Jagdhvā́, ind. p. having eaten, AV. v, 18, 10; TS. ii; TBr. ii; ŚBr. i; Mn.; Yājñ.; MBh. i, 8476.

Jagdhvā́ya, Ved. ind. p., id., RV. x, 146, 5.

जक्ष्म *jakshma*, °*man*, for *yaksh*°, L., Sch.

जग *jaga*, n. = °*gat*, KaushUp. i, 3.

Jagac, in comp. for °*gat*. **-cakshus**, n. 'eye of the universe (= °*gad-eka-c*°),' the sun, Kathās. lix, 51; KāśīKh. vli, 44; BṛNārP. i, 8. **-candra**, m. N. of a Jain Sūri (founder of the Tapā-gaccha, 1229 A.D.) **-candrikā**, f. Bhaṭṭôtpala's Comm. on VarBṛ. (also called Cintā-maṇi). **-citra**, n. a wonder of the universe, R. vii, 34, 9; the universe taken as a picture, Sarvad. viii, 76. **-chandas** (*jág*°), mfn. one to whom the Jagatī metre belongs, connected with it, VS. iv, 87; AV.; ŚāṅkhŚr. xiv.

Jagaj, in comp. for °*gat*. **-jīva**, m. a living being of this world, Rājat. ii, 25. **-jīvana-dāsa**, m. N. of the author of three poems (Jñāna-prakāśa, Prathama-grantha, and Mahā-pralaya).

Jágat, mfn. (√*gam*, redupl., Pāṇ. iii, 2, 178, Vārtt. 3) moving, movable, locomotive, living, RV.; AV. &c.; (=*jāgata*) composed in the Jagatī metre, RV. i, 164, 23; ShaḍvBr. i, 4; Lāṭy. i, 8, 9; m. air, wind, L.; m. pl. people, mankind, Rājat. (C) iii, 494; n. that which moves or is alive, men and animals, animals as opposed to men, men (Naigh. ii, 3), RV.; AV. &c. (°*to madhye*, 'within every-body's sight,' R. vii, 97, 1; 5 & 10); the world, esp. this world, earth, ŚBr.; Mn. &c.; the Jagatī metre, RV. i, 164, 25; 'N. of a Sāman,' see -*sāman*; n. du. heaven and the lower world, Kir. v, 20; n. pl. the worlds (=°*gat-traya*), Prab. i, 10; people, mankind, Kpr. x, 28/29 (Sāh. & Kuval.); (*jágatī*), f. a female animal, RV. i, 157, 5; vi, 72, 4; a cow, Naigh. ii, 11; the plants (or flour as coming from plants), VS. i, 21; ŚBr. i, 2, 2, 2; the earth, ĪśUp.; PraśnUp.; Mn. i, 100; MBh. &c.; the site of a house, L. (Kir. i, 7, Sch.); people, mankind, L.; the world, universe, R. ii, 69, 11; a metre of 4 × 12 syllables, RV. x, 130, 5; AV. viii; xix; ŚBr.; AitBr. &c.; any metre of 4 × 12 syllables; the number 48, Lāṭy. ix; Kāty. xxii; a sacrificial brick named after the Jagatī metre, ŚBr. viii; KātyŚr. xvii; a field planted with Jambū, L. **–kartṛi**, m. 'world-creator,' Brahmā, L. **–kāraṇa**, n. the cause of the universe, Vedāntas.; -*kāraṇa*, n. 'the (cause of the cause, i. e. the) final cause of the universe,' Vishṇu, Vishṇ. i, 61. **–kṛitsna**, n. the whole world, W. **–kshaya**, m. the destruction of the world, W. **–tuṅga**, m. N. of two princes (850 & 900 A.D.) **–traya**, n. the three worlds (heaven, earth, and the lower world), Kathās.; Sāh. **–tri-taya**, n. id., Dhūrtas. ii, 8. **–pati**, m. the lord of the world, Prab. i, 2/3; (°*tas páti*, AV. vii, 17, 1); Brahmā, MBh. i, 36, 20; Śiva, xiii, 588; Kum. v, 59; Vishṇu or Kṛishṇa, Bhag. x, 15; R. i, 14, 24; VarP. clxix, 1; Agni, MBh. i, 8418; the sun, VP. iii, 5, 20; a king, W. **–parāyaṇa**, mfn. chief of the universe (Vishṇu), Vishṇ. iic, 100. **–pitṛi**, m. 'world-father,' Śiva, W. **–prakāśa**, mfn. = -*prathita*, Ragh. iii, 48; m. the light of the world, Bhaktâm. 16. **–pradhāna**, n. 'chief of the world,' Śiva, MBh. vii, 202, 12. **–prabhu**, m. the lord of the world, Prab. i, 24; Brahmā, MBh. iii, 15908; Śiva; Vishṇu, VarP. clxix, 2; N. of an Arhat of the Jainas, L. **–prasiddha**, mfn. known throughout the world, Hemac., Sch. **–prâṇa**, m. 'world-breath,' wind, L.; Rāma, RāmatUp. i, 3, 2. **–prāsāha**, mf(*ā*)n. consisting chiefly of Jagatī verses, AitBr. vi, 12, 15. **–prīti**, f. 'world-joy,' Śiva, MBh. vii, 202, 12. **–samagra**, n. = -*kṛitsna*, W. **–sarva**, n. id., W. **–sâkshin**, m. 'world-witness,' the sun, L. **–sāman**, mfn. having the Jagat (-Sāman) for its Sāman, ĀpŚr. xii, 14, 1. **–siṅha**, m. N. of a prince, Inscr. **–seṭa**, m. N. of a man, Kshitîś. vii. **–srashṭṛi**, m. = -*kartṛi*, W.; Śiva, L. **–svāmin**, m. the lord of the world, Prab. vi, 2; Vishṇu, VāmP. xvi; N. of an image of the sun in Dvādaśâdityâśrama, ŚrīmMāh. xxxi; °*mi-tva*, n. sovereignty of the world, Ratnâv. iv, 20.

Jágatī, f. of °*t*, q.v. **–cara**, m. 'earth-walker,' man, MBh. xii, 6970. **–jāni**, m. 'whose wife is the earth,' a king, ŚārṅgP. **–tala**, n. 'earth-surface,' the ground, soil, Sarvad. iii, 217. **–dhara**, m. 'earth-supporter,' a mountain, R. iii, 68, 45; N. of a Bodhi-sattva, Buddh. L. **–pati**, m. 'earth-lord,' a king, MBh. i, iii; R. i; BhP. v; -*kanyakā*, f. 'king's daughter,' a princess, Kād. vi, 524 (v.l.) **–pāla**, m. 'earth-protector,' a king, MBh. viii, 530; Hit. ii, 11, 8. **–bhartṛi**, m. = -*pati*, R. ii, 103, 17. **–bhuj**, m. 'earth-enjoyer,' a king, Rājat. **–madhya**, n. 'world-centre,' the earth, Bhām. ii, 218. **–ruh**, m. 'earth-grower,' a tree, Kir. vi, 2. **–ruha**, m. id., MBh. **–varāha**, n. N. of a Sāman.

1. **Jagatya**, Nom. °*tyati*, Pāṇ. i, 4, 2, Vārtt. 14, Pat. 2. **Jagatya**, n. (fr. °*tī*), iv, 4, 122.

Jagad, in comp. for °*gat*. **–aṇḍa**, n. the mundane egg, universe. **–aṇḍaka**, n. id., Śiś. ix, 9. **–anta**, m. the end of the world, W. **–antaka**, m. 'world-destroyer,' death, BhP. iv, 5, 6 (°*kântaka*, mfn. destroying death). **–antar-ātman**, m. 'innermost soul of the universe,' Vishṇu, Bhartṛ. iii, 84. **–ambā**, f. the mother of the world, Śatr. ii, 22; = °*mbikā*, Udbh.; -*prādurbhāva*, m. 'appearance of Durgā,' N. of Durgāv. iv. **–ambikā**, f. 'world-mother,' Durgā, Bhagavatīg. **–ātmaka**, mfn. 'whose self is the world,' identical with the world, W. **–ātman**, m. 'world-breath,' wind, R. vi, 82, 153; 'world-soul,' the Supreme Spirit, W. **–ādi-ja**, m. 'first-born of the world,' Śiva. **–ādhāra**, m. support of the universe, Siṅhâs. xv, 4/5; Time (cf. Bhāshāp. 44); Rāma, RāmatUp. i, 5, 8; N. of the Jina Vīra, Śatr. i, 274; wind, L. **–ānanda**, mfn. rejoicing the world, W. **–āyu**, n. 'life-spring of the world,' wind, MBh. iii, 11193. **–āyus**, n. id., xii, 13569. **–īśa**, m. 'world-lord,' Brahmā, BrahmavP. iii, 1, 6; Vishṇu, Gīt. i, 5 ff.; Śiva; N. of a man, Kshitîś. iv, 8; of a scholiast (author of Anumāna-dīdhiti-ṭippanī); -*toshiṇī*, f. N. of a Comm.; -*śataka*, n. N. of a poem (of 100 stanzas). **–īśitṛi**, m. 'world-lord,' Śiva, Siṅhâs.[2] Introd. 1. **–īśvara**, m. world-lord, MBh. i, 811; Prab. v, 9; Śiva, R. iii, 53, 60; Indra, MBh. i, 811; a king, Mn. vii, 23, Kull.; N. of the author of Hāsy. **–uddhāra**, m. salvation of the world, W. **–eka-cakshus**, m. 'sole eye of the universe,' the sun, Siṅhâs. xviii. **–eka-nātha**, m. the sole monarch of the world (Raghu), Ragh. v, 23. **–eka-pāvana**, mfn. the sole purifier of the world, W. **–guru**, m. the father of the world, Ragh. x, 65; Brahmā, BhP. ii, 5, 12; Vishṇu, Hariv. 15699; BhP. i, 8, 25; Śiva, Kum. vi, 15; Rāma (as Vishṇu's incarnation), R. iii, 6, 18. **–gaurī**, f. N. of Manasā(-devī), BrahmavP. ii, 42. **–ghātin**, mfn. destroying the world or mankind, W. **–dala**, m. N. of a king of the Darads, Rājat. viii, 210. **–dīpa**, m. 'world-illuminator,' the sun, Kathās. lxvi, lxxiv. **–deva**, m. N. of a prince (1100 A.D.), Inscr. **–druh**, -*dhruk* or -*dhruṭ*, m. 'people-injurer,' a demon, W. **–dhara**, m. N. of a son of Ratna-dhara and grandson of Vidyā-dhara (author of comments on Mālatîm., Veṇīs., and Kāt.) **–dhātṛi**, m. 'world-creator,' Vishṇu, BrahmaP. ii, 10, 18 & 18, 3; VarP. clxix, 2. **–dhātrī**, f. 'world-nurse,' Sarasvatī, MārkP. xxiii, 30; Durgā, W. **–bala**, m. 'world-strength,' wind, L. **–bimba**, n. = -*aṇḍa*, Bādar. ii, 1, 32 f., Sch. **–bīja**, n. 'world-seed,' Śiva, MBh. vii, 9506. **–bhūshaṇa-koshṭhaka**, n. N. of a work. **–yoni**, m. 'world-womb,' Brahmā; Vishṇu or Kṛishṇa, Hariv. 5880; VarP. clxix, 2; Śiva, MBh. vii, 9506; Prakṛiti, RāmatUp. i, 4, 8; the earth, W. **–vañcaka**, m. 'people-deceiver,' N. of a cheat, Dhūrtan. **–vandya**, mfn. 'to be adored by the world,' Kṛishṇa, MBh. ii, 23. **–vahā**, f. 'bearer of all living beings,' the earth, L. **–vidhi**, m. the arranger of the world, Pañcar. i, 10, 48. **–vināśa**, m. = °*gat-kshaya*, L. **–vaidyaka**, m. 'world-curer,' N. of a physician, Nid., Sch. **–vyāpāra**, m. 'world-business,' creation and support of the world, Bādar. iv, 4, 17.

Jagan, in comp. for °*gat*. **–nātha**, m. 'world-lord,' Vishṇu or Kṛishṇa, MBh. ii, 779; iii, 15529; Rāma (as incarnation of Vishṇu), R. i, 19, 3; Dattâtreya (as incarnation of Vishṇu), MārkP. xviii, 29; du. Vishṇu and Śiva, Hariv. 14394; N. of a celebrated idol of Vishnu and its shrine (at Purī in Orissa, RTL. p. 59), Tantr.; N. of the authors (of Rekhā-gaṇita; of Bhām.; of Rasa-gaṅgādhara; of the Vivāda-bhaṅgârṇava compiled at the end of the last century); (*ā*), f. Durgā, Hariv. 10276; -*kshetra*, n. the district surrounding the Jagan-nātha shrine, W.; -*vallabha-nāṭaka*, n. N. of a drama; -*vijaya*, m. 'Jagan-nātha's victory,' N. of a poem. **–nidhi**, m. 'world-receptacle,' Vishṇu, Hcat. i, 9. **–nivāsa**, m. 'world-abode,' Vishṇu or Kṛishṇa, Bhag. xi, 25 & 37; MBh. vi, 2604; BhP. viii; BrahmâṇḍaP.; Śiva, MBh. xiii, 899; worldly existence, W. **–netra**, n. 'world-eye,' the moon, Kathās. lxxxix, 5; du. the sun and the moon, Kāvyâd. ii, 172 (ŚārṅgP.); Nom. °*trati*, to represent the world's eye (as the moon), Prasannar. vii, 61. **–maṇi**, m. N. of a copyist. **–maya**, mfn. containing the whole world, Hariv.; BhP. viii, 22, 21. **–mātṛi**, f. 'world-mother,' Durgā, Hariv. 10276; Saṃskārak.; Lakshmī, MārkP. xviii, 32. **–mukha** (*jág*°), mfn. (faced by, i. e.) beginning with the Jagatī metre, TS. vii, 2, 8, 2. **–mohana**, n. 'perplexing living beings,' N. of a work. **–mohinī**, f. 'infatuating living beings,' N. of a Surâṅganā, Siṅhâs.

Jaganu, m. a living being, L.; fire, L.

Jagannu, m. a living being, L.; fire, L.

Jaganvás, mf(*gmúshī*)n. pf. p. √*gam*, q.v.

Jagmāná, mfn. pf. p. Ā. √*gam*, q.v.

Jágmi, mfn. (Pāṇ. iii, 2, 171) going, being in constant motion, hastening towards (acc. or loc.), RV.

Jagmivas, mf(*gmúshī*)n. pf. p. √*gam*, q.v.

Jaṅgama, mf(*ā*)n. (Nir. v, 3; ix, 13; √*gam*, Intens.) moving, locomotive (opposed to stationary, *sthāvara* or *sthira*), living, AitUp. v, 3; Mn.; MBh. &c.; (ifc. f. *ā*) a living being, MBh.; BhP. i, 17, 34; (with *visha*, venom) coming from living beings (opposed to poison), MBh. i, 5019; Suśr.; m. pl. N. of a Śaiva sect, Śaṃkar. iv, 28. **–kuṭī**, f. = *bhramat-k*°, L. **–tva**, n. movableness, MBh. xiv, 654. **Jaṅgamêtara**, mfn. immovable, L.

Jaṅgamana, n. course, Nir. v, 19, Sch.

जगद *jagada*, m. an attendant, PārGṛ. iii, 4, 4 & 8 (cf. AV. iii, 12, 7 & ĀśvGṛ. ii, 8, 16).

जगनु *jaganu*, °*gannu*, &c. See *jaga*.

जगर *jagara*, m. = *jāg*°, armour, L.

जगल *jagala*, mfn. fraudulent, L.; m. a kind of spirituous liquor (or fluid suitable for distillation, L.), Car. i, 27; Suśr. i, 45, 10, 10; Bhpr.; Vanguéria spinosa, L.; = °*gara*, W.; n. = *chagaṇa*, L.

जगुरि *jáguri*, mfn. (√*gṛī*, Pāṇ. vii, 1, 103, Kāś.) leading, conducting, RV. x, 108, 1 (Nir. xi, 25).

जग्गिक *jaggika*, N. of a man, Rājat. viii.

जग्ध *jagdhá*, *jágdhi*, &c. See √2. *jaksh*.

जग्मि *jágmi*, °*gmivas*. See *jaga*.

जघन *jaghána* (√*jaṅh*), m. [RV. i, 28, 2; v, 61, 3; vi, 75, 13], n. [AV. xiv, 1, 36; TS. ii; TBr. ii, &c.] the hinder part, buttock, hip and loins, pudenda, mons veneris (ifc. f. *ā* [Pāṇ. iv, 1, 56, Kāś.], MBh. xiii, 5324; R.; Megh.); the hinder part of an altar, Śulbas. iii, 52; rear-guard, MBh. iii, v f., ix; (*ena*), instr. ind. behind (with gen. [ChUp. ii, 24, 3] or acc. [ŚBr. i f., vii, xi] following, once [vii, 2, 2, 4] preceding); so as to turn the back towards, ŚāṅkhGṛ. ii, 1; iv, 12. **–kūpaka**, m. du. = *kakundara*, L. **–gaurava**, n. the weight of the hips, Śak. iii, 5. **–capalā**, f. 'moving the hips,' a libidinous woman, VarBṛS. civ, 3; Pañcat. i, 4, 11; a woman active in dancing, W.; a species of the Āryā metre. **–cyuti** (°*ghána-*), f. (a woman) whose pudendum oozes, TBr. ii, 4, 6, 4; ĀśvŚr. ii, 10, 14. **–tas**, ind. behind, after, Kauś. 75. **–vipulā**, f. (a woman) having stout hips; N. of a metre. **Jaghanârdhá**, m. the hinder part, TS. ii, vi; AitBr. iii, 47; ŚBr. i, iii, viii, x; rear-guard, MBh. v, 5162. **Jaghane-phalā**, f. 'last-ripening,' Ficus oppositifolia, L.

Jaghanin, mfn. having stout hips, Hariv. 9547.

Jaghanyà, mf(*ā*)n. (g. *dig-ādi*; in comp., Pāṇ. ii, 1, 58; ifc., g. *vargyâdi*) hindmost, last, latest, AV. vii, 74, 2; VS.; TBr.; AitBr. &c.; lowest, worst, vilest, least, least important, MBh. &c.; of low origin or rank, (m.) man of the lowest class, Hariv. 5817; R. ii; Pañcat.; BhP. vii, 11, 17; m. N. of the attendant of the model man Mālavya, VarBṛS. lxix, 31 ff.; n. the penis, L.; (*am*), ind. behind, after, last, MBh. iii, 905 f.; R. (G) ii, 112, 31; (*e*), loc. ind. id., MBh. iii, 1303 f.; v, 4506; with √*kṛi*, to leave behind, Hariv. 3087. **–kārin**, mfn. (in med.) attending extremely unskilfully, Suśr. i, 25, 38. **–guṇa**, m. the lowest of the 3 Guṇas (*tamas*), Bhag. xiv, 18; MBh. xiv, 999. **–ja**, mfn. last born, youngest, i, iii; Hariv. 594; m. a younger brother, W.; 'low-born,' a Śūdra, L.; N. of a son of Pradyota. **–tara**, mfn. (compar.) lower, inferior, MBh. xiv, 1137. **–tas**, ind. from behind, R. vi, 7, 35 & 45, 22 & 29; behind, after, last, MBh. iv, 994; R. v, 40, 5. **–prabhava**, mfn. of lowest origin, Mn. viii, 270. **–bhāva**, m. inferiority, L. **–rātre**, loc. ind. at the end of the night, MBh. iii, 10795 & 14750. **–śāyin**, mfn. going to bed last, xii, 8840. **–saṃveśin**, mfn. id., Āp. i, 4, 28. **Jaghanyâyus**, mfn. shortest, Suśr. i, 35, 6.

जघन्वस् *jaghanvas*, mf(*ghnushī*)n. S. √*han*.

Jághni, mfn. (Pāṇ. iii, 2, 171) striking (with acc.), RV. ix, 61, 20; m. a weapon, L. **–vat**, mfn. containing an Intens. form of √*han*, AitBr. i, 25.

Jaghnivás, mf(*ghnushī*)n. pf. p. √*han*, q.v.

Jaghnu, mfn. striking, killing, Uṇ. i, 22.

जघ्रि *jághri*, mfn. (√*ghri*, redupl.) pouring out, sprinkling about, RV. i, 162, 15.

जङ्क्ष् *jaṅksh*, cl. 1. P., v.l. for √*kshaj*.

जङ्ग *jaṅga*, N. of a man, Rājat. viii, 863. **–pūga**, m. wickedness, W. **Jaṅgâri**, see °*ṅghâri*.

जङ्गम *jaṅgama*, °*mana*. See *jaga*.

जङ्गल *jaṅgala*, mfn. arid, sterile, desert,

L.; m. = *-patha,* L.; meat, L.; n. id.; = °*gula,* L.; cf. *dīrgha-, jāṅg°.* **— patha,** m. 'any arid or sterile region, desert,' see *jāṅgalapathika.*

जङ्गाल *jaṅgāla,* m. a dyke, L.

जङ्गिड *jaṅgiḍá,* m. N. of a plant (worn as an amulet), AV. ii, 4, 1 ff.; xix, 34 f.; Kauś. 8.

जङ्गुल *jaṅgula,* n. = *jāṅg°,* venom, L.

जङ्घ *jaṅgha,* m. N. of a Rakshas, R. vi, 69, 12; (*jáṅghā*), f. (√*jaṅh*) the shank (from the ankle to the knee), RV. i, 116, 15 & 118, 8; AV.; VS. &c. (ifc., Pāṇ. vi, 2, 144; f. *ā,* Śrut.; also *ī,* Pāṇ. iv, 1, 55); a part of a bedstead, VarBṛS. lxxix, 30; of a carriage, see *ratha-.*

Jáṅghā, f., see s.v. °*gha.* **— kara,** mfn. 'active with the shanks,' running quickly, m. a runner, courier, Pāṇ. iii, 2, 21. **— °karika,** mfn. id., Daś. vi, 49. **— °kārika,** mfn. m. id., W. **— jaghanya,** mfn. the last with respect to the shanks, MBh. v, 1257 (xii, 4191). **— trāṇa,** n. armour for the shanks, L. **— piṇḍī,** f. the calf, Gal. **— prahata,** n. g. *aksha dyūtâdi* (not in Kāś.) **— prahṛita,** n. ib. **— bandhu,** m. N. of a man, MBh. ii, 111. **— bala,** n. 'strength of the shanks,' running off, flight, Mālav. iii, 10/20. **— mātra,** mf(*ī*)n. 'measuring a shank,' 2½ feet long. **— ratha,** m. N. of a man, pl. his descendants, g. *yaskâdi* (v. l. °*ghe-r°,* Gaṇar., Sch.) **— °ri** (°*ghâr°*), m. N. of a man, MBh. xiii, 256 (°*ṅgâri,* B). **— vihāra,** m. a walk, Divyâv. xxxii, 28. **Jaṅghe-ratha,** see °*ghā-r°.*

Jaṅghāla, m. 'running swiftly, runner,' a class of animals (antelopes &c.), Car. i, 27, 51; Suśr. i, 46; Bhpr. **— tva,** n. the being a good runner (for passing over, *laṅghana*), Sarvad. i, 44 (*a-,* neg.)

Jaṅghikā, f. '= °*ghā.*' See *kap-.*

Jaṅghila, mfn. running swiftly, quick, L., Sch.

जज् *jaj,* cl. 1. P. to fight, Dhātup. vii, 68.

Jaja, m. 'a warrior'; cf. *jājin.* **Jajâujas,** n. 'warrior's strength,' prowess, Śiś. xix, 3.

जज्ज *jajja,* mfn. (etymol.) quick, DaivBr. iii, 17 (*jalacara,* v. l. °*cala,* Nir. vii, 13); m. N. of a man, Rājat. iv, 410; 471 ff.

Jajjala, N. of a man, viii, 1085; 2173.

Jajjalā, ind. (onomat.) with √*kṛi,* to make in an instant, DaivBr. iii, 17 (*jalgalyamāna,* Nir. vii, 13).

जज्ञान *jajñāná,* mfn. pf. p. Ā. √*jñā,* q. v.; m. N. of a man, ĀrshBr.

जज्ञि *jajñi,* mfn. (√*jan,* redupl., Pāṇ. iii, 2, 171 & Vārtt. 3) germinating, shooting, TS. vii, 5, 20, 1; f. seed (? Pāṇ. iii, 2, 171, Kāś.) Siddh.

Jajñivas, mf(*jñushī*)n. pf. p. √*jan,* q. v.

जझ्झती *jajhjhatī,* f. pl. (scil. *āpas*) splashing or rushing waters (Nir. vi, 16), RV. v, 52, 6.

जञ्ज् *jañj,* cl. 1. P. = √*jaj,* Dhātup. vii, 69; p. f. *jáñjatī,* glittering, flashing (Gmn.; = *abhibhavantī,* Sāy.), RV. i, 168, 7.

Jañja, m. g. *uñchâdi.*

Jañjaṇā-bhávat, mfn. glittering, RV. viii, 43, 8.

जञ्जपूक *jañjapūka,* mfn. (√*jap,* Intens.; Pāṇ. iii, 2, 166) muttering prayers repeatedly, Hcar.

जट् *jaṭ,* cl. 1. P. = √*jhaṭ,* Dhātup. ix, 18.

जट *jaṭa,* mfn. wearing twisted locks of hair, g. *arśa-ādi;* m. metrically for °*ṭā,* Hariv. 9551; (*ā*), f. the hair twisted together (as worn by ascetics, by Śiva, and persons in mourning), PārGṛ. ii, 6; Mn. vi, 6; MBh. (ifc. f. *ā,* iii, 16137) &c.; a fibrous root, root (in general), Bhpr. v, 111; ŚārṅgS. i, 46 & 58; N. of several plants (= °*ṭā-vatī,* L.; Mucuna pruritus, L.; Flacourtia cataphracta, L.; = °*ṭā-mūlā,* L.; = *rudra-jaṭā,* L.), Suśr. v f.; N. of a Pāṭha or arrangement of the Vedic text (still more artificial than the Krama, each pair of words being repeated thrice and one repetition being in inverted order), Caraṇ.; (*ī*), f. Nardostachys Jaṭā-māṃsī, L.; (= °*ṭi*) the waved-leaf fig-tree, L.; cf. *tri-, mahā-, vi-; krishṇa-jaṭā.* **— malla,** m. N. of the author of the Jaṭamalla-vilāsa.

Jaṭā, f., see s.v. °*ṭa.* **— kara,** mfn. matting the hair, W. **— kalâpa,** m. a knot of braided hair, Vikr. v, 19; BhP. iii. **— cīra,** m. N. of Śiva, L. **— jāla,** n. = *-kalâpa,* Daś. xii, 20 & 75. **— °jinin** (°*ṭâj°*), mfn. wearing braided hair and covered with a hide, MBh. i, 4917. **— jūṭa,** m. the long tresses of hair twisted on the top of the head, quantity of twisted hair (also applied to that of Śiva, Kathās. i, 18), BhP. v, 17, 3; Mahān.; Kathās. &c. (ifc. f. *ā,* Hcat.) **— jvāla,** m. 'flame-tufted,' a lamp, L. **— ṭaṅka,** m. N. of Śiva, L.; cf. *kaṭaṅkaṭa.* **— °ṭīra** (°*ṭâṭ°*), v. l. for °*ṭā-cīra.* **— dhara,** mfn. = *-dhārin,* R.; Pañcat. i, 4, 5; m. an ascetic, Daś. vii, 203; Śiva, MBh. iii, 1625; BhP. vi, 17, 7; N. of an attendant of Skanda, MBh. ix, 2563; of a Buddha, L.; of a lexicographer; pl. N. of a people in the south of India, VarBṛS. xiv, 13; (*ī*), f. = *rudra-jaṭā,* Bhpr. vii, 10, 8/9. **— dhārin,** mfn. wearing twisted hair, BhP. iv, 2, 29; Vet. i, 23; °*ri-śaiva-mata,* n. the doctrine of the Śaivas who wear twisted hair, Govind. on Bādar. ii, 2, 37. **— °ntā** (°*ṭân°*), f. = °*ṭā-vatī,* Npr.; Flacourtia cataphracta, ib. **— paṭala,** n. N. of a treatise on the Jaṭā(-pāṭha). **— pāṭha,** m. the Jaṭā arrangement of a Vedic text, W. **— bandha,** m. = *-kalâpa,* W. **— bhāra,** m. the mass of braided hair, R. ii. **— maṇḍala,** n. = *-kalâpa,* Hariv. 4565; R. i, iii; Śak. vii, 11. **— māṃsī,** f. = *-vatī,* L. **— mālin,** m. 'garlanded with matted hair,' N. of a Muni, VāyuP. i, 23, 176. **— mūlā,** f. Asparagus racemosus, L. **— vat,** mfn. = *-dhārin,* W.; m. Śiva, Gal.; (*tī*), f. Nardostachys Jaṭā-māṃsī, L. **— valkalin,** mfn. wearing twisted hair and a garment made of bark, Kathās. xciv, 36. **— vallī,** f. a kind of Valleriana, L.; = *rudra-jaṭā,* L. **— śaṃkara,** n. N. of a Tīrtha, Rasik. xii, 22. **— °sura** (°*ṭâs°*), m. N. of a Rakshas (killed by Bhīma-sena), MBh. iii, vii, xiv; pl. N. of a people in the north-east of Madhya-deśa, VarBṛS. xiv, 30. **Jaṭêśvara-tīrtha,** n. N. of a Tīrtha, RevāKh. cvii. **Jaṭôccha,** m. N. of a hill, W.

Jaṭāyu & °**yus,** m. N. of the king of vultures (son of Aruṇa and Śyenī, MBh.; son of Garuḍa, R.; younger brother of Sampāti; promising his aid to Rāma, out of regard for his father Daśa-ratha, but defeated and mortally wounded by Rāvaṇa on attempting to rescue Sītā), MBh. i, 2634; iii, 16043 ff. & 16242 ff.; R. i, iii f.; N. of a mountain, VāyuP. i, 23, 176; bdellium, L.

Jaṭāla, mfn. (g. *sidhmâdi*) = °*ṭā-dhārin,* Hariv. 10594; Caṇḍak. ii, 19; Kathās. liii, 2; cxi; ifc. crested by (flames), liii, 160; m. bdellium, L.; curcuma, L.; Schrebera Swietenioides, L.; the Indian fig-tree, L.; = °*ṭā-vatī,* L.

Jaṭālaka, mfn. = °*ṭā-dhārin,* MārkP. viii, 176; (*ikā*), f. N. of one of the mothers attending on Skanda, MBh. ix, 46, 23 (*jāṭ°,* C).

Jaṭi, f. twisted hair, L.; a mass, multitude, L.; Ficus infectoria, L. **Jaṭika,** 'N.,' see *jāṭikāyana.*

Jaṭin, mfn. = °*ṭā-dhārin,* Mn. xi, 93 & 129; Yājñ.; MBh.; Hariv.; m. an ascetic, Bharaṭ.; Śiva, MBh. vii, 2046 & 2858; N. of one of Skanda's attendants, ix, 2563; a Pratuda bird, Car. i, 27, 56; an elephant 60 years old, L.; Ficus infectoria, L.

Jaṭila, mf(*ā*)n. (g. *picchâdi*) = °*ṭā-dhārin,* Mn. ii f.; MBh.; Hariv. &c.; hairy (the face), MBh. vii, 93, 47; twisted together (the hair), BhP. iii, 33, 14; ifc. crested by, VarBṛS. viii, 53; Pañcat.; Śāntiś. i, 8; Kathās.; Vcar.; m. an ascetic, Kām. vii, 46; Śiva, MBh. xii f.; a goat with certain marks, VarBṛS. lxiv, 9; a lion, L.; N. of a man, Śatr. x, 137; (*ā*), f. = °*ṭā-vatī,* Suśr. i, vi; long pepper, L.; a kind of Artemisia, L.; Acorus Calamus, L.; = *uccaṭā,* L.; N. of a woman (with the patr. Gautamī; mother-in-law of Rādhikā, Gauragan.; said to have had 7 husbands), MBh. i, 7265. **— sthala,** n. N. of a locality, R. iv, 43, 8.

Jaṭilaka, m. N. of a man, pl. his descendants, g. *upakâdi;* (*ikā*), f. (g. *śivâdi*) N. of a woman, Lalit.

Jaṭilaya, Nom. °*yati,* to twist together, form into a clotted mass, Prasaṅg. viii, 4; to crest or fill with (instr.), Bhām. iv, 5.

Jaṭilī, ind. for °*la.* **— √kṛi,** to twist together, form into a clotted mass, W.; to crest or fill with, Pañcat.; Hcar. viii, 15. **— bhāva,** m. the being twisted together, Suśr. ii, 6, 1.

जटुल *jaṭula,* m. = *jaḍ°,* L. (cf. *jatu-maṇi*).

जठर 1. *jaṭhara,* mf(*ā*)n. (v. l. for *baṭh°,* q. v.) hard, firm, Śāntiś. iv, 13 & Sāh. (v. l. *jaratha*); for *jaratha,* old, Bhartṛ. iii, 92; = *baddha,* L.; for *javana,* R. ii, 98, 24; *ati-,* 'very hard' and 'very old,' Śiś. iv, 29; m. N. of a man, Pravar. iv (Mādh.); of a mountain, BhP. v, 16, 28; pl. N. of a people (in the south-east of Madhya-deśa, VarBṛS. xiv, 8), MBh. vi, 350. **— tva,** n. 'hardness,' only *a-* neg., tenderness, Vām. iii, 1, 19.

जठर 2. *jaṭhára,* n. [m.] the stomach, belly, abdomen, bowels, womb, interior of anything, cavity, RV.; AV. &c.; certain morbid affections of the bowels, Car. vi, 1; Suśr. i, vi; (*eṇa*), instr. ind. (opposed to *prishṭha-tas*) so as to turn the face towards, Hit. ii, 3, 3; [cf. γαστήρ? Goth. *kilthei* or *qvithrs?*]. **— gada,** m. a morbid affection of the abdomen or bowels (= *hṛid-roga,* Sch.), VarBṛS. civ, 6 & 13. **— jvalana,** n. 'stomach-heat,' hunger, Bhām. i, 49. **— jvālā,** f. belly-ache, colic, W. **— nud,** m. 'removing the Jaṭhara disease,' Cathartocarpus fistula, L. **— yantraṇā,** f. pain endured (by the embryo) in the womb, W. **— roga,** m. = *-gada,* VarBṛS. civ, 16. **— vyathā,** f. = *-jvālā,* W. **— stha,** mfn. being in the belly or in the womb, W. **— sthāyin,** mfn. id., W. **— sthita,** mfn. id., W. **Jaṭharâgni,** m. digestive stomach-fire, gastric juice, Gṛihyās. i, 11; Kathās. lxxiii, 58; Hcat.; cf. *jāṭhara.* **Jaṭharâmaya,** m. 'stomach-disease,' dropsy, L.

Jaṭharin, mfn. affected with the Jaṭhara disease, Car. v, 6; vi, 18; Suśr. iv, 18, 32.

Jaṭharī-kṛita, mfn. 'contained in the belly,' concealed in the bosom, BhP. iii, 9, 20.

जठर 3. *jáṭhara* (= 2. *j°,* Sāy.), RV. i, 112, 17.

Jáṭhala (= 2. *jaṭhára,* 'cavity [of waters], ocean,' Sāy.), i, 182, 6.

जड *jaḍa,* mf(*ā*)n. (cf. *jáḷhu*) cold, frigid, Pañcat. i, 12, 4; Kāvyâd. ii, 34; Rājat. iv, 41; stiff, torpid, motionless, apathetic, senseless, stunned, paralysed, Ragh. iii, 68; Śak. &c.; stupid, dull, Mn. viii, 394 (also *a-,* neg., 148); Yājñ. ii; MBh. (ifc. 'too stupid for,' iii, 437) &c.; void of life, inanimate, unintelligent, KapS. i, 146; vi, 50; NṛisUp.; Vedântas.; Sarvad.; dumb, Mn. ii, 110; Suśr.; ifc. stunning, stupefying, Śak. iv, 6; m. (g. *aśvâdi*) N. of Sumati (who simulated stupidity), cf. MārkP. x, 9; cold, frost, W.; idiocy, W.; dulness, apathy, W.; 'inanimate,' lifeless matter (opposed to *cetana*); n. water (= *jala*), ŚārṅgP. (Subh.); lead, L.; (*ā*), f. N. of a plant (= *jaṭā,* Mucuna pruritus, Flacourtia cataphracta, L.), Car. vi, 2 (ifc. f. *ā*). **— kriya,** mfn. working slowly, L. **— tā,** f. = *-bhāva,* W.; stiffness, senselessness, apathy, Suśr.; Ragh. ix, 46; Sāh.; stupidity, idiocy, MārkP. x, 13 & 33; inanimateness, Sarvad. iii, 40 & 42 f.; stupefaction, despair, W. **— tva,** n. stiffness, senselessness, Tattvas. 35; Rājat. vi, 26; idiocy, Tattvas. 37; Ratnâv. iii, 12/13. **— dhī,** mfn. stupid-minded, idiotic, Kathās. lxi; Prab.; (*a-,* neg.) BhP. vii, 5, 46. **— prakṛiti,** mfn. id., Ratnâv. ii, 12/13. **— buddhi,** mfn. id., Kathās. lxi, 187; (compar.) iv, 20. **— bharata,** m. 'the stupid Bharata,' N. of a man simulating stupidity, JābālUp.; BhP. v, 9 f. **— bhāva,** m. coolness, Kuval. 504. **— mati,** mfn. = *-dhī,* BhP. v, 9, 8; Veṇīs. ii, 10. **— mūka,** in comp. idiot and dumb, Mn. vii, ix, xi; MBh. iii, 1389; v, 4599; (*mūka-jaḍa,* BhP. i, 4, 6.) **— vipra,** m. 'the idiot Brāhman,' = *-bharata,* VP. **Jaḍâṃśu,** m. 'having cool rays,' the moon, Kuval. 375 (?). **Jaḍâtmaka,** mfn. = °*tman,* Pañcat.; inanimate, unintelligent. **Jaḍâtman,** mfn. 'cold-natured,' and 'stupid,' iii, 12, 11/12; Vcar. **Jaḍâśaya,** mfn. = °*ḍa-dhī,* Kathās. vi, 58 & 132; cxxiv; Kalyāṇam. 5.

Jaḍaya, Nom. °*yati,* to make without feeling for (loc.), Mudr. iii, 4; to render weak, Ratnâv. iv, 13.

Jaḍāya, Nom. °*yate,* to be stiff (the tongue), Subh.

Jaḍita, mfn. rendered lifeless, Bālar. i, 42; Sāh.

Jaḍiman, m. (g. *dṛiḍhâdi*) = °*ḍa-bhāva,* Kād. v f.; stiffness, senselessness, apathy, Mālatīm.; Gīt. vi, 10; Rājat. iv, 110; stupidity, Kathās. lxi, 23.

Jaḍī, ind. for °*ḍa.* **— √kṛi,** to stupefy, Śak. iv, 20/21 (v. l.) **— kṛita,** mfn. rendered torpid or motionless or senseless, stunned, R.; Ragh. ii, 42; Ratnâv.; confounded, rendered stupid, BhP. vi, 3, 25; viii, 12, 35. **— bhāva,** m. stiffness, senselessness, L. **— bhūta,** mfn. become stupid, vi, 18, 28.

जडुल *jaḍula,* m. = *jaṭula,* a freckle, L.

जतु *jatu,* n. lac, gum, Kauś. 13; MBh. i, xii; Suśr.; (*ūs*), f. (Pāṇ. iv, 1, 71, Pat.) a bat, VS. xxiv, 25 & 36; AV. ix, 2, 22; [cf. Lat. *bitumen;* Germ. *Kitt.*] **— kārī,** f. red lac, L.; = *-kṛit,* L. **— kṛit,** f. 'lac-maker,' a kind of Oldenlandia (the lac insect forms its nest in this tree), Bhpr. v, 2, 127. **— krishṇā,** f. id., ib. **— gṛiha,** n. a house plastered with lac and other combustible substances (such a house was built for the reception of the Pāṇḍava princes in Vāraṇāvata by Purocana, at the instigation of Duryodhana, the object being to burn them alive when they were asleep after a festival; warned by Vidura, they discovered the dangerous character of their abode, and dug an underground passage; next having invited an outcaste woman with her five sons, they first stupefied them with wine, and then having burnt Purocana in his own house, set fire to the house of lac, and, leaving the charred bodies of the woman and her sons inside, escaped by the underground passage), MBh. i, 313; 2250 & 5864; (v, 1987, *-geha*); (hence) a place of torture, Divyâv. xxvii (*jantu-g°*); *-parvan*, n. N. of MBh. i, ch. 141–151. **—geha**, n. = *-gṛiha*, q.v. **—dhāman**, n. id., L. **—putraka**, m. 'lac-figure,' a man at chess or backgammon, L.; cf. *jaya-p°*. **—maṇi**, m. 'lac-jewel,' a mole, Suśr. i f., iv. **—maya**, mfn. 'plastered with lac,' *-śaraṇa*, n. = °*tu-geha*, Veṇīs. v, 25. **—mukha**, m. 'lac-faced,' a kind of rice, Suśr. i, 46, 1, 9. **—rasa**, m. 'lac-juice,' lac, L. **—veśman**, n. = *-geha*, MBh. i, 361 & 379. **Jatv-aśmaka**, n. 'lac-stone,' bitumen, L.

Jatuka, m. 'N. of a man,' see *jant°*; n. lac, gum, L.; = *jāt°*, Asa fœtida, L.; (*ā*), f. lac, L.; = °*tu-kṛit*, Bhpr. v, 2, 127; = °*tū*, L.

Jatunī, f. = °*tū*, L.

Jatū, f., see °*tu*. **—karṇa**, m. (g. *gargâdi*, v.l. *jāt°*) 'bat-eared,' N. of a physician (pupil of Bharadvāja Kapishṭhala), Car. i, 1, 29 (v.l. *jātūkarṇya*).

Jatūkā, f. = °*tū*, vi, 9; = °*tu-kṛit*, L.

जतुरक *jaturaka*. See *jantuka*.

जतृण *jatṛiṇa*, m. pl. N. of a family, Pravar. ii, 3, 5.

जत्रु *jatrú*, m. pl. the continuations of the vertebræ, collar-bones & cartilages of the breast-bone (16 are named, ŚBr. xii, 2, 4, 11), RV. viii, 1, 12; AV. xi, 3, 10; VS. xxv, 8; TāṇḍyaBr. ix, 10, 1; n. sg. the collar-bone, Yājñ. iii, 88; MBh.; Hariv.; R.; Suśr.; VarBṛS. (pl.) **Jatruka**, n. the collar-bone, L.

जन् *jan*, cl. 1. [RV.; AV.] & 10. *jánati*, °*te* (Subj. *janat*, RV.; °*nāt*, AV. vi, 81, 3; Ā. °*nata*, RV. x, 123, 7; impf. *ájanat*, RV.; p. *jánat*), *janáyati*, °*te* (in later language only P., Pāṇ. i, 3, 86; Subj. °*náyat*; impf. *ájanayat*; aor. *ájījanat*; p. *janáyat*; inf. *jánayitavaí*, ŚBr. xiv), twice cl. 3 (Subj. *jajánat*, MaitrS. i, 3, 20 & 9, 1 [Kāṭh. ix, 8]; cf. Pāṇ. vi, 1, 192 & vii, 4, 78, Kāś.; pr. *jajanti*, Dhātup. xxv, 24; aor. Ā. *jánishṭa*; Ā. *ájani*, RV. ii, 34, 2; perf. *jajāna*; 3. pl. *jajñúr*, RV. &c.; once *jajanúr*, viii, 97, 10; p. °*jñivas*; Ved. inf. *jánitos*, iv, 6, 7; AitBr.; ŚBr. iii; [Pāṇ. iii, 4, 16]; Ved. ind. p. °*nitvī*, RV. x, 65, 7) to generate, beget, produce, create, cause, RV.; AV. &c.; to produce (a song of praise, &c.), RV.; (cl. 10 or Caus.) to cause to be born, AV. vii, 19, 1; xiii, 1, 19; VarBṛ. xiv, 1; xix, 2; to assign, procure, RV.; VS. xix, 94: cl. 4. *jā́yate* (ep. also °*ti*; impf. *ájāyata*; pr. p. *jā́yamāna*; fut. *janishyate*; aor. *ájanishṭa*; 1. [RV. viii, 6, 10] & 3. sg. *ájani*; 3. sg. *jáni*, i, 141, 1; *jā́ni*, viii, 7, 36; perf. *jajñé*, 2. sg. °*jñishé*, 3. pl. °*jñiré*, p. °*jñāná*) and [RV.] cl. 2. (?) Ā. (2. sg. *janishe*, 2. pl. °*nidhve*, Impv. °*nishvā* [vi, 15, 18], °*nidhvam*, cf. Pāṇ. vii, 2, 78; impf. 3. p. *ajñata* [aor., Pāṇ. ii, 4, 80], AitBr.), twice cl. 1. Ā. (impf. 3. pl. *ajanatā*, RV. iv, 5, 5; p. *jánamāna*, viii, 99, 3) to be born or produced, come into existence, RV.; AV. &c.; to grow (as plants, teeth), AV. iv f.; AitBr. vii, 15; ŚBr. xiv; KātyŚr.; Mn. ix, 38; VarBṛS.; to be born as, be by birth or nature (with double nom.), MBh. i, 11, 15; Pañcat. iv, 1, 5; to be born or destined for (acc.), RV. iv, 5, 5; MuṇḍUp. iii, 1, 10 (v.l. *jayate* for *jāy°*); to be born again, Mn. iv, ix, xi f.; MBh. i, iii, xiii; Hit. Introd. 14; to become, be, RV.; AV. &c.; to be changed into (dat.), Pāṇ. ii, 3, 13, Kāś.; to take place, happen, Vet. i, 11; iv, 25; to be possible or applicable or suitable, Suśr.; to generate, produce, R. iii, 20, 17; Caraṇ.: Pass. *janyate*, to be born or produced, Pāṇ. vi, 4, 43: Desid. *jijanishati*, 42, Kāś.: Intens. *jañjanyate* & *jājāy°*, 43 (cf. Vop. xx, 17); [cf. γίγνομαι; Lat. *gigno*, (*g*)*nascor*; Hib. *genim*, 'I beget, generate.']

Jána, mf(*ī*)n. 'generating,' see *puraṃ-*; m. (g. *vṛishâdi*) creature, living being, man, person, race (*páñca jánās*, 'the five races,' = *p° kṛishṭáyas*, RV. iii, viii ff.; MBh. iii, 14160), people, subjects (the sg. used collectively, e.g. *daívya* or *divyá j°*, 'divine race,' the gods collectively, RV.; *mahat j°*, many people, R. vi, 101, 2; often ifc. denoting one person or a number of persons collectively, e.g. *preshya-*, *bandhu-*, *sakhī-* &c., qq. vv.; with names of peoples, VarBṛS. iv, 22 & v, 74; *ayaṃ janaḥ*, 'this person, these persons,' I, we, MBh. viii, 709; Hariv. 7110; R. ii, 41, 2; Śak. &c.; *esha j°*, id., Kāvyâd. ii, 75), RV. &c.; the person nearest to the speaker (also with *ayam* or *asau*, 'this my lover,' Kāvyâd. ii, 271; Ratnâv. i, $\frac{24}{25}$), Nal. x, 10; Śak.; Mālav.; a common person, one of the people, Kir. ii, 42 & 47; the world beyond the Mahar-loka, BhP. iii, 11, 29; SkandaP.; (°*ná*), m. (g. *aśvâdi*) N. of a man (with the patr. Śārkarâkshya), ŚBr. x; ChUp.; (*ā*), f. 'birth,' *a-jana*, 'the unborn,' Nārāyaṇa, BhP. x, 3, 1. **—ṃ-sahá**, mfn. subduing men (Indra), RV. ii, 21, 3. **—karī**, f. (= *jananī*) red lac, L. **—kalpa**, mf(*ā*)n. similar to mankind, AitBr. vi, 32; ŚāṅkhŚr. xii, 21, 1; f. pl. (scil. *ṛicas*) N. of AV. xx, 128, 6–11, ib. **—kārin**, m. = *-karī*, L. **—gat**, mfn., Pāṇ. i, 4, 2, Vārtt. 14, Pat. **—°gatya**, Nom. (fr. *-gat*) °*tyati*, ib. **—ṃ-gama**, m. a Caṇḍāla (cf. *jalaṃ-g°*), Hcar. vi; Kād. vii, 168 (v.l. *jaran-mātaṅga*); Rājat. vii, 965; (*ā*), f. a Caṇḍāla woman, viii, 1957. **—cakshus**, n. = *jagac-*, 'eye of all creatures,' the sun, Hariv. 8050. **—candra**, m. 'N. of a poet,' for *jala-c°*. **—tā** (°*ná-*), f. (Pāṇ. iv, 2, 43) a number of men, assemblage of people, community, subjects, mankind, AV. v, 18, 12; TS. ii; TBr. i f.; AitBr.; VarBṛS.; Śiś. &c.; generation, W. **—traya**, n. three persons, R. iii, 4, 46. **—trā**, for *jala-*, W. **—dāha-sthāna**, n. a place of cremation, Daś. xii, 2. **—deva**, m. 'man-god,' a king, MBh. xii, 7883; BhP. viii, 19, 2. **—dhā** (*ján°*), mfn. (√*dhai*) nourishing creatures, TBr. i, 1, 1, 1 f. (*-dhāya*, TāṇḍyaBr. i, 4; *-dhāyas*, MaitrS. i, 3, 12 & 27). **—dhāya**, °**yas** (*ján°*), see *-dhā*. **—nātha**, m. 'man-lord,' a king, Kir. ii, 13. **—ṃ-tapa**, m. 'N. of a man,' see *jānaṃtapi*. **—pati**, m. = *-nātha*, Daś. i, 151. **—padá**, m. sg. or pl. a community, nation, people (as opposed to the sovereign), TBr. ii; AitBr. viii, 14; ŚBr. xiii f. &c.; sg. an empire, inhabited country, MBh. &c. (ifc. f. *ā*, R. iii, 61, 27); mankind, W.; *-ghātaka*, m. a plunderer of a country, Buddh. L.; *-maṇḍala*, n. the district formed by a country, Car. iii, 3; *-mahattara*, m. the chief of a country, Daś. viii, 207; °*dâdhipa*, m. 'country-ruler,' a king, R. ii, 63, 48; °*dâyuta*, mfn. crowded with people, W.; °*dêśvara*, m. = °*dâdhipa*, W.; °*dôddhvaṃsanīya*, mfn. treating on the epidemics of a country, Car. iii, 3. **—°padin**, m. 'country-ruler,' a king, Pāṇ. iv, 3, 100. **—pāna**, mfn. being a beverage for men, RV. ix, 110, 5. **—pālaka**, m. guardian of mankind, Kalyāṇam. 30. **—pravāda**, m. 'talk of men,' rumour, report, MBh. ii, 2507 (pl.); Rājat.; Hit. **—priya**, m. 'dear to men,' Śiva; coriander-seed, L.; Moringa pterygosperma, L.; *-phalā*, f. the egg-plant, Gal. **—bāndhava**, m. friend of mankind, Kalyāṇam. 38. **—bālikā**, f. lightning, Gal. **—bhakshá**, mfn. devouring men ['loving men or to be loved by men,' Sāy.], RV. ii, 21, 3. **—bhṛit**, mfn. supporting men, VS. x, 4. **—maraka**, m. 'men-killer,' an epidemic, VarBṛS. **—māra**, m. id., AV. Paris. lxxii, 84; (*ī*), f. id., 98. **—māraṇa**, n. killing of men. **—m-ejayá**, m. (Pāṇ. iii, 2, 28) 'causing men to tremble,' N. of a celebrated king to whom Vaiśampāyana recited the MBh. (great-grandson to Arjuna, as being son and successor to Parikshit who was the son of Arjuna's son Abhimanyu), ŚBr. xi, xiii; AitBr.; ŚāṅkhŚr. xvi; MBh. &c.; N. of a son (of Kuru, i, 3740; Hariv. 1608; of Pūru, MBh. i, 3764; Hariv. 1655; BhP. ix; of Puraṃ-jaya, Hariv. 1671; of Soma-datta, VP. iv, 1, 19; of Su-mati, BhP. ix, 2, 36; of Sṛiñjaya 23, 2); N. of a Nāga, TāṇḍyaBr. xxv; MBh. ii, 362. **—mohinī**, f. 'infatuating men,' N. of a Surâṅganā, Siṇhâs. Concl. **—yópana**, mfn. perplexing or vexing men, RV. x, 86, 22; AV. xii, 2, 15. **—rañjana**, mfn. gratifying men, Gīt. i, 19; n. gratification of people, W.; (*ī*), f. N. of a prayer, Pañcar. iii, 15, 32. **—rava**, m. = *-pravāda*. **—rā́j**, m. = *-nātha*, VS. v, 24. **—rā́jan**, m. id., RV. i, 53, 9. **—loka**, m. 'world of men,' the 5th Loka or next above Mahar-loka (residence of the sons of Brahmā and other godly men), ĀruṇUp.; NṛisUp. i, 5, 6; BhP.; MārkP.; SkandaP.; cf. *janas*. **—vat**, mfn. 'crowded with people,' (*ti*), loc. ind. on a spot filled with people, Car. i, 8, 1, 63. **—vallabha**, m. 'agreeable to men,' the plant Śveta-rohita, L. **—vāda**, m. (g. *kathâdi*) = *-pravāda*, Mn. ii, 179; MBh. ii, xii, xiv; VarBṛS. **—°vādin**, m. a talker, newsmonger, VS. xxx, 17. **—vid**, mfn. possessing men (Agni), Kauś. 78. **—vyavahāra**, m. popular practice or usage, W. **—śrī́**, mfn. coming to men (Pūshan), RV. vi, 55, 6 (Nir. vi, 4). **—śruta**, m. 'known among men,' N. of a man, ChUp. iv, 1, 1, Sch.; (*ā*), f. N. of a woman, AitBr. i, 25, Sāy.; cf. *jānaśruti*. **—śruti**, f. rumour, news, Rājat. vii, 133. **—saṃsad**, f. an assembly of men, MBh. iii, 2729 (pl.); R. **—saṃkshaya**, m. destruction of men, VarBṛS. vli, 30. **—sambādha**, m. a crowd of people, MBh. i, 7125; Kām.; mfn. densely crowded with people, W. **—1. -stha**, mfn. abidi[ng] among men, BhP. vii, 15, 56; see also s.v. *janas*. **—sthāna**, n. 'resort of men,' N. of part of the Daṇḍaka forest in Deccan, MBh. iii, ix, xiii; R.; Ragh. xii f.; *-ruha*, mfn. growing in Jana-sthāna, W. **Janâkīrṇa**, mfn. crowded with people, W. **Janâcāra**, m. popular usage, W. **Janâtiga**, mfn. superhuman, superior, Kir. iii, 2. **Janâdhinātha**, m. = °*na-nātha*, W.; Vishṇu, W. **Janâdhipa**, m. = °*na-nātha*, MBh.; R. (ifc. f. *ā*). **Janânta**, m. a number of men, Sāh. vi, 139; a region (*deśa*), Suśr. i, 46, 2, 38; 'man-destroyer,' Yama, BhP. vi, 8, 16. **Janântika**, 'personal proximity,' (*am*), ind. (as a stage-direction) whispering aside to another, Śak.; Vikr. &c.; (*e*), loc. ind. in the proximity of men, Kathās. lxv, 132. **Janâpavāda**, m. ill report, Pāṇ. ii, 3, 69, Kāś. (pl.) **Janâyana**, mfn. leading to men (a path), AV. xii, 1, 47. **Janârava**, m. = °*na-r°*, Kathās. lxxv, 152. **Janârṇava**, m. 'man-ocean,' a caravan, Nal. xiii, 16. **Janârtha-śabda**, m. a family appellation, gentile noun, W. **Janârdana**, m. (g. *nandy-ādi*) 'exciting or agitating men,' Vishṇu or Kṛishṇa, MBh. iii, 8102; v, 2564; Hariv. 15397; Bhartṛ.; BhP.; Gīt.; N. of several men, Hariv. &c.; of a locality, Tantr.; *-vibudha*, m. N. of a scholiast (author of Bhāvârtha-dīpikā). **Janâlaya**, m. an inhabitant of the Jana-loka, BhP. iii, 11, 31. **Janâv**, nom. *aus*, m. protecting men, Vop. xxvi, 77. **Janâśana**, m. 'man-eater,' a wolf, L. **Janâśraya**, m. 'man-shelter,' inn, caravansary, Rājat. iii, 480. **Janā-sháh**, nom. *-shāṭ*, = °*naṃ-sahá*, RV. i, 54, 11. **Janêndra**, m. = °*na-nātha*, R. ii, 100, 14. **Jane-vāda**, m. = °*na v°*, g. *kathâdi*. **Janêśa**, m. = °*nêndra*, Hariv. 8403; Hcar. v, 405. **Janêśvara**, m. id., MBh. i f.; Hariv. 1828; R. i, iii. **Janêshṭa**, m. 'man-desired,' a kind of jasmine, L.; (*ā*), f. turmeric, L.; the Jatukā plant (Oldenlandia), L.; the medicinal plant *vṛiddhi*, L.; the flower of Jasminum grandiflorum, L. **Janôdāharaṇa**, n. 'man-laudation,' fame, W. **—Janau**, see °*nâv*. **Janâugha**, m. a multitude of people, crowd, R. i, 77, 8; ii, 80, 4.

Janaka, mfn. (Pāṇ. vii, 3, 35, Kāś.) generative, generating, begetting, producing, causing (chiefly ifc.), MBh. iv, 1456; VarBṛS.; Bhāshāp.; Bhpr.; m. a progenitor, father, Hariv. 982; R. vi, 3, 45; Pañcat. &c.; (in music) a kind of measure; (oxyt.) N. of a king of Videha or Mithilā (son of Mithi and father of Udāvasu, R.), ŚBr. xi, xiv; MBh. iii, xii, xiv; Hariv. 9253; of another king of Mithilā (son of Hrasva-roman and father of Sītā), R.; of another king, Rājat. i, 98; of a disciple of Bhagavat, BhP. vi, 3, 20; of several official men, Rājat. vii f.; pl. the descendants of Janaka, MBh. iii, 10637; R. i; Uttarar. i, 16; iv, 9; vi, 42; MārkP.; (*ikā*), f. (as in Pāli) a mother, Divyâv. xviii, 137; a daughter-in-law, W. **—kāṇa**, m. 'the one-eyed Janaka,' N. of a man, Rājat. viii, 881. **—candra**, m. N. of several men, vii f. **—tanayā**, f. 'Janaka's daughter,' Sītā, Megh. 1. **—tā**, f. = *-tva*, Sāh. i, $\frac{2}{3}$, 8; paternity, Kathās. xvii, 57. **—tva**, n. generativeness, Sarvad. ii, 63; generation, i, 38; ii, 133. **—nandinī**, f. = *-tanayā*. **—bhadra**, m. N. of a man, Rājat. viii, 2485. **—rāja**, m. N. of a man, viii, 978 & 1002; Śrīkaṇṭh. xxv (grammarian and Vaidika). **—sapta-rātra**, m. N. of a Saptâha, KātyŚr.; ĀśvŚr. x; ŚāṅkhŚr.; Maś. **—siṇha**, m. N. of a man, Rājat. viii. **—sutā**, f. = *-tanayā*. **Janakâtmajā**, f. id. **Janakâhvaya**, m. Mesua Roxburghii, Gal. **Janakêśvara-tīrtha**, n. N. of a Tīrtha, RevāKh.

Janakīya, mfn. fr. *jána*, g. *gahâdi*, Pāṇ. iv, 3, 60, Kār.

Jánat, mfn. pr. p. √*jan*, q.v.; ind. an exclamation used in ceremonies (like *om*, &c.), Kauś.

Jánad-vat, mfn. containing a form of √*jan*, MaitrS. i, 8, 9.

Jánana, mf(*ī*)n. ifc. generating, begetting, producing, causing, Mn. ix, 81; MBh.; Hariv. &c.; m. a progenitor, creator, RV. ii, 40, 1; n. birth, coming into existence, TāṇḍyaBr. xxi, 9; KātyŚr.; Mn. &c.; 'birth,' i.e. life (*pūrva j°* = °*nântara*),

Kum. i, 54; production, causation, R.; Kum. i, 43; Sāṃkhyak.; Sarvad.; race, lineage, L.; (*ī*), f. a mother, ŚāṅkhŚr. xv; Mn. ix, 192; Yājñ.; Nal. &c.; a queen-mother, W.; a bat, L.; =*jana-karī*, L.; Jasminum auriculatum, L.; Rubia Munjista, L.; the plant *janī*, L.; the plant *kaṭukā*, L.; compassion, L.; cf. *indra-*, *medhā-*. **Jananântara**, n. (another, i.e.) a former life, Śak. v, 2.

Janani, metrically for °*nī*, a mother, VarBṛS. vi, 10; f. birth, W.; the plant *janī*, L.

1. **Jananīya**, Nom. °*yati*, to consider as one's mother, HYog. iii, 9.

2. **Jananīya**, mfn. to be produced, W.

Jánamāna, mfn. pr. p. √*jan*, q.v.; m. N. of a man, g. *gargâdi* (Kāś.; v.l. for *jaramāṇa*).

Jánayati, f. generation, VS. i, 22.

Janayanta, mfn. generating, producing, Vop.

Janayitavya, mfn. to be generated or produced, Prab. i, $\frac{30}{31}$; Sarvad. ii, 57; Sāṃkhyak., Sch.

Janayitṛi, m. (Pāṇ. vi, 4, 53, Kāś.) one who generates or begets or produces, progenitor, father, Mn. ix; MBh. &c.; (*trī*), f. a mother, Rājat. iii, 108.

Janayishṇu, m. a progenitor, MBh. ix, 2222.

Janar, in comp. for °*nas*. **-loka**, m. =*jana-l*°.

Jánas, n. race, class of beings (Lat. *genus*), RV. ii, 2, 4; =*jana-loka*, Vedāntas.; BhP. iii, 13, 25 & 43. 2. **Jana-stha** (fr. °*naḥ-*), mfn. abiding in the Janas (or Jana-loka), VP. i, 3, 24.

Jáni, °*nī*, f. a woman, wife (gen. °*nyur*, RV. x, 10, 3), RV. (pl. also fig. 'the fingers'); VS.; birth, production, Sarvad.; KapS. i, 97, Sch.; a kind of fragrant plant, L.; °*ni*, f. a mother, L.; birth, i.e. life, AgP. xxxviii, 1; birthplace, Hariv. 11979; the rt. *jan*, Bādar. iii, 1, 24, Sch.; cf. *gnā́*. **-kartṛi**, mfn. coming into existence, Pāṇ. i, 4, 30; producing, effecting, Naish. v, 63 (f. °*trī*). **-kāma** (*ján*°), mfn. wishing for a wife, AV. ii, 30, 5. **-** 1. **-tvá**, n. the state of a wife, RV. x, 18, 8. **-tvaná**, n. id., viii, 2, 42. **-dā́**, mfn. giving a wife, iv, 17, 16. **-divasa**, m. birthday, Mcar. vi, 28. **-dhā́**, ?, RV. x, 29, 5. **-nīlikā**, f. the plant Mahā-nīlī, L. **-paddhati**, f. N. of a work. **-mat**, mfn. having a wife or wives (Soma), ŚāṅkhGṛ. i, 9, 9; having an origin, produced, Bādar. iii f., Sch.; creature, man, Mcar. vii, 32. **-vat** (*ján*°), mfn. having a wife, RV.

Janika, mfn. generating, producing, W.

Janita, mfn. born, Hariv. 9238; engendered, begotten, W.; produced, occasioned, MBh. iv, 1236; Pañcat.; Megh. &c.; occurring, W. **-svana**, mfn. making a noise, sounding, W. **Janitôdyama**, mfn. making exertion, energetic, W.

Janitavyà, mfn. to be born or produced, AV. iv, 23, 7. **Janitṛi** or (along with *jajā́na* 4 times) **ján**°, m. (Pāṇ. vi, 4, 53) a progenitor, father, γενετήρ, (Lat.) *genitor*, RV.; VS.; AV.; ChUp.; ŚvetUp.; Pañcat.; (*jánitrī*), f. a mother, γενέτειρα, *genitrix*, RV.; AV.; TS. iv; Gobh.; MBh.; VarBṛS.

Janítra, n. a birthplace, place of origin, home, origin, RV.; AV.; VS.; TBr. ii; MBh. v, 2580; Hariv. 14730; pl. parents, relatives, AitBr. ii, 6; sg. generative or procreative matter, VS. xix, 84; xxi, 55; N. of a Sāman, ĀrshBr.; ŚāṅkhŚr.; Lāṭy.; (du. with *Vasishṭhasya*) another Sāman (consisting of the *janitrâdya* & °*trôttara*), ix, 12, 8; sg. with *uttara*=°*trôttara*, vii, 2, 1.

2. **Jánitva**, mfn.=°*tavyà*, RV. i, 66, 8 & 89, 10; iv, 18, 4; x, 45, 10; AV. ii, 28, 3; m. father, Uṇ., Sch.; m. du. parents, ib.; (*ā*), f. mother, ib.

Jániman, n. generation, birth, origin, RV. ii, 35, 6; iii, 1, 4; iv; x, 142, 2; offspring, v, 3, 3; ix, 68, 5; x, 63, 1; a creature, being, RV.; AV. v, 11, 5; genus, kind, race, RV.; AV. i, 8, 4; ii, 31, 5; vi; [cf. Hib. *geineamhuin*, 'birth, conception.']

Janiya, Nom. (3. pl. °*yánti*) to wish for a wife, AV. iv, 2, 72. **Jánishṭha**, mfn. (superl. of *janitṛi*) most generative, RV. v, 77, 4.

Janishya, mfn. =°*nitavyà*, MBh. xii; R. iii, vii.

Jánī, f., see °*ni*; a daughter-in-law (cf. *jāmi*), L.

1. **Janīya**, Nom. (p. °*yát*) =°*niya*, RV. iv, 17, 16; vii, 96, 4 (cf. Pāṇ. vii, 4, 35, Siddh.); AV. vi, 82, 3.

2. **Janīya**, mfn. See °*nyīya*.

Janu, f. =°*nū́*, L.; the soul, Gal.; cf. *sa-*.

Janús, m. n. (nom. [fr. °*nū́*?] °*nū́s*, RV. vii, 58, 2; ŚBr. iii, 9, 3, 2; acc. °*núsham*, RV. i, 139, 9; 141, 4; ii, 42, 1) birth, production, descent, RV.; AV. vii, 115, 3; 'nativity,' see °*nuḥ-paddhati*; birthplace, ŚBr. iii, 9, 3, 2; a creature, being, RV.; AV.; creation, RV. vii, 86, 1; genus, class, kind, RV. ii, 42, 1 (Nir. ix, 4); (*úshā*), instr. ind. by birth, from birth, by nature, originally, essentially, necessarily, RV.; AV. ix, 4, 24; TS. ii; cf. *aṅga-*. **Januḥ-paddhati**, f. N. of a work on nativities. **Janushândha**, mfn. born blind, Pāṇ. vi, 3, 3, Vārtt. 2. **Janūr-vâsas**, n. the natural garment, ŚBr. v, 3.

Janū́, f. (L.) See °*nús*.

Jano, in comp. for °*nas*. **-loka**, m. =°*na-l*°, KāśīKh. xxii.

Jantú, m. a child, offspring, RV.; Kathās. iic, 58; a creature, living being, man, person (the sg. also used collectively, e.g. *sarva j*°, 'everybody,' Śak. v, $\frac{5}{8}$; *ayaṃ jantuḥ*, 'the man,' KaṭhUp. ii, 20; ŚvetUp. iii, 20; Mn. xii, 99), RV.; Mn. &c.; a kinsman, servant, RV. i, 81, 9 & 94, 5; x, 140, 4; any animal of the lowest organisation, worms, insects, Mn. vi, 68 f.; MBh. xiv, 1136; Suśr.; (n.) HYog. iii, 53 & Subh.; a tree, Gal.; N. of a son of Somaka, MBh. iii, 10473 ff.; Hariv. 1793; BhP. ix, 22, 1; Kathās. xiii, 58 ff.; cf. *kshiti-*, *kshudra-*, *jala-*. **-kambu**, n. a shell inhabited by an animal, L. **-kārī**, f. =*jatu-kṛit*, L. **-gṛiha**, see *jatu-g*°. **-ghna**, mfn. killing worms, Suśr. i, 46, 4, 41; m. =*-mārin*, L.; n. =*-nāśana*, L.; Embelia Ribes, L.; (*ī*), f. id., L. **-jāta-maya**, mfn. =*-mat*, HYog. iii, 35. **-nāśana**, n. 'destroying worms,' Asa fœtida, L. **-pādapa**, m. Mangifera sylvatica, L. **-phala**, m. Ficus glomerata, L. **-mat**, mfn. containing worms or insects, MārkP. xxxii, 19. **-mātṛi**, m. a kind of worm living in the bowels, Car. i, 19, 1, 39; iii, 7; =*-rasa*, Npr. **-mārin**, m. 'worm-killer,' the citron, L. **-rasa**, m. 'insect-essence,' red lac, L. **-hantrī**, f. =*-ghnī*, L.

Jantuka, m. N. of a man, pl. his descendants, g. *upakâdi* (*jat*° & *jant*°, Gaṇar. 28 & 30, *jaturaka*, 30); (*ā*), f. =°*ntu-rasa*, L.; =*jatu-kṛit*, L.

Jantulā, f. Saccharum spontaneum, L.

Jántva, mfn. (=*jánit*°) =°*tavyà*, RV. viii, 89, 6.

Janma, in comp. for °*nman*; n. birth, L., Sch. **-kara**, mfn. ifc. effecting the birth of, Laghuj. iii, 8. **-kāla**, m. time or hour of birth, VarBṛS. vci, 13. **-kīla**, m. 'birth-pillar,' Vishṇu, L. **-kṛit**, m. a progenitor, father, BhP. iii, 13, 7; ix, 22, 1. **-kṛita**, mfn. effected by or resulting from birth, Kād. vi, 1860 (v.l. for *ā-j*°). **-kshetra**, n. birthplace, Kathās. **-gṛiha**, n. =*-bha*, VarYogay. iv, 44. **-citra**, °**traka**, m. N. of a Nāga, Divyâv. xxx. **-cintāmaṇi**, m. 'birth-jewel,' N. of a work on nativities. **-janman**, n. loc. °*ni*, ind. in every (birth or) life, Cāṇ.; °*nmântara*, n. every future life, Pañcat. i, 15, 29. **-jātaka**, n. N. of a work. **-jyeshṭha**, mfn. the eldest by birth, Mn. ix, 126. **-tas**, ind. according to birth, Āp. i, 1, 4; according to the age of life, Mn. ii, 155; ix, 125 f.; MBh. **-tāra** (m., L.) =*-bha*, Hcat. i, 11. **-tithi**, (m. f., L.) birthday, ŚāṅkhGṛ. i, 25. **-da**, mfn. ifc. =*-kara*, Laghuj. iii, 10; a progenitor, father, Śak. vii, 18 (v.l.) **-dina**, n. =*-tithi*, Kum. i, 23. **-nakshatra**, n. =*-bha*, Hcat. i, 8. **-nāman**, n. the name received at birth (i.e. on the 12th day after), W. **-pa**, m. the regent of a planet under which any one is born, VarBr. xv, 3. **-pattra**, n. 'nativity-paper,' horoscope (paper or scroll on which are recorded the year, lunar day, configuration, and relative position of the planets, of any one's birth, table of his fortunes throughout life), W. **-pattrikā**, f. id., Jyot. **-patha**, m. 'birth-path,' the vulva, Gal. **-pādapa**, m. the tree under which any one is born, family tree, Rājat. iv, 175. **-pratishṭhā**, f. 'birth-place,' a mother, Śak. vi, $\frac{1}{10}$. **-prada**, mfn. =*-kara*, VarBṛS. **-pradīpa**, m. N. of a work on nativities (by Vibudha). **-prabhṛiti**, ind. ever since birth, Mn. viii, 90; MBh. v, 4153; R. i. **-bandha**, m. the fetters of transmigration, Bhag. ii, 51. **-bha**, n. the asterism under which any one is born, VarYogay. ix, 10. **-bhāj**, m. 'possessing birth,' a creature, living being, Mṛicch. x, 56 (60); Kalyāṇam. **-bhāshā**, f. mother-tongue, W. **-bhū**, f. native country, Bhpr. ii, 317. **-bhūmi**, f. id., Hariv. 5747; Pañcat.; Prab.; Rājat.; Hit.; *-bhūta*, mfn. become a native country, Kād. iv, 324. **-bhṛit**, mfn. possessing birth, enjoying life, BhP. i, 18, 18; x, 84, 9. **-yoga**, m. a horoscope, W. **-rāśi**, m. the zodiacal sign under which any one is born, VarBṛ. xxiv, 6; °*śy-adhipa*, m. the regent of that zodiacal sign, VarYogay. iv, 45, Sch. **-rogin**, mfn. sickly from birth, W. **-rksha** (*riksha*), n. =*-bha*, Suśr. i, 32, 1; VarBṛS.; VarYogay. ix, 1. **-lagna**, n. =*-rāśi*. **-vaṇśa**, m. relations by birth (opposed to *vidyā-v*°), Pāṇ. ii, 1, 19, Sch. **-vat**, mfn. possessing birth, born, living, Kād. iii, 654 (*-tā*, f. abstr.) **-vartman**, n. =*-patha*, L. **-vasudhā**, f. =*-bhū*, Rājat. iv, 147. **-vailakshaṇya**, n. acting in a manner unbecoming one's birth, W. **-śayyā**, f. the bed on which any one is born, MBh. vi, 5820. **-śodhana**, n. discharging the obligation derived from birth, W. **-samudra**, m. N. of a work on nativities. **-sāphalya**, n. attainment of the object or end of existence, Mn. xii, 93. **-sthāna**, n. =*-kshetra*, W.; =*-bhū*, Pañcat. v, 6, $\frac{3}{4}$; Vet.; the womb, W. **Janmâdhipa**, m. 'lord of birth,' Śiva; =°*nma-pa*, VarBṛS. xxxiv, 11. **Janmântara**, n. 'another birth or life,' a former life, MBh. iii, 2564; Kathās. xxiii, 49; a future life, Pañcat. ii, 6, 42; Caurap.; KapS. i, 7, Sch.; *-gata*, mfn. regenerated, Kathās. iic, 50. **Janmântarita**, mfn. done in a former life, RāmatUp. ii, 4, 26. **Janmântariṇa**, mfn. one's own from a former birth, Sāh. x, $\frac{96}{97}$. **Janmântarīya**, mfn. =°*rita*, Rājat. vi, 85. **Janmândha**, mfn. =°*nushândha*, Bhpr. v, $\frac{3}{4}$ (*-tva*, n. abstr.) **Janmâshṭamī**, f. Kṛishṇa's birth-day (the 8th day in the dark half of month Śrāvaṇa or Bhādra), *-tattva*, n. N. of Smṛitit. viii; *-nirṇaya*, m. N. of a work; *-vrata*, n. N. of a vow described in a tale (which is said to be taken from VP.) **Janmâspada**, n. =°*ma-kshetra*, Hariv. 14653. **Janmêśa**, m. =°*ma-pa*, VarBṛ. xv, 3; VarYogay. iv, 12. **Janmôdaya-rksha**, n. =°*marksha*, 43.

Janmaka, =°*man*, only in comp. **-nātha**, m. =°*ma-pa*, 45, Sch.

Jánman, n. birth, production (*kṛita-*, mfn. 'planted,' Kum. v, 60), origin (ifc. 'born from,' e.g. *śūdra-*, q.v.), RV. iii, 26, 7; vii, 33, 10; AV.; VS. &c.; existence, life, Mn.; Bhag. iv, 5; Yogas. ii, 12 (*dṛishṭâdṛishṭa-j*°, 'present and future life'), &c. (*janma*, acc. ind. through the whole life, HPariś. iv, 7); nativity, VarBṛS. i, 10; re-birth, Sarvad. xi; birthplace, home, RV. ii, 9, 3; viii, 69, 3; x, 5, 7; AV.; VS.; a progenitor, father, Śak. vii, 18; natal star, VarBṛS. iv, 28; (in astrol.) N. of the 1st lunar mansion, civ; a creature, being, RV.; TBr. ii; AitBr. iv, 10; people, RV. ii, 26, 3; iii, 15, 2; the people of a household, kind, race, RV. (*ubhāya j*°, sg., du. & pl., 'both races,' i.e. gods and men or [x, 37, 11] men and animals); nature, quality, i, 70, 2; custom, manner (*pratnéna jánmanā*, 'according to ancient custom'), i, 87, 5; ix, 3, 9; SV. (v.l. *manm*°, RV.); Hariv. 15718 (*dūta-janmanā*, 'like a messenger'); water, Naigh. i, 12. **Janmin**, m. a creature, man, Pañcat. i, 1, 93; ii, 3, 19.

1. **Janya**, mfn. (√*jan*, Pāṇ. iii, 4, 68; iii, 1, 97, Pat.) born, produced, Bhāshāp. 44; BrahmavP.; ifc. born or arising or produced from, occasioned by, Śiś.; Bhāshāp.; Tarkas. &c. (*tā*, f. abstr., Vedāntas.; *-tva*, n. id., KapS., Sch.); m. a father, L.; n. the body, BhP. i, 9, 31; a portent occurring at birth, L.

2. **Jánya**, mfn. (fr. *jána*) belonging to a race or family or to the same country, national, RV. ii, 37, 6 & 39, 1; x, 91, 2; ŚāṅkhŚr. xv, 13, 3; belonging or relating to the people, RV. iv, 55, 5; ix, 49, 2; TBr. i; TāṇḍyaBr.; ShaḍvBr.; m. the friend or companion of a bridegroom, RV. iv, 38, 6; AV. xi, 8, 1 f.; Gobh. ii, 1, 13; MBh. i, iii; Kathās.; a son-in-law, Gal.; a common man, TS. vi, 1, 6, 6; TBr. i, 7, 8, 7; N. of Śiva, MBh. xiii, 1170; v.l. for *jānya*, q.v.; m. n. rumour, report, Pāṇ. iv, 4, 97; n. people, community, nation, RV. ii; x, 42, 6; AV. xiii, 4, 43 (oxyt.); pl. inimical races or men, AitBr. viii, 26; fighting, war, Gaut.; MBh. v, 3195; Ragh. iv, 77; Daś.; a market, L.; (*ā*), f. (g. *utkarâdi*) a bridesmaid, Pāṇ. iv, 4, 82; Ragh. vi, 30; the female friend of a mother, L.; a newly-married wife, Campak. 163 f. & 211; pleasure, L.; affection, W. **-yātrā**, f. bridal journey, Malatim. vi, 2; Campak.

Janyīya, mfn. fr. °*nyā*, g. *utkarâdi*.

Janyu, m. birth (?), Hariv. 7092 (v.l.); a creature, Uṇ.; fire, L.; Brahmā, L.; v.l. for *jahnu*, q.v.

जन्दुरक *janduraka*, a kind of mat or stuff, Divyâv. i, 354.

जन्म *janma*, °*nman*, &c. See √*jan*.

Janmejaya, for *janam-ej*°, BhP.; BrahmavP.

Janya, °*nyīya*, °*nyu*. See above.

जप् *jap*, cl. 1. *jápati* (rarely Ā., ŚāṅkhŚr. iii, 6, 4; MBh. iii, xiii; pf. *jajāpa*; 3. du. *jepatur*, R. i; inf. *japitum*, MBh. xii, 7336; ind. p. °*ptvā*, Mn. xi; R. i; °*pitvā*, Mn. xi; Vet.) to utter in a low voice, whisper, mutter (esp. prayers or incantations), AitBr. ii, 38; ŚBr.; Lāṭy.; KātyŚr.; Kauś.; Mn. &c.; to pray to any one (acc.) in a low voice, MBh. xiii, 750; to invoke or call upon in a low voice, BhP. iv, 7, 29; BhavP. i: Intens. *jañjapyate*, °*pīti* (Pāṇ. vii, 4, 86; p. *pyámāna*) to whisper repeatedly (implying blame, iii, 1, 24), ŚBr. xi, 5, 5, 10.

Jápa, mfn. 'muttering, whispering,' see *karṇe-, ku-*; m. (Pāṇ. iii, 3, 61; oxyt., g. *uñchâdi*) muttering prayers, repeating in a murmuring tone passages from scripture or charms or names of a deity, &c., muttered prayer or spell, AitBr. ii, 38; ŚBr. ii; ŚāṅkhŚr.; Nir. &c. **-tā**, f. the state of one who mutters prayers, MBh. xiii, 1907 (*japatām*, gen. pl. of *japat*, Sch.) **-parāyaṇa**, mfn. devoted to muttering prayers, W. **-mālā**, f. a rosary used for counting muttered prayers. **-yajña**, m. muttering prayers as a religious sacrifice, Mn. ii, 85 f.; Yājñ. i, 101; Bhag.; SkandaP. **-homa**, m. sg. & pl. muttering prayers as a religious offering, Mn. x, 111; xi, 34; MBh. xii, 3756; VarBṛS. vli, 51 & 58; (°*maka*) Rudray. ii, 8, 1; m. du. a muttered prayer and an offering, Śāktān. xii.

Japana, n. muttering prayers, MBh. xii, 7157.

Japanīya, mfn. to be muttered, Mn. ii, 79, Sch.

Japita, mfn. muttered, MBh. xii, 7248.

Japin, mfn. muttering prayers, Yājñ. iii, 286.

Japta, mfn. = °*pita*, MBh. v, 7047; Naish. xi, 26; whispered over, VarBṛS. iil, 72.

Japtavya, mfn. to be muttered, R. vii, 23, 4, 28; VarBṛS. vli, 72; BhP. iv, 24, 31.

Jápya, mfn. id., ŚBr. x; ŚāṅkhŚr.; Mn. xi, 143; VarBṛS.; n. (once m. scil. *mantra*, BhP. iv, 8, 53) a muttered prayer, Mn.; Yājñ.; MBh. &c. **-karman**, n. = °*pana*, Āp. i, 15, 1. **Japyêśvara-tīrtha**, n. N. of a Tīrtha, VāsishṭhalP. iii.

Japyaka, m. N. of a man, Rājat. vii, 495.

जपा *japā*, f. (= *javā*) the China rose, VarBṛS. xxviii, 14; BrahmaP. ii, 1, 7. **-kusuma-saṃnibha**, m. 'resembling the Japā-flower,' the plant *hiṅgūla*, Npr. **Japâkhyā**, f. = °*pā*, L.

जपिल *japila*, N. of a locality, W.

जप्त *japta*, °*ptavya*, &c. See √*jap*.

जबारु *jábāru*, n. = *maṇḍala* (Nir. vi, 17, Sch.), RV. iv, 5, 7.

जबाला *jabālā* (cf. Pāṇ. ii, 4, 58, Pat.), N. of a woman, ChUp. iv, 4, 1.

जभ् 1. *jabh* or *jambh* (cl. 1. *jabhate* or *jambh*°, Dhātup. x, 28; aor. Subj. *jambhishat*) to snap at (gen.), RV. x, 86, 4: Caus. *jambháyati* (p. °*yat*) to crush, destroy, RV.; AV.; VS. xvi, 5: Intens. *jañjabhyáte* (& °*bhīti*, Pāṇ. vii, 4, 86; p. °*bhyámāna* [TS. ii, 5, 2, 4; Nyāyam.; Jaim., Sch.], °*bhāna* [Kauś. 114], °*bhat* [ŚāṅkhŚr. iv, 20, 1]) opening the jaws wide, snapping at (implying blame, Pāṇ. iii, i, 24); cf. *abhi-* & √*jṛimbh*.

Jabdhṛi, mfn. snapping at, vii, 1, 61, Sch.

Jabhya, m. 'snapper,' a kind of animal destructive to grain, AV. vi, 50, 2 (voc.); n. impers. the mouth is to be opened wide, Pāṇ. vii, 1, 61, Kāś.

Jambira, m. See °*bīra*.

Jambīra, m. (= °*mbhīra*) = °*mbhin*, the citron tree, BhP. viii, 2, 13; SkandaP. &c.; = °*raka*, Suśr.; n. a citron, ib. **-nagara**, n. N. of a town, Siṃhās.

Jambīraka, m. a kind of Ocimum, Suśr. i, 46.

Jámbha, m. a tooth, eye-tooth, tusk, (pl.) set of teeth, mouth, jaws, RV.; VS. xi, 79 (du.); xv, 15; AV. iii, 27, 1–6; swallowing, RV. i, 37, 5; (°*bhá*) one who crushes or swallows (as a demon), AV. ii, 4, 2; viii, 1, 16; Kauś.; (g. *śivâdi*) N. of several demons (conquered by Vishṇu or Kṛishṇa, MBh. iii, v, vii; Hariv.; by Indra, MBh.), MBh. i, 2105; iii, 16365; Hariv. 13227; BhP. viii, 10, 21; a leader of the demons in the war against the gods under Indra, MārkP. xviii, 16; N. of a son (of Prahrāda, Hariv. 12461; of Hiraṇya-kaśipu, 12914); of the father-in-law of Hiraṇya-kaśipu, BhP. vi, 18, 11; of Sunda's father, R. i, 27, 7; Indra's thunderbolt, Gal.; a charm (?), MBh. v, 64, 20; = °*bhin*, L.; a quiver, L.; a part, portion, L.; (*ā*), f. (= *jṛimbhā*) opening of the mouth, L.; (*ī*), f. N. of a goddess, Kālac. iii, 132; cf. *ku-, tápur-, tigmá-, tṛishṭa-, vīḷú-; su-jámbha* & *antar-jambhá*; [cf. γαμφηλαί.] **-kuṇḍa**, n. N. of a Tīrtha, KapSaṃh. ix. **-ga**, m. pl. N. of a class of demons (for °*bhaka*?), PadmaP. **-m-jambham**, ind. so as to open the mouth wide (?), Pāṇ. vii, 1, 61, Kāś. **-dvish**, m. 'Jambha-enemy,' Indra, L. **-bhedin**, m. 'Jambha-destroyer,' Indra, Dhūrtan. **-suta** (*jámbh*°), mfn. pressed with the jaws, chewed, RV. x, 80, 2. **Jambhâri**, m. = °*bha-dvish*, Naish.; Kathās. xciii f.; thunderbolt, L.; fire, L.; *-bhuja-stambhana*, n. paralysing Indra's arm (one of Śiva's heroic deeds), Bālar.

Jámbhaka, mfn. (Pāṇ. vii, 1, 61, Kāś.) ifc. crushing, devouring, R. i, 30, 9; yawning (cf. *jṛimbh*°), W.; m. a charm (?), MBh. v, 64, 16; a demon or N. of a demon, VS. xxx, 16; N. of Gaṇêśa, Kathās. lv, 165; of a demon (conquered by Kṛishṇa, MBh. ii, 1111; causing diseases, Hariv. 9557; AgP. xl, 19; attendant of Śiva, L.); pl. N. of several evil spirits supposed to reside in various magical weapons, R. (G) i, 31, 4 & 10; (hence sg.) N. of a verse addressed to them, i, 31, 9; = °*bhin*, L.; (*ā*), f. = °*bhā*, L.; (*ikā*), f. = °*bhī*, Kālac. iii, 165.

Jambhan, ifc. (*tṛiṇa-, su-, soma-, harita-*) = °*bha*, Pāṇ. v, 4, 125.

1. **Jámbhana**, mf(*ī*)n. crushing, destroying, crusher, AV. x, 4, 15; MBh. vi, 807; m. Calotropis gigantea, L.; cf. *kaṇva-, piśāca-, maśaka-, yātu-,* & *vyāghra-jámbh*°. **Jambhara**, m. = °*bhin*, L.

Jambhala, m. id., L.; N. of a spirit, Buddh.; of a man, ib.; (*ā*), f. of a Rākshasī (by meditating on whom women become pregnant), ib. **-datta**, m. N. of the author of Vet.

Jambhalikā, f. a kind of song, Vikr. iv, $\frac{3}{3}$.

Jambhin, m. the citron tree, L.

Jambhīra, m. = °*mbīra*, id., L.; = °*mbīraka*, L., Sch. **-nagara**, v.l. for °*mbīr*°.

Jámbhya, m. an incisor (tooth), grinder, VS. xi, 78; ŚBr. xi, 4, 1, 5; pl. a jaw, TPrāt. ii, 17.

जभ् 2. *jabh* or *jambh*, cl. 1. *jabhati* or *jambh*°, Ā. (Vop.) *jabhate* (aor. *ajambhishṭa*), v.l. for √*yabh* (Dhātup. xxiii, 11) to know carnally, BhP. iii, 20, 26 (inf. *jabhitum*, v.l. *yabh*°).

2. **Jambhana**, n. sexual intercourse, Vop. (v.l.)

जभ्य *jabhya*. See √1. *jabh*.

जम् (1. *jam*), *jmā*, *jmás*. See 2. *kshám*.

जम् 2. *jam* (derived fr. *jamád-agni*), cl. 1. *jámati*, to go, Naigh. ii, 14; Nir. iii, 6; to eat, Dhātup. xiii, 28: Intens. p. *jājamat*, consuming continually, MBh. xiii, 4495.

Jamát, mfn. (derived fr. °*mád-agni*) = *jvalat*, Naigh. i, 17. **Jamana**, n. = *jem*°, L., Sch.

जमज *jama-ja*, mfn. = *yam*°, L.

जमदग्नि *jamád-agni*, m. (cf. √2. *jam*) N. of a Ṛishi (descendant of Bhṛigu, RAnukr.; son of Bhārgava Ṛicīka and father of Paraśu-rāma, MBh. &c.; often named together with Viśvā-mitra as an adversary of Vasishṭha), RV.; VS.; AV. &c. **-tīrtha**, n. N. of a Tīrtha, RevāKh. cccxxvi f. **-datta** (°*mád*°), mfn. given by Jamadagni, RV. iii, 53, 15.

जमश्व *jama-śva*, m. = *yam*°, Kapishṭh. xxxii.

जमालिन् *jamālin*, m. N. of Mahā-vīra's son-in-law (founder of schism 1. of the Jain church).

जम्पती *jam-patī*, m. du. = *dám-p*°, wife and husband, g. *rājadantâdi*; Pāṇ. i, 1, 11, Kāś.

जम्पान *jampāna*, n. a sedan-chair, Bharaṭ. xxv; Jain., Sch.

जम्ब *jamba*, m. mud, clay, Uṇ., Sch.

Jambāla, (m., n., L.), id., Pañcat. i, 13, $\frac{2}{3}$; Kād.; Bālar.; Rājat.; Pārśvan.; Blyxa octandra, ŚārṅgP. xxxii, 9; m. Pandanus odoratissimus, L.

Jambālinī, f. 'muddy,' a river, L.

जम्बिर *jambira*, °*bīra*, &c. See √1. *jabh*.

जम्बु *jambu*, °*bū*, f. the rose apple tree (Eugenia Jambolana or another species), Kauś. 8; MBh. &c.; the shrub *nāga-damanī*, L.; (°*bu*) n. the rose apple fruit, Pāṇ. iv, 3, 165; m. or f. (?; g. *varaṇâdi*) = *-dvīpa*, BhP. v, 1, 32; N. of a fabulous river (flowing from the mountain Meru; formed by the juice of the fruits of the immense Jambu tree on that mountain, cf. MBh. vi, 277 f.), BhP. v, 20, 2; cf. *āḍhaka-, kāka-, go-raksha-, mahā-*. **-dvīpa**, m. the central one of the 7 continents surrounding the mountain Meru (= India, Buddh.; named so either from the Jambu trees abounding in it, or from an enormous Jambu tree on Mount Meru visible like a standard to the whole continent), MBh.; Hariv. &c.; *-prajñapti*, f. '(mythical) geography of Jambu-dvīpa,' N. of Upâṅga vi of the Jaina canon; *-vara-locana*, m. N. of a Samādhi, Kāraṇḍ. xxiii, 148 f. **-dhvaja**, m. 'having the Jambu tree as its standard,' = *-dvīpa*, Lalit. iii, 265; N. of a Nāga, Buddh. L. **-parvata**, m. = *-dvīpa*, MBh. vi, 405. **-prastha**, m. N. of a village, R. ii, 71, 11 (°*mbū-p*°, B). **-mat**, m. 'rich in Jambu trees,' a mountain, W.; a monkey, W.; (*tī*), f. an Apsaras, W. **-mālin**, m. N. of a Rakshas, v f. **-rudra**, m. N. of a Nāga, ŚivaP. **-vana-ja**, n. 'growing in Jambu forests,' the white flower of the China rose, VāmP. **-sara**, the town Jumbooseer (in Gurjara, between Cambay and Baroch). **Jambv-oshṭha**, n. = *jāmbavoshṭha*, Suśr. v, 8, 125.

Jambū, f. = °*bu*, the rose apple tree, MBh. &c.; m. = *-svāmin*, Jain. **-khaṇḍa**, m. n. = °*bu-dvīpa*, MBh. i, 337; vi, 226 & 401; *-vinirmāṇa-parvan*, n. 'section on the extension of the Jambu-dvīpa,' N. of MBh. vi, chs. 1–6. **-dvīpa**, m. = °*bu-d*°; *-prajñapti*, f. = °*bu-d*°. **-nadī**, f. (= *jāmb*°) N. of one of the 7 arms of the heavenly Gaṅgā, vi, 243. **-prastha**, see °*bu-p*°. **-mārga**, m. n. 'way leading to the sacred Jambu on Meru,' N. of a Tīrtha, iii, xiii; Hariv.; VP. ii, 13, 33. **-svāmin**, m. N. of the pupil of Mahā-vīra's pupil Sudharman.

जम्बुक *jambuka*, m. a jackal, MBh.; R.; Pañcat. &c.; a low man, Cāṇ.; Eugenia Jambos, L.; a kind of Bignonia, L.; N. of Varuṇa, L.; of an attendant in Skanda's retinue, MBh. ix, 2576; of a Śūdra, xii, 153, 67 (*śamb*°, C); (*ā*), f. a female jackal, Pañcat. iv, 8, 1. **Jambukêśa**, n. N. of Liṅga, LiṅgaP. i, 1, 3. **Jambukêśvara-tīrtha**, n. N. of a Tīrtha, RevāKh. xxiv.

Jambūka, m. a jackal, Hit. i, 3, $\frac{2}{3}$ (v.l.); a low man, L.; Varuṇa, L.; N. of an attendant of Skanda, MBh. ix, 2578; (*ā*), f. a grape without stones, L.; (*ī*), f. N. of a female attendant of Durgā, W.

जम्बुल *jambula*, m. a kind of disease of the outer ear, Suśr. i, 16, 25 & 35; = °*bu*, Eugenia Jambolana, L.; Pandanus odoratissimus, L.

Jambūla, m. Pandanus odoratissimus, Hariv. 5371; Eugenia Jambolana, L.; n. 'jests addressed to the bridegroom by his female relatives,' see *-mālikā*. **-mālikā**, f. 'Jambūla garland,' jesting compliments addressed to the bridegroom by his female relatives (Sch.; 'brightness of countenance in a bride and bridegroom,' Udvāhat.), Hariv. 10889.

जम्भ् 1. & 2. *jambh*. See √1. & 2. *jabh*.

Jambha, jámbhaka, °**mbhan**. See √1. *jabh*.

Jambhana. See √1. & 2. *jabh*.

Jambhara &c., **jámbhya**. See √1. *jabh*.

जय *jayá*, mfn. (√*ji*) ifc. conquering, winning, see *ṛitam-, kṛitam-, dhanam-jayá, puram-, śatrum-*; m. (Pāṇ. iii, 3, 56, Kāś.) conquest, victory, triumph, winning, being victorious (in battle or in playing with dice or in a lawsuit), AV. vii, 50, 8; ŚBr. vi; Mn. vii (*indriyāṇām j*°, victory over or restraint of the senses) & x; MBh. &c.; cf. *ātma-, prâṇa-, rug-*; m. pl. (parox.) N. of particular verses causing victory (personified as deities, VāyuP. ii, 6, 4 ff.), MaitrS. i, 4, 14; TS. iii; PārGṛ. i, 5; Nyāyam. iii, 4, 24; m. sg. Premna spinosa or longifolia, L.; a yellow variety of Phaseolus Mungo, L.; N. of the 3rd year of the 6th lustrum of the Bṛihaspati cycle, VarBṛS. viii, 38; a kind of flute; (in music) a kind of measure; the sun, MBh. iii, 154; Arjuna (son of Pāṇḍu), 266, 7 & iv, 5, 35; Indra, L.; N. of a Ṛishi (author of RV. x, 180; son of Aṅgiras [RAnukr.] or of Indra; living under the 10th Manu, BhP. viii, 13, 22); of a spirit, VarBṛS liii, 48; Hcat. i, 9, 149 & 172; of an attendant of Vishṇu, BhP. iii, 16, 2; of a Nāga, MBh. v, 3632; ix, 2554; of a Dānava, Hariv. 13093; of a son (of Dhṛita-rāshṭra, MBh. i, vii; of Sṛiñjaya, Hariv. 1514; of Suśruta, VP. iv, 5, 12; of Śruta, BhP. ix, 13, 25; of Saṃjaya, 17, 16; of Saṃkṛiti, 18; of Mañju, 21, 1; of Yuyudhāna, 24, 13; of Kaṅka, 43; of Kṛishṇa, x, 61, 17; of Vatsara by Svar-vīthi, iv, 13, 12; of Viśvāmitra, Hariv. 1462; BhP. ix, 16, 36; of Purūravas by Urvaśī, 15, 1 f.); of an ancient king (11th Cakravartin in Bhārata, L.), MBh. ii, 326; of a Pāṇḍava hero, vii, 6911; of Yudhishṭhira at Virāṭa's court, iv, 176; of Aśoka in a former birth, Divyâv. xxvi, 336 f.; of a carpenter, Rājat. iii, 351; (*ā*), f. Sesbania ægyptiaca, L.; Premna spinosa or longifolia, L.; Terminalia Chebula, L.; *nīla-dūrvā*, L.; for *japā*, Kathās. lxvii, 32; N. of a narcotic substance, W.; the 3rd or 8th or 13th day of either half-month, Sūryapr.; cf. Hcat. i, 3, 360 & Nirṇayas. i, $\frac{333}{334}$; one of the 7 flag-sticks of Indra's banner, VarBṛS. xliii, 40; N. of the *saurā dharmāḥ*, BhavP. i; of Durgā, MBh. iv, vi; Hariv.; Kathās. liii, 170; of a daughter of Daksha (wife of Śiva, MatsyaP. xiii,

32; tutelary deity of the Ārtabhāgas, BrahmaP. ii, 18, 19), R. i, 23, 14; of a Yoginī, Hcat. ii, 1, 694 (v.l. *layā*); of a Śakti, i, 5, 200; of a handmaid of Durgā (wife of Pushpa-danta, Kathās. i, 52; vii, 107; of Hariś-candra, ŚivaP.); (=*tārā*) N. of a Buddh. deity, L.; of the mother of the 12th Arhat of the present Avasarpiṇī, L. **-karṇa**, m. N. of a prince, Pañcad. iii, 1. **-kāṅkshin**, mfn. desirous of victory, W. **-kārikā**, f. Mimosa pudica, Npr. **-kārin**, mfn. gaining a victory, W. **-kīrti**, m. N. of a man. **-kuñjara**, m. a victorious elephant (over rival elephants), Ratnâv. iv, 12. **-kṛit**, m. causing victory, VarBṛS. **-keśi**, m. N. of a man. **-kolāhala**, m.=*-ghosha*, W.; a kind of dice, L. **-kshetra**, n. N. of a locality, RevāKh. cclxxxiii. **-gata**, mfn. conquering, victorious, VarBṛS. xvii, 10. **-garva**, m. pride of conquest, W. **-gupta**, m. N. of a poet, ŚārṅgP. cxxxvi, 8; of a man, Rājat. vi, 287. **-govinda**, m. N. of the author of an Inscr. (A.D. 1668). **-ghaṇṭā**, f. a kind of cymbal. **-ghosha**, m. a shout of victory, Hcat.; (*ā*), f. N. of a Surâṅganā, Siṇhâs. Concl. **-ghoshaṇa**, n. or °**ṇā**, f.=°*sha*, Ragh. xii, 72. **-candra**, m. N. of the author of Gośṛiṅga-svayambhū-caitya-bhaṭṭāra-kôddeśa; of a man, Rājat. viii; of a Gauḍa king, W.; of a king of Kānyakubja, W. **-caryā**, f. N. of a work on omens by Nara-hari. **-ḍhakkā**, f. a large drum of victory, W. **-tīrtha**, m. N. of a commentator; *-bhikshu*, m. id.; *-yati*, m. id. **-tuṅga**, m. N. of an author or work, Nirṇayas. iii; °*gôdaya*, m. N. of a work, ŚārṅgP. iiic, 8. **-da**, mfn. =*-kṛit*, VarBṛS.; (*ā*), f. N. of the tutelary deity of Vāmadeva's family, BrahmaP. ii, 18, 12. **-datta**, m. N. of a king, Kathās. xxi, 54; of a minister of king Jayâpīḍa, Rājat. iv, 511; of the author of Aśva-vaidyaka, ŚārṅgP. lxxix, &c.; of a Bodhi-sattva, Buddh. L.; of a son of Indra, L. **-durgā**, f. a form of Durgā, Tantras. ii; Pheṭk. xiv. **-deva**, m. N. of the authors of Gīt., Prasannar., Candrâloka, and (the grammar) Īshat-tantra. **-devaka**, m.= °*va* (author of Gīt.), Gīt. iii, 10; n. N. of a Muhūrta. **-druma**, m. Vanda Roxburghii, Npr. **-dhara**, m. N. of Śaṃkara's great-grandfather. **-dharman**, m. N. of a Kaurava hero, MBh. vii, 6852. **-dhvaja**, m. a flag of victory; N. of a son of Arjuna Kārtavīrya, Hariv. 1893; VP. iv, 11, 5; BhP. ix, 23, 26 f.; BṛNārP. xxxvii; °*jāya*, Nom. °*jāyate*, to represent a flag of victory, Daś. i, 16. **-dhvani**, m.=*-ghosha*, W. **-nārāyaṇa**, m. N. of the author of the Bengali poem Kāśī-khaṇḍa. **-nīrājana**, n. N. of a military ceremony, Vīrac. viii, 52. **-nṛi-siṇha**, m. a form of Vishṇu, Rasik. xi, 12. **-patākā**, f. a flag of victory, Bālar. vi, 52; a small banner presented to a victorious fighter, Lalit. xii, 103. **-pattra**, n. record of victory (in a lawsuit) given to the victorious party, Smṛitit. x, 12, 4 f.; a sign fastened on the forehead of a horse chosen for an Aśva-medha, W. **-parājaya**, m. du. =°*yâjaya*, Yājñ. ii, 6, Sch.; n. sg. id., Pañcat.; Dhūrtas. ii, $\frac{8}{9}$. **-pāla**, m. 'victory-keeper,' a king, L.; Brahmā, L.; Vishṇu, L.; Croton Jamalgota, Bhpr. v, 3, 201; N. of several kings. **-putraka**, m. a kind of dice, L. **-pura**, n. 'victory-town,' N. of a fortress in Kaśmīr, Rājat. iv, vii; of a town (and small state in Marwur), HPariś. ii, 166. **-prasthāna**, n. march to victory, W. **-priya**, m. 'fond of victory,' N. of a Pāṇḍava hero, MBh. vii, 7011; (*ā*), f. N. of one of the mothers attending on Skanda, ix, 2630. **-bāhu**, m. N. of a man conversant with the 1st Aṅga or Aṅgas, Vardhamānac. i, 50. **-bhaṭa**, m. N. of a man. **-bheri**, m. 'drum of victory,' N. of a man, Vīrac. xv, xxvi. **-maṅgala**, m. a royal elephant, L.; a remedy for fever; (in music) a kind of measure; N. of a Dhruvaka; of an elephant, Kathās. li, 194; of a scholiast on Bhaṭṭ. (°*lā*, f. N. of his Comm.); =*-śabda*, Rājat. iv, 158. **-mati**, m. N. of a Bodhi-sattva, Buddh. L. **-matī**, f. (fr. *-mat*=*-vat*) N. of several women, vii f.; Śatr. **-malla**, m. 'victorious fighter,' a subduer of (in comp.), Veṇīs. vi, $\frac{14}{15}$. **-mādhava**, m. N. of a poet, ŚārṅgP. **-yajña**, m. 'victory-sacrifice,' the Aśva-medha, W. **-ratha**, m. N. of a commentator (author of Alaṃkāra-vimarśinī). **-rāja**, m. N. of several men, Rājat. vii f. **-rāta**, m. N. of a Kaurava hero, MBh. vii, 6710. **-rāma**, m. N. of the author of Nyāya-siddhânta-mālā; of several other men. **-lakshmī**, f. goddess of victory, victory, Rājat. v, 245; N. of a woman, vii, 124; of a work. **-lekha**, m. victory-record, Gīt. viii, 4. **-vat**, mfn. victorious, HPariś. i, 317; (*tī*), f. N. of a Surâṅganā, Siṇhâs. Concl. **-vana**, n. N. of a locality, Vcar. xviii, 70. **-vardhana**, m. N. of a poet, ŚārṅgP. lii, 1. **-varman**, m. N. of a man, Ratnâv. iv, $\frac{8}{9}$; °*ma-deva*, m. N. of a king. **-vaha**, mfn. conferring victory, W. **-vādya**, n. any instrument sounded to proclaim victory, W. **-vārāha-tīrtha**, n. N. of a Tīrtha, RevāKh. ccxviii. **-vāhana**, m. N. of a Samādhi, Kāraṇḍ. xvii, 26. **-vāhinī**, f. 'conferring victory,' N. of Indra's wife, L. **-śaṅkha**, m. a conch sounded to proclaim victory, Daś. i, 17. **-śabda**, m. a cheer of victory, exclamation '*jaya*' repeated, Śak.; VarBṛS.; BhP. viii. **-śarman**, m. N. of an author, Smṛitit. xxx. **-śīla**, mfn.=*-vat*, W. **-śṛiṅga**, n. a horn blown to proclaim victory, W. **-śekhara**, m. N. of a prince, Siṇhâs. xiv, $\frac{4}{5}$; (*ā*), f. N. of a Mūrchanā, Gal. **-śrī**, f. goddess of victory, victory, Rājat. ii, 64; (in music) N. of a measure; of a Nāga virgin, Kāraṇḍ. i, 42; of a woman, HPariś. ii, 83; m. a sword, Gal.; N. of a Buddh. scholar, Kāraṇḍ.[2] **-siṇha**, m. N. of a Kaśmīr king, Rājat. viii; of a man, v, 225; of a son of Rāma-siṇha (1600 A.D.); of several other men; *-deva*, m. king Jaya-siṇha, Kshitīś. vii, 330. **-sena**, m. (=*jaya-t-s*°) N. of a Magadha king, MBh. ii, 121; of a son (of Adīna or Ahīna, BhP. ix, 17, 17; of Sārvabhauma, 22, 10; VP. iv, 20, 3; of Mahêndra-varman, Kathās. xi, 33 ff.); of the father of the Āvantyau, BhP. ix, 24, 38; of a Buddhist; (*ā*), f. N. of a Surâṅganā, Siṇhâs. Concl.; of a female door-keeper, Mālav.; of another woman, HPariś. ii, 82. **-skandha**, m. N. of a minister of king Yudhi-shṭhira, Rājat. iii, 380. **-stambha**, m. column of victory, Ragh. iv, 59; Kathās. xix; Rājat. iii, 479; a trophy, W. **-sthala**, N. of a village, v, 121. **-svāmin**, m. 'victory-lord,' Śiva (?), iii, 350; N. of a scholiast on Chandoga-sūtra and Āśvalāyana-brāhmaṇa, KātyŚr. x, 7, 2, Sch.; Smṛitit. i; °*mi-pura*, n. N. of a town founded by Jushka, Rājat. i, 169; *-virocana*, N. of a sanctuary, v, 448. **Jayâkara**, m. 'mine of victory,' N. of a man, vii, 125. **Jayâjaya**, m. du. victory and defeat, Bhag. ii, 38; n. sg. id., VarYogay. vi, 29. **Jayâtmaja**, m. 'Jaya's (Arjuna's) son,' Abhimanyu, MBh. iii, 10270. **Jayâditya**, m. N. of a king (Vāmana's fellow-author of Kāś.), Mn. i, $\frac{8}{9}$; iii, $\frac{111}{112}$. **Jayânanda**, m. N. of a man, Rājat. vii; *-vāra*, m. id. viii, 3025. **Jayânīka**, m. N. of a Pāṇḍava hero, MBh. vii, 6911 & 7011. **Jayântarāya**, m. victory-hindrance, W. **Jayâpīḍa**, m. N. of a king, Rājat. iv, 402. **Jayârava**, m.=°*ya-ghosha*, W. **Jayârṇava**, m. N. of a work, Nirṇayas. iii, 164 ff. **Jayâvaghosha**, m.=°*yârava*, VarBṛS. xix, 18. **Jayâvaha**, mfn.=°*ya-v*°, R. i, 23, 13; m. a kind of pavilion, Vāstuv.; (*ā*), f. a kind of Croton, L. **Jayâśis**, f. cheer of victory, MBh. iii, 1477; Hariv. 3784; R.; Kum. vii, 47; a prayer for victory, W. **Jayâśrayā**, f. a kind of grass, L. (v.l. *jalâś*°). **Jayâśva**, m. N. of a Pāṇḍava hero, MBh. vii, 7012. **Jayâhvā**, f.=°*yâvahā*, L. **Jayêndra**, m. N. of a Kaśmīr king, Rājat. ii, 63; of a man, iii, 115 f. & 355; *-vihāra*, m. N. of a Vihāra built by the latter, v, 427; vi, 171; *-senā*, f. N. of a woman, Kathās. lxvii, 23. **Jayêśvara**, m. a form of Śiva, KūrmaP. ii; N. of a sanctuary built by Jayā-devī, Rājat. iv, 680. **Jayôddhura**, mfn. exulting in victory, W. **Jayôllāsa-nidhi**, m. N. of a work.

Jayaka, mfn. victorious, g. *ākarshâdi*; m. N. of a man, viii, 685.

Jáyat, mfn. pr. p. √*ji*, q.v. **-sena**, m. (= °*ya-s*°) 'having victorious armies,' N. of a Magadha king, MBh. i, v, ix; Hariv. 6725; of a son (of Sārvabhauma, MBh. i, 3769; of Nadīna, Hariv. 1516; VP. iv, 9, 8; VāyuP.); a N. assumed by a Pāṇḍu prince at Virāṭa's court, MBh. iv, 176; (*ā*), f. N. of one of the mothers attending on Skanda, ix, 2624.

Jayati, m. the rt. *ji*, Pāṇ. i, 4, 26, Kāś.

Jayad, in comp. for °*yat*. **-bala**, m. 'of victorious power,' a N. assumed by a Pāṇḍu prince at Virāṭa's court, MBh. iv, 176. **-ratha**, m. 'having victorious chariots,' N. of a Sindhu-Sauvīra king fighting on the Kaurava's side, i, iii, v, vii; Bhag.; Hariv.; of a son (of Bṛihan-manas, Hariv. 1703 & 1707; BhP. ix, 23, 11; of Bṛihat-kāya, 21, 22; of Bṛihat-karman, VP.; of the 10th Manu, Hariv. 475). N. of a son of Indra, Hariv.; Śak.; Ragh.; VarBṛS.; BhP. vi, 18, 6; VāyuP. ii, 7, 24; of a Rudra, MBh. xii, 7586; of a son of Dharma (=*upêndra*), BhP. vi, 6, 8; of A-krūra's father, MatsyaP. vl, 26; of a Gandharva (Vikramâditya's father), W.; of Bhīma-sena at Virāṭa's court, MBh. iv, 176; of a minister of Daśaratha, R. i, 7, 3; ii, 68, 5; of a Gauḍa king, Rājat. iv, 420 & 455 ff.; of a Kaśmīr Brāhman, iii, 366 ff.; of a writer on grammar; of a mountain, Hariv. 9736; pl. a subdivision of the Anuttara deities, Jain.; n. N. of a town, VāyuP. ii, 27, 2; (*ī*), f. a flag, L.; Sesbania ægyptiaca, L.; barley planted at the commencement of the Daśa-harā and gathered at its close, W.; Kṛishṇa's birthnight (the 8th of the dark half of Śrāvaṇa, the asterism Rohiṇī rising at midnight, Tithyād.), Hariv. 3320; the 9th night of the Karma-māsa, Sūryapr.; the 12th night of month Punar-vasu, Nirṇayas. i, $\frac{331}{332}$; Durgā, Dākshāyaṇī (in Hastinā-pura, MatsyaP. xiii, 28; tutelary deity of the Vasûdrekas, BrahmaP. ii, 18, 21); N. of a daughter of Indra, L.; of Ṛishabha's wife (received from Indra), BhP. v, 4, 8; MatsyaP. vl, 26; of a Yoginī, Hcat. ii, 1, 741; of a Surâṅganā, Siṇhâs. Concl.; of a river, MBh. iii, 5089; of a country, Rājat. viii, 655; of a town, Vīrac. ix. **-svāmin**, m. N. of the author of a treatise on Vedic accent.

Jayana, mf(*ī*)n. victorious, Caṇḍ. iv, 29; n. conquering, subduing, L.; armour for cavalry or elephants &c., L.; (*ī*), f. (=°*yantī*) N. of a daughter of Indra, L. **-yuj**, mfn. caparisoned (a war horse), W.

Jayanta, mf(*ī*)n. victorious, Śiś. vi, 69; m. the moon, L.; N. of a Dhruvaka; Śiva, L.; Skanda, Gal.;

Jayantī, f. of °*ta*, q.v. **-pura**, n. N. of a town, Rāghav. i, 25. **-saptamī**, f. the 7th day in the bright half of Māgha, W.

Jayā, f. of °*ya*, q.v. **-devī**, f. N. of a Buddh. deity (=*jayā*), Rājat. iv, 506; of a woman, 676 & 680. **-bhaṭṭārikā**, f. N. of a locality, vi, 243. **-vatī**, f. (°*ya-v*°) N. of a Surâṅganā, Siṇhâs. Concl.; of one of the mothers attending on Skanda, MBh. ix, 2622. **-siṇha**, m. N. of a man, Rājat. vii, 58.

Jayāyya, mfn. fr. √*ji*, Vop. xxvi, 164.

Jayitṛi, mf(*trī*)n. victorious, MBh. xii, 3753.

Jayin, mfn. (Pāṇ. iii, 2, 157) conquering, conqueror (chiefly ifc.), MBh. 3459; Hariv.; R.; BhP.; victorious (in battle, MBh.; Ragh.; VarBṛS.; BhP.; in a lawsuit, Yājñ. ii; in planetary opposition, Sūryas. vii, 21 ff.; in playing at dice, Kathās. cxxi; in sport, BhP. x); ifc. removing, Bālar.; =°*ya-kṛit*, Pañcat.

Jayishṇu, mfn. victorious, MBh. vii, 1480.

Jayús, mfn. id., RV. i, 117, 16; vi, 62, 7; x.

Jáyya, mfn. (Pāṇ. vi, 1, 81) to be conquered or gained, ŚBr. i, 6, 2, 3; xi, 2, 7, 9; xiv, 4, 3, 24.

जर *jára*, mfn. (√1. *jṛī*) 'becoming old,' see *a-jára*, *ahar-jaram*; cf. *go-jara*; m. the act of wearing out, wasting, RV. i, 164, 11; ii, 34, 10; 1. (*á*), f. (Pāṇ. iii, 3, 104) the act of becoming old, old age, RV. i, 140, 8; v, 41, 17; AV. &c. (personified as a daughter of Death, VP. i, 7, 31); digestion, Car. iii, 1 & 3; vi; Suśr. vi, 46, 10; decrepitude, W.; a kind of date-tree, L.; N. of a Rākshasī (cf. °*rā-saṃdha*), MBh. ii, vii; Hariv. 1810; BhP. ix, 22, 8; cf. *vi-jarā*. **-dvish**, see °*rad-vish*.

Jaraka, n. (=°*raṇa*) Asa fœtida, Npr.

Jaraṭha, mfn. old, Bhartṛ. (Śāntiś. iv, 17); BhP. vi, ix, xi; Rājat. ii, 170; bent, drooping, W.; for *jaṭhara*, hard, solid, Sāh. iv, 9 $\frac{8}{9}$; harsh, cruel, W.; strong, violent, Hcar. ii, 24; Vcar. xi f.; yellowish (old leaves' colour), L.; m. old age, L.

Jaraṭhita, mfn. become violent, Bālar. v, 25.

Jaraṇá, mfn. old, decayed, RV. iv, 33, 3; x, 40, 3; solvent, promoting digestion, Suśr. i, 42 & 45; m. n. cumin-seed, L.; Nigella indica, L.; Asa fœtida, L.; a kind of salt, L.; m.=°*rṇu*, Gal.; Cassia Sophora, L.; n. the becoming old, W.; decomposition, Sarvad. iii, 225 (cf. 221); digestion, Car. iii, 4 & 17; one of the 10 ways in which an eclipse is supposed to end, VarBṛS. v; Costus speciosus or arabicus, L.; 1. (*á*), f. old age, RV. vii, 30, 4; x, 37 & 39; Nigella indica, L. **-druma**, m. Vatica robusta, L.

2. **Jaráṇā**, f. dry wood (?), RV. i, 141, 7; ?, 121, 6.

Jaraṇḍa, mfn. decayed, old, L.

Jaraṇyá, f. decrepitude, 119, 7.

Járat, mf(*atī*)n. (pr. p. √1. *jṛī*, Pāṇ. iii, 2, 104) old, ancient, infirm, decayed, dry (as herbs), no longer frequented (as temples) or in use, RV.; AV. &c. (often in comp. [Pāṇ. ii, 1, 49], Kauś.; ĀśvGr. iv, 2; MBh. &c.); former, APrāt. iv, 53; Sāh.; m.=γέρων, an old man, Śak. (v.l.); VarBṛS. lxxv. **-kakshá**, m. old brambles, TBr. iii, 3, 2, 4; TāṇḍyaBr. xvii, 7, 2. **-karṇa**, m. 'old-ear,' N. of Sarpa Airāvata (author of RV. x, 76). **-kāra**, m. N. of a man, BrahmaP. ii, 12; 18, 19. **-kāru**, m. (g. *śivâdi*) N. of a Ṛishi of Yāyāvara's family, MBh.; BrahmavP. ii, 1 & 43; f. his wife (sister of the Nāga

Vāsuki), MBh.; BrahmavP. ii, 42; *-priyā*, f. Jaratkāru's wife (exercising power over serpents), ib.; °*rv-āśrama*, m. 'Jarat-kāru's hermitage,' N. of a locality, Bhpr. v, 21, 16. **-pitta-śūla**, n. a form of colic, ŚārṅgS. vii, 43.

Jaratikā, f. an old woman, Daś. vii, 314.

Jaratin, m. N. of a man, g. *śubhrâdi*.

Jarad, in comp. for °*rat*. **-ashṭi** (°*rád-*), mfn. attaining great age, very old, RV. x, 85, 36; AV.; VS. xxxiv, 52; ĀśvGṛ.; PārGṛ.; f. longevity, RV. vii, 37, 7; AV. viii, 2, 1. **-gava**, m. (=*go-jara*) an old bull or ox, Ved. (Jaim. i, 3, 31, Sch.); Bṛih. on RV. x, 102, 1; MBh. xiii, 4463; Pañcat.; N. of a vulture, Hit. i, 3, 1 & 4, ½; (*ī*), f. an old cow, W.; °*va-vīthi*, f. 'bull's course,' the moon's path in the asterisms Viśākhā, Anurādhā, and Jyeshṭhā, VarBṛS. ix, 1. **-dāsa**, m. an old servant, ĀśvGṛ. iv, 2, 18. **-yoshā**, f. =°*ratikā*, W. **-vish**, mfn. consuming dry wood (Agni), RV. v, 8, 2 [°*ra-dv*°, 'hating decrepitude,' Gmn.] **-vṛiksha**, m. an old tree, Pāṇ. iv, 3, 156, Vārtt. 3, Pat.

Jaranta, m. an old man, L.; a buffalo, Uṇ., Sch.

Jarantaka, m. a father-in-law, Gal.

Jarayitṛi, mfn. 'consumer,' see *jāra*.

Jarayu, mfn. 'becoming old,' see *a-*.

Jarás, f. (only before vowel-terminations, Pāṇ. vii, 2, 101; other cases fr. °*rā́* s.v. *jára*) the becoming old, decay, old age, RV.; AV.; ŚBr. &c.; m. N. of a son of Vasu-deva by Turī, Hariv. 9203; of a hunter who wounded Kṛishṇa, MBh. xvi, 126 ff.; VP. v, 37, 13 & 62; [cf. γῆρας.] **Jarasa**, ifc. = °*rás* (g. *śarad-ādi*), see *ā-jarasám*, °*sāya*; cf. *vīta-janma-*. **Jarasāna**, m. (Ved. aor. p.) a man, Uṇ.

1. **Jarā́**, f. old age, see s.v. *jára*. **-kāsa**, m. cough caused by old age, Bhpr. vii, 24, 15. **-°tura** (°*rā́t*°), mfn. decrepit from age, L. **-dharma**, m. pl. the laws of old age or decay, Divyâv. xiii, 388. **-°nvita** (°*rā́n*°), mfn. = *-vat*, VarBṛS. lxxvi, 3. **-pariṇata**, mfn. bent down with age, W. **-pushṭa**, m. 'fostered by Jarā,' Jarā-saṃdha, L. **-°bhibhūta** (°*rā́bh*°), mfn. = °*rā́tura*, MBh. i, 3161. **-bhīta**, m. 'afraid of old age,' the god of love, Gal. **-bhīru**, m. id., L. **-mṛityu** (°*rā́-*), mfn. dying from age, AV. ii, xix; m. sg. old age and death, MuṇḍUp. i, 2, 7; du. id., g. *kārta-kaujapâdi*. **-lakshman**, n. 'age-sign,' grey hair, Npr. **-vat**, mfn. aged, Hariv. 1621. **-°vasthā** (°*rā́v*°), f. state of old age, decrepitude, W. **-saṃdha**, m. '(born in halves, but) united by (the Rākshasī) Jarā,' N. of a king of Magadha and Cedi (son of Bṛihad-ratha, father-in-law to Kaṇsa, and enemy of Kṛishṇa; slain in single combat by Bhīma; identified with the Dānava Vipracitti, MBh. i, 2640) i f.; vii; Hariv. 1810; BhP.; N. of a son of Dhṛitarāshṭra, MBh. i, 4548; *-jit*, m. 'Jarāsaṃdha-slayer,' Bhīma, L.; *-pura*, n. 'Jarāsaṃdha's town,' Gayā, Gal.

Jarāyaṇi, m. metron. of °*rā-saṃdha*, L.

Jarā́yu, mfn. withering, dying away (?), RV. x, 106, 6; n. the cast-off skin of a serpent, γῆρας, AV. i, 27, 1; a perishable covering, VS. xvii, 5; (also m. f., L.) the outer skin of the embryo (opposed to *úlba*), after-birth, RV. v, 78, 8; AV.; VS. &c. (*Indrāṇyā ulba-jarāyuṇī*, 'amnion and chorion of Indrāṇī,' N. of two Sāmans); m. froth originating from submarine fire, L.; =*jaṭāyu*, L.; f. N. of one of the mothers attending on Skanda, MBh. ix, 2637; cf. *jyótir-*, *nir-*. **-já**, mfn. viviparous, AV. i, 12, 1; Mn. i, 43; MBh. xiv; Suśr.; BhP.

Jarāyuka, n. secundines, SāmavBr. ii, 6, 10.

Jarita, mfn. (p. p. Caus.) old, decayed, Hariv. 15988; R. ii f.; (*ā*), f. N. of a Śārṅgikā bird (mother of 4 sons at once by the Ṛishi Manda-pāla in the form of a Śārṅgaka; cf. *jaritṛī* at end), MBh. i, 8346 ff. & 8379 ff. **Jaritâri**, m. Manda-pāla's eldest son by Jaritā, 8372 & 8403 ff.

Jarin, mfn. = °*rā-vat*, L. **Jarimán**, m. old age, decrepitude, death from age, RV.; AV.; TS. i, 8, 10.

Jarishṇu, mfn. decaying, RV. x, 151, kh.

Járūtha, m. 'making old (?, cf. °*ra-dvish*),' N. of a demon conquered by Agni, RV. vii, 1, 7 & 9, 6; x, 80, 3; Nir. vi, 17; n. flesh, Uṇ., Sch.; skinniness, W.

Jarjara, mfn. infirm, decrepit, decayed, torn or broken in pieces, perforated, hurt, MBh.; R. &c.; divided (a realm), MBh. xii; Rājat.; Prab.; dull, hollow (sound), VarBṛS.; VarYogay. viii, 12; Kād.; Kathās. xxv, 66; m. = °*raka*, Car. vi, 25, 235; Kathās. lxi, 96; an old man, L.; n. Indra's banner, L.; Blyxa octandra ('benzoin,' W.), L.; (*ā*), f. an old woman, Gal. **-tva**, n. the being decayed, Mṛicch. iv, ½. **Jarjarânanā**, f. 'old-faced,' N. of one of the mothers attending on Skanda, MBh. ix, 2637.

Jarjaraka, m. a broken bamboo, Kathās. lxi.

Jarjarita, mfn. become decrepit or decayed, torn in pieces, worn out, MBh. iii, 10353; Suśr. &c.

Jarjarī, ind. for °*ra*. **-√kṛi**, to break into pieces, R. vi, 83, 54. **-kṛita**, mfn. torn to pieces, split, worn, MBh. **-bhūta**, mfn. id., iii, 434; Vet.

Jarjarīka, mfn. decayed, L.; ragged, L.

Jarṇa, mfn. decayed, L.; m. = °*ṇu*, L.; a tree, L.

Jarṇu, m. 'waning,' the moon, L.

जरटी *jaraṭī*, f. = °*raḍī*, L.

Jaraḍī, f. a kind of grass, L.

जरणिप्रा *jaraṇi-prā́*, mfn. (√3. *jṛī*) moving with noise (?, 'increasing the praiser's wealth,' Sāy.), RV. x, 100. **Jaraṇyú**, mfn. invoking aloud, 61, 23.

Jaramāṇa, m. N. of a man, g. *gargâdi*.

2. **Jarā́**, f. invocation, praise (*stuti*, Nir. x, 8), RV. i, 38, 13; x, 32, 5. **-bodha**, mfn. (Nir. x, 8) attending to invocation or praise, RV. i, 27, 10 (voc.) **-°bodhīya**, n. N. of several Sāmans, TāṇḍyaBr.

Jaritṛí, m. an invoker, praiser, RV.; AV. v, 11, 8; xx, 135, 1 ff.; ĀśvŚr. viii, 3; N. of the author of RV. x, 142, 1 f. (with the patr. Śārṅga; cf. °*ta*).

जरायु *jarā́yu*, °*yuka*. See col. 1.

Jarita &c., **járūtha**. See ib.

जर्च् *jarc* (=√*jarts*), cl. 1. °*cati*, to speak, Dhātup. xxviii, 17; to abuse, ib.; to threaten, ib.

जर्छ् *jarch*, cl. 1, v.l. for √*jarc*.

जर्ज् *jarj*, cl. 1, v.l. for √*jarc*.

जर्जर *jarjara*, °*raka*, &c. See p. 413, col. 3.

जर्जल्प *jarjalpa*. See *nir-*.

जर्झ् *jarjh*, cl. 1, v.l. for √*jarc*.

जर्ण *jarṇa*, °*ṛnu*. See above.

जर्त *jarta*, m. = °*tu*, L.

जर्तिक *jartika*, m. pl. N. of a people (*bāhīka*), MBh. viii, 2033 (v.l. *jārt*°).

जर्तिल *jar-tíla*, m. wild sesamum, TS. v, 4, 3, 2; ŚBr. ix, 1, 1, 3; KātyŚr. xviii, 1, 1. **-yavāgú**, f. juice of wild sesamum, TS. v, 4, 3, 2.

जर्तु *jartu*, m. the vulva, Uṇ. v, 46, Sch.; an elephant, ib.

जर्त्स् *jarts*, cl. 1. °*tsati*, = √*jarc*, Dhātup. xvii, 66; to protect, Vop.

जर्भरि *jarbhári*, mfn. (√*bhṛi*, Intens.; redupl. like in pf.) supporting (Nir. xiii, 5), RV. x, 106, 6.

जर्भुरत् *járbhurat*, °*rāṇa*. See √*bhur*.

जर्य *jarya*. See *a-jaryá*.

जर्वर *jarvara*, m. N. of a Nāga priest, TāṇḍyaBr. xxv, 15, 3.

जर्हिल *jarhila*, m. = °*rtila*, L.

जल् *jal*, cl. 1. °*lati* (pf. *jajāla*, Pāṇ. viii, 4, 54, Sch.) 'to be rich' or 'to cover' (derived fr. *jāla*?), Dhātup. xx, 3; to be sharp, ib.; to be stiff or dull (for *jaḍ*, derived fr. *jaḍa*), ib.: cl. 10. *jālayati*, to cover, xxxii, 10.

जल 1. *jalá*, mfn. = *jaḍa* (cf. √*jal*), stupid (cf. °*lâdhipa*, °*lâśaya*), ŚārṅgP. xxi (v.l.); m. (g. *jvalâdi*) a stupid man, Śiś. v, 37; N. of a man (with the patr. Jātūkarṇya), ŚāṅkhŚr. xvi, 29, 6; n. (also pl.) water, any fluid, Naigh. i, 12; Yājñ. i, 17; MBh. &c. (ifc. f. *ā*); a kind of Andropogon, Bhpr. vii, 10, 52 & 78; 28, 18; the 4th mansion (in astrol.), VarYogay. iv, 26; a cow's embryo (*go-kalaka* or °*lana*), L.; (= *jaḍa*) frigidity (moral or mental or physical), W.; (*ā*), f. N. of a river, MBh. iii, 10556. **-kaṇṭaka**, m. 'water-thorn,' = *-kubjaka*, L.; a crocodile, L. **-kapi**, m. 'water-monkey,' Delphinus gangeticus, Vāsav. 726. **-kapota**, m. 'water-pigeon,' N. of a bird, L. **-kara**, mfn. making or pouring forth water, W.; m. tax derived from water (i.e. from fisheries &c.), W. **-karaṅka**, m. a conch, L.; a cocoa-nut, L.; a lotus-flower, L.; a cloud, L.; a wave, L. **-kalka**, m. 'water-sediment,' mud, L. **-kalmasha**, m. a poisonous fluid, BhP. viii, 7, 43. **-kāka**, m. 'water-crow,' the diver bird, L. **-kāṅksha**, m. 'desiring water,' an elephant, L. **-kāṅkshin**, m. id., L. **-kānta**, m. 'water-lover,' wind, L.; = °*ntâśman*, Uttamac. 35; 181; 230; °*ntâśman*, m. a kind of precious stone, 40. **-kāntāra**, m. 'whose path is water,' Varuṇa, L. **-kāmukā**, f. 'fond of water,' the plant *kuṭumbinī*, L. **-kirāṭa**, m. a shark, L. **-kukkuṭa**, m. a water-fowl, MBh. iii, 9926 & 11579; R. iv; Vet. i, 3; (*ī*), f. the black-headed gull, L. **-kukkubha**, m. the aquatic bird Parra jacana or gœnsis, L. **-kuntala**, m. 'water-hair,' Blyxa octandra, L. **-kubjaka**, m. Trapa bispinosa, L. **-kumāraka**, m. N. of a disease of women. **-kumbha**, m. a water-jar, Pañcat. v, 2, ¾. **-kumbhikā**, f. a jar filled with water, Kathās. vi, 41. **-kūpī**, f. a spring, well, L.; a pond, L.; a whirlpool, W. **-kūrma**, m. the Gangetic porpoise, L. **-kṛit**, mfn. causing rain, VarBṛS. iii, xxxvii. **-ketu**, m. N. of a comet, xi, 46. **-keli**, m. f. frolicking in water, splashing one another, Kathās. xxvi, lxvii; *-varṇana*, n. N. of Hari-nātha's Rāma-vilāsa-kāvya iii. **-keśa**, m. = *-kuntala*, L. **-kriyā**, f. presenting water to deceased relatives, R. i f.; BhP. vi, 16, 16. **-krīḍā**, f. = *-keli*, MBh. i, iii; Hariv. 7120; Pañcat.; BhP. v. **-kshālana-vidhi**, m. N. of a work. **-khaga**, m. an aquatic bird, VarBṛS. iil, 8. **-gandhêbha**, m. 'scented water-elephant,' a kind of mythic animal, Rājat. v, 107. **-gambu**, m. N. of a son of Sūrya, BhavP. i. **-garbha**, m. N. of a son of *-vāhana* (Ānanda in a former birth), Suvarṇapr. xvii f. **-gulma**, m. a turtle, L.; = *-catvara*, L.; a whirlpool, L. **-gṛiha**, n. a house built in or near water, Uṇ. iv, 107, Sch. **-ghaṭī**, f. = *-kumbha*, Bhpr. vii, 16, 24. **-m-ga**, m. the colocynth, L. **-m-gama**, v.l. for *janaṃ-g*°, L., Sch. **-cakra**, n. N. of a mythic region, Virac. xxiv. **-cañcala**, m. 'water-moving,' N. of a fish, W. **-catvara**, n. a square tank, L. **-candra**, m. N. of a poet, Sadukt. iv, 273. **-cara**, m. 'water-goer,' an aquatic animal, R. i, 44, 33; Pañcat.; VarBṛS.; Laghuj.; a fish, VarBṛS. iil, 12; *-jīva*, m. pl. v.l. for °*lajâjīva*; °*râjīva*, m. 'living by fish,' a fisherman, xv, 22. **-cārin**, mfn. living in or near water, m. an aquatic animal, fish, MBh.; R. iii f.; VarBṛS.; BrahmaP. **-ja**, mfn. produced or born or living or growing in water, coming from or peculiar to water, MBh. ii, 94; R. ii, 59, 11; Hariv.; Suśr.; m. an aquatic animal, fish, Gaut.; R.; Suśr. &c.; Barringtonia acutangula, L.; sea-salt, L.; N. of several signs of the zodiac connected with water, Dīp.; (also n., L.) a conch-shell (used as a trumpet, Hariv. 10936; Ragh.; BhP.), MBh. vi, 4996; Hariv. 8056; BhP. viii, 20, 31; n. = *-ja-dravya*, VarBṛS. xiii, xv; = *-ruh*, MBh. ii f.; Hariv.; R. iv; BhP. iii; a kind of ebony, Bhpr. (v.l. °*la-da*); = °*la-kuntala*, L.; = *-vetasa*, L.; (*ā*), f. a kind of Glycyrrhiza, L.; *-kusuma*, n. 'water-flower,' lotus, in comp. °*ma-yoni*, m. 'lotus-born,' Brahmā, MBh. viii, 4647; *jalaja-dravya*, n. any sea-product, pearl, shell, VarBṛS. lxxxvii, 17; *-sumanā*, f. Andropogon aciculatus, Npr.; °*jâkshī*, f. a lotus-eyed woman; °*jâjīva*, m. pl. 'living on fishes,' the inhabitants of the east coast, VarBṛS. xi, 55; °*jâsana*, m. 'lotus-seated,' Brahmā, Kum. ii, 30; °*jêkshaṇā*, f. = °*jâkshī*, Hariv. 3626. **-jantu**, m. an aquatic animal, Hit. i, 7, 32. **-jantukā**, f. a leech, L., Sch. **-janman**, n. 'water-born,' a lotus, L. **-jambukā**, f. a kind of Jambu, Bhpr. v, 6, 69; *-latā*, f. N. of an aquatic plant, Vām. v, 2, 74. **-jāta**, m. = *-vetasa*, Npr. **-°jinī**, f. (fr. *-ja*) 'lotus-group,' *-bandhu*, m. 'lotus-friend,' the sun, Gaṇit. i, 1, 4. **-jihva**, m. 'cold-tongued (?),' a crocodile, L. **-jīvin**, mfn. living in or near water; m. a fisherman, MBh. xii, 7427; (*inī*), f. = *-jantukā*, L. **-jñāna**, n. N. of a Vedântic treatise. **-ḍimba**, m. a bivalve shell, L. **-°taṇḍulīya**, n. N. of a pot-herb, Bhpr. v, 9, 14. **-taraṃga**, m. a wave, Siṇhâs. xxii, 5; a metal cup filled with water producing musical notes, W. **-tā**, f. the state of water, Hariv. 2932. **-tāḍana**, n. 'beating water,' any fruitless action, W. **-tāpika**, m. = °*pin*, L.; the fish Cyprinus Cachius, L. **-tāpin**, m. the fish Clupea alosa, L. **-tāla**, m. id., L. **-tiktikā**, f. Boswellia thurifera, L. **-tumbikā-nyāya**, m. the method of the water and the bottle-gourd. **-turaga**, m. 'water-horse,' a kind of animal, L., Sch. **-trā**, f. 'water-guard,' an umbrella, L. **-trāsa**, m. hydrophobia, Suśr. v, 6, 45. **-°trāsin**, mfn. hydrophobic, ib. **-da**, m. 'water-giver,' a (rain-)cloud, MBh. iii, 1638; R. iii; Suśr. &c.; the ocean, Gal.; Cyperus rotundus, L.; N. of a prince, VP. ii, 4, 60; of a Varsha in Śāka-dvīpa, ib.; m. pl. N. of a school of the AV., Caraṇ.; n. v.l. for *-ja*, q.v.; *-kāla*, m. 'cloud-season,' the rainy season, Śiś. vi, 41; *-kshaya*, m. 'cloud-disappearance,' autumn, Hariv. 3825; *-paṅkti*, f. a line of clouds, W.; *-saṃhati*, f. the gathering of clouds, W.; *-samaya*, m. = *-kāla*, Priy. ii, $\frac{2}{3}$; °*dâgama*, m. 'approach of clouds,' id., Nal. xxi, 4; Kathās.; °*dâtyaya*, m. = °*da-kshaya*, Car. vii, 7, 55; °*dâbha*, mfn. cloud-like, dark, W.; °*dâśana*, m. 'cloud-enjoyer,' Shorea robusta, L. **— dardura**, m. a water-pipe (musical instrument), Hariv. 8427. **— dāna**, n. water-offering (festival in Ujjayinī), Kathās. cxii, 61. **— deva**, n. 'having water as its deity,' the constellation Ashāḍhā, VarBṛS.; VarBṛ. **— devatā**, f. a water-goddess, naiad, Hariv. 13140. **— daivatya**, n. 'having water as its deity,' the constellation Svāti, Gal. **— dravya**, n. = *-ja-dr°*, VarBṛS. v, 42. **— droṇī**, f. a water-bucket, L. **— dvipa**, m. 'water-elephant,' N. of an animal, Vcar. ix, 124. **— dvīpa**, m. N. of an island, R. iv, 40, 33 (*yava-dv°*, B). **— dhara**, m. 'holding water,' a (rain-)cloud, MBh.; R. &c.; the ocean, L.; Cyperus rotundus, L.; Dalbergia ujjeinensis, L.; a metre of 4 × 32 syllabic instants; *-garjita-ghosha-susvara-nakshatra-rāja-saṃkusumitâbhijña*, m. 'having a voice musical as the sound of the thunder of the clouds and conversant with the appearance of the regents of the Nakshatras,' N. of a Buddha, Saddh. xxv; *-mālā*, f. = *jalada-paṅkti*; two metres of 4 × 12 syllables each; °*râbhyudaya*, m. = *jaladâgama*, ŚārṅgP. lxvi, 3. **— dhāra**, m. N. of a mountain, MBh. vi, 417; Hariv. 12405; of a Varsha in Śāka-dvīpa, MBh. vi, 426; (*ā*), f. a stream of water, MBh. vi, ix; BhP. v, 17, 1. **— dhāraṇa**, n. 'holding water,' a ditch, Gal. **— dhi**, m. (Pāṇ. iii, 3, 93, Kāś.) 'water-receptacle,' a lake, W.; the ocean, Pañcat.; Śak.; VarBṛS. &c.; 100 billions; *-kanyakā*, f. = *-jā*, Bhām. iv, 8; *-gā*, f. a river flowing into the ocean, L.; *-jā*, f. 'ocean-daughter,' Lakshmī, L.; *-tā*, f. the state of the ocean, ŚārṅgP. xxix, 12; *-nandinī*, f. = *-jā*, Bhām. iv, 2; *-raśana*, mfn. ocean-girted (the earth), Rājat. i, 46; *-sambhava*, mfn. marine, W. **— dhenu**, f. a cow in the shape of water, MBh. xiii, 71, 41; MatsyaP. liii, 13. **— nakula**, m. an otter, L. **— nara**, m. 'water-man,' id., L., Sch. **— nāḍī**, f. a water-course, W. **— nidhi**, m. 'water-treasure,' the ocean, MBh. iii, 15817; Pañcat.; VarBṛS.; Bhartṛ.; Prab.; N. of a man, Saṃskārak.; *-vacas*, n. pl. 'ocean-words,' = *sāmudrika-śāstra*, Romakas. **— nirgama**, m. a water-course, drain, L. **— nivaha**, m. a quantity of water, W. **— nīlikā**, °**lī**, f. = *-kuntala*, L. **— m-dhama**, m. 'water-blower,' N. of one of Skanda's attendants, MBh. ix, 2559; of a Dānava, Hariv. 12935; (*ā*), f. N. of a daughter of Kṛishṇa, 9184. **— m-dhara**, m. (g. 1. *naḍâdi*) 'water-bearer,' N. of a man, Pravar.; of an Asura (produced by the contact of a flash from Śiva's eye with the ocean, and adopted by the god of the waters; called from having caught the water which flowed from Brahmā's eye), PadmaP. v, 141 ff.; LiṅgaP. i, 97; N. of a particular Mudrā; *-pura*, n. N. of a town, Kathârṇ. xvi. **— paksha-cara**, m. = *-khaga*, Svapnac. **— pakshin**, m. id., Pañcat. iii, 1, $\frac{9}{1}$. **— pati**, m. 'water-lord,' Varuṇa, L. **— pattana**, n. a water-town (forming an island), Śil. **— patha**, m. (g. *devapathâdi*, Kāś.) = *-yātrā*, Ragh. xvii, 81; N. of a Himâlaya mountain, Divyâv. xxx, 306 & 397. **— padavī**, f. = *-nirgama*, Gal. **— paddhati**, f. id., L. **— parṇikā**, f. N. of a plant, Gal. **— paryāya**, m. a kind of andropogon, Gal. **— pātra**, n. a vessel for water, W. **— pāda**, m. N. of a frog-king, Pañcat. iii, 15, $\frac{9}{1}$. **— pāna**, n. the drinking of water, W. **— pārāvata**, m. = *-kapota*, L. **— pitta**, m. n. 'water-bile,' fire, L. **— pippalī**, f. Commelina salicifolia and another species, Bhpr. v, 3, 294 (°*likā*, 295). **— pippikā**, f. a fish, L. **— pīna**, m. N. of a fish, Gal. **— pushpa**, n. an aquatic flower, L. **— pūra**, m. a full bed (of a river), Gīt. xi, 25; N. of a mythic hero, Vīrac. xv, xxx. **— pūrusha**, m. 'water-man,' N. of a mythic being, Kathās. lxiii, 60. **— pūrṇa**, mfn. 'full to overflowing,' with *yoga*, m. irresistible impulse, Hariv. 5196; 5425 & 5429. **— pūrvakam**, ind. after having poured out water, Hcat. i, 5, 1282. **— pṛishṭha-jā**, f. 'water-surface-grower,' = *-kuntala*, L. **— pradāna**, n. 'water-offering,' °*nika*, mfn. relating to a water-offering (a *parvan*), MBh. i, 348. **— prapāta**, m. a water-fall, R. ii, 94, 13. **— pralaya**, m. destruction by water, W. **— pravāha**, m. a current of water, Subh. **— prasaraṇa**, n. 'flowing off from water,' oil, Gal. **— prânta**, m. 'water's edge,' shore, L. **— prāya**, mfn. abounding with water, L.; n. a country abounding with water, W. **— priya**, m. 'fond of water,' a fish, L.; the Cātaka bird, L.; a hog, Gal.; (*ā*), f. N. of Dākshāyaṇī, MatsyaP. xiii, 33. **— plava**, m. = *-plāvana*, Sūryas. i, 18; = *-nakula*, L. **— plāvana**, n. 'water-immersion,' a deluge, W. **— phala**, n. the nut of Trapa bispinosa, Bhpr. v, 6, 91. **— phena**, m. 'water-froth,' os Sepiæ, Npr. **— bandhaka**, m. 'water-barrier,' a dike, L. **— bandhu**, m. 'friend of water,' a fish, L. **— biḍāla**, m. 'water-cat,' = *-nakula*, L. **— bindu**, m. a drop of water; N. of a Tīrtha, VarP. clix; f. N. of a Nāga virgin, Kāraṇḍ. i, 45; *-jā*, f. sugar prepared from Yava-nāla, L. **— bimba**, = *ḍimbikā*, L. **— bilva**, m. = *-valkala*, L.; a turtle, L.; a crab, L.; = *-catvara*, L. **— budbuda**, m. a water-bubble, Yājñ. iii, 8; Pañcat. iii, 16, $\frac{16}{17}$; Kathās. &c. **— brahmī**, f. Hingcha repens, L. **— bhājana**, n. = *-pātra*, R. iii, 4, 49. **— bhū**, mfn. aquatic, W.; m. a cloud, L.; = *-pippalī*, L. **— bhūshaṇa**, m. 'decorating water,' wind, L. **— bhṛit**, m. 'water-bearer,' a cloud, L., Sch. **— makshikā**, f. a water-insect, L. **— magna**, mfn. immersed in water, W. **— madgu**, m. a kingfisher, L. **— madhūka**, m. N. of a tree, L. **— mandira**, n. = *-yantra-m°*, W. **— maya**, mf(*ī*)n. formed or consisting or full of water, Kum. ii, 60; Kathās. ii, 10; Sāh.; Hcat.; = *-magna*, BhP. x, 80, 37. **— markaṭa**, m. = *-kapi*, Gal. **— masi**, m. 'water-ink,' a dark cloud, L. **— mātaṅga**, m. = *-dvipa*, L. **— mātreṇa**, instr. ind. by mere water, W. **— mānusha**, m. = *-pūrusha*, Hcar. vii; Kathās. lxxi, 5 f.; (n., L.) = *-nara*, Kād. iii, 1493; Bālar. vii, $\frac{28}{29}$; (*ī*), f. the female of *-pūrusha*, Vāsav. 214. **— mārga**, m. = *-nirgama*, L. **— mārjāra**, m. = *-biḍāla*, L. **— muc**, mfn. shedding water, VarBṛS. xix, 2; m. a (rain-)cloud, Megh.; Dhūrtas.; Udbh. **— mūrti**, m. Śiva in the form of water, Tithyād. **— mūrtikā**, f. 'water-formed' hail, L. **— moda**, n. 'water-enjoyer,' the root of Andropogon muricatus, L. (v.l. °*lâmoda*). **— m-bala**, n. a stream, W.; collyrium, W. **— yantra**, n. = °*traka*, Hariv. 8425; a clepsydra, VarBṛS.; *-gṛiha*, n. a bath-room with douches, Bhpr. vii, 3, 35; *-cakra*, n. a wheel for raising water, Subh.; *-niketana*, n. = *-gṛiha*, L.; *-mandira*, n. id., Ṛitus. i, 2. **— yantraka**, n. 'watering-engine,' a douche, Hariv. 8432. **— yātrā**, f. a sea voyage, W. **— yāna**, n. 'water-vehicle,' a boat, ship, BhP. iii, 14, 17; x, 68, 24. **— raṅka**, °**ku**, m. a water-fowl, L. **— rañja**, m. id., L. **— raṇḍa**, m. a whirlpool, L.; a drizzle, thin sprinkling of water, L.; a snake, L. **— rasa**, m. sea-salt, L. **— rākshasī**, f. N. of a female demon (mother of the Nāgas who tried to prevent Hanumat's crossing the straits between the continent and Ceylon by attempting to swallow him; he escaped by reducing himself to the size of a thumb, darting through her huge body and coming out at her right ear), MBh. iii, 16255; (called Su-rasā) R. v, 6, 2 ff. **— rāśi**, m. 'water-quantity,' any running water, Vedântas.; a lake, ocean, Bhartṛ.; Kathās. xviii, 2. **— ruṇḍa**, m. = *-raṇḍa*. **— ruh**, m. 'water-growing,' a day-lotus, Bālar. iii, 85. **— ruha**, m. an aquatic animal, VarBṛS. x, 7; n. = *-ruh*, MBh. i, 5005 & 5059; *-kusuma*, n. an aquatic flower, VarYogay. vii, 7; °*hêkshaṇa*, mfn. lotus-eyed, MBh. i, 129, 27. **— rūpa**, m. = *makara*, L. **— rūpaka**, m. id., Gal. **— rekhā**, f. = *-lekhā*, Cāṇ.; a stripe or streak of water, Bhartṛ. (Subh.) **— latā**, f. 'water-creeper,' a wave, L. **— lekhā**, f. a line drawn on water, Cāṇ. **— lohita**, m. 'having water for blood,' N. of a Rakshas, L. **— vat**, mfn. abounding in water, MBh. xii, 3694. **— varaṇṭa**, m. a watery pustule, L. **— vartikā**, f. 'water-quail,' a kind of bird, Gal. **— valkala**, n. 'water-bark,' Pistia Stratiotes, L. **— vallī**, f. = *-kubjaka*, L. **— vādita**, n. 'water-music,' a kind of music in which water is used, Hariv. 8426. **— vādya**, n. a kind of musical instrument played by means of water, 8346; 8427 & 8436. **— vāyasa**, m. = *-kāka*, Svapnac. **— vālaka**, m. 'encircled by (water i.e.) clouds,' N. of the Vindhya range, L.; (*ikā*), f. lightning, L. **— vāluka**, m. = °*laka*, Gal. **— vāsa**, mfn. = °*sin*, MBh. xii, 9280; m. abiding in water (kind of religious austerity), 9281; a kind of bulbous plant, L.; n. = *-moda*, L.; (*ā*), f. a kind of grass, L. **— vāsin**, mfn. living in water, Kathās. lxiii, 52; m. N. of a bulbous plant, Gal. **— vāha**, mfn. carrying water, MBh. ii, 301; m. a cloud, L. **— vāhaka**, m. a water-carrier, Pañcat. iii, $\frac{67}{68}$. **— vāhana**, m. 'water-carrier,' N. of a physician (Gautama Buddha in a former birth), Suvarṇapr. xvii f.; n. flowing of water, W.; (*ī*), f. a water-course, aqueduct, W. **— vishuva**, n. the autumnal equinox, L.; a kind of diagram, Tantr. **— vihaṃgama**, m. a water-fowl, W. **— vīrya**, m. N. of a son of Bharata, Śatr. vi, 289. **— vṛiścika**, m. 'water-scorpion,' a prawn, L. **— vetasa**, m. Calamus Rotang, L. **— vyatha**, m. the fish Esox Kankila, L. **— vyadha**, m. id., L. **— vyāla**, m. a water-snake, L.; a marine monster, L. **— śaya**, °**yana**, m. 'reposing on water (i.e. on his serpent-couch above the waters, during the 4 months of the periodical rains and during the intervals of the submersion of the world),' Vishṇu, L. **— śayyā**, f. lying in water (kind of religious austerity), R. vii, 76, 17. **— śarkarā**, f. 'water-gravel,' hail, BhP. x, 25, 9. **— śāyin**, mfn. lying in water, R. i, 43, 14; m. = *-śaya*; °*yi-tīrtha*, n. N. of a Tīrtha, RevāKh. cxlii. **— śukti**, f. a bivalve shell, L. **— śuci**, mfn. cleansed by water, W. **— śunaka**, m. = *-nakula*, Gal. **— śūka**, m. N. of an animalcule living in mud, Suśr.; Bhpr. **— śosha**, m. drying up of water, drought, W. **— saṃsarga**, m. mixing with water, dilution, W. **— saṃdha**, m. N. of a son of Dhṛita-rāshṭra, MBh. i, iii, y. **— saṃniveśa**, m. a receptacle of water. **— samudra**, m. the sea of fresh water, L. **— samparka**, m. mixture with water, W. **— sambhava**, m. 'water-born,' = *-vetasa*, L. **— sarasa**, n. N. of ?, Pāṇ. v, 4, 94, Kāś. **— sarpiṇī**, f. 'water-glider,' a leech, L. **— sāt**, ind. (with *sam-√pad*, to be turned) into water, Vop. vii, 85. **— sikta**, mfn. water-sprinkled, W. **— sūkara**, m. 'water-hog,' a crocodile, L.; a hog, Npr. **— sūci**, m. the Gangetic porpoise, L.; a crow, L.; = *-vyatha*, L.; a leech, L.; = *-kubjaka*, L. **— sūrya**, °**yaka**, m. the sun reflected in water, Bādar., Sch. **— seka**, m. sprinkling with water, W. **— stambha**, m. solidification of water (magical faculty). **— stambhana**, n. id., GarP. **— stha**, mfn. standing or situated in water, R. iv, 13, 10; BhP. iii, 27, 12; (*ā*), f. a kind of grass, L. **— sthāna**, n. a reservoir, pond, lake, MBh. **— sthāya**, m. id., xii, 4893 f. **— snāna**, n. a water-bath, Subh. **— srāva**, m. a kind of eye-disease, Suśr. vi, 1, 29; ŚārṅgS. vii, 157. **— ha**, n. a small *-yantra-gṛiha*, L. **— haraṇa**, n. a metre of 4 × 32 syllabic instants. **— hastin**, m. = *-dvipa*, Hcar. vii. **— hāra**, m. '= *-vāhaka*,' (*ī*), f. a female water-carrier, Hariv. 3400. **— hāriṇī**, f. = *-nirgama*, Suśr. iii, 7, 1. **— hāsa**, m. 'sea-foam (indurated),' cuttle-fish bone, L. **— hāsaka**, m. id., W. **— hrada**, m. N. of a man, g. *śivâdi*. **Jalâṅśu**, m. = *jaḍâṅśu*, Kuval. 375, Sch. **Jalâkara**, m. water-source, spring, W. **Jalâkāṅksha**, m. = °*la-k°*, L. **Jalâkshī**, f. = °*la-pippalī*, L. **Jalâkhu**, m. 'water-rat,' an otter, L. **Jalâgama**, m. 'water-approach,' rain, Ratnâv. iii, 10. **Jalâñcala**, n. a well, L.; = °*la-kuntala*, L. **Jalâñjali**, m. the hollowed palms filled with water offered to ancestors, Cāṇ.; Amar.; Kathās.; Rājat. iv, 284; Sarvad. (ifc. °*lika*). **Jalâṭana**, m. 'water-goer,' a heron, L.; (*ī*), f. a leech, L. **Jalâḍhya**, mfn. 'rich in water,' watery, marshy, W. **Jalâṇuka**, n. = °*ṇḍaka*, L. **Jalânṭaka**, m. N. of a large aquatic animal, L. **Jalâṇḍaka**, n. 'water-eggs,' the fry of fish, L. **Jalâtmikā**, f. a leech, L.; v.l. for °*lâmbikā*, L. **Jalâtyaya**, m. = °*ladâty°*, R. ii, 45, 22. **Jalâdarśa**, m. 'watery mirror,' water reflecting any object, W. **Jalâdhāra**, m. = °*la-sthāna*, Yājñ. iii, 144; MBh. xii, 4891; N. of a mountain, VP. ii, 4, 62. **Jalâdhidaivata**, n. = °*la-deva*, VarBṛS. lxxii, 10; 'water-deity,' Varuṇa, L. **Jalâdhipa**, m. = °*pati*, Hariv. 13885; 'Varuṇa' and 'lord of the stupid (*jaḍa*),' Naish. ix, 23. **Jalâdhipati**, m. 'water-lord,' Varuṇa, W. **Jalâdhyaksha**, m. id., W. **Jalâdhvan**, m. = °*la-yātrā*, Siṇhâs. vii, $\frac{3}{4}$. **Jalânila**, m. a kind of crab, Gal. **Jalânusāra**, m. going like water, W. **Jalântaka**, mfn. containing water, L.; m. N. of a son of Kṛishṇa, Hariv. 9186. **Jalântam**, ind. (to dig) till reaching water, AgP. xl, 30. **Jalâpasparśana**, n. (touching i.e.) using water, W. **Jalâbhisheka**, m. = °*la-seka*, W. **Jalâmatra**, n. = °*la-droṇī*, Uttamac. 47; 53; 97. **Jalâmoda**, see °*la-m°*. **Jalâmbara**, m. N. of Rāhula-bhadra in a former birth, Suvarṇapr. xvii f. **Jalâmbikā**, f. a well, L. **Jalâmbu-garbhā**, f. N. of Gopā in a former birth, xviii. **Jalâyukā**, f. a leech, Suśr. i, 13, 6. **Jalârka**, m. = °*la-sūrya*, BhP. iii, 27, 1. **Jalârṇava**, m. the rainy season, L.; = °*la-samudra*, W. **Jalârthin**, mfn. desirous of water, thirsty, Mālav. iii, 6. **Jalârdra**, mfn. wet, Śak. i, 31; Megh. 43; m. = °*drā*, L.; (*ā*), f. a wet garment, Bālar. v, 23 & $\frac{50}{51}$; x, 8; Vcar.

iv, 24; a wet cloth (used for cooling), Śiś. i, 65. **Jalârdrikā**, f. ifc. = °drā, Kād. vi, 822. **Jalâlu**, m. a kind of bulbous plant, L. **Jalâluka**, n. = °lūka, L.; (ā), f. = °lāyukā, L. **Jalâlūka**, n. the esculent root of lotus, L. **Jalâlokā**, f. = °lukā, L. **Jalâvatāra**, m. a landing-place at a river's side, L. **Jalâvarta**, m. a whirlpool, W. **Jalâvila**, mfn. stained with water, W. **Jalâśaya**, mfn. lying in water, MBh. iii, 11123; stupid, Kathās. vi, 58 (& 132?); m. a reservoir, pond, lake, ocean, Mn.; MBh. &c.; a fish, L.; = °la-kubjaka, L.; n. = °la-moda, L.; (ā), f. a kind of grass, L.; -pratishṭhā, f. N. of a work; °yântara, n. another lake, W.; °yôtsarga-tattva, n. N. of Smṛitit. xii; °yôtsarga-vidhi, m. N. of a work by Kamalâkara-bhaṭṭa. **Jalâśraya**, m. for °śaya, a pond, Pañcat. i, 13, ½; a water-house, W.; a wolf, Gal.; (ā), f. a kind of crane, L.; a kind of cane, L. **Jalā-shah** (nom. -shāḍ, Kāś. on Pāṇ. [iii, 2, 63] vi, 3, 137 & viii, 3, 56; acc. -shāham, g. sushāmâdi), Ved. mfn. subduing water, W. **Jalâshṭhīlī**, f. a pond, L. **Jalā-sah**, Ved. mfn. = -shah, 56, Kāś. **Jalā-sāha**, mfn. = -shah, iii, 21, 63, Sch. **Jalâsukā**, f. = °lâyukā, L., Sch. **Jalâhati**, f. violent rain-fall, Kathās. xii, 61. **Jalâhvaya**, n. 'water-named,' a lotus, L. **Jalêndra**, m. = °lâdhipati, L.; the ocean, L.; N. of a Jina, L. **Jalêndhana**, m. submarine fire, L. **Jalêbha**, m. = °la-dvipa, VarBṛS. xii, 4; (ī), f. the female of that animal, L. **Jalêlā**, f. N. of one of the mothers attending on Skanda, MBh. ix, 2634. **Jalêśa**, m. = °lâdhipati, Hariv. 13899 f.; BhP. iii, 18, 1; the ocean, viii, 7, 26. **Jalêśvara**, m. = °lâdhipati, MBh. i–iii, ix; Ragh. ix, 24; (cf. RTL. p. 201); the ocean, W.; N. of a sanctuary, MatsyaP. clxxx, 28; clxxxvi, 3; -tîrtha, v.l. for jvāl°. **Jalôcchvāsa**, m. = °la-nirgama, L. **Jalôdara**, n. 'water-belly,' dropsy, MBh. iii, xii; VarBṛ. xxiii, 3; Bhaktâm. 41. **Jalôddhata-gati**, f. 'exulting motion in water,' a metre of 4 × 12 syllables. **Jalôdbhava**, mfn. produced in water, aquatic, marine, MBh.; Suśr.; m. an aquatic animal, Laghuj. ix, 15; N. of a water-demon (slain by Kaśyapa), Rājat. i, 27; 'water-origin,' N. of a place, MBh. ii, 1078; (ā), f. the plant laghu-brāhmī, L.; benzoin, L. **Jalôdbhūta**, mfn. produced from water, W.; (ā), f. = °lâśayā, L. **Jalônnāda**, m. N. of one of the attendants of Śiva, L., Sch. **Jalôpala**, m. = °la-śarkarā, BhP. x, 25, 9, Sch. **Jalôragī**, 'water-snake,' a leech, L., Sch. **Jalâuka**, m. = °kasa, Suśr. i, 29, 79; (ā), f. id., MBh. xii, 3306; Suśr. i, 13; ii, 3; SkandaP.; °kâvacāraṇīya, mfn. treating on the application of leeches, Suśr. i, 13, 1. **Jalâukas**, mfn. living in or near water, m. inhabitant of water, aquatic animal, MBh. xiii, 2650; Hariv. 1215; BhP. i f.; m. N. of a Kaśmīr king, Rājat. ii, 9; f. (said to be used in pl. only) = °kasa, Suśr. i, 8–13; ii; iv, 19. **Jalâukasa**, m. n. 'water-homed,' a leech, L., Sch.; (ā), f. id., ib. **Jalâugha**, m. a quantity of water, W.

2. **Jala**, Nom. °lati, to become water, Śatr. xiv.

Jalaka, n. a conch, W.

Jalāya, Nom. °yate, = 2. jala, Bhartṛ. ii, 78.

Jalikā, °lukā, f. = °lâukā, L., Sch. **Jalūkā**, f. id., L.; = tṛiṇa-, Bādar. iii, 1, 1, Sch.; (cf. jālūka.)

Jale, loc. of °la, q.v. **-cara**, mf(ī)n. living in water, MBh. i, 7852; iii, 17322; R. iv, 50, 18; m. an aquatic animal, MBh. i, iii; R. (ifc. f. ā); a fish, W.; any kind of water-fowl, W. **-cchayā**, f. a kind of Heliotropium, L. **-jāta**, n. 'water-born,' lotus, L. **-ruha**, m. N. of an Orissa king; (ā), f. 'water-grower,' a kind of shrub, L. **-vāha**, m. a diver, PadmaP. iv. **-śaya**, mfn. resting or abiding in water, MBh. i, 1365; Suśr.; m. a fish, L.; = °la-ś°, Hariv. 14348; (saptârṇava-) Ragh. x, 22.

Jaleyu, m. N. of a son of Raudrâśva, MBh. i, 3700; Hariv. 1660; BhP. ix, 20, 4; VP. iv, 19, 1.

Jaloka, m. N. of a Kaśmīr king, Rājat. i, 108; (ā), f. = °lâukā, L., Sch. **Jalokikā**, f. = °lokā, W.

जलडा jalaḍā, f. g. bāhv-ādi (Gaṇar. 203).

जलालदीनाहकवरसाह m. = jalālu 'ddīn akbar shāh; (cf. jallāladīndra.)

जलाष jálāsha, mfn. appeasing, healing, RV. ii, 33, 7 & vii, 35, 6; n. (°shá) water, Naigh. i, 12; happiness (sukha), iii, 6. **-bheshaja** (jál°), mfn. possessed of healing medicines (Rudra), RV. i, 43, 4 & viii, 29, 5; AV. ii, 27, 6.

जलिका jalikā, °lukā, &c. See above.

जल्प् jalp (√lap, redupl.?), cl. 1. jálpati (ep. also Ā.; pf. jajalpa, R.) to speak inarticulately, murmur, ŚBr. xi, 5, 1, 4; to chatter, prattle, W.; to say, speak, converse with (instr. or sârdham), MBh.; R. &c.; to speak about (acc.), MBh. iv, 864; v, 4515; = √arc, to praise, Naigh. iii, 14; (said of the Koil) to sound (its song), Bhartṛ.: Caus. jalpayati, to cause to speak, Pāṇ. i, 4, 52, Vārtt. 3.

Jalpa, m. (g. uñchâdi) talk, speech, discourse (also pl.), MBh. xiii, 4322; Pāṇ. iv, 4, 97; Daś.; BhP.; (pl.) chatter, gossip, x, 47, 13; a kind of disputation (overbearing reply and disputed rejoinder), Nyāyad.; Car. iii, 8; Sarvad.; Madhus.; ŚBr. xiv, Sch.; N. of a Ṛishi, MatsyaP. ix, 16; n. for °lpya, MBh. i, 5066 (C); R. ii, 60, 14; cf. citra-, bahu-.

Jalpaka, mfn. talkative, Bhartṛ. ii, 48; m. a disputant, Car. iii. **Jalpana**, mfn. speaking, g. nandy-ādi; n. (Pāṇ. iii, 3, 115, Kāś.) saying, speaking, VarBṛS. vi; Pañcat.; chattering, W. **Jalpāka**, mfn. (Pāṇ. iii, 2, 155) talkative, Hcar. vii; Bhaṭṭ. vii, 19.

Jálpi, f. inarticulate or low speech, muttering (prayers or formulas), RV. viii, 48, 14; x, 82, 7; discourse spoken in a low voice, AV. xix, 56, 4.

Jalpita, mfn. said, spoken, Pañcat.; addressed, spoken to, Śuk.; n. (Pāṇ. iii, 3, 114, Kāś.) talk, MBh.; R. v, 10, 3; VarBṛS. iiic, 6; Pañcat. &c.

Jalpitṛi, mfn. ifc., see bahu-. **Jalpin**, mfn. ifc. speaking, MBh. v. **Jalpya**, n. gossip, i, 129, 34.

जल्लकिन् jallakin. See acyuta-.

जल्लालदीन्द्र jallāladindra, m. jallālu 'ddīn.

जळ्हु jáḷhu, mfn. 'cool' (cf. jaḍa), dull, RV. viii, 61, 11 (Nir. vi, 25); [cf. Lat. gelu.]

जव javá, mfn. (√ju or jū) swift, AV. xix, 7, 1; m. (parox., Pāṇ. iii, 3, 56, Vartt. 4 & 57) speed, velocity, swiftness, RV. i, 112, 21; x, 111, 9; VS.; AV.; ŚBr. &c.; pl. impulse (of the mind), RV. x, 71, 8; (ât), abl. ind. speedily, at once, Kathās. lxiii, 188; Vcar. xii, 15. **-yukta**, mfn. possessed of fleetness, Nal. xix, 18. **-vat**, mfn. id., ĪśUp., Sch. **Javâgraja**, for yav°, q.v. **Javâdhika**, mf(ā)n. swifter (in course), Kathās. lxvii, 7; extremely swift (a courser), L. **Javânila**, m. 'swift wind,' a hurricane, W.

Jávana, mf(ī)n. (g. dṛiḍhâdi; oxyt., Pāṇ. iii, 2, 150) quick, swift, fleet, RV. i, 51, 2; ŚvetUp. iii, 19; MBh. &c.; m. a fleet horse, L.; a kind of deer, L.; N. of one of Skanda's attendants, MBh. ix, 2577; pl. for yav°, q.v., Kshitîś.; n. speed, velocity, PārGṛ. i, 17; ŚāṅkhGṛ.; MBh. iv, 1414; (ī), f. a curtain, screen, L.; N. of a plant, L.; cf. dhī-jáv°.

Javanikā, f. (for yav°, ? 'borrowed from the Greek') = °nī, a curtain, screen, Hariv. 4648; Śiś. iv, 54; BhP.; the sail of a boat, W.; = °kântara, Sāh. vi, 277. **Javanikântara**, n. an act in a Saṭṭaka.

Javaniman, m. quickness, g. dṛiḍhâdi.

Jávas, n. id., RV.; cf. makshū-, manó-, a-.

Javita, n. running, Lalit. xii, 279.

Javín, mfn. quick, fleet, RV. ii, 15, 6; Yājñ. ii, 109; Kathās. xxv, lxvii; m. a horse, L.; a camel, L.

Javina, mfn. quick, SaddhP. iv; m. the Indian fox, L.; for jahina, MatsyaP. cxciv, 20.

Jávishṭha, mfn. quickest, fleetest, RV. iv, 2, 3; vi, 9, 5; VS. xxxiv, 3; ŚBr. xi; AitBr. i, 5; BhP. xi.

Jáviyas, mfn. quicker, RV. i, viii ff.; ĪśUp.

जवनाल javanāla, n. = yav°, L.

जवस javasa, m. n. = yav°, L., Sch.

जवा javā, f. = japā, MBh.; Hariv.; R.; Megh. 36; saffron, L. **-pushpa**, m. = japā, L.

जवादि javādi, n. a kind of perfume, L.

जवाल javāla, m. = sthāga, L., Sch.

जवित javita, °vín, °vina, &c. See javá.

जशस् jaśas, n. = yaś°, Gal.

जष् jash, cl. 1. P. Ā. to hurt, Dhātup.

जष jashá, m. N. of an aquatic animal (cf. jhashá), AV. xi, 2, 25; TS. v, 5; GopBr. ii, 2, 5.

जस् jas, cl. 1. Ā. (p. jásamāna) to be exhausted or starved, RV. i, 112, 6; vii, 68, 8: P. jásati, to go, Naigh. ii, 14: cl. 4. P. to liberate, Dhātup. xxvi, 102: Caus. jāsayati (aor. ajījasata, 2. du. jajastám) to exhaust, weaken, cause to expire, RV. iv, 50, 11; ŚBr. ii, 2, 2, 19; xii, 4, 3, 9; to hurt (cf. Pāṇ. ii, 3, 56), Dhātup. xxxii; to strike, xxxiii; to contemn, ib.; cf. uj-, ni-; prôjjāsana.

Jásu, f. exhaustion, weakness, RV. x, 33, 2; 'resting-place,' hiding-place (?), x, 68, 6.

Jásuri, mfn. starved, RV. i, 116, 22; iv, 38, 5; v, 61, 7; vi, 13, 5; m. Indra's thunderbolt, Uṇ., Sch.

Jasra. See á-.

Jásvan, mfn. needy, hungry, RV. vi, 44, 11.

जसद jasada, n. zinc, L.

जस्सराज jassa-rāja, N. of a man, Rājat. vii.

जह jaha, mfn. (√3. hā), see śardham-; (ā), f. N. of a plant, L.; (á), ind., see s.v.

Jahaka, mfn. one who abandons, Uṇ., Sch.; m. time, ib.; a boy, L.; the slough of a snake, L.; (jáhakā), f. (= jāhaka) a hedgehog, VS. xxiv; TS.

Jáhat, mfn. pr. p. √3. hā, q.v. **-svârtha**, mf(ā)n. 'losing its original meaning,' (ā), f. (scil. vṛitti) = °hal-lakshaṇā, Pāṇ. ii, 1, 1, Vārtt. 2, Pat.; Sāh. ii, ⅞; cf. a-. **Jahal-lakshaṇā**, f. a particular figure of speech (the word used losing its original meaning), Pratāpar.; Vedântas.

Jahana, see sarva-sattva-pāpa-. **Jáhāka**, mfn. avoiding others, TĀr. i, 3, 1; but cf. RV. viii, 45, 37.

Jahitá, mfn. (Jaina Prākṛit jadha) abandoned, poor, RV. i, 116, 10; iv, 30, 19; viii, 5, 22; cf. pra-.

जहानक jahānaka, v.l. for jih°.

जहि jahi, Impv. √han, q.v. **-joḍa**, mfn. in the habit of hitting one's chin, g. mayūra-vyaṅsakâdi. **-stambha**, mfn. constantly striking against a post, ib. (not in Gaṇar. 121, Sch.)

जहिन jahina, m. N. of a man, Pravar. i, 1 (vv. ll. °hila, javina).

जहु jahu, m. (= yahú) ifc. a young animal, BhP. v, 8, 8; N. of a son of Pushpavat, ix, 22, 7.

जह्नावी jahnāvī, f. Jahnu's family, RV. i, 116, 19; iii, 58, 6.

Jahnú, m. N. of an ancient king and sage (son of Aja-mīḍha, of Su-hotra, of Kuru, of Hotraka; ancestor of the Kuśikas; the Ganges, when brought down from heaven by Bhagī-ratha's austerities, was forced to flow over the earth and to follow him to the ocean and thence to the lower regions in order to water the ashes of Sagara's sons; in its course it inundated the sacrificial ground of Jahnu, who drank up its waters but consented at Bhagī-ratha's prayer to discharge them from his ears; hence the river is regarded as his daughter), MBh. i, xii f.; Hariv.; R. i, 44, 35 ff.; BhP. ix; N. of Vishṇu, L.; of a Ṛishi of the 4th Manv-antara, Hariv. 426 (v.l. janyu); of a Himâlaya cavern (from which the Gaṅgā is bursting forth), Kād. ii, 473; Hcar. iii; pl. Jahnu's race, AitBr. vii, 18; TāṇḍyaBr. xxi, 12, 2; Pravar. iv, 12. **-kanyā**, f. 'Jahnu's daughter,' Gaṅgā, MBh. xiii, 645; Ragh.; Kāvyâd.; Bhartṛ.; (°hnoḥ k°, Megh.) **-tanayā**, f. id., L. **-prajā**, f. id., Gal. **-saptamī**, f. the 7th day in the light half of Vaiśākha, W. **-sutā**, f. = -kanyā, MBh. i, 3913; R. i, 44, 39.

जह्मन् jahman, n. water, Naigh. i, 12.

जह्ल jahla, m. N. of a man, Rājat. viii, 2430; Pravar. i, 1 (Jīvad.)

जा jā, mfn. (Ved. for 2. ja, cf. Pāṇ. iii, 2, 67) ifc. 'born, produced,' see agra-, adri-, apsu-jā &c.; (ā́s), m. f. offspring, pl. descendants, RV. **Jām-dhitá**, mfn. (fr. jāmí?) customary, ŚBr. ii, 6, 2, 7. **Jā-vat**, mfn. granting offspring, RV. viii, 94, 5. **Jā-van**, see pūrva-jāvan. **Jás-pati**, m. (jās, gen. sg.) the head of a family, i, 185, 8; (jás-páti) vii, 38, 6. **Jās-patyá**, n. (for jāyās-p°, VPrāt. iv, 39; cf. APrāt. iv, 64 & 83) RV. the state of the father of a family, v, 28, 3; x, 85, 23.

जांहगिरि jāṅha-giri, m. = jahāṅgīrī.

Jāṅhagīra, the town Dacca, Kshitîś. iii, 24; vii, 18 f. & 267. **-nagara**, n. id., iii, 25; iv, 36; v.

जागत jāgata, mfn. (g. utsâdi) composed in or consisting of or conforming to the Jagatī metre; chiefly praised in that metre, VS.; TS. ii, vii; ŚBr. &c.; m. a deity, RV. vii, 92, 4, Sāy. (cf. VS. xxix, 60); n. (Pāṇ. iv, 2, 55, Vārtt.) the Jagatī metre, Vait. xix, 17. **Jāgatineya**, see jārat°.

जागुड jāguḍa, m. pl. N. of a saffron-cultivating people, MBh. iii, 1991; Śiś.; n. saffron, L.

जागृ *jāgṛi*, cl. 2. °*garti* (cf. Pāṇ. vi, 1, 192; cl. 1. °*garati*, MBh. xii, 7823; 1. sg. irr. °*gṛimi*, 6518; 3. pl. *jā́grati*, AV. &c. [Pāṇ. vi, 1, 189, Kāś.]; Impv. °*gṛihí*, °*gṛitāt*, °*gṛitam*, °*gṛitá*; Subj. °*garat*; Pot. °*gṛiyāt* or °*gṛiy*°, AitBr. viii, 28 &c.; impf. *ájāgar* [RV. x, 104, 9]; p. *jā́grat*; rarely Ā. *jāgramāṇa*, MBh.; pf. Ved. *jāgā́ra* [RV.; AV.], 1. sg. °*gára* [RV. x, 149, 5], p. °*gṛivás* [see s. v.]; pf. class. [Pāṇ. iii, 1, 38; vii, 3, 85; but cf. vi, 1, 8, Vārtt. 1] *jajāgāra* or *jāgarām-cakāra*; fut. 2nd *jāgarishyáti*, TS. &c. [Ā., R. ii, 86, 4]; fut. 1st °*ritā*, Pāṇ. vii, 2, 10, Vārtt. 1, Pat.; aor. *ajāgarīt*, vii, 2, 5; Pass. impers. *ajāgāri*, 3, 85; Prec. *jāgaryāt*, iii, 4, 104, Kāś.) to be awake or watchful, RV.; AV. &c.; to awake, Pañcat. iii, 9, $\frac{4}{1}$; Hit. ii, 3, $\frac{2}{3}$; to watch over, be attentive to or intent on, care for, provide, superintend (with loc. or loc. with *ádhi*), RV.; AV. &c. (with acc., Caurap.); (said of fire) to go on burning, AV. Prāyaśc. i, 5; to be evident, W.; to look on, W.: Caus. (aor. 2. & 3. sg. *ájīgar*, Impv. *jigṛitám*, °*tá*) to awaken, RV.; *jāgarayati* (Pāṇ. vii, 3, 85; aor. Pass. impers. *ajāgari* or °*gāri*, Vop. xviii, 22; xxiv, 6 & 13) id., Hit. ii, 3, $\frac{4}{1}$; [cf. ἐγείρω; Lat. *vigilo*.]

Jāgara, mfn. awake, Pāṇ. vii, 3, 85, Kāś.; m. waking, wakefulness, MBh. viii, 5026; KapS. iii, 26; Ragh. &c.; a vision in a waking state, Yājñ. iii, 172; =*jag*°, L.; (*ā*), f. waking, Pāṇ. iii, 3, 101, Pat.; cf. *ko-*. **Jāgarôtsava**, m. a religious festival celebrated with vigils, Rājat. ii, 141. **Jāgaraka**, m. (Pāṇ. vii, 3, 85, Kāś.) waking, VarBṛS. lx, 15.

Jāgaraṇá, mfn. awake, VS. xxx, 17; n. waking, keeping watch, KātyŚr. iv; Nir.; MBh. &c. (said of fire) going on burning, KātyŚr. xxv; Vait. **Jāgaram**, ind. so as to be awake, Pāṇ. vii, 3, 85, Kāś.

Jāgaritá, mfn. (2, 11 & 3, 85) = °*ta-vat*, Suśr. iii, 8, 1; n. waking, ŚBr. xii, xiv; Suśr. iii, 4, 37. **—vat**, mfn. one who has long been awake or is exhausted with sleeplessness, 37. **—sthāna**, mfn. being awake, MāṇḍUp. 3 & 9. **Jāgaritânta**, m. = °*grad-avasthā*, KaṭhUp. iv, 4.

Jāgaritṛi, mfn. waking, wakeful, L.

Jāgarin, mfn. ifc. id., Pāṇ. vii, 3, 85, Kāś.

Jāgarishṇu, mfn. often sleepless, Suśr. i, 33, 23.

Jāgarū́ka, mf(*ā*)n. (Nir. i, 14; Pāṇ. iii, 2, 165) wakeful, watchful, RV. iii, 54, 7; Suśr.; Ragh. x, 25; Sāh.; Sarvad.; ifc. intent on, occupied with, Ragh. xiv, 85; Hcar. v, 104; ifc. looking on, Prasannar. vi, 2; evident, W. **Jāgartavya**, n. impers. to be awake or awaked, MBh. i, 5925; R. ii, 53, 3. **Jāgarti**, f. waking, vigilance, L., Sch. **Jāgaryā**, f. id., Pāṇ. iii, 3, 101, Pat. **Jāgṛitavya**, n. impers. = °*gart*°, MBh. v, 4610; xiii, 2746. **Jāgṛivás**, mfn. (pf. p.) watchful, RV. vii, 5, 1; x, 91, 1; active, W.

Jā́gṛivi, mfn. (Pāṇ. vii, 3, 85) watchful, attentive, RV.; AV.; PārGṛ. iii, 4; going on burning, not extinguishing, RV.; active, animating (Soma, dice), RV.; VS.; m. a king, Uṇ., Sch.; fire, L.; (*i*), ind. so as to watch, VS. xxi, 36.

Jā́grat, mfn. pr. p. √*jāgṛi*, q. v.; m. waking, Vedāntas. 105; 108; 132; 305. **—svapná**, mfn. in a state of waking and sleep, RV. x, 164, 5; m. du. a state of waking and sleep, Mn. i, 57.

Jāgrad, for °*rat*. **—avasthā**, f. a state of wakefulness, W. **—daśā**, f. id., W. **—duḥshvapnyá**, n. a disagreeable dream in a waking state, AV. xvi, 6, 9.

Jāgran, for °*rat*. **—miśra**, mfn. half awake and half asleep, Gobh. i, 6, 6.

Jāgriyā, f. = °*garyā*, L., Sch.

जाघनी *jā́ghanī*, f. (fr. *jaghána*) a tail, ŚBr. iii f., xii; AitBr. vii; KātyŚr.; Mn.; MBh.; cf. *pṛithu-jāghana*. **—guda**, n. sg. tail and anus, KātyŚr.

जाङ्गल *jāṅgala*, mfn. (fr. *jaṅg*°) arid, sparingly grown with trees and plants (though not unfertile; covered with jungle, W.), Mn. vii, 69; Yājñ. i, 320; Suśr. &c.; found or existing in a jungly district (water, wood, deer), Suśr.; made of arid wood, coming from wild deer, i, iii; Hcat. i, 5, 375; wild, not tame, W.; savage, W.; m. the francoline partridge, Siṇhâs. xxvi, 2; N. of a man, Śatr. x, 138 ff.; pl. N. of a people, MBh. v, 2127; vi, 346 & 364; (cf. *kuru-*); n. venison, Suśr.; meat, Bālar. iii, 3; for °*gula*, q. v.; (*ī*), f. Mucuna pruritus, L.; for °*gulī*, q. v.; cf. *ṛishi-jāṅgalikī*.

Jāṅgalapathika, mfn. going or brought through a *jaṅgala-patha*, Pāṇ. v, 1, 77, Vārtt. 1.

जाङ्गलि *jāṅgali*, m. = °*guli*, L. **Jāṅgalika**, m. = °*gul*°, L., Sch. **Jāṅgalin**, m. id., Gal.

Jāṅgula, n. (= *jaṅg*°) venom, L.; the fruit of the Jālinī, L.; (*ā*), f. knowledge of poisons, Kām. vii, 10; (*ī*), f. id., L. (v.l. °*galī*); Durgā (Gaurī, Gal.), L.; Luffa acutangula, W.

Jāṅguli, m. a snake-charmer, L.

Jāṅgulika, m. id., Hcar. i, 517; KāśīKh. vli, 17.

जाङ्घलायन *jāṅghalāyana*, m. patr., Pravar. v, 4 (Kāty.; v.l. °*ghrāyaṇa*).

Jāṅghāprahatika or °**hṛitika**, mfn. (fr. *jaṅghā-prahata* or °*hṛita*) produced by a blow with the leg, g. *akshadyūtâdi*.

Jāṅghi, metron. fr. *jáṅghā*, g. *bāhv-ādi*.

Jāṅghika, mfn. relating or belonging to the leg, W.; swift of foot, m. a courier, Rājat. vii, 1348; Siṇhâs. Introd. 41; m. a camel, L.; a kind of antelope, L.

जाजनाग *jāja-nāga*, m. N. of a man, Śatr.

जाजमत् *jājamat*, mfn. See √*jam*.

जाजल *jājala*, m. pl. (Pāṇ. vi, 4, 144, Vārtt. 1) Jājalin's pupils (N. of a school of the AV.), Caraṇ.

Jājalāyani, m. patr. fr. °*la* or °*li*, g. *tikâdi* (not in Gaṇap. & Gaṇaratnâv.)

Jājali, m. N. of a teacher, Pravar. v, 4 (?); MBh. xii, 9277 ff.; Hariv. 7999; BhP. iv, 31, 2; VP. iii, 6, 11; VāyuP. i, 61, 52; BrahmavP. i, 16, 12 & 19.

Jājalin, m. id., Pāṇ. vi, 4, 144, Vārtt. 1.

जाजल्ल *jājalla*, m. N. of several princes (A. D. 1114 &c.)

जाजिन् *jājin*, m. = *jaja*, Śiś. xix, 3.

जाज्वल्यमान *jājvalyamāna*. See √*jval*.

जाटलि *jāṭali*, m. f. = *jhāṭ*°, L.

जाटलिका *jāṭalikā*, for *jaṭ*°, q. v.

जाटासुरि *jāṭâsuri*, m. patr. fr. *jaṭâsura*, MBh. vii, 7856. **Jāṭikāyana**, m. (fr. *jaṭika*) N. of the author of AV. vi, 116 (cf. Kauś. 9).

Jāṭilika, mfn. metron. fr. *jaṭilikā*, g. *śivâdi*.

Jāṭya, mfn. = *jaṭā-vat* (Sch.), Nir. i, 14.

जाठर *jāṭhara*, mf(*ī*)n. being on or in or relating to the stomach or belly or womb (*jaṭhára*), MBh. xii, 9661; MārkP. ii, 37; with *agni*, 'stomach-fire,' digestive faculty, MBh. iii, 149; Suśr.; hunger, Pañcat. ii, 6, 50 (iv, 8, 3); BhP. iv; m. 'womb-offspring,' a child, iii, 14, 38; N. of one of Skanda's attendants, MBh. ix, 2564.

Jāṭharya, n. morbid affection of the belly, Suśr.

जाडायन *jāḍāyana*, m. patr. fr. *jaḍa*, g. *aśvâdi* (*tâḍ*°, Kāś.)

Jāḍâra, Pāṇ. iv, 1, 130, Pat. (v.l. *jāṇḍ*°).

Jāḍya, n. (g. *dṛiḍhâdi*) coldness, W.; chilliness, KapS. i, 85; stiffness, inactivity, insensibility, Suśr.; Pratāpar.; Sāh. iii, 156; absence of power of taste (in the tongue), Suśr. iv, 24, 12 & 38, 7; dulness, stupidity, MBh. xii, 6487; Hariv. 15815; Pañcat. &c.; absence of intellect or soul, Vedāntas. **Jāḍyâri**, m. 'enemy of coldness,' the citron tree, L.

जाण्डक *jāṇḍaka*, m. N. of an animal, Car. vi, 21, 115; cf. *śāṇḍika*. **Jāṇḍâra**, v.l. for *jāḍ*°.

जात *jātá*, mfn. (√*jan*; ifc., Pāṇ. vi, 2, 171) born, brought into existence by (loc.), engendered by (instr. or abl.), RV. &c.; grown, produced, arisen, caused, appeared, ib.; ifc. (Pāṇ. ii, 2, 5, Kāś.; 36, Vārtt. 1; vi, 2, 170) see *māsa-*, *saptâha-*, &c.; appearing on or in, VarBṛS. lii, 5 ff.; destined for (dat.), RV. iv, 20, 6; ix, 94, 4; turning to (dat.), Sāh. iii, $\frac{88}{89}$; happened, become, present, apparent, manifest, TS.; VS. &c.; belonging to (gen.), RV. i, 83, 5; viii, 62, 10; ready at hand, Pañcat. ii, 16; possessed of (instr.), MBh. iv, 379; often ifc. instead of in comp. (Pāṇ. ii, 2, 36, Vārtt. 1; vi, 2, 170 f.; g. *āhitâgny-ādi*), e.g. *kiṇa-*, *danta-*, &c., qq. vv.; m. a son, RV. ii, 25, 1; AV. xi, 9, 6; ŚBr. xiv; Pañcat.; a living being (said of men, rarely of gods), RV. iv, 2, 2; v, 15, 2; x, 12, 3; AV. xviii; VS. viii, 36; N. of a son of Brahmā, PadmaP. v; n. a living being, creature, RV.; birth, origin, i, 156, 2 & 163, 1; iii, 31, 3; race, kind, sort, class, species, viii, 39, 6; AV. &c.; a multitude or collection of things forming a class (chiefly ifc., e.g. *karma-*, 'the whole aggregate of actions,' Mn. vii, $\frac{81}{82}$; *sukha-*, 'anything or everything included under the name pleasure,' Gīt. x, 3), Mn. ix; MBh. &c.; individuality, specific condition (*vyakta*), L.; = *-karman*, NārS.; (impers. with double instr.) it turned out or happened that, Rājat. v, 364; (*ā*), f. a daughter, W.; [cf. -γετος; Germ. *Kind*; Lith. *gentis*.] **—karman**, n. a birth-ceremony (consisting in touching a newly-born child's tongue thrice with ghee after appropriate prayers), ŚāṅkhGṛ.; Gṛihyās.; Mn. ii, 27 & 29; Yājñ. i, 11; MBh. &c.; (cf. RTL. pp. 353 & 357.) **—kalâpa**, mfn. having a tail (a peacock). **—kāma**, mfn. fallen in love. **—kopa**, mfn. enraged. **—kautuka**, mfn. delighted. **—kautūhala**, mfn. being eagerly desirous, R. i, 9, 23. **—krodha**, mfn. enraged. **—kshobha**, mfn. agitated. **—tokā**, f. (a woman) who has borne children, L. **—danta**, mfn. (g. *āhitâgny-ādi*) having teeth growing (a child), Mn. v, 70. **—dosha**, mfn. guilty, Mṛicch. viii, 32. **—nashṭa**, mfn. (no sooner) appeared (than) disappeared, Bhartṛ. **—paksha**, mfn. possessing wings, MBh. xii, 9305. **—pāśa**, mfn. fettered, Śak. i, 32 (v.l.) **—putra**, mfn. having a son, (f.) one who has brought forth a son, MānŚr. i, 5, 1; Kathās. **—pratyaya**, mfn. inspired with confidence, Pañcat. i, 4, $\frac{16}{17}$; iii, 9, $\frac{0}{1}$. **—prāya**, mfn. almost happened, Sāh. iii, 195. **—bala**, mfn. become strong, Mn. xii, 101; Car. vi, 2. **—brāhmaṇa-śabda**, mfn. 'grown up with the word *brāhmaṇa*,' constantly devoted to the Brāhmans, Mn. x, 122. **—buddhi**, mfn. become wise, MārkP. lxxiv, 49. **—bhāva**, mfn.? BhP. iii, 23, 37. **—bhī**, f. 'fearful,' N. of a woman, Hariv. (v.l.) **—manmatha**, mfn. = *-kāma*, MBh. **—mātra**, mf(*ā*)n. just or merely born, Mn. ix, 106; MBh. i; just or merely arisen or appeared, Pañcat.; Daś.; VāyuP. **—māsā**, f. (a woman or cow) having borne a month ago (= *māsa-jātā*), Gaṇar. 91, Sch. **—mṛita**, mfn. dying immediately after birth, Vishṇ. xxii, 26. **—rajas**, f. a female who has the catamenia. **—rasa**, mfn. having taste or flavour, Suśr. i, 44 f. **—rūpa**, mfn. beautiful, brilliant, MBh. xiii, 4088; golden, Hcat. i, 11, 494; n. gold, ŚBr. xiv (oxyt.); Naigh. i, 2 (propar.); Kauś.; Lāṭy. &c.; the thorn-apple, W.; *-tā*, f. the state of gold; *-parishkṛita*, mfn. adorned with gold; *-prabha*, mfn. 'shining like gold,' orpiment, Npr.; *-maya*, mf(*ī*)n. golden, AitBr. viii, 13; MBh. &c.; *-śila*, m. N. of a golden mountain, R. iv, 40, 52. **—roma**, mfn. haired, MBh. iii, 10053 (*a-*, neg.) **—rosha**, mfn. = *-kopa*, R. i, 1, 4. **—vat**, mfn. born, Pañcat. i, 5, 6; containing a form of √*jan*, AitBr. i, 16. **—vāsaka**, n. a lying-in-chamber, Kathās. lv, 194. **—vāsa-gṛiha**, n. id., xxiii, 61. **—vidyā́**, f. knowledge of what exists, RV. x, 71, 11 (Nir. i, 8). **—vinashṭa**, mfn. = *-nashṭa*, Pañcat. v, 1, 6. **—vibhrama**, mfn. being in a flurry. **—viśvāsa**, mfn. = *-pratyaya*. **—veda**, mfn. granting wages (Sch.), BhP. v, 7, 13. **—vedas** (°*tá-*), mfn. (fr. √*vid*, cl. 6) 'having whatever is born or created as his property,' 'all-possessor' (or fr. √*vid*, cl. 2. 'knowing [or known by] all created beings;' cf. Nir. vii, 19; ŚBr. ix, 5, 1, 68; MBh. ii, 1146 &c.; N. of Agni), RV.; AV.; VS. &c.; m. fire, MBh. &c.; *-tva*, n. the state of being *jāta-vedas*, AitBr. iii, 36. **—°vedasa**, mfn. belonging or relating to Jāta-vedas (*tṛica*), Nir. vii, 20; (*ī*), f. Durgā, MBh. vi, 802. **—°vedasīya**, n. '= °*sa*,' (scil. *sūkta*) N. of a hymn, ŚBr. xiii, 5, 1, 12; ŚāṅkhŚr. viii, x. **—°vedasya**, mfn. = °*sa*, AitBr. ii. 39; iii, 36. **—vepathu**, mfn. affected with tremor. **—veśman**, n. = *-vāsaka*, Kathās. xvii, lv. **—śilā**, f. a real or massive stone, Gobh. iii, 9, 6. **—śṛiṅga**, mfn. having horns, L. (*a-*, neg.) **—śmaśru**, mfn. one whose beard has grown, g. *āhitâgny-ādi*. **—śrama**, mfn. wearied, exhausted. **—saṃvatsarā**, f. (a woman or cow) having had offspring a year ago (= *saṃvatsara-jātā*), Gaṇar. 91, Sch. **—saṃvṛiddha**, mfn. born and grown up, R. i, 8, 8. **—saṃkalpa**, mfn. feeling a desire for, Naᶦ. iii, 8. **—sa-sneha**, mfn. = *-sneha*, MBh. iii, 11081. **—sādhvasa**, mfn. afraid. **—sena**, m. N. of a man, Pāṇ. iv, 1, 114, Vārtt. 7. **—°senya**, m. patr. fr. *-sena*, ib. **—sneha**, mfn. feeling affection, Kathās. **—spṛiha**, mfn. = *-saṃkalpa*. **—harsha**, mfn. rejoiced. **—hāriṇī**, f. N. of a female demon who carries off new-born children, MārkP. li. **—hārda**, mfn. = *-sneha*. **Jātâgas**, mfn. = °*ta-dosha*. **Jātâpatyā**, f. a woman who has borne a child, L. **Jātâparādha**, mfn. = °*ta-dosha*. **Jātâbhishaṅga**, mfn. defeated, Ragh. ii, 30. **Jātâmarsha**, mfn. = °*ta-kopa*. **Jātâśru**, mfn. being in tears, Amar. 97. **Jātâstha**, mfn. taking into consideration, Kathās. **Jātêshṭi**, f. an oblation given at a child's birth, Vedāntas. 10. **Jātâikabhakti**, mfn. devoted exclusively to, BhP. i, 13, 2. **Jātôksha**, m. a young bullock, Pāṇ. v, 4, 77. **Jātôdaka,** mfn. 'become (full of) water,' dropsy, Bhpr. vii, 53, 28 ff.

Jātaka, mfn. ifc. engendered by, born under (an asterism), Mn. ix, 143; Cāṇ.; m. a new-born child, Kauś.; a mendicant, L.; n. = °*ta-karman*, MBh. i, 949; BhP. v, 14, 33; nativity, astrological calculation of a nativity, VarBṛ. xxvi, 3; BhP. i; Kathās. lxxii, 192; Rājat. vii, 1730; the story of a former birth of Gautama Buddha, Buddh.; Kathās. lxxii, 120; (ifc. after numerals) 'an aggregate of similar things,' see *catur-*. **-dhvani,** m. a leech, W. **-paddhati,** f. N. of works on nativities by Ananta and Keśava. **-muktâvalī,** f. N. of an astrological work by Śiva-dāsa. **Jātakâmbhonidhi,** m. 'ocean of nativities,' N. of an astrol. work by Bhadrabāhu.

Jātāyana, m. patr. fr. *jāta*, g. *aśvâdi*.

Jāti, f. birth, production, AitBr. ii, 39; Mn.; MBh. (also °*tī*, xiii f.) &c.; re-birth, R. i, 62, 17; Kāraṇḍ. xxiii, 193; the form of existence (as man, animal, &c.) fixed by birth, Mn. iv, 148 f.; Yogas. ii, 13; (ifc.) Kathās. xviii, 98; position assigned by birth, rank, caste, family, race, lineage, KātyŚr. xv; Mn.; Yājñ. &c. (°*tī*, MBh. xiv, 2549); kind, genus (opposed to species), species (opposed to individual), class, Lāṭy.; KātyŚr.; Pāṇ. &c. (once °*tī*, ifc., MBh. vi, 456); the generic properties (opposed to the specific ones), Sarvad.; natural disposition to, Car. ii, 1; the character of a species, genuine or true state of anything, Yājñ. ii, 246; MBh. xii, 5334; reduction of fractions to a common denominator; a self-confuting reply (founded merely on similarity or dissimilarity), Nyāyad. v, 1 ff.; Sarvad. xi, 10 & 34; Prab., Sch.; (in rhet.) a particular figure of speech, Sarasv. ii, 1; a class of metres, R. i, 4, 6; Kāvyâd. i, 11; a manner of singing, Hariv.; a fire-place, L.; (= °*tī*) mace, nutmeg, Suśr.; Jasminum grandiflorum, L.; = °*tī-phalā*, L.; = *kampilla*, L.; cf. *antya-, eka-, dvi-*; [cf. Lat. *gens*; Lith. *pri-gentis*.] **-kośa,** m. [Dhanv.] n. [Bhpr. v, 2, 54] a nutmeg; (*ī*), f. mace, L. **-jānapada,** mfn. relating to the (4) castes and to the country, Mn. viii, 41. **-tā,** f. distinction of caste, W.; generic property, W. **-tva,** n. = *-tā*, W.; abstraction, Sarvad. xii, 162. **-dīpaka,** n. a kind of simile in which two statements are made with respect to a generic word, Kāvyâd. ii, 98, Sch. **-dharma,** m. caste, duty, W.; generic or specific property, W. **-dhvaṅsa,** m. loss of caste, W. **-m-dhara,** m. N. of a physician (Śuddhôdana in a former birth), Suvarṇapr. xvi ff. **-pattrī,** f. = *-kośī*, Dhanv.; Bhpr. v, 2, 57. **-parivṛitti,** f. change or succession of births, Āp. ii, 11, 10 f. **-parṇī,** f. = *-pattrī*, Npr. **-phala,** n. = *-kośa*, L. **-brāhmaṇa,** m. a Brāhman by birth (not by knowledge), TāṇḍyaBr. vi, 5, 8, Sch. **-bhāj,** mfn. = *janma-bh°*, ŚārṅgP. **-bhraṅśa,** m. '= *-dhvaṅsa*,' *-kara*, mfn. causing loss of caste, Mn. xi, 68 & 125. **-bhrashṭa,** mfn. fallen from caste, AdhyR. i, 1, 56. **-mat,** mfn. of high birth or rank, R. (G) ii, 75, 21; belonging to a genus, what may be subordinated to a generic idea, Sarvad. x, 9; Kaṇ. i, 1, 18, Sch. (*-tva*, n. abstr.) **-maha,** m. birthday-festival, Buddh. L. **-mātra,** n. mere birth, position in life obtained by mere birth, Hit. i, 4, 2; caste only (but not the performance of especial duties), W.; species, genus, W.; *-jīvin*, mfn. (a Brāhman) who lives only by his caste (without sacerdotal acts), L.; °*trôpajīvin*, mfn. id., Mn. viii, 20; xii, 114. **-mālā,** f. 'caste-garland,' N. of a work on the castes; (cf. RTL. p. 207.) **-lakshaṇa,** n. generic or specific distinction, characteristic, W.; mark of tribe or caste, W. **-vacana,** m. (scil. *śabda*) = *-śabda*, VPrāt., Sch. **-vācaka,** mfn. expressing genus, generic (a name), W. **-viveka,** m. N. of a work. **-vaira,** n. natural enmity, W. **-vailakshaṇya,** n. conduct or quality at variance with birth or tribe, W.; incompatibility, W. **-śabda,** m. a word expressing the idea of species or genus, L. **-śasya,** for *-sasya*, q. v. **-sampanna,** mfn. belonging to a noble family, Nal.; MBh. xiii; R. iii; Jain. **-sasya,** n. = *-kośa*, L. **-sāra,** n. id., L. **-smara,** mf(*ā*)n. recollecting a former existence, MBh. iii, 8180; Hariv. 1209; BhP.; VP.; Kathās.; n. N. of a Tīrtha, MBh. iii, 8106; *-tā*, f. recollection of a former existence, iii, 160; Hcat. i, 7, 692; *-tva*, n. id., MBh. iii, 8107; xiii, 4836; Kathās.; *-hrada*, m. N. of a pond, MBh. iii, 8180. **-smaraṇa,** n. = °*ra-tā*, xii, 6256; Hariv. 1211. **-svabhāva,** m. specific or generic character or nature. **-hīna,** mfn. of low birth or rank, Mn. iv, 141; x, 35.

Jātī, f. = °*ti*, q. v.; Jasminum grandiflorum, Hariv. 7891; Bhartṛ.; BhP. x; Amar.; mace, nutmeg, Suśr.; VarBṛS. **-kośa,** m. (also n., L.) = °*ti-k°*, Suśr. i, 46, 3, 64. **-pattrī,** f. = °*ti-p°*, Bhpr. v, 2, 56. **-phala,** n. = °*ti-ph°*, VarBṛS. xvi, 30; lxxvi, 27 & 33; Pañcad. ii, 66; (*ā*), f. Emblica officinalis, L. **-rasa,** m. gum myrrh, L.; *-phalā*, f. = °*tī-ph°*, Npr.

Jātīya, mfn. ifc. (APrāt. iv, 28; Pāṇ. v, 3, 69 & 4, 9; vi, 3, 35; 42 & 46) belonging to any species or genus or tribe or order or race of, KātyŚr. (*anucara-*) &c. (see *evam-guṇa-, evam-*, &c., *paṭu-, samāna-, sva-*, &c.); ifc. aged (*ashṭa-varsha-*, 8 years), Divyâv. xxxii, 135 f. (cf. 113 & 137); cf. *vi-*.

Jātīyaka, mf(*ā*)n. ifc. *evam-*, of such a kind, Bādar. iv, 2, 13, Sch. **Jātṛī,** f. °*trī*, a mother, AV.

Jāty, in comp. for °*ti*. **-andha,** mfn. blind from birth, MBh. i, xiii; Cāṇ.; Bhartṛ.; *-badhira*, mfn. blind or deaf from birth, Mn. ix, 201. **-apahārin,** mfn. implying loss of caste, Vishṇ. v, 99. **-aśva,** m. a horse of good breed, RV. i, 65, 3, Sāy. **-utkarsha,** m. a higher caste, Yājñ. i, 96. **-utpala,** n. a red and white lotus, Npr.

Jā́tya, mfn. ifc. = °*tīya*, belonging to the family or caste of, MBh. xiii; R. ii, 50, 18; Pañcat.; of the same family, related, ŚBr. i, 8, 3, 6; of a noble family, noble, Ragh. xvii, 4; of good breed, R. ii, 45, 14; legitimate, genuine, γνήσιος, Mn. x, 5; MBh. v; R. ii, 9, 40 (said of gold); Suśr.; (in Gr.) = *nitya*, N. of the Svarita accent resulting in a fixed word (not by Sandhi, see *kshaipra*) from an Udātta originally belonging to a preceding *i* or *u* (e.g. *kvà* fr. *kúa*; *kanyà* fr. *kanía*), Prāt.; MāṇḍŚikshā vii, 5; pleasing, beautiful, L.; best, excellent, W.; (in math.) rectangular. **-ratna-maya,** mfn. consisting of genuine jewels, HPariś. ii, 47.

जातु *jā́tu*, ind. (√*jan?*, cf. *janúshā*, s. v. °*nús*) at all, ever, RV. x, 27, 11; ŚBr. ii, 2, 2, 20 (°*tú*); MBh. v, 7071; Pañcat. i, 1, 6 (*kim tena—jātena*, what is the use at all of him born?); [when *jā́tu* stands at the beginning of a sentence the verb which follows retains its accent, Pāṇ. viii, 1, 47; in connection with the Pot. and *nâvakalpayāmi* &c. (iii, 3, 147) or with the pr. (iii, 3, 142) *jātu* expresses censure, e.g. *jātu vṛishalam yājayen na marshayāmi*, 'I suffer not that he should cause an outcast to sacrifice,' Kāś.; *jātu yājayati vṛishalam*, ought he to cause an outcast to sacrifice? ib.]; possibly, perhaps, MBh. xii, 6739 (with *api* preceding); Kathās. (also with *cid* following); some day, once, once upon a time, Kathās.; Rājat. (also with *cid* following). *Na jātu*, not at all, by no means, never, ŚBr. xiv; Mn.; MBh. &c. (also with *cid* following).

Jātū, in comp. for °*tu*; = *aśáni*, RV. i, 103, 3, Sāy. **-bharman** (°*tū́-*), mfn. ever nourishing or protecting, 3. **-shṭhira** (°*tū́-*), mfn. ever solid, never yielding, ii, 13, 11.

जातुक *jātuka*, m. the plant from which Asa fœtida (*jat°*) is obtained, Car. i, 27, 92 (vv. ll. *yāt°* & *dhāt°*); Suśr. i, 46, 4, 65; n. Asa fœtida, L.

Jātuki, m. pl. Jatuka's descendants, Gaṇar. 28, Sch. (g. *upakâdi*). **Jātusha,** mf(*ī*)n. (Pāṇ. iv, 3, 138) made of or covered with lac or gum (*jatu*), Gobh. iii, 8, 6; MBh. (with *gṛiha* = *jatu-g°*); Pañcat. i, 1, 94; adhesive, Suśr. i, 27, 5.

जातुधान *jātu-dhāna*, for *yāt°*, Kād. ii, 250.

जातुरकि *jāturaki*, m. pl. Jaturaka's descendants, Gaṇar. 30, Sch.

जातुष *jātusha*. See °*tuka*.

जातूकर्ण *jātūkarṇa*, m. (fr. *jat°*? g. *gargâdi*, v. l.) N. of an ancient teacher (one of the 28 transmitters of the Purāṇas, VP. iii, 3, 19; vi, 8, 47 [°*nya*]; VāyuP. i, 1, 8; 23, 201 [°*ṇya*]; DevībhP.; author of a law-book, Yājñ., Sch.; [°*nya*, PārGṛ., Sch.]; N. of a physician), MBh. ii, 109; Hariv. 2364; BhP. vi, 15, 13; (= Agni-veśya) ix, 2, 21; N. of Śiva; (*ī*), f. N. of Bhava-bhūti's mother, Mālatīm. i, $\frac{3}{8}$; mf(*ī*)n. of °*nya*, g. *kaṇvâdi*.

Jātūkarṇya, m. (fr. *jatū-karṇa*, g. *gargâdi*) N. of several preceptors and grammarians (see also °*ṇa*), ŚBr. xiv; KātyŚr. iv, xx, xxv; VPrāt.; ŚāṅkhŚr.; ŚāṅkhGṛ. iv, 10, 3; AitĀr. v, 3; BrahmaP. ii, 12; pl. Jātūkarṇya's family, Pravar. vi, 1 & 6.

जातूभर्मन् *jātū-bharman*, &c. See *jā́tu*.

जातृ *jātṛi*, *jā́tya*. See *jātá*.

1. **Jā́na,** n. birth, origin, birthplace, RV. i, 37, 9 & 95, 3; v, x; AV. vii, 76, 5; ŚBr. iii, 2, 1, 40.

2. **Jāna,** m. (fr. *jána*) patr. of Vṛiśa (= *vaijāna*, 'son of Vijānā,' Sch.), TāṇḍyaBr. xiii, 3; ĀrshBr.

1. **Jānaka,** m. (fr. *janaká*) patr. of Kratu-vid, AitBr. vii, 34; of Āyasthūṇa, BṛĀrUp. (also °*ki*); (*ī*), f. patr. of Sītā, MBh. iii, 15872; R. iii, 51, 6; Ragh. xii, 61; xv, 74; a metre of 4 × 24 syllables.

Jā́naki, m. patr. of Kratu-jit, TS. ii, 3, 8, 1; of Āyasthūṇa, ŚBr. xiv (once °*kī*); of a king, MBh. i, 2675; v, 83; pl. N. of a subdivision of the Tri-garta people, Pāṇ. v, 3, 116, Kāś. (v. l. *jālaki*).

Jānakī, f. of °*ka*, q. v. **-gītā,** f. 'Sītā-song,' N. of a work. **-deha-bhūsha,** m. 'body-ornament of Sītā,' Rāma, RāmatUp. i, 32. **-nātha,** m. 'Sītā's lord,' Rāma, ii, 1, 5, Sch.; *-liṅga*, n. N. of a Liṅga, KapSaṃh.; *-śarman*, m. N. of the author of Siddhânta-mañjarī. **-pariṇaya,** m. 'Sītā's marriage,' N. of a drama. **-mantra,** m. a Mantra addressed to Sītā, RāmatUp. i, 29, Sch. **-rāghava,** n. N. of a drama, Sāh. vi, 98 $\frac{3}{8}$. **-rāma-candra-vilāsa,** m. N. of Mahān. ii. **-vallabha,** m. 'Sītā's lover,' Rāma, Rāmapūjāśar. **-°śa** (°*kīś°*), m. = *-nātha*, AdhyR. i, 1, 1. **-sahasra-nāma-stotra,** n. a hymn containing the 1000 names of Sītā, Tantr. **-svayaṃvara,** m. 'Sītā's husband-choice,' N. of Mahān. i. **-haraṇa,** n. 'carrying off of Sītā,' N. of a poem, Uṇ. iii, 73, Sch.

Jānakīya, m. a prince of the Jānakis, Pāṇ. v, 3, 116, Kāś. **Jānaṃtapi,** m. (fr. *janam-tapa*) patr. of Aty-arāti, AitBr. viii, 23, 9.

Jā́napada, mfn. (g. *utsâdi*) living in the country (*jana-padá*), m. inhabitant of the country, MBh. (Nal. xxvi, 30); R.; Ragh.; BhP.; belonging to or suited for the inhabitants of the country, Mn. viii, 41; R. i, 12, 13; m. one who belongs to a country, subject, ŚBr. xiv; Yājñ. ii, 36; MBh. xii; R.; (*ī*), f. (= *vṛitti*, oxyt., Pāṇ. iv, 1, 42) a popular expression (scil. *ā-khyā*), Lāṭy. viii, 3, 9; N. of an Apsaras, MBh. i, 5076. **Jānapadika,** mfn. relating to a country or to its subjects, xi, 71; xii, 7464 & 12496. **Jānarājya,** n. (fr. *jana-rā́jan*) sovereignty, VS. ix, 40; MaitrS. ii, 6, 6. **Jānavādika,** mfn. knowing popular report (*jana-vāda*), g. *kathâdi*.

Jānaśruti, m. patr. fr. Jana-śruta, ChUp. iv, 1, 1. **Jānaśruteyá,** m. (fr. *jana-śrutá* or *jānaśruti*) N. of Aupāvi or Up°, ŚBr. v, 1, 1, 5 ff.; AitBr. i, 25.

Jānāyana, m. patr. fr. *jana*; g. *aśvâdi*.

Jānârdana, m. patr. fr. *jan°*, Pradyumna, MBh.

Jāni, ifc. (Pāṇ. v, 4, 134) = *jáni*, a wife, Ragh. xv, 61 (*an-anya-*, mfn. 'having no other wife'); Kathās. iic; Rājat. i, 258; cf. *arundhatī-, bhádra-, yúva-, vī-, vittá-, sumáj-, saptá-; a-* & *dvi-jāni*.

1. **Jānī,** f. a mother, L. **Jā́nukā,** f. (a woman) bringing forth, MaitrS. i, 4, 8; ĀpŚr. i, 10, 11.

जानक 2. *jānaka*, m. (√*jñā*) knower (a Buddha), Divyâv. xiii, 348; xxi, 13; pl. the Buddhists, Sūtrakṛit. i, 1, 18 (Prākṛit).

Jānát, mfn. pr. p. P. √*jñā*, q. v. **Jānanti,** m. (fr. *jānát*) N. of a teacher, ĀśvGṛ. iii, 4, 4; BṛNārP. xxxiii. **Jānāná,** mfn. pr. p. Ā. √*jñā*, q. v.

जानी 2. *jānī*, (in colophons) corrupted fr. *yājñika*.

जानु *jā́nu*, n. (rarely m., MBh. iv, 1115; Rājat. iii, 345) the knee, RV. x, 15, 6; AV. ix f.; VS. &c. (°*nubhyām avanim* √*gam*, 'to fall to the ground on one's knees,' MBh. xiii, 935); (as a measure of length) = 32 Aṅgulas, Śulbas.; [cf. γόνυ; Lat. *genu*; Goth. *kniu*; Germ. *Knie*.] **-calana,** n. balancing on the knees, Pañcat. v, 9, $\frac{2}{?}$. **-jaṅgha,** m. N. of a king, MBh. i, 230; xiii, 7684. **-daghná,** mf(*ī*)n. reaching up or down to the knees, TS. v, 6, 8, 3; ŚBr. ix, xii; TĀr. i, 25; BrahmaP.; (*e*), loc. ind. as far up as the knee, ĀpŚr. xv, 13, 3; °*nâmbhas*, mfn. having water up to one's knee, Rājat. viii, 3186. **-pracalana,** n. v. l. for *-cal°*. **-prahṛita,** g. *aksha-dyūtâdi* (not in Gaṇar.); °*tika*, mfn., ib. **-phalaka,** n. the knee-pan, W. **-maṇḍala,** n. id., Buddh. L. **-mātrá,** mfn. reaching up to the knee, ĀśvGṛ. ii, 8; iv, 4; n. the height of the knee, ŚBr. xii, 8, 3, 20. **-śiras,** n. = *-phalaka*, ĀśvŚr. i, 4, 8. **-saṃdhi,** m. the knee-joint, W.

Jānuka, n. (g. *yāvâdi*) the knee, VarBṛS. lviii (in comp.); ifc. (f. *ā*), Hcat. i, 7, 354; (cf. *ūrdhva-, virala-*); m. N. of a man, Śak. vi, $\frac{1}{2}$.

Jānv, in comp. for °*nu*. **-akna,** mfn. = *-âk°*, ĀpŚr. x, 9, 2. **-asthi,** n. the shin-bone, i, 3, 17. **-âkná,** mfn. having the knees bent, ŚBr. iii, 2, 1, 5.

जानुका *jā́nukā*. See *jātṛí*.

Jānevādika, °nov°, = *jānav°*, g. *kathâdi.*

जांधित *jāṃ-dhitá.* See *jā.*

जान्य *jānya*, v. l. for *janya*, q. v.

जाप *jāpa*, m. (√*jap*) 'whispering,' see *karṇa-*; muttering prayers, L.; a muttered prayer, L. (R. i, 51, 27 for *japa*; see also *jāpya*).

Jāpaka, mfn. muttering prayers or names of a deity (in comp.), m. a priest who mutters prayers, MBh. xii, 7153 f.; BhP. ix, 6, 10; Kathās. lxix; NṛisUp.; Hcat.; relating to a muttered prayer, MBh. xii, 7249 & 7336; n., v. l. for *jāyaka*, L.

Jāpin, mfn. ifc. muttering, Yājñ. iii; Kathās.

Jāpya, mfn. to be muttered, BhP. i, 19, 38; (fr. *jāpa*) relating to a muttered prayer, MBh. xii, 7260; n. a prayer to be muttered, muttering of prayers, MBh. xiii, 6232; R. i, 29, 32 (v. l. *jāpa*); BhP. viii, 3, 1.

जापन *jāpana*, n. for *yāp°*, rejection, L.; dismissing, L.; completing, L.

जाबाल 1. *jābāla*, m. = *ajā-pāla*, L.

जाबाल 2. *jābālá*, m. (fr. *jabālā*) metron. of Mahā-śāla, ŚBr. x; of Satya-kāma, xiii f.; AitBr. viii, 7; ChUp.; N. of the author of a law-book, Kull. on Mn. ii, iv f.; Parāś. iii, Sch. (pl.); of the author of a medicinal work, BrahmavP. i, 16, 12 & 18; pl. N. of a school of the Yajur-veda, Caraṇ.; Pravar. iv, 1; cf. *mahā-*. **-śruti**, f. tradition as handed down by the Jābālas, Parāś. ii, Sch.; Mn. vi, $\frac{38}{39}$; Yājñ. iii, $\frac{57}{58}$. **Jābâlôpanishad**, f. N. of an Up., MuktUp. i, 7 & 16; ii.

Jābālāyana, N. of a teacher, BṛĀrUp. iv, 6, 2.

Jābāli, m. patr. fr. *jabāla* (Pāṇ. ii, 4, 58, Vārtt. 1, Pat.), N. of an ancient sage (author of a law-book, PadmaP.; Mn. iv, $\frac{38}{39}$), MBh. iii, 8265; xiii, 254; VarBṛS. viii; Kād.; N. of an infidel Brāhman (priest of Daśa-ratha, who ineffectually tried after his death to shake Rāma's resolution and induce him to take the throne), R. i, 11, 6 & 69, 4; ii, 67, 2. **Jābālîśvara**, n. N. of a Liṅga, KāśīKh. lxv.

Jābālin, m. pl. N. of Jābāla's school, MuktUp. ii, 4.

जामदग्न *jāmadagná*, mf(*ī*)n. derived from or produced by Jamad-agni (or Jāmadagnya, g. *kaṇvâdi*), ŚBr. xiii, 2, 2, 14; ĀśvŚr. iii, 2; m. N. of a Catur-aha, KātyŚr. xxiii, 2; Lāṭy. ix; pl. (g. *kaṇvâdi*) Jamad-agni's descendants, ĀśvŚr. xii, 10.

Jāmadagniya, patr. fr. Jamad-agni, TS. vii, 1.

Jāmadagneya, m. id., R. i, 74, 17.

Jāmadagnya, mfn. belonging or relating to Jamad-agni or to his son Jāmadagnya, MBh. i, 332; Hariv. 2313; R. i, 75, 3; m. (g. *gargâdi*) = °*gniya*, ĀśvGṛ. i, 7; KātyŚr. iii, 3, $\frac{14}{15}$; Rāma (Paraśu-), RAnukr.; MBh. iii, vii; R. i f.; BhP. ix; N. of a Catur-aha, Maś. vii, 5; pl. Jamad-agni's descendants, Pravar. i. **-dvādaśī**, f. the 12th day in the light (?) half of Vaiśākha, VarP. xliv.

Jāmadagnyaka, m. = °*gniya*, AgP. xlii, 24.

Jāmadagnyāyita, n. the act of killing after the manner of Paraśu-Rāma, Rājat. vii, 1506.

जामर्य *jāmarya*, mfn. (milk), RV. iv, 3, 9.

जामल *jāmala*, n. for *yām°*.

जामा *jāmā*, f. a daughter, MBh. xiii, 2474.

Jāmātṛi, m. (*jā-m°*, 'maker of [new] offspring,' Nir. vi, 9; cf. *yām°* & *vi-jām°*) a son-in-law, RV. viii, 2, 20 & (Tvashṭṛi's son-in-law = Vāyu) 26, 21 f.; Yājñ. i, 220; MBh. &c. (acc. sg. °*tāram*, R.; pl. °*taras*, Kathās.); a brother-in-law, R. vii, 24, 30 & 34; a husband, L.; Scindapsus officinalis, L. **-tva**, n. the relationship of a son-in-law, Pañcat. i.

Jāmātṛika, m. = *yām°*, i, 5, $\frac{6}{7}$ (v. l. °*tṛi*).

Jāmí, mfn. related like brother and sister, (f. with [RV. i, iii, ix] or without *svásṛi*) a sister, (rarely m.) a brother, RV. ('sisters,' = fingers; '7 sisters' = 7 acts of devotion in Soma worship, ix, 66, 8; cf. *saptá-*); AV.; related (in general), belonging or peculiar to, customary, usual, (m.) a relative, RV.; (cf. *jām-dhitá*, s. v. *jā*); f. a female relative of the head of a family, esp. the daughter-in-law, Mn. iii, 57 f.; MBh. xiii, xv; BhP. iv, 28, 16; a sister (?), Yājñ. i, 157; a virtuous woman, L.; N. of a goddess, TBr. i, 7, 2, 6; (cf. °*mī*); n. the relation of brother and sister, consanguinity, RV. iii, 54, 9; x, 10, 4; (in Gr. and in liturgy) uniformity, repetition, tautology, TS.; TBr.; ŚBr.; AitBr.; Lāṭy.; Nir.; water, Naigh. i, 12 (v. l. °*mi-vat*); cf. *á-*, *vi-*, *saptá-*, *samāvaj-*, *su-*, *sóma-*; *deva-jāmi*; [cf. Lat. *geminus.*] **-kṛít**, mfn. creating relationship, AV. iv, 19, 1. **-tvá**, n. consanguinity, RV. i, 105, 9 & 166, 13; x, 55, 4 & 64, 13. **-vát**, ind. like a sister or brother, 23, 7; n. for *jāmí*, q. v. **-śaṇsá**, m. curse pronounced by a relative, AV. ii, 10, 1 ff.; ix, 4, 15.

Jāmī, f. = °*mi*, a daughter-in-law, MBh. xii, 8868; N. of an Apsaras, Hariv. iii, 69, 16; for *yām°*, q. v. **Jāmeya**, m. a sister's son, L.

जामित्र *jāmitra*, n. (fr. διάμετρον) the 7th lunar mansion, VarBṛS.; VarBṛ.; Laghuj.; Kum. vii, 1.

जामुन *jāmuna*, mfn. = *yām°*, Ratnak.

जाम्ब *jāmba*, fr. *jamba*, Uṇ. iv, $\frac{95}{96}$. **-vat**, m. N. of a monkey-chief (son of Pitā-maha; father of Jāmba-vatī), MBh. iii, 16115; Hariv. 2065 ff. & 6701; R. iv, vi; BhP. viii; VP.; Śatr. x, 934. **-°vata**, m. patr. fr. *-vat*, g. *arīhaṇâdi*; (*ī*), f. Jāmbavat's daughter (Krishṇa's wife, Śāmba's mother), MBh. iii, xiii; Hariv.; VP.; Śatr. x, 934; = °*bavī*, L. **-°vataka**, = *jāmbavatā nirvṛitta*, g. *arīhaṇâdi.*

1. **Jāmbava**, m. = °*ba-vat*, R. v; Bhaṭṭ. vii, 35.

Jāmbavatī, f. of °*ta* s. v. *jāmba*. **-pati**, m. 'husband of Jāmbavatī,' Krishṇa, Gal. **-vijaya**, m. N. of a poem by Pāṇini, L., Sch. **-haraṇa**, n. N. of a work, Gaṇar., Sch.

जाम्बव 2. *jāmbava*, mfn. coming from the Jambū tree, Suśr. i, 45, 10, 18; n. N. of a town, Pāṇ. ii, 4, 7, Kāś.; (iv, 3, 165) a Jambū fruit, Suśr. i, iv; (= °*būnada*) gold, L.; (*ī*), f. Artemisia vulgaris, Alpinia nutans, L. **Jāmbavoshṭha**, °**vaúshṭha**, n. 'lip (*oshṭha*) made of Jambū wood,' a cauterizing needle or probe, Suśr. (also °*boshṭha* & °*baúshṭha*).

Jāmbavaka, N. of a place, g. *arīhaṇâdi.*

जाम्बिल *jāmbila*, n. (corr. fr. *jānu-bila*) the knee-joint, MaitrS. iii, 15, 3; (°*bīla*) VS. xxv, 3 ['knee-pan,' Sch.] & Kāṭh. v, 13, 1.

जाम्बीर *jāmbīra*, n. = *jam°*, a citron, Sch.

जाम्बील *jāmbīla*, n., s. °*bila*; saliva (?), Vait.

जाम्बुक *jāmbuka*, mfn. coming from a jackal (*jam°*), MBh. xii, 5779.

जाम्बुद्वीपक *jāmbudvīpaka*, mfn. dwelling in Jambū-dvīpa, Kāraṇḍ. iii, 15 f.; xiv, 17; xvii; xxiii.

जाम्बुवत् *jāmbu-vat*, °*tī*, for °*ba-v°*.

जाम्बूनद *jāmbūnada*, mfn. coming from the river (*nadī*) Jambū (kind of gold), n. gold from the Jambū river, any gold, MBh.; Hariv. 13099; R.; BhP. v, 16, 21; mf(*ī*)n. = *-maya*, MBh. i, xii f.; Hariv. 8419; R. v, 7, 19; m. N. of a son of Janam-ejaya, MBh. i, 3745; = *-parvata*, Hariv. 12829; n. a golden ornament, Śiś. iv, 66; thorn-apple, L.; N. of a lake, MBh. v, 3843; (*ī*), f. N. of a river, vi, 338. **-parvata**, m. N. of a mountain, iii, 10835. **-prabha**, mfn. of golden splendour, R. i, 38, 19 (in comp.); m. N. of a Buddha, SaddhP. vi, $\frac{34}{35}$. **-maya**, mf(*ī*)n. made of Jāmbūnada gold, golden, MBh.; Hariv. 6918; R.; Pañcat. iii, 6, $\frac{6}{7}$.

Jāmbeya, m. metron. fr. Jambū, Pāṇ. iv, 1, 114, Vārtt. 2, Pat.

जाम्बोष्ठ *jāmboshṭha* &c. See °*mbava*.

जाम्भ *jāmbha*, patr. fr. *jambha*, g. *śivâdi.*

जायक *jāyaka*, n. a yellow kind of fragrant wood, L. (vv. ll. *jāpaka* & *jāshaka*).

जायद्रथ *jāyadratha*, mfn. belonging to Jayad-ratha, JaimBhār. lxxvi, 1.

Jāyanta, m. (fr. *jay°*) patr. of Bharata, BhP. x.

Jāyantī-putra, m. N. of a teacher, BṛĀrUp. vi.

Jāyanteya, m. metron. fr. *jayantī*, BhP. v, xi.

जायमान *jāyamāna*, mfn. pr. p. √*jan*, q. v.

Jāyam-pati, m. du. (formed after *dám-p°*) = °*yā-p°*, Kāṭh. vi, 4; (cf. °*yām-patika.*)

Jāyā́, f. 'bringing forth (cf. Mn. ix, 8),' a wife, RV.; AV.; ŚBr. &c.; (in astron.) the 7th lunar mansion, VarBṛ.; Laghuj. i, 15. **-ghna**, mfn. a wife-murderer, Pāṇ. iii, 2, 52; m. a mole indicative of a wife's death, 53, Kāś. **-°jīva** (°*yâj°*), mfn. 'earning a living by his wife,' a dancer, L.; cf. Mn. viii, 362. **-tva**, n. the character or attributes of a wife, ix, 8; MBh. i, 3024. **-°nujīvin** (°*yân°*), m. = *-°jīva*, L.; the husband of a harlot, L.; a pauper, L.; the crane Ardea nivea, L.; = *āśvina*, L. **-patī**, m. du. (g. *rājadantâdi*) wife and husband, ŚBr. iv, 6, 7, 9; Kapishṭh. iv, 3; Āp.; Divyâv. xviii, 583. **-m-patika**, n. sg. id., 585 & 592; cf. °*yam-patī*.

जायल *jāyala*, m. pl. = *jājala*, Caraṇ.

जाया *jāyā́*. See above.

जायान्य *jāyā́nya*, m. a kind of disease, AV. vii, 76, 3 ff.; xix, 44, 2; (*jāyénya*, TS. ii, 3 & 5.)

जायिन् *jāyin*, mfn. (√*ji*) ifc. conquering, subduing, ŚBr. xiv; MBh. iii; m. N. of a Dhruvaka.

Jāyú, mfn. = °*yuka*, RV. i, 67, 1; 119, 3 & 135, 8; m. a medicine, Uṇ. i, $\frac{1}{2}$; a physician, ib.

Jā́yuka, mfn. victorious, MaitrS. iii, 1, 9.

जायेन्य *jāyénya*. See *jāyā́nya*.

जार 1. *jā́ra*, mfn. (√*jṛī*) becoming old, RV. x, 106, 7; (°*rá*) m. (= *jarayitṛi*, 'a consumer,' Nir. v, x; Pāṇ. iii, 3, 20, Vārtt. 4) a paramour, lover, RV. (Agni is called 'paramour of the dawn;' also 'of the waters,' i, 46, 4; 'of his parents,' x, 11, 6; &c.); VS.; TBr. i; Lāṭy. i, 4, 4; a confidential friend, RV. x, 7, 5 & 42, 2; a paramour of a married woman, ŚBr. xiv; Lāṭy. i; Yājñ. &c. (ifc. f. *ā*, Rājat. vi, 321; Hit.); (*ī*), f. N. of Durgā, L.; of a plant, L. **-garbha**, m. a child by a paramour, bastard, Nār. (Parāś. i, $\frac{38}{39}$, 1, 31); (*ā*), f. (a woman) pregnant by a paramour, ib. (v. l.) **-ghnī**, f. (a woman) who has killed her paramour, ŚāṅkhGṛ. i, 16, 4; PārGṛ. i, 11, 3. **-ja**, m. = *-garbha*, Pañcat. Introd. 6; Mn. iii, $\frac{158}{159}$. **-janman**, m. id., Bhām. iv, 46. **-jāta**, m. id., VarYogay. iv, 47; a plagiarist. **-jātaka**, mfn. begotten by a paramour, Mn. ix, 143; m. a plagiarist. **-tā**, f. a love-affair with (in comp.), Daś. vii, 64. **-dvaya**, n. a couple of paramours. **-bharā**, f. (g. *pacâdi*) an adulteress, W.

2. **Jāra**, m. (fr. *jara*) patr. of Vṛiśa, RAnukr.

Jāraka, mfn. causing decay, W.; digestive, W.

Jāraṇa, n. causing decay, W.; condiment, a digester, W.; oxydizing of metals; (*ā*), f. id., Sarvad. ix, 33; (*ī*), f. a kind of cumin-seed, L.

Jāratineya, m. patr. fr. Jaratin, g. *śubhrâdi*; metron. fr. Jaratī, g. *kalyāṇy-ādi*. **Jāratkāravá**, m. (g. *śivâdi*) patr. fr. Jaratkāru, ŚBr. xiv, 6, 2.

Jāradgava, mf(*ī*)n. with *vīthi* = *jaradgava-v°*, VarBṛS. ix, 3. **Jāradvṛiksha**, mfn. fr. *jar°*, Pāṇ. iv, 3, 156, Vārtt. 3, Pat. **Jāramāṇa**, n. a kind of dance. **Jāramāṇya**, m. patr. fr. *jar°*, g. *gargâdi.*

Jāraya, Nom. (aor. Pass. °*yâyi*) to cherish, RV. vi, 12, 4. **Jārayán-makha**, mfn.? performing sacrifices (Sāy.; 'm. N. of a man,' Gmn.), x, 172, 2.

Jārāsaṃdhi, m. (fr. *jarā-saṃdha*) patr. of Saha-deva, MBh. ii, v ff. **Jāriṇī**, f. a woman who has a paramour, RV. x, 34, 5. **Jāru-ja**, mfn. = *jarāyu-ja*, AitUp. v, 3. **Jārya**, n. (fr. *jārá*) intimacy, RV. v, 64, 2 ['mfn. to be praised,' fr. √3. *jṛi*, Sāy.]

जारुधि *jārudhi*, m. N. of a mountain, BhP

Jārūthi, f. N. of a town, MBh. iii, 489 (= Hariv. 9136); R. vi, 109, 50.

Jārūthya, mfn. (said of the Aśva-medha) 'in which 3 kinds of Dakshiṇā are given,' or 'rich in meat or in donations of meat (*jārutha*),' MBh. iii, 16601; vii, 2232; xii, 952; Hariv. 2344; R. vi, 113, 10; m. N. of a prince of Ayodhyā, Hcar. vi.

जार्तिक *jārtika*, v. l. for *jart°*.

जार्य *jārya*. See above.

जार्यक *jāryaka*, for *jāhaka*, Rājat. v, 321.

जाल 1. *jāla*, mfn. watery, MBh. iii, 11967.

जाल 2. *jāla*, n. a net (for catching birds, fish &c.), AV. viii, x; KātyŚr.; PārGṛ. &c.; a hair-net, Āp.; a net (fig.), snare, Yājñ. iii, 119; MBh. iii, 25; R. v; Bhartṛ. &c.; (in anat.) the omentum, Bhpr. ii, 310; a cob-web, W.; any reticulated or woven texture, wire-net, mail-coat, wire-helmet, MBh. v ff.; Hariv.; Kum. vii, 59; a lattice, eyelet, R. iii, 61, 13; VarBṛS. lvi, 22; a lattice-window, Mn. viii, 132; Yājñ. i, 361; Vikr. &c.; 'the web or membrane on the feet of water-birds,' see *-pāda*; the finger- and toe-membrane of divine beings and godlike personages, Śak. vii, 16; lion's mane, Kathās. lxxv; a bundle of buds, W.; (chiefly ifc.) collection, multitude, MBh. &c.; deception, illusion, magic, Daś. viii, 42; Kathās. xxiv, 199; pride, W.; for *jāta*, kind, species, ŚvetUp. v, 3; R. ii; m. (g. *jvalâdi*) Nauclea Cadamba, L.; a small cucumber, L., Sch.; (*ī*), f. a kind of cucumber, L.; cf. *áyo-*, *indra-*, *giri-*, *bṛihaj-*. **-karman**, n. 'net-occupation,' fishing, MBh. xiii, 2653. **–kāra**, m. 'web-maker,' a spider, Kathās. lxx, ci. **–kāraka**, m. id., lxx. **–kīṭa**, m. N. of an Udīcya-grāma, g. *palady-ādi;* mfn., ib. **–kshīrya**, n. N. of a plant with a poisonous juice, Suśr. v, 2, 8. **–gardabha**, m. a kind of pimple, ii, 13, 12; iv, 20, 5. **–gavâksha**, m. a lattice-window, Kathās. **–gavâkshaka**, m. id., VarBṛS. lvi, 22; (ifc.) Kathās. lxxxvi. **–goṇikā**, f. a kind of churning-vessel, L. **–daṇḍá**, m. a net-pole, AV. viii, 8, 5 & 12. **–pad** (nom. *pād*), m. 'web-footed,' a goose, L. **–pada**, N. of a locality, g. *varaṇâdi* (v.l. °*dī*); mfn., ib.; (*ī*), f. of *-pāda*, g. *kumbhapady-ādi*. **–pāda**, m. (g. *hasty-ādi*) a web-footed bird (goose &c.), Gaut.; Mn. v, 13; Yājñ. i, 174; Hariv. 8610; Daś.: VarP.; N. of a magician, Kathās. xxvi, 196; *-bhuja*, mfn. having toe- and finger-membranes, MBh. xii, 13339. **–pāśa**, m. pl. the single woven lines of a cob-web, Kathās. lxx. **–pura**, n. N. of a town, lvi. **–prāyā**, f. 'chiefly wire-net,' chain-armour, L. **–baddha**, mfn. caught in a net. **–bandha**, m. a snare, Caṇḍ. ii, 2. **–mālā**, f. a net. **–vat**, mfn. furnished with a net, Suśr. i, 23, 7 (ifc.); Kathās. lx; covered with iron net-work, MBh. vi, 747; furnished with lattice-windows, Ragh. vii, 5; cunning, deceptive, ŚvetUp. iii, 1. **–varvurika**, °**rvūraka**, m. a kind of Varvūra plant, L. **–sarasa**, n. (*saras*)?, Vop. vi, 45 & 51. **–hāsinī**, f. N. of a wife of Kṛishṇa, Hariv. 9179 (v.l. *cāru-h*°). **Jālâksha**, a lattice-window, BhP. viii, 15, 19. **Jālâṅgulika**, mfn. =°*la-pāda-bhuja*, Lalit. vii, 445. **Jālâmukha**, =°*lâksha*, BhP. x, 41, 22. **Jālâvanaddha**, mfn. =°*lâṅgulika*, Divyâv. iii, 18.

Jālaká, n. a net, woven texture, web (also fig., 'a multitude,' e.g. of tears running down the cheeks &c.), ŚBr. xiv, 6, 11, 3; R.; Suśr.; Śak.; Ragh.; Ṛitus.; (ifc.) Kathās.; a lattice, eyelet, Pañcat. iii, 7, 40; a lattice-window (m., L.), Śiś. ix, 39; a bundle of buds, Megh.; Mālav. v, 4; 'a kind of pearl-ornament,' see *-mālin;* a nest, L.; a plantain, L.; illusion, L.; pride, L.; m. N. of a tree, BhP. viii, 2, 18; 1. (*ikā*), f. a net (for catching birds &c.), Kathās. lxi; (cf. *mṛiga-jālikā*); a veil, ŚāṅkhGṛ. i, 14, 1 2/3; a kind of cloth or raiment, W.; chain-armour, R. iii, 28, 26; a spider, L.; plantain, L.; a multitude, Kād. iv, 145; a widow, L.; iron, W.; =*komāsikā*, L. **–gardabha**, m. =°*la-g*°, Car. vi, 17, 92. **–mālin**, mfn. adorned with a kind of pearl-ornament ('veiled,' W.), BhP. viii, 20, 17.

Jālakita, mfn. covered with (in comp.) as with a net, Hcar. viii. **Jālakinī**, f. an ewe, L. **Jālāya**, Nom. °*yate*, to form a net-like enclosure, Gīt. iv, 10.

Jālika, mf(*ī*)n. deceptive, m. a cheat, g. *parpâdi;* m. (g. *vetanâdi*) 'living on his net,' a bird-catcher, Caṇḍ. ii, 2; a spider, L.; =*grāma-jālin*, L.

Jālin, mfn. having a net, W.; retiform, W.; having a window, W.; deceptive, W.; (*inī*), f. (scil. *piḍakā*) N. of certain boils appearing in the Prameha disease, Car. i, 17, 80 & 83; Suśr. ii, 6, 8 & 10; a species of melon (having a reticulated rind), ib.; a painted room or one ornamented with pictures, L. **Jālinī-mukha**, m. N. of a mountain, Kāraṇḍ.

Jālya, mfn. liable to be caught in a net, MBh. xii.

जालकि *jālaki*, v.l. for *jānaki*, q.v.

जालंधर *jālaṃdhara*, m. = *jal*°, N. of an Asura, PadmaP. v, 141 f.; =°*ri*, Ṭoḍ.; a kind of Mudrā, Haṭhapr. iii, 6; pl. N. of the 12 Ādityas when born as men, Vīrac. xxviii; N. of a people (= *tri-garta*, L.), Romakas.; Rājat. iv, 177; viii, 1653; Ratnak.; n. N. of a Tīrtha, MatsyaP. xiii, 46.

Jālaṃdharāyaṇa, patr. fr. *jalaṃ-dhara*, g. *naḍâdi*. °**rāyaṇaka**, mfn. inhabited by the Jālaṃdharāyaṇas, g. *rājanyâdi*. °**ri**, m. N. of a physician.

Jālahrada, m. patr. fr. *jala-h*°, g. *śivâdi*.

जालमानि *jālamāni*, m. pl. N. of a subdivision of the Tri-garta people, Pāṇ. v, 3, 116, Kāś.

Jālamānīya, m. a prince of that people, ib.

जालाष *jālāshá*, n. (fr. *jál*°) a particular drug with soothing qualities, AV. vi, 57, 2.

जालिका 2. *jālikā*, f. =*jal*°, W.

जालीदेश *jālī-deśa*, m. N. of a country, Ratnak.

जालूक *jālūka*, mfn. composed by Jaluka(?) or relating to leeches (*jalūkā*), Pāṇ. iv, 3, 101, Pat.

जालोर *jālora*, m. N. of an Agra-hāra, Rājat. i, 98.

जाल्म *jālma*, mf(*ī*)n. contemptible, vile (livelihood), MBh. v, 4518; xii, 3897; cruel (*krūra*), L.; inconsiderate, L.; (*ás, ī*), m. f. a despised or contemptible man or woman, wretch, AV. iv, 16, 7; xii, 4, 51; ŚāṅkhBr. xxx, 5; Lāṭy.; Vikr. &c. (ifc., Gaṇar. on Pāṇ. ii, 1, 53).

Jālmaka, mfn. despised (a man), MBh. vii, 9023.

जाल्य *jālya*. See col. 1.

जावड *jāvaḍa*, m. N. of a man, Śatr. xiv.

जावत् *jā-vat*, *-van*. See *jā*.

जावनिका *jāvanikā*, f. =*jav*°, a curtain, screen, HPariś. ix, 45.

Jāvanya, n. (fr. *jávana*) swiftness, g. *dṛiḍhâdi*.

Jāvāyani, fr. *jáva*, g. *karṇâdi*.

जाषक *jāshaka*, v.l. for *jāyaka*, q.v.

जाष्कमद *jāshkamadá*, m. a kind of animal, AV. xi, 9, 9.

जासट *jāsaṭa*, m. N. of two men, Rājat. vii, 1525; viii, 540 ff.

जास्पति *jās-pati*, °*tyá*. See *jā*.

जाह *jāha*, n. ifc. (g. 2. *karṇâdi*) the root or point of issue of certain parts of the body, cf. *akshi-*, (*āsya-*), *oshṭha-*, *karṇa-*, *keśa-*, *gulpha-*, *danta-*, *nakha-*, *pāda-*, *pṛishṭha-*, *bhrū-*, *mukha-*.

जाहक *jāhaka*, m. (=*jáhakā*) a hedge-hog, VarBṛS. lxxxvi, 42; Hcar. vii; a chameleon, L.; a leech, L.; a bed, L.

जाहुष *jāhushá*, m. N. of a man protected by the Aśvins, RV. i, 116, 20; vii, 71, 5.

जाह्नव *jāhnava*, m. (fr. *jahnu*) patr. of Viśvā-mitra, TāṇḍyaBr. xxi, 12; of Su-ratha, BhP. ix, 22, 9; N. of a Catur-aha, Maś. vii, 7; (*ī*), f. 'daughter of Jahnu (q.v.),' the Gaṅgā, MBh. iii, v, xiii (metrically °*vi*, 7680); Bhag.; Hariv. &c.

Jāhnavīya, mfn. belonging or relating to the Ganges, MBh. xiii, 1857; Ragh. x, 27.

जि 1. *ji*, cl. 1. *jáyati*, °*te* (impf. *ájayat;* aor. *ajaishīt*, Ved. *djais*, 1. pl. *djaishma*, *jéshma*, 2. sg. *jes* & Ā. *jéshi*, Subj. *jéshat*, °*shas*, °*shāma*, RV.; aor. Ā. *ajeshṭa;* fut. 1st. *jétā*, RV. &c.; fut. 2nd. *jeshyáti*, x, 34, 6 &c.; pf. *jigā́ya* [Pāṇ. vii, 3, 57], *jigetha*, *jigyur;* p. *jigīvás* [°*givás*, TS. i, 7, 8, 4; acc. pl. °*gyúshas*], RV. &c.; Inf. *jishé*, i, 111, 4 & 112, 12; *jétave*, TBr. ii; Class. *jetum:* Pass. *jīyate*, *ajīyata* [Ragh. xi, 65], *ajāyi*, *jāyishyate;* for *jīyate* & cl. 9. *jināti*, see √*jyā*) to win or acquire (by conquest or in gambling), conquer (in battle), vanquish (in a game or lawsuit), defeat, excel, surpass, RV. &c. (with *púnar*, 'to reconquer,' TS. vi, 3, 1, 1); to conquer (the passions), overcome or remove (any desire or difficulties or diseases), Mn.; MBh. &c.; to expel from (abl.), ŚBr. iii, 6, 1, 17; to win anything (acc.) from (acc.), vanquish any one (acc.) in a game (acc.), ŚBr. iii, 6, 1, 28; xiv, 6, 8, 1 & 12; MBh. iii; Daś.; Pāṇ. i, 4, 51; Siddh.; to be victorious, gain the upper hand, RV.; AV.; ŚBr. iii; MuṇḍUp.; Mn. vii, 201; MBh.; often pr. in the sense of an Impv. 'long live!' 'glory to,' Śak.; VarBṛS.; Laghuj.; Bhartṛ. &c.: Caus. *jāpayati* (Pāṇ. vi, 1, 48 & vii, 3, 36) to cause to win, VS. ix, 11 f.; (aor. 2. pl. *djījipata* & *djījap*°) TS. i, 7, 8, 4 & ŚBr. v, 1, 5, 11 f.; ĀśvŚr. ix, 9; to conquer, MBh. vii, 66, 6 (aor. *ajījayat*): Pass. *jāpyate*, to be made to conquer, W.: Desid. *jigīshati*, °*te* (Pāṇ. vii, 3, 57; p. °*shat*, °*shamāṇa*) to wish to win or obtain or conquer or excel, AV. xi, 5, 18; TS. ii; ŚBr.; ŚāṅkhŚr.; MBh. &c.; (Ā.) to seek for prey, RV. x, 4, 3: Intens. *jejīyate*, Pāṇ. vii, 3, 57, Kāś.

2. **Ji**, mfn. conquering, L.; m. a Piśāca, L.

Jigīshā́, f. desire of obtaining, (°*shā́*, Ved. instr.) RV. i, 171, 3 & 186, 4; MBh. iii, 13360; desire of conquering or being victorious, military ambition, i, v; Ragh. xv, 45; BhP. iii, 18; =°*shu-tā*, Kathās. xv, 7 & xxi, 81 (ifc.); Rājat.; eminence, W.; profession or habit of life, W. **Jigīshôtsāha-vat**, mfn. connected with ambition and earnest will, L.

Jigīshita, mfn. wished to be obtained, ŚāṅkhBr.

Jigīshú, mfn. wishing to obtain or gain, seeking for, RV. ii, 38, 6; MBh. i, 6845; BhP. iv, 8, 37; striving to conquer or excel, ambitious, R. i, 13, 21; BhP. &c.; m. N. of a man, g. *gargâdi*. **–tā**, f. desire of excelling, ambition, Kathās. xviii, 85.

Jigyú, mfn. victorious, RV. i, 101, 6.

Jit, mfn. ifc. (Pāṇ. iii, 2, 61) winning, acquiring, cf. *go-* & *svar-jít*, *svarga-*, &c.; conquering, cf. *abhimāti-jít*, *śatru-*, &c.; (in med.) removing, cf. *kāsa-* &c. **–** 1. **-tama**, mfn. ifc., see *svarga-* &c.

Jitá, mfn. won, acquired, conquered, subdued, RV. viii, 76, 4; AV. &c.; overcome or enslaved by (in comp., e.g. *kāma-*, 'under the dominion of lust'), Mn. &c.; given up, discontinued, Mn. iv, 181. **–kāśi**, mfn. the doubled fist, MBh. i, 2, 309, Sch. **–kāśin**, mfn., see s.v. *kāśin*. **–kopa**, mfn. one who has subdued anger. **–krodha**, mfn. id., Mn. viii, 173; R. i, iii. **–klama**, mfn. one who has overcome the sense of fatigue, MBh. **–tara**, mfn. more vanquished, x, 555. **–nemi**, m. a staff made of the wood of the sacred fig-tree (carried during the performance of certain vows), L. **–manas** (°*tá-*), mfn. one who has subdued his heart, MaitrS. i, 10, 16 (Kāṭh. x, 10). **–manyu**, mfn. =*-kopa;* m. Vishṇu, L. **–loka** (°*tá-*), mfn. pl. those who have conquered heaven (a class of manes), ŚBr. xiv, 7, 1, 33 f. **–vatī**, f. 'Victrix,' N. of a daughter of Uśīnara, MBh. i, 3940. **–vrata**, m. 'having overcome his vow,' N. of a son of Havir-dhāna, BhP. iv, 24, 8. **–śatru**, m. '=°*tâmitra*,' N. of a Buddha, Lalit. i, 77; of a king, Jain. (e.g. HPariś. iii, 45; xiii, 181); of the father of the Arhat A-jita, L. **–śiśnôdara**, mfn. one who has overcome lust (lit. the membrum virile) and his appetite (lit. belly), MBh. xiii, 5341. **–śrama**, mfn. one who has trained himself to bear toil, accustomed to fatigues, Hariv. 4544; Cāṇ. **–śvāsa**, mfn. one who has gained power over the act of breathing, BhP. ii, 1, 23. **–saṅga**, mfn. one who has overcome worldly attachments, ib. **–svarga**, mfn. =*-loka*. **–hasta**, mfn. one who has exercised his hand, Car. iii, 8. **Jitâksha**, mfn. one who has subdued his senses, calm, Cāṇ. **Jitâkshara**, mfn. 'one who has mastered his letters,' writing well, Cāṇ. **Jitâtman**, mfn. self-subdued, MBh.; Pañcat. ii, 4, 9/10; (*a-*, neg.) Mn. vii, 34; m. N. of one of the Viśve-devās, MBh. xiii, 4356. **Jitâmitra**, mfn. one who has conquered his enemies, triumphant, MārkP. xxxiv, 113; m. Vishṇu, L. **Jitâri**, m. (=°*ta-śatru*) N. of a Buddha, L.; of a son of Avikshit, MBh. i, 3741; of the father of the Arhat Śam-bhava, L. **Jitâśva**, m. 'one who can subdue horses,' N. of a prince, VP. iv, 5, 12 (v.l.) **Jitâshṭamī**, f.=*jīmūtâshṭ*°, W. **Jitâsana**, mfn. one who has given up using seats, BhP. ii, 1, 23. **Jitâhava**, mfn. one who has won a battle, L. **Jitâhāra**, mfn. one who has overcome the desire for food, TejobUp. 3. **Jitêndriya**, mfn. =°*tâksha*, Mn. ii, vi f.; R. i; m. an ascetic, W.; N. of a man (author of a Nibandha); *-tva*, n. subjugation of the senses, Kpr. vii, 11/12 (and x, 34, Sch.); °*driyâhva*, m. N. of a shrub, L.

Jiti, f. gaining, obtaining, victory, RV. x, 53, 11; AV. x, 6, 16; ŚBr.; AitBr. i, 24; KātyŚr. xix, 5, 4; Lāṭy. v, 4, 19; ŚāṅkhŚr.; KaushUp.; *a-jitasya j*°, N. of a Sāman, ĀrshBr.; cf. *purô-*.

Jitya, mfn. conquerable, W.; m. =*hali*, Pāṇ. iii, 1, 117; (*ā*), f. ifc. 'victory,' see *āji-;* *vāja-jityā*.

Jítvan, mfn. victorious (cf. *sa-jítvan*), Uṇ. iv, 112/113; m. (g. *karṇâdi*) N. of a man, ŚBr. xiv, 6, 10, 5.

Jitvara, mf(*ī*, Pāṇ. iii, 2, 163; cf. *sa-jitvarī*)n. ifc. overcoming, Car. vi, 5, 95; (*ī*), f. 'Victrix,' the city of Benares, Pāṇ. iv, 3, 84, Pat.

जिकन *jikana*, m. N. of a lawyer, Prāyaśc.; Smṛitit. i, iv.

जिगत्नु *jigatnú*, mfn. (√*gam*, redupl.) going quickly, fleet, RV. vii, ix f.; m. breath, Uṇ. iii, 31/32.

Jigamishā, f. intention to go, W.

Jigamishu, mfn. intending to go, MBh.; R. &c.

जिगरिषु *jigarishu*, mfn. (√2. *gṛī*, Desid.) desirous of swallowing, W.

Jigarti, m. a swallower, RV. v, 29, 4.

जिगीषा *jigīshā*, °*shú*, *jigyú*. See cols. 2, 3.

जिघत्नु *jighatnú*, mfn. (√*han*, redupl.) endeavouring to hurt, ii, 30, 9.

जिघत्सा *jighatsā*, f. (√*ghas*, Desid.) desire of eating or consuming, Kathās. lxi; cf. *vi-jighatsā́*.

Jighatsú, mfn. hungry, L.; desirous of consuming, cviii, 106; Bhaktâm. 36; f. N. of an evil demon, AV. ii, 14, 1; (pl.) viii, 2, 20.

जिघांसक *jighāṉsaka*, mfn. (√*han*, Desid.) intending to kill, W.

Jighāṇsā, f. wish or intention to strike or slay or destroy, Mn. xi, 207; MBh. &c.; malice, revenge, W.

Jighāṇsin, mfn. ifc. intending to kill, R. vi, 77.

Jighāṇsīyas, mfn. compar. of °*ṇsu*, W.

Jighāṇsu, mfn. = °*sin* (with acc.), MBh. i, iii; R.; BhP.; Daś.; Kathās.; desirous of destroying or ruining (ifc. or with acc.), Lāṭy. i, 10, 3; Suśr. i, 19, 21; revengeful, W.; m. an enemy, W.

जिघृक्षा *jighṛikshā*, f. (√*grah*, Desid.) wish or intention to take or seize, MBh. vii, 794; Gṛihyās. ii, 27 (v.l.); Ragh. ix, 46; BhP. x, 62, 34.

Jighṛikshu, mfn. (ifc. or with acc.) intending to take or seize, MBh. iv, viii; Hariv. 6463; Śak. i, $\frac{33}{34}$ (v.l.); BhP. x; wishing to rob, MBh. ii, 1952; wishing to take up (water, *jala-*), Pañcat. iii, 12, $\frac{6}{7}$; wishing to gather, MBh. i, 3373; wishing to learn, 5240. **—tā**, f. intention of robbing, Uttamac. 102.

जिघ्र *jighra*, mfn. (√*ghrā*) smelling, Pāṇ. iii, 1, 137; ifc. observing, conjecturing, Sāh. iii, $\frac{8}{9}$.

जिङ्गशल्य *jiṅga-śalya*, = *jihma-ś*°, W.

Jiṅgiṇī, f. = °*ginī*, Car. iii, 8, 3.

Jiṅginī, f. (= *jhiṅg*°) Odina Wodier, Bhpr. v.

Jiṅgī, f. id., ib.; Rubia Munjista, v, 1, 189.

जिजीविषा *jijīvishā*, f. (√*jīv*, Desid.) desire to live, MBh. viii, 1790.

Jijīvishu, mfn. desirous of life, Mn.; MBh. &c.

Jijīshu, mfn. (irr.) id., iii, 14905. **Jijyūshita**, mfn. wishing to live by (instr.), AitBr. vii, 29.

जिज्ञापयिषु *jijñāpayishu*, mfn. (√*jñā*, Caus. Desid.) wishing to make known, Bhaṭṭ. ix, 37.

Jijñāsaka, mfn. (√*jñā*, Desid.) = °*su*, W.

Jijñāsana, n. desire of knowing, investigation, Kathās. v, 136. **Jijñāsanīya**, mfn. = °*sitavya*, W.

Jijñāsā, f. = °*sana*, MBh. ii f., xiii; Hariv.; R.; Pāṇ. i, 3, 21, Vārtt. 3, &c. (*kṛita-jijñāsa*, mfn. having put to the proof any one [gen.], Kathās. cxiii, 78). **—prastāva**, m. N. of a work, Pratāpar., Sch.

Jijñāsita, mfn. investigated, inquired, BhP. i, 5, 3 f.; tested, MBh. xiii, 932.

Jijñāsitavya, mfn. to be investigated, Sarvad.

Jijñāsu, mfn. desirous of knowing, inquiring into, examining, testing, MBh.; R.; BhP. &c.

Jijñāsya, mfn. = °*sitavya*, BhP. ii, 9; Sarvad.

Jijñu, mfn. = °*jñāsu*, R. i, 9, 23.

जिडधन *jiḍadhana*, m. N. of a man.

जित् *jit*, *jitá*, *jíti*. See √*ji*.

जितुम *jituma*, m. (fr. δίδυμοι) the sign Gemini, VarBṛ. i, 8; xxiv, 9; Laghuj. xiii, 1.

2. **Jittama**, **jitma**, m. id., W.

जित्य *jitya*, *jitvan*, °*vara*. See √*ji*.

जिन 1. *jina*, mfn. (√*ji*) victorious, L.; m. 'Victor,' a Buddha, Buddh.; Kathās. lxxii, 99; an Arhat (or chief saint of the Jainas; 24 Jinas are supposed to flourish in each of the 3 Avasarpiṇīs, being born in Āryâvarta), Jain.; Pañcat. v, 1, $\frac{19}{20}$ ff.; VarBṛS. lx; Sarvad.; (hence) the number '24,' Hcat. i, 3, 919; metrically for *jaina*; Vishṇu, Śiś. xix, 112; N. of Hemac. (?); of a Bodhi-sattva; of a son of Yadu, KūrmaP. i, 22, 12. **—kalpa**, m. the ordinances practised by the Jinas (opposed to those of the Sthaviras), Jain. (HPariś. xi, 3). **—°kalpika**, mfn. observing the *jina-kalpa*, Śīl. **—kīrti**, m. N. of a Jain Sūri (author of Campak. and Namaskāra-stava). **—kuśala**, m. N. of a Jain Sūri (A.D. 1281–1333; author of Caitya-vandana-kula-vṛitti). **—candra**, m. N. of 8 Jain Sūris (1. predecessor of the famous Abhaya-deva, author of Saṃvega-raṅga-śālā-prakaraṇa; 2. A.D. 1141–67; 3. 1270–1320; 4. died 1359; 5. 1431–74; 6. 1539–1614; 7. died 1707; 8. 1753–1800). **—jyā**, f. the extent of 24 degrees, Gol. **—datta**, m. N. of a man, HPariś. xiii, 182; of a Jain Sūri (A.D. 1076–1155; teacher of Amara-candra and Jina-bhadra), Sarvad. iii, 269; *-kathā-samuccaya*, m. N. of a collection of tales by Bhadrâcārya; *-caritra*, n. N. of a work. **—dāsa**, m. N. of several men, HPariś. i–iii; of two Jain authors (1. author of a Cūrṇi on Āvaśyaka; 2. author of Dharma-pañcaviṇśatikā). **—deva**, m. an Arhat (of the Jainas), Pañcad. ii, 6; N. of the author of Madana-parājaya. **—dharma**, m. the doctrine of Jina (Mahā-vīra), MatsyaP. xxiv, 47; HYog. iii, 139; N. of a work. **—pati**, m. N. of a Jain Sūri (A.D. 1154–1221; author of several works). **—padma**, m. N. of a Jain Sūri (died A.D. 1350). **—putra**, m. N. of a Bodhi-sattva, Buddh. L. **—prabodha**, m. N. of a Jain Sūri (A.D. 1229–85; author of Pañjikā-durga-pada-prabodha). **—prabha**, m. N. of a Jain Sūri (author of several works). **—bimba-pratishṭhā**, f. 'erection of Jina figures,' N. of a work by Pādalipta-sūri. **—bhakti**, m. N. of a Jain Sūri (A.D. 1714–48). **—bhadra**, m. N. of a famous Jain author (also called °*dra-gaṇi-kshamāśramaṇa*); of the author of a tale (composed A.D. 1148); of a Jain Sūri (died A.D. 1458). **—maṇḍana**, m. N. of the author of Kumārapāla-prabandha. **—māṇikya**, m. N. of a Jain Sūri (A.D. 1493–1556; author of Subāhu-purāṇa). **—mitra**, m. N. of one of the translators of Lalit. **—yajña-kalpa**, m. N. of a work by Āśā-dhara. **—yoni**, m. for *ajin*°, W. **—rakshita**, m. N. of a man, Kathās. lxvii, 76. **—ratna**, m. N. of a Jain Sūri (died A.D. 1655). **—rāja**, m. N. of a Jain Sūri (A.D. 1591–1643; author of a Comm. on Naish.) **—rshi** (*ṛishi*), m. a Jain ascetic, Sarvad. iii, 279. **—labdhi**, m. N. of a Jain Sūri (died A.D. 1350). **—lābha**, m. N. of a Jain Sūri (A.D. 1728–78; author of Ātma-prabodha). **—vaktra**, m. N. of a Buddha, Lalit. i, 71. **—vardhana**, m. N. of the founder of the 5th subdivision of the Kharatara-gaccha of the Jain community (died A.D. 1458; author of Candraprabha-caritra and 4 other Caritras). **—vallabha**, m. N. of a famous Jain author (died A.D. 1111). **—vimala**, m. N. of the author of Śabda-prabheda-ṭīkā (composed A.D. 1598 or 1638?). **—vṛitta**, n. a circle drawn with a radius of 24 degrees and having a pole of the ecliptic for its centre, Gol. **—śataka**, n. N. of a work by Jambu-kavi. **—śata-pañjikā**, f. N. of a work by Samba-sādhu. **—śāsana**, n. the doctrine of Buddha, Rājat. i, 102. **—śekhara**, m. N. of the founder of the 2nd subdivision of the Kharatara-gaccha of the Jain community. **—śrī**, m. N. of a king, Kāraṇḍ.[2] **—sadman**, m. a Jain monastery, L. **—samudra**, m. N. of a Jain Sūri (A.D. 1450–99). **—sahasra-nāma-stotra**, n. N. of a work. **—sāgara**, m. N. of a scholiast on an anthology called Karpūra. **—siṇha**, m. N. of the founder of the 3rd subdivision of the Kharatara-gaccha of the Jain community; of a Jain Sūri (A.D. 1559–1618). **—sena**, m. N. of the author of Trivarṇâcāra-saṃhitā, Harivaṇśa- & Trishashṭilakshaṇa-Purāṇa (completed by Guṇa-bhadra). **—saukhya**, m. N. of a Jain Sūri (A.D. 1683–1724). **—stuti**, f. N. of a poem. **—haṇsa**, m. N. of a Jain Sūri (A.D. 1468–1526; author of a gloss on the 1st Aṅga). **—harsha**, m. N. of the author of Vicārâmṛita-saṃgraha; of a Jain Sūri (consecrated A.D. 1800). **Jinâṇśa-jyā**, f. = °*na-j*°, Gol. **Jinâṅkura**, m. N. of a Bodhi-sattva, Buddh. L. **Jinâdi-vijaya**, m. N. of the author of a gloss on the 3rd Upâṅga (of the Jainas). **Jinâdhāra**, m. N. of a Bodhi-sattva, Buddh. L. **Jinêndra**, m. a Buddha, L.; a Jain saint, Pārśvan.; N. of a grammarian (also called °*dra-buddhi*), author of a treatise called Nyāsa; cf. Śiś. ii, 112; Uṇ. iv, $\frac{143}{144}$; *-caritra*, n. N. of a work by Amara-candra (also called Padmânanda-mahākāvya); *-buddhi*, see before. **Jinêśa**, m. an Arhat (of the Jainas), Kalyāṇam. 15; Pañcad. ii, 6. **Jinêśvara**, m. id., Kalyāṇam. 1; N. of an Arhat (of the Jainas), L.; of two Jain Sūris (1. founding the Kharatara-gaccha A.D. 1024; 2. A.D. 1189–1275). **Jinôttama**, m. = °*nêśa*, HYog. iv, 91. **Jinôdaya**, m. N. of a Jain Sūri (A.D. 1319–76). **Jinôrasa**, m. N. of a Bodhi-sattva, Buddh. L.

Jinana, n. (√*ji*, cl. 9) conquering, Pañcad. i, 38.

जिन 2. *jina*, mfn. (for *jīna* or *jīrṇa*) very old, Uṇ. iii, $\frac{2}{3}$.

जिन्दुराज *jindu-rāja*, m. N. of a man, Rājat. vii, 265 (°*jya*); 271 f.; 370 & 564.

जिन्व् *jinv*, cl. 1. P. *jínvati* (rarely Ā., RV. iii, 2, 11 & [1. sg. °*nvé*] iv, 21, 8; Impv. °*nvatāt*, AV. x, 6, 34; p. °*nvat*; pf. 3. du. *jijinvá-thur*) to move one's self, be active or lively (Naigh. ii, 14), RV.; AV.; to urge on, cause to move quickly, impel, incite, RV.; AV.; ŚāṅkhŚr. viii; to refresh, animate, RV.; VS.; AV.; AitBr. vii, 9; ŚāṅkhŚr. vii; to promote, help, favour, RV.; AV.; to help any one (acc.) to anything (dat.), RV.; KātyŚr. xvii; to receive favourably (prayers or acts of devotion), RV. i, 157; vii f.; x: Caus. (*jinvayati*) v.l. for √*juñc*, q.v.; cf. *ā-*, *pra-*, & *upa-pra-*.

Jinva, mfn. See *dhiyaṃ-jinvá*, *viśva-*.

जिम् *jim*, cl. 1. *jemati*, to eat, Dhātup.

Jimita, n. eating, Jain. Sch. (Prākṛit °*miya*).

Jemana, n. id., BhP. x, 14, 60 (ifc.)

Jemanaka, n. id., Jain.

जिम्भ *jimbha*, for *jṛimbha* (?), in comp. **—jihva-tā**, f. swelling of the tongue, Suśr. 2.

जिरण *jiraṇa*, m. = *jar*°, cumin, L.

जिरि *jiri*, cl. 5. P. °*riṇoti* (Pāṇ. viii, 2, 78, Kāś.) to hurt, Dhātup. xxvii, 31; (cf. *ciri*.)

जिर्वि *jírvi*. See *jívri*.

जिल्लिक *jillika*, m. pl. N. of a people, MBh. vi, 367 (v.l. *jhill*°).

जिवाजीव *jivājīva*, for *jīvaṃj*°, L.

जिव्रि *jívri*, mfn. (Pāṇ. viii, 2, 78, Vārtt. 1; √*jṛī*) old, worn out, decrepit, (du. °*vrī*) RV. i; iv, 19, 2 & 36, 3; viii, x; (Nir. iii, 21); AV. viii, 1, 6 & (*jírvi*) xiv, 1, 21; m. time, Uṇ. v, $\frac{4}{5}$?; a bird, ib.

जिष् *jish*, cl. 1. *jeshati*, to sprinkle, Dhātup.

जिषे *jishé*, Ved. Inf. √*ji*, q.v.

जिष्णु *jishṇú*, mfn. (√*ji*, Pāṇ. iii, 2, 139) victorious, triumphant, winning, RV.; AV.; VS. &c.; (with acc.) vanquishing, conquering, excelling, Bhartṛ. i, 5; Vop. v, 26; (ifc.) winning, conquering, MBh. vi, xiii; m. the sun, L.; Vishṇu, L.; Indra, L.; Arjuna (son of Pāṇḍu), MBh.; BhP. i; N. of a man, Rājat. vi, 155; of a son of Manu Bhautya, Hariv. 495; 'of Brahma-gupta's father,' see *-ja*; of a Vasu, W.; cf. *parā-*. **—gupta**, m. N. of a man. **—ja**, m. 'Jishṇu's son,' Brahma-gupta, Gaṇit. iv, 3, 20.

जिहान *jíhāna*, mfn. pr. p. √2. *hā*, q.v.

Jihānaka, m. the destruction of the world, L.

जिहासा *jihāsā*, f. (√3. *hā*, Desid.) desire of abandoning or giving up, BhP.; Sarvad. iii, 255.

Jihāsu, mfn. desirous of giving up, BhP.; Rājat.

जिहीति *jihīti*, m. pl. N. of a family, Pravar. i, 1 (vv. ll. *jah*°, °*hiti*).

जिहीरषा *jihīrashā*, °*rishu*. See °*rsh*°.

Jihīrshā, f. (√*hṛi*, Desid., Pāṇ. iii, 3, 102, Kāś.) ifc. desire of carrying, BhP. i, 7, 25; desire of seizing, x, 90, 10 (°*rashā*); desire of robbing, iv, 19, 23; wish to remove, iii, 1, 43; desire to carry off or ravish, Kām. iii, 22.

Jihīrshu, mfn. (with acc.) intending to bring, R. ii, 63, 36; wishing to carry off or rob or appropriate, Suparṇ. xx, 2 (°*rishu*); MBh.; Hariv. 14248; Rājat. vi, 106; desirous of removing, v, 401.

Jihīrshya, fut. p. p., Pāṇ. vi, 1, 185, Kāś.

जिह्नु *jihnu*, m. pl. N. of a country, iv, 2, 104, Vārtt. 28, Pat.

जिह्म *jihmá*, mf(ā)n. (Nir. viii, 15) oblique, transverse, athwart, RV. i f.; TS. ii; ŚBr. v; squinting (as the eye), i, 5; Suśr.; VarBṛS. &c.; with √*i* [ŚBr. iii, v; AitBr. v, 9], *gam*, *nir-ṛich* [AV. xii, 4, 53], 1. *as* [ŚBr. xi], to go irregularly, turn off from the right way, miss the aim (abl.); crooked, tortuous, curved, W.; morally crooked, deceitful, false, dishonest, Yājñ. ii, 165; MBh. &c.; slow, lazy, Naish. ii, 102; dim, dulled, Kir.; n. falsehood, dishonesty, PraśnUp. i, 16; MBh.; BhP. i, 14, 4; Tabernæmontana coronaria, L.; (*am*), ind. with √*car*, to miss one's aim, MBh. v, 7361; cf. *ā-*, *vi-*. **—ga**, mfn. = *-gati*, i, 982; moving slowly, L.; a snake, ŚārṅgP. xxii, 9; cf. *a-*. **—gati**, mfn. going tortuously (a snake), Ṛitus. i, 13. **—tā**, f. = *-tva*, W.; falsehood, dishonesty, Hariv. 7335; R. ii, 43, 2. **—tva**, n. crookedness, curvature, W. **—prêkshin**, mfn. squinting, MBh. xii, 6277. **—bāra** (°*má-*), mfn. having an aperture on one side, RV. i, 116, 9; viii, 40, 5. **—mīna**, mfn. appearing in the illusory shape of a fish, BhP. viii, 24, 61. **—mohana**, m. a frog, L. **—yodhin**, mfn. fighting unfairly, MBh. ix, 3366; m. Bhima (who struck an unfair blow at Dur-yodhana), W. **—śalya**, m. 'crooked-thorn,' Acacia Catechu, Dhanv. **—śiras**, mfn. oblique-headed, AitĀr. iii, 2, 4, 10. **—śī**, mfn. lying (athwart i.e.) on the ground, RV. i, 113, 5. **Jihmâksha**, mfn. 'crooked-eyed,' squinting, Suśr. vi, 60, 7. **Jihmâśin**, m. N. of a man, g. *śubhrâdi* (°*śina*, Kāś.) **Jihmêtara**, mfn. 'other than lazy,' not dull, Naish. iii, 63.

Jihmāya, Nom. °*yati*, to turn off from the right way, Nir. i, 11; °*yate*, to be oblique, Vait. x, 17; to be dull, hesitate (with inf.), Hcat. i, 1, 1.

Jihmita, mfn. made crooked, bent, curved, Mṛicch. ix, 12; dulled, obscured, Kād. ii, 157 (v. l. °*ma*).
Jihmī, ind. in comp. — **kara**, mfn. making crooked or oblique, W.; obscuring, W. — **karaṇa**, mfn 'obscuring,' see *candra-sūrya-jihmīkaraṇa-prabha*. — **kṛita**, mfn. made crooked, bent, bowed down (with fear &c.), W.; obscured, Lalit. ix, 17; xxi, 12. — √**bhū**, to be obscured, ix, 21.

जिह्लु *jihlu*, v.l. for °*hnu*.

जिह्व *jihvá*, mfn. (said of Agni) MaitrS. i, 3, 35 (for *yahvá* of Padap. & RV. iii, 2, 9); m. the tongue, Hariv. 6325 f.; (*ā́*), f. (= *juhū́*) id., RV.; AV. &c. (ifc. f. *ā*, MBh. iii, 16137; Hcat.); the tongue or tongues of Agni, i. e. various forms of flame (3 are named, RV. iii, 20, 2; generally 7, VS. xvii, 79; MuṇḍUp. i, 2, 4 [*kālī, karālī, mano-javā, su-lohitā, su-dhūmra-varṇā, sphuliṅginī, viśva-rūpī*]; Hemac.; cf. *saptá-jihva*; also identified with the 7 winds *pra-, ā-, ud-, sam-, vi-, pari-,* & *ni-vaha*); the tongue of a balance, Hcat. i, 5, 163; speech (Naigh. i, 11), RV. iii, 57, 5; the root of Tabernæmontana coronaria, L.; cf. *dvi-, mádhu-, su-; agni-jihvá* &c.; [cf. Lat. *lingua*; Goth. *tuggō*.]
Jihvaka, ifc. (f. *ikā*) the tongue, MBh. iii, 16137 (*a-*, 'tongueless,' f. N. of a Rākshasī); Hcat. i, 7, 279; m. a kind of fever, Śārṅg. Vaidyav.; (*ikā*), f. dimin. fr. °*hvā*, see *adho-, ali-, prati-; upa-jihv°*.
Jihvala, mfn. voracious, Śrāddhat.
Jihvā́, f., see °*hvá*. — **kātya**, m. 'voracious Kātya,' N. of a man, Pāṇ. i, 1, 73, Vārtt. 8. — °**gra** (°*vā́g°*), n. the tip of the tongue, VPrāt.; Suśr.; Hit. — **chedana**, n. cutting off of the tongue, Āp. ii, 27, 14. — **tala**, n. the surface of the tongue, Suśr. ii, 16, 36. — **nirlekhana**, a tongue-scraper, Ashṭāṅg. i, 2, 4. — **nirlekhanika**, id., Buddh. L. — **pa**, m. 'drinking with the tongue,' a dog, L.; a cat, L.; a tiger, L.; a panther or leopard, L.; a bear, L. — **prathana**, n. expansion or too great flattening of the tongue (defect in pronunciation), RPrāt. xiv, 7. — °**maya** (°*vā́m°*), m. a disease of the tongue, ŚārṅgS. vii, 133. — **mala**, n. the fur of the tongue, L. — **mūlá**, n. the root of the tongue, AV. i, 34, 2; Prāt.; Śikshā; Pāṇ. iv, 3, 62. — °**mūlīya**, mfn. (iv, 3, 62) belonging to or uttered from the root of the tongue (viz. *ṛi, ḷri*, the guttural class of consonants, but esp. the Visarga before *k* and *kh*), Prāt.; Pāṇ. viii, 3, 37, Vārtt. 1. — **rada**, m. 'having a tongue-like beak,' a bird, L. — **latā**, f. a long tongue, Hcar. v, 478; viii. — **lih**, m. 'licking with the tongue,' a dog, L. — **laulya**, n. greediness, Pañcat. i f. — **vat** (°*hvā́-*), m. 'having a (greedy) tongue,' N. of a man, ŚBr. xiv, 9, 4, 33. — **śalya**, for °*hma-ś°*. — **śodhana**, n. 'tongue-cleaning,' recitation of particular mystical syllables, Tantr. — **stambha**, m. stiffness of the tongue, ŚārṅgS. vii, 105. — °**svāda** (°*vā́s°*), m. 'tasting with the tongue,' licking, L. **Jihvôdbhava**, m. = °*hvā-mala*, Gal. **Jihvôllekhana**, n. scraping the tongue, W.; (*ī*), f. = °*hvā-nirlekhana*, W. **Jihvôllekhanikā**, f. = °*nī*, W.

जी *jī*, m. 'sir, mister, Mr.' (attached to names as a mark of respect), W.
Jīka, m. id. (in colophons); N. of a plant, Gal.

जीगर्त *jīgarta*. See *a-*.

जीत *jītá*, °*ti*, *jīna*. See √1. *jyā*.

जीमूत *jīmūta*, m. (g. *pṛishódarâdi*) a cloud, RV. vi, 75, 1; AV. xi, 5, 14; VS.; Kāṭh. &c.; a mountain, L.; the sun, MBh. iii, 152; Indra, L.; a nourisher, sustainer, L.; = °*taka*, Suśr. iv, 37, 25; Luffa fœtida or a similar plant, L.; Cyperus rotundus, L.; N. of a metre; of an ancient sage, MBh. v, 3843; of a wrestler, iv, 347; of a son of Vyoman or °ma, Hariv. 1991 f.; BhP. ix, 24, 4. — **ketu**, m. Śiva, VāmP. i; N. of a Vidyā-dhara prince, Kathās. xxii, 17; of the ancestor of a dynasty, Inscr. (A.D. 1095). — **mūla**, n. Curcuma Amhaldi or Zerumbet, L. — **varshin**, mfn. sending down rain from a (passing) cloud, AitBr. ii, 19. — **vāha**, m. N. of a man, SSaṃkar. xi, 21. — **vāhana**, m. (= *megha-v°*) Indra, W.; N. of a son (of Śāli-vāhana, W.; of Jīmūta-ketu, Inscr. (A.D. 1095); Kathās. xxii, 23); of a Vidyā-dhara, Bālar. iv, 7; of the author of Dāyabhāga. — **vāhin**, m. smoke, L. — **svana**, m. 'cloud-sound,' thunder, Nal. xii. **Jīmūtâshṭamī**, f. the 8th day in the dark half of Āśvina (festival in honour of Śāli-vāhana's son Jīmūta-vāhana), W.
Jīmūtaka, m. Lepeocercis serrata, Suśr. i; iv, 18.

जीर 1. *jīrá*, mf(*ā́*)n. (√*jinv*, Uṇ.), quick, speedy, active, RV. (Naigh. ii, 15); driving (with gen.), RV. i, 48, 3; (cf. *gó-*); m. quick movement (of the Soma stones), v, 31, 12; a sword, L. — **dānu** (°*rá-*), mfn. (Pat. on Pāṇ. i, 1, 4, Vārtt. 1 & vi, 1, 66) dropping or sprinkling abundantly, RV.; AV.; ŚāṅkhŚr. i, 14, 3; cf. *jīva-d°*. **Jīrâdhvara**, mfn. having animated rites, RV. x, 36, 3. **Jīrâśva**, mfn. having lively or fleet horses, i, 119; 141; 157; ii, 4, 2.
1. **Jīri**, m. f. quick or flowing water, 17, 3; iii, ix.

जीर 2. *jīra*, m. (√*jṛī*) = °*raṇa*, L.; Panicum miliaceum, L. **Jīraka**, m. n. = °*raṇa*, Suśr. i; iv, 5, 35; vi; VarBṛS. li, 15; (*ikā*), f. = *jīrṇa-pattrikā*, L. **Jīraṇa**, m. = *jīr°*, cumin-seed, L.
2. **Jīri**, f. old age, TāṇḍyaBr. xxv, 17, 3.
Jīrṇá, mfn. (Pāṇ. iii, 2, 104) old, worn out, withered, wasted, decayed, AV. x, 8, 27; TS. i; ŚBr. &c.; ancient (tradition), KātyŚr., Sch.; digested, MBh. iii, 8623; R.; Hariv. &c.; m. an old man, W.; (= *jarṇa*) a tree, L.; = °*raṇa*, L.; n. old age, decrepitude, Rājat. iii, 316; 'digestion,' see *-śakti*; benjamin, L.; (*ā*), f. large cumin-seed, L. — **jvara**, m. a lingering fever with diminishing intensity, Suśr. i, 45 f.; *-hara*, m. 'removing that fever,' N. of a plant, Gal. — °**jvarin**, mfn. affected with the above fever, W. — **ṭīkā**, f. 'ancient Comm.,' N. of a work on astron. — **tā**, f. old age, R. vii, 40, 24. — **tājika**, n. N. of a work. — **tva**, n. = *-tā*, Mṛicch. iii, 17/18; infirmity, decay, W. — **dāru**, m. Argyreia speciosa, L. — **pattra**, m. 'withered-leaved,' a kind of Lodhra tree, Bhpr. v, 1, 216. — **pattrikā**, f. = °*ttra*, a kind of grass, L. — **parṇa**, m. n. '= *-pattra*,' Nauclea Cadamba, L.; *-ja*, n. Cyperus rotundus, Dhanv. iii. — **pushpaka**, n. = *-parṇa-ja*, ib. — **phañji**, f. = *-dāru*, L. — **budhna**, m. = *-pattra*, L. — **budhnaka**, n. = *-parṇa-ja*, L. — **mata**, n. an old (antiquated) opinion. — **vajra**, m. a gem resembling a diamond, L. — **vat**, mfn. old, decayed, W. — **vastra**, n. worn or tattered raiment, W.; mfn. wearing old clothes, W. — **vāṭikā**, f. a ruined house, Mn. ix, 265/266. — **visha**, m. N. of a snake-catcher, Mudr. ii, 1/2. — **śakti**, f. the faculty of digesting anything (loc.)
Jīrṇâmaya-jvara, m. = °*ṇa-jv°*, Kathās. xvii, 36.
Jīrṇôddhāra, m. repairing what is ruined (in a building), Hcat. i, 3, 893; DevīP.; Siṃhās. Introd. 29/30. **Jīrṇôddhṛita**, mfn. repaired, W. **Jīrṇôdyāna**, n. a neglected garden, Mn. ix, 265.
Jīrṇaka, mfn. somewhat old, g. *sthūlâdi*.
Jī́rṇi, mfn. decrepit with age, ŚBr. iv; TBr. iii; ŚāṅkhBr. ii, 9; f. infirmity, decay, L.; digestion, W.
Jīrti, see *a-*. **Jīrvi**, m. = *paśu* or *parśu* (axe or animal), Uṇ. iv, 54/55; a cart, Uṇ. vṛ.; the body, ib.

जील *jīla*, m. = *jīna*, s.v. √1. *jyā*.

जीव *jīv*, cl. 1. *jī́vati* (ep. also Ā.; Subj. °*vāti*, RV. x, 85, 39; AV.; °*vāt*, RV. i, 84, 16; p. *jīvat*; aor. *ajīvīt*; *jīvīt*, AV.; pf. *jijīva*; fut. *jīvishyáti*; Prec. °*vyāsam*, °*vyāsma*, AV.; ŚBr.; inf. *jīvitum*, xiv; MBh. &c.; Ved. °*váse*, RV.; VS.; MBh. i, 732; *jīvitavaí*, AV. vi, 109, 1) to live, be or remain alive, RV. &c.; to revive, Pañcat. iv, 5, 8/9; BhP. iv, 6, 51; (with *punar*) MBh.; to live by (instr.; exceptionally loc., v, 1059 f.), Mn.; Pāṇ. iv, 4, 12; MBh. &c.: Caus. *jīváyati* (ep. also Ā.; aor. *ajījivat* or *ajijīv°*, Pāṇ. vii, 4, 3) to make alive, restore to life, vivify, RV. x, 137, 1; ĀśvŚr. vi, 9; MBh. &c.; to support life, keep alive, MBh. &c.; to nourish, bring up, i, xiii; Kathās. iii, 17 f.; Rājat. v, 72; to shout '*jīva*' (i. e. long live!), Kathās. cxxiv, 113; *jīvāpayati* (cf. °*pita*) to restore to life, Vet. ii, 9/10: Desid. *jijīvishati* (Ā., BhP. xi, 7, 70) to wish to live, KātyŚr. xxii; Lāṭy. viii; ĪśUp.; MBh. &c.; to seek a livelihood, wish to live by (instr.), Mn. x, 121; MBh. v, 702; *jújyūshati*, id., ŚBr. iii, 2, 4, 16 & 5, 3, 11; cf. *jijyūshita*; [cf. Lat. *vivo*; Lith. *gīvénu*.]
Jīvá, mf(*ā́*)n. living, existing, alive, RV. &c.; healthy (blood), Car. viii, 6, 74; ifc. living by (see *jala-cara-, rūpa-*); causing to live, vivifying (see *putra-, -jala*); m. n. any living being, anything living, RV. &c.; life, existence, MBh. iv, vi; Hariv. &c. (ifc. f. *ā*, Kathās.); m. the principle of life, vital breath, the living or personal soul (as distinguished from the universal soul, see *jīvâtman*), RV. i, 164, 30; ChUp.; ŚvetUp.; PraśnUp.; Mn. &c.; N. of a plant, L.; Bṛihaspati (regent of Jupiter), VarBṛS.; Laghuj.; Sūryas.; KāśīKh.; the 3rd lustrum in the 60 years' Bṛihaspati cycle, VarBṛS. viii, 26; N. of one of the 8 Maruts, Yājñ. ii, 102/103, 39; Karṇa, L.; n. N. of a metre, RPrāt. xvii, 4; (*ā*), f. life, L.; the earth, L.; a bow-string, L.; (in geom. = *jyā*) the chord of an arc; the sine of an arc, Sūryas. ii, 57; (cf. *tri-, tri-bha-, dṛig-gati-, lamba-* & *śaṅku-jīvā*); N. of a plant (*jīvantī* or *vacā*, L.), VarBṛS. iil, 39; the tinkling of ornaments, L.; pl. N. of a particular formula, Kauś.; Vait.; cf. *ati-, upa-* & *sam-jīvā*; *a-, kumāra-, ciram-, jagaj-, dur-, nir-, pāpa-, bandhu-, sa-, su-; kshudra-jīvā, yāvaj-jīvam*; [cf. βίος; Lat. *vivus*; Lith. *gīvas*; Goth. *qvius*; Engl. *quick*; Hib. *beo*.] — **kośa**, m. a case (or sheath) enveloping the personal soul, BhP. iv, 22 f.; x. — **koshaṇī**, f., Kauś. 26. — **gṛibh**, m. 'capturing alive,' a bailiff, RV. x, 97, 11. — **grahá**, m. filling (a cup) with living (or unpressed Soma), TS. vi, 6, 9, 2. — **grā́ham**, ind. with √*grah*, (Pāṇ. iii, 4, 36) to capture alive, MaitrS. ii, 2, 12; MBh.; Daś. ix, 181; Kathās. — **ghana**, m. receptacle of everything living, PraśnUp. v, 5; Jain. — **ghātin**, mfn. destroying life (a beast of prey), Subh. — **ghātyā**, f. destruction of life, Kauś. 18. — **ghosha-svāmin**, m. N. of a grammarian. — **ja**, mfn. born-alive, ChUp. vi, 3, 1. — **jīva**, m. a kind of pheasant, L. — **jīvaka**, m. id., Mn. xii, 66; MBh. iii, xii f.; Hariv. 12685; VarBṛS.; BrahmaP.; a Buddh. or Jain ascetic, Gal. — **m-jīva**, m. = *-j°*, L.; the Greek partridge, L.; a mythical bird with two heads, Buddh.; N. of a tree, L. — **m-jīvaka**, m. = *-jīva*, MBh. iii; Hariv. 6957; Lalit.; Suśr.; Kād.; MārkP. — **m-jīvika**, m., id., MBh. v, 4850. — **taṇḍula** (°*vá-*), mfn. germinant rice, MaitrS. i; MānŚr.; m. or n. scil. *odana*, food made of that rice, ĀpŚr. i, 7, 12. — **tokā**, f. a woman whose child or children are living, L. — **tyāga**, m. giving up one's life, voluntary death, Prab. v, 1/2; Sāh. iii, 156. — **tva**, n. the state of life, RāmatUp. i, 14; the state of the individual soul, KapS. vi, 63. — 1. **-da**, m. 'life-giver,' a physician, L.; (*ā*), f. = °*vantī*, L. — 2. **-da**, m. 'life-cutter,' an enemy, L. — **datta**, °**ttaka**, m. N. of a man, Kathās. — **dayā-prakaraṇa**, n. N. of a Jain treatise. — **daśā**, f. mortal existence, W. — **dātrī**, f. 'life-giver,' = *-bhadrā*, L.; Cœlogyne ovalis or Hoya viridiflora, L. — **dāna**, n. 'life-giving,' N. of a manual of med. by Cyavana, BrahmavP. i, 16, 17. — **dānu** (°*vá-*), mfn. for *jīrá-d°*, VS. i, 28; ŚBr. i, 9, 1, 5. — **dāman**, m. N. of a prince. — **dāyaka**, mfn. life-giving, Vet. ii, 10. — **deva**, m. N. of a man. — **dhana**, n. live stock, wealth in flocks and herds, L. — **dhanya** (°*vá-*), mf(*ā*)n. rich in vital powers, RV.; AV. xii, 3, 4 & 25; TBr. ii. — **dhānī**, f. 'receptacle of living beings,' the earth, BhP. iii, 13, 30. — **nā́śa**, mfn. (nom. *-nát*; also *-nak* [= *jīvasya nāśa*], Pāṇ. viii, 2, 63, Kāś.) [a sacrifice] in which living beings are killed, MaitrS. i, 4, 13. — **nātha**, m. N. of a writer on astron.; of a physician. — **nāya**, °**yaka**, m. N. of a poet, ŚārṅgP. lvi, cxxxv. — **nāśam**, ind. with √*naś*, to lose one's life, Pāṇ. iii, 4, 43. — **nikāya**, m. a being endowed with life, BhP. iii, v. — **netrī**, f. a kind of pepper, L. — **m-dharaṇa-caritra**, n. N. of a tale by Bhāskara-kavi. — **pati**, m. a living husband, vi, 19, 24. — **pattra**, n. a fresh leaf, W.; *-pracāyikā*, for *-putra-pr°*. — **patnī**, f. a woman whose husband is alive, ĀśvGṛ. i, 7 & 14; Gobh. ii, 7, 12. — **pitṛi**, mfn. (a son or daughter) whose father is alive, ŚāṅkhŚr. iv. — **pitṛika**, mfn. id., KātyŚr. iv. — **pīta-sarga** (°*vá-*), mfn. whose rays are drunk by living beings, RV. i, 149, 2. — **putra** (°*vá-*), mf(*ā*, Hariv. 7848; R. [B] iv, 19, 11; *ī*, MBh. v, 144, 2; R. [G] iv, 18, 10)n. one whose sons or children are living, RV. x, 36, 9; AV. xii, 3, 35; MBh. &c.; m. N. of a Ṛishi and of the hymn composed by him, ĀśvGṛ. i, 13, 6; N. of a plant, *-pracāyikā*, f. 'gathering of the Jīva-putra plant,' a kind of game, Pāṇ. vi, 2, 74, Kāś. & Siddh. — **putraka**, m. Terminalia Catappa, L.; Putraṃjīva Roxburghii, L. — **purā́**, f. the abode of living beings or men, AV. ii, 9, 3; v, 30, 6. — **pushṭā**, for °*shpā*. — **pushpa**, m. 'life-flower,' N. of a plant (*damanaka* or *phaṇijjhaka*, L.), fig. applied to the head, R. v, 83, 13; (*ā*), f. the plant *bṛihaj-jīvantī*, L. — **pṛishṭā**, f. N. of a plant, L. — **praja**, mf(*ā*)n. having living children, ĀśvGṛ. i, 7, 21. — **priyā**, f. Terminalia Chebula, L. — **barhis** (°*vá-*), mfn. having a fresh bed of sacrificial grass, AV. xi, 7, 7. — **bhadrā**, f. the plant °*vantī* or *vṛiddhi*, L. — **bhūta**, mfn. become alive, endowed with life, W.; forming the life of (gen.), R. i, 4, 23; BhP. v, 24, 19. — **bhójana**, mfn. giving enjoyment to the soul of (gen.), VS. xxiii, 31; n. the pleasure of living beings, AV. iv, 9, 3. — **mandira**, n. = *-kośa*, L. — **maya**, mfn. endowed with life, BhP.

ix, 9, 24. **-miśra**, m. N. of an author, Smṛitit. i. **-meshaka**, m. a kind of portulaca plant, L. **-yājá**, m. the sacrifice of living beings, RV. i, 31, 15. **-yoni**, mfn. enclosing a personal soul (a sentient being), BhP. iii, 9, 19. **-rakta**, n. (living i. e.) menstrual blood, Suśr. i, 14, 4. **-rahita**, mfn. lifeless, W. **-rāja**, m. N. of the author of Caitra-pūrṇimā-kathā; *-dīkshita*, m. N. of an author. **-loká**, m. the world of living beings (opposed to that of the deceased), living beings, mankind, RV. x, 18, 8; AV. xviii, 3, 34; ŚBr. xiii, 8, 4; MBh. &c. **-°laukika**, mfn. peculiar to the world of living beings or men, xii, 8495. **-vat**, mfn. animated, living, viii, 4930; = *jīvana-vat*, ĀpŚr. viii, 14; (*tī*), f. = *-vallī*, Npr. **-vadha**, m. destruction of living beings, Siṇhâs. xxviii, 3. **-vardhanī**, f. 'promoting life,' N. of a plant, L. **-vallī**, f. N. of a bulbous plant, L. **-vicāra**, m. 'disquisition on life,' N. of a Jain work by Śānti-sūri (commented on by Bhāva-sundara, Megha-nandana, and Īśvarâcārya); *-prakaraṇa*, n. id. **-vijaya**, m. N. of a brother of Jinâdi-vijaya. **-vinaya**, m. N. of a work, W. **-vishaya**, m. (dominion i. e.) duration of life, Pañcat. **-vishāṇa**, n. the horn of a living animal, PārGṛ. iii, 7, 2. **-vṛitti**, f. 'livelihood by living beings,' breeding or keeping cattle, L. **-śaṇsá**, mfn. praised by living beings, RV. i, 104, 6; vii, 46, 4. **-śarman**, m. N. of an astronomer, VarBṛS. vii, 9; xi, 1. **-śāka**, m. = *-meshaka*, L. **-śuklā**, f. N. of a bulb, L. **-śesha**, mfn. one who has escaped with his life and nothing more, Pañcat. iii, 1, 9/1. **-śoṇita**, n. healthy blood, Suśr. iv, 34, 10 f. **-śreshṭhā**, f. = *-bhadrā*, L. **-saṃkramaṇa**, n. transmigration of soul, W. **-saṃjña**, m. Kāma-vṛiddhi, L. **-samāsa**, m. N. of a work (commented on by Hemac.) **-sâkshin**, mfn. constituting an evidence of life (with *dhamanī*, f. 'an artery'), ŚārṅgS. iii, 1. **-sādhana**, n. 'means of subsistence,' rice, grain, L. **-sāphalya**, n. realisation of a life's wishes, W. **-siddhi**, m. N. of a man, Mudr. ii, 7/8. **-suta**, mf(*ā*)n. = *-praja*, BhP. vi, 19, 25. **-sū**, f. a mother of living offspring, MBh. i, 7353; R. ii. **-sthāna**, n. any vital part of the body, L. **-hiṇsā**, f. hurting living beings, Siṇhâs. xxviii, 9/1 & 7/8. **Jīvâgāra**, n. = °*va-sthāna*, L. **Jīvâjīvâdhāra-kshetra**, n. the world of living beings and of lifeless matter, L. **Jīvâtman**, m. the living or personal or individual soul (as distinct from the *paramât*°, q. v.), the vital principle, Tarkas.; BhP. vi, viii; Sarvad. iv; vii, 57. **Jīvâdāna**, n. 'taking away all sense of life,' fainting away, swoon, Car. i, viii; Suśr. **Jīvâditya**, m. the living sun, Siṇhâs. xviii, 1. **Jīvâdhāna**, n. preservation of life, W. **Jīvânusiddhi-kulaka**, n. N. of a Jain treatise. **Jīvântaka**, m. 'life-destroyer,' a fowler, L.; murderer, W. **Jīvâbhigama-sūtra**, n. N. of the 3rd Upâṅga of the Jain canon. **Jīvâśa**, mf(*ā*)n. hoping for life, Amar. 90; (*ā*), f. hope of living, BhP. i, 2, 10. **Jīvâśaṅkin**, mfn. believing any one to be alive, Kathās. lxxv. **Jīvâstikāya**, m. the category of 'soul,' Jain. (also Bādar. ii, 2, 35, Sch.) **Jīvêndhana**, n. blazing wood, VarBṛS. **Jīvôtsarga**, m. = °*va-tyāga*, Prab. v, 1/2; Hit. **Jīvôpalambha-prakaraṇa**, n. N. of a Jain treatise. **Jīvôpāya**, m. v. l. for °*vyôp*°. **Jīvôrṇā**, f. wool of a living animal, KātyŚr.

Jīvaka, mfn. living, alive, Hcar. vii; ifc. (f. *ikā*) 'living,' see *cira-*: making a livelihood by (in comp.), MBh. xii f.; Hariv. 4484; Śatr.; (cf. *akshara-*); 'generating,' see *putram-*; ifc. (f. *ā*) long living, for whom long life is desired, Pāṇ. iii, 1, 150, Kāś.; m. a living being, L.; 'living on others,' a servant, L.; an usurer, L.; a beggar, L.; a snake-catcher, L.; a tree, L.; one of the 8 principal drugs called Ashṭavarga (Terminalia tomentosa, L.; Coccinia grandis, L.), Suśr.; VarBṛS.; N. of Kumāra-bhūta, Divyâv. xix, xxxv; (*ikā*), f. living, manner of living, KaṭhUp.; Mn. (iv, 11; x, 82) &c.; livelihood, x, 76; MBh. &c. (ifc. f. *ā*, Rājat. vi, 22); the plant Jīvantī, L.; pl. 'life-giving element,' water, ĀśvŚr. vi, 9.

Jīvat, mfn. pr. p. √*jīv*, q. v. **-toká**, °**kī**, f. = °*va-tokā*, L. **-pati**, f. = °*tnī*, L. **-patikā**, f. id., Mn. iii, 174, Kull. **-patnī**, f. = °*va-p*°, L., Sch. **-pitṛi**, mfn. = °*va-p*°, Āp. (KātyŚr. iv, 1, 27, Sch.) **-pitṛika**, mfn. id., Tithyâd.; occurring during a father's life, PSarv.; *-nirṇaya*, m. N. of a work.

Jīvatha, mfn. long-lived, Uṇ. iii, 112, Sch.; virtuous, L.; m. life, breath, L.; a tortoise, L.; a peacock, L.; a cloud, L.; virtue, W.

Jīvad, in comp. for °*vat*. **-bhartṛikā**, f. = °*va-patnī*, RV. x, 18, 7, Sāy. **-vatsā**, f. = °*va-tokā*, Suśr.

Jīvan, in comp. for °*vat*. **-maraṇa**, n. living-death, Daś. xi, 219. **-mukta**, mfn. emancipated while still alive (i. e. liberated before death from all liability to future births), KapS. iii, 78; Vedântas.; Sarvad. **-mukti**, f. emancipation while still alive, Madhus.; *-viveka*, m. N. of a work by Mādhava. **-mṛita**, mfn. dead while alive (as a lunatic &c.), BhP. v, 10, 8 & (*-tva*, n. abstr.) 12; 14, 12. **-mriyamāṇa**, mfn. living but being about to die, 14, 12. **-vimukta**, mfn. = *-mukta*, Siṇhâs. xx, 6.

Jīvana, mf(*ī*)n. vivifying, giving life, enlivening, ŚBr. ii, 3, 1, 10; MBh. (said of wind, the sun, &c.; of Śiva, xiii, 1236); BhP. x; Kathās.; m. a living being, W.; wind, L.; a son, L.; the plant *kshudra-phalaka*, L.; the plant *jīvaka*, L.; N. of the author of Mānasa-nayana; n. life, RV. i, 48, 10; x, 161, 1; AV.; ŚBr. ix &c.: manner of living, TS. vi, 1, 9, 4; living by (instr. or in comp.), livelihood, means of living, Mn.; Yājñ. iii; MBh. &c.; enlivening, making alive, R. vi, 105; Kathās. lxxvi, 25; Ashṭâṅg.; enlivening a magical formula, Sarvad. xv, 254 & 256; 'life-giving element,' water, BhP. x, 20, 6; Rājat. v, 416; fresh butter, L.; milk, Gal.; marrow, L.; (*ā*), f. N. of a medicinal plant, L.; (*ī*), f. N. of several plants (*jīvantī*, *hāholī*, *ḍoḍī*, *medā*, *mahā-medā*, *yūthī*), L.; (cf. *á-*; *purusha-jīv*°.) **-tā**, f. life, mode of life, W. **-da**, m. 'life-giver,' N. of the leader of a sect, Saṃkar. xxxv. **-yoni**, mfn. having its source in life, Bhāshāp.; m. source of life, W. **-vat**, mfn. possessed of or relating to life, GopBr. ii, 1, 25; ŚāṅkhŚr. iii. **-viḍambana**, n. disappointment in life, living in vain, W. **-hetu**, m. means of subsistence, Mn. x, 116. **Jīvanâghāta**, n. 'life-destroying,' poison, W. **Jīvanânta**, m. end of life, W. **Jīvanârha**, n. 'life-supporting,' milk, Npr.; grain, ib. **Jīvanâvāsa**, m. 'water-abider,' Varuṇa, L. **Jīvanôpāya**, m. = °*na-hetu*, W. **Jīvanâushadha**, n. a life-giving medicine, L.

Jīvanaka, n. food, L.; (*ikā*), f. = °*va-priyā*, L.

Jīvanasyā, f. desire of life, TS. ii; MaitrS. ii, 3, 4.

Jīvani, m. pl. N. of a family, Pravar. v, 1.

Jīvanīya, mfn. vivifying (a class of drugs), Car. i, 1, 107; prepared from Jīvanīya milk, Suśr. vi, 9, 19; n. impers. to be lived, Mn. x, 116, Kull.; a form of milk, Suśr.; water, L.; (*ā*), f. the plant Jīvantī, L.

Jīvantá, mfn. long-lived, L.; m. life, L.; a drug, Uṇ., Sch.; = °*va-śāka*, AV. xix, 39, 3; N. of a man, Pāṇ. iv, 1, 103; g. *karṇâdi*; (*ī*), f. N. of an asterism, MānGṛ. i, 14; of a medicinal and edible plant, AV. viii, 2, 6 & 7, 6; MBh. ii, 98; Suśr.; Cocculus cordifolius, L.; Prosopis spicigera or Mimosa Suma, L.; = °*va-priyā*, L.; a parasitical plant, L.; = *ḍoḍī*, L. **-svāmin**, m. N. of a Jain saint, HPariś. xi, 24.

Jīvantaka, m. = °*va-śāka*, L.; (*ikā*), f. a parasitical plant, L.; a kind of pot-herb, L.; Cocculus cordifolius, L.; = °*va-priyā*, L.

Jīvanti, m. N. of a man and (pl.) his descendants, Pravar. i, 1; also in comp. for °*tī*. **-śāka**, the plant Jīvantī, Suśr. vi, 17, 48. **-śūlām** √**kṛi**, to impale a woman alive, Divyâv. xxvii, 566.

Jīvantika, m. = °*vântaka*, L.; (*ā*), f., see °*taka*.

Jīvantyāyana, m. pl. (fr. °*ti*) N. of a family, Pravar. i, 4 (vv. ll. *jaivantāy*° & *jaivantyāyani*).

Jīvalá, mf(*ā*)n. full of life, animating (water), AV. x, xii, xix; m. N. of a man, ŚBr. ii, 3; Nal. xv, 7; (*ā*), f. Odina Wodier, AV. vi, viii, xix; = °*vālā*, L.

Jīvātu, f. life, RV.; AV. &c. (dat. °*tave*; once °*tvai*, MaitrS. ii, 3, 4); a life-giving drug, HPariś. xiii, 189; m. n. victuals, food (ifc. mfn. 'living on'), Kautukas. **-kāmyā**, f. desire for life, Mṛicch. x, 40. **-mat**, mfn. = °*vana-vat*, ĀśvŚr. ii, 10 & 19.

Jīvāpita, mfn. (Caus.) restored to life, R. vii, 76, 27; Vet. **Jīvālā**, f. (= °*valā*) a kind of pepper, L.

Jīvikā, f., see °*vaka*. **-√kṛi**, to make a livelihood, Pāṇ. i, 4, 79. **-°panna** (°*kâp*°), mfn. one who has obtained a subsistence, W. **-prāpta**, mfn. id., W.

Jīvitá, mfn. living, Ragh. xii, 75; lived through (a period of time), W.; (with or without *punar*) returned to life, MBh. xii, 5686; Pañcat.; Vet.; enlivened, animated, R. v, 66, 24; BhP. viii, 15, 3; n. a living being, RV. i, 113, 6; life, iv, 54, 2; AV. vi, 134, 1; ŚBr. xiv &c.; (ifc. f. *ā*, Kathās.); duration of life, L.; livelihood, Hit. i, 4, 36 (v. l.); cf. *a-*. **-kāla**, m. duration of life, L. **-kshaya**, m. loss of life, death, R. ii. **-gṛidhnu-tā**, f. great desire for life, Kathās. lxxviii, 87. **-jña**, f. 'knowing life,' an artery, L. **-da**, mfn. giving life, Bhpr. vii, 8, 237. **-nātha**, m. 'life-lord,' a husband, Kum. iv, 3. **-priya**, mfn. as dear as life, Amar. 31. **-bhūta**, mfn. 'having lived,' dead, Kād. vi, 1427. **-yópana**, mfn. oppressing living beings, AV. ii, xii. **-vyaya**, m. waste or sacrifice of life, W. **-saṃśaya**, m. risk or danger of life, W. **-sama**, mfn. = *-priya*, Bhartṛ. iii, 10. **-hārin**, mfn. destroying life, W. **Jīvitâkâṅkshin**, mfn. desirous of living, MBh. xii, 4295. **Jīvitâtyaya**, m. = °*ta-saṃśaya*, Mn. x, 104. **Jīvitânta**, m. end of life, death, R. ii, 64, 72; *-kara*, mfn. menacing life, MBh. xii, 5173; *-ga*, mfn. id., R. (B) iv, 7, 9. **Jīvitântaka**, mfn. putting an end to life, iii, 25, 5; iv, 6, 10; m. Śiva. **Jīvitâvabhṛitha**, n. 'life-purification,' end of life, Gobh. i, 3, 13. **Jīvitâśā**, f. hope of life, wish for life, Kāvyâd. ii, 139; Bhaktām.; Hit. **Jīvitêpsu**, mfn. seeking to save one's life, W. **Jīvitêśa**, m. = °*ta-nātha*, Ragh. xi, 20; Yama, ib.; the sun, L.; the moon, L.; a vivifying drug, L.; (*ā*), f. a loved woman, Ratnâv. iii, 17. **Jīvitêśvara**, m. 'life-lord,' Śiva.

Jīvitavya, n. impers. to be lived, Hit.; possibility of living, Pañcat.; Hit.; the life to be expected (till death), duration or (pl.) enjoyments of life, Pañcat.; Kathās. lxxviii, 79; possible return to life, Pañcat. v, 4, 9/1; *-vishaya*, m. duration of life, Introd. 9/10; *-saṃdeha*, m. danger of life, i, 4, 14.

Jīvitu-kāma, mfn. = °*tâkâṅkshin*, GārUp. 1.

Jīvin, mfn. ifc. living (a particular period or at a certain time or in a certain way), Mn.; MBh. &c.; living on or by (loc. [Hariv. 4555; R. i, 9, 61] or in comp.), ĀśvGṛ. iii; Mn. &c.; m. a living being, Pañcat. i, 11, 9/1; BrahmavP. **Jīvi-tva**, n. life, W.

Jīvya, n. impers. to be lived, Cāṇ.; 'life,' see °*vyôpāya*; (*ā*), f. = °*va-priyā*, L.; = *goraksha-dugdhā*, L.; the plant Jīvantī, L. **Jīvyôpāya**, m. means of subsistence, Hariv. 14376 f. (v. l. °*vôp*°).

जु *ju*. See √1. *jū*.

जुकुट *jukuṭa*, (= *jak*°) m. a dog, W.; the Malaya mountain, W.; n. the egg-plant, W.

जुगुपिषु *jugupishu*, mfn. (√*gup*, Desid.) intending to protect, MBh. viii, 1737.

Jugupsana, mfn. = °*psu*, Pāṇ. iii, 2, 149, Kāś.; n. dislike, L.; censure, W.

Jugupsanīya, mfn. disgusting, HPariś. i, 378.

Jugupsā, f. dislike, abhorrence, disgust, MBh.; Pāṇ. i, 4, 24, Vārtt. 1; Mṛicch. i, 14; Yogas. &c.

Jugupsita, mfn. abhorring anything (abl.), Vop. v, 21; disliked, detested, disgusting, MBh.; R. &c.; censured, W.; n. a disgusting or horrible deed, BhP. i, 5, 15; (also *karma-*, id., i, 7, 42); = °*psā*, Sarvad. iii, 270. **-tama**, mfn. most disgusting, Śāntiś. i, 20. **-tva**, n. = °*psā*, Divyâv. xxvii, 13.

Jugupsu, mfn. having a dislike or abhorrence, ŚāṅkhŚr. iii, 20, 5; Pāṇ. ii, 1, 37, Pat. **Jugupsya**, mfn. more disgusting than (abl.), HPariś. i, 381.

जुगुर्वणि *jugurvaṇi*. See √2. *jṛī*.

जुङ्कक *juṅkaka*, m. = *juṅga*, L.

जुङ्ग् *juṅg*, cl. 1. °*gati*, to exclude, Dhātup. v, 51; cf. √*yuṅg*.

Juṅga, m. Argyreia speciosa, L.; (*ā*), f. id., L.

Juṅgaka, m. (= *juṅkaka*) id., L.

Juṅgita, mfn. of degraded caste, Vas. xxi, 10.

जुच् *juc*, cl. 1. 10. P. to speak, Dhātup.

जुट् *juṭ*, cl. 6. °*ṭati*, v. l. for √*juḍ*, q. v.

Juṭaka, n. = *jūṭ*°, L.; (*ikā*), f. id., Hcar. viii.

जुड् *juḍ*, cl. 6. °*ḍati*, to bind, Dhātup. xxviii, 85 (v. l. √*juṭ*); to go, 37 (v. l. √*jun*); cl. 10. *joḍayati*, to send, xxxii, 104.

जुडी *juḍī*, f. N. of a place, Kshitîś. vii, 4.

जुत् *jut* (fr. √*dyut*), cl. 1. *jotate*, to shine, Dhātup. ii, 30.

जुन् *jun*, cl. 6. °*nati*, v. l. for √*juḍ*, q. v.

जुमर *jumara*, m. N. of a scholiast on the Saṃkshipta-sāra; cf. *jaum*°. **-nandin**, m. id.

जुम्बक *jumbaká*, m. N. of a Varuṇa (ŚBr. xiii, 3, 6, 5), VS. xxv, 9.

जुर् 1. *jur* (= √*jṛī*), cl. 4. 6. P. *jūryati* (√*jūr*, Ā. °*te*, Dhātup. xxvi, 47; p. *jūryat* & *jurát*; pf. p. *jujurvás*) to become old or decrepit, decay, perish, RV. i–iii, v, vii; to cause to grow old or perish, i, 182, 3; cf. *a-juryá*. 2. **Júr**, *ūr*, m. an old man (Sāy.), ii, 14, 3 (?, see 2. *jū*); mfn. 'growing old,' see *a-*, *amā-*, *ṛita-*, *dhiyā-* & *sanā-jūr*.

1. **Jūrṇá**, mfn. decayed, old, RV.; (*ī*), f. N. of a snake, AV. ii, 24, 5. **Jūrṇâkhya**, m. Saccharum

cylindricum, L. **Jūrṇâhva**, m. N. of a plant, Car. i, 21, 22. **Jūrṇâhvaya**, m. Andropogon bicolor, L.

Jū́rya, mfn. old, RV. vi, 2, 7; cf. *a-juryá*.

जुल् *jul*, cl. 10. *jolayati*, to grind, Vop.

जुवस् *júvas*. See √*jū*.

जुष 1. *jush*, cl. 6. Ā. °*shá́te* (also P., RV. [°*shát, ájushat*]; MBh. &c.; Subj. °*shāte*; Pot. °*shéta*; 3. pl. °*sherata*, RV.; Impv. °*shátām*; impf. *ajushata*, ii, 37, 4; 1. sg. *ájushe*, AV. vi, 61, 3; p. °*shámāṇa*), cl. 3. P. irr. *jújoshati* (Subj. & p. *jújoshat*; cf. Pāṇ. vii, 3, 87, Vārtt. 2; Impv. 2. pl. °*jushṭana*, RV.), rarely cl. 1. P. *joshati* (Subj. *jóshat*;— aor. p. *jushāṇá*; 3. pl. *ajushran*, i, 71, 1; 2. sg. *jóshi*, ii, iv; 3. sg. *jóshishat*, ii, 35, 1 [cf. Kāś. on Pāṇ. iii, 1, 34 & 4, 7; 94 & 97]; pf. *jujósha*, °*jushé*; p. °*jushvás*, generally °*shāṇá*; ind. p. *jushṭví*, RV.) to be pleased or satisfied or favourable, RV.; AV. &c.; to like, be fond of, delight in (acc. or gen.), enjoy, RV. (with *tanvàm* or °*vàs*, 'to be delighted,' iii, 1, 1; x, 8, 3); AV. &c.; to have pleasure in granting anything (acc.) to (loc.), RV. vi, 14, 1; to have pleasure in (dat.), resolve to (Ved. Inf.), i, 167, 5; iv, 24, 5; ŚBr. iii, 6, 4, 7; to give pleasure to (loc.), RV. x, 105, 8; to choose for (dat.), VS. v, 42; TS. vi; ŚBr. iii, 6, 4, 8; to devote one's self to (acc.), practise, undergo, suffer, BhP. ii, 2, 7; viii, 7, 20; Bhaṭṭ. xvii, 112; to delight in visiting, frequent, visit, inhabit, enter (a carriage &c.), MBh. iii, v, xiv; Bhaṭṭ. xiv, 95; to afflict, MBh. iii: Caus. Ā. (Subj. 2. sg. *joshá́yāse*) to like, love, behave kindly towards (acc.), cherish, RV.; to delight in, approve of (acc.), choose, ŚBr. iii; MBh. xiv, 1289; (P., cf. Dhātup. xxxiv, 28) Bhag. iii, 26; [cf. γεύομαι; Zd. *zaosha*; Hib. *gus*; Goth. *kiusu*; Lat. *gus-tus*.]

2. **Jush**, mfn. ifc. liking, fond of, devoted to (once with acc., BhP. vii, 6, 25; cf. *nikṛitim-*), BhP.; Bhartṛ.; Śāntiś.; Kathās.; dwelling in, Hcar. vii; visiting, approaching, BhP. ii, 7, 25; Madhus.; having, showing, Bālar. iv, 17; ix, 25; Siṇhâs. Introd. 51; xv, 4; Kuval. 169; similar, Hcar. i, 44; cf. *sa-*.

Jusha, mfn. See *alaṃ-*; *prīti-jushā*.

Jushāṇá, m. N. of a sacrificial formula containing the word *jushāṇá* (aor. p.), ŚBr. i; AitBr. i, 17; ŚāṅkhŚr. i, 8, 9. **-vat**, mfn. id., ĀpŚr. vi, 31, Sch.

Júshṭa, mfn. (°*shṭá*, RV. ix, 42, 2; AV. and in later language, Pāṇ. vi, 1, 209 f.) pleased, propitious, RV. ix, 42, 2; liked, wished, loved, welcome, agreeable, usual (cf. Pāṇ. iii, 2, 188, Kār.; with dat. or gen., rarely instr.), RV.; AV.; ŚBr. &c.; frequented, visited, inhabited, MBh.; R.; BhP.; swept over (by the wind), Hariv. 6984; afflicted by (instr. or in comp.), Suśr.; served, obliged, worshipped, W.; practised, W.; furnished with, possessed of (instr. or in comp.), R. iii; BhP.; n. the remnants of a meal, L.; cf. *á-*. **-tama** (*júsh*°), mfn. (superl.) most welcome, RV. **-tara** (*júsh*°), mfn. (compar.) id., viii, 96, 11.

Júshṭi, f. love, service, favour, satisfaction, i, 10, 12; vii, 33, 4; x, 114, 1; AV.; TS. i; ŚāṅkhŚr.; Lāṭy.

Jushya, mfn. fut. p. p., Pāṇ. iii, 1, 109.

जुष्क *jushka*, m. N. of one of the 3 Kaśmīrian Turushka kings, Rājat. i, 168 f. **-pura**, n. N. of a town founded by Jushka, ib.

जुष्कक *jushkaka*, m. = *jūsha*, L.

जुहुराण *juhurāṇá*, mfn. pf. p. Ā. √*hvar*, q. v.; m. the moon, Uṇ. ii, 88, Sch. °**huvāṇa**, m. see °*vāna*; 'invoker,' a sacrificing priest, L. °**huvāna**, m. (pf. p. Ā. √*hve*) 'invoked,' fire, L. (also °*vāṇa*); 'cryer,' a hard-hearted man, L.; a tree, L.

Juhūrāṇa, m. for °*hur*°, L.; for °*huvāna*, fire, L.; a sacrificing priest, L.

जुहू *juhū́*, f. (= *jihvā́*, √*hve*) a tongue (esp. of Agni; 7 are named, RV. i, 58, 7), flame, RV.; personified as wife of Brahmā and goddess of speech (author of x, 109), RAnukr.; (fr. √*hu*, Pāṇ. iii, 2, 178, Vārtt. 3; Uṇ. &c.) a curved wooden ladle (for pouring sacrificial butter into fire), RV.; AV. &c.; that part of the frame enshrining the universal spirit which faces the east, ChUp. iii, 15, 2. **-tvá**, n. the condition of a sacrificial ladle, MaitrS. iii, 1, 1. **-m-agrīya**, m. N. of MaitrS. iii, 1. **-vat**, m. 'tongued,' Agni, L. **Juhv-āsya**, mfn. tongue-mouthed (Agni), RV. i, 12, 6.

Juhūshu, mfn. (√*hu*, Desid.) intending to sacrifice (with acc.), Hcat. i, 3, 939; Siṇhâs. ii, 1.

Juhoti, m. a technical name for those sacrificial ceremonies to which √*hu* (not √*yaj*) is applied, KātyŚr.; Mn. ii, 84; xi, 223, Kull. **Juhoty-ādi**, the (3rd) class of roots beginning with √*hu*, Pāṇ. ii, 4, 75.

Júhvat, °**hvāna**, mfn. pr. p. P. Ā. √*hu*, q. v.

जू 1. *jū* (cf. √*jinv*), cl. 1. Ā., 9. P. *jávate*, *junāti* (√*ju*, cl. 1. P. *javati*, Dhātup. xxii, 60, v. l.; a Sautra rt., Pāṇ. iii, 2, 177; 3, 97 & 4, 80, Kāś.; Subj. 2. sg. *junā́s*; aor. Subj. *jūjuvat*; pf. 3. pl. *jūjuvur*) to press forwards, hurry on, be quick, RV. iii, 33, 1; ŚBr. x; to impel quickly, urge or drive on, incite, RV.; TS. vi; to scare, RV. i, 169, 3; to excite, promote, animate, inspire, RV.: Caus. aor. *ajījavat*, Pāṇ. vii, 4, 80, Sch.: Caus. Desid. *jijāvayishati*, ib., Kāś.; cf. *pra-*.

Júvas, n. quickness, RV. ix, 65, 18.

2. **Jū́**, mfn. (Pāṇ. iii, 2, 177 & 178, Vārtt. 2) quick, speedy, (m.) courser, RV. i, 134, 1 & 140, 4; (ii, 14, 3?, acc. pl.; see 2. *júr*); inciting, driving, VS. ii, 17; ŚBr. x, 3, 5, 2 & 5; f. speed, L.; the atmosphere, L.; a female goblin, L.; Sarasvatī, L.; a spot on the forehead (?) of horses and oxen, Uṇ., Sch.; cf. *api-*, *kaśo-*, *dhī-*, *nabho-*, *mano-*, *yātu-*, *vayo-*, *vasū-*, *viśva-*, *sadyo-*, *sanā-*, & *senā-jū́*.

Jūjuvás, mfn. (pf. p. P.) speedy, RV. iv, 11, 4; v.

Jūjuvāná, mfn. (pf. p. Ā.) id., 29, 9; x, 93, 8.

Jūtá, mfn. impelled, driven, iv, 17, 12; ix; cf. *ádri-*, *índra-*, *dásyu-*, *devá-*, *bráhma-*, *vā́ta-*, *vípra-*.

Jūtí, f. (Pāṇ. iii, 3, 97) going or driving on, quickness, velocity, speed, RV.; AV.; VS. xxi; ŚBr. ii, xii; flowing without interruption, AV. xix, 58, 1; impulse, incitement, instigation, inclination, energy, RV.; VS. ii, 13; ŚBr. xii; = *pra-jñāna*, AitUp. v, 2; m. N. of the author of RV. x, 136, 1; cf. *rátha-*. **-mát**, mfn. impetuous, AV. xii, 1, 58.

जूक *jūka*, fr. ζυγόν, the sign Libra, VarBṛ.

जूट *jūṭa*, m. (fr. *cūḍa*?) twisted hair (of ascetics & Śiva), Mālatīm.; Rājat. iv, 1 & (ifc. f. *ā*) 151.

Jūṭaka, n. id., L.; (*ikā*), f. (= *juṭ*°) id., Gobh., Sch.

जूतिका *jūtikā*, f. a kind of camphor, L.

जूमरनन्दिन् *jūmara-nandin*, m. = *jum*°.

जूर् 1. *jūr*, cl. 4. Ā. See √1. *jur*.

जूर् 2. *jūr* (cf. √*jvar*), cl. 4. Ā. °*ryate*, to hurt, Dhātup.; to be angry with (dat.), Bhaṭṭ. xi, 8.

3. **Jūr**, mfn. fr. √*jvar*, Pāṇ. vi, 4, 20.

Jūra, m. = *hiṇsana*, Śiś. xix, 102; (*ī*), f. saliva, ŚāṅkhBr. xix, 3, Sch.

2. **Jūrṇa**, mfn. fr. √*jvar*, Pāṇ. vi, 4, 20, Sch.

1. **Jūrṇí**, f. glowing fire, blaze, RV. vii, 39, 1; viii, 72, 9; a fiery weapon, i, 129, 8 (Nir. vi, 4); anger, Naigh. ii, 13; = °*rti*, L.; (fr. √1. *jur*, 'decaying'?) the body, L.; (for *jūti*) speed, L.; m. the sun, L.; Brahmā, L. °**ṇin**, mfn. glowing, RV. vi, 63, 4.

Jūrti, f. = *jvara*, fever, Pāṇ. vi, 4, 20, Kāś.

जूर्ण 1. & 2. *jūrṇá*. See 2. *jūr* & p. 423, col. 3.

जूर्णि 2. *jū́rṇi*. See √2. *jṛī*.

जूर्य *jū́rya*. See col. 1.

जूर्व् *jūrv* (cf. √2. *jūr*), cl. 1. P. (p. *jū́rvat*) to consume by heat, singe, RV. i, 191, 9 (Naigh. ii); to hurt, Vop. (Dhātup. xv); cf. *ni-*, *sam-*.

जूष् *jūsh*, cl. 1. P., v. l. for √*yūsh*.

Jūshaṇa, n. Grislea tomentosa, L.

जूष *jūsha*, n. (cf. *jushkaka*) = *yūsha*, L.

जृ 1. *jṛī*, cl. 1. P. See √1. *jṛī*.

जॄ 2. *jṛī*, cl. 1. Ā. (2. du. *jarethe* & Impv. °*thām*; *jarante*, °*rasva*; p. *járamāṇa*) to come near, approach, RV. i–iv, vii f.; x, 40, 3.

जृङ्ग *jṛiṅga*, or °*gi*, m. pl. N. of a people, VarBṛS. iv, 22 (v. l. *bhṛiṅgi*); xiv, 21.

जृम्भ् *jṛimbh* (cf. √*jabh*), cl. 1. Ā. *jṛímbhate* (ep. also P. °*bhati*; p. °*bhamāṇa*; pf. *jajṛimbhe*; ind. p. *jṛimbhitvā*) to open the mouth, yawn, ĀśvGṛ. iii, 6; Mn. &c.; to gape open, open (as a flower), Ṛitus.; Kathās. xxv; to fly back or recoil (as a bow when unstrung), MBh. v, 1909; to unstring a bow, R. iii, 30, 28; to unfold, spread (as a flood &c.), expand, occupy a larger circuit, MBh.; Hariv.; Bhartṛ. iii, 41; Rājat. v, 269; to spread (as sound), v, 363; to feel at ease, Hariv. 12073; Kum. iii, 24; Kathās. vii, 102; Rājat. vi, 283: Caus. (pf. *jṛimbhayām āsa*) to cause to yawn, Hariv. 10632: Intens. *jarījṛimbhate*, to spread everywhere, Dhūrtan. Introd.

Jṛimbha, m. (n., g. *ardharcâdi*) yawning, Suśr. iii, 4, 49; Mn. iv, 43, Kull.; blossoming, Ratnâv. ii, 4 (ifc. f. *ā*); appearance of (in comp.), Subh.; expansion, stretching, W.; m. swelling, L.; N. of a bird, R. ii, 35, 18; (*ā*), f. blossoming, Mālatīm. ix, 16.

Jṛimbhaka, m. 'yawner,' a sort of spirit or demon, MBh. iii, 14548; Hcat. i, 9, 183; (= *jambh*°) N. of certain magical formularies for exorcising the evil spirits supposed to possess weapons, R. i, 30, 7; (*ikā*), f. yawning, MBh. v, 282 f.; Kād.; Kathās.

Jṛimbhaṇa, mfn. causing to yawn, Hariv.; R. i, 56, 7; BhP. iii, x; n. yawning, Suśr.; VarBṛS.; BhP. v; Vedântas.; stretching the limbs, slackness, Ṛitus.; Vet.; bursting open, blossoming, Bhartṛ. i, 24.

Jṛimbhā, f., see °*bha*. **-vat**, mfn. yawning, W.

Jṛimbhita, mfn. opened, expanded, enlarged, increased, MBh. vii, 8198; Kathās. lxiv, lxxi; opened (a flower), L.; unstrung (a bow), R. i, 75, 17 ff.; (fr. Caus.) caused to yawn, Hariv. 10633; exerted, W.; n. yawning, Suśr.; bursting, opening, unfolding, Kathās. xxvi, 89; developing, swelling, W.; exertion, L.; wish, L.; a kind of coitus, L. °**bhin**, mfn. yawning, W.; blossoming, W.; (*inī*), f. Mimosa octandra, L.

जॄ 1. *jṛī* (cf. √*jur*), cl. 1. P. (3. pl. *járanti*; Impv. 2. du. *járatam*; p. *járat*, see s. v.) to make old or decrepit, RV. vi, 24, 7; to cause to grow old, vii, 67, 10; (√1. *jṛī*) to humiliate, L.: cl. 4. P. *jīryati* (AV. &c.; also Ā. °*te*; p. *jīryat*, rarely °*yamāṇa*; once cl. 1. Ā. Subj. 3. pl. *jaranta*, RV. x, 31, 7; cl. 9. *jṛiṇāti*, Dhātup. xxxi, 24; cl. 10. *jārayati*, xxxiv, 9; pf. *jajā́ra*, AV. x, 8, 26 &c.; once *jagāra*, v, 19, 10; 3. pl. *jajarur* & *jerur*, Pāṇ. vi, 4, 124; aor. *ajarat* & *ajārīt*, iii, 1, 38; Subj. 3. pl. *jārishur*, RV.; fut. 1st *jaritā* & °*rītā*, Vop. xi, 2; ind. p. °*ritvā* & °*rītvā*, Pāṇ. vii, 2, 55) to grow old, become decrepit, decay, wear out, wither, be consumed, break up, perish, RV.; AV. &c.; to be dissolved or digested, Yājñ. iii, 111; MBh. i, 1331; Suśr.; VarBṛS.; Bhaṭṭ.: Caus. *jarayati* (ep. also Ā. °*te*; p. °*ráyat*, RV. [once *jār*°, i, 124, 10] &c.) to make old, wear out, consume, RV.; TS. iv; KaṭhUp.; MBh. &c.; to digest, MBh.; R.; Car. i, 21; to cause to be digested, MBh. xii; R.; BhP.

जॄ 2. *jṛī* (= √*gṛī*), cl. 1. Ā. *járate* (p. *járamāṇa*) to crackle (as fire), RV.; (Naigh. iii, 14) to call out to, address, invoke, praise, RV.; cf. γῆρυς.

Jugurvaṇi, mfn. fond of praising, i, 142, 8.

2. **Jū́rṇi**, mfn. invoking, 127, 10.

जेज्झट *jejjaṭa*. See *jaijj*°.

जेत *jeta*, in comp. irr. for °*tṛi*. **-vana**, n. 'Jetṛi's wood,' N. of a grove near Śrāvastī (where Buddha promulgated his doctrines), Buddh. **-°vanīya**, m. pl. N. of a Buddh. school. **-sâhvaya**, mfn. 'called after Jetṛi,' with *vana*, n. = °*ta-vana*, Lalit.

Jetavya, mfn. (√*ji*) to be conquered, conquerable, MBh. ii, 769; Prab. iv, ½; n. impers. to be conquered, R. vi, 91, 7. **Jetu-kāma**, mfn. (fr. inf. °*tum*) desirous of victory, MBh. iii, 133, 22.

Jétṛi, mfn. victorious, triumphant, gaining, (m.) conqueror, RV.; AV. &c.; m. N. of a son of Madhucchandas (author of RV. i, 11), RAnukr.; of a prince who had a grove near Śrāvastī (cf. °*ta-vana*), Buddh.

Jétva, mfn. to be gained, RV. vi, 47, 26; (*jait*°) TāṇḍyaBr. 1. **Jéman**, mfn. victorious, RV. x, 106.

2. **Jemán**, m. victoriousness, VS. xviii, 4; TS. i, 6, 2, 4; vii, 4, 3, 2; TāṇḍyaBr. xiii, 12, 8; xv, 5, 30.

Jeya, mfn. (Kāś. on Pāṇ. iii, 1, 97 & vi, 1, 213) to be conquered, MBh. xv, 220; MārkP. xxvii; xxxix.

Jeshá, m. gaining, RV. i, 100, 11; vi, 44, 18; cf. *uj-*, *kshetra-* & *svar-jeshá*, *vi-*.

जेन्ताक *jentāka*, m. a dry hot bath, Car.

जेन्य *jénya*, mfn. (√*jan*) of noble origin (cf. γενναῖος), RV.; genuine, true (wealth, *vásu*), ii, 5, 1; viii, 101, 6. **Jenyā-vasu**, mfn. having genuine [or 'acquired,' Sāy. fr. √*ji*] wealth, vii, 74, 3; viii.

जेमन *jemana*. See √*jim*.

जेय *jeya*. See above.

जेलक *jelaka*, m. N. of a man, Rājat. vii.

जेष् *jesh*, cl. 1. Ā. to move, Dhātup. xvi.

जेष *jeshá*. See above.

जेह् *jeh* (cf. √*jabh*, *jṛimbh*), cl. 1. Ā. (p. *jéhamāna*) to open the mouth, breathe heavily, be excessively thirsty, RV. i, 163, 6; x; to gape, i, 110, 5; to move ('to strive after,' Vop. & Sāy.), Naigh. ii.

जेहिल *jehila*, m. N. of a Jain Sūri (successor of Nāga), Kalpas. sthavir. xii f.

जै *jai*, cl. 1. *jāyati*, to wane, perish, Dhātup. xxii, 17; cf. √*kshai*.

जैकशून्य *jaikaśūnya*, m. N. of a man, Pravar. i, 1 (vv.ll. *jek°* & *jihvāś°*).

जैगीषव्य *jaigīshavya*, m. patr. fr. *jigīshú* (g. *gargâdi*), N. of an ancient Ṛishi (named along with Asita Devala), MBh. ii, ix, xii f.; Hariv. 952; VarBṛS. iil, 62; BhP. ix, 21, 26. **Jaigīshavyêśvara**, n. N. of a Liṅga in Bārāṇasī, KāśīKh. lxiii.

Jaigīshavyāyaṇi, f. of °*vya*, g. *lohitâdi*.

जैज्जट *jaijjaṭa*, m. (= *jaiyaṭa*) N. of an author on medicine, Ṭoḍar.; Bhpr.; (*jejj°*) Nid., Sch.

जैत्र *jaítra*, mf(ī)n. (fr. √*ji*) victorious, triumphant, superior, RV. i, 102, 3; x, 103, 5; MBh.; Ragh. &c.; leading to victory, RV.; ŚBr. xiii; ĀśvŚr. iv, 13; MBh. &c.; m. a conqueror, W.; N. of a son of Dhṛita-rāshṭra, ix, 1404; n. victory, triumph, superiority, RV.; AV. xx; TBr. ii; (*ī*), f. Sesbania ægyptiaca, L. — **ratha**, m. a triumphant car, Daś.

Jaitrāyaṇa, patr., Pravar. iii, 1 (v. l. *caitr°*).

Jaitrāyaṇi, fr. °*tra*, g. *karṇâdi*.

Jaitriya, n. victory, ĀpŚr. vi, 20. **Jaitva**, mfn., see *jétva*. **Jaitvāyani**, fr. *jitvan*, g. *karṇâdi*.

Jaina, mf(ī)n. relating to the Jinas, Sarvad. iii f.; Pārśvan. ii, 36; m. a worshipper of the Jinas, Jaina, Sarvad. iii, vii, xi; = زين, N. of a prince of Kaśmīr; (*ī*), f. the Jaina doctrine, Hcar. viii. — **taraṃgiṇī**, f. a history of Kaśmīr by Śrī-vara. — **nagara**, n. N. of a town built by prince Jaina. — **pāla**, m. N. of a man. **Jainâyatana**, n. a Jaina monastery, Daś. vii. **Jainâśrama**, m. id., L. **Jainêndra**, m. N. of a grammarian; cf. *jin°*; n. Jinêndra's grammar; *-vyākaraṇa*, n. N. of a grammar by Abhaya-nandi (commented on by Deva-nandi, Abhaya- & Soma-deva).

Jainya, mfn. relating to the Jainas.

Jaipāla, °**laka**, irr. for *jaya-p°*, Croton, Bhpr.

Jaimani, m. patr. fr. *jéman*, Pravar. iv, 1 & vi, 3 (v. l.) **Jaimantāyana**, v. l. for *jīvantyāy°*

Jaimini, m. (= °*mani*) N. of a celebrated sage and philosopher (he was a pupil of Vyāsa [who made over to him the SV., BhP. i, 4, 21; VāyuP.], Sāmav-Br.; MBh. i f., xii; and was Udgātṛi priest at Janamejaya's snake-sacrifice, i, 2046; and was founder of the Pūrva- or Karma-Mīmāṅsā, Pañcat.; Madhus.), ĀśvGṛ. iii, 4; ŚāṅkhGṛ.; Pravar. i, 4; iv, 1; Hariv.; Bādar. &c. — **kaḍāra**, m. = *kaḍāra-jaimini*, the red Jaimini, Pāṇ. ii, 2, 38, Kāś. — **kośa-sūtra**, n. N. of a work. — **bhāgavata**, n. N. of a modern revision of BhP. — **bhārata**, n. N. of a modern revision of MBh. — **sūtra**, n. N. of a work, Prauḍh.

Jaiminīya, mfn. relating to or composed by Jaimini (a Dharma-śāstra), Sarvad. xii, 19; m. an adherent of Jaimini, SŚaṃkar. xvi, 79; pl. N. of a school of the SV., Caraṇ.; n. Jaimini's work, Sarvad. iv, 195. — **nyāya-mālā-vistara**, m. N. of a compendium of the Mīmāṅsā philosophy by Mādhava.

जैमूत *jaimūta*, mfn. relating to the sage Jīmūta, MBh. v, 3845.

जैयट *jaiyaṭa*, N. of Kaiyaṭa's father.

Jaiyyaṭa, v. l. for *jaijjaṭa*.

जैव *jaiva*, mf(ī)n. belonging to the living personal soul (*jīva*), Bādar. ii, 3, 47, Sch.; relating to Jupiter (Thursday, Vishṇ. lxxviii, 5); VarBṛ.; Sūryas.

Jaivantāyaná, m. (Pāṇ. iv, 1, 103) = °*ti*, ŚBr. xiv, 7, 3, 26; Pravar. i, 4 (v. l.)

Jaivantāyani, fr. *jīvanta*, g. *karṇâdi*.

Jaivanti, m. patr. fr. *jīvanta*, Pāṇ. iv, 1, 103.

Jaivantyāyani, v. l. for *jīvantyāyana*.

Jaivala, m. patr. fr. *jīv°*, ŚBr. xiv, 9, 1, 1.

Jaivali, m. id., ChUp. i, 8, 1; v, 3, 1.

Jaivātṛika, mfn. (cf. *jīvā́tu*) long-lived, one for whom long life is desired, Daś. viii, 4 (voc.); thin, lean, L.; m. the moon, Bhām. ii, 76; camphor, L.; a peasant, Uṇ., Sch.; a medicament, L.; a son, L.

Jaivi, fr. *jīva*, g. *sutaṃgamâdi*.

Jaiveya, m. patr. fr. *jīva*, g. *śubhrâdi*.

जैष्णव *jaishṇava*, mfn. fr. *jishṇu*, W.

जैह्नवक *jaihnavaka*, *as*, m. a prince of the Jihnus, Pāṇ. iv, 2, 104, Vārtt. 28, Pat.

जैह्मति *jaihmati*, m. patr., Pravar. i, 1.

Jaihmākani, m. patr., ib. (vv. ll. °*māshmani* [for °*māśmani*?] & *jihmaka*). **Jaihmâśineya**, m. patr. fr. *jihmâśin*, Pāṇ. vi, 4, 174; g. *śubhrâdi*.

Jaihmi, m. patr. fr. *jihmá*, Pravar. vi, 3 (v. l.)

Jaihmya, n. (fr. *jihmá*) 'crookedness,' deceit, falsehood, Mn. xi, 68; Yājñ. iii, 229; Vyavahārat.

जैह्व *jaíhva*, mfn. lying on or relating to the tongue (*jihvā́*), Suparṇ. xvii, 1; Bālar. i, 14.

Jaihvalāyani, patr. fr. *jihvala*, Pravar. ii, 2, 1.

Jaihvākāta, mfn. fr. *jihvā-kātya*, Pāṇ. i, 1, 73, Vārtt. 8. **Jaihvya**, n. the sense of taste in the tongue, BhP. iv, 29, 54; vii, 6, 13 & 15, 18.

जोगू *jógū*, mfn. (√*gu*) praising, RV. x, 53.

जोङ्ग *joṅga*, n. (cf. *juṅga*) aloe wood, L.

Joṅgaka, n. id., Bhpr. v, 2, 21; cf. °*gala*.

जोङ्गट *joṅgaṭa*, m. = *dohada*, L.

जोङ्गल *joṅgala*, m. = °*gaka*, Npr.

जोटिङ्ग *joṭiṅga*, m. an ascetic who subjects himself to severe penances, L.; Śiva, L.

Joṭin, °**ṭiṅga**, m. Śiva, L.

जोड *joḍa*, ifc. the chin (e.g. *a-*, *aśva-*, *eka-*, *khara-*, *go-*, *markaṭa-*, *sūkara-*, *hasti-*; *jahi-*), L.

जोतिक *jotika*, m. N. of a family, Ratnak.

जोनराज *jona-rāja*, m. N. of the author of Rājat. (commenced A.D. 1148).

जोन्नाला *jonnālā*, f. = *yavanāla*, L.

जोमा *jomā*, f. a kind of broth, Divyâv.

जोल *jola*, N. of a mixed caste, BrahmavP. i, 9, 121 (also °*lā jāti*).

जोष *jósha*, m. (√*jush*) satisfaction, approval, pleasure, RV. i, 120, 1; *jósham ā́* or *ánu j°*, 'according to one's pleasure, to one's satisfaction,' RV.; silence, Naish. v, 78; (*am*), ind. (g. *svar-ādi*) according to one's wish or liking, RV.; with √*ās* [MBh. ii, vii f., xii, xv; Śak. v, 1⅛], √1. *as* [Naish. vi, 107; Pārśvan. iii, 168], √*sthā* [KāśīKh.], to remain quiet or silent; cf. *á-*, *sa-jósha*, *yathā-josham*. — **vāká**, m. chattering nonsense, RV. vi, 59, 4.

Joshaka. See *kāla-*, s. v. 2. *kālá*.

Joshaṇa, n. ifc. liking, BhP. iii, 25, 25; 'choosing,' see *bhūmi-joshaṇá*; approval, W.; (*ā*), f. expression of satisfaction by the word *jush*, KātyŚr. v.

Joshayitavya, mfn. to be approved without reflection, Nir. v, 21. **Jóshayitṛi**, mfn. = *joshṭṛí*, ŚBr. ix, 2, 3, 10 (superl. *-tama*); Nir. ix, 41 f. (f. °*ṭrī*).

Joshas. See *ví-*, *sa-jóshas*.

Joshṭṛi & **jóshṭṛi**, mf(nom. du. °*shṭrī*)n. loving, cherishing, fostering, RV. iv, 41, 9; VS.; ĀśvŚr. ii, 16; ŚāṅkhŚr. viii, 18, 6; MānGṛ.; Nir.

Jóshya, mfn. delightful, RV. i, 173, 8; BhP.; cf. *á-*.

जोषा *joshā*, f. = *yoshā*, a woman, L.

जोषिका *joshikā*, f. a cluster of buds, L.

जोषित् *joshit*, °*shitā*, f. = *yoshit*, L.

जोहूत्र *johū́tra*, mfn. (√*hve*) making noise, RV. ii, 10, 1; challenging, 20, 3; neighing, i, 118, 9.

जौमर *jaumara*, n. Jumara's grammar; m. pl. the followers of Jumara, Durgād. on Vop.

जौलायनभक्त *jaulāyana-bhakta*, mfn. inhabited by the Jaulāyanas, g. *aishukāry-ādi*.

जौहव *jauhava*, mfn. relating to the sacrificial ladle (*juhū́*), KātyŚr. vi, 7, 6.

जौहोत्यादिक *jauhotyādika*, mfn. belonging to *juhoty-ādi*, Pāṇ. iii, 1, 56, Siddh.

ज्ञ 1. *jña*, for 1. *jñu*. See *ūrdhva-*.

1. **Jñu**, in comp. & ifc. (see *abhi-* & *asita-jñú*, *ūrdhvá-*, *pra-*, *mitá-*, *saṃ-*) for *jānu*. — **bā́dh**, mfn. bending the knees, RV. vi, 1, 6.

ज्ञ 2. *jñá*, *jñaka*, *jñapita*, &c. See below.

ज्ञा 1. *jñā*, cl. 9. P. Ā. *jānā́ti*, °*nīté* (cf. Pāṇ. i, 3, 76; Subj. °*nā́t*; Impv. °*nītā́t*, 2. sg. °*nīhi*, once irr. *jña*, BhP. x, 89, 46; [fr. cl. 3.] *jijāhi*, MBh. xiii, 4493; 2. pl. irr. °*nata*. ii, 2397; 2. sg. Ā. irr. °*nase*, Divyâv. xviii; p. °*nát*, °*nāná*, irr. °*namāna* [MBh.]; pf. *jajñau*, °*jñe* [Pass., Rājat. v, 481], 3. pl. °*jñúr*, RV. vii, 79, 4; ŚBr. xi; p. °*jñāná*, RV. x, 14, 2; fut. *jñāsyati*, °*te*; aor. *ajñāsīt*, °*sta*, Pass. *ájñāyi*, vi, 65, 1 &c.; Pot. *jñāyā́t* or *jñey°*, Pāṇ. vi, 4, 68; 2. sg. *jñeyas* = γνοίης, RV. ii, 10, 6; inf. *jñā́tum*) to know, have knowledge, become acquainted with (acc.; rarely gen., MBh. iii, 2154; Hariv. 7095), perceive, apprehend, understand (also with inf. [Pāṇ. iii, 4, 65], MBh. ii, v; Daś.), experience, recognise, ascertain, investigate, RV. &c.; to know as, know or perceive that, regard or consider as (with double acc., e.g. *tasya mām tanayām jānīta*, 'know me to be his daughter,' MBh. iii, 2476; with *mṛishā*, 'to consider as untrue,' Ratnâv. ii, 18), Mn. &c.; to acknowledge, approve, allow, VS. xviii, 59 f.; AV. ix, 5, 19; ŚBr. i, xi, xiv; to recognise as one's own, take possession of, SaddhP.; to visit as a friend, AV. x, 1, 25; to remember (with gen.), MBh. xii, 5169; Ā. to engage in (gen., e. g. *sarpisho*, 'to make an oblation with clarified butter'), Pāṇ. i, 3, 45; ii, 3, 51: Caus. *jñapayati*, to teach any one (acc.), ŚāṅkhŚr. xv; *jñāp°* (Pass. *jñāpyate*) to make known, announce, teach anything, MBh. ii, xii; Kāty. & Pat.; to inform any one (gen.) that (double acc.), MBh. i, 5864; Ā. to request, ask, ChUp. ii, 13, 1 (*jñap°*); MBh. iii, 8762 (*jñāp°*): Desid. *jijñāsate* (Pāṇ. i, 3, 57; ep. also P.) to wish to know or become acquainted with or learn, investigate, examine, Mn. ii, 13; MBh. &c.; to wish for information about (acc.), Kathās. xxii, 84; to conjecture, AV. xiv, 1, 56: Caus. Desid. *jijñapayishati* (also °*jñāp°*, Siddh.) & *jñīpsati* (cf. °*psyamāna*), to wish to make known or inform, Pāṇ. vii, 2, 49 & 4, 55; [cf. γνῶ-θι &c.]

2. **Jñá**, mf(*ā*)n. (iii, 1, 135) knowing, familiar with (chiefly in comp.; rarely gen. or loc., MBh. xii, 12028; R. vii, 91, 25), ŚBr. xiv, 7, 2, 3; Mn. &c.; intelligent, having a soul, wise, (m.) a wise and learned man, ŚvetUp.; PraśnUp.; Bādar.; VarBṛ.; BhP. vii; having Jñā as deity, Pāṇ. vi, 4, 163, Pat.; m. the thinking soul (= *purusha*), Sāṃkhyak.; Nyāyad. iii, 2, 20, Sch.; the planet Mercury, VarBṛS.; VarBṛ.; Laghuj.; Sūryas.; the planet Mars, L.; Brahmā, L.; (*ā*), f. N. of a woman, Pāṇ. vi, 4, 163, Pat.; [cf. Lat. *mali-* & *beni-gnu-s*.] — **tā**, f. intelligence, Yājñ. iii, 142; Nyāyad., Sch.; ifc. knowledge of, Nal. xix, 24. — **tva**, n. intelligence, Nyāyad., Sch. — **m-manya**, mfn. thinking one's self wise, Rājat. iii, 491. — **śakti**, f. the intellectual faculty, Bādar. ii, 2, 9.

Jñaka, mf(*akā* or *ikā*)n. dimin. fr. 2. *jñá*, Pāṇ. vii, 3, 47. **Jñapita**, mfn. = °*ptá*, 2, 27.

Jñaptá, mfn. (2, 27) instructed, ŚBr. xi, 5, 3, 8 ff.

Jñapti, f. understanding, apprehension, ascertainment of (in comp.), VarBṛ. i, 2; Kathās.; BhP. x, 89, 2; Sarvad. xi f. (ifc. °*tika*); the exercise of the intellectual faculty, intelligence, BhP. x; Jaim. i, 1, 5, Sch. — **caturtha**, mfn. scil. *karman*, Divyâv. xxvi.

Jñaptika, see °*pti*. 2. **Jñā**, mfn. ifc. 'knowing, familiar with,' see *ṛita-*, *pada-* & *pra-jñá*, *á-sam-*.

3. **Jñā**, f. for *ā-j°* (by irr. Sandhi after *e* and *o*), MBh. i, 3168; iii, 16308.

Jñātá, mfn. known, ascertained, comprehended, perceived, understood, AV. xix, 15, 6; ŚBr. &c. (*ām jñātam*, 'Ah! I know,' Mṛicch. i, ⅛; Śak. &c.); meant (*mayā jñātam*, 'I meant'), Kād. vi, 995; taken for (nom.), Pañcat. i, 2, 2; known as (nom.) to (gen.), Vop. v, 27; m. pl. N. of Mahā-vīra's family, Jain. — **kulīna**, mfn. belonging to a known family, ŚBr. iv, 3, 4, 19. — **tā**, f. the being known or understood, Sarvad. — **nandana**, m. 'son of the Jñāta family,' Mahā-vīra, Jain. — **putra**, m. id., ib. — **mātre**, loc. ind. on its being merely ascertained, Nal. xvi, 4. — **sarvasva**, mfn. all-knowing, Caurap. — **siddhânta**, mfn. completely versed in any science, L. **Jñātā-dharma-kathā**, f. the 6th Aṅga of the Jains. **Jñātânvaya**, m. = °*ta-nandana*, W.

Jñātaka, mfn. known, &c., g. *yāvâdi*.

Jñātavya, mfn. to be known or understood or investigated or inquired after, MBh.; Hariv.; perceptible, 11143; to be considered as, Cāṇ.; Mn., Sch.

Jñāti, m. 'intimately acquainted' (cf. Goth. *knōdi*), a near relation ('paternal relation,' L. & Sch.; cf. *sam-bandhin*), kinsman, RV.; AV. xii, 5, 44; TBr. i &c. — **karman**, n. the act or duty of a kinsman, Gobh. ii, 1, 10. — **kārya**, n. id., Mn. xi, 188; Hariv. 9085. — **tva**, n. consanguinity, relationship, Mn. xi, 173. — **dāsī**, f. a female house-slave, R. ii, 7, 1. — **putra**, m. the son of a relative, Pāṇ. vi, 2, 133; for °*ta-p°*, Buddh. — **prabhuka**, mf(*ā*)n. foremost among relations, Yājñ. ii, ⅛, 28. — **prāya**, mfn. chiefly destined for kinsmen, Mn. iii, 264. — **bhāva**, m. relationship, Hit. ii, 5, 8. — **bheda**, m. dissension among relatives, Hariv. 7304. — **mat**, mfn. having near relations, ŚāṅkhGṛ. i, 9. — **mukhá**, mfn. having the appearance of a relative, AV. xviii, 2, 28. **-vid**, mfn. having or making near relations, Kauś. 78.

Jñātṛí, mfn. one who knows or understands, a knower, ChUp. viii, 5, 1; KaṭhUp. &c.; an acquaintance, (hence) a surety (cf. γνωστήρ), AV. vi, 32, 3; viii, 8, 21; a witness, Mn. viii, 57 (v. l. *sâkshin*). **-tva**, n. knowledge, Sarvad. ix, 49; xv, 127.

Jñāteya, n. (Pāṇ. v, 1, 127) affinity, kindred sentiments, Hcar. i, 534.

Jñā́tra, n. the intellectual faculty, VS. xviii, 7; TS. vii, 2, 4, 2; MaitrS. iv, 2, 8; TāṇḍyaBr. v, 7.

Jñāna, n. knowing, becoming acquainted with, knowledge, (esp.) the higher knowledge (derived from meditation on the one Universal Spirit), ŚāṅkhŚr. xiii; Gobh.; Mn. &c.; 'knowledge about anything, cognizance,' see *-tas* & *a-* (*jñānād a-jñānād vā*, knowingly or ignorantly, xi, 233); conscience, MBh.; =°*nêndriya*, KaṭhUp. vi, 10; engaging in (gen., e. g. *sarpishas*, 'in sacrifice with clarified butter'), Pāṇ. ii, 2, 10, Vārtt., Pat.; N. of a Śakti, Rasik. xiv, 36; RāmatUp. i, 90, Sch.; (*ā*), f. id., Pañcar. iii, 2, 30; Rāmapūjāś. **-kanda**, m. N. of a pupil of Śaṃkarâcārya, Śaṃkar. iv. **-kāṇḍa**, n. (opposed to *karma-k*°) that portion of the Veda which relates to knowledge of the one Spirit, TĀr. x, 1, 19, Sāy. (v. l. *khila-k*°). **-kīrti**, m. N. of a Buddh. teacher. **-ketu**, m. 'having marks of intelligence,' N. of a man, Lalit. xiii, 156; *-dhvaja*, m. N. of a Devaputra, iii, 160. **-khaṇḍa**, N. of part of ŚivaP. **-gamya**, mfn. attainable by the understanding (Śiva). **-garbha**, m. 'filled with knowledge,' N. of a Bodhi-sattva, Buddh. L.; of a scholar, ib. **-gūha**, mf(*ā*)n. concealing the understanding, BhP. iii, 26, 5. **-ghana**, m. pure or mere knowledge or intellect, viii, 3, 12; ix, 8, 23; °*nâcārya*, m. N. of a teacher, W. **-cakshus**, n. the eye of intelligence, inner eye, intellectual vision, Mn. ii, 8; iv, 24; MBh. xiii, 2284; (cf. *-dīrgha*); mfn. seeing with the inner eye, CūlUp. 16. **-candra**, m. N. of a man. **-tattva**, n. true knowledge, W. **-tapas**, n. penance consisting in striving to attain knowledge, W. **-tas**, ind. knowingly, Mn. viii, 288. **-tīrtha**, n. N. of a Tīrtha, W. **-tva**, n. the being knowledge, Sarvad. iii f. **-da**, m. an imparter of knowledge, W. **-datta**, m. 'given by knowledge,' N. of scholar, Buddh. L. **-darpaṇa**, m. 'mirror of knowledge,' Mañjuśrī, L. **-darśana**, n. supreme knowledge, Buddh.; Jain.; m. N. of a Bodhi-sattva, Kāraṇḍ. i, 3. **-dīpa**, m. the lamp of knowledge, W. **-dīrgha**, mfn. far-knowing, far-seeing (the eye, *cakshus*), MBh. xii, 6742. **-durbala**, mfn. deficient in knowledge, W. **-deva**, m. N. of a man, W. **-niścaya**, m. certainty, ascertainment, W. **-nishṭha**, mfn. engaged in cultivating true knowledge, Mn. iii, 134. **-°pata**, mf(*ī*)n. fr. *-pati*, g. *aśvapaty-ādi*. **-pati**, m. the lord of knowledge, ib.; N. of a man, W. **-para**, mfn. wholly devoted to knowledge of Spirit. **-pātra**, n. 'knowledge-vessel,' a man famous through knowledge, Siṃhâs. iii, $\frac{8}{9}$. **-pāvana**, n. 'purifying knowledge,' N. of a Tīrtha, MBh. iii, 7081. **-pūrva**, mfn. preceded by knowledge, well considered, Mn. xii, 89; Car. i, 18; *-kṛita*, mfn. done designedly, R. ii, 64, 22. **-prakāśa**, m. 'knowledge-illumination,' N. of a work by Jagajjīvana-dāsa. **-pradīpa**, m. N. of Yoga-sāra-saṃgraha ii. **-prabha**, m. 'brilliant with knowledge,' N. of a Bodhi-sattva, Buddh. L.; of a man, Buddh. **-pravāda**, m. 'lecture on knowledge,' N. of one of the 14 Pūrvas (or lost Jaina canon). **-prasthāna**, n. 'method of knowledge,' N. of a Buddh. work. **-bodhinī**, f. 'awakening knowledge,' N. of a Vedāntic treatise. **-bhāskara**, m. 'sun of knowledge,' N. of a medical compilation. **-maṇḍapa**, 'knowledge-temple,' N. of a temple, KāśīKh. lxxix. **-maya**, mfn. consisting of knowledge, MuṇḍUp. &c. (*sarva-*, Mn. ii, 7); (*ī*), f. with *mudrā* = °*na-mudrā*, RāmatUp. i, 49. **-mālā**, f. N. of a work, Smṛitit.; Vratapr. **-mudra**, mfn. having the impress of wisdom, wise, W.; (*ā*), f. a kind of Mudrā, Hcat. ii, 1, 765; Vratar. (AgSaṃh.) **-mūrti**, f. knowledge personified, VP. vi, 4, 42. **-meru**, m. knowledge-Meru,' N. of a man, Lalit. xiii, 159. **-yajña**, m. 'sacrifice of knowledge,' N. of Bhāskara-miśra's Comm. on TS. & TĀr. **-yoga**, m. the Yoga as based on the acquisition of true knowledge (opposed to *karma-y*° or the Yoga as based on performance of ceremonial rites), Bhag. iii, 3; VP. vi, 4, 42; NārP.; MatsyaP. **-ratnâvalī**, f. 'knowledge-necklace,' N. of a treatise, Sarvad. vii, 130. **-rāja**, m. 'king of knowledge,' N. of the author of Siddhânta-sundara. **-rādha**, m. pl. N. of a family, Pravar. v, 1. **-lakshaṇā**, f. 'knowledge-marked,' (in logic) intuitive knowledge of anything actually not perceivable by the senses, Bhāshāp. **-vajra**, m. 'knowledge-thunderbolt,' N. of a Buddh. author. **-vat**, mfn. (Pāṇ. viii, 2, 9, Sch.) knowing (that, *iti*), Vedāntas.; Tattvas.; endowed with knowledge or science, intelligent, wise, having spiritual knowledge, MBh.; R. vi, 102, 7; Laghuj. &c.; possessing knowledge (*loka*), ChUp. vii, 7, 2; m. N. of a Bodhi-sattva, Buddh. L. **-varman**, m. N. of a poet, ŚārṅgP. lviii, 1. **-vāpī**, f. 'knowledge-pool,' N. of a Tīrtha, KāśīKh. xxxiii f. **-vijñāna**, in comp., sacred and miscellaneous knowledge, Mn. ix, 41 &c. **-vibhūti-garbha**, m. 'filled with superhuman knowledge,' N. of a Bodhi-sattva, Buddh. L. **-vilāsa-kāvya**, n. N. of a poem. **-vṛiddha**, mfn. advanced in knowledge, R. ii, 45, 8. **-śakti**, f. 'intellectual faculty,' *-mat*, mfn. possessing intellectual faculty, Vedântas. **-śāstra**, n. the science of fortune-telling, Vet. v, $\frac{2}{3}$. **-śrī**, m. N. of a Buddh. author, Sarvad. ii, 84. **-śreshṭha**, mfn. pre-eminent in wisdom, W. **-saṃtati**, f. continuity of knowledge, MāṇḍUp. 10. **-saṃtāna**, m. id., Sarvad. xi, 81. **-sambhāra**, m. a great amount of knowledge, Lalit. iv, 123. **-sāgara**, m. 'knowledge-ocean,' N. of a Jain Sūri (author of a Comm. on Ogha-niryukti, A.D. 1383). **-siddhi**, m. N. of a man, Kathās. liv, 18. **-hasti**, m. N. of a man, Pravar. v, 1. **Jñānâkara**, m. 'knowledge-mine,' N. of a son of a Buddha; of a Buddha. **Jñānâgni**, m. 'knowledge-fire,' distinction between good and bad, GarbhUp. **Jñānâjñāna-kṛita**, mfn. done knowingly or ignorantly, Mn. viii, 145. **Jñānâtman**, m. the intellectual soul, VP. vi, 4, 42; RāmatUp. i, 89; ii, 5; mfn. all-wise, W. **Jñānânanda**, m. 'joy of knowledge,' N. of an author. **Jñānânutpāda**, m. non-production of knowledge, ignorance, W. **Jñānâmṛita**, n. 'knowledge-nectar,' N. of a grammar. **Jñānârṇava**, m. 'knowledge-ocean,' a wise man, BṛNārP. i, 23; N. of a Tantra; of a work (by Śubha-candra), Nirṇayas. i, 515; of a manual on med. by Yama-rāja, BrahmavP. i, 16, 17. **Jñānâvaraṇa**, n. 'knowledge-cover,' error, Sarvad. iii (Jain.) **Jñānâvaraṇīya**, mfn. resulting from error (°*ṇa*; one of the 8 kinds of *karman*), Jain. **Jñānâvalokâlaṃkāra**, m. N. of a Buddh. work. **Jñānâvasthita**, mfn. engaged in cultivating wisdom, W. **Jñānêndra-sarasvatī**, m. N. of a scholiast on Siddh. **Jñānêndriya**, n. 'knowledge-organ,' an organ of sensation, BhP.; Sāy. on ŚBr. ix. **Jñānôttama**, m. N. of an author, W. **Jñānôda-tīrtha**, n. 'Tīrtha of the waters of knowledge,' N. of a Tīrtha, KāśīKh. xxxiii. **Jñānôlkā**, f. 'knowledge-meteor,' N. of a Samādhi, Buddh.

Jñānin, mfn. knowing, endowed with knowledge or intelligence, wise, (opposed to *vi-*) knowing the higher knowledge or knowledge of spirit (Kathās. lxxix), Mn. xii, 103; Hariv. &c.; m. a fortune-teller, astrologer, R. vi, 23, 4; Kathās. xviii, 160; xix, 77; Vet.; 'possessing religious wisdom,' a sage, W. **Jñāni-tva**, n. fortune-telling, Kathās. xix, 75.

Jñānīya, Nom. P. to wish for knowledge, Vop.

Jñāpaka, mf(*ikā*)n. causing to know, teaching, designing, informing, suggesting, Hariv. 6518; Kāty. & Kāś.; BhP. ix, 6, 10; Sāh. &c.; m. a master of requests (particular officer at a Hindū court), Pañcat. iii, $\frac{81}{82}$; n. an expression or rule giving particular information (as a rule of Pāṇ. implying some other grammatical law than that resulting from the mere words of the rule itself), precept, MBh. i, 5846; Pat., Kāś. & Siddh. **-samuccaya**, m. 'Jñāpaka rules (of Pāṇ.),' N. of a work by Purushôttama-deva.

Jñāpana, n. making known, suggesting, Pat. & Kāś.; Rājat. iv, 180. **Jñāpanīya**, mfn. to be made known as (nom.), Kād. vi, 891.

Jñāpita, mfn. informed, ĀśvGṛ. iv, 7, 2; made known, known by (in comp.), Sarvad.; taught, Jaim. i, 1, 2, Sch.; instructed in (acc.), MBh. xiv, 415; Hariv. 10038. **Jñā́pti**, f. for *jñapti*, Buddh. L.

Jñāpya, mfn. to be made known, Sāh. iii, 20.

Jñā́s, m. a near relative, RV. i, 109, 1; cf. *á-*.

Jñīpsā, f. (fr. Desid. of Caus.) asking for information, Dhātup. xxviii, 120. **Jñīpsyamāna**, mfn. (Pass. p.) being desired to be informed, Pāṇ. i, 4, 34.

2. **Jñu**, ifc. (in Prākṛit *savva-ṇṇu*) for 2. *jña*.

Jñeya, mfn. to be known (e. g. *jñeyo mahârṇavo 'tra*, it should be known that there is here a great sea, VarBṛS. xiv, 19; *kathaṃ na jñeyam asmābhir nivartitum*, how should we not know how to leave off, Bhag. i, 39), Mn.; Yājñ.; R. &c.; to be learnt or understood or ascertained or investigated or perceived or inquired about, ŚvetUp. i, 12; MBh. iii, 2737; Nal. &c. **-jña**, m. 'understanding what is to be understood,' the mind, Yājñ. iii, 154. **-tā**, f. intelligibleness, KapS. i, 96, Sch. **-tva**, n. id., Bhāshāp. **-mallaka**, m. pl. N. of a people, MārkP. lvii.

Jñāndanīya, Nom. P. (Desid. *jujñ*° °*yishati*) to wish for the rice of Jñā, Pāṇ. i, 4, 2, Vārtt. 9, Pat.

ज्मन् *jmán* (only loc. *jmán*) = *kshā́man* (cf. *jmā́*, *jmás*, s. v. 2. *kshám*), RV. vii, 21, 6 & 60, 2; VS. xvii, 6; cf. *úpa-*, *uru-*, *dvi-bárha-*, *pṛithu-*, *pári-*. **Jma-yā́**, mfn. (Nir. xii, 43) going on the earth, RV. vii, 39, 3 (opposed to *urā́v antárikshe*).

Jmāyát, mfn. reaching the earth, viii, 68, 3.

ज्य *jya*, *jyakā*. See √1. *jyā* & 3. *jyā́*.

ज्या 1. *jyā* (cf. √*ji*), cl. 9. P. *jināti* (Pot. °*nīyā́t*; p. °*nát*; pf. *jijyaú*; fut. *jyāsyati*, Pāṇ. vi, 1, 16 f.; ind. p. *-jyāya*, 42) Ved. to overpower, oppress, deprive any one (acc.) of property (acc.), RV.; AV. &c.; (derived fr. *jyā́yas*, 'senior') to become old, Dhātup. xxxi, 29: cl. 4. Ā. *jīyate* or Pass. °*yáte*, Ved. to be oppressed or treated badly, be deprived of property (or everything, *sarva-jyānī́m*, TS. vii), RV. &c.: Caus. *jyāpayati*, to call any one old, Pāṇ. iii, 1, 21, Siddh. 46: Desid. (p. *jíjyāsat*) to wish to overpower, RV. x, 152, 5: Intens. *jejīyate*, Pāṇ. vi, 1, 16, Kāś.; cf. *pari-*; βιάω.

Jīta, mfn. oppressed, AV.; old, customary, of old, Jain. (Prākṛit *jīya*); cf. *á-*. **-kalpa-sūtra**, n. 'old Kalpa-sūtra,' N. of a work by Jina-bhadra. **-dhara**, m. Śāṇḍilya. **-vyavahāra-sūtra**, n. N. of a Jain text.

Jīna, mfn. (Pāṇ. viii, 2, 44; vi, 4, 2, Kāś.) old, aged, L.; n. a leather bag ('woollen cover,' Jain. Sch.), Mn. xi, 139 (*jīla*, Gaut. xxii; *jāla*, Sch.)

Jya, mfn. ifc. 'oppressing,' see *brahma-jyá*.

2. **Jyā́**, f. = βία, see *parama-jyā́*; excessive demand, ŚBr. v, 4, 5, 4. **Jyā́na**, n. oppression, iv, 1, 2, 4.

Jyānī́, f. (Pāṇ. iii, 3, 95, Vārtt. 4) id., MaitrS. ii, 2, 10; (cf. *á-*); 'loss,' see *sarva-jyānī́*; disappearance, Mālatīm. ix, 33; infirmity, old age, Vop. xi, 2; a river, L. **Jyā́ya**, see *nṛi-jyāyá*.

Jyā́yas, mfn. (Pāṇ. v, 3, 61 f.; vi, 4, 160) superior, more excellent, greater, larger, stronger, RV. &c. (ifc. [e. g. *vacana-*, 'superior in speech,' Kāś.], Pāṇ. vi, 2, 25); elder, RV. &c.; most excellent, Ragh. xviii, 33; (in law) being of age and answerable for one's conduct, W. **-tva**, n. superiority, Bādar. iii, 3, 57, Sch. **-vat** (*jyā́y*°), mfn. having a superior, AV. iii.

Jyāyasá, mfn. greater in number, ŚBr. xiv, 4, 1.

Jyā́yishṭha, mfn. (irr. superl.) most excellent, first, best, MBh. vii, 3701; Hariv. 7265.

Jyéya, mfn. to be oppressed or deprived of property, ŚBr. xiii, 4, 2; AitBr. vii, 29; (cf. *a-jyeyátā*, *brahma-jyéya*); most excellent, best, KenUp.

Jyéshṭha, mfn. (Pāṇ. v, 3, 61) most excellent, pre-eminent, first, chief, best, greatest, (m.) the chief, RV. &c. (ifc. [e. g. *vacana-*, 'best in speech,' Kāś.], Pāṇ. vi, 2, 25); more excellent than (abl.), MBh. xiii, 7205; (in math. with *pada* or *mūla*) greatest (root [square root] extracted from the quantity operated upon); (Pāṇ. v, 3, 62; °*shṭhá*) eldest, (m.) the eldest brother, RV. iv, 33, 5; x, 11, 2; AV. &c.; m. (scil. *ghaṭa*) the ascending bucket (in a machine for raising water), Kuval. 46; for *jyaishṭha*, VarBṛS.; Rājat.; N. of a man, MBh. xii, 13593; n. what is most excellent, RV. x, 120, 1; AV. (also oxyt.); tin, L.; N. of a Liṅga, LiṅgaP. i, 1, 3; with *pushkara*, see °*shṭha-p*°; (*ā́*), f. (g. *ajâdi*) the 16th (or accord. to modern reckoning 18th) lunar mansion (sacred to Indra), AV. xix, 7, 3 (parox.); TBr. iii, 1, 2; PārGṛ.; MBh. &c. (also pl.); the eldest wife, Mn. ix, 122 & 124; a preferred wife, L.; the 8th year in the Jupiter cycle of 12 years, VarBṛS. viii, 10; the middle finger, L.; a kind of stringed instrument; misfortune (personified as the elder sister of Lakshmī, PadmaP. v; cf. °*shṭha-lakshmī*), BhP. i, 17, 32; N. of a Śakti, Hcat. i, 8, 404; Gaṅgā, L.; (*ā*, L., *ī*), f. a small house-lizard (also *jyaishṭhī*, W.), Tithyād.; (*am*), ind. most, extremely, ŚBr. i, 8, 1, 4. **-kalaśa**, m. N. of Bilhaṇa's father, Vcar. xviii, 79. **-gṛihyá**, m. the eldest member of a family, ŚBr. xii, 4, 1, 4. **-ghnī**, f. = °*shṭhā́*, the 16th lunar mansion, AV. vi, 110, 2; TBr. i, 5, 2, 8. **-jaghanya**, mfn. pl. the elders last, ĀśvGṛ. iv, 4, 12. **-tama** (*jyéshṭh*°), mfn. best or first of all, RV. ii, 16, 1; vi, 67, 1; oldest of all, W. **-tara**, mfn. an elder one, Pañcat. v, 4, $\frac{2}{3}$; (*ā*), f. a woman guarding a young girl, Kathās. lxxv. **-°tarikā**, f. = °*rā*, ib. **-tás**, ind. (reckoning) from the eldest, according to seniority, AV. xi, 3, 32;

ĀpŚr. vi, 7, 8. **–tā**, f. precedence, seniority, primogeniture, Mn.; MBh. iii, 14461; Hariv. 7164. **–tāta**, m. a father's elder brother, L. **–tāti** (°*shṭhá*-), f. (Pāṇ. v, 4, 61) superiority, AV. vi, 39, 1; = -*rā́j*, RV. v, 44, 1. **–tva**, n. = -*tā*, MBh. i, 8372; ŚārṅgP.; Subh. **–pāla**, m. N. of a man, Rājat. viii. **–pushkara**, n. N. of a renowned place of pilgrimage, MBh. iii, xiii; (°*shṭha pushk*°) R. i, 62, 2. **–prathama**, mfn. pl. the elders first, MānGṛ. ii, 7. **–bandhu** (°*shṭhá*-), m. the chief of a family, MaitrS. ii, 2, 10. **–balā**, f. Sida rhomboidea, L. **–brāhmaṇa**, mfn. having the oldest Brāhmaṇa, TāṇḍyaBr. vii, 6, 7. **–bhavikā**, f. an elder brother's wife, Divyâv. ii, 83 & 113. **–bhāryā**, f. id., W.; a senior or chief wife, W. **–yajñá**, m. sacrifice of the eldest, TS. vii; AitBr. iv, 25; the most excellent sacrifice, TāṇḍyaBr. vi, 3, 8. **–rā́j**, m. a sovereign, RV. ii, 23, 1; viii, 16, 3; MaitrS. i, 3, 11. **–lakshmī́**, f. a chief mark, congenital mark (cf. AV. vii, 115, 3), MaitrS. i, 8, 1; TBr. ii, 1, 2, 2 ('indigence personified as the elder sister of Lakshmī,' Sch.). **–lalitā**, f. a particular vow to be observed in month Jyaishṭha, ŚivaP. **–vayas**, mfn. older than (in comp.), Kathās. iic, 28. **–vará**, m. a chief wooer, AV. xi, 8, 1 f. **–varṇa**, m. 'first cast man,' a Brāhman, L.; cf. MBh. xiii, 6571. **–varṇin**, m. id., Kām. ii, 19. **–vṛitti**, mfn. behaving like an eldest brother, Mn. ix, 110; f. the duties of seniority, W. **–śvaśrū**, f. a wife's elder sister, L. **–sāman**, n. the most excellent Sāman, TāṇḍyaBr. xxi, 2, 3; N. of a Sāman, Gobh. iii, 2, 54; MBh. xii f.; mfn. a chanter of that Sāman, Yājñ. i, 219; °*ma-ga*, mfn. id., Āp.; Mn, iii, 185. **–stoma**, m. N. of an Ekâha, ŚāṅkhŚr. xiv. **–sthāna**, n. N. of a place of pilgrimage, MBh. iii, 8204. **Jyeshṭhâṇśa**, m. the eldest brother's share, W.; the best share, W. **Jyeshṭhânujyeshṭhatā**, f. regular succession according to seniority, MBh. i, 2727 & 2742. **Jyeshṭhâmalaka**, m. Azadirachta indica, L. **Jyeshṭhâmbu**, n. the scum of boiled rice or water in which grain has been washed, L. **Jyeshṭhâśrama**, mfn. being in the most excellent order of life (viz. in that of a householder), Mn. iii, 78. **Jyeshṭhâśramin**, mfn. id., W. **Jyeshṭhêśvara**, n. N. of a Liṅga, KāśīKh. lxiii.

Jyeshṭhā́, f. of °*shṭha*, q. v. **–pūjā-vilāsa**, m. N. of a work. **–mūla**, m. the month Jyaishṭha, MBh. xiii, 4609 & 5156; VP. vi, 8, 33 ff. **–°mūlīya**, m. id., L. **–vrata**, n. a kind of observance in honour of Jyeshṭhā, TBr. ii, 1, 2, 2, Sch.

Jyeshṭhinī, f. a woman who has an elder brother, KātyŚr. xxiii, 1, 15, Sch.; cf. *jyaishṭhineyá*.

Jyeshṭhilā, f. N. of a river, MBh. ii, 373.

Jyaishṭha, m. N. of a month (May–June, the full moon standing in the constellation Jyeshṭhā), Lāṭy. x, 5, 18; Mn. viii, 245; Hariv. 7828; KātyŚr., Sch.; (*ī*), f. the full moon in month Jyaishṭha, VarBṛS. xxiii, 1 (cf. *mahā-jyaishṭhī*); see *jyeshṭhī*.

Jyaishṭhasāmika, mfn. fr. *jyeshṭha-sāman*, Gobh. iii, 1, 28. **Jyaishṭhineyá**, m. (g. *kalyāṇy-ādi*) a son of the father's first wife (*jyeshṭhā*), TBr. ii, 1, 8, 1; TāṇḍyaBr. ii, xx; KātyŚr. (fr. *jyeshṭhinī*, Sch.); Gaut. xxviii; Mn. ix, 193; MBh. ii, 1934.

Jyaishṭhya, n. = *jyeshṭha-tā*, RV.; VS. &c.

ज्या 3. *jyā́*, f. a bow-string, βιός, RV.; AV.; VS. &c.; (in geom.) the chord of an arc; = *jyârdha*, Sūryas.; cf. *adhi-, uj-, parama-, vi-* & *sa-jya; eka-, krama-, krānti-*. **–kārá**, m. a bow-string-maker, VS. xxx, 7. **–°kṛishṭi** (*jyâk*°), f. straining a bow-string, Amar. (Vcar.) **–ghoshá**, m. the twang of a bow, AV. v, 21, 9; MBh. xiii, 7471. **–pāśá**, m. a bow-string, AV. xi, 10, 22; Kauś.; MBh. iv, 164. **–piṇḍa**, °*daka*, a sine expressed in figures, Sūryas. ii, 31 f. **–°bāṇeya**, m. pl. N. of a warrior-tribe, & (sg.) a prince of that tribe, g. *yaudheyâdi*. **–magha**, m. N. of Vidarbha's father, Hariv. 1980 ff.; BhP. ix, 23, 33 ff. **–°rdha** (*jyâr*°), m. the sine of an arc, Sūryas. ii, 15; -*piṇḍa*, = *jyā-p*°, 16. **–vāja** (*jyá*-), mfn. having the elasticity of a bow-string, RV. iii, 53, 24. **–hroḍa**, m. a kind of bow (not used for shooting), TāṇḍyaBr. xvii, 1, 14; KātyŚr. xxii; Lāṭy. viii; du. N. of two Sāmans, ĀrshBr. **Jyôtpatti**, f. the calculation of sines, Gol.

Jyakā, f. (in geom.) the chord of an arc.

Jyā́kā, f. a bow-string, RV. x, 133; AV. i, 2, 2.

Jyāyamāna, mfn. like a bow-string, Daś. i, 18.

ज्या 4. *jyā*, f. the earth, L.; a mother, L.

ज्यु *jyu*, cl. 1. Ā. to go (= √*cyu*), Dhātup.

ज्युत् *jyut* (fr. *dyut*), cl. 1. Ā. *jyótate* (Naigh. i, 16; also P., Dhātup. iii, 4, v. l.) to shine, MaitrS. ii, 12, 4, 4; MBh. (v. l.): Caus. *jyotáyati*, to shine upon, illuminate, AV. (iv, 37, 10 &) vii, 16, 1; MBh. (v. l.); cf. *ava-*. **Jyuti-mat**, mfn. v. l. for *dy*°.

Jyotaya-māmaká, m. night-fire (?), AV. iv, 37, 10 (*gandharvá*, AV. Paipp.). **Jyotā**, f. 'the brilliant one,' mystical N. of a cow, VS. viii, 43.

Jyoti (only loc. °*tau*), = °*tis*, TāṇḍyaBr. xvi, 10, 2; cf. *daśa-, śata-*. **–darśana**, ?, GārgiS. **–rata**, m. N. of a Nāga (cf. °*tī-ratha*), Buddh. L. **–rathā**, °**thyā**, see °*tī-rathā*. **–shṭoma**, m. (fr. °*tis-stoma*, Pāṇ. viii, 3, 83) N. of a Soma ceremony (typical form of a whole class of ceremonies consisting originally of 3, and later of 4, 5, or 7 subdivisions, viz. Agni-shṭoma (q. v.), Ukthya, & Ati-rātra, or in addition to these Shodaśin, Aty-agni-shṭoma, Vāja-peya, & Aptor-yāma), TS. vii; ŚBr. x, xiii; AitBr. iii &c. **–°shṭomika**, mfn. fr. °*ma*, KātyŚr. xxiv, 5, 16.

Jyotiḥ, in comp. for °*tis*. **–parāśara**, m. the astronomer Parāśara, Smṛitit. i. **–pitāmaha**, m. Brahmā considered as the grandfather of astron. **–prakāśa**, m. N. of a work on astron., Nirṇayas. **–śāstra**, n. = °*tir-vidyā*, VarBṛS. i, 8 f.; cvi, 4; ŚārṅgP. **–shṭoma**, see °*ti-shṭ*°. **–sāgara**, m. 'luminary-ocean,' N. of a work on astron., Nirṇayas. i, 527 ff.; iii, 645 ff. **–sāman**, n. N. of a Sāman. **–sāra**, m. N. of a work on astron., 720. **–siddhânta**, m. another work on astron.

Jyotika, m. N. of a Nāga, MBh. i, 1558.

Jyotita, mfn. = °*tish-mat*, AgP. cccxxix.

Jyotir, in comp. for °*tis*. **–agra** (*jyót*°), mf(*ā*)n. preceded by light or life, RV. vii; AV. xiv, 2, 31. **–anīka** (*jyót*°), mfn. having a shining face, RV. vii, 35, 4. **–iṅga**, °**gaṇa**, m. 'moving light,' a firefly, L. **–īśa**, °**śvara**, m. N. of the author of Dhūrtas. **–udgamana**, n. the rising of the stars, Pāṇ. i, 3, 40, Pat. **–gaṇa**, m. the heavenly bodies collectively, W. **–garga**, m. the astronomer Garga, Nirṇayas. i, 56 & 58; iii. **–jarāyu** (*jyót*°), mfn. surrounded by a brilliant covering, RV. x, 123, 1. **–jña**, m. 'star-knower,' an astronomer, VarBṛ. xvii, 2. **–jvalanârci-śrī-garbha**, m. N. of a Bodhisattva, Buddh. L. **–dhāman**, m. N. of one of the 7 sages in Tāmasa's Manv-antara, BhP. viii, 1, 28. **–nirbandha**, m. N. of a work on astron., Nirṇayas. i, 41 & 563; ii, 8, 73 f.; iii. **–bīja**, n. 'light-seed,' = -*iṅga*, L. **–bhāga**, mfn. one possessing light, Nir. xii, 1. **–bhāsa-maṇi**, m. a kind of gem, Buddh. L. **–bhāsin**, mfn. brilliant with light, Hariv. 985. **–maṇḍala**, n. the stellar sphere, W. **–mantra**, m. N. of a Mantra, Sarvad. xv, 260 f. **–maya**, mfn. consisting of light, brilliant, MuṇḍUp.; Ragh. x, 24 (Vishṇu) &c.; (also said of Śiva); abounding with stars, starry, xv, 59. **–milin**, m. = -*iṅga* (cf. *nīla-milika*), L. **–mukha**, m. N. of one of Rāma's monkey-followers, R. vi. **–medhâtithi**, m. the astronomer Medhâtithi, Nirṇayas. iii, 706. **–latā**, f. 'light-creeper,' Cardiospermum Halicacabum, L. **–liṅga**, m. N. of several Liṅga temples. **–lekhā**, f. N. of the daughter of a Yaksha, Kathās. lxxiii, 422; -*valayin*, mfn. studded with rows of stars, W. **–loka**, m. the world of light, AV. Pariś. xiv, 1; BhP. v, 23, 8. **–vid**, mfn. = °*tish-kṛit*, TS. i, 4, 34, 1; knowing the stars, (m.) an astronomer, Yājñ. i, 332; Romakas.; Kathās. liv; -*ābharaṇa*, n. N. of a work on astron. **–vidyā**, f. astronomy, Buddh. L. **–vivaraṇa**, n. N. of a work on astron., Nirṇayas. iii, 758 f. **–hastā**, f. 'fire-handed,' Durgā, DevīP.

Jyotiś, in comp. for °*tis*. **–cakra**, n. 'luminary-circle,' the zodiac, BhP.; GarP.; LiṅgaP.; Tithyād. **–candrârka**, m. 'stars, moon and sun,' N. of a work.

Jyotish, in comp. for °*tis*. **–kaṇa**, m. a spark of fire, Ragh. xv, 52. **–kara**, m. 'light-causer,' a kind of flower, Buddh. L. **–karaṇḍaka**, n. N. of a work on astron. (written in Prākṛit by Pāda-lipta-sūri), Sūryapr., Sch. **–kalpa**, mfn. like fire, blazing, W.; -*latā*, f. N. of a work on astrol. **–√kṛi**, (ind. p. *jyótish-kṛitvā*) to illumine, TBr. ii, 1, 3, 9. **–kṛit**, mfn. creating light, RV. i, 50, 4; x, 66, 1; TS. i, 4, 34, 1. **–kaumudī**, f. N. of a work on astron., Smṛitit. i. **–ṭama**, mf(*ā*)n. (superl.) diffusing the most brilliant light, Bhaṭṭ. ix, 85. **–ṭva**, n. luminousness, TāṇḍyaBr. xvi, 1, 1; APrāt. iv, 102; the state of light, BhP. xi, 3, 13. **–paksha** (*jyót*°), mf(*ā*)n. light-winged, Kāṭh.; TS. vii; ŚBr. xi; TāṇḍyaBr. **–prabha**, m. 'brilliant with light,' N. of a flower, Buddh. L.; N. of a Buddha, Buddh.; of a Bodhi-sattva, ib.; of a prince, Kathās. lix, 59. **–prahīṇa**, mfn. deprived of light, blind, MBh. i, 178, 27. **–mat** (*jyót*°), mfn. luminous, brilliant, shining, belonging to the world of light, celestial, RV.; AV. &c. (°*tī trishṭubh*, 'the heavenly Trishṭubh' of 3 × 12 & 1 × 8 syllables, RPrāt.); spiritual, pure, Yogas. i, 36; m. the sun, Daś. viii, 114; = °*shī-mat*, q. v.; the 3rd foot of Brahmā, ChUp. iv, 7, 3 f.; N. of a son (of Manu Svāyambhuva, Hariv. 415; of Manu Sāvarṇa, 467; of Priya-vrata [king of Kuśa-dvīpa], VP.); of a mountain, BhP. v, 20, 4; (*tī*), f. 'star-illumined,' night, L.; a kind of sacrificial brick, VS.; TS. i; a kind of Trishṭubh; = °*shkā*, Suśr.; VarBṛS.

Jyotisha, m. an astronomer, Buddh. L.; the sun, Gal.; a particular magical formula for exorcising the evil spirits supposed to possess weapons, R. i, 30, 6; n. (g. *ukthâdi*) the science of the movements of the heavenly bodies and divisions of time dependant thereon, short tract for fixing the days and hours of the Vedic sacrifices (one of the 6 kinds of Vedâṅga texts), Āp.; MuṇḍUp. i, 1, 5; MBh. xii f. &c.; (*ā*), f. N. of a river, Vishṇ. lxxxv, 33. **–tattva**, n. N. of a work on astron. **–ratna-mālā**, f. another work on astron. **–vidyā**, f. astronomy, W. **–saṃgraha**, m. the whole science of astron., VarBṛ. **Jyotishârṇava**, m. N. of a work on astron., Smṛitit. vii.

Jyotishika, m. (= *jyaut*°, Gaṇar. 306, Sch.) an astronomer, VarBṛ. xiii, 3, Sch.; Siṇhâs. xxv, ½ (v. l.)

Jyotishīka, m. id., Gal.

Jyótishī-mat, mfn. (fr. du. of °*tis*) possessing the two luminaries (moon and sun), AV. xviii, 4, 14 (cf. RV. x, 53, 6); m. N. of one of the 7 suns, TĀr. i, 7, 1 & 16, 1; (°*sh-mat*, VP. vi, 3, 20, Sch.)

Jyotishka, m. Premna spinosa, Suśr. iv; Plumbago zeylanica, L.; the seed of Trigonella fœnum græcum, L.; N. of a Nāga (cf. °*tika*), MBh. v, 3631; of a man, Buddh. (Divyâv. xix); pl. 'the luminaries' regarded as a class of deities (arranged under 5 heads, viz. sun, moon, the planets, fixed stars, and lunar mansions), Jain.; n. N. of a luminous weapon (with which Arjuna destroyed Tamas), MBh. vii, 1325 (*jyautisha*, B); N. of a bright peak of Meru, xii, 10212; (*ā*), f. Cardiospermum Halicacabum, L.

Jyotishyà, mfn. illumined, TS. vi, 4, 2, 2.

Jyótis, n. light (of the sun, dawn, fire, lightning, &c.; also pl.), brightness (of the sky), RV. &c. (*trí-ṇi jyótīṇshi*, light appearing in the 3 worlds, viz. on earth, in the intermediate region, and in the sky or heaven [the last being called *uttamá*, VS. xx; AV. xviii; or *úttara*, i, 9, 1; or *tṛitī́ya*, RV. x, 56, 1], VS. viii, 36; AV. ix, 5, 8; MBh. iii; also personified as 'fire' on earth, 'ether or air' in the intermediate region, and 'sun' in the sky, ŚBr. xi, 5, 8, 2; ŚāṅkhŚr. xvi, 21, 2, &c.; 'fire, sun and moon,' Bhag. xv, 12); fire, flash of lightning, Megh.; Śak.; moonlight, RV. iii, 34, 4; AV. iv, 18, 1; (pl.) ŚBr. x & R. i, 35, 16; eye-light, RV. i, 117, 17; the eye, MBh. i, 6853; Ragh.; BhP. ix; du. sun and moon, Gobh. iii, 3, 18; Śatr. i, 28; pl. the heavenly bodies, planets and stars, Mn.; Bhag. &c. (°*tishām ayana*, n. course or movements of the heavenly bodies, science of those movements [= °*tisha*], Lāṭy. iv, 8, 1; Śiksh.; sg. the light of heaven, celestial world, RV.; VS.; AV.; ŚBr. xiv, 7, 2; light as the divine principle of life or source of intelligence, intelligence, RV. vi, 9, 6; VS. xxiv, 3; AV. xvi; Bhag.; (*paurusha j*°, 'human intelligence') Sarvad.; (*para j*°, 'highest light or truth') RāmatUp. & Sarvad.; light as the type of freedom or bliss or victory (cf. φάος, φῶς & Lat. *lux*), RV.; AV.; VS.; ŚBr. xiv; Suśr.; N. of several Ekâhas, TS. vii; ŚBr. xii f. &c.; of certain formularies containing the word *jyótis*, Lāṭy. i, 8, 13; a metre of 32 short and 16 long syllables; = °*tisha*, science of the movements of the heavenly bodies, L.; a mystical N. for the letter *r*, RāmatUp.; m. fire, L.; the sun, L.; Trigonella fœnum græcum, L.; N. of a Marut, Hariv. 11545; of a son of Manu Svārocisha, 429; of a Prajā-pati, VP.; cf. *dákshiṇā-, śukrá-, sa-, hiraṇya-*, &c. **–tattva**, n. = °*tisha-t*°, Nirṇayas. iii. **–sāt-√kṛi**, = °*tish-√*, Bhaṭṭ. ix, 85.

Jyotī, in comp. for °*tis*. **–ratha** (°*tí*-), mfn. one whose chariot is light, RV. i, 140, 1; ix f.; the pole-star, L.; a kind of serpent, Suśr. v, 4; (*ā*), f. N. of a river (joining the Śoṇa), MBh. iii, 8150 (°*ti-rathyā*); vi, 334; Hariv. 9511 (°*ti-r*°); Ragh. vii, 33. **–rasa**, m. a kind of gem, R. ii, 94, 6; VarBṛS.; Kathās.; mfn. made of that gem, MBh. iv, 24. **–rūpa-svayambhū**, m. Brahmā in the form of light, Buddh. **–rūpêśvara**, n. N. of a Liṅga, KāśīKh. xciv.

Jyótsnā, f. (Pāṇ. v, 2, 114) a moonlight night, TBr. ii, 2, 9, 7; moonlight, MBh.; R. &c. (ifc. f. *ā*, Kathās. cvii); pl. light, splendour, BhP. iii, 28, 21; one of Brahmā's bodies, 20, 39; one of the moon's 16 Kalās, BrahmaP. ii, 15; Durgā, DevīP.; Devīm.; the plant *jyotsnī*, L., Sch.; the plant *ghoshātakī*, L. – **kālī**, f. N. of a daughter of the moon (wife of Varuṇa's son Pushkara), MBh. v, 3534. – **°ādi** (°*nâd*°), a Gaṇa of Kāty. (Pāṇ. v, 2, 103, Vārtt. 2). – **paksha-tantra**, n. N. of a Tantra, Ānand. 31, Sch. – **priya**, m. 'fond of moonlight,' the bird Cakora, L. – **maya**, mfn. consisting of moonlight, Kād.; Hcar. – **vat**, mfn. illuminated by the moon, Ragh. vi, 34; shining, BhP. iv, 21, 26. – **vāpī**, f. 'moonlight-receptacle,' the moon, Alaṃkārav. – **vṛiksha**, m. a lamp-stand, L. **Jyotsnêśa**, m. 'moonlight lord,' the moon, L., Sch.

Jyotsnikā, f. the plant *kośātakī* (or *kṛita-vedhana*, Car., Sch.), L.; N. of a female singer, Mālav.

Jyotsnī, f. (for *jyaut*°) a moonlight night, Naish.; Trichosanthes dioeca, L.; N. of a medical substance, L.

Jyautisha, n. = *jyot*°, science of the movements of the heavenly bodies, Vātsyāy. i, 3; Brahmas.; Madhus.; for *jyotishka*, q.v.; N. of 2 Sāmans, ĀrshBr.

Jyautishika, m. = *jyot*°, g. *ukthâdi*.

Jyautsna, m. (Pāṇ. v, 2, 103, Vārtt. 2) the light half of a month, ŚāṅkhŚr. xiii, 19; Gobh. ii, 8; (*ī*), f. a full moon night, L.; Trichosanthes dioeca, L.

Jyautsnikā, f. a moonlight night, L.

ज्येय *jyéya, jyéshṭha*, &c. See √*jyā*.

ज्यो *jyo*, cl. 1. Ā. *jyavate*, to order, cause any one to observe a vow, Vop. (Dhātup. xxii, 69).

ज्योक् *jyók*, ind. (g. *svar-ādi*) long, for a long time or while, RV.; VS.; AV.; ŚBr.; ChUp. – √**kṛi**, to be long about anything, delay, RV. i, 33, 15; vii, 22, 6; to say 'farewell' (Sch.), Hcar. v (*jyot* for *jyok*; also Caus.). – **tamām**, ind. (superl.) for the longest time, longest, AitBr. ii, 8; ŚBr. x, 2, 6, 5.

Jyokti, f. long life (?), ĀpŚr. xiii, 3, 1.

Jyog, in comp. for *jyók*. – **aparuddha** (*jyóg*-), mfn. expelled a long time, TS. ii, 1, 4, 7. – **āmayāvin** (*jyóg*-), mfn. sick a long time, 1, 1, 3. – **jīvātu**, f. long life, ŚBr. xii, 8, 1, 20; xiii, 8, 3, 1 & 4.

ज्योडि *jyoḍi*. See *kara-, hasta-*.

ज्योता *jyotā*, °*ti*, °*tika*, °*tita*, &c. See √*jyut*.

ज्यौ *jyau*, m. (Ζεύς) planet Jupiter, VarBṛ.

ज्यौतिष *jyautisha*, °*shika*, &c. See above.

ज्रि 1. *jri*, cl. 1. P. *jráyati*, to go, Naigh. ii, 14; to overpower, Dhātup. xxii, 49; cf. *upa-*.

Jraya, see *pṛithu-jráya*. **Jráyas**, n. expanse, space, flat surface (Zd. *zarayo*), RV. i, iv–vi, viii ff.

Jrayasāná, mfn. spreading, expanding, occupying space, v, 66; x, 115. 2. **Jri**, see *uru-* & *pari-jri*.

ज्रि 3. *jri* or *jrī* (= √*jṝi*), cl. 1. 9. 10. *jrayati, jriṇāti, jrāyayati*, to grow old, Dhātup. (v.l.)

ज्वर् *jvar* (cf. √*jval*), cl. 1. °*rati* (cf. 3. *jūr* &c.) to be feverish, xix, 14; Caus. *jvarayati* (Pāṇ. ii, 3, 54) to make feverish (Pass. °*ryate*, 'to become feverish'), Car. vi; Suśr.; cf. *anu-sam-, sam-*.

Jvara, m. (g. *vṛishâdi*) fever (differing according to the different Doshas or humors of the body supposed to be affected by it; 'leader and king of all diseases,' Suśr.), MBh. &c.; fever of the soul, mental pain, affliction, grief, ib. – **kshaya**, m. 'anti-febrile,' Costus speciosus, VarBṛS. lxxviii, 1, Sch. – **ghna**, mfn. febrifuge, Car. vi, 3; Suśr. vi; m. = °*râri*, L.; Chenopodium album, L. – **cikitsā**, f. medical treatment of fever. – **dhūma-ketu**, m. N. of a febrifuge, Bhpr. vii, 1, 219. – **nāśaka**, mfn. = -*hara*. – **nāśinī**, f. = -*hantrī*, Npr.; = °*râri*, ib. – **nirṇaya**, m. N. of a medical work. – **pralāpa**, m. delirious words, Kād. iv, 268. – **brahmâstra**, n. N. of a febrifuge. – **hantrī**, f. 'febrifuge,' Rubia Munjista, L. – **hara**, mfn. febrifuge, Car. vi, 3. **Jvarâgni**, m. feverish heat, W. **Jvarâṅkuśa**, m. a febrifuge; Andropogon Jvarâṅkuśa, W.; N. of a work on med., Ṭoḍar. **Jvarâṅgī**, f. a kind of Croton, L. (v.l. *var*°). **Jvarâtīsāra**, m. diarrhoea with fever, Bhpr. vii, 15, 1 ff. **Jvarânta**, m. 'febrifuge,' a kind of Nimba, Gal. **Jvarântaka**, m. id., L.; Cathartocarpus fistula, L. **Jvarâpaha**, mfn. = °*ra-hara*, Car. vi, 3; Suśr. vi, 39; (*ā*), f. Medicago esculenta, L. **Jvarâri**, m. 'febrifuge,' Cocculus cordifolius, L. **Jvarâśani**, m. N. of a febrifuge.

Jvarita, mfn. (g. *tārakâdi*) feverish, affected with fever, Car. vi, 3; Suśr. i, 11 & 29; vi, 39; Caurap.

Jvarin, mfn. id., Suśr. i, 11; vi, 39; Hcat. i, 7, 315; ŚārṅgP. xxi, 10. **Jvāra**, see *nava-jvārá, pra-*.

ज्वल् *jval*, cl. 1. P. *jválati* (ep. also Ā.; p. °*lat*; aor. *ajvālīt*, Pāṇ. vii, 2, 2; 3. pl. *ajvalishur*, Bhaṭṭ. xv, 106) to burn brightly, blaze, glow, shine, TS. i; ŚBr.; Gobh.; MBh. &c.; to burn (as a wound), Suśr.: Caus. *jvalayati* or *jvāl*°, to set on fire, light, kindle, make radiant, illuminate, GopBr. ii, 5, 5 (Ā.); MBh. &c.: Intens. *jājvalati* (MBh.) or °*lyate* (Pāṇ. iii, 1, 22, Kāś.; p. °*lyamāna*) to flame violently, shine strongly, be brilliant, MBh.; R.; VP. iii, 2, 10; Rājat. i, 154.

Jvala, m. (Pāṇ. iii, 1, 140) flame, W. – **mukhī**, f. 'flame-faced,' N. of a tutelary deity in Lomaśa's family (cf. *jvālâm*°), BrahmaP. ii, 18, 28. **Jvalânana**, mfn. flame-faced, MBh. i, 5933 (v.l.)

Jvalakā, f. a large flame (v.l. *jhalakkā*), L.

Jvalat, mfn. pr. p. √*jval*, q.v.; m. blazing fire, flame, Kām.; (*antī*), f. black mustard, Npr. – **tva**, n. radiance, NṛisUp. ii. – **prabhā**, f. = °*lantī*, Npr.

Jvalan, in comp. for °*lat*. – **maṇi**, mfn. blazing with jewels, W.; m. a brilliant gem, W.

Jvalaná, mfn. (Pāṇ. iii, 2, 150) inflammable, combustible, flaming, ŚBr. xiii, 4, 4, 7; MBh. iii, 12239; shining, 769; m. fire, MaitrS. ii, 9, 1 (*jvál*° or [Padap.] °*lána*); Mn. x, 103; Yājñ.; MBh. &c.; the number 3, Sūryas. ii, 20 f.; corrosive alkali, Suśr.; Plumbago zeylanica (or its root, Npr.), L.; n. blazing, VarBṛS.; (*ā*), f. N. of a daughter of Takshaka (wife of Ṛiceyu or Ṛiksha), Hariv. (*jvālā*, MBh. i, 3778). – **kaṇa**, m. a spark of fire, Mudr. i, 2. – **bhū**, m. 'fire-born,' Kārttikeya, SŚaṃkar. i, 98; Kumārila (incarnation of Kārttikeya), ib. **Jvalanâśman**, m. the sun-stone, L.

Jvalanīya, mfn. fit to be burnt, combustible, W.

Jvalanta-śikharā, f. 'flame-tufted,' N. of a Gandharva virgin, Kāraṇḍ. i, 67.

Jvalita, mfn. lighted, blazing, flaming, shining, MBh. (*triṇeshu jvalitaṃ tvayā*, 'you have lighted flames in the grass,' i.e. you have had an easy work, v, 7089) &c.; (fr. Caus.) set on fire, Mn. vii, 90; n. radiance, Ragh. viii, 53; blazing, MBh. v, 133, 15. – **cakshus**, mfn. fiery-eyed, looking angrily or fiercely, W. – **nayana**, -**netra**, mfn. id., W. **Jvalitânana**, mfn. flame-faced, W.

Jvalitṛi, mfn. shining, NṛisUp. i, 2, 4, 4.

Jvalinī, f. Sanseviera zeylanica, L.

Jvāla, (Pāṇ. iii, 1, 140) mfn. burning, blazing, W.; m. light, torch, Kauś.; flame, MBh.; Hariv. &c.; (*ā*), f. id., ib.; illumination, KātyŚr. iv, Paddh.; causing a flame to blaze, Nyāyam. x, 1, 22; burnt rice, L.; = *jvalanā*, q.v. – **mālâkula**, mfn. 'light-garlanded,' shining brilliantly, TĀr. x, 11, 2.

Jvālā, f. of °*la*, q.v. – **khara-gaḍa**, m. = -*gardabhaka*, L. – **gardabhaka**, m. = *jāla-gardabha*, L. – **jihva**, m. flame-tongued, R. vii; fire, L.; N. of an attendant (of Skanda, MBh. ix, 2563; of Śiva, L., Sch.); N. of a Dānava, Hariv. 12935; of a demon causing diseases, 9559. – **dhvaja**, m. 'flame-marked,' fire, Rājat. iv, 41. – °**nala** (°*lân*°), mfn. with *rasa*, m. N. of a mixture, Bhpr. vii, 18, 83. – **mālin**, mfn. flame-garlanded, R. vii. – **mukha**, m. 'flame-mouthed,' a kind of demon (= *ulkām*°), Mn. xii, 71, Kull.; N. of a Brahma-rākshasa, Kathās. xciv, 71; (*ī*), f. fire or inflammable gas issuing forth from the earth, Bhpr. v, 26, 15; any place from which issues subterranean fire or inflammable gas (a celebrated Jvālā-mukhī, worshipped like others as a form of Durgā, exists in the hills north-east to the Panjāb); N. of a Mantra, GarP. cciv; (°*khī-mālinī*) Tantras. ii. – **rāsabhakâmaya**, m. = -*gardabhaka*, L. – **liṅga**, n. N. of a sanctuary of Śiva, Kathās. i, 28. – **vaktra**, m. 'flame-mouthed,' N. of an attendant of Śiva, BrahmaP. ii, 17. **Jvālêśvara**, n. N. of a Tīrtha, MatsyaP. (v.l.); RevāKh.

Jvālin, mfn. flaming (Śiva), MBh. xiii, 1171; (*inī*), f. a mystical N. of the letter *v*, RāmatUp. i.

झ JHA.

झ 1. *jha*, the 9th consonant (aspirate of the preceding). – **kāra**, m. the sound *jha*, W.

झ 2. *jha*, mfn. asleep, L.; m. playing a tune, beating time, L.; a sound like the splashing of water or clashing of symbols, jingling, clanking, L.; wind accompanied by rain, L.; anything lost or mislaid, L.; Bṛihaspati, L.; N. of a chief of the Daityas, L.; = *jhanṭīśa*, L.; (*ā*), f. a water-fall, L.

झगझगाय *jhagajhagāya*, Nom. Ā. (p. °*yamāna*) to sparkle, flash, DevīP.

झगिति *jhag-iti*, = *jhaṭ-*, Prasannar.

झङ् *jhaṅ*, ind. (onomat.) in comp.; (cf. 2. *jha*). – **kāra**, m. a low murmuring (buzzing of bees &c.), jingling, clanking, Pañcat.; Vikr.; Kād.; Bhartṛ. &c. – **kārita**, n. id., i, 97 (v.l. *taṃ-k*°). – **kārin**, mfn. murmuring, humming, &c., Kād. i, 251; Mālatīm. – **kṛita**, n. pl. = -*kāra*, Caitany.

Jhañjhana, n. jingling, clanking, W.

Jhañjhā, f. the noise of the wind or of falling rain, L.; wind and rain, hurricane, L.; raining in large drops, W.; a stray, W. – °**nila** (°*jhân*°), m. wind with rain, high wind in the rainy season, KāśīKh. lxxxviii, 98. – **marut**, m. id., Amar. – **māruta**, m. id., Pārśvan. vi, 52. – **vāta**, m. id., L.

झट् *jhaṭ*, cl. 1. °*ṭati*, to become entangled or intermixed, Dhātup. ix, 19; cf. *uj-jhaṭita*.

झटि *jhaṭi*, m. a shrub, Uṇ. iv, 117, Sch.

झटिति *jhaṭ-iti*, ind. onomat. (g. *svar-ādi*, not in Kāś.) instantly, at once, Bhartṛ. i, 69 & 95; Ratnâv. i, 6; Śṛiṅgār.; Kathās. vi, 118; ix; Rājat. &c.

झण् *jhaṇ*, cl. 1. °*ṇati*, to sound, Hcar. iv.

Jhaṇaj-jhaṇita, mfn. tinkling, Viddh.; HPariś.

Jhaṇajhaṇāya, Nom. Ā. (p. °*yamāna*) to tinkle, jingle, rattle, Mālatīm. i, 25/26; Kād.; Hcar.

Jhaṇajhaṇâyita, mfn. tinkling, Uttarar. v, 5.

Jhaṇajhaṇā-rava, m. pl. tinkling, Kathās. xxv.

Jhaṇajhaṇī-bhūta, mfn. rattling, MBh. vi.

Jhaṇat-kāra, m. jingling, Prab. ii, 34.

Jhaṇ-iti, v.l. for *jhaṭ-*, Kād. viii, 15.

झण्टि *jhaṇṭi*, see *hima-*. **Jhaṇṭîśa**, m. = 2. *jha*, q.v., L. **Jhaṇṭī**, °**ṇḍī**, f. a kind of grass, L.

झण्डुक *jhaṇḍuka*, m. = °*ḍū*, L.

Jhaṇḍū, f., °**ḍūka**, m. Gomphrena globosa, L.

झनत्कार *jhanat-kāra*, = *jhaṇat-*, W.

झम् *jham*, cl. 1. P. = √*cham, jam*, Dhātup.

झम्प *jhampa*, m., °*pā*, f. a jump (°*paṃ* [Hit.] or °*pāṃ* [HPariś.; Rājat. vii; Siṅhâs. xv, 4/5; xxi, 1/2] √*dā*, to make a jump, ifc. Kathās. lxi, 91), Vcar. xvi.

Jhampaḍa, n. (in music) a kind of measure.

Jhampā, f. of °*pa*, q.v. – **tāla**, m. (in music) a kind of measure; a kind of cymbal. – **nṛitya**, n. a kind of dance. **Jhampâśin**, m. a kingfisher, L.

Jhampāka, °**pāru**, m. 'leaper,' an ape, L.

Jhampin, m. id., L.

झर *jhara*, m. a water-fall, L.; (*ā, ī*), f. id., Prab. iv, 12; (*ī*), f. a river, W.; cf. *nir-*. – **vāhalā**, f. N. of a river.

Jharaṇôdaka, n. water from a cascade, Npr.

Jharat, mfn. flowing or falling down (cf. √*kshar*), Śatr. i, 41 & (?) 44.

झरसी *jharasī*, f. N. of a pot-herb, Npr.

झर्च *jharc, jharch, jharjh*, cl. 1. °*cati*, °*chati*, °*jhati*, to blame (fr. √*bharts*?), Dhātup. xvii, 66 & xxviii, 17 (v.l.); to injure, ib.

झर्झर *jharjhara*, m. a kind of drum, MBh. vi ff.; Pāṇ. iv, 4, 56; Hariv.; R. vi, 99, 23; a strainer, Bhpr. v, 11, 125; = °*raka*, L.; N. of a Daitya (son of Hiraṇyâksha), Hariv. 194; of a river, L.; n. a sound as of splashing or dropping, W.; (*ā*), f. a harlot (cf. *ṛiccharā*), L; (*ī*), f. a kind of drum, Hariv. 13212 & 15885; = °*rikā*, Bhpr. v, 11, 37.

Jharjharaka, m. the Kali-yuga, L.; (*ikā*), f. bean-cake, Bhpr. v, 11, 36. **Jharjharin**, mfn. furnished with a drum (Śiva), MBh. xii, 10406.

झर्झरित *jharjharita*, mfn. (√*jhṝi*) worn, wasted, withered, R. iii, 16, 26; Sarvad.; Priy. i, 10.

झर्झरीक *jharjharīka*, m. n. the body, Uṇ. iv, 20, Sch.; m. a region, Uṇ. vṛ.; a picture, ib.

झलक्का *jhalakkā*. See *jvalakā*.

झलज्झला *jhalajjhalā*, f. (onomat.) the sound of falling drops, Amar. (v.l.); the flapping of an elephant's ears (or of flaccid breasts &c.), Kām.

झलरी *jhalarī*, f. = °*llakī*, L.; a curl, L.

झला *jhalā*, f. a girl, L.; sun-heat, L.; (= *jhillī*) a cricket (also *jhālā*, W.), L.

झलि *jhali*, f. the areca-nut, W.

झल्ल *jhalla*, m. a prize-fighter, cudgel-player (offspring of an outcast Kshatriya), Mn. x, 22; xii, 45; MBh. ii, 102; (*ī*), f. = °*llakī*, L. — **kaṇṭha**, m. = *jhillī-k°*, L. **Jhallaka**, n. cymbals, Tithyād.; (*ī*), f. a kind of drum, L.

झल्लना *jhallanā*, f. N. of a Prākṛit metre.

झल्लरी *jhallarī*, f. a kind of musical instrument, sort of drum or cymbal (cf. *jhalarī, jharjharī*), Hariv. iii, 52, 2; Jain.; Kād.; (ifc. °*rīka*) Hcar.; a curl, L.; moisture, L.; a ball &c. of perfumed substances used for cleaning the hair, L., Sch.; = *śuddha*, L.

झल्लिका *jhallikā*, f. a cloth used for applying colour or perfumes, L. (also *jhill°*, W.; *jhillī*, L.); dirt rubbed off the body by the application of perfumes (also *jhill°* & *jhillīkā*), L.: light, sunshine (also *jhill°*, *jhillī* & *jhillikā*; cf. *jhalā*), L.

झल्लीका *jhallīkā*, f. = *jhillīka*, Svapnac.

झल्लीषक *jhallīshaka*, a kind of musical instrument, Hariv. 8450.

झल्लोल *jhallola*, m. a ball at the lower end of a spindle, L.

झष् *jhash*, cl. 1. °*shati*, to hurt, Dhātup. xvii, 38; (also Ā.) to take, xxi, 26; to cover, ib.

झष *jhashá*, m. a large fish, ŚBr. i, 8, 1, 4; a fish, MBh.; R.; VarBṛS.; BhP.; the sign Pisces, VarBṛ.; VarBṛ.; a forest, forest overgrown with grass, L.; sun-heat, L.; n. a desert, L.; (*ā*), f. Uraria lagopodioides, L. — **ketana**, m. = -*dhvaja*, Bhartṛ.; Ratnâv.; 'the god of love' and 'the sea,' Kuval. 33. — **dhvaja**, m. 'fish-symboled,' the god of love, love, Bhaṭṭ. viii, 48. — **pitta**, n. fish-bile, VarBṛS. l, 24. — **rāja**, m. a large fish, BhP. viii, 18, 2. — **śreshṭha**, m. 'most excellent fish,' the fish Rohita, Bhpr. **Jhashâśana**, m. 'fish-eater,' the Gangetic porpoise, L. **Jhashôdarī**, f. N. of Vyāsa's mother Satyavatī, L.

झां *jhām*, ind. (onomat.) in comp. — **kāra**, m. a low murmuring (of kettle-drums), Alaṃkārat. — **kārin**, mfn. = *jhaṃ-k°*, Mcar. iii, 48. — **kṛita**, n. (cf. *jhaṃ-k°*) a tinkling ornament worn round the toes or feet, L.

झाट *jhāṭa*, m. an arbour, L.; a forest (also n., W.), L.; cleaning sores, L.; (*ā*), f. = °*ṭikā*, L.; a kind of jasmine, L. **Jhāṭâmalā**, f. = °*ṭikā*, L. **Jhāṭâstraka**, m. the water-melon, W.

Jhāṭala, °**li**, m. Bignonia suaveolens, L.

Jhāṭikā, °**ṭikā**, f. Flacourtia cataphracta, L.

झाट्कारिन् *jhāṭ-kārin*, mfn. whistling (the wind), Veṇīs. ii, 18; cf. *jhaṅ-k°* & *jhāṃ-k°*.

झाबुक *jhābuka*, m. = *jhāvuka*, L.

झामक *jhāmaka*, n. (fr. *kshāmá*) a burnt or vitrified brick, L.

झामर *jhāmara*, m. a small whetstone (used for sharpening spindles, needles, &c.), L.

झार्झर *jhārjhara* & °*rika*, m. (fr. *jharjhara*) a drummer, tabor-player, Pāṇ. iv, 4, 56.

झालरी *jhālarī*, for *jhal°*, a kind of drum, W.

झाला *jhālā*, f. = *jhalā*, a cricket, W.

झालि *jhāli*, f. sour or unripe mango fried with salt, mustard, and Asa fœtida, Bhpr. v, 11, 155.

झावु *jhāvu*, m. Tamarix indica, L. **Jhāvuka**, m., °**vū**, f. id., L.

झिङ्गाक *jhiṅgāka*, m. Luffa acutang., L.

झिङ्गिनी *jhiṅginī*, = °*gī*, Bhpr.; a torch, L. **Jhiṅgī**, f. = *jiṅginī*, Bhpr. v, 5, 42.

झिज्झी *jhijjī*, f. = *jiñjhī*, W.

झिञ्झिम *jhiñjhima*, m. a forest on fire, L.

झिञ्झिरा *jhiñjhirā*, f. N. of a shrub, L. **Jhiñjhiriṭā**, °**rishṭā**, °**rīṭā**, f. id., L.

झिञ्झी *jhiñjhī*, f. = *jhillī*, a cricket, W.

झिण्टि *jhiṇṭi*, f. = °*ṭī*, Pañcar. i, 7, 19. **Jhiṇṭikā**, °**ṭī**, f. Barleria cristata, L.

झिरिका *jhirikā*, °*rī*, f. a cricket, L. **Jhirīkā**, °**rukā**, f. id., W. **Jhillarī**, f. id. (?, or = *jhall°*), L. **Jhilli**, f. id., Hariv. 3497; a kind of musical instrument, L.; parchment, W.

Jhillika, m. pl. v.l. for *jill°*, q.v.; (*ā*), f. a cricket, Nal. xii, 1; R.; a cricket's chirp, L.; a kind of vehicle, Hariv. ii, 88, 63; = *jhall°*, q.v., L.; = *jhiṇṭikā*, L.; membrane, parchment, W.

Jhillī, f. a cricket, BhP. v; the wick of a lamp, L.; = *jhallikā*, q.v., L.; rice burnt by cooking in a saucepan, L.; cymbals, W.; parchment, W. — **kaṇṭha**, m. a domestic pigeon, L. **Jhillīka**, m. a cricket, MBh. i, 2849; (*ā*), f. id., L.; = *jhallikā*, q.v., L.

झिल्लिन् *jhillin*, N. of a Vṛishṇi, MBh. i, vii.

झीरिका *jhīrikā*, °*rukā*, f. = *jhir°*, L.

झु *jhu*, cl. 1. Ā., v.l. for √*jyu*.

झुण्ट *jhuṇṭa*, m. a shrub, L.

झुमरि *jhumari*, f. N. of a Rāgiṇī.

Jhumbarī, f. a kind of lute, HPariś. viii, 359 ff.

झूणि *jhūṇi*, f. a kind of betel-nut, L.; a voice boding ill-luck, evil omen, L.; = *kaṭhina*, L.

झूष् *jhūsh*, cl. 1. P., v.l. for √*yūsh*.

झॄ *jhṝ* (= √*jṝ*), cl. 4. 9. *jhīryati*, *jhṛiṇāti*, to become old, Dhātup. xxvi, xxxi; cf. *jharjharita*.

झोड *jhoḍa*, m. the betel-nut tree, L.

झोम्बक *jhombaka*, mfn. making grimaces when singing.

झौलिक *jhaulika*, a small bag, Dhūrtas. ii.

झ्यु *jhyu*, cl. 1. Ā., v.l. for √*jyu*.

ञ ÑA.

ञ 1. *ña*, the palatal nasal (found before palatal consonants). — **kāra**, m. the letter ञ.

ञ 2. *ña*, m. a singer, L.; a jingling sound, L.; a heretic, L.; an ox, L.; the planet Śukra, L.

ट ṬA.

ट 1. *ṭa*, the 1st cerebral consonant (pronounced like *t* in *true*, but properly by keeping back the tip of the tongue and slightly turning it upwards). — **kāra**, m. the letter or sound *ṭ*. — **varga**, m. the cerebral consonants collectively, TPrāt.; Pāṇ.; Kāś. — °**vargīya**, mfn. belonging to the cerebral consonants, (m.) a cerebral, TPrāt. xiii, 14, Sch.

ट 2. *ṭa*, m. sound, L.; a dwarf, L.; a quarter, 4th, L.; n. = *karaṅka*, L.; (*ā*), f. the earth, L.; an oath, confirming an assertion by ordeal &c., L.

टक्क *ṭakka*, m. a niggard (?), Kathās. lxv; (cf. *ṭāka*, *ṭhakka*); m. pl. a Bāhika people, L. (°*kva*). — **deśa**, m. a Bāhika country, Rājat. v, 150. — °**deśīya**, m. 'coming from °*śa*,' Chenopodium album, L.

टक्करा *ṭakkarā*, f. a blow on the head, vf.

टक्किबुद्ध *ṭakki-buddha*, m. N. of a man, vii.

टक्व *ṭakva*, m. pl. See °*kka*.

टक्वर *ṭakvara*, m. N. of Śiva, L.

टगर *ṭagara*, mfn. squint-eyed, L.; m. borax, VarBṛS. xvi, 25; = *helā-vibhrama-gocara*, L.

टङ्क् *ṭaṅk* (derived from °*ka*, 'seal'), cl. 10. °*kayati*, to (seal up, i.e. to) shut, cover, KātyŚr. iv, x.

Ṭaṅka, (m. n., L.) a spade, hoe, hatchet, stone-cutter's chisel, Hariv. 5009 ff.; R. ii, 80, 7; Mṛicch. &c.; a peak or crag shaped like the edge of a hatchet, edge or declivity of a hill, MBh. xii, 8291; R. vii, 5, 24; BhP. viii, x; Bhaṭṭ. i, 8; a leg, L.; borax, L.; pride, L.; m. a sword, L.; a scabbard, L.; a weight of 4 Māshas, ŚārṅgS. i, 19; Vet. iv, ⅛; a stamped coin, Hit.; Feronia elephantum, L.; wrath, L.; (in music) a kind of measure; a man of a particular caste or tribe, Rājat. vii, 1003; n. the fruit of Feronia elephantum, Suśr.; (*ā*), f. a leg, L.; (in music) N. of a Rāgiṇī. — **ṭīka**, m. N. of Śiva, L.; cf. *jaṭā-ṭaṅka*. — **pati**, m. the master of the mint, L., Sch. — **vat**, mfn. having hatchet-like crags (a mountain), R. iii, 55, 44. — **śālā**, f. a mint, W.

Ṭaṅkaka, m. a stamped coin (esp. of silver), L., Sch.; a particular coin, Dhūrtas. i, ⅛; a spade, chisel, Dharmaśarm.; (*ikā*), f. a chisel, Vcar. x, 32. — **pati**, m. = °*ṅka-p°*, L., Sch. — **śālā**, f. = °*ṅka-ś°*, ib.

Ṭaṅkaṇa, m. borax, Kād.; pl. N. of a people (cf. *taṅg°*), R. iv, 44, 20; VarBṛS. xiv. — **kshāra**, m. borax, Suśr. i, 46, 7, 10; KātyŚr. ii, 1, Paddh.; Bhpr.

Ṭaṅkana, m. (= *ṭagara*) borax, L.

टङ्कानक *ṭaṅkānaka*, m. the mulberry, L.

टंकार *ṭaṃ-kāra*, m. (onomat.; cf. *ṭāṃ-k°*) howling, howl, cry, sound, clang, twang, Kād.; BhP. iii, 17, 9; Uttarar.; Rājat. v, 417; Sāh.; notoriety, L.; surprise, L.; (*ī*), f. N. of a shrub, Bhpr. — **rava**, m. cry, sound, Kād. — **vat**, mfn. accompanied by a great noise, Bālar. **Ṭaṃ-kārita**, n., see *jhaṃ-k°*. **Ṭaṃ-kṛita**, n. a clang, Kād. iii, 1291.

टङ्ग *ṭaṅga*, m. n. (= °*ṅka*) a spade, L.; a sword, kind of sword, L.; a leg, L.; m. borax, L.; a weight of 4 Māshas, L. **Ṭaṅgaṇa**, m. n. = °*ṅkaṇa*, borax, L. **Ṭaṅginī**, f. Clypea hernandifolia, L.

टटरीसूर्य *ṭaṭarī-sūrya*, m. a form of the sun (?), Rasik. xi, 44.

टट्टनी *ṭaṭṭanī*, f. a small house-lizard, L.

टट्टरी *ṭaṭṭarī*, f. N. of a musical instrument, L.; a lie, L.; a jest, W.

Ṭaṭṭura, m. the sound of a drum, L. (v.l.)

टणत्कार *ṭaṇat-kāra*, m. pl. = *jhaṇ°*, Alaṃkārat.; HPariś. i, 44.

टण्डन *ṭaṇḍana*, m. N. of a prince, Ṭoḍar.

टल् *ṭal* (= √*tval*, *ḍval*), cl. 1. P. °*lati* (pf. *ṭaṭāla*, Pāṇ. viii, 4, 54, Sch.) to be disturbed, Dhātup. xx, 4: Caus. *ṭālayati*, to disturb, frustrate, Campak. **Ṭala**, = *ṭāla*, g. *jvalâdi*. °**lana**, n. perturbation, W.

टसत् *ṭasat*, ind. (onomat.) an interjection imitating the sound of bursting, Kathās. vc, 78; (°*sad-iti*) cvi, 181. **Ṭas-iti**, ind. id., Bālar. ii, 31.

टाक *ṭāka*, m. = *ṭakka*, a niggard, Rājat. vii, 415; N. of a family, Romakas.; Madanap.; Smṛitik.

टाङ्क *ṭāṅka*, n. a spirituous liquor prepared from the *ṭaṅka* fruit, Mn. xi, 96, Sch.; RTL. p. 193.

टाङ्कर *ṭāṅkara*, m. a match-maker, L.

टांकार *ṭāṃ-kāra*, m. = *ṭaṃ-k°*, Bālar. i, 46 & 49; Rājat. v, 422. **Ṭāṃ-kṛita**, n. pl. id., ii, 99.

टात् *ṭāt*, ind. (onomat.) with √*kṛi*, to cause to jingle or rattle, Prasannar. i, 32.

टापर *ṭāpara*, N. of a village, Muhūrtaṃ.

टार *ṭāra*, m. a horse, L.; a catamite, L.

टाल *ṭāla*, mfn. (= *ṭala*, g. *jvalâdi*) tender (a fruit), Śīl. on Ācār. ii.

टिक् *ṭik* (cf. √*ṭīk*), cl. 1. Ā. to go, Dhātup.

टिक्क *ṭikka*, N. of a man, Rājat. viii, 670 ff.; cf. *bṛihaṭ-*, *sūkshma-*. **Ṭikkikā**, f. the white mark (on the forehead of a horse &c.), VarBṛS. lxv.

टिटिभक *ṭiṭibhaka*, m. = *ṭiṭṭibh°*, L., Sch.

टिटिल *ṭiṭila*, n. a large number (= 100 Naga-balas), Buddh. L.

टिट्टिभ *ṭiṭṭibha*, m. = °*bhaka* (also *ṭiṭibha*, q.v.), Gaut.; Mn. v, 11; Yājñ. i, 172; MBh. xii &c.; N. of a Daitya, ii, 367; of a Dānava (enemy of Indra in the 13th Manv-antara), GarP.; of a bug, Kathās. lx, 128; n. a kind of leprosy, Gal.; (*ī*), f. the female of the Ṭiṭṭibha bird, R. (G) ii, 8, 43.

Ṭiṭṭibhaka, m. the bird Parra jacana, L.

टिण्टिणि *ṭiṇṭiṇi*, m. N. of a man, Haṭhapr. **Ṭiṇṭiṇikā**, °**ṇikā**. See *ṭiṇḍiṇ°*.

टिण्ठा *ṭiṇṭhā*. See *ṭhiṇṭhā*.

टिण्ठिणि *ṭiṇṭhiṇi*, v.l. for °*ṇṭiṇi*.

टिण्डिणिका *ṭiṇḍiṇikā*, f. N. of a plant, Bhpr. (vv.ll. *ṭiṇṭiṇ°*, *ḍhiṇḍhiṇ°*); (*ṭiṇṭiṇīkā*) Npr.

टिण्डिश *ṭiṇḍiśa*, m. = *ḍiṇḍ°*, Bhpr.

टिप् *ṭip*, cl. 10. P. *ṭepayati*. See √*ḍip*.

टिप्पण *ṭippaṇa*, °*naka*, a gloss, comment. **Ṭippaṇī**, °**ppanī**, f. id.

टिरिटिरा *ṭiriṭirā*, f. See *karṇe-*.

टिल्ला *ṭillā*, f. N. of a deity, Rasik. xi, 66.

टीक् *ṭīk* (cf. √*ṭik*), cl. 1. Ā. °*kate*, to move (?, said of a tree), Kāś. on Pāṇ. viii, 3, 34 & 4, 41;

to trip, jump, Mālatīm. ix, 7: Caus. P. *ṭīkayati*, to explain, make clear, Hemac.: Desid. *ṭiṭīkishate*, Pāṇ. viii. 4, 54, Kāś.; cf. *ā-ṭīkana*, *uṭ-ṭikita*.

Ṭīkā, f. a commentary (esp. on another Comm., e.g. Ānanda-giri's *ṭīkā* on Śaṃkara's *bhāshya*).

टीट *ṭīṭa*. See *ava-*.

टीटिभ *ṭīṭibha*, m.=*ṭiṭṭ°*, Kathās. lx, 165 ff.; (*ī*), f. = *ṭiṭṭ°*, li, 78; lx. — **saras**, n. N. of a Tīrtha, li.

टीत्कार *ṭīt-kāra*, m. a crack, Bālar. iii, 78.

टु *ṭu*, m. gold, L.; one who changes his shape at will, W.; love, god of love, W.

टुक्करी *ṭukkarī*, f. a kind of drum.

टुटुक *ṭuṭuka*, m. N. of a pot-herb, L.

टुण्टुक *ṭuṇṭuka*, mfn. small, minute, L.; cruel, harsh, L.; low, W.; m. Calosanthes indica, Car. vi, 25, 66; Suśr. i, 36 & 38; iv; a kind of acacia, L.; the bird Sylvia sutoria, L.; (*ā*), f. = *ṭaṅginī*, L.

टुनाका *ṭunākā*, f. Curculigo orchioides, L.

टुप्टीका *ṭup-ṭīkā*, f. collective N. of the last 8 books of the Tantra-vārttika. **Ṭub-ḍushī**, f. id.

टुल्ल *ṭulla*, m. N. of a man, Rājat. vii.

टेकारी *ṭekārī*, f. = *ṭaṃ-k°*, Bhpr. vii.

टेण्टुक *ṭeṇṭuka*, m. N. of a Bignonia, L.

टेपन *ṭepana*, n. (√*ṭip*) throwing, W.

टेर *ṭera*, mfn. squinting, W. **Ṭerâksha**, mfn. squint-eyed, Buddh. L. **Ṭeraka**, mfn. squinting, L.

टोट *ṭoṭa*, °*ṭī*, v.l. for *ḍoṭ°*, q.v.

टोडर *ṭoḍara*, m. N. of a minister of Akbar Shāh (generally called *-kshmāpati* or *-malla* or °*rêndra*). **Ṭoḍarânanda**, m. 'Ṭoḍara's delight,' N. of a compilation made at Ṭoḍara's desire, Nirṇayas.

टोपर *ṭopara*, a small bag, Dhūrtas. ii, 11/12.

टौक् *ṭauk*, cl. 1. Ā., v.l. for √*ḍhauk*.

टौटेश *ṭauṭêśa*. m. 'Ṭauṭa-lord,' N. of a Kshetra-pāla, RevāKh. cccv.

ट्वल् *ṭval*, cl. 1. P. = √*ṭal*, Dhātup. xx, 5. **Ṭvala, ṭvāla**, g. *jvalâdi*.

ठ ṬHA.

ठ 1. *ṭha*, the aspirate of the preceding consonant. — **kāra**, m. the letter *ṭh*, Pāṇ. viii, 4, 41, Kāś.; °*raya*, Nom. (Desid. *ṭiṭh°°yishati*), 54, Kāś.

ठ 2. *ṭha*, m. a loud noise (*ṭhaṭhaṃ ṭhaṭhaṃ ṭhaṃ ṭhaṭhaṭhaṃ ṭhaṭhaṃ ṭhaḥ*, an imitative sound as of a golden pitcher rolling down steps, Mahān.[2] iii, 5), L.; the moon's disk, L.; a disk, L.; a cypher, L.; a place frequented by all, L.; Śiva, L.

ठंसरी *ṭhaṃsarī*, f. N. of a stringed instrument. ठक्क *ṭhakka*, m. a merchant (= *ṭakka*), Inscr. (1st century A.D.)

ठक्कन *ṭhakkana*, m. N. of a prince, Rājat. vi, 230 ff. & 236 (vv. ll. *ḍhakk°*, *thakk°*).

ठक्कुर *ṭhakkura*, m. a deity, object of reverence, man of rank, chief (the modern 'Thākūr, Tagore' added to names), vii f.; Dhūrtas. i, 18/20.

ठठं *ṭhaṭhaṃ*, *ṭhaṭhaṭhaṃ*. See 2. *ṭha*.

ठात्कार *ṭhāt-kāra*, m. = *ṭāṃ-k°*, Bālar. iii.

ठार *ṭhāra*, rime, KātyŚr. xv, 4, 38, Sch.

ठिण्ठा *ṭhiṇṭhā*, f. a gaming-house, Kathās. xcii, 15 & 21 (*ṭiṇ°*), cxxiv, 211; N. of a woman, Rājat. vii, 103. — **karāla**, m. N. of a gaming-house-keeper, Kathās. cxxi, 71 f.

ठेत्कृत *ṭhet-kṛita*, n. the roaring (of a bull), Alaṃkārat. ठोण्ठपद्धति *ṭhoṇṭha-paddhati*, f. N. of a work, Śūdradh.

ड ḌA.

ड 1. *ḍa*, the 3rd cerebral consonant (pronounced like *d* in *drum* by slightly turning the tip of the tongue upwards; and often in Bengal like a hard *r*). — **kāra**, m. the letter *ḍ*, TPrāt. iv, 38, Sch.

ड 2. *ḍa*, m. a sound, L.; a kind of drum, W.; fear, L.; submarine fire, L.; Śiva, L.; (*ā*), f. a Ḍākinī, L.; a basket &c. carried by a sling, L.

डक्कारी *ḍakkārī*, f. the Cāṇḍāla lute, L.

डङ्गर *ḍaṅgara*, m. = *ḍiṅg°*, L.; throwing (or 'an expression of contempt'), L. (also *ḍiṅg°*); (*ī*), f. a kind of gourd, L. **Ḍaṅgarī**, f. = °*garī*, L.

डप् *ḍap*, cl. 10. Ā. *ḍāpayate*, to accumulate, Dhātup. xxxiii, 4.

डम् *ḍam*, cl. 1. P. (p. °*mat*) to sound (as a drum), Prab. iii, 14.

डम *ḍama*, m. a despised mixed caste (son of a Cāṇḍālī and a Leṭa), BrahmavP.

डमर *ḍamara*, m. (n., L.) a riot, tumult, VarBṛS.; Kathās. c; Pārśvan. iv, 186; cf. *ḍām°*. **Ḍamarin**, m. a sort of drum, BhP. viii, 10, 7. **Ḍamaru**, (m., L.) id., Rājat. ii, 99; Prab. iii, 14; surprise, L. — **yantra**, n. a kind of pan, Bhpr. **Ḍamaruka**, m. (n., L.), °*kā*, f. = °*rin*, Vātsyāy. &c.

डम्प् *ḍamp*, cl. 10. Ā., v.l. for √*ḍap*.

डम्ब् *ḍamb*, cl. 10. °*bayati*, to push, throw, Vop. (Dhātup. xxxii, 132); cf. *vi-*.

डम्बर *ḍambara*, m. great noise, loud assertion of (in comp.), verbosity, Kathās. cvii, 5; Pratāpar.; Sāh.; entanglement, multitude, mass, Mālatīm.; Mcar.; Kathās. lxxi; beauty, Uttarar.; Viddh.; N. of an attendant of Skanda, MBh. ix, 2541; of a Gandharva, Hariv. (v.l. *ḍumb°*); cf. *ā-*. — **nāman**, mfn. having a high-sounding name, Mālatīm. i, 4/5.

डम्बुर *ḍambura*, ?, Hcat. i, 9, 49.

डम्भ् *ḍambh*, cl. 10. Ā., v.l. for √*ḍap*.

Ḍambha, m. N. of a man, Rājat. viii, 1135; (*ā*), f. N. of a weapon, Buddh. L.

डयन *ḍayana*. See √*ḍī*.

डलक *ḍalaka*. See *ḍall°*.

डलन *ḍalana*, m. = *ḍall°*.

डल्लक *ḍallaka*, n. a Dūlī carried on men's shoulders by means of a stick and ropes like the beam and strings of a balance (also *ḍalaka*, W.), BrahmavP.; m. N. of a man, Rājat. vii, 189 & 198.

डल्लन *ḍallana*, m. N. of a scholiast on Suśr.

डवित्थ *ḍavittha*, m. N. of a man (named along with Ḍittha; cf. *ḍāmbhiṭṭa*), Pāṇ. i, 2, 45, Sch. (*kapittha*, Kāś.); Bādar. ii, 4, 20, Sch.; Sāh. ii, 4/5; a wooden antelope, L.

डहाल *ḍahāla*, in Prākṛit for *daśārṇa*, Bālar. iii, 39/40; cf. *ḍāh°*.

डहु *ḍahu*, °*hū*, m. Artocarpus Lakuca, L

डाक *ḍāka*, m. an imp attending Kālī, Kālac. v, 38.

Ḍākinī, f. (of °*ka*, Pāṇ. iv, 2, 51, Pat.) a female imp attending Kālī (feeding on human flesh), BhP. x; BrahmavP.; MārkP.; Kathās. (*ḍāginī*, cii, cviii f.); (cf. *śāk°*); N. of a locality, ŚivaP. i, 38, 18. — **tva**, n. the condition of a female imp, Daś. xi, 302.

Ḍāginī, Prākṛit form for *ḍākinī* (q.v.), Kathās. **Ḍāgineya, °yaka**, N. of a gambler, cxxi, 33 ff.

डांकृति *ḍāṃkṛiti*, f. = *ṭaṃkṛita*, Prab. iii, 14.

डाङ्गरी *ḍāṅgarī*, f. = *ḍaṅg°*, L.

डात्कृति *ḍāt-kṛiti*, f. (= *ḍāṃ-*; *ṭaṃ-kāra*) howling, Mālatīm. v, 19.

डाभी *ḍābhi*, N. of a family, Ratnak.

डामर *ḍāmara*, mfn. 'causing tumult (*ḍam°*),' extraordinary, surprising, Mālatīm. (*-tva*, n. abstr.); Gīt. xii, 23; m. surprise, sight, L.; = *ḍam°*, L.; a lord (probably = baron, knight), Rājat.; a N. of 6 Tantras (*yoga-*, *śiva-*, *durgā-*, *sārasvata-*, *brahma-*, *gandharva-*); of an attendant of Śiva, BrahmaP. — **tantra**, n. N. of a Tantra, Nirṇayas. ii, 7. — **bhairava-tantra**, n. N. of a Tantra.

Ḍāmarava, mfn. coming from a drum, Hastar.

डाम्भिट्ट *ḍāmbhiṭṭa*, m. N. of a man, man of Ḍāmbhiṭṭa's kind (? mentioned along with Ḍittha; cf. *ḍavittha*), Pāṇ. v, 1, 119, Vārtt. 5, Pat. — **tva**, n. an act of a man of Dhāmbhiṭṭa's kind, ib.

डाल *ḍāla*, a branch, Śīl. on Ācār. ii.

डालिम *ḍālima*, m. = *dāḍima*, L., Sch.

डाहल *ḍāhala*, m. pl. N. of a people (= *cedi*, L.; sg. their country, L.), Romakas.; Ratnak. **Ḍāhalâdhīśa**, m. a Ḍāhala prince, Vcar. xviii, 95. **Ḍāhāla**, m. pl. (cf. *ḍah°*) = °*hala*, Vcar. xviii, 93.

डाहुक *ḍāhuka*, m. = *dātyūha*, a gallinule, L.

डिक्करिका *ḍik-karikā*, = *ḍik-karī*, Śīl.

डिङ्गर *ḍiṅgara*, m. a servant, L.; a rogue, cheat, L.; = *ḍaṅg°* (q.v.; 'a fat man,' W.), L.

डिडिमाणक *ḍiḍimāṇaka*, m. N. of a bird of the Pratuda class, Suśr.; (*ḍiṇḍimāṇava*, Car. i, 27.)

डिण्डिक *ḍiṇḍika*, N. of a mouse, MBh. v.

डिण्डिभ *ḍiṇḍibha*, m. a water-snake, L.

डिण्डिम *ḍiṇḍima*, m. a kind of drum, vii, ix; Hariv. (once °*mā*, f., 14836); R. v; Kathās. (once n., xci, 23) &c. (ifc. f. *ā*, Amar.); great noise, murmuring, clamour, loud assertion, Kād.; Bālar.; Vcar. (*-tva*, n. abstr.) &c.; Carissa Carandas, L.; mfn. humming, Kād. ii, 154. **Ḍiṇḍimêśvara-tīrtha**, n. N. of a Tīrtha, RevāKh. cccxi.

डिण्डिमाणव *ḍiṇḍimāṇava*. See *ḍiḍimāṇaka*.

डिण्डिर *ḍiṇḍira*, m. = *hiṇḍ°*, os sepiæ, L. — **modaka**, n. garlic, L. **Ḍiṇḍīra**, (m., L.) = °*ḍira*, Vcar.; (ifc. f. *ā*) Kathās.

डिण्डिश *ḍiṇḍiśa*, = *ṭiṇḍ°* = *tindiśa*, Bhpr.

डिण्डीर *ḍiṇḍīra*. See °*ḍira*.

डित्थ *ḍittha*, m. N. of a man, man of Ḍittha's kind (?; 'a handsome dark-complexioned man conversant with every branch of learning,' L.; cf. *ḍavittha* & *ḍāmbhiṭṭa*), Pāṇ. v, 1, 119, Vārtt. 5, Pat. (also *-tā*, f., *-tva*, n. 'an act of a man of Ḍittha's kind'); i, 2, 45, Kāś.; Bādar. ii, 4, 20, Sch.; Kpr.; Sāh. ii, 4/5; Tarkas. 59; a wooden elephant, L.

डिप् *ḍip*, *ḍimp*, *ḍimbh*, cl. 10. Ā. *ḍepayate*, *ḍimp°*, *ḍimbh°*, to heap together, Dhātup. xxxiii, 4: cl. 4. 6. 10. P. *ḍipyati*, *ḍipati*, *ḍepayati* (v.l. *ṭep°*, Vop.), Ā. *ḍimbayate*, to throw, Dhātup.

डिम् *ḍim* (a Sautra rt.), to injure.

डिम *ḍima*, m. a dramatic exhibition of a siege (as of Tripura-dāha, q.v.), Daśar.; Pratāpar.; Sāh.; a kind of mixed caste, BrahmavP. i, 10, 105.

डिम्प् *ḍimp*, *ḍimb*. See √*ḍip*.

डिम्ब *ḍimba*, (m. n., L.) 'affray, riot,' see °*bâhava*; m. an egg, Mālatīm.; Pañcar.; a chrysalis, W.; the recently-formed embryo, L.; (for °*mbha*) a new-born child, a child, L.; a young animal, W.; an idiot, Rājat. vii, 1074; viii, 1707; a ball, W.; a humming top, Naish. xxii, 53; the body, Śiś. xviii, 77; the lungs, L.; the spleen, L.; the uterus, W.; Ricinus communis, L.; cf. *ujjūta-*, *jala-*. — **yuddha**, n. affray, riot, W. **Ḍimbâhava**, m. id., Mn. v, 95; MBh. i, 1219. **Ḍimbikā**, f. a lustful woman, L.; a bubble, L.; = *moṇaka* or *śoṇ°* (Bignonia indica), L.

डिम्भ् *ḍimbh*. See √*ḍip*.

डिम्भ *ḍimbha*, m. (cf. °*mba*) a new-born child, child, boy, young animal, Śak.; Hāl.; Naish.; Bālar.; Pañcar.; ŚāṅkhGṛ., Sch.; an idiot, Mālatīm.; Sāh.; a young shoot, Naish. viii, 2; an egg, Pañcar.; N. of a Dānava, Hariv. ii, 102, 10; (*ā*), f. an infant, L.; cf. *toya-*. — **cakra**, n. N. of a mystical diagram. **Ḍimbhâḍimbha**, = *ḍimbâhava* (?), Hcat. i, 6.

Ḍimbhaka, m. *ikā*, f. a new-born child, young animal, Śak. (in Prākṛit, v.l.); m. N. of a general of Jarā-saṃdha, MBh. ii, 576 & 601 ff.; Hariv.

डिल्लि *ḍilli*, °*llī*, the town Delhi.

डी *ḍī*, cl. 1. 4. Ā. *ḍayate*, *ḍīyate* (Naigh. ii, 14; Pāṇ. vii, 2, 10, Vārtt. 7, Pat.; pf. *ḍiḍye*, viii, 4, 54, Kāś.; pr. p. *ḍayamāna*, 59, Kāś.; aor. *aḍayishṭa*, Vop.) to fly, Dhātup.; cf. *uḍ-*, *prôḍ-*. **Ḍayana**, n. a bird's flight, L.; a palanquin, L. **Ḍīna**, mfn. (cf. Pāṇ. vii, 2, 14; viii, 2, 45, Kāś.) flown, flying, W.; n. a bird's flight, MBh. viii, 1899 f.; cf. *ati-*, *abhi-*, *ava-*, *ni-*, *nir-*, *parā-*, *pari-*, *punar-*, &c. — **ḍīnaka**, n. flying reiteratedly, ib.

डुडुभ *ḍuḍubha*, m.=*ḍuṇḍ°*, L., Sch.

Ḍuṇḍu, f. id., L.

Ḍuṇḍubha, m. a kind of lizard, i, 984 ff.; vii, 6905 (B; ifc. f. *ā*); Kathās. xiv, 74 & 83 f.

डुण्डुल *ḍuṇḍula*, m. a small owl, L.

डुन्दुक *ḍunduka*, m.=*ḍāhuka*, a gallinule, L.

डुम्ब *ḍumba*, m. v.l. for *ḍomba*, q.v.; cf. *go-*.

डुम्बर *ḍumbara*, v.l. for *ḍamb°*, q.v.

डुल *ḍula*, g. *balâdi*.

डुलि *ḍuli*, f.=*duli*, a turtle, L., Sch.

डुलिका *ḍulikā*, f. a kind of wagtail, L.

डुली *ḍulī*, f. a kind of pot-herb (*cilli*), L.

डुल्य *ḍulya*, g. *balâdi*.

डूलूवैश्वानर *ḍūlū-vaiśvānara*, n. N. of a Tīrtha, Rasik. xi, 79.

डेरिका *ḍerikā*, f. a musk rat, Āp. i, 25, 13.

डोड *ḍoḍa*, m. N. of a royal family, Ratnak.; (*ī*), f.=*kshupa-ḍoḍa-mushṭi*, Pañcad. ii, 71.

Ḍoḍīyā, f. N. of a royal family, Ratnak.

डोडही *ḍoḍahī*, f. a kind of flute.

डोम *ḍoma*, m. a man of low caste (living by singing and music), Tantr.

Ḍomba, m. id., VarBṛS. lxxxvii, 33 (v.l. *ḍumba*); Kathās. xiii, 96 ff.; Rājat. v f.; N. of a man, vii, 1070 & 1136; (*ī*), f. a kind of drama, Daśar. i, 8, Sch.

Ḍombulī, f. (in music) a kind of measure.

डोर *ḍora*, m. n. a string, BhavP.

Ḍoraka, n. (=*ḍor°*) id., ib.

डोरडी *ḍoraḍī*, f. a kind of Solanum, L.

डोला *ḍolā*, f.=*dolā*, a swing, Bālar. vii.

डौण्डुभ *ḍauṇḍubha*, mfn. belonging to a *ḍuṇḍubha*, MBh. i, 1006.

ड्वल् *ḍval* (=√*tval*). See *ā-*.

ढ ḌHA.

ढ 1. *ḍha*, the aspirate of the preceding letter. **—kāra**, m. the letter *ḍh*.

ढ 2. *ḍha*, mfn.=*nir-guṇa*, L.; m. an imitative sound, L.; a large drum, L.; a dog, L.; a dog's tail, L.; a serpent, W.

ढक्क *ḍhakka*, m. a large sacred building, Rājat. iii, v; N. of a locality (cf. *ṭakka*), Mṛicch., Sch. Introd.; (*ā*), f. a large drum (cf. *gaja-*, *jaya-*), Rājat. vi, 133; covering, disappearance, W. **—°deśīya**, mfn. spoken in the district of Ḍhakka, Mṛicch., Sch. Introd.

ढक्कन *ḍhakkana*, n. shutting (of a door), Śil.; m. N. of a man, Rājat. vi, 230 f. (v.l. °*kkama*).

ढक्कारी *ḍhakkārī*, f. N. of the goddess Tārā or Tāriṇī, Kulasadbh.

ढङ्क *ḍhaṅka*, m. N. of a mountain, Śatr. i.

ढड्ढर *ḍhaḍḍhara*, N. of a man, HPariś. xiii.

ढण्टी *ḍhaṇṭī*, f.=*vākya-viśesha*, Rudray.

ढामरा *ḍhāmarā*, f. a goose, Dhanamj.

ढारिका *ḍhārikā*, f. the julus, ĀpGṛ.

ढाल *ḍhāla*, n. 'a shield.' See °*lin*.

Ḍhālin, mfn. armed with a shield, Rudraj.

ढिण्ढिणिका *ḍhiṇḍhiṇikā*. See *ṭiṇṭiṇ°*.

ढुढि *ḍhuḍhi*, v.l. for *ḍhuṇḍhi*.

ढुण्ढ् *ḍhuṇḍh* (a Sautra rt.), to search.

Ḍhuṇḍhana, n. searching, investigating, W.

Ḍhuṇḍhi, m. N. of Gaṇeśa, KāśīKh. **—rāja**, m. N. of the author of a work on nativities; of Bālakṛishṇa's father; of Vināyaka-bhaṭṭa's father (about 1800 A.D.); °*jâkhyāna*, n. N. of GaṇP. ii, 43.

Ḍhuṇḍhikā, f. a gloss (?).

Ḍhuṇḍhita, mfn. sought, inquired, W.

ढेङ्क *ḍheṅka*, m. N. of a bird, Vasantar. viii, 12; (*ī*), f. a kind of dance. **Ḍheṅkikā**, f. (in music) a kind of measure; *-tāla*, m. id.

ढेव्वुका *ḍhevvukā*, f. a coin, Kathârn.

ढोरसमुद्र *ḍhora-samudra*, N. of a locality, Romakas. **Ḍholā-samudra**, =*ḍhora-s°*, W.

Ḍhola, m. a large drum, Rudraj. **—°samudrikā**, f. 'coming from or growing in Ḍhola-samudra (=Ḍhora-s°),' Leea macrophylla, L.

ढोल्लरी *ḍhollarī*, f. a kind of composition.

ढौक् *ḍhauk*, cl. 1. Ā. °*kate* (pf. *ḍuḍhauke* [Pāṇ. vii, 4, 59, Kāś.], Hcar.; Bhaṭṭ.), to approach (with acc.), Kād.; Hcar.; Bhaṭṭ.: Caus. *ḍhaukayati* (aor. *aḍuḍhaukat*, Pāṇ. vii, 4, 2 & 59, Kāś.), to bring near (to, gen.), cause to come near, offer to any one (dat.), Kathās.; Rājat.; Bhaṭṭ.; KātyŚr., Sch.: Desid. *ḍuḍhaukishate*, Pāṇ. vii, 4, 59 & viii, 4, 54, Kāś.: Intens. *ḍoḍhaukyate*, vii, 4, 82, Vārtt. 1, Pat.; cf. *upa-*. **Ḍhaukana**, n. offering, present, Rājat. vi, 166; Śatr. xiv; KātyŚr., Sch.; cf. *upa-*.

Ḍhaukita, mfn. brought near, MBh. xii, 4138.

ण ṆA.

ण 1. *ṇa*, the cerebral nasal, TPrāt. xxi, 14. **—kāra**, m. the letter or sound *ṇ*, vii, 1; xiii, 6.

ण 2. *ṇa*, m. knowledge, L.; certainty, ascertainment, L.; ornament, L.; a water-house, L.; =*nirvṛiti* (invented for the etymology of *kṛishṇa*), MBh. v, 70, 5, Sch.; a bad man, L.; N. of Śiva or of a Buddh. deity, L.; the sound of negation, L.; gift, L.

ण्य *ṇya*, m. (etymological) N. of an ocean in the Brahma-loka, ChUp. viii, 5, 3.

त TA.

त 1. *ta*, the 1st dental consonant. **—kāra**, m. the letter *t*; *-vipulā*, f. N. of a metre. **—para**, mfn. followed by *t*, Pāṇ. i, 1, 70; *-karaṇa*, n. causing *t* to follow, vi, 1, 91, Kāś. **—varga**, m. the dental consonants collectively, TPrāt. **—°vargīya**, mfn. belonging to the dental consonants, xiii, 15.

त 2. *tá*, pronom. base, see *tád*. **—tama**, mfn. (superl.) that one (of many), Pāṇ. v, 3, 93; such a one, BhP. x, 36, 28; just that, AitUp. iii, 12, 13 (=*vyāpta-t°*, Sch.) **—tara**, mfn. (compar.) that one (of two), Pāṇ. v, 3, 92. **—tas** (*tá-*), see s.v.

त 3. *ta*, m. a tail (esp. of a jackal), any tail except that of Bos gaurus, L.; the breast, L.; the womb, L.; the hip, W.; a warrior, L.; a thief, L.; a wicked man, L.; a Mleccha, L.; a Buddha, L.; a jewel, L.; nectar, L.; n. crossing, L.; virtue, L.; (*ā*), f. Lakshmī, L.

तंस् *taṃs* (cl. 1. P. °*sati*, to decorate, Dhātup. xvii, 31; Ā. °*sate* [aor. *ataṃsishṭa*] to decorate one's self, Vop. xxiv, 12; pf. *tatasré*) 'to move,' pour out (fig. a wish), RV. iv, 23, 5: Caus. *taṃsayati* (cl. 10. 'to decorate,' Dhātup. xxxiii, 56; impf. *ataṃsayat*), to draw to and fro, VS. xxiii, 24: Intens. irr. *tantasyati*, 'to afflict' or 'to be distressed' (cf. *vi-*√*taṃs*), g. *kaṇḍv-ādi*; [fr. √*tan*? cf. *tásara*; Goth. *at-þinsan*; Old Germ. *dinsan*, 'to draw.']

तंसु *taṃsu*, m. N. of a prince of the lunar race (son of Mati- or Ranti-nāra), MBh. i, 3704 ff.; 3779 f.; Hariv. 1716 ff.; VP. iv, 19, 1 f.; (*trasu*) VāyuP. ii, 37, 125 & 128. **—rodha**, m. id., BrahmaP.

तक् *tak*, cl. 2. °*kti* (cl. 1. °*kati* ['to laugh' or 'to bear,' Dhātup. v, 2], Naigh. ii, 14; inf. °*kitum*, Nir. ix, 3) to rush along, RV. ix, 16, 1; [cf. *nish-ṭak*, *pari-takana*, *pra-takta*; Lith. *tekù*.]

Tákavāna, mfn. (fr. &) =*táku*, i, 120, 6.

Táku, mfn. rushing along, ix, 97, 52.

Taktá, mfn. id., vi, 32, 5; ix, 32, 4 & 67, 15.

Takya, mfn. fut. Pass. p., Pāṇ. iii, 1, 97, Vārtt. 1, Pat. **Takvá**, mfn. quick, RV. viii, 69, 13.

Tákvan, m. 'rushing,' a bird, bird of prey ['a fleet horse,' Sāy.], i, 66, 2; a thief, Naigh. iii, 24. **Takva-ví**, m. (nom. sg. & pl. *-vís*) a bird, bird of prey, RV. i, x. **Takvavīya**, rapid flight (?), i, 134, 5.

तक *taká*, m (nom. pl. *ās*) fn (*ad*). (dimin. of 2. *tá*) that, 133, 4 & 191, 15; KātyŚr. xiii; Bhadrab.

तकरि *takari*, f.=°*rī*, Kāṭh. xiii, 9 f.

Takarī, f. a particular part of a woman's pudenda, TS. iii, 3, 10, 1; (*tagarī*) AV. Paipp.

तकवान *tákavāna*. See √*tak*.

तकिल *takila*, mfn. fraudulent, L.; (*ā*), f. 'a drug (*aushadha*)' or 'N. of a herb (*oshadhi*),' L.

तकु *táku*. See √*tak*.

तक्कोल *takkola*, m. Pimenta acris, R. iii, 35.

तक्मन् 1. *tákman*, n.=*tok°*, offspring, Naigh.

तक्मन् 2. *takmán*, m. (√*tañc*) 'shrinking,' N. of a disease or of a class of diseases (accompanied by skin-eruptions), AV. i, iv–vi, ix, xi f., xix. **Takmá-nāśana**, mfn. removing the *takmán*, v, 4, 1 f.

Takra, n. (g. *nyaṅkv-ādi*) buttermilk mixed with (a third part of) water, Mn. viii, 326; Yājñ. iii, 37 & 322; Hariv. &c.; (*ā*), f.=°*krâhvā*, L. **—kūrcikā**, f. inspissated buttermilk, Suśr. **—piṇḍa**, m. curd, Bhpr. v, 13, 30. **—bhaktā**, f.=°*krâhvā*, L. **—bhid**, the fruit of Feronia elephantum, Npr. **—māṃsa**, n. meat fried with ghee and eaten with buttermilk, Bhpr. **—sāra**, n. fresh butter, L.

Takrâṭa, m. a churning-stick (cf. *dadhi-cāra*), Vāsav. 157. **Takrâhvā**, f. N. of a shrub, L.

तक्व *takvá*, *tákvan*, °*kva-ví*, &c. See √*tak*.

तक्ष् 1. *taksh*, cl. 1. P. °*kshati* (ep. also Ā.; impf. *tákshat*, *átakshat*, RV.; rarely cl. 2, 3. pl. *tákshati* [Pāṇ. vii, 1, 39, Pat.], RV. i, 162, 6; impf. [aor.?] *atakshma*, 2. pl. *atashṭa*, RV.; once cl. 5. [*takshṇoti*, Pāṇ. iii, 1, 76], Pot. °*kshṇuyur*, Lāṭy. viii; see also *apa-*; aor. *atakshīt*, Pāṇ. vii, 2, 7, Kāś.; 3. pl. °*kshishur*, RV. i, 130, 6; Subj. *takshishat* [Pāṇ. iii, 4, 7, Kāś.], ŚāṅkhŚr. vii; pf. *tatáksha*, once Ā. °*kshé*, RV. v, 33, 4; 3. pl. °*kshúr*, RV. (8 times) &c., once *takshur*, ii, 19, 8; 2. du. *takshathur*, x, 39, 4; pr. p. f. *tákshatī*, i, 164, 41; pf. Pass. p. *tashṭá*, see s. v.) to form by cutting, plane, chisel, chop, RV. &c.; to cut, split, MBh.; Hariv.; Hcar.; to fashion, form (out of wood &c.), make, create, RV.; AV.; to form in the mind, invent, RV.; to make (any one young; double acc.), make able or prepare for (dat.), RV.; (in math.) to reduce by dividing, Gol. xiii, 14 ff.; Līl. &c.; =√*tvac*, Dhātup. xvii, 13; to skin, ib.: Caus. *takshayati* (aor. *atatakshat*), Pāṇ. vii, 4, 93, Kāś.; cf. *tvaksh*. **2. Taksh**, 'paring;' see *kāshṭha-*.

1. Taksha, mfn. 'cutting through,' see *tapas-*; m. ifc. =°*kshan*, VarBṛS. lxxxvii, 20 & 24; (cf. *kauṭa-*, *grāma-*); N. of a Nāga (cf. °*kshaka*), Kauś.; of a son [of Bharata, R. vii, 100 f.; Ragh. xv, 89; BhP. ix, 11, 12; (also °*kshaka*); of Vṛika, 24, 42].

2. Taksha, in comp. for °*kshan*. **—karman**, n. carpenter's work, ĀśvŚr. ii, 1, 13, Sch. **—rathakārá** (*ták°*), m. du. a carpenter and a cartwright, MaitrS. iv, 3, 8. **—vat**, mfn.? (for *kshata-v°*?), MBh. ii, 23, 18. **—śila**, m. pl. the inhabitants of °*lā*, VarBṛS. x, 8 & (in comp.) xvi, 26; (*ā*), f. (Pāṇ. iv, 3, 93; g. *varaṇâdi*) Τάξιλα, city of the Gandhāras (residence of Taksha, R. vii, 101, 11), MBh.; R.; Buddh.; VarBṛS.; Kathās. lxix; °*lā-vatī*, f. N. of a locality, g. *madhv-ādi*. **Takshâyaskāra**, n. sg. a carpenter and a blacksmith, Pāṇ. ii, 4, 10, Kāś.

Takshaká, m. (Pāṇ. viii, 2, 29, Kāś.) 'a cutter,' see *kāshṭha-*, *vṛiksha-*; a carpenter, L.; Viśvakarman, L.; the Sūtra-dhāra or speaker in the prelude of a drama, L., Sch.; N. of a tree, L.; of a Nāga prince (cf. °*ksha*), AV. viii, 10, 29; TāṇḍyaBr. xxv, 15; ŚāṅkhGṛ. iv, 18, 1; Kauś.; MBh. &c.; of a son of Prasena-jit, BhP. ix, 12, 8; see also °*ksha*.

Takshakīyā, f. N. of a place, g. 2. *naḍâdi*.

Takshaṇa, m. a cutter, abrader, W.; (in math.) the divisor employed to reduce a quantity, W.; n. cutting, paring, peeling, abrading, KātyŚr. xxii, 6; Gaut. i, 29; Mn. v, 115 &c.; (N. of a Kalā) Vātsyāy. i, 3, 17; dividing in order to reduce a quantity, Līl.; (*ī*), f. an instrument for cutting or paring, L.

Tákshan, m. (Ved. acc. °*kshaṇam*, class. °*kshāṇam*, Pāṇ. vi, 4, 9, Kāś.) a wood-cutter, carpenter, τέκτων, RV. ix, 112, 1; AV. x, 6, 3; VS. &c.; N. of a teacher, ŚBr. ii, 3, 1, 31; (*kshṇī*), f., g. *gaurâdi* (not in Gaṇar.) **Takshiṇī**, f.=°*kshaṇī*, L.

Takshitṛi, mfn. a cutter, Pāṇ. viii, 2, 29, Kāś.

Tákshya, mfn. to be formed, RV. viii, 102, 8.

तगडवल्ली *tagaḍa-vallī*, for *tagara-*, q.v.

Tagara, n. (m., L.) =°*raka*, Kauś. 16; MBh. xiii, 5042; Buddh.; Suśr.; VarBṛS. lxxvii, 5 ff.; n. =*-pura*, Romakas.; (*ī*), f. = *takarī*, q. v. **—pādika**, n. =°*raka*, L.; (*ā*), f. id., L. **—pādī**, f. id., L. **—pura**, n. N. of a town. **—vallī**, f. Cassia auriculata, Npr. **—śikhin**, m. N. of a man, Lalit. xiii.

Tagaraka, Tabernæmontana coronaria and a fragrant powder prepared from it, VarBṛS. li. °**rika**, m., °**rikī**, f. a seller of Tagara powder, g. *kisarâdi.*

तङ्क् *taṅk*, cl. 1. P. to live in distress, Dhātup.

Taṅka, grief produced by separation from a beloved object, L., Sch.; fear, ib.; v.l. for *ṭaṅka* (a chisel), L.; cf. *ā-, tapas-; pra-taṅkam.*

तङ्ग् *taṅg*, cl. 1. P. °*gati*, to go, Dhātup. v, 41; to stumble, ib.; to tremble, ib.

तङ्गण *taṅgaṇa*, m. pl. N. of a people (in the upper part of the valley of the Sarayū), MBh. ii f., vi f., xiv; Hariv.; VarBṛS. x, xvi f.; cf. *ṭaṅk*°.

तङ्गल्व *taṅgalvà*, m. N. of an evil spirit, AV. viii, 6, 21.

तच्छब्दत्व *tac-chabda-tva* &c. See *tat.*

Taj-ja, **-jaghanyá**, &c. See ib.

तज्वी *tajvī*, f. for *tanvī*, q. v.

तञ्च् 1. *tañc* (=√*tvañc*), cl. 1. °*cati*, to go.

तञ्च् 2. *tañc*, cl. 7. *tanakti*, to contract, Bhaṭṭ. vi, 38; cf. *ā-, abhy-ā-; upâtaṅkyà; takmán* & °*kra*. **Tañj**, v. l. for √2. *tañc*, Dhātup.

तञ्जल *tañjala*, m. the Cātaka bird, Gal.

तट् *taṭ*, cl. 1. P. °*ṭati*, to rumble, ShaḍvBr. v, 7; (derived fr. *taṭa*) to be raised, Dhātup. ix, 21: Caus. *tāṭayati*, v.l. for *tāḍay*°, to strike, xxxii, 43.

तट *taṭa*, m. (exceptionally n., Daśar. ii, 1/10) a slope, declivity, any part of the body which has (as it were) sloping sides (cf. *śroṇi-, stana-*, &c.), a shore, MBh. (said of Śiva, xii, 10381); Hariv. &c. (ifc. f. *ī*, Bhartṛ.); (*ī*), f. (g. *gaurâdi*, Gaṇar. 49) id., Git.; Prab.; Sāh.; cf. *a-, ut-; pura-taṭī*. — **druma**, m. a tree standing on the shore. — **bhū**, f. the shore, Śiś. viii, 19. — **stha**, mfn. standing on a declivity or bank, Naish. iii, 55; = *-sthita*, Mālatīm.; Naish. iii, 55; m. an indifferent person (neither friend nor foe), W.; n. a property distinct from the nature of the body and yet that by which it is known, spiritual essence, Vedântak. — **sthita**, mfn. 'standing aloof,' indifferent, Uttarar. (said of speech). **Taṭâghāta**, m. the butting (of elephants) against banks &c. (*vapra-krīḍā*), Kum. ii, 50.

Taṭaka, n. a shore, Inscr.

Taṭāka, n. (m., L.) a pool, ShaḍvBr. v, 12; R. &c.

Taṭākinī, f. a large pond, MBh. iii, 279, 44.

Taṭāya, Nom. Ā. °*yate*, to appear like a declivity, Alaṃkārav.

Taṭinī, f. (g. *pushkarâdi*) 'having a bank,' a river, Rājat. iii, 339; iv, 548; Śatr. — **pati**, m. 'lord of rivers,' the ocean, i, 50.

Taṭya, mfn. living on slopes (Śiva), MBh. xii.

तटतट *taṭataṭa*, (onomat.) in comp. — **svana**, mfn. rumbling, thundering, VarBṛS. xxxiii, 5.

तड् *taḍ*, cl. 10. *tāḍayati* (perf. °*ḍayām āsa*, Kathās., twice *tatāḍa*, BhP. vi f.; Pass. *tāḍyate*) to beat, strike, knock, strike (with arrows), wound, punish, Nir. iii, 10; Mn. iv, xi; Yājñ. i; MBh. &c.; to strike a musical instrument, MBh.; Hariv. 15092; Mṛicch. v; Kum. &c.; (in astron.) to obscure or eclipse partially, VarBṛS. xxiv, 34; 'to speak' or 'to shine,' Dhātup. xxxiii, 126.

1. **Taḍākā**, f. a stroke, L.; splendour, Uṇ., Sch.

Taḍi, ?, iv, 117, Sch.

Taḍít, ind. = °*ḍitas*, RV. i, 94, 7 (*taḷit*); f. 'stroke (*vadha-karman*, Naigh. ii, 19),' lightning, Nir. iii, 10 f.; Suśr. &c. (ifc. °*ḍita*, Vet. Introd. 20). — **kumāra**, m. pl. = *vidyut-k*°, L. — **prabhā**, f. N. of one of the mothers attending on Skanda, MBh. ix, 2635. — **vat**, mfn. having or emitting lightning, R. v, 40, 4; Vikr. i, 14; VarBṛS.; Kir. v, 4; m. a cloud, Vām. v, 1, 10, Sch.; a kind of Cyperus, W.

Taḍitas (*taḷit*°), ind. closely, near (as if striking against), RV. ii, 23, 9.

Taḍid, in comp. for °*ḍit*. — **garbha**, m. 'containing lightning,' a cloud, ŚvetUp. iv, 4. — **vāsas**, mfn. having lightning-like garments, BhP. i, 12, 8.

Taḍin, in comp. for °*ḍit*. — **maya**, mfn. flashing like lightning, Kum. v, 25; Hcar. viii. — **mālā**, f. a garland of lightning, Śāntiś.; °*lâvalambin*, mfn. having garlands of lightning hanging down, W.

Taḍil, = °*ḍit*. — **latā**, f. forked lightning, Ṛitus. ii, 20. — **lekhā**, f. a streak of lightning, Bhartṛ. iii.

तडग *taḍaga*, m. = °*ḍāga*, a pond, L.

तडतडिति *taḍataḍ-iti*, ind. (onomat.) crack! Bālar. viii, 77; cf. *taṭataṭa*.

Taḍat-kārin, mfn. cracking, iv, 74; v, 11.

तडाक *taḍāka*, m. n. (= *taṭāka*), a tank, pool, L.; 2. (*ā*), f. a shore, L. °**kinī**, for *taṭāk*° (C).

Taḍāga, n. (m., g. *ardharcâdi*) = °*ḍāka*, ŚāṅkhGṛ. v, 2; Mn. iv, vii ff.; Yājñ.; MBh. &c.; a trap, L. — **da**, mfn. making a tank, xiii, 2987. — **bhavanôtsarga**, m. N. of Smṛitit. xii, Smṛitit. Introd. 3. — **bhedaka**, mfn. a tank-breaker, Mn. ix, 279. — **vat**, mfn. = *-da*, MBh. xiii, 2973.

तडि *taḍi*, °*ḍít*, °*ḍitas*. See √*taḍ*.

तडिति *taḍ-iti*, ind. (onomat.) = *taḍataḍ-iti*, Bālar. iv, 59; vi, 69; viii, 67; ix; Vcar. xiii, 40.

तण्ड् *taṇḍ* (= √*taḍ*), cl. 1. Ā. °*ḍate*, to beat, Dhātup. viii, 28.

Taṇḍa, m. N. of a man, g. *gargâdi*. — **vataṇḍa**, m. pl. the descendants of Taṇḍa and Vataṇḍa, g. *kārtakaujapâdi*.

Taṇḍaka, m. n. (g. *ardharcâdi*) a complete preparation, L., Sch.; composition abounding in compound words, L.; the upright post of a house, L.; m. a juggler, L.; the trunk of a tree, L.; foam, L.; a wagtail, L.; cf. *tāṇḍ*°.

Taṇḍā, f. in comp.; cf. *tāṇḍa*. — **pracara**, or **-pratara**, m.? (a term relating to the SV.), Caraṇ. — **lakshaṇa**, n. N. of a Sūtra of the SV.

Taṇḍi, m. N. of a man, Pravar. ii, 4, 1; vii, 2; of a Ṛishi (who saw and praised Śiva), MBh. xiii, 607 & 1037 ff.; ŚivaP. ii, 2; cf. *sudivā-; tāṇḍi*. — **putra**, m. N. of a teacher, VāyuP. i, 61, 37. — **vāha**, m. a barber, Gal.

Taṇḍu, m. N. of an attendant of Śiva (Bharata's teacher in the art of dancing, cf. *tāṇḍava*).

तण्डुरीण *taṇḍurīṇa*, m. one not a citizen, a barbarian, L.; a worm, insect, L.; = °*ṇḍulâmbu*, L.

तण्डुल *taṇḍulá*, m. (g. *ardharcâdi*) grain (after threshing and winnowing), esp. rice, AV. x ff.; ŚBr.; AitBr. &c.; rice used as a weight, Car. vii, 12; VarBṛS.; = °*līka*, L.; m. = °*lu*, L.; (*ā*), f. id., L.; (*ī*), f. a kind of gourd, L.; = °*līka*, L.; the plant *yava-tiktā*, L. — **kaṇa**, m. a rice-grain, Hit. — **kaṇḍana**, n. bran, Suśr. — **kiṇva**, n. g. *rāja-dantâdi*. — **kusuma-bali-prakāra**, or °**li-vik**°, m. pl. N. of a Kalā (q. v.). — **deva**, m. N. of a poet, Bhojapr. 1 62/10 8. — **phalā**, f. long pepper, L. — **vaitālika**, n. N. of the 5th Prakīrṇaka of the Jaina canon. **Taṇḍulâmbu**, n. rice-water or gruel. **Taṇḍulôttha**, °**lôdaka**, n. id., L. **Taṇḍulâugha**, m. a heap of grain, W.; Bambus spinosa, L.

Taṇḍulika, mfn. fr. °*la*, Pāṇ. v, 2, 115, Pat.

Taṇḍulikâśrama, m. N. of a Tīrtha, Vishṇ. lxxxv, 24 (v.l.); MBh. iii, 4084 (vv. ll. °*ḍūl*° & *tandul*°).

Taṇḍulin, mfn. for °*la*, Pāṇ. v, 2, 115, Pat.

Taṇḍulīka, m. Amaranthus polygonoides, L.

Taṇḍulīya, m. (g. *apūpâdi*) id., Suśr.; = °*lu*, L.; iron pyrites, L. °**līyaka**, m. = °*līka*, Suśr.; = °*lu*, L.; (*ikā*), f. id., L. °**ḍulu**, m. Embelia Ribes, L.

Taṇḍulera, m. = °*līka*, L.

Taṇḍūlikâśrama. See °*ḍul*°.

तत् 1. *tat*, for *tád*. See col. 3.

तत् 2. *tat*, 1. *tatá*. See √*tan*.

तत 2. *tatá*, m. (cf. *tāta*) chiefly Ved. a father (familiar expression corresponding to *naná*, mother), RV. viii, 91, 5 f.; ix, 112, 3; AV.; TS. iii; TBr. &c. (voc. [like *tāta*] also term of affection addressed to a son, AitBr. v, 14, 3; vii, 14, 8). — **tata**, m. father of fathers, W. — **druh**, mfn. having hurt one's father, BhP. i, 18, 37. **Tatā-mahá**, m. (formed after &) = *pitā-mahá*, AV. v, 24, 17; xviii, 4, 76; Kauś.; PārGṛ. i, 5; BhP. vi; cf. *pra-*.

ततनुष्टि *tatanúshṭi*. See √*tan*.

ततम *ta-tama, -tara*. See 2. *tá*.

Tátas, ind. (*tá-tas*, correlative of *yá-tas*) used for the abl. (sg., du. & pl.) of *tád* (q. v., Pāṇ. v, 3, 7 f.; vi, 3, 35), RV.; AV.; ĪśUp.; Mn. &c.; from that place, thence, RV.; AV. &c.; in that place, there, MBh. &c.; thither, Mn. vii, 188; R. i, 44, 34; Kathās.; thereupon, then, after that, afterwards (sometimes corresponding to preceding particles like *ágre, puras, pūrvam, prathamam, prāk*, ŚBr. xiv; Mn. ii, 60; Śak.; Pañcat. &c.; corresponding to *prathamá*, RV. i, 83, 5; also correlative of *yád* [x, 85, 5 & 121, 7; AV. xii, 4, 7 ff.], *yátra* [ŚBr. i], *yadā* [Nal. xx; R.], *yadi* [ChUp.; Nal. &c.], *céd* [TUp. ii, 6; Śak. v, 23/8, v.l.]; often superfluous after an ind. p. or after *tadā* or *atha*, Mn. &c.); from that, in consequence of that, for that reason, consequently, AV.; MBh. xii, 13626; R. vi; Hit.; °**taḥ katham**, but how is it then that? Sāh. iii, 2 1/9 0; °**taḥ kshaṇam** or °**ṇāt**, immediately afterwards, Kathās.; °**taḥ pára**, mfn. beyond that, AV. xviii, 2, 32; °*ram*, ind. besides that, further, Pāṇ. vii, 2, 10, Kār.; thereupon, afterwards, MBh. &c. (°*taś ca param*, VP. iv); °**taḥ paścāt**, id., Mn. iii, 116 f.; MBh. &c.; °**taḥ-prabhṛiti**, thenceforth, Nal. ii, 1; Pañcat. &c.; °**tas tataḥ**, (in dram.) what then? what took place after that? Ratnâv.; Hit.; °*tas-tataḥ*, from that and that place, here and there, hither and thither, from all sides, to every place, everywhere, PārGṛ. iii, 13, 6; MBh.; R.; BhP.; (correlative of *yato-yataḥ*, from whatever place, wherever) to that place, Śak. i, 23; BhP.; °**to 'nyatas**, 'to another place than that,' to some other place, Mn. ii, 200; °*to 'nyatra* = *tasmād anyasmin*, L.; °**to 'param**, afterwards, at another time, AitBr. vii, 17, 4; [cf. τότε, τόθεν.] — °**tya**, mf(*ā*)n. (Pāṇ. iv, 2, 104, Pat.) coming from that, proceeding thence, Kir. i, 27; of or belonging to that, W.

1. **Táti**, nom. acc. pl. (Pāṇ. i, 1, 23 ff.) so many, Lat. *tot*, AV. xii, 3. — **dhá**, ind. in so many parts, ib.

Tatithá, mf(*ī*)n. so maniest, ŚBr. i, 8, 1, 5.

Tato, in comp. for °*tas*. — **nidāna**, mfn. caused by that, Vajracch. 8 & 11. — **bṛihatīka**, mfn. having the Bṛihatī metre at that place, ŚāṅkhŚr. xi, 12, 1. — **bhavat**, m. His (or Your) Highness there (cf. *tatra-bh*°), Pāṇ. v, 3, 14, Kāś.

ततामह *tatā-mahá*. See 2. *tatá*.

तति 2. *tati*. See √*tan*.

ततुरि *táturi*, mfn. (√*tṛī*, iii, 2, 171) conquering, RV. i, 145, 3; iv, 39, 2; vi, 22, 2; 24, 2; 68, 7; promoting, ŚBr. i, 8, 1, 22; ŚāṅkhŚr. i, 11, 1.

तत् 1. *tat*, in comp. for *tád*. — **kara**, mf(*ā*)n. doing that, doing any particular work, Pāṇ. iii, 2, 21. — **kartavya**, mfn. proper to be done with reference to any particular circumstance (cf. *iti-k*°), Rājat. vi, 269. — **kartṛi**, m. 'creator of (that, i. e. of) the universe,' N. of the supreme being (with Sikhs), W. — **karma-kārin**, mfn. doing the same work, Mn. ix, 261. — **kārin**, mfn. id., Kāvyâd. ii, 20. — **kāla**, mfn. happening (at that same time, i.e.) immediately, KātyŚr. i, xxv; of that duration, BrahmavP.; m. that time (opposed to *etat-k*°, 'this time'), Vedântas.; the time referred to, KātyŚr. i; VarBṛ.; Laghuj.; (*am*), ind. at that time, at the same time, during that time, Gobh. iii, 3, 28; PārGṛ. ii, 11, 5 f.; VarBṛ.; Kathās. &c.; immediately, Pañcat.; Kathās.; (cf. *tātkālika*); *-dhī*, mfn. having presence of mind, L.; *-lavaṇa*, n. a kind of salt, Nṛ.; °*lôtpanna-dhī*, mfn. = °*la-dhī*, L. — °**kālīna**, mfn. of that time, Daś. iii, 36; simultaneous, BhP. x, 12, 41. — °**kulīna**, mfn. of that family, MBh. v, 7102. — **kriya**, mfn. = *-kara*, L. — **kshaṇa**, m. the same moment, L.; (*am*), ind. at the same moment, directly, immediately, Pañcat.; Kathās. &c. (in comp. °*ṇa-*, Ragh. i, 51; VarBṛS.; Kathās. vi; Hit.); (*āt*), abl. ind. id., Yājñ. ii, 14; R. &c.; (*e*), loc. ind., id., W. — **tad-deśīya**, mfn. belonging to this or that country, Nyāyam. viii, 3, 7, Sch. — **tulya**, mfn. (said of a Prākṛit word) similar or equal to the original Sanskṛit word, Vāgbh. ii, 2. — **tṛitīya**, mfn. doing that for the 3rd time, Pāṇ. vi, 2, 162, Kāś. — **tribhāgaka**, mf(*ikā*)n. forming one-third of that, VarBṛS. lviii. — **tva**, n. true or real state, truth, reality, ŚvetUp.; Mn.; Bhag. &c.; (in phil.) a true principle (in Sāṃkhya phil. 25 in number, viz. *a-vyakta, buddhi, ahaṃ-kāra*, the 5 Tan-mātras, the 5 Mahā-bhūtas, the 11 organs including *manas*, and, lastly, *purusha*, qq.vv.), MBh. xii, 11840; xiv, 984; R. iii, 53, 42; Tattvas.; 24 in number, MBh. xii, 11242; Hariv. 14840 (m.); 23 in number, BhP. iii, 6, 2 ff.; for other numbers cf. xi, 22, 1 ff.; RāmatUp.; with Māheśvaras and Lokâyatikas only 5 [viz. the 5 elements] are admitted, Prab. ii, 1/8; with Buddh. 4, with Jainas 2 or 5 or 7 or 9, Sarvad. ii f.; in Vedânta phil. *tattva* is regarded as made up of *tad* & *tvam*, 'that [art] thou,' and called *mahā-vākya*, the great word by which the identity of the whole world with the one eternal Brahma [*tad*] is expressed); the number 25, Sūryas. ii; the number 24, DevībhP.; ŚBr. vii, 3, 1, 43, Sāy.; an element or elementary property, W.;

the essence or substance of anything, W.; the being that, Jaim. i, 3, 24, Sch.; = *tata-tva*, L.; N. of a musical instrument, L.; (*ena*), instr. ind. according to the true state or nature of anything, in truth, truly, really, accurately, Mn. vii, 68; MBh.; R.; *-kaumudī*, f. 'Tattva-moonlight,' N. of a Comm. on Sāṃkhyak., Sarvad. xiv, 20; *-candra*, m. 'truth-moon,' N. of a Comm. on Prakriyā-kaumudī; 'Tattva-moon,' N. of a Comm. on *-kaumudī*; *-cintāmaṇi*, m. N. of a philos. work by Gaṅgêśa; of another work, Nirṇayas. iii; *-jña*, mfn. ifc. knowing the truth, knowing the true nature of, knowing thoroughly, Mn. xii, 102; MBh. (*a-*, neg., xii, 6623); R. &c.; m. a Brāhman, Npr.; *-jñāna*, n. knowledge of truth, thorough knowledge, insight into the true principles of phil., Sarvad.; *-jñānin*, mfn. = *-jña*, W.; *-taraṃgiṇī*, f. 'truth-river,' N. of a work by Dharma-sāgara; *-tas*, ind. = °*ttvena*, MuṇḍUp. i, 2, 13; Mn.; MBh. &c.; *-tā*, f. truth, reality, W.; *-tyaj*, mfn. mistaking the true state, Viddh. iii, 19; *-traya-maya*, mfn. consisting of the 3 realities, Hcat. i, 11, 893; *-darśa*, m. (= *-dṛiś*) N. of a Ṛishi under Manu Deva-sāvarṇi, BhP. viii, 13, 32; *-darśin*, mfn. = *-dṛiś*, MBh. iii, 1149; Rāmag.; m. N. of one of Manu Raivata's sons, Hariv. 433; of a Brāhman, 1265; *-dīpana*, n. 'Tattva-light,' N. of a work; *-dṛiś*, mfn. perceiving truth, Vedântas.; *-nikasha-grāvan*, m. the touchstone of truth, Hit. i, 9, 12; *-niścaya*, m. 'ascertainment of truth,' right knowledge, Sarvad. vi, 91 & 94; *-nishṭha-tā*, f. veracity, Hemac.; *-nyāsa*, m. 'application of true principles,' N. of a ceremony in honour of Vishṇu (application of mystical letters &c. to parts of the body while prayers are recited), Tantr.; *-prakāśa*, m. 'light of true principles,' N. of a Comm., Sarvad. vii; *-prabodha-prakaraṇa*, n. N. of a work by Haribhadra II (A.D. 1200); *-bindu*, m. 'truth-drop,' N. of a philos. treatise; *-bodha*, m. knowledge or understanding of truth, xii, 46; N. of a work, Tantras. ii; *-bodhinī*, f. 'teaching true principles,' N. of a Comm. on Saṃkshepa-śārīraka; of a Comm. on Siddh. by Jñānêndra-sarasvatī; truth-teaching, cf. RTL. p. 492 & 509; *-bhāva*, m. true being or nature, KaṭhUp. vi; SvetUp. i; *-bhūta*, mfn. true, MBh. xii, 5290; *-muktâvalī*, f. 'necklace of truth,' N. of a work, Sarvad. iv, 110; cf. RTL. p. 123; *-vat*, mfn. possessing the truth or reality of things, MBh. xii, 11480; *-vāda-rahasya*, n. N. of a work, Sarvad. v, 110; *-vid*, mfn. knowing the true nature of (gen.), Bhag. iii, 28; *-vivitsā*, f. desire of knowing the truth, W.; *-viveka*, m. the sifting of established truth; N. of a work on astron. (also *siddhânta-t°*); of another work, Sarvad. v, 6; °*ka-dīpana*, n. 'light of truth-investigation,' N. of a philos. work; *-śambara*, n. N. of a Tantra, Ānand. 31, Sch.; (°*raka*, Āryav.); *-śuddhi*, f. ascertainment or right knowledge of truth, Kathās. lxxv, 194; *-saṃgraha*, m. N. of a work, Sarvad. vii, 88; *-satya-śāstra*, n. N. of a Buddh. work by Guṇa-prabha; *-samāsa*, m. 'Tattva-compendium,' N. of Kapila's Sāṃkhya-sūtras, Tattvas.; *-sāgara*, m. 'truth-ocean,' N. of a work, Smṛitit. xi; Nirṇayas. i, 318; *-sāra*, m. 'truth-essence,' N. of a work, Śāktân. ii; °*vâkhyānôpamā*, f. a simile expressing or stating any truth, Kāvyâd. ii, 36; °*vâdhigata*, mfn. learnt thoroughly, Suśr.; °*vâpahnava-rūpaka*, n. a metaphor denying a truth (as that two eyes are not eyes but bees), Kāvyâd. ii, 95; °*vâbhiyoga*, m. a positive charge or declaration, Yājñ. ii, $\frac{5}{6}$, 4 ff.; °*vârtha*, m. the truth, Sarvad. iii; °*tha-kaumudī*, f. 'truth-light,' N. of a Comm. on Prāyaśc. by Govindânanda; °*tha-vid*, mfn. knowing the exact truth or meaning of (in comp.), Mn. i, 3; (see *veda-*); °*tha-sūtra*, n. N. of a Jaina work by Umā-svāti, Sarvad. iii, 103; °*vâvabodha*, m. perception of truth, W. **—pada**, n. the place of that, Daś. vii, 435; the word *tad*, Vedântas.; m. Ficus religiosa, Npr. **—para**, mf(*ā*)n. following that or thereupon, Megh.; having that as one's highest object or aim, totally devoted or addicted to, attending closely to, eagerly engaged in (loc. [Pāṇ. vi, 2, 66, Kāś.; Pārśvan.] or generally in comp.), SvetUp. i, 7; Mn.; Yājñ.; MBh. &c.; m. $\frac{1}{30}$ of an eye's twinkle, W.; (*ā*), f. $\frac{1}{60}$ of a second of a circle, Āryabh. iii, 2, Sch.; *-tā*, f. scope, design, intention, W.; entire devotion or addiction to (loc.), Hit.; *-tva*, n. id., W.; aiming at, tending to, Daśar. iv, 38 (*a-*, neg.); 'the state of following behind,' inferiority, K[illegible]Śr. i, 4, 16 & 5, 5. **—parāyaṇa**, mfn. addicte[illegible] **—pāṇini**, ind. = *iti-p°*, Pāṇ. ii, 1, 6, Kāś. [illegible] m. the original or supreme spirit (one of the 5 forms of Īśvara [also °*sha-vaktra*], Sarvad. vii), Kāṭh. xvii, 1; TĀr. x, 1, 5 f.; LiṅgaP. i, 13; the servant of him, KātyŚr. vii, 1, 8; N. of a Kalpa period, MatsyaP. liii, 41; a class of compounds (formed like the word *tat-purusha*, 'his servant') in which the last member is qualified by the first without losing (as the last member of Bahu-vrīhi compounds) its grammatical independence (whether as noun or adj. or p.); two subdivisions of these compounds are called Karma-dhāraya and Dvi-gu (qq. vv.); *-vaktra*, m. see before. **—pūrva**, mfn. (cf. Pāṇ. vi, 2, 162) happening for the first time, Mālav. iv, 8; Ragh. xiv; (*am*), ind. that for the first time, Kir. vii, 11; viii, 26; *-tā*, f. happening for the first time, ix, 75; *-sa-ṅga*, mfn. then first restrained, Ragh. ii, 42. **—pṛishṭha**, mfn. combined with that arrangement of Sāmans, ŚāṅkhŚr. xiv, 22, 6. **—prakāra**, mfn. of that kind, W. **—prathama**, mfn. doing that for the first time, Pāṇ. vi, 2, 162, Kāś.; (*am*), ind. = *-pūrvam*, Kir. viii, 30; xvi, 27; *-tas*, ind. id., Divyâv.; *-taram*, ind. that first of all, xxii, 4; xxx, 434. **—prabhāte**, loc. ind. early on the next morning, Vet. i, $\frac{18}{19}$ & $\frac{23}{24}$. **—prabhriti**, mfn. beginning with that, Lāṭy. ii, vii, ix. **—pravara-vat**, mfn. having (his or) their line of ancestors, KātyŚr. i, 6, 13, Sch. **—prêpsu**, m. a particular form of a Desid. Nir. vi, 28; APrāt. iv, 29. **—phala**, mfn. having that as a fruit or reward, W.; having that as a result, W.; the blue water-lily, L.; the plant *kushṭha*, L.; a kind of perfume, L. **—saṃskārârtha-tva**, n. the state of helping to promote that, Jaim. vi, 4, 45 (*a-*, neg.) **—saṃkhyāka**, mfn. of that number, Yājñ. ii, $\frac{6}{7}$. **—sadṛiśa**, mfn. 'fitting or corresponding to that,' see *-sthāna*. **—sama**, mfn. = *-tulya*; ifc. synonymous with, Uṇ. i, 3, Sch. **—samanantaram**, ind. immediately upon that, Kathās. iv, 24; cf. *tad-anant°*. **—sādhu-kārin**, mfn. accomplishing that, Pāṇ. iii, 2, 134. **—sina** (*tát-*), mfn. wishing to acquire or ordering that, RV. i, 61, 4. **—stha**, mfn. being on or in that, Pāṇ. iv, 2, 134; ii, 2, 8, Vārtt. 2; m. a particular mode of multiplication, W.; *-tad-añjana-tā*, f. assuming the colour of any near object, Yogas. i, 41. **—sthāna**, mfn. (= *-sadṛiśa*, Sāy.) for *tasthāná* (q. v.), AitBr. vi, 5, 2. **—spṛishṭin**, mfn. touching them, Gaut. xiv, 30.

Tac, in comp. for *tád*. **—chabda-tva** (*śab°*), n. = *tácchabdya*, TāṇḍyaBr. iv, 8, 15, Sch. **—chīla** (*śīla*), mfn. accustomed to that, Pāṇ. iii, 2, 134; = *sadṛiśa*, similar, Kāvyâd. ii, 64; cf. *tácchīlika*.

Taj, in comp. for *tád*. **—ja**, mfn. sprung from (that, i. e. from) Sanskṛit (as Prākṛit or other words), Vāgbh. ii, 2; *-lân*, mfn. produced, absorbed and breathing in that, ChUp. iii, 14, 1. **—jaghanyá**, mf(*ā*)n. the worst among them, TS. vii, 1, 6, 4. **—jaya**, m. the conquest of that, W. **—ja-lân**, see *-ja*. **—jātīya**, °**yaka**, mfn. of the same kind, (*a-*, neg.) Pāṇ. i, 1, 7, Vārtt. 8 & Pat. **—jña**, mfn. knowing that, (m.) a knowing man, BhP. iii, v (*a-*, q. v.); Rājat. v, 481; ifc. familiar with, Hariv. 8427.

Tátra (also *°trā*, RV.), ind. (*tá-tra*, correlative of *yá-tra*; g. *cādi*, not in Kāś.) used for the loc. (sg., du. & pl.) of *tád* (q. v.; Pāṇ. v, 3, 10; vi, 3, 35), RV.; AV.; Mn. &c.; in that place, there (in comp., Pāṇ. ii, 1, 46), RV. &c.; thither, to that place, ib.; in that, therein, in that case, on that occasion, under those circumstances, then, therefore, (also correlative of *yád* [vi, 57, 4; AV. xii, 1, 34; Nal. &c.], *yadā* [Pañcat. i, 19, 8], *yadi* [Mn. viii f.; Cāṇ.; Hit.], or *ced* [Mn. viii, 295; ix, 205]; *tatra māsa*, 'that month,' i. e. the month that has been spoken of, Kathās. xviii, 208); °**tra tatra**, used for double loc. of *tád*, Nal. v, 8; in that and that place, here and there, everywhere, Mn. vii, 87; MBh.; BhP.; to every place, MBh.; **yatra tatra**, used for the loc. *yasmins tasmin*, in whatever, Mn. iii, 50; vi, 66; xii, 102; in whatever place, anywhere, MBh. xiii, 3686; to any place whatever, v, 5997; at any rate, indiscriminately, xiii, 514; *yatra tatrâpi*, to whatever place, v, 1084; Kathās. xxxvi, 101; [cf. Goth. *thathrō*.] **—cakshur-manas**, mfn. directing one's eyes and mind on him, Gaut. i, 47. **—tya**, mfn. (Pāṇ. iv, 2, 104, Pat.) of that place, being there, BhP.; Kathās.; Rājat. i, 117; Hit. **—bhava**, mfn. employed with that, ĀpŚr. xiv, 5, 1, Sch. **—bhavat**, m., °**tī**, f. (Pāṇ. iv, 1, 166 & v, 3, 14, Kāś.) 'Your Honour there,' (chiefly in dram.) respectful title given to absent persons (once to a present person, Mṛicch. i, $\frac{2}{3}$), R. ii, &c.; cf. *atra-bh°*. **—vāsin**, mfn. dwelling there, i, 25, 21. **—skandha**, m. N. of a deity, Tantr. **—stha**, mfn. dwelling there, situated there, belonging to that place, MBh. iii, 2683; R. ii, iv; Kathās. vii, xxvi.

Táthā, ind. (*tá-thā*, correlative of *yá-thā*, Pāṇ. v, 3, 26; g. *cādi*, Kāś. & Gaṇar.) in that manner, so, thus (the correlative standing in the preceding or in the subsequent clause, e. g. *yathā priyaṃ ta-thâstu*, 'as is agreeable, so let it be'; *tathā praya-tnam ātishṭhed yathâtmānaṃ na pīḍayet*, 'he should so make effort as that he may not injure himself,' Mn. vii, 68; *tathā tathā—yathā*, so much that, VP. iv; also correlative of *iva*, Mn. iii, 181; R. i, 4, 12; of *yena*, Kathās. iii, 18; of *yādṛiśa*, Mn. i, 42; used in forms of adjuration, e. g. *ya-thâham anyaṃ na cintaye tathâyam patatāṃ kshudraḥ parâsuḥ*, 'as surely as I do not think on any other man, so surely let this wretch fall dead,' Nal. xi, 36), RV. &c.; yes, so be it, so it shall be (particle of assent, agreement, or promise; generally followed by *iti*), AV. iii, 4, 5; ŚBr.; AitBr. &c. (*tathêty uktvā*, having said 'so be it' or 'yes,' Nal. &c.); so also, in like manner (e. g. *sukhaṃ seved duḥkhaṃ tathā*, 'let him make use of prosperity and also adversity'), Mn.; MBh. &c.; = *tathā hi*, Nal. xix, 25; °**thā ca**, and likewise, accordingly (introducing quotations), Mn. ix, 19 & 45; Dhūrtas.; Hit.; °**thâpi**, even thus, even so, nevertheless, yet, still, notwithstanding (correlative of *yady api* [R. iii, 3, 3; Dhūrtas. &c.], *api* [Amar.], *api yadi* [Prab.], *kāmam* [Śak.], *varam*), MBh. &c.; *tathâpi tu*, id., Śak.; °**thā hi** (g. *svar-ādi*) for so, for thus (it has been said), for instance, Ragh.; Śak. &c.; °**thâiva**, exactly so, in like manner, Mn. &c.; (with *ca* or *api* following) likewise, Mn. &c.; **atho—tathā**, id., ib.; **yathā-tathā**, in whatever way, in any way, by all means, iv, 17; MBh. i, 45, 17; vii, 6332; Nal.; Naish. ix, 29; **yathā-yathā—tathā-tathā**, in whatever manner or degree—in that manner or degree, the more—the more, Mn.; MBh. (Nal. viii, 14); VarBṛS. xi; Vet.; cf. *yathā-tatham*, *a-* & *vi-tatha*. **—karaṇa**, n. proceeding thus, ĀpŚr. xi, 21, 8, Sch. (*a-*, neg.) **—kāram**, ind. thus (correlative of *yath°*), Pāṇ. iii, 4, 28. **—kṛita**, mfn. thus done or made, W.; made true, VarBṛS. xxxii, 4. **—kratu** (*táth°*), mfn. so intending, ŚBr. xiv, 7, 2, 7. **—gata**, mfn. being in such a state or condition, of such a quality or nature, RPrāt. iii, 5; MBh.; Mālav. v, $\frac{9}{10}$; 'he who comes and goes in the same way [as the Buddhas who preceded him],' Gautama Buddha, Buddh.; Sarvad.; a Buddhist, SSaṃkar. i, 70; x; *-kośa-paripālitā*, f. N. of a Kiṃnara virgin, Kāraṇḍ. i, 83; *-garbha*, m. N. of a Bodhi-sattva, Buddh. L.; *-guṇa-jñānâcintya-vishayâvatāra-nirdeśa*, m. 'direction how to attain to the inconceivable subject of the Tathā-gata's qualities and knowledge,' N. of a Buddh. Sūtra; *-guhyaka*, n. 'Tathāgata-mystery,' N. of a Buddh. work (highly revered in Nepāl); *-bhadra*, m. N. of a pupil of Nāgârjuna. **—guṇa**, mf(*ā*)n. endowed with such qualities, R. ii, 22, 19. **—jātīya**, mfn. of that kind, 15, 13. **—jātīyaka**, mfn. id., Pat. on Śivas. 3 f., Vārtt. 5. **—tā**, f. true state of things, true nature, Vajracch. 17. **—tva**, n. the being so, such a state of things, such a condition, Bhāshāp.; Sāh. vii, $\frac{8}{9}$; Sarvad.; = *-tā*, Mn. x, 57, Sch.; Sāṃkhyak., Sch. **—prabhāva**, mfn. having such power, R. ii, 22, 30. **—bhavi-tavya-tā**, f. the necessity of being so, Kād. iv, 139. **—bhāva**, m. the being so, TPrāt., Sch.; the being of such a nature, true nature, accomplishment, Jain.; Siṃhâs. **—bhāvin**, mfn. about to be of such a kind, Śak. vii, $\frac{33}{34}$. **—bhūta**, mfn. of such qualities or kind or nature, R. i f.; Amar.; Kathās.; Sāh. **—mukha**, mfn. 'so-facing,' turning the face in the same direction, Gobh. iv, 2, 5. °**yatam** (°*thây°*), ind. in the same direction, 4. **—rāja**, m. a Buddha (cf. *-gata*) or Jina, W. **—rūpa**, mf(*ā*)n. so formed, thus shaped, looking thus, Lāṭy. ix, 12; MBh. &c. **—rūpin**, mfn. id., xii, 7344. °**rtha** (°*thâr°*), mfn. 'real,' *-tva*, n. the being real, BṛĀrUp., Sch. **—vādin**, mfn. telling the exact truth, Vishṇ. v, 27; Vajracch. 14; professing to be so, W. **—vidha** (*táth°*), mf(*ā*)n. of such a sort or kind, being in such a condition or state, of such qualities, TBr. ii, 1, 10, 1; Mn. i, viii f. (correlative of *yādṛiśa*, ix, 9); MBh. &c.; (*am*), ind. in this manner, Nal. vii, 15; likewise, Bhāshāp. 94. **—vidhāna**, mfn. following this practice, Hit. iii, 9, $\frac{0}{1}$. **—vīrya**, mfn. of such a strength, MBh. i. **—vrata**, mfn. = *-vidhāna*, Mn. iv, 246. **—śīla**, mfn. behaving thus, MBh. iv, 133; *-samācāra*, mfn. of such a character and behaviour, v, 73, 14 **—svara**, mfn. uttered with the same accent, Lāṭy. vii, 10, 20. **Tathôtsāha**, mfn. making so great efforts, W. **Tathôpama**, mfn. similar to that, MBh. xii, 285 ff.

Tathya, mfn. 'being really so,' true, MBh.; R.; Pañcat.; n. truth, Śak.; Bhartṛ.; (*ena*), ind. according to truth, Mn. viii, 274. — **tas**, ind. id., Rājat. i, 325. — **vacana**, n. a promise, Pañcat. Introd. 1ɣ. — **vādin**, mfn. speaking the truth, BhP. viii, 11, 11.

Tád, (nom. & acc. sg. n. of and base in comp. for 2. *tá* from which latter all the cases of this pron. are formed except nom. sg. m. *sás* or *sá* & f. *sā́*; instr. pl. *tais*, AV. &c.; Ved. *tébhis*, RV.; AV. &c.) m. he, f. she, n. it, that, this (often correlative of *yá* generally standing in the preceding clause, e.g. *yasya buddhiḥ sa balavān*, 'of whom there is intellect he is strong'; sometimes, for the sake of emphasis, connected with the 1st and 2nd personal pronouns, with other demonstratives and with relatives, e.g. *so 'ham*, 'I that very person, I myself' [*tasya = mama*, Nal. xv, 10]; *tāv imau*, 'those very two'; *tad etad ākhyānam*, 'that very tale,' AitBr. vii, 18; *yat tat kāraṇam*, 'that very reason which,' Mn. i, 11; *yā sā śrī*, 'that very fortune which,' MBh. vii, 427), RV. &c.; (*tad*), n. this world (cf. *idam*), R. vi, 102, 25; = Brahma, see *tat-tva*; (*tád*), ind. there, in that place, thither, to that spot (correlative of *yátra* or *yátas*), AV.; AitBr. ii, 11; ŚBr. i, x, xiv.; ChUp.; then, at that time, in that case (correlative of *yadā́*, *yád*, AV.; of *yátra*, ŚBr. xiv; of *yadi*, Nal.; Bhag. &c.; of *céd*, Śak. &c.), RV. iv, 28, 1; AV. &c.; thus, in this manner, with regard to that, ix, xiii; ŚBr.; AitBr.; (*tad etau ślokau bhavataḥ*, 'with reference to that there are these two verses') PraśnUp.; on that account, for that reason, therefore, consequently (sometimes correlative of *yatas*, *yad*, *yena*, 'because,' Daś.; Pañcat.; Kathās. &c.), Mn. ix, 41; MBh. &c.; now (clause-connecting particle), AV. xv; ŚBr.; AitBr.; so also, equally, and AV. xi, xv; **tad tad**, this and that, various, different (e.g. *taṃ taṃ deśaṃ jagāma*, 'he went to this and that place'; *tāsu tāsu yonishu*, 'in different or various birth-places,' Mn. xii, 74); respective, BṛNārP. xiii, 88; *tenaiva tenaiva pathā*, on quite the same path, R. iii, 50, 28; **yad tad**, whosoever, whichsoever, any, every (also with *vā*, Mn. xii, 68 [*yad vā tad vā*, 'this or that, any']; Hariv. 5940; Dhūrtas.; Śak., Sch.; often both pronouns repeated or the interrogative pron. with *cid* added after the relative, e.g. *yad-yat para-vaśaṃ karma tat-tad varjayet*, 'whatever action depends on another, that he should avoid,' Mn. iv, 159; *yat kiṃ-cid—tad*, 'whatever—that,' Mn.); **tan na**, see s.v. *céd*; **tad** (ind.) **api**, 'even then,' nevertheless, notwithstanding, Śak. (v.l.); Bhartṛ.; Prab.; Siṃhâs.; **tad** (ind.) **yathā**, 'in such a manner as follows,' namely, viz., Buddh. (cf. Pāli *seyyathā*; *sá yáthā*, ŚBr.); Jain. (in Prākrit *taṃ jahā*; cf. *sejjahā*); Pat.; Śak.; [cf. ὁ, ἡ, τό; Goth. *sa*, *sō*, *that-a*; Lat. (*is-*)*te*, (*is-*)*ta*, (*is-*)*tud*, *tam*, *tum*, *tunc*.] — **atipāta**, mfn. transgressing that, W. — **anantara**, mf(*ā*)n. nearest to any one (gen.), Nal. xxii, 16; (*am*), ind. immediately upon that, thereupon, then (corresponding to *prāk*, 'before,' Śak. vii, 30; to *prathamam*, 'first,' Mn. viii, 129), MBh. &c. — **anu**, ind. after that, afterwards, Megh.; Ratnâv.; Amar.; Śrut.; Subh. — **anukṛiti**, ind. conformably to that, accordingly, AitBr. vi, 1, 2. — **anusaraṇa**, n. going after that, Sāh. i, ⅜, 58; -*krameṇa*, instr. ind., see s.v. *kráma*. — **anta** (*tád-*), mfn. coming to an end by that, TBr. i, 5, 9, 3; Hit. — **anna** (*tád-*), mfn. accustomed to that food, RV. viii, 47, 16; eating (that i.e.) the same food, R. ii, 103, 30 & 140, 13. — **anya**, mfn. other than that, L. — **anvaya**, mfn. descended from him, VP. iv, 2, 2. — **apatya**, mfn. having offspring from him, Mn. iii, 16 (-*tā*, f. abstr.); -*maya*, mfn. thinking of one's offspring only, Subh. — **apas** (*tád-*), mfn. accustomed to that work or to do that, RV. ii, 13, 3 & 38, 1; viii, 47, 16; ind. in the usual way, v, 47, 2. — **apêksha**, mfn. having regard to that, Gaut. — **artha**, mfn. intended for that, Āp. ii, 14, 3; Pāṇ. ii, 1, 36; i, 3, 72, Kāś.; serving for that, Jaim. i, 2, 1 (*a-*, neg.); having that or the same meaning, Pāṇ. ii, 3, 58; m. (its or) their meaning, Vedântas. 200; (*am*), ind. on that account, with that object, for that end, therefore, Pāṇ. v, 1, 12; R. i, 73, 4; VarBṛS. lxxiv; Kāś.; VP. iv; -*tā*, f. = *tādarthya*, ĀśvŚr. iii, 4, 12, Sch. — **arthaka**, mf(*ikā*)n. denoting that, Naish. iv, 52. — °**arthīya**, mfn. intended for that, undertaken for that end, Bhag. xvii, 27. — °**ardhika**, mfn. half as much, Mn. iii, 1. — **arpaṇa**, n. delivery of that, W. — **arha**, see *a-*. — **avadhi**, ind. from that time, Bhām. ii, 56; up to that period, W. — **avastha**, mfn. so situated, thus circumstanced, in that condition, MBh. iii, 69, 31; Ratnâv.; being in the same condition (as before), undamaged, iv, 19. — **ahe**, loc. ind. on that day, Hemac. — **ākāra**, mfn. having that appearance, W.; -*parijñāna*, n. N. of an art, Gal. — **ātmaka**, mfn. constituting its nature, Car. vi, 12; Sarvad. xv. — **ādi**, ind. from that time forward, Śiś. i, 45; Dharmaśarm. — **āmukha**, n. beginning of that, L. — **íd-artha**, mfn. intent on that particular object, RV. viii, 2, 16; (cf. ii, 39, 1; ix, 1, 5; x, 106, 1). — **id-āsīya**, n. the hymn RV. x, 120, ŚāṅkhŚr. xi. — **ishṭi** (*tád-*), mfn. accompanied by such offerings, AV. xi, 7, 19. — **eka-citta**, mfn. having all the thoughts fixed on that (person or thing), Hit. — **evôpanishad**, f. N. of an Up. (beginning with the words *tad eva*). — **okas** (*tád-*), mfn. rejoicing in that, RV. i, 15, 1; iii, 35, 7; iv, 49, 6; vii, 29, 1. — **ojas** (*tád-*), mfn. endowed with such strength, v, 1, 8. — **gata**, mfn. directed towards him or her or them or that, R. i f.; Kathās. iii, 68; ifc. intent on, Vet. iv, 22; m. (?) the continued multiplication of 4 or more like quantities, W. — **guṇa**, mfn. possessing these qualities, KātyŚr. xiv f.; m. the quality of that or those, xii f.; xvi; xxiii f.; the virtue of (that or) those (persons), Ragh. i, 9; (in rhet.) transferring the qualities of one thing to another (a figure of speech), Sāh. x, 90; Kuval.; Kpr. x, 51; also *a-*, neg. 'a figure of speech in which a quality expected in any object is denied,' 52; -*tva*, n. the having its qualities, Jaim. vi, 7, 16 (*a-*, neg.); -*saṃvijñāna*, n. (a Bahuvrihi compound) in which the qualities implied are perceived along with the thing itself (e.g. *dīrgha-karṇa*, 'long-ear'; opposed to *a-*, e.g. *dṛishṭa-sāgara*, 'one who has seen the ocean'), Bādar. i, 1, 2, Sch.; Sarvad. — **dina**, n. that day, W.; (*am*), ind. on a certain day, W.; during the day, W.; every day, W. — **duḥkha**, n. grief for that or of that, W. — **devata**, mfn. having that deity, KātyŚr. xxiv, 6; ĀpŚr. vii; PārGṛ. iii, 11, 10. — **devatāka**, mfn. id., RV. x, 18, Sāy. — **devatya**, mfn. id., Lāṭy. iv, 4, 21. — **deśya**, mfn. coming from the same country, (m.) a fellow-countryman, MBh. xii, 168, 41; Kām. xiii, 77. — **daivata**, mfn. = -*dev*°, Nir. vii, 1; PārGṛ. iii, 11, 10. — **daivatya**, mf(*ā*)n. id., VarBṛS. ic, 3. — **dvitīya**, mfn. doing that for the 2nd time, Pāṇ. vi, 2, 162, Kāś. — **dhana**, mfn. niggardly, L. — **dharman**, mfn. practising that, iii, 2, 134; accomplishing his business, KātyŚr. i, 6, 12; Jaim. vi, 3, 26; (cf. *tāddharmya*); °*ma-tva*, n. the having his or its peculiarity, KapS. i, 52 (*a-*, neg.) — **dharmin**, mfn. obeying his laws, BhP. iii, 15, 32. — °**dharmya**, mfn. of that kind, v, 14, 2. — **dhāraṇa**, n. N. of an art, Gal. — **dhita** (*hita*), n. sg. & pl. his welfare, Āp. ii; BhP. ii, 9, 7; m. (scil. *pratyaya*) an affix forming nouns from other nouns (opposed to 1. *kṛit*), noun formed thus, derivative noun (*tad-dhita*, mfn. 'good for that or him,' is one of the meanings peculiar to derivative nouns, cf. *maudakika* &c.), Nir. ii, 2; Prāt.; Pāṇ.; ŚāṅkhGṛ.; PārGṛ.; Gobh. ii, 8, 15 (also *a-*, neg. mfn. 'having no Taddhita affix'); -*ḍhuṇḍhī*, f. N. of a gloss on the Taddhita chapter in Hemac.'s grammar by Ānandagaṇi. — **bandhu** (*tád-*), mfn. belonging to that family or race, RV. x, 61, 18. — **bala**, m. or °**lā**, f. a kind of arrow, L. — **bahu**, mfn. doing that often, Pāṇ. vi, 2, 162, Kāś. — **bahula-vihārin**, mfn. id., Divyâv. xvii, 182; 463; 482. — **bhava**, mfn. = *taj-ja*, Mn. iv, 232, Medhāt. — **bhāva**, m. the becoming that, KātySr. iv, 3, 13; Bādar. iii, 4, 40 (*a-*, neg., 'the becoming [not that i.e.] something else'); his intentions, Kām. xi, 29; xviii, 3; ifc. 'becoming,' see *a-bhūta-*. — **bhinna**, mfn. different from that. — **bhūta**, mfn. being in that, Jaim. i, 1, 25. — **rasa**, m. the spirit thereof, W. — **rāja**, m. (scil. *pratyaya*) an affix added to the N. of a race for forming the N. of its chief, Pāṇ. ii, 4, 62; iv, 1, 174; v, 3, 119. — **rūpa**, mf(*ā*)n. thus shaped, so formed, looking thus, KapS. v, 19 & Jaim. vi, 5, 3 (-*tva*, n. abstr.); Pañcat.; Pāṇ. vii, 3, 86, Sch.; of the same quality, Sarvad. xv, 354; Vām. iv, 3, 9 (*a-*, neg. 'of different quality'); *a-*, 'reverse,' Bādar. iii, 4, 40. — **vacaḥ-pratīta**, mfn. believing his words. — **vat**, mfn. having or containing that, VPrāt.; Pāṇ. iv, 4, 125; KapS. i, v; Tarkas. &c.; ind. like that, thus, so (correlative of *yad-vat*, Mn. x, 13; Bhag.; Pañcat.; of *yathā*, 'as,' ŚvetUp. ii, 14 [v. l. for *tad-vā*]; MBh. i, vii &c.), ŚāṅkhGṛ. v, 9, 3 &c.; in like manner, likewise, also, Śrut.; Kathās. vi, xxvi; -*tā*, f. conformity, Vedântas.; Bhāshāp. — **van**, m. pl. N. of a class of Ṛishis (cf. *yad-van*, *tarvan*, *yarv*°), Pat. Introd. on Vārtt. 9. — **vayas**, mfn. of the same age, KātyŚr. xxv, 9, 1. — **vaśá**, mfn. longing for that, RV. ii, 14, 2 & 37, 1. — **vasati**, mfn. dwelling there. — **vā**, ind. = -*vat*, q.v. — **vācaka**, mfn. signifying that. — **vikāra**, m. *a-*, neg. no variety of that, Jaim. vi, 5, 47. — **vid**, mfn. knowing that, familiar with that, AV. ix, 1, 9; ŚBr. xiv; Gobh.; Mn. &c. (also *a-*, neg., xii, 115; MBh. v; BhP. iv; *na-*, neg., v, 4, 13); m. = -*vidya*, VarBṛS. ii, 20; Sarvad.; f. the knowledge of that, KaushUp. i, 2. — **vidya**, mfn. a connoisseur, expert, Nyāyad. iv, 2, 47; Car. i, 25; iii, 8. — **vidha**, mf(*ā*)n. of that kind, conformable to that, Mn. ii, 112; his (or their) like, Suśr. i, 34; Ragh. ii, 22; Kum. v, 73; Mālav.; -*tva*, n. conformity with that, Mn. vii, 17, Sch. — **vishaya**, mf(*ā*)n. belonging to that category, Pāṇ. iv, 2, 66; having that for its object, BṛĀrUp., Sch. — **vishayaka**, mfn. attending to that business, W. — **vīrya-vidvas**, mfn. *a-*, neg., not knowing his manliness, BhP. vi, 17, 10. — **vṛitti**, mfn. living conformably to that, Gaut. — **vrata**, mfn. performing all duties towards (him or) her, Mn. iii, 45; performing the same religious observance, Gaut.

Tadam, ind. ifc. for *tad*, g. *śarad-ādi*.

Tadā́, ind. (Pāṇ. v, 3, 15 & 19 ff.) at that time, then, in that case (often used redundantly, esp. after *tatas* or *purā* or before *atha*, MBh. &c.; correlative of *yád* [AV. xi, 4, 4], *yatra* [ChUp. vi, 8, 1], *yadā* [Mn.; MBh. &c.], *yadi* [Git.; Vet.; Hit.], *yarhi* [BhP. i, 18, 6], *yatas*, 'since' [MBh. xiii, 2231], *céd* [Śak. v (v.l.); Kathās. xi; Śrut.]); °**dā-tadā**, then and then, Sāy. on RV. i, 25, 8; °**dā-prabhṛiti**, from that time forward (correlative of *yadā-pr*°, R. iii, 17, 21; of *yadā*, Śak. vi, ⅛), R.; Ragh. ii, 38; Kathās. ii, 62; **tarhi tadā**, (correlative of *yadi*) then, Vet. iv, 2⅓; **yadā—tadā** (both repeated or the verb being repeated), at any time when—then, Hit.; **yadā-tadā**, at any time whatsoever, always, MBh. i, 6373; Naish. viii, 39. — **tva**, n. (opposed to *ā-yati*) 'state of then,' the present time, Mn. vii; MBh. ii f, v, vii; R. v, 76, 16 & 90, 1.

Tadānīm, in comp. for °*nīm*. — **tana**, mfn. then living, Uttarar. i, ⅔. — **dugdhá**, mfn. (then i.e.) just milked, ŚBr. xi, 1, 4, 3.

Tadā́nīm, ind. (Pāṇ. v, 3, 19) at that time, then (cf. *id*°), RV. x, 129, 1; AV.; MBh. &c. (correlative of *yadā*, VarBṛS. liv; of *yatra* or *yadi*, Śrut.)

Tadīya, mfn. (Pāṇ. i, 1, 74, Kāś.) belonging or relating to or coming from him or her or that or them, his, hers, its, theirs, MBh. viii, 675; R. iv, 21, 35; Ragh. &c.; such, Daś.; BhP. viii, 20, 33 (*na* °*yam aṇv api*, 'not even as little as that, not a bit') &c. — **saṅga**, m. a meeting with her, Pañcat.

Tadrīyañc, m(nom. °*yaṅ*)fn. extending thither, TS. v, 5, 1. °**dryañc**, mfn. id., Pāṇ. vi, 3, 92, Kāś.

Tan, in comp. for *tád*. — **nāmika**, mfn. named thus, iv, 1, 114, Vārtt. 6. — **nāśa**, m. destruction of that. — **nimitta**, mf(*ā*)n. caused by that, Gaut.; Daś.; relating to that, R. ii, 64, 5; conformable to that, MBh. iii, 135, 48; -*tva*, n. the being its cause, Jaim. i, 1, 25; *a-*, neg., 24. — **madhya**, n. 'the midst thereof,' (*āt*), abl. ind. from among them; -*stha*, mfn. situated in the midst of that. — **manas**, mfn. absorbed in mind by that, Car. i, 1. — **maya**, mfn. made up of that, absorbed in or identical with that, MuṇḍUp.; ŚvetUp.; PārGṛ.; MBh. &c.; -*tā*, f. the being absorbed in or identical with that, Kād.; BhP.; Rājat. iii, 498; -*tva*, n. id., MBh. v, 1622 &c.; °*yī-bhāva*, m. id., Sāh. — **mātra**, mfn. = °*traka*, MBh. ix, 1806; Pañcat.; = °*trika*, BhP. iii, 10, 15; n. merely that, only a trifle, Kathās. v, 15; lxiii, 60; Rājat. vi, 1; a rudimentary or subtle element (5 in number, viz. *śabda-*, *sparśa-*, *rūpa-*, *rasa-*, *gandha-*, from which the 5 Mahā-bhūtas or grosser elements are produced, cf. RTL. p. 31 & 33), Yājñ. iii, 179; MBh. i, xiii; Sāṃkhyak.; KapS. &c.; -*tā*, f. the state of a Tan-mātra, MārkP. vi, 46; -*tva*, n. id., BhP. iii, 26, 33 ff.; -*sarga*, m. (in Sāṃkhya phil.) creation of the subtle elements, rudimentary creation. — **mātraka**, mfn. merely that, only so little, Mcar. v, 25. — °**mātrika**, mfn. consisting of Tan-mātras, Sāṃkhyak., Sch.; BhP. xi, 24, 8. — **mānin**, mfn. implying that (which the base indicates, e.g. Nom. P. *aghāya*, 'to act wickedly,' fr. *aghá*), APrā[illegible] — **mukhikayā**, instr. ind. for this re[illegible] — **mūla**, mfn. rooted in (i.e. [illegible]son, Divyâv. [illegible] iv, 2[illegible] caused by) that, Daś.; *-tva*, n. the being based in that, Gaut. vi, 22; the being its root, Kām. xvi, 37.

Tal-lakshaṇa, n. his or her or its or their mark, W.; a particular high number, Lalit. xii, 165.

तदुरी taduri, f. = *tād°*, AV. iv, 15, 15.

तन् 1. tan, cl. 1. 10. *°nati, tānayati*, to believe in, Dhātup.; 'to assist' or 'to afflict with pain,' ib.

तन् 2. tan (= √*stan*), cl. 4. *°nyati* (aor. 2. sg. *tatanas*) to resound, roar, RV. i, 38, 14; vi, 38, 2; [cf. τόνος &c.] **Tanayitnú**, mfn. (= *stan°*) roaring, thundering, iv, 3, 1; x, 66, 11.

Tanyatú, m. thunder, RV. (Ved. instr. *°tā́*, i, 80, 12; perhaps mfn. = *tanayitnú*, iv, 38, 8; vi, 6, 2; x, 65, 13 & 66, 10); AV. v, 13, 3; wind ('a musical instrument,' W.), Uṇ. iv, 2, Sch.; night, ib.

Tanyú, mfn. = *°nayitnú*, RV. v, 63, 2 & 5.

तन् 3. tan, cl. 8. P. Ā. *°nóti, °nuté* (3. pl. *°nváte* [*ā́-* & *vi-tanvaté*, RV.], AV. xii, 1, 13; Impv. *°nu* [*áva-* & *ví-tanuhi*, RV.; cf. Pāṇ. vi, 4, 106, Vārtt. 1, Pat.], RV. i, 120, 11; *°nushva*, RV.; Subj. 2. sg. *°nuthās*, v, 79, 9; 1. du. *°navāvahai*, i, 170, 4; Impf. 3. pl. *atanvata*, x, 90, 6; AV. vii, 5, 4; pf. P. *tatā́na*, once *tāt°*, RV. i, 105, 12; 2. sg. *tatántha* [RV.], class. *tenitha* [Pāṇ. vii, 2, 64, Kāś.]; Ā. 1. 2. 3. sg. [*ā́-*] *tatane*, [*abhí-*]*tatnishe*, [*ví-*]*tatne*, RV.; 3. sg. irr. *tate*, i, 83, 5; 3. pl. *tatniré* [164, 5 *ví-*; AV. xiv, 1, 45] or *ten°* [iv, 14, 4 (*vi-*) &c.; cf. Pāṇ. vi, 4, 99]; aor. P. *átan*, RV. vi, 61, 9; [*ā́-*]*atān*, 67, 6; AV. ix, 4, 1; [*pári-*, *ví-*]*atanat*, RV.; [*anv-ā́*]*atāṅsīt*, VS. xv, 53; *atānīt*, MaitrS.; *tatánat*, [*abhí-*]*°tánāma*, *°tánan*, RV.; 2. pl. *atanishṭa*, Pāṇ. ii, 4, 79, Kāś.; 3. du. *atānishṭām*, Bhaṭṭ. xv, 91; Ā. *atata* or *atanishṭa*, *atathās* or *atanishṭhās*, Pāṇ. ii, 4, 79; 3. pl. *átnata*, RV.; *tatánanta*, i, 52, 11; 1. sg. *atasi*, pl. *ataṅsmahi*, Br.; fut. 2nd *taṅsyáte*, ŚBr.; fut. 1st [*vi-*]*tāyitā*, BhP. viii, 13, 36; p. pr. *tanvát*, *°vānā́*; pf. *tatanvā́s*; ind. p. *tatvā́*, *°tvā́ya*, *-tátya*, Br.; [*vi-*]*tāya*, BhP. vii, 10, 2; inf. *tantum*, Br.; Pass. *tāyáte*, RV. i, 110, 1 & [p. *°yámānā*] x, 17, 7; AV. &c.; *tanyate*, Pāṇ. vi, 4, 44; aor. *atāyi*, Br.) to extend, spread, be diffused (as light) over, shine, extend towards, reach to, RV. &c.; to be protracted, continue, endure, RV.; to stretch (a cord), extend or bend (a bow), spread, spin out, weave, RV. &c.; to emboss, ŚBr. xiv, 7, 2, 5; to prepare (a way for), RV. i, 83, 5; to direct (one's way, *gatim*) towards, Nalôd. i, 20; to propagate (one's self or one's family, *tanūs*, *tantum*), Hariv. 2386; BhP. ii, 3, 8; to (spread, i. e. to) speak (words), Daś. i, 87; to protract, RV. v, 79, 9; Kathās. li, 226; to put forth, show, manifest, display, augment, Ragh. iii, 25; Śak.; Bhartṛ. &c. (Pass. to be put forth or extended, increase, Bhaṭṭ.); to accomplish, perform (a ceremony), RV.; VS. ii, 13; AV. iv, 15, 16; ŚBr. &c.; to sacrifice, xiii, 2, 5, 2; Kauś. 127; to compose (a literary work), Hemac.; Caurap., Sch.; to render (any one thirsty, double acc.), Kuval. 455: Desid. *titanishati*, *°taṅsati*, *°tāṅs°*, Pāṇ. vi, 4, 17; vii, 2, 49, Kāś.: Intens. *tantanyate*, *tantanīti*, vi, 4, 44 & vii, 4, 85, Kāś.; [cf. τάνυμαι, τείνω &c.] **–ādi**, mfn. beginning with √*tan* (the 8th cl. of roots).

2. Tat, mfn. ifc. See *pari-*; cf. *purī-tát*.

2. Tatá, mfn. (vi, 4, 37) extended, stretched, spread, diffused, expanded, RV. &c.; spreading over, extending to, W.; covered over by (instr. or in comp.), Laghuj. ii, 16; Kir. v, 11; Śiś. ix, 23; protracted, W.; bent (a bow), MBh. i, 49, 25; iv, 5, 1; spreading, wide, L.; composed (a tale), i, 2455; performed (a ceremony), RV. &c.; m. wind, L.; n. any stringed instrument, L.; a metre of 4 × 12 syllables. **–cihna**, mfn. having marks drawn along, distinctly marked, W. **–tva**, n. 'protractedness,' slow time (in music), L., Sch. **–pattrī**, f. 'having spreading leaves,' Musa sapientum, L. **–vat**, mfn. containing a derivative of √*tan*, ŚāṅkhBr. xxvi, 8 & 10.

Tatanúshṭi, mfn. 'wishing to show one's self,' fond of ornaments (Nir. vi, 19), RV. v, 34, 3.

2. Tati, f. (Pāṇ. vi, 4, 37, Kāś. v. l.; cf. *tanti*) a mass, crowd, Śak. ii, 6; Śiś. iv, 54 &c. (cf. *tamas-*); the whole mass (of observances, *dharma-*); a sacrificial act, ceremony (cf. *punas-*), ŚāṅkhŚr. vi, 1, 4; a metre of 4 × 12 syllables, Vṛittaratn.

4. Tán, (only dat. *táne* & instr. *tánā*) continuation, uninterrupted succession, RV.; propagation, offspring, posterity, RV. [*tanvā̀ tánā ca* or *tmánā tánā* or *tanvè táne* (*ca*), 'for one's own person and one's children']; (*tánā*, once *tanā́*, x, 93, 12), instr. ind. in uninterrupted succession, one after another, continually, RV. i, 3; 38; 77; ii, 2, 1; viii ff.

Tána, n. offspring, posterity, i, 39, 7; viii, 18, 18 & 25, 2; AV. vii, 73, 5 (*°nāyā* for *°nāya*); (*ā*), f. sg. or Ved. n. pl. id., RV. iii, 25, 1 & 27, 9; ix, 62, 2. **–bāla**, m. pl. N. of a people, MBh. vi, 371.

Tánaya, mfn. propagating a family, belonging to one's own family (often said of *toká*); RV.; AitBr. ii, 7; m. a son, Mn. iii, 16; viii, 275; MBh. (du. 'son and daughter,' iii, 2565); Śak.; Ragh. ii, 64; = *-bhavana*, VarBṛ.; N. of a Vāsishṭha, Hariv. 477 (v. l. *anagha*); pl. N. of a people, MBh. vi, 371; n. posterity, family, race, offspring, child ('grandchild,' opposed to *toká*, 'child,' Nir. x, 7; xii, 6), RV.; VarBṛS. (ifc. f. *ā*, ciii, 1 f.); (*ā*), f. (g. *priyā̀di*) a daughter, Mn. xi, 172 (v. l.), Nal.; R. &c.; the plant *cakra-tulyā*, L. **–bhavana**, n. the 5th lunar mansion, VarBṛS. civ, 27. **–saras**, n. 'offspring-receptacle,' a mother, Divyâv. xxxviii, 18.

Tanayī-kṛita, mfn. made a son, Rājat. iv, 8.

Tánas, n. offspring, RV. v, 70, 4.

Tanikā, f. a cord, Śiś. v, 61.

Tanitṛi, m. an accomplisher, RV. x, 39, 14, Sāy.

Táníman, m. (fr. *°nú*, g. *pṛithv-ādi*; oxyt.) thinness, slenderness, Kād.; Bhartṛ.; shallowness, Vcar. xiii, 6; weakness Bālar. iv, 60; n. the liver, TS. i, 4, 36, 1; ŚBr. iii, 8, 3, 17 & 25.

Tánishṭha, mfn. superl. of *°nú*, smallest, i, vii.

Tánīyas, mfn. compar. of *°nú*, very thin or minute, ii, 2, 2, 9; viii, 7; TāṇḍyaBr.; BhP.; Rājat.

Tanú, mf(*us*, *ūs*, *vī*)n. thin, slender, attenuated, emaciated, small, little, minute, delicate, fine (texture, Ṛitus. i, 7), ŚBr. iii, 5, 4, 21; KātyŚr. viii, 5; MBh. &c. (in comp., g. *kaḍārā̀di*; also = *-dagdha*, Sarvad. xv, 189); (said of a speech or hymn) accomplished (in metre), RV. viii, 1, 18 & (acc. f. *°nvàm*) 76, 12; m. (g. 2. *lohitā̀di*, not in Kāś.) N. of a Ṛishi with a very emaciated body, MBh. xii, 4665; (*us*), f. (once m., Bhām. ii, 79) = *°nū́* (see s. v.), the body, person, self (cf. *dush-ṭanu*, *priyá-*), AitBr. viii, 24, 4 (ifc.); Mn. (*svakā t°*, 'one's own person, iv, 184); MBh.; Hariv. (acc. pl. irr. *°navas*, 3813) &c. (*iyaṃ tanur mama*, 'this my self, i. e. I myself here,' Ratnâv. iv, 4; *°num* √*tyaj* or *hā*, 'to give up one's life,' Mn. vi, 32; BhP. iii; Kathās.); form or manifestation, Śak. i, 1; the skin, L.; = *-gṛiha*, VarBṛ.; Laghuj.; (*vī*), f. a slender or delicate woman, Śak.; Mālav. v; Bhartṛ. &c.; Desmodium gangeticum, L.; Balanites Roxburghii (vv. ll. *tannī*, *°nni*, 'Hemionitis cordifolia'; *tajvī*), L.; a metre of 4 + 24 syllables; N. of a wife of Kṛishṇa (?), Hariv. 6703; [cf. ταvυ-; Lat. *tenuis* &c.] **–kūpa**, m. pore of the skin, W. **–keśa**, mf(*ī*)n. delicate-haired, Laghuj. ii, 13; f. pl., see *kshema-vṛiddhi*. **–kshīra**, m. 'thin-sapped,' Spondias mangifera, L. **–gṛiha**, n. the 1st lunar mansion, v, 12; VarBṛ. vi, 13. **–cchad**, Vop. xxvi, 70. **–cchada**, m. (cf. Pāṇ. vi, 4, 96) = *-tra* (often ifc.), MBh. iii, vii, xii; Ragh. ix, xii; pl. feathers, R. iv, 63, 2. **–cchāya**, m. 'shading little,' a kind of Acacia, Npr. **–ja**, m. = *-ruh*, Jāt. xxx; a son, Pañcat.; BhP. v, 9, 6; (*ā*), f. a daughter, L.; *-tva*, n. sonship, W. **–janman**, m. = *-ja*, HPariś. i f. **–tara**, mfn. = *tánīyas*, Amar. **–tā**, f. thinness, tenuity, littleness, Hariv.; R. v; Megh.; Ragh. &c. **–tyaj**, mfn. giving up one's body, dying, i, 8; = *°nū-t°*, Āp.; MBh. iv, 2354; Ragh. vii; Mālav. v, 1½; BhP. **–tyāga**, mfn. spending little, Hit.; m. risking one's life, R. ii, 40, 6. **–tra**, n. 'body-guard,' armour, MBh. iv, 1009; Suśr.; BhP.; Tantr.; *-vat*, mfn. having armour, R. vi. **–trāṇa**, n. = *-tra*, MBh. iii, vi f.; R. ii. **–trin**, mfn. = *-tra-vat*, Śiś. xix, 99. **–tva**, n. = *-tā*, MBh. xiii, 541; VarBṛS. iii, 16; Sarvad. **–tvak-ka**, mfn. thin-skinned, Suśr. **–tvac**, m. id., (ifc.) Nal. xii, 78; the cinnamon tree, Bhpr. v, 2, 66; Cassia Senna, Npr. **–tvaca**, m. Premna spinosa, L. **–dagdha**, mfn. (said of a Kleśa in Yoga phil.), Sarvad. xv, 192. **–dāna**, n. offering the body (for sexual intercourse); a scanty gift. **–dhī**, mfn. little-minded, Bhaktām. 8. **–pattra**, m. 'thin-leaved,' Terminalia Catappa, Npr.; leafy orpiment, Npr. **–pāda-kshapāṭana**, n. N. of one of 18 ceremonies performed with particular Kuṇḍas, Śārad. v. **–bala**, mf(*ā*)n. 'of small strength,' *a-*, neg., strong, Mudr. vii, 19. **–bīja**, m. 'small-seeded,' the jujube, L. **–bhava**, m. = *-ja*, VarBṛS. vii, 18. **–bhastrā**, f. 'body-bellows,' the nose, L. **–bhāva**, m. = *-tā*, Śak. vii, 8. **–bhūmi**, f. 'stage of personality,' N. of a period in a Śrāvaka's life, Buddh. L. **–bhṛit**, m. any being possessing a body, esp. a human being, Pañcat.; VarBṛS.; Bhartṛ.; BhP.; Prab. **–mat**, mfn. embodied, Kāvyâd. iii, 59. **–madhya**, n. 'body-middle,' the waist, ib.; mf(*ā*)n. = *°dhyama*, Nal. iii, 13; (*ā*), f. a metre of 4 × 6 (– – ◡ ◡ – –) syllables. **–madhyama**, mf(*ā*)n. slender-waisted, MBh. i, 959; Nal.; R. i. **–mūrti**, mfn. thin-shaped, VarBṛS. iv, 20. **–rasa**, m. 'body-fluid,' sweat, L. **–ruh**, n. 'growing on the body,' a hair of the body, L. **–ruha**, n. id., L.; a feather, Śiś. vi, 45. **–latā**, f. a slender body, Prasannar. ii, 19. **–vāta**, m. a highly rarified atmosphere (constituting a kind of hell; opposed to *ghana-v°*), Jain. **–vraṇa**, m. 'body-wound,' elephantiasis, L. **–śarīra**, mfn. delicate-bodied. **–śiras**, f. 'small-headed,' a kind of Ushṇih metre (of 2 × 11 and 1 × 6 syllables). **–satya**, n. a simple truth (?), Divyâv. xxxv, 183. **–saṃcāriṇī**, f. 'moving the body coquettishly (?),' a girl, L. **–sthāna**, n. = *-gṛiha*, Romakas. **–hrada**, m. the rectum, anus, L. **Tanū̀dara**, mf(*ī*)n. thin-waisted, HPariś. ii, 421. **Tanū̀dbhava**, m. = *°nu-ja*, xiii, 39. **Tanū̀na**, m. 'bodiless,' the wind, W. **Tanū̀rja**, m. N. of a son of the 3rd Manu, Hariv.

Tanuka, mfn. (g. *yāvā̀di*) thin, Car. vi, 2 & (said of a liquid) viii, 6; small, Suśr.; m. Grislea tomentosa, Npr.; Terminalia bellerica, ib.; the cinnamon tree, ib.; (*ā*), f. Diospyros embryopteris, ib.

Tanula, mfn. spread, expanded, Uṇ. vṛ.

Tanus, n. (Uṇ. ii, 113) the body, R. v, 93, 23.

1. Tanū, in comp. for *°nú*. **–karaṇa**, n. making thin, attenuation, Yogas. ii, 2; paring, Pāṇ. iii, 1, 76. **–kartṛi**, m. making thin or emaciated, a destroyer, RV. v, 34, 6, Sāy. **–√kṛi**, to make thin, Naish. vii, 82; (ind. p. *-kṛitya*) to diminish, discard (*lajjām*), Ragh. vi, 80. **–kṛita**, mfn. pared, L. **–bhūta**, mfn. become small, diminished, Kathās.

2. Tanū, f. (of *°nú*, q. v.; acc. *°nvàm*, RV. &c.; BhP. iii; *°nuvam* [Pāṇ. vi, 4, 77, Vārtt.], BhP. vii, 9, 37; instr. *°nuvā*, iii f.; gen. abl. *°nvàs*, RV. &c.; loc. *°nvì* & *°nvī̀*, RV.; *°nvām*, AV. &c.; du. *°nū́* [RV. x, 183, 2; AV. iv, 25, 5], *°nvā̀* [RV.], *°núvau* [TBr. i, 1, 7, 3], *°nvau* [see *gharma-*]; pl. nom. & acc. *°nvàs*, RV. &c.; BhP. i; nom. *°núvas*, TBr. i, 1, 7, 3) the body, person, self (often used like a reflexive pron.; cf. *ātmán*), RV. &c.; form or manifestation, RV. &c. (*t° manyos*, 'a sign of wrath,' PārGṛ. iii, 13, 5). **–kṛ́t**, mfn. 'forming the person,' preserving life, RV. i, 31, 9; forming a manifestation of (gen.), ŚāṅkhŚr. vii, 10, 14; caused by one's self, RV. viii, 79, 3. **–krithá**, preservation of the person, 86, 1. **–já**, mfn. produced or born on or from the body, AV. i, 23, 4; belonging to the person, vi, 41, 3 (cf. AitBr. ii, 27); m. a son, MBh. v, viii; Hariv. &c.; N. of a Sādhya, 11536; n. the plumage, wing, MBh. v, 113, 4; (*ā*), f. a daughter, Hariv. 15774; Kum. i, 59. **–jani**, m. a son, W. **–janman**, m. id., Anargh. i, ⅞. **–tala**, m. a measure of length equal to the arms extended, fathom, L. **–tyáj**, mfn. risking one's life, RV. x, 4, 6 & 154, 3 (Nir. iii, 14). **–dūshi**, mfn. destroying the person, AV. xiv, xvi; PārGṛ. ii, 6, 10. **–devatā**, f. a form (of fire) deified, ŚāṅkhŚr. ii, 3, 14. **–deśa**, m. a part of the body, BhP. vii, 13, 12. **–napa**, n. (derived fr. *-nápāt* taken as *-napā́d*, 'eating *tanū-napa*') ghee, L. **–nápāt** (*tánū-*), m. 'son of himself; self-generated (as in lightning or by the attrition of the Araṇis, cf. Nir. viii, 5),' a sacred N. of Fire (chiefly used in some verses of the Āprī hymns), RV. (acc. *°pātam*, x, 92, 2); AV. v, 27, 1; VS. v, 5 (dat. *°ptre*; = TS. i, 2, 10, 2); AitBr. ii, 4; ŚBr. i, 5, 3; iii (gen. *°ptur*, 4, 2, 5, irr. nom. *°ptā* [only etymological, cf. 4, 2, 5] 4, 2, 11); Hit.; fire (in general), Hcar.; N. of Śiva; Plumbago zeylanica, W.; *-vat*, mfn. containing the word *tánū-nápāt*, Nir. viii, 22. **–náptṛi** (*tánū-*), base for the weak cases of *°pāt*, q. v.; cf. *tānūnaptrá*. **–pā́**, m. protecting the person, RV. iv, vi ff.; AV. vi; VS. iii f.; ŚāṅkhŚr. i, 6, 11. **–pā́na**, mf(*ī*)n. id., AV. ii f., xix; TS. v; n. protection of the person, AV. v, 8; viii. **–pāvan**, mfn. = *-pā́*, AitBr. ii, 27. **–pṛishṭha**, m. N. of a Soma sacrifice, ŚāṅkhŚr. x, 8, 33. **–balá**, n. strength of body, one's own strength, AV. ix, 4, 20. **–bhava**, m. = *°nu-ja*. **–rúc**, mfn. brilliant in person, RV. ii, 1, 9; vi, 25, 4; vii, 93, 5. **–ruha**, n. (m., L.) = *°nu-ruh*, MBh.; Hariv. &c. (ifc. f. *ā*, MārkP. xxix, 7); a feather, wing, VarBṛS. lxiii, 1; m. a son, Satr. **–vaśín**, mfn. having power over the person, ruling (Agni, Indra), RV. **–śubhra** (*°nū-*), mfn. decorating the person, v, 34, 3 (cf. *°nūshu śubhrá*, i, 85, 3; Nir. vi, 19). **–havis**, n. an oblation offered to *-devatā*, KātyŚr. iv, 5, 9 & 10, 7; iii, 8, 31, Sch. — **hrada**, m. = °*nu-h*°, W.

Tanti, f. (Pāṇ. vi, 4, 39; Kāś. on iii, 3, 174 & vii, 2, 9) a cord, line, string (esp. a long line to which a series of calves are fastened by smaller cords), RV. vi, 24, 4; BhP.; Sch. on ŚBr. xiii & KātyŚr. xx (ifc.); (°*ntī*) Gobh. iii, 6, 7 & 9; extension, W.; m. a weaver, W.; cf. 2. *tati*. — **cará**, mfn. going with (i.e. led by) a cord, TBr. iii, 3, 2, 5. — **ja**, m. N. of a son of Kanavaka, Hariv. i, 34, 38. — **pāla**, m. 'guardian of (the calves kept together by) a *tanti*,' a N. assumed by Saha-deva at Virāṭa's court, MBh. iv, 68 & 289; N. of a son of Kanavaka, Hariv. i, 34, 38. — °**pālaka**, m. = °*la*, Saha-deva, L.

Tantī, f. = °*ti*, q.v.; see also *vatsa-*. — **yajña**, m. a sacrifice performed for a *tanti*, MānGṛ. ii, 10.

Tántu, m. a thread, cord, string, line, wire, warp (of a web), filament, fibre, RV. &c.; a cobweb, W.; a succession of sacrificial performances, BhP.; any one propagating his family in regular succession, KātyŚr. iii; Āp.; TUp.; MBh. (cf. *kula-*) &c.; a line of descendants, AitBr. vii, 17; any continuity (as of thirst or hope), MBh. xii, 7877; Mālatīm.; N. of a Sāman, ĀrshBr.; = *-nāga*, L.; (g. *gargâdi*) N. of a man, Pravar. iv, 1; cf. *kāshṭha-*, *vara-*, *saptá-*. — **karaṇa**, n. spinning, Sud. on ĀpGṛ. viii, 12. — **karttṛi**, m. 'propagating the succession of a family (*kula-*),' = *kula-tantu* (q.v.), MBh. viii, 3393. — **kārya**, n. 'thread-work,' a web, SarvUp. — **kāshṭha**, n. 'piece of fibrous wood,' a weaver's brush, L. — **kīṭa**, m. a silk-worm, L. — **kṛintana**, n. cutting off the propagation of a family, BhP. vi, 5, 43. — **kriyā**, f. spinning work, Har. on ĀpGṛ. x, 10. — **jāla**, see *kṛimi-*. — **tva**, n. the consisting of threads, Sarvad. xi, 118. — **nāga**, m. a shark, L. — **nābha**, m. 'emitting threads from its navel,' a spider, Bādar. ii, 1, 25, Sch. — **niryāsa**, m. 'having stringy exudations,' the palmyra tree, L. — **parvan**, n. 'thread-festival,' the day of full moon in month Śrāvaṇa (anniversary of Kṛishṇa's investment with the Brāhmanical cord), Tithyād. — **bha**, m. 'thread-like,' Sinapis dichotoma, L.; a calf, L. — **bhūta**, mfn. being the propagator of a family, MBh. iii, 258, 11. — **mat**, mfn. forming threads, 'roping' (as a liquid), Car. vi f.; (*a-*, neg.) Suśr. iii; 'uninterrupted like a thread' (said of an Agni), ĀpŚr. ix, 8, 5; ŚāṅkhGṛ. v, 4, 2; AV.Prāyaśc. ii, 1; (*tī*), f. an oblation offered to that Agni, ĀpŚr. ix, 8, 5, Sch.; N. of Murâri's mother, Anargh. i, ½. — **madhya**, mf(*ā*)n. having a thread-like waist, Priy. iv, 2. — **vardhana**, m. 'race-increaser,' Vishṇu, MBh. xiii, 7033; Śiva. — **vādya**, n. a stringed instrument, W. — **vāna**, n. weaving, Nyāyam. vii, 3, 21, Sch. — **vāpa**, for *-vāya*, L. — **vāya**, m. (Kāś. on Pāṇ. iii, 2, 2 & vi, 2, 76) a weaver, Mn. viii, 397; VarBṛS.; VarBṛ.; (cf. *rajaka-*); a spider, Pāṇ. vi, 2, 77, Kāś.; weaving, L.; *-daṇḍa*, m. a loom, Uṇ. iv, 149, Sch. (v.l.); *-śālā*, f. a weaver's workshop, Gal. — **vigrahā**, f. = *tata-pattrī*, L. — **śālā**, f. = *-vāya-ś*°, L. — **saṃtata**, mfn. woven, L.; sewn, L.; n. wove cloth, W. — **saṃtati**, f. sewing, Vop. xi, 1. — **saṃtāna**, m. weaving of threads, Dhātup. xxvi, 2; KaushUp. i, 3, Sch. — **sāra**, m. 'having a fibrous pith,' the betel-nut tree, L. — **sāraka**, m. id., W.

Tantuka, ifc. a thread, rope, Bhartṛ. i, 95; m. a kind of serpent, Suśr.; the plant °*tu-bha*, L., Sch.; (*ī*), f. a vein, L. **Tantuṇa**, m. = °*tu-nāga*, L.

Tantura, n. the fibrous root of a lotus, L.; m. pl. N. of a family, Pravar. vii, 2 (v.l. °*nnara*).

Tantula, mfn. roping (as slime), Bhpr. vii, 1, 66; n. = °*tura*, the fibrous root of a lotus, L.

Tántra, n. (Pāṇ. vii, 2, 9, Kāś.) a loom, v, 2, 70; the warp, RV. x, 71, 9; AV. x, 7, 42; TBr. ii; TāṇḍyaBr. x, 5; ŚBr. xiv; Kauś.; MBh. i, 806 & 809; the leading or principal or essential part, main point, characteristic feature, model, type, system, framework, ŚBr. xii; TāṇḍyaBr. xxiii, 19, 1; Lāṭy.; KātyŚr. &c. (e.g. *kulasya t*°, 'the principal action in keeping up a family, i.e. propagation,' MBh. xiii, 48, 6; ifc. 'depending on,' cf. *ātma-*, *sva-*, *para-*, &c.); doctrine, rule, theory, scientific work, chapter of such a work (esp. the 1st section of a treatise on astron., VarBṛS. i, 9; Parāśara's work on astron., ii, 3; vii, 8), MBh. &c. (cf. *shashṭi-* &c.); a class of works teaching magical and mystical formularies (mostly in the form of dialogues between Śiva and Durgā and said to treat of 5 subjects, 1. the creation, 2. the destruction of the world, 3. the worship of the gods, 4. the attainment of all objects, esp. of 6 superhuman faculties, 5. the 4 modes of union with the supreme spirit by meditation; cf. RTL. pp. 63, 85, 184, 189, 205 ff.), VarBṛS. xvi, 19; Pañcat.; Daś.; Kathās. xxiii, 63; Sarvad.; a spell, HYog. i, 5; Vcar.; oath or ordeal, L.; N. of a Sāman (also called 'that of Virūpa'), ĀrshBr.; an army (cf. °*trin*), BhP. x, 54, 15; ifc. a row, number, series, troop, Bālar. ii f., vi; = *rājya-t*°, government, Daś. xiii; Śiś. ii, 88; (*para t*°, 'the highest authority') Subh.; a means which leads to two or more results, contrivance, Hariv. ii, 1, 31; a drug (esp. one of specific faculties), chief remedy, cf. °*trâvāpa*; = *paricchada*, L.; = *anta*, L.; wealth, L.; a house, L.; happiness, W.; (*eṇa*), instr. ind. so as to be typical or hold good, KātyŚr. xvi, xx; (*ā*), f. for °*ndrā*, Suśr.; (*īs*, cf. Pāṇ. v, 4, 159, Kāś.; *ī*, L.) f. = °*ntī*, Gobh. iii, 6, 7 & BhP. iii, 15, 8 (v.l. for °*ntī*; see also *vatsa-tantrī*); the wire or string of a lute, ŚāṅkhŚr. xvii; Lāṭy. iv, 1, 2; Kauś. &c. (°*tri*, R. vi, 28, 26); (fig.) the strings of the heart, Hariv. 3210 (v.l.); any tubular vessel of the body, sinew, vein, Pāṇ. v, 4, 159; the plant °*trikā*, L.; a girl with peculiar qualities, L.; N. of a river, L.; cf. *ku-tantrī*. — **kāra**, m. the author of any scientific treatise, Mālav. i, ⅘; Daś. xiii, 87. — **kāshṭha**, n. = °*ntu-k*°, L. — **kaumudī**, f. N. of a work, Tantras. ii. — **gandharva**, n. N. of a work, Śāktân. — **garbha**, m. N. of a work, vii. — **cūḍāmaṇi**, m. N. of a work, Tantras. ii. — **ṭīkā**, f. N. of *-vārttika* i–iv, W. — **tā**, f. the state of anything that serves as a *tantra*, ĀśvŚr. xi, 1; comprehending several rites in one, ceremony in lieu of a number, W. — **tva**, n. dependance on (in comp.), Sarvad. i, 41. — **prakāśa**, m. N. of a work, Vratapr. — **pradīpa**, m. N. of a Comm. on Dhātup. — **bheda**, m. N. of a Tantra, Ānand. 31, Sch. — **mantra-prakāśa**, m. N. of a work, Śāktân. iv. — **ratna**, n. N. of a work by Pārtha-sārathi. — **rāja**, m. N. of a work, Tantras. i; Ānand. 99, Sch. — **rājaka**, m. N. of a medical work by Jābāla, BrahmavP. i, 16, 18. — **vāpa**, for *-vāya*, L. — **vāya**, m. (= °*ntu-v*°) a weaver, R. (G) ii, 90, 15; a spider, L.; m. n. weaving, L. — **vārttika**, n. = *mīmāṃsā-t*°. — **śāstra**, n. N. of a work, Pratāpar., Sch. — **sāra**, m. 'Tantra-essence,' N. of a compilation. — **hṛidaya**, n. N. of a work, Tantras. ii. **Tantrântarīya**, m. pl. the Sāṃkhya philosophers, Bādar. ii, 4, 9, Sch. **Tantrâvāpa**, n. sg. 'attention to the affairs of both one's own and an enemy's country' [Daś. xiii, 92], and 'drugs and their preparation,' Śiś. ii, 88. **Tantrôttara**, n. N. of a work (v.l. *matôtt*°), Ānand. 31, Sch.

Tantraka, mfn. recently from the loom, new and unbleached, Pāṇ. v, 2, 70; ifc. for °*tra*, doctrine, see *pañca-*; (*ikā*), f. Cocculus cordifolius, Bhpr. v, 3, 7; noise in the ears, ŚārṅgS. vii, 142; cf. *apa-*. °**traṇa**, n. the supporting of a family, MBh. v, 3751.

Tantraya, Nom. (fr. °*tra*) °*yati*, to follow as one's rule, xii, 215, 21; to provide for (acc.), Śak. v, 5 (ind. p. °*yitvā*, v.l.; Ā. 'to support a family,' Dhātup. xxxiii, 5); Ā. to regulate, Car. iv, 1; vi, 26.

Tantrāyin, mfn. (said of the sun) drawing out threads or rays (of light), VS. xxxviii, 12.

Tantri, f. = °*trī*, q.v.; v.l. for °*ndri*. — **ja**, v.l. for °*nti-ja*. — **tā**, v.l. for °*ndri-tā*. — **pāla**, v.l. for °*nti-p*°. — **pālaka**, m. N. of Jayad-ratha, L.

Tantrita, mfn. spoken (a spell), Kathās. xxiii, 63; (ifc.) depending on, BhP. xi, 18, 33; *a-*, neg., 'independent,' Gobh. i, 5, 26, Sch.; for *a-tandrita*, MBh.

Tantrin, mfn. having threads, made of threads, spun, wove, W.; chorded (an instrument), W.; m. a musician, W.; a soldier, Rājat. v, 248–339; vi.

Tantrila, mfn. occupied with the affairs of government, Mṛicch. vi, ⅚, Sch.

Tantrillaka, m. N. of a man, Rājat. viii, 2209.

Tantrī, f. of °*tra*, q.v. — **bhāṇḍa**, n. 'chorded instrument,' the Indian lute, Sāh. vi, 214. — **mukha**, m. a peculiar position of the hand, PSarv.

Tantv, in comp. for °*tu*. — **agra**, n. the end of thread, g. *gahâdi*. — °**agrīya**, mfn. fr. °*gra*, ib.

Tandrá, n. a row (ŚBr. viii, 5, 2, 6), VS. xv, 5. — **vāya**, m. for °*ntra-v*°, L., Sch.

Tanv, in comp. for °*nú*. — **aṅga**, m. 'slender-limbed,' N. of a man, Rājat. vii, 260 f.; 635 & 641; (*ī*), f. a delicate-limbed woman, MBh.; Śukas.

Tanvin, m. 'possessed of a body,' N. of a son of Manu Tāmasa, Hariv. 429.

तनक *tanaka* (for *vet*°?), a reward, SaddhP.

तनयित्नु *tanayitnú*. See √2. *tan*.

तनस् *tánas*, °*nikā*, °*nitri*, &c. See √3. *tan*.

तनोनु *tanonu*, a kind of *shashṭika* rice, Npr.

तन्तस्य *tantasya*, Intens. √*taṇs*, q.v.

तन्ति *tantí*, °*tī*, *tántu*, &c. See col. 1.

Tántra, °**traka**, °**traṇa**, &c. See cols. 1, 2.

तन्थी *tanthī*, ind. with √*as*, *kṛi*, *bhū*, g. *ūry-ādi* (Gaṇap.; v.l. *tasthī*).

तन्द् *tand*, cl. 1. Ā. °*date*, to become relaxed, RV. i, 138, 1; cf. *á-tandra*.

Tandr, cl. 1. P. °*drati*, = √*sad*, VS. xv, 5, Mahīdh.; (Subj. °*drat*) to make languid, RV. ii, 30, 7: Caus. °*drâyate*, to grow fatigued, AitBr. vii, 15, 5 (ŚāṅkhŚr. xv, 19); TĀr. iii, 14, 1 & 9 (with inf.).

Tandrayú, mfn. fatigued, lazy, RV. viii, 92, 30.

Tandrā, f. lassitude, exhaustion, laziness, Yājñ. iii, 158; MBh. iii, 3008; xiv, 874; R.; Suśr. &c.

Tandrālu, mfn. (Pāṇ. iii, 2, 158) tired, wearied, sleepy, Suśr. **Tandrāvin**, mfn. id., TĀr. iv, 7, 18.

Tandri, = °*drā*, (ifc.) MBh. xii f. & R. ii, 1, 18; (instr. °*driṇā*) BhP. iii, 20, 40. — **ja**, v.l. for °*nti-ja*. — **pāla**, v.l. for °*nti-p*°.

Tandrika, m. a kind of fever; (*ā*), f. = °*drā*, W.

Tandrita, mfn. = *mūḍha*, L.; see *a-*.

Tandrin, mfn., see *a-*; m. = °*drika*, Bhpr. °**ritā**, f. lassitude, sleepiness, MBh. xii, 4997 & 7958.

Tandrí, *ís* [AV.; MBh. iii, xii], *ī* [iii, xiii], f. = °*drā*, AV. viii, 8, 9; xi, 8, 19; MBh. (ifc. nom. °*drīs*, i, 4474; iii; v, 1358 C; xii); R. (ifc. nom. f. °*drī*, v, 28, 18); BhP.; cf. *saṃbādha-tandrí*.

तन्नि *tanni*, °*nnī*, v.l. for °*nvi*, q.v.

तन्निमित्त *tan-nimitta*. See p. 434, col. 3.

Tan-madhya, **-manas**, &c. See ib.

तन्यतु *tanyatú*, °*nyú*. See √2. *tan*.

तन्व *tanva*, m. N. of the author of a Sāman (cf. 2. *tánva*); (n., ?) a part of the body, Śulbas. ii, 37.

तन्वि *tanvi*, v.l. for °*vī*; °*nvin*; see col. 2.

तप् 1. *tap* (cf. √1. *pat*), cl. 4. Ā. °*pyate*, to rule, Dhātup. xxvi, 50.

Tapa-tā, f. ifc. governing, BhP. iv, 22, 37.

तप् 2. *tap*, cl. 1. *tápati* (rarely Ā.; Subj. °*pāti*, RV. v, 79, 9; p. *tápat*, RV. &c.; cl. 4. p. *tápyat*, VS. xxxix, 12; pf. 1. sg. *tatápa*, RV. vii, 104, 15; 3. sg. °*tāpa*, x, 34, 11; AV. vii, 18, 2 &c.; p. *tepānā*, RV.; fut. *tapsyáti*, Br. &c.; °*te* & *tapishyati*, MBh.) to give out heat, be hot, shine (as the sun), RV. &c.; to make hot or warm, heat, shine upon, ib.; to consume or destroy by heat, ib.; to suffer pain, MBh. viii, 1794; Gīt. vii, 31; (with *paścāt*) to repent of, MBh. viii, 39, 15; to torment one's self, undergo self-mortification, practise austerity (*tapas*), TUp. ii, 6; Mn. i f.; MBh. &c.; to cause pain to, injure, damage, spoil, RV.; AitBr. vii, 17; ŚBr. xiv &c.: Pass. or cl. 4. Ā. *tapyáte* (xiv; or *tápy*°, TBr. ii; p. °*pyámāna*, AV.; *tápy*°, xix, 56, 5; cf. *á-*; aor. *atāpi*, RV. vii, 70, 2; *atapta*, Pāṇ. iii, 1, 65, Kāś.; pf. *tepe*, MBh. &c.; p. °*pānā*, ŚBr.; also P. *tapyati*, °*pyet*, *atapyat*, &c., MBh.; R.; Kathās. x, 4) to be heated or burnt, become hot, RV. &c.; to be purified by austerities (as the soul), Sarvad.; to suffer or feel pain, RV. x, 34, 10 & 95, 17; AV. xix, 56, 5; ŚBr. xiv; MBh. &c.; to suffer pain voluntarily, undergo austerity (*tapas*), AV.; ŚBr.; TBr.; ShaḍvBr.; ŚāṅkhŚr. &c.: Caus. *tāpayati*, °*te* (p. °*páyat*, AV.; Pass. °*pyate*, MBh. &c.; aor. *atītape* & [Subj.] *tatápate*, RV.) to make warm or hot, iv, 2, 6; viii, 72, 4; Kauś.; MBh. &c.; to consume by heat, R. &c.; to cause pain, trouble, distress, AV. xix, 28, 2; MBh. &c.; to torment one's self, undergo penance, iii, 8199: Intens. (p. *tātapyamāna*) to feel violent pain, be in great anxiety, R. i, 11, 8; BhP. ii, 7, 24; [cf. Lat. *tepeo* &c.]

3. **Tap**, mfn. 'warming one's self.' See *agni-tâp*.

Tapa, mfn. ifc. 'consuming by heat,' see *lalā-ṭam-*; 'causing pain or trouble, distressing,' see *janam-* & *param-*; tormented by, Hariv. i, 45, 37; m. heat, warmth (cf. *ā-*), Pañcat. ii, 3, ⅚; the hot season, Śiś. i, 66; the sun, W.; = °*pas*, religious austerity, Car.; Cāṇ.; (cf. *mahā-* & *su-*); a peculiar form of fire (which generated the seven mothers of Skanda), MBh. iii, 14392; Indra, Gal.; N. of an attendant of Śiva, L., Sch.; (*ā*), f. N. of one of the 8 deities of the Bodhi-vṛiksha, Lalit. xxi, 404; cf. *a-*. — **ruj**, f. the pain of bodily austerity, W. — **rtu** (*ritu*), m. the hot season, Naish. i, 41. **Tapâtyaya**,

m. 'end of the heat,' the rainy season, MBh. iii; Śak. iii, 9. **Tapânta**, m. id., MBh. vi, viii; R. vi, 37, 68.

Tapa-ātaṅka, m. = °*pas-taṅka*, Gal.

Tapaḥ, in comp. for °*pas*. — **kara**, m. the fish Polynemus risua or paradiseus, L. — **kṛiśa**, mfn. emaciated by austerities, W. — **kleśa-saha**, mfn. enduring the pain of austerities, Hemac. — **parârdha** (*tápº*), mfn. finishing by *tº*, MaitrS. iii, 4. — **pātra**, n. a man whose austerities have made him a fit recipient of honour, Siṃhâs. iii, §. — **prabhāva**, m. supernatural power (acquired by) austerities, Śak. vii. — **śīla**, mfn. inclined to religious austerities. — **samādhi**, m. the practice of penance, W. — **sādhya**, mfn. to be accomplished by austerities. — **siddha**, mfn. accomplished by penance. — **suta**, m. 'austerity-son,' Yudhi-shṭhira, MBh. iii, 313, 19; (°*pasaḥ suta*, Śiś. ii, 9.) — **sthala**, n. a place of austerity, Hāsy. i, 19; (*ī*), f. Benares, L.

Tapat, mfn. pr. p. √2. *tap*, q. v.; (*tī*), f. 'warming,' N. of a daughter of the Sun by Chāyā (married to Saṃvaraṇa and mother of Kuru), MBh. i; BhP. vi, viii f.; VamP.; = °*pantī*, Rasik.; Kathârṇ.; (*ntī*), f. N. of a river, Divyâv. xxx; cf. *tāpatya*.

Tapatām-pati, m. 'chief of burners,' the sun, W.

Tápana, mfn. warming, burning, shining (the sun), MBh. i, v; R. vi, 79, 57; causing pain or distress, RV. ii, 23, 4; x, 34, 6; AV. iv, xix; m. (g. *nandy-ādi*) the sun, MBh. i, vi, xiii; R. i, 16, 11; Ragh. &c.; heat, L.; the hot season, L.; N. of a hell (cf. *mahā-*), Mn. iv, 89; Buddh.; N. of an Agni, Hariv. 10465; Agastya (cf. *āgneya*), L.; Semecarpus Anacardium, Npr.; = -*cchada* (or 'a white kind of it,' Npr.), L.; Premna spinosa, L.; Cassia Senna, Npr.; the civet cat, Gal.; = -*maṇi*, L.; N. of a Yaksha, MBh. i, 32, 18; of a Rakshas, R. vi; n. (°*ná*) the being hot, burning, heat, TBr. ii, 2, 9, 1 f.; pining, grieving, mental distress, Kāṭh. xxviii, 4; Sāh. iii; (*ī*), f. heat, RV. ii, 23, 14; the root of Bignonia suaveolens, Npr.; = °*pantī*, Divyâv. xxx, 317 & 409; a cooking vessel, Baudh. (TS., Sch.); cf. *gopāla-*, *tripurā-*, *rāma-*. — **kara**, m. a sunbeam, W. — **cchada**, m. the sunflower, L. — **tanaya**, m. 'Sun-son,' Karṇa, W.; (*ā*), f. = -*sutā*, L.; = °*pantī*, W.; = °*pasvishṭā*, L.; °*yeshṭā*, f. id., L. — **dyuti**, mfn. brilliant like the sun, Śiś. i, 42; f. sunshine, L. — **maṇi**, m. the sun-stone, L. — **sutā**, f. 'sun-daughter,' the Yamunā river, Prasannar. v, 33. **Tapanâtmajā**, f. id., L. **Tapanâśman**, m. the sun-stone (*sūrya-kānta*), Dharmaśarm. xvi, 37. **Tapanêshṭa**, n. 'loved by sunbeams,' copper, L. **Tapanôpala**, m. = °*na-maṇi*, Rājat. iii, 296.

Tapanīya, mfn. to be heated, W.; to be suffered (as self-mortification), W.; m. a sort of rice, Car. i, 27; n. gold purified with fire, MBh. iv, vi; R. vi; Ragh. &c. — **maya**, mf(*ī*)n. golden, MBh. vii; Hcat.

Tapanīyaka, n. gold, L. **Tapantaka**, m. N. of a man, Kathās. xxiii. **Tapar-loka**, m. = °*po-lº*, W.

Tapaś, in comp. for °*pas*. — **caraṇa**, n. the practice of austerities, MBh.; R. i; Sarvad.; (°*paścº*, Mn. vi, 75). — **caryā**, f. id., MBh. vii, 1280; Hariv. 14907 f.; MārkP. — **cit**, m. pl. 'accumulating merit by austerities,' N. of a class of deities, TāṇḍyaBr. xxv, 5; °*tām ayana*, n. = *tāpaścitá*, Maś.

Tápas, n. warmth, heat (*pañca tapāṅsi*, the 5 fires to which a devotee exposes himself in the hot season, viz. 4 fires lighted in the four quarters and the sun burning from above, Mn. vi, 23; R.; BhP. iv; BrahmaP.; cf. Ragh. xiii, 41), RV.; AV.; VS.; SāṅkhŚr.; pain, suffering, RV. vii, 82, 7; religious austerity, bodily mortification, penance, severe meditation, special observance (e. g. 'sacred learning' with Brāhmans, 'protection of subjects' with Kshatriyas, 'giving alms to Brāhmans' with Vaiśyas, 'service' with Śūdras, and 'feeding upon herbs and roots' with Ṛishis, Mn. xi, 236), RV. ix, 113, 2; x (personified, 83, 2 f. & 101, 1, 'father of Manyu,' RAnukr.); AV. &c.; (m., L.) N. of a month intervening between winter and spring, VS.; TS. i; ŚBr. iv; Suśr.; Pāṇ. iv, 4, 128, Vārtt. 2, Pat.; Śiś. vi, 63; the hot season, L., Sch.; = °*po-loka*, Vedântas. 120; the 9th lunar mansion (*dharma*), VarBṛ. i, 19; ix, 1 & 4; N. of a Kalpa period, VāyuP. i, 21, 27. — **taksha**, m. 'destroying the power of religious austerity,' Indra (as disturbing the austerities of ascetics lest they should acquire too great power), L. — **taṅka**, m. 'afraid of austerities,' id., L. — **tanu**, mfn. = °*paḥ-kṛiśa*, AitĀr. v, 3, 2, 1. — **tīrtha**, n. N. of a Tīrtha, W. — **pati** (*tápº*), m. the lord of austerities, VS. v, 6 & 40; BhP. iv, 24, 14. — **vat** (*tápº*), mfn. burning, hot, RV. vi, 5, 4; AV. v, 2, 8; SāṅkhŚr. iii, 19, 15; = °*po-vº*, RV. x, 154, 4 f. — **vin**, mfn. (Pāṇ. v, 2, 102) distressed, wretched, poor, miserable, TS. v, 3, 3, 4 (compar. -*vi-tara*); R. ii f.; Śak.; Mālav.; BhP.; Sāh.; practising austerities, (m.) an ascetic, AV. xiii, 2, 25; Kāṭh. xx (compar.), xxiii (superl. -*vi-tama*); ŚBr. (compar. ii) &c.; m. a pauper, W.; = °*paḥ-kara*, L.; a kind of Karañja tree, L.; Nārada, L.; N. of a son of Manu Cākshusha, Hariv. 71; of a Ṛishi of the 12th Manv-antara, 482; BhP. viii, 13, 29; VP.; (*inī*), f. a female devotee, poor wretched woman, Nal.; R. iii, 2, 7; Śak.; Daś.; Nardostachys Jaṭā-māṅsī, L.; Helleborus niger, L.; = *mahā-śrāvaṇikā*, Bhpr.; °*svi-kanyakā* or °*nyā*, f. the daughter of an ascetic, Śak. i, 1⅛ & 24; -*tā*, f. devout austerity, MBh. xiii, 2896; Śatr.; -*pattra*, m. Artemisia, L.; °*svishṭā*, f. Prosopis spicigera, Gal.

Tapasa, m. = °*po-rāja*, Uṇ. iii, Sch.; a bird, ib.

Tapasīvan, mf(*varī*)n. causing pain (?), Kāṭh.

Tapaso-mūrti, m. (= °*po-mº*) N. of a Ṛishi of the 12th Manv-antara, Hariv. 482.

1. **Tapasya**, Nom. °*syati* (Pāṇ. iii, 1, 15) to undergo religious austerities, ŚBr. xiv, 6, 8, 10 (*tápº*); MBh. i, iii, xiii (Ā., cf. 2. *tapasya*); R. &c.

2. **Tapasyà**, mf(*ā*)n. (fr. *tápas*) produced by heat, KātyŚr. xxv; belonging to austerity, Baudh. ii, 5, 1; m. (Pāṇ. iv, 4, 128) the second month of the season intervening between winter and spring (= *phālguna*), VS.; TS. i; ŚBr. iv; Car. viii, 6; Suśr. i; Arjuna (= *phālguna*), L.; N. of a son of Manu Tāmasa, Hariv. 428; n. the flower of Jasminum multiflorum or pubescens, L.; devout austerity (?, °*sye* taken as 1. sg. Ā. of 1. *tapasya* by Nīlak.), MBh. xiii, 10, 13; (*ā*), f. (fr. 1. *tapasya*) id., Hcar.

Tapasyā-matsya, m. = °*paḥ-kara*, W.

Tapā-gaccha, m. the 6th Gaccha of the Śvetâmbara Jains (founded by Jagac-candra, A. D. 1229).

Tapita, mfn. refined (gold), Hariv. 13035.

Tápishṭha, mfn. (superl.) extremely hot, burning, RV.; AV. xi, 1, 16. **Tapishṇu**, mfn. warming, burning (with *deva*, 'the sun'), MBh. xii, 11726.

Tapīyas, mfn. (compar.) most devoted to austerities among (gen.), BhP. ii, 9, 8.

Tápu, mfn. burning hot, RV. ii, 4, 6; ix, 83, 2.

Tapur, in comp. for °*pus*. — **agra** (*tápº*), mf(*ā*)n. burning-pointed (a spear), RV. x, 87, 23. — **jambha** (*tápº*), mfn. burning-jawed (Agni), i, 36, 16 & 58, 5; viii, 23, 4. — **mūrdhan** (*tápº*), mfn. burning-headed (Agni), vii, 3, 1; x, 183, 3; m. N. of the author of RV. x, 183 (son of Bṛihaspati), RAnukr. — **vadha** (*tápº*), mfn. having burning weapons, RV. vii, 104, 5; AV. vi, 20, 1.

Tápushi, mfn. burning (a weapon), RV. iii, 30, 17 (Nir. vi, 3); vi, 52, 3; (m. or f.) a burning weapon, i, 42, 4. **Tápushī**, f. heat of anger, Naigh. ii, 13.

Tapush-pā́, mfn. drinking warm (beverages), RV. iii, 35, 3 ['protecting from pain,' Sāy.]

Tápus, mfn. burning, hot, RV. ii, 30, 4 & 34, 9; vi, 52, 2; m. fire, Uṇ., Sch.; the sun, ib.; 'pain-causer,' an enemy, ib.; n. heat, RV.; AV. i, 13, 3.

Tapo, in comp. for °*pas*. — **gaccha**, m. = °*pā-gº*. — **já**, mfn. born from heat, VS. x, 6; xxxvii, 16; become (a god or saint) through religious austerity, RV. x, 154, 5; AV. vi, 61, 1; MaitrS. iv, 9, 6, 7; AitBr. ii, 27. — **da**, n. 'granting religious merit,' N. of a Tīrtha, Hariv. 9524. — **dāna**, n. id., MBh. xiii, 7650. — **dyuti**, m. 'brilliant with religious merit,' N. of a Ṛishi of the 12th Manv-antara, VP. iii, 2, 34. — **dhana**, mf(*ā*)n. rich in religious austerities, (m.) a great ascetic, Mn. xi, 242; MBh.; Hariv. ii, 69, 62 &c.; m. N. of a son of Manu Tāmasa, i, 7, 23; of a Ṛishi of the 12th Manv-antara, VP. iii, 2, 34; of a Muni, Kathās. cxvii, 125; = °*pasvi-pattra*, L.; (*ā*), f. Sphæranthus mollis, L. — **dharma**, m. N. of a son of the 13th Manu, Hariv. i, 7, 82 (v. l. °*rma-bhṛitha*). — **dhāman**, n. 'place of austerities,' N. of a Tīrtha, Rasik. xi, 37. — **dhṛiti**, m. N. of a Ṛishi of the 12th Manv-antara, Hariv. 483; VP. iii, 2, 34. — **nitya**, mfn. devoting one's self incessantly to religious austerities, MBh. iii, xiv; m. N. of a man (with the patr. Paurušishṭi), TĀr. vii, 9, 1. — **nidhi**, m. 'austerity-treasury,' an eminently pious man, Ragh. i, 56; Śak. (v. l.); [°*pasāṃ nº*, R. (G) i, 67, 3]. — **nishṭha**, mfn. practising austerities, Mn. iii, 134; Yājñ. i, 221. — **'nubhāva**, m. = °*paḥ-prabhº*, W. — **bala**, m. the power acquired by religious austerities, SāṅkhGṛ. iv, 5, 15; Mn. xi, 241; R. i. — **bhaṅga**, m. interruption of religious austerities, Kāvyâd. ii, 325. — **bhṛit**, mfn. undergoing austerities, (m.) an ascetic, Hariv. 4849. — **maya**, mf(*ī*)n. consisting in or composed of religious austerities, 3990; 14430; R. i, 31, 11; BhP. ii; practising religious austerities, Hcat. — **mūrti**, f. an incarnation of religious austerity, R. i, 31, 11; m. = °*paso-mº*, BhP. viii, 13, 29; VP. iii. — **mūla**, mfn. founded on religious austerity, Mn. xi, 235; m. N. of a son of Manu Tāmasa, Hariv. 428. — **yajña**, mfn. sacrificing by austerities, Bhag. iv, 28. — **yukta**, mfn. engaged in austerities, MBh.; VarBṛS. lxxxv. — **rata**, mfn. rejoicing in religious austerity, pious, MBh. i, 36, 3. — **rati**, mfn. id., i, 1838; m. N. of a son of Manu Tāmasa, Hariv. 429; = -*ravi*, VP. iii, 2, 34. — **ravi**, m. 'sun of ascetics,' N. of a Ṛishi of the 12th Manv-antara, Hariv. 482. — **rāja**, m. the moon (as presiding over austerities), L. — **rāśi**, m. an accumulation of religious austerities (Purushôttama), R. i, 31, 11. — **'rthīya**, mfn. destined for austerities, MBh. xi, 760. — **loka**, m. one of the 7 worlds (also called *tapar-lº*, situated above the *jana-lº*), ĀruṇUp.; BhP. ii, 5, 39; KāśīKh. xxii; pl. N. of a family, Pravar. vi, 2. — **vaṭa**, m. Brahmâvarta (in central India), L. — **vat**, mfn. engaged in austerities, MBh. xii, 8548. — **vana**, n. a grove in which religious austerities are performed, Nal. xii, 62; R. i; Śak.; Ragh.; (ifc. f. *ā*) Kathās. xxii. — **vāsa**, m. = °*paḥ-sthala*, Hariv. 5168. — **vidhāna**, n., °**dhi**, m. N. of two Jaina texts. — **vṛiddha**, mfn. rich in religious austerity, MBh. (Nal. xii, 48). — **vrāta**, m. a multitude of austerities, W. — **'śana**, m. 'whose food is austerity,' N. of a Ṛishi of the 12th Manv-antara, Hariv. 482; of a son of Manu Tāmasa, 428.

Taptá, mfn. heated, inflamed, hot, made red-hot, refined (gold &c.), fused, melted, molten, RV.; AV. &c.; distressed, afflicted, worn, R. iii, 55, 15; Megh.; Śak.; (in astrol.) opposed by, VarYogay. ix, 16; practised (as austerities), MBh. v, 7147; R. i, 57, 8; one who has practised austerities, ŚBr.; ChUp.; inflamed with anger, incensed, W.; n. hot water, ŚBr. xiv, 1, 1, 29; (*ám*), ind. in a hot manner, xi, 2, 7, 32. — **kumbha**, m. a heated or red-hot jar, MārkP. xii, 34 f.; xiv, 87; N. of a hell, ib.; (cf. RTL. p. 232). — **kūpa**, m. 'well of heated liquid,' N. of a hell, PadmaP. vi. — **kṛicchra**, m. n. a kind of religious austerity (drinking hot water, milk, and ghee for 3 days each, and inhaling hot air for 3 days), Mn. xi, 157 & 215; Yājñ. iii, 318. — **jāmbūnada-maya**, mf(*ī*)n. made of refined gold, R. i, 15, 8. — **tapas**, mfn. practising austerities, (m.) an ascetic, W. — **tapta**, mfn. made hot repeatedly, Bhpr. v, 26, 3 & 45. — **tāmra**, n. red-hot or melted copper, VarBṛS. vi, 13; BhP. vi, 9, 13. — **pāshāṇa-kuṇḍa**, n. 'pit filled with red-hot stones,' N. of a hell, BrahmavP. — **mudrā**, f. (Vishṇu's) mark burnt (on the skin with red-hot iron),' W. — **rahasa**, n., Pāṇ. v, 4, 81. — **rūpa**, n. 'of refined shape,' silver, Npr. — **rūpaka**, n. id., L. — **lomaśa**, green vitriol, Npr. — **loha**, n. 'glowing iron,' N. of a hell, VP. ii, 6, 11 (cf. RTL. p. 232). — **vāluka**, mfn. having hot gravel, BhP. iii, 30, 23; m. N. of a hell, PadmaP. v, 159, 3; (*ās*), f. pl. hot gravel, Kathās. lxxii, 105. — **vrata** (°*ptá-*), mfn. using hot milk for the initiatory rite, TS. vi, 2, 2, 7; ĀpŚr. xi, 2, 2. — **surā-kuṇḍa**, m. 'jar or hole filled with burning spirituous liquor,' N. of a hell, BrahmavP. — **sūrmi**, f. 'red-hot iron statue,' N. of a hell (in which the wicked are made to embrace red-hot images), BhP. v, 26, 7 (cf. 20 & Mn. xi, 104); -*kuṇḍa*, n. id., BrahmavP. — **hema**, n. refined gold, MBh. iii, 1722; R. i, iii; VarBṛS. cvi, 3; -*maya*, mfn. consisting of refined gold, W. **Taptânna**, n. hot food, hot rice, W. **Taptâbharaṇa**, n. an ornament made of refined gold, R. iii, 58, 19. **Taptâyana**, mf(*ī*)n. dwelling-place of distressed people (the earth), VS. v, 9 (*tiktâyº*, TS. i).

Taptôdaka-svāmin, m. N. of a Tīrtha, SkandaP.

Taptaka, n. a frying-pan, Bhpr.

Taptavya, mfn. to be practised (austerity), MBh.

Tapti, f. heat, Bādar. ii, 2, 10, Sch.

Taptṛi, m. a heater, MBh. i, 8414.

Tapya, mfn. to be refined, Sarvad.; Bādar. ii, 2, 10, Sch. (-*tva*, n., abstr.); performing austerity (= *sattva-maya*, Sch.; said of Śiva), MBh. xii, 10381.

Tapyatí, f. heat, TS. i, 4, 35, 1 (v. l. °*tú*).

Tapyatú, mfn. hot, RV. ii, 24, 9; f., see °*ti*.

तबलाकृति *tabalâkriti*, f. N. of a creeper.

तभ *tabha*, m. = *stº*, a he-goat, L., Sch.

तम् *tam*, cl. 4. *tā́myati* (Pāṇ. vii, 3, 74; rarely Ā., R. ii, 63, 46; Gīt. v, 16; pf. *tatāma*, ŚBr. iv; aor. Pass. *atami*, Pāṇ. vii, 3, 34, Kāś.; Ved. inf. *támitos*, with *á* preceding, 'till exhaustion,' TBr. i, 4, 4, 2; TāṇḍyaBr. xii; Lāṭy.; Āp.; pf. Pass. p. *-tāntá*, q. v.) to gasp for breath (as one suffocating), choke, be suffocated, faint away, be exhausted, perish, be distressed or disturbed or perplexed, RV. ii, 30, 7 (*ná mā tamat* [aor. subj.] 'may I not be exhausted'); Kāṭh.; TBr. &c.; to stop (as breath), become immovable or stiff, Suśr.; Mālatīm.; Amar.; Rājat. v, 344; to desire (cf. 2. °*ma*, °*mata*), Dhātup. xxvi, 93: Caus. *tamáyati* (aor. Pass. *atāmi*, Pāṇ. vi, 4, 93, Kāś.) to suffocate, deprive of breath, ŚBr. iii, 3, 2, 19 & 8, 1, 15; KātyŚr. vi, 5, 18; cf. *á-tameru*.

1. **Tama**, m. (Pāṇ. vii, 3, 34, Kāś.) = *tamas* ('the ascending node,' VarBṛ. [?]; Jyot.), L., Sch.; (= °*māla*) Xanthochymus pictorius, L.; = °*makā*, L.; n. (= °*mas*) darkness, L.; the point of the foot, L.; (*ā*), f. night, L.; Xanthochymus pictorius, L.; (*ī*), f. (g. *gaurâdi*, Gaṇar. 47) night, Śiś. ix, 23; BhP. x, 13, 45; Gol. vii, 10; Naish. vii, 45. **– prabha**, m. = °*maḥ-pr*°, ŚivaP.; (*ā*), f., v. l. for °*maḥ-pr*°, L. **– rāja**, m. = *tava-r*°, L. **Tamâhvaya**, m. the plant *tālīśa-pattra*, Npr.

Tamaḥ, in comp. for °*mas*. **– prabha**, m. N. of a hell, L. (v. l.); (*ā*), f. id., L. **– praveśa**, m. groping in the dark, W.; mental perplexity, W. **– sthita**, n. 'situated in darkness,' N. of a hell, W. **– spṛiś**, mfn. connected with darkness, Kād.

Tamaka, m. (Pāṇ. vii, 3, 34, Kāś.) oppression (of the chest), a kind of asthma, Suśr. i, 43 & 45; vi, 40 & 51; cf. *pra-*; (*ā*), f. Phyllanthus emblica, Npr.

Tamata, mfn. desirous of, Uṇ. iii, 109, Sch.

Tamana, n. the becoming breathless, ŚāṅkhŚr. ii, 7, 7; iv; KātyŚr. iv, 1, 13; cf. *nāga-tamanī*.

Tamam, ind. so as to faint away, Pāṇ. vi, 4, 93.

Támas, n. darkness, gloom (also pl.) RV. (°*maḥ práṇīta*, 'led into darkness,' deprived of the eye's light or sight, i, 117, 17) &c.; the darkness of hell, hell or a particular division of hell, Mn. iv, viii f.; VP. ii, 6, 4; MārkP. xii, 10; the obscuration of the sun or moon in eclipses, attributed to Rāhu (also m., L.), R.; VarBṛS. v, 44; VarBṛ. ii; VarYogay.; Sūryas.; mental darkness, ignorance, illusion, error (in Sāṃkhya phil. one of the 5 forms of *a-vidyā*, MBh. xiv, 1019; Sāṃkhyak. &c.; one of the 3 qualities or constituents of everything in creation [the cause of heaviness, ignorance, illusion, lust, anger, pride, sorrow, dulness, and stolidity; sin, L.; sorrow, Kir. iii; see *guṇa* & cf. RTL. p. 45], Mn. xii, 24 f. & 38; Sāṃkhyak. &c.), RV. v, 31, 9; R. ii; Śak.; Rājat. v, 144; N. of a son (of Śravas, MBh. xiii, 2002; of Daksha, i, Sch.; of Pṛithu-śravas, VP. iv, 12, 2); [cf. *timira*; Lat. *temere* &c.] **– kalpa**, mfn. like darkness, gloomy, W. **– kāṇḍa**, m. (g. *kaskâdi*, not in Kāś.) great or spreading darkness, Śiś. **– tati**, f. id., L. **– vat** (*tám*°), mf(*atī*)n. gloomy, AV. xix, 47, 2; Naigh. i, 7; (*tī*), f. night, L., Sch.; turmeric, T. **– van** (*tám*°), mf(*arī*)n. = *-vat*, TS. ii, 4, 7, 2; cf. *ám*°. **– vinī**, f. = *-vatī*, MBh. iv, 732; Kād.

Tamasá, mfn. dark-coloured, AV. xi, 9, 22; m. darkness, Uṇ., Sch.; a well, Uṇ. vṛ.; n. ifc. for °*mas*, 'darkness,' see *andha-*, °*dhā-*, *ava-*, *vi-*, *sam-*; a city, Uṇ. vṛ.; (*ā*), f. N. of a river (falling into the Ganges below Pratishṭhāna), MBh. iii, 14231; vi, 338; Hariv. 12828; R. i f.; iv, 40, 24; Ragh. ix, 16.

Tamasā-kṛita, mfn., Pāṇ. vi, 3, 3, Kāś.

Tamasā-vana, n. N. of a grove, Divyâv. xxvii.

Tamaska, ifc. = °*mas*, darkness, ChUp. vii, 11, 2; SaṃhUp.; mental darkness, BhP. vii, 1, 11; the quality *tamus* (q. v.), NṛisUp. (*a-*); cf. *nis-*, *vi-*, *sa-*.

Tamāla, m. 'dark-barked (but white-blossomed)' Xanthochymus pictorius, MBh.; Hariv. 12837; R.; Suśr.; Mṛicch. &c.; a sort of black Khadira tree, L.; Cratæva Roxburghii, L.; tobacco, Śikshāp.; sectarial mark on the forehead (made with the juice of the Tamāla fruit), L.; a sword, L.; m. n. (g. *ardharcâdi*) the bark of the bamboo, L.; n. = *-pattra*, L.; (*ī*), f. = *tamakā*, Npr.; Cratæva Roxburghii, L.; = *tāmra-vallī*, L. **– pattra**, n. the leaf of Xanthochymus pictorius, Mṛicch.; Ragh. vi, 64; the leaf of Laurus Cassia, L.; Xanthochymus pictorius, L.; 'a sectarial mark on the forehead,' see *śrī-khaṇḍa-*; *-candana-gandha*, m. 'smelling like Tamāla leaves and sandal wood,' N. of a Buddha.

Tamālaka, (m., n., L.) Xanthochymus pictorius, R. ii, 91, 48 (ifc.); the bark of a bamboo, L.; n. the leaf of Laurus Cassia, L.; Marsilea quadrifolia, L.; (*ā*, *ī*), f. = *tamakā*, Npr.; (*ikā*), f. id., L.; = *tāmra-vallī*, L.; = *tāmra-lipta*, L.; N. of a woman, Kād. v, 427 & 432 (v. l. *taral*°); Vāsav. 573.

Tamālinī, f. a place overgrown with Tamāla trees, g. *pushkarâdi*; = *tāmra-lipta*, L.; = *tamakā*, L. **Tami**, f. = °*mī* (s. v. °*ma*), L.; turmeric, W.

Tamin, mfn., Pāṇ. iii, 2, 141. **Támishīcī**, *īs*, irr. *ayas*, Ved. f. pl. (fr. *tamishy-ac*) oppressing, stunning, confusing, RV. viii, 48, 11; AV. ii, 2, 5.

Támisra, m. = *-paksha*, W.; n. darkness, dark night (also pl.), MBh. iv, 710; BhP. v, 13, 9; Gīt. xi, 12; a dark hell, hell (in general), BhP. iv, 6, 45; anger, L.; (*ā*), f. (Pāṇ. v, 2, 114) a dark night, RV. ii, 27, 14; TBr. ii, 2, 9, 6; MBh. iii; Ragh. &c.; cf. *su-*; *tāmisra*. **– paksha**, m. the dark half of the month, vi, 34; VarBṛS. ix, 36; xxiv.

Tamīśvara, m. the moon, Dharmaśarm. x, 15.

Tamo, in comp. for °*mas*. **– gá**, mfn. roaming in the darkness (Śushṇa), RV. v, 32, 4. **– guṇa**, m. the quality of darkness or ignorance (see *támas*), W. **– °guṇin**, mfn. having the quality of *tamas* predominant, ignorant, proud, W. **– ghna**, m. 'destroying darkness,' the sun, MBh. iii, 193; vii, 6296; the moon, L.; fire, L.; Vishṇu, L.; Śiva; a Buddha ('*bodha*, knowledge,' T.), L. **– jyotis**, m. 'light in darkness,' a fire-fly, L. **– nud**, mfn. dispersing darkness, xiii, 7298; m. light, R. v, 32, 23; the sun (for acc. °*dam*, see °*da*), L.; the moon (for acc. °*dam*, see °*da*), L.; fire, L.; a lamp, L. **– nuda**, mf(*ā*)n. dispersing darkness, Mn. i, 6 & 77; MBh. (*sarva-*, iii, 17114) &c.; m. the sun, 11892; (acc. °*dam*) 17099 & vi, 5765; the moon, Ragh. iii, 33 (acc. °*dam*). **– 'nta-kṛit**, m. 'darkness-finisher,' N. of an attendant of Skanda, MBh. ix, 2560. **– 'ntya**, m. one of the 10 ways in which an eclipse may happen, VarBṛS. v, 43 & 52. **– 'ndhakāra**, N. of a mythical place, Kāraṇḍ. xii; *-bhūmi*, or °*rā bh*°, f. id., ib. **– 'paha**, mfn. removing darkness, Pāṇ. iii, 2, 50; removing ignorance, Daś.; Kir. v, 22; m. the sun, L.; the moon, Ragh. iii, 33 (v. l.); fire, L.; a Buddha ('*bodha*, knowledge,' T.), L. **– bhāga**, mfn. one whose portion is darkness, Nir. xii, 1. **– bhid**, m. 'dispersing darkness,' a fire-fly, L. **– bhūta**, mfn. 'become darkness,' covered with darkness, Mn. i, 5; Bhartṛ. i, 14; ignorant, Mn. xii, 115. **– maṇi**, m. 'darkness-jewel,' a kind of gem, L.; a fire-fly, Vāsav. 442. **– maya**, mf(*ī*)n. consisting or composed of or covered with darkness, VarBṛS. v, 3; BhP. iii; MārkP. &c.; m. the mind enveloped with darkness (one of the 5 forms of *a-vidyā* in Sāṃkhya phil.), viii, 15; °*yī-* √*kṛi*, to cover with darkness, Naish. viii, 65. **– 'ri**, m. 'darkness-enemy,' the sun, Rājat. ii, iv; *-vivara*, 'sun-hole,' a window, vii, 775. **– rūpa**, mf(*ā*)n. consisting of mental darkness or ignorance, NṛisUp. **– °rūpin**, mfn. id., ib., Sch. **– liptī**, f. = *tāma-l*°, L. **– vat**, mfn. = °*mas-v*°, R. iv, 44, 115. **– vāsas**, n. darkness as a cover, Kād. viii, 162. **– vikāra**, m. 'modification of the Guṇa *tamas*,' sickness, L. **– vṛita**, mfn. obscured, W.; overcome with any effect of the Guṇa *tamas*, as rage, fear, &c., W. **– vṛidh**, mfn. rejoicing in darkness, RV. vii, 104, 1. **– vairin**, m. 'darkness-enemy,' fire, Gal. **– hán**, mfn. striking down or dispersing darkness, i, 140, 1; iii, 39, 3; m. fire, Gal.; Vishṇu, ib.; Śiva, ib. **– hara**, m. 'removing darkness,' the moon, L.

Tamrá, mf(*á*)n. oppressing, darkening, x, 73, 5.

तम 2. *tama*, an affix forming the superl. degree of adjectives and rarely of substantives (*kánva-*, &c.), Suśr. i, 20, 11; mfn. most desired, Kir. ii, 14; (*ām*), added (in older language) to adverbs and (in later language) to verbs, intensifying their meaning; ind. in a high degree, much, Naish. viii.

तमङ्ग *tamaṅga*, °*gaka*, m. a platform, L.

तमर *tamara*, n. tin, L.

तमस् *támas*, °*sá*, &c. See col. 1.

Tamāla &c., **tami**, °**min** &c. See ib. & col. 2.

तमुष्टुहीय *tamushṭuhīya*, the hymn RV. vi, 18 (beginning with *tám u shṭuhi*), ŚāṅkhŚr. x, 11, 29.

तम्पा *tampā*, f. a cow (cf. °*mbā*), L.

तम्ब् *tamb*, cl. 1. °*bati*, to go, Vop.

तम्बा *tambā* (fr. *tāmrā*), f. = °*mpā*, L.

तम्बीर *tambīra*, = تمویر, (in astrol.) the 14th Yoga.

तम्र *tamrá*. See col. 2.

तय् *tay*, cl. 1. °*yate* (pf. *teye*), to go towards (acc.) or out of (abl.), Bhaṭṭ. xiv, 75 & 108; (= *tāy*) to protect, Dhātup. xiv, 6.

Taya, m. g. *vṛishâdi*; cf. *tāya*.

तर 1. *tara*, an affix forming the compar. degree of adjectives and rarely (cf. *vṛitra-tára*) of substantives, Suśr. i, 20, 11; (*ām*), added (in older language) to adverbs (see *ati-tarām* &c.) and (in later language) to verbs (Pañcat. i, 14, 7; Ratnâv. iii, 9; Kathās.), intensifying their meaning; ind. with *na*, not at all, BhP. x, 46, 43. **– tama-tas**, ind. more or less, 87, 19; cf. *tāratamya*.

तर 2. *tára*, mfn. (√*tṛī*; g. *pacâdi*) carrying across or beyond, saving (?, said of Śiva), MBh. xii, 10380; ifc. passing over or beyond, W.; 'surpassing, conquering,' see *śoka-tará*, cf. *ratham-tará*; excelling, W.; m. crossing, passage, RV. ii, 13, 12; viii, 96, 1; Mn. viii, 404 & 407; Yājñ. (ifc.); MBh. xii; (*a-*, mfn. 'impassable') Bhaṭṭ. vii, 55; (cf. *dus-*); 'excelling, conquering,' see *dush-ṭara*, *su-tára*, *dus-*; = *-paṇya*, Mn. viii, 406; a raft, W.; a road, L.; N. of a magical spell (against evil spirits supposed to possess certain weapons), R. i, 30, 4; fire, W.; N. of a man, Rājat. vii, 809; (*ī*; also *īs*, L.) f. (g. *gaurâdi*, Gaṇar. 48) a boat, ship (cf. °*ri*), MBh. i, 4228 f.; BhP. iv; Śiś. iii, 76; (cf. *nis-tarīka*); a clothes-basket (also °*ri*), L.; the hem of a garment (also °*ri*), L.; = °*rani-peṭaka*, L.; a club, L.; for *starī* (smoke), W. **– paṇya**, n. ferry-money, freight, Divyâv. **– °paṇyika**, m. one who receives ferry-money or freight, Buddh. L. **– vaṭa**, Cassia auriculata, L. **– vāri**, (m., L.; for *tala-v*°?) a one-edged sword, Hcar. vi; Kalyāṇam.; Pañcad. ii, 77; cf. *tala-vāraṇa*. **– vālikā**, f. (for *tala-v*°?) = *kar*°, id., L., Sch. **– sārika**, see *tala-s*°. **– sthāna**, n. a landing-place, L. **Tarândhu**, m. a large flat-bottomed boat, L. **Tarâlu**, m. id., L.

1. **Taraṃ-ga**, m. (fr. *taram*, ind. √*tṛī*) 'across-goer,' a wave, billow, R. iv, 41, 29 ff.; Jain.; Suśr.; Śak. &c. (ifc. f. *ā*, Pañcat.; Kathās. lxxii); a section of a literary work that contains in its N. a word like 'sea' or 'river' (e.g. of Kathās. & Rājat.); a jumping motion, gallop, waving about, moving to and fro, Hariv. 4298; Gīt. xii, 20; cloth, clothes, Uṇ., Sch.; cf. *ut-*, *carma-*. **– bhīru**, m. '= °*gâpatrasta*,' N. of a son of the 14th Manu, Hariv. 495. **– mālin**, m. 'wave-garlanded,' the sea, Prasannar. vii, $\frac{1}{10}$. **– vatī**, f. 'having waves,' a river, Vcar. vi, 72; N. of a female servant, Vāsav. 374. **Taraṃgâpatrasta**, mfn. afraid of waves, Pāṇ. ii, 1, 38, Kāś.

2. **Taraṃga**, Nom. °*gati*, to move like a billow, wave about, move restlessly to and fro, Kād. vi, 1644 (Pass. p. °*gyamāṇa*); Gīt. ii, 8; cf. *ut-*.

Taraṃgaka, m. a wave, Bālabodh.; (*ikā*), f. N. of a female servant, Viddh. ii, $\frac{8}{?}$; cf. *nārī-*.

Taraṃgaya, Nom. °*yati*, to cause to move to and fro, Bālar. iii, 25 (= Viddh. iii, 27); Sāh. vi.

Taraṃgiṇī, f. of °*gin*. **– nātha**, m. 'river-lord,' the sea, Bālar.; Vcar. xiii. **– bhartṛi**, m. id., 53.

Taraṃgita, mfn. (g. *tārakâdi*) having (folds, *vali-*) as waves, Kathās. lxxxiv, 7; wavy, waving, overflown (by tears), moving restlessly to and fro, MBh. vi, 3851; Mālatīm.; Śāntiś.; Kathās.; Prasannar. &c.; n. waving, moving to and fro, Gīt. iii, 13.

Taraṃgin, mfn. wavy, waving, moving restlessly to and fro, MBh. vi; R. ii, iv; Kathās.; Gīt. v, 19; (*iṇī*), f. (g. *pushkarâdi*) a river, Bhartṛ. iii, 65; N. of a river, Kathās. lxxii, 336; N. of several works, Śaktir.; Nirṇayas. ii, 7; ifc. see *kshīra-* &c.

Taraṇa, m. a raft, boat, L.; 'final landing-place,' heaven, L.; n. crossing over, passing (ifc.), KātyŚr. i, 7, 13; R.; Vikr.; Rājat.; Hit.; overcoming (as of misfortune, gen.), MBh. i, 6054; carrying over, W.; an oar (?), Kauś. 52; (*ī*), f. = °*ṇi*, a boat, Hariv. 14078 (v. l. °*riṇī*); Hibiscus mutabilis, L.; = °*ṇī-vallī*, L.; cf. *ūrdhva-*, *dus-*; *pra-tár*°, *su-*.

Taráṇi, mfn. moving forwards (as the sun &c.), quick, untired, energetic, RV.; AV. xiii, 2, 4 & 36; carrying over, saving, helping, benevolent, RV.; TBr. ii, 7, 13, 2; m. the sun, KapS. iii, 13; BhP. v, viii, x; Rājat.; ŚārṅgP.; Calotropis gigantea, L.; a ray of light, L.; f. = °*ṇī*, a boat, Prab.; Vop.; Śatr.; Aloe perfoliata, L. (also °*ṇī*, Sch.); cf. *go-*, *saṃsāra-*. **– tanayā**, f. 'sun-daughter,' the river Yamunā, Bhām. iv, 7 & 35. **– tvá**, n. zeal, RV. i, 110, 4 & 6 (Nir. xi, 16). **– dhanya**, m. Śiva. **– peṭaka**, m. a baling-vessel, L. **– ratna**, n. 'sun-jewel,' a ruby, L.

Taraṇīya, mfn. to be crossed (a river), R. ii.
Taraṇī-vallī, f. Rosa glandulifera, L.
Taraṇḍa, m. N. of a place, L.; (m. n., L.) the float of a fishing line, float made of bamboos and floated upon jars or hollow gourds inverted, L.; an oar, W.; a raft, boat, HParis. ii, 220; (*ā*, *ī*), f. id., L. **-pādā**, f. 'oar-footed,' a boat, L.
Taraṇḍaka, v.l. for °*rantuka*, q.v.
Taraṇya, Nom. (fr. °*ṇa*) °*ṇyati*, to go, g. *kaṇḍv-ādi* (not in Kāś.).
Tárat, pr. p. & Subj. √*tṝ*, q.v. **-sama**, m. conflagration of chaff (cf. *taratsala*), Gal.; m. or f. pl. = °*mandī*, Vas. xxviii, 11. **-samandī**, f. pl. the hymn RV. ix, 58 (beginning with *tárat sá mandī*), Gaut. **-samandīya**, n. (scil. *sûkta*) id., Mn. xi, 254.
Taratha, see *deva-*. **Tarad**, f. (Siddh. puṃl. 74) a raft, L.; a kind of a duck, L. **Tarád-dveshas**, mfn. conquering enemies (Indra), RV. i, 100, 3.
Tarantá, m. the ocean, L.; a hard shower, Uṇ. k.; a frog, ib.; N. of a man (with the patr. Vaidadaśvi), RV. v, 61, 10; TāṇḍyaBr. xiii, 7 (author of a Sāman); (*ī*), f. a boat, ship, Uṇ. iii, 128, Sch.
Tarantuka, n. N. of a Tīrtha, MBh. iii, 5085; 6022 (vv.ll. *arant°* & *taraṇḍaka*) & 7078; ix, 3032.
Táras, n. rapid progress, velocity, strength, energy, efficacy, RV.; MBh. xii, 5172; R. v, 77, 18; Ragh. xi, 77; a ferry, RV. i, 190, 7; (fig.) v, 54, 15; AV. x, 10, 24; a symbolical N. of the *stoma* of the gods, TāṇḍyaBr. viii, xi, xv; a bank, L.; = *plava-ga*, L.; (*sā*), instr. ind. (g. *svar-ādi*, not in Kāś.) speedily, directly, MBh.; R.; Ragh.; BhP.; Śiś. ix; Kathās.; Prab. iv, 24; (°*rás*), mfn. quick, energetic, SV. i, 4, 2, 4, 1. **-mat**, for *-vat*, q.v. **-vat** (*tár°*), mfn. = *-vín* (Indra), TBr. ii, 8, 4, 1; m. N. of a son of the 14th Manu, Hariv. i, 7, 87 (v.l. °*s-mat*); f. pl. 'the swift ones,' the rivers, Naigh. i, 13. **-vín**, mfn. quick, violent, energetic, bold, RV. viii, 97, 10 & 12 (Indra); VS. xix, 88; MBh.; R.; Śak. &c.; m. a courier, runner, hero, W.; Śiva; the wind, L.; a falcon, Gal.; Garuḍa, L.; N. of a man, Pravar. ii, 2, 2.
Tarasāna, m. a boat, Uṇ. ii, 86, Sch.
Tarāyaṇa. See *tār°*.
Tari, f. = °*rī*, a boat, MBh. i, 4014; xii, 1682; Prab. vi, 7; see also °*rī*, s.v. °*ra*. **-ratha**, m. 'boat-wheel,' an oar, L.
Tarika, m. = °*kin*, Yājñ. ii, 263; a raft, boat, L.; (*ā*), f. id., L.; the skin on the milk, VS. xxxix, 8/9; KātyŚr. xxvi, 7, 51/52. °**kin**, m. a ferry-man, W.
Taritavya, n. impers. it is to be crossed or passed over, ĀśvGṛ. i, 12, 6; MānGṛ. i, 13.
Taritā, f. 'leader,' the fore-finger, L.; garlic (or 'hemp'?), Kulârṇ.; a form of Durgā (cf. *tvar°*), Tantr. **-dhāraṇa-yantra**, n. N. of a mystical diagram, ib. **-pūjā-yantra**, n. another diagram, ib.
Taritṛi, mfn. one who crosses (a river) or who carries over, Pāṇ. vii, 2, 34, Kāś.
Taritra, m. 'a helmsman' (Sch.) or n. 'an oar,' MBh. v, 2436 (*a-*, mfn. without a *t°*).
Tarín, mfn. AV. v, 27, 6 (for *sá īm*, VS. xxvii, 15); (*iṇī*), f. v.l. for °*raṇī*, q.v.
Tarī, f., see °*ra*. **-pa**, see *dus-*, *nis-*.
Tarītṛi, mfn. = °*ritṛi*, Pāṇ. vii, 2, 34, Kāś.
Tarītu, see *dush-tár°*. **Tárīyas**, mfn. (compar.) easily passing through (acc.), RV. v, 41, 12.
Tarīsha, m. a raft, boat, L.; the ocean, L.; a fit or competent person, Uṇ. vṛ.; a fine shape or form ('decorating,' W.), L.; resolution, L.; see also *tavīsha*. **Tarīshaṇi**, Ved. inf. √*tṝ*, q.v.
1. **Táru**, mfn. 'quick' or subst. 'speediness,' (pl.) RV. v, 44, 5 (cf. ii, 39, 3).
1. **Tárutṛi**, mfn. winning, i, 27, 9; 129, 2.
2. **Tarutṛi**, m. (Pāṇ. vii, 2, 34) a conqueror, RV. i; vi, 66, 8; viii; an impeller (of carts), x, 178, 1 (Nir. x, 28); (*trī*), f. adj. a help, MānGṛ. i, 22.
Tárutra, mfn. carrying across (as a horse), RV. i, 117, 9; conquering, triumphant, 174, 1; ii, 11, 15 f.; iii, vi f.; granting victory, superior, iv, vi, viii, x.
Tarush, one base of √*tṝ* (*tarushante* &c.), q.v.
Tárusha, m. a conqueror, overcomer, vi, 15, 3; x, 115, 5; (*ī*). f. victory, SV. i, 4, 1, 4, 5.
Tarushyát, mfn. (pr. p.) attacking, RV. viii, 99, 5 (Naigh. iv, 2; Nir. v, 2). **Tárus**, n. battle, RV. vi, 25, 4; superiority, i, 122, 13; iii, 2, 3.
Tarūtṛi, mfn. = °*ritṛi*, Pāṇ. vii, 2, 34.
Tárūshas, mfn. superior, RV. i, 129, 10.
Tarṇi, m. = °*raṇi*, a boat, L.; the sun, L.
Tartarīka, mfn. (fr. Intens.) being in the habit of crossing (a river), L.; n. a boat, L.
Tartavya, mfn. = °*raṇīya*, MBh. vii, 4706.

Tarman, n. 'passage,' see *su-tárman*; m. n. the top of the sacrificial post (cf. Lat. *terminus*), L.
Tárya, m. N. of a man, RV. v, 44, 12.
1. **Tarsha**, m. = °*rīsha*, a raft, Uṇ. iii, 62, Sch.; the ocean, ib.; the sun, Uṇ. vṛ.

तरक्ष *taraksha*, m. = °*kshu*, VarBṛS. xii, 6; a wolf, Npr.
Tarákshu, m. a hyena, VS. xxiv, 40; MaitrS. iii, 14, 21; GopBr. i, 2, 8; MBh.; Hariv. 9373; R.; Suśr.
Tarakshuka, m. id., L.

तरंग *taraṃ-ga*, &c. See p. 438, col. 3.

तरट *taraṭa*, N. of a medicinal plant, Npr.; (*ī*), f. N. of a thorny plant (cf. *tār°*), L.

तरण *taraṇa*, °*ráṇi*, &c. See p. 438, col. 3.

तरत्सल *taratsala*, m. = °*rat-sama*, W.

तरदी *taradī*, v.l. for °*raṭī*.

तरन्त *tarantá*, °*ntuka*. See col. 1.

तरम्बुज *tarambuja*, n. (borrowed fr. تربز) a water-melon (cf. *kharbūja*), Tantr.

तरल *tarala*, mf(*ā*)n. (√*tṝ*?, cf. *taraṃga*) moving to and fro, trembling, tremulous, MBh. &c.; glittering, R. vi, 4, 33; Ragh. xiii, 76; Śak.; unsteady, vain, Bhartṛ.; Amar.; Rājat. iii, 515; libidinous, L.; liquid, W.; hollow, L.; m. a wave, BhP. x f.; the central gem of a necklace, MBh. viii, 4913; Hariv.; a necklace, L.; a ruby, L.; iron, L.; a level surface (*tala*), L.; the thorn-apple, Npr.; N. of a poet, Bālar. i, 13; ŚārṅgP.; pl. N. of a people, MBh. viii, 237; (*ā*), f. spirituous liquor, L.; a bee, L.; N. of a Yoginī, Hcat. ii, 1, 709; rice-gruel, VarBṛS. lxxvi, 11 (°*la*, n.?). **-tā**, f. = *-tva*, Pañcat.; unsteady activity, Kād. **-tva**, n. tremulousness, unsteadiness, Kpr. x, 33/34. **-nayanī**, f. 'tremulous-eyed,' a metre of 4 × 12 short syllables. **-lekhā**, f. N. of a woman, Rājat. viii, 1445. **-locanā**, f. a tremulous-eyed woman, W.; (cf. R. vi, 4, 34.)
Taralaya, Nom. °*yati*, to cause to tremble, Hcar. v, 205; Amar. 87.
Taralāya, Nom. °*yate*, to tremble, Hcat. ii, 1, 709.
Taralāyita, mfn. made tremulous, agitated, W.; m. a large wave, W.; n. fickleness, W.
Taralikā, f. N. of a female servant, Kād. (see *tamāl°*); Vāsav. 565.
Taralita, mfn. shaking, dangling, undulating, tremulous, Gīt. vii, xi; ŚārṅgP.; n. impers. it has been trembled, Gīt. xii, 15. **-hāra**, mf(*ā*)n. having a tremulous garland, vii, 14.

तरवी *taravī*, (in astrol.) تربيع, quadrature.

तरस् *táras*, °*rás*. See col. 1.

तरस *tarasa*, m. n. sg. & pl. meat, Nyāyam.; Sch. on KātyŚr. ii, v. **-puroḍāśa**, mfn. offering a cake of meat, TāṇḍyaBr. xxv, 7. **-maya**, mfn. consisting of meat (a cake), KātyŚr. xxiv, 5, 20.

तरसत् *tarásat*, for *trás°*, √*trus*, q.v.

तरसान *tarasāna*, &c. See col. 1.

तराम् *tarām*. See 1. *tara*.

तरि *tari*, °*rika*, °*rikin*, &c. See col. 1.

तरु 2. *taru*, m. (g. *vyāghrâdi* [not in Kāś.], cf. *nabhas-*) a tree, Nal. xii, 75; R. vi, 82, 115; Suśr.; Ragh. &c.; N. of a son of Manu Cākshusha, MatsyaP. **-kūṇi**, m. a kind of bird, L. **-koṭara**, n. the hollow of a tree, Hit. **-khaṇḍa**, m. n. (Pāṇ. iv, 2, 38, Kāś. v.l.) = *-shaṇḍa*, Kād. **-gahana**, n. the thicket of woods, ŚārṅgP. **-cchāyā**, f. the shade of a tree, Kathās. lxiii, 9 (ifc. f. *ā*); iic, 36. **-ja**, mfn. produced by a tree (a flower, fruit &c.), W. **-jīvana**, n. (vital organ, i.e.) the root of a tree, L. **-tala**, n. the level ground round the foot of a tree, Kathās.; Hit. **-tā**, f. the state of a tree, MārkP. xxxi, 9; Kathās. lxxii, 235. **-tūlikā**, f. the flying fox (suspending itself from branches like a *tūlikā*, q.v.), L. **-dūlikā**, v.l. for *-tūl°*, W. **-nakha**, m. 'tree-nail,' a thorn, L. **-paṅkti**, f. a row of trees, avenue, W. **-bhuj**, m. 'tree-eater,' the parasitical plant Vanda Roxburghii, L. **-maṇḍapa**, a bower, Kathās. xx, 55. **-mahiman**, m. 'glory of tree-planting,' N. of a section of the Vṛikshāyurveda (on the future rewards of those who plant trees), W. **-mūla**, n. the root of a tree, Kathās. ic, 2. **-mṛiga**, m. 'tree-animal,' an ape, L. **-rāga**, m. n. 'tree-charm,' a bud, L. **-rāja**, m. 'tree-king,' the palmyra-tree, Hcat. ii, 1, 317. **-rājan**, m. 'tree-king,' the Pārijāta, Hariv. 7153 f. **-ruhā**, f. 'growing on trees,' = *-bhuj*, L. **-rohiṇī**, f. id., L. **-vara**, m. 'best of trees,' = *-rājan*, W. **-vallī**, f. a creeper, Kathās. liii, 59; a kind of Oldenlandia (dyeing red), L. **-viṭapa**, m. a branch, W. **-śāyin**, m. 'sleeping on trees,' a bird, L. **-śreshṭha**, m. the best of trees, W. **-shaṇḍa**, n. (cf. *-khaṇḍa*) a group of trees, R. iv, 13, 13; Pañcat. **-sāra**, m. 'tree-essence,' camphor, L.; *-maya*, mfn. consisting of heart-wood, Suśr. iv, 35. **-sthā**, f. = *-ruhā*, L.
Taruśa, mfn. abounding in trees, g. *lomâdi*.

तरुक्ष *táruksha*, m. (g. 2. *lohitâdi*, not in Kāś.) N. of a man, RV. viii, 46, 32; cf. *taluksha*.

तरुण *táruṇa*, mf(*ī* [Pāṇ. iv, 1, 15, Vārtt. 6, Pat.], RV.)n. (√*tṝ*; g. *kapilakâdi*, Gaṇar. 447) 'progressive,' young, tender, juvenile, RV.; AV. &c.; new, fresh, just risen (the sun, cf. *bālâditya*), just begun (heat or a disease), MBh.; R.; Kum. iii, 54; Suśr.; tender (a feeling), Bhartṛ.; m. a youth, MBh. &c.; (cf. *tarṇa*); Ricinus communis, L.; large cumin seed, L.; N. of a particular section in a Tantra work treating of various stages in a Tāntrika's life, Kulârṇ. viii; of a mythical being, MBh. ii, 7, 22; of a Ṛishi in the 11th Manv-antara, Hariv. 477; m. n. the blossom of Trapa bispinosa, L.; n. = °*ṇâsthi*, Suśr.; a sprout (ifc., *kuśa-*), KātyŚr.; PārGṛ. ii, 1, 10; (*ī*), f. (g. *gaurâdi*) a young woman, girl, R.; Suśr. &c.; a kind of pot-herb, i, 46, 4, 39; Aloe perfoliata, L.; Rosa glandulifera or alba, Npr.; Croton polyandrum or Tiglium, L.; [cf. τέρην.] **-jvara**, m. 'slight fever,' a fever that lasts a week, W.; °*rāri*, m. 'enemy of °*ra*,' N. of a drug. **-tā**, f. freshness, vigour, Kād. **-dadhi**, n. coagulated milk five days old, W. **-pītikā**, f. red arsenic, Npr.
Taruṇâbhāsa, m. a kind of cucumber, ib. **Taruṇâsthi**, n. 'soft-bone,' cartilage, Suśr. **Taruṇêndu**, m. the increasing moon, Bhartṛ. iii, 84.
Taruṇaka, m. N. of a Nāga, MBh. i, 2160; n. a sprout, (°*rūṇ°*) AV. x, 4, 2; see *darbha-*; cf. *tarṇ°*.
Taruṇaya, Nom. °*yati*, to make young or fresh, Mālatīm. v, 6.
Taruṇāya, Nom. °*yati*, to bring forth, W.; °*yate*, to become or remain young or fresh, Hariv. 4745; Suśr. iv, 26, 27; Pañcat. v, 1, 14; Bhartṛ. iii, 9.
Taruṇimán, m. youth, juvenility, MaitrS. i, 10, 10; Kāṭh. xxxvi, 5; Śāntiś.; Prasannar. ii, 11.
Taruṇī, f. and ind. of °*ṇa*. **-kaṭâksha-kāma** or °**ksha-māla**, m. Clerodendrum phlomoides, L. **-gaṇa**, m. a number of young women, W. **-jana**, m. a young woman, W. **-√bhū**, to become a youth, Hcar. iv. **-bhūta**, mfn. become a maiden, Daś. vii, 156. **-ratna**, n. = °*raṇi-r°*, Gal.

तरुतृ *tárutṛi*, °*trí*, &c. See col. 1.

तरूट *tarūṭa*, m. the root of a lotus, L.

तरूणक *tarūṇaka*. See °*ruṇ°*.

तरूतृ *tarūtṛi*, *tárūshas*. See col. 1.

तर्क् *tark*, cl. 10. °*kayati* (ep. also °*te*), to conjecture, guess, suspect, infer, try to discover or ascertain, reason or speculate about, MBh. &c.; to consider as (with double acc.), ib.; to reflect, think of, recollect, have in one's mind, intend (with inf., MBh. iii; Mṛicch.; Megh.), MBh.; Hariv.; BhP. iii, 13, 20; to ascertain, R. iii, 25, 12; 'to speak' or 'to shine,' Dhātup.; [cf. *torqueo*, &c.]
Tarka, m. conjecture, MBh. &c.; reasoning, speculation, inquiry, KaṭhUp. ii, 9; PārGṛ. ii, 6, 5; Gaut.; Mn. xii, 106; MBh. &c.; doubt, W.; system or doctrine founded on speculation or reasoning, philosophical system (esp. the Nyāya system, but applicable also to any of the six Darśana, q.v.), BhP. ii, vii f.; Prab.; Vop.; Caraṇ.; Madhus.; the number 6, Sūryas. xii, 87; logic, confutation (esp. that kind of argument which consists in reduction to absurdity), Tarkas.; Sarvad.; Madhus.; wish, desire, L.; supplying an ellipsis, L.; cause, motive, L.; n. a philosophical system, Hcat. i, 7; (*ā*), f. reasoning, inquiry ('= *kāṅkshā*,' Sch.), MBh. iv, 892; cf. *a-*, *ku-*, *dus-*, *rūpa-*. **-karkaśa**, m. N. of a family, Dhūrtan. i. **-karman**, for °*rku-k°*, BhP. x, 45, 36/37; (cf. *-sādhya*). **-kārikā**, f. N. of a Vaiśeshika work by Jīva-rāja Dīkshita. **-kaumudī**, f. N. of a Vaiśeshika work. **-grantha**, m. a treatise on reasoning, manual of logic, Suśr. vi, 19, 15. **-candrikā**, f. N. of an elementary exposition of the

Nyāya phil. **-jñāna**, n. knowledge obtained by reasoning or philosophical inquiry, Bādar. ii, 1, 1½. **-jvālā**, f. 'flame of speculation,' N. of a Buddh. work. **-taraṃgiṇī**, f. N. of a work by Guṇa-ratna. **-dīpikā**, f. N. of a Comm. on Tarkas. **-pañcânana**, m. N. of several writers on Nyāya phil. **-paribhāshā**, f. = *-bhāshā*; *-vṛitti*, f. N. of a Comm. by Vimmi-bhaṭṭa. **-prakāśa**, m. N. of a Comm. by Śrī-kaṇṭha; = *-bhāshā-sāra-mañjarī*. **-pradīpa**, m. N. of a Vaiśeshika manual by Koṇḍa-bhaṭṭa. **-bhāshā**, f. N. of a Nyāya manual by Keśava-bhaṭṭa; *-prakāśa*, m. N. of a Comm. by Go-vardhana; *-prakāśikā*, f. another Comm.; *-bhāva-prakāśikā*, f. another Comm.; *-sāra-mañjarī*, f. another Comm. by Mādhava (of Kāśī). **-mañjarī**, f. N. of a Comm. on *-kārikā* by its author. **-mudrā**, f. a particular position of the hand, BhP. iv, 6, 38. **-yukta**, mfn. conjectured, suspected, R. (G) ii, 109, 16; together with the philosophical systems, MBh. ii, 11, 35. **-ratna**, n. N. of a Vaiśeshika disquisition by Koṇḍa-bhaṭṭa. **-rahasya**, n. N. of a work; *-dīpikā*, f. another N. of Guṇâkara's Shaḍ-darśana-samuccaya-ṭīkā. **-vāg-īśa**, m. N. of several writers on Nyāya phil. **-vid**, m. 'knowing logic,' a philosopher, Bādar. ii, 1, 1½. **-vidyā**, f. 'science of reasoning,' a manual of logic, philosophical treatise, MBh. xiii, 2195; Prab. **-śāstra**, n. id., MBh. xii, 9678 f.; Hariv. 1506; Prab. **-saṃgraha**, m. N. of a manual of the Vaiśeshika branch of the Nyāya phil. by Annam-bhaṭṭa; *-dīpikā*, f. N. of a Comm. on that work by its author. **-samaya**, m. N. of a work, Bādar. i, 1, ⅘. **-sādhya**, n. N. of a Kalā (cf. °*rku-karman*), Gal. **Tarkâṭa**, m. 'inquiry-walker,' a beggar, L. **Tarkânubhāshā**, f. = °*rka-bhāshā-prakāśa*. **Tarkâbhāsa**, m. apparent reasoning or confutation, W. **Tarkâmṛita**, n. 'logic-nectar,' N. of an elementary Vaiśeshika manual by Jagad-īśa Tarkâlaṃkāra Bhaṭṭâcārya; *-cashaka*, N. of a Comm. on that manual by Gaṅgā-rāma Jaṭī; *-taraṃgiṇī*, f. another Comm. on the same by Mukunda Bhaṭṭa Gāḍegila. **Tarkâlaṃkāra**, m. N. of several philosophers.

Tarkaka, m. = °*rkâṭa*, MBh. xii, 1537.

Tarkaṇa, n. conjecturing, Sāh.; reasoning, W.

Tarkaṇīya, mfn. to be suspected, MBh. v, 1093.

Tarkita, mfn. considered as, R. iv, 11, 9; investigated, W.; see *a-*; n. conjecture, Hariv. 9467.

Tarkin, mfn. skilled in speculation, Mn. xii, 111.

Tarku, (m. n., L.; √3. *kṛit*, Nir. ii, 1, but cf. *nish-ṭarkyà*, ἄτρακτος & *torqueo* &c. s. v. √*tark*) a spindle, PārGṛ. i, 1⅘. **-karman**, n. 'spindle-work,' N. of a Kalā (q. v.). **-pāṭhī**, v. l. for *-pīṭhī*. **-piṇḍa**, m. a ball (of clay &c.) at the lower end of a spindle to assist in giving it a rotatory motion, L. **-pīṭha**, m. id., L.; (*ī*), f. id., L. **-lāsaka**, m. a concave shell or saucer serving to hold the lower end of a spindle when whirled round, L. **-śāna**, m. a small whetstone for sharpening spindles, L.

Tarkuka, m. = °*rkaka*, Rājat. iii, 254; cf. *para-piṇḍa-*. **Tarkuṭa**, n. spinning, L.; (*ī*), f. = °*rku*, L.

Tarkya, mfn., see *a-*; *nish-ṭarkyà*.

तर्कारि **tarkāri**, f. = °*rī*, Suśr. vi, 17, 49.

Tarkārī, f. (g. *gaurâdi*) Sesbania ægyptiaca, i, vi; Premna spinosa, VarBṛS. xliv, $\frac{9}{10}$; a kind of gourd, Npr. °**kiṇa**, m. Cassia Tora, L. (v. l. °*kila*).

तर्क्षु **tarkshu**, m. = *tarákshu*, L.

तर्क्ष्य **tarkshya**, m. saltpetre, L.

तर्ज् **tarj**, cl. 1. °*jati* (ep. also Ā.; pf. *tatarja*, Bhaṭṭ.) to threaten, MBh.; R.; to scold, MBh. viii, 1543; Bhaṭṭ. xiv, 80: Caus. *tarjayati* (ep. also Ā.) to threaten, R. iii (Pass. p. °*rjyamāna*); Śak.; Ragh.; to scold, Hariv. 11166; Daś.; BhP. &c.; to frighten, MBh.; R.; Suśr.; Rājat.; to deride, MBh. v, 2485; Bhaṭṭ. vii, 36; for √*tark*, Caus., MBh. iv, 567; [cf. Germ. *drohen* &c.]

Tarjaka, mfn. one who threatens, Pañcar. iv, 3.

Tarjana, n. threatening, scolding, R. iii, v; Ragh. xix, 17; Kum. vi, 45 &c.; (ifc.) frightening, MBh. iii, 12569; derision, W.; putting to shame, surpassing, W.; anger, W.; (*ā*), f. scolding, Sāh.; (*ī*), f. 'threatening finger,' the fore-finger, Kathās. xvii, 88; KātySr., Sch.; = °*nikā*, Hcat. ii, 1.

Tarjanikā, f. a kind of weapon (?), ii, 1, 953.

Tarjanīya, mfn. to be threatened or scolded.

Tarjita, mfn. threatened, R. vi; Ragh. xi, 78; scolded, reviled, Bhaṭṭ.; Rājat. iii, 34: Sāh.; frightened, Hariv. 3911; Suśr.; Rājat. v, 398; n. threat, R.

तर्जिक **tarjika**, m. pl. = *tāj*°, L.

तर्ण **tarṇa**, m. (for °*ruṇa*?) a calf, L.

Tarṇaka, m. id., Kād.; Hcar. ii, 11 (ifc.); Hcat. Rājat. v, 431; any young animal, Dhūrtan. i, 19.

तर्णि **tarṇi**, °*rtarīka*. See p. 439, col. 1.

तर्द् **tard** (= √*tṛid*), cl. 1. P. °*rdati*, to injure, kill, Dhātup. iii, 21. **Tardá**, m. a kind of bird (cf. Lat. *turdus*), AV. vi, 50, 1 f. **Tardā-pati**, m. lord of the female Tarda bird, 3 (voc.)

Tardana, n. opening, hole, ŚBr. iii, 2, 1, 2, Sāy.; sewing with stitches, AitĀr. iii, 2, 5, 4, Sch.

Tardū, f. (√*tṛī*, Uṇ.) a wooden ladle, L.

Tardma, ifc. (*nava-*, *śata-*) for °*dman*, KātyŚr. xv, 5, 27. **-vat**, mfn. 'furnished with (openings, i.e.) stitches,' bound tight, AitĀr. iii, 2, 5, 4. **-samutá**, mfn. sewed with stitches, ŚBr. iii, 2, 1, 2.

Tárdman, n. (√*tṛid*) a hole, cleft, AV. xiv, 1, 40; Kauś. 50 & 76; KātyŚr. vi, 1, 30; vii, 3, 20.

तर्पक **tarpaka**, mfn. ifc. satiating, satisfying, BhP. vii, 15, 10, Sch.

Tárpaṇa, mf(*ī*)n. id., Suśr.; (cf. *ghrāṇa-*); (m. or n.) N. of a plant, iv, 5, 13 & 18; 16, 3; n. satiety, MBh. xiv, 673; satiating, refreshing (esp. of gods and deceased persons [cf. *ṛishi-*, *pitṛi-*] by presenting to them libations of water; a particular ceremony performed with a magical Mantra, Sarvad.; cf. RTL. p. 394 & 409), PārGṛ. iii, 3, 11; Mn. iii, 70; Yājñ. i, 46; MBh. xiii &c.; gladdening (ifc.), BhP. iii, 1, 27; refreshment, food, AV. ix, 6, 6; MBh. xviii, 269 & 275; Car.; Pāṇ. ii, 3, 14, Kāś.; Hcat. (ifc. f. *ā*); fuel, L.; (satiating, i.e.) filling the eyes (with oil &c.), Suśr.; (*ī*), f. N. of a plant, L. **-vidhi**, m. a ch. of Smṛity-artha-sāra. **Tarpaṇêcchu**, m. 'desirous of a Tarpaṇa libation,' Bhīshma, L.

Tarpaṇīya, mfn. to be satisfied, KaṭhUp. i, 27.

Tarpayitavya, mfn. id., Kāṭh. xxxii, 1.

Tarpita, mfn. satisfied, MBh. v; R. i, 53 (*su-*).

Tarpin, mfn. satisfying, W.; offering oblations (to the manes), W.; (*iṇī*), f. Hibiscus mutabilis, L.

तर्पर **tarpara**, m. a bell hanging down from the throat of cattle, g. *kapilakâdi* (Gaṇar. 446).

तर्फितृ **tarphitṛi**, mfn. (√*tṛiph*) one who kills, W.; cf. *turphári* &c.

तर्ब् **tarb**, cl. 1. P. °*bati*, to go, Vop.

तर्बट **tarbaṭa**, m. a year, L.; for °*ra-vaṭa*, L.

तर्मन् **tarman**, *tárya*. See p. 439, col. 2.

तर्वन् **tarvan**, wrong pronunciation for *tad-van*, Pat. on Pāṇ. Introd. Vārtt. 9.

तर्ष 2. **tarsha**, m. (√*tṛish*) thirst, wish, desire for (in comp.), MBh. xii; R. ii, 100, 3; BhP. v, 8, 12 (*ati-*, 'excessive desire'); Desire (son of Arka [the sun] and Vāsanā), vi, 6, 13; (*ā*), f. thirst, desire, xi, 9, 27. **-cetas**, mfn. eagerly desirous of (*arthe* ifc.), viii, 8, 38.

Tarshaṇa, n. thirst, L.; desire, iii, 25, 7.

Tarsham, ind. (Pāṇ. iii, 4, 57). See *dvy-aha-*.

Tarshita, mfn. thirsty, BhP. ix, 6, 27; ifc. desirous of, R. ii, 104, 1; cf. *tṛish*°.

Tarshuka, mfn. thirsty, Gal.

Tarshula, mfn. 'desiring,' *a-tarshulam*, ind. without desire, MBh. xii, 7762.

Tarshyā-vat, mfn. = *tṛish*°, RV. x, 28, 10.

तर्स **tarsa**, n., Pāṇ. viii, 3, 59, Vārtt. 1, Pat.

तर्ह **tarha**. See *śata-tarhá* & *-tárham*.

Tárhaṇa, mf(*ī*)n. (√*tṛih*) crushing, RV. vii, 104, 4; AV. ii, 31, 1; cf. *dasyu-tárh*°.

तर्हि **tárhi**, ind. (fr. *tád-hí*, see *tarvan*; Pāṇ. v, 3, 20 f.) at that time, then, at that moment, in that case (correlative of *yád* [TBr. ii, 1, 10, 1] *yadā́* [AV. iii, 13, 6; BhP.], *yárhi* [TS. i; AitBr. i, 27], *yátra* [ŚBr. ii; BhP. v], *yadi* [Śak. v. l.; Pañcat.; Kathās. &c.], *ced* [Prab.; Sāh.]; often connected with an Impv. [Śak.; Pañcat. &c.] or interrogative pron. [Pat.; Kāś.; Siddh.; Sāh.]), RV. x, 129, 2; AV. &c. (not in MBh. & R.); cf. *etár*°, *kár*°.

तल् **tal**, cl. 1. 10. *talati*, *tālayati* (fr. *tarati*, *tāray*°, √*tṛī*) to accomplish (a vow), L.; to establish, fix (derived fr. 1. *talita*), Dhātup. xxxii, 58.

तल **tala**, (m., L.) n. (√*stṛi*) surface, level, flat roof (of a house), MBh. &c. (chiefly ifc. [f. *ā*, R. v, 13], cf. *nabhas-*, *mahī-* &c.); the part underneath, lower part, base, bottom, Mn. ii, 59; VarBṛS.; Pañcat. &c. (cf. *adhas-*, *taru-* &c.); (m. n.) the palm (of the hand, see *kara-*, *pāṇi-*), R. ii, 104, 17; Śak.; Ragh. vi, 18; the sole (of the foot, *aṅghri-*, *pāda-*), MBh. i; VarBṛS.; (without *kara-* &c.) the palm of the hand (*anyo 'nyasya* or *parasparaṃ talam* or °*lān* √*dā*, to slap each other with the palms of the hands), MBh.; Hariv.; R.; Suśr.; (n., L.; m.) the sole of the foot, R. v, 13, 47; (m.) the fore-arm, L.; = *tāla* (a span, L.; the handle of a sword, L.; the palmyra tree, Viddh. ii, 13); pressing the strings of a lute with the left hand, MBh. viii; m. N. of a hell, ĀruṇUp.; ŚivaP.; (cf. *talâtala*); Śiva, MBh. xiii, 17, 130; N. of a teacher, g. *śaunakâdi*; n. = *-hṛidaya*, L.; = *talka*, L.; = *talaka* (q. v.), L.; = *talla* (q. v.), L.; the root or seed of events, L.; = *-tra*, ĀśvGṛ. iii, 12, 11 (*tala*); MBh.; R.; (*ā*), f. id., L.; N. of a daughter of Raudrâśva, VāyuP. ii, 37, 122; cf. *a-*, *jihvā-*, *ni-*, *nis-*, *pra-*, *mahā-*, *rasā-*, *vi-*, *su-*. **-koṭa**, N. of a plant, Suśr. vi, 51, 43 (v. l.) **-gata**, mfn. 'being in one's palm,' °*taṃ* √*kṛi*, to call together, Vcar. xiv, 11. **-ghāta**, m. a slap with the palm or paw, Hariv. 16027. **-tas**, ind. from the bottom. **-tāla**, m. clapping the hands, MBh. iii f.; Jain. **-tra**, 'arm-guard,' a leathern fence worn by archers on the left arm, iii, vi; Hariv. 13373; *-vat*, mfn. furnished with that fence, 14465. **-trāṇa**, = *-tra*, MBh. iii, vii. **-nishpesha**, m. striking (of the bow-string) against the *tala(-tra)*, v, 48, 52. **-pushpa-puṭa**, n. a particular position in dancing. **-prahāra**, m. = *-ghāta*, R. vi, 76, 37 ff.; Pañcat. iv; N. of a hero (also °*raka*, °*ri*), Vīrac. ix, xvi f., xx. **-baddha**, mfn. = *baddha-tala*, having fastened round one's arm the *tala(-tra)*, MBh. vi, 621; Hariv. 12529 & 13246. **-mīna**, m. v. l. for *nal*°, L., Sch. **-mukha**, m. a particular position of the hands in dancing. **-yukta**, mfn. furnished with a handle, W. **-yuddha**, n. 'palm-fight,' see *-śabda*. **-loka**, m. 'the lower world,' *-pāla*, m. a guardian of that world, BhP. ii, 6, 42. **-vara**, m. = °*lâraksha*, Jain. **-vāraṇa**, n. = *-tra*, Kir. xiv, 29; = *tara-vāri*, W. **-śabda**, m. = *-tāla*, Hariv. 15742; VarBṛS. xliii, 28 (v. l. °*la-yuddha*). **-sampāta**, m. = *-tāla*, R. vi, 70, 44. **-sāraka**, m. a horse's food-receptacle, L. **-sāraṇa**, n. id., Gal. **-sārika**, m. id. or = *uraḥ-paṭṭikā* (Sch.), Hcar. vii. **-stha**, mfn. remaining beneath, W. **-sthita**, mfn. id., W. **-hṛidaya**, n. the centre of the sole of the foot, L. **Talâṅguli-tra-vat**, mfn. furnished with a *tala(-tra)* and *aṅguli-tra*, R. ii, 87, 23. **Talâcī**, f. 'spread on the ground,' a mat, L. **Talâtala**, n. N. of a hell, ĀruṇUp.; BhP. ii, 1 & 5; v; BrahmôttKh. xviii; Vedântas. 121. **Talā-tali**, ind. (to fight) with the palms of the hands, Bālar. x, 19. **Talâraksha**, m. a body-guard (= *aṅga-r*°?), Campak. 286. **Talâsi**, m. pl. strokes with the palms and with swords, MBh. ii, 70, 17. **Talâhvaya**, m. Flacourtia cataphracta, L. **Talêkshaṇa**, m. 'looking downwards,' a hog, L. **Talôdara**, v. l. for *til*°. **Talôdā**, f. 'whose water flows downwards,' a river, L.

Talaka, m. a small cart with burning coals, Hcar. vii; a pot of clay, HPariś. ii, 473; N. of a prince, BhP. xii, 1; n. = *taḍaga*, a pond (also *tala* & *talla*), L.; a kind of salt, Gal.; (*ikā*), f. = °*la-sāraka*, L.

1. **Talita**, mfn. 'bottomed,' fixed, placed, W.

Talin, mfn. = °*la-tra-vat*, MBh. v, 5367; xiv.

तलभ **talabha**, n., Siddh. puṃl. 47.

तलव **talavá**, m. a musician, VS. xxx, 20. **-kāra**, m. pl. N. of a school of the SV.; *-kalpa*, m. the ritual of the Talava-kāras, ĀpŚr. i, 20, 13; *-brāhmaṇa*, n. another N. of JaimBr.; °*rôpanishad*, f. another N. of JaimUp. or KenUp.

तलाशा **talāśā**, f. a kind of tree, AV. vi, 15, 3; Kauś. 8.

तलित 2. **talita**, mfn. fried, Bhpr.

तलिन **talina**, mf(*ā*)n. thin, fine (cf. °*luna*), Vcar. xi, 80; 'slender, meagre,' in comp.; small, little, L.; separate, having spaces, L.; clear, L.; ifc. (fr. °*la*) covered with, xiv, 61; m. N. of a man, Pravar. i, 1 (v. l. *nal*°); n. a couch, Dharmaśarm, v, vii. **Talinôdarī**, f. a slender-waisted woman, Vcar. x, 88.

तलिम **talima**, n. (fr. °*la*?) ground prepared for the site of a dwelling (*kuṭṭima*), Viddh.; a couch, L.; an awning, L.; a sword (cf. °*la-vāraṇa*), L.

तलीद्य **talīdyà**, n. a particular part of the body, AV. vii, 76, 3.

तलुक्ष *taluksha*, m. N. of a man (cf. *tá-ruksha*), g. 2. *lohitâdi* (not in Kāś.)

तलुन *taluna*, mfn. (= *taruṇa*, Pāṇ. iv, 1, 15, Vārtt. 6, Pat.; g. *kapilakâdi*, Gaṇar. 447) young, L.; m. (g. *utsâdi*) a youth, L.; wind, L.; (*ī*), f. (g. *gaurâdi*; proparox., Pāṇ. iv, 1, 15, Vārtt. 6, Pat.) a maiden, L.

तल्क *talka*, n. a forest (cf. *tala*), L.

तल्प *tálpa*, (n., L.) m. (√*trip*) a couch, bed, sofa, AV.; TS. vi; TBr. &c. (ifc. f. *ā*, Rājat. ii, 166; °*lpam ā-√vas*, 'to defile any one's marriage-bed,' ChUp. v, 10, 9; °*lpam adhi-√gam*, 'to have sexual intercourse with' [in comp.], Mn. iii, 250); the seat of a carriage, MBh. iii, 14917; vii, 1626; an upper story, room on the top of a house, turret, i, 7577; = *guru-*, Gaut. xxiii, 12; a raft, boat, L.; a wife, L.; (*ā*), f. a couch, AV. xiii, 1, 17. **—kīṭa**, m. 'bed-insect,' a bug, BrahmavP. **—ga**, mfn. ifc. having sexual intercourse with, Gaut.; MBh. xiii, 4281; see *guru-*. **—giri**, m. N. of a mountain, W. **—ja**, mfn. born (on a marriage-bed, i. e.) of a wife (by an appointed substitute), Mn. ix, 167 & 170. **—śívan**, mf(*varī*)n. resting or lying on a couch, RV. vii, 55, 8. **—sádya**, n. resting on a couch, TBr. i, 2, 6, 5 f.

Talpaka, m. (for *kalp°*, a barber?), Kām. xii.

Talpana, n. the exterior muscles of an elephant's back, L. **Talpala**, m. (g. *kapilakâdi*, Gaṇar. 446; Hemac.) id., Śiś. xviii, 6.

Talpī-kṛita, mfn. made into a couch, Rājat. iii.

Talpe, loc. of °*pa*. **—ja**, mf(*ā*)n. produced on a bed or couch, TĀr. iv, 39, 1. **—śayá**, mf(*ā*)n. = °*pa-śīvan*, AV. iv, 5, 3.

Tálpya, mfn. belonging to a bed, VS. xvi, 44; worthy of a couch, TāṇḍyaBr. xxiii, 4, 5; xxv, 1, 10; = *tālpa*, ŚBr. xiii, 1, 6, 2.

तल्ल *talla*, (Vām. ii, 1, 7) m. = *talaka* (q. v.), L.; n. '= *ālavāla*' or 'a pit,' L. (also *tala*); (*ī*), f. a young woman, L.; Varuṇa's wife, L.; a boat, W.

तल्लक्षण *tal-lakshaṇa*. See p. 435, col. 1.

तल्लज *tallaja*, m. ifc. an excellent specimen of, e. g. *kumārī-*, 'an excellent maiden,' L., Sch.; cf. *go-*; *matallikā*.

तल्लिका *tallikā*, f. = *tālī*, a key, W.

तल्व *talva*, n. scent arising from the rubbing of fragrant substances, W.

तवक *tavaka*, a grammatical base formed for *tāvaka* & °*kīna*, Pāṇ. iv, 3, 3; Vop. vii, 22.

तवक्षीर *tava-kshīra*, m. (for *tvak-ksh°*) manna of bamboo (commonly Tabāshīr), L.; (*ī*), f. a kind of Curcuma (°*rī eka-pattrikā*, 'one-leaved Tavakshīrī,' Curcuma Zedoaria), Npr.

तवप्रिय *tava-priya*, n. the bark of Laurus Cassia, Gal.

तवर *tavara*, a particular high number, L.

तवराज *tava-rāja*, = *-kshīra*, L.

तवश्रवीय *tavaśravīya*, n. N. of a Sāman (made of RV. x, 140, 1, beginning with *Ágne táva śrávo*), SāmavBr. ii, 1, 8.

तवस् *tavás*, mfn. (√*tu*) strong, energetic, courageous, RV. (compar. °*vás-tara* [cf. *távīyas*], i, 30, 7; superl. °*vás-tama*, 190, 5; ii, 33, 3); m. power, strength, courage, RV. iii, 1, 1 & 30, 8; AV. xi, 1, 14; cf. *prá-*, *svá-*. **—vat** (*táv°*), mfn. strong, RV. ix, 97, 46. **Tavā-gá**, mfn. or **-gó**, m. (acc. -*gā́m*) 'strong (a bull)' or 'a strong bull,' iv, 18.

Tavasyà, n. strength, ii, 20, 8.

Tavishá, mfn. strong, energetic, courageous, RV.; m. the ocean, Uṇ., Sch.; heaven, ib.; n. power, strength (also pl.), RV. i, 166, 1 & 9; iii, 12; viii.

Távishī, f. power, strength, violence, courage (also pl.; instr. ind. °*shībhis*, 'powerfully, violently'), RV.; the earth, Uṇ., Sch.; a river, ib.; a heavenly virgin ('N. of a daughter of Indra,' L.), ib. **—mat** (*táv°*), mfn. strong, violent, RV. v, 58, 1. **—vat** (*táv°*), mfn. id., iv, 20, 7; vii, 25, 4; x, 105, 3.

Tavishīya, Nom. P. Ā. (2. sg. °*yáse*, p. °*yát*, °*yámāṇa*) to be strong or violent or courageous, ii, 30, 8; v, 85, 4; viii, 6, 26.

Tavishīyú, mfn. spirited (a horse), 23, 11; violent (the Maruts), 7, 2.

Tavishya, Nom. °*yáte* (p. °*yámāna*) = °*shīya*, ix, 76, 3 & 86, 45; x, 11, 6; AV. xx, 34, 16 (MS. *stav°*). **Tavishyá**, f. violence, RV. ix, 70, 7.

Távīyas, mfn. compar. of °*vás*, stronger, RV. (*tavásas távīyān*, 'stronger than the strong').

Tavīsha, m. (= *tāv°*) the ocean (cf. *tarīsha*), L.; heaven (v.l. *tarīsha*), L.; gold, L.; (*ī*), f. = °*vishī*, N. of a daughter of Indra (v. l. *tarīshī*), L.

Távya, mfn. strong, RV. i, 54, 11; (°*vyà*) TS. ii, 3, 13, 1. **Távyas**, mfn. = °*vīyas*, RV.; cf. *á-*.

तश्ली *taślī*, f. in astron. = تثليث, trigon.

तष्ट *tashṭá*, mfn. (√*taksh*) pared, hewn, made thin, L.; fashioned, formed in mind, produced, RV.; AV. xi, 1, 23; cf. *sú-*, *stóma-*; *vibhva-tashṭá*.

Tashṭi, f. v.l. for *tvashṭi*, q. v.

Táshṭṛi, m. a carpenter, builder of chariots, RV. i, 61, 4; 105, 18; 130, 4; iii f., vii, x; Viśva-karman (cf. *tváshṭṛi*), L.; N. of one of the 12 Ādityas, L.

तस् 1. *tas*, cl. 4. °*syati*, to fade away, perish, Dhātup. xxvi, 103; (cf. √*taṃs*) to cast upwards (or 'to throw down'), ib. (Vop.); to throw, Pāṇ. iii, 4, 61, Kāś. 2. **Tas**, mfn. 'throwing;' see *sukha-*.

Tásara, (m., L.) n. (√*taṃs*?) a shuttle, RV. x, 130, 2; VS. xix, 83 ('the cloth in the loom,' TBr., Sch.)

Tasarikā, f. weaving, Divyâv. vii, 64.

तसीर *tasīra*, in astron. = *tās°*, تسيير.

तस्कर *táskara*, m. (for *tat-k°*, Nir. iii, 14; VPrāt. iii, 51) a thief, robber, RV.; AV.; VS. &c. (ifc. f. *ā*, Hariv. 5180; Kām. iv, 53; cf. *a-taskará*; ifc. used as a term of contempt [Kathās. ci, 140], Gaṇar. 114); Trigonella corniculata, Suśr. iv, 37, 15; Vanguiera spinosa, L.; Ardisia humilis (?), L.; the ear (derived fr. Ragh. i, 27), W.; pl. N. of particular Ketus, VarBṛS. xi, 20; (*ī*), f. a passionate woman, L.; a kind of Mimosa, Npr. **—tā**, f. thievishness, thieving, Ragh. i, 27. **—tva**, n. id., Daś. **—vat**, ind. like a thief, W. **—vṛitti**, m. a purse-cutter, Bhpr. vii, 59, 15. **—snāyu**, m. Leea hirta, L.

Taskarāya, Nom. °*yate*, to behave like a thief, Kathās. lvi, 13.

तस्तुव *tastúva*, n. N. of an antidote against poison (?), AV. v, 13, 11.

तस्थान *tasthāná*, mfn. (pf. p. Ā. √*sthā*) pliable, suiting, ŚBr. iii, 9, 4, 14 f.; xii, 5, 1, 1 f. & 2, 2; (AitBr. vi, 5, 2 *tat-sth°*; cf. vii, 18, 8); cf. *á-*.

Tasthivás, mf(°*thúshī*)n. pf. p. P. √*sthā*, q. v.

Tasthu, mfn. stationary, BhP. vii, 7, 23.

तस्थी *tasthī*. See *tanthī*.

तस्दी *tasdī*, in astron. = تسديس, hexagon.

तस्मात् *tásmāt*, ind. (abl. of 2. *tá*) from that, on that account, therefore (correlative of *yád*, *yasmāt*), AV.; ŚBr.; AitBr.; Mn.; Nal. &c.

Tasyâśitīya, mfn. beginning with *tasyâśita* (an Adhyāya), Car. i, 6.

ताक्षक *tākshaka*, mfn. relating or belonging to Takshakīyā, g. *bilvakâdi*.

Tākshaṇya, m. (fr. *tákshan*) a carpenter's son, Pāṇ. iv, 1, 153, Vārtt. 2. **Tākshaśila**, mf(*ī*)n. coming from Taksha-śilā, g. *takshaśilâdi*.

Tákshṇa, mf(*ī*)n. fit for a carpenter (*tákshan*), ŚāṅkhŚr. ii, 3, 14; m. = °*kshaṇya*, g. *śivâdi*; Pāṇ. iv, 1, 153, Vārtt. 1.

ताच्छब्द्य *tācchabdya*, n. the having that form of a word (*tad śabda*), 2, 60, Pat.; Anup.

Tācchīlika, mfn. (an affix) denoting a particular disposition or custom (*śīla*), Pāṇ. iii, 1, 94, Paribh. 1.

Tācchīlya, n. the being accustomed to that, 2, 11; i, 3, 21, Vārtt. 5; *a-* neg., iii, 2, 79, Kāś.

ताजक् *tājak*, ind. (g. *câdi*) suddenly, TS.; Kāṭh.; MaitrS. i f.; iv, 8, 9; TāṇḍyaBr. xvii, 12.

Tāját, ind. (Naigh. ii, 15) id. AV. viii, 8, 3 (°*jád-bhaṅga*, m. = *eraṇḍa*, Kauś., Sch.)

ताजक *tājaka*, n. N. of certain astronomical books translated or derived from translations from the Arabic and Persian (e.g. *-kalpa-latā*, *-keśavī*, *-kaustubha*, *-cintāmaṇi*, *-tantra*, *-tilaka*, *-dīpaka*, *-paddhati*, *-bhāva*, *-bhūshaṇa*, *-muktâvalī*, *-yoga-sudhâkara*, *-ratna-mālā*, *-śāstra*, *-sarva-sva-sāra*, *-sāra*, *-sudhā-nidhi*, °*kâlaṃkāra*).

Tājika, m. a Persian, pl. the Persians (cf. *tarj°* & *tāyika*), Kathās. xxxvii, 36; Romakas. (also °*jika*); n. = °*jaka* (e. g. *-jyotir-maṇi*, *-praśnâdhyāya*, *-śāstra*, °*kâlaṃkāra*).

ताटङ्क *tāṭaṅka*, (m., L.) n. a kind of ear-ornament, Prasannar. ii, 9.

Tāṭaṅkin, mfn. decorated with °*ka*, iii, 1.

ताटस्थ्य *tāṭasthya*, n. (fr. *taṭa-stha*) standing aloof, indifference, Sch. on KapS. i, 135 & Yogas. i, 33; proximity, W.

ताड *tāḍa*, mfn. (√*taḍ*) 'beating,' see *gha-ṇṭā-*; m. a blow, AV. xix, 32, 2; whipping, W.; sound, noise, L.; a handful of grass &c., L.; a mountain, L.; Lipeocercis serrata, W.; (*ī*), f. a kind of ornament, L.; = °*ḍi*, Rājat. iii, 326; (*am*), ind. *udara-*, so as to beat the stomach or breast, Prab. v, 28. **—gha**, m. a kind of artificer (blacksmith?), Pāṇ. iii, 2, 55. **—ghāta**, mfn. beating or hammering, ib., Kāś. **—pattra**, n. = *tāṭaṅka*, L. **—vakra**, N. of a district, Inscr. (380 A. D.) **Tāḍâvacara**, n. a kind of musical instrument, Lalit. vii, 73 & 298; viii, 12; xiii.

Tāḍaka, m. a murderer, Vcar. xviii, 57; a kind of key, Divyâv. xxxvii; (*ā*), f. N. of a Yakshiṇī (changed into a Rākshasī by Agastya for having disturbed his devotions, afterwards killed by Rāma), R. i, 26, 26 ff. (G 27, 25 ff.); Hariv. 218; Ragh. xi, 14 ff.; VāyuP. ii, 6, 72 f. (wife of Mārica); the large dark-green pumpkin, Npr.; (*ikā*), f. the middle part of the handle of a sword, Gal.

Tāḍakā-phala, n. large cardamoms, L.

Tāḍakāyana, m. N. of a Ṛishi, MBh. xiii, 255.

Tāḍakeya, m. metron. fr. °*kā*, Bālar. iii, $\frac{7}{8}$; $\frac{1}{8}$.

Tāḍaṅka, m. = *tāṭaṅka*, Rājat. vii, 750. °**ṅkī-√kṛi**, to make an ear-ornament out of, Kād. v, 815.

Tāḍana, mfn. beating, striking, hitting, hurting, R. (G) i, 30, 17; BhP. viii, 11, 9; n. striking, beating, thumping, whipping, chastising, hammering (of gold &c.), Yājñ. i, 155; MBh. &c. (often ifc. with the instrument, once [Pañcat.] with the object); (in astron.) touching, partial eclipse, VarBṛS. xxiv, 34; a kind of solemn act (performed with Kuṇḍas, Śārad. v, 3; or with Mantras, Sarvad.); (*ī*), f. a whip, L.

Tāḍanīya, mfn. to be beaten or whipped, Pañcat.; VarBṛS. xliv, 7. °**ḍayitṛi**, mfn. one who strikes any one (gen.), Yājñ. ii, 303. °**ḍi**, f. Corypha Taliera, L.

Tāḍita, mfn. struck, beaten, chastised, R. v, 26, 12; VarBṛS.; Kum. v, 24; Śak. ii, 6; Ragh. &c.

Tāḍī, f. of °*ḍa*, q. v. **—dala**, n. a kind of ear-ornament, Vcar. xii, 12. **—puṭa**, a palm-leaf, Kād.; = *tālī-p°*, q. v. **Tāḍula**, mfn. beating, Uṇ. vr.

Tāḍya, mfn. to be beaten or chastised, Mn. viii, 299; Yājñ. ii, 161; n. = *tāmya*, Gal.

ताडाग *tāḍāga*, mfn. (water) being in or coming from ponds (*taḍ°*), Suśr. i, 45, 1, 1 & 22.

ताण्ड *tāṇḍa*, m. (cf. *taṇḍa*) N. of an old sage (supposed author of °*ṇḍi*), L.; n. = °*ṇḍaka*, Lāṭy. vii, 10, $\frac{1}{1}\frac{7}{8}$. °**ḍaka**, n. part of a Brāhmaṇa, ib.

Tāṇḍava, (m. n., g. *ardharcâdi*; fr. *taṇḍu*?) dancing (esp. with violent gesticulation), frantic dance (of Śiva and his votaries), Mālatīm.; Kathās.; BhP. x; MatsyaP.; Rājat. &c. (cf. RTL. p. 84); (in prosody) a tribrach; Saccharum procerum, L. **—°tālika**, m. 'dancing and clapping the hands (fr. *tāla*),' Śiva's door-keeper Nandin, L. **—priya**, m. 'fond of the Tāṇḍava dance,' Śiva, L.

Tāṇḍavayitṛi, mf(*trī*)n. ifc. one who causes to dance with violent movements, Viddh. ii, $\frac{1}{2}$.

Tāṇḍavikā, f. a dancing mistress, Naish. xxii.

Tāṇḍavita, mfn. 'moving round in a wild dance,' fluttering, Prab. ii, $\frac{6}{8}$; v, $\frac{4}{8}$; Prasannar. i, $\frac{4}{1}$.

Tāṇḍi, n. N. of a manual of the art of dancing (said to be composed by °*ṇḍa*), L., Sch. **Tāṇḍin**, m. N. of a writer on prosody, Chandaḥs.; pl. (Pravar. ii, 2, 2) N. of a school of the SV. (founded by a pupil of Vaiśampāyana, Pāṇ. iv, 3, 104, Kāś.; cf. 2, 66, Kāś.), Sch. on Bādar. iii, 3, 24–28 & (°*nām Up.* = ChUp.) 36. **Tāṇḍi-brāhmaṇa**, n. = °*ṇḍya-br°*.

Tāṇḍya, m. (fr. *taṇḍa*, g. *gargâdi*) patr. of a teacher, ŚBr. vi, 1, 2, 25; VBr.; MBh. ii, xii; n. = *-brāhmaṇa*. **—brāhmaṇa**, n. N. of a Brāhmaṇa of the SV. **Tāṇḍyāyana**, m. patr. fr. °*ṇḍya*, Prasannar. iv, $\frac{6}{9}$ ff.; (*ī*), f. of °*ṇḍya*, g. 2. *lohitâdi*.

तात् *tā́t*, ind. (obs. abl. of 2. *tá*) thus, in this way, RV. vi, 21, 6; x, 95, 16; obs. acc. pl. [!] of 2. *tá*, Pāṇ. vii, 1, 39, Kāś.; cf. *adhás-tāt* &c.

तात *tāta*, m. (cf. 1. *tatá*) a father, MBh. i; R.; Vikr.; Śak. iv, $\frac{1}{8}$ (in comp.) &c.; (*tā́ta*), voc. a term of affection addressed to a junior [ŚBr. xiv; AitBr. vii; ChUp.; MBh. &c.] or senior [i, 6796; Ragh. &c.], addressed to several persons, MBh. i,

6825; v, 5435 (C); in the latter use also (*ās*), voc. pl., ib. (B); i, 6820 f.; iv, 133; [cf. τέττα; Lat. *tata* &c.] — **gu**, mfn. agreeable to a father, L.; m. a paternal uncle, L. — **janayitrī**, f. du. father and mother, W. — **tulya**, mfn. like a father, fatherly, L.; m. a paternal uncle, W. **Tātârya**, m. N. of a prince.

1. **Tātala**, m. a fatherly relative, L. °**ti**, a son, L.

Tātyá, mf(*ā́*)n. fatherly, RV. i, 161, 12; vii, 37, 6.

तातन *tātana*, m. a wagtail, L.

तातल 2. *tātala*, mfn. hot, L.; an iron club, L.; disease, L.; cooking, maturing, L.; heat, W.

तातृपि *tā́tṛipi*, mfn. (√*tṛip*, Intens.) satisfying or delighting much, iii, 40, 2.

तातृषाण *tātṛishāṇá*, pf. p. √*tṛish*, q.v.

तात्कर्म्य *tātkarmya*, n. (fr. *tat-karman*) sameness of occupation, Sāh. ii, 9 $\frac{4}{5}$.

Tātkālika, mf(*ā, ī*, g. *kāśy-ādi*)n. lasting (that time. *tat-kāla*, i. e.) equally long, Yājñ. i, 151; MBh. xii, 12785; happening at that time, Sūryas. vii, 12; Gol. vii, 27 (-*tva*, n. abstr.); R. vii, 36, $\frac{45}{46}$; happening at the same time or immediately, simultaneous, instantly appearing, Daśar. ii, 38; Pratāpar.; Mn. vii, $\frac{182}{183}$; relating to or fit for a particular moment of time, MBh. iii, 22, 20.

Tātkālya, n. simultaneousness, Anup. iii, 2.

Tāttvika, mfn. conformable to or in accordance with reality (*tat-tva*), real, true, Sch. on KapS. & Prab.; knowing the Tattvas or principles (esp. those taught in Jainism), Subh. — **tva**, n. reality, MBh. xii, 308, 1, Sch.; Sāh. x, 38 $\frac{8}{9}$; (*a*-, neg.) Naish., Sch.

Tātparya, mf(*ā*)n. (fr. *tat-para*) aimed at, Sāh.; n. devoting one's self to, Pāṇ. ii, 3, 40, Kāś.; reference to any object (loc.), aim, object, purpose, meaning, purport (esp. of speech or of a work), Bhāshāp.; Vedāntas. &c.; (*ena*), instr. ind. = -*tas*, W. — **tas**, ind. with this intention, Rājat. i, 369. — **nirṇaya**, m. ascertainment of meaning or purport, Vedāntas. 254. — **pariśuddhi**, f. N. of a work by Udayana. — **bodhinī**, f. N. of a Comm. on the philosophical work Citra-dīpa. — **vid**, mfn. knowing the meaning, Kathās. lxii, 212 (*a*-, neg.) **Tātparyârtha**, m. the meaning of a sentence, W.

Tātparyaka, mfn. aiming at, Jaim. i, 14, Sch.

तात्य *tātyá*. See *tāta*.

तात्स्तोम्य *tātstomya*, n. the being formed in that (*tad*) Stoma, Anup. iv, 9; vii, 3.

Tātsthya, n. (fr. *tat-stha*) the residing or being contained in that, Pāṇ. iii, 1, 144, Kāś.; Kām. ii, 15.

Tāthābhāvya, mfn. (fr. *tathā-bhāva*) a N. for the Svarita accent put after an Ava-graha between two Udātta syllables, VPrāt. i, 120; MāṇḍŚ. vii, 10.

Tādarthika, mfn. intended for that, Kauś. 60.

Tādarthya, n. (g. *caturvarṇâdi*) the being intended for that, Jaim. vi, 1 f.; Anup. iii, 8; Pāṇ. ii, 3, 13, Vārtt. 1; Kāś.; the having that meaning, sameness of meaning, iv, 2, 60, Pat.; 'reference to that,' (*ena*), instr. ind. with this intention, L.

Tādavasthya, n. the remaining in the same (*avasthā*) condition, Sāh. vii, $\frac{4}{5}$.

Tādātmaka, mf(*ikā*)n. (fr. *tad-ātman*) denoting the unity of nature, RāmatUp. i, 19.

Tādātmya, n. sameness or identity of nature or character with (instr., loc., or in comp.), BhP.; Sāh.

Tādāyani, m. patr. fr. *tád*, Pāṇ. iv, 1, 93, Vārtt. 13, Pat. **Tādītnā**, ind. (fr. '*tadī-tna* fr. *tadi*,' correlative of *yádi*) at that time, RV. i, 32, 4.

तादुरी *tādurī*, f. (for *tāturi* fr. √*tṛī*, Intens. 'swimmer,' Nir. ix, 7, Sch.; but cf. *dardura*) N. of a female frog, AV. iv, 15, 14.

तादृक्ष *tādṛiksha*, mfn. (for *tad-d*°, Siddh.; Vop. xxvi, 83 f.) such a one, like that, Kāraṇḍ. xi, 70; Vcar. xvi, 53; Rājat. iv, 242.

Tādṛig, in comp. for °*dṛiś*. — **guṇa**, mf(*ā*)n. of such qualities, Mn. ix, 22. — **bhāva**, m. such a condition, MBh. v, 44, 22. — **rūpa**, mf(*ā*)n. of such a shape, such like, Pañcat.; -*vat*, mf(*tī*)n. of such beauty, Nal. i, 13. — **vidha**, mfn. such like, Kathās.

Tādṛiś, mfn. (for *tad-d*°, Pāṇ. iii, 2, 60; vi, 3, 91; nom. m. & f. °*dṛiṅ* [ŚBr.; cf. Pāṇ. vii, 1, 83] or °*dṛik*) such like, such a one, RV. v, 44, 6 (nom. n. °*dṛik*) &c.; (°*dṛik*), ind. in such a manner, Amar.

Tādṛiśa, mf(*ī*)n. (Pāṇ. iii, 2, 60; vi, 3, 91) = °*dṛiś*, ŚBr. xi, 7, 3; Mn. &c.; *yādṛiśa t*° [Pañcat.] or °*śa-t*° [MBh. xiii, 5847], anybody whosoever.

Tāddharmya, n. (fr. *tad-dharman*) sameness of law, analogy, L. **Tāddhita**, mfn. formed with a Tad-dhita affix, Nir. ii, 5.

Tādrūpya, n. sameness of (*rūpa*) form, identity, Pāṇ. vi, 1, 85, Vārtt. 26 (*a*-, neg.); Vām. ii, 2, 17; truth, Kaṇ., Sch. **Tādvidhya**, n. the being such like (*tad-vidha*), Bādar. iii, 3, $\frac{52}{53}$.

तान *tāna*, m. (√3. *tan*) a fibre, Suśr. i, 25; a tone, MBh. ii, 133 & 391; xiii, 3888; Kum. i, 8; a monotonous tone (in reciting, *eka-śruti*), KātyŚr. i, 8, 18; Vait.; Bhāshik.; Nyāyam.; VPrāt., Sch.; an object of sense (or = *tātparya*), L. (cf. *eka*-); [τόνος.] — **karman**, n. tuning the voice previously to singing, W; running over the notes to catch the key, W. — **bhaṭṭa**, m. N. of a man, Uttarar., Sch. — **svara**, mfn. uttered monotonously, Pratijñās.

Tānava, n. (fr. *tanú*, g. *pṛithv-ādi*) thinness, meagreness, smallness, Amar.; Rājat. iv, 25. — **kṛit**, mfn. ifc. diminishing, Bhartṛ.; excelling, Bālar. i.

Tānavya, m. patr. fr. *tanú*, g. 2. *lohitâdi* (not in Kāś.) **Tānavyāyanī**, f. of °*vya*, ib.

Tānuka. See *strī-tānuka-roga*.

Tānūnapāta, mf(*ī*)n. relating or addressed to Tanū-napāt, Lāṭy. vi, 4, 13; Anup. iv, 6; Nidānas.

Tānūnaptrá, n. a ceremony in which Tanū-napāt (-*náptṛi*) is invoked and the oblation touched by the sacrificer and the priests as a form of adjuration, TS. iii, 1, 2, 2; Kapishṭh. xxxviii, 2 (-*tva*, n. abstr.); AitBr. i, 24 (also -*tva*); ŚBr. iii; used in that ceremony, KātyŚr. viii; ŚāṅkhŚr. v; Lāṭy. v; ĀpŚr. — **pātra**, n. a vessel used in that ceremony, Vait.

Tānūnaptrin, m. a coadjutor in the Tānūnaptra ceremony, ĀpŚr. xi; *sá*-, id., MaitrS. iii, 7, 10; AitBr. i, 24; ŚBr. iii, 4, 2, 9; KātyŚr. viii, 1, 26.

तानूर *tānūra*, m. = *tālūra*, L.

तान्त 1. *tā́nta*, m. 'end of *ta*,' a mystical N. of the letter *th*, RāmatUp. i, 78. **Tântânta**, m. 'end of *tā́nta*,' a mystical N. of the letter *d*, ib.

तान्त 2. *tāntá*, mfn. (√*tam*) breathing with difficulty, fainted away, languishing, drooping, TBr. ii, 3, 8, 1; ŚBr. iv, 2, 2, 11; languid (the eye), Amar.; wearied, fatigued, distressed, W.; faded, W.

Tānti, f. suffocation, ĀpŚr. xii, 11, $\frac{8}{9}$.

तान्तव *tāntava*, mf(*ī*)n. made of threads (*tántu*), BhP. x, 64, 4; (*a*-, neg.) Lāṭy. ii, 8, 24; (ifc.) Mn. ii, 42; m. a son, Kum. xvii, 13; n. a woven cloth, Gaut.; Mn.; Gṛihyās.; Pāṇ. vii, 3, 45, Vārtt. 7; Suśr.; weaving, W.; a web, W.

Tāntavya, m. patr. fr. *tántu*, g. 2. *lohitâdi*.

Tāntavyāyanī, f. of °*vya*, ib.

Tāntuvāyya, m. the son of a weaver (*tantuvāya*), Pāṇ. iv, 1, 152, Kāś.

Tāntra, mf(*ī*)n. having wires (*tántra*), stringed (a musical instrument), W.; regulated by a general rule, ĀpŚr. xiv, 12, 5 f.; relating to the Tantras, W.; n. the music of a stringed instrument, R. i, 3.

Tāntrika, mf(*ā*, Suśr. i, 3; *ī*)n. taught in a scientific manual, Tattvas. (°*kī saṃjñā*, 'a technical N.'); taught in the Tantras, mystical, Hār. (Mn. ii, $\frac{1}{2}$); Suśr. &c.; m. one completely versed in any science or system, Bhāshāp.; a follower of the Tantra doctrine, BhP. xii, 11, 2; SSaṃkar.

1. **Tā́nva**, mf(*ā*)n. woven, spun, RV. ix, 14, 4 & 78, 1; (fr. *tanu*) one's own son, iii, 31, 2.

Tānvaṅga, m. patr. fr. *tanv*-, Rājat. vii, 898.

तान्व 2. *tā́nva*, m. patr. fr. *tā́nva* (author of RV. x, 93), 93, 15; n. N. of a Sāman, ĀrshBr.

ताप *tāpa*, m. (√2. *tap*; g. *uñchâdi*) heat, glow, Mn. xii, 76; Śak. &c. (ifc. f. *ā*, Kum. vii, 84); heating, Nyāyam. x, 1, 22; testing (gold) by heat, MBh. xii, 12357; Subh. (°*pana*, GarP.); pain (mental or physical), sorrow, affliction, MBh. &c.; fever, W.; (*ī*), f. the Taptī river ('also the Yamunā river,' L.), Hariv. ii, 109, 30; BhP. v, 19, 18; x, 79, 20; cf. *paścāt*-. — **kshetra**, n. the range of heat (caused by the sun), Sūryapr. — **da**, mfn. ifc. causing pain, VarBṛS. v, 69. — **bhṛit**, mfn., *a*-, neg., not containing heat, Naish. iv, 78. — **sveda**, m. sweat caused by heat, Suśr. iv, 32. — **hari**, f. 'removing heat,' a sort of soup of pulse and grain (first fried with ghee and turmeric and afterwards boiled with salt and sugar), Bhpr. v, 11, 13 f. **Tāpêśvara-tīrtha**, n. N. of a Tīrtha, RevāKh. ccxxiv.

Tāpaka, mfn. heating, inflaming, refining, Sarvad. xv, 14 & 16; causing pain, RV. iii, 35, 3, Sāy.; m. fever, L.; a cooking stove, Hcar. vii; (*ikā*), f. a frying-pan, ib. **Tāpatya**, mfn. relating to Tapatī, MBh. i, 387; m. metron. fr. Tapatī (N. of Kuru, 6505; of Arjuna, 6509; 6514 ff.; 6632 ff.)

Tāpana, mf(*ī*)n. ifc. illuminating, BhP. ii, 9, 8; burning, causing pain, distressing, MBh.; Hariv. 9427; R.; (cf. *indra*-, *candra*-); m. the sun, MBh. v, 1739; the hot season, Npr.; the sun-stone, L.; one of Kāma's arrows, L.; n. burning, Suśr. i, 41, 3; pain, torment, MBh. xiii, 1098; (in dram.) helplessness, perplexity, Sāh. v, 91; N. of a hell, Yājñ. iii, 224; gold, Npr.; (*ā*), f. austerity, HPariś. i, 68; (*ī*), f. N. of several Upanishads; of a river, L.

Tāpanīya, mf(*ā*)n. golden, MBh. i, vii; Hariv.; R.; m. pl. N. of a school of the VS. (to which several Upanishads belong), Caraṇ. (v.l. °*pāyana*). **Tāpanīyôpanishad**, f. N. of several Upanishads.

Tāpayitṛi, mfn. causing pain, Vcar. ix, 22.

Tāpayishṇú, mfn. id., RV. x, 34, 7.

Tāpaścitá, n. (fr. *tapaś-cit*) N. of a Sattra, ĀśvŚr. xii, 5; ŚāṅkhŚr. xiii; KātyŚr.; Lāṭy.; mfn. used in that Sattra (an Agni), ŚBr. x, 2, 5, 3; KātyŚr.

Tāpasá, mfn. (g. *chattrâdi*; Pāṇ. v, 2, 103) a practiser of religious austerities (*tápas*), ŚBr. xiv; Mn. vi, 27 &c.; relating to religious austerity or to an ascetic, R. (G) ii, 52, 5; m. an ascetic, Mn.; Nal. &c.; the moon, Gal.; Ardea nivea, L.; = °*sêkshu*, Suśr. i, 45, 9, 2 & 6; = -*pattra*, L.; patr. of Agni, Gharma, and Manyu, RAnukr.; of a Hotṛi, Tāṇḍya-Br. xxv, 15; n. = -*ja*, L.; (*ī*), f. (g. *gaurâdi*, Gaṇar. 49) a female ascetic, MBh. i, 3006; Śak. iv, $\frac{4}{5}$; Vikr.; Dhūrtas.; Curcuma Zedoaria, Npr.; Nardostachys Jaṭā-māṇsī, ib. — **ja**, n. the leaf of Laurus Cassia, ib. — **taru**, m. 'tree of ascetics,' Terminalia Catappa or Putramjīva Roxburghii, L. — **druma**, m. id., L.; -*saṃnibhā*, f. N. of a shrub, L. — **pattra**, m. Artemisia indica, Npr.; (*ī*), f. id., L. — **priya**, m. 'dear to ascetics,' Buchanania latifolia, L.; (*ā*), f. a kind of sugar-cane, Npr.; a grape, L. — **vṛiksha**, m. = -*taru*, Suśr. i, 38; iv, 18. **Tāpasâdhyushita**, mfn. inhabited by ascetics. **Tāpasâraṇya**, n. a wood of ascetics. **Tāpasêkshu**, m. a kind of sugar-cane, Bhpr. v, 22, 8. **Tāpasêshṭa**, m. = °*sa-priya*, 6, 82.

Tāpasāyani, m. patr. fr. °*sa*, Pāṇ. iv, 1, 158, Vārtt. 4, Pat. **Tāpasya**, n. ascetism, Mn. i, 114; MBh.; R. **Tāpāyana**, m. pl., v. l. for °*panīya*, q.v.

Tāpika, see *jala*-. **Tāpiccha**, m. the Tamāla plant, Mālatim. v; Gīt. xi, 11. **Tāpiñcha**, m. id., Kathās. civ, 90. **Tāpiñja**, m. id., L.; = °*pyaka*, L.

Tāpita, mfn. heated, inflamed, VarBṛS. liv, 115; pained, tormented, distressed, BhP. viii, 5, 13; Gīt.; Rājat. iii f.; Bhaṭṭ.; roused, converted, Divyâv. xxvii.

Tāpin, mfn. ifc. causing pain; exciting, Kir. ii, 42; oppressed by heat, suffering from disease (moral or physical), W.; glowing, W.; (*inī*), f. = °*panī*; a mystical N. of the letter *v*, RāmatUp. i, 79.

Tāpī, f. of °*pa*, q. v. — **ja**, mfn. found near the Taptī river, Suśr. iv, 13, 15; (m.?) a kind of gem, Npr.; (n.?) = -*samudbhava*, ib. — **taṭa**, m. 'bank of the Taptī,' N. of a place, Romakas.; -*deśa*, m. id., Ratnak. — **māhātmya**, n. 'glory of the Taptī,' N. of part of SkandaP. — **samudbhava**, (n.?) pyrites or another mineral substance, Npr. **Tāpy-utthasaṃjñaka**, n. id., ib.

Tāpya, (fr. √*tap*) regret, Divyâv. xviii; m. n. (fr. °*pī*) = °*pī-samudbhava*, Car. vi, 18 & 24; Bhpr. v, 26, 160. **Tāpyaka**, n. = °*pī-samudbhava*, L.

ताबुव *tābúva*, n. an antidote against poison (?), AV. v, 13, 10.

ताम *tāma*, m. (√*tam*) = *bhīshaṇa*, L.; = *dosha*, L.; anxiety, distress, W.; (*ī*), f. = *tamī*, night, L., Sch.; see also °*mī*. — **rasa**, n. a day-lotus, MBh. iii, 11580; Hariv. 5771; R. iii; Ragh. (ifc. f. *ā*, ix, 36) &c.; gold, L.; copper (cf. *tāmra*), L.; a metre of 4 × 12 syllables; m. Ardea nivea, L.; (*ī*), f. a lotus pond, MBh. iv, 220; °*sêkshaṇā*, f. a lotus-eyed woman, Bhām. ii, 153. — **lipta**, m. pl. (= °*mra-l*°) N. of a people and its country, AV. Pariś. lvi, 4; n. N. of a city of that people, L.; (*ī*), f. id., VarBṛS. x, 14; HPariś. ii, 315; Pañcad. iii, 1 & 37. — °**liptaka**, n. = °*ptī*, VarBṛS. xiv, 7 (v. l. °*ptika*).

Tāmam, ind. = *tam*°, Pāṇ. vi, 4, 93.

Tāmara, n. water, L.; ghee, L.

Tāmala, mf(*ī*)n. made of the bark of the Tamāla plant, Āp. i, 2, 37. **Tāmalakī**, f. Flacourtia cataphracta, Suśr. vi, 39, 197 & 203; 51, 25.

Tāmasa, mf(*ī*)n. (fr. *támas*) dark, L.; appertaining to or affected by the quality *tamas* (q. v.), ignorant, various, Mn. xii; Bhag. &c. (°*sī tanū*, 'the form assumed by the deity for the destruction of the world'; °sī śokti, 'the faculty of tamas'); relating to Manu Tāmasa, BhP. viii, 1, 28; m. a malignant person, L.; a snake, L.; an owl, L.; N. of a demon causing diseases, Hariv. 9562; of the 4th Manu, Mn. i, 62; Hariv.; BhP. v, viii; of an attendant of Śiva, L., Sch.; of a man, Pravar. i, 1 (J); n. 'darkness,' see andha-; (ī), f. night, L.; sleep, L.; Durgā, L.; N. of a river, MBh. vi, 339. **-kīlaka**, m. pl. (in astron.) N. of particular Ketus, VarBṛS. iii, 7; xi, 22. **-guṇa**, m. the quality of tamas (q. v.), W. **-tapaḥ-śīla**, m. N. of a Daitya, Gal. **-līnā**, f. (in Sāṃkhya phil.) one of the forms of dissatisfaction, Tattvas. **Tāmasika**, mfn. relating to the quality tamas (q. v.), VarBṛ. ii, 7/8.

Tāmāleya, mfn. fr. tamāla, g. sakhy-ādi.

Tāmi or °**mī**, f. restraining the breath until exhaustion is produced, Kauś. 88.

Tāmisra, (fr. tam° & támisrā, g. jyotsnâdi) mfn. (with paksha) or m. the dark half of the month, Lāṭy. ix; Gobh. iii f.; MBh. iii, 11813; m. 'night-walker,' a Rākshasa, Ragh. xv, 2; (in Sāṃkhya phil.) indignation, anger (one of the 5 forms of A-vidyā), MBh. xiv, 1019; Sāṃkhyak.; Tattvas.; BhP. iii (also n.); MārkP. iii; N. of a hell, Mn. iv, xii; Yājñ. iii, 222; BhP. iii, v; MārkP.; cf. andha-.

तामु tāmu, m. a praiser, Naigh. iii (v. l. st°).

ताम्बल tāmbala, mf(ī)n. made of hemp, Gobh. ii, 10, 10; m. a kind of hemp, ib., Sch.

ताम्बूल tāmbūla (=Prākṛit °bóla fr. tāmra-gula) m. = °bala, W.; n. betel, (esp.) its pungent and aromatic leaf (chewed with the areca-nut and catechu and sometimes caustic lime and spices as a carminative and antacid tonic), Hariv. 8454 & 8457; Suśr.; VarBṛS. &c.; the areca-nut, L.; (ī), f. Piper Betel, Ragh. iv, 42; Kād. &c. **-karaṅka**, m. a betel-box (Pān-dān), Vcar. ix, 82; -vāha, m. a servant carrying his master's betel-box, Hcar.; Vcar. ix; -vāhinī, f. a female servant carrying her master's betel-box, Kād. **-ja**, mfn. 'coming from Piper Betel,' with pattra, betel-leaf, Suśr. iv, 24, 19. **-da**, m. = -karaṅka-vāha, L. **-dāyaka**, m. id., Kām. xii, 46. **-dāyinī**, f. = -karaṅka-vāhinī, Kād. v, 432. **-dhara**, m. = -da, Rājat. viii, 1738. **-pattra**, m. Dioscorea globosa, L.; n. betel-leaf, Suśr. i, 46. **-peṭikā**, f. = -karaṅka, W. **-bhakshaṇa**, n. the eating of betel-leaf, W. **-rāga**, m. Ervum lens, L. **-vallikā**, f. the betel-plant, L. **-vallī**, f. id., Bhartṛ. **-vāhaka**, m. = -da, Pañcat. iii, 8/9. **-vāhinī**, f. = -karaṅka-v°, Hcar. viii. **-vīṭikā**, f. an areca-nut wrapped in a betel-leaf, Kād. v. **Tāmbūlâkta**, mfn. smeared with the juice of chewed betel, Sāh. iii, 8/9. **Tāmbūlâdhikāra**, m. the office of carrying the betel-box for persons of rank, Pañcat. i, 10, 3/4.

Tāmbūlika, m. a seller of betel, R. (G) ii, 90, 23; Kād. iii, 825; Sāh. iii, 1/2. **-sarpa**, m. a kind of snake, Uttamac. 188. **Tāmbūlin**, mfn. having betel, W.; m. = °lika, DharmaP.; = °la-da, W.

ताम्य tāmya, n. = kloman, L.

ताम्र tāmrá, mf(ā)n. (√tam, Uṇ.) of a coppery red colour, VS. xvi (Naigh. iii, 7); MBh. &c. (tāmrā tvac, the 4th of the 7 membranes with which an embryo is covered, Suśr. iii, 4, 2); mf(ī)n. made of copper, R. iii, 21, 17; Suśr.; Mn. vi, 5/4; BhavP.; m. a kind of leprosy with large red spots, Karmavip.; N. of a son of Naraka Bhauma, BhP. x, 59, 12; = -dvīpa, MBh. ii, 1172; Romakas.; n. = -tā, L.; copper, Kauś.; Mn. &c.; a coppery receptacle, MBh. ii, 61, 29; = -dru, W.; (cf. R. ii, 83, 17); (ā), f. Rubia Munjista, Npr.; a red kind of Abrus, ib.; a kind of pepper, L.; N. of a daughter of Daksha (one of the wives of Kaśyapa and mother of various birds), MBh. i, 2620; Hariv.; R. iii; BhP. vi, 6, 25 ff.; VP.; N. of a river, MBh. iii, 12909; vi, 335; (ī), f. a kind of clepsydra (cf. °mra-pātra), L. **-kaṇṭaka**, m. 'red-thorned,' a kind of Acacia, Npr. **-karṇī**, f. 'red-eared,' N. of the female of the quarter-elephant Añjana or Śesha, L. **-kāra**, m. a copper-smith, L. **-kili**, m. a small worm of a red colour, L. **-kuṭṭa**, m. = -kāra, R. (G) ii, 90, 25; (ī), f. a female copper-smith, Paraś., Paddh. **-kuṭṭaka**, m. = °ṭṭa, L.; = -kūṭa, W. **-kuṇḍa**, n. a copper bason, Uṇ. i, 1/14. **-kūṭa**, m. or n. N. of a shrub (tobacco, W.), Kulârṇ. **-kṛimi**, m. cochineal, L. **-krami**, m. id., L. **-garbha**, n. sulphate of copper, L. **-guhā**, f. N. of a mythical cave, Kāraṇḍ. xi. **-cakshus**, m. 'red-eyed,' a kind of pigeon, Npr. **-cūḍa**, mfn. red-crested (a cock), MBh. iii, ix; m. a cock, Suśr. iv, vi; VarBṛS. lxxxviii, 44; Daś.; Blumea lacera, L.; = °ḍaka, PSarv.; Mantram. xix; N. of a Pari-vrājaka, Pañcat. ii, 1, 2/3; (ā), f. N. of one of the mothers attending on Skanda, MBh. ix, 2636; -bhairava, m. a form of Bhairava. **-°cūḍaka**, m. a particular position of the hand. **-ja**, mf(ā)n. made of copper, VarYogay. vi, 4; °jâksha, m. 'copper-eyed,' N. of a son of Kṛishṇa by Satya-bhāmā, Hariv. 9184. **-tanu**, mfn. having a ruddy body, W. **-tapta**, m. N. of a son of Kṛishṇa, BhP. x, 61, 18. **-tā**, f. a coppery red, Kād. vi, 1175. **-tuṇḍa**, m. 'copper-mouthed,' a kind of monkey, Npr. **-trapu-ja**, = °mrârdha, ib. **-tva**, n. 'copper-colour,' redness, R. v, 85, 2. **-dugdhā**, °**gdhī**, f. N. of a small shrub, L. **-dru**, red sandal-wood, Npr. **-dvīpa**, m. 'copper-island,' Ceylon, Divyâv. xxxvi. **-°dvīpaka**, mfn. ceylonic, ib. **-dhātu**, m. red chalk, Npr.; (dhātu tāmra, 'red metal,' copper, R. iii, 21, 17). **-dhūmrá**, mf(ā)n. dark-red, AV. x, 2, 11. **-dhvaja**, m. 'red-bannered,' N. of a man, JaimBh. **-netra**, mfn. red-eyed. **-paksha**, m. N. of a son of Kṛishṇa, VP. v, 32, 2 (vv. ll. -varṇa & pra-paksha); (ā), f. N. of a daughter of Kṛishṇa, Hariv. 9184 (v. l. -parṇī). **-paṭṭa**, m. a copper plate, Yājñ. i, 318 (used for inscribing land-grants &c.); Divyâv. xxxv. **-pattra**, n. a copper plate, W.; m. 'red-leaved,' N. of a pot-herb, L. **-°pattraka**, m. 'red-leaved,' Bauhinia tomentosa, Npr.; Capparis aphylla, ib. **-parṇa**, n. N. of part of Bhārata Varsha (= -dvīpa), Gol. iii, 41; (°mra-varṇa) VP. ii, 3, 6; (ī), f. Rubia Munjista, Npr.; a kind of pond, L.; N. of a river (rising in Malaya; celebrated for its pearls; cf. RTL. p. 324), MBh. iii, 8340; vi, 252; Hariv.; VarBṛS. (once metrically °rṇi, lxxxi, 2); Ragh. iv, 50; BhP. iv f. &c.; (g. varaṇâdi) N. of a town in Ceylon, W.; °rṇī-taṭāka, N. of a locality, Śaṃkar. lxiii. **-parṇi**, for °rṇī, q. v. **-°parṇīya**, m. an inhabitant of Ceylon, esp. a Buddhist. **-pallava**, m. 'red-budded,' Jonesia Aśoka, L. **-pākin**, m. Thespesia populneoides, L. **-pātra**, n. = -kuṇḍa, MBh. xiii, 6026 f.; Suśr. vi, 12, 38; (used as a kind of clepsydra) Sūryas. xiii, 23; -maya, mfn. formed with copper vessels, Hcat. i, 7, 133. **-pādī**, f. 'red-footed,' Cissus pedata, L. **-pushpa**, mfn. decorated with red flowers, Hariv. 12003; m. Kæmpferia rotunda, L.; = °shpaka, L.; (ī), f. Bignonia suaveolens, L.; Grislea tomentosa, L.; Ipomœa Turpethum, L. **-°pushpaka**, m. Bauhinia variegata, Npr.; (ikā), f. Bignonia suaveolens, ib.; Grislea tomentosa, L.; Ipomœa Turpethum, Npr. **-phala**, m. 'red-fruited,' Alangium hexapetalum, L. **-phalaka**, n. = -paṭṭa, W. **-bīja**, m. 'red-seeded,' Dolichos uniflorus, L. **-maya**, mf(ī)n. coppery, Suśr. iv, 29; VarBṛS. lx, 5; Pañcat.; BhP.; MārkP. **-māraṇa**, n. the decomposition of copper and its application as a remedy, W. **-mukha**, mfn. copper-faced, W.; fair-complexioned, W.; m. a European, W. **-mūlā**, f. 'red-rooted,' Rubia Munjista, Npr.; Alhagi Maurorum, ib.; Mimosa pudica, ib. **-mṛiga**, m. the red deer, W. **-mṛishṭânulepin**, mfn. smeared with coppery red unguents, R. ii, 83, 17. **-rajas**, n. copper filings, Car. vi, 25. **-ratha**, mfn. having a dark red carriage, TĀr. i, 12, 4. **-rasā**, f. N. of a daughter of Raudrâśva, VāyuP. ii, 37, 122. **-rasâyanī**, f. = -dugdha, L. **-lipta**, m. pl. N. of a people (living near the western mouth of the Ganges) and its country (vv. ll. tāma-l° &c.), MBh. ii, 1874; Romakas.; a prince of the Tāmra-liptas, MBh. i, 6993; ii, 1098; (ā), f. their capital, Kathās. xiii, 54; (ī), f. id. (= tāma-l°), Kathās.; °pta-rshi, m. N. of a prince, Siṇhâs. **-°liptaka**, m. pl. the Tāmra-lipta people, MBh. vi f.; Hariv. 12838; (ikā), f. = °ptī, Kathās. xviii. **-varṇa**, mfn. copper-coloured, dark-red, TĀr. i, 12, 4; MBh. i; = °rṇaka, L.; = -parṇa, q. v.; see -paksha; (ā), f. the China rose, L.; (ī), f. the blossom of sesamum, W. **-°varṇaka**, m. a kind of grass, L. **-vallī**, f. Rubia Munjista, Bhpr. vii, 83, 8/9; = sūkshma-v°, L. **-vṛiksha**, m. = -bīja, L.; = -dru, L. **-vṛinta**, m. = -bīja, L.; (ā), f. another kind of Dolichos, L. **-śāṭīya**, m. pl. 'red-clothed,' N. of a Buddh. school. **-śāsana**, n. an edict (or grant &c.) inscribed on copper, Daś. ii, 48. **-śikhin**, m. 'red-crested,' a cock, L. **-sāgara**, m. N. of an ocean, Romakas. **-sāra**, n. = -dru, L. **-°sāraka**, n. id., L.; m. a red-blossoming Khadira, L. **-sena**, m. N. of a king, Siṇhâs. **Tāmrâksha**, mf(ī)n. = °mra-netra, MBh. viii, 1908; the Indian cuckoo, L.; N. of a serpent, Divyâv. viii. **Tāmrâkhya**, mfn. called red (a kind of pearl), VarBṛS. lxxxi, 3. **Tāmrâṭavī**, f. 'copper-wood,' N. of a mountain, Divyâv. viii. **Tāmrâbha**, n. = °mra-dru, L. **Tāmrâyasa**, n. 'copper-iron,' a kind of weight, ŚulbPariś. vii, 27. **Tāmrâruṇa**, m. a coppery red dawn, Buddh. L.; n. N of a Tīrtha, MBh. iii, 8132; (ā), f. N. of a river, xiii, 7647. **Tāmrârdha**, n. 'half-copper,' bell-metal, L. **Tāmrā-vatī**, f. 'containing copper,' N. of a river, iii, 14231. **Tāmrâśman**, m. a red stone, ruby, W. **Tāmrâśva**, mfn. having red horses, TĀr. i, 12, 4. **Tāmrôpajīvin**, m. = °mra-kāra, R. (G) ii, 90, 27. **Tāmroshṭha** (osh°), m. du. red lips, Kum. i, 45; MārkP. xxiii, 41; mfn. having red lips, MBh. i, 6073 (su-); m. N. of a Yaksha, iii, 298.

Tāmraka, m. N. of a Gandharva, Gal.; n. copper, Yājñ. i, 296; VarBṛS. civ, 15; (ikā), f. (= °mrī) a kind of clepsydra, L.; Abrus precatorius, L. **Tāmrāku**, m. N. of an Upa-dvīpa (cf. °mra-dvīpa), L. **Tāmrāyaṇa**, m. patr. fr. °mra, N. of a pupil of Yājñavalkya, VāyuP. i, 61, 25; pl. N. of a family, Pravar. i, 3. **Tāmrika**, mfn. coppery, Mn. viii, 136; Yājñ. i, 364; = °mra-kāra, L.; (ā), see °mraka.

Tāmriman, m. = °ra-tā, g. dṛiḍhâdi.

Tāmrī-√kṛi, to dye dark-red, MBh. vii, 8458.

Tāmrya, n. = °ra-tā, g. dṛiḍhâdi.

ताय tāy (derived fr. °yate, Pass. √tan, q. v.), cl. 1. °yate (aor. atāyi or °yishṭa, Pāṇ. iii, 1, 61), to spread, proceed in a continuous stream or line, Dhātup. xiv, 18; (= √trai) to protect, ib.; cf. vi-, saṃ-. **Tāya**, m. g. vṛishâdi (not in Kāś.)

Tāyana, n. proceeding well, successful progress, Pāṇ. i, 3, 38. **Tāyādará**, mfn.?, AV. vi, 72, 2.

Tāyin, m. (for trāy°) a protector (said of Mahāvīra, Jain.; of Buddha, Buddh.)

तायिक tāyika, m. pl. = tājika, L.

तायु tāyú, m. = st°, a thief, RV. i, iv–vii.

तार tārá, mfn. (√tṛī) carrying across, a saviour, protector (Rudra), VS. xvi, 40; ŚiraUp.; (Vishṇu) MBh. xiii, 6986; high (a note), loud, shrill, (m. n.) a high tone, loud or shrill note, TāṇḍyaBr. vii, 1, 7 (compar. -tara & superl. -tama); TPrāt.; Sikshā; MBh. vii; Mṛicch. &c.; mfn. (fr. stṛī?) shining, radiant, Megh.; Amar.; Kathās. lxxiii; Sāh.; clean, clear, L.; good, excellent, well flavoured, L., Sch.; m. 'crossing,' see dus-, su-; 'saving,' a mystical monosyllable (as om), RāmatUp.; SikhUp.; Sarvad.; Tantr.; Andropogon bicolor, L.; N. of Maṇi-rāma (author of a Comm. on Bhām.); of a Daitya (slain by Vishṇu), Hariv.; of one of Rāma's monkey generals (son of Bṛihas-pati, husband of Tārā), MBh. iii, 16372; R. i, iv, vi; pl. a class of gods in the 12th Manv-antara, VP. iii, 2, 33; m. [n. & (ā), f., L.] the clearness or transparency of a pearl, clear pearl, Suśr. v, 3, 19; Gīt. xi, 25; (m. n., L.) = °râbhra, L.; m. n. a star, L.; the pupil of the eye, L.; n. descent to a river, bank (cf. tīra, tīrthá), AV. iv, 37, 3; Pāṇ. vi, 3, 109, Vārtt. 1; silver, BhP. iv, 6, 27; Bhpr. v, 26, 43; (ā), f. (g. bhidâdi) a fixed star, asterism (cf. stṛī), Yājñ. iii, 172; MBh. &c. (ifc. f. ā, Mṛicch. iii, 10); the pupil of the eye (chiefly ifc.), VarBṛS. lviii, 11 &c.; a kind of meteor, vli, 86 & 94; (in Sāṃkhya phil.) one of the 8 Siddhis, Tattvas.; (in music) N. of a Rāga of six notes; a kind of perfume, L.; a form of Dākshāyaṇī (worshipped on the mountain Kishkindha, MatsyaP. xiii, 46; protectress of the Gritsa-madas, BrahmaP. ii, 18, 8; cf. RTL. p. 187); N. of a Buddh. goddess, Vāsav. 433; of Bṛihaspati's wife (carried off by Soma), MBh. v, 3972; Hariv. 1340 ff.; BhP. &c.; of the wife of Buddha Amogha-siddha, Buddh.; of a Śakti, Jain.; of a Yoginī, Hcat. ii, 1, 710; of a female monkey (daughter of Susheṇa, wife of Bālin and mother of Aṅgada), MBh. iii, 16110 ff.; R. i, iv, vi. **-kshiti**, f. N. of a country, VarBṛS. xiv, 21. **-ja**, mfn. made of silver, Hcat. i, 5; n. = -mâkshika, Npr. **-taṇḍula**, m. 'silver-grain,' a kind of Sorghum, L. **-tama**, mfn. very loud, TāṇḍyaBr.; VPrāt. i. **-tāra**, n. (in Sāṃkhya phil.) N. of one of the 8 Siddhis, Sāṃkhyak. 5/1. **-dīrgha**, mfn. loud and lasting long (a tone), Kathās. ci, 57. **-nātha**, m. N. of a Tibetan (living in the beginning of the 17th century; author of a history of Buddhism). **-nāda**, m. a loud or shrill sound. **-paṭṭaka**, m. a kind of sword, Gal. **-patana**, n. the falling of a meteor, W. **-pāla**, m. N. of a lexicographer. **-pushpa**, m. jasmine, L. **-mâ-**

kshika, n. a kind of mineral substance, Bhpr. i f. **–mūla**, n. N. of a locality, Rājat. vii f. **–vimalā**, f. 'silver-clean,' a kind of mineral substance, L. **–śuddhi-kara** [L.], **-kṛit** [Gal.], n. 'silver-refiner,' lead. **–sāra**, m. 'essence of (saving i. e.) mystical syllables,' N. of an Up. **–sthāna**, n. the place in the gamut for the treble notes, W. **–svara**, mfn. sounding loud, Pañcat. i; Kathās. vi, 58. **–hemâbha**, n. 'shining like silver and gold,' N. of a metal, Gal. **Tārâbha**, m. 'resembling silver,' quicksilver, Npr. **Tārâbhra**, m. camphor, L. **Tārâri**, m. 'silver-enemy,' a pyritic ore of iron, L. 1. **Tārâvalī**, f. 'row of tones,' N. of a composition.

Tāraka, mf(*ikā*[Pāṇ. vii, 3, 45, Vārtt. 6], R. ii)n. causing or enabling to pass or go over, carrying over, rescuing, liberating, saving, MBh. xii (Śiva); Jābāl-Up.; ŚivaP. &c. (a particular prayer, *brahman*); belonging to the stars, VS. xxiv, 10 (°*kā*); m. a helmsman, L.; N. of a Daitya (conquered by Indra with the assistance of Skanda), MBh. vi ff. (pl. the children of that Daitya, viii, 1553), xiii; Hariv.; Kum. &c.; of an enemy of Vishṇu, L.; of a friend of Sīmanta, BrahmôttKh. xxx; m. n. a float, raft, L.; n. a star, MBh. v, 5390; Gīt. vii, 24; the pupil of the eye, L.; the eye, L.; a metre of 4 × 13 syllables; (*tārakā*), f. (Pāṇ. vii, 3, 45, Vārtt. 6) a star, AV.; TBr. i, 5, 2, 5; Yājñ. i; MBh. &c. (ifc. f. *ā*); a meteor, falling star, AV. v, 17, 4; the pupil of the eye, MBh. i, 2932; R. iii; Mṛicch. &c.; the eye, L.; coloquintida, L.; = *laghu-vṛindāvana*, Npr.; (= °*rā*) N. of Bṛihas-pati's wife, VP. iv, 6, 9; (*ikā*), f. the juice of palms, Kulārṇ. **–jaya**, m. 'conquest of Tāraka,' N. of PadmaP. i, 41. **–jit**, m. 'Tāraka-conqueror,' Skanda, L. **–tīrtha**, n. N. of a Tīrtha, KāśīKh. xxxiii f. **–tvá**, n. the condition of a star, TBr. i, 5, 2, 5; the being saving, RāmatUp. ii, 2, 6. **–dvādaśī**, f. a particular 12th day, BhavP. ii. **–mantra**, m. 'saving text,' N. of a Mantra, RTL. p. 297. **–ripu**, m. = *-jit*, Mcar. ii, 35. **–vadha**, m. 'Tāraka-slaughter,' N. of ŚivaP. ii, 18. **–vairin**, m. = *-jit*, Gal. **–sūdana**, m. id., Prasannar. iv, 16. **Tārakântaka**, m. id., Kathās. i. **Tārakâri**, m. id., L. **Tārakôpanishad**, f. 'saving Up.,' N. of an Up.

Tārakā, f. of °*ka*, q. v. **–°ksha** (°*kâk*°), mfn. 'star-eyed,' MBh. ix, 2586; m. N. of a Daitya (son of Tāraka), MBh. vii f.; MatsyaP. cxxviii; cxxxvii; see °*râksha*. **–°di** (°*kâd*°), a Gaṇa of Pāṇ. (v, 2, 36; Gaṇar. 388–391). **–maya**, mfn. on account of (Bṛihas-pati's wife) Tārakā (or Tārā; said of the war waged by gods and demons for her rescue), MBh. i f.; vi f.; Hariv.; R. v f.; BhP. ix, 14, 7; m. 'full of stars,' Śiva, MBh. xii, 10424. **–māna**, n. sidereal measure, sidereal time, VarBṛS. iic, 2. **–rāja**, m. 'star-king,' the moon, Kād. v, 106; Hcar. v, 381; viii. **Tārakêśvara**, m. id., iv.

Tārakāyaṇa, m. pl. the descendants of Tāraka, Hariv. 1466; N. of a family, Pravar. iv, 1.

Tārakiṇī, f. 'starry,' night, L.

Tārakita, mfn. (Pāṇ. v, 2, 36) star-spangled (i. e. filled) with (in comp.), Daś.; Kād.; Naish. iv, 49.

Tāraṇa, mf(*ī*)n. causing or enabling to cross, helping over a difficulty, liberating, saving, MBh. xiii, 1232 (Śiva) & 6986 (Vishṇu); Hariv. 7022 & 7941; Kathās. lxvii, 1; m. a float, raft, L.; n. crossing, safe passage; conquering (difficulties), MBh. iv, xiv; R. &c.; carrying across, liberating, saving, MBh. i, iii, ix; N. of a Sāman; the 3rd year of the 4th Jupiter cycle, VarBṛS. viii, 3; Sūryas.; Jyot.; pl. N. of a family, Pravar. ii, 3, 6. °**ni**, f. = *tar*°, a boat, L.

Tāraṇeya, m. patr. of Yāja and Upa-yāja ('born of a virgin,' Sch.), MBh. i, 6363. **Tārayantī**, f. (p. Caus. √*tṛī*) one of the 8 Siddhis (in Sāṃkhya phil.), Tattvas. °**yitṛi**, mfn. a promoter, Nir. x, 28.

Tārā, f. of °*ra*, q. v. **–kavaca**, n. N. of a ch. of Tantras. iii. **–kāruṇya**, n. 'the compassion of Tārā,' N. of R. iv, 20. **–°ksha** (°*râk*°), m. 'star-eyed,' N. of a Daitya (= °*rakâksha*), MBh. viii, 1395; of a king of the Nishadhas (uncle of Dhūmrâksha), Sambh-Māh. ii; of a mountain (also °*rakâksha*), Divyâv. viii. **–gaṇa**, m. a multitude of stars, Hariv. 2661; a caparison (of a horse or elephant) ornamented with stars, Hcat. i, 8, 215 & 9, 2. **–guru**, m. pl. N. of particular authors of Mantras (with Śāktas), Śaktir. v. **–graha**, m. 'star-planet,' one of the 5 lesser planets exclusive of the sun and moon, VarBṛS. lxix, 1. **–cakra**, n. N. of a mystical circle, Rudray. ii, 3, 3. **–candra**, m. N. of a commentator; of a king, Inscr. **–cchāya**, mfn. reflecting the stars, W. **–tīrtha**, n. N. of a Tīrtha, W. **–dharma**, m. N. of a prince of *-pura*, Kathās. **–°dhipa** (°*râdh*°), m. = °*rakā-rāja*, MBh. i, iii, xiii; R.; Kum.; Bhartṛ. **–°dhipati** (°*râdh*°), m. id., W. **–°dhīśa** (°*râdh*°), see °*râpīḍa*. **–pajjhaṭikā**, f. N. of a hymn by Śaṃkara, Tantras. iii. **–pati**, m. = °*râdhipa*, MBh.; Hariv. 10052; R.; Ragh.; AmṛitUp.; 'husband of Tārā,' Bṛihas-pati; Śiva; the monkey Bālin, MBh. iii, 16130; N. of a prince, Kshitîś. ii, 18. **–patha**, m. 'star-path,' the sky, Bālar. viii, 82. **–°paharaṇa** (°*râp*°), n. N. of BrahmavP. iv, 81. **–°pīḍa** (°*râp*°), m. 'star-crowned,' the moon, L.; N. of several princes, Kād.; LiṅgaP. (i, 66, 41) &c. [°*râdhîśa*, KūrmaP. i, 21, 59]; Rājat. iv. **–pura**, n. N. of a town, Kathās. lvi, 41. **–pramāṇa**, n. = °*rakā-māna*, VarBṛS. iic, 2. **–bhūshā**, f. 'star-decorated,' night, L. **–maṇḍala**, n. 'star-circle,' the zodiac, W.; 'eye-circle,' the pupil of the eye, W.; m. a particular kind of Śiva-temple, L. **–mantra**, m. N. of R. iv, 12; of Mantram. iv. **–maya**, mf(*ī*)n. consisting of or representing stars, Śāntiś. iv, 14; Sāh. x, $\frac{8}{18}$. **–mṛiga**, m. 'star-antelope,' the Nakshatra Mṛiga-śīrsha, MBh. iii, 16020; R. iii. **–ramaṇa**, m. = *târâdhipa*, Kād. viii, 3. **–rūpa**, mfn. star-shaped, W. **–vati**, f. a form of Durgā, Śaktir. v; N. of a daughter of Kakutstha (wife of king Candra-śekhara), KālP.; of the wife of Dharma-dhvaja, Vet. **–2.–°valī** (°*râv*°), f. a multitude of stars, Kathās. lxxiii, 340; N. of a figure (in rhetoric), Pratāpar.; of a daughter of the Yaksha prince Maṇi-bhadra, Daś. ix, 43; of other mythical women, Kathās. lxix, lxxxv; cxxiii, 82. **–varsha**, n. 'star-rain,' falling stars, ShaḍvBr. vi, 9. **–°valoka** (°*râv*°), m. N. of a prince, Kathās. cxiii. **–vākya**, n. 'speech of Tārā,' N. of R. iv, 13. **–vilāpa**, m. 'lamentation of Tārā,' N. of R. iv, 17 f. **–vilāsa**, m. N. of a work. **Tārêndra**, m. 'star-prince,' N. of an author.

Tārāyaṇa, m. Ficus religiosa, Lalit. xxiv, 165 & 226; xxv, 1 & 71; pl. N. of a family, Pravar. vi, 2 (v. l. *tar*°). **Tārika**, m. a ferry-man, Vishṇ. v, 131; (n.?) freight, Mn. viii, 407; (*ā*), f., see °*raka*.

Tāriṇī, in comp. **–kalpa**, m. N. of a text, Tantras. ii. **–tantra**, n. N. of a Tantra, Śaktir. ii; iv.

Tārita, mfn. conveyed across, MBh. v, 3921.

Tāritṛi, mfn. (fut. p. Caus. √*tṛī*) being about to save, Hcat. i, 7, 779.

Tārin, mfn. enabling to cross over, saving (said of Durgā), MBh. vi, 797; (*iṇī*), f. a form of Durgā, Tantras. ii; (= °*rā*) N. of a Buddh. goddess, L.

Tāreya, m. 'son of Tārā,' the monkey Aṅgada, R. v, 1, 9 & 2, 4; vi, 6, 21; 16, 75 & 87.

Tārya, mfn. = *taraṇīya*, MBh. xii; R. iii, 30, 40; to be conquered or defeated, BhP. i, 15, 14 (*a-*, neg.); n. impers. it is to be crossed, Pāṇ. iv, 4, 91; n. freight, Mn. viii, 405.

तारटी *tāraṭī*, f. = *tar*°, L.

तारतम्य *tāratamya*, n. (fr. 1. *tara* & 2. *tama*) gradation, proportion, difference, Mṛicch. x, $\frac{5}{8}$; Sāh. i, $\frac{2}{3}$, 31; Udbh.; Kulad.; (*ena*), instr. ind. in different degrees, BhP. v, vii; cf. *tara-tama-tas*.

तारदी *tāradī*, v. l. for °*raṭī*.

तारल *tārala*, mfn. = *tar*°, unsteady, libidinous, L. **Tāralya**, n. unsteadiness, Kād. vi, 470.

तारव *tārava*, mf(*ī*)n. belonging to a tree (*taru*), Bālar. vi, 40.

ताराज् *tā-rāj*, f. a kind of Vi-rāj, RPrāt. xvii, 4 f., Sch.

तारिक *tārika*, °*rita*, &c. See above.

तारुक्षायणि *tārukshāyaṇi*, m. patr. fr. *tá-ruksha*, Pravar. iv, 8 (Kāty.; °*rkshyāy*°, VRJ.)

Tārukshya, m. (g. 2. *lohitâdi*) id., AitĀr. iii, 1, 6, 1. °**kshyāyaṇī**, f. of °*kshya*, g. 2. *lohitâdi*.

तारुण *tāruṇa*, mfn. fr. *tar*°, g. *utsâdi*.

Tāruṇya, n. youth, youthfulness, MBh. xii &c.

तार्क *tārka*, m. pl. N. of a family, Pravar. i.

तार्कव *tārkava*, mfn. fr. *tarku*, Pāṇ. iv, Kāś.

तार्किक *tārkika*, mfn. (fr. *tarka*) related or belonging to logic, W.; m. a dialectician, logician, philosopher, Gāthāsaṃgr.; Vedântas. &c. **–kārikā**, f. N. of a work. **–cūḍāmaṇi**, m. 'crest-jewel of philosophers,' a honorific N. given to Raghu-nātha and others. **–tva**, n. scepticism, philosophy, Prasannar. i, $\frac{1}{17}$. **–rakshā**, 'philosopher's guard,' N. of a work, Sarvad. v, 130. **–śiromaṇi**, m. = *-cūḍām*°.

तार्क्ष *tārksha*, m. (for °*kshya*?) a kind of bird, Suśr. iii, 4, 74; for °*kshya* (N. of a Garuḍa, of Kaśyapa, and of a tree); (*ī*), f. a kind of creeper, L. **–ja, -putra, -suta**, see °*kshya-*. **Tārkshaka**, (ifc.) the fruit of °*kshya-prasava*, Car. i, 27, 128.

Tārkshāka, m. patr. fr. *tṛiksh*°, g. *śivâdi*.

Tā́rkshya, m. N. of a mythical being (originally described as a horse with the epithet *árishṭa-nemi* [RV. i, 89, 6; x, 178, 1; Naigh. i, 14; Kauś. 73], later on taken to be a bird [RV. v, 51, interpol.; ĀśvŚr. x, 7] and identified with Garuḍa [MBh.; Hariv. &c.] or called his elder brother [L.] or father [BhP. vi, 6, 2 & 21; see also *-putra*]; mentioned with Arishṭa-nemi, VS. xv, 18; with Arishṭa-nemi, Garuḍa, Aruṇa and Āruṇi as offspring of Kaśyapa by Vinatā, MBh. i, 2548 & 4830; Hariv. 12468 & 14175; called a Yaksha, VP. ii, 10, 13; a Muni with the N. Arishṭa-nemi, MBh. iii, 12660 & 12665; xii, 10615; pl. a class of demi-gods grouped with the Gandharvas, Yakshas, and Cāraṇas, R. i, 16, 9); N. of the hymn RV. x, 178 (ascribed to Tārkshya Arishṭa-nemi), ĀśvŚr. ix; ŚāṅkhŚr. xi f.; Lāṭy. i; a horse, Naigh. i, 14; a cart, L.; a bird, MBh. vi, 71; Suśr. iv, 28, 5; a snake, L.; = *-prasava*, vi, 51, 19 (°*ksha*, ed.); a sort of antidote, v, 5, 66; gold, L.; = *netrâñca keśa*, Npr.; Śiva; N. of a man, Pravar. ii, 3, 6 (Āp. & Āśv.); pl. N. of a people, MBh. ii, 1871; n. = *-ja*, Suśr. iv, 9, 45. **–ja**, n. a sort of collyrium, vi, 12, 16 (°*ksha-ja*); Bhpr. v, 1, 204. **–dhvaja**, m. 'Garuḍa-symboled,' Vishṇu, L. **–nāyaka**, m. 'bird-leader,' Garuḍa, L. **–nāśaka**, m. 'bird-destroyer,' a kind of falcon, Npr. **–putra**, m. = *-suta*, Suparṇ. xxx, 4; BhP. iii, 2, 24; N. of Suparṇa (author of certain hymns), RAnukr. **–prasava**, m. Vatica robusta, L. **–ratna**, n. a kind of dark jewel, Kathās.; *-maya*, mfn. consisting of that jewel, cxxiii, 131. **–lakshaṇa**, m. 'Garuḍa-marked,' Kṛishṇa (= Vishṇu), MBh. xii, 43, 8. **–śaila**, n. = *-ja*, Suśr. iv, 9. **–sāman**, n. N. of a Sāman, Lāṭy. i, 6, 19. **–suta**, m. 'son of Kaśyapa,' Garuḍa, BhP.

Tārkshyāyaṇa, m. = °*ṇi*, pl. N. of a family, Pravar. i, 6; (*ī*), f. of °*kshya*, g. 2. *lohitâdi*. **–bhakta**, mfn. inhabited by the Tārkshyāyaṇas, g. *aishukāry-ādi*. **Tārkshyāyaṇi**, patr., see °*rukshāy*°.

तार्छ *tārcha*, N. of an amulet, Kauś. 48.

तार्ण *tārṇa*, mfn. made of grass (*tṛiṇa*), MBh. i, v; Suśr. i, 26, 8; levied from grass (a tax), g. *śuṇḍikâdi*; m. & (*ī*), f. patr. fr. *tṛiṇa*, g. *śivâdi*.

Tārṇaka, mfn. fr. *tṛiṇakīyā*, g. *bilvakâdi*.

Tārṇakarṇa, m. patr. fr. *tṛiṇa-k*°, g. *śivâdi*.

Tārṇakarṇi-putra, m. the son of a female descendant of Tṛiṇa-karṇa, Pāṇ. vi, 1, 13, Vārtt. 3, Pat.

Tārṇabindavīya, mfn. fr. *tṛiṇa-bindu*, iv, 2, 28, Vārtt. 1, Pat. °**ṇāyana**, m. patr. fr. *tṛiṇa*, g. 1. *naḍâdi*. **Tārṇi**, pl. id., Pravar. vi, 3 (v. l. °*ṇeya*).

तार्तीय *tārtīya*, mfn. belonging to the 3rd (*tṛit*°), ĀśvŚr. x, 2; BhP. iii, 6, 29; the 3rd, viii, 19, 34; n. a 3rd part, KātyŚr. iv, 7, Paddh.

Tārtīyaka, mfn. belonging to the 3rd, mentioned in the 3rd *kāṇḍa*, Siddh. puṃl. 17, Sch. (v. l. *jātīy*°).

Tārtīyasavana, mfn. belonging to the 3rd Savana, Śikshā. **Tārtīyasavanika**, mf(*ī*)n. id., ĀpŚr. xiv, 19; ŚāṅkhŚr. v, 3, 7. **Tārtīyâhnika**, mfn. belonging to the 3rd day (*ahan*), xv, 8, 3.

Tārtīyika, mfn. (Pāṇ. iv, 2, 7, Pat.) the 3rd, Mālatīm. i, 2. **–tā**, f. the being the 3rd, Naish. iii, 136.

तार्प्य *tārpyá*, n. a garment made of a particular vegetable substance (*tṛipā*, Sāy. on ŚBr.), AV. xviii, 4, 31 (°*pyà*); TS. ii; TBr. i, iii; ŚBr. v, 3, 5, 20; TāṇḍyaBr. xxi; KātyŚr. xv; ŚāṅkhŚr.

तार्य *tārya*. See col. 2.

तार्ष्टघ *tārshṭagha*, m. (fr. *trishṭ*°?) N. of a tree, Kauś. 25 (= *sarshapa*, Sch.); mf(*ī*)n. coming from that tree, AV. v, 29, 15; Śāntik. 21.

ताल *tāla*, m. (Siddh. napuṃs. 25, Sch.) the palmyra tree or fan-palm (Borassus flabelliformis, producing a sort of spirituous liquor; considered as a measure of height, R. iv; vi, 2, 6; Lalit. iii, xxii; forming a banner, MBh. iv, vi, xvi; Hariv.; to pierce seven fan-palms with one shot is held to be a great feat, R. i, 1, 64; AgP. viii, 2), Mn. viii, 246; MBh. &c.; (fr. *tāḍa*) slapping the hands together or against one's arm, xiii, 1397; R. &c.; the flapping of an elephant's ears, Ragh. ix, 71; Kathās. xii; xxi, 1; Prab. i, v; musical time or measure, MBh. &c. (cf. *-jña* & *-śīla*); a dance, Sāh. vi, 277; a cymbal, Pañcat.; BhP. viii, 15, 21; (in prosody) a trochee;

a span measured by the thumb and middle finger, Hcat. i, 3, 855 & 6, 171; (= *tala*) the palm (of the hand), L.; a lock, bolt, W.; (= *tala*) the hilt of a sword, L.; a goldsmith, Gal.; Śiva, MBh. xiii, 1243; pl. N. of a people (cf. *-vana* & *apara-*), VarBṛS. xiv, 22; m. n. orpiment, L.; N. of a hell, VP. ii, 6, 2 & 10; ŚivaP.; n. the nut of the fan-palm, MBh. iii, 8718; Hariv. 3711 (cf. *kākatālīya*); the throne of Durgā (cf. *manas-*), L. (v. l.); mf(*ī*, Pāṇ. iv, 3, 152)n. made of palmyra wood, Mn. xi, 96; (*ā*), f. (g. *kuṇḍâdi*), see *māsa-*; (*ī*), f. (g. *kuṇḍâdi*) N. of a tree (Corypha Taliera, Corypha umbraculifera, Flacourtia cataphracta, Curculigo orchioides, L.), Hariv. 6407; R.; Suśr. &c.; toddy, W.; a fragrant earth, L.; = *tallikā*, L.; a metre of 4 × 3 long syllables; cf. *ucca-*, *ut-*, *eka-*, *kara-*, *kāṇsya-*, *kāma-*, *krośa-*. **–ketu**, m. 'palm-bannered,' Bhīshma, MBh. v f.; Bala-Rāma, VP. iv, 1, 37; N. of an adversary of Kṛishṇa, MBh. iii, 492; Hariv. 9141; 'having the *tāla* hell as a banner,' N. of a Dānava (younger brother of Pātāla-ketu), MārkP. xxii, 6. **–kshīra**, n. = *tava-ksh°*, Npr. **–kshīraka**, n. id., L. **–garbha**, palm-juice, toddy, VarBṛS. l, 24. **–cara**, m. pl. N. of a people, MBh. v, 4751. **–ja**, mfn. coming from the fan-palm, Suśr. i, 46, 3, 41; n. = *-garbha*, L. **–jaṅgha**, mfn. (Pāṇ. vi, 2, 114, Kāś.) having legs as long as a palm-tree, R. v, 12, 35; Hariv. 9553; Tantr.; belonging to the Tāla-jaṅgha tribe, MBh. xiii, 7223; m. a prince of that tribe, iii, 17014; a Rakshas, VarYogay. iii, 21; N. of a Rakshas, R. vi, 84, 12; of a Daitya, Hariv. 12940; of a chief of the Bhūtas, Kathās. cviii, 90; of the ancestor of the Tāla-jaṅgha tribe (descendant of Śaryāti, MBh. xiii, 1946; son of Jaya-dhvaja, VP. iv, 11, 5; BhP. ix, 23, 27); pl. N. of a warrior-tribe, MBh.; Hariv.; R.; BhP. **–jaṭā**, f. the fibres of the palm-tree under the outer bark, W. **–jña**, mfn. knowing the measure (in music), Yājñ. iii, 115. **–druma**, m. the palmyra-tree. **–dhāraka**, m. 'keeping the measure,' a dancer, L. **–dhvaja**, m. '= *-ketu*,' Bala-Rāma, MBh. ix; N. of a mountain, Śatr. i; (*ā*), f. of a town, PadmaP. vi; (*ī*), f. of a river, Śatr. i, 54. **–navamī**, f. the 9th day of the light half of month Bhādra (sacred to Durgā), GarP. **–pattra**, n. 'a palm-leaf,' and 'a kind of ear-ornament,' Kād. ii, 28; Trigonella fœnum græcum, Npr.; (*ī*), f. another plant (Salvinia cucullata, L.; Anethum graveolens, Npr.; = *°la-mūlī*, ib.), Suśr. i, 11, 3 & 36, 29. **–parṇa**, n. = *°lâkhyā*, L.; (*ī*), f. id., L.; Anethum graveolens, L. **–pushpaka**, n. N. of a plant, L. **–pralamba**, m. = *-jaṭā*, L. **–phala**, n. the fruit of the fan-palm, Suśr. i; iv; Gīt. ix, 3. **–baddha**, mfn. measured, rhythmical, W. **–bhaṅga**, m. loss of the measure (in music), Pañcar. i, 12, 9 f. **–bhaṭa**, m. N. of a warrior, Kathās. xiii, 24. **–bhṛit**, m. (= *-dhvaja*) Bala-Rāma, L. **–maya**, mfn. made of the palm, W. **–mardaka**, *°dala*, m. a cymbal, L. **–mātra**, mfn. as big as a palm, MBh. i, iv f.; (*am*), ind. as high as a palm, R. iii, 50, 19. **–mūlikā**, f. Curculigo orchioides, Suśr. iv, 7, 16. **–mūlī**, f. id., Npr. **–yantra**, n. a particular surgical instrument, small pair of pincers, Suśr. i, 7, 1 f. & 7; a lock, lock and key, W. **–recanaka**, m. 'distinguishing the measure (in dancing),' a dancer, L. (v. l. *-vec°*). **–lakshman**, m. = *-bhṛit*, L. **–vana**, n. a grove of palmyra-trees, MBh. vi, 5441; Hariv. 3704; BhP. v (in a hell); m. pl. N. of a people, MBh. ii, 1175. **–vali**, f. a kind of musical composition. **–vādya**, n. clapping the hands together, Kathās. xxv, 136. **–vṛinta**, n. a palm-leaf used as a fan, fan (in general), MBh.; R.; Suśr. &c.; m. a kind of Soma plant, iv, 29, 4; *-nivāsin*, m. N. of a scholiast; *°ntī-√bhū*, to become a fan, Bālar. iii, 13. **–vṛintaka**, n. a fan, L. **–vecanaka**, see *-rec°*. **–śabda**, m. the noise caused by the falling of a palm-fruit, Hariv. 3715; = *-vādya*, 4111 f. **–śila**, mfn. accustomed to beat time in music, Gaut. xv, 18. **–śuddha**, mfn. = *-baddha*, W. **–svana**, m. = *-vādya*, Hariv. 3715. **Tālâkhyā**, f. a kind of perfume, L. **Tālâṅka**, m. = *°la-lakshman*, L.; Śiva, L.; a man marked with auspicious marks, L.; a palm-leaf (used for writing), W.; a book, L.; a saw, L.; a kind of vegetable, L. **Tālâṅga**, m. Cyprinus Rohita, L. **Tālâdi**, a Gaṇa of Pāṇ. (iv, 3, 152; Gaṇar. 261–264 including *rajakâdi*, *palāśâdi* & *bilvâdi*). **Tālâdhyāya**, m. 'time-chapter,' N. of Saṃgīta-darpaṇa vi (treating of musical instruments). **Tālâpacara**, m. = *°la-dhāraka*, R. ii, 3, 17. **Tālâvacara**, m. (cf. *tāḍâv°*) id., vii, 91, 15. **Tālâvacaraṇa**, m. id., Rājat. iii, 335. **Tālôdghāṭinī**, f. a spell used for opening locks, HPariś. ii, 173 & 182. **Tālôpanishad**, f. N. of an Up.

Tālaka, (Siddh. puṃl. 29) m. N. of a venomous insect, Suśr. v, 8, 13; N. of a teacher, VāyuP. i, 61, 45 (v. l. *°lika*); n. orpiment, Bhpr. v, 26, 48 & 221; a fragrant earth, L.; a lock, bolt, L.; a kind of ornament, Buddh. L.; (*ī*), f. = *°la-garbha*, L.; (*ikā*), f. the palm of the hand, Hariv. 9920; = *°la-vādya*, Pañcat. ii, 5, 6; a sign with the hand (?), Bālar. iii, 75; Curculigo orchioides, L.; = *tāmra-vallī*, L. **Tālakâbha**, mfn. 'orpiment-like,' green, L. **Tālakêśvara**, m. N. of a medicinal unguent, Bhpr.

Tālaṅkī-√kṛi. See *tāḍaṅk°*.

Tāli, f. = *tāḍi*, L.; Flacourtia cataphracta, L., Sch.

Tālika, m. the palm of the hand, L. (v. l. for *°kā*, s. v. *°laka*); a cover for binding a parcel of papers or a manuscript, L.; v. l. for *°laka*, q. v.

Tālita, n. = *tulita-paṭa* (dyed or coloured cloth, W.), L.; a string, L.; a musical instrument, L. **–nagara**, n. N. of a town. 1. **Tālin**, mfn. furnished with cymbals (Śiva), Bh. xiii, 1172.

1. **Tālī**, f. of *°la*, q. v. **–paṭṭa**, a kind of ear-ornament, Kād. v, 294. **–pattra**, n. a leaf of the Tālī plant, VarBṛS. xxvii, 3; = *°līśa-p°*, L. **–puṭa**, (– *tāḍī-p°*) – *-paṭṭa*, Kād. iii, 973. **–rasa-ja**, m. sugar made of palm-juice, Gal. **Tālīśa**, m. Flacourtia cataphracta (the leaves of which are used in med.), R. iv, 44, 55; Suśr. i, iv ff.; n. = *-pattra*, L.; *-pattra*, n. the leaf of Flacourtia cataphracta, W.; = *°lī-p°* & *°līśa*, L.; Pinus Webbiana, L. **Tālīśaka**, m. Flacourtia cataphracta, L.

Tālīyaka, a cymbal, R. v, 13, 54.

तालव्य *tālavya.* See *°lu* below.

तालाकट *tālākaṭa*, = *°lik°*, MBh. ii, 1169.

Tālikaṭa, m. pl. N. of a people and its country, VarBṛS. xiv, 11.

तालान *tālāna*, m. pl. N. of a family, Pravar. ii, 4, 1.

तालिन् 2. *tālin*, mfn. (√*tal*) placing upon, Śiś. vi, 66.

तालिन् 3. *tālin*, m. pl. the pupils of Tala, g. *śaunakâdi*.

तालिश *tāliśa*, m. a mountain, Uṇ. k.

ताली 2. *tālī*, ind. (= *dhūli* or colour [*varṇa*, Śākaṭ.] or *uttamârtha* or *vistāra* [Bhoj.], Gaṇar. 96, Sch.) with √*as*, *kṛi*, *bhū*, g. *ūry-ādi*.

तालीश *tālīśa*. See 1. *°lī*.

तालु *tálu*, n., rarely m. [MBh. xiv, 568; Hariv. 14273; BhP. ii] the palate, VS. xxv, 1; Kauś.; RPrāt.; Suśr. &c. **–kaṇṭaka**, 'palate-thorn,' N. of a disease of the palate with children, Npr. **–galapraśosha**, m. morbid dryness of palate and throat, Suśr. ii, 11, 22. **–ja**, mfn. palatal, iv, 22, 57. **–jihva**, m. a crocodile, L.; the uvula, W. **–jihvikā**, f. 'uvula,' N. of a Yoginī, Hcat. ii, 1, 716. **–nāśa**, m. 'destroying the palate (by thorny food),' a camel, Gal. **–pāka**, m. an abscess in the palate, Suśr. ii, 16, 38; iv, 22, 56. **–pāta**, m. 'falling in of the palate,' N. of a disease with children, Npr. **–piḍaka**, another disease of the palate with children, ib. **–pupputa**, m. an indolent swelling of the palate, Suśr. ii, 16, 38; iv, 22, 55. **–mūla**, n. the root of the palate, ii, 16, 39. **–vidradhī**, f. = *-pupputa*, Car. vi, 17. **–viśoshaṇa**, n. the drying of the palate (through much talking), MBh. viii, 4760. **–śosha**, m. morbid dryness of the palate, Suśr. ii, 16. **–sthāna**, mfn. palatal (a letter), RPrāt.; ŚāṅkhŚr.

Tālavya, mfn. (cf. Pāṇ. v, 1, 6) relating to the palate, Suśr. iii, 8, 15; palatal (the letters *i*, *e* & *ai* [called *kaṇṭha-t°*, 'belonging to throat and palate,' Siksh.], *c*, *ch*, *j*, *jh*, *ñ*, *y*, *ś*), Śiksh.; RPrāt.; VPrāt.

Tāluka, n. (g. *yāvâdi*) = *°lu*, Hcat. i, 9, 414 (ifc. f. *ā*); a disease of the palate, Npr.; (*ā*), f. = *°lu*, W.; (*e*), f. du. the two arteries of the palate, TUp. i, 6, 1. **Tālūshaka**, = *°lu*, Yājñ. iii, 87.

तालुक्ष्य *tālukshya*, m. patr. fr. *taluksha*.

Tālukshyāyaṇī, f. of *°kshya*, g. 2. *lohitâdi*.

तालुन *tāluna*, mfn. fr. *tal°*, g. *utsâdi*.

तालुर *tālura*, m. = *°lūra*, W.

Tālūra, m. a whirlpool, Hāl. 37.

तालुवि *tāluvi*. See *nāluhi*.

तालूषक *tālūshaka*. See *°lu*.

तात्प *tālpa*, mfn. (= *tálpya*) born in a marriage-bed (*tálpa*), Kauś. 17.

तावक *tāvaká*, mf(*ī*)n. (fr. *táva* [gen. of 1. *tvá*], Pāṇ. iv, 3, 3) thy, thine, RV. i, 94, 11; MBh. iii, 14621; R. iii, 13, 15; Kum. v, 4; BhP.; Kathās. &c.

Tāvakīna, mfn. (Pāṇ. iv, 3, 3) id., Bhām. i, 4.

तावच् *tāvac*, in comp. for *°vat*. **–chata** (*śata*), mf(*ī*)n. containing so many hundreds, Mn. i, 69; MBh. iii, 188, 23; Hariv. 511; 11309. **–chás** (*śas*), ind. (Vop.) so manifoldly, TS. i, 5, 9, 2.

Tā́vaj-jyok, ind. so long, ŚBr. xi, 5, 1, 2.

Tā́vat, mf(*atī*)n. (fr. 2. *ta*, Pāṇ. v, 2, 39; vi, 3, 91) so great, so large, so much, so far, so long, so many (correlative of *yā́vat*; rarely of *ya* or *yathôkta*, Nal. &c.), RV. &c. (*yāvatā kshaṇena tāvatā*, 'after so long time, in that time,' as soon as, Rājat. v, 110); just a little, Kir. ii, 48; (in alg.) an unknown quantity (also with *yāvat*); ind. (correlative of *yā́vat*) so much, so greatly, to such an extent, in such a number, so far, RV.; AV. &c. (*tā́vat-tāvat*, ŚBr. i, 8, 1, 6); so long, in that time, RV. x, 88, 19; ŚBr. i; Mn. &c.; meanwhile, in the mean time (the correlative *yāvat* being often connected with a neg., e. g. *tāvac chobhate mūrkho yāvat kiṃ-cin na bhāshate*, 'so long a fool shines as long as he says nothing,' Hit.; *śocayishyāmy ātmānaṃ tāvad yāvan me prâptam brāhmaṇyam*, 'so long I will emaciate myself, as long as [i. e. until] I have obtained the state of a Brāhman,' R. i, 64, 19), ŚBr. xiv, 4, 2, 30; ChUp. vi, 14, 2; Mn.; MBh. &c. (also correlative of *purā* [R. i, 28, 21], of *yāvatā na*, of *yāvat* preceded by *purā* [MBh. xiii, 4556], or without any correlative [2727; Kathās.; Hit.]); at once, now, just, first (followed by *anantaram* [Hit.], *aparam* [Pañcat.], *api* [ib.], *idānīm* [Hit.], *uta* [Śak.], *ca* [Daś.; Prab.], *tatas* [Mn. iv, 174; Ragh. vii, 4 f.], *tad-anu* [Megh.], *tu* [Daś. vii; Vedāntas.], *paścāt* [R. ii], *punar* [Pañcat.], *vā*; very often connected with an Impv., rarely [MBh. iv, 888; R. ii, 56, 13] with a Pot., often with the 1st person of pr. or fut., MBh. &c.; the Impv. is sometimes to be supplied [*itas tāvat*, 'just come hither'; *mā tāvat*, 'by no means, God forbid!'], Śak.; Mālav.; Vikr.; Prab.; sometimes *arhasi* with the inf. is used instead, R. i f.); (with *na* or *a-*) not yet, MBh. &c. (followed by *yāvat*, 'while,' Kathās. xxvi, 23; *tāvan na—api na*, 'not only not—but also not,' Kād.); very well! all right, Hcar.; indeed, truly (e. g. *dṛiḍhas tāvad bandhaḥ*, 'the knot is tight I must admit,' Hit.; *gatā tāvat*, 'she is indeed gone,' Kathās. xviii, 241), R. &c.; already (opposed to 'how much more' or 'how much less'), R. iv f.; Śak.; really (= *eva*, sometimes connected with this particle, e. g. *vikrayas tāvad eva saḥ*, 'it is really a sale'), Mn. iii, 53; Hariv. 7110; R. &c.; (*tā*), instr. ind. to that extent, RPrāt. xiii, 13; BhP. v, viii; in that time, in the mean time, meanwhile, Daś.; Kathās. x, 24; Bharaṭ.; (*ti*), loc. ind. so far, ŚBr. viii, 6, 2, 8; so long, in that time, TS. ii, 4; [cf. Lat. *tantus*.] **–kālam**, ind. for so long, Kauś. 141; MBh. iii; Hit. **–kṛitvas**, ind. (Pāṇ. i, 1, 23, Kāś.) so many times, ŚBr. ix, 1, 1, 41 (*tā́vat-kṛit°*); Mn. v, 38; with √*kṛi*, (in math.) to square. **–tāt** (*tā́v°*), just so much, MaitrS. iii. **–priya** (*tā́v°*), mfn. dear to that extent, i. **–phala**, mfn. having such results, Śak. vi, 10. **–sūtra**, n. sg. so many threads, Yājñ.

Tāvatika, mfn. bought for or worth so much, Pāṇ. v, 1, 23. *°***vatitha**, mfn. (2, 53 & 77) the so manieth, KātyŚr. iii, 1, 9. *°***vatka**, mfn. = *°tika*, Pāṇ.

Tāvad, in comp. for *°vat*. **–guṇa**, mfn. having so many qualities, Mn. i, 20. **–guṇita**, mfn. (in math.) squared. **–dvayasa**, mfn. so large, so long, Pāṇ. v, 2, 37, Vārtt. 1. **–dhā**, ind. in that number, in such a number, Bālar. ix, 49. **–varsha**, mfn. so many years old, Lāṭy. ix, 12, 12. **–vīrya-vat** (*tā́v°*), mfn. having so great force or efficacy, ŚBr. i, 2, 3, 7. **–vyakta**, (in alg.) a known number annexed to an unknown quantity.

Tāvan, in comp. for *°vat*. **–mātrá**, mf(*ī*)n. (Pāṇ. v, 2, 37, Vārtt. 1) so much, so many, ŚBr. v; Hariv. 1204; BhP. iv; (*e*), loc. ind. in that distance, v, 24, 4. **–māna** (*tā́v°*), mfn. of that measure, TS. ii, 3, 11, 5. **Tāvanta**, n. so much, Divyâv. i, 5; xxii, 50.

तावर *tāvara*, n. a bow-string, L.

ताविष *tāvisha*, m. (= *tav°*) the ocean, L.; heaven, L.; gold, L.; (*ī*), f. = *tav°*, L.

Tāvisha, m. (= *tav°*) the ocean, L.; heaven, L.; gold, L.; (*ī*), f. N. of a daughter of Indra (or 'of the moon,' *candra-* for *cêndra-*?), L.

तावुर *tāvura*, m. the sign Taurus. **Tāvuri**, m. id. (borrowed fr. ταῦρος), VarBṛ.i. **Tāvuru**, m. id.

तासीर *tāsīra*, = *tas°*, Hāyan.

तासून *tāsūna*, mf(*ī*)n. made of hemp, Gobh. ii, 10, 10 (v. l.); m. a kind of hemp, ib., Sch.

तास्कर्य *tāskarya*, n. = *taskara-tā*, Mn. ix.

तास्पन्द्र *tāspandra*, m. N. of a Ṛishi, Ārsh-Br.; n. N. of two Sāmans, ib.

Tāspindra, n. N. of two Sāmans, ib.

ति *ti* for *íti* (after *kā́*), ŚBr. xi, 6, 1, 3 ff.

तिक् *tik*, cl. 1. *tekate*, to go, Dhātup. iv, 31: cl. 5. *tiknoti* (also *tignoti* fr. √*tig*), id. (cf. √*stigh*), xxvii, 19; to assail, ib.; to wound, ib.; to challenge, L.

तिक *tika*, m. N. of a man, g. 1. *naḍâdi*; Pāṇ. iv, 1, 154. – **kitava**, m. pl. the descendants of Tika and Kitava, ii, 4, 68; *°vâdi*, N. of a Gaṇa of Pāṇ. (ib.; Gaṇar. 32–34). **Tikâdi**, another Gaṇa of Pāṇ. (iv, 1, 154; Gaṇar. 229–231).

Tikīya, mfn. fr. *°ka*, g. *utkarâdi*.

तिक्त *tikta*, *°ktaka*. See below.

तिग् *tig*, cl. 5. *°gnoti*. See √*tik*.

तिगित *tigitá*, *°gmá*. See col. 2.

तिघ् *tigh*, cl. 5. *°ghnoti*, to hurt, kill (= √*tik*), Vop. (Dhātup. xxvii, 26).

तिङ् *tiṅ*, a collective N. for the personal terminations, Pāṇ. – **anta**, n. 'ending with *tiṅ*,' an inflected verbal base. – **sub-anta-caya**, m. 'collection of verbs and nouns (*sub-anta*),' a phrase, Gal.

तिज् *tij*, cl. 1. *téjate* (*°ti*, Dhātup. xxiii, 2; p. *téjamāna*; Ved. inf. *téjase*) to be or become sharp, RV. i, 55, 1; iii, 2, 10 & 8, 11 (*tétijāna*, 'sharp,' VS. v, 43); to sharpen, x, 138, 5: Caus. *tejayati*, id., Dhātup. xxxii, 109; to stir up, excite, R. iii, 31, 36; Ragh. ix, 38: Desid. *títi-kshate* (Pāṇ. iii, 1, 5; 1. pl. *°kshmahe*, MBh. v, 3427; fut. *°kshishyate*, ŚBr. iii; ep. also P., e. g. p. *°kshat*, BhP. iii) 'to desire to become sharp or firm,' to bear with firmness, suffer with courage or patience, endure, RV. ii, 13, 3; iii, 30, 1; AV. viii &c.: Intens. *tétikte* (Pāṇ. vii, 4, 65; p. *°tijāna*, see above) to sharpen, RV. iv, 23, 7; [cf. στίζω; Lat. *dis-tinguo*, &c.]

Tikta, mfn. bitter (one of the 6 modifications of taste, *rasa*), pungent, MBh. xii, xiv; Suśr. &c.; fragrant, Megh.; Śiś. v, 33; m. a bitter taste, pungency, W.; fragrance, W.; Wrightia antidysenterica, L.; Capparis trifoliata, L.; Agathotes Chirayta, Npr.; = *pari-*, ib.; Terminalia Catappa, ib.; a sort of cucumber, ib.; (cf. *anārya-*, *kirāta-*, *cira-*, *mahā-*); n. N. of a medicinal plant, L.; a kind of salt, Npr.; (*ā*), f. N. of a plant (= *-rohiṇī*, L.; Clypea hernandifolia, L.; a water-melon, L.; Artemisia sternutatoria, Bhpr.; = *yava-*, L.; cf. *kāka-*), Suśr. iv, 5, 12. – **kandakā**, *°dikā*, f. Curcuma Zedoaria, L. – **gandhā**, f. 'having a pungent smell,' mustard, Npr. – **guñjā**, f. Pongamia glabra, L. – **ghṛita**, n. ghee prepared with bitter herbs, vi, 11, 2 (cf. *°ktaka*). – **taṇḍulā**, f. long pepper, L. – **tuṇḍī**, f. = *kaṭu-t°*, L. – **tumbī**, f. a bitter gourd (*kaṭu-t°*), L. – **dugdhā**, f. 'having a bitter milky sap,' Odina pinnata, L.; = *kshīriṇī*, L.; = *svarṇa-kshīrī*, L. – **dhātu**, m. 'bitter elementary substance (of the body),' bile, L. – **pattra**, m. 'bitter-leaved,' Momordica mixta, L. – **parvan**, f. Cocculus cordifolius, L.; Hingcha repens, L.; Panicum Dactylon, L.; liquorice, W. – **pushpā**, f. 'bitter-flowered,' Clypea hernandifolia, L.; 'fragrant-flowered,' Bignonia suaveolens, Npr. – **phala**, m. 'bitter-fruited,' = *-marica*, L.; (*ā*), f. a water-melon, L.; = *yava-tiktā*, L.; = *vārtākī*, L. – **bījā**, f. 'bitter-seeded,' = *-tumbī*, L. – **bhadraka**, m. Trichosanthes dioeca, L. – **marica**, m. Strychnos potatorum, L. – **yavā**, f. Andrographis paniculata, L. – **rohiṇikā**, f. = *°ṇī*, L. – **rohiṇī**, f. Helleborus niger, iv, 5, 10 & 16, 15. – **vallī**, f. Sanseviera Roxburghiana, L. – **śāka**, n. a bitter (or a fragrant) pot-herb, Rājat. v, 49; m. Capparis trifoliata, L.; Acacia Catechu, L.; = *pattra-sundara*, L. – **sāra**, m. Acacia Catechu, L.; n. a kind of fragrant grass, L. **Tiktâkhyā**, f. = *°kta-tuṇḍī*, L. **Tiktâṅgā**, f. a kind of creeper, L. **Tiktâmṛitā**, f. Menispermum glabrum, Npr. **Tiktâyana**, mf(*ī*)n. 'possessing the radiance of fire,' see *taptā́y°*. **Tiktâsya**, mfn. having a bitter (taste in the) mouth, ŚārṅgS. vii, 116 (*tā*, f., abstr.).

Tiktaka, mfn. bitter, (n.) anything having a bitter flavour, R. ii; Suśr. (with *sarpis* = *°kta-ghṛita*, iv, 9, 9); m. Terminalia Catappa, Bhpr.; Trichosanthes dioeca, L.; Agathotes Chirayta, L.; a sort of Khadira, L.; (*ā*), f. Cardiospermum halicacabum, Npr.; = *karañja-vallī*, ib.; = *°kta-tumbī*, L.; (*ikā*), f. id., L. **Tiktāya**, Nom. *°yate*, to have a bitter flavour, Naish. iii, 94.

Tigitá, mfn. sharp, RV. i, 143, 5; ii, 30, 9.

Tigmá, mfn. sharp, pointed (a weapon, flame, ray of light), RV.; AV. iv, 27, 7, xiii; ŚāṅkhGṛ. &c.; pungent, acrid, hot, scorching, RV. &c.; violent, intense, fiery, passionate, hasty, ib.; m. Indra's thunderbolt, W.; = *°gmâtman*, VP. iv, 21, 3; pl. N. of the Śūdras in Krauñca-dvîpa, ii, 4, 53 (v. l. *tishya*); n. pungency, L. – **kara**, m. = *-dīdhiti*, L.; the number '12,' Līl. – **ketu**, m. N. of a son of Vatsara by Svar-vithi, BhP. iv, 13, 12. – **ga**, mfn. going or flying swiftly, R. iii, 34, 16. – **gati**, mfn. of (violent i. e.) cruel practices, BhP. iv, 10, 28. – **gu**, mfn. hot-rayed, x, 56, 7. – **jambha** (*°má-*), mfn. having sharp teeth (Agni), RV. i, iv, viii. – **tā** (*°má-*), f. sharpness, ŚBr. ix, 2, 2, 5. – **tejana**, mfn. sharp-edged (an arrow), MBh. vi, 3187. – **tejas** (*°má-*), mfn. id., Hariv. 10703; R. iv, 7, 21; of a violent character, VS. i, xii; AV. xix, 9, 10; MBh.; m. the sun, Kathās. xxix, 121. – **dīdhiti**, m. 'hot-rayed,' the sun, VarBṛ. xi, 17; Kād. – **dyuti**, m. id., Śiś. xx, 28. – **dhāra**, mfn. = *-tejana*, MBh. vii, 47, 15 (v. l. *tiryag-dh°*). – **nemi**, mfn. having a sharp-edged felly, BhP. x, 57, 21. – **bhās**, m. = *-dyuti*, Śiś. xx, 45. – **bhṛishṭi** (*°má-*), mfn. sharp-pointed (Agni), RV. iv, 5, 3. – **manyu**, mfn. of a violent wrath (Śiva), MBh. xiii, 1161. – **mayūkha-mālin**, m. 'garlanded with hot rays,' the sun, VarYogay. iv, 7. – **mūrdhan** (*°má-*), mfn. = *-tejana*, RV. vi, 46, 11. – **yātana**, mfn. causing acute pain or agony (a hell), BhP. vi, 1, 7. – **raśmi**, m. = *-dīdhiti*, VarBṛ.; VarYogay. iv, 11; Śiś. ix, 11. – **ruc**, mfn. (Pāṇ. vi, 3, 116, Siddh.) shining brightly, hot, W.; m. = *°ci*, W. – **ruci**, m. = *-dīdhiti*, Gaṇit. i, 5, 15; Sarasv. – **rocis**, m. id., Prasannar. iv, 46. – **vat** (*°má-*), mfn. containing the word *tigmá*, ŚBr. ix, 2, 2, 5. – **vīrya**, mf(*ā*)n. violent, MBh. i, iii. – **vega**, mf(*ā*)n. id., MBh. – **śṛiṅga** (*°má-*), mfn. sharp-horned, RV. vi f., ix f.; AV. xiii; TBr. iii. – **śocis** (*°má-*), mfn. sharp-rayed (Agni), RV. i, 79, 10. – **heti** (*°má-*), mfn. having sharp weapons (Agni), iv, 4, 4; vi, 74, 4; forming a sharp weapon (Agni's horn), AV. viii, 3, 25. **Tigmâṅśu**, m. = *°ma-dīdhiti*, MBh.; Sūryas.; Kathās.; Gīt.; fire, MBh. i, 8421; Śiva. **Tigmâtman**, m. N. of a prince, MatsyaP. l, 85. **Tigmânīka**, mfn. = *°má-bhṛishṭi*, RV. i, 95, 2. **Tigmâyudha**, mfn. having or casting sharp weapons, ii, v–vii, ix. **Tigmêshu**, mfn. having sharp arrows, x, 84, 1.

Tijila, m. the moon, Uṇ., Sch.; a Rakshas, Uṇ. vṛ.

Titiksha, m. (fr. Desid.) N. of a man, g. *kaṇvâdi*; (*ā*), f. endurance, forbearance, patience, MBh.; Pāṇ. i, 2, 20; Suśr. &c.; Patience (daughter of Daksha; wife of Dharma; mother of Kshema), BhP. iv, 1, 19 ff. **Titikshita**, mfn. endured, W.; patient, L.

Titikshú, mfn. bearing, enduring patiently, forbearing, patient, AV. xii, 1, 48; ŚBr. xiv; MBh.; BhP.; m. N. of a son of Mahā-manas, ix, 23; Hariv.

तिटिभ *tiṭibha*, a particular high number, Buddh. L. **Tiṭilambha**, n. id., Lalit. xii, 158 f.

तिणिस *tiṇisa*, m. = *tiniśa*, KātyŚr., Sch.

तिण्टी *tiṇṭī*, f. Ipomoea Turpethum, L.

तितउ *titaü*, (m., L.; n., Nir. iv, 9) a sieve, cribble, RV. x, 71, 2; Kauś. 26; n. a parasol, Uṇ., Sch.

तितनिषु *titanishu*, mfn. (√*tan*, Desid.) desirous of developing (one's property), Nir. vi, 19.

तितिक्ष *titiksha*, &c. See above.

तितिभ *titibha*, m. cochineal, L.

तितिरि *titiri*, for *titt°*, a partridge, L.

तितिल *titila*, n. sesamum cake, L.; one of the 7 Karaṇas (in astron.), L.; a bowl or bucket, L.

तितीर्षा *titīrshā*, f. (√*tṝ*, Desid.) desire of crossing (ifc.), BhP. ix, 13, 19; desire of final emancipation, W. **Titīrshu**, mfn. desirous of crossing (with acc. or ifc.), MBh. i, 4647; Hariv. 5182; R.; Ragh. i, 2 &c.; desirous of final emancipation, W.

तितील *titīla*, m. a bat, Buddh. L.

तित्तिड *tittiḍa* & *°ḍika*. See *tint°*.

तित्तिर *tittirá*, m. (onomat. fr. the cry *titti*) a partridge, MaitrS. iii, 14, 17; MBh. v, 267 ff.; VP. iii, 5, 12 (cf. BhP. vi, 9, 1 ff.); pl. N. of a people, MBh. vi, 2084. – **ja**, mfn. coming from the Tittiras (horses), 3975. – **vallara**, m. a kind of sword, Gal. **Tittirâṅga**, n. a kind of steel, W.

Tittiri, m. a partridge, VS. xxiv; TS. ii (*°ttirí*); Kāṭh. xii, 10; ŚBr.; Nir.; Mn. &c.; a kind of step (in dancing); the school of the Taittirīyas, Uṇ. k.; N. of a pupil of Yāska (first teacher of the Taittirīya school of the black YV.), ĀtrAnukr.; Pāṇ. iv, 3, 102; MBh. ii, 107; of a Nāga, i, 1560; v, 3629; f. a female partridge, Pāṇ. iv, 1, 65, Kāś.; [cf. κικ-; τέτραξ.] – **tva**, n. the condition of a partridge, MārkP. xv.

Tittirika, m. a partridge, MBh. ix, 2587.

Tittirī-phala, n. Croton Tiglium, L.

तिथ *titha*, m. fire, Uṇ. ii, 12, Sch.; love, ib.; time, L.; autumn, Uṇ. vṛ.

तिथि *tithi*, m. f. (Siddh. stry. 25) a lunar day (30th part of a whole lunation of rather more than 27 solar days; 15 Tithis, during the moon's increase, constitute the light half of the month and the other 15 the dark half; the auspicious Tithis are Nandā, Bhadrā, Vijayā, Pūrṇā, VarBṛS. ic, 2), Gobh. i f.; ŚāṅkhGṛ.; Mn. &c.; the number 15, VarBṛS.; VarBṛ.; Laghuj.; Sūryas.; cf. *janma-*, *dus-*, *mahā-*. – **kshaya**, m. = *try-aha-sparśa*, W.; the day of new moon, W.; pl. = *-pralaya*, W. – **tattva**, n. N. of Smṛitit. vii (commented on by Kāśi-rāma). – **dāna**, n. N. of BhavP. ii, 154. – **devatā**, f. the deity of a lunar day, MānGṛ. i, 10; ii, 2. – **dvaita**, n. N. of a ch. of PSarv. – **dvaidha-prakaraṇa**, n. N. of a work by Śūla-pāṇi. – **niyama**, m. N. of a ch. of Tantras. i. – **nirṇaya**, m. 'disquisition on Tithis,' N. of a work by Ananta-bhaṭṭa; *-saṃkshepa*, *-saṃgraha*, *-sāra*, m. other works on astron. – **pati**, m. the regent of a lunar day, VarBṛS. ic, 1 f. – **pattrī**, f. an almanack, W. – **pālana**, n. observance of the rites appointed for the several lunar days, W. – **prakaraṇa**, n. N. of a ch. of *-sāraṇikā*; of Śrī-pati's Jyotisha-ratna-mālā. – **praṇī**, f. 'Tithi-leader,' the moon, L. – **pralaya**, m. pl. difference between solar and lunar days in any particular period, Āryabh. iii, 6. – **vāra-yoga**, m. pl. N. of a ch. of PSarv. – **viveka**, m. N. of a work, Smṛitit. – **sāraṇikā**, f. N. of a work by Daśa-bala. **Tithīśa**, m. = *°thi-pati*.

Tithī, f. a lunar day, MBh. xiii, 4238.

Tithy, in comp for *°thi*. – **anta-nirṇaya**, m. N. of a ch. of the Smṛity-artha-sāra. – **ardha**, m. n. half of a Tithi, i. e. a Karaṇa (in astron.)

तिनाशक *tināśaka*, = *°niśa*, L.

तिनिका *tinikā*, f. Holcus Sorghum, Npr

तिनिश *tiniśa*, m. Dalbergia Ujjeinensis, R. iii, 17, 7; 21, 15; 79, 37; Suśr. i, iv, vi; cf. *timiśa*.

तिन्तिड *tintiḍa*, m. (also *titt°*, L.) = *°ḍikā*, L.; N. of a Daitya, L.; = *kāla-dāsa*, L.; m. & (*ī*), f. sour sauce (esp. made of the tamarind fruit), L.; (*ī*), f. = *°ḍikā*, VarBṛS. lv, 21; = *ḍimba*, L.

Tintiḍikā, f. the tamarind tree, Car. i, 27.

Tintiḍī, f. of *°ḍa*, q. v. – **dyūta**, n. a kind of game (odd and even played with tamarind seeds), L. – **phala**, n. the sour skin of a Garcinia fruit, L.

Tintiḍīka, m. (*titt°*, Pāṇ. iv, 3, 156, Vārtt. 2, Pat.; *tittirīka*, Suśr. vi, 39, 272) the tamarind tree (also *ā*, f., L., Sch.), (n.) its fruit, Suśr. i, iv; n. sour sauce (esp. made of the tamarind fruit), L.

Tintilikā, *°lī*, f. = *°tiḍikā*, L., Sch.

Tintilīka, n. the tamarind fruit, Car. i, 26 (*°tinīka*, v. l.); (*ā*), f. = *°likā*, ĀpGṛ. vi, 5, Sch.

तिन्दिनी *tindinī*, f. = *°du*, q. v.

तिन्दिश *tindiśa*, m. N. of a plant, L.

तिन्दु *tindu*, m. Diospyros embryopteris, L. (also *°dinī*, Gal.); Strychnos nux vomica (also *°duka*), Npr. – **bilva**, n. N. of a place, Gīt. iii, 10, Sch.

Tinduka, m. Diospyros embryopteris, (n.) its fruit (yielding a kind of resin used as pitch for caulking vessels &c.), MBh.; R.; Suśr.; VarBṛS. &c.; m. = *°du*, q. v.; n. a kind of weight (= *karsha*; = *suvarṇa*, Car. vii, 12), ŚārṅgS. i, 21; Ashṭâṅg.; (*ī*), f. = *°ki*, Suśr. iv, 2, 42 & 21, 8; VarBṛS. lxxix; Kāś.

Tinduki, f. Diospyros embryopteris, L. **Tindukinī,** f. the senna plant, L. **Tindula,** m. = °*duki*, L.

तिप् *tip*, cl. 1. P. *tepati* (Pāṇ. vii, 2, 10, Kār.) to sprinkle, Dhātup. x, 1.

तिप्य *tipya*, N. of a man, Rājat. viii, 15, 5.

तिम् *tim* (= √*stim*), cl. 4. P. °*myati*, to become quiet, Hit.; to become wet (also *tīmy*° fr. √*tīm*), Dhātup.: Intens. *tetimyate*, Pāṇ. vii, 4, Kāś.

Timita, mfn. (= *stim*°) quiet, steady, fixed, R. ii f., v; wet, L. **Tema,** m. = *st*°, the becoming wet, L.

Temana, n. moisture, L.; moistening, L.; a sauce, L.; (*ī*), f. a sort of fire-place, L.

तिम *tima*, m. = °*mi*, a kind of whale, L., Sch.; (*ī*), f. a fish, L.

Timi, m. a kind of whale or fabulous fish of an enormous size, MBh.; Hariv. 4915; R.; VarBṛS. &c.; a fish, Kathās. v, lx; the sign Pisces, VarBṛ., Sch.; the figure of a fish produced by drawing two lines (one intersecting the other at right angles), Sūryas. iii, 3 f.; the ocean, L.; N. of a son of Dūrva (father of Bṛihad-ratha), BhP. ix, 22, 41; f. N. of a daughter of Daksha (wife of Kaśyapa and mother of the sea-monsters), vi, 6, 25 f. **-kośa,** m. 'T°-receptacle,' the ocean, L. **-ghātin,** m. 'fish-killer,' a fisherman, Kathās. lx, 186. **-ṃ-gira,** m. 'T°-swallower,' N. of a Nāga, Kāraṇḍ. i. **-ṃ-gila,** m. (Pāṇ. vi, 3, 70, Vārtt. 7) 'id.,' a large fabulous fish, MBh.; BhP. viii; Vcar. vi; N. of a prince, MBh. ii, 1172; *-gila*, m. (Pāṇ. vi, 3, 70, Vārtt. 7, Pat.) 'Timiṃgila-swallower,' a large fabulous fish, Bālar. vii, 53; °*lāśana*, m. pl. 'eating Timiṃgilas,' N. of a people, VarBṛS. xiv, 16. **-ja,** mfn. coming from the T° (sort of pearl), lxxxi, 23. **-timiṃ-gila,** m. a large fabulous fish, MBh. iii, 12081; Divyâv. xxxv, 346. **-dhvaja,** m. 'T°-bannered,' N. of the Asura Sambara (R. [G] ii, 8, 12) or of one of his sons (R. ii, 44, 11). **-mālin,** m. 'T°-garlanded,' the ocean, W.

तिमिर *timira*, mf(*ā*)n. (fr. *tamar* [Old Germ. *demar*] = *támas*) dark, gloomy, MBh. vi, 2379; R. vi, 16, 104; = *-nayana*, VarBṛ. xx, 1, Sch.; m. a sort of aquatic plant (cf. *-vana*), VarBṛS. lv, 11; n. darkness (also pl.), Yājñ. iii, 172; MBh. &c. (ifc. f. *ā*, R. v, 10, 2; Kathās. xviii); darkness of the eyes, partial blindness (a class of morbid affections of the coats [*paṭala*] of the eye), Suśr. i, iii, v f.; Ashṭâṅg. vi, 13; Rājat. iv, 314; iron-rust, Npr.; N. of a town, R. iv, 40, 26; (*ā*), f. another town, Kathās. xvii, 33; cf. *vi-*, *sa-*. **-cchid,** m. 'darkness-splitter,' the sun, Kir. vi, 36. **-tā,** f. darkness of the eyes, partial blindness, Hāsy. (v. l. °*râkula-tā*). **-nayana,** mfn. suffering from partial blindness, VarBṛ. xx, 1. **-nāśana,** m. 'darkness-destroyer,' the sun, Hcat. i, 11. **-nud,** m. 'darkness-dispeller,' sun, moon, VarBṛS. iv, 45. **-paṭala,** n. the veil of darkness, Prab. vi. **-pratishedha,** m. N. of Ashṭâṅg. vi, 13. **-maya,** mfn. consisting of darkness, Kād.; m. Rāhu, VarBṛS. v, 48. **-ripu,** m. 'darkness-enemy,' the sun, L. **-vana,** n. a multitude of *timira* plants, g. *kshubhnâdi*; Pāṇ. viii, 4, 6, Pat. **Timirâkula,** mfn. affected with partial blindness, Hāsy. ii, 21; *-tā*, f., see °*ra-tā*. **Timirâpagata,** m. N. of a Samādhi, Buddh. L. **Timirâpaha,** mfn. dispelling darkness (fire), MBh. iii, 14113 ff. **Timirâri,** m. = °*ra-ripu*, L., Sch.; *-ripu*, m. 'enemy of the sun,' an owl, Subh. **Timirôdghāṭa,** m. 'removal of darkness,' N. of a Śaiva treatise in verse.

Timiraya, Nom. P. °*yati*, to obscure, BhP. iii, 15, 10; Hit. °**rāya,** Nom. Ā. °*yate*, to appear dark, Mahān. iv, 27. **Timirin,** m. the cochineal, Npr.

तिमिरि *timiri*, m. a kind of fish, L.

तिमिर्घ *timirgha*, m. N. of a Nāga priest, TāṇḍyaBr. xxv, 15, 3.

तिमिला *timilā*, f. N. of a musical instrument, Hcat. i, 6, 322.

तिमिश *timiśa*, m. N. of a tree, R. ii, 94, 8; [B] iii, 15, 16; cf. *tiniśa*. **Timisha,** m. N. of a plant (Beninkasa cerifera, L.; water-melon, L.), Hcat. i, 9, 134 (MatsyaP.); cf. *rāja-*; *dīrgha-timishā*.

तिमीर *timīra*, m. N. of a tree (cf. °*mira*), R. iii, 21, 19; v, 74, 3.

तिम्मय *timmaya*, m. N. of a man.

तिरः *tiraḥ*, in comp. for °*rás*. **-√kṛi,** see °*rás*-√*kṛi*. **-prātiveśya,** m. a near neighbour, Divyâv. xviii, 117; (also *tiraskṛita-pr*°, 134).

Tiraya, Nom. P. (fr. °*rás*) °*yati*, to conceal, hide, prevent from appearing, Mālatim. ix, 30; Śiś. vi, 64; Ratnâv. &c.; to hinder, stop, restrain, Mālatim. i, 35; Ratnâv. &c.; to pervade, Bālar. ii, 57.

Tiraśc, weak base of °*ryáñc*, q. v.

Tiraścá, n. the cross-board of a bedstead, AV. xv, 3, 5 (v. l. °*ścyà*). **-tā** (°*ścá-*), ind. transversely, RV. iv, 18, 2; ix, 14, 6; Suparṇ. xxiii, 1. **-thā** (°*ścá-*), ind. aside, secretly, ŚBr. iii, 7, 3, 7.

Tiraści, loc. of °*ryáñc*, q. v. **-rāji** (*tír*°), mfn. striped across (a serpent), AV. iii, 27, 2; vi f., x, xii.

Tiraścikā, f. = °*ryag-diś* (?), ĀśvŚr. i, 2, 1.

Tiraścī, m. N. of a Ṛishi (descendant of Aṅgiras, author of a Sāman), RV. viii, 95, 4 (gen. °*ścyás*); TāṇḍyaBr. xii, 6, 12 & ĀrshBr. (nom. °*ścī*).

Tiraścīna, mf(*ā*)n. transverse, horizontal, across, RV. x, 129, 5; AV. xix. 16, 2 (?); TS. &c.; (cf. *ā-*). **-nidhana,** n. N. of a Sāman, TāṇḍyaBr. xiv, 3, 21; Lāṭy. vi. **-pṛiśni** (°*ścīna-*), mfn. spotted across, VS. xxiv, 4. **-vaṇśa,** m. a bee-hive, ChUp. iii, 1, 1. **-vāya,** m. the cross-strap (of a couch), AitBr. viii, 12; 17. **Tiraścyà,** n. v. l. for °*ścá*, q. v.

Tirás, ind. (g. *svar-ādi*; √*tṛī*) through (acc.), RV.; AV. xiii, 1, 36; across, beyond, over (acc.), RV.; AV. vii, 38, 5; so as to pass by, apart from, without, against (acc.), RV. (°*rás cittāni*, 'without the knowledge,' vii, 59, 8; °*ró váśam*, 'against the will,' x, 171, 4); apart or secretly from (abl.), AV. xii, 3, 39; ŚBr. i, iii; obliquely, transversely, MārkP. xvii, 3; apart, secretly, TS. ii, 5, 10, 6; AitBr. ii; ŚBr.; [cf. Zd. *tarō*; Lat. *trans*; Goth. *thairh*; Germ. *durch*; Hib. *tar*, *tair*.] **-kara,** mf(*ī*)n. excelling (with gen.), BhP. i, 10, 27. **-karaṇi,** f. (for °*riṇi* = °*riṇī*?) a curtain, R. ii, 15, 20 (v. l. °*rin*). **-karin,** m., see °*raṇi*; (*iṇī*), f. id., Mālav. ii, 1 & 11; Kum. i, 4; Hcar. &c.; a magical veil rendering the wearer invisible, Śak. vi; Vikr. **-kāra,** m. placing aside, concealment, W.; abuse, censure, Hit. i, 2, $\frac{23}{24}$; iv; disdain, Pāṇ. ii, 3, 17, Kāś.; Kathās. xxxii, 55; ŚārṅgP.; a cuirass, Kir. xvii, 49. **-kārin,** mfn. ifc. excelling, Ratnâv. i, 25; (*iṇī*), f. = *-kar*°, L., Sch. **-kuḍya,** mfn. reaching through a wall, Buddh. L. **-√kṛi,** *-karoti* (also °*raḥ k*°, Pāṇ. i, 4, 72; viii, 3, 42; ind. p. *-kṛitya* [also °*raḥ kṛitvā*, ib.], KātyŚr. vi; Mn. iv, 49) to set aside, remove, cover, conceal, ŚBr. &c.; to excel, Ragh. iii, 8; Pañcat.; Bhaṭṭ. &c.; to blame, abuse, treat disrespectfully, despise, BhP.; Hit. **-kṛita,** mfn. concealed, R. ii; Amar.; Bhaṭṭ.; eclipsed, W.; excelled, Pañcat.; censured, reviled, despised, ib. (*a-*, neg.); *-prātiveśya*, m. = *tiraḥ-pr*°, q. v.; *-sambhāsha*, mfn. *a-*, neg. speaking together without abusing each other, MBh. iii, 233, 27. **-kṛiti,** f. reproach, disrespect (ifc.), Daśar. i, 41. **-kriyā,** f. id., Pañcat.; concealment, shelter, R. vi, 116, 27. **-paṭa,** m. = *-kariṇī*, Caurap. 49. **-prākāra,** mfn. = *-kuḍya*, Buddh. L.

Tirasya, Nom. P. °*syati*, to disappear, g. *kaṇḍv-ādi*. **Tiricīna,** mfn. = °*raśc*°, ĀpŚr. ii, 18, 9.

Tiro, in comp. for °*rás*. **-ahniya** (°*ró-*), mfn. = °*hnya*, TS. vii, 3, 13, 1. **-ahnya** (°*ró-*), mfn. (= °*ró-'h*°) 'more than one day old,' prepared the day before yesterday, RV. i, iii, viii. **-gata,** mfn. disappeared, W. **-janám,** ind. apart from men, AV. vii, 38, 5. **-1. -√dhā,** *-dadhāti* (pf. *-dadhe*), to set aside, remove, conquer, RV. vii, ix; AV. viii, xii; MBh. i, 728; BhP.; Sāh. iii, 175 (also Pass. *-dhīyate*, Sch.): Ā. *-dhatte* (pf. *-dadhe*) to hide one's self from (abl.), disappear, KenUp.; Ragh. x f.; BhP. &c. **-2. -dhā,** f. concealment, secrecy, AV. viii, 10, 28. **-dhātavya,** mfn. to be covered or closed (the ear), Mn. ii, 100, Sch. **-dhāna,** n. concealing, L.; a covering (sheath, veil, cloak, &c.), W.; disappearance, Pāṇ. i, 2, 33, Kāś.; BhP. iii, 20, 44. **-bhāvitri,** mf(*trī*)n. disappearing, 27, 23. **-bhāva,** m. disappearance, ChUp. vii, 26, 1; Sāṃkhyak. & KapS., Sch.; Sāh. **-√bhū,** *-bhavati*, to be set aside, disappear, vanish, hide one's self, AV. viii, 1, 7; ŚBr.; Ragh. &c.: Pass. *-bhūyate*, id., KapS. i, 121, Sch.: Caus. *-bhāvayati*, to cause to disappear, dispel, R. i, 44, 9: Intens. (Subj. *-bobhavat*) to try to disappear with (instr.) or conceal anything (instr.), ŚBr. ii, 2, 3, 16. **-varsha,** mfn. protected from rain, MBh. iv, 171. **-hita** (°*ró-*), mfn. removed or withdrawn from sight, concealed, hidden (a meaning), RV. iii, 9, 5; ŚBr. i; AitBr. viii, 27; Mn. &c.; run away, L.; *-tā*, f. disappearance, becoming invisible, Kathās. xxi, 145; *-tva*, n. id., RV. i, 113, 4, Sāy. **-'hnya** (°*ró-*), mfn. = *-ahnya*, ŚBr. xi; TāṇḍyaBr. i, 6; KātyŚr. xii, 6, 10; xxiv; Lāṭy. ii; cf. *tair*°.

1. **Tirya,** for °*yag* in comp. **-ga,** mfn. = °*ryag-*, VarBṛS.: m. 'air-goer,' a Siddha, MBh. xiii, 5755.

Tiryák, ind., see °*yáñc*; in comp. also for °*yáñc*. **-kāram,** ind. having laid aside (after the completion of any work), the work being done, Pāṇ. iii, 4, 60; cf. *tīraya*. **-kṛitya,** ind. id., ib. **-kshipta,** mfn. placed obliquely, L.; said of a form of dislocation (when a part of the joint is forced outwards), Suśr. ii, 15, 2 f. **-tā,** f. animal nature, Rājat. iii, 448. **-tva,** n. id., Mn. xii, 40 & 68; Yājñ. iii; MārkP.; Rājat.; = *-pramāṇa*, KātyŚr. viii, 6, 7, Sch. **-pātana,** n. a kind of process applied esp. to mercury. **-pātin,** mfn. falling obliquely on (loc.), Śiś. x, 40. **-pratimukhâgata,** mfn. come from the side or in front of, Mn. viii, 291. **-pramāṇa,** n. measurement across, breadth, KātyŚr. i f., Sch. (*purastāt-*, 'breadth in front;' *paścāt-*, 'breadth behind.') **-prêkshaṇa,** mfn. = °*kshin*, BhP. v, 26, 36; n. an oblique glance, W. **-prêkshin,** mfn. looking obliquely, MBh. ii, v. **-phalā,** f. Oldenlandia herbacea, L. **-sūtra,** n. a cross-line, W. **-srotas,** mfn. (an animal) in which the current of nutriment tends transversely, R. ii, 35, 19, Sch.; m. n. animals collectively, VP. i, 5, 8; MārkP. viii; NarasP. iii, 25.

Tiryag, in comp. for °*yák* & °*yáñc*. **-anūka,** n. the breadth of the back part of the altar, KātyŚr. xvii, 11, 1, Sch. **-antara,** n. = °*yak-pramāṇa*, L. **-apaccheda,** m. separation made transversely, ii, 4, 37, Sch. **-apâṅga,** mfn. having the outer corners of the eye turned aside, Vṛishabh. i, $1\frac{1}{2}$. **-ayana,** n. 'horizontal course,' the sun's annual revolution (opposed to its diurnal revolution in which it rises and sets vertically), see *tairyagayanika*. **-āgata,** mfn. lying across (at birth; said of a particular position of the child), Suśr. iv, 15, 6. **-āyata,** mfn. stretched out obliquely (a snake), MBh. i. **-īksha,** mfn. = °*yak-prêkshin*, xii, 6575. **-īśa,** m. 'lord of the animals,' Kṛishṇa, vii, 6471. **-ga,** mf(*ā*)n. going obliquely or horizontally, Suśr. i, 14, 1; ii, 1; iii, 9; going towards the north or south, R. (G) ii, 12, 6. **-gata,** mfn. going horizontally (an animal), ii, 35, 17; n. an animal, vii, 110, 19. **-gati,** f. the state of an animal in transmigration, MBh. iii, 1166; *-matin*, n. an animal, xiv, 1138. **-gama,** mfn. going obliquely, vii, 1162. **-gamana,** n. motion sideways, VPrāt. i, Sch. **-gāmin,** m. '= *-gama*,' a crawfish, L. **-guṇana,** n. oblique multiplication. **-grīvam,** ind. so as to have the neck turned aside, Bhām. ii, 130. **-ghātin,** mfn. striking obliquely (an elephant), L. **-ja,** mfn. born or begotten by an animal, Mn. x, 72. **-jana,** m. an animal, BhP. ii, 7, 46. **-jāti,** mfn. belonging to the race of animals, W.; m. an animal, Kād.; f. the brute kind, W. **-jyā,** f. an oblique chord, W. **-dina,** n. flying horizontally, MBh. viii, 41, 26. **-diś,** f. any horizontal region (opposed to nadir and zenith), Hemac. **-dhāra,** mfn. 'having oblique edges,' see *tigma-dh*°. **-nāsa,** mf(*ā*)n. wry-nosed, R. v, 17, 32. **-bila** (°*ryág-*), mfn. having its opening on the side, AV. x, 8, 9. **-bhedā,** f. 'broken sideways,' an oblong brick, Śulbas. **-yavôdara,** n. a barley-corn, W. **-yāta,** mfn. = *-gama*, MBh. vii, 26, 36. **-yāna,** m. = *-gāmin*, L. **-yona,** m. (= *tairy*°) an animal ('bird,' Sch.), Mn. vii, 149. **-yoni,** f. the womb of an animal, animal creation, organic nature (including plants), Mn. iv, 200; MBh. xiii; R. vii, &c.; mfn. born of or as an animal, W.; *-gamana*, n. sexual intercourse with an animal, Prāyaśc.; °*nyanvaya*, m. the animal race, W.; mfn. of the animal race, W. **-vāta-sevā,** f. 'attending the side-wind,' urining or evacuation by stool, Gaut. ii, 27. **-viddha,** mfn. pierced obliquely (a vein in bleeding by an unskilful operator), Suśr. iii, 8, 17. **-visaṃsarpin,** mfn. expanding sideways, Ragh. vi, 15.

Tiryaṅ, in comp. for °*yák* & °*yáñc*. **-nāsa,** see °*yag-n*°. **-niraya,** m. animal nature as a (hell or) punishment for evil deeds, MBh. iii, 12626. **-mānī,** f. = °*yak-pramāṇa*, Śulbas. i, 38; iii, 174.

Tiryáñc, mfn. (fr. *tirás* + *añc*, Pāṇ. vi, 3, 94; nom. m. °*ryáṅ*, n. °*ryák*, f. °*rá́ścī*, also °*ryañcī*, Vop. iv, 12) going or lying crosswise or transversely or obliquely, oblique, transverse (opposed to *anváñc*), horizontal (opposed to *ūrdhvá*), AV.; VS.; TS. &c.; going across, ŚBr. xiv, 9, 3, 2 f.; moving tortuously, W.; curved, crooked, W.; meandering, W.; lying in the middle or between (a tone), xi, 4, 2, 5 ff.; VPrāt. i, 149; m. n. 'going horizontally,' an animal (amphibious animal, bird, &c.), Mn. v, 40;

xii, 57; Yājñ.; MBh. &c.; the organic world (including plants), Jain.; n. = °*ryak-pramāṇa*, Śulbas.; f. the female of any animal, W.; (°*ryák*), ind. across, obliquely, transversely, horizontally, sideways, ŚBr.; KātyŚr.; ŚāṅkhŚr.; VPrāt.; Mn. &c.; (°*raścā*), instr. ind., id., RV. i, 61, 12; ii, 10, 4; x, 79, 4; (°*raścí*), loc. ind., id., ŚBr. ii, 3, 2, 12; KātyŚr. xvii, 8, 14 & 12, 1. **Tiryadryañc**, mfn. = *tiryáñc*, Gal.

तिरिगिच्छि *tirigicchi*, m. N. of a plant, L.

Tiri-jihvikā, N. of a plant, Npr.

Tiriṇī-kaṇṭa, id., ib.

तिरिट *tiriṭa*, m. = °*ṭi*, W.

Tiriṭi, m. the joint of the sugar-cane, L.

तिरिन्दिर *tiríndira*, m. N. of a man, RV. viii, 6, 46; ŚāṅkhŚr. xvi, 11, 20.

तिरिम *tirima*, m. a kind of rice, L.

Tiriya, m. id., L.; cf. 2. *tiryà*.

तिरीट *tirīṭa*, m. Symplocos racemosa, Bhpr. iv; n. a kind of head-dress, tiara, diadem (cf. *kir°*), L.; gold, Uṇ., Sch. °**ṭaka**, m. Symplocos racemosa, Car. vii, 9, 1; a kind of bird, R. iii, 78, 23. °**ṭin**, mfn. furnished with a head-dress, AV. viii, 6, 7.

तिरोअह्निय *tiró-ahniya* &c. See p. 447, col. 2.

तिर्पिरिक *tirpirika*, for *tilvirīka*, q.v.

तिर्य 2. *tiryà*, mfn. for *tilyà*? prepared from sesamum seeds (? *tíla*), AV. iv, 7, 3; cf. *tiriya*.

तिर्यक् *tiryák*, °*ryáñc*. See p. 447, col. 3.

तिल् 1. *til*, cl. 1. *telati*, to go, Dhātup.

तिल् 2. *til* (derived fr. *tíla*), cl. 6. 10. °*lati*, *telayati*, to be unctuous, ib.; to anoint, ib.

Tila, m. Sesamum indicum (its blossom is compared to the nose, Gīt. x, 14; Siṇhās.; cf. *-pushpa*), s° seed (much used in cookery; supposed to have originated from Vishṇu's sweat-drops, Hcat. i, 6, 137 & 142), AV. (°*lá*, xviii, 4, 32); VS.; ŚBr. &c.; a mole, Kālid.; a small particle, MBh. &c.; the right lung, ŚārṅgS. v, 42; pl. N. of a ch. of PSarv.; (cf. *kṛishṇa-*, *carma-*, *shaṇḍha-*). **-kaṭa**, m. the farina of s°, Pāṇ. v, 2, 29, Vārtt. 1. **-kaṇa**, m. a s° seed, Bhartṛ. (v. l. *-khali*). **-kalka**, m. dough made of ground s°, Suśr. i; MārkP. xxxv, 10; *-ja*, s° oil-cake, Npr.; cf. *tail°*. **-kārshika**, mfn. cultivating s°, Kathās. lxi, 7 & 9. **-kālaka**, m. a mole, Suśr. i f., iv; Pāṇ. iii, 2, 52; Pat.; 53, Kāś.; N. of a disease of the penis, Suśr. ii, 14, 16; iv, 21, 16; mfn. having a mole, L., Sch. **-kiṭṭa**, n. = *-kalka-ja*, Bhpr. v, 11, 180; cf. *tail°*. **-khali**, m. id., ib. **-khalī**, f. id., Npr. **-gañji** or °**jin**, n. N. of a Tīrtha, Rasik. xi, 32. **-grāma**, m. N. of a village, Rājat. viii, 2933. **-caturthī**, f. the 4th day of the dark half of Māgha, Vratapr. iv. **-citra-pattraka**, m. N. of a bulbous plant, L. **-cūrṇa**, n. ground s°, Pañcat. ii, 3, $\frac{4}{5}$. **-taṇḍulaka**, n. 'agreeable as rice mixed with s°,' an embrace, L. **-tejāhvā**, f. N. of a plant, Suśr. iv, 2, 92. **-taila**, n. (Pāṇ. v, 2, 29, Vārtt. 4, Pat.) s°-oil, Suśr. i; iv, 31, 2. **-dêśvara-tīrtha**, n. N. of a Tīrtha, RevāKh. cccxxx; cf. *tilakêś°*. **-droṇa-maya**, mfn. consisting of a Droṇa of s°, Hcat. i, 8, 378. **-dvādaśī**, f. the 12th day of a particular month (kept as a festival), Rājat. v, 394; BhavP. ii, 78. **-dhenu**, f. a s° cow (presented to Brāhmans), MBh. xiii, 64, 35 & 71, 40; *-dāna*, n. 'presenting a *tila-dhenu*,' N. of LiṅgaP. ii, 33 & VarP. ic. **-dhenukā**, f. = °*nu*, MBh. iii, 84, 87. **-m-tuda**, m. a s°-grinder, Pāṇ. iii, 2, 28, Vārtt. **-parṇa**, m. the resin of Pinus longifolia, L.; n. a s° leaf, W.; sandal-wood, Bhpr. v, 2, 16; (*ī*), f. the resin of Pinus longifolia, L.; Pterocarpus santalinus, Suśr. i, 39, 8 & 46, 4, 29; olibanum, L. **-°parṇaka**, n. sandal-wood, L., Sch.; (*ikā*), f. a kind of pot-herb, Car. i, 27, 86; Pterocarpus santalinus, Suśr. i, 46, 4, 11. **-°parṇika**, n. sandal-wood, v, 7, 12; the resin of Pinus longifolia, Gal.; (*ā*), f., see °*rṇaka*; cf. *tail°*. **-piccaṭa**, n. = *-kalka-ja*, W. **-piñja**, m. = *-peja*, Pāṇ. iv, 2, 36, Vārtt. 6; white s°, Npr.; (*ī*), f. N. of a plant, AV. ii, 8, 3. **-pīḍa**, m. = *-m-tuda*, MBh. xii; cf. *tail°*. **-pushpa**, n. 's°-flower,' the nose, Kuval. 224. **-pushpaka**, m. Terminalia Bellerica, Npr. **-peja**, m. barren s°, Pāṇ. iv, 2, 36, Vārtt. 6. **-bhāra**, m. pl. N. of a people, MBh. vi, 360. **-bhāvinī**, f. jasmine, Npr. **-bhṛishṭa**, see *-sṛishṭa*. **-maya**, mf(*ī*)n. (Pāṇ. iv, 3, 149) consisting or made of s° seeds, Hcat. i, 6, 182 & 7, 37. **-mayūra**, m. a kind of peacock, L. **-māsha** (°*lá-*), m. pl. s° and beans, ŚBr. xiv, 9, 3, 22. **-miśra** (°*lá-*), mf(*ā*)n. mixed with s°, AV. xviii, 3, 69 (& 4, 26); Kauś. **-miśla**, mfn. id., MānGṛ. i, 21. **-rasa**, m. = *-taila*, L. **-vatsa** (°*lá-*), mf.(*ā*)n. having s°-seeds for children, AV. xviii, 4, 33 f. **-vratin**, mfn. fasting by eating only s°-seeds, Pāṇ. v, 1, 94, Vārtt. 3, Pat.; cf. °*lôdara*. **-śas**, ind. in pieces as small as s°-seeds, Mbh. &c. **-śikhin**, m. = *-mayūra*, Gal. **-sambaddha**, mfn. = *-miśra*, Mn. iv, 75. **-sṛishṭa**, food prepared with s°, MBh. xiii, 104, 70 (°*la-bhṛishṭa*, 'fried s°-seeds,' C.) **-snāyin**, mfn. washing one's self with s°, Hcat. i, 8, 297. **-sneha**, m. = *-taila*, L. **-homa**, m. s°-oblation. **-°homin**, mfn. offering s°-oblations, Hcat. i, 8, 297. **Tilâṅśa**, m. a piece (of land) as small as a s°-seed, Rājat. i, 38. **Tilâṅkita-dala**, m. a kind of bulb, L. **Tilânna**, n. rice with s°-seeds, L. **Tilâpatyā**, f. Nigella indica, L. **Tilâmbu**, n. water with s°, BhP. vii, 8, 44. **Tilôttamā**, f. N. of an Apsaras, MBh. &c.; of a woman, Rājat. vii, 120; a form of Dākshāyaṇī, MatsyaP. xiii, 53; °*mīya*, Nom. P. to represent the Apsaras Tilôttamā, Bhām. ii, 96. **Tilôdaka**, n. (Pāṇ. vi, 2, 96, Kāś.) = °*lâmbu*, Gobh. iv; Mn.; MBh.; MārkP. **Tilôdakin**, mfn. drinking °*ka*, Hcat. i, 8, 297. **Tilôdana**, = °*lâud°*, R. ii, 69, 10. **Tilôdara**, mf(*ā*, *ī*)n. having the stomach filled with s° (cf. °*la-vratin*), Pāṇ. iv, 1, 55, Kāś. **Tilâudana**, n. a s°-dish, ŚBr. xiv, 9, 4, 16; Kauś. 138.

Tilaka, m. (g. *sthūlâdi*) Clerodendrum phlomoides (Symplocos racemosa, L.), MBh. &c.; a freckle (compared to a sesamum-seed), VarBṛS. l, 9; lii, 10; Kathās.; a kind of skin-eruption, L.; (in music) N. of a Dhruvaka; a kind of horse, L.; N. of a prince of Kampanā, Rājat. viii, 577 ff.; m. (n. Pañcad. ii, 57) a mark on the forehead (made with coloured earths, sandal-wood, or unguents, either as an ornament or a sectarial distinction), Yājñ. i, 293; MBh. iii, 11591; R. (ifc. f. *ā*, iii) &c.; the ornament of anything (in comp.), Pañcat. i, 1, 92; Kathās. &c. (ifc. f. *ā*, Rājat. iii, 375); n. id., L.; the right lung, L.; black sochal salt, L.; alliteration, Rājat.; a metre of 4 × 6 syllables; = *tri-śloki*, L.; a kind of observance, Kālanirṇ. Introd. 12; (*ā*), f. a kind of necklace, L.; cf. *eṇa-*, *kha-*, *vasanta-*; *ūrdhva-tilakin*. **-mañjarī**, f. N. of a work. **-rāja**, m. N. of a man, Rājat. vii, 1319. **-latā**, f. N. of a woman, Vāsant. **-vatī**, f. N. of a river, Vām. v, 2, 75. **-vrata**, n. the T° observance, BhavP. ii, 8; Vratapr. i. **-siṇha**, m. N. of a man, Rājat. viii. **Tilakâcārya**, m. N. of a pupil of Śivaprabha (author of Pratyekabuddha-catushṭaya and of comments on Āvaśyaka, Śrāvaka- & Sādhu-pratikramaṇa). **Tilakâvala**, mfn. (cf. Pāṇ. vi, 3, 118) furnished with marks, ŚāṅkhŚr. xvi, 18, 18. **Tilakâśraya**, m. 'T°-receptacle,' the forehead, L. **Tilakêśvara-tīrtha**, n. N. of a Tīrtha, RevāKh. cxiii. **Tilakôttara**, m. N. of a Vidyādhara, Bālar. iv, 7.

Tilakaka, n. N. of a man, Rājat. viii, 469.

Tilakaya, Nom. P. to mark with spots, HPariś. viii, 210; to mark, Bālar. i, 1; vi, 37; to adorn, i, 1; Viddh. ii, 13. **Tilakāyita**, n. impers. it has been acted as an ornament to (gen.), Nalac. i, 20.

Tilakita, mfn. (g. *tārakâdi*) marked, Bālar. vi, 55 & 58; adorned, Kathās. xciii, 17; Rājat. ii, 40.

Tilakin, mfn. marked with the Tilaka.

Tilpiñja, m. (Pāṇ. iv, 2, 36, Vārtt. 7) = °*la-peja*, AV. xii, 2, 54; cf. Kauś. 80.

Tilya, mfn. suited for sesamum cultivation, grown with s°, Pāṇ. v, 1, 7 & 2, 4; n. a s° field, ib.

तिलिङ्ग *tiliṅga*, N. of a country, Romakas.; Ratnak.

तिलित्स *tilitsa*, m. a kind of snake, L.

तिल्पिञ्ज *tilpíñja*, *tilya*. See above.

तिल्पिलिक *tilpilika*, for *tilvilīka*, q.v.

तिल्ल् *till*, cl. 1. P. to go, Dhātup. xv, 27.

तिल्व *tilva*, m. = °*lvaka*, L.

Tilvaka, m. Symplocos racemosa, ŚBr. xiii; KātyŚr. xxi, 3, 20; Gobh. &c.; Terminalia Catappa, Npr.

तिल्विरीक *tilvirīka*. See °*lvilīka*.

तिल्विल *tílvila*, mf(*ā*)n. fertile, RV. v, 62, 7; ĀśvGṛ. ii, 8, 16; ŚāṅkhGṛ. iii, 3, 1; cf. *ibhya-*.

Tilvilāya, Nom. °*yáte*, to be fertile, RV. vii, 78, 5. **Tilvilīka** or °**lvirīka**, m. g. *kapilakâdi*.

तिव्य *tivya*, m. N. of a Brāhman, Rājat.

तिष्ठद् *tishṭhad*, = °*shṭhat*, pr. p. √*sthā*, q.v. **-gu**, ind. (Pāṇ. ii, 1, 17) 'when the cows (*go*) stand to be milked,' after sunset, Bhaṭṭ. iv, 14. **-dhoma**, mfn. (a sacrifice) at which the oblation (*homa*) is offered standing, KātyŚr. i, 2, 6.

तिष्य *tishyà*, m. N. of a heavenly archer (like Kṛiśānu) and of the 6th Nakshatra of the old or 8th of the new order, RV. v, 54, 13; x, 64, 8; TS. (°*shyá*) &c.; the month Pausha, L.; Terminalia tomentosa, L.; = °*shyā*, L.; (Pāṇ. iv, 3, 34; i, 2, 63, Kāś.) 'born under the asterism T°,' a common N. of men, Buddh. (cf. *upa-*); n. (m., L.) the 4th or present age, MBh. vi; Hariv. 3019; mfn. auspicious, fortunate, W.; (*ā*), f. Emblic Myrobalan, L. **-ketu**, m. Śiva. **-gupta**, m. N. of the founder of schism 2. of the Jain community. **-°punarvasavīya**, mfn. relating to the asterisms T° and Punar-vasu, Pāṇ. iv, 2, 6, Kāś. **-punarvasu**, m. du. the asterisms T° and P°, i, 2, 63 & (n. sg.) Kāś. **-pushpā**, f. = *tishyā*, L. **-phalā**, f. id., L. **-rakshitā**, f. N. of Aśoka's 2nd wife, Buddh. (Divyâv. xxvii). **Tishyā-pūrṇamāsá**, m. the day of conjunction of the asterism T° with full moon, TS.

Tishyaka, m. the month Pausha, L.

तिसृ *tisṛi*, f. pl. of *trí*, q.v.; ifc. see *priya-*. **-dhanvá**, n. a bow with 3 arrows, TS.; TBr.; ŚBr.

Tisṛikā, f. N. of a village, Pāṇ. vii, 2, 99, Vārtt. 1. **Tisras-kāram**, ind. so as to change into 3 (Ṛic verses), ĀśvŚr. v, 15, 5. **Tisrā**, f. Andropogon, Npr.

तिहन् *tihan*, m. sickness, Uṇ. vṛ.; = *sadbhāva*, ib.; rice, ib.; a bow, ib.

तीक् *tīk*, cl. 1. Ā. to go, Dhātup. iv, 32.

तीक्ष्ण *tīkshṇá*, mf(*ā*)n. (√*tij*) sharp, hot, pungent, fiery, acid, RV. x, 87, 9; AV. &c.; harsh, rough, rude, Mn. vii, 140; MBh.; R.; VarBṛS.; sharp, keen, Śiś. ii, 109; Pāṇ. v, 2, 76, Kāś.; zealous, vehement, L.; self-abandoning, L.; (with *gati*, 'a planet's course,' or *nakshatra* 'asterism') inauspicious, VarBṛS. vii, 8 & 10; iic, 7 (asterisms Mūla, Ārdrā, Jyeshṭhā, Ā-sleshā); m. nitre, L.; = *-taṇḍulā*, Npr.; black pepper, ib.; black mustard, ib.; = *-gandhaka*, ib.; = *-sārā*, ib.; majoram, ib.; white Kuśa or Darbha grass, ib.; the resin of Boswellia thurifera, ib.; an ascetic, L.; (g. *aśvâdi*) N. of a man, Rājat. viii, 1742 f.; of a Nāga, Buddh. L.; n. pl. sharp language, R. ii, 35, 33; MārkP. xxxiv, 46; sg. steel (cf. *-varman*), Npr.; iron, L.; any weapon, L., Sch.; sea-salt, L.; nitre, L.; Galmei, Npr.; poison, L.; Bignonia suaveolens, L.; Piper Chaba, L.; Asa fœtida, Npr.; battle, L.; pestilence, L.; death, L., Sch.; heat, pungency, W.; haste, W.; (*ā*), f. N. of several plants (Mucuna pruritus, Cardiospermum Halicacabum, black mustard, *atyamla-parṇī*, *mahā-jyotishmatī*, *vacā*, *sarpa-kaṅkālikā*), Npr.; a mystical N. of the letter *p*, Rāmat. i, 77; cf. *a-*, *su-*. **-kaṇṭa**, m. Alhagi Maurorum, L. **-kaṇṭaka**, m. 'sharp-thorn,' Capparis aphylla, Suśr. i, 8, 2; thorn-apple, L.; Terminalia Catappa, L.; Acacia arabica, Npr.; Euphorbia tortilis, ib.; = *varvūra*, L.; (*ā*), f. a kind of Opuntia, L. **-kanda**, m. 'pungent root,' the onion, L. **-kara**, m. 'hot-rayed,' the sun, Kathās. civ, 203. **-karman**, n. a clever work, L.; m. 'sharp in action,' a sword, L.; °*rma-kṛit*, mfn. acting in a clever manner, L. **-kalka**, m. coriander, L. **-kāntā**, f. 'fond of cruelty,' a form of Caṇḍikā, KālP. **-gandha**, m. 'having a pungent smell,' = °*dhaka*, L.; majoram, L.; the resin of Boswellia thurifera, L.; (*ā*), f. N. of several plants (= °*dhaka*, = *-kaṇṭakā*, Sinapis ramosa, *jīvantī*, *vacā*, *śveta-vacā*, L.), Suśr. vi, 23, 2; small cardamoms, L. **-gandhaka**, m. Moringa pterygosperma, L. **-taṇḍulā**, f. long pepper, L. **-tara** (°*ṇá-*), mfn. Compar. sharper, AV. iii, 19, 4; (speech) Mālav. iii, 2; more hot (rays), Ṛitus. i, 18. **-tā**, f. sharpness, R. iii, 19, 7; BhP. vi, 5. **-tuṇḍa**, mf(*ā*)n. sharp-beaked, Suśr. vi, 30, 8. **-taila**, n. 'pungent oil,' the resin of Shorea robusta, L.; the milky juice of Euphorbia lactea, L.; spirituous liquor, L. **-tva**, n. heat, Sūryas. vi, 13. **-daṇshṭrá**, mfn. having sharp teeth or tusks, TĀr. x, 1, 6; MBh.; (*sa-*) VarBṛS.; m. a tiger, L.; N. of a man, Kathās. cix, 55. **-daṇshṭraka**, m. a leopard, Npr. **-daṇḍa**, mfn. directing sharp punishment, Mudr. i, $\frac{22}{23}$. **-dhāra**, mfn. sharp-edged, MBh.; R.; m. a sword, MBh. xii, 6203. **-dhāraka**, m. a kind of weapon, Gal. **-nāsika**, mfn. pointed-nosed, ib. **-pattra**, m. 'pungent-leaved,' coriander, L.; Terminalia Catappa, Npr.; a kind of sugar-cane, ib. **-pushpa**, n. 'pungent flower,' cloves, L.; (*ā*), f.

Pandanus odoratissimus, L.; the clove tree, Npr. **-priya**, m. = *-śūka*, Npr. **-phala**, m. 'pungent-fruited,' coriander, L.; black mustard, Npr.; = *te-jah-phala*, L. **-buddhi**, mfn. sharp-witted. **-mañjarī**, f. the betel plant, Npr. **-mārga**, m. a sword, Śiś. xviii, 20. **-mūla**, m. 'pungent-rooted,' = *-gandhaka*, L.; Alpinia Galanga, L. **-raśmi**, mfn. hot-rayed (the sun), Hariv. 3839. **-rasa**, m. 'pungent liquid,' poison; saltpetre, L.; *-dāyin*, m. a poisoner, Mudr. ii, $\frac{7}{8}$. **-rūpin**, mfn. looking cross, Gaut. xxvi, 12. **-lavaṇa**, mfn. pungent, Suśr. i. **-loha**, n. 'sharp iron,' steel, Bhpr. v, 175. **-vaktra**, mfn. sharp-pointed (arrow), MBh. vii, 123, 30. **-varman**, mfn. steel-cuirassed (?), xii, 4428. **-vipāka**, mfn. pungent during digestion, i, 716. **-visha**, m. virulent poison, xiii, 268; mfn. having virulent poison, W. **-vṛishaṇa**, m. 'strong-testicled,' N. of a bull, Pañcat. ii, 6, $\frac{8}{9}$. **-vega**, m. 'possessing great velocity,' N. of a Rakshas, R. vi, 69, 11. **-śastra**, n. iron or steel, L. **-śigru**, m. = *-gandhaka*, Gal. **-śūka**, m. 'sharp-awned,' barley, L. **-śṛiṅga** (°*ṇá-*), mfn. sharp-horned, AV. xix, 50, 2; (f. °*gī*) iv, 37, 6 & viii, 7, 9. **-sāra**, m. Bassia latifolia, Npr.; = °*rā*, L.; n. iron, Npr.; (*ā*), f. Dalbergia Sissoo, L. **-srotas**, mfn. having a violent current, R. iv. **-hṛidaya-tva**, n. hard-heartedness, MBh. i, 787. **Tīkshṇâṅśu**, mfn. = °*ṇa-raśmi*, R.; Suśr.; m. the sun, VarBṛ.; Laghuj.; Sūryas.; ifc., MBh. i; *-tanaya*, m. 'sun-son,' Saturn, VarBṛ. xi, 6; *-deha-prabhava*, m. id., ii, 12, Sch. **Tīkshṇâgni**, m. 'acrid gastric juice,' dyspepsia, W. **Tīkshṇâgra**, mfn. = °*ṇa-vaktra*, R. iii; (*á-*) ŚBr. v; (*su-*) MBh. i; m. Zingiber Zerumbet. **Tīkshṇâyasa**, n. = °*ṇa-loha*, L. **Tīkshṇârcis**, mfn. = °*ṇa-raśmi*. **Tīkshṇêshu**, mfn. having sharp arrows, AV. iii, 19, 7; v, 18, 9; VS. xvi, 36. **Tīkshṇôpâya**, m. forcible means, L.

Tīkshṇaka, m. Bignonia suaveolens, Npr.; black mustard, ib.; = °*ṇa-taṇḍulā*, ib. **Tī́kshṇīyas**, mfn. Compar. sharper, AV. iii, 19, 4; cf. *tékshṇishṭham*.

तीम् *tīm*, cl. 4. °*myati*, see √*tim*: Caus. *tīmayati*, to wet, Divyâv. xix. **Tīmana**, n. basil, L.

तीर 1. *tīra*, m. tin (cf. *tīvra*), L.; n. a kind of arrow (cf. Pers. تير), Pañcad. ii, 76; (*ī*), f. id., L. **Tīrikā**, f. id., ii, 76.

तीर 2. *tīra*, n. (√*tṛī*, Siddh. puml. 56) a shore, bank, AitBr. &c. (ifc. cf. *ā*, MBh.; R.; Ragh.; ifc., for derivatives cf. Pāṇ. iv, 2, 106 & 104, Vārtt. 2; ifc. ind., for accent cf. vi, 2, 121); the brim of a vessel, ŚBr. vi, xiv. **-graha**, m. pl. N. of a people, MBh. vi, 360. **-ja**, mfn. = *-bhāj*, v; BhP.; m. a tree near a shore, R. ii. **-bhāj**, mfn. growing near a shore, Kād. vi, 681. **-bhukti**, m. Tirhut (province in the east of central Hindūstan), L. **-°bhuktīya**, mfn. coming from Tirhut, Śak. i, $\frac{18}{19}$, Sch. **-ruha**, mfn. = *-bhāj*, R. ii, 95, 4; m. a tree near a shore, 104, 4 & 19 (G). **-stha**, mfn. = *-bhāj*, W. **Tīrâṭa**, m. Symplocos racemosa, W. **Tīrântara**, n. the opposite bank, W.

Tīraṇa, m. Pongamia glabra, Npr.

Tīraya, Nom. P. °*yati*, to finish, Dhātup. xxxv, 58. **Tīrita**, mfn. finished, settled, Mn. ix, 233.

Tīrṇa, mfn. one who has crossed, MBh.; R. (with acc., v, 15, 23); one who has gone over (acc.), Ragh. xiv, 6; Megh. 19; one who has got through (grammar, *vyākaraṇam*), Bādar. iii, 2, 32, Sch.; one who has escaped (with abl.), Hariv. 4066; crossed, R. vi; Śak. vii, 33; Prab. v &c. (*á*, neg., 'endless,' RV. viii, 79, 6); spread, W.; surpassed, W.; fulfilled (a promise), R.; (*ā*), f. a metre of 4 × 4 long syllables. **-padī**, f. Curculigo orchioides, L. **-pratijña**, mfn. one who has fulfilled his promise, Hariv. 7256; R. ii, 21, 46; vi. **Tīrtvā́**, ind. p., see √*tṛī*.

Tīrthá, n. (rarely m., MBh.) a passage, way, road, ford, stairs for landing or for descent into a river, bathing-place, place of pilgrimage on the banks of sacred streams, piece of water, RV. &c.; the path to the altar between the Cātvāla and Utkara, ShaḍvBr. iii, 1; ĀśvŚr. iv, ix; ŚāṅkhŚr.; Lāṭy.; KātyŚr.; a channel, iv, 8, Paddh.; the usual or right way or manner, TS.; ŚBr. xiv, (*á-*, xi); KātyŚr.; MBh. iv, 1411; the right place or moment, ChUp. viii; Anup. &c.; advice, instruction, counsel, adviser, preceptor, MBh. v; Mālav. i, $\frac{12}{13}$; Kir. ii, 3; certain lines or parts of the hand sacred to the deities, Mn. ii; Yājñ. &c.; an object of veneration, sacred object, BhP.; a worthy person, Āp.; Mn. iii, 130; MBh. &c.; a person worthy of receiving anything (gen.), MānGṛ. i, 7; N. of certain counsellors of a king (enumerated in Pañcat. iii, $\frac{67}{68}$), MBh. ii, 171; Ragh. xvii; Śiś. xiv; one of the ten orders of ascetics founded by Śaṃkarâcārya (its members add the word *tīrtha* to their names); a brāhman, Uṇ. vṛ.; = *darśana*, L.; = *yoga*, L.; the vulva, L.; a woman's courses, L.; fire, Uṇ. vṛ.; = *nidāna*, ib. **-kamaṇḍalu**, m. a pot with T°-water, BhP. ix, 10, 43. **-kara**, mfn. creating a passage (through life), MBh. xiii, 7023 (Vishṇu); m. Śiva; a head of a sect, Sarvad. iv, vi, ix; = *-kṛit*, Jain. **-kāka**, m. 'crow at a T°,' an unsteady pupil, Pāṇ. ii, 1, 42, Vārtt., Pat. **-kāśikā**, f. N. of a work by Gaṅgā-dhara. **-kīrti**, mfn. one whose fame is a T° (i. e. carries through life), BhP. iii, 1, 45 & 5, 15. **-kṛit**, m. 'T°-maker,' a Jain Arhat, Jain.; VarBṛ. xv, 4. **-gopāla**, n. N. of a T°, ŚambhMāh. xvi. **-ṃkara**, m. = *-kṛit*, Jain. **-caryā**, f. a visit to any T°, pilgrimage, BhP. ix, 16, 1. **-cintāmaṇi**, m. N. of a work by Vācaspati-miśra, Smṛitit. i, xxv. **-tama**, n. Superl. a T° more sacred than (abl.), MBh. iii, 7018; an object of the highest sanctity, BhP. v. **-deva**, m. Śiva; *-maya*, mf(*ī*)n. containing Tīrthas and gods, Hcat. i, 7, 580. **-dhvāṅksha**, m. = *-kāka*, Pāṇ. ii, 1, 42, Vārtt. **-nirṇaya**, m. N. of a work. **-pati**, m. N. of the head of an ocean-worshipping sect, Śaṃkar. xxxv. **-pad**, nom. *pād*, mfn. having sanctifying feet (Kṛishṇa), BhP. iii, ix. **-pada**, mfn. id., iii, vi. **-pāda**, mfn. id., i, iv, viii, xii. **-°pādīya**, m. an adherent of Kṛishṇa, iv. **-pūjā**, f. washing Kṛishṇa's statue in holy water, W. **-bhūta**, mfn. sanctified, MBh. xiii; BhP. i, 13. **-mahā-hrada**, m. N. of a T°, MBh. xiii, 7654. **-mahiman**, n. N. of a ch. of Śūdradh. **-māhātmya**, n. N. of a ch. of PSarv. **-yātrā**, f. = *-caryā*, MBh.; BhP.; Pañcat. &c.; N. of ŚivaP. ii, 20; *-tattva*, n. N. of Smṛitit. xxx; *-parvan*, n. N. of MBh. iii, chs. 80-156; *-vidhi*, m. N. of a work. **-°yātrin**, mfn. engaged in °*trā*, W. **-rājī**, f. 'line of Tīrthas,' Benares, L. **-vat**, mfn. having water-descents, abounding in Tīrthas, MBh. xiii; R.; (*tī*), f. N. of a river, BhP. v. **-vāka**, m. the hair of the head, L. **-vāyasa**, m. = *-kāka*, Pāṇ. ii, 1, 42, Kāś. **-vāsin**, mfn. dwelling at a T°. **-vidhi**, m. the rites observed at a T°. **-śilā**, f. the stone steps leading to a bathing-place, Śṛiṅgār. 1. **-śravas**, mfn. = *-kīrti*, BhP. ii, viii. **-śrāddha-prayoga**, m. N. of a ch. of Śiva-rāma's Śrāddha-cintāmaṇi. **-sad**, mfn. dwelling at Tīrthas (Rudra), MānGṛ. i, 13. **-seni**, f. N. of one of the mothers in Skanda's retinue, MBh. ix, 2625. **-sevā**, f. = *-caryā*, Cāṇ.; Subh.; worship of the 24 saints, HYog. ii, 16. **-sevin**, m. 'visiting Tīrthas,' Ardea nivea, L. **-saukhya**, n. N. of a work or of part of a work. **Tīrthâsevana**, n. = °*tha-caryā*, Rājat. vi, 309. **Tīrthêśvara**, m. = °*tha-kṛit*, Kalyāṇam. 2. **Tīrthôdaka**, n. T°-water, R. i, 48, 24.

Tīrthaka, mfn. = °*tha-bhūta*, BhP. i, 19, 32; m. = °*thika*, Buddh.; N. of a Nāga, ib.; n. (ifc.) a Tīrtha, Hariv. **Tīrthika**, m. an adherent or head of any other than one's own creed, Buddh.; Jain.

Tīrthī, in comp. for °*tha*. **-karaṇa**, mfn. sanctifying, BhP. v. **-√kṛi**, to sanctify, i, x. **-kṛita**, mfn. sanctified, iii. **-bhūta**, mfn. id., Mn. xi, 197, Kull.

Tī́rthya, mfn. relating to a sacred Tīrtha, VS. xvi, 42; m. = °*thika*, Buddh.; cf. *sa-*; *tairthya*.

तीव् *tīv*, cl. 1. °*vati*, to be fat, Dhātup. xv.

तीवर *tīvara*, m. a hunter (offspring of a Rājaputrī by a Kshatriya), BrahmavP. i; a fisher (for *dhīv*°), L.; the ocean, L.; (*ī*), f. a hunter's wife, i.

तीव्र *tīvrá*, mf(*ā*)n. (fr. *tiv-ra*, √*tu*) strong, severe, violent, intense, hot, pervading, excessive, ardent, sharp, acute, pungent, horrible, RV. &c.; m. sharpness, pungency, Pāṇ. ii, 2, 8, Vārtt. 3, Pat.; for °*vara* (?), g. *rājanyâdi*; Śiva; n. pungency, W.; a shore (for 2. *tīra*?), Uṇ. k.; tin (cf. 1. *tīra*), ib.; steel, L.; iron, L.; (*am*), ind. violently, impetuously, sharply, excessively, W.; (*ā*), f. Helleborus niger, L.; black mustard, L.; basil, L.; *gaṇḍa-dūrvā*, L.; *taraḍī*, L.; *mahā-jyotishmatī*, L.; (in music) N. of a Śruti; of a Mūrchanā; of the river Padmavatī (in the east of Bengal), L. **-kantha** or **-kanda**, m. a pungent kind of Arum, L. **-gati**, mfn. moving rapidly, W.; being in a bad condition, Daś. i, 130; f. rapid gait, 67. **-gandhā**, f. cumin-seed or Ptychotis Ajowan, L. **-jvālā**, f. Grislea tomentosa, L. **-tā**, f. violence, heat, Rājat. i, 41 (*a-*, neg.) **-dāru**, m. N. of a tree, g. *rajatâdi*. **-dyuti**, m. 'hot-rayed,' the sun, Prasannar. vii, 82. **-paurusha**, n. daring heroism. **-mada**, mfn. excessively intoxicating, Car. i, 27. **-mārga**, m. = *tīkshṇa-m*°, Gal. **-ruja**, mfn. causing excessive pain, Suśr. ii, 15, 3 (*-tva*, abstr.) **-rosha-samāvishṭa**, mfn. filled with fierce anger, MBh. iii, 2397. **-vipāka**, v. l. for *tīkshṇa-v*°. **-vedanā**, f. excessive pain, L. **-śoka-samāvishṭa**, mfn. filled with excessive sorrow, 2958. **-śokârta**, mfn. afflicted with poignant grief. **-sava**, m. N. of an Ekâha sacrifice, ŚāṅkhŚr. xiv. **-sút**, mfn. being a pungent juice (Soma), RV. vi, 43, 2; ŚāṅkhŚr.; m. = *-sava*, KātyŚr.; Lāṭy.; Maś.; Vait. **-somá**, m. a variety of the Ukthya libation, TS. vii; = *-sava*, TāṇḍyaBr. xviii. **Tīvrâtitīvra**, mfn. excessively severe (penance), Bhartṛ. iii, 88. **Tīvrânanda**, m. Śiva. **Tīvrânta**, mfn. having a strong effect (Soma), AitBr. ii, 20.

Tīvraya, °*yati*, to strengthen, TāṇḍyaBr. xviii.

Tīvrī́, in comp. for °*vrá*. **-√kṛi**, to make sharp, strengthen, ŚBr. i, 7, 1, 18 & 6, 4, 6; iii, 8, 3, 30. **-√bhū**, to become stronger, increase, Rājat. vi, 99.

तीसट *tīsaṭa*, m. N. of a med. author.

तु 1. *tu*, cl. 2. (*tauti*, Dhātup.; fut. 2nd *totā* or *tavitā*, Vop.) to have authority, be strong, RV. i, 94, 2 (pf. *tūtāva*, cf. Naigh. iv, 1; Pāṇ. vi, 1, 7, Kāś.); to go, Dhātup.; to injure, ib.: Caus. (aor. *tūtot*, 2. sg. °*tos*) to make strong or efficient, RV. ii, 20, 5; vi, 26, 4; cf. *ut-*, *sam-*; *tavás*, &c., *tīvrá*; [Zend *tav*, 'to be able'; Lat. *tumor, tueri, totus*.]

तु 2. *tú* (never found at the beginning of a sentence or verse; metrically also *tū́*, RV.; cf. Pāṇ. vi, 3, 133) pray! I beg, do, now, then, Lat. *dum* used (esp. with the Imper.), RV.; but (also with *evá* or *vai* following), AV. iv, 18, 6; TS.; ŚBr. &c.; and, Mn. ii, 68; or, i, 68; xi, 202; often incorrectly written for *nu*, MBh. (i, 6151 B & C); sometimes used as a mere expletive; **ca—na tu**, though—still not; **na** or **na ca—api tu**, not—but; **kāmam** or **kāmam ca—tu** or **kim tu** or **param tu**, though—still; **kāmam** or **bhūyas** or **varam—na tu**, it is true—but not, ere—than; **kim tu**, still, nevertheless; **na—param tu**, not—however; **tu—tu**, certainly—but, Hit. i, 2, 33.

तुःखार *tuḥkhāra*, = *tukh*°, Rājat. iv, 211.

तुक् *tuk*, m. (fr. *túc*) a boy, L.

तुक *tuka*, m. N. of an astronomer.

तुकाक्षीरी *tukā-kshīrī*, = *tugā-*, Car. vi, 16.

तुक्क *tukka*, m. N. of a man, Rājat. vii f.

तुक्खार *tukkhāra*, m. a Tukhāra horse, Vcar. ix, 116; xviii, 93.

तुक्ष *tuksha*, g. *pakshâdi*.

तुखार *tukhāra* (often spelt *tushāra*, see also *tuḥkh*° & *tukkh*°), m. pl. N. of a people (north-west of Madhya-deśa), AV. Pariś. li; MBh.; R. &c.

तुगा *tugā*, f. (derived fr. *-kshīrī*) Tabāshīr (bamboo manna), Suśr. vi, 52, 20 & 57, 8; (°*gā-khyā*) 45, 30. **-kshīrī**, f. (fr. *tvak-ksh*°) id., i, 12, 13; 38, 32; vi (once metrically °*ri*); cf. *tukā-ksh*°.

तुग्र *túgra*, m. N. of Bhujyu's father (saved by the Aśvins), RV. i; vi, 62; of an enemy of Indra, 20 & 26; x. **Tugriya**, Ved. = °*rya*, Pāṇ. iv, 4, 115. **Túgrya**, m. (fr. °*ra*, 115) patr. of Bhujyu, RV. viii; (*ās*), f. pl. (scil. *víśas*) Tugra's race ['the waters,' Naigh. i, 12], RV. i, 33, 15. **Tugryā-vṛidh**, mfn. favouring the Tugrya (Indra, Soma), viii.

तुग्वन् *túgvan*, n. a ford, viii, 19, 37.

तुङ्ग *tuṅga*, mf(*ā*)n. prominent, erect, lofty, high, MBh. &c.; chief, W.; strong, W.; m. an elevation, height, mountain, R. iv, 44, 20 (cf. *bhṛigu-*); Hit. ii (v. l.); top, peak, W.; (fig.) a throne, BhP. iii, 3, 1; a planet's apsis, VarBṛ. i, vii, x f.; xxi, 1; Laghuj. ix, 20; Rottleria tinctoria, MBh.; R.; Suśr.; the cocoa-nut, L.; = *-mukha*, L.; Mercury, L.; N. of a man, Rājat. vi f.; n. the lotus stamina, L.; (*ā*), f. Mimosa Suma, L.; Tabāshīr, L.; a metre of 4 × 8 syllables; N. of a river in Mysore; (*ī*), f. a kind of Ocimum, L.; turmeric, L.; night, L.; Gaurī, Gal. **-kūṭa**, N. of a Tīrtha, VarP. cxl. **-tva**, n. 'height' and 'passionateness,' Śiś. ii, 48. **-dhanvan**, m. N. of a king of Suhma, Daś. xi, 5. **-nātha**, m. = *bhṛigu-tuṅga*, MBh. i, 215, 2, Nil. **-nābha**, m. N. of a venomous insect, Suśr. v, 8, 14. **-nāsa**, m. long-nosed, Pāṇ. i, 3, 2, Pat. **-nā-**

sikā or °**kī**, f. a long-nosed woman, iv, 1, 55, Kāś. **-prastha**, m. N. of a mountain, MārkP. lvii, 13. **-bala**, m. N. of a warrior, Hit. i, 8, ½. **-bīja**, n. quicksilver, Sūryas. xiii, 17. **-bha**, n. a planet's apsis, VarBṛ. vii, 1 & 6. **-bhadra**, m. a restive elephant, L.; (*ā*), f. the Tumbudra river in Mysore (formed by the junction of the Tuṅgā and Bhadrā), BhP. v; BṛNārP. vi, 32; Rasik. xi, 14 & 34; °*drā-māhātmya*, n. N. of a work. **-mukha**, m. 'long-snouted,' a rhinoceros, L. **-veṇā**, f. N. of a river in the Deccan, MBh. iii, vi. **-śekhara**, m. 'high-peaked,' a mountain, L. **-śaila**, m. N. of a mountain with a temple of Śiva; *-māhātmya*, n. N. of a work. **Tuṅgêśvara**, m. N. of a temple of Śiva, Rājat. ii, 14; °*rāpaṇa*, m. N. of a market-place, vi, 190.

Tuṅgaka, m. Rottleria tinctoria, L.; n. N. of a sacred forest (also °*kâraṇya*), MBh. °**gin**, mfn. being in the apsis (a planet), Jyot.; (*inī*), f. N. of a plant.

Tuṅgiman, m. height, Pañcat. ii, 6, 6; Vcar. xviii.

Tuṅgī, f. of °*ga*. **-nāsa**, m. N. of a venomous insect, Suśr. **-pati**, m. 'night-lord,' the moon, L.

Tuṅgîśa, m. id., L.; the sun, L.; Śiva, Kṛishṇa, L.

तुच् *túc* (only dat. °*cé*), offspring, children, RV. vi, 48, 9; viii, 18, 18 & 27, 14; cf. *túj*, *toká*.

तुच्छ *tuccha*, mfn. empty, vain, small, little, trifling, BhP.; NṛisUp.; Prab.; n. anything trifling, ŚārṅgP. xxxi, 15; chaff, Uṇ. k.; (*ā*), f. the 14th lunar day, Sūryapr. **-tva**, n. emptiness, vanity, Kap. i, 134. **-daya**, mfn. unmerciful, Naish. viii, 24. **-dru**, m. Ricinus communis, L. **-dhānya**, °**yaka**, n. chaff, L. **-prāya**, mfn. unimportant, Prasannar.

Tucchaka, mfn. empty, vain, L.

Tucchaya, Nom. P. to make empty, Mṛicch. x.

Tucchī-kṛita, mfn. despised, BhP. **Tucchyá**, mfn. empty, vain, RV. v, 42; n. emptiness, x, 129.

तुज् 1. *túj*, f. (only acc. °*jam*, dat. °*jé*) = *túc*, iii–v. 1. **Tuji** (only dat. °*jáye*), propagation, v, 46, 7.

तुज् 2. *tuj*, cl. 6. (3. du. Ā. °*jete*; p. P. °*ját*; inf. °*jáse* & *túje*; Pass. p. °*jyámāna*), & *tuñj* (3. pl. P. °*jánti*, Ā. °*játe*; p. °*jāná*, *túñjāna*, & *túñjamāna*), to strike, hit, push, RV.; to press out ('*tūñjati*, to give,' Naigh.; Nir.), RV. i, ix; Ā. to flow forth, iii, 1, 16; to instigate, incite, i, iii; Pass. to be vexed, i, 11, 5: cl. 1. *tojati*, to hurt, Dhātup. vii, 70: Caus. (p. *tujáyat*; aor. Pot. *tutujyāt*, p. *tūtujāna*, q. v.) to promote, RV. i, 143, 6; to move quickly, vii, 104, 7; *tuñjayati*, 'to speak' or 'to shine,' Dhātup. xxxiii, 82; *tuñj*° or *tojayati*, to hurt, xxxii, 30; to be strong, ib.; to give or take, ib.; to abide, ib.; cf. *ā-tují*. 3. **Túj**, mfn. urging, RV.; f. (only instr. °*jā*) shock, impulse, assault, RV.

Tuja, a thunderbolt, Naigh. ii, 20 (v. l. *tuñja*). 2. **Túji**, N. of a man protected by Indra, RV. vi, x. **Tújya**, mfn. to be pushed or impelled, iii, 62, 1; x. **Tuñjá**, m. shock, assault, i, 7, 7; Nir.; cf. *tuja*.

तुञ्जीन *tuñjīna*, m. N. of several kings of Kaśmīr, Rājat. ii, 11; iii, 97 & 386; v, 277.

तुट् *tuṭ*, cl. 6. °*ṭati*, to quarrel, Dhātup.

तुटि *tuṭi*, (m. f., Siddh. strīpuṃs. 2, v. l. *truṭi*) small cardamoms, VarBṛS. lxxviii, 1, Sch.

तुटितुट *tuṭituṭa*, m. Śiva, Hariv. 14882.

तुटुम *tuṭuma*, m. a mouse or rat, L.

तुड् *tuḍ*, cl. 1. 6. *tuḍati*, *toḍ*°, to strike, Dhātup.; to split, ib.; to bring near (v. l.), ib.: Caus., ib.

तुडिग *tuḍiga*, m. N. of a prince, Chandaḥs. vii, 16 & 31, Halāy.

तुडी *tuḍī*, f. N. of a Rāgiṇī.

तुड्ड् *tuḍḍ*, cl. 1. P. to disregard, Dhātup.

तुण् *tuṇ*, cl. 6. P. to curve, xxviii, 42.

तुणि *tuṇi*, °*ṇika*, m. Cedrela Toona, L.

तुण्ड् *tuṇḍ*, cl. 1. Ā. to hurt, viii, 23.

तुण्ड *tuṇḍa*, n. a beak, snout (of a hog &c.), trunk (of an elephant), TĀr. x; MBh &c.; the mouth (used contemptuously), Bādar. ii, 2, 28, Śaṃk.; the point (of an arrow &c.), see *ayas-*, *dhūs-*; the chief, leader, Dhūrtan. i, 4; m. Cucumis utilissimus, L.; Beninkasa cerifera, L.; Śiva, Hariv. 14882; N. of a Rakshas, MBh. iii, 16372; (*ī*), f. a kind of gourd, Cāṇ.; cf. *asthi-*, *kaṅka-*, *kāka-*, *krishṇa-*, *vāyasa-*, *sūkshma-*; *kaṭu-* & *tikta-tuṇḍī*. **-deva**, m. N. of a race or of a class of men, g. *aishukāryādi*; *-bhakta*, mfn. inhabited by °*va*, ib.

Tuṇḍakerikā [L.], °**rī** [Bhpr. v], f. = °*ḍik*°.

Tuṇḍi, m. a beak, snout, Uṇ. k.; f. (also *tundi*, W.) emphysema of the navel (in infants), Suśr. iii, 10, 37; a prominent navel, L. **-cela**, n. a kind of costly garment, Divyâv. xvii, 400.

Túṇḍika, mfn. furnished with a snout, AV. viii, 6, 5; (*ā*), f. the navel (cf. *tund*°), L.; = °*kerī*, L.

Tuṇḍikera, pl. N. of a people, MBh. vii, 691; viii, 138; (*tauṇḍ*°, Hariv.); (*ī*), f. = °*keśī*, Suśr. ii, 2, 4; vi, 48, 25; a large boil on the palate, i f.; iv, 22, 55 & (metrically °*ri*) 62; the cotton plant, L.

Tuṇḍikerin, m. N. of a venomous insect, v, 8, 3.

Tuṇḍikeśī, f. Momordica monadelpha, L.

Tuṇḍibha, mfn. (Uṇ. iv, 117, Sch.) having a prominent navel, L.; see *tund*°. **Tuṇḍila**, mfn. id., L.; talkative, Uṇ. i, 55, Sch.; see *tund*°.

Tuṇḍela, m. N. of a goblin, AV. viii, 6, 17.

तुतात *tutāta*, m. N. of Kumārila, Prab. ii, 3, Sch.; cf. *tautātika*.

तुतुर्वणि *tuturváṇi*, mfn. (√1. *tur*) striving to bring near or obtain, RV. i, 168, 1.

तुत्थ *tuttha*, n. (m., L.) blue vitriol (used as an eye-ointment), Suśr.; fire, L.; n. a collyrium, L.; a rock, Uṇ. k.; (*ā*), f. the indigo plant, L.; small cardamoms, L. **Tutthâñjana**, n. blue vitriol as an ointment, L.

Tutthaka, n. blue vitriol, Suśr. i, 38, 34; vi.

Tutthaya, Nom. P. to cover, Śiś. v, 11.

तुथ *tuthá*, m. VS.; Kāṭh.; TS.; MaitrS.; Kapishṭh.; ŚBr. (= *bráhman*); TāṇḍyaBr.; ŚāṅkhŚr.

तुद् 1. *tud*, cl. 6. P. °*dáti* (p. f. °*datī* or °*dantī*, Pāṇ. vi, 1, 173, Kāś.; pf. *tutóda*; fut. 2nd *totsyati* or *tottā*, vii, 2, 10, Kār.; aor. *atautsīt*) to push, strike, goad, bruise, sting, vex, RV. &c.; Pass. to pain (said of a wound), Car. vi, 13: Caus., see *todita*; [cf. *tóttra* &c.; Τυδ-εύ-ς &c.; Lat. *tundo*.] **-ādi**, the rts. of cl. 6 (beginning with *tud*), Pāṇ. iii, 1, 77. 2. **Tud**, mfn. ifc. 'pricking,' see *vraṇa-*.

Tuda, mfn. ifc. 'striking,' see *aruṃ-*, *tilaṃ-*, *vidhuṃ-*; m. N. of a man, g. *śubhrâdi*; cf. *ut-*.

Tunná, mfn. struck, goaded, hurt, cut, RV. ix, 67, 19 f.; AV. &c.; m. = °*nnaka*, L. **-vāya**, m. a tailor, Mn. iv, 214; Yājñ. i, 163; R. **-sevanī**, f. the suture of a wound, Suśr.; a suture of the skull, Bhpr. ii, 279. **Tunnaka**, m. Cedrela Toona, v, 5, 44.

तुन *túna*, v. l. for *tána*, SV. i, 5, 1, 1, 5.

तुन्द् *tund*, cl. 1. °*dati*, to be active, Dhātup. ii, 32 (v. l.); cf. *ni-√tud*.

तुन्द *tunda*, n. (Pāṇ. v, 2, 117) a protuberant belly, Siṇhâs. xxiii, 1; the belly, L.; mfn. having a protuberant belly, g. *arśa-ādi*; m. the navel, L.; (*ī*), f. id., W. **-kūpikā**, °**pī**, f. 'belly-cavity,' the navel, L. **-parimārja**, mfn. (Pāṇ. iii, 2, 5, Vārtt. 1, Pat.) stroking one's belly, HParis. viii, 281. **-parimārjaka**, mfn. = °*mṛija*, Gai. **-parimṛija**, mfn. (Pāṇ. iii, 2, 5) 'stomach-stroker,' lazy, Anargh. vii, 110. **-vat**, mfn. corpulent, Pāṇ. v, 2, 117, Kāś.

Tundâdi, a gaṇa of Pāṇ. (v, 2, 117.)

Tundi, (v, 2, 139) m. N. of a Gandharva, L.; f., see *tuṇḍi*. **-kara**, m. the navel, L.

Tundika, mfn. = °*da-vat*, 117; (*ā*), f. the navel, L. **Tundita**, mfn. = °*dika*, L. **Tundin**, mfn. id., 117. **Tundibha**, mfn. id., 139; v. l. for *tuṇḍ*°.

Tundila, mfn. (117) id., ŚāṅkhGṛ. iv, 19, 3 (v. l. *tuṇḍ*°); MānGṛ. ii, 10; Hcar. (also *a-*, neg.); = *tuṇḍibha*, L.; m. Gaṇêśa, Gal.; *-phalā*, f. Cucumis utilissimus, L. **Tundilita**, mfn. become corpulent, Naish. iv, 56. **Tundilī-karaṇa**, n. the act of causing to swell, increasing, Bhām. iv, 9.

तुन्न *tunná*, °*nnaka*. See √*tud*.

तुन्यु *tunyu*, m. N. of a tree, Kauś.

तुप् *tup*, तुफ् *tuph*, cl. 1. 6. *topati*, *tup*°, *toph*°, *tuph*°, to hurt, Dhātup.; [cf. *tubh*, *tump*; τύπ-τ-ω, τύμπανον; Lat. *stupeo*; Germ. *stumpf*.]

तुबर *tubara*, mfn. astringent (also *tūb*°, L.), Suśr. i, 45; m. n. an astringent taste, W.; m. = *-yāvanāla*, L.; see *tūb*°; (*ī*), f. Cajanus indicus, L.; alum or alum earth (also *tumb*°, L.; *tūb*°, L., Sch.), Npr.; a bitch (also *tumb*° & *tumburī*), L.; see *tumburu*. **-yāvanāla**, m. a sort of grain, L.

Tubaraka, m. id., Suśr. i, 46, 1, 18; N. of a tree, 45, 7, 11; iv, 9, 4; 13, 18; 31, 5; (*ikā*), f. Cajanus indicus, L.; Sch.; alum or alum earth (also *tūb*°, Sch.), L. **Tubarī-śimba**, m. Cassia Tora, L.

तुभ् *tubh*, cl. 1. 4. *tobhate*, *tubhyati*, to hurt, kill, Dhātup.: cl. 9. (impf. *atubhnāt*) id., Bhaṭṭ. xvii, 79 & 90; [cf. *stubh*; Goth. *thiubs*.]

तुमल *tumala*, for °*mula*, MBh.; Ragh.

तुमिञ्ज *túmiñja*, m. N. of a man, TS. i, 7, 2.

तुमुर *tumura*, = °*mula*, L., Sch.

Tumula, mf(*ā*)n. tumultuous, noisy, Lāṭy. ii, 3, 3; MBh. &c.; n. (Lat.) *tumultus*, tumult, clatter, confusion, MBh. (once m. vii, 154, 21) &c.; m. Terminalia Bellerica, L.

तुम्प् *tump*, तुम्फ् *tumph*, cl. 1. 6. °*pati*, °*phati*, to hurt, Dhātup. xi; xxviii, 26 f.; cf. *pra-stump*.

तुम्ब् *tumb*, cl. 1. °*bati*, to distress, xi, 38: cl. 10. °*bayati*, 'id.,' or 'to be invisible,' xxxii, 114.

तुम्ब *tumba*, m. the gourd Lagenaria vulgaris, Hariv. 3479; R. i; Suśr. iii; (*ī*), f. id., Hariv. 802; Suśr. i, iv; Śāntiś.; Rājat.; Asteracantha longifolia, L.; (*ā*), f. a milk-pail, L. **-vana**, N. of a place, VarBṛS. xiv, 15. **-vīṇa**, m. 'having the T° for a lute,' Śiva, MBh. xiii, 1213. **Tumbaka**, m., °**bi**, °**bikā**, °**binī**, f. the Tumba gourd, L.

Tumbī, f. of °*ba*. **-pushpa**, n. the flower of the T° gourd, L. **-vīṇā**, f. a kind of lute, Hariv. 3618; *-priya*, m. 'fond of that lute,' Śiva, MBh. xii, 10371.

Tumbuka, m. = °*baka* (n., its fruit). **Tumbukin**, mfn. (in music) puffing the cheeks in singing; m. a kind of drum.

तुम्बर *tumbara*, = °*raka*, Kauś. 76; n. its fruit, Madanav.; m. pl. N. of a people, Hariv. 311 (v. l. °*bura*); sg. for °*buru* (Gandharva), Pañcad. i, 63; (*ī*), f. a sort of grain, Madanav. cvii, 46; = *tub*° (q. v.). **Tumbaraka**, m. N. of a tree, lxix, 72.

तुम्बरु *tumbaru*, for °*buru*, MBh. i; BhP.

तुम्बुम *tumbuma*, m. pl. N. of a race, MBh.

तुम्बुर *tumbura*, see °*bara*; (*ī*), see °*ru*, *tubarī*.

Tumburu, m. N. of a pupil of Kalāpin, Pāṇ. iv, 3, 104, Kāś. (Kār.); of a Gandharva, MBh. &c. ('attendant of the 5th Arhat of the present Avasarpiṇī,' Jain.); n. coriander or the fruit of Diospyros embryopteris (also °*rī* & *tubarī*, L.), Suśr. iv; vi, 42, 67 & (metrically °*rū*) 118; Pāṇ. vi, 1, 143, Kāś.

तुम्र *túmra*, mfn. big, strong, RV. iii f.; vi, 22, 5; x, 27 & 89; [cf. *tūtumá*; Lat. *tumidus*.]

तुर् 1. *tur* (cf. *trī*, *tvar*), cl. 6. to hurry, press forwards, vi, 18, 4 (p. °*rát*); TS. ii (Ā. °*rate*): cl. 4 (Imper. *tūrya*) to overpower, RV. viii, 99, 5; Ā. to run, Dhātup.; to hurt, ib.: cl. 3. *tutorti*, to run, ib.: Caus. *turayate* (p. °*ráyat*) to run, press forwards, RV.; SV.: Desid. *tútūrshati*, to strive to press forwards, RV. x, 100, 12; Intens. p. *tárturāṇa*, rushing, pressing each other (waves), ix, 95, 3.

2. **Túr**, mfn. running a race, conquering, i, 112, 4; iv, 38, 7; (*túram*, acc. or ind. 'quickly') promoting, a promoter, v, 82, 1; cf. *ap-*, *āji-*, *pṛitsu-*, *pra-*, *mithas-*, *rajas-*, *ratha-*, &c. **Turas-péya**, n. the racer's or conqueror's drinking, x, 96, 8.

1. **Turá**, mfn. quick, willing, prompt, RV.; AV. vi, 102, 3; strong, powerful, excelling, rich, abundant, RV.; AV. vii, 50, 2; TS. ii; Kauś. 91; m. N. of a preceptor and priest with the patr. Kāvasheya, ŚBr. ix f., xiv; AitBr.; TāṇḍyaBr.; BhP.; (*túram*), ind., see 2. *túr*. **-ga**, m. 'going quickly,' a horse, MBh. i; Pañcat.; Śak. &c.; (hence) the number 7, Chandaḥs. vii, 1, Sch.; the mind, thought, L.; (*ī*), f. a mare, Śatr. xiv; = °*ga-gandhā*, L.; *-kāntā*, f. 'horse-loved,' a mare, °*tā-mukha*, m. 'mare's mouth,' submarine fire (*vaḍabā-mukha*), Śiś. iii, 33; *-kriyā-vat*, mfn. occupied with horses, Dhūrtas. i, 12; *-gandhā*, f. Physalis flexuosa, L.; *-dānava* or *-daitya*, 'horse-titan,' Keśin, Hariv. 4281 ff.; *-nīla-tāla*, m. N. of a gesture, PSarv.; *-paricāraka*, m. = *-raksha*, Kād. v, 804; *-priya*, m. 'liked by horses,' barley, L.; *-brahmacaryaka*, n. 'sexual restraint of horses,' compulsory celibacy, L.; *-mukha*, m. 'horse-faced,' a Kiṃnara, iii, 1474; *-medha*, m. a horse-sacrifice, R. vi; BhP. ix; *-raksha*, m. 'horse-guardian,' a groom, VarBṛS. xv; *-ratha*, m. a cart drawn by horses, Hcat. i, 5, 836; *-līlaka*, m. N. of a time (in music); *-vāhyālī*, f. a riding-school, Kād. iii, 499 (v. l. °*ramg*°); °*gânana*, m. pl. 'horse-faced,' N. of a people, VarBṛS. xiv, 25; °*gâroha*, m. a horseman, xv, 26; °*gôpa-*

cāraka, m. = °ga-raksha, x, 3. **–gâtu** (°rá-), mfn. going quickly, RV. i. 164, 30. **–°gin**, m. a horseman, L. **–m-ga**, m. 'going quickly,' a horse, Suśr.; Pañcat.; Śak. &c.; (hence) the number 7, Sūryas.; Śrut.; the mind, thought, L.; (*ī*), f. a mare, W.; N. of a shrub, L.; = °raga-gandhā, L.; *-gandhā*, f. id., Suśr. vi, 41 & 48; *-dveshaṇī*, f. a she-buffalo, L.; *-nātha*, m. N. of the head of a sect, Śaṃkar. xliii; *-priya*, m. = °rag°, L.; *-mukha*, m. = °rag°, Kād. iii, 1635; *-medha*, m. = °rag°, Ragh. xiii, 61; *-yāyin*, mfn. going on horseback; *-līla*, m. = °rag°; *-vaktra*, *-vadana*, m. = *-mukha*, L.; *-sādin*, m. a horseman, Ragh. vii, 34; *-skandha*, m. a troop of horses, Pāṇ. iv, 2, 51, Kāś.; *-sthāna*, n. a horse-stable, Suśr. iv, 1, 5; °gâri, m. 'horse-enemy,' a buffalo, W.; Nerium odorum, L.; °gâhvā, f. the jujube, Gal.; °gī-bhūya, ind. p. having become a horse, Kād. vi, 1539. **–m-gama**, m. a horse, MBh.; R.; Ragh. &c.; (*ī*), f. a mare, MBh. iv, 254; *-ratha*, m. = °raga-r°, Hcat. i, 5, 838; *-śālā*, f. a horse-stable, VarBṛS. vl, 5. **–m-gin**, m. a horseman, W.; a groom, W.; (*iṇī*), f. a kind of gait (in dancing). **–yā́**, mfn. going quickly, RV. iv, 23, 10. **–śravas**, m. N. of a man, TāṇḍyaBr. ix. 1. **Turâyaṇa**, n. 'Tura's way,' N. of a sacrifice or vow (modification of the full-moon sacrifice), ŚāṅkhBr.; ŚāṅkhŚr.; KātyŚr.; ĀśvŚr.; Pāṇ.; MBh. xiii; cursory reading, Gal. **Turā-shā́h**, nom. *shā́ṭ*, (Pāṇ. iii, 2, 63) overpowering the mighty or overpowering quickly, RV. & VS. xx (Indra); Hariv. 14114 (Vishṇu; voc. *-shāṭ*); m. (acc. *-sāham*; cf. Pāṇ. viii, 3, 56) Indra, Ragh. xv, 40; Kum. ii, 1; BhP. viii, 11, 26.

Turáṇa, mf(*ā*)n. swift, RV. i, 121, 5.

1. **Turaṇya**, (g. *kaṇḍv-ādi*) Nom. °yáti (p. °yát) to be quick or swift, 1; iv, 40, 3; to accelerate, 4; x, 61, 11. 2. **Turaṇya**, m. 'swift,' one of the moon's horses, VāyuP. i, 52, 53. **–sád**, mfn. dwelling among, i. e. belonging to the quick, RV. iv, 40, 2. °ṇyú, mfn. swift, zealous, i, 134, 5; vii f.

2. **Turāyaṇa**, m. (fr. °rá) N. of a man, Pravar. ii, 2, 3 (Kāty.) **Turí**, f. (only dat. °ryaí) = °ryā́, RV. x, 106, 4; 'swift,' a weaver's brush (also *tuli* & °lī), L. **Turī**, f. id., Bādar. ii, 1, 19 & 3, 7, Śaṃk.; Tarkas. 55; a shuttle, Naish. i, 12; (for *tūlī*) a painter's brush (also *tuli*, L., Sch.), W.; N. of a wife of Vasudeva, Hariv. 9203 [= *caturthī* = *śūdrā*, Sch.] **Turípa**, n. (fr. °rí & *ā́p*) seminal fluid, RV. i, iii; vii, 2, 9; VS. xxvii; mfn. spermatic (Tvashṭṛi), xxi, 20; xxii, 20. 1. **Turīya**, Nom. °yáti, to go, Naigh. ii, 14. **Turyá**, f. superior power, TS. ii, 2, 12.

तुर 2. *turá*, mfn. hurt, RV. viii, 79, 2; cf. *ā-*.

तुरक *turaka*, m. pl. the Turks, Romakas. °**rakin**, mfn. Turkish, Kshitīś. vii, 161. °**rakva**, = °ka. °**rashka**, (= °rushka) id., Romakas.; Ratnak.

तुरस्पेय *turas-péya*. See 2. *túr*.

Turâyaṇa, °**rā-shā́h**, °**rí**, °**rī**, °**rípa**. See ib.

तुरीय 2. *turī́ya* (for *ktur*° [Zend *khtuiria*] fr. *catúr*), mfn. (Pāṇ. v, 2, 51, Vārtt. 1) Ved. 4th, RV. &c.; consisting of 4 parts, ŚBr. ix; n. the 4th state of spirit (pure impersonal Spirit or Brahma), Up. (MaitrUp.; NṛisUp. ii, 2, 1 &c.; RTL. 35); Vedântas.; mfn. being in that state of soul, NṛisUp.; *túr*°, a 4th, constituting the 4th part, (n.) a 4th part, AV.; Kāṭh. &c. (with *yantra*, 'a quadrant,' Śaṃkar. xxvii). **–kavaca**, n. N. of a spell. **–bhāga**, m. a 4th part, BhP. v, 16, 30 (v. l.) **–bhāj**, mfn. a sharer of a 4th, AitBr. ii, 25; Mn. iv, 202. **–māna**, n., see *-bhāga*. **–varṇa**, m. '4th caste man,' a Śūdra, L. **Turīyâtīta**, N. of an Up. **Túrīyâditya** for °yam āditya, RV. viii, 52, 7; VS. viii, 3. **Turīyârdha**, m. n. 'half the 4th,' an 8th part, MBh. i, 3862.

Turīyaka, mfn. a 4th (part), Yājñ. ii, 124.

Turya, mfn. (Pāṇ. v, 2, 51, Vārtt. 1) 4th, BhP.; Vet.; Śrut.; forming a 4th part, BhP.; n. the 4th state of soul (see °rīya), vii, 9, 32; Haṭhapr. iv, 45; RāmatUp. ii, 4, 15, Sch.; mfn. being in that state of soul, BhP. vi f. **–bhikshā**, f. the 4th part of alms, Pāṇ. ii, 2, 3. **–yantra**, n. a quadrant, W. **–vā́h**, m. (in strong cases) *vāh*, nom. *vāṭ*, f. °*ryauhī́*, an ox or cow 4 years old, VS.; TS. iv, 3, 3, 2; MaitrS. iii, 11, 11 & 13, 17. **Turyâśra**, mfn. four-cornered, Hcat. i, 3, $\frac{618}{619}$. **Turyauhī́**, see °rya-vā́h.

तुरुष्क *turushka*, m. pl. (= °rashka) the Turks, Kathās.; Rājat.; Prab. &c.; sg. a Turk, Kathās. xxxvii; a Turkish prince, W.; Turkestan, W.; (m. n., L.) olibanum, Jain.; Suśr.; VarBṛS. **–karpūra**, mfn. consisting of olibanum and camphor, Hcat. i, 7, 165. **–gauḍa**, m. (in music) N. of a Rāga. **–datta**, m. N. of a man, Inscr. (A. D. 1105).

तुर्फरि *turphári* & °*phárītu*, mfn. = (*kshipra-*) *hantṛi* (Nir. xiii, 5), RV. x, 106, 6 & 8.

तुर्य *turya*, °*yā́*. See col. 1.

तुर्व् *turv* (cf. √1. *tur*), cl. 1. P. (2. sg. *tū́rvasi*, du. Impv. °*vatam*; p. *tū́rvat*) to overpower, excel, RV. (inf. *turváṇe*, vi, viii, x); to cause to overpower, help to victory, save, vi, viii; cf. *pra-*.

Turvá, m. = °váśa, x, 62, 10. **Turváṇi**, mfn. overpowering, victorious, i, iv f., x. **Turváṇe**, Ved. inf.; see √*turv*. **Turváśa**, m. N. of a hero and ancestor of the Âryan race (named with Yadu; du. *Turvā́śā Yádū*, 'T° and Y°,' iv, 30, 17; pl. T°'s race), RV. **Turvasu**, m. (later form of °śa) N. of a son of Yayāti by Devayānī and brother of Yadu, MBh. i; Hariv. 1604 & 1617; BhP. &c. **Turvī́ti**, m. N. of a man, RV. i; ii, 13, 12; iv, 19, 6.

तुल् *tul*, cl. 10. *tolayati* or *tul*° (only *tul*° also fig.; Ā., MBh.) to lift up, raise, Hariv.; R.; Bhaṭṭ. (fut. Pass. *tolayishyate*); to determine the weight of anything by lifting it up, weigh, compare by weighing and examining, ponder, examine with distrust, MBh. &c.; to make equal in weight, equal, compare (with instr., e. g. *na brāhmaṇais tulaye bhūtam anyat*, 'I do not compare any other being with Brāhmans,' BhP. v; or with an adv. terminating in *-vat*), R.; VarBṛS. &c.; to counterbalance, outweigh, match, possess in the same degree, resemble, reach, Megh.; ŚārṅgP.; (pf. p. *tulita*) Bhartṛ. iii & Ragh. xiii, 75; [cf. Lat. *te-tul-i* &c.; τλῆ-ναι &c.; Goth. *thulan*.] **Tula**, m. (for °lā) the sign Libra, Utp. (on VarBṛ. xi, xvi, xxiii & VarYogay. iv, 55).

Tulaka, m. 'ponderer,' a king's counsellor, Divyâv. xvii. **Tulana**, n. lifting, Mṛicch. ix, 20; weighing, rating, iii, 20; N. of a high number, Buddh. L.; (*ā*), f. rating, ib.; equalness with (instr. or in comp.), Prasannar. ii, 16.

Tulā́, f. a balance, weight, VS. xxx; ŚBr. xi; Mn. &c. (°*layā dhṛi* or °*lām* with Caus. of *adhi-ruh*, 'to hold in or put on a balance, weigh, compare'; °*lām* with Caus. of *adhi-ruh*, 'to risk,' Pañcat. i, 16, 9; °*lām adhi-* or *ā-* or *sam-ā-ruh*, 'to be in a balance,' be equal with [instr.]; the balance as an ordeal, Yājñ. ii; Mṛicch. ix, 43); equal measure, equality, resemblance, Ragh. &c. (°*lām i* or *gam* or *ā-yā* or *ā-lamb* or *dhā*, 'to resemble any one or anything' [instr. or in comp.]; °*lām na bhṛi*, 'to have no equal,' Prasannar. i, 37; °*lām* with Pass. of *nī*, 'to become equal to' [gen.]); = °*la*, Pañcat. i, 14, 14; VarBṛ. &c.; N. of a measure (= 100 Palas), MBh. iii, xiv; VarBṛS.; Suśr.; Ashṭâṅg.; ŚārṅgS. i, 31; a kind of beam in the roof of a house, VarBṛS. liii, 30. **–koṭi**, m. (f., L.) the end of the beam, ŚārṅgP. (*-yashṭi*, Pañcat. i, 3, 20); a foot-ornament of women (also °*ṭī*, f., L., Sch.), Kād.; Vcar.; Prab. iii, 9; N. of a weight, L.; ten millions, L. **–kosha**, m. weighing on a balance, VarBṛS. xxvi, 10. **–guḍa**, m. a kind of ball (used as a missile), MBh. iii, 1718. **–dāna**, n. = *-purusha-d*°, W. **–dhaṭa**, m. a balance cup, W.; an oar, L. **–dhara**, m. 'scale-holder,' = °*la*, VarBṛ.; Laghuj. i. **–°dhānā́** (°*lâdh*°), n. 'putting on a balance,' weighing, ŚBr. xi. **–dhāra**, mfn. bearing a balance, Yājñ. ii, $\frac{102}{}$; m. = *-pragraha*, L.; the beam, W.; a merchant, L.; the bearer of an ordeal balance, Vishṇ. x, 8 f.; = °*la*, L.; N. of a merchant, MBh. xii, 9277 ff. **–dhāraṇa**, n. = °*lâdhānā*, Yājñ. ii, 100. **–°dhiroha** (°*lâdh*°), m. risk, Prasannar. vii, $\frac{8}{9}$. **–°dhirohaṇa** (°*lâdh*°), mfn. resembling, Ragh. xix, 8. **–paddhati**, f. N. of a work by Kamalâkara. **–parīkshā**, f. a balance ordeal, W. **–purusha**, m. & *-dāna*, n. gift of gold &c. equal to a man's weight, AV. Pariś. x; Yājñ. iii (named as a penance); BhavP. ii; MatsyaP. cclxxiii; LiṅgaP. ii, 28; Hcat. i, 4 f; Vishṇu or Kṛishṇa, i, 5, 108. **–pragraha**, °**grāha**, m. the string of a balance, Pāṇ. iii, 3, 52, Kāś. **–bīja**, n. the Guñjā berry (used as a weight), L. **–bhavānī**, f. N. of a town, Śaṃkar. xix. **–bhāra**, m. = *-purusha-dāna*, Hcat. i, 5, 619. **–bhṛit**, m. = *-dhara*; a balance bearer, Bādar. **–yashṭi**, f. 'the beam,' see *-koṭi*. **–vat**, mfn. furnished with a balance, VarBṛ. **–°varârdha**, °**dhya**, mfn. at least as much in weight, SāmavBr. ii, 7, 9. **–sūtra**, n. = *-pragraha*, Pāṇ. iii, 3, 52, Kāś. **Tulita**, mfn. lifted up, Ragh. weighed, VarBṛS.; equalled, compared, lxxx, 12.

Tulima, mfn. what may be weighed, Nār. xi, 3.

Tulya, mf(*ā*)n. (in comp. accent, Pāṇ. vi, 2, 2) equal to, of the same kind or class or number or value, similar, comparable, like (with instr. or gen. [cf. ii, 3, 72] or ifc.; e. g. *tena* [Mn. iv, 86] or *etasya* [KaṭhUp. i, 22] or *etat-* [24], 'equal to him'), KātyŚr.; Lāṭy.; Pāṇ. &c.; fit for (instr.), Sūryas. xiv, 6; even, VarBṛ. iv, 21; n. N. of a dance; (*am*), ind. equally, in like manner, Pāṇ.; MBh.; R.; Hariv.; contemporaneously, Dharmaśarm. xvii, 14. **–kaksha**, mfn. equal to (in comp.), Veṇīs. iii, 25. **–karmaka**, mfn. having the same object (in Gramm.), Pāṇ. iii, 4, 48, Kāś. **–kāla**, mfn. contemporary with (instr.), ĀśvGṛ. i, 3, 9; MBh. iii, 134, 24; *-tva*, n. contemporariness, Pāṇ. iv, 3, 105, Vārtt. 1. **–°kālīya**, mfn. = °*la*, BhP. x. **–°kulya**, m. 'of the same family,' a relative, Bhartṛ. iii, 24. **–guṇa**, mfn. possessing the same qualities, equally good, Āp.; Suśr. **–°jātīya**, mfn. similar, Pāṇ. i & vi, 1, 68, Vārtt. 1, Pat.; iii, 3, 35, Kāś. **–tarka**, m. (in dram.) a guess coming near the truth, Sāh. vi, 172 & 180. **–tā**, f. = *-tva*, MBh.; R.; 'equality of place,' conjunction (in astr.), Sūryas. **–tejas**, mfn. equal in splendour. **–tva**, n. equality, resemblance with (instr. or in comp.), Sūryas.; Prab. ii, 18; (*a-*, neg.) Jaim. ii f. **–darśana**, mfn. regarding with equal or indifferent eyes, BhP. i, 5, 24. **–naktam-dina**, mfn. having equal days and nights, Hemac.; not distinguishing between day and night, Kathās. ci, 289. **–nāman**, mfn. of the same name, MBh. i, 101, 7. **–nindā-stuti**, mfn. indifferent with regard to blame or praise, Bhag. xii, 19. **–pāna**, n. compotation, L. **–bala**, mfn. of equal strength. **–bhāvanā**, f. (in math.) combination of like sets. **–mūlya**, mfn. of equal value. **–yogi-tā**, f. 'combination of equal qualities (of unequal objects),' N. of a simile, Sāh. x, 48 f.; Kuval. **–yogôpamā**, f. id., Kāvyâd. ii, 48. **–rūpa**, mfn. of equal form, analogous, W. **–lakshman**, mfn. having the same characteristic, Sāh. x, 89. **–vaṃśa**, mfn. of equal race with (gen.), Cāṇ. (Hit.) **–vayas**, mfn. of the same age, PārGṛ. iii, 8, 17. **–vikrama**, mfn. of equal prowess. **–vīrya**, mfn. of equal strength. **–vṛitti**, mfn. following the same occupation. **–śas**, ind. in equal parts, Suśr. vi, 12. **–śikha**, m. pl. 'equal-braided,' N. of certain mythical beings, L. **–śuddhi**, f. equal substraction, Bīj. **–śodhana**, n. removal of like magnitudes (on both sides of an equation). **–śruti**, f. standing in the same nominal case, Jaim. ii, 1, 10 (*-tva*, abstr.) **Tulyâkṛiti**, mfn. = °*ya-rūpa*. **Tulyâtulya**, mfn. like and unlike. **Tulyânumāna**, n. like inference, analogy. **Tulyântaram**, ind. in equal intervals, Mṛicch. iii, 18. **Tulyârtha**, mfn. equally rich, Pañcat. i, 8, 33; of the same meaning, Pāṇ. i, 3, 42, Kāś. **Tulyâvasthá**, mfn. being in the same condition with (gen.), Ragh. xii, 80. **Tulyôdyoga**, mfn. equal in labours.

तुलकुचि *tulakuci*, m. N. of a prince (son of Sahalin), Divyâv. xxvi, 391.

तुलभ *tulabha*, °*bhiya*, v.l. for *ul*°.

तुलसारिणी *tula-sāriṇī*, f. a quiver, L.

तुलसि *tulasi*, metrically for °*sī*, BhP. iii, 15, 49. °**sikā**, f. = °*sī*, 19; v, 3, 6 & 7, 10.

Tulasī, f. holy basil (small shrub venerated by Vaishṇavas; commonly Tulsī), BhP.; VāyuP. & PadmaP. (produced from the ocean when churned); BrahmavP. (produced from the hair of the goddess Tulasī, ii, 19.) **–dveshā**, f. a kind of basil, L. **–pattra**, n. 'T° leaf,' a very small gift, W. **–vivāha**, m. the marriage of Vishṇu's image with the T° (festival on the 12th day in the 1st half of month Kārttika), W. **–vṛindāvana**, n. a square pedestal (before a Hindū house-door) planted with Tulasī.

तुलि *tuli*, °*lī*. See *turí* & °*rī*.

तुलिका *tulikā*, f. a wagtail, L.

तुलिनी *tulinī*, °*li-phalā*. See *tūl*°.

तुलिम *tulima*, तुल्य *tulya*. See cols. 2, 3.

तुल्वल *tulvala*. See *taulvali*.

तुवि 1. *tuvi*, f. for *tumbī* (gourd), L.

तुवि 2. *tuví* (√*tu*) = *bahu*, Naigh. iii, 1; only in comp. **–kūrmí**, mfn. powerful in working (Indra), RV. iii, vi, viii. **–kūrmin**, mfn. id., 66, 12. **–kratu**, mfn. id., 68, 2 (voc.) **–kshá**, mfn.? (Indra's bow), 77, 11 [= *bahu-* or *mahā-vikshepa*,

Nir. vi, 33]. **-kshatrá**, mf(*ā*)n. ruling powerfully (Aditi), VS. xxi, 5; AV. vii, 6, 2. **-grá**, mfn. swallowing much (Agni), RV. i, 140, 9. **-grābhá**, mfn. seizing powerfully (Indra), vi, 22, 5. **-grí**, mfn. = *-grá* (Indra), ii, 21, 2. **-grīva**, mfn. powerful-necked, i, v, viii. **-jātá**, mfn. of powerful nature (Indra, Varuṇa, &c.), i-vii, x. **-deshṇa** (°*ví-*), mfn. giving much (Indra), viii, 81, 2. **-dyumná**, mfn. very glorious, powerful (Indra, Agni, the Maruts), i, iii-vi, viii f. **-nṛimṇá**, mfn. very valiant (Indra), i, iv, vi, viii, x. **-pratí**, mfn. resisting powerfully (Indra), i, 30, 9. **-bādhá**, mfn. oppressing many (Indra), 32, 6. **-brahman** (°*ví-*), mfn. very devoted, v, 25, 5. **-maghá**, mfn. = *-deshṇa*, 33, 6. **-manyu**, mfn. very zealous (the Maruts), vii, 58, 2. **-mātrá**, mfn. very efficacious (Indra), viii, 81, 2. **-mrakshá**, mfn. injuring greatly, vi. **-rádhas**, mfn. = *-deshṇa*, iv f., vii. **-vāja** (°*ví-*), mf(*ā*)n. abounding in food, i, vi. **-śagma**, mfn. able to do much (Indra), 44, 2. **-śúshma**, mfn. high-spirited (Indra, Indra-Varuṇa), ii, vi, viii. **-śravas** (°*ví-*), mfn. highly renowned (Agni), iii, v. **-shvaṇás**, mfn. loud-sounding, iv f. **-shváṇi**, mfn. id., i f., v f., viii. **-shván**, mfn. id., 166, 1; i; v, 16, 3; ix, 98, 9.

Tuvish, for °*vis* = *tavás*. **-ṭama** (°*vísh-*), mfn. Superl. strongest, i, v; AV. vi, 33, 3. **-mat** (*túv*°), mfn. powerful, RV.; TS. ii, 3, 14, 4; TBr. iii, 1. **Tuvī**, = °*vi*. **-magha** (°*ví-*), = °*vi-m*°, RV. **-ráva**, mfn. making a terrible noise (in battle), x, 99, 6. **-rávas**, nom. °*vān* (cf. Pāṇ. vii, 1, 83 & 4, 48, Kār.), = °*vi-shvaṇás*, RV. x, 64, 4 & 16. **Tuvy-ójas**, mfn. very powerful, iv, 22, 8.

तुश् 1. *tuś*, cl. 1. *tośate*, to drip, trickle, ix.

तुश् 2. *tuś* (= *tush*), cl. 1. *tośate* (p. *tóśamāna*) to be satisfied or pleased with (instr.), AV. iii, 17, 5; to appease, RV. viii, 15, 11 & 50, 5.

तुष् *tush*, cl. 4. °*shyati* (metrically also °*te*; fut. *tokshyati*, *toshṭā*, and inf. *toshṭum* [MBh. iv, 1562], Pāṇ. vii, 2, 10, Kār. [Siddh.]; aor. *atushat*, Bhaṭṭ. xv, 8; pf. *tutosha*) to become calm, be satisfied or pleased with any one (gen., dat., instr., loc., or acc. with *prati*) or anything (instr.), Śāṅkh-Śr. i, 17, 5; MBh. &c.; to satisfy, please, appease, gratify, i, 4198: Caus. *toshayati* (or metrically °*te*), id., RV. x, 27, 16 (p. f. *tushâyantī*); MBh. &c.; Desid. *tutukshati*, W.: Intens. *totushyate*, *totoshṭi*, W.; cf. *tūshṇīm*. **Tushṭa**, mfn. satisfied, pleased, MBh. &c.; m. N. of a prince, VāyuP. ii, 34, 122.

Tushṭi, f. satisfaction, contentment, Mn.; MBh. &c. (9 kinds are reckoned in Sāṃkhya phil., Kap. iii, 39; Sāṃkhyak. 47 & 50; Tattvas.; 'Satisfaction' personified [Hariv. 9498] as daughter of Daksha and mother of Saṃtosha or Muda, VP. i, 7; BhP. iv, 1, 49 f.; MārkP. l; or as daughter of Paurṇamāsa, VāyuP. i, 28, 8; LiṅgaP.; as a deity sprung from the Kalās of Prakṛiti, BrahmavP. ii, 1; as a Mātṛikā, Bhavadev.; as a Śakti, Hcat. i, 5, 197); N. of a Kalā of the moon, BrahmaP. ii, 15; the plant *vṛiddhi*, L. **-kara**, mfn. causing satisfaction, Mn. xi, 234. **-janana**, mfn. id. **-da**, mfn. id. **-mat**, mfn. satisfied, Hariv. iii, 86, 16, Nīl.; m. N. of a prince, VP. iv, 14, 5; BhP. ix, 24, 23.

Tushya, mfn. = °*shṭi-mat* (Śiva), Hariv. 14882.

तुष *túsha*, m. the chaff of grain or corn or rice &c., AV.; ŚBr.; AitBr. &c.; Terminalia Bellerica, L.; cf. *a-*, *ut-*, *nis-*. **-khaṇḍana**, n. 'chaff-grinding,' useless effort, Hit. iv, 5, 3 (v.l.) **-graha**, m. 'husk-seizer,' fire, L. **-ja**, mfn. produced from chaff, Pāṇ. vi, 2, 82. **-°jaka**, m. N. of a Śūdra, viii, 2, 83, Kāś. **-dhānya**, n. husk-corn, VarBṛS. **-pakva** (*túsh*°), mf(*ā*)n. dried by chaff fire, MaitrS. iii, 2, 4; Kapishṭh.; TS. v; ŚBr. vii; KātyŚr. **-sāra**, m. = *-graha*, L. **Tushâgni**, m. chaff fire, MBh. **Tushânala**, m. id., Dhūrtas. i, 18; a capital punishment consisting in twisting dry straw round a criminal's limbs and setting it on fire, W. **Tushâmbu**, n. sour rice- or barley-gruel, Suśr. i, 45. **Tushôttha**, m. id., L. **Tushôdaka**, n. id. i, iv.

तुषार *tushāra*, mf(*ā*)n. cold, frigid, Ragh.; Naish.; m. sg. & pl. frost, cold, snow, mist, dew, thin rain, MBh. &c.; = *-kaṇa*, Śiś. vi, 24; camphor, Bhpr.; pl. for *tukh*°. **-kaṇa**, m. a dewdrop, icicle, flake of snow, Kathās. xix, 50. **-kara**, m. 'cold-rayed,' the moon, Vcar.; Prasannar. vii, 60; Dhūrtan.; *a-*, 'the sun,' Śiś. ix, 7. **-kiraṇa**, m. = *-kara*, Kād.; Amar. **-giri**, m. 'snow-mountain,' the Himālaya, MBh. xiii, 836. **-gaura**, m. camphor, Ṛitus. i, 6. **-gharaṭṭikā**, f. = *-kara*, Alaṃkārav. **-tvish**, m. id., ib. **-dyuti**, m. id., Naish. **-patana**, n. snow-fall, R. **-mūrti**, m. = *-kara*, Śiś. i. **-raśmi**, m. id., Prab. vi, 31. **-rtu** (*rit*°), m. 'cold season,' winter, Naish. xxii. **-varsha**, m. = *-patana*, Rājat. **-varshin**, mfn. causing snow-fall, Ragh. xiv, 84. **-śikharin**, m. = *-giri*, Hcar.; Rājat. **-śaila**, m. id., Vcar. xiii. **-sruti**, f. = *-patana*, Kum. i, 5. **Tushārâṅśu**, m. = °*ra-kara*, SŚaṃkar. i, 28. **Tushārâdri**, m. = °*ra-giri*, Megh. 104; Bhartṛ. ii, 29; Kathās.

तुषित *tushita*, m. pl. a class of celestial beings, MBh. xiii, 1371; Buddh. &c. (12 in number, Hariv.; VP.; BhP. iv, 1, 8; VāyuP. ii, 6; 36 in number, L.); sg. Vishṇu in the 3rd Manv-antara, Vishṇ. iic, 47; VP. iii, 1, 38; (*ā*), f. N. of the wife of Veda-śiras and mother of the Tushitas, 37; BhP. viii, 1, 21. **-kāyika**, mfn. belonging to the body of the Tushitas, Lalit. v, 6.

तुष्ट *tushṭa*, °*shṭi*, °*shya*. See √*tush*.

तुस् *tus*, cl. 1. *tosati*, to sound, Dhātup.

तुस्त *tusta*, m. n. dust (= *tūs*°), L., Sch.

तुह् *tuh*, cl. 1. *tohati*, to pain, Dhātup.

तुहर *tuhara*, °*hāra*, m. N. of two attendants of Skanda, MBh. ix, 2573.

तुहि *tuhi*, a cuckoo's cry, Subh. 1688.

तुहिन *tuhina*, n. (Siddh. napuṃs. 41) frost, cold, mist, dew, snow, Pañcat. ii, 58; Ṛitus.; Kathās.; Rājat.; Prab.; moonlight, Uṇ. k.; camphor, Npr.; (*ā*), f. the tree *śuka-nāsa*, ib. **-kaṇa**, m. = *tushāra-k*°, Amar. **-kara**, m. = *tushāra-k*°, Kād.; *-sutā*, f. 'moon-daughter,' the river Narmadā, Viddh. iv, 18. **-kiraṇa**, m. = *-kara*, VarBṛ.; *-putra*, m. 'moon-son,' Mercury, VarBṛS. civ. **-kshiti-bhṛit**, m. = *tushāra-giri*, Alaṃkārav. **-kshmā-bhṛit**, m. id., Kathās. cxxiv. **-giri**, m. id., Kād.; Pañcat. (v.l.); *-maya*, mfn. formed by the Himâlaya, Prasannar. iii, 30. **-gu**, m. = *-kara*, VarBṛ. **-dyuti**, m. id., Śiś. ix, 30. **-dīdhiti**, m. id., Vcar. **-mayūkha**, m. id., VP. iii, 7. **-raśmi**, m. id., VarBṛ. **-śarkarā**, f. a piece of ice, ice, Rājat. iii. **-śaila**, m. = *-giri*, Hcar. viii. **Tuhinâṅśu**, m. = °*na-kara*, VarBṛS.; VarBṛ.; camphor, W.; *-taila*, n. camphor-oil, L. **Tuhinâcala**, m. = °*na-giri*, Kathās.; Dev. **Tuhinâdri**, m. id., Ragh. viii, 53; Kathās. lxxiii, 82.

Tuhinaya, Nom. P. to cover with ice, Śiś. vi, 55.

तुहुण्ड *tuhuṇḍa*, m. N. of a Dānava, MBh. i, 2533 & 2655; (son of Dhṛita-rāshṭra) 6983; Hariv.

तूख *tūkha*, m. N. of a man, Kāṭh. Anukr.

तूड् *tūḍ* (= *tuḍ*), cl. 1. °*ḍati*, to split, Dhātup. ix, 67; to slight, disrespect, 72.

तूण् *tūṇ* (cf. *kūṇ*, *cūṇ*), cl. 10. °*ṇayati*, to contract, xxxii, 99; xxxv, 42; °*te* (fr. *tūṇa*) to fill (also *tūlay*°, Vop.), xxxiii, 16.

तूण *tūṇa*, m. (g. *śoṇâdi*; g. *gaurâdi*, v.l.) 'bearer' (√*tul*), a quiver, MBh. &c. (often du.); (*ī*), f. id., KātyŚr.; MBh. &c.; a disease of the anus and the bladder, Suśr.; the Indigo plant, Npr. **-dhāra**, v. l. for °*ṇī-dh*°. **-mukha**, n. the cavity of a quiver, Ragh. vii, 54. **-vat**, mfn. furnished with a quiver, MBh. iii, 703; 8486; 10963; Hariv.

Tūṇaka, ifc. = °*ṇa*, Chandom. 77; n. a metre of 4 × 15 syllables. **Tūṇi**, m. = °*ṇa*, R. ii, 31, 30; f. id., R. (B) iii, 8, 19; m. N. of Yugaṃ-dhara's father, Hariv. 9207; VP. iv, 14, 1 (*kuni*, BhP.; LiṅgaP.; KūrmaP. i, 24, 42). **Tūṇika**, m. = *tuṇ*°, Npr. **Tūṇin**, mfn. = °*ṇa-vat*, Hariv.; R.; m. = °*ṇika*, L.

Tūṇī, f. and ind. fr. °*ṇa*. **-kānta**, m. = °*ṇika*, Gal. **-√kṛi**, to use as a quiver, Ragh. ix, 63. **-dhāra**, m. a quiver-bearer, Pāṇ. vi, 2, 75, Kāś. **-śaya**, mfn. lying in the quiver, MBh. (ifc.); R. vi.

Tūṇīka, m. = °*ṇika*, L. °*ṇīra*, m. = °*ṇa*, MBh.; R.; Mālav. v, 10; *-vat*, mfn. = °*ṇa-v*°, Hariv.; °*rāyamāṇa*, mfn. representing a quiver, Daś. v, 112.

तूणव *tūṇava*, m. a flute, TS. vi; Kāṭh.; ĀpŚr. v, 8, 2; Nir. xiii, 9; ifc., Pāṇ. ii, 2, 34, Vārtt. 1. **-dhmá**, m. a flute-player, VS. xxx, 19 f.

तूत *tūta*, m. the mulberry-tree, Bhpr. v.

तूतक *tūtaka*, n. = *tuttha*, blue vitriol, L.

तूतुजान *tūtujāna*, mfn. (√2. *tuj*) hastening, eager, RV. i, vi f.; (°*ná*) viii & x. **Tūtuji**, mfn. id., iv, vi f., x; °*jí*, m. a promoter of (gen.), 22, 3; cf. *á-*.

तूतुम *tūtumá*, mfn. strong, 50, 6; cf. *túmra*.

तूद *tūda*, m. the cotton tree, L.; = *tūta* (توت), Npr.; Thespesia populneoides, L.; (*ī*), f. N. of a district, Pāṇ. iv, 3, 94.

तूपर *tūpará*, mf(*á*, TS. vii, 5, 1, 2)n. Ved. hornless, (m.) a hornless goat, AV. xi, 9, 22; VS. &c.; blunt (*yūpa*), TBr. i, 3, 7, 2; ĀpŚr. xviii, 1.

Tūbara, m. a hornless bull, L.; a beardless man (*tub*°, Uṇ. k.), L.; = °*raka*, L.; Andropogon bicolor, Gal.; mfn. & (*ī*), f., see *tub*°. **Tūbaraka**, m. a eunuch, MBh. v, vii f.; (*ikā*), f., see *tub*°.

तूय *tū́ya*, mfn. (√1. *tu*) strong, RV. x, 28, 3; (*am*), ind. quick, iii-viii, x; n. water, Naigh. i, 12.

तूर् *tūr*, in comp. for 2. *túr*; mfn. (√*tvar*) hastening, Pāṇ. vi, 4, 20; f. instr. °*rā*, °*rbhis*, hastily, MBh. ii, 72, 10; BhP. ii, 7, 37. **Tūr-ghna**, n. 'racer's death,' N. of the northern part of Kurukshetra, TĀr. v, 1. **Tūr-ṇāśa**, n. id., RV. viii, 32, 4.

Tūrṇa, mfn. (√*turv*, Pāṇ. vi, 4, 21, Kāś.; √*tvar*, 20; vii, 2, 28) = °*rtá*, KātyŚr. x, 1, 9; (*am*), ind. quickly, speedily, viii, xxv; PraśnUp.; Nir.; MBh. &c. **-ga**, mfn. running quickly, BhP. x, 53, 6. **-taram**, ind. more quickly, R. iii, 28. **Tūrṇôdita**, mfn. spoken quickly, L. **Tūrṇaka**, m. 'quickly ripening,' a sort of rice, Car. i, 27, 4.

Tūrṇi, mfn. quick, expeditious, clever, zealous, RV.; TS. ii; ŚBr. i; m. the mind, Uṇ. vṛ.; a Śloka, ib.; dirt, Uṇ. k.; f. speed, L. **Tūrṇy-artha**, mf(*ā*)n. pursuing an object, RV. iii, 52, 5; v, 43.

Tūrtá, mfn. quick, expeditious, ŚBr. vi, 3; cf. *á-*. **Tūrti**, see *viśvá-*. 1. **Tūrya**, see *ap-*, *mitra-* &c. **Tūryantī**, f. N. of a plant, ĀpGṛ. xiv, 14.

तूर *tūra*, m. = 2. °*rya*, L.; cf. *ardha-*; (*ī*), f. a thorn-apple, Bhpr. v, 3, 86.

2. **Tūrya**, n. (m., L.) a musical instrument, Pāṇ.; Mn. vii; MBh. &c. (ifc. f. *ā*, KaṭhUp.; Hariv.); cf. *sa-*. **-khaṇḍa**, **-gaṇḍa**, m. a sort of tabor, L. **-maya**, mfn. musical, Kathās. xxiii, 84. **Tūryâugha**, m. a band of instruments.

तूर्य 3. *tūrya*, mfn. = *tur*°, 4th, Rājat. ii, 91; m. N. of a family, W. **Tūryâṅśa**, m. a 4th part, L.

तूर्वयाण *tū́rvayāṇa*, mfn. (√*turv*) overpowering, RV. i, 174, 3; x, 61, 2; m. N. of a man, i, 53, 10; vi, 18, 13. **Tūrvi**, mfn. superior, ix, 42, 3.

तूल् *tūl*, cl. 1. 10. °*lati*, °*layati*, = *nishkṛish*, Dhātup.; see also *tūṇ*; cf. *anu-tūlaya*.

तूल *tū́la*, n. a tuft of grass or reeds, panicle of a flower or plant, AV. xix, 32, 3; Kāṭh.; TāṇḍyaBr.; ChUp. (*īshīkā-*); Kauś.; Āp.; Pāṇ. (ifc. ind., vi, 2, 121); a pencil, Divyâv. xxxvi; = *tūta*, L.; air, L.; m. the thorn-apple, Npr.; n. (m., L.) cotton, MBh.; R. &c.; (*ā*), f. id., L.; a lamp wick, L.; (*ī*), f. id., L.; cotton, Sāṃkhyak. 17, Gauḍap.; = °*li*, Uṇ., Sch.; = *-paṭī*, Subh.; RāmatUp. i, 86, Sch.; the Indigo plant, L.; cf. *ápa-*, *indra-*, *udak-*, *prāk-*, *bhasma-*, *śaṇa-*, *sa-*, *haṅsa-*. **-kaṇa**, n. 'a cotton flock,' Nom. °*ṇāyate*, to appear worthless, Dhanaṃj. 7. **-kārmuka**, n. 'cotton-bow,' a bow-like instrument used for cleaning cotton, L. **-cāpa**, m. id., L. **-dāham**, ind. (with √*dah*, to consume by fire) like cotton, Mcar. vi, 5. **-nālā**, °**likā**, °**li**, f. 'cotton-tube,' a cotton rock, L. **-paṭikā**, f. = °*ṭī*, Buddh. L. **-paṭī**, f. a cotton quilt, RāmatUp. i, 86, Sch. **-picu**, m. cotton, Divyâv. xvii, xxvii. **-pīṭhī**, f. a spindle, Gal. **-pūrṇa**, mfn. filled with cotton, (*a-*, neg.) MBh. xi, 23, 19. **-phala**, m. Calotropis gigantea, L. **-mūla**, N. of a district on the Candra-bhāgā, Rājat. iv. **-lāsikā**, f. = *-pīṭhī*, Gal. **-vatī**, f. a cotton cover, Bhpr. vii, 10, 63. **-vṛiksha**, m. the cotton tree, L. **-śarkarā**, f. a c° seed, L. **-śodhana**, n. °*dhinī*, f. = *-kārmuka*, Gal. **-secana**, n. 'c°-moistening,' spinning, L.

Tūlaka, n. cotton, Bhāshāp.; (*ikā*), f. a panicle (used as probing-rod), L.; = °*li*, Jñātādh. (in Prākrit); Kum. i, 32; Dharmaśarm.; Vcar.; cf. *akshara-*; a wick, L.; = °*la-paṭī*, Pāṇ. iii, 3, 116, Kāś.; Kathās.; (*su-*) RāmatUp. i, 86; an ingot mould, L., Sch. **Tūli**, f. a painter's brush (cf. *turī*), Uṇ., Sch.; *-phalā*, f. the cotton tree (also *tul*°), L. **Tūlika**, m. a cotton trader, Kathās. lxi. **Tūlinī**, f. the cotton tree (also *tul*°, L.), Bhpr.; a kind of bulb, L.

तूष् *tūsh*, cl. 1. °*shati*, = √*tush*, Dhātup.

तूष *tūsha*, m. n. the border of a garment,

Kāṭh.; TBr.; cf. *kṛishṇá-*, *dāma-*. **Tūshâdhá-na**, n. the place where the border is added, TS. vi.

तूष्णीं *tūshṇīm*, for °*ṇī́m*. — **viprakramaṇa**, n. slipping away silently (without having voted), Buddh. L. — **śaṅsa**, m. a verse which requires silent recitation, AitBr.; ŚāṅkhŚr. — **śīla**, mfn. taciturn, Pāṇ. v, 3, 72, Vārtt. 2, Pat. — **sāra**, mfn. chiefly silent, AitBr. ii, 31, 1. — **sthāna**, n. silence, Kathās. lxxiv. — **homá**, m. an oblation offered silently, TS. vi. — **gaṅga**, n. N. of a Tīrtha, Pāṇ. ii, 2, 29, Pat.; cf. *ushṇī-g°*. — **japa**, m. a prayer muttered silently, ŚāṅkhŚr. ix, 25, 2, Sch. — **daṇḍa**, m. secret punishment, Mcar. iv, ½. — **bhāva**, m. the being silent, silence, MBh. xii, 3840; Sāh. — **bhāvam**, ind. silently, Pāṇ. iii, 4, 63. — **bhūta**, mfn. become silent, MBh. i, 7951; R. i, 70, 18. — **bhūya**, ind. p. (Pāṇ. iii, 4, 63) silently, Pañcat. iii, 14, ½.

Tūshṇīka, mfn. (Pāṇ. v, 3, 72, Vārtt. 2, Pat.) silent, R. (G) ii, 117, 3; Kathās. iic, 60; Mālatīm. i, 19, Sch.; (*am*), ind. silently, MānŚr. i, 7, 5; MBh. v; R. v; (*ām*), ind. (Pāṇ. v, 3, 72, Vārtt. 1, Pat.) id., Bhāgav. (Uṇ. iv, 35, Sch.) **Tūshṇī́m**, ind. (g. *svar-ādi*) silently, quietly, RV. ii, 43, 3; TS. &c. (for °*ṇīṃ babhūva*, 'became silent,' Divyâv.)

तूस्त *tūsta*, n. (Pāṇ. iii, 1, 21; ifc. g. *cūrṇâdi*) dust, iii, 1, 21, Kāś.; Purushôtt. (Uṇ. iii, 86, Sch.); sin, L.; an atom, L.; a braid of hair, L.

तृ *trí* (=*strí*), nom. pl. *tā́ras*, the stars, RV. viii, 55, 2; cf. *tārā*.

तृंहण *triṇhaṇa*, n. (√*tṛih*) crushing, Pāṇ. viii, 4, 2, Kāś.; cf. *tárh°*. °**ṇīya**, to be crushed, ib.

तृक्ष् *trikṣh*, cl. 1. °*kshati*, to go, Dhātup.

तृक्ष *triksha*, m. N. of a man, g. *gargâdi*.

तृक्षस् *trikshas*, for *tváksh°*, Naigh. ii, 9.

तृक्षाक *trikshāka*, N. of a man, g. *śivâdi*.

तृक्षि *trikshí*, m. N. of a man with the patr. Trāsadasyava, RV. vi, 46, 8; viii, 22, 7.

तृख *trikha*, n. nutmeg, L.

तृच *tricá*, m. n. (fr. *trí* & *ṛíc*, Pāṇ. vi, 1, 37, Vārtt. 1) a strophe consisting of 3 verses, AV. xix; TS. i; AitBr.; ŚBr. & KātyŚr. (*tricá*); Nir.; RPrāt.; cf. *try-ṛica*. — **klṛipta**, mfn. arranged in strophes of 3 verses each, ŚāṅkhŚr.; AitBr. iii, 43, Sāy. — **bhāgā**, f. (scil. *ṛic*) verse 1. of the 1st, v. 2. of the 2nd, and v. 3. of the 3rd *paryāya* of a Tṛica, Lāṭy. vi.

Tṛicin, mfn. containing a Tṛica, AitBr. iii, 43.

तृढ *tṛiḍhá*, mfn. (√*tṛih*) crushed, RV. i, vi.

तृण् *triṇ*, cl. 8. °*ṇoti*, °*ṇute*, or *tarṇ°*, °*ṇute*, to eat, Dhātup. 1. **Tṛita**, mfn. eaten, g. *tanoty-ādi*.

तृण *tṛíṇa*, n. (m., g. *ardharcâdi*; ifc. f. *ā*) grass, herb, any gramineous plant, blade of grass, straw (often symbol of minuteness and worthlessness), RV. &c. (ifc. accent, g. *ghoshâdi*); m. N. of a man, g. *śivâdi* & *naḍâdi*; [cf. Goth. *thaurnus*.] — **karṇa**, m. N. of a man, g. *śivâdi* (v.l.); pl. his descendants, g. *yaskâdi*. — **kāṇḍa**, n. a heap of grass, Pāṇ. iv, 2, 51, Kāś. — **kuṅkuma**, n. Kaśmir crocus, L. — **kuñcaka**, n. 'attracting grass (electrically when rubbed),' N. of a gem, Buddh. L. — **kuṭi**, f. a hut of grass or straw, SāmavBr. iii, 9, 1, Sāy. — **kuṭī**, f. id., L. — **kuṭīra**, id., Siṇhâs. — **kuṭīraka**, id., Pañcat. i, 4, ½. — **kūṭa**, m. n. = -*kāṇḍa*, VarBṛS. — **kūrcikā**, f. a whisk, L. — **kūrma**, m. the Tumbī gourd, L. — **ketakī**, f. a kind of Tabāshīr, Npr. — **ketu**, °**tuka**, m. a bamboo, L. — **gaḍa**, m. a sort of sea crab, L. — **gaṇanā**, f. 'valuing at a straw,' thinking anything (loc.) to be of no importance, Vcar. vi, 2. — **gaṇāya**, Nom. °*yate*, to represent a heap of grass, have no value whatever, Prasang. iv, 4. — **gandhā**, f. Batatas paniculata, Npr. — **godhā**, f. a lizard, chamæleon, L. — **gaura**, n. = *kuṅkuma*, L. — **granthi**, f. N. of a plant, L. — **grāhin**, m. 'attracting grass (electrically when rubbed),' sapphire or another gem, L. — **cara**, m. N. of a gem, Npr. — **jambhan**, mfn. graminivorous or having teeth like grass, Pāṇ. v, 4, 125. — **jalāyukā**, f. a caterpillar, ŚBr. xiv. — **jalūkā**, f. id., BhP. iv, 29, 76. — **jantu**, m. a blade of grass, MBh. xii, 261, 21. — **jāti**, f. pl. the different kinds of grass, Mn. i, 48. — **jyotis**, n. N. of a shining grass, Kir. xv, 47, Sch. — 1. -**tā**, f., -**tva**, n. the state of grass, L. — **tvaca**, m. a kind of grass, Gal. — **druma**, m. a palm-tree, L. — **dhānya**, n. wild rice, L. — **dhvaja**, m. = -*ketu*, Bhpr. — **nimbā**, f. the Nepalese Nimba, L. — **pa**, m. 'grass-swallower,' N. of a Gandharva, MBh. i; Hariv. 14157. — **pañca-mūla**, n. an aggregate of 5 roots of gramineous plants (rice, sugar-cane, Darbha, Scirpus Kysoor, Saccharum Sara), Suśr. vi, 48, 23. — **pattrikā**, °**ttrī**, f. a kind of reed, L. — **padī**, f. (a woman) having legs as thin as blades of grass, g. *kumbhapady-ādi*. — **parṇī**, f. = -*pattrī*, Gal. — **pāṇi**, m. N. of a Ṛishi, SV. Anukr. — **pīḍa**, n. 'pressing as close as grass,' hand to hand fighting, MBh. ii, 909. — **purushaka**, m. a straw-man, Kād. — **pulaka**, °**lī**, see -*pūl°*. — **pushpa**, n. = -*kuṅkuma*, L.; (*ī*), f. N. of a plant, L. — **pūla**, a tuft of grass, L.; (*ī*), f. id., Kād. v, 986 (v. l. *pui°*). — **pūlaka**, id., Hcar. vii (v. l. *pul°*). — **pūlika**, N. of a human abortion, Car. iv, 4, 1. — **prāya**, mfn. = -*vat* (a district), R. iii, 15, 41; worth a straw, worthless, W. — **balva-jā**, f. Eleusine indica, L. — **bindu**, m. N. of an ancient sage and prince, MBh. iii f., ix; Ragh.; VP.; BhP.; VāyuP. i, 23, 190; DevībhP.; -*saras*, n. N. of a lake, MBh. iii; cf. *tārṇabindavīya*. — **bīja**, °**jaka**, °**jôttama**, m. Panicum frumentaceum, L. — **bhuj**, mfn. graminivorous, Kathās. lx. — **bhūta**, mfn. become as thin as a blade of grass, R. iv, 9, 95; deprived of all power, MBh. vii, 8303. — **maṇi**, m. = -*kuñcaka*, Subh. 896. — **maya**, mfn. made of grass, ŚārṅgP. (Siṇhâs.) — **mushṭi**, f. a handful of grass. — **rāj**, m. 'king of grasses,' the vine-palm, R. vi. — **rāja**, m. (cf. Bhpr. iv, 35) id., MBh. iv; Hariv. (also °*jan*, 3722); the cocoa-nut tree, L.; a bamboo, Npr.; sugar-cane, ib. — **rājan**, m., see °*ja*. — **lava**, m. a blade of grass, Bhartṛ. — **vat**, mfn. abounding in grass, MBh. xii; Bhartṛ. — **vistara**, m. = -*kāṇḍa*. — **vṛiksha**, m. the fan-palm, Npr.; the date tree, ib.; the cocoa-nut tree, ib.; the areca-nut tree, ib.; Pandanus odoratissimus, ib. — **śīta**, n. N. of a fragrant grass, L.; (*ā*), f. Commelina salicifolia, L. — **śūnya**, m. Jasminum Sambac, Suśr. i, iv; (*śūlya*) v, 7, 19; m. f. n. the fruit of Pandanus odoratissimus, L. — **śūlya**, see -*śūnya*. — **śoṇita**, n. 'grass-blood,' = -*kuṅkuma*, L. — **śoshaka**, m. N. of a serpent, v, 4, 34. — **śauṇḍikā**, f. a kind of Achyranthes, Npr. — **shaṭ-pada**, m. 'grass-infesting six-footed,' a wasp, L. — **saṃvāha**, mfn. grass-moving (wind), Āp. — **sāra**, mfn. 'as weak as grass;' (*ā*), f. Musa sapientum, L.; °*rī-kṛita*, mfn. rendered weak as grass, Kathās. — **siṇha**, m. 'reed-lion,' axe, Pāṇ. vi, 2, 72, Kāś. — **somâṅgiras**, m. N. of one of Yama's 7 sacrificial priests, MBh. xiii, 7112. — **skandá**, m. N. of a man, RV. i, 172, 3. — **stāraka**, m. 'covering with grass,' leaving unremembered, Buddh. L. — **harmya**, m. a bower of grass or straw on the top of a house, L. **Tṛiṇâgni**, m. a grass fire (quickly extinguished), Mn. iii, 168; Pañcat.; burning a criminal wrapped up in straw, W. **Tṛiṇâṅkura**, m. young grass, Bhartṛ. **Tṛiṇâñcana** [Gal.], °**ñjana** [L.], m. = °*ṇa-godhā*. **Tṛiṇâṭavī**, f. a forest abounding in grass, L. **Tṛiṇâḍhya**, m. N. of a grass, L. **Tṛiṇâda**, mfn. = °*ṇa-bhuj*, Subh. **Tṛiṇâdhipa**, m. 'grass-king,' N. of a grass, L. **Tṛiṇânna**, n. = °*ṇa-dhānya*, Npr. **Tṛiṇâmla**, n. N. of a grass, L. **Tṛiṇâri**, m. a kind of Mollugo, Npr. **Tṛiṇâvarta**, m. N. of a Daitya, BhP. x; BrahmavP. iv, 11. **Tṛiṇâśa**, mfn. = °*ṇâda*, Subh. **Tṛiṇâśana**, °**śin**, mfn. id., Kathās. lx. **Tṛiṇâsṛij**, n. = °*ṇa-śoṇita*, L. **Tṛiṇêkshu**, m. N. of a grass, L. **Tṛiṇêndra**, m. = *ṇa-rāj*, MBh. xiii. **Tṛiṇâidha**, m. a fire for which grass is used instead of fuel, ĀpŚr. ix, 9, 12. **Tṛiṇôttama**, m. 'best of grasses,' a kind of Crocus, L. **Tṛiṇôttha**, m. = °*ṇa-kuṅkuma*, L. **Tṛiṇôdaká**, n. sg. grass and water, ŚBr. xiv; ChUp.; MBh. (v. l.); -*bhūmi*, n. sg. grass, water, and a seat, Gaut. v, 35. **Tṛiṇôdbhava**, m. = °*ṇa-dhānya*, L.; = °*ṇôttha*, Npr. **Tṛiṇôlapa**, n. sg. (g. *gavâśvâdi*) grass and shrubs, MBh. v; Kād. **Tṛiṇôlkā**, f. a torch of hay, MBh. v; Hit. i. **Tṛiṇâṅkas**, n. = °*ṇa-kuṭi*, L. **Tṛiṇâushadha**, n. the fragrant bark of Feronia elephantum, L.

Tṛiṇaka, n. a worthless blade of grass, MBh. i.; m. N. of a man, ii, 328. **Tṛiṇakīyā**, f. a grassy place, g. *bilvakâdi*. **Tṛiṇaya**, Nom. °*ti*, to esteem as lightly as straw, Naish. ix, 70. **Tṛiṇasa**, mfn. (Pāṇ. iv, 2, 80) grassy, Vop. **Tṛiṇī-√kṛi**, to make straw of, make light of, MBh. i, 7062; v, vii; Naish. iii, 54; Kathās. xviii, 85; Sāh. **Tṛiṇīya**, g. *utkarâdi*. **Tṛiṇyā**, f. = °*ṇa-kāṇḍa*, g. *pāśâdi*; cf. *a-*.

तृणता 2. *triṇatā*, f. = *tri-ṇ°*, L.

तृणाङ्कु *triṇāṅku*, m. N. of a sage, R. iv.

तृणामल्ल *triṇāmalla*, N. of a temple, Rasik. xi, 15; cf. *tri-m°*. °**ṇāvallī**, f. id., 30.

तृण्ण *trinna*. See *áti-*, *ava-*, *ā́-*, *ví-*, *sám-*.

तृत 1. & 2. *trita*. See √*triṇ* & *tritá*.

Tṛitī́ya, mf(*ā*)n. (fr. *tri*, Pāṇ. v, 2, 55; see also vii, 3, 115; i, 1, 36, Vārtt.) the 3rd, RV. &c.; m. the 3rd consonant of a Varga (*g*, *j*, *ḍ*, *d*, *b*), RPrāt.; VPrāt.; APrāt.; Pāṇ., Vārtt. & Kāś.; (in music) N. of a measure; (*ā*), f. (scil. *tithi*) = °*yikā*, Jyot. &c.; (scil. *vibhakti*) the terminations of the 3rd case, the 3rd case (instrumental), Pāṇ.; APrāt. iii, 19; (*am*), ind. for the 3rd time, thirdly, RV. x, 45, 1; ŚBr. ix, xi; TāṇḍyaBr. &c.; (*ena*), instr. ind. at the 3rd time, PārGṛ. ii, 3, 5; (*tṛitī́ya*) mfn. (Pāṇ. v, 3, 48) forming the 3rd part, (n.) a 3rd part, TS.; TBr.; ŚBr. iii f.; KātyŚr.; Mn. vi, 33; MBh.; [cf. Zend *thritya*, Lat. *tertius*; Goth. *thridja*.] — **karaṇī**, f. the side of a square 3 times smaller than another, Śulb. i, 47. — **tā**, f. the condition of the 3rd consonant of a Varga, RPrāt. xi, 13. — **tva**, n. the condition of being the 3rd, TPrāt., Sch. — **divasa**, m. '3rd day,' the day after to-morrow, Hit. iii, 8, ½. — **prakṛiti**, f. '3rd nature,' a eunuch, L., Sch.; the neuter gender, ib. — **bhikshā**, f. a 3rd part of alms, Pāṇ. ii, 2, 3. — **savaná**, n. the 3rd Soma preparation (in the evening), TS. ii; ŚBr. i–iii; AitBr. vi; KātyŚr.; Nir. vii; °*nīya*, mfn. belonging to °*ná*, ŚāṅkhŚr. — **svara**, n. '3rd tune,' N. of a Sāman. **Tṛitīyâṅśa**, m. a 3rd part, VarBṛS.; mfn. receiving a 3rd as one's share (°*yin*, Sch. on KātyŚr. x, 2, 25 & Nyāyam. iii), Mn. viii, 210.

Tṛitīyaka, mfn. (Pāṇ. v, 2, 81) recurring every 3rd day, tertian (fever), AV. i, v, xix; Suśr.; occurring for the 3rd time, Pāṇ. v, 2, 77, Kāś.; the 3rd, Śrut.; Sāh. vi, 226 & 239; (*ikā*), f. the 3rd day in a half month. — **jvara**, m. tertian ague.

Tṛitīyā, f. & ind. — √**kṛi**, to plough for the 3rd time, Pāṇ. v, 4, 58. — **samāsa**, m. a Tat-purusha compound the former member of which would stand in the instrumental case if separated from the latter, i, 1, 30; vi, 1, 89, Vārtt. 6. **Tṛitīyika**, mfn. v, 1, 48; (*ā*), f. see °*yaka*. **Tṛitīyin**, mfn. holding the 3rd rank, ĀśvŚr.; Lāṭy.; Mn. viii, 210; see °*yâṅśa*.

तृत्सु *trítsu*, m. sg. & pl. N. of a race, RV.

तृद् *trid*, cl. 7. (impf. *atṛiṇat*, pf. *tatarda*, p. Ā. *tatṛidānā́*; aor. *atardīt*, Bhaṭṭ.; fut. *tardishyati*, *tartsy°*, Pāṇ. vii, 2, 57) to cleave, pierce, RV.; Hariv.; Bhaṭṭ.; to split open, let out, set free, RV.; to destroy, Bhaṭṭ. vi, 38: Desid. *titardishati*, °*rtsati*, Pāṇ. vii, 2, 57; cf. √*tard*.

Tṛidilá, mfn. porous, RV. x, 94, 11; cf. *á-*.

तृप् 1. *trip*, cl. 4. *tṛípyati* [AV.; TS. &c.; metrically also °*te*], cl. 5. [Subj. 2. sg. *tṛipṇávas*, Impv. °*nuhi*, °*nutám*, RV. (see also *ā́-tṛipṇuvat*); °*noti*, Dhātup. & g. *kshubhnâdi*], cl. 6. [2. sg. *tṛimpási*, Impv. °*pá*, °*patu*, &c., RV.; ŚBr.; cf. Pāṇ. vii, 1, 59, Vārtt. 1, Pat.; *tṛipati*, Dhātup.; pf. p. Ā. *tātṛipāṇá*, RV. x, 95, 16; P. *tatarpa*; 3. pl. *tātṛipur*, AV. xi, 7, 13; aor. *atṛipat* (iii, 13, 6) or *atrāpsīt*, Pāṇ. iii, 1, 44, Vārtt.; *atarpīt*, *atārpsīt*, Vop.; fut. 1st *tarpishyati* (but cf. Pāṇ. vii, 2, 10, Siddh.), *tarpsy°*, *trapsy°*; Cond. *atrapsyat*, AitUp. iii, 3; fut. 2nd *tarpitā*, °*ptā*, *traptā*, Kāś. on Pāṇ. vi, 1, 59 & vii, 2, 45] to satisfy one's self, become satiated or satisfied, be pleased with (gen., instr., or rarely loc., e.g. *nâgnis tṛipyati kāshṭhānām*, 'fire is not satisfied with wood,' MBh. xiii; *ātṛipyan brāhmaṇā dhánaiḥ*, 'the Brahmans were pleased with wealth,' ŚBr. xiii), RV. &c.; to enjoy (with abl.), Mn. iv, 251; to satisfy, please, Bhaṭṭ. i f.: cl. 1. *tarpati*, to kindle, Dhātup.: Caus. *tarpayati*, rarely °*te* (impf. *atarpayat*, RV. &c.; p. *tarpáyat*, ib.; aor. *atītṛipat*, ŚāṅkhGṛ. iii, 12; BhP.; *dītṛipāma*, VS.; inf. *tárpayitavaí*, ŚBr. i, 7, 3, 28; ĀpŚr. iv, 16, 17) to satiate, satisfy, refresh, gladden, RV. &c.; Ā. to become satiated or satisfied, VS.; AV. vi; to kindle, Dhātup.: Desid. (Subj. *tìtṛipsāt*) to wish to enjoy, RV. x, 87, 19: Caus. Desid. (Pot. *titarpayishet*) to wish to satiate or refresh or satisfy, ŚāṅkhGṛ. i, 2, 7; Gobh. i, 9, 2: Intens. *tarītṛipyate*, *tarītarpti*, °*trapti*, W.; [cf. √*tṛiph*; τέρπω.]

2. **Tṛip**, see *asu-* & *paśu-tṛip*; *śiśnôdara-*.

Tṛipa, mfn. *a-tṛipá*; *asu-*; (*ā*), f. N. of a plant, ŚBr. v, 3, 5, 20, Sāy. **Tṛipát**, ind. with pleasure, to one's satisfaction, RV. ii f., x; m. the moon, Uṇ. k.; a parasol, Uṇ. ii, 85, Sch. **Tṛipála**, mfn. [SV.] or [*am*], ind. [RV. ix, 97, 8] = °*prá* or °*prám*; (*ā*), f. a creeper, Uṇ. i, 106, Sch.; = *tri-*

phalā, Uṇ. vṛ.; *tripála-prabharman,* mfn. (Soma) = *tripra-prahārin* [Nir. v, 12], RV. x, 89, 5. **Tṛi-pāya,** Nom. °*yate* (fr. °*pát*), g. *bhṛiśâdi.* **Tṛipita,** mfn. Pāṇ. vii, 1, 59, Vārtt. 2, Pat. **Tṛipú,** m. a thief (cf. *asu-* & *paśu-tṛip*), Naigh. iii, 24 (v.l. *tripú*).

Tṛiptá, mfn. satiated, satisfied with (gen., instr., or in comp.), AV.; ŚBr. &c.; (*am*), ind. so as to exhibit satiety, AitBr. i, 25, 15; n. N. of a metre, RPrāt. xvii, 5. — **tā,** f. satiety, Kathās. lxii; satisfaction, cxix; *a-,* insatiability, Śiś. ix, 64. **Tṛiptâṇśu,** mfn. having well-nourished shoots, RV. i, 168. **Tṛiptâtman,** mfn. having a contented mind.

Tṛípti, f. satisfaction, contentment, RV. viii, 82, 6 (°*ptí*) & ix, 113, 10; AV. &c.; disgust, Suśr. i, 24, 2; m. N. of a Gandharva, Gal. — **kara,** mfn. giving satisfaction, 46, 9, 7. — **kāraka,** mfn. id. — **kṛit,** mfn. = *a-secana,* L. — **ghna,** mfn. removing disgust. — **da,** mfn. = *-kara.* — **dīpa,** m. N. of Bhpañcad. vii. — **mat,** mfn. satisfied, finding satisfaction in (loc.), ChUp. vii, 10, 2; Rudray. ii, 1, 4. — **yoga,** m. satisfaction, Śiś. ii, 31.

Tṛiptī-√kṛi, to satisfy, gladden, Naish. viii.

Tṛipyat, mfn., *a-* not becoming satiate, Kathās.

Tṛiprá, mf(*ā*)n. KātyŚr. xxv, 11, 30; (*ám*), ind., ŚBr. x, 4, 1, 18; xii, 5; m. = *puroḍāśa* (Uṇ., Sch. & Sāy.; = *ghṛita,* Uṇ. k.), RV. viii, 2, 5; cf. *trapishṭha.* — **daṇśin,** mfn. biting hastily (?), AV. vii, 56, 3.

Tṛiprāya, Nom. °*yate,* g. *sukhâdi.* **Tṛiprālu,** mfn. °*praṃ na sahate,* Pāṇ. v, 2, 122, Vārtt. 6.

Tṛiprin, mfn. g. *sukhâdi.*

तृफ् *tṛiph,* cl. 6. °*phati,* to satisfy (cf. √*tṛip*), Dhātup.; to kill (cf. *tarphitṛi*), W.

तृफला *tṛiphalā.* See *tri-ph*°.

तृफू *tṛiphū,* f. = *sarpa-jāti,* Uṇ. k.

तृभि *tṛíbhi,* m. a ray, TĀr. i, 11, 3.

तृम्प् *tṛimp,* cl. 6. °*pati.* See √*tṛip.*

Tṛimpaṇa, n. the act of pleasing, Pāṇ. viii, 4, 2, Vārtt. 7 f., Pat. °**ṇīya,** mfn. to be pleased, ib.

तृम्फ् *tṛimph* (= √*tṛip*), cl. 6. °*phati,* to satisfy, vii, 1, 59, Vārtt. 1, Pat.

तृवृत् *trivṛit.* See *tri-v*°.

तृष् 1. *tṛish,* cl. 4. °*shyati* (p. *tṛíshyat,* Ā. °*shāṇá,* pf. *tātṛishāṇá,* RV. [*tat*°, vi, 15, 5]; 3. pl. *tātṛishúr,* x, 15, 9; aor. Subj. *tṛishat,* AV. ii, 29, 4; ind. p. °*shṭvā,* xix, 34, 6; °*shitvā* & *tarshitvā,* Pāṇ. i, 2, 25) to be thirsty, thirst, thirst for, RV. &c.: Caus. (aor. 1. pl. *atītṛishāma*) to cause to thirst, iv, 34, 11; [cf. Goth. *thars, thaursus;* τέρσομαι.] 2. **Tṛish,** mfn. 'longing for,' see *artha-;* f. (Siddh. stry. 23) thirst, MBh. xiv; Suśr.; VarBr. &c.; strong desire, L.; Desire as daughter of Love, L.

Tṛishā, f. thirst, Nal. ix, 27; Suśr.; Vet. &c.; strong desire, Hit. i, 6, 34; Desire as daughter of Love, L.; Methonica superba, L. — **bhū,** f. 'thirst-origin,' the bladder, L. — **roga,** m. 'morbid thirst,' N. of a disease, MBh. xii, 11268. — **rta** (°*shâr*°), mfn. suffering from thirst, Sinhâs. vi, 7; Hit. iii, 4, 9/1; affected by desire, i, 6, 34. — **ha,** n. 'thirst-destroying,' water, L.; a kind of anise, L.

Tṛishitá, mfn. (fr. 2. *tṛish,* g. *tārakâdi*) thirsty, thirsting, desirous, RV. i, 16, 5; MBh. &c. (with inf., Hariv. 5033); n. thirst, W.; cf. *á-*. **Tṛishitôttarā,** f. the plant *aśana-parṇī,* L.

Tṛishú, mfn. greedy, eagerly desirous, RV. iv, 4, 1; 7, 11; ind. greedily, rapidly, i, 58; iv, 7, 11; vii, 3, 4; x, 79; 91; 113; 115. — **cyávas,** mfn. moving greedily, vi, 66, 10. — **cyút,** mfn. id., i, 140, 3.

Tṛishṭá, mf(*ā*)n. 'dry,' rough, harsh, rugged, hoarse [cf. Lat. *tussis* fr. *turs-ti-s*], iii, 9, 3; x, 85 & 87; AV. v, 18 f.; vii, 113, 2. — **jambha,** mfn. having rough teeth, vi, 50, 3. — **daṇśman** (°*ṭá-*), mfn. biting roughly, xii, 1, 46. — **dhūma** (°*ṭá-*), mfn. having pungent breath (a snake), xix, 47 & 50. — **vandana,** mf(*ā*)n. having a rough eruption, vii, 113, 1. **Tṛishṭámā,** f. N. of a river, RV. x, 75, 6.

Tṛishṭikā, f. a rough woman, AV. vii, 113, 1 f.

Tṛishṇaka, mfn. desirous, eager for, L.

Tṛishṇáj, mfn. (Nir.; Pāṇ.) thirsty, RV. i, v, vii.

Tṛíshṇā, f. thirst, i, vii, ix; AV.; ŚBr. &c.; desire, avidity (chiefly ifc.), R.; Ragh.; BhP. &c.; Avidity as mother of Dambha (Prab. ii, 1/2), daughter of Death (Mṛityu, VP. i, 7, 31; or Māra, Lalit. xxiv, 20), generated by Vedanā and generating Upādāna (Buddh.); cf. *ati-.* — **kshaya,** m. cessation of desire, tranquillity of mind, L. — **ghna,** mfn. quenching thirst, Suśr. i, 45. — **mārá,** m. dying of thirst, AV. iv, 17, 6 f. — °**ri** (°*ṇâr*°), m. the plant *parpaṭa,* L. — **varūtrī,** f., for *tvashṭā-,* g. *vanaspaty-ādi.*

Tṛishyā́-vat, mfn. = *tarsh*°, RV. vii, 103, 3.

तृषम *tṛishama.* See *tri-sh*°.

तृह् *tṛih,* cl. 7. (Impv. *tṛiṇéḍhu;* Subj. pl. *tṛiṇáhān;* aor. *atṛiham,* AV.; *atarhīt,* Bhaṭṭ.; *atṛikshat,* Durgâd.; pf. *tatarha,* AV.; pr. p. nom. m. *tṛiṇhát,* RV. x, 102, 4; f. du. °*hatī,* ŚBr. xii, 2, 2, 2; ind. p. *tṛiḍhvā́,* Pass. pl. *tṛihyánte,* p. °*hyámāṇa,* AV.; cl. 6. *tṛihati, tṛiṇh*°, Dhātup.) to crush, bruise, RV.; AV.; TS. i, 5, 7, 6; ŚBr.; Bhaṭṭ.: Desid. *titṛikshati, titṛiṇhishati,* Pāṇ. i, 2, 10, Siddh.; cf. *vi-; tárhaṇa, tṛiṇhaṇa, tṛiḍhá.*

तॄ *tṝ,* cl. 1. P. (rarely Ā.) *tárati* (Subj. *tárat,* impf. *átarat,* p. *tárat,* inf. *tarádhyai,* °*rishá́ṇi,* RV.), cl. 5. *tarute* (x, 76, 2; Pot. 1. pl. *turyāma,* v f.), cl. 3. *titarti* (BhP.; p. nom. pl. *títratas,* RV. ii, 31, 2; Pot. *tuturyā́t,* v f., viii), with prepositions Ved. chiefly cl. 6. P. Ā. (*tiráte,* Subj. *tirā́ti,* impf. *átirat,* p. *tirát,* inf. *tíram, tíre,* RV.; —aor. *átārīt,* i, vii; 1. pl. °*rishma* i, vii, °*rima* viii, 13, 21; *tárushante* v, °*ta* i, °*shema* vii [cf. Pāṇ. iii, 1, 85, Kāś.]; Ā. & Pass. *-tāri,* RV.; P. *atārshīt,* BhP.; °*sham,* MBh.; Daś.; pf. *tatā́ra,* RV. &c.; 3. pl. *titirur,* i f.; *teritha,* °*ratur,* Pāṇ. vi, 4, 122; p. *titirvás,* gen. *tatarúshas,* RV.; fut. *tarishyati,* °*rīsh*°, *taritā,* °*rītā* [cf. *pra-tár*°], Pāṇ. vii, 2, 38; *tárutā,* RV. i; Prec. *tīryāt, tarishīshṭa,* Vop.; inf. *tartum,* MBh.; R.; °*rīt*° iv f., °*rit*° MBh. i; Hariv.; R. v; ind. p. *tīrtvā́,* AV.; *-tū́rya,* see *vi-*) to pass across or over, cross over (a river), sail across, RV. &c.; to float, swim, VarBṛS. lxxx, 14; Bhaṭṭ. xii; Cāṇ.; to get through, attain an end or aim, live through (a definite period), study to the end, RV. &c.; to fulfil, accomplish, perform, R. i f.; to surpass, overcome, subdue, escape, RV. &c.; to acquire, gain, viii, 100, 8; MBh. xii; R.; Ā. to contend, compete, RV. i, 132, 5; to carry through or over, save, vii, 18, 6; MBh. i, iii: Caus. *tārayati* (p. °*ráyat*) to carry or lead over or across, Kauś.; MBh. &c.; to cause to arrive at, AV. xviii; PraśnUp. vi, 8; to rescue, save, liberate from (abl.), Mn.; MBh. &c.: Desid. *titīrshati* (also *titarishati,* °*rīsh*°, Pāṇ. vii, 2, 41; p. Ā. *titīrshamāṇa,* MBh. xiii, 2598) to wish to cross or reach by crossing, KaṭhUp.; MBh.; BhP. iv: Intens. *tartarīti* (2. du. °*rīthas;* p. gen. *táritratas* [Pāṇ. vii, 4, 65]; see also *vi-; tātarti,* 92, Sch.) to reach the end by passing or running or living through, RV.; [cf. *tára, tirás, tīrṇá;* Lat. *termo, trans;* Goth. *thairh.*]

तेक्ष्णिष्ठम् *tékshṇishṭham,* ind. (fr. *tīkshṇá*) in a most pungent manner, TBr. i, 5 f.; TĀr. ii.

तेग *tegá* or *stegá,* m. pl., VS. xxv, 1.

तेज् *tej,* °*jati,* to protect, Dhātup. vii, 56.

तेज *teja,* m. (√*tij*) sharpness, Vop. viii, 132; m. N. of a man, Rājat. viii, 1226; (*ā*), f. the 13th night of the Karma-māsa, Sūryapr. — **pattra,** -**pāla,** see °*jaḥ-p*°. — **vatī,** see °*jo-v*°. — **valkala,** m. Zanthoxylon Rhetsa, Bhpr. v, 1, 1/170. — **siṇha,** m. N. of a man (son of Raṇa-dara); cf. °*jaḥ-s*°.

Tejaḥ, = °*jas.* — **pattra,** n. the leaf of Laurus Cassia (also °*ja-p*°, L.), W. — **pāla,** m. N. of a man (also °*ja-p*°). — **prabha,** n. 'gleaming with lustre,' N. of a mythic missile, R. i, 29, 18. — **phala,** m. N. of a tree, L. — **sambhava,** m. (= *agni-s*°) lymph, L. — **siṇha,** m. N. of an astronomer, Hāyan. — **sena,** m. N. of a man, Rājat. viii, 400 f. **Tejâhvā,** f. Scindapsus officinalis, Suśr. iv, 2, 92.

Téjana, n. sharpening, whetting, Dhātup.; inflammation, Suśr. iv, 24; rendering bright, W.; the shaft of an arrow, AV.; Kāṭh.; AitBr. &c.; a reed, bamboo, RV. i, 110, 5; = °*naka,* L.; (*ī*), f. (g. *gaurâdi*) a whetstone, touchstone, L.; a number of reeds or straw &c. twisted or matted together, tuft, mat, Kāṭh. xxii f.; AitBr.; ŚBr.; PārGṛ.; Kauś.; Sanseviera Roxburghiana (also °*jinī,* Npr.), L.; = °*ja-valkala,* Bhpr. v, 1, 170; see also °*jo-'hvā;* cf. *taij*°. °**naka,** m. Saccharum Sara, L. °**nin,** m. = *vikaṭa,* Lāṭy. ix, 2, 27, Sch. °**nī-danta,** m. a prominent tooth (?), 27. **Tejita,** mfn. sharpened, whetted (arrows), MBh. v f.; excited, stimulated, Hariv. 5208; 9644. **Tejinī,** f., see °*janī* & °*jo-vatī.*

Téjas, n. (often pl.) the sharp edge (of a knife &c.), point or top of a flame or ray, glow, glare, splendour, brilliance, light, fire, RV. &c.; clearness of the eyes, VS. xxi; AitBr. &c.; the bright appearance of the human body (in health), beauty, Nal.; Suśr. i, 15; the heating and strengthening faculty of the human frame seated in the bile, 14 & 26; the bile, L.; fiery energy, ardour, vital power, spirit, efficacy, essence, AV. &c.; semen virile, MBh.; R.; Ragh.; Śak.; marrow, L.; the brain, W.; gold, L.; (opposed to *kshamā*) impatience, fierceness, energetic opposition, MBh. iii; VarBṛ.; Sāh. iii, 50 & 54; Daśar. ii, 13; (in Sāṃkhya phil.) = *rajas* (passion); spiritual or moral or magical power or influence, majesty, dignity, glory, authority, AV.; VS. &c.; a venerable or dignified person, person of consequence, MBh. v, xiii; Śak. vii, 15; fresh butter, L.; a mystical N. of the letter *r,* RāmatUp. i, 23; (*ase*), dat. inf. √*tij,* q. v.; cf. *a-, agni-, ugra-* &c. — **ka,** ifc. = °*jas,* RV. i, 116, 8, Sāy. — **kara,** mfn. granting vital power. — **kāma** (*téj*°), mfn. longing for manly strength or vital power, Mn. iv, 44; desiring influence or authority or dignity, TS. ii; AitBr. i; TāṇḍyaBr.; ŚāṅkhŚr.; ĀśvGṛ. — **kāya,** mfn. having light as one's body, Āp. — **timira,** n. du. light and darkness. — **tejas,** m. whose essence is light, W. — **tva,** n. the general notion of *tejas,* Sarvad. x, 42; the nature or essence of light, BhP. iii. — **pada,** n. a mark of dignity, i, 15, 14. — **vat** (*téj*°), mfn. sharp-edged, W.; splendid, bright, glorious, beautiful, AV. xviii; TS. ii f.; TBr.; TāṇḍyaBr.; ChUp.; energetic, spirited, W.; (*tī*), f. N. of a princess, Kathās. xviii; cf. °*jo-v*°. — **vín,** mfn. (Pāṇ. v, 2, 122, Kāś.) sharp (the eye), Bhartṛ.; brilliant, splendid, bright, powerful, energetic, TS. ii f.; TBr. &c.; violent, VarBṛS. ci, 2; inspiring respect, dignified, noble, Mn. &c.; = *-kara,* TUp. ii, 1; m. N. of a son of Indra, MBh. i, 7304; (*inī*), f. Cardiospermum Halicacabum, L.; *mahā-jyotishmatī,* L.; °*svi-tā,* f. energy, MBh. iii; majesty, dignity, Hcar. v, 435; °*svi-tva,* n. brilliancy, MBh. v, 181, 7; Pratāpar.; °*svini-tamā* or °*svinī-t*°, Superl. of f. of °*svin,* Kāṭh. xxiii, 10; TS. vi; °*svi-praśaṇsā,* f. N. of ŚārṅgP. xvii.

Tejasa, n. ifc. = °*jas,* power, MBh. iii, 8681.

Tejasām-adhîśa, m. 'lord of luminaries,' the sun, Hcar. v, 415. **Tejasyà,** mfn. splendid, TS. ii, 3.

Téjishṭha, mf(*ā*)n. (Superl. of *tigmá*) very sharp, RV. i, 53, 8; very hot, i f., vi; very bright, ix f.; ŚBr. i; BhP.; (*am*), ind. with the utmost heat, TāṇḍyaBr. **Téjīyas,** mfn. (Compar.) sharper (the mind), RV. iii, 19, 3; more clever, BhP. x, 33, 30 (BrahmavP.); higher in rank, dignified, BhP. iii f., x.

Tejeyu, N. of a son of Raudrâśva, MBh. i, 3701.

Tejo, = °*jas.* — **ja,** n. blood, Gal. — **jala,** n. 'light-water,' the lens of the eye, Suśr. vi, 1, 16. — **nātha-tīrtha,** n. N. of a Tīrtha, RevāKh. cxxiv. — **nidhi,** mfn. 'treasury of glory,' abounding in glory, W. — **bala-samāyukta,** mfn. endowed with spirit and strength, Nal. xix. — **bindûpanishad,** f. N. of an Up. — **bīja,** n. marrow, Npr. — **bhaṅga,** m. destruction of dignity, disgrace. — **'bhibhavana,** m. N. of a village, R. (B) ii, 68, 17. — **bhīru,** f. 'afraid of light,' shadow, L. — **maṇḍala,** n. a disk or halo of light, PraśnUp. iv, 2. — **mantha,** m. (= *agni-m*°) Premna spinosa, L. — **máya,** mf(*ī*)n. consisting of splendour or light, shining, brilliant, clear (the eye), ŚBr. xiv; ChUp.; ŚvetUp.; Mn. &c. — **mūrti,** mfn. consisting totally of light, iii, 93. — **'mṛita-maya,** mfn. consisting of splendour or nectar, Hcat. i, 6, 253. — **rāśi,** m. 'mass of splendour,' all splendour (mount Meru), MBh. i; (°*jaso r*° iii, 9900); Śiva. — **rūpa,** mfn. consisting wholly of splendour (Brahmā), BrahmavP. — **vat,** mfn. sharp, pungent, W.; bright, VarBṛS. lxxxi, 6; energetic, W.; (*tī*), f. Scindapsus officinalis (°*ja-v*°, Bhpr. v, 1, 170), Suśr. iv, 2; 8; 15; vi; Piper Chaba, L.; *mahā-jyotishmatī,* L.; N. of a root (also °*jinī*), Npr.; of a princess, Kathās. xvii, 34. — **vid,** mfn. possessing splendour or light, TS. iii, 3, 1, 1. — **vṛiksha,** m. = *-mantha,* L. — **vṛitta,** n. dignified behaviour, Mn. ix, 303. — **vṛiddhi,** f. increase of glory. — **hrāsa,** m. = *-bhaṅga.* — **'hvā,** f. (cf. °*jâh*°) = °*ja-valkala,* Bhpr. v, 1, 170; Cardiospermum Halicacabum (also °*janī,* L.), Suśr. iv, 9, 60.

तेजाउर *tejaura,* N. of a place, Rasik. xi.

तेदनी *tedanī,* f. blood or clotted blood, VS. xxv, 2; AV. (?); ŚBr.; TāṇḍyaBr.; ŚāṅkhGṛ. (°*nī*).

तेन 1. *tena,* m. a note or cadence introductory to a song.

तेन 2. *téna,* ind. (instr. of 2. *tá*) in that direction, there (correl. to *yena,* 'in which direction, where'), SaddhP. iv; Pāṇ. ii, 1, 14, Kāś.; in that manner, thus (correl. to *yena,* 'in what manner'),

PārGṛ. ii, 2; Mn. iv, 178; Vop. v, 7; on that account, for that reason, therefore (correl. to *yena* [Mn.; MBh.], *yád* [ŚBr. iv, 1, 5, 7; Mn. i, iii; R. ii], *yasmāt* [MBh.; R.], *yatas* [Sāh. i, 2; Hit.]); *tena hi*, therefore, now then, Śak.; Vikr. i, ⅔.

तेप् *tep*, cl. 1. °*pate*, to distil, ooze, drop, Dhātup. x, 2; to tremble, Kavikalpadr.

तेम *tema*, °*mana*. See √*tim*.

तेर *tera*, °*raṇa*, m. balsamine, L.; cf. *tair*°.

तेल *tela*, m. N. of a high number, Buddh. L.

तेलु *telu*, g. *rājanyâdi*.

तेव् *tev*, cl. 1. °*vate*, to sport, Dhātup. xiv. **Tevana**, n. sport, L.; a pleasure-garden, L.

तैकायन *taikāyana*, m. patr. fr. Tika, g. *naḍâdi*. °**ni**, m. id., Pāṇ. iv, 1, 154. °**nīya**, m. a descendant or pupil of °*ni*, 90, Kāś.

तैक्ष्णायन *taikshṇāyana*, m. patr. fr. Tīkshṇa, g. *aśvâdi*. **Taikshṇya**, n. sharpness (of a knife), Suśr. i, 5; pungency (of drugs), i, iii f.; R.; fierceness, severity, Mn. iv, 163; MBh.; R.; Sāh.; pain, Priyad. i, ⅜. **Taigmya**, n. (fr. *tigmá*) sharpness, pungency, W. **Taijana**, mfn. coming from the plant *tejanī*, Kāṭh. xxi, 10 (ĀpŚr. xvii, 14). **Taijani-tvac**, a kind of lute, Lāṭy. iv. **Taijasá**, mf(*ī*)n. originating from or consisting of light (*téjas*), bright, brilliant, ŚBr. xiv; MāṇḍUp.; MBh. &c.; consisting of any shining substance (as metal), metallic, ĀśvGṛ.; Gaut.; Mn.; KātyŚr., Sch.; said of the gastric juice as coloured by digested food, Suśr. i, 14; passionate, Sāṃkhyak.; Tattvas.; Vedântas.; Suśr.; BhP.; n. metal, L.; vigour, W.; N. of a Tīrtha, MBh. iii, 7035; ix, 2723; (*ī*), f. Scindapsus officinalis, Npr.; long pepper, Gal.; °*sâvartanī*, °*tinī*, f. a crucible, L.

तैतल *taitala*, °*lāyani*, °*li*. See °*til*°.

तैतिक्ष *taitiksha*, mfn. (fr. *titikshā*) patient, g. *chattrâdi*; relating to °*kshya*, g. *kaṇvâdi*. **Taitikshava**, m. patr. fr. *Titikshu*, Hariv. 1681. **Taitikshya**, m. patr. fr. *Titiksha*, g. *gargâdi*.

तैतिल *taitila*, m. N. of a man (v.l. °*tala*), g. *tikâdi*; a rhinoceros, L.; a god, Daś. xii, 129; *kaliṅga*, 129, Sch.; n. (m., Sch.) a pillow, KshurUp.; n. N. of the 4th Karaṇa (in astr.), VarBṛS. iiic, 4 & 6; *-kadrū*, Pāṇ. vi, 2, 42. **Taitilāyani**, m. patr. fr. *Taitila*, g. *tikâdi* (v. l. °*tal*°). **Taitili**, m. N. of a man, Pravar. v, 4 (Kāty.); (°*tali* [in Prākṛit *Teyali*, Jñātādh. xiv; Āv. viii, 182] Jain.) **Taitilin**, m. N. of a man (=°*la*), Pāṇ. vi, 4, 144, Vārtt. 1.

तैत्तिडीक *taittiḍīka*, mf(*ī*)n. prepared with tamarind-sauce, iv, 3, 156, Vārtt. 2, Pat.; 4, 4, Kāś.

तैत्तिर *taittira*, mf(*ī*)n. produced or coming from a partridge (*tittiri*), ĀśvGṛ.; ŚāṅkhGṛ.; R.; Suśr.; sprung from the sage Tittiri, Uṇ. k.; m. a partridge, L.; n. a flock of partridges, L. **Taittiri**, m. N. of a sage (elder brother of Vaiśampāyana, MBh. xii, 12760), Pravar. ii, 2, 3 (v. l. *titt*° pl.); of a son of Kapota-roman, Hariv. 2016; MatsyaP. (not in ed.); (*titt*°) AgP. & BrahmaP. **Taittirika**, m. one who catches partridges, R. (G) ii, 90, 13.

Taittirīya, m. pl. 'pupils of Tittiri,' the Taittirīyas (a school of the Yajur-Veda), Pāṇ. iv, 3, 102; R. ii, 32, 15; VP. &c. **-caraṇa**, n. the school of the T°. **-prātiśākhya**, n. the Prātiśākhya of the T° (commented on by Tri-bhāshya-ratna). **-brāhmaṇa**, n. the Brāhmaṇa of the T°. **-yajur-veda**, m. the YV. according to the T°. **-vārttika**, n. N. of a commentary. **-veda**, m. the Veda according to the T°. **-śākhā**, f. = *-caraṇa*, ĀtrAnukr. **-śākhin**, mfn. belonging to °*khā*, ib., Sch. **-saṃhitā**, f. the Saṃhitā of the T° (chief recension of the Black YV., on the origin of which VP. iii, 5, 1–29 has the following legend: the YV. was first taught by Vaiśampāyana to 27 pupils, among whom was Yājñavalkya; subsequently V. being offended with Y. bade him disgorge the Veda committed to him, which he did in a tangible form; whereupon the other disciples of V. being commanded to pick it up, took the form of partridges, and swallowed the soiled texts, hence named 'black;' the other name *taittirīya* referring to the partridges. Y. then received from the Sun a new or white version of the YV., called from Y.'s patr. *vājasaneyin*). °**yâraṇyaka**, n. the Āraṇyaka of the T°. °**yôpanishad**, f. the Up. of the T°.

Taittirīyaka, mfn. = °*ya-śākhin*, TPrāt.; n. the manual of the T°, Sāy. on RV. i, 65, 2 & 5; iv, 42, 8. °**kôpanishad**, f. = °*rīyôp*°, Sarvad. v.

Taittirya, mfn. coming from a partridge, ĀpGṛ.

तैन्दुक *tainduka*, mf(*ī*)n. derived from Diospyros embryopteris (*tind*°), Suśr. vi, 40, 36.

तैमात *taimātá*, m. N. of a snake, AV. v.

तैमित्य *taimitya*, n. fr. *timita*, dulness, Gal

तैमिर *taimira*, mfn. fr. *timita*, with *roga*, = °*rya*, Suśr. iv, 13. °**rika**, mfn. = *timira nayana*, Kād. iii. °**rya**, n. dimness of the eyes, Hāsy. i, 39.

तैर *taira*, °*raṇa*, m., °*raṇī*, f. = *ter*°, L.

तैरभुक्त *tairabhukta*, mfn. fr. *tīra-bhukti*.

तैरश्च्य *tairaścya*, n. 'melody of the Ṛishi Tiraścī,' N. of a Sāman, TāṇḍyaBr. xii; Lāṭy. vi, 8, 12.

Tairovirāma, m. 'extending beyond (*tirás*) a pause (*vir*°),' the dependant Svarita in a compound when the Udātta upon which it depends stands on the last syllable of the 1st member of the compound, VPrāt. i, 118; (called *prātihata*, TPrāt.) **Tairovyañjana**, m. 'extending beyond the consonant (*vy*°),' the dependant Svarita when separated by one or more consonants from the Udātta syllable upon which it depends, RPrāt. iii, 10; APrāt. iii, 62; VPrāt. i, 117. **Tairo'hnya**, mfn. = *tir*°, ĀśvŚr. v, 5.

तैर्थ *tairtha*, mf(*ī*)n. relating to a Tīrtha, g. *śuṇḍikâdi* & *vyushṭâdi*. °**thaka**, mfn., g. *dhūmâdi*. °**thika**, mfn. (g. *cheddâdi*) = *tīrth*°, addicted or relating to another creed, heterodox, Kāraṇḍ. xi, 62; m. a dignified person, authority, Prab. ii, 1¾; n. water from a Tīrtha, MBh. iii, 8085; = *tīrtha-caryā* (?), xiii, 6066. °**thya**, g. *saṃkāśâdi*.

तैर्यगयनिक *tairyagayanika*, mfn. measured by the revolution (*tiryag-ayana*) of the sun (a year), Lāṭy. iv, 8, 7; Nidānas. v, 12.

Tairyagyona, mfn. = *tir*°, of animal origin, (m.) animal, Mn. vii, 150; Suśr. vi, 39; see °*nya*. °**ni**, mfn. id., MBh. v, 97, 6; relating to the animals (creation), Sāṃkhyak. 54, Gauḍap. °**nya**, mfn. id., 53 (v. l. °*na*); VP. i, 5, 21; MārkP. xlii, 33.

तैल *tailá*, n. (fr. *tíla*) sesamum oil, oil, AV. i, 7, 2 (?); Kauś.; Gobh.; Mn. &c. (ifc. Pāṇ. v, 2, 29, Vārtt. 4, Pat.; ifc. f. *ā*, Kum. vii, 9); olibanum, VarBṛS. lxxvii, 4 & 6. **-kanda**, m. N. of a bulb, L. **-kalka-ja**, m. = *-kiṭṭa*, L. **-kalpanā**, f. N. of ŚārṅgS. xvi, 90–178. **-kāra**, m. an oil-miller, BrahmavP. i. **-kiṭṭa**, n. oil-cake, L. **-kīṭa**, m. N. of an insect, L. **-kuṇḍa** (*tail*°), n. an oil-pot, AV. xx, 136, 16 (v.l. *-kumbha*). **-caurikā**, f. 'stealing oil,' a cock-roach, L. **-tva**, n. oily state, Suśr. i, 45. **-droṇī**, f. a tub filled with oil, R. ii, 66, 14 ff. **-pa**, m. 'oil-drinker,' N. of a man; (*ā*), f. = *-caurikā*, L. **-paka**, see *-pāyika*. **-parṇa**, m. camphor, Gal.; (*ī*), f. sandal, L.; turpentine, L.; olibanum, L. **-parṇaka**, n. N. of a fragrant grass, Bhpr. v, 2, 108; sandal-wood, Npr. **-parṇika**, m. N. of a sandal tree, Hariv. 12680; Bhpr.; n. the wood of that tree, L. **-pātra**, n. an oil-vessel, Gobh. iii, 5, 8. **-pāyika**, m. = *-pā* (or 'N. of a bird,' Sch.), Vishṇ. xliv, 23; Mn. xii, 63 (v. l. *-paka*); (*ā*), f. = *-pā*, MBh. xiv, 5069. **-pāyin**, m. id., xiii; Yājñ. iii, 211; MārkP. xv, 23; ?MBh. vii, 6713; (*inī*), f. id., Npr. **-piñja**, white sesamum, ib. **-pipīlikā**, f. a small red ant, L. **-pīta**, mfn. one who has drunk oil, g. *āhitâgny-ādi*. **-pūra**, m. 'oil-filling,' *a-* [Kum. i, 10] or *apavarjita-* [Bhaktâm. 15], mfn. (a lamp) that wants no oil-filling. **-pesham**, ind. (with √*pish*, to grind) so as to extract oil ('with oil,' Sch.), Pāṇ. iii, 4, 38, Kāś. **-pradīpa**, m. an oil-lamp, Kathās. ic, 4. **-phala**, m. the sesamum plant, Npr.; Terminalia Catappa, L.; Terminalia Bellerica, L. **-bīja**, m. Semecarpus Anacardium, L. **-mālin**, m. or °**lī**, f. a wick, L. **-m-pātā**, f. Pāṇ. iv, 2, 58; vi, 3, 71. **-yantra**, n. an oil-mill, BhP. v (*-cakra*, n. 'wheel of an oil-mill,' 21, 13). **-valli**, f. a kind of Asparagus, L. **-śālikā**, f. = *-yantra*, Gal. **-sādhana**, n. N. of a perfume, L. **-spandā**, f. Cucurbita Pepo, Npr.; Clitoria ternatea, ib.; *kākolī*, ib. **-sphaṭika**, m. N. of a gem, L. **Tailâkhya**, m. olibanum, L. **Tailâguru**, n. a kind of Agallochum, L. **Tailâṭī** f a wasp, L. **Tailâbhyaṅga**, m. anointing with oil. **Tailâmbukā**, f. = °*la-pā*, L. **Tailôtsava**, m. oil-festival (held in honour of Mīnākshī), RTL. p. 442.

Tailaka, n. a small quantity of oil, W. **Tailakya**, n. adorning with the Tilaka, g. *purohitâdi*; the being adorned with the T°, ib. **Tailika**, m. an oil-miller, Mn.; MBh.; VarBṛS.; Vīrac.; cf. *mūrdha-*; (*ī*), f. an oil-man's wife, Parāś. Paddh.; *-cakra*, n. = °*la-yantra-c*°, Divyāv. iv. **Tailin**, m. = °*lika*, L.; (*inī*), f. a wick, L.; = °*la-kīṭa*, L.; °*li-śālā*, f. = °*la-śālikā*, L. **Tailīna**, mfn. grown with sesamum, (n.) a s° field, Pāṇ. v, 2, 4.

तैलङ्ग *tailaṅga*, mfn. relating to the Telinga country; m. pl. its inhabitants, Kuval., Sch.

तैलवक *tailavaka*, mfn. inhabited by the Telus, g. *rājanyâdi*.

तैल्वक *tailvaka*, mfn. coming from or made of the Tilvaka tree, ShaḍvBr. iii, 8; KātyŚr.; Suśr.

तैव्रक *taivraka*, mfn. inhabited by the Tīvras, g. *rājanyâdi*. **Taivradārava**, mfn. coming from or made of the tree Tīvra-dāru, g. *rajatâdi*.

तैष *taisha*, mf(*ī*)n. (Pāṇ. vi, 4, 149) relating to the asterism Tishya, Āp.; m. the month (December–January) in which the full moon stands in the asterism Tishya (= *pausha* & *sahasya*), ŚāṅkhŚr. xiii, 19; (*ī*), f. (scil. *tithi* or *rātri*) the day of full moon in month Taisha, ĀśvŚr.; Gobh.; Anup.

तैसृक *taisṛika*, mfn. made in Tisṛikā, Kāt. ii, 5, 14, Sch.

तोक *toká*, n. (fr. √1. *tuc*) offspring, children, race, child (often joined with *tánaya*; rarely pl., AV. i, v; BhP. vi), RV.; AV.; Kāṭh.; ŚBr., AitBr.; Pāṇ. iii, 3, 1, Kār.; BhP.; a new-born child; ii, x; m. ifc. the offspring of an animal (e.g. *aja-*, a young goat), iii, x; cf. *ava-*, *jīvat-* & *sa-tokā*; √*tvaksh*. **-tā**, f. childhood, 13, 25. **-vat** (°*ká-*), mfn. possessing offspring, RV. iii, 13, 7; (*tī*), f. (a woman) having children, BhP. i. **-sāti** (°*ká-*), f. acquisition of offspring, RV. vi, 18, 6; x, 25, 9; (°*kásya s*°, ii, 30, 5; iv, 24; vi, ix); TBr. i, 2, 1, 1.

Tokāya, Nom. (ind. °*yitvā*) to represent a new-born child, BhP. x. **Tokinī**, f. = °*ka-vatī*, MānGṛ.

Tokma, m. see °*man*; a young shoot, BhP. x; green colour, L.; n. ear-wax, L.; a cloud, L. **Tókman**, m. a young blade of corn, esp. of barley, malt, RV. x, 62, 8; VS.; AitBr. viii, 5 & 16; (°*kma*, m., KātyŚr. xix, 1; BhP. iv); offspring, Naigh. ii, 2.

तोटक *toṭaka* (= *troṭ*°), mfn. quarrelsome, Chandaḥs. vi, 31, Halāy.; m. N. of a venomous insect, Suśr. v, 3; of a pupil of Śaṃkarâcārya, ŚSaṃkar.; n. angry speech, Daśar. i, 40; Pratāpar.; a metre of 4×12 syllables; see also *troṭ*°.

तोड् *toḍ*, cl. 1. °*ḍate*, to disregard, Dhātup.

Todana, n. (√*tuḍ*) splitting (?), viii f., xxviii.

Toḍikā, °*ḍī*, f. (in music) N. of a Rāgiṇī.

तोडरानन्द *toḍarânanda*, for *ṭoḍ*°.

तोडलतन्त्र *toḍala-tantra*, n. N. of a work.

तोतल *totala*, m. N. of a writer on med., Ṭoḍar.; (*ā*), f. N. of a goddess (*tott*°?), W.

Totilā, f. a form of Durgā, Pañcad. ii, 35.

तोते *tóte* [TS. i, 2, 5, 2] & *tóto* [VS. iv, 22] for *táva tava* [MaitrS. i, 2, 4; Kāṭh. ii, 5].

तोत्तला *tottalā*, f. = *totalā*, BrahmaP. ii.

तोत्तायन *tottāyana*, m. pl. N. of a branch of the AV. (v. l. *tautt*°).

तोत्त्र *tottra*, n. (√1. *tud*) a goad for driving cattle or an elephant, MBh.; Pāṇ.; R.; BhP. **-prajita** (*tót*°), mfn. goad-driven, ŚBr. xii, 4, 1, 10.

Todá, m. a driver (of horses &c.), RV. iv, 16, 11; Nir.; Kauś.; 'instigator, exciter,' the Sun, RV. i, 150, 1; vi, 6 & 12; pricking pain, BhP. iii, 18, 6; Suśr.; *Gotamasya t*°, N. of a Sāman. **-parṇī**, f. 'prick leaf,' a bad kind of grain, i, 46, 1, 18.

Todana, n. = *tottra*, L.; pricking pain, i, 22, 5; (m.) N. of a tree and (n.) its fruit, 46, 3, 25 & 29.

Todita, mfn. goaded, R. ii, 74, 31.

Todya, n. a kind of cymbal; cf. *ā-*.

तोमर *tomara*, m. n. (g. *ardharcâdi*) a lance, javelin, MBh. &c.; m. pl. N. of a people, vi, 377; sg. N. of the ancestor of a commentator on Devīm.; n. a metre of 4×9 syllables. **-graha**, m. a lance-bearer, Pāṇ. iii, 2, 9, Vārtt. 1; lance-throwing, Divyāv. iii, 59; viii. **-dhara**, m. a lance-bearer, L.; fire, L.

तोमराण *tomarāṇa*, N. of a man, Rājat. v.

तोमरिका *tomarikā*, f. = *tūbar*°, L.

तोय **tóya**, n (ifc. f. *ā*) water, Naigh. i, 12; Mn. v, viii f.; MBh. &c. (°*yaṃ √kṛi* with gen., 'to make offerings of water to the dead,' xviii, 32; (*ā*), f. N. of a river in Śālmala-dvīpa, VP. ii, 4, 28; of another in India). **-kaṇa**, m. a drop of water. **-karman**, n. 'water-ceremony,' ablution of the body, oblation of water to the dead,' MBh. i, xii. **-kāma**, m. 'fond of water,' Calamus fasciculatus, L. **-kumbhā**, f. = *-vṛiksha*, Npr. **-kṛicchra**, m. n. swallowing nothing but water (sort of fast), Yājñ., Sch. **-kṛit**, mfn. causing rain, VarBṛS. ix, 43. **-krīḍā**, f. 'water-sport,' splashing about in water, Megh. 34; cf. *jala-kr*°. **-garbha**, 'containing water,' the cocoa-nut, Npr. **-cara**, mfn. moving in water, (m.) an aquatic animal, MBh.; Hariv.; MārkP. **-ja**, mfn. water-born, Hariv.; 'lotus,' °*jâkshī*, f. a lotus-eyed woman, Daś. iv, 79. **-ḍimba**, °**mbha**, m. hail, L. **-da**, m. 'water-giver,' a rain-cloud, R.; Ragh. &c.; Cyperus rotundus, L.; ghee, L.; °*dâtyaya*, m. 'cloud-departure,' the autumn, R. ii; VarBṛS. xliv, 23. **-dāna**, n. N. of a gesture, PSarv. **-dhara**, mfn. containing water, R. ii; m. a rain-cloud, L.; Cyperus rotundus, L.; Marsilea quadrifolia, L. **-dhāra**, m. a stream of water, Hariv.; (*ā*), f. id., MBh.; R. **-dhi**, m. 'water-receptacle,' the ocean, Sūryas. xii; cf. *kshīra-t*°; *-priya*, n. 'fond of the sea (produced in maritime countries),' cloves, L. **-nidhi**, m. = *-dhi*, L. **-nīvī**, f. ocean-girdled (the earth), BhP. i. **-pāta**, m. 'waterfall,' rain, VarBṛS. lxxxix, 19. **-pāshāṇa-ja-mala**, n. calamine, Npr. **-pippalī**, f. Jussiæa repens, L. **-pushpī**, f. Bignonia suaveolens, L. **-prashṭhā**, f. id., W. **-prasādana**, m. 'water-purifyer,' Strychnos potatorum, L. **-phalā**, f. Cucumis utilissimus, L. **-maya**, mf(*ī*)n. consisting of water, MBh.; Hariv. **-mala**, n. sea-foam, Npr. **-muc**, m. 'water-yielder,' a cloud, R. iii, 79, 4. **-yantra**, n. a water-clock, Sūryas. xiii. **-rasa**, m. moisture, water, MBh. viii. **-rāj**, m. 'water-king,' the ocean, Hariv. **-rāśi**, m. 'heap of water,' a pond, lake, R. ii, 63, 17; the ocean, Kād. **-vat**, mfn. surrounded by water, MBh. xii; (*tī*), f. Cocculus cordifolius, Npr. **-vallikā**, f. id., ib. **-vallī**, f. Momordica Charantia, L. **-vāha**, m. 'water-carrier,' a rain-cloud, Bālar. ix, 30. **-vṛiksha**, m. Blyxa Saivala, Npr. **-vṛitti**, m. Achyranthes aquatica, ib. **-vyatikara**, m. blending of the waters (of two rivers). **-śuktikā**, f. a bivalve shell, oyster, L. **-śūka**, m. = *vṛiksha*, Npr. **-sarpikā**, f. a frog, ib. **-sūcaka**, m. id., L. **Toyâgni**, m. submarine fire, MBh. xii, 5178. **Toyâñjali**, m. the hollowed hands joined and filled with water (offered to the dead), Mudr. iv, ½. **Toyâdhāra**, m. a water reservoir, lake, river, Śak. i, 14. **Toyâdhivāsinī**, f. = °*ya-pushpī*, L. **Toyâpāmārga**, m. = °*ya-vṛitti*, Npr. **Toyâmbudhi**, m. the sea of fresh water, PadmaP. v. **Toyâlaya**, m. = °*ya-dhi*; N. of a constellation, VarBṛ. xii. **Toyâśaya**, m. = °*yâdhāra*, VarBṛS.; Ṛitus.; Dhūrtas. **Toyêśa**, m. 'water-lord,' Varuṇa, VP. v, 18. **Toyôtsarga**, m. discharge of water, rain, Megh. **Toyôdbhavā**, f. = °*ya-vṛitti*, Npr.

Toyikā, f. N. of a place (known by a festival [*maha*] called after it), Divyâv. vi, 101; xxxi, 146.

तोरण **toraṇa**, n. (g. *ardharcadi*) an arch, arched doorway, portal, festooned decorations over doorways (with boughs of trees, garlands, &c.), MBh. &c. (ifc. f. *ā*); a mound near a bathing-place, W.; a triangle supporting a large balance; m. Śiva, xiii, 1232; n. the neck, L.; cf. *ut-*, *kapāṭa-*, *kautuka-*. **-māla**, N. of a place, Rasik. xii, 24; Romakas.

तोरमाण **toramāṇa**, N. of a prince, Rājat.

तोल **tola**, mfn. (√*tul*) 'poising one's self,' see *ghana-*; m. n. = °*laka*, W.; (*ā*), f. 'weighing (?),' Vop. **Tolaka**, (m. n., L.) a weight of gold or silver (in books = 16 Māshas, in practise only = 12 M°), Rājat. iv, 201; (*ikā*), f. a wall round a watch-tower, BhP. x, 76, 10. **Tolana**, n. lifting up, R. i, 66 f.; Sāh. v, ½; weighing, Sch. on KātyŚr. i, 3 & Yājñ.; Subh. **Tolya**, mfn. to be weighed, Hcat. i, 5, 113.

तोश **tośá**, mfn. (√1. *tuś*) distilling, trickling, RV. iii, 12, 4; granting, i, 169, 5 (°*śá-tama*, Superl.). **Tośás**, mfn. id., viii, 38, 2.

तोष **tosha**, m. (√*tush*) satisfaction, contentment, pleasure, joy (with loc., gen., or ifc.), MBh. &c.; Contentment as a son of Bhaga-vat and one of the 12 Tushitas, BhP. iv, 1, 7. °**shaka**, mfn. 'pleasing,' see *sura-*. °**shaṇa**, mf(*ī*)n. satisfying, gratifying, appeasing, pleasing, MBh.; BhP.; n. the act of satisfying or appeasing or delighting, i, 2, 13 (ifc.); (*ī*), f. Durgā, Hariv. 10238; cf. *su-*. °**shaṇīya**, mfn. to be pleased, W.; pleasing, Lalit. v, 195. °**shayitavya**, mfn. to be pleased, MBh. ix. °**shayitṛi**, mfn. ifc. one who pleases (others, *para-*), Śiś. xvi, 28 (v.l.). °**shita**, mfn. satisfied, gratified, pleased, MBh.; R.; BhP.; Śak. vii, 1; Kathās. °**shin**, mfn. ifc. satisfied with, liking, MBh. xiii; Hariv.; satisfying, pleasing, R. iv; Kum. v, 7. °**shya**, mfn. = °*shayitavya*, MBh.

तोसल **tosala**, m. pl. N. of a people, AV.-Pariś. lvi, 4; sg. N. of a wrestler (also °*laka*), Hariv. ii, 30, 48 ff.; BhP. x, 36; 42; 44, 27. **Tosaliputra**, m. N. of a Jain teacher, HPariś. xiii, 38.

तौक्षायण **taukshāyaṇa**, fr. Tuksha, g. *pakshâdi*.

तौक्षिक **taukshika**, m. (fr. τοξότης) the sign Sagittarius, VarBṛ. i, 8.

तौग्र्य **taugryá**, m. 'son of Tugra,' Bhujyu, RV. i, 117 f.; 158; 180 & 182; viii, 5, 22; x, 39, 4.

तौच्छ्य **taucchya**, n. (fr. *tuccha*) emptiness, meanness, worthlessness, Dhātup. vii, 3.

तौण्डिकेर **tauṇḍikera**. See *tuṇḍ*°.

तौतातित **tautātita**, mfn. taught or composed by Tutātita (or Kumārila), Prab. ii, 3 (v. l. °*tātika*, fr. Tutāta); m. an adherent of T°, Sarvad. iii, 52; xiii, 110; SSaṃkar. x, 119.

तौतिक **tautika**, m. the pearl-oyster, L.; n. a pearl, L.

तौत्तायन **tauttāyana**. See *tott*°.

तौद **taúda**, n. (fr. *tuda* or *toda*) N. of a Sāman; (*ī*), f. N. of a plant (?), AV. x, 4, 24.

तौदादिक **taudādika**, mfn. belonging to the *tud-ādi* roots (cl. 6), Siddh.

तौदेय 1. **taudeya**, m. pl. (fr. *tuda*, g. *śubhrâdi*) N. of a family, Pravar. ii, 1, 2 (v. l. *taul*°).

तौदेय 2. **taudeya**, mfn. produced in or coming from the district called Tūdī, Pāṇ. iv, 3, 94.

तौबरक **taubaraka**, mfn. coming from the plant Tub°, Suśr. i, 46, 3, 58 & 10, 5; vi, 16, 6.

तौभ **taubha**, n. N. of a Sāman, ĀrshBr.

तौम्बुरव **taumburava**, n. the story of (Śiva and) Tumburu, Bālar. ii, ⅛. °**vin**, m. pl. the pupils of T°, Pāṇ. iv, 3, 104, Kāś.

तौर **taura**, n. = *turâyaṇa*, Lāṭy. x; Maś.

Tauraṃgika, m. (fr. *turaṃ-ga*) a horseman, Kir., Sch. **Taurâyāṇa**, mfn. hastening, Nir. v, 15. **Tauraśravasa**, n. (fr. *tura-śravas*) N. of a Sāman, TāṇḍyaBr. ix, 4, 10; Lāṭy. vii, 3, 3 f.; KātyŚr. xxv, 14, 14. **Taurâyaṇika**, mfn. performing the *turâyaṇa*, Pāṇ. v, 1, 72.

तौरव **taururava**, n. the fruit of the Tururu tree, g. *plakshâdi* (Kāś.).

तौरुष्किक **taurushkika**, mfn. (fr. *turushka*) Turkish, Kuṭṭanim. 64.

तौर्य **taurya**, mfn. coming from a musical instrument (*tūrya*), Dharmaśarm. vi, 25. **-trika**, n. 'triple symphony,' song, dance, and instrumental music, Mn. vii, 47.

तौर्वश **taurvaśá**, m. (fr. *turváśa*) a kind of horse, ŚBr. xiii, 5, 4, 16.

तौल **taula**, n. = *tulā*, a balance, W.

तौलकेशि **taulakeśi**, °*śin*, m. (fr. *tūla-keśa*, 'cotton-haired'), N. of a man, Pravar. i, 1.

1. **Taulika**, °**kika**, m. (fr. *tūlikā*) a painter, L.

तौलिक 2. **taulika**, cf. *uda-*, *daśa-*, *viṅśati-*.

Taulin, m. = *tulā-dhara*, VarYogay. iv, 50.

Taulya, n. weight, Hcat.; equality, TPrāt., Sch.

तौल्वलायन **taulvalāyana**, m. patr. fr. °*li*, Pāṇ. iv, 1, 101. **Taulvali**, m. N. of a teacher, ĀśvŚr. ii, v; Pravar. ii, 2, 1; cf. *ajā-*; °*ly-ādi*, N. of a Gaṇa of Pāṇ. (ii, 4, 61; Gaṇar. 171–173).

तौविलिका **tauvilikā**, f. N. of an animal (?), AV. vi, 16, 3.

तौषायण **taushāyaṇa**, fr. *tusha*, g. *pakshâdi*.

तौषार **taushāra**, mfn. sprung from snow (*tush*°), snowy, Suśr. i, 45, 1, 1; n. snow, cold, W.

त्त **-tta**, mfn. fr. √1. & 3. *dā*.

-tti, f. 'gift' (fr. √1. *dā*). See *bhága-*.

त्मन् **tmán** (= *ātmán*), m. the vital breath, RV. i, 63, 8 (acc. *tmánam*); ĀśvŚr. vi, 9, 1 (acc. *tmānam*); one's own person, self, RV.; '*tman* after *e* or *o* for *ātman*, KaṭhUp. iii, 12; MBh. i–iii; BhP. vii, 9, 32; *tmánā*, instr. & (at the end of a Pāda) *tmán*, loc. ind. used as an emphatic particle (like μέν and μήν) 'yet, really, indeed, even, at least, certainly, also,' RV.; VS. vi, 11; xi, 31; TS. ii, 1, 11, 2; AV. v, 27, 11; *utá tmánā* or *tmánā ca*, 'and also, and certainly,' *iva* or *ná tmánā*, 'just as,' *ádha tmánā*, 'and even,' RV.

Tmányā, ind. (fr. loc. *tmáni* + *á*?) only in the Vanas-pati verse of some Āprī hymns = *tmánā*, i, 188, 10; x, 110, 10; VS. xx, 45; xxix, 10.

त्य **tyá**, see *tyád*. **-japa** (*tyá-*), m. that (i.e. a lower kind of) muttering (opposed to *mahā-japá*), MaitrS. ii, 9, 1, 12.

त्यग्नायिस् **tyagnāyis**, N. of a Sāman, Lāṭy.

त्यज् 1. **tyaj**, cl. 1. °*jati* (metrically also *te*; pf. Ved. *tityája*, Class. *tat*°, Pāṇ. vi, 1, 36; *tatyaja*, BhP. iii, 4; fut. *tyakshyati*, Pāṇ. vii, 2, 10, Kār.; *tyajishy*°, R. ii, vii; MārkP.; aor. *atyâkshīt*; inf. *tyaktum*) to leave, abandon, quit, RV. x, 71, 6; Mn.; MBh. &c.; to leave a place, go away from, Mn. vi, 77; MBh. &c.; to let go, dismiss, discharge, VarBṛS. xvii, 22; Bhaṭṭ.; to give up, surrender, resign, part from, renounce, ĪśUp. 1; Mn.; MBh. &c. (*tanum* or *deham* or *kalevaram*, 'to abandon the body, die,' Mn. vi; MBh. &c.; *prāṇān* or *śvāsam* or *jīvitam*, 'to give up breath or life, risk or lose one's life,' MBh.; R. &c.); P. Ā. to shun, avoid, get rid of, free one's self from (any passion &c.), MBh. &c.; to give away, distribute, offer (as a sacrifice or oblation to a deity; *tyajate* etymologically = σέβεται), Mn.; Yājñ.; MBh. &c.; to set aside, leave unnoticed, disregard, ŚāṅkhŚr.; Mn. iii; MBh. i, 3098; Hit. ii, 3, 30; (ind. p. *tyaktvā*) to except, VarBṛS.; Caurap., Sch.; Pass. *tyajyate*, to be abandoned by, get rid of (instr.), Pañcat. i, 10, ⅔: Caus. *tyājayati* (aor. *atityajat*, Bhaṭṭ.) to cause anyone to quit, MBh. xiii, 288; to cause anyone to give up, Kathās. lxxxiii, 34; to expel, turn out, xx, 126; to cause any one to lose, deprive of (instr.), Bhaṭṭ. xv, 120; to empty the body by evacuations, Bhpr.: Desid. *tityakshati*, to be about to lose (one's life, *prāṇān*), Car. v, 10 & 12.

Tyakta, mfn. left, abandoned. **-jīvita**, mfn. one who has given up all expectation of life, ready to abandon life, Bhag. i, 19; Nal. ii, 16 (in comp.); R. iv. **-prāṇa**, mfn. id., MBh. v, 7204. **-lajja**, mfn. abandoning shame, shameless, BhP. v, 26, 23. **-vat**, mfn. having left. **-vidhi**, mfn. transgressing rules, ix, 6, 9. **-śrī**, mfn. abandoned by fortune. **Tyaktâgni**, mfn. (a Brahman) neglecting the household-fire, Mn. iii, 153. **Tyaktâtman**, mfn. despairing, Gaut. xv. **Tyaktavya**, mfn. to be left or abandoned, Mn. ix, 239; to be kept off from (abl.), VarBṛS.; to be given up or sacrificed, MBh. i, 6183 & 6195; R.; to be given up in despair, Subh. **Tyaktu-kāma**, mfn. wishing to leave. **Tyaktṛi**, mfn. abandoner of any one (gen.), Mn. iii, 245, Sch.; one who abandons or sacrifices (his life, *prāṇān*), MBh. vii, 378.

2. **Tyaj**, mfn. ifc. leaving, abandoning, W.; giving up, offering, BhP. viii; Rājat. iv; cf. *tanu-*, *tanū-*, *su-*. **Tyaja**, see *dus-*. **Tyajana**, n. leaving, abandoning, W.; giving, W.; excepting, exclusion, W.; expelling, AV. Paipp. xix, 12, 4. **Tyajanīya**, mfn. to be left or abandoned, W.; to be avoided or excepted, W. **Tyájas**, n. abandonment, difficulty, danger, RV.; alienation, aversion, envy (= *krodha*, Naigh. ii, 13), RV.; °*jás*, m. 'offshoot,' a descendant, x, 10, 3. **Tyajita**, mfn. = *tyakta*, Hariv. ii, 2, 22.

Tyāgá, m. (Pāṇ. vi, 1, 216) leaving, abandoning, forsaking, Mn. &c.; quitting (a place, *deśa-*), Pañcat.; discharging, secretion, MBh. xiv, 630; VarBṛS.; giving up, resigning, gift, donation, distribution, KātyŚr.; Mn. &c.; sacrificing one's life, RV. iv, 24, 3; liberality, Mn. ii, 97; R. &c.; a sage, L.; cf. *ātma-*, *tanu-*, *deha-*, *prāṇa-*, *śarīra-*. **-gatā**, f. N. of a Nāga virgin, Kāraṇḍ. i, 47. **-yuta**, mfn. liberal, Laghuj. **-śīla**, mfn. id.; *-tā*, f. liberality, Hit.

Tyāgin, mfn. (Pāṇ. iii, 2, 142) = *tyājaka*, Mn. iii, 245 (with gen.); Yājñ. & Śak. v, 28 (ifc.); giving up, resigning (ifc.), Bhag. xviii, 11; one who has resigned (as an ascetic who abandons worldly objects), MBh. iii, 77; sacrificing, giving up (life, *ātmanaḥ*), Mn. 89; liberal, (m.) donor, R. vi; Pañcat.; Kathās.; m. a hero, L.; °*gi-tā*, f. liberality, Hit. i. **Tyāgima**, mfn., W. **Tyājaka**, mfn. one who abandons or expels, Yājñ. ii, 198. **Tyājana**, n. abandoning (worldly attachments, *saṅgānām*), BhP. xi, 20, 26. **Tyājita**, mfn. made to abandon (with acc.), Kathās. lxxxvi, 13; made to give up, MārkP. lxxxix, 19; deprived of (acc.), MBh. xiii; Kum. vii, 14; Megh. &c.; expelled, Pañcad. iii, 60; caused to be disregarded, Ragh. vi, 56. **Tyājya**, mfn. (Pāṇ. vii, 3, 66, Vārtt.) to be left or abandoned or quitted or shunned or expelled or removed, Mn. ix, 83; MBh. &c.; to be given up, Bhag. &c.; to be sacrificed, Daś. vii, 211; to be excepted, W.; n. part of an asterism or its duration considered as unlucky, W.

त्यद् *tyád*, nom. *syá(s)*, *syā́*, *tyád*, (g. *sarvâdi*) that (often used like an article, e.g. *tyát Paṇīnā́m vásu*, 'that i.e. the wealth of the Paṇis,' RV. ix, 111, 2; sometimes strengthened by *cid*; often put after *utá* or after another demonstrative in the beginning of a sentence), RV.; AV. vii, 14, 1; ŚBr. xiv (*tyásya = máma*, 4, 1, 26; n. *tyám* for *tyád*, 5, 3, 1 & [in the etymology of *satyám*] KaushUp.); TUp. ii, 6; *tyád*, ind. indeed, namely, as it is known (always preceded by *ha*), RV. [cf. Old Germ. *der*.]

Tyatra, ind. 'there;' *-tya*, mfn. being there, Vop. vii, 111. **Tyadam**, ind. ifc. = *tyad*, g. *śarad-ādi*. **Tyāda**, m. (patr. fr. *tyad*) the son of that person, Pāṇ. iv, 1, 156, Siddh. **Tyādāyani**, m. id., ib. (*tyad*° ed., but cf. *tād*°, *yād*°). **Tyādṛiś**, °**śa**, mfn. such a one as that, iii, 2, 60.

त्युग्र *tyúgra*, m. for *túgra*, TĀr. i, 10, 2.

त्र 1. *tra*, mf(*ā*)n. (√*trai*, Pāṇ. iii, 2, 3) ifc. 'protecting,' see *aṅsa-*, *aṅguli-*, *ātapa-*, *kaṭi-*, *giri-*, *go-*, *tanu-*, *tala-*, *tvak-*, *vadha-*; *kṛita-* & *jala-trā*.

त्र 2. *tra*, = *tri*, 'three,' see *dvi-*.

त्रंस् *traṇs*, cl. 1. 10. °*sati*, °*sayati*, 'to speak' or 'to shine,' Dhātup. xxxiii, 88.

त्रख् *trakh*, cl. 1. °*khati*, to go, v, 30.

त्रङ्ख् *traṅk*, °*ṅkh*, °*ṅg*, cl. 1. id., iv f.

त्रङ्ग *traṅga*, m. °*gā*, f. a kind of town or N. of a town, L.; cf. *dr*°, *udr*°, *kudr*°.

त्रटत् *traṭat*, ind. (onomat.) — **kāra**, m. crackling (of fire), Alaṃkārat. — **traṭ-iti**, ind. crack! HPariś. iv, xi. **Traṭatraṭa**, ind. id., Pañcad.

त्रद *tradá*, m. (√*trid*) one who cleaves or opens, RV. viii, 45, 25.

त्रन्द् *trand*, cl. 1. to be busy, Dhātup. iii.

त्रप् *trap*, cl. 1. °*pate* (pf. *trepe*, Pāṇ. vi, 4, 122) to become perplexed, be ashamed, Rājat. iii, 94: Caus. *trapayati* or *trāp*°, id., Dhātup.; *trap*°, to make perplexed or ashamed, Śāntiś. iv, 15; cf. *apa-*, *vy-apa-*; *tripála* & *tripra* (?).

Trapā, f. (Pāṇ. iii, 3, 104) perplexity, bashfulness, shame, MBh. ii; BhP.; Ratnâv. &c.; (ifc. f. *ā*, Sāh.); an unchaste woman, L.; family, L.; fame, L. — **nvita** (°*pân*°), mfn. bashful. — **yukta**, mfn. id. — **raṇḍā**, f. a harlot, L. — **vat**, mfn. = *-yukta*. — **hīna**, mfn. shameless.

त्रपाक *trapāka*, m. pl. N. of a barbarous tribe, Uṇ. k.

त्रपिष्ठ *trapishṭha*, mfn. Superl. fr. *tṛiprá*, Pāṇ. vi, 4, 157. **Trapīyas**, mfn. Compar., ib.

त्रपु *trápu*, n. (1, 177, Kāś.) tin, AV. xi, 3, 8; VS. xviii; Kapishṭh.; ChUp.; Mn. &c. — **karkaṭī**, f. a kind of cucumber, L. — **karṇin**, m. 'having tin ear-ornaments,' Bhava-nandin, Avadānaś. — **paṭṭa**, m., °**ṭṭikā**, f. N. of an ear-ornament, L.

Trapula, n. tin, L., Sch. **Trapusha**, m. N. of a merchant, Lalit. xxiv; n. tin, L., Sch.; see °*pusa*. **Trápus**, n. tin, TS. iv, 7, 5, 1. **Trapusa**, n. id., L.; the fruit of °*sī* (also °*pusha*, L.), Kauś.; Suśr.; (*ī*), f. coloquintida (and other cucumbers, L.), vi, 47.

त्रप्स्य *trapsya*. See *drapsya*.

त्रय *trayá*, mf(*ī*)n. (fr. *trí*, Pāṇ. v, 2, 43) triple, threefold, consisting of 3, of 3 kinds, RV. x, 45, 2; AV. iv, 11, 2; VS. &c. (°*yī vidyā́*, 'the triple sacred science,' reciting hymns, performing sacrifices, and chanting [RV., YV., and SV.], ŚBr.; AitBr. &c.; n. a triad (chiefly ifc.), ChUp.; KaṭhUp.; Mn. &c.; (*ī*), f. id., see *śata-*; = °*yī́ vidyā́*, Gaut.; Mn. &c.; the Buddh. triad (Buddha, Dharma, and Saṃgha), Hcar. viii; summit, Bālar. i, 28; a woman whose husband and children are living, L.; Venonia anthelminthica, L.; *su-mati*, L.

Trayaḥ, = °*yas*. — **pañcāśat** (*tráy*°), f. (Pāṇ. vi, 2, 35 & 3, 49) 53, ŚBr. xii, 3, 5, 12. — **shashṭi**, f. 63, Pāṇ. — **śata-śatârdha**, mf(*ā*)n. 350, R. (B) ii, 39, 36. — **saptati**, f. 73, Pāṇ.

Trayaś, = °*yas*. — **catvāriṇśa**, mfn. the 43rd (ch. of MBh. i–iii). — **catvāriṇśat**, f. 43, Pāṇ.

Tráyas, pl. of *trí*; in comp. with any decad except *aśīti* and interchangeable with *trí* before *catvāriṅśát* &c., Pāṇ. vi, 3, 48 f.; [cf. τρισ-καί-δεκα for τρεῖς-κ°; Lat. *trēdecim* for *trēs-decem*.] — **triṇśá**, mf(*ī́*)n. the 33rd, ŚBr. (du. 'the 32nd and 33rd,' iv, xi); (chs. of MBh. & R.); + 33, SBr. xiii, 5, 4, 12 f.; consisting of 33 parts (*stóma*, sometimes to be supplied), VS.; AV.; TBr.; ŚBr.; TāṇḍyaBr.; MaitrUp.; numbering 33 (the gods), VS. xx; AV.; ŚBr.; ŚāṅkhŚr. iv; celebrated with the °*śá* Stoma, VS.; ŚBr.; KātyŚr.; ŚāṅkhŚr.; °*śa-pati*, m. 'lord of the gods,' Indra, L.; °*śá-vartani*, mfn. forming the path for the °*śá* Stoma, TS. iv; °*śá-stoma*, mfn. containing the °*śá* Stoma, ŚBr. xiii; ŚāṅkhŚr. x. — **triṇśat** (*tráy*°), f. (Pāṇ. vi, 2, 35 & 3, 49) 33, VS. xiv; AV. &c. (acc. °*śat*, R. iii, 20, 15; pl. °*śatas*, MBh. i, 2601); °*śad-akshara* (*tráy*°), mf(*ā*)n. having 33 syllables, ŚBr.; AitBr.; °*śad-rātra*, n. an observance lasting 33 days, KātyŚr.; ŚāṅkhŚr.; *Prajāpates trayastriṅśat-sammita*, n. N. of a Sāman. — **triṇśati**, f. 33, AitBr. — **triṇśin**, mfn. containing 33, TBr. i.

Trayī́, f. of *yá*. — **tanu**, m. = *-deha*, Hcat. i, 8, 425; Śiva; = *-mukha*, Gal. — **deha**, m. 'having the 3 Vedas for a body,' the sun, 11, 374. — **dharma**, m. the duty enjoined by the 3 Vedas, MBh. iii; Bhag. ix; MārkP. xxi. — **dhāma-vat**, m. = *-deha*, VP. iii, 5, 15. — **bhāshya**, n. a commentary on the 3 Vedas, SSaṃkar. xiii, 63. — **maya**, mf(*ī*)n. consisting of or containing or resting on the 3 Vedas, BhP. (the sun, v, 20, 4; the sun's chariot, 21, 12); MārkP. xxix; KūrmaP. i, 20, 66 (Rudra); Siṇhâs. xviii. — **mukha**, m. 'having the 3 Vedas in his mouth,' a Brahman, L. — **vidá**, mfn. knowing the triple science, TBr. i, 2, 1, 26.

Trayo, = °*yas*. — **daśa** (*tráy*°), mfn. (Pāṇ. vi, 2, 35 & 3, 48) 13, VS. xiv, 29 (instr. °*śábhis*); ŚBr.; Mn. ix; °*śá*, mf(*ī*)n. the 13th, VS.; AV.; ŚBr.; R.; VarBṛS.; (*śata*, 100) + 13, ŚāṅkhŚr.; consisting of 13 parts (*stóma*), VS.; Lāṭy.; (*ī*), f. the 13th day of a half-moon, Mn. &c.; N. of a kind of gesture, PSarv.; *-dvīpa-vatī*, mfn. consisting of 13 islands (the earth), MBh. iii, 3, 52 & 134, 20; *-dhā́*, ind. into 13 parts, ŚBr. x; Rājat. v; *-māsika*, mfn. consisting of 13 months, Kāraṇḍ. xix, 96; *-rātra*, n. an observance lasting 13 days, KātyŚr. xii, Sch.; *-rcá*, mfn. containing 13 Ṛic verses (a hymn), AV. xix, 23, 10; *-varjya-saptamī*, f. N. of a 7th day, BhavP. ii, 41; *-vārshika*, mfn. 13 years old, MBh. vii, 197, 7; *-vidha*, mfn. of 13 kinds, Car. vi, 3; Sāṃkhyak.; *tráyodaśâkshara*, mfn. having 13 syllables, VS. ix; *tráyodaśâratni*, mfn. 13 yards long, ŚBr. iii, xiii; °*śâha*, m. = °*śa-rātra*, R. (G) ii, 86, 4. — °**daśaka**, n. the number 13, Shaḍguruś. — °**daśama**, m. the 13th, BhP. i, 3, 17. — °**daśika**, mfn. happening on the 13th day of a half-moon, R. (G) ii, 86, 1. — °**daśin**, mfn. containing 13, Lāṭy.; Nidānas. — **navati**, f. 93, Pāṇ. — **viṇśá**, mf(*ī*)n. the 23rd, VS.; ŚBr.; VarBṛS.; (chs. of MBh. & R.); consisting of 23 parts (*stóma*), Lāṭy. — **viṇśat**, f. 23, BhP. xii, 13. — **viṇśati** (*tráy*°), f. (Pāṇ.) id., VS.; ŚBr.; KātyŚr.; BhP. x (instr. °*tibhis*); *-tattva*, n. pl. 23 Tattvas, iii; *-tama*, mfn. the 23rd (ch. of R. iii f.); *-dāru*, mfn. consisting of 23 pieces of wood, ĀpŚr. vii, 7, 7; *-dhā́*, ind. into 23 parts, ŚBr. x, 4; *-rātra*, n. an observance lasting 23 days, KātyŚr.; ŚāṅkhŚr. — °**viṇśatika**, mfn. consisting of 23 (*gaṇa*), BhP. iii.

Trayy-anta, m. = *vedânta*, Sarvad. xiii, 171.

Trayyāruṇa, m. (for *try-aruṇa*) N. of a prince (son of Tri-dhanvan, Hariv. 716 ff.; VP. iv, 3, 13; LiṅgaP. i, 66, 2; KūrmaP. i, 21, 1; of Uru-kshaya, VP. iv, 19, 10; °*ṇi*, BhP. ix, 21, 19; VāyuP. ii, 37, 159; *try-aruṇa*, MatsyaP. il, 39). °**ṇi**, m. N. of the Vyāsa of the 15th Dvāpara, BhP. xii, 7, 5; KūrmaP. i, 52, 6; VāyuP. i, 23, 155 (*try-āruṇi*); (°*ṇa*) VP. iii, 3, 15 & DevībhP. i, 3; see °*ṇa*.

त्रययाय्य *trayayā́yya*, mfn. (√*trai*) to be protected (= *trātavya*, Sāy.), RV. vi, 2, 7.

त्रस् 1. *tras*, cl. 10. P. *trāsayati* (ind. p. °*sayitvā*) to seize, Mṛicch. iii, 17/18; to prevent, Dhātup.

त्रस् 2. *tras*, cl. 1. *trásati* (Pāṇ. iii, 1, 70), 4. *trasyati* (MBh. &c.; ep. also Ā.; pf. 3. *tatrasur* [BhP. vi] or *tresur* [Devīm. ix, 21], Pāṇ. vi, 4, 124) to tremble, quiver, be afraid of (abl., gen., rarely instr.), RV. vi, 14, 4 & (p. f. *tarásantī*) x, 85, 8; AV. v, 21, 8; ŚBr. &c.: Caus. *trāsayati* (ep. also Ā.) to cause to tremble, frighten, scare, MBh. &c.; [cf. Zend √*tares*; τρέω; Lat. *terreo*.]

Trasa, mfn. moving, n. the collective body of moving or living beings (opposed to *sthāvara*), MBh. xii f.; Jain.; m. 'quivering,' the heart, L.; n. a wood, L. — **dasyu** (°*sá-*), m. (formed like Φερεκύδης &c.) 'before whom the Dasyus tremble,' N. of a prince (son of Puru-kutsa; celebrated for his liberality and favoured by the gods; author of RV. iv, 42), i, iv f., vii f., x; TS.; TāṇḍyaBr.; MBh.; Hariv.; VP. iv, 3, 13. — **reṇu**, m. the mote or atom of dust moving in a sun-beam (considered as an ideal weight either of the lowest denomination [Mn. viii, 132 f.; Yājñ. i, 361] or equal to 3 [BrahmavP. iv, 96, 49; BhP. iii, 11, 5] or 30 [Vaidyakaparibh.] invisible atoms); f. N. of a wife of the sun, L.

Trasad-dasyu, m. for °*sa-d*°, BhP. ix, 6, 33 ff. **Trasana**, n. a quivering ornament (?), Kauś. 14. **Trasara**, m. for *tás*°, a shuttle, Bālar. iii, 85. **Trasura**, mfn. timid, fearful, Uṇ. vṛ. **Trasta**, mfn. quivering, trembling, frighted, MBh. &c.; (in music) quick; [Lat. *tristis*.] **Trasnu**, mfn. (Pāṇ. iii, 2, 140) = °*sura*, Bhaṭṭ. vi, 7; Rājat. v; cf. *á-*.

त्रा *trā́*, m. (√*trai*) a protector, defender, RV. i, 100, 7; iv, 24, 3; cf. *án-agni-*; 1. *tra*.

Trāṇa, mfn. protected, Pāṇ. viii, 2, 56; n. protecting, preserving, protection, defence, shelter, help (often ifc.), ChUp.; Mn.; MBh. &c.; protection for the body, armour, helmet &c., iii, 12092; = *trāyamāṇā*, L.; (*ā*), f. id., L.; cf. *aṅguli-*, *udara-*, *uras-* &c. — **kartṛi**, m. a protector, saviour, W. — **kārin**, m. id., W. — **sārin**, mfn. having an excellent helmet, Kām. xiii, 12. **Trāṇana**, n. protecting, RāmatUp.

Trāta, mfn. (Pāṇ. viii, 2, 56) 'protected,' see *bhava*; m. (vi, 1, 205, Kāś.) N. of a man, VBr. i, 3; n. protection, W.; see °*tra*. **Trātavya**, mfn. to be protected or guarded, MBh. iii, vii. **Trātṛí**, m. a protector, defender, one who saves from (abl. or gen.), RV. (with *devá* applied to Bhaga or Savitṛi); VS.; AV.; TS. (Indra); MBh. &c. **Trātra**, mfn. addressed to Trātṛi (Indra), ĀpŚr. iii, 15, 10, Sch.; n. 'defence,' *Indrasya*, N. of a Sāman, ĀrshBr.

Trā́man, n. protection, RV. i, 53, 10; v, 46, 6. **Trāyantikā**, f. = °*ti*, Suśr. iv. **Trāyantī**, f. (fr. p. °*yat*) = °*yamāṇā*, vi; (metrically °*ti*) Car. vi, 17. **Trā́yamāṇa**, mfn. preserving, protecting, RV.; AV. &c.; (*ā́*), f. Ficus heterophylla, vi, 107, 1 f.; viii, 2, 6; Suśr. i, 38 & 42; iv, vi; VarBṛS. xliv, 10 (°*ṇa*, m. or n.) & iii, 39. **Trāyamāṇikā**, f. id., L.

त्राटक *trāṭaka*, n. (an ascetic's) method of fixing the eye on one object, Hathapr. ii, 32 f.

त्रापुष *trāpusha*, mfn. (Pāṇ. iv, 3, 138) made of tin (*trápus*), Kād.; n. tin, Gal.; silver, L. °**pusa**, mf(*ī*)n. coming from the plant Trapusī, Śāntik.

त्राप्य *trāpya*, mfn. fr. √*trap*, Vop. xxvi, 12.

त्रायोदश *trāyodaśa*, mfn. relating to the *trayodaśī*, g. *saṃdhivelâdi*.

त्रास *trāsa*, m. fear, terror, anxiety, MBh. &c.; a flaw in a jewel, L. — **kara**, mfn. causing fear, alarming. — **kṛit**, mfn. id., VarBṛS. civ, 4. — **dāyin**, mfn. id., Hemac.

Trā́sadasyava, m. patr. fr. Trasa-dasyu, RV. viii, 19, 32 & (°*vá*) 22, 7; x, 33, 4; n. N. of a Sāman.

Trāsana, mf(*ī*)n. terrifying, alarming, frightening (with gen. or ifc.), MBh. ('Śiva,' xiii, 1207); Hariv.; R.; n. frightening, alarming, MBh. iv; Daś. vii; Kathās.; cause of alarm or fright, Hariv.; BhP. °**sanīya**, mfn. frightening, Hariv. 2430; to be frightened, W. °**sin**, mfn. fearful, MBh. xii, 5904.

त्रि *trí*, m. *tráyas*, f. nom. acc. *tisrás*, n. *trī́ṇi* [*trī́*, RV.; ŚBr. xi], 3, RV. &c. (*tribhís* & *tisṛíbhis*, &c., RV.; only once *tríbhis* [viii, 59, 5] with the later accentuation, cf. Pāṇ. vi, 1, 177 & 180 f.; gen. *trīṇā́m* [RV. x, 185, 1; cf. Pāṇ. vii, 1, 53, Kāś.] & *tisṛīṇā́m* [RV. viii, 19, 37 & 101, 6], later on [fr. °*yá*] *trayāṇā́m* [AitBr.; Mn.] & *tisṛiṇā́m* [RV. v, 69, 2 against metre; cf. Pāṇ. vi, 4,

4 f.]; ifc., vii, 2, 99 f., Kāś.); [cf. τρεῖς, Lat. *tres;* Goth. *threis;* &c.] **– kakúd**, mfn. having 3 peaks or points or horns, TS. vii (°*kúd evá samānắnām* [°*kup sam*° TāṇḍyaBr. xxii, 14] 'thrice excelling one's equals'); AV. v, 23, 9; m. N. of a Himâlaya mountain (cf. *tri-kūṭa*), iv, 9, 8, ŚBr. iii; Pāṇ. v, 4, 147; [°*kúbh*, VS. xv; Kāṭh. xxiii]; of a Daśâha ceremony, TS. vii; ŚāṅkhŚr.; Vait.; [°*kubh*, TāṇḍyaBr. xxii; KātyŚr.; ĀśvŚr.; Maś.]; Vishṇu or Kṛishṇa, MBh. xii f.; Hariv. 14115; Brahmā, R. vii, 36, 7; N. of a prince, BhP. ix, 17. **– kakuda**, mfn. (Pāṇ. v, 4, 147, Kāś.) three-peaked, MBh. xii. **– kakúbh**, mfn. three-pointed, (Indra's thunderbolt) RV. i, 121; m. Indra, TāṇḍyaBr. viii, 1; see °*kúd*. **– kaṭa**, m. Asteracantha longifolia, L. **– kaṭu**, °**ṭuka**, n. the 3 spices (black and long pepper and dry ginger), Suśr.; cf. *kaṭu-traya*. **– kaṇṭa**, n. the 3 thorny plants (3 kinds of Solanum), L.; = *-kaṭa*, L.; *pattra-gupta*, L.; N. of a fish, L. **– kaṇṭaka**, m. (g. *rajatâdi*) 'three-thorn,' = *-kaṭa*, Suśr.; N. of a venomous insect, v, 8; N. of a fish (Silurus), L.; a kind of weapon, R. iii, 28, 25. **– kadruka** (*trí-*), m. pl. the 3 Soma vessels, RV. 1 f., viii, x; the first 3 days of the Abhi-plava festival, ŚBr. xiii, 5; KātyŚr.; ĀśvŚr.; Lāṭy.; mfn. containing the word *trí-kadruka* (RV. ii, 22, 1), TāṇḍyaBr. xvi, 3; °*drukīya*, mfn. id., ŚāṅkhŚr. (*pratipad*); RPrāt. xvii, 29 (scil. *ṛic*). **– kapardin**, mfn. wearing 3 braids of hair, Gṛihyās. ii, 40. **– kapāla**, mfn. distributed in 3 receptacles, AitBr. i, 1. **– karaṇī**, f. the side of a square 3 times as great as another (i. e. the diagonal of a quadrangle, the sides of which are formed by the side and the diagonal of the smaller square), Śulbas. **– karṇa**, mf(*ī*)n. having 3 ears, R. v. **– karman**, mfn. performing (a Brāhman's) 3 chief duties (viz. performing ceremonies, repeating the Veda, and gifts), MBh. xiii; °*ma-kṛit*, mfn. id., KaṭhUp. **– karsha**, n. = *-kārshika*, Npr. **– kalā**, f. N. of a female deity produced by the union of 3 gods for the destruction of Andhaka, VarP. xc ff. **– kaliṅga**, m. pl. N. of a people, Sāh. iv, 9⅛. **– kaśá**, mfn. having 3 whips (a chariot), RV. ii, 18, 1. **– kāṇḍa** (*trí-*), mf(*ā*)n. consisting of three parts or divisions (an arrow or asterism), AitBr. iii, 33; ŚBr. ii; 3 Kāṇḍas in measure (48 cubits long, W.), Vop. vi, 55; n. N. of a work, KātyŚr. iii, 2, 1, Sch.; of Amarasiṇha's dictionary (commented on by °*ḍa-cintāmaṇi* & *-viveka* and supplemented by *-śesha*); *-maṇḍana*, n. N. of a work. **– kāya**, m. 'having 3 bodies,' a Buddha, MWB. 246. **– kārshika**, n. the 3 astringent substances (dry ginger, Ati-vishā, and Mustā), L. **– kāla**, n. the 3 times or tenses (pf., pr., fut.), ŚvetUp.; BhP. v; RāmatUp.; mfn. relating to them, Sāṃkhyak. 33; m. a Buddha, W.; (*am*), ind. 3 times, thrice, BhP. v; in the morning, at noon, and in the evening, MBh. xiii; (°*la-*), Kām.; *-jña*, mfn. knowing the 3 times, omniscient, R. i; VarBṛS.; m. a Buddha, L.; *-darśin*, mfn. omniscient, R. i; VarBṛS.; a sage, L.; *-nātha*, m. N. of a Yogin, Siṇhās. xx, ♀; *-rūpa*, mfn. three-shaped at the 3 times (of day, i. e. the sun), VP. iii, 5, 19; *-vid*, mfn. omniscient, R. v; a Buddha, L.; an Arhat of the Jainas, L. **– kuṇḍeśvara**, n. N. of a Tantra, Ānandal. 31, Sch. **– kumārīka**, mfn. (the place) where the 3 virgins (Umā, Eka-parṇā, and Eka-pāṭalā) reside, Hariv. 948. **– kulā**, f. the plant *yava-tiktā*, Car. vii, 11. **– kūṭa**, mfn. having 3 peaks or humps or elevations, MBh. xii; N. of a mountain (= *-kakúd*), ii, 1484 (Hariv. 12782); BhP. v; of another mountain, viii, 2, 1; of a peak of mount Meru, VP. ii, 2, 26; of a mountain in Ceylon on the top of which Laṅkā was situated, MBh. iii; R.; Pañcat. v; n. sea-salt prepared by evaporation, L.; *-lavaṇa*, n. id., L.; *-vat*, m. N. of a mountain, MBh. xiv. **– kūrcaka**, n. a sort of knife with 3 edges, Suśr. i, 8, 1. **– kṛitvas**, ind. 3 times, Hcat. i, 10, 106. **– koṇa**, mf(*ā*)n. (fr. τρίγωνον) triangular, MBh. xiv; VarBṛS.; Phetk.; forming a triangle, VarBṛS.; n. a triangle, RāmatUp. i, 29; = °*ṇa-bhavana*, VarBṛS.; VarBṛ.; Laghuj.; (*ā*), f. Trapa bispinosa, Npr.; *-phala*, n. id., L.; *-bhavana*, n. the 5th and 9th mansion, VarBṛS. **– °koṇaka**, n. a triangle, RāmatUp. i, 50. **– kauśeya**, n. 'thrice silken,' a kind of garment, MBh. xiii. **– krama**, m. a Krama word composed of 3 members (the middle one being a single vowel), RPrāt. xi, 10; VPrāt. iv, 182. **– kshāra**, n. pl. (sg., L.) the 3 acrid substances (natron, saltpetre, and borax), Bhpr. v, 26, 234. **– kshura**, m. = *-kaṭa*, L. **– ksheptṛi**, m. = *-pura-ghna*, Bālar. iii, 81. **– kha**, n. 'having 3 cavities,' a cucumber, L. **– khaṭva**, n., °*ṭvī*, f. 3 beds collectively, L. **– khaṇḍa**, the inhabited earth as divided into 3 portions (the first 2 continents and half of the 3rd), Śatr. x, 318; xiv, 309. **– kharva**, m. pl. N. of a Vedic school, TāṇḍyaBr. ii, 8; n. a particular high number, MBh. ii, 1749 & 1826. **– gaṅga**, n. N. of a Tīrtha, iii; xiii. **– gaṇa**, m. the triad of duties (*dharma*, *kāma*, and *artha*), Kir. i, 11. **– gata**, n. 'tripled,' (in dram.) triple meaning given to the same word, Bhar. xviii, 115; Daśar. iii, 16; Pratāpar.; Sāh. vi. **– gandhaka**, n. = *-jāta*, Npr. **– gambhīra**, see *g*°. **– garta**, pl. (g. *yaudheyâdi*) N. of a people inhabiting modern Lahore, AV. Pariś. lvi, 8; MBh. (ifc. f. *ā*, vii, 688); Hariv. &c.; sg. a T° prince, MBh. &c.; the T° country, Daś. xi, 119; a particular method of calculation, L.; (*ā*), f. a lascivious woman, L.; a woman, L.; a kind of cricket, L.; a pearl, L.; N. of a town, Kathās. lxxiii, 21; *-shashṭha*, m. pl. a collective N. of six warrior tribes, Pāṇ. v, 3, 116, Kāś. **– °gartaka**, m. pl. the T° people, BhP. x. **– °gartika**, m. the T° country, L. **– guṇa**, n. sg. the 3 Guṇas (*sattva*, *rajas*, & *tamas*), BhP. iv; m. pl. id., Tattvas.; mf(*ā*)n. containing them, ŚvetUp.; Mn. i, 15; Sāṃkhyak.; Kap.; consisting of 3 threads or strings, ŚāṅkhŚr.; KātyŚr.; Kum. v, 10; threefold, thrice as great or as much, triple, KātyŚr.; Mn.; (*sapta tri-guṇāni dināni*, 3 × 7 days) Ragh. ii, 25; (*am*), ind. in 3 ways, Caraṇ.; *-parivāra*, n. the trident, Kir. xviii, 45; °*ṇā-karṇa*, mfn. whose ear-lobes are slit into 3 divisions (as a mark of distinction), Pāṇ. vi, 3, 115, Kāś.; °*ṇā-kṛita*, mfn. = *tṛitīyā-k*°, L.; °*ṇâkhya*, mfn. said of different mixtures and of a kind of oil, Rasêndrac.; Rasar.; °*ṇâtmaka*, mfn. possessing the 3 Guṇas, Vedântas. 37; °*ṇī-kṛitya*, ind. p. making threefold, AgP. xxxiii, 5. **– gūḍha**, °**ḍhaka**, n. a dance of men in female attire, Sāh. vi, 213 & 219. **– grāmī**, f. '3 villages,' N. of a place, Rājat. iv f. **– grāhin**, mfn. extending to the length of 3 (padyās). **– ghana**, m. 3^3 (= 27), Laghuj. i, xiii. **– cakrá**, mfn. having 3 wheels, RV. i, iv, viii, x (scil. *rátha*, 85, 14). **– cakshus**, mfn. three-eyed (Kṛishṇa, more properly Śiva), MBh. xii, 1505. **– catura**, mfn. (Pāṇ. v, 4, 77, Vārtt.) 3 or 4, Daś. vii; Kathās.; Sāh. **– caturdaśa**, mfn. du. the 13th and 14th, Śrut. **– catvāriṇśa**, mf(*ī*)n. the 43rd (ch. of MBh. iv ff.; Hariv.; R.) **– catvāriṇśat**, f. 43, Pāṇ. vi. **– cít**, mfn. consisting of 3 layers of fuel, ŚBr. vii; KātyŚr. **– citīka** (*trí-*), mfn. id., TS. v, 2, 3, 6. **– cīvara**, n. the 3 vestments of a Buddh. monk, MWB. 83. **– jagat**, n. sg. = *jagat traya*, BhP. viii; Caurap.; Kathās.; Vet.; pl., Ānand., Sch. Introd. 1; (*tī*), f. id., BhP. v; °*gaj-jananī*, f. 'the 3 worlds' mother,' Pārvatī, Kathās. i, 14; °*gad-īśvara*, m. lord of the 3 worlds (a Jina), Bhaktâm. 14; °*gan-mohinī*, f. 'beguiling the 3 worlds,' Durgā (?), BrahmaP. ii, 18, 18. **– jaṭa**, mf(*ā*)n. = *-kapardin*, MBh. iii, (Śiva) xii; m. N. of a Brāhman, R. ii; (*ā*), f. Ægle Marmelos, Jñānabhair.; N. of a Rākshasī (who was friendly to Sītā), R. iii, v f.; Ragh. xii, 74; of a Nāga virgin, Kāraṇḍ. i, 43; °*ṭā-svapna-darśana*, n. 'dream of Tri-jaṭā,' N. of R. v, 23. **– jaya**, mf(*ā*)n. the 13th, Dharmaśarm. vi, 13. **– jāta**, °**taka**, n. the 3 spices (mace, cardamoms, and cinnamon), Suśr.; Daś. **– jīvā**, f. the sine of 3 signs or 90 degrees, radius, Sūryas. **– jyā**, f. id., ib. **– ṇata**, mfn. bent in 3 places (a bow), R. vi, 20, 28; (*ā*), f. a bow, Śiś. xix, 61. **– ṇavá**, mfn. consisting of 3 × 9 parts (*stóma*), VS.; TS.; TBr.; ŚBr.; TāṇḍyaBr.; connected with the T° *stóma*, VS.; ŚBr.; ŚāṅkhŚr.; Nidānas.; in comp. 27, BhP. ix; *-rātra*, mfn. lasting 27 days, x; °*vá-vartani*, mfn. forming the path for the T° *stóma*, TS. iv, 3, 3, 2; *-sāhasra*, mf(*ī*)n. 27000, BhP. ix; °*vâtmaka*, mfn. 27fold, Jyot. 11, Sch. (Garga). **– ṇāka**, for *-nāka*. **– ṇāciketa**, mfn. one who has thrice kindled the Nāciketa fire or studied the Nāciketa section of Kāṭh., Āp.; KaṭhUp.; Mn.; Yājñ.; MBh. (Nārāyaṇa, xii); VP. iii, 15, 1; MārkP.; m. pl. N. of 3 Anuvākas of Kāṭh., Mn. iii, 185, Kull. **– ṇāman**, mfn. having 3 names (Agni?), AV. vi, 74, 3; cf. TS. ii, 1, 11, 3. **– ṇidhana**, n. N. of a Sāman, TāṇḍyaBr. (v. l. *nidh*°); ShaḍvBr.; Lāṭy.; *Agneh*, ĀrshBr. **– ṇītā**, f. 'thrice married (to Soma, Gandharva, and Agni),' a wife, Npr. **– ṇemi**, mfn. with 3 fellies, BhP. iii, 8, 20 (v. l. *-nemi*). **– taksha**, n. an association of 3 carpenters, L.; (*ī*), f. id., L. **– tanti**, mfn. having 3 chords (a lute), Sch. on ŚBr. & KātyŚr. **– tántu**, mfn. thrice woven (?), RV. x, 30, 9. **– tantrikā**, f. (a lute) having 3 chords. **– tas**, ind. on 3 sides, W. **– tā**, f. a triad, Nir. **– tāmra**, mfn. red on 3 parts of the body, R. (B) v, 35, 17. **– trika**, mfn.? (Rāma), 32, 13. **– tri-koṇa**, n. (= *tri-k*°) the 9th mansion, VarBṛ.; Laghuj. **– tva**, n. = *-tā*, MBh. xiv; BhP. i, 15. **– daṇḍa**, n. = °*ṇḍaka*, Mn. &c.; triple control (i. e. of thoughts, words, and acts), xii, 11. **– daṇḍaka**, n. the 3 staves of a Parivrājaka, MBh. xii; Up. **– daṇḍin**, m. 'carrying the 3 staves tied together,' a Parivrājaka, Yājñ. iii, 58; MBh. &c.; a triple commander (i. e. controlling his own thoughts, words and deeds), Mn. xii, 10; MārkP. xli. **– dat**, mfn. (Pāṇ. vi, 2, 197) grown as old as to possess three teeth, v, 4, 141, Kāś. **– danta**, mfn. having 3 teeth, ib.; (*ī*), f. the plant *mahā-medā*, Bhpr. v, 1, 130. **– damatha-vastu-kuśala**, m. 'skilled in the threefold self-control (cf. *-daṇḍa*),' Buddha, Divyâv. ix, 13; xix, 50. **– dalā**, f. 'three-leaved,' Cissus pedata, L. **– dalikā**, f. Mimosa abstergens, L. **– daśa**, mf(*ā*)n. 3 × 10 (= 30), MBh. i, 4445; m. pl. (cf. Pāṇ. ii, 2, 25; v, 4, 73; vi, 3, 48, Kāś. & *dvi-d*°) the 3 × 10 (in round number for 3 × 11) deities (12 Ādityas, 8 Vasus, 11 Rudras, and 2 Aśvins; cf. RV. ix, 92, 24), MBh. &c.; du. the Aśvins, iii, 10345; mfn. divine, R. iii, 41, 21; n. heaven, MBh. xiii, 3327 (*tri-diva*, B); *-guru*, m. 'thirty-god-preceptor,' Bṛihaspati (regent of Jupiter), VarBṛS.; VarBṛ.; *-gopa*, m. = *indra-g*°, a fire-fly, Ragh. xi, 42; *-gopaka*, m. id., Npr.; *-tā*, f. divine nature, Bālar.; *-tva*, n. id., Ragh. xviii, 30; *-dīrghikā*, f. 'heavenly lake,' Gaṅgā, L.; *-nadī*, f. 'heavenly river,' Gaṅgā, W.; *-pati*, m. 'lord of the gods,' Indra, Mṛicch.; Ratnâv. iv, 11; VP. v, 18; *-puṃgava*, m. 'god-chief,' Vishṇu, R. i, 14, 42; *-pratipaksha*, m. = °*śâri*; *-mañjarī*, f. 'heavenly plant,' the Tulasī, L.; *-vadhū*, f. 'wife of the gods,' an Apsaras, W.; *-vanitā*, f. id., Megh.; *-śaila*, m. 'heavenly mountain,' the Kailāsa, Kathās. cxiv; *-śreshṭha*, mfn. best of gods (Brahmā, Agni), R. vi, 102 f.; *-sarshapa*, m. = *deva-s*°, Npr.; °*śâṅkuśa*, m. 'divine goad,' a thunderbolt, L.; °*śâṅganā*, f. = °*śa-vadhū*, Bhaktâm. 15; °*śâcārya*, m. = °*śa-guru*, L.; °*śâdhipa*, m. a lord of the gods, 28; °*śâdhipati*, m. Śiva; °*śâyana*, m. 'resort of the gods,' Nārāyaṇa, Hariv.; °*śâyudha*, n. 'divine weapon,' the rainbow, Ragh. ix, 54; the thunderbolt, L.; °*śâri*, m. an enemy of the gods, Asura, R. vi, 36, 78; °*śâlaya*, m. 'abode of the gods,' heaven, MBh. iii; R. i; Vet.; the mountain Su-meru, L.; a heaven-dweller, god, MBh. iii, 1725; °*śâvāsa*, m. = °*śâlaya*, heaven, L.; °*śâhāra*, m. 'divine food,' nectar, L.; °*śī-bhūta*, mfn. become divine, Ragh. xv, 102; °*śêndra*, m. 'god-chief,' Indra, Pañcat. i; °*śêndra-śatru*, m. 'Indra's foe,' Rāvaṇa, R. vi, 36, 6; °*śêśa*, m. = °*śêndra*, MBh. iii; °*śêśadvish*, m. = °*śâri*, MBh.; °*śêśvara*, m. = °*śêndra*, MBh.; R. ii; Śiva, MBh.; pl. Indra, Agni, Varuṇa, and Yama, Nal. iv, 31; (*ī*), f. Durgā, DevīP.; N. of a female attendant of Durgā, W.; °*śêśvara-dvish*, m. = °*śêndra-śatru*, R. i, 14, 47. **– dina-spṛiś**, m. conjunction of 3 lunations with one solar day, Jyot. **– divá**, n. (m., L.) the 3rd or most sacred heaven, heaven (in general), RV. ix, 113, 9 & AV. (with gen. *divás*); GopBr.; PraśnUp.; Mn. &c.; (*ā*), f. cardamoms, Npr.; N. of a river in India, MBh. vi, 324; xiii, 7654; of a river in the Plaksha-dvīpa, VP. ii, 4, 11; (°*vī*) BrahmâṇḍaP. [Hcat. i, 5, 1070]; *-gata*, mfn. 'heaven-departed,' dead, Vcar. vi, 62; °*vâdhīśa*, °*vêśa*, m. 'lord of heaven,' a god, L.; °*vêśāna*, m. id., Gal.; °*vêśvara*, m. 'lord of heaven,' Indra, R. i; °*vôdbhavā*, f. large cardamoms, L.; °*vâukas*, m. 'heaven-residing,' a god, Vcar. xv, 72. **– divasa**, mfn. tertian (fever), AgP. xxxi, 18. **– dṛiś**, m. = *-netra*, Śiva, L. **– dosha**, in comp., disorder of the 3 humours of the body; mfn. causing the T°, Suśr. i, 45, 10, 11 & 46, 4, 28; *-kṛit*, mfn. id., 45, 8, 10; *-ghna*, mfn. removing the T°, 45, 1, 16; *-ja*, mfn. resulting from the T°, L.; *-śamana*, mfn. = *-ghna*, 46, 4, 32; *-hārin*, mfn. id. (a kind of mixture) Rasêndrac.; °*shâpaha*, m. 'keeping off 3 kinds of sins (cf. *-daṇḍa*),' Buddha, Buddh. L. **– dvāra**, mf(*ā*)n. 'having 3 doors,' reachable in 3 ways, MBh. iii. **– dhanvan**, m. N. of the father of Trayyāruṇa (q. v.). **– dharman**, m. Śiva, R. vii. **– dhā** (*trí-*), ind. (VPrāt. ii, 44) in 3 ways, in 3 parts, in 3 places, triply, RV. i f., iv; ChUp.; MBh. &c.; *-√kṛi*, to treble, xiii, 6467; *-tva*, n. tripartition, ChUp. vi, 3, 3, Śaṃk.; (*e*), loc. ind. in 3 cases, APrāt., Sch.; *-mūrti*, f. a girl 3 years of age representing Durgā at her festivals. **– dhắtu**, mfn. consisting of 3 parts, triple, threefold (used like Lat. *triplex* to denote excessive), RV.; ŚBr. v, 5, 5, 6; m. (scil. *puroḍâśa*) N. of an oblation, TS. ii, 3, 6, 1 (*-tvá*, n. abstr.); Gaṇêśa, L.; N. of a man, TāṇḍyaBr.

xiii, 3, 12, Sch.; n. the triple world, RV.; the aggregate of the 3 minerals or of the 3 humours, W.; *tridhātu-śriṅga*, mfn. having a tripartite horn (Agni), v, 43, 13. **-°dhātuka**, mfn. consisting of 3 humours, BhP. x; m. Gaṇeśa, L. **-dhāman**, n. = *-divá*, BhP. iii, 24, 20; mfn. shining in the 3 worlds, 8, 31; VP. ii, 8, 54 ('triple-gloried'); tripartite, MBh. xiii; m. Vishṇu, xii; Hariv.; R. vii; BhP. vi; Brahmā, R. vii, 36, 7; Śiva, L.; fire, Agni, L.; death, L.; N. of the Vyāsa (= Vishṇu) of the 10th Dvāpara, VP. iii, 3, 13; VāyuP. i, 23, 136; DevībhP. i, 3; KūrmaP. i, 52, 4. **-dhāra**, mf(*ā*)n. three-streamed (Gaṅgā), Hariv. 3189; (*ā*), f. Euphorbia antiquorum, Gal.; *-snuhī*, f. id., Npr.; the plant *dhārā-snuhī*, L. **-dhāraka**, m. 'three-edged' Scirpus Kysoor, L.; = °*rā*, Npr. **-nagarī-tīrtha**, n. N. of a Tīrtha, Rasik. xi, 28. **-nayana**, m. = *-driś*, MBh. xiv; R.; PāṇŚikshā; Megh. &c.; n. N. of a town, Kṛishṇakrīḍ.; (*ā*), f. Durgā, DevīP. **-navata**, mfn. the 93rd (chs. of MBh.) **-navati**, f. 93, Pāṇ. vi; *-tama*, mfn. = °*vata* (chs. of R.) **-nava-'ha**, n. pl. (metrically for °*vāha*, cf. *tri-ṇavá*) 27 days, BhP. x, 83, 10. **-nāká**, n. = *-divá*, RV. ix, 113, 9; AV. ix, 5, 10; BhP. vi. **-nābha**, mfn. whose navel supports the 3 worlds (Vishṇu), viii, 17, 26. **-nā́bhi**, mfn. three-naved (a wheel), RV. i, 164, 2; MBh. xiii; BhP. **-nāli**, mfn. 3 × 24 minutes long, Sāh. vi, 303. **-nidhana**, see *-nidh°* **-nivit-ka**, mfn. containing 3 Nivid verses, AitĀr. i, 5, 2, 4. **-nishka**, mfn. worth 3 Nishkas, Pāṇ. v, 1, 30. **-netra**, m. 'three-eyed,' Śiva, MBh. &c.; (with *rasa*) N. of different mixtures, Rasêndrac.; Bhpr. vii, 8, 157; 'Śiva's asterism,' Ārdrā, VarBṛS. xv, 29; N. of a prince, MatsyaP. cclxx, 27; (*ā*), f. Durgā, Kathās. cvii; the root of Yam, Gal.; (*ī*), f. id., L.; *-cūḍāmaṇi*, m. 'Śiva's crest,' the moon, L.; *-phala*, m. the cocoa-nut tree, Gal.; °*trôdbhava*, m. 'Śiva's son,' Kumāra, Alaṃkārar. **-nemi**, see *-ṇemi*. **-naishkika**, mfn. = *-nishka*, Pāṇ. **-paksha**, n. 3 fortnights, ŚāṅkhGṛ. iv, 3; VarBṛS. xxxii, 32. **-pakshaka**, m. Butea frondosa, L. **-pacchas** (*pad* + *śas*), ind. by 3 Pādas, ŚāṅkhŚr. xi. **-pañcaka**, mfn. pl. of 3 × 5 kinds, Yājñ. ii, 181/182, 11 **-pañcāśá**, mf(*ī*)n. the 53rd (chs. of MBh. & R.); numbering 53 (dice), RV. x, 34, 8; AV. xix. **-pañcāśat**, f. 53, Pāṇ. vi; *-tama*, mfn. the 53rd (ch. of MBh. ii). **-paṭu**, n. 3 saline substances (stone-salt, Viḍ-lavaṇa, and black salt), Npr. **-patat**, in comp. = *-dhāra*, BhP. xi, 6, 13. **-patāka**, mfn. (with *kara*, *hasta*, the hand) with 3 fingers stretched out (in dram. introductory to words meant *janântikam*), Bālar. iii, 4/5; Sāh. vi, 139; PSarv.; Hastar.; (°*ka-kara*) Daśar.; (with *lalāṭa*, the forehead) marked naturally with 3 wrinkles, L. **-pati**, f. N. of a Tīrtha, Rasik. xi, 25. **-pattra**, m. 'three-leaf,' Ægle Marmelos, BṛihaddhP.; N. of a bulb, Npr. **-pattraka**, m. = *-pakshaka*, L. **-patha**, in comp. '= *-jagat*;' n. a place where 3 roads meet, L.; mf(*ā*)n. reached by 3 roads (Mathurā), Rasik. xi, 21; *-gā*, f. 'flowing through heaven, earth, and the lower regions,' the Ganges, MBh. &c.; *-gāminī*, f. id., i, 3903; R. **-pathaka**, m. (in music) a kind of composition. **-pā́d**, m(*pā́d*)f(*pād* [Pāṇ. iv f.]; *pádī*, g. *kumbhapady-ādi*)n. three-footed, RV. x, 117, 8; VS.; ChUp.; Ragh. (Dharma); BhP. (Vishṇu, Yajña, Jvara); making 3 steps, ĀśvGṛ.; ŚāṅkhGṛ.; having 3 divisions (a stanza), ŚBr. xiv; BhP. (Sāvitrī, Gāyatrī); Chandaḥs.; trinomial; three-fourths, RV. x, 90, 3 f.; m. N. of a Daitya, MBh. ix, 2693; (*dī*), f. an elephant's fetter, Ragh. iv, 48; Dharmaśarm. xi, 51; a kind of elephant's gait, Kād.; Vcar. xv; Cissus pedata, L.; N. of a Prākṛit metre; of a composition (in music). **-pada**, mfn. three-footed, MBh. vi, 71; extending over 3 squares, Hcat.; (Pāṇ. iv, 1, 9) having 3 divisions (a stanza), VS. & ŚBr. (f. *tripadā*); TS. (f. °*pádā*); AitBr. &c.; measuring 3 feet, KātyŚr.; containing 3 words, VPrāt.; APrāt., Sch.; n. 3 words, VPrāt.; (*ā*), f. Cissus pedata, L.; the Gāyatrī metre, Gal.; *-prabhṛiti*, mfn. containing 3 or more words, TPrāt. **-padikā**, f. a tripod stand, Tantras. **-padya**, mf(*ā*)n. tripartite, Jyot. (YV) 15. **-panna**, m. N. of one of the moon's horses, L., Sch. **-parikrānta**, mfn. one who has overcome the 3 internal foes (*kāma*, *krodha*, and *lobha*), MBh. xiii, 6455. **-parivarta**, mfn. (the wheel of the law) turning thrice, Lalit. xiii, 14; Divyâv. xxvii, 189; xxxv, 218. **-parṇa**, m. = *-pakshaka*, L.; (*ā*), f. wild hemp, Npr.; (*ī*), f. Desmodium gangeticum, Bhpr. vii, 2, 16; the wild cotton tree, v, 3, 31; = °*ṇā*, Npr.; Sanseviera zeylanica, L.; N. of a bulb, L. **-parṇikā**, f. id., L.; Carpopogon pruriens, Npr.; Alhagi Maurorum, L. **-parus**, mfn. consisting of 3 divisions, BhP. **-paryāya**, mfn. having 3 turns (a *stóma*), KātyŚr. ix f. **-parva**, mfn. consisting of 3 parts (an arrow, cf. *-kāṇḍa*), Hariv. 12238. **-parvata**, '3 mountains,' N. of a place. **-parvan**, mfn. = °*va*, MBh. iv, 43, 18. **-pala**, mf(*ā*)n. weighing 3 Palas, Yājñ. ii, 179. **-paśu**, mfn. having 3 victims, KātyŚr. xv. **-pastyá**, mfn. having 3 dwellings (Agni), RV. viii, 39, 8. **-pājasyá**, mfn. having 3 flanks, iii, 56, 3. **-pāta**, m. intersection of a prolonged side and perpendicular (in a quadrangular figure), figure formed by such intersection. **-pātikā**, f. a beak, Gal. **-pāṭhin**, m. familiar with the 3 Vedas (epithet of a commentator on Vās. and of several copyists). **-pāṇa**, mfn. (irreg.) made of the plant Tri-parṇī, KātyŚr. xv, 5, 9. **-pāda**, m. an asterism of which three-fourths are included under one zodiacal sign, W.; = *-padikā*, Kauś.; (*ī*), f. a kind of Mimosa, Npr.; *-vigraha*, mfn. three-footed, Hariv. 2626. **-pād**, see *-pā́d*; *-vibhūti-kathana*, n. N. of PadmaP. v, 29. **-pādaka**, mf(*ikā*)n. three-footed, R. v; (*ikā*), f. Cissus pedata, L.; = °*dī*, Npr. **-piṭa**, mfn. knowing °*ṭaka*, Divyâv. xvii; xxxv. **-piṭaka**, n. the 3 baskets or collections of sacred writings (Sūtra-, Vinaya-, and Abhidharma p°), Buddh.; mfn. = °*ṭa*, Divyâv. ii, 575. **-piṇḍaka**, mfn. consisting of °*ṇḍī*, Śrāddhac. **-piṇḍī**, f. the 3 sacrificial cakes (cf. Mn. iii, 215). **-piba**, mfn. drinking with 3 members of the body (with the 2 pendent ears and tongue, as a long-eared goat), 271, Kull. **-pishṭapa**, n. (m., Uṇ., Sch.) = *-divá*, Indra's heaven, MBh. i, 7580 & 7657; R. i, vi; MārkP. xviii, 27; the sky, L.; cf. *-visht°*; *-sad*, m. 'heaven-dweller,' a god, L. **-puṭa**, mfn. threefold, Buddh. L.; m. a kind of pulse, VarBṛS.; = *-kaṭa*, L.; N. of a measure of length (*hasta-bheda*), L.; (in music) a kind of measure; a shore, L.; (*ā*), f. Arabian jasmine, L.; Durgā, Tantras. ii f.; (*ā*, *ī*), f. = *-pushā*, L.; large cardamoms, L. **-puṭaka**, mfn. triangular (a wound), Suśr. i, 22; m. a kind of pulse, 46. **-puṭin**, m. Ricinus communis, L.; °*ṭi-phala*, id., L. **-puṇḍra**, °*ḍraka*, n. a triple sectarial mark consisting of 3 lines or marks on the forehead (or on back, heart, shoulders &c., RTL. 400), Vas.; Hariv.; BrahmāṇḍaP.; Tithyād. **-puṇḍrin**, mfn. furnished with °*ra*, SSaṃkar. xi, 30. **-puṇḍhra**, n. = °*dra*, ŚāṅkhGṛ. ii, 10; BrahmôttKh. xxviii. **-pur**, f. pl. 'Τρίπολις,' the 3 strong cities, triple fortification, BhP. vii. **-purá**, n. sg. id. (built of gold, silver, and iron, in the sky, air, and earth, by Maya for the Asuras, and burnt by Śiva, MBh. &c.; cf. TS. vi, 2, 3, 1), ŚBr. vi, 3, 3, 25; AitBr. ii, 11; ŚāṅkhBr., N. of an Up.; of a town, Kshitîś. iii, 17; m. Śiva; Śaktir. v; the Asura Bāṇa, RevāKh.; (*ā*), f. a kind of cardamoms (cf. *-puṭā*), Gal.; a kind of rice, ib.; a kind of sorcery, Śārad. xii; N. of an Up.; Durgā, KālP.; Tantras.; Pañcad.; (*ī*), f. N. of an Up.; of the capital of the Cedis, MBh. iii, 254, 10; VarBṛS. xiv, 9; Bālar. iii, 38; *-kumāra*, m. N. of a pupil of Śaṃkarâcārya, Śaṃkar. lxx; *-ghātin*, m. 'destroyer of T°,' Śiva, Kathās. cxv; *-ghna*, m. id., MBh.; R. i; *-jit*, m. id., W.; *-dahana*, m. id., L.; n. N. of a drama; *-dāha*, m. 'burning of T°,' N. of PadmaP. iv, 5; of a drama; *-druh*, m. 'enemy of T°,' Śiva, Bālar.; *-dvish*, m. id., Ragh. xvii, 14; *-pramāthin*, m. = *-ghna*, Dhanamj. 37; *-bhairava*, m. N. of a mixture, Bhpr.; (*ī*), f. Durgā, KālP.; Śārad. xii; *-mallikā*, f. a kind of jasmine, L.; *-mālī*, f. id., L.; *-vadha*, m. 'destruction of T°' (°*rasya v°*, MBh. vii, 9570), N. of ŚivaP. ii, 5–7; *-vijaya*, m. conquest of T°, Megh. 56; N. of LiṅgaP. i, 71 f.; *-vijayin*, m. 'T°-conqueror,' Śiva, Mudr. i, 2; *-vidhvaṃsaka*, m. id., Buddh. L.; *-sundarī*, f. Durgā, Rudray. ii, 1; Tantras. iii f.; *-han*, m. = *-ghna*, R. vi; BhP. iv; *-hara*, m. id., Prasannar. ii, 35; Hāsy.; N. of LiṅgaP. i, 72; °*râdhipati*, m. 'T°-lord,' Maya, BhP. v, viii; °*rântaká*, m. = °*ra-ghna*, MBh. ii; Hariv. 1579; ŚatarUp. (interpol.); Kathās. ciii; °*rântakara*, m. id., MBh. ii, 754; °*rânta-krit*, m. id., Āryav.; Rāma's bow, Mcar. i, 52; °*rârāti*, m. = °*ra-druh*, Kathās. lvi; °*rāri*, m. id., Suśr. vi; Kathās. ix, 7; °*rārṇava*, m. N. of a work, Sch. on Ānand. 1 & 3; °*rārdana*, m. = °*ra-ghna*, MBh. iii; °*rêśâdri*, m. N. of a mountain, Rājat. v; °*rêśvara*, N. of a place, v f.; °*rôpākhyāna*, n. N. of ŚivaP. iii, 52–54. **-purā**, see °*ra*; *-tapana*, n. *-tāpanī*, f. N. of an Up.; *-bhairavī*, f. = °*ra-bh°*, Tantr.; *-sāra*, m. N. of a work, Tantras. ii; *-samuccaya*, m. N. of a work, Tantr. **-purāṇaka**, mf(*ikā*)n. (a coin) worth 3 Purāṇas. **-purāṇīya**, mfn. id., Mn. xi, 228, Kull. **-purī**, see °*ra*; *-kshetra*, n. the district of Tripurī; *prakaraṇa*, n. N. of a Vedântic work (ascribed to Śaṃkara). **-purusha**, n. sg. 3 generations, Gaut.; (*ī*), f. id., ĀpŚr. x, Sch. Introd.; (*am*), ind. through 3 generations, ŚāṅkhŚr.; PārGṛ.; °*shá*, mfn. having the length of 3 men, ŚBr. x; (*-pūr°*) TBr. i; having 3 assistants, ĀśvŚr. iv, 1. **-pushā**, f. dark-blossomed Convolvulus Turpethum, L. **-pushkara**, mfn. decorated with 3 lotus flowers, Lāṭy. ix, 2, 9; pl. 'the 3 lakes,' N. of a Tīrtha, Ragh. xviii, 30; m. N. of a man, Siṃhâs. ix, 2/3. **-pūrushá**, see *-pur°*. **-pṛishṭhá**, mfn. having 3 backs or surfaces (Soma compared with a chariot or bull or horse), RV. vii, ix; m. Vishṇu, BhP. vii f.; the first of the black Vāsu-devas, Jain. L.; n. = *-divá*, AV. ix, 5, 10; BhP. i f. **-paurusha**, mf(*ī*)n. extending over 3 generations, KātyŚr., Sch. **-pratishṭhita** (*trí-*), mfn. having a threefold footing, AV. x, 2, 32. **-pralamba**, °*bin*, mfn. having 3 pendent parts of the body, R. v. **-prasruta**, mfn. having 3 fluid streams flowing from the forehead (a rutting elephant), ii; Hcar. vii. **-prātihārya-sampanna**, mfn. 'possessed of magical power of 3 kinds,' a Buddha, Buddh. L. **-plaksha**, m. pl. 'the 3 fig-trees,' a place near the Yamunā where the Dṛishad-vatī disappears, TāṇḍyaBr. xxv, 13; ŚāṅkhŚr. xiii; °*kshâvaharaṇa*, n. id., KātyŚr. xxiv; Lāṭy. x. **-phala**, mfn. having 3 fruits, Kām. viii, 42; (*ā*), f. (Pāṇ. iv, 1, 64, Vārtt. 3) the 3 Myrobalans (fruits of Terminalia Chebula, T° Bellerica, and Phyllanthus Emblica; also *triph°*, L.), Suśr.; VarBṛS. xvi; Kathās. lxx; KātyŚr., Sch.; the 3 sweet fruits (grape, pomegranate, and date), Npr.; the 3 fragrant fruits (nutmeg, areca-nut, and cloves), ib.; (*ī*), f. id., L. **-bandhana**, m. N. of a son of Aruṇa, BhP. ix, 7, 4 (v.l. *ni-b°*). **-bandhú**, mfn. being the friend of the 3 worlds (Indra), RV. vii, 37, 7. **-barhis**, mfn. having 3 seats of sacrificial grass, i, 181, 8. **-bāhu**, m. 'three-armed,' N. of a goblin, Hariv. 14852; a kind of fighting, 15980. **-bīja**, m. 'three-seeded,' Panicum frumentaceum, L. **-brahman**, mfn. with Brahmā, Vishṇu, and Śiva, DhyānabUp. **-bha**, mfn. containing 3 zodiacal signs, Sūryas. xiv; n. 3 zodiacal signs, quadrant, 90 degrees, vii; *-jīvā*, *-jyā*, *-maurvikā*, f. = *tri-j°*, iii; *tribhôna-lagna*, n. 'part of the ecliptic which does not reach the eastern point by 90 degrees,' the highest point of the ecliptic above the horizon, v, Sch. **-bhaṅgi**, m. (in music) a kind of measure. **-bhaṅgī**, f. a metre of 4 × 32 syllabic instants. **-bhaṇḍī**, f. = *-pushā*, Suśr. (metrically °*ḍi*, vi, 56). **-bhava**, mfn. said of a kind of fever, Bhpr. vii, 8, 70. **-bhāga**, m. the 3rd part, Hariv.; VarBṛS.; Rājat.; KātyŚr., Sch.; the 3rd part (of the eye sending a particular side-glance), Kād.; Hcar. vii; Bālar. iii, 49; the 3rd part of a zodiacal sign, VarBṛ.; three-fourths, Pañcar. i, 14, 50. **-bhāj**, mfn. receiving 3 shares, AitBr. ii, 24. **-bhāṇḍī**, f. = *-bhaṇḍī*, Car. vii, 7. **-bhānu**, m. N. of a descendant of Yayāti and father of Karam-dhama, BhP. ix; (*-sānu*, VāyuP. ii, 37, 1 f.) **-bhāva**, g. *brāhmaṇâdi*. **-bhāshya-ratna**, n. N. of a commentary on TPrāt. **-bhinna**, m. (in music) N. of a measure. **-bhukti-rāja**, m. N. of a Tīrtha, Rasik. xii, 2. **-bhúj**, mfn. threefold, AV. viii, 9, 2. **-bhuja**, mfn. triangular; m. a triangle, Āryabh. ii, 11. **-bhuvana**, n. (Pāṇ. ii, 4, 30, Vārtt. 3, Sch.) = *-jagat*, Bhartṛ.; BhP. &c.; N. of a town, Kathās. lvi; m. N. of a prince, ib.; Rājat. vi f.; *-guru*, m. 'the 3 worlds' master,' Śiva, Megh.; *-pati*, m. Vishṇu, Dhūrtas. i, 13; *-pāla-deva*, m. N. of a prince, Dūtāṅg. i, 2/3; *-prabhā*, f. N. of the daughter of a Dānava, Kathās. cxviii; *-malla-deva*, m. the hero of Vcar.; *-māṇikya-carita*, n. N. of a work, Ganar.; °*nâbhoga*, m. the extension of the 3 worlds, Prasannar. i, 8/9; °*nêśvara*, m. = °*na-guru*, ŚivaP. ii, 28; Indra, BrahmaP.; °*nêśvara-liṅga*, n. N. of a Liṅga, KapSaṃh. **-bhūma**, mfn. three-storied, Pāṇ. v, 4, 75, Sch. **-bhauma**, mfn. id., Hcat. i, 9, 330. **-maṇḍala-pariśuddha**, mfn ?, Buddh. L. **-maṇḍalā**, f. (scil. *lūtā*), N. of a venomous spider, Suśr. v. **-mada**, m. the 3 narcotic plants (Cyperus rotundus, Plumbago zeylanica, and Embelia Ribes); the threefold haughtiness, BhP. iii, 1, 43. **-madhu**, mfn. knowing or reciting the 3 verses beginning with *mádhu* (RV. i, 90, 6–8), Gaut.; Yājñ. i; VP. iii, 15, 1; MārkP. xxxi; n. = °*dhura*, L. **-madhura**, n. the 3 sweet substances (sugar, honey, ghee), VarBṛS.; Śārad. ix; (*madhura-traya*, Tantras. iv). **-mántu**, mfn. 'offering threefold advice' or m. 'N. of a man,' RV. i, 112, 4.

–mala, mfn. affected by 3 kinds of uncleanness, GarbhUp. 1. **–malla**, N. of a sacred place, Rasik. xi, 25; *-candra*, m. N. of a prince. **–mātṛi**, mfn. having 3 mothers (m. 'creator of the 3 worlds,' Sāy.), RV. iii, 56,5. **–mātra**, mf(*ā*)n. = °*trā-kāla*, RPrāt.; APrāt.; ŚāṅkhŚr.; 3 in number, MBh. vii; °*trā-kāla*, mfn. containing or sounding 3 syllabic instants, Bhāshik. ii, 32, Sch.; °*trika*, m. (unmetrically for °*tra*) the syllable *om*, Prapañcas. (Rāmat-Up. ii, 2, 3, Sch.) **–mārikā**, f. 'three-killer,' N. of a woman, Kathās. lxvi. **–mārga**, in comp. = *-patha*; mfn. with 3 ways, DhyānabUp. 17; (*ī*), f. 3 ways, L.; *-gamana*, n. going by 3 ways (through heaven, earth, and the lower regions), R. (G) i, 45, 40; *-gā*, f. = *tripatha-gā*, Ragh. xiii, 20; Śiś. xii. **–mukuṭa**, m. 'three-peaked,' the Tri-kūṭa mountain, L. **–mukha**, m. 'three-faced,' the 3rd Arhat of the present Avasarpiṇī, L.; (*ā*), f. Śākya-muni's mother, L. **–muni**, mfn. (grammar) produced by the 3 Munis (Pāṇ., Kāty., Pat.), Pāṇ. ii, 1, 19, Kāś.; Madhus. **–mūḍha**, °**ḍhaka**, n. = *-gūḍha*, Bhar. xviii. **–mūrti**, mfn. having 3 forms or shapes (as Brahmā, Vishṇu, Śiva), Kum. ii, 4; Gaṅgêś.; Rāmat-Up. i, 16, Sch.; in comp. Brahmā, Vishṇu, Śiva, Hcat. i, 11, 547; m. the sun (cf. *trayī-deha*), 8, 221; a Buddha, L.; one of the 8 Vidyêśvaras, 8, 406; 11, 857; ii, 1, 941; Śaktir. v; (°*tika*) Sarvad. vii, 75. **–mūrdha**, mfn. three-headed, Pāṇ. v f. **–mūrdhán**, mfn. id., RV. i, 146, 1; m. N. of a Rakshas, Uttarar. ii, 15. **–yajña**, see *triy-aksha*. **–yava**, mfn. weighing 3 barleycorns, Mn. viii, 134; Śulbas. **–yashṭi**, m. Oldenlandia biflora (?), L. **–yāna**, n. the 3 Vehicles (leading to Nirvāṇa), Buddh. **–yāma**, mf(*ā*)n. (the night) containing 3 watches (or 9 hours), R. (G) ii, 10, 7; (*ā*), f. night, Hariv. 5768; R. &c.; turmeric, W.; = *-pushā*, Uṇ. k.; the Indigo plant, ib.; the river Yamunā, ib. **–yāmaka**, n. sin, L. **–yukta**, mfn. (a cart) drawn by 3, KātyŚr. xv. **–yugá**, n. (= *-purusha*) 3 generations (Nir.; 'spring, rainy-season, and autumn,' ŚBr. vii), RV. x, 97, 1; mfn. appearing in the first 3 Yugas (Kṛishṇa), MBh.; BhP. **–yugma**, mfn. possessing 3 pairs (*yaśo-vīrye, aiśvarya-śriyau, jñāna-vairāgye*), R. vii. **–yūpa**, mfn. with 3 sacrificial posts, KātyŚr. **–yojaná**, n. 3 Yojanas, AV. vi, 131, 3. **–yoni**, mfn. (a lawsuit) resulting from 3 reasons (anger, covetousness, or infatuation), W. **–ratna**, n. the 3 gems: Buddha, the law, and the monkish brotherhood, Buddh. **–rasaka**, n. 'triple-flavoured,' a spirituous liquor, Śiś. x, 12 (Sāh. iii, $\frac{148}{149}$); see *-saraka*. **–rātrá**, n. sg. 3 (nights or) days, ŚBr.; KātyŚr.; Kauś.; (pl., MBh. iii, 82, 18); mfn. lasting (3 nights or) days, ŚBr. xiii; ŚāṅkhŚr.; m. a sacrificial performance of 3 days, TāṇḍyaBr.; cf. *aśva-*, *garga-*, *baida-*; (*am*), ind. for 3 days, during 3 days, KātyŚr.; ĀśvGṛ.; Mn. &c.; (*āt*, *ena*), ind. after 3 days, v; °*trais tribhiḥ*, after 3 × 3 days, 64; °*trâvaram*, ind. at least 3 days, KātyŚr. iv, 11, 3; Gaut. **–rātrīṇā**, f. (a woman) 3 days after her courses, ĀpŚr. ix, 2, 3. **–rāva**, m. N. of a son of Garuḍa, MBh. v, 101, 11 (v.l. *-vāra*). **–rāśi-pa**, mfn. governing 3 zodiacal signs. **–rūpa** (*tri-*), mfn. three-formed, NṛisUp. ii, 9, 6; three-coloured, ŚBr. iv, xiii; KātyŚr.; having 3 syllabic instants, TPrāt., Sch. **–rekha**, mf(*ā*)n. three-lined (the neck), L.; m. a conch (or some other animal), L.; °*khâṅkita*, m. N. of a fish, Gal.; °*khā-puṭa*, a sexangle, RāmatUp. i, 58. **–lava**, m. a third part, Līl. **–lavaṇa**, n. = *-paṭu*, L. **–liṅga**, mfn. possessing the 3 Guṇas (cf. *-guṇa*), BhP. iii; = °*gaka*; n. 'the 3 Liṅgas,' the country Telinga; (*ī*), f. the 3 genders (in Gram.), L. **–liṅgaka**, mfn. having 3 genders, adjective, L. **–loka**, n. sg. [MBh. xiii; Hariv. 11303], m. pl. [R. iii] the 3 worlds (= *-patha*); m. sg. the inhabitants of the 3 worlds, BhP. iii, 2, 13; (*ī*), f. the 3 worlds, i–iii; Rājat.; Prab.; *-nātha*, m. 'T°-lord,' Indra, Ragh. iii, 45; Śiva, Kum. v, 77; *-rakshin*, mfn. protecting the 3 worlds, Vikr. i, 5; *-vaśaṃ-kara*, m. N. of a Lokêśvara; *-vīra*, m. N. of a Buddh. deity; *-sāra*, m. N. of a work; °*kâtman*, m. 'T°-soul,' Śiva; °*kêśa*, m. 'T°-lord,' Vishṇu, Siṇhâs.; Siva, MBh. xiv; the sun, L. **–lokī**, f. of °*ka*; *-kṛiti*, f. the creation of the 3 worlds, Dhūrtan.; *-jit*, mfn. conquering the 3 worlds, Dhanaṃj. 4; *-nātha*, m. 'T°-lord,' Vishṇu, Śāntiś.; *-pati*, m. id., Siṇhâs. xii, 3; *-rāja*, m. Indra, Gal. **–locana**, mfn. three-eyed (Śiva), DhyānabUp.; KaivUp.; R. i; Ragh. &c.; m. (with *rasa*) a kind of mixture, Rasar.; m. N. of a poet, ŚārṅgP.; = *-dāsa*, Hemac., Sch.; = *-pāla*, Rājat. vii; Kshitîś.; (*ā*), f. a disloyal wife, L.; N. of a goddess (also °*nī*, W.), BrahmaP. ii, 18, 20; *-tīrtha*, n. N. of a Tīrtha, KapSaṃh.; *-dāsa*, m. N. of a grammarian; *-pāla*, m. N. of a prince, Rājat. vii; °*nâshṭamī*, f. the 8th day in the dark half of month Jyaishṭha, W.; °*nêśvara-tīrtha*, n. N. of a Tīrtha, RevāKh. clxxxviii. **–loha**, n. the 3 metals (copper, brass, and bell-metal), Hcat. i, 11; mf(*ī*)n. made of one of the 3 metals (v. l. *-lauh*°), Tantras. i. **–lohaka**, n. the 3 metals (gold, silver, copper), L. **–lauha**, see *-loha*. **–vakrā**, f. 'thrice crooked,' N. of a woman, BhP. x, 42, 3. **–vaṇa-saṃjñikā**, °**ṇī**, f. (in music) N. of a Rāgiṇī. **–vat** (*trí-*), mfn. (Pāṇ. vi, 1, 176, Vārtt. 2; viii, 2, 15, Kāś.) containing the word *tri*, TS. ii, 4, 11, 2. **–vatsá**, mf(*ā*)n. 3 years old (ox or cow), VS.; TāṇḍyaBr.; Lāṭy.; Kāty. **–vandhurá**, mfn. (Pāṇ. vi, 2, 199, Vārtt., Pat.) having 3 seats (the Aśvins' chariot), RV. i, vii–ix. **–vayas** (*tri-*), mfn. having threefold food (or texture?), ii, 31, 5. **–várūtha**, mfn. protecting in 3 ways, RV.; AV. vii–ix; (°*thá*) VS. & TBr. ii. **–varga**, m. the three things, KātyŚr.; Lāṭy. &c. (= *-gaṇa*, Mn.; Yājñ.; MBh. &c.; = *-guṇa*, L.; the 3 conditions, 'progress, stationariness, and decline,' xii, 2664; the 3 higher castes, xiii; = *-madhura*, Suśr. vi, 41; = *-kaṭu*, L.; = *-phalā*, L.); *-cintana*, n. N. of a ch. of Psarv.; *-pārīṇa*, mfn. having passed through the 3 conditions or attained the *tri-gaṇa*, Bhaṭṭ. ii, 46. **–varṇa**, mfn. three-coloured, ŚāṅkhGṛ.; *-kṛit*, m. the chameleon, Npr. **–varṇaka**, m. n. = *-kaṭa*, L.; n. = *-kaṭu*, Suśr. i, 44; the 3 Myrobalans (*-phalā*), L. **–vártu**, mfn. threefold, RV. vii, 101, 2. **–vartman**, mfn. going by 3 paths, ŚvetUp. v, 7; °*tma-gā*, f. = *tripatha-gā*, MBh. xiii, 1842. **–varsha**, mfn. = *-vatsá*, Lāṭy. viii; n. 3 years, Suśr. ii, 1; *a-*, not yet 3 years old, Mn. v, 70; *trivarsha-pūrva*, mfn. known less than 3 years, Āp. **–varshaka**, mf(*ikā*)n. = *-vatsá*, Hemac. **–°varshīya**, mfn. used for 3 years, MBh. xiii, 4467. **–vali**, mfn. having 3 folds or incisions, KātyŚr. vii, 3, 29; f. in comp. the 3 folds over a woman's navel (regarded as a beauty), VarBṛS. lxx, 5; Ṛitus.; GarP. **–valī**, f. id., MBh. iii, 1824; Hariv. 3625; Bhartṛ.; the anus, L.; N. of a drum; *-vat*, see *-valīka*. **–°valīka**, mfn. (Rāma) having 3 folds (on the belly or neck), R. v, 32, 12 (v.l. °*lī-vat*); n. the anus, W. **–vācika**, mfn. effected by 3 words, Pañcat. iv, 5, $\frac{0}{1}$. **–vāra**, see *-rāva*; (*am*), ind. thrice, Śāktân. ii. **–vārshika**, mfn. 3 years old, Pañcat. iii, 2, $\frac{17}{18}$. **–vikrama**, n. the 3 steps (of Vishṇu), R. vi; Kum. (in comp.); mfn. or m. who strided over the 3 worlds in 3 steps (Vishṇu), Hariv. 2641; R. i &c.; m. N. of a Brāhman, Śukas.; of the author of a work (called after him Traivikramī), Nirṇayas. iii; of a medical author and of a mixture (called after him), Rasêndrac.; = *-bhaṭṭa*; *-tīrtha*, n. N. of a Tīrtha, RevāKh. cclxxi; *-deva*, m. N. of an author, Rasar.; *-bhaṭṭa*, m. N. of the author of Nalac.; *-sena*, m. N. of a prince, Kathās.; °*mâcārya*, m. N. of an astronomer. **–vitastá**, mfn. 3 spans long, TBr. i, 5, 10, 1; n. 3 spans, ĀpŚr. vii, 4; 2. **–vidya**, mfn. containing the 3 Vedas (Śiva; cf. *trayī-tanu*); (*ā*), f. threefold knowledge (cf. *trayī vidyā*), Pāṇ. iv, 1, 88, Pat. **–vidha** (*trí-*), mfn. of 3 kinds, triple, threefold, ŚBr. xii; ŚāṅkhŚr.; Mn. &c.; *-damatha-vastu-kuśala*, m. = *tri-dam*°, Divyâv. viii, 79. **–vinata**, mfn. bent in 3 ways, R. v, 32, 13 (v.l. *try-avan*°). **–vibudhī**, f. 3 deities, Naish. **–vishṭapa**, n. = *-pishṭ*°, GopBr.; Yājñ.; MBh. &c.; N. of a Liṅga, LiṅgaP. i, 1, 4; for °*shṭabdha*, Saṃny-Up. iv, 1; *-sad*, m. = *-pishṭ*°, L. **–vishṭabdha**, n. the 3 staves of a Parivrājaka (= *-daṇḍa*), MBh. xii. **–vishṭabdhaka**, n. id., Pat. on Pāṇ. i, 1, 1, Vārtt. 8; ii, 1, 1, Vārtt. 4; & iii, 2, 124, Vārtt. 2. **–vishṭí**, ind. thrice, RV. iv, 6, 4 & 15, 2; *-dhātu*, mfn. threefold, i, 102, 8. **–vista**, mfn. weighing 3 Vistas, Pāṇ. v, 1, 31. **–vṛít**, mfn. threefold, triple, triform, consisting of 3 parts or folds &c., RV. &c.; connected with the Tri-vṛit Stoma, ŚBr. xiii; KātyŚr.; ŚāṅkhŚr.; (n. pl. *-vṛinti*) ĀśvŚr.; m. (with or without *stóma*) a threefold Stoma (in which first the three 1st verses of each Tṛica of RV. ix, 11 are sung together, then the 2nd verses, and lastly the 3rd), VS. &c.; m. a triple cord, ŚāṅkhGṛ.; Mn. iii, 43; an amulet of 3 strings, AV. v, 28; N. of a Vyāsa (see *-vṛisha*); f. = °*tā*, Suśr. (generally written *tri-v*°); *trivṛic-chiras*, mfn. T°-headed, MBh. xii, 1632; xiii, 7379; *trivṛit-karaṇa*, n. making threefold, Vedântas. 116 (ChUp. vi, 3, 2 f.); *trivṛit-tā*, f. triplicity, ŚBr. vi; *-parṇī*, f. Hingcha repens, L.; *trivṛit-prāya*, mfn. similar to the T°, xii, 3, 1, 5; *-stoma*, mfn. connected with the T° Stoma, Hariv. 7435. **–vṛitā**, f. Ipomœa Turpethum, Suśr.; VarBṛS. **–vṛitti**, f. livelihood through 3 things (sacrifice, study, and alms), MBh. xiii, 1541. **–vṛinta**, m. = *-pakshaka*, Npr. **–vṛintikā**, f. = *-vṛitā*, L. **–vṛishá**, mfn. having 3 bulls, AV. v, 16, 3; m. N. of the Vyāsa in the 11th Dvāpara, DevībhP. i, 3; KūrmaP. i, 52, 5 (v.l. *ṛishabha*); (°*shan*) VP. iii, 3, 14; (°*vṛit*) VāyuP. i, 23, 140. **–vṛishan**, m. N. of Try-aruṇa's father (cf. *traivṛishṇá*), RV. v, 27, 1, Sāy.; see °*sha*. **–veṇi**, f. = °*ṇī*, Uṇ., Sch. **–veṇikā**, f. N. of a grammar. **–veṇī**, f. (g. *śivâdi*) 'triple-braided,' the place of confluence (Prayāga, now Allāhābād) of the Ganges with the Yamunā (Jumnā) and the subterranean Sarasvatī; N. of another place. **–veṇu**, mfn. three-bannered (a chariot), BhP. iv, 26, 1; m. N. of part of a chariot, MBh. iii f., vii (also °*ṇuka*)–ix; BhP. xi. **–veda**, in comp. the 3 Vedas, KātyŚr. xxv; (*ī*), f. id., L.; mfn. familiar with the 3 Vedas, Mn. ii, 118; m. = *trayī-deha*, Hcat. i; °*dī-tanu*, m. (with *deva*) id., Bālar. iii, 85. **–vedin**, mfn. familiar with the 3 Vedas, W.; = *trayī-mūrti-mat*, R. vii. **–velā**, f. = *-vṛitā*, L. **–vaistika**, mfn. = *-vista*, Pāṇ. **–vyāma**, mf(*ā*)n. 3 cords long, KātyŚr. vi, 3, 5. **–vrata** (*trí-*), mfn. eating thrice a day, TS. vi, 2, 5, 3. **–śakala**, m. having 3 Śakalas, Pāṇ. vi, 2, 47, Kāś. **–śakti**, f. = *-kalā*, VarP. xc ff. **–śaṅku**, m. N. of a sage, TUp. i, 10; of a king of Ayodhyā (aspiring to ascend to heaven in his mortal body, he first requested Vasishṭha to perform a great sacrifice for him; on V.'s refusing he applied to V.'s hundred sons, who cursed and degraded him to the rank of a Caṇḍāla [hence called a Caṇḍāla king, Divyâv. xxxiii]; Viśvā-mitra then undertook the sacrifice for him and invited all the gods, who declined to come and thereby so enraged the sage that, by his own power, he transported T° to heaven; on his being hurled down again headforemost by the gods, he was arrested in his course by Viśvā-mitra and remained suspended in the sky, forming the southern cross constellation, R. i, 57 (59 G) ff. [son of Pṛithu]; Hariv. 730 ff. & VP. iv, 3, 13 f. [son of Trayyāruṇa]; [son of Tri-bandhana] BhP. ix, 7), MBh. i, xiii &c.; a cat, L.; the civet-cat, Npr.; a grasshopper, L.; a fire-fly, L.; = °*ṅkha*, L.; N. of a mythical mountain, Divyâv. viii, 293 ff.; f. N. of a mythical river, 223 & 295; (°*kā*) 298; m. pl. N. of thorns, 293; *-ja*, m. 'T°'s son,' Hari-ścandra, L.; *-tilaka*, mf(*ā*)n. adorned with the T° constellation (the southern region, *diś*), Kād.; *-yājin*, m. 'sacrificing for T°,' Viśvā-mitra, L. **–śaṅkuka**, m. a wag-tail, Gal.; (*ā*), f., see °*ṅku*. **–śaṅkha**, m. the Cātaka bird, Gal. **–śatá**, mfn. 103, ŚāṅkhBr. xiv; ŚāṅkhŚr.; 300, RV. i, 164, 48; AV. xi, 5, 2; the 300th (chs. of MBh. iii, xii & R. [G] ii, vi); = °*taka*, Hariv. 512 (f. *ī*); Kām.; n. 300, MBh. xiii; R. i, vii; (*ī*), f. 300, MBh. xiv; Jyot. (YV.) 29; °*taṃ-shashṭi-parvan*, mfn. consisting of 360 sections, BhP. iii; °*ta-tama*, mfn. the 300th (ch. of Hariv.) **–śataka**, mf(*ikā*)n. consisting of 300, Buddh. **–śaraṇa**, n. 'threefold refuge,' = *-ratna*, Buddh.; the three-refuge formula of Buddhists, MWB. 78. **–śarīra**, m. three-bodied, NṛisUp. ii, 1, 4. **–śarīrin**, mfn. id. (Vishṇu), Hariv. 14982. **–śarkarā**, f. 3 kinds of sugar (*guḍôtpannā*, *himôtthā*, *madhurā*), L. **–śalá**, mfn. 3 bristles long, TBr. i, 5, 10, 1; (*ā*), f. the mother of Mahāvīra, Jain. **–śalya**, mfn. three-pointed (an arrow), MBh. vii, 202, 82. **–śas**, ind. by threes, RPrāt. xviii. **–śākha**, mf(*ā*)n. three-wrinkled (*bhru-kuṭī*), MBh. viii; Kathās. cii, 72; *-pattra*, m. Ægle Marmelos, L. **–śāṇa**, °**ṇya**, mfn. weighing 3 Śāṇas, Pāṇ. v, 1, 36. **–śānu**, m. for *-bhānu*, Hariv.; BrahmaP. **–śāla**, n. a house with 3 halls, MatsyaP. ccliii. **–śālaka**, n. id., VarBṛS. liii, 37 f. **–śikha**, mf(*ā*)n. three-pointed, trident-shaped, BhP. iii, v f.; three-flamed, Hariv. 12292; = *-śākha*, MBh. i; Hariv.; Pañcat. i, 15, $\frac{24}{26}$; iv, 4, $\frac{4}{5}$; m. = *-śākha-pattra*, L.; a Rakshas, L.; Indra in Tāmasa's Manv-antara, BhP. viii, 1; n. a trident, Kathās. lv, ci, cvii; a three-pointed tiara, L.; (*ī*), f. N. of an Up. **–śikhara**, m. 'three-peaked,' (with *śaila*) N. of a mountain, R. iv, 44, 50. **–śikhi-dalā**, f. 'trident-leaved,' N. of a bulb, L. **–śira**, mfn. (for °*ras*) three-pointed, MBh. xiii, 7379 (v.l. *catur-aśva*); m., see °*ras*; (*ā*), f. Clypea hernandifolia, L.; *-giri*, m. N. of a mountain, SkandaP. **–śiras**, mfn. three-headed (Tvāshṭra, author of RV. x, 8), TāṇḍyaBr. xvii; Bṛih.; KaushUp.; MBh.; Kām.; (Jvara) BhP. x, 63, 22; three-pointed, MBh. xiii; R. iv; m. N. of an Asura killed by Vishṇu, MBh. ix, 1755; of a Rākshasa killed by Rāma, R.; Ragh.; (°*ra*) BhP. ix, 10, 9; n.(with *rakshas*) id., R. i, 1,45; a Rakshas, L.; Kubera, L. **– śila**, n. 3 stones, Kauś. **– śīrsha**, mfn. three-headed, MBh. (Śiva, xii); Hariv.; *-guhā* & °*shâkhya-g*°, f. N. of a cavern in Kailāsa, Kathās. cviii f.; °*sha-vat*, mfn. having 3 crowns (or vertices), R.(B) v, 35, 18. **– śīrshaka**, n. a trident, L. **– śīrshán**, mfn. three-headed (Tvāshṭra, *dāsa*, &c.), RV. x; AV. v, 23, 9; Kāṭh.; ŚBr.(*trí-ś*°); ŚāṅkhŚr. xiv. **– śukra** (*tri-*), mfn. triply pure, TBr. ii. **– śukriya**, mfn. id., Kāṭh.; ShaḍvBr.; ŚāṅkhŚr. **– śukla**, m.(=°*kra*) Śiva, MBh. **– śúc**, mfn. triply shining, VS. xxxviii; (*-śrut*, ĀśvŚr. v, 13, 6). **– śūla**, n. a trident, MBh. &c. (Śiva's weapon, iii, 5009; Hariv.; MatsyaP. xi, 29); m. N. of a mountain; *-khāta*, n. N. of a Tīrtha, MBh. iii; *-gaṅgā*, f. N. of a river; *-purī*, f. N. of a town; *-vara-pāṇin* & *-hasta*, mfn. bearing the trident in his hand (Śiva), xii, xiv; °*lâṅka*, m. 'trident-marked,' Śiva, Shaḍguruś.; °*lāya*, Nom. Ā. to resemble Śiva's trident, Veṇis. i, §. **– śūlikā**, f. a small trident, Kād. **– śūlin**, m. 'bearing the trident,' Śiva, W.; (*inī*), f. Durgā, Hariv. 9428; Tantras. ii. **– śṛiṅga**, m. 'three-horned,' a triangle, Sārasam.; N. of a mountain (=*-kūṭa*, L.), Hariv. 12853; R.; BhP.; the membrum virile, MantraBr. i, 1, 4, Sch. **– śṛiṅgin**, m. the fish Cyprinus Rohita, L. **– śóka**, mfn. =*-śúc*, RV. x, 29, 2; m. N. of a Ṛishi (author of viii, 45), i, 112, 12; viii, 45, 30; AV. iv, 29, 6. **– śyeta**, mf(*ā*)n. =*triḥ-śveta*, MānŚr. i, 7, 2. **– śrut**, see *-śúc*. **– śruti**, mfn. (in music) containing 3 intervals. **– shaṃyuktá** (*sam-*), mfn. triply connected, ŚBr. xii; (n. scil. *havis* or *kárman*) v & KātyŚr. xv. **– shaṃvatsara**, mfn. lasting 3 years, KātyŚr.; (*-saṃv*°) Lāṭy. & ŚāṅkhŚr. **– shatya** (*trí-*), mfn. trebly truthful (in thought, word, and deed), MaitrS.; TS. vi; TBr. iii; Kāṭh. (also *-satya*); ShaḍvBr. **– shadhasthá**, mf(*ā*)n. having a triple seat (*sadh*° = *barhis*), RV. (also °*dhástha*, vi); n. a triple seat, v, x. **– shaṃdhi** (*trí-*), mfn. 'having 3 joints (*saṃdhi*),' composed of 3 parts, AV. xi, 9 f. (also m. a kind of snake); ŚBr. xi; AitBr. i, 25; Kauś.; n. N. of a Sāman. **– shaptá**, pl. m(*ā́s*)fn. =*-saptá*, AV. i, xiii; Kāṭh. xxxvii; °*ptīya*, n. the hymn AV. i, 1, Kauś. **– shama**, mfn. 'triply even,' small, Naigh. iii, 2 (v.l.) **– shavaṇa**, mfn. connected with 3 Soma libations, ŚBr. xii, 2 (*-sav*°); ŚāṅkhŚr.; n. pl. the 3 Soma libations, MBh. iii (*-sav*°); sg. (with or without *snāna*) the 3 ablutions (at dawn, noon, and sunset (also *triḥ-snāna*, Kām. ii, 28), xiii; Mn. &c. (*-sav*°, MārkP. xxiii); (*am*), ind. at dawn, noon, and sunset, Āp.; MānGṛ.; m. N. of a man, BrahmaP. ii, 12 & 18, 19; *-snāyin*, mfn. performing the 3 ablutions, MBh. xiii; Yājñ. iii. **– shash**, mfn. pl. 3 × 6, BhP. xii, 7, 24. **– shashṭa**, mf(*ī*)n. the 63rd (chs. of MBh.) **– shashṭi**, f. 63, Pāṇ. vi; *-tama*, mfn. = °*shṭa* (chs. of MBh. ii & R.); *-dhā*, ind. in 63 parts, Suśr. i; *-śalākā-purusha-carita*, n. 'lives of the 63 great personages,' N. of a work by Hemac. **– shāhasra** (*trí-*), mfn. (=*-sāh*°) consisting of 3000, TS. v; Śulbas. **– shuvarcaka**, see *-suv*°. **– shṭā-várūtrī**, see *tvasht*°. **– shṭúk** &c. (in the nom. and before consonantic terminations as well as in comp.) for *-shṭúp* &c.; *trishṭúñ-mukha*, mfn. beginning with a Tri-shṭubh, TS. vii. **– shṭúp-chandas**, mfn. having Tri-shṭubh as metre, MaitrS. ii, 3, 3; AV. vi, 48, 3. **– shṭúbh**, f. a metre of 4 × 11 syllables (RPrāt. xvi, 41 ff.; Nir. vii, 12), RV. viii ff.; VS. &c. (°*bhām arkau*, N. of 2 Sāmans); (in the later metrical system) any metre of 4 × 11 syllables. **– shṭoma**, mfn. containing 3 Stomas, ŚāṅkhŚr. xvi; m. N. of an Ekāha sacrifice, xv; KātyŚr. xv, 9. **– shṭhá**, mfn. (Pāṇ. viii, 3, 97) = *-vandhurá*, RV. i, 34, 5. **– shṭhín**, mfn. = *-pratishṭhita*, VS. xxx, 14. **– saṃvatsara**, see *-shaṃv*°. **– satya**, see *shatya*; n. a triple oath, Pañcat. (v.l.) **– saṃdhi**, mfn., see *-shaṃdhi*; f. =°*dhya-kusumā*, L. **– saṃdhika**, mfn. occurring at the 3 divisions of the day, Yavanêśv. **– saṃdhī**, f. =°*dhya-kusumā*, Npr. **– saṃdhya**, n. the 3 divisions of the day (dawn, noon, and sunset), Tithyād; (*ī*), f. id., L., Sch.; (*ā*), f. id., W.; *-kusumā*, L.; Durgā, MatsyaP. xiii, 37; (*am*), ind. at dawn, noon, and sunset, ŚāṅkhGṛ.; PārGṛ.; MBh. iii.; Kathās.; Śatr.; *-kusumā*, f. Hibiscus rosa sinensis, L. **– saptá**, mfn. pl. 3 × 7, RV. i, 133, 6 & TS. v (instr. °*ptais*); MBh. ix (instr. °*ptabhis*); (in comp.) Hcat. i, 6, 331; see *triḥ-s*°. **– saptaka**, in comp. 3 × 7, VarBṛS. lvi. **– saptata**, mfn. the 73rd (chs. of MBh. & Hariv.) **– saptati**, f. (Pāṇ. vi) 73, KātyŚr., Sch.; *-tama*, mfn. = °*ptata* (chs. of MBh. ii & R.) **– sama**, mfn. having 3 equal sides (a quadrangle); having 3 equal parts of the body, R.(B) v, 35, 17; n. an aggregate of equal parts of 3 substances (yellow myrobalan, ginger, and molasses), L. **– samṛiddha** (for *triḥ-s*°), mfn. (a cow) triply fortunate (not obstinate, milk-giving, and fertile), Hcat. i, 7. **– sara**, m. n. = *kṛis*°, L.; a triple pearl-string (in Prākṛit *tis*° & *tisaraya* [*tri-saraka*], Jain.), Pañcad.; (*ī*), f. N. of a stringed instrument. **– saraka**, see °*ra*; n. 'thrice enjoying spirituous liquors,' v.l. for *-rasaka*. **– sarga**, m. the creation of the 3 Guṇas, BhP. i, 1, 1. **– savana**, see *-shav*°. **– sāṃvatsara**, mfn. = *-vatsá*, ŚāṅkhBr. **– sādhana**, mf(*ā*)n. having a threefold causality, Ragh. iii, 13. **– sānu**, see *-bhānu*. **– sāman**, mfn. singing 3 Sāmans, MBh. xii. **– sāmā**, f. N. of a river, VP. ii, 3, 13; BhP. v, 19. **– sāmya**, n. equilibrium of the 3 Guṇas, ii, 7, 40. **– sāhasra**, n. 3000, x, 58, 50; mf(*ī*)n. consisting of 3000, KātySr.; *-mahā-sāhasra*, m. (with or without *loka-dhātu*) N. of a world, Lalit. xix, xxi; *-mahāsāhasrika*, mfn. governing that world, xix. **– sitā**, f. = *-śarkarā*, L. **– sītya**, mfn. thrice ploughed, L. **– sugandha**, m. n. = *-jāta*, Hcat. ii. **– sugandhi**, (n., L.), °*dhika*, id., Suśr. vi; Bhpr. **– sundara**, m. N. of a mixture, Rasêndrac. **– suparṇa** (*trí-*), m. n. N. of RV. x, 114, 3–5 (or of TĀr. x, 48–50), TĀr. x, 48–50; mfn. familiar with or reciting those verses, Āp. ii; Gaut.; Mn. iii, 185; Yājñ. i (°*rṇaka*); MBh. xiii; VP. iii, 15, 1; MārkP. **– suvarcaka**, m. 'triply splendid,' N. of a man, MBh. iii (*-shuv*° B). **– sūtra**, mfn. having 3 threads, MaitrUp. vi; CūlUp.; (*ī*), f. 3 Sūtras, Nyāyas., Sch.; °*trī-karaṇa*, n. N. of a performance, Śarad. v, 5. **– saugandhya**, n. = *-sugandha*, Suśr. i, 44, 19. **– sauparṇa**, mfn. relating to the Tri-suparṇa verses, MBh. xii. **– skandha**, n. 'consisting of 3 Skandhas,' the Jyotiḥ-śāstra, Āryabh., Sch. Introd.; *-patha-daiśika*, m. Buddha, Buddh. L. **– skandhaka**, N. of a Buddh. Sūtra, Buddh. L. **– stana**, mfn. milked from 3 nipples, KātyŚr.; (*ī*), f. (a woman) having 3 breasts, MBh. iii; Pañcat. v; (a cow) having 3 nipples, Hcat. i, 7, 469. **– sthalī**, f. the 3 (sacred) places; *-setu*, m. N. of a work. **– sthāna**, mfn. having 3 dwelling-places, DhyānabUp.; extending through the 3 worlds, Nir. ix, 25; n. *Mahêśvarasya*, N. of a Tīrtha, MBh. xiii, 702. **– sthūṇa**, mfn. having (the humours as the) 3 supports, v, 1070; Suśr. i, 21, 1; Laghuj. ii, 16. **– srotas**, f. 'three-streamed,' the Ganges, Śak. vii; Kum. vii, 15; Ragh. x, 64; N. of another river, L. **– srotasī**, f. N. of a river, MBh. ii, 375. **– halikā-grāma**, m. N. of a Tīrtha, Vishṇ. lxxxv, 24. **– halya**, mfn. = *-sītya*, L. **– havish-ka**, mf(*ā*)n. = °*vis*, ĀśvŚr., Sch. **– havis** (*trí-*), mfn. connected with 3 oblations, ŚBr. xiii; ĀśvŚr. ii. **– hāyana**, mf(*ī*)n. = *-vatsá*, KātyŚr.; Kauś.; Anup.; Śulbas.; Yājñ.; MBh. iii f., vii; ? BrahmavP. **Trîndriya**, mfn. having 3 organs of sensation, Hemac. **Trîrāvatika**, mfn. watered by 3 Irāvatī rivers, Pāṇ. i, 4, 1, Vārtt. 19, Pat. **Trishu**, mfn. furnished with 3 arrows, ŚāṅkhŚr. **Trishuka**, mfn. id., KātyŚr. xxv, 4, 47. **Trishṭaká**, mfn. furnished with 3 bricks, ŚBr. x, 5, 2, 21.

Triṇśa mf(*ī*)n., the 30th (chs. of MBh. & R.); + 30, Pāṇ. v, 2, 46; m. 'a Stoma consisting of 30 parts,' mfn. connected with that Stoma, TāṇḍyaBr.; Lāṭy.; m. = °*śâṅśa*, Laghuj. **Triṇśâṅśa**, °*śaka*, m. $\frac{1}{30}$ of a zodiacal sign, degree, VarBṛ.; Laghuj. iv.

Triṇśaka, mfn. consisting of 30 parts, MBh. iii, 10644; bought for or worth 30 &c., Pāṇ. v, 1, 24; n. 30, Supadm.; (*ikā*), f. N. of a work, Param., Sch. **Triṇśác-chloki**, f. '30 Ślokas,' N. of a work. **Triṇśac-chata** (°*t-ś*°), n. 130, RV. vi, 27, 6.

Triṇśát, f. (Pāṇ. v, 1, 59) 30, RV. &c. (pl., MBh. vi, xiii; with the objects in the same case, once [Rājat. i, 286] in the gen.; acc. °*śat*, Hcat. i, 8). **– tamá**, mf(*ī*)n. the 30th, ŚBr. viii–x; (chs. of MBh. xii, xv & Hariv.) **– tvá**, n. the condition of 30, MaitrS. i, 10; Kāṭh. xxxvi, 10. **– pattra**, n. 'thirty-leaved,' the blossom of Nymphæa esculenta, L. **– sāhasra**, mf(*ā*)n. pl. 30,000, R.(G) ii, 100, 44.

Triṇśati, f. 30, Kām. viii, 38; Rājat. i, 348 (with gen.) **Triṇśatka**, n. id., Kām. viii, 37.

Triṇśad, = °*śát*. **– akshara** (°*śád-*), mf(*ā*)n. having 30 syllables, ŚBr. iii, vii. **– aṅga** (°*śád-*), mfn. having 30 parts, AV. xiii, 3, 8. **– ara** (°*śád-*), mfn. having 30 fellies, iv, 35, 4. **– yogâvali**, f. N. of a work. **– rātra**, n. a ceremony lasting 30 days, ŚāṅkhŚr. xiii. **– viṇśa**, mfn. pl. between 20 and 30, Rājat. v, 214; viii, 1084. **– vikrama** (°*śád-*), mf(*ā*)n. 30 paces long, ŚBr. iii, 5, 1, 7. **– varsha**, mfn. 30 years old, Mn. ix, 94.

Triṇśin, mfn. (Pāṇ. v, 2, 37, Kār., Pat.) containing 30, TāṇḍyaBr. xvi, xxiv (Vi-rāj); Lāṭy. x, 10 (month).

Triḥ, = *trís*. **– pratihāram**, ind. so as to touch thrice, Kauś. **– prasruta-mada**, mfn. = *tri-prasruta*, MBh. i, 151, 4. **– śukla**, mfn. 'triply white,' having 3 white lines, Kauś. 29. **– śrāvaṇa**, n. N. of a work, Āp. **– śreṇi**, mfn. forming 3 rows, AitBr. iii, 39, 2. **– śveta**, mf(*ā*)n. white on 3 spots, ŚāṅkhGṛ. i, 22, 8; Gobh. ii, 7, 8. **– shamṛiddha**, mfn. 'well furnished with 3 things,' only abstr. *-tvá* (also *triḥ-sam*°, Pāṇ. viii, 3, 106, Kāś.), TS. ii, 4, 11, 5. **– sapta**, mfn. pl. = *tri-s*°, ĀpGṛ. ix, 5; *-kṛitvas*, ind. 21 times, MBh. i; Hariv. (v.l. *tri-s*°); R. v; BhP. i. **– samṛiddha-tva**, see *-sham*°. **– saha-vacana**, n. N. of a text, Āp. **– snāna**, n., see *tri-shavaṇa*.

Triká, mfn. triple, threefold, forming a triad, RV. x, 59, 9; Lāṭy. (Stoma; cf. *eka-*); Śulbas. i; Suśr. &c.; happening the 3rd time, Pāṇ. v, 2, 77; (with or without *śata*) 3 per cent., Mn. viii, 152, Kull.; m. (n., L.) a place where 3 roads meet, Hariv.; Jain.; m. = *tri-kaṭa*, Npr.; Trapa bispinosa, ib.; n. a triad (cf. *kaṭu-*, *taurya-*, *tri-*, *pañca-*), Mn. ii, vii; Pat. & Kāś.; VarBṛS.; the loins, regio sacra, hips, Hariv.; Pañcat.; Suśr. (also 'the part between the shoulder-blades') &c.; the triple Vyāhṛiti, W.; (*ā*), f. a triangular frame across the mouth of a well, L. **– traya**, n. the 3 triads (*tri-phalā*, *-kaṭu*, & *-mada*), L. **– vedanā**, f. pain in the loins, Suśr. **– sāra**, N. of a work. **– sthāna**, n. the loins, L. **– hṛidaya**, n. N. of a work. **Trikâgni-kālá**, m. Rudra, SatarUp. (interpol.) **Trikâika**, m. = *ekatrika*, ŚāṅkhŚr. xiv, 42, 7. **Tricá**, see *tṛicá*.

Tritá, m. 'third' (τρίτος), N. of a Vedic deity (associated with the Maruts, Vāyu, and Indra; fighting like the latter with Tvashṭra, Vṛitra, and other demons; called Āptya [q. v.], 'water-deity,' and supposed to reside in the remotest regions of the world, whence [RV. viii, 47, 13–15; AV.] the idea of wishing to remove calamity to T°, and the view of the Tritas being the keepers of nectar [RV. vi, 44, 23], similarly [RV. ii, 34, 10; TS. i; TBr. i] the notion of Trita's bestowing long life; also conceived as an inferior deity conquering the demons by order and with the help of Indra [RV. ii; viii, 52, 1; x]; fallen into a well he begged aid from the gods [i, 105, 17; x, 8, 7]; as to this last myth Sāy. on i, 105 relates that 3 Ṛishis, Ekata, Dvita, and Trita, parched with thirst, looked about and found a well, and when T° began to draw water, the other two, desirous of his property, pushed him down and closed up the well with a wheel; shut up there, T° composed a hymn to the gods, and managed miraculously to prepare the sacrificial Soma, that he might drink it himself, or offer it to the deities and so be extricated: this is alluded to in RV. ix, 34, 4 [cf. 32, 2; 38, 2; 102, 2] and described in MBh. ix, 2095; also Nir. iv, 6 makes him a Ṛishi and he is the supposed author of RV. i, 105; viii, 36; ix, 33 f. & 102; x, 1–7: in epic legends [MBh. ix, xii f.] Ekata, Dvita, and T° are described as 3 brothers, sons of Gautama or of Prajā-pati or Brahmā; elsewhere T° is one of the 12 sons of Manu Cākshusha by Naḍvalā, BhP. iv, 13, 16; cf. *trai tanā*; Zend *Thrita*; Τρίτων, τριτο-γενής, &c.); n. triplet of young (three-twin), TS., Sch. **– kūpa**, m. 'T°'s well,' N. of a Tīrtha, BhP. x, 78, 19.

Tritaya, n. (Pāṇ. v, 2, 42 f.) a triad, Yājñ. &c.

Triy, for *try*. **– aksha**, see *try-*. **– adhvan**, n. the 3 times (pf., p., fut.), Buddh. L. **– ambaka**, see *try-*. **– avastha**, mfn. having 3 conditions, BhP. xi. **– ávi**, see *try-*. **– ṛica**, n. = *tṛicá*, Kāṭh. xxxiv, 1.

Trir, = *trís*. **– akshara**, mfn. consisting of 3 sounds, DhyānabUp. **– áśri**, mfn. three-cornered, RV. i, 152, 2. **– unnata**, mfn. having 3 parts of the body stretched upwards, ŚvetUp. ii, 8. **– vyūha**, mfn. triply appearing, MBh. xii, 348, 57.

Trís, ind. (Pāṇ. v, 4, 18) thrice, 3 times, RV. (*saptá*, 3 × 7, i, iv, vii ff.; *áhnas* or *áhan*, 'thrice a day,' i, iii f., ix f.; cf. Pāṇ. ii, 3, 64); ŚBr.; KātyŚr.; Mn. (*abdasya*, 'thrice a year,' iii, xi) &c.; before gutturals and palatals [cf. RV. viii, 91, 7] *ḥ* may be substituted by *sh*, Pāṇ. viii, 3, 43. **– tāvā**, f. (a Vedi) 3 times as great (fr. *tāvat*), Pāṇ. v, 4, 84.

त्रिङ्ख् *triṅkh*, cl. 1. P. for *traṅkh*, W.

त्रिच *tricá*. See *tṛicá*.

त्रिण *triṇa*, n. for *tṛiṇa*, grass, VarP.

त्रिणत *tri-ṇata*, *-ṇavá*, &c. See *trí*.

त्रिपु **tripú.** See *tṛipú.*

त्रियूह **triyūha,** m. a chestnut-coloured horse, L.; cf. *ukanāha, urāha, kiyāha, kokāha.*

त्रिल्लक **trillaka,** N. of a man, Rājat. viii, 1684; 1709; 2497. **°lla-sena,** another man's N., vii.

त्रीशट **trīśaṭa,** m. = *tīsaṭa.*

त्रुट् **truṭ,** cl. 6. 4. °*ṭati,* °*ṭyati* (Pāṇ. iii, 1, 70) to be torn or split, tear, break, fall asunder, Bhartṛ.; Mālatīm.; Bālar.; Rājat. (pf. *tutroṭa*); Hit.; Kuval.: Caus. *troṭayati* (ind. °*yitvā;* Ā. °*yate,* Dhātup. xxxiii, 25) to tear, break, Pañcat. ii, 6, 88/88; v, 10, 1/2; Rājat. vi, 248; Pañcad.; cf. *ut-.*

Truṭi, f. (Siddh. stry. 26) an atom (= 7 Reṇus, Lalit. xii, 176); a very minute space of time, MBh. i, 1292; Hariv. 9529; VarBṛS. ii, 1/2; Sūryas.; BhP. iii, 11, 6; x; small cardamoms, Suśr. vi; doubt, L.; cutting, breaking, W.; loss, destruction, W.; breaking a promise, W.; N. of one of the mothers attending on Skanda, MBh. ix, 2635; see *troṭi.* — **pattra,** n. (?), Kapishṭh. xxx, 7. — **bīja,** m. Arum Colocasia, L. — **śas,** ind. in very short spaces of time, MBh. v, xii. **Truṭy-avayava,** m. half a T°, VarBṛS. ii, 1/1.

Truṭita, mfn. broken, divided, chapped, Pañcat.; Uttarar. i, 29; Kathās.; Sāh. iii, 88/88; n. *mṛiṇālikā* & *bāhu-rakshikā,* Śil. **Truṭī,** f. = °*ṭi,* L., Sch.

त्रुप् **trup,** cl. 1. *tropati,* to hurt, Dhātup. **Truph, trump,** °**ph,** *trophati, trump*°, °*ph*°, id.

त्रेणी **treṇī** See *try-eṇī.*

त्रेता **tretā,** f. (fr. *trayá*) a triad, triplet, MBh. xiv, 2759; the 3 sacred fires (= *agni-*), v, 1559; Hariv. 1410; trey (throw at dice or the side of a die marked with 3 spots), VS. xxx, 18; TS. iv; Mṛicch. ii, 9; 'age of triads,' the 2nd Yuga (or silver age), AitBr.; MuṇḍUp.; ŚāṅkhŚr.; Mn. &c. — **°gni** (°*tāg*°), m. = *agni-tretā,* Hariv. 1409; MBh. xiii; Ragh. xiii; -*hotra,* n. id., MBh. xii, 6001. — **chandas,** n. pl. a class of metres, Nidānas. i, 6, 3. — **tva,** n. the condition of the fire-triad, Hariv. 11863. — **°ya** (*tāya*), m. the cast trey, ChUp., Sch. — **yuga,** n. the T° age, MBh. &c. — **stoma,** m. pl. a class of Stomas, Nidānas. i, 9. **Tretinī,** f. the threefold flame of the 3 fires of the altar, RV. x, 105, 9.

Tredhā, ind. = *tri-dhā,* RV.; VS. &c. — **bhāva,** m. dwelling in 3 places, Nir. vii, xii. — **vihitá,** mfn. divided into 3 parts, ŚBr. — **saṃnaddhá,** mfn. triply bound, MaitrS. i. — **sthita,** mfn. = *-vihitá,* Ragh.

त्रै **trai,** cl. 1. Ā. *trāyate* (Impv. °*yatām,* 2. sg. °*yasva* & *trāsva,* pl. °*yadhvam* & *trādhvam,* RV.; ep. *trāti, trātu, trāhi;* aor. Subj. *trāsate,* 2. du. *trāsāthe,* Prec. *trāsīthām,* RV.; inf. *trātum,* MBh. &c.; ind. p. *trātvā,* BhP. ii, 7, 9) to protect, preserve, cherish, defend, rescue from (gen. or abl.); cf. *pari-, sam-.*

त्रैंश **traiṇśa,** n. a Brāhmaṇa containing 30 (*triṇśát*) Adhyāyas (ŚāṅkhBr.), Pāṇ. v, 1, 62. **°śika,** mf(*ā*)n. consisting of 30, ĀtrAnukr. i, 16; 23; 25.

Traikakudá, mfn. coming from the mountain Tri-kakud, AV.; ŚBr.; TĀr.; KātyŚr. **°kakubha,** mfn. coming from the mountain Tri-kakubh, MānGṛ. i, 11; n. N. of a Sāman, TāṇḍyaBr.; Lāṭy. **°kaṇṭaka,** mfn. coming from the plant Tri-kaṇṭaka, g. *rajatâdi.* **°kālika,** mf(*ī*)n. relating to the 3 tenses (pf., pr., fut.), MBh. xii; BhP. iii, xi; KāśīKh.; Tarkas. **°kālya,** n. the 3 tenses (pf., pr., fut.), VPrāt.; MBh. xii; Hariv.; dawn, noon, and sunset, Yājñ. iii, 308; growth, maintenance, and decay, Hariv. 7446. **°kuntaka,** a kind of ornament, Buddh. L.

Traigarta, mfn. = °*taka,* MBh. iv, 1117; m. (g. *yaudheyâdi;* Pāṇ. iv, 1, 111) a Trigarta prince, MBh. iv, vi; Rājat. v; pl. the Trigartas, VarBṛS. x, xvi f.; (*ī*), f. (g. *yaudheyâdi*) a Trigarta princess, MBh. i. **°taka,** mfn. belonging to the Trigartas, vii, 726; xiv; VarBṛS. iv, 24; Pāṇ. iv, 2, 124, Kāś. **°tāyana,** mfn., **°naka,** n. fr. °*ta,* g. *arīhaṇâdi.*

Traiguṇika, mfn. relating to the 3 Guṇas, W.; thrice repeated, W. **°ṇya,** n. the state of consisting of 3 threads, tripleness, Mn. ii, 42, Kull.; 3 qualities (*śaitya, saugandhya, māndya*), Śivarātrivr.; the 3 Guṇas, MBh.; Sāṃkhyak. 14; 18; Tattvas.; Mālav. i, 4; MārkP. l, 3; mfn. having the 3 Guṇas, BhP. xi, 25, 30; -*vat,* mfn. id., Sarvad. xiv, 63.

Traicīvarika, mfn. possessing the *tri-cīvara,* L.

Traitá, m. (fr. *tritá*) a triplet (one of three at a birth), TS. ii, 1, 1, 6; MaitrS. ii, 5, 1; n. 'relating to Trita,' N. of a Sāman, TāṇḍyaBr. xiv; Lāṭy. vii, 3. **°taná,** m. N. of a deity (connected with Trita; = Zend *Thraetaona,* Pers. *Feridun*), RV. i, 158, 5.

Traidaśika, mfn. relating to the (*tri-daśa*) gods, Mn. ii, 58 (°*śaka,* Hcat. iii, 1, 10).

Traidha, mfn. (fr. *tri-dhā* or *tredhā*) triple, Pāṇ. v, 3, 45, Vārtt., Sch.; (*am*), ind. (v, 3, 45) = *tredhā,* KātyŚr.; ŚāṅkhŚr.; Lāṭy.; Kauś.; MBh.

Traidhātavī, f. (scil. *ishṭi*) N. of a closing ceremony (fr. *tri-dhātu*), ŚBr. v, xiii; KātyŚr.; ŚāṅkhŚr. **°vīya,** n. (scil. *karman*) id., TS. ii, 4, 11; (*ā*), f. id., Nyāyam. ix, Sch. **°vyā,** f. id., MaitrS. ii, 4, 3.

Traidhātuka, n. the 3 worlds, SaddhP. iv. **°tva,** m. 'son of Tri-dhātu,' = *traivṛishṇá,* TāṇḍyaBr.

Trainishkika, mfn. = *tri-nishka,* Pāṇ. v, 1, 30.

Traipakshika, mfn. lasting 3 half months, Prāyaśc. **Traipatha,** n. N. of a manner of sitting, BṛNārP. xxxi, 115. **°pada,** n. three-fourths, TāṇḍyaBr. xvi, 13, 12; ŚāṅkhŚr. xiv, 41, 11.

Traipārāyaṇika, mfn. performing the Pārāyaṇa 3 times, Pāṇ. v, 1, 20, Vārtt. 2, Pat. **Traipishṭapa,** n. (fr. *tri-p*°) N. of a Liṅga, KāśīKh.

Traipura, mfn. relating to Tri-pura, Śārad. xii; n. Śiva's conquest of T°, Bālar. ii, 1/2; m. pl. the inhabitants of T°, Hariv. 7443; the inhabitants of Tripurī or the Cedis, MBh. vi, 3855; sg. a Cedi prince, ii, 1164. **°rīya,** n. N. of an Up.

Traipurusha, mfn. = *tri-paur*°, xiii, 4322.

Traiphala, mfn. coming from (*tri-phalā*) the 3 myrobalans, Suśr. iv, 5 & 9; vi, 17 & 39. **Traibali,** m. (fr. *tri-bala*) N. of a man, MBh. ii, 108.

Traibhāvya, n. threefold nature, g. *brāhmaṇâdi.*

Traimātura, mfn. having 3 (*mātṛi*) mothers, Pāṇ. vi, 3, 48, Kāś. **°māsika,** mfn. 3 months old, lasting 3 months, quarterly, BhP. ii, 7, 27; Mn. xi, 127, Kull. **°māsī,** mfn. 3 months, Divyâv. xix. **°māsya,** n. id., KātyŚr. xx, 3, 6. **Traiyaksha,** mfn. belonging to (*try-*) Śiva, Bālar. vii, 30

Traiyambaká, mfn. relating or belonging or sacred to Try-ambaka, VS. xxiv; Lāṭy.; KātyŚr & Gobh. iii, 10, 14 (scil. *apūpa,* 'cake'); MBh. vii, 169 & 2778. — **mantra,** m. N. of a Mantra, Śārad. xxiii. — **saras,** n. N. of a lake, ŚrīmMāh. xiv f.

Traiyalinda, mfn. fr. *try-,* Pāṇ. vii, 3, 3, Kār., Pat.

Traiyāhāvaka, mfn. coming from or relating to a *try-āhāva* village, g. *dhūmâdi.*

Trairātrika, mfn. of 3 days, 15, Vārtt. 2, Pat.

Trairāśika, mfn. 'relating to 3 (*rāśi*) numbers,' with or without *gaṇita* or *karman,* the rule of three (in arithm.; cf. *krama-, viloma-, vyasta-*), Laghuj., Sch.; Sūryapr., Sch.; relating to 3 zodiacal signs, Hāyan. **°śya,** n. sg. the 3 groups, Nyāyad. iv, 1, 3.

Trairūpya, n. tripleness of (*rūpa*) form, threefold change of form, Pāṇ. vii, 3, 49, Sch. (not in Kāś.)

Trailāṭa, a sort of horse-fly, Buddh. L.

Trailiṅga, mfn. having 3 (*liṅga*) sexes, MBh. xii, 11353 (v.l. °*gya,* n. 'triplicity of sex').

Trailokya, n. (g. *caturvarṇâdi*) the 3 Lokas or worlds, Mn. xi, 237; MBh. &c.; a mystic N. of some part of the body; m. N. of a man, Rājat. vii f. — **kartṛi,** m. 'T°-creator,' Śiva, MBh. — **cintāmaṇi-rasa,** m. N. of a mixture. — **ḍambara,** N. of a med. work. — **dīpikā,** f. N. of a Jaina work. — **devī,** f. N. of the wife of King Yaśaḥ-kara, Rājat. vi. — **nātha,** m. 'T°-lord,' Rāma, R. i, 76, 19; N. of a mixture. — **prakāśa,** m. N. of an astron. work. — **prabhava,** m. 'T°-son,' Rāma, Ragh. x, 54. — **prabhā,** f. N. of the daughter of a Dānava, Kathās. cviii. — **bandhu,** m. 'T°-friend,' the sun, Prasannar. vi, 39. — **bhaya-kāraka,** mfn. causing fear to the 3 worlds. — **mālin,** m. N. of a Daitya, Kathās. cviii. — **rāja,** m. N. of a man, Rājat. vii f. — **rājya,** n. T°-sovereignty, Bhartṛ. — **vikramin,** m. 'striding through the 3 worlds,' N. of a Bodhi-sattva, SaddhP. i. — **vijayā,** f. 'T°-conqueror,' a sort of hemp (from which an intoxicating infusion is prepared), L. — **sāgara,** m. N. of a work, Dvaitanirn. — **sāra,** N. of a work, Hcat. i, 3, 932 ff. — **sundara,** m. N. of a mixture, Rasar.; (*ī*), f. N. of a work, Gaṇar. **Trailokyâdhipati-tva,** **°patya,** n. for °*kya-rājya.*

Trailocana, n. fr. *tri-l*°, = *traipishṭapa,* KāśīKh.

Traivaṇa, m. (g. *śivâdi*) metron. fr. *tri-veṇī,* Pravar. vi, 2 (v.l. °*varṇa*). **Traiváṇi,** m. id., ŚBr. xiv, 5, 5 & 7, 4. **°vaṇīya,** fr. °*ṇa,* g. *utkarâdi.*

Traivargika, mf(*ī*)n. relating to *tri-gaṇa,* BhP. ii f., vi, xi f. **°gya,** mfn. belonging to *tri-gaṇa,* iv.

Traivarṇa, m. a member of the first 3 (*varṇa*) castes, Hcat. **°rṇika,** m. id., Mn.; Āryabh., Sch.

Traivarshika, n. a triennial performance, ĀśvŚr. xii, 5, 6; mfn. sufficient for 3 years, Pāṇ. vii, 3, 16, Kāś. **°vsssh**°, mfn. id., Gaut. Mn.; Yājñ.; MBh.

Traivikrama, mfn. belonging to (*tri-v*°) Vishṇu, Ragh. vii, 32; m. a kind of cohabitation, Hāl. 411, Sch.; n. (Vishṇu's) act of taking the 3 strides, Hariv. 3168; (*ī*), f., see *tri-vikrama.*

Traivida, v.l. for *trayī-v*°, Sch. on TS. & KātyŚr.

Traividya, mfn. (Pāṇ. iv, 2, 60, Pat.) familiar with *tri-vidyā,* Lāṭy. viii, 6, 29; Mn.; Yājñ.; MBh.; n. = *tri-vidyā,* Āp.; Gaut. Gṛihyās.; Mn. &c.; an assembly of Brāhmans familiar with *tri-vidyā,* Yājñ.; Hariv. 9578; MārkP. xxiii, 35. **°dyaka,** mfn. practised by Brāhmans familiar with *tri-vidyā,* Āp. i, 1, 23 & 2, 6; n. = *tri-vidyā,* MānGṛ. i, 23.

Traividhya, n. triplicity, Bādar. i, 31; Suśr. v; KapS. i, 70; Bhāshāp. &c.; mfn. triple, BhP. vi, 3, 4.

Traivishṭapa, m. pl. 'inhabitants of *tri-v*°,' the gods, Ratnâv. iv, 22; BhP. i f. **°peya,** m. pl. id., viii.

Traivṛita, mfn. coming from (*tri-vṛit*) Ipomœa Turpethum, Suśr. i, 44, 3; vi, 17, 3 & 26, 8. **°vṛishṇá,** m. (fr. *tri-vṛishan*) patr. of Try-aruṇa, RV. v, 27, 1. **°vedika,** mf(*ī*)n. relating to the 3 Vedas, Mn. iii, 1; VāyuP. i, 1, 65.

Traiśaṅkava, mfn. belonging to Tri-śaṅku, Hcar.; Bālar.; m. patr. of Hari-ścandra, Hariv. 755; BhP. ix. **°śabdya,** n. 3 kinds of (*śabda*) expression, Pat. on Pāṇ. i, 4, 74, Vārtt. 4 & iii, 1, 44, Vārtt. 7. **°śāna,** mf(*ī*)n. = *tri-ś*°, Pāṇ. **°śāni,** m. patr. fr. *tri-śānu,* Hariv. **°śāmba,** for °*śāni,* VP. iv, 16, 2. **°śāli,** id., AgP. **°śīrsha,** mf(*ā*)n. relating to (i. e. committed against) the three-headed (*tri-śīrshan*) Viśva-rūpa (a murder), MBh. v, 335. **°śṛiṅga,** m. patr. fr. *tri-ś*°, Pravar. vi, 4 (°*gāyaṇa,* MatsyaP.); n. 'coming from *tri-ś*°,' (with *ājya*) semen virile, MantraBr. — **°śoka,** n. 'Tri-śoka's melody,' N. of a Sāman, TāṇḍyaBr. viii, xii, xviii, xxi; Lāṭy. vi, 11.

Traishṭubha, mf(*ī*)n. (g. *utsâdi*) relating to or composed in the Tri-shṭubh metre, RV. v, 29, 6; VS. &c.; n. (= *tri-shṭubh,* Pāṇ. iv, 2, 55, Vārtt., Pat.) the Tri-shṭubh metre, RV. i, 164, 23 f.; ii, 43, 1.

Traisamika, mfn. (fr. *samā*) triennial, Pāṇ. vii, 3, 15, Vārtt. 2, Pat. **°sānu,** v.l. for °*śāni.* **°srotasa,** mfn. belonging to (*tri-srotas*) the Ganges, Ragh. xvi, 34. **°svarya,** n. (g. *caturvarṇâdi*) the 3 accents, Pāṇ. i, 2, 33, Kāś.; Nyāyam. ix, 2, 15; Sch. on VPrāt. i, 129; 132 & Bhāshik. ii, 36.

Traihāyaṇá, n. (v.l. °*yana,* Pāṇ. v, 1, 130, Kāś.) a period of 3 years, AV. x, 5, 22; xii, 4, 16.

त्रोटक **troṭaka** (= *toṭ*°), mfn. destroying (fr. √*truṭ*), Chandaḥs. vi, 31, Sch.; m. N. of a venomous insect, Suśr. v, 8; of a pupil of Śaṃkarâcārya, SŚaṃkar. xii; n. a kind of drama, Vikr. i, 1/2; Sāh. vi, 273 (v.l. *toṭ*°); angry speech, 99; (*ī*), f. (in music) N. of a Rāgiṇī, L. **°ṭi,** f. a beak, L.; the mouth of a fish, L.; N. of a bird, L.; = *kaṅka-,* L.; the Kaṭphala tree (also *truṭi,* Npr.), L.; -*hasta,* m. 'beak-handed,' a bird, L. **°ṭita,** mfn. broken, Kathās.

त्रोतल **trotala,** n. N. of a Tantra, Ānand. 31, Sch.; cf. *toḍala.* **°lôttara,** n. another Tantra, ib.

त्रोत्र **trotra,** n. a weapon, Uṇ., Sch.; (= *tôttra*) a goad, W.; N. of a disease, Uṇ. vṛ.; *ārūpa-kriyā,* ib.

त्रौक् **trauk** (= *ḍhauk*), cl. 1. Ā. (pf. *tutrauke,* Kāś.) to go, Dhātup. iv, 25: Caus. aor. *atutraukat,* Pāṇ. vii, 4, 59, Kāś.: Desid. *tutrokishate,* ib.: Intens. *totraukyate,* 82, Vārtt. 1, Pat.

त्र्य **try,** before vowels = *tri,* sometimes resolved into *triy,* q. v. — **aṇśa,** m. sg. 3 shares, Mn. ix, 151; mfn. having 3 shares, Jyot., Sch.; m. a 3rd part, VarBṛS.; Laghuj.; the 3rd part of a zodiacal sign (= *dṛikāṇa*) xii, 2 ff. & VarBṛ. xxiii, 14 f. (also *-nātha,* m. 'the regent of a Dṛikāṇa'). — **aksha,** mf(*ī* or [Hcat. i, 5, 1202] *ā*)n. three-eyed, MBh. ii f.; Hariv.; Kathās. cxviii; m. Śiva, MBh.; Hariv. 15415 (*triy-,* v.l. *tri-yajña*); BhP.; Kathās.; Kaśyapa, Gal.; N. of an Asura, BhP. vii, 2, 4; -*patnī,* f. 'Śiva's wife,' Pārvatī, Hariv. 10000. — **akshaka,** m. Śiva, ŚivaP. — **akshan,** m. id., MBh. xiv, 193. — **âkshara,** mfn. (or n. a word) consisting of 3 sounds or syllables, VS. ix; ŚBr. vi, xiv; TāṇḍyaBr.; Lāṭy.; Mn. xi, 266; m. a matchmaker ('a genealogist,' W.), L. — **aṅkaṭa,** v.l. for *-aṅgaṭa.* — **aṅgá,** n. pl. the 3 portions of a victim belonging to Svishṭakṛit (upper part of the right fore-foot, part of the left thigh, and part of the intestines), TS. vi; ŚBr. iii; Kauś.; KātyŚr., Sch.; sg. a tripartite army (chariots, cavalry, and infantry), MBh. viii, 2526; (ix, 1388?). — **aṅgaṭa,** n. 3 strings suspended to either end of a pole for carrying burdens, L.; a kind of collyrium,

L.; m. Śiva, L. — **aṅgulá**, n. 3 fingers' breadth, ŚBr. iii, 3, 2, 4 & 7, 1, 25; xiv; KātyŚr. vii; -*áṅg*°, mfn. 3 fingers broad, ŚBr. i, 2, 5, 9; KātyŚr. ii, vi. — °**aṅgyà**, mfn. belonging to the -*aṅgá* portions, ŚBr. iii. — **añjana**, n. the 3 kinds of collyrium (*kālâñj°*, *pushpâñj°*, *rasâñj°*), L. — **añjala**, n. 3 handfuls, Pāṇ. v, 4, 102. — **añjali**, m. a handful belonging to 3 persons, 102, Kāś.; mfn. bought for 3 handfuls, ib. — **adhipati**, m. the lord of the 3 Guṇas or of the 3 worlds (Kṛishṇa), BhP. iii, 16, 24 (v. l.) — **adhishṭhāna**, mfn. having 3 stations, Mn. xii, 4. — **adhîśa**, m. = °*dhipati*, BhP. iii f., viii. — **adhva-gā**, f. = *tri-patha-gā*, W. — **anīká**, mfn. three-faced, RV. iii, 56, 3; Kāṭh. xxx, 2; triple-arrayed, AitBr. iii, 39, 2; Pāṇ. iv, 1, 21, Siddh. (f. *ā*); (*ā*), f. N. of a ceremony, ĀpŚr. xxi, 14. — **anta**, n. with *Tvāshṭrī-sāman*, N. of a Sāman. — **abda**, n. 3 years, Mn. viii; mf(*ā*)n. 3 years old, L.; (*am*), ind. during 3 years, xi; -*pûrva*, mfn. existing for 3 years, ii, 134; cf. Āp. i, 14, 13. — **àmbaka**, m. 'three-eyed' (originally probably 'three-mothered' fr. the threefold expression *ámbe ámbiké 'mbālike*, VS. &c.; cf. *tri-mātṛi* & *traimātura*) Rudra or (later on) Śiva, RV. vii, 59, 12; VS. &c. (*triy-*, Kapishṭh. viii, 10; R. vii; Kum. iii, 44; cf. Pāṇ. vi, 4, 77, Vārtt., Pat.); N. of one of the 11 Rudras, MBh. iii; Hariv.; VP. i, 15, 123; NarasP. v, 9; pl. (= *traiy°*) the cakes sacred to Rudra Try-ambaka, TS. iii; TBr. i; Kāṭh.; ŚBr.; ŚāṅkhBr.; KātyŚr.; ĀśvŚr.; sg. the ceremony in which those cakes are offered, ŚāṅkhŚr. xiv, 10, 21; n. N. of a Liṅga, ŚivaP. i, 38, 19; mfn. knowing the 3 Vedas or pervading the 3 worlds, TejobUp. 6; (*ā*), f. Pārvatī, DevīP.; -*parvata*, m. N. of a mountain, Vaidyaj.; -*māhātmya*, n. N. of part of PadmaP. iv; -*vṛishabha*, m. Śiva's bull, Kād.; -*sakha*, m. 'Śiva's friend,' Kubera, L.; °*kêśvara-purī*, f. = *śaiva-nagara*. — **ambuka**, a kind of fly, Buddh. L. — **ara**, mfn. having 3 fellies, AV. x, 2, 32. — **aratni**, mfn. 3 arms long, Kauś. — **àruṇa**, m. N. of a man, RV. v, 27, 1 f.; TāṇḍyaBr. xiii, 3; later on called *trayyār°*, q. v. — **àrusha**, mf(*ī*)n. marked red in 3 places, RV. viii, 46, 22. — **artha**, mfn. having 3 meanings, L. — **alinda**, N. of a village, Pāṇ. vii, 3, 3, Kār., Pat. — **avanata**, see *tri-vin°*. — **avara**, mfn. pl. at least 3, Mn. iii, viii; Yājñ. ii, 69; (*am*), ind. at least thrice, Gaut.; Mn. xi, 81; °*rârdhyam*, ind. id., ĀpŚr. iii, 16, 9; ĀpGṛ. xxi, 9. — **ávi**, m. '3 sheep times old,' a calf 18 months old, RV. iii, 55, 14; VS. (f. °*vī́*, xviii, 26); MaitrS.; cf. *páñcâvi*. — **aśīta**, mf(*ī*)n. the 83rd (chs. of MBh. & Hariv.) — **aśīti**, f. 83, Pāṇ. vi; -*tama*, mfn. the 83rd (chs. of R.) — **aśra**, mfn. triangular, Suśr. iv, 2, 3; n. a triangle, RāmatUp. i, 52; m. a triplet, Sāh. vi, 283; a kind of jasmine, L.; -*kuṇḍa*, n. N. of a mystical diagram, Tantr.; -*phalā*, f. Boswellia thurifera, L. — **ashṭaka**, mfn. containing 3 Ashṭakā days, Gobh. iii, 10, 7; n. N. of a vessel, Suśr. i, 45. — **ashṭa-varsha**, mfn. 3 × 8 years old, Mn. ix, 94. — **asra**, = -*aśra*. — **ahá**, m. 3 days, ŚBr. &c. [chiefly (*am*), ind. 'during 3 days,' (*āt*, *e*, *ena*), ind. 'after 3 days']; mfn. = °*hina*, R. i, 13, 43; m. a performance lasting 3 days, ŚBr. iv, xii; ĀśvŚr.; KātyŚr.; -*vṛitta*, mfn. happened 3 days ago, Pāṇ. iii, 2, 115, Pat.; -*sparśa*, m., -*spṛiśa*, n. = *tri-dina-spṛiś*, Jyot.; °*hâhika*, mfn. furnished with food for 3 days, Mn. iv, 7. — °**ahīna**, mfn. lasting 3 days, Lāṭy. viii. — **ahna**, mfn. happened after 3 days, Vop. vi, 38 f. — **āyushá**, n. (Pāṇ. v, 4, 77) threefold vital power ('threefold period of life, i. e. childhood, youth, and old age,' Sch.), VS. iii, 62; cf. ŚBr. xii, 9, 1, 8. — **āruṇi**, see *trayyāruṇa*. — **ārsheya**, mfn. having 3 sacred ancestors, MānŚr. xi; Pravar.; m. pl. a blind, a deaf, and a dumb person, W. — **ālikhitá**, mfn. indented or marked in 3 places (a brick), TS. v; ŚBr. vi; Śulbas.; °*tá-vat*, mfn. consisting of bricks so marked, ŚBr. viii. — **āvrit**, mfn. consisting of 3 series, xii f.; TBr. ii, 1. — **âśir**, mfn. mixed with 3 products of milk, RV. v, 27, 5. — **āhala**, m. 'triple-crower (cf. *āhâlak*),' a cock, Suśr. i, 46. — **āhāva**, mfn. having 3 watering-places, g. *dhūmâdi*. — **āhika**, mfn. = *tri-divasa*, Aparāj.; = -*ahâhika*, Yājñ. i, 128 (v. l. -*aih°*). — **uttarī-bhāva**, m. progression by 3, Lāṭy. vi, 5, 17. — **udâyá**, m. thrice approaching the altar (at dawn, noon, and sunset), RV. iv, 37, 3. — **ùddhi**, mfn. having a triple stand, TS. v; MaitrS. i, 6, 8; ĀpŚr. v, 22, 6. — **udhán**, mfn. three-uddered, RV. iii, 56, 3. — **ùnnata**, mfn. having 3 elevations, TS. vi. — **upasat-ka**, mfn. containing 3 *upasád* ceremonies, ĀpŚr. xv. — **ushaṇa**, n. = -*ūsh°*, L. — **ūshaṇa**, n. = *tri-kaṭu*, Suśr. — **ṛica**, n. = *tri-cá*, Mn.; Yājñ. — **eṇī**, f. (the *śalalī* bristle) being variegated in 3 places, KātyŚr. v; ĀpŚr. viii & ĀpGṛ. (*treṇī*); ĀśvGṛ. i, 14, 4; PārGṛ. i, 15, 4; ii, 1, 10. — **èṇī**, f. id., ŚBr. ii, 6, 4, 5. — **aihika**, see -*āh°*.

Tryakshāyaṇa, for *tryāksh°*, Gaṇar. 269, Sch.

Tryāksh°, m. fr. *try-aksha*, g. *aishukāry-ādi*.

त्व 1. *tva*, mfn(*tvad*). one, several, RV.; *tva — tva*, one — the other, RV.; AV. viii, 9, 9; *tvad*, partly, RV. x, 72, 9; ŚāṅkhBr. xvii, 4; *tvad — tvad*, partly — partly, RV. vii, 101, 3; ŚBr.

Tvadānīm, ind. sometimes, MaitrS. iv, 2, 2.

त्व 2. *tvá*, base of the 2nd personal pron.: nom. *tvám*, acc. *tvā́m*, instr. *tváyā* [& *tvā́*, RV., also in comp., see *tvā́-datta*, -*dāta*, -*vṛidha* &c.], dat. *túbhyam* [& °*bhya*, RV.; PārGṛ. i, 6, 2], abl. *tvát* or *tvád* [& *tvat-tas*, MBh. &c.], gen. *táva*, loc. *tvé* [RV.; cf. RPrāt. i, 19 & g. *câdi*], *tváyi* [AV. &c.]; enclitic forms are acc. *tvā* [RV.; AV.], gen. dat. *te* [RV. &c.; = τοι]; [cf. Lat. *tu* &c.] — **yata** (*tvá-*), mfn. given by thee, vii, 20, 10.

3. **Tvá**, mfn. thy, your, ii, 20, 2.

Tvam, for *tvam*. — **kāra**, m. addressing with 'thou' (disrespectfully), Mn. xi, 205. — **kṛitya**, ind. addressing with 'thou,' Yājñ. iii, 292.

Tvakat, dimin. for *tvat*, in comp. — **pitṛika**, mfn. = *tvát-pitṛi*, Pāṇ. i, 1, 29, Pat.

Tvakam, familiar dimin. for *tvám*, ib.; Bhadrab. i, 64 & (instr. *tvayakā*) iv, 9.

Tvat, in comp. for 2. *tvá*. — **kṛita**, mfn. made or composed by thee, R. i, 2, 40; made like you, 44, 47. — **tanāt**, abl. ind. from you, TāṇḍyaBr. xiv. — **tara**, mfn. Compar. more yours, Pāṇ. vii, 2, 98, Kāś. — **tas**, see s. v. 2. *tvá*. — **pitṛi** (*tvát-*), m(pl. °*tāras*)fn. having thee as a father, TS. i. — **prati-kshin**, mfn. waiting on thee, Nal. xvii, 37. — **pra-sūta** (*tvát-*), mfn. instigated by thee, ŚBr. iv, 1, 4, 4. — **saṃgama**, m. union with thee.

Tvatka, = *tvakat*. — **pitṛika**, = *tvakat-*, Pat.

Tvad, = *tvat*. — **anya**, mfn. other than thee, Nal. i, 20; xii, 14; Ragh. iii, 63. — **artham**, °**the**, ind. on thy account, about thee. — **gṛiha**, n. thy house. — **devatyà**, mfn. having thee as deity, ŚBr. viii, 4. — **dhita**, mfn. suitable (*hita*) for thee, Pāṇ. vii, 2, 98, Kāś. — **bhaya**, n. dread of thee, MBh. iii. — √**bhū**, to become thou, Pāṇ. i, 4, 108, Pat. — **yoni** (*tvád-*), mfn. proceeding from thee, AV. xiii, 1, 2. — **vidha**, mfn. like thee, MBh. iii; R. ii f.; Kathās. cix. — **viyoga**, m. separation from thee. — **vivācana** (*tvád-*), mfn. having thee as an umpire, TS. i.

Tvadīya, mfn. thy, your, thine, yours, MBh. &c.

Tvadya, Nom. °*yati*, to wish thee, Pāṇ. vii, 2, 98, Kāś.; °*yate*, to act like thou, ib.

Tvadrík, ind. towards thee, RV. v, 3, 12; x, 43, 2.

Tvan, = *tvat*. — **manya**, mfn. thinking to be thou, Pāṇ. vi, 3, 68, Kāś. — **maya**, mfn. consisting of thee, Hariv.; Vcar. — **tā**, f. identity with thee, Naish.

Tvā́m-kāma, mfn. longing for thee, RV. viii, 11, 7.

Tvātputra, m. pl. the pupils of (*tvat-p°*) your son, Pāṇ. i, 1, 74, Pat.

Tvā́-datta, mfn. given by thee, RV. ii, 33, 2; viii, 92, 18. **Tvā́-dāta**, mfn. id., i, 10; iii, v. **Tvā́-dūta**, mfn. having thee as a messenger, ii, v. **Tvā-dṛiś**, nom. -*dṛik*, mfn. like thee, of thy kind, KaṭhUp.; MBh. v; BhP. i, 17. **Tvā-dṛiśa**, mf(*ī*)n. id., MBh.; R. &c. **Tvā-dṛiśaka**, mfn. id., MBh. v, 4399. **Tvā-nid**, mfn. hating thee, RV. viii, 70, 10. **Tvā́m-āhuti**, mfn. offering oblations to thee, TS. i, 5, 10, 2. **Tvāyát**, mfn. = *tvā́m-kāma*, RV. **Tvāyā́**, ind. out of love towards thee, for thee, i–viii. **Tvāyú**, mfn. = °*yát*, i, iii f., vi–viii, x. **Tvā́-vat**, mfn. (Pāṇ. v, 2, 39, Vārtt.) similar to thee, as rich or mighty or great as thou, worthy of thee, RV. **Tvā́-vasu**, mfn. having thee as a possession, vii, 32, 14. **Tvā́-vṛidha**, mf(*ā*)n. favoured by thee, i, x. **Tvéshita**, mfn. sent by thee, viii, 77, 10. **Tvóta**, mfn. helped or protected or loved by thee, i–vi, viii ff.; cf. *indra-*. **Tvóti**, mfn. id., v, 65, 5; ix, 66 & 76.

त्वक्ष् *tvaksh* (= √*taksh* & related to 2. *tvác*), cl. 1. °*kshati*, to create, produce, Nir. viii, 13; to pare, Dhātup.; to skin, ib.; to cover, ib.; [cf. *pra-tvakshâṇa*; Zend *thwakhsh*, τυκ, τυχ.]

Tvákshas, n. energy, vigour, RV. i, 100, 15; iv, 27, 2; vi, 18, 9; viii, 20, 6. **Tvákshīyas**, mfn. very vigorous, ii, 33, 6; cf. Zend *thwakhshista*.

त्वङ्ग् *tvaṅg*, cl. 1. *gati*, to wave, tremble, jump, leap, gallop, Daś. x, 36; Bālar. viii, 77; Kathās. xviii, 7; lxxxv, 11; to flare, Vcar. xviii, 81.

त्वच् 1. *tvac*, cl. 6. °*cati*, to cover, Dhātup.

Tvak, in comp. for 2. *tvác*. — **kaṇḍura**, m. a skin-wound, sore, L. — **kshīrā**, f. 'bark-milk,' bamboo manna (Tabāshīr), L. — **kshīrī**, f. id., Suśr. i, 44, 14. — **chada**, m. Lipeocercis serrata, L. — **cheda**, m. a skin-wound, cut. — **chedana**, n. cutting the skin. — **taraṃgaka**, m. 'skin-wave,' a wrinkle, Npr. — **to-bila**, see *tvag-b°*. — **tra**, n. 'skin-fence,' armour, Bhaṭṭ. xiv, 94; cf. *nish-ṭv°*. — **trāṇa**, n. protection of the skin, Pāṇ. i, 2, 45, Vārtt. 11, Pat. — **pattra**, m. Laurus Cassia, MBh. xii; n. = °*ttraka*, Suśr.; (*ī*), f. *hiṅgu-pattrī*, L.; Malabathron, Npr. — **pattraka**, n. the bark or leaf of Laurus Cassia, Bhpr. vii, 1, 202. — **pariputana**, n. desquamation, Suśr. i, 17, 3; ii, 12, 5. — **parṇī**, f. = -*pattrī*, L. — **palita**, n. leprosy, Gal. — **pāka**, m. 'skin-inflammation,' N. of a disease, 14, 1 & 11. — **pārushya**, n. roughness of the skin, 5, 1; iv, 5, 2. — **pushpa**, n. = *tvag-aṅkura*, L.; blotch, scab, L.; (*ī*), f. id., L. — **pushpikā**, f. id., L. — **śūnya-tā**, f. want of sensation in the skin, Bhpr. — **sāra**, mfn. having an excellent or sound skin, Laghuj. ii, 16; Suśr. i, 35; m. a bamboo, MBh.; R.; Suśr. &c.; Laurus Cassia (the plant and the bark), L.; Bignonia indica, L.; (*ā*), f. Tabāshīr, L.; -*bhedinī*, f. the plant *kshudra-cañcu*, L.; -*vyavahāra-vat*, mfn. occupied with bamboo work, Mn. x, 37. — **sugandha**, m. an orange, Bhpr.; (*ā*), f. the bark of Feronia elephantum, L. — **sraja**, n. sg. skin and wreath, Pāṇ. v, 4, 106, Laghuk. — **svādvī**, f. = -*sugandha*, Npr.

Tvag, = 2. *tvác*. — **aṅkura**, m. 'skin-bristling,' horripilation, L. — **asthi-bhūta**, mfn. become mere skin and bones, MBh. xiii, 29, 6. — **indriya**, n. the sense of touch, W. — **uttarâsaṅga-vat**, mfn. having an upper garment made of bark, Kum. v, 16. — **ut-thā**, f. 'skin-produced,' chyle, Gal. — **ela**, n. Cassia bark and cardamoms, Suśr. i, 44. — **gandha**, m. = *tvak-sug°*, L. — **ja**, n. 'skin-born,' the hairs on the body, L.; blood, L. — **jala**, n. 'skin-water,' sweat, Gal. — **dosha**, m. skin-disease, leprosy, MBh. v, 5064; Suśr. i, 45; Sāy.; Hcat.; °*shâpahā*, f. 'leprosy-curer,' Vernonia anthelminthica, L.; °*shâri*, m. 'leprosy-enemy,' N. of a bulb, L. — °**doshin**, mfn. having skin-disease, leprous, MBh. v, 5056. — **bila**, mf(*ā*)n. having the cavity on the bark side (a ladle), KātyŚr. i, 3; *tvak-to-b°*, ĀpŚr. i. — **bheda**, m. the chapping of the skin, Suśr. ii, 1. — **bhedaka**, m. one who scratches the skin, Mn. viii, 284. — **roga**, m. = -*dosha*. — **vat**, mfn. furnished with a skin or bark, Pāṇ. v, 3, 65, Kāś.

Tvagā-kshīrī, f. = *tvak-ksh°*, L.

Tvaṅ, = 2. *tvác*. — **maya**, mfn. made of skin or bark, viii, 4, 45, Vārtt., Sch.; iv, 3, 144, Siddh. — **mala**, n. the hairs of the body, L. — **māṅsâsthi-maya**, mfn. consisting of skin, flesh and bones, Bhartṛ. i, 77.

2. **Tvác**, f. skin (of men, serpents &c.), hide (of goats, cows &c.), RV. &c. (*kṛishṇā́*, 'the black man,' i, 130, 8); a cow's hide (used in pressing out the Soma), i, iii, ix; VS. xix, 82; a leather bag, RV. v, 33, 7; (fig. 'a cloud') i & ix; bark, rind, peel, RV. &c.; Cassia bark, VarBṛS. lxxvii, 6; 12; 24; 32; cinnamon, cinnamon tree, L.; a cover (of a horse), RV. viii, 1, 32; surface (of the earth), i, 145, 5; x, 68, 4; AV. vi, 21, 1; TBr. i, 5, 5, 4; with *kṛishṇā́* or *ásiknī*, 'the black cover,' darkness, RV. ix, 41, 1 & 73, 5; a mystical N. of the letter *ya*, RāmatUp. i, 77.

Tvaca, n. skin (ifc. see *mukta-*, *mṛidu-*), Uṇ. ii, 63, Sch.; cinnamon, cinnamon tree, R. iii, 39, 22; Suśr.; Cassia bark, L.; (*ā*), f. skin, L.; cf. *guḍa-*; *tanu-* & *pṛithak-tvacā*. °**cana**, n. skinning, Dhātup. xvii, 13. °**caya**, Nom. °*yati*, to skin, Pāṇ. iii, 1, 25. °**cas**, see *sá-*, *sūrya-*, *hiraṇya-*. °**casyà**, mfn. being in the skin, AV. ii, 33, 7. °**cā-pattra**, n. Cassia bark, L. °**cāyani**, m. patr. fr. °*c*, Pāṇ. iv, 1, 95, Vārtt. 1, Pat. °**cita**, mfn. skinned, HPariś. ii, 23. °**cishṭha**, mfn. having the best or an excellent skin, Pāṇ. v, 3, 65, Kāś. °**ci-sāra**, m. (vi, 3, 9, Kāś.) = *tvak-s°*, a bamboo, Bhpr. v, 3, 153. °**cīyas**, mfn. having a better skin, Pāṇ. v, 3, 65, Kāś. °**cya**, mfn. conducive to healthiness of skin, Suśr. i, 45, 7, 3; 46, 2, 11.

Tvāca, mfn. relating to (*tvác*) the skin, L.

त्वञ्च् *tvañc* (= 1. *tañc*), cl. 1. to go, Dhātup.; (= 2. *tañc*) cl. 7. *tvanakti*, to contract, Kavikalpat.

त्वत् *tvát* (or *tvád*) &c. See col. 2.

त्वर् *tvar*, cl. 1. *tvárate* (ep. also °*ti*; pf. *tatvare*, Ragh.; aor. 2. pl. *atvaridhvam*, °*ridhvam*, °*riddhvam*, Vop.; Subj. 2. sg. *tvarishṭhās*, Pāṇ. i, 3, 21, Siddh.) to hurry, make haste, move with speed,

Kāṭh.; ŚBr.; ŚāṅkhŚr.; MBh. &c.: Caus. *tvarayati* (Impv. °*ráya*; aor. *atatvarat*, Pāṇ. vii, 4, 95) to cause to hasten, quicken, urge forward (with acc., dat. or inf.), AV. xii, 3, 31; MBh. &c.; *tvār*°, to convert quickly into the state (*bhāva*, dat.) of, Bādar. ii, 1, 24, Śaṃk.; cf. √*tur*.

Tvara, only (*ena*), instr. ind. hastily, BhP. x, 13, 62.

Tvaraṇá, mf(*ā́*)n. produced by hurrying (sweat), AV. xi, 8, 28; n. making haste, W. °**ṇīya**, mfn. requiring haste, MBh. vii, 5842.

Tvarā, f. haste, speed, MBh.; R. &c. (°*rām* √*kṛi* with gen. 'to make haste with,' Kathās. xx, 199); (*ayā*), instr. ind. hastily, quickly, R.; Suśr.; Śak. vi, $\frac{3}{8}$. **-yukta**, mfn. expeditious, BrahmaP. i, 56, 17. **-°roha** (°*rā́r*°), m. 'ascending quickly,' a pigeon, Npr. **-vat**, mfn. expeditious, MBh.; R.

Tvarāyasya, Nom. P. to hurry, g. *kaṇḍv-ādi*.

Tvari, f. haste, L. °**rita**, mfn. (Pāṇ. iii, 2, 187) hasty, quick, swift, expeditious, MBh. &c.; n. impers. hurried, W.; n. haste (see *sa-tvaritam*), L.; (*am*), ind. quickly, swiftly, MBh.; R.; Śak. iii, $\frac{1}{2}$; Kāraṇḍ.; (*ā*), f. Durgā and a magical formula called after her, Tantras. iv; Śārad. x; *-gati*, f. 'swift motion,' a metre; *ram*, ind. more quickly, Prab. vi, $\frac{1}{2}$; *-vikrama*, of 4 × 10 syllables, Chandaḥs. vi, 10 ff., Sch.; *-ta*, mfn. stepping quickly, Hariv. 3182; 4507; R. i, vii; °*tōdita*, mfn. = *tūrṇōd*°, L.; cf. *tūrtá*, °*rṇa*. **ri-taka**, m. = *tūrṇaka*, Suśr. i, 46; (*ā*), f. id., Npr.

त्वष्ट *tvashṭa*, mfn. (√*tvaksh*) = *tashṭa*, L.

Tváshṭā-várūtrī, du. 'Tvashṭṛi and his Help (cf. RV. vii, 34, 22),' N. of two Asura priests, Kapishṭh. vli, 4; Kāṭh. xxx, 1 (*trish*°); MaitrS. iv, 8, 1 (*trish*° & *tṛish*°). **Tvashṭi**, f. carpentry, Mn. x, 48. **Tváshṭī-matī**, °**shṭu-mat**, see °*shṭri-m*°

Tváshṭṛi, m. a carpenter, maker of carriages (= *táshṭri*), AV. xii, 3, 33; 'creator of living beings,' the heavenly builder, N. of a god (called *su-kṛít*, *-pāṇi*, *-gábhasti*, *-jániman*, *sv-ápas*, *apásām apástama*, *viśvá-rūpa* &c., RV.; maker of divine implements, esp. of Indra's thunderbolt and teacher of the Ṛibhus, i, iv–vi, x; Hariv. 12146 f.; R. ii, 91, 12; former of the bodies of men and animals, hence called 'first-born' and invoked for the sake of offspring, esp. in the Āprī hymns, RV.; AV. &c.; MBh. iv, 1178; Hariv. 587 ff.; Ragh. vi, 32; associated with the similar deities Dhātṛi, Savitṛi, Prajā-pati, Pūshan, and surrounded by divine females [*gnā́s*, *janáyas*, *devā́nām pátnīs*; cf. *tváshṭā-várūtrī*] recipients of his generative energy, RV.; ŚBr. i; KātyŚr. iii; supposed author of RV. x, 184 with the epithet Garbha-pati, RAnukr.; father of Saraṇyū [Su-reṇu, Hariv.; Sva-reṇu, L.] whose double twin-children by Vivasvat [or Vāyu?, RV. viii, 26, 21 f.] are Yama-Yamī and the Aśvins, x, 17, 1 f.; Nir. xii, 10; Bṛih.; Hariv. 545 ff.; VP.; also father of Tri-śiras or Viśva-rūpa, ib.; overpowered by Indra who recovers the Soma [RV. iii f.] concealed by him because Indra had killed his son Viśva-rūpa, TS. ii; ŚBr. i, v, xii; regent of the Nakshatra Citrā, TBr.; ŚāṅkhGṛ.; Śāntik.; VarBṛS. iic, 4; of the 5th cycle of Jupiter, viii, 23; of an eclipse, iii, 6; *Tvashṭur ātithya*, N. of a Sāman, ĀrshBr.); a form of the sun, MBh. iii, 146; Hariv. 13143; BhP. iii, 6, 15; (styled *mahā-graha*) Parāś.; N. of the 12th Muhūrta, Sūryapr.; of an Āditya, MBh. i; Hariv.; BhP. vi, 6, 37; VP. i, 15, 130; ii, 10, 16; of a Rudra, i, 15, 122; of a son of Manasyu or Bhauvana, ii, 1, 40; BhP. v, 15, 13. **-devatya**, mfn. having T° as deity, PārGṛ. iii, 15, 5. **-mat** (*tváṣh*°), mfn. connected with or accompanied by T°, RV. vi, 52, 11; VS. xxxvii, 20; (°*tri-m*°) MaitrS. & Kapishṭh.; (°*ṭu-m*°) ĀpŚr.; f. [cf. Pāṇ. iv, 1, 34, Vārtt. 1, Pat.] °*ṭrī-matī* TĀr., °*ṭī-m*° TS. i, 2, 5, 2 & ĀpŚr. **Tvāshṭi**, f. (for °*ṭrī*) Durgā, DevīP.

Tvāshṭrá, mfn. belonging to or coming from Tvashṭṛi, RV. i, 117, 22; AV.; VS. &c. (*putrá*, 'son of T°,' Prab. ii, 31); having T° as regent, VarBṛS. viii, 37; Jyot. (YV.) 6, Sch.; m. the son of T° (Viśva-rūpa, RV. &c.; Ābhūti, ŚBr. xiv; Vṛitra, BhP. vi, 9, 17; xi, 12, 5; Tri-śiras, RAnukr.); N. of an eclipse, VarBṛS. iiic, 2; n. T°'s energy, creative power, RV. iii, 7, 4; BhP. viii, 11, 35; the asterism Citrā, VarBṛS.; (*ī*), f. 'daughter of T°,' Saraṇyū (Vivasvat's wife), Nir. xii, 10; MBh. i, 2599; Hariv. 545 f.; the asterism Citrā, L.; a small car, L.; pl. 'daughters of T°,' certain divine female beings, TāṇḍyaBr. xii, 5. °**ri-sāman**, n. N. of a Sāman (also °*ryāḥ s*°; also *anta-tvāshṭrī*), Lāṭy. °**reya**, N. of a family, Pravar.

त्वाव *tvā́vá*, = *tú vā́vá*, ŚBr. xi f.; cf. *tvaí*.

त्विष् 1. *tvish* (cl. 1. *tveshati*, °*te*, Dhātup.; aor. *atvikshat* [cf. Pāṇ. vii, 2, 10, Kār.], Vop.; pl. *ā́tvishur*, °*shanta*, *ā́titvishanta*; pf. *titvishé*, p. °*shāṇá*) Ā. to be violently agitated or moved or excited or troubled, RV.; (P.) Bhaṭṭ.; P. Ā. to excite, instigate, RV. i, x; to shine, glitter, viii, 96, 15; Nir.; BhP. x, 46, 45 (pr. p. *tvishyat*); cf. *ava-*.

Tviṭ-pati, m. 'light-lord,' the sun, Gal.

2. **Tvísh**, f. violent agitation, vehemence, violence, fury, perplexity, RV. iv f., viii, x; VS.; light, brilliance, glitter, splendour, beauty, authority, RV. viii, 43, 3; MBh. &c.; colour, VarBṛS. xxxii, 21; lxiv, 3; Suśr.; Ratnâv.; Kathās.; speech, L.

Tvishā, f. light, splendour, L.; N. of a daughter of Marīci by Sambhūti, VāyuP. i, 28, 8; LiṅgaP.

Tvishām-īśa, **-pati**, m. = *tviṭ-p*°, L.

Tvíshi, f. vehemence, impetuosity, energy, RV. v, 8, 5; AV.; VS.; TS.; splendour, light, brilliancy, beauty, RV. i, ix f.; AV.; VS.; ŚBr.; TāṇḍyaBr.; N. of an Ekâha, Vait. **-mat** (*tvíshi*°), see °*shī-m*°.

Tvishitá, mfn. violently agitated, RV. x, 84, 2.

Tvíshī-mat, mfn. vehemently excited, vehement, energetic, RV.; shining, brilliant, beautiful, iii, vi; °*shi-m*°, ŚBr. xi; ŚāṅkhŚr.; KātyŚr.; Kauś.

Tveshá, mf(*ā́*)n. vehement, impetuous, causing fear, awful, RV.; brilliant, glittering, RV. **-dyumna** (°*shá-*), mfn. having glittering brilliancy, i, 37, 4. **-nṛimṇa** (°*shá-*), mfn. of brilliant power, x, 120, 1; AV. v, 11, 1. **-pratīka** (°*shá-*), mf(*ā*)n. of brilliant appearance, RV. i, 66, 7 & 167, 5. **-yāma** (°*shá-*), mfn. impetuous in course, 166, 5. **-ratha**, mfn. having rushing or brilliant chariots, v, 61, 13. **-saṃdṛiś** (°*shá-*), mfn. = *-pratīka*, i, 85; v f., x.

Tveshátha, m. fury, violence, i, 141, 8.

Tveshás, n. energy, impulse, 61, 11. **Tveshin**, mfn. impetuous, vii, 60, 10 (°*shi*, nom. f. of °*shá*?).

Tveshyà, mfn. terrifying, awful, 58, 2.

त्वेषित *tvéshita*. See p. 463, col. 2.

त्वै *tvaí*, ind. (g. *cādi* & Pāṇ. vi, 1, 94, Vārtt. 1, Pat.) = *tú vai*, TS. ii f.; ŚBr. ix f.; cf. *tvā́vá*.

त्वोत *tvóta*, °*ti*. See p. 463, col. 2.

त्सर् *tsar*, cl. 1. *tsárati* (Subj. & p. *tsárat*; pf. *tatsāra* & aor. *átsār*, RV.; *atsārīt*, Pāṇ. vii, 2, 2; pf. pl. *tatsarur*, vi, 4, 120, Kāś.) to go or approach stealthily, creep on, sneak, RV.; AV.; ŚBr.; TāṇḍyaBr.; Kauś.; Anup.; cf. *abhi-*, *ava-*, *upa-*.

Tsarā, f. approaching stealthily, Nyāyam., Sch.

Tsáru, m. a crawling animal, RV. vii, 50, 1; the stalk of a leaf (see *palāśa-*), handle of a vessel, Suśr.; the hilt of a sword, MBh.; R.; Hariv.; Ragh.; cf. *sumati-*. **-mat**, mfn. having a handle, ĀpŚr. xii, 2, 8. **-mārga**, m. sword-fight, MBh. i, 5341. **Tsaruka**, mfn. making hilts of swords, g. *ākarshâdi*.

Tsāra, see *ku-*. °**rin**, mfn. approaching stealthily, hidden, RV. i, 134, 5; AV. x, 1; TS. vi. °**ruka**, mfn. skilful in handling (*tsaru*) a sword, MBh. i, 5271.

थ THA.

थ 1. *tha*, aspirate of the preceding letter. **-kāra**, m. the letter or sound *th*.

2. **Tha**, m. a mountain, L.; a protector, L.; a sign of danger, L.; N. of a disease, L.; eating, L.; n. preservation, L.; fear, L.; an auspicious prayer, L.

थक्कन *thakkana*, m. See *ṭhakk*°, Rājat.

थक्रिय *thakriya*, m. N. of a man, iv, 493.

थक्वियक *thakviyaka*, N. of a man, v, 151.

थरथराय *tharatharāya*, Nom. Ā. (p. °*yamāna*) to grow giddy, tumble, Kāraṇḍ. xi, 130.

थर्व् *tharv*, cl. 1. P. to go, Nir. xi, 18.

थल्योरक *thalyoraka*, N. of a village, Rājat.

थुड् *thuḍ*, cl. 6. °*ḍáti*, to cover, Dhātup.

थुत्कार *thut-kāra*, m. = *thūt-k*°, W.

Thutthu-kāraka, mfn. one who smacks his lips in eating (not admitted into the Buddh. brotherhood), L.

Thuthu, = *thūthū*. **-kṛit**, m. N. of a bird, Npr.

थुर्व् *thurv*, cl. 1. p. *thúrvat*, (Agni) hurting (Dhātup. xv, 62; cf. √*turv*), MaitrS. ii, 10, 1.

थूत् *thūt*, ind. (fr. *shṭhyūta*?). **-kāra**, m. the sound made in spitting, Rājat. vii f. **-kṛita**, n. id., vii, 1116. **-kṛitya**, ind. spitting, ib.

Thūthū, imitative sound of spitting, Sûktik.

थैथै *thaithai*, (in music) imitative sound of a musical instrument.

थोडन *thoḍana*, n. fr. √*thuḍ*, W.

थौणेय *thauṇeya*, °*yaka*, n. = *sth*°, Car. vi f.

द DA.

द 1. *da*, the 3rd and soft letter of the 4th or dental class. **-kāra**, m. the letter or sound *d*.

द 2. *da*, mf(*ā*)n. (√1. *dā*) ifc. (Pāṇ. iii, 2, 3) giving, granting, offering, effecting, producing (e.g. *abhīshṭa-*, 'giving any desired object,' Pañcat. ii, 50; *gaja-vāji-vriddhi-*, 'promoting the welfare of elephants and horses,' VarBṛS. xviii, 5), Mn.; MBh. &c. (cf. *agni-*; *a-doma-dá*; *anna-*, *artha-*, *garbha-*, *janma-* &c.); m. n. a gift, L.; (*ā*), f. id., L.

द 3. *da*, mfn. (√*do*) ifc., see *anala-*, 2. *jīva-*; m. n. the act of cutting off, L.; (*ā*), f. id., L.

द 4. *da*, mfn. (√4. *dā*) ifc. See *ṛiśya-dá*.

द 5. *da*, = *dát*, cf. *a-panna-*, *panna-*; *sho-ḍa*.

द 6. *da*, m. a mountain, L.; n. a wife (derived fr. *dám-patī*), L.; (*ā*), f. heat, pain, L.

दंश् 1. *daṅś* or *daṉs*, cl. 1. 10. P. °*śati*, °*śayati* or °*s*°, 'to speak' or 'to shine,' Dhātup. xxxiii, 91; cl. 1. P. & 10. Ā. (fr. Prâkṛit *daṉse*) to show, 2 f.

दंश् 2. *daṉś*, cl. 1. (originally 6.) *dáśati* (Pāṇ. vi, 4, 25; Ā., MBh. i, 1798 & Hariv. 4302; p. *dáśat*, RV. &c.; pf. *dadaṉśa*; pl. °*śur*, R. i, 45, 20; p. *dadaśvā́s*, RV. iv, 38, 6; fut. *daṅkshyati*, Bhaṭṭ.; *daṉshṭā*, Pāṇ. vii, 2, 10, Kār.; 1. pl. *daśishyāmas*, MBh. i, 1605; aor. *adāṅkshīt*, Vop.; pl. °*shur*, Bhaṭṭ.; ind. p. *daṉshṭvā*, TāṇḍyaBr.; cl. 1. *daṉśati*, Cāṇ.) to bite, RV.; AV.; ŚBr. &c.: Caus. to cause to bite, Kauś.; to cause to be bitten by (instr.), MBh. i, 2243; iii, 544; Suśr. iv, 14, 6 & 12: Intens. *dandaśyate*, °*śīti*, Pāṇ. iii, 1, 24; vii, 4, 86; *dandashṭi*, °*daṉshṭi*, Vop. xx, 19; p. *dándaśāna* (cf. °*śū́ka*) repeatedly biting, RV. x, 95, 9: Caus. of Intens. (ind. p. *dandaśayitvā*) causing to be bitten by (instr.), Daś. i, 142; [cf. δάκνω; Goth. *tahyan*.]

Daṉśa, mfn. 'biting,' see *mṛiga-*; m. a bite, sting, the spot bitten (by a snake &c.), Suśr.; Mālav. iv, 4 & $\frac{4}{5}$, 3; Gīt. x, 11; Kathās. lx, 131; snake-bite, W.; pungency, W.; a flaw (in a jewel), L.; a tooth, L.; a stinging insect, gnat, gad-fly, ChUp.; Mn. xii, 62; Yājñ. iii, 215; MBh. &c.; N. of an Asura, xii, 93; armour, mail, BhP. i, iii; a joint of the body, L.; (*ī*), f. a small gad-fly, L.; cf. *kshamā-*, *vṛisha-*. **-nāśinī**, f. 'sting-curing,' a kind of insect, L. **-bhīru**, °**ruka**, m. 'afraid of gad-flies,' a buffalo, L. **-maśaka**, n. sg. gad-flies and gnats, Mn. i, 40 & 45; (in comp.) Jain. & Pañcat. iii, 2, 9. **-mūla**, m. 'pungent-root,' Hyperanthera Moringa, L. **-vadana**, m. 'sharp-beaked,' a heron, L.

Daṉśaka, mfn. 'biting,' see *dṛiḍha-*, *mṛiga-*; m. 'a tooth,' see *puru-*; a gad-fly, L.; a common fly, Npr.; N. of a prince of Kampana, Rājat. viii, 178; (*ikā*), f. a kind of stinging fly, Npr. °**śana**, n. the act of biting, bite, MBh. xiv, 754; Sāh.; the being bitten by (instr.), MBh. viii, 4252; armour, mail, i, iii, viii; Devīm. ii, 27. °**śita**, mfn. bitten, Vet. ii, $\frac{4}{5}$; armed, mailed, MBh.; R. iii; BhP. vi; protected, MBh.; Hariv.; adorned, 5432; ready for (loc.), MBh. xii, 644; fitting closely (like armour), standing closely together, crowded, iv; v, 7184 (*saṃś*° B); Hariv.; n. a bite, L. °**śin**, mfn. 'biting,' see *tripra-daṉśin*; m. a dog, Npr.; a wasp, ib.

Dáṉśuka, mfn. biting (with acc.), Kāṭh.; TS.; TBr.

Daṉśera, for *daś*°, Uṇ. i, 58. °**śman**, n. a bite or the spot bitten, Kauś. 29 & 32; cf. *tṛishṭá-*.

Daṉshṭrí, m. a biter, AV. x, 4, 26.

Dáṉshṭra, m. a large tooth, tusk, fang, RV. ii, 13, 4; x, 87, 3; AV. &c.; (*ā*), f. (g. *ajâdi* & Pāṇ. iii, 2, 182) id., Śiksh.; MBh. &c.; cf. *áyo-*, *ashṭa-*, *ashṭā-*, *cátur-*, *tīkshṇa-*, *bhagna-*, *raudra-*, *su-*.

Daṉshṭrā, f. of °*ra*. **-karāla**, mfn. having terrible tusks, i, 5929; *-vat*, mfn. id., R. (B) iv, 22, 29. **-daṇḍa**, m. a hog's tusk, Dhanaṃj. 1. **-nivāsin**, m. N. of a Yaksha, Divyâv. xxix. **-°yudha** (°*ray*°), mfn. using tusks as weapons (dogs), R. ii, 70, 23; m. a wild boar, Npr. **-visha**, mfn. having venom in the teeth, Suśr. v, 3, 3. **-sena**, m. N. of a Buddh. scholar, Buddh. L. **Danshṭrāla**, mfn. tusked, Hariv.; R.; m. N. of a Rakshas, v, 12, 13.

Danshṭrika, mfn. tusked, g. *vrīhy-ādi*; (*ā*), f. = *dāḍhikā*, L.; N. of a plant, Npr. °**ṭrin**, mfn. (g. *vrīhy-ādi*) tusked, m. an animal with tusks, Mn.; Yājñ.; MBh. &c.; m. Śiva, xiv, 205; a wild boar, L.; a hyena, Npr.; a snake, Hariv. 12496.

दंस् 1. *dans*, cl. 1. 10. See √1 *danś*.

दंस् 2. *dans*, cl. 10. (Subj. 2. sg. °*sáyas*, = nom. pl. of °*sí*, Nir. iv, 25) to destroy (?), RV. x, 138, 1; cl. 1. P. 10. Ā. (for 2. *danś*) to bite, Dhātup.

Dansána, n. a surprising or wonderful deed, marvellous power or skill, RV. i, 166, 13; (*ā*), f. id., i, iii–viii (often instr. °*sánā*), x. °**sánā-vat**, mfn. endowed with wonderful skill or power, i, iii; ŚāṅkhŚr. viii, 17. °**sayitṛi**, m. a destroyer, Nir. vi, 26, Sch.

Dánsas, n. = °*sána*, RV.; cf. *puru-* & *su-dánsas*.

Dansí, m. or f. '= *karman*,' see s. v. 2. *dans*.

Dánsishṭha, mfn. (Superl. of °*su* or *dasrá*) of very wonderful strength, i, 182, 2; viii; x, 143, 3.

Dánsu, mfn. only in comp., = δασύς, Lat. *densus* (for the change of meaning cf. *gurú* & βαρύς &c.); ind. wonderfully, i, 134, 4 & 141, 4. –**jūta** (*dánsu-*), mfn. wonderfully quick, 122, 10. –**patnī** (*dánsu-*), f. having a powerful lord (cf. Pāṇ. iv, 1, 34, Vārtt. 1, Pat.), iv, 19, 7 & (*dánsu-pát*°), vi, 3, 7.

दंह् *danh*, cl. 10. °*hayati*, to shine, burn, Vop.

दक *daka*, n. = *ud*°, water, Phetk. xvii; cf. *dagârgala*. –**rākshasa**, m. a water-Rakshasa, Divyâv. viii, 262 ff. –**lâvaṇika**, mfn. prepared with water and salt, L. **Dakôdara**, n. a dropsical belly (cf. *udák*°), Suśr. i, 25, 8; ii, 7; iii, 8; v, 2, 36.

दक्ष् *daksh*, cl. 1. P. (Impv. 2. pl. *dákshatā*) to act to the satisfaction of (dat.; Nir. i, 7), RV. vii; Ā. *dákshate* (p. *dákshamāṇa*; pf. *dadakshe*) to be able or strong, 16, 6; AV. i f.; ŚBr. ii, iv; to grow, increase, Dhātup. xvi, 7; to act quickly, ib.; to go, xix, 8; to hurt, ib.: Caus. *dakshâyati* (aor. *adadakshat*), to make able or strong, ŚBr. ii, iv, viii, xi.

Dáksha, mf(*ā*)n. able, fit, adroit, expert, clever, dexterous, industrious, intelligent, RV. &c.; strong, heightening or strengthening the intellectual faculties (Soma), ix f.; passable (the Ganges), MBh. xiii, 1844; suitable, BhP. iv, 6, 44; Bhartṛ. iii, 64; right (opposed to left), RāmatUp. i, 22; Phetk. i; m. ability, fitness, mental power, talent (cf. *-kratú*), strength of will, energy, disposition, RV.; AV.; VS.; evil disposition, RV. iv, 3, 13; x, 139, 6; a particular form of temple, Hcat. ii, 1, 390; a general lover, W.; a cock, Car. i, vi; N. of a plant, L.; fire, L.; Śiva's bull, L.; N. of an Āditya (identified with Prajā-pati, TS. iii; ŚBr. ii; father of Kṛittikā, Śāntik.), RV. i f., x; Nir. ii, xi; N. of one of the Prajā-patis (MBh. xii, 7534; Hariv.; VP. i, 7, 5 & 22, 4; BhP. iii, 12, 22; MatsyaP. cvl, 15; KūrmaP. &c.; Śak. vii, 27; born from Brahmā's right thumb, MBh. i, xii; Hariv. &c.; or from A-ja, 'the unborn,' BhP. iv, 1, 47; or son of Pra-cetas or of the 10 Pra-cetasas, whence called Prācetasa, MBh. i, xii f.; Hariv. 101; VP. i, 15; father of 24 daughters by Pra-sūti, VP. i, 7, 17 ff.; BhP. &c.; of 50 [or 60, MBh. xii, 6136; R. iii, 20, 10; or 44, Hariv. 11521 ff.] daughters of whom 27 become the Moon's wives, forming the lunar asterisms, and 13 [or 17, BhP.; or 8, R.] those of Kaśyapa, becoming by this latter the mothers of gods, demons, men, and animals, while 10 are married to Dharma, Mn. ix, 128 f.; MBh. i, ix; xii, 7537 ff.; Hariv.; VP. &c.; celebrating a great sacrifice [hence *Dakshasyâyana*, 'N. of a sacrifice,' Mn. vi, 10] to obtain a son, he omitted, with the disapproval of Dadhīca, to invite Śiva, who ordered Vīra-bhadra to spoil the sacrifice, Hariv. 12212 [identified with Vishṇu] ff.; VāyuP. i, 30 = BrahmaP. i; LiṅgaP.; MatsyaP. xiii; VāmP. ii–v; ŚivaP. i, 8; KāśīKh. lxxxvii ff.; named among the Viśve-devās, Hariv. 11542; VāyuP.; Bṛihasp. [Hcat.] &c.); N. of a son of Garuḍa, MBh. v, 3597; of a man with the patr. Pārvati, ŚBr. ii, 4, 4, 6; of a law-giver, Yājñ. i, 5; Mn. ix, 88, Sch. &c.; of a son of Uśī-nara, BhP. ix, 23, 2; of one of the 5 Kānyakubja Brāhmans from whom the Bengal Brāhmans are said to have sprung, Kshitîś. i, 13 & 41; (*ā*), f. the earth, L.; cf. *a-tūrta-*, *dīnā-*, *samānā-*; *su-dáksha*; *mārga-dakshaka*; *dākshāyaṇá*; δεξιός; Lat. *dex-ter*; Goth. *taihsvs*. –**kanyā**, f. a daughter of D°, MBh. i; Durgā, L. –**kratú**, m. du. = *krátū-dákshau*, TBr. i, 5; ĀśvGṛ.; *dáksh*°, mfn. able-minded, VS. iv, 11; ŚBr. iii. –**jā**, f. 'D°'s daughter,' Durgā, L.; pl. the Moon's wives, HPariś. ii, 88; -*pati*, m. 'lord of Durgā,' Śiva, W.; = °*kshâtmajā-p*°, L. –**ṇidhana**, n. N. of a Sāman, TāṇḍyaBr. xiv. –**tā**, f. dexterity, ability, Kām. v, 15; Sāh. iii, 51. –**tāti** (*dáksh*°), f. id., AV. viii, 1, 6. –**nidhana**, n. = -*ṇidh*°. –**pati** (*dáksh*°), m. lord of the faculties, RV. i, 95, 6; cf. 56, 2. –**pitṛi** (*dáksh*°), m. 'id.' or 'having D° as father' (Mitra & Varuṇa, the gods &c.), vi–viii (du. °*tarā*, pl. °*taras*); VS.; TS. i, 2 (pl. °*tāras*); ŚāṅkhŚr. –**putra**, see -*sāvarṇa*. –**makha-mathana**, n. 'destruction of D°'s sacrifice,' N. of LiṅgaP. i, 99 f. –**mathana**, m. 'destroyer of D°,' Śiva, Hcar. iii. –**yajña**, m. Daksha's sacrifice; -*prabhañjana*, m. 'destroyer of D°'s sacrifice,' Śiva; -*vidhvaṅsa*, m. '= °*ksha-makha-manthana*,' N. of KūrmaP. i, 15; -*vidhvaṅsana*, n. N. of PadmaP. i, 5 & ŚivaP. ii, 11; -*vināśinī*, f. Durgā, W. –**vihitā**, f. (scil. *gāthā*) a song composed by D°, Yājñ. iii, 114. –**vṛidh**, mfn. rejoicing in cleverness, TS. iii, 5, 8. –**śāpa**, m. 'curse of D°,' N. of PadmaP. iii, 33. –**sādhana**, mfn. effective of cleverness, RV. ix. –**sāvarṇa**, m. N. of the 9th Manu, VP. iii, 2, 20; -*putra sāv*° or simply -*putra*, MārkP. xciv, 4 & 10. –**sāvarṇi**, m. id., BhP. viii, 13, 18. –**suta**, m. a son of D°, god (cf. -*pitṛi*), R. v, 43, 14; (*ā*), f. a daughter of D°; pl. the Moon's wives, Ragh. iii, 33. –**stha**, mf(*ā*)n. being (on the right i.e.) south, Hcat. i, 3, 934. –**smṛiti**, f. N. of a law-book. **Dakshâṇḍa**, n. a hen's egg, Bhpr. v, 30, 73; vii, 76, 219. **Dakshâtmajā-pati**, m. 'lord of D°'s daughters,' the Moon, Vām. **Dakshâdhvara**, m. = °*ksha-yajña*; -*dhvaṅsaka*, m. = °*ksha-yajña-prabhañjana*, L.; -*dhvaṅsa-kṛit*, m. id., L.; -*dhvaṅsana*, m. id., Prab. ii, 28. **Dakshâri**, m. 'D°'s foe,' Śiva. **Dakshêśvara-liṅga**, n. N. of a Liṅga, KāśīKh. lxxxix.

Dákshas, mfn. able, dexterous, RV. i f., vi; viii, 13.

Dakshâyya, mfn. to be satisfied by skill, i f., vii.

Dakshi, m. pl. N. of a family, Pravar. iii, 3.

Dákshiṇa (also °*ṇá*, ŚBr.), mf(*ā*)n. (declined as a pron. when denoting relative position ['right' or 'southern'], KātyŚr.; ĀśvGṛ. &c.; cf. Pāṇ. i, 1, 34; vii, 1, 16; but not necessarily in abl. & loc. sg. m. n. [°*ne*, KātyŚr.; Mn. ii, 63] and nom. pl. m. except Hariv. 12390) able, clever, dexterous, Pāṇ. i, 1, 34, Kāś.; Śatr. (ifc.); right (not left), RV.; AV.; VS. &c. (°*ṇam parī*, 'to walk round a person with the right side towards him,' BhP. iv, 12, 25; °*ṇam* √*kṛi*, 'to place any one on the right side as a mark of respect,' i, viii); south, southern (as being on the right side of a person looking eastward), situated to the south, turned or directed southward, AV.; VS. &c.; coming from south (wind), Suśr.; Ragh. iv, 8; (with *āmnāya*) the southern sacred text (of the Tāntrikas), Kulârṇ. iii; straightforward, candid, sincere, pleasing, compliant, MBh. iv, 167; R.; Śak. iv, 18; Sāh. iii, 35; Pratâpar.; BrahmaP.; m. the right (hand or arm), RV. i, viii, x; TS. v; the horse on the right side of the pole of a carriage, i, x; VS. ix, 8; Śiva; m. or n. the south, Nal. ix, 23; R. iv; n. the right-hand or higher doctrine of the Śāktas, Kulârṇ. ii; (*am*), ind. to the right, R. ii, 92, 13; (*ā*), f. (scil. *gó*) 'able to calve and give milk,' a prolific cow, good milch-cow, RV.; AV.; a fee or present to the officiating priest (consisting originally of a cow, cf. KātyŚr. xv; Lāṭy. viii, 1, 2), RV. &c.; Donation to the priest (personified along with Brahmaṇas-pati, Indra, and Soma, i, 18, 5; x, 103, 8; authoress of x, 107, RAnukr.; wife of Sacrifice [Ragh. i, 31; BhP. ii, 7, 2], both being children of Ruci and Ākūti, iv, 1, 4 f.; VP. i, 7, 18 f.); reward, RV. viii, 24, 21; (offered to the Guru), MBh. v; Ragh. v, 20; Kathās. iv, 93 f.; (°*ṇām ā-*√*diś*, 'to thank,' Divyâv. vii, 104; Caus. 'to earn thanks,' i); a gift, donation (cf. *abhaya-*, *prâṇa-*, *rati-*), Mn. iii; R. ii; (scil. *diś*) the south, Deccan, L.; a figure of Durgā having the right side prominent, W.; completion of any rite (*pratishṭhā*), L.; (*e*), loc. ind. on the right side, Hemac.; (*āt*), abl. ind. from or on the right side, Pāṇ. v, 3, 4; from the south, southward, ib.; (*ena*), instr. ind. on the right or south (35), on the right side of or southward from (acc.; ii, 3, 31), ŚBr.; KātyŚr.; MBh. &c. (with √*kṛi*, to place or leave on the right, BhP. v, 21, 8); (*ais*), instr. ind. to the right, Kauś. 77; [cf. Lith. *désziné*, f. 'the right hand.'] –**kālikā**, f. a form of Durgā worshipped by the Tāntrikas, W. –**kālī-māhātmya**, n. N. of a work. –**jānv-akna**, mfn. having the right knee bent, Gobh. i, 3, 1. –**tás**, ind. (Pāṇ. v, 3, 28) from the right or south, on the right side or southward from (gen.), RV. &c. (with √*as* or *bhū*, 'to stand at the right side of, assist,' viii, 100, 2; x, 83, 7; AV. xviii; with √*kṛi* = °*ṇena* with √*kṛi*, BhP. v, 23, 1; with *purástāt* or °*ras*, south-east, ŚBr. xiii; MBh. ii); °*ta-upacāra*, mfn. having the entrance on the south, ĀpŚr. xi, 9, 4; °*ta-upavītin*, mfn. wearing the sacred thread on the right, iii, 17, 11; °*tás-kaparda*, mfn. wearing the braid on the right side of the head, RV. vii, 33, 1; (°*ṇā-k*°, Gṛihyās. ii, 40); °*taḥ-sád*, mfn. = °*ṇa-s*°, MaitrS. i, 4, 6; °*to-nyāya*, mfn. where the southern direction is the rule, ŚāṅkhŚr. ii, iv. –**trā**, ind. on the right side, RV. vi, 18, 9. –**tva**, n. uprightness, honesty, Hemac. –**dagh**, see -*sád*. –**dvārika**, mfn. (an asterism) propitious to a military expedition to the south, VarYogay. v, 1, Sch. –**dhurīṇa**, mfn. harnessed on the right side of the pole, Pāṇ. iv, 4, 78, Kāś. –**pañcāla**, mfn. belonging or relating to the southern Pañcālas (realm), BhP. iv, 25, 50. –**paścāt**, ind. (Pāṇ. v, 3, 32, Vārtt. 2, Pat.) south-west from (gen.), Vait. –**paścârdha**, m. (Pāṇ. v, 3, 32, Vārtt. 3, Pat.) the south-western side, ŚāṅkhGṛ. i, 9, 6. –**paścima**, mf(*ā*)n. south-western, ĀśvGṛ.; MBh. iii, 16823; xvii, 44. –**pāñcālaka**, mfn. = -*pañcāla*, Pāṇ. vii, 3, 13, Kāś. –**pūrva**, mf(*ā*)n. (ii, 2, 26, Kāś.) south-eastern, KātyŚr.; (*ena*), instr. ind. south-east from (acc.), viii, 6, 20; (*ā*), f. (scil. *diś*) the south-east, Kauś.; ĀśvGṛ. iv, 1 f.; Gobh. iv, 2, 3; BhP.; °*rvâyata*, mf(*ā*)n. extending south-eastward, KātyŚr. xxv; °*rvârdha*, m. the south-eastern side, iix; Kauś. –**pūrvaka**, mfn. = °*rva*, Hcat. i, 11, 711. –**prâk-pravaṇa**, mfn. sloping south-eastwards, ŚāṅkhŚr. iv, 14, 6. –**prâcī**, f. = -*pūrvā*, R. vi, 96, 11. –**bhāga**, m. the southern hemisphere (°*ṇa bh*°, i, 60, 20), W. –**mānasa**, n. N. of a Tīrtha near Benares. –**mārga**, m. the southern course (of a planet), VarYogay. iv, 49. –**rāḍhā**, f. southern Rāḍhā (in Bengal), Prab. ii, $\frac{2}{3}$ & $\frac{8}{9}$. –**lipi**, f. the southern way of writing, Lalit. x, 31. –**sád**, mfn. sitting on the right or southern side, VS. xxxviii; (°*ṇā-s*°) ix, 35; (°*ṇa-dhak*, nom. fr. -*dagh*, Lāṭy. v, 7, 3.) –**savyá**, mfn. du. right and left, AV. xii, 1, 28. –**stha**, m. 'standing on the right of his master,' a charioteer, L. **Dakshiṇâgní**, m. the southern fire of the altar (= *anvāhārya-pácana*), AV.; ĀśvŚr.; KātyŚr.; Lāṭy.; ChUp.; ĀśvGṛ.; VP. v, 34; BhP. iv. **Dakshiṇâgra**, mfn. having the points turned to the south, ŚBr. xii; KātyŚr.; ŚāṅkhŚr.; Gobh.; MBh.; R. **Dakshiṇâc**, m(acc. °*ṇâñcam*)fn. southward, Kauś. 87. **Dakshiṇâcala**, m. 'southern mountain,' the Malaya range, L. **Dakshiṇâcāra**, mfn. upright in conduct, MBh. iv, 167; = °*rin*; -*tantra*, n. N. of a Tāntric work. **Dakshiṇâcārin**, mfn. worshipping Śakti according to the right-hand ritual; °*ri-tantra*, n. = °*ra-t*°. **Dakshiṇâdhipati**, m. the lord of the Deccan, Vet. v, $\frac{1}{2}$. **Dakshiṇântikā**, f. N. of a metre. **Dakshiṇâpara**, mf(*ā*)n. south-western, KātyŚr.; Lāṭy.; Kauś.; ĀśvGṛ.; Āp.; °*râbhimukha*, mfn. turned to the south-west, Vishṇ. lxi, 12. **Dakshiṇâpavarga**, mfn. terminating in the south, Kauś. 87; ĀpGṛ. xxi, 9. **Dakshiṇâbdhi**, m. the southern ocean, VP. v, 23, 2 (v. l. for °*ṇā-patha*). **Dakshiṇâbhimukha**, mf(*ā*)n. having the face turned southwards, Mn. iv, 50; Hcat. i, 11, 7; flowing southwards, Suśr. i, 45; -*sthita*, mfn. standing with the face southwards, MārkP. **Dakshiṇâyana**, n. 'southward way,' way to Yama's quarter, MBh. xii, 996; 'sun's progress south of the equator,' the winter half-year, Gaut.; Mn. i, 67; MBh.; VarBṛS.; Pañcat.; BhP. v, 21, 3; mfn. situated in the sun's winter course (as an asterism), 23, 5 f. **Dakshiṇâranya**, n. 'southern forest,' N. of a forest, Hit. i, 2, $\frac{0}{1}$. **Dakshiṇârus**, mfn. wounded on the right side, L. **Dakshiṇârdhá**, m. the right or southern side, TS.; TBr.; ŚBr.; KātyŚr.; MBh.; R.; -*paścârdha*, m. = °*ṇa-p*°, MānŚr. vi, 2, 5; -*pūrvârdha*, m. = °*ṇa-p*°, i, 1, 2 & 7, 6; ĀpGṛ. ii, 6; °*ṇârdhâparârdha*, m. = °*ṇa-paścardha*, ŚāṅkhŚr. xviii, 24, 18. **Dakshiṇârdhya**, mfn. being on the right or southern side, TS. ii, vi; ŚBr.; -*pūrvârdhya*, mfn. being on the south-western side, Lāṭy. i, 10, 3. **Dakshiṇâvacara**, mfn. (an embryo) moving in the right part (of the womb), Lalit. vi, 7. **Dakshiṇâvarta**, mfn. turning (from the left) to the right (a conch-shell, Sāh.; *kuṇḍala*, BhP. v, 23, 5; a fruit, Bhpr. v, 1, 139; a woman's navel, Subh.); moving in the southern course (the sun), MBh. vi, 5671; m. a conch-shell opening to the right, Divyâv. viii, 490. **Dakshiṇâvartaka**, mf(*ikā*)n. turned to the right or southwards, MBh. xiii; AgP. xl, 28;

Hcat. i, 3, 964; (ī), f. Tragia involucrata, L. **Dakshiṇâśā**, f. 'southern quarter,' *-pati*, m. 'lord of D°,' Yama, Hemac.; *-rati*, f. 'delight of D°,' Canopy, ib. **Dakshiṇêtara**, mfn. 'other than right,' left, Kum. iv, 19. **Dakshiṇêti**, f. (=°*ṇâyana*) the sun's progress south of the equator, Jyot. (YV) 9. **Dakshiṇêrma**, mfn. broken on the right side (a cart), Pāṇ. v, 4, 126, Kāś. **Dakshiṇêrman**, mfn. (126) = °*ṇârus*, Bālar. vii, 11. **Dakshiṇôttara**, mf(*ā*)n. having the right lying on the other (the two hands), Gobh. i, 7, 4; right and left, ĀśvGṛ. iii, 2; southern and northern, KātyŚr.; MārkP.; (in comp.) Hcat. i, 3, 903 $\frac{a}{b}$; °*râyata*, mf(*ā*)n. extending from south to north, $\frac{875}{876}$; 903 $\frac{b}{}$; 9, 141 $\frac{a}{b}$; °*râyāma*, mfn. id., 5, 929. **Dakshiṇôttarin**, mfn. overhanging on the right side, ŚāṅkhŚr. i, xvii. **Dakshiṇôttāna**, mfn. having the right hand turned upwards, KātyŚr. viii, 2, 9; (the hands) of which the right is turned upwards, ŚāṅkhŚr. v, 8, 5; Gobh. iv, 3. **Dakshiṇôdag-dvāra**, mf(*ā*)n. having doors north and south, Āp. ii, 25, 5. **Dakshiṇôpakrama**, mfn. beginning on the right, MānŚr. i, 4, 1.

Dakshiṇā, f. of °*ṇa*, q. v.; °*ṇā* (old. instr.) ind. on the right or south (Pāṇ. v, 3, 36), on the right side of or southward from (abl.: ii, 3, 29), RV. ii, 27, 11; x, 17, 9; AV. (also *dáksh*°); VS.; TBr.; ŚBr.; KātyŚr.; ŚāṅkhŚr.; Lāṭy.; ChUp.; Kauś. **-kaparda**, see °*ṇatás-k*°. **-kāla**, m. the time of receiving the sacrificial fee, KātyŚr.; ŚāṅkhŚr. **-gavī**, f. pl. the cows given as a sacrificial fee, ĀpŚr. xii, 19, 6, Sch. **-jyotis** (*dáksh*°), mfn. brilliant by the sacrificial gift, AV. ix, 5, 22 ff. **-°tinayana** (°*ṇât*°), m. the Mantra with which the Dakshiṇā cows are driven southwards, ĀpŚr. xiii, 6, 9. **-tvá**, n. the state of the sacrificial gift, MaitrS. iv, 8, 3. **-°deśana** (°*ṇâd*°), n. thanksgiving, Divyâv. xviii, 200; (*ā*), f. id., xiii, 247. **-dvāra**, n. a door on the south, MānGṛ. ii, 11; mfn. having a door on the south, Kauś.; Gobh. **-nyāya**, mfn. = °*ṇato-ny*°, ŚāṅkhŚr. i, 1, 14. **-patha**, m. path of the Dakshiṇā cow (between the Śālā and the Sadas), ŚāṅkhŚr.; ĀśvŚr.; KātyŚr.; Lāṭy.; (°*ṇā-saṃcara*, Vait.) the southern region, Deccan, MBh.; Hariv. 5289; VarBṛS.; Suśr.; BhP.; Kathās.; Vet.; Hit.; see °*ṇâbdhi*. **-°pathika**, mfn. belonging to the Deccan, Hariv. 6144. **-pratyac**, mf(*tīcī*)n. 'south-western,' (*tīcī*), f. south-west, Gaut.; (with *diś*) MānGṛ. ii, 1, Sch.; (*tyak*), ind. south-westwards, 1; °*tyak-pravaṇa*, mfn. sloping south-westwards, ĀpGṛ. xvii, 1; °*tyag-apavarga*, mfn. terminating in the south-west, Kauś. 1. **-pravaṇa** (°*ṇā*°), mf(*ā*)n. sloping southwards, ŚBr.; KātyŚr.; ĀśvGṛ.; MānGṛ. ii, 11; Mn. iii; Yājñ. **-prashṭi**, m. the horse harnessed on the right side of the yoke-horses, ŚBr. v, 1, 4; ix, 4, 2; KātyŚr. **-praharaṇa** (°*ṇā*-), mfn. hurled to the right, MaitrS. iii, 2, 10. **-prāg-agra**, mfn. having the points turned to the south-east, ĀpŚr. xiv, 32, 3; ĀpGṛ. i, 15. **-bandha**, m. 'bondage of ritual reward,' one of the 3 states of bondage (in Sāṃkhya phil.), Tattvas. **-mukha**, mf(*ī*)n. standing with the face to the right or south, ŚāṅkhŚr.; KātyŚr.; Lāṭy.; ĀśvGṛ.; Mn.; R. **-mūrti**, m. a Tāntric form of Śiva; N. of a copyist of the 17th cent.; *-prayoga*, m. N. of a ch. of Tantras. iv; *-mantra*, m. N. of Śārad. xix; *-saṃhitā*, f. N. of a work, Tantras.; Ānand. 31, Sch.; *-stava*, m. or *-stotra*, n. 10 verses ascribed to Śaṃkara (explained by Viśva-rūpa or Surêśvara in a commentary with gloss by Rāma-tīrtha); °*ty-upanishad*, f. N. of an Up. **-yugyá**, m. the right yoke-horse, ŚBr. v, ix. **-°rha** (°*ṇâr*°), mfn. deserving the sacrificial fee, L. **-lipi**, v. l. for °*ṇa-l*°. **-vat** (*dáksh*°), mfn. giving sacrificial presents, RV. (Indra, iii, vi, ix); AV. xviii; abounding in sacrificial rewards (sacrifice), ŚBr.; Lāṭy.; MBh. **-váh**, mf(nom. *-vâṭ*)n. being borne to the right of the fire (the ladle), RV. iii, 6, 1. **-vṛít**, mfn. turning or going round to the right, i, 144, 1 (the ladle); ŚBr. vi–viii; TBr. i; ŚāṅkhŚr.; Kauś. **-vṛitta**, mfn. twisted from the left to the right, Āp. **-śiras**, mfn. having the head southwards, KātyŚr. xxii, 6, 4 & 15; Gobh. iii, 10, 27. **-śroṇi**, f. the right buttock, KātyŚr. xvii, 8, 24. **-saṃcara**, m., see *-patha*. **-sád**, see °*ṇa-s*°.

Dakshiṇāt, see °*ṇa*. **-sád**, mfn. sitting to the south, MaitrS. ii, 6. °**nād-vātá**, m. the south wind, 7.

Dakshiṇāhi, ind. far to the right or in the south (of, abl., Pāṇ. ii, 3, 29), v, 3, 37. °**ṇít**, ind. with the right hand, RV. v, 36, 4; cf. *pra-*. °**ṇī-√kri**, = °*ṇena* with √*kṛi*, BhP. iii, 24, 41; to give anything (acc.) as a sacrificial fee, Bālar. ii, 23. °**ṇíya**, mfn. (Pāṇ. v, 1, 69) = °*nyà*, AV. viii, 10, 4; ŚBr. iii f.; Hariv.; VarBṛS.; Mālav. ii, $\frac{10}{11}$; venerable, Lalit. xxvi, 26; Kāraṇḍ. xxiii, 205 & 208 f.; cf. *a-*. °**ṇyà**, mfn. (Pāṇ. v, 1, 69) worthy of the sacrificial fee, fit for a sacrificial gift, TBr. i, 3, 3; ii, 1; cf. *a-*.

दक्षत् **dákshat, dakshi**. See √*dah*.

Dákshu, °**kshús**, mfn. burning, blazing, RV. i f.

दगार्गल **dagârgala**, n. 'water-key (*daga* = *daka*),' examining the soil in searching for wells or rules for doing so, VarBṛS. liv; (*udag*°) cvii; N. of liv.

दगु **dāgu**, m. N., see *dāgavyāyani*.

दग्ध **dagdhá**, mfn. (√*dah*) burnt, scorched, consumed by fire, AV. iv, xviii; KātyŚr.; Mn. &c.; tormented, pained, consumed by grief or hunger, distressed, Ṛitus. i, 10; Amar. 24; Rājat.; dry, insipid, Śiksh.; inauspicious, PSarv.; miserable, execrable, Daś. vii, 290; Kād.; n. cauterisation (cf. *agni-*), Suśr. i, 11 f.; (*ā*), f. (scil. *diś*) the quarter where the sun remains overhead, L.; (scil. *tithi*) N. of certain inauspicious days; = *-ruhā*, L. **-kāka**, m. 'inauspicious crow,' a raven, L. **-jaṭhara**, n. the hungry stomach, Bhartṛ. iii, 22. **-putra** (°*dhá-*), mf(*ā*)n. whose son is burnt, Suparṇ. ix, 2. **-matsya**, m. a grilled fish, Bhpr. v, 10, 127. **-mandira-sāra**, mfn. one who has burned the best of mansions. **-maraṇa**, m. N. of an author, ŚārṅgP. cvi, 5. **-yoni**, mfn. having its source or origin destroyed. **-ratha**, m. N. of a Gandharva, W. **-ruha**, m. 'growing in ashes,' Clerodendrum phlomoides, L.; (*ā*), f. N. of a plant, L. **-varṇaka**, N. of a grass, Npr. **-vraṇa**, m. a burn, singe. **Dagdhâkshara**, an inauspicious letter (in a word), W. **Dagdhêshṭakā**, f. a burnt brick, L. **Dagdhôdara**, n. = °*dha-jaṭhara*, Hit. i, 4, 13.

Dagdhavya, mfn. to be burnt, Mn.; Yājñ.; MBh.

Dágdhṛi, m. one who burns (with acc.), RV. v, 9, 4; °*dhṛi*, a burner of (gen.), ŚBr. ii, 2; Mālav.

दघ् **dagh**, cl. 5. (Pot. °*ghnuyāt*; Prec. 3. sg. °*ghyās*; aor. Subj. 1. pl. °*ghma*) with *paścā* or °*cāt*, to fall short of (cf. *á-paścā-daghvan*), RV. i, 123, 5; vii, 56, 21; with *adhas*, to reach below the regular height, Kāṭh. viii, 12; to strike, Dhātup. xxvii, 26; to protect (cf. √*daṅgh*), ib.: cl. 4. *dághyati*, to go, Naigh. ii, 4; to flow, Nir. i, 9; cf. *ati-, ā-; pra-dághas*; δέχομαι. **Daghná**, mf(*ā*, *ī*)n. ifc. (Pāṇ. iv, 1, 15; v, 2, 37) 'reaching up to,' cf. *aṃsa-, aśva-, ā-, upa-kaksha-, upastha-, ūru-, kaṇṭha-, kulpha-, gulpha-, jānu-, nābhi-, mukha-, stana-*.

दङ्क्ष्णु **daṅkshṇú**, mfn. (√2. *daṃś*, 139, Vārtt. 4, Pat.) mordaceous, VS. xv; MaitrS. ii, 8, 10.

दङ्घ् **daṅgh**, cl. 1. °*ghati*, to keep off (derived fr. *daghná*), Dhātup.; to protect (cf. √*dagh*), ib.

दच्छद **dac-chada**, m. = *danta-cch*°, BhP.

दडी **daḍī**, v. l. for *dāḍī*, Kāś.

दण्ड **daṇḍá**, (= δένδρο-ν, hence cognate with *dāru* & √*drī*) m. (n. [cf. *ikshu-*], g. *ardharcâdi*) a stick, staff, rod, pole, cudgel, club, RV. &c. (staff given at investiture with the sacred thread, ŚBr. &c.; 'penis [with *vaitasá*],' xi, 5, 1, 1; 'trunk,' see *śuṇḍā-*; 'arm' or 'leg,' see *dor-, bāhu-*; 'tusk,' see *daṃshṭrā-*); = °*ḍakâsana*, BṛNārP. xxxi, 115 (n.); a stalk, stem (of a tree; cf. *ikshu-, ud-, khara-*), MBh. ii, 2390; the staff of a banner, 2079; iv, xiv; the handle (of a ladle, sauce-pan, fly-flap, parasol &c.), AitBr.; ŚBr. &c.; the steam of a plough, L.; 'a mast,' see *mahā-daṇḍa-dhara*; the cross-bar of a lute which holds the strings, ŚāṅkhŚr. xvii; the stick with which a lute is played, L.; a churning-stick (cf. °*ḍâhata*), L.; a pole as a measure of length (= 4 Hastas), VarBṛS. xxiv, 9; MārkP. il; N. of a measure of time (= 60 Vi-kalās), BrahmavP. ii; VarP.; BhavP.; N. of a staff-like appearance in the sky ('N. of a planet,' L.; cf. *-bhāsa*), VarBṛS.; N. of a constellation, xx, 2; VarBṛ.; Laghuj.; a form of military array (cf. *-vyūha*), L.; a line (cf. *-pāta*); a staff or sceptre as a symbol of power and sovereignty (cf. *nyasta-*), application of power, violence, Mn. vii f.; MBh.; power over (gen. or in comp.), control, restraint (cf. *vāg-, mano-, kāya-* [*karma-*, MārkP. xli, 22]; *tri-daṇḍin*), Subh.; embodied power, army (*kośa-*, du. 'treasure and army,' Mn. ix, 294; MBh.; Kir. ii, 12), Mn. vii; Ragh. xvii, 62; the rod as a symbol of judicial authority and punishment, punishment (corporal, verbal, and fiscal; chastisement and imprisonment, reprimand, fine), TāṇḍyaBr. xvii, 1; Mn.; MBh. &c. (cf. *guptá* & *gūḍha-*); pride, L.; m. a horse, L.; Punishment (son of Dharma and Kriyā, VP. i, 7, 27; MārkP. l); Yama, L.; Śiva, MBh. xii, 10361; N. of an attendant of the Sun, iii, 198; (g. *śivâdi* & *śaunakâdi*) N. of a man with the patr. Aupara, MaitrS. iii, 8, 7; TS. vi, 2, 9, 4; of a prince slain by Arjuna (brother of *-dhara*, identified with the Asura Krodha-hantṛi), MBh. i f., viii; of a Rakshas, R. vii, 5, 39; see °*ḍaka*; (*ā*), f. Hedysarum lagopodioides, Npr. **-kandaka**, m. N. of a bulb, L. **-kapālin**, mfn. carrying a staff and a skull, Hcat. ii, 1, 704. **-kamaṇḍalu**, m. a jar with a handle, Divyâv. i, 262 & 301; xviii, 343 (n.); xxxii, 63. **-kartṛi**, m. a punisher. **-karman**, n. punishment, Yājñ. ii, 275. **-kala**, n. N. of a metre. **-kalita-vat**, ind. like one driven by a stick, ĀpŚr. xi, 12, 6, Sch. **-kāka**, for *dagdha-k*°, W. **-kāshṭha**, n. a wooden staff, MBh. i; R. vii; Hariv.; Mṛicch. i, $\frac{41}{42}$; Śak. ii, $\frac{0}{1}$; vi, $\frac{8}{9}$; Mālav. iv, $\frac{15}{16}$. **-kuśa** or **-kūla**, m. pl. N. of a people, R. iv, 40, 25. **-ketu**, m. N. of a man, MBh. vii; BṛNārP. xxxvii. **-gaurī**, f. N. of an Apsaras, MBh. iii, 1784. **-grahaṇa**, n. 'taking the staff,' becoming an ascetic, W. **-grāha**, m. 'staff-bearer,' g. *revaty-ādi*. **-ghaṭanā**, f. 'waving a stick' and 'prostrating one's self (before an idol),' Siṇhās. Introd. 13. **-ghna**, mfn. striking with a stick, committing an assault, Mn. viii, 386. **-cakra**, n. = *-sthāna*, Mālav. i, $\frac{7}{8}$; Daś. viii, 205; N. of a mythical weapon, R. i, 29, 5. **-cchadana**, n. a room for utensils, Buddh. L. **-jita**, mfn. subdued by punishment. **-ḍhakkā**, f. N. of a drum or gong on which the hours are struck, L. **-tāḍana**, n. punishing with a stick, Āp. **-tāmrī**, f. = *t*°, L. **-tva**, n. the state of a stick, Bhāshāp. **-dāsa**, m. a slave or one enslaved for (non-payment of a) fine, Mn. viii, 415. **-dhara**, mfn. 'rod-bearer,' punisher (of, gen.), ix, 245; MBh. xii; R. vi; BhP.; m. a king, ix; Ragh. ix, 3; Rājat. iv; Yama, 655; a judge, vii, 1458; = *-mukha*, Daś. viii, 209; a door-keeper, Dharmaśarm. ii, 76; a mendicant, W.; a potter, W.; °*râdhipati*, m. a king who has full administrative powers, Rājat. iv, 655. **-dhāra**, mfn. = °*raka*, MBh. iii, 1596 (Yama); Kām.; Rājat. iv; a king, L.; Yama, L.; N. of a prince slain by Arjuna (brother of Daṇḍa and identified with the Asura Krodha-vardhana), MBh. i f., viii; of a son of Dhṛita-rāshṭra, i, 2738; pl. N. of a people, R. (G) ii, 88, 7. **-dhāraka**, mfn. 'rod-bearer,' administering justice, MBh. xii, 2510. **-dhāraṇa**, n. carrying a staff, PārGṛ. ii, 5, 11; applying the rod, punishment, MBh. i, iii; R. iv. **-dhārin**, mfn. = °*raka*, BhP. vi, 3, 5. **-dhṛik**, mfn. ifc. governing, iv, 21, 12. **-nāyaka**, m. 'rod-applier,' a judge, Hit. ii, 9, $\frac{0}{1}$ & $\frac{4}{5}$; = *-mukha*, Jain.; VarBṛS. lxxiii, 4; Rājat. vii; N. of an attendant of the Sun, L., Sch.; *-purusha*, m. a policeman, Caurap., Sch. **-nidhāna**, n. 'laying aside the rod,' pardoning, indulgence, MBh. xii, 6559 & 9964. **-nipātana**, n. application of the rod, punishing (with gen.), Kām. xiii, 17. **-niyoga**, m. infliction of punishment, Gaut. xii, 51. **-nīti**, f. application of the rod, administration of justice, judicature (as a science), Mn. vii, 43; Yājñ. i, 310; MBh. &c.; N. of a work, Ragh. i, 26, Sch.; Durgā, DevīP.; *-mat*, mfn. familiar with judicature, MBh. xii, 2699. **-netṛi**, m. 'rod-applier,' see *adhi-*; *-tva*, n. judicature, Mn. xii, 100 (BhP. iv, 22, 45). **-pa**, m. N. of a man, g. *naḍâdi*. **-pakshaka**, m. N. of a position of the hands, Hastar. **-parāyaṇa**, mfn. wanting a stick (for walking), Kāraṇḍ. xvi, 16. **-pāṃsula**, m. a door-keeper, L. **-pāṇi** (°*ḍá-*), mfn. (g. *āhitâgny-ādi*) staff-handed, ŚBr. xi; Kathās. liv; m. a policeman, Hāsy.; Yama, ShaḍvBr. v, 4; BhP. i, v; N. of the leader of 2 of Śiva's troops, KāśīKh. xxxii; of the father of Buddha's wife Go-pā, Lalit. xii; Suvarṇapr. xviii; of a Kāśi king, PadmaP.; of a physician, Bhpr. vii, 8, 137; of a prince (grandfather of Kshemaka), BhP. ix, 22, 42; VāyuP. ii, 37, 270 ff.; MatsyaP. l, 87; BrahmâṇḍaP.; (*khaṇḍ*° VP. iv, 21, 4.) **-pāta**, m. = *-nipātana*, v, 22, 17; a kind of fever, Bhpr. vii, 8, 82; dropping a line (in a manuscript); *-nipāta*, m. N. of a position of the feet in dancing, VP. v, 7, 46 (v. l. *caṇḍ*°). **-pātana**, n. = *-nip*°, Kām. viii, 76. **-pātin**, mfn. punishing (with loc.), R. i, 7, 13. **-pārushya**, n. actual violence, harsh punishment, Gaut.; Mn. viii, 278 & 301; Pañcat.; *-vat*, mfn. inflicting harsh punishment, Kām. xiv, 13. **-pāla**, °**laka**, m. 'superintendent of punishment or judicature,' see *pṛithivī-*; a door-keeper, W.; N. of a fish, L. **-pāśaka**, m. 'holding a noose to catch offenders, a policeman, Pañcat. ii, 4, $\frac{2}{3}$; Mudr. i, $\frac{8}{11}$. **-piṅgalaka**, m. pl. N. of a people to the north of Madhya-deśa, VarBṛS. xiv, 27. **-poṇa** (i.e. *pavana*), a strainer with a handle, Buddh. L. **-prajita** (°*ḍá*-), mfn. driven with a stick, ŚBr. xii, 4, 1, 10. **-praṇayana**, n. 'infliction of punishment,' N. of a ch. of PSarv. **-praṇāma**, m. a prostration of the body at full length (like a stick), Daś. ii, 29. **-pradāna**, n. donation of a staff (at investiture with the thread), ŚāṅkhGṛ. ii, 11, 4. **-bāhu**, m. N. of an attendant of Skanda, MBh. ix, 2575. **-bhaṅga**, m. omission of punishment, BhP. vi, 3, 2. **-bhaya**, n. dread of punishment, Nal. iv, 10. **-bhāj**, mfn. undergoing punishment (through, gen.), BhP. x, 64, 42; Yājñ. ii, $\frac{6}{5}$, 35. **-bhāsa**, m. N. of an appearance in the sky, Buddh. L. **-bhīti**, f. = *-bhaya*, Kām. ii, 43 (Hit.) **-bhṛit**, mfn. carrying a staff, W.; a potter, L.; Yama, VarVogay. vi, 21. **-matsya**, m. N. of a fish, Bhpr. v, 10, 118. **-mānava**, m. (Pāṇ. iv, 3, 130; 2, 104, Vārtt. 23, Pat.) 'staff-pupil,' a young Brāhman after *-pradāna*, R. ii, 32, 18. **-mātaṅga**, Tabernæmontana coronaria, Npr. **-mātha**, Pāṇ. iv, 4, 37, Kāś. **-mukha**, m. 'leader of a column or army,' a captain, general, Buddh. L. **-mukhya**, m. id., Kām. xvii, 49. **-yātrā**, f. a procession, bridal procession, L.; a military expedition, Hcar. iv, vi f. **-yāma**, m. a day, L.; Yama, L.; = *dakshiṇâśā-rati*, L. **-yoga**, m. = *-niy*°, Kām. ii, 43 (Hit.) **-leśa**, n. a small fine, Mn. viii, 51. **-vat**, mfn. (Pāṇ. v, 2, 115, Kāś.) carrying a staff, Hcat. i, 11, 566; furnished with a handle, KātyŚr. xxvi; having a large army, Ragh. xvii; Kām. xiii, 37; ind. like a stick, Vishṇ. xxviii, 5; (with *pra-ṇamya*, prostrating the body) in a straight line, AdhyR. Introd. 5. **-vadhá**, m. 'death by punishment,' capital punishment, ŚBr. v, 4, 4, 7. **-vācika**, mfn. actual or verbal (assault), Mn. viii, 6. **-vādin**, mfn. pronouncing judicial reprimand, W.; m. a door-keeper, L. **-vārita**, mfn. forbidden by threat of punishment, Pāṇ. ii, 1, 24, Vārtt. 5, Pat. **-vāladhi**, m. 'stick-tailed,' an elephant, L. **-vāsika**, m. a door-keeper, Buddh. L. **-vāsin**, m. id., L.; 'a village-head,' *a-daṇḍavāsika*, mfn. having no head (a village), Hcat. i, 9, 60 (AgP.) **-vāhin**, m. a policeman, Daś. xi, 249. **-vikalpa**, m. 'alternative of punishment,' discretionary punishment or fine, Mn. ix, 228. **-vishaya**, m. the region of Daṇḍaka, R. vii, 81, 18. **-vishkambha**, m. a stake to which is fastened the cord of a churning-stick. **-vīrya**, m. N. of a prince, Śatr. vi, 289. **-vṛikshaka**, m. Tithymalus antiquorum, L. **-vyūha**, m. arraying an army in columns, Mn. vii, 187. **-vrata-dhara**, mfn. = *-dhāraka*, BhP. iv, 13, 22. **-śatru, -śarman**, m. N. of two princes, Hariv. i, 38, 3. **-śrī**, for *caṇḍ*° (N. of a prince), VāyuP. ii, 37, 350. **-saṃkhyā**, f. N. of a ch. of PSarv. **-sena**, m. N. of a son of Vishvak-sena, Hariv. 1070; of another prince (= *-dhāra*), MBh. i, 544. **-sthāna**, n. a division of an army, Divyâv. xxxvi. **-hasta**, mfn. staff-handed, MBh. vi, 4959 (Yama); m. a door-keeper, W.; n. = *-mātaṅga*, L.; (*ā*, L.; *ī*, Bhpr. v, 2, 29), f. id. **Daṇḍâkhya**, m. called after a staff (see °*ḍaka*); called Daṇḍa, L., Sch.; n. a two-sided hall facing north and east, VarBṛS. liii, 39 & 41; N. of a Tīrtha, MBh. iii, 8157. **Daṇḍâghāta**, m. a blow with a stick, Kathās. liv, 203. **Daṇḍâjina**, n. sg. staff and dress of skin as mere outward signs of devotion, hypocrisy, deceit, Pāṇ. v, 2, 76. **Daṇḍâdaṇḍi**, ind. (4, 127 & ii, 2, 27, Kāś.) stick against stick (in fighting), Mn. iv, 121, Kull. **Daṇḍâdhipa, °pati**, m. a chief judge, Kathās. **Daṇḍânīka**, n. = °*ḍa-sthāna*, Mālav. v, 2. **Daṇḍâpatānaka**, m. tetanus, Suśr. ii, 1, 51; Bhpr. vii, 36, 172. **Daṇḍâpūpa**, 'stick and cake,' *-nyāya*, m. a method of reasoning in which a self-evident truth is illustrated by saying that a mouse which has eaten a stick is sure to eat a cake, Dāyakramas.; °*pūpāyita*, mfn. self-evident, Sch. **Daṇḍâpūpikā**, f. = °*pūpa-nyāya*, Sāh. x, 84. **Daṇḍâmitrā**, for *dattâm*°. **Daṇḍârta**, n. N. of a Tīrtha, MBh. iii, 8141. **Daṇḍâlasikā**, f. = °*ḍakâlasaka*, Npr. **Daṇḍâlu**, n. Dioscorea alata, W. **Daṇḍâvayava**, m. = °*ḍânīka*, Daś. viii, 11. **Daṇḍâśrama**, m. 'staff-condition,' asceticism, W.; °*min*, m. an ascetic, W. **Daṇḍâsana**, n. = °*ḍakâs*°, HYog. iv, 123 & 130; Yogas. ii, 46, Sch.; N. of an arrow, L. **Daṇḍâstra**, n. N. of a mythical weapon, R. i, 56, 9. **Daṇḍâhata**, n. 'struck by a churning-stick,' butter-milk, Bhpr. v, 13, 43. **Daṇḍêśa**, m. = °*ḍa-mukha*, Gal. **Daṇḍôtpala**, m. n. & (*ā*), f. N. of a plant, L. **Daṇḍôdyama**, m. lifting the stick against, threatening (ifc.), Yājñ. iii, 293; pl. application of power, R. v, 24, 34; Pañcat. i, 16, 9. **Daṇḍôpaghātam**, ind. so as to strike with a stick, Pāṇ. iii, 4, 48, Kāś.

Daṇḍaka (g. *ṛiśyâdi*), m. (n., g. *ardharcâdi*) ifc. 'a staff,' see *tri-*; a handle (of a parasol), L.; the beam (of a plough), L.; the staff of a banner, MBh. vii, ix; (Pāṇ. 3, 87, Kāś.) N. of a plant, Suśr. v, 7, 1; a row, line, ŚāṅkhŚr., Sch.; a class of metres the stanzas of which may extend from 4 × 27 to 4 × 999 syllables, Chandaḥs. vii, 33-36; HanRām-Up. 15; a kind of spasm, Car. vi, 28; Bhpr. vii, 36, 171 & 227; (°*ḍâkhya*) $\frac{171}{2}$; N. of a work relating to VS.; m. N. of a son of Ikshvāku (whose country was laid waste by the curse of Bhārgava, whose daughter he had violated; his kingdom in consequence became the °*kâraṇya*), MBh. xii (allusion only); Hariv. 637; BhP. ix, 6, 4; Kām. (v.l. *dāṇḍakya*); °*ṇḍa*, R. vii, 79, 15; VP. iv, 2, 4; VāyuP. ii, 26, 9; PadmaP. i; N. of a silly man, Bharat. xxv; of an Asura, Virac. x; pl. the inhabitants of °*kâraṇya*, MBh. ii, xiii; R.; Ragh.; VarBṛS.; n. = °*kâraṇya*, MBh. xiii; R.; BhP. ix, 11, 19; Prasannar. vii, 77 (pl.); (*ā*), f. id., R.; Ragh. xiii (colophon); VarBṛS.; Mcar. iv, $\frac{4}{5}$; (*ikā*), f. a stick, staff, Mn. v, 99, Kull. (ifc.); a line, Naish. i, 21, Sch.; a rope, L.; a string of pearls, L. **Daṇḍakâraṇya**, n. the Daṇḍaka forest in the Deccan, MBh. iii, 8183; Hariv. 638; R.; Ragh.; Hit.; *-prasthāna*, n. N. of Abhirāmam. iv. **Daṇḍakâlasaka**, m. a kind of dysentery, Car. vi, 10; Rājat. vii. **Daṇḍakā-vana**, n. = °*kâraṇya*, R. ii, 30; VarBṛS. xiv, 16. **Daṇḍakâsana**, n. lying prostrate on the ground, Sarvad. xv, 301.

Dáṇḍana, m. a cane (?), AV. xii, 2, 54; n. beating, chastising, punishing, Yājñ. (also *a-*); MBh. xii, 431; Kām.; Kulârṇ. i, 78; cf. *a-dharma-*. **-vidhi**, m. the practice of inflicting punishment, Bālar. v, 63.

Daṇḍanīya, mfn. to be punished, Yājñ.; Bālar. v.

Daṇḍaya, Nom. °*yati*, to chastise, punish (with acc. of fine, Mn. ix, 234; Pat. on Pāṇ. i, 1, 1, Vārtt. 12 & 7, Vārtt. 1; on ii, vi, viii, cf. i, 4, 51, Siddh. & Vop. v, 6), Mn. viii f.; Yājñ. i f.; MBh. xii &c.

Daṇḍāya, Nom. (p. °*yamāna*) to stand erect, W.

Daṇḍāra, m. 'having a flag-staff,' a carriage, L.; 'having oars,' a boat, L.; a potter's wheel (cf. °*ḍa-bhṛit*), L.; 'having a staff,' a bow, L.; an elephant in rut, L. °**raka**, ifc. the pole of a well (or °*ḍâraka*, 'stick and spokes of a water-wheel'?), Kād. v, 840. **Daṇḍi**, m. pl. N. of a family, Pravar. vii, 2.

Daṇḍika, mfn. (g. *purohitâdi*) carrying a stick, Pāṇ. v, 2, 115, Kāś.; iii, 1, 7, Kār., Sch.; = *dāṇḍ*°, MBh. vi, 439; m. a policeman, Gaut.; N. of a fish, L.

Daṇḍita, mfn. punished, Pañcat. i, 1, 74; Hit.

Daṇḍin, mfn. (Pāṇ. v, 2, 115, Kāś.) carrying a stick, ŚBr. xiii; KātySr.; ŚāṅkhŚr.; Mn. &c.; m. a Brāhman in the 4th stage of his life (= *tri-*), Kālid.; N. of an order of ascetics founded by Śaṃkarâcārya, W.; a door-keeper, policeman, Nal. iv, 25; Kād. i, 225; an oarsman, W.; Yama, Kām. ii, 36; Mañju-śrī, L.; (g. *naḍâdi*) N. of a son of Dhṛita-rāshṭra, MBh. i, 2738; of a door-keeper of the Sun, R. vii, 23, 2, 9 & 11; of the author of Daś., Kāvyâd. and some 3rd work; Artemisia Abrotanum, L.; pl. N. of a family, Pravar. ii, 2, 2. °**ḍi-datta**, m. du. Daṇḍin & Datta, Pāṇ. viii, 2, 2, Vārtt. 2, Pat. (not in ed.) °**ḍi-mat**, mfn. having club-bearers (an army), iii, 1, 7, Kār., Sch. °**ḍi-muṇḍa**, m. staffed-handed and bald (Śiva), MBh. xii, 10358.

Daṇḍiman, m. abstr. of °*ḍá*, g. *pṛithv-ādi*.

Daṇḍya, mfn. = °*ḍanīya*, Āp.; Gaut.; Pāṇ. v, 1, 66; Mn. &c. (with acc. of fine, viii; Yājñ. i, 66; ii).

दत् *dát*, m. (taking the form *dánta* in the strong cases, Pāṇ. vi, 1, 63) a tooth, RV. (nom. *dán*, x, 115, 2); AV.; VS.; ŚBr.; ĀśvGṛ.; BhP.; often ifc. (Pāṇ. v, 4, 141-145), see *a-* &c.; *a-dat-ka*; *dac-chada*; [cf. ὀδόντ-, Lat. *dens* &c.] **-vát**, mfn. furnished with teeth, RV. i, 189, 5; AV. iv, 3, 4; (*tī*), f. with *rájju*, 'rope with teeth,' a snake, 2; vii, 108, 1; xix, 47, 8. **Dad-āyudha**, mfn. using the teeth as a weapon, BhP. x, 17, 6.

दत्त 1. *datta*, mfn. (√*de*) protected, L.; honoured, L.

दत्त 2. *dattá*, mfn. (√1. *dā*) given, granted, presented, RV. i f., viii, x; AV. &c.; placed, extended, W.; (with *putra*) = °*ttrima*, MBh. xiii, 2616; m. a short form [Pāṇ. v, 3, 83, Kār., Pat.] of names so terminating (*yajña-, deva-, jaya-* &c.) which chiefly are given to Vaiśya men, vi, 2, 148; v, 3, 78 ff., Kāś.; Mn. ii, 32, Kull.; Sāh. vi, 141; (Pāṇ. vi, 1, 205, Kāś.) N. of an ascetic, Tāṇḍya-Br. xxv, 15, 3 (snake-priest); MBh. xii, 10875; BhP. iv, 19, 6; = °*ttâtreya*, 1, 15; vi, 15, 14; N. of a son of Rājâdhideya Sūra, Hariv. 2033; of a sage in the 2nd Manv-antara, 417; of the 7th Vāsudeva, Jain. L.; of the 8th Tīrtha-kara of the past Utsarpiṇī, ib.; n. a gift, donation, ChUp. v; BhP. i, 5, 22; (*ā*), f. N. of a woman, Pat.; Kāś. (see *dātteya*); (names so terminating given to *veśyās*, Sāh. vi, 141); cf. *á-*. **-karṇa**, mfn. ifc. giving ear to, listening to, Kād. iii, 759. **-kshaṇa**, mfn. to whom occasion or a festival has been given, BhP. iii, 3, 21. **-gītā**, f. N. of a work. **-daṇḍin**, m. du. D° & D°, Pāṇ. viii, 2, 2, Vārtt. 2, Pat. (not in ed.) **-drishṭi**, mfn. directing the eye towards, looking on (loc.), Śak. i, 7 (v.l.); Kathās. lxxvii, 22. **-nṛityôpahāra**, mfn. presented with the compliment of a dance, Megh. 32. **-pūrvôkta-śāpa-bhī**, mfn. causing fear by a previously uttered curse, Kathās. lxxxiii, 23. **-prâṇa**, mfn. sacrificing life. **-bhujaṃga-stotra**, n. N. of a hymn ascribed to Śaṃkarâcārya. **-mahiman**, m. another work ascribed to him. **-mārga**, mfn. having the road ceded, Megh. 45 (v.l.) **-vat**, mfn. one who has given. **-vara**, mfn. presented with the choice of a boon, Hariv.; R. i, 1, 22; granted as a boon, vi, 19, 61. **-śatru, -śarman**, for *daṇḍa-*. **-śulkā**, f. (a bride) for whom a dowry has been paid, Mn. ix, 97. **-hasta**, mfn. ifc. having a hand given for support, supported by, Sarvad. iv, 39; shaking hands, W. **Dattâksha**, mf(*ī*)n. = °*tta-drishṭi*, Sāh. iii, 114. **Dattâkshara**, mf(*ā*)n. having one syllable added, x, $\frac{1}{2}\frac{4}{}$. **Dattâtaṅka**, mfn. causing fear to (gen.), Ratnâv. ii, 2. **Dattâtman**, mfn. (with *putra*, a son deserted by his parents) who gives himself (for adoption as a child), Yājñ. ii, 131; m. N. of one of the Viśve-devās, MBh. xiii, 4359. **Dattâtri**, see *dambholi*. **Dattâtreya**, m. N. of a sage (son of Atri by Anasūyā who favoured Arjuna Kārtavīrya), MBh. iii, xii f.; Hariv.; BhP. ix, 23, 23 (Brahmā, Vishṇu, and Śiva propitiated by his penance became in portions of themselves severally his sons Soma, Datta, and Dur-vāsas; hence worshipped as representing the Triad); VP. i, 10, 10; iv, 11, 3; MārkP. xvi ff.; BṛNārP. xxi; N. of an author, VP. iii, 9, 31, Sch.; Ānand. 2 & 96, Sch.; pl. N. of a family, Pravar. iii, 1; °*yâshṭôttara-śata-nāma-stotra*, n. N. of a ch. of BrahmâṇḍaP.; °*yôpanishad*, f. N. of an Up. **Dattâtreyīya**, n. 'story of °*treya*,' N. of MārkP. xix. **Dattâdatta**, mfn. given and received. **Dattâdara**, mfn. showing respect; treated with respect. **Dattânapakarman**, n. non-delivery of gifts, W.; cf. Mn. viii, 4. **Dattâpahṛita**, mfn. given and taken again, W.; cf. Yājñ. ii, 176. **Dattâpradānika**, mfn. relating to the non-delivery of a gift, $\frac{176}{}$. **Dattâmitra**, m. N. of a Sauvīra prince, MBh. i, 5537; (*ā*), f. N. of a place (cf. *dattâmitrīya*), R. iv, 43, 20 (v.l. *daṇḍâm*°). **Dattâvadhāna**, mfn. attentive, Pañcat. ii, 2, $\frac{1}{2}$; Kathās. xxiv, 98. **Dattâsana**, mfn. having a seat given. **Dattairaṇḍapallaka**, N. of a district in the Deccan. **Dattôttara**, mfn. answered, Sarvad. xv, 211 (*-tva*, n. abstr.) **Dattôpanishad**, f. N. of an Up.

Dattaka, mfn. (with *putra*) = °*ttrima*, Pravar.; Yājñ. ii, 130; Mn. ix, 141, Kull.; m. a form of names terminating in *-datta*, Pāṇ. v, 3, 83, Kār., Pat.; N. of an author, Vātsyāy. Introd. & ii, 10, 44; of Māgha's father, Śiś. (colophon). **-candrikā**, f. N. of a work. **-mīmāṅsā**, f. another work.

Dattā, f. of °*ttá*. **-kārishagandhyā**, f. du. D° & K°, Pāṇ. ii, 4, 26, Vārtt. 6, Pat. **-gārgyâyaṇī**, f. du. D° & G°, ib. **Datti**, f. (vii, 4, 46) a gift, Ragh. **Dattika**, °**ttiya**, °**ttila**, m. forms of names terminating in *-datta*, Pāṇ. v, 3, 83, Kār., Sch. **Datteya**, m. Indra, L. °**ttogni**, °**ttoni**, see *dambholi*.

Dáttra, n. (Indra's) gift, RV. iii, 36, 9; iv, 17, 6; viii, 49, 2. **-vat** (*dátt*°), mfn. rich in gifts, vi, 50, 8.

Dattrima, mfn. received by gift (son, slave), Mn.

Dattvā, ind. p. √*dā*, q. v.; cf. *á-*. **-dāna** (°*ttvâd*°), n. resumption of a gift, Buddh. L.

Dad, cl. 1. °*dati*, see √*dā*; mfn. ifc. see *āyurdád*. **Dada**, mf(*ā*)n. (Pāṇ. iii, 1, 139) 'giving,' see *abhayam-*; *dhanam-dadā*. **Dadana**, n. giving, L.

Dadāti, m. a gift, Gaut. v, 19.

Dadi, mfn. giving, bestowing (with acc.), RV. i f., iv, 24, 1; vi, 23, 4 (Pāṇ. ii, 3, 69, Kāś.); viii; x, 133, 3.

Daditṛi, m. a giver (preserver?), VS. vii, 14.

दददस् *dadadás*, ind. (onomat.) imitative sound of a thunder's roaring, ŚBr. xiv, 8, 2, 4.

ददरि *dadari*, N. of a river, Rasik. xii, 4.

ददायुध *dad-āyudha*. See *dát*.

दद्रृत् *dadṛit*, mfn. (√*dṛī*) bursting or causing to burst, Pāṇ. iii, 2, 178, Vārtt. 3, Pat.

Dadru, a tortoise, Uṇ. vr.; f. (also *dara°*, Uṇ. k.) = *°drū*, Suśr. i, 11 & 45; v, 8. **– kushṭha**, n. id., ii, 5; iv, 31. **– ghna**, m. (also *dara°*) = *°drū-*, L.; Psoralea corylifolia, L. **– nāśinī**, f. 'removing leprosy,' N. of an insect, L. (v. l. *dard°*). **– roga**, m. = *dadrū*, Hcat. i, 8, 455 & 11, 245. **– rogin**, mfn. leprous (also *dard°*, L.), 8, 444; 11, 232 & 244.

Dadruka, m. = *°drū*, L. **°druṇa**, mfn. (g. *pāmâdi*) leprous (also *dard°*, L.), 8, 456.

Dadrū, f. (Pāṇ. v, 2, 100, Vārtt. 1 & Pat.) a cutaneous eruption, kind of leprosy (also *dard°*, Uṇ. i, 92 & *dardū*, Sch.), Suśr. iv, 9; VarBṛS. xxxii, 14. **– ghna**, mfn. 'removing leprosy,' Cassia Tora or alata, L. **– rogin**, mfn. = *°dru-*, L., Sch. (v. l. *dard°*).

Dadrūṇa, mfn. = *°druṇa*, L., Sch. (also *dard°*).

दद्रृशानपवि *dadṛiśānâ-pavi*, mfn. (√*dṛiś*) having visible fellies, RV. x, 3, 6.

दध् *dadh* (redupl. of √*dhā*), cl. 1. *°dhate*, to hold, Dhātup. ii, 7; to give, ib.: Intens. 2. sg. Impv. *dādaddhi*, Pāṇ. viii, 2, 37, Kāś.

Dadha, mfn. (iii, 1, 139) 'giving,' see *iḍā-*, *ilā-*.

Dadhana, n. 'putting,' see *antar-*.

1. **Dádhi**, mfn. (2, 171, Vārtt. 3) giving, RV. x, 46, 1; preserving (with acc.), Vop.; n. a house, L.

Dadhán, see 2. *dádhi*. **– vát**, mfn. containing coagulated milk, RV. vi, 48, 18.

2. **Dádhi**, n. (replaced in the weakest forms by *°dhán* [Pāṇ. vii, 1, 75]: instr. &c. *°dhnā́*, *°dhné*, *°dhnás*; loc. *°dhani*, ĀśvGṛ. i, 24, 5 & ŚvetUp. i, 5, or *°dhni*, [ifc.] Suśr. vi, 40, 150) coagulated milk, thick sour milk (regarded as a remedy; differing from curds in not having the whey separated from it), RV. &c.; turpentine, L.; the resin of Shorea robusta, L. **– karṇa**, m. 'milk-ear,' N. of a cat, Pañcat. iii, 2, 5/6 & 9/10 (Hit. ii); v. l. for *adh°*. **– kulyā**, f. a stream of *d°*, R. i, 53, 3. **– kūrcikā**, f. mixture of boiled and *d°* milk, Madanav. **– kra**, m. N. of a man, Pravar. vi, 3 (Kāty.) **– krā́**, m. (Naigh. i, 14; Nir. ii, 27 f. & x, 31) N. of a divine horse (personification of the morning Sun; addressed in RV. iv, 38-40; vii, 44), iii, 20; x, 101, 1; *°krā́-vatī*, f. (scil. *ṛic*) the verse iv, 39, 6 (AV. xx, 137, 3), MaitrS. i, 5, 13. **– krā́van**, m. = *-krā́*, RV. iv, 39 f.; vii, 41 & 44; TS. ii. **– graha**, m. a cup with *d°*, Jaim. iv, 4, 8; *-pātra*, n. the vessel used for taking up *d°*, ĀpŚr. xii, 2, 1. **– ghana**, m. 'thickened *d°*,' curds, Pāṇ. iii, 3, 77, Kāś. **– gharmá**, m. a warm oblation of *d°*, ŚBr. xiv; KātyŚr.; ĀśvŚr.; ŚāṅkhŚr.; Lāṭy.; *-homa*, m. id., Vait. **– cāra**, m. a churning-stick, L. **– ja**, mfn. produced from or on *d°*, L.; n. fresh butter, L. **– drapsá**, m. a globule of thickened *d°*, ŚBr. ix; ĀśvGṛ. i, 17, 7. **– dhānī**, f. a vessel for holding *d°*, Āp. **– dhenu**, f. a cow represented by *d°* (offered to priests), VarP. cvi; BhavP. ii, 168. **– nadī**, f. N. of a river, KapSaṃh. xx. **– payas**, n. du. *d°* and milk, Pāṇ. ii, 4, 14. **– parṇa**, m. N. of a man, BrahmaP. ii, 12 & 18, 26. **– piṇḍa**, m. = *-ghana*, Gal. **– puccha**, m. 'milk-tail,' N. of a jackal, Pañcat. iii, 14, 4/5. **– pushpikā**, f. 'milk-flower,' Clitoria Ternatea, L. **– pushpī**, f. the plant *kola-śimbī*, L. **– pūpaka**, m. N. of a cake made of *d°*, Madanav. **– pūraṇa**, m. N. of a Nāga, L., Sch. **– pūrva-mukha**, see *-m°*. **– pṛishātaka**, N. of a mixture made with *d°*, PārGṛ. ii, 16, 3. **– phala**, m. Feronia elephantum (its fruit having the acid taste of *d°*), L. **– bhaksha**, m. food prepared from *d°*, Lāṭy. ii, xii; mfn. eating *d°*, Pañcar. iv, 8, 41. **– bhāṇḍa**, n. = *-dhānī*, Hit. iii, 5, 1/2. **– maṇḍa**, m. whey, Rasar.; *°dôda*, mfn. having whey as liquid (an ocean), BhP. v; *°dôdaka*, mfn. id., MBh. vi, 443; VP. ii, 4, 57 f. **– mantha**, m. a beverage obtained by churning *d°*, Kauś. 40; ĀśvGṛ. ii, 5, 2 (pl.) **– manthana**, n. the churning of *d°*. **– mukha**, m. 'milk-faced,' a kind of snake, Suśr. v, 4; N. of a Nāga, MBh. i, v; Hariv. 9503; of a Yaksha, W.; of a monkey (brother-in-law of Su-grīva), MBh. iii, 16275; R. v, 1 & 59; (*-pūrva-m°*) 63, 20; vi, 6 & (metrically *°dhī-*) 7, 32; (also *°dhi-vaktra*, v f.) **– vaktra**, see *-mukha*. **– vat** (*dádh°*), mfn. prepared with *d°*, AV. xviii, 4, 17. **– vāmana**, m. 'milk-dwarf,' m. N. of a mystic person, Tantras. ii, iv. **– vāri**, mfn. having *d°* as liquid (an ocean), Hemac. **– vāhana**, m. N. of a prince (son of Aṅga and father of Divi-ratha), MBh. xii, 1796; Hariv. 1693 f.; VāyuP. ii, 37, 100; MatsyaP. iii, 91 f.; (*adh°* AgP.); of a king of Campā, Jain. **– vidarbha**, for *daśī-*. **– śara**, m. = *-maṇḍa*, W. **– śoṇa**, m. a monkey, L. **– saktu**, m. pl. barley-meal with *d°*, Kauś.; ĀśvGṛ. iii, 5, 5 & 10; MBh. xiii, 5049. **– samudra**, m. the *d°* ocean (cf. *-vāri*), Sāṃkhyas. vi, 52, Anir. **– sambhava**, mfn. produced by *d°*, Mn. v, 10; n. fresh butter, Gal. **– sāra**, n. id., L. **– skanda**, n. N. of a Tīrtha, RevāKh. **– sneha**, m. = *-maṇḍa*, L. **– sveda**, m. butter-milk, L.

Dadhika, ifc. for *°dhi*, g. *ura-ādi*.

Dadhittha, m. = *°dhi-phala*, Gobh. i, 5, 15 (the wood of which is not allowed to be used in sacrifices); = *-rasa*, Suśr. vi, 21, 4. **– rasa**, m. the resin of D°, 49, 24. **Dadhitthâkhya**, m. n. id., L.

Dadhishāyya, n. (for *didh°*) clarified butter, Uṇ.

Dadhisya, Nom. *°yati*, = *°dhīya*, Pāṇ. vii, 1, 51, Siddh. **°dhyasya**, Nom. *°yati*, id., ib.

Dadhīca, m. = *°dhy-ác* (devoted himself to death that Indra might slay Vṛitra with the thunderbolt fabricated by Tvashṭṛi out of his bones), MBh. i, iii, ix (father of Sārasvata by Sarasvatī, 2929 ff.), xii; (blamed Daksha, q. v.), VāyuP. i, 30, 103 ff.; KūrmaP. i, 15, 6 ff. (v. l. *°ci*); author with the patr. Pāthnya, Anukr. on Kāṭh. xvi, 4. **– kshupa-saṃvāda**, m. dialogue between D° & Ksh°, LiṅgaP. i, 35.

Dadhīci, m. = *°ca*, MBh. xii, 10283 ff. (blaming Daksha); VarBṛS. lxxx, 3. **°cy-asthi**, n. 'D°'s bones,' the thunderbolt, L.; the diamond, L.

Dadhī-mukha. See *dadhi-m°*.

Dadhīya, Nom. (Pāṇ. viii, 4, 68, Vārtt. 3, Pat.; Pot. *°yāt*) to like *dádhi*, ĀpŚr. (KātyŚr., Sch.)

Dadhy, in comp. for *°dhi*. **– agra**, n. = *°dhi-maṇḍa*, W. **– ác**, m. (nom. *-áṅ*, acc. *-áñcam*; dat. *°dhīcé*, gen. *°dhīcás*; cf. Pāṇ. vi, 1, 170) 'sprinkling *dádhi*' (cf. *°dhi-krā́* & *ghṛitâcī*) N. of a mythical Ṛishi or sacrificer (RV. i, 80, 16 & [called Aṅgiras] 139, 9; [*āṅgirasa*] TāṇḍyaBr. xii, 8; son of Atharvan [cf. *ātharvaṇá*], RV. vi, 16, 14; BhP. iv, 1, 42; having the head of a horse and teaching the Aśvins to find in Tvashṭṛi's house the *mádhu* or Soma, RV. i, 116 f. & 119; ix, 108, 4; favoured by Indra [x, 48, 2] who slays 99 Vṛitras or foes with a thunderbolt made of his bones, i, 84, 13; BhP. vi, 11, 20; viii, 20, 7; propounder of the Brāhmaṇa called *mádhu*, ŚBr. iv, xiv; BhP. vi, 9, 50 ff.) **– anna**, n. rice prepared with *d°*, Yājñ. i, 288. **– ākara**, m. = *°dhi-samudra*, L. **āśir** (*dádh°*), mfn. mixed with *d°* (Soma), RV. i, v, vii; ix, 22, 3; 63, 15; 101, 12. **– āhva**, *°hvaya*, m. the resin of Pinus longifolia, L. **– uttara**, n. = *-agra*, Hariv. 4216; Suśr. i, 43, 4 f.; (*ā*), f. bulb-milk, Gal.; *-ga*, n. = *°dhy-uttara*, L. **– uda**, mfn. = *°dhi-vāri*, L. **– ódana**, m. (Pāṇ. ii, 1, 34, Kāś.) boiled rice mixed with *d°*, ŚBr. xiv; Yājñ. i, 303.

दधिषु *dadhishú*, *°shū-pati*. See *didh°*.

दधृष् *dadhṛish*, mfn. (√*dhṛish*) bold, Bhaṭṭ. vi, 117 (nom. *°dhṛik*); (*°dhṛík*), ind. (Pāṇ. iii, 2, 59) strongly, boldly, RV. v, 66, 3; viii, 82, 2; x, 16, 7. **°shá**, mfn. bold, iii, 42, 6. **°shi**, see *dā́dh°*. **°shváṇi**, mfn. bold, viii, 61, 3.

दध्न *dadhna*, m. N. of Yama, L.

दध्यच् *dadhy-ác*, *-anna*, &c. See above.

दध्यानी *dadhyānī*, f. N. of a plant, L.

दन् *dán*, *dánas*. See *dát*, 2. & 1. *dam*.

दनायुस् *danāyus*, *°yū́*. See *dánu*.

दनीध्वंस *danīdhvansa*, mfn. (fr. Intens. of √*dhvaṇs*), Pāṇ. ii, 4, 74, Kāś.

दनु *dánu*, f. N. of a daughter of Daksha (by Kaśyapa [or *Danā́yū*, ŚBr. i, 6, 3, 9], mother of the Dānavas), MBh. i, 2520 ff.; Hariv.; R. iii, 20; VP. &c.; VarBṛS.; m. N. of a son of Śrī (also called Dānava; originally very handsome, but changed into a monster [*kabandha*] by Indra for having offended him), R. iii f. **– kabandha**, m. the monster D°, Mcar. iv, 1/2. **– ja**, m. 'born from D°,' a Dānava, BhP. vi, 9, 39; *-dvish*, m. 'Dānava-enemy,' a god, L., Sch.; *°jā-ri*, m. id., W.; *°jêndra*, m. a Dānava prince, Vcar. **– sambhava**, m. = *-ja*, MārkP. **– sūnu**, m. id., L.

Danā́yus, f. N. of a daughter of Daksha (named with Danu), MBh. *°yū́*, m., see s. v. *dánu*.

दन्त *dánta*, m. (fr. &) = *dát*, RV. vi, 75, 11; AV. &c. (n., R. vi, 82, 28; ifc. *ā* [Kathās. xxi; Caurap.] or *ī* [MBh. ix; Mṛicch. x, 13; VarBṛS.; Ghaṭ.], Pāṇ. iv, 1, 55); the number 32, Gaṇit.; an elephant's tusk, ivory, MBh.; R. &c.; the point (of an arrow? *atharī*), RV. iv, 6, 8; the peak or ridge of a mountain, Haravij. iv, 32; Dharmaśarm. vii, 32; an arbour Śiś. iv, 40; a pin used in playing a lute, Haravij. i, 9; (*ī*), f. = *°tikā*, Suśr.; VarBṛS.; (in music) N. of a composition; cf. *ibha-dantā*; *kuḍmala-* & *krūra-dantī* &c. **– karshaṇa**, m. 'teeth-injuring,' the lime, L. **– kāra**, m. an ivory worker, R. ii. **– kāshṭha**, n. a small piece of the wood (of particular trees) used for cleaning the teeth, MBh. xiii &c.; cleaning the teeth with the *danta-kāshṭha*, 4996; VarP.; m. N. of various trees the wood of which is used for cleaning the teeth (Flacourtia sapida, L.; Asclepias gigantea, Ficus indica, Acacia Catechu, Pongamia glabra, Terminalia alata), Npr.; *°shṭhâbhakshaṇa*, n. 'omitting to use the *d°*,' N. of VarP. cxxxi. **– kāshṭhaka**, m. Tabernæmontana coronaria, L. **– kumāra**, m. N. of a man. **– kūra**, N. of a place, MBh. v, 23, 24 & 48, 76. **– krūra**, m. N. of a prince, vii, 70, 5. **– grāhi-tā**, f. the state of injuring the teeth, Suśr. i, 45. **– gharsha**, m. chattering of the teeth, MārkP. xliii, 22. **– ghāṭa**, *°ṭaka*, m. = *-kāra*, Kathās. lxxv (Vet. i, 8/9). **– ghāta**, m. a bite, Sāh. iii, 8 b. **– cāla**, m. looseness of the teeth, Suśr. iv, 39. **– cchada**, m. (Kāś. on Pāṇ. iii, 3, 118 & vi, 4, 96) 'tooth-cover,' a lip, Bhartṛ.; Ṛitus. &c.; (*ā*), f. Momordica monadelpha (its red fruit being compared to the lips), Npr.; *°dôpamā*, f. id., L. **– cchadana**, n. = *°da*, Gal. **– cchedana**, n. biting through, Bhpr. v, 11, 168. **– janman**, n. growth of the teeth, Yājñ. iii, 23. **– jāta**, mf(*ā*, Pāṇ. iv, 1, 52, Vārtt. 1)n. (vi, 2, 171; g. *āhitâgny-ādi*) = *jāta-danta*, Mn. v, 58; (*a-*, neg.) ĀśvGṛ. iv, 4, 24. **– jāha**, n. the root of a tooth, g. *karṇâdi*. **– darśana**, n. (a dog's) showing the teeth, MBh. v, 2652. **– dyut**, f. brightness of the teeth, Bālar. v, 66. **– dhāva**, m. cleaning the teeth, BhP. xi, 27, 35. **– dhāvana**, n. id., Kauś.; Gaut.; Mn. iv; Yājñ. i; MBh. &c.; = *-pavana*, R. ii; Suśr. iv, 22; Pāṇ. vi, 2, 150, Kāś.; GarP.; N. of a ch. of PSarv.; m. Acacia Catechu, L.; Mimusops Elengi, L.; a kind of *karañja*, L.; *-prakaraṇa*, n. N. of Parāś. i, 48/49, 5; *-vidhi*. m. N. of Smṛitik. iv, 2, 1; of a ch. of Smṛityarth.; of Bhpr. iv, 24 ff. **– dhāvanaka**, m. N. of a tree, Kauś. 36. **– nishkāsita**, mfn. showing the teeth (a jackal), Hit. iii, 7, 4/5 (v. l.) **– pattra**, n. a kind of ear-ring, Kum. vii, 23; Kād.; Hcar. i, 387; Bālar. v, 76; Nom. *°ttrati*, to represent that ear-ring, Prasannar. vii, 61. **– pattraka**, n. a kind of jasmine (its petals being compared to the teeth), L.; (*ikā*), f. an ivory ear-ring, Śiś. i, 60; a comb, MBh. i, 3, 157, Sch. **– pavana**, n. 'tooth-cleaner,' a small piece of wood (= *-kāshṭha*), Car. i, 5; Suśr. iv, 24. **– pāta**, m. the falling out of the teeth, VarBṛS. lxvi, 5. **– pāli**, f. an ivory hilt (of a sword), Vāsav. 487. **– pālī**, f. the gums, VarBṛS. lxviii, 97. **– pāvana**, n. = *-dhāva*, Pañcad. ii, 45. **– pupputa**, m. gumboil, Suśr. i, 25. **– pupputaka**, m. id., ii, 16; iv, 22. **– pura**, n. 'city of Buddha's tooth,' the capital of Kaliṅga, Jain. &c. **– pushpa**, n. Strychnos potatorum, L. **– prakshālana**, n. = *-dhāva*, Āp.; Gobh.; = *-pavana*, KātyŚr. viii, 9; Āp.; PārGṛ. **– praveshṭa**, a case round an elephant's tusk, Śiś. xviii, 47. **– phala**, m. Feronia elephantum, L.; n. = *-pushpa*, L.; (*ā*), f. long pepper, L.; N. of a gourd, Gal. **– bīja**, m. pomegranate, L.; (*ā*), f. id., L.; N. of a gourd, L. **– bījaka**, m. = *°ja*, L. **– bhaṅga**, m. fracture of the teeth, Suśr. ii, 16; Pañcat. i; Kām. xiv; Pañcad. **– bhāga**, m. the fore-part of an elephant's head (where the tusks appear), L.; part of a tooth, W. **– madhya**, n. the space between an elephant's tusks, Gal. **– maya**, mfn. made of ivory, Mn. v, 121. **– mala**, n. impurity of the teeth, L. **– māṇsa**, n. the gums, Suśr. i, 35; ii, 16. **– mūlá**, n. = *-jāha*, VS. xxv, 1; VPrāt.; APrāt.; Suśr.; = *-śopha*, L. **– mūlikā**, f. = *dantikā*, L. **– °mūlīya**, mfn. belonging to *°lá*, dental (letter), RPrāt. i, v. **– racanā**, f. = *-dhāva*, Kathās. lxxv. **– rajas**, n. = *-mala*, Kauś. 31. **– roga**, m. tooth-ache, Suśr. iv, 22. **– °rogin**, mfn. suffering from *°ga*, 24. **– lekhaka**, m. one who lives by painting the teeth, Kāś. on Pāṇ. ii, 2, 17 & vi, 2, 73. **– vaktra**, for *-vakra*. **– vakra**, m. N. of a Karūsha prince (also called *vakradanta* & *vakra*; described as a Dānava or Asura), MBh. i f.; Hariv.; VP. iv, 14, 11; v, 26, 7; BhP. iii, vii, ix; VāyuP. ii, 34, 145; BrahmaP.; Kām. **– vat**, mfn. having teeth, Pāṇ. v, 2, 106, Kāś. **– varṇa**, mfn. 'tooth-coloured,' brilliant, MBh. viii, 63, 11. **– valka**, n. the enamel of the teeth, Suśr. ii, 16. **– vastra**, m. n. = *-cchada*, L. **– vāṇijya**, n. ivory trade (forbidden to Jain laymen), HYog. iii, 98 &

105. — **vāsas**, (m., W.) = *-cchada*, Kum. v, 34. — **vighāta**, m. = *-gh°*, Ṛitus. iv, 12. — **vidradhī**, f. an abscess of the teeth, Car. vi, 18. — **vīṇā**, f. 'tooth-guitar,' *°ṇām vādayat*, mfn. 'playing the *°ṇā*,' chattering with the teeth, Pañcat. i, 18, ½. — **veshṭa**, m. = *°ṭana*, MBh. vii, 3639; the gums, Yājñ. iii, 96 (du. 'the gums of the upper and lower jaw'); MBh. vii f. (of an elephant); Suśr. i, 5; ii, 16; tumour of the gums, i, 23 & 25; ii, 16, 15. — **veshṭaka**, m. id., 11; du. the gums of the upper and lower jaw, Car. iv, 7. — **veshṭana**, n. = *-praveshṭa*, Śiś. xviii, 47, Sch. — **vaidarbha**, m. looseness of the teeth through external injury, Suśr. i, 11; ii, 16; iv, 22. — **vyasana**, n. fracture or decay of the teeth or of a tusk. — **vyāpāra**, m. ivory work, Kād. — **śaṅku**, n. a pair of pincers for drawing teeth, Suśr. i, 8. — **śaṭha**, mfn. 'bad for the teeth,' acid, L.; m. acidity, L.; N. of several trees with acid fruits & (n.) N. of the fruits (= *-karshaṇa*, Citrus Aurantium, = *-phala*, Averrhoa Carambola, L.), 42 & 46; (*ā*), f. Oxalis pusilla, L. — **śarkarā**, f. tartar of the teeth, 23; ii, 16. — **śāṇa**, m. tooth-powder, L. — **śirā**, f. a back tooth, L.; the gums, W. — **śuddhi**, f. = *-dhāva*. — **śūla**, m. n. = *-roga*, MBh. xii; GarP. — **śodhana**, n. = *-dhāva*, Bhpr. iv, ½; (*ī*), f. a tooth-pick, W.; *-cūrṇa*, n. tooth-powder, 25. — **śopha**, m. swelling of the gums, L. — **ślishṭa**, mfn. entangled in the teeth, W. — **saṃgharsha**, m. gnashing the teeth, MārkP. xxxiv, 72. — **sadman**, n. 'tooth-abode,' the mouth, Gal. — **skavana**, n. picking the teeth, Āp. — **harsha**, m. morbid sensitiveness of the teeth, Suśr. i, 42; ii, 16; iv, 22; = *-gh°*, VāyuP. i, 19, 19. — **harshaka**, **°shaṇa**, m. = *-karshaṇa*, L. — **hastin**, mfn. having tusks and a trunk, R. i, 6, 24. — **hīna**, mfn. toothless. **Dantâgra**, n. the top of a tooth, VPrāt. i, 81. **Dantâgrīya**, mfn. fr. *°gra*, g. *gahâdi*. **Dantâghāta**, m. = *°ta-gh°*, W.; = *°ta-karshaṇa*, L. **Dantâñji**, mfn. showing the teeth, MantraBr. ii, 4, 6. **Dantâda**, mfn. corroding the teeth, Suśr. vi, 54. **Dantā-danti**, mfn. (cf. Pāṇ. v, 4, 127) tooth against tooth, MBh. viii, 2377. **Dantântara**, n. 'space between the teeth,' *-gata*, mfn. = *°nta-ślishṭa*, Suśr. i; *°tar-adhishṭhita*, mfn. id., Mn. v, 141. **Dantâyudha**, m. 'tusk-weaponed,' a hog, L. **Dantârbuda**, m. n. = *°ta-śopha*, L. **Dantâlaya**, m. = *°ta-sadman*, L. **Dantâli**, f. a row of teeth. **Dantâlikā**, f. a horse's bridle, Śiś. v, 56. **Dantâlī**, f. id., L. **Dantâvali**, f. = *°tâli*, Bhartṛ. iii, 74. **Dantâślishṭa**, mfn. = *°ta-ś°*, Mn. v, 141, Kull. **Dantôcchishṭa**, n. the remains of food lodged between the teeth, Gṛihyās. ii, 89. **Dantôdbheda**, m. appearance of the teeth, dentition, W. **Dantôlūkhala**, n. 'tooth-hole,' alveole, Car. iv, 7, 1. **Dantôlūkhalika**, mfn. 'using the teeth as a mortar,' eating unground grain (an ascetic), Mn. vi, 17; Yājñ. iii, 49; MBh. ix, 2182; xiii, 647. **Dantôlūkhalin**, mfn. id., ix, 2166; R. (G) i, 52, 26; iii, 10, 3. **Dant'oshṭhaka**, for *°taushṭh°*. **Dantaushṭhaka**, mfn. paying attention to one's teeth and lips, Pāṇ. v, 2, 66, Kāś.

Dantaka, ifc. 'a tooth,' see *a-, kṛimi-, śyāva-*; m. a projection in a rock, L.; 'a pin projecting from a wall,' see *nāga-*; mfn. paying attention to one's teeth, Pāṇ. v, 2, 66, Sch.; (*ikā*), f. Croton polyandrum (yielding a pungent oil), L.

Dantāvala, m. (113; vi, 3, 118) 'tusked,' an elephant, Mn. vii, 106, Kull.; N. of a man, GopBr. i, 2, 5.

Danti, for *°tin*, q. v. — **jā**, f. = *°tikā*, L. — **danta**, m. 'an elephant's tusk,' *-maya*, mfn. made of ivory, MBh. viii, 1021. — **durga**, m. N. of a man. — **daitya**, m. N. of a Daitya, Bālar. x, 30. — **mada**, m. the juice flowing from a rutting elephant's temples, L. — **vaktra**, m. 'elephant-faced,' Gaṇeśa, iv, 16. — **stha**, mfn. seated on an elephant, Kum. xvi, 2.

Dantin, mfn. tusked (Gaṇeśa), MaitrS. ii, 9, 1 (*°ti*, TĀr. x, 1, 5); m. an elephant, MBh.; R. &c.; a mountain, L.; (*inī*), f. = *°tikā*, L. **°tila**, m. N. of a man, Pañcat. i, 3, ½. **°tura**, mf(*ā*, Vop.)n. (Pāṇ. v, 2, 106) having projecting teeth, Kathās. xii, xx, cxxiii; KātyŚr. xx, Sch.; jagged, uneven, Naish. vii, 13 (*-tā*, f. abstr.); ifc. = *°rita*, Kād.; Hcar. i, 121; ii, 224; Kathās. xviii; Vcar.; ugly, Kād. v, 1047 (*-tā*, f. abstr.); *-cchada*, m. 'prickly-leaved,' the lime tree, L. **°turaka**, mfn. having prominent teeth, VarBṛS. lxix, 20; m. pl. N. of a people (east of Madhya-deśa), xiv, 6. **°turaya**, Nom. *°yati*, to fill with (instr.), Hcar. ii, 488. **°turita**, mfn. ifc. filled with, full of, Kād. iii, 1250; v, 843. **°tūla**, mfn. having teeth, g. *sidhmâdi*. **°teya**, m. Indra (v. l. *datt°*), L.

Dantya, mf(*ā*, Pāṇ. vi, 1, 213, Sch.)n. dental (a letter), Prāt.; Kāś.; Vop.; being on the teeth, Pāṇ. iv, 3, 55, Kāś.; Hemac.; suitable to the teeth, Suśr. i, 46; Pāṇ. v, 1, 6, Kāś.; cf. *a-*. **Danty'oshṭhya** or **°tyaush°**, mfn. denti-labial, Śiksh. 25; Pāṇ. vii, Kāś.

दन्दश *dandaśa*, m. (√*daṇś*) a tooth, W.

Dandaśūka, mf n. (iii, 2, 166) mordacious, VS.; TS.; ŚBr.; MBh.; malignant, v, 1245; Car. iii, 8; m. a snake, Yājñ. iii, 197; MBh. xiv; BhP. iv–vii; N. of a hell infested by serpents, v, 26; of a Rākshasa, L.

दन्द्रमण *dandramaṇa*, mfn. fr. Intens. of √*dram*, Pāṇ. iii, 2, 150.

दन्ध्वन *dandhvana*, m. (√*dhvan*, Intens.) 'whistler,' a kind of cane, MBh. xii, 86, 14.

दन्व् *danv*, cl. 1. P., to go, Dhātup. xv, 88.

दभ् *dabh* or *dambh*, cl. 1. (Subj. *dábhat* & *°bhāti*, RV.; pl. *°bhanti*, vii, *°bhan*, i f., x & AV.; Pot. *°bheyam*, TS. i, 6, 2, 4) & 5. *dabhnóti* ('to go,' Naigh. ii, 14; Impv. *°nuhi*, AV. x, 3, 3; cf. *ā-*;—Pass. *dabhyate*, RV. i, 41, 1; pf. *dadābha*, v, 32, 7; *°dámbha* [Pāṇ. i, 2, 6, Siddh.], AV. v, 29; pl. *debhur* [Pāṇ. vi, 4, 120, Vārtt. 4, Pat.], RV. i, 147, 3 = iv, 4, 13; x, 89, 5; also *dadambhur* & 2. sg. *debhitha* or *dadambhitha*, Pāṇ. i, 2, 6, Siddh.; aor. pl. *dadabhanta*, RV. i, 148, 2; *adambhishur*, Bhaṭṭ. xv, 3) to hurt, injure, destroy, RV.; AV.; TS.; ŚBr.; ShaḍvBr.; Bhaṭṭ.; to deceive, abandon, RV. i, 84, 20; VS. iv f., viii: Caus. (Subj. & p. *dambháyat*; 2. sg. *°yas*, *°ya*) to destroy, RV.; AV.; *dambhayati* or *dābh°*, to impel, Dhātup. xxxii, 132; *dambhayate*, to accumulate, xxx, 4: Desid. *dípsati* (Subj. [AV. iv, 36, 1 f.] & p. *dípsat*) to intend to injure or destroy, RV.; AV.; VS. xi, 80; *dhips°*, *dhīps°*, *didambhishati*, Pāṇ. vii, 2, 49 & 4, 56 (i, 2, 10, Pat.)

Dabdha, see *á-*. **Dábdhi**, f. injury, TS.; Kāṭh.

Dábha, mfn. deceiving, RV. v, 19, 4; (*āya*), dat. inf. to deceive, 44, 2; vii, 91, 2; ix, 73, 8; AV. iv; cf. *a-*.

Dabhī́ti, m. an injurer, enemy, RV. iv, 41, 4; N. of a man (favoured by Indra, ii, iv, vi f., x; by the Aśvins, i, 112, 23). **°bhna**, see *dura-dabhná*.

Dábhya, mfn. deceivable, x, 108, 4; deceitful, 61, 2.

Dabhrá, mf(*ā*)n. little, small, deficient, i, iv, vii f., x; ŚāṅkhGṛ. iii, 13, 5; KenUp.; cf. *dahra*; m. the ocean, Uṇ., Sch.; n. distress, RV. vii, 104, 10; (*ám*), ind. scarcely, i, 113, 5; cf. *á-*. — **cetas** (*°rá-*), mfn. little-minded, viii, x. — **buddhi**, mfn. id., BhP. vi, 7.

दम् 1. *dam*, cl. 4. *dāmyati* (Pāṇ. vii, 3, 74; ind. p. *dāntvā* & *damitvā*, 2, 56; aor. Pass. *adami*, 3, 34, Kāś.; P. *°mīt*, Bhaṭṭ. xv, 37) to be tamed or tranquillised, ŚBr. xiv, 8, 2, 2 (Impv. *dā́myata*); to tame, subdue, conquer, MBh. vii, 2379 & BhP. iii, 3, 4 (ind. p. *damitvā*); Bhaṭṭ.: cl. 9. irreg. (? Subj. 2. sg. *dānas*) id., RV. i, 174, 2: Caus. *damayati* (p. *°máyat*; Ā., Pāṇ. i, 3, 89) to subdue, overpower, RV. vii, 6; x, 74, 5; AV. v, 20, 1; MBh.; Rājat.; Desid., see √*dān*; [cf. δάμνημι, δμώς; Lat. *domare* &c.]

2. **Dám**, a house, RV. x, 46, 7 (gen. pl. *damā́m*); *pátir dán* (gen. sg.) = *dám-patis*, 99, 6; 105, 2; i, 149, 1; 153, 4; *pátī dán* = *dám-patī*, 120, 6; *śíśur dán*, 'a child of the house,' x, 61, 20; [cf. δῶ &c.] — **pati** (*dám-*), m. (= δεσ-πότης) the lord of the house (Agni, Indra, the Aśvins), i; ii, 39, 2 (cf. Pāṇ. i, 1, 11, Kāś.); v, viii; (*ī*), du. (g. *rājadantâdi*, the comp. taken as a Dvandva and *dam* in the sense of 'wife') 'the two masters,' husband and wife, v, viii, x; AV.; Gobh. &c. (said of birds, VarBṛS. vc; Hit.)

Dáma, m. (or n.) house, home (δόμος, Lat. *domus*), RV.; AV. vii (also *puru-dáma*, q. v.); VS. viii, 24; mfn. ifc. 'taming, subduing,' see *ariṃ-, gāṃ-, baliṃ-*; m. self-command, self-restraint, self-control, ŚBr. xiv, 8, 2, 4 (*°má*, but cf. Pāṇ. vii, 3, 34, Kāś.); TUp.; KenUp.; Mn. &c.; taming, L.; punishment, fine, viii f.; Yājñ. ii, 4; BhP.; N. of a brother of Damayantī, Nal. i, 9; of a Maha-rshi, MBh. xiii, 1762; of a son of Daksha, i, Sch.; of a grandson [or son, BhP. ix, 2, 29] of Marutta, VP. iv, 1, 20; MārkP. cxxxiv; VāyuP.; cf. *dur-, su-*. — **kartṛi**, m. a ruler, W. — **ghosha**, m. N. of a Cedi prince (father of Śiśu-pāla), MBh. i–iii; Hariv.; VP. iv, 14, 13; BhP. vii, ix; *-ja*, m. 'son of D°,' Śiśu-pāla, Śiś. ii, 60; *-suta*, m. id., xvi, 1. — **maya**, mfn. consisting of self-control, ŚāṅkhBr. ix, 1. — **śarīrin**, mfn. keeping one's body in self-control, BhP. iii, 31, 19. — **svasṛi**, f. 'Dama's sister,' Damayantī, Naish. viii f.

Damaka, mfn. (Pāṇ. vii, 3, 34, Kāś.) ifc. taming, a tamer, Mn. iii, 162; MBh. xiii, 1651. **°matra**, see *mahā-*. **°matha**, m. (Uṇ. iii, 114, Sch.) 'self-control,' see *tri-*; punishment, L. **°mathu**, m. self-control, L.; punishment, W.

Damana, mf(*ī*)n. ifc. taming, subduing, overpowering, MBh. viii; Bhartṛ.; self-controlled, passionless, L.; m. a tamer of horses, charioteer, BhP. iv, 26, 2; (g. *nandy-ādi*) Artemisia indica, Mantram. xxiii; N. of a Samādhi, Kāraṇḍ. xvii, 18; of Yāmāyana (author of RV. x, 16), RAnukr.; of a son of Vasu-deva by Rohiṇī, Hariv. 1951; of a Brahmarshi, Nal. i, 6; VāyuP. i, 23, 115; of a son of Bharadvāja, KāśīKh. lxxiv; of an old king, MBh. i, 224; of a Vidarbha king, Nal. i, 9; n. taming, subduing, punishing, MBh.; R.; Śak.; BhP.; BrahmavP.; self-restraint, W.; (*ī*), f. Solanum Jacquini, L.; N. of a Śakti, Hcat. i, 8, 405. — **bhañjikā**, f. 'breaking *damana* flowers,' a kind of sport, Vātsyāy. i, 4.

Damanaka, m. Artemisia indica, VarBṛS. lxxvii, 13; BhavP. ii; N. of a man, Bharat. iii; of a jackal, Pañcat. i, ½ ff.; Kathās. lx, 19 ff.; (n.?) N. of a metre of 4 times 6 short syllables; of another of 4 lines of 10 short syllables and one long each.

Damanīya, mfn. tamable, to be restrained, W.

Damanya, Nom. (Subj. *°yat*) to subdue, RV. x, 99.

Damayantī, f. 'subduing (men),' N. of Nala's wife (daughter of Bhīma king of Vidarbha), Nal.; a kind of jasmine, L.; *-kathā*, f. N. of Nalac.; *-kāvya*, n. N. of a poem, Prauḍh.; *-pariṇaya*, m. N. of a drama. **°yantikā**, f. N. of the mother of a Sch. on Veṇīs. **°yitṛi**, m. a tamer, MBh. xiii, 7041 (Vishṇu); Śiva.

Damāya, Nom. (pl. *°yantu*) to control one's self, TUp. i, 4, 2; (p. *°yát*) to subdue, RV. vi, 18, 3; 47, 16.

Damita, mfn. tamed, subdued, Pāṇ. vii, 2, 27.

Damitṛi, m. = *°mayitṛi*, RV. ii, 23, 11; iii, 34, 10; v, 34, 6. **Damin**, mfn. (Pāṇ. iii, 2, 141) tamed, self-controlled, MBh. iii, 5016; 'taming,' see *kāma-daminī*; n. N. of a Tīrtha, 5014; m. pl. the Brāhmans of Śaka-dvīpa, VP. ii, 4, 39.

Damunas, (Uṇ. iv) m. (for *°mūn°*) fire, Agni, L.

Dámūnas, mfn. belonging or devoted or dear to the house or family (Agni &c.), RV. (pl. the Ṛibhus v, 42, 12); AV. xix; m. a friend of the house (Agni, Savitṛi, Indra, Dīrgha-nītha), RV.; AV. vii; ŚāṅkhŚr.

1. **Damya**, mfn. tamable, Mn. viii, 146; BhP. xi; m. a young bullock that has to be tamed, MBh. xii f.; Hariv.; R.; Ragh.; Vikr. — **sārathi**, m. 'guide of those who have to be restrained,' N. of a Buddha, L.

2. **Dámya**, mfn. being in a house, homely, RV.

दमदमाय *damadamāya*, (onomat.) P. Ā. *°yati*, *°yate*, Pāṇ. iii, 1, 13, Vārtt. 1, Pat. (not in ed.)

दमावन्दु *damāvandu*, N. of a mountain in Persia called Demavend, Romakas.

दम्पति *dám-pati*. See 2. *dám*.

दम्भ् *dambh*. See √*dabh*.

Dambha, m. deceit, fraud, feigning, hypocrisy, Mn. iv, 163; MBh. &c.; Deceit (son of A-dharma and Mṛishā, BhP. iv, 8, 2), Prab. ii; Indra's thunderbolt, L.; Śiva; N. of a prince (*darbha*, AgP.; *rambha*, VP.), PadmaP. — **caryā**, f. deceit, hypocrisy, L. — **muni**, m. a hypocritical Muni, Kathās. lxxii, 263. — **yajña**, m. a hypocritical sacrifice, BhP. v, 26, 25. **Dambhôdbhava**, m. N. of a prince (who fought with hermits but was worsted), MBh.; Kām. i.

Dambhaka, mfn. ifc. deceiving, Mn. iv, 195.

Dambhana, mfn. ifc. 'damaging,' see *amitra-* & *sapatna-dámbh°*; n. deceiving, 198; MBh. xii, 2111.

Dambhin, mfn. acting deceitfully, (m.) a deceiver, hypocrite, Yājñ. i, 130; BhP. xii, 6, 30; cf. *a-*.

Dambholi, m. Indra's thunderbolt, Bālar. iv, 51; ix, ½; Kathās. xciv, 11; Prasannar. iv, 10; v, 53; Sāh.; Agastya (Ṛishi of the 1st Manv-antara), VP. i, 10, 9; (*dattogni*) iii, 1, 11; (*°ttoni*) BrahmaP. & (v. l. *dānt°*) Hariv. 417; (*°ttātri*) VāyuP.; (*°ttātreya*) PadmaP. — **pāṇi**, m. '*d°*-handed,' Indra, Naish. xvii, 42; Bālar. x, 39. — **pāta**, m. the falling of Indra's thunderbolt, vii, 50; *°tāya*, Nom. *°yate*, to fall down like Indra's thunderbolt, Rājat. viii, 1615.

दय् *day*, cl. 1. Ā. *dáyate* (p. *dáyamāna*, RV. &c.; aor. *adayishṭa*, Bhaṭṭ.; pf. *°yām cakre*, Pāṇ. iii, 1, 37) to divide, impart, allot (with gen., ii, 3, 52; acc., RV.); to partake, possess, RV.; Nir.; to divide asunder, destroy, consume, RV. vi, 6, 5; x, 80, 2; to take part in, sympathise with, have pity on (acc., vii, 23, 5; AV.; ŚBr. xiv; Bhaṭṭ.; gen., Daś.; Bhaṭṭ.; Kathās. cxxi, 104); to repent, RV. vii, 100, 1; to go, Dhātup.: Caus. (Pot. *dayayet*) to have pity on (gen.), BhP. ii, 7, 42: Intens. *dandayyate*, *dād°*, Vop. xx, 8 f.; cf. *ava-, nir-ava-, vi-*.

Dayā́, f. sympathy, compassion, pity for (loc., MBh.;

Pañcat.; Bhartṛ.&c.; gen.,R.; Hariv.8486; in comp., MBh.xiv; Hit.i,6,41), ŚBr.xiv &c.(°*yām* √*kṛi*, 'to take pity on' [loc., MBh.; Hit. i, 2, 7; gen., Vop.]); Pity (daughter of Daksha and mother of A-bhaya, BhP. iv, 1, 49 f.), Hariv. 14035; cf. *a-dayá; nir-*, & *sa-daya*. **-kara**, mfn. showing pity (Śiva). **-kūrca**, m. 'store of pity,' a Buddha, L. **-kṛit**, mfn. pitiful. **-nidhi**, m. 'treasure of mercy,' a very compassionate person. **-°nvita** (°*yān*°), mfn. full of pity. **-yukta**, mfn. id. **-rāma**, m. N. of several men, Śaṃkaracetov. i, 130 &c. **-vat**, mfn. pitiful, taking pity on (gen., MBh. xiii; loc., ii; R. ii); (*tī*), f. N. of a Śruti (in music). **-vīra**, m. a hero in compassion, very merciful man, Siṇhâs. **-śaṃkara**, m. N. of a man. **-śīla**, mfn. compassionate. **Dayôrmi**, mfn. having compassion for (its) waves, Hit.

Dayālu, mfn. (Pāṇ. iii, 2, 158) = °*yā-vat*, MBh. &c. (with loc., Ragh. ii, 57); *-tā*, f. pity, Kād.; Kathās. civ; *-tva*, n. id., Kām. (with loc.) °**luka**, mfn. = °*lu*.

Dayita, mfn. cherished, beloved, dear, MBh.; R.; protected, Bhaṭṭ. x, 9; m. a husband, lover, Śak. iii, 18/19 (v.l.); (*ā*), f. a wife, beloved woman, Ragh. ii, 30; Megh. 4; Śiś. ix, 70; Kathās.; Dhūrtas. ii, 13.

Dayitā, f. of °*ta*. **-°dhīna** (°*tādh*°), mfn. subject to a wife. **-maya**, mfn. wholly devoted to a beloved woman, Kathās. ci, 276.

Dayitāyamāna, mfn. lovely, Haravij. ii, 8.

Dayitnu, mfn.?, Lāṭy. vii, 10, 13.

दर *dara* (Pāṇ. iii, 3, 58), mfn. (√*dṝ*) ifc. cleaving, breaking,' see *puram-dará, bhagam-*; m. (g. *ardharcâdi, uñchâdi*) = °*rī*, R. ii, 96, 4; a conch-shell, BhP. i, vf., x; Kramadîp.; m. the navel, Gal.; 'stream,' see *asṛig-*; fear, MBh. v, 4622; n. poison (v.l. *dhara*), L.; (*ī*), f. a hole in the ground, cave, MBh.; R.; Hariv.; Kum. &c.; (*am*), ind. a little, Bhartṛ. iii, 24. **-kaṇṭikā**, f. 'little-thorn,' Asparagus racemosa, L. **-kara**, m. 'hole-maker,' a staff, Gal. **-timira**, n. the darkness of fear, Gīt. x, 2. **-manthara**, mfn. a little slow, xi, 3. **-mukulita**, mfn. a little budded, ii, 17; Sāh. iii, 14/14. **-vidalita**, mfn. slightly opened, Gīt. i, 35. **-vrīḍā**, f. slight shame, Sāh. iii, 60. **-ślatha**, mfn. a little loose, Gīt. xii, 13. **-hāra**, m. N. of a plant (v.l.), L. **Darêndra**, m. Vishṇu's conch, W.

Daraṇa, n. cleaving, rending, breaking, ŚāṅkhŚr. xiii; Kauś.; ShaḍvBr. v, 3; VarBṛS.; falling away (of flesh), Suśr. v, 1, 50. °**ṇi**, m. f. surf, Uṇ. ii, 103, Sch. °**ṇīya**, mfn. *a-*, 'unbreakable,' Nir. ix, 9.

Darat-pura, n. the city of the Darads, Rājat. vii, 916; viii, 1155; (*ī*), f. id., vii, 913.

Daratha, m. a cave, Uṇ. iii, Sch.; taking flight, ib.

Darad, m. (g. *sindhv-ādi*) see °*da*; f. (Pāṇ. iv, 1, 120, Pat.) = °*rat-pura*, L., Sch.; the heart, Uṇ., Sch.; a bank, ib.; a mountain, L.; a precipice, L.; fear, L. °**da**, m. pl. N. of a people (living above Peshāwar; also called °*d*, Rājat.), Mn. x, 44; MBh.; Hariv. 6441; R. iv; VarBṛS.; VāyuP. i, 45, 118; sg. a Darada prince (also °*d*, Rājat. vii, 914), MBh. i, 2694; Hariv.; fear, L.; n. red lead, Bhpr. v, 26, 93; vii, 1, 227; *-lipi*, f. writing peculiar to the Daradas, Lalit. x, 32.

Darasāna, m. = *dyotva*, Uṇ. ii, 86, Sch.

Darāyya, mfn. fut. Pass. p. √*dṝ*, Vop. xxvi, 164.

Dari, mfn. 'splitting, opening,' see *go-*; m. N. of a Nāga, MBh. i, 2157; f. metrically for °*rī*, vii, 8409. °**rita**, mfn. timid, L. °**rin**, mfn. Pāṇ. iii, 2, 157.

Darī, f. of °*ra*. **-bhṛit**, m. 'having caves,' a mountain, Kir. xviii, 2. **-mat**, mfn. abounding with caves, R. (B) iv, 40, 35. **-mukha**, n. a mouth like a cave, MBh. vii, 6437; the opening of a cave, ib.; a cave representing a mouth, Kum. i, 8; Ragh. xiii, 47; m. 'cave-mouthed,' N. of a monkey, R. iv; of a Pratyeka-buddha, Jāt. 378. **-vat**, mfn. = *-mat*, R.

Dárīman, destruction, RV. i, 129, 8.

Dártri, mfn. breaking, RV. vi, 66, 8; °*trí*, m. a breaker, i, 130, 10; viii, 98, 6. **Dartnú**, m. id. vi, 20, 3.

Dardara, mfn. broken, burst, L.; m. 'having caves,' a mountain, L.; a ravine (?), R. (B) iv, 43, 27; a kind of drum, L.; (*ī*), f. N. of a river, L. °**rāmra**, m. a sort of sauce, L. °**rīka**, m. N. of a tree, L. °**rīka**, m. a frog, Uṇ. vṛ.; a cloud, ib.; N. of a musical instrument (also °*rvar*°), ib.; n. any musical instrument, ib.

Dardura, m. a frog (cf. *kūpa-*), Mn. xii, 64; MBh.; R. &c.; a flute (cf. *jala-*), Mṛicch. iii, 18/18; BhP. i, 10, 15; the sound of a drum, L.; a cloud, L.; a kind of rice, Car. i, 27; N. of a southern mountain (often named with Malaya), MBh. ii f.; Hariv.; R.; Ragh.; VarBṛS.; of a man, BhP. ii, 7, 34; of a singing master, Kathās. lxxi, 73; = °*raka*, Mṛicch. ii, 1/12; n. a kind of talc, Bhpr.; an assemblage of villages, L.; (*ā*, *ī*), f. Durgā, L. **-cchadā**, f. the plant *brāhmī*, Npr. **-parṇī**, f. id., ib. **-puṭa**, m. the mouth of a pipe, W. **Dardurâmra**, m. = °*dar*°, L.

Darduraka, m. N. of a gamester, Mṛicch. ii, 4 ff.

Dardū, see *dadru*. °**dru**, m. N. of a bird, Car. i, 27; see *dadr*°. °**druṇa**, °**drū**, °**drūṇa**, see *dadr*°.

दरिद्र *dáridra*, mf(*ā*)n. (√*drā*, Intens., Pāṇ. vi, 4, 114, Vārtt. 2) roving, strolling, TS. iii, 1, 1, 2 (°*rídra*); VS. xvi, 47; ŚBr. i, 6, 1, 18; Tāṇḍya-Br.; poor, needy, deprived of (instr., Kathās. lxxiii; in comp., lxiv; Bhartṛ. iv, 11), (m.) a beggar, Mn. ix, 230; R. &c. (ifc. f. *ā*, Kathās. xc, 26); cf. *mahā-*. **-tā**, f. indigence, penury, state of being deprived of (in comp.), Pañcat. ii; Mṛicch.; Bhartṛ.; Naish. &c. **-tva**, n. id., Rājat. **-nindā**, f. N. of ŚārṅgP. xxv.

Daridrat, mfn. (pr.p.) poor, Daś. vii, 155. °**drāṇa**, n. = °*dra-tā*, Pāṇ. vi, 4, 114, Vārtt. 2, Kār. °**drāyaka**, mfn. poor, ib. °**drita**, mfn. id., 52, Siddh. °**dritṛi**, mfn. (fut. p., vii, 2, 10, Vārtt. 7, Pat.) id., W. °**drin**, mfn. id., Siṇhâs. xxi, 1/2. °**drī**, ind.; *-kriya*, ind. causing any one to rove, ŚBr. xi, 3, 3, 4; *-bhūta*, mfn. impoverished, Kathās. cxiv, 94.

दरोदर *darodara*. See *dur*°.

दर्तृ *dártri*, °*tnú*, *dardara*, &c. See col. 1.

दर्प *darpa*, m. (√2. *dṛip*) pride, arrogance, haughtiness, insolence, conceit, Mn. viii; MBh. &c. (pl., Śāntiś. iv, 22); Pride (son of A-dharma and Śrī, MBh. xii, 3388; MārkP. l, 25; of Dharma, VP. i, 7, 26; BhP. iv, 1, 51; musk, Hcat. i, 7, 1311; cf. *ati-, sa-*. **-cchid**, mfn. ifc. destroying the pride of, Hemac. **-da**, m. Śiva. **-dhmāta**, mfn. puffed up with pride, W. **-nārāyaṇa**, m. N. of a king, Kathârṇ. vi. **-pattraka**, N. of a grass, Npr. **-pūrṇa**, mfn. full of pride, R. i, 55, 19. **-sāra**, m. N. of a man, Daś. **-ha**, mfn. pride-destroying, W. **-han**, m. Śiva. **-hara**, mfn. = *-ha*, Subh. **Darpârambha**, m. beginning of pride, L. **Darpôpaśānti**, f. allaying pride, Hit. ii, 12, 17.

Darpaka, mfn. ifc. making proud, W.; m. pride, Vāsav. 511; the god of love, L.

Darpaṇa, m. (g. *nandy-ādi*) 'causing vanity,' a mirror, Hariv. 8317; R. ii; Śak. &c.; ifc. 'Mirror' (in names of works), e.g. *ātaṅka-, dāna-, sāhitya-*; = *dāna-*, Smṛitit. iv; N. of a measure (in music); of a mountain (seat of Kubêra), KālP.; of Śiva, MBh. xiii, 1194; n. the eye, L.; repetition, VarBṛS. iii, 11, Sch.; kindling, W.; Nom. P. °*ṇati*, to represent a mirror. **-kāra**, m. the author of Sāh., Kāvyac. **-maya**, mfn. consisting of mirrors, Hcar. iv.

Darpaṇikā, f. a mirror, Naish. v, 106.

Darpita, mfn. made proud, Mn. viii; MBh.; Hariv.; R.; proud (horses, frogs), MBh. iii; Suśr.; Bhartṛ. **-pura**, n. N. of a town, Rājat. iv, 183; viii, 1942.

Darpin, mfn. ifc. proud of, Hariv. 15606.

दर्भ *darbhá*, m. (√2. *dṛibh*) a tuft or bunch of grass (esp. of Kuśa grass; used for sacrificial purposes), RV. i, 191, 3; AV. &c.; N. of a grass (different from Kuśa and Kāśa, Suśr. i, 38; Saccharum cylindricum, W.), Lalit. xvii, 89; Suśr.; (Pāṇ. iv, 1, 102; g. *kurv-ādi*, v.l.) N. of a man, Pravar. ii, 3, 1 (Āśv.; Kāty. &c.); 'of a prince,' see *dambha*. **-kuṇḍikā**, f. a jar with *d*°, Hariv. 14836. **-kusuma**, N. of an insect, Bhpr. vii, 19, 9; ŚārṅgS. vii, 15. **-guru-mushṭi**, see *g*°. **-cīra**, n. a dress of *d*°, MBh. iii, 1538. **-taruṇaká**, n. a young shoot of *d*°, ŚBr. iii; AitBr. vii, 33, 1; ĀśvGṛ. iv, 6. **-pattra**, m. Saccharum spontaneum, L. **-pavitrá**, n. *d*° used for cleaning, ŚBr. iii; *-pāṇi*, mfn. having °*tra* in the hand, Pāṇ. i, 1, 1, Vārtt. 7, Pat. **-piñjūlá**, n. a bunch of grass, MaitrS. iv, 8, 7 (Kapishṭh. vli, 8); Kaṭh. xxiii, 1; AitBr. i, 3, 8; ŚāṅkhBr. xviii, 8; MānŚr.; ŚāṅkhGṛ. vi (*-vat*, mfn.); PārGṛ. i, 15, 4; (*ī*), f. id., Kauś.; Gobh. ii, 7, 5; Gṛihyās. i, 94. **-puñjīlá**, n. id., TS vi; TBr. i f. **-pushpa**, n. = *-kusuma*, Car. i, 19; Suśr. vi, 54; N. of a snake, v, 4. **-pūtika**, for °*tīka*, Vām. (Gaṇar. 132, Sch.) & Gaṇaratnāv. **-pūtīka**, n. sg. *d*° & *p*°, g. *gavâśvâdi*. **-pūla**, m. a bunch of (Kuśa) grass, KātyŚr. v, 5, 8, Sch. **-baṭu**, m. a puppet made of *d*°, Gobh. i, 6, 21. **-máya**, mf(*ī*)n. (g. *śarâdi*) made of *d*°, TBr. i; ŚBr. xiii; Pañcat.; Kāś.; BhP. **-mushṭí**, m. f. = *-guru-m*°, ŚBr. ix; TBr. iii; KātyŚr.; ĀśvGṛ.; Gobh. iv, 2, 20. **-mūlī**, f. N. of a plant, Pāṇ. iv, 1, 64, Kāś. **-rajju**, f. a rope made of *d*°, MānGṛ. i, 11. **-lavaṇa**, n. an instrument for cutting grass, Kauś. 8. **-śara**, n. sg. *d*° & *ś*° grass, g. *gavâśvâdi*. **-saṃstara**, m. a bed made of *d*°, R. ii, v; Kathās. xxii, liv. **-sūci**, f. the point of *d*° grass, ŚāṅkhGṛ. i, 22, 8. **-stambá**, m. = *-pūla*, TS. v; TBr. ii, 7, 17; AitBr. v, 23, 9; ŚBr. vii, 2, 3, 1; ĀśvŚr. ii, 14, 16; MānŚr. **Darbhânūpa**, g. *kshubhnâdi*. **Darbhâhvaya**, m. Saccharum Munja, L. **Darbhêshīkā**, f. a stalk of *d*° grass, MānGṛ. i, 11.

Darbhaka, m. N. of a prince, VP. iv, 24, 3; BhP. xii, 1, 5. °**bhaṇa**, n. a mat of grass, Baudh. (ĀpŚr. xi, 8, 5, Sch.) °**bhara**, m. (g. *aśmâdi*) Perdix chinensis, Bhpr. v, 10, 60. °**bhi** or °**bhin**, m. N. of a man, MBh. iii, 7024 & 7027.

दर्भट *darbhaṭa*, n. = *dārvaṭa*, L.

दर्म *darmá*, m. (√*dṝ*) a demolisher, RV. iii, 45, 2. °**mán**, m. id., i, 61, 5; 132, 6; x; ŚāṅkhŚr. viii.

Darya, mfn. fr. °*ra*, g. *gav-ādi*.

Daryaka, m. N. of a man, Rājat. viii, 866.

Darva, m. = °*vi*, a ladle (cf. *pūrṇa-darvá*), ŚāṅkhGṛ. iv, 15, 19; the hood of a snake, Uṇ., Sch.; a Rakshas, ib.; a mischievous man, rapacious animal, Uṇ. vṛ.; see °*vi*; pl. N. of a people (cf. *dārva*), MBh. ii, 1869; vi, 362; xiii, 2158; (*ā*), f. N. of a daughter of Uśīnara, Hariv. 1675 ff.; VāyuP. ii, 37, 19.

Darvarīka, m. wind, Uṇ. vṛ.; Indra, ib.; see °*rdar*°.

Dárvi, f. 'wooden (cf. *drú*),' a ladle, RV. v, x; AV. (voc. °*ve*, iii, 10, 7; cf. Pāṇ. vii, 3, 109, Vārtt. 2, Pat.); the hood of a snake (cf. *vi-darvya*), AV. x, 4, 13; m. N. of a son of Uśīnara, VP. iv, 18, 1 (v.l. °*va*). **-bhṛit**, m. = °*vī-kara*, Śiś. xx, 42. **-homá**, m. an oblation made with a ladle, TS. iii; ŚBr. v; KātyŚr.; Kauś. **-°homin**, mfn. offering °*má*, Nir. i, 14.

Darvika, m. a ladle, L.; (*ā*), f. id., L.; see *dārv*°.

Dárvidā, f. a sort of woodpecker, MaitrS. iii; VS.

Dárvī, f. = °*vi*, a ladle, VS. ii, 49 (voc. °*vi*; cf. Pāṇ. vii, 3, 109, Vārtt. 2); Kauś.; ĀśvGṛ.; PārGṛ.; Gobh.; MBh. &c.; the hood of a snake, L.; N. of a country, vi, 362. **-kara**, m. a hooded snake (class of snakes with 26 species), Suśr. i, 46; v, 4; Daś. vii, 165; Ashṭâṅg. vi, 36. **-pralepa**, m. N. of an unguent, Car. i, 3. **-saṃkramaṇa**, n. N. of a Tîrtha, MBh. iii, 8023. **-homa**, m. = °*vi-*, ii, 537; ŚBr. xiv, 6, 8, 9, Sāy.; cf. *dārvīhaumika*. °**vyudāyuvana**, n. remnants clinging to the spoon, ĀpŚr.

Dárvya, m. = °*vi-homa*, ŚBr.

दर्वट *darvaṭa*, m. = *garvāṭa*, L.

दर्श *darśá*, mfn. (√*dṛiś*) ifc. 'looking at, viewing,' see *avasāna-, ādinava-*, & *vadhū-darśá, tattva-*; 'showing,' see *ātma-*; m. 'appearance,' see *chādir-darśá, dur-, priya-*; (g. *pacâdi*) the moon when just become visible, day of new moon, half-monthly sacrifice performed on that day, AV.; (parox.) TS., TBr. & ŚBr. xi; Kauś.; ĀśvGṛ. &c. (n., MBh. iii, 14206); (Day of) New Moon (son of Dhātṛi, BhP. vi, 18, 3; of Krishṇa, x, 61, 14; N. of a Sādhya, VāyuP. ii, 5, 6); du. = *-pūrṇamāsâ*, TS., Sch. **-pa**, m. pl. 'drinking the new moon oblation,' a class of gods, MBh. xiii, 1372. **-pūrṇamāsá**, m. du. (the days of) new and full moon, ceremonies on these days (preceding all other ceremonies), TS. i f.; TBr. ii; ŚBr. i f.; AitBr. &c.; *-devatā*; f. the deity presiding on those days, ŚāṅkhGṛ. i, 3; *-prayoga*, m. *-prāyaścitti*, f. N. of works; *-yājin*, mfn. = °*sín*, TS. ii; ŚBr. x; °*sāyana*, n. = °*sêshṭi*, ŚāṅkhŚr. iii, 11, 4; Vait.; °*sêshṭi*, f. a new and full moon sacrifice. **-°pūrṇamāsin**, mfn. offering °*sêshṭi*, MaitrS. i, 5, 13. **-paurṇamāsa**, in comp.; *-prāyaścitta-vidhi, -vidhi*, m. *-hautra*, n. N. of works; °*sêshṭi*, f. = *darśa-pūrṇ*°. **-yāga**, m. a new moon sacrifice. **-yāminī**, f. the new moon night, L. **-vipad**, m. 'having the misfortune to be hardly visible when new,' the moon, L. **-śrāddha**, n. a Śrāddha performed on new moon, VP. iii, Sch.

Darśaka, mfn. seeing (with gen.), Pāṇ. ii, 3, 70, Kāś.; looking at (acc.), MBh. xiii, 5097; ifc. looking for, i, 5559; 'examining,' see *aksha-*; showing, pointing out (with gen., Kum. vi, 52; Hit. Introd. 10; ifc., Mṛicch. iv, 20; BhP. i, 13, 38; Rājat. i; with *lohitasya*, making blood appear by striking any one), Mn. viii, 284; m. a door-keeper, L.; a skilful man, W.; N. of a prince, VāyuP. ii, 37, 312; pl. N. of a people, MBh. vi, 361.

Darśatá, mf(*ā́*)n. visible, striking the eye, conspicuous, beautiful, RV.; AV. iv, vii, xviii; ŚBr. xiv, 8; m. the sun, Uṇ., Sch.; the moon, ib.; cf. *viśvá-*. **-śrī**, mfn. of conspicuous beauty, RV. x, 91, 2.

Dárśana, mf(*ī*)n. showing, Pāṇ. v, 2, 6; ifc. seeing, looking at (see *tulya-, deva-, sama-*), Ragh. xi, 93; 'knowing,' see *dharma-*; exhibiting, teaching, MBh. i, 583; BhP. v, 4, 11; n. seeing, observing, looking, noticing, observation, perception, RV. i, 116.

23; ŚBr. xiv; ŚāṅkhGṛ. v, 5; MBh. &c.; ocular perception, Suśr. iv, 27; the eye-sight, vi, 17; inspection, examination, Yājñ. i, 328; Hariv. 5460; visiting, Yājñ. i, 84; Kathās. iii, 8; audience, meeting (with gen., Cāṇ.; instr. with or without *saha*, Vet.; in comp., Ragh. xii, 60), Śak. v, $\frac{5}{6}$; vii, $\frac{25}{26}$; Rājat. vi, 43; experiencing, BhP. i, 8, 25; foreseeing, Ragh. viii, 71; contemplating, Mn. viii, 9 & 23; apprehension, judgment, Śak. iii, $\frac{6}{7}$; discernment, understanding, intellect, Mn. vi, 74; Yājñ. i, 8; Bhag. &c.; opinion, Mālav. v, $\frac{13}{14}$; Kām. ii, 6; intention (cf. *pāpa-*), R. i, 58, 18; view, doctrine, philosophical system (6 in number, viz. [Pūrva-] Mīmāṃsā by Jaim.; Uttara-Mīmāṃsā by Bādar.; Nyāya by Gotama; Vaiśeshika by Kaṇâda; Sāṃkhya by Kap.; Yoga by Pat.), MBh. xii, 11045 f.; BhP. &c.; the eye, Suśr. v, 8; Śak. iv, 6; Prab. iii, 10; the becoming visible or known, presence, ĀśvGṛ. iii, 7; Mn. ii, 101; iv; Yājñ. i, 131; ii, 170; MBh. &c.; appearance (before the judge), Mn. viii, 158; Yājñ. ii, 53; Kām.; the being mentioned (in any authoritative text), Kāty-Śr. i, xxvi; Lāṭy. vi, ix; Bādar. i, 1, 25; MBh. xiv, 2700; a vision, dream, Hariv. 1285; Hit. iii, 9, $\frac{0}{1}$; ifc. appearance, aspect, semblance, Mn. ii, 47; MBh. (Nal. ii, 3; xii, 18 & 44); R.; Ragh. iii, 57; colour, L.; showing (cf. *danta-*), Bhartṛ. ii, 26; Dhūrtas. i, $\frac{10}{11}$; a mirror, L.; a sacrifice, L.; = *dharma*, L.; (*ī*), f. Durgā, Hariv. 10238; N. of an insect, Npr.; cf. *a-*, *su-*. **—gṛiha,** n. an audience-chamber, Mn. vii, 145, Kull. **—gocara,** m. the range of sight, Ratnâv. iii, $\frac{3}{4}$. **—patha,** m. id., Pañcat. i, 5, $\frac{3}{4}$; Prab. ii, $\frac{4}{5}$; iv, $\frac{26}{27}$; cf. *a-*. **—pāla,** m. N. of a man, Rājat. vii. **—pratibhū,** m. bail for appearance, Yājñ. ii, 54. **—prātibhāvya,** n. surety for appearance, Mn. viii, 160. **—bhūmi,** f. 'range of perception,' N. of a period in a monk's life, Buddh. L. **—lālasa,** mfn. ifc. desirous of beholding, MBh. **—viveka,** m. N. of a work. **—vishaya,** mfn. being in any one's range of sight, Pāṇ. iii, 2, 111, Vārtt. 2. **Darśanâgni,** m. the fire in the body that causes ocular sensation, GarbhUp. **Darśanântara-gata,** mfn. come within the range of sight, Mṛicch. iii, 12. **Darśanârtha,** mfn. intending to see any one, Āp.; (*am*), ind. to visit, Kād. **Darśanâvaraṇa,** n. obscuration of one's (philosophical) views, Jain. (Sarvad. iii, 195 ff.); °*nīya*, mfn. originating from °*ṇa*, ib.; Bādar. ii, 2, 33, Govind. **Darśanêpsu,** mfn. = °*na-lālasa*. **Darśanôjjvalā,** f. 'of brilliant aspect,' great white jasmine.

Darśanīya, mfn. visible, R. i, v; worthy of being seen, good-looking, beautiful, TS. ii, 7, 9; ŚBr. xiii; ShaḍvBr.; ChUp.; ŚāṅkhGṛ.; MBh. &c. (superl. *-tama*, ii; R. iii; BhP. iv); to be shown, Kathās. lxxi, 20; to be made to appear (before the judge), Mn. viii, 158, Kull.; m. Asclepias gigantea, Npr.; cf. *a-*. **—mānin,** mfn. thinking any one (gen.) to be good-looking, Pāṇ. vi, 3, 36, Kāś.; thought to be g° by (gen.), iii, 2, 82 f., Kāś.; = °*yam-manya*, ib. **—°m-manya,** mfn. thinking one's self to be g°, ib.

Darśanīyā, f. of °*ya*. **—kānta,** m. having a good-looking wife or mistress, Gaṇar. 139, Sch. **—sama,** mfn. indifferent towards a good-looking woman, ib.

Darśam-darśam, ind. at every sight, Kathās.

Darśayitavya, mfn. to be shown, Bādar. iii, 2, 21, Śaṃk. °**tu-kāma,** mfn. wishing to show.

Darśayitṛi, mfn. showing, a shower, guide, MBh. vi, 129; Ragh. iii, 46; a door-keeper, L., Sch.

Darśāpita, mfn. made to see, shown, Siṇhâs. i, $\frac{5}{6}$.

Darśita, mfn. shown, displayed, exposed to view, R. i; Megh. &c.; explained, Hariv. 7289 &c. **—dvār,** m. a door-keeper, Gal. **—vat,** mfn. having shown.

Darśin, mfn. ifc. seeing, looking at, observing, examining, finding, MBh. viii, 1757; R. &c.; knowing, understanding, (G) ii, 64, 3; Śak. i, $\frac{16}{17}$; Ragh. xiv, 71; Kum. ii, 13; Hit. i; receiving, Mṛicch. ii, 7; experiencing, R. iii, 65, 11; composer (of a hymn, *sûkta-*); looking, appearing, iv, 40, 48; showing, exhibiting, teaching, MBh.; Śak. iv, $\frac{21}{22}$; Kathās. lvi, 203; inflicting (cf. *pāpa-*), R. ii, 75, 12; Hariv.

Darśivas (only ifc. nom. m. °*vān* at the end of Ślokas), one who has seen (irreg. pf. p.), MBh. viii, 1756–1771 (*Arjuna-*); knowing, *tattva-*, i, 5637, *tattvârtha-*, iv, 902, *dharma-*, i, 6157; *sarva-*, Sūryas. xii; *dīrgha-*, MBh. v, 4380; cf. *pratyaksha-*.

Dárśya, mfn. worthy of being seen, RV. v, 52, 11.

दल् *dal* (= √*dṛī*), cl. 1. °*lati* (pf. *dadāla*, Bhaṭṭ. xiv; aor. pl. *adālishur*, xv) to crack, fly open, split, open (as a bud), Suśr. ii, 16; Śiś. ix, 15; Bhām. i, 4; Amar.; Gīt.; Dhūrtas.: Caus. *dālayati*, to cause to burst, Suśr.; Bhaṭṭ.: *dal°*, id., Anargh.; Gīt. i, 8, Sch.; to expel, Mālatīm. viii, 1; Kathās. lviii, 8; cii, 58; cf. *ava-*, *ud-*, *vi-*.

Dala, n. (m., L.) a piece torn or split off, fragment (cf. *aṇḍa-*, *carma-*, *dvi-*, *veṇu-*), Suśr. v, 3, 22; vi, 5, 4; Śiś. iv, 44 (ifc. f. *ā*); Naish. vii, 31; 'part,' a degree, VarBṛ. xvii, 4; a half (cf. *adhara-*, *ahar-*, *dyu-*), VarBṛS.; Suśr. i, 7; Sūryas.; a hemistich; 'unfolding itself,' a small shoot, blade, petal, leaf (often ifc. in names of plants), MBh.; R. &c.; cinnamon leaf, L.; unclean gold, Bhpr. v, 26, 2; a clump, heap, L.; a detachment, W.; = *utsedha*, °*dhavad-vastu*, *avadravya* (*apad°*, W.), L.; dividing, splitting, W.; m. N. of a prince, MBh. iii, 13178; VP. iv, 4, 47. **—kapāṭa,** m. a folded petal or leaf. **—komala,** the lotus, Npr. **—kośa,** m. a kind of jasmine, Kād. iii, 389. **—ja,** mfn. produced from petals (honey), L., Sch. **—taru,** m. Corypha Taliera, L. **—nirmoka,** m. 'leaf-shedding,' Betula Bhojpattra, L. **—pati,** m. N. of a prince, Inscr.; = °*lâdhîśvara*. **—pushpā,** °**pī,** f. Pandanus odoratissimus, L. **—mālinī,** f. leaf-cabbage, Npr. **—modaka,** m. petal-honey, Gal. **—yoga,** m. N. of a constellation, Laghuj. x, 1, Sch. **—vīṭaka,** n. N. of an ear-ornament, Kuṭṭanīm. 65. **—śas,** ind. (√*yā* to go) to pieces, Kathās. xix, 109; lxviii, 167. **—śālinī,** f. N. of a pot-herb, Npr. **—sāyasī,** f. white basil, ib. **—sāriṇī,** f. Colocasia antiquorum, L. **—sūci,** m. 'leaf-needle,' a thorn, L. **—snasā,** f. the fibre of a leaf, L. **Dalâkhya,** m. = °*la-yoga*, Laghuj. x, 2; VarBṛ. xii, 2 f. **Dalâgra-lohita,** a sort of spinage, L. **Dalâḍhaka,** m. Pistia Stratiotes, Jasminum multiflorum or pubescens, wild sesamum, Mesua ferrea, Acacia Sirissa, L.; red chalk, L.; foam or sea-foam, L.; a ditch, L.; the head of a village, L.; an elephant's ear, L.; a hurricane, L. **Dalâḍhya,** m. mud, L. **Dalâdi-tva,** n. the state of a leaf, &c., Kāvyâd. ii, 70. **Dalâdhîśvara,** m. N. of the author of Nṛisiṇha-prasāda. **Dalâmala,** m. (for °*mla*?) the plants *damanaka*, *maruvaka*, & *madana* (? *damana*), L. **Dalâmla,** n. sorrel, L. **Dale-gandhi,** m. 'fragrance in the leaf,' Alstonia scholaris, L. **Dalôdbhava,** mfn. = °*la-ja*, Suśr.

Dalad-dhṛidaya, mfn. broken-hearted, W.

Dalana, mf(*ī*)n. splitting, tearing asunder, dispelling, BhP. vii, 10, 59; Bhartṛ. iii, 47; Vidvanm.; n. breaking (of the heart), Gīt. v, 2; destruction, Naish. iv, 116; Kathās. lxxv, 62; causing to burst, splitting, Bhartṛ.; Kathās.; Rājat.; Gīt.; (*ī*), f. a clod of earth, L.; cf. *nir-*; *māṅsa-*. °**li,** f. id., Uṇ., Sch. °**lika,** n. timber, L. °**lita,** mfn. (g. *kṛitâdi*, Gaṇap.) burst, split, broken, torn asunder, MBh. viii, 4633; VarBṛS.; Bhartṛ. &c.; unfolded, blown, Sāh. x, 66 $\frac{a}{b}$; halved, Sūryas. iv, 12; divided into degrees, xiii, 5 f.; driven asunder, scattered, dispersed, destroyed, Kām.; Bhaktâm. 1 & 18; Caurap.; Prab. v f.; BrahmôttKh. iv, 59; ground, Śiś. vi, 35; displayed, Prab. ii, 35; cf. *saṃ-*. °**lin,** mfn. fr. °*la*, g. *sukhâdi*. °**li-kṛita,** mfn. halved, Sūryas. xii, 84.

Dalmi, m. (Uṇ. iv, 47) Indra (cf. *darmá*), L.; Indra's thunderbolt, g. *yavâdi*; *-mat*, mfn. having a thunderbolt, ib. **Dalya,** mfn. fr. °*la*, g. *balâdi*.

दलतृ *dalatṛi*, g. *arīhaṇâdi*.

दलप *dalapa*, m. (ifc., g. *cūrṇâdi*) a weapon, Uṇ. iii, 142, Sch.; gold, ib.

दल्भ *dalbha*, m. a wheel, 151, Sch.; fraud, Uṇ. k.; N. of a Ṛishi, g. *kaṇvâdi*. °**bhya,** see *dāl°*.

दव *dava*, m. (√2. *du*) a wood on fire, BhP. viii, 6, 13; fire, L., Sch.; burning, heat, Car. i, 20; fever, W.; a forest, L.; cf. *dāva*. **—dagdhaka,** N. of a grass, L. **—dahana,** m. the fire in a burning forest, BhP. v, 8, 22; Prasannar. vii, 23; (°*naka*, vi, 32); Nītir.; Kuval. **—dāna,** n. setting fire on a forest, HYog. iii, 99 & 112. **Davâgni,** m. = °*va-dahana*, MBh. vii; Ragh.; Megh.; BhP. i, 10, 2 (ifc.) &c.; cf. *dāv°*. **Davânala,** m. id., iii, 30, 23; Kathās. lvi, 413 (ifc. f. *ā*); cf. *dāv°*.

Davathu, m. (Pāṇ. iii, 3, 89) heat, pain, Dhūrtan. i, 14; inflammation (of the bile, eyes &c.), Car. i, 20.

दवय *davaya*, Nom. °*yati*, to make distant, Bhaṭṭ. ii, 55.

Davishṭha, mfn. (superl. fr. *dūrá*, Pāṇ. vi, 4, 156) remotest, Rājat.; (*am*), ind. very far away, RV. vi, 51, 13. **Dávīyas,** mfn. (compar., Pāṇ.) very long (way), Bhartṛ. i, 68; very distant, Rājat. iv, 369; Kathās. xvi, xxv; *dūrâd d°*, 'farther than far,' very distant, lx, 172; cxxiii, 14; ind. farther away, AV. x, 8, 8; farther, ŚBr. iii, 6, 2, 3; *dūrâd dáv°*, farthest away, RV. vi, 47, 29; Kathās. lxv, 21; *dávīyasi páras*, in a more remote time, ŚBr. x, 4, 2, 26.

दवर *davara*, °**raka,** m. a string, Jain.

दश 1. *daśa*, ifc. for °*śā* (*apa-*, *udag-* &c.)

दश 2. *daśa*, ifc. (*tri-*, *dvi-*, *nir-*) & in comp. for °*śan*; (*ās*), f. pl. 'Decads,' N. of 10 Jain texts (*upâsaka-* &c.) consisting of 10 chs. each. **—kakshya** (*dáś°*), mfn. having 10 girths, RV. x, 94, 7. **—kaṇṭha,** m. (parox., Pāṇ. vi, 2, 114) 'ten-necked,' Rāvaṇa, Bālar. ii, $\frac{12}{13}$; *-jit*, m. 'enemy of R°,' Rāma, L.; *-nigraha*, m. N. of Anargh. vi; °*ṭhâri*, m. = °*ṭha-jit*, Ragh. viii, 29; °*ṭhāya*, Nom. °*yate*, to act like Rāvaṇa, Bālar. iii, $\frac{37}{38}$. **—kandhara,** m. = *-kaṇṭha*, MBh. iii; BhP.; Bālar.; HYog. **—kanyā-tīrtha,** n. the Tīrtha of the 10 Virgins, RevāKh. cccvi. **—karma-paddhati,** f. N. of a work on the 10 ceremonies prescribed to the 3 twice-born classes. **—kāma-ja-vyasana,** n. the 10 vices arising from love of pleasure (see Mn. vii, 47). **—kumāra-carita** or °**tra,** n. 'adventures of the 10 princes,' N. of a work by Daṇḍin. **—kshiti-garbha,** m. N. of a Buddh. Sūtra. **—kshīra,** mfn. mixed with 10 parts of milk, Suśr. vi, 21 & 24; n. a compound of 10 parts of milk with 1 part of some other substance, iv, 22, 14; (*ksh° daśa-guṇa*, 16). **—gaṇī,** f. the 10 classes of roots, Pāṇ. i, 3, 1, Sch. **—gārgya,** mfn. bought for (the prize of) 10 women of Garga's family, ii, 4, 62, Vārtt. 2, Pat. **—gīti,** °**tikā,** f. N. of a work by Āryabh. **—gu,** mfn. possessing 10 cows, MBh. xiii, 78, 11. **—guṇa,** mfn. tenfold, 10 times larger or more, i, 45 f.; Mn. viii; see *-kshīra*; (*am*), ind. tenfold, Yājñ. i, 141. **—guṇita,** mfn. multiplied by 10, Bālar. ix, 53. **—goṇi,** mfn. having 10 sacks, Pāṇ. i, 1, 52, Kāś. **—grāma,** g. 1. *kumudâdi* & *kāśy-ādi*; (*ī*), f. 10 villages, Yājñ. ii, 272; MBh. xii, 87, 3; *-pati*, m. a chief of 10 villages, Mn. vii, 115. **—°grāmika,** mfn. g. 1. *kumudâdi*. **—grāmin,** m. = °*ma-pati*, W. **—grīva,** m. (Pāṇ. vi, 2, 114, Kāś.) = *-kaṇṭha*, MBh. iii, 15895; R. i, 16, 18; iii; BhP.; N. of a demon, MBh. ii, 367; Hariv.; of a son of Damaghosha, 6601; of an enemy of Vṛisha, GarP. **—gva** (*dáś°*), m. 'Decimus,' N. of an Aṅgiras, RV. iv, 51, 4; viii, 12, 2; x, 62, 6; (pl.) his family (named with that of Nava-gva; worshipping Indra), i, 62, 4; ii, 34, 12; iii, 39, 5; v, 29, 12. **—gvin,** mfn. tenfold, viii, 1, 9. **—catushka,** n. N. of a sport, Siṇhâs. xxvii, $\frac{3}{4}$. **—candra,** mfn. having 10 moon-like spots, BhP. iv, 15, 17. **—cchadin,** mfn. ten-leaved, x, 2, 27. **—jyoti,** °**tis,** m. N. of a son of Su-bhrāj, MBh. i, 44 f. **—ṭīkā-sarvasva,** n. N. of a work, Pratāpar., Sch. **—tas,** ind. from 10, Mn. viii f. **—taulika,** m. N. of a weight, Suśr. iv, 13. **—tva,** n. the state of 10, Jaim. iii, 7, 27. **—daśâvayava,** mfn. containing 10 parts each, Car. i, 4. **—daśin,** mfn. consisting of repeated decades, ŚāṅkhBr.; TāṇḍyaBr.; ŚāṅkhŚr.; ŚāṅkhGṛ. **—dāsa,** m. pl. N. of a people, MBh. iii, 134, 17. **—diś,** f. sg. the 10 regions (including that overhead and underneath), Vet. i, $\frac{25}{26}$; Pañcad.; °*dig-vyavalokana*, m. N. of a Samādhi, Kāraṇḍ. xvii, 8. **—dṛishṭânta-kathā,** f. N. of a work. **—dyu** (*dáś°*), m. N. of a man favoured by Indra, RV. i, 33, 14; vi, 26, 4. **—dhanus,** m. N. of an ancestor of Śākya-muni, W. **—dharma-gata,** mfn. addicted to the practices of the 10 (kinds of mental non-restraint), Hariv. 744 & 1153. **—dhá,** ind. in 10 parts, tenfold, TBr.; ŚBr.; ŚāṅkhŚr.; Mn. &c. **—dhīva,** mf(*ā*)n. bought for (the prize of) 10 (*dhīvarī*) clever women, Pāṇ. iv, 1, 36, Vārtt. 2, Pat. **—nāmaka,** see *-mānika*. **—nāli,** mfn. 10 × 24 minutes long, Sāh. vi, 304. **—m-daśin,** mfn. = *-daś°*, ŚBr. iv, xi. **—pa,** m. = *-grāmin*, MBh. xii, 3266. **—paksha** (*dáś°*), mf(*ā*)n. having 10 side posts, AV. ix, 3, 21. **—paṭu,** mfn. = *-dhīva* (fr. *paṭvī*), Pāṇ. iv, 1, 36, Vārtt. 2, Pat. **—pada,** mf(*ā*)n. 10 feet long and broad, ĀpŚr. vii, 3, 10. **—padma** (B) or °**ma-vat** (G), mfn. having 10 lotus-like parts of the body, R. v. **—padya,** mf(*ā*)n. = °*da*, KātyŚr. v, 3, 33. **—parvī,** f. '10 Parvans (or chs.),' N. of a work, HPariś. i, 5. **—pala,** n. sg. 10 Palas, Mn. viii, 397; mf(*ā*)n. weighing 10 Palas, Yājñ. ii, 179. **—paśu,** mfn. intended for 10 oxen, ŚāṅkhŚr. xvi. **—pādī,** f. '10 chs.,' N. of a grammatical work, Prauḍh. **—pāramitā-dhara,** m. 'possessing the 10 perfections,' a Buddha, L. **—piṇḍa-śrāddha,** n. a funeral ceremony in which one and on each successive day one more Piṇḍa is offered until the number amounts to 10, W. **—pura,**

n. a kind of Cyperus rotundus (also *-pūra*, Sch.), L.; 'Decapolis,' the modern Man-dasor (in Malwa), Megh. 47; VarBṛS. xiv, 13; HPariś. xii f.; (*ī*), f. id., Kād. **— puraṃdara,** N. of a town or district, Siṅhās.² xxix. **— purusham,** ind. through a series of 10 ancestors, ĀśvŚr.; ŚāṅkhŚr.; °*shám-rājya*, n. a kingdom inherited through a series of 10 ancestors, ŚBr. xii, 9, 3; °*shânūkam*, ind. backwards through 10 generations, Pāṇ. iv, 1, 93, Vārtt. 5, Pat. **— pūra,** see *-pura*. **— pūrusha,** mfn. being the 10th in the succession of generations, MBh. xiii, 4297. **— pūrva-ratha,** see *-ratha*. **— pūrvin,** m. 'knowing 10 (of the 14) Pūrvas,' N. of 7 Jain patriarchs. **— pūlī,** f. 10 bunches, Pāṇ. ii, 1, 51, Vārtt. 6, Pat. **— péya,** m. N. of a Soma libation (part of a Rāja-sūya), ŚBr. v; TāṇḍyaBr.; ĀśvŚr.; ŚāṅkhŚr.; KātyŚr. **— pramati** (*dáś°*), mfn. (Agni) taken care of by the 10 (fingers), RV. i, 141, 2. **— phala-vrata,** n. N. of an observance, Vratapr. viii. **— baddha,** mfn. pl. bound in numbers of 10, Hariv. 3507. **— bandha,** m. a 10th part, Mn. viii, 107. **— bandhaka,** ifc. = °*dha*, Yājñ. ii, 76. **— bala,** m. 'possessing 10 powers,' N. of a Buddha, L.; *-kāśyapa*, m. N. of one of the first 5 pupils of Śākya-muni; *-balin*, mfn. possessing the 10 powers, Divyâv. viii, 81; ix, 17. **— bāhu,** m. 'ten-armed,' Śiva, L. **— bṛihat,** m(nom. °*hat*)fn. having 10 large parts of the body, R. (B) v, 35, 20. **— brāhmaṇa,** N. of Jāt. 495. **— bhujā,** f. 'ten-armed,' Durgā, KālP. **— bhuji** (*dáś°*), mfn. = *-guṇa*, RV. i, 52, 11. **— bhūmi,** N. of a Buddh. Sūtra; *-ga*, m. 'traversing the 10 stages,' a Buddha, L.; °*mīśa*, m. id., L.; °*mīśvara*, m. = °*mi*. **— bhūmika,** = °*mi*, Buddh. L. **— mahā-vidyā,** f. 'possessing the 10 great sciences,' Durgā, W. **— mānika,** m. pl. N. of a people, VāyuP. i, 45, 117; (*-nāmaka*, MatsyaP. cxiii, 42). **— māya** (*dáś°*), mfn. having 10 tricks, RV. vi, 20, 8. **— mārikā,** f. 'killer of 10,' N. of a woman, Kathās. lxvi, 86. **— māla,** n. 10 garlands, L.; (*ī*), f. id., L. **— mālika,** = *-mānika*, MBh. vi, 374. **— māsya** (*dáś°*), mfn. 10 months old (the child just before birth; cf. *á-*), RV. v, 78, 7 f.; AV. i, iii; ĀśvGṛ.; BhP.; let loose for 10 months (a horse), ŚBr. xiii, 5, 4, 22. **— mukha,** m. = *-kaṇṭha*, Megh.; Gīt.; Prab.; Sāh.; n. pl. 10 mouths, BhP. ix; (*ī*), f. id., Bālar. i, 33; v, 17; *-ripu*, m. 'enemy of Rāvaṇa,' Rāma, Ragh. xiv, 87; *-vadha*, m. 'slaughter of Rāvaṇa,' N. of a poem (different from Setub.?), Kāvyâd. i, 34, Sch.; °*khântaka*, m. = °*śa-ripu*, L. **— mūtraka,** n. the urine of 10 (elephant, buffalo, camel, cow, goat, sheep, horse, donkey, man, and woman), L.; cf. Suśr. i, 45, 11, 1 & 12. **— mūla,** n. a tonic medicine prepared from 10 roots (*tri-kaṇṭaka*, both kinds of *bṛihatī*, *pṛithak-parṇī*, *vidārī-gandhā*, *bilva*, *agni-mantha*, *tuṇṭuka*, *pāṭalā*, & *kāśmarī*), i, 38; iv, 37; (*ī*), f. id., 15; Car. vi, 22. **— yantra** (*dáś°*), mfn. = °*śâbhīśu*, RV. x, 94, 8; having 10 water-raising machines, vi, 44, 24. **— yoktra** (*dáś°*), mfn. having 10 girths, x, 94, 7. **— yoga-bhaṅga,** m. a method of fixing the position of a Nakshatra, Jyot. **— yojana** (*dáś°*), mfn. 10 times fastened, RV. x, 94, 7; n. a distance of 10 Yojanas, R. i, 1, 63; (*ī*), f. id., Kathās. xciv, 14. **— ratha** (*dáś°*), mfn. having 10 chariots, RV. i, 126, 4; m. N. of Rāma's father (descendant of Ikshvāku, sovereign of Ayodhyā), R. i; ii, 63 f. (death of D°); Jāt. 461; Hariv. 821 f.; Ragh. viii, 29 (*-pūrva-ratha*); BhP. ix, 10, 1; VP. iv, 4, 40 & 18, 3; N. of an ancestor of Rāma's father, 4, 38; of a son of Nava-ratha, 12, 16; BhP. ix, 24, 4; Hariv. 1993; of Roma- or Loma-pāda, 1696; VP. iv, 18, 3; of a son of Su-yaśas, 24, 8 (*dáś°*, v.l.) & Inscr. (in Prākṛit *Dasalatha*); n. the body, Npr.; *-tattva*, n. N. of a work; *-yajñârambha*, m. N. of PadmaP. iv, 14; *-lalitā-vrata*, n. N. of an observance, Vratapr. iv; *-vijaya*, m. N. of PadmaP. iv, 12. **— raśmi-śata,** m. = *-śata-r°*, Ragh. viii, 29. **— rātrá,** mfn. lasting 10 days, ŚBr. xiii; KātyŚr. xxi; m. a 10 days' ceremony, TāṇḍyaBr.; KātyŚr. xxiii; ŚāṅkhŚr.; N. of a 10 days' ceremony (forming the chief part of the Dvādaśâha), ŚBr. xii; KātyŚr.; 10 days, xxv; ŚāṅkhŚr.; Kauś.; Gobh.; Mn.; R. (n., iii, 2, 12); MārkP.; *-parvan*, n. N. of a Sāman. **— rūpa,** in comp. the 10 forms of Vishṇu (hence °*pa-bhṛit*, m. 'N. of Vishṇu,' L.), Daśar. i, 2; the 10 kinds of dramas, Bhar. xix, 46; n. N. of a work on rhetorical and dramatic composition (also called °*pâloka* & °*pâvaloka*, m.) **— rūpaka,** n. id., Mall. on Kum. & Śiś.; Ānand. 51, Sch.; the 10 kinds of dramas, Vām. i. **— rcá,** n. a hymn of 10 Ric verses, AV. xix, 23, 7; Kāṭh. xxi, 10; TS. v, 4, 6, 4; KātyŚr. xx, 6, 18. **— rshabha** (*dáś°*), mf(*ā*)n. consisting of 10 (*rish°*) bulls, TS. ii, 1, 4, 1. **— lakshaṇa,** n. 10 marks or attributes, W.; mfn. relating to 10 objects, BhP. ii, 9, 43; (*ī*), f. '10 chs.,' N. of Kaṇâda's Sūtras, Sarvad. x, 8. **— lakshaṇaka,** mfn. tenfold, Mn. vi, 91 & 94. **— vaktra,** m. N. of a magical formula pronounced over weapons, R. (G) i, 31, 6. **— vadana,** m. = *-kaṇṭha*, Bhaṭṭ. ix, 137. **— varga,** m. a collection of 10, KātyŚr. xxii; mfn. forming a collection of 10, Divyâv. i, 325. **— varsha,** mfn. 10 years old, Āp.; Mn. ii, 135. **— varshin,** mfn. id., MBh. xiii, 8, 21. **— varshīya,** mfn. id., Pañcar. i, 3, 9. **— vājin,** m. 'having 10 horses,' the moon, L. **— vāra,** mfn. 10 times repeated, Pañcar. i, 8, 31. **— vārshika,** mf(*ī*)n. = *-varsha*, R. iv, 48, 12; lasting 10 years, Pañcat. iii, 2, 5; happening after 10 years, Yājñ. ii, 24. **— vidha,** mfn. of 10 kinds, tenfold, Jain.; Sāṃkhyak.; BhP. iii; *-snāna-mantra*, m. pl. N. of particular hymns, ĀśvMantraS. **— vīra** (*dáś°*), mfn. granting 10 men, VS.; TāṇḍyaBr. **— vṛiksha,** m. N. of a tree, AV. ii, 9, 1. **— vṛishá,** mfn. possessing 10 bulls, v, 16, 10. **— vaikālika,** n. N. of a Jain text, HPariś. v, 85. **— vraja** (*dáś°*), m. 'having 10 cow-sheds,' N. of a man, RV. viii, 8 & 49 f. **— śatá,** mfn. numbering 10 hundred, AV. v, 18, 10; n. 110, ŚāṅkhŚr. xi; Lāṭy. ix; 1000, MBh. iii, xiii; Padyas.; (*ī*), f. 1000, Naish. v, 19; Rājat. vi, 38; *-kara-dhārin*, mfn. thousand-rayed (the moon), Hit. i, 2, 16; *-tama*, mfn. the 110th (ch. of R. [G] ii & vi); *-nayana*, m. 'thousand-eyed,' Indra, Lalit. xv, 162 & 202; *-raśmi*, m. 'thousand-rayed,' the sun, L., Sch.; °*tâksha*, mfn. thousand-eyed (Indra), MBh. vii, xiii; Daś. xi, 121; °*tâṅghri*, m. 'thousand-footed,' Asparagus racemosus, Npr.; °*târa*, n. Vishnu's thousand-fellied disc, BhP. iii, 28, 27. **— śala** (*dáś°*), a distance of 10 Śalas, AV. viii, 7, 28. **— śākha** (*dáś°*), mfn. having 1000 fingers, RV. x, 137, 7. **— śipra** (*dáś°*), m. N. of a man, viii, 52, 2. **— śiras,** m. 'ten-headed,' Rāvaṇa, L., Sch.; 'ten-peaked,' N. of a mountain, R. iv, 43, 51. **— śīrsha** (*dáś°*), mfn. ten-headed, AV. iv, 6, 1; MBh. i, 2162; m. Rāvaṇa, R. iv, 10, 22; N. of a magical formula pronounced over weapons, i, 30, 5. **— ślokī,** f. ten Ślokas (on Vedânta phil. by Śaṃkara), KāśīKh. lxxxvii, 33, Sch. **— sani,** mfn. winning 10, MantraBr. i, 7, 6. **— saptā,** f. N. of a Vishṭuti of the Saptadaśa-stoma, TāṇḍyaBr. ii, 7. **— sahâika,** mfn. 10 + 1, RPrāt. xvi, 36. **— sāhasra,** mfn. = °*srika*, MBh. i f., iv; R. vi; n. 10000, Hariv. **— sāhasrika,** mfn. numbering 10000, 6312. **— stobha,** n. N. of a Sāman. **— harā,** f. 'taking away the 10 sins,' the Gaṅgā; a festival in honour of the Gaṅgā (on the 10th day of Jyaishṭha, Vratapr. x; now held in honour of Durgā in month Āśvin), PSarv.; *-kathā*, f., *-stotra*, n. N. of 2 works. **— hala,** mf(*ā*)n. consisting of 10 ploughs, Hcat. i, 5, 889. **— hotṛi** (*dáś°*), m. N. of MaitrS. i, 9, 1 = Kāṭh. ix, 8 = TĀr. iii, 1 f. (symbolizing the 10 parts of a sacrifice), TBr. ii; TāṇḍyaBr. xxv; Lāṭy. x; ŚāṅkhŚr.; MānŚr. i. **Daśâṅśa,** m. a 10th part, Śāktân. xii; Hcat. i, 10 f. **Daśâksha,** m. N. of a formula pronounced over weapons, R. i, 30, 5. **Dáśâkshara,** mf(*ā*)n. containing 10 syllables, VS. ix, 33; TS. v, 4, 6, 4; ŚBr. **Daśâgni,** mfn. worshipping 10 Agnāyīs, Pat. on Pāṇ. i, 1, 58, Vārtt. 2 & iv, 1, 36, Vārtt. 2. **Daśâṅgulá,** n. a length of 10 fingers, RV. x, 90, 1; mfn. 10 fingers long, Mn. viii, 271; n. a water-melon, Npr. **Daśâdhipati,** m. a commander of 10 men, MBh. xii, 3712. **Daśânana,** m. = °*śa-kaṇṭha*, R. iii; vi, 5, 21; Ragh. x, 76. **Daśânika,** m. Croton polyandrum or Tiglium, L. **Daśânīkinī,** f. 'ten-arrayed,' a complete army, L. **Daśânugāna,** n. N. of several Sāmans, ĀrshBr. **Daśântarushyá,** n. a distance of 10 stations, RV. x, 51, 3. **Daśâbdâkhya,** mfn. existing for 10 years, Mn. ii, 134; cf. Āp. i, 14, 13. **Dáśâbhīśu,** mfn. having 10 bridles, RV. x, 94, 7. **Dáśâritra,** m. having 10 *aritra* parts (a chariot), ii, 18, 1. **Daśârṇa,** mfn. having 10 syllables, VS. iii, 41, Sch.; m. pl. (g. *vimuktâdi*) 'Ten Lakes,' N. of a people (south-east of Madhya-deśa, VarBṛS.), MBh.; Hariv.; R.; Megh.; sg. a Daśârṇa king, MBh. v, 7519; n. the Daśârṇa country, Pāṇ. vi, 1, 89, Vārtt. 8, Pat. (*daśa* + *ṛiṇa*); (*ā*), f. the Dasān river (rising in Bhopal and emptying into the Betwa); cf. *dāś°*. **Daśârṇeyu,** m. N. of a son of Raudrâśva, Hariv. 1660. **Daśârdha,** mfn. pl. 'half of ten,' five, Mn. i, 27; MBh. i; *-tā*, f. (= *pañca-tva*) dissolution of the body into the 5 elements, iii, 209, 26; *-bāṇa*, m. 'five-arrowed,' Kāma, Naish. viii, 73; *-vayas*, mfn. 5 years old, BhP. v, 15, 30. **Daśârha,** (g. *vimuktâdi* & *prajñâdi*) m. pl. (g. *parśv-ādi*) N. of a warrior tribe, MBh. iii; BhP. i, 11, 12; sg. of its ancestor (being of Yadu's family), ix, 24, 3; VP. iv, 12, 16; VāyuP. ii, 33, 40; LiṅgaP. i, 68, 42 f.; MatsyaP. xliv, 40; AgP.; BrahmaP.; Hariv. 1991; Kṛishṇa, MBh. xiii, 7003 (*dāś°*, B); = °*śa-bhūmi-ga*, L.; (*ī*), f. a Daśârha princess, g. *parśv-ādi*; cf. *su-*. **Daśârhaka,** m. pl. (g. *yāvâdi*, Gaṇar. 187) the Daśârhas, BhP. ix, 24, 62. **Daśâlaṃkāra-mañjarī,** f. N. of a work. **Daśâvatāra,** m. (= °*śa-rūpa*) Vishṇu, L.; n. N. of an observance (performed on the 10th day of the light half of Bhādrapada, Vratapr. x), BhavP. ii, 60; *-carita*, n. N. of a work. **Daśâvara,** mfn. pl. at least 10, Gaut. xxviii, 48 f.; mf(*ā*)n. sg. consisting of at least 10, Mn. xii, 110 f.; m. N. of an evil spirit, MBh. ii, 367. **Daśâvarta,** mfn. having 10 crowns, R. v, 32, 12. **Daśâśva,** m. = °*śa-vājin*, L.; N. of a son of Ikshvāku, MBh. xiii, 89 f. **Daśâśvamedha,** n. the Tīrtha of the 10 horse-sacrifices, iii, 5084; RevāKh. ccviii & cclvii; KāśīKh. lii; ŚambhMāh. v; cf. *dāś°*. **Daśâśvamedhika,** n. id., MBh. iii, 6034; Hariv. 9522. **Dáśâsya,** mfn. ten-mouthed, AV. iv, 6, 1; m. Rāvaṇa, R. iii, 55, 12; Sāh. vi, 2⁄3; *-jit*, m. 'conqueror of Rāvaṇa,' Rāma, L.; °*syântaka*, m. id., RāmatUp. i, 32. **Daśâha,** m. 10 days, ŚBr. xiii; ĀśvGṛ.; Mn.; R.; a ceremony lasting 10 days, KātyŚr. xxiii; Lāṭy. x, 10. **Daśêndra,** mfn. worshipping the 10 Indrāṇīs, Pat. on Pāṇ. i, 1, 58, Vārtt. 2 & iv, 1, 36, Vārtt. 2; i, 2, 49, Kāś. **Daśêndriya,** n. pl. the 10 organs (*ind°*, q. v.), W. **Daśêśa,** m. = °*śa-pa*, Mn. vii, 116. **Daśâikâdaśika,** mf(*ī*)n. 'taking 11 for 10,' lending money at 10 per cent., Pāṇ. iv, 4, 31. **Dáś'oṇi,** m. N. of a man protected by Indra, RV. vi, 20, 4 & 8; x, 96, 12. **Dáś'oṇya,** m. id., viii, 52, 2. **Daśôpanishad-bhāshya,** n. N. of a Comm. by Ānanda-tīrtha.

Daśaka, mfn. consisting of 10, having 10 parts, RPrāt.; Mn.; Chandaḥs.; Kāś.; Kām.; (with *śata*) 10 per cent., Yājñ. ii; m. one in a decad of chs. (of the Sāma-tantra); n. a decad, Śāntiś. iv, 7; Kathās. cii, 108; KātyŚr. xvii, 6, 3, Sch. **— māsika,** mfn. hired for 10 months, Pāṇ. v, 4, 116, Vārtt. 4, Pat.

Daśát, (1, 60) mfn. consisting of 10, Kāś.; f. a decad, MaitrS. i; TS. vii; TBr. i; ŚBr.; TāṇḍyaBr.

Dáśataya, mf(*ī*)n. (Pāṇ. v, 2, 42) consisting of 10, tenfold, RV. i; (*ī*), f. N. of a Comm.; pl. (scil. *ṛicas*) the 10 Maṇḍalas of RV., Lāṭy. x; Nir.; cf. *dāś°*.

Daśati, f. a decad of verses in SV. (nom. °*ti*, v. l. °*tyā*); 100 (only nom. acc. °*tir daśa*, '1000'), MBh.

Daśan, pl. (g. *svasr-ādi*, Gaṇar. 42) ten (nom. acc. *dáśa*, RV. &c.; instr. [*dáśa*, x, 101, 10 &] *daśábhis*, loc. °*śásu*, RV. &c.; both forms & °*śabhyas* in Class. also oxyt., Pāṇ. vi, 1, 177 ff.); cf. *á-*, δέκα.

Daśamá, mf(*ī*)n. the 10th, RV. i (with *yugá* = °*mí*, 158, 6); x; AV. v; xiii; VS. &c.; n. with *áhan*, the last day of the Daśa-rātra ceremony, TBr. ii; ŚBr. xii; TāṇḍyaBr.; ŚāṅkhŚr.; (without *ahan*) Lāṭy.; (proparox., Pāṇ. v, 3, 49) a 10th part, Mn. viii f.; (*ám*), ind. for the 10th time, RV. viii, 24, 23; TBr. ii; (*ī*), f. the 10th stage of human life (age from 91 to 100 years), AV. iii, 4, 7; TāṇḍyaBr.; Gaut.; Mn. ii; (scil. *tithi*) the 10th day of the half-moon, iii, 276; MBh. &c.; the 10th day after birth, Pat. Introd. 73; [cf. Lat. *decimus*.] **— bhāva,** m. the culminating point, or that point in which the meridian crosses a given circle, Sūryas., Sch. **Daśamin,** mfn. 91–100 years old, ŚāṅkhBr. xiii, 3, Sch.

Daśin, mfn. having 10 parts, ŚBr. xiii; AitBr.; Lāṭy.; Maś.; RPrāt.; m. = °*śa-grāmin*, Mn. vii, 119.

दशन *daśana* (√*daṅś*) m. (n., L., Sch.) a tooth, Mn. &c. (ifc. f. *ā*, iii, 10; MBh. xii; Megh. &c.); a bite, Vātsyāy. i, 1, 2; m. a peak, L.; n. (= *daṅś°*) armour, L. **— cchada,** m. = *danta-*, MBh.; Hariv.; R.; BhP. **— pada,** n. 'teeth-mark,' a bite, Gīt. viii, 6. **— bīja,** the pomegranate, Npr. **— vasana,** n. = *-cchada*, Prasannar. ii, 9; °*nâṅga-rāga*, m. pl. N. of a Kalā (q. v.), Vātsyāy. i, 3, 17. **— vāsas,** n. = *-vasana*, L. **— vyaya,** m. loss of the teeth, W. **Daśanâṅśu,** m. pl. brightness of the teeth, Kum. vi, 25. **Daśanâṅka,** m. = °*na-pada*, W. **Daśanâḍhyā,** f. Oxalis corniculata, L. **Daśanôcchishṭa,** m. a kiss, L.; a sigh, L.; a lip, L.

दशस्य *daśasya*, Nom. (fr. °*sas* = Lat. *decus*; cf. √*dāś* & *yáśas*) °*yáti* (Impv. °*yá*, °*ya*; p. °*yát*) to render service, serve, worship, favour, oblige (with acc.), RV.; to accord, do favour to (dat.), RV.

Daśasyá, ind. to please any one (dat.), vii, 99, 3.

दशा *daśā,* f. (√*daṇś?*) the fringe of a garment, loose ends of any piece of cloth, skirt or hem, KātyŚr. iv, 1, 17 (*ūrṇā-*); Lāṭy. viii, 6, 22; Kauś.; ŚāṅkhGṛ. ii, 12, 5; Mn. &c.; a wick, Gobh. iv, 2, 32 (*kshauma-*); Kum. iv, 30; Bhartṛ. iii, 1; state or condition of life, period of life (youth, manhood, &c.), condition, circumstances, R.; Pañcat.; Megh. &c.; the fate of men as depending on the position of the planets, aspect or position of the planets (at birth &c.), VarBṛS.; VarBṛ.; Laghuj.; the mind, L.; cf. *vastra-*; 1. *daśa.* **—°karsha, °shin** (°*śā́k*°), m. 'wick-drawing,' a lamp, L. **—°nta** (°*śā́n*°), m. the end of a wick, Ragh. xii, 1; the end of life, ib.; Hariv. 4394. **—pati,** m. the planet governing a man's life, VarBṛ., Sch. **—°panna** (°*śā́p*°), mfn. being in a particular state or condition. **—paripāka,** m. a change in a man's fate, Mcar. vii, 1/2. **—pavitrá,** n. a fringed filtering cloth, ŚBr. iv, 2, 2, 11; Lāṭy. i, 9. **—pāka,** m. the fulfilment of fate, VarBṛS. vc, 61. **—phala,** n. result of condition of life, future fate of a man, lxx, 26; N. of wk. **—maya,** m. Śiva, L. **—°ruhā** (°*śā́r*°), f. 'sticking to fringes,' N. of a plant, L. **—lakshaṇa,** n. N. of a ch. of PSarv. **—vat,** mfn. having fringes, ĀpŚr. xii, 14, 11. **—viśesha,** m. any particular state, Sāh. iii, 189; Hit. i, 7, 1/2. **Daśéndhana,** m. 'wick-kindling,' a lamp, L.

दशीविदर्भ *daśī-vidarbha,* m. pl. N. of a people (v.l. *dadhi-*), MBh. vi, 372.

दशेर *daśera,* mfn. (√*daṇś*) mordaceous, injuring, Uṇ., Sch.; attacking or killing any one when asleep, L.; m. a beast of prey, W. **°raka,** m. an ass (cf. *dasra*), MBh. viii, 1852; pl. N. of a people (= *maru*; cf. *dāś*°; sg. their country, L.), iii, 134, 17 (°*śair*° derived fr. 2. *daśa*); vii, 397; VarBṛS. v, 67; cf. *agniveśa-*; *-gaḍeraka,* m. pl. the descendants of D° & G°, g. *tika-kitavâdi* (Gaṇar. 34).

दशोणि *dáś'oṇi,* °*nya.* See 2. *daśa.*

दशोनसि *dáśonasi,* N. of a snake, AV. x, 4.

दष्ट *dashṭa,* mfn. (√*daṇś*) bitten, stung, Mn. xi; MBh. &c. (said of a wrong pronunciation, PāṇŚ. [RV.] 35); n. a bite, Suśr. i, 13, 6.

दस् *das,* cl. 1. 4. (p. *dásamāna*; impf. pl. *adasyan*) to suffer want, become exhausted, RV. i, 134, 5 (Nir. i, 9); TS. i, 6, 11, 3; = *upa-√kship,* Dhātup.: Caus. Ā. (1. sg. °*saye*; Subj. pl. °*sayanta*) to exhaust, iv, 2, 5, 4; RV. v, 45, 3; cf. *apa-, upa-, anúpa-, pra-, vi-*; *sam-dadasvás, draviṇo-dás*; δεῖ. **Dása,** m. a demon, vi, 21, 11.

Dasta, mfn. = *dāsita,* Pāṇ. vii, 2, 27; Vop. xxvi.

दस्म *dasmá,* mfn. (√*daṇs*) accomplishing wonderful deeds, wonderful, extraordinary, RV.; m. a sacrificer, L.; fire, L.; a thief, rogue (cf. °*syu*), L. **—tama** (°*smá-*), mfn. most wonderful, ii, 20, 6. **—varcas** (°*smá-*), mfn. of wonderful appearance, RV.

Dasmát-√kṛi, to make wonderful, i, 74, 4.

Dásmya, mfn. wonderful, viii, 24, 20.

Dasrá, mfn. accomplishing wonderful deeds, giving marvellous aid (chiefly said of the Aśvins), RV.; m. N. of one of the Aśvins, Bṛih.; MBh.; Hariv. 601; du. the Aśvins, L.; sg. the number 2, Sūryas. i; = *-devatā,* viii, 9; a robber, thief, Uṇ., Sch.; an ass (cf. *daśeraka*), L.; n. the cold season, Uṇ. vṛ. **—devatā,** f. 'having the Aśvins as deity,' the Nakshatra Aśvinī, L. **—sū,** f. 'mother of the Aśvins,' Saṃjñā, L.

दस्यु *dásyu,* m. (√*das*) enemy of the gods (e.g. *śámbara, śúshṇa, cúmuri, dhúni*; all conquered by Indra, Agni, &c.), impious man (called *a-śraddhá, a-yajñá, á-yajyu, á-pṛiṇat, a-vratá, anyá-vrata, a-karmán*), barbarian (called *a-nā́s* or *an-ā́s* 'ugly-faced,' *ádhara* 'inferior,' *á-mānusha* 'inhuman'), robber (called *dhanín*), RV.; AV. &c.; any outcast or Hindū who has become so by neglect of the essential rites, Mn.; not accepted as a witness, viii, 66; cf. *trasá-* (*dásyave vṛika,* m. 'wolf to the Dasyu,' N. of a man, RV. viii, 51; 55 f; *dásyave sáhas,* n. violence to the D° (N. of Turvīti), i, 36, 18). **—jīvin,** mfn. living a robber's life, MBh. xii, 2433. **—jūta** (*dás*°), mfn. instigated by Dasyus, RV. vi, 24, 8. **—tárhaṇa,** mfn. crushing the Dasyus, ix, 47, 2. **—sāt-√bhū,** to become a prey to robbers, MBh. xii. **—hátya,** n. a fight with the Dasyus, RV. i, x; cf. *śushṇa-h*°. **—hán,** m(nom. °*hā́,* instr. °*ghnā́*)fn. destroying the Dasyus (Indra i, vi, viii; Indra's gift, x, 47, 4; *manyú,* 83, 3; *mánas,* iv, 16, 10); °*hán-tama,* mfn. (superl.) most destructive to the Dasyus, vi, 16, 15 & viii, 39, 8 (Agni); x, 170, 2 (Light); Hariv. (Budha); cf. Pāṇ. viii, 2, 17, Kāś.

दस्र *dasrá.* See *dasmá.*

दह् 1. *dah,* cl. 1. P. *dahati* (ep. also Ā.; p. *dáhat*; impf. *ádahat*; aor. *adhāk,* RV. ii, 15, 4; 1. sg. °*ksham,* MBh. vii; 3. pl. °*kshur,* Kathās.; Subj. *dhāk,* RV. i, 158, 4; 2. sg. *dhakshi,* iv, 4, 4; p. *dhákshat* [also nom. m.], vi, 3, 4; x, 91, 7; *dákshat,* i, 130, 8; fut. *dhakshyati* [Pāṇ. vii, 2, 10, Siddh. Kār. 6], MBh. [Pot. *dhakshyet,* i, 8383] &c.; *dahishy*°, i, 2120; BhP. iv; Prasaṅg. xix, 7; inf. *dagdhum*) to burn, consume by fire, scorch, roast, RV. &c.; to cauterise, Suśr.; to consume, destroy completely, Mn. vii, 9; MBh. &c.; to torment, torture, pain, distress, disturb, grieve, MBh. &c.: Pass. *dahyate* (°*ti,* MānGṛ. ii, 15; MBh. i f., xii f.) to be burnt, burn, be in flames, AV.; Nir. &c.; to be consumed by fire or destroyed, Mn. vi, 71; to be inflamed (a wound), Suśr. i, 28; to be consumed by internal heat or grief, suffer pain, be distressed or vexed, MBh. &c.: Caus. *dāhayati,* to cause to burn or be burned, Mn.; Yājñ. i, 89; MBh. &c.; to cause to be cooked, Hariv. 15523 (aor. pl. *adīdahan*): Desid. *didhakshati* (cf. °*kshā,* °*kshu*) to be about to burn or consume or destroy, MBh. i–iv; R. (p. °*kshamāṇa*): Desid. Caus. (p. °*kshayat*) to cause any one to make efforts to burn, Bhaṭṭ. iii, 33: Intens. *dandahīti,* °*hyate* (Pāṇ. iii, 1, 24; vii, 4, 86) to burn or destroy completely, Hariv. 8726; BhP. vi, 8, 21 (Impv. °*dagdhi*), Śiś.; Prasannar. vi, 32 & 48; Ā. to be burnt completely, Hariv. 7040; BhP.; Pañcat. i, 8, 2/3; [cf. Lith. *degù,* 'I am hot;' Goth. *dag-s*; Old Germ. *tāh-t,* 'a wick'].

2. **Dah,** mfn. 'burning,' see *uśá-.* **Dahati,** m. N. of an attendant of Skanda, MBh. ix, 2536.

Dahadahā, f. N. of one of the mothers attending on Skanda, 2638.

Dahana, mf(*ī*)n. burning, consuming by fire, scorching, destroying (chiefly ifc.), Hariv.; BhP.; Bhartṛ.; (said of the *dhāraṇā* of fire) Goraksh. 164; m. fire (of three kinds), Agni, Kauś.; MBh. &c. (ifc. f. *ā,* Horāś.); the numeral three, VarBṛS.; Sūryas.; one of the 5 forms of fire in the Svāhā-kāra, Hariv. 10465; a pigeon, L; Plumbago zeylanica, L.; Anacardium officinarum, L.; N. of an attendant of Skanda, MBh. ix, 2536; N. of a Rudra, i; MatsyaP.; n. burning, consuming by fire, Kauś. 80; R. vii; Ragh. &c.; cauterising, Suśr.; sour gruel, Npr.; (*ā*), f. N. of part of the moon's course, VarBṛS. ix, 1–3, Sch.; (*ī*), f. Sanseviera Roxburghiana, L. **—karman,** n. the act of burning, Dhūrtas, i, 22. **—ketana,** m. 'mark of burning,' smoke, L. **—garbha,** mf(*ā*)n. filled with the fire (of wrath), Daś. vi, 21. **—tā,** f. the state of fire, ŚārṅgP. xxix, 11. **—priyā,** f. the wife of Agni, L. **—rksha** (*ṛik*°), n. the constellation Kṛittikā, VarBṛS. x, 19. **Dahanâguru,** n. a kind of Agallochum, L. **Dahanârāti,** m. 'fire-enemy,' water, L. **Dahanôpakaraṇa,** n. the means for cauterising, Suśr. i, 12, 2. **Dahanôpala,** m. the sun-gem, L. **Dahanôlkā,** f. a firebrand, L.

Dahanīya, mfn. to be burnt, combustible, W. **—tā,** f. combustibility, W. **—tva,** n. id., W.

दहर *dahara,* mfn. (fr. *dabhrá*) small, fine, thin, ChUp. viii, 1, 1; KātyŚr. xiv; KenUp. (v.l. *dabhra*); BhP. x; young in age, Lalit. vii, 72; SaddhP.; m. a younger brother, L.; a child, W.; a young animal, W.; a mouse, Gaut.; Yājñ. iii, 274/1. **—pṛishṭha,** n. N. of TS. v, 1, 11 & 2, 11 f., Ātr-Anukr. i, 24. **—sūtra,** n. N. of a Buddh. Sūtra.

Daharaka, mfn. short (day), ŚāṅkhBr. xix, 3; Naigh. iii, 2.

1. **Dahra,** mfn. small, fine, thin, NṛUp.; Ap. i, 9, 23 (°*re' para-rātre,* 'in the shorter half of the night'); (*ám*), ind. little, TS. vii, 5, 3, 1; n. the cavity of the heart, BhP. iii; vi, 9. **Dahrāgni,** m. Agastya in a former birth, iv, 1, 36.

दह्र 2. *dahra,* m. a wood on fire, Uṇ. vṛ.; fire, ib.

दा 1. *dā,* cl. 3. *dádāti* (pl. °*dati,* RV. &c.; Ā. *datte,* Pañcat. i, 4, 18/0 & 12, 7; Subh.; 1. sg. *dadmi,* MBh. xii; Hariv.; R. i f.; Impv. *dádātu,* pl. °*datu*; 2. sg. *daddhí* RV. i f., iv, vi, viii, x; *dehí* [Pāṇ. vi, 4, 119], RV. iii f., viii, x; AV. v, xviii f. &c.; 2. pl. *dádāta* RV. vii, 57, 6, °*tana* x, 36, 10, *dattá* 51, 8; VS.; AV. &c.; 2. du. °*ttám,* RV. i, 34, 6; AV. &c.; Pot. *dadyā́t,* AV. &c.; impf. *ádadāt*; pl. *ádadur,* RV. vi, x; AV. v, 18, 1; 2. du. *ádattam,* RV. &c.; 2. pl. °*ttana* i, 139, 7, *ádadāta* x, 64, 12; Subj. *dádat* ii, v, vii f., x, °*das* vii f., °*dan* AV. vi, 24, 1; p. m. nom. sg. *dádat,* pl. °*tas,* RV. &c.; p. Ā. *dádāna,* v, 33, 9; °*nā,* i, 148, 2; v, 2, 3; sg. *dadati,* ii, 35, 10; MBh. iii, 13422; pl. °*danti,* xii f.; Impv. °*da,* ix; MārkP.; °*data,* Siṃhâs.; Pot. °*det,* Parāś. vi, 19; impf. *ádadat,* AV. xii, 4, 23; MBh.; R.; Ā. sg. *dádate,* RV. i, 24, 7; AV. x, 8, 36; pl. °*dante,* 35; VS. viii, 31; Impv. sg. °*datām,* RV. iii, 53, 17; °*dasva,* MBh.; Hariv. &c.; impf. pl. *ádadanta,* RV. vii, 33, 11; AV. xiv; p. *dádamāna,* RV. i, 41, 9; iv, 26, 6; — aor. *ádāt* [Pāṇ. ii, 4, 77], *dā́t, ádur, dúr* &c.; Subj. 2. du. *dā́sathas,* RV. viii, 40, 1 [cf. Naigh. ii, 30]; Pot. 1. pl. *deshma,* VS. ii, 32; pf. *dadaú,* °*dúr,* °*dáthur,* °*datur,* °*dá,* RV. &c.; Pass. °*dé,* iv, 34 & 37; AV. x, 2, 16; *dadade,* °*dāte,* °*dire,* Pāṇ. vi, 4, 126, Kāś.; p. gen. *dadúshas* RV. i, viii, °*shām* vi; nom. °*dvā́n,* x, 132, 3; °*dāvā́n,* AV. v, 11, 1; acc. °*divā́ṃsam,* ix, 5, 10 [cf. Vop. xxvi, 133]; fut. p. *dasyát,* AV. vi, 71, 3, Ā. °*syate,* °*syante,* 1. sg. °*sye,* MBh.; Hariv.; R.; MārkP.; Prec. *deyāt,* Pāṇ. vi, 4, 67; inf. *dāváne,* RV.; *dā́tos,* vii, 4, 6; °*tave,* vii–ix; AV. iii, 20, 5; *dā́tavaí* [Pāṇ. vi, 1, 200, Siddh.], RV. iv, 21, 9; °*tum,* v; AV. &c.; ind. p. *dattvā́ya* [Pāṇ. vii, 1, 47, Kāś.], RV. x, 85, 33; °*ttvā́,* AV. &c.; *-dāya* [Pāṇ. vi, 4, 69], RV. &c.: Pass. *dīyate* [Pāṇ. vi, 4, 62]; p. °*yámāna,* AV. ix; aor. *adāyi,* Pāṇ. vii, 3, 33, Kāś.; Prec. *dāsīshṭa, dāyis*°, vi, 4, 62), cl. 1. *dāti* (RV. iv–viii; Impv. °*tu,* 15, 11; cf. Pāṇ. vi, 1, 8, Vārtt. 3, Pat.; ii, 4, 76, Kāś.) to give, bestow, grant, yield, impart, present, offer to (dat., in later language also gen. or loc.), RV. &c.; to give (a daughter, *kanyām*) in marriage, Mn. v, ix; Yājñ.; MBh. &c.; to hand over, Mn. viii, 186 & 234; (with *haste*) Kathās.; to give back, 222 f.; MBh. iii; Pañcat.; VP.; Kathās. lxxiv; to pay (*daṇḍam,* 'a fine,' Mn. viii f.; *ṛiṇam,* 'a debt,' viii; Yājñ. ii, 45); to give up, cede (*āsanam,* 'one's seat'), Mn. iv, 154; (*panthānam* or *mārgam,* 'to give up the road, allow to pass') viii, 275 & R. v, 94, 8; to sell (with instr. of the price), i; Nal. xiv, 21; VarBṛS. xlii, 11; to sacrifice (*ātmānam,* 'one's self,' Kathās. xxii, 227; *āt*° *khedāya,* 'to give one's self up to grief,' v, 57); to offer (an oblation &c.), Mn.; Yājñ.; R. &c.; to communicate, teach, utter (blessings, *āśishas,* Śak.; MārkP.), give (answer, *prati-vacas,*°*canam, praty-uttaram,* Nal.; Śak. &c.), speak (*satyaṃ vacas,* the truth, Yājñ. ii, 200; *vācam,* to address a speech to [dat.] Śak. vi, 5); to permit, allow (with inf.), MBh. i; Śak. vi, 22; to permit sexual intercourse, ŚBr. xiv, 9, 4, 7; to place, put, apply (in med.), Mn.; Yājñ.; MBh. &c.; to add, Pañcat. ii, 6, 5; Sūryas.; VarBṛS.; Laghuj.; with *varam,* 'to grant a boon,' ŚBr. xi; KātySr.; MBh. &c.; *śokam,* 'to cause grief,' xiii; R. ii; *avakāśam,* 'to give room or space, allow to enter,' Yājñ. ii, 276; Mṛicch.; Ragh. &c.; *prāṇān* or *jīvitam,* 'to spare any one's life,' MBh.; Kathās. xviii, 275; *talam* or °*lān,* to slap with the palms of the hands, MBh. iii, ix; Hariv. 15741; °*la-prahāram,* to strike with the palm, Pañcat. iv, 2, 1/2; *tālam,* to beat time with the hands, MBh. i; Bhaṭṭ.; *saṃjñām,* to make a sign, Mṛicch.; *saṃketakam,* to make an appointment, Pañcat. ii, 4, 2/3; *samayam,* to propose an agreement, Kathās. xviii, 139; *upamām,* to compare with [gen.], Cāṇ.; *paṭaham,* to proclaim with the drum, Kathās. lxxiii, 357; *śabdam,* to make a noise, call out, Vet. iv, 2/3; *śāpam,* to utter a curse, MBh.; R. &c.; *gālīḥ,* id., Bhartṛ.; *anuyātrām,* to accompany, Kathās. xviii, 197; *āliṅganam, parirambhaṇam,* to embrace, 209; Git. iii, 8; *jhampam,* to jump, Hit.; *śrāddham,* to perform a Śrāddha, MBh. xiv; R. ii; *vratakam,* to accomplish a vow, Hariv.; *yuddham, niy*°, *saṃgrāmam,* to give battle, fight with, MBh.; Hariv.; R.; *ājñām, ādeśam,* to give an order, command, i; BrahmaP.; Vet.; *saṃdeśam,* to give information, Kathās. xvii, 161; *prayogam,* to give a dramatic representation, Mālav. i, 1/2; *vṛitim,* to fence in, Mn. viii, 240, Kull.; *darśanam,* to show one's self, Prab. iii, 1/2; *dṛishṭim, dṛiśam, akshi, cakshus,* to fix the eyes on (loc.), Śak. i, 6; Kathās.; Dhūrtas.; Śṛiṅgārat.; Sāh.; *karṇam,* to give ear, listen, Śak.; Kathās.; *manas,* to direct the mind to (loc.), MBh. xii, 2526; *kare* *kapolam*, to rest the cheek on the hand, Kāraṇḍ. xviii, 73; *nigaḍāni*, to put on or apply fetters, Mṛicch. vii, ½; *pāvakam*, to set on fire; *agnīn*, to consume by fire, Mn. v, 168; *śāram*, to move a chess-man, Daś. vii, 137; *argalam*, to draw a bolt, bar, Kathās.; Rājat. vi, 96; *jānu*, to kneel upon (gen.), MBh. iii f.; *padam*, to tread upon [loc.], Bhartṛ.; Hit. ii, 12, 25; SŚaṃkar. i, 38; to direct the steps, Amar. 74; *visham*, to poison, Pañcar. i, 14, 80 (with acc.!); *garam*, id., VP. iv, 3, 16 (with gen.); — Ā. to carry, hold, keep, preserve, RV.; AV.; VS.; 'to show,' SV. i, 2, 1, 4, 7 (aor. *adadishṭa*; *aded°* fr. √*diś*, RV.): Caus. *dāpayati* (Pāṇ. vii, 3, 36; aor. *adīdapat*, 4, 1 & 58, Kāś.) to cause to give or be given, cause to bestow or present or give up, oblige to pay, make restore, VS. ix, 24; AV. iii, 20, 8; Mn. &c.; to demand from (abl.), Mn. viii, 47; to cause to utter or speak, Hariv. 15782; Yājñ. ii, ½; *ghoshaṇām*, to cause to be made known, Kathās. lxiv, 86; to cause to place or advance, xii, 160; to cause to perform, v, 112; to cause to be put on (loc.), MBh. i, 5724: Desid. *ditsati* (Pāṇ. vii, 4, 54 & 58; p. *didāsat*, RV. x, 151, 2; *ditsat*, ii, vii–ix; AV. v, 7, 6; MBh.; Pot. °*tseyam*, RV. viii; MBh.; pf. 2. sg. *didāsitha*, AitBr. viii, 21; ŚāṅkhŚr. xvi, 16; cf. ŚBr. xiii, 7, 1, 15) to wish to give, be ready to bestow, RV. &c.; to wish to give in marriage, MBh. &c.: Intens. *dedīyate*, Pāṇ. vi, 4, 66, Kāś.; [cf. δίδωμι; Lat. *do*; &c.]

2. **Dā́**, m. a giver, RV. v, 41, 1 (dat. *dé*); vi, 16, 26 (nom. *dā́s*); ifc. 'giving, granting,' see *an-aśva-*, *a-bhiksha-*, *aśva-*, *ātma-*, &c. *-dā́*; *án-āśīr-*.

Dāka, m. a donor, Uṇ. iii, 40, Sch.; a sacrificer, ib.

1. **Dāta**, mfn. 'given,' see *tvā́-*. °**tavya**, mfn. to be given, AitBr.; Mn. &c.; to be communicated, ŚvetUp.; Pañcat. i; MārkP.; to be given in marriage, Dāyabh. (Paiṭh.); Kathās.; to be paid or restored, Mn. viii; Pāṇ. iii, 3, 171, Kāś.; to be placed upon (loc.), Mn. v, 136; VarBṛS.; to be made, Bhpr. vii, 18, 74. 1. **Dāti**, see *havyá-*; *-vāra* (*dā́t°*), mfn. liking to give, RV. i, 167, 8; iii, 51, 9; v, 58, 2.

1. **Dā́tṛi** (with acc.; once without, RV. iv, 31, 7), °**tṛí** (with or without gen.; exceptionally with acc., ŚBr. xi, 5, 1, 12), m. giving, a giver, donor, liberal, RV. &c.; one who gives a daughter (gen.) in marriage (cf. *kanyā-*), Kum. vi, 1; a father or brother who gives a daughter or sister in marriage, MānGṛ. i, 8; Mn. iii, 172; Paiṭh.; R.; one who offers (his wife, gen.), L.; a creditor, Mn. viii, 161; the arranger of a meal, iii, 236; granting, permitting (ifc. or with gen.), v, viii, xi; MBh. &c.; a founder (of a household, *kuṭumbānām*), xiii, 1663; [cf. *a-*, *ṛiṇa-*, *brahma-*; δωτήρ, δοτήρ, Lat. *dator*, *daturus*.] **-tā**, f. the being a giver, liberality, Rājat.; Sāh. iii. ⁶⁄₈. **-tva**, n. id., Hariv. 14414; Ragh.; Cāṇ. **-nirūpaṇa**, n. N. of a ch. of PSarv. **-pura**, n. N. of a town, Śaṃkaracetov. i.

Dātta, m. a well made by Datta, Pāṇ. iv, 2, 74, Kāś. **Dāttâmitrī**, f. N. of a town built by Dattāmitra, 76, Kāś.; °*trīya*, mfn. fr. °*trī*, 123, Kāś.

Dātteya, m. metron. fr. Dattā, 1, 121, Kāś.

Dātva, m. a giver, Uṇ.; n. a sacrificial act, ib.

Dāda, m. (√*dad*) gift, donation, MBh. ix, 2117; 2269 (B. *dāya*); Śiś. xix, 114. **-da**, mfn. gift-giving, Śiś. x, ib.

Dādin, mfn. giving, a giver, W.

1. **Dā́na**, n. the act of giving, RV.; ŚBr.; MBh. &c.; giving in marriage (cf. *kanyā-*); giving up (cf. *prāṇa-*, *ātma-*, *śarīra-*, Pañc. ii); communicating, imparting, teaching (cf. *brahma-*); paying back, restoring, Mn.; Yājñ.; adding, addition (VarBṛS.); donation, gift [Lat. *donum*], RV.; ŚBr. &c. (°*nam dā*, to offer a g°; Mn.; Yājñ.; Hit. &c.; °*nam prayam*, to bestow a g°, Mn. iv, 234); oblation (cf. *udaka-*, *havir-*); liberality (cf. 2. *dāna*); bribery, Mn. vii, 198 (cf. *upâya*). **-kamalâkara**, m., **-kalpa-taru**, m. N. of wks. **-kāma** (*dā́°*), mfn. fond of giving, liberal, TS.; TBr. **-kusumâñjali**, m., **-keli-kaumudī**, f., **-kaumudī**, f., **-kaustubha**, m. or n., **-kriyā-kaumudī**, f. N. of wks. **-khaṇḍa**, m. N. of part 1 of Hemâdri's wk. **-candrikā**, f. N. of wk. **-cyuta**, m. 'one who has abandoned liberality,' N. of a man (g. *kārtakaujapâdi*). **-tas**, ind. through gifts, by liberality, MW. **-darpaṇa**, m., **-dinakara**, m. N. of wks. **-dharma**, m. duty of liberality, Mn.; Hit.; *-kathana*, n., *-vidhi*, m., °*mâdhyâya*, m. N. of wks on alms-giving. °**ṃ-dadā**, f. N. of an Apsaras or of a female Gandharva, Kāraṇḍ. **-pati**, m. 'liberality-lord,' munificent man, MBh.; R.; N. of A-krūra, MBh.; Hariv.; of a Daitya, Hariv. **-pattra**, n. deed of gift, MW. **-paddhati**, f. N. of a wk on the 16 offerings, RTL. 415. **-para**, mfn. devoted to liberality; *-tā*, f. liberality, Nāg. v, 29. **-paribhāshā**, f. N. of wk. **-pātra**, n. 'object of charity,' N. of a ch. of PSarv. **-pāramitā**, f. perfection of liberality, Kāraṇḍ.; Naish. **-pārijāta**, m., **-prakaraṇa**, n., **-prakāśa**, m., **-pradīpa**, m. N. of wks. **-prātibhāvya**, n. security for payment, W. **-bhāgavata**, n. N. of wk. **-bhinna**, mfn. set at variance by bribes, Hit. iv, 39. **-mañjarī**, f., **-manohara**, m. N. of wks. **-maya**, mf(*ī*)n. consisting in liberality, L. **-mayūkha**, m. N. of wk. **-yogya**, mfn. worthy of a gift, Daś. **-vajra**, m. 'whose weapon is liberality' (said of Vaiśyas), MBh. i, 6487. **-vat** (*dā́°*), mfn. having or bestowing gifts, liberal, RV. viii, 32, 12; MBh. xiii, 55. **-varman**, m. 'whose armour is liberality,' N. of a merchant, Kathās. **-vaśī-√kṛi**, to make subject by bribery, id. **-vār**, n. libation of water, Kāv. **-vidhi**, m. N. of wk. **-vīra**, m. 'liberality-hero,' munificent man, Kathās. **-vyatyāsa**, m. giving to a wrong person, W. **-vrata**, mfn. devoted to liberality; m. pl. N. of inhabitants of Śaka-dvīpa, Bh. v, 20, 28. **-śālā**, f. hall for alms-giving, Subh. 127. **-śālin**, mfn. rich in gifts; wet with rut-fluid, Siṅhâs., Introd. 9. **-śīla**, mfn. liberally disposed, Yājñ.; MBh.; m. N. of a translator of Lalit. **-śūra**, m. = *-vīra*, Kathās.; N. of a Bodhisattva (v. l. *sūra*), Buddh. **-śauṇḍa**, mfn. 'intoxicated with giving,' very liberal, L. **-sāgara**, m. 'gift-ocean,' N. of wk. **-stuti**, f. 'praise of liberality,' N. of a kind of hymn. **-hīna**, mfn. deprived of gifts, MW. **-hemâdri**, m. = *-khaṇḍa*. **Dānâdhikāra**, m. N. of a Buddh. wk. **Dānâpnas**, mfn. abounding in gifts, Rv. x, 22, 11. **Dānôddyota**, m. N. of wk.

Dānaka, n. a paltry gift; (*ā*), f. a partic. coin = 4 Paṇa, Sch.; N. of a drama. °**nika**, mfn. relating to a gift, &c. (only ifc.; cf. *adhyayana-*, *udaka-*, *vara-*).

Dānin, mfn. giving, liberal, BhP.; having or receiving gifts (cf. *agre-*).

Dānīya, mfn. worthy of gifts or offerings, Pāṇ. iii, 3, 113, Kāś.; n. gift, donation, W.

Dānu, mfn. liberal (Uṇ. iii, 32); courageous, L.; m. prosperity, contentment, L.; air, wind, L.

Dāpana, n. (fr. √1. *dā*, Caus.) forcing to give or pay (ifc.), L. °**panīya**, mfn. to be made to give or pay, Kull.; to be got or procured from (*sakāśât*, Pañc. i, ¹⁄₄). °**payitavya**, mfn. to be obliged to give or pay, Kull. °**payitvā**, ind.p. having fined, W. °**pita**, mfn. caused to give (acc.) to (dat.), Kathās. xxii, 149; caused to be given, got, procured, obtained, Pañc. i, ⁴⁄₄; Rājat. vi, 50; condemned to pay, fined, L. (v. l. *dāyita*). °**pya**, mfn. to be caused to give or pay, Mn., Yājñ.

1. **Dāmán**, m. a giver, donor, RV.; a liberal man, MBh. xii, 3479; (*dā́°*) n. giving, a gift, RV. (cf. *a-*, *su-*). 1. **Dā́manvat**, mfn. furnished with gifts, RV. v, 79, 4.

1. **Dāya**, mfn. (Pāṇ. iii, 1, 139; 141) giving, presenting (cf. *śata-*, *go-*); m. gift, present, donation, MBh.; R. &c.; nuptial fee, L. (cf. *su-*); gift at the ceremony of initiation, W.; handing over, delivery, Mn. viii, 165; n. game, play, Pañcad.

1. **Dāyaka**, mf(*ikā*)n. giving, granting, bestowing; imparting, communicating, uttering, telling; fulfilling, causing, effecting, MBh.; Hariv.; Daś. &c. (generally ifc.; cf. *agni-*, *uttara-*, *jñāna-*, *visha-*).

Dāyita. See under *dāpana*.

Dāyin, mfn. (ifc.) giving, granting, communicating; yielding, ceding, allowing, permitting; causing, effecting, producing, performing, ChUp.; Mn.; MBh.; Bhartṛ. &c.; having to pay, owing (acc.), Pāṇ. ii, 3, 70; iii, 3, 170, Kāś.

Dāyī-√kṛi, to make a gift, Mālatīm. viii, 6.

1. **Dāru**, mfn. liberal, L. (cf. Pāṇ. iii, 2, 159); m., see 2. *dāru*.

Dāvat. See *prāṇa-*.

Dāván, only dat. °*váne* (mostly as inf.) in order to give or to receive, RV.; mfn. (ifc.) giving, granting, RV.; AV. &c.; (°*varī*), f. in *go-*, *śata-*.

दा 3. *dā*. For √*do*, to cut, q.v.

2. **Dāta**, mfn. cut off, mowed (*barhis*), Pāṇ. vii, 4, 46, Sch.

2. **Dāti**, f. sickle, scythe, Gal.

Dā́tu, n. part, division, allotted portion or task, RV. x, 99, 1; ifc. divisible, after a numeral = fold (cf. *su-*, *śata-*, *sahasra-*).

2. **Dātṛi**, m. mowing, a mower (with acc.), RV. v, 7, 7.

Dā́tra, n. a sort of sickle or crooked knife, RV.; Āpast.; MBh. &c.; (*dātrá*) allotted portion, share, possession, RV.

2. **Dā́na**, n. cutting off, splitting, dividing, L.; pasture, meadow, RV.; rut-fluid (which flows from an elephant's temples), MBh.; Hariv. &c.; (*dāná*) m. (only in RV., but cf. *vasu-*) distribution of food or of a sacrificial meal; imparting, communicating, liberality; part, share, possession; distributor, dispenser, RV. vii, 27, 4. **Dānâúkas**, m. delighting in a sacrificial meal (Indra), RV. i, 65, 1.

Dānavá, m. (fr. 2. *dā́nu*) a class of demons often identified with the Daityas or Asuras and held to be implacable enemies of the gods or Devas, RV.; AV.; ŚBr.; Mn.; MBh. &c. (described as children of Danu and Kaśyapa, sometimes reckoned as 40 in number, MBh. i, 252; sometimes as 100 &c.); (*ī*), f. a female D°; mf(*ī*)n. belonging to the D°, MBh.; R. &c. **-guru**, m. preceptor of the D°, regent of planet Venus, Var. **-pati**, m. king of the D°, N. of Rāhu, Bhartṛ. **-pūjita**, mfn. worshipped by the D°; m. regent of Venus, Var. **-priyā**, f. the betel plant, L. **-vairin**, m. enemy of the D°, N. of Śiva, Siṅhâs. **Dānavâri**, m. id., L.; N. of Indra, R. ii, iii, 9; pl. the gods, L. **Dānavêndra**, m. chief of the D°, MW.

Dānaveya, m. a Dānava or demon, MBh.; Hariv.

2. **Dā́nu**, mfn. valiant, victor, conqueror, W.; m. a class of demons (cf. *dānava*), RV. (f., i, 54, 7); ŚBr.; n. a fluid, drop, dew (°*nas pátī*, m. du. N. of Mitra-Varuṇa or of the Aśvins, RV. viii, 256; 8, 16; cf. *ārdrá-*, *jīrá-*). **-citra** (*dā́°*), mfn. brilliant with dew or moisture, RV. **-dá**, mfn. trickling, ib. **-pinvá**, mfn. swelling with drops (Soma), ib. **-mat** (*dā́°*), mfn. trickling, fluid, ib.

2. **Dā́man**, n. or f. allotment, share, RV.

2. **Dāyá**, m. share, portion, inheritance, RV.; TS. &c. (*dāyâd upâgata*, obtained through inheritance, Mit.; *dāyam upâiti pitus*, he obtains his father's inheritance, Br.); division, part (ifc. = fold, cf. *śatá-*); dismembering, destruction, L.; irony, L.; place, site, L. **-kāla**, m. time of dividing an inheritance, Yājñ. **-krama-saṃgraha**, m., **-tattva**, n. N. of wks.; °*tva-kṛit*, m. N. of an author. **-nirṇaya**, m. N. of wk. **-bandhu**, m. partner in inheritance, brother, L. **-bhāga**, m. partition of inheritance, Mn. ix, 103; N. of wk.; *-ṭīkā*, f. and *-tattva*, n. N. of wks. **-rahasya**, n. N. of wk. **-vibhāga**, m. division of property, W. **-hara**, m. receiver of inheritance, heir (cf. *brahma-*). **Dāyâdá**, m. id. (with gen. or loc. of thing or ifc., Pāṇ. ii, 3, 37, vi, 2, 5) AV.; ŚBr.; Mn.; Yājñ.; a son or distant descendant or kinsman, MBh.; Pañc.; (*ā*, *ī*), f. heiress, daughter, AgP.; *-vat*, mfn. having an heir, MBh. **Dāyâdya**, n. inheritance (g. *brāhmaṇâdi*), GṛS.; Mn.; MBh. &c.; *-tā*, f. near relationship, affinity, MBh. i, 7509. **Dāyâdhikāra-krama-saṃgraha**, m. N. of wk. **Dāyâpavartana**, n. forfeiture of property, Mn. ix, 79. **Dāyârha**, mfn. claimable as (or capable of being claimed as) inheritance, MW.

Dāyaka, m. heir, kinsman, GṛS.

Dāyâdava, m. id., W.

दा 4. *dā*, cl. 4. P. *dyáti* (cf. *ā-* √4. *dā*), to bind, only in *dīshva*, VS. xxxviii, 3 [cf. δέω, δίδημι].

1. **Dāma**, in comp. for *dāman*, p. 475. **-kaṇṭha**, m. 'having a rope round neck,' N. of a man; pl. his descendants (g. *upakâdi*). **-granthi**, m. N. assumed by Nakula, MBh. iv, 1020 (cf. *granthika*). **-candra**, m. N. of a man, MBh. vii, 7009. **-carita** or **śrīdāma-carita** (or °*tra*), n. N. of a drama, W. **-jāta-śrī**, m. N. of a prince (on coins). **-tūsha**, mfn. having threads for fringes, TāṇḍyaBr. **-daśa**, mfn. id., Lāṭy. **-lih**, mfn. licking or wishing to lick a rope. **-lihya**, Nom. P., °*ti*, to wish to lick a rope, Pāṇ. viii, 2, 37, Kāś. **-siṅha**, m. N. of a prince. **Dāmâñcana** (L.), °**cala** (Śiś. v, 61), n. a foot-rope. **Dāmôdara**, m. 'having a rope round waist,' N. of Kṛishṇa, MBh.; Hariv.; of 12th month, VarBṛS.; of 9th Arhat of past Ut-sarpiṇī, L.; of 2 kings of Kaśmīra, Rājat. &c.; of a river (held sacred by the Santāls), MW.; *-gupta*, m. N. of a poet, Rājat. iv, 495; *-tantra*, n. N. of wk.; *-datta* & *-deva*, m. N. of 2 men; *-paddhati*, f. N. of wk.; *-bhūti*, m. N. of a man; *-miśra*, m. N. of author of one recension of the Hanūman-nāṭaka; °*râraṇya*, n. N. of a forest, Rājat. vi, 183; °*rīya*, mfn. relating to (king) Dāmodara, Rājat. i, 157. **Dāmôshṇīsha**, m. N. of

an ancient sage, MBh. (v.l. °nīva & °nīśa); °shi, m. patr. fr. °sha; °shya, m. patr. fr. °shi (g. kurv-ādi).

2. **Dāma**, n. (ifc., where also -ka) wreath, garland, MBh.; Hariv.; (ā́), f. id., RV. viii, 61, 6.

3. **Dā́man**, n. (m., L.) string, cord, rope, fetter, RV.; AV.; ŚBr.; MBh. &c.; girdle; chaplet, wreath, garland for forehead, MBh.; Hariv.; Kāv.; large bandage, Suśr.; a partic. constellation, VarBṛS.; N. of a friend of Kṛishṇa = śrī-d° (cf. below); ifc. either in proper N. (cf. ā́śā-d°) or in adj. (where, after a numeral, the fem. must end in ī, e.g. dvi-dāmnī, Pāṇ. iv, 1, 27). [Cf. Gk. δῆμα in διά-δημα; δεμνον in κρή-δεμνον.] °**manī**, f. (ifc. also °nīka) a long rope to which calves are tied by means of shorter ropes, Hariv. — **Dā́man-vat**, mfn. furnished with cords, RV. vi, 24, 4.

दा 5. dā. For √de, q.v.

6. **Dā**, f. (√de), protection, defence, L.

दा 7. dā. For √dai, q.v.

8. **Dā**, f. (√dai) cleansing, purifying, L.

3. **Dāta**, mfn. cleansed, purified, Pāṇ. vii, 4, 46 (cf. ava-, vyava-).

3. **Dāna**, n. purification, L.

दाक्ष dāksha, mf(ī)n. (fr. daksha) relating to Daksha (Hariv.) or to Dākshi (Pāṇ. iv, 2, 112); southern, dwelling in the south, SŚaṃkar.; m. or n. the south (in °shasyâyana, n. the sun's progress towards s°, the winter solstice and sacrifice then performed, Mn. vi, 10 [v.l. daksh°]); m. pl. N. of the disciples of a partic. school (see kumārī-d°). °**shaka**, mfn. inhabited by the Dākshis (g. rājanyâdi); n. a number of descendants of Daksha, L.

Dākshāyaṇá, mf(ī)n. coming from or relating to Daksha, VS.; m. a son or descendant of D°, VS.; ŚBr. &c.; a partic. sacrifice (cf. -yajña); (ī), f. N. of any daughter of D° (Aditi, Diti, Kadrū &c.), MBh.; R.; BhP. &c. (pl. the 27 lunar mansions considered as daughters of D° and wives of the Moon, among whom Rohiṇī is the favourite, L.); Croton Polyandrum, L.; n. the posterity of D°, BhP. iv, 1; gold or a gold ornament (cf. -hastá, below); = dākshasyâyana (under dāksha). — **bhakta**, n. district inhabited by Dākshas (g. aishukāryâdi). — **yajña**, m. a partic. sacrifice, Br.; °ñika, mf(ī)n. relating to it, ŚāṅkhŚr.; °ñin, mfn. id., ŚBr. — **hastá**, mfn. having gold in the hand, ŚBr. vi, 7, 4, 2. **Dākshāyaṇī-pa, -pati, -ramaṇa**, m. the protector, husband, lover of D° (i.e. Durgā or Rohiṇī), Śiva or the Moon, L. **Dākshāyaṇy-agni-praveśa**, m. N. of a ch. of ŚivaP.

Dākshāyaṇin, mfn. wearing golden ornaments, Yājñ. i, 133; m. a Brāhman student, W. °**ṇya**, m. the son of the Dākshāyaṇī Aditi, the Sun, MBh. xiii, 6831. °**yiṇī**, f. w. r. for °yaṇī (above).

Dākshi, m. a son of Daksha, Pāṇ. iv, 1, 93; (ī), f. a daughter of D°, i, 65. — **kanthā**, f. N. of a village, Pāṇ. ii, 4, 20; °thīya, mfn. relating to it, iv, 2, 142. — **karsha**, m. N. of a village, vi, 2, 129. — **karshū**, f. N. of a place; °shuka, mfn. iv, 2, 104, Vārtt. 7, Pat. — **kūla**, n. N. of a village, vi, 2, 129. — **grāma**, m., **-nagara**, n., **-palada**, m. or n., **-hrada**, m. N. of places; °mīya, °rīya, &c., mfn. relating to Dākshi-grāma, °nagara &c., iv, 2, 142. **Dākshī-putra**, m. metro .. of Pāṇini, L.

Dāksheya, m. 'son of Dākshī,' metron. of Pāṇini, L. (cf. Pāṇ. iv, 1, 120); (ī), f. 'daughter of Dākshī' (?), metron. of the mother of parrots, MBh. xiii, 275 (cf. R. iii, 20, 17, 18).

Dākshya, n. (fr. dáksha) cleverness, skill, fitness, capability, industry, MBh.; Kāv. &c.

दाक्षाय्य dākshāyya, m. a vulture, L.

दाक्षिण dākshiṇá, mf(ī)n. (fr. dákshiṇā, f.) belonging or relating to a sacrificial fee, ŚBr., ŚāṅkhŚr.; relating to the south, W.; (ā), f. the southern country, i.e. the Deccan (see below, -ja); n. a collection of sacrificial fees (g. bhikshâdi); pl. N. of a Kāṇḍa of TS. — **śāla**, mfn. relating to a hall situated to the south, Pāṇ. iv, 2, 107, Kāś. — **homa**, m. the oblation connected with the sacrificial fee, Vait. xxi, 23.

Dākshiṇâgnika, mf(ī)n. performed in the southern fire, MānŚr. **Dākshiṇā-ja**, m. inhabitant of the Deccan, Nir. vi, 9; (f. ī), iv, 5. — **pathaka**, mf(ī)n. relating to Dakshiṇā-patha (g. dhūmâdi). **Dākshiṇârdhika**, mf(ī)n. = dakshiṇârdhyà, Pat.

Dākshiṇātya, mf(ā)n. (fr. dakshiṇā, ind., Pāṇ. iv, 2, 98) southerly, southern, belonging to or living in or coming from the south or Deccan, MBh.; Hariv. &c.; (also °tyaka, mf[°tyikā]n. Pāṇ. vii, 3, 44, Vārtt. 5, Pat.); m. (or n.?) the south, Hariv. 6200; cocoa-nut, L.; pl. inhabitants of the Deccan, MBh.; Hariv.

Dākshiṇika, mf(ī)n. connected with a sacrificial fee, Sch.

Dākshiṇīya, mfn. = dakshiṇīya, L. (v. l.)

Dākshiṇya, mfn. belonging to or worthy of a sacrificial fee, L.; n. dexterity, skill, officiousness, gallantry, kindness, consideration, piety (with loc., gen. or ifc.), Hariv.; K. &c.; the ritual of the right hand Śāktas, L.; N. of a Tantra. — **vat**, mfn. amiable, kind; °vad-dara, mfn. having a kind wife; **-tā**, Prasaṅg. — **sampanna**, mfn. coming from the south; possessing kindness, Kāvyâd. ii, 174.

दागव्यायनि dāgavyāyani, m. 'son of Dagu,' N. of a man, Pāṇ. iv, 1, 155, Vārtt. 1, Pat.

दाडक dāḍaka, m. tooth, tusk (cf. dāḍhā).

दाडिम dāḍima, mf(ī)n. the pomegranate tree, MBh.; Hariv.; Suśr. (n. also its fruit; °māni daśi, to bite pomegranates, said of a hard or unwelcome task, Vām. iii, 2, 14); small cardamoms, L.; mfn. being on the pomeg° tree, Suśr. — **pattraka**, m. Soyimida Febrifuga or Amoora Rohitaka, L. — **pushpa**, m. id., L. (also -ka); n. the flower of the pomeg° tree, Suśr. — **priya** & **-bhakshaṇa**, m. 'liking and eating pomeg°,' parrot, L. — **bhaṭṭa**, m. N. of a poet, Cat. °**mī-vat**, mfn. planted with pomeg° trees, Pāṇ. viii, 2, 9, Kāś. °**mī-sāra**, m. = dāḍima, L. **Dāḍimba**, m. the pomeg° tree, L.

दाडी dāḍī, f. a kind of plant and its fruit (g. harītaky-ādi; cf. doḍī and dālī).

दाढा dāḍhā, f. (= and prob. fr. daṇshṭrā) large tooth, tusk, L.; wish, desire, L.; number, multitude, L. °**ḍhikā**, f. (fr. daṇshṭrikā) the beard, the whiskers, Mn. viii, 283; tooth, tusk, L.

दाण्ड 1. dāṇḍa, mf(ī)n. relating to a stick or to punishment, W.; m. patr. fr. daṇḍa (g. śivâdi); (ā), f. a partic. game with sticks, Pāṇ. iv, 2, 57, Kāś.; n. the being a staff (g. pṛithv-ādi); multitude of staff-bearers, vi, 4, 164, Sch. — **grāhika**, m. patr. fr. daṇḍa-grāha (g. revaty-ādi). — **pāṇika**, m. (fr. daṇḍa-pāṇi) relating to a police officer, Sch. on Hāla 536. — **pātā**, f. (fr. daṇḍa-pāta, scil. tithi) 'stick-throwing,' a partic. festival, Pāṇ. iv, 2, 58, Kāś. (cf. tailam-, śyainam-). — **pāyana**, m. patr. fr. daṇḍa-pa (g. naḍâdi). — **pāśika**, m. = daṇḍa-pāśaka, Deśīn. ii, 99. — **māthika**, mf(ī)n. (fr. daṇḍa-mātha) churning with a straight stick (?), Pāṇ. iv, 4, 37, Kāś. **Dāṇḍâjinika**, mf(ī)n. (fr. daṇḍâjina) carrying a staff and skin (as mere outward signs of religion), m. cheat, rogue, hypocrite, Pāṇ. v, 2, 76.

Dāṇḍaka, m. N. of a Bhoja (v. l. °kya).

Dāṇḍaki, m. patr. fr. daṇḍaka; pl. N. of a tribe belonging to the Tri-gartas, Pāṇ. v, 3, 116, Kāś. °**ḍakiya**, m. a prince of the Dāṇḍakis, ib. °**ḍakya**, m. N. of a prince, Kām. i, 56 (v. l. °daka).

Dāṇḍāyana, m. patr. fr. daṇḍa (?), only in comp. — **sthalaka**, mf(ī)n. relating to °sthalī (g. dhūmâdi). — **sthalī**, f. N. of a village, Pāṇ. vi, 2, 129, Kāś.

Dāṇḍika, mf(ī)n. inflicting punishment, punishing, MBh. xii, 2135; m. punisher, Pāṇ. iv, 4, 12, Sch. °**kya**, n. the office of a rod-bearer or policeman (g. purohitâdi).

Dāṇḍin, m. pl. the school of Daṇḍa (g. śaunakâdi). °**ṇḍināyana**, m. patr. fr. daṇḍin, Pāṇ. vi, 4, 174.

दात 4. dāta, m. pl. N. of a school of AV.

दात्यूह dātyūha, m. a gallinule, Mn.; MBh.; R. &c.; Cuculus Melanoleucus, L.; a cloud, L. °**tyūhaka**, m. a little gallinule, R. iii, 79, 11. °**tyauhá**, m. a gallinule, VS. xxiv, 25, 39; MaitrS. iii, 14, 6 (accord. to Pāṇ. vii, 3, 1 fr. ditya-vah).

दादा dādā, dādâkhya-bhaṭṭa or dādā-bhāī, m. N. of several authors.

दादू dādū, m. N. of founder of a sect, RTL. 178; 268. — **panthin**, m. pl. his followers, ib.

दाधिक dādhika, mf(ī)n. (fr. dadhi) made of or mixed or sprinkled with coagulated milk, Pāṇ. iv, 2, 18; 3, 22. 26; carrying about or selling it, 4, 8; eating anything with it, Siddh. ib.; m. N. of a princely race; n. a kind of broth, Suśr.; ifc. f. ā, ib.

दाधिक्र dādhikra, mf(ī)n. relating to Dadhi-krā, AitBr. vi, 36; n. (agnes) N. of a Sāman, ĀrshBr.

दाधित्थ dādhittha, mf(ī)n. (fr. dadhittha) relating to Feronia Elephantum, P. iv, 3, 140, Kāś.; n. its resin, Suśr.

दाधीच dādhīca, mf(ī)n. relating to Dadhīci or Dadhyac; m. patr. of Cyavana, TāṇḍBr.

दाधृवि dā́dhṛivi, mfn (√dhṛi) able to bear (bhā́radhyai), RV. vi, 66, 3.

दाधृषि dā́dhṛishi, mfn. (√dhṛish) courageous, bold, RV.; AV.

दाध्रेयक dādhreyaka, m. a patr. (also pl.), Pravar.

दान् dān (Dhātup. xxiii, 25), cl. 1. P. Ā. and 10. P. dānati, °te and nayati, to cut off; Desid. P. Ā. dīdāṅsati, °te, to be or make straight, Pāṇ. iii, 1, 6.

दान्त 1. dāntá, mfn. (√dam) tamed, broken in, restrained, subdued; mild, patient, Br.; Mn.; MBh. &c.; liberal, L.; m. a tamed ox or steer (cf. damya), Rājat. v, 432; a donor, giver, W.; Ficus Indica or = damanaka, L.; N. of a son of Bhīma, Nal. 1, 9; of a bull, Kathās. xvi, 295; pl. of a school of the AV.; (ā), f. of an Apsaras, MBh. xiii, 1425. **-deva**, **-bhadra**, and **-sena**, m. N. of men.

Dānti, f. self-restraint, patience, L.

Dāntvā, ind. p. (Pāṇ. vii, 2, 56) having subdued or tamed.

दान्त 2. dānta, mf(ī)n. (fr. danta) made of ivory, MBh.; R.; Suśr. °**taka** & °**tika**, mf(ī)n. id., R.

दान्त 3. dā̂nta, mfn. ending in dā, MānGr. i, 18; Gobh. ii, 8, 16.

दाभ dābha, mf(ī)n. hurting, injuring, TS. ii, 4, 3, 1. °**bhya**, mfn., see a-dābhya.

दामन dāmana, mf(ī)n. (fr. damana) relating to the Artemisia flower. — **parvan**, n. the 14th day in light half of the month Caitra (a festival on which flowers are gathered), L. **Dāmani**, m. patr. fr. Damana, pl. N. of a warrior tribe, P. v, 3, 116; °manīya, m. a prince of the Dāmanis, ib.

दामलिप्त dāmalipta, m. pl. N. of a people, VP. ii, 2, 177; n. and (ā), f. N. of a town, Daśak. (cf. tāma- or tāmra-).

दामोद dāmoda, m. pl. N. of a school of AV.

दाम्पत्य dāmpatya, n. (fr. dam-patī) state of husband and wife, matrimonial relationship, Pur.

दाम्भ dāmbha, mf(ī)n. (fr. dambha) deceitful, hypocritical, Nalac.

Dāmbhika, mf(ī)n. id.; m. a cheat, hypocrite, Mn.; MBh.; Hariv.; Ardea Nivea, L. (cf. baka).

दाम्भोल dāmbhola, see a- (add.)

दाय् dāy, cl. 1. Ā. dāyate (Dhātup. xiv, 9) to give.

दार 1. dāra, mf(ī)n. (√dṛī) tearing up, rending (cf. bhū-); m. rent, cleft, hole, TāṇḍyaBr. xv, 3, 7 (cf. udara-, karbu-, a-dāra-sṛit); (ī), f. id., Suśr. °**raṇa**, mf(ī)n. tearing, splitting, rending (w. gen. or ifc.), MBh.; (ī), f. N. of Durgā, Hariv.; n. the act of tearing &c.; bursting, flying open; a means of opening, Suśr.; the clearing-nut plant, L.

1. **Dāraka**, mf(ikā)n. breaking, tearing, splitting (cf. loha- and śatru-); m. a hog, L.; N. of Kṛishṇa's charioteer (cf. 1. dāruka), L.; (ikā), f. rent, chink (cf. pāda-).

Dāri, mfn. splitting, tearing asunder (cf. veṇu-).

Dārita, mfn. torn, rent, divided, MBh. &c.

1. **Dārin**, mfn. id., with gen. (or ifc.), MBh.

2. **Dārú**, mfn. breaking, splitting (Indra), RV. vii, 6, 1; m. an artist, L.

1. **Dāruka**, m. N. of Kṛishṇa's charioteer, MBh.; of an incarnation of Śiva, VāyuP. °**ruki**, m. (patr. fr. °ka) N. of Pradyumna's charioteer, MBh.

दार 2. dāra, m. pl. (probably not connected with 1. dāra and √dṛī, but cf. Pāṇ. iii, 3, 20, Vārtt. 4) a wife (wives), GṛS.; Mn.; MBh. &c. (°ān-√kṛi or pra-kṛi, take to wife, marry, MBh.; cf. kṛita-); rarely m. sg. (Āp. i, 14, 24; Gaut. xxii, 29), f. sg. (BhP. vii, 14, 11) and n. pl. (Pañc. i, 450). — **karman**, n. taking a wife, marrying, Mn. iii, 5.

12. **-kriyā**, f. id., MBh.; R. **-gava**, n. a wife and cows, Pāṇ. v, 4, 77. **-grahaṇa**, =-*karman*, MBh. **-tyāgin**, m. a repudiator of his wife, Śak. 130. **-parigraha**, m. =-*karman*, Mn. ix, 336; °*hin*, m. one who takes a wife, L. **-bali-bhuj**, w. r. for *dvāra-b*°. **-rakshitaka**, mfn. relating to the protection of women. **-lakshaṇa**, n. sign of wifehood, Mn. viii, 237. **-saṃgraha**, m. =-*karman*, MBh. **-sambandha**, m. union with a wife, marriage, MBh. i, 7240. **-suta**, n. sg. wife and child, Yājñ. ii, 175. **-Dārânukramaṇa**, n. N. of a ch. of the PSarv. **Dārâdhigamana**, n. 'wife-going,' marriage, Mn. i, 112. **Dārâdhīna**, mfn. dependent on a wife, Mn. ix, 28. **Dārôpasaṃgraha**, m. 'wife-taking,' marriage, Yâjñ. i, 56.

2. **Dāraka**, m. (rather connected with 2. *dāra* than with √*dṛī*) a boy, son, child, MBh.; Mṛicch.; Pañc.; Suśr.; young animal, Pur.; (*ikā*), f. a girl, daughter, Hariv.; Kathās. (*akī*, BhP. iv, 28, 21); harlot, L.; (*akau*), m. du. a boy and girl, Nal. **Dārakâcārya**, m. 'boy-preceptor,' schoolmaster, Lalit. **Dārikā-dāna**, n. gift of a daughter in marriage, Kām. ix, 6.

2. **Dārin**, m. 'having a wife or wives,' a husband, W.

दारद *dārada*, mf(*ī*)n. coming from the country of the Darads or Daradas (*g. sindhv-ādi*); m. a kind of poison, L.; quicksilver, L.; the ocean, L.; m. and n. vermilion, L.; m. pl. N. of a people (probably w. r. for *darada*, MBh.)

दारिद्र *dāridra*, n. probably w. r. for °**drya**, n. poverty, Mricch.; VarBṛ.; Pañc.; Hit.

दारिल *dārila*, m. N. of Sch. on Kauś.

दारु 3. *dāru*, m. n. (*g. ardharcâdi*) a piece of wood, wood, timber, RV.; AV.; TS.; Br.; Up.; MBh.; R. &c. (usually n., m. only Hariv. 15522); n. Pinus Devadāru, Suśr.; ore, L. [connected with 4. *dru* and *taru*; cf. also Zd. *dauru*; Gk. δόρυ, δρῦς; Goth. *triu*; Germ. *trewo*; Engl. *tree*]. **-kaccha**, m. or n. N. of a district; °*cchaka*, mfn. relating to it, Pāṇ. iv, 2, 126, Kāś. **-kadalī**, f. a kind of wild plantain (=*vana-*), L. **-karṇin**, m. 'having wooden earrings,' N. of Bhavila, Buddh. **-karman**, n. wood-carving, Kād. **-kṛitya**, n. anything to be made of wood, Pañc. i, 108. **-gandhā**, f. a kind of perfume, L. **-garbhā**, f. wooden puppet, doll, L. **-ja**, mfn. made of wood, wooden, AgP. Hcat.; m. a kind of drum, L. **-tīrtha**, n. N. of a Tīrtha, ŚivaP. **-niśā**, f. a species of Curcuma, Car. **-pattrī**, f. Balanites Roxburghii, L. **-parvata**, m. N. of a palace, Veṇīs. i, $\frac{4}{5}$. **-pātrá**, n. a wooden vessel, MānŚr. **-pītā**, f. =-*niśā*, L. **-puttrikā**, f. (Kathās.), **-puttrī**, f. (L.) =-*garbhā*. **-phala**, m. or n. Pistachio (tree and nut); °*laka*, n. window-shutter, HPariś. **-brahma-rasa**, m. a partic. medicine. **-matsyâhvaya**, m. a lizard, L. **-maya**, mf(*ī*)n. made of wood, wooden (°*yi nārī*, *yoshā* or *strī*, a wooden doll, MBh.; *citi*, a funeral pile, BhP. iv, 28, 50). **-mukhyâhvaya** or °**hva**, m. = *matsyâhvaya*, L. **-muca**, m. or n. (med.) white arsenic. **-mūkhā** (*shā*?), f. id., Bhpr. iii, 25. **-yantra**, n. a wooden puppet moved by strings, MBh. v, 5405. **-varman**, m. N. of a man, Mudrâr. **-vaha**, mfn. bearing or carrying timber, Pāṇ. vi, 3, 121, Vārtt. **-śailamaya**, mf(*ī*)n. wooden or stony, AgP. **-shaṭka**, n. a partic. mixture, Bhpr. iv, 34. **-sitā**, f. cinnamon in sticks, Bhpr. i, 188. **-strī**, f. a wooden doll, L. **-haridrā**, f. =-*niśā*, Suśr. **-hasta** or °**taka**, m. a wooden spoon or ladle, L. **Dārv-āghāṭa** (VS.) and **-āghāta** (L.) m. the woodpecker. **Dārv-āhāra**, m. a collector of wood, VS. xxx, 12.

Dārava, mf(*ī*)n. wooden, made of wood or coming from wood, Mn.; MBh. &c. °**vīya**, mfn. id., Vām. v, 2, 55, Bālar. ii, $\frac{3}{4}$.

2. **Dāruka**, n. Pinus Devadaru, L.; (*ā*), f. a wooden doll or puppet, L. °**kā-vana**, n. N. of a wood, ŚivaP. °**kêśvaratīrtha**, n. N. of a Tīrtha, ib.

Dāruṇá and (Uṇ. iii, 53) **dā́ruṇa**, mf(*ā*, once *ī*)n. hard, harsh (opp. *mṛidu*), ŚBr.; MBh.; Suśr.; rough, sharp, severe, cruel, pitiless; dreadful, frightful; intense, violent, Mn.; MBh.; R.; Śak.; Pañc. &c.; (in comp. or °*am* before a vb. to express excellence or superiority, cf. g. *kāshṭhâdi*); m. Plumbago Zeylanica, L.; n. harshness, severity, horror, MBh.; °*ṇaka*, n. N. of a disease of the roots of the hair, Suśr.; °*nya*, n. harshness (of sound, TPrat. ii, 10). **-karman**, n. violent treatment (of diseases), Suśr. **-tā**, f. harshness, dreadfulness, MBh.; VarBṛS. **-vapus**, mfn. of frightful shape, MBh. **Daruṇâkṛiti**, mfn. id., Nal. **Dāruṇâtman**, mfn. hard-hearted, cruel, Śak. **Dāruṇâdhyāpaka**, m. an indefatigable teacher, Pāṇ. viii, 1, 67, Kāś.

Dāruṇāya, Nom. Ā. °*yate*, to act harshly or cruelly, Naish. i, 80.

Dārva, mf(*ī*)n. wooden, Pur.; m. pl. N. of a people (generally associated with the Abhi-sāras), MBh.; Hariv. &c.; (*ī*), f. Curcuma Aromatica or Xanthorrhiza, also a kind of collyrium extracted from it, Suśr.; =*deva-dāru*, L.; =*go-jihvikā*, L. **Dārvi-pattrikā**, f. N. of a plant =*go-jihvā*, L. **Dārvi-homika**, mfn. =°*vīhaumika*, Comm. on Nyāyam. viii, 4, 2. **Dārvī-kvāthôdbhava**, n. collyrium prepared from Curcuma Aromatica or Xanthorrhiza, L. **Dārvīhaumika**, mf(*ī*)n. (fr. *darvīhoma*) relating to an oblation made with a ladle, Suśr.

Dārvaka, mf(*ikā*)n. relating to the Dārvas, Pāṇ. iv, 2, 125, Kāś.; (*ikā*), f. N. of a plant =*go-jihvā*, L.; collyrium prepared from Curcuma Aromatica or Xanthorrhiza, L.; N. of a river, VāyuP. iv, 24, 18.

दारोदर *dārôdara*, mf(*ī*)n. (fr. *darôdara*) connected with gambling, Nalôd. iii, 7.

दार्घसत्त्र *dārghasattra*, mf(*ī*)n. (fr. *dīrgha-*) connected with a long sacrifice, Pāṇ. vii, 3, 1.

दार्ढच्युत *dārḍhacyuta*, m. patr. fr. *dṛiḍha-cyuta*, Pravar.; n. N. of a Sāman, Lāṭy. vii, 4, 1.

दार्ढ्य *dārḍhya*, n. (fr. *dṛiḍha*) hardness, fixedness, stability, strength, corroboration, Suśr.; Kām.; Rājat.

दार्तेय *dārteya*, m. patr. (fr. *dṛiti*), Kāṭh.; TāṇḍyaBr.

दार्दुर *dārdura*, mf(*ī*)n. (fr. *dardura*) relating to a cloud, Hariv. 4162; a frog's (bite), Car. vi, 23; belonging to the mountain Dardura, R. ii, 15, 33; n. a conch-shell the valve of which opens to the right, L.; lac, L.; water, L.; the ways of a frog, L. °**duraka** or °**rika**, mf(*ikā*)n. belonging to a frog, BhP. ii, 3, 20.

दार्भ *dārbha*, mf(*ī*)n. made of Darbha grass, Lāṭy. °**bhāyana** and °**bhi**, m. patr. fr. Darbha, Pāṇ. iv, 1, 102, Sch. °**bhya** or °**bhyà**, m. id. (g. *kurv-ādi*), RV. v, 61, 17 (applied to Śyāvâśva); TS. ii, 6, 2, 3.

दार्वट *dārvaṭa*, n. (fr. Pers. دربار) a court or council-house, L. (cf. *darbhaṭa*).

दार्वण्ड *dārvaṇḍa*, m. a peacock, L.

दार्वन् *dārvan*, m. N. of a son of Uśīnara, VP. (cf. *darvā*).

दार्श *dārśa*, mf(*ī*)n. (fr. *darśa*) relating to the new moon or the n° m° sacrifice, Kauś. 24; m. (scil. *yajña*) the n° m° s°, Mn. vi, 9. °**śa-paurṇamāsika**, mf(*ī*)n. belonging to the Darśa-pūrṇamāsa sacrifice, ŚāṅkhŚr. v, 18, 7. °**śika**, mf(*ī*)n. and °**śya**, mf(*ā*)n. relating to the new moon or the n° m° sacrifice, Comm. on ĀpSr. x, 21, 6 and TS. iii, 2, 2, 3.

दार्शनिक *dārśanika*, mf(*ī*)n. (fr. *darśana*) acquainted or connected with the Darśanas or philosophical systems, L.

दार्षद *dārshada*, mf(*ī*)n. (fr. *dṛishad*) ground on a stone, Pāṇ. iv, 2, 92, Sch.; stony, mineral, W. °**shadvata**, n. (fr. *dṛishadvatī*) N. of a Sattra, ŚrS.

दार्ष्टान्त *dārshṭânta*, mf(*ī*)n. (fr. *dṛishṭânta*) explained by an example or simile, L. °**tika**, mf(*ī*)n. id., Saṃk. on Bādar. ii, 3, 24; one who uses an example or simile as a proof, Sch.

Dārshṭivishayika, mf(*ī*)n. (fr. *dṛishṭi* and *vishaya*) perceptible by the eye, Nir. vii, 8.

दाल *dāla*, n. (fr. *dala*) a kind of honey produced from petals (cf. *dala-ja*), L.; (*ā*), f. colocynth, Bhpr.; (*ī*), f. a kind of plant =*deva-dālī*, L.; m. a sort of grain = Paspalum Frumentaceum, W. (cf. *rajju-*). °**laka**, see *rajju-*; (*ikā*), f. colocynth, Bhpr.

Dālaki, m. N. of a preceptor, VāyuP.

Dālana, n. (√*dal*) decay (of the teeth), Suśr.

दालभ्य *dālabhya* = *dālbhya*.

दालव *dālava*, m. a sort of poison, L.

दालिम *dālima*, m. the pomegranate tree (cf. *dāḍima*). **-phala**, n. a pomeg°, Amar. 13.

दाल्भ *dālbha*, mf(*ī*)n. relating to Dālbhya (see below), Pāṇ. iv, 2, 111 (g. *kaṇvâdi*). °**bhi**, m. (fr. *dalbha*) patr. of Vaka, Kāṭh. °**bhya**, m. (fr. *dalbha*, cf. iv, i, 105) patr. of Keśin, TāṇḍyaBr. xiii, 10, 8; of Vaka, ChUp. i, 2, 13; of Caikitāyana, ChUp. i, 8, 1; N. of a grammarian, VPrāt. iv, 15; *-ghosha*, m. N. of an ancient sage, MBh. iii, 8383; *-pariśishṭa*, n. N. of wk. °**bhyaka**, m. N. of an ancient sage, BrahmaP.

दाल्मि *dālmi*, m. N. of Indra, L. (cf. *dalmi*).

दाव *dāvá*, m. (fr. √2. *du*, Pāṇ. iii, 1, 142) conflagration, esp. a forest conflagration, ŚBr.; MBh. &c.; fire, heat; distress, L.; m. n. a forest, MBh. (always connected with fire), Ragh. ii, 8. **-dahana-jvālā-kalāpāya**, Nom. Ā. °*yate*, to resemble the sheet of flame in a burning forest, Gīt. iv, 10. **-pá**, m. one who keeps watch over a forest on fire, VS. xxx, 16. **-parita**, mfn. surrounded by fire, VarBṛS. xxiv, 15. **-latā**, f. a creeper in a burning f°, BhP. iv, 8, 16. **-vivarjita**, mfn. free from fire. **-su**, m. N. of an Āṅgirasa, TāṇḍyaBr.; *-nidhana*, n. N. of a Sāman, ib. **Dāvâgni**, m. fire in a forest, MBh., Hariv. **Dāvânila**, m. id., Pañc., Kathās.

दाविक *dāvika*, mfn. coming from the river Devikā (water), Pāṇ. vii, 3, 1, Sch. **Dāvikā-kūla**, mfn. (rice &c.) coming from the banks (*kūla*) of the Devikā, ib.

दाश् 1. *dāś* (the finite forms only in RV. and once in ŚBr., see below), cl. 1. P. *dāśati*, i, 93, 10; 151, 7 &c., Ā. °*te*, Dhātup. xxi, 18 (rarely cl. 2. 5. P. *dāshṭi*, i, 127, 4; *dāśnóti*, viii, 4, 6 [the latter also = √*dās*]; pf. *dadā́śa*, i, 36, 4 &c.; Subj. *dádāśati*, °*śas*, °*śat*, i, 156, 2; 94, 15; 91, 20 &c.; p. *dadāśvás* [dat. °*śúshe*, i, 112, 20 &c.], *dāśivás* [only SV. i, 2, 1, 1, 1] and *dāśvás* [see below]), to serve or honour a god (dat. or acc.) with (instr.), i, 68, 6; vii, 14, 3 &c.; v, 41, 16; viii, 19, 4; offer or present (acc.) to (dat.), grant, give, bestow, i, 93, 3; ii, 19, 4 &c.: Caus. P. *dāśayati*, offer, present, ŚBr. i, 6, 2, 5. [Cf. *daśasya*, and Gk. δωκ in ἔ-δωκ-α, δέ-δωκ-α.]

2. **Dā́ś**, f. worship, veneration, RV. i, 127, 7; m. worshipper, vi, 16, 26 (cf. *dū-* and *puro-*). **Dāśas-pati**, m. lord of oblations, one who offers much, Sch.; *-patya*, mf(*ā*)n. offering much milk (cow), TāṇḍyaBr. xiii, 5, 26, 27; n. N. of a Sāman, ib.

1. **Dāśa**. See *puro-*.

Dāśu, mfn. worshipping, sacrificing (cf. *á-*).

Dāśvâdhvara, mfn. intent on sacrificial oblations, RV.

Dāśura, m. N. of a man (v. l. °*śūra*).

Dā́śuri, mfn. making offerings, devout, pious, RV. viii, 4, 12 (cf. *á-*).

Dāśva, mfn. (corrupted fr. *dāśvás*) liberal, munificent, L.

Dāśvás (p. pf. fr. √1. *dāś*), honouring or serving the gods, devout, pious, RV., AV., VS.; gracious, RV. i, 3, 7 (the gods); 110, 2 (Savitṛi); x, 65, 5, 6 (Varuṇa); 104, 6 (Indra); giving, granting (with acc. or ifc.), BhP.

2. **Dā́śa** or (Uṇ. v, 11) **dāśá** (written also *dāsa*), m. fisherman, ferryman, mariner, VS. xxx, 16; Mṛicch. viii, 408, 9; MBh.; Hariv. &c.; the son of a Nishāda by a woman of the Āyogava caste, Mn. x, 34; servant, slave, L.; (*ī*), f. fisherwoman, female slave, L. **-tva**, n. the condition of a fisherman, Kathās. **-nandinī**, f. the fisherman's daughter, N. of Satyāvatī (mother of Vyāsa), L. **-pati**, m. the chief of fishermen, Kathās. lii, 337 (printed *dās*°).

Dāśaka, m. fisherman (?), N. of a son of Bhajamāna, Hariv.; *-putra*, m. the son of a fisherman, Sch. on Pāṇ. vi, 2, 132 (Kāś. *dāmaka-*). °**śeya**, m. (fr. *dāśī*) the son of a fisherman's wife, L.; (*ī*), f. = *dāśa-nandinī*, MBh. i, 4015 (also written *dāseya*, f. *ī*). °**śera**, m. fisherman (v. l. *dās*°), L.; camel, L. °**śeraka**, m. fisherman, Kathās. cxxvi, 204; pl. N. of a people (= *daś*), MBh. vi, 2080.

दाश 3. *dāśa*, the Vṛiddhi form of 2. *daśa* in comp. **-kaṇṭha**, mf(*ī*)n. belonging to Daśakaṇṭha, i.e. Rāvaṇa, Bālar. x, 37. **-grāmika**, mf(*ī* and *ā*)n. (g. *kumudâdi* & *kāśy-ādi*). **-pura**, mf(*ī*)n. coming from Daśa-pura; n. (also °*pūra*) a kind of fragrant grass (cf. *daśa-*), Bhpr. **-phalī**, f., Pāṇ. iv, 1, 64, Sch. (Kāś. *dāsī-*). **-mūlika**, mf(*ī*)n. coming from the Daśa-mūla, Car.

—ratha, mf(*ī*)n. (a road) affording space for ten waggons, MBh. xii, 242; belonging to or coming from Daśa-ratha; m. patr. of Rāma, R. v, 80, 23. **—rathi,** m. a descendant of Daśa-ratha, patr. of Rāma, MBh.; R. &c.; of Lakshmaṇa, L.; of Catur-aṅga, Hariv. 1697; (with Jainas) N. of the 8th Black Vāsu-deva, L.; du. Rāma and Lakshmaṇa, R. vi, 16, 97; Ragh. xii, 76; xiv, 1. **—rathī-tantra,** n. N. of wk. **—rājñá,** n. the fight with the ten kings, RV.; AV. **—rātrika** (*dā°*), mf(*ī*)n. celebrated in the same manner as the Daśa-rātra, ŚBr. xii, 1, 2, 2. **—rūpya,** n. N. of a village; °*yaka,* mfn. relating to it, Pāṇ. iv, 2, 104; Vārtt. 26, Pat. **—vāja,** n. N. of two Sāmans, ĀrshBr. **Dāśârṇa,** mf(*ī*)n. containing the word Daśārṇa, treating of it (g. *vimuktâdi*); m. a prince of the D°, MBh. v, 7458, pl. N. of a people (=*daś°*), MBh. v, 7515; °*rāja* & *dāśārṇêśa,* m. a king of the D°, ib. and vi, 2080; °*rṇaka,* mf(*ikā*)n. Daśarnic, MBh. ii, 1063; v. **Dāśârha,** mf(*ī*)n. containing the word Daśārha, treating of it (g. *vimuktâdi*); belonging to D°, i.e. Kṛishṇa, MBh. ii, 84; Hariv. 6810; m. a prince of the D°, N. of Krishna (MBh.) and of a king of Mathurā (SkandaP.); (*ī*), f. a princess of the D°, MBh. i, 3786; m. pl. N. of a people (= *daś°*), MBh. i, 7513 (also *-ka,* m. pl., BhP. iii, 1, 29. **Dāśâśvamedha,** w. r. for *daś°* (q. v.) **Dāśân-danika,** mf(*ī*)n. Pāṇ. iv, 3, 68, Sch.; m. (scil. *yajña*) N. of a partic. sacrificial rite; (*ī*), f. the priest's fee at it, Pāṇ. v, 1, 95, Sch.

Dāśat, w. r. for *daśat.*

Dāśataya, mf(*ī*)n. (fr. *daś°*) tenfold, belonging to the text of RV. (consisting of 10 Maṇḍalas), RV. Prāt. xvii, 25; f. pl. (= *daś°*) the 10 M°, xvi, 54; ŚāṅkhŚr. xii, 2, 16, 22; du. ŚāṅkhBr. viii, 7.

दाशर्म *dāśarma,* m. N. of a man, Kāṭh.

दाश्विवस् *dāśivas, dāśvas.* See √1. *dāś.*

दाशेय *dāśeya, dāśera.* See above.

दास् 1. *dās,* cl. 1. P. Ā. *dāsati,* °*te,* to give (Dhātup. xxi, 28), cl. 5. P. *dāsnoti* (v. l. for *dāś,* Vop. ib. xxvii, 32), to hurt, injure. (There occurs only *dāsati* with *abhi;* see s. v.)

1. **Dāsá,** m. fiend, demon; N. of certain evil beings conquered by Indra (e.g. Namuci, Pipru, Śambara, Varcin &c.), RV.; savage, barbarian, infidel (also *dắsa,* opp. to *ārya;* cf. *dasyu*); slave, servant, RV.; AV.; Mn. &c.; a Śūdra, L., Sch.; one to whom gifts may be made, W.; a fisherman (v. l. for *dāśa*); ifc. of names, esp. of Śūdras and Kāya-sthas (but cf. also *kāli-*); (*ī*), f. a female servant or slave, AV.; ŚBr.; Mn.; MBh. &c.; harlot, L.; Sch.; N. of a plant (= *nīlā* or *pītā jhiṇṭī, kāka-jaṅghā, nīlâmlāna* &c.), L.; an altar, L.; N. of a river, L.; (*dắsa*), mf(*ī*)n. fiendish, demoniacal, barbarous, impious, RV. **—karma-kara,** m. a servant doing his work, Āp. **—ketu,** m. N. of a son of Manu Daksha-sāvarṇa, VP. iii, 2, 23. **—jana,** m. slave, servant, Kālid.; Kathās. &c. **—jīvana,** mfn. living like a slave, Mn. x, 32. **—tā,** f. slavery, servitude, Veṇīs. 175; Kathās. lxxii, 34. **—tva,** n. id. MBh.; R.; sense of dependence, humbleness, Sarvad. **—dāsī,** f. the female slave of a slave, Mn. ix, 179; *-jana,* m. a male and a female slave, VarBṛ. li, 25. **—nandinī,** see *dāsa-.* **—patnī** (°*sá-*), f. pl. having the demons as masters, being in the power of demons, (*āpas,* RV. i, 32, 11 &c.; *puras,* RV. ii, 12, 16). **—pravarga** (°*sá-*), mfn. (wealth) connected with a multitude of servants, RV. i, 92, 8. **—bhārya,** n. sg. servants and wives, ChUp. vii, 24, 2. **—bhāva,** m. condition of a slave, servitude, MBh. **—mitra,** m. N. of a man; °**trāyaṇa** & °**tri,** m. descendant of Dāsa-mitra (*-bhakta,* n. the district inhabited by them, g. *aishukāry-ādi*); °**trika,** mf(*ā* and *ī*)n. relating to D° (g. *kaṣy-ādi*). **—mithuna,** n. a couple of slaves, KāṭyŚr., Lāṭy.; Mn. **—varga,** m. the whole collection of slaves or servants, Mn. **—veśa** (°*sá-*), m. probably N. of a man, RV. ii, 13, 8. **—śarman,** m. N. of a Sch. on ŚāṅkhŚr. **—śiras** & **sarasa,** n. N. of two Sāmans, ĀrshBr. **Dāsasya-kula,** n. low people, the mob, Pāṇ. vi, 3, 21, Sch. **Dāsânudāsa,** m. a slave of a slave (sometimes applied by a humble speaker to himself), MW.

Dāsaka, m. N. of a man (cf. *dāś°*), g. *aśvâdi;* (*ikā*), f. female slave, L. °**kāyana,** m. patr. fr. *dāsaka,* ib.

Dāsāya, Nom. P. Ā., °*yati,* °*te,* to become a slave, g. *lohitâdi.*

Dāsāyana, m. the son of a slave or of a man called Dāsa, g. *naḍâdi.*

1. **Dāsī-√kṛi,** to make any one a slave, enslave, Kathās. xxii, 184. **—√bhū,** to become the slave of (gen.), Naish. viii, 71.

2. **Dāsī** (also °*sikā,* ifc.), f. of 1. *dāsa* (q.v.). **—jana,** m. a female slave, VarBṛ. **—tva,** n. the condition of a female slave, MBh. i, 1088. **—dāna-vidhi,** m. N. of 146th ch. of the BhavishyôttaraP. **—dāsa,** n. sg. (g. *gavâśvâdi*) female and male slaves, MBh; R.; m. pl. MBh. ii, 2510. **—putra,** (BrahmavPur.) or °**syāḥputra** (Pāṇ. vi, 3, 22), m. 'the son of a female slave,' a low wretch or miscreant (as an abusive word often in the plays). **—brāhmaṇa,** m. a Brāhman who goes after a female slave, Pāṇ. vi, 2, 29, Kāś. **—bhāva,** m. the condition of a female slave, MBh. **—māṇavaka,** m. female slaves and boys, g. *gavâśvâdi.* **—śrotriya,** m. = *-brāhmaṇa,* Pāṇ. vi, 2, 29, Sch. **—sabha,** n. a company of female slaves, L. **—suta** or **dāsyāḥ-suta,** m. = *-putra,* Rājat. v, 397; BhP. iii, 1, 15.

1. **Dāseya,** m. (fr. *dāsī*) the son of a female slave, Pāṇ. iv, 1, 31, Kāś.; slave, servant, L.

2. **Dāseya.** See *daseya.*

Dāsera, m. = 1. *dāseya,* Pāṇ., ib.; a fisherman (cf. *dāś°*), L.; a camel, L. °**raka,** m. = 1. *dāseya,* L.; a fisherman (cf. *dāś°*); a camel, Śiś. v, 66; Pañc. iv, $\frac{68}{69}$; N. of a man, pl. ifc. his descendants, Pāṇ. ii, 4, 68, Kāś.; of a people (cf. *dāś°*), VarBṛS. xiv, 26; (*ī*), f. a female camel, Pañc. i, $\frac{412}{413}$. °**raki,** m. patr. fr. *dāseraka,* Pāṇ ii, 4, 68, Kāś.

Dāsyà, n. servitude, slavery, service, ŚBr.; Mn. &c.

Dắsvat, mfn. (√*dās* or 1. *dā* ?) disposed to give, liberal, RV.

दास 2. *dāsa,* m. a knowing man, esp. a knower of the universal spirit, L.

दासनीय *dāsanīya,* m. pl. N. of a people, MBh. ii, 1825.

दासनु *dāsanu,* m. N. of a semi-divine being, TāṇḍBr. i, 7, 8, 9.

दासमीय *dāsamīya,* m. pl. N. of a people, MBh. viii, 2056 &c.

दासमेय *dāsameya,* m. pl. N. of a people to the north of Madhya-deśa, VarBṛS. xiv, 28 (Sch. *dāś°*).

दास्र *dāsra,* mf(*ī*)n. relating to the Aśvin Dasra, Jyot.

दाह *dāha,* m. (fr. √*dah*) burning, combustion, conflagration, heat, KātyŚr.; Mn.; Yājñ.; MBh.; R. &c.; place of cremation, Vas. xix, 26; glowing, redness (of the sky, cf. *dig-*), Mn.; MBh.; VarBṛS. &c.; cauterizing, cautery (of a wound), Suśr.; Mālav. iv, 4; internal heat, fever, Suśr.; pl. N. of a people (v. l. for *vaideha*), VāyuP. 1; °*haka,* mf(*ī*)n. burning, setting on fire, Yājñ. ii, 282; BhP. xi, 10, 8; m. Plumbago Zeylanica. **—kāshṭha,** n. a kind of Agallochum used as a perfume, L. **—jvara,** m. inflammatory fever, Kathās.; Daśak. **—dā,** f. Piper Betle, L. **—maya,** mf(*ī*)n. consisting of heat, inflammable; *-tva,* n. inflammableness, Sāh. **—vat,** mfn. heated, on fire, W. **—sara,** m., **-saras,** n., **-sthala,** n. a place where dead bodies are burnt, L. **—haraṇa,** n. 'removing heat,' the root of Andropogon Muricatus. **Dāhâguru,** n. = *dāha-kāshṭha.* **Dāhâtmaka,** mf(*ikā*)n. of an inflammable nature, easily kindled or burning, Śak. ii, 7. **Dāhâtman,** mfn. id.; Kāvyâd. ii, 177. **Dāhâdhikāra,** m. N. of a ch. of a medical work by Vṛinda.

Dāhana, n. (fr. the Caus.) causing to burn or be burnt, reducing to ashes, MBh. i, 403; BhP. xii, 12, 40; cauterizing, W.; (*ī*), f. Grislea Tomentosa, L. **Dāhanâguru,** w. r. for *dah°.*

Dāhin, mfn. burning, setting on fire; tormenting, paining, Mn.; MBh.; Bhartṛ. &c.

Dắhuka, mfn. burning (acc.), TBr. i, 1, 2, 2; causing a conflagration, ĀpŚr. v, 3, 4; m. a conflagration, ĀśvGṛ. ii, 8, 14.

दिकम् *dikam,* ind., g. *câdi.*

दिक्क 1. *dikka,* ifc. = 2. *diś.*

दिक्क 2. *dikka,* m. = *karabha* (v.l. *dhikka* and *vikka*), W.

दिक्कन्या *dik-kanyā,* &c. See under 2. *diś.*

दिगन्त *dig-anta,* &c. See ib.

दिग्ध *digdhá,* mfn. (√*dih*) smeared, anointed; soiled, defiled; poisoned, AV.; ŚBr.; Mn.; MBh.; Kāv. &c.; m. a poisoned arrow, R. ii, 30, 23 (cf. below); fire, L.; oil, L.; a tale, L. **—viddha** (*dí°*), mfn. pierced by a p° a°, ŚBr. xiv, 9, 4, 8. **—saha-śaya,** mfn. lying in mud or along with any soiled person, Pāṇ. iii, 2, 15; Vārtt. 2, Pat. **—hata,** mfn. hit by a poisoned arrow, R. ii, 144, 33. **—hasta,** mfn. (a hunter) having (in his hand) or using poisoned arrows, MBh. v, 1473; having the hands smeared or soiled, MW. **Digdhâṅga,** mf(*ī*)n. having the limbs anointed or smeared with (ifc.), MBh.; R. &c.

दिङ्क *diṅka,* m. the nit of a louse, L.

दिङ्नाग *diṅ-nāga,* &c. See under 2. *diś.*

दिण्डि *diṇḍi* or *diṇḍin,* m. N. of a man connected with the worship of the sun or of Śiva (he is called also *gaṇa-nāyaka* or *tripurântaka*), BhavP. (cf. *ḍhuṇḍhi*).

दिण्डीय *diṇḍīya,* m. N. of a man, MW.

दिण्डीर *diṇḍīra,* v. l. for *hiṇḍīra.*

दिण्ण *diṇṇa,* a Prākṛit form for *datta.* See *deva-.*

दित 1. *dita,* mfn. (√3. *dā*) bound (cf. *ud-, ni-, sam-*).

1. **Diti,** f. N. of a deity answering to A-diti (q. v.) as Sura to A-sura and without any distinct character, AV. vii, 7, 1 &c.; VS. xviii, 22; in ep. daughter of Daksha and wife of Kaśyapa and mother of the Daityas (see s. v.), MBh.; Hariv.; Pur.; (the Maruts are also described as her progeny or derived from the embryo in her womb divided into pieces by Indra), Hariv. 239; R. i, 46, 1; cf. Pañc. ii, 40. **—ja,** m. son of D°, a Daitya, MBh.; BhP.; °*jârāti,* m. enemy of the Daityas, N. of Vishṇu, Rājat. iv, 199. **—tanaya, -nandana,** m. = *-ja,* Hariv.; BhP. **—suta,** m. id.; Sāh.; *-guru,* m. the planet Venus, Var.

Ditya, m. a son of Diti (w. r. for *daitya*).

दित 2. *dita,* mfn. (√*do,* Pāṇ. vii, 4, 40) cut, torn, divided, BhP. vi, 6, 23 (cf. *nir-*).

2. **Diti,** f. cutting, splitting, dividing, L.; distributing, liberality (also personified, cf. 1. *diti*), RV.; m. N. of a king, L.; a king, W.

दित्यवह् *ditya-vah,* m. (in strong cases °*vāh,* nom. °*vāṭ;* instr. *dityauhā*); f. °*tyauhī* (Pāṇ. iii, 2, 64; vi, 4, 132, Kāś.) a two-year-old steer or cow, VS.; TS. (Prob. from *ditya* = *dvitīya* + *vah,* cf. *turya-vah.*)

Dityauhī, f., see above.

दित्सा *ditsā,* f. (√1. *dā,* Desid.) desire or intention of giving, Rājat. iii, 252. °**sita,** mfn. wished to be given, MBh. iii, 8627. °**sú,** mfn. wishing to give or grant or perform (acc.); RV. v, 39, 3; MBh.; Kathās. °**sya,** mfn. what one is willing to give, Pāṇ. iii, 1, 97, Pat. **Diditsu,** mfn. ready to give or sacrifice (acc.), MBh. v, 187.

दिदम्भिषु *didambhishu,* mfn. (√*dambh,* Desid.) wishing to deceive, Bhaṭṭ.

दिदिवि *didivi* = *dīdivi,* the sky, L.

दिदीवि *didivi* = *dīdivi,* boiled rice, L.

दिदृक्षा *didṛikshā,* f. (√*dṛiś,* Desid.) desire of seeing, MBh.; Kathās. **—vat,** mfn. having a desire to see, W. °**shita,** mfn. what one has wished to see; n. the wish to see, BhP. xv, 31. °**shitṛi,** mfn. desirous of seeing (acc.), ŚBr.

Didṛikshu, mfn. id., RV.; wishing to examine or try, Mn. viii, 1. °**shéṇya** & °**shéya,** mfn. what one likes or wishes to see, worth seeing, attractive, RV.

दिदेविषु *didevishu,* mfn. (√*div,* Desid.) desirous of playing, Bhaṭṭ. ix, 32.

दिद्दा *diddā,* f. N. of a princess of Kaśmīra, Rājat. vi, 177 &c. **—kshema,** m. 'promoting welfare of Diddā,' N. of Kshema-gupta, Rājat. vi, 177. **—pāla,** m. 'protector of D°,' N. of a man, ib. 146. **—pura,** n. N. of a town built by D°, ib. 300. **—svāmin,** m. N. of a temple built by D°, ib.

दिद्दिभ *diddibha,* prob. w. r. for *ṭiṭṭibha.*

दिद्यु *didyu,* m. (√2. *div* or 1. *di*) a missile, weapon, arrow, RV.; AV.; VS. (cf. *aśma-*); the sky, heaven, L. °**dyút,** mfn. shining, glittering, RV. vii,

6, 7; f. an arrow, missile, thunderbolt of Indra, RV.; flame, ib. vi, 66, 10; N. of an Apsaras, AV. ii, 2, 4.

दिद्योतिषु didyotishu, mfn. (√dyut, Desid.) wishing to shine, Bhaṭṭ. vii, 107.

दिधक्ष् didhaksh, mfn. nom. °dhak (√dah, Desid.), wishing to burn, Vop. iii, 151. °**kshā**, f. desire to burn, MBh.; BhP. °**kshu**, mfn. desirous of burning, MBh.; R.; BhP.

दिधि didhi, f. (prob. w. r.) firmness, stability, W.

दिधिक्ष् didhiksh, mfn. nom. °dhik (√dih, Desid.) wishing so smear, Vop. iii, 151.

दिधिषाय्य didhishā́yya, mfn. (√dhā, Desid.) 'to be tried to be gained,' to be sought (Agni), RV. ii, 4, 1 (= *dhārayitṛi*, supporter, Sāy.)

Didhishū́, mfn. wishing to gain or obtain, striving after, seeking, RV.; m. a suitor, RV. x, 18, 8; a husband, BhP. ix, 9, 34; the second husband of a woman twice married (also °*shū*), L.; (*u* or *ū*), f. a widow remarried or an elder sister married after the younger (both of whom having the choice of their husbands may be compared to suitors). °**shū-pati**, m. the husband of a woman so married, Kāṭh. xxxi, 7; Gaut.; Vas. °**shūpapati**, m. her paramour, MBh. xii, 1211. (Cf. *agre-didhishu* and *edidhishuḥ-pati*.)

Didhīshu, f. = *didishū*, L.

दिधीर्षा didhīrshā, f. (√dhṛi, Desid.) the wish to hold or support, Bālar. i, 48.

दिन 1. diná, mfn. (√do) cut, divided, mowed, RV. viii, 67, 10 (cf. *svayam-*).

दिन 2. dina (√3. dā). See *a-sam-*.

दिन 3. dína (accented only Naigh. i, 9), m. n. (g. *ardharcâdi*, only occurring as n.) a day, Mn.; Ragh.; Pañcat. &c. (ifc. also in Vedic texts), ifc. f. *ā*, Rājat. i, 347. [Cf. Lat. *peren-dinus*, *nūndinus* &c.; Got. *sin-teins*; Lit. *dēna*; O.Pr. acc. sgl. *deinan*; Slav. *dĭnĭ*.] **-kara**, mf(*ī*)n. making day or light; m. the sun, Kāv. &c.; N. of an Āditya, RāmatUp.; of the author of the wk. Candrârkī; of a Sch. on Śiś. (*miśra-d°*); of other men; (*ī*), f. (scil. *ṭīkā*) N. of Comm. on the Bhāshāp. and Siddhânta-muktāvalī; °*ra-ṭippaṇī*, f. N. of a Comm.; °*ra-tanaya*, m. 'son of the sun,' the planet Saturn, Var.; °*ra-deva*, m. N. of a poet; °*ra-bhaṭṭa*, m. N. of an author; °*ṭīya*, n. his wk.; °*rātmaja*, m. 'daughter of the sun,' patr. of the river Yamunā; °*rīya*, n., °*rôddyota*, m. N. of wks. **-kartavya**, n. 'day-duty,' ceremonies to be performed daily, Kathās. **-kartṛi**, m. 'day-maker,' the sun, Hariv. **-kārya**, n. = *-kartavya*, Kathās. **-kṛit**, m. = *-kartṛi*, MBh.; VarBṛS. &c.; *-suta*, m. = *-kara-tanaya*, VarYogay.; °*d-divasa*, m. Sunday, ib. **-kṛitya**, n. = *-kartavya*, Kathās. lii, 410 (printed *diva-k°*). **-keśava** & **-kesara** (also written °*śara*, m. 'day-hair,' darkness, L. **-kshaya**, m. 'day-decline,' evening, Kām.; = *tithi-*, Hcat. i, 3; N. of a ch. of PSarv. **-gaṇa**, m. = *ahar-*, Gaṇit.; °*ṇita*, n. N. of wk. **-graha**, m. day-planet, Hcat. i, 7. **-caryā**, f. daily-work, Kathās. **-cchidrā**, n. change of moon at the beginning or end of a half-day; a day; a constellation or a lunar mansion, Hcat. i, 3, 5. **-jyotis**, n. daylight, sunshine, L. **-duḥkhita**, mfn. 'afflicted by day,' m. the Cakra-vāka bird, L. **-naktam**, ind. by day and night, MārkP. **-nātha**, m. 'day-lord,' the sun, Vcar. xiv, 64. **-niś**, f. du. day and night, VarBṛS. xxxii, 7. **-pa**, m. the regent of a week-day, Āryabh. iii, 16. **-pati**, m. id., Gaṇit.; 'day-lord,' the sun, Bhartṛ.; Rājat. **-pākin**, mfn. being digested within a day, Bhpr. **-pāṭikā**, f. a day's wages, Vet. iv, $\frac{1}{2}$ (v. l.) **-praṇī**, m. 'day-leader,' the sun (cf. *tithi-*), L. **-prabhā**, f. = *-jyotis*, L. **-bandhu**, m. 'day-friend,' the sun, L. **-bala**, m. 'day-strength,' N. of the 5th–8th, 11th and 12th signs of the zodiac collectively, L. **-bhartṛi**, m. = *-nātha*, Vcar. xi, 1, 12. **-maṇi**, m. 'day-jewel,' the sun, Gīt.; Bālar.; *-sārathi*, m. the sun's charioteer, Aruṇa, Bālar. vi, $\frac{8}{8}$. **-mala**, n. 'day-refuse (?),' a month, L. **-mukha**, n. 'day-face,' daybreak, Daś. **-mūrdhan**, m. 'day-head,' the eastern mountain (cf. *udayá*), L. **-ratna**, n. = *-maṇi*, L. **-rāja**, m. 'day-king,' the sun, Svapnac. i, 18. **-rāśi**, m. a term of days, L. (cf. *ahar-gaṇa*). **-vāra**, m. week-day, Gaṇit. **-vyāsa-dala**, n. 'day-radius,' the radius of a circle made by an asterism in its daily revolution, Sūryas. ii, 60. **-saṃcaya**, m. = *-rāśi*, Gol. ii, 12. **-spṛiś**, n. a lunar day coinciding with three week-days, Hcat. i, 3. **Dinâṇśa** & °**śaka**, m. 'day-portion,' day-time, L. **Dinâgama**, m. daybreak, Hariv. 4287. **Dinâṇḍa**, n. 'day-egg' (i. e. d°- veil or - cover), darkness, L. **Dinâtyaya**, m. = °*na-kshaya*, L. **Dinâdi**, m. daybreak, dawn, Śiś. xi, 52. **Dinâdhinātha** & **dinâdhīśa**, m. 'day-lord,' the sun, Daś.; Pañc. **Dinânta**, m. 'day-end,' sunset, evening, Kālid. **Dinântaka**, m. 'day-destroyer,' darkness, L. **Dinârambha**, m. daybreak, W. **Dinârdha**, m. 'day-half,' noon, Kalpat.; half a day, MBh. vii, 6036; half the days or time, Siṇhâs. **Dinâvasāna**, n. 'day-close,' evening, Kālid. **Dinâstra**, n. 'day-missile,' N. of a magical formula, Mantram. **Dineśa**, m. = °*na-pati*, VarBṛS.; °*śātmaja*, m. 'son of the Sun,' the planet Saturn, ib. **Dineśvara**, m. = °*na-nātha*, Hariv.; R.; Bhartṛ. **Dinaika**, m. one day, MW. **Dinôdaya**, m. daybreak, dawn, Subh. **Dinôpavāsin**, mfn. fasting by day, Hāsy. i, 17. **Dinâugha**, m. = *dina-rāśi*, Gaṇit. **Dinikā**, f. a day's wages, L.

Dinī-√kṛi, to reduce to days, Sūryas.

दिन्दिम dindima, m. N. of a man, W.

दिन्न dinna, prob. = *diṇṇa* (q. v.) **-sūri**, m. N. of a man, W. **Dinnā-grāma**, m. N. of a village, Rājat. viii; (cf. *dharma-*.)

दिन्व् dinv, cl. 1. P. *dinvati*, to gladden, Dhātup.

दिप् dip, cl. 1. Ā. *depate*, ib. (v. l. *tip*).

दिप्सु dipsú, mfn. (√dabh, Desid.) intending to hurt or injure, RV.

दिम्प् dimp, cl. 10. Ā. *dimpayate*, to accumulate, Vop. in Dhātup.

दिम्भ् dimbh, cl. 10. Ā. *dimbhayate*, id., P. °*ti*, to order, direct, id.

दिय díya, mfn. deserving of gifts (= *deya* or *dānârha*, Durga on Nir. iii, 15), RV. viii, 19, 37; (prob. n.), a gift; *diyā́nām páti*, m. lord of gifts, a very liberal man.

दिर् dir (√dṛī) in *kalaśa-dír* (q. v.)

दिरिपक diripaka, m. or n. a ball for playing with, L.

दिलीप dili-pa, m. (fr. *dilī* = modern Delhi [cf. *ḍillī*] + *pa*, a protector?) N. of certain kings (esp. of an ancestor of Rāma, son of Aṇśumat and father of Bhagī-ratha), MBh.; Hariv. &c.

दिलीर dilīra, m. or n. = *śilindhraka*, a mushroom, L.

दिल्ह dilha, m. N. of a man (also *-bhaṭṭāra*), Rājat. viii; (cf. *dihlā*.)

दिव् 1. div, cl. 1. P. *-devati*, cl. 10. P. *-devayati*, to cause to lament, to pain, vex; to ask, beg; to go; Ā. °*te*, to suffer pain, Dhātup. xxxiii, 51, 32.

दिव् 2. div, cl. 4. *dī́vyati*, °*te*, RV.; Br. &c. (perf. *didéva*, AV.; fut. *devishyati*; cond. *adevishyat*, MBh.; Daś.; aor. *adevīt*, MBh.; infin. *devitum*, MBh. &c.; ind. p. *devitvā*, Pāṇ. i, 2, 18; *-dīvya*, RV. x, 42, 9) to cast, throw, esp. dice, i. e. play, gamble (*akshais*, RV. x, 34, 13; MBh. iii, 2260; *akshān*, Pāṇ. i, 4, 43), with (instr., MBh. ii, 2509), for (instr., ii, 2061 &c.; acc., MaitrS. i, 6, 11; ŚBr. v, 4, 4, 23; dat., MBh. iv, 534; ii, 2468; gen. [*śatasya*], Pāṇ. ii, 3, 58); to lay a wager, bet with (*sârdham*), upon (dat.), MBh. i, 1192; to play, sport, joke, trifle with (acc., AV. v, 29); to have free scope, spread, increase (Pañc. ii, 193, B. *vardhati*); to shine, be bright [Zd. *dīv*; (?) Lit. *dyvas*], BhP. iii, 20, 22; to praise, rejoice, be drunk or mad; to sleep; to wish for; to go, Dhātup.: Caus. *devayati*, to cause to play (Sch.) or to sport, BhP. iii, 20, 22: Desid. *didevishati* and *dudyūshati*, Pāṇ vii, 2, 49, Kāś.: Caus. of Desid. *dudyūshayati*, to incite to play, Bhaṭṭ. v, 49: Intens. *dedivīti*, *dedyeti*, *dedeti* &c., Vop. xx, 17.

3. **Dív**, **dyú** (nom. *dyaús*; voc. *dyàus* [RV. vi, 51, 5; AV. vi, 4, 3]; acc. *dyā́m*, *dívam*; instr. *divā́* or *dívā* [see below]; dat. *dive* [*dyave*, MBh. i, 3934]; abl. gen. *divás* [rarely *dyós*, e. g. RV. iv, 27, 3; i, 115, 5]; loc. *diví*, *dyávi*; du. *dyā́vā*, s. v. [*dyávī* as voc. only iv, 56, 5]; pl. nom. *dyávas* [*dívas* only ix, 118, 11]; acc. *dyū́n* [rarely *dívas*, *divás*, e. g. i, 194, 2; iv, 3, 8]; instr. *dyúbhis*; native grammarians give as stems *div* and *dyo*; the latter is declined through all cases like *go*, but really does not occur except in forms mentioned above and in *dyo-salila*, MBh. viii, 4658, while *div* and *dyu* regularly alternate before vow. and cons.), m. (rarely f.) in Ved., f. in later Skr. heaven, the sky (regarded in Ved. as rising in three tiers [*avama*, *madhyama*, *uttama* or *tṛitīya*, RV. v, 60, 6 &c.], and generally as the father (*dyaúsh pitā́*, while the earth is the mother [cf. *dyā́vā-pṛithivī*], and Ushas the daughter), rarely as a goddess, daughter of Prajā-pati, AitBr. iii, 33; ŚBr. i, 7, 4, 1); m. (rarely n.) day (esp. in pl. and in such forms as *divā́*, by day (cf. s. v.); *dyávi-dyavi*, daily, every day; *ánu dyū́n*, day by day, daily; *dyúbhis* and *úpa dyúbhis*, by day or in the course of days, a long time, RV.; m. brightness, sheen, glow (only *dyúbhis*), RV. i, 53, 4; iii, 3, 2 &c.; fire (nom. *dyus*), L. [Cf. *dyú*; Gk. Ζεύς, Διϝός &c. = *dyaús*, *divás*; Lat. *Jou*, *Ju* in *Ju-piter*, *Jovis*, *Jovi* &c. = *dyavas*, *dyavi*; O. E. *Tīw*; O. H. G. *Zīu*; O. N. *Týr*.] **-ít**, mfn. going to the sky, RV. x, 76, 6. **-ítmat**, mfn. going in or to the sky, heavenly, RV. iv, 31, 11 &c.; °*matā*, instr. heavenwards, RV. i, 26, 2. **-ishṭi** (*dív-*), f. longing for heaven, devotion, worship, sacrifice (generally loc. plur.), RV. **-īśa**, m. lord in heaven, pl. N. of the Ādityas, Vasu and Rudra, Hcat. i, 6. (For other comp. see under *divás*, *divā*, 2. *diví*, *divo* and 3. *dyú*.)

Divá, n. heaven, sky, MBh.; Hariv.; day, esp. in *divé-dive*, day by day, daily, RV. and ifc. (g. *śarad-ādi*); wood, L. [Cf. *áhar-*, *tri-*, *naktam-*, *bṛihad-*, *rātrim-*, *su-*; cf. also δίϝο in ἔν-διος; Lat. (?) *biduum*.] **-kshas** (°*vá-*), mfn. living in heaven, heavenly, RV. **-m-gama**, mfn. going or leading to heaven, MBh. (?fr. *divam*, acc. of 3. *div* + *g°*). **-darśa**, m. pl. N. of a school of AV. **-ratha**, w. r. for *divi-* (q. v.) **-spṛiś**, mfn. (nom. *spṛik*) heaven-touching, MBh. **Divâtithi**, °**vâdi**, °**vârka**, see under *divā*; °**vâvasāna** = (& prob. w. r. for) *dinâv°*, L. **Div'okas**, m. (cf. °*vâu°*) a god or the Cātaka bird, L. **Divôdbhava**, mfn. 'sky-born,' (*ā*), f. cardamoms, L. **Divôlkā**, f. 'sky-firebrand,' a meteor (cf. °*vyô°*), MBh. i, 1416. **Divâukas**, m. 'sky-dweller,' a deity, Mn.; MBh.; Kālid. &c.; planet, Gaṇit.; the Cātaka; a deer; a bee; an elephant, L.; °*kaḥ-pati*, m. N. of Indra, Prasannar. **Divâukasa**, m. (= °*kas*) a god, L., N. of a Yaksha, Divyâv.

Divan, m. a day, L. (cf. *prati-*).

Divás, gen. of 3. *dív* in comp. **-°vaḥ-śyenī**, f. N. of partic. sacrifices, Kāṭh. °**vas-pati**, m. 'sky-lord,' N. of Indra, Nahusha and Vishṇu, MBh.; of the Indra of the 13th Manv-antara, BhP. viii, 13, 32. 33. °**vas-pṛithivyau**, f. du. heaven and earth, Pāṇ. vi, 3, 30 (gen. °*vás-pṛithivyós*, RV. ii, 2, 3; x, 3, 7; 35, 2; cf. *dyā́vā-pṛithivyau*).

Divasa, m. (or n., g. *ardharcâdi*, L.) heaven, TBr. i, 7, 6, 6; a day, MBh.; Kāv. &c. [Cf. δίϝες in εὐδιέστερος, εὐδιεινός for εὐδιεσνός.] **-kara**, m. 'day-maker,' the sun, R.; Hariv. &c. **-kṛit**, m. id., MBh.; Var. **-kriyā**, f. the religious performances of the day, Kathās. liv, 136. **-kshaya**, mfn. 'day-end,' evening, MBh. i, 699. **-cara**, mfn. 'day-walking' (opp. to *niśā-cara*), VarBṛS. **-cchidra**, n. = *dina-*, Hcat. i, 3. **-tithi**, m. the day-part of a lunar day, Sūryapr. **-nātha** & **-bhartṛi**, m. 'day-lord,' the sun, Var. **-nirīkshaka**, m. a kind of ascetic, Buddh. **-mukha**, n. 'day-face,' daybreak, dawn, Ragh. v, 76. **-mudrā**, f. 'day's coin,' a day's wages, Buddh. **-vāra**, m. week-day, Var. **-vigama**, m. the departure of the day, Megh. 77. **-vyāpāra**, m. the day-work (washing &c.), Kād. **Divasâtyaya**, m. the passing away of day, evening, MW. **Divasântara**, mfn. only one day old, MBh. xi, 98. **Divasâvasāna**, n. 'day-close,' evening, MW. **Divaseśvara**, m. 'day-lord,' the sun, Bhartṛ.

Divasī-√kṛi, to convert the night into day, Mṛicch. iv, 3.

Divā, ind. (for *divā́*, instr. of 3. *div*) g. *svar-ādi*, by day (often opposed to *náktam*), RV.; used also as subst., e. g. *divā bhavati*, ChUp. iii, 11, 3; (with *rātris*) MBh. ii, 154 &c.; esp. in beginning of comp. **-kará**, m. 'day-maker,' the sun, AV.; MBh.; R. &c. (with *niśā-* among the sons of Garuḍa, MBh. v, 3599); a crow (cf. *divâṭana*, below), L.;

Calotropis Gigantea (cf. *arká*), L.; N. of an Āditya, RāmatUp.; of a Rakshas, VP.; of a prince, VP. (= *divârka*, BhP.); of the founder of the Sūrya-bhakta sect; of other men (also *-bhaṭṭa*); *-mitra*, m. N. of a man, Hcar. 201; *-vatsa*, m. N. of an author; *-vara-locana*, m. a partic. Samādhi, Kāraṇḍ.; *-suta*, m. 'son of the sun,' the planet Saturn, VarBṛS.; (*ā*), f. 'daughter of the sun,' N. of the river Yamunā, ib.; *-karôddyota*, m. N. of a wk. **—kīrti** (or °*âk*°), m. a Caṇḍāla, Mn. v, 85; a barber, L.; an owl, L. **—kīrtya**, mfn. to be recited by day; n. N. of partic. recitations, Br.; (a day) having such a r°, AitBr. iv, 18; m. a Caṇḍāla (in *antar-di*°, add.) **—kṛita**, mfn. done by day, MW. **—gaṇa**, m. = *ahar-*, Gaṇit. **—cara**, mfn. going by day, Mn.; Var. **—cārin**, mfn. id., Gṛihyas. **—°tana** (°*vât*°), mfn. id., m. a crow, L. **—°tithi** (°*vât*°), m. a guest coming in the day-time, VP. **—°di** (°*vâdi* or °*vâdi*?), m. beginning of day, morning, Gaut. **—naktam**, adv. (older *dívā náktam*) by day and night, Subh. 104; (as a subst. form) day and night, BhP. v, 22, 5. **—nidrā**, f. sleeping by day. **—niśam**, ind. day and night, Kathās. lxxvi, 11. **—°ndha** (°*vân*°), mfn. blind by day, m. an owl, Pañc.; (*ā*), f. a kind of bird (= *valgulā*), L.; °**ndhakī**, f. the musk-rat, L. **—pati**, m. 'day-lord,' N. of the 13th month, Kāṭh. **—pushṭa**, m. 'day-nourished,' the sun, L. **—pradīpa**, m. 'day-lamp,' i.e. an obscure man, L. **—bhīta**, mfn. timid by day; m. an owl, Kum. i, 12; a thief, L.; a flower closing itself by day, L. **—bhīti**, f. 'having fear by day,' an owl, L. **—bhūta**, mfn. turned into day, become bright (night), MBh. xiv, 1757. **—maṇi**, m. 'day-jewel,' the sun, L. **—madhya**, n. midday, noon, L. **—manya**, mfn. passing for day, appearing as day (night), Pāṇ. vi, 3, 66, Kāś. **—maithunin**, mfn. cohabiting by day, MārkP. xiv, 74. **—rātram**, ind. = *-niśam*, Mn. v, 80, MBh. &c.; as a subst. day and night, MBh. iii, 816. **—°rka** (°*vâr*°?), m. N. of a prince (cf. *divâ-kara*). **—vasu**, mfn. beautiful by day (?), RV. viii, 34, 1. **—vihāra**, m. rest by day, Divyâv. **—śaya**, mfn. sleeping by day, Ragh. xix, 34. **—śayatā**, f. sleep by day, Rājat. v, 252. **—śayyā**, f. id., Kshem. ii, 18. **—saṃketa**, m. appointment (of lovers) by day, Mālav. iv, [illegible]. **—saṃcara**, mfn. = *-cara*, Var. **—supta**, mfn. asleep by day, MW. **—svapana**, n. sleeping by day, Suśr. **—svapna**, m. (n. only MBh. xiii, 5094) sleep by day, Mn.; MBh.; Suśr. **—svāpa**, m. id., Suśr.; mfn. sleeping by day, (*ā*), f. a kind of night-bird (= *valgulā*), L.

Divātana, mf(*ī*)n. (Pāṇ. iv, 3, 23) daily, diurnal, Kum. iv, 46. °**tara** (*dí*°), mfn. id., RV. i, 127, 5.

1. **Divi**, m. the blue jay (= *kikīdivi*), L.

2. **Diví**, loc. of 3. *dív* in comp. **—kshaya**, mfn. heaven-dwelling, VāyuP. **—kshit**, mfn. id., RV. x, 92, 12; ChUp. ii, 24, 14. **—gata**, mfn. being in heaven, m. a god, Hariv. **—gamana**, m. 'sky-traveller,' a planet, star; *-ratna*, n. 'star-jewel,' the sun, Prasaṅg. **—cara** (*diví-*), mfn. moving in the sky (as a planet), AV. xix, 9, 7. **—cārin**, mfn. id., m. an inhabitant of the sky, MBh.; Hariv.; R. **—ja**, mfn. (Pāṇ. vi, 3, 15) heaven-born, celestial; m. a god, BhP. **—já**, mfn. 'sky-born,' RV. **—jāta**, mfn. id., m. N. of a son of Purū-ravas, VāyuP. **—yáj**, mfn. praying to heaven, RV. ix, 97, 26. **—yoni** (*diví-*), mfn. sky-born (Agni), RV. x, 88, 7. **—ratha**, m. N. of several men (v.l. *diva-*), MBh.; Hariv.; Pur. **—śrit**, mfn. going to heaven, AV. xi, 7, 23. **—shád**, mfn. sitting or dwelling in heaven, AV.; VS.; m. a god, R.; Gīt.; Dhūrtas.; *-adhvan*, m. the gods' path, atmosphere, Daśak. **—shṭambhá**, mfn. resting on the sky, AV. xix, 32, 7. **—shṭha**, mfn. dwelling in heaven, celestial, MBh.; Hariv. **—sád** and **stha** = *-shád* and *-shṭha*. **—spṛiś**, mfn. heaven-touching, RV.; MBh.; BhP. **—spṛiśat**, mfn. id., BhP. vii, 8, 22. **Diviśa**, see *div-īsa* under 3. *dív*.

Divī, f. a species of insect (= *upa-jihvikā*), L.

Divo, in comp. for °*vas*. **—já**, mfn. born or descended from heaven (Ushas), RV. vi, 65, 1. **—dāsa** (*dí*°), m. 'heaven's slave,' N. of Bharad-vāja (celebrated for his liberality and protected by Indra and the Aśvins, RV. i, 112, 14; 116, 18 &c.; the son of Vadhry-aśva, RV. vi, 61, 5; his father is also called Bhadra-sva, Bahv-aśva &c., and his son Mitra-yu or Mitrā-yu, Hariv.; Pur.); of the father of Su-dās, RV. vii, 18, 28; of a king of Kāśi surnamed Dhanvantari, founder of the Indian school of medicine, Suśr.; of the father of Pra-tardana, MBh. xiii; Hariv.; Pur.; of a descendant of Bhīma-sena, Kāṭh. vii &c.; °*sêśvara-liṅga*, n. N. of a Liṅga, SkandaP.; °*sôpâkhyāna*, n. 'the episode of D°' in PadmaP. **—dúh**, mfn. milking from the sky, SV. (v.l.) **—rúc**, mfn. shining from heaven, RV. iii, 7, 5.

1. **Divya**, Nom. P. °*yati*, to long for heaven, Pāṇ. viii, 2, 77, Sch.

2. **Divyá** (*divya*, Pāṇ. iv, 2, 101), mfn. divine, heavenly, celestial (opp. to *pārthiva*, *āntarīksha* or *mānusha*), RV.; AV.; ŚBr.; Kauś.; MBh. &c.; supernatural, wonderful, magical (*aṅgāra*, RV. x, 34, 9; *aushadha*, Bhartṛ. ii, 18; *vāsas*, Nal. xiv, 24; cf. *-cakshus*, *-jñāna* &c. below); charming, beautiful, agreeable, R.; Kathās. &c.; m. a kind of animal (= *dhanvana*), VarBṛS. lxxxviii, 9; barley, L.; bdellium, L.; N. of a prince, Pur.; of the author of RV. x, 107 &c.; (*ā*), f. N. of plants (= *harītakī*, *bandhyā*, *karkoṭakī*, *śatāvarī*, *mahā-medā* &c.), L.; a kind of perfume = *surā*, L.; N. of a Buddh. deity, Kālac.; of an Apsaras, Sch.; n. the divine world or anything d°; pl. the celestial regions, the sky, heaven, RV.; an ordeal (10 kinds, viz. *tulā*, *agni*, *jala*, *visha*, *kośa*, *taṇḍula*, *tapta-māsha*, *phāla*, *dharmâdharma*, *tulasī*, cf. ss. vv.), Yājñ. ii, 22, 95; Pañc. i, [illegible], 451, 452 &c.; oath, solemn promise, Hit. iv, [illegible]; cloves, L.; a sort of sandal, L.; N. of a grammar. [Cf. Gk. δῖος for διϝιος; Lat. *dīus* for *divius* in *sub dīo*.] **—kaṭa**, n. N. of a town, MBh. ii. **—kānana**, n. celestial grove; *-darśanā*, mfn. in aspect like to it, Nal. xii, 61. **—kārin**, mfn. undergoing an ordeal, taking an oath, W. **—kuṇḍa**, n. N. of a lake, KālP. **—kriyā**, f. the application of an ordeal, Rājat. iv, 94. **—gandha**, m. 'having a divine odour,' sulphur, L.; (*ā*), f. large cardamoms, L.; a kind of vegetable (= *mahā-cañcu*), L.; n. cloves, L. **—gāyana**, m. 'd° songster,' a Gandharva, L. **—cakshus**, n. a d° eye, supernatural vision, Daś.; Buddh.; mfn. having a d° eye, Ragh. iii, 45; fair-eyed, L.; having (only) the d° eye, (in other respects) blind, L.; m. a monkey, L.; a kind of perfume, L. **—jñāna**, n. d° knowledge; mfn. possessing it, MBh. i, 1784. **—tattva**, n. 'd° truth,' N. of a wk. **—tā**, f. divinity, d° nature, Naish. **—tumbī**, f. a kind of plant, Gal. **—tejas**, n. a kind of plant, L. **—tva**, n. = *-tā*, Kathās. **—darśana**, mfn. of a divine aspect, MBh. iii, 17075. **—darśin**, mfn. having a d° vision, MBh. xv, 566. **—dṛiś**, mfn. seeing d° things, Kathās.; m. an astrologer, Var. **—dṛishṭi**, f. = *-cakshus*, n. Kathās. **—devī**, f. N. of a goddess, Buddh. **—deha**, m. a d° body, MW. **—dohada**, n. d° desire, the object of a deity's desire, L.; mfn. fit for an offering or oblation, L. **—dharmin**, mfn. 'having a d° nature,' virtuous, agreeable, W. **—nadī**, f. a d° stream, ŚivaP. **—nārī**, f. a d° female, an Apsaras, R.; Kathās. **—pañcâmṛita**, n. 'the five d° ambrosias,' viz. ghee, milk, coagulated milk, honey, and sugar, L. **—pāṭala**, m. 'having a d° pale-red colour,' N. of a plant, MBh. i, 2374. **—purusha**, m. 'a d° man,' ghost, Uttarar. ii, [illegible]. **—pushpa**, m. Nerium Odorum, L.; (*ā*), f. a kind of plant, L.; °*pikā*, f. a kind of Calotropis, L. **—prajñāna**, n. = *-jñāna*, n.; *-śālin*, mfn. = id., mfn., Kathās. lxxv, 136. **—prabhāva**, mfn. having celestial power, MW. **—praśna**, m. inquiring into d° phenomena, augury, MBh. v, 1906. **—mantra**, m. 'the d° syllable,' Om, AmṛitUp. 20. **—māna**, n. measuring time according to the days and years of the gods, Sūryas. **—mānusha**, m. 'd° man,' demi-god, Kathās. i, 47. **—yamunā**, f. 'the d° Jamnā,' N. of a river in Kāma-rūpa, KālP. **—ratna**, n. 'd° gem,' the fabulous gem Cintā-maṇi, L. **—ratha**, m. 'd° car,' vehicle of the gods, L. **—rasa**, m. 'd° fluid,' quicksilver, L.; °*sêndra-sāra*, m. N. of a wk. **—rūpa** & °**pin**, mfn. of a d° aspect, beautiful, handsome, MBh.; Kathās. **—latā**, f. 'the d° creeper,' Sanseviera Zeylanica (= *mūrvā*), L. **—varma-bhṛit**, mfn. wearing d° armour, MBh. iii, 17167. **—vastra**, m. 'divinely dressed,' a kind of flower (= *sūrya-śobhā*), L. **—vākya**, n. a d° voice. **—vijñānavat**, mfn. = *-jñāna*, mfn., Kathās. lxxvii, 6. **—śrotra**, n. 'a d° ear' (which hears everything), Buddh. **—saṃkāśa**, mfn. having a d° appearance, R. **—saṃgraha**, m. N. of a wk. **—sānu**, m. 'd° eminence,' N. of one of the Viśve Devās, MBh. xiii, 4355. **—sāra**, m. 'having d° juice or resin,' Thorea Robusta, L. **—sūri**, m. N. of a man; *-carita*, n., *-prabhāva-dīpikā*, f. N. of two wks. **—strī**, f. a d° female, an Apsaras, Var.; Kathās. **—srag-anulepin**, mfn. adorned with d° garlands and unguents, Hcat. i, 8. **Divyâṃśu**, m. 'having d° rays,' the sun, MBh. iv, 390. **Divyâkṛiti**, mfn. of d° form, very beautiful, Kathās. lxxvii, 68. **Divyâṅganā**, f. = °*vya-strī*, Daś. **Divyâdivya**, mfn. d° and not d° (i.e. partly divine partly human), L.; (*ā*), f. the heroine of a poem (as Sītā &c.) of mixed origin or character, a goddess, W. **Divyâvadāna**, n. 'd° achievements,' N. of a well-known Buddh. wk. from Nepāl (written in Sanskṛit). **Divyôdaka**, n. 'd° water,' i.e. rain-water, L. **Divyôpapāduka**, mf(*ī*)n. divinely born, celestial, supernatural, L. **Divyâugha**, m. pl. 'the d° hosts,' forms of Śiva and Durgā (with the Sāktas), L. **Divyâushadha**, n. heavenly herbs or medicine, a magical potion, Bhartṛ. ii, 13. **Divyâushadhi**, f. red arsenic, Bhpr.

Divyaka, m. a kind of serpent, Suśr.; another kind of animal (= *divya*, *dhanvana*), VarBṛS. lxxxviii, 18.

Divyelaka, m. a kind of serpent, Suśr. (= *divyaka*?).

Dív, f. (only dat. *dīvé*, loc. *dīvi*, RV.; acc. *dyúvam*, dat. *dyuvé*, AV.) gambling, playing with dice. °**vana**, n. id. (cf. *devana*). °**vyat**, mfn. playing, gambling; m. a gambler by profession, Sāh.

Divi, m. the blue jay, L. (cf. *divi*).

दिविर *divira*, m. a husband's brother (= *devara*), Gal.; chief clerk or secretary (also *-pati*), Sch. **—kiśora**, m. N. of a poet.

दिश् 1. *diś*, cl. 3. P. *dídeshṭi* (Imper. *dídeshṭu*, RV.; cl. 6. *diśáti*, °*te* [later the only Pres. stem]; pf. *didéśa*, *didiśé*; fut. *dekshyati*, °*te* [*deshṭā*, Siddh.]; aor. *adikshat*, ŚBr. &c.; *adikshi*, *ádishṭa*, RV.; inf. *deshṭum*, MBh. etc.; *diśe*, RV.) to point out, show, exhibit, RV. viii, 82, 15; to produce, bring forward (as a witness in a court of justice), Mn. viii; to promote, effect, accomplish, Kir. i, 18; to assign, grant, bestow upon (dat., RV. ii, 41, 17; AV. xiv, 2, 13; gen., MBh. iii, 14278; xiii, 1843; loc., R. i, 2, 28); to pay (tribute), Hariv. 16061; to order, command, bid (inf.), Kir. v, 28; Pass. *diśyate*, MBh. &c.: Caus. *deśayati*, °*te*; aor. *adīdiśat*, to show, point out, assign, MBh.; R.; to direct, order, command, ib.; teach, communicate, tell, inform, confess, Buddh.: Desid. *didikshati*, °*te*, to wish to show &c.: Intens. *dédishṭe*, 3. pl. °*śate*, (p. f. pl. °*śatīs*) to show, exhibit, manifest, RV.; to order, command, ib.: Pass. *dediśyate*, to show or approve one's self, AV.; VS. [Cf. Z. *dis*; Gk. δείκνυμι; Lat. *dīco*, *in-dīcare* &c.; Goth. *teihan*; O. E. *tēon* (fr. *tīhan*).]

Dik, in comp. for 2. *diś*, p. 480. **—kanyā**, f. a quarter of the sky deified as a young virgin, Bhartṛ. iii, 93 (v. l. *kāntā*). **—kara**, mf(*ī*)n. youthful, juvenile (lit. making, i. e. changing q° continually, restless); m. a youth, L.; = *aruṇa* (as making a q° for the sun), L.; = *śambhu* (granter of space, promoter?), L.; (*ī*), f. a young woman, L.; *-vāsinī*, f. a form of Devī, VP. **—karika**, mfn. (ifc.) = *-karin* and (at once) = *-karikā*, f. the mark of a bite or of a nail, Śiś. iv, 9; (*ā*), f. N. of a river, KālP. **—karin**, m. 'elephant of the q°,' one of the mythical elephants which stand in the four or eight quarters of the sky and support the earth, BhP. **—kāntā** (Bhartṛ. iii, 93), **-kāmini**, f. (Rājat. iii, 382) = *-kanyā*. **—kuñjara**, m. = *-karin*, Sāh. **—kumāra**, m. pl. 'the youths of the q°,' a class of deities (with Jainas), L. **—cakra**, n. the circuit of the q° of the compass, the horizon, Ratn. iii, 5; the compass, the whole world, VarBṛS.; *-vāla*, n. the whole range of sight, the scenery all around, Kād. **—chabda** (for *śabda*), m. a word denoting a direction, Pāṇ. ii, 3, 29. **—taṭa**, m. the line of the horizon, remotest distance, Rājat.; Kathās. **—tás**, ind. from the regions of the sky, ŚBr. **—tulya**, mfn. having the same direction, Sūryas.; *-tā*, f. ib. **—pati**, m. a regent or guardian of a q° of the sky (often identified with *loka-pāla*, q. v.), VarBṛS.; Gīt. **—patha**, m. 'the path of the horizon,' the surrounding region or q°, Rājat. v, 341. **—pāla**, m. = *-pati*, Rājat. iv, 225. **—pravibhāga**, m. a q° direction, Sch. on VarBṛS. **—prêkshaṇa**, n. looking round in all directions (from fear &c.), Sāh. **—śūla**, n. 'sky-spear,' any inauspicious planetary conjunction; N. of partic. days on which it is not allowed to travel in certain directions, L.; *-lakshaṇa*, n. N. of ch. of the PSarv. **—sama**, mfn. = *-tulya*, Sūryas. **—sādhana-yantra**, n. N. of wk. **—sāmya**, n. sameness of direction, Sūryas. **—sudṛiś** (SSaṃkar.) and **-sundarī** (Gīt.), f. = *-kanyā*. **—srakti**, mfn. having the angles or corners towards the quarters of the compass, Sch. on KātyŚr. **—svāmin**, m. = *-pati*, VarBṛS.

Dig, in comp. for 2. *diś*. **—aṅganā**, f. = *dik-kanyā*, Kuval. **—adhipa**, m. = *dik-pati*, Naish. vi, 112. **—anta**, m. 'the end of the horizon,' remote distance, Bhartṛ. i, 37; mfn. being in r° d°, MBh. x, 260. **–antara**, n. another region, a foreign country, Ragh. ii, 15, Rājat. &c.; a quarter of the sky; (also pl.) space, the atmosphere, Kād. **–ambara**, mfn. 'sky-clothed,' i.e. quite naked, Bhartṛ. iii, 90; Pañc. v, 14; m. (also *-ka*) a naked mendicant (esp. of the Jaina or Bauddha sect, cf. 1. *kshapaṇa*), Prab.; Vet. &c.; MWB. 530 &c.; N. of Śiva or Skanda, L.; of a grammarian, Gaṇar.; darkness, L.; (*ī*), f. N. of Durgā, L. (cf. *-vastra* and *-vāsas*); °*ra-tva*, n. entire nakedness, Kum. v, 72. **–avasthāna**, n. air, Gal. **–āgata**, mfn. come from a distant q°, Yājñ. ii, 254. **–ibha**, m. = *dik-karin*, BhP. v, 14, 39. **–īśa** (Var.) & **-īśvara** (MBh.), m. = *dik-pati*. **–gaja**, m. = *dik-karin*, MBh.; R. &c. **–grahaṇa**, n. observing and fixing the quarters of the compass, Var. BṛS. xxiv, 9. **–jaya**, m. the conquest of various countries in all directions, Rājat. iv, 183 (cf. *-vijaya*). **–jyā́**, f. the azimuth cosine of a place, Gaṇit. **–dantin**, m. = *dik-karin*, Śatr. **–darśana**, n. the act of looking to every q°, a general survey, MW. **–darśin**, mfn. looking round on all sides, having a general view, ib. **–dāha**, m. glowing, i.e. preternatural redness of the horizon, Mn. iv, 115, Yājñ.; MBh. &c. **–devatā**, f. = *dik-pati*, BhP. **–deśa**, m. a distant region or country, Rājat. iv, 308; 417; in g. region, country, Hit. i, $\frac{1}{2}$. **–daivata**, n. = *-devatā*, MBh. vii, 7293. **–nāga**, see *diṅ-*. **–bandha**, m. = *-grahaṇa*, Kathās. lxxiii, 116. **–bhāga**, m. = *dik-pravibh°*, R. iv, 47, Pañc. ii, $\frac{12}{13}$. **–bheda**, m. difference of direction, Sūryas. **–bhrama**, m. perplexity about points of the compass; mistaking the way or direction, Vcar. v, 66. **–maṇḍala**, see *diṅ-*. **–yātrā**, f. a procession in different directions, Siṅhâs. Introd. 3. **–lābha**, m. profit or gain in a distant region, Yājñ. ii, 254. **–vakra-saṃstha**, mfn. standing apart from the right direction, VarYogay. viii, 1. **–vadhū**, f. = *-aṅganā*, Kād. **–vasana**, m. a Jaina, ŚSaṃkar.; n. nakedness, Pratāpar. **–vastra**, mfn. = *-ambara*; m. N. of Śiva, L.; of a grammarian (= *deva-nandin*), Gaṇar. **–vāraṇa**, m. = *dik-karin*, MBh. **–vāsas**, mfn. = *-ambara*, Mn. xi, 201; MBh.; BhP.; m. a naked mendicant, L.; N. of Śiva, MBh. xiii, 695 &c.; of a grammarian, Gaṇar. **–vijaya**, m. = *dig-jaya*; N. of a section of the MBh. (ii, 983–1203) describing the victories of Yudhi-shṭhira; of a wk. by Śaṃkarâcārya describing his controversial victories over various sects; *-krama*, m. going forth to conquer the world, invasion, W. **–vidik-stha**, mfn. situated towards the cardinal and intermediate points, encompassing, MW. **–vidhāna**, n. N. of a ch. of the Tantras. **–vibhāga**, m. q°, point, direction, Vikr. i, $\frac{4}{5}$; Ratn. iv, 5. **–vibhāvita**, mfn. celebrated or known in all q°rs, W. **–virati**, f. the not passing beyond boundaries in any direction, Jain. **–vilokana**, n. = *dik-prekshaṇa*, Kām. vii, 25. **–vyāghāraṇa**, n. sprinkling of the q°rs of the sky, PārGṛ. iii, 8, 9. **–vyāpin**, mfn. spreading through all space or every q°, W. **–vrata**, n. = *-virati*, Jain.

Diṅ, in comp. for 2. *diś*. **–nāga**, m. = *dik-karin*, MBh.; N. of a Buddh. author (v. l. *dig-n°*) &c. **–nātha**, m. = *dik-pati*, Var. **–maṇḍala**, n. = *dik-cakra*, Bhartṛ.; Var. (v. l. *dig-m°*). **–mātaṅga**, m. = *-nāga*, Rājat. **–mātra**, n. a mere direction or indication, Kāvyâd. ii, 96. **–mārga**, m. a country road or a r° to a distant c°, MW. **–mukha**, mf(*ī*)n. facing any point or q°, W.; n. any q° or point of the heavens, Kāv.; place, spot, Sūryas.; *-maṇḍala*, n. pl. the countries all around, Subh. 123. **–mūḍha**, mfn. confused about the q°rs of the compass, R. iii, 60, 3; anything about the direction of which one is doubtful, VarBṛS. liii, 115. **–moha**, m. = *dig-bhrama*, Kām. xiv, 24.

2. **Diś**, f. quarter or region pointed at, direction, cardinal point, RV.; AV.; ŚBr. &c. (four in number, viz. *prācī*, east; *dakshiṇā*, south; *pratīcī*, west; and *udīcī*, north, AV. xv, 2, 1; ĀśvGṛ. iv, 8 &c.; sometimes a 5th, *dhruvā*, AV. viii, 9, 15; ŚBr. ix, 4, 3, 10; and a 6th, *ūrdhvā*, AV. iii, 27, 1; ŚBr. xiv, 6, 11, 5; and a 7th, *vy-adhvā*, AV. iv, 40, 1; ŚBr. ix, 5, 2, 8; but oftener 8 are given, i.e. the 4 cardinal and the 4 intermediate quarters, S.E., S.W., N.W., and N.E., Mn. i, 13 [cf. *upa-*]; and even a 9th and 10th, *tiryak* or *adhas* and *ūrdhvam*, ŚBr. vi, 2, 2, 34, MBh. i, 729; *diśām pati* [cf. *dik-pati*, below] = Soma, RV. ix, 113, 2, or = Rudra, VS. xvi, 17); quarter, region, direction, place, part (pl., rarely sg. the whole world, e.g. *diśi diśi*, in all directions, everywhere, Bhartṛ. i, 86; *digbhyas*, from every q°, BhP. i, 15, 8; *diśo diśas*, hither and thither, Pañc. ii, $\frac{116}{117}$; *diśo 'valokya*, looking into the q° of the sky, i.e. into the air, Ratn. iv, $\frac{4}{5}$; *diśo 'ntāt*, from the extremities of the world, ib., Introd. 6); country, esp. foreign country, abroad (cf. *dig-āgata* & *-lābha*, below); space (beside *kāla*), Kap. ii, 12; the numeral 10 (cf. above), Śrutab.; Sūryas.; a hint, reference, instance, example, Suśr.; Sāh.; Schol.; precept, order, manner, RV. [cf. δίκη; O. H. G. *zeiga* (see also *diśā*)]; mark of a bite, L.; N. of a river, MBh. vi, 327.

Diśo = *diśas* (gen. of 2. *diś*) in comp. **–daṇḍa**, m. 'sky-staff,' a partic. appearance in the sky. **–dāha**, m. = *dig-*, Divyâv. **–bhāga**, w. r. for **-bhāj**, mfn. one who runs away in all directions, Pañc. (B) iv, 15, $\frac{114}{115}$. **–yāyin**, mfn. spreading in all directions, Kād.

Diśam, ind. = 2. *diś*, ifc. (g. *śarad-ādi*).

Diśas, f. region, quarter &c., L.

Diśā, f. direction, region, quarter or point of the compass, MBh. iv, 1716 &c., Har. 2243 (cf. *antara-* and *avântara-*); N. of the wife of Rudra-Bhīma, VP. **–gaja**, m. = *dik-karin*, Hariv.; R. **–cakshus**, m. 'sky-vision,' N. of a son of Garuḍa, MBh. v, 3595. **–pāla**, m. = *dik-*, Hariv. 273; = *dik-karin*, R. i, 41, 16 &c.

Díśya, mfn. relating to the quarters of the sky or to the horizon, being there, ĀśvGṛ.; Kauś.; relating to space, Kaṇ. ii, 2, 10; foreign, outlandish, Śiś. iii, 76; (*ā*), f. N. of a kind of brick, ŚBr.; KātyŚr.

Dishṭá, mfn. shown, pointed out, appointed, assigned (*dishṭā gatis*, 'the appointed way,' i.e. death, R. ii, 103, 8); fixed, settled; directed, bidden, RV.; AV.; MBh.; R. &c.; m. time, L.; a sort of Curcuma, L.; N. of a son of Manu Vaivasvata, Pur.; n. appointed place, ChUp. v, 9, 2; aim, goal, TBr. ii, 4, 2, 2 &c.; allotment, assignment, decree; fate, destiny, AV. x, 3, 16; MBh.; direction, order, command, BhP. v, 1, 11 &c.; Rājat. iv, 121; a description according to space and time (i.e. of a natural phenomenon), Sāh. **–kārin**, mfn. executing an order or acting according to fate, BhP. iv, 28, 1. **–dṛiś**, mfn. looking at fate or at one's lot, BhP. iv, 21, 22. **–para**, mfn. relying on fate, fatalist, MBh. iii, 1214. **–bhāva**, m. 'appointed state,' i.e. death, MBh. v, 4529. **–bhuj**, mfn. reaping the appointed results of one's works, BhP. vii, 13, 39. **Dishṭânta**, m. 'appointed end,' i.e. death, MBh.; R. &c.

Dishṭi, f. direction, prescription, TāṇḍyaBr. xxv, 18; auspicious juncture, good fortune, happiness (esp. instr. °*tyā*, thank heaven! I congratulate you on your good luck! often with *vardhase*, you are fortunate), MBh.; Kāv. &c.; a kind of measure of length, Kauś.; Sch. on Kāty. Śr. **–vṛiddhi**, f. congratulation, Kād.; Hcar.

दिश् 3. *diś*, a vulgar form for *dṛiś*, to see, Pāṇ. i, 3, 1, Vārtt. 13, Pat.

दिष्णु *dishṇu*, mfn. = *deshṇu*, liberal.

दिह् 1. *dih*, cl. 2. P. Ā. *degdhi*, *digdhe*, Dhātup. xxiv, 5 (Subj. *-dehat*, RV. vii, 50, 2; pf. *dideha*, *didihe*, MBh.; fut. *dhekshyati*, *degdhā*, Siddh.; aor. *adhikshat*, °*ta*, 3. pl. °*shur*, JaimBr.; *adigdha*, Pāṇ. vii, 3, 73) to anoint, smear, plaster, ŚBr.; KātyŚr.; Mn.; MBh.; R. &c.; increase, accumulate, L.: Caus. *dehayati*, °*te*, MBh. &c.; aor. *adīdihat*: Desid. *didhikshati*, °*te*; *dhīkshate* (ŚBr.), to wish to anoint one's self: Intens. *dedihyate*, *dedegdhi*. [Fr. orig. *dhigh*; cf. θιγγάνω, ἔ-θιγ-ον, τεῖχος, τοῖχος; Lat. *fingo*, *figulus*, *figura*; Goth. *deigan*, *gadigis*; O.E. *dāh*; E. *dough*; Germ. *Teig*.]

2. **Dih**. See *su-*.

दिह्ला *dihlā*, f. N. of a woman, Rājat. vii, 332 (cf. *dilha*).

दी 1. *dī* (cf. √*ḍī*), cl. 4. P. Ā. *dīyati*, °*te*, to soar, fly, RV.; SV.: Intens. inf. *dédīyitavai*, to fly away, ŚBr. [Cf. *ḍī*; Gk. δίεμαι, δίνη, δινεύω, δῖνος.]

दी 2. *dī* (*dīdī* or *dīdi*), cl. 3. P. 3. pl. *dīdyati* (Impv. *dīdihi* and *dīdihi*, RV.; impf. *ádīdet*, ib.; pf. *dīdāya* or (ŚBr.) *dīdaya*; *dīdetha*, *dīdiyus*, ib.; Subj. *dīdáyati*, °*yat*, ib.; *dīdayat*, RV. x, 30, 4; 95, 12; *dīdāyat*, AV. iii, 8, 3; *dīdayante*, ib. xviii, 3, 23; Prec. *dīdyāsam*, TBr.; p. Pres. P. *dīdiat*, Ā. *dīdiāna*, p. pf. *dīdivás*) RV. to shine, be bright; to shine forth, excel, please, be admired, RV.; AV.; Br.; bestow upon (loc. or dat.) by shining, RV. ii, 2, 6; i, 93, 10. [Cf. δέατο, δέελος, δῆλος.]

Dīti, f. splendour, brightness (see *su-*).

Dīdi, mfn. shining, bright; only in **dīdy-agni**, mfn. having bright fires (said of the Aśvins), RV. i, 15, 11; viii, 57, 2.

Dīditi, f. = *diti* (see *su-dīditi*).

Dī́divi, mfn. shining, bright, RV. i, 1, 8; risen (as a star), L.; m. a N. of Bṛihas-pati, the planet Jupiter, L.; heaven, final emancipation (cf. *didivi*), L.; m. n. boiled rice, food, L. (cf. *didīvi*); = *artha*, L.

दी 3. *dī*, cl. 4. Ā. *dīyate*, to decay, perish (Dhātup. xxvi, 25; *didīye*; *dāsyate*, *dātā*; *adāsta*, Pāṇ. vi, 4, 63; i, 50): Caus. *dāpayati*, Vop.: Desid. *didīshate* and *didāsate*, ib.

4. **Dī**, f. decay, ruin. **–da**, mfn. causing ruin, destroying, W.

Dīná, mfn. (fr. √3. *dī*?) scarce, scanty, RV.; depressed, afflicted, timid, sad; miserable, wretched, Mn.; MBh.; Kāv. &c.; (*am*), ind. sadly, miserably, Śiksh. 35; n. distress, wretchedness, Hariv.; Pañc.; Tabernæmontana Coronaria, L.; (*ā*), f. the female of a mouse or shrew, L. **–citta** and **-cetana**, mfn. 'distressed in mind,' dejected, Kāv. **–tā** (°*ná-*), f. scarcity, weakness, RV. vii, 89, 3. **–daksha** (°*ná-*), mfn. of weak understanding, RV. x, 2, 5. **–dāsa**, m. a N. applied to a Śūdra, Kull. **–dīna**, mfn. very wretched or miserable, Bhām. **–dhī**, mfn. = *-citta*, MW. **–nātha** and °*tha-sūri*, m. N. of authors, Cat. **–manas** and **-mānasa**, mfn. = *-citta*, MBh. **–mukha**, mf(*ī*)n. 'sad-faced,' looking melancholy, W. **–rūpa**, mfn. of melancholy aspect, dejected, MBh. i, 1817. **–locana**, m. (*dīpta-*?) a cat, L. **–vatsala**, mfn. kind to the poor, MW. **–vadana**, mfn. = *-mukha*, Daś. **–varṇa**, mfn. discoloured, pale, MBh. iii, 15677. **–sattva**, mfn. = *-citta*, R. **–sādhaka**, m. 'causing woe,' N. of Śiva, MBh. xiii, 1152. **Dīnâkrandana-stotra**, n. N. of Stotras. **Dīnânukampana**, mfn. pitying the poor, MW. **Dīnâsya**, mfn. = °*na-vadana*, Bhartṛ. iii, 22. **Dīnaka**, mfn. very miserable or dejected; (*am*), ind. very miserably, MBh. iii, 12260.

दीक्ष् *dīksh* (Desid. of √*daksh*?), cl. 1. Ā. *dīkshate*, Dhātup. xvi, 8 (pf. *didīkshé*; fut. *dīkshishyáte*; aor. *adidīkshas* and *adīkshishṭa*, Br.; ind. p. *dīkshitvā*, ChUp.) to consecrate or dedicate one's self (esp. for the performance of the Soma-sacrifice), Br.; Up.; Pur.; to dedicate one's self to a monastic order, Buddh.: Caus. *dīkshayati*, °*te*, to consecrate, initiate, TS.; Br.; pf. *didīkshur*, TāṇḍyaBr. xxiv, 18; to consecrate as a king, MBh.; Hariv.; to make ready, prepare, MBh.: Desid. *didīkshishate*, to wish to be consecrated, AitBr. iv, 25.

Dīkshaka, m. a priest, spiritual guide; N. of a king, Virac.

Dīkshaṇa, n. consecrating one's self or causing one's self to be consecrated, consecration, initiation, ŚrS.; MBh.; (*ā*), f. id., VarBṛS. xcviii, 14. °**shaṇīya**, mfn. (fr. √*dīksh*) to be consecrated or initiated; (fr. *dīkshaṇa*) relating to consecration, Br.; (*ā*), f. (Vait.) = °*yeshṭi*, f. the sacrifice of consecration or initiation, Br.; ŚrS.

Dīkshayitṛi, m. consecrator, AitBr. i, 4.

Dīkshā́, f. preparation or consecration for a religious ceremony, undertaking religious observances for a partic. purpose and the observances themselves, AV.; VS.; Br.; ŚrS. &c.; dedication, initiation (personified as the wife of Soma, RV. 25, 26, of Rudra Ugra or R° Vāmadeva, Pur.); any serious preparation (as for battle), MBh.; Hariv.; Kāv.; self-devotion to a person or god, complete resignation or restriction to, exclusive occupation with (comp.; cf. *viraha-*, *śāka-*, *śṛiṅgāra-*). **–karaṇa**, n. performance of consecration, Sarvad. **–kārin**, mfn. consecrating, initiating, ib. **–krama-ratna**, n. 'the jewel of the regular order of initiation,' N. of wk. **–guru**, m. a teacher of initiation, Bālar. x, 41. **–°ṅga-svasti-vācana** (°*kshâṅg°*), n. N. of wk. **–tattva**, n. 'essence of initiation,' N. of wk. **–°nta** (°*kshânta°*), m. the end of a D° = *avabhṛitha*, L. **–pati** (°*kshā́-*), m. 'consecration-lord,' i.e. Soma, VS. v, 6. **–pattra**, n. N. of wk. **–paddhati**, f. N. of wk. **–pāla**, m. guardian of initiation (Agni or Vishṇu), Br. **–prakaraṇa**, n. N. of wk. **–phala**, n. 'the fruit of initiation,' N. of a ch. of the PSarv. **–maya**, mf(*ī*)n. consisting in initiation, Hariv. 2115. **–mahôtsava**, m., **-māsâdi-vicāra**, m., **-ratna**, n., **-vidhāna**, n., **-vidhi**, m., **-vinoda**, m., **-viveka**, m., **-saṃskāra**, m., **-sūkta**, n., **-setu**, n., N. of wks.

Dīkshitá, mf(*ī*, GopBr. i, 5, 24)n. consecrated, initiated into (dat., loc., instr., or comp.) AV.; TS.; Br.; ŚrS.; Mn.; MBh. &c.; prepared, ready for (dat., instr. or comp.), MBh., R. (°*tam-√kṛi*, to initiate, instruct, Kathās. xx, 198); performed (as the Dīkshā ceremony), W.; m. a priest engaged in a D° (*-tva*, n. Jaim.); a pupil of (affixed, and rarely prefixed to the N. of a teacher, and given as a N. to a Brāhman to denote his being a pupil of that t°, e.g. *Bhaṭṭoji-*, *Śam-kara-*; sometimes the teacher's N. is dropped and D° is used alone). **— dhuṇḍhi-rāja**, m., **-bāla-kṛishṇa**, m., **-yajña-datta**, m. N. of men, Cat. **— vasana**, n. the garment of an initiated person, ŚBr. **— vādá**, m. the statement that a person is initiated, TS. **— vimitá**, n. a temporary dwelling for a person about to be initiated, Kāṭh. xiii, 1; AitBr. 1, 3 (cf. *prācīna-vaṅśa*). **— vrata**, n. the vow of an initiated person, KātyŚr. iv, 6, 13. **— sāmarāja**, m. N. of the author of Dhūrta-nartaka. **Dīkshitâvedana**, n. = °*ta-vāda*, Vait. xi, 12.

Dīkshitāyanī, f. N. of the wife of Dīkshita-yajñadatta, L. °**tīya**, mfn. written by a Dīkshita; n. N. of such a work.

Dīkshitṛi, m. a consecrator, Pāṇ. iii, 2, 153.

Dīkshin, mfn. (ifc.) one who has been initiated (cf. *gaṇa-*).

दीदी *dīdī* or *dīdi*. See √2. *dī*.

दीधी 1. *dīdhī* (connected with √2. *dī*), cl. 2. Ā. *dīdhīte*, to shine, be bright, Dhātup. xxiv, 68; P. *ádīdhet*, 3. pl. *adīdhayur*, to appear as, resemble (nom.), RV. v, 40, 5; x, 98, 7.

1. **Dī́dhiti**, f. brightness, splendour, light, a ray, Naigh. i, 5; MBh.; Kālid. &c.; majesty, power, Bhartṛ. ii, 2; N. of wks., esp. ifc. **— prakāśa**, m., **-pratyaksha-ṭīkā**, f., **-māthurī**, f., N. of Comms. **— mat**, mfn. having splendour, shining, brilliant, ŚāṅkhGṛ. vi, 3; m. the sun, Kum. ii, 2; vii, 10; N. of a Muni, Kathās. lix, 93. **— raudrī**, f., **-vyākhyā**, f. N. of wks.

दीधी 2. *dīdhī* (cf. √1. *dhī* and √*dhyai*), cl. 2. Ā. *dīdhīte*, 1. sg. *dīdhye* (RV. v, 33, 1), p. Pres. *dī́dhyat* (RV. ii, 20, 1) and *dī́dhyāna* (RV., often with *manasā*) to perceive, think, be intent upon; to wish, desire. 2. **Dī́dhiti**, f. religious reflection, devotion, inspiration, RV. i, 186, 11 &c.

दीन *dīná*, mfn. See under √3. *dī*.

दीनार *dīnāra*, m. (fr. δηνάριον, *denarius*) a gold coin or a certain weight of gold (variously stated as 2 Kāshṭhas, 1 Pala of 32 Rettis or the large Pala of 108 Suvarṇas), Pañc.; Rājat. iv; a gold ornament, L.; a seal, L. °**raka**, m., °**rikā**, f. (Hariv.), and **dīnnāra**, m. (Rājat.) id.

दीप *dīp*, cl. 4. Ā. *dīpyate* (*dīpyáte*, TBr., *dīpyati*, MBh., pf. *didīpe*, Ragh. v, 47; fut. *dīpishyate*, *dīpitā*; aor. *adīpi*, *adīpishṭa*, inf. *dīpitum*, Pāṇ. vii, 2, 8, Sch.; iii, 1, 61) to blaze, flare, shine, be luminous or illustrious, AV.; Br.; Mn.; MBh.; Kālid. &c.; glow, burn (also with anger, Bhaṭṭ.): Caus. *dīpáyati*, °*te*, aor. *adīdipat* or *adidīpat* (Pāṇ. vii, 4, 3) to kindle, set on fire, inflame, TāṇḍyaBr. xvi, 1; ĀśvGṛ. iv, 6; Kauś. 60 &c.; illuminate, make illustrious, MBh.; Hariv. &c.; excite, rouse, ib.: Desid. *didīpishate*: Intens. *dedīpyate*, to blaze fiercely, shine intensely, be very bright, MBh.; BhP.; p. *dedīpyantī*, MBh. vii, 8138.

Dīpa, m. a light, lamp, lantern, ĀśvGṛ.; Mn.; MBh. &c. **— karpūra-ja**, m. a kind of camphor, Gal. **— kalikā**, f. N. of a Comm. on Yājñ. **— kiṭṭa**, n. lamp-black, soot, L. **— kūpī**, f., **-khorī**, f. the wick of a l°, L. **— m-kara**, m. 'light-causer,' N. of a mythical Buddha, MWB. 136; *-jñāna*, m. having the knowledge of a B°, N. of a man, Buddh. **— da**, mfn. one who gives a lamp, Mn. iv, 229. **— dāna**, n. 'giving light,' N. of a ch. of the PSarv.; *-paddhati*, f., *-ratna*, n., *-vidhi*, m. N. of wks. **— dhvaja**, m. 'lamp-sign,' soot, L. **— pādapa**, m. 'l°-tree,' a candlestick, L. **— pushpa**, m. 'l°-flower,' Michelia Campaka, L. **— pūjā**, f., *-vidhāna*, n., **-prakāśa**, m. N. of wks. **— bhājana**, n. 'light-receptacle,' a lamp, Ragh. xix, 51. **— mallī**, f. a l°, Gal. **— mālā**, f. a row of l°s, an illumination, MBh. xiii, 4727; Caurap. 18. **— mālikā**, f. id.; N. of wk.; °*lôtsava*, m. 'the feast of lights,' N. of the 125th ch. of the BhavP. ii. **— māhātmya**, n. 'the glory of the festival of lights,' N. of a ch. of the BhavP. i. **— vat**, mfn. 'containing lights,' illuminating; (*ī*), f. N. of a river, KālP. **— varti**, f. the wick of a lamp, Daś. **— vidhāna**, n., **-vidhi**, m. N. of wks. **— vṛiksha**, m. = *-pādapa*; lantern, light, MBh.; R.; Pinus Longifolia or Devadāru, L. **— vyākaraṇa**, n. N. of wk. **— śatru**, m. 'lamp-foe,' a moth, L. **— śikhā**, f. the flame of a l°, Kathās. xviii, 77; the point of a shining body, Līl. 95; l°-black, soot, L.; °*khôpanishad*, f. N. of an Up. **— śṛiṅkhalā**, f. a row of lamps, L. **— śrāddha-vidhi**, m., **-sāra**, m., **-stambha-devatā-pūjā**, f. N. of wks. **Dīpâṅkura**, m. the flame or light of a l°, Bhartṛ. iii, 81. **Dīpânvitā**, f. (sc. *tithi*) 'furnished with l°s,' N. of the Dīwālī festival, BhavP. **Dīpârādhana**, n. worshipping an idol by waving a l° before it, MW. **Dīpâlī**, f. 'a row of l°s,' a festival with illuminations on the day of new moon in the month Āśvina or Kārttika (Dīwālī), RTL. 432; °*lika-kalpa*, m. N. of wk. **Dīpâloka**, m. lamp-light, a burning l° or torch, ŚārṅgP. **Dīpâvali**, f. a row of lights, nocturnal illumination, BhP. iv, 21, 4, also = *dīpâlī*; °*valī-prayoga*, m. N. of wk. **Dīpâsura**, m. N. of an Asura, Virac. xvi. **Dīpôcchishṭa**, n. 'l°-sediment,' soot. **Dīpôtsava**, m. a festival of lights, BhavP.

Dīpaka, mfn. kindling, inflaming, illuminating, Pañc. iii, 27, $\frac{221}{222}$; exciting, stimulating (digestion), Suśr.; skilful in managing a lamp (g. *ākarshâdi*); m. a light, lamp, Hariv., Bhartṛ., BhP.; the shining body, Līlāv.; N. of two plants having digestive properties, Ptychotis Ajowan or Celosia cristata, L.; a bird of prey, L.; (in music) N. of a Rāga; a kind of measure; N. of Kāma (the inflamer), L.; of a son of Garuḍa (MBh. v, 3596) &c.; m. or n. saffron, L.; (*ikā*), f. a light, lamp, lantern, Hariv.; Kāv. &c.; moonlight, W.; 'illustrator' or 'illustration' at the end of titles of books (cf. *kula-*, *gūḍhârtha-*, *trailokya-*) and also alone, N. of wks. (see below); Ptychotis Ajowan or the root of Calmus, L.; (in music) N. of a Rāgiṇī; n. a partic. class of rhet. figures (throwing light upon an idea), Sāh.; Kuval.; N. of a metre. **— mālā**, f. N. of a metre. **— vyākaraṇa**, n. N. of wk.

Dīpana, mf(*ī*)n. kindling, inflaming, setting on fire, MBh.; Hariv.; Kālid.; digestive, stimulating (cf. *agni-* and *anala-*), Suśr.; m. N. of certain digestive plants (= *mayūra-śikhā*, *śāliñca-śāka* or *kāsa-marda*), L.; an onion, L.; (*ī*), f. Trigonella Fœnum Græcum, Bhpr.; Ptychotis Ajowan; Clypea Hernandifolia, L.; a mystical formula described in the Tantra-sāra; (in music) a kind of composition; N. of a female attendant of Devī, W.; n. the act of kindling &c., R.; Pañc.; Daś.; promoting digestion, Suśr.; a digestive or tonic, Suśr.; the root of Tabernæmontana Coronaria (cf. *dīna*), L.; a partic. process to which minerals are subjected, Sarvad.; a partic. procedure with a magic formula, ib. **Dīpanīya**, mfn. to be kindled or lighted or excited or stimulated; relating to tonic medicines; promoting digestion, Suśr.; Car.; m. Ptychotis Ajowan, L.; n. a digestive, Suśr. **Dīpayat**, mfn. illuminating, inflaming, W.

Dīpikā, f. of *dīpaka*, q.v. **— ṭīkā**, f. N. of a Comm. **— taila**, n. the oil of Ptychotis Ajowan, Suśr. **— dhāriṇī**, f. a female lamp-carrier, Kād. **— prakāśa**, m., °**śikā**, f., **-vivaraṇa**, n., **-vyākhyā**, f. N. of Comms.

Dīpita, mfn. set on fire, inflamed, excited, illuminated, manifested, MBh.; R. &c. **Dīpitṛi**, m. an illuminator, enlightener, Pāṇ. iii, 2, 153.

Dīpin, mfn. kindling, inflaming, exciting (ifc. Kathās. lxxxii, 29); (*inī*), f. a mystical formula (cf. *dīpana*, f.).

Dīpta, mfn. blazing, flaming, hot, shining, bright, brilliant, splendid; MuṇḍUp. ii, 1, 1; MBh., R. &c.; excited, agitated (*krodha-*, MBh. v, 7207); (in augury) exposed to the sun (also *āditya-*, MBh. iii, 15669); being on the wrong side, inauspicious (opp. to *śānta*), Hariv., Suśr., VarBṛS.; clear, shrill (?applied to the inauspicious voice of an animal and opp. to *pūrṇa*), VarBṛS. lxxxviii, 11; xci, 1; Suśr.; m. a lion (from his bright colour), L.; the citron tree, L.; inflammation of the nose, Suśr.; (*ā*), f. Methonica Superba, L.; Cardiospermum Halicacabum, L.; = *sātalā*, L.; red arsenic, L.; (in music) a partic. tone; a partic. Śakti, Hcat. i, 5; n. Asa Fœtida, L.; gold, L. **— kiraṇa**, mfn. 'hot-rayed,' the sun, Mṛicch. viii, 23. **— kīrti**, mfn. 'bright-famed;' N. of Skanda, MBh. iii, 14630. **— ketu**, m. 'bright-bannered,' N. of a king, MBh. i, 231; of a son of Manu Daksha-sāvarṇi, BhP. viii, 13, 18. **— jihvā**, f. 'red-tongued,' a fox, L. **— tapas**, mfn. fervent in devotion, of glowing piety, BrahmaP. **— tejas**, mfn. radiant with glory, ib. **— tva**, n. flaming, shining, Sāh. **— nayana**, m. 'having glittering eyes,' N. of an owl, Kathās. **— piṅgala**, m. 'bright and yellowish,' a lion, L. **— pushpā**, f. 'bright-flowered,' Tragia Involucrata, L. **— rasa**, m. 'having a yellow liquid,' an earth-worm, L.; *-tva*, n. the predominance of fiery passions, Vām. iii, 2, 14. **— rūpin**, m. a partic. personification, Gaut. **— roman**, m. 'red-haired,' N. of one of the Viśve Devās, MBh. xiii, 4356. **— locana**, m. 'having glittering eyes,' a cat, L. **— loha**, n. the shining metal, brass, L. **— varṇa**, mfn. 'red-coloured,' N. of Skanda, MBh. iii. **— vīrya**, mfn. of fiery strength, MBh. i, 2915. **— śakti**, m. 'having a glittering spear,' N. of Skanda, ib. **— śikha**, mfn. 'bright-flamed' (fire), Kathās. lxxiii, m. N. of a Yaksha, ib. **— svāmin**, m. N. of the father of Śabara-svāmin, Cat. **Dīptâṅśu**, m. 'hot-rayed,' the sun. **Dīptâksha**, mf(*ī*)n. having bright or glittering eyes, MBh. iii, 16138; m. a cat, L.; a peacock, W.; N. of an owl, Pañc.; pl. N. of a people, MBh. v. **Dīptâgni**, m. blazing fire, MBh. iii, 706; N. of Agastya, L. (cf. *dahrâgni* and *satyâgni*); mfn. having the gastric fire well kindled, i.e. digesting well, Suśr., Hcat.; *-tā*, f. goodness of digestion, ib. **Dīptâṅga**, m. 'having a brilliant body,' a peacock, L. **Dīptâtman**, mfn. having a fiery nature, MBh. v, 7040. **Dīptâsya**, mfn. 'having fiery jaws,' a serpent, ib. 7169. **Dīptôda**, n. 'having brilliant water,' N. of a Tīrtha, MBh. iii, 8685. **Dīptôpala**, m. 'brilliant stone,' the sun gem (= *sūrya-kānta*); a crystalline lens, L. **Dīptâujas**, mfn. glowing with energy, VarBṛS. xxxii, 15.

Dīptaka, m. or n. a kind of disease of the nose, L.; n. gold, L.

Dī́pti, f. brightness, light, splendour, beauty, ŚBr.; Mn. (cf. *gṛiha-*) &c.; the flash-like flight of an arrow, L.; lac, L.; brass, L.; m. N. of one of the Viśve Devās. **— kara**, mf(*ā* or *ī*)n. irradiating, illuminating, MW. **— ketu**, m. N. of a son of Manu Daksha-sāvarṇi (cf. *dīpta-*), VP. **— mat**, mfn. bright, splendid, brilliant, MBh.; Kāv. &c.; m. N. of a son of Kṛishṇa, Hit.; (*ī*), f. (in music) N. of a Śruti.

Dīptika, mfn. (ifc.) = *dī́pti*; m. a species of plant, L. °**kêśvara-tīrtha** (°*kêśv°*?), n. N. of a Tīrtha, ŚivaP.

Dīpya, mfn. to be kindled or inflamed or stimulated, W.; promoting digestion, L.; m. Celosia Cristata; Ptychotis Ajowan; cumin-seed, L.; n. white cumin-seed, L. **Dīpyaka**, m. a species of plant, Suśr.; m. Celosia Cristata, m. or n. Ptychotis Ajowan; n. Apium Involucratum, L.; n. a figure of rhetoric, L.

Dīpra, mfn. flaming, shining, radiant, Kathās. xxv, 135; m. fire, L.

दीर्घ *dīrghá*, mf(*ā*)n. (compar. *drā́ghīyas*, superl. *drā́ghishṭha* [qq. vv.]; rarely *dīrghatara* [Pañc. iv, $\frac{10}{14}$] and °*tama* [BhP. vii, 5, 44]) long (in space and time), lofty, high, tall; deep, RV.; AV.; Br. &c.; long (in prosody), Prāt., Mn. &c.; (*ám*) ind. long, for a long time (superl. °*atamam*, BhP. iii, 1, 37); m. a long vowel, Gobh. ii, 8, 15, KātyŚr. &c.; a camel, L.; Saccharum Sara; Shorea Robusta, = *utkaṭa*, *rāma-śara* &c. L.; a mystical N. of the letter *a*, Up.; the 5th or 6th or 7th or 8th sign of the zodiac, Jyot.; N. of a prince of Magadha, MBh. i, 4451; of Śiva, MBh. xiii, 1158; (*ā*), f. an oblong tank (cf. °*ghikā*), R. v, 16, 27; a kind of plant = *-pattrā*, L.; a mystical N. of the letter *n*, Up.; n. a species of grass, L.; N. of a Sāman, ĀrshBr. [Fr. √*drāgh*; cf. also Gr. δυλιχός; Sl. *dlŭgŭ*.] **— kaṇā**, f. white cumin, L. **— kaṇṭa**, °**ṭaka**, m. 'long-thorned,' N. of a plant (= *varvūra*), L. **— kaṇṭha**, m. 'l°-necked,' N. of a Dānava, Har. (v. l. *-bāhu*). **— kaṇṭhaka**, m. Ardea Nivea, L. **— kandaka**, n. 'having long bulbs,' a kind of radish (= *mūlaka*); (*ikā*), f. Curculigo Orchioides (= *mushalī*), L. **— kam-dharā**, f. = *-kaṇṭhaka*, L. **— karṇa**, m. 'l°-ear,' N. of a cat, Hit. **— karshaṇa**, n. a sort of Svara, SaṃhUp., Pushpas. **— kāṇḍa**, m. 'having l° joints,' the root of Scirpus Kysoor, L.; (*ā*), f. a sort of creeper, L. **— kāya**, mfn. 'l°-bodied,' tall, MW. **— kāla**, m. a l° time, Mn. viii, 145, MBh.; *-jīvin*, mfn. l°-lived, MW. **— kāshṭha**, n. a l° piece of timber, spar, beam, W. **— kīla** or °**laka**, m. 'l°-stemmed,' Alangium Hexapetalum (= *aṅkoṭa*), L. **— kūraka**, n. 'l°

rice,' a kind of r° (= *rājânna*), L. **-kūrca**, mfn. 'l°-bearded,' MBh. vii, 4749. **-keśa**, mf(*ī*)n. 'l°-haired;' m. a bear, L.; pl. N. of a people. **-kośā**, °*śikā*, and °*śī*, f. a kind of muscle shell, a cockle, L. **-gati**, m. 'making l° journeys,' a camel, L. **-gāmin**, mfn. going or flying far, MBh. vii, 3672. **-granthi**, m. 'having l° knots or joints,' Scindapsus Officinalis (= *gaja-pippalī*), L. **-grīva**, mfn. 'l°-necked;' m. a camel, L.; a kind of curlew, L.; pl. N. of a people, VarBṛS. xiv, 23. **-ghāṭika**, m. 'l°-necked,' a camel, L. **-cañcu**, m. 'l°-beaked,' a kind of bird, L. **-caturaśra**, mfn. shaped like an oblong square or parallelogram, Sāy.; m. an oblong, Śulbas. i, 36. **-cchada**, mfn. 'l°-leaved;' m. Tectonia Grandis or sugar-cane, L. **-jaṅgala**, m. a kind of fish (= *bhaṅgana*), L. **-jaṅgha**, m. 'l°-legged,' a camel, L.; Ardea Nivea, L.; N. of a Yaksha, Kathās. ii, 20. **-jānuka**, m. 'l°-kneed,' Ardea Sibirica, L. **-jihva**, mfn. 'long-tongued;' m. a snake, L.; N. of a Dānava, MBh. i; Hariv.; (*ā*), f. N. of a Rākshasī, MBh.; R.; of one of the mothers attending on Skanda, MBh. ix, 2641; (*ī*), f. (Pāṇ. iv, 1, 59) N. of an evil spirit, Br. **-jihvya**, mfn. 'l°-tongued,' RV. ix, 101, 1. **-jīraka**, m. cumin, Bhpr. **-jīvantī**, f. N. of a med. wk. **-jīvin**, mfn. l°-lived, Cāṇ. 9. **-tanu**, mf(*vī*)n. 'having a l° body,' tall; (*vī*), f. a kind of Aroidea, L. **-tantu** (°*ghá-*), mfn. forming a l° thread or row, RV. x, 69, 7. **-tapas**, mfn. performing l° penances, R.; Hariv.; m. N. of several Ṛishis (also v. l. for °*tamas*), Hariv.; Pur.; °*pa-ākhyāna*, and °*paḥ-svarga-gamana*, n. 'the story of a l° penance,' and 'going to heaven by l° penance,' N. of 2 chapters of the ŚivaP. **-tama**, mfn. longest. **-tamas** (°*ghá-*), m. N. of a Ṛishi with the patron. Aucathya and the metron. Māmateya, RV. i, 158, 1; 6 (author of the hymns RV. i. 140–164; father of Kakshīvat, Sāy. on RV. i, 125, 1; through Bṛihas-pati's curse born blind, MBh. i, 4192 &c.; xii, 13182; father of Dhanvan-tari, Pur.; has by Su-deshṇā, Bali's wife, five sons, Aṅga, Bhaṅga, Kaliṅga, Puṇḍra, and Suhma, MBh.; Pur.); pl. his descendants; °*tamaso 'rka*, m., °*so vrata*, n. N. of two Sāmans (cf. *-tapas* and *dairghatamasa*). **-tara**, mfn. longer. **-taru**, m. 'the lofty tree,' the Tāl or palm tree, L. **-tā**, f. (Suśr.; Var.) and **tva**, n. (BhP.) length, longness. **-timishā**, f. Cucumis Utilissimus, L. **-tīkshṇa-mukha**, mf(*ī*)n. having a l° and pointed mouth (leech), Suśr. **-tuṇḍa**, mf(*ī* and *ā*)n. 'l°-snouted,' MBh. ix, 2649; (*ā*), f. the musk-rat, L. **-tṛiṇa**, n. a kind of grass (= *palli-vāha*), L. **-daṇḍa**, mf(*ī*)n. l°-stemmed, Kauś. 15; m. Ricinus Communis, Bhpr.; the palm tree, L.; (*ī*), f. a kind of small shrub (= *go-rakshī*), L.; °*ḍaka*, m. Ricinus Communis, L. **-danta**, mf(*ī*)n. 'l°-toothed,' MBh. ix, 2649. **-darśana**, mfn. far-seeing, provident, sagacious, wise, BhP. x, 29, 2. **-darśin**, mfn. id., MBh.; R. &c.; m. a bear, L.; a vulture, L.; N. of a minister, Kathās. lxxxvi, 5; of a monkey, R. v, 73, 43 (cf. *dūra-*); °*śitā*, f., °*śitva*, n. far-sightedness, providence, Kām. viii, 10; iv, 8. **-darśivas** (MBh. v, 4380), **-dṛiśvan** (Kathās. lxi, 131) and **-dṛishṭi** (L.), mfn. = *-darśana*. **-dru**, m. = *-taru*, L. **-druma**, m. 'the lofty tree,' Salmalia Malabarica, L. **-dveshin**, mfn. cherishing long hatred, implacable, MW. **-nakha**, mf(*ī*)n. having l° nails, MBh. ix, 2649; m. N. of a man, Buddh.; (*ī*), f. Diospyros Embryopteris, L. **-nāda**, mfn. l°-sounding; m. a dog, L.; a cock, L.; a conch-shell, L. **-nāla**, m. 'l°-stalked,' N. of several kinds of grass (= *vṛitta-gunḍa* and *yāvanāla*); n. = *-rohishaka*, L. **-nidrā**, f. l° sleep, Ragh. xii, 81; death, Hcar. **-niśvasya**, ind. sighing or having sighed deeply, W. **-niśvāsa**, m. a l° or deep-drawn sigh, Mālatīm. vii, ½. **-nītha** (°*ghá-*), m. N. of a man, RV. viii, 50, 10. **-paksha**, m. 'l°-winged,' the fork-tailed shrike, L. **-paṭolikā**, f. a kind of cucurbitaceous fruit, L. **-pattra**, mfn. 'l°-leaved;' m. a kind of sugar-cane, Suśr.; a species of ebony tree, Bhpr.; the palm tree, L.; a kind of onion, L.; some other bulbous plant (= *vishṇu-kanda*), L.; several kinds of grass, L.; (*ā*), f. a kind of plant related to the Hemionitis Cordifolia, L.; Pandanus Odoratissimus, L.; = *ḍoḍī*, *gandha-pattrā* &c., L.; (*ī*), f. = *palāśī* or *mahā-cañcu*, L. **-pattraka**, m. a kind of sugar-cane, Suśr.; a kind of garlic (= *rakta-lasuna*), L.; Ricinus Communis, L.; Barringtonia Acutangula, L.; a kind of reed, L.; Capparis Aphylla, L.; = *jalaja-madhūka*, L.; (*ikā*), f. Desmodium Gangeticum, L.; Aloe Indica, L.; = *palāśī*, L. **-pad** or **pād**, mfn. 'l°-legged;' m. a heron, L. **-parṇa**, mfn. l°-leaved; (*ī*), f. a species of plant related to the Hemionitis Cordifolia, L. **-parvan**, m. 'having l° knots or joints,' sugar-cane, L. **-pallava**, m. 'having l° shoots or tendrils,' Cannabis Sativa or Crotolaria Juncea, L. **-pavana**, mfn. 'l°-winded;' m. an elephant, L. (cf. *-māruta*). **-pāṭha**, m. 'the l° reading,' a kind of recitation of the VS. in which the consonants are often doubled, Cat. **-pāda** = *-pad*, L. **-pādapa**, m. = *-taru* or the Areca-nut tree, L. **-pādyā**, f. a kind of brick, Śulbas. iii, 177. **-pushpa**, m. 'having l° flowers,' Michelia Champaka or Calotropis Gigantea, L. **-pṛishṭha**, mfn. 'l°-backed;' m. a snake, L. **-prajña**, mfn. having a far-seeing mind; m. N. of a king, MBh. **-prayajyu** (°*ghá-*), mfn. persevering in offerings and sacrifices, RV. vii, 82, 1; receiving constant offerings or worship (Vishṇu-Varuṇa), TBr. ii, 8, 4, 5. **-prayatna**, m. persevering effort, MW. **-prasadman** (°*ghá-*), mfn. offering extensive seats (the earth), RV. viii, 10, 1; 25, 20. **-prâṇa**, mfn. having l° breath, ĀpSr. vi, 20, 2. **-prêkshin**, mfn. = *-darśana*, MBh. vii, 5467. **-phala**, mfn. having l° fruit; m. N. of plants (Cathartocarpus Fistula, Butea Frondosa, Asclepias Gigantea), L.; (*ā*), f. a red-colouring Oldenlandia; a vine with reddish grapes; Odina Pennata; a kind of cucumber, L. **-phalaka**, m. Agati Grandiflora, L. **-bāhu**, mfn. l°-armed, MBh. iii, 2454; R. ii, 42, 18 &c.; m. N. of one of the attendants on Śiva, Hariv.; of a Dānava, ib. (v. l. *-kaṇṭha*); of a son of Dhṛita-rāshṭra, MBh. i; of a son or grandson of Dilīpa, Pur.; *-garvita*, m. 'proud of having l° arms,' N. of a demon, Lalit. **-bījā**, f. 'having l° seed,' N. of a plant, Gal. **-bhuja**, mfn. 'l°-armed;' m. N. of one of the attendants on Śiva, L. **-māruta**, = *-pavana*, L. **-mukha**, mf(*ī*)n. l°-mouthed, l°-beaked, l°-faced, TĀr. iv, 32, 1; m. N. of a Yaksha (?), Buddh.; (*ī*), f. Parra Jacana or Goensis, ĀpŚr. xv, 19, 4, Sch.; the musk-rat, L. **-mūla**, n. 'l°-root,' the root of Andropogon Muricatus; mf(*ā* and *ī*)n. having l° roots; m. a kind of Bilva or creeper, L.; (*ā*), f. Desmodium Gangeticum or Ichnocarpus Frutescens, Suśr.; (*ī*), f. Alhagi Maurorum, Leea Hirta, Solanum Indicum, L. **-mūlaka**, n. a kind of radish, L.; (*ikā*), f. Desmodium Gangeticum, L. **-yajña**, m. 'performing a l° sacrifice,' N. of a king of Ayodhyā, MBh. ii, 1076. **-yaśas** (°*ghá-*), mfn. renowned far and wide, RV. v, 61, 9. **-yāthá**, m. or n. a l° course or journey, RV. ii, 15, 3; v, 45, 9. **-yāma**, mfn. having l° watches (as the night), Megh. **-raṅgā**, f. 'having a lasting colour,' turmeric, L. **-rata**, m. 'l° in copulation,' a dog, W. (cf. *-surata*). **-rada**, m. 'l°-tusked,' a hog, L. **-rasana**, m. 'l°-tongued,' a serpent, L. **-rāgā**, f. = *-raṅgā*, L. **-rātram**, ind. for a l° time or period, Lalit.; Divyâv. **-rātrika**, mfn. 'l°-lasting' (fever), Bhpr. **-rāva**, m. 'making a prolonged noise or yell,' N. of a jackal, Hit. **-rūpa**, mfn. having a l° form, having the form of a l° vowel, MW. **-rogin**, mfn. l° ill or sick, W. **-roma**, m. '= next;' N. of a son of Dhṛita-rāshṭra, MBh. **-roman**, mfn. 'l°-haired;' m. a bear, L.; N. of one of the attendants on Śiva, Hariv. **-rosha**, mfn. l° in anger, bearing a grudge, ŚārṅgP.; *-tā*, f., Mālav. iv, 1, 2. **-roshaṇa**, mfn. = *-rosha*, Subh. 203. **-rohishaka**, m. a kind of fragrant grass, L. **-latā-druma**, m. Shorea Robusta, L. **-locana**, mfn. l°-eyed, Hariv.; m. N. of a son of Dhṛita-rāshṭra, MBh. **-lohita-yashṭikā**, f. 'having a l° red stem,' red sugar-cane, L. **-vaṅśa**, mfn. having a l° reed; being of an ancient family, W.; m. Amphidonax Karka, L. **-vaktra**, m. 'l°-faced,' an elephant, L. **-vacchikā** (fr. *vatsa* ?, L.) or **-varchikā**, f. (W.) a crocodile or alligator. **-vat**, ind. like a l° vowel, W. **-varṇa**, m. a l° vowel, W. **-vartman**, n. = *-yātha*, W. **-varshā-bhū**, f. a white-flowered Punar-navā, L. **-vālā**, f. 'l°-tailed,' the bos grunniens, L. **-viśva-vedasa-kaivalya-dīpikā**, f. N. of wk. **-vṛiksha**, m. = *-taru*, L. **-vṛitta-phalā** (*vrinta-*?), f. a kind of gourd, L. **-vṛinta**, m. 'l°-stalked,' Colosanthes Indica; (*ā*), f. = *indra-cirbhiṭī*, L. **-vṛintaka**, m. Colosanthes Indica and a variety of it, L.; (*ikā*), f. Mimosa Octandra, L. **-veṇu**, m. pl. N. of a people, MBh. ii. **-vyādhi**, mfn. suffering from a l° illness, L. **-śara**, m. 'having a l° reed,' Andropogon Bicolor, L. **-śākha**, mfn. having l° branches; m. Shorea Robusta, L.; °*khikā*, f. a kind of shrub, L. **-śimbika**, m. 'having a l° pod,' black mustard, L. **-śira**, m. 'having a l° head or beak,' a kind of bird, L. **-śūka**, °**kaka**, m. 'having l° awns or beards,' a sort of rice, L. **-śṛiṅga**, mfn. l°-horned, Kāv. **-śmaśru** (°*ghá-*), mfn. l°-bearded, AV. xi, 5, 6. **-śravas** (°*ghá-*), mfn. renowned far and wide; m. N. of men, RV.; TāṇḍyaBr. xv, 3. **-śrút**, mfn. hearing from afar, RV. x, 114, 2; heard or renowned far and wide (superl. °*tama*), RV.; TS. **-saktha**, mf(*ī*)n. having l° thighs, P. v, 4, 113, Kāś.; °*thi*, mfn. having l° shafts, ib. **-sattrá**, n. a l°-continued Soma sacrifice, ŚBr., MBh. &c.; N. of a Tīrtha, MBh. iii, 5050; mfn. = °*trín*, mfn. occupied with a prolonged Soma rite, ŚBr., BhP. **-saṁdhya**, mfn. performing l° prayers or rites at the different twilights; *-tva*, n., Mn. iv, 94. **-sasya**, m. 'having l° fruit,' Diospyros Embryopteris, L. **-surata**, m. = *-rata*, L. **-sūtra**, mfn. 'spinning a l° yarn,' slow, dilatory, procrastinating, MBh.; R. &c.; *-tā*, f. (ib.), *-tva*, n. (Gal.) procrastination, dilatoriness. **-sūtrin**, mfn. = °*tra*, Bhag. xviii, 28; °*tritā*, f. = °*tratā*, Hit. i, 29 (v. l.) **-skandha**, m. = *-taru*, L. **-svara**, m. = *-varṇa*, W. **Dīrghâṅhri**, m. 'having l° roots,' Desmodium Gangeticum, L. **Dīrghâkāra**, mfn. l°-formed, oblong, MW. **Dīrghâksha**, mf(*ī*)n. l°-eyed, Mālav. ii, 3. **Dīrghâgama**, m. N. of a Buddh. wk. **Dīrghâṅka-grāma**, m. N. of a village. **Dīrghâṅgī**, f. (Bhpr.) and °**ṅghri**, m. (L.) = °*ṇhri*. **Dīrghá-dhī**, mfn. having a far-seeing mind, RV. ii, 27, 4. **Dīrghâdhva**, m. a l° way or journey, AitBr. vi, 23; *-ga*, mfn. going l° journeys; m. a camel, a letter-carrier or messenger, L. **Dīrghânala**, n. a mystical N. of the syllable *rā*, RāmatUp. **Dīrghânuparivartin**, mfn. having a l° after-effect, L. **Dīrghâpâṅga**, mfn. having l° outer corners of the eyes; m. N. of an antelope, Śak. v, 2/21. **Dīrghâpêkshin**, mfn. very regardful or considerate, MBh. vii, 5467 (B. *dīrgha-pr°*). **Dīrghâpsas**, mfn. having a l° fore-part (a waggon), RV. i, 122, 15. **Dīrghâmaya**, mfn. l° sick, Hit. iv, 36. **Dīrghâyu**, mfn. l°-lived, viii, 70, 7; *-tvá*, n. ib. x, 62, 2; ŚBr. &c.; *-śocis* (°*ghâyu-*), mfn. shining through a l° life (Agni), RV. v, 18, 3. **Dīrghâyudha**, m. (!) l° weapon, spear, L.; mfn. having l° weapons (tusks), m. a hog, L. **Dīrghâyus**, mfn. l°-lived, RV., MBh. &c.; wished to be l°-lived, R. iii, 1, 11 (cf. *āyushmat*); m. a crow, L.; N. of 2 trees (*jīvaka* and *śālmali*), L.; of Mārkaṇḍeya, L.; °*shka*, mfn. l°-lived, Bhpr.; °*sh-ṭva*, n. long-livedness, a l° life, Hariv. 886 (cf. °*yu-tva*); °*shya*, n. id., m. N. of a tree (= *śveta-mandāraka*), L. **Dīrghâraṇyá**, n. a l° tract of wild or desert country, Br. **Dīrghâlarka**, m. = °*ghâyushya*, m., L. **Dīrghâsya**, mfn. l°-faced, Hariv.; m. N. of a people, Var. **Dīrghâhan**, mf(*hnī*)n. having l° days, Pāṇ. viii, 2, 69, Vārtt. 1, Pat.; viii, 4, 7, id. **Dīrghêrvāru**, m. a kind of cucumber (= *ḍaṅgarī*), L. **Dīrghôcchvāsam**, ind. with a deep-drawn sigh, Megh. 99. **Dīrghôt-kaṇṭha-manas**, mfn. having the heart full of an old longing, BhP. iv, 9, 43.

Dīrghaya, Nom. P. °*yati*, to be long, tarry, procrastinate, R.

Dīrghikā, f. an oblong lake or pond, MBh., Suśr.; Kāv.

Dīrghī, ind. in comp. for °*gha*. **-√kṛi**, to lengthen, prolong, Kālid. **-√bhū**, to become l°; **-bhāva**, m. lengthening (of a vowel), VS. Prāt.; **-bhūta**, lengthened (a vowel), Pāṇ. vii, 4, 72, Sch.

दीर्ण *dīrṇa*, mfn. (√*dṛī*) torn, rent, sundered, SāṅkhŚr. xiii, 12, 1; R. ii, 39, 29; scattered, dispersed (army), MBh. vi, 144, 146; frightened, afraid, MBh. v, 4622, 4627.

दीव् *dīv*, *dīvi*, *dīvyat*. See under √2. *div*.

दु 1. *du* (or *dū*), cl. 1. P. (Dhātup. xxii, 46) *davati* (pf. *dudāva*; fut. *doshyati*, *dotā*; aor. *adāvīt* or *adaushīt*, Vop.), to go: Caus. *dāvayati* or *davayati* (see s. v.) Actually occurring only in Subj. aor. *davishāṇi*, RV. x, 34, 5, '*na d° ebhiḥ*,' (?) I will not go, i.e. have intercourse with them (the dice). [Cf. δύω, δύνω, δεύομαι.]

दु 2. *du* (also written *dū*), cl. 5. P. 4. Ā. (Dhātup. xxvii, 10; xxvi, 24) *dunoti*, *dūyate* (ep. also °*ti*; pf. *dudāva*; fut. *doshyati*; aor. *adaushīt*; inf.

dotum), to be burnt, to be consumed with internal heat or sorrow (Pres. *dunoti*, MBh. iii, 10069; BhP. iii, 2, 17; Gīt. iii, 9; but oftener *dūyate*, which is at once Pass.), MBh.; Suśr.; Kāv. &c.; (only *dunóti*) to burn, consume with fire, cause internal heat, pain, or sorrow, afflict, distress, AV. ix, 4, 18; MBh.; VarBṛS.; Kāv.: Caus. *dāvayati*, aor. *adūduvat:* Desid. *dudūshati:* Intens. *dodūyate, dodoti.* [Cf. δαίω for δαϝιω; δύη, pain; Lit. *davyti*, to torment; Sl. *daviti*, to worry.]

Dut, f. anxiety, uneasiness. **Dud-da** and **duddādin,** mfn. giving pain, cruel, wicked, L.

Duta, mfn. pained, afflicted, Śiś. vi, 59.

Dunvat, mfn. afflicting, injuring, W.

दुः *duḥ*, in comp. for *dus* (p. 488; for *duḥ-k°*, *duḥ-p°*, see *dush-k°*, *dush-p°*). **-śáṉsa,** mfn. wishing or threatening evil, malicious, wicked, RV.; AV. &c. **-śaka,** mfn. impracticable, impossible; *-tva*, n., Comm. **-śakta** and **°ti,** mfn. powerless, Pāṇ. v, 4, 121, Sch. **-śala,** m. N. of a son of Dhṛita-rāshṭra, MBh. i; (*ā*), f. of the only daughter of Dh°, wife of Jayad-ratha, ib. **-śasta,** mfn. badly recited; n. a bad recitation, Br. **-śākam,** ind. ill with vegetables, Pāṇ. ii, 1, 6, Sch. **-śāsa,** mfn. difficult to be controlled, Vop. **-śāsana,** mfn. id., Pāṇ. iii, 3, 130, Vārtt. 1, Pat.; m. N. of a son of Dhṛita-rāshṭra, MBh. i. **-śā́sus,** mfn. malevolent, RV. x, 33, 1. **-śikshita,** mfn. ill-bred, impertinent, Bālar. ii, $\frac{22}{83}$. **-śishya,** m. a bad scholar, Kathās. **-śī́ma,** mfn. bad to lie upon, ŚāṅkhBr. ii, 7; m. N. of a man, RV. x, 93, 14. **-śīrta-tanu,** mfn. having an indestructible body, MaitrS. i, 8, 6. **-śīla,** mfn. badly disposed, ill-behaved, MBh.; R. &c. (*-tā*, f. Kull.); (*ā*), f. N. of a woman, Kathās.; *-citta*, mfn. bad-hearted, Subhāsh. **-śṛiṅgī,** f. a disloyal wife, L. **-śṛita** (*dúḥ-*), mfn. not well cooked, underdone, MaitrS. i, 4, 13. **-śéva,** mfn. envious, malignant, RV. i, 42, 2. **-śodha,** mfn. difficult to be cleaned, Suśr. **-śosha,** mfn. difficult to be dried, MBh. vii, 856. **-śrava,** mfn. unpleasant to be heard; n. and *-tva*, n. cacophony, Sāh. **-śruta,** mfn. badly or wrongly heard, R. iii, 41, 10 &c. **-shanta,** m. older form for *dushyanta* (q.v.) **-1. -shama,** n. a partic. weight (= 6 Dāṇaka), Car. viii, 1 (printed *°ḥ-kh°*). **-2. -shámā,** n. a bad year, ŚBr. iii, 2, 1, 10; AitBr. ii, 29; (*am*), ind. unevenly, improperly; at a wrong time (g. *tishṭhadgv-ādi*); (*ā*), f. (with Jainas) N. of two spokes in the wheel of time (viz. the 5th in the Ava-sarpiṇī and the 2nd in the Ut-s°), L.; *°ma-sushamā*, f. (with Jainas) id. (the 4th and 3rd resp.), L. **-sháha,** mfn. irresistible, RV. ix, 91, 5 (cf. *duḥ-s°*). **-shupta,** mfn. sleeping badly, having bad dreams, L. **-shṭuta,** n. faulty recitation of a Stotra, AitBr. iii, 38. **-shṭutí** or (*dúḥ-*) **shṭuti,** f. a faulty or bad hymn, RV. i, 53, 1 &c. **-shṭhu,** mfn. ill-behaved, Uṇ. i, 26, Sch.; ind. badly (g. *svar-ādi*). **-shparśa,** see *-sparśa.* **-shvanta,** w.r. for *dushy°*. **-shvápnya,** n. bad sleep or dreams, RV.; AV. **-saṃrakshya,** mfn. difficult to be guarded, Nīlak. **-saṃlakshya,** mfn. difficult to be observed or recognised, Rājat. **-saṃskāra,** m. a bad custom or practice, ib. **-saṃsthita,** mfn. deformed, R. ii, 8, 40. **-saktha** or **°thi,** mfn. having deformed thighs, Pāṇ. v, 4, 121, Kāś. **-saṅga,** m. bad inclination, BhP. **-saṃcāra,** mfn. difficult to be walked or passed, Pañc. i, 189; Bālar. vi, $\frac{33}{34}$. **-saṃcintya,** mfn. difficult to be conceived or imagined, Rājat. **-sattva,** n. evil being, noxious animal; *-vat*, mfn. filled with wild beasts (wood), R. ii, 28, 17. **-saṃdhāna,** mfn. d° to be united, Pañc. ii, 36. **-saṃdheya,** mfn. id., MBh. v, 5827. **-sama,** mfn. unequal, uneven, unfit, perverse, bad, L. (cf. *duḥsh°*). **-samatikrama,** mfn. d° to be surmounted, L. **-samartha,** mfn. d° to be conceived, Sarvad. **-samīkshya,** mfn. d° to be perceived, MBh. vii, 1928. **-sampāda** (Daś.) and **°dya** (Śaṃk., *-tva*, n.), mfn. d° to be attained or arrived at. **-sarpa,** m. a vicious serpent, Kathās. **-saha,** mfn. d° to be borne, unbearable, irresistible (*-tva*, n.; comp. *-tara*), MBh.; Kāv. &c.; m. N. an evil demon, MārkP.; of a son of Dhṛita-rāshṭra, MBh. i; of Puru-kutsa, Pur.; (*ā*), f. N. of Śrī, MBh. xii, 8154; of a shrub (= *nāga-damanī*), L. **-sahāya,** mfn. having bad companions, forsaken by all, MBh. v, 1861. **-sākshin,** m. a false witness, R. iii, 18, 34. **-sādhya,** mfn. difficult to be performed or accomplished, Hariv.; Kām.; Pañc. &c.; d° to be managed or dealt with, Pañc. i, $\frac{258}{259}$; d° to be reconciled, Bhartṛ. i, 49; d° to be cured, Hariv. 16132; d° to be conquered, MW. **-sevya,** mfn. d° to be managed, intractable, MBh. xiii, 2225. **-strī,** f. a bad woman (g. *yuvâdi*). **-stha,** mfn. 'standing badly,' unsteady, disquieted (lit. and fig.); uneasy, unhappy, poor, miserable, Pur.; Rājat.; ignorant, unwise, a fool, L.; covetous, W.; (*am*), ind. badly, ill; with √*sthā*, to be unwell, Amar. 29. **-sthita,** mfn. = *-stha*, Kathās.; Pur.; Rājat.; n. an improper manner of standing, MBh. iii, 14669. **-sthiti,** f. ill condition, Kathās. lxxi, 240. **-stheya,** mfn. difficult to be stood; n. d° standing, MBh. xii, 11090. **-snāna,** n. defective or inauspicious ablution, Hariv. 3413. **-sparśa,** mfn. difficult to be touched or unpleasant to the touch, MBh.; BhP.; m. Alhagi Maurorum (also *°śaka*, Car.); Guilandina Bonduc, L.; (*ā*), f. A° M°; Solanum Jacquini; Mucuna Pruritus; Cassyta Filiformis, Suśr.; Bhpr.; L. **-spṛiśa,** mfn. difficult or unpleasant to be touched, Hariv. 3645. **-spṛishṭa,** n. slight contact, the action of the tongue which produces the sounds *y, r, l, v*, RV. Prāt.; m. a sound thus produced, Śiksh. **-sphoṭa,** m. 'difficult to be burst,' a sort of weapon, L. **-smara,** mfn. unpleasant to be remembered, Uttarar. vi, 32. **-svana,** mfn. sounding badly, cacophonous, MBh. v, 7241. **-svapna,** m. a bad dream, GS.; *-darśana*, n. seeing a b° d°, ŚāṅkhGṛ.; *-nāśa*, m. removal of b° d°s, BhP.; mfn. = next, Hariv.; *-nāśana* and *°śin*, mfn. removing b° d°s, MBh.; Hariv.; *-pratibodhana*, mfn. difficult to be awakened from sleep, R. v, 81, 53; *-śānti*, f. (lit. = the next) N. of wk.; *°pnôpaśānti*, f. the cessation of a b° d°, BhP. viii, 4, 15.

दुःख 1. *duḥkhá*, mfn. (according to grammarians properly written *dush-kha* and said to be from *dus* and *kha* [cf. *su-khá*]; but more probably a Prākritized form for *duḥ-stha*, q.v.) uneasy, uncomfortable, unpleasant, difficult, R.; Hariv. (compar. *-tara*, MBh.; R.); n. (ifc. f. *ā*) uneasiness, pain, sorrow, trouble, difficulty, ŚBr. xiv, 7, 2, 15; Mn.; MBh. &c. (personified as the son of Naraka and Vedanā, VP.); (*am*), ind. with difficulty, scarcely, hardly (also *āt* and *ena*), MBh.; R.; impers. it is difficult to or to be (inf. with an acc. or nom., R. vii, 6, 38; Bhag. v, 6); *duḥkham* -√*ās*, to be sad or uneasy, Ratn. iv, $\frac{19}{20}$; -√*kṛi*, to cause or feel pain, Yājñ. ii, 218; MBh. xii, 5298. **-kara,** mf(*ī*)n. causing pain to (gen.), afflicting, MBh. i, 6131. **-kārin,** mfn. id., Ratn. iv, $\frac{16}{17}$. **-gata,** n. adversity, calamity, MBh. xii, 5202. **-graha,** mfn. difficult to be conceived, Ratn. iv, $\frac{12}{13}$. **-cārin,** mfn. going with pain, distressed, R. iii, 23, 14. **-cchinna,** mfn. cut with difficulty, tough, hard; pained, distressed, W. **-cchedya,** mfn. to be cut or overcome with difficulty, Hit. iv, 24. **-jāta,** mfn. suffering pain, distressed, Pāṇ. iv, 1, 52, Vārtt. 5, Pat.; vi, 2, 170. **-jīvin,** mfn. living in pain or distress, Mn. xi, 9. **-tara,** n. greater pain, a greater evil than (abl.), Nal. xi, 17 (cf. above). **-tā,** f. uneasiness, pain, discomfort, ChUp. vii, 26; R. **-dagdha,** mfn. 'burnt by affliction,' pained, distressed, W. **-duḥkha,** n. (instr.) with great difficulty, Megh. 90; *-tā*, f. the uneasiness connected with pain, SaddhP. **-duḥkhin,** mfn. having sorrow upon sorrow, BhP. xi, 11, 19. **-dohyā,** f. difficult to be milked (cow), L. **-nivaha,** mfn. carrying pain with or after it, painful (thirst), BhP. ix, 19, 16; m. a multitude of pains or evils, ib. iii, 9, 9. **-parîtâṅga,** mfn. whose limbs are surrounded or filled with pain, MBh.; *°tâtman*, mfn. whose soul is affected with anguish, ib. **-pātra,** n. a vessel or receptacle (= object) for sorrow, Jain. **-prāya** or **-bahula,** mfn. full of trouble and pain, W. **-bodha,** mfn. difficult to be understood, Nyāyas. i, 1, 37. **-bhāgin,** mfn. having pain as one's portion, unhappy, Mn. iv, 157. **-bhāj,** mfn. id., Veṇis. iv, $\frac{110}{111}$. **-bheshaja,** mf(*ī*)n. healing woe (Kṛishṇa), MBh. xii, 1624. **-maya,** mf(*ī*)n. consisting in suffering; *-tva*, n. Sāh. **-maraṇa,** mfn. having a painful death, Mālatīm. viii, $\frac{8}{9}$. **-moksha,** m. deliverance from pain, MW. **-moha,** m. perplexity from pain or sorrow, despair, Daś. **-yantra,** n. application of pain, torture, ib. **-yoga,** m. infliction of pain, Mn. vi, 24. **-yoni,** m. or f. a source of misery, Bhag. v, 22. **-labdhikā,** f. 'gained with difficulty,' N. of a princess, Kathās. **-lavya,** mfn. hard to be cut or pierced (aim), Bālar. iv, 11. **-loka,** m. 'the world of pain' (= *saṃsāra*), L. **-vasati,** f. and **-vāsa,** m. a difficult abode, MBh. **-vega,** m. a violent grief, Kāv. **-vyābhāshita,** mfn. pronounced with difficulty, MBh. xiii, 4485. **-śīla,** mfn. bad-tempered, irritable, MBh.; *-tva*, n. irritability, Suśr. **-śoka-paritrāṇa,** n. a shelter from pain and sorrow (Kṛishṇa), MBh. xii, 1681. **-śoka-vat,** mfn. feeling pain and sorrow, R. iv, 19, 11. **-śoka-samanvita,** mfn. id., MW. **-saṃyoga,** m. = *duḥkha-yoga*, W. **-saṃvardhita,** mfn. reared with difficulty, W. **-saṃsthiti,** mfn. in a wretched condition, poor, miserable, W. **-saṃsparśa,** mfn. unpleasant to the touch, MBh. v, 2046. **-saṃcāra,** mfn. passing unhappily (time), R. iii, 22, 10. **-samāyukta,** mfn. accompanied with pain, affected by anguish, MW. **-sāgara,** m. 'ocean of pain,' great sorrow; the world, W. **-sparśa,** mfn. = *-saṃsp°*, Kull. ii, 98. **-han,** mfn. removing pain, W. **Duḥkhâkara,** m. a multitude of sorrows, Daś. **Duḥkhâkula,** mfn. filled with sorrow, Kathās. **Duḥkhâcāra,** mfn. difficult to be dealt with, hard to manage, MBh. iv, 274. **Duḥkhâtita,** mfn. freed or escaped from pain, W. **Duḥkhâtmaka,** mfn. whose essence is sorrow; *-tva*, n. Sarvad. **Duḥkhânarha,** mfn. deserving no pain, MBh. iii, 998. **Duḥkhânta,** m. 'the end of pain or trouble,' (with the Māhêśvaras) final emancipation, Madhus. **Duḥkhânvita,** mfn. accompanied with pain, filled with grief, distressed, W. **Duḥkhâbhijña,** mfn. familiar with pain or sorrow, MBh. i, 745. **Duḥkhârta,** mfn. visited by pain, distressed, MBh. i, 1860. **Duḥkhâlīḍha,** mfn. consumed with grief, MW. **Duḥkhâsikā,** f. a condition of uneasiness or discomfort, Subh. 156; Kād. **Duḥkhôcchedya,** mfn. = *duḥkha-cch°* (v. l.) **Duḥkhôttara,** mfn. followed by pain, Śak. v, $\frac{8}{9}$. **Duḥkhôdarka,** mfn. having pain as result, BhP. xi, 20, 28. **Duḥkhôpaghāta,** m. violent pain or grief, MBh. xii, 7460. **Duḥkhôpacarya,** mfn. = *°khâcāra*, Mudr. iii, 5. **Duḥkhôpahata-cetas,** mfn. having the heart stricken with sorrow, MBh. xiii, 1801. **Duḥkhôpêta,** mfn. affected by pain, suffering distress, MW.

2. **Duḥkha,** Nom. P. *°khati*, to pain, SaddhP. **°khaya,** Nom. P. *°yati*, (Dhātup. xxxv, 76), id.

Duḥkhā- √kṛi, to cause pain, afflict, distress, Śiś. ii, 11. **°khāya,** Nom. Ā. *°yate*, to feel pain, be distressed, Mālav. v, 3.

Duḥkhita, mfn. pained, distressed; afflicted, unhappy, Mn.; MBh.; R. &c.; *-citta*, mfn. grieved in mind, MW.

Duḥkhin, mfn. pained, afflicted, grieved, Kathās.; Hit. &c. **°khitā,** f., Kathās.; **°khitva,** n. Vedântas.

Duḥkhīya, Nom. P. *°yati*, to feel pain, be distressed, Hit. ii, 25.

Duḥkhya, Nom. P. *°yati*, to cause pain (g. *kaṇvâdi*).

दुकूल *dukūla*, m. a kind of plant, Hariv. 12680; n. very fine cloth or raiment made of the inner bark of this plant, MBh.; Hariv.; Suśr.; Kāv. &c. (different from *kshauma*, MBh. xiii, 7175, opp. to *valkala*, Bhartṛ. iii, 54). **-paṭṭa,** m. a head-band of fine cloth, Hariv. 7041. **-vat,** mfn. wearing a garment of fine cloth, Ragh. xvii, 25. **Dugūla,** n. = *°kūla*, n., L. (Megh. 64 as v. l.)

दुग्ध *dugdhá*, mfn. (√2. *duh*) milked, milked out, extracted, RV.; AV. &c.; sucked out, impoverished, Daś.; milked together, accumulated, filled, full, BhP.; L.; n. milk, AV.; TS.; ŚBr.; Suśr.; Pañc. &c.; the milky juice of plants, sap (cf. *go-raksha-* and *tāmra-*); (*ī*), f. a kind of Asclepias (= *kshīrāvikā*), L. **-kūpikā,** f. a cake made of ground rice and filled with coagulated m°, Bhpr. **-caru,** m. m°-food, Gal. **-tā,** f. and **-tva,** n. milkiness, milky nature, W. **-tālīya,** n. the froth of m°, cream, L.; m° and mangoes, mango fool, W. **-tumbī,** f. a kind of gourd, L. **-da,** mfn. giving m°, Pañc., Intr. 5; increasing m°, Bhpr. **-doha,** mfn. milked out, KaṭhUp. i, 3. **-padī** (*°dhá-*), f. whose footstep is m°, Suparṇ. ix, 4. **-pācana,** n. a kind of salt (= *vajraka*), L.; a vessel for boiling m°, W. **-pātra,** n. a m°-pan, MW. **-pāyin,** mfn. drinking m°, ib. **-pāshāṇa,** n. calcareous spar, L. **-pucchī** and **-peyā,** f. a kind of Curcuma, L. **-poshya,** m. a suckling, MW. **-phena,** m. the froth of m°, cream, L.; (*ī*), f. a kind of small shrub (= *gojā-parṇī, payaḥ-pheni*, &c.), L. **-bandhaka,** m. the pledging of m°, L. **-bījā,** f. rice mixed with m°, L.; a kind of gourd, L. **-bhṛit,** m. bearing or yielding m°, MaitrS. i, 6, 1. **-mukha**, mfn. having m° in the mouth, very young, HPariś. **-vaṭī**, f. a partic. mixture against diarrhœa (med.) **-samudra**, m. the sea of m°, L. **-sindhu**, m. id., Mālatīm. iii, 1/7. **-srotas**, n. a stream of m°, ib. iii, 14. **Dugdhâksha**, m. 'having m°-white eyes,' a partic. precious stone, L. **Dugdhâgra**, n. upper part or surface of m°, cream, L. **Dugdhâbdhi**, m. the sea of m°, Rājat. iii, 276; Kathās.; *-tanayā*, f. N. of Lakshmī, Kavik. **Dugdhâmbudhi**, m. = °*dhâbdhi*, Prab. iv, 8/0. **Dugdhâmra**, n. m° and mangoes, mango fool, L. **Dugdhâśman**, m. calcareous spar, L. **Dugdhôdadhi**, m. the sea of milk, Naish.

Dugdhikā, f. (written also °*dhīkā*) a sort of Asclepias or Oxystelma Esculentum (med.)

Dugdhin, mfn. having milk, milky, W.; n. calcareous spar, L. °**dhinikā**, f. red-flowered Apâmārga, L.

Dugha, mfn. milking, yielding (ifc.); (*dúghā*), f. a milch-cow, RV.; VS.

दुच्छक *ducchaka*, m. a kind of fragrance or a hall of fragrances (= *gandha-kuṭī*), L.

दुच्छुना *ducchúnā*, f. (prob. fr. *dus* and *śunā*) misfortune, calamity, harm, mischief (often personified as a demon), RV.; AV.; VS.; °**nāya**, Nom. Ā. °*yáte*, to wish to harm, be evil disposed, RV.

दुडि *duḍi*, f. a small tortoise, L. (cf. *duli*).

दुण्डुक *duṇḍuka*, mfn. fraudulent, malicious, L.

दुण्डुभ *duṇḍubha* and °*bhi*, m. a kind of lizard, MBh. vii, 6905; Suśr.; Var. (= *duṇḍubha*; cf. also *dundubha* and °*bhika*).

दुण्ढा *duṇḍhā*, f. N. of a Rākshasī, W.

दुत्थोत्थदवीर *dutthótthadavīra* (astrol.), N. of the 13th Yoga.

दुद *duda*, m. N. of a mountain, MBh. xiii, 7658.

दुदुह *duduha*, m. (√2. *duh*?) N. of a prince, Hariv.; Pur.

दुद्धर *duddhara*, m. (for *dur-dh*°?) a kind of rope-ladder, Pañcad.

दुद्यूषु *dudyūshu*, mfn. (√2. *div*, Desid.) wishto play with (acc.), Bhaṭṭ. ix, 32.

दुद्रुक्षु *dudrukshu*, w. r. for दुध्रुक्षु q. v.

दुद्रुम *dudruma*, w. r. for दुर्द्रुम q. v.

दुध् *dudh*, cl. 1. P. *dódhati* (Nigh. ii, 12), to be angry, hurt, injure; Pres. p. *dódhat*, impetuous, wild, fierce, RV.

Dúdhi, mfn. violent, impetuous, injurious, RV.

Dúdhita, mfn. troubled, perplexed, turbid, RV.

Dudhrá, mfn. = *dúdhi*, RV. **-kṛít**, mfn. exciting, boisterous (the Maruts), RV. i, 64, 11. **-vāc** (°*dhrá-*), mfn. speaking boisterously or confusedly, RV. vii, 21, 2.

दुधुक्षु *dudhukshu*, mfn. (√2. *duh*, Desid.) wishing to milk, MBh. vii, 2409.

दुध्रुक्षु *dudhrukshu*, mfn. (√*druh*, Desid.) wishing to harm, malicious, Rājat. vii, 1267.

दुन्दम *dundama*, m. a drum, L.

दुन्दु *dundu*, m. id., L.; N. of Vasu-deva, L. **-nābha** (*nāda*?), m. a kind of spell (= *dundubhi-svana*), R. **-māra**, m. = *dhundhu-* (q. v.), L.

दुन्दुभ *dundubha*, m. an unvenomous watersnake, Sāy. (cf. *duṇḍubha* and °*bhi*); N. of Śiva, ŚivaP.; pl. of a Vedic school, Hcat. i, 7; a drum (cf. *anaka-*).

दुन्दुभि *dundubhí*, mf. a sort of large kettledrum, RV.; Br.; MBh.; Kāv. &c.; a sort of poison, L.; N. of the 56th year in the Jupiter cycle of 60 years, Var.; Sūryas.; of Kṛishṇa, MBh. xii, 1511; of Varuṇa, L.; of Asuras, a Rakshas, a Yaksha &c., R.; Hariv.; Kathās.; of a son of Andhaka and grandson of Anu &c., Pur.; f. a drum, AV. vi, 38, 4 (also °*bhī*, MBh. iii, 786); (*ī*), f. a partic. throw of the dice in gambling, L.; N. of a Gandharvī, MBh.; n. N. of a partic. Varsha in Krauñca-dvīpa, VP. **-grīva**, mfn. 'drum-necked' (ox), MBh. viii, 1805. **-darpa-han**, m. 'breaking the pride of D°,' N. of Vālin, Gal. **-nirhrāda**, m. 'drumsounding,' N. of a Dānava. **-vadha**, m. N. of the 89th ch. of the GaṇP. **-vimocanīya**, mfn. (*homa*) relating to the uncovering of a drum, ĀpŚr. xviii, 5. **-svana**, m. 'drum-sound,' a kind of magical formula against evil spirits supposed to possess weapons, R. **-svara**, m. 'having drum-like voice,' N. of a man; *-rāja*, m. N. of sev. Buddhas. **Dundubhîśvara**, m. N. of a Buddha. **Dundubhy-āghātá**, m. a drummer, ŚBr.

Dundubhika, m. a kind of venomous insect, Suśr. °**bhyà**, mfn. only in *cakra-*.

Dundumāya, Nom. Ā., only in °*yita*, n. the sound of a drum, Uttarar. vi, 2.

दुफार *duphāra*, m. N. of a place, Romakas.

दुमती *dumatī*, f. N. of a river, L.

दुमेल *dumela*, n. a partic. high number, Buddh.

दुम्बक *dumbaka*, m. the thick-tailed sheep, Bhpr.

दुम्मदुमाक *dummadumāka*, m. N. of a village.

दुर् 1. *dúr*, f. (only *dúras*, acc. nom., and *duras*, acc. pl.) = *dvār*, a door (cf. 2. *dura*). **Duraḥ-prabhṛiti**, mfn. beginning with the doors, ĀpŚr. **Duro-dara**, m. 'door-opener' (cf. *dura-dabhna*), a dice-player, gamester, MBh. ii, 2000 &c.; dice-box, viii, 3763; a stake, L.; n. (m.?) playing, gaming, a game at dice, MBh.; Kāv. (written also *daro-*). **Duḥ-sādhin**, m. a door-keeper.

1. **Dura** = 1. *dur*, only in *śata-* (q. v.) **-dabhná**, mfn. 'eluding doors,' not to be kept by bolts and bars, AV. xii, 4, 4, 19.

2. **Durá**, m. (perhaps √*dṛī*) 'one who opens or unlocks,' giver, granter (= *dātṛi*, Sāy.), RV. i, 53, 2; vi, 35, 5.

Duroṇá, n. residence, dwelling, home, RV. **-yú**, mfn. fond of a house or of home, viii, 49, 19. **-sád**, mfn. residing in a house, iv, 40, 5.

Dúrya, mfn. belonging to the door or house, RV.; m. pl. a residence (cf. Lat. fores), ib.

Duryoṇá, n. = *duroṇá*, ib.

दुर् 2. *dur*, in comp. for *dus* (p. 488), denoting 'bad' or 'difficult' &c.; *durishṭha*, (superl.) very bad or difficult or wicked; n. great crime or wickedness, L. **-aksha**, m. (fr. 2. *aksha*) a bad or fraudulent die, W.; (°*shá*), mf(*ī*)n. (fr. 4. *aksha*) weak-eyed, ŚBr. **-akshara**, n. an evil word, Naish. ix, 63. **-atikrama**, mfn. hard or difficult to be overcome, insurmountable, inevitable, Mn. xi, 238; R.; Pañc. &c.; m. N. of a Brāhman (regarded as son of Śiva), VāyuP.; N. of Śiva; °*maṇīya*, mfn. impassable, Bāl. vi, 1/8. **-atyaya**, mfn. = *-atikrama*, KaṭhUp. iii, 14; MBh.; R. &c.; inaccessible, MBh. xiii, 4880; inscrutable, unfathomable, R. iii, 71, 15; BhP.; °*yānukramaṇa*, mfn. whose ways are past finding out (God), MW. **-atyétu**, mfn. = *-atikrama*, RV. vii, 65, 3. **-adṛishṭa**, n. ill luck, L. **-admanī**, f. bad or noxious food, VS. ii, 20. **-adhiga**, mfn. difficult to be obtained, BhP. iii, 23, 8; °*gama*, id., inscrutable, unfathomable, Kir. v, 18. **-adhishṭhita**, mfn. badly managed or executed, MBh. vii, 3314; n. staying anywhere improperly, ib. xii, 3084. **-adhîta**, mfn. badly read or learnt, Cāṇ. **-adhîyāna**, mfn. learning badly, GopBr. i, 1, 31. **-adhîśvara**, m. a bad king, L. **-adhyaya**, mfn. difficult of attainment, Śiś. xii, 11; °*yayana*, mfn. = °*adhīyāna*, MW. **-adhyavasāya**, m. a bad or foolish beginning, Bhartṛ. **-adhyeya**, mfn. difficult to be studied or learnt; *-tva*, n. Cat. **-adhva**, m. a bad road, Naish. ix, 33. **-anujñāta**, mfn. badly allowed or granted, BhP. x, 64, 35. **-anuneya**, mfn. difficult to be won over; *-tā*, f. Jātakam. **-anupālana**, mfn. d° to be kept or preserved, MBh. xiii, 1929. **-anubodha**, mfn. d° to be recollected, L. **-anuvartya**, mfn. d° to follow, Jātakam. **-anushṭhita**, mfn. badly done or acted, R.; °*shṭheya*, mfn. d° to perform, MBh. **-anta**, mfn. having no end, infinite; having a bad end, miserable, Mn.; MBh. &c.; *-kṛicchra*, m. or n. infinite danger, BhP. i, 15, 11; *-kṛit*, mfn. doing what is endless or suffering endless pains, MBh. x, 15; *-cintā*, f. infinite sorrow, BhP. iv, 28, 8; *-deva*, m. the god who removes difficulties (Gaṇêśa), Cāṇ.; *-paryanta*, mfn. having a bad end, Prasannar.; *-bhāva*, mfn. exceedingly passionate, BhP. i, 11, 33; *-moha*, mfn. whose infatuation has a bad ending or has no end, BhP. vii, 6, 13; *-vīrya*, mfn. having endless energy, BhP. i, 3, 38; *-śakti*, mfn. having endless power, ib. vii, 8, 40. **-antaka**, mfn. = *-anta* (Śiva), MBh. xiii, 724. **-anvaya**, mfn. difficult to be passed along (road), R. ii, 92, 3; d° to be accomplished or performed, MBh., Hariv.; d° to be found out or fathomed, R.; not corresponding or suitable, BhP. x, 84, 14; m. a false concord (in gram.); a consequence wrongly deduced from given premises, MW. **-anveshya**, mfn. d° to be searched out or through, R. iv, 48, 6. **-apacāra**, mfn. d° to be displeased or offended, W. **-apavāda**, m. ill report, slander, Subh. **-apâsa**, mfn. d° to be cast off, Naish. v, 130. **-abhi**, n. (wrongly opp. to *surabhi*) stench, MaitrS. ii, 1, 3. **-abhigraha**, mfn. d° to be laid hold of, W.; m. Achyranthes Aspera, L.; (*ā*), f. Mucuna Pruritus; Alhagi Maurorum, L. **-abhiprâya**, mfn. having a bad intention, BhP. x, 42, 20. **-abhibhava**, mfn. hard to be overcome or surpassed, Kād. **-abhimānin**, mfn. disagreeably or intolerably proud, Prab. iii, 1/7. **-abhiraksha**, mfn. d° to be watched or kept; *-tā*, f. Daś. **-abhisaṃdhi**, m. = *-abhiprâya*, Sch. on Mṛicch. v, 27. **-abhisambhava**, mfn. d° to be performed, beset with difficulties, Jātakam. **-avagama**, mfn. d° to be understood, incomprehensible, BhP. v, 13, 26. **-avagāha**, mfn. d° to be fathomed or found out, Śak. (Pi.) i, 2/4/5; d° to be entered, inaccessible, Jātakam. **-avagraha**, mfn. d° to be kept back or restrained, Kām. viii, 66; m. wicked obstinacy, stubbornness, BhP. iv, 19, 35; *-grāha* (B.) or *-grāhya*, mfn. d° to be attained (BhP. vii, 1, 19). **-avacchada**, mfn. d° to be veiled or hidden, ib. x, 62, 27. **-avatāra**, mfn. d° to be reached by descending, Kathās. lxv, 17. **-avadhāraka**, mfn. deciding or judging badly, ib. lxxii, 215. **-avadhāraṇa**, mfn. difficult to be defined, Parvad.; °*dhārya*, mfn. d° to be understood, ib. lviii, 66. **-avabodha**, mfn. id., BhP. x, 49, 29; *-tā*, f. Sāy. **-avaroha**, mfn. = *-avatāra*, Rājat. vi, 49. **-avalepa**, m. disagreeable arrogance, Prasannar. **-avavada**, n. (impers.) difficult to speak ill of (gen.), AitBr. v, 22. **-avasita**, mfn. d° to be ascertained, unfathomed, BhP. xii, 12, 66. **-avastha**, mfn. badly situated; (*ā*), f. a bad situation, Prab. vi, 1/2; °*sthita*, mfn. not firmly established, BhP. x, 76, 22. **-avâpa**, mfn. d° to be attained or accomplished, MBh. vii, 727; Śak. i, 2/7. **-avêkshita**, n. an improper look, a forbidden glance, MBh. iii, 14669. **-ahna**, m. a bad day, L. **-ākṛiti**, mfn. badly formed, disfigured, misshapen, R.; Hariv. **-ākranda**, mfn. having bad (or no) friends, Pañc. iv, 31. **-ākrama**, mfn. d° to be ascended or approached, MBh.; R. **-ākramaṇa**, n. unfair attack; difficult approach, MW. **-ākrānta**, mfn. unjustly attacked; difficult of access, ib. **-ākrāma**, mfn. d° to be passed, invincible, R.; metric. = °*krama*, ib. (B.) **-ākrośam**, ind. while badly scolding, R. iv, 9, 19. **-āgata**, m. 'badly come,' N. of a man, Buddh. **-āgama**, m. bad income, improper gain, MBh. v, 1513. **-āgraha**, m. = *-avagraha*, m. BhP. iii, 5, 43. **-ācara**, mfn. d° to be practised or performed, MBh. xii, 656; d° to be treated or cured, incurable, Suśr.; °*rita*, n. misfortune, ill luck, MBh. vii, 6336. **-ācāra**, m. bad behaviour, ill conduct, MBh.; mfn. ill-conducted, wicked, Mn.; MBh. &c.; °*rin*, mfn. id. **-āḍhya**, mfn. not rich, poor, W.; *-m-kara*, mfn. d° to be made rich, Pāṇ. iii, 3, 127, Sch.; *-m-bhava*, mfn. becoming rich with difficulty, ib. **-ātman**, mfn. evil-natured, wicked, bad, Mn.; MBh. &c.; °*ma-tā*, f. meanness, wickedness, MBh. i, 2010; °*ma-vat*, mfn. = °*man*, MBh. i, 2017 &c. **-ādāna**, mfn. d° to be laid hold of, ShaḍvBr. iii, 10. **-ādṛishṭi**, mfn. bad-looking, Cāṇ. **-ādeya**, mfn. d° to be taken away or seized, MBh. v, 5201. **-ādhana**, m. N. of a son of Dhṛitarāshṭra, MBh. i, 2736 (cf. next). **-ādhara**, mfn. d° to be withstood, irresistible, invincible, inaccessible, MBh.; m. N. of a son of Dhṛita-rāshṭra, MBh. i, 4549 (cf. the prec.) **-ādhársha**, mfn. d° to be attacked or approached, dangerous, invincible, irresistible, RV.; AV.; MBh. &c.; haughty, arrogant, W.; m. white mustard, L.; (*ā*), f. a kind of shrub (= *kuṭumbinī*), L. **-ādhāra**, mfn. d° to be conceived, Nīlak. on MBh. xiii, 724. **-ādhi**, m. distress or anxiety of mind, Kir. i, 28; indignation, Bhadrab. i, 34. **-ādhí**, mfn. meditating evil, malignant, RV. **-ānama**, mfn. hard to bend (as a bow), R. i, 77, 14; Ragh. xi, 38. **-āneya**, mfn. d° to be brought near, HPariś. **-ā́pa**, mfn. d° to be attained or approached, inaccessible, ŚBr.; Mn.; MBh. &c.; m. N. of a Dānava, Hariv. **-āpaná**, mfn. d° to be overtaken, RV. x, 95, 2. **-āpādana**, mfn. d° to be brought about, BhP. iii, 23, 42. **-āpūra**, mfn. d° to be filled or satisfied, vii, 6, 8. **-ābādha**, mfn. not to be assaulted with impunity (Śiva), MBh. xiii, 724. **-āmoda**, m. bad scent, stench, Kathās. lxxxii, 22. **-āmnāya**, mfn. d° to be handed down, MBh. xiv, 1441. **-ā́yya**, v.l. for *-ā́vī*. **-āraksha** or °**shya**, mfn. d° to be protected, R. ii, 52, 72. **-ārādha** or °**dhya**, mfn. d° to be propitiated or won or overcome, Kāv. **-āri-han** (for *ar*°), m. 'killing wicked enemies,' N. of Vishṇu, MBh. xiii, 7032. **-āruha**, mfn. d° to be ascended or mounted, MBh.; R.; m. a cocoa-nut tree or Aegle Marmelos, L.; (*ā*), f. Phoenix Sylvestris, L. **-ārūḍha**, mfn. ascended with difficulty, MW. **-āropa**, mfn. d° to be strung (bow), Bālar. i, $\frac{4}{1}\frac{9}{7}$. **-āroha**, mfn. d° to be ascended, MBh.; R. (*-tā*, f. Kād.); m. the palm or date tree, L.; (*ā*), f. the silk-cotton tree, L.; °*hanīya*, mfn. d° to be ascended, MW. **-ālakshya**, mfn. d° to be perceived, MBh.; Kāv. **-ālabha**, mfn. d° to be handled, W.; *ā*, (f.) Alhagi Maurorum, Suśr. **-ālamba**, mfn. d° to be laid hold of or attained, R. v, 73, 6. **-ālambha**, mfn. d° or unfit to be touched or handled, MBh. xiii, 4707; (*ā*), f. = *-ālabhā*, L. **-ālāpa**, m. curse, imprecation, abuse, L. **-āloka**, mfn. d° to be perceived, Kāv.; not to be looked at, painfully bright; m. dazzling splendour, W. **-āvara**, v.l. for °*vāra*, R. (B.) **-āvarta**, mfn. d° to be turned (from an opinion &c.), MBh. xii, 597. **-āvaha**, mfn. d° to be brought or led towards (comp.), MBh. xii, 12459. **-āvāra**, mfn. d° to be covered or filled up, R. ii, 105, 3; d° to be restrained, invincible, MBh. vii, 1480. **-āvāsin**, mfn. having a bad dwelling, Cāṇ. **-āvī́** (acc. °*vyàm*), mfn. d° to be passed through, RV. ix, 41, 2. **-1. -āśā**, m. N. of an Ekāha, ŚāṅkhŚr. **-2. -āśa**, mfn. having bad expectations, Prab. iii, 5; (*ā*), f. bad expectation, vain hope, despair, Rājat.; BhP. **-āśaṇsin**, mfn. foreboding evil, Vṛishabhân. **-āśaya**, mfn. evil-minded, malicious, Prab. ii, $\frac{2}{1}\frac{8}{3}$; BhP.; m. the subtle body which is not destroyed by death, Sch. **-āśir** (*dúr-*), mfn. badly mixed (Soma), RV. viii, 2, 5. **-āśis**, mfn. having evil wishes or intentions, BhP. **-āśraya**, mfn. d° to be practised, TejobUp. 2. **-1. -āsa**, mfn. d° to be driven out or expelled, W. **-2. -āsa**, mfn. d° to be abided or associated with, Śiś. v, 19. **-āsada**, mfn. d° or dangerous to be approached, MBh.; Kāv.; Pur.; d° to be found or met with, unheard of, unparalleled, MBh.; R.; difficult to be accomplished (v.l. °*saha*); m. N. of Śiva, mystical N. of a sword, MBh. xii, 6203. **-āsaha**, mfn. d° to be accomplished, MBh. iii, 12255 (v.l. °*sada*); m. mystical N. of a sword (v. prec.), Gal. **-āsita**, n. a bad manner of sitting, MBh. iii, 14669; xii, 3084. **-āseva**, mfn. d° to be dealt with or associated with, R. iii, 23, 15. **-āhara**, mfn. d° to be offered (sacrifice), MBh. ii, 664. **-āhā́**, ind. (opp. to *sv-āhā*) ill luck, misfortune, AV. **-√i**, cl. 1. Ā. *dur-ayate* or *dul-ayate*, Siddh., only in deriv. **-itá** (*dúr-*, RV. i, 125, 7), n. bad course, difficulty, danger, discomfort, evil, sin (also personified), RV.; AV.; Hariv.; Kāv. &c.; mfn. difficult, bad, AV. xii, 2, 28; wicked, sinful, L.; *-kshaya*, m. destruction of sin, BhP.; N. of a man, ib.; *-damanī*, f. Mimosa Suma, L.; °*tâtman*, mfn. evil-minded, malicious, Subh. 147; °*târi*, f. 'enemy of sin,' N. of a Jaina goddess; °*târṇava*, m. 'ocean of sins,' N. of a king, Kautukar. **-iti**, f. bad course, difficulty, distress, TBr. **-1. -ishṭa**, n. (√3. *ish*) 'bad wish,' curse, sorcery, (cf. °*īshaṇā*); *-kṛit*, mfn. performing a magic spell to injure another, VP. **-2. -ishṭa** (*dúr-*), mfn. (√*yaj*) badly sacrificed (opp. to *sv-ishṭa*), Br. **-ishṭi** (*dúr-*), f. defect or failure in a sacrifice, AV.; VS. **-īksha**, mfn. difficult to be seen; *-tā*, f. Śiś. xvii, 10. **-īśa**, m. a bad master, Prab. v, 18. **-īshaṇā** (for *esh*°), f. imprecation, L. (cf. *-ishṭi*). **-īha**, mfn. ill-meant, SSaṃkar. **-uktá**, mfn. 'badly spoken,' harsh, injurious; harshly addressed, Pañc. i, 100; n. bad or harsh word, Br.; GS.; MBh. &c.; °*ktôkta*, mfn. ill spoken of, AitBr. ii, 17, 6. **-ukti**, f. harsh or injurious speech (personified as a daughter of Krodha and Hiṇsā and sister and wife of Kali), BhP. **-uccheda**, mfn. d° to be extirpated or destroyed, Prab. iv, $\frac{2}{1}\frac{6}{8}$; °*dya*, mfn. id., Pañc.; d° to be cut through (knot), Prab. v, $\frac{2}{1}\frac{1}{8}$. **-uta**, mfn. badly woven, L. **-1. -uttara**, mfn. (fr. 1. *uttara*) unanswerable, W. **-2. -uttara**, mfn. (fr. 2. *uttara* or Prākṛit for *dus-tara*) d° to be crossed or overcome, Kathās. xxvi, 10; Kull. on Mn. ix, 161. **-utsaha** or °**sāha**, mfn. d° to bear or resist, MBh. &c. **-udaya**, mfn. appearing with difficulty, not easily manifested, BhP. iii, 15, 50. **-udarka**, mfn. having bad or no consequences, Naish. v, 41. **-udāhara**, mfn. d° to be pronounced or uttered, Śiś. ii, 73. **-udvaha**, mfn. hard to bear, MBh. &c. **-upakrama**, mfn. d° of access or approach, W.; d° of cure, Suśr. **-upacāra**, mfn. id., Pañc.; Car. **-upadishṭa**, mfn. badly instructed. **-upadeśa**, m. bad instruction, Pat. **-upapāda**, mfn. d° to be performed, Kād.; d° to be demonstrated, Sarvad. **-upayukta**, mfn. wrongly applied, DaivBr. iv. **-upalaksha**, mfn. d° to be perceived, Daś. **-upasada**, mfn. d° of approach, Kir. vii, 9. **-upasarpin**, mfn. approaching incautiously, Mn. vii, 9. **-upasthāna**, mfn. = *-upasada*, W. **-upā́pa**, mfn. d° of attainment, ŚBr. **-upāya**, m. a bad means or expedient, MW. **-ūha**, mfn. d° to be inferred or understood; *-tva*, n. Sch. **-éva**, mfn. ill-disposed, malignant; m. evil-doer, criminal, RV.; AV. **-ókam**, ind. unpleasantly, RV. vii, 4, 3; °*ka-śocis*, mfn. glowing unpleasantly (too bright or hot), ib. i, 66, 5. **-ósha** and °**shas**, mfn. slow, lazy, RV. **-ga**, see *Durga* (p. 487). **-gā**, see *Durgā* (p. 487). **-gata**, mfn. faring ill, unfortunate, miserable, MBh. &c.; N. of a poet, Cat.; *-tā*, f. ill luck, misery, Pañc. i, 297. **-gati**, mfn. = *-gata*, R. vii, 88, 3; f. misfortune, distress, poverty, want of (gen.), MBh.; Kāv. &c.; hell, L.; *-nāśinī*, f. 'removing distress,' N. of Durgā, BrahmavP. **-gandha**, m. bad smell, stink, Kauś.; mfn. ill-smelling, stinking, Hariv.; Suśr.; m. the mango-tree (= *āmra*), L.; an onion, Bhpr.; n. sochal-salt, L.; *-kāra*, m. the anus, Car.; *-tā*, f. badness of smell, Suśr. **-gándhi**, mfn. ill-smelling, stinking, AV.; ChUp.; Mn. &c. **-gama**, mfn. difficult to be traversed or travelled over, impassable, inaccessible, unattainable, MBh.; Hariv.; Kāv.; m. or n. a d° situation; m. N. of a son of Vasu-deva and Pauravī, VP.; of Dhṛita, ib., &c.; *-mārga-nirgama*, mfn. of d° access and issue, Pañc. i, 427; *durgamârtha-bodhinī*, f. N. of a Comm. **-gamanīya** (Sch.) & **-gamya** (R.), mfn. = *-gama*. **-gaya**, m. (√*ji*?) N. of an author. **-gala**, m. pl. N. of a people, MBh. vi, 359. **-gáha**, n. (√*gāh*) an impassable or impervious place, difficulty, danger, RV.; m. N. of a man, ib. viii, 54, 12. **-gādha** (Hariv.), **-gādha** (Suśr.), and **-gāhya** (*-tva*, n. Pañc. i, 317), mfn. unfathomable. **-gṛibhi**, mfn. difficult to be seized or laid hold of, RV. i, 140, 6; *-śvan*, mfn. continually swelling, RV. i, 52, 6. **-gṛibhīya**, Nom. Ā. °*yate*, to be seized with difficulty, RV. v, 9, 4. **-goshṭhī**, f. evil association, conspiracy, Rājat. vi, 170. **-graha**, m. 'seizing badly,' the evil demon of illness, spasm, cramp, Suśr.; Kathās.; obstinacy, insisting upon (loc.), whim, monomania, Kathās. lviii, 62 &c.; Naish. ix, 41; mfn. d° to be seized or caught or attained or won or accomplished or understood, Kāṭh. xxxi, 15; MBh.; Kāv. &c. **-grāhya**, mfn. = *-graha*, mfn., MBh.; Hariv. &c.; *-tva*, n. Pañc. i, 317; *-hṛidaya*, mfn. whose heart is d° to be gained, R. ii, 39, 22. **-ghaṭa**, mfn. hard to be accomplished, difficult, Rājat. iv, 364; BhP. (*-tva*, n. vii, 15, 58); m. or n. N. of a gram. work; °*ṭa-kāvya*, n. N. of a poem; °*ṭa-ghāṭana*, m. or n., °*ṭa-vṛitti*, f., °*ṭârtha-prakāśikā*, f., °*ṭôdghāṭa*, m. N. of Comms. **-ghosha**, m. 'harsh-sounding, roaring,' a bear, L. **-jana**, m. a bad man, villain, scoundrel, Mn.; Kāv. &c.; m. pl. bad people, Sch.; mfn. malicious, wicked, Kathās.; *-tā*, f. & *-tva*, n. wickedness, villainy, L.; *-nindā*, f., *-mukha-capeṭikā*, f., *-mukha-padma-pādukā*, f., *-mukha-mahā-capeṭikā*, f. N. of wks.; *-malla*, N. of a prince, Inscr. **-janāya**, Nom. Ā. °*yate*, to be a wicked man, Pañc. i, 5. **-janī-√kṛi**, 'to make into a bad man,' insult, wrong, Ratn. iii, $\frac{1}{1}\frac{7}{6}$; iv, $\frac{1}{1}\frac{8}{7}$. **-jaya**, mfn. d° to be conquered or won, invincible, irresistible, Mn.; MBh. &c.; m. N. of a Dānava, MBh.; of an assemblage of D°s, Śak. vi, $\frac{2}{3}\frac{8}{1}$; of a Rakshas, R.; of sev. heroes, MBh.; Pur.; (*ā*), f. N. of a place, MBh. iii, 8540. **-jayanta**, m. N. of a mountain, VP. **-jara**, mfn. not decaying or mouldering, BhP. x, 6, 10; 64, 32; indigestible, Suśr.; d° to be enjoyed, Rājat. v, 19; m. or n. N. of a place, KālP. **-jala**, n. bad or noisome water, Bhpr. **-jāta**, mfn. badly born, ill-starred, miserable, wretched, MBh.; R.; wicked, bad, wrong, false, Rājat. iii, 142; with *bhartṛi* false lover, paramour, ib. 507; n. misfortune, calamity, Ragh. xiii, 72; disparity, impropriety, W. **-jāti**, f. misfortune, ill condition, Mālav. v, 11; mfn. bad-natured, wicked, MBh. &c.; °*tīya*, mfn. id., Hariv. **-jīva**, mfn. difficult to live; n. impers. a d° life, R. ii, 57, 20 &c. **-jeya**, mfn. d° to be conquered, BhP. x, 72, 10. **-jñāna**, mfn. d° to be known, MBh.; *-tva*, Kull. on Mn. iv, 1. **-jñeya**, mfn. d° to be understood or found out; m. N. of Śiva, MBh., Hariv. **-ṇaya**, w. r. for *-naya*. **-ṇā́śa**, mfn. unattainable, inaccessible, AV. v, 11, 6 (cf. *dū-ṇ*°, *dū-ṇāśa*). **-ṇashṭa**, mfn. unattained, MW. **-ṇāmacātana**, mfn. driving away the demons called Durṇāman, AV. viii, 6, 3. **-ṇā́man**, mf(*mnī*)n. having a bad name; m. N. of partic. evil demons causing diseases (or according to Nir. vi, 12, N. of a worm; cf. *-nāman*), RV.; AV.; °*ma-hán*, mfn. destroying the Dur-ṇāmans. **-ṇihitâishin**, mfn. tracing out what is badly kept, AV. xi, 9, 15. **-ṇīta** & °**ti**, see *-nīta* & °*ti*. **-dagdha**, mfn. burning or cauterising badly, Suśr. **-datta**, mfn. badly given, Pāṇ. vii, 4, 47, Sch. **-dama**, mfn. hard to be subdued, MBh. xii, 3310; m. N. of a son of Vasu-deva and Rohiṇī, Hariv.; of a prince, son of Bhadra-śreṇya, ib.; Pur.; of a Brāhman, VP. **-damana**, mfn. = *-dama*; m. N. of a prince, son of Satānīka, BhP. **-damya**, mfn. indomitable, obstinate, MBh. xii, 2951. **-dara**, mfn. tearing badly, distressing, W.; m. battle, Gal. (cf. *duro-*); a kind of drug, W. **-darśa**, mfn. difficult to be seen or met with, KaṭhUp.; Āpast.; MBh.; R. &c.; disagreeable or painful to the sight, MBh.; Hariv. &c.; *-tā*, f. MBh. viii, 861; °*śatāya*, Nom. Ā. °*yate*, to have a bad or disgusting appearance, MW. **-darśana**, mfn. = *-darśa*, Suśr.; BhP. **-daśā**, f. bad situation, misfortune, Kathās. **-dānta**, mfn. badly tamed, untamable, uncontrolled, MBh.; Hariv.; m. a calf, L.; strife, quarrel, L.; N. of a lion, Hit. **-dāru**, n. bad wood, Car. **-dina**, n. a rainy or cloudy day, bad weather, Kauś. 38; MBh.; Kāv.; mfn. cloudy, rainy, dark, MBh. viii, 4771; R.; Hariv.; *-grasta-bhāskara*, mfn. having the sun obscured by dark clouds, MW.; *durdināya*, Nom. Ā. °*yate*, to become covered with clouds, Pāṇ. iii, 1, 17, Vārtt. 1, Pat. **-divasa**, m. a bad or rainy day, Pañc. **-duruṭa**, m. an abusive word, Gaṇar. (v.l. *-duruta*, cf. *-dhurūṭa*); atheist; = *karaṭa*, L. **-duhā**, f. difficult to be milked (cow), MBh. v, 1128. **-dūrânta**, mfn. very long (path), Sch. **-dṛiś**, mfn. seeing badly, BhP. iv, 3, 17. **-dṛiśa**, mfn. = *-darśa*, MBh. **-dṛiśīka**, mfn. looking bad, RV. vii, 50, 1. **-dṛishṭa**, mfn. ill-seen (lit. & fig.), ill-examined or unjustly decided (lawsuit), Yājñ. ii, 305; looked at with an evil eye, W. **-deśa**, m. a bad or unwholesome place; *-ja*, mfn. coming from it (water), Bhpr. **-daiva**, n. bad luck, misfortune, Hit.; *-vat*, mfn. unfortunate, ib. **-dolī**, f. a knot difficult to be undone, Sch. on Hāla, 149. **-dohā**, f. difficult to be milked, ĀpŚr. **-dyūta**, n. a bad or unfair game; *-devin*, mfn. playing unfairly, cheating at play, MBh. iv, 532; *-vedin* (prob. w. r. for *devin*), m. N. of Śakuni, Gal. **-druma**, m. a green onion, L. **-dhára**, mfn. difficult to be carried or borne or suffered, unrestrainable, irresistible, RV. i, 57, 1; MBh.; Hariv. &c.; d° to be administered (punishment), Mn. vii, 28; d° to be kept in memory or recollected, MBh. xiii, 3618; inevitable, absolutely necessary (suffix), Vām. v, 2, 51; m. quicksilver, L.; N. of two plants (*ṛishabha* & *bhallātaka*), L.; a kind of hell, L.; N. of a son of Dhṛita-rāshṭra (cf. *-dharsha*), MBh.; of one of Śambara's generals, Hariv.; of Mahisha, L.; (*ā*), f. N. of a partic. constellation (cf. *durudharā*); of Candra-gupta's wife, HPariś.; °*rā-yogâdhyāya*, m. N. of a ch. of the Mīna-rāja-jātaka. **-dhárītu** & **-dhártu**, mfn. unrestrainable, irresistible, RV. **-dharuṭa** = *-dhurūṭa*, W. **-dharma**, mfn. having or obeying bad laws, MBh. viii, 2066. **-dharsha**, mfn. d° to be assaulted or laid hold of, inviolable, inaccessible, unconquerable, dangerous, dreadful, awful, MBh.; R. &c. (*-tā*, f. MBh.; *-tva*, n. BhP.); haughty, distant, W.; m. N. of a son of Dhṛita-rāshṭra (cf. *-dhara*), MBh. i; of a Rākshasa, R. v; of a mountain in Kuśa-dvîpa, MBh. vi, 451; (*ā*), f. N. of two plants (= *nāga-damanī* & *kanthārī*), L.; *-kumāra-bhūta*, m. 'one who has become an inviolable youth,' N. of a Bodhi-sattva. **-dharshaṇa**, mfn. inaccessible, dangerous, R. iv, 9, 55 &c. **-dhā́**, f. bad order, disarrangement, RV. x, 109, 4 (cf. *-dhita*). **-dhārya**, mfn. difficult to be borne, MBh. iii, 99, 41; with *manasā*, d° to be recollected, ib. xiii, 4483. **-dhāva**, mfn. d° to be cleaned or purified, Pat.

-dhita (*dúr-*), mfn. badly arranged, untidy, RV. i, 140, 11. **-dhī**, mfn. weak-minded, stupid, silly, MBh. v, 4590; BhP. ii, 15, 13; having bad intentions, malignant, Nir. x, 5 (cf. *dū-ḍhī*). **-dhúr**, mfn. badly yoked or harnessed, RV. v, 56, 4. **-dhurūṭa**, m. (for °*ūḍha*?, cf. *dhūr-vodhṛi*) a pupil who does not obey his teacher without exercising his own judgment (cf. *-durūṭa*), L. **-dhyāna**, n. evil thoughts, HPariś. **-naya**, m. bad or imprudent conduct, MBh.; Hariv. &c. **-narêndra**, m. a miserable sorcerer or conjurer, Hcar.; L. **-nāman**, m. 'having a bad name,' N. of a Yaksha, BrahmaP.; f. (=m. or °*mnī*) a cockle, L.; hemorrhoids, piles, L. (cf. *-ṇāman*); °*mâri*, m. 'enemy of p°,' the bulbous root of Amorphophallus Campanulatus, L.; °*maka*, n. hemorrhoids; °*mikā*, f. a cockle, L. **-nigraha**, mfn. difficult to be restrained or conquered, MBh. **-nimita**, mfn. ill-measured, irregular (steps), Ragh. vii, 10. **-nimitta**, n. a bad omen, MBh. ii, 818; Śak. v, $\frac{1}{2}$. **-niyántu**, mfn. d° to be checked or held back, RV. **-nirīksha**, °**kshaṇa**, °**kshya**, mfn. d° to be looked at or seen, MBh.; R. &c. **-nivartya**, mfn. d° to be turned back (flying army), MBh. vi, 145; = *-nivṛitta*, xiii, 3504. **-nivāra**, mfn. d° to be kept back, unrestrainable, irrepressible, MBh., Kāv. &c.; *-tva*, n. Kull. **-nivārya**, mfn. id., MBh.; Hariv. &c. **-nivṛitta**, mfn. d° to be returned from, R. iv, 22, 36. **-nivedya**, mfn. d° to be related; *-tva*, n. Jātakam. **-nishedha**, mfn. d° to be warded off, Bālar. ii, $\frac{3}{3}\frac{4}{8}$. **-nishkramaṇa**, n., **-nishprapatana**, n. (wrongly written °*tara*), **-niḥsaraṇa**, n. d° escape, ChUp. v, 10, 6, Śaṃk. **-nīta**, mfn. ill-conducted, wrong; n. misconduct, impolicy, folly, ill-luck, MBh.; Hariv.; Pañcat. ii, 21; *-bhāva*, m. bad behaviour, improper conduct, MBh. v, 6007. **-nīti**, f. maladministration, impolicy, Jātakam. **-nṛipa**, m. a bad king, Rājat. v, 416. **-nyasta**, mfn. badly arranged, Mālatīm. ix, 41; badly used (said of a spell), Divyâv. 27. **-baddha**, mfn. badly fastened, Suśr. **-bandha**, mfn. d° to be composed, Vām. i, 3, 22. **-bala**, mfn. of little strength, weak, feeble, Mn.; MBh. &c.; thin, slender (waist), R. iii, 52, 31; emaciated, lean (cow); sick, unwell, Kāty. Śr. xxv, 7, 1; MBh. iv, 182; scanty, small, little, MBh.; Kāv.; Pur.; m. an impotent man, weakling, Mn. iii, 151 (v.l. *-vāla*); a kind of bird (w.r. for *-bali*); N. of a prince, VP.; of an author, Cat.; (*ā*), f. a species of plant (= *ambu-śirīshikā*), Bhpr.; (*ī*), f. N. of wk.; *-balatā*, f. weakness, thinness, Kāv.; Pañc.; *durbalâgni*, mfn. having a weak digestion (°*ni-tā*, f. Suśr.); °*lâyāsa*, mfn. 'weak of effort,' ineffective, MW.; °*lêndriya*, mfn. having feeble (i.e. unrestrained) organs of sense, MW.; °*lita*, mfn. weakened, rendered ineffective, Kathās. cv, 91; °*lī-√bhū*, to become weak or ineffective, ib. cvii, 52 (read *-bhūtās*); °*lī-bhāva*, m. the becoming weak (of the voice), Car.; °*līyas*, mfn. weaker, feeble, MBh.; Mn. iii, 79. **-bali**, m. (VarBṛS. lxxxviii, 88, 28, v.l. °*la*) & °**lika**, m. (ib., 7) a kind of bird (= *bhāṇḍīka*). **-bāla**, see *-vāla*. **-bīriṇa** (*dúr-*), mfn. bristly, rough (beard), ŚBr. **-buddhi**, f. weak-mindedness, silliness, MBh.; mfn. silly, foolish, ignorant, malignant, MBh.; R. &c. **-budha**, mfn. weak-minded, silly, MBh. xi, 166. **-bodha**, mfn. difficult to be understood, unfathomable, R. iv, 17, 6; BhP. &c.; *-pada-bhañjikā*, f. N. of a Comm. on Megh.; *-pada-bhañjinī*, f. of a Comm. on MBh. **-bodhya**, mfn. = *-bodha*, Sch. on Mṛicch. iv, 8. **-brāhmaṇa** (*dúr-*), m. a bad Brāhman, TS. **-bhaksha** or °**shya**, mfn. to be eaten with difficulty, W. **-bhága**, mfn. 'having a bad portion,' unfortunate, unlucky, Suśr.; VarBṛS.; Pañc.; BhP.; disgusting, repugnant, ugly (esp. a woman), AV. x, 1, 10; MBh.; Hariv. &c.; (*ā*), f. a bad or ill-tempered woman, a shrew, W.; personified = Old Age, daughter of Time, BhP. iv, 27, 10; *-tva*, n. ill fortune, BhP. **-bhagna**, mfn. badly broken, Suśr. **-bhaṅga**, mfn. d° to be broken or loosened, Hariv. **-bhaṇa**, mfn. d° to be mentioned; *-tva*, n. Parāś. **-bhara**, mfn. d° to be borne or supported or maintained, R.; Pañc.; BhP.; heavily laden with (comp.), Śāntiś. i, 24; Kathās. cxii, 156. **-bhartṛi**, m. a bad husband, Kathās. **-bhāgya**, mfn. unfortunate, unlucky, Tattvas.; n. ill luck, MW. **-bhāryā**, f. a bad wife, Kathās. **-bhāvanā**, f. an evil thought, bad inclination, MW. **-bhāvya**, mfn. d° to be called to mind, MārkP. x, 7. **-bhāsha**, mfn. speaking ill, AgP.; m. injurious words, BhP. **-bhāshita**, mfn. badly spoken or uttered, with *vāc*, f. = prec. m., MBh. v, 1171. **-bhāshin**, mfn. speaking ill, abusing, insulting, ib. 751. **-bhiksha**, n. (rarely m.) scarcity of provisions, dearth, famine, want, distress, TĀr. i, 4, 3; Mn.; MBh. &c.; *-tva*, n. Pañc. ii, 54, 55; *-vyasanin*, mfn. suffering from the calamity of famine, Hit. iv, 44; *-śamana*, m. 'alleviator of famine,' a king, L. **-bhida**, mfn. d° to be broken or torn asunder, MBh. **-bhishajya** (*dúr-*), n. d° cure, ŚBr. xiv, 7, 1, 5. **-bhūtá**, n. ill luck, harm, AV.; TBr. **-bhṛiti**, f. scanty maintenance or subsistence, RV. vii, 1, 22. **-bheda** or °**dya**, mfn. = *-bhida*, MBh.; Hariv. &c. **-bhogā**, f. = *bhikshukī*, Gal. **-bhrātṛi**, m. a bad brother, MBh. iii, 996. **-makha** & **-maṅgala**, see *a-dur-m°*. **-maṅku**, mfn. refractory, obstinate, disobedient, L. **-mata-khaṇḍana**, n. N. of wk. **-matí**, f. bad disposition of mind, envy, hatred, RV.; VS.; AV.; false opinion or notions, Cāṇ.; mfn. weak-minded, silly, ignorant (rarely 'malicious,' 'wicked'), m. fool, blockhead (rarely 'scoundrel,' 'villain'), Mn.; MBh. &c.; N. of the 55th year of the cycle of Jupiter (lasting 60 years), Var.; Sūryas.; of a demon, Lalit.; of a blockhead, Bharat. **-matī-kṛita**, mfn. (fr. *matyà* & √*kṛi*) badly harrowed or rolled, AitBr. iii, 38. **-mada**, m. mad conception or illusion, foolish pride or arrogance, Pur.; (*-máda*), mfn. drunken, fierce, mad, infatuated by (comp.), RV.; MBh. &c.; m. N. of a son of Dhṛita-rāshṭra, MBh. i; of a son of Dhṛita (father of Pracetas); of a son of Bhadra-sena (father of Dhanaka); of a son of Vasu-deva and Rohiṇī or Pauravī, Pur.; °*da-vīra-mānin*, mfn. foolishly fancying (one's self) a hero, BhP. iii, 17, 28; °*dândha*, mfn. 'blinded by mad illusion,' besotted, v, 12, 16; °*din*, m. drinker, drunkard, Pat. **-manas**, n. bad disposition, perversity of mind, R. ii, 31, 20; mfn. [cf. δυσ-μενής] in bad or low spirits, sad, melancholy, MBh.; R. &c. (*-tā*, f. sadness, Sch.); N. of a man (cf. *daur-manasāyana*); °*ska*, mfn. = *-manas*, mfn.; *-tā*, f. Kathās. cxiv, 35. **-manāya**, Nom. Ā. °*yate*, to be or become troubled or sad, Kāv. **-manushya**, m. a wicked man, villain, MBh. viii, 2117. **-mántu**, mfn. d° to be understood, RV. x, 12, 6. **-mantra**, m. bad advice, Bhartṛ. ii, 34 (v.l. *daurmantrya*); °*trita*, mfn. badly advised; n. = prec., MBh.; °*trin*, m. bad adviser or minister, Kathās. lxxii, 220; mfn. having bad ministers, Pañc. iii, 244. **-mánman**, mfn. evil-minded, RV. viii, 49, 7. **-mára**, mfn. dying hard, tenacious of life, ŚBr.; MBh.; n. a hard death (w. instr. of pers.), MBh. xiv, 2364; (*ā*), f. a kind of Dūrvā grass or Asparagus Racemosus, L. **-maraṇa** (MW.) & **-maratva** (MBh.), n. any violent or unnatural death. **-marāyú**, mfn. difficult to be put to death, TS. **-maryāda**, mfn. knowing no limits, having evil ways, wicked; *-tā*, f., Uttarar. iv, $\frac{2}{2}\frac{3}{4}$. **-márṣha**, mfn. not easily to be forgotten, RV. viii, 45, 18 &c.; unbearable, insupportable, unmanageable, BhP. vi, 5, 42 &c.; m. N. of the Asura Bali, viii, 10, 32. **-marshaṇa**, mfn. unmanageable, unbearable, insupportable; MBh.; R.; m. N. of a son of Dhṛita-rāshṭra, MBh. i &c.; of a son of Śṛiñjaya, BhP. ix, 24, 41; of Vishṇu, MBh. xiii, 6971; °*shita*, mfn. made refractory, MBh. xiv, 2314. **-mallikā** or **-mallī**, f. a kind of minor drama, Sāh. **-mātsarya**, n. evil envy, Bhartṛ. iii, 31. **-māyin** or °**yú**, mfn. using bad arts, BhP. viii, 11, 6; RV. iii, 30, 15. **-mitrá**, mfn. unfriendly; m. N. of the author of RV. x, 105; of a prince, VP.; (*ā*), f. N. of a woman (g. *bāhv-ādi*); °*triyá*, mfn. unfriendly, VS. vi, 22. **-milā** or °**likā**, f. N. of sev. forms of metre. **-mukha**, mf(*ī*)n. ugly-faced, MBh.; R. &c.; foul-mouthed, abusive, scurrilous, Bhartṛ. ii, 59; m. a horse, L.; a serpent, L.; N. of the 29th year of the cycle of Jupiter (lasting 60 years), Var.; Sūryas.; of a prince of the Pañcālas, AitBr. viii, 23; of a son of Dhṛita-rāshṭra, MBh. i &c.; of an astronomer, L.; of a serpent-demon, MBh.; Hariv.; of a Rakshas, R.; BhP.; of a Yaksha, BrahmaP.; of a monkey, R.; of a general of the Asura Mahisha, L.; °*khâcārya*, m. N. of an author. **-muhūrta**, m. n. an unauspicious hour or moment, MBh. xii, 6735. **-mūlya**, mfn. dear in price, L. **-medha** or **-medhas** (Pāṇ. v, 4, 122), mfn. dull-witted, stupid, ignorant, MBh.; R. &c.; °*dhas-tva*, n. foolishness, stupidity, Suśr.; °*dhā-vin*, mfn. = *-medha*, MBh. xii, 9486. **-maitra**, mfn. unfriendly, hostile, BhP. vii, 5, 27. **-moca**, mfn. hard to unloose; *-hasta-grāha*, mfn. 'whose hand's grasp is hard to unloose,' holding fast, Śak. vii, $\frac{1}{1}\frac{7}{7}\frac{0}{7}$. **-mohā**, f. Capparis Sepiaria, L. **-yavanam**, ind. bad for or with the Yavanas, Pāṇ. ii, i, 6; Kāś. **-yaśas**, n. disgrace, Naish. i, 88. **-yāman**, m. 'going badly,' N. of a prince, VP. (v.l. *-dama*). **-yuga**, n. a bad age, Sch. **-yúj**, mfn. d° to be yoked, RV. x, 44, 7. **-yoga**, m. bad contrivance, crime, MBh. i, 1316; Uttarar. vi, $\frac{1}{1}\frac{8}{9}$. **-yodha**, mfn. d° to be conquered, Vop. **-yodhana**, mfn. id. (*-tā*, f. MBh. iv, 2103); N. of the eldest son of Dhṛita-rāshṭra (leader of the Kauravas in their war with the Pāṇḍavas), MBh.; Hariv. &c. (cf. *su-y°*); of a son of Su-durjaya, MBh. xiii, 96; *-rakshā-bandhana*, n. N. of wk.; *-vīrya-jñāna-mudrā*, f. 'mark of knowledge of invincible heroism,' a partic. intertwining of the fingers, L.; °*nâvaraja*, m. 'the younger brother of D°,' N. of Duḥ-śāsana, G. **-yoni**, mfn. of low or impure origin, Mn. x, 59. **-lakshaṇa**, mfn. badly marked, MW. **-lakshya**, mfn. hardly visible, Daś.; Rājat.; n. a bad aim, Ratn. iii, 2. **-laṅghana**, mfn. difficult to be surmounted or overcome, Kull.; *-śakti*, mfn. of insurmountable power, MW. **-laṅghya**, mfn. = *-laṅghana*; (*-tā*, f. Daśar. iv, 13); d° to be transgressed (command), Rājat. v, 395. **-labha**, mfn. d° to be obtained or found, hard, scarce, rare (comp. *-tara*), Mn.; MBh.; Kāv. &c.; hard to be (with inf. MBh. iii, 1728); extraordinary, eminent, L.; dear, beloved (also *-ka*), Kāraṇḍ.; m. Curcuma Amhaldi or Zerumbet, L.; N. of a man, Cat.; (*ā*), f. Alhagi Maurorum or = *śveta-kaṇṭa-kārī*, L.; *-tā*, f. (Rājat.), *-tva*, n. (Var.) scarceness, rarity; *-darśana*, mfn. out of sight, invisible, Mālav.; *-rāja*, m. N. of the father of Jagad-deva, Cat.; *-vardhana*, m. N. of a king of Kaśmīra, Rāj. iii, 489. **-labhaka**, mfn. = °*bha*; m. N. of a king of Kaśmīra (also called Pratāpâditya), Rājat. iv, 7; *-svāmin*, m. N. of a temple built by Dur-vardhana, Rājat. iv, 6. **-lalita**, mfn. ill-mannered, wayward; spoilt by, weary of, disgusted with (comp.), Kāv. (°*ka* & *-lasita*, v.l., Śak. vii, $\frac{1}{1}\frac{8}{9}$); n. waywardness, naughty or roguish tricks, Hariv. **-lābha**, mfn. = *-labha*, MBh. xii, 11168. **-likhita**, mfn. badly scarified, Suśr. **-lipi**, m. 'the fatal writing' (of Destiny on man's forehead), ŚārṅgP. **-lekhya**, n. a false or forged document, Yājñ. ii, 91. **-vaca**, mfn. d° to be spoken or explained or asserted or answered, MBh.; R. &c. (*-tva*, n. Sarvad.); speaking ill or in pain, W.; n. abuse, censure; evil or unlucky speech, W. **-vacaka**, mfn. d° to be answered (?); *-yoga*, m. pl. a partic. art, Sch. on BhP. x, 45, 36. **-vacana**, n. pl. bad or harsh language, Ratn. iii, $\frac{1}{1}\frac{0}{1}$. **-vacas**, n. id., MBh.; Pur.; mfn. using bad or harsh l°, R.; d° to be explained or answered; *-tva*, n. VāyuP. **-vañca**, mfn. d° to be deceived. **-vaṇij**, m. a wicked merchant, Kathās. ci, 333. **-vadaka**, mfn. speaking badly, stammering, Cat. **-varāha** (*dúr-*), m. a tame hog, ŚBr. xii; Āśv. Śr. ix, 10, 15, Sch. **-varṇa**, m. bad colour, impurity, Bh. xii, 3, 47; (*várṇa*), mfn. of a bad colour or species or class, inferior, TBr.; MBh. &c.; n. silver (opp. to *su-varṇa*, gold), L. (also *-ka*, n.); the fragrant bark of Feronia Elephantum, L. **-vártu**, mfn. difficult to be kept back, irresistible, RV. **-vala**, see *bala*. **-vasa**, n. (impers.) d° to be resided in (loc.), MBh. iv, 93; mfn. d° to be passed or spent (time), 7; d° to be stayed with, causing ill luck by one's presence, R. vii, 86, 12; 17. **-vasati**, f. bad dwelling, MBh.; Ragh. **-vaha**, mfn. hard to bear, MBh.; Hariv.; Kāv. **-vahaka**, m. N. of a poet, Cat. **-vākya**, n. harsh or abusive language, W. **-vāc**, f. id., MBh.; (*vâc*), mfn. having a bad voice, AV. iv, 17, 5; speaking ill, Kāv.; *-vāg-bhāva*, m. abusiveness, MBh. xiii, 2259 (C. *-bhava*). **-vācaka-yoga**, v.l. for *vac°*, Cat. **-vācika**, n. a bad commission, Naish. ix, 62. **-vācya**, mfn. hard (to be uttered); n. a h° word, Pur.; bad news, R. **-vāta**, m. 'bad wind,' a fart, L; °*tāya*, Nom. P. °*yati*, to break wind or fart against (acc.), BhP. xi, 23, 39. **-vāda**, m. slander, abuse, reproach, ŚārṅgP. (v.l.); mfn. speaking ill, L. **-vānta**, mfn. having badly vomited (also said of a leech that has not ejected blood), Suśr. **-vāra**, mfn. hard to be restrained, irrepressible, irresistible, MBh.; Kāv. &c. (*-tva*, n. Suśr.); °*raṇa*, mfn. id., ib.; m. pl. N. of a tribe of the Kāmbojas, MBh. vii, 4333 (v.l. °*vāri*); °*raṇīya*, °*rita*, °*rya*, mfn. = *-vāra*, MBh. (°*rya-tva*, n., ib.) **-vārttā**, f. bad news, Ragh. xii, 51, Sch. **-vāla**, mfn. bald-headed, Mn. iii, 151 (Comm. 'red-haired' or 'afflicted with a skin-disease'). **-vāsa**, m. (cf. *-vāsas*) prob. = °*sâcārya*, m. N. of a Ṛishi, Cat.; °*sa-purāṇa*, n. N. of a Pur.; °*sêśvara*, n. N. of a Liṅga, SkandaP.; °*sôpanishad*, f. N. of a section of ŚivaP. **-vāsanā**,

f. bad inclination, Prab. vi, $\frac{1}{1}\frac{1}{2}$. **-vāsas**, mfn. badly clad, naked, RV. vii, 1, 19; MBh. xiii, 1176 (Śiva); m. N. of a Ṛishi or saint (son of Atri by Anasūyā, and thought to be an incarnation of Śiva, known for his irascibility), MBh.; Śak. iv, 7; Pur. &c.; °*sa-upapurāṇa*, n., °*sa-upâkhyāna*, n., °*so-darpa-bhaṅga*, m., °*so-dvi-śatī*, f., °*so-mata-tantra*, n., °*so-mahiman*, m., °*so-vākya*, n. N. of wks. **-vāhita**, n. a heavy load or burden, Rājat. iv, 18. **-vikatthana**, mfn. boasting in an arrogant or offensive manner, Daś. **-vikalpa**, m. unfounded irresolution, Daś.; mfn. very uncertain, Sch. **-vigāha**, mfn. = -*avag*°, Kāv.; Pañc.; difficult, dangerous, Prasannar. (also -*vigāhya*, MBh. xiii, 1840); m. N. of a son of Dhṛita-rāshṭra, MBh. i. **-vicāra**, m. an ill-placed hesitation, Daś.; mfn. very irresolute; -*tva*, n. Hcat. **-vicintita**, mfn. ill thought or found out, Var. **-vicintya**, mfn. hardly conceivable, MBh. **-viceshṭa**, mfn. ill-behaved, ib. **-vijñāna**, n. understanding with difficulty; (°*nd*), mfn. = next, ŚBr. **-vijñeya**, mfn. hardly conceivable, unintelligible, Āśv.; MBh. &c. **-vitarka** or °**kya**, mfn. difficult to be discussed or understood, BhP. **-vida**, mfn. d° to be known or discovered, MBh. **-vidagdha**, mfn. wrongly taught, wrong-headed, silly, Mṛicch. v, $\frac{1}{1}\frac{5}{6}$; Bhartṛ. &c. **-vidātra**, mfn. 'ill-disposed,' envious, ungracious, RV. **-vidya**, mfn. uneducated, ignorant, Rājat. i, 356. **-vidvas** (*dúr-*), mfn. evil-minded, malignant, RV. **-vidha**, mfn. acting in a bad manner, badly circumstanced, mean, poor, miserable, R.; SSaṃk.; stupid, silly (w. r. for -*vidya*?), L. **-vidhi**, m. 'bad fate,' misfortune, Kathās. xxi, 29. **-vinaya**, m. imprudent conduct, Pañc. v, $\frac{7}{8}$. **-vinīta**, mfn. badly educated, ill-conducted, undisciplined, mean, wicked, obstinate, restive, MBh., Kāv. &c. (°*taka*, id., Kathās. xx, 9); m. N. of a sage (associated with Durvāsas &c.), VarBṛS. xlviii, 63; of a prince. **-vipāka**, m. an evil consequence or result (esp. of actions in former births matured by time), Hit. i, $\frac{4}{4}\frac{8}{9}$; mfn. having evil consequences (esp. as result of actions in former births), Uttarar. i, 44. **-vibhāga**, m. pl. 'd° to be disunited,' N. of a people, MBh. ii. **-vibhāva** or °**vana** or °**vya**, mfn. d° to be perceived or understood, Kāv. **-vibhāsha**, mfn. d° to be uttered; n. harsh language, MBh. ii, 2187. **-vimarśa**, mfn. d° to be tried or examined, BhP. x, 49, 29. **-vimocana**, m. 'd° to be set free,' N. of a son of Dhṛita-rāshṭra, MBh. i. **-virecya**, mfn. d° to be purged, Suśr. **-virocana**, m. 'shining badly' (?), N. of a son of Dhṛita-rāshṭra, MBh. i. **-vilasita**, n. a wayward or rude or naughty trick, ill-mannered act, Prab. vi, $\frac{9}{10}$; Bālar. iv, 60. **-vivaktṛi**, m. one who answers wrongly, MBh. v, 1212. **-vivāha**, m. bad marriage, misalliance, Mn. iii, 41. **-vivecana**, mfn. d° to be judged or decided, Saṃk. on Bādar. **-viśa**, mfn. d° to be entered, R. vi, 19, 16. **-visha**, m. 'd° to be pervaded or approached,' N. of Śiva, MBh. xii, 10432. **-vishaha**, mfn. d° to be borne or supported, intolerable, irresistible, impracticable, MBh.; R.; BhP. (°*shahya*, id., MBh.; R.); m. N. of Śiva, MBh. xii, 10431; of a son of Dhṛita-rāshṭra, MBh. i. **-vṛitta**, n. bad conduct, meanness, MBh.; mfn. behaving badly, vile, mean; m. rogue, villain, MBh.; R. &c. **-vṛitti**, f. distress, misery, want, MBh.; R.; vice, crime, Hit. iii, 21 (v. l. *vṛitta*); juggling, fraud, W. **-vṛishala**, m. a bad Śūdra, L. **-vṛishṭi**, f. want of rain, drought, Jātakam. **-1. -veda**, mfn. (√1. -*vid*) having bad or little knowledge, ignorant, MBh. iii, 13437; difficult to be known, R. iv, 46, 2. **-2. -véda**, mfn. (√3. *vid*) d° to be found, ŚBr. **-vaira**, mfn. living in bad enmity, BhP. x, 13, 60. **-vyavasita**, n. an evil intention, Mudrār. iii, $\frac{1}{1}\frac{3}{4}$. **-vyavasthāpaka**, mfn. deciding or judging badly, Rājat. vi, 54. **-vyavahāra**, m. wrong judgment (in law), Kull. **-vyavahṛiti**, f. ill-report or rumour, Mcar. iii, 36. **-vyasana**, n. bad propensity, vice, Kathās. lxxiii, 73. **-vyāhṛita**, mfn. spoken badly or ill; n. a bad or unfit expression, MBh.; R. **-vrajita**, n. bad or improper manner of going, MBh. iii, 14669. **-vrata**, mfn. not obedient to rules, transgressing rules (cf. *daur-vratya*). **-háṇā**, f. (√*han*) mischief, harm, RV.; °*haṇāya*, Nom. P., p. °*yát*, meditating harm, ib. x, 134, 2; °*ṇāyú*, mfn. id., ib. iv, 30, 8; °*háṇā-vat*, mfn. inauspicious, pernicious, RV. viii, 2, 20; 18, 14. **-hanā** &c., see *haṇā*. **-hanu**, mf(*ū*)n. 'ugly-jawed,' RV.; TĀr. **-hala** or **-hali**, mfn. having a bad plough, Pāṇ. v, 4, 121, Kāś. **-hārd**, mfn. evil-minded, malignant, AV. **-hita** (*dúr-*), mfn. ill-conditioned, miserable, RV. viii, 19, 26; hostile, troublesome, AV. iv, 36, 9. **-huta**, mfn. badly offered (as sacrifice), MBh. xii, 559. **-hṛiṇāya**, Nom. P., p. °*yát*, furious, enraged, SV. (v.l. for *haṇ*°, RV.); °*yú*, mfn. id., i, 84, 16; vii, 59, 8. **-hṛita**, mfn. removed with difficulty, Car. **-hṛid**, mfn. bad-hearted, wicked; m. enemy, MBh. **-hṛidaya**, mfn. id. (g. *yuvâdi*; cf. *daur-h*°). **-hṛishīka**, mfn. having bad or uncontrolled organs of sense, MBh. iii, 13951.

Durasya, Nom. P. °*yáti*, to wish to hurt or injure, AV. i, 29, 2 &c.; °*syú*, mfn. wishing to do harm, AV. v, 3, 2; ĀpŚr. vi, 21, 1.

Durgá, mfn. (2. *dur* & √*gam*) difficult of access or approach, impassable, unattainable, AV.; Mn.; MBh. &c.; m. bdellium, L.; N. of an Asura (supposed to have been slain by the goddess Durgā, Skanda P.) and of sev. men (g. *naḍâdi*, Pāṇ. iv, 1, 99), esp. of the commentator on Yāska's Nirukta; also abridged for *durga-gupta, durgā-dāsa* &c. (see below); (*ā*), f. see *Durgā*; n. (m. only Pañc. v, 76; B n.) a difficult or narrow passage, a place difficult of access, citadel, stronghold (cf. *ab-, giri-* &c.); rough ground, roughness, difficulty, danger, distress, RV.; AV.; Mn.; MBh. &c. **-karman**, n. fortification, MBh.; R. **-kāraka**, m. 'making difficult or impassable,' the Bhojpatra or birch tree, L. **-gupta** (for °*gā-g*°, Pāṇ. vi, 3, 83), m. N. of a grammarian, Col. **-ghāta**, m. or n. N. of a fort, Rājat. **-ghna**, mfn. removing difficulties; (*ā*), f. N. of Durgā, Hariv. 6426. **-ṭīkā**, f. Durga's commentary (on Yāska's Nirukta &c.). **-taraṇī** & °**riṇī**, f. 'conveying over difficulties,' N. of the Sāvitrī-verse, MBh. ii, 451; Hariv. 14078. **-tā**, f. impassableness, R. iv, 27, 16. **-datta** (for °*gā-d*°, Pāṇ. vi, 3, 63), m. N. of a man, Cat. **-deśa**, m. an impassable region, Kāv. **-nāga**, m. N. of a man, L. **-nivāsin**, mfn. dwelling in a stronghold, W. **-pati** & **-pāla**, m. the commandant or governor of a fortress, Pañc.; BhP. **-pada-prabodha**, m. N. of a Comm. **-piśāca**, m. N. of a Mātaṅga, Kathās. **-pura**, n. a fortified city, W. **-pushpī**, f. N. of a plant (= *keśa-pushpā*), L. **-mārga**, m. a defile, a difficult pass or way, W. **-laṅghana**, m. 'making one's way through d° places,' a camel, L. **-vākya-prabodha**, m. 'knowledge of d° words,' N. of a work. **-vāsa**, m. staying over-night in unhospitable places, MBh. iii, 12344. **-vṛitti**, f. N. of wk. **-vyasana**, n. defect in a fortress (its being ill-guarded &c.), W. **-śaila**, m. N. of a mountain, MBh. **-saṃcara** or °**cāra**, m. difficult passage, defile, L.; Sch. **-sampad**, f. perfection or excellence of a fortress, W. **-saha**, mfn. overcoming difficulties or dangers, Hariv. 5018. **-siṇha** (for °*gā-s*°, P. vi, 3, 63), m. N. of a grammarian and of an astronomer, Cat.; (*ī*), f. D°'s commentary on the Kātantra. **-sena**, m. N. of an author, Cat. **Durgâkramaṇa**, n. the taking of a fort, MW. **Durgâcārya**, m. N. of a commentator on Yāska's Nirukta (= *durga*). **Durgâdhikārin** & °**dhyaksha**, m. the governor of a fortress, L. **Durgântarâtithi**, m. guest of the inside of a stronghold, a prisoner, MW. **Durgârohaṇa**, mfn. difficult to be ascended, R. **Durgâvarodha**, m. investing or besieging a fortress, W. **Durgâśrayaṇa**, n. taking refuge in a fortress, W.

Durgā, f. (of °*ga*, q.v.) the Indigo plant or Clitoria Ternatea, L.; a singing bird (= *śyāmā*), L.; N. of two rivers, MBh. vi, 337; 'the inaccessible or terrific goddess,' N. of the daughter of Himavat and wife of Śiva (also called Umā, Pārvatī &c., and mother of Kārttikeya and Gaṇêśa, cf. -*pūjā*), TĀr. x, 2, 3 (*d*° *devī*); MBh. &c.; of a princess, Rājat. iv, 659, and of other women. **-kavaca**, m. or n. N. of wk. **-kuṇḍa**, n. N. of a pool, W. **-tattva**, n. N. of wk. **-datta**, m. N. of the author of the Vṛitta-muktâvali. **-dāsa**, m. N. of Sch. on Vopadeva; of a physician, Cat.; of a prince, Kshitîś. **-navamī**, f. the ninth day of the light half of Kārttika (sacred to D°), L. **-pañcâṅga**, n. N. of wk. **-pūjā**, f. the chief festival in honour of D°, held in Bengal in the month Aśvin or about October, RTL. 197, 431; N. of a ch. of the PSarv. **-bhakti-taraṃgiṇī**, f., **-mahat-tva**, n., **-māhātmya**, n. (cf. *devīm*°), and **-°mṛita-rahasya** (°*gâm*°), n. N. of wks. **-yantra**, n. N. of a mystical diagram in the Tantra-sāra. **-°rāma** (°*gâr*°), m. N. of an author, Cat. **-°rcana-māhātmya** (°*gâr*°), n. N. of wk. **-vati**, f. N. of a princess, Inscr. **-vallabha**, m. a kind of perfume, Gal. **-vilāsa**, m. N. of a poem, Cat. **-°shṭamī** (°*gâsht*°), f. N. of a partic. eighth day connected with D°, Cat. **-saṃdeha-bhedikā**, f. N. of wk. **-sāvitrī**, f. (°*tri* only Vas. xxviii, 11) N. of RV. i, 99, 1, Vishṇ. lvi, 9. **-stava**, m., **-stuti**, f., **-stotra**, n. 'praise of D°,' N. of wks. **-°hlāda** (°*gâhl*°), m. a kind of perfume, Gal. (cf. °*gā-vallabha*). **Durgôtsava**, m., -*tattva*, n. N. of two treatises.

Durgi, f. N. of a deity (also = *durgā*) TĀr. x, 1, 7.

Durgilā, f. N. of a woman, HPariś.

Duś, in comp. for *dus* (p. 488). **-cakshas**, mfn. evil-eyed, TBr. **-√car**, to act wrongly or badly towards (acc.), to behave badly, MW. **-cara**, mfn. difficult to be gone or passed; d° to be performed, MBh.; Hariv.; K.; Pur. (-*tva*, n. R. v, 86, 14); going with trouble or difficulty; acting ill, behaving wickedly, W.; m. a bear; a bivalve shell (prob. both as moving slowly), L.; -*cārin*, mfn. practising very difficult penance, MW. **-carita** (*dúś-*), n. misbehaviour, misdoing, ill-conduct, wickedness, VS. iv, 28; Mn.; MBh. &c.; pl. (Buddh.) the 10 chief sins (viz. murder, theft, adultery, lying, calumny, lewdness, evil speech, covetousness, envy, heresy; cf. MWB. 126); mfn. misbehaving, wicked, Kathās (also °*tin*, Lāṭy. iv, 3, 10). **-carmaka**, n. leprosy, L. **-cárman**, mfn. affected with a skin-disease, leprous, TS.; TBr.; Yājñ.; having no prepuce, L. **-cāritra** (MBh.) and **-cārin** (Kathās.), mfn. = -*carita*. **-cikitsa**, mfn. difficult to be cured, BhP. iv, 30, 38; (*ā*), f. (med.) a wrong treatment, Kull.; °*tsita*, mfn. = °*tsa*, ib.; °*tsya*, mfn. id., Suśr.; Car. (superl. -*tama*, Suśr.; n. -*tva*, Kull.) **-cit**, mfn. thinking evil, AV. **-citta**, mfn. melancholy, sad, Kāraṇḍ. **-cintita**, n. a bad or foolish thought, Kathās. **-cintin**, mfn. 'thinking evil thoughts,' N. of a Māra-putra, Lalit. **-cintya**, mfn. difficult to be understood, MBh. **-ceshṭa**, f. misconduct, error, K.; °*ṭita*, n. id., ib.; mfn. misbehaving, doing evil, W. **-cyavaná**, mfn. d° to be felled, unshaken, RV.; AV.; m. N. of Indra, Pratāp. **-cyāva**, mfn. id.; °*vana*, mfn. shaking the unshaken, MBh. viii, 1506 = -*cyavana*, W. **-chada**, mfn. badly covering (the body), R. ii, 32, 31; hardly covered, tattered, W. **-chāya**, mfn. having a bad complexion, looking unwell, Car. **-chid**, mfn. difficult to be cut or destroyed (enemy), Kām. xiv, 68. **-chinna**, mfn. badly cut out or extracted (thorn), MBh. xii, 5307.

1. Dush, in comp. for *dus* (p. 488). **-kara**, mfn. hard to be done or borne, difficult, arduous, Br.; Mn.; MBh. &c. (often with inf.; °*ram yad* or *yadi*, with indic. or Pot. and also with inf. = hardly, scarcely, MBh.; R.); rare, extraordinary, MBh.; Kathās.; doing wrong, behaving ill, wicked, bad, W.; n. difficult act, difficulty, ib.; austerity, Divyâv. 392; aether, air, L.; the tree of plenty, W.; -*karman* (v. l. *dushkarma-kārin*), mfn. doing difficult things, clever, Daś.; -*kārin*, mfn. id.; experiencing difficulties, R. &c. (°*ritā*, f. MBh. xii, 5886); -*caryā*, f. hard penance, N. of a ch. of Lalit.; -*sādhana*, n. means of overcoming difficulties, Daś. **-karaṇa**, n. a difficult or miserable work, Kāś. on Pāṇ. vi, 2, 14. **-karṇa**, m. N. of a son of Dhṛita-rāshṭra, MBh. i. **-karman**, n. wickedness, sin; any difficult or painful act, MBh.; mfn. acting wickedly, criminal, ib.; °*ma-sūdana*, mf(*ī*)n. destroying criminals, Śatr. **-kalevara**, n. 'the bad or miserable body,' BhP. **-kāyastha-kula**, n. 'the miserable writer-caste,' Rājat. **-kāla**, m. an evil time, HPariś.; 'bad or all-destroying Time,' R.; N. of Śiva, MBh. xii, 10418. **-kīrti**, f. dishonour, BhP.; mfn. infamous, of bad repute, ib. **-kula**, n. a low family or race, Mn.; MBh.; R.; mfn. of a low family, low-born, Hariv.; Bhartṛ. (-*tā*, f. Sāh.); °*līna*, mfn. id., MBh.; R.; m. a sort of perfume, L. **-kuhaka**, mfn. incredulous, Divyâv. 7; 9 &c. **-kṛit**, mfn. acting wickedly, criminal, evil-doer, RV.; AV.; MBh. **-kṛita** (*dúsh-*), mfn. wrongly or wickedly done, badly arranged or organized or applied, ŚBr. viii, 6, 2, 18; MBh. &c.; (°*tá*), n. evil action, sin, guilt, RV.; ŚBr.; ChUp.; Mn.; MBh. &c.; a partic. class of sins, Divyâv. 544; -*kárman*, mfn. acting wickedly, criminal, Mn.; Yājñ.; R.; n. wicked deed, wickedness, W.; °*ta-bahish-kṛita*, mfn. free from sin, W.; °*tâtman*, mfn. evil-minded, wicked, base, BhP. **-kṛiti**, mfn. acting wickedly, an evil-doer, MBh.; R.; °*tin*, id., ib. **-kṛishṭa**, mfn. badly ploughed, ill-cultivated, AitBr. iii, 38. **-krama**, mfn. ill-arranged, unmethodical (-*tā*, f. Kāvyapr.); difficult of access; going ill, W. **-kriyā**, f. evil act, a misdemeanour, MW. **-krīta**, mf(*ā*)n. badly or dearly bought, Nār. **-kha** &c., see *duḥkha*. **-khadira**, m. a tree related to the Acacia

Catechu, L. **-ṭanu**, mfn. having an ugly body, AV. iv, 7, 3. **-ṭara**, mfn. difficult to be passed or overcome or endured; unconquerable, irresistible; incomparable, excellent, RV.; AV. (cf. *dus-t°*); *-tárītu*, mfn. id., RV.; TS.; N. of a man, ŚBr. xii, 9, 3, 1. **-ṭuta** (*dushṭuta*), see *duḥ-shṭuta*; *-°ti*, see *duḥ-shṭuti* (under *duḥ*). **-paca**, mfn. difficult to be digested, L. **-patana**, n. falling badly, L. **-pattra**, n. a kind of perfume (= *cora*), L. **-páda**, mfn. unfathomable or inaccessible (river), RV. i, 53, 9. **-parājaya**, m. 'd° to be conquered,' N. of a son of Dhṛita-rāshṭra, MBh. i. **-parigraha**, mfn. d° to be seized or kept, Kām. **-pariṇāma**, w. r. for *°māna*, mfn. of undefined extent, Kauś. 139. **-parimṛishṭa**, mfn. badly considered, Suśr. **-parihántu**, mfn. d° to be removed or destroyed, RV. ii, 27, 6. **-parîkshya**, mfn. d° to be investigated or examined, MBh. **-parśa** (*dushparśa*) = *duḥ-sparśa* (see *duḥ*). **-pāna**, mfn. d° to be drunk, Pāṇ. iii, 3, 128, Kāś. **-pāra**, mfn. d° to be crossed or overcome or accomplished, MBh. &c. **-pārshṇi-graha** or **-grāha**, mfn. having a dangerous enemy in the rear, Kām. **-pīta**, mfn. badly drunk, Pāṇ. viii, 3, 41, Kāś. **-putra**, m. a bad son, MBh. **-purusha**, m. a bad man (g. *brāhmaṇâdi*). **-pūra**, mfn. difficult to be filled or satisfied, MBh. &c. **-peshaṇa**, mfn. d° to be pounded or crushed, ĀpŚr. viii, 5, 40, Comm. **-posha**, mfn. d° to be nourished; *-tā*, f. L. **-prakampa** and *°pya*, mfn. d° to be shaken or agitated, immovable, MBh.; Hariv. **-prakāśa**, mfn. 'lighting badly,' obscure, dark, MBh. **-prakṛiti**, f. a mean nature or bad character, Kād.; mfn. evil-natured, bad-tempered, MBh. **-prakriyā**, f. little authority, Rājat. viii, 4. **-praja** (BhP.) and **°jas** (Pāṇ. v, 4, 122), mfn. having bad offspring. **-prajña**, mfn. weak-minded, stupid, MBh.; *-tva*, n. stupidity, Prab. vi, 1/8. **-prajñāna**, n. want of understanding, weak intellect, MBh.; (*°ná*), mfn. = *-prajña*, TBr. **-praṇīta**, mfn. badly led or conducted, ill-managed, MBh.; R.; n. ill-conduct or behaviour, MBh. **-pratara**, mfn. difficult to be passed or overcome, MBh.; R. **-pratigráha**, mfn. d° to be taken or laid hold of, AV. x, 10, 28. **-prativāraṇa**, mfn. d° to be averted, R. iii, 31, 49. **-prativîkshaṇīya** or **°kshya**, mfn. d° to be looked at, dazzling, MBh.; R. **-pratyabhijña**, mfn. d° to be recognised, Caṇḍ. **-prada**, mfn. causing pain or sorrow, R. (B.) ii, 106, 29. **-pradharsha**, mfn. not to be assailed or touched, intangible, MBh.; R.; m. N. of a son of Dhṛita-rāshṭra, MBh. vi; (*ā*), f. Alhagi Maurorum or Phœnix Sylvestris, L.; *°shaṇa*, mf(*ī*)n. id., MBh.; R.; m. N. of a son of Dhṛita-rāshṭra, MBh. i.; (*ī*), f. Melangena Incurva, L. *°shiṇī*, f. N. of various egg-plants, Bhpr.; v. r. for prec., L. *°dhṛishya*, mfn. = *°dharsha*, MBh.; R. **-prapadana**, mfn. difficult to be attained or entered, Sāy. on RV. i, 59, 3. **-prabodha**, mfn. awaking with difficulty, Bhpr. **-prabhañjana**, m. hurricane, Mcar. vii, 12. **-pramaya**, mfn. d° to be measured, W. **-prayukta**, mfn. falsely used, Vām. v, 2, 55. **-pralambha**, mfn. d° to be deceived, Āp. **-pravāda**, m. ill speech, slander, Kathās. **-pravṛitti**, f. bad news, Ragh. **-praveśa**, mfn. difficult to be entered, MBh.; R.; d° to be introduced, Suśr.; (*ā*), f. a species of Opuntia, L. **-prasaha**, mfn. d° to be borne or supported or suffered, irresistible; terrible, frightful, MBh.; Kāv.; m. N. of a Jaina teacher, Śatr. **-prasāda** (MBh.) and **°dana** (BhP.), mfn. d° to be propitiated. **-prasādhana** (MBh.) and **°dhya** (Kām.), mfn. d° to be managed or dealt with. **-prasāha**, w. r. for *°saha*. **-prasū**, f. bringing forth (children) with difficulty, Suśr. **-praharsha**, m. 'bad rejoicing,' N. of a son of Dhṛita-rāshṭra, MBh. i. **-prâpa** or **°paṇa** or **°pya**, mfn. hard to attain, inaccessible, remote, MBh.; K.; Pur. &c. **-prâpta**, w. r. for *-prâpa*. **-prâví**, mfn. 'badly heeding,' unkind, unfriendly, RV. iv, 25, 6. **-prīti**, f. displeasure (cf. *jana-*, add.) **-prêksha** or **°kshaṇīya** or **°kshya**, mfn. difficult to be looked at, disagreeable to the sight, MBh.; Kāv. &c. **-prêkshita**, mfn. badly looked at, VarBṛS. ii, 23. **-vápnya** (*dushvápnya*), see *duḥ-shv°*.

Dushṭhu. See *duḥ-shṭhu* under *duḥ*.

Dushmanta, w. r. for *Dushyanta* below.

Dushyanta, m. (fr. *dus* + √*so*? or p. of √*dush*?, older form *duḥ-shanta*) N. of a prince of the lunar race (descendant of Puru, husband of Śakuntalā and father of Bharata), MBh.; Śak.; Pur.

Dushvanta, w. r. for *Dushyanta* above.

Dus, ind. a prefix to nouns and rarely to verbs or adverbs (Pāṇ. ii, 1, 6; 2, 18; Vārtt. 2, Pat.; iii, 3, 126 &c.) implying evil, bad, difficult, hard; badly, hardly; slight, inferior &c. (opp. to *su*), often = Engl. *in-* or *un-* [cf. √*2. dush*; Zd. *dush-*; Gr. δυσ-; Goth. *tuz-*; O.H.G. *zur-*]. It becomes *dur* (q.v.) before vowels and soft consonants; *dū* (q.v.) before *r* and sometimes before *d, dh, n*, which become *ḍ, ḍh, ṇ*; remains unchanged before *t, th* (in older language however *shṭ, shṭh*); becomes *dush* (q.v.), rarely *duḥ* before *k, kh; p, ph*; *duś* (q.v.) before *c, ch*; *duḥ* (q.v.), rarely *duś, dush, dus*, before *ś, sh, s*. **-tapa**, mfn. difficult to be endured (penance), Śatr. **-tara**, mfn. (cf. *sh-ṭ°*) difficult to be passed or overcome, unconquerable, invincible, MBh.; Kāv. &c. **-taraṇa**, mf(*ī*)n. id., MBh. **-tarka**, m. false reasoning, wrong argument, BhP.; *-mūla*, mfn. founded on it, MW. **-tarkya**, mfn. difficult to be supposed or reasoned about, ib. **-tāra** and **-tīrṇa**, mfn. = *-tara*, MBh. **-tithi**, m. an inauspicious lunar day, MBh. xii, 6735. **-tīrtha**, mfn. offering a bad ford or descent (river), MBh. v, 7363. **-tosha**, mfn. difficult to be satisfied, MBh., BhP. **-tyajya**, mfn. difficult to be relinquished or quitted, MBh.; R. &c. **-tyājya**, mfn. id., Śāntiś.

Dustha, dusthita, duspṛishṭa. See *duḥ-stha* &c. under *duḥ*.

1. Dū, in comp. for *dus* above. **-ḍábha** or **-ḍábha**, mfn. difficult to be deceived, RV. **-ḍáś**, mfn. not worshipping, irreligious, RV. **-ḍāśa**, mfn. id., Pāṇ. vi, 3, 109, Vārtt. 5, Pat. **-ḍhí**, mfn. malevolent, RV. **-ḍhya**, mfn. id., Pāṇ., ib. **-ṇáśa**, mfn. unattainable, inaccessible, RV. iii, 56, 8. **-ṇāśa**, mfn. (fr. √*1. naś*) id., RV. vi, 27, 8; Pāṇ. ib.; N. of an Ekâha, ŚrS.; (fr. √*2. naś*) imperishable, incessant, perpetual. **-rakta**, mfn. badly coloured or dyed, Pāṇ. viii, 3, 14, Kāś. **-rakshya**, mfn. difficult to be guarded or preserved, Mṛicch. iv, 1/8. **-rada**, mfn. difficult to be scratched, hard, Śiś. xix, 106. **-rādha**, mfn. difficult to be accomplished, TāṇḍyaBr. xx, 11. **-rūḍha**, mfn. badly grown or cicatrized; *-°tva*, n., Suśr. **-roha**, mfn. difficult to be ascended or reached, AitBr. iv, 20. **-rohaṇa**, mfn. id.; n. N. of a difficult recitation of a verse in 7 ways (1 Pāda, 2 Pādas, 3 Pādas, the whole verse, 3 Pādas, 2 Pādas, 1 Pāda), MaitrS.; VS. &c.; *°ṇīya*, mfn. recited in that way, ŚāṅkhBr.

दुराक *durāka*, m. N. of a barbarous tribe, L.

दुरु *duru*, m. N. of a mountain, MBh. xiii, 7658.

दुरुःफ *duruḥpha*, m. (astrol.) N. of the 15th Yoga (v.l. *durapha* and *durupha*).

दुरुधरा *durudharā*, f. a peculiar position of the moon (δορυφορία), Var.

दुरोदर *duro-dara*. See under 1. *dur*.

दुर्दुरूट *durdurūṭa* and *durdh°*. See under 2. *dur*.

दुर्द्रिता *durdritā*, f. a kind of creeping plant, L.

दुर्व् *durv*, cl. 1. P. *dūrvati*, to hurt, injure, kill, Dhātup. xv, 63 (cf. √*dhurv*).

दुर्वारि *durvāri*. See *-vāraṇa* under 2. *dur*.

दुल् *dul*, cl. 10. P. *dolayati*, to swing, throw up, shake to and fro, Bhartṛ. iii, 43 (cf. *tul, dola, dolāya*).

Dulā́, f. 'shaking,' one of the 7 Kṛittikās, TS., Comm.

दुलयते *dul-ayate* = *dur-ayate*. See *dur-*√*i* under 2. *dur*.

दुलारभट्टाचार्य *dulāra-bhaṭṭâcārya*, m. N. of an author, Cat.

दुलि *duli*, m. N. of a sage, L.; (*ī*), f. a small or female tortoise, L. (Cf. *dauleya*.)

दुलिदुह *duliduha*, m. N. of a prince, MBh.; Hariv.

दुलोक *duloka*, m. N. of a poet, Cat.

दुल्लल *dullala* (?) = *romaśa*, L.

दुवन्यसद् *duvanya-sád*, mfn. (fr. √*1. du*) dwelling among the distant (Dadhi-krāvan), RV. iv, 40, 2 (Sāy. among the worshippers, cf. 2. *dúvas*).

1. **Duvás**, mfn. stirring, restless (Soma), RV. i, 168, 3. **Duvasana**, mfn. id. (eagle), iv, 6, 10.

दुवस् 2. *dúvas*, n. (fr. 3. *dū*, a collateral form to *dā* as *gū* to *gā*, *pū* to *pā*, *sthū* to *sthā*; cf. *agre-gū*, *-pū*, *sthavira*) gift, oblation, worship, honour, reverence, RV. i, 14, 1 &c. (165, 14 *duvás*, prob. gift, liberality). **-√kṛi**, to worship (loc.), RV. **-vat** (*dúv°*), mfn. offering or enjoying worship, VS.

Duvasya, Nom. P. *°yáti*, to honour, worship, celebrate, reward, RV. iii, 2, 8 &c.; give as a reward, i, 119, 10. *°syú*, mfn. worshipping, reverential, viii, 91, 2.

Duvo, in comp. for *dúvas* above. **-√dhā**, to worship (loc.), RV. **-yā́**, f. (instr.) worship, RV. v, 36, 3. **-yú**, mfn. worshipping, honouring, vi, 36, 5; (*ú*), ind. reverently, 51, 4; out of acknowledgment, as a reward, vii, 18, 14; 25.

दुश्चिक्य *duścikya*, n. N. of the 3rd lunar mansion, Var.

दुष् 2. *dush*, cl. 4. P. *dushyati* (*°te*, MBh.; pf. *dudosha*; fut. *dokshyati*, *doshṭā*, Siddh.; aor. *adushat*, Pāṇ. iii, 1, 55; *adukshat*, Vop.) to become bad or corrupted, to be defiled or impure, to be ruined, perish; to sin, commit a fault, be wrong, AitBr.; ChUp.; MBh. &c.: Caus. *dūshâyati* (ep. also *°te*), see under *dūsha*; *doshayati* (Pāṇ. vi, 4, 91), to spoil or corrupt (the mind).

Dushṭa, mfn. spoilt, corrupted; defective, faulty; wrong, false; bad, wicked; malignant, offensive, inimical; guilty, culpable, ŚrS.; Mn.; Yājñ.; Suśr.; MBh. &c.; sinning through or defiled with (cf. *karma-*, *mano-*, *yoni-*, *vāg-*); m. a villain, rogue; a kind of noxious animal, Vishṇ. xii, 2; (*ā*), f. a bad or unchaste woman, L.; n. sin, offence, crime, guilt, Hariv., R. (cf. *śruti-*); Costus Speciosus or Arabicus, L. **-gaja**, m. a vicious elephant, MW. **-caritra**, mfn. ill-conducted, evil-doer, Pañc. i, 2 1/8 . **-cārin**, mfn. id., MBh.; R. &c. **-cetas**, mfn. evil-minded, malevolent, Mn.; R. **-tā**, f. or **-tva**, n. badness, wickedness; falsehood; defilement, violation, R.; Mṛicch.; Pañc. **-damana**, n. 'taming of the bad,' N. of wk.; *-kāvya*, n. N. of a poem. **-durjana**, m. villain, reprobate, Kāv. **-dhī**, mfn. = *-cetas*, MW. **-nāśinī**, f. N. of a deity, Cat. **-baṭuka**, m. a bad fellow, villain, Mṛicch. i, 4/4. **-buddhi**, mfn. ill-disposed against (*upari*), Pañc.; m. N. of a villain, Kathās. **-bhāva**, mfn. evil-natured, malignant, vicious, Āp.; MBh.; R.; *-tā*, f. R. i, 3, 11. **-mati**, mfn. = *-cetas*, MW. **-mānasa**, mf(*ī*)n. id., ib. **-yoni-prâpti-vicāra**, m., **-rajo-darśana-śānti**, f. N. of wks. **-lāṅgala**, n. N. of a partic. form of the moon, Var. **-vāc**, mfn. uttering bad language, Mn. viii, 386. **-vānara**, m. a vicious monkey, Ratn. ii, 3/4. **-vṛisha**, m. a vicious or stubborn ox, W. **-vraṇa**, m. a dull boil or sore; a sinus, W. **-hṛidaya**, mfn. bad-hearted, Daś.

Dushṭâtura, mfn. a bad or disobedient patient, Kaṭh. lx, 120 **Dushṭâtman**, mfn. evil-minded, malevolent, MBh.; *°ṭântarātman*, id. **Dushṭânvita**, mfn. defiled, rendered impure, W.

Dúshṭi, f. corruption, defilement, depravity, AV.; growing worse (of a wound &c.), Suśr.; Car. *°ṭīya*, Nom. P. *°yati*, to become bad or corrupted, Pāṇ. vii, 4, 36, Sch.

Dūsha, mfn. defiling, corrupting (ifc.; cf. *kora-*, *paṅkti-*). **Dūshaka**, mf(*ikā*)n. corrupting, spoiling, disgracing, seducing, Mn.; MBh.; R. &c. (*°shika* only Divyâv.); offending, transgressing (gen. or comp.), Hariv. 5635; Mṛicch. ix, 40; sinful, wicked, MBh. xii, 1236 &c.; m. offender, seducer, disparager (*vedānām*, MBh. xiii, 1639; *prakṛitinām*, Mn. ix, 232); (*ikā*), f. impurity or impure secretion of the eyes, Mn.; Suśr.; a kind of rice, Suśr.; pencil or paint-brush, L.

Dū́shaṇa, mf(*ī*)n. corrupting, spoiling, vitiating, violating, AV.; ŚāṅkhGṛ. &c.; counteracting, sinning against (comp.), R. ii, 109, 7 (cf. *arāti-d°*, *kula-d°*, *kṛityā-d°*, *khara-d°*, *loka-d°*, *visha-d°*, *vishkandha-d°*); m. N. of a Rakshas (general of Rāvaṇa), MBh.; R. &c.; of a Daitya slain by Śiva, ŚivaP.; (*ā*), f. N. of the wife of Bhauvana and mother of Tvashṭṛi, BhP. v, 15, 13; n. the act of corrupting &c. (see above), Mn.; MBh. &c.; dishonouring, detracting, disparaging, MBh.; Mṛicch.; Kathās. &c.; objection, adverse argument, refutation, Sarvad.; Jaim.; Kap., Schol.; fault, offence, guilt, sin, Mn.; Kāv.; Hit. &c. (cf. *artha-d°*, *sukṛita-d°*, *strī-d°*). **-tā**, f. the being a fault,

ŚārṅgP.; *-vādin*, m. opponent, adversary (in a disputation), Nyāyas., Comm. °**ṇâri**, m. 'the enemy of D°,' N. of Rāma, L. °**ṇâvaha**, mfn. occasioning guilt, MW. °**ṇôddhāra**, m. N. of wk. °**shaṇīya**, mfn. = 1. °*shya*, L.

Dūsháya, Nom. P. °*yati* (ep. also °*te*) to corrupt, spoil, contaminate, vitiate (of moral corruption also *doshayati*, see 2. *dush*), AV.; Mn.; MBh.; Kāv. &c.; to dishonour or violate (a woman), Mn. viii, 364; MBh. &c.; (astrol.) to cause evil or misfortune, Var.; to adulterate, falsify, MBh. xiii, 1683; to object, refute, disprove, blame, ib.; Kathās. &c.; to retract or break (*vācam*, one's word), MBh. xii, 7256; to find fault with, accuse, MBh.; R.; (*paras-param*, each other), Pañc. i, $\frac{445}{446}$; to offend, hurt, injure (gen.), R. ii, 74, 3; MBh. iv, 2228 &c. °**shayat**, mfn. making bad, corrupting, defiling, MW. °**shayāṇa**, mfn. id., W. °**shayitṛi**, m. corrupter (see *kanyā-d°*). °**shayitnu**, m. id., Vop.

Dūshi, mfn. corrupting, ruining, destroying (ifc.; cf. *arāti-d°*, *ātma-d°*, *kṛityā-d°*, *tanū-d°*); f. a poisonous substance, AV.; = next, L. **Dūshī** (or °*shikā*), f. the rheum of the eyes (cf. °*shikā* under °*shaka*), AV.; ŚBr.; Suśr.; *-visha*, n. a vegetable poison spoilt through age or decomposition, Suśr.; mfn. slightly poisonous, Car.; °*shâri*, m. a kind of antidote, Suśr. **Dūshy-udara**, n. a disease of the abdomen caused by poisonous substances; °*rin*, mfn. affected with this disease, Suśr. (°*shyod°*, a wrong formation for °*shy-ud°*).

Dūshita, mfn. spoiled, corrupted, contaminated, defiled, violated, hurt, injured, Mn.; MBh.; Kāv. &c.; censured, blamed, MBh.; Kathās.; calumniated, blemished, compromised, falsely accused of (often in comp., see *manyu-*, *śatrûpajāpa-*), Mn. vi, 66 (v.l. *bhūshita*), viii, 64 &c.; MBh.; Bhartṛ.; Pañc. &c.; (*ā*), f. a girl who has been violated or deflowered, W. **-tva**, n. Sarvad.

Dūshin, mfn. corrupting, polluting, violating (ifc.; cf. *kanyā-*), MBh.; Yājñ.

1. **Dūshya**, mfn. corruptible, liable to be soiled or defiled or disgraced or ruined, MBh.; Kām.; reprehensible, culpable, vile, bad; m. wicked man, a villain, R.; Kām.; n. matter, pus; poison, L. **-yukta**, mfn. associated with a vile rascal, Kām. xiii, 70.

Dūshyat, mfn. offending, Yājñ. ii, 296 (for °*shayat*?).

दुस्सथ *dussatha*, m. (w. r. or Prākr. for *duḥ-saktha*?) a cock or dog, L.

दुस्सनि *dussani*, m. (*dus* + *sani*, gift or giver?) N. of a man, Rājat. iv, 167.

दुह् 1. *duh*, cl. 1. P. *dohati*, to pain, Dhātup.

दुह् 2. *duh* (orig. *dugh*, cf. *dúghāna*, *dugha* &c., and the initial *dh* of some forms), cl. 2. P. Ā. *dogdhi*; *dugdhe* or *duhé*, RV. &c. (pl. Ā. *duhaté*, ix, 19, 5 &c.; *duhrate*, i, 134, 6 &c.; *duhré*, vii, 101, 1 &c.; impf. P. *ádhok*, iii, 19, 7; *duhúr*, ii, 34, 10 &c.; Ā. *adugdha* [according to Pāṇ. vii, 3, 73 aor.], pl. *aduhran*, AV. viii, 10, 14; 3 sg. *aduha*, pl. °*hra*, MaitrS. [cf. Pāṇ. vii, 1, 8; 41, Kāś.]; Impv. *dhukshva*, RV.; AV.; 3 sg. *duhām*, RV. i, 164, 27; pl. *duhrām*, °*rátām*, AV.; *dhugdhvam*, ĀśvŚr.; Subj. *dohat* [3 pl. °*hān*, Br.], °*hate*, RV.; Pot. *duhīyat*, RV. ii, 11, 21; °*yán*, i, 120, 9; Ā. °*hīta*, ii, 18, 8; p. P. *duhát*, Ā. *duhāná*, *dúhāna*, and *dúgh°*, RV.); cl. 6. P. Ā. *duháti*, °*te*, RV. &c.; cl. 4. *duhyati*, °*te*, MBh.; pf. *dudóha* [°*hitha*, RV. ii, 3, 16], *duduhé*, 3 pl. *duduhur* [*dudūhur*, BhP. v, 15, 9], RV. &c.; Ā. *duduhre*, RV. iii, 57, 2 &c. [ix, 70, 1, SV. °*hrire*]; fut. *dhokshyati*, °*te*, Pāṇ. viii, 2, 37, Kāś.; aor. *ádhukshat*, °*shata* [3 sg. ix, 2, 3, pl. 110, 8], *adukshat*, i, 33, 10; *dukshata*, 3 sg. i, 160, 3; Impv. *dhukshásva*, RV.; Pot. *dhukshīmáhi*, TS. i, 6, 4, 3; inf. *dogdhum*, MBh. &c.; *dogdhos*, ŚBr.; *duhádhyai* and *doháse*, RV.; ind. p. *dugdhvā*, ŚBr.) to milk (a cow or an udder), fig. take advantage of (cf. ἀμέλγεσθαι), enjoy; to milk or squeeze out, extract (milk, Soma, e.g. any good thing); draw anything out of another thing (with 2 acc.), RV. &c. &c.; (mostly Ā.) to give milk, yield any desired object (acc., rarely gen.), RV. &c. &c.: Pass. *duhyáte*, aor. *adohi* (Pāṇ. iii, 1, 63, Kāś.) to be milked, to be drawn or extracted from, RV.; AV.; MBh. &c.: Caus. *dohdyati*, °*te*, aor. *adūduhat*, Pass. *dohyáte*, to cause to milk or be milked; to milk, milk out, extract, ŚBr.; Vait.; Mn.; BhP.: Desid. *dúdukshati* (RV.), *dudhukshati* (Bhartṛ. ii, 38, cf. *dudhukshu*), to wish to milk.

3. **Duh**, mfn. (nom. *dhuk*) milking; yielding, granting (cf. *kāma-*, *go-* &c.) **Duha**, mfn. id. ifc.

Duhitṛi, f. a daughter (the milker or drawing milk from her mother [cf. Zd. *dughdar*, Gk. θυγάτηρ, Goth. *dauhtar*, Lith. *duktė*, Slav. *dushti*]). °**tā-mātṛi**, f. du. daughter and mother, Kathās. xcviii, 54. °**tuḥ-pati**, m. a daughter's husband, Pāṇ. vi, 3, 24, Kāś. °**tṛi-tva**, n. the condition of a daughter, MBh.; Pur. **-pati**, m. = °*tuḥ-p°*, Pāṇ. ib. **-mat**, mfn. having a daughter, GS.

Duhya, mfn. to be milked, milkable, W.

दुह्यु *duhyu*, w. r. for *druhyu*.

दू 2. *dū*, f. (fr. √2. *du*) pain, distress. **-da**, mfn. afflicting, harassing, L. (For 1. *dū*, see p. 488, col. 2.)

1. **Dūtaka**, m. N. of Agni in the form of a forest conflagration, Gṛihyas. (cf. *dava*, *dāva*).

Dūná, mfn. (Pāṇ. viii, 2, 45) burnt, afflicted, distressed, AV.; MBh. &c.

Dūyana, n. heat (of the body), fever, Car.

दू 3. *dū* = 2. *dúvas*, only nom. acc. pl. *dúvas*, RV. (cf. *á-dū*).

दूत *dūtá*, m. (prob. fr. √1. *du*; cf. *dūrá*) a messenger, envoy, ambassador, negotiator, RV.; AV.; ŚBr.; MBh. &c. (°*taya*, Nom. P. °*yati*, to employ as m° or a°, Naish); (*ī*), f. female messenger, esp. procuress, go-between, RV.; MBh.; Kāv. &c.; a kind of bird (= *sārikā*), L.; N. of a female attendant on Durgā, W. **-karman**, n. business or duty of a m°, MBh.; Pañc. **-ghnī**, f. 'm°-killer,' N. of a plant, L. **-tva**, n. the office or state of a m°, Pañc. **-parîkshā**, f. N. of wk. **-mukha**, mf(*ī*)n. 'having an ambassador as mouth,' speaking by an a°, Śiś. ii, 82. **-mocana**, n. 'liberation of an a°,' N. of a ch. of the GaṇP. **-lakshaṇa**, n. N. of wk. **-vat**, mfn. having a messenger, Kaush-Up. ii, 1. **-vākya**, n. and *-prabandha*, m. N. of wks. **-sampreshaṇa**, n. the sending forth ambassadors, Mn. vii, 153. **Dūtâṅgada**, m. 'Aṅgada as messenger,' N. of an act of the Mahā-nāṭaka; n. of a Chāyā-nāṭaka by Subhaṭa. **Dūti-tva**, w. r. for °*tī-tva*, n. the office or state of a procuress, Śukas. **Dutī-prakāśa**, m., °**tī-lakshaṇa**, n., °**ty-upahāsa**, m. N. of wks.

2. **Dūtaka**, m. a messenger, ambassador (cf. *deva-*); (*ikā*), f. a female m°, confidante, Pañc.; Vet.; a gossiping or mischief-making woman, Rājat. °**tikā**, f. = prec. f., L. °**tya**, n. the state or office of an ambassador; an embassy, message, RV.; Hcar. &c.

दून *dūna*. See under 2. *dū*.

दूप्र *dūpra*, mfn. strong, L. (cf. *dṛipra*).

दूर् *dūr*, N. of the Prâṇa or vital breath regarded as a deity, ŚBr.

दूर *dūrá*, mf(*ā*)n. (prob. fr. √1. *du*, but see Uṇ. ii, 21; compar. *dávīyas*, superl. *davishṭha*, qq.vv.) distant, far, remote, long (way); n. distance, remoteness (in space and time), a long way, ŚBr.; MBh.; Kāv. &c.; (*ám*), ind. far. far from (gen. or abl., Pāṇ. ii, 3, 34, Kāś.), a long way off or a long period back, RV.; AV.; ŚBr &c. (also *dūrád dūrám*, AV. xii, 2, 14); far above (*ut-patati*, Hit. i, $\frac{101}{102}$) or below (*ambhasi*, Kathās. x, 29); far, i.e. much, in a high degree (*dūram un-manī-kṛita*, Prab. iii, $\frac{21}{22}$); *dūraṃ-√kṛi*, to surpass, exceed, Ragh. xvii, 18; °*ṃ-karaṇa*, mf(*ī*)n. making far or distant, removing, Vop. (v.l.); °*ṃ-gata*, mfn. = °*ra-g°*, Śaṃk.; °*ṃ-gamá*, mfn. going far away, VS. xxxiv, 1; (*ā*), f. (scil. *bhūmi*) one of the 10 stages in the life of a Śrāvaka, L.; (*eṇa*), ind. (Pāṇ. ii, 3, 35) far, from afar, by far, MBh.; Kāv. &c.; compar. °*ra-tareṇa*, VP. iii, 7, 26, 33; (*āt*), ind. (Pāṇ. ib.) from a distance, from afar, RV.; AV.; MBh. &c.; far from (abl.), Mn. iv, 151; a long way back or from a remote period, iii, 130; in comp. with a pp., e.g. *dūrád-āgata*, come from afar, Pāṇ. ii, 1, 39; vi, 1, 2; 2, 144, Kāś.; (*e*), ind. (Pāṇ. ii, 3, 36, Kāś.) in a distant place, far, far away, RV. i, 24, 9; iv, 4, 3 (opp. *ánti*) &c., AV.; ŚBr.; TśUp. 5 (opp. *antike*); Mn.; MBh. &c.; compar. °*ra-tare*, some way from (abl.), Mn. xi, 128; *dūre-√kṛi*, to discard, Amar. 67; *dūre-√bhū* or *-√gam*, to be far away or gone off, Kathās; Vet.; °*re tishṭhatu*, let it be far, i.e. let it be unmentioned, never mind, Kathās. vi, 37. **-ādis** (*dūrá-* for °*ré-ā°*), mfn. announcing far and wide, RV. i, 139, 10. **-ādhī** (*dūrá-* for °*ré-ā°*), mfn. whose thoughts are far away, vi, 9, 6. **-upa-śabdas** (*dūrá-* for °*ré-up°*), mfn. sounding to a distance, vii, 21, 2. **-khātôdaka**, mfn. (said of a place) where water is only found after deep digging, Gobh. iv, 7, 8, Comm. **-ga**, mfn. going or being far, remote, Hariv.; Rājat. **-gata**, mfn. gone far away, R. **-gamana**, n. the going or travelling far, Kāv. **-gā**, mfn. = *-ga*, TāṇḍyaBr. **-gāmin**, mfn. going far, R.; m. an arrow, W. **-gṛiha**, mfn. whose house is distant, far from home, R. **-grahaṇa**, n. seizing or perceiving objects from afar (a supernatural faculty), BhP. **-cara**, mfn. walking or being far, R.; keeping away from (abl.), Jātakam. **-ja**, mfn. born or living in a distant place, MBh. **-tás**, ind. from afar, at a distance, aloof from, far off, AV.; Mn.; MBh.; Kāv. &c.; *dūrato-√bhū*, to keep away, ŚārṅgP. **-tā**, f. (W.), *-tva*, n. (Bhāshāp.) remoteness, distance. **-darśana**, m. 'far-seeing,' a vulture, L.; n. long-sightedness; foresight, W.; mfn. visible only from afar, BhP. i, 11, 8. **-darśin**, mfn. far-seeing; long-sighted (fig.), R.; m. a seer, prophet (cf. *dīrgha-d°*); a vulture, L.; N. of a v° who was prime-minister of Citra-varṇa, MW. **-dṛiś**, mfn. id.; m. a vulture; a learned man, L. **-dṛishṭi**, f. long-sightedness, foresight, discernment, W. **-patha**, m. a long way; °*thaṃ gata*, living far off, MBh. i, 801. **-pāta**, m. a long flight, MBh.; falling from a great height; mfn. shooting from afar, MBh.; R. (cf. *durâp°*). **-pātana**, n. the act of shooting to a distance, MBh. **-pātin**, mfn. flying far or a long way, MBh.; R.; shooting to a distance, hitting from afar, ib. (°*ti-tā*, f. and °*ti-tva*, n., MBh.) **-pātra**, mfn. having a wide channel or bed (river), R. ii, 73, 2 (v.l. *-pāra*). **-pāra**, mfn. having the opposite shore far off, very broad or wide, R. ii, 71, 2 &c. (cf. prec.); difficult of access or attainment, MBh. xi, 138; m. a very broad river, MBh.; BhP.; (*ā*), f. N. of the Ganges, MW. (cf. *dush-p°*). **-prasārin**, mfn. reaching far, Bhpr. **-bandhu**, mfn. having one's kinsmen distant, banished from wife and kindred, MBh.; Megh. **-bhāj**, mfn. 'possessing distance,' distant, W. **-bhāva**, m. remoteness, distance, Megh. **-bhinna**, mfn. pierced from a distance, wounded deeply, W. **-bheda**, m. the act of piercing from a distance, L. **-mūla**, m. Saccharum Munjia or Alhagi Maurorum, L. **-m-bhavishṇu** or **-bhāvuka**, mfn. moving to a distance, Vop. **-yāyin**, mfn. going far, W. **-vartin**, mfn. being in the distance, far removed, Kālid. **-vastraka**, mfn. having the clothes removed, naked, W. **-vāsin**, mfn. residing in a distant land, W. **-vidāritânana**, mfn. having the mouth widely open, Ṛitus. i, 14 (v.l. *bhūri-*). **-vibhinna**, mfn. 'far separated,' not related, W. **-vilambin**, mfn. hanging far down, Śak. v, 12 (v.l. *bhūri-*). **-vedha**, m. the act of striking from afar, L.; °*dhin*, mfn. piercing from afar (as a missile, weapon), L. **-śūnya**, mfn. leading through a long desert (way), Gal. **-śravaṇa**, n. hearing from afar, Pañcar. **-śravas** (°*rá*), mfn. far-renowned, AV. (cf. °*re-śr°*). **-saṃstha**, mfn. being in the distance, remote, Megh.; °*sthāna*, n. residing at a distance, W. **-sūrya**, mfn. having the sun distant, R. **-stha**, mfn. = *saṃstha*, Mn.; MBh. &c.; *-tva*, n. Kathās. xiii, 80. **-sthāyin**, mfn. id., MW. **-sthita**, mfn. id., Ratn. **-svarga**, mfn. having heaven distant, far off from h°, BhP. viii, 21, 33 (v.l. °*re-sv°*). **Dūrâgata**, mfn. come from afar, Cāṇ. **Dūrâdhirohin**, v. l. for °*rârohin*, q. v. **Dūrântara**, n. a wide space, long interval; °*rita*, mfn. separated by a w° sp°, MW. **Dūrâpaṇika**, mfn. frequenting distant markets, Dharmaśarm. **Dūrâpāta**, °**tin** = °*ra-vedha*, °*dhin*, L. **Dūrâpêta**, mfn. not even distantly to be thought of, quite out of the question, Kād.; *-tva*, n. Comm. **Dūrâplāva**, mfn. leaping far, W. **Dūrârūḍha**, mfn. mounted high, far gone or advanced, Vikr. iv, $\frac{65}{66}$. **Dūrârohin**, mfn. id., Śak. v, $\frac{115}{116}$. **Dūrârtha**, m. remote or recondite object, MW. **Dūrâloka**, m. sight from afar; °*ke sthita*, standing very far off, Vikr. iv, 46. **Dūrâvasthita**, mfn. standing or being afar off, W. **Dūrêritêkshaṇa**, mfn. 'who sends his glances far apart,' squint-eyed, L. **Dūrêshu-pātin**, mfn. shooting arrows to a distance, MBh. vii, 264. **Dūrôtsārita**, mfn. driven far away, removed, banished, Vikr. iv, 23; *-tva*, n. Sarvad. **Dūrônnamita**, mfn. raised aloft, stretched far out, ib. 18.

Dūraya, Nom. P. °*yati*, to be far from (abl.),

Vām. v, 2, 79; to keep distant, remove, Kum. viii, 31 (v. l. *dhūnayati*).

Dūrī, ind. in comp. for *dūra*. **–karaṇa**, n. the making distant, removing, W. **–√kṛi**, to make distant, remove, repel, Pāṇ. i, 3, 37, Sch.; *-kṛita*, mfn. repelled, surpassed, exceeded, Kāv. **–√bhū** to withdraw, retire, stand back; *-bhūta*, mfn. distant, removed, far off, Kāv.; Pur.

Dūre, loc. of *dūra* (q. v.) in comp. **–anta**, mfn. ending in the remote distance, boundless (heaven and earth), RV.; AV. **–amitra** (°*ré-*), mfn. whose enemies are far away, VS. xvii, 83. **–artha** (°*ré-*), mfn. whose aim is far off, RV. vii, 63, 4. **–gavyūti** (°*ré-*), mfn. whose domain is or reaches far, AV. iv, 28, 3. **–cara**, mfn. going or being far, distant, Kām. **–janânta-nilaya**, mfn. living far away from men, Suśr. **–tya**, mfn. being far off, distant, Pāṇ. iv, 2, 104, Vārtt. 1, Pat. **–dṛiś**, mfn. visible far and wide, RV. **–paśyā**, f. 'far-seeing,' N. of an Apsaras, TBr. iii, 7, 12, 3. **–pānīya-gocara**, mfn. having remote watering places (said of animals), Suśr. **–bāndhava**, m. a distant kinsman, Vas. xv, 7. **–bhā** (°*ré-*), mfn. shining to a distance, RV. i, 65, 10. **–yama**, mfn. one from whom Yama is distant, BhP. iii, 15, 25. **–vadhá**, mfn. far-striking, VS. xvi, 40. **–śravas**, mfn. far-renowned, ŚāṅkhŚr. viii, 17, 11 (cf. °*ra-śr*°); m. N. of a man (see *daureśravasa*). **–śruta**, m. N. of a man (cf. *daure-*). **–heti** (°*ré-*), mfn. whose arrows fly to a distance, PārGṛ. iii, 14; m. a partic. form of Agni, TS.; Comm.

दूरक्त *dū-rakta*, *-rakshya* &c. See 1. *dū*.

दूर्य *dūrya*, n. (fr. 1. *dur*?) feces, ordure; a kind of Curcuma (= *śaṭī*), L.

दूर्व *dūrva*, m. N. of a prince who was son of Nṛipam-jaya and father of Timi, BhP. ix, 22, 41.

दूर्वा *dū́rvā*, f. (√*durv*?) bent grass, panic grass, Dūrb grass, Panicum Dactylon, RV.; VS.; Br.; MBh. &c. (cf. *ali-*, *gaṇḍa-*, *granthi-*, *mālā-*). **–kāṇḍa**, n. a quantity or heap of D° grass, Pāṇ. iv, 2, 51, Kāś. **–°kshī** (°*vâk*°), f. N. of the wife of Vṛika, BhP. ix, 24, 42. **–gaṇa-pati-vrata**, n. N. of a partic. observance, Cat.; *-kathā*, f. N. of wk. **–loshṭa**, n. lump of earth from a D° field, MānGṛ. i, 7. **–vaṇa** or °**na**, n. a thicket of D° grass, Pāṇ. viii, 4, 6, Kāś. **–vat**, mfn. intertwined or joined with D° grass, Kum. vii, 14. **–vināyaka-vrata**, n. N. of wk. **–vrata**, n. N. of a partic. observance, Cat. **–°shṭamī** (°*vâsh*°), f. N. of a festival on the 8th day of the light half of the month Bhādra on which the D° is worshipped as a deity, BhavP. **–vrata-kathā**, f. N. of wk. **–soma**, m. a species of Soma plant. **Dūrvêshṭakā**, f. D° grass used like bricks in erecting an altar, ŚBr.; TS.

दूर्श *dūrśá*, n. a kind of woven cloth or vesture, AV. (cf. *dūśya*, 2. *dūshya*).

दूलाल *dūlāla*, m. N. of an author; °**li-pattra** and °**liya**, n. N. of wks, Cat.

दूलास *dūlāsa* (?), m. a bow, W.

दूलिका *dūlikā* and *dūlī*, f. the Indigo plant, L. (cf. *tūlī*, *dolā*, *taru-dūlikā*).

दूश्य *dūśya*, n. a tent (cf. *dūrśa*, 2. *dūshya*).

दूष *dūsha*, °*shaka*, °*shaṇa*, °*shita*. See under √2. *dush*.

दूष्य 2 *dūshya*, n. a tent, Śiś. v, 21; clothes or a kind of cloth, cotton, calico, Divyâv. (cf. *kalpa-*, *dūrśa* and *dūśya*); (*ā*), f. an elephant's leathern girth (cf. *cūshā*, °*shyā*, *kakshyā*).

दूस *dūsa*. See *avi-d*°.

दृ *dṛi*, cl. 6. Ā. *driyáte* (ep. also °*ti*), to respect, honour (Dhātup. xxviii, 118); occurring only with prep. *ā*, cf. *ā-√dṛi*; Desid. *didarishate*, Pāṇ. vii, 2, 75.

Dṛita, mfn. respected, honoured, W.; (*ā*), f. cumin, L.

दृंह *dṛiṅh* or *dṛih*, cl. 1. P. *dṛíṅhati*, to make firm, fix, strengthen, RV.; AV.; VS. &c. (p. *dṛiṅhántam*, AV. xii, 29); Ā. °*te*, to be firm or strong, RV. &c. (trans. = P. only in *dṛiṅhéthe*, RV. vi, 67, 6, and *dṛiṅhāmahai*, ŚBr. ii, 1, 1, 9); cl. 4. P. Ā. only Impf. *dṛihya* and °*hyasva*, be strong, RV.; cl. 1. *darhati*, to grow, Dhātup. xvii, 84; pf. *dadarha* or *dadṛiṅha*; p. Ā. *dādṛiháṇá*, fixing, holding, RV. i, 130, 4; iv, 26, 6; fixed, firm, i, 85, 10; aor. *ádadṛihanta*, they were fixed or firm, x, 82, 1: Caus. P. Ā. *dṛiṅhayati*, °*te*, to make firm, fix, establish, AV.; Kauś.; Gobh.

Dṛiṅha in *bhūmi-d*° (q. v.) **Dṛíṅhaṇa**, n. making firm, fastening, strengthening, AV. vi, 136, 1 (cf. *keśa-d*°); means of st°, TBr. ii, 8, 3, 8. °**hitá** (or *dṛihita*, Pāṇ. vii, 2, 20, Sch.), mfn. made firm, fortified; n. stronghold, RV. °**hitṛí**, m. strengthener, fortifier, ib., TBr.

Dṛiḍha (or **dṛiḷhá**), mfn. fixed, firm, hard, strong, solid, massive, RV.; AV.; ŚBr.; MBh. &c.; firmly fastened, shut fast, tight, close (e.g. ship, 52, 5; bonds, fetters, chains, Hit. i, 97/98; Mṛicch. vii, 6/7; fist, MBh. iv, 1976); whole, complete (opp. to *bhinna*), MBh. xiii, 7453; difficult to be bent (bow, ChUp. i, 3, 5); steady, resolute, persevering, Hariv.; Kathās.; confirmed, established, certain, sure, Mn.; MBh.; Kāv. &c.; intense, violent, mighty, MBh.; Kāv. &c.; (in mathem.) reduced to the last term or smallest number by a common divisor; m. (in music) a kind of Rūpaka; N. of a son of the 13th Manu, Hariv.; of a son of Dhṛita-rāshṭra, MBh. vii; (*ā*), f. N. of a Buddh. goddess; n. anything fixed or firm or solid; stronghold, fortress, RV. &c.; iron, L.; (*ám*), ind. firmly, fast, AV.; MBh.; R. &c. (comp. *-taram*, Prab. iv, 11); steadily, perseveringly, thoroughly, much, very well, MBh.; Kāv.; BhP. &c. **–kaṇṭaka**, m. 'hard-thorned,' a kind of plant, L.; (*ā*), f. Phoenix Sylvestris, L. **–kāṇḍa**, m. 'strong-stemmed,' a bamboo, L.; (*ā*), f. a kind of creeping plant, L.; n. a kind of fragrant grass, L. **–kārin**, mfn. 'acting firmly,' resolute, persevering, Mn.; Gaut. **–kuṭṭaka**, m. (math.) a multiplier admitting of no further simplification or reduction. **–krodha**, mfn. having violent anger, MBh. iii, 1972. **–kshatra**, m. 'having strong prowess,' N. of a son of Dhṛita-rāshṭra, MBh. i. **–kshurā**, w. r. for *dṛiḍhéksh*°, q. v. **–gātrikā**, f. 'having hard particles,' granulated sugar, L. **–granthi**, m. 'hard-knotted,' a bamboo, L. **–grāhin**, mfn. seizing firmly, pursuing an object with untiring energy, MBh. xii, 7184. **–cchada**, m. 'hard-leaved,' m. Borassus Flabelliformis, L.: n. a kind of fragrant grass, L. **–cyuta** (also °*ḍhā-c*° and *dṛiḷha-c*°), m. N. of a son of Agastya or author of a hymn of the RV.; Prav.; BhP. (cf. *dārḍha-c*°). **–jñāna**, n. certain knowledge, firm conviction, MW. **–°tara**, mfn. compar. firmer, harder; °*rī-√kṛi*, to strengthen, confirm, Daś. **–taru**, m. 'strong tree,' Grislea Tomentosa, L. **–tā**, f., **-tva**, n. firmness, hardness, solidity, strength; steadiness, perseverance, MBh.; Kāv. &c. **–tṛiṇa**, n. 'strong grass,' Saccharum Munjia, L.; (*ā*), f. Eleusine Indica, L. **–toraṇârgala**, mfn. having the bars of the gates firmly fastened (town), R. i, 6, 26. **–tvac**, m. 'tough-barked,' a kind of reed, L. **–daṅśaka**, m. 'strong-toothed,' a shark, L. **–dasyu**, m. N. of an old sage, also named Idhmavāha (son of Dṛiḍha-cyuta, see above), Kād.; BhP. (cf. *dṛiḍhasyu*). **–dvāra**, mfn. having strong or well-secured gates, R. i, 5, 10. **–dhana**, m. 'having secure wealth,' N. of Gautama Buddha, Lalit. **–dhanus**, m. 'having a strong bow,' N. of an ancestor of Gautama (v. l. *-hanu* and °*ḍhâśva*), VP. **–dhanvan**, mfn. having a strong bow, MBh. iii, 13553; m. a good archer, ib. i, 6995. **–dhanvin**, mfn. id., MBh. iii, 1348 &c.; furnished with strong archers, R. v, 72, 13. **–dhur**, mfn. having a strong pole or beam, Pāṇ. v, 7, 74, Kāś. **–dhṛiti**, mfn. 'strong-willed,' resolute, Āpast. **–nābha**, m. a spell for restraining magical weapons, R. i, 30, 5. **–niścaya**, mfn. 'having fixed certainty,' certain, undoubted, W. **–nīra**, m. 'strong-juiced,' the cocoa-nut tree, L. **–netra**, m. 'strong-eyed,' N. of a son of Viśvā-mitra, R. i. **–nemi**, m. N. of a prince (son of Satya-dhṛiti), Hariv.; Pur. **–pattra**, m. 'strong-leaved,' a bamboo, L.; (*ī*), f. Eleusine Indica, L. **–pāda**, m. 'firm-footed,' N. of Brahmā, Hariv.; (*ā*), f. Andrographis Paniculata, L.; (*ī*), f. Phyllanthus Niruri, L. **–pratijña**, mfn. firm in keeping a promise or agreement, Śak. ii, 1/2 (v. l.) **–pratyaya**, m. firm confidence, Bhartṛ. iii, 14. **–praroha**, m. 'growing strongly,' Ficus Infectoria, L. **–prahāra**, m. a hard or violent stroke, Śak. i, 32, Sch. **–prahārin**, mfn. striking hard, shooting surely (°*ritā*, f. Mcar. i, 30/31; Divyâv. 58 &c.); m. N. of a man, HYog. **–phala**, m. 'having hard fruit,' the cocoa-nut tree, L. **–baddha**, mfn. firmly bound, tied tightly, W. **–bandhana-baddha**, mfn. caught fast in a snare, MW. **–bandhinī**, f. 'winding closely round,' a kind of creeper (= *śyāmā*), L. **–bala**, m. 'of firm strength,' N. of a medical author. **–bīja**, m. 'having hard seeds,' Cassia Tora, L.; Zizyphus Jujuba, L.; Acacia Arabica, L. **–buddhi**, m. 'firm-minded,' N. of a man, Kathās. **–bhakti**, mfn. 'firm in devotion,' faithful, R. (*-tā*, f. Kām.); °*ktika* and °*kti-mat*, mfn. id., R. **–mati**, mfn. firm-minded, strong-willed, resolute, Bhag. xviii, 64. **–manyu**, mfn. having intense anger or grief, Ragh. xi, 46. **–mushṭi**, m. a strong fist, Kathās. cix, 148; a sword, L. (cf. *gāḍha-m*°); N. of a man, Kathās.; mfn. strong-fisted, whose grasp is difficult to unloose, MBh.; Hariv. (*-tā*, f. MW.); close-fisted, i.e. miserly, niggardly, L. **–mūla**, m. 'having a hard root,' the cocoa-nut tree, L.; Saccharum Munjia, L.; another kind of grass (= *manthānaka*), L. **–raṅgā**, f. 'having a fast colour,' alum, L. **–ratha**, m. 'having a strong chariot,' N. of a son of Dhṛita-rāshṭra, MBh. i, vii (°*thâśraya*, i, 4551, prob. id.); of a son of Jayad-ratha and father of Viśva-jit, Hariv.; of the father of the 10th Arhat of the present Ava-sarpiṇī, L. **–ruci**, m. 'of great glory,' N. of a prince and of a Varsha in Kuśa-dvīpa, BhP. **–latā**, f. 'having strong branches,' a kind of plant, L. **–loman**, mfn. coarse-haired, bristled; m. coarse hair, bristles; a hog, L. **–vajra**, m. 'having a strong thunderbolt,' N. of a king of the Asuras, L. **–vapus**, mfn. 'strong-bodied,' hale and hearty, Subh. **–varman**, m. 'having strong armour,' N. of a son of Dhṛita-rāshṭra, MBh. i; of a king of Prayāga, Priy. **–valka**, m. 'hard-barked,' the Areca-palm, L.; (*ā*), f. Hibiscus Cannabinus, L. **–valkala**, m. 'id.', Artocarpus Locucha, L. **–vāda-parākrama**, mfn. firm in words and acts, MBh. xii, 201. **–vikrama**, mfn. of firm fortitude, MBh. i, 7636. **–vṛiksha**, m. 'firm tree,' the cocoa-nut, L. **–vedhana**, n. piercing strongly, MBh. vii, 2635. **–vairin**, m. a relentless foe, MW. **–vrata**, mfn. 'firm-vowed,' firm in austerity or resolution, Mn.; MBh. &c.; persevering in, intent upon, devoted to (loc. or comp.), R. **–śaktika**, mfn. of great power; strong-willed, L. **–saṃdha**, m. 'faithful to engagements,' N. of a son of Dhṛita-rāshṭra, MBh. i. **–saṃdhi**, m. firmly united, closely joined; strong-knit, thick-set; close, compact, L. **–samādhāna**, mfn. paying fixed attention, Nāg. v, 27/28. **–sūtrikā**, f. 'having strong fibres,' Sanseviera Zeylanica, L. **–sena**, m. 'having a strong army,' N. of a prince, Pur. **–sauhṛida**, mf(*ī*)n. firm in friendship, constant, Pañc.; Hit. **–skandha**, m. 'strong-stemmed,' a sort of Mimusops, L. **–sthūṇa**, mfn. having firm posts or columns, R. **–hanu**, m. 'strong-jawed,' N. of a prince, BhP. (cf. °*ḍha-dh*°). **–hasta**, m. 'strong-handed,' N. of a son of Dhṛita-rāshṭra, MBh. i. **Dṛiḍhâksha**, m. 'strong-eyed,' N. of a prince, Hariv. (v. l. °*ḍhâśva*). **Dṛiḍhâṅga**, mf(*ā* or *ī*)n. 'firm-bodied,' hard, strong; n. a diamond, L. **Dṛiḍhânutāpa**, mfn. deep repentance, Kum. iii, 8. **Dṛiḍhâyu** or °**yus**, m. 'firm-lived,' N. of the son of Purū-ravas and Urvaśī, MBh. i; of a prince, ib. v; of one of the 7 sages of the south, ib. xiii; of a son of the 3rd Manu Sāvarṇa. **Dṛiḍhâyudha**, mfn. having strong weapons, MBh.; m. N. of Śiva; of a son of Dhṛita-rāshṭra, MBh. i. **Dṛiḍhâśva**, m. 'strong-horsed,' N. of a son of Dhundhu-māra, MBh. &c.; of a son of Kāśya, Pur. (v. l. °*ḍha-dhanus* and *-hanu*). **Dṛiḍhêkshurā**, f. Eleusine Indica, L. **Dṛiḍhêshudhi**, m. 'having a strong quiver,' N. of a prince, MBh. i, 231.

Dṛiḍhaya, Nom. P. °*yati* = °*ḍhī-√kṛi*, Kāv.; Sch. (cf. *draḍhaya*). °**ḍhavya**, w. r. for °**ḍhâyus** (q. v.), MBh. xiii, 7112. °**ḍhasyu**, m. N. of an ancient sage (= °*ḍha-dasyu*, q. v.), MBh. iii, 8640. °**ḍhishṭha**, w. r. for *draḍh*°. °**ḍheyu**, m. N. of one of the 7 sages of the west, MBh. xiii, 7114.

Dṛiḍhī, ind., in comp. for °*ḍha*. **–karaṇa**, n., **-kāra**, m. strengthening, corroboration, confirmation, MBh.; R. **–√kṛi**, to make firm or fast, to strengthen, corroborate, confirm, Kāv.; Sch. **–√bhū**, to become strong, increase, Pañc. iii, 258.

दृक *dṛika*, n. a hole, opening, L.

दृकाण *dṛikāṇa*, m. (δέκανος) the third part of a sign of the zodiac or a demi-god presiding over it, Var. (v. l. *dṛikkāṇa*, *drekk*°, *dreshk*°).

दृक्कर्ण *dṛik-karṇa* &c. See 2. *dṛiś*.

दृक्ष *dṛiksha*, mf(*ī*)n. looking like, appearing as (in *amū-*, *ī-*, *kī-*, *tā-*; cf. 2. *dṛiś* and *dṛiśa*).

दृगञ्चल *drig-añcala* &c. See 2. *dṛiś.*

दृग्भू *drigbhū*, f. a thunderbolt, L.; the sun, L.; a serpent, L. (cf. *drinphū, drimphū, drinbhū, drimbhū*).

दृङ्नीरज *driṅ-nīraja* &c. See 2. *dṛiś.*

दृडक *dṛiḍaka*, m. a fire-place or hole made in the ground for cooking, W.

दृडु *dṛiḍu*, m. or f. (mus.) a kind of dance.

दृढ *dṛiḍha.* See under √*dṛiṇh* &c.

दृति *dṛíti*, m. (fr. √*dṛī*) a skin of leather, a leather bag for holding water and other fluids (fig. = a cloud), skin, hide, a pair of bellows, RV.; AV.; Br.; Mn.; MBh. &c.; a fish, L.; N. of a man with the patr. Aindrôti or °drôta, TāṇḍyaBr. [cf. *dārteya*; Gk. δέρμα]. **–kuṇḍa-tapaścit** (only °*citām ayana*, n.), N. of a Sattra, ŚrS. **–dhāraka**, m. a kind of plant, L. **–vātavata** (only °*vator ayana*, n.), N. of a Sattra, ŚrS. **–hari**, mfn. carrying a leather skin or bags (said of cattle), Pāṇ. iii, 2, 25; m. a dog, L. **–hāra**, mfn. id. (but not said of cattle), Pāṇ. ib.; m. a carrier of skins and bags, a water-carrier &c., W.

दृध्र *dṛidhrá*, mfn. (√*dhṛi*) seizing or fastening tightly, RV. iv, 1, 15.

दृन् *dṛin*, ind. an interjection (prob. made to explain *dṛinbhū*), L.

दृन्फू *dṛinphū*, m. a kind of snake, Uṇ. i, 93, Sch. (v.l. *dṛimphū*).

दृन्भू *dṛinbhū*, m. (Pāṇ. vi, 4, 84, Vārtt. 1, Pat.) a thunderbolt, L.; the sun, L.; (f., W.) a snake; L.; a wheel, L. **Dṛimbhū**, id., Uṇ. i, 93, Sch. (cf. *dṛigbhū* &c.)

दृप् 1. *dṛip* or *dṛiph*, cl. 6. P. *dṛipati* or *dṛimp°*; *dṛiph°* or *dṛimph°*, to pain, torture, Dhātup. xxviii, 28.

दृप् 2. *dṛip*, cl. 4. P. *dṛipyati* (*darpati* only ĀpDh. i, 13, 4; fut. *drápsyati* or *darpishyati*, Br.; *darpitā*, °*ptā*, and *draptā*, Pāṇ. vii, 2, 45; pf. *dadarpa*; aor. *adṛipat*, Br.; *adrāpsīt*, Pāṇ. iii, 1, 44, Vārtt. 7; *adarpīt* and *adārpsīt*, Vop.) to be mad or foolish, to rave, Br.; to be extravagant or wild, to be arrogant or proud, to be wildly delighted, MBh.; Kāv. &c.; to light, kindle, inflame (*darpati* or *darpayati*, Dhātup. xxxiv, 14, v.l. for *chṛid*): Caus. *darpayati*, to make mad or proud or arrogant, Pañc.; Kathās.

Dṛipta, mfn. mad, wild, proud, arrogant (*-tara*, compar.), MBh.; Kāv. &c. (cf. *á-d°* and *a-dṛiptá*). **–bālāki**, m. N. of a man with the patr. Gārgya, ŚBr. **Dṛiptâtman**, mfn. 'haughty-minded' (Kṛishṇa), MBh. xii, 1661.

Dṛipti. See *prá-d°*.

Dṛipyat, mfn. being proud or arrogant, W. (cf. *á-d°*).

Dṛipra, mfn. strong, Uṇ. ii, 13, Sch. (cf. *dūpra*); proud, arrogant, W.

दृभ् 1. *dṛibh*, cl. 1. 10. P. *darbhati* and *darbhayati*, to fear, be afraid, Dhātup. xxxiv, 15.

दृभ् 2. *dṛibh*, cl. 6. P. *dṛibháti* (ŚBr.); 1. 10. P. *darbhati* and *darbhayati* (Dhātup. xxxiv, 16), to string or tie together, tie in a bunch.

Dṛibdha, mfn. strung, tied, L. (cf. *saṃ-d°*). °**bdhi**, f. stringing together, arranging, L.

दृभीक *dṛíbhīka*, m. N. of a demon slain by Indra, RV.

दृमिचण्डेश्वर *dṛimicaṇḍêśvara*, n. N. of a Liṅga, MatsyaP. (v.l. *kṛim°*).

दृम्प् *dṛimp* or *dṛimph*. See 1. *dṛip.*

दृम्फू *dṛimphū* or °*bhū*. See *dṛinphū* &c.

दृवन् *dṛiván* (√*dṛī*?), mfn. piercing (arrow), VS. x, 8.

दृश् 1. *dṛiś* (Pres. forms supplied by √*paś*, q. v.; pf. P. *dadárśa*, RV. &c. [2 sg. *dadarśitha* and *dadrashṭha*, Pāṇ. vii, 2, 65]; Ā. *dadṛiśé*, AV. [*dádṛiśe*, 3 pl. °*dṛiśre*, RV.; °*śrire*, TBr.]; p. P. *dadṛiśvás*, RV.; °*śivas*, Up.; *darśivas*, q. v.; Ā. *dádṛiśāna*, RV.; fut. P. *drakshyáti*, Br. &c.; Ā. °*shyate* and fut. 2. *drashṭā*, MBh.; aor. P. *adarśam*, °*śas*, °*śat*, 3 pl. °*śur*, Br.; 1 pl. *adarśma*, TS.; *adṛiśma*, JaimBr.; Subj. *darśam*, °*śat*, °*śathas*, RV.; AV.; Ā. 3 pl. *ádṛiśran*, VS.; AV.; Br.; °*śram*, RV.; p. *dṛiśāná* or *dṛ́iśāna* [cf. s. v.], RV.; P. *dṛiśan*, 3 pl. *ádṛiśan*, Br.; Pot. *dṛiśéyam*, RV.; °*śema*, AV.; P. *adrākshit* and *adrāk*, Br.; Ā. 3 pl. *ádṛikshata*; Subj. 2 sg. *dṛikshase*, RV.; inf. *dṛiśé* and *dṛiśáye*, RV.; *dráshṭum*, AV. &c.; ind. p. *dṛishṭvā́*, AV. &c. [MBh. also *dṛiśya*], °*ṭvāya*, RV.; *-dṛ́iśya*, RV.; *-darśam*, Daś.) to see, behold, look at, regard, consider, RV.; AV.; ŚBr.; MBh. &c.; to see, i. e. wait on, visit, MBh.; R.; to see with the mind, learn, understand, MBh.; Kāv. &c.; to notice, care for, look into, try, examine, Yājñ.; Pañc.; to see by divine intuition, think or find out, compose, contrive (hymns, rites, &c.), Br.; Nir. ii, 11: Pass. *dṛiśyáte* (ep. also °*ti*), aor. *adárśi*, RV. &c. to be seen, become visible, appear, RV.; AV.; ŚBr.; MBh. &c.; to be shown or manifested, appear as (*iva*), prove, Mn.; MBh.; Kāv. &c.: Caus. P. Ā. *darśayati*, °*te*, AV. &c.; aor. *adīdṛiśat*, Br.; *adadarśat*, Pāṇ. vii, 4, 7, to cause to see or be seen, to show a thing (Ā. esp. of something belonging to one's self) or person (P. and Ā. with or scil. *ātmānam*, also one's self), to (acc., AV. iv, 20, 6; ŚBr. &c.; gen., Mn. iv, 59; MBh. &c.; dat., R. ii, 31, 33; Ragh. &c.; instr. after Ā. refl., Pāṇ. i, 4, 53, Kāś.); to show = prove, demonstrate, Mn.; MBh.; Kāv. &c.; to produce (money), i. e. pay, Mn. viii, 155; (a witness), 158: Desid. Ā. *dídṛikshate* (ep. also °*ti*) to wish to see, long for (acc.), RV. iii, 30, 13; ŚBr.; MBh. &c.: Desid. of Caus. *didarśayishati*, to wish to show, Śaṃk.; *adidarśayishīt*, Nid.: Intens. *darīdṛiśyate*, to be always visible, Bhojapr.; *darīdarshṭi* or *dard°*, Pāṇ. vii, 4, 90; 91. [Cf. Gk. δέρκομαι, δέδορκα, ἔδρακον; Goth. *tarhjan.*]

Dṛik, in comp. for 2. *dṛiś.* **Dṛik-karṇa**, m. 'eye-eared,' a snake, L. **–karman**, n. an operation by which any planet of a certain latitude (*vikshepa*) is referred to the ecliptic, Sūryas. **–kāṇa**, m. see *dṛikāṇa*. **–krodha**, m. the wrathfulness of the aspect (of a planet), Sūryas. **–kshatra**, prob. w. r. for *-chattra*, q. v. **–kshaya**, m. decay of sight, growing dim-sighted, MW. **–kshepa**, m. the sine of the zenith-distance of the highest or central point of the ecliptic at a given time, Sūryas. **–chattra**, n. 'eye-cover,' eye-lid, Rājat. viii, 133. **–tulya**, mfn. (astron.) being in accordance with an observed spot, Sūryas.; *-tā*, f. ib. **–patha**, m. range of sight; °*thaṃ* √*i* or *gam*, to appear, become visible, Kālid.; Rājat. **–pāta**, m. the letting fall a glance, a look, esp. a downward l°, Var.; Rājat. **–prasādā**, f. 'eye-cleaner,' a blue stone used for a collyrium (= *kulatthā*), L. **–priyā**, f. 'eye-delight,' beauty, splendour, L. **–śakti**, f. (with the Pāśupatas) a supernatural power of sight, Sarvad. **–śruti**, m. = *-karṇa*, L. **–saṃgama**, m. sight of and meeting with (gen.), Pañc. iv, 35.

Dṛig, in comp. for 2. *dṛiś.* **–añcala**, m. a sidelong glance, Prasannar. (cf. *nayanâñc°* and *locanâñc°*). **–adhyaksha**, m. 'sight-ruler,' the sun, L. **–anta**, m. the outer corner of the eye, Prasannar. **–gati**, f. the cosine of the zenith-distance or the sine of the highest or central point of the ecliptic at a given time, Āryabh.; Sūryas.; *-jīvā*, f. (Sūryas.); *-jyā*, f. (Schol. on Āryabh.) id. **–gocara**, m. range of sight, horizon, Rājat. **–gola**, m. a small circle on the axis of the earth within the greater circles of the armillary sphere and accompanying each planetary circle, W.; *-varṇana*, n. N. of wk. **–jala**, n. 'eye-water,' tears, L. **–jyā**, f. the sine of the zenith-distance or the cosine of the altitude, Sūryas. **–dṛiśya-prakaraṇa**, n., **-dṛiśya-viveka**, m. N. of wks. **–bhakti**, f. look of love, Dhūrtas. **–bhū**, see *dṛigbhū*. **–ruj**, f. disease of the eye, L. **–rudh**, mfn. obstructing the sight, Śiś. xix, 76. **–lambana**, n. vertical parallax, Sūryas.; Sch. **–visha**, mfn. having poison in the eyes, L.; m. a Nāga or serpent, W. (cf. *dṛig-*). **–vihīna**, mfn. 'deprived of sight,' blind, Gal. **–vṛitta**, n. vertical circle, Sūryas.; Sch.

Dṛiṅ, in comp. for 2. *dṛiś.* **–nīraja**, mfn. whose eyes are like the lotus, MW. **–maṇḍala**, n. vertical circle, Azimuth, Āryabh.

2. **Dṛiś**, m. (nom. *k*, Ved. *ṅ*, Pāṇ. vii, 1, 83) seeing, viewing, looking at; knowing, discerning, Yājñ.; MBh. &c. (ifc., cf. *āyurveda-d°*, *dishṭa-d°*, *prithag-d°*, *mántra-d°*, *sama-d°*, *sarva-d°*, *sūrya-d°*); f. sight, view (dat. *dṛiśé* as inf., cf. √1. *dṛiś*); look, appearance (in *ī-d°*, *kī-d°*, *tā-d°*); the eye, R.; Var. &c. (also n., BhP. iv, 4, 24); theory, doctrine, Vcar.; (astrol.) the aspect of a planet or the observed spot. [Cf. Gk. δρα for δρακ in ὑπόδρα.]

Dṛiśa, m. look, appearance (cf. *ī-d°*, *kī-d°*, *tā-d°* &c.); (*am*), ind. = 2. *dṛiś*, ifc. (g. *śarad-ādi*); (*ā*), f. the eye, L. **Dṛiśâkâṅkshya**, n. 'desirable to the eye,' a lotus, L. **Dṛiśâsphuṭa-mālā** (or °*śā-sph°*?), f. N. of wk. **Dṛiśôpama**, n. 'resembling the eye,' Nelumbium Speciosum.

Dṛiśati, f. look, appearance, RV. vi, 3, 3.

Dṛiśāna, m. (cf. 1. *dṛiś*) a Brāhman or spiritual teacher, L.; N. of a Ṛishi with the patr. Bhārgava, Kāṭh.; of a demon, L.; n. light, brightness, L.

Dṛiśālu, m. the sun, L.

Dṛiśi, f. seeing, the power of seeing, Vedāntas. (dat. °*śáye* as inf., cf. 1. *dṛiś*); the eye, BhP. (also °*śī*, L.); a Śāstra, W. **–mat**, mfn. seeing, beholding, BhP.

Dṛiśīka, mfn. worthy to be seen, splendid, RV.; (*ā́*), f. look, appearance, ib. (cf. *citra-*, *dur-*, *su-*). °**kú**, m. beholder, TS.

Dṛiśénya, mfn. = *dṛiśīka*, RV. x, 88, 7.

Dṛiśna. See *ánati-* (add.)

1. **Dṛiśya**, mfn. visible, conspicuous, RV.; MBh.; Kāv. &c.; to be looked at, worth seeing, beautiful, pleasing, Hariv.; Kāv.; Pur.; m. (arithm.) a given quantity or number; n. any visible object, Mālav. i, 9; the v° world, RTL. 119; N. of a town = *-pura*, Brahmap. **–jāti**, f. (arithm.) reduction of a given quantity with fractions affirmative or negative. **–tā**, f. (Daśar.), **-tva**, n. (Var.) visibility, vision, sight. **–pura**, n. N. of a town (see above). **–śravya**, mfn. being seen or heard; *-tva*, n. Sāh. **–sthāpita**, mfn. placed conspicuously, Kathās. xxiv, 92. **Dṛiśyâdṛiśya**, mfn. visible and invisible; (*ā*), f. N. of Sinīvālī, MBh. iii, 14126. **Dṛiśyêtara**, mfn. 'other than visible,' invisible; *-tā*, f. Naish.

2. **Dṛiśya**, ind. (for *dṛishṭvā*) having seen, MBh.

Dṛiśvan, mf(°*varī*)n. seeing or having seen, familiar with (ifc.), Kām.; Ragh. **–°va-tva**, n. Bhaṭṭ.

Dṛishṭá, mfn. seen, looked at, beheld, perceived, noticed, Mn.; MBh.; Kāv. &c.; visible, apparent, AV.; VS.; considered, regarded, treated, used, Śak. iii, 7; Pañc. i, 191/192; appeared, manifested, occurring, existing, found, real, Kāv.; Pañc.; Hit.; experienced, learnt, known, understood, MBh.; Kāv. &c.; seen in the mind, devised, imagined, MBh.; R.; allotted, destined, ib.; settled, decided, fixed, acknowledged, valid, Mn.; Yājñ.; MBh. &c.; n. perception, observation, Sāṃkhyak.; Tattvas.; (scil. *bhaya*) a real or obvious danger. **–karman**, mfn. whose actions are seen or proved, tried by practice, MBh.; Rājat.; who has seen the practice of others, Suśr.; Bhpr. **–kashṭa**, mfn. who has experienced calamity, Rājat. **–kūṭa**, n. riddle, enigma, W. **–cara**, mf(*ī*)n. seen before, not quite unknown, Jātakam. **–tas**, ind. as something seen, Gobh. iii, 5, 27. **–tva**, n. the being seen or learnt or examined, Var.; Kap. **–duḥkha**, mfn. = *-kashṭa*, R. **–dosha**, mfn. found out faulty or sinful or guilty, Mn.; Yājñ. &c. **–drashṭavya**, mfn. who has seen what was to be seen, Dhanaṃj. 7/4. **–dharma**, mfn. who has seen Dharma; m. this world, mundane existence, the present, Divyâv.; °*mika*, mfn. belonging to it, Buddh. **–dharman**, v. l. for *-śarman*. **–nashṭa**, mfn. seen and (at once) disappeared, Kathās. &c.; *-tā*, f. Rājat. (cf. *kshaṇa-dṛ°-n°*). **–pushpā**, f. a girl arrived at puberty (having experienced the menses), Gal. **–pūrva**, mfn. seen before, MBh.; °*vin*, mfn. having known by sight before, HPariś. **–pratyaya**, mfn. having confidence manifested, Pañc. i, 193/194. **–bhakti**, mfn. whose service has been beheld, Megh. **–mātra**, mfn. just or merely seen, Ratn. ii, 6/7. **–rajas** (L.) and °**skā** (Gal.), f. = *-pushpā*. **–ratha**, m. N. of a king, MBh. xiii, 7678 (v.l. *dṛiḍha-* and *dhṛishṭa-*). **–rūpā**, f. N. of a female attendant on Devī, W. **–vat**, mfn. having seen or beheld, MBh. **–vīrya** (*dṛishṭá-*), mfn. of tried strength, RV. ii, 23, 14. **–vyatikara**, mfn. who has experienced misfortune, Hit. **–śarman**, m. N. of a prince, VP. (v.l. *-dharman*). **–śruta**, mfn. seen and heard, Mn. viii, 75. **–sāra**, mfn. = *-vīrya*, Kām. **–hāni**, f. disparagement of the evidence of the senses, Sāṃkhyas. **Dṛishṭâdṛishṭa**, mfn. visible and invisible, relating to the present and future life, Rājat. i, 130; n. as subst., MBh. i, 6170; Pañc. iii, 242. **Dṛishṭânta**, m. (n. only R. ii, 109, 37) 'the end or aim of what is seen,' example, paragon, standard, allegory, type, MBh.; R. &c.; instance, exemplification (rhet.); a Śāstra, L.; a partic. high number, L.; death, L. (cf. *dishṭ°*); *-kalikā*, f. N. of wk.; *-tas*, ind. as a standard or example or precedent, MBh. ii, 70; *-vat*, mfn. containing examples or comparisons, Jātakam.; *-śataka*, n. 'a hundred examples,' N. of wk., MW.; *dṛishṭântaya*, Nom. P. *°yati*, to adduce as an example, Hcat.; *°ntita*, mfn. adduced as an example or comparison, Sch. on Prab. vi, 12. **Dṛishṭârishṭa,** mfn. in whom the symptoms of death are visible, Bhpr. **Dṛishṭârtha,** mfn. having the aim or object apparent, obvious, practical (opp. to *a-d°*, transcendental), Śaṃk.; serving for a pattern or standard, Gaut.; knowing the matter or the real nature of anything, R.; Rājat.; *-tattvajña*, mfn. knowing the true state or circumstances of the case, MW.

Dṛishṭi, f. seeing, viewing, beholding (also with the mental eye), Br.; Up. &c.; sight, the faculty of seeing, ŚBr.; Mn.; Suśr. &c.; the mind's eye, wisdom, intelligence, BhP.; L.; regard, consideration, L.; view, notion, Bhag.; Kap.; (with Buddhists) a wrong view; theory, doctrine, system, Jātakam.; eye, look, glance, Mn.; MBh.; Kāv. &c. (*°ṭiṃ dā* with loc. turn the eye to, look at, Śṛiṅgār. 15); the pupil of the eye, Suśr.; aspect of the stars (e.g. *śubha-*), Var. **-kṛit** or **-kṛita,** m. or n. 'suitable to the faculty of seeing,' Hibiscus Mutabilis, L. **-kshama,** mfn. 'sight-bearing,' worth seeing, Vikr. iv, 21. **-kshepa,** m. casting glances, Kāv. **-gata,** n. theory, doctrine, Divyâv. 164. **-guṇa,** m. mark for the sight, aim, L. **-guru,** m. 'sight-lord,' N. of Śiva, MBh. **-gocara,** m. range of sight, Pañc.; mfn. visible, MW. **-dāna,** n. 'aspect-giving,' appearance, Daś. **-dosha,** m. the evil influence of the human eye, RTL. 128. **-nipāta,** m. 'falling of the sight,' look, glance, Mn.; Var. **-pa,** mfn. drinking with the eyes, MBh. xiii, 1372. **-patha,** m. the path or range of sight, MBh.; R. &c. **-pathin,** m. (nom. *panthās*), id., Hariv. 6289. **-pāta,** m. = *-nip°*, Kālid.; Kathās. &c. **-pūta,** mfn. purified (i. e. protected from impurity) by the sight, Mn. vi, 46. **-pūtanā,** f. N. of an evil demon, Cat. **-prasāda,** m. the favour of a look, Hit. **-phala,** n. 'the results of the aspect of the planets,' N. of ch. of VarBṛS.; *-bhāvâdhyāya*, m. N. of wk. **-bandhu,** m. 'friend of sight,' a fire-fly, L. **-bāṇa,** m. 'eye-arrow,' a glance, leer, MW. **-maṇḍala,** n. the pupil of the eye, Suśr.; the circle or circuit of sight, MW. **-mat,** mfn. having eyes or intellect, wise, knowing, MBh.; Kām. **-mārga,** m. = *-patha*, Kathās. **-rāga,** m. expression of the eyes, Śak. ii, 1/2. **-roga,** m. disease of the eyes, Cat. **-vāda,** m. N. of the 12th Aṅga of the Jainas. **-vikshepa,** m. = *-kshepa*, Śak. (Chézy) 16, 1. **-vidyā,** f. the science of vision, optics, MW. **-vibhrama,** m. 'eye-rolling,' ogling, Śak. i, 23. **-visha** (also *°shṭi-*), mfn. 'having poison in the eyes,' poisoning by the mere look, MBh.; R.; m. a snake, W. (cf. *dṛig-*). **-sambheda,** m. 'mixing glances,' mutual glance, Mālatim. vii, 1/2.

Dṛishṭika, mfn. falsely believing in (comp.), Vajracch.

Dṛishṭin, mfn. having an insight into or familiar with anything; having the looks or thoughts directed upon anything, MW.

Dṛishṭvá and *°ṭvāya*. See 1. *dṛiś*.

दृशद् *dṛiśad, dṛiśadvatī* = *dṛishad, dṛishadvatī* below.

Dṛishac, in comp. for *dṛishad* below. **-chārada** (for *°shat-śā°*), mfn. fresh from the mill-stone, newly-ground, Pāṇ. vi, 2, 9, Kāś.

Dṛishat, in comp. for *dṛishad* below. **-kaṇa,** m. small stone, pebble, Kāvyapr. **-putra,** m. the upper and smaller mill-stone, Gobh. **-sāra,** n. 'stone-hard,' iron, L.

दृषद् *dṛishád*, f. (√*dṛī?*, Uṇ. i, 130) a rock, large stone, mill-stone, esp. the lower m°-st° (which rests on the *upalā*), RV.; AV.; VS.; ŚBr.; GS.; Kāv. &c. **-aśman,** m. = *°t-putra*, BhP. x, 9, 6. **-upala,** n. a grindstone for condiments, MW.; also = (*ā*), f. du. the upper and lower millstone, ŚBr. i, 1, 1, 22. **-vat,** mfn. rocky, stony, Pāṇ. viii, 2, 10, Kāś.; m. N. of the father of Varāṅgī (wife of Saṃyāti), MBh. i, 3767; (*atī*), f. (*°shád-v°*, also read *°śad-v°*), N. of a river which flows into the Saras-vatī, RV. iii, 23, 4; TāṇḍyaBr.; Mn.; MBh. &c.; the mother of Ashṭaka and wife of Viśvā-mitra, Hariv.; the m° of Pratardana and w° of Divo-dāsa, ib.; the m° of Śibi Auśīnara and w° of Nṛipa, ib.; m° of Prasena-jit (called also Haimavatī, prob. as N. of a river), ib.; of Durgā, L.

Dṛishada = *°shad* in *°dôlûkhala*, n. sg. mill-stone and mortar, Hariv. 6509. **°daka,** Pāṇ. i, 1, 4, Vārtt. 6, Pat. **°dya,** Nom. Ā. *°dyate*; *°dyitā* or *°ditā*, Pāṇ. vi, 4, 50, Kāś.

Dṛishadi, loc. of *dṛishad* in comp. **-māshaka,** m. (with the eastern people) a tax raised from mill-stones, Pāṇ. vi, 3, 10, Kāś.

Dṛishan, in comp. for *dṛishad*. **-nau,** f. a ship made of stone, Subh.

दृष्ट *dṛishṭa*. See above.

दृष्या *dṛishyā*, f. = *dūshyā*, L.

दृह् *dṛih*. See √*dṛiṇh* and *dhṛik*.

दॄ *dṛī*, cl. 9. P. *dṛiṇāti*, Pot. *-dṛiṇīyāt*, ŚBr.; cl. 2. P. 2. sg. Subj. *dárshi*, 2. 3. sg. *dárt*, impf. 2. sg. *adar*, RV. (pf. *dadāra* [2. sg. *dadaritha*, Pāṇ. vi, 4, 126, Sch.; 3 pl. *dadrur* or *dadarur*, vii, 4, 12, Sch.]; aor. *adarat* [Ved. *adārīt*], Pāṇ. iii, 1, 59, Sch.; Subj. P. *darshasi*, *dárshat*; Ā. *darshate*; Pot. *°shīshṭa*, RV.; Prec. *dīryāt*, Hariv. 15177) to burst, break asunder, split open, RV.; Hariv. (cf. above); to cause to burst, tear, rend, divide, RV.; MBh.; BhP.: Pass. *dīryate* (*°ti*, MBh.), p. *dīryamāṇa* and *dīryat*; pf. *dadre* (ŚāṅkhŚr. xiv, 27, 2) to be split, break open, fall asunder, decay, Br.; MBh.; Suśr.; Kāv.; to be dispersed or scattered (as an army), MBh.; R.; to be frightened or afraid (also *darati*), Dhātup. xix, 47: Caus. P. *darayati*, to split, tear, break open, RV.; P. Ā. *dārayati*, *°te*; aor. *adadarat* (Pāṇ. vii, 4. 95) to tear asunder, divide by splitting or digging, MBh.; Kāv. &c.; to scatter, disperse, MBh.: Intens. P. *dárdarti* or *dādarti*; Impv. 2. sg. *dādṛihi*; Subj. 3. sg. *dardirat*; impf. 2. 3. sg. *ádardar*, 3. pl. *adardirur* = Caus.; RV. [Cf. Gk. δέρω and δαίρω; Lith. *dirù*; Slav. *drati*; Goth. *tairan*; Angl. Sax. *teran*; Engl. *to tear*; Germ. *zerren*, *zehren*.]

दे *de*, cl. 1. Ā. *dayate*, Dhātup. xxii, 66; pf. *digye*, Pāṇ. vii, 4, 9, to protect, defend: Desid. *ditsate*, 54. [Cf. 1. *datta*; 4. 5. *dā*.]

देउलिय *deüliya*, n. (Prākr. for *devakulya*?) N. of a Grāma, Kshitîś.

देङ्गपाल *deṅga-pāla*, m. N. of a man, Rājat.

देण्टिका *deṇṭikā*. See *nāga-*.

देदीप्यमान *dedīpyamāna* (√*dīp*, Intens.) shining intensely, glowing, blazing, MBh. &c.

देदीयितवै *dédīyitavaí*, dat. inf. of √1. *dī*, Intens.

देय *déya*, mfn. (√1. *dā*) to be given or presented or granted or shown; fit or proper for a gift, AV.; TS.; Mn.; MBh. &c.; to be or being given in matrimony (cf. *brahma-*); to be delivered or handed over, Mn. viii, 185; to be ceded (road), Mn. ii, 138; to be returned, Vikr. iv, 33; to be paid (as a debt, wages, taxes &c.) Mn.; Yājñ.; to be laid or set to (as fire), MBh.; Bhpr.; n. giving, gift (cf. *a-*, *bala-*, *magha-*, *rādho-*, *vasu-*, *vaira-*); tax, tribute, MBh. xii, 3308; water (?), L. **-dharma,** m. 'the duty of giving,' charity, Buddh.

देलिम *delima*, m. or n. N. of a place, Cat.

देव् *dev*. See √1. 2. *div*.

1. **Devana,** n. lamentation, wailing, grief, sorrow, L.

देव *devá*, mf(*ī*)n. (fr. 3. *div*) heavenly, divine (also said of terrestrial things of high excellence), RV.; AV.; VS.; ŚBr. (superl. m. *devá-tama*, RV. iv, 22, 3 &c.; f. *devi-tamā*, ii, 41, 16); m. (according to Pāṇ. iii, 3, 120 *déva*) a deity, god, RV. &c. &c.; (rarely applied to) evil demons, AV. iii, 15, 5; TS. iii, 5, 4, 1; (pl. the gods as the heavenly or shining ones; *víśve devā́s*, all the gods, RV. ii, 3, 4 &c., or a partic. class of deities [see under *víśva*], often reckoned as 33, either 11 for each of the 3 worlds, RV. i, 139, 11 &c. [cf. *tri-daśa*], or 8 Vasus, 11 Rudras, and 12 Ādityas [to which the 2 Aśvins must be added], Br.; cf. also Divyâv. 68; with Jainas 4 classes, viz. *Bhavanâdhīśa*, *Vyantara*, *Jyotishka*, and *Vaimānika*; *devā́nām pátnyas*, the wives of the gods, RV.; VS.; Br. [cf. *deva-patnī* below]); N. of the number 33 (see above), Gaṇit.; N. of Indra as the god of the sky and giver of rain, MBh.; R. &c.; a cloud, L.; (with Jainas) the 22nd Arhat of the future Ut-sarpiṇī; the image of a god, an idol, Vishṇ.; a god on earth or among men, either Brāhman, priest, RV.; AV. (cf. *bhū-d°*), or king, prince (as a title of honour, esp. in the voc. 'your majesty' or 'your honour'; also ifc., e.g. *śrī-harsha-d°*, *vikramâṅka-d°*, king Śrī-h° or Vikr°, and in names as *purushôttama-d°* [lit. having Vishṇu as one's deity; cf. *atithi-d°*, *ācārya-d°*, *pitṛi-d°*, *mātṛi-d°*]; rarely preceding the name, e.g. *deva-caṇḍamahāsena*, Kathās. xiii, 48), Kāv., Pañc. &c. (cf. *kshiti-*, *nara-*, &c.); a husband's brother (cf. *devṛi* and *devara*), W.; a fool, dolt, L.; a child, L.; a man following any partic. line or business, L.; a spear-man, lancer, L.; emulation, wish to excel or overcome, L.; sport, play, L.; a sword, Gal.; N. of men, VP.; of a disciple of Nāgârjuna, MWB. 192; dimin. for *devadatta*, Pāṇ. v, 3, 83, Vārtt. 4, Sch.; (n., L.) an organ of sense, MuṇḍUp. iii, 1, 8; 2, 7; (*ā*), f. Hibiscus Mutabilis or Marsilia Quadrifolia; (*ī*), f. see s. v. [Cf. Lat. *dīvus*, *deus*; Lit. *dë́vas*; Old Pruss. *deiwas*.] **-ṛishabha,** m. 'a bull among the gods,' N. of a son of Dharma and Bhānu, BhP. vi, 6, 5. **-ṛishi,** m. 'a Ṛishi among the gods,' N. of Nārada, 16, 1 (cf. *°varshi*). **-kaḍa,** m. (for *kṛita*?) N. of a Grāma, MW. (cf. *devī-kṛiti*). **-kanyakā,** f. a celestial maiden, a nymph, Kāv. **-kanyā,** f. id., MBh.; R. **-kamala-pura,** n. N. of a town, Kathās. **-kardama,** m. 'divine paste,' a fragrant p° of sandal, agallochum, camphor, and safflower, L. **-karmá,** m. master of divine or sacred work, RV. x, 130, 1. **-karman,** n. religious act or rite, worship of the gods, ŚāṅkhŚr.; *°ma-kṛit*, mfn. performing it, MBh. **-kalaśa,** m. N. of a man, Rājat. **-kalpa,** mfn. god-like, MBh. i, 3124. **-kavaca,** n. divine armour, MW. (cf. *devī-*). **-kāñcana,** m. 'divine gold,' the tree Bauhinea Purpurea, L. **-kānta,** m. 'god-loved'(?), magnet, L. (cf. *candra-*, *sūrya-*). **-kāma** (*°vá-k°*), mfn. loving the gods, pious, RV. **-kārya,** n. = *-karman*, Mn.; MBh.; any matter concerning the gods, divine command, Ragh. xii, 103. **-kāshṭha,** n. 'divine wood,' Pinus Devadāru or some other kind of pine, Suśr. **-kirī,** f. (in music) N. of a Rāgiṇī regarded as wife of Megha-rāga (cf. *-girī*, *deśa-kari*, *goṇḍa-kirī*, *rāma-k°*). **-kilbishá,** n. offence against the gods, RV. x, 97, 16. **-kīrti,** m. N. of an astronomer, Cat. **-kuṇḍa,** n. a natural spring, L.; Sch. **-kuru,** m. N. of a people and country (associated with the *uttara-k°*), L.; Sch. **-kurumbā,** f. N. of a plant (= *mahādroṇa*), L. **-kula,** n. 'deity-house,' a temple, ŚāṅkhGṛ.; Kāv.; Var. &c.; *°lâvāsa*, m. pl. buildings belonging to a t°, Kathās.; *°lika*, m. attendant on a t°, L.; (*ā*), f. a small t°, chapel, Pañcad. **-kulyā,** f. 'river of the gods,' personif. as a daughter of Pūrṇiman and grand-daughter of Marīci, BhP.; N. of the wife of Ud-gītha, ib. **-kusuma,** n. 'divine flower,' cloves, Bhpr. **-kūṭa,** n. 'd° peak,' N. of a mountain, VāyuP. **-kṛita** (*°vá-k°*), mfn. made or done by the gods, RV.; AV.; ŚBr. &c. **-kṛitya,** n. = *-kārya*, MBh.; BhP. **-kośá,** m. d° cask or receptacle, AV.; TāṇḍyaBr. **-krī,** f. (in music) N. of a Rāga (cf. *-kirī*). **-kshatra** (*°vá-k°*), n. domain of the gods, RV. v, 64, 7 (*-kshetra?*); m. N. of a prince (son of Deva-rāta), Hariv.; Pur. **-kshetra,** n. domain of the g°, Br. **-kshema,** m. N. of the author of the Vijñāna-kāya, Buddh. **-khāta,** mfn. 'dug by the g°,' hollow by nature; n. (m., Sch.) a natural pond or reservoir, VāyuP.; a cave or cavern, W. (*-ka*, n. id., L.); *-tīrtha*, n. N. of a Tīrtha, ŚivaP.; *-bila*, n. cavern, chasm, W. **-gaṇá,** m. a troop or class of gods, VS.; MBh. &c.; *-deva*, m. N. of a poet, Cat.; *°ṇikā*, f. 'd° courtezan,' Apsaras, L.; *°ṇêśvara*, m. 'lord of the troop of gods,' N. of Indra, MBh. **-gandharva,** m. pl. gods and Gandharvas, Āpast.; the divine G° (opp. to *manushya-*), Taitt. Up.; MBh.; R. (Nārada so called, Hariv. 9633); n. a mode of singing, 8449 (cf. *-gāndhāra*). **-gandhā,** f. 'having d° fragrance,' a kind of medic. plant (= *mahāmodā*), L. **-garjana,** n. 'celestial roaring,' thunder, L. **-garbha,** m. divine child, MBh.; Hariv.; (*ā*), f. N. of a river in Kuśa-dvīpa, BhP. **-gava,** m. pl. the bulls of the gods, ĀpŚr. xi, 7, 6; (*°vī*), f. pl. the cows of the g°, MaitrS. i, 6, 3; N. of partic. verses or formulas, ĀpŚr. iv, 10, 4. **-gāndhāra,** n. or m. a partic. mode of singing, Hariv. 8689 (cf. *-gandharva*); (*ī*), f. (in music) N. of a Rāgiṇī. **-gāyana**, m. 'celestial songster,' a Gandharva, L. **-giri**, m. 'd° hill,' N. of a mountain, Suśr.; Pur. (cf. *-pūrva*); N. of Daulat-ābād (situated between mountains), Cat. **-girī**, f. (in music) N. of a Rāgiṇī (cf. *-kirī*). **-gupta**, mfn. 'god-guarded,' BhP.; m. N. of a man, Rājat. **-guru**, m. the father or preceptor of the gods, i.e. Kaśyapa (Hariv.; Śak.) or Bṛihaspati (L.); god and preceptor (at the beg. of comp.), Siṇhās. **-guhī**, f. N. of a place, BhP. **-guhya**, n. a secret known only to the g°, MBh.; Hariv.; R. (cf. *-rahasya*). **-gṛihá**, n. house of the g°, TBr.; R.; temple, chapel, R.; Suśr.; Var. &c.; palace of a king, Mālav. v, 1/4. **-gopā** (°*vá*-), mfn. having the g° for guardians, RV. i, 53, 11 &c.; (*ā*), f. divine protectress, RV. x, 36, 16; AV. vii, 20, 5. **-grantha**, m. N. of wk. **-granthí**, m. a d° knot or tie, Kapishṭh. **-graha**, m. 'd° seizer,' a class of demons who cause harmless madness, Suśr.; MBh. **-ghosha**, m. N. of a man, Kathās. **-m-gamá**, mf(*ā*)n. going to the gods, TS.; ŚBr. **-çakrá**, n. a d° wheel, Br.; (with Śāktas) 'the holy circle,' N. of a mystical diagram, RTL. 196. **-candra**, m. N. of a man, W. **-carita**, n. the course of action or practices of the gods, MW. **-caryā**, f. service of the g°; °*ryôpaśobhita*, mfn. beautified by it (as a hermitage), MBh. iii, 11045. **-cikitsaka**, m. divine physician; du. the two Aśvins, L. **-cittá**, n. the will of the gods, ŚBr. **-cchanda**, m. a necklace of pearls (composed of 100 or 103 or 81 or 108 strings), VarBṛS. lxxxi, 32, L.; *-prāsāda*, m. a temple consecrated to a god, MW. **-cchandas** and °**dasá**, n. a d° metre, Nid.; Kāṭh. **-já**, mfn. god-born, divine (as a Sāman), ŚBr.; m. N. of a prince (son of Saṃyama), BhP. **-jagdha** and °**dhaka**, n. 'god-eaten,' a kind of fragrant grass (= *kattṛiṇa*), L. **-janá**, m. (generally pl.) a troop or collection of gods or demons or serpents &c., AV.; VS. &c. (cf. *daiva-*, *itara-*); *-vid*, mfn. knowing gods &c., ŚBr.; *-vidyā*, f. knowledge of serpents &c., ŚBr.; ChUp. **-jananī**, f. the mother of the gods, Śak. (Pi.) vi, 177/8. **-japa**, m. N. of a Vidyā-dhara, Kathās. **-jaya**, m. N. of a poet, Bhojapr. **-jā́**, mfn. 'god-born,' RV.; AV. **-jāta** (°*vá*-), mfn. id., ib.; (*jātá*), n. a class or race of gods, Br. **-jāmi** (°*vá*-), mfn. peculiar to the gods, RV. vii, 23, 2; (*jāmí*), f. a sister of the g°, AV. vi, 46, 2. **-jushṭa** (°*vá*-), mfn. agreeable to the g°, RV. **-jūta** (°*vá*-), mfn. 'god-sped,' incited or inspired or procured by the g°, RV. **-jūti** (*dé*°!), m. N. of an Āditya, TS. **-tara**, m. N. of a man (g. *śubhrâdi*). **-taratha** and **-taras**, m. N. of teachers, VBr. **-taru**, m. divine tree, the old or sacred tree of a village (cf. *caitya* and *dyu-t*°), L.; N. of the 5 trees of Svarga (*mandāra*, *pārijātaka*, *saṃtāna*, *kalpa-vṛiksha*, *hari-candana*). **-tarpaṇa**, n. 'refreshing of the gods,' offerings of water, part of the Sandhyā ceremony, RTL. 409. **-talpa**, m. couch of the gods, TāṇḍyaBr. **-tā**, see *Devátā*. **-tāda**, m. Lipeocercis Serrata, L. (also °*ḍaka*, m. or °*ḍī*, f.); Luffa Fœtida or a similar plant, L.; fire, L.; N. of Rāhu, L. **-tāt** or **tāti** (°*vá*-), f. divine service, RV. i, 28, 2; iii, 19, 1 &c.; divinity, the gods collectively, RV. i, 95, 8; iii, 19, 4 &c. **-tālaka**, m. Lipeocercis Serrata, Car. (cf. *-tāḍ*°). **-tīrtha**, n. 'd° Tīrtha,' N. of a bathing-place, ŚivaP.; right moment for (worshipping) the gods, Anup.; the part of the hands sacred to the g° (i.e. the tips of the fingers), MārkP.; *-maya*, mf(*ī*)n. full of divine Tīrthas, Kathās.; *-svāmin*, m. the ascetic N. of Viśvêsvara-datta-mitra, Cat. **-tumula**, n. 'd° noise,' thunder, MānGṛ. i, 4. **-°tta** (°*vá*-, for *devá-datta*), mfn. god-given, RV. **-trā́**, ind. among or to the gods, RV.; VS.; AV.; ŚBr. **-trāta**, m. 'god-protected,' N. of a Sch. on ĀśvŚr., Cat. **-tvá**, n. godhead, divinity (cf. *-tā́*), RV.; TBr.; Mn.; MBh. &c. **-datta**, mfn. god-given, Mn.; MBh. &c.; m. N. of Arjuna's conch-shell, MBh.; of one of the vital airs (which is exhaled in yawning), Vedântas.; N. of a cousin (or younger brother) and opponent of Gautama Buddha, MWB. 52 &c.; of a son of Uru-śravas and father of Agni-veśya, BhP.; of a son of the Brāhman Govinda-datta, Kathās.; of a son of Hari-datta, ib.; of a son of king Jaya-datta, ib.; of sev. authors, Cat.; of a Nāga, BhP.; of a Grāma of the Bāhīkas, Pāṇ. i, 1, 75, Sch.; a common N. for men used in gr., phil. &c.; (*ā*), f. N. of the mother of Deva-datta who was the cousin of Gautama Buddha (see above); of a courtezan, Kathās.; °*ttaka*, m. pl. the party led by D°, Pāṇ. v, 2, 78, Kāś.; (*ikā*), f. dimin. for *-dattā*, vii, 3, 45, Vārtt. 4, Pat.; °*tta-cara*, mfn. formerly in the possession of D°, v, 3, 54, Kāś.; °*tta-maya*, mf(*ī*)n. consisting of D°, iv, 2, 104, Vārtt. 16, Pat.; °*tta-rūpya*, mfn. = *-cara*, v, 3, 54, Kāś.; °*tta-śatha*, m. N. of a preceptor, g. *śaunakâdi* in Kāś.; °*ttâgraja*, m. 'the elder brother of D°,' N. of Gautama Buddha, Buddh. (cf. above); °*ttīya*, m. pl. the pupils of D°, Pāṇ. i, 1, 73, Vārtt. 5, Pat. **-dantin**, m. N. of Śiva (?), Kathās. iii, 5. **-damanikā** or °**manī**, f. N. of a woman, Pañcad. **-darśa**, m. N. of a teacher of AV., Col.; (*ī*), f. of a school of AV., Āryav. **-darśana**, mfn. seeing the gods, familiar with them, MBh.; m. N. of Nārada, BP. ii, 8, 1; of a Brāhman, Kathās.; n. appearance of a god, Siṇhās. **-darśanin**, w. r. for *daiva-d*°. **-darśin**, mfn. = °*śana*, R.; m. N. of a school of AV., Kauś. **-dānī**, f. a kind of creeper (= *ghoshakâkṛiti*), L. **-dāru**, m.n. Pinus Devadāru or Deodar (also Avaria Longifolia and Erythrosylon Sideroxyloides), MBh.; Kāv.; Pur. &c.; *-vana-māhātmya*, n. N. of wk.; *-maya*, mf(*ī*)n. made of its wood, MBh.; R. **-dālikā** or °**dālī**, f. a kind of pumpkin, Suśr.; Bhpr. **-dāsa**, m. a servant of a monastery (Buddh.); N. of a merchant's son, Kathās.; of the brother of Śārṅgadhara's mother (also °*sa-deva*), Cat.; of the son of a Kālidāsa, ib.; of sev. authors, Cat.; (*ī*), f. a temple Nāch-girl, RTL. 451; the wild citron tree, L. **-dinna**, m. corrupt form for *-datta*, Pat. (Ben.) Introd. **-dinna**, m. id., N. of a son of Devadatta, HPariś. **-dīpa**, m. 'divine lamp,' the eye, L. **-dundubhi**, m. 'd° drum,' holy basil with red flowers, L.; N. of Indra, L. **-durga**, mfn. inaccessible to the gods, R. **-dūtá**, m. divine messenger, TS. &c. (also °*taka*, MBh.); (*ī*), f. female messenger of the gods, W.; the wild citron tree, L. **-dūti**, w. r. for *-hūti*. **-deva**, m. 'the god of gods,' N. of Brahmā, MBh. i, 1628; of Rudra-Śiva, 7324; of Vishṇu-Kṛishṇa, Bhag. x, 15; of Gaṇêśa, Kathās. xx, 55; du. Brahmā and Śiva, MBh. viii, 4456; pl. the Brāhmans, BhP. iii, 16, 17; (*ī*), f. N. of Durgā, Hcat. i; °*vêśa*, m. 'lord of the chiefs of the gods,' N. of Śiva, MBh. i, 8123; of Indra, iii, 17191; of Vishṇu, xii, 12864. **-daivatya**, mfn. 'having the g° as deity,' destined for the g°, Mn. ii, 189. **-dyumna**, m. 'glory of the g°,' N. of a prince (son of Devatā-jit and father of Parame-shṭhin), BhP. **-droṇī**, f. an idol procession (orig. ablution; cf. *droṇī*), L.; Phlomis Ceylanica, L. **-dryàc**, mf(*īcī*)n. turned towards the gods, RV. **-dhara**, m. (*bhāgavatâcārya*) N. of Sch. on GṛS. **-dharma**, m. religious duty or office, MW. **-dharman**, m. N. of a king, VP. **-dhānī**, f. 'divine abode,' N. of Indra's city on the Mānasôttara (east of Meru), BhP. **-dhānya**, n. 'god's grain,' Andropogon Saccharatus, A. Sorgum, Holcus S° or S° Cernuum, L. **-dhāman**, n. = *-gṛiha*, AgP. **-dhishṇya**, n. seat (i.e. chariot) of a god, BhP. **-dhūpa**, m. 'd° incense,' the resin of Shorea Robusta, Bhpr.; bdellium, L. **-nakshatrá**, n. N. of the first 14 Nakshatras in the southern quarter (opp. to *yama-*), TBr.; m. N. of a king, VP. (v.l. for °*va-kshatra*). **-nadī**, f. 'd° river,' N. of several sacred rivers, Mn.; MBh.; R. &c. **-nandā**, f. 'gods' joy,' N. of a celestial woman, Siṇhās.; °*din*, m. 'rejoicing the gods,' N. of one of Indra's doorkeepers, L.; of a grammarian, Cat. **-nala**, m. 'god's reed,' Arundo Bengalensis, L. (cf. *-nāla*). **-nāgarī**, f. 'divine city writing,' N. of the character in which Sanskṛit is usually written (prob. from its having originated in some city), Col.; MWB. 66, 1. **-nātha**, m. 'lord of the g°,' N. of Śiva, Śivag.; of sev. authors (also *-ṭhakkura*, *-tarka-pañcânana*, and *-pāṭhaka*). **-nābha**, m. N. of a man, Cat. **-nāmá**, m. pl. N. of partic. formulas, TĀr. v, 7, 1. **-nāman**, m. N. of a king and a Varsha in Kuśa-dvīpa, BhP. **-nāyaka**, m. N. of a man, Rājat.; *-pañcāśat* and *-stuti*, f. N. of wks. **-nāla**, m. = *-nala*, L. **-nikāya**, m. host or assembly of gods, Mn. i, 36; MBh. i, 4804; heaven, paradise, W. **-nid**, mfn. hating the g°, a god-hater, RV. **-nindaka**, mfn. id.; atheist or atheism, MW. **-nindā**, f. heresy, atheism, MW. **-nibandha**, m. N. of wk. **-nirmālya**, n. a garland remaining from a sacrifice, Var. **-nirmita**, mfn. 'god-made,' created, natural, W.; (*ā*), f. Cocculus Cordifolius, Bhpr. **-niśrayaṇī** or °**śreṇī**, f. 'ladder towards the gods,' N. of a partic. penance, Baudh. iii, 9, 18. **-nītha**, m. a formula consisting of 17 Pādas, Vait. **-pañca-rātra**, m. N. of a Pañcâha, Cat. **-paṇḍita**, m. N. of an author, Cat. **-pati**, m. 'lord of gods,' N. of Indra, MBh.; R.; pl. the most excellent of gods, BhP.; *-mantrin*, m. 'I°'s counsellor,' N. of Bṛihas-pati, the planet Jupiter, Var. **-pattana**, n. N. of a town, Cat. **-patnī** (°*vá*-), f. having a god as husband, the wife of a god, RV.; MBh.; sweet potato (= *madhv-āluka*), L. **-patha**, m. 'gods' path,' heaven, ChUp.; MBh.; the Milky Way, L.; N. of place of pilgrimage (cf. Pāṇ. v, 3, 100), MBh. iii, 8187 (also *-tīrtha*, n., ŚivaP.); °*thīya*, mfn. being on the celestial path, Kāṭh.; relating to or coming from Deva-patha (above), MW. **-padá**, n. a word containing a god's name, ŚBr. xi, 56, 9; = *-pāda*, W. **-parishad**, f. an assembly of deities, MW. **-parṇa**, n. 'divine leaf,' N. of a medic. plant (= *sura-*), L. **-pallī-paṭṭana**, n. N. of a town, Col. **-paśu**, m. any animal consecrated to a deity, Mn. **-pāṇi**, m. 'god-handed,' N. of a class of Asuras, MaitrS. **-pātrá**, n. cup or drink of the gods, Br. **-pātrin**, mfn. partaking of the divine cup, TāṇḍyaBr. **-pāda**, m. pl. 'the feet of a god or king,' the royal presence or person, 'His Majesty,' Pañc. i, 111/2 &c.; *-mūla*, n. id., Prab. ii, 3/4. **-pā́na**, mfn. serving the gods for a beverage, RV.; AV. **-pāla**, m. 'god-defender,' N. of sev. princes, Śatr.; of a mountain, BhP.; of an author (son of Hari-pāla), Cat. **-pālita**, m. 'god-protected,' N. of a man, Pāṇ. vi, 2, 148, Kāś. **-piyú**, mfn. reviling or despising the gods, AV. **-putra**, m. the son of a god, Hariv. (also °*traka*, Kathās.); N. of Śiva, Kāraṇḍ.; (°*vá*-), mfn. having gods as children (said of heaven and earth), RV. i, 106, 3; 159, 1 &c.; (°*trī* or °*trikā*), f. Trigonella Corniculata, L.; *-māra*, m. N. of one of the four Māras, Buddh. **-pur**, f. (nom. *-pūr*) = *-purā*, TāṇḍyaBr. xxii, 17; = *-pura*, n. Cat. **-pura**, n. Indra's residence, R. v, 73, 8; (*ā*), f. divine fortress, AV., TS. **-purī-māhātmya**, n. N. of wk. **-purohita**, m. domestic priest of the gods, Hariv. 13208; N. of Bṛihas-pati, i.e. the planet Jupiter, Var., Sch. **-pushpa**, n. 'divine flower,' cloves, L. **-pūjaka**, m. worshipper of the gods, MW. **-pūjā**, f. worship of the gods (esp. the daily w° in the domestic sanctuary), RTL. 394; N. of wk. (also *-vidhi*, m., Cat.) **-pūjita**, mfn. worshipped by the gods, MBh. **-pūjya**, m. 'to be honoured by the gods,' N. of Bṛihas-pati, i.e. the planet Jupiter, Var. **-pūrva**, mfn. 'preceded by the word *deva*,' with *giri* = *deva-giri*, Megh. 42. **-pūrvakam**, ind. beginning with the gods, Mn. iii, 209. **-prakāśinī**, f. N. of wk. **-pratikṛiti**, f. (Pāṇ. v, 3, 99, Sch., where wrongly *prakṛ*°) and **-pratimā**, f. (VarBṛS. xxxiii, 20) image of a deity, idol. **-pratishṭhā**, f., *-tattva*, n., & *-prayoga*, m. N. of wks. **-prabha**, m. 'having divine splendour,' N. of a Gandharva, Kathās.; (*ā*), f. of the daughter of a Siddha, ib. **-prayāga**, m. 'd° place of sacrifice,' N. of a sacred bathing-place, Cat. **-praśna**, m. 'consulting the gods,' fortune-telling, L. (cf. *daiva-*). **-prasāda**, m. 'having the d° favour,' N. of a man, Rājat. **-prasūta** (°*vá*-), mfn. god-produced (water), AV. vi, 102. **-prastha**, m. N. of the city of Senā-bindu, MBh. ii, 1022. **-priya**, mfn. 'dear to the gods;' stupid, silly, Gal. (cf. *devānām-*); m. N. of Śiva, Śivag.; of two plants (= *pīta-bhṛiṅgarāja* and *baka-pushpa*), L. **-psaras** (°*vá*-), mfn. serving the gods as a feast or enjoyment, RV. **-bandhu** (°*vá*-), mfn. related to the gods, RV.; m. N. of a Ṛishi, Kāṭh. **-bala**, m. 'having d° strength,' N. of a general, Kathās.; (*ā*), f. Sida Rhomboidea, L. **-bali**, m. oblation to the gods, Uṇ. iv, 123, Sch. **-bāhu**, m. 'the arm of the gods,' N. of an ancient Ṛishi, Hariv.; of a son of Hṛidika, BhP. **-bodha**, m. 'having d° knowledge,' N. of a poet and a Sch. on MBh., Cat. **-bodhi**, m. 'god-inspired,' N. of a poet, Cat. **-bodhi-sattva**, m. N. of a Buddh. saint. **-brahman**, m. 'a Brāhman among the gods,' N. of Nārada, L. (cf. *-rshi*); of Devala, Gal. **-brāhmaṇa**, m. a Brāhman esteemed by the gods, Pāṇ. ii, 1, 69, Siddh.; °*ṇasāt-√kṛi*, to present to the gods and Brāhmans, Hcat. i, 7 (wrongly °*sata-kṛi*). **-bhakta** (°*vá*-), mfn. distributed by the gods, RV. **-bhakti**, f. service of the gods, Siṇhās. **-bhaṭṭa**, m. N. of a man, Cat. **-bhadra**, m. N. of an author, Cat. **-bhavana**, n. 'divine abode,' heaven, L.; temple, Kathās.; Ficus Religiosa, L. **-bhāga**, m. 'the portion of the gods,' the northern hemisphere (opp. to *asura-*), Sūryas.; (°*gá*), N. of a teacher called also Śrauta or Śrautarsha, Br.; of a son of Sūra and brother of Vasu-deva, Hariv.; BhP. **-bhāshya-snāna-vidhi-paddhati**, f. N. of wk. **-bhishaj**, m. physician of the gods (the Aśvins), MBh. i, 721. **-bhīti**, f. fear of the gods (?), g. *dāsī-bhārâdi*.

— bhū, m. a god or (f.?) heaven, L. **— bhūta**, mfn. having become a god, Kāv. **— bhūti**, m. N. of the last prince of the Śuṅga dynasty, Pur. (v. l. °*mi* and °*ri*); f. the Ganges of the sky, L. **— bhūmi**, v. l. for prec. m. **— bhūya**, n. godhead, divinity, L. (°*yaṃ gata*, mfn. gone to d°, i. e. dead, Hcar.) **— bhūri**, v. l. for °*ti*, m. **— bhoga**, m. pleasure of the gods, heavenly joy, Bhag. ix, 20. **— bhojya**, n. 'food of gods,' Amṛita; nectar, L., Sch. **— bhrāj**, m. (nom. *ṭ*) 'shining like a god,' N. of a son of Mahya, son of Vivasvat (the sun), MBh. i, 43. **— mañjara**, n. the jewel on Vishṇu's breast, L. (cf. *-kaustubha*). **— maṇí**, m. divine amulet, AV. viii, 5, 20; = prec., L.; a twist of hair on a horse's neck, Śiś. v, 4, Sch.; N. of a drug belonging to the Ashṭa-varga (= *mahā-medā*), L.; N. of Śiva, L. **— maṇḍala**, m. N. of a partic. Samādhi, Kāraṇḍ. **— mata**, m. 'god-approved,' N. of a Ṛishi, MBh. xiv, 711. **— mati**, m. N. of a man, Pravar.; f. of a woman, Kathās. **— madhu**, n. divine honey, ChUp. iii, 1, 1. **— manushyà** (AV.) or °**shyá** (ŚBr.), m. pl. gods and men. **— maya**, mf(*ī*)n. consisting of or containing the gods, Hariv.; BhP. **— malimluc**, m. 'robber of the gods,' an Asura, TāṇḍyaBr. xiv, 4. **— māta**, m. N. of a man, Cat. **— mātṛi**, f. pl. the mother of the gods, MBh. xiii, 626; sg. N. of Aditi or of Dākshāyaṇī, Hariv.; Pur. **— mātṛika**, mfn. 'having the god (Indra) or clouds as foster-mother,' moistened only by rain-water (as corn, land), MBh. ii, 211; R. ii, 109, 23 (cf. *nadī-*). **— mādana**, mfn. gladdening or inspiring the gods (Soma), RV. **— māná**, n. dwelling of the gods, ib. **— mānaka**, m. = *-mañjara*, L. **— māya**, m. N. of a prince, Kathās.; (*ā*), f. d° illusion, R. i, 1, 26. **— mārga**, m. 'the way of the gods,' the air or sky, Gal.; = anus, R. v, 61, 4, Sch. (cf. Pañc. Introd. $\frac{1}{1}$). **— mālā**, f. 'divine garland,' N. of an Apsaras, Kathās. **— māsa**, m. 'the month of the gods,' the 8th m° of pregnancy, L. **— mitra**, m. 'having the gods as friends,' N. of an ancient teacher called also Śākalya, Pur.; of the father of Vishṇu-mitra, Cat.; (*ā*), f. N. of one of the Mātṛis attending on Skanda, MBh. **— mithuna**, n. cohabitation of the gods, AitBr. i, 22. **— miśra**, m. N. of an author, Cat. **— mīḍha** (VP. *-ka*), m. 'god-begotten (?),' N. of a Yādava and grandfather of Vasu-deva (cf. next), MBh.; of a descendant of Nimi and Janaka, R.; BhPur. **— mīḍhusha**, m. N. of the grandfather of Vasu-deva (cf. prec.), Hariv. **— muni**, m. heavenly or d° Muni, TāṇḍyaBr.; N. of a son of Iram-mada and author of RV. x, 146, RV. Anukr. **— yáj**, mfn. sacrificing to the gods (Agni), VS. i, 17. **— yájana**, mf(*ī*)n. id., AV. xii, 2, 42; serving for an oblation, x, 5, 15; n. place of offering, AV.; VS.; Br.; *-tvá*, n. MaitrS. iii, 8, 3; °*na-vat*, mfn. having a p° of o°, ShaḍvBr. ii, 10. **— yaji**, mfn. = *-yaj*, Bhaṭṭ.; m. a worshipper of the gods, a Muni, W. **— yajñá**, m. sacrifice to the gods (esp. the Homa or burnt s°, one of the 5 great oblations), ŚBr.; ĀśvGṛ.; Mn.; N. of a man (cf. *daiva-yajñi*). **— yájya**, n. or **-yajyá**, f. worship of the gods, a sacrifice, RV.; Br. &c. (instr. also °*jyā́*, RV. x, 30, 11 &c.) **— yaśás**, n. divine glory, TS. iii, 1, 9, 1; °*śín*, mfn. of d° g°, ib. **— yā́**, mfn. going to the gods, longing for them, RV. **— yājin**, mfn. sacrificing to the gods, ŚBr.; m. N. of one of the attendants of Skanda, MBh.; of a Dānava, Hariv. (v. l. *-yātrin*). **— yājñika**, m. N. of an author (= *yājñika-deva*), Cat. **— yātu**, m. 'a heavenly Yātu,' Kāṭh. (v. r. °*ta*; cf. *daiva-yātava*). **— yātrā**, f. an idol procession, Mālav. v, $\frac{1}{1}$. **— yātrin**, see *-yājin*. **— yā́na**, mf(*ī*)n. = *-yā*, RV.; AV.; VS.; leading to the gods, serving them as a way (*adhvan*, *pathin* &c.), ib.; Br.; Up.; MBh.; n. way leading to the gods, MBh.; BhP.; the vehicle of a god, L.; (*ī*), f. N. of a daughter of Uśanas or Śukrācārya (wife of Yayāti and mother of Yadu and Turvasu), MBh.; Hariv.; Pur.; of a wife of Skanda, RTL. 214. **— yānīya**, mfn. leading to the gods, Sāy. on RV. x, 18, 2. **— yávan**, mf(*varī*)n. going to the gods, RV. vii, 10, 2. **— yukta** (°*vá-*), mfn. (horses) yoked by the gods, 67, 8. **— yuga**, n. 'the age of the gods,' the first age of the world (= *kṛita*), MBh.; any age or period of the gods comprising the 4 ages of mankind, MW. **— yoní**, m. f. place or origin of a god, a d° birth-place, Br.; the sacred wood used for kindling fire, Gṛihyās. i, 81 &c.; mfn. of d° origin; m. a demi-god or demon, Devīm. v, 60. **— yoshā**, f. the wife of a god, MBh.; Hariv. **— rakta-daṇśī**, f. (in music) N. of a Rāgiṇī. **— rakshita**, m. 'god-protected,' N. of a son of Devaka, Hariv.; of a prince of the Kosalas, VP.; of a Brāhman, Kathās.; (*ā*), f. of a daughter of Devaka and one of the wives of Vasu-deva, Hariv.; Pur. **— rata**, mfn. delighting in the gods, pious, Pañc. **— rati**, f. 'gods' delight,' N. of an Apsaras, Kathās. **— rathá**, m. the car or vehicle of a god, AV.; TS.; Br.; a car for carrying the images of the gods in a procession, L. (cf. *daiva-*); N. of a man, Pravar.; °*thâhnyá*, n. a day's journey for the sun's chariot, SBr.; BṛĀrUp. **— rahasya**, n. divine mystery (cf. *-guhya*), MBh. **— rāj**, m. 'king of the gods,' N. of Indra, MBh.; R.; of Nahusha, MBh. xiii, 4788 &c. **— rājá**, m. d° ruler, TBr.; king of the gods, N. of Indra, MBh.; R. &c.; N. of a king, MBh.; of a Ṛishi, Var.; of a Buddha, Buddh.; the father of Śārṅgadhara, and sev. authors, Cat.; *-prabandha*, m., *-mahishī-stotra*, n. N. of wks.; *-yajvan*, m. N. of a Sch. on Naighaṇṭuka and also of his grandfather; *-sama-dyuti*, mfn. equal in glory to the king of the gods, MW. **— rājan**, m. a prince of a Brāhmanical family, TāṇḍyaBr. xviii, 10, 5. **— rājya**, n. sovereignty over the gods, MBh.; R.; Kathās. **— rāta**, m. 'god-given,' N. of Śunaḥ-śepa after being received into the family of Viśvā-mitra, AitBr. vii, 17; MBh. &c. (pl. his descendants, Pravar.); N. of a king who was the son of Su-ketu and descendant of Nimi, R.; Pur.; of a king who was son of Karambhi, Pur.; of another king, MBh. ii, 121; of Parikshit, BhP.; of the father of Yājña-valkya, ib. xii, 6, 64 (cf. *daiva-rāti*); a sort of crane, L. **— rāma** (*-bhaṭṭa*), m. N. of sev. authors, Cat. **— rāshṭra**, n. 'the empire of the gods,' N. of an empire in the Deccan. **— rūpā**, f. 'of divine form,' N. of an Apsaras, Kathās.; °*pin*, mfn. having a d° form, god-like, MBh. **— retasa**, mfn. sprung from d° seed, AitĀr. iii, 17. **— rshi**, m. (*deva* + *ṛishi*) a Ṛishi, a saint of the celestial class, as Nārada, Atri &c., MBh. (xiv, 781 *sapta saptarshayaḥ* for *s° devarsh°*); R.; Pur. &c. (cf. *brahmarshi* and *rājarshi*); N. of Śiva, MBh. xiii, 1259; *-carita*, n. the deeds of d° sages, MBh. xii, 7663; *-tva*, n. state or rank of a d° s°, BhP. i, 3, 8; *-pitṛi-vallabha*, m. sesamum, Gal.; *-varya*, m. chief of sages, MW. **— lakshmá**, n. d° characteristic, TS.; the Brāhmanical cord, Gal. **— latā**, f. 'divine creeper,' double jasmine, L. **— lāṅgulikā**, f. Tragia Involucrata, L. **— lāti**, g. *dāsībhārâdi*. **— liṅga**, n. the image or statue of a deity, BhP. iii, 17, 13. **— lekhā**, f. 'having a d° outline,' N. of a princess, Rājat. **— loká**, m. the world or sphere of any divinity; heaven or paradise; any one of the 3 or 21 (TS.) or 7 (MatsyaP.) superior worlds, Br.; Mn.; MBh. &c. (for the 6 d° lokas of Buddh. see MWB. 206 &c.); °*ke gata*, mfn. gone to the gods, dead, MBh. xiii, 2994; *-pāla*, m. 'protector of the world of the gods,' N. of Indra, Kathās. cxv, 25. **— vaktra**, n. 'the mouth of the gods,' N. of Agni as the devouring flame, L. **— vacanā**, f. 'having d° speech,' N. of a Gandharvī, Kāraṇḍ. **— 1. -vat** (°*vá-*), mfn. guarded or surrounded by gods (also °*vā́-v°*), RV.; m. N. of a man, ib. vii, 18, 22 (the grandfather of Su-dās, Sāy.); of a son of A-krūra, Pur.; of Devaka who was a son of Āhuka, Hariv.; of the 12th Manu, BhP. viii, 13, 28 (cf. *-vāyu*); (*vatī*), f. N. of a daughter of the Gandharva Grāma-ṇī, R. vii, 3, 3. **— 2. -vat**, ind. like (in, with &c.) a god, KātyŚr. **— vadhá**, m. a weapon of the gods, AV. vi, 13, 1. **— vadhū**, f. the wife of a god, MW. **— vandá**, mfn. praising the gods, RV. x, 15, 5. **— vara**, m. a superior or supreme deity, W.; n. a divine boon or blessing, ib. **— varṇini**, f. N. of a daughter of Bharad-vāja, R. vii, 3, 3. **— vartman**, n. 'd° path,' the atmosphere, L. **— vardhaki**, m. 'd° architect,' N. of Viśva-karman, L. **— vardhana**, m. N. of a son of Devaka, Pur. **— várman**, n. armour of the gods, AV.; m. 'having d° armour,' N. of a prince, VP.; of the author of the Tomara-vaṇśa (1350), Cat. **— varya**, m. best or chief of the gods (Śiva), MBh. vii, 9470. **— varsha**, m. N. of a prince; n. (?) of a Varsha in the Dvīpa Śālmala called after him, BhP. v, 20, 9. **— vallabha**, m. Rottlera Tinctoria, L. **— vāṇī**, f. a d° voice, MW. **— vāta** (°*vá-*), mfn. agreeable to the gods, RV.; m. N. of a man, ib. iii, 23, 2. **— vāyu**, m. N. of the 12th Manu, Hariv. 484 (cf. 1. *-vat*). **— vāhana**, mfn. (horse) carrying the gods, RV. **— vijaya-gaṇi**, m. N. of a teacher, Cat. **— víd**, mfn. knowing the gods, ŚBr. **— vidyā**, f. divine science (= *nirukta*, Saṃk.) **— vibhāga**, m. 'quarter of the gods,' the northern hemisphere, Sūryas. **— vimala-gaṇi**, m. N. of a poet, Cat. **— víś** (Br.) or **-viśā́** (MaitrS.), f. the gods collectively. **— ví** (or °*vā́-v°*), mfn. (superl. *-tama*) gratifying the g°, RV. **— vīti** (°*vá-v°*), f. a feast or enjoyment for the g°, RV.; N. of a daughter of Meru and wife of a son of Agnīdhra, BhP. **— vṛiksha**, m. 'd° tree,' a tree of paradise (cf. *-taru*), L.; Alstonia Scholaris, L.; bdellium (= *guggulu*), L. **— vṛitti**, f. Deva's (i. e. Purushottama-D°'s) Comm. on Uṇ. **— veśman**, n. 'house of the gods,' temple, chapel, Kathās. **— vyacas** (°*vá-*), mfn. affording space for the gods, receiving them, RV. **— vratá**, n. any religious observation or vow, ŚBr.; Lāṭy. &c.; the favourite food of the g°, TāṇḍyaBr. xviii, 2; N. of sev. Sāmans, SāmavBr.; mfn. devoted to the g°, religious, MBh.; Hariv.; Pur.; m. N. of Bhīshma, MBh.; of Skanda, Mṛicch. iii, $\frac{1}{1}$. **— vratin**, mfn. obeying or serving the g°, MBh. **— śakti**, m. 'having divine strength,' N. of a king, Pañc. **— śata-bhāshya**, n. N. of wk. **— śatru**, m. foe of the gods, an Asura or Rakshas, MBh.; R.; (°*vá-*), mfn. having the g° as foes, RV. vi, 59, 1. **— śabda**, m. the N. of a god, Jaim.; d° sound, i. e. thunder, Dhātup. xxxv, 8. **— śarman**, m. 'having the g° as refuge,' N. of an old sage, MBh.; of an Arhat (author of the Vijñāna-kāya-śāstra), MWB. 419; of a minister of Jayâpīḍa (king of Kaśmīra), Rājat.; Kathās. &c. **— śas**, ind. deity after deity, RV. iii, 21, 5. **— śābara-tantra**, n. N. of wk. **— śilpa**, n. work of divine art, AitBr. vi, 27. **— śilpin**, m. 'the artist of the gods,' N. of Tvashṭṛi, L. **— śiśu**, m. = *-garbha*, MBh. **— śishṭa** (°*vá-*), mfn. taught or directed by the g°, RV. i, 113, 3. **— śunī**, f. 'divine dog,' N. of Saramā, MBh. i, 671. **— śūra**, m. 'd° hero,' N. of a man, Cat. **— śekhara**, m. 'd° diadem,' Artemisia Indica, L. **— śesha**, n. the remnants of a god's sacrifice, MBh. xiii, 2019. **— śravas** (°*vá-*), m. 'having d° renown,' N. of a Bhārata, RV. iii, 23, 2. 3; of a son of Yama and author of RV. x, 17, Anukr.; of a son of Viśvā-mitra, Hariv.; of a son of Śūra and brother of Vasu-deva, ib.; Pur. **— śrī**, mfn. approaching the gods, worshipping, VS. xvii, 56, Mahīdh.; m. N. of a Ṛishi, VP.; *-garbha*, m. N. of a Bodhi-sattva, Buddh. **— śrút**, mfn. audible to or heard by the gods, RV.; VS. **— śruta**, m. 'having divine knowledge,' = lord, god (*īśvara*), L.; N. of Nārada, L.; (with Jainas) N. of 6th Arhat of future Ut-sarpiṇī; n. a sacred treatise or manual, L. **— śrū́**, mfn. known to the gods, TĀr.; m. barber of the g°, TS., Sch. **— śreṇī**, f. Sanseviera Zeylanica, L. **— śreshṭha**, m. 'best of the g°,' N. of a son of the 12th Manu, Hariv.; BhP. **— saṃsád**, f. assembly of the g°, TBr. **— saṃhitā**, f. the Saṃhitā of the gods, SaṃhUp. vi, 4. **— sakha**, m. friend or companion of the g°, VS. xxiii, 49. **— sakhi**, m. 'id.,' N. of a mountain, R. (B.) iv, 43, 17. **— saṃgīta-yonin**, m. (?) N. of Nārada, Hariv. 4347. **— sattra**, n. a long festival in honour of the g°, MBh. **— sattva**, mfn. having the nature of a god, R. **— satyá**, n. divine truth, established order of the gods, ŚBr. **— sád**, mfn. living among the g°, VS. ix, 2. **— sádana**, mfn. serving as a seat for the g°, AV. v, 4, 3. **— sadman**, n. a god's seat, MBh.; Hariv. **— saṃdha**, mfn. connected with the g°, divine, W. **— saṃnidhi**, m. presence of the g°, MW. **— sabha**, n. N. of a town, Kathās.; (*ā*), f. a hall serving as a meeting-place for the gods, ib.; a gambling-house, L. **— sabhya**, m. keeper of a gambling-house, L.; a gambler; frequenter of clubs or assemblies; deity's attendant, W. **— sarasa**, n. 'pool of the gods,' N. of a place, Rājat. **— sarshapa**, m. 'd° mustard,' a kind of m°, L. **— savá**, m. a kind of sacrifice, Kāṭh. **— saha**, m. N. of a mountain, Suśr.; (*ā*), f. N. of plants (= *saha-devī* or (?) *bhikshā-sūtra*), L. **— sākshya**, n. testimony of the gods; loc. before the g° as witnesses, Nid. **— sāgara-gaṇi**, m. N. of an author (1630), Cat. **— sāt-√kṛi**, to offer to the g°, Bhaṭṭ.; **-√bhū**, to become a god, MBh. **— sāyujya**, n. union with or reception among the g°, deification, L. **— sāvarṇi**, m. N. of the 13th Manu, BhP. **— siṇha**, 'god-lion,' N. of Śiva, Śivag.; of an author, Cat. **— siddhi**, m. N. of a man, Kathās. **— sunda**, m. N. of a lake, Suśr. **— sumatí**, f. favour of the gods, RV. x, 98, 5. **— sumanas**, n. 'divine flower,' a species of f°, L. **— sushi**, m. a divine tube or vital air (5 in number, viz. *prâṇa*, *vy-āna*, *apâna*, *sam-āna*, *ud-āna*), ChUp. iii, 13, 1. **— sū**, m. (with or scil. *deva*) N. of 8 deities (viz. Agni gṛiha-pati, Soma vanas-pati, Savitṛi satya-prasava, Rudra paśu-pati, Bṛihas-pati vâcas-pati, Indra jyeshṭha, Mitra satya, and Varuṇa dharma-pati), VS.; TS.; Br. &c. **— sūka-kshetra**, n. N. of a region of the northern

Pañcālas, W. **–sūda**, m. N. of a village, Pāṇ. vi, 2, 129, Kās. **–sūri**, m. N. of a man, Cat. **–sṛishṭa** (°*vá-*), mfn. discharged or caused or created by a god, ŚBr.; (*ā*), f. a kind of intoxicating drink, L. **–sena**, m. N. of a king of Śrāvastī, Kathās.; of a king of Pauṇḍra-vardhana, ib.; of a cowherd, ib.; of a Buddh. Arhat; (*ā́*), f. a host of celestials, RV.; AV.; Br. &c. (pl. the hosts of Deva or Īśāna, ĀpGṛh. xx, 5; *-pati* [L.] and *-priya* [MBh.], m. N. of Skanda); N. of a daughter of Prajā-pati or niece (daughter, L.) of Indra and wife of Skanda, MBh.; Pur.; a particle of *mūla-prakṛiti*, W.; N. of Comm. on Kum. **–soma**, °**maka**, m. N. of a man, Kathās. **–stava**, m. N. of a prince, VP. **–stút**, mfn. praising the gods, RV. v, 50, 5. **–strī**, f. the wife of a deity, MW. **–sthalī**, m. N. of an author, Cat. **–sthāna**, m. N. of an ancient Ṛishi, MBh.; n. of 2 Sāmans (*varuṇasya* and *bṛihad-deva-*), ĀrshBr. **–smitā**, f. 'having a divine smile,' N. of the daughter of a merchant, Kathās. **–sva**, n. d° property, Mn. xi, 20; 26. **–svâpaharaṇa**, n. plunder of d° property, sacrilege, MW. **–svāmin**, m. 'lord of the gods,' N. of sev. Brāhmans, Kathās.; Vet.; of an astronomer, VarBṛS. vii, 7; of a Sch. on ĀśvŚr. &c., Cat. **–havís**, n. oblation to the gods, VS.; ŚBr. **–havya**, n. id., MBh.; m. N. of a Ṛishi, ib. **–hiṇsaka**, m. enemy of the gods, MW. **–hita** (°*vá-*), mfn. arranged or appointed or settled by the g°, RV.; m. the good or welfare of the g°; °*târthāya*, ind. for the sake of the g°, MBh. xiii, 13965. **–hiti** (°*vá-*), f. d° ordinance or arrangement, ib. **–hū**, mfn. invoking the g° (superl. *-tama*), RV.; VS.; m. N. of a man, g. *gargâdi*; f. (scil. *dvār*) N. of the northern aperture of the human body, i.e. of the left ear (which is turned northwards if the face is directed towards the east), BhP. iv, 25, 51 &c. (cf. *pitṛi-*). **–hūti** (°*vá-*), f. invocation of the gods, RV.; AV. &c. (also °*tī*, BhP. ix, 24, 31); N. of a daughter of Manu Svayam-bhū and wife of Kardama, BhP. ii, 7, 3 &c. (°*tī*, iii, 21, 3). **–hūya**, n. invocation of the g°, RV.; ŚBr. **–hédana** or **-hélana**, n. offence against the g°, AV.; VS.; N. of AV. vi, 114, Kauś. **–hetí**, f. d° weapon, AV. **–hotra**, m. N. of the father of Yogêśvara (a partial incarnation [aṇśa] of Hari), BhP. viii, 13, 33. **–hrada**, m. 'the d° lake,' N. of a sacred bathing-place, MBh. **Devâṇśa**, m. a portion, i.e. partial incarnation of a god, Kathās. **Devâkrīḍa**, m. playing-place of the g°, Hariv. **Devâkshara**, mfn. whose syllables are divine beings, TBr. **Devâgama-stotra**, n., °**mâlaṃkṛiti**, f. N. of wks. **Devâgāra**, n. 'house of the g°,' temple, R.; Kathās. **Devâṅkī-pūjā**, f. N. of wk. **Devâṅga**, m. N. of an emanation from Sadā-śiva's body (inventor of weaving); *-caritra*, n. N. of wk. **Devâṅganā**, f. a divine female, Siṇhâs. **Devâc**, mf(*âcī*)n. directed towards the gods, RV. i, 127, 1. **Devâcārya**, m. 'd° teacher,' N. of a man, W.; of sev. authors, Cat.; *-dig-vijaya*, m. N. of wk. **Devâjīva** & °**vin**, m. a man subsisting by attending on an idol and receiving its offerings, L. **Devâñjana**, n. divine ointment, AV. xix, 44, 6. **Devâṭa**, m. N. of a sacred bathing-place, VarP. (cf. *patny-āṭa*). **Devâtitha**, w. r. for *daiv°*. **Devâtithi**, m. 'guest of the g°,' N. of a Kāṇva and author of RV. viii, 4, TāṇḍyaBr. ix, 2; of a prince who was son of A-krodhana (or Krodhana, BhP. ix, 22, 11) and Karambhā, MBh. i, 3775. **Devâtideva**, m. a god surpassing all other gods, MBh.; N. of Śiva, MBh. xiii, 1259; of Vishṇu, Hariv. 8814; of Śākya-muni, Buddh. **Devâtman**, m. the divine soul, ŚvetUp. i, 3; Ficus Religiosa, L.; mfn. being of d° nature, containing a deity, sacred, W.; °*tma-śakti*, f. the power of the d° soul, ŚvetUp., ib. **Devâtmā**, f. the mother of the gods, L. (cf. *devatâtmā*). **Devâdhideva**, m. 'god over gods,' an Arhat, Jain. **Devâdhipa**, m. 'king of the g°,' N. of Indra, MBh. v, 297; of a king identified with the Asura Nikumbha, i, 2663. **Devâdhipati**, m. 'id.,' N. of Śiva, MBh. xiii, 1204. **Devânanda**, m. 'delight of the gods,' N. of a man, W.; of sev. authors (also *-sūri*), Cat.; (*ā*), f. N. of the 15th night of the Karma-māsa (see s.v.), Sūryapr.; N. of a divine female, Siṇhâs. **Devânīka**, n. an army of celestials, MBh.; m. N. of a king (son of Kshema-dhanvan), Hariv.; Ragh.; Pur.; of a son of the 11th Manu, Hariv.; of a mountain, BhP. **Devânukrama**, m. 'series or order of the gods,' N. of wk. **Devânucara**, m. a follower or attendant of a god, Ragh. **Devânuyâyin**, m. id., Kull. **Devânta**, m. N. of a son of Hṛidika, Hariv. **Devântaka**, m. N. of a Rakshas, R.; of a Daitya, GaṇP.; *-vadha*, m. 'destruction of D°,' N. of 71st ch. of GaṇP. ii. **Devândhas**, n. 'd° food,' ambrosia, L. **Devânna**, n. id., L.; food offered (first) to the gods, Mn. v, 7. **Devâpi**, m. 'friend of the g°,' N. of a Ṛishi who was son of Ṛishṭi-sheṇa, RV. x (according to a later legend he is a son of king Pratīpa, resigns his kingdom, retires to the woods and is supposed to be still alive, MBh.; Pur. &c.) **Devâbhimukha**, m. a partic. Samādhi, Kāraṇḍ. **Devâbhīshṭā**, f. 'desired by the g°,' Piper Betel, L. **Devâyatana**, n. 'the dwelling of a god,' a temple, Mn. &c. **Devâyúdha**, n. 'weapon of the g°,' N. of Indra, TBr.; the rainbow, L. **Devâyushá**, n. the life-time of a god, ŚBr. **Devâraṇya**, n. divine grove, MBh.; Ragh. **Devârādhana**, n., °**nā**, f. worship of the gods, MW. **Devâri**, m. 'foe of the g°,' an Asura, MBh.; *-pa*, m. 'protector of the A°' (?), the sea, Nīlak. on MBh. iv, 1712; *-bala-sūdana*, m. 'destroyer of the army of the A°,' N. of Vishṇu, Vishṇ. i, 49. **Devârcaka**, m. worshipper of the gods, MW. **Devârcana**, n. worship of gods, idolatry, Pañc. (also °*nā*, f., MW.); *-krama-paddhati*, f. N. of wk. **Devârpaṇa**, n. an offering to the g°, MBh. xiii, 4202 (cf. *mad-arp°*). **Devârya**, m. N. of the last Arhat of the present Ava-sarpiṇī, Jain. **Devârha**, mfn. worthy of the g°, divine, W.; m. a kind of medic. plant, L.; N. of a prince, VP.; (*ā*), f. Sida Rhomboidea, L. **Devârhaṇa**, m. N. of a prince, VP. **Devâlaya**, m. 'residence of the g°,' heaven, L.; temple, Pañc.; MārkP.; *-pratishṭhā*, f., *-pratishṭhā-vidhi*, m., *-lakshaṇa*, n., °*yôtsavâdi-krama*, m. N. of wks. **Devá-vat** = *devá-v°*. **Devâvataraṇa**, n. 'descent of the gods,' N. of a poem. **Devâvatāra**, m. 'id.,' N. of a place, L. **Devâvasatha**, m. 'habitation of the gods,' temple, Rājat. **Devâvāsa**, m. id., L.; Ficus Religiosa, L. **Devâvī́** = *deva-vī*. **Devā-vṛídh** (for °*va-v°*), mfn. gladdening the g°, ŚBr. xi; m. N. of a mountain, Hariv. 12855 (nom. *-vṛit*; v. l. *-vṛidha*). **Devâvṛidha**, m. N. of a prince who was father of Babhru (cf. *daivā-v°*), MBh.; Hariv.; Pur. (v. l. *-vṛiddha*); of a mountain (see *-vṛidh*). **Devâśva**, m. divine horse, ŚāṅkhBr. v, 2; Indra's horse Uccaiḥ-śravas, L. **Devâsurá**, m. pl. the gods and the Asuras, ŚBr.; MBh.; R. &c.; mfn. (with *yuddha*, *raṇa* &c. the war) of the g° and A°, MBh.; R.; BhP.; *-gaṇâgraṇī*, °*ṇâdhyaksha*, °*ṇâśraya*; *-guru*; *-namaskṛita*; *-pati*; *-mahā-mātra*; *-mahâśraya*; *-mahêśvara*; *-vara-prada*; *-vinirmātṛi*; °*surêśvara*, m. N. of Śiva, MBh. xiii, 1233; 1257–60. **Devâhāra**, m. 'd° food,' ambrosia, L. **Devâhvaya**, m. 'called Deva,' N. of a prince, MBh. i, 228. **Devi-** and **devī-**, see *Devī́*. **Devêj**, mfn. (nom. *ṭ*) sacrificing to the gods, Vop. **Devêjya**, m. 'teacher of the g°,' N. of Bṛihas-pati, i.e. the planet Jupiter, L. **Devêddha**, mfn. kindled by the g° (*agni*), RV.; Br. (opp. *manv-iddha*). **Devêndra**, m. 'chief of the g°,' N. of Indra or Śiva, MBh.; R.; of sev. authors, Cat.; *-kīrti-deva*, m. N. of a man, Cat.; *-buddhi*, m. N. of a learned Buddhist, L.; *-samaya*, m. N. of a Buddh. wk.; *-sūri*, m. N. of a Jaina writer (1240), Cat.; °*drâśrama*, m. N. of an author, ib. **Devêśa**, m. 'chief of the g°,' N. of Brahmā or Vishṇu or Śiva or Indra, MBh.; Kāv.; king, prince, MBh. xiii, 1832; (*ī*), f. N. of Durgā or of Devakī, Cat.; *-tīrtha*, n. N. of a Tīrtha, ŚivaP. **Devêśvara**, m. 'sovereign of the g°,' N. of Śiva, R.; of a pupil of Śaṃkarâcārya, Cat.; of another author, ib.; *-paṇḍita*, m. N. of a poet, ib. **Devêshita**, mfn. sent or impelled by the g°, RV.; AV. **Deveshú**, m. divine arrow, MaitrS. **Devêshṭa**, mfn. wished by or acceptable to the g°, W.; m. a sort of drug (also *ā*, f.); the resin of Shorea Robusta, Gal.; bdellium, L.; (*ā*), f. the wild lime tree, L. (see also m.) **Devâinasá**, n. the curse of the g°, AV. **Devôdyāna**, n. 'grove of the g°,' sacred grove, L. **Devôpâsaka**, m. worshipper of the g°, MW. **Devâukas**, n. 'd° abode,' mount Meru, Sūryas. **Devasya-tva-ka**, mfn. containing the words *devasya tvā* (as an Adhyāya or Anuvāka), g. *goshad-ādi*. **Devānām-priya**, mfn. 'beloved of the gods,' simple, foolish, Pāṇ. vi, 3, 21, Vārtt. 3; L. **Deve-śaya**, mfn. resting on a god (Vishṇu), MBh. xii, 12864.

Devaka, mf(*ikā*)n. who or what sports or plays, W.; divine, celestial, id.; m. (*dév°*) a god, deity (at the end of an adj. comp.), MBh. ii, 1396 &c. (cf. *daivaka*); N. of a man (?), RV. vii, 18, 20, Sāy.; of a Gandharva (at once a prince, son of Āhuka and father of Devakī [below], MBh. i, 4480; v, 80 &c.; Hariv.; Pur.); of a son of Yudhi-shṭhira and Yaudheyī or Pauravī (cf. °*vikā* below), Pur.; familiar N. for *deva-dattaka*, Pāṇ. v, 3, 83, Pat.; pl. N. of the Śūdras in Krauñca-dvīpa, BhP. v, 20, 22; (*ā*), f. fam. for *deva-dattikā*, Pāṇ. vii, 3, 45, Vārtt. 4, Pat.; (*dévikā*), f. N. of a class of goddesses of an inferior order, Br. (pl. the oblations made to them, viz. to Anu-mati, Rākā, Sinīvālī, Kuhū, and to Dhātṛi, TS.; cf. *-havis*, AitBr.; Vait.); of the wife of Yudhi-shṭhira and mother of Yaudheya, MBh. i, 3828; of a river, MBh. iii, 5044 (cf. *dāvika*); of a country, VarBṛS. xi, 35; the thorn-apple, Bhpr.; (*devakī*), f., see below. **–bhoja-putrī**, f. patron. of Devakī, BhP. iii, 1, 33. **Devakâtmajā**, f. id., L.

Devakī, f. N. of a daughter of Devaka (see above) who was wife of Vasu-deva and mother of Kṛishṇa, MBh.; Hariv.; Pur. (identified with *A-diti*, Hariv.; with *Dākshāyaṇī*, MatsyaP.) **–nandana** (or °*kin°*), **-putra**, **-mātṛi**, **-sūnu**, m. N. of Kṛishṇa, ChUp.; MBh.; Hariv.

Devakīya, mfn. (g. *gahâdi*) divine, belonging or relating to a divinity, W. °**kya**, mfn. id.; godlike, corresponding to the number of the gods (said of the metre Anushṭubh), ŚāṅkhBr. xxvii, 3 (v. l. °*tya*).

Devátā, f. godhead, divinity (abstr. & concr.), RV.; AV.; Br. &c.; image of a deity, idol, Mn. iv, 130; MBh.; Pur. (ifc. *-ka*, Kull. viii, 105); N. of the organs of sense (cf. *deva*), ŚBr. ii, 5, 2, 2 &c.; (*ā*), ind. with divinity, i.e. with a god (gods) or among the gods, RV.; AV. **–°gāra** (°*tâg°*), n. 'gods' house,' temple, chapel, Mn.; R. **–gṛiha**, n. id., R.; Kathās. **–jit**, m. 'g°-conqueror,' N. of a son of Su-mati and grandson of Bharata, BhP. **–tas**, ind. on the part of a deity, ŚāṅkhŚr. i, 16, 15. **–°tman** (°*tât°*), mfn. having a divine soul, Kum. i, 1; m. N. of Śiva, MBh. xiii, 1260. **–°tmā** (°*tât°*), f. mother of the gods, L. (cf. *devâtmā*). **–tva**, n. state of divinity, Nyāyam.; *-nirṇaya*, m. N. of wk. **–darśana**, n. manifestation of a deity, NṛisUp. **–dvaṃdva**, n. a compound whose members are two or more names of deities, Pāṇ. **–°dhipa** (°*tâdh°*), m. 'deity-chief,' N. of Indra, L. **–°dhyāya** (°*tâdh°*), n. (scil. *brāhmaṇa*) N. of a Br. of the SV. **–°nukrama** (°*tân°*), m., °**maṇī**, f. index of the Vedic deities. **–pāramya**, n. N. of wk. **–pūjana**, n. worship of a d° (cf. *deva-pūjā*), Parāś. **–praṇidhāna**, n. devotion to a d°, L. **–pratimā**, f. 'god-image,' an idol, MBh. vi, 60. **–pratishṭhā-vidhi**, m. N. of wk. **–bādha** (or °*tâb°*), m. molestation of the gods, MBh. i, 7579. **–°bhyarcana** (°*tâbh°*), n. worship of an idol or a deity, Mn. ii, 176; *-para*, mfn. devoted to it, Nal. xii, 58. **–maṇi**, m. 'divine jewel,' N. of a medic. plant, Bhpr. **–mandira**, n. = *-gṛiha*, Mālatīm. vi, 8/9. **–maya**, mf(*ī*)n. containing all deities, KaṭhUp. iv, 7. **–mithuna**, n. the cohabitation of deities, MW. **–mūrti-prakaraṇa**, n. N. of a wk. on sculpture. **–°yatana** (°*tây°*), n. = *-gṛiha*, Mn.; MBh. &c. **–°rādhana** (°*târ°*), n. homage to the gods, Siṇhâs. **–°rcana** (°*târ°*), n. worship of the g°, Kāv.; *-krama* & *-vidhi*, m. N. of sev. wks. **–°laya** (°*tâl°*), m. (Var.); **-veśman**, n. (R.) = *-gṛiha*. **–vāda-vicāra**, m., **-vāri-pūjā**, f. N. of wks. **–śesha**, m. = *deva-ś°* (q.v.) **–°śraya** (°*tâś°*), mfn. relating to a g°, MānGṛ. **–sahāyin**, mfn. accompanied (only) by the g°, i.e. alone, Śak. (Pi.) iii, 88/89. **–sthāpana-vidhi**, m. N. of wk. **–snāna**, n. ablution of an idol, MatsyaP. **–svarūpa-vicāra**, m. N. of wk. **Devatêjyā**, f. sacrifice to a deity, KātyŚr. **Devatôpadeśana**, n. designation of the d° worshipped in any rite, ĀpŚr.

Devatyà, mfn. (ifc.) having as one's deity, sacred to a d° (cf. *eka-*, *kiṃ-*, *bahu-*, *soma-*; *daivatya*); (*ā*), f. a species of animal (?), AV. i, 22, 3.

Devan, m. brother-in-law (= *devṛi*), L.

2. **Devana**, m. a die, dice for gambling, L.; (*ā*), f. sport, pastime, L.; service, L.; n. (*dév°*) shining, splendour, Kull. viii, 92; gaming, a game at dice, RV. x, 43, 5; MBh.; R. &c.; play, sport, pastime, L.; pleasure-ground, garden, L.; a lotus, L.; praise, L.; desire, emulation, L.; affair, business, profession, L.; going, motion, L.

Devaya, Nom. P., only p. °*yát*, loving or serving the gods, religious, RV. (cf. *á-*); divine or shining (?), BhP. iii, 20, 22. °**yú**, mfn. devoted to the g°, pious, RV.

Devara, m. = *devṛi*, ĀśvGṛ.; Mn.; MBh. &c.; husband, lover, BhP. iv, 26, 26. **–ghnī**, f. killing one's brother-in-law, ŚāṅkhGṛ. i, 16. **–vatī**, f. having a brother-in-law, Gaut.

1. **Devala**, m. an attendant upon an idol (who subsists on the offerings made to it; oftener °*laka*, Mn. iii, 152; 180; MBh.); a virtuous or pious man, Uṇ. i, 108, Sch.; N. of a descendant of Kaśyapa and one of the authors of RV. ix; of Asita or a son of A°, MBh.; Pur.; of a man mentioned with A°, Prav.; of an astronomer, Var.; of a legislator (also *-bhaṭṭa*), Madhus.; Kull.; of a son of Pratyūsha, MBh.; Hariv.; of an elder brother of Dhaumya, MBh.; of the husband of Eka-parṇā, Hariv.; of the father of Saṃnati (the wife of Brahma-datta), ib.; of the grandfather of Pāṇ., Col.; of a son of Viśvā-mitra (pl. his descendants), Hariv.; of a son of Kṛiśāśva by Dhishaṇā, BhP. **–smṛiti**, f. Devala's law-book, Cat.

2. **Devala** = *devara* (q.v.)

Devāya, Nom.P., only p.°*yát* = °*vayát*, Maitr. & KapS.; Kāṭh. °*yú* or °*yū́* (only acc. sg. f. °*yúvam*) = °*vayú*, MaitrS.; Ār.

Devālā, f. (in music) N. of a Rāgiṇī.

Devi, in comp. for °*vī*. **–tama**, see *deva*. **–dāsa**, m. N. of sev. men, Cat.; of a Sch. on Vop., Col.

Devika, mf(*ī*)n. appertaining to or derived from a deity, W.; m. fam. N. for *deva-datta*, Pāṇ. v, 3, 78, Kāś.; (*ikā*), f. see *devaka*.

Devitavya, mfn. to be gambled (impers.), MBh.; n. gambling, ib. **Devitṛi**, m. gambler, ib. **Devitvā**, ind. p. having gambled (see √2. *div*).

Devin, mfn. gambling, a gambler, MBh. (cf. *aksha-*, *durdyūta-*, *sādhu-*).

Deviya, m. fam. N. for *deva-datta*, Pāṇ. v, 3, 79, Kāś.

Devila, m. id., ib.; mfn. righteous, virtuous (= *dhārmika*), Uṇ. i, 57, Sch.; appertaining to a deity, divine, W.

Devī́, f. (cf. *devá*) a female deity, goddess, RV.; AitBr.; MBh. &c. (e.g. Ushas, RV. vii, 75, 5; Sarasvatī, v, 41, 17; Sāvitrī, the wife of Brahmā, MBh.; Durgā, the wife of Śiva, MBh.; Hariv.; Kāv. &c.; the 4 goddesses of Buddhists are Rocanī, Māmakī, Pāṇḍurā and Tārā, Dharmas. iv); N. of a nymph beloved by the Sun, L.; of an Apsaras, MBh. i, 4818; (with Jainas) the mother of 18th Arhat of present Ava-sarpiṇī, L.; queen, princess, lady (the consecrated wife or daughter of a king, but also any woman of high rank), MBh.; Kāv. &c.; a kind of bird (= śyāmā), L.; a partic. supernatural power (= *kuṇḍalinī*), Cat.; worship, reverence, W.; N. of plants (colocynth, a species of cyperus, Medicago Esculenta &c.), L. **–kalpa**, m., **-kavaca**, n., **-kālôttara**, n. N. of wks. **–kṛiti**, f. 'the queen's creation,' N. of a grove, Kathās. **–koṭa**, n. 'Durgā's stronghold,' N. of a town (prob. Devicotta on the Coromandel coast), L. **–krīḍā**, f. Durgā's playground, Bṛih. **–garbha-gṛiha**, n. D°'s sanctuary, Kathās. **–gṛiha**, n. D°'s shrine, ib.; apartment of a queen, Kām. **–tantra**, n. N. of a Tantra. **–tva**, n. the state or rank of a goddess or queen, Kathās. **–datta**, m. N. of the father of Rāma-sevaka and grandfather of Kṛishṇa-mitra, Cat. **–dāsa**, m. N. of sev. authors (also *-cakra-vartin* & *-paṇḍita*), Cat. **–dhāman**, n. temple of Durgā, Rājat. **–nava-ratna**, n. N. of a Stotra. **–nāmâvalī**, f., **-nitya-pūjā-vidhi**, m. N. of wks. **–m-dhiyaka**, mfn. containing the words *devīṃ dhiyā* (as an Adhyāya or Anuvāka), g. *goshad-ādi*. **–pañca-ratna**, n., **-pañca-śatī**, f., **-para-pūjā-vidhi**, m., **-paricaryā**, f. N. of wks. **–pāda-dvaya**, n. 'the two feet of Durgā,' N. of a bathing-place, Cat. **–purāṇa**, n. N. of an Upa-purāṇa; °*ṇīya*, mfn. belonging to it, Cat. **–pūjana-bhāskara**, m., **-pūjā-paddhati**, f., **-pūjā-prakaraṇa**, n., **-pūjā-vidhi**, m. N. of wks. **–bhavana**, n. = *-dhāman*, Kathās. **–bhāgavata-purāṇa**, n., **-bhāgavata-sthiti**, f. N. of wks. **–bhāva**, m. the dignity of a queen, Vām. **–bhujaṃga**, m. or n. N. of a Stotra. **–bheda-giri**, m. N. of a mountain, Rājat. **–mata**, n. N. of a Tantra. **–mahā-deva**, n. N. of an Ullāpya (kind of play). **–mahiman**, m. N. of a Stotra. **–māna-nirṇaya**, m., **-mānasa-pūjana**, n., **-mānasa-pūjā-vidhi**, m. N. of wks. **–māhātmya**, n. N. of ch. of MārkP.; *-pāṭha-vidhi*, m., *-mantra-vibhāga-krama*, m. N. of wks. **–yāmala-tantra** & **-rahasya**, n. N. of wks. **–r-āpaka** (Gaṇar.) or °**pasaka** (g. *goshad-ādi*), mfn. containing the words *devīr āpas* (cf. *-m-dhiyaka*). **–śataka**, **-śata-nāma-stotra** & **-sahasra-nāman**, n. N. of wks. **–sahāya** & **-siṃha-deva**, m. N. of authors, Cat. **–sūkta**, n., **-stuti**, f., **-stotra**, n., **-svarūpa-stuti**, f., **-hṛidaya**, n. N. of Stotras.

Devīka, ifc. = *devī*; see *sa-*.

Devṛí, m. a husband's brother (esp. his younger brother), RV.; AV. (prob. as the player, because he has less to do than his elder b°); the husband of a woman previously married, W. [Cf. Arm. *taigr*; Gk. δαήρ; Lat. *levir*; Angl. S. *tacur*; Germ. *zeihhur*; Lith. *dêveris*; Slav. *dĕverĭ*.] **–kāma** (°*vṛí-*), mfn. loving one's brother-in-law. **–ghnī**, see *á-devṛi-ghnī*.

Devy, in comp. for *devī* before vowels. **–aparādha-kshamāpaṇa-stotra**, **-ashṭaka**, **-ashṭôttara** & **-āgamana-tantra**, n.; **-ātharvaṇa-śirshôpanishad**, f. N. of wks. **–āyatana**, n. = °*vī-dhāman*, Rājat. **–āryā-śataka**, n., **-āvaraṇa-pūjā** & **-upanishad**, f. N. of wks.

Devyà, n. divine power, godhead, RV.

देवट *devaṭa*, m. (√*dev*?, Uṇ. iv, 81, Sch.) artist, artisan.

देवट्टी *devaṭṭī*, f. a sort of gull (= *gaṅgā-cillī*), L.

देवण्णभट्ट *devaṇṇa-bhaṭṭa*, m. N. of an author, Cat.

देश *deśá*, m. (√1. *diś*) point, region, spot, place, part, portion, VS.; AitBr.; Śr. & GṛS.; Mn. &c.; province, country, kingdom, R.; Hit.; Kathās.; Vet.; institute, ordinance, W. (*deśam ā* √*vas* or *ni-* √*viś*, to settle in a place, Mn.; °*śe*, in the proper place [esp. with *kāle*], MBh.; Hit. Often ifc. [f. *ā*, Ragh. vii, 47; Ṛit. i, 27] esp. after a word denoting a country or a part of the body, e.g. *kāmboja-*, *magadha-*; *aṅsa-*, *kaṇṭha-*, *skandha-*; *ātmīya-*, one's own country or home); (*ī*), f. see *Deśī*. **–kaṇṭaka**, m. 'country's thorn,' public calamity, Jātakam. **–kārī**, f. (in music) N. of a Rāgiṇī. **–kāla**, m. du. place and time, Mn. iii, 126 &c.; (sg.) p° and t° for (gen.), Mṛicch. iii, 1/15; *-jña* (Kād.) and *-vid* (Car.), mfn. knowing p° and t°; *-vibhāga*, m. apportioning of p° and t°, MW.; *-virodhin*, mfn. neglecting p° and t°, Pañc.; *-vyatīta*, mfn. regardless of p° and t°, MBh.; *-vyavasthita*, mfn. regulated by p° and t°, W. **–cyuti**, f. banishment or flight from one's country, Daśar., Sch. **–ja** or **-jāta**, mfn. 'country-born,' native, born or produced in the right place, genuine (as horses, elephants &c.), MBh.; Hariv.; R. **–jña**, mfn. knowing a district, familiar with places, R. **–dṛishṭa**, mfn. seen (i.e. usual or customary) in a country, Mn. viii, 3; locally considered, judged as to place, W. **–dharma**, m. law or usage of a c°, Mn. i, 118. **–nirṇaya**, m. 'description of c°,' N. of wk. **–pālī**, f. (in music) N. of a Rāga. **–bha**, n. the asterism dominating a c°, Var. **–bhaṅga**, m. ruin of a c°, Kathās. **–bhāshā**, f. the language or dialect of a c°, MBh.; Kathās.; *-vijñāna*, n. its knowledge (one of the 64 Kalās), Cat.; °*shântara*, n. a foreign l° or d°, Mṛicch. iii, 19. **–bhramaṇa**, n. wandering about a country, peregrination, touring, MW. **–mānika**, m. pl. N. of a people (v. l. *daśa-*), VP. **–rakshin**, m. protector of a country, king, Daś. **–rāja-carita**, n. 'history of native princes,' N. of wk. **–rūpa**, n. conformity with place, propriety, fitness, MBh. xii, 3961. **–vāsin**, mfn. residing in a country, MW. **–vibhraṅśa**, m. = *-bhaṅga*, Var. **–vṛitta**, n. a circle depending upon its relative position to the place of the observer, Sūryas., Sch. **–vyavahāra**, m. custom or usage of a country, W. **–saukhya**, n. N. of a ch. of the Ṭoḍarânanda. **–stha**, mfn. situated or living in a c°, MW. **–svāmin**, m. lord or prince of a c°, Siṃhās. **Deśâkramaṇa**, n. invasion of a c°, Kull. vii, 207. **Deśâkhya**, m. (in music) N. of a Rāga; (*ā*), f. of a Rāgiṇī (also °*khyikā*). **Deśâcāra**, m. local usage or custom, MW. **Deśâṭana**, n. roaming through a land, travelling, Subh. **Deśâtithi**, m. 'land-guest,' foreigner, MBh.; Hariv. **Deśântara**, n. another country, abroad, Mn. v, 78; longitude, the difference from the prime meridian, Sūryas.; *-gamana*, n. going abroad, travelling, Mṛicch. ii, 0/9; *-phala*, n. the equation for difference of meridian, MW.; *-bhāṇḍâna-yana*, n. importing wares from foreign countries, MW.; *-mṛita-kriyā-nirūpaṇa*, n. N. of wk.; *-stha*, mfn. being in a f° c°, MānŚr.; °*ntarita*, mfn. living in a f° c°, Gaut.; °*ntarin*, mfn. belonging to a f° c°, a foreigner, Śatr. **Deśâpêkshā**, f. spying or inspecting a land, W. **Deśâvakāśika**, n. (with Jainas) a partic. vow or observance; *-vrata*, n. id. **Deśôpadeśa**, m. N. of a poem (cf. °*śa-nirṇaya*). **Deśôpasargá**, m. distress of a country, calamity in a c°, AV. xix, 9, 9.

Deśaka, mfn. (ifc.) showing, pointing out; m. shower, indicator (*san-mārga-*, MārkP. xix, 17; *dharma-*, Pañc. iii, 104/105, v. l. °*mâd*°); ruler, instructor, L. **–paṭu**, n. a mushroom, Kauś.

Deśanā, f. direction, instruction, SaddhP.; Śatr.

Deśika, mfn. familiar with a place, a guide (lit. and fig.), MBh. i, 3599 (v. l. *daiś*°, cf. *a-*[add.]); m. a Guru or spiritual teacher, MBh.; AgP.; a traveller, L. **–vijaya**, m., °**kôpanishad**, f. N. of wks.

Deśita, mfn. shown, directed, instructed, MBh.; R. &c.

Deśin, mfn. showing, instructing, guiding, MBh. &c.; of or belonging to a country, L.; (*inī*), f. the index or forefinger, Yājñ. i, 19; BhP.

Deśī, f. (sc. *bhāshā*) the vulgar dialect of a country (opp. to *saṃskṛita*), provincialism; *-tva*, n., Kāvyâd.; Deśin.; L.; a vulgar mode of singing, Cat.; dance (opp. to *mārga*, pantomime), Daśar.; (in music) N. of a Rāgiṇī. **–kaṭṭari**, f. (in music) a kind of dance (mus.) **–kośa**, m. a vocabulary of provincialisms, Cat. **–tāla**, n. (in music) a kind of measure. **–nāma-mālā**, f. N. of a dictionary of provincialisms by Hemac. **–nṛitya**, n. (in music) country dance. **–prakāśa**, m. N. of a dictionary of provincialisms, Sch. on Mṛicch. **–varāḍī**, f. (in music) N. of a Rāga. **–śabda-saṃgraha**, m. = *-nāma-mālā*, Cat.

Deśīya, mfn. peculiar or belonging to or inhabiting a country, provincial, native (esp. ifc., e.g. *Māgadha-*, a native of Magadha, ŚrS.); bordering on, resembling, almost, nearly (ifc. and regarded as a suffix, Pāṇ. v, 3, 67; cf. *pañca-varshaka-*, *paṭu-*, *shaḍ-varsha-*). **–rājaśekhara-kośa**, m. N. of wk. **–varāḍī**, f. = °*śī-v*°, Cat. **–śabda-saṃgraha**, m. = °*śī-ś*°, Cat.

Deśya, mfn. to be pointed or picked out, excellent in its kind, standard, Pat.; being on the spot or present, witness, Mn. viii, 52 (?, v. l. *deśa*); = *deśīya*, in all meanings, MBh.; Hariv. (*-tva*, Deśin.); Pāṇ. v, 3, 67 (cf. *ṭad-*, *nānā-*, *paṭu-*, *vanāyu-*, *vitasti-*, *śiśu-*); born in the country, indigenous, a true native, R. (cf. *deśa-ja*); n. the proposition or statement (= *pūrva-paksha*), L.; the fact or charge to be proved or substantiated, W. **–nighaṇṭu**, m., **-nidarśana**, n. N. of glossaries. **–bhikshu**, m. a native mendicant, Rājat. iii, 9.

Deshṭavya, mfn. to be pointed out or shown or declared, R.

Deshṭṛi, m. pointer, indicator (*kupatha-*, BhP. vi, 7, 14); (*ṭrī́*), f. N. of a divine female, RV.; AV.

Deshṭrā, n. indication, direction, RV.

देष्ठ *déshṭha*, mfn. (fr. √1. *dā*) giving most or best, RV.

Deshṇá, n. giving, a gift, RV. (cf. *kumāra-*, *cāru-*, *tuvi-* &c.), RV.

Deshṇu, mfn. giving, liberal, L.; = *dur-dama* or *dur-gama*, L.; m. (fr. √*dai*) a washerman.

देह *deha*, m. n. (√*dih*, to plaster, mould, fashion) the body, TĀr.; KātyŚr.; Mn. &c.; (in a triad with *manas* and *vāc*), Mn. i, 104 &c.; (°*haṃ dhāraya*, to support the body, i.e. exist, Nal.); form, shape, mass, bulk (as of a cloud; ifc. f. *ā*), Var.; person, individual, Subh.; appearance, manifestation, ifc. having the appearance of (*saṃdeha-*, Bālar. iii, 4/11); N. of a country, L.; (*ī*), f. mound, bank, rampart, surrounding wall, RV. **–kara**, m. 'body-former,' a father, MBh. **–kartṛi**, m. id., MW.; N. of the sun, MBh. **–kṛit**, m. a father, BhP.; N. of Śiva, MBh. **–kośa**, m. 'b°-covering,' skin or wing, L. (cf. *-dhi*). **–kshaya**, m. 'b°-decay,' sickness, disease, L. **–gata**, mfn. 'gone into a b°,' incarnate, MW. **–grahaṇa**, n. assuming a b° or visible form, ib. **–catushṭaya-vyavasthā-lakshaṇa**, n. N. of wk. **–cara**, mfn. being on or in a b°, bodily (as disease), BhP. **–caryā**, f. care of the b°, Kathās. **–cyuta**, mfn. separated from the b° (as excrement or the spirit), W. **–ja**, m. 'b°-born,' a son, BhP. (cf. *tanu-*); the god of love, Daś. **–tantra**, mfn. whose chief kind of existence is corporeal, BhP. iii, 33, 5. **–tyāga**, m. relinquishing the b°, death, Mn. x, 62; Kāv. &c. **–tva**, n. the state or condition of a b°, Āpast. **–da**, m. 'b°-(life?)giving,' quicksilver, L. (cf. *pāra-*). **–dāha**, m. 'b°-heat,' fever, Mālatīm. **–dīpa**, m. 'b°-lamp,' the eye, L. **–dharma**, m. function or law of the b°, MW. **–dhātṛi**, m. (for *dhātu*?) chief part or element of the b°, Car. (cf. *dhātu*). **–dhāraka**, m. 'b°-supporter,' bone, L. — **dhāraṇa**, n. 'supporting the b°,' living, life, existence, MBh. — **dhārin**, mfn. having a b°, living, alive, Daś. — **dhi**, m. 'b°-receptacle,' wing, L. — **dhṛik**, m. (nom.) 'sustaining the b°(?),' air, wind, Suśr. — **patana**, n. (MBh.), **-pāta**, m. (Kathās.) 'decay of the b°,' death. — **bandha**, mfn. furnished with a b°, Hariv. 9030 (*baddha*?). — **bhāj**, m. 'possessed of a b°,' corporeal, m. living creature (esp. man), Kāv.; BhP. — **bhuj**, m. 'possessing a b°,' N. of Śiva, MBh. xiii, 1067. — **bhṛit**, mfn. 'carrying a b°,' embodied, corporeal; m. a living creature (esp. man), MBh.; Ragh.; Pur.; N. of Śiva, MBh. xiii, 1067 (cf. *-bhuj*); life, vitality, W. — **bheda**, m. 'destruction of the b°,' death, ŚvetUp.; MBh. — **madhya**, n. 'middle of the b°,' waist, RāmatUp. — **mātrâvaśeshita**, mfn. having merely the b° left, BhP. — **mānin**, mfn. proud of the b°, MW. — **m-bhara**, mfn. intent (only) upon nourishing the b° or prolonging life, BhP. v, 26, 3; *-vārttika*, id.; 5, 3; voracious, gluttonous, MW. (cf. *udaram-bh°*). — **yātrā**, f. supporting the b° or prolonging life, BhP.; Vedântas.; food, nourishment, L.; passing away of the b°, dying, death, L. — **raksha**, f. 'care of the b°,' chastity, MBh. iii, 17092. — **lakshaṇa**, n. 'b°-mark,' mole, L. — **vat**, mfn. furnished with a b°, embodied, R.; m. a living creature, man, MBh.; BhP. — **varman**, n. 'b°-armour,' the skin, Gal. — **vāyu**, m. 'b°-wind,' vital air, L. — **visarjana**, n. 'quitting the b°,' death, MW. — **vṛitti**, f. support of the b°, Kathās. — **vṛinta**, n. 'b°-stalk,' navel, Gal. — **śaṅku**, m. a pillar of stone (?), KātyŚr. xxi, 3, 31, Schol. — **saṃcāriṇī**, f. 'issued from or passing through (her father's) b° (?),' a daughter, L. — **sāra**, m. 'b°-essence,' marrow, L. — **siddhi-sādhana**, n. N. of wk. — **sukha**, mfn. agreeable to the b°, Var. — **sthasvarôdaya**, m. N. of wk. **Dehâtmavāda**, m. 'assertion that the soul is b°,' materialism, Madhus.; *°din*, m. materialist, Cārvāka, L. **Dehânta**, m. end of the b°, death, BhP. **Dehântara**, n. another b°, MW.; *-prâpti*, f. obtaining another b°, transmigration, id. **Dehâri**, m. 'foe of the b°,' N. of Śiva, MBh. xiii, 1179, Sch. (as v. l. for *kāhali*). **Dehâvaraṇa**, n. 'b°-screen,' armour, dress, MBh. **Dehâvasāna**, n. = *°hânta*, Siṃhâs. **Dehâsava**, m. 'b°-liquid,' urine, Gal. **Dehêśvara**, m. 'lord of the b°,' the soul, MārkP. **Dehôtkampa**, m. trembling of the b°, Mālatim. v, 19. **Dehôdbhava** or **°bhūta**, mfn. born in the b°, innate, MW.

Dehalā, f. spirituous liquor, L.

Dehalī, f. (rarely *°li*) the threshold of a door or a raised terrace in front of it, GṛS.; Kāv.; Pur. — **mukta-pushpa**, n. a flower dropped on the threshold, Megh. 85. **Dehalîśa-stuti**, f., **°śastotra**, n. 'praise of the lord of the threshold,' N. of two hymns.

Dehikā, f. a sort of ant or insect which throws up the earth, MārkP. (cf. *ud-*, *upa-*).

Dehin, mfn. having a body, corporeal; m. a living creature, man, Mn.; MBh.; Kāv. &c.; m. the spirit, soul (enveloped in the b°), Up.; Bhag.; Suśr.; BhP.; (*inī*), f. the earth, L.

दै *dai*, cl. 1. P. *dāyati*, to purify, cleanse, Dhātup. xxii, 26 (cf. √5. *dā*).

दैक्ष *daiksha*, mf(ī)n. (fr. *dīkshā*) relating to initiation or inauguration &c., Lāṭy.

दैगम्बर *daigambara*, mf(ī)n. relating to the Dig-ambaras, VP.

दैड *daiḍá*, m. (*i*), f. patron., MaitrS.

दैतेय *daiteya*, m. (fr. *diti*) a son or descendant of Diti, an Asura, MBh.; Hariv.; R. &c.; N. of Rāhu, Var.; (*ī*), f. a female descendant of D°, R. vii, 58, 5, Sch.; mf(*ī*)n. proceeding from or belonging to the Daiteyas, MBh.; Hariv.

Daitya, m. a son of Diti, a demon, Mn.; MBh. &c.; mf(*ā*)n. belonging to the Daityas, MBh.; R.; (*ā*), f. N. of plants (= *caṇḍâushadhi* and *murā*), L.; spirituous liquor, L. — **guru**, m. 'preceptor of the Daityas,' N. of Śukra, the planet Venus, Var. — **dānava-mardana**, m. 'crusher of D°s and Dānavas,' N. of Indra, MW. — **deva**, m. 'god of the Daityas,' Varuṇa; Wind, L. — **dvīpa**, m. 'refuge of the D°(?),' N. of a son of Garuḍa, MBh. — **nāśana**, m. 'D°-destroyer,' N. of Vishṇu, MBh. — **nishūdana**, m. 'id.', N. of Indra, Jātakam. — **nisūdana**, m. 'id.', N. of Vishṇu, Pur. — **pa** and **-pati**, m. 'D°-prince,' N. of Bali, MBh.; Kathās. — **purodhas**, **-purohita**, **-pūjya**, m. = *-guru*, Var.; L. — **mātṛi**, f. 'mother of the D°s,' Diti, L. (pl., Hariv. 9498). — **meda-ja**, m. 'produced from the marrow of a D°,' a kind of bdellium, L.; (*ā*), f. the earth (supposed to be produced from the marrow of Madhu and Kaiṭabha), L. — **yuga**, n. an age of the D°s (= 4 ages of man), L. — **ṛtvij** (*°ya-ṛit°*), m. = *-guru*, Var.; Sch. — **senā**, f. N. of a daughter of Prajā-pati and sister of Deva-senā, MBh. — **han**, m. 'Daitya-slayer,' N. of Śiva, MBh.; of Indra, Hcat. — **hantṛi**, m. 'id.,' N. of Vishṇu, Kāv. **Daityântaka**, m. 'D°-destroyer,' Ratn. **Daityâri**, m. 'foe of the D°s,' a god (esp. Vishṇu), Prab. ii, 28; *-paṇḍita*, m. N. of a poet, Cat. **Daityâho-rātra**, m. a day and night of the D°s (= a year of man), L. **Daityêjya**, m. = *°tya-guru*, Var. **Daityêndra**, m. 'D°-prince,' N. of Pātāla-ketu, Prab. iii, 4; *-pūjya*, m. = *°tyêjya*, Var.

Daityāya, Nom. Ā. *°yate*, to represent a Daitya, BhP. x, 30, 16.

दैधिषव्य *daidhishavya*, m. (fr. *didhishū*) prob. the son of a woman by her second husband, ŚrS.

दैन 1. *daina*, mf(*ī*)n. (fr. *dina*) relating to a day, diurnal, daily, L. — **m-dina**, mf(*ī*)n. happening daily, quotidian, Pur.; *-dāna-kāṇḍa*, m. & n., *-sad-ācāra-darpaṇa*, m. N. of wks; *-pralaya*, m. destruction of the world after the lapse of 15 years of Brahmā's age, Pur.

Dainika, mf(*ī*)n. daily, diurnal, L.; (*ī*), f. a day's hire or wages, W.

दैन 2. *daina*, n. (fr. *dīna*) = the next, L.

Dainya, n. wretchedness, affliction, depression, miserable state, MBh.; Kāv.; Suśr. &c.; meanness, covetousness, W.

दैप *daipa*, mf(*ī*)n. (fr. *dīpa*) relating or belonging to a lamp, Śiś. xi, 18.

दैयाम्पाति *daiyāmpāti*, m. patr. fr. *dyām-pāta*, ŚBr.

दैर्घ 1. *dairgha* or (oftener) *°ghya*, n. (fr. *dīrgha*) length, longness, MBh.; Var.; Suśr.; Pur.

2. **Dairgha**, Vṛiddhi form of *dīrgha* in comp. — **tama**, m. = next, m., BhP. — **tamasa**, mf(*ī*)n. relating to Dīrgha-tamas, Lāṭy.; m. patr. fr. D°, ĀśvŚr.; n. N. of sev. Sāmans, ĀrshBr. — **rātrika**, mf(*ī*)n. long, chronic (disease), Car. — **varatra**, mfn. (with *kūpa*) founded by Dīrgha-varatra, Pāṇ. iv, 2, 73, Kāś. — **śravasa**, mf(*ī*)n. relating to Dīrgha-śravas, ŚrS.; n. N. of 2 Sāmans, ĀrshBr.

दैलीपि *dailīpi*, m. patr. fr. Dilīpa, q.v.

दैव 1. *daíva* or *daivá*, mf(*ī*)n. (fr. *devá*) belonging to or coming from the gods, divine, celestial, AV.; Br.; Mn.; MBh. &c.; sacred to the gods (*tīrtha*, n. the tips of the fingers, Mn. ii, 59; cf. s.v.; *°vī dik*, f. the north, L.; cf. 2. *diś*); royal (*vāc*), Rājat. v, 205; depending on fate, fatal, Kāv.; m. (with or without *vivāha*) a form of marriage, the gift of a daughter at a sacrifice to the officiating priest, Mn. iii, 21; 28; the knowledge of portents, Saṃk.; patr. of Atharvan, ŚBr.; pl. the attendants of a deity, TaṇḍBr. xvii, 1, 1; (*ī*), f. a woman married according to the Daiva rite, Vishṇ. xxiv, 30; a division of medicine, the medical use of charms, prayers &c., W.; n. a deity (cf. *kula-*), BhP. iii, 1, 35 &c.; (scil. *karman*, *kārya* &c.) a religious offering or rite, Yājñ.; MBh.; divine power or will, destiny, fate, chance (*°vāt*, ind. by chance, accidentally), AV.; Mn.; MBh. &c. — **karman**, n. oblations to the gods, religious rite, W. — **kṛita**, mfn. caused by divine power or nature, natural (opp. to 'artificial'), Suśr. — **kovida**, mfn. acquainted with the destinies of men; m.f. (*ā*) a fatalist, fortune-teller, L. — **gati**, f. 'course of destiny,' fortune (*°tyā* = *daivāt*), Megh. — **cintaka**, m. 'reflecting on fate,' astrologer, N. of Śiva, MBh.; Var.; Kāv.; fatalist, W. — **cintana**, n. (MW.), **-cintā**, f. (W.) fatalism or astrology. — **jña**, mfn. knowing fate or men's destinies; m. = *-cintaka*, N. of Śiva, Yājñ.; MBh.; Kāv. &c.; *-tva*, n. Var.; (*jñā*), f. female fortune-teller, L.; *-kalā-nidhi* & *-cintā-maṇi*, m., *-jātaka*, n., *-dīpa-kalikā* & *dīpikā*, f., *-bhūshaṇa*, n., *-manohara*, m., *-mukha-maṇḍana*, n., *-vallabha*, m. (or *°bhā*, f.), *-vidhi-vilāsa* & *-vilāsa*, m. N. of wks.; *-śarman*, m. N. of Viśva-nātha (son of Gopāla), Cat.; *-śiro-maṇi*, m. N. of wk.; *-sanmuni*, m. N. of an astrologer, L.; *°jñâlaṃkṛiti*, f. N. of wk. — **tantra**, mfn. subject to fate, MW. — **tas**, ind. by f° or chance, Kathās.; BhP. — 1. **-datta**, mfn. (for 2. see 2. *daiva*) given by f° or fortune, innate, natural, Daś. — **dīpa**, m. 'the heavenly lamp,' the eye, L. (cf. *deva-*, *deha-*). — **dur-vipāka**, m. the evil ripening of destiny through the effect of deeds done in the present or former births, Hit. — **dosha**, m. the fault or evil result of deeds, evil fate, MW. — **nirmita**, mfn. = *-kṛita*, MBh. — **para**, mfn. trusting to f°, fatalist, Kām.; Hit.; Pur. (also *°rāyaṇa*, R.); fated, willed, predestined, W. — **parîkshā**, f. N. of wk. — **praśna**, m. inquiring of f°, astrology (cf. *deva-*); a supernatural voice heard at night (cf. *upa-śruti*), L. — **yajña-piṇḍa-sūrya**, m. N. of an author, Cat. (w. r. for *deva-*?). — **yuga**, n. an age of the gods (cf. *daitya-*), MW. — **yuta**, mfn. favoured by fate, Var. — **yoga**, m. juncture of fate, fortune, chance; (*ena* & *āt*) ind. by chance, accidentally, Hariv.; Kathās.; Vet. — 1. **-rakshita**, mfn. (for 2. see 2. *daiva*) guarded by the gods, MW. — **ratha**, m. divine chariot (w. r. for *deva-*?), MBh. i, 634. — **rājya**, w. r. for *deva-*. — **lekhaka**, m. fortune-teller, astrologer, L. — **laukika**, mf(*ī*)n. celestial and worldly, MW. — **vaśa**, m. the will or power of destiny; (*āt*), ind. by chance, fatally, Dhūrtas. — **vāṇī**, f. a voice from heaven, W. — **vid**, mfn. destiny-knowing; m. an astrologer, Var.; Rājat. — **vidhi**, m. course of fate, Pañc. iii, 238. — **śrāddha**, n. a partic. Śrāddha. — **sampanna**, mfn. favoured by destiny; *-tā*, f., Kām. — **hata**, mfn. stricken by d°, ill-fated, R. — **hataka**, mfn. id.; cursed by d°, Amar.; n. a blow of d°, Prab.; cursed D°, Ratn. iv, ½. — **hīna**, mfn. forsaken by fortune, Var. **Daivâtyaya**, m. danger or evil resulting from unusual natural phenomena, Var. **Daivâdy-anta**, mfn. beginning and ending with a ceremony in honour of the gods (opp. to *pitrādy°*), Mn. iii, 205. **Daivâdhīna**, mfn. subject to fate, MW. **Daivânurodhin**, mfn. obedient to fate or to the will of the gods, W. **Daivânvita**, mfn. favoured by destiny, Var. **Daivâyatta**, mfn. dependent upon d°, W. **Daivâhō-rātra**, n. a day and night of the gods (= a year of men), W. (cf. *daityâho-*). **Daivêjya**, m. sacred to the planet Jupiter (topaz), L. **Daivôḍhā**, f. a woman married according to the Daiva ritual (see above); *-ja*, m. the son of such a w°, Mn. iii, 38. **Daivôdyāna**, n. divine grove, R. (cf. *devôdy°*). **Daivôpahata** (W.) & **°taka** (Kām.), mfn. struck by fate, ill-fated (cf. *daiva-h°*).

2. **Daiva**, Vṛiddhi form of *deva* in comp. — **kshatri**, m. patr. fr. Deva-kshatra, Hariv. 1994. — **jana** (*dai°*), mf(*ī*)n. belonging to the gods collectively, RV. x, 2, 22. — **tarasa**, m. patr. fr. Deva-taras, ĀśvŚr. xii, 10. — **tareya**, m. patr. fr. Deva-tara, g. *śubhrâdi*. — 2. **-datta**, mf(*ī*)n. being in the village Deva-datta, Pāṇ. i, 1, 75, Sch.; m. pl. the pupils of D°, 73. Vārtt. 5, Pat. (cf. *deva-dattīya*); *-śaṭhin*, m. pl. id., g. *śaunakâdi*, Kāś. — **datti**, m. patr. fr. Deva-datta, Pat.; *°dattika*, mf(*ī*)n. relating to D°, g. *kāśy-ādi*. — **darśanin**, m. pl. the pupils of Deva-darśana, g. *śaunakâdi*. — **dārava**, mf(*ī*)n. made of the tree Deva-dāru or being on it, Pāṇ. iv, 3, 139, Kāś. — **mati** & **-mitri**, m. patr. fr. Deva-mata & -mitra, g. *taulvaly-ādi*. — **mānushaka**, mfn. belonging to gods and men, Mn. xi, 235. — **yajñi**, m. patr. fr. Deva-yajña, g. *taulvaly-âdi* (f. *ī* or *yā*, Pāṇ. iv, 1, 81). — **yātava**, m. patr. fr. Deva-yātu; *°vaka*, mf(*ī*)n. inhabited by the Daivayātavas, g. *rājanyâdi*. — **yāneya**, m., metron. fr. Deva-yānī, MBh. i, 3163. — 2. **-rakshita**, m. patr. fr. Deva-r° (also pl.), VP. — **rathāyani**, m. patr. fr. Deva-ratha, g. *tikâdi*. — **rāja**, n. N. of a Sāman; *°jaka*, mfn. made by Deva-rāja, g. *kalâlâdi*; *°jika*, mf(*ā* & *ī*)n., g. *kāśy-ādi*. — **rāti**, m. patr. fr. Deva-rāta, N. of Janaka, MBh. xii, 11546; of Yājñavalkya, ŚBr. xiv, 4, 2, 5, Sch. — **vātá**, mf(*ī*)n. relating to Deva-vāta, RV.; m. patr. of Śriñjaya, ib. — **śarmi**, m. patr. fr. Deva-śarman, g. *bāhv-ādi*; *°mīya*, mfn. g. *gahâdi*. — **sthāni**, m. patr. fr. Deva-sthāna, g. *pailâdi*. — **hava**, mf(*ī*)n., g. *kaṇvâdi*. — **havya**, m. patron. fr. Deva-hū, g. *gargâdi*. **Daivātitha**, mf(*ī*)n. relating to Devātithi; n. N. of a Sāman, Lāṭy. **Daivānīka**, n. (fr. *devân°*) N. of a Sāman. **Daivāpá**, m. patr. fr. Devāpi, N. of Indrota, ŚBr. xiii, 5, 4, 1. **Daivāripa**, m. (fr. *devâri-pa*) a shell, MBh. iv, 1712. **Daivāvṛidh**, n. (fr. *dev°*) a partic. formula, Vait. **Daivāvṛidha**, m. patr. fr. Devā-vṛidha, N. of Babhru, AitBr. vii, 34. **Daivāsurá**, mf(*ī*)n. relating to the gods and Asuras, ŚBr.; cf. Pāṇ. iv, 3, 88, Vārtt.;

existing between the g° and A° (*vaira*, 'hostility'), 125, Vārtt.; containing the word *devâsura* (as an Adhyāya or Anuvāka), g. *vimuktâdi*.

Daivaka, mf(*ī*)n. (ifc.) = *daiva*, a deity (cf. *sa-*); (*ī*), f. = *devakī*, the mother of Krishṇa, L. °**kī-nandana**, m. N. of an author, W.; v.l. for *devakī-n*°, L.

Daivata, mf(*ī*)n. (fr. *devatā*) relating to the gods or to a partic. deity, divine, Śr. and GṛS.; m. N. of a prince, VP.; n. (m., g. *ardharcâdi*) a god, a deity (often coll. 'the deities,' esp. as celebrated in one hymn, cf. g. *prajñâdi*) Śr. & GṛS.; Up.; Mn.; MBh. &c.; image of a god, idol, Kauś.; Mn.; BhP.; mf(*ā*)n. ifc. having as one's deity, worshipping (cf. *ab-* [add.], *tad-*, *bhartṛi-*). — **kāṇḍa**, n. N. of Nir. vii–xii. — **pati**, m. 'lord of gods,' N. of Indra, R. — **para**, mfn. worshipper of the g°s, Nal. — **pratimā**, f. the image of a deity, AdbhBr. — **sarit**, f. 'divine stream,' the Ganges, Dhūrtan. ii, 27.

Daivatya, mf(*ā*)n. (fr. *devatā*) ifc. having as one's deity, addressed or sacred to some d°, Yājñ.; Mn.; MBh. &c. (cf. *devatya*).

Daivala, m. patr. fr. Devala, TāṇḍBr. °**laka**, m. = *devalaka*, L. °**li**, m. patr. fr. Devala, g. *taulvaly-ādi*, Kāś.

Daivika, mf(*ī*)n. peculiar or relating to the gods, coming from gods, divine, Mn.; Pur.; n. a fatal accident or chance, Yājñ. ii, 66; a partic. Śrāddha (on behalf of the gods, esp. the Viśve Devās), RTL. 305. — **dharma-nirūpaṇa**, n. N. of wk.

Daivya, mf(*ā* and *ī*)n. divine, RV. (esp. °*vyā hótārā*, the two divine priests); AV. &c.; m. N. of a messenger of the Asuras, TS.; n. divine power or effect, AV. iv, 27, 6; fortune, fate, L. — **hotṛi**, m. pl. the divine priests (cf. above), ĀpŚr. iii, 7, 10.

दैवन्त्यायन *daivantyāyana*, m. (patr. fr.?) N. of a man, pl. his descendants, ĀśvŚr. xii, 10.

दैवसक *daivasaka*, mf(*ikā*)n. (fr. *divasa*) happening in one day, MBh. iii, 13255.

दैवाकरि *daivākari*, m. (fr. *divā-kara*) 'son of the Sun,' patr. of Yama and Śani (the planet Saturn), L.; (*ī*), f. 'daughter of the Sun,' patr. of the river Yamunā, L. **Daivādika**, mf(*ī*)n. belonging to the div-ādis, i.e. to the 4th class of roots, Pāṇ. viii, 3, 65, Sch. **Daivodāsa**, mf(*ī*)n. relating to Divo-dāsa, RV.; m. patr. fr. D°, Pravar.; °*dāsi*, m. patr. of Pratardana, ŚāṅkhBr.; of Parucchepa, RV. Anukr.

दैशिक *daiśika*, mf(ī)n. (fr. *deśa*) relating to space (opp. to *kālika*, Bhāshāp.) or to any place or country; local, provincial, national, MBh.; R.; a native, Rājat.; knowing a place, a guide, MBh.; showing, directing, spiritual guide or teacher, MBh.; Hariv. (cf. *deśika* and *deśya*); n. a kind of dance, Mall. on Megh. 35.

दैशेय *daiśeya*, m. metron. fr. 2. *diś*, g. *śubhrâdi*.

दैष्टिक *daishṭika*, mf(ī)n. (fr. *dishṭi*) fated, predestined, W.; m. predestinarian, fatalist, Pāṇ. iv, 4, 60, Kāś. — **tā**, f., -**tva**, n. fatalism, predestinarianism, destiny, MW.

दैहिक *daihika*, mf(ī)n. (fr. *deha*) bodily, corporeal, PhP. °**hya**, mf(*ā*)n. being in the body (*ātman*), ib.; m. the soul, ib.

दो *do*, cl. 2. 4. P. *dāti*, RV. &c.; *dyáti*, AV. &c. (pf. 3 pl. Ā. -*dadire*, ŚBr. iii, 4, 2, 5; aor. *adāsīt* and *adāt*, Pāṇ. ii, 4, 78; Prec. *deyāt*, vi, 4, 67; *dāyāt*, Kāṭh.; -*dishīya*, RV.; cf. *ava-√do*) to cut, divide, reap, mow, RV.; AV.; ŚBr. &c.: Pass. *dīyate*, prob. to be cast down or dejected, Bhojapr.; Rājat.: Desid. *ditsati*, Pāṇ. vii, 4, 54: Intens. *dedīyate*, vi, 4, 66 (cf. *√day* and 3. *dā*).

दोःशालिन् *doḥ-śālin*, &c. See *doḥ*, p. 499.

दोग *doga*, m. a bull(?), W.

दोग्धव्य *dogdhavya*, mfn. (fr. *√duh*) to be milked, MBh.

Dogdhu-kāma, mfn. wishing to milk or to suck out, i. e. to strip or impoverish, Daś.

Dogdhṛi, m. a milker, AV.; MBh. &c. (cf. *a-*); a cowherd, L.; a calf, L.; a poet who writes for reward, L.; (*dógdhrī*), f. giving milk (a cow, wet-nurse &c.), VS.; Suśr. &c.; mfn. yielding milk or profit of any kind, MBh.; Kāv.

Dógdhos, abl. inf. of *√2. duh*, ŚBr.

Dogdhra, n. milk-pail, ĀpŚr.

Dógha, mfn. milking, or m. milker, milking, RV. v, 15, 5 (cf. *madhu-*, *su-*).

दोडी *doḍī*, f. a species of plant and its fruit, g. *harītaky-ādi* (cf. *ḍoḍī*, *ḍāḍī*).

दोड्डयाचार्य *doḍḍayâcārya*, m. N. of a teacher, Cat.

दोदुल्यमान *dodulyamāna*, mfn. (*√dul*, Intens.) swinging or being swung repeatedly or violently, W.

दोध *dodha*, m. (for *dogdhṛi*?) a calf, L.

दोधक *dodhaka*, mfn. robbing one's own master, L.; n. a form of metre (also -*vṛitta*, n.), Śrutab.; Chandom.; -*śloka-ṭīkā*, f. N. of Comm.

दोधत् *dodhat*. See *√dudh*.

दोधूयमान *dodhūyamāna*, mfn. (*√dhū*, Intens.) shaking or trembling violently, MBh.

दोमन् *doman*, n. (*√2. du*) pain, inconvenience (see *a-doma-dá* and *-dhá*).

दोरक *doraka*, n. rope, strap of leather, KātyŚr., Sch.; m. f. (*ikā*), a string for fastening the wires of a lute, W.

दोरान्दोलन *dor-āndolana*, &c. See *dos*.

दोल *dola*, m. (*√dul*) swinging, oscillating, MBh. i, 1214; a festival (on the 14th of Phālguna) when images of the boy Krishṇa are swung, W.; a partic. position of the closed hand, Cat.; (*ā*), f., see below. — **parvata**, m. N. of a mountain, L. — **maṇḍapa**, m. or n. a swing, L. — **yātrā**, see °*lā-y*°. — **yāna**, n. a swing, L. **Dolâdri**, m. = °*la-parvata*, L.

Dolā, f. litter, hammock, palanquin, swing (fig. = fluctuation, incertitude, doubt), MBh.; Kāv. &c. (rarely °*la*, m. or *ī*, f.); the Indigo plant, L. — °**kula-dhī** (°*lāk*°, Rājat.) and -**cala-citta-vṛitti** (Ragh.), mfn. one whose mind is agitated like a swing. — **ghara** and °**raka**, m. or n. a hall with a s°, Mālav. iii, $\frac{1}{1}\frac{4}{8}$. — °**dhirūḍha** (°*lādh*°), mfn. mounted on a s°, MW.; restless, disquieted, Kathās.; — °**ndolana** (°*lând*°), n. fluctuating in doubt like a s°, Prab. ii, 34 (v.l. *dor-ând*°). — **yantra**, n. drugs tied up in a cloth and boiled out over a fire, Bhpr. — **yātrā**, f. 'swing festival,' RTL. 430 (cf. *dola*); -*viveka*, m. N. of wk. — **yuddha**, n. a doubtful fight; Śiś. xviii, 80. — °**rūḍha** (°*lār*°) = °*lādhir*°, Kād., Pañc. — **rohaṇa-paddhati** (°*lār*°), f. N. of wk. — **lola**, mfn. restless like a s°, uncertain, Prab. v, 30. — **Dolôtsava**, m. = °*lā-yātrā*, W.

Dolāya, Nom. Ā. °*yate*, to rock about like a swing, move to and fro; be doubtful or uncertain, MBh.; Kathās. &c. °**yamāna**, mfn. oscillating, wavering; -*mati*, mfn. doubtful in mind, Hit. °**yita**, mfn. swung about, rocking; -*śravaṇa-kuṇḍala*, mfn. one whose earrings swing to and fro, Cat.

Dolikā, f. a litter, swing, cradle, L.

Dolita, mfn. swung, shaken, tossed (-*citta*, Śatr.); m. a buffalo, Gal.

दोष 1. *dosha*, m. evening, darkness (only BhP., where personified as one of the 8 Vasus and husband of Night, vi, 6, 11; 14); (*ā́*), f., see next.

1. **Doshā́**, f. darkness, night, RV.; AV. &c. (*ā́m* & *ā́* [instr.; cf. g. *svar-ādi*], ind. in the evening, at dusk, at night); Night personified (and regarded with Prabhā as wife of Pushpârṇa and mother of Pradosha or Evening, Niśitha [!] or Midnight and Vyushṭa or Day-break), BhP. iv, 13, 13; 14 (cf. *doshás*, *paścā-dosha*, *pra-dosha*, *prati-dosham*). — 1. -**kara**, m. 'night-maker,' the moon, Śatr. — **kleśī**, f. 'fading in the evening,' a kind of plant, L. — **tana**, mf(*ī*)n. (fr. *doshā*, ind.) nocturnal, at evening, Ragh. xiii, 76. — **tilaka**, m. 'night-ornament,' a lamp, L. — **bhūta**, mfn. (fr. *doshā*, ind.) having become n°, turned into n° (day), Uṇ. iv, 174, Sch. — **manya**, mfn. (fr. *doshā*, ind.) considered as n°, passing for n° (day), Śiś. iv, 62; cf. Pāṇ. vi, 3, 66, Kāś. — **ramaṇa**, m. 'N°'s lover,' the moon, Dhūrtan. ii, 22. — **vastṛi**, m. illuminer of the dark (Agni), RV. **Doshâsya**, m. 'face of the night,' a lamp, L.

Doshás, n. evening, dusk, AV. xvi, 4, 6.

दोष 2. *dosha*, m., rarely n. (*√dush*) fault, vice, deficiency, want, inconvenience, disadvantage, Up.; Mn.; MBh.; Kāv. &c.; badness, wickedness, sinfulness, Mn.; R.; offence, transgression, guilt, crime (acc. with *√ṛi* or *labh*, to incur guilt), ŚrS., Mn.; MBh. &c.; damage, harm, bad consequence, detrimental effect (*nâsha doshaḥ*, there is no harm; *ko 'tra d*°, what does it matter?), Mn.; MBh.; Kāv. &c.; accusation, reproach (°*sham √kṛi* or °*shena √gam* with acc., to accuse), R.; alteration, affection, morbid element, disease (esp. of the 3 humours of the body, viz. *pitta*, *vāyu*, and *śleshman* [cf. *tri-dosha* and *dhātu*], applied also to the humours themselves), Suśr.; (also °*shaka*) a calf, L. — **kara**, mf(*ī*)n. causing evil or harm, pernicious, Var. — **kārin** and -**kṛit**, mfn. id., ib. — **kalpana**, n. attributing blame, reprehending, W. — **guṇa**, n. bad and good qualities, Mn. ix, 330; °*ṇī-karaṇa*, n. turning a fault into a merit, Kuval., Sch. — **guṇin**, mfn. having good and bad qualities; °*ṇi-tva*, n., Mn. viii, 338; Sch. — **grasta**, mfn. involved in guilt, guilty, MW. — **grāhin**, mfn. fault-finding, censorious, susceptible of evil, L. (cf. *guṇa-*). — **ghna**, mf(*ī*)n. removing the bad humours, Suśr. — **jitkāra**, m. N. of wk. — **jña**, mfn. knowing the faults of (comp.), Kāv.; knowing what is evil or to be avoided, prudent, wise, Ragh. i, 93; m. a physician, L.; a Pandit, teacher, discerning man, W. — **tas**, ind. from a fault or defect; -*to √brū*, to accuse of a fault, R. ii, 61, 34. — **traya**, n. vitiation of the 3 humours (above); any combination of 3 defects, W.; -*ghna*, (f. *ī*) and -*hara*, mfn. removing the 3 bad h°, Suśr. — **tva**, n. faultiness, deficiency, Sāh. — **dūshita**, mfn. disfigured by a fault; -*tva*, n. Sarvad. — **dṛishṭi**, f. looking at faults, f°-finding, MW. — **dvaya**, n. a combination of two evils, Pracaṇḍ. i, 68. — **nirghāta**, m. expiation of a crime, penance, Āpast. — **parihāra**, m. N. of wk. — **prasaṅga**, m. attaching blame, condemnation, W. — **phala**, n. the fruit or consequence of a sin, Āp.; mfn. sinful, wicked, ib. — **bala-pravṛitta**, mfn. proceeding from the influence of bad humours (a disease), Suśr. — **bhakti**, f. tendency to a disease, Car. — **bhāj**, mfn. possessing faults or doing wrong, Yājñ.; a villain, Kautukas. i, 23. — **bhīti**, f. fear of offence, MW. — **bheda**, m. a partic. disease of the 3 humours, Suśr.; °*dīya*, mfn. relating to it, Cat. — **maya**, mf(*ī*)n. consisting of faults, Subh. — **vat**, mfn. having f°, faulty, defective, blemished, Mn.; MBh. &c.; guilty of an offence, Āp.; MBh.; connected with crime or guilt, sinful, wicked, Gaut.; Āp.; Mn.; noxious, dangerous, R. — **śamana**, mfn. = -*ghna*, Suśr. — **sthāna**, n. the seat of disorder of the humours, ib. — **hara**, mfn. = -*ghna*, ib. 2. **Doshâkara**, m. a mine or heap of faults, Kathās. **Doshâkshara**, n. 'word of blame,' accusation, Śak. **Doshânudarśin**, mfn. perceiving faults, MBh. i, 3068. **Doshânuvāda**, m. talking over faults, tale-bearing, MW. **Doshânta**, mfn. containing a fault, Pat. on Pāṇ. i, 1, 58. **Doshâpatti**, f. incurring a f°, MW. **Doshâropa**, m. imputing f°s, accusation, L. **Doshâikadṛiś**, mfn. seeing only f°s, censorious, L. **Doshôcchrāya**, m. the rise or accumulation of vitiated humours, Suśr. **Doshôdaka**, n. water caused by dropsy, ib. **Doshôddhāra**, m. N. of wk. **Doshôpacaya**, m. = °*shôcchrāya*, Suśr. **Doshôllāsa**, m. N. of wk.

Doshaṇa, n. imputation of a crime, accusation, MW. °**shala**, mfn. of a faulty nature, defective, corrupt, Suśr. °**shika**, mf(*ī*)n. faulty, defective, bad; m. disease, W. °**shin**, mfn. faulty, defiled, contaminated, Kāv.; Pur.; guilty of an offence, Gaut.

Doshāya, Nom. Ā. °*yate*, to seem or appear like a fault, Bhavabh.

दोषन् *doshán*, n. (occurring only in nom. du. *dosháṇī*, AV.; AitBr.; gen. sg. *doshṇás*, ŚBr.; instr. *doshṇā*, loc. *doshṇi* [or *doshaṇi-*, see below], gen. du. *doshṇos*, Rājat.; acc. pl. [m.!] *doshṇas*, Pāṇ. vi, 1, 63; the other forms are supplied by *dos*, q. v.) the fore-arm, the lower part of the fore-foot of an animal; the arm in general. **Doshaṇi-śrish**, mfn. leaning or hanging on the arm, AV. vi, 9, 2.

Doshaṇyà, mfn. being in or belonging to the arm, RV.; AV.

2. **Doshā**, f. (for 1. see 1. *dosha*) the arm, L.

Dós, n. (m. only R. vi, 1, 3; nom. acc. sg. *dós*, ŚBr.; du. *doshī*, Kauś.; *dorbhyām*, MBh.; Kāv.; pl. °*bhis*, Mālav.; *doḥshu*, BhP.) the fore-arm, the arm &c. = *doshan* (q. v.); the part of an arc defining its sine, Sūryas.; the side of a triangle or square, W. (cf. *bāhu* and *bhuja*).

Doḥ, in comp. for *dos*. **-śālin**, mfn. having strong arms, Kathās. **-śiñjinī**, f. = *dor-jyā*, Gaṇit. **-śekhara**, n. 'arm-top,' shoulder, L. **-sahasra-bhṛit**, m. '1000-armed,' N. of Arjuna Kārtavīrya, L.

Dor, in comp. for *dos*. **-ândolana**, n. swinging the arm, Prab. ii, 34 (v.l. *dolând°*). **-gaḍu**, mfn. having a crippled arm, L. **-graha**, mfn. 'seizing with the arms,' strong, L.; m. pain in the arm, W. **-jyā**, f. the sine of the base, Sūryas. **-daṇḍa**, m. 'arm-stick,' a long arm, Kāv. **-nikartana**, n. amputation of the arm, R. **-bāhavá**, n. pl. fore- and upper-arms, ŚBr. **-madhya**, n. the middle of the arm, W. **-mūla**, n. 'arm-root,' i.e. the armpit, Naish. **-latikā**, f. 'arm-creeper' (cf. *-daṇḍa*); *-darśanīya* (Subh.) or *-bhīma* (ŚārṅgP.), m. N. of the poet Bhīma.

Dosh-mat, mfn. having arms, HPariś. **Dostha** (for *doḥ-*), mfn. placed on the arm, W.; m. servant (cf. *pārśva-stha*), service, L.; player, play, L.

दोह **dóha**, mfn. (√2. *duh*) milking, i.e. yielding, granting (ifc.), BhP.; m. milking or milk, RV.; AV.; ŚBr. &c.; deriving advantage from (gen. or comp.), profit, gain, success, Daś.; Pur.; a milk-pail, MBh.; BhP.; *manaso d°*, N. of a Sāman; (*ā*), f. N. of a Prākṛit metre, Chandom. **-kāma** (*dó°*), mfn. desirous to be milked, TS.; Kāṭh. **-ja**, n. 'produced by milking,' milk, L. **Dohâdohīya**, n. N. of a Sāman, ĀrshBr. **Dohâpanaya**, m. milk, L.

Dohaka, m(*ikā*)fn., see *go-*.

Dohána, mf(*ā*)n. giving milk, a milker, RV.; giving milk, yielding profit (cf. *kāma-*, *bahu-*), MBh.; Hariv.; (*ī*), f. milk-pail, Kauś. (also *°nikā*, Hcat.); n. (also *dóh°*) milking, RV.; ŚBr. &c. (cf. *go-*); the result of m°, KātyŚr.; (also *°naka*, Hcat.) milk-pail, MBh.; Suśr.; BhP. (cf. *kāṅsya-*). **°nīya**, mfn. to be milked, MW.

Dóhas, n. milking; dat. *°háse*, as inf., RV. **°hita**, mfn. made to yield milk, milked, ŚBr. **°hin**, mfn. milking, yielding milk or desires (cf. *kāma-dohinī*). **°hīyas**, mfn. giving more or much milk, Pāṇ. v, 3, 59, Kāś.

Dóhya, mfn. to be milked, milkable, MaitrS.; n. an animal that gives milk, Yājñ. ii, 177 (cf. *duhya*, *duḥkha-dohya*, *sukha-dohā*).

दोहडिका **dohaḍikā**, f. a kind of Prākṛit metre (= *dohā*), Chandom.

दोहद **dohada**, m. (also n., L.; probably Prākṛit for *daurhṛida*, lit. sickness of heart, nausea) the longing of a pregnant woman for partic. objects (fig. said of plants which at budding time long to be touched by the foot or by the mouth [Ragh. xix, 12] of a lovely woman); any morbid desire or wish for (loc. or comp., f. *ā*), Yājñ.; R.; Kālid.; Pañc.; Kathās. &c.; pregnancy; a kind of fragrant substance used as manure, Naish. i, 82, Sch. **-duḥkha-śīlatā**, f. 'tendency to morbid desires,' pregnancy, Ragh. iii, 6. **-prakāra**, m. N. of a wk. on pregnancy. **-lakshaṇa**, n. 'having morbid longing as its mark,' a fetus or embryo, Ragh.; the period of passing from one season of life to another, L. **-vatī** and **°dânvitā**, f. having a pregnant woman's longing for anything, L. **°din**, mfn. eagerly longing for (loc. or comp.), Vāsav.; Kād.; Kathās.; m. the Aśoka tree, L.

Dohala, **°lavatī**, and **°lin** = *dohada* &c.

दौः **dauḥ**, Vṛiddhi form of *duḥ*, in comp. for *dus*, q.v. **-śaleya**, m. prob. metron. fr. Duḥ-śalā, Cat. **-śāsana**, mf(*ī*)n. belonging to Duḥ-śāsana, Pracaṇḍ. ii, 41; *°ni*, m. patr. fr. D°, MBh. xiv, 1825. **-śīlya**, n. bad character or disposition, wickedness, MBh.; R. &c. **-shanti** (*dáuḥ-*), m. patr. fr. Duḥ-shanta, Br. **-shṭhava**, n. (fr. *duḥ-shṭhu*) badness, wickedness, L. **-shvapnya**, n. evil dreams, AV. iv, 17, 5. **-stra**, n. (fr. *duḥ-strī*) discord between women (g. *yuvâdi*). **-sthya**, n. (fr. *duḥ-stha*) bad condition, Sarvad.

Daur, Vṛiddhi of *dur* for *dus*. **-ātmya**, n. bad-heartedness, wickedness, depravity, MBh.; Kāv. &c.; *°myaka*, mfn. wicked, evil (deed), R. **-ārddhi** (*daúr-*), f. (√*ṛidh*) want of success, TBr. **-itá**, n. mischief, harm, ŚBr. **-ga**, see *daurga*. **-gatya**, n. distress, misery, poverty, MBh. &c. **-gandha** (Divyâv.) and **°dhi** (W.), m.; **°dhya** (MBh.), n. bad smell, fetor. **-gahá**, m. 'descendant of Dur-gaha,' patr. of Puru-kutsa (Naigh. 'horse'), RV. iv, 42, 8. **-jana**, mf(*ī*)n. consisting of bad people (company), Nalac.; *°nya*, n. wickedness, depravity; evil, wrong, Hit.; BhP.; ill-will, envy, Śārṅg-P. **-jīvitya** (*daúr-*), n. a miserable existence, AV. iv, 17, 3. **-bala**, (v.l. for) **°lya**, n. weakness, impotence, MBh. &c. **-brāhmaṇya**, n. the state of being a bad Brāhman, KātyŚr.; Sch. **-bhāgineya**, m. the son of a woman disliked by her husband (g. *kalyāṇy-ādi*); (*ī*), f. the daughter of a disliked woman. **-bhāgya**, n. (fr. *dur-bhaga* or *-bhagā*) ill-luck, misfortune, Yājñ. i, 282; (*daúr-*), unhappiness of a woman disliked by her husband, AV.; MBh. &c. **-bhiksha**, n. famine, TāṇḍyaBr., Sch. **-bhrātra**, n. discord between brothers, g. *yuvâdi*. **-madya**, n. brawl, fight, L. **-manasâyana**, m. patr. fr. Dur-manas, g. *aśvâdi*. **-manasya**, n. dejectedness, melancholy, despair, Var.; Pañc. &c. **-mantrya**, n. bad consultation or advice, Bhartṛ. ii, 34 (v.l. *dur-mantra*). **-mitri**, m. metron. fr. *dur-mitrā* (g. *bāhv-ādi*). **-mukhi**, m. patr. fr. *dur-mukha*, MBh. vii, 7008 &c. **-yodhana**, mf(*ī*)n. belonging or relating to Dur-yodhana, MBh. iv, 1712 &c.; *°ni*, m. patr. fr. D°, vi, 2367. **-labhya**, n. difficulty of attainment, rarity, MW. **-vacasya**, n. evil speech, L. **-varṇika**, n. bad mark, Divyâv. **-vāsa** or **°sasa**, mf(*ī*)n. relating to Dur-vāsas, Madhus.; n. (scil. *purāṇa*) N. of an Upa-purāṇa. **-vratya** (*daúr-*), n. disobedience, ill conduct, VS. **-hārda**, n. badness of mind, wickedness, enmity, g. *yuvâdi*. **-hṛida**, n. id., MBh. v, 751; m. villain, Nīlak.; morbid longing of pregnant women, L. **-hṛidinī**, f. a p° w°, Bhpr.

Dauś, Vṛiddhi of *duś* for *dus*. **-carmya**, n. a disease of the skin or of the prepuce, Mn. xi, 49, Kull. **-carya**, n. ill conduct, wickedness, R. vi, 103, 20.

Daush, Vṛiddhi of *dush* for *dus*. **-kula** and **°leya**, mf(*ī*)n. sprung from a bad or low race, MBh.; R. **-kulya**, mfn. id., MBh. iii, 12629; n. low extraction, BhP. i, 18, 8. **-kṛitya**, n. badness, wickedness, TāṇḍBr.; Lāṭy. **Daushṭhava**, see *dauḥ-sh°* (above). **Daushpurushya**, n. the state of a bad man, g. *yuvâdi*.

दौकूल **daukūla**, mf(*ī*)n. (fr. *dukūla*) covered with fine cloth (also *°kūlaka* or *°gūla*), L.; n. a cloth made of Dukūla, Var.

दौत्य **dautya**, n. (fr. *dūta*) the state or function of a messenger, message, mission, MBh.; Hariv. &c. (*°yaka*, n., BhP.)

दौरुधर **daurudhara**, mfn. (fr. *durudharā*), Var.

दौरेश्रवस **daureśravasa**, m. (fr. *dūre-śravas*) patr. of the serpent-priest Pṛithu-śravas, TāṇḍyaBr. **Daureśruta**, m. (fr. *dūre-śruta*) patr. of the serpent-priest Timirgha, ib.

दौर्ग **daurga**, mf(*ī*)n. relating to Durga or Durgā; m. pl. the school of Durga, Cat.; n. a wk. by Durga, ib. **-siṅha**, mf(*ī*)n. belonging to or composed by Durga-siṅha, Cat. **Daurgāyaṇa**, m. fr. Durga, g. *naḍâdi*.

Daurgya, n. difficulty, inaccessibility, W.

दौर्वीण **daurvīṇa**, n. (fr. *dūrvā*) the sap or juice of bent grass, L.; = *mṛishṭa-parṇa* (a clean leaf, W.) or *ishṭa-parṇa*, L.

दौलेय **dauleya**, m. (fr. *duli*) a turtle or tortoise, L.

दौल्मि **daulmi**, m. N. of Indra (cf. *dalmi* and *dālmi*).

दौवारिक **dauvārika**, m. (fr. *dvār* or *dvāra*) door-keeper, warder, porter, Śak.; Pañc.; Rājat. (*°kī*, f., Ragh. vi, 59); a kind of demon or genius, Var.; Hcat.

दौवालिक **dauvālika**, m. pl. N. of a people, MBh. ii, 1874.

दौष्क **daushka**, mf(*ī*)n. (fr. *dos*) one who swims or crosses a stream by the help of his arms, Pāṇ. vii, 3, 51; Pat.; going on the arms, Uṇ. ii, 69, Sch.

दौष्ट्य **daushṭya**, n. (fr. *dushṭa*) depravity, wickedness, Var.

दौष्यन्त **daushyanta**, mf(*ī*)n. relating to Dushyanta, MBh.; m. N. of a mixed caste, Gaut.; *°ti*, m. patr. of Bharata, MBh.; Śak. &c. (w.r. *daushv°*).

Daushmanta, **°ti**, w.r. for prec.

दौहदिक **dauhadika**, m. (fr. *dohada*) a landscape gardener, Naish.; morbid or ardent desire, ib.

Dauhṛida and **°dinī** (Suśr.) = *daurhṛ°* (see *daur* under *dauḥ*).

दौहिक **dauhika**, mf(*ī*)n. (fr. *doha*) g. *chedâdi*.

दौहित्र **dauhitra**, m. (fr. *duhitṛi*) a daughter's son, Mn.; MBh. &c.; N. of a prince, VP. (v.l. *°trya*); (*ī*), f. a d°'s d°, MBh.; R.; n. a rhinoceros, L.; sesamum-seed, L.; ghee from a brownish cow, L. **-dauhitra**, m. the son of the daughter of the daughter's son, MBh. i, 5026. **-vat**, mfn. having a daughter's son, MBh.

Dauhitraka, mf(*ī*)n. relating to a daughter's son, ib.

Dauhitrāyaṇa, m. the son of a daughter's son, g. *haritâdi*.

द्य **dya**, **dyas**. See *a-dyá*, *sa-dyás*.

Dyām-pāta, **dyávā**. See under 2. *dyú*.

Dyāvan. See *vṛishṭi-*.

द्यु 1. **dyu**, cl. 2. P. *dyauti* (Dhātup. xxiv, 31; pf. *dudyāva*, 3 pl. *dudyuvur*) to go against, attack, assail, Bhaṭṭ. **Dyut**, mfn. advancing against, (ifc.), ib.

द्यु 2. **dyú**, for 3. *div* as inflected stem and in comp. before consonants. **-karṇârdha**, m. = *dina-vyāsa-dala*, Sūryas. **-kāma**, m. N. of a man (cf. *dyaukāmi*). **-kshá**, mf(*ā́*)n. (fr. 1. *ksha*) heavenly, celestial, light, brilliant, RV.; *-vacas* (*kshá-*), mfn. uttering heavenly words, vi, 15, 4. **-ga**, m. 'sky-goer,' a bird, L. (cf. *khe-cara*). **-gaṇa**, m. = *dina-rāśi*, Sūryas. **-gát**, ind. (√*gam*?) through the sky (Naigh. quickly), RV. viii, 86, 4. **-cara**, mfn. walking or moving in heaven, an inhabitant of h°, Hariv.; Rājat.; m. a Vidyā-dhara, Kathās. (*°rī* √*bhū*, to become a V°, ib.); a planet, Gol. **-cārin**, m. a Vidyā-dhara, Kathās. **-jana**, m. a god, Pur. **-jaya**, m. conquest or attainment of heaven, BhP. **-jīvā** (Gol.) and **-jyā** (Sūryas., Sch.), f. 'sky-diameter,' the d° of a circle made by an asterism in its daily revolution. **-taru**, m. the tree of heaven, BhP. **-dantin**, m. heavenly elephant (cf. *dik-karin*), Dharmaśarm. **-dala**, n. 'sky-half,' noon, Sūryas. **-dhāman**, m. having one's abode in heaven, a god, Pur. **-dhuni**, f. 'heavenly river,' the Ganges, BhP. **-nadī**, f. id., ib.; *-saṃgama*, m. N. of a place of pilgrimage, Rasik. **-nivāsa**, m. heavenly abode, heaven, W.; inhabitant of h°, a deity, ib. (also *°sin*, Siddhântas.); *°si-bhūya*, n. the becoming a deity. **-niś** or **-niśa**, day and night (only *°śi*, Var.; *°śos*, Mn.; *°śam*, Yājñ.; *°śe*, du., Sūryas.) **-pati**, m. 'sky-lord,' a god (pl.), BhP.; the sun, L.; N. of Indra, L. **-patha**, m. 'sky-path,' the upper part of the sky, Rājat. **-piṇḍa**, m. or n. = *ahar-gaṇa*, Sūryas. **-puraṃdhri**, f. = *-yoshit*, Rājat. **-bhakta** (*dyú-*), mfn. distributed by heaven, RV. **-maṇi**, m. 'sky-jewel,' the sun, Hcat.; N. of Śiva, MW.; calcined copper, Bhpr. **-mát**, mfn. bright, light, brilliant, splendid, excellent, RV.; VS.; BhP.; clear, loud, shrill, RV.; AV.; brisk, energetic, strong, ib.; m. N. of a son of Vasishṭha, BhP.; of Divo-dāsa (= Pratardana), ib.; of Manu Svārocisha, ib.; N. of a minister of Śalva, ib.; n. eye, ib. iv, 25, 47; ind. clearly, brightly, loudly, RV.; *-sena*, m. N. of a prince of Śālva, father of Satyavat, MBh.; R.; *°d-gāman*, mfn. loud-singing, SV. **-maya**, mf(*ī*)n. light, clear; (*ī*), f. N. of a daughter of Tvashṭṛi and wife of the Sun, L. **-maryāda** (or *-vat*), mfn. having the sky as boundary (*°da-tva* and *°da-vat-tva*, n., Śaṃk.) **-mārga**, m. = *-patha*, Kathās. **-maithuna**, n. cohabitation by day, AV.Pariś. (cf. *divā-maithunin*). **-maurvī**, f. = *-jīvā*, Gaṇit. **-yoshit**, f. 'heavenly woman,' an Apsaras, Kathās. **-ratna**, n. 'sky-jewel,' the sun, Kāvyapr. **-rātra**, n. day and night, Gaṇit.; *-vṛitta*, n. diurnal circle, Gol. **-rāśi**, m. = *ahar-gaṇa*, ib. **-loka**, m. the h° world, BṛĀrUp. (cf. *dyaur-l°*). **-vadhū**, f. = *-yoshit*, Kathās. **-van**, m. the sun, heaven, Uṇ. **-vanī**, f. heavenly grove, SŚaṃkar. **-shad**, m. 'sitting in h°,' a god, Rājat.; a planet, Gol. **-sad** and **-sadman**, m. a god, L. (cf. prec.) **-sambhava**, mfn. originating by day, Var. **-saras**, n. the lake of the sky, Kathās. **-sarit** (Bhartṛ.) and **-sindhu** (Kathās.), f. = *-nadī*. **-strī**, f. = *-yoshit*, Kathās.

Dyām-pāta, m. (fr. *dyām*, acc. of *div*, *dyu* + *p°*) N. of a man (cf. *daiyāmpāti*).

Dyávā (du. of *div*, *dyu*, 'heaven,' generally connected with another du. meaning earth, but also alone) heaven and earth, RV. ii, 6, 4; vii, 65, 2 &c.; night and day, i, 113, 2. **-kshame**, f. du. heaven and earth, L. **-kshāmā** (*dyā́°*), f. du. id., RV. **-pṛithivī** (*dyā́°*), f. du. id., RV.; AV. &c. (°*vyaú*, Suparn); *-vat*, mfn. connected with h° & e°, RV.; °*thivī́ya*, mfn. relating or sacred to them (also *vyà*), Br.; n. (scil. *sū́kta*) a partic. hymn, ŚāṅkhBr. **-bhū́mī** (*dyā́°*), f. du. heaven and earth, RV.; AV. &c.

Dyumná, n. splendour, glory, majesty, power, strength, RV.; AV.; ŚrS.; MBh. i, 6406; enthusiasm, inspiration, RV.; VS.; wealth, possession (= *dhana*, Naigh. ii, 10), Daś.; food, L.; N. of a Sāman, ĀrshBr.; m. N. of the author of RV. v, 53; of a son of Manu and Naḍvalā, BhP. **-vat** (°*mná-*), mfn. inspired or clearly sounding, RV. iii, 29, 15; strong, powerful, v, 28, 4 &c. **-várdhana**, mfn. increasing strength, ix, 31, 2. **-śravas** (°*mná-*), mfn. producing a strong or clear sound, v, 54, 1. **-sāti** (°*mná-*), f. receiving inspiration or power, i, 131, 1. **-hūti** (°*mná-*), f. inspired invocation, i, 129, 7 &c. **Dyumnā-sah** (strong *-sāh*), mfn. bearing strength, i, 121, 8. **Dyumno-dā** (fr. a stem °*mnas*), mfn. granting splendour, NārUp.

Dyumni, m. N. of a prince, VP. °**mnín**, mfn. majestic, strong, powerful, inspired, fierce, RV. °**mnīka**, m. N. of a son of Vasishṭha and author of RV. viii, 76.

Dyus. See *anye-*, *apare-* &c.

Dyo, Guṇa form of *dyu* in comp. **-kāra**, m. 'maker of brightness,' builder of splendid edifices, Nīlak. on MBh. xii, 1799 (v. l. *jyā-*). **-druma**, m. the heavenly tree = *kalpa-d°*, Naish. **-bhūmi**, m. 'moving between heaven and earth,' a bird, L.; (*ī*), f. du. h° and e°, W. **-shad**, m. 'sitting in h°,' a deity, L.

Dyau, Vṛiddhi form of *dyu* in comp. **-kāmi**, m. patr. fr. Dyu-kāma. **-śaṅsita** (*dyaú-*), mfn. impelled or incited by heaven, AV. x, 3, 25. **Dyaur-dā**, mfn. giving h°, ĀpŚr. xvii, 5. **-loká**, m. the heavenly world, ŚBr. xiv, 6, 1, 9.

द्युक *dyuka* & °*kāri*, w. r. for *ghūka* & °*kāri*.

द्युत 1. *dyut*, cl. 1. Ā. *dyótate*, AV.; MBh. (also °*ti*) &c. (pf. *didyute*, p. °*tāná*, RV. [cf. Pāṇ. vii, 4, 67], *didyóta*, AV.; °*dyutur*, TS.; aor. *adyutat* and *ádidyutat*, Br.; *ádyaut*, RV.; Br., *adyotishṭa*, Pāṇ. i, 3, 91; iii, 1, 55, Kāś., p. P. *dyutat*, A. °*tānā* or *dyútāna*, RV.; fut. *dyotishyati*, Br.; ind. p. *dyutitvā* or *dyot°*, Pāṇ. i, 2, 26, Kāś.; *-dyutya*, AitBr.) to shine, be bright or brilliant: Caus. *dyotayati* (°*te*, Bhaṭṭ.) to make bright, illuminate, irradiate, MBh.; Kāv.; to cause to appear, make clear or manifest, express, mean, ShaḍvBr.; Lāṭy.; Śaṃk.; Sāh.: Desid. *didyutishati* or *didyot°*, Pāṇ. i, 2, 26, Kāś.: Intens. *dávidyot*, 3 pl. °*dyutati*, RV.; AV.; Br.; *dedyutyate*, Pāṇ. vii, 4, 67, Kāś., to shine, glitter, be bright or brilliant.

2. **Dyút**, f. shining, splendour, ray of light, RV.; MBh. &c. (cf. *danta-*). °**tat**, mfn. shining; °*tád-yāman*, mfn. having a shining path, RV. °**tāná**, mfn. shining, bright, RV.; m. N. of a Ṛishi (with the patr. Māruta or °ti, author of RV. viii, 85) and the hymn ascribed to him.

Dyuti, f. splendour (as a goddess, Hariv. 14035), brightness, lustre, majesty, dignity, Mn.; MBh.; Var.; Kāv. &c.; (dram.) a threatening attitude, Daśar.; Sāh.; m. N. of a Ṛishi under Manu Meru-sāvarṇa, Hariv.; of a son of Manu Tāmasa, ib. **-kara**, mf(*ī*)n. producing splendour, illuminating, bright, handsome, W.; m. the polar star or (in myth.) the divine sage Dhruva, L. **-dhara**, m. N. of a poet, Cat. **-mat**, mfn. resplendent, bright, Var.; Rājat.; splendid, majestic, dignified, MBh.; R. &c.; m. N. of a prince of the Madras and father-in-law of Saha-deva, MBh.; of a prince of the Sālvas and father of Ṛicīka, ib.; of a son of Madirâśva and father of Su-vīra, ib.; of a son of Priya-vrata and king of Krauñca-dvīpa, Pur.; of a son of Prâṇa (Pāṇḍu), VP.; of a Ṛishi under the first Manu Meru-sāvarṇa (Hariv.) or under Manu Dākshasāvarṇi, BhP.; of a son of Manu Svāyam-bhuva, Hariv.; of a mountain, MBh.; (*ī*), f. N. of a woman, Cat. **-mati**, mfn. of brilliant understanding, clear-minded, R. iii, 78, 16.

Dyutita, mfn. enlightened, illuminated, shining (cf. *dyotita* and Pāṇ. i, 2, 21, Kāś.)

Dyutilā, f. Hemionitis Cordifolia, L.

1. **Dyota**, m. light, brilliance (cf. *kha-*, *cintya-*, *nakha-*); sunshine, heat, W.; (*ā*), f. a squinting or a red-eyed or a red-haired woman, GṛS., Comm. °**taka**, mfn. shining, illuminating (cf. *kha-*); (ifc.) making clear, explaining, Rājat. iii, 158; expressing, meaning, Sarvad.; *-tva*, n. ib.

1. **Dyótana** or **dyotaná**, mf(*ā* or *ī*)n. shining, glittering, RV.; illuminating, enlightening (cf. *kha-*); explaining, meaning, MW.; m. a lamp, Uṇ. ii, 78, Sch.; N. of a man, RV. vi, 20, 8 (Sāy.); n. shining, being bright, Śaṃk.; Kull.; illumination, BhP.; making manifest, explaining, showing, Śaṃk.; Sarvad.; seeing, sight, L. °**tanaka**, mf(*ikā*)n. making manifest, explaining; (*ikā*), f. explanation (ifc.), Cat. °**taní**, f. splendour, brightness, RV. °**tita**, mfn. shone upon, illustrated, bright (cf. *dyut°*); *-prabha*, mfn. resplendent, W. °**tin**, mfn. shining, brilliant, Megh. 18; meaning, expressing (ifc.), Sarvad.

Dyotis, n. light, brightness; a star; °*ir-iṅgaṇa*, m. a shining insect, fire-fly, L.; °*ish-patha*, m. 'star-path,' the upper part of the air, Ragh. xiii, 18 (v. l. *jyotish-*).

Dyotman. See *su-d°*.

Dyotya, mfn. to be expressed or explained, Pāṇ. ii, 3, 26; 27, Kāś.

Dyauta, n. N. of sev. Sāmans, ĀrshBr. °**tāna**, n. N. of a Sāman, TāṇḍBr.; Lāṭy. °**ttra**, n. light, splendour, Uṇ. iv, 160; forked lightning, W.

द्युत 3. *dyut*, Caus. *dyotayati*, to break, tear open, AV. iv, 23, 5 (cf. *abhivi-*, *ā-*).

Dyuttá, mfn. broken, torn or rent asunder, AV. iv, 12, 2; xii, 3, 22.

2. **Dyota** and °**tana.** See *hṛid-d°*.

द्युत *dyuta*, n. N of the 7th mansion (= δυτόν), Var. (v. l. *dyuna* or *dyūna*).

द्युन *dyuna.* See prec.

द्यू *dyū*, mfn. (fr. √2. *div*) playing or sporting with, delighting in (cf. *aksha-*, *eka-*, *kama-*, *mṛiga-*); f. game at dice (only *dyúvam* & *dyuvé*), AV. vii, 50, 9; 109, 5 (cf. *dív*).

Dyūtá, n. (m. only MBh. ii, 2119; cf. Pāṇ. ii, 4, 31) play, gaming, gambling (esp. with dice, but also with any inanimate object), AV.; ŚrS.; Mn.; MBh. &c.; (fig.) battle or fight, contest for (comp.), MBh. iii, 3037 &c.; the prize or booty won in battle, ib. vii, 3966; ix, 760. **-kara**, m. a gambler, Mṛicch.; *-maṇḍalī*, f. a gambler's circle (cf. *dyūta-maṇḍala*), ib. ii, 8/9. **-kāra**, m. = *-kara*, Pañc.; = next, L. **-kāraka**, m. the keeper of a gaming-house, L. **-kiṃkarī**, f. = *-dāsī*, Pracaṇḍ. ii, 42. **-kṛit**, m. a gambler, L. **-krīḍā**, f. playing with dice, gambling, MW. **-jita**, mfn. won at dice, MBh. **-tā**, f. = *-krīḍā*, MBh. xii, 2519. **-dāsa**, m. a slave won at dice, Veṇīs. v, 33/34; (*ī*), f. a female sl° won at dice, 29. **-dharma**, m. the laws concerning gambling, Mn. ix, 220. **-palāyita**, mfn. one who has run away from a game, Mṛicch. **-pūrṇimā** or **-paurṇimī**, f. the day of full moon in Kārttika (spent in games of chance in honour of Lakshmī), L. **-pratipad**, f. the first day of the bright half of the month Kārttika (celebrated by gambling), L. **-priya**, mfn. fond of gambling, MW. **-phalaka**, n. gambling-board, Pañcad. **-bīja**, n. a cowrie (a small shell used as a coin and in playing), L. **-bhūmi**, f. gambling-ground, playing-place, KātyŚr. **-maṇḍala**, n. a circle or party of gamblers; a gambling-house, Nār. xvi, 5, 6; MBh. ii, 2615; a circle drawn round a gambler (to make him pay), Mṛicch, ii, 8/9. **-lekhaka**, m. or n. a gambling-bill, Mṛicch, ii, 1 8/9. **-vartman**, n. method of g°, Daś. **-viśesha**, m. pl. 'different kinds of g°,' N. of ch. of Vātsyāy. **-vṛitti**, m. a professional gambler; the keeper of a g°-house, Mn. iii, 160. **-vaitaṅsika**, m. pl. men who live by g° and bird-catching, R. ii, 90, 28. **-śālā**, f. (Kathās.), **-sadana**, n. (BhP.), **-sabhā**, f. (W.), **-samāja**, m. (Daś.) a g°-house; an assembly of gamblers. **-samāhvaya-prakaraṇa**, n. 'a treatise on the law-suits arising from g°,' N. of ch. of Viśvêśvara's Su-bodhinī. **Dyūtâdhikārin**, m. the keeper of a g°-house, W. **Dyūtâdhyaksha**, m. superintendent of g°, Daś.

Dyūtya and °**tvā.** See *a-dyūtyá* and 2. *div.*

द्यून 1. *dyūna*, mfn. (fr. √1. and 2. *div*) lamenting, sorrowful, Bhojapr. (cf. *pári-*); playing, sportive, W.

द्यून 2. *dyūna* (ifc. also *-ka*), n. the 7th sign of the zodiac reckoning from that which the sun has entered, Var. (cf. *dyuta* & *dyuna*).

द्यै 1. *dyai*, cl. 1. P. *dyāyati* (Dhātup. xxii, 9), to despise, ill-treat.

2. **Dyai**, ind. fie! for shame! W.

द्यो *dyo*, *dyota* &c. See under *dyu* and 1. *dyut*.

द्यौष्पितृ *dyaush-pitṛi.* See under 3. *div*.

द्र *drá*, m. (fr. 2. *drā?*) AV. xi, 7, 3 (cf. *ut-tara-drá* [or *-drú?*], *kṛishṇa-*, *madhu-*).

द्रकट *drakaṭa* or *dragaḍa*, m. a kettle-drum for awakening sleepers, L.

द्रङ्क्षण *draṅkshaṇa*, n. a measure of weight (= *tolaka*), ŚārṅgS.

द्रङ्ग *draṅga*, m. a town, city, Śatr.; Rājat.; (*ā*), f. id., Rājat. (cf. *udr°* [for *ud-dr°*], *ku-dr°*; *traṅga*).

द्रढय *dradhaya* (fr. *dṛiḍha*), Nom. P. °*yati*, to make firm, fasten, tighten, strengthen, Uttarar. ii, 27; confirm, assert, L.; Sch.; to stop, restrain, Śārṅg. (cf. *dṛiḍhaya*).

Draḍhika, m. N. of a man, Pañc. °**ḍhiman**, m. firm place, stronghold against persecutors, Sch. on Yājñ. iii, 227; firmness, resolution, Bālar.; Kathās.; BhP.; affirmation, assertion, Śaṃk.

Draḍhishṭha and °**ḍhīyas**, mfn. superl. and compar. of *dṛiḍha*, Pāṇ. vi, 4, 161, Pat.

Drádhas, n. (for °*ḍhas?*) garment, TS. iii, 2, 2, 2.

द्रप्स *drapsá*, m. (√2. *dru?*) a drop (as of Soma, rain, semen &c.), RV.; ŚBr.; Gṛ. & ŚrS.; a spark of fire, RV. i, 94, 11; x, 11, 4; the moon (cf. *indu*), vii, 87, 6; flag, banner, iv, 13, 2; n. thin or diluted curds, L. **-vat**, mfn. (°*psá-*) besprinkled, AV.; containing the word *drapsa*, ĀpŚr. **Drapsín**, mfn. falling in drops, RV. i, 64, 2; flowing thickly, ŚBr. xi, 4, 1, 15; distilling, MW. **Drapsya**, n. thin or diluted curds, L.

द्रबुद्ध *drabuddha*, m. or n. a partic. high number, Buddh.

द्रम *dram*, cl. 1. P. *drámati* (Naigh. ii, 14) to run about, roam, wander, Dhātup. xiii, 23; pf. *dadramur*, Bhaṭṭ.: Intens. *dandramyate*, id., KaṭhUp. ii, 5. [Cf. √*drā* and 2. *dru*; Gk. ἔ-δραμ-ον, δέ-δρομ-α, δρόμος.]

द्रमिट *dramiṭa* or °*ta*, m. N. of a serpent-king, L.

द्रमिड *dramiḍa*, m. pl. N. of a school of grammarians (opposed to the Āryas), Cat. (cf. next and *draviḍa*). **-bhāshya**, n. N. of Comm. on the Brahma-sūtra.

द्रमिल *dramila*, m. N. of a country (also = *draviḍa*), L.; of a lexicographer (v. l. *drim°*); pl. his school, L.; Cat.

द्रम्म *dramma*, fr. and = Gk. δραχμή, Cat.; Col.

द्रव *dravá*, mfn. (fr. √2. *dru*) running (as a horse), RV. iv, 40, 2; flowing, fluid, dropping, dripping, trickling or overflowing with (comp.), Kāṭh.; Mn.; MBh.; Kāv.; fused, liquefied, melted, W.; m. going, quick motion, flight, Hariv.; play, sport, Jātakam.; distilling, trickling, fluidity, Bhāshāp.; juice, essence, decoction; stream or gush of (comp.), Kāv.; (dram.) the flying out against one's superior, Daśar.; Sāh.; N. of one of the Viśve Devās, Hcat. **-ja**, m. treacle, L. **-tā**, f. (Kād.; Śiś.), **-tva** (Hit.) and **-tvaka** (Bhāshāp.), n. natural or artificial fluid condition of a substance, fluidity, wetness. **-dravya**, n. a fluid substance, Suśr. **-prāya**, mfn. chiefly fluid (food), ib. **-maya**, mf(*ī*)n. liquid, soft, Mālatīm. iii, 4. **-mūrti**, f. fluid condition, Pāṇ. vi, 1, 24. **-rasā**, f. 'having fluid essence,' lac, gum, extract, L. **-vasu**, m. N. of a prince, VP. **-sveda**, m. a hot bath, Suśr. **Dravâdhāra**, m. 'fluid-holder,' a small vessel or receiver, L. **Dravêtara**, mfn. 'other than fluid,' hard, solid, congealed, Kir. xvii, 60. **Dravôttara**, mfn. chiefly fluid, very fluid, Suśr.

Dravaka, mfn. running, Vop. °**vaṇa**, n. running, TBr.; Hariv.; melting, becoming fluid, ŚārṅgP.; dropping, exuding, W.; heat, W.

Drávat, mfn. running, swift, RV. &c.; trickling, oozing, W.; (*antī*), f. a river, L.; Anthericum Juberosum, Suśr.; (*át*), ind. quickly, speedily. **Dravác-cakra**, mfn. having rapid wheels, RV. viii, 34, 18. **Dravat-pattrī**, f. a kind of shrub (= *śimṛiḍī*), L. **Dravát-pāṇi**, mfn. swift-footed, RV. viii,

5, 35; having swift horses, i, 3, 1. **Dravád-aśva,** mfn. drawn by swift horses, iv, 43, 2.

Dravatya, Nom. P. °*yati*, to become fluid, L.

Dravamāṇa, mfn. running, flowing, fluid, melted, MBh. &c.

Dravaya, Nom. Ā. °*yate*, to run, flow, RV. x, 148, 5.

Dravará, mfn. running quickly, RV. iv, 40, 2.

Dravasya, Nom. P. °*yati* (fr. *dravas* [√*dru*?], g. *kaṇḍv-ādi*), to harass one's self, toil, serve.

Draví, m. a smelter, one who melts metal, RV. vi, 3, 4.

Dráviṇa, n. movable property (as opp. to house and field), substance, goods (m. pl. BhP. v, 14, 12), wealth, money, RV.; AV.; Mn.; MBh. &c.; essence, substantiality, strength, power, RV.; AV.; ŚBr.; R. &c.; N. of a Sāman, ĀrshBr.; m. N. of a son of Vasu Dhara (or Dhava), MBh.; Hariv.; VP.; of a son of Pṛithu, BhP.; of a mountain, ib.; pl. the inhabitants of a Varsha in Krauñca-dvīpa, ib. **–nāśana,** m. 'destroying vigour,' Hyperanthera Moringa, L. **–rāśi,** m. a heap of wealth or riches, Hcar. **–vat,** mfn. possessing or bestowing goods, TāṇḍBr.; strong, powerful, MBh.; Hariv. **Draviṇâgama,** m. acquirement of property or wealth, Pañc. ii, 12 (B. °*ṇôdaya*). **Draviṇâdhipati,** m. 'lord of wealth,' N. of Kubera, R. **Draviṇêśvara,** m. = °*ṇâdhipati*, Pañc.; possessor of wealth, Subh. **Draviṇôdaya,** see °*ṇâgama*.

Draviṇaka, m. N. of a son of Agni, BhP.

Dráviṇas, n. movable property, substance &c. (= *dráviṇa*), RV. i, 15, 7 &c.; concr. bestower of wealth (said of Agni; Sāy. 'moving, ever moving'), iii, 7, 10; m. N. of a son of Pṛithu (= *draviṇa*), BhP. iv, 24, 2. **Dráviṇas-vat,** mfn. possessing or bestowing goods, RV. ix, 85, 1.

Draviṇasyú, mfn. desiring or bestowing goods, RV.

Draviṇiya, Nom. P. °*yati*, Pāṇ. vii, 4, 36, Sch.

Draviṇo, in comp. for °*ṇas*. **–dá, -dás, -dā́,** mfn. granting wealth or any desired good, RV.; AV.; VS. **–vid,** mfn. id., RV. ix, 97, 25.

Dravitṛí, m. runner, RV. vi, 12, 3, Sāy. °**vitnú,** mfn. running, quick, RV.

Dravī, in comp. for *drava*. **–karaṇa,** n. liquefaction, melting, L. **–√kṛi,** to liquefy, melt, L. **–bhāva,** m. melting, i. e. becoming soft or moved, Sāh. **–√bhū,** to become fluid, MBh.; Suśr.; Mṛicch.

Dravya, n. a substance, thing, object, Up.; Mn.; MBh. &c.; the ingredients or materials of anything, MBh.; R.; medicinal substance or drug, Suśr.; (phil.) elementary substance (9 in the Nyāya, viz. *pṛithivī, ap, tejas, vāyu, ākāśa kāla, diś, ātman, manas;* 6 with Jainas, viz. *jīva, dharma, adharma, pudgala, kāla, ākāśa*); (Gr.) single object or person, individual (cf. *eka-*); fit object or person (cf. *ā-*); object of possession, wealth, goods, money, Mn.; Yājñ.; MBh. &c.; gold, R. vii, 18, 34, Sch.; bell-metal, brass, L.; ointment, L.; spirituous liquour, L.; a stake, a wager, W. **–kiraṇâvalī,** f. N. of wk. **–kṛiśa,** mfn. poor in goods, Āp. **–gaṇa,** m. a class of similar substances, Suśr. **–garvita,** mfn. proud of money, Mṛicch. iii, 1. **–guṇa,** m. N. of wk.; *-dīpikā*, f., *-paryāya*, *-vicāra* & *-viveka*, m., *-śata-ślokī*, f., *-saṃgraha*, m., °*ṇâkara*, °*ṇâdarśa-nighaṇṭu* & °*ṇâdhirāja*, m. N. of wks. **–jāta,** n. a kind of substance, VP. iv, 4, 19 &c.; all kinds of things, Mālatīm. vi, 18/19. **–tas,** ind. in substance, according to s° &c., MW. **–tva,** n. substantiality, substance, Sarvad.; *-jāti-māna-vicāra*, m. N. of wk. **–dīpaka,** n. a kind of simile, Kāvyâd. ii, 101, Sch. **–devatā,** f. the deity of a substance, KātyŚr.; Hcat. **–dvaita,** n. duality of s°, instrumental cause (?), MW. **–nirūpaṇa,** n. N. of wk. **–niścaya,** m. N. of ch. of Bhaṭṭôtpala's Comm. on VarBṛS. **–patākā,** f., **-padârtha,** m. N. of wks. **–parigraha,** m. the acquirement or possession of property or wealth, R. **–pūjā,** f. N. of ch. of the PSarv. **–prakarsha,** m. the excellence of a matter, Pāṇ. v, 4, 11. **–prakalpana,** n. procuring materials for a sacrifice, ĀpŚr. **–prakāśikā,** f. N. of wk. **–prakṛiti,** f. the nature of a matter, MW.; pl. the constituent elements or necessary attributes (of a king), Pañc. i, 48; Kull. vii, 155. **–prayojana,** n. use or employment of any article, W. **–bhāshā** & *-ṭīkā*, f. N. of 2 Comms. **–maya,** mf(*ī*)n. material, substantial, MBh.; R. **–mātra,** n. only the money, Pañc. (B.) iv, 11, 24 (v. l. °*trā*). **–yajña,** mfn. offering a material sacrifice, Bhag. **–ratnâvalī,** f. N. of wk. **–lakshaṇa,** n. characteristic of a thing or person, definition, Kaṇ. **–vat,** mfn. inherent in the substance, Kaṇ.; rich, wealthy, KātyŚr.; Suśr.; MBh.; R.; *-tva*, n. wealth, opulence, Jaim. **–vardhana,** m. N. of an author, Var. **–vācaka,** mfn. expressive of a (single) thing or person; m. a substantive, MW. **–vādin,** mfn. = prec. (opp. to *jāti-*), RāmatUp. **–vṛiddhi,** f. increase of wealth, Mn. **–śabda,** m. = *-vācaka*, Sāh. **–śuddhi,** f. cleansing of soiled articles, Mn.; Gaut.; N. of wk.; *-dīpikā*, f. of a Comm. on it. **–śodhana-vidhāna,** n. N. of wk. **–saṃskāra,** m. consecration of articles for a sacrifice; purification or cleansing of soiled or defiled articles, W. **–saṃgraha,** m. N. of wk. **–saṃcaya,** m. accumulation of property or wealth, W. **–samuddeśa,** m. N. of ch. of the Vākyapadīya. **–sāra-saṃgraha,** m. N. of wk. **–siddhi,** f. acquirement of wealth; success by wealth, W. **–hasta,** mfn. holding anything in the hand, Mn. v, 143. **Dravyâtmaka,** mfn. substantial, containing a substance, BhP. **Dravyâtma-kārya-siddhi,** f. effecting one's object by means of wealth, MW. **Dravyâdarśa,** m. N. of wk. **Dravyântara,** n. another thing, g. *mayūra-vyaṃsakâdi*. **Dravyârjana,** n. acquirement of property or wealth. **Dravyâśrita,** mfn. inherent in a substance, L. **Dravyâugha,** m. abundance of wealth, Sāh.

Dravyaka, m. a carrier or taker of anything, Pāṇ. v, 1, 50.

द्रविड **dravida,** m. N. of a people (regarded as degraded Kshatriyas and said to be descendants of Draviḍa, son of Vṛishabha-svāmin, Śatr.) and of a district on the east coast of the Deccan, Mn.; Var.; MBh. &c.; collect. N. for 5 peoples, viz. the Āndhras, Karṇāṭakas, Gurjaras, Tailaṅgas, and Mahārāshṭras (cf. *drāviḍa* below); N. of a son of Kṛishṇa, BhP.; of an author, Cat.; pl. of a school of grammarians, ib.; (*ī*), f. (with *strī*) a Dravidian female, Cat.; (in music) N. of a Rāgiṇī. **–gauḍaka,** m. (in music) N. of a Rāga. **–deśa,** m. the country of the Dravidians, Cat.; °*śīya*, mfn. coming from or born in it, ib. **–bhāshya,** n. N. of Comm. **–śiśu,** m. 'son of Draviḍa,' N. of an author, Cat. **Draviḍâcārya,** m. N. of a teacher. **Draviḍôpanishad,** f. N. of an Up.; °*shac-chekhara*, m., °*shat-tātparya-ratnâvali*, f., °*shat-sāra*, m., °*shat-sāra-ratnâvalī-vyākhyā*, f. N. of wks. relating to it.

Drāviḍa, mf(*ī*)n. Drāvidian, a Drāvida, MBh.; Rājat. &c.; m. pl. the D° people, MBh. R.; Pur.; also collect. N. for the above 5 peoples, and of the 5 chief D° languages, Tamil, Telugu, Kanarese, Malayālam and Tulu; m. sg. a patr. fr. Draviḍa, Śatr.; N. of a Sch. on the Amara-kośa, Col.; a partic. number, L.; Curcuma Zedoaria or a kindred plant, Bhpr.; (*ī*), f. a Dravidian woman, Vcar.; small cardamoms, Bhpr. **–gauḍaka,** m. = *draviḍa-g°*. **–jāti,** f. N. of wk. **–bhūtika,** m. Curcuma Zedoaria. **–lipi,** f. the Drāvidian writing or character, Lalit. **–veda-pārāyaṇa-pramāṇa,** n. N. of work.

Drāviḍaka, m. Curcuma Zedoaria, L.; n. a kind of salt, L.

द्रव्य 2. **dravya,** mfn. (fr. 4. *dru*) derived from or relating to a tree, Pāṇ. iv, 3, 161; tree-like or corresponding to a tree, ŚāṅkhBr. x, 2; n. lac, gum, resin, L.

द्रष्टव्य **drashṭavyà,** mfn. (fr. √*dṛiś*) to be seen, visible, apparent, ŚBr.; MBh.; Kāv. &c.; to be examined or investigated, Yājñ.; to be regarded or considered as (nom.), MBh.; R.

Drashṭu, inf.-stem of √*dṛiś* in comp. **–kāma,** mfn. wishing to see, desirous of seeing, Mālatīm. ii, 5/6. **–manas,** mfn. having a mind to see, wishing to see, Vikr. ii, 17. **–śakya,** mfn. able to be seen, MW.

Drashṭṛi, m. one who sees, AV.; ŚBr.; MBh. &c. (also as 2nd sg. fut., MBh. i, 1685); one who sees well, R. ii, 80, 3; one who examines or decides in a court of law, a judge, Yājñ.; Mṛicch. **–tva,** n. the faculty of seeing, Kap.; Sāṃkhyak.; BhP.

द्रह **draha,** m. = *hrada*, a deep lake, L.

द्रह्य **drahya,** m. (fr. √*dṛih*) N. of a man (cf. *drāhyāyaṇa*).

Drahyát, ind. firmly, strongly, RV. ii, 11, 5.

द्रा 1. **drā.** See *drai*.

Drāṇa. See *an-ava-*, *ni-*, *vi-*.

द्रा 2. **drā,** cl. 2. P. *drāti* (Impv. *drā́tu*, *drā́ntu*, RV.; AV.; pf. *dadrau*, p. Ā. *dadrāṇá*, RV.; aor. *adrāsīt;* Subj. *drāsat*, ib.), to run, make haste: Caus. *drāpayati* (Desid. of Caus. *didrāpayishati*), ŚBr.; aor. *adidrapat*, Siddh.: Intens. *dáridrāti*, TS.; 3 pl. *daridrati*, Hit.; to run hither and thither; to be in need or poor: Desid. of Intens. *didaridrāsati* & *didaridrishati*, Pāṇ. vi, 4, 114, Vārtt. 2, Pat. [Cf. √2. *dru* & *dram;* Gk. διδρά-σκω, δρᾶ-ναι.]

Drāk, ind. (fr. √2. *drā* + *añc* or fr. √*dṛiś*) quickly, speedily, shortly, soon, Hariv.; Pañc. &c. **–kendra,** n. eccentricity, the distance of a planet from the point of its greatest velocity, Gaṇit. **–pratimaṇḍala,** n. a second eccentric circle, Gol. **Drāg-bhṛitaka,** n. water just drawn from a well, L.

Drāṇa, mfn. run, flown, Up.

द्राक्षा **drākshā,** f. vine, grape, Hariv.; Suśr.; Kāv. &c.; mfn. (*as, ī, am*) made of grapes, Kull. xi, 95. **–ghṛita,** n. a partic. medicine, Rasar. **–prastha,** n. N. of a city, g. *mālâdi*. **–mat,** mfn. furnished with grapes, g. *yavâdi*. **–rasa,** m. grape-juice, wine, MW. **–°rāmêśvara** (°*kshâr*°), m. 'lord of the vineyard,' N. of Śiva, RTL. 446, 5. **–rishṭa,** m. (in med.) a partic. beverage. **–latā,** f. vine, vine-tendril, MW. **–vana,** n. vineyard, Hariv. **–valaya-bhūmi,** f. a place furnished with vineyards, Ragh. **–vāruṇī,** f., **-°sava** (°*kshâs*°), m. liquor made of grapes, L.

द्राख् **drākh,** cl. 1. P. *drākhati*, to become dry or arid; to be able or competent; to adorn; to prohibit or prevent, Dhātup. v, 10 (cf. *dhrākh*).

द्राघ् **drāgh,** cl. 1. Ā. *drāghate*, to be able; to stretch, lengthen; to exert one's self; to be tired; to tire, torment; to roam, stroll, Dhātup. iv, 40: Caus. *drāghayati*, to lengthen (also prosod., RPrāt.), extend, stretch, Rājat.; Bhaṭṭ.; to be long or slow, tarry, delay, R.

Drāghita, mfn. lengthened (metrically), RPrāt.

Drāghimán, m. length, VS.; a degree of longitude, L.; °*ma-vat*, mfn. long, lengthy, W.

Drā́ghishṭha, mfn. (superl. fr. *dīrgha*, q. v.) longest, RV. &c.; m. a bear, L.; n. a kind of fragrant grass, L. °**ghīyas,** mfn. (compar. fr. *dīrgha*, q. v.) longer, RV. &c.

Drāghmán, m. = °*ghimán*, RV.; MaitrS.; instr. °*ghmā́*, ind. in length or along, RV. x, 70, 6.

द्राङ्क्ष् **drāṅksh,** cl. 1. P. *drāṅkshati*, to utter a discordant sound, croak or caw; to desire, long for, Dhātup. xvii, 19 (cf. *dhrāṅksh*).

द्राङ्गवध **drāṅgavadha,** m. N. of a man, Pravar.

द्राड् **drāḍ,** cl. 1. Ā. *drāḍate*, to split, divide; to go to pieces, Dhātup. viii, 35 (cf. *dhrāḍ*).

द्राप **drāpa,** m. (only L.) mud, mire; heaven, sky; fool, idiot; N. of Śiva with his hair twisted or matted; a small shell, Cypraea Moneta.

द्रापि 1. **drāpí,** m. mantle, garment, RV.; AV.

द्रापि 2. **drāpi,** mfn. (Caus. of √2. *drā*) causing to run (said of Rudra), VS. xvi, 47, Mahīdh.

द्रामिडी **drāmiḍī,** f. small cardamoms, Var. BṛS. lxxviii, 1, Sch. (v. l. *drāviḍī*).

द्रामिल **drāmila,** m. 'born in Dramila,' N. of Cāṇakya, L. (v. l. *dromiṇa*).

द्राव **drāva,** m. (fr. √2. *dru*) going quickly, speed, flight; fusing, liquefaction; heat, L. **–kanda,** m. a kind of bulbous plant, L. **–kara,** m. a kind of borax; a flux, L.

Drāvaka, mfn. (fr. √2. *dru*, Caus.; only L.) causing to run; captivating, enchanting; cunning; m. a pursuer or chaser; a thief; a wit, clever man; a libertine; a loadstone; a flux to assist the fusion of metals; distilled mineral acids; a kind of Rasa or sentiment; (*ikā*), f. saliva (as flowing); n. bee's wax (as melting); a drug employed in diseases of spleen.

Drāvaṇa, mfn. causing to run, putting to flight, MBh.; Hariv.; n. the act of causing to run &c., Hariv.; fusing, distilling, L.; softening, touching, Anaṅgar.; the clearing-nut, L. **–bāṇa,** mfn. whose arrow puts to flight (Kāma-deva), RTL. 200.

Drāvayát-sakha, mfn. (p. Caus. of √2. *dru* + *sakhi*) speeding the comrade (i. e. carrying the rider quickly away, said of a horse), RV. x, 39, 10.

Drāvayāṇa, mfn. putting to flight, MBh. vi

5199. °**vayitnú**, mfn. melting, RV. ix, 69, 6. °**vita**, mfn. made to run or fly, chased, BhP.; melted, liquefied, L.; softened, mollified, L. °**vin**, mfn. getting in motion (cf. *laghu-*); dissolving, removing (cf. *pitta-*, *mala-*, *māṅsa-*). °**vya**, mfn. to be made to run or put to flight, W.; fusible, liquefiable.

द्राविड *drāviḍa*. See p. 501, col. 2.

द्राविणोदस *drāviṇodasá*, mf(ī)n. (fr. *draviṇo-das*) coming from or belonging to or destined for those who present gifts (i. e. the sacrificers), RV. ii, 37, 4; Vait. xx, 5; relating to Draviṇo-das (Agni), Nir. viii, 2.

द्राविल *drāvila*, m. = *vātsyāyana*, Gal.

द्राह् *drāh*, cl. 1. Ā. *drāhate*, to wake; to deposit, put down, Dhātup. xvi, 45.

द्राह्यायण *drāhyāyaṇa*, m. (fr. *drahya*) patr. of an author of certain Sūtras, VBr. 1. **-gṛihya**, n. or **-sūtra**, n. pl. D°'s wks.

Drāhyāyaṇaka, n. the Sūtra of Drāhyāyaṇa. °**yaṇi**, m. patr. fr. D°. °**yaṇīya**, mfn. relating to D°, composed by him, L.

द्रिमिल *drimila*. See *dramila*.

द्रु 1. *dru*, cl. 5. P. *druṇoti*, to hurt, injure, Dhātup. xxvii, 33 (pf. *dudrāva*, Bhaṭṭ.); to repent; to go, Vop. (cf. 1. *drū*).

द्रु 2. *dru*, 1. P. (Dhātup. xxii, 47; ep. also Ā.) *drávati*, °*te*, RV. &c. &c. (pf. *dudrāva*, Br.; °*drotha*, °*druma*, Pāṇ. vii, 2, 13; °*druvur*, MBh.; R. &c.; aor. *adudruvat*, Br.; °*drot*, Subj. *dudrávat*, RV.; fut. *droshyati*, Br.; inf. *-drotum*, Śatr.; ind. p. *drutvā* & *-drutya*, Br.) to run, hasten, flee, RV.; AV.; ŚBr.; MBh.; Kāv. &c.; to run up to (acc.), attack, assault, MBh.; R.; to become fluid, dissolve, melt, Pañc.; Vet.; BhP.: Caus. *drāváyati* (ep. also °*te*; *dravayate*, see under *dravá*) to cause to run, make flow, RV. viii, 4, 11; to make fluid, melt, vi, 4, 3; to drive away, put to flight, MBh. (Pass. *drāvyate*, vii, 3515); R.; BhP.: Desid. *dudrūshati*, Gr.: Desid. of Caus. *dudrāvayishati* or *did*°, Pāṇ. vii, 4, 81: Intens. *dodrūyate* or *dodroti*, Gr. (*dodrāva*, TS.). [Cf. 2. *drā* & *dram*; Zd. *dru*, *drvant*.]

3. **Dru**, mfn. running, going (cf. *mita-*, *raghu-*, *śatā-*); f. going, motion, L.

Druta, mfn. quick, speedy, swift, MBh.; R.; quickly or indistinctly spoken, Gīt.; flown, run away or asunder, Kāv.; Pur.; dissolved, melted, fluid, Kāv.; m. a scorpion, L.; a tree (cf. *druṇa* & *druma*), L.; n. a partic. faulty pronunciation of vowels, Pat.; (*am*), ind. quickly, rapidly, without delay, Mn.; MBh. &c. **-gati**, mfn. going quickly, hastening, Daś. **-caurya**, n. a theft rapidly committed, Deśīn. **-tara**, mfn. (compar.) quicker, swifter (*-gati*, mfn. quicker in motion, Megh.); (*am*), ind. very quickly, as quickly as possible, Kāv. **-tva**, n. melting, softening, touching, Sāh. **-pada**, n. a quick pace or step, W.; a form of metre, Col.; (*am*), ind. quickly, MBh.; Var.; Śak. **-bodha**, m. 'quick understanding,' N. of a grammar. **-bodhikā**, f. N. of a modern Comm. on Ragh. **-madhyā**, f. 'quick in the middle,' a kind of metre, Col. **-meru**, m. (in music) a kind of measure. **-yāna**, n. swift going, running, Suśr. **-varāha-kula**, n. a herd of running boars, Ragh. **-vāhana**, mfn. having swift chariots or horses, R. **-vikrama**, mfn. having a quick step, BhP. **-vilambita**, n. 'quick and slow motion alternately,' Chandom.; a kind of metre (also *-ka*), Śrutab.

Druti, f. melting (cf. *garbha-*); being softened or touched, Sāh.; N. of the wife of Nakta and mother of Gaya, BhP.

द्रु 4. *drú*, m.n. (= 3. *dāru*) wood or any wooden implement (as a cup, an oar &c.), RV.; TBr.; Mn.; m. a tree or branch, HPariś. (cf. *indra-*, *su-*, *harid-*, *hari-*). **-kilima**, n. Pinus Deodora, L. **-gha**, m. N. of a man, g. *śivâdi*, Kāś. **-ghaṇá**, m. a wooden mace, RV.; AV. &c.; axe, hatchet (also °*na*), L.; Kaempferia Rotunda, L.; N. of Brahmā, L. **-ghnī**, f. a hatchet for cutting wood, Kauś. **-ṇasa**, mfn. 'tree-nosed,' i.e. large-n°, L. **-ṇaha** (or *-naha*, W.), m. scabbard, sheath of a sword, L. **-nakha**, m. 'tree-nail,' thorn, L. **-padá**, n. a wooden pillar, a post (to which captives are tied), any pillar or column, RV.; VS.; AV.; m. N. of a king of the Pañcālas (son of Pṛishata and father of Dhṛishṭa-dyumna, of Śikhaṇḍin or Śikhaṇḍinī, and of Kṛishṇā, the wife of the Pāṇḍu princes, hence called Draupadī), MBh.; Hariv.; Pur.; (*ā*), f. (with or scil. *sāvitrī* or *ṛic*) N. of a sacred formula, TBr.; Vishṇ.; *-putra*, m. patr. of Dhṛishṭa-dyumna, Bhag.; °*dât-majā*, f. patr. of Kṛishṇā or Draupadī (cf. above), who is sometimes identified with Umā, SkandaP.; °*dâditya*, m. a form of the Sun, ib. **-pāda**, mf(*padī*)n. large-footed, g. *kumbha-pady-ādi*; (*padī*), f. a splay-footed female, MW. **-mat**, mfn. furnished with wood, g. *yavâdi*. **-mara**, m. 'tree-death,' a thorn, L. **-shád** or **-shadvan**, mfn. sitting in or on a piece of wood or a tree, RV.; TS.; TBr. **-sallaka**, m. Buchanania Latifolia, L.

Drv-ànna, mfn. one whose food is wood, RV.

Druma, m. a tree, MBh.; Kāv. &c. (sometimes also any plant; according to some esp. a tree of Indra's paradise = *pārijāta*); N. of a prince of the Kim-purushas, MBh.; Hariv.; of a son of Kṛishṇa and Rukmiṇī, Hariv.; (*ā*), f. N. of a river, VP. **-kiṃ-nara-prabha**, m. N. of a prince of the Gandharvas. **-kiṃ-nara-rāja**, m. Druma, prince of the Kiṃ-naras; *-paripṛicchā*, f. 'the questioning of D° &c.,' N. of a Buddh. work. **-kulya**, m. N. of a place, R. **-khaṇḍa**, m.n. a group of trees, Hariv. (v. l. *shaṇḍa*). **-da**, m. N. of a man, MBh. **-nakha**, m. = *dru-n*°, L. **-maya**, mf(*ī*)n. made of wood, wooden, Nir. **-ratna-śâkhā-prabha**, m. N. of a prince of the Kiṃ-naras, L. **-vat**, mfn. overgrown with trees, woody, MBh.; Ragh. **-valka**, m. or n. the bark of a tree, R. **-vāsin**, m. 'tree-dweller,' ape, R. (B.). **-vyādhi**, m. 'tree-disease,' lac, resin, L. **-śīrsha**, n. 'tree-head,' a sort of decoration on the upper part of a building or wall, L. **-śreshṭha**, m. 'the best of trees,' N of the palm-tree (= *tāla*), L. **-shaṇḍa**, m.n. = *-khaṇḍa*, Hariv.; R. **-sena**, m. N. of a king (identified with the Asura Gavishṭha), MBh. **Drumâgra**, n. tree-top, R. **Drumâmaya**, m. = °*ma-vyādhi*, L. **Drumâri**, m. 'enemy of trees,' an elephant, L. **Drumâlaya**, m. a place of shelter or dwelling in trees, MW. **Drumâśraya**, mfn. seeking shelter in trees, W.; m. lizard, chameleon, L. **Drumêśvara**, m. 't°-king,' the Pārijāta, Hariv.; the palm-tree, L.; N. of the Moon, L. **Drumôtpala**, m. Pterospermum Acerifolium, L.

Drumara. See under 4. *dru*.

Drumāya, Nom. Ā. °*yate*, to pass for or be like a tree, Hit.

Drumiṇī, f. an assemblage of trees, a forest, g. *khalâdi* (P. iv, 2, 51). °**mila**, m. N. of a Dānava (prince of Saubha), Hariv.; of a son of Ṛishabha, BhP.; of a cowherd (husband of Kalāvatī and father of Nārada), BrahmavP.

Druváya, m. a wooden vessel or dish; the wooden part of a drum, AV.; m. n. a wooden measure (Pāṇ. iv, 3, 162), L.

द्रुग्ध *drugdhá*. See under √1. *druh*.

द्रुड् *druḍ*, cl. 1. and 6. P. *droḍati* and *druḍati*, to sink, perish, Dhātup. xxviii, 100 (v. l.).

द्रुण् *druṇ*, cl. 6. P. *druṇati*, to make crooked, bend; to go, move; to hurt, kill, Dhātup. xxviii, 47 (cf. 1. *dru* and 1. *drū*).

Druṇa (only L.), m. a scorpion; a bee; a defamer; (*ī*), f. a small or female tortoise; water-trough (also °*ṇi*; cf. *droṇa* and °*ṇī*); centipede; (*ā*), f. bow-string; n. bow; sword. **-ha**, see *druṇaha* under 4. *dru*.

द्रुम्भूली *drumbhūlī*, f. a kind of reed, stalk, MaitrS. iii, 8, 3.

द्रुम्म् *drumm*, cl. 1. P. *drummati*, to go, Naigh. ii, 14.

द्रुह् 1. *druh*, cl. 4. P. *drúhyati* (ep. and metr. also Ā. °*te*), Br.; MBh.; R. &c. (pf. *dudróha*, RV., °*hitha*, AV.; aor. *adruhat*, Gr., Subj. 2 sg. *druhas*, MBh., 3 pl. *druhan* [with *mā*], RV.; 2 sg. *adrukshas*, AitBr.; fut. *dhrokshyati*, MaitrS., *drohishyati*, Pāṇ. vii, 2, 45; *drogdhā*, *droḍhā* or *drohitā*, Gr.; inf. *drogdhavai*, Kāṭh.; ind.p. *drugdhvā*, *drohitvā*, *druhitvā*, Gr.; *-druhya*, MaitrS.) to hurt, seek to harm, be hostile to (dat.; rarely gen. [R. ii, 99, 23; Hit. ii, 121], loc. [BhP. iv, 2, 21] or acc. [Mn. ii, 144]); absol. to bear malice or hatred, MBh.; Hit.; to be a foe or rival, Kāvyâd. ii, 61: Caus. *drohayati*: Desid. *dudrohishati*, *dudruh*°, Gr.; *dudrukshat*, Kāṭh. (cf. *abhi-* & *dudhrukshu*). [Orig. *dhrugh*; cf. Zd. *druj*; Germ. *triogan*, *trügen*.]

Drugdhá, mfn. one who has tried to harm, hurtful, malicious, RV. v, 40, 7; n. offence, misdeed, vii, 86, 5; impers. harm has been done, Rājat. v, 298.

2. **Drúh**, mfn. (nom. *dhruk* or *dhruṭ*, Pāṇ. viii, 2, 33; wrongly *druk*; cf. *nidrā-*) injuring, hurtful, hostile to (gen. or comp.), Mn.; MBh.; Pur.; m.f. injurer, foe, fiend, demon, RV.; Kāṭh.; f. injury, harm, offence, RV.; AV. [Cf. Zd. *druj*; Germ. *gidrog*, *gethroc*.] **Druham-tara**, mfn. (√*tṛī*) overcoming the injurer or demon, RV. i, 127, 3.

Druhú, m.f. = 2. *drúh*, AV. °**hya**, m. N. of a man; g. *śivâdi*, pl. his descendants; g. *yaskâdi* (also v.l. for the next, Hariv.) °**hyú**, m. pl. N. of a people, RV.; sg. N. of a son of Yayāti and brother of Yadu &c.; MBh. (w.r. *dúhyu*); Hariv. (v.l. *druhya*); Pur.

Drúhvan, mfn. hurting, injuring, RV.; AV.

Drogdhavyà, mfn. to be injured, ŚBr.; MBh.

Drogdhṛi, m. injurer, ill-wisher, MBh.; Rājat.

Drógha, in °*ghāya vácase* for *drogha-vacase*, using injurious or malicious words, RV. vi, 62, 9. **-mitra** (*drógha-*), m. a mischievous friend, x, 89, 12. **-vâc**, mfn. = *-vacas* (above), 104, 14.

Droha, m. injury, mischief, harm, perfidy, treachery, wrong, offence, Mn.; MBh.; R. &c. **-cintana**, n. injurious design, L. **-para**, mfn. full of malice, Rājat. **-buddhi**, mfn. maliciously-minded, malevolent, MW. **-bhāva**, m. hostile disposition, Mn. ix, 17. **-vacana**, n. injurious language, MBh. **-vṛitti**, mfn. malicious, wicked, Rājat.

Drohâṭa (°*hâta*?) m. a false man; a hunter; a form of metre (L.).

Drohita, mfn. hostile, maliciously inclined, L. °**hin**, mfn. hurting, harming; perfidious against, hostile to (gen. or comp.), MBh.; R. &c.

द्रुह *druha*, m. a son, L.; a lake, L. (cf. *draha*); (*ī*), f. a daughter, L.

द्रुहण *druhaṇa*, m. (either fr. √1. *druh* or = *dru-ghaṇa*) N. of Brahmā, L. °**hiṇa**, m. id.; Rājat.; N. of Śiva or Vishṇu, Hariv. (w.r. °*hina*).

द्रू 1. *drū*, cl. 9. P. *drūṇāti*, to hurl, throw, MaitrS. (v.l. *druṇ*°); cl. 5. P. *drūṇoti*, to kill or to go, Dhātup. xxvii, 33 (v.l.)

द्रू 2. *drū*, mfn. taking any shape at will, L.; f. (?) gold, Uṇ. ii, 57.

द्रूघण *drū-ghaṇa*, m. = *dru-ghana*, L.

द्रूड् *drūḍ*, cl. 1. *drūḍati* (°*ḷati*), to go, Naigh. ii, 14.

द्रूण *drūṇa*, m. a scorpion, L.; n. a bow, L. (cf. *druṇa*).

द्रेक् *drek*, cl. 1. Ā. *drekate*, to sound; to be in high spirits; to grow or increase, Dhātup. iv, 4 (cf. *dhrek*).

द्रेका *drekā*, f. Melia Sempervirens, Bhpr.

द्रेक्क *drekka* or *drekkāṇa* or *dreshkāṇa* = *dṛikāṇa*, L. **Dreshkāṇâdhyāya**, m. N. of ch. of VarBṛS.

द्रेश्य *dreśya*, mfn. (prob. fr. √*driś* = *dṛiś*) visible; cf. *a-*.

द्रै *drai* or *drā* (Dhātup. xxii, 10 and xxiv, 46), cl. 1. P. Ā. *drāyati*, °*te* (cf. *ni-*) or cl. 2. P. *drāti* (pf. *-dadrau*, Naish.; aor. *adrāsīt*, Br.; fut. *drāsyáti*, ib.) to sleep. [Cf. Gk. ἔδραθον, Lat. *dormio*].

द्रोग्धव्य *drogdhavyà* &c. See above.

द्रोण *dróṇa*, n. (fr. 4. *dru*) a wooden vessel, bucket, trough &c.; a Soma vessel [cf. Zd. *draona*], RV.; MBh. &c. (ifc. f. *ā*, Hcat.); m. n. a measure of capacity (= 4 Āḍhakas = 16 Pushkalas = 128 Kuñcis = 1024 Mushṭis, or = 200 Palas = $\frac{1}{16}$ Kumbha, or = $\frac{1}{16}$ Khārī = 4 Āḍhakas, or = 2 Āḍhakas = ½ Śūrpa = 64 Śeras, or = 32 Śeras), Mn.; Yājñ.; MBh.; Suśr. &c.; a measure for measuring fields (as much land as is sown with a D° of corn), Col.; n. an altar shaped like a trough, Śulbas. iii, 216; m. a lake or large piece of water of 400 poles length, L.; a kind of cloud (from which the rain streams forth as from a bucket), L. (cf. *-megha* and

-vṛishṭi below); a raven or crow, L. (cf. *-kāka*); a scorpion (cf. *druṇa*); a kind of plant (prob. Leucas Linifolia), L.; N. of one of the 8 Vasus (husband of Abhimati and father of Harsha, Śoka, Bhaya &c.), BhP.; of a Brāhman said to have been generated by Bharad-vāja in a bucket (the military preceptor of both the Kuru and Pāṇḍu princes; afterwards king of a part of Pañcāla and general of the Kurus, the husband of Kṛipī and father of Aśvatthāman), MBh.; Hariv.; Pur. &c.; of one of the 4 sons of Mandapāla and Jaritā (born as birds), MBh. i, 8345 &c. (as author of RV. x, 142, 3, 4, with the patr. Śārṅga); of a Brāhman, Pañc.; of sev. other men, VP.; of sev. mountains, ib.; (*ā*), f. a kind of shrub, L.; N. of a daughter of Siṅha-hanu, Buddh.; (*ī*), f. a wooden trough or tub, MBh.; Hariv.; R. &c.; any vessel or implement made of wood, L.; a measure of capacity (= 2 Śūrpas = 128 Śeras), L.; a valley, Mālatim. ix, 1/2; Pur.; a kind of creeper, Bhpr.; of coloquintida (= *indra-cirbiṭī*), L.; of salt, L.; N. of a country, of a mountain and of a river, L. **-kalaśá**, m. a large wooden vessel for the Soma, VS.; TS.; Br. &c. **-kāka** or **-kākala**, m. a raven, L. (cf. above). **-kshīrā**, f. (a cow) yielding a Dr° of milk, L. **-gandhikā**, f. a kind of plant (= *rāsnā*), L. **-ghā**, f. = (and corrupted from?) *-dughā*, L. **-cit**, mfn. arranged in a trough form, ŚBr.; Śulbas. **-citi**, f. arrangement in tr°-form, MaitrS. **-dugdhā** or **-dughā**, f. = *-kshīrā*, L. **-padī**, f. 'tr°-footed,' L. **-parṇī**, f. 'tr°-leaved,' Musa Sapientum, L. **-parvan**, n. 'D° section,' N. of MBh. vii. **-pushpa**, n. flower of Leucas Linifolia, L. (cf. above). **-pushpī**, f. Phlomis Zeylanica or other plant, Bhpr. **-maya**, mf(*ī*)n. made of the D° measure, Hcat.; consisting only of D°s, MBh. **-mānā**, f. = *-kshīrā*, L. **-mukha**, n. the chief of 400 villages, Divyâv. (°*khya*, ib.); the end of a valley (v.l. °*nī-m*°). **-megha**, m. a kind of cloud (see above), Mṛicch. x, 25. **-m-paca**, mfn. 'cooking a D°,' liberal in entertaining, L. **-ripu**, m. 'D°'s foe,' N. of Dhṛishṭa-dyumna, Gal. **-vṛishṭi**, f. rain streaming forth as from a trough, Mṛicch. x, 37 (cf. *droṇa* and *-megha*). **-śarmapada**, n. N. of a Tīrtha, MBh. **-sâc**, mfn. clinging to the trough, united with it (Soma), RV. x, 44, 3. **-siṅha**, m. N. of a prince of the Vallabhī dynasty, Inscr. **-stūpa**, m. N. of a Stūpa (said to contain a D° holding relics of Gautama Buddha), Buddh. **Droṇâcārya**, m. D° as teacher of the Kuru and Pāṇḍu princes, L. **Droṇâsa**, m. 'trough-mouthed,' N. of a demon who causes diseases, PārGṛ. i, 16 (long-nosed, Sch.; cf. *dru-ṇasa*). **Dróṇâhāva**, mfn. having a D° for a bucket (= streaming abundantly), RV. x, 101, 7. **Droṇôdana**, m. N. of a son of Siṅha-hanu and uncle of Buddha, Lalit.

Droṇaka, m. pl. 'the inhabitants of a valley,' N. of a people, VP.; (*ikā*), f. trough, tub, L.; the tongue bent in the form of a trough (to pronounce *sh*), AV. Prāt. i, 23; the indigo plant, L.

Droṇi, f. trough, tub, L.; a valley, Nalac.; N. of a country, L.

Droṇī, f. of *droṇa*, q.v. **-ja**, n. = *-lavaṇa*, L. **-dala**, m. Pandanus Odoratissimus, L. **-padī**, f. = °*ṇa-p*°, L. **-mukha**, see °*ṇa-m*°. **-lavaṇa**, n. a kind of salt coming from Droṇī, L. **Droṇyaśva**, mfn. having troughs (i.e. clouds) for horses, RV. x, 99, 4. **Droṇy-āmaya**, m. a kind of disease (= *arishṭy-āmaya*), KātyŚr. xx, 3, 16, Sch.

Droṇeya, n. = °*ṇī-lavaṇa*, L. **Drónya**, mfn. belonging to or longing for the manger, RV. x, 50, 4.

Drauṇa, mf(*ī*)n. containing a Droṇa, Pāṇ. v, 1, 52, Vārtt., Pat. °**ṇāyana** (Pāṇ. iv, 1, 103), °**ṇāyani** (MBh.), m. patr. of Aśvatthāman. °**ṇi**, m. id., Pāṇ. iv, 1, 103; MBh.; Hariv. &c.; N. of Vyāsa in a future Dvāpara, VP. °**ṇika**, mf(*ī*)n. = *drauṇa*, g. *nishkâdi*; (with or scil. *kshetra*) a field sown with a D° of grain, Pāṇ. v, 1, 45, Kāś. °**ṇī** (MBh. v, 2119) w.r. for *droṇī*. °**ṇeya**, n. a kind of salt, L.

द्रोमिण *dromiṇa*, m. N. of Cāṇakya, L. (cf. *drāmila*).

द्रोह *droha* &c. See above.

द्रौघण *draughaṇa* (Bṛih.) and °*ṇaka* (g. *arīhaṇâdi*) fr. *dru-ghaṇa*.

द्रौपद *draupada*, mf(*ī*)n. belonging to or descendant from Drupada; (*ī*), f., see below. **Draupadâditya**, v.l. for *drup*°, q.v. **Draupadāyani**, fr. *drupada*, Pāṇ. iv, 2, 80, g. *karṇâdi*.

Draupadi-ja, m. pl. (for °*dī*-) the sons of D°, Bh. viii, 4202.

Draupadī, f. patr. of Kṛishṇā (wife of the Pāṇḍu princes), MBh.; Hariv. &c. (identified with Umā, SkandaP.) **-pramātha**, m. = *-haraṇa*. **-vastrâharaṇa**, n. 'the seizure of D°'s garments,' N. of a poem. **-svayam-vara**, m. N. of a drama. **-haraṇa**, n. 'the forcible abduction of D°,' N. of ch. of MBh. iii.

Draupadeya, m. pl. metron. of the 5 sons of Draupadī (viz. of Prativindhya, son of Yudhi-shṭhira; of Suta-soma, son of Bhīma; of Śruta-kīrti or Śruta-karman, son of Arjuna; of Śatânīka, son of Nakula; and of Śruta-sena, son of Sahadeva), MBh.; MārkP.

द्रौहिक *drauhika*, mfn. fr. *droha* (g. *chedâdi*).

द्रौह्य *drauhya* (g. *śivâdi*) and °*hyava* (Pāṇ. iv, 1, 168, Sch.) patr. fr. Druhyu.

द्व *dva*, original stem of *dvi*, q.v. (nom. acc. du. m. *dvā* or *dvau*, f. n. *dvé*; instr. dat. abl. *dvā́bhyām*, gen. loc. *dváyos*) two, RV. &c. &c.; both (with *api*, Ragh. xii, 93); loc. *dvayos* in two genders (masc. and fem.) or in two numbers (sing. and plur.), Gr.; L. [Cf. *dvā* and *dvi*; Zd. *dva*; Gk. δύο, δύω and δι = δϝι; Lat. *duŏ* and *bi* = *dvi*; Lith. *du*, *dvi*; Slav. *dŭva*; Goth. *tvai*, *tva* &c.]

Dvaká, mfn. du. two and two, twofold, RV. x, 59, 9.

द्वंद *dvaṃda*, n. (corrupted fr. *dvaṃdva*) pair, couple, L.; m. a clock or plate on which the hours are struck, W.

द्वंद्व *dvaṃdvá*, n. (the repeated nom. of *dva*) pair, couple, male and female, TS.; Br.; MBh.; Kāv. &c. (*ám*, *e*, or *ena*, ind. by two, face to face, secretly); a pair of opposites (e.g. heat and cold, joy and sorrow &c.), Up.; Mn.; MBh.; R. &c.; strife, quarrel, contest, fight (esp. between two persons, a duel), MBh.; R.; Hit.; stronghold, fortress, L.; m. (scil. *samāsa*; rarely n.) a copulative compound (or any c° in which the members if uncompounded would be in the same case and connected by the conjunction 'and,' cf. *devatā-*, *nakshatra-*), Pāṇ. ii, 2, 29; 4, 2; m. N. of sev. Ekāhas, KātyŚr.; the sign of the zodiac Gemini, Gol.; (in music) a kind of measure; a species of disease, a complication of two disorders, a compound affection of two humours, L. **-cara** (L.) and **-cārin** (Ragh.), m. 'living in couples,' the ruddy goose, Anas Casarca. **-ja**, mfn. proceeding from a pair or from discord or from a morbid affection of two humours, W. **-duḥkha**, n. pain arising from opposite alternations (as heat and cold &c.), Śiś. iv, 64. **-bhāva**, m. antagonism, discord, Ṛitus. **-bhinna**, n. separation of the sexes, W. **-bhūta**, mfn. become doubtful, irresolute, uncertain of (loc.), MBh. i, 1867 (v.l. °*dvī-bh*°). **-moha**, m. trouble excited by doubt, MW. **-yuddha**, n. duel, single combat, W.; *-varṇana*, n. N. of 41st ch. of GaṇP. ii. **-yodhin**, mfn. fighting in couples or by single combat, BhP. **-lakshaṇa-vāda**, m., **-vicāra**, m. N. of wks. **-śas**, ind. two by two, in couples, MBh.; R. &c. **-samprahāra**, m. = *-yuddha*, Uttarar. **-sahishṇu-tā**, f. (Vedânt.), **-tva**, n. (MBh.) ability to support opposites (as happiness and misery &c.) **Dvaṃdvâtīta**, mfn. gone beyond or freed from opposites (see above), W. **Dvaṃdvâdi-kośa**, m. N. of a dictionary. **Dvaṃdvârāma**, mfn. liking to live in couples, MBh. **Dvaṃdvâlāpa**, m. dialogue between two persons, private conversation, Pañc.

Dvaṃdvin, mfn. forming a couple, ŚBr.; opposed to one another, contradictory, antagonistic, Prab.

Dvaṃdvī-√bhū, to become joined in couples, BhP.; to engage in single combat, MBh.; to hesitate or be doubtful (cf. °*dva-bhūta*).

द्वय *dvayá*, mf(*ī*)n. (fr. and in comp = *dvi*) twofold, double, of 2 kinds or sorts, RV.; AV.; Br.; MBh. &c. (°*ye*, m. pl. Śiś. iii, 57); (*ī*), f. couple, pair, Naish.; Rājat.; n. id.; two things, both (e.g. *tejo-*, the 2 luminaries, Śak. iv, 2), Yājñ.; MBh.; Kāv. &c. (ifc. *ā*, R. i, 29, 14); twofold nature, falsehood, RV. i, 147, 4 &c.; the masc. and fem. gender, Gr.; (*am*), ind. between, Śiś. iii, 3. [Cf. Zd. *dvaya*; Gk. δοιός.] **-dvaya-samāpatti**, f. copulation, L. **-bhāratī**, f. N. of a woman, Cat. **-vādin**, mfn. double-tongued, insincere, MW. **-sata**, see *dve-s*°. **-hīna**, mfn. destitute of both genders, neuter, L. **Dvayâgni**, m. Plumbago Zeylanica. **Dvayâtiga**, mfn. one who has overcome the two (bad qualities, i.e. passion and ignorance) or the opposites (see under *dvaṃdva*), L.; m. a saint, a holy or virtuous man, W. **Dvayâtmaka**, mfn. having a twofold nature, appearing in a t° manner, L. **Dvayôpanishad**, f. N. of an Up.

Dvayat, **dvayas**. See *á-d*°.

Dvayasa, mf(*ī*)n. (ifc.) having the length or breadth or depth of, reaching up to, Kāv.; Hcat.

Dvayāvin, mfn. false, dishonest, RV.; AV. °**yin**, m. comrade, fellow (cf. *asad-dvayin*, add.) °**yú**, mfn. = °*yāvin*, RV.

द्वर *dvará* and °*rí* (or °*rín*), mfn. (fr. √*dvṛi*) obstructing, RV. i, 52, 3 (Sāy.)

द्वा *dvā*, old nom. du. of *dva*, substituted for *dvi* in comp. before other numerals &c. **-catvāriṅśa**, mf(*ī*)n. the 42nd; °*śat* (MBh.) and °*śati* (Rājat.), f. 42. **-ja**, m. son of two fathers, BhP. ix, 20, 38 (wrong explanation of *bharad-vāja*). **-triṅśá**, mf(*ī*)n. the 32nd, MBh.; consisting of 32, Br.; Lāṭy.; 32, in °*śāra*, mfn. having 32 spokes, RāmatUp. **-triṅśat** (*dvā́-*), f. 32; °*śac-chāla-bhañjikā*, f. pl. 32 statues, Siṅhâs.; N. of wk.; °*śat-karma-paddhati*, f. N. of wk.; °*śat-pattra*, mfn. having 32 petals, NṛisUp.; °*śad-akshara* (*dvā́-*, TS.) and °*rin* (L.), mfn. consisting of 32 syllables; °*śad-aparādha-stotra*, n. N. of part of the VarP.; °*śad-ara*, mfn. = °*śāra*; °*śad-upanishad*, f. N. of an Up.; °*śad-rātra*, n. (sc. *sattra*) a sacrifice lasting 32 days, ŚrS.; °*śal-lakshaṇika* (Siṅhâs.) and °*nôpêta* (Hit.), mfn. 'having 32 auspicious marks upon the body,' illustrious, great. **-triṅśati**, f. collection of 32 (w. r. for °*śat* in *siṅhâsana-t*°). **-triṅśatikā** or °**tkā** (Siṅhâs.) and °**śikā** (in *bharaṭaka-dvātṛ*°, Cat.), f. aggregate or collection of 32. **-daśa** and **-daśan**, see below. **-navata**, mf(*ī*)n. the 92nd, MBh.; °*ti*, f. 92, Pāṇ. vi, 3, 49. **-pañcāśá**, mf(*ī*)n. the 52nd, MBh.; R. (du. the 51st and 52nd, ŚāṅkhBr. xviii, 3); accompanied or increased by 52, ŚBr. **-pañcāśat**, f. 52, Hariv.; Rājat.; °*śad-akshara*, mfn. consisting of 52 syllables, Nidānas. **-pára**, m. n. that die or side of a die which is marked with two spots, VS.; TS.; Kāṭh.; MBh.; the Die personified, Nal. vi, 1; 'the age with the number two,' N. of the 3rd of the 4 Yugas or ages of the world (comprising 2400 years; the Y° itself = 2000, and each twilight = 200 years; it is also personified as a god), AitBr.; Mn.; MBh. &c.; RTL. 111; 433; N. of a myth. being, MBh. i, 2713; doubt, uncertainty, L.; *-cchandas*, n. pl. a partic. class of metre, Nidānas.; *-stoma*, m. pl. of Stomas, ib. **-viṅśá**, mf(*ī*)n. the 22nd, Br.; Up.; Mn.; consisting of 22, VS. **-viṅśati**, f. (*dvā́-*) 22, ŚBr.; MBh. &c.; *-tama*, mf(*ī*)n. the 22nd, MBh.; R.; *-dhā́*, ind. 22fold, ŚBr.; *-rātra*, n. (sc. *sattra*) a sacrifice lasting 22 days, ŚrS.; *-śata*, n. 122; *-śatama*, mf(*ī*)n. the 122nd, MBh.; R.; °*ty-akshara*, mfn. consisting of 22 syllables, Nidānas. **-shashṭá**, mf(*ī*)n. the 62nd, MBh.; joined with 62, ŚBr. **-shashṭi**, f. 62, MBh.; *-tama*, mf(*ī*)n. the 62nd, R. **-saptata**, mf(*ī*)n. the 72nd, MBh. **-saptati** (*dvā́-*), f. 72; °*tishṭaka*, mfn. consisting of 72 bricks, ŚBr.

1. **Dvā-daśá**, mf(*ī*)n. the twelfth, VS.; ŚBr.; Mn.; MBh. &c. (du. the eleventh and twelfth, Kāṭh.); ifc. (f. *ā*) forming 12 with (cf. *aśva-*, add.); consisting of 12, 12fold, RV.; ŚBr.; increased by 12, KātyŚr.; (*ī́*), f. (sc. *rātri* or *tithi*) the 12th day of the half-month; n. a collection or aggregate of 12, ŚBr. **Dvādaśâṅśa**, m. the 12th part or division (esp. of a constellation), Var.

Dvā-daśaka, mf(*ī*)n. the twelfth, MBh.; consisting of 12 (syllables), RV.; Prāt.; with *dama* (a fine) amounting to 12 (Paṇas), Mn.; n. the number or an aggregate of 12, Yājñ. °**śika**, mfn. having the length of 12, Śulbas.; happening on the 12th day or on the 12th day of a half-month, R.

Dvā́-daśan, pl. (nom. acc. *dvā́-daśa*, instr. *dvādaśábhis*, dat. abl. °*śábhyas*, loc. °*śásu*, gen. °*śā́nām*, according to Pāṇ. vi, 1, 179, 180 in Class. also °*śabhís*, °*śabhyás*, °*śasú*) twelve, RV. &c. [Cf. Zd. *dva-daśan*; Gk. δώ-δεκα; Lat. *duo-decim*.]

2. **Dvā-daśa** for *-daśan*, in comp. **-kapāla**, mf(*ī*)n. distributed on 12 potsherds, ŚBr. **-kara**, m. '12-handed or 12-rayed,' N. of Kārttikeya, L.; of Bṛihas-pati or the planet Jupiter, L. **-gavá**, n. a team of 12 bulls, TS.; ŚBr. **-gṛihītá**, mfn. drawn 12 times (as water), ŚBr. **-gopāla-nirṇaya-**

bhakti, f., **-jyotir-liṅga-stotra**, n. N. of wks. **-tā**, f., **-tva**, n. the aggregate of 12, KātyŚr., Sch. **-dhā**, ind. 12fold, AV. &c. **-nāma-pañjara**, n. N. of a Stotra. **-nidhana**, n. N. of a Sāman, ĀrshBr. **-pañjarikā-stotra**, n. N. of a Stotra. **-pattra**, mfn. having 12 petals, NṛisUp. **-pattraka**, n. N. of a Yoga or partic. religious observance in which the 12 syllables *oṃ namo bhagavate vāsudevāya* are connected with the 12 signs of the zodiac and with the 12 months, VāmP. **-pada**, mf(*ā*)n. consisting of 12 words, Mālatīm., Sch. **-pushkara**, mfn. consisting of 12 lotus flowers, TāṇḍyaBr. **-bhavana**, n., **-bhāva**, m., °*va-phala*, n., °*va-vicāra*, m. N. of wks. **-bhuja**, m. 'having 12 arms,' N. of one of Skanda's attendants, MBh. **-ma**, mf(*ī*)n. the 12th, MBh.; BhP. (cf. 1. *dvā-daśa*). **-mañjarī** or °**rikā**, f. N. of a work by Śaṃkarâcārya. **-mahā-vākya**, n. pl. 'the 12 great words,' N. of a wk. on the Vedânta; *-nirṇaya*, m., *-vivaraṇa*, n. N. of Comms. on it; °*kyâvalī*, f. prob. = *mahā-vākya*. **-mahā-siddhânta-nirūpaṇa**, n. N. of wk. **-mātra**, mfn. consisting of 12 metrical instants, AmṛitUp. **-māsa-deya-dāna-ratnâkara**, m. N. of wk. **-māsika**, mfn. consisting of 12 months, Kāraṇḍ. **-mūla**, m. 'having 12 roots,' N. of Vishṇu, L. **-yātrā-tattva**, n. N. of a work. **-yoga**, v. l. for °*śây*°, q. v. **-rātra**, n. a period of 12 nights (days), ĀśvGṛ.; mfn. lasting 12 nights (days), KātyŚr. **-rāśi-phala**, n. N. of wk. **-rcá** (°*śa* + *ṛicā*), mfn. containing 12 verses, ŚrS. **-lakshaṇī**, f. = °*śâdhyāyī* (q. v.) **-liṅga-stavana**, °*ga-stotra*, & °*gôdbhava*, n. N. of wks. **-locana**, m. '12-eyed,' N. of Skanda, L. **-vatsarī**, f. a period of 12 years, HPariś. **-varga**, m. an aggregate of 12, Cat.; °*gīyā*, f. pl. 12 female heretics, Divyâv. **-vārshika** (v. l. *var*°), mf(*ī*)n. 12 years old, lasting 12 years, Mn.; *-vrata*, n. a vow for 12 years, MW. **-vidha** (*dvá-*), mfn. 12fold, ŚBr.; *-putra-mīmāṅsā*, f. N. of wk. **-śata** (*dvá-*), n. 112; in comp. also 1200 (= *ī*, f., Rājat.); *-tama*, mf(*ī*)n. the 112th; *-dakshiṇa*, mfn. (a sacrifice) at which 1200 are given as a fee, ĀpŚr. **-saṃskāra**, m. pl. 'the 12 ceremonies,' N. of wk. **-sāhasra**, mf(*ī*)n. consisting of 1200, MārkP. **-siddhânta**, m. N. of wk. on the Vedânta. **-stotra**, n. pl. 'the 12 Stotras,' N. of wk. **Dvādaśâṅśu**, m. 'the 12-rayed,' N. of Bṛihas-pati or the planet Jupiter, L. **Dvādaśâkāra** (Divyâv.), **dvādaśâkṛiti** (RV.), mfn. having 12 shapes. **Dvādaśâksha**, mf(*ī*)n. 12-eyed; m. N. of Skanda, L. (cf. °*śa-locana*); of one of his attendants, MBh.; of a Buddha (cf. °*śâkhya*), L. **Dvādaśâkshara** (*dvá-*), mf(*ā*)n. containing 12 syllables, VS.; ŚBr.; *-mantra*, m. the prayer of 12 s° addressed to Vishṇu (cf. *dvādaśa-pattraka*), PadmaP.; *-mālā* (Cat.) & *-vidyā* (BhP.), f. probably id. **Dvādaśâkhya**, m. 'the 12-named?' a Buddha, L. (cf. °*śâksha*). **Dvādaśâṅgī**, f. the collective Jaina sacred writings (consisting of 12 parts), L. **Dvādaśâṅgula**, mfn. having the breadth of 12 fingers, L.; *-sāriṇī*, f. N. of wk. **Dvādaśâtman** or °**tmaka**, m. 'appearing in 12 forms,' the sun (in each month), MBh.; L. **Dvādaśâditya**, (in comp.) the 12 Ādityas; *-tīrtha*, n. N. of a Tīrtha, ŚivaP.; *-stava*, m. N. of wk.; °*tyâśrama*, m. N. of a hermitage, SkandaP. **Dvādaśâdhyāyī**, f. N. of Jaimini's Mīmāṅsā (consisting of 12 Adhyāyas). **Dvādaśânta-prakaraṇa**, n. N. of wk. **Dvādaśânyika**, mfn. one who has made 12 mistakes in reading, Pāṇ. iv, 4, 64, Kāś. **Dvādaśâbda**, mfn. lasting 12 years, VP.; °*bdânanta-râvalokana-vidhi*, m. N. of wk. **Dvādaśâyus**, m. 'whose life lasts 12 (years),' a dog, L. **Dvādaśayogá**, mfn. yoked with 12 (bulls), MaitrS.; ŚāṅkhŚr. **Dvádaśâra**, mfn. having 12 spokes (as the wheel or cycle of the year), RV.; MBh. **Dvádaśâratni**, mfn. 12 cubits long, ŚBr. **Dvādaśârka**, m. N. of wk. **Dvādaśârcis**, m. = °*śâṅśu*. **Dvādaśâvarta**, m. a form of salutation involving 12 circumambulations, HPariś. **Dvādaśâsra**, n. or °**sri**, f. a dodecagon, a dodecagonal figure, Col. (written also °*śra*, °*śri*). **Dvādaśâhá**, mfn. lasting 12 days; a period or ceremony of 12 days, AV.; ŚBr.; Mn.; MBh.; *-prayoga*, m., *-prayoga-paddhati*, & *-prayoga-vṛitti*, f., *-praśna*, m., *-mahā-vrata-prayoga*, m., *-maitrāvaruṇa-prayoga*, m., *-hautra*, n., °*śâhâṇḍa-bilā*, f. N. of wks. **Dvādaśâhika** (KātyŚr., Sch.) & °**hīya** (TBr., Sch.), mfn. relating to a period or ceremony of 12 days. **Dvādaśôdyāma**, mfn. having 12 traces or strings, Kap.

Dvā-daśika, see above. **-daśin**, mfn. consisting of 12, twelvefold, RV. Prāt.; ŚāṅkhŚr.

Dvā-daśī, f. of 1. *dvā-daśa* in comp. **-tīrtha**, n. N. of a Tīrtha, ŚivaP. **-māhātmya**, n. N. of wk. **-vrata**, n. a partic. observance on the 12th day of a half-month, BhP. °**śy-udyāpana**, n. N. of wk.

द्वांद्विक *dvāṃdvika*, mfn. (fr. *dvaṃdva*) proceeding from a compound affection of two humours, Car.

द्वाः *dvāḥ*, in comp. for *dvār*. **-stha** (MBh.; Kāv.) and **-sthita** (L.), mfn. standing at the gate or door; m. door-keeper, porter, warder (written also *dvā-sth*°).

Dvār (fr. √*dvṛi*?), gate, door, entrance or issue, fig. expedient, means, opportunity (instr. °*rā*, ifc. by means of, by), RV.; AV.; ŚBr.; Mn.; MBh., Kāv. &c. [Cf. 1. *dur*, 1. *dura* and *dvāra*; Gk. θύρα; Lat. *fores*; Slav. *dvĭrĭ*; Lit. *dùrys*; Got. *daur*; Old Sax. *dor* &c.] **-bāhu**, m. door-post, ĀpŚr. **-vat**, mfn. having many doors; (*ī*) f. = *dvāra-vatī*, BhP.

Dvā́ra, n. door, gate, passage, entrance, ŚBr.; ĀśvGṛ.; Mn.; MBh. &c.; opening, aperture (esp. of the human body, cf. *nava-*), Up.; Suśr. &c.; a way, means, medium (instr. °*reṇa*, ifc. by means of, with regard or according to), MBh.; Kāv.; Pañc. &c. (the Māheśvaras hold that there are 6 Dvāras or means of obtaining religious ecstasy, Sarvad.); m. N. of a Gandharva, R.; (*ī*), f. door, ŚāṅkhŚr. **-kaṇṭaka**, m. 'door-thorn,' the bolt of a d°, L.; a d° or gate, L. **-kapāṭa**, m. or n. the leaf of a d°, L. **-koshṭaka**, m. gate-chamber, Divyâv. **-japasûkta**, n. pl. N. of partic. hymns. **-tā**, f. the being the way to or the occasion of (comp.), Ragh.; Kād.; a door, gate; an entrance, way, access, MW. **-tva**, n. the being caused or produced by (comp.), Saṃk. **-darśin**, m. a d°-watcher, d°-keeper, R. **-dātu** & **-dāru**, m. Tectona Grandis, Bhpr. **-nāyaka**, m. d°-keeper, porter, warder, Rājat. **-pa**, m. id., AitBr.; ChUp. **-paksha** (ĀśvGṛ.), °**kshaka** (Kād.), m. d°-panel; d°, gate. **-paṭṭa**, m. id., Kathās. **-pati**, m. = *-pa*, MBh. **-pāla**, m. id., MBh.; Hariv. &c. (*ī*, f. g. *revaty-ādi*); N. of various Yakshas and of sacred places connected with them, MBh.; *-mantra*, m. a kind of hymn. **-pālaka**, m. door-keeper; (°*likā*, f., Kād.) **-pālika**, m. metron. fr. *-pālī* (g. *revaty-ādi*). **-piṇḍī**, f. the threshold of a d°, L. **-pidhā́na**, n. (m., ŚBr.) d°-bolt; closure, end, Mālav. ii, 11. **-phalaka**, n. = *-kapāṭa*, ŚāṅkhGṛ. **-bandhâvaraṇa**, mfn. one who hides himself behind a bolted d°, Hariv. **-bali-bhuj**, m. 'eater of offering at d°,' Ardea nivea; a crow or a sparrow, L. **-bāhu**, m. d°-post, Lāṭy. (ifc. *-ka*, Hariv.) **-mahima-varṇana**, n. N. of ch. 127 of GaṇP. ii. **-mukha**, n. 'd°-mouth,' opening, Mṛicch. iv, $\frac{2}{2}$. **-yantra**, n. d°-bolt, L. **-yātrā-vidhi**, m. N. of wk. **-rakshaka** (Kālid.) & **-rakshin** (Kathās.), m. d°-keeper. **-lakshaṇa-paṭala**, m. or n. N. of wk. **-vaṅśa**, m. the cross-beam of a d°, MānGṛ. **-vat**, mfn. 'many-gated;' (*ī*), f. N. of the capital of Kṛishṇa, MBh.; Hariv.; °*tī-nirmāṇa* & °*tī-māhātmya*, n. N. of wks. **-vartman**, n. gateway, MW. **-vṛitta**, n. black pepper, L. **-śākhā**, f. door-post, L. **-śobhā**, f. a beautiful portal, Mṛicch. iv. $\frac{2}{2}$. **-stambha**, m. = *-śākhā*, L. **-stha**, mfn. standing at the d°; m. d°-keeper, porter, MBh.; Hariv. &c. **-sthita**, mfn. id., Pañcad. **-sthūṇā**, f. d°-post, ĀpŚr. **Dvārâdhipa** (Rājat.) & °**râdhyaksha** (MBh.), m. = °*ra-rakshin*. **Dvārâpidhāna** (Sch.) = °*ra-p*°. **Dvārâbhimānin**, mfn. assuming the character of (sacrificial) doors, MW. **Dvārârari**, m. leaf of a door, Rājat. **Dvārāvatī**, f. = °*ra-v*°, VarP.; *-māhātmya*, n. N. of wk. (= *dvārakā-m*°).

Dvāraka, n. door, gate, MBh.; ifc. occasioned or caused by, Saṃk.; (*akā*), f. 'many-gated,' N. of the capital of Kṛishṇa (on the western point of Gūjarāt, supposed to have been submerged by the sea), MBh.; Hariv.; Pur. &c. (*ikā*, f. id., L.; RTL. 55, 1; 113; 400, 2).

Dvārakā, f. of prec. **-dāsa**, m. 'slave of Dvārakā,' N. of a man, Cat. **-nātha-yajvan**, m. 'worshipper of the lord of D°,' N. of Sch. on Śulbas. **-praveśa**, m. 'entrance into D°,' N. of ch. 103 of BrahmavP. iv. **-māhātmya**, n. 'glory of D°,' N. of wk. (= *dvāravatī-m*°). **Dvārakârambha**, m. 'commencement of D°,' N. of ch. 102 of BrahmavP. iv. **Dvārakêśa**, m. 'lord of D°,' N. of Kṛishṇa, L.

Dvārika, m. door-keeper, warder, Pañc. iii. 85; N. of one of the Sun's 18 attendants, L. (*ikā*, f., see *dvāraka*). °**rin**, m. d°-keeper, MBh. i. 4906. °**rya**, mfn. belonging to or being at a door, GṛS.; Śr.S.; (*ā*), f. (scil. *sthūṇā*) d°-post, ib.

Dvārī-√kṛi, to employ as a medium or means or mediator, Mudr. iv, $\frac{3}{4}$.

द्वि *dvi*, du. two (nom. *dvau*, see *dva*). **-ka**, m. 'having 2 k's in one's name' (cf. *kāka*), a crow, Vām. v, 1, 15; Anas Casarca, L.; *-kāra*, m. id., L. **-kakud**, m. '2-humped,' a camel, L. **-kapāla** (*dvi-*), mfn. distributed on 2 potsherds or consisting of 2 skull-bones, ŚBr. **-kara**, mf(*ī*)n. doing 2 things or making 2 of anything, W. (cf. Pāṇ. iii, 2, 21, Kāś.) **-karaṇī**, f. the diagonal of a square, Śulbas. **-karmaka**, mfn. having 2 objects or accusatives, Pāṇ. ii. 3, 68, Kāś. **-karma-vāda**, m. N. of wk. **-kāṇḍa**, mf(*ī*)n. consisting of 2 strings (rope); (f. *ā*) containing 2 Kāṇḍas (kind of measure), Pāṇ. iv, 1, 23, Kāś. **-kārshāpaṇa** & °**ṇika**, mfn. worth 2 Kārshāpaṇas, v, 1, 29, Kāś. **-kālam**, ind. at 2 times, ĀpŚr., Sch. **-kubja**, mfn. 2-humped, L. **-kulija**, mf(*ā*, *ī*)n., **-kulijika**, mf(*ī*)n. & **-kulijīna**, mf(*ā*)n. containing 2 Kulijas (see s. v.), Pāṇ. v, 1, 55, Kāś. **-kūbara**, mfn. (carriage) having 2 poles, BhP. **-koṇa**, mfn. '2-cornered,' ĀpŚr.; Sch. **-kauḍavika**, mfn. containing 2 Kuḍavas (see s. v.), Pāṇ. vii, 3, 17, Sch. **-krama**, m. a Krama (see s. v.) consisting of 2 elements, RV. Prāt. xi, 3, 8. **-khaṇḍikā**, f. a couplet, MW. **-khārika**, mfn. worth 2 Khāris, Pāṇ. v, 1, 33, Sch. **-khura**, mfn. having 2 (i. e. cloven) hoofs, TĀr., Comm. **-gat**, m. N. of a Bhārgava, TāṇḍyaBr. **-gata**, mfn. ambiguous, Pat. **-gava**, mfn. yoked with 2 oxen or cows, Parāś. **-gu**, m. (sc. *samāsa*) N. of a Tatpurusha compound in which the 1st member is a numeral (being formed like *dvi-gu*, 'worth 2 cows'), Pāṇ. ii, 1, 52 &c. **-guṇá** (or *dvi-g*°), mfn. double, twofold, of 2 kinds, ŚBr.; ŚrS. &c.; doubled, i. e. folded (garment), ŚBr.; twice as large or as much as (abl.), Yājñ. ii, 4; (comp.), Mn. viii. 59; compar. *-tara*, Kād.; *-taram*, ind. Ratn. i, 16; *-tā*, f. Var.; *-tva*, n. Amar.; °*ṇaya*, NomP. °*yati*, to double, multiply by 2, Sch.; °*ṇita*, mfn. doubled, Mṛicch.; Ratn.; Kir. °*ṇā*, ind., with √*kṛi*, to plough twice, Pāṇ. v, 4, 59, Kāś.; °*ṇā-karṇa*, mfn. having an ear divided by a slit (cattle), vi, 3, 115, Kāś.; °*ṇāya*, °*yate*, to become double, Kād.; °*ṇī-√kṛi*, to double, make twofold, Śiś.; Kād.; °*ṇī-√bhū*, to become double, grow, increase, Kād. **-gūḍha**, n. a kind of song, Sāh. **-cakra**, m. N. of a Dānava, Hariv. (C. *-vaktra*); a partic. phenomenon in the sky, MBh. **-catur-aśraka**, m. N. of a partic. gesture or posture, Vikr. (v. l. *catur-asr*°). **-catvāri**, n. pl. two or four, RāmatUp. **-catvāriṅśa**, mf(*ī*)n. the 42nd, MBh. **-catvāriṅśat**, f. 42, Pāṇ. vi, 3, 49 (cf. *dvā-*). **-catvāriṅśika**, w. r. for **cātv**°. **-candra**, mfn. having 2 moons, Viddh. **-caraṇa**, mfn. 2-legged, Śāntiś. **-cātvāriṅśika**, mfn. consisting of 2, L. **-cūḍa**, mfn. having 2 protuberances (brick), KātyŚr. **-cchinna**, mfn. cut into two, bisected, MW. **-já**, see *Dvijá*. **-jánman**, mfn. having a double birth or b°-place or nature, RV.; a member of the first three classes (esp. a Brāhman), Mn.; MBh. &c.; a tooth (as twice grown), L.; any oviparous animal (as bird, snake &c.), L. **-jā́**, mfn. twice-born, RV. **-jāti**, mfn. id.; m. an Āryan, esp. a Brāhman; Mn.; Yājñ.; MBh. &c.; a bird or snake &c., L. (cf. *-janman*); *-mukhya*, m. 'first of the twice-born,' a Brāhman, Mn. iii, 286; *-sāt*, ind. for or to Brāhmans; with *-√kṛi*, to make a present of (acc.) for B°, Rājat. v, 120. **-jātīya**, mfn. relating to the twice-born, i. e. to the first 3 castes; of twofold nature or mixed origin, mongrel; m. a mule, L. **-jāni**, mfn. having 2 wives, RV. **-jihva** (*dvi-*), mfn. double-tongued (lit. and fig.), AV.; MBh. &c. (*-tā*, f., *-tva*, n., Kāv.); m. a partic. disease of the tongue, Suśr.; a snake, MBh.; R. &c.; informer, thief, scoundrel, villain, W.; N. of a Rakshas, R. **-jyā**, f. the sine of an arc, W.; *-mārga*, m. a horizontal line, ib. **-ṭha** or **-ḍha**, m. N. of the Visarga (as having 2 points) and of Svāhā (wife of Agni), L. **-1. -tā**, f. doubleness, the number 2, duality, MW. **-tra**, mfn. pl. 2 or 3, Kāv. &c. **-trayas-triṅśat**, f. 2 × 33, Lāṭy. **-tri** = *-tra*, esp. in comp.; *-caturam*, ind. twice or thrice or four times, Daś; *-catur-bhāga*, m. pl. $\frac{1}{2}$, $\frac{1}{3}$ or

½, VarBṛS. xxxii, 7; *-catush-pañcaka*, mfn. increased by 2, 3, 4 or 5; with *śata*, n. 2, 3, 4 or 5 per cent., Yājñ. ii, 37; *-divasa-nivāsa*, m. abode for 2 or 3 days, Prab. ii, ⅛. **—triveṇu**, mfn. (chariot) furnished with 2 Triveṇus (s. v.), MBh. vii, 1569. **—tris**, ind. twice or three times, Jātakam. **—tva**, n. = duality (phil.); dual, Pāṇ. ii, 3, 46, Kāś.; reduplication, Sch. on i, 1, 58, 59 &c.; *-tva*, n. the being duality or dualism, Sarvad. **—daṇḍi**, ind. (fr. *daṇḍa*) with 2 sticks, stick against stick, single stick, quarter staff, W. (cf. Pāṇ. v, 4, 128, Kāś.) **—daṇḍin**, m. 'carrying 2 staves,' a kind of mendicant (Buddh.) **—dat**, mfn. having (only) 2 teeth (as a mark of age; cf. Lat. *bi-dens*), Pāṇ. v, 4, 141, Sch. **—datta**, m. N. of a man (cf. *dvaidatti*). **—danta**, mfn. = *-dat*; m. elephant, Gal. **—dala**, mfn. split in two, forked, Hariv.; m. fork, ib.; (*ā*), f. Bauhinia Tomentosa, L. **—daśa**, mfn. pl. 20, Pāṇ. ii, 2, 25, Sch. **—dāmnī**, f. (a cow) tied with 2 ropes, L. **—diva**, mfn. lasting 2 days; m. a ceremony of that length, TāṇḍBr. **—devata**, mfn. relating or belonging to 2 deities, ŚrS.; n. the constellation Viśākhā (presided over by Agni and Indra; cf. *-daivatyā*), VarBṛS. **—devatya**, mfn. = prec. mfn.; Br.; m. (scil. *graha*) a ladleful for 2 deities, ib.; *-pātra*, n. pl. the ladles used for such libations, ĀpŚr. **—deha**, m. '2-bodied,' N. of Gaṇeśa (s. v.), L. **—daivatyā**, f. = *-devata*, n., L. **—droṇa**, n. sg. 2 Droṇas; °*ṇena*, (to buy or sell) by the measure holding 2 D°s, Pāṇ. ii, 3, 18, Kāś. **—dha**, mfn. divided in 2, split asunder, forked, Gṛihyās. **—dhā** (*dvi-*), ind. in 2 ways or parts, twofold, divided, RV.; Mn.; MBh. &c.; *-karaṇa*, n. the dividing into 2, making twofold, arranging in two ways, L.; -°*kāra* (*-dhâk*°), mfn. of 2 kinds, twofold, Pañc.; *-kāram*, ind. dividing into 2 parts, Pāṇ. iii, 4, 62, Kāś.; *-√kṛi*, to divide, MBh.; Kāv.; *-gati*, m. 'going in 2 ways,' a crab or crocodile, L.; *-√gam*, to be divided or split, Kathās.; -°*tmaka* (*-dhâtm*°), n. nutmeg (as being of 2 kinds?), L.; *-bhāvam*, ind. being divided into 2 parts, Pāṇ. iii, 4, 62, Kāś.; *-√bhū*, to be divided or separated, MBh.; Kāv.; *-bhūtâkṛiti*, mfn. of a twofold shape (leech), Suśr.; *-lekhya*, mfn. to be written in 2 ways, W.; m. Phoenix Paludosa, L.; *-sthita*, mfn. existing double or in 2 forms, Śak. vi, ½. **—dhātu**, mfn. (musical piece) consisting of 2 parts, twofold; m. N. of Gaṇeśa (cf. *-deha*), L. **—dhāra**, mfn. (water) forming 2 streams, RV. **—dhūr-vaha**, m. a draught-ox carrying loads in the 2nd year, Līl. **—nagnaka**, m. 'doubly naked,' a person having no prepuce, L. **—nayanī**, f. the two eyes, Naish. **—nava-kṛitvas**, ind. 18 times, BhP. **—navata**, mf(*ī*)n. the 92nd, MBh. **—navati**, f. 92, ib.; *-tama*, mfn. the 92nd, ib. **—nāman** (*dvi-*), mf(*mnī*)n. having 2 names, Br. **—nārāśaṇsa**, mf(*ī*)n. twice furnished with the vessels called N°, AitBr. **—nidhana**, n. N. of a Sāman, L. **—nishka**, mf(*ā*)n. or **-naishkika**, mf(*ī*)n. worth 2 Nishkas, Pāṇ. v, 1, 30. **—netra**, mfn. 'two-eyed,' Pañcad.; *-bhedin*, mfn. knocking out a person's 2 eyes, Yājñ. **—pa**, m. elephant (lit. drinking twice, sc. with his trunk and with his mouth), Mn.; MBh.; R. &c. (ifc. f. *ā*); N. of the number 8, Gaṇit.; Mesua Ferrea, L.; *-dāna*, n. the rut-fluid of an elephant, Ragh.; *-pati*, m. 'prince of elephants,' a large e°, Ratn.; *-mada*, m. = *-dāna*, L.; -°*pâri*, m. 'foe of elephants,' a lion, BhP.; -°*pâsya*, m. 'having an e°'s face,' N. of Gaṇeśa, L.; -°*pêndra*, m. = *-pa-pati*, Ragh.; -°*pêndra-dāna*, n. the rut-fluid of a large e°, Var.; -°*pêśvara*, m. = -°*pêndra*, Mālatim. **—paksha** (*dvi-*), mfn. having 2 side-posts, AV. **—pañcadvayasâṅgula**, mfn. having the height, depth &c. of 10 finger-breadths, Hcat. **—pañca-mūla**, n., °**lī**, f. = *daśa-mūla*, Suśr.; Car. **—pañca-viṇśa**, n. du. 2 × 25, AitBr. **—pañcāśa**, mf(*ī*)n. the 52nd, MBh.; n. 2 × 50, AitBr. **—pañcāśat**, f. 52, Pāṇ. vi, 3, 49 (cf. *dvā-*); °*śat-tama*, mf(*ī*)n. the 52nd, MBh. **—paṇya**, mfn. worth 2 Paṇas, Pāṇ. v, 1, 34, Kāś. **—pattraka**, m. '2-leaved,' a kind of bulbous plant, L. **—patnīka**, m. having 2 wives, Nyāyam., Sch. **—patha**, m. a place where 2 roads meet, crossway, L.; (*ā*), f. a kind of metre, Col. **—pád** (or *dví-*, Pāṇ. vi, 2, 197), m. (*pắd*, RV.) f. (*padī*, ib., or *pād*, g. *kumbha-pady-ādi*) n. (*pắd* or *pád*, RV.), two-footed, bipedal, biped (m. man; n. sg. men, mankind), RV.; AV.; Br.; MBh. &c.; consisting of 2 Pādas (m. a metre of that kind), RV.; ŚBr.; (*padī*), f. a kind of Prākrit metre, Col.; a song composed in this m°, Kād. (°*dī-khaṇḍa*, Ratn. i, 1⅜; 1⁴⁄₇);

taking 2 steps, ĀśvGṛ. i, 7, 19. **—pada** (*dvi-*), mf(*ā*)n. 2-footed, MBh.; Kathās.; consisting of 2 Pādas, VS.; ŚBr. &c.; containing 2 words, VPrāt.; binomial, Col.; m. a biped, (contemptuously) a man, Kathās. vi, 63; a brick 2 Pādas long, Śulbas.; N. of partic. signs of the zodiac, L.; (*ā*), f. a stanza consisting of 2 Pādas, TS.; ŚBr.; RPrāt.; n. a kind of metre, Col.; a combination of 2 words, VPrāt.; *-pati*, m. 'lord of men,' a king, prince, BhP.; *-rāśi*, m. any one of the signs Gemini, Libra, Aquarius, Virgo, and half of Sagittarius; °*dântara* or °*dâbhyāsa* (with *rathaṃtara*), N. of a Sāman. **—padikā**, f. = *dvau pādau*, prob. double amount, Pāṇ. v, 4, 2, Kāś. (cf. *-pādya*); a kind of metre (= °*dī*), Col.; a partic. manner of singing (?), Vikr. iv, ½ &c. **—parāka**, see *dvai-p*° under *dvai*. **—parârdhika**, mfn. equal to 50 of Brahmā's years (cf. *parârdha*), MārkP. **—pari**, ind. except 2, Pāṇ. ii, 1, 10, Kāś. **—parṇa**, mf(*ī*)n. 2-leaved, opposite-leaved; (*ī*), f. wild jew's thorn, L. **—paśu**, mfn. (sacrifice) at which 2 animals are killed, ĀśvŚr.; *-tva*, n. ib., Comm. **—pāt-tā**, f., **-pāt-tva**, n. (cf. *-pad*) 2-footedness, bipartiteness, W. **—pātra**, n. sg. a couple of vessels, Vop.; mf(*ī*)n. containing 2 Pātras (kind of measure), Pāṇ. v, 1, 54, Sch.; °*trika*, mf(*ī*)n. and °*triṇa*, mf(*ā*)n. id., ib. **—pād**, see *-pad*. **—pāda** (*dvi-*), mfn. 2-footed, ŚBr.; MBh. &c. **—pādaka**, mfn. twofold; with *puṇya-kshetra*, n. N. of Buddha, Divyâv. **—pādikā**, f. a kind of song (cf. *-padikā*), R. vii, 6, 58. **—pādya**, mfn. worth double, amounting to double, Pāṇ. v, 1, 34; n. a double penalty, L. **—pāyin**, m. 'drinking twice,' an elephant, R. iii, 20, 26 (cf. *-pa*). **—pāyya**, mfn., Pāṇ. vi, 2, 122, Kāś. **—pitṛi**, mfn. having 2 fathers or ancestors, Baudh.; °*tṛika*, mfn. (a Srāddha) relating to 2 ancestors, Cat. **—puṭa**, mf(*ī*)n. folded double, L.; (*ī*), f. a kind of jasmine, L. **—purusha**, mf(*ā* or *ī*)n. having the length of 2 men; (*ā*, f.) bought with 2 men, Pāṇ. iv, 1, 24; (*am*), ind. through 2 generations, AitBr. viii, 7. **—pṛishṭha**, m. (with Jainas) the 2nd black Vāsudeva. **—paurusha**, mf(*ī*)n. having the length of 2 men, Sūryapr. **—pratika**, mf(*ī*)n. bought &c. with 2 Kārshāpaṇas, Pāṇ. v, 1, 29, Kāś. **—pratishṭha** (*dvi-*), mfn. 2-legged, Br. **—pratihāra**, mfn. (liturg.) connected with 2 Pratihāras (s. v.), Lāṭy. **—pravācana**, mfn. having a double name, ĀśvŚr. **—pravrājinī**, f. running after 2 men, ĀśvGṛ. **—praîsha**, mfn. issuing 2 invitations, AitBr. **—bándhu**, m. N. of a man, RV. **—bárha-jman**, mfn. (fr. *barha* = °*has*) having a double course or path, RV. **—bárhas**, mfn. (°*hās* also n. & ind.) doubly close or thick or strong; in g. doubled (as opposed to single), mighty, large, great, RV. **—bāṇī**, f. sg. 2 arrows, Naish. **—bāhu**, mfn. 2-armed; m. man, Kathās. liii, 94. **—bāhuka**, m. 'the 2-armed one,' N. of one of the attendants of Śiva, Hariv. **—bindu**, m. 'double-dot,' the sign of the Visarga, Vop. **—bhallaka**, n. a kind of arrow-point, ŚārṅgP. **—bhāga** (*dvi-*), m. double portion or share, TS.; a partic. sin, L.; *-dhaná*, n. double the goods or property, AV. xii, 2, 35. **—bhāta**, n. twilight; *-tva*, n. HPariś. **—bhādra**, mfn. having 2 months called Bhādra, Rājat. **—bhārya**, m. having 2 wives, Kāty.; Var.; -°*ryâgni*, m. N. of wk. **—bhāva**, see *dvai-bhāvya*. **—bhuja**, mfn. '2-armed,' Hcat.; n. an angle, W.; *-rāma-dhyāna*, n. N. of wk. **—bhūma**, mfn. '2-floored,' Pāṇ. v, 4, 75, Vārtt. **—bhauma**, mf(*ī*)n. id., Hcat. **—mantha**, mfn., Pāṇ. vi, 2, 122, Kāś. **—maya**, mf(*ī*)n. made or consisting of 2 parts of (gen.), v, 2, 47, Kāś. **—mātṛi**, mfn. having 2 mothers (as fire produced by 2 rubbing sticks), RV.; *-ja*, mfn. born from 2 mothers or in 2 ways, W. (cf. *dvaimātura*). **—mātra**, mfn. doubly as great, MānŚr. and Gṛ.; containing 2 syllabic instants, Prāt. (also °*trika*, Śiksh.); (*ā*), f. sg. 2 s° instants, RPrāt. **—mārga**, m. (Gal.) °**gī**, f. (Bharat.) cross-way. **—māshya**, mfn. weighing or worth 2 Māshas, Pāṇ. v, 1, 34. **—mīḍha**, m. N. of a son of Hastin (Bṛihat) and grandson of Su-hotra, Hariv.; Pur. **—mukha**, mf(*ī*)n. 2-mouthed, 2-faced, Hcat.; m. a kind of worm, Suśr.; of snake, L.; (*ā*), f. leech, L.; a water-jar with two mouths, L.; °*khâhi* or °*khôraga*, m. a kind of serpent, L. **—muni**, mfn. produced by 2 sages, Pāṇ. ii, 1, 19, Sch. (cf. *tri-*). **—musali** (written also °*shali*), ind. with 2 clubs, club against club (in fighting), g. *dvidaṇḍy-ādi*. **—mūrdha**, mf(*ī*)n. 2-headed, Pāṇ. v, 4, 115. **—mūrdhan** (*dvi-*), mfn. id., vi, 2, 197; m. N. of an Asura, AV.; MBh.; Hariv. **—yaja**, mfn.

twice containing (the word) *yaja*; *-tva*, n., ĀpŚr., Sch. **—yajus** (*dvi-*), f. a partic. brick, ŚBr. **—yama**, '2 tones,' circumflex, TPrāt. **—yamunam**, ind. at the confluence of the 2 Jumnās, Pāṇ. ii, 1, 20, Kāś. **—yāmī**, f. 2 night-watches = 6 hours, HPariś. **—yodha**, m. 'fighting with 2,' N. of Kṛishṇa's charioteer (v. l. °*dhin*); (*ī*), f. a kind of metre, Col. **—ra**, m. = *-repha*, L. **—rada**, mfn. 2-tusked, L.; m. an elephant, MBh.; Kāv. &c.; *-pati*, m. a large e°, BhP.; *-karâgra*, n. the tip of an e°'s trunk, MW.; *-rata*, m. a partic. Samādhi, Kāraṇḍ.; °*dântaka*, m. 'destroyer of the e°,' lion, L.; °*dârāti*, m. 'foe of the e°,' the fabulous animal Śarabha, L.; °*dâśana*, n. 'food of the e°,' Ficus Religiosa; °*dâsya*, m. 'e°-faced,' N. of Gaṇeśa, Bālar. **—rasana**, mfn. 'double-tongued'; m. snake, L. **—rājá**, n. battle between 2 kings, AV. **—rātrá**, mfn. lasting 2 days; m. a period or festival of that length, AV.; ŚrS. **—rātrīṇa**, mfn. to be accomplished in 2 nights, Lāṭy. **—rūpá**, mfn. biform, bicolour, twofold, VS.; TS; ŚBr.; Daś.; spelt or written in 2 ways; m. a word so spelt, variety of interpretation or reading, W.; *-kośa*, m. a dictionary of words written in 2 ways, Cat.; *-tā*, f. doubleness of form or expression, L. **—retas** (*dvi-*), mfn. (a male ass) doubly impregnating (sc. mare and she-ass), Br.; (a mare) doubly impregnated (sc. by horse and male ass), TāṇḍyaBr.; a kind of hermaphrodite, Car. **—repha**, m. 'shaped like 2 r's or having 2 r's in its name (*bhramara*)?,' a large black bee, Var.; Kāv. &c.; *-gaṇa-saṃkulā*, f. Rosa Glandulifera, L.; *-gaṇa-sammitā*, f. a kind of rose, MW.; *-caya*, m. (Caurap.), *-mālā*, f. (Kum.), *-vṛinda*, n. (MW.), a flight or swarm of bees. **—laksha**, n. a distance of 200,000 (sc. Yojanas), Kāv. **—lakshaṇa**, mfn. twofold, of 2 kinds, Mn. **—laya**, m. (in music) double time (?), Vikr. iv, ³⁄₈. **—vaktrá**, mfn. 2-faced, 2-mouthed, Suparṇ.; m. N. of a Dānava, Hariv. **—vacana**, n. the dual and its endings, Pāṇ. i, 4, 102 &c.; °*nânta*, m. a d°-termination, MW. **—vacas**, n. = *-vacana*, RPrāt. **—vajraka**, m. a 16-angled column, Var. **—varṇa**, mfn. bicolour, GṛS.; n. doubling of a consonant, TPrāt.; *-ratha*, m. N. of an ancestor of Śākya-muni, L. **—varsha**, mfn. 2 years old; (*ā*), f. a 2 y° o° cow, L. **—varshaka**, mf(*ikā*)n., **-varshīṇa**, mf(*ā*)n. = prec. mfn., L. **—vastra**, mfn. clothed with 2 garments, MānGṛ. **—vācin**, mfn. expressing or denoting 2 (a dual suffix), Kāt. **—vārshika**, mf(*ī*)n. 2 years old, Pāṇ. vii, 3, 16, Kāś. (cf. *ūna-*, add.) **—vāhikā**, f. a swing or litter, L. **—viṇśatikīna**, mfn. worth 2 × 20, L. **—vida**, m. N. of a monkey (slain by Vishṇu, or an ally of Rāma and son of the Aśvins), MBh.; Hariv.; Pur.; °*dâri*, m. 'Dvi-vida's foe,' N. of Vishṇu, L. **—vidha**, mfn. twofold, of 2 kinds, ŚāṅkhŚr.; Mn.; Suśr. &c.; (*ā*), ind. in 2 parts or ways (*vibhinna*), R. vii, 7, 54. **—vivāhin**, mfn. allied with 2 by matrimony; °*hitâ-sapiṇḍī-karaṇa*, n. N. of ch. of PSarv. **—vista**, mfn. worth 2 Vistas, Pāṇ. v, 1, 31. **—vṛintaya**, Nom. Ā. °*yate*, to appear to have 2 stalks, Viddh. **—vṛishá**, mfn. having 2 bulls, AV. **—veda**, mfn. familiar with 2 Vedas, iv, 1, 88, Sch.; *-gaṅga*, m. N. of Sch., Cat. **—vedin**, mfn. = *-veda*, Pāṇ. iv, 1, 88, Sch. **—vesarā**, f. a kind of light carriage drawn by 2 mules, L. **—vaistika**, mf(*ī*)n. = *-vista*, Pāṇ. v, 1, 31. **—vyāma**, mfn. 2 fathoms long, KātyŚr. **—vyāyāma**, mfn. id., ĀpŚr. **—vraṇīya**, mfn. relating to the twofold wounds, Suśr. **—vrata** (*dvi-*), mfn. eating twice a day, TS. **—śata**, mf(*ī*)n. consisting of 200, containing 200, Mn. viii, 257; the 200th, MBh.; (*ī*), f. 200, Āryabh.; n. 200, Pāṇ. vi, 3, 47, Vārtt.; 102, Nidānas.; *-ka*, mfn. worth 200, bought for 200, Pāṇ. v, 1, 24, Sch.; *-tama*, mf(*ī*)n. the 200th, Hariv.; °*tôttara-sāhasra*, mf(*ī*)n. consisting of 1200, Cat.; °*tikā*, f. an amount of 200, Pāṇ. v, 4, 1; 2, Kāś.; °*tya*, mfn. = *-śataka*, Pāṇ. v, 1, 34, Vārtt. **—śapha**, mfn. cloven-hoofed; m. a cloven-hoofed animal, Mn.; Yājñ. **—śarīra**, m. '2-bodied,' N. of Gaṇeśa, L. **—śavas** (*dvi-*), mfn. having or granting twofold strength, RV. ix, 104, 2. **—śas**, ind. 2 by 2, in pairs, KātyŚr.; Suśr. **—śākha**, mfn. 2-branched, forked, Kauś.; °*khaka*, mf(*ikā*)n. id., Gṛihyās., Comm. **—śāṇa**, °**ṇika** (ŚārṅgS.), or °**ṇya**, mfn. worth 2 Śāṇas, Pāṇ. v, 1, 36. **—śāla**, mfn. containing 2 rooms, Var.; n. a 2-roomed house, MatsyaP. **—śikha**, mfn. two-pointed, forked, BhP. **—śiras** (Pañc.) and °**ska** (Var.), mfn. 2-headed. **—śīrsha** and °**shaka**, mfn. id., L.; (°*shaka*), m. N. of Agni, L. **—śukla**, mfn. doubly pure (sc. on father's and mother's side), R.; *-vat*, mfn. id., R. (B.), Comm. **—śūrpa**, mfn. containing 2 Śūrpas or winnowing baskets, Pāṇ. v, 1, 28, Sch. — **śūla**, mfn. 2-pronged, forked, ŚrS. — **śṛiṅga**, mfn. having 2 horns or points, KātyŚrS., Sch. — **śṛiṅgikā**, f. a kind of plant, L. — **śṛiṅgin**, m. '2-horned,' a kind of fish, L. — **śaurpika**, mfn. = *-śūrpa*, Pāṇ. v, 1, 20, Vārtt. 2, Pat. — **śruti**, mfn. (in music) comprehending 2 intervals. — **shaṃhita**, mfn. (for *-saṃh°*) twice folded, Br. — **shaṇḍika**, m. (*-khaṇḍ?*) a garment sheltering from wind and cold, L. — **shaṃdhi**, mfn. (cf. *-saṃdhi*) composed of 2 parts, AitBr.; admitting a twofold Sandhi, RPrāt. — **shash**, mfn. pl. 2 × 6, 12, BhP. — **shashṭa**, mf(*ī*)n. the 62nd, ch. of MBh. — **shashṭi**, f. 62, ib. (cf. Pāṇ. vi, 3, 49 and *dvā-*); *-tama*, mf(*ī*)n. the 62nd, ch. of MBh. and R.; *-vākya*, n. N. of wk. — **shāshṭika**, mf(*ī*)n. consisting of 62, worth 62 &c., Pāṇ. v, 1, 57; vii, 3, 15, Kāś. — **shāhasra** (*dvi-*), mf(*ī*)n. consisting of 2000, TS. (cf. *-sāh°*). — **shûkta**, mfn. having 2 Sûktas, SāṅkhBr. — **shṭha**, mfn. staying in 2 places, Sūryas.; AgP. (*-tā*, f.); ambiguous (words), Pat., Introd. — **saṃvatsarīṇa**, mfn. accomplished in 2 years, Pāṇ. v, 1, 87, Kāś. — **saṃstha** or °**sthita**, mfn. standing on 2 fields, AgP. — **sattva-lakshaṇa**, n. N. of wk. — **saṃdhi**, mfn. = *-shaṃdhi*, Pāṇ. viii, 3, 106, Kāś. — **saṃdhya**, mfn. having a morning and an evening twilight, Suśr. — **saptata**, mf(*ī*)n. the 72nd, ch. of MBh. — **saptati**, f. 72, Mn. vii, 172 (cf. Pāṇ. vi, 3, 49 and *dvā-*); *-tama*, mf(*ī*)n. the 72nd, ch. of MBh. and R. — **sapta-dhā**, ind. in (into) 14 parts, BhP. — **saptan**, mfn. pl. 2 × 7, 14, RāmatUp.; °*pta-saṃkhyāka*, mfn. id., Pañcad. — **sama**, mfn. consisting of 2 equal portions; having 2 equal sides; *-caturaśra* or *-tribhuja*, m. an isosceles quadrangle or triangle, alg. — **samīna**, mfn. 2 years old, v, 1, 86, Sch. — **sahasra**, mfn. worth 2000, Pāṇ. iv, 3, 156; v, 1, 29, Kāś.; n. 2000, vi, 3, 47, Vārtt., Pat. (cf. *-shāh°* and *-sāh°*); °*srāksha*, m. 'the 2000-eyed one,' N. of the serpent-king Śesha, Hariv. — **sāṃvatsarika**, mf(*ī*)n. = *-saṃvatsarīṇa*, Pāṇ. v, 1, 87, Kāś. — **sāptatika**, mf(*ī*)n. worth 72, Pāṇ. vii, 3, 15, Kāś. — **sāhasra**, mf(*ī*)n. = *-sahasra*, KātyŚr.; n. 2000, MārkP. — **sītya**, mfn. twice ploughed, L. — **suvarṇa** or **-sauvarṇika**, mfn. worth 2 Suvarṇas, Pāṇ. v, 1, 29, Vārtt., Pat. — **sūrya**, mfn. having 2 suns, Kād. — **stanā** (*dvi-*) and °**nī**, f. having 2 udders or 2 pegs, ŚBr.; KātyŚr., Comm. (cf. Pāṇ. vi, 2, 164). — **sthūṇa**, m. (sc. *daṇḍa*) a partic. form of military array, Kām. — **srakti**, mfn. 2-cornered; n. a vessel so shaped for making libations to the Aśvins, ĀpŚr. — **sva-bhāva**, mfn. having a double nature or character, MW. — **svara**, mfn. 2-syllabled, TPrāt. — **han**, m. 'striking twice, i.e. with tusks and teeth,' an elephant, L. — **halya**, mfn. twice ploughed, L. (cf. *-sītya*). — **havis**, mfn. connected with 2 oblations, SāṅkhŚr. — **hasta**, mf(*ā*)n. 2 hands long, Hcat. — **hāyana**, mf(*ī*)n. 2 years old, Mn. xi, 134; (*ī*), f. a 2-year-old cow, L. — **hiṃkāra**, m. N. of 2 Sāmans, ĀrshBr. — **hīna**, mfn. destitute of both genders (i.e. of the masc. and the fem.), neuter; n. the neuter gender, L. — **hūta-vat**, mfn. containing an invocation of 2 gods, AitBr. — **hṛidayā**, f. 'double-hearted,' pregnant, Suśr. — **hotṛi** (*dvi-*), m. a double Hotṛi (Agni), TĀr. **Dviḍa**, n. N. of a Sāman, Kāth. **Dvîndriya**, n. 2 organs of sense (*-grāhya*, mfn. perceptible by 2 senses, sc. sight and touch, Bhāshāp.); mfn. having 2 senses (touch and taste), L. **Dvīpá** &c., see s.v. **Dvirāvatīka**, mfn. (place) possessing 2 Irāvatīs, Pat. **Dvy-aṅsa** &c., see p. 507, col. 3.

Dviḥ-, in comp., see under *dvis-*, p. 507, col. 3.

2. **Dvika**, mfn. consisting of two, 2-fold, Lāṭy.; Suśr.; two, VarBṛS. xiii, 3; happening the 2nd time, Pāṇ. v, 2, 77, Kāś.; increased by 2 (e.g. °*kaṃ śatam* 102, i.e. 2 per cent.), Mn. viii, 141. — **pṛishṭha**, m. the 2-humped camel, L.

Dvi-já, mfn. twice-born; m. a man of any one of the first 3 classes, any Āryan, (esp.) a Brāhman (re-born through investiture with the sacred thread, cf. *upa-nayana*), AV.; Mn.; MBh. &c.; a bird or any oviparous animal (appearing first as an egg), Mn.; MBh. &c.; a tooth (as growing twice), Suśr.; Bhartṛ.; Var. (n., BhP. ii, 1, 31); coriander seed or Xanthoxylum Alatum, L.; (*ā*), f. Piper Aurantiacum, Bhpr.; Clerodendrum Siphonantus, L.; = *pālaṅkī*, L. (cf. *-jā* & *-jāti*). — **kalpa-latā**, f. N. of wk. — **kutsita**, m. 'despised by Brāhmans,' Cordia Latifolia and Myxa, L. — **ketu**, m. a kind of citron, L. — **cchatra**, n. N. of a place, Cat. — **jetṛi**, m. N. of a Brāhman, ib. — **tva**, n. 'the being twice-born;' the condition or rank of a Brāhman or of any one of the first 3 classes; Vishṇ.; BhP.; Rājat. — **dāsa**, m. 'slave of the twice-born,' a Śūdra, L. — **deva**, m. 'god among the twice-born,' a Brāhman, a sage, BhP.; *-deva*, m. 'god among B°s,' a very pious or excellent B°, MW. — **nayana**, n. N. of wk. — **nishevita**, mfn. inhabited by birds, MW. — **pati**, m. 'chief of twice-born,' the moon (as produced first from Atri's eye and again from the ocean of milk), Hariv. 12491. — **prapā**, f. 'watering-place for birds,' a basin for water round the foot of a tree (= *ālavāla*), L. — **priya**, mfn. dear to a Brāhman (Āryan); m. a kind of Khadira, L.; (*ā*), the Soma-plant, L. — **bandhu**, m. 'a mere twice-born,' a B° &c. only by name, L. (cf. *kshatra-*). — **bruva**, m. called or calling one's self (but not being) a B°, L. — **maya**, mf(*ī*)n. consisting of B°s, Cāṇ. — **malla**, m. N. of a man, Cat. — **mukhya**, m. 'first among the twice-born,' a Brāhman, MBh. — **rāja**, m. = *-pati*, Hcat.; the moon; N. of a Brāhman, Śrikaṇṭh.; N. of Garuḍa (king of birds), L.; of Ananta (serpent-king), L.; camphor, L.; °*jôdaya*, m. N. of wk. — **ropaṇī**, f. a kind of pill, Rasêndrac. — **rshabha** (°*ja* + *ṛish°*), m. 'bull (i.e. best) among the twice-born,' a Brāhman, MBh. — **rshi** (°*ja* + *ṛishi*), m. a priestly sage (= *brahma-rshi*), VP. — **liṅgin**, mfn. wearing the insignia of a B°, Mn. ix, 224; a Kshatriya, L.; an impostor, a pretended B°, W. — **vara**, m. = *-mukhya*, MBh. — **varya**, m. an excellent or superior B°, W. — **vāhana**, m. 'having a bird (Garuḍa) as vehicle,' N. of Kṛishṇa, Hariv. — **vraṇa**, m. gum-boil, L. — **śapta**, m. 'cursed by Brāhmans,' prohibited (on certain occasions), Dolichos Catjang, L. — **śreshṭha** and **-sattama**, m. = *-mukhya*, MBh. — **sevaka**, m. = *-dāsa*, L. — **sevā**, f. service of the twice-born (by Śūdras), W. — **sneha**, m. 'favourite of Brāhmans,' Butea Frondosa, L. **Dvijâgrya**, m. = °*ja-mukhya*, Mn. iii, 35 &c.; a chief or respectable Brāhman, W. **Dvijâṅgikā** or °**ṅgī**, f. a kind of medicinal plant (= *kaṭukā*), L. **Dvijâmbā**, f. N. of a princess, L. **Dvijâlaya**, m. 'the residence of birds,' the hollow trunk of a tree, L.; the r° of Brāhmans, W. **Dvijêndra**, m. = °*ja-mukhya*, MBh.; = °*ja-pati*, Inscr.; N. of Garuḍa, Suparṇ. **Dvijêndraka**, m. = *-jaketu*, L. **Dvijêśa**, m. = °*ja-pati*, L. **Dvijêśvara**, m. 'chief of twice-born,' a Brāhman; the moon, Kāvyâd. ii, 175; N. of Śiva, L. **Dvijôttama**, m. = °*ja-mukhya*, Mn.; Yājñ.; MBh. **Dvijôpāsaka**, m. = °*ja-dāsa*, L.

Dvijāya, Nom. Ā. °*yate*, to become or be born again as a Brāhman, Hcat.

Dvijāyanī, f. the thread worn over the shoulder and marking the first 3 or twice-born classes, L.

Dviji-√bhū, to make one's self a Brāhman, Vīrac.

Dvitá, m. 'second,' N. of an Āptya (s.v.; cf. *tritá*), RV.; VS.; ŚBr.; (according to some he is the author of RV. ix, 103; to others, son of Atri and author of v, 18, Anukr.) — **vana**, m. N. of a man (cf. *dvaitavana*).

Dvitaya, mfn. consisting of two, twofold, double, BhP.; Pāṇ. v, 2, 42; pl. (*e* or *ās*, i, 1, 33, Kāś.) two, both (each thought of as a plurality, e.g. mountains and trees), Ragh. viii, 89; n. a pair or couple, Yājñ.; Kāv.; Pur.

Dvitā, ind. (Nir. v, 3) doubly so, i.e. just so, by all means, indeed, certainly, especially (often in relat. clauses and connected with *adha* or *aha*), RV.

Dvitīya, mf(*ā*)n. (fr. *dvi*, Pāṇ. v, 2, 54; decl. i, 1, 36, Vārtt. 3, Pat., cf. vii, 3, 115) second, RV. &c. &c.; (*am*), ind. for the second time, KaṭhUp.; MBh. &c.; m. companion, fellow (friend or foe), ŚBr.; MBh. &c.; ifc. doubled or accompanied by, furnished with (cf. *a-*, *chāyā-*, *dhanur-* &c.); the 2nd in a family (i.e. a son, L.; cf. AitBr. vii, 29); the 2nd letter of a Varga, i.e. the surd aspirate, Prāt.; Pāṇ. &c.; (*ā*), f. female companion or friend, Kāth. xcviii, 33; wife (a second self), L.; (sc. *vibhakti*) the 2nd case, the accusative or its terminations, Pāṇ. ii, 1, 24 &c.; (sc. *tithi*) the 2nd day of a half-month, Rātn. iv, $\frac{3}{8}$; (*dvítīya*), mfn. (Pāṇ. v, 3, 49) forming the 2nd part or half of anything, with *bhāga*, m. half of (gen.), Mn. iv, 1 &c.; n. the half (at the beginning or end of a comp.), Pāṇ. ib., ii, 2, 3, Kāś. — **kula-dhāraka**, m. a son (cf. above), Gal. — **cakravarti-lakshaṇa**, n. N. of wk.; *-dīdhiti-ṭīkā*, f., *-prakāśa*, m., *-rahasya*, n., °*ṇânugama*, m. N. of wks. — **tantra**, n. N. of wk. — **tā**, f. state of being second, MW. — **tāla**, m. (in music) a kind of measure. — **triphalā**, f. the 2nd set of 3 fruits (viz grape, date, and the fruit of Gmelina Arborea), L. — **tvá**, n. = *-tā*, MaitrS. — **pragalbha-lakshaṇa**, n., *-ṇânugama*, m. N. of wks. — **miśra-lakshaṇa**, n., *-prakāśa*, m., *-vivecana*, n., °*ṇânugama*, m. N. of wks. — **vat** (°*tīya-v°*), mfn. having as a second or companion, accompanied by (instr.), ŚBr.; MBh. — **vayas**, mfn. having arrived at the 2nd period of life, L. — **svara**, n. N. of a Sāman. — **svalakshaṇa**, n. N. of wk.; *-ṭīkā* & *-dīdhiti-ṭīkā*, f., *-rahasya*, n., °*ṇânugama* & °*ṇâloka*, m. N. of wks. **Dvitīyâdi-vyutpatti-vāda**, m. N. of wk. **Dvitīyâbhā**, f. Curcuma Aromatica or Xanthorrhiza, L.

Dvitīyaka, mfn. second, the second, AgP.; (*dvít°*) happening the 2nd time, Pāṇ. v, 2, 77, Kāś.; recurring every other day (fever), 2, 81, Kāś.

1. **Dvitīyā**, f. of °*tīya*. — **kalpa**, m. N. of wk. — **candra**, m. the moon of the 2nd day of the half-month, the young moon, Ratn. iv, $\frac{3}{8}$. — **tantra**, n. N. of wk. — °**rcana-kalpa-latā** and -°**rcana-candrikā** (°*yârc°*), f. N. of wks.

2. **Dvitīyā**, ind. -√**kṛi**, to plough the second time, Pāṇ. v, 4, 58, Kāś.

Dvitīyika, mfn. Pāṇ. v, 1, 48. °**yin**, mfn. standing in the 2nd place or rank, ĀśvŚr.; receiving the half as portion or share, Nyāyam., Comm. °**yūka**, mfn. second, W.

Dvir, in comp. for *dvis* below. — **aṅsaka**, mfn. 2-shouldered, L. — **anugāna**, n. N. of a Sāman, Ārsh Br. — **abhyasta**, mfn. twice repeated, L. — **abhyāsâkūpara**, n. N. of a Sāman, L. — **aśana**, n. eating twice a day, L. — **āgamana**, n. 'twice coming,' the ceremony of the second entrance of the bride into her husband's house after a visit to that of her father, L.; *-prakaraṇa*, n. N. of wk. — **āpa**, m. '(?) drinking twice' (sc. with trunk and mouth), elephant, L. (cf. *dvi-pa*). — **āmushyāyaṇa**, mfn. = *dvy-ām°*, Nār. — **āshāḍha**, m. an intercalary Āshāḍha month, Jyot. — **iḍa**, mfn. containing the word *iḍā* twice; (with *pada-stobha*, m.) N. of a Sāman, TāṇḍyaBr. — **ukta**, mfn. twice said, repeated, doubled, reduplicated, VPrāt.; said or told in 2 ways, W.; n. repetition, Siddh. — **ukti**, f. repetition, tautology, telling anything in two or various ways, W.; (Gr.) repetition of a syllable; twofold way of expression or of spelling a word; *-kośa*, N. of a dictionary; *-prakriyā*, f. N. of ch. of the Madhya-siddhânta-kaumudī. — **uccārita**, n. the repetition of a piece of music, Mṛicch. iii, 5. — **udātta**, mfn. doubly accented, VPrāt. — **ūḍhā**, f. (a woman) twice married, L. — **oshṭhya**, mfn. containing 2 labials; *-tva*, n., VPrāt., Comm. — **nagna**, mfn. doubly naked or defective (i.e. whose ancestors on both sides have during 3 generations omitted all Veda-study and kindling of the sacred fire), Gobh. — **bhāva**, m. doubling, reduplication, Vop.; double-dealing, deceit, Pañc. (B.) iii, 65. — **vacana**, n. repetition, reduplication, APrāt.; Pāṇ. &c. — **vyūha**, mfn. appearing twofold, MBh. 13603.

1. **Dvish**, in comp. for *dvis* below. — **ṭamām** and **-ṭarām**, ind. (superl. & comp.), Pāṇ. viii, 2, 27, Sch. **Dvish-pakva**, mfn. twice cooked, warmed up, Gobh.

Dvis, ind. (Pāṇ. v, 4, 18; cf. viii, 3, 43) twice, RV. &c. (*dvir ahnaḥ*, *ahnā*, or *ahni*, twice a day, Pāṇ. ii, 3, 64, Kāś. [Cf. Zd. *bis*; Gk. δίς; Lat. *bis*.] **Dviḥ-sama**, mfn. twice as large, Yājñ. **Dviḥ-svara**, mfn. doubly accented, Prāt. **Dvistāvā**, f. (fr. *tāvat*) twice as large (a Vedi), Pāṇ. v, 4, 84.

द्विष् 2. **dvish**, cl. 2. P. Ā. *dvéshṭi*, *dvishṭé* (ep. also *dvishati*, °*te*; Subj. *dvéshat*, AV.; impf. *advet*, 3. pl. *advishur* & °*shan*, Pāṇ. iii, 4, 112; pf. *didvesha*, ŚBr.; aor. *dvikshat*, °*shata* (3. sg.), AV.; fut. *dvekshyati*, *dveshṭā*, Siddh., Pāṇ. vii, 2, 10; inf. *dveshṭum*, MBh.; *dvéshṭos*, ŚBr.) to hate, show hatred against (acc.; rarely dat. or gen.), be hostile or unfriendly, RV.; AV.; ŚBr.; Mn.; MBh.; Kāv. &c.; to be a rival or a match for, Kāvyâd. ii, 61: Pass. *dvishyate*; aor. *adveshi*, Gr.: Caus. *dveshayati*, Kāv.: Desid. *didvikshati*, °*te*, Gr.; Intens. *dedvishyate*, *dedveshṭi* or *dedvishīti*, Gr. [Cf. Zd. *ḍbish*; Gk. ὀ-δύσ-ασθαι; Germ. *Zwist*.]

Dviṭ, in comp. for 3. *dvish*. — **sevā**, f. service of a foe, treachery, W. — **sevin**, mfn. serving an enemy, traitor, Mn. ix, 232.

3. **Dvish** (nom. *dviṭ*), hostility, hatred, dislike; (also m.) foe, enemy, RV.; AV. &c.; mfn. hostile, hating, disliking (ifc.), ŚBr.; Mn.; MBh.; Kāv. &c.

Dvisha, mfn. (ifc.) hostile, hating (cf. *-tā* and

-*tva*); hateful or unpleasant to, Hariv.; m. foe, enemy, L. **-tā**, f. (MW.), **-tva**, n. (Var.) hostility, hatred (see above). **-m-tapa**, mfn. vexing an enemy, revenging, retaliating, Pāṇ. iii, 2, 39; vi, 3, 67; 4, 94.

Dvishát, mfn. (p. Pres. of √1. *dvish*) hating or detesting, hostile, unfriendly, foe, enemy (with acc. or gen., Pāṇ. ii, 3, 69, Vārtt. 5, Pat.), ŚBr.; Mn.; MBh. &c. °**tī-tāpa**, mfn. harassing female foes, L.

1. **Dvishṭa**, mfn. hated, disliked, odious, hostile, Yājñ.; Mn.; MBh. &c. **-tva**, n. odiousness, Naish.

Dvésha, m. hatred, dislike, repugnance, enmity to (comp.), ŚBr.; Mn.; MBh. &c. (°*shaṃ-√kṛi*, to show enmity against (dat.), Pañc. iii, 160). **-parimuktā**, f. 'free from hatred,' N. of a Gandharva maid, Kāraṇḍ. **-parimocana**, m. a partic. Samādhi, ib. **-stha**, mfn. betraying dislike or aversion, Gīt.

Dveshaṇa, mfn. hating, disliking; foe, enemy, MBh.; n. dislike or hatred against (gen. or comp.), Suśr.; MBh.

Dveshaṇīya, mfn. = °*shya*.

Dvéshas, n. aversion, dislike, hostility; foe, enemy, RV.; AV.; VS. **Dvesho-yávana** (MaitrS.) and **-yút** (RV.), mfn. removing hostility.

Dveshin, mfn. hating, disliking, hostile, malignant against (gen. or comp.), MBh.; Hariv.; Suśr.; Kāv. &c.; m. foe, enemy, ŚārṅgP.

Dveshṭum & °**ṭos**. See √2. *dvish*.

Dveshṭṛi, mfn. one who hates or dislikes (comp.), enemy, foe, MBh.; Hariv.; Suśr.

Dvéshya, mfn. to be hated or disliked, odious, detestable; foe, enemy, AV.; ŚBr.; MBh. &c.; n. nutmeg, Gal. **-tā**, f. (Pañc.), **-tva**, n. (Bhpr.) odiousness, disfavour. **-pāpaka**, mfn. detesting sin, MBh. xii, 3168.

द्विषण्डिक *dvishaṇḍika*. See under *dvi*.

द्विषदा *dvishadā*, f. Polianthes Tuberosa, L.

द्विषा *dvishā*, f. cardamoms, L.

द्विष्ट 2. *dvishṭa*, n. (for *dvy-ashṭa*) copper, L.

द्वीप *dvīpá*, m. n. (fr. *dvi* + *ap*, Pāṇ. v, 4, 74; vi, 3, 97) an island, peninsula, sandbank, RV.; ŚBr.; MBh. &c.; a division of the terrestrial world (either 7 [Jambu, Plaksha or Go-medaka, Śālmali, Kuśa, Krauñca, Śāka and Pushkara, MBh. vi, 604 &c.; Hariv.; Pur. &c.] or 4 [Bhadrāśva, Ketu-māla, Jambu-dvīpa and Uttarāḥ Kuravaḥ, MBh. vi, 208, Hariv.; Kāv. &c.; cf. Dharmas. cxx] or 13 [the latter four + 9, viz. Indra-dvīpa, Kaserū-mat, Tāmra-varṇa, Gabhasti-mat, Nāga-dvīpa, Saumya, Gāndharva, Vāruna and Bhārata, which are enumerated VP. ii, 3, 6; 7, as forming Bhārata-varsha] or 18 [among which the Upa-dvīpas are said to be included, Naish. i, 5, Sch.]; they are situated round the mountain Meru, and separated from each other by distinct concentric circumambient oceans; *ayaṃ dvīpaḥ* = *jambu-dv*°, BhP. v, 16, 5 or = *bhārata-dv*°, VP. ii, 3, 7); m. place of refuge, shelter, protection or protector, MBh.; Kāraṇḍ.; a tiger's skin, L.; cubebs, L. (cf. *-sambhava*). **-karpūraka** or **-karpūra-ja**, m. camphor from China, L. **-kumāra**, m. (with Jainas) N. of a class of deities, L. **-kharjurī**, f. a kind of date, L. **-cchandira**, m. or n. N. of a place, Cat. **-ja**, n. = *-kharjurī*, L. **-rāja**, m. N. of a partic. Samādhi, Kāraṇḍ. **-vat**, mfn. abounding in islands, MBh.; m. the ocean, L.; a river, L.; (*ī*), f. a river, Dharmaś.; the earth, L. **-vyavasthā**, f. N. of wk. **-śatru**, m. Asparagus Racemosus, Car. (cf. °*pi-ś*°). **-śreshṭha**, m. the best of islands, MW. **-sambhava**, m. the largest sort of raisin, cubebs, L.; Vernonia Anthelminthica, L.; (*ā*), f. a kind of date, L. **Dvīpântara-vacā**, f. Smilax China, Bhpr. **Dvīpêśa**, m. lord of an island, viceroy, Pracaṇḍ.

Dvīpi, in comp. = °*pin*. **-karṇi**, m. 'tiger-eared,' N. of a prince, Kathās. **-nakha**, m. Unguis odoratus, L. **-śatru**, m. Asparagus Racemosus (cf. *dvīpikā* & next).

Dvīpikā, f. Asparagus Racemosus, Car. (cf. *dvīpa-śatru* and *dvīpya*).

Dvīpin, mfn. having islands or spots like islands, L.; (*ín*), m. tiger, ounce or panther, leopard, AV.; Hariv.; MBh. &c.; (*nī*), f. the sea or a river, Bālar. iii, 48; a kind of plant, L.

Dvīpya, mfn. living on an island, VS.; m. cubebs (cf. *dvīpa-sambhava*), L.; a sort of crow, L.; N. of Vyāsa (cf. *dvaipāyana*), L.; (*ā*), f. Asparagus Racemosus (cf. *dvīpikā* and *dvīpi-śatru*), L.

द्वृ *dvṛi*, cl. 1. P. *dvarati* (Dhātup. xxii, 36) to obstruct; to cover; to disregard; to appropriate.

द्वेधा *dve-dhā*, ind. (fr. *dvaya*; cf. *tre-dhā*) in two parts or ways, twice, Br.; MBh. &c. **-kāram**, ind. changing into two, ĀśvŚr. **-kṛita**, mfn. broken in two, Bālar. iv, 53. **-kriyā**, f. breaking or splitting in two, Mcar. ii, 33.

Dve-dhī, ind. in two, asunder; *-kṛita*, AV. Pariś.

Dve-sata, mfn. 'in two places equal,' having the same length above and below the navel (v. l. *dvaya-s*°), Lāṭy. i, 1, 7.

द्वेष *dvesha*, &c. See above.

द्वै *dvai*, Vṛiddhi form for *dvi* in comp. **-kulijika**, mf(*ī*)n. containing 2 Kulijas (kind of measure), L. **-gata**, mfn. (fr. *dvi-gat*) N. of a Sāman, TāṇḍyaBr. **-guṇika**, mf(*ī*)n. (fr. *dvi-guṇa*) one who requires the double or cent per cent interest; m. usurer, L. **-guṇya**, n. doubling or the double, Mn.; MBh. &c.; duality, W.; the possession of 2 out of the 3 qualities, W. **-jāta**, mfn. (fr. *dvi-jāti*) belonging to the twice-born, consisting of them, Mn. viii, 374. **-ta**, see *Dvaitá*. **-datti**, m. patr. fr. *dvi-datta*, Pāṇ. iv, 1, 88, Sch. (w.r. *daiva-datti*). **-dha**, see *Dvaidha*. **-paksha** and °**shya**, n. 2 factions or parties, MBh. **-pada**, m. a combination or compound of 2 words, RPrāt. (*-śas*, ind. ib., Sch.); 2 Pādas, Vait.; mfn. relating to a stanza consisting of 2 Pādas, ŚaṅkhBr. **-padika**, mf(*ī*)n. familiar with the Dvi-padā, g. *ukthâdi*. **-parāka**, m. (fr. *dvi-p*°) N. of a Tri-rātra, ŚāṅkhŚr. **-pārāyaṇika**, mf(*ī*)n. one who performs the Pārāyaṇa twice, Pāṇ. v, 1, 20, Vārtt. 2, Pat. **-bhāvya**, n. double nature; division or separation into two, g. *brāhmaṇâdi*. **-matya**, m. patron. (also pl.), Prav. **-mātura**, mf(*ī*)n. (fr. *dvi-mātṛi*, Pāṇ. iv, 1, 115) having 2 mothers (with *bhrātṛi*, m. step-brother), Kathās.; Rājat.; m. N. of Gaṇêśa, L.; of Tarasaṃdha, L. **-mātṛika**, mf(*ī*)n. nourished by (2 mothers, i. e. by) rain and rivers (as a country, cf. *deva-m*° and *nadī-m*°), L. **-māsya**, mfn. (fr. *dvi-māsa*) lasting 2 months, Gaut. **-mitri**, mfn. (fr. *dvi-mitra*) born of 2 friends, L. **-yogya**, n. (fr. *dvi-yoga*) a combination or connection with two, Pāṇ. v, 1, 30, Vārtt. 1. **-ratha**, n. (*yuddha*) 'chariot-duel,' a single combat in chariots, any s° c°, MBh., Hariv.; R.; mf(*ī*)n. relating to any s° c° in chariots, ch. of R.; m. an adversary, MBh.; BhP. **-rājya**, n. a dominion divided between 2 princes, Mālav. v, $1\frac{2}{3}$; Rājat.; the boundaries of 2 states, a frontier, Naish. viii, 59. **-rātrika**, mf(*ī*)n. of or belonging to a period of 2 nights, Pāṇ. v, 1, 87, Kāś. **-rūpya**, n. duality of form, double appearance or nature, BhP. **-liṅgya**, n. duplicity of sex, Sch. **-vacana**, mf(*ī*)n. relating to the dual, ĀśvŚr. **-varshika**, mf(*ī*)n. biennial, happening after 2 years, W. (cf. Pāṇ. vii, 3, 16). **-vidhya**, n. twofold state or nature or character, duplicity, variance, MBh.; Suśr. &c. **-śāṇa**, mf(*ī*)n. worth 2 Śāṇas. **-saṃdhya**, n. morning and evening twilight, Kāv. **-samika**, mf(*ī*)n. 2 years old, Pāṇ. vii, 3, 15, Vārtt. 2, Pat. **-hāyana**, n. a period or the age of 2 years, L.

Dvaitá, n. (fr. 1. *dvi-tā*) duality, duplicity, dualism (cf. *-vāda*), doubt, ŚBr.; Kap.; Prab.; BhP. &c. **-nirṇaya**, m. (*-ṭīkā* and *-phakkikā*, f., *-śiva-pūjā-saṃgraha* and *-siddhânta-saṃgraha*, m.), **-pariśishṭa** and **-bhūshaṇa**, n. N. of philos. wks. **-bhṛita**, m. pl. N. of a philos. school, Cat. **-vāda**, m. dualism, Cat. **-vādin**, m. 'dualist,' assertor of dualism (a philosopher who asserts the 2 principles or the existence of the human soul as separate from the Supreme Being), L. (cf. *a-dv*°). **-viveka**, m. N. of wk. **-vaitathyôpanishad**, f. N. of an Upan. **-siddhânta-saṃgraha**, m., **-siddhi**, f. N. of wks. **Dvaitâdvaitamārga**, m. the path of dualism and non-dualism; *-paribhrashṭa*, mfn. having missed it, Prab. ii, $\frac{4}{5}$.

Dvaitavaná, m. (fr. *dvita-vana*) patr. of the king Dhvasan, ŚBr.; (*dvait*°), mfn. belonging or relating to Dhvasan Dvaitavana, ŚBr.; MBh.; n. (with or sc. *vana*) N. of a forest, MBh. iii, 453 &c., Kir. i, 1.

Dvaitin, m. = *dvaita-vādin*, Śaṃk.

Dvaitīyaka, mf(*ī*)n. recurring every second day (fever; cf. *dvitīyaka*), L. °**tīyīka**, mf(*ī*)n. the second (cf. Pāṇ. iv, 2, 7, Vārtt. 1, Pat.); *-tā*, f. Naish. ii, 110.

Dvaidha, mf(*ī*)n. (fr. *dvi-dhā*) twofold, double, Pāṇ. v, 3, 45, Vārtt. 1, Pat. (cf. *a-*); n. a twofold form or state, duality, duplicity, division, separation into two parts, contest, dispute, doubt, uncertainty, Lāṭy.; Mn.; MBh. &c.; double resource, secondary array or reserve, Mn. vii, 161, 167; (*am*), ind. (Pāṇ. v, 3, 45) into two portions, in two parts or ways, doubly, AitBr.; KātyŚr.; Hariv. **-m-kāram**, ind. = *dvidhā-k*°, Pāṇ. iii, 4, 62, Sch. **-sūtra**, n. N. of ch. xxii–xxv of Baudh.

Dvaidhī, in comp. for °*dha*. **-karaṇa**, n. making into two, separating, Dhātup.; W. **-kṛita**, mfn. separated, made twofold, W.; brought into a dilemma, MW. **-bhāva**, m. duality, double nature, MBh.; dilemma, doubt, uncertainty, ib.; double-dealing, falsehood, deceit, Yājn.; Pañc.; Kām.; separation (esp. of an army, one of the six kinds of royal policy), Mn. vii, 160; exciting dissension or causing the separation of allies, W. **-√bhū**, to become separated or divided into two parts, to be disunited, MBh.; Hariv.; Kāv.; *-bhūta*, mfn. separated, disunited, MBh.

Dvaidhya, n. duplicity, falsehood, Kām.; diversity, variance, discrepancy, MW.

द्वैप *dvaipa*, mf(*ī*)n. (fr. *dvīpá*) being or living or happening on an island, an islander, Śiś., Sch.; g. *kacchâdi*; (fr. *dvīpin*) belonging to a tiger or panther, Suśr.; m. (with or scil. *ratha*) a car covered with a tiger's skin, Pāṇ. iv, 2, 12; L.

Dvaipaka, mf(*ī*)n. living on an island, an islander, Pāṇ. iv, 2, 127; 133 &c.

Dvaipāyana, m. (Pāṇ. iv, 1, 99) 'island-born,' N. of Vyāsa (author or compiler of the Vedas and Purāṇas, the place of his nativity being a small island in the Ganges), MBh.; Hariv. &c.; mf(*ī*)n. relating to Dvaipāyana, MBh.

Dvaipya, mf(*ā*)n. (Pāṇ. iv, 3, 10; 1, 16, Pat.) of or belonging to an island, islander, Śiś. iii, 76. **-bhaimāyana**, m. pl. N. of a tribe belonging to the Andhaka-Vṛishṇis, Pāṇ. vi, 2, 34, Sch.

द्वैयहकाल्य *dvaiyahakālya*, n. abstr. fr. *dvy-aha-kāla*, Jaim. **Dvaiyahnika**, mf(*ī*)n. (fr. *dvy-ahan*) of or belonging to 2 days, Pāṇ. v, 1, 87, Kāś. **Dvaiyāhāvaka**, mf(*ī*)n. fr. *dvy-āhāva*, L.

द्वैषणीया *dvaishaṇīyā*, f. a sort of betel pepper, L. (cf. *dveshaṇīya*, *dveshya*).

द्व्य् *dvy*, in comp. before vowels for *dvi*, p. 504. **-aṅśa**, m. sg. 2 shares, Mn.; (*ī*), f. id., Gaut.; mfn. having 2 shares or parts, Jyot. **-aksha**, mf(*ī*)n. 2-eyed, MBh.; m. pl. N. of a people, ib. **-akshara**, n. sg. 2 syllables, TS.; mf(*ā*)n. 2-syllabled, ŚBr. (*aksharā*, TS.); n. a 2-syllabled word, ib. &c.; N. of a Sāman; *-nāma-mālā*, f. N. of a dictionary. **-agni**, mfn. twice containing the word *agni*, AitBr. **-agra**, mf(*ā*)n. 2-pointed, ending in 2 extremities, MW. **-aṅga**, w. r. for *try-aṅga*, MBh. ix, 1388 (B. *vy-aṅga*). **-aṅgulá**, n. 2 fingers' breadth, ŚBr. (°*la utkarsham*, °*lenôtk*° or °*lôtk*°, in such intervals, Pāṇ. iii, 4, 51, Kāś.); mfn. 2 fingers broad; *-śṛiṅga*, mfn. having horns of 2 fingers' breadth (said to denote the age of a horned animal), Pāṇ. vi, 2, 115, Kāś. **-añjala**, n. 2 handfuls, Pāṇ. v, 4, 102. **-aṇuka**, n. a combination of 2 atoms (the first step in the formation of substances when they become perceptible), Śaṃk.; °*kīya*, Nom. P. °*yati*, to become twice as thin, Alaṃkāraś.; °*kôdara*, mf(*ī*)n. having a very thin body, Naish. iv, 3. **-adhika**, mf(*ā*)n. 2 more, Mn.; Gaut. **-anīká**, mf(*á*)n. forming 2 rows, TS. **-antara**, mf(*ā*)n. separated by 2 intermediate links, Gaut. **-anya**, mf(*ā*)n. accompanied &c. by 2 others; n. the 2 others collectively, W. **-abhiyoga**, m. a twofold accusation, Nār. **-artha**, mf(*ā*)n. having 2 senses, ambiguous, equivocal, Sāh.; having 2 objects, W.; n. double meaning, double entendre, W.; *-kośa*, m. N. of a dictionary of ambiguous words. **-ardha**, mfn. $1\frac{1}{2}$, Sūryap. **-asita**, mf(*ī*)n. the 82nd (chs. of MBh.) **-aśīti**, f. 82, Pāṇ. vi, 3, 47; *-tama*, mfn. the 82nd (chs. of MBh.) **-ashṭa**, n. (fr. *ashṭan*?) copper, L. (cf. 2. *dvishṭa*). **-ashṭa-sahasra** or **-sāhasra**, n. 16000, BhP. **-ahá**, m. a period of 2 days, ŚBr.; Lāṭy. &c.; (*am*), ind. during 2 days, Gaut.; (*e* and *āt*), ind. after 2 days, Suśr.; Pāṇ. ii, 3, 7, Kāś.; mfn. lasting 2 days; m. such a festival or ceremony, ŚBr.; ŚrS.; *-kāla*, mf(*ā*)n. falling on 2 days, Jaim., Comm.; *-vṛitta*, mfn. happened 2 days ago, Pāṇ. iii, 2, 115, Pat.; *-tarshaṃ* or °*haṃ t*°, ind. having caused any one to be thirsty for 2 days, 4, 57, Kāś.; °*hâtyāsam* or °*haṃ atyāsam*, ind. always overleaping 2 days, every 3rd day, ib. **-ahan** (only loc. °*hni*), 2 days, Vop. **-ahīna,** mfn. to be accomplished in 2 days; *-tva*, n. Lāṭy. **-ākshāyaṇa,** m., g. *aishukāry-ādi.* **-ācita,** mf(*ā*)n., °**tika,** mf(*ī*)n., °**tīna,** mf(*ī*)n. containing 2 waggon-loads, Pāṇ. v, 1, 54, Sch. **-āḍhaka,** mf(*ā*)n., °**kika,** mf(*ī*)n., °**kīna,** mf(*ā*)n. containing 2 Āḍhaka-measures, ib. **-ātmaka,** mfn. 'double-natured;' m. pl. the signs of the zodiac Gemini, Virgo, Sagittarius and Pisces, Jyot. **-ādhāna,** n. the placing or kindling of the sacred fire by 2 persons, Jaim. **-āmushyāyaṇa,** °**ṇaka,** m. descended from 2 persons, being the Āmushyāyaṇa (s. v.) to 2 people, Nār.; MārkP.; a boy who remains heir to his father though adopted by another, W. **-āmnāta,** mfn. twice mentioned, Jaim. **-āyusha,** n. a double life, 2 lives, Pāṇ. v, 4, 77. **-ārsheya,** mfn. having 2 holy ancestors, L. **-āśraya-kośa-vṛitti,** f. N. of wk. **-āsyà,** mfn. two-mouthed, AV. **-āhāva,** mfn. having 2 watering-places, g. *dhūmâdi.* **-āhika,** mf(*ī*)n. recurring every other day (fever), AgP. **-uktha,** mfn. reciting 2 Ukthas (s. v.), AitBr. **-udātta,** mfn. doubly accented; n. a doubly accented word, L. **-udāsa,** mfn. having 2 elevations of sound or accent, Tāṇḍya-Br. **-ūraṇa,** mf(*ā*)n. having 2 lambs, ŚBr. **-ṛica,** m. a strophe consisting of 2 verses, RPrāt.; ĀśvŚr. **-ekântara,** mfn. separated by two or by one (degree), Mn. x, 7. **-oga** (for *dvi-yoga*), mfn. (carriage) drawn by 2 pairs, TāṇḍyaBr. **-opaśa,** mf(*ā*)n. having 2 appendages, ib.

ध DHA.

ध 1. *dha*, aspirate of the preceding letter, **-kāra,** m. the letter or sound *dh.*

ध 2. *dha*, mf(*ā*)n. (√1. *dhā*; cf. 2. *dhā*) ifc. placing, putting; holding, possessing, having; bestowing, granting, causing &c. (cf. *a-doma-dhá, garbha-dhá*); m. N. of Brahmā or Kubera, L.; (in music) the 6th note of the gamut; virtue, merit, L.; n. wealth, property, L.; (*ā*), f. in 2. *tiro-dhā́*; *dur-dhā́* (qq. vv.)

धक् 1. *dhak*, nom. fr. *dagh* or *dah* (cf. *dakshiṇa-dagh* and *uśá-dah*).

धक् 2. *dhak*, an exclamation of wrath, Uttarar. iv, 23.

धकित् *dhakit*, ind. = *dhik*, Pāṇ. v, 3, 72, Kāś.

धक्क् *dhakk*, cl. 10. P. *dhakkayati*, to destroy, annihilate, Dhātup. xxxii, 55.

धक्षत् *dhákshat* and *dhákshu*, mfn. (√*dah*) = *dákshat* and *dákshu*, RV.

धगद्धगिति *dhagaddhag-iti*, ind. (onomat.) crack! crack! HPariś.

धगिति *dhag-iti*, ind. (onom.) in a moment, at once, Kād.

धञ्जोक *dhañoka*, m. N. of a poet, Cat.

धट *dhaṭa*, m. (prob. fr. √*dhṛi* like *bhaṭa* fr. √*bhṛi*) a balance or the scale of a b°, Hcat. (cf. *tulā-*); ordeal by the b°, Mit.; the sign of the zodiac Libra, Jyot.; (*ī*), f. old cloth or raiment; a piece of cloth worn over the privities, L. **Dhaṭi-dāna,** n. giving an old cloth to a woman after impregnation, MW.

Dhaṭaka, m. a kind of weight = 14 Vallas or 42 Raktikās, Līl.

धटिका *dhaṭikā*, *dhaṭin*, and *dhaṭôtkaca*, w. r. for *ghaṭikā* &c.

धडिइव *dhaḍieva*, m. N. of a man, Inscr.

धण् *dhaṇ*, cl. 1. P. *dhaṇati*, to sound, Dhātup. xiii, 11 (cf. √1. *dhan, dhvan*).

धत्तूर *dhattūra*, m. the white thorn-apple, Datura Alba (used as a poison), Suśr. (also °*raka*, m., °*kā*, f.); Bhpr.; Kāv.; gold, Kāv.; n. the fruit of Datura Alba, Kathās.

धन् 1. *dhan*, cl. 1. P. *dhanati*, to sound, L. (cf. √*dhaṇ* and *dhvan*).

धन् 2. *dhan*, cl. 3. P. *dadhánti* (Pāṇ. vi, 1, 192) to cause to run or move quickly (p. *dadhánat, dadhanvás*; Pot. *dadhanyur*, RV.); to bear fruit, Dhātup. xxv, 23: Caus. *dhanáyati*, °*te*, to cause to move or run; to move or run, RV. (cf. *dhanv* and *dhánishṭha*).

Dhána, n. the prize of a contest or the contest itself (lit. a running match, race, or the thing raced for; *hitám dhánam*, a proposed prize or contest; *dhanaṃ √ji*, to win the p° or the fight), RV.; booty, prey (*dhanam √bhṛi* Ā., to carry off the prize or booty), RV.; AV.; any valued object, (esp.) wealth, riches, (movable) property, money, treasure, gift, RV. &c. &c.; capital (opp. to *vriddhi* interest), Yājñ. ii, 58; = *go-dhana*, Hariv. 3886; (arithm.) the affirmative quantity or plus (opp. to *ṛiṇa, kshaya, vyaya, hāni*); N. of the 2nd mansion, Var.; m. N. of a merchant, HPariś.; Siṇhâs. **-kāma** (*dhána-*) and **-kāmyá,** mfn. desirous of wealth, covetous, AV. **-keli,** m. 'sporting with w°,' N. of Kubera, L. **-kośa,** m. treasure of w° or money, R. **-krītī** (or °**tā**), f. a woman bought with m°, MW. **-kshaya,** m. loss of m° or property, Var.; Pañc.; N. of a man, Vet. **-garva,** m. 'purse-proud,' N. of a man, Daś. **-garvita,** mfn. proud of money, MW. **-giri,** m. 'm°-mountain,' N. of a man, HPariś. **-gupta,** mfn. (for *g°-dh°*) one who guards his m° carefully; m. N. of a merchant's son, Pañc. ii, $\frac{153}{154}$ (*-tā*, f. $\frac{154}{155}$). **-goptṛi,** mfn. = prec. mfn., Kāv. **-candra,** N. of an author. **-cchū,** m. the Numidian crane (= *karetavyā*), L. **-cyuta,** mfn. fallen from wealth, poor, W. **-jāta,** mfn. arising from wealth, produced by w°, W.; n. pl. goods of every kind, Mn. ix, 114. **-jit,** mfn. winning a prize or booty, victorious, wealth-acquiring, RV.; AV.; VS.; m. N. of an Ekâha, ŚāṅkhŚr. **-ṃ-jayá,** mfn. = prec. mfn., RV.; AV.; TBr.; m. fire, Kāṭh.; a partic. vital air supposed to nourish the body, Vedāntas.; Plumbago Zeylanica, L.; N. of Arjuna, MBh.; Hariv.; the 9th day of the Karma-māsa (s. v.), the plant Terminalia Arjuna, L.; N. of a serpent-demon, MBh.; Hariv.; BhP.; of a Vyāsa, VP.; of a king of Kaliṅga, Kathārṇ.; of a king of Kausthalapura, L.; of the author of the Daśa-rūpaka &c. (see below); of a merchant, SkandaP.; of a Brāhman, pl. his descendants, Pravar.; *-kośa*, m., *-nāma-mālā*, f., and *-nighaṇṭu*, m. N. of dictionaries; *-vijaya*, m. 'the victory of Dhanaṃ-jaya or Arjuna,' N. of a Vyāyoga by Kāñcana; *-saṃgraha*, m. N. of wk.; *-sena*, m. N. of a poet, Cat. **-tama,** m. (with *dāya*) an exceedingly rich donation, TāṇḍyaBr. **-tṛipti,** f. sufficiency of money, Pañc. **-tṛishṇā,** f. thirst for m°, covetousness, MW. **-tyaj,** mfn. resigning wealth, ib. **-da,** mf(*ā*)n. 'w°-giving,' liberal, Kām.; m. Barringtonia Acutangula, L.; N. of Kubera, MBh.; R. &c.; a Guhyaka, L.; N. of a servant of Padma-pāṇi, W.; of sev. men, Siṇhâs.; of a monkey, RāmatUp.; of a mountain, MBh.; (*ā*), f. N. of one of the Mātṛis attending on Skanda, MBh.; of a Tantra deity, Tantras.; n. a kind of house, Gal.; *-tīrtha*, n. N. of a Tīrtha, ŚivaP.; *-deva*, m. N. of a poet, Cat.; *-stotra*, n. N. of a Stotra; °*dâkshī*, f. a kind of tree (= *kuberâkshī*), L.; °*dânuja*, m. the younger brother of Kubera, N. of Rāvaṇa, R.; °*dā-pūjā-yantra*, n. N. of a mystical diagram, Tantras.; °*dā-mantra*, m. N. of a partic. prayer, ib.; °*dāya*, Nom. P. °*yate*, to resemble Kubera, Jātakam.; °*dâvāsa*, m. K°'s residence, N. of the mountain Kailāsa, L.; °*dā-stotra*, n. N. of a Stotra; °*dêśvara*, m. 'wealth-giving lord,' N. of Kubera, Kathās.; °*dêśvara-tīrtha*, n. N. of a Tīrtha, ŚivaP. **-daṇḍa,** m. fine, amercement, Mn.; Yājñ. **-datta,** m. 'w°-given,' N. of sev. merchants, Mṛicch.; Kathās.; Vet. **-darpa,** m. pride of w°, MW. **-dā́,** mfn. prize-giving, giving booty or treasures, RV.; AV. (cf. *-da*). **-dāyin,** mfn. giving rewards or treasures, SaṃhUp.; m. N. of Agni, L. **-deva,** m. N. of a minister and author, Cat.; of another man, Pañc. **-dharma** or °**man,** m. N. of a king, VP.; °*manī*, n. du. (*Prajā-pateḥ*) N. of 2 Sāmans, ĀrshBr. **-dhānī** (*dhána-*), f. receptacle for valuable articles, TĀr. **-dhānya,** n. money and grain (°*nyâdhika*, mfn. rich in m° and g°, MW.); a spell for restraining certain magical weapons, R. **-nāśa,** m. loss of wealth or property, Kāv. **-netṛi,** m. 'bringer of w°,' prince, king, Gal. **-ṃ-dadā,** f. 'w°-granting,' N. of a Buddh. deity. **-pati** (*dhána-*), m. lord of w° (with or scil. *dhanānām*), AV.; a rich man, Kāv.; a king, Gal.; N. of Kubera, ŚāṅkhGṛ.; MBh.; Kāv.; N. of sev. authors, Cat. (also *-miśra* and *-sūri*). **-para,** mf(*ā*)n. fond of money, Vām. **-pālá,** m. guardian of treasure, treasurer, AV.; king, Gal.; N. of a grammarian; of the author of the Pāiya-lacchī &c, Cat.; of other men, HPariś. **-piśācikā** or °**cī,** f. thirst for wealth, avarice, L. **-priya,** mfn. fond of w°, MW.; (*ā*), f. N. of a plant, L. (prob. w. r. for *ghana-*). **-bhakshá,** m. pl. booty and enjoyments, RV. x, 102. **-1. -mada,** m. pride of money, Kathās.; *-vat*, mfn. proud of money, Kāv. **-mitra,** m. N. of sev. men, Śak.; Daś.; **-mūla,** n. principal, capital, L.; mfn. proceeding from or founded on wealth, Hit. **-mūlya,** n. w°-root, capital; *-tā*, f., Jātakam. **-mohana,** m. N. of a merchant's son, Kathās. **-yauvana-śālin,** mfn. endowed with w° and youth, Kathās. **-raksha,** m. keeping money, not spending it, Kāv. **-rakshaka,** m. N. of Kubera, R. **-rūpa,** n. a partic. kind of property, Gaut. **-rca** (RV.); **-rci** (SV.), mfn. shining with booty (fr. *-ṛica, -ṛici*; √*arc*). **-rṇa** (for *-ṛiṇa*), n. (in arithm.) positive and negative quantities, MW. **-lubdha,** mfn. greedy of wealth, avaricious, Var. **-lobha,** m. desire of w°, covetousness, Kathās. **-lobhin,** mfn. = *-lubdha*, MW. **-va,** Nom. (fr. the next) P., °*vati*, to become rich, Kulārṇ. **-vat,** mfn. wealthy, rich; m. a rich man, Mn.; R. &c.; the sea or ocean, Kāvyâd. iii, 117; (*ī*), f. the constellation Dhanishṭhā, L.; N. of a Vidyā-dharī and a merchant's daughter, Kathās. **-varjita,** mfn. destitute of w°, poor, Pañc. **-varman,** m. N. of a man, Kuṭṭanīm. **-viparyaya,** m. = *-nāśa*, Kāv. **-vibhāga,** m. distribution of w°, MW. **-vṛiddha,** mfn. rich in money, Kāv. **-vṛiddhi,** f. increase of property, MW. **-vyaya,** m. the spending of m° or treasure, extravagance, Kathās. **-śrī,** f. N. of a woman, HPariś. **-saṃcaya,** m. (Mn.), °**yana,** n. (Kāv.) collection of m°, riches. **-saṃcayin,** mfn. having a c° of m°; m. a rich man, Var. **-sáni,** mfn. granting or winning wealth, AV.; ChUp. **-sampatti** (Hit.), °**pad** (Var.), f. accumulation or abundance of w°. **-sammata,** m. N. of a prince, Divyâv. **-sā́,** mfn. = *-sáni*, RV.; AV.; AitBr. **-sāti** (*dhána-*), f. acquisition of w°, RV.; AV.; VS. **-sādhana,** n. id., Siṇhâs. **-sū,** m. 'w°-producer,' the fork-tailed shrike, L. **-stha,** mfn. 'living in w°,' wealthy, rich, MBh. **-sthāna,** n. 'receptacle for w°,' treasury; (astron.) the 2nd mansion; °*nâdhikārin*, m. 'superintendent of t°,' a treasurer, Rājat. **-spṛit,** mfn. carrying away the prize or booty, RV. **-svāmin,** m. owner of money, capitalist, Kāś. on Pāṇ. i, 4, 35. **-hara,** mfn. m°-stealing; m. a thief or an heir, L.; a kind of plant, Bhpr.; (*ī*), f. a kind of perfume commonly called Chora, ib. **-harin,** mfn. = prec. mfn., MW. **-hāraka,** mfn. with money, Divyâv. **-hārin,** mfn. = *-hara*, MW. **-hārya,** mfn. to be won by money, Mṛicch. i, 23. **-hīna,** mfn. = *-varjita*, Kāv.; *-tā*, f. poverty, ib. **-hṛit,** mfn. = *-hara*, Kāv.; m. a thief, MW.; a kind of bulbous plant, L. **Dhanâgama,** m. (ifc. f. *ā*) accession of wealth, gain, Mn.; Var. &c. **Dhanâḍhya,** mfn. opulent, rich, Kāv.; *-tā*, f. riches, wealth, Rājat. **Dhanâdāna,** n. acceptance of money, Mn. xi, 69; *-nibandhana*, mfn. contingent on the possession or non-possession of wealth, ib. **Dhanâdhikāra,** m. title or right to property, ib. **Dhanâdhikārin,** m. heir; = the next, W. **Dhanâdhikṛita,** m. 'placed over treasures,' a treasurer, W. **Dhanâdhigoptṛi,** m. 'guardian of t°,' N. of Kubera, MBh. **Dhanâdhipa,** m. 'lord of t°,' N. of Kubera, Hariv. **Dhanâdhipati,** m. id., Kathās.; Kir.; °*patya*, n. dominion over t°, MBh. **Dhanâdhyaksha,** m. 'overseer of t°,' treasurer, R.; N. of Kubera, MBh.; Hariv. **Dhanândha,** mfn. blinded by riches, MW. **Dhanânvita,** mfn. endowed with riches, wealthy, Var. **Dhanâpahāra,** m. taking away of property, fine, amercement; plunder, W. **Dhanâpti,** f. acquisition of wealth, Pañc. **Dhanâyus,** m. N. of a son of Purū-ravas, MBh. (cf. *van*°). **Dhanârghá,** mfn. deserving a reward or prize, TS. **Dhanârcita,** mfn. 'honoured by w°,' rich, opulent, W. **Dhanârjana,** n. acquisition of w° or property, W. **Dhanârthin,** mfn. 'w°-seeking,' covetous, miserly, Mn.; Kāv. **Dhanâśā,** f. longing after w°, desire for riches, Hariv.; Hit.; hope of gaining wealth, Kāv. **Dhanêcchā,** f. desire for w°, Kāv. **Dhanêś,** m. 'w°-lord,' a rich man, Siṇhâs. **Dhanêśa,** m. id., Var.; N. of Kubera, ib.; Hariv. (*-tva*, n., Jātakam.); N. of Vopadeva's teacher, Cat. **Dhanêśvara,** m. 'treasure-lord,' N. of Kubera, MBh.; N. of a Brāhman, PadmaP.; of Vopadeva's teacher (cf. prec.) &c., Cat.; (*ī*), f. a rich woman or the wife of Kubera, BhP. vi, 19, 25. **Dhanâiśvarya,** n. dominion over riches, Mn. **Dhanâishin,** mfn. longing for t°, wishing for money, Jātakam.; m. a creditor who claims his m°, Mn. viii, 60. **Dhanôshman** (or °*nôsh*°), m. burning desire for m° or for wealth, Mn. ix, 231.

Dhanaka, m. avarice, covetousness, L.; N. of a Yādava (son of Dur-dama or Dur-mada), Pur.; of another man, Daś.

Dhanāya, Nom. P. Ā. °*yati*, °*te*, to wish for wealth or money, be desirous of (gen., dat. or acc.), VS.; MBh.; Kir. °**yā**, f. desire of w°, covetousness, L. °**yú**, mfn. acquiring m°, AV.

Dhanika, mfn. wealthy, opulent, Pañc.; Dhūrtas. (-*tā*, f. wealth, opulence, Kāv.); good, virtuous, L.; m. a rich man, owner, creditor, Mn.; Yājñ.; a husband, L.; N. of Sch. on Daśar.; m. n. coriander, L.; (*ā*), f. a virtuous or excellent woman; any young woman or wife, L.; Panicum Italicum, L.

Dhanin, mfn. possessing wealth or treasures, wealthy, rich, well off, RV.; MBh. &c.; m. a rich man, owner, creditor, Mn.; Yājñ.; N. of Kubera, L.; of a messenger of the Kapas, MBh.

Dhánishṭha, mfn. (superl. of √2. *dhan*) very swift, RV. x, 73, 1; (fr. *dhana*) very rich, ŚāṅkhŚr. viii, 20, 4; (*ā*), f. sg. and pl. the more modern N. of the Nakshatra Śravishṭhā or 24th lunar mansion, ŚāṅkhGṛ.; MBh. &c.

Dhanīkā, f. = *dhanikā*, a young woman, L.

Dhanīya, Nom. P. °*yati*, to wish for riches, Pāṇ. vii, 4, 34, Kāś.

Dhanīyaka or °**neyaka**, n. coriander seed (= *dhanyāka*), L.

1. **Dhanū**, m. a store of grain, L. (for 2. see *dhanu*).

Dhaneya, m. N. of a son of Raudrâśva, Hariv.

Dhánya, mfn. bringing or bestowing wealth, opulent, rich (ifc. full of), RV. &c. &c.; fortunate, happy, auspicious, Mn.; MBh. &c.; good, virtuous, L. (cf. *dhanika*); wholesome, healthy, Car.; m. infidel, atheist, W.; a spell for using or restraining magical weapons, R.; Vatica Robusta, L.; N. of a man, Rājat. (cf. Pāṇ. iv, 1, 110, g. *aśvâdi*); of the Vaiśyas in Krauñca-dvīpa, VP.; (*ā*), f. a nurse, L.; Emblic Myrobalan, L.; N. of Dhruva's wife, VP.; (also n.) coriander, L.; n. treasure, wealth, L. — **tā**, f. fortune, good luck, opulence, MBh. — **tithi**, m. an auspicious or a particular day, L. — **tva**, n. = -*tā*, f., MW. — **m-manya**, mfn. thinking one's self fortunate, Daś. — **vāda**, m. thanksgiving, praise, applause, MW. — **stotra**, n. 'the praise of the blessed,' N. of a poem ascribed to Śaṃkarâcārya, Cat. **Dhanyâśi**, f., see *dhanāśrī* below. **Dhanyâshṭaka**, n. = °*nya-stotra*, Cat. **Dhanyôdaya**, m. N. of a man, Rājat.

Dhanyaka, m. N. of a man, Daś.

Dhanyāka, n. Coriandrum Sativum, L.

धनस्यक *dhanasyaka*, m. Asteracantha Longifolia, L.

धनाश्री *dhanāśrī* or *dhanyâsi* (in music) N. of a Rāgiṇī.

धनीराम *dhanīrāma*, m. N. of an author, Cat.

धनु *dhanu*, m. or (Uṇ. i, 82) 2. *dhanū*, f. (fr. √2. *dhan*?) a bow, Hit.; Śāntiś.; a measure of 4 Hastas or cubits, L. (cf. *dhanv-antara* below); the sign of the zodiac Sagittarius, Priy. i, 5; Buchanania Latifolia, L.; Semecarpus Anacardium, L.; (*dhánu* or *dhanū*), f. a dry sandbank, a sandy shore [cf. Engl. *bight*, Germ. *Bucht*], RV.; AV. i, 17 (nom. °*nūs*). — **ketakī**, f. a kind of flower, L. — **gupta**, m. N. of a man, L. — **rāja**, m. N. of one of the ancestors of Śākya-muni, L. — **rāśi**, m. the sign of the zodiac Sagittarius, L. — **śreṇī**, f. Sanseviera Zeylanica, L. — **stambha**, see *dhanuḥ-st*°. — **hastā**, f. N. of a being attendant on Devī, W. **Dhanv-aṅga**, see *dhanvaga*. **Dhanv-antara**, n. the space or distance of a Dhanu or 4 Hastas, MBh. viii, 4224; N. of Śiva, vii, 9536 (Nīlak. 'bow-string'; but cf. °*tari*). **Dhánvarṇas**, mfn. overflowing the dry land, RV. v, 45, 2.

Dhanuḥ, in comp. for °*nus*. — **kāṇḍa**, -**khaṇḍa**, -**paṭa** = *dhanush-k*°, -*kh*°, -*p*° (below). — **śata**, n. 100 Dhanus or 400 Hastas or cubits, Mn. viii, 237. — **śākhā**, f. = °*nur-guṇā* (below), L. — **śālā**, f. bow-room, Hariv. — **śreṇī**, f. = *dhanu-ś*° or = *mahêndra-vāruṇī*. — **saṃstha**, mfn. shaped like a bow, MBh. — **stambha**, m. a kind of spasmodic contraction of the body, Suśr.

Dhanur, in comp. for °*nus*. — **ākāra** or -**ākṛiti**, mfn. bow-shaped, curved, bent, W. — **ārtnī**, f. the end of a bow (where the string is fastened), ŚBr. — **āsana**, n. a partic. mode of sitting, Cat. — **guṇa**, m. a bow-string, W.; (*ā*), f. Sanseviera Zeylanica (from the leaves of which a tough thread is extracted of which b°-strings were made), L. — **graha**, m. bearing a b°, an archer, R.; the art of managing a b°, MBh.; N. of a son of Dhṛita-rāshṭra, ib. — **grāha** (MBh.), °**hin** (Śak.), m. an archer. — **jyā**, f. a bow-string, ĀśvGṛ.; Hariv.; -*tala-śabda*, m. the mere twanging noise of the b°-st°, MW. — **durga**, mfn. made inaccessible or protected by a desert; n. a place so protected, MBh. xii, 3332; Mn. vii, 70 (v. l. *dhanva*-). — **druma**, m. 'b° tree,' the bamboo (used for bows), L. — **dvitīya**, mfn. furnished with a b°, MW. — **dhara**, m. = -*graha*, Mn.; MBh.; R. &c. (also as N. of Śiva); the sign of the zodiac Sagittarius, Var.; N. of a son of Dhṛita-rāshṭra, MBh. — **dhārin** (R.), -**bhṛit** (Ragh.), m. bow-man, archer. — **makha**, v. l. for -*maha*. — **madhya**, n. the middle part of a b° (= *lastaka*), L. — **maha**, m. the consecration of a b°, Hariv. — **mārga**, m. 'b°-line,' curve, L. — **mālā**, f. = -*guṇā*, L. — **māsa-māhātmya**, n. N. of wk. — **yantra**, n. (Bālar.), -**yashṭi**, f. (Daś.) a bow (lit. b°-instrument, b°-stick). — **yāsa**, m. Alhagi Maurorum, L. — **yogyā**, f. b°-exercise, archery, Bālar. — **latā**, f. a bow (lit. b°-creeper), Kathās.; = *soma-vallī*, L. — **vaktra**, m. 'b°-mouth,' N. of one of Skanda's attendants, MBh. — **vakra**, mfn. crooked like a b°, Suśr. — **vāta**, m. a kind of disease, Cat. — **vidyā**, f. 'b°-science,' archery, Vet.; -*dīpikā*, f., °*dyârambha-prayoga*, m. N. of wks. — **vṛiksha**, m. 'b°-plant,' the bamboo; Ficus Religiosa; Semecarpus Anacardium; Isora Corylifolia, L.; a measure of 4 cubits, L.; (geom.) an arc, W. — **veda**, m. the science of archery, an a°-treatise (regarded as an Upa-veda connected with the Yajur-veda, and derived from Viśvāmitra or Bhṛigu), MBh.; Hariv. &c.; N. of a wk. by Śārṅga-datta, Cat.; -*cintā-maṇi*, m. N. of wk.; -*para* or -*parâyaṇa*, mfn. devoted to archery; -*prakaraṇa*, n.; -*sāra*, m. N. of wks. — **vedin**, mfn. versed in a°; m. N. of Śiva, Śivag. — **hasta**, mfn. bow in hand, having a bow, W.

Dhanush, in comp. for °*nus*. — **kapāla**, n., g. *kaskâdi*. — 1. -**kara**, m. a bow-maker, L.; (*ī*), f. a kind of flower, L. — 2. -**kara**, mfn. b° in hand, armed with a b°, L. — **karshaṇa**, n. bending a b°, Ragh. vii. sq. — **kāṇḍa**, n. sg. b° and arrow, Hit. — **kāra** and -**kṛit**, m. a b°-maker, VS. — **koṭi** or °**ṭī**, f. the curved end of a b°, MBh.; Kāv. etc. — **khaṇḍa**, n. a portion of a b°, Megh. 15. — **khātā**, f. N. of a river, Kāś. on Pāṇ. vi, 2, 146. — **paṭa**, m. Buchanania Latifolia, L. — **pāṇi**, mfn. b° in hand, armed with a b°, MBh.; R. — **mat**, mfn. armed with a b°, an archer, MBh.; R. &c.; m. N. of a mountain to the north of Madhya-deśa, Var.; (*ī*), f. N. of the tutelary deity in the family of Vyāghra-pād, BrahmaP.; -*tā*, f. archery, Bhartṛ. i, 13.

Dhanusha, m. N. of a Ṛishi (°*shâkhya*, MBh. xii, 12758). **Dhanushâksha** (or °*shâksha*?) id., iii, 10741.

Dhanushka, mfn. ifc. = *dhanus*, see *sa*-; n. a small bow, Lāṭy. viii, 6, 8.

Dhánus, n. (m. g. *ardharcâdi*; cf. *dhanu*) a bow, RV. &c. &c.; a measure of length = 4 Hastas or $\frac{1}{2000}$ Gavyūti, Mn.; Yājñ. &c.; (geom.) an arc or part of a circle; (astron.) an arc or quadrant for ascertaining the sun's altitude and zenith-distance; a fiddle-stick; the sign of the zodiac Sagittarius, Sūryas.; Var.; Buchanania Latifolia, L.; N. of Śiva, MBh. vii, 9536 (armed with a bow, L., or = *dhanuḥ-svarūpa*, Nīlak.); a desert, arid land (cf. °*nur-durga*). **Dhanustambha**, see °*nuḥ-st*°.

धन्ध *dhandha*, n. indisposition, L. (cf. *dhāndhya*).

धन्य *dhanya*, *dhanyaka* etc. See col. 1.

धन्व् *dhanv*, cl. 1. P. Ā. *dhanvati*, °*te* (Impv. *dhaniva*, metric. for *dhanva*, SV.; pf. *dadhanvé*, °*viré*, p. *dadhanvás*; aor. *ádhanvishur*) to run or flow; cause to run or flow, RV. (Cf. √2. *dhan*; *dhav* and 1. *dhāv*.)

Dhánutṛi, mfn. running, moving quickly, RV.

Dhanva, n. = *dhánvan* (Uṇ. iv, 95, Sch.; esp. at the beginning and at the end of comp.; cf. *ishu*-, *tisṛi*-, *priya*-; also *ā*, f. in *dhanvābhis*, Hariv. 7315, v. l. °*vibhis*); m. N. of a man, Rājat. v, 51; 56. — **ga**, see s. v. — **cará**, mfn. going in a desert land, RV. v, 36, 1. — **cyút**, mfn. shaking the ground, i, 168, 5. — **ja**, mfn. growing on dry soil, produced on barren land, Suśr. — **taru**, m. 'desert tree,' a kind of Soma plant, L. — **durga**, mfn., see *dhanur-d*°. — **dhi**, m. a bow-case, ŚāṅkhŚr. — **pati**, m. g. *aśvapaty-ādi*. — **yavāsa**, °**saka**, m. Alhagi Maurorum, L. — **yāsa**, °**saka**, m. id., Car. **Dhanvâcārya**, m. teacher of archery (Śiva), MBh.

Dhánvan, n. a bow, RV. &c. (esp. ifc.; cf. *asthi*-, *ugra*-, *kshipra*- &c., and Pāṇ. v, 4, 132 &c.; Vām. v, 2, 67); rain-bow, MānGṛ. i, 4; the sign of the zodiac Sagittarius, Jyot.; (also m.) dry soil, shore (*samudrasya*; cf. *dhanu*); a desert, a waste, RV. &c. &c.; m. Alhagi Maurorum, L.; N. of a country, BhP. (Cf. *dhanu*, °*nus*.)

Dhanvan-tari, m. (for °*vani-t*°) 'moving in a curve,' N. of a deity to whom oblations were offered in the north-east quarter, Kauś. 74; Mn. iii, 85, MBh. xiii, 4662 (where °*tare* w. r. for °*tareḥ*); of the sun, MBh. iii, 155; the physician of the gods (produced at the churning of the ocean with a cup of Amṛita in his hands, the supposed author of the Āyur-veda, who in a later existence is also called Divo-dāsa, king of Kāśi, and considered to be the founder of the Hindū school of medicine), MBh.; Hariv.; R.; Suśr.; Pur.; Rājat. vii, 1392 (*dhānv*°); N. of the author of a medical dictionary (perhaps the same mentioned among the 9 gems of the court of Vikramâditya), Cat. — **guṇâguṇa-yoga-śata**, n., -**grantha**, m. N. of wks. — **grastā**, f. Helleborus Niger, L. — **darpa-bhaṅga**, m. 'the breaking of Dh°'s pride,' N. of a ch. of BrahmavP. iv. — **nighaṇṭu**, m., -**pañcaka**, n. N. of wks. — **yajña**, m. the sacrifice offered to Dh°, ĀśvGṛ. i, 3, 12. — **vilāsa** and -**sāra-nidhi**, m. N. of wks.

Dhanvantarīya, mfn. composed by Dh° (also read *dhānv*°), Cat.

Dhanvanyà, mfn. being in dry soil or barren land, AV.; TĀr.

Dhanvā, in comp. for °*van*. — **yin** or -**vin**, mfn. carrying or bearing a bow, VS. — **sáh** (*sāh*), mfn. skilled in archery, RV. i, 127, 3.

Dhanvāyana. See *bhīma-dh*°.

Dhanvin, mfn. (Vām. v, 2, 59) armed with a bow, a b°-man, MBh. &c. &c. (cf. *ishu*-, *dṛiḍha*-, *bahu*-); cunning, shrewd, L.; m. the sign of the zodiac Sagittarius, Var.; N. of Śiva, MBh.; of Vishṇu, L.; of Arjuna, L.; Terminalia Arjuna; Mimusops Elengi; Alhagi Maurorum, L.; N. of a son of Manu Tāmasa, Hariv.; of a Sch. on DrāhyŚr. (also °*vi-svāmin*); °*vi-bhāshya*, n. the Comm. of Dhanvin.

धन्वग *dhanvaga* or °*vaṅga*, m. Grewia Elastica, Bhpr.; n. its fruit.

धन्वन *dhanvana*, m. n., id., L.; m. a kind of animal, VarBṛS. lxxxviii, 9; v. l. °*vina*.

धम् *dham* or *dhmā*, cl. 1. P. *dhámati* (Ā. °*te*, Up.; MBh.; p. *dhmāntas* = *dhamantas*, BhP. x, 12, 7; perf. *dadhmau*, 3. pl. Ā. °*mire*, MBh.; aor. *adhmāsīt*, Kāv.; Prec. *dhmāyāt* or *dhmeyāt*, Gr.; fut. *dhamishyati*, MBh.; *dhmāsyati*, *dhmātā*, Gr.; ind. p. -*dhmāya*, Br.) to blow (either intrans. as wind [applied also to the bubbling Soma, RV. ix, 73] or trans., as to blow a conch-shell or any wind instrument), RV. &c. &c.; to blow into (loc.), MBh. i, 813; to breathe out, exhale, RV. ii, 34, 1; MBh. xiv, 1732; to kindle a fire by blowing, RV. ii, 24, 7; MBh. ii, 2483; to melt or manufacture (metal) by blowing, RV. &c. &c.; to blow or cast away, MBh. v, 7209: Pass. *dhamyate*, ep. also °*ti*, *dhmāyáte*, °*ti* (ŚBr.; MBh.) to be blown &c.: Caus. *dhmāpayati*, MBh. (aor. *adidhmapat*, Gr.; Pass. *dhmāpyate*, MBh.) to cause to blow or melt; to consume by fire, reduce to cinder, MBh.; Suśr.: Desid. *didhmāsati*, Gr.: Intens. *dedhmīyate*, Pāṇ. vii, 4, 31; *dādhmāyate*, p. °*yamāna* being violently blown (conch-shell), BhP. i, 11, 2. [Cf. Slav. *dumo* 'smoke'.]

Dhama, mfn. blowing, melting (ifc.; cf. *karaṃ*-, *khariṃ*-, *jalaṃ*- &c.); m. (only L.) the moon; N. of Brahman; of Yama; of Kṛishṇa.

Dhamaka, m. 'a blower,' blacksmith (as blowing the forge), Uṇ. ii, 35, Sch.

Dhama-dhama, m. 'blower,' N. of a demon that causes disease, Hariv.; of an attendant of Śiva, L.; (*ā*), f. N. of one of the Mātṛis attending on Skanda, MBh.; (*ā*), ind. blowing repeatedly or the sort of sound made by blowing with a bellows or trumpet, MW.

Dhamana, mfn. blowing with a bellows, L.; blowing i. e. scaring away (cf. *māyā*-); cruel, L.;

m. reed, Bhpr.; Azadirachta Indica, L.; m. or n. a partic. high number, Buddh.; n. melting (of ore).

Dhamáni, f. the act of blowing or piping, RV. ii, 11, 8; (also °*nī*) a pipe or tube, (esp.) a canal of the human body, any tubular vessel, as a vein, nerve &c., AV.; ChUp.; MBh.; Suśr. &c. (24 t° vessels starting from the heart or from the navel are supposed to carry the *rasa* or chyle through the body); the throat, neck, L.; N. of Hrāda's wife (the mother of Vātāpi and Ilvala), BhP.; (*ī*), f. a sort of perfume, Bhpr.; turmeric or Hemionitis Cordifolia, L. – **saṃtata** and °**nī-rajju-saṃtata**, mfn. 'having the veins strained like cords,' emaciated, lank, Hariv.

Dhamanīla, mfn. full-veined, having prominent veins, g. *sidhmâdi.*

Dhamara or **dhamātra**, m. or n. a partic. high number, Buddh. (cf. *dhamana*).

Dhami, mfn. blowing, puffing; f. the act of blowing (see *antram-*).

Dhamitá, mfn. blown, kindled, RV.

Dhamitra, n. an implement for kindling fire, L. (cf. *dhav°*).

Dhamin. See *kāmaṃ-dh°.*

Dhamyat or °**yamāna**, mfn. being blown or melted, W.

धमधमाय *dhamadhamāya*, Nom. Ā. *yate*, to quake, tremble, Mālatīm. vii, ½.

धम्मट *dhammaṭa*, m. N. of a man, Rājat.

धम्मल *dhammala*, m. the breast ornamented with gold or jewels (cf. °*milla*), W.

धम्मिका *dhammikā*, f. N. of a woman, Rājat.

धम्मिल्ल *dhammilla*, m., ifc. °*laka*, mf(*ā*)n. a woman's braided and ornamented hair wound round the head, Kathās.; Sāh. &c. (Śatr. i, 58, w. r. *dhamilla*); N. of a Brāhman. – **caritra**, n. N. of wk.

धय *dhaya*, mf(*ā*)n. (√*dhe*) sucking, sipping, drinking; (often ifc.; cf. *āsyaṃ-, karaṃ-, ghaṭiṃ-*); with gen., Naish. i, 82.

Dháyadvat, mfn. containing the word *dhayati* &c., TBr.

Dhayantikā, f. (dimin. of °*ntī*) sucking, AV. Paipp.

धर *dhara*, mf(*ā*)n. (√*dhṛi*) bearing, supporting (scil. the world, said of Kṛishṇa and Śiva), MBh.; ifc. holding, bearing, carrying, wearing, possessing, having, keeping (also in memory), sustaining, preserving, observing (cf. *aṅśu-, aksha-, kulaṃ-* &c.), MBh.; R. &c.; m. a mountain, Kir. xv, 12; (cf. *kshiti-, bhū-* &c.); a flock of cotton, L.; a frivolous or dissolute man (= *viṭa*), L.; a sword, Gal.; N. of a Vasu, MBh.; of a follower of the Pāṇḍavas, ib.; of the king of the tortoises, L.; of the father of Padma-prabha (6th Arhat of pres. Ava-sarpiṇī), L.; (*ā*), f. 'bearer, supporter,' the earth, Mn.; MBh.; Kāv. &c.; the uterus or womb, Bhpr.; a vein or tubular vessel of the body, L.; marrow, L.; a mass of gold or heap of valuables (representing the earth and given to Brāhmans), W.; one of the 8 forms of Sarasvatī, id.; N. of one of the wives of Kaśyapa (mother of the land and water-birds, prob. = the Earth), Hariv. 232 (v. l. *irā*); n. poison, L. (v. l. *dara*). – **paṭṭa** and **-sena**, m. N. of 2 princes of the Valabhī dynasty, Inscr. – **saṃstha**, mfn. mountain-like, MW. **Dharâdhārā**, f. 'support of the mountains,' the earth, L.

Dháraṇa, mf(*ī*)n. bearing, supporting, VS.; TĀr.; m. a dike or bank, L.; the world, L.; the sun, L.; the female breast, L.; rice-corn, L.; N. of a king of the Nāgas, Śatr.; m. or n. a sort of weight variously reckoned as = 10 Palas, = 16 silver Māshakas, = 1 silver Purāṇa, = $\frac{1}{10}$ Śatamāna, = 19 Nishpāva, = $\frac{2}{5}$ Karsha, = $\frac{1}{10}$ Pala, = 24 Raktikā, Mn.; Yājñ.; Suśr.; Var. &c.; n. the act of bearing, holding, &c., Kāv.; bringing, procuring (cf. *kāma-*); support, prop, stay (cf. *pṛithivī-, savana-*); a partic. high number, Buddh. (cf. *dhamana, dhamara*); (*ī*), f., see s. v. – **priyā**, f. N. of the goddess executing the commands of the 19th Arhat, Jain.

Dharaṇi, f. (cf. the next) the earth (personif. as the wife of Dhruva), MBh.; R.; BhP. &c. – **kośa**, m. N. of the Dictionary of Dharaṇi-dāsa. – **goṇiga**, m. N. of a man, Cat. – **grāma**, m. N. of a village. – **ja**, m. 'earth-born,' a tree, Daś.; 'son of the earth,' metron. of the planet Mars, Var. – **tala**, n. the surface of the earth; *-taitila*, m. a god on earth, a Brāhman, Daś. – **dāsa**, m. N. of a lexicographer, Cat. – **dhara**, m. 'earth-bearer,' N. of Vishṇu or Kṛishṇa, VP. (cf. *pṛithu-dharaṇi-dh°*); a mountain, MBh. (cf. °*ṇī-dh°*). – **pati** (Prasaṅg.), **-bhuj** (Vcar.), **-bhṛit** (Rāj.), m. a prince or king. – **maṇḍa**, m. or n. N. of a place, Lalit. – **suta**, m. metron. of the planet Mars, Var., Sch. (cf. *-ja*). – **stha**, mfn. being or staying on earth, MW.

Dharaṇī, f. (cf. °*ṇa* and °*ṇi*) the earth, the soil or ground, MBh.; Kāv.; Pur.; a vein or tubular vessel of the body, L.; = *-kanda*, L.; a beam or rafter for a roof, L.; N. of a Dictionary (cf. °*ṇi-kośa*). – **kanda**, m. a kind of bulbous plant or esculent root, L. – **kīlaka**, m. a mountain, L. – **tala**, n. the surface of the earth; *-śrī*, m. N. of a prince of the Kiṃnaras, L. – **dhara**, mfn. bearing or sustaining the earth; m. N. of Vishṇu or Kṛishṇa, L.; of Śiva, MBh.; of Śesha, Hariv.; of the mythic. elephants fabled to support the earth, MBh.; a mountain, MBh. &c.; a tortoise, L.; a king, Rājat.; N. of a man of the family of Maunin and son of Maheśvara, Inscr.; of the father of Saśi-dhara, ib.; of the father of Vāsudeva and grandfather of the author Hari-nātha, Cat.; of the father of Dayā-śaṃkara, ib.; of a Sch. on Mn., Kull.; of a poet and other authors (also with *pantha*), Cat.; of a Bodhi-sattva (also read °*ṇiṃ-dh°*), Buddh. – **dhṛit**, m. 'earth-bearer,' N. of Śesha, Hariv. 6766 (v. l. *-bhṛit*). – **dhra**, m. id., a mountain, Vām. v, 2, 36. – **nārāyaṇa-stotra**, n. N. of a Stotra. – **ṃ-dhara**, see °*ṇī-dh°* (above). – **pūra**, m. 'earth-flooding,' the ocean, L. – **plava**, m. 'having the earth as ship,' id., ib. – **bandha**, m. 'earth-bond,' id., Bālar. iv, 77. – **bhṛit**, m. a mountain, Hariv. 13616 (cf. *-dhṛit*). – **maṇḍala**, n. 'earth-sphere,' the globe, Pañc. – **ruha**, m. 'earth-growing,' a tree, R. – **varāha**, m. N. of a king, Kathās.; *-saṃvāda*, m. N. of wk. – **vrata**, n. N. of a partic. observance, Cat. – °**śvara** (°*ṇîśv°*), m. 'earth-lord,' N. of Śiva, L.; *-rāja*, m. N. of a Bodhi-sattva, Lalit. – **suta**, m. metron. of Aṅgiras or the planet Mars, L.; (*ā*), f. of Sītā, L. – **sura**, m. 'god on earth,' a Brāhman, RāmatUp.

Dharaṇīya, mfn. to be held or borne (cf. *śiro-*).

Dharā, f. of °*ra*, q. v. – **kadamba**, m. Nauclea Cadamba, L. – **turāshāh** (*sāh*), m. prince, king, Naish. iii, 95. – °**tmaja** (°*rātm°*), m. metron. of the planet Mars, L. – **dhara**, m. 'earth-bearer,' N. of Vishṇu or Kṛishṇa, MBh.; BhP.; (ifc. f. *ā*) mountain, MBh.; R. &c.; °*rêndra*, m. 'm°-king,' N. of Himâlaya, Śiś. i, 5. – **dhava**, m. 'earth-lord,' king, Rājat. vii, 337. – °**dhārā** (°*rādh°*), f. the earth, L. – °**dhipa** (°*râdh°*), m. id., MBh. – **pati**, m. id., Daś.; N. of Vishṇu, BhP. – **putra**, m. metron. of the planet Mars, MBh. – **bandha**, m. = *dharaṇī-b°*, Bālar. vii, 46. – **bhuj**, m. 'earth-enjoyer,' a king, Rājat. – **bhṛit**, m. 'earth-bearer,' a mountain, MBh. – °**mara** (°*râm°*), m. 'a god on earth,' a Brāhman, MārkP. – **śaya**, mf(*ī*)n. sleeping on the earth, Mn. vi, 26. – **sūnu**, m. = *-putra*, L. **Dharôddhāra**, m. deliverance of the world, W. **Dharôpastha**, m. the surface of the earth, L.

Dhariṇi, m. N. of an Āgastya, Pravar.

Dháritrī, f. a female bearer or supporter, VS.; TS.; Hariv.; the earth, Var.; Kāv.; Pur. – **dhara**, m. 'earth-holder,' mountain, Kir. – **putra**, m. metron. of the planet Mars, Var. Yogay. – **bhṛit**, m. prince, king, ib., Sch. – **sutrāman**, m. id., Dhūrtan.

Dhariman, m. a balance, weight (cf. °*ma-meya*); form, figure, Uṇ., Sch. °**ma-meya**, mfn. measurable by weight, Mn. viii, 321.

Dharītu. See *dur-dhárītu.*

Dhárīman, m. = *dharman*; only loc. °*maṇi*, according to custom or law or precept, RV.

1. **Dharúṇa**, mf(*ī*)n. bearing, holding, supporter, RV.; VS.; AV.; m. N. of the supposed author of RV. v, 15; of Brahmā, L.; heaven, L.; (also n.) water, L.; opinion, L.; (*ī*), f. capacious, as subst. receptacle, AV. iii, 12, 3; n. basis, foundation, firm ground (also pl.); the firm soil of the earth; prop, stay, receptacle, RV.; AV. – **hvara** (°*rúṇa-*), mfn. trembling in its foundations or receptacle, RV. i, 54, 10.

Dharṇasa, mfn. holding, supporting; strong, powerful, able, Kāṭh.; ĀpŚr. °**nasí**, mfn. id. (a synonym of *bala*, Naigh. ii, 9); full of spirit (as Soma), RV.; TBr.; n. support, RV. i, 105, 6.

Dharṇi, m. supporter, keeper (of riches), i, 127, 7.

Dhartavya, mfn. to be upheld or supported; to be held or had or possessed; to be placed or fixed, W.

Dhartu. See *dur-dhártu.*

Dhartṛí, m. bearer, supporter, RV.; AV.; &c. (f. °*trī*, VS.; TS.); (°*tári*), loc. inf. in bearing or supporting or preserving, RV. ii, 23, 17; ix, 86, 42.

Dhartrá, n. prop, support, stay, VS.; TS.; ŚāṅkhŚr.; a house, L.; sacrifice, merit, L.

1. **Dhárma**, m. (rarely n., g. *ardharcâdi*; the older form of the RV. is *dhárman*, q. v.) that which is established or firm, steadfast decree, statute, ordinance, law; usage, practice, customary observance or prescribed conduct, duty; right, justice (often as a synonym of punishment); virtue, morality, religion, religious merit, good works (*dhármeṇa* or °*māt*, ind. according to right or rule, rightly, justly, according to the nature of anything; cf. below; °*me sthita*, mfn. holding to the law, doing one's duty), AV. &c. &c.; Law or Justice personif. (as Indra, ŚBr. &c.; as Yama, MBh.; as born from the right breast of Yama and father of Śama, Kāma and Harsha, ib.; as Vishṇu, Hariv.; as Prajā-pati and son-in-law of Daksha, Hariv.; Mn. &c.; as one of the attendants of the Sun, L.; as a Bull, Mn. viii, 16; as a Dove, Kathās. vii, 89, &c.); the law or doctrine of Buddhism (as distinguished from the *saṅgha* or monastic order, MWB. 70); the ethical precepts of Buddhism (or the principal *dharma* called *sūtra*, as distinguished from the *abhi-dharma* or 'further dharma' and from the *vinaya* or 'discipline,' these three constituting the canon of Southern B°, MWB. 61); the law of Northern B° (in 9 canonical scriptures, viz. Prajñā-pāramitā, Gaṇḍa-vyūha, Daśa-bhūmîśvara, Samādhi-rāja, Laṅkâvatāra, Saddharma-puṇḍarīka, Tathāgata-guhyaka, Lalita-vistara, Suvarṇa-prabhāsa, ib. 69); nature, character, peculiar condition or essential quality, property, mark, peculiarity (= *sva-bhāva*, L.; cf. *daśa-dh°-gata*, ŚBr. &c. &c.; *upamânôpameyayor dh°*, the tertium comparationis, Pāṇ. ii, 1, 55, Sch.); a partic. ceremony, MBh. xiv, 2623; sacrifice, L.; the ninth mansion, Var.; an Upanishad, L.; associating with the virtuous, L.; religious abstraction, devotion, L.; = *upamā*, L. (cf. above); a bow, Dharmaś.; a Soma-drinker, L.; N. of the 15th Arhat of the present Ava-sarpiṇī, L.; of a son of Anu and father of Ghṛita, Hariv.; of a s° of Gāndhāra and f° of Dhṛita, Pur.; of a s° of Haihaya and f° of Netra, BhP.; of a s° of Pṛithu-śravas and f° of Uśanas, ib.; of a s° of Su-vrata, VP. (cf. *dharma-sūtra*); of a s° of Dīrgha-tapas, VāyuP.; of a king of Kaśmīra, Rāj. iv, 678; of another man, ib. vii, 85; of a lexicographer &c. (also *-paṇḍita, -bhaṭṭa* and *-śāstrin*), Cat. [Cf. Lat. *firmus*, Lith. *dermė̃*.] – **kañcuka**, m. or n. armour or garb of virtue; *-praveśin*, mfn. putting it on, Śak. v, $\frac{1}{2}$. – **kathaka**, m. propounder of the law (v. l. °*thika*), Buddh. – **kathā**, f. discourse upon l° &c., MW. – **karôpâdhyāya**, m. N. of an author, Cat. – **karman**, n. work of duty, pious action, BrahmavP.; Subh. – **kāṅkshiṇī**, f. N. of a Gandharvī and a Kiṃ-narī, Kāraṇḍ. – **kāṇḍa**, m. n. N. of wk. – **kāma**, mfn. loving justice, observing right, R.; m. N. of a demon (son of Pāpīyas), Lalit.; °*mârtha*, m. pl. virtue, pleasure, and wealth, Mn. vii, 151; °*mârtha-sambaddha*, mfn. joined with or containing v°, p°, and w°, MW.; °*mârtha-sambandha*, m. alliance for v°, p°, and w°, i. e. matrimony, MBh. i, 3007. – **kāya**, m. 'law-body,' N. of one of the 3 bodies of a Buddha, Vajracch.; MWB. 246; 'having the l° for body,' a Buddha, L.; a Jaina saint, W.; N. of Avalokiteśvara, Buddh.; of a god of the Bodhi tree, Lalit. – **kāra**, m. 'law-doer,' N. of a man, MW. – **kāraṇa**, n. cause of virtue, ib. – **kārya**, n. any act of duty or religion, good work, virtuous conduct, Mn.; Yājñ.; Śak. – **kāla**, m. (*kāya?*) a Jina, Gal. – **kīrti**, m. 'glory of the l°,' N. of a philosopher and poet, Cat.; of a grammarian, ib.; of a king, Pur. – **kīla**, m. royal edict or grant (also *-ka*), L.; husband, Gal. – **kūṭa**, m. N. of Sch. on R., Cat. – **kūpa**, m. 'holy well,' N. of a Tīrtha, SkandaP. – **kṛicchra**, n. a difficult point of duty or right, MBh. – 1. **-kṛit**, mfn. (2. see under 3. *Dharma*) doing one's duty, virtuous, MBh. – **kṛitya**, n. fulfilment of duty, virtue, any moral or religious observance, Āpast.; Hariv. – **ketu**, m. 'having justice for a banner,' N. of a son of Su-ketu and father of Satya-ketu, Hariv.; Pur.; a Buddha, Lalit.; a Jaina saint, W. – **kośa** or °**sha**, m. the treasury or collective body of laws and duties, Mn. i, 99; N. of wk., Cat. – **kośa-vyākhyā**, f. N. of a Buddh. wk. – **kriyā**, f. observance of duties, pious work, righteous conduct, Mn.; Var.; Kām.; Śak. – **kshetra**, n. 'law-field'

= *kuru-kshetra*, q.v., Bhag. i. 1; m. a man of piety and virtue, W.; N. of a man, VP. — **khaṇḍa,** m. N. of wk. — **gañja,** m. the treasury of law, Kāraṇḍ.; N. of a library consisting of sacred books, Buddh. — **gavesha,** m. 'virtue seeking,' N. of a man, Avadānaś. — **gahanâbhyudgata-rāja,** m. 'a prince who has penetrated the depths of the law,' N. of a Buddha. — **gup,** mfn. protecting or observing the law, MBh. — **gupta,** m. 'l°-protected,' N. of men, Kathās.; SkandaP. (also *-miśra*), of a poet, Cat.; of a Buddh. school; *-carita*, n. N. of wk. — **gopa,** m. N. of a king, Kathās. — **ghaṭa,** m. a jar of fragrant water offered daily in the month Vaiśākha, L.; *-vrata-kathā*, f. N. of wk. — **ghosha,** m. N. of an author, Car. — **ghna,** mf(*ī*)n. 'destroying law or right,' unlawful, immoral, Yājñ.; m. Terminalia Bellerica (whose seeds are used as dice), L. — **cakra,** n. the wheel or range of the law, MBh.; Buddh.; Jain.; a partic. mythical weapon, Hariv.; R.; m. 'having or turning the wh° of the l°,' a Buddha, L.; *-bhṛit*, m. 'holding the wh° of the l°,' a Buddha or Jaina, L. — **cakshus,** n. the eye of the l°, Vajracch.; mfn. having an eye for the l° or for what is right, R. — **candra,** m. 'l°-moon,' N. of a man, L. — **cara,** m. 'l°-observer,' N. of a Deva-putra, Lalit. — **caraṇa,** n. (MBh.), **-caryā,** f. (Āpast.) observance of the l°, performance of duty. — **cārin,** mfn. observing the l°, fulfilling one's duties, virtuous, dutiful, moral, MBh.; R. &c.; m. N. of Śiva, MBh.; of a Deva-putra, Lalit.; of a deity of the Bodhi tree, ib.; (*iṇī*), f. a female helpmate in the fulfilment of duties; an honest wife, a virtuous woman, Vikr. v, $\frac{1}{20}$; L. (cf. *saha-dharma-c°*). — **cintaka,** mfn. meditating on the law, familiar with it, MBh. — **cintana,** n. (L.), **-cintā,** f. (Lalit.) consideration of the l° or duty, virtuous reflection. — **cintin,** mfn. = *-cintaka*, Lalit. — **cchala,** m. fraudulent transgression of l° or duty, MBh. — **ja,** mfn. produced by a sense of duty, Mn. ix, 107; m. = the next. — **janman,** m. 'son of Dharma, i. e. Yama,' N. of Yudhi-shṭhira, BhP. — **jijñāsā,** f. 'inquiry into the l°,' N. of a Pariśishṭa of Kāty. — **jīvana,** mfn. living by fulfilment of duties; m. a Brāhman who lives according to rule, Mn. ix, 273. — **jña,** mfn. knowing the l° or what is right, Mn.; Var.; MBh. &c.; *-tama*, mfn. superl. R. ii, 112, 31. — **jñāna,** n. knowledge of l° or duty, Hit. — **tattva,** n. the real essence of the l° (*-tas*, ind. in a manner entirely corresponding to the l°, MBh. viii, 229); N. of a wk. by Kamalakara; of a modern wk., RTL. 510, n. 1; *-prakāśa*, m. N. of wk.; *-vid*, mfn. knowing the truths of laws or religion, MW.; *-saṃgraha*, *°tvârtha-cintāmaṇi*, m. N. of wks. — **tantra,** n. sg. and pl. the beginning and end of the law, summum jus, Gaut.; MBh.; m. N. of a man, VP. — **tas,** ind. according to l° or rule, rightly, justly, Mn.; MBh.; R.; Pañc.; from a virtuous motive, Mn. viii, 103; ifc. = *dharmāt*, from the rules of, VP. iii, 7, 20. — **tā,** f. essence, inherent nature, Buddh.; the being law or right, Jātakam.; (*tayā*), ind. ifc. by way or means of, Divyâv. — **tīrtha,** n. N. of a Tīrtha, MBh. — **tyāga,** m. abandonment of religion, apostacy, MW. — **trāta,** m. 'l°-protected,' N. of a Buddh. author. — **tva,** n. inherent nature, peculiar property, Kap.; Sāh.; morality, piety, W. — **da,** mfn. giving or granting virtue, Hariv.; m. N. of one of the attendants of Skanda, MBh. — **dakshiṇā,** f. fee for instruction in the law, Kāraṇḍ. — **datta,** m. N. of a poet and a writer on rhetoric, Cat. — **darśana,** n. knowledge of duty or l°, MW. — **darśin,** mfn. seeing what is right, R. (B.), Comm. — **dāna,** n. a gift made from duty, L.; *-paddhati*, f. N. of wk. — **dāra,** m. pl. a lawful wife, Kathās. — **dāsa,** m. 'duty-slave,' N. of a man, Buddh.; of sev. authors (a poet, a grammarian and a Sch. on Karpūra-mañjarī), Cat. — **dinnā,** f. (Pāli = *dattā*) 'given by religion,' N. of a female, Buddh. — **dīpa,** m., **-dīpikā,** f. N. of wks. — **dughā,** f. a cow milked for a sacrifice, BhP. — **dṛiḍhâbhedya-sunilambha,** m. N. of a king of the Garuḍas, L. — **dṛiś,** mfn. seeing the right, regarding piety, MW. — **dṛishṭi,** mfn. id., MBh. — **deva,** m. the god of justice, MBh. — **deśaka,** m. teacher of the law, Pañc. iii, $\frac{104}{105}$ (v. l. *°mâd°*). — **deśanā,** f. instruction in the l°, ib. (B.; v. l. *°môpad°*); with Buddhists = sermon, Kāraṇḍ.; Lalit. — **dogdhrī,** f. a cow whose milk is destined for sacrifice, VP. (cf. *-dughā*). — **dravī,** f. 'having l° or virtue for its waters,' N. of the Ganges, L. — **druh,** mfn. violating the l° or right, Mcar. ii, 7. — **droṇa,** m. or n. 'l°-vessel,' N. of the l°-books of Mn., Vas., Yājñ. and Gaut., Sch. on Gobh. Śrāddhak. — **drohin,** mfn. = *-druh*; m. a Rākshasa, L. — **dvāra,** n. pl. the virtues or duties as a means of acquiring the highest wisdom, Car. — **dveshin,** m. Terminalia Bellerica, L. (cf. *-ghna*). — **dvaita-nirṇaya,** m. N. of wk. — **dhara,** m. 'l°-supporter,' N. of a partic. Samādhi; of a prince of the Kimnaras; of a Bodhi-sattva, Buddh. — **dhātu,** m. 'the element of l° or of existence,' one of the 18 Dhātus of the Buddhists; a Buddha (whose essence is l°), L.; *-niyata*, m. a partic. Samādhi, L.; *-parirakshiṇī*, f. N. of a Kiṃ-narī, Kāraṇḍ.; *-vāg-īśvara*, m. N. of a Buddh. deity. — **dhātrī,** f. female l°-supporter &c. (said of the water), Hariv. — **dhāraya,** mfn. maintaining the l°, MaitrS. — **dhurya,** mfn. foremost in justice, Kām. — **dhṛik,** m. N. of a son of Śva-phalka, Hariv.; VP. (lit. = next or fr. √*dhṛish*?). — **dhṛit,** mfn. observing the l° &c., AV. — **dhenu,** f. = *-dogdhrī*, VP. — **dhvaja,** mfn. 'whose banner is l°,' feigning virtue, hypocritical, an impostor, BhP. (also *-vat* and *°jika*, MBh.; *°jin*, Mn. iv, 195); m. N. of the sun, MBh. iii, 149; of a king of Mithilā (son of Kuśa-dhvaja, father of Amita-dhvaja and Kṛita-dhvaja), Pur.; of a brother of Kuśa-dhvaja, ib.; of a king of Kāñcana-pura, ib.; of another person, Lalit. — **nada,** m. N. of a sacred lake, SkandaP. — **nandana,** m. 'Dharma's joy or son,' N. of Yudhi-shṭhira; pl. the sons of Pāṇḍu, BhP. i, 9, 12 (cf. *-ja*, *-janman* &c.) — **nandin,** m. N. of a Buddh. author. — **nātha,** m. legal protector, R. — **nābha,** m. 'l°-centre,' N. of Vishṇu, L.; of a king, Cat. — **nāśā,** f. 'law-ruin,' N. of a fictitious city, Kautukas. — **nitya,** mfn. constant in duty, MBh. — **nibandha,** m. attachment to l°, virtue, piety, W. (*°dhin*, mfn. pious, holy, ib.); N. of wk. — **niveśa,** m. religious devotion, MW. — **nishṭha,** mfn. grounded on or devoted to virtue, Mṛicch. x, 53. — **nishpatti,** f. fulfilment of duty, moral or religious observance, W. — **netra,** m. 'l°-eyed,' N. of a grandson of Dhṛita-rāshṭra, MBh.; of a son of Taṃsu and father of Dushmanta, Hariv.; Pur.; of a son of Haihaya, ib.; of a son of Su-vrata, BhP., VP. (v. l. *-sūtra*). — **m-dada,** mfn. giving the l°, Kāraṇḍ.; (*ā*), f. N. of a Gandharvī, ib. — **pañcaviṇśatikā,** f. N. of wk. — **paṭṭa,** m. the band of l° or duty, L. — **paṭṭana,** v. l. for *-pattana*, q. v. — **pati** (*dhárma-*), m. the lord or guardian of l° and order, VS.; ŚBr. — **pattana,** n. 'the city of the law,' N. of the city of Śrāvastī (v. l. *-paṭṭana*, VarBṛS. xiv, 14), L.; pepper, Bhpr. — **pattra,** n. Ficus Glomerata, L. — **patnī,** f. a lawful wife, Mn.; Yājñ.; MBh.; Kāv. (cf. *-dāra*). — **patha,** m. = next, R.; N. of a merchant, L. — **pathin,** m. (nom. *-panthās*) the way of duty or virtue, R. — **para,** mfn. intent on virtue, pious, righteous, Āpast.; Var.; MBh.; Kāv. — **parâyaṇa,** mfn., id., MBh.; R. — **parīkshā,** f. 'inquiry into the l°,' N. of wk. — **paryāya,** m. N. of partic. Buddh. wks., Lalit.; Kāraṇḍ. — **pāṭhaka,** m. a teacher of l°, lawyer, Mn. xii, 111. — **pāla,** m. 'l°-guardian,' fig. = punishment or sword, MBh. xii, 4429; 6204; N. of a minister of king Daśa-ratha, R.; of a great scholar, Buddh.; of a prince, Inscr.; of a poet, Cat. — **pāśa,** m. 'band of l° or duty,' N. of a partic. mythical weapon, R. — **pīṭha,** m. 'l°-seat,' N. of a place in Vārāṇasī, SkandaP.; (*ā*), f. N. of a serpent-maiden, Kāraṇḍ. — **pīḍā,** f. transgression of l° or duty, Daś. — **putra,** m. a son begot from a sense of duty, L.; N. of Yudhi-shṭhira (cf. *-janman*), Mṛicch. i, 39; of the 11th Manu, VP.; du. of the Ṛishis Nara and Nārāyaṇa, Pur.; *°traka*, m. adopted son (cf. *pārvatī-dharma-putraka*). — **pura,** n. 'l°-city,' N. of Ayodhyā, R.; of a town situated on the Narmadā river, W. — **puraskāra,** mfn. placing duty above all, Āpast. — **purāṇa,** n. N. of wk. — **pūta,** mfn. purified by virtue, most virtuous, Daś. — **prakāśa,** m. N. of wk. — **pracāra,** m. 'the course of l° or right,' fig. = sword, L. — **pratirūpaka,** m. counterfeit of virtue, Mn. xi, 9. — **pradīpa,** m. 'light of the law,' N. of several wks.; *-vyākhyāna*, n. N. of a Comm. — **pradhāna,** mfn. eminent in piety, Mn. iv, 243. — **prabhāsa,** m. 'illuminator of the law,' N. of a Buddha. — **pramāṇa-paricceheda,** m. N. of wk. — **pravaktṛi,** m. teacher of l°, Mn. — **pravacana,** n. promulgation of the law, Buddh. — **pravṛitti,** f. practice of virtue, pious act, Rājat.; N. of wk. — **praśna,** m. 'inquiry into the l°,' N. of wk.; *-vyākhyā*, f. N. of a Comm. on it. — **prastha,** m. 'habitation of the god Dharma,' N. of a place of pilgrimage, MBh. — **priya,** m. 'l°-friend,' N. of a Gandharva prince, Kāraṇḍ.; of a Buddh. scholar. — **prêksha,** mfn. having an eye for what is right R. — **plava,** m. boat of virtue (a son), MBh. i, 3097. — **bala,** m. 'l°-strength,' N. of a man, Buddh. — **bāṇijika** &c., see *-vāṇ°*. — **bāhya,** mfn. 'outside the law,' contrary to what is right, ...W. — **bindu,** m. 'a drop of the l°,' N. of wk. — **buddhi,** mfn. having a virtuous mind, Pañc.; N. of a merchant, Kathās. — **bhaginī,** f. a female that has the rights of a sister, Kathās.; a sister in respect of religion, Mṛicch. viii, $\frac{4}{8}$ (cf. *-bhrātṛi*). — **bhagna,** mfn. one who has neglected his duty, Hariv. — **bhāgin,** mfn. possessed of virtue, virtuous, Hit. — **bhāṇaka,** m. l°-expounder, preacher, Buddh.; lecturer, public reader of the MBh. and other sacred wks., W. — **bhikshuka,** m. a mendicant from virtuous motives, Mn. xi, 2. — **bhīru,** mfn. forgetful (lit. afraid) of duty, Kautukar.; *°ruka*, mfn. tremblingly alive to d°, MW. — **bhṛit,** m. 'l°-supporter,' N. of princes and other men, MBh. &c. &c. (cf. *-dhṛit*). — **bhṛita,** m. N. of a son of the 13th Manu, Hariv. (v. l. *-bhṛitha*). — **bhrātṛi,** m. a brother in respect of religion or piety, Yājñ. (cf. *-bhaginī*). — **mati,** m. 'pious-minded,' N. of a prince and of a god of the Bodhi tree. — **maya,** mf(*ī*)n. consisting merely in law or virtue, moral, righteous, ŚBr.; MBh.; BhP. — **mahāmātra,** m. a minister in matters of religion, Buddh. — **mātra,** mfn. depending only on modality or on the method, only attributive, KātyŚr. (*-tva*, n. ib.); n. mere modality, the manner or method, Jaim.; Kāś. on Pāṇ. ii, 3, 33. — **mārga,** m. the path of virtue or duty, Pañc. — **mitra,** m. 'friend of the law,' N. of a man, Buddh. — **mīmāṇsā,** f. N. of the Pūrva-mīmāṇsā of Jaimini; *-paribhāshā*, f., *-saṃgraha* and *-sāra-saṃgraha*, m. N. of wks. — **mūla,** n. the foundation of law and religion, the Vedas, Gaut. — **mṛij,** m. (nom. *mṛik*), v. l. for *-dhṛik*, Hariv. — **megha,** m. a partic. Samādhi, Yogas. (*-dhyāna*, n. a partic. state of mind connected with it, ib., Sch.); (*ā*), f. N. of one of the 10 Bhūmis, Buddh. — **meru,** m. N. of Comm. on Ragh. — **yajña,** m. sacrifice of virtue, an unbloody s°, Jātakam. — **yaśas,** m. 'glory of the l°,' N. of a man, L. — **yukta,** mfn. righteous, Āpast.; accordant with the law, ib.; R. — **yuga,** n. 'age of religion,' the Kṛita-yuga, Hariv. — **yuj,** mfn. = *-yukta*, L. — **yuddha,** n. an honest fight, Kāv. — **yogêśvara,** m. N. of a poet. — **yoni,** m. the womb or source of l°, N. of Vishṇu, Vishṇ. — **rakshitā,** f. 'l°-protected,' N. of a female, Daś. — **rata,** mfn. 'delighting in virtue,' virtuous, Kāv. — **rati,** mfn. id., Ragh.; N. of a demon, Lalit. — **ratna,** n., *-mañjūshā*, f., *°tnâkara*, m. N. of wks. — **ratha,** m. 'law-chariot,' N. of a son of Sagara, Hariv.; of Divi-ratha, Pur.; *°thâbhirūḍha*, m. a partic. Samādhi, Kāraṇḍ. — **rasâyana** and **-rahasya,** n. N. of wks. — **rāj,** m. 'king of justice,' N. of Yama, Mn.; BhP.; of Yudhi-shṭhira, MBh.; of a king of the herons (son of Kaśyapa and an Apsaras), MBh. xii, 6350 (cf. *rāja-dharman* and *dharmâṅga*). — **rāja,** m. 'id.' a just or righteous king, Hariv.; any king or prince, L.; a Buddha, L.; N. of Yama, MBh.; Hariv.; Daś. &c. (*-tā*, f., MBh.); of Yudhi-shṭhira, MBh.; Hariv. (*-purogama*, mfn. headed by Y°, MW.); Law conceived as a king, Kāraṇḍ.; N. of sev. authors (also *-dīkshita* [*°tīya*, n. his wk.], *-putra*, *-bhaṭṭa*, *°jâdhvari-vara* and *°jâdhvarîndra*, m.) — **rājan,** m. 'id.,' N. of Yudhi-shṭhira, MBh. — **rājikā,** f. a Stūpa, Buddh. — **rātrī,** f., w. r. for *-dhātrī*, Hariv. — **ruci,** mfn. delighting in or devoted to virtue, Āpast.; m. N. of a Dānava, Kathās.; of a god of the Bodhi tree, Lalit.; of a man, Buddh. — **rodhin,** mfn. opposed to l°, illegal, immoral, W. — **lakshaṇa,** n. an essential mark of l° or ethics (as place, time &c.), ib. — **lopa,** m. violation of l°, neglect of duty, irreligion, MBh.; absence of an attribute, Sāh. — 1. **-vat,** mfn. (2. see under 3. *Dharma*) virtuous, pious, just, L.; (*atī*), f. N. of a Mudrā, Buddh.; N. of women, Kathās. — **vatsala,** mfn. tenderly alive to duty, loving piety, MW. — **vartin,** mfn. 'abiding in duty,' righteous, ib. — **vardhana,** mfn. increasing right or virtue (Śiva), MBh.; N. of a king of Śrāvastī, Daś.; of a poet, Cat.; n. N. of a town, R. — **varman,** n. 'shield or armour of justice,' N. of Kṛishṇa, BhP. — **vasu-prada,** mfn. granting virtue and wealth (Vishṇu), Vishṇ. — **vācas-pati,** m. N. of Sch. on Kāvyâd., Cat. — **vāṇijaka** (MBh.), **°jika** (L.), **°jyaka** (MBh.), m. one who tries to make a profit out of his virtue like a merchant. — **vāda,** m. discussion or argument about l° or duty, R.; *°din*, mfn. discussing l° or d°, MBh.; Pañc. — **vāsara,** m. 'day of religious duties,' the day of full moon, L.; yesterday (= *pūrve-dyus*), L. (cf. *dharmâha*). — **vāha,**

m. 'whose vehicle is the l°,' just, virtuous, MBh. **-vāhana,** m. 'id.;' N. of Śiva, L. **-vāhya,** see *-bāhya.* **-vicāra,** m. 'discussion of l° or duty;' *-śāstra,* n., *-saṃgraha,* m. N. of wks. **-vijaya,** m. the victory of justice or virtue, Rājat.; N. of a drama, Cat.; *-gaṇi,* m. N. of Sch. on Kir., Cat. **-vid,** mfn. knowing the l° or duty, virtuous, pious, Gaut.; MBh. **-vidyā,** f. knowledge of the l° or right, L. **-vidharman,** n. pl. (*prajāpater dharma-v°*) N. of 4 Sāmans, ĀrshBr. **-vidhi,** m. course of l°, legal precept or injunction, Mn. x, 131. **-viplava,** m. violation of l° or duty, wickedness, Kir. **-virodha-vat,** mfn. = *-rodhin,* R. (B.) **-vivaraṇa,** n., **-vivṛiti,** f. 'explanation of the l°,' N. of wks. **-vivardhana,** m. 'promoter of l° or right,' N. of a son of Aśoka (= *kunāla*), Buddh. **-viveka,** m. 'discussion on the l°,' N. of wks.; *-vākya,* n. N. of a short poem ascribed to Halâyudha. **-vivecana,** n. judicial investigation, Mn. viii, 21. **-vṛitti,** f. 'explanation of the l°,' N. of ch. of ŚārṅgP. **-vṛiddha,** mfn. 'advanced in virtue,' MBh.; N. of a son of Śva-phalka, BhP. (cf. *-dhṛik* and *-bhṛit*); of other men, VP. **-vaitaṇsika,** m. 'merit-catcher,' one who gives away money unlawfully acquired in the hope of acquiring merit, L. **-vyatikrama,** m. transgression of the l°, Āpast.; Gaut. **-vyavasthā,** m. judicial decision, decisive sentence, Gaut. **-vyādha,** m. 'the righteous hunter,' N. of a Brāhman changed into a hunter in consequence of a curse, MBh. iii; Sukas. (according to the VarP. of a Brāhman-killer born as a hunter from the body of Vasu, king of Kaśmīra). **-śarīra,** n. a body or collection of virtues or sacred relics, Jātakam.; a kind of small Buddh. Stūpa. **-śarman,** m. 'refuge of l° or virtue,' N. of a preceptor; *°mâbhyudaya,* m. N. of wk. **-śāṭa-praticchanna,** mfn. clothed with the garb of righteousness, naked, Divyâv. **-śālā,** f. court of justice, tribunal, W.; charitable asylum, hospital, esp. religious asylum, L.; RTL. 153. **-śāsana,** n. l°-book, code of laws, MBh. **-śāstra,** n. id.; *-kārikā,* f., *-dīpikā,* f., *-nibandha,* m., *-vacana,* n., *-saṃgraha,* m. (and *°ha-śloka,* m. pl.), *-sarvasva,* n., *-sudhā-nidhi,* m., *°strôddhṛita-vacana,* n. pl. N. of wks. **-śāstrin,** m. an adherent of the l°-books; pl. N. of a partic. school, Hcar. **-śīla,** mfn. of a virtuous disposition, just, pious, MBh.; Kāv.; m. N. of a man, Kathās.; of a woman, Śukas. **-śuddhi,** f. a correct knowledge of the law, Mn. xii, 103. **-śravaṇa,** n. the hearing of a sermon, Buddh. **-śreshṭhin,** m. N. of a Buddh. Arhat. **-saṃyukta,** mfn. lawful, legal, Sch. on Yājñ. **-saṃśrita,** mfn. virtuous, pious, Var. **-saṃhitā,** f. code or collection of l° (as Manu, Yājñ. &c.); N. of a partic. wk., Cat. **-saṃkathā,** f. pl. pious conversation, Kād. **-saṅga,** m. devotion to justice or virtue; hypocrisy, W. **-saṃgara,** m. = *-yuddha,* MBh. **-saṃgīti,** f. 'discussion about the l°,' a Buddh. council; N. of wk. **-saṃgraha,** m. N. of a collection of Buddh. technical terms; *-nivṛitti,* f. N. of a Jaina wk. **-saṃcaya,** m. store of good wks., Mṛicch. viii, 1. **-saṃjña,** mfn. having the sense of duty; *-tva,* n. (Jātakam.) and *°jñā,* f. (MBh.) the sense of duty. **-satya-vrata,** mfn. devoted to truth and virtue, R. **-satya-vrateyu,** m. pl. = Dharmeyu, Satyeyu and Vrateyu, BhP. ix, 20, 4. **-saṃtāna-sū,** mfn. producing virtuous offspring or actions, MW. **-sabhā,** f. court of justice, tribunal, L. **-samaya,** m. a legal obligation, Mn. ix, 273. **-sampradāya-dīpikā,** f. N. of wk. **-sahāya,** m. a companion in religious duties, Sāh. **-sāgara,** m. 'ocean of justice,' N. of an author. **-sāṃkathya,** n. discussion about the law, Kāraṇḍ. **-sādhana,** n. fulfilment of duties, Siṇhâs.; means of the f° of d°, any act or virtue essential to a system of duties, Kām. **-sāra,** m. 'law-essence,' N. of wk.; *-samuccaya,* m. 'collection of laws,' N. of work. **-sārathi,** m. 'charioteer of Dharma,' N. of a son of Tri-kakud, BhP. **-sāvarṇi,** *°ṇika,* m. N. of the 11th Manu, Pur. **-siṇha,** m. 'lion of virtue,' N. of a man, L. **-sindhu,** m. 'ocean of law,' N. of sev. wks.; *-sāra,* m. 'essence of the ocean of l°,' N. of wk. **-suta,** m. 'son of Dharma,' N. of Yudhi-shṭhira, BhP. **-subodhinī,** f. N. of wk. **-sū,** mfn. promoting order or justice, TBr.; m. the fork-tailed shrike, L. **-sūkta,** n. N. of wk. **-sūtra,** n. a Sūtra wk. treating on l° and custom (*-kāra,* m. the author of a S° wk., Uttarar. iv, ½; *-vyākhyā,* f. N. of wk.); m. N. of a son of Su-vrata, BhP. **-setu,** m. barrier of l° or justice, MBh.; Hariv.; R.; N. of Śiva, Śivag.; of a son of Āryaka, BhP. **-sena,** m. N. of a king, Vet.; of an author, Cat. **-sevana,** n. fulfilment of duties, Hit. **-skandha,** m. 'l°-collection,' N. of wk.; chief section of a wk. relating to laws, Saṃk. **-stha,** m. 'abiding in the l°,' a judge, Mn. viii, 27. **-sthala,** n. 'place of justice,' N. of a town, Vet. **-sthavira,** m. 'firm in l°,' N. of a man, Buddh. **-sthiti-tā,** f. the constant nature of Dharma, ib. **-sthūṇā-rāja,** m. chief pillar of the l°, PārGṛ. **-smāraka,** m. l°-teacher. **-smṛiti,** f. N. of wk. **-svāmin,** m. 'lord of l° and right,' N. of a Buddha; of a sanctuary built by Dharma (king of Kaśmīra), Rājat. iv, 696. **-hantṛi,** mf(*trī*)n. transgressing the law or justice, MBh. **-hāni,** f. neglect of duty, Āpast. **-hīna,** mfn. standing outside the l°, Gaut. **Dharmâkara,** m. 'mine of virtue or l°,' N. of a poet, Cat.; of the 99th Buddha; of a disciple of B° Lokêśvara-rāja; of a Buddh. translator. **Dharmâkshara,** n. pl. 'letters of the law,' formula or confession of faith, Mṛicch. viii, ⁴⁄₁₂. **Dharmâkshepa,** m. objection to the commonly accepted property or nature of anything, Kāvyâd. ii, 128. **Dharmâkhyāna,** n. explanation of duties, Cāṇ. **Dharmâgama,** m. 'l°-tradition,' a l°-book, MārkP. (cf. *siddhânta-dh°*). **Dharmâṅga,** m. 'whose body is the l°,' N. of Vishṇu, Vishṇ.; (*ā*), f. a heron, L. (cf. *dharma-rāj*). **Dharmâṅgada,** m. 'having the l° for ornament,' N. of a king (son of Priyaṃ-kara), Kshitîś.; of another man, Cat. **Dharmâcārya,** m. teacher of l° or customs, ĀśvGṛ.; *-stuti,* f. N. of wk. **Dharmâtikrama,** m. transgression of the l°, Āpast. **Dharmâtmaja,** m. = *°ma-suta,* Vet. **Dharmâtma-tā,** f. religious-mindedness, justice, virtue, MBh.; R. **Dharmâtman,** mfn. religious-minded, just, virtuous, dutiful, MBh.; R.; Var.; m. a saint, religious person; N. of Kumāra-pāla, L. **Dharmâditya,** m. 'sun of justice,' N. of a Buddh. king, Inscr. **Dharmâdeśaka,** see *°ma-d°.* **Dharmâdharma,** m. du. right and wrong, justice and injustice, MW.; *-jña,* mfn. knowing r° and w°, Mn. i, 26; *-parîkshaṇa,* n., *°kshā,* f. the test of r° and w°, a kind of ordeal by drawing lots or slips of black and white paper, Sch. on Yājñ.; *-prabodhinī* and *-vyavasthā,* f. N. of wks.; *-senā-hanana,* n. N. of ch. of the GaṇP. **Dharmâdhikaraṇa,** n. administration or court of justice, Pañc. (*-sthāna,* n. a law-court, ib.); m. a judge, magistrate, MatsyaP. **Dharmâdhikāra,** m. administration of the l°s, Śak.; N. of wk.; *-kāraṇika* (Pañc.) and *°nin* (L.), m. a judge; *°rika,* mfn. relating to the chapter on the l°, Cat.; *°rin,* mfn. administrator of the l°, chief officer of justice, judge, magistrate, Pañc.; Rājat. (*°ri-purusha,* m. officer of a law-court, Vet.); a judge of morals, censor, preacher, Siṇhâs. **Dharmâdhikṛita,** m. a judge, Pañc. **Dharmâdhishṭhāna,** n. a court of justice, ib. **Dharmâdhyaksha,** m. 'overseer of justice,' minister of j°, judge, magistrate, Cāṇ.; Rājat. **Dharmâdhvan,** m. the way of justice or virtue, Prab.; *°dhva-bodha,* m. N. of wk. **Dharmânala,** m. fire of j°, N. of a man, Kautukar. **Dharmânukāṅkshin,** mfn. striving after j° or what is right, R. **Dharmânushṭhāna,** n. fulfilment of duty, virtuous or moral conduct, Āpast. **Dharmânusāra,** m. conformity to l° or virtue, course or practice of duty, W. **Dharmânusmṛiti,** f. continual meditation on the l°, Lalit.; *°ty-upasthāna,* n. N. of wk. **Dharmândhu,** m. 'well of virtue,' 'sacred well,' N. of a Tīrtha, SkandaP. **Dharmânvaya,** m. obedience to l°, Divyâv. **Dharmâpêta,** mfn. departing from virtue, wicked, unrighteous; n. immorality, vice, W. **Dharmâbhijana-vat,** mfn. righteous and of noble origin, R. **Dharmâbhimanas,** mfn. directing the mind to virtue or religion, virtuous, W. **Dharmâbhimukha,** m. 'turned to virtue,' N. of a partic. Samādhi, Kāraṇḍ.; (*ā*), f. N. of an Apsaras, ib. **Dharmâbhisheka-kriyā,** f. any ablution prescribed as a religious duty, Śak. **Dharmâmṛita,** n. 'l°-nectar,' N. of wk.; *-mahôdadhi,* m. 'the ocean of l°-nectar,' N. of work. **Dharmâmbodhi,** m. 'l°-ocean,' N. of wk. **Dharmâyatana,** n. the sphere or objects of Manas; *°nika,* mfn. relating to them, Buddh. **Dharmâyana,** n. course of law, lawsuit, Bhar. **Dharmâraṇya,** n. 'grove of religion,' sacred g° or wood, Śak.; N. of a sacred forest in Madhya-deśa, Var.; MBh.; of a town founded by Amūrta-rajas, R.; N. of wk.; *-kulâcāra-nirṇaya,* m., *-khaṇḍa,* m. or n., *-māhâtmya,* n. N. of wks. **Dharmârṇava,** m. N. of wk. (cf. *°mâmbodhi*). **Dharmârtha,** m. du. religious merit and wealth, Mn. ii, 112 &c.; (*am*), ind. for religious purposes, according to right or rule or duty, MW.; *-kāma-moksha,* m. pl. religious merit, wealth, pleasure and final emancipation (the 4 objects of existence), MW.; *-darśin,* mfn. having an eye to duty and interest or to religion and wealth, MW.; *-pratibaddhatā,* f. attachment to d° and i° or to r° and w°, ib.; *-yukta,* mfn. conformable to duty and interest, Āpast.; *°rthika,* mfn. striving after righteousness, just, pious, L.; *°rthīya,* mfn. relating to law or duty, MBh. **Dharmâlīka,** mfn. having a false character, MW. **Dharmâloka,** m. 'light of the law,' N. of wk., Kāraṇḍ.; *-mukha,* n. introduction to the light of the l°, Lalit. **Dharmâvâpti,** f. acquirement of religious merit, R. **Dharmâviruddham,** ind. according (lit. not opposed) to law or duty, MBh. i, 3501. **Dharmâśoka,** m. 'the Aśoka of justice,' N. of king A° (the grandson of Candra-gupta); of a poet; *-datta,* m. N. of a poet. **Dharmâśrita,** mfn. seeking virtue, just, pious, Var. **Dharmâsana,** n. the throne of justice, judgment-seat, Mn.; MBh.; Kāv. &c.; *-gata,* mfn. seated on it, MW. **Dharmâstikāya,** m. the category or predicament of virtue, Jain. **Dharmâha,** m. yesterday, L. (cf. *°ma-vāsara*). **Dharmâhṛita,** mfn. acquired in a legal manner, Āpast. **Dharmêndra,** m. 'lord of justice,' N. of Yama, MBh. **Dharmêpsu,** mfn. wishing to gain religious merit, Mn. x, 127. **Dharmêśa,** m. = *°mêndra,* SkandaP. **Dharmêśvara,** m. id., ib. (*-tīrtha,* n., ŚivaP.; *-liṅga,* n., SkandaP.); N. of a Deva-putra, Lalit.; of sev. men, ib.; of sev. authors (also *°ra-daivajña* & *°râgni-hotrin*), Cat. **Dharmôccaya,** m. 'accumulation of law,' N. of a palace, Buddh. **Dharmôttamā,** f. N. of a Comm. **Dharmôttara,** mfn. entirely devoted to justice or virtue, Gaut.; Ragh.; m. N. of a Buddh. teacher (*°rīya,* m. pl. his scholars), n. predominance of virtue (over wealth and pleasure), MBh; N. of wks. (cf. *vishṇu-dh°* and *śiva-dh°*). **Dharmôpaghātaka,** mfn. 'law-killing,' unlawful, MBh. i, 2979. **Dharmôpadeśa,** m. instruction in l° or duty, religious or moral instruction, Mn.; Āpast.; the laws collectively, Mn. xii, 106; the statement of modality, Jaim. (cf. *°ma-mātra*); N. of a Jaina wk.; *°deśaka,* m. teacher of the l°, spiritual preceptor, L.; *°deśanā,* f. v. l. for *°ma-deśanā,* q. v. **Dharmôpadha,** mfn. making a pretence of religion, hypocritical, MW. **Dharmôpamā,** f. a simile in which two things are compared with regard to a common characteristic peculiarity, Kāvyâd. ii, 15. **Dharmôpêta,** mfn. endowed with virtues, MW.

2. **Dharma,** Nom. P. *°mati,* to become law, Vop.

3. **Dhárma,** in comp. for *°man,* q. v. **-2. -kṛit,** m. maintainer of order (Indra), RV. viii. 87, 1. **-2. -vat** (*dhárma-*), mfn. accompanied by Dharman or the law (Aśvins), viii, 35, 13.

Dharmaka, ifc. = 1. *dhárma;* m. N. of a man, Inscr.

Dharmán, m. bearer, supporter, arranger, RV.; N. of a son of Bṛihad-rāja and father of Kṛitaṃ-jaya, VP.; (*dhárman*), n. (older than *dhárma,* q.v., in later language mostly ifc.; cf. below) support, prop, hold, RV.; VS.; established order of things, steadfast decree (of a god, esp. of Mitra-Varuṇa), any arrangement or disposition; will, pleasure; law, rule, duty; practice, custom, mode, manner (*dhármaṇā,* *°mabhis;* *°maṇas pári* in regular order, naturally; *svāya dharmaṇe* at one's own pleasure; *dharmaṇi* with the permission of, *ádhi dh°* against the will of [gen.]), RV.; AV.; VS.; (esp. ifc.) nature, quality, characteristic mark or attribute, ŚBr. (cf. *an-ucchitti-*); MBh. (cf. *uñcha-* [add.], *kshatra-*, *phala-*, *phena-*); Var. (cf. *dasyu-* [add.]); Kap. (cf. *cid-dh°* [add.]); Kāv. (cf. *vināśa-*).

Dharmayu, mfn. righteous, virtuous, L.

Dharmāya, Nom. P. Ā. *°yati, °te,* to become law, Vop.

Dharmika, w. r. for *dhārmika.*

Dharmin, mfn. knowing or obeying the law, faithful to duty, virtuous, pious, just, Gaut.; MBh.; R.; endowed with any characteristic mark or peculiar property, Hariv.; Kāvyâd. (cf. below); Sāh.; (ifc.) following the laws or duties of, having the rights or attributes or peculiarities of, having anything as a characteristic mark, subject to any state or condition, Mn.; MBh.; Kāv.; Pur. &c.; m. the bearer of any characteristic mark or attribute, object, thing, Kap.; N. of the 14th Vyāsa, DevībhP.; of a king, VP.; (*iṇī*), f. a kind of perfume, L.; N. of a woman (cf. *dhārmiṇeya*). **°mi-tā,** f. the being endowed with any ch° m° or a° (ifc.), Sarvad.; *°tâva-*

ccheda, m., °*tâvacchedakatā-vāda* &°*vādârtha*, m., °*tâvacchedaka-pratyāsatti*, f., °*tti-nirūpaṇa*, n., °*tâvacchedaka-rahasya*, n., °*tâvacchedaka-vāda*, m. N. of wks. °**mi-tva**, n. virtuousness, justice, faithfulness to duty, Kām.; (ifc.) the being obliged to, Gaut.; the being endowed with or obnoxious to, Suśr.; Kāv.; Pur. °**my-âkshepa**, m. objection to the bearer of any characteristic or peculiarity, Kāvyâd. ii, 130.

Dharmishṭha, mfn. (superl.) very virtuous or righteous, completely lawful or legal, Mn.; MBh.; Kāv. &c. — **tā**, f. great virtuousness or righteousness, MBh. i, 2987.

Dharmīyas, mfn. (compar.) more virtuous &c.; very pious or moral &c., W.

Dharmeyu, m. N. of a son of Raudrāśva, MBh.; BhP.

Dharmya, mfn. legal, legitimate; usual, customary, Mn.; MBh.; Kāv. &c.; just, virtuous, righteous, Mṛicch. ix, 5; endowed with qualities or properties, 'propertied,' KaṭhUp. ii, 13 (cf. *tad-*); suitable to (gen.), Pāṇ. iv, 4, 47; N. of a man (cf. *dhārmyāyaṇa*); n. a customary donation, vi, 2, 65. — **vivāha**, m. a legal marriage, Mn. iii, 22. **Dharmyâmṛita**, n. the nectar of law or faith, Bhag. xii, 20.

धरुण 2. *dharúṇa*, m. (√*dhe*?) a sucking calf, VS. viii, 51 (cf. *dhāru*).

धर्कट *dharkaṭa*, m. N. of a teacher, Cat.

धर्बक *dharbaka*, m. N. of a son of Ajātaśatru, VP.

धर्म *dharma.* See p. 510, col. 3.

धर्मण *dharmaṇa*, m. a kind of snake, L.; a kind of tree, Grewia Elastica, L.

धर्मय्यदीक्षित *dharmayya-dīkshita*, m. N. of a man, Cat.

धर्मीपुत्र *dharmī-putra*, m. an actor, a player (v. l. *dhātrī-p°*).

धर्ष *dharsha*, m. (√*dhṛish*) boldness, insolence, arrogance, MBh. i, 7040 (cf. *dur-*); impatience, W.; paralysing, rendering weak or impotent, ib.; violation (of a woman), ib.; injury, wrong, insult; restraint, ib.; a eunuch, ib. (cf. below). — **kāriṇī**, f. a violated virgin, W. — **vara**, m. a eunuch (prob. w. r. for *varsha-dhara*), W.

Dharshaka, mfn. attacking, assailing (ifc.), Hariv. 8844; overbearing, MW.; violating, seducing, ib.; m. seducer, adulterer, ib.; dancer, actor, mime, L.

Dharshaṇa, mfn. offending, hurting, assaulting, MW.; n. & (*ā*), f. assault, outrage, offence, violation, seduction, MBh.; Hariv.; Pañc. &c.; overpowering, L.; copulation, L.; (*ī*), f. a wanton or unchaste woman, a harlot, Uṇ. ii, 105, Sch.; L. **Dharshaṇâtman**, m. having a violent nature, N. of Śiva, MBh.

Dharshaṇīya, mfn. liable to be attacked or assaulted, violable, conquerable, MBh.; Hariv.; R.

Dharshita, mfn. overpowered, violated, ill-treated, MBh.; Hariv.; Pur.; n. contumely, insolence, W.; copulation, ib.; (*ā*), f. an unchaste woman, L.

Dharshin, mfn. attacking, assaulting, ill-treating (ifc.), Hariv.; proud, arrogant, W.; cohabiting, ib.; (*iṇī*), f. a disloyal or unchaste woman, L. (cf. °*shaṇī*).

धलण्ड *dhalaṇḍa*, m. a kind of small thorny tree, L.

धलिल *dhalila*, m. or n. N. of a valley in which the capital of Udyāna is said to have been situated, L.

धव् *dhav*, cl. 1. Ā. *dhavate*, to run, flow, RV. [Cf. 2. *dhan* & 1. *dhāv*; Gk. θεϝ in θέω, θεύσομαι, θοός.]

Dhávīyas, mfn. (comp.) running fast, RV. vi, 12, 5.

धव 1. *dhavá*, m. Grislea Tomentosa or Anogeissus Latifolia, AV.; MBh. &c.; Suśr.; Bhpr.

धव 2. *dhavá*, m. (accent. only Naigh.; said by some to be fr. √*dhū*, but more probably a secondary formation fr. *vi-dhávā*, q. v.) a man, Naigh. ii, 3; Pañc. ii, 109; a husband, BhP. i, 16, 20; lord, possessor, Hariv. 14952; rogue, cheat, L.; N. of a Vasu (w. r. for *dhara*?), VP.

धवनी *dhavanī*, f. Desmodium Gangeticum or a similar plant, L.

धवर *dhavara*, n. a partic. high number, Buddh.

धवल *dhavala*, mf(*ā*)n. (fr. √2. *dhāv*? cf. Uṇ. i, 108, Sch.) white, dazzling wh°, Var.; Kāv., Pur. &c.; handsome, beautiful, L.; m. white (the colour), L.; a kind of dove, Bhpr.; an old or excellent bull, Hcar.; a kind of camphor, L.; Anogeissus Latifolia, L.; (in music) N. of a Rāga; N. of a man, Kathās.; of one of the elephants of the quarters, R.; of a dog; (*ā* & *ī*), f. a white cow, Kād.; (*ī*), f. wh° hair (as a kind of disease), L.; N. of a river, L.; n. wh° pepper, L.; a kind of metre (= °*lâṅka*), Col.; N. of a town, Kathās. — **giri**, m. 'the wh° or snowy mountain,' N. of one of the highest peaks of the Himâlayas (commonly *dhoula-giri* or *dhola-gir*). — **gṛiha**, n. the upper story of a house (painted wh°), Pañc.; Hcar. — **candra**, m. N. of the patron of Nārāyaṇa (the author of Hit.), Caṭ. — **tā**, f. (Kathās.), -**tva**, n. (Inscr.) whiteness. — **nibandha**, m. N. of wk. — **paksha**, m. 'wh°-winged,' a goose, L. (-*vihaṃgama*, id. Śiś. vi, 45); the light half of the month, L. — **mukha**, m. 'wh°-mouthed,' N. of a man, Kathās. — **mṛittikā**, f. 'wh° earth,' chalk, L. — **yāvanāla**, m. wh° Yāvanāla, L. — **smṛiti**, f. N. of wk. **Dhavalâṅka**, m. a kind of metre (= *dhavala*, n.), Col. **Dhavalâshṭaka**, n. N. of a poem. **Dhavalêtara-taṇḍula**, m. Andropogon Bicolor, Gal. **Dhavalôtpala**, n. the wh° esculent water-lily, L.

Dhavalaya, Nom. P. °*yati*, to make white, illuminate, Kād., Prasannar.; °*lita*, mfn. whitened, illuminated, Bhartṛ.

Dhavalāya, Nom. Ā. °*yate*, to become white, shine brightly, Kād.; Hcar.; °*yita*, mfn. become white, ib.

Dhavaliman, m. white colour, whiteness, Śiś. iv, 65.

Dhavalī, in comp. for °*vala*. — **kṛita**, mfn. made white, W. — **bhūta**, mfn. become wh°, Hcar.

धवाणक *dhavāṇaka*, m. (√*dhū*) wind, Uṇ. iii, 83, Sch.

Dhavitavyà, mfn. to be fanned, ŚBr.

Dhavítra, n. a fan (made of skin or leather, esp. for blowing the sacrificial fire), ŚBr.; TĀr.; Āp. Śr. — **daṇḍa**, m. the handle of a fan, MānŚr.

धा 1. *dhā*, cl. 3. P. Ā. *dádhāti*, *dhatté*, RV. &c. &c. (P. du. *dadhvás*, *dhatthás*, *dhattás* [Pāṇ. viii, 2, 38]; pl. *dadhmási* or °*más*, *dhatthá*, *dádhati*; impf. *ádadhāt*, pl. °*dhur*, 2. pl. *ádhatta* or *ádadhāta*, RV. vii, 33, 4; Subj. *dádhat* or °*dhāt* [Pāṇ. vii, 3, 70, Kāś.], °*dhas*, °*dhatas*, °*dhan*; Pot. *dadhyā́t*; Impv. *dádhātu*, pl. °*dhatu*; 2. sg. *dhehí* [fr. *dhaddhi*; cf. Pāṇ. vi, 4, 119] or *dhattā́t*, RV. iii, 8, 1; 2. pl. *dhattá*, i, 64, 15, *dhattana*, i, 20, 7, *dádhāta*, vii, 32, 13, or °*tana*, x, 36, 13 [cf. Pāṇ. vii, 1, 45, Sch.]; p. *dádhat*, °*ti*, m. pl. °*tas*; Ā. 1. sg. *dadhé* [at once 3. sg. = *dhatté*, RV. i, 149, 5 &c. and = pf. Ā.], 2. sg. *dhátse*, viii, 85, 5 or *dhatsé*, AV. v, 7, 2; 2. 3. du. *dadhā́the*, °*dhā́te*; 2. pl. °*dhidhvé* [cf. pf.]; 3. pl. *dádhate*, RV. v, 41, 2; impf. *ádhatta*, °*tthās*; Subj. *dádhase*, viii, 32, 6 [Pāṇ. iii, 4, 96, Kāś.]; Pot. *dádhīta*, RV. i, 40, 2 or *dadhītá*, v, 66, 1; Impv. 2. sg. *dhatsva*, x, 87, 2 or *dadhishva*, iii, 40, 5 &c.; 2. pl. *dhaddhvam* [Pāṇ. viii, 2, 38, Kāś.] or *dadhidhvam*, RV. vii, 34, 10, &c.; 3. pl. *dadhatām*, AV. viii, 8, 3; p. *dádhāna*); rarely cl. 1. P. Ā. *dadhati*, °*te*, RV.; MBh.; only thrice cl. 2. P. *dhā́ti*, RV.; and once cl. 4. Ā. Pot. *dhāyeta*, MaitrUp. (pf. P. *dadhaú*, °*dhātha*, °*dhatur*, °*dhimá*, °*dhur*, RV. &c.; Ā. *dadhé* [cf. pr.], *dadhishé* or *dhishe*, RV. i, 56, 6; 2. 3. du. *dadhā́the*, °*dhā́te*, 2. pl. *dadhidhvé* [cf. pr.]; 3. pl. *dadhiré*, *dadhre*, x, 82, 5; 6, or *dhire*, i, 166, 10 &c.; p. *dádhāna* [cf. pr.]; aor. P. *ádhāt*, *dhā́t*, *dhā́s*; *adhur*, *dhúr*, RV. &c.; Pot. *dheyām*, °*yur*; *dhetana*, RV.; TBr.; 2. sg. *dhāyīs*, RV. i, 147, 5; Impv. *dhā́tu* [cf. Pāṇ. vi, 1, 8, Vārtt. 3, Pat.]; 2. pl. *dhā́ta* or °*tana*, 3. pl. *dhāntu*, RV.; Ā. *adhita*, °*thās*, *adhītām*, *adhīmahi*, *dhīmahi*, *dhīmahe*, *dhāmahe*, RV.; 3. sg. *ahita*, *hita*, AV.; TĀr.; Subj. *dhéthe*, RV. i, 158, 2, *dhaithe*, vi, 67, 7; Impv. *dhishvá*, ii, 11, 18, &c.; P. *adhat*, SV.; *dhat*, RV.; P. *dhāsur*, Subj. °*sathas* and °*satha*, RV.; Ā. *adhishi*, °*shata*, Br.; Pot. *dhishīya*, ib. [P. vii, 4, 45]; *dheshīya*, MaitrS.; fut. *dhāsyati*, °*te* or *dhātā*, Br. &c.; inf. *dhā́tum*, Br. &c.; Ved. also °*tave*, °*tavaí*, °*tos*; *dhiyádhyai*, RV.; Class. also -*dhitum*; ind. p. *dhitvā́*, Br.; *hitvā* [Pāṇ. vii, 4, 42], -*dhāya* and -*dhā́m*, AV.: Pass. *dhīyáte*, RV. &c. [Pāṇ. vi, 4, 66], p. *dhīyámāna*, RV. i, 155, 2; aor. *ádhāyi*, *dhā́yi*, RV. [Pāṇ. vii, 3, 33, Kāś.]; Prec. *dhāsishṭa* or *dhāyishīshṭa* [vi, 4, 62]) to put, place, set, lay in or on (loc.), RV. &c. &c. (with *daṇḍam*, to inflict punishment on [with loc., MBh. v, 1075, with gen., R. v, 28, 7]; with *tat-padavyām padam*, to put one's foot in another's footstep, i. e. imitate, equal, Kāvyâd. ii. 64); to take or bring or help to (loc. or dat.; with *āré*, to remove), RV.; AV.; ŚBr.; (Ā.) to direct or fix the mind or attention (*cintām*, *manas*, *matim*, *samādhim* &c.) upon, think of (loc. or dat.), fix or resolve upon (loc., dat., acc. with *prati* or a sentence closed with *iti*), RV.; Mn.; MBh.; Kāv.; BhP.; to destine for, bestow on, present or impart to (loc., dat. or gen.), RV.; Br.; MBh. &c. (Pass. to be given or granted, fall to one's [dat.] lot or share, RV. i, 81, 3); to appoint, establish, constitute, RV.; ŚBr.; to render (with double acc.), RV. vii, 31, 12; Bhartṛ. iii, 82; to make, produce, generate, create, cause, effect, perform, execute, RV.; TBr.; ŚvetUp. &c. (aor. with *pūrayām*, *mantrayām*, *varayām* &c. = *pūrayām* &c. *cakāra*); to seize, take hold of, hold, bear, support, wear, put on (clothes), RV.; AV.; Kāv.; BhP. &c.; (Ā.) to accept, obtain, conceive (esp. in the womb), get, take (with *ókas* or *cánas*, to take pleasure or delight in [loc. or dat.]), RV.; AV.; Br.; to assume, have, possess, show, exhibit, incur, undergo, RV.; Hariv.; Kāv.; Hit. etc.: Caus. -*dhāpayati*, Pāṇ. vii. 3, 36 (see *antar-dhā*, *śrad-dhā* &c.): Desid. *dhítsati*, °*te* (Pāṇ. vii, 4, 54), to wish to put in or lay on (loc.), RV.; AitBr. (Class. Pass. *dhitsyate*; *dhitsya* see s. v.); *dídhishati*, °*te*, to wish to give or present, RV.; (Ā.) to wish to gain, strive after (p. *dídhishāṇa*, x, 114, 1), ib.: with *avadyám*, to bid defiance, ib. iv, 18, 7 (cf. *didhishā́yya*, *didhishú*): Intens. *dedhīyate*, Pāṇ. vi, 4, 66. [Cf. Zd. *dā*, *dadaiti*; Gk. θε-, θη-, τίθημι; Lith. *dedù*, *dė́ti*; Slav. *dedją*, *děti*; Old Sax. *duan*, *dôn*, Angl. Sax. *dôn*, Engl. *to do*; Germ. *tuan*; *tuon*, *thun*.]

2. **Dhā**, mfn. putting, placing, bestowing, holding, having, causing &c. (ifc.; cf. 2. *dha*); m. placer, bestower, holder, supporter &c.; N. of Brahmā or Bṛihas-pati, L.; (*ā*), f., see 2. *dha*; instr. (= nom.) perhaps in the suffix *dhā* (which forms adverbs from numerals, e. g. *eka-dhā́*, *dvi-dhā́* &c.)

Dhāka, m. an ox, Uṇ. iii, 40, Sch.; a receptacle (= *ādhāra*; v. l. *āhāra*, food), ib.; a post, L.; (*ā*), f., Pāṇ. vii, 4, 13, Vārtt. 1, Pat. [cf. θήκη].

1. **Dhātu**, m. layer, stratum, KātyŚr.; Kauś.; constituent part, ingredient (esp. [& in RV. only] ifc., where often = 'fold,' e. g. *tri-dhā́tu*, threefold &c.; cf. *trivishṭi-*, *sapta-*, *su-*), RV.; TS.; ŚBr. &c.; element, primitive matter (= *mahā-bhūta*, L.), MBh.; Hariv. &c. (usually reckoned as 5, viz. *kha* or *ākāśa*, *anila*, *tejas*, *jala*, *bhū*; to which is added *Brahma*, Yājñ. iii, 145; or *Vijñāna*, Buddh.); a constituent element or essential ingredient of the body (distinct from the 5 mentioned above and conceived either as 3 humours [called also *dosha*] phlegm, wind and bile, BhP. [cf. *purīsha*, *māṇsa*, *manas*, ChāndUp. vi, 5, 1]; or as the 5 organs of sense, *indriyāṇi* [cf. s. v. & MBh. xii, 6842, where *śrotra*, *ghrāṇa*, *āsya*, *hṛidaya* & *koshṭha* are mentioned as the 5 dh° of the human body born from the ether] & the 5 properties of the elements perceived by them, *gandha*, *rasa*, *rūpa*, *sparśa* & *śabda*, L.; or the 7 fluids or secretions, chyle, blood, flesh, fat, bone, marrow, semen, Suśr. [L. *rasâdi* or *rasa-raktâdi*, of which sometimes 10 are given, the above 7 and hair, skin, sinews, BhP.]); primary element of the earth, i. e. metal, mineral, ore (esp. a mineral of a red colour), Mn.; MBh. &c.; element of words, i. e. grammatical or verbal root or stem, Nir.; Prāt.; MBh. &c. (with the southern Buddhists *dhātu* means either the 6 elements [see above], Dharmas. xxv; or the 18 elementary spheres [*dhātu-loka*], ib. lviii; or the ashes of the body, relics, L. [cf. -*garbha*]). — **kathā**, f., -**kalpa**, m., -**kāya**, m., -**kāvya**, n. N. of wks. -**kāsīsa**, n. red sulphate of iron, L. — **kuśala**, mfn. skilled in metals, metallurgist, Var. — **kośa**, m., -**krama-mālā**, f. N. of wks. on verbal roots. — **kriyā**, f. metallurgy, Var. — **kshaya**, m. waste of the humours, consumption; -*kāsa*, m. a consumptive cough, L. — **gaṇa**, m. 'list of roots,' N. of wk. — **garbha**, m. (with Buddh.) receptacle for ashes or relics, a Dāgaba or Dāgoba (Sinhalese corruption of Pāli Dhātu-gabbha), MWB. xxxv; -*kumbha*, m. a relic-urn, Hcar. — **grāhin**, m. calamine, L. — **ghoshā**, f. N. of wk. on verbal roots. — **ghna**, m.

'destroying the humours,' sour gruel, L. — **candrikā**, f., -**candrôdaya**, m., -**cintā-maṇi**, m. N. of wks. — **cūrṇa**, n. mineral powder, Suśr. — **ja**, mfn. produced or derived from a verbal root; m. or n. bitumen, L. — **taraṃginī** & -**dīpikā**, f. N. of gramm. wks. — **drāvaka**, n. 'dissolving metals,' borax, Bhpr. — **nāśana**, n. = *-ghna*, L. — **nidāna**, n. N. of a med. wk. — **pa**, m. 'chief of the 7 fluids,' elementary juice or chyle, L. — **paryāya-dīpikā** & -**paryāya-mañjūshā**, f. N. of wks. on grammatical or verbal roots. — **pāṭha**, m. 'recital of g° r°,' N. of an ancient list of roots ascribed to Pāṇini. — **pārāyaṇa** or °**ṇīya**, n., -**vṛitti**, f. N. of wks. on verbal roots. — **pushpikā** & °**pī**, f. Grislea Tomentosa, L. (cf. *dhātṛi-*). — **pūjā**, f., -**prakaraṇa**, n., -**prakāśa**, m., -**pratyaya-pañcaka**, n., -**pratyaya-pañjikā**, f., -**pradīpa**, m., -**pradīpikā**, f. N. of wks. — **prasakta**, mfn. devoted to alchemy, Var. — **priyā**, f. N. of a Kiṃnarī, Kāraṇḍ. — **bhṛit**, m. 'earth-bearer,' a mountain, L.; a robust man, W.; mfn. promoting the animal secretions, ib. — **mañjarī**, f. 'root-garland,' N. of a gramm. wk. — **mat**, mfn. containing elements, BhP.; abounding in minerals or metals, MBh.; Hariv.; R.; *-tā*, f., Kum. i, 4. — **maya**, mf(*ī*)n. metallic, Kāv. — **mala**, n. impure excretion from the fluids of the body, fæces, BhP.; lead (the most impure of metals), L. — **mākshika**, n. sulphuret of iron, L. — **māraṇa**, n. N. of a med. wk. — **mārin**, m. 'dissolving metals,' sulphur, L.; (*iṇī*), f. borax, ib. — **mālā** & -**ratna-mañjarī**, f. N. of wks. on gramm. roots. — **ratna-mālā**, f. N. of a med. wk. — **ratnâkara**, m., -**ratnâvalī**, f., -**rahasya**, n. N. of wks. on gramm. roots. — **rājaka**, n. 'chief fluid of the body,' semen, L. — **rūpa**, n., -**rūpâdarśa**, m., -**rūpâvalī**, f. N. of wks. on verbal roots. — **lakshaṇa**, n. N. of a wk. on some Vedic verbs. — **vallabha**, n. 'friend of metals,' borax, L. — **vāda**, m. metallurgy, alchemy, Kād.; °*din*, m. assayer, metallurgist, Kāv. — **vikāra**, m. = *-kshaya*, MW. — **vish**, f. = *-mala*, lead, L. — **visha**, n. a mineral poison, Suśr. — **vṛitti**, f. Comm. on verbal roots, (with *mādhavīyā*) Sāyaṇa's Comm. on Dhātup. — **vairin**, m. 'metal-enemy,' sulphur, L. — **śekhara**, n. 'chief of minerals,' green vitriol, L. — **śodhana**, m. or n. lead, L. — **saṃgraha** & -**samāsa**, m. N. of wks. on verbal roots. — **sambhava**, m. or n. lead. — **sādhana**, n. 'complete scheme of verbal roots,' N. of a wk. containing paradigms of conjugation. — **sāmya**, n. equilibrium of the bodily humours, good health, MW. — **stūpa**, m. (with Buddh.) 'relic-receptacle,' a Dāgaba, MWB. 504; Kāraṇḍ. — **han**, m. 'destroying metals,' sulphur, L. **Dhātûpala**, m. 'mineral-like stone,' chalk. **Dhātv-artha**, m. 'having the sense of a root,' a verb, MW. **Dhātv-avaropaṇa**, n. depositing of relics (inside a Dāgaba or Stūpa), Kāraṇḍ. (printed °*tvâva*° & *dhyānâva*°). **Dhātv-ākara**, m. a mine; °*râkhya*, n. pl. minerals, VarBṛS. civ, 12.

Dhātuka (ifc.) = 1. *dhātu*; m. or n. bitumen, L.

Dhātula, mfn. full of (comp.), HPariś.

Dhātṛi, m. establisher, founder, creator, bearer, supporter (cf. *vasu-*), orderer, arranger, RV. &c. &c.; N. of a divine being who personifies these functions (in Vedic times presiding over generation, matrimony, health, wealth, time & season, & associated or identified with Savitṛi, Prajā-pati, Tvashṭṛi, Bṛihaspati, Mitra, Aryaman, Vishṇu &c., RV. x; AV.; TS.; ŚBr. &c.; later chiefly the creator and maintainer of the world = Brahmā or Prajā-pati, MBh.; Kāv.; Pur.; in ep. one of the 12 Ādityas and brother of Vi-dhātṛi & Lakshmī, son of Brahmā, MBh.; or of Bhṛigu & Khyāti, Pur.; Fate personified, Kāv.); one of the 49 winds, VahniP.; paramour, adulterer, Daś.; the 10th or 44th year in the cycle of Jupiter, Cat.; N. of a Ṛishi in the 4th Manv-antara, Hariv. (C. *dhāman*); of an author, Cat.; (*trī*), f., see *dhātrī*. [Cf. Zd. *dātar*; Gk. θετήρ; Slav. *dĕteli*.] — **putra**, m. 'Brahmā's son,' N. of Sanat-kumāra, L. — **pushpikā** & °**pī**, f. Grislea Tomentosa, L. (cf. *dhātu-*). — **bhavana**, n. Brahmā's heaven, Var.

Dhātṛikā, w. r. for °*trikā*.

1. **Dhātra**, n. receptacle, vessel, L.

2. **Dhātrá**, mf(*ī*)n. belonging to Dhātṛi, ŚBr.

Dhātri, f. (metric.) = °*trī*, Emblica Officinalis, Suśr.

Dhātrikā, f. wet-nurse or = prec., L.

Dhātrī, f. 'female supporter,' a nurse, MBh.; Kāv. &c.; midwife, Hit. iv, 61; mother, Yājñ. iii, 82; the earth, Var.; MBh.; Hariv. &c.; Emblica Officinalis, Var.; Suśr. (some derive it fr. √*dhe*, cf. *dhāyas* & Pāṇ. iii, 2, 181). — **dhara**, m. 'earth-bearer,' mountain, Var. — **pattra**, n. the leaf of Flacourtia Cataphracta, L. — **putra**, m. 'the son of a nurse,' an actor, L. (v. l. for *dharmī-p*°). — **phala**, n. the fruit of Emblica Officinalis, W. — **modaka**, m. a kind of pastille (in med.) — °**śvarī** (°*trīśv*°), f. Grislea Tomentosa, L.

Dhātreyikā, f. foster-sister (a sort of confidante), MBh.; Bālar.; wet-nurse, L.; female slave, Nīlak. — °**yī**, f. foster-sister, Daśar. ii, 27; wet-nurse, L.

Dhā́na, mfn. containing, holding (cf. *uda-*); n. receptacle, case, seat (cf. *agni-*, *kshura-*, *rajju-* &c.; °*nam aktós* prob. = womb or bosom of the night, RV. iii, 7, 6); (*ī*), f. = n. (cf. *aṅgāra-*, *gopāla-*, *rāja-* &c.); the site of a habitation, L.; coriander, L.; N. of a river, L.; (*ā́*), f., see s. v.

1. **Dhānaka**, n. coriander, Bhpr.; (*ā*), f. pl. dimin. fr. next, L.

Dhānā́, f. corn, grain (originally the grains of seed from their being 'laid' into and 'conceived' by the earth, cf. √1. *dhā*, but usually = fried barley or rice or any grain fried and reduced to powder), RV. &c. &c.; coriander, L.; bud, shoot, L. — **cūrṇa**, n. the meal or flower of fried barley &c., L. — °**ntar-vat** (*dhānā́nt*° or *dhānā́nt*°), m. N. of a Gandharva, ŚBr. — °**pūpa** (°*nā́p*°), m. a cake of fried barley &c., MBh. — **phala-vrata-kathā**, f. N. of wk. — **bharjana**, n. the frying or parching of grain, KātyŚr. — **mushṭi**, f. a handful of g°, MBh. — **ruh** (°*nā́-*), mfn. growing from a grain, ŚBr. — **vat** (°*nā́-*), mfn. accompanied by g° (as Soma), RV. — **somá**, m. pl. grains with Soma, TS.; ŚBr.

Dhānākā, f. pl. = *dhānā*, L.

Dhānika, f. See *aṅgāra-dh*°.

Dhānin, m. Careya Arborea or Salvadora Persica, L.

Dhānī, f. See *dhāna* (above).

Dhāneya & °**yaka**, n. coriander, Bhpr.; MBh. 13, 5468 (B ?).

1. **Dhānyà**, mfn. consisting or made of grain, RV.; AV.; n. corn, grain, ib. &c. &c. (according to Suśr. only *śālayaḥ*, *shashṭikāḥ* & *vrīhayaḥ*, the other grains being *ku-dhānya*, q. v.); a measure = 4 sesamum seeds, L.; coriander (also *ā*, f.), L.; Cyperus Rotundus, L.; a kind of house, Gal. — **kaṭaka**, N. of a country, L. — **kartana**, n. 'corn-reaping,' N. of ch. of PSarv. — **kalka**, m. bran, chaff, straw, W. — **kūṭa**, m. or n. granary, Var. — **kośa** or °**sha**, m. store of grain, R.; ear of corn, Gal. — **koshṭaka**, n. = *-kūṭa*, L. — **kshetra**, n. a corn-field, rice-field, MW. — **khala**, m. threshing-floor, KātyŚr. — **gava**, m. c° heaped up in the shape of or equal in size to a bull, Pāṇ. vi, 2, 62, Kāś. — **camasa**, m. rice flattened by threshing, L. — **cārin**, mfn. eating grains (bird), Bhpr. — **caura**, m. a stealer of corn, Mn. xi, 50. — **jīvin**, mfn. living on grains; m. a bird l° on g°, R. — **tā**, f., w. r. for *dhanya-tā*. — **tilvila** (°*nyà-*), mfn. abounding in corn, ŚBr. — **tvac**, f. husk of c°, L. — **da**, mfn. giving or distributing c°, Mn. — **dhana**, n. sg. c° & wealth; *-tas*, ind. on account of possessing c° & w°, Mn. ii, 155; *-vat*, mfn. rich in c° & w°, Hcat. — **dhenu**, f. a heap of rice (like a cow) to be presented to a Brāhman, MW. (cf. *-gava*). — **pañcaka**, n. the 5 sorts of grain (*śāli-dhānya*, *vrīhi-*, *śūka-*, *śimbī-*, *kshudra-*), L. — **pata**, mfn. & -**pati**, m., g. *aśva-paty-ādi*, Pāṇ. iv, 1, 84. — **parvata-dāna-vidhi**, m. N. of ch. of PSarv. — **pātra**, n. a vessel for corn, Lāṭy. — **pāla**, m. N. of a family, Cat. — **pūla**, m. a bunch of corn-stalks, ĀśvŚr., Comm. — **bīja**, n. coriander, L. — **maya**, mf(*ī*)n. consisting of corn or rice, Hcat. — **mātṛi**, m. a measurer of c°, L. — **māna**, n. 'c°-measure,' as much c° as a man can eat at once, VP. (v. l.) — **māya**, m. = *-mātṛi*, L.; corn-dealer, ib. — **māsha**, m. a partic. measure, Car. — **miśra**, mfn. mixing or adulterating corn, Yājñ.; (*ā*), f. a mixture of different sorts of grain, Deśīn. — **rāja**, m. 'g°-king,' barley, L. — **ropaṇa**, n. 'g°-planting,' N. of ch. of PSarv. — **vat**, mfn. rich in g°, L.; ind. like g°, Mn. v, 119. — **vani**, (?) a heap of g°, L. — **vapana**, n. 'g°-sowing,' N. of ch. of PSarv. — **vardhana**, n. usury with g°, L. — **vīja**, see *-bīja*. — **vīra**, m. 'g°-chief,' Phaseolus Radiatus, L. — **śīrshaka**, n. the ear of corn, L. — **śūka**, n. the awn or beard of c°, L. — **śaila-dāna**, n. N. of ch. of MatsyaP. (cf. *-parvata-dāna-vidhi*). — **śreshṭha**, n. 'the best of c°,' a kind of rice, L. — **saṃgraha**, m. a store or magazine of grain, W. — **sāra**, m. 'essence of g°,' threshed corn, L. **Dhānyâṃśa**, m. a grain of corn, L. **Dhānyā-kṛit** (for °*nya-kṛ*° or = °*nyâkṛ*°), m. cultivator of g°, RV. x, 94, 13. **Dhānyâcala**, m. a pile of g° for presentation to Brāhmans, W. (cf. °*nya-parvata* & *-śaila*). **Dhānyâdá**, mfn. eating corn, Br. **Dhānyâbhra** & °**raka**, n. a partic. preparation of talc, Bhpr. **Dhānyâmla**, n. sour rice-gruel, Suśr. **Dhānyâri**, m. 'enemy of corn,' a mouse, L. **Dhānyârgha**, m. the price of c°, Var. **Dhānyârtha**, m. wealth in rice or grain, W. **Dhānyâsthi**, n. threshed corn, L. **Dhānyôttama**, m. 'the best of grain,' rice, L.

Dhānyaka (ifc. for *dhānya*), grain, corn, Mn.; MBh.; m. N. of a man, Daś.; Rājat.; n. = *dhānyāka*, coriander (cf. *dhanyāka*).

Dhānyeya, n. coriander, Gal.

1. **Dhāma**, m. pl. N. of a class of superhuman beings, MBh.; n. abode &c. = *dhāman*, L.

2. **Dhāma**, in comp. for °*man*, below. — **keśin**, mfn. 'ray-haired' (the sun), MBh. iii, 193. — **chád**, mfn. hiding (i. e. changing) his abode; m. N. of Agni, TS.; VS.; of a Vashaṭ-kāra, AitBr. iii, 7; of VS. xviii, 76, ŚBr. — **dhā́**, m. causer of order or founder of homesteads, RV. ix, 86, 28. — **nidhi**, m. 'treasure of splendour,' the sun, L. — **bhāj**, mfn. possessing seats (the gods), ŚāṅkhBr. x, 6. — **mānin**, mfn. believing in a place, i. e. in a material existence, BhP. iii, 11, 38. — **vat**, mfn. powerful, strong, Kir. i, 43. — **śas**, ind. according to place or order, RV. i, 164, 15. — **sā́c**, mfn. keeping a certain place (Indra), RV. iii, 51, 2 ('possessing riches,' Sāy.) **Dhāmâdhipa**, m. 'lord of rays,' the sun, Prab. iv, $\frac{3}{3}\frac{0}{1}$.

Dhā́man, n. dwelling-place, house, abode, domain, RV. &c. &c. (esp. seat of the gods, cf. *madhyamaṃ dhāma Vishṇoḥ*, Śak. [Pi. iv, 5]; site of the sacred fire and the Soma, RV. &c.; with *priyam*, favourite residence, VS.; Br.); favourite thing or person, delight, pleasure, VS.; AV.; Br.; the inmates of a house or members of a family, class, troop, band, host (also pl.), RV. &c.; law, rule, established order (esp. of Mitra-Varuṇa), RV.; AV.; state, condition, Prab. i, 30; manner, mode, tone, form, appearance (esp. in sacrifice, song &c.), RV.; VS.; effect, power, strength, majesty, glory, splendour, light, RV. &c.; MBh.; Kāv.; Pur.; m. N. of one of the 7 Ṛishis of the 4th Manv-antara (v. l. *dhātṛi*), Hariv. [Cf. Gk. θημον in εὐ-θήμων; θαμά, θωμός &c.; Lat. *fam-ulus*; Angl. Sax. *dôm*; Goth. *domas*; Germ. *tuom* & suff. *-tum*.]

Dhāya, mfn. having, possessing &c. (also *-ka*, Pāṇ. vii, 3, 33, Kāś.); m. layer, stratum, Kauś.

1. **Dhāyu**, mfn. giving, liberal (Indra), RV. iii, 30, 7.

Dhāyya, mfn., g. *dig-ādi* (Kāś. °*yā*); m. a Purohita or family priest, W.; (*ā*), f. (scil. *ṛic*) an additional verse inserted in certain hymns, TS.; Br. &c.

1. **Dhāsí**, f. dwelling-place, seat, home, RV.

धाटी *dhāṭi*, f. assault, L. — **pañcaka** and -**rahasya**, n. N. of wks.

धाडुनृत्य *dhāḍu-nṛitya*, n. a kind of dance (mus.)

धाणक *dhāṇaka*, m. (√1. *dhā*? cf. Uṇ. iii, 83) a weight of gold, part of a Dīnāra (cf. 2. *dhān*°), L.; (*dhāṇikā*), f. pudendum muliebre (?), TS. (Comm. 'a pregnant woman'); AV.; (°*ṇikī*), f., see *maṇḍūra-dh*°.

धातक *dhātaka*, n. = *dhāṭi*, Gal.

धातकि *dhātaki*, m. N. of one of the 2 sons of Vīti-hotra Praiyavrata (king of a Varsha of Pushkara-dvīpa), Pur.; (*ī*), f. Grislea Tomentosa, Suśr. — °**ki-tīrtha**, n. N. of a Tīrtha, ŚivaP. — °**kī-khaṇḍa** & -**shaṇḍa**, n. N. of a Varsha of Pushkara-dvīpa ruled by Dhātaki, Pur.

धातु 2. *dhātu*, mfn. (√*dhe*) to be sucked in or drunk (*havis*), RV. v, 44, 3, f. = *dhenu*, milch cow, Lāṭy. vii, 5, 9.

Dhā́yas, mfn. nourishing, refreshing, strengthening, sustaining, satisfying (cf. *ari-*, *kāra-*, *go-* &c.); n. the act of nourishing &c., RV. **Dhāyin**, see *amṛita-dh*° (add.) 2. **Dhāyú**, mfn. voracious, RV. vii, 36, 4.

Dhārú, mfn. sucking (acc.), AV. iv, 18, 2 (cf. Pāṇ. iii, 2, 159).

2. **Dhāsí**, m. milk-beverage; any drink, nourishment, refreshment, RV. **Dhāsyú**, mfn. desirous of drinking or eating, AV.

धातु 3. *dhātu*, n. (with *rauhiṇa*) N. of a Sāman, ĀrshBr.

धातृ *dhātṛí*, *dhātrī*, &c. See col. 1.

धानक 2. *dhānaka*, m. a partic. coin of a certain weight (=4 *Kārshāpaṇas*), Car.; Hcat.

धानंजय्य *dhānaṃjayya*, m. patron. fr. *dhanam-jaya*, N. of a teacher, Lāṭy.; mfn. relating to Dhānaṃjayya, ib.

धानद *dhānada*, mf(ī)n. relating to Dhanada i.e. Kubera, ShaḍvBr. v, 1.

धानपत *dhānapata*, mf(ī)n. relating to Dhana-pati i.e. Kubera, g. *aśva-paty-ādi*.

धानश्री *dhānaśrī*, f. (in music) N. of a Rāga.

Dhānasī, f. (in music) N. of a Rāgiṇī.

धानाक *dhānāka*, m. patr. of Luśa (fr. *dhanāka*), RV. Anukr.; n. N. of 2 Sāmans, ĀrshBr.

धानुर्दण्डिक *dhānurdaṇḍika*, mf(ī)n. (fr. *dhanus* + *daṇḍa*) living by bow and club, Pāṇ. iv, 4, 12, Sch.

Dhānurveda, m. = *dhanur-veda*, HPariś.

Dhānushka, mf(*ī*)n. armed with a bow; m. bowman, archer, MBh. (-*tā*, f. Bhartṛ. i, 13, v. l.); (*ā*), f. Achyranthes Aspera, L.

Dhānushkari, N. of a plant (prob. w. r. for *dhanush-k*), Lalit.

Dhānushya, m. 'suitable for bows,' a bamboo, L.

धान्त *dhānta* (or *dhvānta*?), mystical N. of the letter *n*, Up.

धान्धा *dhāndhā*, f. small cardamoms, L.

धान्ध्य *dhāndhya*, n. indisposition, L. (cf. *dhandha*).

धान्य 2. *dhānya*, n. (fr. *dhana*) the being rich, richness, Dhātup. xx, 3.

धान्यायन *dhānyāyana*, m. patr. fr. *dhanya*, g. *aśvâdi*.

धान्व *dhānva*, mf(ī)n. (fr. *dhanvan*) = *dhanva-ja*, Car.; (°*vá*), m. patr. of Asita (chief of the Asuras), ŚBr.

1. **Dhānvana**, mf(*ī*)n. situated in a desert, Kām.; m. = prec. m., ŚāṅkhŚr.

धान्वन 2. *dhānvana*, mf(ī)n. made from the wood of the Dhanvana tree, ŚāṅkhŚr.; Suśr.

धान्वन्तर *dhānvantara* (Suśr.) or °*rīya* (Cat.) or °*rya* (MBh.), mfn. relating to or proceeding from Dhanvan-tari (see s.v.)

धान्वपत *dhānvapata*, mf(ī)n. relating to Dhanva-pati, g. *aśva paty-ādi*.

धामक *dhāmaka*, m. a sort of weight (= *māshaka*), L.

धामनिका *dhāmanikā*, f. (fr. *dhamanī*?) Solanum Jacquini, L.

Dhāmanī, f. Hemionitis Cordifolia, L.; any tubular vessel of the body (= *dhamani*), ib.

धामार्ग *dhāmārga*, m. a kind of plant, Car. (prob. = next). °**gava**, m. Luffa Foetida or a similar plant, Suśr.; Achyranthes Aspera, L.; patr. of Vadiśa, Car.

धार 1. *dhāra*, mf(ī)n. (√*dhṛi*) holding, supporting, containing (ifc.; cf. *karṇa-*, *chattra-*, *tulā-* &c.); m. N. of Vishṇu, L.; debt, L.

1. **Dhāraka**, mfn. = prec. (ifc.; cf. *kula-*, *deha-*, *nāma-* &c.); keeping in the memory (with gen.), Kāraṇḍ.; m. a receptacle or vessel for anything, Suśr.; a water-pot, L.; (*ikā*), f. prop, pillar, Hcat.; a division of time (=6 Kshaṇas = ½ Muhūrta), L.; (*dhārakā*), f. the vulva of a female, VS.; ŚBr.

Dhāraṇa, mf(*ī*)n. holding, bearing, keeping (in remembrance), retention, preserving, protecting, maintaining, possessing, having (ifc. or with gen.), TĀr.; MBh.; Suśr.; BhP.; assuming the shape of (gen.), resembling, MBh. xiii, 739; m. N. of Śiva, MBh.; of a son of Kaśyapa, ib.; of a prince of the Candravatsas, ib.; du. the two female breasts, L.; (*dhāraṇa*), n. the act of holding, bearing &c., ŚBr.; Mn.; Yājñ.; MBh. &c.; wearing (see *liṅga-*); suffering, enduring, R.; keeping in remembrance, memory, TĀr.; Mn.; MBh.; Hariv.; immovable concentration of the mind upon (loc.), Vedântas.; restraining (cf. *śvāsa-*); keeping back i.e. pronouncing imperfectly, Prāt.; (*ā* & *ī*), f., see *dhāraṇā* & °*ṇī*. — **pātra**, n. a kind of vessel or receptacle, Buddh. — **mātṛikā**, f. one of the 64 arts, BhP., Sch. — **yantra**, n. a kind of amulet, Tantras. — **lakshaṇa**, n. N. of wk. **Dhāraṇâdhyayana**, n. the conservative method of reading (i. e. the rehearsing of a work to keep it in memory, as opp. to *grahaṇâdh*°, the acquisitive method), L. **Dharaṇânvita**, mfn. endowed with a good memory, Kām.

Dhāraṇaka, mfn. holding, containing, consisting of (cf. *a-*, *pañca-*); m. a debtor, Yājñ. ii, 63.

Dhāraṇā, f. (cf. °*ṇa*, col. 1) the act of holding, bearing, wearing, supporting, maintaining, MBh.; R.; retaining, keeping back (also in remembrance), a good memory, KaṭhUp.; GṛS.; MBh.; BhP.; collection or concentration of the mind (joined with the retention of breath), Mn.; MBh.; Suśr.; Kāv.; Pur. &c.; cf. MWB. 239 (°*ṇām* √*dhṛi*, to exercise concentration, Yājñ.; °*ṇām gataḥ*, having composed one's self, R.); understanding, intellect, Yājñ. iii, 73; firmness, steadfastness, righteousness, L.; fixed precept or settled rule, certainty, Mn.; MBh.; pl. the 8th to the 11th day in the light half of month Jyaishṭha, Var. — °**tmaka** (°*ṇât*°), mf(*ikā*)n. that whose nature consists in bearing itself, Sūryas.; one who easily collects or composes himself, Suśr. — **pāraṇa-vrata**, n. N. of wk. — **maya**, mf(*ī*)n. consisting in abstraction of the mind, BhP. — **yukta**, mfn. connected with abstr° of the m°, MBh. — **yoga**, m. abstr° of the m°, deep devotion, MW. — **vat**, mfn. connected with memory, L.

Dhāraṇi, m. patr. (fr. *dhāraṇa*?), g. *taulvaly-ādi*.

Dhāraṇī, f. any tubular vessel of the body, L.; the earth, Gal.; a partic. bulbous plant, ib.; a mystical verse or charm used as a kind of prayer to assuage pain &c., MWB. 154; 351 &c. (4 kinds of Dh°s according to Dharmas. lii); row or line (w. r. for *dhoraṇī*), L.; N. of a daughter of Sva-dhā, VP. — **mati**, m. (?) N. of a Samādhi, L. — **mukha-sarva-jagat-praṇidhi-saṃdhāraṇa-garbha**, m. N. of a Bodhi-sattva. — **rāja**, m. N. of a Buddh. wk.

Dhāraṇīya, mfn. to be held or borne or sustained &c.; (*ā*) f. a partic. bulbous plant (= *dharaṇī-kanda*), L.

Dhāraya, mfn. holding, bearing &c. (Pāṇ. iii. 1, 138); owing a sum (gen.) to (dat.), L.

Dhārayat, mf(*antī*)n. holding, possessing, maintaining &c. (cf. below); acquainted with, versed in, W. — **kavi** (°*yát-k*°), mfn. supporting or cherishing sages, RV. — **kshiti** (°*yát-ksh*°), mfn. bearing or sustaining creatures, ib. **Dhāráyad-vat**, mfn. possessing the quality of sustaining or supporting (Ādityas), TS.

Dhārayāṇa, mfn. bearing, holding, supporting, containing &c., MW. (cf. Vām. v, 2, 83).

Dhārayitavya, mfn. to be borne or held, Var.; Prab.; to be perceived or understood, Saṃk. °**rayitṛi**, m. holder, bearer, restrainer, MBh.; R.; who keeps anything in remembrance, TĀr.; (*trī*), f. the earth, L. °**rayishṇu**, mfn. capable of bearing or accustomed to bear, Pāṇ. iii, 2, 137, Kāś.; -*tā*, f. patience, Kām.

Dhāri, mfn. holding, bearing, Sch.

Dhārita, mfn. borne (also in the womb), held, supported &c., TĀr.: MBh.; n. (also °*taka*) a horse's trot, W. (w. r. for *dhorita*, °*taka*).

1. **Dhārin**, mfn. bearing, wearing, holding, possessing, keeping in one's memory, maintaining, observing (with gen. or ifc.), Mn.; MBh.; Kāv. &c.; = *poshka* (?), Hariv. 11986 (Nīlak.); m. Careya Arborea or Salvadora Persica, L.; (*iṇī*), f. the earth, L. (cf. *bhūta-*); N. of a daughter of Sva-dhā, BhP. (cf. °*raṇī*); N. of a deity, Jain.; of the wife of Agni-mitra, Mālav.; of other women, HPariś.; pl. a collect. N. of the 74 wives of the gods, VahniP.

1. **Dhārya**, mfn. to be borne or worn or carried &c., MBh. (-*tva*, n., L.); (*daṇḍa*) to be inflicted or imposed on (dat.), ib. v, 7526; to be kept (also in the memory), to be upheld or maintained, MBh.; Hariv.; Suśr. &c.; to be observed or followed (order, vow, &c.), Hariv.; to be called to mind (*cetasi*) or attended to, Kāv.; to be suffered or put up with (said of a servant), Pañc.; to be kept back or restrained, MBh.; n. clothes, BhP.

Dhāryamāṇa, mfn. being held, maintained &c. — **tva**, n. possession, property, W.

धार 2. *dhāra*, m. or n. (√1. *dhāv*) stream, gush (cf. *taila-* [add.] & *toya-*); mfn. coming down in a stream or as rain, Suśr.; Bhpr. — **pūta** (*dhā*°), mfn. pure as a stream of water (Ādityas), RV. ii, 27, 2; 9. — **lopaka**, m. or n. N. of a partic. observance, Cat. — **vāká**, mfn. whose praises are pure or gush forth like water, v, 44, 5.

Dhārayú, mfn. streaming, dripping (Soma), RV. ix, 67, 1.

1. **Dhā́rā**, f. stream or current of water; (cf. *tri-*, *dvi-*, *śata-*, *sahasra-*), flood, gush, jet, drop (of any liquid), shower, rain (also fig. of arrows, flowers, &c.; *vásor dh*°, 'source of good,' N. of a partic. libation to Agni, AV.; ŚBr., MBh.; of a sacred bathing-place, MBh.; of Agni's wife, BhP.); a leak or hole in a pitcher &c., L.; the pace of a horse, Śiś. v, 60 (5 enumerated, viz. *dhorita*, *valgita*, *pluta*, *ut-tejita*, *ut-tērita*, or *ā-skandita*, *recita* for the two latter, L.; with *paramā*, the quickest pace, Kathās. xxxi, 39); uniformity, sameness (as of flowing water?), L.; custom, usage, W.; continuous line or series (cf. *vana-*); fig. line of a family, L.; N. of a sacred bathing-place (also with *māheśvarī*, cf. above), MBh.; of a town (the residence of Bhoja), Cat. — **kadamba**, m. Nauclea Cordifolia, Kād. (also °*baka* L.); N. of a poet, Cat. — **gṛiha**, n. a bath-room with flowing water, shower-bath, Suśr.; Kāv.; -*tva*, n. Vcar. — **graha**, m. a cup filled from flowing Soma, KātyŚr. — **ghosha**, m. the noise of milk flowing into a bucket, ĀpŚr. — °**ṅkura** (°*rāṅk*), m. a rain-drop, L.; hail, VarBṛS. xxxii, 21; advancing before the line of an army to defy an enemy, L. — 1. -**ṅga** (°*rāṅga*), m. a sacred bathing-place, L. — °**ṭa** (°*rāṭa*), m. the Cātaka bird (fond of rain-drops), L.; a horse (going in paces, see above), L.; a cloud (filled with drops), L.; a furious elephant (emitting rut-fluid), L. — 1. -**dhara**, m. 'water-bearer,' a cloud, MBh.; Hariv. &c.; °*rāgama*, m. 'cloud-coming,' the rainy season, Kād.; °*rātyaya*, m. 'c°-ceasing,' autumn, Car.; °*rôdyāna*, n. c°-garden,' N. of a grove, Priyad. — **dhvaṃsa**, N. of a poem, Cat. — **dhvani**, m. the sound of falling rain or flowing water, W. — **nipāta**, m. rain-shower, Pañc. — °**nuyāja** (°*rān*°), m. a secondary sacrifice connected with a libation, KātyŚr., Sch. — **pāta**, m. (only pl.) = -*nipāta*, Mṛicch.; Megh. — **yantra**, n. 'water-machine,' a fountain, Kāv.; -*gṛiha*, n. a bath-room with fountains, Kathās. — **yāja**, m. a sacrifice connected with a libation, KātyŚr., Sch. — **vatī**, f. N. of a town, PadmaP. — **vani**, m. wind, L. (cf. next). — **vará**, mfn. fond of showers (Maruts), RV. ii, 34, 1 (cf. prec.) — **varta** (°*rāv*°), m. whirlpool; (*ena*, ind.) fluently, quickly, Hcat. — **varsha**, m.n. a torrent of rain, Kāv. — **vāsa**, m. N. of a town, Pañcad. — **śīta**, mfn. (milk) cooled after having been milked, Bhpr. — °**śru** (°*rāśru*), n. a flood of tears, Amar. — **sampāta**, m. = -*nipāta*, Prab. — °**sāra** (°*rās*°), m. id., Kāv.; Hit. — **sūra**, m. or n. N. of a place situated on the river Go-dāvarī, Cat. **Dhārêśvara**, m. the lord of Dhārā i.e. King Bhoja, Cat. **Dhārôrmi**, m. or f. a rolling or heaving wave, MBh. **Dhārôshṇa**, mfn. warm from the cow (milk), Suśr.

Dhārāya, Nom. Ā. °*yate*, to be like a stream, Amar. 10, Sch.

Dhārāla, mfn., g. *sidhmâdi*.

धार 3. *dhāra*, m. a sort of stone, L.; edge, boundary, L. (cf. 2. *dhārā*); deep place, depth, W. (to 1. *dhāra*?).

2. **Dhāraka**, ifc. = prec. or next; cf. *tri-*.

धारा 2. *dhārā*, f. (√2. *dhāv*) margin, sharp edge, rim, blade (esp. of a sword, knife, &c.; fig. applied to the flame of fire), RV.; ŚBr.; MBh.; Kāv. &c.; the edge of a mountain, L.; the rim of a wheel, Ragh. xiii, 15; the fence or hedge of a garden, L.; the van of an army, L.; the tip of the ear, L.; highest point, summit (cf. °*rādhirūḍha*); glory, excellence, L.; night, L.; turmeric, L. — °**gra** (°*rāg*°), n. the broad-edged head of an arrow, L. — 2. °**ṅga** (°*rāṅ*°), m. sword, L. — **jala**, n. blood dripping from the edge of a sword, Kād.; Prasannar. — °**ñcala** (°*rāñ*°), m. the e° of a s°, Prasannar. — 2. -**dhara**, m. sword, L.; — °**dhirūḍha** (°*rādh*°), mfn. elevated to the highest point or pitch, Kathās. vi, 62. — °**ntara-cara** (°*rânt*°), mfn. 'moving among swords,' daring, audacious, impudent, R. (v. l. *dharânt*° & *hārânt*°). — **patha**, m. 'rim-path,' i. e. the rut (of a wheel), Dharmaś.; the reach of a blade; °*tham prâpay*, to cause to perish by the blade of (gen.), Veṇis. iii, 7. — **payas**, n. = -*jala*, Vcar. — **phala**, m. N. of a tree with prickly fruits (= *madana*), L. — °**mbhas** (°*râm*°), n. = -*ra-jala*, Prasannar. — **vat**, mfn. having an edge, edged, Kām.; (*vatī*), f., see 1. *dhārā*. — **visha**, m. 'having a poisoned edge,' a sword, scimitar, L. **-salila**, n. = *-jala*, Dharmaś. **-snuhī**, f. N. of a plant, L.

धार्त *dhārta*, Vṛiddhi form of *dhṛita*, in comp. **-rājña**, m. patr. fr. Dhṛita-rājan, Pāṇ. vi, 4, 135 (mfn. Vop.); (*ī*), f., g. *dhūmâdi* to iv, 2, 127; °*jñaka*, mfn. ib. **-rāshṭra**, mf(*ī*)n. belonging to Dhṛita-rāshṭra, MBh.; m. a son of Dhṛ°, a Kuru (cf. *nir-*), esp. patr. of Dur-yodhana (ifc. f. *ā*), ib.; a kind of snake, L.; (fr. *dhṛita-rāshṭrī*) a sort of goose with black legs and bill, Hariv.; Kād.; *-padī*, f. N. of a plant, L. **-rāshṭri**, m. N. of a serpent-demon, Kauś.

Dhārteyá, m. pl. (prob. fr. *dhṛita*), N. of a warlike tribe; sg. a prince of this tribe, f. *ī*, g. *yaudheyâdi*.

धार्म 1. *dhārmá*, mf(*ī*)n. (fr. *dharma*) relating to justice or virtue, ŚBr.; belonging to Dharma (god of justice), MBh.

2. **Dhārma**, Vṛiddhi form of *dharma* in comp. **-pata**, mf(*ī*)n. relating to Dharma-pati, g. *asva-paty-ādi*. **-pattana**, n. black pepper, L. **-vidya**, mfn. familiar with the law, a lawyer, jurist, Pāṇ. iv, 2, 60, Vārtt. 4, Pat.

Dhārmika, mf(*ī*)n. righteous, virtuous, pious, just, Up.; Mn.; MBh. &c.; resting on right, conformable to justice (mind, words &c.), R.; m. judge, L.; a bigot, Kād.; juggler, Ratn.; a Bodhi-sattva, L. **-tā**, f. (Rājat.), **-tva** (Kull.) & °**kya** (g. *purohitâdi*), n. righteousness, justice, virtue.

Dhārmiṇa, n. an assemblage of virtuous men, g. *bhikshâdi* (iv, 2, 38).

Dhārmiṇeya, metr. fr. *dharmiṇī*, g. *śubhrâdi*.

Dhārmuka, mfn. just, righteous, MānŚr. i, 6, 1.

Dhārmya, w. r. for *dharmya*.

Dhārmyāyaṇa, m. patr. fr. *dharmya*, g. *aśvâdi*.

धार्ष्ट *dhārshṭa*, mf(*ī*)n. (BhP.), °*ṭaka* (Hariv. [v. l. °*shṇaka*]; VP.) proceeding or descended fr. Dhṛishṭa.

Dhārshṭadyumna or °**mni**, m. patr. fr. Dhṛishṭa-dyumna, MBh.

Dhārshṭya, n. boldness, audacity, violence, Var.; R.; Suśr. &c.

Dhārshṇaka (w. r. for °**ṇava**), mfn. descended fr. Dhṛishṇu, Hariv. 642 (v. l. °*ṭaka*; cf. above).

धाव् 1. *dhāv*, cl. 1. P. Ā. *dhā́vati*, °*te* (pf. *dadhāva*, °*ve*, Gr.; aor. *adadhāvat*, RV.; *adhāvīt*, Br.; Prec. *dhāvyāsam*, Gr.; fut. *dhāvishyati*, Kāv., °*te* & *dhāvitā*, Gr.; ind. p. *dhāvitvā* & °*vya*, Kāv.; *dhautvā*, Gr.) to run, flow, stream, move, glide, swim, RV. &c. &c.; to run after (with or scil. *paścāt*), Mn.; MBh. &c. = seek for (acc.), Kir. ii, 29; run towards (*-abhimukham*), Hit., run a race (*ājim*) Br., run as fast as possible (*sarvam javam*) ib.; run to and fro (*itas cêtas ca*), MBh.; Hit.; run away, flee, RV.; AV.; to advance or rush against (acc.), MBh.; R.; (*prati*), Kathās.: Caus. *dhāvâyati* (aor. *adīdhavat*, Gr.) to make run, impel, Pañc.; to drive in a chariot, (with instr. of the vehicle and acc. of the way), Br.; to jump, dance, RV. x, 146, 2. (Cf. √2. *dhan, dhanv, dhav*; 1. *dhū*.)

Dhāvaka, mfn. running; *purato dh*°, m. forerunner, R. **Dhāvat**, mf(*ntī*)n. running, quick.

1. **Dhāvana**, n. running, Suśr.; galloping, Sāh.; attack, assault, Rājat.

Dhā́vamāna, mfn. running, going quickly, RV.

1. **Dhāvita**, mfn. running, having begun to run, Kath. iii, 52. °**vitṛi**, m. runner, courser, MBh. °**vin**, mfn. running, going quickly, Naish.

धाव् 2. *dhāv*, cl. 1. P. Ā. *dhāvati*, °*te* (pf. *dadhāva*, Bhaṭṭ.; aor. *-adhāvishṭa*, RV. ix, 70, 8; ind. p. *dhautvā*, Prab. iv, 23 [v. l. *dhūtvā*] & *-dhāvya*, Kauś.) to rinse, cleanse, wash, purify, polish, make bright (Ā. also to rub one's self with, rub into one's own person), RV. &c. &c.: Pass. *dhāvyate* (pf. 3. pl. *-dadhāvire*), Śiś.: Caus. *dhāvayati*, °*te*, to cleanse, wash, Br.; Mn.; MBh. &c.; cause to be washed, L.: Desid. *didhāvishati*, °*te*; Intens. *dādhāvyate*, Gr.

Dhāva, mfn. washing, cleansing (ifc.; cf. *asi-*, *caila-*); m., see *danta-*. °**vaka**, mfn. id.; m. a washerman, Kathās.

2. **Dhāvana**, mfn., see *bila-*; n. washing, cleansing, rubbing off or in, Suśr.; MBh.; R. (cf. *manaḥśilā-candana-dh*° & *mīna-dh*°*-toya*); having a garment washed by a man that is not one's kin, Buddh.

Dhāvanī, f. Uraria Lagopodioides, Bhpr.; °**ni**, f. Solanum Jacquini or Grislea Tomentosa, L.; °**nikā**, f. Solanum Jacquini, L.

2. **Dhāvita**, mfn. purified, clean, MBh.

धावल्य *dhāvalya*, n. (fr. *dhavala*) whiteness, Śiś. iv, 65, Sch.

धासस् *dhāsas*, m. (√1. *dhā*?) a mountain, Uṇ. iv, 220, Sch.

धि 1. *dhi*, cl. 6. P. *dhiyati* (*didhāya*, *dheshyati* &c.) to hold (Dhātup. xxviii, 113). Prob. abstracted fr. √1. *dhā*, of which it is the weak form.

2. **Dhi**, m. receptacle (only ifc.; cf. *ambu-*, *ishu-* &c.)

1. **Dhita**, mfn. (cf. *hitá* and √1. *dhā*) put, placed, bestowed &c., Hariv. 7799 (cf. *dur-*, *nema-*, *mitra-* &c.) °**tā-van**, mfn. rich in gifts, liberal (Agni), RV. iii, 27, 2; lucrative (sacrifice), 40, 3.

Dhiti, f. See *nemá-*, *mitrá-*, *vaná-*, *vásu-*.

Dhitsya, mfn. (fr. Desid. of √1. *dhā*), Pāṇ. iii, 1, 97, Sch.

धि 3. *dhi* or *dhinv*, cl. 5. P. *dhinoti* (aor. *adhinvīt*, Br.; pf. *didhinva*; fut. *dhinvishyati*, *dhinvitā*, Gr.) to nourish, satiate, satisfy, Br.; to delight, please, Kāv.

2. **Dhita**, mfn. satisfied, pleased, MW.

धि 4. *dhi* = 2. *ádhi* (e.g. in *dhi-shṭhita* [MBh.; BhP.] for *adhi-shṭhita*, q.v.; cf. *pi* = *ápi*, *va* = *áva*).

धिक् *dhik*, ind., used as a prefix or as an interj. of reproach, menace or displeasure = fie! shame! out upon! what a pity! &c. (with acc., rarely gen., voc. or nom.), Up.; Lāṭy.; MBh.; Kāv. &c. (also *dhig dhik*, *aho dhik*, *hā dhik*, *hā dhik kashṭam*, *hā hā dhik* &c.; *dhik tvām* or *tava* [also with *astu*] shame upon you!) **-kāra**, m. reproach, contempt, scoffing, BhP. **-√kṛi**, to reproach, reprimand, curse, MBh.; R. &c. **-kṛita**, mfn. reproached &c.; mocked, derided, Daś.; n. pl. reproach, contempt, ib. **-kriyā**, f. = prec. n. pl., L. **-pārushya**, n. excessive abuse, W.

Dhig, in comp. for *dhik*. **-daṇḍa**, m. reprimand, censure, Mn.; Yājñ.; MBh. **-vāda**, m. reproachful speech, censure, Jātakam.

धिक्क *dhikka*, m. a twenty-year-old elephant, Gal. (cf. 2. *dikka*).

धिक्ष् *dhiksh* (Desid. of √1. *dah*? cf. *dhuksh*), cl. 1. Ā. *dhikshate*, to kindle; to live; to be weary or harassed, Dhātup. xvi, 2.

धिग्वण *dhigvaṇa*, m. (Prākṛit = *dhig-varṇa*?) a man of low or mixed caste (sprung from a Brāhman and an Āyogava woman), Mn. x, 15.

धित *dhita* and *dhitsya*. See above.

धिन्व् *dhinv*. See √3. *dhi*.

धिप्सु *dhipsu*, mfn. (Desid. of √*dambh*) wishing to trick or deceive, deceptive, Bhaṭṭ.

धियंजिन्व *dhiyam-jinvá*, &c. See √1. *dhī*.

धिष् 1. *dhish*, cl. 3. P. *didheshṭi*, to sound, Dhātup. xxv, 22. (Probably invented to explain *dhishaṇā*, speech, hymn; according to Nir. viii, 3 = √1. *dhā*, from which it seems to be a kind of Desid. = *didhishati*.)

2. **Dhish**, only instr. °*shā*, (?) mindfully, zealously, RV. i, 173, 8; iv, 21, 6 (= *prajñā*, *karman*, *stuti*, Sāy.)

Dhisha. See *narám-*.

Dhisháṇa, mfn. intelligent, wise, Hcat.; m. N. of an evil being, AV. ii, 14, 1; of Bṛihas-pati (the regent of the planet Jupiter, also °*nâdhipa*, Matsya-P.), Hcar.; of the pl° J° itself, L.; of a Nārāyaṇa, Cat.; of an astronomer, L.; of a writer on Tājaka wks., Cat.; any Guru or spiritual preceptor, W.; (*ā*), f. a sort of Soma-vessel, a cup, goblet, bowl, fig. the S° juice itself and its effects, RV. (du. the two bowls or worlds, i.e. heaven and earth; pl. h°, e° & the intermediate atmosphere, ib.); knowledge, intelligence (generally ifc.), VarBṛS. civ, 29; BhP. (cf. *agādha-* [add.], *bodha-*, *viśuddha-*); speech, praise, hymn, L.; dwelling-place, abode, seat, BhP.; N. of a deity presiding over wealth and gain (also in pl.), RV.; MBh.; of the wife of Havir-dhāna and daughter of Agni, Hariv.; VP.; of the w° of Kriśāśva and mother of Veda-śira, Devala, Vayuna & Manu, BhP.; n. understanding, intellect, BhP. viii, 5, 39.

1. **Dhishaṇya**, mfn. formed by Yāska (Nir. viii, 3) to explain *dhishṇya*.

2. **Dhishaṇya**, Nom. P.; only p. °*ṇyat*, attentive, zealous, RV. iv, 21, 6.

Dhishṭya and °**ṭhya**, w. r. for *dhishṇya*.

Dhishṇiya, m. = °*ṇya*, 'earth heap'; pl. N. of genii watching the Soma, TS., Comm.

Dhishṇīya, mfn. intended for or belonging to the Dhishṇyas or fire-places, KātyŚr.

Dhishṇya, mfn. mindful, attentive, benevolent, liberal (Aśvins), RV. i, 3, 2; 89, 4 &c.; devout, pious (voice, hymn), x, 114, 9; m. (f. *ā* only RV. iv, 3, 6; n. MBh. i, 7944) a sort of subordinate or side-altar (generally a heap of earth covered with sand on which the fire is placed, and of which 8 are enumerated, viz. besides the *Āgnīdhrīya* [in the Āgnīdhra] those in the Sadas [see s. v.] belonging to the *Hotṛi*, the *Maitrā-varuṇa* or *Pra-śastṛi*, the *Brāhmaṇâcchaṅsin*, the *Potṛi*, *Neshṭṛi* & *Acchā-vāka*; and the *Mārjālīya*), Br.; ŚrS. &c. (cf. *klṛipta-*) &c.; N. of Uśanas, i.e. the planet Venus, L. (cf. *dhishaṇa*); (*ā*) f. a meteor, Var. (n. only MBh. v, 7272); n. site, place, abode, region, house, MBh.; Kāv.; Pur. &c.; the seat of a god, i. e. a quarter of the sky, VP.; star, asterism (looking like the fire on the side-altars), Var.; the orb of an asterism (on which its light seems to centre), MBh.; VP.; power, strength, L.; mfn. placed upon a mound of earth serving as an altar, AV.; Br. &c.; m. (with or scil. *agni*) a fire so placed, VS.; TS. &c. **-pa**, m. the guardian of a quarter of the sky, BhP. **-vat**, mfn. having a Dhishṇya or side-altar, ŚrS. **-homa**, m. a sacrifice offered in a Dh°, Vait. **Dhishṇyâdhipati**, m. = *-pa*, VP.

धी 1. *dhī*, cl. 3. Ā. *dīdhīte*, &c., RV. (cf. √*dīdhī*; the forms *dhīmahi* and *ádhāyi* belong rather to √1. *dhā*; pf. *dīdhaya*, °*dhima*, °*dhiyur* or °*dhyur*, °*dhire*, RV.; AV.; Br.) to perceive, think, reflect; wish, desire: Intens. *dedhyat*, TS.

Dhiya, Nom. P. °*yati* (fr. 2. *dhī*), Pat.

Dhiyam &c., obl. cases of 2. *dhī* in comp. **-jinvá**, mfn. exciting meditation or devotion, RV. **-dhā**, mfn. reflecting, devout, pious, wise, RV. **Dhiyā-júr**, mfn. worn out or grown old in devotion, RV. v, 43, 15. **Dhiyām-pati**, m. 'lord of the thoughts,' the soul, L.; N. of Mañju-ghosha, L. **Dhiyā-vasu**, mfn. rich in devotion, RV.

Dhiyasāna, mfn. attentive, mindful, RV.

Dhiyāya, Nom. Ā. °*yate*, to be attentive or devout; p. °*yat*, mindful, RV. °**yú**, mfn. thoughtful, devout, pious, ib.

2. **Dhī́**, f. thought, (esp.) religious thought, reflection, meditation, devotion, prayer (pl. Holy Thoughts personif.), RV.; understanding, intelligence, wisdom (personif. as the wife of Rudra-Manyu, BhP.), knowledge, science, art; mind, disposition, intention, design (ifc. intent upon, Kāv.); notion, opinion, the taking for (comp.), RV. &c. &c. (*yáthā dhiyā́* or *dhiyā́ ná*, according to thy wisdom or will; *itthā́ dhiyā́* or *dhīyaḥ*, willingly, lit. such is thy will, RV.); N. of the 5th house from the Lagna, Var. **-karman**, n. the object of perception or understanding, Sarvad. **-koṭi**, f. N. of wk. **-jaḍa**, m. N. of a man, Cat. **-jávana** or **-jū́**, mfn. inspiring the mind or rousing devotion, RV. **-°ndriya** (*dhīnd°*), n. an organ of perception, L. **-mat**, mfn. intelligent, wise, learned, sensible, Mn.; MBh. &c.; m. N. of Bṛihas-pati, L.; of a son of Virāj, VP.; of a Ṛishi in the 4th Manv-antara, ib.; of a son of Purū-ravas, MBh.; a Bodhi-sattva, L. **-maraṇa**, m. (*miśra-dhī-m°*) N. of a man, Cat. **-raṇa** (*dhī-*), mfn. delighting in devotion, RV. **-rāja**, m. N. of one of the attendants of Śiva, L. **-vat** (*dhī-*), mfn. intelligent or devout, RV. **-vibhrama**, m. 'error of thought,' hallucination, Bhpr. **-vṛiddhi-da**, m. or n. N. of wk., Cat. (also *śishya-dhī-vṛ°*). **-śakti**, f. mental or intellectual faculty, L. **-śodhinī**, f. N. of wk. **-sakha** (L.) or **-saciva** (Rājat.), m. wise counsellor, minister. **-harā**, f. a kind of sweet gourd, L.

1. **Dhītá**, mfn. reflected on, thought about; n. pl. thoughts, meditations, RV.

1. **Dhītí**, f. thought, idea, reflection, intention, devotion, prayer (pl. also personified; cf. 2. *dhī*), RV.; TBr. &c.; pl. wisdom, understanding (Naigh. ii, 5 & Sāy. 'the fingers'), RV.

Dhītika, m. N. of a Buddh. patriarchal saint.

1. **Dhīdā**, f. intelligence, understanding, L.

1. **Dhīra**, mf(*ī* or *ā*)n. intelligent, wise, skilful, clever, familiar with, versed in (loc.), RV. &c. &c. (compar. *dhīra-tara*, AV.; R.); m. N. of a Buddha, L.; of sev. men with the patr. Śātaparṇeya, ŚBr. **— 1. -tā**, f., 1. **-tva**, n. wisdom, discretion, Cāṇ. **— rañjanikā**, f. N. of Comm. on Kum. **Dhīrêndra**, m. N. of an author, Cat. **Dhīrêśa-miśra**, m. N. of a teacher, ib. **Dhīrêśvara**, m. N. of the father of Jyotir-iśvara (author of Dhūrtas.)

Dhī́van, mf(*varī*)n. skilful, clever, AV.; m. an artisan, Uṇ., Sch.; a fisherman, L. (cf. next).

Dhīvara, m. a very clever man, Subh.; (also °*raka*) a fisherman, MBh., Kāv. &c. (as a mixed caste, Gaut. iv, 19); (*ī*), f. (cf. prec.) a fisherman's wife, Kathās.; a sort of harpoon for catching fish, Uṇ., Sch.; a fish-basket, ib.; n. iron, L.

धी 3. *dhī*, cl. 4. Ā. *dhīyate*, to contain, hold (Pass. of √1. *dhā*?); to slight, disregard; to propitiate (?), Dhātup. xxvi, 37.

धी 4. *dhī́*, f. for *dī*, splendour, RV. iii, 34, 5; vi, 3, 3.

धीक्ष् *dhīksh* (Desid. of √*dih*), cl. 1. Ā. *dhīkshate*, to wish to anoint, ŚBr.

धीत 2. *dhītá* (√*dhe*), sucked, drunk, AV.; Br. **— rasa**, mfn. whose juice has been sucked out, Br.

2. **Dhīti**, f. drinking; thirst, L.

धीता *dhītā* (Buddh.) and 2. *dhīdā* (Mṛicch.; Ratn.), f. (Pāli & Prākṛit forms for *duhitā*) daughter.

धीतीका *dhitīkā*, f. (√1. *dhā*?) layer, Car. (v. l. *dīrghikā*).

धीतोकक *dhītokaka*, m. N. of a poet, Cat.

धीन *dhīna* (?), n. iron, L.

धीर 2. *dhīra*, mf(*ā*)n. (√*dhṛi* or *dhā*? cf. Uṇ. ii, 24) steady, constant, firm, resolute, brave, energetic, courageous, self-possessed, composed, calm, grave, Hariv.; Kāv.; Pur.; deep, low, dull (as sound), Kālid.; Amar. &c.; gentle, soft, L.; well-conducted, well-bred, L.; (*am*), ind. steadily, firmly &c.; m. the ocean, sea (as an image of constancy?); N. of Bali, L.; of other men, Rājat.; f. N. of sev. medic. plants (*kākolī*, *kshīra-kāk*°, *mahā-jyotishmatī*, *medā*, *śveta-vacā*, Rosa Glandulifera), Bhpr.; L.; an intoxicating beverage, L.; a woman who keeps down all expression of resentment or jealousy, Sāh.; N. of a woman, Cat.; n. saffron, L. (not always, esp. in comp., separable from 1. *dhīra*). **— govinda-śarman**, m. N. of an author (c. 1800), Cat. **— cetas**, mfn. strong-minded, self-possessed, courageous, Ragh.; Kathās. **— 2. -tā**, f., 2. **-tva**, n. firmness, fortitude, courage, Kāv.; Pañc., Hit.; suppression of jealous emotions (in women), W.; jealousy, MW. **— dhvani**, m. a deep sound, MW. **— nāga**, m. (*bhadanta*) N. of a poet, Cat. **— pattrī**, f. a partic. bulbous plant, L. **— praśānta**, mfn. deep and calm (*-svara*, mfn. having a d° and c° voice, Sak. ii, 12/13); constant and calm (hero), Sāh.; Bhar. (also °*taka*). **— bhāva**, m. constancy, firmness, Daś. **— lalita**, mfn. firm and brave, but reckless and sportive (hero of a play), Sāh.; (*ā*), f. a kind of metre, Cat. **— śānta**, mfn. brave and calm, Daśar. **— śiva**, m. N. of a man, Cat. **— sattva**, mfn. steadfast, resolute, Kathās. **— skandha**, m. 'strong-shouldered,' a buffalo, L. **Dhīrâdhīrā**, f. a jealous woman who alternately expresses and suppresses her jealousy, Sāh. **Dhīrôdātta**, mfn. brave and noble-minded (hero of a play), Daśar.; Bhar.; Sāh. **Dhīrôddhata**, mfn. brave but haughty, ib. **Dhīrôshṇin**, m. 'brave and fiery,' N. of one of the Viśve Devās, MBh.

Dhīraya, Nom. P. °*yati*, to encourage or comfort, Kathās.

Dhīrī-√kṛi, id., Jātakam.

Dhīrya, mfn. = 2. *dhīra*, ŚāṅkhBr. xix, 3; (*dhīryà*), n. intelligence, prudence, RV. ii, 27, 11.

धीरावी *dhīrāvī*, f. N. of a plant (= *pīta-śiṃsapā*), L.

धीलटी *dhīlaṭī*, f. daughter (cf. *dhītā*, °*dā*), L.

धीवर *dhīvara*. See above.

धु 1. *dhu* = 1. *dhū*, q. v.

2. **Dhu**, f. shaking, trembling, L.

Dhuta, mfn. shaken, agitated; shaken off, removed, abandoned, MBh.; R. &c. **— guṇa** = *dhūta-g*° (q. v.), SaddhP. **— pāpa**, mfn. purified from sin, R.; BhP.

Dhunana, n. shaking, agitation, W. **Dhunāna**, mfn. shaking, agitating, ib. **Dhunvat** (MBh., Kāv. &c.) & °**nvāna** (KātyŚr.), mfn. id.

Dhuvaka, m. one who gets rid of a fetus (= *garbha-mocaka*), Uṇ. ii, 32, Sch.; (*ā*), f. the introductory stanza of a song (forming afterwards the burthen of each verse), W. (cf. g. *prêkshâdi*). °**kin** & °**kila**, mfn., see g. *prêkshâdi* & *picchâdi*.

Dhúvana, m. fire (Vedic), Uṇ. ii, 80, Sch.; n. shaking, agitation, ŚBr.; place of execution, ŚāṅkhGṛ. iv, 12, Sch.

Dhuvitra, n. = *dhavítra*, L.

धु 3. *dhu* = 2. *duh* in *sabar-dhú*, q. v. (cf. 2. *dhru*).

धुक *dhuka*, m. a kind of plant (commonly Bhuyabora or Rānabora), L.; (*ā*), f. id., ib.

धुक्का *dhukkā*, f. (in music) a kind of flute.

धुक्ष् *dhuksh*, cl. 1. Ā. *dhukshate*, &c. (Dhātup. xvi, 1) to kindle; to be weary; to live (occurs only with *sam*).

धुङ्क्षा *dhúṅkshā*, f. a kind of bird, VS. xxiv, 31.

धुन *dhuna*, mfn. (√*dhvan*) roaring, only in °*néti*, mfn. having a roaring course, RV. iv, 50, 2.

Dhunaya, Nom. P. °*yati*, to roar, flow noisily, RV.

Dhúni, mfn. roaring, sounding, boisterous (the Maruts, rivers, the Soma &c.), RV.; VS.; TĀr.; m. N. of a demon slain by Indra, RV.; of a son of the Vasu Āpa, BhP.; (*ī*), f. river (cf. *dyu-dhuni*). **— mat** (*dhú*°), mfn. roaring, noisy, RV. **— vrata** (*dhú*°), mfn. roaring habitually, ib. **Dhúnī-cúmuri**, m. du. the 2 demons Dh° & C°, ib. vi, 20, 13. **Dhunī-nātha**, m. 'lord of the rivers,' the ocean, L.

धुन्धु *dhundhu*, m. N. of an Asura slain by Kuvalâśva (or °layâśva), the father of Sunda, MBh.; Hariv.; R.; Pur.; v. l. for *cuñcu*, VP. **— mat**, mfn. N. of a son of Kevala, ib. (v. l. *bundh*°). **— māra**, m. 'slayer of Dh°,' N. of Kuvalâśva, MBh. &c. (*-tva*, n. Hariv. 672); a son of Tri-śaṅku & father of Yuvanâśva, R.; Daś.; the cochineal insect, L.; a kind of plant (= *gṛiha-dhūma*), L.; a house-lizard (?), W.; the smoke of a house (?), ib.; °*rôpâkhyāna*, n. N. of 3rd ch. of PadmaP. iii. **— han**, m. N. of Kuvalâśva (see above), BhP.

Dhundhuka, n. a partic. defect (or a place full of holes) in a piece of wood, VarBṛS. lxxix, 32; 37.

धुन्धुरि *dhundhuri* (or °*rī*), a partic. musical instrument, BhP. x, 75, 9.

धुमधुमाय *dhumadhumāya*, °*yate*, w. r. for *ghumagh*°, q. v.

धुर् *dhúr*, f. (m. only MBh. xiii, 2876; nom. & stem before a cons. *dhūr*; fr. √*dhṛi*) a yoke; (fig.) burden, load, RV. (v, 43, 8 ?) &c. &c.; pole or shaft of a carriage (esp. their forepart); a peg, pin (cf. *aksha-*); top, summit, front, place of honour (loc. at the head, in front, in presence of), MBh.; Kāv. &c.; a finger, L.; N. of 6 partic. verses of the Bahish-pavamāna, ShaḍvBr.; Lāṭy.; (°*roh śamye* or *sāmanī*, du., & °*rām sāma*, n. N. of Sāmans, ĀrshBr.); (only L.) reflection, recollection; a spark of fire; part, portion; wealth; N. of the Ganges.

Dhuram-dhara, mfn. bearing a yoke or a burden (lit. & fig.), fit to be harnessed, MBh.; Pañc.; helping another (gen.) out of need, Hit.; m. a beast of burden, L.; chief, leader, MBh.; Kāv.; a man of business, W.; N. of Śiva, Śivag.; of a Rakshas, R.; Grislea Tomentosa, L.; pl. N. of a people, MBh.; VP. **Dhūrgata**, **-vaha** &c., see 2. *dhūr*.

Dhúra, m. yoke, pole, burden, peg of the axle (esp. ifc.), MBh. &c.; mfn. having anything as chief (foremost) part or ingredient, distinguished by (ifc.), Bālar. i, 11; (*ā*), f. burden, load, Pañc.; Kathās.; pole, shaft, Pañc. i, 22/23. °**rā-nikshepaṇa** (?), N. of a Caitya of the Mallas, Divyâv. 201. °**rā-vaha**, mfn. bearing a burden, Hariv. 8459.

Dhurikā, f. a small axle-pin, KātyŚr., Sch.

Dhuriṇa, mfn. fit to be harnessed, L.; charged with, bearing (lit. & fig.), W.; m. a beast of burden, L.; a man of business, W.; leader, chief, Pañc.; Hit. (cf. *uttara-*, *eka-*, *dakshiṇa-*, *sarva-*).

Dhurīya, mfn. fit for a burden, L.; charged with important duties, L.; m. a beast of burden, L.; a man of business or affairs, W.

Dhúrya, mfn. (w. r. *dhūrya*) fit o be harnessed, able to draw or bear (Pāṇ. iv, 4, 77); being at the head of, foremost, best, AV.; MBh. &c.; eminently fit for or distinguished by (comp.), Bālar. iii, 2/3; m. beast of burden, horse, bullock &c., Mn.; MBh. &c.; minister, chargé d'affaires, W. (with *mantrin*, Kathās. ix, 14); leader, chief (cf. *kula-*), MBh. &c.; a kind of medic. plant (= *ṛishabha*), L.; n. forepart of a pole, R.; N. of all Stotras except the 3 Pavamānas, KātyŚr., Sch. **— tā**, f. the state of being a burden-bearer, the office of a minister &c.; first place, leadership, Śiś. i. 41. **— vat**, ind. like a beast of burden, MBh. **— vāha**, m. the load of a draught-ox, Āpast.; beast for draught, MBh. **Dhuryâsana**, n. seat of honour, ib. **Dhuryêtara**, mfn. 'other than the first,' the charioteer (as opp. to the hero), ib.

धुरा *dhurā́*, ind. (√*dhvṛi*) violently, hurtfully, ŚBr.

धुरि *dhuri*, m. N. of a son of the Vasu Āpa, VP.

धुर्व् *dhurv* = *dhūrv*, q. v.

धुवक *dhuvaka*, &c. See under 1. *dhu*.

धुशुल्या *dhuśulyā*, f. N. of a river, VP.

धुस्तुर *dhustura* (L.) and °*tūra* (Kathās.; Uṇ. iv, 90, Sch.; ifc. also °*raka*) thorn-apple (cf. *dhattūra*).

धू 1. *dhū*, cl. 5. P. Ā. *dhūnóti*, °*nuté*, RV.; AV.; *dhunoti*, °*nute*, Br. &c. &c.; cl. 6. P. (Dhātup. xxvii, 9) *dhuvati*, AV.; Br. (cf. *ni-*; Pot. *dhūvet*, Kāṭh.); cl. 9. P. Ā. (xxxi, 17) Pot. *dhunīyāt*, Suśr.; p. Ā. *dhunāna*, BhP.; cl. 1. P. (xxxiv, 29) *dhavati*; cl. 2. Ā., 3. pl. *dhuvate* (*dhunváte*?), ŚBr.; p. *dhuvāná*, TS. (pf. *dudhāva*, MBh., °*dhuve*, AV.; *dudhuvitá* & *dū́dhot*, RV.; aor. *adhūshṭa*, 3. pl. °*shata*, ib.; *adhoshṭa*, *adhavishṭa*; *adhaushīt*, *adhāvīt*, Gr.; fut. *dhavishyati*, °*te*, Br. &c.; *dhoshyati*, °*te*, *dhotā* & *dhavitā*, Gr.; ind. p. *dhūtvā*, AitBr., *-dhū́ya*, AV. &c.; inf. *dhavitum*, Gr.) to shake, agitate, cause to tremble, RV. &c. &c.; to shake down from (e.g. fruits [acc.] from a tree [acc.]), RV. ix, 97, 53; (oftener Ā.) to shake off, remove, liberate one's self from (acc.), Br.; Up.; MBh. &c.; to fan, kindle (a fire), KātyŚr.; MBh. &c.; to treat roughly, hurt, injure, destroy, Kāv.; Pur.; to strive against, resist, Pañc. i, 42; Pass. *dhūyáte*, AV. &c. (p. *dhūyat*, MBh.): Caus. *dhāvayati* (Dhāt. xxxiv, 29) & *dhūnayati* (see *dhūna*): Desid. *dudhūshati*, °*te*, Gr.; Intens. *dodhavīti*, RV.; MBh. (p. *dódhuvat dávidhvat*, RV.); *dodhūyate*, p. °*yamāna* & °*yat*, MBh.; to shake or move violently (trans. & intr.); to shake off or down; to fan or kindle. [Cf. √*dhav* and *dhāv*; Gk. θύω, θύνω, θυμός.]

2. **Dhū**, f. shaking, agitating, L.

Dhūka, m. wind, L.; rogue, L.; time, L.; Mimusops Elengi, Car.

Dhūtá, mfn. shaken, stirred, agitated, RV. &c. &c. (said of the Soma = 'rinsed,' SV. *dhauta*); fanned, kindled, Ṛitus.; shaken off, removed, destroyed (see below); judged, L.; reproached, ib.; n. morality, Buddh.; (*ā*), f. a wife, W. **— kalmasha**, mfn. 'whose sins are shaken off,' pure, R. **— guṇa**, m. ascetic practice or precept, Divyâv. (there are 12 according to Dharmas. lxiii). **— pāpa**, mfn. = *-kalmasha*, R.; destroying sin, MW.; (*ā*), f. N. of 2 rivers, VP. **— pāpaka**, **-pāpa-tīrtha** & **-pāpêśvara-tīrtha**, n. N. of Tīrthas, Pur. **— pāpman**, mfn. = *-pāpa*, MBh.

Dhū́ti, m. shaker, agitator (Maruts), RV.; N. of an Āditya, VP.; shaking, moving to and fro, fanning, Vop.

Dhūna, mfn. (Pāṇ. viii, 2, 44) shaken, agitated; distressed by heat or thirst, W. °**nana**, m. wind, L.; n. shaking, agitation, Śiś.; Rajat. °**naya**, Nom. P. °*yati*, to shake, agitate, Pāṇ. vii, 3, 37, Vārtt. 1, Pat. °**ni**, f. shaking, agitation, L. °**nvat**, pr. p. of √*dhū*; m. a partic. personification, Gaut. xxvi, 12.

Dhūpa, m. sg. pl. (fr. *dhū* as *pushpa* fr. √*push*, *stūpa* fr. √*stu*) incense, perfume, aromatic vapour or smoke proceeding from gum or resin, the g° & r° themselves, Kāṭh.; GṛS.; Yājñ.; MBh.; Kāv. &c.; one of the 16 acts of homage or offerings in the Pancâyatara ceremony, RTL. 415. **— kaṭacchuka**, m. a small spoon with frankincense, Kāraṇḍ. **— tṛiṇa**, n. grass serving as incense, ĀpŚr. **— dāna**, n. N. of ch. of PSarv. **— dhūpita**, mfn. made fragrant or fumigated with incense, MW. **— netra**, n. a pipe for smoking, Car. (cf. *dhūma-*). **—pātra,** n. a vessel for incense, a perfume box, R. **—varti,** f. a kind of cigarette, Kād. **—vṛiksha,** °**shaka,** m. Pinus Longifolia, L. **Dhūpâguru,** n. a kind of Agallochum, L. **Dhūpâṅga,** m. turpentine from Pinus Longifolia, L. **Dhūpâṅgada,** m., °**pârha,** n. 2 kinds of Agallochum, L. **Dhūpôshman,** m. the heat or smoke of burnt frankincense, Kum.

Dhūpaka, m. = *dhūpa*, esp. ifc. (see *kṛitrima-, sa-*); preparer of incense, perfumer, R. (cf. °*pika*).

Dhūpana, n. incensing, fumigation, KātyŚr.; MBh.; Suśr.; (also m.) perfume, incense, Mn.; MBh.; (in astrol.) the obscuration of a comet (cf. °*paya*). **—dhūpita,** mfn. = *dhūpa-dh*°, MBh. **Dhūpanâguru** (R.; Pañc.), °**nâṅga** (Suśr.) = *dhūpâguru* and °*pâṅga*.

Dhūpaya, Nom. P. °*páyati*, to fumigate, perfume, VS.; TS.; ŚBr.; MBh. &c.; (astrol.) to obscure with mist, be about to eclipse, Var.; R.; to speak or to shine, Dhātup. xxxiii, 99. °**payitavya,** mfn. to be incensed or fumigated, Var. °**pita,** mfn. incensed, perfumed, MBh.; R.; suffering pain or fatigue, L.

Dhūpāya, Nom. P. °*yati*, to fumigate, perfume with incense, Kāv. °**pāyita,** mfn. incensed, perfumed; vexed, pained, L.

Dhūpi, m. N. of a class of winds causing rain, TĀr. °**pika,** m. preparer of incense, perfumer, R. °**pin,** mfn. perfuming, making fragrant, Naish. °**pya,** mfn. to be fumigated with (comp.), Var.; m. or n. Unguis Odoratus, L.

Dhūmá, m. (√*dhū* or 1. *dhvan*) smoke, vapour, mist, RV. &c. &c.; smoke as a sternutatory (in 5 forms), Suśr.; a place prepared for the building of a house, Jyot.; wheat, L.; a kind of incense, L.; a saint, W.; N. of a man, g. *gargâdi*; (*ā*), f. a kind of plant, L. [Cf. Lat. *fumus*.] **—ketana,** m. 'smoke-marked,' fire, Ragh.; meteor, a comet, L.; Ketu or the personified descending node, W. **—ketu** (°*má-*), mfn. having sm° as banner or sign (Agni, RV.; the sun, MBh.); m. fire, MBh.; a comet or falling star, ib.; Hariv.; Kāv. &c.; the personified descending node, W.; N. of the sun, MBh.; of a Yaksha, Kathās.; w. r. for *dhūmra-k*°. **—gandhi** (°*má-*), mfn. smelling of sm°, RV.; °*dhika*, m. a kind of fragrant grass, Bhpr. **—graha,** m. N. of Rāhu, Mālatīm. ii, 8. **—ja,** n. a kind of caustic potash, L. **—jāla,** n. a mass of clouds or of smoke, MBh.; R. **—tā,** f. state of being sm°, BhP. **—tānta** (*má-*), mfn. choked by sm°, TBr. **—darśin,** mfn. seeing sm° (in the eye, a disease), Suśr. **—dhūmra,** mfn. dark like smoke, Suśr.; Kāv. **—dhvaja,** m. 'smoke-marked,' fire, Sarvad. **—nirgamana,** n. 'smoke-outlet,' chimney, Hcat. **—netra,** n. = *dhūpa-n*°, Car.; m. N. of a mountain, Divyâv. **—pa,** mfn. drinking or inhaling (only) sm°, ib. (cf. *-prâśa*). **—patha,** m. 'way of sm°,' sacrifice, seeking salvation by works, BhP. (= *karma-mârga*, Sch.) **—pallava,** m. streak of sm°, Hcar. **—pāta,** m. flight of (i. e. ascending) sm°, Ratn. **—pāna,** n. inhalation of sm° or vapour, Car.; tobacco-smoking, L.; *-vidhi*, m. N. of ch. of the ŚārṅgS. **—prabhā,** f. 'having sm° as light,' N. of a hell, L. **—prâśa,** mfn. feeding only on vapour (as an ascetic), MBh. (cf. *-pa*). **—maya,** mf(*ī*)n. consisting only of sm° or vapour, MBh. **—mahishī,** f. 'smoke's wife,' fog, mist, L. **—yoni,** m. 'smoke-engendered,' 'vapour-born,' a cloud, L.; Cyperus Rotundus, ib. **—rakta** (°*má*), mfn. coloured with smoke, ŚBr. **—rāji,** f. column of sm°, Hariv. **—lava,** m. puff of sm°, Var. **—lekhā,** f. = *-rāji*, Dhanaṃj.; N. of the daughter of a Yaksha, Kathās. **—vat,** mfn. smoky, steaming, Suśr.; Tarkas.; containing the word *dhūma*, Kāṭh.; *-tva*, n. smokiness, Bhāshāp.; °*d-gati*, mfn. moving like sm°, MBh. **—varcas,** m. 'shining like sm°,' N. of a man, MBh. **—varṇa,** m. 'sm°-coloured,' N. of a serpent-king, Hariv. **—varti,** f. = *-rāji*, Hariv.; = *dhūpa-v*°, Car. **—vartman,** n. = *-patha*, BhP. **—śikhā,** f. = *-rāji*, AV.; Venis.; fee, salary, reward, Vas. **—saṃhati,** f. = *-rāji*, L. **Dhūmâkāra,** mfn. having the form of sm°, W. **Dhūmâkshá,** mf(*ī*)n. dim-eyed, AV. (cf. °*ma-darśin*). **Dhūmâṅga,** m. or n. = *śiṅśapā*, L. **Dhūmânubandha,** m. a thick cloud of sm°, Ratn. **Dhūmâbha,** mfn. smoke-coloured, L.; m. purple, W. **Dhūmā-vatī,** f. N. of a place of pilgrimage, MBh.; *-dīpa-dāna-pūjā*, f., *-paṭala*, m. or n., *-pūjā-paddhati*, f. N. of wks.; *-manu* & *-mantra*, m. N. of partic. magical formulas, Cat. **Dhūmâvali,** f. a wreath or cloud of smoke, W. **Dhūmôttha,** n. = *-ma-ja*, L. **Dhūmôdgama,** m. issuing or ascending sm°, Ratn.; Daś. **Dhūmôdgāra,** m. id., Megh.; a kind of disease, L. **Dhūmôpahata,** mfn. 'smoke-struck,' suffocated by sm°, Suśr. **Dhūmôrṇā,** f. 'smoke-wool,' N. of the wife of Yama, MBh. (*-pati*, m. = Y°, L.); of the wife of Mārkaṇḍeya, ib. (cf. *dhūmrôrṇā*). **Dhūmôshṇa-yoni,** m. = *-ma-yoni*, R.

Dhūmaka, ifc. = *dhūma*, smoke; m. a kind of pot-herb, Car.; (*ikā*), f. smoke, Kathās.; fog, mist, L.; w. r. for *bhūmikā*. **—pushpā,** f. a species of nettle, L.

Dhūmana, n. (astrol.) the obscuration (of a comet; cf. *dhūpana*).

Dhūmaya, Nom. P. °*yati* (Pass. °*myate*, v. l. °*pyate*), to cover with smoke, obscure with mist, eclipse, R. °**mita,** mfn. tasting of sm°, L.; obscured, darkened; (*ā*), f. (scil. *diś*) that quarter towards which the sun turns first, VarBṛS. xc, 3.

Dhūmarī, f. mist, fog, L.

Dhūmala, mfn. smoke-coloured, purple, L.; m. a colour compounded of black and red, W.; a kind of musical instrument (?), L.

Dhūmāya, Nom. P. Ā. °*yati*, °*te*, to smoke, steam, Br.; Var.; MBh. &c.: Caus. °*yayati*, to cause to sm° or st°, MBh. °**māyana,** n. smoking, heat, fever, Suśr. °**māyita,** n. smoking, steaming, MBh.

Dhūmin, mfn. smoking, steaming, RV.; (*ī*), f. one of the seven tongues of Agni, Gṛihyās.; N. of the wife of Aja-mīḍha, MBh.; of another woman, Daś.; (with *diś*) = *dhūmitā*, Var.

Dhūmyā, f. thick smoke, cloud of sm°, Mālatīm. **Dhūmyâṭa,** m. the fork-tailed shrike, L. (cf. °*mrâṭa*).

Dhūmrá, mf(*ā*)n. smoke-coloured, smoky, dark-coloured, grey, dark-red, purple, VS.; Br. &c. &c.; dim, obscured (see below); m. a camel, TS.; a mixture of red and black, purple (the colour), W.; incense (= *turushka*), L.; (in astrol.) the 28th Yoga; N. of one of Skanda's attendants, MBh.; of a Dānava, Hariv.; of Śiva, MBh.; of a monkey or bear, R.; of an author & other men, Cat. (cf. *dhūmrāyaṇa* & *dhaumr*°); pl. of a family of Ṛishis, R.; (*ā*), f. a kind of gourd (= *śaśâṇḍulī*), L.; N. of the mother of the Vasu Dhara, MBh.; of Durgā, Devīm.; n. wickedness, sin, W. **—ketu,** m. 'grey-bannered,' N. of a son of Bharata, BhP.; of a son of Tṛiṇa-bindu, ib. **—keśa,** m. 'dark-haired,' N. of a son of Pṛithu and Arcis, BhP.; of a son of Kṛiśâśva and Arcis, ib.; of a Dānava, ib. **—giri,** m. N. of a mountain, R. **—jaṭila,** mfn. dark and tortuous (snake), Suśr. **—jānu,** mfn. having grey knees, L. **—dhī,** mfn. of dimmed or troubled intellect, BhP. **—nikāśa** (°*rá-*), mfn. greyish, VS. **—pattrā,** f. 'dark-leaved,' N. of a shrub (= *dhūmrâhvā*, *sulabhā*, &c.), L. **—mūlikā,** f. 'dark-rooted,' a kind of grass, L. **—ruc,** mfn. of a purple or grey colour, Śiś. **—rohita** (°*rá-*), mfn. greyish-red, VS. **—lalāma** (°*rá-*), mfn. having a grey spot, TS. **—locana,** m. 'dark-eyed,' a pigeon, L.; N. of a general of the Asura Śumbha, MārkP. **—lohita,** mfn. dark-red, deep purple, MBh. **—varṇa,** mfn. 'smoke-coloured,' dark, grey, dark-red, MBh.; R.; m. incense, L.; N. of a son of Aja-mīḍha and Dhūminī, Hariv.; of a mountain, ib.; (*ā*), f. N. of one of the 7 tongues of Agni, Gṛihyās. (cf. *su-dhūmra-v*°); *-ka*, m. the Indian fox, L.; °*nā-manu*, m. N. of a magic formula, Cat. **—vidyā,** f. N. of a form of magic, ib. **—vṛitta-phalā,** f. a kind of gourd, L. **—śikha,** m. N. of a Rakshas, Kathās. **—śūka** or **-śūla,** m. a camel, L. **—saṃrakta-locana,** mfn. having dark-red or greyish-red eyes, MW. **—Dhūmrâksha,** mf(*ī*)n. grey-eyed, R.; m. N. of a Rakshas, MBh.; R.; of a son of Hemacandra (grandson of Triṇa-bindu, cf. °*râśva*), BhP.; of a king of the Nishadhas, SkandaP. **Dhūmrâkshi,** m. a pearl of a bad colour, L. **Dhūmrâṭa,** m. the fork-tailed shrike, L. (cf. °*myâṭa*). **Dhūmrânīka,** m. N. of a son of Medhâtithi & a Varsha called after him, BhP. **Dhūmrâbha,** m. 'smoke-coloured (?),' air, wind, L. **Dhūmrâśva,** m. 'having dark horses,' N. of a son of Su-candra (son of Hemacandra) & father of Sṛiñjaya, R.; VP. (cf. °*râksha*). **Dhūmrâhvā,** f. = °*ra-pattra*, L. **Dhūmrôrṇā,** f. N. of a divine female, VahniP. (°*môrṇā*).

Dhūmraka, m. 'the grey animal,' a camel, L.; (*ikā*), f. Dalbergia Sissoo, ib.

Dhūmraya, Nom. P. °*yati*, to make dark-coloured or grey, Mudr. v, 22.

Dhūmrāyaṇa, m. patr. fr. *dhūmra*, Pravar. (cf. *dhaumr*°).

Dhūmrimán, m. dark colour, obscurity, TS.; Kāṭh.

Dhūmrī-√kṛi, to make dark-coloured or grey, Kām.

Dhūli, f. (W. also m.; √*dhū*?) dust (also the dusty soil), powder, pollen, Var.; Pañc.; Kāv.; Pur. &c. (also °*lī*, f., L. & in comp., see below); a partic. number, W. **—kuṭṭima,** n., **-kedāra,** m. a mound, rampart of earth, L. **—guccha** & °**aka,** m. the red powder thrown about at the Holi festival, RTL. 430. **—dhūmra,** mfn. smoke-coloured or dark with dust, BhP. **—dhvaja,** m. 'dust-bannered,' air or wind, L. **—paṭala,** n. cloud of dust, Kull. iv, 102. **—pushpikā,** f. Pandanus Odoratissimus, L. **—maya,** mf(*ī*)n. covered with dust, MW. **—mushṭi,** m. a handful of d°, ib.; **—prakshepa,** m. the throwing of h°s of d°, ib. **—hastaya,** Nom. P. °*yati*, to take d° into the hand, Naish. °**lī-kadamba,** m. a kind of Kadamba & other plants, L. °**lī-jaṅgha,** m. a crow, L. °**lī-patala,** n. & **-maya,** mf(*ī*)n., see above °*li-p*° &c. °**lī-varsha,** m. n. falling (lit. rain of) dust, Kull. iv, 115.

Dhūlaya, Nom. P. °*yati*, to sprinkle with dust or powder. °**lana,** n. covering with dust, Bhpr. °**lita,** mfn. sprinkled with (instr.), ib.

Dhulikā, f. pollen of flowers, L.; fog, mist, L.; a kind of game, Siṃhās.

धूण *dhūṇa*, m. the resin of Shorea Robusta, L.

Dhūnaka, m. id.; any resin, L.

धूत्कार *dhūt-kāra*, m. roaring, thundering, Bālar. vii, 82.

धूप् *dhūp* (Dhātup. xi, 2; xxxiii, 99). See *dhūpaya* & °*pāya* above.

Dhūma. See above.

धूमस *dhūmasa*, m. Tectona Grandis, L.; (*ī*), f. a kind of flour or cake made of baked beans, L.

धूमीका *dhūmīkā*, f. a partic. bird of prey, Car. (v. l. °*mākā*).

धूर् 1. *dhūr*, cl. 4. Ā. *dhūryate*, to hurt or kill (cf. *dhūrv*); to move or approach, Dhātup. xxvi, 44.

धूर् 2. *dhūr*, in comp. for *dhur*. **—gata,** mfn. being on the pole or foremost part of a chariot; (ifc.) being at the head, foremost or chief of, MBh.; the driver of an elephant, Kir. vii, 24. **—gṛihītá,** mfn. seized by the yoke, ŚBr. **—jaṭa,** m. N. of an attendant of Śiva, Kathās. (cf. next). **—jaṭi,** m. 'having matted locks like a burden,' N. of Rudra-Śiva, MBh.; Kathās.; Hit. &c. (°*ṭin*, MBh. xiii, 7510); N. of a poet (also *-rāja*), Cat. **—dhara,** mfn. bearing a burden, managing affairs, L.; m. beast of burden, L.; leader, chief, Kād. **—yuja,** m. a carriage, Nilak. **—vat,** mfn. having a load, laden, MW. (cf. Pāṇ. viii, 2, 15, Kāś.) **—vaha,** mfn. = *-dhara*, mfn.; m. a beast of burden, L. **—voḍhṛi,** id., Pañc. (B.) i, ११. **—shád,** mfn. being on the pole of a carriage; being foremost; m. driver of a carriage, guide, chief, RV. **—shāh,** mfn. bearing the yoke, VS.

Dhūrushád, m. (TBr.) = *dhūr-shád*.

Dhūrya, w. r. for *dhurya*.

धूर्ण *dhūrṇa*, m. the resin of Shorea Robusta, L. (cf. *dhūṇa*, *dhūnaka*).

धूर्व् *dhūrv* or *dhurv* (Dhātup. xv, 64), cl. 1. P. *dhūrvati*, RV.; VS.; Br. (aor. *adhūrvīt*, ŚBr.; inf. *dhūrvitum*, ib.; pf. *dudhūrva*; fut. *dhūrvishyati*, °*vitā*, Gr.) to bend, cause to fall, hurt, injure, RV. &c.; Bhaṭṭ. (cf. *dhvṛi*).

Dhūrta, mfn. (√*dhūrv* or *dhvṛi*) cunning, crafty, fraudulent, subtle, mischievous; m. a rogue, cheat, deceiver, swindler, sharper, gambler, Yājñ.; MBh.; Kāv. &c. (also ifc.; cf. *kaṭha-* and Pāṇ. ii, 1, 65); N. of Skanda, AV. Pariś.; the thorn-apple, L.; a partic. fragrant plant, L.; (*ā*), f. a sort of nightshade, L.; n. rust or iron-filings, L.; black salt, L. **—kitava,** m. a gamester, sharper, Yājñ. **—kṛit,** m. thorn-apple, L.; knave, rogue, cheat, W. **—carita,** n. the tricks of rogues (pl., Kathās.); N. of a play. **—jantu,** m. 'cunning creature,' man, L. **—tā,** f., **-tva,** n. knavery, roguery, Kāv. **—nartaka,** n. N. of a drama. **—pralāpa,** m. rogues' talk, R. **—maṇḍala,** n. of a party of rogues or gamblers, Yājñ. **—mānushā,** f. N. of a plant (= *rāsnā*), L. **—racanā,** f. rogues' tricks, roguery, Kathās. **—rāja,** m.

the chief of rogues, MW. **-lavaṇa,** n. a kind of salt, L. **-viḍambana** and **-samāgama,** n. N. of dramas. **-svāmin,** m. N. of a Sch.; °*mi-bhāshya,* n. of his wk.

Dhūrtaka, mfn. cunning, crafty; a cheat, rogue, MBh.; Kāv.; m. a jackal, L.; N. of a Nāga, MBh.

Dhūrti, f. injury, damage, harm, RV.; N. of Rudra, MaitrS. (v. l. °*ta,* ĀpŚr.)

Dhūrtila, see *aksha-*.

Dhū́rvan, n. causing to fall, hurting (dat. °*ṇe* as inf.) RV. ix, 61, 30.

धूर्वा *dhū́rvā,* f. (ŚBr.) = *dūrvā.*

धूर्वी *dhūrvī,* f. (L.) = *dhur,* the forepart or pole of a carriage.

धूश् *dhūś* or *dhūsh* or *dhūs* (Dhātup. xxxii, 97), cl. 10. P. *dhūśayati* &c., to embellish.

धूषर *dhūshara,* w. r. for next.

धूसर *dhūsara,* mf(ā)n. (√*dhvaṇs* or *dhvas;* cf. *dhvasira*) dust-coloured, grey, Kāv.; Rājat. &c. (-*tva,* n. Dhūrtas.); m. grey (the colour), W.; an ass, L.; an oilman, ib.; a pigeon, ib.; a partic. plant, Var. (sweet vetch, Gal.); (*ā*), f. a kind of shrub, L.; (*ī*), f. N. of a Kiṃ-narī. **-cchadā,** f. a kind of plant (= *śveta-vuhnā*), L. **-pattrikā,** f. Tragia Involucrata or Heliophytum Indicum, L.

Dhūsaraka, m. N. of a jackal, Pañc.

Dhūsarita, mfn. made grey, greyish, Uṇ. iii, 73, Sch.

Dhūsariman, m. grey or dusty-white (the colour), Hcar.

धूस्तूर *dhūstūra,* m. = *dhustūra,* the thorn-apple, L.

धृ *dhṛi,* cl. 1. P. Ā. *dharati,* °*te* (Dhātup. xxii, 3; Ā. Pot. *dhareran,* ĀpŚr.), but more commonly in the same sense the Caus. form *dhārayati,* °*te* (perf. P. *dādhā́ra,* °*dhártha* [Impv. *dadhartu,* AV. Paipp.]; Ā. *dadhré,* 3. pl. °*dhriré,* RV. &c. &c.; aor. *adhāram,* R.; *adhṛita, dhṛithās,* AV.; *dā́dharat,* RV. &c. &c. [*didhar, didhṛitam,* °*ta,* RV.; 3. pl. °*rata,* ŚBr.]; *adārshīt,* Gr.; fut. *dharishyati,* MBh.; °*shyé,* AV.; *dhartā,* BhP.; inf. *dhartum,* Kāv., °*tavai,* Br. [*dhartári,* see under °*tṛi*]; ind. p. *dhṛitvā, -dhṛitya,* Br.) to hold, bear (also = bring forth), carry, maintain, preserve, keep, possess, have, use, employ, practise, undergo, RV. &c. &c.; (with or scil. *ātmānam, jīvitam, prāṇān, deham, śarīram* &c.) to preserve soul or body, continue living, survive, MBh.; Kāv. &c. (esp. fut. *dharishyati;* cf. Pass. below); to hold back, keep down, stop, restrain, suppress, resist, Br.; MBh.; Kāv. &c.; to place or fix in, bestow or confer on (loc.), RV.; AV.; Br. &c.; destine for (dat.; Ā. also to be destined for or belong to), RV.; present to (gen.), Kāraṇḍ.; to direct or turn (attention, mind, &c.) towards, fix or resolve upon (loc. or dat.), Up.; Yājñ.; MBh.; Ā. to be ready or prepared for, ŚBr.; P. Ā. to owe anything (acc.) to (dat. or gen.), MBh. (cf. Pāṇ. i, 4, 35); to prolong (in pronunciation); AitBr.; RPrāt.; to quote, cite, L.; (with *garbham*) to conceive, be pregnant (older °*bham* √*bhṛi*), MBh.; Kāv. &c.; (with *daṇḍam*) to inflict punishment on (loc.), MBh.; R.; BhP. (also *damam*); (with *keśān* or *śmaśru*) to let the hair or beard grow, MBh.; (with *raśmīn* [ib.] or *praharān* [Śak.]) to draw the reins tight; (with *dharmam*) to fulfil a duty, R.; (with *vratám*) to observe or keep a vow, RV. &c. &c.; (with *dhāraṇām*) to practise self-control, Yājñ.; (with *tapas*) to perform penance, BhP.; (with *mūrdhnā* or °*dhni, śirasā* or °*si*) to bear on the head, honour highly, Kāv.; (with or scil. *tulayā*) to hold in a balance, weigh, measure, MBh.; Kāv. &c.; (with or scil. *manasā*) to bear in mind, recollect, remember, ib.; (with *samaye*) to hold to an agreement, cause to make a compact, Pañc. i, $\frac{125}{126}$ (B. *dṛishṭvā* for *dhṛitvā*): Pass. *dhriyáte* (ep. also °*yati;* pf. *dadhré* &c. = Ā.; aor. *adhāri*) to be borne &c.; to be firm, keep steady, RV. &c. &c.; continue living, exist, remain, Br.; MBh.; Kāv. &c. (also *dhāryate,* R.); to begin, resolve upon, undertake (dat.; acc. or inf.), AV. ŚBr., ChUp.: Caus. *dhāráyati,* °*te,* see above: Desid. *didhīrshati* (see °*shā*), *didharishate,* Pāṇ. vii, 2, 75; *didhārayishati,* to wish to keep up or preserve (*ātmānam*), Gobh. iii, 5, 30: Intens. *dárdharti* (RV.) and *dādharti* (3. pl. °*dhrati,* TS.; cf. Pāṇ. vii, 4, 65) to hold fast, bear firmly, fasten. [Cf. Zd. *dar;* Gk. θρό-νος, θρᾶ-νος, θρή-σασθαι; Lat. *frē-tus, frē-num.*]

Dhṛik (only nom. sg.) = (& v. l. for) **dhṛit,** mfn. holding, bearing, supporting, wearing, having, possessing, &c. (only ifc.)

Dhṛitá, mfn. held, borne, maintained, supported, kept, possessed; used, practised, observed, RV. &c. &c.; measured, weighed (with or scil. *tulayā*), MBh.; worn (as clothes, shoes, beard, &c.), Mn.; MBh.; Kāv.; kept back, detained (*kare,* by the hand), Hit.; drawn tight (reins), Śak.; turned towards or fixed upon, ready or prepared for, resolved on (loc. or dat.), MBh.; R.; continuing, existing, being, ib.; prolonged (in pronunciation), Prāt. (*am,* ind. solemnly, slowly, Pañc. iii, $\frac{72}{73}$); (with *antare*) deposited as surety, pledged, ib. iv, $\frac{31}{32}$; quoted, cited by (comp.), L.; m. N. of a son of the 13th Manu, Hariv. (v. l. *bhṛitha*); of a descendant of Druhyu and son of Dharma, Pur. (cf. *dhārteya*); n. a partic. manner of fighting, Hariv. **-kanaka-māla,** mfn. wearing a golden collar or wreath, MW. **-kārmukêshu,** mfn. armed with bow and arrows, W. **-ketu,** m. N. of a son of the 9th Manu, VP. **-kleśa,** m. undergoing hardships, Rājat. **-garbhā,** f. 'bearing a fetus,' pregnant, Kathās. vii, 83. **-cāpa,** mfn. armed with a bow, R. **-tāla,** m. = *vetāla,* Kathās. lxxxix, 115. **-daksha** (°*tá-*), mfn. of collected mind, attentive or constant, RV. **-daṇḍa,** mfn. carrying the rod, inflicting punishment, BhP.; one on whom p° has been or is being inflicted, punished by (instr.), Mn. viii, 318. **-dīdhiti,** m. 'constant in splendour,' fire, L. **-devā** or °**vī,** f. N. of a daughter of Devaka, Pur. **-dvaidhī-bhāva,** mfn. held in doubt or suspense, Śak. i, $\frac{25}{26}$. **-dhanus,** m. = *-cāpa,* Vām. v, 2, 67. **-niścaya,** mfn. firmly resolute or intent upon (dat.), MBh. **-paṭa,** mfn. covered or overspread with a cloth &c., W. **-pūrva,** mfn. worn before (as an ornament), Mudr. **-praja,** mfn. having descendants, Ragh. **-matī,** w. r. for *dhṛiti-m°*. **-rājan,** m. N. of a man, L. (see *dhārta-rājña*). **-rāshṭra,** m. whose empire is firm, a powerful king, L.; N. of a Nāga also called Airāvata, AV.; Br.; MBh. &c.; of a Deva-gandharva sometimes identified with King Dh° (below), MBh. (with Buddhists, N. of a king of the Gandharvas & one of the 4 Mahārājas [Lalit.] or Lokapālas [Dharmas. vii]; MWB. 206); of a son of the Daitya Bali, Hariv.; of a king of Kāśi, ŚBr. (with the patr. *vaicitravīrya,* Kāṭh.); of the eldest son of Vyāsa by the widow of Vicitra-vīrya (brother of Pāṇḍu & Vidura and born blind, husband of Gāndhārī and father of 100 sons of whom the eldest was Dur-yodhana; sometimes identified with Dhṛita-rāshṭra & Haṇsa, 2 chiefs of the Gandharvas), MBh.; of a son of Janam-ejaya, ib.; of a king of the geese (cf. Haṇsa, above), Jātakam.; a partic. bird, L.; pl. the 100 sons of King Dh° (enumerated MBh. i, 4540); (*ī*), f. N. of a daughter of Tāmrā (mother of geese and other water-birds), MBh.; R.; Pur.; °*tra-ja,* m. son of Dh°, N. of Dur-yodhana &c., Pracaṇḍ.; °*trânuja,* m. younger brother of Dh°, N. of Pāṇḍu, Gal. **-vat,** mfn. one who has held or taken or conveyed, Git.; Hit.; one who has firmly resolved upon (dat.), Kathās.; (*ī*), f. N. of a river, MBh. (also v. l. for *ghṛita-vatī*). **-varman,** m. 'wearing armour,' N. of a warrior on the side of the Kurus, MBh. **-vrata** (°*tá-*), mfn. of fixed law or order (Agni, Indra, Savitṛi, the Ādityas, &c.), RV.; ŚBr.; maintaining law or order, Gaut.; firmly resolute, MBh.; being accustomed to (inf.), ib.; devoted, attached, faithful, MBh.; R.; BhP.; m. N. of Rudra, BhP.; of a son of Dhṛiti, Hariv.; Pur. **-śarīra,** mfn. 'retaining a body,' continuing to live, existing, Kap. **-śrī,** f. a kind of metre, Col. **-saṃkalpa,** mfn. (with loc.) = *-niścaya,* MBh. **-saṃdhi,** m. 'keeping compacts,' N. of a son of Susaṃdhi and father of Bharata, R. **-siṇha,** v. l. for °*ti-s°*. **-havya,** v. l. for *vīta-h°*. **-heti,** mfn. bearing weapons, armed, W. **Dhṛitâtman,** mfn. firm-minded, steady, calm, Kāv. **Dhṛitâmbhas,** mfn. containing water, W. **Dhṛitârcis,** m. 'of constant splendour,' N. of Vishṇu, Vishṇ. **Dhṛitêshudhi,** mfn. carrying a quiver, MW. **Dhṛitâika-veṇi,** mfn. bearing a single braid of hair (as a sign of mourning), Śak. vii, 21. **Dhṛitôtseka,** mfn. possessing pride, haughty, arrogant, Rājat.

Dhṛitaka, m. N. of a Buddh. saint or patriarch; v. l. for *vṛika,* VP.

Dhṛiti, f. holding, seizing, keeping, supporting (cf. *carshaṇī-, vi-*), firmness, constancy, resolution, will, command, RV. &c. &c.; satisfaction, content, joy, MBh.; Kāv. &c. (°*tiṃ* √*kṛi,* to keep ground or stand still, MBh. vii, 4540; to find pleasure or satisfaction, Ratn. iv, $\frac{4}{5}$; °*tiṃ* √*bandh,* to show firmness, Amar. 67; to fix the mind on, Mn. v, 47); Resolution or Satisfaction personified as a daughter of Daksha and wife of Dharma (MBh.; Hariv.; Pur.) or as a Śakti (Hcat. &c.); N. of partic. evening oblations at the Aśvamedha, ŚBr.; any offering or sacrifice, W.; of sev. kinds of metre & of a class of metres consisting of 4 × 18 syllables, Col.; of the numeral 18, Var.; Gaṇit.; of one of the astrol. Yogas, L.; of a mythical garden, Gol.; of one of the 16 Kalās of the moon, Pur.; of a goddess (daughter of a Kalā of Prakṛiti & wife of Kapila), ib.; of the wife of Rudra-Manu, ib.; of the 13th of the 16 Mātṛikās, L.; m. with *kshatrasya = kshatra-dh°,* Lāṭy.; N. of one of the Viśve Devās, MBh.; of a preceptor, Cat.; of a son of Vijaya & father of Dhṛita-vrata, Hariv.; Pur.; of a son of Vīta-havya & father of Bahulâśva, Pur.; of a son of Babhru, L.; of a Varsha in Kuśa-dvīpa, VP. **-gṛihīta,** mfn. armed with constancy and resolution, Bhag. **-paripūrṇa,** m. N. of a Bodhi-sattva. **-paritâtman,** mfn. joyful in mind, Pañc. **-mat,** mfn. steadfast, calm, resolute (-*tā,* f.), Mn.; MBh.; Suśr. &c.; satisfied, content, MBh.; Ragh.; m. N. of a form of Agni, MBh.; of a son of Manu Raivata & Savarṇa, Hariv.; of one of the Saptarshis in the 13th Manv-antara, ib.; of a son of Kīrti-mat (son of Aṅgiras), VP.; of a son of Yavīnara, Hariv.; of a Brāhman, ib.; (*ī*), f. N. of a river (v. l. °*ta-m°*), VP.; n. N. of a Varsha in Kuśa-dvīpa, MBh. **-maya,** mf(*ī*)n. consisting of constancy or contentment, MBh.; Kāv. **-mālin,** m. a partic. magic. formula spoken over weapons, R. **-mush,** mfn. 'fortitude-stealing,' disheartening, agitating, W. **-yoga,** m. N. of an astrol. and mystical Yoga, L. **-siṇha,** m. (v. l. °*ta-s°*) N. of an author (said to have assisted Purushôttama in composing the Hārâvalī), Cat.

Dhṛitvan, m. 'supporter,' N. of Vishṇu, Uṇ. iv, 113, Sch.; (only L.) a clever man; a Brahman; virtue; the sea; the sky (cf. *kshema-*); (*arī*), f. the earth, L.

Dhṛitvā́, ind. having held or borne (see √*dhṛi*).

धृज् *dhṛij* or *dhṛiñj,* cl. 1. P. *dharjati, dhṛiñjati,* to go, move, Dhātup. vii, 42, 43 (cf. √*dhraj, dhrij*).

धृष् *dhṛish,* cl. 5. P. *dhṛishṇóti,* RV. &c. &c.; cl. 1. P. *dhárshati,* VS.; R. (p. *dhṛishát,* °*shámāṇa,* RV.; °*shāṇá,* AV.; perf. *dadhársha,* RV. &c. &c.; 3. pl. *dādhṛishur,* AV.; Subj. *dadharshat,* °*shati,* °*shīt,* RV.; *dadhṛishate,* °*shanta,* AV.; p. *dadhṛishvás,* RV.; aor. *adhṛishas,* ŚBr., *adharshishur,* TĀr.; fut. *dharshishyati,* °*shitā,* Gr.; ind. p. *-dhṛishya,* Br.; inf. *-dhṛíshas,* °*shi,* RV.), to be bold or courageous or confident or proud, RV.; AV.; VS.; to dare or venture (inf. in *tum,* Pāṇ. iii, 4, 65); to dare to attack, treat with indignity (acc.), Br.; MBh.; to surpass (?), AV. iii, 3, 2: Caus. *dharshayati* (Dhātup. xxxiv, 43; aor. *adīdhṛishat* or *adadharshat,* Gr.) to venture on attacking; to offend, violate (a woman), overpower, overcome, Br.; MBh.; Kāv. &c.: Desid. *didharshishati:* Intens. *darīdhṛishyate* or *darīdharshṭi,* Gr. [Cf. Zd. *daresh;* Gk. θάρσος, θαρσέω; Lit. *dristu;* Goth. *ga-dars,* Angl. Sax. *dors-te,* Engl. *durs-t.*]

Dhṛisháj, m. bold, a hero, RV. v, 19, 5.

1. **Dhṛishát,** mfn. bold, courageous, confident; (*á*), ind. boldly, courageously, strongly, RV. °**shád-varṇa,** mfn. of bold race or nature (Agni), RV. x, 87, 22. °**shad-vín,** mfn. = *-shát,* RV. v, 52, 2. °**shan-manas,** mfn. bold-minded, RV.

Dhṛishitá, mfn. bold, brave, daring, RV.; AV.; (*á*, ind., RV. viii, 52, 3 = (or w. r. for) °*shatá* (see above).

Dhṛishu, mfn. clever, Uṇ. i, 24, Sch.; deep, L.; proud, W.; m. heap, multitude, L.

Dhṛishṭá, mfn. bold, daring, confident, audacious, impudent, RV.; AV.; (cf. *á-, án-ā-*); MBh.; Kāv. &c.; secured, obtained, W.; profligate, abandoned, ib. (ifc. it gives a bad sense to the first member of the comp., Pāṇ. ii, 1, 53; Gaṇar. ii. 114); m. a faithless husband, ib.; a magic. formula spoken over weapons, R.; N. of a son of Manu Vaivasvata, Hariv. (C. °*shṇu*); Pur. (cf. *dhārshṭa*); of a son of Kunti, Hariv.; of a son of Bhajamāna, ib. (C. °*shṇa*); (*ā*), f. a disloyal or unchaste woman, W.; (*am*), ind.

boldly, courageously, fearlessly, ŚBr.; Lāṭy.; R. **-ketu**, m. N. of a king of Cedi, MBh.; of a king of Videhā or Mithilā (son of Su-dhṛiti), R.; BhP.; of a son of Satya-dhṛiti, VP.; of the son of Sukumāra, Hariv.; of his father, BhP.; of a son of Dhṛishṭa-dyumna, Hariv.; Pur.; of a king of the Kaikayas, BhP.; of a son of Manu, Hariv. **-tama**, mfn. very bold or confident, Daś. **-tā**, f. (Śiś.) **-tva**, n. (MBh.; Pañc.) boldness, courage, impudence. **-dyumna**, m. N. of a son of Dru-pada (killed by Aśvatthāman), MBh.; Hariv. &c. **-dhī** or **-buddhi**, m. 'bold-minded,' N. of a man, Cat. **-parākrama**, mfn. of daring valour, R. **-mānin**, mfn. having a high opinion of one's self, R. (B. °*na*). **-ratha**, m. N. of a prince, MBh. xiii, 7676 (v. l. *dṛishṭa-r°*). **-vādin**, mfn. speaking boldly, Hariv. **-śarman**, m. N. of a son of Svaphalka, VP. **Dhṛishṭôkta**, m. N. of a son of Arjuna Kārtavīrya, Hariv. (C. °*shṇôktā*).

Dhṛishṭaka, m. N. of a prince, Hariv. (C. °*shṇuka*); VP. **-kathā**, f. N. of wk.

Dhṛishṭi, mfn. bold, VS. i, 17 (Mahīdh.); f. boldness, ŚāṅkhŚr.; m. a pair of tongs, TĀr.; Kāty Śr.; N. of a son of Hiraṇya-kasipu, BhP.; of a minister of King Daśa-ratha, R.

Dhṛishṇa, °**ṇôkta**, w.r. for °*shṭa*, °*ṭôkta*.

Dhṛishṇaj, mfn. bold, confident, impudent, L. (cf. °*shāj*).

Dhṛishṇi, m. ray of light, L.

Dhṛishṇú, mfn. bold, courageous, fierce, violent, strong (Indra, Soma, the Maruts; fire, weapons &c.), RV.; AV.; VS.; impudent, shameless, L.; (*ú*), ind. boldly, strongly, with force, RV. &c., ŚBr. (cf. *dadhṛish*); m. N. of a son of Manu Vaivasvata, MBh.; Hariv. (v. l. °*shṭa*); of a son of Manu Sāvarṇa, Hariv.; of a son of Kavi, MBh.; of a son of Kukura, Hariv.; n. (*Kaśyapasya*) N. of a Sāman, ĀrshBr. **-tva**, n. boldness, courage, MBh. **-sheṇa** (°*ṇú-*), mfn. having a resistless weapon (Indra or the Maruts), RV.; leading a valiant army (drum), AV. v, 20, 9. **Dhṛishṇv-ôjas**, mfn. endowed with resistless might (Indra or the Maruts), RV.

Dhṛishṇuka, m. N. of a prince (v. l. °*shṭaka*), Hariv.

Dhṛishṇuyā́, ind. boldly, strongly, firmly, RV.

Dhṛishya, mfn. assailable, to be attacked, MBh.

धृषद् 2. *dhṛishád* = *dṛishád*, RV. viii, 52, 4.

धॄ *dhṝ*, cl. 9. P. *dhṛiṇāti*, to be or grow old (Dhātup. xxxi, 24 v. l. for *jṝ* or *jhṝ*).

धे *dhe*, cl. 1. P. (Dhāt. xxii, 6) *dháyati*, RV. &c. &c. (pf. *dadhau*, 3. pl. °*dhúr*, RV.; aor. *-adhāt*, AV. x, 4, 26; *adhāsīt* or *adadhat*, Pāṇ. ii, 4, 78; iii, 1, 49; Prec. *dheyāt*, vi, 4, 67; fut. *dhāsyati*, MBh., *dhātā*, Gr.; dat. inf. *dhā́tave*, RV.; ind. p. *dhītvā́* & *-dhīya*, ŚBr.; *-dhāya*, Gr.) to suck, drink, suck or drink in, take to one's self, absorb, appropriate, RV. &c. &c.: Pass. *dhīyate*, Gr.: Caus. *dhāpáyate* (cf. Pāṇ. i, 3, 89, Vārtt. 1, Pat.) to give suck, nourish, RV.; °*ti*, ŚBr. (cf. *anu-* √*dhe*); aor. *adīdhapat*, Gr.: Desid. *dhitsati*, Pāṇ. vii, 4, 54: Intens. *dedhīyate*, *dādheti*, & *dādhāti*, Gr. [Cf. Gk. θῆ-σασθαι, γαλαθηνός, θη-λή; Lat. *fē-lare*; Goth. *dadd-jan*; Germ. *tā-an*, *tā-jan*.]

Dhena, m. the ocean or a river, L.; (*dhénā*), f. a milch cow, pl. any beverage made of milk, RV.; a mare (?), i, 101, 10; v, 30, 9; river, L.; speech, voice (?), i, 2, 3 (Sāy.; cf. Naigh. i, 11); N. of the wife of Bṛihaspati, TĀr.; Vait.; (*ī*), f. a river, L.

Dhenikā, f. coriander, Bhpr. (v. l. °*nukā*).

Dhenú, mfn. milch, yielding or giving milk; f. a milch cow or any cow, RV. &c. &c. (ifc. of names of animals also denoting the female of any species; cf. *khaḍga-*, *go-*, *vaḍava-*); any offering or present to Brāhmans instead or in the shape of a cow (mostly ifc. [cf. *ghṛita-*, *jala-*, *tila-* &c.], where it also forms diminutives; cf. *asi-*, *khaḍga-*); metaph. = the earth, MBh. xiii, 3165; pl. any beverage made of milk, RV. iv, 22, 6 &c.; n. N. of a Sāman, ĀrshBr. (also *marutām dh°* & *dhenu-payasī*, du.) **-go-duha**, n. cow and milker, Pāṇ. v, 4, 106, Kāś. **-tva**, n. the state of being a cow, Hcat. **-dakshiṇa**, mfn. (sacrifice) whereat a cow is given as a fee, ŚrS. **-dugdha**, n. cow's milk, L.; a kind of gourd, L.; **-kara**, m. Daucus Carota, L. **-bhavyā**, f. about to become a milch cow, Gaut.; Āpast. **-makshikā**, f. horse-fly, gad-fly, L. **-mát**, mfn. containing or yielding a nourishing beverage, RV.; containing the word *dhenu*, AitBr.; (*ī*), f. N. of the wife of Deva-dyumna, BhP. **-m-bhávyā**, f. = °*nu-bh°*, MaitrS. (Pāṇ. vi, 3, 70; Vārtt. 3). **-shṭarī**, f. (fr. *starī*) a milch cow ceasing to give milk, MaitrS.; Kāṭh. **Dhenv-anaḍuhá**, n. sg. or m. du. milch cow and bull, ŚBr.; Gaut. (cf. Pāṇ. v, 4. 77).

Dhenuka, m. a kind of coitus, L. (cf. *dhain°*); N. of an Asura slain by Kṛishṇa or Bala-bhadra, MBh.; Hariv.; Pur.; of a son of Dur-dama, VP.; pl. N. of a people, MBh.; (*dhénukā*), f. milch cow, cow; any female animal (also a woman), AV.; Br.; Śr. & GṛS.; MBh. &c.; = *dṛishṭa-pushpā*, Gal.; = *dhenu*, ifc. to form dimin., L.; a vein which when cut bleeds only at intervals, Suśr.; coriander, Bhpr. (v. l. *dhenikā*); N. of the wife of Kīrti-mat (son of Aṅgiras), VP.; of a river, ib.; n. N. of a herd of milch cows, L.; N. of a place of pilgrimage, MBh. **-dhvaṅsin**, m. 'slayer of Dhenuka,' Kṛishṇa, L. **-vadha**, m. the killing of Dh°; N. of ch. of BrahmavP. iv. **-sūdana**, m. = *-dhvaṅsin*, L. **Dhenukā-dugdha**, n. cow's milk, L.; a kind of gourd, L. **Dhenukâri**, m. 'enemy of Dh°,' Kṛishṇa, L.; a kind of small tree, L. **Dhenukâśrama**, m. N. of a hermitage, MBh.

Dhenushyā, f. a cow whose milk has been pledged, L. (cf. Pāṇ. iv, 4, 89). °**shyita**, mfn. one who has pledged the milk of his cows (?), g. *tārakâdi*.

Dhenūka. See *bahu-*.

Dhainava. See g. *utsâdi* & *bid-âdi*.

Dhainuka, n. a herd of cows, L.; a kind of coitus, L.

धेमात्र *dhemātra*, m. or n. a partic. high number (Buddh.), v.r. for *dhamātra* (see *dhamara*).

धेय *dheya*, mfn. (√1. *dhā*) to be held or taken &c.; to be created or what is created, MBh. xii, 13108; to be applied or put in practice, Śiś. v, 60; n. giving, imparting (ifc., cf. *nāma-*, *bhāga-*, *mitra-* &c., Pāṇ. v, 4, 36, Vārtt. 2, 3). **Dheyêśvara**, m. N. of an author, Cat.

Dheshṭha, mfn. (superl.) giving the most, most liberal, RV.

धैर्य 1. *dhairya*, n. (1. *dhīra*) intelligence, forethought (opp. to *mālvya*), VS.; Kāṭh.

धैर्य 2. *dhairya*, n. (2. *dhīra*) firmness, constancy, calmness, patience, gravity, fortitude, courage, (°*ryam-*√*kṛi* or *ava-lamb* or *ā-lamb*, to compose one's self, gather courage) MBh.; Kāv. &c.; precision of diction, Śiksh. **-kalita**, mfn. assuming firmness or composure, steady, calm, Śiś. ix, 59. **-tā**, f. constancy, perseverance, Pañcar. (for *dhīratā*?). **-dhara**, mfn. possessed of firmness or constancy, Kāv. **-dhvaṅsa**, m. failure of courage, MW. **-pāramitā**, f. highest perfection of perseverance, Kāraṇḍ. **-mitra**, m. N. of a poet, Cat. **-yukta** (Hariv.), **-vat** (R.; Rājat.), mfn. possessed of firmness or patience, firm, steady. **-vṛitti**, f. steady conduct, composure (Vikr. v, 9 read *ujjhita-dhairya-vṛittir*, v. l. *vṛittam*); mfn. of steady conduct, steadily behaved, MW.

धैवत *dhaivata*, n. the sixth note of the gamut, MBh. xii, 6859.

धैवत्य *dhaivatya*, n. (fr. *dhīvan*, Pāṇ. vi, 4, 174) skilfulness (?).

धैवर *dhaivará*, mf(ī)n. belonging or relating to a fisherman, VS.

धोईकवि *dhoī-kavi*, m. N. of a poet (prob. = *dhoyin*), Cat.

धोड *dhoḍa*, m. a sort of snake (commonly Dhora), L.

धोयिन् *dhoyin*, or °*yī* or °*yīka*, m. N. of a poet (cf. *dhoī-kavi*), Cat.

धोर् *dhor*, cl. 1. P. (pf. *dudhora*, fut. *dhoritā*; Caus. aor. *adudhorat*, Gr.) to run, trot, be quick or alert, Dhātup. xv, 45.

Dhoraṇa, n. any vehicle, L.; a horse's trot, L.; going well or quickly, W.; (*ī*), f. an uninterrupted series, tradition, Vcar. °**rita** or °**ritaka**, n. a horse's trot, L.

धौत *dhauta*, mfn. (√2. *dhāv*) washed, cleansed, purified, TāṇḍBr.; Suśr.; Kāv. &c.; washed off, removed, destroyed, Kālid.; Śiś.; Bhaṭṭ. (cf. *dhūtá*); polished, bright, white, shining, MBh., Kāv. &c.; (*ī*), f. washing, Siṅhās.; n. id., Cāṇ.; silver, L. **-kaṭa**, m. a bag of coarse cloth, L. **-kushṭha**, n. a kind of leprosy, Gal. **-kośaja** or **-kauśeya**, n. bleached or purified silk (= *pattrôrṇa*), L. **-khaṇḍī**, f. sugar-candy, L. **-danta**, mfn. having clean teeth, MBh. **-pāpman**, mfn. purified from sin, Caraṇ. **-bali**, f. a kind of collyrium, L. (cf. °*tâñjanī*). **-mūla**, mfn. (a tree) having its roots washed by (instr.), Śak. (Pi.) i, 14. **-mūlaka**, m. N. of a prince of the Cīnas, MBh. **-śila**, n. 'bright stone,' rock crystal, L. **Dhautâñjanī** or °**lī**, f. a sort of collyrium (= *try-aṅkaṭa* or °*ṅgaṭa*), L. **Dhautâtman**, mfn. pure-hearted, BhP. **Dhautâpâṅga**, mfn. having the corners of the eyes illumined, Megh. 45.

Dhautaka, mfn. made of bleached or purified silk, Pat.

Dhautaya (?) or °**teya**, n. rock-salt, L. (cf. *dhauta-śila*).

Dhautī, f. a kind of penance (consisting in washing a strip of white cloth, swallowing it and then drawing it out of the mouth), Cat.

धौतरी *dhautárī*, f. (√1. *dhū*, Sāy.) shaking, RV. vi, 44, 7.

धौति 2. *dhautí*, f. (√1. *dhāv*) spring, well, rivulet, RV. ii, 13, 5.

धौन्धुमार *dhaundhumāra*, mf(ī)n. treating of Dhundhu-māra (as an episode), MBh. °**māri**, m. patr. fr. Dhundhu-māra, Hariv.

धौमक *dhaumaka*, m. (fr. *dhūma*, Pāṇ. iv, 2, 127) N. of a district, W.

Dhaumāyana, m. patr. fr. Dhūma, g. *aśvâdi*. °**mīya**, mfn. smoky, MW. (cf. g. *kṛiśâśvâdi*).

Dhaumya, m. (patr. fr. *dhūma*, g. *gargâdi*) N. of an ancient Ṛishi, MBh.; Hariv.; Pur.; of a son of Vyāghra-pāda, MBh.; of a younger brother of Devala and family priest of the Pāṇḍavas, ib.; of a pupil of Vālmīki, R.; of sev. authors, Cat.; *-śikshā* & *-smṛiti*, f. N. of wks.

Dhaumra, m. (fr. *dhūmra*) patr. of Dantāvala, GopBr.; N. of an ancient Ṛishi, MBh.; n. grey (the colour), L.; a partic. place for building, L. (cf. *dhūma*). °**rāyaṇa**, m. patr. fr. *dhūmra*, g. *aśvâdi* (cf. *dhūmrāyaṇa*).

धौमत *dhaumata*, m. or n. myrrh, L. °**tāyana**, °**naka**, g. *arīhaṇâdi* (not in Kāś.)

धौर *dhaura*, m. Grislea Tomentosa, Bhpr. °**râditya-tīrtha**, n. N. of a Tīrtha, ŚivaP.

धौरितक *dhauritaka* and *dhaurya*, n. a horse's trot, L. (cf. *dhorita*, °*taka*).

धौरेय *dhaureya*, mf(ī)n. (fr. *dhur*) fit to be harnessed or for a burden, L.; being foremost, at the head of (cf. *purusha-*); m. beast of burden, draught-horse, L. (also °*yaka*, Veṇis. iv, 1/0).

धौर्जट *dhaurjaṭa*, mf(ī)n. (fr. *dhūr-jaṭa*) belonging to Śiva, Bālar. viii, 45.

धौर्तक *dhaurtaka*, n. (fr. *dhūrta*) roguery, knavery, fraud, g. *manojñâdi*. °**tika**, mf(*ī*)n. belonging to a cheat, knavish, fraudulent, W.; n. fraud, dishonesty, ib. °**teya**, m. pl. N. of a warlike tribe; sg. a prince of this tribe, g. *yaudheyâdi*, iv, 1, 178 (Kāś. *dhārteya* & *ghārt°*). °**tya**, n. fraud, dishonesty, Daśar. ii, 20.

धौवकि *dhauvaki*, m. metron. fr. Dhuvakā, g. *bāhv-ādi*.

धौष्य *dhaushya*, m. pl. a partic. school of the Yajur-veda, AV. Paipp.

ध्मा 1. *dhmā*. See √*dham*.

Dhma, mfn. blowing, a blower (cf. *tūṇa-*, *śaṅka-*).

2. **Dhmā**, m. (?) blowing. **-kāra**, m. a blacksmith, L.

Dhmātá, mfn. blown, blown up or into, RV. &c. &c.; inflamed, excited, W.; n. a partic. wrong pronunciation of vowels, Pat. °**tavya**, mfn. to be blown or kindled, Kull.

Dhmā́tṛi, m. a blower, smelter or melter (of metal), RV. v, 9, 5; (*dhmātṛí*), n. a contrivance for blowing or melting, ib.

Dhmāna, n. blowing, puffing, swelling, Suśr.

Dhmāpana, (Caus. of √*dham*) n. the act of reducing to (powder, &c.) or any contrivance for it, Car. °**pita**, mfn. reduced to ashes, burnt to a cinder (*kshauma*), Suśr.

Dhmāyat, mf(*antī*)n. or °**yamāna**, mfn. being blown, being melted &c., MW.

ध्माङ्क्ष् *dhmāṅksh*, v. r. for *dhvāṅksh*, Vop.

Dhmāṅksha, m., w.r. for *dhvaṅksha*, a crow.

ध्मामन् *dhmāman*, w. r. for *dhyāman*, Uṇ. iv, 152.

ध्या *dhyā, dhyāta, dhyāna.* See under √*dhyai*, below.

ध्याम *dhyāma*, mfn. dark-coloured, black, L. (cf. *śyāma*); n. any or a partic. fragrant grass, Suśr.; Artemisia Indica, L. °**mī-karaṇa**, n. making dark-coloured, blackening, L.; burning, consuming, L. °**mī-kṛita**, mfn. made dark-coloured, blackened, L.

Dhyāmaka, n. a part. kind of grass, Suśr.; Bhpr.

Dhyāmala, mfn. dark-coloured, black, impure, unclean, Dharmaś. °**li-√kṛi**, to make dirty, soil, pollute, ib.

ध्युषित *dhyushita*, mfn. dazzling white, Kāraṇḍ. °**tâsva**, m. N. of a prince, Ragh. xviii, 22 (v.l. *vyushit*°).

ध्यै *dhyai*, cl. 1. P. *dhyāyati* (ep. also °*te* or cl. 2. *dhyāti*; Impv. *dhyāhi*; Pot. *dhyāyāt*, Br.; °*yīta*, Up.; perf. *dadhyau*, Br. &c.; aor. *ádhyāsīt*, Br.; 3. pl. *dhyāsur*, MBh.; fut. *dhyāsyati*, ib.; *dhyātā*, Br.; ind. p. *dhyātvā*, ib.; *-dhyāya*, MBh.; *dhyāyam*, Kathās.) to think of, imagine, contemplate, meditate on, call to mind, recollect (with or scil. *manasā* or °*si, cetasā, dhiyā, hṛidaye* &c.), Br.; Gṛ. & ŚrS.; MBh.; Kāv. &c.; to brood mischief against (acc.), TS.; (alone) to be thoughtful or meditative, MBh.; Kāv. &c.; to let the head hang down (said of an animal), Car.: Pass. *dhyāyate*, to be thought of, &c., ib.; Caus. *dhyāpayati*, Gr.: Desid. *didhyāsate*, ŚBr.: Intens. *dādhyāyate, dādhyāti, dādhyeti*, Gr.

Dhyā́, f. thinking, meditation, RV.

Dhyāta, mfn. thought of, meditated on, Br.; Up.; MBh. &c. **-mātra**, mfn. merely thought of; °*trâgata*, °*trôpagāmin*, °*trôpanata* & *trôpasthita*, mfn. appearing when merely thought of, R.; Kathās.

Dhyātavya, mfn. to be thought of or reflected upon, Vop.; Kull. **Dhyātṛi**, m. one who reflects upon, a thinker, Hariv.; Kum.; BhP.; *-dhyātavyatva*, n. = *dhyātṛitva* + *dhyātavyatva*, Saṃk.

Dhyātva, n. thought, reflection, L.

Dhyāna, n. meditation, thought, reflection, (esp.) profound and abstract religious meditation, (°*nam āpad, ā-√sthā* or °*nam-√gam*, to indulge in r° m°) ChUp.; Mn.; MBh.; Kāv. &c. (with Buddhists divided into 4 stages, MWB. 209; Dharmas. lxxii; but also into 3, ib. cix); mental representation of the personal attributes of a deity, W.; insensibility, dulness, Bhpr.; (°*ná*), m. N. of a partic. personification, MaitrS.; of the 11th day of the light half in Brahmā's month, Pur. **-gamya**, mfn. attainable by meditation, MW. **-gocara**, m.pl. a partic. class of deities, Lalit. **-cakshus**, n. the eye of m°, R. **-ccheda**, m. interruption of thought or m°, Bhartṛ. **-japya**, m.pl. N. of a race, Hariv. (v.l. *kara-j*° & *dhyāna-pushṭa*). **-tatpara**, mfn. lost in m°, thoughtful, MBh. **-taraṃga-ṭīkā**, f. N. of Comm. **-dīpa**, m., °**pikā**, f. N. of wks. **-dṛishṭi**, mfn. seeing with the mind's eye, R. **-dyuti**, m. N. of a man, Buddh. **-dhīra** (Daś.), **-nitya** (MBh.), **-nishṭha** (R.), **-para** (MBh.), mfn. engaged in meditation, thoughtful. **-pāramitā**, f. perfection of m°, Kāraṇḍ.; MWB. 128. **-pushṭa**, see *-japya*. **-pūta**, mfn. purified by m°, BhP. **-phala**, n. 'fruit of m°,' N. of ch. of PSarv. **-bindûpanishad**, f. N. of an Up. **-bhaṅga**, m. = *-ccheda*, MW. **-maya**, mf(*ī*)n. consisting of m°, Hariv. **-mātra**, n. mere m°, thought alone, MW. **-mudrā**, f. a prescribed attitude in which to meditate on a deity, ib. **-yoga**, m. profound m° (or 'm° and abstraction'), Svet Up.; Mn.; N. of a kind of magic, Cat.; *-sāra*, m. N. of an extract from PadmaP.; °*gin*, mfn. absorbed in meditation, Hcat. **-lakshaṇa**, n. 'mark of m°,' N. of ch. of PSarv. **-vat**, mfn. intent on religious m°, MBh. **-vallarī**, f., **-śataka**, n. N. of wks. **-śīlā**, f. N. of a Buddh. goddess. **-stimita-locana**, mfn. having an eye rigid by m°, Ragh. **-stha** (MW.), **-sthita** (Kathās.), mfn. absorbed in m°. **Dhyānâgāra**, m. or n. a room to indulge in m°, Jātakam. **Dhyānâmbā**, f. N. of a woman, Cat. **Dhyānâlaṃkāra**, m. N. of a partic. Samādhi, Kāraṇḍ. **Dhyānâvacara**, m. pl. N. of a class of Buddh. deities (cf. °*na-gocara*). **Dhyānâśraya-ṭīkā**, f. N. of wk. **Dhyānâhāra**, m. the nutriment of m°, Dharmas. lxx.

Dhyānika, mfn. proceeding from religious meditation, Mn. vi, 82.

Dhyāni, in comp. for °*nin*. **-buddha** & **-bodhi-sattva**, m. a spiritual (not material) Buddha or Bodhi-sattva, MWB. 203.

Dhyānin, mfn. contemplative, engaged in religious meditation, MBh. °**nīya**, mfn. = *dhyeya*, Vop.

Dhyāyat, mf(*antī*)n. thinking, meditating, imagining, Mn.; MBh.; R. °**yati**, m. N. of √*dhyai*, Saṃk. °**yam**, ind. (repeated) meditating on (acc.), Kathās. °**yamāna**, mfn. being reflected or meditated upon, Mn.; R. °**yin**, mfn. absorbed in meditation, quite intent upon or engrossed in (comp.), Hcat.

Dhyeya, mfn. to be meditated on, fit for meditation, to be pondered or imagined, Yājñ.; MBh.; Kāv. &c.

ध्र *dhra*, mf(ī)n. (√*dhṛi*) = *dhara*, ifc.; cf. *aṅsa-dhrī, mahī-dhra*, &c.

ध्रज् *dhraj, dhrañj* or *dhrāj*, cl. 1. P. (Nigh. ii, 14; Dhātup. vii, 38, &c.) *dhrájati* RV. (*dhrañjati* or *dhriñjati*, Gr.; p. Ā. *dhrājamāna*, MaitrS.; aor. Pot. Ā. *dhrājishīya*, ib.) to move, go, glide, fly, sweep on. (Cf. *dhṛij* & *dhrij*.)

Dhrajati. See *citrá-*.

Dhrájas, n. gliding course or motion, RV.

Dhraji, id. (g. *yavâdi*). **Dhrájī-mat**, mfn. gliding, moving, RV.

Dhrā́j, f. the power to glide or move, MaitrS. **Dhrājá**, m. one who glides or moves, ib. **Dhrā́ji**, f. = *dhrájas*, ib. (also *dhrājī*); impulse, force (of a passion), AV.; whirlwind, L.

ध्रण् *dhraṇ*, cl. 1. P. °*ṇati*, to sound, Dhātup. xiii, 16 (cf. *dhvan, dhvraṇ*).

ध्रस् *dhras*, cl. 9. and 10. P. *dhrasnāti, dhrāsayati*, to glean or to cast upwards, xxxi, 52; xxxiii, 68 (cf. *udhras*).

ध्रा *dhrā*, cl. 2. and 1. P. *dhrāti* or *dhrati, dhrayati* &c. to go, Naigh. ii, 14.

ध्राक्षा *dhrākshā*, v.l. for *drākshā*. **-mat**, mfn. g. *yavâdi*.

ध्राख् *dhrākh*, °*khati* = *drākh*, Dhātup. v, 11.

ध्राघ् *dhrāgh*, °*ghate* (perf. *dadhrāghe*, Pāṇ. viii, 4, 54, Sch.) = *drāgh*, Dhātup. iv, 40; 41.

ध्राङ्क्ष् *dhrāṅksh*, °*kshati* = *dhvāṅksh*, xvii, 20 (cf. *dhmāṅksh*).

ध्राड् *dhrāḍ*, °*ḍate* = *drāḍ*, viii, 36.

Dhrāḍi, m. gathering flowers, Uṇ. iv, 117, Sch.

ध्रि *dhri* (√*dhṛi*) in *á-dhri*, q.v.

Dhriyamāṇa, mfn. being held or sustained &c.; continuing to live, existing, alive, Mn.; MBh. &c.

ध्रिज् *dhrij*, cl. 1. P. *dhrejati*, to go, move, Dhātup. vii, 46 (Vop.); cf. *dhraj* & *dhṛij*.

ध्रु 1. *dhru*, cl. 6. P. *dhruváti* (Naigh. ii, 14) to go; to be firm or fixed (also cl. 1. P. *dhravati*, Dhātup. xxii, 45; p. *dhruvat*, knowing, Bhaṭṭ.; perf. *dudhrāva*, be killed, ib.)

ध्रु 2. *dhru*. See *ásmṛita-dhru*.

ध्रु 3. *dhru*. See *dhvṛi*.

Dhrut. See *varuṇa-dhrút*.

Dhrúti, f. misleading, seduction, RV. vii, 86, 6.

ध्रुपदाख्यनृत्य *dhrupadâkhya-nṛitya*, n. (in music) a kind of dance (for *drup*°?).

ध्रुव् *dhruv*, °*vati*, v.l. for 1. *dhru*, Dhātup. xxviii, 107.

ध्रुव *dhruvá*, mf(*á*)n. (prob. fr. √*dhṛi*, but cf. √*dhru* & *dhruv*) fixed, firm, immovable, unchangeable, constant, lasting, permanent, eternal, RV. &c. &c. (e.g. the earth, a mountain, a pillar, a vow &c.; with *svâṅga*, n. an inseparable member of the body, Pāṇ. vi, 2, 177; with *dhenu*, f. a cow which stands quiet when milked, AV. xii, 1, 45; with *diś*, f. the point of the heavens directly under the feet [reckoned among the quarters of the sky, cf. 2. *diś*], AV.; Br.; with *smṛiti*, f. a strong or retentive memory, ChUp. vii, 26, 2; cf. also under *karaṇa* & *nakshatra*); staying with (loc.), RV. ix, 101, 12; settled, certain, sure, Mn.; MBh.; Kāv. &c.; ifc. = *pāpa*, L.; m. the polar star (personified as son of Uttāna-pāda and grandson of Manu), GṛS.; MBh. &c.; celestial pole, Sūryas.; the unchangeable longitude of fixed stars, a constant arc, ib.; a knot, VS. v, 21; 30; a post, stake, L.; the Indian fig-tree, L.; tip of the nose (?), L.; a partic. water-bird, ib.; the remaining (i.e. preserved) Graha which having been drawn in the morning is not offered till evening, ŚBr.; Vait.; (in music) the introductory verse of a song (recurring as a kind of burthen) or a partic. time or measure (*tāla-viśesha*); any epoch to which a computation of dates is referred, W.; N. of an astrol. Yoga; of the syllable Om, RāmatUp.; of Brahmā, L.; of Vishṇu, MBh.; of Śiva, Śivag.; of a serpent supporting the earth, GṛS.; TĀr.; of a Vasu, MBh.; Hariv.; Pur.; of a son of Vasu-deva and Rohiṇī, BhP.; of an Āṅgirasa (supposed author of RV. x, 173), Anukr.; of a son of Nahusha, MBh.; of a follower of the Pāṇḍus, ib.; of a son of Ranti-nāra (or Ranti-bhāra), Pur.; (*ā*), f. the largest of the 3 sacrificial ladles, AV. xviii, 4, 5, 6 (with *juhū* & *upabhṛit*), VS.; ŚBr. &c.; (scil. *vṛitti*) a partic. mode of life, Baudh.; (scil. *strī*) a virtuous woman, L.; Desmodium Gangeticum, L.; Sanseviera Zeylanica, L.; (in music) the introductory verse (cf. above); n. the fixed point (from which a departure takes place), Pāṇ. i, 4, 24; the enduring sound (supposed to be heard after the Abhinidhāna), RPrāt.; air, atmosphere, L.; a kind of house, Gal.; (*am*), ind. firmly, constantly, certainly, surely, Mn.; Yājñ.; MBh.; Kāv. &c.; (*āya*), ind. for ever, Hariv. [Cf. Zd. *drva*.] **-ketu**, m. a kind of meteor, Var. **-kshít**, mfn. resting firmly, VS. **-kshiti** (°*vá-*), mfn. having a firm position or abode, VS.; BhP.; m. a partic. personification, TĀr. **-kshetra**, n. N. of a place, W. **-kshema** (°*vá-*), mfn. firmly fixed, immovable, RV. **-gati**, f. a firm position, BhP.; mfn. going firmly, ib. **-gīta-nṛitya**, n. (in music) a partic. dance. **-gopá**, m. protector of the Grahas called Dhruva, Br.; KātyŚr. **-cakra** & **-carita**, n. N. of wks. **-cyút**, mfn. shaking the immovable, RV. **-tāraka**, n. (Var.; Sch.), **-tārā**, f. (Sūryas.) the polar star. **-tva**, n. (in music) quick time or measure. **-devī**, f. N. of a princess, L. **-naḍi** or °**ḍī**, f. N. of wk. **-nṛitya**, n. (in music) a partic. dance (cf. *-gīta-n*°). **-paṭu**, m. N. of a prince, L. **-pada**, n. N. of wk. **-pāla**, m. N. of an author, Cat. **-bhāga**, m. the unchangeable longitude of fixed stars, Gaṇit.; Sch. **-bhramaṇa**, n.; *-yantra*, n.; °*nâdhikāra*, m. N. of wks. **-maṇḍala**, n. the polar region. **-mānasa**, n. N. of wk. **-yashṭi**, f. the axis of the poles, Gol. **-yoni** (°*vá-*), mfn. having a firm resting-place, VS. **-ratnā**, f. N. of one of the Mātṛis attending on Skanda, MBh. **-rāja**, m. N. of a prince, L. **-rāhu**, m. a form of Rāhu, Var. **-lakshaṇa**, n. 'the mark of recurring verses,' N. of ch. of PSarv. **-śīla**, mfn. having a fixed residence, Gaut. **-sád**, mfn. resting on firm ground, VS. **-saṃdhi**, m. 'whose alliance is sure,' N. of a son of Su-saṃdhi or Su-sh° & father of Bharata, R.; of a son of Pushya, Ragh.; Pur. **-siddhi**, m. 'through whom cure is sure,' N. of a physician, Mālav. **-sûkta**, n. N. of wk. **-sena**, m. N. of 2 Valabhī princes, Inscr. **-stuti**, f. N. of wk. **-sthālī**, f. the vessel for the Graha called Dhruva, TBr.; Lāṭy. **Dhruvâkshara**, n. 'the eternal syllable' Om as N. of Vishṇu, MBh. **Dhruvânanda**, m. N. of an author (with *miśra*), Cat.; *-mata-vyākhyā*, f. N. of Comm. on Dh°'s wk. **Dhruvâvarta**, m. the point on the crown of the head from which the hairs radiate, Var. **Dhruvâśva**, m. N. of a prince, MatsyaP. (cf. Zd. *drvâspa*); of a partic. sacrificial act, MānGṛ.

Dhruvaka, m. the unchangeable longitude of fixed stars, Sūryas.; post, pale, stake, L.; (in music) = *dhruvā*, f.; N. of an attendant of Skanda, MBh.; (*ā*), f. (in music) = *dhruvā*, f. (cf. *dhuvakā*); N. of a woman, g. *bāhv-ādi*. **-bhāga**, m. (astron.) = *dhruvaka*, Gaṇit, Sch. **Dhruvakin** & °**kila**, mfn., see g. *prêkshâdi* & *picchâdi*.

Dhruváse, ind. (dat. as inf.) to stop or rest, RV. i, 70, 1.

Dhruvâḍaka, n. a kind of dance (°*vâṭaka*?).

Dhruví, mfn. firmly fixed, firm (mountains), RV. vii, 35, 8.

Dhrauva, mf(*ī*)n. belonging to Dhruva or the

polar star, MārkP.; being in the ladle called Dhruvā (with or m. scil. *ājya*), ŚrS.

Dhrauvaki, m. metron. fr. Dhruvakā, g. *bāhv-ādi.*

Dhrauvapada-ṭīkā, f. N. of a Comm.

Dhrauvya, n. fixedness, firmness, immovableness, Pāṇ. iii, 4, 76; duration, ŚāṅkhŚr.; Kauś.; certainty, necessity, Saṃk.; mfn. conferring firmness or duration, BhP.

ध्रुवाडक *dhruvāḍaka.* See above.

ध्रेक् *dhrek,* cl. 1. Ā. *dhrekate,* to sound, Dhātup. iv, 5 (cf. *drek*).

ध्रै *dhrai,* cl. 1. P. *dhrāyati,* to be pleased or satisfied, Dhātup. xxii, 11; cl. 2. &c. *dhrāti, dhrāti, dhrāyati,* see *dhrā.*

ध्रौपद *dhraupada,* n. (in music) a kind of dance (cf. *dhrupadâkhya-nṛitya*).

ध्रौव *dhrauva,* &c. See under *dhruva.*

ध्वंस *dhvaṇs* or *dhvas,* cl. 1. P. Ā. *dhvaṇsati* (to go, Naigh. ii, 14), °*te* (Dhātup. xviii, 16; perf. *dadhvaṇsur,* Up.; *dadhvaṇsire,* MBh. [also *dhvaṇsire*]; Bhaṭṭ.; *-dadhvase,* RV.; aor. *-dhvasán,* RV. viii, 54, 5; *adhvaṇsishṭa,* Gr.; fut. *dhvaṇsishyate,* °*sitā,* ib.; ind. p. *-dhvasya,* MBh.), to fall to pieces or to dust, decay, be ruined, perish, RV. &c. &c.; to be gone, vanish (only Impv. *dhvaṇsa,* °*sata,* °*satām*), MBh.; Hariv.; R.; to scatter, cover &c. (only *dhvasta,* q.v.): Pass. *dhvasyate* (Pāṇ. vi, 4, 24; Kāś.); °*ti* (GopBr.) to be destroyed, perish: Caus. *dhvaṇsáyati,* °*te,* to scatter, TBr.; to destroy, disperse, disturb, R.; Daś.; to violate (a woman), Kathās.; *dhvasáyati,* to scintillate, sparkle (Agni), RV. i, 140, 3; 5: Desid. *didhvaṇsishate,* Gr.: Intens. *danīdhvasyate,* °*dhvaṇsīti,* Pāṇ. vii, 4, 84, Kāś. [Cf. Germ. *dunst, tunst;* Angl. Sax. *dûst,* Engl. *dust.*]

Dhvaṇsá, m. falling down, perishing, destruction, loss, ruin, TBr. Var.; Kāv. &c.; (*ī*), f. a mote in a sun-beam, L. **-kārin,** mfn. (ifc.) destroying, Hit. i, 17; violating, Kathās. cvi, 166, &c.

Dhvaṇsaka, mfn. destroying, removing (cf. *dakshâdhvara-*); m. a partic. disease (caused by over-drinking), Car.

Dhvaṇsakalā-√kṛi, g. *ūry-ādi.*

Dhvaṇsana, mfn. = °*saka,* MBh. (cf. *dakshâdhvara-*); sputtering, Nir. ii, 9; n. destruction, ruin, R.; BhP.

Dhvaṇsi, m. $\frac{1}{100}$ part of a Muhūrta, ŚāṅkhŚr.

Dhvaṇsita, mfn. destroyed, ruined, lost, violated, Kathās.

Dhvaṇsin, mfn. perishing, disappearing, Megh. 109; destroying, removing, Hariv.; Var. &c.; m. = *dhvaṇsī,* L.; a kind of Pīlu-tree, L.

ध्वज 1. *dhvaj* or *dhvañj,* cl. 1. P. *dhvajati, dhvañjati,* to go, move, Dhātup. vii, 44; 45 (prob. Nom. fr. next).

2. **Dhvaj** (in *kṛita-dhváj*), banner (fr. *dhū+aj?*).

Dhvajá, m. (n. only Hariv. 9245 & g. *ardharcâdi;* fr. 2. *dhvaj*) a banner, flag, standard (ifc. f. *ā*), RV. &c. &c.; a flag-staff, W.; mark, emblem, ensign, characteristic, sign, MBh.; Hariv.; attribute of a deity (cf. *makara-, vṛishabha-* &c.); the sign of any trade (esp. of a distillery or tavern) & the business there carried on, Mn. iv, 85; a distiller or vendor of spirituous liquors, L.; (ifc.) the ornament of (e.g. *kula-dhvaja*), L.; the organ of generation (of any animal, male or female), Suśr.; L. (cf. *pum-, strī-*); a skull carried on a staff (as a penance for the murder of a Brāhman, W.; as a mark of ascetics and Yogīs, MW.); N. of a tree (= *-vṛiksha*), Cat.; a place prepared in a peculiar way for building, L. (in pros.) an iambic; (in Gr.) a partic. kind of Krama-pāṭha; (in astrol.) N. of a Yoga; pride, arrogance, hypocrisy, L.; N. of a Grāma, Pāṇ. iv, 2, 109, Sch. **-gṛiha,** n. a room in which banners are kept or from which b° wave, Hariv. **-grīva,** m. 'b°-(i. e. high-)necked,' N. of a Rakshas, R. **-druma,** m. the palm tree (used for making flag-staffs), L.; mfn. having banners for trees, R. **-navamī,** f. a partic. festival, Cat. **-paṭa,** m. b°-cloth,' a flag, Kāv. &c. **-patākin,** mfn. furnished with b°s and t°s, Hcat. **-praharaṇa,** m. 'b°-striking,' air, wind, L. **-bhaṅga,** m. fracture or fall of a b°, W.; fall of the male organ, impotence, Suśr. **-yantra,** n. °b-instrument,' any contrivance for fastening a flag-staff, MBh.; R. **-yashṭi,** f. flag-staff, Mn.; MBh.; R. **-rājin,** mfn. displaying flags or banners, MW. **-vat,** mfn. decorated with b°s (town), R.; bearing a mark or sign (esp. that of a criminal), Yājñ. iii, 243; m. a standard-bearer, MBh.; a vendor of spirituous liquors, Mn. iv, 84 (cf. *dhvajá* above); a Brāhman who having slain another carries the skull of the murdered man by way of penance, W.; (*ī*), f. N. of a divine female (the daughter of Hari-medhas), MBh.; of a divine attendant of a Bodhi-sattva, Lalit. **-vada,** m. N. of a man, g. *tikâdi,* Kāś. **-vṛiksha,** m. Caryota Urens, L. **-samucchraya,** m. raising a flag, Buddh. **-hṛita,** mfn. = °*jâhṛita,* L. **Dhvajâṇśuka,** m. = °*ja-paṭa,* W. **Dhvajâkāra,** mf(*ā*)n. furnished with a banner (flag-staff), Hariv. **Dhvajâgra,** n. the top of a standard (see below); m. a partic. Samādhi, Kāraṇḍ.; a partic. Roma-vivara, ib.; *-keyūra,* m. 'the ring on the top of a standard,' N. of a partic. Samādhi, Buddh.; *-niśā-maṇi,* m.; °*gra-vatī,* f. N. of 2 modes of reckoning, Lalit. **Dhvajâropaṇa,** n. raising a flag, Cat. **Dhvajâroha,** m. a kind of ornament on a f°, MBh. vi, 619 (w.r. *gajâr*°, B.) **Dhvajârohaṇa,** n. (°*ropaṇa?*) N. of wk. **Dhvajâhṛita,** mfn. plundered on the battle-field (where the standard is), Mn. viii, 415. **Dhvajôcchrāya,** m. erecting a banner, L.; = °*jônnati,* Suśr. **Dhvajôtthāna,** n. = °*jôcchrāya,* N. of a festival in honour of Indra, L. **Dhvajôtthāpana,** n. = °*jôcchrāya; -mantra,* m. N. of wk. **Dhvajônnati,** f. erection of the male organ, Bhpr.

Dhvaji or °**jī,** g. *yavâdi* & *bāhv-âdi.*

Dhvajika. See *dharma-.*

Dhvajin, mfn. having or bearing a banner, MBh.; R.; (ifc.) having anything as a mark (esp. for a committed crime), MBh.; m. a standard-bearer, ib.; any one having an emblem or sign, (esp.) a vendor of spirituous liquors, Yājñ. i, 141; (only L.) a chariot; a mountain; a snake; a peacock; a horse; a Brāhman; (*inī*), f. 'a bannered host,' an army, MBh.; Kāv. &c. °**inī-pati** (R.), °**inī-pāla** (BhP.), m. leader of an army. °**iny-utsava-saṃketa,** m. N. of a people, MBh. vi.

Dhvajī, in comp. for °*ja.* **-karaṇa,** n. raising a standard or making anything a plea, W. **-√kṛi,** to raise a standard; to make a plea or pretext (ind. p. *-kṛitya,* Hit. ii, 95).

ध्वञ्ज् *dhvañj,* °*jati.* See 1. *dhvaj.*

ध्वण् *dhvaṇ,* cl. 1. P. *dhvaṇati,* to sound, Dhātup. xiii, 10 (cf. 2. *dhvan*).

ध्वन् 1. *dhvan* (only aor. *ádhvanīt*), to become covered or extinguished (as anger), RV.: Caus. *ádhvănayat,* aor. *dhvanayīt,* to envelop, wrap up, darken, ib. [Cf. 2. *dhvāntá;* Lith. *dumju, dumti,* to cover, wrap up; Angl. Sax. *dvinan, dvan,* to be extinguished, vanish; *dun,* dark-brown, dark.]

ध्वन् 2. *dhvan,* cl. 1. P. *dhvanati* (perf. *dadhvāna, dadhvanur,* Bhaṭṭ.; fut. *dhvanishyati,* °*nitā,* Gr.) to sound, roar, make a noise, echo, reverberate, Kāv. &c.; to mean, imply, (esp. Pass. *dhvanyate,* it is meant, it is implied): Caus. *dhvănayati,* Dhātup. (aor. *adidhvanat* or *adadh*°, Gr.), to cause to sound, make resound (cf. °*nayat* below); *dhvanayati,* to allude to, hint at, Mṛicch., Comm.: Intens. in *dandhvana,* q. v. [Cf. 1. *dhvāntá:* Lith. *dundĕti,* to sound, call; Angl. Sax. *dynian,* to thunder.]

Dhvaná, m. N. of a wind, TĀr.; sound, tune, L.; N. of a man, g. *aśvâdi.* **-modin,** m. 'delighting by its sound,' a bee, L.

Dhvanana, n. sounding, humming, singing (cf. *karṇa-*); hinting at, allusion, Sāh.

Dhvanáyat, m. 'causing to sound, resounding,' N. of a wind, TĀr.

Dhvaní, m. sound, echo, noise, voice, tone, tune, thunder, AV. &c. &c.; the sound of a drum, W.; empty sound without reality, MW.; a word, L.; allusion, hint, implied meaning, poetical style, Sāh.; N. of wk.; N. of one of the Viśve Devās, VP.; of a son of the Vasu Āpa, ib. **-kāra** & **-kṛit,** m. N. of an author, Cat. **-gāthā-pañjikā,** f. N. of wk. **-graha,** m. 'sound-catcher,' the ear, L. **-tva,** n. figurative allusion, poetical style, Sāh. **-dhvaṇsa,** m. N. of wk. **-nātha,** m. N. of a man, Cat. **-nālā,** f. N. of sev. musical instruments, L. **-pradīpa,** m. N. of wk. **-bodhaka** or **-bodhana,** m. a kind of grass (= *rohisha*), L. **-mat,** mfn. containing a hint or an allusion; *-tā,* f. Pratāp. **-vikāra,** m. change of voice, L. **-viveka** & **-siddhânta-saṃgraha,** m. N. of wks.

Dhvanita, mfn. caused to sound, Śatr.; alluded to, implied, W.; n. sg. or pl. sound, thunder, Kād.

Dhvany, in comp. for °*ni.* **-artha,** m. implied meaning or truth, MW. **-ācārya,** m. N. of an author = *Ānanda-vardana.* **-ātmaka,** mfn. inarticulate (sound), Tarkas. **-āloka,** m. or **-ālocana,** n. N. of wk.

Dhvanyà, m. N. of a man, RV. v, 33, 10.

ध्वरस् *dhvarás,* f. (√*dhvṛi*) destructive, mischievous, N. of partic. female demons or noxious beings, RV.

Dhvará, f. bending, causing to fall, MaitrS.

Dhvartavya (see *a-,* add.) & **dhvarya** (Pāṇ. iii, 1, 123), to be bent or thrown down.

ध्वस् 1. *dhvas.* See *dhvaṇs.*

2. **Dhvas,** mfn. (nom. *t,* Pāṇ. viii, 2, 72) causing to fall, throwing down (cf. *parṇa-*).

Dhvasán, m. N. of a king of the Matsyas, ŚBr.

Dhvasáni, m. sprinkler (a cloud), RV. i, 164, 29. °**sánti,** m. N. of a man, 112, 23.

Dhvasirá, mfn. sprinkled, spattered, covered, vii, 83, 3 (cf. *dhūsara*).

Dhvasta, mfn. fallen, destroyed, perished, lost, Br. &c. &c.; eclipsed, obscured, Var.; scattered or covered with (instr. or comp.), MBh.; Kāv. &c. **-kamala,** mfn. (a pond) which has lost its lotus-flowers, R. **-dhī,** m. one whose senses are lost (through passion &c.), Rājat. **-preman,** mfn. whose love has vanished, Amar. 12. **-mūrdhaja,** mfn. whose hair has fallen out, R. **-rajaḥ-sattva-tamo-mala,** mfn. freed from the impurity of passion, goodness & darkness, BhP. **Dhvastâksha,** mf(*ī*)n. whose eyes are sunk (as in death), BhP.

Dhvasti, f. ceasing, destruction, Bālar. iv. 9; cessation of all the consequences of actions (one of the 4 states to which the Yogin attains), MārkP.

Dhvasmán, m. polluting, darkening, RV. (destroying, Sāy.) **-vat,** mfn. covered, obscured, ib.; n. water, Naigh. i, 12.

Dhvasrá, mfn. = °*sirá,* RV.; decaying, falling off, ib.; m. N. of a man, ib.

ध्वाक्षा *dhvākshā,* f. N. of a plant and its fruit, L. (v. l. *dhvāṅkshā*).

ध्वाङ्क्ष् *dhvāṅksh,* cl. 1. P. *dhvāṅkshati,* to utter the cry of birds, to caw, croak, &c.; to desire, Dhātup. xvii, 21 (cf. *dhmāṅksh* & *dhrāṅksh*).

Dhvāṅksha, m. a crow, AV. &c. &c. (cf. *tīrtha-*); Ardea Nivea, L.; a beggar, L.; a house; (in astrol.) N. of a Yoga; N. of a Nāga, L.; (*ā*), f. a kind of plant & its fruit, g. *harītaky-ādi,* Kāś.; (*ī*), f. a partic. medicinal plant, L. **-jaṅghā,** f. Leea Hirta, L. **-jambū,** f. a kind of plant (= *kākaj*°), L. **-tīrtha,** n. a bathing-place for crows, BhP. **-tuṇḍa-phala,** m.; **-tuṇḍā** & °**ḍī,** f. Ardisia Solanacea, L. **-dantī** & **-nakhī,** f. Capparis Sepiaria, L. **-nāman,** m. a species of dark Udumbara, L.; (°*mnī*), f. Ficus Oppositifolia, L. **-nāśanī,** f. a kind of plant (= *hapushā*), L. **-nāsā** & °**sikā,** f. Ardisia Solanacea, L. **-pushṭa,** m. 'brought up by crows,' the Kokila or Indian cuckoo (cf. *kāka-p*°), L. **-mācī,** f. Solanum Indicum, L. **-vallī,** f. Ardisia Solanacea, L.; Pongamia Glabra, L.; = next, L. **Dhvāṅkshâdanī,** f. Capparis Sepiaria, L. **Dhvāṅkshârāti,** m. 'crow-enemy,' an owl, L.

Dhvāṅkshikā, °**ksholikā** & °**ksholī,** f. a partic. medicinal plant, L.

ध्वान *dhvāna,* m. (√2. *dhvan*) humming, murmuring (one of the 7 kinds of speech or *vācaḥ sthānāni,* a degree louder than *upâṇśu,* q.v.), TPrāt.; any sound or tone, Rājat.; Kathās (cf. *prati-*).

Dhvānāyana, m. patr. fr. Dhvana, g. *aśvâdi.*

Dhvānita, mfn. caused to sound; **-dundubhi,** m. a sounding drum, Śatr.

1. **Dhvāntá,** m. N. of a wind, TS.

ध्वान्त 2. *dhvāntá,* mfn. (√1. *dhvan,* cf. Pāṇ. vii, 2, 18), covered, veiled, dark; n. darkness, night, RV. &c. &c. **-citta,** m. a fire-fly, L. (v. l. *-vitta*). **-jāla,** n. the net of darkness or the cover of night, Daś. **-dīpikā,** f. N. of wk. **-śātrava,** m. 'enemy of d°,' Bignonia Indica, L.; = next, W. **Dhvāntârāti,** m. 'id.,' the sun or any luminary, L. **Dhvāntônmesha,** m. = °*nta-citta,* L.

ध्वृ *dhvṛi,* cl. 1. P *dhvárati* (Naigh. ii, 19;

Dhātup. xxii, 41; perf. *dadhvāra*, Gr.; aor. *adhvārshīt*, ib.; 3. pl. Ā. *ádhūrshata*, RV.; Prec. *dhvṛishīshṭa*, Bhaṭṭ.; *dhvarish°*, Gr.; fut. *dhvarishyati, dhvartā*, ib.) to bend, cause to fall, hurt, injure, RV.; TS.: Caus. *dhvārayati*, Gr.: Intens. *dādhvaryate*, Pāṇ. vii, 4, 30, Kāś.: Desid. *dudhūrshati* & *didhvarishati*, Vop. [Cf. *dhūrv*; Goth. *dvals*; Angl. S. *dwellan*; Engl. *dull, dolt*; Germ. *toll*.]

Dhvṛit, mfn. bending, felling, killing (ifc.; cf. *satya-*).

ध्वण् *dhvaṇ*, cl. 1. P. *dhvaṇati*, to sound, Dhātup. xiii, 16 (v. r. for *dhraṇ*).

न NA.

न 1. *na*, the dental nasal (found at the beginning of words and before or after dental consonants as well as between vowels; subject to conversion into ण, Pāṇ. viii, 4, 1-39). — 1. **-kāra**, m. the sound or letter *n*, Gr.; (in prosody) a tribrach; *-vipulā*, f. a kind of metre.

न 2. *ná*, ind. not, no, nor, neither, RV. (*nā*, x, 34, 8) &c. &c. (as well in simple negation as in wishing, requesting and commanding, except in prohibition before an Impv. or an augmentless aor. [cf. 1. *mā*]; in successive sentences or clauses either simply repeated, e.g. Mn. iv, 34; or strengthened by another particle, esp. at the second place or further on in the sentence, e.g. by *u* [cf. *nó*], *utá, api, cāpi, vā, vâpi* or *atha vā*, RV. i, 170, 1; 151, 9; Nal. iii, 24, &c.; it may even be replaced by *ca, vā, api ca, api vā*, &c. alone, as Mn. ii, 98; Nal. i, 14, &c.; often joined with other particles, beside those mentioned above e.g. with a following *tu, tv eva, tv eva tu, cêd*, q.v., *khalu*, q.v., *ha* [cf. g. *câdi* and Pāṇ. viii, 1, 31] &c.; before round or collective numbers and after any numeral in the instr. or abl. it expresses deficiency, e.g. *ekayā na viṇśati*, not 20 by 1, i.e. 19, ŚBr.; *pañcabhir na catvāri śatāni*, 395, ib.; with another *na* or an *a* priv. it generally forms a strong affirmation [cf. Vām. v, 1, 9], e.g. *nêyaṃ na vakshyati*, she will most certainly declare, Śak. iii, 9; *nâdaṇḍyo 'sti*, he must certainly be punished, Mn. viii, 335; it may also, like *a*, form compounds, Vām. v, 2, 13 [cf. below]); that not, lest, for fear lest (with Pot.), MBh.; R.; Daś. &c.; like, as, as it were (only in Veda and later artificial language, e.g. *gauro na tṛishitaḥ piba*, drink like [lit. 'not,' i.e. 'although not being'] a thirsty deer; in this sense it does not coalesce metrically with a following vowel). [Cf. Gk. νη-; Lat. *nĕ-*; Angl. Sax. *ne*, 'not;' Engl. *no*, &c.] — 2. **-kāra**, m. the negation *na*, the word No, Naish. — **kiṃcana**, mfn. having nothing, very poor, MBh.; Pañc. (cf. *a-k°*). — **kiṃcid**, n. nothing, Kathās.; *-api-saṃkalpa*, m. no desire for anything, Kāv. — **kim**, ind. = *na-kīm*, g. *câdi*. — **kis** (*ná-*), ind. no one, nobody, RV.; = next, ib. (g. *câdi*; cf. Naigh. iii, 12). — **kīm** (*ná-*), ind. not, not at all, never, ib. (cf. ib.). — **kutaścid**, ind. from nowhere, in *-bhaya*, mfn. = *a-k°-bh°*, BhP. — **ga**, m., see *nága*. — **câtha-vāda** (?), m. N. of wk. — **ciketa** (metric.) & **-ciketas** (*ná-*), m. (√4. *cit*) N. of a man, TBr.; KaṭhUp. — **cira**, mfn. not long (in time), MBh.; (*am*), ind. not long, for a short time; (*ena, āt, āya*), ind. id., shortly, soon; *-kālam*, ind. = *°ram*, MBh.; Kāv. &c. — **tad-vid**, mfn. not knowing that, BhP. — **tamām** (?, MaitrS.), **-tarām** (ŚBr.), ind. not at all, never. — 1. **-dīna**, mfn. not small or insignificant, Kathās. — **dūshita**, mfn. uncorrupted; *-dhī*, mfn. of unc° mind, BhP. — **dṛiśya**, mfn. invisible; *-tva*, n. PadmaP. — **nu**, see *nanú*. — **para**, m. or n. N. of wk. — **parājit**, m. 'not yielding,' N. of Śiva, MBh. vii, 2877 (Nīlak.) — **puṇs** (only *°sā*, BhP.) and **-puṇsa** (only *°sāya*, MBh.), not a man, a eunuch. — **puṇsaka** (*ná-*), mf(*ā*)n. neither male nor female; a hermaphrodite; a eunuch; a weakling, coward, MaitrS.; Br.; Up.; MBh. &c.; neuter, n. a word in the n° gender or the n° g° itself, ŚBr.; Prāt.; Pāṇ. &c.; *-pāda*, m. N. of ch. of the Su-bodhā; *-liṅga*, mfn. of the neuter gender, Cat.; *-liṅga-saṃgraha*, m. N. of ch. of the Nāmaliṅgânuśāsana. — **bhīta**, mfn. not afraid, fearless; *-vat*, ind. Hariv. — **bhrāj**, m. (nom. *ṭ*) N. of a divine Soma-keeper, MaitrS.; a cloud, L. — **mātra**, m. or n. N. of a partic. high number, Buddh. — **muca** & **°ci**, see *Namuca, °ci*. — **murá**, m. or n. the not dying (?), AV. — **mṛita**, mfn. not dead, alive (memory), BhP. — **yuta**, m. pl. a myriad, Lalit. (cf. *a-y°*). — **rishyat**, m. N. of a son of Manu Vaivasvata, MBh.; Hariv.; Pur.; *°yanta*, m. id., ib.; of a son of Marutta, VP. — **roga**, mf(*ā*)n. not ill, well, Hcat. — **liptâṅga**, mfn. whose body is not anointed, R. (B.) — **vidya** (MBh. i, 3246), **-vidvas** (BhP.), mfn. ignorant. — **śakti**, f. inability, Kālac. — **śubha**, mfn. unpleasant, inauspicious, MBh. — **śesha**, mfn. without remainder, entire, all, RāmatUp. — **saṃvid**, f. unconsciousness, forgetfulness, Kāv. — **sukara**, mf(*ā* or *ī*)n. not easy to be done, difficult, MBh. — **sparśana**, n. non-contact. — **hí**, see *na-hí*. **Nâgni-dūshita**, mfn. unhurt by fire, Mn. ii, 47. **Nâti** (for *na* + *ati*, in comp.; cf. *an-ati-*), not very or much, not too; *-kalyāṇa*, mfn. not very beautiful or noble, Daś.; *-kṛicchra*, mfn. n° v° painful or difficult; (*āt*), ind. easily, MBh.; *-kovida*, mfn. n° v° familiar with or clever in (loc.), ib.; *-krūra-mṛidu*, mfn. (bow) neither too strong nor too weak, Vishṇ.; *-gādha*, mfn. not very shallow, rather deep, MBh.; *-cira*, mfn. n° v° long (time), ib.; (*e*), ind. shortly, soon, R.; *-cchina*, mfn. not too much torn or rent, Suśr.; *-jalpaka*, mfn. n° t° garrulous, MBh.; *-tīvra*, mfn. n° t° violent or intense, moderate, ib.; *-tṛipti*, f. absence of over-saturation, Yājñ.; *-dīrgha*, mfn. not too long, Sah.; (*am*), ind. id., MBh.; *-dūra*, mfn. n° t° far or distant, (*am*, Hit.; *e* or *āt*, R. with abl. or gen.) not far away (*°ra-ga*, mfn. n° t° distant, Kathās.; *°ra-nirīkshin*, mfn. not seeing very far, R.; *°ra-vartin*, mfn. not abiding v° f°, Vṛishabhân.; *°ra-sthita*, mfn. id., VP.); *-doshala*, mfn. not of too bad quality or nature, Suśr.; *-drava*, mfn. not too liquid, ib.; *-drutam*, ind. n° t° quick, Vishṇ.; *-dhanin*, mfn. n° t° rich, AgP.; *-nirbhagna*, mfn. n° t° much bent, R.; *-nirvṛitti*, f. n° t° m° ease, Kathās.; *-nīca*, mfn. n° t° low, Bhag.; *-parikara*, mfn. having little attendance, Daś.; *-parisphuṭa*, mfn. not fully displayed, Śak.; *-paryāpta*, mfn. not too abundant, Ragh.; *-pushṭa*, mfn. n° t° much provided with (instr.), Daś.; *-pṛithu*, mf(*u*)n. n° t° broad, Var.; *-prakupita*, mfn. n° t° angry, Daś.; *-pracura-padya-vat*, mfn. containing n° t° many verses, Sāh.; *-pramanas*, mfn. not in very good spirits, MBh.; *-prasiddha*, mfn. n° t° well known, ib.; *-prasīdat*, mf(*antī*)n. not quite serene, BhP.; *-prīta*, mfn. not much pleased, ib.; *-bhārika*, mfn. not too weighty, Mudr.; *-bhinna*, mfn. n° t° much slit, Suśr.; not very different from (abl.), Śak.; *-bhogin*, mfn. n° t° m° given to enjoyments, MārkP.; *-mahat*, mfn. n° t° large, Car.; n° t° long (time), MBh.; *-mātram*, ind. not too much, Mudr.; *-mānin*, mfn. n° t° proud or arrogant (*°ni-tā*, f., Bhag.); *-mudā-vat*, mfn. not very glad or joyful, MārkP.; *-ramaṇīya*, mfn. n° v° pleasant (*-tā*, f., Mudr.); *-rūpa*, mfn. n° v° pretty, MBh.; *-rohiṇī*, f. not too red, ib.; *-laghu-vipula*, mfn. neither too short nor too long, Var.; *-lampaṭa*, mfn. not too greedy or lustful, BhP.; *-lalita*, mfn. n° v° pleasing or beautiful, Cat.; *-lomaśa*, mfn. n° t° hairy, MBh.; *-vatsala*, mfn. n° t° tender, unfriendly, MārkP.; *-vātala*, mfn. n° t° much producing wind (in the body), Suśr.; *-vāda*, m. n° t° harsh language, MBh.; *-vilambita* (*am*, ind. Vishṇ.) or *-vilambin* (*°bi-tā*, f. L.), mfn. n° t° slow or tardy; *-viśadam*, ind. (to kiss) n° t° apparently, Daś.; *-vistāra-saṃkaṭa*, mfn. neither too wide nor too narrow, Kām.; *-vṛitta*, mfn. not very distant from (abl., e.g. *yauvanāt*, from youth, i.e. very young), MārkP.; *-vṛiddha*, mfn. n° v° old (*vayasā*, of years), ib.; *-vyakta*, mfn. n° v° clear or distinct, Var.; *-vyasta*, mfn. not too far separated, TPrāt.; *-śītôshṇa*, mfn. neither too cold nor too warm, Ragh.; *-śobhita*, mfn. not making much show, unsightly, MBh.; *-śrānta*, mfn. not too much tired, MārkP.; *-ślishṭa*, mfn. not very close or tight, Śak.; *-samañjasa*, mf(*ā* or *ī*)n. not quite right or proper, MBh.; *-sāndra*, mfn. not too tough, Suśr.; *-svalpa*, mfn. n° t° short, Sāh.; *-sva-stha*, mfn. n° v° well, MBh.; *-hṛishṭa*, mfn. n° v° glad, MBh. **Nâty** = *nâti* before vowels; *-antadūra*, mfn. n° v° distant or remote, Kathās.; *-apacita*, mfn. not too thin or emaciated, Car.; *-ākīrṇa*, mfn. n° t° crowded, rather empty (street), R.; *-ādṛita*, mfn. not much respected, rather neglected, Daś.; *-ucca*, mfn. n° t° high, L.; *-ucchrita*, mfn. id., Bhag.; *-upapanna*, mfn. not quite natural or normal, Daś.; *-upasaṃhṛita*, mfn. not too much brought together, TPrāt. **Nâdara**, m. disrespect, L. 1. **Nâdeya**, mfn. not to be taken &c., MW. **Nâdhita**, mfn. unread, Hit. **Nânurakta**, mfn. not attached, unkind, Pañc. ii, 46 (v. l.) **Nântarīyaka**, mfn. not external, contained or inherent in (comp.), Vām. ii, 1, 8; Pat. (*-tva*, n. Pat.) **Nânyatra**, ind. except (with acc. or abl.), Divyâv. **Nâbhijāta**, mfn. not well-born, ignoble, Kāv. **Nâbhidhāvat**, m. one who does not give assistance, Mn. ix. 274. **Nâbhimāna**, m. absence of pride, modesty, humbleness, MBh. (v.l. *an-abh°*); Mālav. **Nâbhilakshita**, mfn. unperceived, unseen, Yājñ. (v. l. *an-abh°*). **Nâruṃ-tuda**, mfn. not hurting (a wound or a weak point), harmless, MBh. vii, 2763. **Nârya-tikta**, m. = *an-ārya-t°*, q.v. **Nâsatya**, see s.v. **Nâsti**, ind. (*na* + *asti*) it is not, there is not; *-tā*, f., *-tva*, n. non-existence, Śaṃk.; *-mūrti*, mfn. incorporeal, Naish; *-vāda*, m. assertion of non-ex°, atheism, Hariv. **Nâstika**, mf(*ī*)n. atheistical, infidel; m. an atheist or unbeliever (opp. to *āstika*, q.v.), Mn.; MBh. &c.; *-tā*, f. (MW.), *-tva*, n. (W.) disbelief, atheism; *°kya*, n. id. (with *karmaṇām*, denying the consequence of works), Mn. iii, 65; *-mata*, n. an atheistical opinion, MW.; *-vṛitti*, mfn. leading the life of an atheist or receiving sustenance from an ath°, Vishṇ. **Nêd**, see s.v. **Naika**, mf(*ā*)n. not one, more than one, various, manifold, numerous, many (also pl.), Yājñ.; Mn. &c.; *-cara*, mf(*ī*)n. going in troops, gregarious (animal), BhP.; *-dṛiś*, m. 'many-eyed,' N. of a son of Viśvāmitra, MBh.; *-dravyôccaya-vat*, mfn. furnished with plenty of various goods, ib.; *-dhā*, ind. manifoldly, in various ways or parts, MBh.; Hariv. &c.; *-puṭa*, mfn. showing many rents or gaps, torn (cloud), Var.; *-pṛishṭha*, m. pl. 'many-backed,' N. of a people, MBh. (v. l. *°shṭa*); VP.; *-bhāvâśraya*, mfn. 'not abiding in one condition,' changeable, fickle, unsteady, MW.; *-bheda*, mfn. of many kinds, various, manifold, L.; *-māya*, mfn. using many artifices or stratagems, MBh.; *-rūpa*, mf(*ā*)n. multiform, various, R.; *-rshi* (for *-ṛishi*), m. N. of a man; pl. his family, Pravar.; *-varṇa*, mfn. many-coloured, MBh.; *-vikalpa*, mfn. manifold, various, Daś.; *-vidha*, mfn. id., Var.; *-śas*, ind. repeatedly, often, Var.; Kāv.; *-śastramaya*, mf(*ī*)n. consisting of various missiles (rain), R.; *°kâtman*, mfn. of manifold nature (Śiva), Śivag. **Naiva-**, **Nô**, see s.v. **Nôtpādita**, mfn. ungenerated; *-tva*, n., VP. **Nôpasthātṛi** (Yājñ., Sch.) and *°***sthāyin** (Smṛitit.), not at hand, absent.

न 3. *na* (L.), mfn. thin, spare; vacant, empty; identical; unvexed, unbroken; m. band, fetter; jewel, pearl; war; gift; welfare; N. of Buddha; N. of Gaṇeśa; = *prastuta*; = *dviraṇḍa* (?); (*ā*), f. the navel; a musical instrument; knowledge.

नंश *náṇśa*, m. (√1. *naś, naṇś*) acquisition, RV. i, 122, 12.

Náṇśana. See *svapna-n°*.

नंशुक *naṇśuka*, mf(*ā*)n. (√2. *naś*) perishing, Kāṭh.; = *aṇu*, Uṇ. ii, 30; injurious, destructive, W.

Naṇshṭavya, mfn. (Pāṇ. vii, 1, 60) to be injured or killed, W.

Naṇshṭṛi, mfn. (ib.) an injurer, injurious, destructive, W.

नंहस *naṇhasa*, m. a god smiling on or kind to his worshipper, MBh. i, 6450, v.l. (Nīlak.)

नःक्षुद्र *naḥ-kshudra*. See under 3. *nás*.

नक् *nák*, ind. (g. *svar-ādi*, as nomin. RV. vii, 71, 1) night.

नक *naka*, m. N. of a man (son of Dāruka), VāyuP.; n. N. of sev. Sāmans.

नकिम् *nakim*, *°kis* &c. See under 2. *ná*.

नकुच *nakuca*, v.l. for *lakuca*.

नकुट *nakuṭa*, n. the nose, L.

नकुल *nakulá*, mfn. (in spite of Pāṇ. vi, 3, 75 prob. not fr. *na* + *kula*) of a partic. colour (perhaps that of the ichneumon), TS.; RPrāt.; m. the Bengal mungoose or Viverra Ichneumon (enemy of mice and of serpents from whose venom it protects itself by a medic. plant; cf. *nākulī*), AV.; MBh. &c.; a son, L.; a partic. musical instrument, Lalit.; N. of Śiva, L.; of a son of the Aśvins and Mādrī (twin-brother of Saha-deva & fourth of the Pāṇḍu princes), MBh.; Hariv.; Pur.; of a Vedic poet with the patr. Vāma-deva (*°vya*) or Vaiśvāmitra (*°lasya vāma-*

devasya prêṅkha, m. N. of a Sāman), ĀrshBr.; of a physician (author of a wk. on horses), Cat.; (*ā*), f. N. of Śiva's wife, L.; (*ī*), f., see below; n. a myst. N. of the sound *h*, L. **—tva**, n. the state of an ichneumon, MBh. **Nakulâdyā**, f. the i° plant, L. **Nakulândhatā**, f., °**lândhya**, n. 'i°-blindness,' a kind of disease of the eyes, Suśr. **Nakulêśa**, v.l. for °*līśa* (below). **Nakulêshṭā** or °**shṭakā**, f. 'liked by the i°,' a kind of medic. plant (cf. above), L. **Nakul'oshṭhī**, f. (in music) a partic. stringed instrument.

Nakulaka, m. or n. an ornament shaped like an ichneumon, L.; m. a kind of purse (?), Divyâv.; (°*likā*), f. a female i°, Kād.

Nakulī, f. a female ichneumon, MantraBr.; MBh.; Salmalia Malabarica, L.; Nardostachys Jatamansi, L.; saffron, L.; = *śaṅkhinī*, L. **—vāg-īśvarī-mantra-vidhāna**, n. N. of wk. **—°śa** (°*līśa*), m. a form of Bhairava, L.; a myst. N. of the sound *h*, ib.; *-darśana*, n. N. of wk.; *-pāśupata*, m. pl. a partic. sect, Sarvad.; *-yoga-pārāyaṇa*, n. N. of wk.

नक्क् *nakk*, cl. 10. P. *nakkayati*, to destroy, kill, Dhātup. xxxii, 54.

नक्त 1. *nákta*, n. night, RV.; AV. (*náktā*, f. only in *naktayā*, q.v., and as du. with *ushā́sā*; cf. °*sā-naktā* & *naktôshāsā*); eating only at n° (as a sort of penance), Yājñ.; Hcat.; (*am*), ind. by night (often opp. to *divā*), RV. &c. &c.; m. N. of a son of Pṛithu, VP.; of a son of Pṛithu-sheṇa and Ākūti, BhP.; (*ā*), f. (cf. above) Methonica Superba, L. [Cf. *nak* & *nakti*; Zd. *nakht-uru, nakht-ru*; Gk. νύξ; Lat. *nox*; Lith. *naktis*; Slav. *nošti*; Goth. *nahts*; Angl.Sax. *neaht, niht*, Engl. *night*, Germ. *Nacht*.] **—kāla-nirṇaya**, m. N. of wk. **—cārin** (L.), mfn. walking at night; m. an owl; cat; thief; a Rakshas (cf. *naktam-c°*). **—prabhava**, v.l. for *naktam-pr°*. **—bhojana**, n. the eating only at n° (cf. above), Hcat.; supper, W.; °*jin*, mfn. eating at n°, BhavP.; °*ji-tva*, n. Kathās. **—mukhā**, f. evening, n°, L. (for *-mushā*?). **—vat**, mfn. eating only at n°, Hcat. **—vrata**, n. 'n°-observance,' eating at n° (& fasting by day), W. **Naktândha**, mfn. blind at n°, Suśr.; °*tândhya*, n., ib. **Naktâśin**, mfn. eating only at n°, Vishṇ. **Náktôshā́sā**, f. du. n° and morning, RV.

Naktán (only °*tábhis*), night, RV. vii, 104, 18.

Náktam (*m* before labials), ind., see 1. *nákta*. **—samaya**, m. night-time, Naish. **—homá**, m. n°-oblation, TS. **—cara**, mf(*ī*)n. walking about at n°; m. any n°-animal or creature, GṛS.; Gaut.; MBh. &c.; nocturnal demon, Rakshas, MBh.; Var. &c. (°*rêśvara*, m. the lord of the rovers or fiends, MBh.); the bdellium tree, W.; (*ī*), f. a female demon, Kathās. **—caryā**, f. the walking about at n°, MBh. **—cārin**, mfn. = *-cara*, GṛS.; Gaut.; Mn.; m. a cat, L. **—jātá**, mf(*ā́*)n. grown at n° (herb), AV. **—dina**, n. sg. n° and day, Mālav. v, 13; (*am*), ind. = next, Kathās.; Pañc. **—divam**, ind. by n° and day, L. **Naktam-prabhava**, mfn. produced at n°, Var. (v.l. °*ta-pr°*). **Naktam-bhāga**, mfn. having a nocturnal part, Var. **Naktam-bhogin**, mfn. = °*ta-bh*, MBh. iii, 13734 (v.l.)

Naktayā́, ind. at night, RV. iv, 11, 1.

Nákti, f. night, RV. ii, 2, 2.

नक्त 2. *nakta* or *nakla* (?) n. (in astron.) N. of the fifth Yoga (= نقل).

नक्तक *naktaka*, m. dirty or ragged cloth, rag, wiper &c., L. (v.r. for *laktaka*).

नक्तमाल *naktamāla* or °*laka*, m. Pongamia Glabra, L.

नक्र *nakra*, m. (according to Pāṇ. vi, 3, 75 fr. *na* + *kra*) crocodile, alligator, Mn.; MBh. &c. (ifc. f. *ā*); the sign of the zodiac Scorpio, Gol.; (*ā*), f. a swarm of bees or wasps, L.; n. the nose (also *ā*, f.), L.; a partic. disease of the nose, L.; the upper timber of a door-frame, L. (cf. *nā́kra* and Pāṇ. vi, 3, 75). **—ketana**, m. N. of the god of love, Daś. (cf. *makara-k°*). **—cakra**, n. a multitude of crocodiles, Pañcad. **—makshikā**, f. a kind of fly, L. **—rāj** or **-rājaka**, m. a shark or any other large sea animal (lit. king of the Nakras), L. **—hāraka**, m. id. (lit. seizer of the N°s), L.

नक्ष् *naksh*, cl. 1. P. Ā. *nákshati*, °*te* (perf. *nanakshúr*, °*kshé*, RV.; aor. *anakshīt*, Gr.; fut. *nakshishyati, nakshitā*, ib.) to come near, approach, arrive at, get, attain, RV.; AV.; VS. (cf. 1. *naś*; *inaksh*).

Nakshat, mf(*antī*)n. approaching. °**shad-dā-bhá**, mfn. striking down any one that approaches (Indra), RV. vi, 22, 2.

Nákshatra, n. (m. only RV. vi, 67, 6; prob. fr. √*naksh*, cf. *naksh dyām*, i, 33, 14 &c.) a star or any heavenly body; also applied to the sun; n. sg. sometimes collectively 'the stars,' e.g. vii, 86, 1, RV. &c. &c.; an asterism or constellation through which the moon passes, a lunar mansion, AV. &c. &c. (27, later 28, viz. Śravishṭhā or Dhanishṭhā, Śata-bhishaj, Pūrva-bhādrapāda, Uttara-bh°, Revatī, Aśvinī, Bharaṇī, Kṛittikā, Rohiṇī or Brāhmī, Mṛiga-śiras or Āgrahāyaṇī, Ārdrā, Punarvasū or Yāmakau, Pushya or Sidhya, Āśleshā, Maghā, Pūrva-phalguni, Uttara-ph°, Hasta, Citrā, Svātī, Viśākhā or Rādhā, Anurādhā, Jyeshṭha, Mūla, Pūrvâshāḍhā, Uttarâsh°, Abhijit, Śravaṇa; according to VarBṛS. Revatī, Uttara-phalgunī, °ra-bhādrapāda & °râshāḍha are called *dhruvāṇi*, fixed; in the Vedas the Nakshatras are considered as abodes of the gods or of pious persons after death, Sāy. on RV. i, 50, 2; later as wives of the moon and daughters of Daksha, MBh.; Hariv. &c.; according to Jainas the sun, moon, Grahas, Nakshatras and Tārās form the Jyotishkas); a pearl, L. **—kalpa**, m. N. of a Pariś. of AV. **—kānti-vistāra**, m. the white Yāvanāla flower. **—kūrma**, m. (or *-cāra*, m., *-vibhāga*, m.) N. of ch. xiv of VarBṛS. **—kośa**, m. N. of a list of stars. **—graha-yuty-adhikāra**, m. N. of ch. of Sūryas. **—grahôtpāta**, m. N. of the 63rd Pariś. of AV. **—grāma-yājaka**, m. = °*tra-y°*, MBh. **—cakra**, n. a partic. diagram, Tantras.; the N°s collectively, W.; the sphere of the fixed stars, MW. **—cintā-maṇi** & **-cūḍā-m°**, m. N. of wks. **—já**, mfn. star-born, m. son of the stars, AV. **—jātaka** & °**kâdi-bhāva-phala**, n. N. of wks. **—tārā-rājâditya**, m. a partic. Samādhi, Buddh. **—darśá**, m. star-gazer, VS. **—dāna-vidhi**, m. N. of wk. **—devata**, mfn. having the N°s as deities, ĀśvGṛ. **—devatā-kathana** & **-dohada-śāntika**, n. N. of wks. **—dvamdva**, n. a N° compound (as *tishya-punarvasu*), Pāṇ. i, 2, 63. **—nātha**, m. 'lord of the N°s,' the moon, Hariv. **—nāman**, n., **-nighaṇṭu** & **-nirṇaya**, m. N. of wks. **—nemi**, m. the pole-star, L.; the moon, L.; N. of Vishṇu, MBh.; f. the N° Revatī. **—nyāsa**, m. N. of ch. of PSarv. **—pa**, m. = *-nātha*, L. **—paṭalôpâya-dāna**, n. N. of wk. **—pati**, m. = *-pa*; *-nandana*, m. the planet Mercury, Vāstuv. **—patha**, m. 'star-path,' the starry sky, Hcar.; *-varcas*, n. its splendour, R. **—pāṭhaka**, m. 'star-reader,' astrologer, Cat. **—pāta**, m. N. of wk. **—purusha**, m. (astrol.) a human figure representing the N°s (also *-ka*); a ceremony in which such a figure is worshipped; N. of ch. of the VāmP.; *-vrata*, n. N. of a partic. observance & of ch. of the MatsyaP. **—pūjita**, mfn. 'star-honoured,' auspicious, MW. **—prakaraṇa**, n., **-praśna**, m., **-phala**, n., **-bhakti**, f., **-bhukta-ghaṭī-cakra**, n. N. of wks. **—maṇḍala**, n. star-cluster, Cat. **—mārga**, m. = *-patha*, MBh. **—mālā**, f. star-circle, star-group, R.; the N°s collectively, Var.; a necklace of 27 pearls, ib.; a partic. ornament for an elephant's head, Kād. (°*lāya*, Nom. Ā. °*yate*, ib.); a kind of dance, W.; N. of sev. wks. **—mālikā**, f., **-yajña**, m. N. of wks. **—yājaka**, mfn. offering oblations to the N°s, MBh. **—yoga**, m. conjunction of (moon with the) N°s, ib.; *-dāna*, n. N. of wk.; °*gin*, mfn. connected with N°s, MBh.; Hariv.; f. pl. chief stars in the N°s, L. **—rāja**, m. 'king of the stars,' AV.; the moon, MBh.; R.; N. of a Bodhi-sattva, Buddh.; *-prabhāva-bhāsa-garbha*, m. N. of a B°-s°, ib.; *-vikrīḍita*, m. a partic. Samādhi, ib.; *-saṃkusumitâbhijña*, m. N. of a B°-s°, ib. **—loká**, m. pl. the world of the N°s, ŚBr.; sg. the starry region, firmament, MW. **—vartman**, n. = *-patha*, L. **—vāda-mālikā**, **-vādâvalī**, f. N. of wks. **—vidyā**, f. 'star-knowledge,' astronomy, ChUp.; Mn. **—vidhāna**, n. N. of wk. **—vīthī**, f. path of the N°s, MBh. **—vṛiksha**, m. a tree consecrated to a N°, L. **—vṛishṭi**, f. 'star-shower,' shooting stars, L. **—vyūha**, m. = *-bhakti*. **—śavas** (*nákṣh°*), mfn. equal to stars in number, RV. x, 22, 10 (Sāy. 'going to the gods'). **—śānti**, f., **-śuddhi-prakaraṇa**, n. N. of wks. **—saṃvatsara**, m. a particular form of year, Var. **—sattra**, n. = *nakshatrêshṭi*; N. of wk.; *-prayoga*, m., *-hautra*, n., °*trêshṭi-prayoga*, m., °*trêshṭi-hautra-prayoga*, m. N. of wks. **—samuccaya**, m. 'assemblage of N°s,' N. of wk. **—sūcaka**, m. 'star-indicator,' astrologer, Var. **—stoma**, m. N. of a partic. Ekâha, ŚāṅkhŚr. **—sthāpana**, n. N. of wk. **Nakshatrâdhipa**, m. the regent of a N°, Cat.; °*pati*, m. 'chief of N°s,' N. of Pushya, Lalit. **Nakshatrâbhidhāna**, n. N. of wk. **Nakshatrâśraya**, mfn. relating to a star or N°, MānGṛ. **Nakshatrêśa**, m. = °*tra-nātha*, Caurap. **Nakshatrêshṭakā́**, f. N. of partic. sacrificial bricks, TS.; ĀpŚr. **Nakshatrêshṭi**, f. a sacrifice to the N°s; N. of wk.; *-nirūpaṇa*, n., *-paddhati*, f., *-prayoga*, m., *-homa*, m., *-hautra*, n. N. of wks. **Nakshatrôpajīvin**, m. 'subsisting by the N°s,' astrologer, Yājñ. iii, 289, Sch.

Nakshatrin, m. 'having or holding the stars,' N. of Vishṇu, MBh. xiii, 6996 (cf. °*tra-nemi*).

Nakshatríya, mfn. relating to the stars or Nakshatras, containing a number equal to that of the N°s, i.e. 27, AV.; VS. &c.

Nakshya, mfn. to be approached, RV. vii, 15, 7.

नख् *nakh* or *naṅkh*, cl. 4. & 1. P. *nakhyati*, *nakhati* & *naṅkhati*, to go, move, Naigh. ii, 14; Dhātup. v, 20, 21.

नख *nakhá*, m. n. (fr. √*nagh* [?], cf. *nagha-māra*; prob. not fr. *na* + *kha* in spite of Pāṇ. vi, 3, 75; ifc. f. *ī*) a finger-nail, toe-nail, claw, talon, the spur of a cock, RV. &c. &c. (°*khāni* √*kṛi* or √*klṛip*, to cut the nails, Kauś.; Mn.); = 20, Sūryas.; n. and (*ī*), f. Unguis Odoratus, VarBṛS.; Hcat.; m. part, portion. [Cf. Gk. ὄνυξ, stem ὀ-νυχ; Lat. *unguis*; Lit. *nágas*; Slav. *nogŭtĭ*; Angl.Sax. *naegel*; Engl. *nail*; Germ. *Nagel*.] **—kuṭṭa**, m. 'nail-cutter,' barber, L.; N. of an author, Sāh. **—khādin**, mfn. biting (lit. eating) the n°s, Mn.; MBh. **—gucha-phalā**, f. a kind of pulse, L. **—ccheda**, m. (MW.); °*dana*, n. (Mn.; Suśr.) n°-cutting. **—cchedya**, mfn. to be slit by the n°s, Bhpr. **—jāha**, n. n°-root, L. **—dāraṇa**, m. 'tearing with the claws,' falcon, hawk, L. **—nikṛintana**, m. or n. n°-scissors, ChUp. **—nirbhinna** (°*khá-n°*), mfn. split asunder with the n°s, TS.; Pāṇ. vi, 2, 48, Kāś. **—nishpāvikā** or °**pāvī**, f. a kind of pulse, L. **—nyāsa**, m. inserting the claws, Ragh. **—pada**, n. n°-mark, scratch, Megh.; Unguis Odoratus, VarBṛS. Sch. **—parṇī**, f. a kind of plant (= *vṛiścika*), L. **—puñja-phalā**, f. a kind of pulse, L. **—pushpī**, f. Trigonella Corniculata, L. **—pūrvikā**, f. = *-nishpāvī*, L. **—praca**, n., g. *mayūra-vyaṃsakâdi*. **—phalinī**, f. a kind of pulse, L. **—bhinna**, mfn. scratched or torn off with a n°, W. **—muca**, n. 'n°-looser,' bow, L. **—m-paca**, mf(*ā*)n. n°-scalding, Pāṇ. iii, 2, 34, Kāś.; scanty, shallow (water), Kāv. **—rajanī**, f. a kind of plant and its fruit, L. **—rañjanī**, f. n°-scissors, L. **—lekhaka**, m. n°-painter, L. **—lekhā**, f. a scratch with the nail, n°-painting, MW. **—vādana** (Āpast.) & **-vādya** (L.), n. 'n°-music,' noise made with the finger-nails. **—vilekhā**, f. a scratch, W. **—visha**, mfn. having venom in the n°s or claws, L. **—vishkira**, m. 'tearing or rending with the claws,' scratcher, Mn. v, 13. **—vṛiksha**, m. a kind of tree, L. **—vraṇa**, n. 'n°-wound,' scratch, W. **—śaṅkha**, m. a small shell, L. **Nakhâṃśu**, m. elegance or brightness of the finger-n°s, W. **Nakhâgrá**, n. n°-point, ŚBr. **Nakhâghāta**, m. = °*kha-vraṇa*, L. **Nakhâṅka**, m. n°-mark, Kāv.; Unguis Odoratus, L. **Nakhâṅga**, n. a kind of perfume, L. **Nakhâcchoṭanikā**, f. (√*cuṭ*) making a noise with the n°s (as a token of applause or approval), HPariś. **Nakhā-nakhi**, ind. n° against n°, close fighting (with mutual scratching), MBh. viii, 2377 (cf. *keśā-keśi*). **Nakhâyudha**, mfn. 'claw-armed,' Pañc. ii, $\frac{61}{51}$; *-tva*, n. ib. $\frac{323}{325}$, m. a lion; tiger; cock, L.; monkey, R. **Nakhâri**, m. N. of an attendant of Śiva, L. **Nakhârtha**, m. a kind of perfume, Gal. **Nakhâli** or °**likā**, f. a small shell (cf. °*kha-śaṅkha*). **Nakhâvapūta**, mfn. purified with the nails; pl. N. of partic. grains, MaitrS. **Nakhâśin**, m. 'eating with claws,' an owl, L.

Nakhaka, m. N. of a Nāga-rāja, L.

Nakhará, mfn. shaped like a claw, curved, crooked, ŚBr., MBh.; m. a curved knife, MBh.; Daś.; m., f(*ā*) or n. nail, claw, Var.; Pañc. &c. nail-scratch, Cat.; (*ī*), f. Unguis Odoratus, L. **—rajanī**, f. v.l. for *nakha-r°*, g. *harītaky-ādi*, Kāś. **Nakharâyudha**, m. a lion; tiger; cock, L. (cf. *nakhấy°*). **Nakharâhva**, m. Nerium Odorum, L.

Nakhālu, m. a kind of tree (= *nakha-vṛiksha*), L.

Nakhín, mfn. having nails or claws; thorny, prickly, ŚBr.; m. a clawed animal, lion, L.

नग ná-ga, m. 'not moving' (cf. á-ga), a mountain (ifc. f. ā; cf. sa-naga), AV.&c. &c.; the number 7 (because of the 7 principal mountains; cf. kula-giri), Sūryas.; any tree or plant, MBh.; Kāv. &c.; a serpent, L.; the sun, L. **-karṇī**, f. Clitoria Ternatea, L. **-ja**, mfn. mountain-born, mountaineer; m. elephant, L.; (ā), f. a kind of plant, L. **-nadī**, f. 'm°-river,' N. of a river, Megh. **-nandinī**, f. 'm°-daughter,' N. of Durgā (d° of Himâlaya), L. **-nimna-gā**, f. 'm°-river,' torrent, Śiś. ii, 104. **-pati**, m. 'm°-chief,' the Himâlaya, L. **-bhid**, m. 'rock-splitter,' (L.) an axe; a crow; Indra; a kind of plant. **-bhū**, mfn. = -ja; m. a kind of plant, L. **-mūrdhan**, m. 'm°-crest,' W. **-randhra-kara**, m. 'm°-splitter,' N. of Kārttikeya, Ragh. ix, 2. **-vat**, mfn. abounding in mountains or trees, R. **-vāhana**, m. 'm°-borne,' N. of Śiva, Śivag. **-vṛittika**, m. (and °kā, f.) a kind of plant, Suśr. **-śreshṭhá**, m. the finest tree, Suparṇ. **-svarūpiṇī**, f. a kind of metre, Śrutab. **Nagâgra**, n. m°-top, MBh. **Nagâṭana**, m. 'tree-wanderer,' monkey, L. **Nagâdhipa**, m. = °ga-pati, L. **Nagâdhirāja**, m. id., MW. **Nagâpagā**, f. = °ganimnagā, Śiś. ii, 100. **Nagâri**, m. N. of a man, MBh. iv, 1294. **Nagâlikā**, see nagānikā. **Nagâvāsa**, m. 'tree-dweller,' a peacock, L. **Nagâśman**, m. a piece of rock, Śiś. xv, 10. **Nagâśraya**, mfn. living in mountains, W.; m. a kind of plant, L. **Nagâhvaya**, m. N. of a man, MBh. iv, 1294. **Nagêndra**, m. 'm°-lord,' N. of Himâlaya, Ragh. ii, 28; of Kailāsa, Megh. 63; of Nishadha, Ragh. xviii, 1. **Nagêśa**, m. id., N. of a partic. m°, Śatr.; of Kailāsa or of Śiva, MW. **Nagêśvara**, m. id., N. of Himâlaya, L. **Nagôcchrāya**, m. m°-elevation, W. **Nagôdara**, n. m°-rift, BhP. **Nagâukas**, m. 'mountain- or tree-dweller,' (L.) lion; the fabulous animal Śarabha; a crow (cf. agâukas); any bird.

नगणा nagaṇā, f. Cardiospermum Halicacabum, L. (v. l. nagnā).

नगर nágara, n. (m. only MBh. iii, 3014; ifc. f. ā, Hariv. 2951; prob. not fr. naga + ra, but cf. g. aśamâdi; the n cannot be cerebralized, g. kshubhnâdi) a town, city, N. of sev. cities, TĀr.; Mn.; MBh. &c.; (ī), f., see below. **-kāka**, m. 'a town-crow,' a term of contempt, L. **-koṭi**, N. of a town (Nagar-kot), and of another place, Cat. **-khaṇḍa**, N. of ch. of the SkandaP. **-gāmin**, mfn. (road) going or leading to a t°, Mālatīm. i, 37. **-ghāta**, m. 't°-destroying, (also -ka), an elephant, L. **-catush-patha**, m. or n. meeting of 4 ways in a t°, MānGṛ. **-jana**, m. pl. towns-folk, sg. a citizen, Hit. **-daivata**, n. presiding deity of a t°; -vat, ind. Mṛicch. i, 19. **-dvāra**, n. t°-gate, Hit.; -kūṭaka, n. a kind of fence on a t°-g°, L. **-dhana-vihāra** or **-dhana-saṃghârāma**, m. N. of a Buddh. monastery. **-pati**, m. t°-chief, L. **-pura**, n. N. of a t°, L. **-pradakshiṇā**, f. carrying an idol round a t° in procession, MW. **-prânta**, m. the outskirts of a t°, ib. **-bāhu**, m. 't°-arm,' N. of a man, L. **-bāhya**, mfn. situated without the town, MW. **-maṇḍanā**, f. 't°-ornament,' a courtezan, Vāsav. **-mardin**, m. 't°-crusher,' N. of a man, g. bāhv-ādi. **-mālin**, mfn. garlanded with cities, MW. **-mustā**, f. = °rôttha. **-rakshâdhikṛita**, m. the chief of the t°-guard, Mṛicch. **-rakshin**, m. t°-watchman, ib. **-vāyasa**, m. = -kāka, L. **-vāsin**, mfn. 't°-dwelling,' a citizen, MW. **-vṛiddha**, m. t°-senior, Daś. **-sammita**, mfn. equal to a t°, MW. **-stha**, m. = -vāsin, Hit. **-svāmin**, m. 't°-chief,' N. of a man, Kathās. **-hāra**, 't°-taking,' N. of a kingdom, L. **Nagarâdhikṛita** (Rājat.), °râdhipa & °pati (Kathās.), °râdhyaksha (Hariv.), m. t°-chief, head police-officer. **Nagarâbhyāśa**, m. neighbourhood of a t°, MW. **Nagarôtthā**, f. a kind of plant, L. **Nagarôpânta**, n. = ra-prânta, MW. **Nagarâukas**, m. = °ra-vāsin, Rājat. **Nagarâushadhi**, f. Musa Sapientum, L.

Nagarāya, Nom. Ā. °yate, to look like a town, MBh.; Hariv.

Nagarin, m. lord of a town, Car.; N. of a man, AitBr. v, 30. °ry-anna, n. food given by the lord of a town, Mn. iv, 213.

Nagarī, f. = °ra, Mn.; MBh. &c. **-nirodha**, m. N. of ch. of GaṇP. ii. **-baka**, m. 'town-crane,' a crow, L. **-yukti**, f. N. of ch. of the Yukti-kalpataru. **-rakshin**, m. town-watchman, MBh.

Nagarīya, mfn. belonging to a town, civic, urban, Kāv.

नगानिका nagānikā, °nī or nagālikā, f. a kind of metre, Col.

नग्न nagna. See under √naj below.

नग्नहु nagnáhu (or °hū, L.), m. ferment, a drug used for fermenting spirituous liquor, VS.; ŚBr.

नघमार nagha-mārá & naghā-rishá, m. N. of the plant kushṭha = Costus Speciosus, AV. (cf. nakhá).

नघुष naghusha, m. N. of a man = nahusha, MaitrUp.; Ragh.; n. Tabernaemontana Coronaria, Bhpr.

नङ्ख् naṅkh. See √nakh.

नचिकेत na-ciketa, na-cira &c. See under 2. na, p. 523.

नज् naj, cl. 6. Ā. najate, to be ashamed (v. l. for lajj, Dhātup. xxviii, 10; probably invented to explain nagna).

Nagná, mf(ā́)n. naked, new, bare, desolate, desert, RV. &c. &c.; m. a naked mendicant (esp. a Bauddha, but also a mere hypocrite), Var.; VP.; a bard accompanying an army, L.; N. of Śiva, Śivag.; of a poet, Cat.; (ā́), f. a naked (wanton) woman, AV. v, 7, 8; a girl before menstruation (allowed to go naked), Pañc. iii, 217; Cardiospermum Halicacabum, L. (cf. nagaṇā); = vāc (v. l. for nanā), Naigh. i, 11, Sch. [Cf. Zd. maghna for naghna; Lith. nûgas; Slav. nagŭ; Goth. nagaths; Angl.Sax. nacod; Engl. naked; Germ. nackt.] **-kshapaṇaka**, m. a naked mendicant, Kād.; mfn. (place) containing (only) n°m°s, Cāṇ. **-m-karaṇa**, mf(ī)n. making n°, Pāṇ. iii, 2, 56. **-caryā**, f. vow to go n°, Divyâv. **-jit**, m. N. of a prince of the Gandhāras (father of one of Kṛishṇa's wives), Br.; MBh.; of a writer on architecture (?), VarBṛS. lviii, 4; 15; of a poet, Cat. **-tā** (°gná-), f. (RV.; ŚBr.), **-tva**, n. (Hit.) nakedness. **-dhara**, m. N. of Sch. on Ragh.; Cat. **-nīlapaṭâdika**, n. nick-name of Kaṇâda's wks., Cat. **-bhūpati-graha**, m. N. of a drama. **-mushita**, mfn. stripped bare, g. rājadantâdi. **-m-bhavishṇu**, mfn. (Pāṇ. iii, 2, 57) = -m-bhâvuka, mfn. (ib.) becoming naked, uncovering one's self in a shameless manner, TS.; Kāṭh. **-vṛitti**, f. N. of Comm. on Uṇ. **-vrata-dhara**, mfn. observing the vow of a n° mendicant (Śiva), Śivag. **-śramaṇa** (VarBṛS., Sch.) & **-śravaṇa** (Kāraṇḍ.), m. a n° ascetic. **Nagnâcārya**, m. a bard, VarBṛS., Sch. (cf. nagná above). **Nagnâṭa** & °ṭaka, m. a n° wanderer, (esp.) a Buddh. or Jain. mendicant, Rājat.; L.

Nágnaka, mf(ikā)n. naked, wanton, AV.; HPariś.; m. a n° mendicant, Pañc.; a bard, L.; (ikā), f. a n° or wanton woman, L.; a girl before menstruation, MBh.; Pañc.

Nagnī, in comp. for °na. **-karaṇa**, n. stripping, undressing, W. **-√kṛi**, to render naked; **-kṛita**, mfn. converted into a n° mendicant, Bhartṛ. i, 64.

नञ् nañ, ind. N. of the negat. particle na, negation, Pāṇ. ii, 1, 60; Vām. v, 2, 13 &c. **-artha**, m. the meaning of na; -nirṇaya & -vāda, m. (°da-ṭīkā & vivṛiti, f.) N. of wks. & Comms. **-vāda**, m. N. of wk.; -ṭippaṇī, f., -viveka, m. N. of Comm.'s on it. **-viveka**, **-śiro-maṇi**, **-samāsa** & **-sūtrârtha-vāda**, m. N. of wks.

नञ्जराज nañja-rāja, m. N. of a king and author (?). **-yaśo-bhūshaṇa**, n. N. of wk.

नट् naṭ (Prākṛ. for nṛit, q.v.), cl. 1. P. naṭati (Dhātup. xix, 19; ix, 23) to dance, Kāv.; to hurt or injure, Vop. (cf. un-√naṭ): Caus. nāṭayati (Dhātup. xxxii, 12) to represent anything (acc.) dramatically, act, perform, imitate, Mṛicch.; Śak. &c.; to fall (cf. √naḍ); to shine, Vop.

Naṭa, m. (fr. prec.; but cf. Uṇ. iv, 104) actor, dancer, mime, MBh.; Kāv. &c.; N. of a partic. caste (sons of degraded Kshatriyas, Mn. x, 22); Colosanthes Indica, L.; Jonesia Asoka, L.; a sort of reed (= kishku-parvan), L.; (in music) N. of a Rāga; N. of a man (who with his brother Bhaṭa built a Vihāra), Buddh.; (ā), f. Caesalpina Banducella, L.; (ī), f. an actress (g. gaurâdi), Śak.; Sāh. &c.; a dancer, Nauch girl, courtezan, L.; a partic. fragrant plant, Bhpr.; red arsenic, L.; (in music) N. of a Rāgiṇī. **-gaṅg'oka**, m. N. of a poet, Cat. **-gati**, f. a kind of metre, Col. **-caryā**, f. an actor's performance, BhP. **-tā**, f. office or condition of an a°, Hariv. **-nārāyaṇa**, m. (in music) N. of a Rāga. **-pattrikā**, f. Solanum Melongena, L. **-parṇa**, n. 'a°s wing,' the skin, W. **-baṭu**, m. a young a°, L. **-bhaṭika-vihāra**, m., **-bhaṭikā**, f. 'temple of Naṭa & Bhaṭa,' N. of a t°, Buddh. **-bhūshaṇa** and **-maṇḍana**, n. 'a°'s ornament,' orpiment, L. **-raṅga**, m. 'a°'s arena,' anything illusory, Buddh. **-vara** (W.) or **-śreshṭha** (MW.), m. chief a° or dancer. **-saṃjñaka**, m. orpiment, L. an a° or d°, W. (cf. -bhūshaṇa). **-sūtra**, n. rules for a°s, Pāṇ. iv, 3, 110. **Naṭântikā**, f. 'a°-killing, a°-spoiling,' shame, modesty, L. (v. l. °ndhikā). **Naṭêśvara**, m. 'lord of dancers,' N. of Śiva, W.

Naṭaka, m. an actor, L. **-melaka**, n. 'company of actors,' N. of a comedy.

Naṭana, n. dancing, dance, pantomime, Kautukas. °nânanda-nātha, m. N. of an author, Cat.

Naṭanīya, mfn. to be danced, Gīt.

Naṭita, mfn. disgusted with, tired of (instr.), HPariś.; n. acting, representation, MW.

Naṭī, f., see naṭa, above. **-suta**, m. the son of a dancing girl, MW.

Naṭyā, f. a company of actors, g. pāśâdi.

नट्ट naṭṭa or °ṭaka, m., °ṭā, f. (in music) N. of a Rāgiṇī. **-kalyāṇa** & **-nārāyaṇa** (cf. naṭa-n°), m. id. **-paṭṭa-grāma**, m. N. of a village, Cat. **-mallārikā**, **-varāṭikā** & **-hambīrā**, f. N. of Rāgiṇīs.

नड् 1. naḍ, cl. 10. P. nāḍayati, to fall, Vop. in Dhātup. xxxii, 12 (cf. √naṭ).

2. **Naḍ**, in comp. and word-formation for naḍa. **-antikā**, f. 'reed-destroying,' N. of a river, Vishṇ. (cf. naḍânt°). **-bhuvaka**, m. N. of a poet, Cat. **-vat**, mfn. covered with reeds, Pāṇ. iv, 2, 87. **-vala**, mf(ā)n. = -vat, iv, 2, 88; n. a quantity of r°s, r°-bed, MBh.; Ragh.; (ā), f. id., VS.; N. of the wife of Manu Cākshusha, Hariv.; Pur. (v. l. navalā; cf. nāḍvaleya). **-vābhū** (?), f. = kuṭṭima, L.

Naḍá or nalá, m. (L. also n.) a species of reed, Arundo Tibialis or Karka, RV.; AV.; ŚBr.; N. of a prince with the patr. Naishidha, ŚBr. (= Nala Naishadha, Sch.); of a Nāga, L.; of a partic. tribe whose employment is making a sort of glass bracelet, W. (cf. nala). **-kūbara**, m. N. of a son of Kubera, Kathās. (cf. nala-). **-neri**, f. (in music) a kind of dance. **-prāya**, mfn. abounding in reeds, L. **-bhakta**, mfn. inhabited by Naḍa (?), g. aishukāry-ādi (v. l. naḍa-). **-maya**, mf(ī)n. consisting or made of r°, Kauś. **-mīna**, m. 'r°-fish,' a kind of sprat, L. **-vana**, n. 'r°-thicket,' L.; N. of a place, Rājat. **-saṃhati**, f. 'id.,' L. **Naḍâgāra**, n. r°-hut, MW. **Naḍâ-giri**, m. (g. kiṃśulakâdi) N. of an elephant, Kathās.

Naḍaka, n. the hollow of a bone, KātyŚr. °ḍakīya, mfn. abounding in reeds, Pāṇ. iv, 2, 91. °ḍaśa, mfn. id., g. tṛiṇâdi.

Naḍinī, f. a reed bed, g. pushkarâdi. °ḍila, mfn. reedy, covered with reeds, g. kāśâdi.

Naḍyā, f. a reed bed, L.

नडह naḍaha, mfn. lovely, beautiful (prob. w. r. for laḍaha).

नडुवाह naḍu-vāha, m. N. of a poet, Cat. (for naḍ-v° or naḍa-v°?).

नत् nat, mfn. (√nam) bowing, bowing one's self (ifc.), MW.

Natá, mfn. bent, bowed, curved, inclined, inclining, RV. &c. &c.; bowing to, saluting (acc. or gen.), BhP. vi, 9, 40; v, 18, 4; depressed, sunk, flat; deep, hanging down, MBh.; Kāv. &c.; ifc. bent down by or turned towards (cf. vāma-, add.); cerebralized (as the letter n, cf. nati), RPrāt.; m. n. Tabernaemontana Coronaria, L.; n. zenith-distance at meridian transit, Sūryas.; hour-angle or distance in time from meridian, ib.; inclination, ib. **-kaṃdhara**, mfn. bowing (the neck), MW. **-kāla**, m. hour-angle (see above), Sūryas., Sch. **-ghaṭikā**, f. id., ib. **-jyā**, f. the sine of the hour-angle, MW. **-druma**, m. = latā-sāla (bower?), L. **-nāḍikā** or **-nāḍī**, f. = -kāla, L.; any hour of birth after noon or before midnight, W. **-nābhi**, mfn. 'deep-naveled,' thin, slender, Kum. i, 38. **-nāsika**, mfn. flat-nosed, Var. **-parvan**, mfn. (arrow) flat-jointed, smooth, MBh. v, 7143; Śak. vii, 162 (read adhunā nata°). **-bhāga**, m. zenith-distance at meridian transit, Sūryas. **-bhrū**, mfn. having arched brows or bending the brows, frowning, Vikr. iv, 28. **-mukha**, mf(ī)n. bending down the face, looking down, Rājat. **–mūrdhan**, mfn. bending or hanging down the head, W. **–Natâṅsa**, m. = °*ta-bhāga*, Sūryas. **Natâgra-nāsa**, mfn. = °*ta-nāsika*, Var. **Natâṅga**, mf(*ī*)n. bent, curved, bowed, stooping, W.; (*ī*), f. a (smooth- or round-limbed) woman, Mālatim. i, 38. **Natôdara**, mfn. = °*ta-nābhi*, MBh. vii, 2735. **Natônnata**, mfn. depressed and elevated; *-bhūmi-bhāga*, mfn. (path) with d° and e° portions of ground, Śak. iv, 14; *-bhrū*, mfn. depressing and elevating the eye-brows, frowning, MW.

Nati, f. bending, bowing, stooping, modesty, humility, Kāv.; Śatr. &c.; inclination or parallax in latitude, Sūryas.; curvature, crookedness, W.; the change of a dental letter to a cerebral, Prāt. **–tati**, f. excessive humbleness, Kāv. **Naty-akshara**, n. a letter subject to cerebralization (e.g. the letter *n*), Prāt.

नतमंहस् *na-tam-aṅhas*, the beginning of RV. x, 126 (cf. Mn. xi, 252).

नतमाम् *na-tamām* & *na-tarām*. See 2. *na*.

नत्यूह *natyūha*, m. prob. = *dātyūha*, R. (B.)

नत्र *natra*, n. (in music) a kind of dance.

नद् *nad*, cl. 1. P. (Dhātup. iii, 17) *nádati* (ep. also °*te*; pf. *nanāda*, *nedur*, *nedire*, MBh.; aor. *anādīt*, Gr.; fut. *nadishyati*, °*ditā*, ib.) to sound, thunder, roar, cry, howl &c. (also with *nādám*, *śabdam*, *svanam* &c.), AV. &c. &c.: Pass. *nadyate*, MBh.: Caus. *nadáyati*, °*te*, to make resound or vibrate, RV.; *nādayati*, °*te*, to make resonant, fill with noises or cries, MBh., Kāv. &c.; aor. *anīnadat*, Gr.; Pass. *nādyate*, MBh.: Desid. *ninadishati*, Gr.: Intens. 3. pl. *nānadati*, p. *nānadat*, RV.; 3. sg. *nānadyate*, p. °*dyamāna*, Br.; MBh. to vibrate or sound violently, to roar, howl, cry, neigh &c.

Nadá, m. a roarer, bellower, thunderer, crier, neigher &c. (as a cloud, horse, bull, met. a man, i, 179, 4), RV.; N. of RV. viii, 58, 2 (beginning with *nadam*), ŚBr.; ŚāṅkhŚr.; a river (if thought of as male, ifc. ind. *-nadam*; cf. *nadī*), Mn.; MBh. &c.; = *naḍa*, reed, RV. i, 32, 8; (*ī*), f., see *Nadī*. **–dhra**, mfn. (for *dhara*?) possessing rivers, Kāv. **–nadī**, (in comp.) the male and female rivers; *-pati*, m. 'lord of m° and f° rivers,' N. of the Sindhu, Hariv.; of the ocean, MBh.; R.; *-bhartṛi*, m. 'id.,' the ocean, MBh. **–bhakta**, see *naḍa-bh°*. **–bhartṛi**, m. 'lord of rivers,' the ocean, Śis. **–rāja**, m. id.; *-sutā*, f. N. of Śrī, Śiś. ix, 30.

Nadat, mf(*antī*)n. sounding, resounding, roaring; m. N. of an Āṅgirasa, ĀrshBr.

Nadathu, m. noise, clamour, din, ChUp. iii, 13, 8.

Nadana, mfn. sounding, Nir. v, 2. **°nimán**, mfn. humming, murmuring, AV. v, 23, 8. **°nú**, m. noise, din, RV. viii, 21, 14; the sound of approbation, MW.; war, battle, Naigh. ii, 17; a cloud (*nadánu*), Uṇ. iii, 52, Sch.; a lion, L.; *-mát*, mfn. roaring, thundering, RV. vi, 18, 2.

Nadara, mfn., g. *aśmâdi*.

Nadasya, Nom. Ā. °*syate* to roar, Divyâv.

Nadi, m. a crier, caller, RV. v, 74, 2 (= *stuti*, Sāy.); ifc., see *nadī*. **–ja**, m. (for °*dī-*) Lablab Vulgaris, L.

Nadikā, see next.

Nadī, f. flowing water, a river (commonly personified as a female; but see *nadá* above), RV. &c. &c. (ifc. *nadikā*; cf. *ku-nadikā* and *giri-*; ind. *-nadi*; cf. *upa-nadi* [beside *-nadam*, fr. *nadá*, Pāṇ. v, 4, 110]); N. of 2 kinds of metre, Col.; of partic. fem. stems ending in *ī* or *ū* (as *nadī* itself), Pāṇ. i, 4, 3, &c. **–kadamba**, m. N. of a plant, L. **–kānta**, m. 'lover of rivers,' the ocean, L.; Vitex Negundo or Barringtonia Acutangula, L.; (*ā*), f. Eugenia Jambolana or Leea Hirta, L.; a creeper (= *latā*), L. **–kāśyapa**, m. N. of a contemporary of Śākya-muni, Buddh. **–kūla**, n. bank of a r°, Cāṇ.; *-priya*, m. Calamus Rotang, L. **–kshetrâdi-māhātmya**, n. N. of ch. of SkandaP. **–ja**, mfn. r°-born, coming from a r° (horses), MBh.; m. patr. of Bhīshma, ib.; N. of plants (Terminalia Arjuna, Barringtonia Acutangula, Lablab Vulgaris, or a species of reed = *yāvanāla-śara*), L.; antimony, Suśr.; (*ā*), f. = next; n. a lotus, W. **–jāta**, m. Premna Spinosa or Longifolia, L. **–jña**, mfn. knowing the course of r°s, MW. **–taṭa**, m. = *-kūla*, Var. **–tara**, mfn. crossing a river, L.; m. swimming across a r°, Yājñ.; *-sthala* or *-sthāna*, n. landing-place, ferry, L. **–tīra**, n. = *-kūla*, Kāv. **–datta**, m. 'r°-given,' N. of a Bodhi-sattva. **–doha**, m. r°-toll or tribute, L. **–dhara**, m. 'bearer of the r° (Ganges),' N. of Śiva, Sivag. **–2. -°na** (°*dīna*), m. 'lord of r°s,' the ocean, Kathās.; N. of Varuṇa, Kāv.; of a son of Saha-deva and father of Jagat-sena, Hariv. **–nada**, m. pl. (Mn. vi, 90) or n. sg. (MBh. viii, 4068) = *nada-nadī* (above). **–nātha**, m. 'lord of r°s,' the ocean, Kāv. **–nishpāva**, m. Lablab Vulgaris, L. **–paṅka**, m. or n. 'r°-mud,' the marshy bank of a r°, R. **–pati**, m. lord of flowing waters, VS.; the ocean, R.; sea-water, ŚBr. **–pūra**, m. 'r°-flood,' a swollen r°, Amar. **–bhallātaka**, m. a kind of plant (= *bhojanaka*), Suśr., Sch. **–bhava**, n. 'r°-born,' r°-salt. **–mātṛika**, mfn. 'r°-nourished,' well watered, L.; *-tā*, Naish. **–mārga**, m. course of a r°, R. **–mukha**, n. mouth of a r°, R.; a kind of grain (cf. *nandī-m°*), MW. **–raya**, m. the current of a r°, ib. **–vakra**, n., **-vaṅka**, m. the bend or arm of a r°, L. **–vaṭa**, m. a kind of tree (= *vaṭī*), L. **–vāsa**, m. standing in a r° (a form of penance), Kāv. **–vṛit**, mfn. stream-obstructing (Vṛitra), RV. **–vega**, m. = *-raya*, W. **–velā**, f. the current or tide of a r°, ib. **–°śa** (°*dīśa*), m. 'lord of the r°s,' the ocean, Pañc. **–shṇa**, mfn. (√*snā*) familiar with (lit. bathing in) r°s, Ragh.; Bhaṭṭ.; skilful, experienced, clever (cf. *ati-n°*, add.) **–saṃtāra**, m. crossing a r°, L. **–sarja**, m. Terminalia Arjuna. **Nady-ambujīvana**, mfn. (country) thriving by r°-water, L. **Nady-āmra**, m. a kind of plant, L.

Nadīya, m. or n. N. of a locality, W.

Nadeyī, w. r. for *nādeyī*, q.v.

नदाल *nadāla*, n. a potsherd (cf. *kumbhī-*, add.)

नद्ध *naddhá*, mfn. (√*nah*) bound, tied, bound on or round, put on, fastened to (comp.), AV. &c. &c.; joined, connected, covered, wound, inlaid, interwoven (with instr. or ifc.), MBh.; Kāv.; obstructed or impeded (*oshṭhābhyām*, by the lips, said of a faulty pronunciation), RPrāt.; n. tie, band, fetter, knot, string, trace, AV. &c. **–vimoksha**, m. the getting loose or breaking of a trace, GṛS.; deliverance from fastenings or fetters, MW.

Naddhavya, mfn. to be bound or tied &c., Pāṇ. viii, 2, 34, Kāś.

Naddhi, f. binding, fastening (cf. *barsa-*).

Naddhrī, f. a strip of leather, L.

Nad-bhyas. See 2. *náh*.

ननन्दृ *nanandṛi* (L.) or *nánāndṛi* (RV. x, 85, 46), f. a husband's sister. **Nanāndṛi-pati** or °**duh-pati**, m. the husband of a h°'s sister, L.

नना *nanā*, f. fam. expression for 'mother,' RV. ix, 112, 3 (cf. 2. *tatá*); = *vāc*, Naigh. i, 11.

ननु *na-nú*, ind. (2. *ná* + *nu*) not, not at all, never, RV.; AV.; (interr.) not? is it not? = nonne, AV.; ŚBr. &c. &c. (hence often =) certainly, surely, indeed, no doubt (esp. in questions amounting to an affirmation, e.g. *nanv ahaṃ te priyaḥ*, am I not your friend, i.e. certainly I am your fr°, Daś. [so also *na ca*, there can be no doubt, Pāṇ. ii, 3, 11; 29, Kāś.], or to a request, e.g. *nanu gacchāmi bhoḥ*, surely I may go, Pāṇ. viii, 1, 43, Kāś., and even as a responsive particle, e.g. *akārshīḥ kaṭam – nanu karomi bhoḥ*, indeed I have made it, ib.; with another interr. or an Impv. = pray, please, e.g. *nanu ko bhavān*, pray who are you? Mṛicch. x, $\frac{48}{49}$; *nanûcyatām*, please tell, ib. $\frac{52}{53}$; in argument often as an inceptive particle implying doubt or objection, 'now it may be said, well, but then' &c., esp. in *nanv astu* or *nanu mā bhūt–tathâpi*, well, be it so or not so—nevertheless); a vocat. particle implying kindness or reproach or perplexity &c., L.

नन्तव्य *nantavya*, mfn. (√*nam*) to be bent or bowed; to be saluted or honoured, W.

Nantṛi, mfn. bending, bowing; changing a dental to a cerebral, RPrāt.

Nántva, mfn. to be bent, RV. ii, 24, 2.

नन्द् *nand*, cl. 1. P. (Dhātup. iii, 30) *nándati*, ep. also °*te* (pf. *nananda*, MBh.; fut. *nandishyate*, ib., °*dishyati* and °*ditā* Gr.; aor. *anandīt*; inf. *nanditum*, ib.) to rejoice, delight, to be pleased or satisfied with, be glad of (instr., rarely abl.), RV. &c. &c.: Pass. *nandyate*, MBh. &c.: Caus. *nandayati*, °*te*, aor. *ananandat*, to make glad, gladden, Up.; MBh. &c.: Desid. *ninandishati*, Gr.: Intens. *nānandyate*, Pāṇ. vi, 4, 24, Kāś.

Nánda, m. joy, delight, happiness (also pl.), AV.; VS. &c.; (in mus.) a flute 7 inches long; N. of one of Yudhi-shṭhira's 2 drums, MBh.; of one of Kubera's 9 gems, L.; a son (in *gopa-*, add.; cf. *nandana*); N. of Vishṇu, MBh.; of one of Skanda's attendants, ib.; of a Nāga, ib.; (also *-ka*); of a Buddh. deity, Lalit.; of an attendant on Daksha, BhP.; of a son of Dhṛita-rāshṭra (also *-ka*), MBh.; of a step-brother and disciple of Gautama Buddha, MWB. 441; of a son of Vasu-deva, Pur.; of the foster-father of Kṛishṇa and ancestor of Durgā, MBh.; Hariv.; Pur. &c. (also *-ka*, L.); of a leader of the Sātvatas, BhP.; of a king of Pāṭali-putra and founder of a dynasty consisting of 9 successive princes, HPariś.; Pur.; Kathās.; Pañc. &c.; of the number 9 (because of the 9 Nandas), Jyot.; of sev. scholars and authors, Cat.; of a mountain, BhP. (cf. *-parvata* & *nandi-giri*); (*ā*), f. Delight, Felicity (personif. as wife of Harsha; cf. *nandi*), MBh. i, 2597; prosperity, happiness, L.; a small earthen water-jar (also °*dikā*), L.; a husband's sister (cf. *nanāndṛi*), L.; N. of the 3 auspicious Tithis (1st, 6th, and 11th day of the fortnight), VarBṛS. ic, 2 (also °*dikā*, L.); of the 7th day in Mārgaśirsha, Hcat.; (in music) of a Mūrchanā; of Gaurī, Hcat.; of an Apsaras, Hariv.; of a daughter of Vibhīshaṇa, L.; of a girl connected with Śākya-muni, Buddh.; of the mother of 10th Arhat of present Ava-sarpiṇī, L.; of the wife of Gopāla-varman, Rājat.; of a river flowing near Kubera's city Alakā, MBh.; BhP.; (*ī*), f. Cedrela Toona, Suśr.; a kind of song or musical instrument, MānGṛ.; N. of the 6th day in a month's light half, ib.; of Durgā, DevīP.; of Indra's city, W.; n. a kind of house, Gal. **–kiśora**, m. N. of an author, Cat. **–kumāra**, m. 'Nanda's son,' patr. of Kṛishṇa, Bhām.; N. of an author, Cat. **–gopa**, m. the cowherd N°, Hariv.; *-kula*, n. his family (°*le jātā* or °*lôdbhavā*, f. 'descended from N°s f°,' Durgā, MBh.); *-kumāra*, m. 'son of N°,' N. of Kṛishṇa, BhP. **–gopitā**, f. N. of a plant (= *rāsnā*), L. **–dāsa**, m. N. of an author, Cat. **–deva**, m. N. of a king, ib. **–nandana**, m. = *-kumāra*, L.; (*ī*), f. 'N°'s daughter,' N. of Durgā, ib. **–nātha** and **-paṇḍita**, m. N. of authors, Cat. **–padra**, m. or n. N. of a town, ib. **–parvata**, m. king N° compared with a mountain, Kām. **–pāla**, m. 'guardian of the treasure N°,' i.e. Varuṇa, L. (cf. above). **–putra**, m. = *-kumāra* (°*trôtsava*, m. N. of ch. of BrahmavP. iv); (*ī*), f. = *-kumārī*. **–prabhañjana-varman**, m. N. of a man, L. **–prayāga**, m. N. of a place (at the confluence of 2 rivers whose names contain *nanda*), Rasik. **–balā**, f. N. of a girl connected with Gautama Buddha, Lalit. **–mitra** (?), m. N. of a man, ib. **–rāma**, **-lāla**, **-vardhana** and **-śarman**, m. N. of authors, Cat. **–sāra**, m. N. of a king, VP. **–suta**, m. = *-kumāra*, Bhām. **–sundara**, m. N. of an author, Cat. **–sūnu**, m. = *-suta*, Vṛishabhân. **Nandâtmaja**, m. id., Gīt.; (*ā*), f. N. of Durgā, L. **Nandâśrama**, m. N. of a hermitage, MBh. **Nandôpananda**, m. N. of a Nāga, L.; voc. (used as an exclamation of sorrow) alas! woe is me! Divyâv.; *-saṃjñā*, f. du. N. of 2 Kumārīs on Indra's standard, VarBṛS. xliii, 39. **Nandôpâkhyāna**, n. N. of wk.

Nandaka, mfn. delighting in (comp.), MBh.; rejoicing, gladdening, making happy (esp. a family), L.; m. joy, delight, L.; a frog, L.; N. of Kṛishṇa's sword, MBh.; (°*kin*, m. its possessor, i.e. Kṛishṇa, ib.); of a bull, Pañc.; of a village, Rājat. (cf. also under *nanda*, m.); (*ikā*), f. N. of Indra's pleasure-ground, L. (cf. ib., f. *ā*).

Nandaki, m. (√*nand*?) long pepper, L.

Nandathu, m. joy, delight, happiness, L.

Nandana, mf(*ā*)n. (the initial *n* is not changeable to *ṇ*, g. *kshubhnâdi*) rejoicing, gladdening (cf. °*daka*), MBh.; Var.; Pañc.; m. a son, Yājñ.; MBh.; Kāv. &c. (ifc. also °*naka*, MBh.); a frog (cf. °*daka*), L.; a kind of poisonous plant, Suśr. (also f., Sch.); a partic. form of temple, Var.; (in music) a kind of measure; N. of Vishṇu or Śiva, MBh.; of an attendant of Skanda, ib.; of a Siddha, BhP.; of a Buddh. deity, Lalit. (v.l. *nanda*); (with Jainas) of the 7th of the 9 white Balas; of a mountain, Pur.; of sev. authors (also *-bhaṭṭâcārya* & *-miśra*), Cat.; of the 26th year in a Jupiter cycle of 60 years, Var.; (*ā*), f. a daughter (cf. *kula-*); n. gladdening or gladness, MBh.; a divine garden, (esp.) Indra's paradise,

MBh.; Kāv. &c.; N. of a sword, R. (cf. °*daka*); N. of a metre, Col. **-kānana**, n. N. of a wood, Rasik. **-ja**, m. 'grown in the divine garden,' yellow sandal-wood, L. **-druma**, m. tree of the d° g°, Kum. **-mālā**, f. N. of a garland worn by Kṛishṇa, L. **-vana**, n. divine grove, R. **Nandanôdbhava**, m. = °*na-ja*, Gal.

Nandanta, mf(*ī*)n. rejoicing, gladdening; m. son, friend, king; (*ī*), f. daughter, L.

Nandayat, mf(*antī*)n. = prec. mfn. °**dayanta**, mf(*ī*)n. id., L.; (*ī*), f. N. of a woman, Kathās. °**dayitṛi**, mfn. giving joy, making happy, MW.

Nandā, f. of *nanda*, q.v. **-tīrtha**, n. N. of a Tīrtha, Cat. **-purāṇa**, n. N. of an Upapur. (cf. *nandī-p*°). **-prācī-māhātmya**, n. N. of wk. **-hrada-tīrtha**, n. N. of a Tīrtha, Cat.

Nandi, m. 'the happy one,' N. of Vishṇu, MBh.; of Śiva, ib.; of an attendant of Śiva, TĀr.; MBh. &c.; of a Gandharva, MBh.; of a man, Pravar.; the speaker of a prologue, W. (w.r. for *nāndin*); f. joy, happiness, welfare, MBh. &c. (also m. n., L.); Joy personified as daughter of Heaven or as wife of Kāma and mother of Harsha, Pur.; n. = *dyūta* & *dyūtâṅga*, L.; (with Jainas) a class of sacred writings (m. or f.?), MWB. 533. **-kara**, mfn. causing joy or happiness (with gen.), MBh. ii, 740; m. son of (comp.), MBh. (cf. *nandana*); N. of Śiva, ib. **-kuṇḍa**, m. or n. N. of a sacred bathing-place, ib. **-kshetra**, n. a district frequented by gods, Rājat. **-giri**, m. N. of a mountain; *-māhātmya*, n. N. of wk. **-gupta**, m. N. of a prince of Kaśmīra, Rājat. **-grāma**, m. N. of a village near Daulat-ābād (where Bharata resided during Rāma's banishment), MBh.; Kāv. &c.; *-darśana*, n. N. of ch. of PadmaP. **-ghosha**, m. cry or music of joy, (esp.) the proclamation of a panegyrist or herald, MBh.; R.; Arjuna's chariot, L.; *-vijaya*, m. N. of a drama. **-ja**, n. Lablab Vulgaris, Gal. **-taru**, m. Anogeissus Latifolia, Bhpr. **-tūrya**, n. a musical instrument played on joyful occasions, MBh.; Hariv. **-deva**, m. N. of a man, Kathās.; °*vī*, f. common N. of one of the loftiest Himalayan peaks, MW. **-dharma**, m. Nandi's or Nandin's precepts, Cat. **-nāgaraka**, mfn. N. of a partic. written character, Hcat. **-nāgarī**, f. a partic. kind of writing, L. **-pada-cchandas**, n. N. of a wk. on Prākṛit metres (in Prākṛ.), Cat. **-pura-māhātmya**, n. N. of wk. **-purāṇa**, n. N. of a Pur. (cf. *nandikêśvara-p*° & *nandîśvara-p*°). **-bharata**, m. or n. N. of a wk. on music. **-mukha**, m. a species of rice, Suśr.; N. of a man, Rājat.; *-sughosha*, m. N. of a man (°*shâvadāna*, n. N. of wk., Buddh.) **-yaśas**, m. N. of a prince, VP. **-rudra**, m. N. of Śiva in a joyful or serene form, Rājat. **-vardha**, m. N. of a prince (cf. next), R. **-vardhana**, mfn. increasing pleasure, promoting happiness (with gen.), MBh.; BhP.; m. son, MBh.; R.; friend, L.; the end of a half-month, the day of full moon or of new moon, L.; a partic. form of temple, Var. (cf. *nandana* & °*din*); (in music) a kind of measure; N. of Śiva, MBh.; of a prince (son of Udāvasu), R.; VP.; of a son of Janaka, VP.; of a son of Udayâśva, L.; of a son of Rājaka, BhP.; of a son of A-jaya, ib.; of a brother of Mahāvīra, W.; n. N. of a town, Siṇhâs. **-varman**, m. N. of a man, L. **-vāralaka**, m. a species of fish, Suśr. **-vivardhana**, mfn. = *-vardhana*, mfn., R. **-vṛiksha**, °**aka**, m. Cedrela Toona, Bhpr. (cf. °*dī-vṛ*°). **-vega**, m. pl. N. of a people, MBh. **-śikhā**, f. N. of wk. **-sheṇa**, m. = *-sena*, in °*ṇêśvara*, n. N. of a Liṅga, PadmaP. **-sena**, m. N. of an attendant of Skanda, MBh. **-svāmin**, m. N. of a grammarian, Cat. **Nandîśa**, m. (°*ndi* or °*ndin* or °*ndī* + *īśa*?) N. of an attendant of Śiva, Rājat.; of Śiva himself, W.; (in music) a kind of measure. **Nandîśvara**, m. (°*ndi* or °*ndin* or °*ndī* + *īśv*°) N. of Śiva, MBh.; N. of the chief of Ś°'s attendants, BhP. (cf. *nandin*); of one of Kubera's attendants, MBh.; N. of a place held sacred by the Jainas, Śatr.; of an author, Cat.; (in music) a kind of measure; *-purāṇa*, *-māhātmya*, n., °*rôtpatti*, f. N. of wks. **Nandy-āvarta**, m. a kind of diagram, MBh.; Var. (cf. °*ndikâv*°); anything so formed (e.g. a dish or vessel), MBh. vii, 2930 (Nīlak.), a palace or temple, VarBṛS. lii, 32 (also n., L.); a cake, MnGṛh.; a species of large fish, L.; Tabernaemontana Coronaria, L.; the holy fig-tree, L.; any tree, L.; a kind of shell, L.; cf. MWB. 523; (in music) a partic. attitude in dancing. **Nandy-upapurāṇa** & **-upâkhyāna**, n. N. of wks.

Nandika, mfn. Cedrela Toona, L.; N. of one of Śiva's attendants, Cat.; of a pupil of Gautama Buddha (chief of the village Uru-vilvā), Lalit. °**kâcārya-tantra**, n. N. of a medic. wk. °**kâvarta**, m. a kind of diagram, Lalit. (= *nandy-āv*°); a species of plant, Var. °**kêśa**, m. N. of a holy place, ŚivaP.; *-liṅga*, n. N. of ch. of the ŚivaP. °**kêśvara**, m. N. of one of Śiva's attendants, Hariv. (= *nandi*, °*ndin*); of an author, Cat.; *-kārikā* or *-kāśikā*, f. N. of a mystic. interpretation of the Śiva-sūtras; *-tārâvalī*, f. N. of wk.; *tīrtha*, n. N. of a sacred bathing-place, ŚivaP.; *-purāṇa*, n. N. of an Upapur.; *-saṃhitā*, f. N. of wk.; °*râbhisheka*, m. N. of ch. of LiṅgaP.; °*rôtpatti*, f. N. of ch. of ŚivaP.

Nandin, mfn. (initial *n* cannot be cerebralized, g. *kshubhnâdi*) rejoicing, gladdening (ifc.), MBh.; Kāv.; delighting in, liking, ib.; m. son (ifc.; cf. *bhāskara-n*°); the speaker of a prologue (cf. *nāndin*, L.); N. of sev. plants (the Indian fig-tree, Thespesia Opulneoides &c.), L.; a partic. form of temple, Var. (cf. °*ndi-vardhana*); N. of an attendant of Śiva, MBh.; Hariv. &c. (cf. *nandi*, °*ndîśa*, °*ndikêśvara*); of Śiva's bull, W.; of sev. authors, Cat.

Nandinī, f. a daughter, MBh. &c.; a husband's sister (= *nanāndṛi*), L.; N. of Durgā, MatsyaP.; of Gaṅgā, L.; of the river Bāṇa-nāśa, BrahmâP.; of one of the Mātṛis atttending on Skanda, MBh.; of a fabulous cow (mother of Śurabhi and property of the sage Vasishṭha), MBh.; Ragh.; of the mother of Vyāḍi, L.; N. of sev. plants (= *tulasī*, *jaṭāmāṇsī* &c.), L.; a kind of perfume (*reṇukā*), Bhpr.; a kind of metre, Col.; (in music) a partic. composition; N. of a locality, MBh.; of Comm. on Mn. **-tanaya**, m. metron. of Vyāḍi, L. (cf. above). **-tīrtha**, n. N. of a sacred bathing-place, SkandaP. **-putra**, m. metron. of Kaṇâda, Gal. **-suta**, m. = *-tanaya*, L.

Nandī, f. of *nanda*, q.v. **-carita**, n. N. of wk. **-pati**, m. N. of a man, Cat. **-pura**, n. N. of a town, Cat. **-purāṇa**, n. N. of a Pur. **-mukha** (cf. °*ndi-m*°), m. N. of Śiva, MBh.; a kind of water-bird, Bhpr.; a species of rice, Suśr.; pl. a kind of Manes, L. (w. r. for *nāndī-m*°); (*ī*), f. sleep, L. **-vṛiksha**, m. N. of sev. plants (Bignonia Suaveolens, Cedrela Toona &c.), L. **-saras**, n. N. of Indra's lake, L.

नन्दीक *nandīka* (?), m. a cock, L.

नन्दीट *nandīṭa*, m. a bald-headed man, L.

नन्देरी *nanderī*, f. a kind of metre.

नन्नम *nannama* (√*nam*). See *ku-n*°.

Nannamyamāna, mfn. (fr. the Intens.) bending or bowing very low, W.

नन्नयभट्ट *nannaya-bhaṭṭa*, m. N. of an author, Cat.

नपराजित् *na-parājit*, *na-puṇs* &c. See 2. *ná*.

नपात् *nápāt*, *náptṛi*, m. (the former stem only in the strong cases and earlier lang.; the latter in Class., but acc. *naptāram* appears in TS. & AitBr.) descendant, offspring, son (in this meaning esp. in RV., e.g. *apāṃ n*°, *ūrjo n*°, *divo n*°, *vimuco n*° &c.); grandson (in later lang. restricted to this sense), RV. &c. &c.; N. of one of the Viśve devās, MBh. xiii, 4362; path of the gods (?), Mahīdh. on VS. xix, 56; granddaughter (?), Uṇ. ii, 96, Sch.; (*tī*), f., RV.; AV. (ix, 1; 3 nom. °*tīs*) daughter, granddaughter (pl. often fig. 'the fingers, hands' &c.); (*trī*), f. granddaughter, SVĀr.; L. [Prob. neither = *na* + *pat* (Uṇ. ii, 96) nor *na* + *pāt* (Pāṇ. vi, 3, 75), and of very questionable connection with √*nabh* or *nah*; cf. Zd. *napāt*, *naptar*; Gk. νέποδες, ἀνεψιός; Lat. *nepōt-em*; Angl.Sax. *nefa*; HGerm. *nëvo*, *nëve*, *Neffe*.]

Napātka, mfn. relating to a grandson (applied to a partic. sacrif. fire), Kāṭh.

Naptṛikā, f. a species of bird, Suśr.

नभ् 1. *nabh*, cl. 1. Ā. *nábhate*, to burst, be torn or rent asunder, RV. viii, 39, 1; x, 133, 1; impf. P. *nábhas*, to break or destroy (?), i, 174, 8 (cf. Dhātup. xviii, 13, Naigh. ii, 19); cl. 4. 9. P. *nabhyati*, *nabhnāti* (Dhātup. xxvi, 130, xxxi, 48), to hurt, injure (pf. Ā. *nebhe*, Bhaṭṭ.): Caus. *nabhayati*, to cause to burst, tear open, AitBr.

2. **Nabh**, f. or m. injury (Sāy.) or injurer, RV. i, 174, 8 (only acc. pl. *nábhas*; but cf. 1. *nabh* above).

Nabha, m. (rather fr. √*nabh* denoting 'bursting forth' or 'expanding' than fr. √*nah* 'connecting,' scil. heaven and earth) the sky, atmosphere (= *nabhas*), L.; the month Śrāvaṇa, Car.; N. of a son of Manu Svārocisha or of the 3rd M° (together with Nabhasya), Hariv.; of one of 7 sages of the 6th Manv-antara, ib.; of a demon (son of Vipra-citti by Siṇhikā), ib.; VP.; of a son of Nala (Nishadha) and father of Puṇḍarīka (cf. *nabhas*), Hariv.; BhP.; (*ā*), f. a spitting-pot (?), L.; N. of the city of the sun, W. **-kānana**, m. pl. N. of a people, MBh. **-ga**, m. N. of a son of Manu Vaivasvata, Pur. (cf. *nabhāga*, *nābhāga*). **Nabhâṅkas**, m. inhabiting the sky or atmosphere, BhP.

Nabhaḥ, in comp. for °*bhas*. **-ketana**, m. 'sky-banner,' the sun, L. **-krānta** and °**tin**, m. 'sky-walker' (from the lion-like shape of certain clouds), a lion, L. **-pāntha**, m. 'sky-traveller,' the sun, L. **-prabheda** or °**dana**, m. N. of a descendant of Virūpa and author of RV. x, 112, RV. Anukr. **-prāṇa**, m. 'sky-breath,' air, wind, L. **-śabda-maya**, mf(*ī*)n. consisting of the word *nabhas*, Ragh. **-śrit**, mfn. reaching to the sky, Kir. **-śvāsa**, m. = *-prâṇa*, L. **-sad**, m. 'sky-dweller,' a god, Śiś.; a planet, Gaṇit. **-saras**, n. 'sky-lake,' the clouds, L. **-sarit**, f. 'sky-river,' the milky way or = next, L. **-sindhu**, f. the celestial Ganges; *-putra*, m. patr. of Bhīma, Pracaṇḍ. **-sena**, f. N. of a woman, HPariś. **-stha**, mfn. 'sky-staying,' aerial, celestial, W. **-sthala**, mfn. 'sky-residing' (said of Śiva), MBh.; n. (Kāvyâd.) and (*ī*), f. (Rājat.) the celestial vault, firmament. **-sthita**, mfn. = *-stha*; m. N. of a hell, L. **-spṛiś**, mfn. 'sky-touching,' attaining heaven, MBh.; R. &c.

Nabhanú, m., °**nū́**, f. a spring (lit. = next), RV.

Nabhanyà, mfn. springing forth (as a hymn, horse &c.), ib.

Nabhas, in comp. for °*bhas*. **-cakshus**, n. 'eye of the sky,' the sun, L. **-camasa**, m. 'goblet of the sky,' the moon, L.; a kind of cake, L.; magic, conjuring, L. **-cara**, mf(*ī*)n. 'sky-going,' aerial, celestial, Kāv.; m. a god, Ragh.; a Vidyādhara, Kathās.; a bird, L.; a cloud, L.; the wind, L. **-cyuta**, mfn. fallen from the sky, MBh.

Nábhas, n. (cf. *nabha*) mist, clouds, vapour (esp. of the Soma), RV.; AV.; ŚBr.; the sky or atmosphere (du. heaven and earth, AV.); MBh.; Kāv. &c.; ether (as an element), BhP.; (m., L.) N. of a month in the rainy season (= *śrāvaṇa*, July–August), ŚBr.; Ragh.; Suśr.; the sun, Naigh. i, 4; period of life, age, L.; m. clouds, rainy season, L.; the nose or smell (= *ghrāṇa*), L.; a rope made of lotus fibres, L.; a spitting-pot, L.; N. of a prince (son of Nala and father of Puṇḍarīka), Ragh.; VP. [Cf. Gk. νέφος, νεφέλη; Lat. *nĕbula*; Slav. *nebo*; Germ. *nëbul*, *nëbel*, *Nebel*; Angl.Sax. *nifol*, 'dark.'] **-tala**, n. 'sky-surface,' firmament, Var.; MBh. &c.; N. of the 10th solar mansion, Var. **-tas**, ind. from the sky, Var.; Ragh. **-máya**, mf(*ī*)n. vaporous, misty, hazy, RV. **-1. -vat**, mfn. id., RV.; AV.; young, L.; m. wind, MBh.; Kāv. &c.; N. of a son of Naraka Bhauma, BhP.; (*atī*), f. N. of the wife of Antar-dhāna and mother of Havir-dhāna, BhP. **-2. -vat**, ind. like vapour, MW.

Nabhasá, mfn. vapoury, misty, AV.; m. sky, atmosphere, L.; the rainy season, L.; the ocean, L.; N. of a Ṛishi of the 10th Manv-antara, Hariv.; of a Dānava, ib. (v.l. *rabhasa* & *raśmisa*); of a son of Nala, Vp. **-m-gama**, m. 'sky-goer,' a bird, L.

Nabhasyà, mfn. foggy, misty, ŚāṅkhŚr.; m. N. of a month in the rainy season (= *bhādra*, August–September), VS.; ŚBr.; Hariv. &c.; of a son of Manu Svārocisha or of the 3rd Manu, Hariv.; of Śiva, Śivag.

Nabho, in comp. for °*bhas*. **-ga**, m. 'sky-goer,' a planet, Gaṇit.; N. of a Ṛishi of the 10th Manv-antara, Hariv. **-gaja**, m. 'sky-elephant,' a cloud, L. **-gati**, f. 'sky-going,' soaring, flying, L. **-'ṅgaṇa**, n. celestial vault, firmament, Vāsav. **-jā́**, mfn. produced from vapour, RV. **-jū́**, mfn. impelling the clouds, ib. **-da**, m. N. of one of the Viśve devās, MBh. **-duha**, **-dvīpa**, **-dhūma**, **-dhvaja**, m. a cloud, L. **-dṛishṭi**, mfn. 'sky-looking,' blind; looking up to heaven, MW. **-nadī**, f. 'sky-river,' the celestial Ganges, L. **-nabhasya-tva**, n. the state of the rainy months Nabhas and Nabhasya, Naish. **-maṇi**, m. 'sky-jewel,' the sun, L. **-maṇḍala**, n. 'sky-circle,' firmament; *-dīpa*, m. 'firmament-lamp,' the moon, L. **-madhya**, n. 'sky-centre,' the zenith, Āryabh. **-mudrā**, f. a partic. position of the fingers, Cat. **-'mbu-pa**, m. 'drinking sky-water or rain,' the Cātaka bird, L. **-yoni**, m. 'sky-born,' N. of Śiva, Śivag. **-rajas**, n. 'sky-dust,' darkness, L. **-rūpa** (*ná°*), mfn. 'cloud-coloured,' gloomy, dark, VS.; (*-rūpá*), m. N. of a mythic. being, Suparṇ. **-reṇu**, f. 'sky-dust,' fog, mist, L. **-laya**, m. 'sky-dissolved,' smoke, L. **-lih**, mfn. 'sky-licking,' lofty, towering, W. **-vaṭa**, m. 'sky-expanse,' atmosphere, L. **-vid**, mfn. knowing the sky, abiding in it, RV. x, 46, 1. **-vīthī**, f. 'sky-road,' the sun's path, BhP.

Nabhya, mfn. foggy, moist, cloudy, ŚāṅkhGṛ.

नभाक *nabhāka*, m. N. of the author of RV. viii, 39-41 (*-vát*, N°'s hymn, AitBr. vi, 24; ind. like N°, RV. viii, 40, 4; 5); n. = *nabhas* or *tamas*, Uṇ.; L.

नभाग *nabhāga*, m. N. of a son of Manu Vaivasvata, VP. (cf. *nabha-ga*, *nābhāga*).

नभि *nabhi*, m. a wheel, W.

2. **Nábhya**, n. the centre part of a wheel, the nave, AV.; Br. &c.; the middle (*-stha*, mfn. standing in the m°), ŚBr.; mfn. (according to g. *gav-ādi* fr. *nābhi*) belonging to or fit for a nave, Uṇ. iv, 125, Sch.

नभीत *na-bhīta*, *na-bhrāj* &c. See 2. *ná*.

नम् *nam*, cl. 1. P. *námati* (Dhātup. xxiii, 12), °*te* (mostly intrans.; cf. Pāṇ. iii, 1, 89; pr. p. Ā. *namāna*, R.; pf. P. *nanāma*, RV. &c.; 2. sg. *nemitha* or *nanantha*, Vop.; Subj. *nanámas*, RV.; 3. pl. *nemur*, Kāv.; Ā. *neme*, RV.; 3. pl. *-nanāmire*, MBh.; aor. P. *anān*, Kāṭh.; *anansīt*, Daś.; Ā. *anansta*, Gr.; 3. pl. *anansata*, Br.; Subj. *nansai*, *nansante*, RV.; fut. *nansyati*, Br.; *namishyati*, Hariv.; *nantā*, Siddh.; inf. *-námam*, *-náme*, RV.; *nantum*, *namitum*, Kāv.; ind. p. *natvā*, BhP.; Kathās.; *-natya*, Br.; *-namya*, MBh.) to bend or bow (either trans. or oftener intr.), to bow to, subject or submit one's self (with gen., dat. or acc.), RV. &c. &c.; (with *hiruk*) to turn away, keep aside, AV. iv, 1, 3; to turn towards, i.e. to aim at (gen.) with (instr.), RV. i, 165, 6; to yield or give way, keep quiet or be silent, Bālar. vi, 12; (in gram.) to change a dental letter into a cerebral, RPrāt.: Pass. *namyate*, to be bent or bowed; yield or submit to, TUp. iii, 10, 4: Caus. *namáyati*, RV. &c. &c. (*nāmayati*, Up. &c.; *nāmyati* [!], Mṛicch. i, 30; aor. *anīnamat*, RV.; Pass. *nāmyate*, °*ti*, MBh. &c.) to cause to bow or sink, incline, RV. &c. &c.; (with *cāpam*) to bend a bow, MBh.; Hariv. &c.; to turn away or ward off, RV.; to aim at (gen.), ix, 97, 15; (in gram.) to change a dental letter into a cerebral, RPrāt.: Desid. *ninansati*, Gr.: Intens. *nánnamīti*, RV.; *nannamyate*, KātyŚr. (3. sg. *námnate*, impf. *anamnata*, p. *námnamāna*, RV.) to bow or submit one's self to (dat.), RV.; Br. [Cf. Zd. *nam*, *nemaiti*; Gk. νέμω, νέμος, νόμος; Lat. *nemus*; Goth., Old Sax., Angl. Sax. *niman*; HGerm. *nëman*, *nëmen*, *nehmen*.]

1. **Náma**, m. pasture-ground, RV. iii, 39, 6.

2. **Nama** = °*mas* in **náma-ukti**, f. homage, veneration, RV. i, 189, 1 &c.

Namaka, m. (prob.) N. of an author. **-bhāshya** & **-camaka-bhāshya**, n. N. of Comms.

Namat, mf(*ntī*)n. bending, bowing, stooping, Kāv.; Pur.

1. **Namata**, mf(*ā*)n. bent, crooked, Uṇ. iii, 110, Sch.; m. master, lord; actor, mime, L.; a cloud, W.

Namana, mfn. bending, bowing (ifc.), Śiś. vi, 30 (cf. *nṛi-*); n. bowing down, sinking, MārkP.; bending (a bow), Sāh. °**nīya**, mfn. to be bowed down to, venerable; *-pāda*, BhP.

Namayat, mf(*ntī*)n. bending, inclining, Kathās. °**yitavya**, mfn. to be bent (bow), Prasannar. °**yishṇu**, mfn. bowing, bending, RV.

Námas, n. bow, obeisance, reverential salutation, adoration (by gesture or word; often with dat., e.g. *Rāmāya namaḥ*, salutation or glory to Rāma, often ind. [g. *svar-ādi*]; *namas-√kṛi*, to utter a salutation, do homage; ind. p. °*mas-kṛítya* [AV.; TS. &c.] or °*mas-kṛitvā* [MBh.; BhP.]; *námas-kṛita*, worshipped, adored), RV. &c. &c.; food, Naigh. ii, 7; a thunderbolt, ii, 20; gift, donation, L.; m. (?) an inarticulate cry, L. **-kartṛi**, mfn. worshipping, a worshipper, MBh. **-kārá**, m. the exclamation 'namas,' adoration, homage, AV.; Br.; &c.; a sort of poison, L.; (*ī*), f. a kind of plant; °*ra-vat*, mfn. containing the word 'namas-kāra,' AitBr.; °*ra-vidhi* & °*ra-stava*, m. N. of wks. **-kārya**, mfn. to be worshipped or adored, venerable, MBh.; Hariv. **-kṛiti** (Kād.), **-kriyā** (MBh.), f. adoration, homage. **-vat** (*ná°*), mfn. paying or inspiring veneration, RV. **-vin**, mfn. worshipping, reverential, ib.

Namasa, mfn. favourable, kind, Uṇ. iii. 117; m. (?) agreement, W. °**sāná**, mfn. paying obeisance, worshipping, AV. °**sita**, mfn. (prob. w. r. for °*syita*, see next) reverenced, worshipped, Br.

1. **Namasya**, Nom. P. °*yati* (ep. also °*te*), to pay homage, worship, be humble or deferential, RV. &c. &c. (p. °*syat*; ind. p. °*sya*). °**syā́**, f. reverence, adoration, RV. x, 104, 7. °**syita**, mfn., see under *namasa*. °**syú**, mfn. bowing down (in *á-n°*, q.v.); doing homage, worshipping, RV.; m. N. of a son of Pravīra, BhP.

2. **Namasyà**, mfn. deserving or paying homage, venerable or humble, RV. &c. &c.

Namita, mfn. bowed, bent down, Kāv.

Namo, in comp. for °*mas*. **-guru**, m. spiritual teacher, a Brāhman, L. **-vāka**, m. uttering the 'namas,' homage, obeisance, RV.; AV. &c. **-vṛikti** (*ná°*), f. reverential cleansing (of the Barhis), RV.; TS.; *-vat*, mfn. containing the word 'namo-vṛikti,' ĀpŚr. **-vṛídh**, mfn. honoured by adoration, RV. **-vṛidhá**, mfn. worshipping, glorifying, ib.

Namya, mfn. to be bowed down to, venerable, MW.; changeable to a cerebral letter, RPrāt.; (*ā*), f. the night, Naigh. i, 7.

Namrá, mf(*ā*)n. bowing, inclining; bowed, bent, curved; hanging down, sunk; bowing to (comp.); submissive, reverential, humble, RV. &c. &c.; (*ā*), f. N. of 2 verses addressed to Agni, ŚrS. **-tā**, f., **-tva**, n. state or condition of bowing or hanging down; bowing to (loc. or comp.); submissiveness, humbleness, meekness, Kāv. **-nāsika**, mfn. flat-nosed, L. **-prakṛiti**, mfn. of a gentle or submissive disposition, MW. **-mukha**, mf(*ī*)n. having the face bent down, looking down, W. **-mūrti**, mfn. having the form bent, stooping, bowed, W. **Namrâṅga**, mf(*ī*)n. bending the body, bowed, stooping, MW.

Namraka, mfn. bowed down, stooping, L.; m. Calamus Rotang, Bhpr.

Namrita, mfn. bent down, made to sink, Inscr.

Namrī-√kṛi, to bend or bring down, humiliate, ib.

नमत 2. *namata*, n. felt, woollen stuff, L. (cf. 2. *navata*).

नमात्र *na-mātra*, *na-mura* &c. See 2. *ná*.

नमि *nami*, m. N. of a Jain. author (1069), Cat.

नमी *námī*, n. N. of a man, RV.

नमुच *namuca*, m. N. of an ancient sage, MBh. xiii, 7112 (cf. next).

Namuci, m. (according to Pāṇ. vi, 3, 75 = *na* + *m°*, 'not loosing,' scil. the heavenly waters, i.e. 'preventing rain') N. of a demon slain by Indra and the Aśvins, RV.; VS.; Br.; MBh. &c.; of the god of love, L. **-ghna** (MBh.), **-dvish** (Śiś.), m. 'hater or killer of Namuci,' N. of Indra. **-sūdana**, m. 'destroyer of N°,' id.; *-sārathi*, m. Indra's charioteer Mātali, Bālar. **-han**, m. = *-ghna*, MBh.

नमेरु *nameru*, m. Elaeocarpus Ganitrus, L.

नमैय *namaiya*, m. N. of a poet, Cat. (v.l. *nammaiya*).

नम्ब् *namb*, cl. 1. P. *nambati*, to go, Vop in Dhātup. xi, 35.

नम्बिकारिका *nambi-kārikā*, f. N. of wk.

नम्मैय *nammaiya*. See *namaiya*.

नय् *nay*, cl. 1. Ā. *nayate*, to go; to protect, Dhātup. xiv, 7.

नय *naya*, m. (√1. *nī*) leading (of an army), R.; conduct, behaviour, (esp.) prudent c° or b°, good management, polity, civil and military government, MBh.; Kāv. &c.; wisdom, prudence, reason (*naya* ibc. or *nayeshu*, in a prudent manner, MBh.), R.; BhP.; plan, design, MBh.; Pañc.; Kathās.; leading thought, maxim, principle, system, method, doctrine, R.; Sāh.; Bhāshāp.; Sarvad.; a kind of game and a sort of dice or men for playing it, L.; N. of a son of Dharma and Kriyā, Pur.; of a son of 13th Manu, Hariv.; guide, conductor, L.; mfn. fit, right, proper, L. **-kovida**, mfn. skilled in policy, prudent, BhP. **-ga**, mfn. behaving properly or prudently, MBh. **-cakshus**, n. the eye of prudence, R.; mfn. wise, prudent, Ragh. **-candra**, m. N. of a dram. poet, Cat.; *-sūri*, m. N. of the author of the Hammīra-carita, ib. **-jā**, f. N. of a woman, ib. **-jña**, mfn. = *-kovida*, R.; Pañc.; m. a follower of any system, MW. **-datta**, m. N. of a man, Kuttanīm. **-dyumaṇi**, m., **-nirūpaṇa**, n. N. of wks. **-netṛi**, m. a master in policy or politics, L. **-pāla**, m. N. of a king, Vet.; of another man, Inscr. **-pīṭhī**, f. a board for playing, L. **-prakāśikā**, f. N. of wk. **-prayoga**, m. political wisdom or address, W. **-bodhikā**, **-maṇi-mañjarī**, **-māṇi-mālikā**, **-mayūkha-mālikā**, f.; **-mārtaṇḍa**, m.; **-ratna**, n.; **-ratna-mālā**, f.; **-locana**, n. N. of wks. **-vat**, mfn. versed in polity, prudent, Kāv.; containing some form of √*nī* (as a Ṛik), TS. **-vartman**, n. 'path of policy,' political wisdom, Kir. **-vid**, mfn. = *-kovida*, Kāv.; m. a politician, statesman, MW. **-viveka**, m. N. of wk.; *-dīpikā*, *-śaṅkā-dīpikā*, f.; °*kâlaṃkāra*, m. N. of Comms. **-viśārada**, mfn. = *-vid*, R. **-vīthi**, f. N. of wk. **-vedin**, mfn. = *-vid*, Gal. **-śālin**, mfn. endowed with political wisdom or prudence, Kathās. **-śāstra**, n. the doctrines of p° w°, R.; Pañc. **-saṃgraha**, m. 'summary of p° w°,' N. of wk. **-sādhana**, n. political conduct, R. **-sāra**, m. 'essence of polity,' chief of a village, W.; N. of wk. **-sāhasônnati-mat**, mfn. requiring a high degree of prudence and resolution, Pañc. iii, 264. **-siddhi**, f. political success, W.

Nayaka, mfn. clever in policy, L.

Nayat, mf(*antī*)n. leading, guiding &c. (see √*nī*); informing, certifying, obtaining, W.

Nayana, m. N. of a man, Rājat.; (*ā* or *ī*), f. the pupil of the eye, L.; n. leading, directing, managing, conducting; carrying, bringing, Hariv.; Kāv.; Pañc. &c.; (*kālasya*) fixing, MBh. i, 2580, Nīlak.; drawing, moving (a man or piece in a game, cf. *naya* and *naya-pīṭhī*), L.; (pl.) prudent conduct, polity, BhP. x, 50, 34; 'the leading organ,' the eye (ifc. f. *ā* or *ī*), MBh.; Kāv.; Suśr. &c. **-gocara**, mfn. being within the eye's range, visible (*-tva*, Naish., Sch.; °*rī-√kṛi*, to perceive or behold, Vās.) **-candrikā**, f. moonshine, anything looking bright to the eyes, Daś.; N. of wk. **-carita**, n. play of the eyes, ogling, Pracaṇḍ. **-chada**, m. eye-covering, an eyelid, L. **-jala**, n. 'eye-water,' tears, Kād. **-tva**, n. condition of the eyes, sight, Veṇis. vi, 3/8. **-patha**, m. (Vedāntas.), **-padavī**, f. (Kāv.) range or field of sight. **-puṭa**, m. or n. the eyelid, Var. **-prabandha**, m. the outer corner of the eye, ib. **-prasādinī**, f. N. of wk. **-prīti**, f. 'eye-delight,' lovely sight, L. **-plava**, m. swimming of the eyes, Suśr. **-budbuda**, n. eyeball, ib. **-bhūshaṇa**, n. N. of wk. **-vat**, mfn. having eyes, Mālatīm. **-vāri**, n. = *-jala*, Śiś. **-vishaya**, m. 'range of sight,' the horizon, Megh.; *-°yī-bhāva*, m. the being within sight, Naish. **-śāṇa**, m. a partic. ointment for the eye, Bhpr. **-salila**, n. = *-jala*, Megh.; Kād. **-sukha**, m. N. of an author, Cat. **Nayanâñcala**, m. eye-corner, R.; side-glance, Prasannar. **Nayanâñjana**, n. any ointment for the eye, R. **Nayanâñjala**, w. r. for °*nâñcala*. **Nayanânanda**, m. = *-prīti*, Ratn.; N. of Sch. on the Amara-kośa (also *-śarman*), Cat. **Nayanânta**, m. eye-corner, Kāv. **Nayanâmṛita**, n. a partic. ointment for the eyes, Rasêndrac. **Nayanâmbu**, n. = °*na-jala*, Kir. **Nayanôtsava**, m. 'eye-festival,' any lovely sight or object, L.; a lamp, L. **Nayanôda**, n. 'eye-water,' tears, MW. (also °*daka*, Kād.); *-bindu*, m. tear-drop, Vikr. **Nayanôpânta**, m. eye-corner, L. **Nayanâushadha**, a partic. ointment for the eyes, L.

Nayitavya, mfn. to be conducted or brought, Hariv.

Náyishṭha, m. leading in the best manner, RV. x, 126, 3.

नय्यग्रोध *náyyagrodha*, mf(*ī*)n. (fr. *nyagrodha*) relating to the sacred fig-tree, TS. (v.l. *naiyagr°*).

नर *nára*, m. (cf. *nṛi*) a man, a male, a person (pl. men, people), TS. &c. &c.; husband, Mn. ix, 76; hero, VarBṛS. iv, 31; Bālar. viii, 56; a man or piece at chess or draughts &c., L.; the pin or gnomon of a sun-dial, Sūryas. (cf. *-yantra*); person, personal termination, Kāś. on Pāṇ. iii, 1, 85 (cf. *purusha*); the primeval Man or eternal Spirit pervading the universe (always associated with Nārāyaṇa, 'son of the pr° man'; both are considered either as gods or sages and accordingly called *devau*, *ṛishī*, *tāpasau* &c.; in ep. poetry they are the sons of Dharma by Mūrti or A-hiṇsā and emanations of Vishṇu, Arjuna being identified with Nara, and Kṛishṇa with Nārāyaṇa), Mn. (cf. *-sūnu*); MBh.; Hariv.; Pur.; (pl.) a class of myth. beings allied to the Gandharvas and Kiṃ-naras, MBh.; Pur.; N. of a son of Manu Tāmasa, BhP.; of a s° of Viśvā-mitra, Hariv.; of a s° of Gaya and father of Virāj, VP.; of a s° of Su-dhṛiti and f° of Kevala, Pur.; of a s° of Bhavan-manyu (Manyu) and f° of Saṃkṛiti, ib.; of Bharadvāja (author of RV. vi, 35 and 36), Anukr.; of 2 kings of Kaśmīra, Rājat.; of one of the 10 horses of the Moon, L.; (*ī*), f. a woman (= *nārī*), L.; n. a kind of fragrant grass. — **kapāla**, n. a man's skull, Pañc. — **kāka**, m. a crow-like m°, Daś. — **kīlaka**, m. a man who has murdered his preceptor, L. — **kesarin**, m. 'm°-lion,' Vishṇu in his 4th Avatāra, Cat. — **gaṇa-pati-vijaya**, m. N. of wk. — **grāha**, m. 'm°-crocodile,' N. of a kind of Kirāta, R. — **candra**, m. N. of a Jaina writer, Cat. — **cihna**, n. 'm°-sign,' moustaches, Gal. — **jāṅgala**, n. m°'s flesh, Mālatim. — **tā**, f., **-tva**, n. manhood, humanity, human condition, Pur. — **troṭakâcārya**, m. N. of a man, Cat. — **da**, see *narada*. — **datta**, m. N. of a Brāhman (nephew of the Ṛishi Asita), Lalit.; (*ā*), f. N. of a goddess executing the commands of the 20th Arhat of present Ava-sarpiṇī, L.; of one of the 16 Vidyā-devīs, L. — **danta**, m. a man's tooth, Kathās. — **deva**, m. 'm°-god,' a king, Mn.; MBh. &c. (*-tva*, n. BhP.); N. of an author, Cat.; *-deva*, m. god among kings, supreme sovereign, BhP.; *-putra*, m. the son of a m° and a god, MW — **dvish**, m. 'm°-hater,' a Rakshas, Bhaṭṭ. — **nagara**, n. N. of a town, L. — **nātha**, m. 'm°-protector,' a king, R.; Pur. &c.; *-mārga*, m. 'king's road,' high street, Rājat.; °*thâsana*, n. throne or dignity of a k°, ib. — **nāman**, m. a kind of tree, L. — **nāyaka**, m. 'man-leader,' king, Inscr. — **nārāyaṇa**, m. N. of Kṛishṇa, MBh.; BhP.; N. of an author, Cat.; du. Nara and Nārāyaṇa (see above), MBh.; °*ṇânanda-kāvya*, n. N. of a poem, Cat. — **nārī-vilakshaṇā**, f. 'having the signs of m° and woman,' a hermaphrodite, Gal. — **m-dhisha** (*naráṃ-*), m. 'watching or heeding men (?),' N. of Vishṇu, VS.; ŚBr.; of Pūshan, VS.; TĀr. — **pa**, m. 'm°-protector,' a king, Dhūrtan. — **pati**, m. 'm°-lord,' a king, Var.; Kāv. &c.; N. of one of the 4 myth. kings of Jambu-dvīpa, L.; of an author, Cat.; *-jaya-caryā*, f., °*ryā-sāra*, m. N. of wks.; *-patha*, m. = *-nātha-mārga*, Megh.; *-vijaya*, m. N. of wk. — **paśu**, m. 'm°-beast,' a brute in human form, BhP.; a m° as sacrificial victim, Jātakam. — **pāla**, m. = *-pa*, Pañc. — **pālinī**, f. = *-māninī*, Gal. — **puṃgava**, m. 'm°-bull,' an excellent hero, Bhag. — **pūtanā-śānti**, f. N. of wk. — **priya**, mfn. favourable to mankind, W.; m. N. of a tree, L. — **bali**, m. a human sacrifice, Siṇhâs. — **brahma-deva**, m. N. of a king, Cat. — **bhuj**, mfn. man-eating, cannibal, MW. — **bhū** or **-bhūmi**, f. 'land of men,' N. of Bhārata-varsha, L. — **māṇsa**, n. m°'s flesh, Siṇhâs. — **mānikā** and **-māninī**, f. a m°-like woman, a w° with a beard, L. — **mālā**, f. a string or girdle of human skulls, Devīm. — **mālinī**, f., w. r. for *-māninī*. — **mūrchana**, n. N. of ch. of the PadmaP. — **medha**, m. = *-bali*, MBh.; R. — **mohinī**, f. N. of a Surâṅganā, Siṇhâs. — **m-manya**, mfn. thinking one's self a man, passing for a m°, Pāṇ. vi, 3, 68, Sch. — **yantra**, n. 'gnomon-instrument,' a sun-dial, Sūryas. — **yāṇa** or **-yāna**, n. a carriage drawn by men, MBh.; Pañc.; BhP. — **ratha**, w. r. for *nava-r°*. — **rāja**, m. 'king of m°,' a king, R.; °*jya*, n. kingship, royalty, Caurap. — **rūpa**, n. human form; mf(*ī*)n. m°-like (also °*pin*), W. — **rshaba**, m. (°*ra + ṛish*°) 'm°-bull,' a king, MW. — **loka**, m. 'men's world,' the earth; mortals, men, BhP.; *-pāla*, m. = *nara-pa*, Ragh.; *-vīra*, m. a human hero, Bhag. — **vat**, ind. like a m°, MW. — **vara**, m. an excellent m°; *-vrishabha*, m. an e° hero (like a bull); °*rôttama*, m. the best of e° men, id. — **varman**, m. N. of a prince of Mālava in the 12th century, Rājat. &c.; °*ma-nṛipati-kathā*, f. N. of wk. — **vāhana**, m. 'borne or drawn by men,' N. of Kubera, MBh. &c.; of a prince (successor of Śāli-vāhana), Inscr.; of a prince of the Dārvâbhisāras, Rājat.; of a minister of king Kshema-gupta, ib.; *-janana*, n. N. of ch. of Kathās.; *-datta*, m. N. of a son of king Udayana, Kathās.; *-datta-carita-maya*, mf(*ī*)n. containing the adventures of prince Naravāhana-datta, ib.; *-dattīya*, mfn. relating to him, ib. — **vāhin**, mfn. drawn or carried by men, Nal. — **vishāṇa**, n. 'm°'s horn,' i.e. anything non-existent, Nyāyam. — **vishvaṇa**, m. 'm°-devourer,' a Rakshas, L. — **vīra**, m. an heroic or excellent m°, MBh.; *-loka*, m. the bravest of men or mankind, Kāv. — **vṛittâshṭaka**, n. N. of wk. — **vyāghra**, m. = next, MBh.; pl. N. of a myth. people, R. — **śārdūla**, m. 'm°-tiger,' an eminent or illustrious man, MBh. — **śṛiṅga**, n. = *-vishāṇa*, W. — **śreshṭha**, m. the best of men, MW. — **saṃvāda-sundara**, m. or n. N. of wk. — **saṃsarga**, m. intercourse of men, human society, MW. — **sakha**, m. 'Nara's friend,' N. of Nārāyaṇa, Vikr. — **saṃghārāma**, m. N. of a Buddh. monastery. — **sarājīya**, n. N. of a poem. — **sāra**, m. sal ammoniac, L. — **siṇha**, m. 'man-lion,' great warrior, MBh.; R.; N. of Vishṇu in his 4th Ava-tāra (when he was half m° half l°), Kāv.; Pur.; N. of the father of king Bhairava, Cat.; of sev. princes and authors (also *-kavi*, *-kavi-rāja*, *-ṭhakkura*, *-dīkshita*, *-deva*, *-paṇḍita*, *-bhaṭṭa*, *-miśra*, *-muni*, *-yati*, *-yatīndra*, *-rāja*, *-vājapeyin* (or °*hâgnicid-vāj*°), *-śāstrin*, *-sarasvatī*, *-sūri*, *-sena*, *-°hâcārya*), Cat.; *-kalpa*, m. N. of wk.; *-cūrṇa*, n. N. of a partic. aphrodisiac, L.; *-dvādaśī*, f. N. of the 12th day in the light half of the month Phālguna (°*śī-vrata*, n. a ceremony then performed, N. of wk.), Cat.; *-nakha-stotra* and *-pañca-ratna*, n. N. of Stotras; *-pārijāta*, m., *-purāṇa*, n., *-bhaṭṭīya*, n., *-bhāratī-vilāsa*, m., *-bhujaṃga*, m., *-bhūpāla-caritra*, n. N. of wks.; *-yantra*, n. N. of a mystic. diagram, Tantras.; *-rājīya*, n., °*harshabha-kshetra-māhātmya*, n. N. of wks.; *-varman*, m. N. of a man, L.; *-śāstri-prakāśikā*, f.; *-sahasra-nāman*, n. pl.; *-stuti*, f. N. of wks. — **skandha**, m. a multitude of men, L. — **haya**, v.l. for *nāra-h°*. — **hari**, m. N. of Vishṇu as 'man-lion' (cf. *-siṇha*), Gīt.; BhP.; of sev. authors (also *-tīrtha*, *-bhaṭṭa*, *-śāstrin*, *-sūri*, °*ry-upâdhyāya*), Cat.; of another man, Kshitîś.; *-deva*, m. N. of a prince, Inscr. **Narâṅga**, m. n. 'm°-member,' the penis, L.; m. eruption on the face, L. (cf. *naraṅga*); mf(*ī*)n. having a human body (also *-ka*), Hcat. **Narâṅghri**, mfn. having human feet, ib. **Narâca**, m. (√*añc*) a kind of metre, Col. (v.l. *nār*°); (*ī*), f. a species of plant (?), AV.; N. of a wife of Kṛishṇa, Hariv. **Narâdhama**, m. a low or vile man, a wretch, Bhag. **Narâdhāra**, m. 'asylum or receptacle of men,' N. of Śiva, L.; (*ā*), f. the earth, L. **Narâdhipa**, m. = next, Mn.; MBh. &c.; Cathartocarpus Fistula, Suśr.; °*dhipati*, m. 'lord of men,' king, prince, R.; Var. **Narânta**, m. N. of a son of Hṛidika, Hariv. **Narântaka**, m. 'm°-destroyer,' death; N. of a Rakshas, R.; Pur.; *-nigraha-varṇana*, n.; *-nirgama*, m. N. of of GaṇP. i, 59 and 57. **Narâyaṇa**, w.r. for *Nār*°. **Narâśa**, m. 'm°-eater,' a Rakshas or demon, Bhaṭṭ. **Nárā-śáṇsa** (°*râś*°?), m. 'the desire or praise of men (?),' a mystic. N. of Agni (esp. in the Āprī hymns, besides or instead of Tanū-nápāt, q.v.), RV.; VS.; TS.; Br.; (rarely) of Pūshan, e.g. RV. i, 164, 3; x. 64, 3; *-paṅkti*, w. r. for *nārā-ś°-p°*. **Narâśana**, m. = *narâśa*, R. **Narêtara**, m. 'different from men,' a god, BhP. iv, 6, 9; a beast or b°-like man, ib. iii, 13, 49. **Narêndra**, m. 'm°-lord,' king, prince, Mn.; MBh. &c.; a physician, master of charms or antidotes, Daś. (cf. *dur-n*°); = *narêndra-druma*, Suśr. (cf. *narâdhipa*); = *vārttika* or *rājika*, L.; N. of a poet, Cat.; of another man, Kshitîś.; a kind of metre, Col.; *-kanyā*, f. a princess, Ragh.; *-tā*, f. (Priy.), *-tva*, n. (Rājat.) kingship, royalty; *-deva*, m. N. of a king, W.; *-druma*, m. Cathartocarpus Fistula, Suśr.; *-nagarī* (?), m. N. of a grammarian, Cat.; *-putra*, m. a prince, Var.; *-mārga*, m. 'king's road,' high street, R.; *-svāmin*, m. N. of a temple built by Narêndrâditya, Rājat.; °*drâcārya*, m. N. of a grammarian, Cat.; °*drâditya*, m. N. of 2 kings of Kaśmīra, Rājat.; °*drâhva*, n. Agallochum, L. **Narêśa**, m. 'lord of men,' king, MBh. **Narêśvara**, m. id., ib.; N. of an author, Cat.; *-parīkshā*, f., *-viveka*, m. N. of wks. **Narôttama**, m. best of men, MBh.; Hariv.; N. of Vishṇu or Buddha, L.; of Sch. on the Adhyātma-rāmāyaṇa, Cat.; *-dāsa*, m. N. of an author, ib.; *-kīrti-leśa-mātra-darśaka*, m. or n. N. of wk.; °*mâraṇya-śishya*, m. N. of an author, Cat.

Nari, in comp. for °*ra*. — √**bhū**, to become a man, HPariś.

Nárya, mfn. manly, human; strong, powerful, heroic (as Indra, the Maruts &c.); suitable or agreeable to men (as food, riches &c.), RV.; AV.; VS.; Br.; m. a man, a person, RV. (cf. Nir. xi, 36); N. of a man, RV. i, 54, 6; 112, 9 (Sāy.); n. a manly or heroic deed (with or scil. *ápas*), RV.; a gift for men, ib. **Náryâpas**, mfn. performing manly deeds, RV.; VS.

नरक *náraka* (Nir.; *naráka*, TĀr.), m. or n. hell, place of torment, Mn.; MBh. &c.; (distinguished from *pātāla*, q.v.; personif. as a son of Anṛita and Nirṛiti or Nirkṛiti, MārkP.; there are many different hells, generally 21, Mn. iv, 88–90; Yājñ.; Pur. &c.); m. N. of a demon (son of Vishṇu and Bhūmi or the Earth, and therefore called Bhauma, haunting Prāg-jyotisha and slain by Kṛishṇa), MBh.; Pur.; Rājat. &c.; of a son of Vipra-citti, VP.; = *deva-rātri-prabheda* (?), L.; m. or n. N. of a place of pilgrimage, MBh. (v.l. *anaraka*); (*ikā*), f. Pāṇ. vii, 3, 44, Vārtt. 4, Pat. — **kuṇḍa**, n. a pit in hell for tormenting the wicked (86 in number), BrahmavP. — **jit**, m. 'vanquisher of the demon N°,' N. of Vishṇu-Kṛishṇa, Hcar. — **tiryak-saṃśodhana**, n. a partic. Samādhi, Kāraṇḍ. — **devatā**, f. 'the deity of hell,' N. of Nirṛiti, L. — **pāta**, m. the falling into h°, Pañc. — **bhūmi**, f. a division of h°, L. — **ripu**, m. 'foe of Naraka,' N. of Kṛishṇa, Veṇ. (cf. *-jit*). — **rūpin**, mfn. 'h°-formed,' hellish, MW. — **varga**, m. 'h°-chapter,' N. of ch. of Amara-siṇha's Liṅgânuśāsana. — **varṇana**, n. 'description of h°,' N. of ch. of the Revā-māhātmya. — **vāsa**, m. abode in h°, Hcar. — **vedanā**, f. N. of wk. — **stha**, mfn. living or being in h°, BhP.; (*ā*), f. the river of h° Vaitaraṇī, L. — **svarga-prāpti-prakāra-varṇana**, n. 'description of the mode of obtaining heaven and h°,' N. of ch. of the Māgha-māhātmya. **Narakântaka**, m. 'destroyer of the demon N°,' N. of Kṛishṇa, L. **Narakâmaya**, m. = *prêta*, the soul after death, a ghost, L. **Narakâri**, m. = °*ka-ripu*, L. **Narakârṇava**, m. the hellish sea, Hcat. — **Narakâvāsa**, m. an inhabitant of h°, L. **Narakâsura-dhvaṇsa**, m., **ra-vijaya**, m. and °*ra-vyāyoga*, m. N. of wks. **Narakôttaraṇa**, n. N. of a Stotra. **Narakaukas**, m. = °*kâvāsa*, MārkP.

Narakāya, Nom. Ā. °*yate*, to resemble or be similar to hell, MārkP.

नरङ्ग *naraṅga*, w r. for *nāraṅga*, L.

नरद *narada*, m. N. of a Brāhman, Lalit.; m. or n. (prob.) = *nálada*, g. *kiśarâdi*. °**dika**, mfn. dealing in the substance called Narada, ib.

नराशंस *nárā-śáṇsa*. See under *nara*.

नरिष्टा *naríshṭā* (AV.), °*shṭhā* (VS.), f. joking, chattering, pastime (cf. *narma*, *man*).

नरिष्यत् *na-rishyat*, °*shyanta* &c. See under 2. *ná*.

नरीय *narīya*, m. N. of a son of Bhaṅga-kāra, Hariv. (v.l. *nāreya*, *tāreya*).

नरुण *narúṇa*, m. (√*nṛi*?) leader (said of Pūshan). TĀr.

नर्क *narka*, n. the nose, Gal.

Narkuṭa, n. id., ib. (cf. *nakuṭa*); °*ṭaka*, n. id., L.; a kind of metre, Var. (cf. *nardaṭaka*).

नर्त *narta*, mfn. (√*nṛit*) dancing (cf. *ni-tya-*); m. dance, g. *chedâdi*.

Nartaka, mfn. causing to dance (fr. Caus.), Sāh; m. dancer, singer, actor (often with *naṭa*), MBh.; Var.; Kāv.; Pur. &c.; a dancing-master (fr. Caus.), MBh.; a bard, herald, W.; an elephant, L.; a peacock, W.; a kind of reed, L.; (*ī*), f. (cf. Pāṇ. iii, 1, 145, Kāś.) a female dancer, actress, singing girl, Kāv.; Pur. &c. (*-tva*, n. Vcar.); a female elephant, L.; a peahen, W.; a kind of perfume, L.; n. a partic. myth. weapon, MBh. **Nartakaka**, m., °**kikā**, f. dimin. fr. *nartaka*, Pat.

Nartana, m. (initial *n* not changeable to *ṇ*, g. *kshubhnâdi*) dancer, MBh.; Hariv.; n. dancing, acting (metric. also *ā*, f.; cf. °*nā-gṛiha*, below). — **nirṇaya**, m. N. of wk. — **priya**, m. 'fond of dancing,' a peacock, L. — **śālā**, f. dancing-room, MBh. — **sthāna**, n. dancing-place. **Nartanâgāra** and °**nā-gṛiha**, n. = °*na-śālā*, MBh.

Nartayitṛi, mfn. causing to dance (with acc.), Vcar.; m. dancing-master, Mālav. ii, 24; $\frac{29}{30}$ (cf. °*taka*). **Nartita**, mfn. made to dance, dandled, Kāv.; n. dance, MBh.; *-bhrū-lata*, mfn. a face the eyebrows of which are dancing or moving to and fro, Bhartṛ.; *-mayūra*, mfn. possessing dancing peacocks, ib. **Nartitavya**, n. the being obliged to dance, necessity of dancing, Ratn. i, 1/2.

Nartin, mfn. dancing (cf. *vaṅśa-n°*).

Nartū, f. actress, dancing girl, L.

नर्द् *nard*, cl. 1. P. (Dhātup. iii, 19) *nardati* (ep. also *°te*; pf. *nanarda*, MBh.; aor. *anardīt*, Gr.; *anardishur*, Bhaṭṭ.; fut. *nardishyati*, *°ditā*, Gr.; inf. *narditum*, ib.; ind. p. *-nardam*, MBh.) to bellow, roar, shriek, sound, Br. &c. &c.; to go, move, Gr.: Caus. *-nardayati*, GopBr.

Narda, mfn. bellowing, roaring (cf. *go-n°*). **°dat**, mf(*antī*)n. roaring, sounding, praising, proclaiming, MBh. &c. **°dana**, m. 'roarer,' N. of a Nāga-rāja, L.; n. sounding, roaring, Var.; celebrating, praising aloud, W. **°daniya**, mfn. to be sounded; to be celebrated or praised aloud, ib. **°dita**, mfn. roared, bellowed &c.; n. bellowing, roaring, sounding, R.; Hit.; m. a kind of die or a throw at dice, Mṛicch. ii, 7 (= *nādī* or *nāndī*, Sch.; prob. the chief die; cf. *vrisha*, Nal. vii, 6). **°din**, mfn. roaring, sounding (cf. *gehe-n°*).

नर्दटक *nardaṭaka*, n. a kind of metre, Col. (w.r. *nardh°*; cf. *narkuṭaka*).

नर्दबुद *nardabuda*, mfn. = *garbhasya śabdayitā, niśāmakaḥ*, TS., Sch.

नर्ब् *narb*, cl. 1. P. *narbati*, to go, move, Dhātup. xi, 34 (cf. *namb*).

नर्म 1. *narmá*, m. sport, pastime, VS. (cf. *narman*, *narishṭā*).

2. **Narma**, in comp. for *°man*. **-kīla**, m. a husband, L. **-garbha**, mfn. containing a joke, not meant seriously, Bālar.; m. (dram.) an action of the hero in an unrecognizable form, Sāh.; Bhar. **-da**, mfn. causing mirth or pleasure, delightful, Naish.; m. a jester, the companion of a person's sports or amusements, L.; N. of a man, Cat.; (*ā*), f., see *Narmadā*. **-dyuti**, mfn. bright with joy, happy, merry, W.; f. enjoyment of a joke or any amusement, Daśar.; Sch. **-yukta**, mfn. sportive, jocose (word), MBh. **-vatī**, f. N. of a drama, Sāh. **-saṃyukta**, mfn. sportive, droll, MBh. **-saciva**, m. 'amusement-companion,' promoter of the a° of a prince, Kām. **-sācivya**, n. superintendence of a prince's a°s, W. **-suhṛid**, m. = *-saciva*, Kathās. **-sphañja** or **-sphiñja** (Daśar.), **-sphūrja** (Sāh.; Bhar.), m. (dram.) the first meeting of lovers beginning with joy but ending in alarm. **-sphoṭa**, m. (dram.) the first symptoms of love, ib. **Narmârtham**, ind. for sport, MBh. **Narmâlāpa**, m. a jocular conversation, Hcat. **Narmâika-sodara**, mfn. having pleasure or mirth as one's only brother, thinking only of sport, Kathās. **Narmôkti**, f. a facetious expression, Rājat.

Narmaṭha, m. (only L.) a jester; a libertine; sport; coition; the nipple; the chin.

Narma-dā, f. of *-da* (above), 'pleasure-giver,' N. of a river (the modern Nerbudda), MBh. &c. (she is personified as the wife of Puru-kutsa and mother of Trasa-dasyu, or as a sister of the Ura-gas i.e. serpents, or as a daughter of the Soma-pas); of a Gandharvī, R.; a kind of plant, L. **-khaṇḍa**, m. or n. N. of ch. of the SkandaP. **-taṭa-deśa**, m. N. of a district, MW. **-tīra-gamana**, n. N. of ch. of the R. **-tīrtha**, n. N. of a sacred bathing-place, ŚivaP. **-māhātmya**, n., **-laharī**, f., **-°shṭaka** (*°dāsht°*), n., **-sundarī-rāsa**, m. N. of wks. **Narmadêśvara**, m. (prob.) a form of Śiva; *-tīrtha*, n. N. of sev. Tīrthas, ŚivaP.; *-parīkshā*, f. N. of wk.; *-māhātmya*, n. N. of ch. of ŚivaP.; *-liṅga*, n. N. of a Liṅga; of ch. of SkandaP.

Narman, n. sport, play, amusement, pleasure, pastime, pleasantry, dallying, jest, joke, wit, humour, (*°māṇi* √*kṛi*, to joke; *°maṇā*, ind. in jest, for sport), MBh.; Kāv. &c.

Narmaya, Nom. P. *°yati*, to gladden or exhilarate by jests or sports, Kām.

Narmāyita, n. sport, pastime, Bālar.

नर्मट *narmaṭa*, m. a potsherd; the sun, L.

नर्मरा *narmarā*, f. (L.) cavity or valley; a bellows; an old woman past menstruation; a kind of plant.

नल् *nal*, cl. 1. P. to smell or to bind, Dhātup. xx, 8 (confusion of *gandhe* and *bandhe*?); cl. 10. P. *nālayati*, to speak or shine, xxxiii, 127; to bind or confine, W.

नल *nala*, m. (cf. *naḍá*, *naḷá*) a species of reed, Amphidonax Karka (8-12 feet high), Gobh.; MBh. &c.; a measure of length, MBh. (v.l. *tala*); a partic. form of constellation in which all the planets or stars are grouped in double mansions, Var.; the 50th year of the cycle of Jupiter which lasts 60 years, Cat.; N. of a divine being mentioned with Yama, Karmapr. (= *pitṛi-deva* or *-daiva*, L.; a deified progenitor, W.); of a Daitya, BrahmaP.; of a king of the Nishadhas (son of Vīra-sena and husband of Damayantī), MBh.; Pur.; of a son of Nishadha and father of Nabha or Nabhas, Hariv.; Ragh.; VP.; of a descendant of the latter Nala (s° of Su-dhanvan and f° of Uktha), Hariv.; VP.; of a son of Yadu, Pur.; of a monkey-chief (son of Tvashṭṛi or Viśva-karman; cf. *-setu*), MBh.; R.; of a medic. author, Cat.; (*ī*), f. a kind of perfume or red arsenic, L. (cf. *naṭī*); n. the blossom of Nelumbium Speciosum, L. (cf. *nalina*, *°nī*); smell, odour, L. (cf. √*nal*). **-kānana**, m. pl. N. of a people, MBh.; VP. (= *naḷakān°*? v.l. *nalakālaka*, *nabhakānana*). **-kīla**, m. the knee, L. **-kūbara**, m. N. of a son of Kubera, MBh.; *-saṃhitā*, f. N. of wk. **-giri**, m. N. of Pradyota's elephant, Megh. **-campū**, f. N. of an artificial poem (half prose half verse) = Damayantī-kathā. **-carita** & **°tra**, n. N. of a poem and a drama. **-1.-da** (*ná°*), m. or n. Nardostachys Jatamansi, Indian spikenard, AV.; Suśr. &c. (also *ā*, f., L.; cf. *narada*); the root of Andropogon Muricatus, Naish. (*-tva*, n. ib.); the blossom of Hibiscus Rosa Sinensis, L.; the honey or nectar of a flower, L.; (*ā*), f. N. of a daughter of Raudrâśva, Hariv.; (*ī*), f. N. of an Apsaras, AV.; *°dika*, mf(*ī*)n. dealing in Indian spikenard, g. *kiśorâdi*. **-2.-da**, mfn. bringing near king Nala, Naish (*-tva*, n. ib.) **-paṭṭikā**, f. a mat made with reeds, L. **-pāka-śāstra**, n. N. of a manual on cookery. **-pura**, n. N. of a town, Inscr.; of N°'s town = Nishadhā, Gal. **-priyā**, f. 'beloved of Nala,' N. of Damayantī, ib. **-bhūmipāla-nāṭaka**, n. N. of a drama. **-mālin**, m. 'reed-garlanded,' N. of an ocean, Jātak. **-mīna**, m. a kind of fish, L. (v.l. *tala-m°*). **-yādava-rāghava-pāṇḍavīya** & **-varṇana**, n. N. of 2 poems. **-setu**, m. 'N°s bridge,' the causeway constructed by the monkey Nala for Rāma from the continent to Laṅkā (the modern Adam's Bridge), MBh.; R.; Suśr. **-sena**, m. N. of a prince, L. **-stotra**, n. N. of a poem. **Nalânanda**, m. 'N°'s joy,' N. of a drama. **Nalêdhma**, m. reeds serving as fuel. **Nalêśvara-tīrtha**, n. N. of a sacred bathing-place, ŚivaP. **Nalôttama**, m. Arundo Bengalensis, L. **Nalôdaya**, m. 'N°'s rise,' N. of an artificial poem ascribed to Kālidāsa. **Nalôpâkhyāna**, n. 'the story of N°' in MBh. iii, 6, 52-77.

Nalaka, n. a bone (hollow like a reed); any long bone of the body, e.g. the tibia or the radius of the arm, Suśr.; a partic. ornament for the nose, Caṇḍ.; (*ikā*), f. a tube or tubular organ of the body (= *nāḍī*), L.; a quiver, Naish.; Dolichos Lablab, Var.; Polianthes Tuberosa or Daemia Extensa, L.; a kind of fragrant substance, L.; *°ikā-bandha-paddhati*, f. N. of wk. **Nalakinī**, f. a leg, L.; the knee-cap or -pan, W.

Nalita, m. a species of vegetable (= *nālitā*), L.

Nalina, n. (fr. *nala* because of its hollow stalk?) a lotus flower or water-lily, Nelumbium Speciosum (ifc. f. *ā*), MBh.; Kāv. &c.; the Indigo plant, L.; water, L. **-dala**, n. a leaf of the lotus flower (cf. *nalinī-dala* and *nava-nalina-dalāya*); m. the Indian crane, L. (cf. *pushkara*); Carissa Carandas, L.; N. of a man, Pravar. **-nābha**, m. 'lotus-naveled,' N. of Vishṇu-Kṛishṇa, Kād. **Nalinâsana**, m. 'the l°-throned,' N. of Brahmā, ib. (w. r. *°nâśana*). **Naline-śaya**, m. reclining on a l°, N. of Vishṇu, L.; (*ī*), f., see below.

Nalini, metric. for *°nī* in **-dala** = *°nī-d°*, Gīt. ix, 6.

1. **Nalinī**, f. (fr. *nalina* above or fr. *nala* 'lotus' as *ab-jinī* fr. *ab-ja*, *padminī* fr. *padma* &c.) a lotus, Nelumbium Speciosum (the plant or its stalk), an assemblage of l° flowers or a l° pond, MBh.; Kāv.; Pur. &c.; the Ganges of heaven or rather an arm of it, ib.; a myst. N. of one of the nostrils, BhP.; a partic. class of women (= *padminī*), Cat.; a kind of fragrant substance (= *nalikā*), L.; the fermented and intoxicating juice of the cocoa-nut, L.; N. of the wife of Aja-mīḍha and mother of Nīla, BhP.; of 2 rivers, VP. **-khaṇḍa**, n. an assemblage of lotus flowers, Kāś. on Pāṇ. iv, 2, 51. **-gulma**, n. N. of an Adhyayana, HPariś.; of a Vimāna, ib. **-dala**, n. a leaf of the lotus plant, Kāv.; *-maya*, mf(*ī*)n. consisting of l° leaves, Daś. **-nandana**, n. N. of a garden of Kubera, R. **-pattra**, n. = *-dala*, Kāv. **-padma-kośa**, m. N. of a partic. position of the hands, Cat. **-ruha**, m. 'lotus-born,' N. of Brahmā, L.; n. the fibres of a l°-stalk, L.

Nalinīka, ifc. = 1. *nalinī*, BhP. v, 8, 22; (*ā*), f. a partic. pot-herb, Car.

2. **Nalinī**, f. having king Nala, Naish.

Nalīya, mfn. relating to Nala, ib.

नल्ल *nalla*, w.r. for *nalva*.

नल्लादीक्षित *nallā-dīkshita*, *-paṇḍita*, *-budha*, m. N. of authors, Cat.

नल्व *nalva*, m. a furlong, a measure of distance = 400 (or 104?) cubits, MBh.; Hariv.; R. (w. r. *nala*, *nalla*). **-vartma-ga**, mfn. going the distance of a Nalva; (*ā*), f. Leea Hirta or the orange tree, L.

Nalvaṇa, n. a measure of capacity, ŚārṅgS.

नल्वणगोन्नलकामाभट्ट *nalvaṇgônnalakāmā-bhaṭṭa* (?), m. N. of an author, Cat.

नव 1. *náva*, mf(*ā*)n. (prob. fr. 1. *nú*) new, fresh, recent, young, modern (opp. to *sana*, *purāṇa*), RV. &c. &c. (often in comp. with a subst., e.g. *navânna*, cf. Pāṇ. ii, 1, 49; or with a pp. in the sense of 'newly, just, lately,' e.g. *navôdita*, below); m. a young monk, a novice, Buddh.; a crow, L.; a red-flowered Punar-navā, L.; N. of a son of Uśīnara and Navā, Hariv.; of a son of Viloman, VP.; (*ā*), f. N. of a woman (see above), Hariv.; n. new grain, Kauś. [Cf. Zd. *nava*; Gk. νέος for νέϝος; Lat. *novus*; Lith. *naŭjas*; Slav. *nŏvŭ*; Goth. *niujis*; Angl. S. *nîwe*; HGerm. *niuwi*; *niuwe*, *neu*; Engl. *new*.] **-karmika**, mfn. superintendent of the construction of an edifice, Buddh. **-kārikā**, f. a newly-married woman, L. (w. r. for *-varikā*?); a new Kārikā (q. v.), L. **-kālaka**, mf(*ikā*)n. of recent time or young age; (*ikā*), f. a young woman (either one recently married or one in whom menstruation has recently commenced), W. **-kālidāsa**, m. 'a new Kālidāsa,' N. of Mādhava as author of Śaṃkar. (cf. *abhinava-k°*). **-kṛit** (ŚaṅkhGṛ.), prob. w. r. for **-gát**, mfn. first-bearing, AV.; TS. **-1.-graha**, mfn. (for 2. see 4. *náva*) recently caught, Kād. **-ghāsa**, m. new food, Vait. **-cchātra**, m. n° scholar, novice, W. **-ja**, mfn. 'recently born,' new, young (moon), MBh. **-jâ** and (*náva-*) **-jāta**, mfn. 'id.,' fresh, new, RV. **-jvara-ripu-rasa** and **-jvarêbha-siṅha**, m. N. of partic. medicaments, Rasêndrac. **-jvārá**, m. new pain or sorrow, RV. **-tara** (*náva-*), mfn. (compar.) newer, younger, fresher, ŚBr. (cf. *návīyas*). **-tā**, f. freshness, novelty, Kum. **-1.-tva**, n. (for 2. see 4. *nava*) id., Rājat. **-dala**, n. the fresh leaf of a lotus or any young leaf, W. **-dāvá**, m. recently burnt pasture land; *°vyà*, mfn. growing on it, TS. **-dvīpa**, m. 'the new island,' N. of a place now called Nuddea (at the confluence of the Bhāgīrathī and the Jalangī rivers), Kshitīś.; *-parikramā*, f. N. of wk. **-nagara**, n. 'new town,' N. of a town, L. **-nalina-dalāya**, Nom. Ā. *°yate* (p. *°yamāna*), to resemble the leaf of a fresh lotus blossom, BhP. **-nava**, mfn. always new; most various or manifold, Vcar.; HPariś. **-nātha-yogin**, m. N. of an author, Cat. **-nī**, f. (BrahmavP.) = next. **-nīta** (*náva-*), n. fresh butter, Br.; MBh.; Suśr. &c.; *-kavi*, m. N. of an author, Cat.; *-khoṭī*, f. a kind of tree, Car., Comm.; *-gaṇa-pati*, m. N. of a form of Gaṇêśa, RTL. 218; *-ja*, n. ghee (= *ghṛita*), Gal.; *-jātaka*, n. N. of wk.; *-dhenu*, f. a quantity of butter presented to Brāhmans (cf. under *dhenu*), W.; *-nibandha*, m. N. of wk.; *-pṛiśni*, mfn. having spots as yellow as butter, TāṇḍBr.; *-maya*, mf(*ī*)n. consisting of fresh b°, Hcat.; *-sama*, mfn. 'b°-like,' soft, gentle (voice), Pañc. **-nītaka**, n. clarified butter, L. **-pattrikā**, f. N. of a partic. play or sport, Cat. (a fictitious marriage, Sch.) **-pariṇayā**, f. recently married, Kāvyapr. **-parṇâdi-bhakshaṇa**, n. 'eating of new leaves, &c.,' N. of ch. of PSarv. **-pallava**, n. a new shoot, young sprout, W. **-prasūtā**, f. any female who has lately brought forth, L. **-prâśana**, n. eating of new corn, PārGṛ. **-phalikā**, f. a newly-married woman, L.; a girl in whom menstruation has recently begun, L. **-baddha**, mfn. lately caught, recently bound, R.; Ragh. — 1. **-má**, mfn. = *nava-tama*, RV. v, 57, 3 (Sāy.) — **mallikā** or **-mallī**, f. Jasminum Sambac, Kāv. — **mālikā**, f. id., ib.; Var.; Suśr.; N. of a daughter of Dharma-vardhana (king of Śrāvasti), Daś. — **mālinī**, f. N. of a kind of metre, Col. — **mālī**, f. = *-mallikā*, L. — **megha**, m. a new cloud or one just appearing, MW. — **yajña**, m. an offering of the first-fruits of the harvest, Gobh. — **yauvana**, n. fresh youth, bloom of y°, Bhartṛ.; mf(*ā*)n. (Śṛiṅgār.) = *-vat* (MW.), mfn. blooming with the freshness of y°. — **raktaka**, n. a newly-dyed garment, W. — **raṅga**, see under 4. *náva*. — **rajas**, f. a girl who has only recently menstruated, L. — **rāja**, m. N. of an author (son of Deva-siṃha), Cat. — **rāshṭra**, n. N. of a kingdom, MBh.; Hariv.; pl. its inhabitants, MBh. — **vadhū**, f. = next, Kāv.; a daughter-in-law, L. — **varikā**, f. a newly-married woman, L. (cf. *-kārikā*). — **vastra**, n. new cloth, L. — **vāstva**, see under 4. *nava*. — **śaśi-bhṛit**, m. 'bearing the new moon-crescent,' N. of Śiva, Megh. — **śrāddha**, n. the first series of Śrāddhas collectively (offered on the 1st, 3rd, 5th, 7th, 9th, and 11th day after a person's death), W. — **saṃghārāma**, m. N. of a monastery, Buddh. — **sasya**, n. the first-fruits of the year's harvest; °*syêshṭi*, f. a sacrifice of f° f°, Mn. iv, 26; 27. — **sū** (RV.), **-sūtikā** (L.), f. a cow that has recently calved (the latter also 'a woman r° delivered,' W.) — **sthāna**, m. 'having (always) a new place (?),' the wind, L. — **sva-stara**, m. a bed or couch of fresh grass, ĀpGṛ. **Navâgata**, mfn. just come, Kām. **Navânna**, n. new rice or grain; first-fruits, AitBr.; Mn.; a ceremony observed on first eating n° rice &c., MW.; *-bhakshaṇa*, n. 'eating of n° grain,' N. of ch. of the PSarv.; *-vidhi*, m., *-sthālī-pāka-mantra*, m. pl.; *-hautra*, n. N. of wks.; °*nnêshṭi*, f. = *nava-sasyêshṭi*, L. **Navâmbara**, n. new and unbleached cloth, W. **Navâmbu**, n. fresh water, MW. **Navârma**, n. N. of a place, L. **Návâvasāna**, n. a new dwelling, MaitrS. **Navâvasitá**, n. (prob.) id., ŚBr., KātyŚr. 1. **Navâhá**, m. 'a n° day,' first d° of a fortnight, L. **Navêtara**, mfn. 'other than n°,' old, Ragh. **Navôḍhā**, f. a newly-married woman, Kāv. **Navôdaya**, mfn. newly risen (moon), Ragh. **Navôdita**, mfn. id. (sun), MBh. **Navôddhṛita**, n. fresh butter, L. **Navonava-vyākhyā** (!) and **Navâucitya-vicāra-carcā**, f. N. of wks.

1. **Navaka**, mf(*ikā*)n. new, fresh, young, Vās.; m. a novice, Divyâv.; (*ikā*), f. = *nava-śabda-yukta*, L.

Návishṭha, mfn. (superl.) the newest, youngest, last (Agni, Indra &c.), RV.

Navī, in comp. for 1. *nava*. — **karaṇa**, n. making new, renewing, W. — **√kṛi** (pp. *kṛita*) to make new, revive, MBh.; Kāv. &c. — **bhāva**, m. becoming new, renovation, Kathās. — **√bhū** (pp. *bhūta*) to become new, be renewed or revived, Kāv.; Kathās.

Navīna, mf(*ā*)n. new, fresh, young, Kāv. — **candra**, m. the new moon, MW. — **nirmāṇa**, n., **-mata-vicāra** and **-vāda**, m. N. of wks. — **vedântin**, m. a modern Vedânta philosopher, Sch.

Návīya, mfn. new, young, RV. iii, 36, 3.

Návīyas, mfn. (compar.) new, fresh, young, recent, being or doing or appearing lately, RV.; (*as*, *asā*), ind. recently, lately, ib.

1. **Návya**, mf(*ā*)n. = °*vīya*, RV. &c. &c.; (with *strī*), f. a newly-married woman; (*ā*), f. a red-flowered Punar-navā, L. — **dharmitâvaccheda-ka-vādârtha**, m., **-nirmāṇa**, n., **-mata-rahasya**, n., **-mata-vāda** or **-mata-vicāra**, m., **-mata-vādârtha**, m., **-mukti-vāda-ṭippaṇī**, f. N. of wks. — **vat**, ind. ever anew, BhP. — **vardhamāna**, m. N. of an author, Cat. **Navyâkṛiti**, m. N. of Krishṇa, Dhūrtan. **Navyânumiti-parāmarśa-kārya-kāraṇa-bhāva-vicāra** & **Navyânumiti-parāmarśa-vicāra**, m. N. of wks.

Návyas, mfn. = *návīyas*, RV. (gen. pl. °*sīnām* for °*sām*, v, 53, 10; 58, 1); (*as*, *asā*, *ase*), ind. recently, lately; anew, ib.

नव 2. *nava*, m. (√2. *nu*) praise, celebration, L.

Navana, n. (ifc. f. *ā*) the act of praising, laudation, Nalôd.

Návishṭi, f. song of praise, hymn, RV. viii, 2, 17.

2. **Návya**, mfn. to be praised, laudable, RV. (*navyá*, AV. ii, 5, 2).

नव 3. *nava*, m. (√5. *nu*) sneezing, Car.

नव 4. *náva*, in *tri-ṇava*, q.v., & in comp. = °*van*. — **kaṇḍikā-śrāddha-sūtra**, n. N. of the 6th Pariś. of Kāty. (= *śrāddha-kalpa-s°*). — **kapāla** (*ná°*), mfn. distributed in 9 dishes, ŚBr. — **kara**, m. '9-handed (?),' N. of a poet, Cat. (cf. *-hasta*). — **kṛitvas**, ind. 9 times, Vedântas. — **koṭi**, f., **-khaṇḍa-yoga-sahasra**, n. N. of wks. — **guṇita**, mfn. multiplied by 9, L. — 2. **-graha**, m. pl. the 9 planets (i.e. sun, moon, 5 planets with Rāhu and Ketu), W.; *-kavaca*, m. or n., *-gaṇita*, *-cakra*, n., *-cintā-maṇi*, m., *-daśā-lakshaṇa*, *-dāna*, *-dhyāna*, n., *-dhyāna-prakāra*, m., *-nāmâvali*, *-paddhati*, *-pūjā*, *-pūjā-paddhati*, f., *-pūjā-vidhi*, *-prayoga*, *-praśna*, m., *-phala*, n., *-bali-dāna-prayoga*, m., *-makha*, m., *-makha-śānti*, f., *-maṅgalâshṭaka*, n., *-mantra*, m. pl., *-yantrôddharaṇa-krama*, *-yāga*, m., *-vidhāna*, n., *-śānti*, f., *-sûkta*, n., *-stava*, m., *-stuti*, f., *-stotra*, *-sthāpana*, n., *-homa*, m., °*hâdhidevatā-sthāpana*, °*hâdhipatyâdhidevatā-sthāpana*, n., °*hânayana-koshṭhaka*, n. pl. N. of wks. — **gva** (*ná°*), mf(*ā*)n. (√*gam*) going by 9, consisting of 9, 9-fold; m. pl. N. of a myth. family described as sharing in Indra's battles &c.; m. sg. one of this f°, RV. (cf. *daśa-gva*). — **catvāriṅśa**, mf(*ī*)n. the 49th; °*śat*, f. 49. — **cchadi** (*ná°*), mfn. having 9 roofs, TS. — **tattva**, n., *-prakaraṇa*, n., *-bāla-bodha*, *-bālâvabodha*, or *-bodha*, m., *-sūtra*, n. N. of wks. — **tantu**, m. N. of a son of Viśvā-mitra, MBh. — **tardma**, mfn. having 9 holes, KātyŚr. — **tāntava**, mf(*ī*)n. consisting of 9 threads, Gṛhyās. — 2. **-tva**, n. an aggregate of 9, Sarvad. — **daśá**, mf(*ī*)n. the 19th, R.; consisting of 19, VS. — **daśán** or (*náva-*) **-daśan**, mfn. pl. 19, VS. — **dīdhiti**, m. '9-rayed,' the planet Mars or its regent, L. (cf. *navârcis*). — **durgā**, f. Durgā in her 9 forms (viz. Kumārikā, Tri-mūrti, Kalyāṇī, Rohiṇī, Kālī, Caṇḍikā, Śāmbhavī, Durgā, Bhadrā), L. — **deva-kula**, n. N. of a town, L. — **dolā**, f. a litter borne by 9 men, W. — **dvāra**, n. pl. the 9 doors or apertures (of the body; cf. 3. *khá*), Subh.; (*ná°*), mfn. 9-doored, AV.; Up. &c.; n. the body, Kum. — **dhā**, ind. into 9 parts, in 9 ways, 9 times &c., AV.; Up. &c. — **navati**, f. 99 (in RV. for any large number); *-tama*, mf(*ī*)n. the 99th, R. — **pañcāśa**, mf(*ī*)n. the 59th; °*śat*, f. 59; *-pad* (*ná°*), mfn. (nom. *pāt*, *padī*, *pat*) 9-footed, RV. — **pāshāṇa-darbha-śayana-saṃkalpa**, m. N. of wk. — **bhāga**, m. the 9th part (esp. of an asterism or of a lunar mansion), Var. (cf. *navâṅśa*). — **maṇi-mālā**, f. N. of wk. — **mukha**, mf(*ī*)n. having 9 apertures or openings, BhP. (cf. *-dvāra*). — **yoga-kallola**, m. N. of wk. (= *nyāya-ratnâkara*). — **raṅga**, n. a gift to 5 and acceptance by 4 persons of the best Kāyastha families, L.; a kind of garment (also *-ka*), L. (fr. 1. *nava*?); *-kula*, mfn. having the privilege of marrying into 9 distinct families (?), MW. — **ratna**, n. 9 precious gems (viz. pearl, ruby, topaz, diamond, emerald, lapis lazuli, coral, sapphire, and Go-medha; they are supposed to be related to the 9 planets), L. (cf. MWB. 528); the 9 jewels (i.e. the 9 men of letters at the court of Vikramâditya, viz. Dhanvantari, Kshapaṇaka, Amara-siṃha, Śaṅku, Vetāla-bhaṭṭa, Ghaṭa-karpara, Kāli-dāsa, Vara-ruci, and Varāha-mihira), L.; N. of a collection of 9 stanzas and other wks.; *-jyotir-gaṇita*, n., *-dāna*, n., *-dhātu-vivāda*, m., *-parîkshā*, *-mālā*, *-mālikā*, f., °*tnêśvara-tantra*, n. N. of wks. — **ratha**, m. N. of a son of Bhīma-ratha and father of Daśa-ratha, Hariv.; BhP. — **rasa** (in comp.), the 9 sentiments or passions (dram.); *-taraṃgiṇī*, f., *-ratna-hāra*, m. N. of wks. — **rātra**, m. a period of 9 days, AitBr.; ŚrS.; a Soma sacrifice with 9 Sutyā days, KātyŚr.; 9 days in the middle of the Gavām-ayana, ŚāṅkhŚr.; n. (also °*trika*) the 9 days from the 1st of the light half of month Āśvina to the 9th (devoted to the worship of Durgā), RTL. 431; *-kṛitya*, n., *-ghaṭa-sthāpana-vidhi*, m., *-nirṇaya*, m., *-pūjā-vidhāna*, n., *-pradīpa*, m., *-vrata*, n., *-havana-vidhi*, m. N. of wks. — **rāśika**, m. or n. the rule of proportion with 9 terms comprising 4 proportions, MW. — **rāshṭra**, see under 1. *nava*. — **rcá** (°*va* + *ṛica*), mfn. consisting of 9 verses, AV. — **varṇa-mālā**, f., **-varsha-mahôtsava**, m. N. of wks. — **vārshika**, mfn. 9 years old; *-deśīya*, mfn. about 9 y° old, Pañcad. — **vāstva** (*ná°*), m. 'having 9 dwelling-places,' N. of a myth. being, RV. — **viṅśa**, mf(*ī*)n. the 29th, R.; *-śati* (*ná°*), f. 29, VS. — **vitṛiṇṇa**, mfn. perforated in 9 places, ŚBr. — **vidha**, mfn. 9-fold, consisting of 9 parts, Kauś.; BhP. — **viveka-dīpikā**, f. N. of wk. — **vṛishá**, mfn. having 9 bulls, AV. — **vyūha**, m. N. of Vishṇu, L. (cf. *catur-v°*). — **śakti**, m. 'having 9 faculties,' N. of Vishṇu or Śiva, L. — **śata**, n. 109; *-tama*, mf(*ī*)n. the 109th, R. — **śas**, ind. 9 by 9, by nines, W. — **śāyaka**, m. N. given to any of 9 inferior castes (viz. cowherd, gardener, oilman, weaver, confectioner, water-carrier, potter, blacksmith, and barber), W. — **shaṭka**, mfn. consisting of 9 × 6 (strings &c.), Var. — **shashṭi**, f. 69; *-tama*, mf(*ī*)n. the 69th, R. — **saṃyojana-visaṃyojanaka**, m. N. of Buddha, Divyâv. — **saṃghārāma**, see under 1. *nava*. — **saptati**, f. 79; *-tama*, mf(*ī*)n. the 79th, R. — **sapta-daśa**, m. N. of an Atirātra, ŚrS. — **sara**, m. or n. a kind of ornament consisting of pearls, Pañcad. — **sāhasâṅka-carita**, n. 'the 9 [or new?] deeds of king Sāhasâṅka,' N. of a poem by Śrī-Harsha. — **sāhasra**, mf(*ī*)n. consisting of 9000, Cat. — **stobha**, n. (with *âyus*), N. of a Sāman. — **srakti** (*ná°*), mfn. '9-cornered,' consisting of 9 parts (as a hymn), RV. viii, 65, 12. — **hasta**, m. N. of an author, Cat. (cf. *-kara*). **Navâṅśa** or °*śaka*, m. = °*va-bhāga*, Var.; °*ka-pa*, m. the regent of a N°, ib. **Navâkshara**, mf(*ā* or *ī*)n. consisting of 9 syllables, ŚBr.; °*rī-kalpa*, m. N. of wk. **Navâṅkura**, m. N. of wk. **Navâṅgā**, f. a kind of gall-nut, L. (v.l. *latâṅgī*). **Navâtmaka**, mfn. consisting of 9 parts, L. **Navânupūrva-samāpatti-kuśala**, m. N. of Buddha, Divyâv. **Navâyasa**, n. a medic. preparation containing 9 parts of iron, Rasar. **Návâratni**, mfn. 9 ells long, ŚBr. **Navârcis**, m. = °*va-dīdhiti*, VP. **Navârṇava** (in comp.), the 9 seas; *-paddhati*, f., *-prakaraṇa*, n. N. of wks. **Navâśīti**, f. 89; *-tama*, mf(*ī*)n. the 89th, R. **Navâśra**, mfn. 9-cornered; *-kuṇḍa*, Cat. — **Navâha**, m. the first day of a half-month, L.; = °*va-rātra*, m. ShaḍvBr.; Lāṭy. **Navâhnika-bhāshya**, n. (prob.) = the Mahā-bhāshya of Patañjali, Cat. (cf. *bh°-n°*).

2. **Navaka**, mfn. consisting of 9, RPrāt.; MBh.; n. the aggregate of 9, Var.; Car. &c.

1. **Navata**, mf(*ī*)n. the 90th, Rājat. (cf. *eka-*, *dvā-* &c.)

Navati, (L. also °*tī*) f. 90, RV. &c. &c. — **tama**, mf(*ī*)n. the 90th, MBh.; R. — **dhanus**, m. N. of an ancestor of Gautama Buddha, Inscr. — **dhā**, ind. 90-fold, W. — **prakrama** (°*ti-*), mf(*ā*)n. 90 steps long, ŚBr. — **ratha**, m. N. of an ancestor of Gautama Buddha, Inscr. — **rupati-māhātmya** (?), n. N. of wk. — **śata**, n. 190, L. — **śas**, ind. 90 by 90.

Navatikā, f. (fr. *navati*) a paint-brush containing 90 hairs, L.

Návan, pl. (nom. acc. *náva*; instr. *navábhis*, abl. dat. °*bhyas*, loc. °*su*; Class. also *navabhis*, °*bhyás*, °*sú*; gen. *navānā́m*, Pāṇ. vi, 1, 177 &c.) nine, RV. &c. &c. [Cf. Zd. *navan*; Gk. ἐννέα for ἐ-νϝεα fr. ἐ-νεϝα; Lat. *nŏvem*; Goth. and OldHGerm. *niun*, OSax. and Angl. Sax. *nigun*, NHGerm. *neun*, Eng. *nine*.]

2. **Navamá**, mf(*ī*)n. the ninth, AV. &c. &c. (cf. 1. *navamá* under 1. *nava*); of 9 kinds, ninefold, Hcat.; (*ī*), f. (sc. *tithi*) the 9th day of a lunar half-month. °**mâṅśa**, m. (in astrol.) = *navâṅśa*.

Navamaka, mfn. the ninth, Śrut.

Navin, mfn. consisting of nine, Lāṭy.

नवत 2. *navata*, m. an elephant's painted or variegated housings; woollen cloth; a cover, blanket, wrapper, L. (cf. 2. *namata*).

नवर *navara*, m. or n. N. of a partic. high number, Buddh. — **saundarya-bhaṭṭa**, m. N. of an author, Cat.

नवरम् *navaram*, ind. (Prākr.) only, L.

नविद्वस् *na-vidvas*, *na-vipulā*. See under 2. and 1. *nā*.

नवेद *náveda* (only RV. i, 165, 13) and *ná-vedas*, mfn. observing, cognizant (with gen.), RV. (Clearly not from the negat. *na*, but cf. Pāṇ. vi, 3, 75.)

नव्य 1. and 2. *navya*. See above.

नश् 1. *naś* or *naṅś*, cl. 1. P. Ā. *náśati*, °*te* (aor. *ānaṭ*, *-naṭ*; *-anashṭām*, *-nak* [in *pra-ṇak*], Impv. *-nákshi*; Ā. 1. sg. *nâṅśi*, Prec. *naśīmahi*; inf. *-náśe*), to reach, attain, meet with, find, RV. [Cf. 1. *aś* and *naksh*; Lat. *nac-tus sum*; Lith *nèszti*; Slav. *nesti*; Goth. *ganóhs*; Germ. *genug*; Angl. Sax. *genôh*; Eng. *enough*.]

1. **Naśa**. See *dur-naśa*, *dū-naśa*.

Naśâya, Nom. P. °*yati*, to reach, attain to (acc.), RV. x, 10, 6.

नश् 2. *naś*, cl. 4. P. (Dhātup. xxvi, 85) *náśyati* (rarely °*te* and 1. P. *náśati*, °*te*; pf. *nanāśa*, 3. pl. *neśur*; aor. *anaśat*, MBh. &c.; *aneśat*, *néśat*, RV.; Br. [cf. Pat. on Pāṇ. vi, 4, 120]; fut. *naśishyati*, AV.; *naṅkshyati*, °*te* [cond. *anaṅkshyata*], MBh.; *naśitā*, ib.; *naṉshṭā*, Pāṇ. vii, 2, 45; *naṅgdhā*, Vop.; inf. *naśitum*, *naṉshṭum*, Gr.; ind. p. *naśitvā*, *nashṭvā*, *naṉshṭvā*, ib.) to be lost, perish, disappear, be gone, run away, RV. &c. &c.; to come to nothing, be frustrated or unsuccessful, Mn.; MBh.; Kāv. &c.: Caus. *nāśáyati*, ep. also °*te* (aor. *-anīnaśat*; dat. inf. *-nāśayadhyai*, RV.) to cause to be lost or disappear, drive away, expel, remove, destroy, efface, RV. &c. &c.; to lose (also from memory), give up, MBh.; Kāv.; Pañc.; to violate, deflower (a girl), Daś.; Kull.; to extinguish (a fire), BhP.; to disappear (in *mā nīnaśaḥ* and °*naśuḥ*), MBh.: Desid. *ninaśishati* or *ninaṅkshati*, Pāṇ. vii, 1, 60; 2, 45 (cf. *ninaṅkshu*); Desid. of Caus. *ninā́śayishati*, to wish to destroy, Daś.: Intens. *nānaśyate* or *nānaṉshṭi*, Gr. [Cf. Gk. *νεκρός*; Lat. *nex*, *nocere*].

3. **Naś**, mfn. perishing (in *jīva-*, q. v.)

2. **Naśa**, m. destruction, MW. (cf. 2. *nāśa*).

Naśana, n. disappearing, escaping, L.; loss, BhP.

Naśitṛi, mfn. one who disappears or destroys, L. (cf. *naṉshṭṛi*).

Naśyat, mf(*antī*)n. perishing, being destroyed &c. — **prasūti** or °**tikā**, f. a female bearing a dead child, L.

Naśvara, mf(*ī*)n. perishing, perishable, transitory, Kāv.; Pur. &c.; destructive, mischievous, W. — **tva**, n. perishableness, transitoriness, Daś.

Nashṭá, mfn. lost, disappeared, perished, destroyed, lost sight of, invisible; escaped (also *-vat*, mfn. MBh.), run away from (abl.), fled (impers. with instr. of subj. Ratn. ii. 3), RV. &c. &c.; spoiled, damaged, corrupted, wasted, unsuccessful, fruitless, in vain, Mn.; Yājñ.; MBh. &c.; deprived of (instr.), R. i, 14, 18 (in comp. = 'without,' '-less,' 'un-'; see below); one who has lost a lawsuit, Mṛicch. ix, 4. — **kāryārtha**, mfn. one who has lost interest in what is to be done, R. (B.) — **kriya**, mfn. ungrateful, Pañc. iii, 245 (lit. on whom a benefit is lost; cf. MBh. i, 6116). — **gaṇita**, n. N. of wk. — **candra**, m. 'moonless,' N. of the 4th day in both halves of Bhādra, L. — **caryā**, f. playing at hide and seek, Nalac. — **cetana**, mfn. one who has lost consciousness, insensible, MBh.; Suśr. — **ceshṭa**, mf(*ā*)n. one who has lost the power of motion, rigid, fainted, insensible, MBh.; Kathās.; *-tā*, f. rigidity, swooning, L. — **janman** and **-jātaka**, n. 'a lost nativity,' subsequent calculation of a l° n°, Var.; N. of wk. (also *-vidhāna*, N.) — **dṛishṭi**, mfn. sightless, blind, BhP. — **dhī**, mfn. unmindful or forgetful (of an offence), Rājat. v, 299. — **nidra**, mfn. sleepless, Pañc. — **pattrikā**, f. N. of wk. — **pishṭa**, mfn. dissolved into powder, Bhpr.; °*ṭī-√kṛi*, to d° into p°, ib. — **praśna**, m. N. of wk. — **bīja**, mfn. destitute of the seminal secretion, impotent, L. — **mati**, mfn. one who has lost his senses, BhP. — **mārgaṇa**, n. seeking any l° object, Var. — **rājya**, n. N. of a district to the north-east of Madhya-deśa, ib. — **rūpa**, mfn. 'whose form is lost,' invisible, MBh.; (*ā* or *ī*), f. N. of a metre, RPrāt. — **visha** (°*ṭá-*), mfn. (a snake) whose venom is lost, AV. — **védana**, mf(*ī*)n. finding any l° object, ŚBr. — **samsmṛiti**, mfn. unmindful or forgetful of (gen.), Bhaṭṭ. — **saṃjña**, mf(*ā*)n. = *-cetana*, MBh.; — **hīna-vikala-vikṛita-svara**, mfn. whose voice has been lost or become feeble or deficient or changed; *-tā*, f. Suśr. — **smṛiti**, mfn. one who has l° his memory, forgetful, MW. **Nashṭâgni**, m. (a householder) whose fire has been extinguished, L. **Nashṭâtaṅkam**, ind. without fear (v. l. for °*tâśaṅka*). **Nashṭâtman**, mfn. deprived of mind or sense, MBh. **Nashṭâpti-sūtra**, n. 'line or series of lost property,' booty, L. **Nashṭârtha**, mfn. one who has lost his property, reduced, poor, Kathās. **Nashṭâśaṅka**, mfn. fearless, dauntless, Śak. (Pi.) i, 14. **Nashṭâśva-dagdha-ratha-vat**, ind. like one whose horse was lost and one whose waggon was burnt (who therefore helped each other), Pat. on Pāṇ. i, 1, 50, Vārtt. 16. **Nashṭâsu**, mfn. one whose vital spirits have disappeared, AV. **Nashṭêndu-kalā**, f. (night) in which the moon is invisible, L. **Nashṭendriya**, mfn. = °*ṭa-bīja*, deprived of one's senses, MW. **Nashṭaishá** (ŚBr.), °**shin** (AitBr.), mfn. seeking what has been lost. **Nashṭaishya**, n. the act of seeking what has been lost, AitBr. **Nashṭôddishṭa-prabodhaka-dhrauvapada-ṭīkā**, f. N. of a wk. on music. **Nashṭôbhaya-loka**, mfn. one for whom both worlds are lost, Kād.

Nashṭi, f. loss, destruction, ruin, BhP.

नशाक *naśāka*, m. a kind of crow, L.

नष्ट *nashṭa*. See above.

नस् 1. *nas*, encl. form for acc. gen. dat. pl. of the 1st pers. pron. (Pāṇ. viii, 1, 21), us, of us, to us; in Veda changeable into *ṇas* (4, 27; 28). [Cf. Zd. *na*, our; Gk. *νῶϊ*, *νώ*; Lat. *nos*, *nos-ter*; Old Lat. dat. *nis*.]

नस् 2. *nas*, cl. 1. Ā. (Dhātup. xvi, 26) *násate* (aor. Pot. *nasīmahi*, RV. ii, 16, 8; pf. *nese*; fut. *nasitā*, Gr.) to approach, resort to, join, copulate (esp. as husband and wife), RV.; to be crooked or fraudulent, Dhātup. [Cf. Gk. *νέ(σ)ομαι*, *να-(σ)ίω*, *νόσ-τος*; Goth. *ga-nizan*, *nas-jan*; Angl. S. *genesan*; HGerm. *ginesan*, *genesen*.]

नस् 3. *nás* or *nūs*, f. (the strong stem occurs only in du. *nā́sā*, RV. ii, 39, 6, the weak stem only in *nasā́*, *nasi*, *nasós* [cf. Pāṇ. vi, 1, 63] and in comp.) the nose, RV.; AV.; VS.; TS.; BhP. [Cf. *nāsā*, *nāsikā*; Lat. *nas-turcium*, *nāres*; Lith. *nósis*; Slav. *nosŭ*; Germ. *Nase*; Angl. Sax. *nosu*; Eng. *nose*, *nostril* = *nose-thrill*, nose-hole.] **Naḥ-kshudra**, mf(*ā*)n. small-nosed, L. **Nas-tas**, ind. from or into the nose, Br. &c. &c.; *-taḥ-karaṇa*, see *nasta-k°*; *-taḥ-karman*, n. 'the putting into the n°,' taking snuff, Car. **Nasy-otá**, mfn. (√*ve*) fastened or tied by the n°, led by a n°-cord, TS.; MBh.; BhP. **Nas-vát**, mfn. nosed, AV.

Nasa (ifc.) the nose (cf. *apī-n°*, *urū-ṇ°*, *kumbhī-n°* &c.); (*ā*) f. id., L.

Nasi, id. (?); see *kumbhī-n°*.

Nasta, m. the nose, L.; (*ā*), f. a hole bored through the septum of the n°, L.; n. a sternutatory, snuff, L. — **karaṇa**, n. instrument used by Bhikshus for injecting the n°, L. (°*taḥ-k°*? cf. above). — **tas**, ind. = (and prob. fr.) *nas-tás* (cf. *pat-ta-tas* fr. *pat-tas*), MBh. **Nast'ota**, mfn. = *nasy-ota*, L.

Nastaka, m. the septum of the nose (of cattle for draught) or a hole bored in it, MBh. xii, 9377.

Nastita, mfn. nozzled (cf. *nast'ota* and *nasy-ota*), L.

Násya, mfn. belonging to or being in the nose (as breath), ŚBr.; (*ā*), f. n°-cord, Yājñ., Sch. (cf. *nāsya*); the nose, L.; n. the hairs in the n°, VS.; a sternutatory, errhine, MBh.; R.; Suśr. — **karman**, n. the application of a sternutatory, Suśr. — **bhairava**, m. (scil. *rasa*) a partic. medicament, Rasêndrac. — **vidhi**, m. 'rules about sternutatories,' N. of ch. of ŚārṅgS.

Nasyita, mfn. = *nasy-ota*, Gal.

नसंविद् *na-saṃvid*, *na-sukara* &c. See 2. *ná*.

नह् 1. *nah*, cl. 4. P. Ā. (Dhātup. xxvi, 57) *náhyati*, °*te* (Pot. *-nahet*, MBh.; *na-hyur*, AitBr.; p. Ā. *náhyamāna* [also with pass. meaning], RV. &c.; pf. *nanāha*, *nehe*; fut. *nat-syati*, *naddhā*, Siddh. [cf. Pāṇ. viii, 2, 34]; aor. *anātsīt*, Bhaṭṭ.; *anaddha*, Vop.; ind. p. *naddhvā*, Gr.; *-náhya*, Br. &c.; inf. *-naddhum*, Kāv.) to bind, tie, fasten, bind on or round or together; (Ā.) to put on (as armour &c.), arm one's self, RV. &c. &c.: Pass. *nahyate*, p. °*hyamāna* (see above); Caus. *nāhayati* (aor. *anīnahat*, Gr.) to cause to bind together, BhavP.: Desid. *ninatsati*, °*te*, Gr.: Intens. *nānahyate*, *nānaddhi*, ib. [Prob. for *nagh*; cf. Lat. *nectere*, Germ. *Nestel* (?).]

2. **Náh** (only in *nádbhyas*, RV. x, 60, 6; but cf. *akshā-náh*) a bond, tie.

Náhasra, n. bolt, nail, crotchet, RV.; AV.; bond, fetter (cf. *un-n°*); putting on, girding round, Viddh.

Náhus, m. neighbour, fellow-creature, man, (comp. °*hush-ṭara*, nearer than a n°, x, 49, 8); (collect., also pl.) neighbourhood, mankind, RV. (cf. Naigh. ii, 2).

Náhusha, m. = *náhus*, RV. i, 31, 11; v, 12, 6; (prob.) N. of a man, viii, 46, 27; of a son of Manu and author of RV. ix, 101, Anukr.; of an ancient king (son of Āyu or Āyus [cf. RV. i. 31, 11] and father of Yayāti; he took possession of Indra's throne, but was afterwards deposed and changed into a serpent, Mn. vii, 41; MBh.; R. &c. (cf. RTL. 240); according to R. i, 72, 30 and ii, 119, 30 he is a son of Ambarīsha and father of Nābhāga); of a serpent-demon, MBh.; Hariv.; of a Marut, Hariv.; of Vishṇu-Kṛishṇa, MBh. — **carita**, 'Nahusha's life,' N. of ch. of the PadmaP. **Nahushâkhya**, n. the flower of Tabernaemontana Coronaria, L. **Nahushât-maja**, m. N. of king Yayāti (cf. above), W.

Nahushyà, mfn. relating to man, human, RV. ix, 88, 2; 91, 2; descended from Nahusha (?), x, 63, 1.

नहि *na-hí* (*ná-hi*, MaitrS. and ŚBr.), ind. (g. *cādi*) for not, surely not, by no means, not at all (often strengthened by other particles, as *aṅgá*, *nú*, *sma*), RV. &c. &c. (*nahikam*, g. *cādi*). — **mā-tra**, m. or n. a partic. high number (v. l. *mantra*), Buddh. (cf. *na-mātra* under 2. *ná*).

ना *nā́*. See 2. *ná*.

नाक *nā́ka*, m. (√*nam* [?]; according to Br. and Nir. fr. 2. *ná* + 2. *áka*, 'where there is no pain' [?]; cf. Pāṇ. vi, 3, 75 and below mfn.) vault of heaven (with or scil. *divás*), firmament, sky (generally conceived as threefold, cf. *tri-diva*, *tri-nāka*, and AV. xix, 27, 4; in VS. xvii, 67 there is a fivefold scale, viz. *pṛithivī*, *antari-ksha*, *div*, *divo-nāka*, and *svar-jyotis*), RV. &c. &c.; the sun, Naigh. i, 4; N. of a Maudgalya, ŚBr. &c.; of a myth. weapon of Arjuna, MBh.; of a dynasty, VP.; mfn. painless, ChUp. ii, 10, 5. — **cara**, mfn. walking in the sky, MBh. — **nadī**, f. 'the river of heaven,' the heavenly Gaṅgā, Vcar.; the earthly G°, Naish. — **nātha** or °**thaka**, m. 'sky-lord,' N. of Indra, L. — **nāyaka**, m. id., Bālar.; Naish.; *-purohita*, m. 'Indra's chief priest,' N. of Bṛihas-pati or the planet Jupiter, L. — **nārī**, f. 'heavenly female,' an Apsaras, Kathās. — **pati**, m. 'sky-lord,' a god, BhP. — **pālá**, m. 'sky-guardian,' a god, AV. — **puraṃdhri**, f. = *-nārī*, Bālar. — **pṛishṭha**, n. 'sky-ceiling,' the uppermost heaven, Āpast.; MBh. (°*ṭhya*, mfn. being in it, R.); m. N. of a man, Kāś. on Pāṇ. vi, 2, 114. — **loka**, m. the heavenly world, MBh. — **vanitā**, f. = *-nārī*, L. — **sád**, mfn. sitting or dwelling in the sky, VS.; ŚBr.; m. a deity, Hariv.; Bhaṭṭ.; N. of 9 Ekāhas, ŚrS.; f. N. of a kind of Ishṭakā, ŚBr.; Śulbas. (*sat-tvá*, n., TS.) — **strī**, f. = *-nārī*, Kathās.

Nākâdhipa, m. = °*ka-nātha*; *-nāyikā*, f. pl. the courtezans of Indra, i. e. the Apsaras, Naish. **Nākâpagā**, f. the heavenly Gaṅgā, Inscr. **Nākêśa**, m. = °*ka-nātha*, L. **Nākêśvara**, m., -°*ka-pati*, Hariv. **Nāk'oka**, m. N. of a poet, Cat. **Nākâukas**, m. = °*ka-sád*, m., R.

Nākin, m. 'having (i. e. dwelling in) heaven,' a god, Pur. — °**ki-nātha** (Śatr.) and °**ki-nāyaka** (Siṇhâs.), m. 'chief of the gods,' N. of Indra.

नाकु *nā́ku*, m. (√*nam* [?], Uṇ. i, 19) ant-hill, Nalac.; mountain, L.; N. of a Muni, L. — **sad-man**, m. a snake, W.

नाकुल *nākula*, mf(*ī*)n. (fr. *nak°*) ichneumon-like, g. *śarkarâdi*; m. patr. fr. Nakula, RPrāt. (cf. Pāṇ. iv, 1, 114, Sch.); pl. N. of a people, MBh.; (*ī*), f. the ichneumon plant (supposed to furnish the i° with an antidote when bitten by a snake), Suśr. (cf. *nakulêshṭā*); Piper Chaba, L.; = *yava-tiktā* (L.), *sarpa-gandhā* (Bh.), and other plants. **Nākulândhya**, n. = *nak°*, Suśr.

Nākulaka, mfn. worshipping Nakula, Pāṇ. iv, 3, 99; Kāś.

Nākuli, m. descendant of Nakula, patr. of Śatânika, MBh.

नाक्र *nā́kra*, m. a kind of aquatic animal, VS.; TS. (cf. *nakra*).

नाक्षत्र *nākshatra*, mf(*ī*)n. relating to the Nakshatras, starry, sidereal, Lāṭy.; Var. &c.; m. astronomer, astrologer, MBh.; n. a month computed by the moon's passage through the 27 mansions, or of 30 days of 60 Ghaṭis each, W.

Nākshatrika, mf(*ī*)n. = prec. mfn., Jyot.; m. a month of 27 days (each day being the period of the moon's passage through a mansion), W.; (*ī*), f. the state or condition to which a person is subjected agreeably to the asterism presiding over his nativity, ib.

नाग *nāgá*, m. (prob. neither fr. *na-ga* nor fr. *nagna*) a snake, (esp.) Coluber Naga, ŚBr.; MBh. &c.; (f. *ī*, Suparṇ.) a Nāga or serpent-demon (the race of Kadrū or Su-rasā inhabiting the waters or the city Bhoga-vatī under the earth; they are supposed to have a human face with serpent-like lower extremities [see esp. Nāg. v, 17; RTL. 233 &c.]; their kings are Sesha, Vāsuki, and Takshaka, ib. 323; 7 or 8 of the Nāgas are particularly mentioned, MBh.; Kāv. &c.; with Buddhists they are also represented as ordinary men, MWB. 220); N. of the numbers 7 (Sūryas.) or 8 (Hcat.); a cruel man, L.; one of the 5 airs of the human body (which is expelled by eructation), Vedântas.; (sg. also collect.) an elephant (f. *ī*, ifc. f. *ā*), Kāv.; BhP. etc.; the best or most excellent of any kind (ifc.), L. (cf. *ṛi-shabha, vyāghra* &c.); shark, L.; cloud, L.; N. of sev. plants (Mesua Roxburghii, Rottlera Tinctoria &c.), L.; N. of a serpent-demon, VP.; of a Sādhya, Hariv.; of a teacher, Buddh.; of a dynasty of 9 or 10 princes, VP.; of sev. authors (also *-śarman* and *-bhaṭṭa*), Col.; of sev. other men, Rājat.; of a mountain, Pur.; of a district, L.; = *-danta* (below), L.; (*ā* and *ī*), f. N. of sev. women, Rājat.; (*ī*), f. N. of a metre, Col. (cf. above); n. (m., L.) tin, lead, Bhpr.; a kind of talc, ib.; a kind of coitus, L.; N. of the 3rd invariable Karaṇa (see s. v.), Sūryas.; Var.; of the effects of that period on anything happening during it, W.; of a district of Bhārata-varsha, Gol.; mf(*ā* or *ī*)n. formed of snakes, relating to serpents or s°-demons, snaky, serpentine, serpent-like, MBh. &c. (with *āsana*, n. a partic. attitude in sitting, Cat.; *ā*, f. [scil. *vīthī*] = *nāga-v°*, below, Var.); belonging to an elephant, elephantine (as urine), Suśr. **–kanda**, m. a kind of bulbous plant, L. **–kanyakā** (L.), **-kanyā** (Kāraṇḍ.), f. a serpent-virgin (cf. MWB. 220; RTL. 233). **–karṇa**, m. red Ricinus, L. **–kiñjalka**, n. the blossom of Mesua Roxburghii, L. **–kuṇḍala-kuṇḍalin**, mfn. wearing a coiled serpent for an earring, MBh. **–kumāra**, m. prince of the serpent-demons, Divyâv.; pl. N. of a class of deities among the Bhavanâdhīśas guarding the treasures of Kubera, L.; (*ī*), f. Rubia Munjista, L.; (also °*rikā*) Cocculus Cordifolius, L. **–keśa**, m. N. of a minister of king Nāgêśa, Buddh. **–kesara**, m. Mesua Roxburghii, Vāsant.; n. its blossom, Suśr. (*-cūrṇaka*, L.); a kind of steel, L. **–khaṇḍa**, n. N. of one of the 9 divisions of Bhārata-varsha, Rājat. (w. r. *-cchanda*; cf. *-dvīpa*). **–gandhā**, f. a kind of bulbous plant, L. **–garbha**, n. red lead, ib. **–campaka**, m. a kind of Campaka, L. **–cūḍa**, m. 'serpent-crested,' N. of Śiva, Śivag. **–cchattrā**, f. Tiaridium Indicum, L. **–ja**, n. 's°-born,' red lead, tin, L. **–jihvā**, f. 's°-tongue,' a species of creeper, L.; °*vikā*, f. red arsenic, L. **–jīvana**, n. tin, L.; *-śatru*, m. 'foe of tin,' orpiment, L. **–tamanī**, f. = *-yashṭi*, L. **–tīrtha**, n. N. of a Tīrtha, ŚivaP.; *-māhātmya*, n. N. of wk. **–datta**, mfn. given by Nāgas or serpents, MBh. i, 5033 (v. l. *-danta*); m. N. of a son of Dhṛita-rāshṭra, MBh.; of a man related to Gautama Buddha, Lalit.; of a king of Āryāvarta, contemporary of Samudra-gupta, Inscr. **–danta**, m. elephant's tusk or ivory, MBh.; a peg in the wall to hang things upon, Pañc.; Kathās.; (*ā*), f. N. of an Apsaras, R. (v. l. *-dattā*); (*ī*), f. Tiaridium Indicum, Suśr.; Heliotropium Indicum, L.; *-maya*, mf(*ī*)n. made of ivory, Hcat. **–dantaka**, m. = *-danta*, m., Var.; Hit.; (*ikā*), f. Tragia Involucrata, L. **–damanī**, f. s°-spell, Artemisia Vulgaris, or Alpinia Nutans, L. **–dalôpama**, n. Xylocarpus Granatum, L. **–dāsaka**, m. (°*saka*?) N. of a prince, Buddh. **–deṇṭikā**, f. (for *-dantikā*?) the betel plant, L. **–deva**, m. a serpent-king, W.; N. of sev. authors (also *-bhaṭṭa*); °*vâhnika*, n. N. of wk.; °*vīya*, mfn. written by Nāga-deva; n. N°'s wk. **–dru**, m. a species of Euphorbia (used in offerings to the snake-goddess Manasā), W. **–dvīpa**, n. N. of a Dvīpa in Jambū-khaṇḍa or Bhārata-varsha, MBh. (cf. *nāga-khaṇḍa*). **–dhanvan**, m. (!) N. of a Tīrtha (cf. *-vartman*, MBh., B.) **–dharīya**, n. N. of wk. **–dhvani**, m. (in music) N. of a Rāga. **–nakshatra**, n. N. of the lunar mansion Aśleshā, Var. **–nātha**, m. serpent-chief, Inscr.; N. of sev. authors, Cat.; n. = °*thêśa-liṅga*, n. N. of a Liṅga sacred to Śiva, Cat. **–nābha** (?), m. of a man, Cat. **-nāmaka**, n. tin, L.; the blossom of Mesua Roxburghii, Gal. **–nāman**, m. holy basil (= *tulasī*), L. **–nāyaka**, m. serpent-chief, Rājat. **–nāsā**, f. the trunk of an elephant; °*sôru*, f. a round-thighed woman, R. (cf. *karabhôru*). **–niryūha**, m. a peg in a wall (= *-danta*), L. **–pañcamī**, f. a partic. festival sacred to the Nāgas (the 5th day in the light half of month Śrāvaṇa or in the dark h° of m° Āshāḍha), L.; RTL. 323; *-vrata*, n., °*ta-kathā*, f. N. of wks. **–pati**, m. a serpent-chief, MBh. **–pattrā**, f. = *-damanī*, Bhpr. **–pada**, m. a kind of coitus, L. **–parṇī**, f. the betel plant, L. **–pāla**, m. N. of a man, Rājat.; of a prince of Sāśikya, Daś. **–pāśa**, m. a sort of magical noose (used in battles), Mahīdh. on VS. vi, 8 (cf. MBh. viii, 2586 &c.); a kind of metre (= *-bandha*), L.; N. of Varuṇa's weapon, L.; of a man, Cat.; °*śaka*, m. a kind of coitus, L. **–putra**, m. a young serpent-demon, Pañcad. **–pura**, n. N. of a town (= *hāstina-pura*), AVPariś.; MBh.; °*rī*, f. (prob.) id. in °*rī-māhātmya*, n. N. of wk. **–pushpa**, m. N. of sev. plants, MBh.; Hariv.; Suśr. &c. (= Mesua Roxburghii, Rottlera Tinctoria, and Michelia Champaka, L.); (*ī*), f. = *-damanī*, Bhpr.; n. the blossom of Mesua Roxb°, Var.; *-phalā*, f. Benincasa Cerifera, L.; °*pikā*, f. yellow jasmine, L. **–paiya** (?), m. N. of a poet, Cat. **–pota**, m. = *-putra*, Hariv. (v. l. *pannagêndra*). **–pratishṭhā**, f., **-vidhi**, m. N. of wks. **–phala**, m. Trichosanthes Dioeca, L.; (*ā*), f. Momordica Monadelpha, Var. **–bandha**, m. a snake as a chain or fetter, Kathās.; N. of a metre resembling the coilings of a s°, Pratāp. (cf. *-pāśa*). **–bandhaka**, m. elephant-catcher, L. **–bandhu**, m. 'e°-friend,' Ficus Religiosa, L. **–bala**, m. 'having the strength of an e°,' N. of Bhīma, L.; (*ā*), f. Uraria Lagopodioides, Suśr.; Sida Spinosa, L.; n. a partic. high number, Lalit. **–bali**, m. an oblation to the Nāgas (a partic. marriage ceremony), ĀpGṛ. ii, 15, Sch.; N. of a work attributed to Śaunaka, Cat. **–buddha**, m. N. of an ancient teacher, Buddh. **–buddhi**, m. N. of a medical author; *-nighaṇṭu*, m. N. of his wk. **–bodha** or °**dhin**, m. N. of an author, Cat. **–bhaginī**, f. 'serpent's sister,' N. of the goddess Manasā, BrahmavP. (cf. *-mātṛi*). **–bhid**, m. 'elephant-destroyer,' a species of snake (v. l. for *-bhṛit*?), L. **–bhūshaṇa**, m. 'decorated with serpents,' N. of Śiva, Śivag. (cf. *-cūḍa*); N. of an author, Cat. **–bhṛit**, m. a species of snake, Amphisbaena, L. (cf. *-bhid*). **–bhoga**, m. a species of snake (or the coiling of a s°?), R. v, 74, 31. **–maṇḍalika**, m. a keeper or catcher of snakes, L. **–matī**, f. Ocimum Sanctum, L. **–maya**, mf(*ī*)n. consisting of or in elephants, Hariv. **–malla**, m. 'athlete among the e°,' N. of Indra's e° Airāvata, L. **–mātṛi**, f. 'serpent-mother,' N. of Su-rasā, R.; of the goddess Manasā, L.; red arsenic, L. **–māra**, m. a species of pot-herb, L. **–mudra**, m. N. of a Buddhist Sthavira; (*ā*), f. a seal-ring showing a serpent, Mālav. **–mauñjin**, mfn. (fr. *muñjā*) wearing a snake as girdle, MBh. **–yajñôpavīta**, n. a serpent as the sacred thread; mfn., °*ta-vat* (Hcat.) °*tin* (MBh.), mfn. possessing it. **–yashṭi** and °**ṭikā**, f. a post serving as water-mark, L. **–rakta**, n. red lead, L. **–raṅga** and °**gaka**, m. an orange-tree, Śrīkaṇṭh.; L. **–raṭṭa**, m. N. of a man, Rājat. viii, 1137 (v. l. *-vaṭṭa*). **–rāj**, m. serpent-king, MBh. **–rāja**, m. id., ib. (also °*jan*); a large or noble elephant, ib.; N. of an author (also *-keśava*); *-nāṭaka*, n., *-paddhati*, f., *-śataka*, n. N. of wks.; °*jāya*, Nom. Ā. °*yate*, to become a serpent-king, Vās. **–ruka**, m. (fr. *-vṛiksha*?) the orange-tree, L. (cf. *-raṅga*). **–rūpa-dhṛik**, m. N. of an author of Mantras (among the Śāktas), Cat. **–reṇu**, m. red lead, L. **–latā**, f. Piper Betle, Bālar.; the penis, L.; N. of a woman, Rājat. **–lekhā**, f. N. of a woman, ib. **–loka**, m. the world of serpents or s°-demons (called Pātāla and thought to be under the earth), MBh.; Hariv. &c.; the race of these beings collectively, ib.; *-pati*, m. a s°-chief, BhP. **–vaṭṭa**, m., see *-raṭṭa*. **–vat**, mfn. consisting of serpents (MW.) or of elephants, MBh. **–vatman**, w. r. for *-vartman* or *-dhanvan*. **–vadha** (with *rasa*), m. a remedy against leprosy for the preparation of which a snake is used, Bhpr. **–vadhū**, f. female elephant, R. **–vana**, n. (in comp.) e°s and forests or a f° of e°s, Vishṇ. iii, 16; N. of a place, L. **–vartman**, m. (!) N. of a Tīrtha, MBh. ix. 2148 (B. *-dhanvan*). **–vardhana** and **-varman**, m. N. of men, L. **–vallarī**, f. Piper Betle, Bhpr. **–vallī**, f. id., R. (also °*li*, Śiś. ix, 35, °*likā*, L.); N. of wk. (also *-kalpa*, m.) **–vaśā**, f. = *-vadhū*, Mudr. **–vārika**, m. (L.) royal elephant; e°-driver; a peacock; N. of Garuḍa; the chief person in a court or assembly. **–vāsa**, m. 'abode of snakes,' N. of a lake supposed to have been formed by the valley of Nepal, Buddh. **–vīthī**, f. a row of serpents, MBh.; 's° path,' the moon's path through the asterisms Svāti (or Aśvinī), Bharaṇī and Kṛittikā, Var. (cf. *nāgā*, f. and *gaja-v°*); N. of a daughter of Dharma and Yāmī or of Kaśyapa and Yāminī, Hariv.; Pur. **–vṛiksha**, m. a kind of tree, R. (cf. *-ruka*). **–vyādhi-nirṇaya**, m. N. of wk. **–śata**, m. N. of a mountain, MBh. **–śabdī**, f. (in music) N. of a Rāga. **–śarman**, m. N. of a Purohita, Bhadrab. **–śuṇḍī**, f. a kind of cucumber, L. **–śūra**, m. N. of a man, Kathās. **–śrī**, f. N. of a princess, ib. **–sambhava**, n. red lead, L. **–sambhūta**, mfn. produced from serpents (said of a kind of pearl), Var. **–sâhvaya** (with *nagara*), n. 'the town called after elephants,' i. e. Hāstina-pura, MBh. **–sugandhā**, f. the ichneumon plant (cf. *nākulī*), Bhpr. **–sena**, m. N. of a Buddh. Sthavira, MWB. 141; 192, n. 1x; of a king of Āryā-varta and contemporary of Samudra-gupta, Inscr. **–stokaka**, n. a species of poisonous plant, L. **–sthala**, n. N. of a village near Mathurā, Kathās. **–sphoṭā**, f. Croton Polyandrum or Tiaridium Indicum, L. **–svāmin**, m. N. of a man, Kathās. **–hanu**, m. Unguis Odoratus, L. **–hantrī**, f. a kind of plant, L. **–hrada**, m. a lake inhabited by snakes or serpent-demons, R. **Nāgâkhya**, m. Mesua Roxburghii, L. **Nāgâṅga**, n. N. of the town Hāstina-pura, W. **Nāgâṅganā**, f. female elephant, L.; v. l. for next. **Nāgâñcanā**, f. an e°'s trunk, L.; = *nāga-yashṭi*, L. **Nāgâñcalā**, f. = °*ga-yashṭi*, L. **Nāgâñjanā**, f. female e°, L.; = prec., L. **Nāgâdhipa**, m. 'serpent-prince,' N. of Śesha, L. **Nāgâdhipati**, m. 'id.,' N. of Virūḍhaka, L. **Nāgâdhirāja**, m. the king of the elephants, Vikr. **Nāgânana**, w. r. for °*gâśana*. **Nāgânanda**, or °**dīya**, n. 'the serpents' joy,' N. of a Buddh. play ascribed to king Harsha. **Nāgântaka**, m. 's°-destroyer,' N. of Garuḍa, L. **Nāgâbharaṇa**, n. N. of wk. **Nāgâbhibhu**, m. N. of a Buddha (°*bhū*, of another man), Lalit. **Nāgârāti**, m. = °*ga-hantrī*, L. **Nāgâri**, m. 'serpent-foe,' N. of Garuḍa, Rājat.; Pañc.; *-giri-vivara-kalpa*, m. N. of wk.; *-tantra-homa*, m. a kind of sacrifice, Saṃskārak. **Nāgârūḍha**, mfn. mounted or riding upon an elephant, W. **Nāgârjuna**, m. N. of an ancient Buddh. teacher of the rank of a Bodhi-sattva, MWB. 192; (*-carita, -jātaka, -tantra*, °*nīya* and °*nīya-dharma-śāstra*, n. N. of wks.); (*ī*), f. N. of a rock-cavern, Inscr. **Nāgâlābu**, f. a kind of gourd, L. **Nāgâvalokita**, n. elephant-look (turning the whole body, as a mark of Buddha), Divyâv. **Nāgâśana**, m. 'snake-eater,' a peacock, Kāv.; N. of Garuḍa, Pañc. **Nāgâhva**, n. 'the town called after elephants,' Hāstina-pura, L.; (*ā*), f. Mesua Roxburghii, Rasar.; a kind of Champaka, L.; a kind of bulbous plant, L. **Nāgâhvaya** (with *pura*), n. = prec. n. (cf. *nāga-sâhv°*), MBh.; m. a kind of plant, R.; N. of Tathāgata-bhadra, L. **Nāgêndra**, m. serpent-chief, MBh.; Suśr.; a large or noble elephant, Kāv.; (*ī*), f. N. of a river, Śatr. **Nāgêśa**, m. N. of a prince, Buddh.; of a man called also *daiva-jña*, Cat.; of Patañjali, L.; (also *-bhaṭṭa*) = *nāgoji-bh°* (°*śa-vivaraṇa*, n. N. of wk.); n. N. of a Liṅga in Dārukā-vana, ŚivaP. **Nāgêśvara**, m. a kind of plant, Pañcar.; N. of a man, Rājat.; (*ī*), f. N. of the goddess Manasā, Cat.; n. N. of a Liṅga, ŚivaP.; *-tīrtha*, n. N. of sev. sacred bathing-places, ib. **Nāgôda**, n. (*nāga* + *uda* or corrupted fr. next) armour for the front of the body, L. **Nāgôdara**, m. N. of a medical author, L.; n. a kind of decay of the fetus in the womb, Car.; = prec., L. **Nāgôdbheda**, m. N. of a sacred spot where the river Sarasvatī reappears, MBh. **Nāgôpavītin**, mfn. = *nāga yajñôp°*, Hcat.

Nāgaka, m. N. of a man, Rājat.

Nāgin, mfn. covered with or surrounded by serpents, Hariv.; (*ī*), f. Piper Betle, L.; a kind of bulbous plant, L.

Nāgila, m. N. of a man, Śatr.; (*ā*), f. N. of a woman, HPariś.

1. **Nāgī**, f. of *nāga*. **–ja**, n. the blossom of Mesua Roxburghii, L.

2. **Nāgī**, in comp. for *nāga*. **–√bhū**, to be changed into a serpent-demon, Rājat.

नागम्मा *nāgammā*, f. (Prākr. for *na-agamyā*?) N. of a poetess, Cat.

नागय्य *nāgayya*, m. N. of an author, Cat.

नागर *nāgara*, mf(*ī*)n. (fr. *nagara*) town-born, t°-bred, relating or belonging to a t° or city, t°-like, civic, MBh.; Kāv. &c.; spoken in a t° (said of a partic. Apabhraṅśa dialect; cf. *upa-n°*), Sāh.; polite, civil, Śak. v, ½ (v. l. for °*rika*); clever, dexterous, cunning, Dhūrtan.; bad, vile, L.; nameless, L.; m. a citizen, MBh. &c.; (= *paura*) a prince engaged in war under partic. circumstances (opp. to *yāyin* &c. and also applied to planets opposed to each other), Var.; a husband's brother, L.; a lecturer, L.; an orange, L. (cf. *nāga-raṅga*); toil, fatigue, L.; desire of final beatitude, L.; denial of knowledge, L.; (*ī*), f. Euphorbia Antiquorum, L.;

= *deva-nāgarī*, Col.; a clever or intriguing woman, W.; n. dry ginger, Suśr.; the root of Cyperus Pertenuis, L.; a partic. written character, Hcat.; a kind of coitus, L.; N. of sev. places, L. — **khaṇḍa**, n. N. of ch. of SkandaP. — **ghana**, m. = -*mustā*, L. — **tā**, f. cleverness, dexterity, Dhūrtan. — **nṛipati**, m. a prince engaged in war under partic. circumstances (also applied to planets in opposition to each other), Var. — **mustā**, f. a species of Cyperus grass, L.; °*taka*, n. its grain, Bhpr. — **yāyi-graha**, m. pl. planets opposed to each other in various partic. ways, Var. (cf. above). — **sarvasva**, n. N. of wk. — **sena**, m. N. of a prince, Hcar. — **strī**, f. townswoman, female citizen, R. **Nāgarâvalambikā**, f. (prob.) N. of a woman, Buddh. **Nāgarâhva**, n. dry ginger, L. **Nāgarôtthā**, f. = °*ra-mustā*, L.

Nāgaraka, mf(*ikā*)n. living in a town (opp. to *āraṇyaka*), L.; clever, cunning, L.; m. a citizen, L.; chief of a town, police-officer, Śak. (v.l. for °*rika*); applied to planets opposed to each other, Var. (cf. *nāgara-nṛipati* and -*yāyi-graha*); an artist, W.; a thief, W.; (*ikā*) f. N. of a female slave, Mālav.; n. dry ginger, Suśr.; a kind of metre, Col.

Nāgarika, mfn. born or living in a town, civic, Kāv.; Pur.; polite, courtly, Śak. (cf. -*vṛitti*, below); clever, cunning, Pañc.; m. inhabitant of a town, (esp.) chief of a t°, police-officer, Śak. (v.l. °*raka*); n. the toll raised from a t°, Pāṇ. iv, 3, 75, Sch. — **pura**, n. N. of a town, Cat. — **bala**, n. the guard of a police-officer, Daś. — **vṛitti**, f. a courtly manner or style, Śak. v. ½.

Nāgareyaka, mfn. belonging to a town, city-like, civic, g. *kattry-ādi*.

Nāgarya, n. town-life, shrewdness, g. *purohitâdi*.

नागरमर्दि *nāgaramardi*, m. patron. fr. *nagara-mardin*, g. *bāhv-ādi*.

नागरीट *nāgarīṭa*, prob. w.r. for *nāgavīṭa*, m. intriguer, match-maker, L.

नागुली *nāgulī*, f. N. of a town, Col.

नागोजि *nāgoji*, m. N. of a grammarian (also °*jī* or °*jī-bhaṭṭa* [cf. *nāgêśa*], author of a gloss on Kaiyaṭa's Comm. on Pat. [= *nāgêśa-vivaraṇa*], of a gram. wk. called Paribhāshêndu-śekhara &c.); -*paddhati*, f. N. of wk.; -*bhaṭṭīya*, n. a work of N-Bh°.

नागोब *nāgoba*, m. N. of an author (1780), Cat.

नाग्नजित *nāgnajitá*, m. a descendant of Nagna-jit, ŚBr.; (*ī*), f. a daughter of Nagna-jit (N. of one of the wives of Kṛishṇa), Hariv. (w. r. *nagnājitī*); BhP. x, 61, 13 (where metri causa °*jiti*).

नाचिक *nācika*, m. N. of a son of Viśvāmitra, MBh.

नाचिकेत *nāciketá*, mf(*ī*)n. relating to Naciketa or Na-ciketas, KaṭhUp.; TĀr.; m. (with *agni*) a partic. fire, ib.; (sc. *agni*) any fire, L. (w. r. *nāciketu* or *nācchiketa*); N. of an ancient sage (son of Uddālaki), MBh. (cf. *tri-ṇāciketa*). — **prayoga**, m., °**tôpâkhyāna**, n. N. of wks.

नाचिराज *nācirāja* and *nācoka*, m. N. of poets, Cat.

नाचीन *nācīna*, m. N. of a people, MBh.

नाज्जक *nājjaka*, m. N. of a man, Rājat.

नाट *nāṭa*, m. or n. (√*naṭ*; g. *ardharcâdi*) dancing, acting, a dance, L.; m. (in music) N. of a Rāga; of a serpent-demon, Buddh. (cf. *naṭa*); pl. of a people, Rājat. (= *karṇāṭaka*, L.); (*ī*), f. (scil. *bhāshā*) the language of the Nāṭas. — **bhaṭika-vihāra**, m. N. of a monastery, Buddh. (v. l. *naṭa-bh°*). — **sūtra**, n. N. of wk. **Nāṭâmra**, m. the water-melon, L.

Nāṭaka, mf(*ī*)n. acting, dancing, W.; m. an actor, dancer, mime, R.; N. of a mountain, KālP.; (*ikā*), f. a kind of Upa-rūpaka or drama of the second order, Sāh. &c.; any show or representation, Bālar. vii, 76; (in music) N. of a Rāgiṇī; (*akī*), f. the court of Indra, L.; n. any play or drama, Hariv.; Kāv. &c. (personif. as m. MBh. ii, 453); a kind of play, the first of the Rūpakas or dramas of the first order, Sāh. &c. — **candrikā**, f., -**dīpa**, m., -**paribhāshā**, f., -**prakāśa**, m. N. of wks. — **prapañca**, m. course or arrangement of a drama, W. — **ratna-kośa**, m., -**lakshaṇa**, n. N. of wks. — **vidhi**, m. mimic art, dramatic action, MW. **Nāṭakâkhyāyika-darśana**, n. N. of one of the 64 Kalās, L. **Nāṭakâvatāra**, m. N. of wk.

1. **Nāṭakī**. See °*ṭaka*, above.

2. **Nāṭakī**, ind. for °*ṭaka*; with √*kṛi*, to make into a play, Hariv.

Nāṭakīya, mfn. dramatic, Śiś. ii, 8; (*ā*), f. an actress or dancing girl, Bhar.; Daś.

Nāṭakeya, m. pl. N. of a people, MBh.

Nāṭayitavya, mfn. to be played (a drama), Ratnâv.; Bālar.

Nāṭāra, m. the son of an actress, L.

Nāṭikā, f. of °*ṭaka*, q. v.

Nāṭita, n. mimic representation, a gesture (in comp. also °*taka*), Kālid.; Ratnâv.; Bālar. &c.

Nāṭin, mfn. dancing; see *saṃdhyā-n°*.

Nāṭeya or **Nāṭera**, m. the son of an actress or a dancing girl, L. (cf. °*ṭāra*).

Nāṭya, n. dancing, mimic representation, dramatic art, Kāv.; Pur. &c. (°*ṭyena*, ind. with a gesture, Kālid. &c.); the costume of an actor, BhP. (cf. below). — **darpaṇa**, m. N. of wk. — **dhara**, mfn. wearing an actor's costume, BhP. i, 8, 19. — **dharmikā** or -**dharmī**, f. the ruler of dramatic representation, L. — **pradīpa**, m. N. of wk. — **priya**, mfn. fond of dancing (Śiva), L. — **rāsaka**, n. a kind of play consisting of one act, Sāh. — **lakshaṇa**, n., -**locana**, n. (and °*na-kāra*, m.) N. of wks. — **varga**, m. N. of ch. of the Nāma-liṅgânuśāsana by Amarasiṃha. — **veda**, m. the science of dancing or mimic representation, Caṇḍ.; Daśar. — **vedī**, f. stage, scene, Kathās. — **śālā**, f. dancing-room, GaruḍaP.; a theatre, W. — **śāstra**, n. = -*veda*, Mālav.; -*pravaktṛi*, m. the author of a work on dramatic art, L. — **śekhara**, m. N. of wk. **Nāṭyâgāra**, n. dancing-room, Bhar. **Nāṭyâcārya**, m. dancing-master, Mṛicch.; °*ryaka*, n. the office of a d°-m°, Pañc. **Nāṭyâlābu**, f. a kind of gourd, Gal. (v. l. *nāgâl°*). **Nāṭyôkti**, f. dramatic phraseology, Sāh. **Nāṭyôcita**, mfn. (song) fit for a dramatic representation, Dhūrtas.

नाड *nāḍa*, n. (fr. *naḍa*) = *nāla*, a hollow stalk, L.; (*ā*), f. N. of a partic. verse, Vait. — **pít**, m. or n. N. of a place, ŚBr.; (*ī*), f., see below.

Nāḍāyana, m. a more remote descendant of Naḍa, Pāṇ. iv, 1, 99; -*naka*, mfn. iv, 3, 80, Sch.

1. **Nāḍi**, m. the son of Naḍa, Pāṇ. iv, 1, 99, Kāś.

2. **Nāḍi**, f. any tube or pipe, (esp.) a tubular organ (as a vein or artery of the body), BhP. (cf. *nāḍī*). — **cīra**, n. a weaver's shuttle, L. — **ṃ-dhama**, mfn. swelling the veins, causing a quicker pulse, agitating, Kād.; Bālar.; terrifying, W.; m. a goldsmith, L. (cf. *pāñca-janya-nāḍiṃ-dh°*). — **ṃ-dhaya**, mfn. drinking or sucking through a tube, L. — **pattra**, n. Colocasia Antiquorum, L. — **maṇḍala**, n. the celestial equator, L.

Nāḍika, mfn. ifc., id., BhP.; (*ā*), f. a hollow stalk, Jyot.; any tubular organ (as a vein or artery of the body), KātyŚr., Sch.; a measure of time = ½ Muhūrta, Var.; Mālatīm. &c.; a measure of length = ½ Daṇḍa, MārkP.; v. l. for *nālikā*, Kām. v, 51; n. Ocimum Sanctum, Bhpr. °**kā-datta**, m. N. of an author, Cat. °**kā-vṛitta**, n. equinoctial circle, Gol.

Nāḍī́, f. (fr. *nāḍa*, nom. °*ḍīs*, RV. x, 135, 7) the tubular stalk of any plant or any tubular organ (as a vein or artery of the body); any pipe or tube, RV. &c. &c.; a flute, RV.; Kāṭh.; the box of a wheel, TS.; Kāṭh.; a fistulous sore, Suśr.; the pulse, W.; any hole or crevice, Kathās.; a sort of bent grass (= *gaṇḍa-dūrvā*), L.; a strap of leather, thong, L.; a measure of time = ½ Muhūrta, Var.; a juggling trick, deception, L. — **kalāpaka**, m. a species of plant, Bhpr. — **grantha**, m., -**cakra**, n. N. of wks. — **caraṇa**, m. 'stalk-legged,' a bird, L. — **jaṅgha**, m. 'id.,' a crow; N. of a fabulous crane, MBh.; of a Muni, L. (cf. *nāli-j°*). — **jñāna**, n.; -*dīpikā*, f. N. of wks. — **taraṃga**, m. a kind of poison (= *kākola*), L.; an astrologer, W.; a ravisher, debaucher (= *rata-hiṇḍaka*, cf. *nārī-t°*), W. — **tikta**, m. a species of Nimba, L. — **datta**, m. N. of an author, Cat. (cf. *nāḍikā-d°*). — **deha**, m. 'stalk-bodied,' N. of an attendant of Śiva (= *bhṛiṅgin*), L. (cf. -*vigraha*). — **nakshatra**, n. the planet of a person's nativity (= *janma-n°*), L.; -*mālā*, f. N. of wk. — **nidāna**, n. N. of wk. — **ṃ-dhama**, w. r. for *nāḍiṃ-dh°* (above). — **parīkshā**, f. feeling a vein or the pulse, Bhpr.; N. of wk.; °*kshâdi-cikitsā-kathana*, n. N. of wk. — **pātra**, n. a kind of water-clock, L. — **prakaraṇa**, n., -**prakāśa**, m. N. of wks. — **yantra**, n. any tubular instrument (in surgery), Suśr. — **valaya**, n. equinoctial circle, Gol. — **vigraha**, m. = -*deha*, L. — **vijñāna** or °**nīya**, n. N. of wk. — **vṛitta**, n. = -*valaya*, Gol.; Sch. — **vraṇa**, m. an ulcer, fistula, L. — **śāka**, m. a species of vegetable (= *nāḍīka*), Bhpr. — **śāstra**, n., -**śuddhi**, f., -**saṃkhyā**, f., -**saṃcāra**, m., -**saṃjñāna**, n., -**samuccaya**, m. N. of wks. — **sneha**, m. = -*deha*, L. — **sveda**, m. steam-bath through tubes, Car. — **hiṅgu**, n. the resin of Gardenia Gummifera, L.

Nāḍīka, mfn. ifc. = *nāḍī*, L.; m. Corchorus Olitorius and another pot-herb, Bh.; (*ā́*), f. the wind-pipe or throat, AV.

नाडिकेल *nāḍikela* or *nāḍīkela*, m. = *nārikela*, the cocoa-nut palm, L.

नाडीच *nāḍīca*, m. Colocasia Antiquorum, L. (cf. *nāḍikā-pattra*).

नाड्वलेय *nāḍvaleya*, m. metron. fr. *naḍvalā*, Hariv.

नाणक *nāṇaka*, n. a coin or anything stamped with an impression, Yājñ.; Mṛicch.; Hcat. — **parīkshā**, f. the testing of coin, assaying, W. — **parīkshin**, m. 'coin-tester,' assayer, ib.

नातङ्कोविल्स्थलमाहात्म्य *nātaṅkovilsthala-māhātmya*, n. N. of ch. of BhavP.

नातानतिक *nātānatika*, mfn. fr. *nata* + *anata*, Pat.

नातिकल्याण *nâti-kalyāṇa*, *nâti-kovida* &c. See 2. *nâ*.

नात्र *nātra*, prob. w.r. for *nāntra*, q.v.

नाथ *nāth*, cl. 1. Ā. (Dhātup. ii, 6) *nā́thate*, TS.; Kāṭh. &c. (°*ti*, MBh.; Kathās.; pf. *nanātha*; aor. *anāthīt*; fut. *nāthishyati* or *nāthitā*, Gr.; inf. *nāthitum*, Kathās.; ind. p. -*nāthya*, Prab.) to seek aid, approach with prayers or requests (loc.), TS.; Kāṭh.; to ask, solicit, beg for (gen. of thing, MBh. iii, 126, 30; cf. Pāṇ. ii, 3, 55; dat. of th°, Vop.; with 2 acc. Naish. iii, 25); to have power, be master, Dhātup.: Caus. *nāthayati*, to cause a person to ask for anything, i. e. to grant a request (acc.), BhP. (B.) ii, 9, 25. [Cf. √*nādh*; Goth. *ni-thān*, Old Sax. *ginātha*, *nātha*; HGerm. *genâde*, *gnade*.]

Nāthá, n. refuge, help, AV.; TBr.; m. a protector, patron, possessor, owner, lord (often ifc., esp. in names of gods and men, e. g. *govinda-*, *jagan-* &c.; but also mf[*ā*]n. possessed of, occupied by, furnished with, cf. *sa-*); a husband (esp. in voc.), MBh.; Kāv. &c.; a rope passed through the nose of a draft ox, L.; N. of sev. authors, Cat. — **kāma** (°*thá-*), mfn. seeking help, AV. — **kumāra**, m. N. of a poet, Cat. — **tva**, n. protectorship, patronage, R. — **malla**, m. N. of a man, Cat.; -*brahmacārin*, m. N. of an author, ib. — **vat**, mfn. having a protector or master, dependant, subject, R. (-*tā*, f. MBh.); (*ī*), f. having a husband, MBh.; R.; Var. &c. — **víd** or -**vindu**, mfn. (√3. *vid*) possessing or granting protection, AV.; TāṇḍBr. — **siṃha**, m. N. of an author, Cat. — **stuti**, f. N. of a poem (called also *ātma-mandira-stotra*), ib. — **hari**, mfn. carrying a master (as cattle), Pāṇ. iii, 2, 25. — **hāra**, mfn. id. (but not said of cattle), ib.; cf. iii, 2, 1. **Nāthânanda-muni**, m. N. of an author, Cat. **Nāth'oka** (?), m. N. of a poet, ib.

Nāthamāna, mfn. seeking help, suppliant, MBh. &c.

Nāthāya, °*yati*, w.r. for *nāthayati*; see √*nāth*, Caus.

Nāthitá, mfn. one who needs help, oppressed, suppliant, RV.; TS.; n. supplication, demand, request, BhP.

Nāthin, mfn. having a protector or master, Hariv.; R.

नाद *nādá*, m. (√*nad*) a loud sound, roaring, bellowing, crying, RV. &c. &c.; any sound or tone, Prāt.; R. &c. (= *śabda*, L.); (in the Yoga) the nasal sound represented by a semicircle and used as an abbreviation in mystical words, BhP.; a praiser (= *stotṛi*), Naigh. iii, 16. — **kārikā**, f. N. of wk. — **tā**, f. the quality of sounding, RPrāt. — **dīpaka**, m. or n. N. of wk. — **purāṇa**, n., -**bindûpanishad**, f. N. of wks. — **vat**, mfn. pronounced with sound (as letters), sonant, Kāś.

Nādi, mfn. sounding, roaring, PārGṛ.

Nādita, mfn. made to resound; ifc. sounding with, reverberant, MBh. &c.; n. sound, noise, ib.

Nādin, mfn. sounding, resonant, howling, roaring &c.; ifc. = prec., MBh.; Kāv. &c.; pronounced with sound, sonant, Śiksh.; m. N. of a Dānava, Hariv.; of a Brāhman changed into an antelope, ib.

नादर *nâdara*, 1. *nâdeya* &c. See 2. *ná.*

नादिक *nādika*, m. N. of a country, Buddh.

नादिग *nādiga*, m. N. of a man, Cat.

नादेय 2. *nādeyá*, mf(*ī*)n. (fr. *nadī*) coming from or belonging to a river, fluvial, aquatic, VS.; R.; Suśr.; m. Saccharum Spontaneum or Calamus Rotang, L.; (*ī*), f. N. of sev. plants (Tesbania Aegyptiaca, Premna Spinosa &c.), L.; n. rock-salt, Suśr.; antimony, L.

Nādyá, mfn. = prec. mfn., RV. ii, 35, 1 (?); TS.

नाध् *nādh*, cl. 1. Ā. (Dhātup. ii, 5) *nādhate*, occurring only in p. *nā́dhamana*, seeking help, asking, begging, RV. (cf. *nāth*).

Nā́dhas, n. (prob.) = *nātha*, help, refuge, RV. x, 65, 5.

Nādhitá, mfn. oppressed, needy, suppliant, RV. i, 118, 8; 182, 7.

नान *nāna*, m. N. of a man (also *-bhaṭṭa*), Cat.; (*ā*), f. coin (= *nāṇaka*), Hcat.

नानकचन्द्रोदय *nānaka-candrôdaya*, m. or n. N. of a poem by Deva-rāja.

नानद *nānada*, n. N. of a Sāman, Br. (w.r. *nānanda*).

नानर्दमान *nānardamāna*, mfn. (√*nard*, Intens.) sounding loudly, roaring lustily, Hariv.

नाना 1. *nā́nā*, ind. (Pāṇ. v. 2, 27; g. *svarâdi*) differently, variously, distinctly, separately, (often used as an adj. = various, different, distinct from [with instr., e.g. *viśvaṃ na nānā Śambhunā*, 'the Universe is not distinct from Ś°,' Vop.; rarely mfn., e.g. *nārīshu nānāsu*, Pañcar.] esp. in comp.; cf. below), RV. &c. &c.; = *vinā*, without (with instr., abl. or acc.), Pāṇ. ii, 3, 32. **-kanda**, m. a species of bulbous plant, L. **-karaṇa**, n. variation, Divyâv. **-karman**, mfn. one who has performed many sacrifices, Āpast. **-kāmá**, m. pl. many desires or wishes, ŚBr. **-°kāra** (°*nā́k°*), mfn. manifold, various, Var.; Rājat. **-kāram** (or *-kṛitya*, or *-kṛitvā*), ind. Pāṇ. iii, 4, 62; Kāś. **-kshetra-māhātmya**, n. N. of wk. **-gati**, m. 'moving in different ways,' the wind, Kir. **-gotra**, m. belonging to different families, MānGṛ. **-graha**, m. taking separately (used to explain *avagraha*), RPrāt. **-cetas** (*nā́nā-*), mfn. of different mind, ŚBr. **-jana**, m. pl. d° people or tribes, TāṇḍBr. **-jātīya**, mfn. belonging to d° kinds or classes, Pat. on Pāṇ. v, 2, 21. **-tanu**, mfn. one who has assumed d° bodies, BhP. **-tantra**, mfn. performed separately, ĀpŚr. **-°tma-** (°*nâtma*) different souls (in comp.); *-paksha*, m. the assertion that there are differences, KapS.; *-vādin*, m. one who so asserts, ib. **-°tyaya** (°*nât°*), mfn. various, manifold, ChUp. **-tva**, n. difference, variety, manifoldness, Br.; MBh. &c.; *-vāda-tattva*, n. N. of wk. **-dāna**, n. pl. 'various presents,' N. of ch. of PSarv. **-dig-deśa**, m. sg. the regions or countries of the different quarters; (*āt*), ind. from everywhere, Ratn.; Hit. **-dikshita**, m. N. of sev. authors, Cat. **-devata** (ĀpŚr., Sch.), **-devatya** (AitBr.), mfn. relating or addressed to different gods. **-deśa**, m. sg. d° regions or countries, MBh.; R.; °*śīya* (Hcar.) or °*śya* (MBh.), mfn. coming from d° c° (as princes). **-dharman** (*nā́nā-*), mfn. having d° customs, AV. **-dhātu** (in comp.), various minerals or gramm. roots; *-prakriyā*, f. N. of a gramm. wk.; *-śata*, n. a hundred v° m°, MW.; *-samākīrṇa*, mfn. filled with v° m°, ib. **-dhishṇya** (*nā́nā-*), mfn. having d° earth-mounds or side-altars, ŚBr. **-dhī** (*nā́nā-*), mfn. (pl.) having d° minds or views, RV. **-dhvani**, m. any musical instrument with more than one tone, L. **-°nargha-mahā-ratna-maya** (°*nân°*), mf(*ī*)n. consisting of d° precious jewels, Kathās. **-nāma-nirūpaṇa**, n. N. of ch. of GaṇP. **-pakshi-gaṇâkīrṇa**, mfn. filled with flocks of various birds, MW. **-pattrakā**, f. N. of a partic. personification, MānGṛ. **-pada**, n. a different or independent word, Prāt. (*-vat*, ind., ib.); °*dīya*, mfn. belonging to it, TPrāt. **-pāṭhaka**, m. N. of an author, Cat. **-prakāra**, mfn. various, manifold, R.; Suśr. **-prabhṛiti** (*nā́nā-*), mfn. beginning differently, ŚBr. **-prastāva** (*nā́nā-*), mfn. having a different prelude (as a Sāman), ib. **-phala-maya**, mf(*ī*)n. consisting of various fruits, Hcat. **-bīja**, n. pl. v° kinds of grain, ŚrS. **-buddhi-ruc**, mfn. one whose mind delights in v° things, MBh. **-brahma-sāma-tva**, n. manifoldness of the Brahma-sāman, Lāṭy. **-bhaṭṭa**, m. N. of an author (= *nāna-bh°*), MW. **-bhāva**, mf(*ā*)n. various, manifold, Vajracch. **-bhūta**, mfn. id.; TPrāt., Sch. **-manas** (*nā́nā-*), mfn. of v° minds, TS. **-mantrâugha-siddhi-mat**, mfn. having plenty of v° magic formulas, Kathās. **-mṛiga-gaṇa**, m. pl. flocks of v° animals, MW. **-°yudha-lakshaṇa** (°*nây°*), n. N. of wk. **-yoga**, m. manifoldness, Kap. **-ratnâkara-vat**, mfn. having a mine of various jewels, Var. **-rathám**, ind. in v° or separate chariots, RV. **-rasa**, mfn. containing v° passions or emotions (as a drama), Mālav. **-°rūpa**, n. pl. v° forms or shapes, R.; (*nā́nā-*), mfn. multiform, manifold, AV.; Br.; Mn. &c. (°*pá-tā*, f. ŚBr.); *-samutthāna*, mfn. following v° occupations, R. **-°rtha** (°*nâr°*), mfn. having a different aim or object, KaṭhUp.; containing some other sense (as a new sentence), VPrāt.; having d° meanings (as a word of d° m°), Gi.; L.; *-kośa*, m. *-dhvani-mañjarī*, f., *-mañjarī*, f., *-ratna-tilaka*, m. or n., *-ratna-mālā*, f., *-śabda-kośa*, m., *-śabda-ratna*, n., *-śabdânuśāsana*, n., *-saṃgraha*, m. N. of dictionaries; *-saṃdigdhârtha-vicāra*, m. N. of a Nyāya wk. **-liṅga**, mfn. different, various; *-tva*, n., TĀr. **-varṇa**, m. pl. v° colours, R.; mf(*ā*)n. many-coloured, variegated, Var.; Suśr.; Hcat.; *-tva*, n., MBh.; °*nâkṛiti*, mfn. pl. of different colours or shapes, Bhag. **-vāda-saṃgraha-grantha**, m. N. of wk. **-vidha**, mfn. of various sorts, multiform, manifold, Mn.; MBh. &c.; *-śānti*, f. N. of wk. **-vishyá**, mfn. consisting of more than one village or tribe, MaitrS. **-vīrya** (*nā́nā-*), mf(*ā*)n. having different powers or effects (as herbs), AV.; Br.; *-tā*, f. TāṇḍBr. **-vṛikshīya**, mfn. coming from d° trees, ĀpŚr. **-vṛitta-maya**, mf(*ī*)n. composed in d° metres, Sāh. **-veshâkṛiti-mat**, mfn. of d° garb and shape, MBh. **-vrata** (*nā́nā-*), mfn. having d° customs or observances, TS. **-śāstra** (in comp.) d° sciences or scientific works; °*strârtha-nirṇaya*, m. N. of wk.; °*strīya*, mfn. taken from d° wks., Hcat. **-saṃvāsika**, mfn. living in d° places, belonging to d° communities, Buddh. **-samutthāna**, mfn. of d° duration, TĀr. **-sāma-vat**, ind. like d° Sāmans, Lāṭy. **-sūrya**, m. pl. d° suns, TĀr. (*-tva*, n. ib.); (*nā́nā-*), mf(*ā*)n. illuminated by d° suns, RV. **-strī**, f. pl. women belonging to d° castes, Mn. **Nā́nôlba**, mfn. pl. having more than one membrane or cover, ŚBr. **Nānâushadha** (in comp.), various herbs or drugs; *-pariccheda* and *-vidhi*, m. N. of wks.

Nānānám, ind. differently, in various ways, RV.

नानान्द्र *nānāndra*, m. (fr. *nanāndṛi*) a husband's sister's son, g. *bidâdi*. °**drāyaṇa**, m. patron. fr. *nānāndra*, g. *haritâdi*.

नानू *nānū*, m. N. of a man, Cat.

नान्त्र *nāntra*, n. (√*nam*) praise, eulogy, Uṇ. iv, 159, Sch.; wonder, L.; m. a sage, L.; N. of Śiva, L.

नान्द *nānda*, mf(*ī*)n. relating to Nanda (*upapurāṇa*), Madhus.

Nāndaná, n. (√*nand* or *nandana*) a pleasure-garden, paradise, SV.; AitUp.

Nāndi for °*ndī* in comp. **-kara**, m. = °*dī-k°*, L. **-datta**, m. N. of an author, Cat. (cf. Pāṇ. vi, 3, 63, Kāś.)

Nāndika, n. = °*ndī-śrāddha*, Saṃskārak.

Nāndin, m. = °*ndī-kara*, L.

Nāndī, f. (√*nand*) joy, satisfaction, pleasure, RV.; MBh.; eulogium or praise of a deity, (esp.) a kind of blessing pronounced as a prologue to a drama, Mṛicch.; Kālid.; Sāh.; Pratāp. &c.; (in music) a partic. measure; = *dvādaśa-tūrya-nirghosha*, L. **-kara**, m. (in dram.) the speaker of the prologue; a proper N., Kāś. on Pāṇ. vi, 3, 63. **-ghosha**, m. a proper N., ib. **-nāda** (Mudr.) and **-ninâda** (Kathās.), m. shout of joy. **-paṭa**, m. the lid or cover of a well, L. **-pura**, n. N. of an eastern town, Pāṇ. v, 4, 74, Kāś.; °*raka*, mfn. iv, 2, 122, Kāś.; **-bhājana**, n. a partic. water-vessel, Uttamac. **-mukha**, mf(*ī*)n. having a cheerful face, Siṃhâs.; (°*khī rātri*, f. end of night, daybreak, Lalit.); m. pl. (with or scil. *pitaras*; also °*khāḥ pitṛi-gaṇāḥ*) a class of deceased ancestors to whom a partic. Śrāddha, is offered (according to some the 3 ancestors preceding the great-grandfather), GṛS.; Yājñ.; Pur. &c.; = *nāndī-paṭa*, L.; (*ī*), f. a female ancestor sharing in the N° Śrāddha, W.; a kind of grain, Suśr.; N. of a metre, Col.; n. (Hcat.) = *-śrāddha*, n. a Śrāddha offered to a class of deceased ancestors (cf. above), Cat.; °*dha-nirūpaṇa*, n., °*dha-paddhati*, f., °*dha-prayoga*, m. N. of wks. **-rava**, m. shout of joy, MBh. **-viśāla**, m. a proper N., Pāṇ. vi, 3, 63, Kāś. **-śrāddha**, n. = *nāndī-mukha-śr°*, Cat.

Nāndīka, m. a post in a door-way set up for good luck, W.

Nānduka, m. N. of a man, Pañc.

नान्यदेव *nānya-deva*, m. N. of a poet, Cat.

नापि *nâpi*. See under 2. *ná*.

नापित *nāpitá*, m. (Uṇ. iii, 87 *nāp°*; √*snā?*) a barber, a shaver, ŚBr.; ŚrGṛS.; Mn. &c.; RTL. 374, 459; (*ī*), f. the wife of a barber. (Cf. *vaptṛi*.) **-gṛiha**, n. a barber's shop, L. **-bhāṇḍa**, n. shaving tackle, L. **-vāstu**, n. a b°'s dwelling; °*stuka*, mf(*ī*)n. Pāṇ. iv, 2, 104, Vārtt. **-śālā** and °*likā*, f. a b°'s shop, L.

Nāpitāyani, m. the son or offspring of a barber, Pāṇ. iv, 1, 158.

Nāpitya, m. id., Pāṇ. iv, 1, 152, Kāś.; n. the trade or business of a barber, W.

नाभ् *nā́bh*, f. (√1. *nabh*) an opening, fissure, spring, RV. ix, 74, 6.

Nābha, ifc. (mfn.) = *nābhi*, nave, navel, central point (cf. *abja-nābha*, *vajra-n°*, *su-n°* &c.); m. N. of Śiva, MBh.; of a son of Śruta and father of Sindhu-dvīpa, BhP.

Nā́bhā, loc. of *nābhi* (for *-bhan*). **-nédishṭha** (*nā́°*), m. N. of a son of Manu Vaivasvata and author of RV. x, 61; 62, TS.; Br.; mfn. (also °*shṭhīya*) relating to or composed by N°, Br.

Nā́bhi, f. (prob. fr. √1. *nabh*, 'to burst asunder or into a hole'; ifc. f. *i* or *ī*, Vām. v, 49) the navel (also n°-string, cf. *-kṛintana*), a navel-like cavity, RV. &c. &c. (in later language also m. and °*bhī*, f.); the nave of a wheel, ib. (also m., L., and °*bhī*, f.); centre, central point, p° of junction or of departure, home, origin, esp. common o°, affinity, relationship; a near relation or friend, ib. (m., L.); musk (= *mṛiga-n°*), L.; m. or f. musk-deer, Megh. 53 (?); BhP.; m. a chief (= central point) of (gen.), Ragh. xviii, 19 (cf. *maṇḍala-nābhi-tā*); a sovereign or lord paramount (= *mukhya-rāj*), L.; a Kshatriya, L.; N. of a grandson of Priya-vrata (son of Agnidhra and father of Ṛishabha), Pur.; of the father of Ṛishabha (first Arhat of the present Avasarpiṇi), L. [Cf. Angl. Sax. *nafu*, *nafela*; Germ. *naba*, *Nabe*, *nabolo*, *Nabel*; Eng. *nave*, *navel*.] **-kaṇṭaka**, m., **-kūpikā**, f. a protruding or ruptured navel, L. **-kṛintana**, n. the cutting of the n°-string, Gobh. **-gandha**, m. the odour of musk or of the m°-deer, Megh. 53. **-guḍaka**, m. = *-kaṇṭaka*, L. **-gupta**, m. N. of a son of Hiraṇya-retas and of a Varsha in Kuśa-dvīpa ruled by him, BhP. **-golaka**, m. = *-kaṇṭaka*, L. **-cakra**, n. (magical) navel-circle, Cat. **-cchedana**, n. = *-kṛintana*, W. **-ja**, m. 'navel-born,' = next, L.; n°-dirt, Gal. **-janman**, 'id.,' N. of Brahmā (said to have first appeared on the lotus sprung from the n° of Vishṇu), L. **-2. -jāta**, mfn. (for 1. see 2. *ná*), sprung from a navel, Vcar. (v. l.) **-tva**, n. the state or condition of being a n°, AitBr. **-daghná**, mf(*ā*)n. reaching up to the n°, ŚBr.; Yājñ.; *-pāda*, mf(*ā*)n. (a chair) with legs so high, ĀpŚr. **-nāḍī**, f. the navel string, L. (cf. *garba-n°*). **-nāla**, n. or °**lā**, f. id. (only mf[*ā*]n. ifc.), Ragh. v, 7. **-bhū**, m. = *-janman*, Siṃhâs. **-mātra**, mf(*ī*)n. = *-daghna*, L. **-mūla**, n. the part of the body immediately under the n°, Var. **-vardhana**, n. (√*vardh*) = *-kṛintana*, Mn. ii. 29; (√*vṛidh*) umbilical hernia, L.; corpulency, L. **-varsha**, m. n. the Varsha governed by Nābhi (son of Agnidhra), Pur. **Nābhy-āvarta**, m. the cavity of the navel, W.

Nābhika, ifc. (mfn.) = *nābhi*, navel, Hcat.; nave of a wheel, MBh.; (*ā*), f. a navel-like cavity, ŚBr.; Achyranthes Atropurpurea, L. **-pura**, n. N. of a town of the Uttara-kurus, BrahmaP.

Nābhila, mfn. g. *sidhmâdi*, Uṇ. iv, 125, Sch.

Nābhīla, n. (only L.) the groin of a woman; a prominent or ruptured navel; the cavity of the n°; pain, distress.

Nābheya, m. patr. of Ṛishabha (first Arhat of the Jainas), Śatr.

Nābhya, mfn. sprung from or being in the navel, umbilical, BhP.; m. N. of Śiva (with *nābha*), MBh.; n. a kind of sacrifice, MānGṛ.

नाभक *nābhaka*, m. Terminalia Chebula, L.

नाभस *nābhasa*, mf(*ī*)n. (fr. *nabhas*) celestial, heavenly, appearing in the sky, Var.; (with *yoga*) N. of certain constellations, ib. (according to Bhaṭṭôtpala 2, divided into 4 classes, viz. 3 Āśraya-, 2 Dala-, 20 Ākṛiti- and 7 Saṃkhyā-yogas). **-yogâdhyāya**, m. N. of 12th ch. of VarBṛS. and 10th ch. of Laghuj.

नाभाक *nābhāka*, mf(*ī*)n. belonging to or composed by Nabhāka, AitBr.; (°*ká*), m. (= *nabhāka*) N. of a Ṛishi of the Kaṇva family, RV. viii, 41, 2; patron. fr. *nabh*°, g. *śivâdi*.

नाभाग *nābhāga*, m. (cf. *nabha-ga*, *nabhāga*) N. of a son of Manu Vaivasvata, MBh.; Hariv.; Pur.; patron. of Ambarīsha, MBh.; N. of a son of Manu and father of Ambarīsha, Hariv.; of a s° of Nabhāga and f° of A°, Pur.; of a s° of Śruta and f° of A°, Hariv.; of a s° of Nedishṭha or Arishṭa or Dishṭa and f° of Bhalandana, Pur.; of a s° of Yayāti (grandson of Ambarīsha) and f° of Aja, R.; of a grandson of Amb° and f° of Aja, ib. **-dishṭa** and **-nedishṭha**, w. r. for *nābhā-nédishṭha* (above). **Nābhāgârishṭa**, m. N. of a son of Manu Vaivasvata, MBh.; Hariv.; VP.

Nābhāgi, m. patron. of Ambarīsha, MBh.; Hariv.

नाभिजात *nābhijāta*, *nābhimāna* &c. See under 2. *ná*.

नाम 1. *nā́ma*, ind. (acc. of *nā́man*) by name i. e. named, called, RV. &c. &c. (also with *nāmatas* and *nāmnā*); indeed, certainly, really, of course, ib.; quasi, only in appearance, Jātak.; however, nevertheless, ib.; after an interr. = then, pray, e.g. *kiṃ n*°, *kathaṃ n*°, *kadā n*°, what then? pray, what? &c., MBh.; Kāv. &c.; after an Impv. = may it be so, no matter, e.g. Śak. v, 8; *api n*° at the beginning of a sentence = perhaps, I dare say, e.g. *apy esha nāma phalam icchati*, this man wants perhaps a reward, Mṛicch. viii, 25; with Pot. often = would that, e.g. *api nāmâivaṃ syāt*, would that it were so, Vikr. v, $\frac{1}{2}\frac{8}{0}$; opp. to *mā n*° with Pot. would that not, I should think not, e.g. *mā nāma akāryam kuryāt*, I hope he will not do something wrong, Mṛicch. iii, 26.

2. **Nāma**, in comp. for *nāman*, q. v. (sometimes ifc. as in *satya-*, q.v.) **-karaṇa**, m. a nominal suffix, Nir.; n. the calling of a person (gen.) by the name of (*nāmnā*), Sarvad.; the ceremony of naming a child after birth, Kauś. &c.; RTL. 370; (°*raṇam* √*kṛi*, to perform this c°), BhP.; *-prayoga*, m. N. of wk. **-karman**, n. name-giving (cf. prec.), R. **-kīrtana**, n. mentioning the name of (gen.), Yājñ., Sch.; (esp.) incessant repetition of the name of a god, RTL. 141; *-māhātmya*, n. N. of wk. **-kaumudī**, f. N. of wk. **-kaustubha**, m. or n. N. of a Stotra. **-gṛihya**, ind. while mentioning the name, ĀpŚr. **-gotra**, n. du. personal and family name, Gaut.; Kauś. **-graha**, m. mentioning a name, naming, Amar. **-grahaṇa**, n. (ŚrS.; Mn.; Kāv. &c.), **-grāhá**, m. (AV.; Lāṭy.), id. **-grā́ham**, ind. = *-gṛihya*, ŚBr.; Kauś. **-candrikā**, f., **-caraṇa-bhāshya**, n., **-caraṇa-vārttika**, n., **-cintā-maṇi**, m. N. of wks. **-caura**, m. the stealer of (i. e. assumer of) another person's name, L. **-jāti-graha**, m. (Mn.); **-jāti-grahaṇa**, n. (Kull.) mentioning the name and race. **-tīrtha**, m. N. of an author, Cat. **-deva**, m. N. of a man, L. **-dvādaśī**, f. a ceremony consisting in worshipping Durgā under one of her 12 appellations (Gaurī, Kālī, Umā, Bhadrā, Durgā, Kānti, Sarasvatī, Maṅgalā, Vaishṇavī, Lakshmī, Śivā, Nārāyaṇī), W. **-dhá** or **-dhā́**, m. name-giver, RV.; AV. **-dhātu**, m. a verbal base derived from a noun, Pāṇ. **-dhāraka**, mfn. bearing only the name of (nom.), Pañc. ii, 91. **-dhārin**, mfn. bearing the name of, being called (ifc.), Kathās.; = prec., Gobh. **-dhéya**, n. a name, title, appellation (often ifc.; cf. *kim-n*°, *puṃ-n*° &c.), RV. &c. &c.; the ceremony of giving a name to a child, Mn. ii, 123 (also *-karaṇa*, n. Gobh.); *-tas*, ind. by name, MW.; *-pāda-kaustubha*, m. or n. N. of wk. **-nāmika**, m. N. of Vishṇu, MBh. **-nighaṇṭu**, m., **-nidhāna**, n. N. of glossaries. **-niyata-praveśa**, m. N. of a Samādhi, L. **-nirdeśa**, m. pointing out by name, MW. **-nau**, f. a ship only by n° (not real), BhP. **-paṭhana-stotra**, n. N. of a Stotra. **-pada**, n. name, BhP. **-pārāyaṇa**, n., **-prapañca**, m. N. of glossaries. **-pūrva**, mfn. having a noun as first element, ĀpGṛ. **-bibhratín**, mfn. bearing only the name, AV. **-mātra**, mfn. = having only the name of (nom.), Pañc. i, 87; n. the mere n°, Śak.; Pañc.; (*eṇa*) ind. nominally, merely, MW.; °*trâvaśeshita*, mfn. having only the n° left i. e. dead, R. **-mātrikā-nighaṇṭu**, m. N. of a vocabulary. **-mālā**, f. N. of sev. glossaries (also *-kośa*, m. and °*likā*, f.); *-saṃgraha*, m. N. of a Stotra. **-māhātmya**, n. N. of wk. **-mudrā**, f. a seal-ring with a name (engraved on it), Śak. **-yajña**, m. a sacrifice only in n°, Bhag. **-yāthārthya-nirṇaya**, m. N. of wk. **-ratna-vivaraṇa**, n., **-ratnâkara**, m., **-ratnâvalī**, f. N. of wks. **-rasāyana** and **-rasôdaya**, m. or n. N. of Stotras. **-rūpá**, n. du. name and form, Br.; Up. &c. (°*pâtmaka*, mfn.); = individual being, MWB. 102. **-liṅga**, n. the gender of nouns or a wk. treating thereof, L.; °*gâkhyā-komudī*(!), f., °*gânuśāsana*, n. N. of wks. **-vat**, mfn. having a name, ĀpŚr., Sch. **-varjita** or **-vivarjita**, mfn. nameless, stupid, L. **-vācaka**, mf(*ikā*)n. expressing a name; (gram.) a proper n°, MW. **-vidhi**, m. N. of ch. of ŚivaP. **-vismṛiti**, f. forgetting the name (of any one), MW. **-vyūha**, m. N. of a Samādhi, L. **-śuṇḍī**, f. a kind of gourd, L. **-śesha**, mfn. having only the name left i. e. dead, Uttarar.; m. death, W. **-saṃkīrtana**, n. the glorification or incessant repetition of the name of a god, RTL. 105; N. of ch. of ŚivaP. **-saṃgraha**, m. collection of nouns; *-nighaṇṭu*, m., *-mālā*, f. N. of vocabularies. **-sārôddhara**, m. N. of a glossary of nouns. **-siddhânta**, m., **-sūtra**, n. pl. N. of a philos. and of a gramm. wk. **Nāmâkshara**, n. pl. the syllables forming a name, n°-writing, Vikr. **Nāmâkhyātika**, mfn. relating to nouns and verbs, Pāṇ. iv, 3, 71, Vārtt. **Nāmâṅka**, mfn. marked with a name, Ragh. (also °*ṅkita*, Vikr.); *-śobhita*, mfn. adorned with the mark of the n° or with n° and cipher, MW. **Nāmâdeśam**, ind. by announcing one's n°, ĀpGṛ. **Nāmânuśāsana**, n. N. of a dictionary of nouns. **Nāmâparādha-nirasana-stotra**, n. N. of a Stotra. **Nāmâvalī**, f. N. of a dictionary. **Nāmâhuti-vidhi**, m. N. of wk.

1. **Nāmaka**, mf(*ikā*)n. ifc. = *nāman*, name, Hariv.; Kāv. &c. (cf. *aṅghri-*, *kṛita-* &c.)

Nāmatas, ind. = abl. of *nāman*, BhP. v, 12, 8; by name, namely (often with 1. *nāma*), Mn.; MBh.; Kāv. &c.; with √*kṛi*, to give a person (acc.) a n°, call by the n° of (acc.), MBh.; with √*prach*, to inquire after the n° of (acc.), Śak. vii, $\frac{1}{2}\frac{2}{1}$.

Nāmáthā, ind. by name, AV.

Nā́man, n. (prob. neither fr. √*jñā* nor fr. √*mnā* [cf. Uṇ. iv, 150]; ifc. f. either = m. or °*mnī*) a characteristic mark or sign, form, nature, kind, manner, RV.; VS.; AV.; name, appellation, RV. &c. &c.; personal name (as opp. to *gotra*, family n°; cf. *nāma-gotra* above), Kāś. on Pāṇ. viii, 2, 23 (often ifc. = named, called, e.g. *Vishṇu-śarma-nāmā paṇḍitaḥ*, a sage named V°); merely the n° (as opp. to reality; cf. *nāma-dhāraka*, *-mātra*, *-śesha* &c.), a noun (as opp. to a verb), Nir.; Prāt.; substance, essence (in the Mīmāṅsā phil. opp. to *guṇa*, accidental quality); a good or great name, renown, fame (only ifc.; cf. *śva-*, *sumántu-*); water, Naigh. i, 11; *nā́mnā*, ind. by name (also joined with 1. *nāma*); with √*kṛi* (Kāv.) or *vi-dhā* (Kathās.) to call by a name; *nāma* (q. v.) with √*grabh* (*grah*) to mention or address by n°, RV. &c. &c.; with √*bhṛi*, to bear or have a n°, ib.; with √*kṛi* (Br., Mn. &c.), √*dā* or *dhā* (GṛS), to give a n°, call. [Cf. Zd. *nāman*; Gk. ὄ-νομα; Lat. *nōmen*; Goth. *namō*; Germ. *namo* &c.; Eng. *name*.]

1. **Nāmika**, mfn. relating to a name or to a noun, Pāṇ. iv, 3, 72.

1. **Nāmin**, mfn. having a name, RāmatUp.

नामतिक *nāmatika*, mf(*ī*)n. (fr. 2. *namata*) dressed in woollen cloth, L.

नामि *nāmi*, m. N. of Vishṇu, L.

नामित *nāmita*, mfn. (√*nam*, Caus.) bent, bowed, R.; Mṛicch.

2. **Nāmin**, mfn. bending, (esp.) changing a dental to a cerebral (said of all vowels except *a* and *ā*), Prāt.

Nāmya, mfn. to be bent (as a bow), bendable, pliant, MBh. &c.

नाम्ब *nāmbá*, m. a species of grain, MaitrS.; ŚBr. (*āmbá*, TS.; Kāṭh.); mf(*ī*)n. consisting of Nāmba, KātyŚr.

नाम्र *nāmra*, v.l. for *namra*, ĀśvŚr.

नाय *nāyá*, m. (√*nī*) a leader, guide, RV. vi, 24, 10; 46, 11 (pr. N., Sāy.; cf. *aśva-*, *go-*); guidance, direction, L.; policy, means, expedient, Bhaṭṭ., Sch.

Nāyaka, m. a guide, leader, chief, lord, principal, MBh.; Kāv. &c. (with or scil. *sainyasya*, a general, commander; ifc. f. *akā*, cf. *a-nāyaka*); a husband, BhP.; (in dram.) the lover or hero; the central gem of a necklace (implying also 'a general,' cf. *nāyakāya* and *mahā-nāyaka*); a paradigm or example (in gram.); N. of Gautama Buddha, Buddh.; of a Brāhman, Rājat.; of an author (also *bhaṭṭa-n*°), Cat.; m. or n. a kind of musk, L. (cf. *nāyikā-cūrṇa*); (*ikā*), f., see *Nāyikā*; *-tva*, n. leadership, R. **-ratna**, n. N. of a Comm. **Nāyakâdhipa**, m. 'chief of leaders,' sovereign, king, L.

Nāyakāya, Nom. Ā. °*yate*, to play the part of a leader; to act the part of the central gem of a necklace, Śiś. ii, 92.

Nāyikā, f. (of °*yaka*, q. v.) a noble lady, Vet.; mistress, courtezan (cf. *nākâdhipa-*); the heroine in a drama, Sāh. &c.; an inferior form or Śakti of Durgā (of which there are 8, viz. Ugra-caṇḍā, Pra-caṇḍā, Caṇḍôgrā, Caṇḍa-nāyikā, Ati-caṇḍā, Cāmuṇḍā, Caṇḍā, and Caṇḍa-vatī; cf. *kula-n*°), Cat.; a class of female personifications representing illegitimate sexual love (they are called Balinī, Kāmêśvarī, Vimalā, Aruṇā, Medinī, Jayinī, Sarvêśvarī, Kaulêśī), RTL. 188; = next, L. **-cūrṇa**, n. a partic. medicament, Rasar. **-sādhana**, n. N. of wk.

Nāyin, mfn. guiding (cf. *ayuta-*).

नायन *nāyana*, mf(*ī*)n. (fr. *nayana*) relating to the eye, ocular, Nyāyas., Sch.

नार् *nār*, Vṛiddhi form of *nṛi* in comp. **-kalpi**, m. (patron.), **-kuṭa**, mf(*ī*)n., **-namana**, m. (patron.), **-patya**, mfn., fr. *nṛi-kalpa*, *-kuṭa*, *-namana*, *-pati*, Pat. **-mata**, m. patron. fr. *nṛi-mat*, Pāṇ. viii, 2, 9, Vārtt. **-mará**, m. (fr. *nṛi-m*°) N. of a demon, RV. ii, 13, 8. **-medha**, m. (fr. *nṛi-m*°) patr. of Śaka-pūta, RV. Anukr.; n. N. of a Sāman, TāṇḍBr. **-shadá**, m. (fr. *nṛi-shád*) patr. of Kaṇva, RV. i, 117, 8; N. of a demon, x, 61, 13.

नार *nārá*, mf(*ī*)n. (fr. *nara*) relating to or proceeding from men, human, mortal, Mn.; Kāv.; spiritual (?), W.; m. a man, TĀr. (v. l.); (pl.) water (also sg. n. and *ā*, f. L.), Mn. i, 10 (prob. invented to explain *nārāyaṇa*); = *Nārāyaṇa*, L.; a calf, L.; (*ī*), f., see *nārī*; n. a multitude of men, L.; dry ginger, L. **-kapāla**, n. a human skull; *-kuṇḍala-vat*, mfn. wearing h° skulls as an ornament for the ears, Prab. iv, 1. **-kīṭa**, m. a kind of worm, L.; one who disappoints expectations excited by himself, L. **-candra**, m. N. of an author (cf. *nara-c*°); *-paddhati*, f. N. of his wk. **-jīvana**, n. gold, L. **-haya**, n. (with *yuddha-*) a fight between man and horse, Hariv. (v. l. *nara-h*°). **Nārôpāyana** (?), m. N. of a man, Pravar.

Nārāyaṇá, m. (patr. fr. *nára*, q. v.) the son of the original Man (with whom he is generally associated, e.g. Mn. i, 10; he is identified with Brahmā, ib. 11; with Vishṇu or Kṛishṇa, TĀr.; MBh. &c.; the Apsaras Urvaśī is said to have sprung from his thigh, Hariv. 4601; elsewhere he is regarded as a Kāśyapa or Āṅgirasa, also as chief of the Sādhyas, and with Jainas as the 8th of the 9 black Vāsudevas); the Purusha-hymn (RV. x, 90, said to have been composed by N°), ŚBr.; ŚāṅkhŚr.; (as synonym of Vishṇu) N. of the 2nd month (reckoning from Mārgaśīrsha), Var.; a mystical N. of the letter *ā*, Up.; N. of a son of Ajā-mila, BhP.; of a son of Bhū-mitra or Bhūmi-mitra (a prince of the dynasty of the Kāṇvāyanas), Pur.; of a son of Nara-hari, Kshitîś.; of sev. men, authors and commentators (also with *ācārya*, *kavi*, *gārgya*, *cakra-cūḍāmaṇi*, *daiva-vid*, *dharmâdhikārin*, *paṇḍita*, *paṇḍita-dharmâdhikārin paṇḍitâcārya*, *parivrāj*, *bhaṭṭa* [cf. below, and *bhaṭṭa-n*°], *bhaṭṭâcārya*, *bhaṭṭâraḍa*, *bhāratī*, *bhishaj*, *muni*, *yati*, *yatîśvara*, *rāya*, *vandya*, *vādîśvara*, *vidyā-vinoda*, *vaishṇava-muni*, *śarman*, *sarasvatī*, *sarva-jña*, *sārvabhauma*); mf(*ī*)n. relating or belonging to Nārāyaṇa or Kṛishṇa, MBh. &c. (m. pl. the warriors of K°, iv, 147); n. (with *kshetra*) N. of the ground on the banks of the Ganges for a distance of 4 cubits from the water, L.; (with *cūrṇa*) a partic. medicinal powder, Bhpr.; (with *taila*) a medic. oil expressed from various plants, ib.; (ī), f., see s.v. **-kaṇṭha**, m. N. of an author, Sarvad. **-kalpa**, m., **-kavaca**, m. or n., **-gītā**, f. N. of wks. **-gupta** (?), m. N. of a prince, Inscr. **-cakravartin**, m. N. of a grammarian, °*ti-kośa*, m. N. of his wk. **-caritra-mālā**, f. N. of wk. **-cūrṇa**, see above. **-tattva-vāda**, m. N. of wk. **-tāra**, m. N. of an author, Col. **-tīrtha**, m. N. of an author (also °*ṇa-bhikshu* or °*ṇa-muni*), Cat.; of a sacred bathing-place, ŚivaP.; *-taraṃga*, m. N. of wk. **-taila**, see above. **-datta**, m. N. of a poet, Cat. **-dāsa**, m. N. of sev. authors (also *-kavirāja* or *-siddha*), Cat. **-dīkshita** and *-sūnu*, m. N. of authors, ib. **-deva**, m. the god Nārāyaṇa, L.; N. of sev. authors, Cat. **-dharma-sāra-saṃgraha**, m., **-nāma-vivaraṇa**, n., **-paddhati**, f., **-prabodhôtsava**, m. N. of wks. **-priya**, m. 'friend of Nārāyaṇa,' N. of Śiva, L.; yellow sandal-wood, L. **-bali**, m. 'oblation to N°,' a partic. funeral ceremony; N. of wk. (also *-prayoga*, m., *-vidhi*, m., *-samarthana*, n., *-svayam-prayojana-sañcikā*, f.) **-bhaṭṭi**, f., **-bhaṭṭīya**, n. N. of wks. **-mantrârtha**, m. N. of wk. **-maya**, mf(ī)n. consisting in Nārāyaṇa, representing him, Pur. **-miśra**, m. N. of an author; °*śrīya*, n. N. of a wk. **-rāja** and **-labdhi**, m. N. of authors. **-varṇana** and **-varman**, n., **-vārttika**, n., **-vilāsa**, m., **-vṛitti**, f., **-śabda-vādârtha** or **-śabdârtha**, m. N. of wks. **-śesha**, m. N. of an author (also *śesha-n°*), Cat. **-śrī-garbha**, m. N. of a Bodhi-sattva, Buddh. **-śruti**, f. (prob.) = °*ṇô-panishad*, Sarvad. **-saṃhitā**, f. N. of a Pauranic wk. **-saras**, n. N°'s lake, BhP.; °*ro-vara-māhātmya*, n. N. of wk. **-sāra-saṃgraha**, m., **-sūtra**, n. N. of wks. **-sūri**, m. N. of a man, Cat. **-stava-rāja**, m., **-stotra**, n., **-smṛiti**, f. N. of wks. **-svāmin**, m. N. of a poet. **-hṛidaya**, n. N. of a Stotra. **Nārāyaṇâtharvaṇaśīrshôpanishad**, f. N. of an Up. **Nārāyaṇâvalī**, f. N. of a wk. on partic. funeral ceremonies. **Nārāyaṇâśrama**, m. N°'s hermitage, BhP.; N. of sev. authors, Cat.; °*mīya*, n. N. of wk. **Nārāyaṇâshṭôttara-śata-stotra**, n. N. of a Stotra. **Nārāyaṇêndra**, m. N. of an author (also *-sarasvatī* and *-svāmin*), Cat. **Nārāyaṇôpanishad**, f. N. of an Up.; °*shaṭ-ṭīkā*, f., °*shaṭ-sāra*, m., °*shaḍ-artha-prakāśa*, m., °*shaḍ-dīpikā*, f. of Comms. on it.

Nārāyaṇāya, Nom. Ā. °*yate*, to be or act like Nārāyaṇa, Pañc.

Nārāyaṇi, m. N. of a son of Viśvā-mitra, Hariv.

Nārāyaṇī, f. (of °*ṇa*, q.v.) patr. of Indra-senā (the wife of Mudgala), MBh.; Hariv.; N. of Durgā, Hariv.; of Lakshmī, L.; of Gaṅgā and Gaṇḍakī, L. **-praśnâvalī**, f., **-vilāsa**, m. N. of wks.

Nārāyaṇīya, mfn. relating to Nārāyaṇa (also *-ka*, AgP.), treating of him, MBh.; n. N. of sev. wks. **-tantra**, n., **-bīja**, n., **-vyākhyā** (and *-bhakti-dīpikā*), f., and °**yôpanishad**, f. N. of wks.

Nāri, f. = *nārī* below. **-shṭhá**, m. du. 'the fire of digestion and the wind of breath,' TS.; *-homa*, m., Sch.

Nārika, mf(ī)n. watery, aqueous, L.; spiritual, L. (cf. *nārá*).

Nārī, f. (of °*rá*, q.v.) a woman, a wife (in older language also *nárī*), RV. &c. &c.; a female or any object regarded as feminine, VS.; TĀr.; sacrifice, Naigh.; N. of a daughter of Meru, BhP.; of 2 kinds of metre, Col. **-kavaca**, m. 'having women for armour,' N. of Mūlaka (king of the solar line and son of Aśvaka), Pur. **-kuñjara**, m. (?), Pañcad. **-taraṃgaka**, m. a libertine, catamite, L. (cf. *nāḍī-t°*). **-tīrtha**, n. pl. N. of 5 sacred bathing-places of women, MBh. **-dūshaṇa**, n. any woman's vice (6 usually reckoned, viz. drinking spirits, keeping bad company, quitting a husband, rambling abroad, sleeping and dwelling in a strange house), W. **-nātha**, mfn. having a woman for possessor or owner (as a house), Mṛicch. iv, 3. **-pattana**, n. N. of a town, Cat. **-parâyaṇa**, mfn. devoted to women, MW. **-pura**, n. gynæceum, MBh. **-prasaṅga**, m. addiction to women, W. **-maya**, mf(ī)n. consisting only or totally of women, Bhartṛ.; Kād. **-mukha**, m. pl. N. of a people to the south-east of Madhyadeśa, Var. **-yāna**, n. a woman's conveyance, a litter &c., Mn. iii, 12. **-ratna**, n. a jewel of w°, an excellent w°, MW. **-vākya**, n. the word of a wife, ib. **Nārîshṭā**, f. 'dear to women,' Arabian jasmine, L. **Nārī-shṭha**, mfn. devoted to w°, fond of them, ŚāṅkhŚr.

Nārīka, ifc. (mfn.) = *nārī*, woman, wife, R.; n. (in Sāṃkhya) one of the 9 kinds of Tushṭi.

Nārīya, Nom. Ā. °*yate*, to become a woman, Kpr.

Nāreya, m. (prob. fr. *nārī*) N. of a son of Bhaṅga-kāra, Hariv.

Nāryá, m. N. of a man, RV.; n. the being a man, Bhadrab.

नारक *nāraka*, mf(ī)n. (fr. *naraka*) relating to hell, hellish, infernal; (with *loká*), m. hell, AV. (also *nāraká*, m., VS.); m. inhabitant of hell, Pur.

Nārakika, mf(ī)n. hellish; m. an inhabitant of hell, L. °**kin**, mfn. hellish, being in or condemned to hell; m. = prec. m., L. °**kīya**, mfn. hellish, infernal; m. = prec. m., L.

नारङ्ग *nāraṅga*, m. the orange-tree (cf. *nāga-raṅga*), Suśr. &c. (also *ī*, f., ŚārṅgP.); the juice of the pepper plant, L.; a libertine, L.; a living being, L.; a twin, L.; n. a carrot, L. **-pattraka**, m. a yellow carrot, L.

नारद *nárada* or *nāradá*, m. N. of a Ṛishi (a Kāṇva or Kāśyapa, author of RV. viii, 13; ix, 104; 105, Anukr.; as a Devarshi often associated with Parvata and supposed to be a messenger between gods and men, MBh.; Hariv.; Kāv. &c.; among the 10 Prajā-patis as a son of Brahmā, Mn. i, 35; in later mythology he is a friend of Kṛishṇa and is regarded as inventor of the Vīṇā or lute; in ep. poetry he is called a Deva-gandharva or a Gandharva-rāja or simply Gandharva); of a son of Viśvā-mitra, MBh.; of one of the 24 mythic. Buddhas, MWB. 136; of sev. men, Lalit.; HPariś.; of sev. authors, Cat. (cf. below); of a mountain, BhP.; (*ā*), f. the root of sugar-cane, L.; mf(ī)n. relating to Nārada, composed by him, Cat. **-gītā**, f., **-tantra**, n., **-pañca-rātra**, n., **-parivrājakôpanishad**, f., **-purāṇa**, n., **-bindûpanishad**, f., **-vacana**, n., **-vilāsa-kāvya**, n., **-śataka**, n., **-śikshā**, f., **-saṃhitā**, f., **-stotra**, n., **-smṛiti**, f. N. of wks. **Nāradêśvara-tīrtha**, n. N. of a sacred bathing-place, Cat. **Nāradôpadeśa**, m. N. of ch. of the GaṇP. **Nāradôpanishad**, f. N. of an Up.; *-dīpikā*, f. of a Comm. on it. **Nāradôpapurāṇa**, n. N. of an Upapur.

Nāradin, m. N. of a son of Viśvā-mitra, MBh.

Nāradīya, mfn., relating to or composed by Nārada, Cat. (also °*yaka*, ib.); n. N. of sev. wks., Kād. **-krama**, m. N. of wk. **-mahā-sthāna**, n. N. of a place, Cat. **-sapta-sahasra**, n. N. of wk. **-purāṇa** and °**dīyôpapurāṇa**, n. N. of a Pur. and an Upapur.

नारद्वासव *nāradvāsava*, n. N. of a Sāman, ĀrshBr. (prob. for *-nārada-v°*).

नारसिंह *nārasiṇha*, mf(ī)n. (fr. *nara-siṇha*) relating or belonging to the man-lion (Vishṇu in his 4th Avatāra), MBh.; Hariv. &c.; m. the 16th Kalpa or period of the world (cf. s.v.), L.; = *nara-siṇha*, Vishṇu as m°-l°, TĀr.; BhP.; N. of a man, Inscr.; n. N. of a town, L. **-cūrṇa**, n. a partic. aphrodisiac, L. (cf. *nara-s°-c°*). **-tantra**, n. N. of a Tantra. **-purāṇa**, n. N. of a Pur. **-shaṭ-cakry-upanishad**, f. N. of an Up. **Nārasiṇhīya**, n. N. of a wk. on rhet. **Nārasiṇhôpanishad**, f., **Nārasiṇhôpapurāṇa**, n. N. of an Up. and an Upapur.

नाराच *nārāca*, m. (fr.?) an iron arrow, any a°, MBh.; Kāv. &c. (cf. *ardha-*); water-elephant (= *jalêbha*), L.; a bad or cloudy day (?), L.; (*ī*), f. a goldsmith's scales; n. a kind of metre, Col. (cf. *nar°*); a partic. medicament, Car. **-ghṛita** and **-cūrṇa**, n., and **-rasa**, m. N. of partic. medicaments (cf. above). **-dur-dina**, n. a shower (lit. bad weather i.e. storm) of arrows, Ragh.

Nārācaka, n. a kind of metre; (*ikā*), f. = °*cī*, L.; a kind of metre.

नारायण *nārāyaṇa*. See above.

नाराशंस *nārāśaṇsá*, mf(ī)n. (fr. *nárā-śáṇsa*) relating to the praise of a man or men, laudatory, eulogistic (as a hymn, tale &c.), TS.; Br.; Yājñ. &c.; relating or sacred to Agni Narā-ś° (applied to the Soma, RV.; to a Ṛic, TBr. &c.); m. N. of partic. Soma libations, VS.; TBr. &c.; m. pl. of a class of Pitṛis or Manes, ib.; (*ī*), f. N. of partic. verses or formulas, n. a tale or legend in honour of liberal men, L. **-paṅkti**, mfn. (sacrifice) performed with 5 Soma-libations called Nārāśaṇsas, AitBr. ii, 24, 3 (w. r. *nar° p°*).

नाराशर्य *nārāśarya*, m. N. of a man, Col. (v. l. *pār°*).

नारिकेर *nārikera*, m. the cocoa-nut tree, the cocoa-nut, Suśr. &c.

Nārikela, m. id., MBh. &c. (L. also °*li* or °*lī*, f.) **-kshāra**, m. a partic. medicament, L. **-dvīpa**, m. N. of an island, ib.

नारिङ्ग *nāriṅga*, m. (Car.), °*gī*, f. (ŚārṅgP.) the orange-tree. **-kanda**, m. a yellow carrot, L. (cf. *nāraṅga-pattraka*).

नारिष्ट *nārishṭa* and *nārishṭa-homa* (Nyāyam.) = *nāri-shṭha* and *-homa* (see under *nārī*).

नारी *nārī*, f. See above.

नारीकेल *nārīkela*, m. = *nārik°*; N. of an island, Kathās.; (*ī*), f. the cocoa-nut or a fermented liquor made from the milk of it, L.

नारीच *nārīca*, n. Corchorus Capsularis, L.

नारोजिपण्डित *nāroji-paṇḍita*, m. N. of an author, Cat.

नार्कल्पि *nār-kalpi*, °*kuṭa* &c. See *nār*, p. 536, col. 3.

नार्तिक *nārtika*, mf(ī)n. fr. *narta*, g. *chedâdi*.

नार्मद *nārmada*, mf(ī)n. belonging to the river Narma-dā (*pra-vāha*), Kathās.; m. metron. of a man, Hariv. 8019.

नार्मिणी *nármiṇī* (fr. *na* + *armin* [?] 'not in ruins'), N. of a town, RV. i, 149, 3.

नार्यङ्ग *nāryaṅga*, m. = *nāraṅga*, the orange-tree, L.

नाल *nāla*, mfn. (fr. *nala*, cf. *nāḍa*) consisting or made of reeds, BhP.; m. (g. *ardharcâdi*), f. (*ā* or *ī*, L.) and n. a hollow stalk, (esp.) of the lotus, MBh.; Kāv. &c.; any tube or tubular vessel or vein &c. of the body, ib.; m. or n. the navel-string, Gobh., Sch.; m. N. of a poet, Cat.; (*ā*), f. N. of a river, MBh.; VP. (v.l. *nīlā*); (*ī*), f. an instrument for perforating an elephant's ear, L.; the stalk of a pot-herb, L.; a piece of metal on which the hours are struck = *ghaṭī*, W.; a lotus-flower, L. (cf. *nālīka*); n. the urethra, Suśr.; a handle (only mf[*ā*]n. ifc.), MBh. vii, 75; a partic. ornament on a chariot, R. vi, 75, 28; yellow orpiment, L. **-vaṇśa**, m. = *nala*, a reed, L. **-veshṭana-śānti-prayoga**, m. N. of wk. **Nālâstra**, n. any tubular weapon (e.g. gun, cannon &c.), L.

Nālaka, ifc. (mfn.) a stalk, (esp.) a lotus-st° (cf. *cāru-n°*); (*ikā*), f. id., L.; N. of sev. plants (also *-pushpa*, n.), Suśr.; L.; an instrument for perforating an elephant's ears, L.; = *ghaṭī* (cf. *nāla*), Jātakam.; a period of 24 minutes, Rājat. iv, 570; hint, insinuation, enigmatical expression, Kām. v, 51.

Nālakinī, f. a multitude of lotus flowers, a lotus lake, L.

Nālāya, Nom. Ā. °*yate*, to represent the handle (of an axe); °*yita*, mfn. BhP.

Nālāyana, m., patr., also pl. Saṃskārak.

Nālī, f. = *nāḍī*, any tubular vessel or vein &c. of the body, L.; ifc. = °*likā*, a period of 24 minutes, Sāh. °**li-jaṅgha**, m. a crow, L. (cf. *nāḍī-j°*). °**li-jaṅgha**, m. N. of a man, Daś. °**li-vraṇa**, m. = *nāḍī-vr°*, L.

Nālika, mfn. (with *āsana*) a partic. manner of sitting, Cat.; ifc. a period of 24 minutes (cf. *shaṇ-n°*); m. a trader with (?), Pañcad.; a buffalo, L.; (*ā*), f., see under °*laka*; n. = *nālâstra*, L.; a lotus flower, L.; m. or n. myrrh, L.; a kind of wind instrument, L.

Nālinī, f. a mystic. N. of one nostril, BhP.

Nālīka, m. a kind of arrow or spear, MBh.; R. &c.; body, limb, L.; m. n. a lotus flower, L.; n. (ib.) = °**kinī**, f. a multitude of l° flowers, a l° lake, g. *pushkarâdi*.

Nālya, mfn. (fr. *nala*), g. *saṃkāśâdi*.

नालन्द *nālanda*, m. N. of a village near Rāja-gṛiha containing a celebrated Buddh. monastery, MWB. 169 &c.

Nālandara, m. N. of a Buddh. monastery, L.

नालागिरि *nālāgiri*, m. N. of an elephant connected with Gautama Buddha, MWB. 406.

नालिकेर *nālikera*, m. the cocoa-nut tree or the c°-nut, Var.; Suśr. (also °*kela* as v.l.); Kāv. (also °*kerī*, f., Bālar.); N. of a district to the south-east of Madhya-deśa, Var.

नालिता nālitā, f. Arum Colocasia, L.

नालीप nālīpa, m. Nauclea Cadamba (?), L.

नाव 1. nāvá, m. (√4. nu) a shout of joy or triumph, RV.

नाव 2. nāva=nau, a boat, a ship (in comp., cf. ardha-n°, dvi-n°; Pāṇ. v, 4, 99, 100); (á), f. id., RV. i, 97, 8. **-prabhráṅśana**, n. N. of a place, AV. **Nāvājá**, m. a boatman, sailor, ŚBr. **Nāvôpajīvana** and °**vin**, m. id., MBh.

Nāvika, mf(ī)n. belonging to a ship or boat, W.; m. a helmsman, pilot, sailor (ifc. f. ā), MBh.; R. &c.; n. N. of a Sāman. **-nāyaka** and **-pati**, m. 'sailor-chief,' the captain of a vessel, Daś.

Nāvin, m. a boatman, sailor, L.

1. **Nāvya**, Nom. P. °yati, to wish for a ship, L.

2. **Nāvyà**, mf(ā)n. navigable, accessible by a boat or ship, AV.; MBh. &c.; m. a shipman, sailor, ĀpGṛ.; (ā), f. a navigable river, RV.; ŚBr.; n. id., Kāś. on Pāṇ. ii, 3, 18.

नावन nāvana, n. (√5. nu; cf. 3. nava) a sternutatory, ŚārṅgS. °**nīya**, mfn. good as a st°, Car.

नावनीत nāvanīta, mf(ī)n. (fr. nava-nīta) coming from butter, Nyāyam.; mild as b°, MBh.

नावमिक nāvamika, mf(ī)n. (fr. navama) the ninth, R.

नावयज्ञिक nāvayajñika, mfn. (fr. nava-yajña), with kāla, m. the time of offering the first-fruits &c. of the harvest, Pāṇ. iv, 2, 35, Vārtt. 1.

नावर nāvara, m. N. of a family, Cat.

नावाकार nāv-ākāra, nāv-āroha, nāvy-udaka. See 2. nau.

नाव्य 3. nāvya, n. (fr. 1. náva) newness, novelty, L.

नाश 1. nāśa, m. (√1. naś) attainment (see dūṇ°).

नाश 2. nāśa, m. (√2. naś) the being lost, loss, disappearance, destruction, annihilation, ruin, death, Br.; Mn.; MBh. &c. (ifc. destroying, annihilating, cf. karma-nāśā, graha-nāśa, duḥ-svapna-n°); flight, desertion, W.; (arithm.) elimination, ib.; (ī), f. N. of a river near Benares, L. **-tas**, ind. =nāśāt, from death, MW. **-śata** (?), m. N. of a Buddh. patriarch.

Nāśaka, mf(ikā)n. destroying, annihilating, removing (with gen. or comp.), MBh. &c. (cf. ku-n°, kṛita-n°); wasting, prodigal of (cf. artha-n°).

Nāśana, mf(ī)n. destroying &c. = prec. (with gen. or ifc.), VS.; MBh. &c.; n. destruction, removal; causing to be lost or perish, Āpast.; MBh.; R. &c.; forgetting (adhītasya), Yājñ. iii, 228. **-kara**, mf(ī)n. destroying (ifc.), Kāv. **Nāśanīya**, n. (scil. karman) expulsion from the order, Buddh.

Nāśayitṛi, mf(trī) n. destroying, remover, VS.

Nāśita, mfn. destroyed, ruined, lost, Yājñ.; banished, expulsed, an outcast (see next). **-saṃgraha**, m. intercourse with an outcast, Buddh.

Nāśin, mfn. perishing, perishable, Mn.; Prab. (cf. a-n°); ifc. destroying, removing, MBh.; Hariv. &c.

Nāśuka, mf(ā)n. disappearing, perishing, being lost, TS.

Nāśya, mfn. liable to be destroyed or removed or banished, Bhāshāp.; Kap. (-tva, n.)

Nāshṭika, mf(ī)n. (fr. nashṭa) relating to anything lost, W.; m. the (former) owner of any l° object, Mn. viii, 202.

Nāshṭrā́, f. danger, destruction, evil demon, AV.; VS.; ŚBr.

नाशिर nāśira, m. or n. a pressed Soma-stalk, Āryav.

नास 1. nās, cl. 1. Ā. nāsate, to sound, Dhātup. xvi, 24.

नास् 2. nā́s, the strong stem of 3. nás, q. v.

Nā́sā, f. the nose (either du., e. g. AV. v, 23, 3, or sg., Mn.; MBh. &c.; ifc. f. ā, MBh.; R. &c.); proboscis (cf. gaja-n°); =-dāru (below), L.; Gendarussa Vulgaris, L. (cf. 3. nas and nāsikā). **-°gra** (°sâg°), n. the tip of the nose, Gaut.; Suśr. **-chidra**, n. a nostril, L. **-chinnī**, f. a species of bird with a divided beak, L. **-jvara**, m. a kind of disease of the nose (=nakra), L. **-dakshiṇâvarta**, m. wearing the nose-ring in the right nostril (marking women who have children or money), W. **-dāru**, n. a piece of wood projecting like a nose over a door, L. **-nāha**, m. obstruction of the n°, Suśr. **-°ntika** (°sânt°), mfn. (a stick) reaching to the n°, Mn. ii, 46 (cf. keśânt°). **-pariśosha**, m. heat and dryness of the n°, Suśr. **-parisrāva**, m. 'n°-flow,' running at the n°, ib. **-pāka**, m. a kind of inflammation of the n°, ib. (cf. ghrāṇa-p°). **-puṭa**, m. wing of the n°, nostril, ib.; Var.; Hcat.; -maryādā, f. septum of the nose, Suśr. **-pratīnāha**, m. =nāsā-nāha, Suśr. **-pramāṇa**, n. size of the n°, ib. **-bhaṅga**, m. falling in of the n°, ib. **-mūla**, n. the root of the n°, Cat. **-yoni**, m. a weak or passionless man who has no desire for cohabitation without smelling the genitals, Bhpr. **-rakta-pitta**, n. nose-bleeding, L. **-randhra**, n. 'n° aperture,' nostril, Śiś. v, 54, Sch. **-roga**, m. disease of the n°, Suśr. **-°rbuda** (°sârb°) and **-°rśas** (°sârś°), n. polypus of the n°, ib. **-vaṇśa**, m. the bridge of the n°, ib.; Pañc. **-°vabhaṅga** (°sâv°), m. =nāsā-bhaṅga, Suśr. **-vāmâvarta**, m. wearing the nose-ring in the left nostril (a mark of sorrow or childlessness), W. **-viroka**, m. 'nose-cavity,' nostril, Śiś. v, 54 (cf. -randhra). **-vivara**, n. id., BhP. **-vedha**, m. perforation of the nose (of cattle), Hemac. **-śosha**, m. dryness of the n°, W. **-saṃvedana**, m. Momordica Charantia, L. **-srāva**, m. =-parisrāva, Suśr. **Nasôttha**, n. snot, Gal.

Nāsālu, m. N. of a tree, L.

Nāsika, m. or n. N. of a place (cf. below and nāsikya); in some comp. =°sikā. **-kshetra-māhātmya**, n. N. of wk. **-tryambaka**, m. or n. (also nāsika alone) N. of a locality; -tīrtha, n. N. of a sacred bathing-place, Cat. **-m-dhama**, mfn. blowing through the nose, Pāṇ. iii, 2, 29; vi. 3, 66. **-m-dhaya**, mfn. drinking through the n°, ib. **-vat** (nā́s°), mfn. having a n°, nosed, TS.

Nā́sikā, f. a nostril; (older du.) the nose, RV. &c. &c. (ifc. f. ā or ī, Pāṇ. iv, 1, 55); the proboscis of an elephant, BhP.; =nāsā-dāru, L.; N. of Aśvinī (mother of the two Aśvins), L. **-°gra** (°kâg°), n. the point of the nose, Bhag. (-tas, ind.) **-chidra**, n. (MānŚr.), **-chinnī**, f. (L.), **-pāka** and **-puṭa**, m. (Suśr.) =nāsā-chidra &c. **-mala**, n. 'nose-dirt,' nose-mucus, snot, Śak., Sch. **-mūla**, n. =nāsā-m°, L. **-rajju**, f. a nose-string, Mṛicch. vi, ⁹⁄₁. **-srotas**, n. a nostril, Gobh. (w. r. -sr°).

Nāsikya, mf(ā)n. being in or coming from the nose, ChUp.; Vait.; uttered through the n°, nasal, Prāt.; Hcat.; m. any nasal sound, Śiksh.; a partic. n° s° related to the so-called Yamas, Prāt.; du. the two Aśvins (=nāsatyau), L.; pl. N. of a people in Dakshiṇā-patha, Var.; AVPariś.; n. the nose (also -ka), L.; N. of a town, Pāṇ. vi, 1, 63, Vārtt. 3.

Nāsya, n. the nose-cord (of a draught-ox &c.), Mn. viii, 291; (prob.) an errhine (in next). **-grāsam**, ind. putting into the mouth as if it were an e° (to be put into the nose), swallowing easily, Hariv. 15996.

नासत्य nā́satya, mfn. (prob. fr. √2. nas, Caus.) helpful, kind, friendly (mostly m. du. as N. of the Aśvins, RV.; later m. sg. N. of one of the A°s, the other being then called Dasra); relating or belonging to the A°s, MBh.; (ā), f. the constellation Aśvinī, L. (The derivations fr. na + asatya or fr. nāsā + tya or fr. nā + satya are very improbable.)

नासिर nāsira or nāsīra, n. the van of an army, Kād.; Hcar.; m. a champion who advances before the line, L.

नास्तिक nāstika &c. See under 2. ná.

नास्तितद nāstitada or nāstida, m. the mango tree.

नाह nāha, m. (√nah) binding, tying, L.; obstruction (cf. nāsā-n°); trap or snare for catching deer, L.

नाहल nāhala, m. a man of a barbarous or outcast tribe; pl. N. of a non-Āryan people (=mleccha), L.

नाहुष 1. nā́husha, mf(ī)n. (fr. náhus) neighbouring, kindred; m. neighbour, kinsman, RV.

2. **Nāhusha**, m. (fr. nahusha) patron. of Yayāti, MBh.; R. &c.; N. of a serpent-demon, VāyuP.

Nāhushi, m. patr. of Yayāti, L.

नाह्नाभाइ nāhnābhāï, m. N. of Rāma-kṛishṇa (son of Dāmodara), Cat.

नि 1. ní, ind. down, back, in, into, within (except AV. x, 8, 7 always prefixed either to verbs or to nouns; in the latter case it has also the meaning of negation or privation [cf. 'down-hearted' = 'heartless']; sometimes w. r. for nis); it may also express kshepa, dāna, upa-rama, ā-śraya, moksha &c., L. [Cf. Zd. ni; Gk. ἐ-νί; Slav. ni-zu; Germ. ni-dar, ni-der, nieder; Angl. Sax. ni-ther, Eng. ne-ther, be-neath.]

नि 2. ni (for nī), mfn. See ṛita-ní.

नि 3. ni, (in music) the 7th note (for nishadha).

निंस् niṇs, cl. 2. Ā. (Dhātup. xxiv, 15) niṇste, Bhaṭṭ. (niṇsate, niṇsata and p. niṇsāna, RV.; niṇsse, niṇssva, Kāś. on Pāṇ. viii, 3, 58; pf. niniṇse, aor. aniṇsishṭa, fut. niṇsishyate, niṇsitā, Gr.) to touch closely, kiss, salute. (Perhaps fr. ninaṇs, Des. of √nam, like lips fr. li-laps &c.; cf. √niksh.)

Niṇsin, mfn. touching, kissing (ifc.; cf. netra-).

निः niḥ, for nis (q. v.) before a sibilant and rarely before k, kh; p, ph. **-kshatra**, mf(ā)n. having no military caste, BhP. (°tre, ind. when there was no m° c°, ib.); -karaṇa, n. depriving of the m° c°, ib.; °triya, mfn. =°tra, mfn., Bālar. **-śaṅka**, mf(ā)n. free from fear or risk, not afraid of (comp.); careless, secure, Hariv.; Kāv. &c. (also °ṅkita, Pañc.); (am), ind. fearlessly, securely, easily, MBh.; R. &c.; m. (in music) a kind of measure or dance; (ā), f. absence of fear or hesitation; (ayā), ind. without f° or h°, ŚārṅgP.; -līla, m. (in music) a kind of dance; -supta, mfn. sleeping calmly, Śāntiś. **-śatru**, mfn. free from enemies, Kathās. **-śabda**, mf(ā)n. noiseless, silent, still, MBh.; R. &c.; m. or n. silence (°daṃ √kṛi, to make no noise), R.; (am), ind. noiselessly, MBh. (cf. ni-ś°); -niścala, mfn. (night) noiseless and motionless, Kathās.; -padam, ind. with soundless i. e. inaudible steps, R.; -saṃvṛitta, mfn. become noiseless, R.; -stimita, mfn. =-niścala, MBh.; -sravat, mfn. (tear) flowing noiselessly, Rājat. **-śama**, m. uneasiness, anxiety, L. **-śaraṇa**, mf(ā)n. defenceless, unprotected, Rājat. **-śarkara**, mfn. free from pebbles (as a bathing-place), R. **-śalāka**, mfn. free from grass &c., lonely, solitary, Mn. vii, 147. **-śalka** and °**kaka**, mfn. (fish) having no scales, L. **-śalya**, mfn. freed from an arrow or from thorns or from pain, MBh. &c. (v. l. vi-ś°); (am), ind. without pain, easily, willingly, Daś. **-śastra**, mfn. weaponless, unarmed, Rājat. **-śākha**, mfn. branchless; -tā, f. Kād.; °khī-√kṛi, to deprive of branches, ib. **-śukra**, mfn. without fire or energy, AitBr. viii, 23. **-śūka**, mfn. without a beard or awns (as corn), Bhpr.; merciless, cruel, Hcar.; Siṇhās.; m. beardless rice without any awn, L. **-śūnya**, mfn. quite empty, R. **-śṛiṅga**, mf(ā)n. hornless, Hcat. **-śesha**, mf(ā)n. without remainder, (either =) finished, passed away (kalpa), Hariv. (°shaṃ √kṛi, to destroy completely, MBh.); (or =) complete, whole, entire, all, MBh.; R. &c.; at beg. of comp. (= am or eṇa, ind.) totally, completely; -kṛit, mfn. eating one's meals without any remainder, Vishṇ.; -tas, ind. wholly, entirely, Rājat.; Suśr.; -tā, f. complete destruction, MBh.; Pañc.; -bhagna, mfn. totally broken, Hariv.; -mushita, mfn. totally robbed out, Kathās.; °shaṇa, mf(ā)n. =niḥ-śesha, MW.; °shaya, Nom. P. °yati, to destroy totally, Prab. ii, 33; °shita, mfn. having nothing left, totally consumed or finished or destroyed, R.; Pañc.; Rājat. **-śoka**, mfn. free from sorrow or care, Hariv.; Rājat. **-śodhya**, mfn. not to be cleansed or purified; clean, pure, L. **-śmaśru**, mfn. beardless, L. (w. r. ni-ś°). **-śrami** and **-śrayaṇī**, w. r. for ni-ś°. **-śrī**, w. r. for niḥ-svī. **-śrīka**, mfn. deprived of beauty, ugly, MBh.; unfortunate, inglorious, ib.; Pur.; -tā, f. misfortune, want of good luck, MW. **-śreṇī**, f. =ni-śreṇī, L.; the wild date tree, L.; °ṇikā, f. a ladder, Dharmaśarm.; a kind of grass, L.; °ṇi-pushpaka, m. a species of thorn-apple, L. **-śreyaṇī**, f. =ni-śrayaṇī, Gal. **-śreyasa**, mf(ī)n. 'having no better,' best, most excellent, MBh.; R. &c.; m. N. of Śiva, L.; n. the best i. e. ultimate bliss, final beatitude or knowledge that brings it, KaushUp.; Mn.; MBh. &c.; belief, faith, L.; apprehension, conception, L. -kara, mfn. conferring final happiness or emancipation, W. — **shaṅga**, w. r. for *-saṅga.* — **shaṃdhi**, g. *sushāmādi.* — **shāmam**, ind. at the wrong time, unseasonably, L. (cf. Pāṇ. viii, 3, 88). — **shyandana**, n. a trickling or flowing down, streaming, dropping, Sāy. (= *ni-syanda*, m.) — **saṃśaya**, mfn. undoubted, certain, MBh.; R. &c. (also °*yita*, Kād.); not doubtful, not doubting or suspecting, MBh.; Ragh.; (*am*), ind. undoubtedly, surely, MBh.; R. — **saṃskāra**, mfn. uneducated, ill-mannered; *-tā*, f., Kād. — **saṃkaksha**, mfn. not perplexed or confused, L. (w. r. *ni-s*°). — **saṃkalpa**, mfn. having no determination or will, Nyāyas. — **saṃkshobha**, mfn. unshaken, Jātakam. — **saṃkhya**, mfn. innumerable, numberless, Inscr. — **saṅga**, m. absence of attachment, entire concentration, BhP.; mfn. unobstructed, moving freely, MBh.; unconnected, separated, detached, Kap.; not attached or devoted, indifferent to (loc.), Prab.; Vedānt.; free from worldly attachment, unselfish, disinterested, MBh.; Hariv.&c.; (*am* or *ena*), ind. without interest, without reflection, at random, R. ii, 21, 12 (w. r. for *-śaṅkam*?); BhP. iv, 8, 31; m. N. of a man, Cat.; *-tā*, f., *-tva*, n. absence of attachment, unselfishness, indifference, Pur. &c. — **saciva**, mfn. without a minister or councillor, Subh. — **saṃcāra**, mfn. not moving about, not leaving one's home, Rājat.; m. not taking a walk, Mālatīm. — **saṃjña**, mfn. senseless, unconscious, MBh.; R. &c. — **sattva**, mfn. without existence, unsubstantial (*-tva*, n.), Vajracch.; unenergetic, weak, impotent, wretched, miserable (*-tā*, f.), MBh.; Kāv. &c.; deprived of living beings, Pañc.; insignificant, mean, low, W.; n. want of power or energy, insignificance; non-existence, W. — **satya**, mfn. untrue, false; *-tā*, f. falsehood, insincerity, Kām.; Hit. — **saṃtati**, mfn. destitute of offspring, childless, Rājat. — **saṃtāna**, mfn. id., MW. — **saṃdigdha**, mfn. not doubtful, certain; (*am*), ind., MBh. &c. — **saṃdeha**, mf(*ā*)n.; (*am*), ind. = prec., Kathās.; Kull. — **saṃdhi**, mfn. having no joints perceptible, well knit, compact, close, firm, Bālar. — **sapatna**, mf(*ā*)n. having no rival, not sharing the possession of anything with another, MBh.; R.; not claimed by another, belonging exclusively to one possessor, ib.; unrivalled, unparalleled (*-tā*, f.), Kād.; having no enemies, MW. — **samā**, f. 'matchless,' N. of a Surâṅganā, Siṅhâs. — **sampāta**, mfn. affording no passage, blocked up, Hariv.; m. thick darkness, midnight, L. — **sambandha**, mfn. without relatives, MW. — **sambādha**, mfn. not crowded, lonely, solitary; *-velā*, f. a time when there is no crowding in the streets, Daś. — **sambhrama**, mfn. not perplexed, unembarrassed (with infin.), Rājat. — **saraṇi**, mfn. pathless, impracticable, Hcar. — **sarpa**, mfn. free from snakes, Pañc. — **salila**, mfn. waterless, Rājat. — **saha**, mf(*ā*)n. not able to support or resist (comp.); powerless, weak (*-tā*, f., *-tva*, n.), Kāv.; Rājat.; Kathās. (comp. *-tara*, Śiś.); intolerable, irresistible, W. — **sahāya**, mfn. without helpers, unassisted, Mālatīm. — **sâdhāra**, mfn. supportless; (*am*), ind. Śiś. xviii, 46. — **sâdhvasa**, mf(*ā*)n. fearless, bold, Hariv.; Kāv.; (*am*), ind. fearlessly, boldly, Rājat.; *-tā*, f. (Jātakam.), *-tva*, n. (R.) fearlessness, boldness. — **sāmarthya**, mfn. unfit, unsuitable, MBh. — **sāmānya**, mfn. extraordinary, uncommon, Rājat. — **sāra**, mf(*ā*)n. sapless, pithless, worthless, vain, unsubstantial (*-tā*, f., *-tva*, n.), Hariv.; Var.; Kāv.; Pur.; m. Trophis Aspera or a kind of Śyonāka, L.; (in music) a kind of time (also *sāru* and °*ruka*); (*ā*), f. Musa Sapientum, L.; °*raka*, n. a kind of diarrhœa, Bhpr. — **sālá**, mf(*ā́*)n. being out of the house, AV. — **sīman**, mfn. unbounded, immeasurable, infinite, grand, Kāv. — **sukha**, mfn. joyless, sad, unhappy, MBh.; disagreeable, distressing, W. — **sugrīva**, mf(*ā*)n. freed from Sugrīva, R. — **suvarṇaka**, mfn. deprived of gold, Mṛicch. ix, $\frac{7}{2}$. — **sūtra**, mfn. without thread, Naish.; helpless, ib. — **sūnu**, mfn. sonless, Viddh. — **somaka**, mfn. moonless, Veṇis. — **stambha**, mfn. having no posts or pillars, Kām.; having no support or help, BhP. — **stuti**, mfn. praising nothing, MBh. — **sthāman**, mfn. powerless, weak, Deśīn. — **sneha**, mf(*ā*)n. not unctuous or greasy, Mn.; Pañc.; not wet, dry, R.; insensible, cold, unfeeling (with *prati*), Kāv.; Pañc. (*-tva*, n.); not longing for, indifferent, MBh.; not loved, uncared for, hated, disagreeable, Kathās.; Pañc.; m. ungreasing, Dhātup.; (*ā*), f. Linum Usitatissimum, L.; *-phalā*, f. Solanum Diffusum, L. — **spanda** (cf. *nish-p*°), mfn. motionless, Kathās.; Naish.; *-tva*, n. Sāh. (also *ni-sp*°). — **sparśa**, mfn. hard, rough, Kād.; *-gātra*, mfn. rough-limbed, Divyāv. — **spṛiha**, mf(*ā*)n. free from desire, not longing for (loc. or comp.), abstaining from (abl.), Mn.; MBh. &c. (*-tā*, f. Yājñ.); (*am*), ind., Pāṇ. viii, 3, 110, Kāś. — **sphura**, mfn. (heart) not throbbing, Mālatīm. x, $\frac{1}{1}\frac{3}{2}$. — **syanda** = *ni-s*°. — **sva**, mfn. deprived of one's own, indigent, poor, Mn.; MBh. &c.; *-tā*, f. poverty, Var. — 1. **-svana**, mfn. soundless, Kathās. — **svabhāva**, m. want of property, poverty, Śāntiś.; mfn. 'unpropertied,' void of peculiarities, Sarvad. — **svādu**, mfn. insipid, tasteless, W. — **svâdhyāya-vashaṭkāra**, mfn. neither studying the Vedas nor offering burnt sacrifices, VP. — **svāmikā**, f. having no lord or husband, Kathās. — **svī-kṛita**, mfn. (*svī* in comp. for *-sva*) deprived of one's property, impoverished, Var. — **svī-bhūta**, mfn. id., Daś.

Nir for *nis* (q. v.) before vowels and soft consonants. — **aṅśa**, mfn. having no degrees (of latit. or long.); *-tva*, n. Sūryas. — **aṅśaka**, mfn. receiving no share, Yājñ. — **aṅśu**, mfn. rayless, MBh. — **aksha**, mfn. having no dice, W.; having no latitude, ib.; m. the place of no 1° i.e. the terrestrial equator, Sūryas.; *-deśa*, m. the equatorial region, ib. — **akshara**, mfn. not knowing the letters, HPariś. — **agni**, °**nika**, mfn. having no (consecrated) fire, MBh. — **agra** or **-agraka**, mfn. divisible without remainder, Līl. — **agha**, mf(*ā*)n. sinless, free from faults, Rājat. — **aṅkuśa**, mfn. unchecked (lit. not held by a hook), uncontrolled, independent, free, unruly, extravagant (*am*, ind.; *-tā*, f., *-tva*, n.), MBh.; Kāv. &c.; °*śaya*, Nom. P. *yati*, to unfetter, Kād. — **aṅga**, mf(*ā* or *ī*)n. incomplete, Sāh.; having no resources or expedients, Hit. — **aṅgula**, mfn., Pāṇ. v, 4, 86, Kāś. — **aṅguli**, mfn. fingerless, Kāv. — **ajina**, mfn. without a skin or hide, L. — **añjana**, mf(*ā*)n. unpainted, spotless, pure, simple, Up.; MBh. &c.; void of passion or emotion, W.; m. N. of Śiva, Śivag.; of an attendant of Ś°, Hariv.; of sev. authors, Cat. (also with *yati*; °*nâshṭaka*, n. N. of wk.) n. the Supreme Being, W.; (*ā*), f. the day of full moon, L.; N. of Durgā, L. — **atiśaya**, mfn. unsurpassed (*-tva*, n.), Hariv.; Pañc. &c. — **aticāra**, mfn. inviolable, HPariś. — **atyaya**, mf(*ā*)n. free from danger, secure, infallible (*-tva*, n.), Kāv. &c.; unblamable, faultless, Kir.; causing no pain, Suśr. — **adhishṭhāna**, mfn. having no resting-place or basis, supportless, untenable, MBh.; R.; independent, Śaṃk. — **adhva**, mfn. one who has lost his way, L. — **anukrośa**, mf(*ā*)n. pitiless, hard-hearted (*-tā*, f.), MBh.; R.; m. mercilessness, cruelty, R.; *-kārin*, mfn. acting pitilessly, MBh.; *-tas*, ind. in a cruel manner, Pañc.; *-yukta*, mfn. uncompassionate, hard-hearted, R. — **anuga**, mfn. having no followers, unattended, Rājat. — **anugraha**, mfn. ungracious, unkind, BhP. — **anunāsika**, mfn. not marked with the Anunāsika, not nasal, Vop. — **anubandha**, mfn. showing no secondary or symptomatic affection, Car.; °*dhaka*, mfn. having no indicatory letter, Pat. — **anumāna**, mfn. not bound to conclusions or consequences, Tattvas. — **anuyojya**, mfn. unblamable, faultless; °*jyânuyoga*, m. the blaming of anything faultless, Nyāyas.; Sarvad. — **anurodha**, mfn. unfavourable, unfriendly, unamiable (*-tva*, n.), Kāv.; unkind towards, regardless of (loc.), Ratnâv. — **anuśaya**, mfn. without the consequences or results of acts, Śaṃk. — **antara**, mf(*ā*)n. having no interval (in space or time), close, compact, dense, uninterrupted, perpetual, constant (*-tā*, f.), MBh.; Kāv. &c.; faithful, true, Pañc.; abounding in, full of (comp.), R.; Sāh.; not other or different, identical, MBh.; R. &c.; not hidden from view, W.; (*am*), ind. closely, tightly, firmly, Ṛit.; Suśr.; constantly, continually, MBh.; Kāv. &c.; immediately, at once, Kām.; Vet.; *-gṛiha-vāsin*, mfn. living in the next house, Kull.; *-payodharā*, f. having closely contiguous breasts (clouds), Mṛicch. v, 15; *-viśesha*, mfn. (pl.) being without difference in regard to (loc.), being treated alike, MBh.; *-śarīra*, mfn. one whose body is densely transfixed with (arrows), R.; °*râbhyāsa*, m. constant repetition or study, diligent exercise or practice, Prab.; °*rôtkaṇṭhā*, f. continual longing for, Ratn.; °*rôdbhinna*, mfn. densely sprouted, ib. — **antarāla**, mfn. without an intervening space, close, narrow; *-tā*, f., Śiś., Sch. — **andhas**, mfn. foodless, hungry, BhP. — **anna**, mfn. wanting food, starving, MBh.; Suśr.; giving or yielding no food, BhP.; (°*nne*), ind. during a famine, ib. — **anvaya**, mfn. having no offspring, childless, Rājat.; unconnected, unrelated, Mn. viii, 198; 331; illogical, unmethodical, W.; not committed in the presence of others, Mn. viii, 332; without retinue, unaccompanied, Bhaṭṭ. — **apa**, mfn. waterless, R. — **apakrama**, mfn. not to be escaped from, GopBr. — **apatya**, mfn. childless; *-tva*, n., Car. — **apatrapa**, mf(*ā*)n. shameless, impudent, confident, MBh.; R.; Suśr. &c. — **aparādha**, mf(*ā*)n. unoffending, guiltless, blameless (*-tā*, f.), Vikr.; Kathās. &c.; m. faultlessness, innocence; *-vat*, mfn. innocent, R. — **apavarta**, mfn. not returning, W.; (in arithm.) = next. — **apavartana**, mfn. not to be divided by a common divisor, Gol. — **apavāda**, mfn. blameless, BhP.; not admitting of any exception (also *-ka*), Pat. — **apahnava**, mfn. unconcealed, Sāh. — **apāya**, mfn. imperishable, MBh. (also °*yin*, Kāv.); infallible, R.; Suśr.; free from harm or evil, MW. — **apêksha**, mf(*ā*)n. regardless of, indifferent to, independent of (loc. or comp.); desireless, careless, indifferent, disinterested, Mn.; MBh.; Kāv. &c. (also *-ka*, BhP.); (*am*), ind. regardlessly, accidentally, MBh.; Daś.; (*ā*), f. (R.) *-tā*, f., (Kathās.), *-tva*, n. (RāmatUp.) disregard, indifference, independence; °*kshita*, mfn. regardless, Prab.; disregarded, Daś.; °*kshin*, mfn. indifferent, independent, MBh.; °*kshya*, mfn. not to be regarded, Bhartṛ. — **abhiprâya**, mfn. purposeless, Kathās. — **abhibhava**, mfn. not subject to humiliation or disgrace, Bhartṛ.; not to be surpassed, MW. — **abhimāna**, mfn. free from pride, BhP. — **abhilapya**, mfn. unutterable, inexpressible, Sarvad. — **abhilāsha**, mfn. not desirous of, indifferent to (comp.), Śak. — **abhisaṃdhāna**, n. absence of design, Sāṃkhyas., Sch.; °*saṃdhin*, mfn. free from egoistic designs, Saṃk. — **abhīmāna**, mfn. = *-abhim*°, MBh.; unconscious, ib. — **abhyaṅga**, mfn. unanointed, not rubbed in, Car. — **abhra**, mfn. cloudless, MBh.; (°*e*), ind. when the sky is c°, ib.; Suśr. — **amarsha**, mfn. not impatient, apathetic, MBh.; R. (v. l. *nir-ām*°). — **amitra**, mfn. free from enemies, ib.; m. N. of a son of Nakula, MBh.; of a son of the king of Tri-garta, ib.; of a son of Khaṇḍa-pāṇi (or Daṇḍa-p°), Pur. (w. r. *nir-ām*°); of a son of Ayutâyus, ib.; of a sage considered as Śiva's son, ib. (v. l. *nir-ām*°). — **ambara**, mf(*ā*)n. undressed, naked, MBh.; Kathās. — **ambu**, mfn. abstaining from water, BhP.; destitute of w°, MBh. — **argala**, mfn. unbarred, unimpeded, free, irresistible, MBh.; Kāv. &c.; (*am*), ind. freely, Rājat.; *-vāc*, mfn. of unrestrained language, Viddh. — **arti**, mfn. painless, Car. — **artha**, mf(*ā*)n. void of wealth, poor, Mṛicch.; useless, vain (*-kalaha*, a useless quarrel, MBh.); meaningless (*-tā*, MārkP.); (a consonant) having no following vowel, VPrāt., Sch.; m. (°*thá*) loss, detriment, TĀr.; pl. nonsense, R. — **arthaka**, mf(*ikā*)n. useless, vain, unsuccessful, MBh.; Kāv. &c. (*am*, ind., R.; Bhartṛ.; *-tva*, n., Mṛicch.); unmeaning, nonsensical, MBh.; (said of a consonant) = *-artha*, VPrāt., Sch.; n. (in phil.) a nonsensical objection; (in rhet.) an expletive. — **arbuda**, m. or n. N. of a hell in which the wicked are punished by excessive cold, Buddh. — **alaṃkāra**, mfn. unornamented, R. (B.), Sch. — **alaṃkṛiti**, f. (in rhet.) want of ornaments, simplicity. — **avá**, mfn. unprotected, RV. i, 122, 11, Sāy. (only gen. *-avásya*, perhaps one who calls, fr. √*ru*? or ind. p. fr. √*so*?). — **avakāśa**, mf(*ā*)n. wanting room, crowded (said of a hell), BhP.; out of place or time, unseasonable, inconvenient, Hcar.; *-tā*, f., Kād.; °*śī*-√*kṛi*, to remove from its place, Ragh. ix, 28 (C.), Sch. — **avagraha**, mfn. unrestrained, independent, free, MBh.; Kāv. &c. (°*he*, ind. where there is room to move freely, MBh.); self-willed, headstrong, W. — **avadosha-tva**, n. (?), Kauś., Sch. — **avadya**, mf(*ā*)n. unblamable, unobjectionable, Up.; MBh. &c. (*-tva*, n., BhP.); n. blamelessness, excellence (*-vat*, mfn., MBh.); n. or m. a partic. high number, Lalit. — **avadhi**, mfn. unlimited, Bhavabh.; Rājat.; endless, infinite, Sarvad. (also °*dhika*). — **avayava**, mfn. having no limbs or members; not consisting of parts, indivisible (*-tva*, n.), Saṃk.; Sarvad. &c. — **avarodha**, mfn. unrestrained, unopposed, BhP. — **avalamba**, mfn. supportless (lit. and fig.), Śak.; °*bana*, mf(*ā*)n. id., ib. (v. l.); belonging to nobody, Hcar.; n. want of a prop or of reliance, MW. — **avaśesha**, mfn. without a residue, complete, whole, R. &c.; (°*sheṇa* and °*sha-tas*), ind. completely, totally, fully, Hariv. — **avasāda**, mf(*ā*)n. not cast down, cheerful, Gīt.; anxious, eager, W. — **avaskṛita**, mfn. (prob.) clean, pure, MBh. (cf. *an-avaskara*). — **avastāra**, mfn. not strewn or covered, bare, BhP. — **avahālikā**, f. a fence, hedge, outer wall, L. — **avyaya**, mf(*ā*)n. undecaying, eternal, W. – **aśana,** mfn. abstaining from food, Hariv.; n. going without food, fasting, L. – **aśva,** mfn. without horses, Kathās.; *-purusha,* mf(*ā*)n. w° h° and men, MBh. – **astra,** mfn. weaponless, R.; Caurap. – **asthi,** mfn. boneless (as flesh), Suśr. – **ahaṃstambha,** mfn. free from the fetters of egotism, BhP. – **ahaṃkāra,** mfn. free from egotism, unselfish, humble, MBh.; BhP.; m. a partic. heaven, Hcat.; °*kārin,* mfn. free from the sentiment of egotism, BhP.; °*kṛita,* mfn. having no self-consciousness or personality, BhP.; = next, MBh.; BhP.; °*kṛiti,* mfn. free from egotism or pride, humble, Bhartṛ.; BhP.; °*kriya,* mfn. having no personality or individuality, BhP.; (*ā*), f. absence of egotism or selfishness, ib. – **aham,** mfn. devoid of self-conceit or selfishness, BhP.; *-mati* and *-māna,* mfn. free from the sentiment of egotism, ib. – **ahna,** m., Pāṇ. viii, 4, 7, Kāś. – **ākāṅksha,** mfn. expecting or wishing nothing, desireless, hopeless, Kathās.; Pur. (also °*kshin,* MBh.); wanting nothing to fill up, complete (*vākya*), KātyŚr.; Sāh. – 1. **-ākāra,** mfn. formless, shapeless, incorporeal (*brahman*), making no appearance or show, insignificant, unimportant, MBh.; R. &c.; having no object (cf. below); m. N. of Śiva, Śivag.; of Vishṇu, L.; heaven, L.; the universal spirit, god, L.; *-jñāna-vāda,* m. the doctrine that the perception of the outer world does not arise from images impressed on the mind, Sarvad.; *-locana,* n. a vacant (lit. objectless) look, Mṛicch., Sch. – **ākāśa,** mfn. having no free space, completely filled, R. – **ākula,** mfn. not too much beset, little frequented, Kathās.; not disarranged, Gīt.; unconfused, clear, calm, steady (*am,* ind.), Var.; Kāv.; Pañc.; n. perspicuity, clearness, calmness, Var.; *-dvāra,* mf(*ā*)n. (city) whose gates are not too much crowded, Kathās.; °*lârtham,* ind. for the sake of clearness, Var. – **ākṛiti,** mfn. formless, shapeless (Vishṇu), Hariv.; deformed, ugly, MārkP.; m. a person who neglects his religious duties, (esp.) a Brāhman who has not duly read the Vedas, Gaut.; Mn.; MBh. etc. – 1. **-ākṛitin,** mfn. making no show &c. = *-ākāra* (above), MBh. (v. l. *kṛiti*). – **ākranda,** mf(*ā*)n. having no friend or protector, Hariv.; finding no help from (loc.), Jātakam.; affording no shelter or protection, Kathās.; m. or n. a place that affords no p°, MBh. – **ākrośa,** mfn. unaccused, unreviled, W. – **āgama,** mfn. not founded on revelation, MBh. – **āgas,** mfn. sinless, innocent, Ragh.; Rājat. – **āgāra,** mfn. houseless, shelterless. – **āgraha,** mfn. not insisting upon, not obstinate, Rājat. – **ācāra,** mfn. without approved usages or customs, lawless, barbarian, Hcat. – **ājīvya,** mf(*ā*)n. not yielding subsistence, Kām. – **āḍambara,** mfn. without drums; *-sundara,* mfn. beautiful w° d° i.e. w° praise, b° in itself, Rājat. – **ātaṅka,** mf(*ā*)n. free from fear or pain, not feeling or causing it, MBh.; Kāv. &c.; m. N. of Śiva, Śivag. – **ātapa,** mf(*ā*)n. not penetrated by the sun's rays, shady, Hariv.; (*ā*), f. the night, L. – **ātapatra,** mfn. without umbrella, Hcat. – **ātithya,** mfn. inhospitable, lonely, Kathās. – **ātmaka,** mfn. having no separate soul or no individual existence, BhP.; °*tman* or °*tma-vat,* mfn. id., MBh.; °*tma-tva,* n., Vajracch. – **ādara,** mfn. showing no respect, disrespectful, Rājat. – **ādāna,** mfn. taking or receiving nothing, MBh.; m. N. of Buddha, L. – **ādhāna** (*nir-*), mfn. unbridled, TBr. (cf. *antar-ādh*°). – **ādhāra,** mfn. without a receptacle or a support, MBh.; *-tva,* n., Sarvad. – **ādhi,** mfn. free from anxiety, secure, Kām. – **ānanda,** mf(*ā*)n. joyless, sorrowful, sad, melancholy, MBh.; R. &c.; *-kara,* mf(*ī*)n. causing no pleasure, afflicting, MBh.; Hariv. – **āntra,** mfn. eviscerated, having the entrails hanging out, AitBr. – **āpad,** f. no misfortune, security, prosperity, MBh.; mfn. prosperous, fortunate, secure, Ragh.; Śatr. – **ābādha,** mf(*ā*)n. undisturbed, unmolested, secure, MBh.; Hariv.; (*am,* ind. incontestably, Sarvad.) not disturbing, not molesting, harmless, guileless, ib.; frivolously or unreally vexatious (as a cause of complaint), Yājñ., Sch.; *-kara,* mfn. not causing injury or pain, Hariv. – **ābhāsa,** mfn. without fallacious appearance, HaṇsUp. – **āmaya,** m. freedom from illness, health, welfare, MBh.; (*am,* ind. in °*mayam Devadattāya,* or °*ttasya,* good health or hail to D°!, Pāṇ. ii, 3, 73, Kāś.); mfn. free from illness, healthy, well, MBh.; R.; Suśr. &c.; causing health, wholesome, MBh. xii, 6569; complete, entire, Hariv.; infallible, secure, MBh.; R; untainted, pure, L.; m. a wild goat, L.; a hog, a boar, L.; N. of a king, MBh. – **āmarda,** m. 'not oppressing,' N. of a king, MBh. – **āmarsha,** **-āmitra,** see *-am*°. – **āmisha,** mfn. fleshless, Bhartṛ.; receiving no booty or wages, MBh.; free from sensual desires or covetousness, Mn. vi, 49; not striving after any reward, Lalit.; °*shâśin,* mfn. eating no flesh, Hit. – **āya,** mfn. having or yielding no income, profitless, W.; *-vyaya-vat,* m. having neither income nor expenditure, an idler who lives from hand to mouth, W. – 1. **-āyata,** mfn. unextended, contracted, compact, W.; *-tva,* n. shortness, compactness, Kir. viii, 17. – **āyati,** mfn. one who has no future, one whose end or destruction is at hand, ib. ii, 15. – **āyāsa,** mfn. not causing trouble or fatigue, easy, MBh.; kind, Divyâv. – **āyudha,** mfn. weaponless, unarmed, Mn.; Hariv. – **ārambha,** mfn. not undertaking enterprises, abstaining from all work, MBh. – **ālamba,** mfn. = *-aval*°; self-supported, independent; friendless, alone, Mn.; MBh. &c. (*am,* ind., R.; *-tva,* n., Hcar.); m. N. of a philosopher (worshipping the empty air as deity), Cat.; (*ā*), f. spikenard, L.; *-°bôpanishad,* f. N. of wk. – **ālambana,** mfn. supportless or self-supported, not resting on another, free, MBh.; R. – **ālasya,** mfn. not slothful, MW. – **ālāpa,** mfn. not talking, Kathās. – **āloka,** mfn. not looking about, R.; deprived of light, dark or blind, MBh.; Mālatīm.; Kām.; ifc. looking at, investigating, scrutinizing (cf. *ātma-n*°), MBh. – **āvaraṇa,** mfn. unveiled, manifest, evident, Veṇis. – **āvarsha,** mfn. (a tree) sheltering from rain, Hariv. – **āśa,** mf(*ā*)n. without any hope or wish or desire, indifferent, Kap.; Kāv.; Rājat. &c. (*āśāṃ nir-āśāṃ √kṛi,* to make hope hopeless i.e. giving up all hope, MBh. xii, 6647; cf. 6520); despairing or despondent of (with loc., dat., acc. and *prati,* abl., or comp.), MBh.; R. &c.; (*ā*), f. hopelessness, despair, Subh.; Hcar.; *-ka,* mfn. despairing of (abl.), MBh. viii, 3761; *-kara,* mfn. taking away all hope, making impossible (in comp.), Gīt. xii, 20; *-guṭikā,* w.r. for °*sa-g*° (see under 2. **nir-āsa,** p. 553); *-tā,* f. (Bhām.), *-tva,* n. (Pañc. B.) hopelessness, despair; °*śâsanna,* mfn. nearly driven to despair, Hcar.; °*śin,* mfn. hopeless, despairing, MBh. (°*śi-tva,* n. hopelessness, Kām.; v. l. for °*śa-tva,* Pañc.); °*śī-bhāva,* m. despair, L.; *-°śī-bhūta,* mfn. become hopeless, despairing, MW. – **āśaṅka,** mf(*ā*)n. fearless, being not afraid of (loc. for infin.), Cāṇ.; (*am*), ind. without fear or hesitation, Śaṃk.; °*kya,* mfn. not to be apprehended, Daś. – **āśaya,** mfn. (wound) not deep, Suśr. (v. l. for *-āśraya*). – **āśis,** mfn. hopeless, despairing, MBh.; Kāv. &c. (°*śīs-tva,* n., MBh. xii, 12440); free from desire, indifferent, Kum. v, 76; without a blessing, W. – **āśrama,** mfn. not being in one of the four periods or stages of a Brāhman's life, Kull. (°*min,* id., ib.); *-pada,* mfn. (a wood) having no hermitages in it, Kathās. – **āśraya,** mfn. shelterless, R.; supportless, having or offering no prop or stay, destitute, alone, MBh.; Kāv. &c.; not deep (v. l. °*śaya*), lying open, Suśr. – 1. **-āsa,** m. seatless, shelterless, MBh. – **āsaṅga,** mfn. unhindered (in the use of one's forces), Car. – **āsitva,** w. r. for *-āśitva,* or *-āśatva* (above), Pañc. – **āsu** (!), mfn., v. l. for *-ambu,* MBh. – **āstha,** mf(*ā*)n. not interested in anything, not intent upon (comp.), Kathās. – **āspada,** mfn. restless, homeless, portionless, objectless, MW. – **āsrava,** mfn. sinless, Divyâv. (printed °*śrava*). – **āsvāda,** mfn. tasteless, insipid, unsavoury, MBh.; Hariv.; *-rasa,* mfn. (herbs) not tasting of anything, MBh. – **āsvādya,** mfn. giving no enjoyment; *-tama,* mfn. most unsavoury, R. – **āhāra,** m. want of food, fasting, Yājñ.; mf(*ā*)n. having no food or abstaining from it, MBh.; Hariv. &c.; *-tā,* f. foodlessness, fasting, MBh.; Kathās. – **iṅga,** mfn. immovable, not flickering, MBh. – **iccha,** mfn. without wish or desire, indifferent, ib. – **indriya** (*nir-*), mf(*ā*)n. impotent, destitute of manly vigour or strength, AV.; ŚBr. &c.; barren (a cow), KaṭhUp.; infirm, weak, frail, Mn. ix, 18 (or = *pramāṇa-rahita,* Kull.); having no organs of sense, L. – **indhana,** mfn. destitute of fuel, MBh.; Hariv. &c. – **iti,** mfn. free from calamities or afflictions, Ragh.; *-ka,* mf(*ā*)n. auspicious, R. – **īśa,** see *-īsha.* – **īśvara,** mfn. godless, atheistic; *-vāda,* m. ath° doctrine, MW.; *-vādin,* mfn. holding ath° d°, ib.; *-sāṃkhya-śāstra,* n. the Sāṃkhya doctrine in a restricted sense (excluding the Yoga-Sāṃkhya), Sarvad. – **īsha,** n. the body of a plough, or mfn. without a pole or shaft, L. (v. l. *-īśa*). – **īha,** mfn. motionless, inactive, desireless, indifferent, unanxious, MBh.; Kāv. &c.; (*ā*), f. (BhP.) = *-tā,* f. (MBh.), *-tva,* n. (MW.), °*hâvasthā,* f. (Sāh.) absence of effort or desire, indifference. – **ucchvāsa,** mf(*ā*)n. not breathing, breathless, MBh.; Suśr. &c.; narrow, contracted, crowded, W.; m. breathlessness (*-nipīḍita,* mfn. afflicted by b°); m. or n. N. of a partic. hell where the wicked cannot breathe, L. – **utkaṇṭha,** mfn. free from longing or desire, Śak. – **uttara,** mfn. having no superior, L.; answerless, silenced, Hariv.; Kathās. &c.; n. = *-tantra,* n. N. of a Tantra; °*rī-√kṛi,* to make unable to answer, silence, Kathās. – **uttha,** mfn. irrecoverable, Bhpr. – **utpāta,** mf(*ā*)n. free from portents, Hariv. – **utsava,** mfn. having no festivals, Ragh.; BhP.; °*vârambha,* mfn. making or showing no preparation for a festival, Śak. – **utsāha,** m. absence of exertion, indolence, Hariv.; mf(*ā*)n. without energy or courage, indolent, indifferent, MBh.; R. &c.; despondent of (loc.), MBh. vii, 1836; *-tā,* f., Pañc. – **utsuka,** mfn. careless, indifferent, tranquil, MBh.; Kāv.; m. N. of a son of Manu Raivata, Hariv.; of one of the Saptarshis under the 13th Manu, ib. – **udaka,** mfn. waterless, Pāṇ. vi, 2, 184; BhP.; Hcat. (w. r. *-ūd*°). – **udara,** mfn. having no belly or trunk, Kāv. – **uddeśam,** ind. without any statement, Kād. – **uddrāva,** mfn. immovable, undecaying, W. – **uddhati,** mfn. (chariot) not jolting, Śak. vii, 10 (v. l.) – **udyama,** mfn. effortless, inactive, lazy, MBh. &c. – **udyoga,** mfn. id., ib.; disheartened, R.; causeless (?), MW. – **udvigna,** mfn. unexcited, sedate, calm, MBh.; R.; *-manas,* mfn. undisturbed in mind, ib. – **udvega,** mfn. = *-udvigna,* ib. – **unmāda,** mfn. free from pride or arrogance, Sāh. – **upakārin,** mfn. not assisting, inofficious, Subh. – **upakrama,** mfn. not to be cured, incurable, Car.; having no commencement, BhP. – **upakriya,** mfn. not useful or profitable, Kathās. – **upadrava,** mfn. free from affliction or danger, neither inflicting nor incurring adversity, harmless, peaceful, secure, happy, MBh.; Kāv. &c.; (also *-upadruta*) not inauspicious (as stars), Var.; *-tā,* f. absence of danger, security, Kull. – **upadhi,** mfn. guileless, blameless, honest, secure, Kāv.; *-jīvana,* mfn. leading an honest life (*-tā,* f., Dhūrtas.); *-pālita-prakṛitika,* mfn. (prob.) one whose subjects are protected from danger or harm, Inscr.; *-śesha,* mfn. one in whom no remainder of guile is left, Buddh.; (said of Nirvāṇa), Divyâv. – **upapatti,** mfn. unfit, unsuitable; *-tva,* n. ib. – **upapada,** mfn. having no epithet, Mṛicch. x, 1/5; not connected with a subordinate word, Sch. – **upaplava,** mfn. untroubled, unmolested, unharmed, Śak. iii, 1/2 (v. l. *-upadrava*); m. 'not causing adversity,' N. of Śiva, Śivag. – **upabhoga,** mfn. not enjoying, Sāṃkhyak. – **upama,** mf(*ā*)n. peerless, unequalled, incomparable, Hariv.; Kāv. &c.; m. N. of a man, L.; (*ā*), f. N. of a Surāṅganā, Siṇhâs. – **upayoga,** mfn. useless, unserviceable, Hcar. – **upala,** mfn. stoneless, g. *nirudakâdi.* – **upalepa,** mfn. unsmeared, L. – **upasarga,** mfn. free from portents, auspicious, Var. – **upasṛishṭa,** mfn. undamaged, ib. – **upaskṛita,** mfn. unimpaired by (instr.), simple, pure, MBh. – **upasthāyaka,** mfn. unattended, Divyâv. – **upahata,** mfn. unhurt, uninjured; harmless, auspicious, Var. – **upahita,** mfn. (in phil.) without Upa-dhi or Upā-dhi (see s. v.) – **upâkhya,** mf(*ā*)n. destitute of all qualification, Sarvad.; immaterial, unreal, false, non-existent, L.; indescribable, inexpressible, Naish.; *-tva,* n., Śaṃk. – **upâdāna,** mfn. free from desire or clinging to life, Divyâv. (cf. MWB. 44; 102 &c.) – **upâdhi** (VP.) and °**dhika** (BhP.), mfn. without attributes or qualities, absolute. – **upâya,** mfn. without expedients, helpless, unsuccessful, Kām. – **upêksha,** mfn. not neglectful; free from trick or fraud, W. – **ushṇatā,** f. want of heat, coldness, rigidity; °*tāṃ √nī,* to bring to c°, kill, Daś. – **ushṇīsha,** mfn. without a turban or head-dress, bareheaded, Rājat. – **ushman,** &c., w. r. for *-ūshm*°. – 1. **-ūḍha,** mfn. unmarried, W. – **ūdaka, -ūpama, -ūpâkhya,** w. r. for *-ud*°, *-up* &c. – **ūshman,** mfn. devoid of heat, cold, MBh.; Hariv. (°*maka,* Jātakam.); °*ma-tva,* n. coldness, MBh. – 1. **-ūha,** m. a complete sentence, one having no ellipsis, W. – **ṛiṇa** (Siṇhâs.), °**ṇin** (Nār., Sch.), mfn. free from debts. – 1. **-eka,** mfn. excluding 'one,' Jyot. – **enas,** mfn. free from guilt, Śiś. – **oshṭhya,** n. absence of all labials, ib., Sch. – **aushadha,** mfn. incurable, Pracaṇḍ. – **gandha,** mfn. void of smell, inodorous, Suśr.; Kāv. &c.; *-tā,* f. scentlessness, Kum.; *-pushpī,* f. Salmalia Malabarica, L. – **garbha,** mfn. having no germ or sprout in it, AP. – **garva,** mfn. free from pride, humble, Rājat. – **garha,** mf(*ā*)n. blameless, Kathās. – **ga-**

vâksha, mfn. windowless, Kām. **-gahana**, mfn. 'knowing no difficulties,' intrepid, Vcar. **-guṇa**, mf(*ā*)n. having no cord or string, Kāv.; having no good qualities or virtues, bad, worthless, vicious, MBh.; R. &c.; devoid of all qualities or properties, Up.; MBh. &c.; having no epithet, KātyŚr., Sch.; (said of the Supreme Being), W.; *-ka*, mfn. having no qualities, RāmatUp.; *-tattva*, n. N. of wk.; *-tā*, f., *-tva*, n. absence of qualities or properties; want of good q°, wickedness, viciousness, MBh.; Kāv.; Pur.; *-mānasa*, mfn. of bad or vicious mind, Kāv.; °*ṇâtmaka*, mfn. having no q°, MBh. **-gulika**, mfn. having no pill, Kathās. **-gulma**, mf(*ā*)n. shrubless, MBh. **-gṛiha**, mf(*ī*)n. houseless, Pañc. **-gaurava**, mf(*ā*)n. without dignity; (*am*), ind., Rājat. **-grantha**, mfn. free from all ties or hindrances, BhP.; without possessions, poor, L.; a saint who has withdrawn from the world and lives either as a hermit or a religious mendicant wandering about naked, Var.; Buddh.; a fool, idiot, L.; a gambler, L.; murder, manslaughter, Gal.; °*thaka*, mfn. unattended, deserted, alone, L.; fruitless, L.; clever, expert, L.; m. a naked Jaina or Buddhist mendicant, L.; n. (?) Jainism or Buddhism, MW.; °*thana*, n. killing, slaughter, L.; °*tha-śāstra*, n. N. of wk.; °*thi*, mfn. free from knots, knotless, L.; without blemish, perfect (°*thi-ramaṇīyatā*, Caṇḍak.); °*thika*, mfn. clever, conversant, L.; = *hīna*, L.; m. = °*thaka*, m. **-ghaṭa**, n. a great fair, crowded market, free market; a place where there is no quay or steps, L. **-ghṛiṇa**, mf(*ā*)n. unmerciful, cruel, MBh.; Kāv. &c.; shameless, immodest, W.; (*am*), ind. cruelly, MBh.; (*ā*), f. (in *sa-nir-ghṛiṇa*), *-tā*, f. (Bhartṛ.), *-tva*, n. (MārkP.) pitilessness, cruelty. **-1. -ghosha**, mf(*ā*)n. soundless, noiseless, MBh.; °*shâkshara-vimukta*, m. N. of a Samādhi. **-jana**, mf(*ā*)n. unpeopled, lonely, desolate, MBh.; R.; m. or n. solitude, desert, R.; Rājat.; *-tā*, f. (Rājat.), *-tva*, n. (Sāh.) depopulation, voidness; *-vana*, n. a lonely or unfrequented forest, MW. **-jantu**, mfn. free from living creatures (worms &c.), HYog. **-jara**, mfn. (in some cases °*ras*, Pāṇ. vii, 2, 101) not becoming old, young, fresh, BhP.; imperishable, immortal, W.; m. a god, Rājat.; (*ā*), f. Cocculus Cordifolius or Anethum Graveolens, L.; n. ambrosia or nectar, L.; *-paṇya-yoshit*, f. 'immortal courtezan,' an Apsaras, Vcar.; *-sarshapa*, m. a species of mustard, L. **-jarāyu** (*nir-*), mfn. (snake) that has cast its skin, AV. **-jarjalpa** (*nir-*), mfn. tattered, VS. (Mahīdh.; v.l. TS. *-jālmaka*). **-jala**, mf(*ā*)n. waterless, dry (m. or n. a dry country, desert, waste, MBh.; R.); not mixed with water (as buttermilk), L.; °*la-toyadâbha*, mfn. of the colour of a waterless cloud i.e. white, fair, MW.; °*la-mīnāya*, Nom. Ā. °*yate*, to be like a fish without water, Bhām.; °*lâikādaśī*, f. the 11th day in the light half of the month Jyaishṭha (on which even the drinking of water is forbidden), Col. **-jalada**, mf(*ā*)n. cloudless, Subh. **-jāḍya**, mfn. free from coldness, L. **-jālmaka** (*nir-*), mfn. maneless, TS., Sch. (cf. *-jarjalpa*). **-jijñāsa**, mfn. not desirous of knowing or understanding, Nyāyas., Sch. **-jihva**, mfn. tongueless, MBh.; n. a frog, L. **-jīva**, mf(*ā*)n. lifeless, dead, MBh. &c.; *-karaṇa*, n. killing, striking dead (with gen.), Kathās. xvii, 15 (w.r. *-kār*°); °*vita*, mfn. = *-jīva*; °*ta-tva*, n., Vajracch. **-jñāti**, mfn. having no kinsfolk, MBh. **-jñāna**, mf(*ā*)n. ignorant, stupid, silly, Kathās. **-jyotis**, mfn. lightless, dark, Hcar. **-jvara**, mfn. feverless, healthy, L. **-daṅśin**, mfn. (snake) not biting or stinging, AitBr. **-daṭa** or **-dada**, mfn. (Prākr. for *dṛita* fr. √*dṛi*, cf. *ā-dṛi*?) unkind, malicious, censorious, slanderous; useless, unnecessary; mad, intoxicated, L. **-daṇḍa**, mfn. not punishing, MBh.; m. a Sūdra, L. (as the staffless?). **-danta**, mfn. (elephant) having no teeth or tusks, Subh. **-daya**, mf(*ā*)n. pitiless, unkind, cruel, hard, violent, excessive, MBh.; Kāv. &c.; unpitied by any, Mn. ix, 239; (*am*), ind. unmercifully, passionately, violently, greatly, Kāv. (°*ya-taram*, Bhartṛ. i, 64); *-tva*, n. unmercifulness, cruelty, Kāv.; °*ya-danta-daṅśa*, m. unmerciful or passionate biting (with the teeth), Git.; °*ya-rati-śramâlasa*, mf(*ā*)n. tired by p° amorous sports, Ragh. xix, 32; °*yâślesha*, m. a p° embrace, Megh. 105. **-1. -dara**, mfn. (fr. √*dṛi*[?]; cf. *-daṭa*) pitiless, hard, shameless; (*am*), ind. excessively, strongly, L. **-daraṇa**, mf(*ā*)n. free from clefts or holes, Kām. **-daśa**, mfn. more than ten days old, happened more than ten days ago (*-tā*, f. ĀpGṛ.), AitBr.; Mn. &c. (cf. *a-nir-d*°). **-daśana**, mfn. toothless, Hit.; °*nâkshi-jihva*, mfn. deprived of teeth and eyes and tongue, MBh. **-dasyu**, mfn. (a place) free from robbers, MBh.; Hariv. **-1. -dahana**, mfn. (for 2. see *nir-dah*) not burning, W. **-dākshiṇya**, mfn. uncourteous, Kād. **-dāridrya**, mfn. free from poverty, wealthy, Kathās. **-duḥkha**, mfn. painless, not feeling or causing pain, MBh.; Kathās.; *-tva*, n. painlessness, Bhāshāp. **-durdina**, mfn. 'free from bad weather,' serene, bright, Dhanaṃj. **-deva** (*nir-*), mfn. abandoned by the gods, TS.; without gods or idols, Subh. **-dainya**, mfn. free from misery, comfortable, at ease, Kathās.; Rājat. **-dosha**, mf(*ā*)n. faultless, defectless, guiltless, innocent, MBh.; Kāv. &c.; infallible, Sarvad.; *-kula-sârâvali*, f. N. of wk.; *-tā*, f. faultlessness, Sch.; °*shī-karaṇa*, n. rendering innocuous, paralyzing, Bhpr.; °*shī-kṛita*, mfn. cleared from guilt, MW. **-dravya**, mfn. immaterial, MBh.; without property, poor. **-druma**, mfn. treeless; °*mī-√kṛi*, to deprive of trees, Vcar. **-droha**, mfn. not hostile or malicious, friendly, Rājat. **-dvaṃdva**, mfn. indifferent to the alternatives or opposite pairs (of feelings, as pleasure and pain), neither glad nor sorry &c., MBh.; Hariv.; Pur.; not standing in mutual relation, independent (as *brahman*), MBh. i, 3315; xii, 489 = xiv, 314; free from envy or jealousy, MBh.; Kathās.; not contested, indisputed, MBh.; not double, W.; not acknowledging two principles, ib. **-dhana**, mfn. without property, poor, MBh.; Kāv. &c.; (an enterprise) undertaken without money, Cāṇ.; m. an old bull, L.; *-tā*, f. (Mṛicch.), *-tva*, n. (MBh.; Pañc.) poverty, indigence; °*nī-√kṛi* (Daś.) to make poor; °*nī-√bhū* (Kull.) to become poor. **-dharma**, mfn. unrighteous, lawless, impious, Kathās.; 'unpropertied,' Kap. (*-tva*, n.); m. unrighteousness, in °*ma-mūrkhatā*, f. unr° and foolishness, Kathās.; °*mârtha*, mfn. unjust and useless, MBh. **-dhārtarāshṭra**, mfn. having no descendants of Dhṛitarāshṭra, free from them, MBh. **-dhūma**, mfn. smokeless, Mālatīm.; *-tva*, n., DevībhP. **-namaskāra**, mf(*ā*)n. offering no homage (e.g. to the gods), not respecting any one, uncourteous, MBh.; R. &c.; unrespected, despised by all, Mn.; Bhaṭṭ. **-nara**, mfn. abandoned by men, deserted, Hariv. **-nāṇaka**, mfn. coinless, penniless, Mṛicch. ii, 6. **-nātha**, mfn. protectorless, without a lord or guardian, Kād.; *-tā*, f., MBh. **-nābhi**, mfn. (without i.e.) not reaching to the navel; *-kauśeya*, n. a silken garment not reaching to the n°, Kum. **-nāyaka**, mfn. having no leader or ruler, anarchic (as a country), Subh.; *-tva*, n., Nīlak. **-nidra**, mfn. sleepless; *-tā*, f., Rājat. **-nimitta**, mfn. without reason or motive, causeless, Nyāyas., Sch. (*-tva*, n., Saṃk.); having no egoistic motive, disinterested, Kād.; (*am*), ind. without cause, Var.; °*ta-kṛita*, mfn. produced without a visible cause, ib. **-nimesha**, mfn. not twinkling (*cakshus*), Śatr.; not closing the eye, Naish. **-nirodha**, mf(*ā*)n. unobstructed, Rājat. **-nīḍa**, mfn. having no nest, BhP. **-bandhu**, mfn. without relations or friends, MBh. **-barha**, mfn. (a peacock) without tail-feathers, Vās. **-bala**, mfn. powerless, weak, Hit. **-bāṇa**, mfn. arrowless, L. **-1. -bādha**, mfn. free from vexation or annoyance, Kathās. **-bīja**, mfn. seedless, impotent (*-tva*, n., Tattvas.); (*ā*), f. a sort of grape without seeds or stones, L. **-buddhi**, mfn. senseless, ignorant, stupid, Mṛicch.; Pañc. **-busa**, mfn. free from chaff; °*sī-kṛita*, mfn. freed from chaff, husked, L. **-bodha**, v.l. for *-buddhi*, q.v. **-1. -bhakta**, mfn. (medicine) taken without eating, Suśr. **-bhaya**, n. fearlessness, security, Hcat.; mf(*ā*)n. fearless, not afraid of (comp.); free from danger, secure, tranquil (*am*, ind. fearlessly &c.), Mn.; MBh.; Kāv. &c.; m. N. of a son of the 13th Manu, Hariv.; *-bhīma*, N. of a play; *-rāma-bhaṭṭa*, m. N. of an author, Cat. **-bhara**, mf(*ā*)n. 'without weight or measure,' excessive, vehement, violent; deep, sound (as sleep), ardent (as an embrace), Kāv. &c.; full of, abounding in, Kathās.; Pur. &c. (also °*rita* with instr., Cat.); (*am*), ind. excessively, violently, very much, deeply, soundly, Kathās.; Hit.; °*ra-nidrā*, f. sound sleep, Hit.; °*ra-parirambha*, m. a passionate embrace, Git.; °*ra-praṇayitā*, f. deep affection, Amar.; °*ra-rahaḥ-krīḍa*, f. excessive amorous sport, Bhartṛ.; °*ra-sambhoga*, m. excessive enjoyment, Rājat. **-bhastraka**, mf(*akā* or *ikā*)n., Pāṇ. vii, 3, 47, Kāś. **-bhāga**, mfn. not consisting of parts; *-tva*, n., Kap. **-bhāgya**, mfn. unfortunate, L. **-1. -bhinna**, mfn. undistinguished, equal, like, W. **-bhī**, mfn. fearless, not afraid. **-bhīka**, mfn. id., Car. **-bhīta**, mfn. id., R.; BhP. **-bhugna**, mfn. not bent, straight, flat, W. **-bhuja**, mf(*ā*)n. N. of a kind of Saṃdhi or Saṃhitā, RPrāt.; n. = *saṃhitā*, AitĀr. **-bhṛiti**, mfn. without wages, hireless, L. **-1. -bheda**, mf(*ā*)n. uninterrupted, Hariv. **-bhedya**, mfn. having no cleft or fissure, Kām.; missing the aim, R. **-bhoga**, mfn. not devoted to pleasure or enjoyment, MBh. **-makshika**, mfn. free from flies, g. *nir-udakâdi*; (*am*), n. or ind. the being free from flies i.e. from troublesome people, complete solitude, °*kaṃ vartate*, Pāṇ. ii, 1, 6, Kāś.; °*kaṃ kṛitam*, Śak. **-majja**, mfn. marrowless, fatless, meagre, Hariv. **-maṇḍūka**, mfn. frogless, destitute of frogs, MW. **-matsara**, mfn. without envy or jealousy, unselfish, Rājat.; BhP. **-matsya**, mfn. fishless; *-tā*, f., Pañc. **-mada**, mfn. unintoxicated, sober, quiet, humble, modest, MBh.; Rājat.; Kathās.; (elephant) not in rut, Var. **-madhyā**, mfn. having no middle, TS.; (*ā*), f. a partic. fragrant substance (prob. w.r. for *nirmathyā*). **-manaska**, mfn. mindless, having no Manas; *-tā*, f., Kām. **-manuja**, mfn. unpeopled, uninhabited, desolate, BhP. **-manushya**, mf(*ā*)n. id., R. (with *mātaṅga*, m. an elephant without riders, MBh.); *-mṛiga*, mfn. (a forest) without men or deer, R. **-mantu**, mfn. faultless, innocent, HYog. **-mantra**, mfn. (a ceremony) unaccompanied by holy texts, MBh.; not familiar with h° t°, MBh. xii, 1339 (= Mn. ii, 158, where v.l. *an-ṛica*). **-manyu**, mfn. free from anger or resentment, MBh.; Kathās.; m. N. of a hunter, Hariv. **-mama**, mf(*ā*)n. unselfish, disinterested, (esp.) free from all worldly connections, MBh.; R. &c.; regardless of, indifferent to (loc.), ib.; m. (with Jainas) N. of the 15th Arhat of the future Ut-sarpiṇī; N. of Śiva, Śivag.; *-tā*, f. (Kāv.), 1. *-tva*, n. (Pur.) complete unselfishness or indifference (see *nis*); 2. *-tva*, mfn. free from selfishness, indifferent, Kull. **-maryāda**, mfn. boundless, immeasurable, innumerable, Var.; MBh.; unlimited, unrestrained, unruly, wicked, criminal, MBh.; R. &c.; (*am*), ind. confusedly, topsy-turvy, MBh.; n. confusion, disturbance of boundaries or rules, ib.; a kind of fight, Hariv. **-mala**, mf(*ā*)n. spotless, unsullied, clean, pure, shining, resplendent, bright, Up.; MBh.; Kāv. &c.; sinless, virtuous, Mn. viii, 318; m. N. of Skanda, AV. Pariś.; pl. N. of a sect, W.; n. talc, L.; = *nir-mālya*, n., L.; °*la-gada*, mfn. having a bright mace, MBh.; °*la-tā*, f. (Hariv.), °*la-tva*, n. (Bhag.; Var.) stainlessness, cleanness, purity; °*la-tīrtha*, n. N. of a Tīrtha, W.; °*la-prakāśa*, m. N. of wk.; °*la-bhaṭṭa*, m. N. of an author, Cat.; °*lâñjana*, n. N. of ch. of the Prakaraṇa-pañcikā; °*lâtma-vat*, mfn. having a pure mind, Hcat.; °*lī-karaṇa*, n. cleansing, purification, Pat.; °*lī-kṛita*, mfn. freed from impurity, cleansed, cleared, Vās; °*lôpala*, m. crystal, L. **-malīmasa**, mfn. spotless, clean, pure, L. **-maśaka**, mfn. free from gnats or mosquitoes, g. *nir-udakâdi*. **-māṅsa**, mfn. fleshless, emaciated, MBh.; R. &c. **-mādhyastha**, n. absence of impartiality, interest, sympathy, R. (B.) **-māna**, mfn. without self-confidence, free from pride, MBh.; Kāv. **-mānusha**, mf(*ā*)n. unpeopled, desolate, Kād.; Kathās.; (*e*), ind. in a solitary place, Rājat.; °*shī-√kṛi*, to depopulate, Priy. **-māya** (*nir-*), mfn. powerless, weak, TS. **-1. -mārga**, mfn. roadless, pathless, Kām. **-mālī**, f. = °*lyā* (next). **-mālya**, mfn. cast out or left from a garland, useless, unfit, Gṛihyās.; Vajracch. (*-tā*, f.); worn the day before, Daś.; = *nir-mala*, L.; (*ā*), f. Trigonella Corniculata, L.; n. the remains of an offering to a deity, flowers left at a sacrificial ceremony, MBh.; the remains i.e. a feeble reflex of (gen.), Bālar. i, 40; stainlessness, purity, W.; *-dāman*, n. a garland made of flowers left at a sacrifice, Ṛitus. iv, 15. **-mithya**, mfn. not false, true, HYog. **-muṇḍa**, m. 'very bald' (?), a eunuch, Bhar. **-mūla**, mfn. rootless (as a tree), MBh.; baseless, unfounded, BhP.; eradicated, W.; °*la-tā*, f. rootlessness, baselessness, Prab.; °*lana*, m. an uprooter, Damayantīk.; n. uprooting, extirpating, Bhartṛ.; °*laya*, Nom. P. °*yati*, to uproot, eradicate, annihilate, Kād. **-mūshaka**, mfn. free from mice, Kathās. **-mṛiga**, mfn. deerless, R. **-megha**, mf(*ā*)n. cloudless, BhP. **-medha**, mfn. without understanding, stupid; °*dhâśrama*, m. N. of a man, Cat. **-mogha**, v.l. for next. **-moha**, mfn. 'free from illusion,' N. of Śiva, Śivag.; of a son of the fifth Manu, Hariv.; of one of the Saptarshis under the 13th Manu, ib. (cf. *nir-moka*, below). **—yatna**, mfn. inactive, immovable, lazy, Hariv.; *-tā*, f. inactivity, ib. **—yantraṇa**, mfn. unrestrained, uncontrolled, self-willed, independent, Kāv.; Suśr.; (also °*trita*, W.); (*am*), ind. without restraint, Ṛitus.; Rājat.; *-pradeśâvasthita*, mfn. being at a place where no restraint is needed, Kull. **—yaśaska**, mfn. inglorious, MBh. **—yādava**, mfn. freed from the Yādavas, Hariv. **—1. -yukti**, f. want of union or connection (esp. in gram.); unfitness, impropriety, W.; mfn. unfounded, illogical, wrong, Gol.; °*tika*, mfn. id., °*tika-tva*, n. L. **—yūtha**, mfn. separated or strayed from the herd (as an elephant), Hariv. **—yoga-kshema**, mfn. free from care or anxiety about acquisition or possession, Bh. ii, 45. **—lakshaṇa**, mf(*ā*)n. having no special marks, undistinguished, insignificant, plain, ill-featured, R.; Kathās.; unworthy, fit for nothing, Kād.; unspotted, W. **—lakshya**, mfn. inobservable, invisible, Kathās. **—lajja**, mf(*ā*)n. shameless, impudent (*-tā*, f.), MBh.; Kāv. &c. **—lavaṇa**, mfn. graceless (figure), Subh. **—liṅga**, mfn. having no characteristic marks, indefinable (as *ātman*, *brahman*), MBh. **—lipta**, m. 'unsmeared, undefiled,' N. of Kṛishṇa, BrahmavP.; a sage, W. **—lepa**, mfn. unsmeared, free from fatty substances, Mn. v, 112; stainless, sinless, L.; not attached to anything, L.; (*am*), ind. completely (so as to leave nothing that clings or sticks), Śaṃk.; m. N. of Śiva, Śivag.; a sage, W. **—lobha**, mfn. free from desire, unavaricious, Rājat.; *-tva*, n. Sinhās. **—loma**, mfn. hairless, smooth, Kauś. **—loha**, n. myrrh, L. **—vaṇśa**, mfn. having no family, standing alone, Hit. **—1. -vacana**, mfn. not speaking, silent, Śukas.; unobjectionable, blameless, MBh.; (*am*), ind. silently, Kum. vii, 19. **—vana**, m. or n. a country without forests, L.; mfn. = *-vana;* (°*ne*), ind. in the open country, Pāṇ. vi, 2, 178; viii, 4, 5, Kāś. **—vatsala**, mf(*ā*)n. not lovingly clinging to (esp. to children, with loc.), Veṇis. v, 3; vi, 17. **—vatsa-śiśu-puṃgava**, mfn. deprived of calves and young bulls, Hariv. **—vana**, mfn. having no wood, being out of a w° or in the open country, MBh. v, 863 (cf. *-vana*). **—vara**, mfn. excellent, L. **—varuṇám**, ind. without falling into Varuṇa's power, TS. (cf. *a-v*°); *-ṇá-tā*, f. (JBr.); °*ṇa-tvá*, n. (TS.) deliverance from V°'s p°. **—varti**, mfn. wickless, Kād. **—valkala**, mfn. barkless, Mṛicch. i, 51. **—vaśa**, mfn. having no free will, dependent on another; *-tā*, f. Hcar. **—vashaṭkāra-maṅgala**, mfn. destitute of sacrifices and festivities, Kathās. **—vasu**, mfn. without property, poor; *-tva*, n. Rājat. **—vastra**, mfn. unclothed; °*strī-√kṛi*, to rob a person of his clothes, Subh. **—vākya**, mf(*ā*)n. speechless, R. **—vāc**, mfn. id., BhP. **—1. -vācya**, mfn. unobjectionable, blameless; improper to be said, W. **—vāṇī**, f. (with Jainas) N. of a deity who executes the commands of the 16th Arhat of the present Ava-sarpiṇī. **—1. -vāta**, mfn. free from wind, sheltered, still, Pañc.; m. a calm, a place sheltered from wind; *-stha*, mfn. standing sheltered from the w°, MBh.; Hariv. **—1. -vāda**, m. absence of dispute or railing, W. **—vānara**, mfn. free from monkeys, R. **—vāyasa**, mfn. free from crows, Pañc. **—vārāṇasi**, mfn. one who has left Vārāṇasī, Pāṇ. vi, 2, 2. Vārtt. 3, Pat. **—1. -vāsana**, mfn. without fancy or imagination, Sāh. **—vikalpa**, mfn. (or °*pana*, L.) not admitting an alternative, free from change or differences, Tejob-Up.; Vedântas.; admitting no doubt, not wavering, Bhartṛ. (*am*), ind. without hesitation or reflection, Pañc.; *-vāda* and *-vicāra*, m. N. of wks. **—vikalpaka**, mfn. = *-vikalpa*, BhP.; Bhāshāp.; Vedântas.; n. knowledge not depending upon or derived from the senses, W. **—vikāra**, mfn. unchanged, unchangeable, uniform, normal, MBh. (also *-vat*); Kāv.; Suśr.; *-tā*, f. MBh. **—vikāsa**, mfn. not opening or expanded, unblown; *-tva*, n., Mallin. **—vighaṭṭam**, ind. without any hindrance from (in comp.), Jātakam. **—vighna**, mf(*ā*)n. uninterrupted, unhindered, Hariv.; Kāv.; (*am* and *ena*), ind. unobstructedly, freely, Rājat.; Sāh. **—vicāra**, mf(*ā*)n. not needing any consideration, Yogas.; not reflecting or considering, Rājat.; (*am*), ind. without reflection, inconsiderately, R. **—vicikitsa**, mf(*ā*)n. without reflecting much (*am*, ind.), Kull.; indubitable, Sarvad. **—viceshṭa**, mfn. motionless, insensible, MBh.; R. **—vitarka**, mfn. unreflecting, inconsiderate, Yogas. **—vidya**, mfn. unlearned, uneducated, Kām. **—vidhitsa**, mfn. not wishing to do, having no designs, MBh. **—vinoda**, mfn. having no pastime, void of solace or diversion, Megh.; Vcar. **—vindhyā**, f. 'being outside or coming from the Vindhya,' N. of a river, Var.; Kālid. &c. **—vibandha**, mfn. offering no obstacles, quite fit for (gen.), Bālar. vii, $\frac{1}{2}\frac{4}{}$; inoffensive, harmless, ib. ix, 53. **—vimarśa**, mfn. (also written °*sha*) unreflecting, inconsiderate, Kathās.; not having the Saṃdhi called Vimarśa, Sāh. **—virodha**, mf(*ā*)n. not being opposed to (comp.), Jātakam. **—vivara**, mfn. having no opening or rent, close, contiguous, Kathās.; *-tā*, f. close, contiguousness (as of female breasts); agreement, understanding, Śiś. ix, 44. **—vivāda**, mfn. having no context, agreeing, MBh.; incontestable, Sāh.; °*dī-√kṛi*, to cause to agree, conciliate, L. **—viveka**, mfn. undiscriminating, inconsiderate, foolish, Subh.; *-tā*, f. (Pañcad.), *-tva*, n. (Kathās.) want of judgment, indiscretion. **—viśaṅka**, mf(*ā*)n. fearless, confident, Mn.; MBh. &c.; (*am* and *ena*), ind. without fear or hesitation, Suśr.; R.; -°*kita*, mfn. = °*ka;* (*am*), ind., Hariv. **—viśesha**, mf(*ā*)n. showing or making no difference, undiscriminating, without distinction, MBh.; R. &c.; not different from, same, like (comp.), Kālid.; (with *viśesha*, m. not the least difference, Bhartṛ. iii, 54); unqualified, absolute, Sarvad.; (*am* and *eṇa*), ind. equally, alike, the same as (comp.), MBh.; Kāv. &c.; n. absence of difference, indiscriminateness, likeness, MBh. vi, 5519; °*shaṇa*, mfn. having no attributes, BhP.; °*sha-tā*, f. (Bhām.), °*sha-tva*, n. (MBh.) = °*sha*, n.; °*sha-vat*, mfn. not different, indiscriminate, xii, 7516; °*shâkṛiti*, mfn. whose forms are precisely alike, MW. **—visha**, mf(*ā*)n. non-venomous (as a snake), MBh.; R. &c.; °*shī-√kṛi*, to deliver from poison, Bālar.; Vet.; (*a* and *ī*), f. Kyllingia Monocephala, L. **—vishaṅga**, mfn. not attached to anything, indifferent, BhP. **—vishaya**, mfn. having no dwelling-place or expelled from it (also °*yī-kṛita*), banished from (comp.), Kāv.; supportless, hanging in the air, Hariv. 3645; having no object or sphere of action, Sāh. (*-tva*, n. Saṃk.); not attached to sensual objects, Kap.; BhP.; °*yôparāga*, mfn. unharmed by objects of sense, MW. **—vishāṇa**, mfn. having no tusks (as an elephant), MBh. **—visarga**, mfn. without Visarga, Mṛicch., Sch. **—vihaṃga**, mfn. (wood) birdless, Hariv. **—vihāra**, mfn. having no pleasure, ib. **—vīja**, see *-bīja*. **—vīra** (*nír-*), mfn. deprived of men or heroes, TS. (°*rá-tā*, f. MaitrS.); unheroic, cowardly, W.; (*ā*), f. a woman whose husband and sons are dead, L.; N. of a river, MBh.; n. N. of a place of pilgrimage, ib. **—vīrudh**, mfn. deprived of plants, BhP. **—vīrya** (*nír-*), mfn. powerless, unmanly, impotent; m. a weakling, TBr.; ŚBr.; MBh. &c.; *-tā*, f. unmanliness, powerlessness, impotence, exhaustion, Āpast.; BhP. **—vṛiksha**, mfn. destitute of trees, MBh.; *-toya*, mfn. treeless and waterless, Kathās.; *-mṛiga-pakshin*, mfn. without trees or deer or birds, MBh. **—1. -vṛitti**, mfn. having no occupation, destitute, W. **—vṛisha**, mfn. having no bulls, Hariv. **—vega**, mfn. without violent motion, quiet, calm, R.; Suśr. **—vetana**, mfn. unsalaried, Rājat. **—1. -veda**, mfn. not having the Vedas, infidel, unscriptural, W. **—vepana**, mfn. not trembling or flickering, Var. **—vaira**, n. absence of enmity, Bh. (also °*riṇa*, Tarkas.); mfn. free from enmity, peaceable, amicable, Var.; MBh. &c.; (*am*), ind. peaceably, without enmity, R.; m. N. of a hunter, Hariv.; *-tā*, f. concord, MBh.; Hariv. **—vailakshya**, mfn. shameless, L. **—vyagra**, mfn. unconfused, calm, BhP. **—vyañjana**, mfn. without condiment, MBh.; Hariv.; (*e*), ind. in a plain manner, directly, Pañc. **—vyatha**, mfn. free from pain, quiet, calm, MBh.; Rājat. **—vyathana**, mfn. id., Naish.; n. a hole, cavern (as undisturbed), ib. **—vyapatrapa**, mfn. shameless, Jātakam. **—vyapêksha**, mf(*ā*)n. disregarding, indifferent to (loc. or comp.), Kāv.; Rājat. **—vyalīka**, mfn. not causing pain, (either =) not offending, harmless (as a word), BhP.; (or =) easy, hearty, willingly done (as a gift), MBh.; not feeling pain or uneasiness, willing, ready, sincere, undissembling, MBh.; R. &c.; °*kena cetasā* or *hṛidā*, with a willing or easy heart or mind, MBh.; (°*kam* or °*ka-tas*), ind. sincerely, willingly, BhP. **—vyavadhāna**, mfn. (ground) uncovered, bare, Hcar. **—vyavastha**, mfn. not staying in a certain place, moving hither and thither, Daś. **—vyasana**, mfn. free from bad inclinations, Kathās. **—vyākula**, mfn. not troubled or excited, calm; *-tā*, f. calmness, tranquillity, Pañc. **—vyāghra**, mfn. not haunted or infested by tigers, MBh. **—vyāja**, mfn. free from deceit or ambiguity, undisputed; exact, honest, sincere, pure, MBh.; Kāv. &c.; (*am*), ind. exactly, plainly, honestly, ib.; *-tā*, f. honesty, plainness, candour, Bhartṛ.; °*jī-kṛita*, mfn. made plain, freed from deceit or illusion, Śāntiś. **—vyādhi**, mfn. free from sickness, healthy, strong, MBh.; Car. **—vyāpāra**, mfn. free from occupation, not busy, at leisure, passive, Kāv. &c.; *-tva*, n. (Saṃk.) = *-sthiti*, f. (L.) want of occupation, leisure. **—vyāvṛitti**, mfn. (emancipation) not involving any return (to worldly existence), Sarvad. **—vraṇa**, mfn. unwounded, unhurt, MBh.; BhP.; undamaged, without notches or rents, Mn.; MBh.; AgP. **—vrata**, mfn. neglecting religious observances or vows, MBh. **—vrīḍa**, mfn. shameless, impudent, Kathās. **—hasta** (*nír-*), mfn. handless, AV. (cf. *nair-h*°). **—hima**, n. (or *am*, ind.) cessation of winter, Pāṇ. ii, 1, 6, Kāś. **—heti**, mfn. weaponless, unarmed; Yājñ. **—hetu**, mfn. causeless, reasonless, MBh.; *-tā*, f., *-tva*, n. want of a cause or reason, Sāh. **—hrī** or **-hrīka**, mfn. shameless, impudent, bold, daring, MBh. **—hlāda**, mfn. joyless, uncomfortable, uneasy, Mālav. i, $\frac{1}{1}\frac{1}{}$.

1. **Niś** for *nis* (q.v.) before *c*, *ch*. **—cakrika**, mfn. without tricks or deceit, honest, Subh. **—cakshus**, mfn. eyeless, blind, MBh. **—catvāriṇśa**, mfn. pl. more than forty, Vop. **—cala**, mf(*ā*)n. motionless, immovable, fixed, steady, invariable, unchangeable, MBh.; Kāv. &c.; (*ā*), f. the earth, L.; Desmodium Gangeticum, L.; °*la-kara* and °*la-dāsa-svāmin*, m. N. of authors; °*lâṅga*, m. 'firm-limbed, firm,' Ardea Nivea, L.; a rock, mountain, L. **—cāmara**, mfn. without a chowrie, Hcar. **—citta**, m. N. of a Samādhi, L. **—cinta**, mfn. not thinking, thoughtless, careless, unconcerned, MBh.; Kāv. &c. **—cetana**, mfn. unconscious, unreasonable, Hariv.; R. &c.; *-tā*, f., Kād. **—cetas**, mfn. out of one's senses, MBh.; R. **—ceshṭa**, mfn. incapable of motion, motionless, powerless, helpless, MBh.; Kāv.; Suśr. &c.; (*am*), ind. without motion, MBh.; (*ā*), f. motionless; °*ṭā-karaṇa*, mfn. causing it (N. of one of the arrows of the god of love), L.; °*ṭī-√bhū*, to become motionless, Kathās. **—caura**, mfn. free from robbers or thieves, Rājat. **—cyavana**, m. 'unperishing (?),' a partic. form of fire, MBh.; N. of one of the Saptarshis in the 2nd Manv-antara, Hariv. **—chandas**, mfn. not studying Vedic texts, Mn. iii, 7. **—chāya**, mfn. shadeless, Deśîn. **—chidra**, mfn. having no rents or holes, without weak points or defects, unhurt, uninterrupted, Var.; Kāv.; Pur. **—cheda**, mfn. indivisible, reduced by the common divisor to the least term, Col.

Nish for *nis* (q.v.) before *k*, *kh*; *p*, *ph*. **—kaṇṭaka**, mfn. free from thorns or enemies, unhurt, untroubled, secure, MBh.; Kāv. &c.; m. N. of Śiva, Śivag.; (*ikā*), f. N. of 2 Comms. **—kaṇṭha**, m. Crataeva Roxburghii, L. **—kanishṭha** or °*ṭhika*, mfn. (a fist) with the little finger stretched out, L. **—kanda**, mfn. without edible roots, Śāntiś. **—kapaṭa**, mfn. guileless, free from deceit or fraud, MW. **—kampa**, mfn. not shaking or tremulous, motionless, immovable, Kāv.; Kathās.; *-tā*, f., Ragh. **—kara**, mfn. free from taxes, Vas. **—karuṇa**, mf(*ā*)n. pitiless, unmerciful, cruel (*-tā*, f.), Hariv.; Kāv. &c.; °*ṇī-√kṛi*, to make pitiless or cruel, Kathās. **—karūsha**, mfn. free from dirt, R. **—karṇa**, mf(*ā*)n. not curved (*gadā*), MBh. (Nīl.; perhaps 'without an ear or handle'). **—karman**, mfn. inactive, Kull.; exempt from or neglecting religious or worldly acts, W. **—kala**, mfn. without parts, undivided, Up.; MBh. &c.; waned, diminished, decayed, infirm, MBh.; Daś.; seedless, impotent, L.; m. an old man, W.; N. of Śiva, Śivag.; a receptacle, L.; pudendum muliebre, L.; (*ā* or *ī*, g. *gaurâdi*), f. a woman past childbearing or menstruation, L.; *-tva*, n. indivisibility, the state of the absolute Brahma, MBh. **—kalaṅka**, mfn. stainless, immaculate, Rājat.; m. N. of Śiva, Śivag.; *-tīrtha*, n. N. of a sacred bathing-place, Cat. **—kali**, m. a spell for weapons, R. (B.) **—kalmasha**, mf(*ā*)n. stainless, sinless, pure, MBh.; Hariv. &c.; °*shī-√bhū*, to become stainless &c., Yājñ. **—kashāya**, mfn. free from dirt or impure passions, MBh.; m. N. of 13th Arhat of future Ut-sarpiṇī, L. **—kāṅksha**, mfn. free from doubts, L. **—kānta**, mfn. not lovely, ugly, Kathās. **—kāma** (*nísh-*), mfn. desireless, disinterested, unselfish, ŚBr.; Mn. &c.; *-cārin*, mfn. acting without interest or selfishness, MārkP. **—kāmuka**, mf(*ā*)n. free from worldly desires, Kād. **-kāraṇa,** mf(*ā*)n. causeless, unnecessary, MBh.; BhP.; disinterested (as a friend), Hit.; groundless, not proceeding from any cause, Kathās.; Pur. &c.; (*am* and *āt*), ind. causelessly, without a reason or any special motive, MBh.; Kāv. &c. **-kārya,** mfn. to no purpose, worthless, vain, Kāv. **-kālaka,** m. (g. *nir-udakâdi*) one who has shaven his hair, Vas.; an ascetic shaven and smeared with ghee or clarified butter, L. (cf. next). **-kālika,** mfn. one who has no more time to live, whose term of life is elapsed, MBh. viii, 3628 (g. *nirudakâdi*). **-kiṃcana,** mf(*ā*)n. having nothing, poor, Rājat.; BhP.; *-tva,* n. poverty, MBh. **-kilbisha,** mfn. free from sin, Kathās. **-kutūhala,** mfn. having no curiosity, incurious, L. **-kula,** mf(*ā*)n. without family, having no kindred, Mn. viii, 28 (°*laṃ-√kṛi,* to make family-less, exterminate, R.); shelled, husked, Car.; *-tā,* f. dying out, perishing, Pañc.; *-tvac,* mfn. stripped off, husked, Bhpr.; °*lā-* or °*lī-√kṛi,* to shell, strip off, husk, Daś.; Var. &c.; °*līna,* mfn. of low family, plebeian, Kāv. **-kūja,** mfn. noiseless, still, MBh.; R. **-kūṭa,** mfn. free from deceit, guileless, R. **-kṛipa,** mfn. pitiless, cruel, Prasann. **-kevala,** mf(*ā*)n. belonging exclusively, MBh.; °*lya* (*nish-*), mfn. id., VS.; Br.; (with or scil. *śastra* and *uktha*), n. N. of a partic. recitation connected with the midday oblation and belonging to Indra exclusively, ib. **-kaitava,** mfn. undeceitful, honest, Kathās. **-kaivalya,** mfn. mere, pure, absolute, MBh.; (a fight) singular in its kind, ib. (Nīlak.) **-kośa,** mfn. unsheathed, Mcar. **-kaurava,** mf(*ā* MBh., *ī* BhP.)n. deprived of or freed from the Kauravas. **-kauśāmbi,** mfn. one who has left Kauśāmbi, Pāṇ. vi, 2, 2, Vārtt. 3, Pat. **-kriya,** mfn. = *-karman,* Up.; MBh. &c.; n. 'the actionless One,' the Supreme Spirit, W.; *-tā,* f. inactivity, neglect of (comp.), MBh.; °*yâtman,* mfn. lazy, inactive; °*tma-tā,* f. inactivity, non-performance of religious acts or prescribed duties, Mn.; MBh. **-krodha,** mfn. free from wrath, not angry with (gen.), Śak. **-kleśa,** mfn. free from pain or moral faults, MWB. 124, 133; *-leśa,* mfn. not suffering the least pain, quite happy, Bhartṛ. **-pakva** (*nish-*), mf(*ā*)n. well cooked or boiled, TS.; ŚBr.; well ripened, L. **-paṅka,** mf(*ā*)n. free from mud, clear, pure, MBh.; R. **-patāka,** mfn. having no flag or banner; *-dhvaja,* m. a flag-staff without a banner, MW. **-pati-sutā,** f. having no husband and no sons, L. **-pattra,** mfn. leafless, MBh.; R.; unfeathered, featherless (cf. °*trā-√kṛi* and *a-nishpattram*); m. or n. the clove tree, L.; °*traka,* mfn. leafless; (*ikā*), f. Capparis Aphylla, L.; °*traya,* Nom. P. °*yati,* to deprive of leaves, MBh.; °*trā-√kṛi,* to pierce with an arrow so that the feathers come through on the other side (opp. to *sa-pattrā-√kṛi*), Daś.; to cause excessive pain, wound severely (fig.), Bhām.; °*trākṛiti,* f. causing excessive bodily pain, L. **-pathya,** mfn. unwell, ill, Rājat. **-pad,** mf(*ī*)n. footless, g. *kumbhapady-ādi.* **-pada,** mfn. id.; (with *yāna*), n. a vehicle moving without feet (as a ship &c.), L. **-1. -panda** (fr. *nis + sp*°; cf. Vām. v, 2, 89), mf(*ā*)n. motionless, immovable, MBh.; R. &c. (also w. r. for *nishyanda*); °*da-tarī-√bhū,* to become more or quite motionless, Naish.; °*dī-√kṛi,* to keep quiet, not move, Mṛicch. **-payoda,** mfn. cloudless, R. **-parākrama,** mfn. powerless, weak, Bhaṭṭ. **-parāmarśa,** mfn. incapable of thinking, without advice, helpless, Mālav. iv, $\frac{2}{3}$. **-parikara,** mfn. without preparations or provisions, Kathās. **-parigraha,** mfn. having no property, MBh.; Hariv. &c.; m. an ascetic without family or dependants, W. **-paricaya,** mfn. not becoming familiar, Kād. **-paricchada,** mfn. having no retinue or court, Kull. **-paridāha,** mfn. incombustible, L. **-parihārya,** mfn. not to be omitted, by all means to be applied, Car. **-parīksha,** mfn. not examining or testing accurately, MBh. **-parīhāra,** mfn. not avoiding, not observing caution; (*am*), ind. not so as to avoid, Suśr. **-parusha,** mfn. (music) not harsh, soft, Divyâv. **-paryanta,** mfn. boundless, unlimited, Rājat. **-paryāya**°, out of order, Bālar. **-palāva,** mf(*ā*)n. free from chaff (fig.), Buddh. **-pāṇḍava,** mf(*ā*)n. freed from the Pāṇḍavas, Veṇis. **-pāpa,** mf(*ā*)n. sinless, guiltless, Rājat. **-pāra,** mfn. boundless, unbounded, R. **-pālaka,** mfn. without guardian, unprotected, Rājat. **-pitṛika,** mfn. fatherless, Campak. **-putra,** mfn. sonless, childless, Hit.; *-jīvana,* n. life without a son, ib.; °*trī-√kṛi,* to deprive of sons, Bhām. **-pudgala,** mfn. without soul or personality; *-tva,* n., Vajracch. **-purāṇa,** mfn. not existing before, unheard of, new, Hariv. **-purīsha,** mfn. free from excrement, ĀśvŚr.; Bhpr.; °*shī-bhāva,* m. discharge of e°, Gaut. **-purusha,** mfn. deprived of men, desolate, MBh.; one who has not produced male children, Mn. iii, 7; not male, feminine or neuter, W.; m. a weakling or coward, W. **-pulāka,** mfn. free from chaff or useless grain (°*kīkṛita,* freed from chaff by winnowing, Kull.); m. N. of the 14th Arhat of future Ut-sarpiṇī, L. **-pūtigandhika,** mfn. not stinking, fragrant, Divyāv. **-posha,** mfn. not being nourished, Vajracch. **-paurusha,** mfn. devoid of manhood, unmanly, Prab. ii, 18 (printed *niḥ-p*°); °*shâmarsha,* mfn. devoid of manhood and wrath, Kathās. **-prakampa,** mf(*ā*)n. immovable, MBh.; m. N. of one of the Saptarshis in the 13th Manv-antara, Hariv. **-prakāraka,** mfn. without distinction or specification, Tarkas. **-prakāśa,** mfn. not transparent, lightless, dark, MBh. **-prakrama,** mfn. unruly, rash, L. **-pragala,** mfn. not dripping, dry, L. **-pracāra,** mfn. not moving, remaining in one place, fixed or concentrated (as mind), MBh. **-prajña,** mfn. ignorant, stupid, Kathās. **-praṇaya,** mfn. without affection, cold, Uttarar.; *-tā,* f., *-tva,* n. want of confidence or affection, coldness, reserve, Jātakam. **-pratāpa,** mf(*ā*)n. void of dignity, mean, base, Mṛicch.; Pañc. **-pratikriya,** mfn. incurable, irremediable, Daś.; *-tā,* f., Kād. **-pratigraha,** mfn. not accepting gifts; *-tā,* f., Kām. **-pratigha,** mfn. unhindered, unimpeded, Ragh. **-pratidvaṃdva,** mfn. having no adversary or match, unopposed, unequalled, MBh. **-pratipaksha,** mfn. without an adversary or opponent; *-tā,* f., Kull. **-pratibandha,** mfn. unimpeded, unopposed, Sarvad. **-pratibha,** mf(*ā*)n. devoid of splendour, Hariv.; stupid, dull, L.; °*bhaṃ-√kṛi,* to reduce to silence, Jātakam. **-pratibhāna,** mfn. not bold, cowardly, L. **-pratīkāra,** mfn. = *-pratikriya,* unobstructed, uninterrupted; (*am*), ind., MBh. **-pratīpa,** mfn. unopposed, unhindered, unconcerned, ib. **-pratyāśa,** mfn. hopeless, despondent of (loc. or comp.), Kād.; °*śī-√bhū,* to give up all hope in (*prati*), Ratnâv. **-pratyūha,** mfn. unimpeded, irremediable, Mālatim.; (*am*), ind., Rājat. **-pradeśa,** mfn. having no certain place, Śaṃk. **-pradhāna,** mf(*ā*)n. deprived of a chief or leaders, R. **-prapañca,** mfn. subject to no expansion or manifoldness, BhP.; pure, honest, L.; *-sad-ātman,* mfn. being of real essence without expansion (°*tma-tva,* n.), Śaṃk.; °*câtman,* m. N. of Śiva, Śivag. **-prabha,** mf(*ā*)n. deprived of light or radiance, lustreless, gloomy, dark (*-tā,* f. R.; *-tva,* n. Suśr.); m. N. of a Dānava, Hariv. **-prabhāva,** mfn. powerless; *-tva,* n., Kathās. **-pramāṇaka,** mfn. without authority, Kull. **-pramāda,** mfn. not negligent or careless, Hcat. **-prayatna,** mfn. abstaining from exertion, inactive, Hariv. **-prayojana,** mfn. having no motive, impartial, indifferent, MBh.; Kād.; harmless, Yājñ., Sch.; groundless, needless, unnecessary (*am,* ind.; *-tā,* f.; *-tva,* n.), Hariv.; Daś.; Hit. &c. **-pravaṇi** and **-pravāṇa,** (L.) = next. **-pravāṇi,** mfn. fresh from the loom, quite new (cloth &c.), Daś.; Pāṇ. v, 4, 160. **-prâṇa,** mfn. breathless, lifeless, quite exhausted, MBh.; Hariv.; *-tā,* f., Sāh. **-prīti,** mfn. not taking delight in, not pleased with (loc.), Gaut.; MBh. **-prītika,** mfn. not connected with joy or delight, Lalit. **-phala,** mf(*ā*)n. bearing no fruit, fruitless, barren, resultless, successless, useless, vain, Mn.; MBh.; Var.; Kāv. &c.; seedless, impotent, W.; (*ā*), f. a woman past childbearing or menstruation (also *ī,* v. l. *nish-kalā*), L.; a species of Momordica, L.; *-tva,* n. unfruitfulness, uselessness, Mṛicch. iv, 9; °*laya,* Nom. P. °*yati,* to render fruitless, Kull.; °*lī-√kṛi,* to make fruitless, neglect, Mṛicch.; v. l. for *nish-kulī-√kṛi,* VarBṛS. lv, 29. **-phena,** mfn. foamless, frothless, Suśr.; n. opium, L. (cf. *a-ph*°).

Nis, ind. out, forth, away &c. (rarely used as an independent word [e. g. AV. vi, 18, 3; vii, 115, 3; xvi, 2, 1], but mostly as a prefix to verbs and their derivatives [cf. *niḥ-√kshi* &c. below], or to nouns not immediately connected with verbs, in which case it has the sense 'out of,' 'away from' [cf. *nirvana, nish-kauśāmbi* &c.] or that of a privative or negative adverb = 3. *a,* 'without,' 'destitute of,' 'free from,' 'un-' [cf. *nir-artha, nir-mala* &c.], or that of a strengthening particle 'thoroughly,' 'entirely,' 'very' [cf. *niḥ-śūnya, nish-kevala, nir-muṇḍa*]; it is liable to be changed to *niḥ, nir, niś, nish* and *nī;* cf. above and below). **-tattva,** mfn. not comprehended in the 24 Tattvas or principles, MBh. **-tantu,** mfn. having no offspring, childless, ib. **-tantra,** w. r. for **-tandra,** mfn. not lazy, fresh, healthy; *-tā,* f., Sāh. **-tandri** and **-tandrī** (nom. *īs*), mfn. id., R. **-tamaska,** mfn. free from darkness, not gloomy, light, Śak. **-tamisra,** mfn. id., Prasann. **-tambha,** mfn. = *niḥ-st*°. **-taraṃga,** mf(*ā*)n. motionless, still, Naish. **-tarīka** and **-tarīpa,** g. *nirudakâdi.* **-tarkya,** mfn. unimaginable, inconceivable, MBh. **-tala,** mfn. not flat, round, globular, Kum.; trembling, moving, L.; down, below, W. **-tāntava,** mfn. not wearing a woven garment, SāmavBr. **-timira,** mf(*ā*)n. = *-tamaska,* MBh.; Hariv. **-tula,** mfn. matchless, incomparable, Dharmaśarm.; v. l. for *-tala,* R. (B.) **-tusha,** mf(*ā*)n. freed from chaff or husk, KātyŚr.; Suśr.; (fig.) purified, cleansed; simplified, Rājat.; Siṃhâs.; *-kshīra* or °*rin,* m. wheat, L.; *-tva,* n. = *nir-doshatva,* n., Śrikaṇṭh.; *-ratna,* n. crystal, L.; °*shita,* mfn. (L.) freed from husk; simplified; abandoned; °*shī-√kṛi,* to free from husk i. e. lessen, diminish, Viddh. **-tṛiṇa-kaṇṭaka,** mfn. cleared or freed from grass and thorns, R. **-tṛish,** mfn. desireless, satisfied, Kād. **-tṛishṇa,** mfn. free from desire, Divyâv. **-tejas,** mfn. destitute of fire or energy, impotent, spiritless, dull, MBh.; Kāv. &c. **-toya,** mf(*ā*)n. waterless, R.; Kathās. &c.; *-tṛiṇapādapa,* mf(*ā*)n. without water or grass or trees, Kathās. **-transa,** mfn. fearless, W. (prob. w. r. for *-triṇśa*). **-trapa,** mfn. shameless, MBh. **-triṇśa,** mfn. more than thirty (pl.), L.; merciless, cruel, Kāv.; Pañc.; m. a sword, MBh.; Kathās.; Suśr. &c.; a sacrificial knife, W.; a partic. stage in the retrograde motion of the planet Mars, Var. (= °*śa-musala,* ib.); *-karkaśa,* mfn. cruel and hard, Kāv.; *-tva,* n. cruelty, Rājat.; *-dharmin,* mfn. resembling a sword, Rājat.; *-dhārin,* m. a s°-bearer, MatsyaP.; *-pattraka,* m. (Car.); °*trikā,* f. (L.) Euphorbia (Antiquorum or Tortilis); *-bhṛit,* m. = *-dhārin,* MW.; °*śin,* mfn. bearing a s°, ĀśvŚr. **-truṭi,** f. cardamoms, L. **-traiguṇya,** mfn. destitute of the three Guṇas (*sattva, rajas, tamas;* see *guṇa*), Bhag. ii, 45. **-tvak-paksha,** mfn. deprived of skin and fins, R. (B.)

1. **Nī** for *nis* (q. v.) before *r.* **-rakta,** mfn. colourless, faded, L. **-raṅgikā** (Deśīn.) or °**ṅgī** (HPariś.), f. a veil. **-1. -raja,** mfn. free from dust, MBh.; free from passion, Kāv.; Pur. &c.; m. (with *viraja*) N. of Śiva, MBh.; °*jas,* mfn. = prec. mfn., R.; having no pollen, L.; f. a woman not menstruating, W.; °*jaska,* mf(*ā*)n. = *-raja,* mfn., MBh.; R. &c.; °*jas-tama* (R.) or °*maska* (L.), mfn. free from passion and darkness; °*jas-tamasā,* f. absence of p° and d°, Yājñ.; °*jasva,* mfn. free from dust, W.; °*jī-√kṛi,* to make free from dust (*-kārita,* mfn. fr. Caus.), Bhaṭṭ. **-rata,** mfn. not delighting in, indifferent (= *virata*), L. **-1. -rada,** mfn. toothless, Kāv. **-randhra,** mf(*ā*)n. having no holes or openings, imperforate, close, thick, dense, uninterrupted, Kum.; Uttarar.; Sāh.; firmly closed, Bālar. iii, 36; *-tva,* n. closeness, close connection, Śiś., Sch.; °*dhrita,* mfn. thickly set with, abounding in (comp.), Prasannar.; uninterrupted, Naish. **-rava,** mf(*ā*)n. soundless, Ragh. **-raśana,** see *a-nī-r*°. **-rasa,** mf(*ā*)n. without juice, sapless, dried up, withered (*-tva,* n.), Hariv.; Kāv. &c.; flavourless, tasteless, Bhartṛ. iii, 16; insipid, without charm, dull (*-tā,* f.), Kāv.; Pañc.; Sāh. &c.; m. the pomegranate, W. **-rāga,** mfn. colourless, Kathās.; free from passion, Bhartṛ. **-ruc,** mfn. lustreless, dim, Śiś. xi, 27 (according to Pāṇ. vi, 3, 116 fr. *ni + ruc*). **-ruj,** mfn. free from sickness, well, in health, Hit.; Suśr. **-ruja,** mf(*ā*)n. id., MBh.; R. &c.; n. a species of Costus, L. **-rūpa,** mfn. shapeless; m. air, wind, L.; a god, L.; n. heaven, ether, L. **-1. -reṇuka,** mf(*ā*)n. free from dust, Prasann. **-2. -reṇuka,** mfn. without Reṇukā, ib. **-roga,** mfn. free from sickness, healthy, well, Suśr., Pañc. (*-tā,* f.); *-durbhiksha,* mfn. not visited by disease or famine, Kathās.; °*gyatā,* w. r. for °*gatā.*

निःक्षि *niḥ-√1. kshi,* P. *-kshiṇoti,* to destroy, remove (an illness), AV.

निःक्षिप *niḥ-√kship,* prob. w. r. for *ni-√kship,* q. v. °**kshipta,** mfn. thrown away, spent (as time), R. °**kshipya,** ind. p. having thrown away or spent (time); having wiped away (tears), MBh.; R. °**kshepa,** m. throwing or sending away, removing, Kull.

निःशस् niḥ-śás, f. (√śaṃs) refusing, declining (?), RV. x, 164, 3.

निःशाण niḥ-śāṇa, m. or n. march, procession, Sāh. (Pers. نشان ?).

निःशास niḥ-√śās (pf. Subj. -śaśās), to drive away, expel, RV. i, 80, 1.

निःशिष् niḥ-√śish; Caus. -śeshayati, -śeshita &c. See niḥ-śesha under niḥ, p. 538, col. 3.

निःशी niḥ-√śī, only pr. p. Ā. -śayāna, mfn. starting up from sleep, BhP.

निःशुच् niḥ-√śuc, Intens. Ā. -śośucanta, to shine forth, RV. vii, 1, 4.

निःशृङ्खण niḥ-śriṅkhaṇa, n. blowing the nose, Āpast. (cf. śriṅkhāṇikā).

निःशॄ niḥ-√śṝ, P. -śṛiṇāti (Impv. -śṛiṇīhi), to break, crush, AV.

निःश्वस् niḥ-√śvas, P. -śvasiti (pf. -śaśvāsa), to hiss (said of a serpent), R.; to snort (said of an elephant), ib.; to breathe, exhale, Suśr., inhale, MārkP.; to sigh, MBh.; Kāv. &c. **°śvasana**, n. breathing out or sighing, W. **°śvasita**, mfn. breathed or breathing out, sighing; n. expiration, Ragh.; a sigh, Kum.; Vikr. **°śvasya**, ind. having breathed out or sighed, sighing, R.; Kālid. &c. **°śvāsa**, m. (ifc. f. ā) = °śvasita, n., Mn.; MBh. &c. (often v. l. or w. r. ni-śv°); -parama, mf(ā)n. quite addicted to sighing, melancholy, Nal.; -saṃhitā, f. N. of a code of laws supposed to have been revealed by Rudra-Śiva, Pur.

निःषिच् niḥ-shic (√sic), P. -shiñcati (Pāṇ. viii, 3, 65, Vārtt. 1, Pat.), to pour away, AitBr. **°shikta**, mfn. poured away i.e. shaken off, removed (as a sin or crime), Nir. **°shecana**, n. a contrivance for pouring out; -vat, mfn., ĀpŚr.

निःषिध् 1. niḥ-shidh (√2. sidh), P. -shedhati (Pāṇ. viii, 3, 65, Vārtt. 1, Pat.), to frighten away, VS. 2. **Niḥ-shidh**, see puru-n°

निःषिध् 3. niḥ-shídh, f. (√1. sidh) granting, bestowal, gift, oblation, RV. **°shídhvan**, mf(varī)n. granting, munificent, ib.

निःषु niḥ-shu (√3. su), P. -shuṇoti, Pāṇ. viii, 3, 65, Vārtt. 1, Pat.

निःषू niḥ-shū (√1. sū), P. -shuvati (Pāṇ. ib.), to drive or frighten away, AV. **°shūti**, f., Pāṇ. viii, 3, 88.

निःष्टन् niḥ-shṭan (√stan; cf. VPrāt. iii, 68, P. ni-shṭanati for niḥ-sht°, p. ni-shṭanat for niḥ-sht°, MBh.; 2. sg. Impv. niḥ-shṭanihi, RV. vi, 47, 30), to roar out, thunder, sound, cry.

निःष्ठा niḥ-shṭhā (√sthā; cf. Pāṇ. viii, 3, 65), P. nis-tishṭhati, to grow forth, rise, RV.; bring to an end, finish, make ready, prepare, ChUp.: Caus. ni-shṭhāpayati (for niḥ-shṭh°), to drive out into (loc.), Kauś.; to prepare, make ready, KātyŚr. **Niḥ-shṭhita** (or ni-shṭh°), mfn. grown forth, RV.; finished, accomplished, ready, ŚBr.; MBh. &c.

निःष्ठिव् niḥ-√shṭhiv, P. -shṭhīvati or °vyati, to spit, ŚBr.; to draw lines with spittle, Daś.

निःष्वप् niḥ-shvap (√svap), P. -shvapiti, cf. Pāṇ. viii, 3, 88. **°shupta**, mfn., ib.

निःसृ niḥ-√sṛi, P. -sarati (pr. p. Ā. -saramāṇa, MBh.), to go out, come forth, depart, withdraw, Mn.; MBh. &c.: Caus. -sārayati, to cause to go out, turn out, expel (abl. with or without bahis), MBh.; R. &c.; to conclude, finish, BhP. **°sara**, mfn. issuing out; -tva, n. = pitta-roga, L. **°saraṇa**, n. going forth or out, MBh.; Pañc.; issue, egress, gate, L.; means, expedient, remedy to get rid of (comp.), MBh.; departure, death, final beatitude, L.; -vat (niḥ-sár°), mfn. flowing out, liquid, ŚBr. **°sāra**, m. going forth or out, MBh. **°sāraṇa**, n. turning out, expelling, Rājat.; egress or road of egress, L. **°sārita**, mfn. turned out, expelled, dismissed, MBh. &c. **°sāru** or **°sāruka**, m. (in music) a kind of measure. **°sārya**, mfn. to be expelled or excluded, Kull. **°sṛita**, mfn. gone out or forth (with abl. or comp.), departed, Up.; MBh.; Hit.; prominent (eyes), Hariv.; prolapsus (yoni), Kāv.; v.l. for niḥ-stṛita, q.v.; n. a kind of sword-dance (in which a sword is drawn out of a person's hands), Hariv.

निःसृज् niḥ-√sṛij, P. Ā. -sṛijáti, °te, to pour out, shed forth, RV.; VS.; to let loose, set free, RV.; AV.; to separate (as words), RPrāt.; to remove, destroy (as sorrow), ŚBr.

निःसृप् niḥ-√sṛip, P. -sárpati, to sneak or steal away, ŚrS.; to start, set out on a journey, R.

निःस्तृत niḥ-stṛita, mfn. (√stṛi) crumbled off from (abl.), Gṛihyās. (v. l. niḥ-sṛita).

निःस्पृ niḥ-√spṛi, P. -spṛiṇoti (2. du. aor. -spartam, RV. vii, 71, 5), to rescue from (abl.)

निःस्फुर् niḥ-√sphur, P. -sphuráti, to jerk or hurl away, RV.

निःस्यन्द् niḥ-syand or -shyand (√syand; Pāṇ. viii, 3, 72). **°syanda**, v.l. or w.r. for ni-sy°.

निःस्रु niḥ-√sru, P. -srávati, to flow out or off, ŚBr.; rise from (abl.), Cat.; to disappear or be lost to or from (abl.), Āpast.: Caus. -srāvayati, to cause to flow out (as a pond), MBh.; to cause to disappear from or be lost to or from (abl.), Āpast. **°srava**, m. remainder, surplus, overplus (with abl.), Yājñ. ii, 251. **°srāva**, m. the causing to flow out, expending, expense, Kām.; the moisture or water of boiled rice, L. (cf. ni-srāva). **°sruta**, mfn. flowed out or off, Suśr.; passed away (time), L.

निःस्वृ niḥ-√svṛi, P. -svárati, to sing or chant away i.e. expel by singing or chanting, Kāṭh.

निक nika, n. (with prajā-pateḥ) N. of a Sāman, ĀrshBr.

निकक्ष ni-kakshá, m. the arm-pit, ŚBr. &c.

निकट ni-kaṭa, mf(ā)n. being at the side, near; m. or n. nearness, proximity (°ṭam, ind. near to, towards, with gen. or comp.; °ṭe, id., near, at hand; °ṭāt, away from), R.; Pañc.; Kathās. &c. **-ga**, mfn. near, at hand, Var. **-vartin** (Pañc.) and **-stha** (Daś.), mfn. id.
Nikaṭī, in comp. for nikaṭa. **-bhūya**, ind. p. having become near; **-bhūta**, mfn. become near, approached, Kathās.

निकथितिन् nikathitin, mfn. (fr. ni-kathita, √kath), g. ishṭādi.

निकम् ni-√kam (Pot. -kāmayet, BhP.; p. Ā. -kāmáyamāna, TS.; pf. cakame, ŚBr.; inf. -kamam, Kāṭh.), to long or wish for, lust after (acc.) **°kāmá**, m. desire, wish, pleasure, RV.; VS.; AV.; ibc. = (am), ind. according to wish or desire, to one's heart's content, abundantly, excessively, Var.; Mṛicch. &c. (cf. yadā-nikāmam); (ní-k°), mfn. desirous, covetous, greedy, RV.; m. N. of an Agni, ŚāṅkhGṛ.; -kāma, mfn. covetous, BhP.; -jala, mfn. (a river) yielding abundant water, Śak. vi, 16; -tapta, mfn. excessively burnt, Kum.; -dhāraṇa, mfn. bearing according to wish, TBr.; -niraṅkuśa, mfn. freely ruling over (gen.), Gīt. vii, 40; -bhāma-bhāshya, n. N. of wk.; -varsha, mfn. having plenty of rain, MBh.; -varshin, mfn. raining according to wish, ib.; -sukhin, mfn. exceedingly happy, Śiś. iv, 54. **°kāman** (ní-), mfn. desirous, eager, RV. **°kāmana**, n. desire, Lāṭy.

निकर ni-kara, m. (√kṛi) a heap, pile, a flock or multitude, a bundle, mass, collection (mfn. ifc. f. ā), MBh.; Kāv. &c.; (L.) pith, sap, essence; suitable gift, a honorarium; a treasure, the best of anything, a treasure belonging to Kubera. 1. **Nikāra**, m. (L.) piling up or winnowing corn; tossing or lifting up.

निकर्तव्य ni-kartavya, ni-kartana, ni-karsha &c. See ni-kṛi, ni-kṛit, ni-kṛish &c.

निकष् ni-√kash, -kashati, °te, to scratch, rub, Car. **°kasha**, m. rubbing in, smearing, Mālav. ii, f.; a roller or harrow, Āpast.; the touchstone, MBh.; Kāv. &c.; N. of wk.; (ā), f. N. of the mother of Rāvaṇa, (R.) or of all the Rākshasas (°shâtmaja, m. a Rakshas, L.); n. the streak of gold or test made on the touchstone, MBh. xii, 7471 (Nilak.); °sha-grāvan (Hit.), °sha-pāshāṇa (ib.), °shâśman (BhP.), °shôpala (Hariv.), m. the touchstone. **°kashaṇa**, n. rubbing off, ĀpŚr., Sch.; m. or n. the touchstone, BhP. **°kashā**, ind. (g. svar-ādi) near to (with acc.), proximate, Hariv. 16038; Śiś. i, 68, &c.; in the middle, between, L. **°kashāya**, Nom. Ā. °yate, to serve as a touchstone; °yamāna, mfn. serving as a test or standard for (comp.), Daś. **°kāsha**, m. scratching, rubbing, grinding, pounding, Mcar.; Kir.; (am), ind. having pounded or mixed together (cf. hiraṇya-nik°).

निकस nikasa, °sâtmaja = ni-kasha, °shât° (above), L.

निकाणम् ni-kāṇam (√kaṇ); °ṇam akshi, ind. having closed the eyes, Pāṇ. iii, 4, 54, Sch. (cf. akshi-nikāṇam).

निकाय ni-kāyá (√1. ci) a heap, an assemblage, a group, class, association (esp. of persons who perform the same duties), Mn.; MBh. &c.; congregation, school, Buddh.; collection (of Buddh. Sūtras, there are 5, MWB. 62, 63); habitation, dwelling, hiding-place, R. (cf. Pāṇ. iii, 3, 41); the body, ŚvetUp.; the air, wind, VS. xv, 5 (Mahīdh.); aim, mark, L.; the Supreme Being, L. **°kāyântarīya**, mfn. belonging to another school, Buddh. **°kāyin**, m. N. of a partic. sacrifice, L. **°kāyya**, m. or n. a dwelling-house, L.

निकार 1. and 2. ni-kāra, °raṇa, &c. See under ni-kara and ni-kṛi.

निकावल्गा nikāvalgā, f. N. of a woman (or of two women, Nikā & V°?), Rājat. vii, 482.

निकाश ni-kāśa, m. (√kāś) horizon, range of sight, proximity (°śam me, before my eyes, to me), BhP.; ifc. having the appearance of, similar, like, MBh. &c. (cf. nī-k°, pra-k° &c.)

निकाष ni-kāsha. See ni-kash.

निकास ni-kāsa, w.r. for °kāśa.

निकिल्बिष ni-kilbishá, n. freeing from sin, deliverance from evil, RV.

निकुञ्च् ni-√kuñc, Caus. -kuñcayati, to draw in, contract (opp. to 'stretch out'), Car. **°kuciti**, f. contraction (?), Pāṇ. vii, 2, 9, Vārtt. 1, Pat. **°kucya-karṇi**, ind. with the ears hanging down, ib. v, 4, 128, Sch. **°kuñca**, m. a key, Gal. **°kuñcaka**, m. Calamus Rotang, Bhpr.; a measure of capacity equal to ¼ of a Kuḍava, L. **°kuñcana**, n. shrinking together, contraction, Car. **°kuñcita**, mfn. contracted, W.

निकुञ्ज ni-kuñja, m. (n., L.) an arbour, a bower, thicket, MBh.; Kāv. &c. **°jikâmlā**, f. a species of plant (= kuñjikā), L.

निकुट्टन ni-kuṭṭana, n. (√kuṭṭ) pounding, crushing down, Var.

निकुब्ज ni-kubja, mfn. curved, bent, Lalit. **°kubjana**, n. upsetting (a vessel), L.

निकुम्भ ni-kumbha, m. Croton Polyandrum (also ī, f., L.); N. of a Dānava (son of Prahlāda and brother of Kumbha, father of Sunda and Upasunda), MBh.; of a Rākshasa, R.; of a son of Kumbha-karṇa, L.; of an attendant of either Śiva (Hariv.) or Skanda (MBh.); of one of the Viśve Devās, Hariv. (viskumbhu C.); of a hero on the side of the Kurus, MBh.; of a king of A-yodhyā (son of Hary-aśva and father of Saṃhatâśva or Varhaṇâśva), Hariv.; Pur.; °bhâkhya-bīja, n. Croton Jamalgota, L. **°kumbhita**, n. a kind of time in music. **°kumbhila**, m. or (ā), f. (fr. kumbha?), a place where oblations are offered, (esp.) a grove at the western gate of Laṅkā for the performance of sacrificial rites; (according to others) an image of Bhadra-kālī on the west side of Laṅkā, R.

निकुरम्ब nikuramba (Mālatīm.), °rumba (Viddh.), °baka (Kāśīkh.), m. or n. a flock, mass, multitude.

निकुलीनका ni-kulīnakā, f. a partic. mode of flying, MBh. viii, 1902, Nilak. (v.l. °nikā).

निकूज् ni-√kūj, P. Ā. -kūjati, °te, to warble, moan, groan, R.; BhP. **°kūjita**, mfn. warbled, sung, BhP. (°taṃ haṅsaiḥ). **°kūjitavya**, n. moaning, groaning, Jātakam.

निकूड् ni-√kūḍ, P. -kūḍayati (ind. p. -kūḍya), to burn, set on fire, ĀpŚr.

निकूण् ni-√kūṇ, P. -kūṇati, Caus. °ṇayati, to close, contract. **°kūṇita**, mfn. closed, shut (esp. an eye), Deśīn.

निकूल *ni-kūla*, mfn. going down hill (in *utkūla-n°*, q.v.) — **vṛiksha**, m. N. of a tree, R.

निकृ *ni-√1.kṛi*. P. Ā. *-karoti, -kurute* (dat. inf. *ní-kartave*, RV. viii, 78, 5), to bring down, humiliate, subdue, overcome, RV.; AV.; VS.; ŚBr.: Desid. *-cikīrshati*, to wish to overcome, AV. **°kartavya**, mfn. to be acted badly or basely, to be injured, MW. **°kartu**, m.(?) a sword, Kāv. **°kartṛi**, m. one who acts badly or basely, MBh. (v.l. *vi-k°*). **°kāra**, m. bringing down, humiliation, wrong, offence, injury, MBh.; Kāv. &c.; wickedness, malice, W.; opposition, contradiction, W.; = next, Gal. **°kāraṇa**, n. killing, slaughter, L. **°kārin**, m. injurer, oppressor, VS. **°kṛita**, mfn. brought down, humiliated, offended, injured, tricked, deceived, MBh.; R. &c.; low, base, wicked, ib.; removed, set aside, dismissed, W.; n. lowering, humbling, humiliation, Bhartṛ. ii, 30 (v.l. *°ti*); *-prajña* (MBh.), *-mati* (BhP.), mfn. depraved in mind. **°kṛiti**, mfn. deceitful, dishonest, MBh. xii, 6269; iii, 11810 (Nīlak.); m. N. of one of the 8 Vasus, Hariv. (v.l. *nir-ṛiti*); f. low conduct, baseness, dishonesty, fraud, wickedness, MBh.; R. &c. (personified as a daughter of A-dharma and mother of Lobha [MBh.], or as a sister of Lobha and daughter of Dambha [BhP.]); abuse, reproach; rejection, removal; poverty, indigence, W.; *-jīvana*, mfn. subsisting by fraud or dishonesty, acting deceitfully, MBh.; *-prajña*, mfn. versed in dishonesty, well acquainted with vice, MBh. (cf. *°ta-pr°*); *°tim-jush*, mfn. delighting in dishonesty or vice, BhP. **°kṛitin** (MBh.) and **°kṛiti-mat** (Subh.), mfn. dishonest, low, base, wicked. **°kṛityā**, f. wickedness, dishonesty, MBh.; MārkP. **°kṛítvan**, mfn. deceitful (as dice), RV. x, 34, 7.

निकृत् *ni-√1. kṛit*, P. Ā. *-kṛintati, °te*, to cut or hew down, cut away, cut or chop off, cut through or to pieces, massacre, KātyŚr.; MBh.; R.; Suśr. &c.; Ā. *°te*, (also) to cut one's self (or one's nails &c.), TS.; ŚBr.: Caus. *-kartayati*, to cause to cut or cut down, ŚāṅkhŚr. **°kartana**, mfn. cutting away, robbing, impoverishing, MBh. (Nīlak.); n. cutting down or off, MBh.; R.; plucking, impoverishing (see above). **°kṛitta**, mfn. cut off, cut up, MBh.; R.; *-mūla*, mfn. cut up by the roots, Suśr. **°kṛintana**, mf(*ī*)n. cutting down or off, destroying (ifc.), MBh.; R.; m. N. of a hell, MārkP.; n. cutting, cutting off (hair, the neck &c.), KātyŚr.; MBh.; massacring, destruction (of enemies), MBh.; an instrument for cutting (cf. *nakha-*). **°kṛintin**, mfn. tearing asunder (ifc.), Kāśikh.

निकृष् *ni-√1. kṛish*, P. *-karshati*, to draw or drag down, TS.; ŚBr.; *-kṛishati*, to plough in (*phalam kshetreshu*), AV Paipp.: Pass. *-kṛishyate*, to be borne down by the stream of a river, MBh. i, 3616. **°karsha**, m. lowering, reducing, decreasing, Śaṃk.; w.r. for *ni-kasha*, Mālav. ii, 7. **°karshaṇa**, n. an open place in or near a town, L.; a court at the entrance of a house, W.; a neighbourhood, W.; = *ni-kashaṇa*, MBh. **°kṛishṭa**, mfn. debased, vile, low, despised, outcast, MBh.; Kāv. &c.; near, n. nearness, Kathās.; Suśr.; *-bhūta*, mfn. appearing low or small in comparison with (gen.), MBh.; *°ṭâśaya*, mfn. base-minded (*°ya-tā*, f.), Daś.; *°ṭī-√kṛi*, to surpass, excel, Kāv. ii, 37, Sch.; *°ṭôpâdhi*, mfn. having something inferior as a condition (*°dhitā*, f.), Vedāntas.

निकेचाय *ni-kecāya*, m. (√1. *ci*) piling or collecting repeatedly, W.

निकेत *ni-keta*, m., rarely n. (√4. *cit*) a mark, sign, MBh. iii, 12541 (*tapâtyaya-n°*, 'mark of departure of heat,' said of a cloud); a house, habitation, MBh.; Kāv. &c.; seat of one of the constituent elements of the body, Car.; a bee-hive (?), MBh. xi, 140; a stage in the religious life of a Brāhman, iii, 13411; state of being, Divyâv. **°ketana**, n. a house, mansion, habitation, temple, Mn.; MBh. &c.; m. an onion, L.

निकोच *ni-koca*, m. (√*kuc*, to contract) closing (*akshi-*, of the eyes), Pat. **°caka**, m. Alangium Decapetalum; n. its fruit, Bhpr. (also *nikoṭhaka*, L.) **°cana**, n. = *nikoca*, Kull.

निकोथक *ni-kothaka*, m. (√*kuth*), N. of a teacher with the epithet Bhāyajātya.

निकोश्य *ni-kośyà*, m. or n. a partic. part of the entrails of sacrificial animals, TS. (cf. *kośya*).

निक्त *nikta*. See under *nij* below.

निक्रन्द् *ni-√krand*, cl. 1. P. *-krandati* (aor. *ny-akrandīt*), to cry from above (as a bird on a tree), Nir. ix, 4: Caus. *-krandayati*, to cause to roar, RV. x, 102, 5. **°krandita**, mfn. cried or roared (said of a faulty recitation), Saṃhitôp.

निक्रम् *ni-√kram*, P. *-krāmati* (aor. *ny-akramīt*), to put down the feet, tread down (acc.), RV.; to enter (loc.), AV.; TS. **°krámaṇa**, n. putting down the feet, footstep, footfall, RV.; AV.; TS.

निक्रीड् *ni-√krīḍ*, Caus. *-krīḍayati*, to cease or finish (playing), ShaḍvBr. (Sch. = *vi-√ram*). **°krīḍa**, m. play, sport, with *marutām*, N. of a Sāman, ĀrshBr.

निक्वण *ni-kvaṇa* (Kir.) or *ni-kvāṇa* (Śiś.), m. (√*kvaṇ*) sound, L.

निक्ष् *niksh*, cl. 1. P. *níkshati*, to pierce, AV.; to kiss, Dhātup. xvii, 7 (cf. *niṇs*).

Niksha, mfn. kissing (ifc. cf. *pushpa-n°*); (*ā*), f. a nit (prob. w.r. for *likshā*), L.

निक्षत्रिय *ni-kshatriya*, mfn. where the warriors are overthrown, Dharmaśarm.

निक्षिप् *ni-√kship*, P. *-kshipati*, to throw or cast or put or lay down, throw &c. in or upon (loc. or *upari*), Yājñ.; MBh.; R. &c.; to pour in (*kshīram śarāve*), Pañc. iii, $\frac{1}{1}\frac{3}{1}\frac{1}{1}$; to deliver anything (acc.) to (loc., esp. *haste*), to give or hand over, deposit, intrust, Mn.; Yājñ.; MBh. &c.; to instal, appoint to (loc.), R.; to lay aside, give up, leave, abandon, cast off, repel, MBh.; R. &c.; to put down figures, count, cipher, Lalit. **°kshipta**, mfn. thrown down or upon &c.; deposited, pawned, pledged; rejected, abandoned, given away, sent off, Mn.; MBh.; Kāv. &c.; appointed, installed, R.; inclining towards (comp.), Sarvad.; *-bhāra*, mfn. having put the load upon (comp.), Pañc. i, $\frac{1}{1}\frac{8}{8}\frac{7}{8}$; *-vāda*, mfn. one who has ceased talking or left off boasting, MBh.; Hariv. **°kshepa**, m. putting down, HYog. (esp. of the feet, Kālid.); throwing or casting on (loc. or comp.), Megh.; Sāh.; a deposit, pledge, trust, anything pawned, Mn.; Yājñ.; MBh.; Kāv. &c.; abandoning, throwing or sending away, W.; wiping, drying, ib.; *-cintāmaṇi*, *-dīpa*, m., *-rakshā*, f. N. of wks.; *-lipi*, f. a partic. mode of writing, Lalit. **°kshepaṇa**, n. putting down (the feet), Kum.; a means by which or a place in which anything is kept, Suśr. **°kshepita**, mfn. (fr. Caus.) caused to be set down in writing, committed to w°, inscribed, Ragh. **°kshepin**, mfn. being in possession of a deposit, Pañc. (B.) i, 14. **°ksheptṛi**, m. a depositor, a pawner or pledger, Mn. **°kshepya**, mfn. to be put down or deposited, Kathās.; to be thrust into (loc.), Mn.

निक्षुभा *ni-kshubhā*, f. (√*kshubh*), N. of the mother of Maga, BhavP.

निक्ष्विद् *ni-√kshvid* (only Vedic inf. *ni-kshvídas*), to destroy by creaking, MaitrS.

निखट्वा *ni-khaṭvā*, f. a kind of chair or couch, Gal.

निखन् *ni-√khan*, P. *-khanati*, to dig into (the ground), bury, RV. &c. &c.; to fix, implant, erect (as a post, column &c.), Kāv.; to dig or root up, BhP.; to infix, pierce (with an arrow &c.), MBh.; R. &c.: Caus. *khānayati*, see *ni-khānita* below. **°khanana**, n. digging in, burying, Śaṃk.; Kull. **°khāta** (*ní-*), mfn. dug in, buried, fixed in the ground, RV. &c. &c.; dug up, excavated, W. **°khātaka** (*ní-*), mfn. dug in a little, AV. **°khāna**, m. digging in, L. (cf. *naikhānya*). **°khānita**, mfn. infixed, implanted, Suśr. **°kheya**, mfn. to be thrust into, Vishṇ.

निखर *ni-khara*(?), mfn. N. of Agni, ŚāṅkhGṛ.

निखर्व *ni-kharva*, mfn. dwarfish, a dwarf, L.; n. a billion, MBh.; R. **°vaka**, m. or n. 1000 millions, TāṇḍBr. **°vaṭa**, m. N. of a Rakshas, MBh. **°vāda**, m. or n. = *°vaka*, ŚāṅkhŚr.

निखिद् *ni-√khid*, P. *-khidáti*, to press down, RV. iv, 28, 2.

निखिल *ni-khila*, mf(*ā*)n. complete, all, whole, entire, Up.; Mn.; MBh. &c.; (*ena*), ind. completely, totally, MBh.; R. &c. (cf. *a-kh°*).

निखुर्यप *nikhurya-pá*(?), m. N. of Vishṇu, TS.

निग *niga*, mfn. bound, fettered(?), Kāṭh.

निगड *ni-gaḍa*, m. (g. *ardharcâdi*) and n. (fr. √*gaḍ* = *gal*?) an iron chain for the feet, (esp.) the heel chains for an elephant or a noose for catching the feet and throwing an animal down, any fetter or shackle, Hariv.; Kāv. &c.; N. of a teacher (*-kshveḍana*, n. N. of wk.); mfn. bound or fettered on the feet, Mn. iv. 210. **°gaḍana**, n. putting in irons or fetters, Daś. **°gaḍaya**, Nom. P. *°yati*, to put in fetters, bind, ib. **°gaḍita**, mfn. chained, fettered, Kād.

निगण *ni-gaṇa*, m. (fr. *ni-garaṇa*?), the smoke of a burnt offering, L.

निगद् *ni-√gad*, P. *-gadati* (aor. *ny-agadīt*, Bhaṭṭ.), to recite, proclaim, announce, declare, tell, speak, ŚrS.; MBh.; R. &c.; to speak to, address (acc.), to say anything (acc.) to (acc.), Kāv.; to enumerate, cite, quote, Suśr.; to call (esp. Pass. *-gadyate*, to be called or named), MBh.; Kāv.; Suśr. &c.: Caus. *-gādayati*, to cause to recite, ŚāṅkhŚr.: Intens. *-jāgadyate*, (with pass. meaning) to assert firmly or repeatedly, Sarvad. **°gadá**, m. reciting, audible recitation, a prayer or sacrificial formula recited aloud, Br.; ŚrS. &c.; mention, mentioning, Bādar.; speech, discourse, W.; N. of wk.; m. or n. a partic. potion, Car.; *-vyākhyāta*, mfn. explained i.e. clear by mere mentioning, Nir. **°gadana**, n. reciting from memory, SāmavBr., Sch. **°gadita**, mfn. recited, told, spoken, MBh. &c.; n. speech, BhP.; *-vat*, mfn. having said or spoken, Bhaṭṭ.; *°ditin*, mfn. one who has spoken, g. *ishṭâdi*. **°gāda**, m. recitation, L.; *°din*, mfn. reciting, telling, speaking, Suśr. **°gādya**, mfn. to be told or communicated to (loc.), Naish.

निगम् *ni-√gam*, P. *-gacchati* (often w.r. *-yacchati*), to settle down upon or near (acc. or loc.), RV.; AV.; inire feminam, RV.; to enter, resort to, undergo, incur, become (with acc., e.g. *śāntim*, to become pacified, Bhag.); to enter, i.e. be inserted, ŚāṅkhŚr. (cf. *ni-gama* below); to acquire knowledge, W.: Caus. *°gamayati*, to cause to enter, insert, ĀśvŚr.; to conclude, sum up, Kir. i, 25, Sch. **°gantavya**, mfn. to be studied or learned, Āpast. **°gama**, m. insertion (esp. of the name of a deity into a liturgical formula), ŚrS.; the place or passage (esp. of the Vedas) where a word occurs or the actual word quoted from such a passage, Nir.; the root (as the source from which a word comes; hence ifc. 'derived from'), ib.; the Veda or the Vedic text, Hariv.; Pāṇ.; Pur. &c.; any work auxiliary to and explanatory of the Vedas, Mn. iv, 19 (Kull.); a sacred precept, the words of a god or holy man, MBh.; Pur. &c.; doctrine, instruction in, art of (comp.), Bālar.; certainty, assurance, L.; trade, traffic, W.; a town, city, market-place, Āpast.; Car.; Lalit.; a road, L.; a caravan or company of merchants (ifc. f. *ā*), R.; Daś.; = *-pariśishṭa*, Cat.; n. a partic. number, Buddh.; *-kalpa-druma*, m., *-kalpa-latā*, f., *-kalpa-sāra*, m. N. of wks.; *-jña*, mfn. familiar with the holy texts, Var.; *-tattva-sāra*, m., *-pariśishṭa*, n., *-latā*, f., *-sāra*, m., N. of wks.; *-sthāna*, n. place of insertion (cf. above), ŚrS.; *°mâkhya-kośa* and *°mântârtha-ratnâkara*, m. **°gamana**, n. insertion, quotation of words (from the Veda) and the word quoted, Nir.; the summing up of an argument or conclusion in a syllogism, deduction, Tarkas.; going in or into, W. **°gamin**, mfn. familiar with or versed in the Vedas, MW.

निगर *ni-gara*, *°raṇa* &c. See *ni-√gṛī*.

निगर्ह् *ni-√garh*, Ā. *-garhate*, (prob.) to blame, censure, find fault with, Pāṇ. i, 4, 32, Kāś.; P. *-garhayati*, to disdain, despise (acc.), MBh. (v.l. *vi-g°*).

निगल् *ni-√1. gal*, Intens. *-galgalīti*, to emit moisture, VS.

निगल् *ni-√2. gal*, *-galati*, to swallow, devour, Bhartṛ. **°galana**, n. swallowing, eating, L. **°gāla**, m. the throat or neck of a horse, Śiś. v, 4, Sch. (cf. 2. *gala*, *ni-garaṇa*); *-vat*, m. a horse, W. **°gālaka**, mfn. = *°gāraka*, Pāṇ. viii, 2, 21, Kāś.

निगल *ni-gala*, m. n. = *ni-gaḍa* above, L.

निगा *ni-√1. gā* (aor. *ny-agāt*, *ni-gām*), to enter, come or get into, attach one's self to (acc.), RV.; AV.; MBh.

निगु *nigu* (L.), mfn. pleasing, charming; m. the mind (=*manas*); dirt (√4. *gu*?); a root; painting.

निगुत् *ni-gút*, m. (√3. *gu*?) an enemy, RV. x, 128, 6, Sāy. (cf. *naiguta*).

निगुप् *ni-√2. gup*, inf. *-gopitum*, to conceal, Kir. xv, 19.

निगुह् *ni-√guh*, P. Ā. *-gūhati*, °*te* (aor. *ny-agūḍha* or *ny-aghukshata*, Pāṇ. vii, 3, 73, Kāś.), to cover, conceal, hide, MBh.; R. &c.: Caus. *-gūhayati* (Pāṇ. vi, 4, 89), id., Pañc. v, 8/9 (B. *-gūhan* for °*hayan*). °**gūḍha**, mfn. concealed, hidden, secret, obscure (lit. and fig.), RV. (*nī-gūḷha*) &c. &c.; (*am*), ind. privately, secretly, Kathās.; *-kārya*, mfn. secret in operation, MW.; *-cārin*, mfn. walking concealed or in disguise, Mn. ix, 260; *-tara*, mfn. well c° or hidden, Pañc.; *-niścaya*, mfn. whose design is c°, MBh.; *-roman*, mfn. having c° hair, Suśr.; °*ḍhârtha*, mfn. having a hidden or mysterious sense, abstruse, occult; °*ḍhârtha-dīpikā* and °*ḍhârtha-mañjūshikā*, f. N. of wks. °**gūḍhaka**, m. a species of wild bean, L. °**gūhaka**, mfn. hiding, concealing, L. °**gūhana**, n. the act of h° or c°, Kāv. °**gūhanīya**, mfn. to be hidden or covered and protected, W. °**gūhin**, see *sādhu-nigūhin*.

निगृहीत *ni-gṛihīta*, °*ti*. See *ni-grah* below.

निगृ *ni-√2. gṛī*, P. *-girati* or *-gilati*, Pāṇ. viii, 2, 21 (*-griṇāti*, PārGṛ.; aor. *-gārīt*, RV.; fut. *-garishyati*, Kathās.; inf. *-giritum*, ib.); to swallow, ingurgitate, devour, RV. &c. &c.; to swallow i.e. totally appropriate, Kathās.: Pass. *-gīryate*, p. °*yamāna* (with act. meaning), MBh. i, 8238 &c.: Caus. *-gārayati* or *-gālayati* (cf. *ni-√gal*, above); Pass. *-gāryate* or *-gālyate*, Pāṇ. viii, 2, 21: Intens. *-jegilyate*, iii, 1, 24, Kāś. °**gara**, m. eating, swallowing, W. °**garaṇa**, n. id., Śaṃk.; m. the throat, L.; the smoke of a burnt offering, L. (cf. *ni-gaṇa* above). °**gāra**, m. swallowing, L. °**gāraka**, mfn. swallowing (cf. *ni-gālaka* above). °**giraṇa**, n. swallowing up, devouring, Kathās. °**gīrṇa**, mfn. swallowed, devoured &c.; left out, not expressed (cf. *a-nig*°); *-tva*, n., Sāh.; *-vat*, mfn., Kathās.

निगै *ni-√gai*, P. *-gāyati*, to accompany with song, sing, chant, ŚBr. °**gīta**, mfn. sung, proclaimed, Mn. ix. 19.

निग्रन्थ् *ni-√granth*, see *punar-nigrantham*. °**granthana**, n. (w.r. for *ni-kṛ*°?; cf. *nir-gr*°) killing, slaughter, L. °**granthi**, m. the cover of a book, Hcat.

निग्रह् *ni-√grah*, P. Ā. *-gṛihṇāti*, °*ṇīte* (dat. inf. *-grábhe*, RV.), to hold down, lower, depress, RV.; TS.; KātyŚr.; to keep or hold back, draw near, attract, RV.; AV.; ŚBr. &c.; to seize, catch, hold, hold fast, stop, restrain, suppress, curb, tame, punish; Mn.; MBh. &c.; to contract, close (as the eyes), Mṛicch. ii, 1/2: Caus. *-grāhayati*, to cause to be apprehended or seized, Daś.: Caus. of Desid. *-jighṛikshayati* (p. °*shayat*), to cause any one to desire to overpower or excel, Bhaṭṭ. °**gṛihīta**, mfn. held down or back, seized, caught, checked, MBh. &c.; harassed, assailed, attacked, W.; n. (in music) a partic. method of beating a drum. °**gṛihīti**, f. restraint, check; overpowering, Kathās. °**gṛihītṛi**, w. r. for *-grah*°. 1. °**gṛihya**, mfn. to be held back &c.; deserving reproof or correction, Pāṇ. viii, 2, 94. 2. °**gṛihya**, ind. p. having held back or taken or arrested or confined, R. &c.; having restrained or coerced, by coercion, MW. °**grabhītṛi**, m. one who holds fast or binds, AitBr. °**graha**, m. keeping down or back, restraining, binding, coercion, suppression, subjugation, Mn.; MBh. &c.; defeat, overthrow, destruction, Kāv.; seizing, catching, arresting, holding fast, MBh.; R. &c.; suppression of an illness i. e. healing, cure, Suśr.; confinement, imprisonment, any punishment or chastisement, Mn.; MBh.; R.; Pañc. &c. (*vadha-nigr*°, pain of death, Kathās.); reprimand, blame, L.; aversion, ill-will, dislike, disgust, L.; anything for catching hold of, a handle (ifc. f. *ā*), Suśr.; a place or occasion for being caught hold of, (esp. in Nyāya phil.) an occasion for refutation, a weak point in an argument or fault in a syllogism (cf. *-sthāna*); a boundary, limit, L.; N. of Śiva and Vishṇu-Kṛishṇa, MBh.; *-sādhana* and *-stotra*, n. N. of wks.; *-sthāna*, n. (in phil.) the position of being unfit to carry on an argument from impossibility of agreeing about first principles; *-sthāna-sūtra-ṭīkā*, f., °*hâshṭaka*, n. N. of wks. °**grahaṇa**, mfn. holding down, suppressing (ifc.), Suśr.; n. subduing, suppression, ib.; capture, imprisonment, punishment, MBh.; war, fight, Dhanamj. °**grahītavya**, mfn. to be punished, Hit. °**grahītṛi**, m. one who seizes or lays hold of, Daś.; one who keeps back or prevents, BhP. °**grābhá**, m. pressing down, letting sink, VS.; suppressing (the voice, opp. to *ud-grābha*, elevating), Pāṇ. iii. 3, 36, Vārtt. 3; N. of a verse recited when the Soma plants are pressed, ŚBr.; of a partic. gift or oblation, Hcat. °**grābhyà**, mfn. (with *āpas*) the water with which the Soma plants are sprinkled before they are pressed, VS.; ŚBr. °**grāha**, m. punishment, chastisement, Bhaṭṭ. (esp. used in imprecations, e.g. *ni-grāhas te bhūyāt*, confusion seize thee, Pāṇ. iii, 3, 45, Kāś.) °**grāhaka**, mfn. suppressing, injuring (*-tva*, n., Kāvyâd. ii, 27, Sch.) °**grāhya**, mfn. to be (or being) suppressed or punished, MBh.; Hariv. &c.

निघ *ni-gha*, mfn. (√*han*) as high as broad (=*vishvak-sama*), L.; (?) equally distant (as trees), Pāṇ. iii, 3, 87, Kāś.; m. anything whose height and circumference are equal (as a circle a ball &c.), W.; sin (cf. *a-gha*), L. **Nighânigha**, mfn. of different forms or sizes, W.

निघण्ट *ni-ghaṇṭa*, m. (√*ghaṇṭ*, to speak?; cf. *ghaṇṭā*, a bell) a collection of words, vocabulary, Cat.; N. of a Dānava, Kathās. °**ṭi**, m. a glossary, Cat. °**ṭikā**, f. a species of bulbous plant, L. °**ṭu**, m. a glossary (also *-ka*), N. of sev. wks.; (mostly pl.) N. of the Vedic glossary explained by Yāska in his Nirukta; *-kośa*, m., *-khaṇḍa-nirvacana*, n., *-bhāshya*, n., *-rāja* and *-śesha*, m., *-saṃgraha-nidāna*, n., *-samaya* and *-sāra*, m. N. of wks.

निघर्ष *ni-gharsha*, °*shaṇa*. See *ni-ghṛish* below.

निघस *ni-ghasa*, m. (√*ghas*) eating, food, L.

निघात *ni-ghāta*, m. (fr. Caus. of *ni-√han*) a blow, stroke, Gaut.; Kāv.; suppression or absence of accent, AVPrāt.; (*am*), ind. having struck, MW. °**ti**, f. an iron club or hammer, L. °**tin**, mfn. striking down, killing, destroying (ifc.), MBh.; Hariv.

निघुष् *ni-√2. ghush*, Caus. *-ghoshayati*, to tread down, crush, destroy, RV.

निघुष्ट *ni-ghushṭa*, n. (√1. *ghush*) sound, noise.

निघृष् *ni-√2. ghṛish*, P. *-gharshati*, to rub into, rub down, grind, wear away, MBh.; to try, examine, ib. °**gharsha**, m. rubbing, pounding, crushing, Kāv.; v.l. for *ni-kasha*, Mālav. ii, 7. °**gharshaṇa**, n. rubbing, grinding, trituration, MBh. °**ghṛishṭa**, mfn. rubbed, ground, worn away, subdued, MBh. °**ghṛishva**, mfn. rubbed off, excoriated; worn away, harassed, afflicted, TaittĀr., Sch.; small, insignificant, Naigh.; m. a hoof, Uṇ. i, 153, Sch.; an ass, a mule or a boar, L.; n. the mark of a hoof, Uṇ. ib.

निघ्न *ni-ghna*, mf(*ā*)n. (√*han*) dependent, subservient, docile, obedient; (ifc.) dependent on, ruled by, devoted to, full of, Kāv. &c. (*-tā*, f. Kathās.); (after a numeral) multiplied with, Sūryas.; m. N. of a son of An-araṇya and father of An-amitra, Hariv.; of a son of An-amitra, ib. °**ghnaka**, mfn. dependent, L. °**ghnat**, °**ghnamāna** and °**ghnāna**, mfn. slaying, killing, MBh.; R. &c.

निचक *nicaka*, m. N. of a man, Pat. (cf. *naicakya*).

निचक्नु *nicaknu*, m. N. of a prince, VP. (v.l. *nicakru*).

निचक्रया *ní-cakrayā*, ind. with down-rolling chariots or without chariots, RV. viii, 7, 29.

निचक्षुस् *ni-cakshus*, m. N. of a prince, Hariv. (v. l. *vi-c*°).

निचङ्कुण *nicaṅkuṇa*, v.l. for *nicumpuṇa*.

निचन्द्र *ni-candra*, m. N. of a Dānava, MBh.

निचमन *ni-camana*, n. (√*cam*) sipping, Nir.

निचय *ni-caya* &c. See under 1. *ni-ci* below.

निचल् *ni-√cal*, Intens. *calcalīti*, to stir, quiver, MaitrS.

निचाङ्कुण *nicāṅkuṇa*, v.l. for *nicuṅkuṇa*.

निचाय् *ni-√cāy* (only ind. p. *-cáyyā*) to regard with reverence, honour, worship, RV.; observe, perceive, ib.; Daś.

निचि *ni-√1. ci*, to pile up, heap up, collect, only in deriv. (cf. *ni-kāya* &c. above). °**caya**, m. piling up, heaping up, heap, mass, quantity, store, provisions (cf. *alpa-n*°, *shaṇ-māsa-n*°); collection, multitude, assemblage (rarely of living beings, cf. *vadhū-n*°), Mn.; MBh.; Kāv. &c.; *-gulma*, m. a swelling of the abdomen caused by an excess of the 3 humours, Car.; °*yôdarin*, mfn. suffering from it (lit. having such an abdomen), ib. °**cayaka**, mfn. skilful in piling up, g. *ākarshâdi*. °**cayin**, mfn. heaped up, plentiful, abundant, Kir. °**cāya**, m. a heap (as a measure), L. 1. °**cita**, mfn. piled up, heaped up, erected; covered, overspread with, full of (with instr. or ifc.), MBh.; Kāv. &c.; constipated (as the bowels), Suśr.; m. pl. N. of a warrior-tribe (cf. *naicitya*); (*ā*), f. N. of a river, MBh. °**cekīya**, m. (fr. Intens.) continual or repeated piling up, Siddh. °**ceya**, mfn. to be piled or heaped up, MBh.

निचि *ni-√2. ci*, P. *-ciketi* (pf. *-cikāya*, 3. pl. °*kyur*), to perceive, notice, observe, recognise, RV.; AV.; ŚBr.: Desid. *-cikīshate*, to observe, watch, guard, RV.; VS. 2. °**citá**, mfn. observed, beheld, appearing, RV. ii, 12, 13. °**cirá**, mfn. attentive, vigilant, RV. °**cetṛi** (*nī-* without acc., *ni-cetṛ́i* with acc.), observing, observer, ib.

निचिकी *niciki*, f. an excellent cow, L. (cf. *naicikī*).

निचुङ्कुण *nicuṅkuṇa*, m., v. r. for *nicumpuṇá* below; N. of a Vāruṇi, Kāṭh., Anukr.

निचुद् *ni-√cud*, Caus. *-codayati*, to afford or procure quickly, RV. viii, 24, 25.

निचुम्पुण *ni-cumpuṇá*, m. (√*cup*?) prob. a gush, flood (*apām*), RV. viii, 93, 22; N. of a Śaunaḥśepa, Kāṭh., Anukr.

निचुल *ni-cula*, m. (√*cul*) an upper garment, overcoat, L.; N. of a tree (Barringtonia Acutangula), Kāv.; Suśr.; Calamus Rotang, L.; N. of a poet. °**culaka**, m. outer garment, L.; case, box, Bālar. vi, 42. °**culita**, mfn. being in a case, cased, ib. iv, 53; (ifc.) covered with, Prasann. °**cūla**, m. an outer garment, L.; Barringtonia Acutangula, L. °**cola**, m. id.; Kāv.; Car.; a case or box, Vcar. °**colaka**, m. an outer garment (also n.); a cuirass, L.; m. or n. a box or case, Hcar.

निचृत् 1. *ni-√cṛit*, P. *-cṛitáti*, to infix, insert, Kauś. 2. **Ni-cṛit**, f. a defective metre, Nidānas. (w. r. *ni-vṛit*).

निचेरु *ni-cerú*, mfn. (√*car*) gliding, creeping, RV.; VS.

निच्छवि *nicchavi*, f. N. of a district (=*tīra-bhukti*, the modern Tirhut), L. (cf. *licchavi*).

निच्छिद्र *ni-cchidra*, w.r. for *niś-ch*°, q.v.

निच्छिवि *nicchivi*, m. N. of one of the degraded castes sprung from the outcast or Vrātya Kshatriyas, Mn. x, 22.

निच्छेद *nicched*a, w.r. for *niś-ch*°, q.v.

निज् *nij*, cl. 2. Ā. *niṅkte*, Dhātup. xxiv, 16; cl. 3. P. Ā: *nenekti*, *nenikte* (Intens.?; cf. below), Dhātup. xxv, 11 (from the pres. stem only 2 pl. Impv. *ninikta*, RV., p. *nijānā*, ib., *nije* = *ninije*, BhP.; pf. *nineja*, *ninije*, Gr.; fut. *nekshyati*, *nektā*, ib.; aor. *anijam*, °*jan*, AV.; *anaikshīt*, *nikshi*, ib.; ind. p. *niktvā*, Br.; *-nijya*, ib.; dat. inf. *-nije*, RV.), to wash, cleanse, purify (Ā. one's self), RV.; ŚBr. &c.; to nourish, Dhātup.: Pass. *nijyate*, to be washed &c., MBh.: Caus. *nejayati*, Br.; aor. *anīnijat*, Gr.: Desid. *ninikshati*, Gr.: Intens. *nénekti*, *neniktě* (cf. above; Pot. *nenijyāt*, Mn. viii, 396; *nenijīti*, *nenijyate*, Gr.), to wash (one's self). [Cf. Gk. νίζω for νιγ-ζω; Angl. Sax. *nicor*; Germ. *Nix, Nixe.*]

Niktá, mfn. washed, cleansed, purified, sprinkled, RV.; ŚBr. — **hasta** (°*ktá*), mfn. clean-handed, RV.

निज *ni-já*, mf(*ā*)n. (√*jan*) innate, native, of one's own party or country (with *ripu*, m. an enemy in one's own country, Hit.; m. pl. one's own people, Rājat.); constant, continual, AV.; Br.; Mn.; MBh. &c. (in later Sanskṛit used as a reflex. possess. pron. = *sva*, my own, his own, our own &c.) — **karman**, n. one's own work; °*ma-bandhana*, mfn. fettered by one's own works, MW. — **ghāsa**, m. 'devouring his own,' N. of a demon, Hariv. — **dhṛiti**, f. N. of a river in Śāka-dvīpa, BhP. — **paksha**, m. one's own party or adherents, Kathās. — **mukta**, mfn. liberated for ever, Kap. — **lābha-pūrṇa**, mfn. engrossed in self-interest, self-satisfied, MW. — **vinoda**, m. N. of wk. — **śatru**, m. an enemy being in one's own self, an innate e°, R. — **sva**, n. one's own property, MW. **Nijâkshara-mīmāṇsā**, f. N. of wk. **Nijâtmânanda-nātha**, m. N. of an author, Cat. **Nijânandânubhūti-prakaraṇa**, n. N. of wk. **Nijârtham**, ind. for one's own sake, for one's self, MW.

निजघ्नि *ni-jaghni*, mfn. (√*han*) striking down, overpowering, RV.

निजानुका *ni-jānukā*, f. shaking or trembling of the knees, TaittĀr.

निजि *niji*, g. *yavâdi*; *-mat*, mfn. ib.

निजिघृक्षयत् *ni-jighṛikshayat*. See *ni-grah* above.

निजुह्नूषु *ni-juhnūshu*, mfn. (Desid. of *ni-√hnu*) wishing to conceal or deny, W.

निजूर्व *ni-√jūrv*, P. *-jūrvati*, to consume by fire, RV. °**júr**, f. singeing, burning, destroying by fire, RV. ii, 29, 6.

निञ्ज् *niñj*, cl. 2. Ā. *niṅkte* &c. See *nij*.

निटल *niṭala*, °*ṭāla* or °*ṭila*, n. the forehead, Kāv. **Niṭalâksha**, m. 'having an eye on the f°,' N. of Śiva, L. **Niṭila-taṭa-cumbita**, mfn. kissed on the f°, Daś. **Niṭilâksha** (L.) or °**lâkshaṇa** (Daś.), m. N. of Śiva (cf. above).

निट्टल *niṭṭala*, m. N. of a family of Brāhmans, Cat.

निडीन *ni-ḍīna*, n. (√*ḍī*) the downward flight or swoop of a bird or a partic. mode of flying, MBh.

निण्यक् *ni-ṇík*, ind. (prob. fr. *ni* and connected with *ni-ṇya*) secretly, mysteriously, RV. iv, 5, 8.

निण्डिका *niṇḍikā*, f. Ipomoea Turpethum, L. (prob. w. r. for *tiṇḍ*°; cf. *tiṇṭī*).

निण्य *ni-ṇyá*, mfn. (fr. *ni*; cf. *ni-ṇík*) interior, hidden, concealed, mysterious, RV.; n. a secret, mystery, ib.; (*ám*), ind. secretly, mysteriously, ib.

नितततपस् *nitatatapas*, ind. an onomatop. word to denote the speech of a stutterer, Kāṭh.

नितन् *ni-√tan*, P. Ā. *-tanoti*, *-tanute*, to pervade, penetrate, pierce, RV.; cause to go or grow downwards, AV.; AitBr. °**tatní**, f. N. of one of the 7 Kṛittikās, TS. °**tatní**, f. id., Kāṭh.; a species of plant, AV. °**tāná**, m. the shoot (of a plant) which grows downwards, AV.; N. of a man with the patr. Māruta, Kāṭh.

नितप् *ni-√tap*, P. *-tapati*, to emit heat downwards (impers., ChUp. vii, 11, 1); to consume by fire, AV.; ĀpŚr.

नितम् *ni-√tam*, Caus. *-tamayati*, to choke, suffocate, Kāṭh. °**tānta**, mfn. extraordinary, excessive, considerable, important; ibc. and (*am*), ind. very much, in a high degree, Kāv. &c.; *-kathiṇa*, mfn. very hard, Vikr.; *-rakta*, mfn. very red, ib.; *-vṛikshīya* (v. l. °*ntâvṛ*°) and °*ntīya*, mfn., g. *utkarâdi*.

नितम्ब *nitamba*, m. the buttocks or hinder parts (esp. of a woman; mostly du.; ifc. f. *ā*; *-tā*, f.); (fig.) the ridge or side or swell of a mountain, the sloping bank or shore of a river, MBh.; Kāv. &c.; the shoulder, L.; the sounding-board of the Vīṇā, Kāv.; a partic. position of the hands in dancing, Cat.; (*ā*), f. a form of Durgā, Cat.; *-prabhava*, mfn. (river) coming from the slope of a mountain, BhP. — **bimba**, mfn. having Bimba-like round hips, MW. — **maya**, mf(*ī*)n. formed of or by buttocks, Naish. — **vat**, mfn. having beautiful b° or hips, καλλίπυγος, Vikr.; Gīt.; (*ī*), f. N. of a woman, Daś. — **sthala**, n. (Ratnâv.); **-sthalī**, f. (Bhartṛ.) the region of the b° or hips. **Nitambin**, mfn. having b° (mostly ifc., cf. *su-n*°); having beautiful hips, Kālid.; having beautiful sides (as a mountain), Rājat.; (*ī*), f. a woman with large and handsome hips, Kālid.; Bhartṛ.

नितम्भू *nitambhū*, m. N. of a man, MBh.

नितराम् *ni-tarām*, ind. (*ni* with the compar. suffix) downwards, TBr.; in a low tone, Śāṅkh. Br.; completely, wholly, entirely; by all means, at all events; especially, in a high degree, Kāv.; Pur.; explicitly, Kull.

नितल *ni-tala*, n. one of the 7 divisions of the lower regions, Up.; Pur.

नितिक्त *ní-tikta*, mfn. (√*tig*) excited, roused up, RV. x, 111, 9. **Ní-tikti**, ind. quickly, speedily, ib. vi, 4, 5.

नितुण्ड *ni-tuṇḍa*, m. N. of a man (cf. *naituṇḍi*).

नितुद् *ni-√tud*, P. Ā. *-tudáti*, °*te* (*-tundate*, RV. i, 58, 1; [*ni* w. r. for *nú*?]), to pierce, penetrate, RV.; AV. °**tunna**, see *punar-n*°. °**toda**, m. piercing, a hole, KātyŚr. °**todin**, mfn. piercing, penetrating, RV.; AV.

नितुश् *ni-√1. tuś*, Ā. *-tośate*, to drip down (trans. and intrans.), sprinkle, grant, distribute, RV.; to kill, Naigh. ii, 19: Caus. *-tośayati*, to grant, distribute, RV. viii, 55, 8; to kill, Naigh. °**tóśana**, mfn. sprinkling, distributing, granter of (gen.), RV.

नितृद् *ni-√tṛid*, P. Ā. *-tṛiṇatti*, *-tṛintte*, to pierce, cleave, split, AV.

नितृप् *ni-√tṛip*, P. *-tṛimpati*, RV. viii, 70, 10 (*ná* for *ní*?).

नितॄ *ni-√tṝi* (*-tirah*, RV. viii, 32, 3; *-tārishah*, ix, 79, 5; *-tārīt*, i, 152, 3), to dispel, subdue, overpower. °**tīraṇa**, n. decision, L.

नित्य *nítya*, mf(*ā*)n. (fr. *ni*; cf. *ni-ja*) innate, native, MBh. iii, 13941; one's own (opp. to *araṇa*), RV.; continual, perpetual, eternal, RV. &c. &c.; ifc. constantly dwelling or engaged in, intent upon, devoted or used to (cf. *tapo-n*°, *dharma-n*°, *dhyāna-n*°, *śastra-n*°), Mn.; MBh. &c.; ordinary, usual, invariable, fixed, necessary, obligatory (opp. to *kāmya*, *naimittika* &c.), Br.; ŚrS.; Mn. &c. (with *samāsa*, m. a compound the meaning of which is not expressed by its members when not compounded, Pāṇ. ii, 1, 3, Sch.; with *svarita*, m. = *jātya*, the independent Svarita, TPrāt. ii, 8); m. the sea, ocean, L.; (*ā*), f. a plough-share, Gal.; N. of Durgā, BrahmavP.; of a Śakti, Tantras.; of the goddess Manasā, L.; n. constant and indispensable rite or act, W.; (*am*), ind. always, constantly, regularly, by all means, RV. &c. &c. (*na nityam*, never; *nityam an-ādāta*, never a receiver, Mn. vi, 8). — **karman**, n. a constant act or duty (as observance of the 5 great acts of worship), any daily and necessary rite, Jaim., Sch.; N. of wk.; °*ma-paddhati*, *-prakāśikā*, *-latā*, f., *-vidhi*, m.; °*mânushṭhāna-krama*, m. N. of wks. — **kālam**, ind. always, at all times, Mn. ii, 58; 73. — **kṛitya**, n. a regular and necessary act or ceremony, Hit. — **kriyā**, f. id.; N. of wk. — **gati**, mfn. moving continually, MBh.; m. wind, or the god of wind, L. — **japa-vidhāna**, n. N. of wk. — **jāta**, mfn. constantly born, Bhag. ii, 26. — **jvara**, m. uninterrupted fever, L. — **tarpaṇa**, n. N. of wk. — **tā**, f. perpetuity, continuance, continual repetition of (comp.), MBh.; Suśr.; necessity, MārkP. — **tva**, n. id.; KātyŚr.; Bhag.; Suśr. &c. — **dā**, ind. always, perpetually, constantly, MBh.; BhP. (cf. g. *svarâdi*). — **dāna**, n. daily alms-giving, W.; °*nâdi-paddhati*, f. N. of wk. — **dhṛit**, mfn. constantly bearing or maintaining; observing daily duties (?), MW. — **dhṛita**, mfn. constantly maintained or kept up, ŚāṅkhŚr. — **narta**, mfn. constantly dancing (Śiva), MBh. — **nātha**, m. N. of an author (also *-siddha*), Cat. — **naimittika**, n. (with or scil. *karman*) any regularly recurring occasional act or ceremony or any rite constantly performed to accomplish some object (as Śrāddhas at fixed lunar periods), W. — **pari-vṛita**, m. N. of a Buddha. — **parīkshaṇa**, n. constant investigation or inspection, MW. — **pāda**, m. = *-nātha*, Cat. — **pushṭa**, mf(*ā*)n. always well-supplied, TĀr. — **pūjā**, f. N of wk.; *-yantra*, n. a kind of amulet, Cat. — **pramudita**, mfn. always delighted or satisfied, MBh. — **prayoga-ratnâkara**, m. N. of wk. — **pralaya**, m. the constant dissolution of living beings, W. — **buddhi**, mfn. considering anything (loc.) as constant or eternal, BhP. — **bhāva**, m. eternity, Suśr. — **maya**, mf(*ī*)n. formed or consisting of anything eternal, MBh. — **mukta**, mfn. emancipated for ever (*-tva*, n.), Kap. — **yātrā**, f. N. of wk. — **yukta**, mfn. always busy or intent upon (loc.), Mn.; Gaut. — **yuj**, mfn. having the mind always fixed upon one object, BhP. — **yauvana**, mfn. always young; (*ā*), f. N. of Draupadī; n. perpetual youth, L. — **rtu** (for *-ṛitu*), mfn. regularly recurring at the seasons, annual, MW. — **līlā-sthāpana**, n. N. of wk. — **vatsa** (°*tyá*), mf(*ā*)n. always possessing a calf, AV.; (*ā*), f. a partic. form of Sāma supplication, Lāṭy.; n. N. of sev. Sāmans, ĀrshBr. — **varsha-deva**, m. N. of a man, L. — **vitrasta**, m. 'always scared,' N. of an antelope, Hariv. — **vidhi**, m. N. of wk. — **vaikuṇṭha**, m. N. of a partic. residence of Vishṇu in heaven, BrahmavP. — **vyaya**, mfn. always expending; (*ā*), f. ever laying out, MW. — **vrata**, n. a perpetual observance (lasting for life), Gobh. — **śaṅkita**, mfn. perpetually alarmed, always suspicious, Hit. — **śaya**, mfn. always sleeping or reclining, MBh. — **śas**, ind. always, constantly, eternally, Mn.; MBh. &c. — **śrāddha**, n. a daily or constant Śrāddha, RTL. 305. — **śrī**, mfn. of lasting beauty, Bhām. — **saṃhṛishṭa**, mfn. always exulting or triumphant; always rivalling one another (cf. *saṃghṛishṭa*), MW. — **saṃnyāsin**, m. always an ascetic, Bhag. — **sama**, m. the assertion that all things remain the same, Sarvad. — **samāsa**, m., see above. — **siddha**, mfn. 'ever perfect,' a Jaina predicate of the soul, MW. — **sevaka**, mfn. always serving others, Pañc. — **stotra** (*ní*°), mfn. receiving perpetual praise, RV. — **stha**, mfn. always abiding in (loc.), MBh. — **snāyin**, mfn. constantly bathing or making ablutions, Vishṇ.; Hit. — **svâdhyāyin**, mfn. always engaged in the study of the Veda (°*yi-tā*, f.), MBh. — **hotṛi** (*ní*°), mfn. always sacrificing, RV. — **homa**, perpetual sacrifice, in *-prāyaścitta*, n., *-vidhi*, m., °*mâdi-prakīrṇaka*, n., °*mâdi-vidhi*, m. N. of wks. **Nityâgnihotra**, n. N. of wk. **Nityâcāra**, m. constant good conduct; *-pradīpa* and *-vidhi*, m. N. of wks. **Nityā-tantra**, n. N. of wk. **Nityânadhyāya**, m. invariable suspension of repetition of the Vedas (as on the day of full moon &c.), W. **Nityânanda**, m. 'eternal happiness,' N. of sev. authors (also *-nātha*, *-mano'bhirāma*, *-rāma*, *-śarman*, °*dânucara* and °*dâśrama*); *yugalâshṭaka*, n. N. of wk.; *-rasa*, m. 'essence of eternal joy,' N. of a partic. medic. preparation, Rasar.; *-rasôdadhi*, m. 'ocean of the ess° &c.,' God, MW. **Nityânitya**, mfn. eternal and perishable, permanent and temporary, W. **Nityânugṛihīta**, mfn. constantly maintained or kept (fire), ĀśvGṛ. **Nityânubaddha**, mfn. always approached or resorted to; (*ā*), f. (with *devatā*) tutelary deity, Divyâv. **Nityânushṭhāna-pūjā-paddhati**, f., **Nityânusaṃdhāna**, n., **Nityânna-dāna-māhātmya**, n. N. of wks. **Nityâyukta**, m. 'always active,' N. of a Bodhi-sattva, Lalit. (cf. °*tyôdy*° below). **Nityârādhana**, n., *-krama* and *-vidhi*, m. N. of wks. **Nityâritra** (*ní*°), mf(*ā*)n. having its own oars (as a ship), moving by itself, RV. **Nityârtha-sāmānya-pañcapaṭhī**, f. N. of wk. **Nityôtkshipta-hasta**, m. 'who always raises his hand,' N. of a Bodhi-sattva, L. **Nityôtsava**, m. (ibc.) constant or regular festivals, R.; N. of wk. (also *-vidhi*, m.) **Nityôdaka** (KātyŚr.) and °**kin** (ŚāṅkhGṛ.), mfn. always furnished with water. **Nityôdita**, mfn. risen by itself (as knowledge), Bhartṛ.; m. a partic. medic. preparation, Rasêndrac.; N. of a man, Kathās. **Nityôdyukta**, m. 'always energetic,' N. of a Bodhi-sattva (cf. *nityây*°).

निद् 1. *nid*. See √*nind* and √2. *ned*.

2. **Nid**, f. mocking, ridiculing, contempt; mocker,

scoffer, blamer, enemy, RV. **Nidā́**, f. blame, contempt, ib. 1. **Nidānā́**, mfn. reproached, ridiculed, ib. **Nidyámāna**, mfn. id., ib. **Nedya**, see *á-nedya*.

निद *nida*, m. or n. poison, venom, L.

निदण्ड *ni-daṇḍa*, mfn. one who has laid down the stick (i. e. does not use force, cf. *nyasta-d°*), Pāṇ. vi, 2, 192, Kāś.

निदत्त *ni-datta* or *nītta*, mfn. fr. *ni-√1. dā*, Pāṇ. vi, 3, 124, Sch.; Kārikā on vii, 4, 47.

निदद्रु *nidadru*, m. a man, L. (according to W. fr. *nida + dru*).

निदर्शक *ni-darśaka*, *°śana*, &c. See *ni-√dṛiś*.

निदह् *ni-√dah*, P. *-dahati* (Pass. *-dahyate*, MBh.; aor. *-dhakshi*, RV.), to burn down, consume by fire. **°dāghá**, m. (g. *nyaṅkv-ādi*) heat, warmth, the hot season (May and June), summer, ŚBr.; MBh. &c.; internal heat, Ṛit. i, 4; sweat, perspiration, L.; N. of a man (pl. of his descendants, g. *upakâdi*); of a son of Pulastya, VP.; *-kara*, m. 'heat-causer' or 'hot-rayed,' the sun, L.; *-kāla*, m. the 'time of heat,' summer, MBh.; Kāv.; *-dhāman*, m. 'having hot radiance' or 'abode of heat,' the sun, Śiś. i, 24; *-ruci*, m. 'hot-rayed,' id., Kāv.; *-vārshika*, mfn. (months) belonging to the hot and the rainy season, MBh. vii, 1311; *-sindhu*, m. a river in hot weather, one nearly dry, W.; *°ghâvadhi*, m. the hot season, Ragh. xvi, 52.

निदा *ni-√4. dā*, P. *-dyati*, to bind on, fasten, RV. **°dātṛi**, m. one who fastens or ties up, RV. viii, 61, 5. **°dā́na**, n. a band, rope, halter, RV. vi, 32, 6; MBh.; a first or primary cause (cf. *ni-bandhana*), RV. x, 114, 2; Br.; Kāṭh.; original form or essence (*ena*, ind. originally, essentially, properly), Br.; (with Buddh.) a cause of existence (12 in number), MWB. 56; 103; any cause or motive, Divyâv.; the cause of a disease and enquiry into it, pathology (= *nidāna-sthāna*, q. v.), L.; = *nidāna-sūtra*, Cat.; cessation, end, L.; purification, correctness, L.; claiming the reward of penitential acts, L.; *-tattva*, n., *-pradīpa*, m. N. of wks.; *-vat* (*nidā́na-*), mfn. founded on a cause, essential, TBr.; Kāṭh.; *-vid*, mfn. knowing the causes or symptoms of a disease, BhP.; *-saṃgraha*, m. N. of a medic. wk.; *-sūtra*, n. N. of a wk. on metres and Vedic Stomas; *-sthāna*, n. the subject of the causes of diseases, pathology (one of the 5 departments of medic. science), Suśr.; *-dānârtha-kara*, mfn. operating as a cause, Bhpr. **°dita** (*ní-*), mfn. bound, fettered, RV. v, 2, 7; hidden, concealed, ib. viii, 92, 11.

निदाघ *ni-dāgha*. See *ni-dah*.

निदिग्ध *ní-digdha*, mfn. (*√dih*) smeared, plastered; clinging to, ŚBr.; heaped or piled up, L.; (*ā*), f. cardamoms. **°digdhikā**, f. Solanum Jacquini, Suśr. (cf. *nir-dagdhikā* and *nir-digdh°*); cardamoms, L.

निदिद्रासु *ni-didrāsu*. See under *ni-drā*, col. 2.

निदिध्यासन *ni-didhyāsana*. See *ni-dhyai*.

निदिश् *ni-√diś*, P. *-diśati*, to direct, order, point out &c. (only in deriv.) **°dishṭa**, mfn. (Pañc. v. 1/2), w. r. for *nir-d°*. **°deśa**, m. order, command, direction (*°śam √kṛi* or *pālaya* or *upa-pālaya* or *°śe √vṛit* or *√sthā*, to execute orders, be obedient), MBh.; Kāv. &c.; talk, conversation, L.; vicinity, neighbourhood (*e*, ind. near, close by, Kull. on Mn. ii, 197; others 'in a lower place'); = *bhājana*, L.; *-kārin*, *-kṛit*, *-bhāj*, *-vartin*, mfn. executing the orders of, obedient to (gen. or comp.), MBh. &c. **°deśin**, mfn. showing, directing, pointing out, W.; (*inī*), f. region, quarter, point of the compass, L. **°deśya**, mfn. to be ordered or told, MW. **°deshṭṛi**, m. who or what points out or orders; explaining, advising, commanding, W.

निदी *ni-√2. dī* (Impv. *-didīhi*, RV. i, 113, 7), to shine down upon, bestow anything (acc.) on (dat.) by shining down.

निदुश *niduśa*, m. a fish, L.

निदृश् *ni-√dṛiś*, Caus. *-darśayati*, to cause to see, show, point out, introduce, indicate, MBh.; Kāv. &c.; to impart knowledge, teach, instruct, advise, ib.; to announce, proclaim, BhP.; to show one's self i. e. to appear (in a vision) to (acc.), Hariv. **°darśaka**, mfn. seeing into, perceiving, MBh.; proclaiming, announcing, ib.; Daś. **°darśana**, mf(*ī*)n. pointing to, showing, indicating, announcing, proclaiming, teaching, Hariv.; BhP.; suiting, pleasing (*sarva-loka-nid°*; v. l. *°ka-nidarśin* and *-vidarśin*), R. ii, 108, 18; (*ā*), f. a partic. form of a simile or comparison (e. g. Ragh. i, 2), Kpr.; Sāh. &c.; n. seeing, view, appearance, sight, vision (cf. *svapna-nid°*), MBh.; Suśr. &c.; pointing to, showing, indicating, Mn.; MBh.; proof, evidence, Pañc.; instance, example, illustration, ŚrS.; Mn.; MBh.; Kāv. &c. (*-tva*, n., Naish.; *°nârtham*, ind. for instance, MBh.); refutation of a stated argument, Sāh.; N. of the third member of a complete syllogism (= *udāharaṇa*), MW.; a prognostic, sign, mark, omen, MBh.; Hariv.; Suśr. (ifc. f. *ā*, showing, betraying, R.); a scheme, system, Suśr.; injunction, precept, ordinance, authority, text, W. **°darśayitavya**, mfn. to be pointed out or put forth or shown, Pat. **°darśita**, mfn. shown, presented, offered (as a seat), Rājat.; illustrated, exemplified, Mn.; MBh. &c. **°darśin**, mfn. seeing, having an insight into, familiar with, knowing, MBh.; suiting, pleasing (v. l. *nidarśana*; cf. above).

निदेश *ni-deśa*. See *ni-diś* above.

निद्रा *ni-√1. drā* (or *√drai*), P. Ā. *-drāyati*, *°te* (*-drāti*, Śāntiś.; pf. *-dadrau*, Naish.), to fall asleep, sleep, slumber, ŚBr.; MBh.; Kāv. &c. **°drā́**, f. sleep, slumber, sleepiness, sloth, RV.; MBh.; Kāv. &c.; the budding state of a flower (hence *°drāṃ √tyaj*, to bloom), ŚārṅgP.; a mystic. N. of the letter *bh*, Up.; *-kara*, mfn. making sleepy, Hariv.; Suśr.; *-kshaṇa*, m. or n. a moment of sleep, BhP.; *-°gama* (*°drâg°*), approach or time of s°, Śāntiś.; *-caura*, m. stealer of s°, Mṛicch.; *-°tura* (*°drât°*), mfn. sleepy, languid, Cat.; *-daridra*, mfn. suffering from want of sleep, Vcar.; m. N. of a poet, Cat.; *-daridrī-√kṛi*, to deprive of s°, Kpr.; *-druh* (mfn. nom. *dhruk*, Pāṇ. viii, 2, 37; cf. Vām. v, 2, 88), disturbing s°; *-°ntarita* (*°drânt°*), mfn. asleep, Pañc.; *-°ndha* (*°drân°*), mfn. blind with sleep, dead asleep, fast asleep, MBh.; *-bhaṅga*, m. rousing from s°, awaking, W.; *-°bhibhūta* (*°drâbh°*), mfn. subdued by s°, sleeping, Suśr.; *-maya*, mf(*ī*)n. consisting in s°, Hariv.; *-yoga*, m. a state of such deep meditation as to resemble sleep, ib. (cf. *yoga-nidrā*); *-°lasa* (*°drâl°*), mf(*ā*)n. slothful from drowsiness, fast asleep, Hit.; *-°lasya* (*°drâl°*), n. sleepiness, long sleeping, MBh.; Var.; *-vaśa*, mfn. overpowered by sleep, Vet.; *-vṛiksha*, m. 'sleep-plant,' darkness, L.; *-saṃjanana*, n. 'producing s°,' phlegm, the phlegmatic humour, L. **°drāṇa**, mfn. asleep, sleeping, Rājat.; shut up, closed (as a blossom), L. **°drāt**, mf(*ātī* or *āntī*)n. sleeping, MBh. &c. **°drāyamāṇa**, mfn. id., Hariv. **°drālu**, mfn. sleeping, sleepy, drowsy, Yājñ.; MBh.; Suśr. &c.; m. N. of Vishṇu, L.; f. Solanum Melongena, L.; = *vana-barbarikā*, L.; a kind of perfume, L.; *-tva*, n. sleepiness, drowsiness, L. **°drita**, mfn. sleeping, asleep, Naish. (cf. g. *tārakâdi*); *-vat*, mfn. one who has slept, ib., Sch.

Ni-didrāsu, (fr. Desid.) wishing to sleep, sleepy, Rājat. viii, 2130 (printed *vinidr°*).

निधन 1. *ni-dhana*, mfn. (for 2. see col. 3) having no property, poor, L. **-tā**, f. poverty, Mṛicch. i, 13; Hit. i. 128.

निधा *ni-√1. dhā*, P. Ā. *-dadhāti*, *-dhatte*, to put or lay down, deposit, lay up, preserve (Ā. for one's self); to intrust, commit, present to (dat. or loc.); put into, fix in (loc., or loc. with *antár*, or *antar* ifc.), RV. &c. &c.; put or lay before a person (dat.), KenUp.; (with *bhūmau* [Hit.] or *avaṭe* [R.]) to bury; (with *śirasi*, rarely *°sā*) to esteem highly, R.; Kālid.; Pañc.; (with *dṛiśam*) to fix the eyes upon (loc.), Kathās.; (with *manas*) to fix or direct the thoughts upon or towards i. e. resolve, determine to (dat.), Hariv.; (with *manasi*, *°sā* or *hṛidaye*) to keep in mind, bear in mind, remember, lay to heart, Kāv.; Pur.; (with *hṛidayam*) to give one's heart to (loc.); (with *ātmānam*) to intrust one's self to (loc.), Kathās.; (with *kriyām*) to take pains with (loc.), Hit.; (with *karmaṇi*) to appoint a person to a work, Rājat.; to keep down, restrain, Kāv.; Pur.; to end, close, ŚBr.: Pass. *-dhīyate*, to be put or laid down &c.; to be contained or situated or absorbed in, to rest in (loc.), RV.; AV. &c. &c.; Caus. *-dhāpayati*, to cause to be put or laid down &c.; Vait.; R.; Hcat.; to cause to be deposited or preserved, Mn. viii, 30; to lay up, preserve, Car.; to appoint, BhP.: Desid. *-dhitsate*, to intend to put down &c., Naish.: Intens. *ni-dedhyat*(?), to settle down, VS.; MaitrS. 2. **°dhána** (for 1. see col. 2), n. (m. only Hariv. 4846; g. *ardharcâdi*) settling down, residence or place of r°, domicile, receptacle, AV.; Suśr.; BhP.; conclusion, end, death, destruction, loss, annihilation, Mn.; Var.; MBh. &c.; (in music) the concluding passage of a Sāman which is sung in chorus; any finale, AV.; TS.; Br. &c.; N. of the 8th mansion, Var.; race, family, L.; m. the head of a family, W.; (*ā*), f. pl. N. of partic. verses or formulas, Kauś.; *-kāma*, n. N. of sev. Sāmans, TāṇḍBr.; Lāṭy.; *-kārin*, mfn. causing death, destroying, W.; *-kriyā*, f. a funeral ceremony, Hariv.; *-pati*, m. lord of the end or of destruction, TĀr.; *-bhūta*, mfn. (in music) forming a finale, Lāṭy.; *-vat* (*°dhána-*), mfn. having a finale, VS.; TāṇḍBr. &c.; *-sūtra*, n., *-sūtra-vṛitti*, f. N. of wks.; *°nôttama*, m. N. of Śiva, R. 2. **°dhā́**, f. a net or snare, RV.; *-pati* (*°dhā́-*), m. possessor or bearer of snares, ib. **°dhātavya**, mfn. to be put down or deposited or concealed or delivered or directed towards, Mn.; MBh. &c. **°dhātṛi**, m. one who lays down i. e. imprints or leaves (a footmark), RV. v, 30, 2. **°dhātos** (*ní-*), abl. inf. (with *ā*) to the end, until death, RV. **°dhā́na**, n. putting or laying down, depositing, keeping, preserving, KātyŚr.; MBh. &c.; laying aside (cf. *daṇḍa-n°*); placing (the sacrificial fire), KātyŚr.; place for depositing anything, receptacle (rarely m.; ifc. f. *ī*; cf. *garbha-n°*), RV. &c. &c.; a place of cessation or rest, W.; anything laid up, a store, hoard, treasure (esp. the t° of Kubera), Mn.; Mṛicch.; Ragh. &c. (*-tā*, f., Jātakam.); (*ī*), f. N. of a formula, TBr.; ĀpŚr.; mfn. containing anything (gen.) in itself, TĀr.; *-kumbha*, m. a pot or jar containing a treasure, Sāh.; *°nī-√kṛi*, to pile up, Hcat.; *°nêśa*, m. 'lord of treasure,' a Yaksha, Śatr. **°dhānaka**, mfn., g. *ṛiśyâdi*. **°dhānya**, mfn. fit for being laid or put down, RV. **°dhāpaka**, m. (fr. Caus.) one who causes a weapon to be put down (?); burnt timber; charcoal; the castor oil plant, W. **°dhāpya**, ind. (fr. Caus.) having caused to be placed or fixed in, having installed or appointed, MW. **°dhāya**, ind. having fixed or placed in or on; with *manasi*, fixing or laying up in the mind; reflecting, Hit. **°dhāyam**, see *ghṛita-n°*. **°dhi**, m. setting down or serving up (food, &c.), RV. i. 183, 4 &c.; the bottom of the Ukhā, ŚBr.; a place for deposits or storing up, a receptacle (esp. *apāṃ nidhi*, r° of waters, the ocean, sea, also N. of a Sāman; *kalānāṃ n°*, the full moon), MBh.; Kāv. &c.; a store, hoard, treasure, RV. &c. &c. (in later language esp. the divine treasures belonging to Kubera, nine of which are enumerated, viz. Padma, Mahāpadma, Śaṅkha, Makara, Kacchapa, Mukunda, Nanda, Nīla and Kharva, they are also personified as attendants either of Kubera or of Lakshmī; cf. *nidhi-datta* and *-pālita* below); the sea, L.; (with *daiva*) the science of chronology, ChUp. vii, 1, 2 (Saṃk.); N. of a partic. medic. plant (= *jīvikā*), L.; a kind of perfume (= *nalikā*), L.; *-guhyakâdhipa*, m. 'lord of the treasures and Guhyakas,' Kubera, Kir. v, 20; *-gopá*, m. guardian of t°, ŚBr.; *-datta*, m. N. of a merchant, Kathās.; *-dīpikā*, f. N. of wk.; *-nātha*, m. 'lord of t°,' N. of Kubera, L.; of an author, Cat.; *-pa*, m. = *-gopa*, Mn.; MBh.; any guardian or protector (as *yajñasya*, *vedasya*), ĀśvGṛ. i, 22, 21; *-pati* (*°dhí-*), m. lord of t°, AV.; VS.; N. of Kubera, Hariv.; of a rich merchant, Vet.; *-pati-datta*, m. N. of a merchant, Daś.; *-pā́* (AV.; TBr.), *-pāla* (MBh.), m. guardian of treasure; *-pālita*, m. N. of a merchant, Daś.; *-prabhu*, m. lord of treasures, N. of Kubera, MW.; *-bhṛit*, m. bearer of t°, id., Dharmaśarm.; *-mát*, mfn. containing t° or forming a store, abundant, RV.; *-maya*, mf(*ī*)n. consisting of t°, Hcat.; *-rāma*, m. N. of an author, Cat.; *-vāda*, m. the art of finding t°, Kād.; *-vāsa*, m. 'place of t°,' N. of a town, L.; *°dhīśa* (*-tva*, n., R.), *°dhīśvara* (Dharmaśarm.), m. 'lord of t°,' N. of Kubera; *°dhy-arthin*, mfn. seeking t°, MW. **°dheya**, mfn. to be placed in or on, to be deposited or kept or preserved, Hariv.; Car. &c. **Nihita**, see s. v. p. 564.

निधारय *ni-dhārayá*. See *ni-dhṛi*.

निधाव् *ni-√2. dhāv*, Ā. *-dhāvate* (aor. *adhā-*

vishta), to rub into one's person, TS.; to press one's self on, cling to (loc.), RV.

निधि *ni-dhí.* See under *ni-dhā.*

निधू *ni-√dhū*, P. *-dhūnoti* (*-dhuváti*, AV.; TS.; Pot. *-dhūvet*, Kāth.), to throw down, deliver over, AV.; to shake to and fro, agitate, Hariv. °**dhuvana**, n. shaking, trembling, agitation, L.; sexual intercourse, Git.; Hāsy.; sport, play, L.

निधृ *ni-√dhṛi* (only pf. *-dadhre*), to bend or yield to (dat.) RV. i, 37, 7: Caus. *dhārayati* (aor. *-dīdhar*), to place down in, bring to (loc.), RV.; establish, appoint, render (with double acc.), ib.; to preserve, keep, BhP. °**dhārayá**, mfn. establishing or having established (acc.), RV. viii, 41, 4. °**dhṛiti**, m. N. of a son of Vṛishṇi, AgP.

निध्यै *ni-√dhyai*, P. *-dhyāyati* (pf. *-dadhyau*, °*dhyur*), to observe, perceive; to meditate, think of, remember (acc.), AitBr.; BhP.: Desid. *-didhyāsate*, to wish to meditate on, think of attentively, ŚBr.

Ni-didhyāsana, n. profound and repeated meditation, Prab.; Vedântas. °**didhyāsitavya**, mfn. to be thought about or attended to, ŚBr. °**didhyāsu**, mfn. desirous of meditating on or attending to, BhP.

Ni-dhyapti, f. reflection, philosophical meditation, L. °**dhyāta**, mfn. meditated or thought on, Vajracch. °**dhyāna**, n. intuition, seeing, sight, L.

निध्रुव *ni-dhruva*, m. N. of a man, Pravar.: pl. his descendants, ĀśvŚr. (cf. *naidhruva*, °*vi*).

Ní-dhruvi, mfn. constant, persevering, faithful, RV.; m. N. of a Kāśyapa and author of RV. ix, 63, Anukr.

निध्वंस् *ni-√dhvaṇs*, Caus. *-dhvasayati*, to scatter, overthrow, destroy, RV. x, 73, 6.

निध्वान *ni-dhvāna*, m. (√2. *dhvan*) sound, L.

निनङ्क्षु *ninaṅkshu* (Desid. of √2. *naś*), wishing to perish or die, Bhaṭṭ.

निनद् *ni-√nad*, P. *-nadati*, to sound, cry out, resound, MBh.; R. &c.: Caus. *-nādayati*, to cause to sound or resound, fill with noise or cries &c., ib. °**nada**, m. (n., ChUp. iii, 13, 8), °**nāda**, m. sound, noise, crying, humming, MBh.; Kāv. &c. °**nādita**, mfn. filled with noise, resonant with (instr.), ib.; n. = prec., ib. °**nādin**, mfn. sounding, resounding, crying, resonant with (instr. or comp.), MBh.; R. &c.; ifc. causing to sound, playing (a musical instrument), MBh.; Hariv.

निनद्ध *ní-naddha*, mfn. (√*nah*) fastened on, tied to (loc.), RV. vi, 75, 5.

Ni-nāhya (or °**nāhyà**), m. a water-jar put into the ground, ŚBr.

निनयन *ni-nayana*, °*yanīya.* See *ni-nī* below.

निनर्तशत्रु *ninarta-śatru*, w.r. for *nivṛitta-s*°.

निनर्तिषा *ninartishā*, f. (√*nṛit*) desire of dancing, Hcar.

निनर्द् *ni-√nard*, P. *-nardati*, to sound, prolong a note in chanting, slur or trill, ShaḍvBr. (cf. *ava-√nard*): Caus. *-nardayati*, GopBr.

Ni-narda, m. a slur or trill, ĀśvŚr.

निनित्सु *ninitsú.* See under √*nind.*

निनी *ni-√nī*, P. Ā. *-nayati*, °*te* (Subj. aor. *-neshat*), to lead to, carry or bring towards (dat. or loc.), bring or cause to (dat. inf.), RV.; AV. &c.; to incline, bend, BhP.; to pour down, pour out or in, TS.; ŚBr.; Yājñ. &c.; to cause to enter, BhP.; to offer as a sacrifice, ib.; to carry out, accomplish, perform, ib.; to spend (time), MW. °**nayana**, n. pouring down or out, Kauś. (cf. *svadhā-n*°); carrying out, performance, MW. °**nayanīya**, see *svadhā-ninayanīya.*

निनीषा *ninīshā* (fr. Desid. of √1. *nī*), desire of bringing or carrying or taking away, MBh. °**shu**, mfn. wishing to take or carry or bring or lead to (acc. or acc. with *prati*) or spend (time), MBh.; Kād.; Rājat.

निनृत् *ni-√nṛit*, P. *-nṛityati*, to repeat (lit. dance again) a portion of a verse or syllable, ŚāṅkhBr. °**nṛitta**, mfn. repeated (as above), AitBr.; *-vat*, mfn. having repetition, ib. °**nṛitti**, f. repetition, ŚāṅkhBr.

निन्द् *nind* or *nid*, cl. 1. P. *níndati*, ep. also °*te* (the form *nid* only in 3. pl. pf. *ninidús*, in the Desid. and in some deriv., see under 1. *nid* and *ninitsú* below; pf. *nininda*, MBh.; aor. *áninदishur*, RV.; *nindishat*, AV.; Pot. *nindyāt*, Up.; fut. *nindishyati*, Vop.; *ninditā*, MBh.; ind. p. *-nindya*, ib.), to blame, censure, revile, despise, ridicule, RV. &c. &c.: Desid. *nínitsati*, °*te*, to wish to blame &c., RV.; ĀśvŚr. [Cf. Gk. ὄ-νειδος.]

Ninitsú, mfn. (fr. Desid.) wishing to blame, RV.

Ninda, only in **-tala**, mfn. = *nindita-hasta*, having a maimed hand, L. (also *nimna-t*°, W.)

Nindaka, mfn. blaming, abusive, censorious; (mostly ifc.) a blamer or scorner (cf. *brāhmaṇa-*, *veda-*), Mn.; MBh. &c. °**dana**, n. reproach, censure, blame, Pāṇ.

Nindanīya, mfn. blamable, reprehensible, Hariv.

Nindā́, f. blame, censure, reproach, reviling, defamation, controversy, injury, outrage, AV.; Mn.; MBh. &c.; (with Buddh.) one of the eight worldly conditions, Dharmas. lxi; *-stuti*, f. ironical praise, irony, L.; °*dôpamā*, f. a comparison which involves reproof, Kāvyâd. ii, 30.

Ninditá, mfn. blamed, censured, abused, defamed, low, despicable, prohibited, forbidden, RV.; Br. &c.

Ninditâśva, m. N. of a man, RV. viii, 1, 30.

Ninditṛi, m. scorner, scoffer, RV.

Nindin, mfn. blaming, censuring, reproaching (ifc.), Kāvyâd.

Nindu, f. a woman bearing a dead child, L.

Nindyà (or *nindya*), mfn. = °*danīya*, RV.; ŚBr.; Mn. &c.; *-tā*, f. blamableness, disgrace, Mn.

निन्व् *ninv*, cl. 1. °*vati* (Dhātup. xv, 81; v. l. *sinv*), to wet or to attend (prob. a confusion between *secane* and *sevane*).

निप *ni-pa.* See under *ni-pā* below.

निपक्षति *ní-pakshati*, f. the second rib, VS.

निपठ *ni-paṭha*, m. (√*paṭh*) recitation, study, Pāṇ. iii, 3, 64, Kāś. °**ṭhana**, n. (L.), °**ṭhiti**, f. (Pat. on Pāṇ. vii, 2, 9) id. °**ṭhitin**, mfn., g. *ishṭâdi.* **Nipāṭha**, m. = *-paṭha*, Pāṇ. iii, 3, 64.

निपत् *ni-√pat*, P. *-patati* (ep. also °*te*), to fly down, settle down, descend on (loc.), alight, MBh.; Kāv. &c.; to rush upon, attack, assail (acc. or loc.), Ratnâv.; Kathās.; to fall down, fall upon or into (lit. and fig., with *upari*, acc. or loc.; with *pādayoḥ*, to throw one's self at a person's [gen.] feet, Kum.; Kathās.); to fall into ruin or decay, be lost, AV.; MBh.; Suśr. &c.; to be miscarried (as the fetus), BhP.; to befall, happen, take place, occur, fall to the share of (loc.), Mn.; MBh.; Suśr. &c.; to enter, be inserted, get a place, Pāṇ.; Nir.: Caus. *-pātayati* (aor. *-apīpatat*, RV.), to cause to fall down, or on (loc.), throw down, fell, kill, destroy, RV. &c. &c.; to spit out, Pañc. iii, 60; to inlay, emboss, MBh. iv, 1325; to fix (the teeth) in (loc.), MBh.; to direct (the eyes) towards (loc.), MārkP.; to impute (a fault) to (gen.), Kathās.; to raise (taxes) from (abl.), MBh.; (in gram.) to put down as a special or irregular form, consider as anomalous or irregular. °**patana**, n. falling down, falling, descending, MBh.; Hariv.; (*garbhiṇyā garbhasya*) the lying-in of a pregnant woman, VarBṛS. li, 35; flying, MBh. °**patita**, mfn. flown or fallen down, descended (*nabho-n*°, from heaven), fallen upon or into (loc.), MBh.; Kāv. &c.; decayed, sunk, withered, Dhūrtas. °**patya**, ind. having fallen down &c., MBh.; *-rohiṇī*, f. (prob.) falling and ascending, g. *mayūra-vyaṇsakâdi.* °**patyā**, f. any slippery ground; a field of battle, L. °**pāta**, m. falling down, descending, alighting (lit. and fig.), falling from (abl.) into or upon (comp.), rushing upon, attacking (comp.), Mn.; MBh. &c.; decay, destruction, ruin, death, ib.; (from the Caus.) casting, hurling, discharging, Kum. iii, 15; accidental occurrence or mention, Nir.; ĀśvŚr.; (in gram.) irregular form, irregularity, exception (cf. *para-*, *pūrva-*); a particle (all adverbs including conjunctions and interjections), Nir.; Prāt.; Pāṇ. i, 4, 56; *-tva*, n. the state of being a particle, MW.; *-pratīkāra*, m. the repelling of assaults, ib.; °*tâvyayôpasarga*, m. pl. N. of wk. °**pātaka**, ifc. = *pātaka*, a bad deed, a sin, MBh. v, 4053. °**pātana**, mfn. (fr. Caus.) throwing down, killing, destroying, knocking out (an eye), MBh.; n. causing to descend or fall, throwing down, letting drop or sink, Mn.; Yājñ.; R. (cf. *daṇḍa-n*°); putting on, applying (as a knife), touching with (comp.), Suśr.; overthrowing, destroying, killing, Mn.; MBh.; (in gram.) accidental mention or use of a word, putting down as an irregularity; an irregular form or exception, Prāt.; Pāṇ., Sch.; Vop.; = *ni-patana*, falling down (of a fire-brand), Yājñ. i, 145; alighting (said of a bird), Pañc. ii. 57. °**pātanīya**, mfn. to be caused to fall; (with *daṇḍa*, m. 'punishment must be inflicted),' Sāh. °**pātita**, mfn. made to fall or descend on (loc.); overthrown, beaten down, destroyed, killed, MBh. &c.; (in gram.) irregular, exceptional. °**pātin**, mfn. falling or flying down, MBh.; falling or alighting on (comp., Ragh. ix, 40; *upari*, Vikr. v, 15); striking down, destroying, MBh.; Ragh. 1. °**pātya**, ind. throwing down, overthrowing, destroying, killing, MBh.; BhP. 2. °**pātya**, mfn. to be cast down or overthrown; (in gram.) to be put down or mentioned as an irregularity. °**pātyamāna**, mfn. being thrown down, being precipitated into (loc.), Prab. vi, ⅞.

निपद् *ni-√pad*, Ā. *-padyate*, to lie down, rest, lie down with (acc.), RV.; ŚBr.: Caus. *-pādayati*, to throw down, fell, ib.

निपरण *ni-paraṇa.* See *ni-√pṛī.*

निपलाशम् *ní-palāśam*, ind. (as softly or silently as) the falling of leaves, ŚBr.

निपा *ni-√1. pā*, P. *-pibati*, to drink or suck in, kiss, Kāv.; to absorb, dry up, BhP.: Caus. *-pāyayati*, cause to imbibe or suck in, ib. 1. °**pa**, m. a water-jar, Nauclea Cadamba, L. 1. °**pāna** (or °*naka*, W.), n. drinking, imbibing, MBh.; BhP.; any place or trough for watering cattle, a well, pool, tank; Mn.; MBh. &c.; a milk-pail, L.; *-kartṛi*, m. one who makes a tank, Mn. iv, 211; *-vat*, mfn. abounding in pools or tanks, Ragh.; *-saras*, n. a pool or lake for watering cattle, Kād. °**pīta**, mfn. drunk in, absorbed, imbibed, drunk up, Kāv.; *-kusuma*, mfn. (a tree) whose blossoms are sucked by (instr.), ŚārṅgP.; *-toya*, mfn. (a river) whose water has been drunk by (instr.), R.; *-sāra*, mfn. (a lip) whose moisture has been sucked in (that has been kissed), Ṛit. °**pīti**, f. drinking, L. °**pīyamāna**, mfn. being drunk in or imbibed, Kathās.

निपा *ni-√2. pā*, P. *-pāti*, to guard or protect from (abl.); to observe, watch over, RV.; AV.: Caus. *-pālayati*, to protect, guard, govern, MW. 2. °**pa**, mfn. protecting (cf. *āke-n*°), RV.; m. a lord, chief, L. °**paka**, mfn. intelligent, wise (cf. Pāli), L.; m. chief, Divyâv. 2. °**pāna**, n. place of refuge, Jātakam.; °*nī√kṛi*, ib.

निपाक *ni-pāka* (√*pac*), cooking, maturing, ripening, L.

निपाठ *ni-pāṭha.* See *ni-paṭha* above.

निपात *ni-pāta.* See under *ni-pat.*

निपाद *ni-pādá*, m. (fr. *pāda*) low ground, a valley, RV.

निपित्सु *ni-pitsu*, mfn. (√*pat*, Desid.) going or about to fall, Hariv.

निपिष्ट *ní-pishṭa*, mfn. (√*pish*) crushed, destroyed, AV.

निपीड् *ni-√pīḍ*, Caus. *-pīḍayati*, to press close to or against, press together, impress; to oppress, afflict, plague, trouble, MBh.; Kāv. &c.; (in astron.) to eclipse, Var. °**pīḍana**, n. squeezing, pressing, hurting, giving pain, L.; (*ā*) f. oppression, Sāh. °**pīḍayat**, mf(*antī*)n. pressing, pressing together; (*dantān dantaiḥ*) gnashing the teeth, Pañc. °**pīḍita**, mfn. squeezed, pressed, embraced; pained, hurt, Mn.; MBh. &c.; °*ḍitâlaktaka-vat*, ind. like pressed lac, MW. °**pīḍya**, ind. having squeezed or pressed or embraced or hurt, MBh.; Kāv. &c.

Ni-pīlana, n. pressing out, HPariś. (= *ni-pīḍana*).

निपीय् *ni√pīy*, P. *-pīyati*, to revile, abuse, TBr.

निपु *nipu*, m. N. of a man, Kshitîś.

निपुण *nipuṇa*, mf(*ā*)n. (said to be from a √*puṇ*), clever, adroit, skilful, sharp, acute, Mn.; MBh.; Suśr.; Kāv. &c.; skilled in, conversant with, capable of (mostly comp. [cf. Pāṇ. ii, 1, 31 and g. *śauṇḍâdi*]; but also infin. [Kāv.], loc. [Var.], gen. [Vop. v, 29] or instr. [Pāṇ. ii, 1, 31]); kind or friendly towards (loc. or *prati*, Pāṇ. ii, 3, 43); delicate, tender, Jātak.; perfect, complete, absolute (as purity, devotion &c.), Mn.; BhP.; (*am*), ind. in a clever or delicate manner, MBh.; Kāv.; completely, perfectly, absolutely, exactly, precisely, R. (also *nipuṇa* ibc. Pāṇ. vi, 2, 24, and °*ṇena*, MBh.; BhP.) **–tara**, mfn. more clever or perfect &c.; (*am*), ind. = next, Pañc. **–tas**, ind. wholly, completely, MBh. **–tā**, f. skilfulness, adroitness, carefulness, accuracy, Kāv.; Pañc. **–dṛiś**, mfn. sharp-sighted, clever, knowing, MW. **Nipuṇikā**, f. N. of a waiting-maid, Kālid.

निपुथ् *ni-√puth*, Caus. *-pothayati*, to dash down, Hariv.

निपुर् *ni-púr*, f. the subtle body, VS.; AV. (= *sūkshma-deha*, Mahidh.)

निपूत *ní-pūta*, mfn. (√*pū*) strained, filtered, purified, RV.

निपॄ *ni-√pṝī*, P. *-pṛiṇāti* (Pot. *-pṛiṇuyāt*, Lāṭy.), to put down, pour out, offer (esp. to deceased relatives), AV.; ŚBr. &c.: Intens. *-popūryate*, Pat. °**paraṇa**, n. the putting down or offering (of rice &c. to deceased relatives), Nir.; ĀśvŚr., Sch. °**pāraka**, mfn. one who puts down &c., Pat. °**pṛita** (ĀśvŚr.) and °**pūrta** (Pat.) mfn. put down, poured out, offered.

निप्रथ *ni-√prath* (Caus. aor. *-paprathan*), to spread or increase, RV. ii. 11, 8.

निप्रयत्न *ni-prayatna*, w. r. for *nish-pr°*, Hariv.

निप्रहन् *ni-pra-√han*, P. *-hanti*, to hurt or destroy (with gen.), Pāṇ. ii, 3, 56, Kāś.

निप्रियाय *ni-priyāya* (fr. *ni-priya*), Nom. Ā. °*yáte*, to keep in one's possession, not to be willing to give up (acc.), AV.

निफला *ni-phalā*, f. Cardiospermum Halicacabum, L.

निफालन *ni-phālana*, n. seeing, sight, L. (prob. w. r. for *ni-bh°*).

निफेन *ni-phena*, n. opium, L. (cf. *a-ph°*).

निबन्ध् *ni-√bandh*, P. *-badhnāti*, to bind on, tie, fasten to (loc.), AV.; Kauś.; MBh. &c.; to enchain, fetter (lit. and fig.), Mn.; MBh.; R. &c.; to contract, unite, join, close, obstruct, Kāv.; Kathās.; to compose, draw up, write down, Mn.; Var.; R. &c.; to catch, win, acquire, MBh.; Pañc.; to hold fast, restrain, check, MBh.; Ragh.; to put or fix upon (foot, eye &c., i.e. undertake, begin, with loc.), Hariv.; Kāv.; Pañc.; to fix, place, locate, Rājat.; to show, exhibit, Sāh.: Pass. *-badhyate*, to be bound &c., Mn.; MBh. &c. °**baddha**, mfn. bound, fettered, chained, tied or fastened to, fixed on (loc.); covered with, veiled in (instr.), MBh.; dependent on (instr.), Mn.; MBh. &c.; relating to, contained in (loc.), MBh.; Hariv.; composed or consisting of, accompanied by, furnished with, adorned or inlaid with (comp.), Mn.; MBh.; Kāv. &c.; shut up, closed, obstructed, Kathās.; constructed, built, ib.; composed, written down, R.; Kālid. &c.; used, employed (as a word), Sāh.; called as a witness (*a-n°*, Mn. viii, 76); confined, costive, W.; committed, intrusted, MW.; m. (in music) a partic. instrument. °**baddhavya** (!), mfn. necessarily connected with (instr.), Sāh. °**band-dhṛi**, m. binder, fastener, author, composer, Bālar. i, 11 (printed *nibaddhṛi*). °**bandha**, m. binding on, tying, fastening, R.; chain, fetter, bondage, MBh.; BhP.; attachment to, intentness on, L.; basis, root, origin, MBh. ii. 2532; a grant of property, an assignment of cattle or money, Yājñ. i. 317; fixed property, ib. ii. 121; restraint, obstruction, L.; constipation or suppression of urine, Suśr. (v. l. for *vi-b°*); any literary composition or work, Cat.; N. of a partic. wk., ib.; Azadirachta Indica, L.; n. song, singing, L.; *-candrôdaya* and *-tattva-dīpa*, m. N. of wks.; *-dāna*, n. grant of property, assignment or gift of a corrody, MW.; *-nava-nīta*, m. or n. N. of wk.; *-rāja*, m. N. of an author, Cat.; *-vivṛiti-yojanā*, f., *-śiromany-ukta-nir-ṇaya*, m.pl., *-saṃgraha*, m., *-sarvasva*, n., *-sāra*, m. N. of wks. °**bandhaka**, mfn., g. *ṛiśyâdi* (v. l. °*dhanaka*). °**bandhana**, mf(*ī*)n. binding, fastening, fettering, MBh.; BhP.; m. N. of a son of Aruṇa, BhP. (v. l. *tri-b°*); (*ī*), f. band, bond, fetter, MBh.; Suśr.; n. tying, fastening, binding together, ligation, Mn.; Suśr.; holding fast, restraining, MBh.; Kāv. &c.; constructing, building (as a bridge), MBh.; band, fetter (lit. and fig.), support, stay, ib.; Kāv.; Kathās.; BhP.; cause, origin, basis, foundation, Mn.; MBh. &c. (often ifc. = supported by, fastened to, based or dependent on, connected with, relating to); seat, receptacle (cf. *ishu-n°*); the peg of a lute, L.; a grant, an assignment or royal gift, Śiś. ii, 112; composition, arrangement, Kum.; a literary composition or treatise, Śiś. ii, 112; (in gram.) syntax; a commentary; *-grantha*, m. N. of a class of wks. °**bandhanaka**, see °*dhaka* above. °**bandhanīya**, mfn. good or friendly relation; acc. with √*kṛi*, to be on good terms with (instr.), Hcar. (v. l. *nir-b°*). °**bandhika**, see *aśva-nib°*. °**bandhita**, mfn. bound, fastened, confined, tied, W. °**bandhin**, mfn. binding, confining, fettering, MBh.; Kāv.; (ifc.) joined by, connected with, MBh., Suśr.; causing, being the cause of, Yogas.

निबर्हण *ni-barhaṇa*. See *ni-bṛih* below.

निबल *nibala*, m. or n. a partic. number, Buddh.

निबाढ *ní-bāḍha* or °*bāḷha*, mfn. (√*baṇh*) forced down, thrown into (loc.), RV. i, 106, 6.

निबाध् *ni-√bādh*, Ā. *-bādhate*, to press down or together, confine, obstruct, oppress, RV.

Ni-bādha. See *a-nibādhá*.

निबिड *ni-biḍa* or *ni-viḍa*, mf(*ā*)n. (prob. fr. *biḍa* = *bila*, a hole; cf. *ni-khila*) without spaces or interstices, close, compact, thick, dense, firm, MBh.; Kāv. &c.; full of, abounding in (instr. or comp.), Hariv.; Śak. vii, 11 (v. l. for *ni-cita*); low, Kād.; crooked-nosed, Pāṇ. v, 2, 32, Kāś.; m. N. of a mountain, MBh. vi, 460; n. crooked-nosedness, Pāṇ. v, 2, 32, Kāś.

Nibiḍaya, Nom. P. °*yati*, to make tight, embrace firmly, Bālar. ii, 62. °**ḍita**, mfn. made tight, become thick or heavy, Mālatīm.; pressed close to, Bālar. v, 19.

Nibiḍī-√kṛi, to make tight or firm, bend (a bow), Vcar.

Nibirīsa, mfn. = *ni-biḍa*, Kāv. (*-ni-tamba*, Śiś. vii, 20); Pāṇ. v, 2, 32, Kāś. (W. *niviḍīsha*).

निबुध् *ni-√budh*, P. *-bodhati* (aor. *-bódhishat*, RV.), to learn or hear anything (acc.) from any one (gen., rarely *sakāśāt*), to attend or listen to (esp. Impv. *nibodha*, °*dhata*; rarely °*dhasva*, °*dhadhvam*); to know, understand, consider as (often with double acc.), RV.; AV.; Mn.; MBh. &c.: Caus. *-bodhayati*, to cause to know or learn, to inform, tell, BhP. °**boddhavya**, mfn. to be learnt; to be regarded or considered as (with nomin.), Var. °**boddhṛi**, mfn. knowing, wise, Gal.

निबुसीकृत *ni-busi-kṛita*, mfn. freed from chaff, husked, Kuval. (cf. *nir-b°*).

निबृह् *ni-√bṛih* (*vṛih*), P. *-bṛihati* (aor. *-barhīt*), to throw down, overthrow, crush, destroy, RV.: Caus. *-barhayati*, id., ib.; MBh. &c. °**barhaṇa**, mfn. crushing, destroying, removing, MBh.; R. &c.; n. destruction, annihilation, ib. °**barhita**, mfn. destroyed, removed; °*tâṇhas*, mfn. destroying sin, Śiś. i, 29.

निभ *ni-bha*, mf(*ā*)n. (√*bhā*) resembling, like, similar (ifc.), MBh.; R. &c. (sometimes pleonast. after adj., e.g. *cāru-nibhânana*, 'hand-some-faced,' Hariv., or comp. with a synonym, e.g. *naga-nibhôpama*, 'mountain-like,' MBh.; *padma-pattrâbha-nibha*, 'like a lotus-leaf,' ib.); m. or n. appearance, pretext (only ifc. instr., Daś.; abl., Kathās.). **–tā**, f. similarity, likeness, RPrāt.

निभञ्ज् *ni-√bhañj*, P. *-bhanakti* (aor. *ny-a-bhāṅkshīt*), to break or dash to pieces, Bhaṭṭ. °**bhañjana**, n. breaking to pieces or asunder, AV.

निभर्त्सन *ni-bhartsana*, °*tsayat*, w. r. for *nir-bh°*.

निभल् *ni-√bhal*, P. Ā. *-bhālayati*, °*te*, to perceive, see, ChUp.; Bālar. °**bhālana**, n. seeing, perception, L. (w. r. *ni-ph°*).

निभसद् *ni-bhasad*, mfn. (prob.) having the hinder parts directed downwards, TāṇḍyaBr.

निभिद् *ni-√bhid* (Pass. *-bhidyate*), to be opened, open, BhP. (v. l. *anu-bh°*).

निभुज् *ni-√1. bhuj*, P. *-bhujati*, to bend (head and knees), Pat.

निभूत *ni-bhūta*, mfn. (√*bhū*) past, gone, L.; quite frightened, A.

निभूयप *nibhūyapa* (?), m. N. of Vishṇu, VS.

निभृत *ní-bhṛita*, mfn. (√*bhṛi*) borne or placed down, hidden, secret, MBh.; Kav. &c.; nearly set (as the moon), Ragh.; firm, immovable, Hariv.; Kāv.; Pur.; shut, closed (as a door), L.; fixed, settled, decided, RV.; fixed or intent upon (comp.), Kād.; filled with, full of (instr. or comp.), BhP.; attached, faithful, MBh.; MārkP.; still, silent, Kum.; quiet, humble, modest, mild, gentle, MBh.; R. &c.; free from passions, undisturbed (= *śānta*), Hcar.; lonely, solitary, Gīt.; (*ā*), f. a kind of riddle, Kāvyâd.; (*am*), ind. secretly, privately, silently, quietly, Mn.; Kāv.; Pañc. &c.; n. humility, modesty, MBh. v, 1493 (Nīlak. 'secrecy, silence'). **–sthita**, mfn. standing out of sight, unperceived, Kathās. **Nibhṛitâgata**, mfn. secretly arrived, ib. **Nibhṛitâcāra**, mfn. of resolute conduct, firm, R. **Nibhṛitâtman**, mfn. resolute-minded, resolute, BhP. **Nibhṛitârtha**, mfn. having a secret meaning, occult, Śiś. **Nibhṛitôrdhva-karṇa**, mfn. having the ears fixed and erect (said of horses), Śak. i, 8.

Nibhṛitī-√kṛi, to keep quiet or unmoved, Kāv.

निभ्रंश् *ni-√bhraṇś*, Caus. *-bhrāśayati*, to cause to fall, strike down, fell, RV. x, 116, 5. °**bhṛishṭa**, see *a-nibhṛ°*.

निम *nima*, m. a pin, stake (?), W.

निमज्ज् *ni-√majj*, P. Ā. *-majjati*, °*te* (p. *-majjat* and °*jjamāna*, MBh.; pf. *-mamajja*, MārkP.; fut. *-majjishyati*, MBh.; *-maṅkshye*, Ait.Br.; aor. *-amāṅkshīt*, Bhaṭṭ.; *-majjīḥ*, MBh.), to sink down, dive, sink or plunge or penetrate into, bathe in (loc.), Br.; Mn.; MBh. &c.; to sink in its cavity (the eye), Suśr.; to disappear, perish, MBh.; Kāv. &c.; to immerse or submerge in water, cause to sink or perish, MBh.: Caus. *-majjayati*, to cause to dive under water, Mn. viii, 114; (with *samare*, *saṃgrāme* &c.) to cause to penetrate into a battle, lead into the thick of a fight, MBh. °**magna**, mfn. sunk, fallen into (water &c.); submerged, plunged, or immersed in, penetrated or fixed into (loc. or comp.), Br.; Up.; MBh. &c.; gone down, set (as the sun), Ragh.; Gīt.; (with *para-lokāya*) entered into the other world, MBh.; sunk in, depressed, not prominent, deep, Suśr. (cf. below); overwhelmed, covered, MW.; *-nābhi* or *-madhyā*, f. (a woman) having a depressed navel or a slender waist, Vikr. °**magnaka**, mfn. sinking or entering deep into the flesh, MBh. i, 5601. °**majjathu**, m. the act of diving or entering into, plunging; (with *talpe*) going to bed, Bhaṭṭ. °**majjana**, mf(*ī*)n. causing a person (gen.) to enter or plunge into (water &c.), MBh.; n. bathing, diving, sinking, immersion, MBh.; Kāv. &c. °**majjita**, mfn. plunged into the water, drowned, MBh.

निमथ् *ni-√math* (ind.p. *-mathya*), to strike down, kill, R.

निमद् *ni-√mad*, P. *-mādayati*, to pronounce distinctly but slowly, Sāy. °**mada**, m. pronunciation which is distinct but slow (one of the 7 *vācaḥ sthānāni* or degrees of pronunciation), TPrāt.

निमन् *ni-√man* (aor. Ā. *-amaṃsata*), to regard or consider as (with double acc.), BhP.

निमन्त्र् *ni-√mantr*, Ā. *-mantrayate* (°*ti*), to invite, summon, call to (loc. or infin.), Mn.; Yājñ.; MBh. &c.; to invite or entertain with (instr.) or offer anything to (acc.), ĀśvGṛ.; MBh. &c. °**mantraka**, m. an inviter, MBh. °**mantraṇa**, n. invitation, calling, a summons, Yājñ.; MBh.; R. °**mantrita**, mfn. invited (esp. to a feast, with instr., e. g. *vivāhena*, Pañcar.; cf. Pañc. iii, 139);

summoned, called, convoked, Mn.; MBh. &c. 1. °**mantrya**, mfn. to be invited or called, MBh. xii, 3340. 2. °**mantrya**, ind. having invited, by means of an invitation, Rājat. i, 66.

निमन्यु *ni-manyu*, mfn. not angry, unresentful, appeased, AV.

निमय *ni-maya*. See under *ni-me*.

निमर्दक *ni-mardaka*. See under *ni-mṛid*.

निमा *ni-√mā*, Ā. *-mimīte* (pf. *-mamire*, RV. iii, 38, 7), to measure, adjust, RV. &c. &c. (cf. *ni-me*). 1. °**mātavya**, mfn. to be (or being) measured, Pat. °**māna**, n. measure, Pāṇ. v, 2, 47 (cf. *a-nim°*), price, Siddh. 1. °**mita**, mfn. measured (cf. *cakshur-n°*, *dur-n°*); caused, BhP. (v.l. *nir-m°*). 1. °**meya**, mfn. to be measured, measurable, Pāṇ. v, 2, 47, Vārtt. 5.

निमार्जन *ni-mārjana*. See under *ni-mṛij*.

निमि 1. *nimi*, m. N. of sev. kings of Videha, Mn.; MBh. &c.; of a son of Dattâtreya, MBh.; of a son of Ikshvāku, Pur. (having lost his body through the curse of Vasishṭha he occupied the eyes of all living beings, hence the opening and shutting of men's eyelids; cf. *ni-misha* and see VP. iv, 5); of 21st Jaina Arhat of present Ava-sarpiṇī (identified with the former Nimi), L.; of a son of Bhajamāna, VP.; of a son of Daṇḍa-pāṇi, BhP.; of a Dānava, Hariv. (v.l. *ḍimbha*); the closing or winking of the eyes, twinkling, BhP. ix, 24, 64. **—ṃ-dhara**, m. N. of a prince, Lalit. **Nimîśvara**, m. (with Jainas) N. of 16th Arhat of past Ut-sarpiṇī.

निमि 2. *ni-√1. mi*, P. *-minoti* (pf. *-mimāya*, Pass. *-mīyate*), to fix or dig in, erect, raise, RV.; AV.; Br. &c.; to perceive, notice, understand (?), AV. iv, 16, 5. 2. °**mita**, mfn. fixed, raised, erected, RV.; AV.; TBr. °**miti**, f. (?) settlement, RV. v, 62, 7.

निमित्त *nimitta*, n. (possibly connected with *ni-√mā* above) a butt, mark, target, MBh.; sign, omen, Mn.; Yājñ.; MBh. &c. (cf. *dur-n°*); cause, motive, ground, reason, Up.; Kap.; Var.; Mn.; MBh.; Kāv. &c. (in all oblique cases = because of, on account of, cf. Pāṇ. ii, 3, 23, Pat.; mfn. ifc. caused or occasioned by; °*ttaṃ-√yā*, to be the cause of anything, Kād.); (in phil.) instrumental or efficient cause (opp. to *upâdāna*, the operative or material cause), Vedântas.; Bhāshāp.; = *āgantu*; *deha*; *ādeśa*; *parvan*, L. **—kāraṇa**, n. instrumental or efficient cause (esp. the Deity as the agent in creation), W.; *-tā*, f., MW. **—kāla**, m. the period or moment of time which may be regarded as causing any event; *-tā*, f., KātyŚr., Sch. **—kṛit**, m. 'omen-maker,' a crow, raven, L. **—jña**, mfn. acquainted with omens, MW. **—jñāna**, n. 'knowledge of omens or signs,' N. of ch. of the Kāma-sūtra by Vātsyāyana; cf. RTL. 397. **—tā**, f., **-tva**, n. (in phil.) the state of being a cause, causality, instrumentality. **—dharma**, m. expiation, any occasional or special penance or rite or obligation, W. **—nidāna**, n. N. of wk. **—nimittin**, mfn. operating and operated upon, Sch. on P. viii, 3, 9. **—naimittika**, n. du. cause and effect, Śak. vii, 30. **—bhūta**, mfn. become or being a cause or reason or means, MW. **—mātra**, n. the mere efficient cause or instrument, Bhag.; Veṇīs. **—vid**, m. 'omen-knower,' an astrologer, L. **—vedhin**, mfn. hitting a mark, MBh. **—saptamī**, f. a seventh case (locative) indicating the cause or motive, Kāś. on Pāṇ. i, 1, 57. **—hetu**, m. the efficient cause; *-tva*, n., Bhāshāp. **Nimittâyus**, mfn. one whose age is dependent on some cause, MBh. **Nimittârtha**, m. (in gram.) the infinitive mood, MW. **Nimittâvṛitti**, f. dependence upon a special cause or occasion, W. **Nimittâvêksha**, mfn. considering the cause, ĀpGṛ.

Nimittaka, mfn. caused or occasioned or produced by (ifc.), Kāp.; Sch. on Pāṇ. i, 1, 16; n. kissing, a kiss, L. °**ttāyamāna**, mfn. (fr. an unusual Nom. °*ttāya*) causing, producing, MW.

Nimittin, mfn. operated on or influenced by a cause, having a cause or reason, TPrāt., Sch.; Pāṇ., Sch. (cf. *nimitta-n°* above).

Nimittī, for °*tta* in comp. **—√kṛi**, to make anything a cause, use as a cause or means, Daś.; BhP. **—kṛitya**, ind. in consequence of, by the fault of (acc.), Kād. **—bhū**, to become a cause or reason for (loc.), Sāh.

निमिश्र *ni-miśra*, m. N. of a man (cf. *naimiśra*).

Ní-miśla, mf(*ā*)n. devoted or attached to (loc.), RV. **—tama**, mfn. most attached to (loc.), ŚBr.

निमिष् *ni-√mish*, P. *-mishati* (aor. *-amīmishat*), to shut the eyelids, wink, fall asleep, RV. &c. &c.; to be shut (said of the eyelids), R.; (fut. *-mishyati?*) Daś. (cf. *a-nimishat*). °**mish**, f. winking or twinkling of the eye (cf. *a-nimish*); shutting the eyes, falling asleep, RV.; AV. (cf. 1. *nimi*). °**misha**, m. twinkling, shutting the eye (also considered as a measure of time, a moment, MBh.; R.; as a disease, Suśr.); N. of a son of Garuḍa, MBh.; of Vishṇu, L.; *-kshetra*, n. N. of a district, Cat.; °*shântara*, n. the interval of a moment; (*eṇa*), in a m°, MBh.; Kāv. °**mishita**, n. shutting of the eyes, Pat. °**meshá**, m. shutting the eye, twinkling, winking, TS.; Mn.; Yājñ.; MBh. &c. (also as a measure of time i.e. a moment; °*shād iva*, in a m°, MBh.; R.&c.; °*shaṃ nimesham*, every m°, ŚBr.; as a disease, Suśr.); N. of a Yaksha, MBh.; *-kṛit*, f. 'twinkler,' lightning, L.; *-tás*, ind. with regard to the shutting of the eyes, VS.; *-dyut* or *-ruc*, m. a fire-fly, L.; *-mātra*, n. merely an instant; (*eṇa*), ind. in barely a moment, MBh.; °*shântara*, n. = *nimish°* (cf. under *cārin*); °*shârdhāt*, ind. in half a twinkling of the eye, in less than an instant, Ragh. °**meshaka**, m. twinkling of the eye; a fire-fly, W. °**meshaṇa**, mf(*ī*)n. causing twinkling &c., Suśr.; n. shutting the eyes, twinkling, BhP.

निमिह् *ni-√mih*, P. *-mehati* (Intens. *-mémihat*), to pour down urine, moisten with urine, wet, TS.; ŚBr.

निमील् *ni-√mīl*, P. *-mīlati*, to shut the eyes, fall asleep; to close (as flowers), die, disappear, Mn.; MBh.; Kāv. &c.: Caus. *-mīlayati* (°*te*), to close (the eyes, eyelids, blossoms &c.), MBh.; Kāv. &c. (cf. *ni-mīlita* below). °**mīlaka**, mf(*ikā*)n. shutting the eyes; (*ikā*), f., see below. °**mīlana**, n. shutting the eyes, Kāv. (met. = death, L.); closing (of a flower), Sāh. (cf. *padma-*); (in astron.) complete obscuration, a total eclipse, Sūryas. °**mīlā**, f. shutting the eyes, Naish. °**mīlikā**, f. id. (cf. *ibha-nimīlikā* and *gaja-n°*); fraud, trick, W. °**mīlita**, mfn. having closed the eyes, MBh.; Kāv.; closed (as eyes, flowers; n. also impers., e.g. °*tam puṇḍarīkaiḥ*), twinkled, blinked, Kāv.; Suśr.; disappeared (cf. below); (fr. Caus.) caused to shut the eyes i.e. killed, Pañc. iii, 269; *-dṛiś*, mfn. having the eyes closed, Ragh. (C.) xix, 28; *-nakshatra*, mfn. having the stars obscured (as the sky), Hariv. 2660; *-mukha*, mf(*ī*)n. (Ragh. xix, 28, C. *-dṛiś*, cf. above) and °*tâksha*, mf(*ī*)n. (Suśr.) = *-dṛiś*. °**mīlin**, mfn. having the eyelids shut (as a face), Naish.

निमीव् *ni-√mīv* (only pres. p. f. *-mīvantī*), to press on, press down, AV. v, 7, 7.

निमुष्टि *ni-mushṭi*, m. or f. 'less than a handful,' a kind of measure, Kauś. °**ṭika**, mfn. smaller than a closed hand, AitĀr.

निमूलम् *ni-mūlam*, ind. down to the root, Pāṇ. iii, 4, 34. °**la-kāsham**, ind. id., ib., Kāś.

निमृ *ni-√mṛi* (2. sg. Impv. *-mṛiṇīhi*), to crush, AV. x, 1, 17.

निमृज् *ni-√mṛij*, P. Ā. *-mārshṭi*, *-mṛishṭe*, *-mṛijati*, °*te* &c. (Pot. *-mṛijyāt*, Mn.; *-mṛiñjyāt*, ŚBr.; Impv. *-mṛiḍhvam*, TS.; pf. *-māmṛijur*, °*je*, RV. [for *mimṛikshur*, RV. i, 64, 4 read *mimikshur* and see under *ni-myaksh*]; aor. *-amṛikshāma*, ib.; *-amṛishṭa*, ŚBr.), to rub in or upon (loc.), wipe off; Ā. to cleanse one's self, TS.; ŚBr.; Śr. & GṛS.; Mn. &c.; to lead or bring or attach to (loc.); Ā. to take to one's self, appropriate, RV. °**mārjana**, n. wiping off, ĀpGṛ., Sch. °**mṛigra** (*ni-*), mf(*ā*)n. attached or devoted to (loc. with *ā*), RV. ii, 38, 2.

निमृद् *ni-√mṛid*, P. *-mṛidnāti*, to crush, dash to pieces, ĀpŚr.; to rub off, ŚBr. °**mardaka**, m. a kind of food, Car. °**mṛid**, m. a crusher, destroyer, ĀpŚr.

निमे *ni-√me*, Ā. *-mayate* (ep. also °*ti*; Pass. *-mīyate*), to change, exchange for (instr.), barter, MBh.; Pañc. °**maya**, m. barter, change, exchange, MBh. 2. °**mātavya**, mfn. to be exchanged or bartered, Mn. x, 94. 2. °**meya**, mfn. to be exchanged; m. barter, exchange, L. (cf. *naimeya*).

निमेष *ni-mesha*. See under 1. *ni-mish*.

निम्न *nimná*, n. (fr. *ni* or *√nam?*) depth, low ground, cavity, depression, RV. &c. &c. (*âls*, ind. downwards, x, 78, 5; 148, 5); mf(*ā*)n. deep (lit. and fig.), low, depressed, sunk, Var.; Kāv. &c.; (ifc.) inclined towards, L.; m. N. of a prince, BhP. **—gata**, mfn. going in deep or low places; MārkP.; n. a low place, Inscr. **—gā**, f. 'going downwards, descending,' a river, mountain-stream, Mn.; MBh. &c.; *-pati*, m. 'lord of rivers,' the ocean, Śiś.; *-suta*, m. 'river-born,' N. of Bhīshma, ib. **—tala**, see *ninda-t°*. **—tā**, f., **-tva**, n. depth, lowness, profundity, W. **—deśa**, m. a low or deep place, R. **—nābhi**, mfn. 'deep-naveled,' slender, thin, Kālid. (cf. *nimagna-n°*). **—pravaṇa**, mfn. flowing downwards, Mallin. on Kum. v, 5. **—bhāga**, m. = *-deśa*, R. **—lalāṭa**, mfn. having a low forehead, VarBṛS. **Nimnâbhimukha**, mfn. (water) tending i.e. flowing downwards, Kum. v, 5 (cf. *-pravaṇa* above). **Nimnônnata**, mfn. low and high, depressed and elevated (applied to women), Mālatīm. iv, 10.

Nimnaya, Nom. P. °*yati*, to humble i.e. outstrip, surpass, Nalac.

Nimnita, mfn. deep, depressed, sunk, MBh.

निम्ब *nimba*, m. the Nimb or Neemb tree, Azadirachta Indica (its fruit is bitter and its leaves are chewed at funeral ceremonies), Gobh.; Var.; Suśr.; Kāv. (also *-ka*). **—kara**, v.l. for *nimbaraka*. **—taru**, m. Erythrina Fulgens or Melia Sempervirens (considered as one of the trees of paradise), Bhpr. **—taila**, n. the oil from the Nimb tree, Mālatīm. v, ½. **—deva**, m. N. of a man, L. **—pañcaka**, n. the 5 products (viz. leaves, bark, blossom, fruit, and root) of the Nimb tree, L. **—bīja**, m. Mimusops Hexandra, L. **—māla**, m. a partic. plant, Car. **—rajas**, n. a partic. high number, Buddh. **—vatī**, f. N. of a woman, Daś. **Nimbâditya**, m. N. of the founder of a Vaishṇava sect, RTL. 146. **Nimbârka**, m. id.; *-karavīrârcana-vrata*, n. N. of a partic. vow and of ch. of BhavP.

Nimbū and **nimbūka**, m. the common lime, Citrus Acida (v.l. *nisbū*), L. °**ka-phala-pānaka**, n. lemonade, Bhpr.

निम्बरक *nimbaraka*, m. Melia Bukayun, BhPr.

निम्यक्ष् *ni-√myaksh*, P. *-myakshati* (pf. 3. du. *-mimikshatur*; 3. pl. *-mimikshur*, Ā. °*kshire*), to hold, wield (thunderbolt &c.), RV. vii, 20, 4, viii, 50, 5; (Ā.) to be contained or present in (loc.), x, 96, 5; to be fixed on (loc.), i, 64, 4 (read *mimikshur* for *mimṛikshur*).

निम्रुच् *ni-√mruc*, P. *-mrocati*, to set, disappear (as the sun), AV.; TS.; AitBr.; Kāṭh.; TĀr. °**mrukti** (*ní-*), f. sunset, evening, TS.; Kāṭh. °**mrúc**, f. id., RV.; AV. &c.; mfn. slack, loose, AV. iv, 3, 6. °**mrocana**, n. = prec. f., ĀpŚr., Sch.

निम्लुच् *ni-√mluc*, P. *-mlocati* = 1. *ni-mruc*, ŚBr.; ChUp.; to set upon (with acc.; cf. *abhi-ni-mluc*), Mn. ii, 220. °**mlukti**, f. disappearance in (loc.), Saṃk. °**mloca**, m. setting of the sun, BhP.; (*ā*), f. N. of an Apsaras, VP. °**mlocanī**, f. N. of Varuṇa's city situated on the mountain Mānasottara towards the west, BhP. °**mloci**, m. N. of a prince, son of Bhajamāna, ib.

नियत् *ni-√yat*, Ā. *-yatate*, to arrive at, come to (loc.), RV. i, 186, 11.

नियत *ni-yata*, °*ti*, &c. See under *ni-yam*.

नियन्त्र् *ni-√yantr*, P. *-yantrayati* (inf. *-yantrayitum*), to restrain, Kāv. &c. °**yantraṇa**, n. restraining, checking, governing, Rājat.; restricting to a certain sense, defining, definition, Sāh.; (*ā*), f. shutting up, closure, HPariś.; control, restraint (*a-n°*), Kathās. °**yantrita**, mfn. restrained, checked, fettered, Kāv; dammed up, embanked, Rājat.; restricted to a certain sense (as a word), Kpr.; governed by, depending on (instr. or comp.), Sāh.; Kathās.; Vedântas.

नियम् *ni-√yam*, P. *-yacchati*, to stop

(trans.), hold back, detain with (loc.); (Ā.) to stop (intrans.), stay, remain, RV.; to keep back, refuse; (Ā.) to fail, be wanting, ib.; to fasten, tie to (loc.), bind up (hair &c.), ib. &c. &c.; to hold over, extend (*śarma*), AV.; to hold downwards (the hand), TS.; to bring near, procure, bestow, grant, offer, present (rain, gifts &c.), RV.; AV.; Br. &c.; to hold in, keep down, restrain, control, govern, regulate (as breath, the voice, the organs of sense &c.), Mn.; MBh. &c.; to suppress or conceal (one's nature), Mn. x, 59; to destroy, annihilate (opp. to √*sṛij*), BhP.; to restrict (food &c.; cf. below); to fix upon, settle, determine, establish, Sarvad.; Kathās.; BhP.; Kāś. on Pāṇ. ii, 3, 66; (in gram.) to lower, pronounce low i.e. with the Anudātta, RPrāt.: Caus. *-yamayati*, to restrain, curb, check, suppress, restrict, MBh.; Kāv. &c. °**yata** (*ni-*), mfn. held back or in, fastened, tied to (loc.), RV.; put together (hands), R.; restrained, checked, curbed, suppressed, restricted, controlled, Mn.; MBh. &c.; limited in number, Ratnâv. iii, 3; connected with, dependent on (loc.), Mn. iv, 256; contained or joined in (loc.), R. iii, 70, 5; disciplined, self-governed, abstemious, temperate; constant, steady, quite concentrated upon or devoted to (loc.), MBh.; Kāv. &c.; fixed, established, settled, sure, regular, invariable, positive, definite, GṛŚrS.; Mn.; MBh. &c.; customary, usual (cf. *a-n*°, MBh. iii, 15416); (in gram.) pronounced with the Anudātta, RPrāt.; m. N. of the Saṃdhi of *ās* before sonants, ib.; (*am*), ind. always, constantly, decidedly, inevitably, surely; n. pl. (in Sāṃkhya) the organs of sense; *-kāla*, mfn. limited in time, temporary, Kāś. on Pāṇ. i, 4, 44; *-bhojana*, mfn. abstemious in food, temperate, R.; *-mānasa*, mfn. of subdued mind or spirit, W.; *-maithuna*, mfn. abstaining from cohabitation, R.; *-vāc*, mfn. limited as to the use of words, Nir. i, 15; *-vibhaktika*, mfn. limited as to case, standing always in the same case, Pāṇ. i, 2, 44, Sch.; *-vishaya-vartin*, mfn. steadily abiding in one's own sphere, MW.; *-vrata*, mfn. constant in the observance of vows, regular in observances, pious, religious, MBh.; °*yatâñjali*, mfn. putting the joined hands to the forehead, R.; °*yatâtman*, mfn. self-controlled, self-restrained, Mn.; R.; °*yatânupūrvya*, mfn. limited as to the order of words, Nir. i, 15; °*yatâpti*, f. (in dram.) sure expectation of attaining an object by overcoming a partic. obstacle, Sāh.; °*yatâśin*, mfn. = *-ta-bhojana*, Yājñ.; °*yatâhāra*, mfn. id.; Mn. (*śva-māṃsa-n*°, eating only dog's flesh, R.); °*yatêndriya*, mfn. having the passions subdued or restrained, Mn.; MBh. &c. °**yati**, f. the fixed order of things, necessity, destiny, fate, ŚāṅkhBr.; ŚvetUp.; MBh. &c. (sometimes personified as a goddess, Niyati and Āyati being regarded as daughters of Meru and wives of Dhātṛi and Vidhātṛi, BhP.; VP.); restraint, restriction; religious duty or obligation; self-command, self-restraint, L.; (*ī*), f. N. of Durgā, DeviP. °**yantavya**, mfn. to be restrained or checked or controlled or forced, Mn.; MBh. &c.; *-tva*, n., Saṃk. °**yantu**, see *dur-niyántu*. °**yantṛí**, m. who or what holds in or restrains or governs or tames, &c., MBh.; R. &c. (*-tva*, n., Vedântas.); m. a restrainer, governor, tamer (esp. of horses), charioteer, MBh.; Ragh. °**yama**, m. restraining, checking, holding back, preventing, controlling, Mn.; MBh. &c.; keeping down, lowering (as the voice), RPrāt.; limitation, restriction (*ena*, ind. with restrictions i.e. under certain conditions, Car.); reduction or restriction to (with loc. or *prati*), determination, definition, GṛŚrS.; Prāt.; MBh.; Rājat.; any fixed rule or law, necessity, obligation (*ena* and *āt*, ind. as a rule, necessarily, invariably, surely), Var.; R.; Suśr. &c.; agreement, contract, promise, vow, R.; Kathās.; any act of voluntary penance or meritorious piety (esp. a lesser vow or minor observance dependent on external conditions and not so obligatory as *yama*, q. v.), TĀr.; Mn.; MBh.; Kāv. &c.; a partic. process applied to minerals (esp. to quicksilver, w. r. °*yāma*), Cat.; (in rhet.) a common-place, any conventional expression or usual comparison; (in Mīm. phil.) a rule or precept (laying down or specifying something otherwise optional); restraint of the mind (the 2nd of the 8 steps of meditation in Yoga); performing five positive duties, MWB. 239; N. of Vishṇu, MBh.; Necessity or Law personified as a son of Dharma and Dhṛiti, Pur.; *-dharma*, m. a law prescribing restraints, Mn. ii, 3; *-nishṭhā*, f. rigid observance of prescribed rites, MW.; *-pattra*, n. a written agreement or stipulation, ib.; *-para*, mfn. observing fixed rules; relating to or corroborative of a rule, W.; *-pāla*, m. 'observer of vows,' N. of a sage (from whom the Nepalese derive the N. Nepāl); *-bhaṅga*, m. breach of a stipulation or contract, MW.; *-laṅghana*, n. trangression of a fixed rule or obligation, Kāp.; *-vat*, mfn. practising religious observances, MBh.; (*ī*), f. a woman in her monthly courses, Suśr.; *-sthiti*, f. state of self-restraint, ascetism, L.; *-hetu*, m. a regulating cause, Sarvad.; °*yamânanda*, m. another N. of Nimbârka, Cat.; °*yamôpamā*, f. a simile which expressly states that something can be compared only with something else, Kāv. ii, 19. °**yamana**, mfn. subduing, taming, overpowering, Hariv.; n. the act of subduing &c., MBh.; Kāv. &c.; restriction, limitation, definition, Rājat.; Kpr.; Sāh.; precept, fixed practice or rule, W.; coercion, humiliation, MW. °**yamita**, mfn. checked, restrained, bound by, confined in, fastened to (comp.), MBh.; Kāv. &c.; stopped, suppressed, Kālid.; fixed on, determined, destined to be (inf.), Rājat.; Pañcar.; governed, guided; regulated, prescribed, W.; stipulated, agreed upon, MW. 1. °**yamya**, ind. having restrained or checked or bound &c., MBh.; R. &c. 2. °**yamya**, mfn. to be restrained &c., ib.; to be (or being) limited or restricted or defined, Śaṃk. °**yāma**, m. = *niyama*, Pāṇ. iii, 3, 63; a sailor, boatman (cf. next and *nir-yāma*). °**yāmaka**, mf(*ikā*)n. restraining, checking, subduing, controlling, governing, MBh.; Kām.; Sarvad.; restrictive, limiting, defining (*-tā*, f., *-tva*, n.), BhP.; Sarvad.; m. a guide or ruler, Sarvad.; a charioteer, L.; a sailor or boatman, L. °**yāmana**, (prob.) w. r. for *ni-yamana*.

नियियन् *ni-yayín.* See under *ni-yā.*

नियव *ni-yavá.* See under *ni-yu.*

निया *ni-√yā*, P. *-yāti*, to pass over (with a carriage), RV. v, 35, 5; 42, 10; 54, 5; to come down to (acc.), 75, 5; to fall into, incur (acc.), ĀśvGṛ. i, 13, 7. °**yayín**, mfn. going over, passing over (as a carriage), RV. x, 60, 2. °**yā́na**, n. a way, access, RV.; AV.; Br.

नियातन *ni-yātana*, w. r. for *ni-pātana.*

नियु *ni-√2. yu*, P. Ā. *-yauti* or *-yuváti*, °*te* (1. sg. Ā. *-yuve*; Impv. 2. du. P. *-yuyotam*; ind. p. *-yūya*), to bind on, fasten, RV.; TBr.; to bring near, procure, bestow, RV.; TS.: Intens. 3. sg. *-yoyuve*, RV. x, 93, 9. °**yavá**, m. compact order, continuous line or series, RV. x, 30, 10. °**yút** (*ni-yút*), f. = prec., ib.; team of horses (esp. of Vāyu's h°), ib.; VS.; TS.; pl. series of words, verses, a poem, RV.; *-vat* (°*yút-*), mfn. drawn by a team of horses (as a carriage, Vāyu, Indra, the Maruts), RV.; forming a series, flowing continuously or abundantly (as Soma), ib.; containing the word *niyut* or *niyut-vat* (as a verse or hymn), TS.; ŚBr.; *-vatīya*, mfn. belonging to Niyutvat i.e. Vāyu, ŚBr. °**yúd-ratha**, mfn. one whose car is drawn by a team of horses, RV. x, 26, 1. °**yuta** (*ní-*), mfn. fixed, fastened, RV. i, 121, 3; m. or n. a very high number, generally a million, Br.; Pur.

नियुज् *ni-√yuj*, P. Ā. *-yunakti*, *-yuṅkte*, to bind on, tie or fasten to (loc.), AV.; ŚBr.; MBh. &c.; (with *dhuri*) to tie to the pole of a carriage i.e. yoke, harness, R.; (met.) to place in front i.e. employ in the hardest work, ib. (also *guru-dhūrshu*, MBh.); to join, put together (esp. the hands in a certain position; cf. *kapota*), Sch. on Śak.; to attach to i.e. make dependent on (dat. or loc.), AV.; ŚBr.; to enjoin, order, command, coerce, impel, appoint, instal (double acc.), trust or charge with, direct or commission or authorize to (loc., dat., *artham* ifc., or infin.), Mn.; MBh. &c.; to confer or intrust anything (acc.) upon or to (loc.), R.; BhP.; to place at, put in the way (with loc.), MBh.; to direct towards, fix (mind or eyes upon, with loc.), ib.; to use, employ, GṛS.: Caus. *-yojayati*, to harness (horses &c.), put or tie to (loc.), Pañc.; Hit.; to set or lay (a trap or snare &c.), Hit.; to enjoin, urge, impel, coerce, appoint or instal as (double acc.), appoint to (loc.), direct or compel or request or command to (dat., loc., acc. with *prati*, or *artham* ifc.); commit or intrust anything (acc.) to (loc.), Mn.; MBh.; Kāv. &c.; to put in any place or state (loc.), ib.; to confer or bestow upon (loc.), Kāv.; Pañc.; Pur.; to use, employ (reason &c.), Pañc. i, 413; to accomplish, perform (a rite), Mn. iii, 204; to endow or furnish with, cause to partake of (instr.), Var.; Kāv.; Pañc. °**yukta**, mfn. bound on, bound, chained, fettered, AitBr.; tied or fastened or attached or directed to, put or placed or fixed on (loc.), MBh.; R. &c.; appointed, directed, ordered, commissioned, charged, intrusted (loc.; dat.; *artham* ifc.; inf. or comp.), Mn.; MBh.; Kāv. &c.; used or employed for (loc.), Mn. v, 16; prescribed, fixed, settled; (*am*), ind. by all means, necessarily, Pāṇ. iv, 4, 66; m. a functionary, official, Hit. °**yuktaka**, mfn. appointed, elected, placed in authority, L. °**yukti**, f. injunction, order, command, charge, office, Kull. °**yujya**, ind. having joined or attached or harnessed or appointed &c., R.; Pur. &c. °**yoktavya**, mfn. to be placed in or put to (loc.; *ātmā sukhe °vyah*, we shall enjoy ourselves, R.); to be appointed or authorized or charged or intrusted with (loc.), Mn.; Yājñ.; MBh. &c.; to be harassed or prosecuted, Mn. viii, 186 (v. l. *abhi-yokt*°). °**yoktṛi**, m. one who joins or fastens or attaches, AitBr.; a ruler, lord, master, Ragh. °**yoga**, m. tying or fastening to (cf. *-pāśa* below); employment, use, application, Lāṭy.; Mṛicch.; injunction, order, command (*āt* or *ena*, ind. by order of, ifc.), commission, charge, appointed task or duty, business (esp. the appointing a brother or any near kinsman to raise up issue to a deceased husband by marrying his widow), Mn. (esp. ix, 59 &c.); MBh.; Kāv.; Suśr. &c.; necessity (*ena*, ind. necessarily, certainly, surely, Ragh.), obligation, fate, destiny, Kāv.; *-karaṇa*, n. making a command, commanding, Pāṇ. iii, 3, 161, Sch.; *-kṛit*, m. executing another's command, Yājñ.; Sch.; *-tas*, ind. according to order or command, MW.; *-pāśa*, m. the trace on a carriage (lit. string for tying [sc. the horses to it]), Hariv.; *-prayojana*, n. the object of any appointment, authorized act or duty, W.; *-vidhi*, m. the form of appointing to any act or duty, ib.; *-saṃsthita*, mfn. being in an office or commission, Pañc.; *-stha*, mfn. being under another's command, obedient to (gen.), R.; °*yogârtha*, m. the object of an authorized act or appointment, Mn. ix, 61; 62. °**yogin**, mfn. appointed, employed; m. a functionary, official, minister, Hit. ii, 94; °*gy-arthagrahôpâya*, m. the resource of confiscating the property of men in office, ib. 100. °**yogya**, in *a-n*° w. r. for *a-niyoga*, q. v.; m. lord, master, Vop. °**yojaka**, mfn. in *sarva-n*°, q. v.; (*ikā*), f. N. of a daughter of the demon Duḥ-saha, MārkP. °**yójana**, n. the act of tying or fastening (as to the sacrificial post), ŚBr.; that with which anything is tied or fastened, AV.; enjoining, urging, impelling, commanding, directing, appointing to (loc.), MBh. &c.; (*ī*), f. a halter, KātyŚr. °**yojanīya**, mfn. = *niyoktavya* above, Kull. °**yojayitavya**, mfn. to be appointed or directed to (loc.), Kāraṇḍ.; to be punished with (instr.), Pañc. v, 6/7. °**yojita**, mfn. put, placed, laid, (jewel) set in (comp.); connected with, attached to, fixed on (comp.); appointed, authorized; enjoined, directed, commanded; urged, impelled, Mn.; MBh. &c. °**yojya**, mfn. to be fastened or attached to, Pañc.; to be endowed or furnished with (instr.), Cāṇ.; to be enjoined (*a-n*°), MBh. i, 3267; to be committed or intrusted, Hcat.; to be appointed or employed or directed or commanded, Mn.; MBh. &c.; m. a functionary, official, servant, Śak.; BhP.; °*jyânvaya-nirūpaṇa*, n. N. of wk.

नियुत *ni-yuta.* See under *ni-yu*, col. 2.

नियुध् *ni-√yudh*, Ā. *-yudhyate* (rarely °*ti*), to fight, MBh.; Hariv. &c. °**yutsā**, f. (prob. for *ni-yuyutsā*, fr. Desid.) N. of the wife of Prastāva and mother of Vibhu, BhP. °**yuddha**, n. fighting (esp. with fists), pugilistic combat, close or personal struggle, MBh.; Hariv.; Var.; Suśr. &c.; *-kuśala*, or *-śīla*, mfn. skilled in fighting, MBh.; *-bhū*, f. place for pugilists, L. °**yoddhṛi**, m. id. or a cock, L. °**yodhaka**, m. a combatant, wrestler, pugilist, MBh.

निरज् *nir-√aj*, P. *-ajati* (dat. inf. *-áje*), to drive out or away, RV.; AV. °**aja**, see *su-nirája*. °**āja**, m. marching off, Kāṭh.

निरञ्छन *ni-rañchana*, n. (*rañch* = *lañch*) a mark or knot in a measuring line, KātyŚr., Sch.

निरण *ni-√raṇ* (only *-raṇyáthas*), to rejoice or delight in (instr.), RV. i, 112, 18.

निरत *ni-rata*, °*ti.* See *ni-ram.*

निरध् *ni-√radh* (only Caus. impf. *-árandhayas*), to deliver up, surrender, RV. vii, 19, 2.

निरभ्यवेक्ष् *nir-abhy-avêksh* (*√īksh*), to search through, examine thoroughly, Kāraṇḍ.

निरम् *ni-√ram*, Ā. *-ramate* (aor. 3. pl. *-araṅsata*), to rest, come to rest, cease, AV.: Caus. *-rāmayati* (aor. *-arīramat*), to cause to rest, stop, detain, RV.; (*-ramayati*) to gladden, give pleasure (by sexual union), BhP. °**rata**, mfn. pleased, satisfied, delighting in, attached or devoted to, quite intent upon, deeply engaged in or occupied with (loc., instr. or comp.), Mn.; Var.; MBh.; Kāv. &c. °**rati**, f. delighting in, attachment to (comp.), Var. 1. °**ramaṇa** (cf. 2. *nir-am*°, next), n. resting, ceasing, Nir. ii, 7. °**rāmin**, mfn. waiting, lurking, RV. ii, 23, 16.

निरमण 2. *nir-ámaṇa*, mfn. (*nis + √am?*) worn out, exhausted, ŚBr.

निरय *nir-aya*, m. (either fr. *nis + √i* = egression, sc. from earthly life, or fr. *nir + aya* 'without happiness') Niraya or Hell (personified as a child of fear and death, BhP.), Mn.; MBh.; Kāv. &c. **-pati**, m. the king of hell, BhP. **Nirayâvali-sūtra**, n. N. of wk.

Nir-áyana, n. (*√i*) egression, RV.

Nir-ayín, m. an inhabitant of hell, BhP.

निरर्द् *nir-√ard*, P. *-ardati*, to stream forth, ŚBr.

निरवत्त *nir-ávatta*, °*tti*. See *nir-ava-do*.

निरवदय् *nir-ava-√day*, Ā. *-dayate*, to satisfy any one (acc.) with (acc. or instr.) or with respect to (abl.), TS.; Br.

निरवदो *nir-ava-√do*, P. *-dāti* or *-dyati* (ind. p. *-dāya*), to distribute or divide completely, give any one his share, appease or satisfy with (double acc.), TS. °**ávatta**, mfn. distributed, completely divided or allotted; *-bali*, mfn. whereof oblations have been distributed all round, ŚBr. °**ávatti**, f. (TBr.; Kāṭh.), °**avadāna**, n. (Jaim.; ĀpŚr.) allotment or distribution of shares.

निरवद्य *nir-avadya*, *-avayava* &c. See *nir*, p. 539, col. 3.

निरवधे *nir-ava-√dhe*, P. *-dhayati*, to suck out, ĀpŚr.

निरवयज् *nir-ava-√yaj*, Ā. *-yajate*, to satisfy a god (acc.) by means of sacrifice in preference to another god (abl.), Kāṭh.

निरवसो *nir-ava-√so*, Caus. *-sāyayati*, to establish, settle, furnish with (instr.), TS.; TBr. °**avasita**, mfn. expelled, rejected, Pāṇ. ii, 4, 10.

निरवह *niravaha*, m. (fr. *nis + ava + √han?*) a kind of sword, Gal.

निरविन्द *niravinda*, m. (for *nir-arav*°?) N. of a mountain, MBh.

निरवेक्ष् *nir-avêksh* (*√īksh*), to observe, perceive. °**avêkshya**, ind. having observed or perceived, Mṛicch. v, 30.

निरष्ट *nír-ashṭa* (*√aksh*), emasculated, deprived of vigour, RV.; ŚBr. (cf. *mahā-n*°).

निरस् *nir-√2. as*, P. Ā. *-asyati*, °*te* (inf. *asitum*, MBh.; aor. *-āsthat*, Bhaṭṭ.), to cast out, throw or drive away, expel, remove, banish from (abl.), ŚBr.; ŚrS.; Mn.; MBh. &c.; to ward off, keep away, MBh.; Kāv. &c.; to strip off (also Ā.), Pāṇ. i, 3, 29, Vārtt. 3; Pat.; to stretch out (*hastau*, also Ā.), Vop.; to reject, refuse, decline (as a suitor, an offer, &c.), Sāh.; to destroy, annihilate, Yājñ.; MBh.; Hit. °**asana**, mf(*ī*)n. casting out, driving away, expelling, removing, rejecting, Śiś.; BhP.; Suśr.; n. the act of casting out &c., ŚāṅkhŚr.; BhP.; Sarvad.; vomiting, spitting out, L.; banishment from (abl.), MBh.; denying, refusal, contradiction, Kap. & Jaim., Sch.; scattering, dispersing, Vedāntas.; destruction, extermination, L. °**asanīya**, mfn. to be driven out or expelled, Kull.; to be rejected or refused, Naish., Sch. °**asta** (R. also °*asita*), mfn. cast out or off, expelled, banished, rejected, removed, refuted, destroyed, ŚBr.; Mn.; MBh. &c.; shot off (as an arrow), L.; spit out, vomited, L.; pronounced hurriedly or dropped in pronouncing (*a-n*°, ChUp. ii, 22, 3); n. dropping or leaving out (considered a fault in pronunciation), Pat.; *-bheda*, mfn. having all difference removed, identical, MW.; *-rāga*, mfn. one who has abandoned worldly desires or has devoted himself to religious penance, ib.; *-saṃkhya*, mfn. innumerable (lit. refusing calculation), Dhanaṃj.; *-sukhôdaya*, mf(*ā*)n. hopelessly unfortunate (lit. whose fortune has given up rising), Amar. °**astâpad**, mfn. having misfortune removed, happy, Dhūrtas. °**asti**, f. removal, destruction, Car. 1. °**asya**, mfn. to be expelled or driven out, Kām. 2. °**asya**, ind. having cast or thrown out, having rejected or expelled &c., MBh.; R. 2. **Nir-āsa** (for 1. see p. 540, col. 2), m. casting or throwing out, expulsion, exclusion, removal, refusal, rejection, contradiction, refutation, Mn.; MBh. &c.; spitting out, vomiting (cf. below); dropping, leaving out (of a sound), RPrāt.; *-guṭikā*, f. a pill to produce vomiting, Cat. **Nir-āsaka**, mfn. refusing, turning off, Naish., Sch. **Nir-āsana**, n. = *nir-asana*, L.

निरह् *nir-√ah* (only pf. *-āha*, °*hur*), to utter, pronounce, express, ŚBr.

निराक *nirāka*, m. (only L., prob. w. r. for *ni-pāka*) cooking; sweat; the recompence of a bad action.

निराकृ *nir-ā-√1. kṛi*, P. *-karoti*, to separate or divide off, ChUp.; to drive away, turn or keep off, repudiate, remove, reject, omit, refuse, spurn, oppose, contradict, MBh.; Kāv. &c. °**karaṇa**, n. separating (in *a-nirāk*°), Sarvad.; driving away, turning out, expelling, removing, repudiating (of a woman), opposing, contradicting, denying, Kālid.; Sarvad. &c.; forgetting (in *a-nirāk*°), TĀr.; PārGṛ.; neglecting the chief sacrificial or religious duties, W. °**karaṇīya**, mfn. to be opposed or refuted, Śaṃk. °**karishṇu**, mfn. rejecting, repudiating, Ragh.; obstructive, envious, hindering or preventing from (abl.), Rājat.; forgetful, PārGṛ.; *-tā*, f. envy, malevolence, Suśr. °**kartavya**, mfn. = °*karaṇīya*, Śaṃk. °**kartṛi**, mfn. contradicting, refuting, Śaṃk.; repudiating, repudiator of (gen.), Hcat.; contemner, despiser (esp. of the Veda and religion), MBh. 2. °**kāra** (for 1. see p. 540, col. 1), m. rebuke, reproach, censure, L. °**kṛita**, mfn. pushed or driven away, repudiated, expelled, banished, rejected, removed; frustrated, destroyed; omitted, forgot; refuted; despised, made light of, MBh.; Kāv. &c.; deprived of (comp.), Bhaṭṭ.; *-nimesha*, mfn. (eye) forgetting to wink, Śak. (Pi.) ii, 11 (41); °*tânyôttara*, mfn. excluding every answer, irrefutable (*-tva*, n.), L. 2. °**kṛiti** (for 1. see p. 540, col. 1), obstruction, impediment, interruption, Sāh.; repudiation, rejection, contradiction, refutation, L.; forgetting (see *sarva-n*°), BhP.; mfn. impeding, obstructing, L.; m. N. of a son of the first Manu Sāvarṇi, Hariv. 2. °**kṛitin** (for 1. see p. 540, col. 1), mfn. one who has forgotten what he has learned (*a-nirāk*°), ĀśvŚr.; cf. g. *ishṭâdi*. °**kriyā**, f. expulsion, removal, MBh.; contradiction, refutation, L.

निराक्रम् *nir-ā-√kram*, P. *-krāmati*, to come forth, go out of (abl.), MBh.; Ragh.

निराग *ni-rāga*, mfn. passionless, dispassionate, ŚāṅkhBr. (cf. *nī-r*°).

निरागम *nir-āgama*, *nir-āgas*, &c. See p. 540, col. 1.

निराचक्ष् *nir-ā-√caksh*, Ā. *-cashṭe*, to refute, reject, Sarvad.

निराचिकीर्षु *nir-ā-cikīrshu* (Desid. of √1. *kṛi*), desirous of contradicting or refuting, Śaṃk.

निराज *nir-āja*. See under *nir-aj*.

निराणद्ध *nir-ā-ṇaddha*, mfn. (*√nah*), Pāṇ. viii, 4, 2, Kāś.

निरादिष्ट *nir-ā-dishṭa*, mfn. (*√diś*) paid off (as a debt), Mn. viii, 162. °**deśa**, m. complete payment or discharge of a debt, W.

निराधा *nir-ā-√dhā*, *-dadhāti*, to take out of, take away, AV.; Br.

निरामालु *nirāmālu*, m. (*nis + āma + ālu?*) Feronia Elephantum, L.

निरामित्र *nir-āmitra*, w. r. for *nir-am*° (see *nir*, p. 540, col. 2).

निरामिन् *ni-rāmín*. See under *ni-ram*.

निरायम् *nir-ā-√yam*, P. *-yacchati* (ind. p. *-yatya*), to bring or get out, AV.; ŚBr. 2. °**yata** (for 1. see p. 540, col. 2), mfn. stretched out, extended; *-pūrva-kāya*, mfn. having the fore-part of the body stretched out, Śak. i, 8.

निरालक *nirālaka*, m. a species of fish, L.

निरावह् *nir-ā-√vah*, P. *-vahati*, to carry off, TāṇḍBr.; to fetch, bring, AV.

निराविश् *nir-ā-√viś*, P. *-viśati*, to retire, keep away from (abl.), MBh.

निरास 1. 2. *nir-āsa*. See under *nir* and *nir-as*.

निराह *nir-āha*, m. (prob. fr. next) call, exclamation, TāṇḍBr.

Nir-āhava, m. (*√hve*) id.; *-vat*, mfn. accompanied by an exclamation, ib. (v. l. °*hā-vat*).

निरि *nir-√i*, P. *-eti* (1. sg. Subj. *-ayā*, RV.; dat. inf. *-étave*, ib.; Ā. *nir-ayate* or *nil-ayate*, Siddh. on P. viii, 2, 19), to go out, come forth, go off, depart (said of persons and things), RV.; MBh. &c.

निरिङ्गिनी *niriṅginī*, f. a veil, L. (cf. *nī-raṅgi*).

निरी *ni-√rī*, P. Ā. *-riṇāti*, °*ṇīte*, to dissolve, scatter, tear, rend, destroy, RV.; AV.; to unveil, discover (Ā.), RV. i, 124, 7; v, 80, 6; to rush forth, escape (Ā.), ix, 14, 4.

निरीक्ष् *nir-√īksh*, Ā. *-īkshate* (°*ti*), to look at or towards, behold, regard, observe (also the stars), perceive, Var.; MBh.; Kāv. &c. °**īkshaka**, mfn. looking at, seeing, viewing, BhP.; seeing = visiting (*a-n*°), Rājat. °**īkshaṇa**, mfn. looking at, regarding (ifc.), BhP.; n. look, looking at, observing; sight, view (ifc. f. *ā*; cf. *dur-n*°); the aspect of the planets, Var.; R.; Suśr. &c. °**īkshā**, f. looking at, regarding; (*ayā*), ind. with regard to (comp.), R.; hope, expectation, W. °**īkshitavya**, mfn. to be looked at, Kāraṇḍ. °**īkshin**, mfn. looking, seeing (see *nâtidūra-n*°). 1. °**īkshya**, mfn. to be looked at or regarded or considered, MBh.; R.; BhP. 2. °**īkshya**, ind. having looked at or viewed, R.; Kathās. °**īkshyamāṇa**, mfn. being looked at &c.; looking, MBh. i, 7694.

निरुक्त *nir-ukta*, mfn. (*√vac*) uttered, pronounced, expressed, explained, defined, Br.; Up.; MBh. &c.; declared for (nom.), MBh.; explicitly mentioned or enjoined, ĀśvGṛ.; containing the name of a god (as a verse), ŚāṅkhBr.; distinct, loud (opp. to *upâṅśu*), ŚBr.; interpreted i.e. become manifest, fulfilled, accomplished (as a word), MBh. ix, 1316; n. explanation or etymological interpretation of a word, ChUp. viii, 3, 3; MBh. i, 266 &c.; N. of sev. wks., esp. of a Comm. on the Nighaṇṭus by Yāska. **-kāra**, m. N. of Sch. on Megh. (quoted by Mallin.) **-kṛit**, m. 'Nirukta-composer,' N. of Yāska, Jyot.; of a pupil of Śāka-pūṇi, VP. **-ga**, m. 'penetrater of mysteries,' N. of Brahmā, MBh. **-ja**, m. N. of a class of sons, MBh. xiii, 2615. **-pariśishṭa**, n. N. of wk. **-bhāshya**, n. N. of Comm. (prob. = *-vṛitti*). **-vat**, mfn. 'author of the Nirukta,' N. of Yāska, Bṛih. **-vṛitti**, f. N. of a Comm. on Yāska's Nirukta by Durgâcārya.

Nir-ukti, f. etymological interpretation of a word, MBh.; BhP.; (in rhet.) an artificial explanation or derivation of a word, Kuval.; (in dram.) communication of an event that has taken place, Sāh.; N. of Yāska's Comm. on the Nighaṇṭus; of a Comm. on the Tarka-saṃgraha &c. **-khaṇḍa**, m. or n. N. of ch. of Tarkas. **-prakāśa**, m., **-lakshaṇa**, n. N. of wks.

निरुक्ष् *nir-√uksh*, P. *-ukshati*, to remove by sprinkling, ŚBr.

निरुज *ni-ruja*, mfn. healthy, wholesome, MBh.; Hcat.; °*jī-√kṛi*, to make healthy, Hcat. (cf. *nī-r*°).

निरुञ्छन *nir-uñchana*, n. (*√uñch*) = *nī-rājana*, Kum. xiii, 18 (v. l. *nir-mañchana*).

निरुत *nir-uta*, mfn. (*√ve*), Pāṇ. vi, 3, 2, Sch.

निरुध् *ni-√rudh*, P. Ā. *-ruṇaddhi*, *-runddhe*, to hold back, stop, hinder, shut up, confine, restrain, check, suppress, destroy, RV. &c. &c.;

to keep away, ward off, remove, RV.; Br.; to surround or invest (a place), Rājat.; BhP.; to close (lit. 'a door' or fig. 'heart, mind' &c.), MBh.; Kāv. &c.; to catch or overtake, Mṛicch. i, 20: Caus. *-rodhayati*, to shut or cause to be shut, Rājat. **°ruddha**, mfn. held back, withheld, held fast, stopped, shut, closed, confined, restrained, checked, kept off, removed, suppressed, RV. (*ni-ruddha*, i, 32, 11; *ni-ruddhá*, x, 28, 10) &c. &c.; rejected (=*apa-ruddha*), TāṇḍBr.; Kāṭh.; covered, veiled, MBh.; Hariv. &c.; filled with, full of (instr. or comp.), R.; Kathās.; BhP.; m. N. of a prince (v.l. *a-nir°*, q.v.); *-kaṇṭha*, mfn. having the breath obstructed, suffocated, MW.; *-guda*, m. contraction or obstruction of the rectum, Suśr.; *-prakaśa*, m. stricture of the urethra, ib.; *-vat*, mfn. having (= he has) invested or besieged, Rājat.; BhP.; *-śama-vṛitti*, mfn. 'whose state of repose is interrupted,' wearied, tired, W. **°rudhyamāna**, being checked or reined in, MW. **°rundhat**, mfn. checking, hindering, suppressing &c., Śak. **°rundhāná**, mfn. obstructing, hindering, preventing, keeping off &c., RV.; AV.; ŚBr.; MBh. &c. **°roddhavya**, mfn. to be shut in or confined; to be enclosed with a fence or hedge, MBh. **°rodha**, m. confinement, locking up, imprisonment (*-tas*, Mn. viii, 375); investment, siege, Cat.; enclosing, covering up, Var.; Kāv. &c.; restraint, check, control, suppression, destruction, Mn.; MBh. &c.; (in dram.) disappointment, frustration of hope, Daśar.; (with Buddh.) suppression or annihilation of pain (one of the 4 principles), Lalit.; MWB. 43, 56, 137 &c.; a partic. process to which minerals (esp. quicksilver) are subjected, Cat.; hurting, injuring (=*ni-graha*), L.; aversion, disfavour, dislike, W.; N. of a man, Lalit.; *-jñāna*, n. (with Buddh.) one of the 10 kinds of knowledge, Dharmas. 93; *-lakshaṇa* (*°ṇa-vivaraṇa*), *-varṇana*, n., *-vivṛiti*, f. N. of wks. **°rodhaka**, mfn. obstructing, confining, hindering (ifc.), MBh. &c. **°ródhana**, mfn. id., Suśr.; n. confining, imprisonment, Mn. viii, 310; keeping back, restraining, subduing, suppressing, MBh. &c.; denying, refusing, AV.; (in dram.) = *°rodha*; Daśar. **°rodhin**, mfn. obstructing, hindering, Suśr.

निरुप्ति *nir-upti*, f. (√*2. vap*) scattering, pouring out, offering, KātyŚr., Sch. **°úpya**, mfn. to be scattered or poured out, ŚBr.

निरुब्ज् *nir-√ubj*, P. *-ubjati* (impf. *-aubjas*), to cause to flow down, let loose, RV. i, 56, 5 &c.

निरुह् *ni-√ruh*, Caus. *-ropayati*, to transplant, transfer from (abl.) to (loc.), Rājat. 2. **°rūḍha** (cf. *nir-ūḍha*, p. 540, col. 3), mfn. grown up, BhP.; conventional, accepted (as a word or its meaning, opp. to *yaugika*, q.v.), Dāyabh.; Sarvad.; m. (in rhet.) the force or application of words according to their natural or received meanings, W.; (in logic) the inherence of any property in the term implying it (as of redness in the word 'red' &c.), ib.; *-mūla*, mfn. firmly rooted, BhP.; *-lakshaṇā*, f. (in rhet.) the secondary use of a word which is based not on the particular intention of the speaker but on its accepted and popular usage.

निरूप् *ni-√rūp*, P. *-rūpayati*, to perform, represent on the stage, act, gesticulate, indicate or exhibit by gestures (e.g. *ratha-vegam*, the swiftness of a carriage; *vṛiksha-secanam*, the watering of a tree, Śak.); to perceive, notice, find out, ascertain, Hariv.; Kāv. &c.; to investigate, examine, search, try, consider, reflect upon, Kāv.; Suśr.; Sarvad. &c.; to state, define, Pañc.; Pur.; Śaṃk.; to select, choose, appoint as (double acc.), appoint to (loc., dat. or inf.), Kāv.; Pañc. &c. **°rūpaka**, mfn. observing, observer, Śaṃk.; =next mfn., TPrāt., Sch. **°rūpaṇa**, mfn. stating, determining, defining (ifc.), ch. of Sāh.; (*ā*), f. the act of stating &c., Śaṃk.; n. id., Pur.; Śaṃk.; Kull.; looking into, searching, investigation, examination, Sarvad.; sight, appearance, form, shape, MBh. **°rūpaṇīya**, mfn. to be looked for or discussed or investigated &c., W. **°rūpayitavya**, mfn. to be ascertained or determined, BhP. **°pita**, mfn. seen, observed, considered, weighed, discovered, ascertained, determined, defined; Kāv.; Pur. &c.; appointed, elected, chosen, BhP.; Pañc.; pointed against, shot off, BhP.; n. the state of having been discussed or ascertained, Hcat. **°rūpiti**, f. statement, definition, Śaṃk. 1. **°rūpya**, ind. performing, acting, gesticulating, Śak.; having seen, considered &c. 2. **°rūpya**, mfn. to be seen or defined or ascertained, MBh.; not yet certain, questionable, Vām.; *-tā*, f., *-tva*, n., W.

निरूह् *nir-√1. ūh*, P. Ā. *-ūhati*, *°te* (inf. *nir-ūhitavaí*, ŚBr.; ind. p. *-uhya*, ib.; Pass. pr. p. *-uhyamāna*, KātyŚr.), to push or draw out, put aside or apart, remove, AV.; ŚBr.; ŚrS.: Caus. *-ūhayati*, to cause to draw out or purge, Suśr. 3. **°ūḍha**, mfn. drawn out, put aside, separate, Gaut.; purged, Car.; Suśr.; eviscerated (cf. comp.); *-paśu-paddhati*, f. N. of wk.; *-paśu-bandha*, m. 'the offering of an eviscerated animal' or 'separate off° of an a°,' N. of one of the regular Havir-yajñas, Gaut. &c. (*°dha-prayoga*, *°dha-maitrāvaruṇa-prayoga*, *°dha-hautra-prayoga*, m. N. of wks.); *-śiras* (*nír-*), mfn. with the head laid apart, ŚBr. — **ūḍhi**, f. fame, celebrity (lit. spreading, divulging?), Kir. ii, 6. 1. **°ūha**, m. a purging clyster, an enema not of an oily kind, Suśr.; =*ni-graha*, L.; *-vasti-vidhi*, m. N. of ch. of ŚārṅgS.; *°hâdhikāra*, m. N. of ch. of a medic. wk. by Vṛinda. 1. **°ūhaṇa**, n. causing to purge with a clyster, Suśr.; a purging cl°, Car. **°ūhita**, mfn. purged, Suśr.

निरूह 2. *nir-ūha*, m. (*nir-√2. ūh*) logic, disputation, W.; certainty, ascertainment, ib.; mfn. =*niś-cita*, L. 2. **ūhaṇa**, n. ascertainment, W.

निरृ *nir-√ṛi* (aor. *-ārata*, Subj. *-arāma*, RV.; ind. p. *-ṛitya*, AV.), to go out or off, fall away from, be deprived of (abl. or gen.), RV. i, 4, 5; vii, 56, 21 &c.; to separate, disjoin, AV. x, 2, 2: Caus. *-arpayati*, to cause to go to pieces or decay, to dissolve, destroy, ruin, ŚBr. **°ṛita** (*nír-*), mfn. dissolved, decayed, debilitated, RV. i, 119, 7; m. N. of Rudra, VāyuP. **°ṛiti** (*nír-*), f. dissolution, destruction, calamity, evil, adversity, RV. &c. &c. (personif. as the goddess of death and corruption and often associated with Mṛityu, A-rāti &c., RV.; AV.; VS.; variously regarded as the wife of A-dharma, mother of Bhaya, Mahā-bhaya and Mṛityu [MBh.] or as a daughter of A-dharma and Hiṇsā and mother of Naraka and Bhaya [MārkP.]; binds mortals with her cords, AV.; Br. &c.; is regent of the south [AV.] and of the asterism Mūla [Var.]); the bottom or lower depths of the earth (as the seat of putrefaction), AV.; VS.; ŚBr.; m. death or the genius of death, BhP.; N. of a Rudra, MBh.; Hariv.; Pur.; of one of the 8 Vasus, Hariv. (v.l. *ni-kṛiti*); *-gṛihīta* (*nír-ṛ°*), mfn. seized by Nir-ṛiti, ŚBr.; *-pāśá*, m. the fetters of N°, TS. **°ṛithá**, m. destruction, RV.; AV.; personif. as the destroyer, AV. vi, 93, 1; N. of a partic. Agni, xii, 2, 14; of the Sāma-veda, Uṇ. ii, 8, Sch.

निरृछ् *nir-√ṛich*, P. *-ṛichati*, to go asunder or pass away, AV.; ŚBr.; to be deprived of (abl.), TāṇḍBr.

निरृज् *nir-√ṛij*, P. *-arjati*, to let out, deliver, TS.

निरे *nir-ê* (=*nir-ā-√i*, only Impv. *nir-âitu*), to go off, depart, AV. x, 4, 21; 22.

निरेक 2. *ni-reká*, m. (√*ric*) prominence, superiority, pre-eminence over (gen.), RV.; (*é*), ind. above all, in a high degree, ib.

निरेभ *ni-rebha*, mfn. soundless, noiseless, W.

निरोद्धव्य *ni-roddhavya*, *ni-rodha*, &c. See *ni-rudh*, p. 553, col. 3.

निर्गम् *nir-√gam*, P. *-gacchati* (Subj. *-gamāni*, pf. p. *-jaganvān*, RV.; ind. p. *-gatya*, MBh. &c., *-gamya*, MārkP.), to go out, come forth (often with *bahis*), depart from (abl.), set out, start, RV. &c. &c.; to come out or appear (as a bud), Śak.; to go away, disappear, Rājat.; Pañc.; to enter into any state, undergo (acc.), MBh.; (with *nidrām*) to fall asleep, Kathās.: Caus. *-gamayati*, to cause or order to set out, BhP.: Desid. *-jigamishate*, to wish to set out, ib. **°ga**, m. a country, region, district, province, L. (cf. Pāṇ. iii, 2, 48, Vārtt. 4, Pat.). **°gata**, mfn. gone out, come forth (with abl. or ifc.; cf. Pāṇ. ii, 1, 37, Pat.), appeared, become visible, MBh.; Kāv. &c.; disappeared, extinct, Rājat.; Vedāntas.; freed from (abl.), L.; *-nikhila-kalmasha-tā*, f. the state of being entirely freed from sin, Vedântas.; *-viśaṅka*, mfn. freed from fear, fearless, Pañc. **°gama**, m. going forth, setting out, departure, Var.; R. &c.; escaping from (abl.), Vedântas.; disappearing, vanishing, cessation, end, MBh.; Kāv.; Suśr. &c.; exit, issue, outlet, R.; Pañc.; a door, L.; export-place (of goods), Mn. viii, 401 (opp. *ā-gama*). **°gamana**, n. going out, coming forth from (comp.), MBh.; Var.; issue, outlet, a door, L.

निर्गलित *nir-galita*, mfn. (√*gal*) flowed out, dissolved, melted, Ragh.

निर्गा *nir-√gā* (only Subj. *-gāt*, RV.; impf. *-agāt*, Kathās.; BhP.; Bhaṭṭ.), to go out, come forth.

निर्गीर्ण *nir-gīrṇa*, mfn. (√*gṛī*) vomited forth, R.

निर्गुण *nir-guṇa*, &c. See p. 541, col. 1.

निर्गुण्टी *nirguṇṭī* (L.) or *°ṇḍī* (Suśr.), f. Vitex Negundo; *°ṇḍī*, f. the root of a lotus, L.

निर्गुप् *nir-√gup* (only pf. *-jugopa*), to guard, protect, Bhaṭṭ.

निर्गूढ *nir-gūḍha*, m. (√*guh*) the hollow of a tree, L.

निर्ग्रन्थ *nir-grantha*, &c. See p. 541, col. 1.

निर्ग्राह्य *nir-grāhya*, mfn. (√*grah*) to be traced or found out, perceivable, Kār. on Pāṇ.

निर्घण्ट *nir-ghaṇṭa*, *°ṇṭu*, *°ṇṭuka* =(and prob. w.r. for) *ni-ghaṇṭa* &c., collection of words, vocabulary.

निर्घर्षण *nir-gharshaṇa* &c. See *nir-ghṛish*.

निर्घात *nir-ghāta*, m. (fr. Caus. of √*han*) removal, destruction, TS.; Āpast.; whirlwind, hurricane, thunderstorm, earthquake &c. (ifc. f. *ā*), Gaut.; Mn.; MBh. &c.; N. of a Dānava, Kathās.; *-kara*, mfn. removing, destroying, Car.; *-duḥsaha*, mfn. difficult to be destroyed or overcome (sorrow), Kathās.; *-lakshaṇa*, n. N. of 60 Pariś. of AV. **°ghātana**, n. forcing out, bringing out, Suśr. **°ghātaya**, Nom. P. *°yati*, to draw or force out, Suśr.; to cause to be destroyed or killed, MBh. **°ghātya**, mfn. to be forced or brought out (*a-nirgh°*), Suśr.

निर्घुष्ट *nir-ghushṭa*, mfn. (√*ghush*) sounded, resounded.

2. **Nir-ghosha** (for 1. see p. 541, col. 1), m. (ifc. f. *ā*) sound, noise, rattling, tramping, MBh.; Kāv. &c.; *°shâkshara-vimukta*, m. N. of a Samādhi, L.

निर्घूरिणी *nir-ghūriṇī*, f. a river, L. (prob. w.r. for *nir-jhariṇī*).

निर्घृष् *nir-√ghṛish*, P. *-gharshati* (only ind. p. *-ghṛishya*), to rub against or on (loc.), R. **°gharshaṇa**, n. rubbing, friction, Sāy. **°gharshaṇaka**, mfn. fit for rubbing or cleaning the teeth, Hit.

निर्जात *nir-jāta*, mfn. (√*jan*) come forth, appeared, visible (ifc. in inverted order), Lalit.

निर्जि *nir-√ji*, P. *-jayati* (pf. *-jigāya*, ind. p. *-jitya*), to conquer, win (in battle, play &c.), acquire; subdue, vanquish, surpass, Mn.; MBh.; Kāv. &c. **°jaya**, m. conquest, complete victory, subduing, mastering, MBh.; Kāv.; Suśr. &c. **°jita**, mfn. conquered, subdued, gained, won, ib.; claimed i.e. due (as interest on money), Mn. viii, 154; *-varman*, m. N. of a man, Rājat.; *°tāri-gaṇa*, mfn. one who has conquered hosts of enemies, MW.; *°têndriya* and *°driya-grāma*, mfn. one who has subdued (the whole assemblage of) his passions or feelings (the latter also m. 'a Muni, a saint'), W. **°jiti**, f. =*-jaya*, Śāntiś. **°jetṛi**, m. a conqueror, vanquisher, R.

निर्जिगमिषु *nir-jigamishu*, mfn. (√*gam*) wishing to go out or come forth, Kād.; Hcar.

निर्जिहीर्षु *nir-jihīrshu*, mfn. (√*hṛi*) wishing to take off or remove, BhP.

निर्जुष्ट *nir-jushṭa*, mfn. (√*jush*) frequented, inhabited, ib.

निर्जॄ *nir-√jṛī*, Caus. *-jarayati*, to wear down, rub to pieces, crush, ib. 2. **°jara** (for 1. see p. 541), mfn. completely wearing down or destroying, Col.; m. (with Jainas) the gradual destruction of all actions (also *ā*, f. and °*raṇa*, n.), HYog.; Sarvad.; *-prakaraṇâdi*, N. of wk.

निर्झर *nir-jhara*, m. (cf. *jhara*, *jharat*) a waterfall, cataract, mountain torrent, cascade, MBh.; Kāv. &c. (also n., R. iv, 13, 6; *ī*, f., L.; [ifc. f. *ā*, Śāntiś.], and °*raṇa*, n., Pañcad.); burning chaff, L.; an elephant, L.; N. of one of the horses of the Sun, L. (cf. *nirṇara*); (*ī*), f. a river, L. °**riṇ**, m. a mountain, L.; (*iṇī*), f. a torrent, river, Kād.; Kathās.

निर्झाटित *nir-jhāṭita*, mfn. (Caus. of √*jhaṭ*) burst, Deśīn.

निर्डीन *nir-ḍīna*, n. (√*ḍī*) a partic. mode of flying, MBh.

निर्णम् *nir-ṇam* (√*nam*), only Caus. *-ṇāmayati*, to put out (tongue), Divyâv. °**ṇata**, mfn. bent outwards, prominent, Kāṭh. (opp. to *upa-nata*, q.v.); *-tama*, mfn. bending or bowing very low, being far below another person, Nir. viii, 5; °*tôdara*, mfn. having a prominent belly, MBh. °**ṇamana**, n. bending, Śulbas., Sch. °**ṇāmá**, m. id., Śulbas.; turning and winding (*vṛitrasya*), Nir. ii, 16; joint of a wing, ŚBr.

निर्णय *nirṇaya* &c. See *nir-ṇī*.

निर्णर *nirṇara*, m. N. of one of the horses of the Sun, L. (cf. *nirjhara*).

निर्णिज् *nir-ṇij* (√*nij*), P. *-ṇenekti* (Subj. *-ṇenijati*; Ā. *nenikte*, Br.; dat. inf. *-ṇíje*, RV.), (P.) to wash off, cleanse, Br.; ChUp.; (Ā.) id., TS.; to wash or dress or adorn one's self, RV. &c. &c. °**ṇikta**, mfn. washed, cleaned, polished, purified, pure; *-bāhu-valaya*, mfn. with polished bracelets, BhP.; *-manas*, mfn. pure-hearted, MBh. °**ṇikti**, f. (Mcar.), °**ṇeka**, m. (Mn.) washing, ablution, expiation. °**ṇij**, f. a shining dress or ornament, any bright garment &c., RV. °**ṇega**, see *pātra-nirṇega*. °**ṇejaka**, m. a washerman, washer, Mn. °**ṇejana**, n. washing, cleansing, Gaut.; expiation, atonement for an offence, Mn.; water for washing or rinsing (see *patrī-nirṇejana*).

निर्णी *nir-ṇī* (√*nī*), P. Ā. *-ṇayati*, °*te*, to lead or take away, carry off, AV.; Kauś.; to find out, investigate, ascertain, settle, decide, fix on, R.; Daś.; Hit. &c. °**ṇaya**, m. taking off, removing, Mn.; MBh.; Kāv. &c.; complete ascertainment, decision, determination, settlement, ib.; (in logic) deduction, inference, conclusion, demonstration; application of a conclusive argument; (in law) sentence, verdict (cf. *-pāda* below); (in rhet.) narration of events, Sāh.; discussion, consideration (= *vicāra*), L.; *-kamalâkara*, m., *-kaumudī*, f., *-kaustubha*, m. or n., *-candrikā*, f., *-tattva*, n., *-taraṇi*, m. or f., *-darpaṇa*, m., *-dīpa* and °*paka*, m., °*pikā*, f. N. of wks.; *-pāda*, m. the fourth (and last) part of a lawsuit, sentence, decree, verdict, L.; *-bindu*, m., *-bhāskara*, m., *-mañjarī*, f., *-ratna*, n., *-ratna-dīpikā*, f., *-ratnâkara*, m., *-vivaraṇa*, n., *-saṃgraha*, m., *-samudāya*, m., *-sāra*, m., *-siddhānta*, m., *-sindhu*, m., °*yâmṛita*, n., °*yârṇava*, m., °*yârtha-pradīpa*, m., °*yôddhāra*, m. N. of wks.; °*yôpamā*, f. a comparison based upon an inference, Kāvyâd. ii, 27. °**ṇayana**, n. = *-ṇaya*, L. — **ṇāyaka**, mfn. settling, conclusive, Nyāyam., Comm. °**ṇāyana**, n. rendering certain, W.; the outer angle of the elephant's eye, L. °**ṇīta**, mfn. traced out, ascertained, settled, decided, MBh. &c. °**ṇetṛi**, mfn. settling, deciding, Pāṇ. i, 3, 23, Sch.; m. a judge, Kathās.; a voucher, W.; a guide, ib.; *-tva*, n. proof, verification, ib. °**ṇeya**, mfn. to be ascertained or determined, ib.; w.r. for *nir-ṇaya* (also in *nir-ṇeya-sindhu* for *nir-ṇaya-s*°).

निर्णुद् *nir-ṇud* (√*nud*), P. *-ṇudati* (w. r. *nud*°), to push out, drive away, reject, repudiate, AV.; AitBr.; MBh. &c. °**ṇoda**, m. removal, banishment, Gobh.

निर्दंश् *nir-√daṇś*, P. *-daśati* (pres. p. *-daśat* and °*śamāna*, ind. p. *-daśya*), to bite through, bite, gnash or grind the teeth, MBh.; Hariv.

निर्दर 2. *nir-dara*, m. (√*dṛī*) a cave, cavern, R. (v. l. °*ri*); *-vāsin*, mfn. inhabiting a cave, ib.

निर्दलन *nir-dalana*, n. (√*dal*) splitting, cleaving asunder, breaking, Vcar.; Rājat.

निर्दह् *nir-√duh*, P. Ā. *-dahati*, °*te* (inf. *-dahas*, Br.), to burn out, burn up, consume by fire, destroy completely, RV. &c. &c.: Caus. *-dāhayati*, to cause to burn up or set on fire, Rājat. 2. °**dagdha**, mfn. burnt, burnt up, MBh.; Hariv. &c. °**dagdhikā**, f. = *ni-digdhikā* or *nir-digdhikā*. °**dahana**, mf(*ī*)n. burning up, consuming, AV.; m. Semecarpus Anacardium, L.; (*ā*), f. Sanseviera Roxburghiana, Suśr.; n. burning, ib. °**dāhá**, mfn. burning, AV.; m. N. of a partic. Agni, ib.; the act of burning up (see *á-nirdāha*). °**dāhuka**, mfn. burning (see *a-nirdāhuka*).

निर्दातृ *nir-dātṛi*, m. (√*dai*) a weeder, reaper, Mn.; MBh.

निर्दारित *nir-dārita*. See *nir-√dṛī*.

निर्दिग्ध *nir-digdha*, mfn. (√*dih*) anointed, smeared; well-fed, stout, lusty, L.; (*ā*), f. Solanum Jacquini (also °*dhikā*), L.

निर्दिधारयिषा *nir-didhārayishā*, f. (fr. Desid. of Caus. of *nir-√dhṛi*) desire of investigating or ascertaining, ŚBr., Sch.

निर्दिश् *nir-√diś*, P. *-diśati* (aor. *-adikshat*, Daś.; Bhaṭṭ. ind. p. *-diśya*, Śak.; Mālav.; inf. *-deshṭum*, MBh.), to point to (acc.), show, Mṛicch.; Śak. &c.; to assign anything to, destine for (dat. or gen.), Hariv.; R. &c.; to indicate, state, name, define, specify, Br.; Mn.; MBh. &c.; to take for, regard as (with double acc.), Mn.; Vet.; to announce, proclaim, foretell, prophesy, MBh.; Var.; to recommend, advise, suggest (with double acc.), Hit.: Desid. *-didikshati*, to wish to point out or define more closely, Śaṃk. °**dishṭa**, mfn. pointed out, shown, indicated, declared, announced, foretold, enjoined, TS.; Mn.; MBh. &c.; ordered, meant or determined for, appointed to (dat.), Var.; learned, wise (= *paṇḍita*), Gal. °**deśa**, m. pointing out, indicating, directing, order, command, instruction (often ifc.), Mn.; Kāv.; Pur.; description, specification, special mention, details or particulars, GṛŚrS.; R.; Suśr. &c.; vicinity, proximity, L.; certainty, ascertainment, W.; a partic. number, Buddh.; *-kārin*, mfn. executing orders, obedient, BhP.; *-pālana*, n. obeying a command, R. °**deśaka**, mfn. pointing out, showing, indicating; describing, defining, TPrāt.; ordering, MW. °**deśanīya** (MW.), °**deśya** (Mn.; MBh. &c.), mfn. to be pointed out or determined or described or proclaimed or foretold. °**deshṭṛi**, mfn. who or what points out or shows or defines, L.; m. an authority, a guide, W.

निर्दी *nir-√dī* (only impf. *-adiyam*), to fly away, RV. iv, 27, 1 (cf. *nir-ḍīna*).

निर्दुह् *nir-√duh*, P. *-duhati* (aor. *-adhukshat*, 3. pl. *-dhukshan*, Ā. *-adhukshata*, RV.), to milk out, extract, RV.; MBh. °**dugdha**, mfn. milked or drawn out, extracted, Kathās.

निर्दॄ *nir-√dṛī* (only pf. *-dadāra*), to tear or rend asunder, BhP.: Caus. *-dārayati*, id., Hariv.; to cause to be dug up, Rājat. °**dārita**, mfn. torn asunder, split open, Hariv.

निर्द्युत् *nir-√dyut*, Caus. *-dyotayati*, to illustrate, explain, TāṇḍBr.

निर्द्रु *nir-√dru*, P. *-dravati*, to run out or away, AV.

निर्धम् *nir-√dham* (*dhmā*), P. *-dhamati*, to blow away, blow out of, RV.; TĀr.; Suśr.

निर्धा *nir-√dhā*, P. *-dadhāti*, to take or find out, RV. x, 160, 4.

निर्धाटय *nir-dhāṭaya*, Nom. P. °*yati*, to use ill, Śīl.

निर्धाव् *nir-√1. dhāv*, P. *-dhāvati*, to stream forth or spring or run or escape from (abl.), ŚBr.; Hariv.

निर्धू *nir-√dhū*, P. Ā. *-dhūnoti*, -°*nute*, to shake, agitate, shake out or off, scatter, remove, destroy, expel, reject, Br.; MBh.; R. &c. °**dhūta**, mfn. shaken, agitated &c., Mn.; MBh. &c. (also *-dhūta*); harassed, tormented, R.; deprived or bereft of (comp.), Hariv.; suffered, undergone, W.; m. a man abandoned by his relatives or friends, ib.; *-pāpa*, mfn. one whose sins are wholly shaken off or removed, MW.; *-saktu* (*nír-dh*°), mfn. (bag) having the barley-meal shaken out, ŚBr. °**dhūnana**, n. heaving, fluctuating (of the sea), Kum.

निर्धृ *nir-√dhṛi* (only Pass. aor. *-adhāri*, Śiś. ix, 20), to settle, ascertain: Caus. *-dhārayati*, to hold back (the breath), VPrāt., Sch.; to take or pick out, particularize (determine, Pass. pres. p. *-dhāryamāṇa*), Pāṇ. ii, 3, 42, Sch.: Desid. of Caus. *-didhārayishati*, to wish to ascertain or define, Śaṃk. °**dhāra**, m. (Vop.; L.), °*dhāraṇa*, n. (Var.; Śaṃk.; Pāṇ., Sch.; Vop.) taking out or specifying one out of many, particularizing, defining, settling, certainty, ascertainment. °**dhāraṇīya**, mfn. to be ascertained or determined, W. °**dhārayitṛi**, m. one who settles or decides, Śaṃk. °**dhārita**, mfn. determined, ascertained, settled, accurately stated or told, ib. °**dhāritavya** and °**dhārya**, mfn. = °*dhāraṇīya*. °**dhṛiti**, v.l. for *vidhṛiti*, VP.

निर्धे *nir-√dhe*, *-dhayati*, to drink or suck up, absorb, AV.; ŚBr.

निर्धौत *nir-dhauta* (√2. *dhāv*), washed off, cleansed, purified, polished, bright, MBh.; Kāv.

निर्ध्मापन *nir-dhmāpana*, n. (*nir-√dham*) blowing away, Suśr.

निर्ध्यै *nir-√dhyai* (pres. p. *-dhyāyat*, Rājat.; ind. p. *-dhyāya*, R.), to think of, reflect upon. °**dhyāta**, mfn. thought of, meditated, MW.

निर्नश् *nir-√2. naś*, only Caus. *-nāśayati* (aor. *-anīnaśat*), to drive away, remove, destroy, RV.; AV. °**nashṭa**, mfn. lost, disappeared, Rājat. °**nāśana**, mfn. removing, expelling, destroying, Hit.; n. the act of removing &c., MBh. °**nāśin**, mfn. = °*śana*, mfn., Śatr.

निर्बन्ध् *nir-√bandh*, P. *-badhnāti*, to fix or fasten upon, attach one's self to, insist upon, persist in, urge, MBh.; Pur. °**baddha**, mfn. fixed or fastened upon (loc.), BhPur.; clung to, pressed hard, urged, Daś.; Naish. °**bandha**, m. objection, Gaut.; insisting upon (loc. or comp.), pertinacity, obstinacy, perseverance, MBh.; Kāv. &c. (ibc., °*dhāt*, °*dhena*, °*dhatas*, ind. perseveringly, with or by perseverance; °*dhaṃ √kṛi*, to urge [gen.], Kathās. i, 25; to show obstinacy against [instr.], MBh. xiii, 5034); the attributing anything to, accusing of (comp.), Mn. xi, 56; *-para*, mf(*ā*)n. intent upon, desirous of (comp.), Kum. v, 66; *-pṛishṭa*, mfn. urgently asked, importuned, Ragh. xiv, 32. °**bandhanīya**, w.r. for *ni-b*°. °**bandhin**, mfn. insisting upon (loc. or comp.), MBh.; °*dhi-tā*, f., Jātak.

निर्बर्हण *nir-barhaṇa*, n. = *ni-b*°, L.

निर्बाध् *nir-√bādh*, Ā. *-bādhate*, to keep off, ward off, Kāṭh. °**bādhá**, m. a knob, prominence (as that which keeps off or defends?), TS.; ŚBr. (°*dhe √kṛi*, [prob.] to set aside, remove, TS.; °*dhavá*, n., ib.) °**bādhín**, mfn. removing all (impediments), TS. °**bādhya**, mfn. able to remove all (impediments), ĀpŚr.

निर्ब्रू *nir-√brū*, P. *-braviti*, to speak out, pronounce (loud or clearly), Br.; RPrāt.; to interpret, explain, Nir.

निर्भज् *nir-√bhaj*, P. Ā. *-bhajati*, °*te* (2. sg. aor. Subj. *-bhāk*), to exclude from participation or coparceny with (abl.), to content or satisfy with (instr.), RV.; AV.; Br.: Caus. *-bhājayati*, (in law) to exclude from sharing in, disinherit. 2. °**bhakta**, mfn. excluded from participation, MW. °**bhājya**, mfn. to be excluded from p° or sharing in, Mn. ix, 207.

निर्भञ्ज् *nir-√bhañj*, P. *-bhanakti* (2. sg. impf. *-abhanas*; Impv. *-bandhi*, AV. iii, 6, 7), to break or split asunder, defeat, AV.; R. (w. r. *-bhajanti* for *bhañj*°, v, 73, 37). °**bhagna**, mfn. broken asunder or down, bent, MBh.; R. °**bhajyamāna**, mfn. being broken in pieces, BhP.

निर्भट *nirbhaṭa*, mfn. hard, firm, L. (v. r. *nirvaha*, perhaps w.r. for *nibhaṭa* = *ni-bhṛita*, q. v.)

निर्भर्त्स् *nir-√bharts*, P. *-bhartsayati* (ind. p. *-bhartsya*), to threaten, menace, rebuke, blame, MBh.; Kāv. &c.; to mock, deride, (met. =) outstrip, surpass, Kāv.; Hit. °**bhartsana**, n. threatening, reproach, blame, MBh.; Rājat. (also *ā*, f.); red paint, lac, L.; *-daṇḍa-mohita*, mfn. bewildered by the threat of punishment, MBh. °**bhartsita**, mfn. threatened, menaced, reviled, abused, Kathās.; Pur.; *-vat*, mfn., Pañc.

निर्भल् *nir-√bhal* (only pr.p.f. *-bhālayantī* in Prākr., Mālav. i, ½, v.l. *-dhyāyantī*), to see, perceive, notice = (and perhaps w.r. for) *ni-bh°*.

निर्भस् *nir-√bhas*, *-bapsati*, to bite off, chew, TBr.; Kāṭh.

निर्भा *nir-√bhā*, P. *-bhāti* (pf. *-babhau*), to shine forth, appear, arise, Mn.; Kāv.; Pur.; to look like, seem to be (*iva*), MBh. viii, 3141. °**bhāta**, mfn. shone or shining forth, appeared, arisen, MBh.; Kāv. &c.

निर्भास् *nir-√bhās*, Caus. *-bhāsayati*, to illuminate, Hariv. °**bhāsa**, m. appearance, Sarvad. (ifc. f. *ā* = *nibha*, similar, like, Kāraṇḍ., printed °*bhāsha*). °**bhāsana**, n. illuminating, illustrating, making manifest, Sarvad. °**bhāsita**, mfn. illuminated, illumined, Hariv.; = *dīpta*, L.

निर्भिद् *nir-√bhid*, P.Ā. *-bhinatti* (2.sg.Subj. aor. *-bhed*, RV. i, 104, 8; pf. *-bibheda*, MBh. &c.; *-bibhide*, Hariv.; ind. p. *-bhidya*, ŚBr.; MBh. &c.), to cleave or split asunder, divide, open, pierce, hurt, wound, destroy, RV. &c. &c.; (with *locane*) to put out, MBh.; (with *kham*) to form an aperture, excavate, BhP.; (with *granthim*) to loose, untie, ib.; to penetrate i.e. find out, investigate, discover, MBh.; Kāv. &c.: Pass. *-bhidyate*, to be broken asunder, cleave or split open (intrans.), Up.; Suśr.; BhP. °**bhinna**, mfn. broken asunder, budded, blossomed; divided, separated, disunited; pierced, penetrated; found out, betrayed, Br.; MBh.; Kāv. &c.; *-tanu*, mfn. having the body pierced through or transfixed, MW. °**bheda**, m. breaking asunder, splitting, bursting (trans. and intrans.), R.; Suśr.; split, rent, channel (of a river), Hariv.; betraying, revealing, Mālav. iv, ½. °**bhedin**, mfn. splitting, piercing, Kathās. 2. °**bhedya** (for 1. see p. 541, col. 3), mfn. to be split asunder.

निर्भुज् *nir-√1. bhuj*, P. *bhujati*, to bend awry, distort (mouth, eyes &c.), Yājñ.; Suśr. °**bhugna**, mfn. bent awry, distorted, MBh.; Suśr.

निर्भू *nir-√bhū* (only aor. *-bhūt*, he disappeared, 'was off'), RV. iv, 19, 9; viii, 68, 2. °**bhūti** (*nír-*), f. disappearing, vanishing, AV.

निर्भृ *nir-√bhṛi* (only pf. *-jabhāra*), to take or draw out, RV. x, 68, 8; 9. °**bhṛita**, (prob.) w.r. for *ni-bh°* (cf. *nir-bhaṭa*).

निर्मज्ज् *nir-√majj*, P. *-majjati* (pf. *-mamajja*), to sink under, sink into, MBh.; Hariv.; to inundate, deluge (Pot. *-majjyāt*), ŚBr. °**magna**, mfn. to sink under (opp. to *un-magna*), Sāh.; sunk into i.e. firmly fixed upon (comp.), R. °**majā** (*nír-*), f. watering-place, pond (?), RV. viii, 4, 20 (Sāy. '*nir-maj*, mfn. = *śuddha*').

निर्मञ्च् *nir-√mañc* (ind.p. *-mañcya*), to perform the ceremony of lustration with anything (acc.), Naish. °**mañcana**, n. = *nī-rājana*, ib. Sch. (w.r. °*mañchana*, Kum. xiii, 18, with v.l. °*uñchana*).

निर्मथ् *nir-√math* or *manth*, P.Ā. *-manthati*, °*te*, RV.; *-mathati*, °*te*, MBh.; *-mathnāti*, Kāṭh. (fut. *-mathishyati*, ind. p. *-mathya*, MBh.; Kāv. &c.); to grind (fire) out of (wood), to produce (fire) by rubbing (wood together), rub or churn anything out of anything (double acc.), RV.; ŚBr. &c.; to stir or churn (the sea), MBh.; R.; to tear or draw or shake out of, extract, MBh.; Kāv.; Pur.; to shake, agitate (the mind), MBh.; to grind down, crush, destroy, MBh.; Hariv. &c.: Pass. *-mathyate* (p. °*yamāna*), to be rubbed or churned &c., MBh.; Hariv. °**matha**, m. rubbing; *-dāru* = *nirmantha-d°*, L. °**mathana**, n. rubbing, churning, making butter, lighting a fire by rubbing two pieces of wood together or by churning, Up.; MBh.; Suśr.; Kām. °**mathita**, mfn. stirred about, churned, agitated, crushed, destroyed, MBh.; Kāv. &c.; wiped off, Mṛicch.; m. a fire newly lighted by rubbing (wood), KātyŚr. 1. °**mathya**, mfn. to be (or being newly) excited by friction, Vait.; (*ā*), f. a partic. fragrant bark, L. 2. °**mathya**, ind. having ground or churned &c., MBh.; Kāv.; having discriminated or particularized, W.; forcibly, by force, Kathās. °**mantha**, m. rubbing; *-kāshṭha* or *-dāru*, n. the wood or stick used for kindling fire by friction; a churning stick, L. °**manthana**, n. rubbing together (esp. for kindling fire), churning, friction, Vait.; Suśr. °**manthyà**, mfn. to be (or being) stirred or churned or excited by friction (as fire), TS.; ŚrS.; to be distinguished or discriminated, W.; *-dāru*, n. the wood for kindling fire by fr°, L. °**māthin**, mfn. grinding down, crushing or stamping to pieces, churning, rubbing, Rājat.

निर्मद् *nir-√mad*, Caus. *-mādayati*, to wash, Divyâv.

निर्मा *nir-√mā*, Ā. *-mimīte*, TS.; AV.; Br.; *-māti*, Kāv.; Pur. (pf. *-mame*, Mn.; MBh.; ind. p. *-māya*, Prab.; inf. *-mātum*, Rājat.); to mete out, measure, AV.; to build, make out of (abl.), form, fabricate, produce, create, TS.; Br., Mn. &c.; (with *citram*) to paint, Śak.; Daś.; (with *kośam*) to compose or write, Cat.; (with *giram*) to utter, Kull.; (with *nītim*) to show, betray, MBh.: Pass. *-mīyate* (pf. *-mame*, Rājat. v, 425; aor. *-amāyi*, Cat.), to be measured out &c.: Caus. *-māpayati*, to cause to be made or built, Rājat.; Kathās.: Desid. *-mitsati*, to wish to make or build, Naish. °**mā**, f. value, measure, equivalent, Lāṭy. °**māṇa**, n. measuring, measure, reach, extent (often, mfn. ifc.); Hariv.; R.; forming, making, creating, creation, building, composition, work (ifc. 'made of,' Suśr.), MBh.; Kāv. &c.; (with Buddh.) transformation; pith, the best of anything (= *sāra*), L.; = *asamañjasa*, L.; *-kāya*, m. the body of transformations, Buddh.; MWB. 247; *-kāraka*, m. creator, Vishṇ.; *-rata*, m. pl. 'finding pleasure in creating,' N. of a class of gods, MBh.; *-rati-deva*, m. pl. 'id.' or 'enjoying pleasures provided by themselves,' a class of beings inhabiting the fifth heaven, VP.; Lalit.; MWB. 208. °**mātṛi**, m. (*trī*, f.) maker, builder, creator, author, MBh.; Hariv. &c.; *-tā*, f., *-tva*, n. creatorship &c., Śaṃk. °**mita** (*nír-*), mfn. constructed, built, fashioned, formed, created, made by (instr. or comp.) out of (abl., instr. or comp.), ŚBr.; Mn.; MBh. &c.; (law) fixed, settled, Mn. ix, 46; (ceremony) performed, celebrated, R. (B) i, 14, 42; (sacrificial animal) put apart, separated, isolated (= *nir-ūḍha*), ĀśvŚr.; m. pl. (with Buddhists) a class of deities, Lalit. °**miti**, f. formation, creation, making, Rājat.; adding, addition (of a word), Kpr. vii, 10. °**mitsu**, mfn. wishing to create (with acc.), Kāv. °**mimitsā** (!), f. desire of creating, Yogas., Sch.

निर्माख्य *nir-mākhya* (!), m. N. of a man, Cat. (v.l. *tigmâtman* and *nirmād*).

निर्मि *nir-√mi*, P. *-minoti*, to make by miracle, Divyâv. °**mita**, see 1. *nir-mā*.

निर्मुच् *nir-√muc*, P. *-muñcati*, to loosen, free from (abl.), liberate, RV. &c. &c.: Pass. *-mucyate* (aor. *-amoci*, ŚBr.), to be freed or free one's self from, get rid of (abl.), RV.; ŚBr.; MBh. &c.; to be deprived of (instr.), Rājat.; to be abandoned or given up (as life &c.), ib.; (sc. *tvacas*) to cast off (said of a serpent casting its skin), Mṛicch. iii, 9: Caus. *-mocayati*, to loosen or liberate from (abl.), Hariv.; to redeem (a pawn) from (abl.), Vishṇ. °**mukta**, mfn. loosed, separated, sundered, liberated or saved or escaped or free from, deprived of (instr., abl. or comp.), MBh.; Kāv. &c.; given up, lost, disappeared, vanished (esp. ibc.; cf. below); flung, hurled, MBh.; BhP.; (a serpent) that has lately cast its skin, MBh.; free from every attachment (= *niḥ-saṅga*), L.; deprived of all, possessing nothing (= *nish-parigraha*), ib.; *-kalmasha*, mfn. freed from sin, MBh.; *-deha*, mfn. one who is freed from his body (or bodily desires), ib.; *-saṅga*, mfn. one who has given up all (worldly) attachments, BhP. °**mukti** (*nír-*), f. liberation, deliverance from (abl. or comp.), AV.; Kathās.; = *tyāga* or *dāna*, Sch. on BhP. x, 17, 18. °**moka**, m. setting loose or free, liberating, L.; a cast-off skin (esp. of a snake), MBh.; Kāv. &c. (*-paṭṭa*, m. a piece of cast-off skin, Ragh. xvi, 17); armour, mail, L.; sky, atmosphere, L.; N. of a son of the 8th Manu, BhP.; of a Ṛishi under the 13th Manu, ib. (cf. *nir-moha*, p. 541, col. 3). °**moktṛi**, m. a looser, solver (as of doubts), MBh. °**moksha**, m. liberation, deliverance from (gen. or comp.), MBh.; Kāv. °**mocaka**, mfn. setting free, liberating, L.; n. the cast-off skin of a snake, Car. °**mocana**, n. deliverance, MBh.

निर्मुट *nirmuṭa*, m. (only L.) a tree; a free market or fair; the sun; = *kharpara*; n. an arbour, Gal.

निर्मुण्ड *nir-muṇḍa*. See p. 541, col. 3.

निर्मुष् *nir-√mush*, *-mushṇāti*, to snatch away, Vait.

निर्मुह् *nir-√muh*, Caus. *-mohayati* (ind. p. *-mohya*), to confuse, bewilder, MBh.

निर्मृज् *nir-√mṛij*, P. *-mārshṭi*, &c. (Pot. *-mṛijyur*, Kāṭh.; Impv. *-mṛiḍḍhi*, AV.; p. Ā. *-mṛijāna*, Kauś.; pf. *-mamārja*, Pur.; Subj. aor. *-mṛikshatam*, RV.; ind. p. *-mṛijya*, MBh.), to rub or wipe off, sweep out, destroy. 2. °**mārga**, m. wiping off (cf. *á-nirm°*, add.); that which is stripped or wiped off, refuse, TBr. °**márguka**, mfn. drawing off, withdrawing from (abl.), TS. °**mārjana**, n. wiping off, sweeping, cleaning, MBh. °**mārjanīya**, mfn. to be cleaned, R. °**mārshṭi**, f. N. of the wife of Duḥ-saha, MārkP. (w. r. °*māshṭi*). °**mṛishṭa**, mfn. rubbed out, wiped off, destroyed, Kāv.

निर्म्रेतुक *nir-mretuka*, mf(*ā*)n. (√*mrit*) fading away, withering, TāṇḍBr. (v.l. °*metuka*, °*mṛītuka*).

निर्म्लुक्ति *nir-mlukti*, w. r. for *ni-m°*.

निर्यत् 1. *nir-yat*, mfn. (*nir-√i*) going forth, coming out, issuing, MBh.; Kāv. &c.

निर्यत् 2. *nir-√yat*, Caus. *-yātayati*, to snatch away, carry off, take or fetch out of (abl.), get, procure, MBh.; Hariv.; Kāv.; to give back, restore, make restitution, Mn.; MBh. &c.; to give as a present, Lalit.; Divyâv.; (*vairam*) to return or show enmity, take revenge, MBh.; R.; Divyâv.; to forgive, pardon, set free, MW. °**yātaka**, mfn. bearing away, carrying off, removing (ifc.; cf. *preta-*, *mṛita-*). °**yātana**, n. giving back, returning, restoring, delivery of a deposit, replacing anything lost, payment of a debt (with gen. or comp.; cf. *vaira-*), Hariv.; R. &c.; gift, donation, L.; revenge, killing, slaughter, L. °**yātita**, mfn. restored, returned, requited, MBh.; Hariv.; past, spent (as years), R. 1. °**yātya**, ind. having restored &c., Kathās. 2. °**yātya**, mfn. to be restored or delivered &c., MBh.; Hariv.

निर्या *nir-√yā*, P. *-yāti*, to go out, come forth, go from (abl.) to or into (acc.), set out for (dat., [e.g. *yuddhāya*, MBh.; *dig-jayāya*, Rājat.] or *artham* [e.g. *bhikshârtham*, Pañc.]), MBh.; Kāv. &c.; (with *mṛigayām*) to go hunting, MBh.; to depart from life, die, Car.; to pass away (as time), Kāv.; to weed (a field), MBh.: Caus. *-yāpayati*, to cause to go out &c., MBh.; R.; to drive away, expel from (abl.), BhP. °**yā́**, f. getting out of order, disturbance, defect (esp. of a rite), TS.; TāṇḍBr. °**yāṇa**, n. going forth or out, exit, issue; setting out, decamping (of an army), going out (of cattle to the pasture ground), MBh.; Kāv. &c.; departure, vanishing, disappearance, Rājat.; Sāh.; departure from life, death, MBh.; Hariv.; Var.; final emancipation (w. r. for *nir-vāṇa*?), L.; a road leading out of a town, L.; the outer corner of an elephant's eye, Daś.; Śiś. (cf. *nir-ṇāyana*); a rope for tying cattle, a foot-rope; *-hasta*, mfn. having a foot-rope in the hand, Śiś. xii, 41. °**yāṇika**, mfn. conducive to emancipation, Lalit. °**yāta**, mfn. gone out or forth, issued, &c.; laid aside (as money), MBh.; completely familiar or conversant with (loc. or comp.), Lalit. (v. l. *nir-jāta*). °**yāti**, f. departure, dying, final emancipation, Buddh. °**yātṛi**, m. a weeder (of a field), MBh. (cf. *nir-dātṛi*). °**yāpaṇa**, n. (fr. Caus.) expelling, banishing, BhP. °**yāpita**, mfn. caused to go out &c.; removed, destroyed, BhP.; undertaken, begun, ib. °**yiyāsu**, mfn. (fr. Desid.) wishing or trying to go out, Suśr.

निर्याच् *nir-√yāc*, P. Ā. *-yācati*, °*te*, to beg of or solicit from (abl.), to ask, entreat, request (with double acc.), AV.; TS.; TāṇḍBr.

निर्याम *nir-yāma*, m. (√*yam*) a sailor, pilot,

L. (cf. *ni-y*°). °**yāmaka**, m. an assistant, HPariś. °**yāmaṇā**, f. assistance, ib.

निर्यास *nir-yāsá*, m. (n., g. *ardharcâdi*; √*yas*) exudation of trees or plants, juice, resin, milk (ifc. f. *ā*), Gaut.; Mn.; MBh.; Suśr. &c.; any thick fluid substance, Hariv.; extract, decoction, L. (also °*syā*, f., Vishṇ., Sch.); °*sika*, mfn., g. *kumudâdi* on Pāṇ. iv, 2, 80.

निर्यु *nir-*√*4. yu* (only Ā. pres. p. *-yuvāṇá*, mfn.), to keep away, ward off, RV. iv, 48, 2.

निर्युक्त *nir-yukta*, mfn. (√*yuj*) constructed, built, erected, raised, Hariv.; (ifc.) directed towards (v. l. *nir-mukta*), ib.; (in music) limited as to metre and measure (v. l. *ni-y*°). 2. °**yukti** (for 1. see p. 542, col. 1), f. (with Jainas) explanation of a sacred text (cf. *nir-ukti*). °**yoga**, m. (prob.) a decoration, Hariv.; a rope for tying cows, BhP., Sch.

निर्यूष *nir-yūsha*, m. extract, juice &c. = *nir-yāsa*, L.

निर्यूह *nir-yūha*, n. (m., L.; often v. l. and prob. only w. r. for *nir-vyūha*) prominence, projection; a kind of pinnacle or turret, MBh.; Hariv.; R. (ifc. f. *ā*); a helmet, crest or any similar head-ornament, MBh.; Hariv. (= *āpīḍa*, L.); a peg or bracket, L.; wood placed in a wall for doves to build upon, W.; a door, gate, Hariv.; m. extract, juice, decoction, R.; Suśr. (cf. *nir-yāsa*, *nir-yūsha*).

निर्येष *nir-*√*yesh*, *-yeshati*, to boil or bubble forth, TS.

निर्योल *nir-yola*, m. (fr.?) a partic. part of a plough, Kṛishis.

निर्लयनी *nir-layanī*, w. r. for *nir-vl*°.

निर्लाञ्छन *nir-lāñchana*, n. (√*lāñch*) the marking of domestic animals by perforating the nose &c., HYog.

निर्लिख *nir-*√*likh*, P. *-likhati*, to scratch, scarify, Suśr.; to scratch or scrape off, Āpast. °**lekhana**, n. an instrument for scraping off, a scraper, Suśr. (cf. *jihvā-nirl*°).

निर्लिह् *nir-*√*lih*, P. *-leḍhi*, to lick off, sip off or away, ĀpŚr.

निर्लुञ्चन *nir-luñcana*, n. (√*luñc*) pulling out or off, tearing off, peeling, KātyŚr., Sch.

निर्लुठ् *nir-*√*1. luṭh*, Caus. *-loṭhayati*, to roll down (trans.), Rājat. °**luṭhita**, mfn. rolled down, ib.; come forth, prolapsed (from the womb), Pat.

निर्लुठ् *nir-*√*2. luṭh*, *-loṭhayati*, to rob, steal, Rājat.

निर्लुड् *nir-*√*luḍ*. See *a-nirloḍita*.

निर्लुण्ठ् *nir-*√*luṇṭh*, *-luṇṭhati* (only p. *-luṇṭhyamāna*), to rob, plunder. °**luṇṭhana**, n. robbing, plundering, Sāh.; w. r. for *nir-luñcana*. °**luṇṭhita**, mfn. robbed, plundered, Rājat.

निर्लुप् *nir-*√*lup*, P. *-lumpati* (only ind. p. *-lupya*), to draw out, extract, MaitrS. °**lopa**, m. plundering, plunder, spoil; °*lopâpahāraka*, mfn. one who carries off by robbery, L.; cf. *ni-lup*.

निर्लून *nir-lūna*, mfn. (√*lū*) cut through or off, Śiś.; Bālar.; Kathās.

निर्लोच् *nir-loc* (only ind. p. *-locya*), to meditate, ponder, Kathās.

निर्ल्वयनी *nir-lvayanī*, w. r. for *nir-vl*°.

निर्वच् *nir-*√*vac* (aor. *-avocat*, AV.; ŚBr.; but mostly used in Pass. *-ucyate*, *-ucyamāna*; cf. *nir-ukta*), to speak out, express clearly or distinctly, declare, interpret, explain, Br.; Mn.; MBh. &c.; to derive from (abl.), Hariv.; to order off, warn off, drive away, tell any one to go away from (abl.), AV. °**vaktavya**, mfn. to be interpreted or explained, Nir. 2. °**vacana**, n. speaking out, pronouncing, ŚāṅkhŚr.; a saying or proverb, MBh.; interpretation, explanation, etymology, MBh. °**vacanīya**, m. = next (cf. *a-nirv*°). 2. °**vācya** (for 1. see p. 542, col. 1), mfn. to be explained, RPrāt.; Mallin.

निर्वञ्च् *nir-*√*vañc*, Ā. *-vañcate*, to deceive, Śṛiṅgār.

निर्वद् *nir-*√*vad*, P. Ā. *-vadati*, °*te* (aor. *-avādisham*, *-vādishṭam*), to order off, warn off, expel or drive away, VS.; to speak out, utter, AV.; to abuse, revile, MBh.; to deny, MW. 2. °**vāda** (for 1. see p. 542, col. 1), m. obloquy, censure, MBh.; Ragh.; rumour, report, L.; = *niścita-vāda*, or *nishṭhita-v*°, L.; w. r. for *nir-vāha*, Rājat. viii, 565.

निर्वध् *nir-*√*vadh*, to split off or asunder, sever, separate, Br.

निर्वप् *nir-*√*vap*, P. Ā. *-vapati*, °*te* (pf. *-vavāpa*, R., *-uvāpa*, Bhaṭṭ., *-ūpe*, RV.; fut. *-vapsyati*, TBr., *-vapishyati*, Hariv.; R.), to pour out, sprinkle, scatter, to offer, present (esp. sacrificial food, the funeral oblation or libation to deceased relatives); to choose or select for (dat. or gen.), to distribute (e. g. grain for sacrif. purposes); to perform (a sacrifice or a funeral oblation &c.), RV. &c. &c.; (with *kṛishim*) to practise or exercise agriculture, MBh.: Caus. *-vāpayati*, to sow out, Pañc.; to choose or select (for the gods), MBh. °**vápaṇa**, n. pouring out, sprinkling, scattering, KātyŚr.; offering (esp. the funeral oblation or libation), Mn.; MBh. &c.; that by which a libation is made (as a ladle or vessel), ŚBr.; gift, donation, alms, BhP.; mfn. relating to libations, Gṛihyās.; (ifc.) scattering, pouring out, bestowing, MBh. °**vapaṇīya** and °**vaptavya**, mfn. to be scattered out or offered, Nyāyam., Sch. 1. °**vāpa**, m. scattering, pouring out, offering, oblation (esp. in honour of a deceased ancestor), MBh.; Kāv. &c.; sacrificial rice, RTL. 367; gift, alms, Pañc. 1. °**vāpaṇa**, n. (fr. Caus.) scattering, sowing, throwing in or down, Pañc.; Suśr.; offering, presenting funeral oblations, giving, L. 1. °**vāpita**, mfn. scattered, sown, Pañc. 1. °**vāpya**, mfn. to be scattered or offered, Yājñ. 2. °**vāpya**, ind. having offered or distributed or selected, MBh.

निर्वम् *nir-*√*vam*, P. *-vamati*, to vomit, spit out, eject, MBh.; Hariv. °**vānta**, mfn. emitted, Divyâv.

निर्वर्ण् *nir-*√*varṇ*, P. *-varṇayati* (ind. p. *-varṇya*), to look at, contemplate, Mṛicch.; Kālid. &c.; to describe, depict, represent, Suśr. °**varṇana**, n. looking at, regarding, sight, L. °**varṇanīya**, mfn. to be looked at or regarded (*a-nirv*°), Śak.

निर्वर्तक *nir-vartaka*, *nir-vartana*, &c. See under *nir-vṛit*.

निर्वस् *nir-*√*5. vas*, P. *-vasati*, to dwell, finish dwelling (with *vāsam* &c.), MBh.; to dwell abroad, MW.: Caus. *-vāsayati*, to expel from (abl.), banish, Mn.; MBh. &c.; to dismiss, BhP. °**vāsa**, m. leaving one's home, expulsion from (abl.), banishment, MBh.; R.; killing, slaughter, L. 1. °**vāsana**, n. (fr. Caus.) expelling from home, banishment, MBh.; R. &c.; leading out to some other place, Kām.; killing, slaughter, Rājat. (cf. *ud-vās*°). °**vāsanīya** (MBh.), °**vāsya** (Mn.; Yājñ.; Mṛicch.), mfn. to be driven away or banished. °**vāsita**, mfn. expelled, banished, dismissed, spent (as time), Rājat.; BhP. &c.

निर्वह् *nir-*√*vah*, P. *-vahati* (fut. *-voḍhā*, ŚBr.), to lead out of, save from (abl.), RV.; AV.; to carry off, remove, AV.; ŚBr.; Lāṭy.; to flow out of (abl.), MānGṛ.; to bring about, accomplish, Suśr.; to be brought about, succeed; to attain one's object, be successful, overcome obstacles, Kathās.; Sarvad. &c.; to subsist, live on or by (instr.), Campak.; to be fit or meet, HPariś.: Caus. *-vāhayati*, to perform, accomplish, Kathās.; Hit.; to pass, spend (time), Pañc. °**vahaṇa**, n. end, issue, completion, Kāv.; Rājat.; the catastrophe of a drama, Daśar. °**vahitṛi**, m. accomplisher, producer of (gen.), ChUp. viii, 14. °**vāha**, m. carrying on, accomplishing, performing, completion, Kāv.; describing, narrating, Sāh.; steadfastness, perseverance, Mudr.; sufficiency, subsistence, livelihood, Rājat.; Kull. °**vāhaka**, mf(*ikā*)n. accomplishing, performing, effecting (ifc.), Sāh. (*-tā*, f.); Sāy.; (*ikā*), f. diarrhœa, Bhpr. °**vāhaṇa**, mfn. (fr. Caus.) carrying off, removing, destroying (ifc.), Var.; n. = °*vahaṇa*, L. °**vāhin**, mfn. leading or carrying out, discharging (as a wound), Suśr. °**vāhya**, mfn. to be carried on or accomplished or performed, Kathās. °**voḍhṛi**, see p. 558, col. 2.

निर्वा *nir-*√*vā*, P. *-vāti* (pf. *-vavau*), to blow (as wind), R.; to cease to blow, to be blown out or extinguished; to be allayed or refreshed or exhilarated, MBh.; Kāv. &c.: Caus. *-vāpayati*, to put out, extinguish, allay, cool, refresh, delight, RV. &c. &c. °**vāṇa**, mfn. blown or put out, extinguished (as a lamp or fire), set (as the sun), calmed, quieted, tamed (cf. *a-nirv*°), dead, deceased (lit. having the fire of life extinguished), lost, disappeared, MBh.; Kāv. &c.; immersed, plunged, L.; immovable, L.; *-bhūyishṭha*, mfn. nearly extinguished or vanished, Kum. ii, 53; n. blowing out, extinction, cessation, setting, vanishing, disappearance (°*ṇaṃ* √*kṛi*, to make away with anything i. e. not to keep one's promise); extinction of the flame of life, dissolution, death or final emancipation from matter and re-union with the Supreme Spirit, MBh. &c. &c.; (with Buddhists and Jainas) absolute extinction or annihilation (= *śūnya*, L.) of individual existence or of all desires and passions, MWB. 137–139 &c.; perfect calm or repose or happiness, highest bliss or beatitude, MBh.; Kāv. &c.; N. of an Upanishad; instructing in sciences, L.; bathing of an elephant, L.; the post to which an elephant is tied, Gal.; offering oblations (for 1. *nir-vāpaṇa*?), L.; *-kara*, m. 'causing extinction of all sense of individuality,' a partic. Samādhi, Kāraṇḍ.; *-kāṇḍa*, m. or n. N. of wk.; *-tantra*, see *bṛihan-nirvāṇat*° and *mahā-n*°; *-da*, mfn. bestowing final beatitude, MBh.; *-daśaka*, n. N. of wk.; *-dīkshita*, m. N. of a grammarian, Cat.; *-dhātu*, m. the region of Nirvāṇa, Vajracch.; Kāraṇḍ.; *-purāṇa*, n. offering oblations to the dead, Rājat.; *-prakaraṇa*, n. N. of wk.; *-priyā*, f. N. of a Gandharvī, Kāraṇḍ.; *-maṇḍapa*, m. N. of a temple, SkandaP.; *-mantra*, n. N. of a mystical formula, Cat.; *-maya*, mf(*ī*)n. full of bliss, VP.; *-mastaka*, m. liberation, deliverance, W.; *-yoga-paṭala-stotra* and *-yogôttara*, n. N. of wks.; *-ruci*, m. pl. 'delighting in final beatitude,' N. of a class of deities under the 11th Manu, BhP. (cf. *nirmāṇa-rati*); *-lakshaṇa*, mfn. having complete bliss as its characteristic mark, MW.; *-shaṭka*, n. N. of a Stotra; *-saṃcodana*, m. a partic. Samādhi, Kāraṇḍ.; *-sūtra*, n. N. of partic. Buddh. Sūtras; °*ṇôpanishad*, f. N. of an Upanishad. °**vāṇin**, m. (with Jainas) N. of 2nd Arhat of past Utsarpiṇī, L. °**vāta**, see under *nir*, p. 542, col. 3. 2. °**vāpa**, m. extinction (of a fire or light), W.; killing, slaughter. °**vāpaka**, mfn. putting out, extinguishing (ifc.), Car.; Vishṇ. 2. °**vāpaṇa**, mfn. cooling, refrigerant, Car.; n. the act of cooling or refreshing or quenching or delighting, Kāv.; Suśr.; extinguishing, extinction, annihilation, Mṛicch.; Rājat.; killing, slaughter, L. °**vāpayitṛi**, m. extinguisher, quencher, refresher, Śak. 2. °**vāpita**, mfn. extinguished, quenched, allayed, cooled, Ragh.; Mālatīm.; Kathās.; killed, W. 3. °**vāpya**, ind. having extinguished or quenched or refreshed or delighted, W.

निर्वाक *nirvāka*. See *karṇa-* (add.)

निर्वाञ्च् *nirvāñc*, mfn. outward, exterior, ŚāṅkhBr. (fr. *nir* + *ava* + *añc*, Sch.)

निर्विक्रम् *nir-vi-*√*kram*, *-krāmati* (pf. *-cakrāma*), to step out, MBh.

निर्विद् *nir-*√*3. vid*, P. *-vindati* (Ā. *-vide*, ind. p. *-vidya*), to find out, RV. x, 129, 4; (Ā.) to get rid of, do away with (gen. or acc.), RV.; ŚBr.: Pass. *-vidyate*, to be despondent or depressed, be disgusted with (abl. or instr., rarely acc.), ŚāṅkhBr.; MBh. &c.: Caus. *-vedayati*, to cause despair, MBh. xii, 2658. °**viṇṇa**, mfn. (wrongly *-vinna*; cf. Pāṇ. viii, 4, 29, Vārtt. 1, Pat.) despondent, depressed, sorrowful, afraid, loathing, disgusted with (abl., instr., gen., loc. or comp.), MBh.; Kathās.; Pur. &c.; abused, degraded, humble, W.; known, certain, ib.; *-cetas*, mfn. depressed in mind, meek, resigned, Bhag. °**vid**, f. despondency, despair, Kathās. 2. °**vedá** (for 1. see p. 542, col. 3), m. id., complete indifference, disregard of worldly objects, ŚBr.; Up.; MBh. &c.; loathing, disgust for (loc., gen. or comp.), MBh.; R. &c.; *-duḥ-saham*, ind. in a despairingly insupportable manner, Mālatīm.; *-vat*, mfn. despondent, resigned, indifferent, Pañc.

निर्विद्ध *nir-viddha*. See *nir-vyadh*.

निर्विभास् *nir-vi-*√*bhās*, Caus. *-bhāsayati*, to illumine, enlighten, MW.

निर्विवह् *nir-vi-*√*vah*, P. *-vahati*, to carry out, export, expel, MW.

निर्विविक्षत् *nir-vivikshat*, mfn. (fr. Desid. of *nir-viś*) wishing to enter a common dwelling, BhP.

निर्विवित्सु nir-vivitsu, mfn. (fr. Desid. of *nir-√3. vid*) desirous of disuniting (*surâsurān*), MBh. ii, 141.

निर्विश् nir-√viś, P.-*viśati* (inf.-*veshṭum*), to enter into (acc. or loc.); (esp.) to settle in a home, become a householder (also with *griheshu*); to marry, Kāv.; Pur.; to pay, render, offer (*bhartṛi-piṇḍam*), MBh.; to enjoy, delight in (acc.), Hariv.; Kāv. &c.; to go out or forth, W.; to embellish, MW.; to reward, ib. °**vishṭa**, mfn. entered, sticking in (loc. or comp.), BhP.; sitting, Ragh. xii, 68 (C. *niv*°); married (see *a-nirv*°, add.); paid off, rendered (see ib.); enjoyed, Kāv.; earned, gained, Gaut. °**veśa**, m. payment, returning, offering; wages, reward, Mn. vi, 45 (v.l. *nirdeśa* and *nid*°); R.; Daś.; atonement, expiation, Āpast. (cf. *a-nirv*°, add.); entering, attaining, enjoying, L.; fainting, swooning, L. °**veśanīya**, mfn. to be gained or enjoyed, Ragh. °**veśya**, mfn. to be paid or rendered, MBh. °**veshṭavya**, mfn. to be rewarded or paid, MBh.; to be embellished, Hariv.; to be entered into, MW.

निर्विशॄ nir-vi-√śṝi, Pass.-*śīryate*, to peel or drop off, fall asunder, R.

निर्वृ nir-√1. vṛi (of verbal forms only ind. p. *a-nirvṛitya*, 'not finding satisfaction or delight,' BhP.) °**vārita**, mfn. (fr. Caus.) warded off, Prab. iv, ३४. °**vṛita**, mfn. satisfied, happy, tranquil, at ease, at rest, Mn.; MBh.; Kāv. &c.; extinguished, terminated, ceased, Veṇ. vi, 1; MārkP.; emancipated, W.; n. a house, W. °**vṛiti**, f. complete satisfaction or happiness, bliss, pleasure, delight, MBh.; Kāv. &c.; emancipation, final beatitude (= *nir-vāṇa*), Bhām. (cf. MWB. 137); attainment of rest, Suśr.; extinction (of a lamp), Kād.; destruction, death, L.; w.r. for 1. *nir-vṛitti*, Hit. iv, ६; m. N. of a man, Hariv.; of a son of Vṛishṇi, Pur.; *-cakshus*, m. N. of a Ṛishi, MārkP.; *-mat*, mfn. quite satisfied, happy, Mālatīm.; *-śatru*, w.r. for *ni-vṛitta-ś*°, Hariv.; *-sthāna*, n. place of eternal bliss, Śak. vii, १३ (w.r. *nir-vṛitti*).

निर्वृ nir-√2. vṛi, Ā. *-vṛiṇīte*, to choose, select, RV.; TS.

निर्वृत् nir-√vṛit, Ā. *-vartate* (P. only in fut. *-vartsyāmi*, to cause to roll out or cast (as dice), MBh. iv, 24 [B.]; fut. *-vartsyati* and cond. *-avartsyat*, to take place, happen, Bhaṭṭ.), to come forth, originate, develop, become, ŚBr.; Up. &c.; to be accomplished or effected or finished, come off, take place (cf. above), Mn.; MBh.; Kāv. &c.; often w.r. for *ni-vṛit*, q.v.: Caus. *-vartayati* (ind. p. *-vartya*; Pass. *-vartyate*), to cause to come forth, bring out, turn out, do away with, remove, Hariv.; Rājat.; to bring about, complete, finish, perform, make, produce, create, RV. &c. &c.; to gladden, satisfy (*a-nirvartya* v.l. for *a-nirvṛitya*), BhP. °**vartaka**, mfn. (fr. Caus.) bringing about, accomplishing, performing, finishing, Saṃk.; Pat.; v.l. for *niv*°. °**vartana**, n. completion, execution, Saṃk.; v.l. for *niv*°. °**vartitavya**, mfn. to be performed (in Prākr.), Ratnâv. 2. °**vartin**, mfn. accomplishing (ifc.), Śak. v, २१ (v.l. *niv*°). °**vartya**, mfn. to be brought about or accomplished or effected (*-tva*, n.), Daśar.; Rājat.; Saṃk.; to be uttered or pronounced, VPrāt., Sch. °**vṛitta**, mfn. sprung forth, originated, developed, grown out (fruit), accomplished, finished, done, ready, Mn.; MBh.; Kāv. &c.; *-cūḍaka*, mfn. one on whom tonsure has been performed, Mn. v, 67; *-mātra*, mfn. just finished (day), R.; *-śatru*, w.r. for *nivṛitta-ś*°. 2. °**vṛitti**, f. originating, development, growth, completion, termination, Mn.; MBh. &c. (often w.r. for *nivṛitti* or *nirvṛiti*).

निर्वृष्ट nir-vṛishṭa, mfn. (√*vṛish*) that has ceased to rain (as a cloud), Vām. iv, 2, 10; m. or n. = next. °**vṛishṭi**, f. cessation of rain, a rain that has just ceased, Hariv.

निर्वेद 1. and 2. nir-veda. See p. 542, col. 2, and *nir-vid*.

निर्वेध nir-vedha, °*dhima*. See *nir-vyadh*.

निर्वेश nir-veśa, °*śanīya* &c. See *nir-viś*.

निर्वेष्ट् nir-√veshṭ, Caus. *-veshṭayati*, to unwind, take off, L. °**veshṭana**, n. a weaver's shuttle, L. °**veshṭita**, mfn. denuded, Nir. v, 8.

निर्वै nir-√vai, P.-*vāyati*, to be extinguished, go out (as fire), TS. (cf. *nir-vā*).

निर्वोढृ nir-voḍhṛi, mfn. (*nir-√vah*) accomplishing, performing, Hcar. (also as fut. p. of *nir-√vah*, q.v.)

निर्व्यञ्जक nir-vyañjaka, mfn. (√*añj*) indicating, betraying (with gen.), Mcar. v, 62. 2. °**vyañjana** (only *e*, ind.), explicitly, Pañc. iv, ३३.

निर्व्यध् nir-√vyadh, P. *-vidhyati* (ind. p. *-vidhya*), to pierce through or into, hit, wound, beat, kill, RV.; MBh. &c. °**viddha**, mfn. wounded, killed, R.; separated from each other, isolated, MBh. °**vedha**, m. penetration, insight, Divyâv.; *-bhāgīya*, mfn. relating to it, L. °**vedhima**, mfn. (with *karṇa*) a partic. deformity of the ear, Suśr.

निर्व्युषित nir-vy-ushita, mfn. (*nir-vi-√5. vas*) spent, passed away, MBh.

निर्व्यूढ nir-vy-ūḍha, mfn. (√1. *ūh*) pushed out, expelled from (abl.), MBh.; arrayed in order of battle, BhP.; carried out, finished, completed, Mālatīm.; Kathās.; succeeded, successful, lucky, Bālar.; left, abandoned, Priy. i, 6; n. bringing about, accomplishing (v.l. for *nirvāha*), Bhartṛ. ii, 39. °**vyūḍhi**, f. end, issue, Rājat.; highest point or degree, ib. °**vyūha**, n. (m., Siddh.) a turret, MBh.; Hariv.; a helmet or its ornament, a crest, ib.; a door, gate, Hariv.; a peg to hang things upon, L.; decoction, L. (cf. *niryūha*).

निर्व्रज् nir-√vraj, P. *-vrajati*, to come or proceed out, Kauś.

निर्व्रणित nir-vraṇita, mfn. (√2. *vraṇ*) whose wounds have been healed, Kathās. (cf. *nir-vraṇa*, p. 542, col. 3).

निर्व्रश्च् nir-√vraśc (only ind. p. *-vṛiścya*, ĀpŚr., Sch.), to uproot. °**vraska**, mfn. uprooted, extirpated, KātyŚr.

निर्व्ली nir-√vlī, P. *-vlīnāti*, to tilt, turn over, ĀpŚr. °**vlayanī**, f. the cast-off skin of a snake, L. (cf. *ahi-nirvl*°).

निर्हककविवल्लभ nirhaka-kavivallabha, m. N. of the author of a glossary, Cat.

निर्हन् nir-√han, P. *-hanti*, to strike off, expel, remove, strike or knock out (eye, tooth &c.), hew down, kill, destroy, RV. &c. &c.: Caus. *-ghātayati*, to take out, remove, Suśr.; to kill, destroy, MBh. **Nirghāta** (fr. Caus.), see s.v. **Nirhata**, mfn. struck down (cf. *ulkā-nirh*°).

निर्हा nir-√2. hā (only pr. p. Ā. *nir-jihāna*), to rise out of (abl.), ascend, Rājat.

निर्हाद nir-hāda, m. (√*had*) evacuation, voiding excrement, MBh.; Var.

निर्हृ nir-√hṛi, P. Ā. *-harati*, °*te*, to take out or off, draw or pull out, extract from (abl.), expel, remove, destroy, RV. &c. &c.; to export (goods), Mn.; to carry out (a dead body), ib.; Yājñ.; to let (blood), Suśr.; to purge, ib.; (Ā.) to exclude or deliver from (abl.), TS.; ŚBr.; to shake off, get rid of (acc.), Āpast.; MBh.; Kāv. &c.; to change or interchange (clothes), Mn. viii, 396; to fix, Śulbas.; to get, receive, SaddhP.: Caus. *-hārayati*, to cause (a dead body) to be carried out, Kull. on Mn. v, 104: Desid. *-jihīrshati*, to wish to take off or subtract, Sulbas. (cf. *nir-jihīrshu*). °**haraṇa**, n. taking out, extracting, expelling, removing, destroying, MBh.; Suśr.; Pur.; carrying out (esp. a dead body), MBh.; R. &c. °**haraṇīya** (Kull.), °**hartavya** (Suśr.), mfn. to be taken away or removed. °**hāra**, m. = *haraṇa*, BhP.; setting aside or accumulation of a private store, a hoard, Mn. ix, 199; evacuation or voiding of excrement (opp. to *ā-hāra*), MBh. xiii, 1796; deduction, Śulbas.; completion, L.; diffusive fragrance, W. (cf. *hārin*). °**hāraka**, mfn. carrying out (as a dead body; cf. *prêta-nirh*°); purifying, L. °**hāraṇa**, n. (fr. Caus.) causing (a dead body) to be carried out, Kull. °**hārin**, mfn. diffusively fragrant, MBh. xii, 6848; taking forth or out, W.; having wealth, ib. °**hṛita**, mfn. taken or carried forth or out, extracted, removed &c., MBh.; Suśr.; Rājat.; BhP. °**hṛiti**, f. taking away, removal, Kām. 1. °**hṛitya**, mfn. to be taken or left out, TBr. 2. °**hṛitya**, ind. having taken out or extracted, W.

निर्ह्रस् nir-√hras, Ā.-*hrasate*, to be shortened, become short (as a vowel), RPrāt. °**hrasita**, mfn. shortened, Nir. °**hrasta**, mfn. abridged, diminished, ĀśvŚr. °**hrāsa**, m. shortening, abbreviation, ib.

निर्ह्राद् nir-√hrād, Caus. *-hrādayati*, to cause to sound, beat (a drum), Kāṭh. °**hrāda**, m. sound, noise, humming, murmuring, roaring &c. (ifc. f. *ā*), MBh.; Kāv.; Pur. °**hrādana**, n. sound, cry, Kpr. °**hrādin**, mfn. sounding, humming, roaring, Kāv.; Kathās.

निर्ह्वे nir-√hve, P. *-hvayati*, to call off, TS.; AV.

निल् nil, cl. 6. P. *nilati*, to understand with difficulty; to be impassable or impenetrable, Dhātup. xxviii, 68.

निलङ्गु nilaṅgu, m. a species of worm, TS. (v.l. for *nīl*°).

निलय् nilay, °*yate*, see *nir-√i*. 1. **Nilayana**, n. the act of going out, Pāṇ. vii, 2, 46, Sch. (prob. ident. with 2. *ni-l*° below).

निलय ni-laya &c. See *ni-lī*.

निलिप् ni-√lip, P. Ā. *-limpati*, °*te* (3. pl. aor. Ā. *-alipsata*), to besmear, anoint (Ā. one's self), ŚBr.; to cause to disappear (Ā. to disappear, become invisible), RV.; AV. °**limpá**, m. N. of a class of supernatural beings, TS.; AV.; a troop of Maruts, TĀr.; a god, L.; (*ā*), f. a cow, L.; a milk-pail, Gal.; *-nirjharī*, f. N. of Gaṅgā, L.; *-pāṃsulā*, f. an Apsaras, Vcar. °**limpikā**, f. a cow, L.

निली ni-√lī, Ā. *-līyate* (rarely P., e.g. Pot. *-līyet*), MBh. &c. or *-láyate*, RV.; AV. (cf. *ni-rī*; impf. *-alāyata*, TS.; pf. *-lilye*, 3. pl. °*yire* or °*yur*, Br.; *-layām cakre*, ŚBr.; aor. *-aleshṭa*, Br.; 3. pl. *-aleshata*, Bhaṭṭ.; ind. p. *-lấya*, TBr.; *-līya*, Hariv.; inf. *-letum*, Śiś.); to settle down (esp. applied to the alighting of birds), alight, descend, MBh.; Kāv. &c.; to become settled or fixed, Rājat. iii, 426; to hide one's self, conceal one's self from (abl.), disappear, perish, RV. &c. &c. °**laya**, m. rest, resting-place (cf. *a-nil*°); hiding- or dwelling-place, den, lair, nest; house, residence, abode (often ifc. [f. *ā*] = living in, inhabiting, inhabited by), MBh.; Var.; Kāv. &c.; *-sundara*, m. N. of a man, Cat. 2. °**láyana**, n. settling down, alighting in or on (loc.), Var.; Suśr.; hiding-place &c. = prec., TBr.; MBh. &c. °**lấya**, m. place of refuge, AV. iv, 16, 2. °**lāyana**, n. hiding one's self; *-krīḍā*, f. playing at hide and seek, BhP. °**lāyin**, mfn. descending or alighting in, inhabiting (comp.), Śiś.; °*lāyi-tā*, f., ib. °**līna** (*ní-*), mfn. clinging to, sitting on, hidden in (loc. or comp.), AV.; Var.; Kāv. &c.; quite intent upon or devoted to (loc.), Bhartṛ. (v.l. *vil*°); resorted to, sought for shelter by (instr.), R.; fused into, involved, encompassed, wrapt up, W.; destroyed, perished, ib.; transformed, changed, ib. °**līnaka**, mfn. shrunk up (while being cooked, as milk), Pat. (cf. g. *ṛishyādi*); m. or n. (?) N. of a village in the north country (cf. *nailīnaka*). °**liyamāna**, mfn. hiding, lying concealed in (loc.), BhP.

निलुप् ni-√lup (only ind. p. *-lopam*, robbing), prob. w.r. for *nir-lup*, L.

निव niva, g. *brāhmaṇâdi*, Kāś.

निवक्षस् ní-vakshas, mfn. having a sunken breast (said of the sacrificial victim), TS.

निवच् ni-√vac (only aor. *-avocat*), to speak, say, BhP.; = Caus., MBh.: Caus. *-vācayati*, to abuse, revile, L. °**vácana**, n. expression, address, RV.; proverbial expression, ib.; ŚBr.; °*ne-√kṛi* (ind. p. *-kṛitvā* or *-kṛitya*), to obstruct the speech, cease to speak, Pāṇ. i, 4, 76, Kāś.

निवत् ni-vát, f. depth, any deep place or valley (opp. to *ud-vát*, q.v.), RV.; AV.; TS.; TBr.; (°*tā*), ind. downhill, downwards, RV.; AV.

निवद् ni-√vad, Caus. Ā.-*vādayate*, to make resound (as a drum &c.), MBh.

निवध् *ni-√vadh* (aor. *-avadhīt*), to strike down, kill, MBh.; R. &c.; to fix in, hurl down upon (loc.), RV. iv, 41, 4.

निवना *ni-vanā́*, ind. downwards, downhill, RV. (cf. *ni-vatā*).

निवप् *ni-√2. vap*, P. *-vapati* (fut. *-vapsyati*; ind. p. *ny-upya*; Pass. *ny-upyate*), to throw down, overthrow, RV.; VS.; to fill up (a sacrificial mound), Br.; GṛŚrS.; to throw down, scatter, sow, offer (esp. to deceased progenitors), ib.; Mn.; MBh.; Kāv. &c. °**vapana**, n. scattering or throwing down, pouring out, KātyŚr.; an offering to deceased progenitors, MBh. xiii, 4373; Śak. vi, 24 (cf. *nir-vapaṇa*). °**vapta**, mfn. = *ny-upta*, R. °**vāpa**, m. seed (pl. grains of corn) or a sown field, MBh.; an oblation or offering (esp. to deceased relatives or at the Śrāddha), ib.; Kāv. &c.; throwing down, killing, slaughter, Gal.; *-datti*, f. sacrificial gift, Ragh.; *-mālya*, n. funeral wreath (°*lya-tā*, f.), ib.; °*pāñjali*, m. two handfuls of water as a libation to deceased ancestors, ib.; Mudr.; (°*li-dāna*, n., Rājat.); °*pânna*, n. sacrificial food, MBh.; °*pôdaka*, n. a libation of water offered to deceased progenitors, Mṛicch. x, 17 (read °*ka-bhojana*). °**vāpaka**, m. a sower, R. °**vāpin**, mfn. throwing, scattering &c., g. *grahâdi*. **Ny-ùpta**, mfn. thrown down, cast (dice), scattered, sown, offered, RV. &c. &c.

निवर *ni-vara* &c. See *ni-vṛi*.

निवर्त *ni-varta* &c. See *ni-vṛit*.

निवर्हण *ni-varhaṇa*. See *ni-barhaṇa*.

निवस् *ni-√4. vas*, Ā. *-vaste*, to put on over another garment, KātyŚr.; to gird round (as a sword), MBh., R. (ind. p. *-vasya*); to clothe or dress one's self (aor. *-avasishṭa*, Impv. *-vaddhvam*), Bhaṭṭ.; to change one's clothes, MW.: Caus. *-vāsayati*, to put on (a garment), dress, clothe, MBh.; R. °**vasana**, n. putting on (a garment), R.; cloth, garment (cf. *kaṭī-niv*°), Var.; Kāv. &c.; an under garment, L. °**vasita**, mfn. clothed in (instr.), R. **vāsa**, m. clothing, dress (ifc. = prec.), Hariv. °**vāsana**, n. (fr. Caus.) a kind of raiment, Buddh. °**vāsin**, mfn. dressed in, wearing (ifc.), MBh.; Kāv.

निवस् *ni-√5. vas*, P. *-vasati* (rarely °*te*; fut. *-vatsyati*), to sojourn, pass or spend time, dwell or live or be in (loc.), Mn.; MBh. &c.; to keep one's ground, withstand (*-vāsate* for *-vas*°?), RV. x, 37, 3; to inhabit (acc.), MBh.; BhP.; to incur or undergo (acc.), MBh.; to cohabit, approach sexually (*Rohiṇīm*), MBh. ix, 2023: Caus. *-vāsayati* (pf. °*sayām āsa*), to cause to stay, receive as a guest, BhP.; to make inhabited, populate, MBh.; to choose as a dwelling-place, inhabit, R.; to put or place upon (loc.), BhP. °**vasati**, f. habitation, abode, L. °**vasatha**, m. a village, L. °**vasana**, n. dwelling, habitation, L. °**vasita**, mfn. dwelled, lived (n. impers.), L. °**vastavya**, mfn. to be lived (n. impers.), MBh.; to be spent, ib. °**vāsa**, m. living, dwelling, residing, passing the night; dwelling-place, abode, house, habitation, night-quarters, MBh.; R. &c.; *-bhavana*, n. sleeping-room, Kathās.; *-bhūmi*, f. place of residence, ŚārṅgP.; *-bhūya*, n. habitation or inhabiting, W.; *-racanā*, f. an edifice, Mṛicch. iii, 23; *-rājan*, m. the king of the country in which one dwells, Yājñ. iii, 25; *-vṛiksha*, m. 'dwelling tree,' a tree on which a bird has its nest, Vikr. v, ½. °**vāsana**, n. (fr. Caus.) living, residing, sojourn, abode, Cāṇ.; R.; passing or spending time, R. °**vāsin**, mfn. dwelling or living or being or sticking in (comp.); m. an inhabitant, Mn.; MBh.; Kāv. &c.

निवह् *ni-√vah*, P. Ā. *-vahati*, °*te*, to lead down, lead or bring to (dat. or loc.), RV.; ŚBr.; to flow, MBh. xii, 10318; to carry, support (see below): Caus. *-vāhayati* (Pass. *vāhyate*), to set in motion, Hariv. °**vaha**, mf(*ā*)n. bringing, causing, BhP. (cf. *duḥkha-*, *puṇya-*); m. multitude, quantity, heap (also pl.), Var.; Kāv. &c.; killing, slaughter, Gal.; N. of one of the 7 winds and of one of the 7 tongues of fire (?), L. °**vāhá**, m. leading down (opp. *abhy-ava-roha*), ŚBr.

निवाकु *nivāku*, m. N. of a man, g. *bāhv-ādi*.

निवाच् *ni-vāc*, mfn. = *nihita-vāc*, Pāṇ. vi, 2, 192, Kāś.

निवात 1. *ni-vātá*, mf(*ā*)n. (√2. *vā*) sheltered from the wind, calm, MBh.; Kāv. &c.; n. a place sheltered from the w°, absence of w°, calm, stillness, ŚBr.; ŚrGṛS.; MBh. &c. (often ifc. after the word expressing the sheltering object, Pāṇ. vi, 2, 8).

निवात 2. *ni-vātá*, mfn. (√*van*; cf. 3. *á-vāta*) unhurt, uninjured, safe, secure (n. security), VS.; AV.; ŚBr. &c.; dense, compact, L.; m. asylum, refuge, L.; an impenetrable coat of mail, ib.; *-kavaca*, m. one whose armour is imp°, N. of the grandson of Hiraṇya-kaśipu; pl. of a class of Dānavas or Daityas, MBh.; R.; Pur. °**vānyà** or °**vānyà-vatsā**, f. a cow that suckles an adopted calf, ŚBr. (= *abhi-v*°); °*nyā-vatsa*, m. a calf so suckled, KātyŚr.

निवाप *ni-vāpa* &c. See *ni-vap*.

निवार *ni-vāra* &c. See *ni-vṛi*.

निवावरी *nivāvarī*, f. (with *sikatā*), pl. N. of a Ṛishi-gaṇa, Anukr. on RV. ix, 86, 11–20.

निवाश *ni-vāśá*, mfn. (√*vāś*) roaring, thundering, AV.

निविड *ni-viḍa* &c. See *ni-biḍa*.

निविद् *ni-√1. vid* (aor. *-avedishur*, BhP.; inf. *-veditum*, with v.l. °*dayitum*, Śak.), to tell, communicate, proclaim, report, relate: Caus. *-vedayati*, °*te* (pf. *-vedayām āsa*, ind. p. °*dayitvā* or °*dya*), id. (with dat., gen. or loc.), Mn.; MBh.; Kāv. &c.; to offer, present, give, deliver, Br.; GṛS. &c.; (with *ātmānam*) to offer or present one's self (as a slave &c.), ŚBr.; Mn. &c.; to proclaim i.e. introduce one's self, R.; Śak.; Kathās.; (with *dosham*) to throw the blame upon (dat.), Pañc. (B.) iii, 163. °**vid**, f. instruction, information, RV. (cf. Naigh. i, 11); N. of partic. sentences or short formularies inserted in a liturgy and containing epithets or short invocations of the gods, AV.; VS.; Br.; ŚrS. &c.; *-chaṃśam* (°*vic-ch*° for °*vid-ś*°), ind. reciting in the manner of the Nivids, ŚāṅkhŚr.; *-adhyāya*, m. N. of wk.; *-dhā́na*, mfn. containing the N°s, Br.; n. inserting the N°s, Sāy.; *-dhānīya*, mfn. = *-dhāna*, mfn., ŚrS. °**vedaka**, mf(*ikā*)n. (fr. Caus.) communicating, relating, MBh. °**vedana**, mfn. announcing, proclaiming, Hariv.; m. N. of Śiva, MBh.; n. making known, publishing, announcement, communication, information (*ātma-niv*°, presentation or introduction of one's self), MBh.; R. &c.; delivering, entrusting, offering, dedicating, MBh.; Rājat.; BhP.; (in dram.) the reminding a person of a neglected duty, Sāh. °**vedayishu**, mfn. (fr. Desid. of Caus.) wishing to report or to relate about (acc.), MBh. (B. *vived*°). °**vedita**, mfn. made known, announced, told, represented, entrusted, presented, given, MBh.; R.; Kathās. &c. °**vedin**, mfn. knowing, aware of (comp.), Mālatim.; communicating, reporting, MBh.; R.; offering, presenting, BhP. °**vedya**, mfn. to be communicated or related or presented or delivered, MBh.; Rājat.; Hcat.; n. an offering of food for an idol (for *naivedya*), Rājat.

निविद्ध *ni-viddha*. See *ni-vyadh*.

निविरीस *nivirīsa*. See *nibirīsa* under *ni-biḍa*.

निविवृत्सत् *ni-vivṛitsat*, °*tsu*. See *ni-vṛit*.

निविश् *ni-√viś*, Ā. *-viśate* (rarely P. °*ti*; cf. Pāṇ. i, 3, 17; aor. *-aviśran*, *-avikshata*, RV.; pf. *-viviśre*, ib.), to enter or penetrate into (acc. or loc.); to alight, descend; to come to rest, settle down or in a home, RV. &c. &c.; to encamp, Mn.; MBh.; to sit down upon (loc.), Śiś.; Pañc.; to resort to (acc.), BhP.; to settle, take a wife, MBh.; to be founded (said of a town), ib.; to be fixed or intent on (loc., said of the mind), Mn.; MBh.; Kāv.; to sink down, cease, disappear, vanish, RV.: Caus. *-veśayati*, to bring to rest, RV.; TBr.; to cause to enter, introduce; to cause to sit or lie or settle down on (loc.), MBh.; Hariv. &c.; to cause (a man) to marry, Śak.; to draw up or encamp (an army), MBh.; Kāv.; to build, erect, found, populate (a house, temple, town &c.), Mn.; MBh.; R.; Var. &c.; to lead or bring or put or transfer, to bestow on (loc.), R.; Rājat.; BhP.; to throw or hurl upon, shoot at (loc.), MBh.; R.; to fix in, fasten to (loc.), put on (clothes), appoint to (an office), turn or direct towards (mind, eye &c.), MBh.; Kāv. &c.; to inscribe (*paṭṭe*), MārkP.; to write down (*nāma sva-haste*), Yājñ.; to paint (*citre*), Śak.; to call to mind, impress (*manasi*, *hṛidaye* &c.), Var.; Kāv.; Pur.: Desid. *-vivikshate*, Pāṇ. i, 3, 62, Kāś. °**vishṭa** (*ni-*), mfn. settled down, come to rest, VS.; AV.; drawn up, encamped (army), MBh.; Kāv.; placed, located, appointed (guardians), R.; entered, penetrated into (also with *antar*), lying or resting or sticking or staying in (loc. or comp.), RV. &c. &c.; seated or sitting upon or in (loc. or comp.), Kāv.; Rājat.; Pañc. (Ragh. xii, 68, v. l. *nirv*°); situated (town), Hariv.; R.; married (*a-niv*°), MBh. i, 7241 (cf. *nir-vishṭa* under *nir-viś*); turned to, intent upon (loc. or comp.), Mn.; MBh. &c.; begun, AitBr.; founded (as a town, tank &c.), Mn.; Hariv.; occupied, settled, cultivated (country), Mn.; R.; Ragh.; endowed with (instr.), R.; *-cakra*, mf(*ā*)n. one who has entered anybody's domain, ĀśvGṛ. °**vishṭi**, f. coming to rest, PārGṛ. °**veśá**, m. (the initial *n* not subject to cerebralisation, g. *kshubhnâdi*) entering, settling in a place, encamping, halting, MBh.; Kāv. &c.; a dwelling-place, habitation of any kind (as a house, camp, palace &c.), RV. ix, 69, 7; MBh.; Kāv. &c. (°*śam* √*kṛi*, to take up one's residence, settle, encamp); founding a household, matrimony, Āpast.; Gaut.; MBh.; founding a town, R.; (with *sthāne*) putting in order, arrangement, Vcar.; pressing against, Mālatim. vii, ½; impression, mark (of fingers), Śak. (Pi.) vi, 14; depositing, delivering, L.; military array, L.; ornament, decoration, L.; *-deśa*, m. a dwelling-place, L.; *-vat*, mfn. lying in or on, resting on (ifc.), Kum. °**véśana**, mf(*ī*)n. entering (ifc.), Hariv.; (fr. Caus.) bringing to rest, providing with a resting-place, RV.; TS.; AV.; m. N. of a Vṛishṇi, Hariv.; n. (ifc. f. *ā*) entering, entrance into (comp.), RV.; Kauś.; going or bringing to rest, ib.; MBh.; Hariv. (°*naṃ* √*kṛi*, to settle, encamp; [*sainya-*] encampment of an army); putting down (the feet), Śatr.; introducing, employing, Sāh.; fixing, impressing, Sarvad.; cultivating, populating (of a land, a desert &c.), R.; Kām.; founding a household, marrying, marriage, BhP.; hiding or dwelling-place of any kind, nest, lair, camp, house, home, RV. &c. &c.; town, R. °**veśanīya**, mfn. to be entered or fixed or raised, Kāv.; Hcat.; to be engaged in, W. °**veśayitavya**, mfn. to be put or placed, Śaṃk. °**veśita**, mfn. made to enter, placed in or upon, turned to, fixed or intent upon, engaged in &c., MBh.; Kāv. &c. °**veśin**, mfn. resting in, lying in or on or near, Kāv.; Śaṃk.; based upon, KātyŚr., Sch. °**veśya**, mfn. to be founded (as a town), Hariv.; to be married (as a man), MBh.; w.r. for *nirv*° (see *nir-viś*). °**veshṭavya**, mfn. to be put into (loc.), MBh. v, 1026 (B.); n. impers. (it is) to be married, one should marry, MBh. xiii, 5090.

निवी *ni-√vī* (Intens. *-veveti*), to force a way into, rush among (loc.), RV.

निवीत *ni-vīta*, °*tin*. See *ni-vye*.

निवीर्य *ni-vīrya*, mf(*ā*)n. impotent, Kathās. (cf. *nir-v*° under *nir*).

निवृ *ni-√1. vṛi* (only pf. *-vavāra*, 3. pl. *-vavrur*), to ward off, restrain, R.; Bhaṭṭ.; to surround, Bhaṭṭ.: Caus. *-vārayati*, °*te* (inf. *-vāritum*; ind. p. *-vārya*; Pass. *-vāryate*), id., MBh.; Kāv. &c.; to hold back from (abl., rarely acc.), prohibit, hinder, stop, prevent, withhold, suppress, forbid, ib.; to put off, remove, destroy, Kathās.; BhP.; to exclude or banish from (abl.), Mn.; Rājat. °**vará**, m. covering, protection or a protector, RV. viii, 93, 15 (Sāy. 'a preventer, obstructer'); (*ā*), f. a virgin, unmarried girl, Pāṇ. iii, 3, 48, Sch. (fr. *ni* + *vara*, 'having no husband,' W.) °**varaṇa**, n. hindrance, disturbance, trouble, SaddhP. (cf. *sarva-niv*°*-vishkambhin*). °**vāra**, m. keeping off, hindering, impediment (cf. *dur-niv*°); (*ā*), f. N. of a river, MBh.; VP. (v. l. *niv*°). °**vāraka**, mfn. keeping off, defending (ifc.), Daś.; Rājat.; m. a defender, MBh. °**vāraṇa**, mfn. = prec. mfn., MBh.; Hariv.; Suśr.; n. keeping back, preventing, hindering, opposing, refuting, ib.; Pañc.; BhP. °**vāraṇīya**, mfn. to be kept off or defended or prevented &c., Yājñ., Sch. °**vārita**, mfn. kept off, hindered, forbidden, prevented, MBh.; Kāv. &c. °**vārin**, mfn. warding off, holding back, HYog. °**vārya**, mfn. = °*vāraṇīya*, MBh.; R. °**vṛita** (*ni-*), mfn. held back, withheld, RV.; surrounded, enclosed, L.; m. or f. or n. (= *ni-vīta*) a veil, mantle, wrapper, L.; n. = next, L. °**vṛiti**, f. covering, enclosing, L.

निवृज् *ni-√vṛij*, P. *-vṛiṇakti* (Impv. *-vṛindhi;* 2. 3. sg. impf. *-avṛiṇak*), to throw down, cause to fall, RV.

निवृत् *ni-√vṛit*, Ā. *-vartate* (ind. p. *-vṛitya*, AV.; infin. *-vartitum*, MBh.; rarely P., e.g. Pot. *-vartet*, MBh.; Hariv.; impf. or subj. *-vartat*, RV.; pf. *-vāvṛitur*, ib.; fut. *-vartishyati*, MBh.; *-vartsyan*, Bhaṭṭ.; aor. *-avṛitat*, ib.), to turn back, stop (trans. and intrans.), RV. &c.; to return from (abl.) to (acc. with or without *prati* or dat.); to return into life, revive, be born again, MBh.; Kāv. &c.; to turn away, retreat, flee, escape, abstain or desist from, get rid of (abl.), ib.; to fall back, rebound, R.; to leave off (*sāmi*, in the midst or when anything is half finished, ŚBr.), cease, end, disappear, vanish, TS.; ŚBr.; Up. &c.; to be withheld from, not belong to (abl.); to be omitted, not to occur, Lāṭy.; Mn.; MBh.; to be ineffective or useless, MBh.; Kathās.; to be wanting, not to exist (*yato vāco nivartante*, for which there are no words), TUp.; to pass over to (loc.), MBh.; to be turned upon (loc. or *tatra*), ib.: Caus. *-vartayati*, °*te* (Ā. Pot. *-vartayīta*, ĀśvŚr.; Pass. *-vartyate*, Ragh.), to turn downwards, let sink (the head), TBr.; to turn back i.e. shorten (the hair), Br.; to lead or bring back, reconduct, return, AV. &c. &c.; to turn away, avert or keep back from (abl.), MBh.; Kāv. &c.; to give up, abandon, suppress, withhold, refuse, deny; to annul, remove, destroy, Mn.; MBh.; Kāv.; Pur.; to bring to an end i.e. perform, accomplish (a sacrifice &c.), R.; BhP.; to procure, bestow, Hariv.; MārkP.; to desist from (abl.), MBh.; R. °**varta**, mfn. causing to turn back, RV. °**vartaka**, mf(*ikā*)n. turning back, flying (*a-niv*°), Hariv.; causing to cease, abolishing, removing, MBh.; Saṃk. (*-tva*, n.); desisting from, stopping, ceasing, MW. °**vártana**, mfn. causing to turn back, RV.; n. turning back, returning, turning the back i.e. retreating, fleeing, AV.; MBh. &c. (*mṛityum kṛitvā nivartanam*, making retreat equivalent to death i.e. desisting from fighting only in death, MBh. vi, vii; w.r. *kṛitvā mṛityu-niv*°); ceasing, not happening or occurring, being prevented, MBh.; Hariv. &c.; desisting or abstaining from (abl.), MBh.; BhP.; desisting from work, inactivity (opp. to *pra-vartana*), Kām.; causing to return, bringing back (esp. the shooting off and bringing back of weapons), MBh.; Kāv.; turning back (the hair), KātyŚr.; a means of returning, RV.; AV.; averting or keeping back from (abl.), Vedântas.; reforming, repenting, W.; a measure of land (20 rods or 200 cubits or 40,000 Hastas square), Hcat.; *-stūpa*, m. N. of a Stūpa erected at the spot where the charioteer of Buddha returned. °**vartanīya**, mfn. to be brought back, Mālav. v, 1/2 (w.r. *nir-v*°); to be prevented or hindered, MBh. °**vartayitavya**, mfn. to be kept back or detained, R. °**vartita**, mfn. turned or brought back, averted, prevented, given up, abandoned, suppressed, removed, MBh.; Kāv.; Pur.; *-pūrva*, mfn. one who has turned away before, MW.; °*tâkhilâhāra*, mfn. one who has abstained from all food, BhP. °**vartitavya**, mfn. to be brought back, MBh. °**vartin**, mfn. turning back, retreating, fleeing (mostly *a-niv*°, q.v.); abstaining from (comp.), MBh.; allowing or causing to return (*a-niv*°), Hariv.; w.r. for *nir-v*°, q.v. °**vartya**, mfn. to be turned back (see *dur-niv*°); annulled, declared to be invalid, Pat. °**vivṛitsat** (W.), °**vivṛitsu** (Saṃk.), mfn. (fr. Desid.) desirous of returning or desisting. °**vṛit**, w.r. for *ni-cṛit*. °**vṛitta**, mfn. (often w.r. for *nir-vṛitta*, *vi-vṛitta*, *ni-vṛita*) turned back, returned to (acc.), MBh.; rebounded from (abl.), R.; retreated, fled (in battle), MBh.; set (as the sun), R.; averted from, indifferent to, having renounced or given up (abl. or comp.), MBh.; Kāv. &c.; abstracted from this world, quiet, BhP.; Hcat.; rid or deprived of (abl.), MBh.; R.; passed away, gone, ceased, disappeared, vanished, ib.; (with *karman*, n. an action) causing a cessation (of mundane existence), Mn. xii, 88 (opp. to *pravṛitta*); ceased to be valid or binding (as a rule), Pat.; Kāś.; omitted, left out (cf. comp. below); finished, completed, W.; desisting from or repenting of any improper conduct, ib.; n. return (see *durniv*°); *-kāraṇa*, mfn. without further cause or motive; m. a virtuous man, one uninfluenced by worldly desires, W.; *-kṛishi-gorakshа*, mfn. ceasing from agriculture and the tending of cattle, MBh.; *-dakshiṇá*, f. a gift renounced or despised by another, ŚBr.; *-deva-kārya*, mfn. ceasing from sacrificial rites, MW.; *-māṇsa*, mfn. one who abstains from eating meat, Uttarar.; *-yajña-svâdhyāya*, mfn. ceasing from sacrifices and the repetition of prayers, MBh.; *-yauvana*, mfn. whose youth has returned, restored to y°, Ragh.; *-rāga*, mfn. of subdued appetites or passions, W.; *-laulya*, mfn. whose desire is averted from, not desirous of (comp.), Ragh.; *-vṛitti*, mfn. ceasing from any practice or occupation, W.; *-śatru*, m. 'having one's foes kept off,' N. of a king, Hariv.; *-saṃtāpa*, mfn. one whose heat or pain has ceased, Suśr.; *-hṛidaya*, mfn. with relenting heart, MBh.; one whose heart is averted from or indifferent to (*prati*), Mālav. ii, 14; °*ttâtman*, m. 'one whose spirit is abstracted,' a sage, W.; N. of Vishṇu, ib.; °*ttêndriya*, mfn. one whose senses or desires are averted from (comp.), Ragh. °**vṛitti**, f. (often w.r. for *nir-v*°) returning, return, MBh.; Ragh.; ceasing, cessation, disappearance, ŚrS.; Up.; MBh. &c.; leaving off, abstaining or desisting from (abl.), Mn.; MBh.; Bhartṛ. &c.; escaping from (abl.), Pañc. ii, 87 (w.r. °*ttaḥ*); ceasing from worldly acts, inactivity, rest, repose (opp. to *pra-vṛitti*), Bhag.; Prab.; (in dram.) citation of an example, Sāh.; suspension, ceasing to be valid (as of a rule), Pāṇ., Sch.; destruction, perdition, RāmatUp.; denial, refusal, W.; abolition, prevention, ib.

निवृह् *ni-vṛih*. See *ni-bṛih*.

निवेदक *ni-vedaka*, °*dana* &c. See 1. *ni-vid*.

निवेश *ni-veśa*, °*śana* &c. See *ni-viś*.

निवेष्ट् *ni-√vesht*, Caus. *-veshṭayati*, °*te*, to grasp (also with *haste*), cover, AV.; TS.; Kāṭh.; Br.; to wind round, R. °**veshṭa**, m. a cover, envelope; du. (with *Vasishṭhasya*) N. of Sāmans, ĀrshBr. °**veshṭana**, n. covering, wrapping, clothing, Kauś. °**veshṭita**, mfn. wound round, girt by (instr. or in comp.), Var.; R.

निवेषी *ni-veshī*, f. (√*vish*) prob. a kind of cake ('kind of bone' B.), Kauś.; (pl., AV. ix, 7, 4?). °**veshyá**, m. a whirlpool, a water-spout, ŚBr.; a whirlwind or any similar phenomenon, VS.; hoarfrost, Mahīdh.; (°*shyà*), mfn. whirling, belonging to a whirlpool or eddy, VS.; KātyŚr.

निव्यध् *ni-√vyadh*, P. *-vidhyati* (ep. also °*te*), to throw down, break or push in, RV.; AV.; ŚBr.; to pierce through, shoot at, hit, wound, RV.; MBh. °**viddha** (*ní-*), mfn. pierced, wounded, thrown down, RV. °**vyādha**, m. opening, aperture (esp. of a window), ŚāṅkhŚr. °**vyādhin**, mfn. piercing, opening, VS.

निव्यूढ *ni-vyūḍha*, n. (√1. *ūh*) perseverance, resolution (cf. *nir-v*°).

निव्ये *ni-√vye* (ind. p. *-vīya*), to put on (round the neck), BhP. °**vīta**, mfn. hung or adorned with (instr.), ib.; having the Brāhmanical thread round the neck, ShaḍvBr.; Lāṭy.; n. wearing the Br°th° like a necklace round the neck; the th° so worn, TS.; KātyŚr.; mf(*ā* or *ī*?)n. a veil, mantle, wrapper (cf. *ni-vṛita*). °**vītin**, mfn. wearing the th° round the neck in worshipping the Ṛishis, Mn. ii, 63; RTL. 379; 410.

निव्रश्च् *ni-√vraśc*, P. *-vṛiścati*, to cut down, RV.; TBr.

निश् 1. *niś* for *nis*, in comp. See p. 542, col. 3.

निश् 2. *niś*, cl. 1. P. *neśati*, to meditate upon, be absorbed in meditation, Dhātup. xvii, 73.

निश् 3. *niś*, f. (occurring only in some weak cases as *niśi*, °*śas*, °*śau*, °*śos* [and *niḍbhyas* Pāṇ. vi, 1, 63], for or with *niśā*, and prob. connected with *nak*, *nakta;* cf. also *dyu-*, *mahā-*) night, Mn.; MBh.; Var.; Śak. &c.; *niśi niśi*, every night, Mn. iv, 129.

Niśa, n. (or *am*, ind.) ifc. for *niśā* (cf. *a-*, *ahar-*, *divā-*, *niśā-*, *śva-*, and Pāṇ. ii, 4, 25).

Niśā, f. night, GṛŚrS.; Mn.; MBh. &c.; a vision, dream, MBh.; turmeric, Curcuma (of 2 species, prob. C° Zedoaria and C° Longa), Suśr.; = *-bala*, Jyot. **-kara**, m. (ifc. f. *ā*) 'night-maker,' the moon (with *Divā-kara* among the sons of Garuḍa), MBh.; R. &c.; N. of a Ṛishi, R.; of the numeral 1, Sūryas.; a cock, L.; *-kalā-mauli*, m. 'bearing a crescent as diadem,' N. of Śiva, Kathās. **-kānta**, m. 'the beloved of Night,' N. of the moon, Kathās. **-kāla**, m. time of n°, MW. **-kshaya**, m. close of n°, R. **-°gama** (°*śâg*°), m. the beginning of n°, Kathās.; Pañc. **-gṛiha**, n. sleeping-room, R. **-cara**, mfn. n°-walking, moving about by n°, R.; m. a fiend or Rākshasa, MBh.; Kāv. &c.; a jackal, Suśr.; an owl, L.; Anas Casarca, L.; a snake, L.; a kind of Granthi-parṇa, Bhpr.; N. of Śiva, Śivag. (cf. RTL. 106, n. 1.); (*ī*), f. a female fiend, MBh.; R. &c.; a woman going to meet her lover at night, Ragh. xi, 20 (where also = female fiend); a bat, L.; N. of a plant (= *keśinī*), L.; *-pati*, m. 'lord of n°-walkers,' N. of Śiva, MBh.; *-pūjā-paddhati*, f. N. of wk.; °*rêśa*, m. N. of Rāvaṇa, R. **-carman**, n. 'skin of n°,' darkness, L. **-chada**, m. a species of plant, Suśr. **-jala**, n. 'n°-water,' dew, L. **-°ṭa** (°*śâṭa*), m. 'n°-rover,' an owl, L.; a demon, ghost, W.; *-ka*, m. bdellium, L. (cf. *kauśika*). **-°ṭana** (°*śâṭ*°), m. an owl, L.; N. of an author, Cat.; (*ī*), f. a species of moth, L. **-°tikrama** (°*śât*°), m. the passing away of n°, MW. **-°tyaya** (°*śât*°), m. 'n°-close,' daybreak, L. **-darśin**, m. 'seeing at n°,' an owl, L. **-°di** (°*śâdi*), m. 'beginning of n°,' twilight, L. **-°dhīśa** (°*śâdh*°), **-nātha**, m. 'n°-lord,' the moon, Kāv. **-nārāyaṇa**, m. N. of a poet, Cat. **-niśam**, ind. n° by n° i.e. every n° or day, always, MBh. **-2. -°nta** (°*śânta*), m. or n. 'n°-close,' daybreak, Mn. iv, 99. **-°ndha** (*śândha*), mfn. blind at n°, Var.; (*ā*), f. a species of creeper, L. **-pati**, m. = *-nātha*, Var.; camphor, L. **-putra**, m. pl. 'sons of n°,' N. of a class of demons, Hariv. **-pushpa**, n. 'flower of n°,' the white water-lily, L.; hoar-frost, dew, W. **-prāṇêśvara**, m. = *-nātha*, Bhartṛ. **-bala**, n. a collect. N. of the signs of the zodiac Aries, Taurus, Gemini, Cancer, Sagittarius, Capricornus, Jyot. **-bhaṅgā**, f. a species of plant, L. **-maṇi**, m. 'n°-jewel,' the moon, L. **-miśra**, m. N. of an author, Cat. **-mukha**, n. the face or the beginning of n°, MBh.; Kāv. **-mṛiga**, m. 'n°-deer,' a jackal, L. **-ratna**, m. or n. = *-maṇi*, L. **-°rtha** (°*śârth*°), n. = *-gṛiha*, L. **-°rdha-kāla** (°*śârdh*°), m. first part of the n° (opp. to next), Var. **-vasāna** (°*śâv*°), m. the second part i.e. the end of n°, ib. **-vihāra**, m. 'n°-walker,' a fiend or Rākshasa, Bhaṭṭ. **-vṛinda**, n. a number of n°s, W. **-vedin**, m. 'n°-knower,' a cock, L. **-hasa**, m. 'n°-smiler,' the white water-lily, L. **-°hvā** (°*śâh*°), f. turmeric, L. **Niśêśa**, m. = °*śā-nātha*, L. **Niśôlita**, m. 'shining at n°,' Ardea Nivea, L. **Niśôtsarga**, m. = °*śâtyaya*, L. **Niśôpaśāya**, m. 'resting at n°,' W. **Niśôshita**, mfn. (√5. *vas*) having remained overnight, Bhpr.

1. **Niśi**, loc. of *niś*, in comp. **-pāla**, m. a kind of metre, Col. **-pushpā**, °**pikā** and °**pī**, f. Nyctanthes Arbor Tristis, L.

निशठ *ni-śaṭha*, mfn. not false, honest, BhP.; m. N. of a Vṛishṇi, a son of Bala-rāma by Revatī, MBh.; Hariv.; VP. (v.l. *nishaṭha*, *nisaṭha*, *nisatha*).

निशब्द *ni-śabda*, mfn. speechless, silent, Kir. (cf. *niḥ-ś*).

निशम् *ni-√śam*, P. *-śāmyati*, to be extinguished, Dharmaś.; Divyâv.: Caus. *-śamayati*, to appease, make quiet, AV. vi, 52, 3; 111, 2; to cool down, Sāy. on RV. x, 39, 9; *-śāmayati* (ep. also *-śāmyate;* p. *-śamyamāna* with act. meaning, R. [B.] ii, 66, 10; ind. p. *-śāmya* and *-śamayya* [Śiś. xvi, 38; cf. Vām. v, 2, 76]), to observe, perceive, hear, learn, MBh.; Kāv. &c. °**śamana**, n. perceiving, hearing, L. °**śamaya**, mfn. perceiving i.e. coming into contact with, reaching to (comp.), Prasannar. 2. °**śānta**, mfn. allayed, tranquil, calm, L.; customary, traditional, ĀśvŚr. (cf. *yathā-n*°); n. a house, dwelling, habitation, Kāv.; a harem, seraglio, Dharmaś.; *-nārī*, f. a woman living in the inner apartments, W.; *-vṛiksha*, m. a tree near a house (?), g. *utkarâdi* (v.l. °*ntâvṛ*° and °*nta*, *vṛ*°); °*ntīya*, mfn. ib.; °*ntôdyāna*, n. a garden near a house, Daś. °**śāma**, m. observing, perceiving, Vop. °**śāmana**, n. id., Lāṭy. °**śāmayitavya**, mfn. to be perceived, perceivable, ib., Sch. °**śāmita**, mfn. perceived, heard, learnt, MBh.; Hariv.

निशरण *ni-śaraṇa* &c. See *ni-śṛī*.

निशाण *ni-śāṇa, ni-śāta*. See *ni-śo*.

निशातय *ni-śātaya* (cf. √*śad*), Nom. P. °*yati*, to cut down, MārkP.

निशाद *ni-śāda*, m. a man of low caste, L. (= *ni-shāda*). **-tva**, n. the state or condition of a m° of l° c°, W. °**dā-putra** (?), m. a pestle, L. °**dāśilā**, f. a mortar, L.

निशादन *niśādana*, m. = *niśāvana*, L.

निशायिन् *ni-śāyin* (√2. *śī*), mfn. prob. lying down, sleeping, g. *grahādi*.

निशावन *niśāvana*, m. hemp, L. (cf. *śaṇa*).

निशास् *ni-√śās*, P. -*śāsti* (aor. -*aśishat*), to order off, order to go off, separate from (instr.), AV.; to take anything (acc.) from (abl.), TS.; to adjudge or present to (dat.), RV. iv, 2, 7.

निशि 2. *ni-√śi* (for 1. see p. 560), P. -*śiśāti* (Ā. p. -*śiśāna*), to sharpen, whet; to excite, strengthen; prepare or present (food &c.) for strengthening, RV. (cf. *ni-śo*). °**śita** (*ní-*), mfn. sharpened, sharp (lit. and fig.), KaṭhUp.; MBh. &c.; stimulated, excited, eager for (loc.); strengthened; prepared, presented, RV.; n. iron, steel, L.; -*nipāta*, mfn. sharp-falling (arrow), Śak.; °*tâṅkuśa*, m. or n. a sharp or pointed hook, Bhartṛ. °**śiti** (*ní-*), f. exciting, stimulating, refreshing, RV.

निशिता *niśitā*, f. night, TS. (cf. *niś, a-niśita*, and next).

निशिथ *niśitha*, m. (m.c.) = next; N. of one of the 3 sons of Doshā (night), BhP. (v.l. °*śītha*).

निशीथ *ni-śītha*, m., rarely n. (√*śī*) midnight, night, MBh.; -*dīpa*, m. night-lamp, Ragh.; -*paryāya*, m. N. of wk. °**thikā**, f. = *svâdhyāya*, L. °**thinī**, f. night; -*nātha* (L.) and -*pati* (Vcar.), m. 'husband of n°,' the moon. °**thyā**, f. night, L.

निशुच् *ni-śuc*, P. -*śocati* (impers.), to be burning hot, ChUp.

निशुभ् *ni-√śubh* (or *śumbh*), P. -*śumbhati*, to tread down, Bālar. viii, 53. °**śumbha**, m. killing, slaughter, Mālatīm.; N. of a Dānava (brother of Śumbha), Hariv.; Pur. (also -*ka*, R.); -*mathanī* and -*mardinī*, f. 'destroyer of Ni-śumbha,' N. of Durgā, L. °**śumbhana**, n. killing, Bālar. °**śumbhin**, m. N. of Vajra-ṭika, L.; an inferior deity of the Buddhists, W

निशुष्म *ni-śushma*, mfn. cracking downwards or not cracking (said of fire, opp. to *ucchushma*), TS.

निशृम्भ *ni-śṛimbhá*, mfn. (√*śrambh*) treading or proceeding firmly, RV. vi, 55, 6.

निशॄ *ni-√śṝ* (ind. p. -*sirya*), to break off, VS. °**śărana**, n. killing, slaughter, L. °**śāruka**, m. (in music) a kind of measure.

निशो *ni-√śo*, P. -*śyati* (Ā. p. -*śyāna* or -*śāna*, AitBr.; ŚāṅkhŚr.), to sharpen, whet, Nir. iv, 18 (cf. *ni-śi*). °**śāta**, mfn. sharpened, polished, whetted, sharp, Kāv.; Pur. &c. °**śāna**, n. sharpening, whetting, Dhāt.; Vop.; observing, perceiving, Suśr.; L. (w.r. *niśāṇa*); -*paṭṭa*, m. a whet-stone, Dharmaś.

निशोत्रा *ni-śotrā*, f. (√*śu*?) Ipomoea Turpethum, Bhpr. (cf. *ni-sṛitā*).

निश्चत् *niś-√cat*, Caus. -*cātayate*, to scare or drive away, AV.

निश्चप्रच *niś-ca-pra-ca*, prob. backwards and forwards, g. *mayūra-vyaṅsakâdi* (cf. *ācaparāca* and *ācôpaca*).

निश्चय *niś-caya* &c. See *niś-ci*.

निश्चर् *niś-√car*, P. -*carati* (pf. 3. pl. -*cerur*, inf. -*caritum*), to come forth, go out, issue out, proceed, appear, rise (as sounds), RV. &c. &c.: Caus. -*cārayati*, to cause to issue or come forth, Lalit. °**cara**, m. N. of one of the Saptarshis in the 2nd Manv-antara, Hariv. °**cāraka**, m. (only L.) voiding excrement; air, wind; obstinacy, wilfulness. °**cārayitavya**, mfn. to be issued or made known, Car.

निश्चि *niś-√2. ci*, P. -*cinoti* (Impv. -*cinu*, Hariv.; pf. -*cikāya*, Bhaṭṭ.; aor. Ā. *nir-aceshṭa*, Śiś.; Pass. *nir-acāyi*, ib.; Bhaṭṭ.; ind. p. *niś-citya*, MBh. &c.), to ascertain, investigate, decide, settle, fix upon, determine, resolve, MBh.; Kāv. &c. °**caya**, m. inquiry, ascertainment, fixed opinion, conviction, certainty, positiveness (*iti niścayaḥ*, 'this is a fixed opinion;' °*yaṃ √jñā*, 'to ascertain the certainty about anything;' °*yena* or °*yāt*, ind. certainly), Mn.; MBh.; R. &c.; resolution, resolve, fixed intention, design, purpose, aim (°*yaṃ √kṛi*, to resolve upon, determine to [dat., loc. or inf.]), MBh.; Kāv. &c.; (in rhet.) N. of a partic. figure, Sāh.; -*kṛit*, mfn. giving a certain meaning, Sarasv.; -*datta*, m. N. of a merchant, Kathās.; -*rūpa*, mfn. 'having the form of certainty,' being certain, MW. °**cayin**, mfn. of firm opinion or resolution, HPariś. (cf. *kṛita-niśc°*). °**cāyaka**, mfn. who or what ascertains and determines, determining, decisive (-*tva*, n.), TPrāt., Sch. °**cita**, mfn. one who has come to a conclusion or formed a certain opinion, determined to, resolute upon (dat., loc., *artham* ifc. or comp.), MBh.; Kāv.; Suśr. &c.; ascertained, determined, settled, decided, Up.; MBh. (superl. -*tama*); R. &c.; (*am*), ind. decidedly, positively, Kāv.; Kathās.; Pañc.; n. certainty, decision, resolution, design, R.; (*ā*), f. N. of a river, MBh.; VP.; °*târtha*, mfn. one who has formed a certain opinion about (loc.), judging rightly (compar. -*tara*), R. (B.) °**citi**, f. ascertainment, fixing, settling, L. (cf. *pāṭha-niśc°*). °**citya**, ind. having ascertained or decided, feeling assured or convinced or resolute, MBh.; Kāv. &c. °**cīyamāna**, mfn. being in the course of ascertainment, being under investigation or concluded, W. °**cetavya**, mfn. to be ascertained or established, Nyāyam., Sch. °**ceya**, see *a-niśc°* (add.)

निश्चिर *niścira*, m. N. of a Ṛishi in the 2nd Manv-antara (v.l. for °*cara*); (*ā*), f. N. of a river (v.l. for °*citā*).

निश्चुक्कण *niś-cukkaṇa*, n. (√*cukk*?) a sort of tooth-powder which destroys the tartar but blackens the teeth, L. (also written -*cūkvaṇa* and -*cuṅkaṭa*).

निश्चुत् *ni-√ścut*, Ā. -*ścotate*, to ooze, drop, Mālatīm.: Caus. (ind. p. -*ścotya*) to cause to ooze or drop, Kāśīkh. °**ścutita**, mfn. oozed or dripped from (comp.), Suśr.

निश्चृत् *niś-√cṛit* (ind. p. -*cṛitya*), to loosen, untie, AitBr.

निश्न *niśna*, g. *brāhmaṇâdi* (not in Kāś.)

निश्नथ् *ni-√śnath* (Impv. -*śnathihi*; Caus. aor. -*śiśnathat*), to push or strike down, RV.

निश्मश्रु *niśmaśru*, w.r. for *niḥ-śm°*.

निश्रथ् *ni-√śrath*, only ind. p. -*śrathya*, having fastened or harnessed, Nir. vi, 4.

निश्रम *ni-śrama*, m. (√*śram*) labour bestowed upon anything, continued practice, MBh.

निश्रय *ni-śraya* &c. See *ni-śri*.

निश्राविन् *niśrāvin*, mfn. (√*śru*), g. *grahâdi*.

निश्रि *ni-√śri*, P. -*śrayati* (aor. -*aśret*), to lean on or against, ŚBr.; to lay or cast down, RV. °**śraya**, m. refuge, resource (= *āśraya*), L. (the 4 resources of a Buddhist, see MWB. 80). °**śrayaṇī**, f. a ladder, staircase, ŚBr.; KātyŚr. (also written *niḥ-śrayaṇī* or °*yiṇī*). °**śritya**, ind. going to, Divyâv. °**śreṇī**, f. id., MBh.; Ragh. &c. (also written *ni-śreṇi, niḥ-śreṇī*).

निश्रीक *niśrīka*, w.r. for *niḥ-śr°*.

निश्लिष् *ni-√ślish*, Caus. -*śleshayati*, to fasten, paste on or up, ŚBr. °**ślish**, mfn. clinging, sticking, MantraBr.

निश्वस् *ni-√śvas*, P. -*śvasiti*, ep. also °*sati* (pf. -*śaśvāsa*, aor. or impf. *ny-aśvasat*, MBh.; °*śvasīt*, Daś.; ind. p. -*śvasya*), to draw in the breath, inspire; to hiss, snort &c., MBh.; Kāv. &c. (often v.l. *niḥ-śv°*). °**śvasita** (*ní-*), n. breath, expiration or inspiration, ŚBr.; Śiś. °**śvāsa**, m. id.; a sigh, R.; Sāh.; Suśr. (opp. *uc-chvāsa*).

निष् 1. *nish* for *nis* in comp. See p. 542, col. 3.

निष् 2. *nish*, cl. 1. P. *neshati*, to moisten, sprinkle, Dhātup. xvii, 49.

निषच् *ni-shac* (√*sac*), Ā. -*shacate*, to be closely connected or associated, RV. viii, 25, 11.

निषञ्ज् *ni-shañj* (√*sañj*), only aor. Ā. -*asakta*, to hang or put on, RV.; Pass. -*ashaṅgi*, to hang i.e. be fastened on, ŚBr. °**shakta** (*ní-*), mfn. hung or hanging on, fixed in, fastened to (loc. or comp.), ŚBr.; Kālid.; Var. °**shaṅga**, m. clinging to, attachment, L.; a quiver, MBh.; Kāv. (°*gi-√bhū*, to become a quiver, Daś.); a sword, L.; -*dhi*, m. the sheath of a sword, VS. (Mahīdh.) °**shaṅgathi** (L.), mfn. embracing; m. an embrace; a bowman; a charioteer; a car; the shoulder; grass. °**shaṅgin**, mfn. having a quiver (or sword?), AV. &c. &c.; cleaving, clinging, sticking, attached to, Śiś. v, 39; xii, 26; m. a bowman, warrior, L.; N. of a son of Dhṛitarāshṭra, MBh. °**shañja**, see *ku-nish°*.

निषठ *nishaṭha*, w.r. for *ni-śaṭha*.

निषद् *ni-shad* (√*sad*), P. -*shīdati*, Ved. also -*shadati* (impf. *ny-ashīdat* or *ny-asīdat*; Ved. also -*asadat*; pf. P. -*shasāda*, -*shedur*, Ā. -*shedire*, RV. &c. &c.; aor. P. -*shatsi*, -*shatsat*; Pass. *ny-asādi*, RV.; ind. p. -*shadya*, ib.; Ved. inf. -*shāde*, ib.; for *s* and *sh* cf. Pāṇ. viii, 3, 66 &c.), to sit or lie down or rest upon (loc.), RV. &c. &c.; to sink or go down (as a ship), Hariv.; to be afflicted, suffer pain, MW.; to perform or celebrate by sitting (*sattram*), Br.; (P. Ā.) to set, found, establish, appoint, RV.: Caus. -*shādayati*, °*te*, to cause to sit down, set down, appoint, RV. °**shaṇṇá**, mfn. sitting, seated, sitting or lying or resting or leaning upon (loc. or comp.), ŚBr.; Hariv.; R. &c.; performed by sitting (as a Sattra), TS.; sat upon (as a seat), R.; sunk down, afflicted, distressed, MW. °**shaṇṇaka**, mfn. sitting, seated, W.; n. a seat, L.; a kind of pot-herb, L. °**shattá** (or *ní-sh°*), mfn. sitting, seated, RV. °**shatti** (*ní-*), f. sitting, resting, RV. iv, 21, 9. °**shatsnú**, mfn. sitting fast, ib. x, 162, 3. °**shád**, mfn. sitting inactive, ŚāṅkhŚr.; sitting (esp. near the altar at a sacrificial rite), RV.; ŚBr.; N. of a kind of literary composition, MBh. xii, 1613. °**shada**, m. a musical note (= *ni-shāda*), L.; w.r. for *nishadha*. °**shádana**, n. sitting down, dwelling, residing, RV. &c. (cf. *ushṭra-nish°*, *krauñca-nish°*). °**shadyā**, f. a small bed or couch, L.; the hall of a merchant, L.; a market-place, Śiś. xviii, 15. °**shadvará**, mfn. sitting (near the altar), VS.; sitting lazily, AitBr.; ŚāṅkhŚr.; m. mud, mire (in which one sinks), L.; the god of love, L.; (*ā* or *ī*), f. night, L. °**shādá**, m. N. of a wild non-Āryan tribe in India (described as hunters, fishermen, robbers &c.), VS.; Br.; MBh. &c.; = *bhilla*, 'the Bheels,' Kathās.; Mahīdh.; a man of any degraded tribe, an out-caste (esp. the son of a Brāhman by a Śūdra woman), Mn. x, 8; the progenitor of the N°s (said to have sprung from the thigh of Vena), MBh.; Hariv.; (in music) N. of the first (more properly the last or 7th) note of the gamut, MBh. xiv, 1419; N. of a Kalpa, VāyuP.; (*ī*), f. N. of a female of the N° tribe (-*tva*, n.), MBh.; Kathās.; -*karshu* (or *ū*?), N. of a region, Pāṇ. iv, 2, 119, Sch.; -*grāma*, m. a village of the N°, Lāṭy.; KātyŚr.; -*tva*, n. state or condition of a N°, R.; -*rāshṭra*, n. the country of the N°s (to the south-east of Madhya-deśa), Var.; -*vat*, m. = *nishāda* (in music), MBh. xii, 6859; -*saṅgha*, m. multitude or tribe of the N°s, Var.; -*sthapati*, m. chief of the N°s; -*strī*, f. a N° woman, Mn. x, 39. °**shādita**, mfn. (fr. Caus.) made to sit or kneel down, Mālatīm.; °*tin*, mfn. = *nishāditam anena*, g. *ishṭâdi*. °**shādin**, mfn. sitting down, sitting or lying or resting on or in, Ragh.; Kathās.; m. an elephant-keeper or driver, Śiś. v, 41 (cf. °*shādita*); N. of Eka-lavya, VP.

निषध *nishadha*, m. N. of a mountain or chain of mountains (described as lying immediately south of Ilāvṛita and north of the Himālaya), MBh.; Pur.; m. (pl.) N. of a people and their country governed by Nala, ib.; the sovereign of the Nishadhas (N. of a son of Janam-ejaya; of Kuśa the father of Nala; of a grandson of Kuśa &c.), ib.; a partic. position of the closed hand, Cat.; a bull, L.; (in music) a partic. note (cf. *ni-shāda*); (*ā*), f. N. of Nala's capital, L.; of a river, VP.; mfn. hard, W. **-vaṅśa**, m. the race of Nishadha, MBh. **Nishadhâdhipa** or °**dhipati** or °**dhêndra** or

°**dhêśvara**, m. 'lord of N°,' N. of Nala, MBh. &c. **Nishadhâśva**, m. N. of a son of Kuru, BhP. **Nishadhêndra-kâvya**, n. 'the poem of the prince of N°,' N. of a poem.

निषमम् *ni-shamam*, ind. (fr. *ni+sama*), Pāṇ. vi, 2, 121, Sch.

निषय *ni-shaya*, m. (√*si*), Kāś. on Pāṇ. viii, 3, 70.

निषर्ग *ni-sharga*, w.r. for *ni-sarga*.

निषह् *ni-shah* (√*sah*), Ā. *-shahate* (impf. *ny-ashahata* and *ny-asahata*, fut. *ni-soḍhā*), Pāṇ. viii, 3, 70; 71; 115, Sch. (cf. *nī-shah*).

निषाद *ni-shāda* &c. See *ni-shad*.

निषिच् *ni-shic* (√*sic*), P. *-shiñcati* (impf. *ny-ashiñcat*, pf. *ni-shisheca*; cf. Pāṇ. viii, 3, 65), to sprinkle down, pour upon or into, infuse, instil, irrigate, RV. &c. &c.; to dip into, Bhpr.: Caus. *-shecayati*, to irrigate, wet, moisten, R.; Suśr.: Intens. *-sesicyate*, Pāṇ. viii, 3, 112, Sch. °**shikta** (*ní-*), mfn. sprinkled, infused, irrigated, RV. &c. &c.; *-pā́*, mfn. protecting the infused (semen), RV. vii, 36, 9. °**sheka**, m. sprinkling, infusion, aspersion, dripping, distilling, Kāv.; seminal infusion, impregnation and the ceremony connected with it, Mn.; Var.; Suśr.; water for washing, dirty water, wash (impurities caused by seminal effusion?), Mn. iv, 151; *-prakāra* and *-vicāra*, m., *-svarā*, f. N. of wks. °**shektavya**, mfn. to be poured upon (loc.), Hariv. °**shektṛi**, m. impregnator, begetter, BhP. °**shécana**, n. pouring out, sprinkling, irrigation, AV. &c. &c. °**shecitṛi**, m. one who sprinkles or pours into, an instiller, infuser, MBh.

निषिध् *ni-shidh* (√2. *sidh*), P. *-shedhati* (impf. *ny-ashedhat*; aor. *ny-ashedhīt*; pf. *ni-shishedha*; Pass. *ni-shidhyate*, impf. *ny-ashidhyata*, aor. *ny-ashedhi*; ind. p. *ni-shidhya*, inf. *ni-sheddhum*; cf. Pāṇ. viii, 3, 65, Sch.), to drive away, RV.; AV.; to ward off, keep back, prevent from (abl.), AitBr.; MBh.; Kāv. &c.; to forbid, prohibit, object to (acc.), Kathās.; BhP.; to keep down, suppress, outdo, surpass, Kāvyâd. ii, 64: Caus. *-shedhayati*, to keep off, prohibit, forbid, Pañc.; BhP.; to deny, W. °**shiddha**, mfn. warded off, kept back, restrained, checked, prevented from, forbidden to (inf.), ŚBr.; Mn.; MBh. &c.; *-vat*, mfn. having warded off, Kathās. °**shiddhi**, f. warding off, prohibition, defence, Daś. °**sheddhavya**, mfn. to be kept back or obstructed, Śak. °**sheddhṛi**, mfn. who or what keeps back or restrains or prevents, ŚBr.; MBh.; Hariv. °**sheddhra**, see *a-nisheddhrá*. °**shedha**, m. warding or keeping off, hindering, prevention, prohibition, Yājñ.; Var.; Suśr.; contradiction, negation, denial, Śak. vii, ११ (v.l. for *vi-vāda*); Vām. v, 1, 8; discontinuance, exception, W.; (with *Aṅgirasām* &c.) N. of Sāmans, ĀrshBr.; *-vāda*, m. N. of wk. °**shedhaka**, mfn. keeping back, preventing, prohibiting, MārkP.; TPrāt., Sch. °**shedhana**, n. the act of warding off or defending, prevention, Suśr. °**shedhin**, mfn. defending, keeping back or down, excelling, surpassing, Ragh. °**shedhya**, mfn. to be kept back or prohibited or hindered, Yājñ.

निषिध *nishidha*, m. pl. N. of a people (v.l. for *nishadha*; cf. *naishidha*).

निषिव् *ni-shiv* (√*siv*), P. *-shīvyati* (impf. *ny-ashīvyat*, Pāṇ. viii, 3, 70 &c.; aor. *ny-ashevīt* or *ny-asevīt*, Vop.; Caus. aor. *ny-asīshivat*, Pāṇ. viii, 3, 116, Sch.) °**shyūta** (*ní-*), mfn. sewn in, embroidered, ŚBr.

निषुत *ni-shuta*, mfn. (√3. *su*) laid or thrown into, AitBr.

निषूद् *ni-shūd* (√*sūd*), Caus. *-shūdayati*, to kill, slay, MBh.; R. &c. °**shūda**, m. killing, slaughter, Gal. °**shūdaka**, m. (ifc.) killer, slayer, destroyer, Yājñ.; MBh. °**shūdana**, m. id., MBh.; Ragh.; removing, destroying, Suśr.; n. killing, slaughter, W. °**shūdita**, mfn. killed, slain, destroyed, MBh.; R.; (with *śūlāyām*) impaled, Kathās.

निषेव् *ni-shev* (√*sev*), Ā. *-shevate* (impf. *ny-ashevata*, pf. *ni-shisheve*, Pāṇ. viii, 3, 70 &c.; ind. p. *-shevya*), to stay in, abide or have intercourse with (loc.), RV.; AV.; (with acc.) to frequent, inhabit, visit, serve, attend, honour, worship, follow, approach, enjoy (also sexually), incur, pursue, practise, perform, cultivate, use, employ, Mn.; MBh. &c.: Caus. *-shevayati*, to fall into (hell &c.), Pañc. (B.) iii, 155; Desid. *-shishevishate*, Pāṇ. viii, 3, 70, Kāś. °**sheva**, mfn. practising, exercising, observing (ifc.), MBh.; (*ā*), f. exercising, practice, service, BhP.; use, employment, ib.; worship, adoration, ib. °**shevaka**, mfn. visiting, frequenting, using, employing, observing, enjoying (ifc.), MBh.; BhP. °**shevaṇa**, n. visiting, frequenting, living in, practice, performance, use, employment, adherence or devotion to, honour, worship (gen. or comp.), MBh.; Yājñ.; Suśr. &c. °**shevaṇīya**, mfn. to be served or followed or obeyed, W. °**shevamāṇa**, mfn. being or situated or flowing near (as a river), R. (B.) ii, 68, 12. °**shevita**, mfn. visited, frequented, occupied, held, practised, observed, approached resorted to, attended, served, honoured, obeyed, Mn.; MBh.; Kāv. &c. °**shevitavya**, mfn. to be practised or observed or used or enjoyed, MBh.; Śak.; Var. °**shevitṛi**, m. practiser, observer, enjoyer, MBh.; R. °**shevin**, mfn. practising, observing, enjoying (ifc.), MBh.; Hariv. &c. °**shevya**, mfn. to be frequented or enjoyed, MBh.; Hariv.; to be used or applied, Car.; to be honoured, BhP.

निषो *ni-sho* (√*so*), P. *-shyati* (impf. *ny-ashyat*, Pāṇ. viii, 3, 65, Sch.; aor. *ny-ashāt* or °*shāsīt*, Vop.) °**shita**, mfn., Pāṇ. viii, 3, 70.

निष्क् *nishk*, cl. 10. Ā. *nishkayate*, to measure, weigh, Dhātup. xxxiii, 13; (prob. artificially formed to explain the next, or Nom. fr. it.)

Nishká, m., rarely n. (Uṇ. iii, 45, g. *ardharcâdi*) a golden ornament for the neck or breast (also used as money), RV. &c. &c.; later a partic. coin varying in value at different times (= 1 Dīnāra of 32 small or 16 large Rettis, = 1 Karsha or Suvarṇa of 16 Māshas, = 1 Pala of 4 or 5 Su-varṇas, = 1 larger Pala or Dīnāra variously reckoned at 108 or 150 Su-varṇas, = 4 Māshas, = 16 Drammas; also a weight of silver of 4 Su-varṇas); a golden vessel, L.; gold, L.; m. a Cāṇḍāla, L.; (*ā*), f. a measure of length, MārkP. — **kaṇṭha**, mf(*ī*)n. = *-grīva*, AitBr.; ŚrS.; MBh. &c.; m. (or n.?) a golden ornament, MBh. — **grīva**, mfn. wearing a g° o° round the neck, RV.; AV. **Nishkâdi-pramāṇa**, n. N. of wk. **Nishkín**, mfn. = *nishka-grīva*, ŚBr.

निष्कम्भ *ni-shkambha*, m. (√*skabh*), w. r. for *vi-shk°* in *vajra-vishk°*. **Ni-shkambhu**, m. N. of a partic. divine being (v.l. *ni-kumbha* and *nish-k°*).

निष्कर *nish-kara*, w.r. for *nish-kira*.

निष्कर्तृ *nish-kartṛi*. See *nish-kṛi*.

निष्कर्ष *nish-karsha*, °*shaṇa* &c. See *nish-kṛish*.

निष्कल् *nish-√2. kal* (only ind. p. *-kālya*), to drive out or away, Kathās. °**kali**, m. a partic. spell (for weapons), R. (B.) °**kālana**, n. driving out (cattle), Gobh.

निष्कस् *nish-√kas*, Caus. *-kāsayati* (also written *-kāś°* and *niḥ-kās°*), to drive or turn out, expel, Kāv.; Pañc.; Vet. °**kāsa**, m. issue, egress (cf. °*śa*), R.; a portico, verandah, L. (w.r. °*śa*); w.r. for *kāsha*. °**kāsana**, n. driving away, L. °**kāsanīya**, mfn. to be driven away or turned out, KātyŚr., Comm. (w.r. °*kāś°*). °**kāsita**, mfn. expelled, turned out, Vet. (also written °*śita*; Divyāv. °*kasita*); placed, deposited, L.; placed over, appointed, L.; opened out, blown, expanded (for °*śita*?), W. °**kāsin**, mfn. who or what expels, L.; (*inī*), f. a female slave not restrained by her master, L.

निष्कावम् *nishkâvam*. See *niḥ-shkāvam*.

निष्काश् *nish-√kāś*, Caus. *-kāśayati* = (and perhaps w. r. for) *-kāsayati* (see *nish-kas*), KātyŚr., Comm. °**kāśa**, m. issue, egress, Hcat.; disappearance, L. (cf. °*sa*). °**kāśanīya**, mfn., for °*kāsanīya*, above. °**kāśita**, mfn., see *danta-nishk°*; v.l. for °*kāsita* (see *nish-kas*).

निष्काष *nish-kāsha*, m. (√*kash*) scrapings, what is scraped off from a pan, MaitrS.

निष्किर *nish-kira*, m. (√*kṝ*) N. of a Brahmanical school or of a race, TāṇḍBr. (w.r. °*kara*). °**kirīya**, m. id., ib.

निष्कुट *nish-kuṭa*, m. n. (ifc. f. *ā*) a pleasure-grove near a house (also *-ka*), MBh.; R.; Var.; m. (L.) a field; the hollow of a tree (cf. *-kuha*); a door; the female apartments, Zenana; N. of a mountain, MBh.; n. a hole of a particular shape in the frame of a bedstead (v.l. *niḥ-kuṭa*), VarBṛS.

Nish-kuṭī, f. large or small cardamoms, Bhpr.; L. (cf. *nis-truṭī*).

Nish-kuṭikā, f. N. of one of the Mātṛis attending on Skanda, MBh.

निष्कुपित *nish-kupita*, m. (√*kup*) N. of a Marut, Hariv. (v.l. *nish-kushita*).

निष्कुम्भ *nish-kumbha*, m. Croton Polyandrum (= *ni-k°*), L.; N. of one of the Viśve Devās, Hariv.; Pur.; (*ā*), f. N. of the mother of the Magas, BhavP.

निष्कुष् *nish-√kush*, P. *-kushati* (fut. *koshitā* or *-koshṭā*; inf. *-koshitum* or *-koshṭum* &c., Pāṇ. vii, 2, 46; 47), to pull out, extract; to injure or hurt by tearing, BhP.; to shell, husk (see below). °**kushita**, mfn. torn off, stripped off, extracted, forced out, torn, lacerated, Kāv.; N. of a Marut, Hariv. (v.l. °*kupita*). °**kosha**, m. tearing off or out, extracting, husking, shelling, Pāṇ. v, 4, 62. °**koshaṇa**, n. id., Suśr. °**koshaṇaka**, mfn. fit for picking, serving for a tooth-pick, Pañc. °**koshitavya**, mfn. to be forced out or extracted, Bhaṭṭ. (also °*koshṭ°*, Pāṇ. vii, 2, 46, Sch.)

निष्कुह *nish-kuha*, m. = *nish-kuṭa*, the hollow of a tree, L.

निष्कृ *nish-√1. kṛi*, P. Ā. *-karoti*, *-kurute* &c. (2 pl. *-kṛitha*, impf. *-askṛita* [Padap. and Prāt. *-akṛita*], *-kranta*, RV.; Impv. *-kuru*, AV. *-kṛidhi*, ib.; *-kṛiṇotana*, RV. pres. p. *-kṛiṇvāna*, ib.; aor. Pass. *nir-akāri*, Bhaṭṭ.), to bring out, extract, drive away, expel, remove, RV.; AV.; ŚBr.; to break in pieces, Bhaṭṭ.; to arrange, set in order, prepare, RV.; TS. (cf. *ish-kṛi*); to restore, cure, RV.; AV. °**kāraṇa**, n. taking off, killing, L. °**kṛit**, mfn., see *yajña-nishkṛit*. °**kṛitá**, mfn. done away, removed, expelled, atoned, expiated (cf. *a-nishkṛita*); made ready, prepared; n. atonement, expiation, BhP.; a fixed place, place of rendezvous, RV.; °*tâhāva*, mfn. furnished with a trough, TS. °**kṛiti** (*nísh-*), f. complete development (see *garbha-nishkṛiti*); restoration, cure, RV.; acquittance, requital, atonement, expiation, RV. &c. &c.; removal, doing away, escaping, avoiding, neglecting, L.; w.r. for *ni-kṛiti*, BhP.; m. a form of Agni, MBh.

निष्कृत् *nish-√kṛit*, P. *-kṛintati* (ep. also Ā.; ind. p. *-kṛitya*), to cut off or out, divide, separate, hew asunder, massacre, RV.; ŚBr.; MBh.

निष्कृष् *nish-√kṛish*, P. *-karshati* (pf. *-cakarsha*; ind. p. *-kṛishya*; inf. *-krashṭum*), to draw out, extract, ŚBr.; MBh.; Suśr.; Rājat.; = Caus., BhP.: Caus. *-karshayati*, to tear in pieces, destroy, ib. °**karsha**, m. drawing out, extracting, MBh.; extract or essence of anything, chief or main point, Mn.; MBh. (*āt*, ind. chiefly for the sake of [comp.], °*shān niścayāt*, briefly and exactly, MBh.); measuring, Dhātup. xv, 20; ascertainment, L.; n. oppressing subjects by taxes, MBh. ii, 526 (Nīlak.) °**karshaṇa**, n. drawing out, extracting, taking off, Ragh. °**karshin**, m. N. of one of the Maruts, Hariv. (v.l. °*kushita*). °**kṛishṭa**, mfn. drawn or pulled out, extracted, Suśr. °**kṛishyamāṇa**, mfn. (arrow) being extracted, R. °**kṛishya-vidhāna**, n. an implicit or peremptory precept, Āryabh., pref.

निष्क्रम् *nish-√kram*, P. Ā. *-krāmati*, *-kramate* (*-kramati*, R., ind. p. *-kramya*; inf. *krāmitum*, *-kramitum* or *-krāntum*), to go out, come forth, go or come from (abl., rarely gen.), depart, RV. &c. &c.; to leave (worldly life), Divyâv.; (in dram.) to make an exit: Caus. *-krāmayati* (Pass. *-krāmyate*), to cause to go out, drive or let out, deliver, ŚBr.; Kāv. &c. °**krama**, m. going out, coming forth, an exit, departing from (abl.), R.; Kathās.; the first carrying out (of a child; cf. next), Yājñ.; degradation, loss of caste, inferiority of tribe, L.; intellectual faculty, L. °**kramaṇa**, n. going forth or out, departing, KātySr.; R.; Pañc.; taking a child for the first time out of the house in the fourth month after birth to see the sun, Mn. ii, 34; RTL. 253; 258; (also °*ṇikā*, f., PārGṛ.) ceasing, disappearing, Cat.; *-prayoga*, m. N. of wk. °**kramaṇita,** mfn. (a child) taken out for the first time, g. *tārakâdi.* °**krānta,** mfn. gone out, departed, come forth, MBh. &c.; (dram.) exit, exeunt.

निष्क्री *nish-√krī*, P. Ā. *-krīṇāti, -krīṇīte*, to buy off, redeem or ransom from (abl.; Ā. also 'one's self,' with or sc. *ātmānam*), TS.; AV.; Br. °**kraya,** m. redemption, ransom, Suparn.; Kāv.; compensation, equivalent (in money), GobhŚrāddh., Comm.; price, reward, hire, wages, Mn.; MBh. &c.; return, acquittance, Śiś. i, 50. °**kráyaṇa,** mfn. redeeming, ransoming (ifc.), Br.; n. redemption, buying off, Mṛicch.; ransom, TS. °**krīti** (*nish-*), f. redeeming, redemption, ŚBr.

निष्क्रोध *nish-krodha, nish-kleśa* &c. See under *nish*, p. 543, col. 1.

निष्क्वथ् *nish-√kvath*, Caus. *-kvāthayati* (only ind. p. *-kvāthya*), to boil down, thicken by boiling, Suśr. °**kvātha,** m. a decoction, broth, soup, ib.

निष्खन् *nish √khan*, P. Ā. *-khanati*, °*te*, to dig out or up, ŚBr.

निष्खिद् *nish-√khid*, P. *-khidati* (inf. *-khídam*, AV. v, 18, 7), to loosen, get loose, Kāṭh.

निष्टक्वन् *nish-ṭakvan*, mf(*varī*)n. (*√tak?*) prob. 'running away,' AV. v, 22, 6.

निष्टङ्क् *nish-ṭaṅk* (only Pass. aor. *nir-aṭaṅki*), to express one's self, express in words, Sarvad. (cf. to 'coin' words).

निष्टन् *ni-shṭan* (for *niḥ-shṭan?*, *√stan;* cf. VPrāt. iii, 68), P. *-shṭanati* (rarely Ā.; p. *-shṭanat*), to roar, thunder, sound or cry loudly, RV.; MBh. &c. °**shṭana,** m. groan, sigh, R. °**shṭānaka,** mfn. speaking loud, R.; m. roar, murmur, rustling, MBh.; N. of a serpent-demon, MBh. (v.l. °*shṭhānaka*).

निष्टप् *nish-ṭap* (*√tap*), to singe, scorch, MBh.; to heat thoroughly, melt (as gold, according to Pāṇ. viii, 3, 102 *nis-tap*, if the action is repeated), anneal, purify by heat, free from impurities, TBr.; MBh.; R. &c.; to roast, fry, R.; Hariv. °**ṭapana,** n. burning, L. °**ṭapta** (*nish-*), mfn. burnt, scorched, heated thoroughly, melted (as gold), well cooked or dressed, VS.; TBr.; MBh. &c.

निष्टर्क्य *nish-ṭarkyà*, mfn. (*√tark;* cf. *tarku*) to be opened by unscrewing or loosened by untwisting, TS.; Kāṭh.; ĀpŚr. &c.

निष्टवैश्य *nishṭa-vaiśya* (?), m. N. of a man, Rājat.

निष्टि *nishṭi*, f. = *grīvā-bandha*, TĀr., Sch. °**grī**, f. (*√2. grī?*) N. of Indra's mother, RV. x, 101, 12.

निष्टु *ni-shṭu* (*√stu*), P. *-shṭauti* (*ny-ashṭaut* and *-astaut*), Pāṇ. viii, 3, 70.

निष्टुर् *nish-ṭúr*, mfn. (*√tṝ*) throwing down, overthrowing, RV.

निष्ट्य *níshṭya*, mfn. (fr. *nis+tya;* cf. Pāṇ. iv, 2, 104; viii, 3, 101) external, foreign, strange, RV.; AV.; VS.; ŚBr.; m. a Caṇḍāla or Mleccha, L.; (*ā*), f. N. of a lunar mansion (= *svāti*), TBr.; ĀpGṛ.

निष्ट्यै *ni-shṭyai* (*√styai*), Ā. *-shṭyāyate*, °*shṭyāyatām;* ind. p. *-shṭyāya*), to stick to by coagulation or condensation, to grow or crowd together, VS.; TS.

निष्ठा *ni-shṭhā* (*√sthā;* aor. *ny-ashṭhāt*, pf. *ni-tasthau*, Vop.): Caus. (aor. *ny-atishṭhipat*) to fix in (loc.), ŚBr.; to give forth, emit, yield, HPar. °**shṭha,** mfn. (in some senses = or w.r. for *niḥ + stha*) being in or on, situated on, grounded or resting on, depending on, relating or referring to (usually ifc.), Mn.; MBh. &c.; intent on, devoted to, ib. (cf. *dharma-, satya-*); conducive to, effecting (dat.), Bālar. v, 51; *-loka*, m. pl. dependent people i.e. servants, Rājat. vii, 114. 1. °**shṭhā,** f. (ifc. f. *ā*) state, condition, position, Bhag.; firmness, steadiness, attachment, devotion, application, skill in, familiarity with, certain knowledge of (loc.), MBh.; Kāv.; Pur.; decision about (gen.), Rājat.; decisive sentence, judgment, Gaut.; Āp.; completion, perfection, culminating or extreme point, Mn.; Āp.; MBh. &c.; conclusion, end, termination, death (ifc. 'ending with'), MBh.; Kāv. &c.; asking, begging, L.; trouble, distress, L.; (in gram.) N. of the p.p. affixes *ta* and *tavat;* (in dram.) the end or catastrophe, W.; *-gata*, mfn. gone to or attaining perfection; m. pl. a class of Buddh. deities, Lalit.; *-nta* (°*ṭhânta*), m. end, conclusion, MBh.; BhP. (v.l. *dishṭânta*); *-va*, mfn. concluding, deciding, AitBr.; *-vat*, mfn. perfect, complete, consummate, R.; *-śūnya*, mfn. devoid of firmness, unsteady, irresolute, Mālatīm. 2. °**shṭhá** (Padap. *niḥ-shṭhā*), mfn. excelling, eminent, RV. °**shṭhāna,** n. sauce, condiment, L. °**shṭhānaka,** w.r. for *ni-shṭānaka.* °**shṭhita** (*ni-*, sometimes for *niḥ-*), mfn. being in or on (loc.), R.; BhP.; fallen from the hand, HPar.; grown forth, RV.; complete, perfect, consummate, ŚBr.; attached or devoted to, conversant with, skilled in (loc.), MBh.; R. &c.; firm, fixed; certain, ascertained, W.; *-cīvara* (?), mfn., Divyâv.

निष्ठिव् *ni-√shṭhiv* (or *shṭhīv*), P. *-shṭhīvati* (impf. *ny-ashṭhīvat*, MBh.; pf. *ni-tishṭhivuḥ*, Bhaṭṭ.; ind. p. *-shṭhīvya*, Mn.), to spit, spit out, eject from the mouth. 2. °**shṭhita** (!), mfn. spit upon, BhP. °**shṭhīva,** m. n. spitting, spitting out, L. °**shṭhīvana,** n. spitting, saliva, MBh.; Suśr.; *-śarāva*, m. spitting-box, spittoon, Bhartṛ. °**shṭhīvikā,** f. (Car.), °**shṭhīvita,** n. (Gaut.; Var.; °*tā*, f., Hariv.), °**shṭheva,** m. (and °*vana*, n., L.) = °*shṭhīva.* °**shṭhūta** and °**shṭhūti,** w.r. for °*shṭhy*° (see next). °**shṭhyūta,** mfn. spit out, ejected from the mouth, emitted, sent forth, KātyŚr.; Kāv. &c.; n. spittle, Mn.; Yājñ. °**shṭhyūti,** f. spitting, spitting out, L.

निष्ठुर *ni-shṭhura*, mfn. (*√sthā?*) hard, rough, harsh, severe, cruel (said of persons and things, esp. words), MBh.; Kāv. &c.; *-tā*, f. (Mn.; Kāv. &c.), *-tva*, n. (Caurap.) harshness of speech, coarseness; *-bhāshin*, mfn. speaking harshly, Cāṇ.; *-mānasa*, mfn. cruel-minded, MārkP. °**shṭhuraka,** m. N. of a man, Kathās. °**shṭhurika,** m. N. of a Nāga, MBh. (v.l. °*shṭhūr*°). °**shṭhūrin,** mfn. rough, coarse, L.

निष्ठ्य *nishṭhya*, n. making a cracking noise with the fingers, Āpast.

निष्ठ्यूत *ni-shṭhyūta*, °*ti.* See *ni-shṭhiv.*

निष्णा *ni-shṇā* (*√snā*), only Pot. *-shṇāyāt*, to be absorbed in (loc.), BhP. °**shṇa,** mfn. clever, skilful, versed or experienced in (comp.), Bhaṭṭ. (cf. *ni-śna, nadī-shṇa*, and next). °**shṇāta,** mfn. deeply versed in, skilful, clever, learned (with loc. or ifc.), MBh.; Kāv.; Pur.; agreed upon, Yājñ.; Mālatīm.; *-tva*, n. skill in, familiarity with (*prati*), Kull. x, 85. **Ni-snāta,** mfn., see Pāṇ. viii, 3, 89.

निष्पक्व *nísh-pakva* &c. See p. 543, col. 1.

निष्पत् *nish-√pat*, P. *-patati* (pf. 3. pl. *-petur*, ind. p. *-patya*), to fly out of (abl.), rush out, jump out, fall out, issue, depart, hasten away, RV. &c. &c.: Caus. *-pātayati*, to cause to fall out, ruin, destroy, AV.; R. °**patana,** n. rushing out, issuing quickly, R. °**patita,** mfn. flown or fallen out &c., Hariv. °**patishṇu,** mfn. rushing or running or hastening out, MBh. °**pāta,** m. throbbing, any short or quick motion, BhP. °**pātita,** mfn. (fr. Caus.) caused to fall, ruined, destroyed, R.

निष्पद् *nish-√pad*, Ā. *-padyate*, to fall out (Subj. *-padyātai*), ŚBr.; to come forth, issue, arise, be brought about or effected, become ripe, ripen, Mn.; MBh. &c.: Caus. *-pādayati*, °*te*, to bring about, accomplish, perform, do, make (with *rājyam*, 'to reign'), cause to ripen, MBh.; R.; Var. &c. °**patti,** f. going forth or out, being brought about or effected, completion, consummation, Hariv.; R.; Var.; coming or being derived from (*dhātoḥ*), Sarvad.; a partic. state of ecstasy, Cat. °**pád,** f. excrement, ordure, RV.; TS. °**panna,** mfn. gone forth or sprung up, arisen, descended from (abl., rarely instr.), R.; Var.; (in gram.) derived from (abl.), Sarvad.; brought about, effected, succeeded, completed, finished, ready, Kathās.; Rājat.; Hit. &c. °**pādaka,** mf(*ikā*)n. (fr. Caus.) accomplishing, developing, effective (*-tva*, n.), Sāh. °**pādana,** n. effecting, causing, producing, L. °**pādanīya,** mfn. to be effected or brought about or achieved, Hcat. °**pādita,** mfn. done, effected, prepared, achieved, Pur.; Vet. °**pāditavya,** mfn. = °*pādanīya*, MW. °**pādya,** mfn. id., Sāh.; *-tva*, n., TPrāt., Comm.

निष्पन्द 2. *ni-shpanda* (for 1. see p. 543), m. (*√spand*) motion; *-hīna*, mfn. motionless, MBh.

निष्पलाय् *nish-palây* (= *nish-parā-√ay* or *i*), P. °*yati*, to run away, Divyâv.

निष्पा *nish-√1. pā*, P. *-pibati*, to drink out or up, drink from (abl.), TS. °**pāna,** n. drinking out or up, Pāṇ. viii, 4, 35. °**pīta,** mfn. drunk out or up, ŚBr.; emptied by drinking, dried or sucked up, exhausted, R.; Kathās. °**peya,** mfn. being drunk out or up, L.

निष्पा *nish-√3. pā*, P. *-pāti*, to protect from (abl.), RV. x, 126, 2.

निष्पिश् *nish-√piś*, P. *-piṅśati*, to tear the flesh of an animal from the skin, RV. i, 110, 8.

निष्पिष् *nish-√pish*, P. *-pinashṭi* (Pot. *-pisheyam*, MBh.; pf. *-pipesha*, ib.; ind. p. *-pishya*, ib.; *-pesham*, Bālar. iv, 65), to stamp or beat (linen with stones in washing), ŚBr. (inf. *nish-peshṭavai*); to pound, crush, rub, grind (*sva-caraṇau*, to stamp one's feet; *karaṃ* °*reṇa*, to rub the hands together; *dantair*°*tān* or *dantān*°*teshu*, to gnash the teeth), MBh.; Hariv.; R. &c.: Caus. *-peshayati*, to crush, destroy, Prab. ii, 33 (v.l. *niḥ-śesh*°). °**pishṭa,** mfn. stamped, ground, pounded, crushed, beaten, oppressed, MBh. &c. °**pesha,** m. rubbing together, grinding, striking or clashing and the sound produced by it, MBh.; Kāv. &c. °**peshaṇa,** n. id., MBh.

निष्पीड् *nish-√pīḍ*, P. *-pīḍayati* (ind. p. *-pīḍya;* Pass. *-pīḍyate*), to press or squeeze out, press together or against, ĀśvGṛ.; MBh.; Suśr. &c.; to contract (in pronouncing), Śiksh. °**pīḍa** (R. ii, 62, 17), w.r. for *nish-pīta.* °**pīḍana,** n. pressing, squeezing, Mālatīm.; wringing out (of a cloth), AV.Pariś.

निष्पू *nish-√pū*, P. *-punāti*, to winnow, fan, purify, ŚBr.; KātyŚr.; Suśr. &c. °**pavana,** n. winnowing, fanning, KātyŚr., Sch. °**pāva,** m. id., L.; the wind caused by the winnowing sieve, L.; Dolichos Sinensis or a similar species, Bhpr.; straw, chaff, L.; (*ī*), f. a species of pulse (perhaps Dolichos Lablab), L.; mfn. = *nir-vikalpa*, L. °**pāvaka,** m. a species of pulse, L. °**pāvala,** mfn., g. *sidhmâdi.*

निष्पूर्त *nish-pūrta*, mfn. (*√pṝ*) poured out, MBh.

निष्पृ *nish-√1. pṛi*, P. *-piparti* (2. pl. *-piprithaḥ*, Impv. *-pipartana*, Subj. aor. *-parshat*), to bring out, rescue or deliver from (abl.), RV.; to come out (Impv. *nísh-para*, v.l. *nishvara*), TS.: Caus. *-pārayati*, to help out, rescue, RV.

निष्फार *ni-shphāra*, m. (*√sphar*), see *jṛimbha-nishpāra* (add.)

निष्फुर् *ni-shphur* or *ni-sphur* (*√sphur*), see Pāṇ. viii, 3, 76.

निष्फुल् *ni-shphul* or *ni-sphul* (*√sphul*), ib.

निष्यन्द् *ni-shyand* &c. See *ni-syand.*

निष्यूत *ni-shyūta.* See *ni-shiv.*

निष्वञ्ज् *ni-shvañj* (*√svañj*), Ā. *-shvajate* (impf. *ny-ashvajata* or *ny-asvajata*, Pāṇ. viii, 3, 70 &c.; aor. *ny-ashvaṅkta* or *ny-asvaṅkta*, Vop.)

निष्वप् *ni-shvap.* See *ni-svap.*

निष्षपिन् *nish-shapin*, mfn. (fr. *nis+sapa* = *pasa*) libidinous, lustful, RV. i, 104, 5.

निष्षह् *nish-shah* (or *-shāh*, nom. *-shāṭ*), mfn. (*√sah*) overpowering, mighty, RV.

निष्षिध् *nish-shídh*, f. (*√1. sidh*) granting, bestowing, gift, donation, RV. **-shidhvan,** mf(*varī*)n. granting, presenting, ib.

निस् *nis.* See p. 543, col. 2.

निसंकक्ष *ni-saṃkaksha*, w.r. for *niḥ-s*°.

निसंज्ञ *ni-saṃjña*, w.r. for *niḥ-s*°.

निसन्दि *nisandi*, m. N. of a Daitya, R.

निसंपात *ni-sampāta*, m. = *niḥ-s*°, L.

निसर *ni-sará* (*√sṛi*), VS. xxx, 14.

निसर्ग *ni-sarga*, m. (√*sṛij*) evacuation, voiding excrement, MBh.; giving away, granting, bestowing, a favour or grant, Mn.; MBh. &c.; relinquishing, abandoning, W.; creation, MBh.; Hariv.; natural state or condition or form or character, nature (*nisarga* ibc., °*geṇa*, °*gāt* or °*ga-tas*, ind. by nature, naturally, spontaneously), MBh.; Kāv. &c. **-ja**, mfn. innate, inborn, produced at creation, natural, Mn.; MBh. **-nipuṇa**, mfn. naturally clever, Mālav. **-padva**, mf(*ī*)n. n° inclined to, feeling attracted towards (loc.), Daś. **-bhāva**, m. natural state or condition, Var. **-bhinna**, mfn. naturally distinct, MW. **-vinīta**, mfn. n° discreet, ib. **-śālīna**, mfn. n° timid or modest, Mālav. **-siddha**, mfn. effected by nature, natural, Bhartṛ. **-sauhṛida**, n. natural friendship, f° from infancy, Mālatīm.

Ni-srishṭa, mfn. hurled, thrown, cast, R.; Hariv.; BhP.; sent forth, dismissed, set free, Mn.; MBh.; allowed, authorized, ib.; kindled (as fire), BhP.; intrusted, committed, transferred, granted, bestowed, MBh.; Hariv.; R.; fabricated or made of (instr.), BhP.; = *madhya-stha*, L. **-vat**, mfn. one who has granted or bestowed, MBh. **Nisṛishṭârtha**, mf(*ā*)n. intrusted with something, authorized, Mālatīm.; m. a chargé d'affaires, agent, messenger, Kām.; Sāh.

निसर्प *ni-sarpa*. See *naisarpa*.

निसार *ni-sāra* (√*sṛi*?) = *saṃgha*, *sāra* or *nyāya-dātavya-vitta*, L. (prob. w. r. for *ni-kara*).

निसिन्धु *ni-sindhu* or °*dhuka*, m. Vitex Negundo, L. (cf. *sindhu*, *sindhu-vāra*).

निसुन्द *ni-sunda*, m. N. of an Asura slain by Kṛishṇa, MBh.; Hariv. (cf. *sunda*, *upa-s*°).

निसुम्भ *ni-sumbha*. See *ni-ś*°.

निसुसूष् *ni-susūsh*, mfn. (√3. *su*), Pāṇ. viii, 3, 117, Sch. (cf. *abhi-s*°).

निसूदक *ni-sūdaka*, °*dana*. See *ni-shūd*.

निसृत *ni-sṛita*, mfn. (prob. m. c. for *niḥ-s*°, √*sṛi*) gone away, disappeared, Rājat.; come forth i.e. unsheathed (as a sword), Vcar.; (*ā*), f. Ipomoea Turpethum, L.; N. of a river, VP. (v.l. *niś-citā*).

निसृष्ट *ni-sṛishṭa*. See above.

निसेवितव्य *ni-sevitavya*, w. r. for *ni-sh*°.

निस्तक्ष् *nis-*√*taksh*, P. *-takshati* (2. pl. aor. *-atashṭa*), to carve out, fashion, create, form, make from (abl.), RV.; AV.; ŚāṅkhŚr.; to cut, wound (by insults), MW.

निस्तनी *ni-stanī*, f. (fr. *stana*, 'breast?') a pill, bolus, a sort of force-meat ball, L.

निस्तप् *nis-*√*tap*. See *nish-ṭap*.

निस्तब्ध *ni-stabdha*, mfn. (√*stabh*) paralyzed, numbed; stopped, fixed, W. (see *a-nist*°). **Ni-stambha**, see *niḥ-st*°.

निस्तरण *nis-taraṇa*, *nis-tāra* &c. See *nis-tṛī*.

निस्तर्ह *nis-tarha*, m. (Gal.), °*haṇa*, n. (L.) crushing, destroying (√*tṛih*).

निस्तुति *ni-stuti*. See *niḥ-stuti*.

निस्तुद् *nis-*√*tud*, P. *-tudati* (Pass. *-tudyate*), to pierce, prick, sting, Car.; Suśr. °**toda**, m., °**todana**, n. piercing, pricking, stinging, Suśr.

निस्तृ *ni-*√*stṛi* (only 3. sg. aor. *-ástar*), to throw down, overthrow, RV. (cf. *a-nishṭṛita*).

निस्तॄ *nis-*√*tṛī*, P. *-tarati* (ind. p. *-tīrya*, inf. *-tartum*), to come forth from, get out of, escape from (abl.), MBh.; to pass over or through, cross (sea &c.), pass or spend (time); to overcome or master (an enemy), MBh.; Kāv. &c.; to fulfil, accomplish, perform (promise, vow &c.), ib.; to suffer for, expiate (acc.), R.; BhP.; (with *abhiyogam*) to clear one's self from an accusation, Yājñ.: Caus. *-tārayati*, to rescue, save, deliver from (abl.), Mn. iii, 98; to overcome, overpower, Cat.; Desid. *-titīrshati* &c., to wish to cross or pass over (acc.), BhP. °**taraṇa**, n. passing over, going forth, coming out (of danger), rescue, deliverance, Kull.; a means of success or rescue, L. °**taraṇīya** (Daś.), °**tartavya** (MBh.; Kād.), mfn. to be passed over or overcome or conquered. °**tāra**, m. crossing, passing over, rescue, deliverance, Bhartṛ.; acquittance, requital, payment, discharge of a debt, Hit.; means, expedient, W.; final liberation, ib.; *-bīja*, n. a means of crossing (the ocean of life), a cause of final liberation, BrahmavP. °**tāraka**, mf(*ikā*)n. rescuing, delivering, a saviour, MW. °**tāraṇa**, n. (fr. Caus.) crossing, passing over, overcoming, BhP.; rescuing, liberating, MW. °**tārayitṛi**, mfn. = °*tāraka*, Jātakam. °**titīrshat**, mf(*antī*)n. desirous to cross (the ocean of life), wishing for salvation or liberation, W. °**tīrṇa**, mfn. crossed, passed over, spent, gone through, fulfilled, accomplished; escaped, rescued, delivered, saved, MBh.; Kāv. &c.

निस्त्यज् *nis-*√*tyaj* (only *-tyakta-vat*, mfn.), to drive away, expel, R.

निस्त्रस् *nis-*√*trus* (only impf. *nir-atrasan*), to fly, run away, RV. viii, 48, 11.

निस्त्रुटी *nis-truṭī*, f. cardamoms, L. (cf. *nish-kuṭi*).

निस्त्रैणपुष्पक *nistraiṇa-pushpaka*, m. a species of thorn-apple, L. (prob. w. r. for *niḥ-śreṇi-pushpaka*).

निस्नात *ni-snāta*. See *ni-shṇā*.

निस्नाव *ni-snāva*, m. (√*snu*?) residue of articles &c. after a sale or market, W.

निस्नेह *ni-sneha*, w. r. for *niḥ-sneha*.

निस्पन्द *ni-spanda* = 1. 2. *ni-shpanda*; also w. r. for *ni-syanda*.

निस्पृश् *ni-*√*spṛiś*, P. *-spṛiśati* (Vedic inf. *-spṛíśe*), to touch softly, caress, fondle, RV.

निस्पृह् *ni-spṛíh*, mfn. (√*spṛih*) greedy for, desirous of (loc.), RV. x, 95, 9 (nom. *-spṛík*).

निस्पृह *ni-spṛiha*, w. r. for *niḥ-spṛiha*.

निस्यन्द् *ni-*√*syand*, Ā. *-syandate* (or *-shy*°: cf. Pāṇ. viii, 3, 72), to flow or trickle down, flow into (loc.), BhP.; to make any fluid drop or drip or trickle down (only *-syandate*, Pāṇ. ib.; Vop.) °**syanda** (or °*shy*°), mfn. flowing or dripping down, Ragh.; Śiś.; m. a flowing or trickling down or forth, issuing, stream, gush, a discharge (of any fluid), MBh.; Kāv.; Suśr.; necessary consequence or result, Buddh. °**syandin** (or °*shy*°), mfn. flowing or dripping down or out, (ifc.) flowing with, Kāv.; Suśr.

निस्रु *ni-*√*sru*, Ā. *-sravate* (also for *niḥ-sr*°), to flow down or forth, spring or arise from (abl.), Cāṇ.: Caus. to make water flow down from (acc.) upon (loc.), Baudh. °**srava** (also for *niḥ-sr*°), m. flowing down or out, stream, torrent, MBh. °**srāva**, m. id., Hariv.; the scum of boiled rice, L. (cf. *niḥ-sr*°). °**sruta** (or *niḥ-sr*°?), mfn. flowed down or out, Suśr.

निस्वन् *ni-*√*svan*, P. *-svanati*, to make a noise in eating, Vop. 1. °**svana**, m. (ifc. f. *ā*) sound, noise, voice, Yājñ.; MBh.; R. &c. (cf. *niḥ-sv*°). °**svanita**, n., °**svāna**, m. id., MBh.

2. **Ni-svaná**, m. N. of Agni (v.l. for *ni-svara*), TĀr.

निस्वप् *ni-*√*svap* (Impv. *-svapa*; pf. *-sushupur*), to fall asleep (also = meet death, die, vii, 18, 14), RV.: Caus. *-svāpayati* (*-shv*°), to cause to sleep, lull asleep, RV.; AV.; ŚBr.; to kill, RV. vii, 19, 4.

निस्वर *ni-svará*, mfn. soundless, noiseless; (*am*), ind. noiselessly, RV.; m. N. of Agni, AV.; TĀr. (v.l. *ni-svaná*).

निह् *nih*, m. = *ni-hantṛi*, AV.; VS. (Mahīdh.)

निहन् *ni-*√*han*, P. *-hanti* (Impv. *-jahi*, RV.; p. *-ghnat*, TS. &c.; 3. sg. Ā. *-jighnate*, RV.; p. *-jighnamāna*, MBh.; pf. *-jaghāna*, RV. &c.; 3. pl. *-jaghnur*, °*nire*, MBh.; R.; fut. *-hanishyati*, °*te*, *-haṅsyati*, MBh.; p. *-hanishyát*, RV.; ind. p. *-hatya*, KātyŚr. [cf. *a-nihatya*]; inf. *-hantave*, RV.; *-hantum*, R.), to strike or fix in, hurl in or upon or against (loc.), RV. &c. &c.; to make an attempt upon, attack, assail (acc., loc. or gen.), AV.; KātyŚr.; MBh.; to strike or hew down (also = mow, L.), kill, overwhelm, destroy, RV. &c. &c. (also applied to planets, Var.); to hit, touch (lit. and fig.), MBh.; BhP.; to beat (a drum), Bhaṭṭ.; to punish, visit, afflict, Kāv.; Pur.; to attach to (Pass. *-hanyate*, to be fixed upon, with loc.), AV.; to drop, lower, let sink (hands, wings &c.), AV.; VPrāt.; to speak with the unaccented tone i.e. with the Anudātta, RPrāt.; ĀśvŚr.; (in arithm.) to multiply, Āryabh., Comm.: Caus., see *ni-ghāta*, °*taya*. °**hata** (*ní-*), mfn. hurled, thrown, RV.; hit, touched (lit. and fig.), MBh.; Kāv.; struck down, smitten, slain, killed, destroyed, lost, gone, ib. &c.; having the unaccented tone or Anudātta (*-tva*, n.), TPrāt.; *-bhūyishṭha*, mfn. having the greater number killed, R.; *-sena*, mfn. having (their) armies smitten or destroyed, MW.; °*târtha*, mfn. (word) whose meaning is out of use or obsolete (*-tā*, f., *-tva*, n.), Sāh.; °*ôshṭra*, mfn. having the camels killed, whose camels have been slain, MW. °**han**, m. a killer, destroyer (ifc.), MBh.; R. °**hanana**, n. killing, slaughter, L. °**hantavya**, mfn. to be struck down or killed or destroyed, MBh.; Pañc. °**hantṛi**, m. a killer, destroyer, Mn.; MBh. &c.; one who removes or expels or hinders, Vikr.; Suśr.; N. of Śiva, MBh.

निहव *ni-hava*. See *ni-hve*.

निहा *ni-*√2. *hā*, Ā. *-jihīte* (3. pl. Impv. *-jihatām*), to descend, stoop, yield, RV.; ĀśvŚr.: Desid. *jihīshate*, to wish to stoop or yield, AV.

Nihākā, f. 'coming down,' a storm, whirlwind, RV.; an iguana, the Gangetic alligator, L. (according to Uṇ. iii, 42 fr. next).

निहा *ni-*√3. *hā*, only Pass. *-hīyate*, to be deficient or wanting or lost, RV.; to be deprived of (instr.), Jātak. °**hīna**, mfn. low, vile, mean, MBh.; Kāv.; *-tara*, mfn. lower, worse, Āpast.; *-varṇa*, mf(*ā*)n. of low caste or origin, MBh.

निहार *ni-hāra* &c. See *ni-*√*hṛi*.

निहिंसन *ni-hiṅsana*, n. (√*hiṅs*) killing, slaughter, L.

निहित *ní-hita*, mfn. (√1. *dhā*) laid, placed, deposited, fixed or kept in (loc.), RV. &c. &c.; delivered, given, bestowed, intrusted, ib.; laid down or aside, removed (see below), laid (as dust by rain), Ghaṭ.; encamped (as an army), Bhaṭṭ.; uttered in a deep tone, VPrāt. (cf. *ni-hata*). **-daṇḍa**, mfn. one who has laid aside the rod, who shows clemency, MW. **-nayana**, mf(*ā*)n. having the eyes fixed or directed upon (loc.), Megh. **-bhāga** (*níh*°), mfn. one whose share has been laid aside, MaitrS.

निहीन *ni-hīna*. See *ni-*√3. *hā*.

निहृ *ni-*√*hṛi*, P. *-harati* (ind. p. *-hāram*), to offer (as a gift or reward), VS.; AV.; TāṇḍyaBr. °**hāra**, m. excrement, Vishṇ. (cf. *nir-h*°); mist, L. (cf. *nī-h*° under 5. *nī*). °**hārin**, w. r. for *nir-h*°.

निहृष् *ni-*√*hṛish*, P. *-hṛishyati*, to sink down (as a flame), AitBr. (opp. to *ud-dhṛish*).

निह्नु *ni-*√*hnu*, Ā. *-hnavate* (rarely P. °*ti*), to make reparation or amends to (dat.) for (acc.); to beg pardon for (cf. below), Br.; GṛŚrS.; to disown, deny, dissimulate, conceal, evade, Mn.; MBh.; Kāv. &c. °**hnava**, m. begging pardon, making amends or reparation (a kind of ceremony at which the Ṛitvij lay their hands upon the Prastara and recite VS. v, 7), Sāy. on AitBr. i, 26 (also °*hnavana*, Gobh.); atonement, expiation, amends for (gen.), Mn. ix, 21; denial, concealment, secrecy, mistrust, suspicion, Yājñ.; MBh.; Kāv.; contradiction, MBh.; eclipsing, obscuring, surpassing, Kāvyâd.; wickedness, W.; N. of a Sāman, ĀrshBr.; *-vādin*, m. a defendant or witness who prevaricates or tries to hide the truth, W.; °*vôttara*, n. an evasive reply or defence, ib. °**hnuta**, mfn. denied, disowned, concealed, hidden, secreted, given out for something else, Ratnâv.; Kathās.; Rājat. °**hnuti**, f. denial, dissimulation, reserve, secrecy, concealment, Kāv. °**hnuvana**, n. id., Gobh.; v.l. for °*hnavana*, ib. °**hnuvāna**, mfn. dissimulating, prevaricating, insinuating, W.

निह्राद् *ni-*√*hrād*, Caus. *-hrādayati*, to cause to sound, beat (as a drum), MaitrS. (cf. *nir-hr*°). °**hrāda**, m. sound, noise, Ragh.; BhP. (cf. *nir-hr*°); *-vat*, mfn. sounding, pealing, Kir. °**hrādita**, n. roaring, BhP. °**hrādin**, mfn. sounding, pealing, MW.

निह्वे *ni-*√*hve*, Ā. *-hvayate* (Pāṇ. i, 1, 30;

3. pl. *-juhvate,* impf. *-ahvanta;* Pass. *-hūyate,* RV.), to call down or near, invoke, RV.; AV.; AitBr. **°hava,** m. invocation, calling, Br.; ŚrS.; ChUp.; (with *Vasishṭhasya* or *Vasishṭha-*) N. of a Sāman, ĀrshBr. (cf. *ni-hnava*).

नी 2. *nī* (for 1. see p. 543, col. 3), cl. 1. P. Ā. (Dhātup. xxii. 5) *nayati,* °*te* (pf. P. *ni-nāya,* 2. sg. *ninetha,* RV., 1. pl. *ninima,* TS.; Subj. *ninīthás,* Pot. *ninīyāt,* RV.; Impv. *ninetu,* MaitrS.; Ā. *ninye,* Br. &c.; *-nayām āsa,* MBh.; *-nayām cakre,* R.; aor. P. 3. du. *anītām,* Subj. *néshi, nethā,* RV.; *anaishīt,* Subj. *neshati,* °*shat,* 3. pl. Ā. *aneshata,* ib.; *anayīt,* AV.; fut. *neshyati,* AV.; °*te,* Br.; *nayishyati,* °*te,* MBh.; R.; *netā,* *nayitā,* ib.; ind. p. *nītvā,* Br. &c.; *nayitvā,* MBh.; *-nīya,* AV. &c.; inf. *nesháṇi,* RV.; *nétavai,* °*tos* and *nayitum,* Br.; *nétum,* ib. &c. &c.), to lead, guide, conduct, direct, govern (also with *agram* and gen.; cf. *agra-ṇī*), RV. &c. &c.; to lead &c. towards or to (acc. with or without *prati,* dat., loc. or *artham* ifc.), ib.; to lead or keep away, exclude from (abl.), AitBr.; (Ā.) to carry off for one's self (as a victor, owner &c.), AV.; TĀr.; MBh.; (Ā., rarely P.) to lead home i. e. marry, MBh.; R.; to bring into any state or condition (with acc., e.g. with *vaśam,* to bring into subjection, subdue [Ā., RV. x, 84, 3; AV. v, 19, 5; P., Ragh. viii, 19]; with *śūdra-tām,* to reduce to a Śūdra, Mn. iii, 15; with *sākshyam* [Ā.], to admit as a witness, viii, 197; with *vyāghra-tām,* to change into a tiger, Hit.; with *vikrayam,* to sell, Yājñ.; with *paritosham,* to satisfy, Pañc.; with *duḥkham,* to pain, Amar.; rarely with loc., e.g. *duhitṛi-tve,* to make a person one's daughter, R. i, 44, 38; or with an adv. in *-sāt,* e.g. *bhasma-sāt,* to reduce to ashes, Pañc. i, 1⁸⁄₉; to draw (a line &c.), ŚāṅkhŚr.; Sūryas.; to pass or spend (time), Yājñ.; Kāv. &c.; (with *daṇḍam*) to bear the rod i.e. inflict punishment, Mn.; Yājñ.; (with *vyavahāram*) to conduct a process, Yājñ.; (with *kriyām*) to conduct a ceremony, preside over a religious act, MBh.; to trace, track, find out, ascertain, settle, decide (with *anyathā,* 'wrongly'), Mn.; Yājñ.; MBh. &c.; (Ā.) to be foremost or chief, Pāṇ. i, 3, 36: Caus. *nāyayati,* °*te,* to cause to lead &c.; to cause to be led by (instr.), Mn. v, 104 (cf. Pāṇ. i, 4, 52, Vārtt. 5, Pat.): Desid. *ninīshati,* °*te* (AV. xix, 50, 5, w.r. *nineshati*), to wish to lead or bring or carry to or into (acc. or dat.), AV.; Up.; MBh. &c.; to wish to carry away, R.; to wish to spend or pass (time), Naish.; to wish to exclude from (abl.), AitBr.; to wish to find out or ascertain, investigate, MBh.: Intens. *nenīyáte,* to lead as a captive, have in one's power, rule, govern, TS.; VS.; MBh.

3. **Nī,** mfn. leading, guiding, a leader or guide (mostly ifc., cf. Pāṇ. iii, 2, 61 and *agra-ṇī, agre-ṇī;* but also alone, cf. vi, 4, 77; 82 &c.)

Nīka, m. N. of a tree, Uṇ. iii, 47, Sch.; (*ā*), f. a channel for irrigation, L.

1. **Nītá,** mfn. (for 2. see 4. *nī*) led, guided, brought &c., RV. &c. &c.; gained, obtained, W.; well-behaved, correct, modest, ib.; n. wealth, corn, grain, L.; = *nava-nīta,* ĀpŚr. **—dakshiṇa,** mfn. one whose sacrificial fee has been carried off, L. **—miśrá,** mfn. not yet entirely made into butter, TBr. **Nītârtha,** mfn. of plain or clear meaning, Nyāyas., Sch.

Nīti, f. leading or bringing, guidance, management, L.; conduct, (esp.) right or wise or moral c° or behaviour, prudence, policy (also personif.), political wisdom or science, moral philosophy or precept (also pl.), Mn.; MBh.; Kāv. &c.; relation to, dependence on (*itarêtarayoḥ*), MBh.; presenting, offering (?), Pāṇ. v, 3, 77; acquirement, acquisition, W. **—kathā,** f. any work on moral or political science, W. **—kamalâkara** and **-kalpa-taru,** m. N. of wks. **—kuśala,** mfn. conversant with pol° sc° or policy, Hit. **—garbhita-śāstra,** n. N. of wk. **—ghosha,** m. N. of the car of Bṛihaspati, L. **—jña,** mfn. = *-kuśala;* m. a statesman, politician, Mn.; Var.; Rājat. **—tantra,** n. = *āvāpa,* L. **—taraṃga,** m., **-dīpikā,** f. N. of wks. **—dosha,** m. error of conduct, mistake in policy, MW. **—nipuṇa** (Bhartṛ.), **-nishṇa** (MW.), mfn. = *-kuśala.* **—paṭala,** n. a chapter or book on policy, Daś. **—prakāśa** and **-pradīpa,** m. N. of wks. **—bīja,** n. a germ or source of intrigue, MW. **—mañjarī,** f. N. of wk. **—mat,** mfn. of moral or prudent behaviour, eminent for political wisdom (compar. *-mat-tara*), MBh.; Hariv.; R.; describing pol° w°, Kathās. **—mayūkha,** m. N. of ch. of the Bhagavad-bhāskara. **—mukula,** n. N. of wk. **—yukta,** mfn. intrusted with policy, being at the head of government, MBh. **—ratna,** n., **-ratnâkara,** m., **-latā,** f. N. of wks. **—vartanī,** f. the path of prudence or wisdom, Vcar. (printed °*tinī*). **—varman,** m. N. of a poet, L. **—vākya,** n. pl. words of wisdom; °*kyâmṛita,* n. N. of wk. **—vid,** mfn. = *-jña,* Hit. **—vidyā,** f. moral or political science, ib. **—vilāsa** and **-viveka,** m. N. of wks. **—vishaya,** m. the sphere of morality or prudent conduct, MW. **—vedin,** mfn. = *-jña,* L. **—vyatikrama,** m. error of conduct or policy, Rājat. **—śataka,** n. the 100 verses on morality by Bhartṛ. **—śāstra,** n. the science of or a work on political ethics or morals, Kathās.; *-samuccaya,* m. N. of wk. **—saṃhitā,** f., **-saṃkalana,** n., **-saṃgraha,** m. N. of wks. **—saṃdhi,** m. essence of all policy, Pañc. (B.) **—samuccaya,** m., **-sāra,** m. n., **-sāra-saṃgraha,** m., **-sumāvali** (!), f. N. of wks.

Nītha, m. leading or a leader, L.; N. of a man, MBh.; (*nīthā*), f. way, trick, art, stratagem, RV.; also = (*nīthá*), n. a mode in music, musical mode or air, song, hymn, ib.; water, L. **Nīthā-vid,** mfn. knowing musical modes, skilled in sacred song, RV. (Prāt. °*tha-v°*).

Nīthya. See *grāma-ṇīthya.*

Netavya, netṛi &c. See p. 568, col. 3.

नी 4. *nī,* P. *ny-eti* (3. pl. *ni-yanti;* p. *-yat;* impf. *ny-āyan,* ind. p. *nī́tya*), to go into (cf. *ny-āya*), enter, come or fall into, incur (acc.), RV.; AV.; TS.; ŚBr.; to undergo the nature of i. e. to be changed into (°*bhāvam*), RPrāt. 2. **Nītá,** mfn. entered, gone or come to (*mṛityor antikam*), RV.; AV.

नी 5. *nī,* in comp. = 1. *ni* (p. 538, col. 3). **—karshin,** mfn. (√*kṛish*) spreading the tail (as a peacock), Lāṭy. **—kāra,** m. (√1. *kṛi*) disrespect, contempt, degradation, Hcar. **—kāśa,** m. (√*kāś*) appearance, look, mien (ifc. = like, resembling), MBh.; certainty, ascertainment, L. **—kulaka,** m. N. of a man, Pravar. **—kleda,** m. (√*klid*) moistening (?), Pāṇ. vi. 3, 122, Sch. **—dhra,** see *nīdhra.* **—nāhá,** m. (√*nah*) a girth, AV. **—mānuja,** m. N. of a Vaishṇava teacher, Cat. **—vāka,** m. (√*vac*) the increased demand for grain in times of dearth, dearth, scarcity, L. **—vārā,** v.l. for *ni-vārā* (see under *ni-vṛi*). **—vāha,** m. (√*vah*) diminution, decrease (of days), GopBr. (cf. *ni-v°*). **—vid,** f. = *ni-v°,* AV. **—vi,** see *nī-vī.* **—vṛit** (L.), **-vṛiti** (HPariś.), f. an inhabited country, a realm. **—veshyā,** mfn. = *ni-v°,* MaitrS. **—śāra,** m. (√*śṛī*) a warm cloth or outer garment, Pat.; curtains, (esp.) mosquito c°, an outer tent or screen, L. **—shāh,** mfn. (fr. *ni-shah*) overpowering, AV. **—hārá,** m. (once n.) mist, fog, hoar-frost, heavy dew, RV. &c. &c. (cf. *ni-hāra* under *ni-hṛi*); evacuation (cf. *nir-h°*); *-kara,* m. 'dew-maker' or 'cold-rayed,' the moon, Daś.; *-cakshus,* mfn. one whose eyes are veiled by mist, BhP.; *-maya,* mf(*ī*)n. consisting of m°, Kād.; °*rāya,* Nom. Ā. °*yate,* to become or make m°, Pāṇ. iii, 1, 17, Vārtt. 2, Pat. °*rī-√kṛi,* to convert into m°, Mcar.

नीक्षण *nī́kshaṇa,* n. (√*nīksh* = *niksh*) a stick for stirring up a cauldron, a kind of ladle, RV. i, 162, 13 (cf. *nekshaṇa* and *mekshaṇa*).

नीच *nīca,* mf(*ā*)n. (*ni* + 2. *añc*) low, not high, short, dwarfish, Mn.; MBh. &c.; deep, depressed (navel), Pañc.; short (hair, nails), Suśr.; deep, lowered (voice), Prāt.; low, vile, inferior (socially or morally), base, mean (as a man or action or thought), Var.; MBh.; Kāv. &c.; m. a kind of perfume (= *coraka*), L.; n. (in astrol.) the lowest point of a planet (= ταπείνωμα), the 7th house from the culminating point, Var. (cf. 2. *ny-añc*). **—kadamba,** m. N. of a plant, L. **—karman,** mfn. having a low occupation (as a servant), Vet. **—kula,** n. a low family; °*lôdgata* (Mṛicch.) and °*lôdbhava* (Var.), descended from a l° f°. **—keśa-nakha,** mfn. having short hair and nails, Suśr. **—keśaśmaśru-nakha,** mfn. having sh° h° and beard and n°, Yājñ. **—ga,** mfn. going low, descending (as a river), Hit.; belonging to a low man, ib.; = *-gata,* Var.; (*ā*), f. a river, L.; n. water. **—gata,** mfn. being at the lowest point (as a planet), Var. **—gāmin,** mfn. going towards low ground (said of rivers), following low courses (said of women), Subh. **—gṛiha,** n. the house in which a planet stands at its lowest point, Var. **—jāti,** mfn. of low birth, Subh. **—tā,** f. lowness (lit. and fig.), baseness, inferiority, MBh.; Kāv.; °*tayā√yā,* to stoop, Ratnāv. ii, 3. **—tva,** n. lowness, social inferiority, Var.; lowering of tone, VPrāt. **—nakha-roman,** mfn. having short nails and hair, Suśr. **—patha,** m. a descending path, Kāv. **—bhojya,** m. 'food of low men,' an onion, L. **—yonin,** mfn. of low origin, Hariv. **—rata,** mfn. delighting in mean things, Var. **—rksha** (for *ṛiksha*), m. = *-gṛiha,* ib. **—vajra,** n. 'inferior diamond,' a sort of gem, L. **—śākha,** see *Naicāśākhá.* **Nīcâyaka,** m., °**kīya,** mfn. (?) g. *ut-karâdi.* **Nīcâvagāha,** mfn. (a tank) in which low people bathe, Kāv. **Nīcôkti,** f. a low or vulgar expression, MW. **Nīcôcca-vṛitta,** n. an epicycle, Col. **Nīcôpagata,** mfn. situated low in the sky, Var.

Nīcaka, mf(*ikā*)n. low, short, L.; soft, gentle (as the voice, a gait &c.), MBh.; vile, mean, W.; (*akā, akī* and *ikā*), f. an excellent cow; (*ais*), ind. low, below, little, W. (Pāṇ. v, 3, 71, Kāś.)

Nīcakin, m. the head of an ox, L.

Nīcā́, ind. below, down, downwards, RV.; AV. **—meḍhra,** m. one whose penis hangs low, TāṇḍBr.; Lāṭy. **—vayas** (°*cā́-*), mfn. one whose strength has failed, RV.

Nīcā́t, ind. from below, RV.

Nīcī-√kṛi, to lower, pronounce without an accent, RPrāt., Sch.

Nīcīna, mfn. below, being low, downward, hanging or flowing down, cast down, RV. &c. &c., **—bāra** (°*cīna-*), mfn. having its opening below, RV.

Nīcaiḥ, in comp. for °*cais.* **—kara,** mfn. causing a low or deep tone, giving depth of voice, TPrāt. **—kāram, -kṛitya** and **-kṛitvā,** ind. in a low tone, softly, gently, L.

Nīcair, in comp. for °*cais.* **—ākhya,** mfn. named 'low,' ML. **—mukha,** mfn. with downcast countenance, L.

Nīcais, ind. low, below, down, downwards, underneath, AV.; ŚBr.; MBh. &c.; also used adjectively, e.g. *nīcair adṛiśyata,* he appeared lower or shorter, Ragh.; cf. *uccais* (*nīcair nīcais-tarām,* deeper and deeper, Kām.); humbly, modestly, Kāv.; softly, gently, ib.; in a low or deep tone, VPrāt.; Pāṇ. i, 2, 30; N. of a mountain (called also *Vāmana-giri* or *Kharva*), Megh. **—tarām,** ind. lower, deeper, softer, gentler, AitBr.; TPrāt.

1. **Nīcya,** m. pl. 'living below,' N. of certain nations in the west, AitBr.

2. **Nīcya,** Nom. P. °*cyati,* to be in a low situation, be a slave, Siddh.

नीड *nīḍá* (*nīlá*), m. n. (*ni* + √*sad*) any place for settling down, resting-place, abode, (esp.) a bird's nest, RV. &c. &c.; the interior or seat of a carriage, ŚBr.; MBh. &c.; place, spot (= *sthāna*), L. [Cf. Lat. *nīdus;* Germ. *Nest;* Eng. *nest.*] **—garbha,** m. the interior of a nest, Hit. **—ja,** m. 'nest-born,' a bird; *-jêndra,* m. 'chief of birds,' N. of Garuḍa, L. **Nīḍôdbhava,** m. = °*ḍa-ja,* L.

Nīḍaka, m. or n. the nest of a bird, MBh.

Nīḍaya, Nom. Ā. °*ḍáyate* (for °*ḍayate*), to bring to rest, RV. vi, 35, 2 (Sāy. 'bring together,' i.e. 'cause to come to close fighting').

Nīḍi (*nīḷi*), m. house-mate, RV. x, 92, 6.

नीत *nīta, nīti* &c. See √*nī.*

नीत्त *nītta.* See *ni-datta,* p. 548, col. 1.

नीध्र *nīdhra,* n. (*ni* + √*dhṛi* ?) the eaves of a roof, Rājat.; a wood, L.; the circumference of a wheel, L.; the moon or the lunar mansion Revatī, L. (cf. *nīvra*).

नीप *nīpa,* mfn. (fr. *ni* + *ap;* cf. *dvīpa* and Pāṇ. vi, 3, 97, Sch.) situated low, deep, Kāṭh.; m. the foot of a mountain, Mahīdh.; Nauclea Cadamba (n. its fruit and flower, Megh.); Ixora Bandhucca or a species of Aśoka, L.; N. of a son of Kṛitin and father of Ugrâyudha, BhP.; pl. of a regal family descended from Nīpa (son of Pāra), MBh.; Hariv. &c.; (*ā*), f. N. of a river, VP. **—rāja,** m. or n. the fruit of the Nipa, L. **Nīpâtithi,** m. N. of a descendant of Kaṇva and author of RV. viii, 34.

Nīpya, mfn. being low or on the ground, VS.

नीर् *nīr* (*ni* + √*ir*), Caus. (only impf. *ny-airayat*), to hurl down upon (loc.), RV. vi, 56, 3 (cf. *ny-ēr*).

नीर *nīrá*, n. (√*nī?*) water, MBh.; Kāv. &c. (cf. Naigh. i, 12); juice, liquor, L.; =*griha*, L. (=or w. r. for *nīḍa*, *nīla?*); N. of a teacher, Cat. [Cf. Zd. *nira*.] — **graha**, m. taking up water in a ladle (see under *graha*). — **cara**, m. 'moving in w°,' a fish or any aquatic animal, Bhām. — 2. -**ja**, m. n. (for 1. see p. 543, col. 3) 'w°-born,' a w°-lily, lotus, MBh.; Kāv. &c.; m. an otter, L.; a species of grass, L.; n. a species of Costus, Suśr.; a pearl, L.; -*jâkshī*, f. a lotus-eyed or beautiful woman, Vcar. — **jâta**, mfn. 'water-born,' produced from w°, aquatic, MBh. — **taraṃga**, m. a w°-wave, L. — **tīraja**, m. 'w°-shore-born,' Kuśa grass, L. — 2. -**da**, m. (for 1. see p. 543, col. 3) 'w°-giver,' a cloud, Kāv.; Cyperus Rotundus, L.; -°*din*, mfn. cloudy, Śiś. — **dhi** or -**nidhi**, m. 'w°-receptacle,' the ocean, Prasann. — **patatrin**, m. 'w°-bird,' Ragh. — **priya**, m. 'w°-friend,' Calamus Rotang, L. — **rāśi**, m. 'w°-mass,' the ocean, Śiś. — **ruha**, n. 'w°-grown,' the w°-lily, lotus. **Nīrâkhu**, m. 'w°-rat,' an otter, L.

नीरक्त *nī-rakta*, 1. *nī-raja* &c. See 1. *nī*.

नीराज् *nī-rāj* (*nis* + √*rāj*), Caus. -*rājayati*, to cause to shine upon, illuminate, irradiate, Prab.; to perform the Nīrājana ceremony on (acc.), ib.; Uttarar. °**rājana**, n. lustration of arms (a ceremony performed by kings in the month Āśvina or in Kārttika before taking the field), Var.; Hariv.; Kāv. &c.; waving lights before an idol as an act of adoration, W.; -*giri*, m. N. of an author, Cat.; -*dvādaśī-vrata*, n. N. of a partic. observance, Cat.; -*padyâli-lakshaṇa-vibhakti*, f., -*prakāśa*, m. N. of wks.; -*vidhi*, m. the Nīrājana ceremony, Ragh.; N. of 43rd ch. of VarBṛS.; -*stotra*, n. N. of a Stotra. °**rājita**, mfn. shone upon, illuminated, irradiated, Prab.; Uttarar.; lustrated, consecrated, Var.; Kām. °**rājya**, mfn. clear, pure, limpid, Kāśīkh.

नीरिन्दु *nīrindu*, m. a species of plant, L. (Trophis Aspera, W.)

नीरी *nī-rī* (*nis* + √*rī*), P. Ā. -*riṇāti*, -*riṇīte*, to loosen, separate from (abl.), RV. i, 161, 7; to allure, seduce, ib. i, 179, 4.

नीरुच् *nī-ruc* (*nis* + √*ruc*), only pf. -*rurucur*, to drive away by shining, RV. viii, 3, 20.

नीरोह *nī-rohá*, m. (*nis* + √*ruh*) shooting out, growing, TS.

नील् *nīl*, cl. 1. P. (Dhātup. xv, 15) *nīlati*, to be dark, dye dark, Bālar. (either Nom. fr. next or invented to explain it).

Nīla, mf(*ā* or *ī*; cf. Pāṇ. iv, 1, 42, Vārtt.; Vām. v, 2, 48)n. of a dark colour, (esp.) d°-blue or d°-green or black, RV. &c. &c.; dyed with indigo, Pāṇ. iv, 2, 2, Vārtt. 2, Pat.; m. the sapphire, L. (with *maṇi*, R. iii, 58, 26); the Indian fig-tree (=*vaṭa*), L.; =*nīla-vṛiksha*, L.; a species of bird, the blue or hill Maina, L.; an ox or bull of a dark colour, L.; one of the 9 Nidhis or divine treasures of Kubera, L.; N. of a man, g. *tikâdi*; of the prince of Māhishmatī, MBh.; of a son of Yadu, Hariv.; of a son of Aja-mīḍha, BhP.; of a son of Bhuvana-rāja, Rājat.; of an historian of Kaśmīra, ib.; of sev. authors (also -*bhaṭṭa*), Cat.; N. of Mañju-śrī, L.; of a Nāga, MBh.; Rājat.; of one of the monkey-chiefs attending on Rāma (said to be a son of Agni), MBh.; R. &c.; the mountain Nīla or the blue m° (immediately north of Ilāvṛita or the central division; cf. *nīlâdri*), MBh.; Hariv.; Pur.; (*ā*), f. the indigo plant (Indigofera Tinctoria), L. (cf. *nīlī*); a species of Boerhavia with blue blossoms, L.; black cumin, L.; a species of blue fly, L.; (du.) the two arteries in front of the neck, L.; a black and blue mark on the skin, L.; N. of a goddess, W.; (in music) of a Rāgiṇī (personif. as wife of Mallāra); of a river, MBh. (v. l. *nālā*); (*ī*), f. the indigo plant or dye, Mn.; Var.; Suśr. &c. Blyxa Octandra, L.; a species of blue fly, L.; a kind of disease, L.; N. of the wife of Aja-mīḍha, MBh.; Hariv. (v. l. *nalinī* and *nīlinī*); n. dark (the colour), darkness, TS.; KaushUp.; any dark substance, ŚBr.; ChUp.; =*tālī-pattra* and *tālīśa*, L.; indigo, Yājñ. iii, 38; black salt, L.; blue vitriol, L.; antimony, L.; poison, L.; a partic. position in dancing, L.; a kind of metre, Col. — **kaṇā**, f. a species of cumin, L. — **kaṇṭha**, mfn. blue-necked, MBh.; m. a peacock, MBh.; Kāv.; Suśr.; a species of gallinule or water-hen (=*dātyūha*), L.; a wagtail, L.; a sparrow, L.; the blue-necked jay, L.; Ardea Sibirica, L.; a species of plant (=*pīta-sāra*), L.; N. of Śiva (as having a black throat from swallowing the poison produced at the churning of the ocean), R.; Hit. &c.; N. of the celebrated Sch. on MBh. and of other authors (also -*dīkshita*, -*nāga-nātha*, -*bhaṭṭa*, -*bhāratī*, -*miśra*, -*śarman*, -*śāstrin*, -*śivâcārya*, -*sūnu*, -*sūri*, °*ṭhâcārya*), Cat.; (*ī*), f. a pea-hen, R. v, 11, 23; N. of sev. Comms. composed by a Nīla-kaṇṭha, Cat.; n. a radish, L.; N. of a Tīrtha, Cat.; -*kośa*, m., -*campū* (or -*vijaya-campū*), f., -*jātaka*, n., -*tantra*, n., -*dīkshitīya*, n., -*prakāśa*, m., -*prakāśikā*, f., -*bhāshya*, n., -*mālā*, f., -*stava*, m., -*stotra*, n., -*sthāna-māhātmya*, n., N. of wks.; °*ṭhâksha*, n. the berry or seed of Elaeocarpus Ganitrus, L.; °*ṭhīya*, n., °*ṭhôdâharaṇa*, n. N. of wks. — **kanda**, m. a species of bulbous plant, L. — **kapitthaka**, m. a kind of mango, L. — **kamala**, n. a blue water-lily, L. — **kāca**, mf(*ā*)n. made of blue crystal, VarYogay. — **kāyika**, m. pl. 'blue-bodied' or 'dark-bodied,' N. of a class of deities, Lalit. — **kuṇḍa**, n. N. of a Tīrtha, MatsyaP. — **kuntalā**, f. N. of a female friend of Durgā, L. — **kuraṇṭaka** or -**kuruṇṭaka**, m., -**kusumā**, f. (prob.) Barleria Caerulea, L. — **kṛitsna**, n. one of the 10 mystical exercises called Kṛitsna, Divyâv. — **keśī**, f. the indigo plant, L. — **krāntā**, f. Clitoria Ternatea, L. — **krauñca**, m. the blue heron, L. — **gaṅgā**, f. N. of a river, ŚivaP. — **gaṇêśa**, m. the blue Gaṇêśa, L. — **gandhika**, n. the blue ruby, L. — **garbha**, m. or n. (prob.) a young Blyxa Octandra, Hariv. (v. l. *nala-g°*). — **gala**, m. 'blue-necked,' N. of Śiva (cf. -*kaṇṭha*), Hariv.; -*māla*, mfn. wearing a garland round (his) blue neck, NīlarUp. — **giri**, m. N. of a mountain, Cat.; -*karṇikā*, f. a blue variety of Clitoria Ternatea, L. — **grīva** (*nī́°*), m. 'blue-necked,' N. of Śiva, VS.; MBh.; of a prince, Kathârṇ. — **ghora**, m. = -*pora*, L. — **candra**, m. N. of a prince, Cat. — **carman**, m. Grewia Asiatica, L. — **colaka-vat**, mfn. wearing a blue jacket, Viddh. — **cchada**, m. 'dark-leaved,' the date tree, L.; 'blue-winged,' N. of Garuḍa, L. — **cchavin**, m. or -**cchavī**, f. a kind of bird, L. — **ja**, n. 'produced in the blue mountains,' blue steel, L.; (*ā*), f. N. of the river Vitastā, Rājat. — **jhiṇṭī**, f. prob. Barleria Caerulea, L. — **tantra**, n. N. of a Tantra. — **taru**, m. the cocoa-nut tree, L. — **tā**, f. blueness, a dark colour, Kām.; Suśr. — **tārā-sarasvatī-stotra**, n. N. of a Stotra. — **tāla**, m. Xanthochymus Pictorius or Paludosa, L. — **toyada**, m. a dark cloud, TĀr. — **daṇḍa**, m. 'carrying a black staff,' (with Buddh.) N. of one of the 10 gods of anger, Dharmas. 11. — **dūrvā**, f. a species of Dūrvā or Dūrb grass, Bhpr. — **druma**, m. a species of tree, L.; mfn. consisting of Indian fig-trees, L. — **dhvaja**, m. Xanthochymus Pictorius, L.; N. of a prince of Māhishmatī, JaimBr. — **nakhá**, mfn. black-clawed (?), AV. xix, 22, 4. — **nicolin**, mfn. wearing a black mantle, Rājat. — **nirguṇḍī**, f. a species of blue Nirguṇḍī, L. — **niryāsaka**, m. a species of tree (=*nīlâsana*), L. — **nīraja**, n. the blue water-lily, Kāv. — **pakshman**, mfn. having black eyelashes, Bhartṛ. — **paṅka**, m. n. darkness, L.; black mud, W.; -*ja*, n. a blue water-lily, L. — **paṭa**, m. a dark garment, Hit. — **paṭala**, n. a dark film or membrane over the eye of a blind person, Pañc.; mfn. very dark or black, W. — **paṭṭa**, m. N. of a poet, Cat. — **pattra**, m. 'dark-leaved,' Scirpus Kysor, L.; the pomegranate tree, L.; Bauhinia Tomentosa, L. = *nīlâsana*, L.; (*ā*), f. Premna Herbacea, L.; (*ī*), f. indigo, L.; n. = next, L. — **padma**, n. the blue water-lily, L. — **parṇa**, m. 'dark-leaved,' Grewia Orientalis, L. — **pācana**, n. steeping or maceration of indigo, W.; -*bhāṇḍa*, n. an i°-vat, ib. — **piṅgala**, mf(*ā*)n. dark-brown, L. — **piccha**, m. 'black-tailed,' a falcon, L. — **piṭa**, m. a collection of annals and royal edicts, Buddh. — **piṇḍa**, n. a kind of steel, L. — **pishṭauḍī** (!), f. a species of shrub, L. — **pīta**, mfn. dark-green (*śādvala*), R. — **punarnavā**, f. a species of Punar-navā with blue blossoms, L. — **pura**, n. N. of a town, Rājat. — **purāṇa**, n. N. of a Pur. — **pushpa**, m. 'blue-flowered,' a species of Eclipta, L.; =*nīlâmlāna*, L.; (*ā*), f. Clitoria Ternatea, L.; (*ī*), f. id., L.; Convolvulus Argenteus, L.; n. a kind of fragrant plant, Bhpr. — **pushpikā**, f. the indigo plant, L.; Linum Usitatissimum, L. — **pṛishṭha**, m. 'black-backed,' N. of Agni, RV.; m. Cyprinus Denticulatus (a kind of fish), L. — **pora** and -**paura**, m. a species of sugar-cane, L. (cf. -*ghora*). — **phalā**, f. the egg-plant, L. — **bīja**, m. a kind of Terminalia, L. — **buhnā**, f. Convolvulus Argenteus, L. — **bha**, m. 'of bluish or dim appearance,' the moon, L.; a cloud, L.; a bee, L. (cf. *nīlâbha*). — **bhū**, f. N. of a river, Rājat. — **bhṛiṅgarāja**, m. a species of Verbesina with blue blossoms, L. — **maksha** (Kauś.), -**makshikā** (Suśr.), f. a kind of blue fly or bee. — **maṇi**, m. a sapphire, Dhūrtan. — **mata** (or -*purāṇa*), n. N. of a Pur. — **maya**, mf(*ī*)n. consisting of sapphires, Hcat. — **mallikā**, f. Aegle Marmelos, L. — **mahisha**, m. a buffalo of a dark colour, TS., Comm. — **mādhava**, m. N. of Vishṇu or Kṛishṇa, L. — **māsha**, m. Dolichos Catjang, L. — **mīlika**, m. a shining winged insect, L. — **mṛittikā**, f. iron pyrites, L. — **meha**, m. blue diabetes, Car.; °*hin*, mfn. voiding bluish urine, ib.; Suśr. — **yashṭikā**, f. a species of dark sugar-cane, L. — **ratna**, °**naka**, n. the sapphire, Gīt.; L. — **rāji**, f. a dark line or mass, darkness, Ṛitus. — **rudrôpanishad**, f. N. of an Up. — **rūpaka**, m. Thespesia Populneoides, L. — **loha**, n. blue steel, L. — **lohitá**, mfn. dark-blue and red, purple, dark-red, RV. &c. &c.; m. N. of Śiva, MBh.; Kāv.; Pur.; N. of a Kalpa (see s. v.), L.; a mixture of blue and red, a purple colour, W.; (*ā*), f. a kind of vegetable, L.; N. of a goddess (the wife of Śiva), BrahmaP.; °*tâksha*, m. 'having dark-red eyes,' Śiva, Śivag.; °*tântevâsin*, m. Ś°'s pupil, i. e. Paraśu-rāma, Bālar. — **vajra**, m. N. of a Gaṇa of Ś°, Hariv. — **vat** (*nī́°*), mfn. blackish, dark, RV.; m. N. of a mountain, Śatr. — **varṇa**, mfn. blue-coloured, blue, Hit.; m. or n. a radish, L.; m. Grewia Asiatica, L.; (*ā*), f. the indigo plant, L. — **varshābhū**, f. = -*punarnavā*. — **vallī**, f. Vanda Roxburghii, L. — **vasana**, n. a blue garment, Kathās.; m. the planet Saturn, L. — **vastra**, n. = prec. n., GāruḍaP.; m. N. of Bala-rāma, L.; (*ā*), f. N. of Durgā, L. — **vānara**, m. a species of blue monkey, MW. — **vāsas**, mfn. dressed in dark-blue clothes, BhP.; m. the planet Saturn, L. — **vṛiksha**, m. a species of tree, L. — **vṛinta**, m. or n. a fan, L. — **vṛintaka**, m. a species of tree, L. — **vṛisha**, m. a dark-coloured bull, Yājñ.; (*ā*), f. Solanum Melongena, L. — **vrata**, n. a kind of religious ceremony, MatsyaP. — **śikhaṇḍa** (*nī́°*), mfn. having black tufts or locks of hair (Rudra-Śiva), AV. — **śigru**, m. Moringa Pterygosperma, L. — **śīrshṇī** (*nī́°*), f. 'black-headed,' a kind of animal, TS. — **shaṇḍa**, m. a dark-coloured bull at liberty, MBh. — **saṃdhāna-bhāṇḍa**, n. a vat for the mixing i. e. preparing of indigo, Hit. — **saṃdhyā**, f. = -*giri-karṇikā*, L. — **sarasvatī**, f. N. of a goddess (=*tārā*), L.; -*paddhati*, f. N. of wk.; -*manu*, m. N. of an incantation or magic formula, Cat. — **saroruha**, n. a blue water-lily; °*hâkshī*, f. a lotus-eyed or beautiful woman, Vcar. — **sāra**, m. a kind of tree (=*nīlâsana* or *tinduka*), L. — **sindhuka**, m. Vitex Negundo, L. — **skandā** or -**skandhā** or -**spandā**, f. the dark Go-karṇī, L. — **svarūpa**, n. a kind of metre, Col. **Nīlâṅśuka**, n. a blue garment, Kāv. **Nīlâksha**, m. 'blue-eyed,' a goose, L. **Nīlâṅkita-dala**, (prob.) w. r. for *til°*. **Nīlâṅga**, mfn. 'dark-bodied,' R.; m. the Indian crane or Coracias Indica, L.; N. of a poet, Cat. **Nīlâcala**, prob. w. r. for *līl°*. **Nīlâñjana**, n. black antimony, R.; an unguent made of ant° and blue vitriol, L. (v. r. °*lâśmaja*); (*ā*), f. lightning; (*ī*), f. a kind of shrub, L. **Nīlâñjasā**, f. lightning (cf. prec.), L.; N. of an Apsaras and a river, L. **Nīlâṇḍaja**, m. a kind of deer, Hcar. **Nīlâda**, m. N. of a Yaksha, Divyâv. (for °*lôda*?). **Nīlâdri**, m. the mountain Nīla; -*karṇikā* or -*parājitā*, f. a blue species of Clitoria Ternatea, L. -*mahôdaya*, m., -*māhātmya*, n. N. of wks. **Nīlā-pariṇaya**, m. N. of a drama. **Nīlâbja**, n. a blue water-lily, L. **Nīlâbha**, mf(*ā*)n. bluish; m. a cloud, L.; N. of a mountain, Kālac. (cf. *nīla-bha*). **Nīlâbhra**, m. a dark cloud, W.; -*saṃvṛita*, mfn. obscured or concealed by dark clouds, MW. **Nīlâmbara**, m. 'dressed in a blue garment,' a Rakshas, L.; the planet Saturn, L.; N. of Bala-rāma, L. (cf. *nīla-vasana* and -*vastra*); N. of a poet and sev. other authors (also with *âcārya*, *upâdhyāya*, *purohita* and *miśra*); n. black or dark-blue raiment, W.; = *tālīśa-pattra*, L. **Nīlâmbujanman**, n. the blue water-lily, L. **Nīlâmbhoja**, n. id., Subh. **Nīlâmlāna**, m., °**mlī**, f. N. of plants, L. **Nīlâyudha**, m. pl. N. of a people, MBh. (v. l. *līl°*). **Nīlâruṇa**, m. 'the dark-red' or first dawn of day,

L. **Nīlâli-kula-saṃkula**, m. 'full of swarms of blue bees,' Rosa Glandulifera, L. **Nīlâlu**, m. a species of bulbous plant, L. **Nīlâśoka**, m. an Aśoka with blue blossoms, R.; Var. **Nīlâśmaja**, see *nīlâñjana*. **Nīlâśman**, m. 'blue-stone,' a sapphire, Śiś. **Nīlâśva**, m. N. of a district, Rājat. **Nīlâsana**, m. a species of tree, L.; (°*lâs*°?) a kind of coitus, L. **Nīlâsura**, m. N. of an author, L. **Nīlêśvara**, n. N. of a town on the Malabar coast (Νελκύνδα). **Nīlôtpala**, n. a blue lotus, Nymphaea Cyanea, MBh.; Kāv. &c.; *-gandha*, m. a partic. Samādhi, Kāraṇḍ.; *-maya*, mf(*ī*)n. formed or consisting of blue lotuses, MBh.; R. &c.; °*lin*, m. n. of Mañju-śrī, L.; (*ī*), f. a pond with blue water-lilies, L. **Nīlôtsarga-paddhati**, f. N. of wk. **Nīlôda**, m. 'containing blue water,' N. of a sea or river, Pāṇ. vi, 3, 57, Sch. **Nīlôdvāha**, m., *-paddhati*, f., *-vidhi*, m. N. of wks. **Nīlôpakāśa**, mfn. blackish-looking, ĀpŚr. **Nīlôpala**, m. a blue stone, a sapphire, Śiś.

Nīlaka, mfn. blue (esp. as N. of the third unknown quantity or of its square), Col.; m. Terminalia Tomentosa, L.; a male bee, Var.; Antilope Picta, L.; a dark-coloured horse, L.; (*ikā*), f. Blyxa Octandra, MBh.; a partic. medicinal plant, Suśr.; the indigo plant, L.; Nyctanthes Arbor Tristis, L.; Vitex Negundo, L.; a kind of malady (black and blue marks in the face), Suśr.; a partic. disease of the lens of the eye (also °*likā-kāca*, m.), Suśr.; N. of a river, MBh.; n. blue steel, L.

Nīlāya, Nom. P. Ā. °*yati* and °*te*, to begin to become blue or dark-coloured, Kād. (cf. Pāṇ. iii, 1, 13).

Nīlāśi, f. (*nīla* + ?) Vitex Negundo, L.

Nīlinī, f. the indigo plant, Suśr. (*-phala*, n. ib.); a species of Convolvulus with blue blossoms, L.; N. of the wife of Aja-mīḍha, Hariv. (cf. *nīlī*, *nalinī*).

Nīliman, m. blueness, blackness, darkness, Kāv.

Nīlī, f. of *nīla*, q.v. **-bhāṇḍa**, n. an indigo vat, Hit. **-rasa**, m. liquid i°, Pañc. **-rāga**, m. an affection as unchangeable as the colour of i°, Sāh.; mfn. having the c° of i° or constant in affection, L. **-roga**, m. (prob.) = *nīlikā-kāca* (see *nīlaka*), Suśr. **-varṇa**, mfn. having the colour of i°, Pañc.; Hit. = *-śṛigāla-vat*, ind. like the blue jackal, Hit. **-vastra**, n. a garment dyed with indigo, Cat. **-saṃdhāna-bhāṇḍa**, n. = *nīla-s°-bh°*.

नीलङ्गु *nīlaṅgu*, m. (according to Uṇ. i, 37 *nīlaṅgú*, fr. *ni* + √*lag*) a species of worm, VS.; a species of fly or bee, L.; a jackal, L.; = *pra-sūta* or *pra-sūna*, L.

Nīlâṅgu, m. id., L.

नीलागलसाला *nīlāgalasālā*, f., AV. vi, 16, 4.

नीव् *nīv*, cl. 1. P. *nīvati*, to become fat, Dhāt. xv, 58 (cf. √*tīv*, *pīv*, *mīv*).

नीव *nīva*, m. a species of tree, Gobh.

नीवन् *nīvan*, m. N. of one of the 10 horses of the Moon, L.

नीवर *nīvara*, m. (√*nī*?; cf. Uṇ. iii, 1) a trader; an inhabitant; a beggar; mud; n. water, L.

नीवाक *nī-vāka*, *nīvāha*, *nīvṛit* &c. See under 5. *nī*.

नीवार *nīvāra*, m. (ifc. f. *ā*) wild rice (sg. the plant; pl. the grains), VS.; ŚBr.; MBh. &c.; (*ā*), f. N. of a river, MBh.; VP. (v. l. *ni-v*°). **-prasṛitim-paca** or **-mushṭim-paca**, mfn. cooking only a handful of wild rice, extremely frugal in eating, Bālar.

नीवि *nīvi* or *nīvī*, f. (prob. fr. *ni* + √*vye*) a piece of cloth wrapped round the waist (esp. as worn by women; but cf. Vām. i, 3, 5), a kind of skirt or petticoat, VS.; AV.; ŚBr.; MBh. &c.; a band or cord for tying together folded Kuśa-grass in making offerings at the funeral rites of a Śūdra, L.; a hostage, L.; capital, principal stock, Daś. **Nīvi-bhāryà**, mfn. to be worn in a skirt or apron, AV.

नीव्र *nīvra*, m. (*ni* + √*vṛi*?) = *nīdhra* (q.v.), L.

नीशार *nī-śāra*, *nī-shah*, *nī-hāra* &c. See 5. *nī*, p. 565, col. 2.

नु 1. *nú* (in RV. also *nū́*; esp. at the beginning of a verse, where often = *nú* + *u*), ind. now, still, just, at once; so now, now then, RV.; AV.; Br.; Up.; indeed, certainly, surely, RV. &c. &c.; cf. Pāṇ. iii, 2, 121, Sch. (often connected with other particles, esp. with negatives, e.g. *nahí nú*, 'by no means,' *nákir nú*, 'no one or nothing at all,' *mā́ nú*, 'in order that surely not;' often also *gha nu*, *ha nu*, *in nu*, *nu kam* &c. [*nū́ cit*, either 'for ever, evermore; at once, forthwith' or 'never, never more;' so also *nū* alone, RV. vii, 100, 1]; with relat. = -cunque or -soever; sometimes it lays stress upon a preceding word, esp. an interr. pronoun or particle, and is then often connected with *khalu*, RV. &c. &c.; it is also employed in questions, esp. in sentences of two or more clauses [cf. Pāṇ. viii, 2, 98, Kāś.] where *nu* is either always repeated [Śak. vi, 9] or omitted in the first place [ib. i, 8] or in the second place and further replaced by *svid*, *yadi vā* &c., and strengthened by *vā*, *atha vā* &c.) [Cf. 1. *náva*, *nū́tana*, *nūnám*; Zd. *nū*; Gk. νύ, νῦν; Lat. *nun-c*; Germ. *nu*, *nun*; Angl.Sax. *nu*, *nū*; Eng. *now*.]

नु 2. *nu*, m. a weapon, L.; time, L.

नु 3. *nu*, cl. 1. Ā. *navate* (*nauti* with *apa*), to go, Naigh. ii, 14: Caus. *nāvayati*, to move from the place, remove, ShaḍvBr.

नु 4. *nu* or *nū*, cl. 2. 6. P. (Dhāt. xxiv, 26; xxviii, 104) *nauti*, *nuvati*, (pres. also *návate*, °*ti*, RV. &c.; p. P. *nuvát*, *návat*, Ā. *návamāna*, RV.; pf. *nunāva*, Kāv.; aor. *ánūnot*, *anūshi*, °*shata*, *anavishṭa*, RV.; *anaushīt*, *anāvīt*, *anuvīt*, Gr.; fut. *navishyati*, *nuv*°; *navitā*, *nuv*°; ib.; ind. p. *-nutya*, *-nāvam*, Br.; inf. *navitum*, v. l. *nuv*°, Bhaṭṭ.), to sound, shout, exult; praise, commend, RV. &c. &c.: Pass. *nūyate*, MBh. &c.: Caus. *nāvayati*, aor. *anūnavat*, Gr.: Desid. *nunūshati*, ib.: Desid. of Caus. *nunāvayishati*, ib.: Intens. *nónavīti*, *nonumas* (impf. *anonavur*, Subj. *návīnot*; pf. *nónāva*, *nonuvur*, RV.; *nonūyate*, *nonoti*, Gr.), to sound loudly, roar, thunder, RV.

5. **Nu**, m. praise, eulogium, L.

Nuta, mfn. praised, commended, Pur.; Bhaṭṭ. **-mitra**, m. 'having praised friends,' N. of a man, Daś.

Nuti, f. praise, laudation; worship, reverence, Bhartṛ.; Bālar.; Naish.

Nūta, mfn. = *nuta*, L.

नु 6. *nu*, Caus. *nāvayati*, to cause to be drawn into the nose, Car. (cf. 3 *nava*).

नु 7. *nu* (ifc.) = *nau*, a ship, BhP.

नुड् *nuḍ*, cl. 6. P. *nuḍati*, to hurt, strike, kill, Dhāt. xxviii, 92 (Vop.)

नुद् *nud*, cl. 6. P. Ā. (Dhātup. xxviii, 2; 132) *nudáti*, °*te* (pf. *nunoda*, Kāv.; *nunudé*, 3. pl. °*dre*, RV. &c.; aor. P. *anautsīt*, Gr.; Ā. *anutthās*, RV.; *nudishṭhās*, AV.; Prec. *-nudyāt*, Bhag.; fut. *-notsyati*, MBh.; °*te*, Br. &c.; *nottā*, Gr.; ind. p. *-nudya*, ŚāṅkhGṛ.; inf. *-núde*, RV.; *-nudas*, Kāṭh.; *-nodam*, RV.), to push, thrust, impel, move, remove, RV. &c. &c.: Caus. *nodayati* (Pass. *nodyate*), to push on, urge, incite, Up.; MBh.; Kāv. &c.: Intens. *nonudyate*, to push or drive away repeatedly, AitBr.

Nuttá, mfn. pushed or driven away, AV.; despatched, sent, ordered, W.; m. N. of a plant, ib.

Nutti, f. driving away, removing, destroying, BhP.

2. **Nud** or **nuda**, mfn. pushing, impelling, driving away, removing, Up.; MBh.; Kāv. &c. (ifc. or with acc.)

Nudita, mfn. = *nutta* or *nunna*, MBh.

Nunutsu, mfn. (fr. Desid.) desirous of impelling or inciting or removing, Naish.

Nunna, mfn. = *nutta*, MBh.; R.

Nodita, mfn. (fr. Caus.) incited, impelled, ib.

नूतन *nū́tana*, mf(*ā*)n. (fr. 1. *nú* or *nū́*), belonging to 'now' or the present day, new, novel, recent, modern, young, fresh (opp. to *pūrva*, *purāṇa* &c.), RV. &c. &c.; (with *vayas*, n. youth, juvenility, Hcar.); new i.e. curious, strange, Bālar. vii, 69; Hit. ii, $\frac{128}{129}$. **-gajâroha-prakāra**, m. N. of wk. **-tari**, f. N. of Comm. on the Rasa-taraṃgiṇī. **-tā**, f., **-tva**, n. newness, novelty, W. **-pratishṭhā-prayoga**, m., **-mūrti-pratishṭhā**, f. N. of wks. **-yauvana**, mfn. young, fresh, Kathās. **-śruti-gītā-vyākhyā**, f. N. of wk. **Nūtanâśvâroha-prayoga**, m. N. of wk. **Nūtanêśvara**, m. a young king, Ragh. **Nūtanêshṭi-prayoga**, m. N. of wk.

Nūtanaya, Nom. P. °*yati*, to make new, renew, BhP.

Nū́tna, mf(*ā*)n. = *nū́tana*, RV.; BhP. **-vayas**, mfn. in the bloom of youth, in the spring of life, BhP.

Nūnám, ind. now, at present, just, immediately, at once; for the future; now then, therefore; (esp. in later lang.) certainly, assuredly, indeed (also in questions, e.g. *kadā n*°, when indeed? *kva n*°, where indeed?), RV. &c. &c. **Nūna-bhāva**, m. (for °*nam-bh*°) probability; (*āt*), ind. probably, MBh. iii, 59.

नूद *nūda*, m. a kind of mulberry tree, L. (prob. w.r. for *tūda*).

नूपुर *nūpura*, m. n. (ifc. f. *ā*) an ornament for the toes or ankles or feet, an anklet, MBh.; Kāv. &c.; m. N. of a descendant of Ikshvāku, L. **-vat**, mfn. adorned with anklets or foot-ornaments, Amar. **Nūpurôttamā**, f. N. of a Kiṃ-narī, Kāraṇḍ.

Nūpurin, mfn. = *nūpura-vat*, Priy.

नृ *nṛí*, m. (acc. *náram*, dat. *náre*, gen. abl. *náras*, loc. *nári*; du. *narā*, *nárau*; pl. nom. voc. *náras*, acc. *nṝín* [may also stand for other cases; for the final *n* before *p* cf. Pāṇ. viii, 3, 10], instr. *nṛíbhis* or *nṛibhís*; dat. abl. *nṛíbhyas* or *nṛibhyás*, loc. *nṛíshu* or *nṛishú* [vi, 1, 184], gen. *narā́m*, *nṛiṇā́m* or *nṝṇā́m* [vi, 4, 6]) a man, hero (used also of gods), person; mankind, people (mostly pl.), RV. &c. &c.; (in gram.) a masculine word (nom. *nā*), L.; the pin or gnomon of a sun-dial, Col.; a piece at chess, W. [Cf. *nara*; Zd. *nar*; Gk. ἀ-νήρ, stem -νερ; Old Lat. *ner*, st. *nerōn*, Lat. *Nero*.] **-kalevara**, m. a human body, dead body, Kathās. **-kalpa**, m. N. of a man (cf. *nārkalpi*). **-kāra**, manly deed, heroism, Subh. **-kukkura**, m. 'man-dog,' a dog of a man, Rājat. **-kula-devā**, f. N. of a woman, Bhadrab. **-kesari** (NṛisUp.) and °**rin** (Cat.), m. 'man-lion,' Vishṇu in his 4th Avatāra (written also *-keś*°). **-ga**, m. N. of an ancient king, MBh.; of a grandson of Ogha-vat, ib.; of a son of Uśīnara by Nṛi-gā (ancestor of the Yaudheyas), Hariv.; of a son of Manu, VP.; of the father of Su-mati, BhP.; of a king (the patron of the philosopher Vācaspati-miśra); (°*gasya sāma*, n. N. of a Sāman, ĀrshBr.); (*ā*), f. N. of the wife of Uśīnara and mother of Nṛi-ga, Hariv.; *-tīrtha*, n. N. of a Tīrtha, Cat.; *-nṛipati-pāshāṇa-yajña-yūpa-praśasti*, f., *-moksha-prakaraṇa*, n., *-śāpa*, m., *-śvabhra-praveśa*, m., °*gâkhyāna* and °*gôpâkhyāna*, n. N. of wks. and chs. of wks. **-cákshas**, mfn. beholding or watching men (said of gods), RV.; AV.; VS.; TS.; looking after men i.e. leading or guiding them (as a Ṛishi), RV. iii, 53, 9; 10; m. 'waiting for men,' a Rākshasa, Pāṇ. ii, 4, 54, Vārtt. 10, Pat. **-cakshus**, mfn. seeing with human eyes, Hariv.; m. N. of a prince (a grandson or son of Su-nītha), Pur. **-candra**, m. 'man-moon,' N. of a prince (a son of Ranti-nāra), Pur. **-jala**, m. 'man-water,' human urine, L. **-jit**, mfn. conquering men, RV. ii, 21, 1; m. N. of an Ekâha, ŚāṅkhŚr. **-jyāyá**, m. the conquering of men, MaitrS. **-tama** (*nṛ́-*), mf(*ā*)n. most manly or strong, RV. vi, 19, 10. **-tā**, f. manhood, Śiś. **-durga**, mfn. protected by men; n. a place so protected, Mn. vii, 70. **-deva**, m. 'man-god,' a king, MBh.; R.; (*ī*), f. a princess, queen, BhP. **-dharman**, m. 'acting as a man,' N. of Kubera, L. **-dhūta** (*nṛ́-*), mfn. shaken about or stirred by men (as the Soma), RV. **-namana**, mfn. bending men, g. *kshubhnâdi*; m. N. of a man (cf. *nār-namani*). **-pa**, see p. 568, col. 2. **-pañcânana** and °**cásya**, m. = *-kesarin*, Sarvad. **-páti**, m. 'lord of men,' king, prince, sovereign, RV. (where also with *nṛiṇā́m*) &c. &c.; N. of Kubera, L.; *-kanyakā*, f. a princess, Kathās.; *-dvāra*, n. 'king's door,' the entrance of a palace, VarYogay.; *-nīti-garbhita-vṛitta*, n. N. of a modern wk.; *-patha*, m. 'king's road,' chief street, Daś. **-pátnī**, f. a king's wife, queen, RV. **-paśu**, m. 'man-beast,' a brute of a man, Veṇīs.; a man serving as a sacrificial victim, BhP. **-pā́ṇa**, mfn. giving drink to men, RV. **-pā́tṛi**, m. protector of men, ib. **-pā́yya**, mfn. (√3. *pā*) men-protecting; n. a large edifice, hall, ib. **-pāla**, m. 'men-protector,' a king, Bhartṛ.; BhP. **-píti** (*nṛ́-*), f. protection of men, RV. **-péśas**, mfn. formed by or consisting of men, RV. iii, 4, 5. **-prajā́**, f. pl. the children of men, Pañc. **-bandhu**, m. N. of a prince, VP. **-bāhú**, m. a man's arm, RV. **-bhartṛi**, m. = *-páti*, Var. **-bhṛita**, m. N. of a prince, VP.

-máṇas, mfn. mindful of or kind to men, RV.; °*ṇasya*, Nom. Ā. °*syate*, to be kind to men, ib. **-maṇi,** m. N. of a demon said to seize on children, PārGṛ. **-mat,** mfn. abounding in men; m. N. of a man, L. **-mana,** g. *kshubhnâdi* (v.l. for *-namana*). **-mara,** mfn. men-killing, L. (cf. *nārmara*). **-māṅsa,** n. the flesh of men; °*śâsana*, n. eating of it, Kathās. **-mâdana,** mfn. gladdening men, RV. **-mithuna,** n. 'a pair of men,' the sign of the zodiac Gemini (cf. *-yugma*). **-megha,** m. a man compared to a cloud yielding rain, MārkP. **-medha,** m. man-sacrifice (cf. *-yajña*); (*-médha* or *-medhas*) m. N. of a man (author of RV. viii, 87; 88), RV.; SV.Anukr. **-yajña,** m. sacrifice or homage to be offered to men, hospitality (one of the 5 Mahā-yajñas, RTL. 411); Mn.; MārkP. **-yugma,** n., **-yuj** (VarBṛS. i, 11), the sign of the zodiac Gemini. **-loka,** m. the world of men, the earth, MBh.; Hariv. &c.; *-pâla*, m. earth-protector, BhP. **- 1. -vát,** ind. like men, strongly, richly, abundantly, RV. **- 2. -vát,** mfn. having men, belonging to or fit for or consisting of men &c., RV.; *-sakhi* (*nṛivát-*), mfn. (a sacrifice) having many associates who take part in it, ib. **-vara,** m. best or chief of men, sovereign, king, Mudr. **-varāha,** m. man-boar (Vishṇu in his 3rd Avatāra), AgP. **-vâhaṇa** or **-vâhas,** mfn. conveying men, RV. **-vāhya,** n. a palankeen, Hcat. **-veshṭana,** m. 'encircled with (the bones of) men,' N. of Śiva, L. **-śaṅsa** (*nṛí-*), m. N. of a god, RV. ix, 81, 5 (cf. *narā-ś°* under *nara*); mf(*ā*)n. injuring men, mischievous, noxious, cruel, base, RV. &c. &c.; *-kārin* or *-kṛit*, mfn. acting cruelly, mischievous, MBh.; *-tā*, f. mischievousness, baseness, Kathās.; Rājat.; *-vat*, mfn. malicious, vile, MBh.; *-varṇa* or *-vādin*, mfn. using low speech, ib.; *-vṛitta*, mfn. practising mischief, W.; °*sita*, n. = °*satā*, BhP.; °*sya*, mf(*ā*)n. malicious, mischievous, vile, MBh.; n. = °*sita*, ib. **-śastrá,** mfn. praised by men, TBr. (Comm.) **-śṛiṅga,** n. 'man's horn' (as an example of what cannot exist), an impossibility, Kap. **-shâc,** mfn. favouring or befriending men, RV. **-shadgu,** m. N. of a Ṛishi, R. (v.l. *ruśaṅgu*). **-shád,** mfn. sitting or dwelling among men, RV.; VS.; AitBr.; m. N. of the father of Kaṇva, RV.; (prob. f.) = *buddhi*, BhP. **-shádana,** n. assemblage or residence of men, RV. **-shádman** (SV.), **-shádvan** (RV.), **-shadvara** (AitBr.; but cf. *ni-shadvará* under *ni-shad*), mfn. sitting or dwelling among men. **-shâh,** mfn. overcoming men, RV. **-shâhya,** mfn. overpowering men, ib.; n. the overpowering of men, ib. **-shâ,** mfn. (√*san*) procuring men, ib. (cf. Pāṇ. iii, 2, 67). **-shāti,** f. the capturing or procuring of men, ib. **-shūta** (*nṛí-*), mfn. impelled or incited by men, ib. **-siṅha,** m. 'man-lion,' a great or illustrious man, MBh.; R.; (also *-ka*) Vishṇu in his 4th Avatāra (cf. *nara-s°*), ib. &c.; a prayer to V° as m°-l°, AgP. (*-tva*, n.); a kind of coitus, L.; N. of sev. authors (also *-cakravartin*, *-ṭhakkura*, *-deva*, *-daivajña*, *-pañcânana*, *-pañcânanabhaṭṭâcārya*, *-purī-parivrāj*, *-bhaṭṭâcārya*, *-mūrty-ācārya*, *-vājapeyin*, *-śāstrin*, *-sarasvatī*, *-sūri*, °*hâcārya*, °*hâcārya-śishya*, °*hânanda*, °*hâraṇya-muni* and °*hâśrama*), Cat.; *-karaṇa*, n., *-kalpa* and *-kavaca*, m., *-gaṇita*, n. N. of wks.; *-gāyatrī*, f. N. of a metre; *-caturdaśī*, f. the 14th day in the light half of the month Vaiśākha (a festival), Col.; *-campū*, f., *-carita*, n., *-jayantī*, f. *-jayantī-kalpa*, m., *-tāpanī* and *-tāpanīyôpanishad*, f. N. of wks.; *-dvādaśī*, f. the 12th day in the light half of the month Phālguna, W.; *-pañcaratnamālā*, f. *-pañjara*, n., *-paṭala*, n., *-paddhati*, f., *-para*, m. or n., *-paricaryā*, f., *-paricaryā-pratishṭhā-kalpa*, m., *-purāṇa*, n., *-pūjā-paddhati*, f., *-pūrva-tāpanīya*, n., *-prakāśikā*, f., *-prasāda*, m., *-prādur-bhāva*, m., *-bīja-stotra*, n., *-bhaṭṭīya*, n., *-mantra*, m., *-mantra-paddhati*, f.; *-mantra-rāja-puraścaraṇa-vidhi*, m., *-mahataś-caritra*, n., *-mahiman*, m., *-mālā-mantra*, m., *-māhātmya*, n., *-rshabha-kshetra-māhātmya* (for *ṛish°*), n., *-vajra-pañjara*, n. N. of wks.; *-vana*, n. N. of a district in the north-west of Madhya-deśa, Var.; *-sarvasva*, n., *-sahasra-nāman*, n., *-sahasra-nāma-stotra*, n., *-stava-rāja*, m., *-stuti*, f., *-stotra*, n., °*hâdi-sāman*, n. pl., °*hârādhana*, n., °*hâshṭaka*, n., °*hâshṭôttara-śata-nāman*, n., °*hīya*, n., °*hôttara-tāpanīya*, n., °*hôdaya*, m. N. of wks. **-sena,** n., **-senâ,** f. an army of men, L. **-soma,** m. 'man-moon,' a great or illustrious man, Ragh. **-hán,** mfn. (dat. *-ghné*) killing men, RV. **-hari,** m. 'man-lion,' Vishṇu in his 4th Avatāra, Rājat.; BhP.; N. of sev. authors, Cat. **Nṛíṅh-praṇetra,** mfn. leading men, TBr. **Nṛ-adhīśa,** m. 'lord of men,' prince, king, Vāgbh. **Nṛ-asthi-mālin,** mfn. wearing a garland of human bones, m. N. of Śiva, L. **Nrārthi,** Pāṇ. vii, 3, 3, Sch.

Nṛi-pa, m. (√3. *pā*) protector of men, prince, king, sovereign, ŚāṅkhŚr.; Mn.; MBh. &c.; (in music) a kind of measure; N. of the numeral 16, Gaṇit. **-kanda,** m. a species of onion, L. **-kārya,** n. the affairs or business of a king, Yājñ., Sch. **-kriyā,** f. 'k°'s business,' government; °*yāṃ* √*kṛi*, Caus. to reign, Hariv. **-gṛiha,** n. 'k°'s house,' a palace, Var.; Rājat. **-cihna,** n. 'k°'s sign,' a white umbrella, Gal. **-jana,** m. 'royal people,' princes, kings, Ratnâv. **-ṃ-jaya,** m. N. of 2 princes, a son of Su-vīra, Hariv.; a son of Medhāvin, BhP. **-tāla,** m. (in music) a kind of measure. **-tva,** n. royalty, dominion, Hariv.; *-tvaṃ* √*kṛi*, to reign, Var. **-dīpa,** m. a king compared to a lamp, Pañc. **-druma,** m. 'k°'s tree,' Cathartocarpus Fistula or Mimusops Hexandra, L. **-dvish,** mfn. k°-hating, MW. **-nīti,** f. royal policy, k°-craft, ib. **-palāṇḍu,** m. = *-kanda*, L. **-priya,** m. (only L.) 'dear to kings,' a kind of parrot; Bambusa Spinosa; a species of Saccharum Sara; rice; a species of onion; the mango tree; (*ā*), f. Pandanus Odoratissimus; a species of date tree; *-phalā*, f. Solanum Melongena, L. **-badara,** m. a species of jujube; n. its fruit, L. **-bhūshaṇī,** f. N. of wk. **-mandira,** n. = *-gṛiha*, Rājat. **-māṅgalyaka,** n. Tabernaemontana Coronaria, L. **-māna,** w. r. for *nṛipâbhīra*. **-māsha,** m. Dolichos Catjang, L. **-yoga,** m. N. of partic. constellations, VarYogay. **-lakshman,** n. = *-cihna*, L. **-liṅga,** n. an emblem or mark of royalty; *-dhara*, mfn. assuming the insignia of r°, BhP. **-vallabha,** m. 'dear to a king,' a kind of mango, L.; (*ā*), f. a k°'s wife, a queen, L.; a species of flower, L. **-vṛiksha,** m. N. of a tree (= *rāja-v°*), Suśr. **-veśman,** n. a royal court, law-court, VarYogay. **-śāsana,** n. a royal edict, MW. **-śreshṭha,** m. a kind of jujube, L. **-saṃśraya,** m. service of princes, W. **-sabha,** n. an assembly of princes or a royal palace, L. **-suta,** m. a king's son, prince, L.; (*ā*), f. a k°'s daughter, L.; the musk-rat, Var. **-snushā,** f. the daughter-in-law of a king, MW. **Nṛipâṅsa,** m. a k°'s share ($\frac{1}{6}$, $\frac{1}{8}$ &c. of grain, fruit &c.), royal revenue, L. **Nṛipâkṛishṭa,** n. a partic. favourable position of the pieces in the game Catur-aṅga, L. **Nṛipâṅgaṇa** or °**na,** n. a royal court, Bhartṛ.; Kpr.; (°*nā*), f. a princess, queen, Daś. **Nṛipâtmaja,** mfn. of royal birth; m. a king's son, a prince, R.; a species of mango, L.; (*ā*), f. a princess, Naish.; a bitter gourd, L. **Nṛipâdhvara,** m. a sort of sacrifice (= *rājasūya*), L. **Nṛipânucara,** m. a king's attendant, a minister, Var. **Nṛipânna,** n. a sort of rice, L. **Nṛipânyatva,** n. change of government, Var. **Nṛipâbhīra,** n. music played at a king's meals, L. (v.l. *nṛipa-māna*). **Nṛipâmaya,** m. 'king's disease,' consumption, L. **Nṛipâryaman,** m. a sun among princes, Rājat. **Nṛipâlaya,** m. a king's residence, a palace, R. **Nṛipâvarta,** m. a kind of gem (= *rājâvarta*), L. **Nṛipâsana,** n. royal seat, a throne, MBh. &c. **Nṛipâspada,** n. 'a king's place,' a palace, Rājat. **Nṛipâhvaya,** m. a species of onion, L. **Nṛipêcchā,** f. the royal pleasure, MW. **Nṛipêshṭa,** m. a kind of onion, L. (cf. *nṛipa-priya*). **Nṛipôcita,** m. 'suited to a king, kingly,' Dolichos Catjang (= *rāja-māsha*), L.

Nṛimṇá, n. manhood (virtus), power, strength, courage, RV.; VS.; AV.; Kāṭh.; TĀr.; = *dhana*, Naigh. ii, 10; mfn. = *sukha-kara*, BhP., Comm.; (*ā*), f. N. of a river (v.l. *nṛimaṇā*), ib. (B.) **-várdhana,** mfn. enhancing courage, RV. **Nṛimṇāyi,** a sacrificial exclamation, TĀr.

नृत् 1. *nṛit*, cl. 4. P. (Dhātup. xxvi, 9) *nṛ́ityati* (ep. also °*te*; pf. *nanarta*, *nanṛitur*, MBh.; aor. *anartishur*, RV.; *-nṛitur* [cf. *ā-*√*nṛit*]; p. *nṛitámāna* [?], ib. v, 33, 6; fut. *nartishyati*, MBh. &c.; *nartsyati* and *nartitā*, Gr.; inf. *nartitum* and *narttum*, MBh. &c.; ind. p. *nartitvā*, ib., *-nartam*, Br.), to dance, RV. &c. &c.; to act on the stage, represent (acc.), Hariv. &c.; to dance about (acc.), R.: Caus. *nartáyati*, °*te*, to cause to dance, RV. &c. &c.: Desid. *ninṛitsati* and *ninartishati*, Pāṇ. vii, 2, 57: Intens. *narī-nartti*, Var.; Kāv.; *narīnṛityate*, °*ti*, Kāv.; *narnartti*, *narnṛitīti*, *narīnṛitīti*, Gr., to dance about or cause to dance about (cf. *naṭ*).

Narta, °**taka,** &c. See s.v.

2. **Nṛit,** f. dancing, gesticulation, AV.

Nṛiti, f. id., RV.; grand or solemn appearance, show, ib.

Nṛitú, mfn. dancing, gesticulating, lively, active (said of Indra, the Aśvins, and the Maruts), RV.; (*ú*), m. (nom. *ûs*) a dancer, an actor, RV. &c. &c.; a worm, L.; the earth, L.; mfn. long, L.

Nṛittá, n. dancing, acting, gesticulation, AV.; ŚBr. &c. &c. **-jña,** mfn. knowing to dance, Var. **-prayoga,** m. N. of wk. **-maya,** mf(*ī*)n. consisting in dance, Kathās.

Nṛitya, n. dancing, acting, gesticulation, pantomime, MBh.; Var.; Kāv. &c. **-gīta,** n. du. d° and singing, KaṭhUp.; *-vādya*, n. pl. d°, s°, and instrumental music, MW. **-priya,** m. 'fond of d°,' a peacock, L.; N. of Śiva, RTL. 84; (*ā*), f. N. of one of the Mātṛis attending on Skanda, MBh. **-vilāsa,** m. N. of wk. **-śālā,** f. a d°-room, L. **-śāstra,** n. the science or art of d°, Hcat. **-sarvasva,** n. N. of wk. **-sthāna,** n. a place for d°. **-hasta,** m. the position of the hands in d°, Cat. **Nṛityâdhyāya,** m. N. of wk. **Nṛityêkshaṇa,** n. looking at a dance or pantomime, L.

नृपीट *nṛipīṭa*, n. water, Naigh. i, 12 (v.l. for *kṛipīṭa*).

नृमणा *nṛimaṇā*, f. N. of a river, BhP. (v.l. for *nṛimṇā*).

नॄ *nṝi*, cl. 9. P. *nṛiṇāti*, to lead, Dhātup. xxxi, 25.

नॄँःप्रणेत्र *nṝiṅh-praṇetra*. See *nṛi*.

नेक्षण *nekshaṇa*, n. (√*niksh*) a sharp stick or spear, a fork or similar cooking implement, AV.; Kauś. (cf. *nikshaṇa* and *mekshaṇa*).

नेग *nega*, m. pl. N. of a school of the Sāmaveda (cf. *naigeya*).

नेजक *nejaka*, m. (√*nij*) a washerman, Mn.; Yājñ.

Nejana, n. washing, cleansing, MBh.; washing-place, ib.

नेजमेष *nejamesha*, m. N. of a demon inimical to children, GṛS. (cf. *naigamesha*).

नेतव्य *netavya*, mfn. (√*nī*) to be led or guided &c.; to be led away; to be led towards or to or into (acc.), MBh.; Kāv. &c.; to be applied, Śaṃk.; to be examined, ib.

Netī, f. the drawing of a thread through the nose and mouth (as a kind of penance), Cat.

Nétṛi, mfn. leading, guiding, one who leads or will lead, RV. x, 26, 5; m. bringer, offerer (with acc.; cf. Pāṇ. ii, 3, 69), MBh.; (*netṛí*), m. leader, guide, conductor (with gen. or ifc.), RV. &c. &c.; (with *daṇḍasya*) 'rod-applier,' inflicter of punishment, Mn. vii, 25 (cf. *daṇḍa-n°*); the leader or chief of an army, Var.; N. of Vishṇu, RTL. 106, n.; the hero of a drama (= *nāyaka*), Daśar.; Sāh.; a master, owner, W.; the numeral 2, MW. (cf. *netra*); Azadirachta Indica, L.; (*netrī́*), f. a female leader (with gen. or ifc.), RV.; TS.; MBh. &c.; a river, L.; a vein, L.; N. of Lakshmī, L. **-tva,** n. the office or business of a leader, BhP. **-mat,** mfn. containing the word *netṛi*, AitBr.

Netra, m. a leader, guide (with gen., R. [B.] iii, 66, 10; mostly ifc., e.g. *tvaṃ-netra*, 'having you for guide,' MBh. ii, 2486 [f. *ā*, ib. ix, 222]; cf. Pāṇ. v, 4, 116, Vārtt. 2, 3, Pat.), AitUp.; MBh.; BhP.; N. of a son of Dharma and father of Kuntī, BhP.; of a son of Su-mati, MatsyaP.; (°*trá*), n. (and m., Siddh.) leading, guiding, conducting, AV. x, 10, 22; (ifc. f. *ā*), the eye (as the guiding organ, also *-ka*, HCat.; cf. *nayana*); the numeral 2, Sūryas. (cf. *netṛi*); the string by which a churning-stick is whirled round, MBh.; a pipe-tube, Car.; an injection-pipe, Suśr.; the root of a tree, Kād.; a kind of cloth, Hcar.; a veil, R.; Ragh.; a carriage, L.; a river, L. **-kanīnikā,** f. the pupil of the eye, L. **-kārmaṇa,** n. a spell for the eyes, Vcar. **-kośa,** m. the eyeball or the bud of a flower, R. (also written *-kosha*). **-gocara,** mfn. within the range of the eyes, visible, BhP. **-capala,** mfn. restless with the eyes, Mn. iv, 177. **-cchada,** m. the eyelid, L. **-ja,** mfn.

'eye-born' (with or sc. *vāri*), n. a tear, R.; W. **-jala**, n. = prec. n.; *-srava*, m. a flood of tears, R. **-tā**, f. the state of being an eye; *-tām √yā*, to become an eye, Amar. **-tribhāga-brahma-yaśasvin**, m. N. of an author, Cat. **-niṇsin**, mfn. (sleep) kissing or touching the eye, Daś. **-pattra**, n. the eye-brows, Svapnac. **-paryanta**, m. the outer corner of the e°, L. **-pāka**, m. inflammation of the e°, Suśr. **-piṇḍa**, m. the eyeball, L.; a cat, L. **-pushkarā**, f. a species of creeper, L. **-peya**, mfn. to be drunk in or enjoyed by the eyes, Vāsav. **-praṇayin**, mfn. desirous of a person's e°, i.e. coming before the e° of, face to face with (gen.), Vcar. **-prabandha**, m. = (and v. l. for) *nayana-pr°*, q. v. **-bandha**, m. 'eye-binding,' hood-winking; playing at hide-and-seek, BhP. **-bhava**, m., **-mala**, n. excretion of the eye, Gal. **-manaḥ-svabhāva**, m. pl. eyes, mind, and soul, MW. **-mīlā**, f. Autographis Paniculata, L. **-mush**, mfn. stealing or captivating the eye, MBh. **-yoni**, m. N. of Indra (whose body, after his adultery with Ahalyā, was covered with marks which resembled the female organ and then were made to resemble eyes; cf. *sahasrâksha*), L.; the moon (as produced from the eye of Atri), L. **-rañjana**, n. 'eye-colouring,' collyrium, L. **-ruj**, f. eye-disease, L. **-roga**, m. id., Suśr.; mfn. afflicted with e°-d°, (*-tā*, f.), Var.; *-cikitsā*, f. healing e°-d°, N. of wk.; *-han*, m. 'destroying e°-d°,' Tragia Involucrata, L. **-roman**, n. the eyelash, L. **-vasti**, m. an injection-pipe with a receptacle attached to it, Suśr. **-vastra**, n. a veil over the eye, Kāśikh. **-vār** or **-vāri**, n. eye-water, tears, Kāv. **-vish**, f. excretion of the eye, Suśr. **-visha**, mfn. having poison in the eyes, MBh. **-saṃvejana**, n. fixing an injection-pipe, Suśr. **-stambha**, m. rigidity of the eyes, ib. **-hārin**, mfn. = *-mush*, L. **-hita**, mfn. good or wholesome for the e°, Bhpr. **Netrâñjana**, n. e°-ointment, collyrium, Śriṅgār.; N. of wk. **Netrâtithi**, mfn. one who has become visible (lit. an e°-guest), Dhūrtan. **Netrânta**, m. = °*tra-paryanta*, MW. **Netrâbhishyanda**, m. running of the e°, Suśr. **Netrâmaya**, m. ophthalmia, ib. **Netrâmbu** (L.), °**mbhas** (Rājat.), n. = °*tra-vāri*. **Netrâri**, m. 'e°-foe,' Euphorbia Antiquorum, L. **Netrôtsava**, m. 'e°-feast,' any beautiful object, Dhūrtas. **Netrôddyota**, m., **Netrôpanishad**, f. N. of wks. **Netrôpama**, n. the almond fruit (resembling the eye); *-phala*, m. the almond tree, Bhpr. **Netrôpâdhyāya**, m. N. of an author, Cat. **Netrâushadha**, n. 'eye-medicine,' green sulphate of iron, L.; (*ī*), f. Odina Pinnata, L.

Netrika, n. a clyster-pipe; a ladle, L.

Netrya, mfn. good or wholesome for the eyes, Bhpr.

नेद् 1. *néd* (fr. *ná* + *íd*), not, not indeed (= *nâiva*, Sāy.), RV. viii, 5, 39; AV. &c.; in order that not, lest (with Subj., Pot. or Impv.; the verb accented, cf. Pāṇ. viii, 1, 30), RV.; AV.; VS.; Br. [Cf. Zd. *noid*, 'not.']

नेद् 2. *ned*, cl. 1. P. *nedati*, to go, flow (cf. *ati-ned* and Naigh. ii, 14), to censure, blame, Dhātup. xxi, 8 (cf. √1. *nid* and *nind*); to be near, ib. (prob. an artificial meaning to explain *nedishṭha* &c.)

Nedaya (fr. *neda*, see next), Nom. P. °*yati*, to bring near, Bhaṭṭ.

Nédishṭha, mf(*ā*)n. (superl. of *neda* substituted for *antika*, Pāṇ. v, 3, 63) the nearest, next, very near, RV. &c. &c. (*am*, ind. next, in the first place, ib.; *āt*, ind. from the neighbourhood, AitBr.; Kāth.); = *nipuṇa*, L.; m. Alangium Hexapetalum, L.; N. of a son of Manu Vaivasvata, VP. **-tama** (*néd°*), mfn. the nearest of all, RV.; (*ām*), ind., ŚBr.

Nedishṭhin, mfn. very near, very nearly related, TāṇḍBr.; SrS.

Nédiyas, mfn. (compar. of *neda*; cf. *nedishṭha* and Pāṇ. v, 3, 63) nearer, very near, RV.; Ait. Br.; (*as*), ind. near, hither, RV.; AV.; Br. °**yas-tā**, f. nearness, neighbourhood, ŚāṅkhBr. °**yo-maraṇa**, mfn. whose death is near or imminent, Rājat. iv, 31.

नेन्य *nenya*, mfn. (Intens. of √*nī*) taking or obtaining frequently (?), W.

नेप *nepa*, m. (√*nī*?) the family priest, Uṇ. iii, 23, Sch.; n. water, L.

नेपथ्य *nepathya*, n. (and m., L.) an ornament, decoration, costume (esp. of an actor), attire (ifc. f. *ā*), MBh.; Kāv. &c. (°*thyam √kṛi* or *grah* or *rac* or *vi-dhā*, 'to make the toilet'); n. (in dram.) the place behind the stage (separated by the curtain from the *raṅga*), the postscenium, the tiring-room; (*e*), ind. behind the scenes (see esp. MW. Śak. p. 3, n. 2). **-gṛiha**, n. a toilet room, Mālav. **-grahaṇa**, n. making the t°, Ragh. **-prayoga**, m. the art of t°-making (one of the 64 Kalās), Cat. **-bhṛit**, mfn. wearing a costume, ib. **-vidhāna**, n. = *-grahaṇa*, Ragh.; Śak. **-samprayoga**, m. = *-prayoga*, Cat. **-savana**, n. a ceremony performed in full toilet, Mālav. (B. *nepathya-s°*). **Nepathyâbhimukham**, ind. towards the tiring-room, Śak., Introd.

नेपाल *nepāla*, m. N. of a country and (pl.) of a people, Nepal or the Nepalese, Var.; Rājat. &c.; a species of sugar-cane, L.; (*ī*), f. red arsenic, L.; the wild date-tree or its fruit, L.; n. copper, L. **-jā** or **-jātā**, f. red arsenic, Suśr. **-nimba**, m. a kind of tree, L. **-pāla** (Cat.), **-pālaka** (Rājat.), m. a king of Nepal. **-māhātmya**, n. N. of wk. **-mūlaka**, n. a radish, Bhpr. **-vishaya**, m. the country of Nepal, Rājat.

Nepālaka, n. copper, L.; (*ikā*), f. red arsenic, L.

नेम *néma*, mfn. (fr. *na* + *ima* [?]; loc. *némasmin*, nom. pl. *néme* and °*mās*, cf. Pāṇ. i, 1, 33) one, several; *néma-néma*, the one–the other, RV. (unaccented, vi, 16, 18); (ibc.) half (cf. Nir. iii, 20); m. N. of a Ṛishi with the patr. Bhārgava (author of RV. viii, 89); (only L.) portion; time; limit; boundary; the foundation of a wall (cf. *nemi*); a hole; upper part, above; deceit; acting, dancing; evening; a root; food, rice; n. a partic. high number, Buddh. [Cf. Zd. *naima*.] **-candra**, m. 'half-moon,' N. of a prince, L. **-dhita** (°*má-*), Pāṇ. vii, 4, 45; cf. Sāy. on RV. i, 72, 4 (the only form °*tā* is prob. loc. of next). **-dhiti** (°*má-*), f. separation, conflict; (*tā*), ind. apart, aside, RV. **-nātha** (or *nitya-n°*), m. N. of an author, Cat. **-pishṭa** (*néma-*), mfn. half ground (*-tā*, f.), MaitrS. **-śāha**, m. N. of an author (cf. *nemi-ś°*). **-spṛishṭa**, mfn. half touched, Śiksh. **Nêmâditya**, m. N. of Trivikrama-bhaṭṭa's father, Cat.

नेमन्निष् *nemann-ísh*, mfn. (prob. loc. *neman* [√2. *nī*] and √3. *ish*) following guidance, striving after, seeking to reach or overtake (sc. Indra, said of praises), RV. i, 56, 2 (Sāy. praisers 'moving reverentially or bearing oblations').

नेमि *nemí*, f. (√*nam*) the felly of a wheel (also °*mī*, L.), any circumference or edge or rim (ifc. 'encircled' or 'surrounded by'), RV. &c. &c.; a windlass or framework for the rope of a well (also °*mī*), L.; a thunderbolt, L.; the foundation of a wall, Gal. (cf. *nema*); m. Dalbergia Ougeinensis, L.; N. of a Daitya, BhP.; of a Cakra-vartin, Buddh. (cf. *nimi*); of 22nd Arhat of present Ut-sarpiṇī, L. **-ghosha**, m. the noise of (the felly of) a wheel, the din of a carriage, Mṛicch. **-cakra**, m. a prince descended from Parī-kshit (said to have removed the capital of India to Kauśāmbī after the inundation of Hāstina-pura), BhP. **-caritra**, n. N. of wk. **-dhvani**, m. = *-ghosha*, Veṇis. **-nātha**, m. N. of a man, W. **-ninada**, m. = *-ghosha*, MBh. **-m-dhara**, m. (with Buddh.) N. of one of the mountains, Dharmas. 125. **-purāṇa** and **-rājarshi-caritra**, n. N. of wks. **-vṛiksha**, m. Acacia Catechu, L. **-vṛitti**, mfn. following the track of a person's wheels, entirely conforming to (gen.), Ragh. **-śabda**, m. = *-ghosha*, Mṛicch. **-śāha**, m. N. of an author (cf. *nêma-ś°*). **-svana**, m. = *-ghosha*, MBh.

Nemita, m. N. of a prince, Buddh.

Nemin, m. Dalbergia Ougeinensis, L.; N. of the 22nd Arhat of present Ut-sarpiṇī, L. (cf. *nemi*, m.)

नेय *neya*, mfn. (√*nī*) to be led or guided or managed or governed; to be led away or to be led to (loc.), MBh.; Kāv. &c.; to be brought into any state or condition (e.g. *śāntim*, *kshība-tām*), Megh.; Kathās.; to be moved (*śāra*), Pāṇ. v, 2, 9; to be applied or inflicted (*daṇḍa*), Kām.; to be spent or passed (*kāla*), Rājat.; Pañc.; to be guessed (see *neyârtha* below). **-dhī**, mfn. of manageable or tractable character, Rājat. **-pāla**, m. N. of a prince, Buddh. **Neyârtha** or °**thaka**, mfn. (a word or sentence) having a sense that can only be guessed, Vām. ii, 1, 13; *-tā*, f., *-tva*, n., Sāh.

नेरणिवादार्थ *nerani-vādârtha*, m. N. of a gramm. treatise by Nāgeśa.

नेरि *neri*, m. or f. a kind of dance (mus.)

नेरुङ्गल *neruṅgala*, m. N. of a prince, Col.

नेरेल्ल *nerella*, m. N. of a race, Cat.

नेल *nela*, *nelu*, and *nevalla*, m. a partic. number, Buddh.

नेष् *nesh*, cl. 1. Ā. *neshate*, to go, move, Dhātup. xvi, 16 (*neshatu*, *neshṭāt*, Pāṇ. iii, 2, 135, Vārtt. 4, Pat.)

नेष *nésha* (√*nī*), only in superl. instr. pl. *nésha-tamais*, ind. with the best guides or guidance, RV. i, 141, 12.

Nesháṇi, loc. inf. of √*nī*.

Neshṭā = °*ṭri* in comp. **-potārau**, m. du. the Neshṭṛi (see next) and the Potṛi. **Neshṭôdgātārau**, m. du. the Neshṭṛi and the Udgātṛi, Pāṇ. vi, 3, 25, Kāś.

Néshṭṛi, m. (prob. fr. √*nī*, aor. stem *nesh*; but cf. Pāṇ. iii, 2, 135, Vārtt. 2 &c.) one of the chief officiating priests at a Soma sacrifice, he who leads forward the wife of the sacrificer and prepares the Surā (Tvashṭṛi so called, RV. i, 15, 3), RV.; Br.; ŚrS. &c. **-tva-prayoga** or **-prayoga**, m. N. of wks.

Neshṭrá, n. the Soma vessel of the Neshṭṛi, RV. (cf. Nir. viii, 3); the office of the N°, KātyŚr.

Neshṭrīya, mf(*ā*)n. belonging to the Neshṭṛi, relating to him, AitBr.

नेष्टु *neshṭu*, m. a lump of earth or clay, a clod, MBh. xiii, 1541; Nīlak. (perhaps w. r. for *loshṭu*, *loshṭa*).

नै *nai*, Vṛiddhi form of *ni* in comp. **-kaṭika**, mfn. near, neighbouring, Hcar.; Bhaṭṭ. (cf. Pāṇ. iv, 4, 73). **-kaṭya**, n. nearness, neighbourhood, Kathās. **-kashī**, f. N. of Rāvaṇa's mother, AgP. (cf. *ni-kasha*). **-kasheya**, m. a Rākshasa (v. l. °*seya*). **-kṛitika** (Mn.; MBh. &c.), **-kṛitin** (Var.), mfn. dishonest, fallacious, low, vile. **-khānya**, mfn. liable to be buried, ShaḍvBr. **-gama**, mf(*ī*)n. relating to the Veda or Vedic words or quotations (a N. given to the collection of 278 separate words occurring in the Nigama or Veda and commented on by Yāska; they are arranged in one chapter of three sections), Vedic, Nir.; BhP.; m. an interpreter of the sacred writings, Pāṇ. v, 4, 118, Pat.; an Upanishad, L.; = *dṛiti*, L.; a way, means, expedient, MBh. xii, 3685; prudent conduct, L.; a citizen, townsman, SaddhP.; a trader, merchant, Yājñ.; MBh.; R. &c.; N. of an ancient teacher, Cat.; *-kāṇḍa*, m. or n. N. of the three chapters of the Nirukta where the Nigamas or Vedic words are explained by Yāska; °*mâbhidhāna*, n. N. of wk.; *-gamika*, mfn. relating to the Veda, Vedic, Kār. on Pāṇ. vii, 1, 1; *-gameya*, m., see s. v. **-gutá**, m. destroyer of enemies (or of Nigut), RV. **-ghaṇṭuka**, mfn. mentioned by the way or incidentally, Nir.; m. author of a glossary, ĀpŚr., Sch.; n. N. of the 3 chapters or collections of Vedic words commented upon by Yāska; °*kâikâdhyāya*, m. N. of a glossary by Bāhlikeya-miśra. **-citya**, m. a prince of the Nicitas, Pāṇ. iv, 1, 172, Sch. **-ja**, mfn. own, one's own, Hariv.; BhP. **-tala**, mfn. (fr. *ni-tala*); *-sadman*, n. Mcar. v, 18. **-tuṇḍi**, m. patr. fr. *ni-tuṇḍa*, Pravar. **-tośá**, mfn. (fr. *ni-tośa*, √*tuś*) munificent, liberal, RV. x, 106, 6. **-dāgha** (*nai-*), mf(*ī*)n. relating to the hot season, summer-like, scorching, Megh. (also °*ghika*, BhP., and °*ghīya*, TāṇḍBr.); m. the hot season, AV.; TBr.; ŚBr. (°*ghá*) &c. **-dāna**, m. an etymologist, Nir.; a pathologist, Śiś., Sch. **-deśika**, m. 'executing orders,' a servant, BhP. **-dra**, mf(*ī*)n. (fr. *ni-drā*, f.) sleepy, somniferous, W.; closed (like the petals of a lotus), Śiś. vi, 43. **-dhana**, mfn. (fr. 2. *ni-dhana*) subject to death, perishable, deadly, funereal, final, Hariv.; R. &c.; (in astrol. with or sc. *gṛiha*) the 8th house, the house of death, Var. **-dhāna**, mf(*ī*)n. (a boundary) indicated by putting down various objects, Nār. (cf. g. *saṃkalâdi*). **-dhānya**, n., g. *brāhmaṇâdi*, Kāś. **-dheya** (Pāṇ. iv, 1, 122, Sch.), **-dhruva** (also pl., Pravar.), **-dhruvi** (*nai-*, ŚBr.), patr. fr. *ni-dhi* and *-dhruva*. **-pātika**, mfn. only mentioned incidentally or by the way, Bṛih.

-pātya, n., g. *brāhmaṇâdi*. **-puṇa**, mfn. = *ni-puṇa* (ifc.), Jātak.; n. = next. **-puṇya** (cf. g. *brāhmaṇâdi*), n. dexterity, experience in (gen. or comp.), skill or anything which requires skill; completeness, totality (*ena*, ind. totally, exactly), Mn.; MBh.; R. &c. **-baddhaka**, mfn., g. *varāhâdi*. **-biḍya**, n. closeness, compactness, continuity, Rājat.; (in music) a partic. quality (prob. fulness) of a blown sound. **-bhṛitya**, n. stillness, silentness, MBh. **-magnaka**, mfn., g. *varāhâdi*. **-mantraṇaka**, n. a banquet, feast, L. **-maya**, m. a trader, merchant, Śiś., Sch. **-miśa** (BhP.), °**śīya** (TāṇḍBr.) = °*misha*, °*shīya*. **-miśri**, m. patron. fr. *ni-miśri*, g. *taulvaly-ādi*. **-misha**, mf(*ī*)n. momentary, transient, W.; n. N. of a forest and a sacred Tīrtha (where Sauti related the MBh., and so called because in it an army of Asuras was destroyed in a twinkling), MBh. i, 1026, Hariv. &c.; m. pl. the inhabitants of the Naimisha wood, MBh.; *-kānana*, n. the N° w°, ib.; *-kuñja*, n. N. of a Tīrtha, ib.; *-nṛipa*, m. a king of N°, Var.; °*shâyana*, mfn. living in N°, BhP. (°*shâyaṇa*?); °*shâraṇya*, n. the N° w°, MW.; °*shi*, m., g. *taulvaly-ādi*; °*shīya*, mfn. relating to or being in N°, MBh.; BhP.; m. pl. the inhabitants of N°, ŚāṅkhBr.; °*sheya*, mfn. = prec. mfn., MBh.; °*shya*, m. pl. = °*shīya*, m. pl., Kāṭh. **-meya**, m. = *ni-maya*, barter, exchange, L. **-yatya**, n. the being settled or established, Śāṇḍ., Comm.; necessity, obligation, Rājat.; self-command, L. **-yamika**, mfn. settled, enjoined, prescribed, Āpast. (w. r. *naiyy*°). **-līnaka**, mfn. (fr. *ni-līna*), Pāṇ. iv, 2, 110, Kāś. **-vātâyana**, mfn. (fr. *ni-vāta*), g. *pakshâdi*. **-vāsika**, mfn. dwelling, L.; (suffix) indicating a dwelling-place or abode, Pat. (cf. g. *guḍâdi*); (*ā*), f. deity dwelling (in a tree), Divyâv. **-vida**, mf(*ī*)n. containing a Nivid, Kaush-Ār. **-vedya**, n. an offering of eatables presented to a deity or idol, BhP. (cf. RTL. 144; 415); *-prakaraṇa*, n., *-prasāda-māhātmya*, n., *-vidhi*, m. N. of wks. **-veśa**, mfn., g. *saṃkalâdi*. **-veśika**, n. any vessel or implement belonging to the furniture of a house, Yājñ.; a present to a Brāhman householder, a girl so given or ornaments with her, &c., W. **-śitya**, n. sharpness, Śiś., Sch. **-śreyasa**, w. r. for *naiḥ-śr*°. **-śvāsa**, m. N. of wk. **-shadyika**, m. (with Buddh.) N. of one of the 12 Dhūta-guṇas or ascetic practices, Dharmas. 63. **-shāda**, mf(*ī*)n. belonging to the Nishādas, BhP.; m. a N°, VS.; ŚāṅkhBr.; a hunter or bird-catcher, Jātak.; pl. the N° people, MBh.; °*daka*, n., g. *kulālâdi*; °*da-karshuka*, mfn. Pāṇ. iv, 2, 119; °*daki* (iv, 1, 97, Vārtt. 1, Pat.) and °*dâyana* (g. *haritâdi*), m. patr. fr. *ni-shāda*; °*di*, f. a prince of N°, MBh. **-shedhikī**, f. the obtruding one's self upon a person's notice (to prevent his surprise), HPariś. **-shṭhika** (or *naiḥ-*; see 2. *ni-shṭhā*), mf(*ī*)n. forming the end, final, last, MBh.; Hariv.; Ragh.; definitive, fixed, firm, MBh.; R.; Yājñ.; highest, perfect, complete, MBh.; Kāv.; Pur. (*-sundara*, mfn. perfectly beautiful, Kum. v, 62); completely versed in or familiar with (comp.), Var.; belonging to the character or office of a perpetual student, W.; m. a perpetual religious student or Brāhman who observes the vow of chastity, Rājat.; BhP. **-shṭhurya**, n. harshness, severity, MBh.; Kāv.; Hit. **-shṭhya**, n. (cf. *-shṭhika*) constancy, adherence to rule, firm belief, MW. **-shṇihya**, n. (fr. *ni-shṇih* = *niḥ-snih*?) getting rid of, freeing one's self from (abl.), ĀśvŚr. **-sarga**, mfn. innate, natural, BhP. **-sargika**, mfn. id., Mālatīm.; w. r. for *naiḥ-s*°, q. v.; *-daśaka*, n. N. of wk. **-sarpa**, m. (fr. unused *ni-s*°) N. of one of the 9 treasures (with Jainas). **-snehya** and **-svya**, w. r. for *naiḥsn*° and *-svya*.

नैः *naiḥ*, Vṛiddhi form of *niḥ* (for *nis*) in comp. **-śreyasa**, mf(*ī*)n. leading to happiness or future beatitude, Mn. (°*sika*, xii, 88); MBh.; n. N. of a wood in the world of Vishṇu, BhP. **-saṅgya**, n. absence of attachment, indifference, Jātak. **-sargika**, mfn. cast off, put off, Divyâv.; N. of partic. transgressions punished with the confiscation of something belonging to the transgressor, Buddh. **-snehya**, n. absence of love or affection, Mn. ix, 15. **-spṛihya**, n. absence of longing for anything, Kāv. **-svabhāvya**, n. (fr. *niḥ-svabhāva*), L. **-svya**, n. (fr. *niḥ-sva*) absence of property, destitution, poverty, Var.

Nair, Vṛiddhi form of *nir* (for *nis*) in comp. **-añjanā**, f. N. of a river (Nilajan) falling into the Ganges in Magadha (Behar), Lalit. **-antarya**, n. uninterruptedness, close succession, continuousness, compactness, Daś.; Yogas. (°*yeṇa*, ind. uninterruptedly, continually, Śaṃk.; Pañc.); immediate consequence, Sarvad. **-apêksha**, mfn. = (prob. w. r. for) *nir-ap*°, BhP., Sch.; n., w. r. for next. **-apêkshya**, n. disregard, indifference, Kap.; Kull.; complete independence, Nyāyam. **-ayika**, mfn. hellish, an inhabitant of hell, L. **-arthya**, n. meaninglessness, nonsense, MārkP. **-ākāṅkshya**, n. absence of need of supplying a word or sentence, Śaṃk. **-ātma**, n., w. r. for next. **-ātmya**, n. (fr. *nir-ātman*), Lalit. (cf. Dharmas. cxvi). **-āśya**, n. hopelessness, non-expectancy, despair at (*prati* or comp.), MBh.; R. &c. **-āsya**, m. N. of a magical formula pronounced over weapons, R. **-ukta**, mfn. based on etymology, explained etymologically, MBh.; relating to the Nirukta (q. v.), explaining it, g. *ṛigayanâdi*; m. (also *-uktika*, g. *ukthâdi*) a knower of the derivation of words, an etymologist, Nir.; Mn. **-ūhika**, mfn. (fr. 1. *nir-ūha*) purging, cleaning out, Suśr. **-ṛitá**, mf(*ī́*)n. belonging or consecrated to Nirṛiti (q. v.), AV.; ŚBr. &c.; south-western, Mn.; MBh.; Suśr. &c.; belonging to the Rākshasas, MBh. (see m.); relating to the lunar mansion Nairṛita (Mūla), Cat.; m. a child of Nirṛiti, a Rākshasa or demon, MBh.; R. &c. (*-kanyā*, f. a Rākshasa girl, R.; *-rāja*, m. the R°-king, ib.); N. of one of the Loka-pālas (the ruler of the south-west quarter, L.; cf. Dharmas. 8); of a Rudra, Hariv. (C. *nir-ṛiti*); pl. N. of a people, MBh.; (*ī*), f. (with or sc. *diś*) the south-west quarter, Mn.; MBh.; Var.; N. of Durgā, Devīm.; n. the lunar mansion Mūla, Var. **-ṛiti**, m. N. of a demon, MBh.; a Rākshasa, L. **-ṛiteya**, mf(*ā*)n. descended from or belonging to Nirṛiti, Suśr. **-ṛitya**, mfn. belonging or consecrated to N°, Kauś.; Yājñ.; south-western, Cat. **-gandhya**, n. absence of smell, inodorousness, Mallin. on Kum. iii, 28. **-guṇya**, n. absence of qualities or properties, MBh.; BhP.; want of good qu° or excellencies, MBh.; Pañc.; mfn. having no connection with qu°, BhP. **-granthya**, n. (fr. *nir-grantha*), Bhadrab. **-ghṛiṇya**, n. pitilessness, cruelty, Mālav.; Kathās. **-jara**, mf(*ī*)n. divine, Kāśīkh. **-jhara**, mfn. belonging to a waterfall, to be found there, Bālar. **-daśya**, n. getting over the first ten days (said of a new-born child), surmounting any dangerous time or bad influence, TāṇḍBr. **-deśika**, mf(*ī*)n. (fr. *nir-deśa*), Pat. **-dhanya**, n. want of property, poverty, Kathās. **-bādhyà**, mfn. = *nir-b*°, AV. **-malya**, n. stainlessness (lit. and fig.), purity, MBh.; Śatr. **-māṇika**, mfn. miraculous, Divyâv. **-yāṇika**, mf(*ī*)n. treating of the manner of dying (N. of ch. of VarBṛS.); conducive to emancipation, Lalit. (cf. Dharmas. 100); *-tā*, f., L. **-lajjya**, n. shamelessness, impudence, Suśr. **-vāṇika**, mf(*ī*)n. relating to Nirvāṇa, where N° takes place &c.; Kāraṇḍ.; °*mārgâvataraṇa*, n. entering the path of N° (one of the 4 *vaiśāradyani* or subjects of confidence of a Buddha), Dharmas. 77. **-vāhika**, mfn. conducting or leading out, carrying (water &c.) out; (with *dvāra*), n. a sluice, Var. **-vedhika**, mfn. piercing, penetrating; *-prajña*, mfn. having a p° mind, sagacious, L. **-hastá**, mfn. (a weapon) intended for handless demons, AV.

Naiś, Vṛiddhi form of *niś* (for *nis*) in comp. **-calya**, n. fixedness, immovableness, MW. **-citya**, n. determination, certainty, W.; a fixed ceremony or festival (as a birth, investiture, marriage &c.), ib. **-cintya**, n. freedom from anxiety, absence of care, Bhartṛ.

Naish, Vṛiddhi form of *nish* (for *nis*) in comp. **-karmya**, n. inactivity, abstinence or exemption from acts and their consequences, MBh.; BhP.; mf(*ā*)n. relating to it, BhP.; *-siddhi*, f. N. of wk., a refutation of the Mīmāṇsā system. **-kāmya**, n. suppression of desire, profound contemplation, MWB. 128. **-kiṃcanya**, n. absence of property, poverty, Rājat. **-kṛitika**, w. r. for *nai-kṛ*°. **-kramaṇa**, mfn. (oblation) offered or (rite) performed when a new-born child is taken out of the house for the first time, g. *vyushṭâdi*. **-kramya**, n. indifference (esp. to worldly pleasures), resignation, Jātak. (w. r. for *naish-karmya* or *-kāmya*?), MWB. **-purīshya**, n. evacuation of excrement, Āpast. **-purushya**, n., Pāṇ. viii, 3, 41, Vārtt. 1, Pat. **-peshika**, mfn., g. *saṃtāpâdi*; *-tva*, n., L. **-premya**, n. absence of any inclination, Car. **-phalya**, n. absence of fruit or effect, uselessness, MBh.

Nais, Vṛiddhi form of *nis* in comp. **-triṇśika**, mfn. armed with a sword, L.

नैक *naíka* &c. See p. 523, col. 3.

नैकत *naikata*, mfn. (fr. *naikatī*, f., N. of a village in the north of India), Pāṇ. iv, 2, 110, g. *palady-ādi*.

नैगमेय *naigameya*, m. a form of Skanda (considered also as his son and play-fellow), MBh.; Suśr. (cf. next).

नैगमेष *naigamesha*, m. N. of a demon with the head of a ram (supposed to seize or injure children), AV. (cf. prec. and *nejamesha*).

नैगेय *naigeya*, m. (fr. *nega*) N. of a school of the Sāma-veda, Āryav.

नैचक्य *naicakya*, m. patr. fr. *nicaka*, Pat.

नैचाशाख *naicāśākhá*, m. prob. N. of Pramagandha (patr. fr. *nīcā-ś*°?), RV. iii, 53, 14; n. N. of a town, Sāy.

नैचिक *naicika*, n. the head of an ox, L.; (*ī*), f. an excellent cow, L. (cf. *nīcaka*, °*kin*).

नैचुदार *naicudāra*, mfn. made of the tree Nicudāra, TāṇḍBr.

नैचुल *naicula*, mfn. coming from the Nicula tree (Barringtonia Acutangula), Suśr.

नैजमेष *naijamesha*, mfn. consecrated to Nejamesha, MānGṛ.

नैतन्धव *naitandhava*, m. sg. and pl. N. of a place on the Sarasvatī, TāṇḍBr.; ŚrS.

नैत्य *naitya*, mfn. (fr. *nitya*) continually done or to be done, regularly repeated, g. *vyushṭâdi*; n. eternity, perpetuity, W. **-śabdika**, mfn., Pāṇ. iv, 4, 1, Vārtt. 1, Pat.

Naityaka, mfn. to be always or regularly done (not occasionally; cf. *naimittika*), constantly repeated, invariable, obligatory, Mn.; MBh. &c.; n. the food regularly offered to an idol, MBh.

Naityika, mfn. = °*tyaka*, mfn., Mn.; MBh.

नैनार *naināra* and °*râcārya*, m. N. of an author, Cat.

नैप *naipa*, mf(ī)n. (fr. *nīpa*) coming from the Nauclea Cadamba, L. **Naipātitha**, m. (fr. *nipātithi*) N. of Sāmans, TāṇḍBr.; ĀrshBr. **Naipya**, n. patr. fr. *nīpa*, Pat.

नैपथ्यसवन *naipathya-savana*, v. l. for *nep*°, q. v.

नैपाल *naipāla*, mf(ī)n. produced &c. in Nepal; m. a species of sugar-cane, Suśr.; a species of Nimba tree, L.; (*ī*), f. red arsenic, Madanav.; Suśr.; N. of sev. plants (Arabian jasmine, Jasminum Sambac, Nyctanthes Arbor Tristis, and the indigo plant), L.

Naipālika, mfn. = prec. mfn.; n. copper, L.

Naipālīya, mfn. = prec. mfn. **-devatā**, f. a partic. deity; *-kalyāṇa-pañcaviṇśatikā*, f. N. of a Buddh. wk.

नैबुक *naibuka*, n. N. of partic. rites to be performed at full moon, Kālanirṇ.

नैमित्त *naimitta*, mfn. (fr. *ni-mitta*) relating to or explanatory of signs, g. *ṛigayanâdi*; m. an interpreter of prognostics, fortune-teller, L. (also °*ttaka*, Divyâv.)

Naimittika, mf(*ī*)n. produced by any or by some partic. cause, occasional, special, accidental (opp. to *nitya*), KātyŚr.; Mn.; MBh. &c. (*-tva*, n. Kap., Sch.); m. = prec. m., g. *ukthâdi*, Divyâv.; n. an effect (see *nimitta-n*°); = next, W. **-karman**, n., **-kriyā**, f. an occasional or periodical ceremony or rite (as observed on the birth of a child &c.), ib. **-prakaraṇa**, n., **-prayoga** and **-prayoga-ratnâkara**, m. N. of wks. **-śrāddha**, n. a special funeral rite, RTL. 305.

नैमिष *naimisha* &c. See under *nai*, col. 1.

नैम्ब *naimba*, mfn. relating to or coming from the Nimba tree (Azadirachta Indica), Var.

नैयग्रोध *naíyagrodha*, mfn. (fr. *nyag-rodha*; cf. Pāṇ. vii, 3, 5) belonging to or made of the Indian fig-tree, TS.; Br.; n. the fruit of it, g. *plakshâdi* (cf. *naiyyagrodha*).

नैयङ्कव *naiyaṅkava*, mfn. (fr. *ny-aṅku*) belonging to or coming from the antelope called Nyaṅku, Uṇ. i, 18, Sch.

नैयाय *naiyāya*, mfn. (fr. *ny-āya*) treating of the Nyāya philosophy (q.v.), explaining it &c., g. *ṛigayanâdi*.

Naiyāyika, mfn. knowing the Nyāya philosophy; m. a follower of the N° system of investigation, MBh.; R. &c.

नैयासिक *naiyāsika*, mfn., g. *ukthâdi*.

नैय्यग्रोध *naiyyagrodha*, *naiyyamika*, *naiyyāyika*, w.r. for *naiyagrodha* &c.

नैरुज्य *nairujya*, n. (fr. *nī-ruja*) health, Kull. on Mn. xi, 237.

नैलकण्ठि *nailakaṇṭhi*, m. patr. fr. Nīlakaṇṭha, L. °**ṭhīya**, mfn. composed by N°, MBh. (under chapters or books).

नैलायनि *nailāyani*, m. patr. fr. Nīla, g. *tikâdi*.

नैल्य *nailya*, n. (fr. *nīla*) dark-blue (the colour), L.

नैव *naiva*, ind. (= 2. *ná* + *eva*) in comp. — **śāśvato-nâśāśvatas-ca** (sc. *loka*), not eternal and not transitory, Dharmas. 137. — **saṃjñā-nâsaṃjñānâyatana**, n. a place where there is no thinking and no not-thinking, ib. 59; °*tanôpaga*, m. one who resorts to this place, one of the four classes of gods of the formless world, ib. 129. — **saṃjñā-samādhi**, m. meditation in which there is no reflection, L. — **saṃjñi-nâivâ-saṃjñin**, mfn. without reflection and (or) not without reflection, Vajracch. **Naivântavān-nânantavāṇś-ca** (sc. *loka*), not finite and not infinite, Dharmas. 137.

नैवकि *naivaki* and *naivati*, m., g. *taulvaly-ādi*.

नैवाकव *naivākava* and °*kavīya*, mfn.; °*kavi*, m. (fr. *ni-vāku*), g. *utkarâdi* and *bāhv-ādi*.

नैवार *naivārá*, mfn. (fr. *nīvāra*) consisting in or made of wild rice (as food), TS.; TBr.; ŚrS.

नैव्य *naivya*, n. (fr. *niva*), g. *brāhmaṇâdi*.

नैश *naiśa* or °*śika*, mf(ī)n. (fr. *niśā*) relating to night, happening at night, nightly, nocturnal, Mn.; Yājñ.; MBh.; Kāv. &c.; walking or studying at night, Pāṇ. iv, 3, 51; 52, Sch.

Naiśākara, mf(ī)n. (fr. *niśā-kara*) caused by or belonging to the moon &c., Hariv.

नैष *naisha*, m. N. of a country, Pat.

नैषध *naishadha*, mf(ī)n. relating to Nishadha, m. a species of grain, Suśr. (-*ka*, m., Car.); a prince of the Nishadhas (esp. N. of Nala), MBh.; Kāv. &c.; m. pl. N. of a people (= *nishadha*), MBh.; VP.; of a dynasty, BhP.; n. N. of an artificial epic poem by Śrī-harsha (treating of Nala's adventures). — **kāvya** or **-carita**, n. = prec. n. — **prakāśa**, m. N. of Comm. on Naish. **Naishadhânanda-nāṭaka**, n. N. of a drama.

Naishadhīya, mfn. relating to Nala Naishadha; n. = next. — **carita**, n. = *naishadha*, n. — **prakāśa**, m. = °*dha-pr*°.

Naishadhya, mfn. belonging or peculiar to the Nishadhas, MBh.; m. a N° prince, Pāṇ. iv, 1, 172, Kāś.

Naishidhá, m. (older form for *naishadha*) N. of Naḍa (q.v.), ŚBr.

नैष्क *naishka*, Vṛiddhi form of *nishká*. — **śatika** and **-sahasrika**, mfn. containing or worth 100 (1000) Nishkas, Pāṇ. v, 2, 119, Kāś. **Naishkika**, mfn. worth a N°, bought with a N° &c., Pāṇ. v, 1, 20 &c.; m. a mint-master, L.

नैहार *naihāra*, mfn. (fr. *nī-hāra*) produced by mist or fog, BhP.

नो *nó*, ind. (fr. 2. *ná* + *u*) and not, RV.; ŚBr.; MBh.; Kāv. &c. (in later language also = *na*, 'not,' for which it is generally used to suit the verse; *nô cêd*, see under *cêd*; *nô vā*, 'or not').

Nót (or *nôd*), ind. (*ná* + *ut*?) almost, nearly, ŚBr.

नोटी *noṭī*, f., g. *gaurâdi*.

नोण *noṇa*, m. N. of a merchant, Rājat.

नोद *noda*, m. (√*nud*) pushing away, repelling, Vop. in Dhātup.

Nodana, mfn. driving away, removing, Kāvyâd.; n. = *noda*, BhP.; impelling, impulse, ib.

Nodin, mfn. driving away, Ragh.

Nodya, mfn. to be impelled or driven away or removed, MW.

नोधस् *nodhás*, m. (according to Uṇ. iv, 225 fr. √4. *nu*?) N. of a Ṛishi also called Gautama (RV. Anukr.) or Kākshīvata (TāṇḍBr.), RV. i, 61, 14; 64, 1; 124, 4 (cf. Nir. iv, 16).

Naudhasá, m. patr. of Eka-dyū (q.v.), RV. Anukr.; n. N. of a Sāman, AV.; Br. &c. — **śyaita** and **-śyaita-yoni**, n. N. of Sāmans, ĀrshBr.

नोधा *nodhā*, ind. (fr. *nava-dhā*) ninefold, in 9 parts, BhP.

नोन *nona*, m. N. of a man (also -*ka*), Rājat.; (*ā*), f. N. of a woman, ib. — **ratha**, m. N. of a man, ib.

नोनुव *nonuva*, mfn. (√4. *nu*, Intens.) sounding, resounding, Nir. vi, 30 (*sadā-n*°).

नौ 1. *nau*, encl. acc. dat. gen. du. of 1st pers. pron. (cf. Pāṇ. viii, 1, 20), RV. &c. &c. (VS. also *nau*; cf. VPrāt. iii, 85).

नौ 2. *naú*, f. a ship, boat, vessel, RV. &c. &c.; (in astrol.) N. of a partic. appearance of the moon or of a constellation, Var.; = *vāc*, Nir. i, 11 (either because prayer is a vessel leading to heaven or fr. √4. *nu*, 'to praise'). [Cf. 2. *nāva* and 7. *nu*; Gk. ναῦς, ναύ-της &c.; Lat. *nāvis*, *nau-ta*, *nau-fragus* &c.; Icel. *nór*; (?) Germ. *Nachen*.] — **karṇa**, m. the helm of a ship (cf. below); (*ī*), f. N. of one of the Mātṛis attending on Skanda, MBh.; -*dhāra*, m. a helmsman, Var.; (fig.) governor, ruler, manager, Kād. — **karman**, n. the occupation or business of a sailor, Mn. x, 34. — **krama**, m. a bridge of boats, Divyâv. — **cakrī-vat**, m. an owner of ships and waggons, Gaut. — **cara**, mfn. going in a ship; m. a sailor, Ragh. — **jīvika**, m. 'living in a ship,' a sailor, boatman, Var. — **tārya**, mfn. passable in a ship, navigable, L. — **daṇḍa**, m. 'boat-pole,' an oar, L. (cf. *naukā-d*°). — **nidhirāma**, m. N. of a man, Cat. — **netṛi**, m. 'ship-conductor,' a helmsman, ĀpGṛ., Sch. — **bandhana**, n. 'ship-anchorage,' N. of the highest peak of the Himālayas (to which in the great flood Manu fastened his ship), MBh.; -*māhātmya*, n. N. of wk. — √**bhū**, to be or become a ship, L. — **maṇḍá**, n. the essence or chief part of a ship; (*e*), du. the two sides (or the rudders?) of a ship, ŚBr. — **yāna**, n. going in a ship, navigation, Rājat.; = -*krama*, Divyâv.; a ship, R. — **yāyin**, mfn. going in a boat, a passenger or freight, Mn. viii, 409. — **vāha**, m. = -*netṛi*, L. — **vyasana**, n. shipwreck, naufrage, Śak. — **shecana**, n., g. *sushāmâdi* (Kāś. -*shevaṇa*). — **saṃkrama**, m. going in a ship or a bridge of boats, Divyâv.

Nāv, in comp. for 2. *nau* before vowels. — **ākāra**, mfn. boat-shaped, cymbiform, MW. — **āroha**, m. a passenger on board ship, a sailor, L. (Cf. under 2. *nāva*, p. 538, col. 1.)

Nāvy = loc. *nāvi* fr. 2. *nau* before vowels. — **udaka**, n. water in the hold of a ship, KātyŚr.

Nauka, ifc. (f. *ā*) = 2. *nau*, MBh. (cf. g. *ura-ādi*).

Naukā, f. a small boat or ship, MBh.; R. &c.; the rook or castle (in the game Catur-aṅga), L.; N. of sev. Comms. — °**kṛishṭa** (°*kākṛ*°), n. N. of a favourable position in the game Catur-aṅga, L. — **daṇḍa**, m. 'boat-pole,' an oar, L. — **dāna**, n. N. of wk.

नौकाय *naukāya*, m. pl. N. of a school (v.l. for *naigeya*).

नौतन *nautana*, mfn. (fr. and) = *nūtana*, Bhadrab.

नौधस *naudhasá* &c. See *nodhás*.

नौपुर *naupura*, mfn. fr. *nūpura*, Śṛiṅgār.

नौलिक *naulika*, n., *naulī*, f. a kind of self-penance, Cat.

न्य *nyá* (nom. *nyas*), AV. xi, 7, 4.

न्यक् *nyak*, *ny-àkna*, *nyag* &c. See under 1. and 2. *ny-añc*.

न्यक्त *ny-àkta*. See *ny-añj*.

न्यक्ष *ny-aksha*, *ny-aṅka*, *ny-aṅku* &c. See *ny-añj*.

न्यङ्कोतक *nyaṅkotaka*, m. N. of a man, Rājat.

न्यङ्ग *ny-aṅga* &c. See *ny-añj*.

न्यच्छ *nyaccha*, n. a mole or spot upon the body, Suśr.

न्यञ्च् 1. *ny-*√*añc*, P. -*añcati*, to sink, bend or hang down, Bālar.; Kathās.; to pass away, fade, perish, Bhām.: Caus. -*añcayati*, to press down or in, HPariś. °**àkna**, mfn. bent down, TBr. °**aṅká**, m. du. a partic. part of a carriage, TS.; TBr. °**aṅku**, m. id., TāṇḍBr.; a deer, an antelope, VS.; MBh. &c.; N. of a Muni and a Cakra-vartin, L.; -*bhūruha*, m. Bignonia Indica, L.; -*śiras* (with *kakum-nicṛit*), f.; -*sāriṇī* (with *bṛihatī*), f. N. of two kinds of metre, RPrāt. °**áñcana**, mf(*ī*)n. curve, recess, hollow, hiding-place, RV.; AV. (°*nâśhin*, mfn. seeking a h°-pl°, MaitrS.); a partic. mark on a measuring-cord, Śulb.; (*ī*), f. the lap, AV. °**añoita**, mfn. bent down, L.

Ny-ácam, ind. bending down, ŚBr.

Nyak, in comp. for 2. *ny-añc* below. — **karaṇa**, n. lowering, degrading, treating with disrespect, W. — **kāra**, m. humiliation, contempt, disregard, Hariv.; BhP. — **kṛita**, mfn. humbled, treated with contempt or contumely, Rājat.; Kathās. — **kṛiti**, f. = -*kāra*, Bālar.; Pañcad. — **kṛitya**, ind. having humbled, by humbling, Rājat.

Nyaksha, mfn. (hardly fr. *ni* + *aksha*; but cf. Pāṇ. vi, 2, 192, Sch.) low, inferior, L.; whole, entire, L. (cf. 2. *ny-añc*); m. a buffalo, L.; N. of Paraśurāma, L.; n. entireness (*eṇa*, ind. entirely), L.; grass, L.

Nyag, in comp. for 2. *ny-añc*. — **jāti**, mfn. of a low or inferior race, W. — **bhāva**, m. being brought or coming down, Sarvad.; being sunk or absorbed in (loc.), ib.; = next, Śaṃk. — **bhāvana**, n. humiliation, contempt, Pāṇ. i, 3, 70, Sch. — **bhāvayitṛi**, m. one who lowers or humbles, Daś. — **bhūta**, mfn. being low, humble, MBh. — **bhūtvā**, ind. having humbled (or by humbling) one's self, ib. — **rodha**, m. (√*rudh* = *ruh*) 'growing down wards' the Banyan or Indian fig-tree, Ficus Indica (it belongs to the *kshīra-vṛikshas*, q.v.; fibres descend from its branches to the earth and there take root and form new stems), AV. &c. &c.; Prosopis Spicigera or Mimosa Suma, L.; a fathom (measured by the arms extended), L.; N. of a son of Kṛishṇa, BhP.; of a son of Ugra-sena (also °*dhaka*), Hariv.; Pur.; of a Brāhman, a monastery and a village, Lalit.; (*ā*), f. Salvinia Cucullata or some other plant, Car.; (*ī* or °*dhikā*), f. id., L.; -*kshīra*, n. the milky juice of the Indian fig-tree, Suśr.; -*parimaṇḍala*, mfn. being a fathom in circumference, MatsyaP.; °*la-tā*, f. the having a waist like a fig-tree, (with Buddh. one of the 32 signs of perfection, Dharmas. 83); (*ā*), f. an elegant woman, L.; -*pāda*, m. N. of a man; °*dhaka*, mfn., g. *ṛiśyâdi* (cf. also above); °*dhika*, and °*dhin*, mfn., g. *kumudâdi* and *prêkshâdi*.

2. **Ny-añc** (fr. *ni* + 2. *añc*), mf(*nīcī*)n(*ny-ak*). going or directed downwards, bent down, RV. &c. &c.; lying with the face downwards (opp. to *ut-tāna*), ŚBr.; depressed, deep, low (sound, voice &c.), ib.; humble, vile, contemptible (cf. *nyak* &c. above); slow, lazy, L.; whole, entire, L.; (*nīcā*), ind., see under *nīca*; (*ny-àk*), ind. downwards, down, RV.; ŚBr.; humbly; with √*kṛi*, to bring down, humble; (*nyag*) with √*bhū*, to humble one's self, be humble or modest: Caus. -*bhāvayati* = √*kṛi*, Pāṇ. i, 3, 70, Sch. (cf. *nyak*- and *nyag*- above).

न्यञ्ज् *ny-*√*añj*, P. -*anakti* (pf. Ā. -*ānaje*, ind. p. -*ajya*), to anoint, besmear, AV.; Kāty.; Ā. to creep in, conceal one's self among (loc.), RV.

Ny-àkta, mfn. anointed, decorated (?), AV. xiv, 2, 33 (RV. *vy-àkta*); imbued with, having the nature of (gen.), ŚBr.

Ny-aṅgá, m. anything inherent in, a mark, sign, TBr.; ŚBr.; ĀpŚr.; anything which resembles or is like, a kind of (gen. or comp.), ŚBr.; Lāṭy.; (ifc. having anything as secondary, mentioning it only accidentally, ŚāṅkhŚr.); invective, insinuation, sarcastic language, Nār.

न्यञ्जलिका *ny-añjalikā*, f. an Añjali which is directed downwards, TĀr.

न्यन्त *ny-anta*, m. or n. proximity (cf. Pāṇ. vi, 2, 181, Sch.); °*te* (ĀpŚr.) and °*téna* (ŚBr. &c.), near, near to.

न्यय *ny-aya*, m. (fr. 4. *nī*) going off, destruction, loss, waste, Pāṇ. iii, 3, 37, Sch.; L.

Ny-áyana, n. entry, entrance- or gathering-place, receptacle, RV.

न्यर्ण *ny-arṇa*, mfn. waterless, ŚāṅkhŚr.

न्यर्ण्ण *ny-àrṇṇa*, mfn. (√*ard*) dissolved, gone, ŚBr. (W. 'asked, solicited; injured').

न्यर्थ *ny-arthá*, n. going amiss, failure, destruction, RV.

न्यर्पय *ny-arpaya*, °*pita*. See *ny-ṛi*.

न्यर्बुद *ny-àrbuda*, n. one hundred millions, AV. &c.

Ny-àrbudi, m. N. of a divine being of combative propensities, AV.

न्यवग्रह *ny-avagraha*, m. the accentless vowel at the end of the first member of a compound, VPrāt.

न्यवचर् *ny-ava-√car*, P. -*carati*, to enter into, penetrate, MW.

न्यवसृज् *ny-ava-√sṛij*, P. -*sṛijati*, to pour out, shed forth, R.

न्यवेक्ष् *ny-avêksh* (√*īksh*, *īkshate*), to consider, deliberate, MBh.

न्यस् *ny-√2. as*, P. -*asyati* or -*asati*, to throw or cast or lay or put down (with loc., e.g. *bhuvi*, on the earth), AV. &c. &c.; to take off, MBh.; R.; to give up, resign (as life), R.; to set in the ground, plant (*prarohān*, shoots), Bālar.; (with loc.) to throw or hurl upon, pour or shed on or in, put or place or fix or insert in, turn or direct to, deposit with, intrust or commit to; to settle arrange, MBh.; Kāv. &c. (with *citre*, 'to place in a picture,' paint, depict; with *śirasi*, 'to place on the head,' receive with reverence; with *manasi*, 'to call to mind,' reflect, ponder; with *pathi*, 'to lay on the road,' give up); to bring forward, mention, Mall.: Caus. (pf. *nyāsayām āsa* or °*sayām cakre*) to cause to put or lay down, MBh. °**asana**, n. putting down, depositing, placing, arranging, Sāh.; bringing forward, mentioning, Kāvyâd. °**asanīya**, mfn. to be put or placed, AgP. °**asta**, mfn. thrown or cast or laid down, put, placed, fixed, inserted, applied, deposited, committed; given up, resigned, Mn.; MBh.; Kāv.; stretched out, lying, R.; exposed (*krayāya*, for sale), L.; mystically touched, Mālatīm. v, 2; put on, donned, ib. 22; having the low tone (as a vowel), RPrāt.; short, Śrutab.; -*cihna*, mf(*ā*)n. one who has relinquished one's marks or characteristics, destitute of external signs, Ragh. ii, 7; -*daṇḍa*, mfn. 'one who has laid down the rod,' meek, harmless, R.; -*deha*, mfn. 'one who has laid down the body,' dead, ib.; -*śastra*, mfn. 'one who has laid down the weapons,' averse from strife, peaceful, Mn. iii, 192; m. the Pitṛis or deified progenitors, L.; -*vāda*, mfn. one who has ceased to speak, ceasing to speak about (*prati*), Hariv.; °*târtvijya*, mfn. where the Ṛitvij have laid down their office, ŚāṅkhŚr. °**astaka**, mf(*ikā*)n., AV. vi, 139, 1. °**astavya**, mfn. to be put down or placed or fixed or established, Vāstuv.; Hcat. 1. °**asya**, mfn. to be laid down or deposited or delivered or appointed to (loc.), MBh. 2. °**asya**, ind. having laid down or deposited &c., ib.

Ny-āsa, m. putting down or in, placing, fixing, inserting, applying, impressing, drawing, painting, writing down, MBh.; Kāv. &c. (cf. *akshara-*, *khura-*, *caraṇa-*, *nakha-*, *pada-*, *pāda-*, *bīja-*, *rekhā-*); putting away, taking off, laying aside, MBh.; Hariv.; Daś.; BhP. (cf. *deha-*, *śarīra-*, *śastra-*); abandoning, resigning, Up.; Bhag.; BhP.; depositing, intrusting, delivering; any deposit or pledge, Mn.; Yājñ.; MBh. &c.; written or literal text (cf. *yathā-nyāsam*), Pat.; lowering (the voice), RPrāt.; (in music) the final tone; bringing forward, introducing (cf. *arthântara-*); consigning or intrusting anything to the mind, W.; mental appropriation or assignment of various parts of the body to tutelary deities, RTL. 205 &c.; N. of sev. wks., (esp.) of a Comm. on Kāś.; -*kāra* or -*kṛit*, m. the author of the Comm. on Kāś. called Nyāsa, i.e. Jinêndra-buddhi; -*khaṇḍa*, m. or n., -*khaṇḍana*, n., -*tilaka*, m. or n., -*tūlikā*, f., -*daśaka*, n. N. of wks.; -*dhāraka* or °*rin*, m. the holder of a deposit, Mn.; -*prakaraṇa*, n. N. of wk.; -*bhūta*, mfn. being (or that which is) a deposit, MBh.; -*lopa*, m. wasting a d°, ib.; -*viṇśati*, f., -*vidyā-darpaṇa*, m., -*vidyā-vilāsa*, m., -*vidhāna*, n., -*viśesha*, m., -*śataka*, n. N. of wks.; -*hara*, m. robber of a deposit, BhP.; °*sâdeśa-vivaraṇa*, n. N. of wk.; °*sâpahnava*, m. repudiation of a d°, MW.; °*sôddyota*, m. N. of wk. °**āsika**, mfn., g. *parpâdi*. °**āsita**, mfn. (fr. Caus.) caused to lay or put down, BhP. °**āsin**, mfn. one who has abandoned all worldly concerns, ib. °**āsī-√kṛi**, to make a deposit, deposit anything with a person, Kum.; Kathās.; Rājat.

न्यह्न *ny-ahná*, m. or n. the closing day (only loc.), AV.

न्याकृ *ny-ā-√1. kṛi* (only Impv. -*kuru*), to hold back, RV. x, 19, 2.

न्याक्य *nyākya*, n. fried rice, L.

न्यागम् *ny-ā-√gam* (only Impv. -*gatam*), to come down towards, RV. viii, 5, 13.

न्याग्रोधमूल *nyāgrodhamūla* (Pāṇ. vii, 3, 5, Sch.) or °*mūlika* (Vop. vii, 4; 18), mfn. (fr. *nyagr*°) being or situated at the roots of the Ficus Indica.

न्याङ्कव *nyāṅkava*, mfn. = *naiyaṅkava*, Uṇ. i, 18, Sch.

न्याचम् *ny-ắcam*. See 1. *ny-añc*.

न्याद *ny-āda*, m. (√*ad*) eating, feeding, Pāṇ. iii, 3, 60.

न्याधा *ny-ā-√1. dhā* (only pf. -*dadhur*), to put down, fix, establish, appoint, RV. viii, 73, 2.

न्याधृ *ny-ā-√dhṛi*, only pf. Ā. -*dadhre*, to be directed towards or fixed upon (loc.), RV. viii, 17, 13.

न्यानी *ny-ā-√2. nī* (Pot. -*nayet*), to bring back, restore, AV. vii, 38, 5.

न्याम *nyāma*, m. = *ni-yāma*, *ni-yama*, L.

न्याय *ny-āyá*, m. (fr. 4. *nī*) that into which a thing goes back i.e. an original type, standard, method, rule, (esp.) a general or universal rule, model, axiom, system, plan, manner, right or fit manner or way, fitness, propriety, TS.; Br.; Mn.; MBh. &c. (*nyāyena* and °*yāt*, ind. either 'in the right manner, regularly, duly,' or ifc. 'after the manner of, by way of'); a lawsuit, legal proceeding, judicial sentence, judgment, Mṛicch.; Pañc.; a logical or syllogistic argument or inference (consisting of a combination of enthymeme and syllogism, and so having, according to the Naiyāyikas 5 members, viz. *pratijñā*, *hetu*, *udāharaṇa*, *upanaya*, *nigamana*, or according to the Vedântins 3 members); a system of philosophy delivered by Gotama or Gautama (it is one of the six *Darśanas*, q.v., and is perhaps so called, because it 'goes into' all subjects physical and metaphysical according to the above syllogistic method treated of in one division of the system; its branch is called Vaiśeshika); likeness, analogy, a popular maxim or apposite illustration (cf. *kākâkshi-*, *ghuṇâkshara-*, *daṇḍâpūpa-* &c.); (*am*), ind. after a finite verb expresses either censure or repetition, Pāṇ. viii, 1, 27. — **kaṇikā**, f., -**kandalī**, f., -**karaṇḍa**, n., -**kalānidhi**, m., -**kalāpa**, m., -**kalikā**, f., -**kalpa-latā** or °**tikā**, f., -**kāśikā**, f., -**kiraṇâvalī**, f., -**kutūhala**, n., -**kuliśa**, m. or n., -**kusuma-mañjarī**, f., -**kusumâñjali**, m. (-*kārikā*, f., -*prakāśa*, m., -*vikāśa*, m., -*viveka*, m.) N. of wks. — **kokila** (?), m. N. of a Buddh. teacher. — **kośa**, m., -**kaumudī**, f., -**kaustubha**, m. or n., -**kroḍa**, m. (-*pattra*, n.), -**khaṇḍana-khaṇḍa-khādya**, n., -**grantha**, m., -**candrikā**, f., -**cintāmaṇi**, m., -**cūḍāmaṇi**, m. (-*prabhā*, f.), -**tattva**, n. (-*parīkshā*, f., -*vivaraṇa*, n., -*viloka*, m.), -**tantra**, n. (-*bodhinī*, f.), -**taraṃgiṇī**, f. N. of wks. — **tas**, ind. in a fitting manner, as is fit or proper, according to right or justice, Mn.; Yājñ.; R. — **tā**, f. (ŚāṅkhŚr.), -**tva**, n. (MW.), fitness, propriety. — **tātparya-dīpikā**, f., -**tri-sūtrī-vārttika**, n., -**darpaṇa**, m., -**dīpa**, m. (-*vyākhyā*, f., °*pâvalī*, f.), -**dīpikā**, f. N. of wks. — **deva**, m. N. of an author, Cat. — **dvayakāraṇatā-vāda**, m., -**dvāraka-śāstra**, n., -**naya**, m., -**nibhandha**, m. (-*prakāśa*, m.), -**nirṇaya**, m. N. of wks. — **nirvapaṇa**, mfn. bestowing justly; m. N. of Śiva, MBh. xiii, 1239. — **pañcâdhyāyī**, f. = -*sūtra*. — **pañcânana**, m. N. of Jaya-rāma, Cat. — **pañcāśat**, f. N. of wk. — **patha**, m. pl. the different philosophical systems, BhP. — **padârtha-mālā**, f., -**pariccheda**, m., -**pariśishṭa**, n. (-*prakāśa*, m.), -**pariśuddhi**, f., -**pārijāta**, m., -**pushpâñjali**, m., -**prakaraṇa**, n., -**prakāśa**, m., -**prakāśikā**, f., -**pradīpa**, m., -**pradīpikā**, f., -**pramāṇa-mañjarī-ṭīkā**, f., -**praveśa**, m. (-*tāraka-śāstra*, n.) N. of wks. — **prasthāna-mārga**, m. pl. the roads leading towards (i.e. the works treating of) the different philosophical systems (cf. -*patha*). — **bindu**, m. (-*ṭīkā*, f.), -**bodhinī**, f., -**bhāshya**, n., -**bhāskara**, m., -**bhūshaṇa**, n., -**makaranda**, m. (-*vivardhinī*, f., -*vivṛiti*, f., -*vivecinī*, f.), -**mañjarī**, f. (-*grantha-bhaṅga*, m., -*sāra*, m.), -**mañjūshā**, f., -**mata-khaṇḍana**, n., -**manoramā**, f., -**mahôdadhi**, m., -**mātṛikā**, f., -**mārtaṇḍa**, m., -**mālā**, f. (-*vaiyāsikī*, f., -*vārttika-saṃgraha*, m., -*vistara*, m.), -**mālikā**, f., -**mīmāṇsā-prakaraṇa**, n., -**mīmāṇsā-rahasya**, n., -**muktâvalī**, f. (-*kiraṇa*, n., -*prakāśa*, m.), -**mūla-paribhāshā**, f., -**rakshāmaṇi**, m., -**ratna**, n. (-*kośavādârtha*, m., -*ṭīkā*, f., -*prakaraṇa*, n., -*prakāśikā*, f., -*mālā*, f., °*tnâkara*, m., °*tnâvalī*, f.), -**rahasya**, n., -**lakshaṇa-vicāra**, m., -**līlāvatī**, f. (-*kaṇṭhâbharaṇa*, n., -*prakāśa*, m. [-*dīdhiti*, f., -*dīdhiti-viveka*, m., -*rahasya*, n.], -*bhāva-prakāśa*, m., -*rahasya*, n., -*vibhūti*, f., -*viveka*, m.) N. of wks. — **vat**, mfn. acting rightly, behaving properly, MBh.; R. — **vartin**, mfn. well behaved, acting with propriety, Mn.; Yājñ. — **vastu-sāra**, m. N. of wk. — **vāgīśa** and -**vācaspati**, m. N. of 2 authors on rhet. — **vāda**, m. N. of wk. — **vādin**, mfn. speaking properly, R. — **vārttika**, n. (-*tātparya-ṭīkā*, f., -*tātparya-pariśuddhi*, f.) N. of wks. — **vid**, m. one who knows what is fit or proper, Āpast. — **vidyā**, f. 'science of what is right,' logic, Nyāyas., Comm. — **vilāsa**, m., -**vivaraṇa**, n., -**viveka**, m. (-*dīpikā*, f.) N. of wks. — **vihita**, mfn. prescribed by rule, Lāṭy. — **vṛitta**, mfn. = -*vartin*, Mn.; R. — **vṛitti**, f. N. of wk. — **śāstra**, n. the doctrine of the Nyāya school of philosophy, Sarvad. — **śikshā**, f. = -*vidyā*, MBh. -**śikhāmaṇi**, m., -**śiromaṇi**, m., -**śuddhi**, f. N. of wks. — **saṃhita**, mfn. fit, proper, Āpast. — **saṃketa**, m. (-*tilakā*, f.), -**saṃkshepa**, m., -**saṃgraha**, m. (-*dīpikā*, f.), -**sad-artha-saṃgraha**, m. N. of wks. — **sambaddha**, mfn. connected with reason, rational, logical (as an argument), R. — **sāra**, m. (-*ṭīkā*, f., -*dīpikā*, f., -*pada-pañjikā*, f., -*saṃgraha*, m., °*râvalī*, f.) N. of wks. — **sāriṇī**, f. right or fit behaviour, L.; a woman acting or judging rightly, W. — **siddhâñjana**, n., -**siddhânta**, m. (-*candrikā*, f., -*tattva* and °*tvâmṛita*, n., -*dīpa*, m., -*mañjarī*, f. [-*dīpikā*, f., -*prakāśa*, m., -*bhūshā*, f., -*sāra*, m.], -*mālā*, f., -*muktâvalī*, f.) N. of wks.; °*nta-pañcânana*, m. N. of a Viśva-nātha, Cat.; °*nta-vāgīśa*, m. N. of a Gadā-dhara, ib. — **sudhā**, f. N. of wk. — **sūtra**, n. the aphorisms of the Nyāya philosophy by Gautama; -*vṛitti*, f. a commentary on these aphorisms, I.W. 71. — **svarūpa-nirūpaṇa**, n. N. of wk. **Nyāyâgata**, mfn. rightly come in or acquired (as money), MBh. **Nyāyâcāra**, mfn. acting justly, virtuous, W. **Nyāyâcārya**, m. N. of Śivâditya-miśra, Cat. **Nyāyâdhāra**, m. 'receptacle of justice,' an example of virtue or propriety, W. **Nyāyâdhva-dīpikā**, f., **Nyāyânusāra-śāstra**, n. N. of wks. **Nyāyânveshaṇa**, n. seeking for justice, Pañc. **Nyāyâbhāsa**, m. semblance of a reason, sophism, Nyāyas., Comm. **Nyāyâmṛita**, n. (-*taraṃgiṇī*, f.) N. of wks. **Nyāyârjita**, mfn. honestly earned or acquired, Daś. **Nyāyârtha-dīpikā**, f., **Nyāyârtha-laghu-subodhinī**, f. N. of wks. **Nyāyâlaṃkāra**, m. 'ornament of justice,' N. of Śrī-govinda and of Śrī-mahêśvara (also -*bhaṭṭa*), Cat. **Nyāyâvakrakramaṇa**, mfn. walking rightly on the straight path (-*tā*, f.), Lalit. **Nyāyâvatāra**, m., **Nyāyâvalī-dīdhiti**, f. N. of wks. **Nyāyôpeta**, mfn. rightly admitted, ŚāṅkhGṛ.

Nyāyika, n. logic, VP.

Nyāyin, mfn. = *nyāya-vat*, L.

Nyāyya, mf(*ā*)n. regular, customary, usual, correct, right, fit, proper (often with an infin. which then has a pass. sense), Lāṭy.; Mn.; MBh. &c.; also w.r. for *nyāya*. — **tva**, n. fitness, propriety, Kaiy. — **daṇḍa**, mfn. punishing justly (-*tva*, n.), Gaut.

न्यालून *ny-ā-lūna*, mfn. (√*lū*) cut off, Hariv. (v.l. *vy-ā-l*°).

न्याविश् *ny-ā-√viś* (only pf. *-viviśur*), to enter into (loc.), RV. x, 56, 4.

न्यावृत् *ny-ā-√vṛit*, Caus. *-vartayati*, to make a person desist from (abl.), keep back, prevent, Kathās.

न्याव्यध् *ny-ā-√vyadh*, P. *-vidhyati*, to cause to burst forth, let loose, set free, MW.

न्यास *ny-āsa* &c. See under *ny-as.*

न्यासद् *ny-ā-√sad*, P. *-sīdati* (pf. *-sasāda*, ind. p. *-sadya*), to sit down near or in or upon (loc. or acc.), RV. **Ny-ā-shatta** (or *-á-ni-sh°*), sitting down or on, seated on; dived into (loc.), ib.

न्युङ्ख *nyuṅkha*, m. = *nyūṅkha*, L.; mfn. proper, right; pleasing, agreeable, L.

न्युच् *ny-√uc*, P. *-ucyati* (pf. *-uvoca*), to delight or take pleasure in (acc. or loc.), RV.; to like to stay in or with (loc.), AV.

Ny-oka, mfn. (prob.) = next, Kāś. on Pāṇ. vii, 3, 64. **°okas**, mfn. belonging to home, domestic, wont, comfortable, RV.; AitBr. **°ocanī**, f. (prob.) a kind of woman's ornament (Sāy. 'female slave'), RV. x, 85, 6. **°ocará**, mfn. (prob.) belonging to or fit for a place, AV. v, 22, 5.

न्युद् *ny-√2. ud* or *und* (only p. Ā. *-undamāna*), to dip, sprinkle, ŚāṅkhBr. **°ùtta**, mfn. dipped in, sprinkled with (loc.), SBr.

न्युप्त *ny-upta, ny-upya.* See *ni-vap.*

न्युब्ज् *ny-√ubj*, P. *-ubjati*, to bend or press or throw upside down, upset, overthrow, SV.; AV.; Br. **°ubja**, mfn. turned or bent downwards, lying with the face downwards, looking downwards, KātyŚr.; MBh.; Hariv.; Suśr.; hump-backed, crooked-backed (as the result of disease, cf. Pāṇ. vii, 3, 61), L.; convex, W.; m. N. of the Nyag-rodha tree in Kuru-kshetra, AitBr.; n. the fruit of the Averrhoa Carambola, L.; m. or n. = *śrāddhâdi-pātra-bheda, darbhamaya-śruc* or *kuśa-śruc*, L.; *-khaḍga*, m. a crooked sword, a sabre, L. **°ubjaka**, mf(*ikā*)n. = next, Comm. on TāṇḍBr. **°ubji-mat**, mfn. bent, crooked, TāṇḍBr.

न्युभ् *ny-√ubh*, P. *-ubhnāti* (impf. *-aubhnāt*), to keep down or together, RV. iv, 19, 4.

न्युष् *ny-√ush*, P. *-oshati* (Impv. *-oshatāt*), to burn down, consume or destroy utterly, RV.; AV.

न्यूङ्ख *nyūṅkha*, m. the insertion of the sound *o* (in different places with difference of quantity and accentuation) in the recitation of hymns, Br.; ŚrS. &c. (cf. Pāṇ. i, 2, 34, Sch.); (*am*), ind. with the Nyūṅkha, ŚāṅkhŚr.

Nyūṅkhanīya, mfn. to be inserted, ŚāṅkhŚr.

Nyūṅkhamānaka, mfn. stumbling, ŚāṅkhBr.

Nyūṅkhaya, Nom. P. *°yati*, to insert the Nyūṅkha, Br.; ŚrS.; Ā. (*nyūṅkhayate*) to growl (as a hungry animal), RV. x, 94, 3.

Nyūṅkhya, mfn. = *°khanīya*, AitBr.

न्यून *ny-ūna*, mf(*ā*)n. (fr. *ni* with *ūna*) less, diminished, defective, deficient (opp. to *ati-rikta, adhika, pūrṇa*), destitute or deprived of (instr. or comp.), inferior to (abl.), Br.; GṛŚrS.; MBh.; Suśr. &c.; (with *pādaiḥ*) having a defect in the feet, BhP.; low, vile, base, mean, MBh.; Var.; Pur.; (*am*), ind. less, Hariv.; Var.; n. euphem. = vulva, TS.; ŚBr.; want or omission of one of the 5 members in a Nyāya argument, Nyāyas. **-tara**, mfn. falling below a standard, Divyâv.; (*am*), ind. still less, Var.; lower or deeper, MārkP. **-tā**, f. (MBh. &c.), **-tva**, n. (Madhus.) inferiority to (abl.); want, deficiency, incompleteness. **-pañcāśad-bhāva**, m. 'having 49 (not full 50) properties of human nature,' an idiot, L. **-padatā**, f., **°tva**, n. want of one word in a sentence, Sāh. **-bhāva**, m. inferiority, deficiency, MBh. **Nyūnâksharā**, mf(*ā*)n. defective in letters or syllables, ŚBr. **Nyūnâṅga**, mf(*ā*)n. defective in a limb or organ, maimed, mutilated, imperfect, W. **Nyūnâdhika**, mfn. less or more, unequal; n. inequality, difference, ŚāṅkhGṛ.; *-vibhakta*, mfn. one who has received too little or too much at the division of an inheritance, Yājñ.; *-vibhāga*, m. unequal partition, W.; *°kâṅga*, mfn. having less or more limbs or organs (than necessary), Suśr.; *°kya*, n. want or surplus (e.g. of an organ), Hcat. **Nyūnâha**, m. = *kshayâha*, Gaṇit. **Nyūnêndriya**, mfn. wanting some organ or sense, deficient, imperfect (as blind, deaf &c.), W.

Nyūnaya, Nom. P. *°yati*, to lessen, diminish, Bhaṭṭ., Sch.

Nyūni, in comp. for *nyūna*. **-√kṛi**, to make less, lessen, diminish, Bhaṭṭ., Sch. **-bhāva**, m. state of deficiency, incompleteness, L.

न्यूह् *ny-√1. ūh*, Ā. *-ūhate*, to push in for one's self, drive into one's own stable, TāṇḍBr.

न्यूह् *ny-√2. ūh*, Ā. *-ohate*, to heed or to appear, RV. v, 52, 11.

न्यृ *ny-√4. ṛi*, P. *-ṛiṇvati*, to lay down, put or place in (loc.), RV.: Caus. *-arpayati*, to throw down, ib.; AV. **Nyàrpita**, mfn. thrown down, AV.

न्यृञ्ज् *ny-√ṛiñj*, Ā. *-ṛiñjate*, to reach, attain, overpower, subdue, RV.

न्यृष् *ny-√2. ṛish*, P. *-ṛishati*, to push or stuff into (acc.), cover, fill, RV.; ŚBr. **°ṛishṭa**, mfn. filled or endowed with (instr.), RV.

न्ये *nyé* (*ny-ā-√i*, only ind. p. *-êtya*), to fall into (acc.), BṛĀrUp.

न्येज् *ny-√ej*, P. *-ejati*, to tremble, Kir. xv, 22.

न्येर् *nyêr* (*ny-ā-√īr*, only pf. Ā. *nyêriré*), to direct or address (a wish or desire) to (loc.), R.; to appoint as (acc.), ib. (cf. *nīr*).

न्योक *ny-oka* &c. See *ny-uc.*

न्योजस् *ny-ojas*, mfn., Uṇ. iv, 222, Sch.

नृधीश *nr-adhīśa.* See *nṛí.*

न्वै *nvaí*, ind. (for *nú-vaí*) indeed, certainly, Br. (cf. Pāṇ. vi, 1, 94, Vārtt. 1, Pat.)

प PA.

प 1. *pa*, the first labial consonant. **-kāra**, m. the letter or sound *pa*. **-varga**, m. 'the *p* series,' the labial series of consonants.

प 2. *pa*, mf(*pā* and *pī*)n. (√1. *pā*) drinking (cf. *aṅhri-, aneka-* &c.; also *paka* in *taila-paka*); m. or (*pā*) f. the act of drinking, L.

प 3. *pa*, mfn. (√3. *pā*) guarding, protecting, ruling (ifc.; cf. *aja-, kula-* &c.; also *paka* in *hasti-paka*); (*ā*), f. guarding, protecting, L.

प 4. *pa*, m. (in music for *pañcama*) the fifth note of the gamut.

प 5. *pa*, m. (only L.) wind; a leaf; = *pūta*; (*ā*), f. = *pūta* and *pūritaka*.

पंश् *pams* or *pans*, cl. 1. and 10. P. *pansati* or *°sati, pansayati* or *°sayati*, to destroy, Dhātup. xxxii, 73.

पंसक *pansaka, °sana*, prob. w. r. for *pāṅsaka, °sana.*

पकथ *pakatha*, w. r. for *paktha.*

पक्कटी *pakkaṭī*, f. Thespesia Populnea, L.

पक्कण *pakkaṇa*, m. n. the hut of a Cāṇḍāla or any outcast, a village inhabited by savages or barbarians, MBh.; Kād.

पक्तपौड *pakta-pauḍa*, w. r. for *pakhauḍa.*

पक्तव्य *paktavya, pakti, paktha, pakva* &c. See under √2. *pac*, p. 575.

पक्वश *pakvaśa*, m. a Cāṇḍāla, L. (cf. *pakkaṇa, pukkaśa*).

पक्वापक्वा *pakvāpakvā*, onomat. (imitative of the cry of birds), MBh.

पक्ष् *paksh*, cl. 1. and 10. P. (Dhātup. xvii, 14; xxxii, 17) *pakshati, °shayati*, to take, seize (*parigrahe*, Dhāt.); to take a part or side, W.

Pakshá, m. (ifc. f. *ā* or *ī*) a wing, pinion (in one passage, n.), RV. &c. &c.; a symbol. N. of the number two, Var.; Hcat.; a feather, the feathers on both sides of an arrow (cf. *gārdhra-p°*); the fin of a fish (cf. *nis-tvak-p°*); the shoulder; the flank or side or the half of anything, RV. &c. &c.; the side or wing of a building, AV.; the wing or flank of an army, MBh.; Hariv.; the half of a lunar month (the first half from new moon to full moon was called *pūrva* or *āpūryamāṇa*, later *śukla* or *śuddha*; the other half *apara* or *apa-kshīyamāṇa*, later *kṛishṇa* or *tāmisra*; each fortnight consists of 15 Tithis or lunar days called *prathamā, dvitīyā* &c.), Br.; GṛŚrS.; MBh.; Var. &c.; a side, party, faction; multitude, number, troop, set, class of beings; partisan, adherent, follower, friend (*śatru-*, 'the enemy's side' or 'a partisan of the enemy;' *mahā-*, 'one who has many adherents'), MBh.; Kāv. &c.; side, i.e. position, place, stead (*°kshe*, ifc. instead of or by way of), ib.; quantity (see *keśa-*); one of two cases or one side of an argument, an alternative (*°kshe*, 'on the other hand,' with *atra*, 'in this case,' *pakshântare*, 'in the other case'), Pāṇ., Sch.; a point or matter under discussion, a thesis, a particular theory, a position advanced or an argument to be maintained (cf. *pūrva-, uttara-*); an action or lawsuit, Yājñ., Sch.; (in logic) the proposition to be proved in a syllogism, Tarkas.; Bhāshāp.; any supposition or view, motion, idea, opinion (*mukhyaḥ pakshaḥ*, 'an excellent idea,' Śak., Sch.), MBh.; Kāv. &c.; the sun, Sāy. on RV. iii, 53, 16; N. of sev. men, VP.; (in alg.) a primary division or the side of an equation in a primary division; the wall of a house or any wall, L.; an army, L.; favour, L.; contradiction, rejoinder, L.; the ash-pit of a fire-place, L.; a royal elephant, L.; a limb or member of the body, L.; the feathers of the tail of a peacock, a tail, L.; proximity, neighbourhood, L.; a bracelet, L.; purity, perfection, L.; mfn. = *pācaka, bādhaka*, Sāy. on RV. vi, 47, 19. [Cf. OGerm. *fahs*; Angl.Sax. *feax*.] **-kṛit**, m. a partisan, follower, VāmP. **-kshaya**, m. the end of a half month, Var. **-kshepa**, m. the stroke or beat of a wing, Bhpr. (v. l. *pakshôtk°*). **-gama**, mfn. moving with w°s, flying; m. a bird, R. **-gupta**, m. 'w°-protected,' a species of bird, L. **-grahaṇa**, n. taking the side of (gen.), Kām. **-grāha** (Hariv.), **°hin** (R.), mfn. one who takes the side or chooses the party of (gen. or comp.) **-ghāta**, see *pakshâgh°*. **-ghna** (with *tri-śālaka*), n. (a house) wanting (lit. killing) a side i.e. having three halls towards east and south and north (but not one towards the west), Var. **-m-gama**, mfn. = *°ksha-g*, R. **-cara**, m. = *-gama*, m. (cf. *jala-paksha-c°*); an elephant that has strayed from the herd, Kād.; the moon, L. **-cchid**, m. 'cutter of the wings' (of mountains), N. of Indra, Kālid. **-ja**, m. 'produced in half a month,' the moon (also *-janman*), L.; N. of partic. clouds, VP. **-tā**, f. partisanship, adherence to a party (*°tām √gam*, with gen. 'to take the side of'), MBh.; (in phil.) the taking up a side or argument; maintaining or defending a thesis; the essential nature of a proposition; the being the premiss to be proved; N. of sev. wks.; *-kroḍa*, m., *-grantha*, m., *-ṭippaṇī* and *-ṭīkā*, f., *-rahasya*, n., *-vāda*, m., *-vādârtha*, m., *-vicāra*, m., *-siddhânta-grantha*, m. N. of wks. **-tva**, n. the being a part of (comp.), Śaṃk.; the being the premiss to be proved, Tarkas.; the being a lawsuit, Yājñ., Sch.; = *-tā*, L. **-dvaya**, n. both sides of an argument, W.; a month (lit. 2 half months), ib. **-dvāra**, n. a side or inner or back door, private entrance, Mṛicch. **-dhara**, mfn. having wings (cf. m.); taking the side of, clinging to (gen. or loc.), MBh.; m. a bird, Hariv.; an elephant that has strayed from the herd, L.; the moon, L. (cf. *-cara*); N. of Jayadeva (author of the Tattva-cintāmaṇy-āloka), Cat.; (*ī*), f. N. of wk.; *-miśra*, m. N. of an author; *-vyākhyā*, f., *°rôddhāra*, f. N. of wks. **-dharmatā-vāda**, m. N. of wk. **-nāḍī**, f. a quill, Suśr. **-nikshepa**, m. the placing on the side of, counting among (comp.), Sarvad. **-pāta**, m. 'falling of the feathers,' the moulting of birds, L.; flying, soaring, Ratnâv. ii, 7; adopting a side or argument, siding with, partiality or inclination for (loc., gen., acc. with *prati*, or comp.), MBh.; Kāv. &c. (also Ratnâv. ii, 7); a partisan, adherent, W.; *-kṛita-sneha*, mfn. manifesting party attachment, sympathising, MW. **-pātin**, mfn. flying; ifc. siding with, favouring, Kāv.; Pañc.; *°ti-tā*, f., Rājat.; Naish.; *°ti-tva*, n., MW. **-pāli**, f. a wing, Caṇḍak.; a private or back door, L. **-pucchá**, n. wings and tail, ŚBr.; *°cchá-vat*, mfn. having w° and t°, ib. **-puṭa**, m. a wing (lit. 'the hollow of the w°s'), Hariv.; Kād. **-poshaṇa**, mfn. favouring a party, factious, BhP. **-pradosha-vrata**, n. N. of wk. **-pradyota**, m. N. of a partic.

position of the hands in dancing, Cat. **-bala,** n. strength of wing, MW. **-bindu,** m. 'wing-spot, a heron, L. **-bhāga,** m. the side or flank, (esp.) the flank of an elephant, L. **-bhukti,** f. the course traversed by the sun in a fortnight, BhP. **-bheda,** m. distinction between two sides of an argument; the difference between the two halves of a lunar month, MW. **-mūla,** n. the root or articulation of a wing, L. **-yāga,** m. N. of wk. **-racanā,** f. forming a party or faction; *-naipuṇya,* n. skill in forming &c., Daś. **-rātri,** f. a kind of play or sport, Cat. **-vañcitaka,** n. a partic. position of the hands in dancing, ib. **-vat** (°*kshá-*), mfn. winged, having wings or flanks, ŚBr.; MBh. &c.; belonging to a party, having adherents or followers, MBh. (Nilak. 'belonging to a good family, well-born'). **-vadha,** m. 'side stroke,' paralysis of one side, Car.; Bhpr. **-vāda,** m. expression of opinion, stating a case, MBh. **-vāhana,** m. 'whose vehicles are wings,' a bird, L. **-vikala,** mfn. having mutilated w°s, Mṛicch. **-vyāpin,** mfn. embracing the whole of an argument, MW. **-śas,** ind. by or for half months or fortnights, MBh. **-sammita,** mfn. corresponding to the (size of the) wings, KātySr. **-sundara,** m. Symplocos Racemosa, L. **-hatá,** mfn. paralysed on one side, ŚBr. **-hara,** m. a recreant, traitor, MBh. **-homa,** m. an oblation lasting for a fortnight or to be offered every f°, L.; *-vidhi,* m., *-samasya-vidhāna,* n. N. of wks. **Pakshâkāra,** mfn. wing-shaped, MW. **Pakshâghāta,** m. = °*ksha-vadha,* Car.; Suśr.; refutation of an argument or view, W. **Pakshâdi,** m. the first day of a half month, PārGṛ. **Pakshâdhyāya,** m. casuistry, logic, Divyâv. **Pakshânta,** m. the end of the wings of an army arranged in the shape of a bird, MBh.; the last or 15th Tithi of either half month, new or full moon, Gobh.; Mn. &c. **Pakshântara,** n. an individual or particular case, L.; another side or view of an argument, Śak., Sch. **Pakshâbhāsa,** m. a seeming or fallacious argument, a fallacy, a false plaint, Yājñ., Sch. **Pakshâvalī,** f. N. of wk. **Pakshâvasara,** m. (L.), °*vasāna,* n. (Var.) the last Tithi or day of either half month, day of new or full moon. **Pakshâshṭamī,** f. the 8th Tithi or day of either half month, PārGṛ. **Pakshâhati,** f. a stroke with the wings, MW. **Pakshâhāra,** m. one who eats food only once in a half month, MBh. **Pakshêśvara,** m. N. of an author (prob. = °*sha-dhara*), Cat. **Pakshôtkshepa,** m., v.l. for °*ksha-kshepa.* **Pakshôdgrāhin,** mfn. = °*ksha-grāhin,* MW.

Pakshaka, m. a wing (ifc.; cf. *sa-*); N. of the number two, Hcat.; a fan, Gal.; a side door, L.; a side, Śiś.; a partisan, L.

Pakshatí, f. the root or pit of a bird's wing, VS.; Kāv.; Rājat. (cf. Pāṇ. v, 2, 25); the feathers or plumage of a bird, Kād.; Bālar. (ifc.; *-tā,* f.); the first Tithi or day of the half month (also °*tī*), L. **-puṭa,** m. pl. the expanded wings, Caṇḍ. (cf. *paksha-p°*).

Pákshas, n. a wing, Uṇ. iv, 219, Sch.; a side, RV. vi, 47, 19; the side part of a carriage, AV.; ŚāṅkhBr.; Gobh.; the leaf or side-post of a door, VS.; TBr.; Kāṭh.; the wing of an army, ŚāṅkhBr.; a half or any division, ŚrS.; a half month, TāṇḍBr.; the side or shore of a river, ib.; ŚāṅkhŚr.

Pakshālikā, f. N. of one of the Mātṛis attending on Skanda, MBh.

Pakshālu, m. a bird, L.

1. **Pakshi,** m. a bird (only acc. sg. °*kshim,* R. [B.] iii, 14, 2; pl. °*kshīn,* MBh. xii, 9306).

2. **Pakshi,** in comp. for °*kshin.* **-kīṭa,** m. a species of small bird, MW. **-jyotisha,** n. N. of wk. **-tīrtha,** n. N. of a sacred bathing-place, Cat. **-tva,** n. the state or condition of a bird, Kathās. **-pati,** m. 'prince of b°s,' N. of Sampāti, R. **-pānīya-śālikā,** f. a trough or reservoir for watering b°s, L. **-puṃgava,** m. 'bull among b°s,' N. of Garuḍa, Hariv.; of Jaṭāyu, R. **-pravara,** m. 'most excellent among b°'s,' N. of Garuḍa, Hariv. **-bālaka,** m. a young b°, MW. **-manushyâlaya-lakshaṇa,** n. N. of wk. **-mārga,** m. 'bird's path,' the air, Gal. **-mṛiga-tā,** f. the form or condition of a b° or of a beast, Mn. xii, 9. **-rāj** or **-rāja,** m. 'king of b°s,' N. of Garuḍa or of Jaṭāyu, R.; Kathās. **-rājya,** n. the sovereignty of the feathered tribes, MW. **-śārdūla,** m. (in music) a kind of dance. **-śālā,** f. 'bird-house,' an aviary or a nest, L. **-śāvaka,** m. a young b°, MW. **-siṇha** (L.), *-svāmin* (Hit.), m. 'lion or lord among b°s,' N. of Garuḍa. **Pakshîndra,** m. = °*kshi-rāj,* R.; Ragh.; Kathās. **Pakshîśa,** m. id., R.

Pakshin, mfn. winged (lit. and fig.), RV. &c. &c.; (ifc.) taking the side of, siding with, Hariv.; m. a bird or any winged animal, RV. &c. &c.; the bird Garuḍa as one of the 18 attendants of the Sun, L.; N. of Śiva, MBh.; a day with the 2 nights enclosing it, L.; an arrow, L.; a partic. sacrificial act, TāṇḍBr.; (*iṇī*), f. a female bird, Hariv.; (with or sc. *rātri*) a night with the 2 days enclosing it, Gobh.; Gaut.; the day of full moon, L.; N. of a Śākini, L.

Pakshila, m. N. of the saint Vātsyāyana, L. **-svāmin,** m. id. (as identified with Cāṇakya), Sarvad.

Pakshī-√kṛi, to appropriate, become master of anything, Hcar.

Pakshīya, mfn. taking the side or party of, siding with (comp.), Hariv.

Pakshu, m. N. of a serpent-demon, L. (w. r. for *vakshu*?).

1. **Pakshma,** m. or n. an eye-lash (in gen. pl. °*māṇām,* MBh. iv, 390); n. lead, Gal.

2. **Pakshma,** in comp. for °*man.* **-kopa,** m. irritation in the eye from the eyelashes turning inwards (Entropium), Suśr. **-pāta,** m. 'falling of the eyelashes,' closing of the eyes, Ragh. **-prakopa,** m. = *-kopa,* Suśr. **-yūkā,** f. a louse in the eyelashes, L. **-sampāta,** m. = *-pāta; -ja* (with *kāla*), m. an instant, MBh. **-spanda,** m. quivering of the eyelashes, Kāvyâd. ii, 149. **Pakshmâksha,** mfn. suffering from Entropium (cf. above), L.

Pákshman, n. (sg. and pl.) the eyelashes (°*ṇo nipātena,* 'in the twinkling of an eye, in an instant,' MBh.; cf. *pakshma-pāta* &c. above), TS.; ŚBr. &c. &c.; the hair (of a deer), Śiś. i, 8; the filament of a flower, ib. v, 85; a thin thread, L.; the leaf of a flower, Kād.; a wing, L.; a whisker, MW.

Pakshmala, mf(*ā*)n. having long eyelashes, Kāv.; Suśr.; having long or thick hair, hairy, shaggy, Śiś.; downy, soft, Kād.; Bālar. **-dṛiś,** f. (a woman) having long eyelashes, Viddh.

Pakshyà, mf(*ā*)n. being in or belonging to the wings (cf. below); changing every half month, RV. iii, 53, 16 (Sāy. 'descended from Paksha i.e. the sun'); produced or occurring in a fortnight, W.; (ifc.) siding or taking part with, Kathās. **-vayas,** mfn. whose strength lies in his (its) wings, Śulbas.

पक्ष्णु *pakshṇu.* See p. 575, col. 2.

पखोद *pakhoda* and *pakhaudu,* m. Capparis Divaricata, L.

पगारा *pagārā,* f. N. of a place, Inscr.

पङ्क *páṅka,* m. n. (g. *ardharcâdi;* said to be fr. √1. *pac,* 'to spread') mud, mire, dirt, clay (ifc. f. *ā*), Suparṇ.; Mn.; MBh. &c.; ointment, unguent (in comp.; cf. *kuṅkuma-, candana-* &c.), Kāv.; BhP.; moral impurity, sin, L. **-karvaṭa,** m. mud on the banks of a river, soft mud, L. **-kīra,** m. an aquatic bird, lap-wing, L. **-krīḍa** and **-krīḍanaka,** m. 'sporting in mud,' a pig, L. **-gaḍaka,** m., **-gaṇḍī** and **-gati,** f. a small fish, Macrognathus Pancalus, L. **-grāha,** m. the marine monster Makara, L. **-cchid,** m. 'mud-destroyer,' Strychnos Potatorum (the fruit of which is used for purifying foul water), Mālav. **-ja,** n. (ifc. f. *ā*) 'mud-born,' a species of lotus, Nelumbium Speciosum (whose flower closes in the evening), MBh.; Kāv. &c. (in Kathās. once *ā,* f.); m. N. of Brahmā, Cat. (for *paṅkaja-ja*); mfn. lotus-eyed, Jātakam.; *-janman,* m. 'lotus-born,' N. of Brahmā, Hariv.; *-nayanā,* f. a l°-eyed woman, Bhām.; *-nābha,* m. 'having a l° springing from his navel,' N. of Vishṇu, Ragh.; BhP.; *-netra,* mfn. 'l°-eyed' (said of Vishṇu), BhP.; *-pattra-netra,* m. having eyes like l°-leaves, MW.; *-mālin,* mfn. wearing a l°-crown (Vishṇu), BhP.; *-lāvam,* ind. (fr. √*lū*) cutting off like a l°-flower, Bālar.; *-vat,* mfn. furnished with a l°, Nīlak. on MBh.; °*jâkshī,* f. = °*ja-nayanā,* Amar.; °*jâṅghri,* mfn. whose feet are adorned with l°-flowers (Vishṇu), BhP.; °*jâvalī,* f. N. of a metre, Col. (cf. *paṅkâvalī*); °*jâsana-stha,* mfn. sitting on a l°-throne (Brahmā), Var.; °*jin,* mfn. furnished with a l°, MBh.; (*nī*), f. Nelumbium Speciosum (the plant or a group or the flexible stalk of such lotuses), also a l°-pond (= °*nī-saras*), Kāv.; Pur. **-janman,** n. = *-ja,* n., L. **-jāta,** n. id.; = *pāpa-samūha,* Dharmaś. **-jit,** m. N. of a son of Garuḍa, MBh. **-tā,** f. the nature or property of mud, muddiness, Śiś. **-dantá,** mfn. having mud or clay between the teeth, Suparṇ. **-digdha,** mfn. mud-smeared; *-śarīra,* m. 'having a m°-sm° body,' N. of a Dānava, Hariv.; °*dhâṅga,* m. 'having m°-sm° limbs,' N. of a being attending on Skanda, MBh. **-prabhā,** f. (with Jainas) N. of one of the 7 divisions of hell (where mud takes the place of light), L. **-bhāj,** mfn. sunk in the mire, W. **-bhāraka,** mfn. laden with mud, muddy, W. **-bhāva,** m. = *-tā,* Ragh. **-magna** (*paṅká-*), mfn. immersed in m°, Suparṇ. **-majjana,** n. immersion in m°, MW. **-maṇḍuka** (!), m. a bivalve conch, L. (w. r. °*dūka*). **-maya,** mf(*ī*)n. full of mud, muddy, MW. **-ruh** and **-ruha,** n. = *-ja,* n. L.; °*hiṇī,* f. (Vcar.) = *-jinī.* **-lagna,** mfn. sticking in mud, Bhpr. **-vat,** mfn. muddy, covered with mud, Hariv.; R. **-vāri,** n., v.l. for *pakva-v°.* **-vāsa,** m. 'mud-dweller,' a crab, L. **-śukti,** f. 'm°-shell,' the stair-case shell, L. **-śūraṇa,** m. 'm°-root,' the fibrous eatable root of a lotus (also written *-shūraṇa* or *-sūr°*). **Paṅkâkta,** mfn. smeared with mud, Hit. **Paṅkâvalī,** f. N. of a metre, Col. (cf. *paṅkajâv°*).

Paṅkaya, Nom. P. °*yati,* to make muddy, trouble, Kir. xi, 19; to besmear, Hcar.

Paṅkāra, m. (only L.) Blyxa Octandra; Trapa Bispinosa; a dam, dike; stairs, a ladder.

Paṅkin, mfn. muddy, ifc. covered with anything as with mud, MBh. (cf. *mala-*).

Paṅkila, mf(*ā*)n. = prec., MBh.; Hariv.; thick, condensed, L.; m. a boat, canoe, L.

Paṅke, loc. of *paṅka* in comp. **-ja,** n. = °*ka-ja,* L. **-ruh,** n. id., Prasann. **-ruha,** n. id., Dhūrtas.; BhP.; m. the Indian crane, L.; *-vasati,* m. l°-dweller, N. of Brahmā, Vcar.; °*hâkshī,* f. a l°-eyed woman, Bhām.; °*hiṇī,* f. Nelumbium Speciosum, ib. **-śaya,** mfn. resting or dwelling in mud, Suśr.

पङ्कण *paṅkaṇa,* w. r. for *pakkaṇa.*

पङ्क्ति *paṅkti* (also °*ktī,* m. c. and in comp.), f. (fr. *pañcan*) a row or set or collection of five, the number 5, AV.; Br. &c.; a sort of fivefold metre consisting of 5 Pādas of 8 syllables each, ib.; any stanza of 4 × 10 syllables, Col. (= *chandas,* L.); the number 10, Hcat. (cf. *-grīva* &c. below); any row or set or series or number, a group, collection, flock, troop, assembly, company (e.g. of persons eating together or belonging to the same caste), Mn.; MBh.; Kāv. &c.; the earth, L.; w. r. for *pakti,* q. v. **-kaṭa,** m. a species of grass, ĀpGṛ., Sch. **-kaṇṭaka,** m. a white-flowering Achyranthes, L. **-kanda,** m. a partic. bulbous plant, L. **-krama,** m. order, succession, Hit. **-grīva,** m. 'ten-necked,' N. of Rāvaṇa, L. **-cara,** m. 'going in lines,' an osprey, L. **-dūsha** (MBh.), °**shaka** (Var.), °**shaṇa** (Āpast.), mfn. 'defiling society,' (any person) improper to associate with. **-dosha,** m. 'society-bane,' anything which defiles a social circle, MBh. **-pāvana,** mfn. purifying society, respectable (opp. to *-dūsha*), Mn.; MBh. &c.; *-pāvana,* mfn. doing honour to a social circle, TS., Sch. **-bīja,** m. Acacia Arabica, L. **-mālā,** f. a species of plant, Gal. **-ratha,** m. 'having 10 chariots,' N. of Daśaratha (Rāma's father), Ragh.; Pur. **-rādhas** (°*ktl-*), mfn. containing fivefold (or numbers of) gifts, RV. **-vihaṃgama-nāma-bhṛit,** m. = *-paṅkti-ratha* or *daśa-r°,* Vām. ii, 1, 13. **-śas,** ind. by rows or numbers, Śiś. xiv, 33.

Paṅktikā, f. the number ten, a decade, Hcat.; a row, line (in *akshara-p°*), Bhartṛ.

Paṅktī, for *paṅkti* in comp. **-kṛita,** mfn. combined into groups, Hariv. **-hara,** see *pāṅktīhari.*

Paṅkty-uttarā, f. a kind of metre, RPrāt.

पङ्गु *paṅgu,* mf(*vī* or *ū*)n. (fr. √*paj*?; cf. Uṇ. i, 37, Sch.) lame, halt, crippled in the legs, AVPar.; Yājñ.; MBh. &c.; N. of those elements of the body which are themselves without motion (but are moved by the wind), Bhpr.; m. N. of the planet Saturn (as moving slowly), Cat. (cf. *-vāsara*); of Nirjita-varman, Rājat. **-graha,** m. the sea-monster Makara (cf. *paṅka-g°*), W.; one of the signs of the zodiac (cf. *makara*), MW. **-tā,** f. lameness, motionlessness; *-hāriṇī,* f. 'destroying lameness,' a species of shrub, L.; Mn. xi, 51. **-tva,** n. = *-tā,* Tattvas. **-bhāva,** m. = *-tā,* Vcar. **-vakra-karma-prakāśa,** m. N. of wk. **-vāsara,** m. Saturday, Kāśīkh.

Paṅguka, mfn. = *paṅgu,* lame, MBh.

Paṅgula, mfn. id., L.; n. (?) lameness, Suśr.; m. a horse of a glassy or silvery white colour, L.

Paṅgūyita, n. limping, lameness, Śrīkaṇṭh.

पच् 1. *pac* or *pañc*, cl. 1. P. Ā. *pacati*, °*te*, or *pañcati*, °*te*, to spread out, make clear or evident, Dhātup. vi, 14: Caus. *-pañcayati* (xxxii, 108), see *pra-pañcaya*.

1. **Pañca**, mf(*ā*)n. spread out, Uttarar.; m. (in music) a kind of measure.

पच् 2. *pac*, cl. 1. P. Ā. (Dhātup. xxiii, 27) *pácati*, °*te* (cl. 4. Ā. *pácyate*, cf. below; p. *pacāna*, MBh. iii, 13239 [cf. *kim-pa-cāna*]; pf. *papāca* [2. sg. *papaktha* or *pecitha*, Pāṇ. vi, 4, 121, Sch.], *pecur; pece, pecire* [*ápe-ciran*, AV.; *peciran*, Pat. on Pāṇ. vi, 4, 120]; aor. *pákshat*, RV.; *apākshīt, apakta*, Gr.; Prec. *pacyāt*, ib.; fut. *pakshyati*, °*te* or *paktā*, Br.; ind. p. *paktvā́*, AV.; MBh.; inf. *páktave*, AV.; Br.; *paktum*, Pāṇ. viii, 2, 30, Sch.), to cook, bake, roast, boil (Ā. also 'for one's self'), RV. &c. &c.; (with double acc.) to cook anything out of (e.g. *taṇḍulān odanam pacati*, 'he cooks porridge out of rice-grains'), Siddh.; to bake or burn (bricks), ŚBr.; to digest, Suśr.; to ripen, mature, bring to perfection or completion, RV. &c. &c.; (with double acc.) to develop or change into (e.g. *puṇyâ-puṇyaṃ sukhâsukham*, 'merit and demerit into weal or woe'), Vop.; (intrans.) to become ripe or mature, Bhpr.: Pass. *pacyáte* (°*ti*, MBh.; aor. *apāci*, Gr.), to be cooked or burnt or melted or digested or ripened or developed, RV. &c. &c.; to be tormented, Divyâv.; also intrans. = *pácyate* (cf. above), to become ripe or mature, to develop or ripen, RV.; VS.; Br. (with acc. of the fruit that is borne or ripens, Maitr.; Kāth.; cf. Pāṇ. iii, 1, 87, Vārtt. 14, Pat.; *lokā́ḥ pácyamānāḥ*, 'the developing world,' ŚBr.): Caus. *pācayati*, °*te*, Br. (aor. *apīpacat*, Gr.; Pass. *pācyate*, p. °*cyamāna*, MBh.); to cause to cook or be cooked (Ā. 'for one's self'), to have cooked or to cook, ŚBr.; MBh. &c. (cf. Pāṇ. i, 3, 74; 4, 52, Sch.); to cause to ripen, TBr.; to bring to completion or to an end, cure, heal, Suśr.: Desid. *pipakshati*, Gr.: Intens. *pāpacīti*, Gr.; *pāpacyate*, to be much cooked, to cook very much or burn excessively, to be much afflicted, BhP.; Suśr.: Desid. of intens. *pāpacishati*, °*te*, Gr. [Cf. Gk. πέσσω for πεκ-jω; Lat. *coquo*; Slav. *peką, pešti*.]

Paktavya, mfn. to be cooked or baked, MBh.; to be matured or digested, W.

Paktí (VS. *pákti*), f. cooking, preparing food, Mn. ix, 11 (*anna-p*°); food or any dish of cooked food, RV.; VS.; digesting, digestion, Mn.; Yājñ.; Suśr.; place of digestion (= *-sthāna*), Suśr.; ripening, development (cf. *loka-*), having results or consequences, Var.; Kāv.; purification, MBh. xii, 9745 (Nīlak.); respectability, dignity, fame, Suśr. **–dṛishṭi**, f. du. digestive organs and sight, Mn. xii, 120. **–nāśana**, mfn. spoiling digestion, Suśr. **–śūla**, n. violent pain or inflammation of the bowels proceeding from indigestion, colic, L. **–sthāna**, n. place of digestion, Suśr.

Paktṛi, mfn. who or what cooks or roasts or bakes (with gen.), AV.; ŚBr.; MBh. &c.; digestive, promoting digestion, Suśr.; m. or n. the digestive fire, force of digestion, Car. °**tra**, n. the state of a householder who possesses a sacred fire or that fire perpetually maintained by him, Uṇ. iv, 166. °**trima**, mfn. obtained by cooking, Pāṇ. iii, 3, 88; iv, 4, 20; ripe, HPariś.; cooked, W.

Pakthá, m. N. of a man protected by the Aśvins, RV. (°*thasya Saubharasya*, N. of 2 Sāmans, ĀrshBr.); pl. N. of a people, ib. °**thín**, m. 'who cooks the oblation' (Sāy.; prob. N. of a man), ib.

Pakvá, mf(*ā*)n. (considered as p.p. of √2. *pac*; cf. Pāṇ. viii, 2, 52) cooked, roasted, baked, boiled, prepared on a fire (opp. to *āma*), RV. &c. &c. (also applied to the milk in an udder); warmed (cf. *dvish-*), Gobh.; Mn. &c.; baked or burnt (as bricks or earthenware pots), ŚBr.; Var. &c.; ripe, mature (lit. and fig.), RV. &c. &c. (also applied to a tree with ripe fruits); grey, hoary (as the hair), Dhūrtas.; accomplished, perfect, fully developed (as the understanding, character &c.), MBh.; BhP.; ripe for decay, near to death, decrepit, perishing, decaying, ib.; digested, W.; n. cooked food, dish, RV.; AV.; ŚBr.; ripe corn, AV.; the ashes of a burnt corpse, ib. **–kashāya**, mfn. whose passion has become extinguished, BhP. **–kṛit**, mfn. cooking, maturing, dressing food; m. Azadirachta Indica, L. **–keśa**, mfn. grey-haired, W. **–gātra**, mfn. having a decrepit or infirm body, Divyâv. **–tā**, f. ripeness, maturity, greyness (of the hair), L. **–rasa**, m. wine or any intoxicating liquor made of the juice of the sugar cane, Bhpr. **–vat**, mfn. one who has cooked &c., MW. **–vāri**, n. sour rice-gruel (= *kāñjika*), L.; boiling or distilled water, W. (v.l. *paṅka-v*°). **–sasyôpamônnati**, m. a species of Kadamba, L. **–harita-lūna**, mfn. cut (grain), ripe but not dry, L. **Pakvâtīsāra**, m. chronic dysentery, Bhpr. **Pakvâdhāna**, n. the receptacle for digested food, the stomach, abdomen, Suśr. **Pakvânna**, n. cooked or dressed food, Mn.; Var. &c. **Pakvâśaya**, m. = °*vâdhāna*, MBh.; Suśr. (cf. *āmâś*°). **Pakvâsin**, mfn. eating only cooked food, Pracaṇḍ. i, 19. **Pakvêshṭaka**, mfn. made of burnt bricks, Mṛicch.; *-cita*, n. a building constructed with burnt bricks, Yājñ. **Pakvêshṭakā**, f. a burnt or baked brick, Var.; *-maya*, mf(*ī*)n. made of burnt bricks, Hcat.

Pakvaká, m. (?), AV. xx, 130, 6.

Pakshṇu, mfn. who or what cooks or matures, Vop.

3. **Pac**, mfn. (ifc.; nom. *-pak*, Pāṇ. vi, 4, 15, Sch.) cooking, baking.

1. **Paca**, mfn. id. (cf. *alpam-, ishṭi-, kim-* &c.); m. and (*ā*), f. the act of cooking &c., L. **–paca**, m. 'continually bringing to maturity' (?), N. of Śiva, MBh. **–m-pacā**, f. Curcuma Aromatica or Xanthorrhiza, Bhpr. (v.l. *-bacā*, L.)

2. **Paca**, 2. sg. Impv. of √*pac*. **–prakūṭā** and **-lavaṇā**, f., g. *mayūra-vyaṃsakâdi*.

Pacaka, m. a cook, cooking, baking, L.

Pacat, mf(*ntī*)n. cooking, roasting &c. **–puṭa**, m. Hibiscus Phoeniceus, L.

1. **Pacatá**, mfn. cooked, boiled &c., RV.; VS.; ŚāṅkhBr.; m. fire, L.; the sun, L.; N. of Indra, L.; n. cooked food (= *pakti*), Nir. vi, 16.

2. **Pacata**, 2. pl. Impv. of √*pac*. **–bhṛijjatā**, f. (2. pl. Impv. of √*pac* and √*bhṛijj*) continual baking and roasting, g. *mayūra-vyaṃsakâdi*.

Pacati-kalpam, ind. (?), Pāṇ. v, 3, 67, Sch.

Pacatyà, mfn. cooked, dressed, RV. iii, 52, 2.

Pacana, mfn. cooking, maturing (cf. *anvāhārya-, enī-*); m. fire, L.; (*ā*), f. becoming ripe, ripening, L.; (*ī*), f. the wild citron tree, L. (v.l. *pavanī*); n. (*pác*°) a means or instrument for cooking, RV.; ŚBr.; cooking, roasting, maturing, becoming cooked or ripe, MBh.; Suśr.; BhP. **–kriyā**, f. cooking, dressing food, Gaut. **Pacanâgāra**, n. 'cooking room,' a kitchen, ĀpGṛ., Sch. **Pacanâgni**, m. a fire for boiling, ib.

Pacanikā, f. a pan, L.

Pacamānaka, mfn. accustomed to cook one's food, Baudh.

Paci, m. fire, L.; cooking, maturing, L.

Pacelima, mfn. being soon cooked, cooking or ripening quickly, Pāṇ. iii, 1, 96, Vārtt. 1, Pat.; Kull. on Mn. iv, 172; m. (L.) Phaseolus Mungo or a similar species of bean; fire; the sun. °**luka**, m. a cook, L.

Pacya, mfn. becoming ripe, ripening (see *kṛish-ṭa-pacya*).

पच्चनिका *paccanikā* or *paccanī*, f. a partic. part of a plough, Kṛishis.

पच्छब्द् *pac-chabda, pac-chas* &c. See under 3. *pad*, p. 583.

पज् *paj* or *pañj*, to become stiff or rigid, only pf. Ā. *pāpaje* with *apa*, he started back from (loc.), RV. x, 105, 3. [Cf. Gk. πήγνυμι; Lat. *pango*.]

Pajrá, mf(*ā́*)n. solid, stout, fat, strong, RV. [cf. Gk. πηγός]; m. N. of Kakshīvat and other men, ib.; (*ā*), f. the Soma plant, ib.; n. N. of a Sāman, Lāṭy. **–hoshin**, mfn. having fat or rich oblations (Indra-Agni), RV. vi, 59, 4 (cf. Nir. v, 22).

Pajriyá, m. N. of Kakshīvat, RV.

Pañjaka, m. N. of a man, Rājat.

Pañjara, n. a cage, aviary, dove-cot, net, MBh.; Kāv. &c.; a skeleton, the ribs, Prab.; Caṇḍ. (also m., L.); N. of partic. prayers and formularies, VāmP.; m. (L.) the body, Udbh.; the Kali-yuga, L.; a purificatory ceremony performed on cows, L.; a kind of bulbous plant (v. l. *pañjala*). **–kapiñjala**, m. a partridge in a cage, Mṛicch. **–kapota**, m. a pigeon in a c°, ib. **–kesarin**, m. a lion in a c°, Kād. **–cālana-nyāya**, m. the rule (exemplified by the story) of shaking the c° (by 11 birds who united their strength for this purpose although they differed in other ways), Śaṃk. **–bhāj**, mfn. 'keeping the c°,' remaining in it, Kād. **–śuka**, m. a parrot in a c°, Mṛicch. **Pañjarâkheṭa**, m. a sort of basket or wicker trap in which fish are caught, L.

Pañjaraka, m. or n. a cage, aviary &c., MBh.; Pañc.

पजोक *pajoka*, m. N. of a poet, Cat.

पज्ज *paj-ja*. See 3. *pad*.

पज्झटिका *pajjhaṭikā*, f. (*pad*+?) a small bell, Chandom.; a kind of metre, ib.

पञ्च् *pañc*. See √1. *pac*, col. 1.

1. **Pañca**. See under 1. *pac*, ib.

पञ्च 2. *pañca*, in comp. for *pañcan* (see p. 578). **–kapāla** (*páñca-*), mf(*ī*)n. prepared or offered in five cups or bowls, m. (with or sc. *puro-ḍāśa*) an oblation so offered, ŚBr.; ŚrS. **–karṇa**, mfn. branded in the ear with the number 5 (as cattle), Pāṇ. vi, 3, 115; m. N. of a man, TĀr. **–karpaṭa**, m. pl. N. of a people, MBh. **–karma**, n. (L.), **-karman**, n. (Suśr.), **-karmī**, f. (L.) the 5 kinds of treatment (in medicine, viz. giving emetics, purgative medicines, sternutatories, and enemas of two kinds, oily and not oily); °*ma-vidhi* and °*mâdhikāra*, m. N. of medic. wks. **–kalpa**, m. one who studies or has studied 5 Kalpas (esp. those belonging to the AV.), L.; (*ī*), f. N. of wk. **–kalyāṇaka**, m. a horse with white feet and a white mouth, Hcat. **–kashāya**, m. (?), a decoction from the fruits of 5 plants (the Jambū, Śālmali, Vāṭyāla, Bakula and Badara), L.; *-ja* and °*yôttha*, mfn. produced from the above decoction, Suśr. **–kāṭhaka-prayoga-vṛitti**, f. N. of wk. **–kāpittha**, mfn. prepared with the 5 products of Feronia Elephantum, Suśr. **–kārukī**, f. the 5 artisans in a village, L. **–kāla-kriyā-dīpa**, m., **-kāla-paddhati**, f., **-kāla-pravartana**, n. N. of wks. **–kūrca**, n. = *-gavya*, Kāśikh. **–kṛitya**, n. the 5 actions by which the supreme power manifests itself (viz. *sṛishṭi, sthiti, saṃhāra, tirobhāva* and *anugraha-karaṇa*), Sarvad.; (m.) a species of plant, L. **–kṛitvas**, ind. 5 times, Lāṭy.; KātyŚr.; Suśr. **–kṛishṇa**, m. 'having 5 black spots,' a species of poisonous insect, Suśr. **–kṛishṇala**, n. 5 Kṛishṇalas or coins so called, Gaut.; °*laka*, mfn. comprising 5 K°s, MW. **–koṇa**, m. a pentagon, Col. **–kola** or °**laka**, n. the 5 spices (viz. long pepper, its root, Piper Chaba, plumbago and dry ginger), Car.; Bhpr. **–kośa**, (ibc.) the 5 sheaths supposed to invest the soul, W. (cf. *kośa*); *-viveka* and *-saṃnyāsâcāra*, m. N. of wks. **–krama**, m. a particular Krama (or method of reciting the Vedic text) consisting of 5 members (see *pāṭha*), L.; N. of a Buddh. wk. (also *-ṭippaṇī*, f.) **–krośa**, m. or °*śī*, f. a distance of 5 Krośas, the ground extending to that distance round Benares (cf. RTL. 218, 1; 435); °*śa-mañjarī*, f. (°*rī-sudarśana*, n.), °*śa-māhātmya*, n., °*śa-yātrā*, f., or °*śī-yātrā-vidhi*, m. N. of wks. **–kroshṭṛi**, mfn. = *pañcabhiḥ kroshṭṛībhiḥ krītaḥ*, Pat. **–kleśa-bheda**, mf(*ā*)n. afflicted by the 5 kinds of pain, ŚvetUp. **–kshāra**, n. = *-lavaṇa*, q.v. **–khaṭva**, n., °*vī*, f. a collection of 5 bedsteads, L. **–gaṅga**, n. (C.), **-gaṅgā**, f. (B.) N. of a locality, MBh. **–gaṇa-yoga**, m. a collect. N. of 5 plants (viz. *vidārī-gandhā, bṛihatī, pṛiśni-parṇī, nidigdhikā* and *sva-daṃsh-ṭrā*), L. **–gaṇḍaka**, mfn. (prob.) consisting of 5 parts (said of the Dharma-cakra), Divyâv. **–gata**, mfn. 'arrived at 5,' raised to the 5th power, Col. **–gati-samatikrānta**, m. 'having passed through the 5 forms of existence,' N. of Gautama Buddha, Divyâv. (some reckon 6 forms, see MWB. 121). **–gava**, n., **-gavī**, f. a collection of 5 cows; °*va-dhana*, mfn. one whose property consists of 5 cows, L. **–gavya**, n. the 5 products of the cow (viz. milk, coagulated or sour milk, butter, and the liquid and solid excreta), L.; N. of wk.; *-ghṛita*, n. N. of a partic. mixture, Rasar.; *-melana-prakāra*, m. N. of wk.; °*vyâpâna-vat*, mfn. having an anus made of the Pañca-gavya, Hcat. **–gārgya**, mfn. = *pañcabhir gārgībhiḥ krītaḥ*, Pat. **–gu**, mfn. bought with 5 cows, Pāṇ. i, 2, 44, Vārtt. 3, Pat. **–guṇa**, mfn. fivefold; having 5 virtues or good qualities, MBh. **–gupta**, m. covered or protected in a fivefold manner,' a tortoise (as drawing in its 4 feet and head; cf. *pañcâṅga-g*°), L.; the materialistic system of the Cārvākas, L. **–gupti**, f. Medicago Esculenta, L. **–gṛihītá**, mfn. taken or taken up 5 times, ŚBr.; KātyŚr.; °*tin*, mfn. one who has taken up 5 times, Lāṭy., Sch. **–goṇi**, mfn. 'carrying 5 loads,' bearing a heavy burden, Vajras. (cf. Pāṇ. i, 2, 50, Vārtt. 1, Pat.) **–gauḍa-brāhmaṇa-jāti, -granthī, -graha-yoga-śānti,** f. N. of wks. **–grāmī,** f. a collection of 5 villages, Yājñ. **–ghāta,** m. (in music) a kind of measure. **–cakshus,** m. 'five-eyed,' N. of the Buddha (who was supposed to have the *mānsa-c°, dharma-c°, prajñā-c°, divya-c°* and *Buddha-c°*, i. e. the carnal eye, the eye of religion, the eye of intellect, the divine eye and the eye of Buddha), MW. (cf. Dharmas. lxvi). **–catvāriṇsa,** mf(*ī*)n. the 45th (ch. of MBh. and R.) **–catvāriṇsat** (*pá°*), f. 45, ŚBr. **–candra,** m. N. of a man, Rājat. **–cāmara,** n. N. of 2 kinds of metre, Col.; *-stotra,* n. N. of a hymn by Śaṃkara. **–citīka** (*pá°*), mfn. piled up in 5 tiers or layers, ŚBr.; Kāṭh.; ĀpŚr. &c. **–cīra,** m. a Buddh. saint also named Mañjuśrī (the teacher of Buddhism in Nepal, MWB. 202, n. 1), W. **–cūḍa** (*pá°*), mf(*ā*)n. having 5 protuberances (cf. f.); (also *-ka*) having 5 crests or tufts of hair, Kathās.; (*ā*), f. = *-coḍā,* ŚBr.; N. of an Apsaras, MBh.; R.; *°ḍā-maṇi,* m. N. of wk. (also *°ṇi-ṭīkā*). **–coḍā,** f. a brick with 5 protuberances, TS.; ĀpŚr.; Śulb. **–cola,** m. or n. N. of a part of the Himālaya range, L. **–janá,** m. (pl.) the 5 classes of beings (viz. gods, men, Gandharvas and Apsaras, serpents, and Pitṛis), TS.; ŚBr. &c.; man, mankind, Hcar. (*°nêndra,* m. prince, king, Rājat.); (ibc.) the 5 elements, MBh.; N. of a demon slain by Kṛishṇa, MBh.; R. &c. (cf. *pāñcajanya*); of a son of Saṃhrāda by Kṛiti, BhP.; of a Prajāpati, ib.; of a son of Sagara by Keśinī, Hariv.; of a son of Sṛiñjaya and father of Soma-datta, ib.; (*ī*), f. an assemblage of 5 persons, L.; N. of a daughter of Viśva-rūpa and wife of Bharata, BhP. (v. l. *pāñcajanī*); *°nīna,* mfn. devoted or consecrated to the 5 races, TS.; TBr. (also *°nīya,* AitBr.; ŚāṅkhŚr.; cf. Pāṇ. v, i, 9, Vārtt. 4, Pat.); m. an actor, a buffoon, L.; the chief of 5 men, W. **–jitam-te,** N. of a Stotra. **–jñāna,** m. 'possessing fivefold knowledge,' a Buddha, L. **–ḍākinī,** f. N. of a female attendant on Devī, W. **–taksha,** n., **°kshī,** f. a collection of 5 carpenters, L. **–tattva,** n. the 5 elements collectively (cf. *tattva*), L.; (in the Tantras) the 5 essentials (= *pañca-makāra,* q. v.); *-prakāśa,* m., *°tvâtmaka-stotra,* n. N. of wks. **–tantra,** n. N. of the well-known collection of moral stories and fables in 5 books from which the Hitopadeśa is partly taken (also *-ka*); of a poem by Dharma-paṇḍita; *-kāvya-darpaṇa,* m. N. of wk. **–tanmātra,** n. sg. the 5 subtle rudiments of the 5 elements, Kap. **–tapa,** mfn. = *-tapas,* mfn. **–tapas,** n. (ibc.) the 5 fires (to which an ascetic who practices self-mortification exposes himself, viz. one fire towards each of the 4 quarters, and the sun overhead); mfn. sitting between the 5 fires, Mn. vi, 23 (cf. MWB. 30, n. 2); *°po'nvita,* mfn. id., R. **–tā,** f. fivefoldness, fivefold state or amount, Mn. viii, 151; an aggregate or a collection of 5 things, (esp.) the 5 elements, viz. earth, air, fire, water and *ākāśa* ether, and dissolution into them i. e. death (*-tām* with √*gam, yā* &c., to die, with *upa-*√*nī,* to kill), Kāv.; Suśr.; Pur. **–tāra,** mfn. five-starred, MW. **–tikta,** n. 5 bitter things (viz. *nimba, amṛitā, vṛisha, paṭola,* and *nidigdhikā*), Bhpr.; *-ghṛita,* n. a partic. mixture, Rasav. **–tīrthī,** f. any five principal places of pilgrimage (esp. Viśrānti, Saukara, Naimisha, Prayāga, and Pushkara), VarP.; N. of a sacred bathing-place, Kathās.; bathing on the day of the equinox (?), W. **–triṇśá,** mf(*ī*)n. the 35th, ŚBr.; + 35, Jyot. **–triṇśat** (*pá°*), 35, ŚBr., ch. of MBh.; *°śac-chlokī* and *°śat-pīṭhikā,* f. N. of wks. **–triṇśati,** f. 35, Rājat. **–triṇśika,** mfn. having the length of 35, Śulb. **–trika,** mfn. (pl.) 5 × 3, MBh. **–tva,** n. fivefoldness; the 5 elements, BhP.; dissolution, death (*pañca-tvaṃ gata,* mfn. dead, Hit.; cf. *-tā*), Yājñ.; R.; Var. &c. **–daka** (?), m. pl. N. of a people, MBh. **–daṇḍa,** mfn. having 5 sticks, Pañcad.; *-cchattra-prabandha,* m. N. of a tale. **–1. -daśa,** mf(*ī*)n. the 15th, AV. &c. &c.; + 15, ŚāṅkhŚr.; consisting of 15, RV. &c. &c.; containing or representing the Pañca-daśa Stoma, connected with it, Br.; (*ī*), f. (sc. *tithi*) the 15th day of a half month, the day of full or new moon, TBr.; Yājñ.; Var.; N. of sev. wks. (also *°śī-tantra,* n., *-prakaraṇa,* n., *-yantra-vidhāna,* n., *-viveka,* m., *-vyākhyā,* f., *-samāsa,* m.) **–2. -daśa,** for *°śan* in comp.; *-karman,* n. N. of wk.; *-kṛitvas,* ind. 15 times, Lāṭy.; *-cchadi* (*pá°*), mfn. having 15 roofs, TS.; *-dhā,* ind. in or into 15 parts or ways, MārkP.; *-mālā-mantra-vidhi,* m. N. of wk.; *-rātra,* m. a period of 15 nights, a fortnight, Pāṇ. iii, 3, 137, Kāś.; *-rcá* (for *-ṛica*), mfn. consisting of 15 verses, AV.; Br.; *-vat* (*°śá-*), mfn. possessing the Pañca-daśa Stoma, ŚBr.; *-varṇa-mālikā,* f. N. of a Stotra; *-vartani,* mfn. forming the path of a Pañca-daśa Stoma, TS.; *-vārshika,* mf(*ī*)n. 15 years old, Pañc.; N. of a kind of Cāturmāsya, ĀpŚr.; *°śâkshara* (*pá°*), mfn. consisting of 15 syllables, VS.; *°śâha,* m. a period of 15 days, Mn. v, 83; *°śâhika,* mf(*ī*)n. lasting 15 days, Yājñ. iii, 323. **–daśan** (*pá°*), mfn. pl. (gen. *°śānām,* ŚBr.; instr. *°śabhis,* L.) 15, RV. &c. &c. **–daśama,** mf(*ī*)n. the 15th, KūrmaP. **–daśika,** mfn. having the length of 15, Śulb. **–daśin,** mfn. consisting of 15 parts, ŚBr. **–dāman,** mf(*mnī*)n. having 5 cords, Pāṇ. iv, 1, 29, Kāś. **–dīrgha,** n. sg. the 5 long parts of the body (viz. the arms, eyes, belly [knees, Buddh.], nose, and breast), L. **–daivata,** mfn. having 5 deities (organs of sense), YogaśUp. **–daivatya,** n. a partic. gift to Brāhmans (at the offering of which 5 deities are thought to be present), Hcat. **–drāviḍa-jāti,** f. N. of wk. (cf. *pañca-gauḍa-brāhmaṇa-j°*). **–drauṇika,** mf(*ī*)n. containing 5 Droṇas (a partic. measure of capacity), MBh. **–dhanus,** m. N. of a prince, VP. **–dhā́,** ind. in 5 ways or parts, fivefold, AV. &c. &c.; *-bandhyā-prakāśa* (?), m. N. of wk. **–dhāraṇaka,** mfn. upheld or subsisting by the 5 elements, MBh. **–dhīva,** mf(*ā*)n. = *pañcabhir dhīvarībhiḥ krītaḥ,* Pat. **–nakha,** mfn. '5-clawed,' having 5 nails, Var.; m. a 5-clawed animal, Mn.; MBh.; R.; an elephant, L.; a lion, Gal.; a tiger, L. (also *°khin,* Gal.); a tortoise, L. **–nada,** n. the Pañjāb or country of 5 rivers (viz. the Śata-dru, Vipāśā, Irāvatī, Candra-bhāgā, and Vitastā, i. e. the Sutlej, Beās, Rāvī, Chenāb, and Jhelum or Behut), MBh.; R.; Rājat. (also *ī,* f., Hcat.); N. of sev. Tīrthas (esp. of one near the junction of the Kiraṇā and Dhūta-pāpā with the Ganges after the union of the latter river with the Yamunā and Sarasvatī), MBh.; SkandaP.; m. or n. N. of a river produced by the junction of the 5 rivers of the Pañjāb and which falls into the Sindhu, L.; m. a prince of Pañca-nada, MBh. (pl. the inhabitants of P°-n°, MBh.); N. of an Asura, Hariv.; of a teacher, VāmP.; *-kshetra-māhātmya,* n. N. of wk.; *-tīrtha,* n. N. of a sacred bathing-place (cf. above); *-māhātmya,* n. N. of wk. **–nalīya,** n. N. of wk. **–navata,** mf(*ī*)n. the 95th (ch. of MBh. and Hariv.); + 95 (*°te dina-śate,* on the 195th day), VarBṛS. xxi, 7. **–navati,** f. 95 (ch. of MBh.); *-tama,* mf(*ī*)n. 95th; the 95th (ch. of R.) **–nātha,** m. N. of an author, Cat. **–nāman** (*pá°*), mf(*mnī*)n. having 5 names, AV.; *°mâvalī,* f. N. of wk. **–nāli,** mfn. lasting 3 × 24 minutes, Sāh. **–nidhana,** n. N. of sev. Sāmans, ĀrshBr. **–nimba,** n. sg. the 5 products (viz. the flowers, fruit, leaves, bark, and root) of the Azadirachta Indica, L. **–nirgranthī-sūtra,** n. N. of wk. **–nīrājana,** n. waving 4 things (viz. a lamp, lotus, cloth, mango or betel leaf) before an idol and then falling prostrate, W. **–pakshin,** m. or n. (?), N. of a small wk. containing auguries ascribed to Śiva (in which the 5 vowels *a, i, u, e, o* are connected with 5 birds), L.; *°kshi-śāstra,* n. N. of a wk. on augury. **–pakshī,** f. N. of sev. wks. on astrology; *-ṭīkā,* f. N. of sev. Comms. **–pañcaka** (R.), **-pañcan** (BhP.), 5 × 5 (ibc.) **–pañca-nakha,** m. species of 5 animals allowed to be killed and eaten (viz. the hare, porcupine, alligator, rhinoceros, and tortoise), W. **–pañcāśa,** mf(*ī*)n. the 55th (ch. of MBh.) **–pañcāśat** (*pá°*), f. 55, ŚBr. &c. &c. **–pañcin** (*pá°*), mfn. fivefold, Br. **–paṭala,** m. or n., **°likā,** f. N. of wks. **–paṭu,** mfn. = *pañcabhiḥ paṭvībhiḥ krītaḥ,* Pat. **–pattra,** mfn. having 5 feathers, R.; m. '5-leaved,' a species of Caṇḍāla-kanda, L. **–pada** (*pá°*), mf(*ā*)n. containing 5 Padas, ŚBr.; (*ī*), f. taking 5 steps, consisting of 5 feet or steps or parts, TS.; GṛS. (fr. *-pad?*); 'only 5 steps,' a cold or unfriendly relationship (opp. to *sāptapadīna,* q. v.), Bahc. ii, 123; the 5 strong cases (viz. nom. and voc. sg. du. pl.; acc. sg. du.), APrāt.; N. of a river in Śāka-dvīpa, BhP.; *°dârthī,* f., *°dī-vivṛiti,* f. N. of wks. **–parishad,** f. an assembly taking place every 5th year, Buddh. **–parṇikā** or **°ṇī,** f. a species of small shrub, L. **–parva,** mf(*ā*)n. (river) having 5 windings, ŚvetUp. **–parvata,** n. 'the 5 peaks' (of the Himālayas), L. **–parvan,** mfn. 5-knotted (as an arrow), R.; m. a stick with 5 knots, Kauś.; *°va-* and *°vī-māhātmya,* n., *°vīya-vidhi,* m. N. of wks. **–pala** (Yājñ.), **-palika** (KātyŚr., Sch.), mfn. weighing 5 Palas; *°lī,* f. a weight of 5 P°s, Kathās. **–pallava,** n. the aggregate of 5 sprigs or shoots of the Āmra, Jambū, Kapittha, Bīja-pūraka, and Bilva (according to others, of the Āmra, Aśvattha, Vaṭa, Parkaṭī, and Yajñôdumbara; or of the Panasa, Āmra, Aśvattha, Vaṭa, and Bakula, L.; or of the spondias, rose-apple, Bel or marmelos, citron, and wood-apple, W.) **–paśu,** m. (!) sg. the 5 sacrificial animals, KātyŚr.; mfn. destined for the 5 s° a°s, Vait. **–pātra,** n. a partic. vessel for purifying water used at the Ācamana (q. v.), RTL. xxi; n. 5 cups or vessels collectively or a Śrāddha in which offerings are made in 5 vessels, L. **–pāda** (*pá°*), mfn. 5-footed, RV.; AV.; (*ī*), f. N. of a wk. on the Uṇ-ādis. **–pādikā,** f. N. of a philos. wk.; *-ṭīkā,* f., *-ṭīkā-tattva-dīpana,* n., *-°dhyāsa-bhāshya-vyākhyā* (*°kâdh°*), f., *-vivaraṇa,* n. (*°ṇa-prakāśikā,* f.), *-vyākhyā,* f., *-śāstra-darpaṇa,* m. N. of Comms. **–pitta,** n. the gall or bile of 5 animals (viz. the boar, goat, buffalo, fish, and peacock), L. **–pura,** n. N. of a city, Śukas. **–purāṇīya,** mfn. worth 5 Purāṇas (a partic. coin), Kull. on Mn. xi, 227. **–purusham,** ind. through 5 generations of men, ĀpŚr., Sch. **–pushpamaya,** mf(*ī*)n. formed or consisting of 5 flowers, Kathās. **–pūlī,** f. 5 bunches, Pāṇ. ii, 1, 51, Vārtt. 6, Pat. **–prakaraṇa,** n., **°ṇī,** f. N. of wks. **–prayāga,** m. a kind of oblation, RTL. 367. **–prayoga,** m. N. of wk. **–prastha,** mfn. having 5 elevations or rising grounds (said of a forest), BhP. **–praharaṇa,** mfn. having 5 carriage-boxes, ib. **–prâṇa,** m. pl. the 5 vital airs (supposed to be in the body); *°ṇâhuti-khaṇḍa,* m. or n. (?) N. of wk. **–prādeśa,** mf(*ā*)n. 5 spans long, KātyŚr. **–prāsāda,** m. a temple with 4 pinnacles and a steeple, W. **–phuṭṭika,** m. 'weaving 5 Phuṭṭikās (s. v.) in a day,' N. of a Śūdra, Kathās. **–baddha,** mfn. pl. joined into 5, Hariv. **–bandha,** m. a fine equal to the 5th part of anything lost or stolen, Yājñ. **–bandhura,** see *-vandh°.* **–bala,** n. the 5 forces (viz. faith, energy, recollection, self-concentration, reason), MWB. 50. **–balā,** f. the 5 plants called Balā (viz. *balā, nāga-b°, mahā-b°, ati-b°,* and *rāja-b°*), L. **–bāṇa,** m. 'having 5 arrows,' N. of the god of love, Kālid.; Daś. &c.; *-vijaya* and *-vilāsa,* m. N. of wks. **–bāṇī,** f. the 5 arrows (of the god of love), Naish. **–bāhu,** m. '5-armed,' N. of one of the attendants of Śiva, Hariv. **–bindu-prasṛita,** n. N. of a partic. movement in dancing, Daś. **–bila** (*pá°*), mfn. having 5 openings, ŚBr. **–bīja,** n. a collection of 5 kinds of seeds (viz. of Cardiospermum Halicacabum, Trigonella Foenum Graecum, Asteracantha Longifolia, Ligusticum Ajowan, and cumin-seed; or of Trapusa, Karkaṭī, Dāḍima, Padma, and Vānarī; or of Sinapis Racemosa, Ligusticum Ajowan, cumin-seed, sesamum from Khorasan, and poppy), L. **–bodha,** m. N. of wk. **–brahma-mantra,** m., **-brahma-vidyôpanishad** or **-brahmôpanishad,** f. N. of wks. **–bhaṅga,** m. pl. boughs of 5 partic. trees, Hcat. **–bhaṭṭīya,** n. N. of wk. **–bhadra,** mfn. having 5 good qualities or auspicious marks, Hcar.; consisting of 5 good ingredients (as a decoction), ŚārṅgS.; vicious, L.; m. a kind of pavilion, Vāstuv.; n. a partic. mixture, Bhpr. **–bhāra,** mfn. having the weight of 5 Bhāras, Siṇhâs. **–bhāshā-maṇi,** m. N. of wk. **–bhuja,** m. 5-armed, pentagonal; m. N. of Gaṇêśa, Gal.; a pentagon, W. **–bhūta,** n. pl. the 5 elements (earth, air, fire, water, and ākāśa), Kap.; *-parityakta,* mfn. deserted by the 5 el° (as a dead body), MW.; *-vādârtha* and *-viveka,* m. N. of wks.; *°tâtmaka,* mfn. consisting of 5 el° (as the human body), Suśr. **–bhūryābhimukhā** (!), f. N. of an Apsaras, Kāraṇḍ. **–bhṛiṅga,** m. or n. N. of the 5 plants Deva-dālī, Śamī, Bhaṅgā, Nirguṇḍī, and Tamāla-pattra, L. **–bhautika,** w. r. for *pāñcabh°.* **–ma-kāra,** n. the 5 essentials of the left-hand Tantra ritual (the words for which begin with the letter *m,* viz. *madya,* wine; *māṇsa,* meat; *matsya,* fish; *mudrā,* intertwining of the fingers; and *maithuna,* sexual union), W. (cf. *-tattva* and RTL. 192). **–mantra-tanu,** m. 'whose body consists of 5 Mantras,' N. of Śiva (with Śaivas), Sarvad. **–maya,** mf(*ī*)n. consisting of 5 (elements), MārkP. **–mahākalpa,** m. N. of Vishṇu, MBh. xii, 338. **–mahāpātakin,** mfn. guilty of the 5 great sins (see *mahā-pātaka*), MW. **–mahābhū-**

ta-maya, mf(*ī*)n. consisting of 5 elements, Hcat. **-mahāyajña,** m. pl. the 5 great devotional acts of the Hindūs (see *mahā-y°*), W.; *-vidhi,* m. N. of wk. **-mahisha,** n. the 5 products of the buffalo cow (cf. *pañca-gavya*), Suśr. **-māshaka** (f. *ī* [!], Gaut.) and °**shika** (Mn.), mfn. consisting of or amounting to 5 Māshas. **-1. -māsya,** mfn. (for 2. see under *pañcama*) happening every 5 months or containing 5 months, AitBr. **-mithyātva-ṭīkā,** f. N. of wk. **-mukha,** mf(*ī*)n. 5-faced or 5-headed (also applied to Prajā-pati), KaushUp.; m. N. of Śiva, L.; a lion, L.; an arrow with 5 points, R.; (*ī*), f. Gendarussa Vulgaris, L. **-mudrā,** f. 5 gestures to be made in presenting offerings to an idol, W. **-mushṭī,** f. Trigonella Corniculata, L. **-mushṭika,** m. a partic. decoction, Bhpr. **-mūtra,** n. sg. the urine of 5 (female animals, viz. the cow, goat, sheep, buffalo, and ass), L. **-mūrti** and °**tika,** mfn. having a fivefold form (applied to a partic. offering to Brāhmans), Hcat. **-mūla,** m. N. of an attendant of Durgā, Kathās.; n. (also °*laka*) and (*ī*), f. a class or group of 5 roots or plants with tuberous roots (according to Suśr. there are 5 classes each containing 5 medicinal plants, viz. *kanīyas* or *alpam* or *kshudrakam, mahat, vallī-saṃjñaḥ* [sc. *gaṇaḥ*], *kaṇṭaka-s°,* and *triṇa-s°,* i.e. the smaller and the larger cl°, the creepers, the thorny plants and the 5 kinds of grass; other groups are also enumerated), Suśr.; Bhpr. &c. **-meni,** mfn. having 5 missiles, AitBr. **-yakshā,** f. N. of a Tīrtha, MBh. **-yajña,** m. pl. the 5 religious acts or oblations of a house-keeper (cf. *pañca-mahāyajña*); *-paribhrashṭa,* m. a Brāhman who omits to perform the 5 religious acts, MW. **-yāma** (*pá°*), mfn. having 5 courses (as a sacrifice), RV.; N. of a son of Ātapa (who was son of Vibhāvasu and Ushā), BhP. **-yuga,** n. a cycle of 5 years, a lustrum, MBh. **-yojaná,** n. (AV.), °**nī,** f. (Rājat.) a way or distance of 5 Yojanas. **-rakshaka,** m. a species of plant, L. **-rakshā,** f. N. of wk. **-ratna,** n. a collection of 5 jewels or precious things (viz. gold, diamond, sapphire, ruby, and pearl, Hcat.; or gold, silver, coral, pearl, and Rāga-paṭṭa, L.); N. of sev. wks.; pl. the 5 gems or most admired episodes of the MBh.; MW.; *-kalā,* f., *-kiraṇâvali,* f., *-prakāśa,* m. N. of wks.; *-maya,* mf(*ī*)n. consisting of the 5 jewels, Hcat.; *-mālikā,* f., *-stava,* m., °*nâkara-stotra,* n. N. of Stotras. **-raśmi** (*páñca-*), mfn. (a chariot) having 5 strings or traces, RV. **-rasā,** f. the Emblic Myrobolan tree, L. **-rāji-phala,** m. Trichosanthes Dioeca, L. **-rātra** or °**traka,** m. a period of 5 days (nights), Kauś.; Mn. &c.; (°*trá*), mfn. lasting 5 days, ŚBr.; MBh. (also °*traka,* Pañc.); m. N. of an Ahīna (see 1. *áh°*) which lasts 5 days, TāṇḍBr.; ŚrS.; N. of the sacred books of various Vaishṇava sects (also pl.), MBh.; R. &c.; *-dīpikā,* f., *-naivedya-vidhāna,* n., *-pakvânna vidhāna,* n., *-prāyaścitta,* n., *-rakshā,* f. N. of wks. **-rātrika,** w. r. for *pāñcar°.* **-rāśika,** mfn. relating to the 5 ratios or proportions of numbers; n. the rule of 5, the rule of proportion with 5 terms, Col. **-rudra,** m. N. of an author; °*drīya,* n., °*drôpanishad-bhāshya,* n. N. of wks. **-rūpa-kośa,** m. N. of wk. **-rcá** (for *-ṛica*), mfn. consisting of 5 verses; m. a stanza consisting of 5 verses, AV.; ŚāṅkhGṛ. **-lakshaṇa,** mfn. possessing 5 characteristics (said of the Purāṇas, which ought strictly to comprehend 5 topics, viz. the creation of the universe, its destruction and renovation, the genealogy of gods and patriarchs, the reigns of the Manus, and the history of the solar and lunar races); n. a Purāṇa or mythological poem, W.; *-vidhi,* m. N. of wk. **-lakshaṇī,** f. N. of sev. wks. (also *-kroḍa,* m., *-ṭīkā,* f., *-prakāśa,* m., *-vivecana,* n., °*ny-anugama,* m.) **-lambaka,** n. N. of Kathās. xiv. **-lavaṇa,** n. 5 kinds of salt (viz. *kāca, saindhava, sāmudra, viḍa,* and *sauvarcala*), Suśr. **-lāṅgala,** (ibc.) a gift of as much land as can be cultivated with 5 ploughs (also *-ka,* Hcat.; MatsyaP.); *-dāna-vidhi,* m. N. of wk. **-loha,** n. a metallic alloy containing 5 metals (viz. copper, brass, tin, lead, and iron), L. **-lohaka,** n. the 5 metals (viz. gold, silver, copper, tin, and lead), L. **-vaktra,** mfn. 5-faced, Hariv.; R.; m. N. of Śiva, Dhūrtas.; of one of the attendants of Skanda, MBh.; a lion, L.; (*ā*), f. N. of Durgā, Cat.; *-rasa,* m. a partic. mixture, Bhpr.; *-stotra,* n. N. of a Stotra. **-vaṭa,** m. '5-threaded,' the Brāhmanical cord (but cf. RTL. 361), L.; N. of a man, Rājat.; (*ī*), f. the 5 fig-trees (N. applied to Aśvattha, Bilva, Vaṭa, Dhātrī, and Aśoka), SkandaP.; (also n.) N. of a part of the great southern forest where the Godāvarī rises and where the banished Rāma resided, MBh.; R.; Ragh.; °*ṭa-* or °*ṭī-māhātmya,* n. N. of wk. **-vadana-stotra,** n. N. of a Stotra (cf. *pañca-vaktra-st°*). **-vandhura,** mfn. having 5 seats, BhP. (cf. *tri-v°*). **-varga,** m. a class or group or series of 5, e.g. the 5 constituent elements of the body (cf. 1. *dhātu*), R. ii, 118, 27; the 5 classes of spies (viz. a pilgrim or rogue, an ascetic who has violated his vows, a distressed agriculturist, a decayed merchant, a fictitious devotee), Kull. vii, 154; the 5 organs of sense, the 5 devotional acts &c. (also *ī,* f.); mfn. proceeding in 5 lines or at 5 times, KātySr. **-varṇa,** mfn. '5-coloured,' L. (Mṛicch. i, 7/8?); fivefold, of 5 kinds (*-tā,* f.), Hcat.; m. N. of a mountain, Hariv.; of a forest, ib. (v. l. *pāñc°*). **-vardhana,** m. a species of plant, L. **-varsha** (KātyŚr.), °**shaka** (MBh.), mfn. 5 years old; °*sha-deśīya* (L.) and °*shaka-deśīya* (MBh.), mfn. about 5 years old. **-varshika-maha,** m. a kind of festival or ceremony, L. **-varshīya,** mfn. 5 years old, Śatr. **-vali,** mfn. having 5 folds or incisions, KātySr. **-valkala,** n. a collection of the bark of 5 kinds of trees (viz. the Indian, glomerous, holy, and waved-leaf fig-tree, and Calamus Rotang, i.e. Nyag-rodha, Udumbara, Aśvattha, Plaksha, and Vetasa; but other trees are sometimes substituted), Rasar. **-vallabhā,** f. 'dear to 5,' N. of Draupadī, Gal. **-vastu,** n.(?), N. of wk. **-vātīya,** m. a partic. oblation offered to the 5 winds at the Rāja-sūya, ŚBr. **-vāda,** m. N. of wk.; *-kroḍa-pattra,* n., *-ṭīkā,* f. N. of wks. **-vārshika,** mf(*ī*)n. 5 years old, recurring every 5 years; n. and *-maha,* m. (prob.) = *pañca-varshika-maha,* Divyâv.; L. **-vāhin,** mfn. yoked with 5, drawn by 5 (as a carriage), AV. **-viṅsá,** mf(*ī*)n. the 25th, ŚBr. &c.; containing or consisting of 25, ib.; representing the Pañca-viṅśa Stoma, belonging to it, celebrated with it, &c., Br.; ŚāṅkhŚr.; m. a Stoma consisting of 25 parts, VS.; ŚBr.; N. of Vishṇu regarded as the 25th Tattva, BhP.; *-brāhmaṇa,* n. a Brāhmaṇa consisting of 25 books, N. of the TāṇḍyaBr. **-viṅśaka,** mfn. the 25th, BhP.; consisting of 25, L.; (with *vayasā*) 25 years old, R. **-viṅsat,** f. 25, Hcat. **-viṅsati** (*pá°*), f. id., VS.; ŚBr.; a collection of 25 (also °*tī* and °*tikā*; see *vetāla-*); *-gaṇa,* m. a multitude of 25, Kap.; *-tama* or °*ti-ma,* mf(*ī*)n. the 25th, MBh.; *-rātra,* mfn. lasting 25 nights (days), KātySr.; *-sāhasrikā,* f. N. of a Prajñā-pāramitā, L. **-viṅśatika,** mfn. (a fine) consisting of or amounting to 25 (Paṇas), Yājñ. ii, 205; n. the number 25, MBh.; (*ā*), f., see *-viṅsati.* **-vikrama,** mfn. (a carriage) moving in a fivefold manner, BhP. **-vigrāham,** ind. by distributing 5 times or by a fivefold distribution, ĀśvŚr. **-vijaya,** m. N. of wk. **-vidha** (*páñca-* or *pañcá-*), mfn. of 5 kinds, fivefold, ŚBr.; *-nāma-bhāshya,* n., *-sūtra,* n. N. of wks. **-vidheya,** n. = *-vidha-sūtra.* **-vīra-goshṭha,** n. (prob.) an assembly-room named 'the 5 heroes,' i.e. the 5 sons of Pāṇḍu, Daś. **-vṛiksha,** n. sg. or m. pl. 'the 5 trees' (of Svarga, viz. Mandāra, Pārijātaka, Saṃtāna, Kalpa-vṛiksha, and Hari-candana), MW. **-vṛit** (ŚāṅkhGṛ.) and **-vṛitam** (Gobh.), ind. fivefold, 5 times. **-śata,** mf(*ī*)n. 500 (pl.), MBh.; BhP.; (a fine) amounting to 500, Yājñ.; fined 500 (Paṇas), Mn.; the 500th (°*te kāle,* in the 500th year), MBh.; n. 105, Lāṭy.; 500, Mn.; MBh.; (*ī*), f. 500, Kathās.; a period of 500 years, Vajracch.; N. of wk.; *-tama,* mf(*ī*)n. the 105th (ch. of R.); °*tī-prabandha,* m. N. of wk. **-śatika,** mfn. 500 (feet &c.) high, Hcat. **-śara,** m. = *-bāṇa,* Prab. (*ī,* f. = *-bāṇī,* Naish.); *-nirṇaya,* m., *-vijaya,* m., *-vyākhyā,* f. N. of wks. **-śarāva,** mfn. (a measure) containing 5 Śarāvas (q. v.), Jaim. **-śala** (*pá°*), m. or n. (?) a distance of 5 Śalas (q. v.), AV. **-śas,** ind. by fives, 5 by 5, BhP. **-śasya,** see *-sasya.* **-śākha,** mfn. 5-branched, 5-fingered, R.; m. the hand, Dhūrtan. **-śāradīya,** m. N. of a Pañcâha representing 5 years, Br.; ŚrS. **-śāstra,** n. N. of the sacred books of various Vaishṇava sects, Hcat. (cf. *-rātra*). **-śikha,** mfn. '5-crested,' having 5 tufts of hair on the head (as an ascetic), MBh. (°*khī-kṛita,* mfn. made an a°, Bhartṛ.); m. a lion, L.; N. of a Sāṃkhya teacher (called also *-muni,* a pupil of Āsuri), MBh.; VāyuP. &c.; of an attendant of Śiva, Kathās.; of a Gandharva, L. **-śikhin,** mfn. = *-śikha,* mfn., AV. Pariś. **-śirīsha,** m. a medicine composed of 5 parts (viz. root, bark, leaf, flower, and fruit) of the Acacia Sirissa, Car. **-śila,** mf(*ā*)n. consisting of 5 rocks, Cat. **-śīrsha,** mf(*ā*)n. 5-headed, MBh.; 5-eared (as corn, sc. on one stalk), ib.; m. N. of a mountain, Buddh. **-śīla,** n. the 5 chief rules of conduct for Buddhists, MWB. 89; 126. **-śukla,** m. 'having 5 white spots,' a species of venomous insect, Suśr. **-sūraṇa,** n. the 5 (bulbous plants called) Śūraṇas (q. v.), L. **-śairīshaka,** n. the 5 products of the Acacia Sirissa (cf. *-śirīsha*), L. **-śaila,** m. N. of a mountain, MārkP. **-ślokī,** f. N. of wk. **-sha,** mf(*ā*)n. pl. 5 or 6, Kāv. **-shashṭa,** mf(*ī*)n. the 65th (ch. of MBh. and Hariv.) **-shashṭi,** f. 65 (ch. of MBh.); *-tama,* mf(*ī*)n. the 65th (ch. of MBh. and R.) **-saṃskāra,** m. '5 rites,' N. of wk.; *-prayoga,* m., *-mahiman,* m., *-vidhi,* m. N. of wks. **-sattra,** n. N. of a place, Rājat. **-saṃdhi,** m. N. of wk. **-sapta** (in comp. for °*ptan*), 5 × 7, 35, MārkP. **-saptata,** mf(*ī*)n. the 75th (ch. of MBh. and Hariv.) **-saptati,** f. 75 (ch. of MBh.); *-tama,* mf(*ī*)n. the 75th (ch. of MBh. and R.) **-samāsīya,** n. N. of wk. **-savana,** n. (a sacrifice) containing 5 Savanas (q. v.), ĀpŚr. **-sasya,** n. sg. 5 species of grain (viz. Dhānya, Mudga, Tila, Yava, and Śveta-sarshapa or Māsha), L. **-sahasrī,** f. sg. (ifc. *-ka,* mfn.) 5000, Kathās. **-sāṃvatsarika,** mf(*ī*)n. 'recurring every 5 years,' N. of a kind of Cāturmāsya, ĀpŚr., Sch. **-sāmaka, -sāyaka,** n. (?) N. of wks. **-sāra,** mfn. consisting of 5 parts or ingredients, Suśr.; n. (?) N. of wk. **-siddhânta,** m. N. of the Bhāsvatī-karaṇa (q. v.) **-siddhântikā,** f. N. of an astron. wk. by Varāha-mihira (founded on the 5 older astron. wks., and called by Var. himself Karaṇa). **-siddhâushadhika,** mfn. consisting of 5 kinds of medic. plants, L. **-siddhâushadhī,** f. the 5 medic. plants, ib. **-sugandhaka,** n. a collection of 5 kinds of aromatic vegetable substances (viz. cloves, nutmeg, camphor, aloe wood, and Kakkola, q. v.), L. **-sûkta,** n. '5 Vedic hymns,' N. of wk. **-sūtra,** n. (and *ī,* f.) '5 Sūtras,' N. of wk. **-sūnā,** m. pl. 5 things in a house by which animal life may be accidentally destroyed (viz. the fire-place, slab for grinding condiments, broom, pestle and mortar, and water-pot), W.; RTL. 418. **-skandha** (ibc.) = °*dhī*; *-vimocaka,* m. N. of Buddha, Divyâv. **-skandhaka,** n. N. of wk. **-skandhī,** f. sg. the 5 Skandhas (s. v.) or constituent elements, Buddh. **-stava,** m. (and *-vyākhyā,* f.), **-stavī,** f. N. of wks. **-smṛiti,** f. '5 law-books,' N. of wk. **-srotas,** n. = *manas,* Niiak. **-svarā,** f. N. of an astrol. wk. on divination; *-nirṇaya,* m. N. of Comm.; °*rôdaya,* m. N. of wk. **-svastyayana,** n. N. of wk. **-havis,** mfn. furnished with 5 oblations, ŚāṅkhŚr. **-hasta,** m. '5-handed,' N. of a son of Manu, VP.; of a place, Rājat. **-hāyana,** mfn. 5 years old, BhP. **-hāva,** m. N. of a son of Manu Rohita, Hariv. (v. l. *-hotra*). **-hotṛi** (*pá°*), mfn. attended by 5 priests (?), RV. v, 42, 1; m. (sc. *mantra*) N. of a partic. formula in which 5 deities are named (as Hotṛi, Adhvaryu &c.), Br.; ŚrS. **-hotra,** see *-hāva.* **-hrada-tīrtha,** n. N. of a place of pilgrimage, SkandaP. **Pañcâṅśa,** m. the 5th part, 1/5, Var. **Pañcâksha,** m. '5-eyed,' N. of a Gaṇa of Śiva, Hariv. **Pañcâkshara,** mfn. consisting of 5 syllables, VS.; AitBr. &c.; m. N. of a poet; (*ī*), f. see s. v.; *-kalpa,* m. N. of wk.; *-maya,* mf(*ī*)n. consisting of 5 s°, Hcat.; *-māhātmya,* n. N. of wk.; *-śas,* ind. by 5 s°, Lāṭy. **Pañcâksharī,** f. 5 s°, Viddh.; *-yantrôpadeśa,* m., *-vidhāna,* n., *-shaṭprayoga,* m., *-stotra,* n. N. of wks. **Pañcâkhyāna,** n. = °*ca-tantra* (q. v.); *-vārttika,* n. N. of wk. **Pañcâgni** (mostly in comp.) = °*ca-tapas* (q. v.), n. the 5 sacred fires (viz. Anvāhārya-pacana or Dakshiṇa, Gārhapatya, Āhavanīya, Sabhya, and Āvasathya); 5 mystic fires supposed to be present in the body, W.; mfn. = °*ca-tapas,* mfn., Kathās.; maintaining the 5 sacred fires, KaṭhUp.; Mn. &c.; acquainted with the doctrine of the 5 mystic fires, W.; *-ka,* n. N. of a partic. observance, MānŚr.; *-tva,* n. a collection or aggregate of 5 fires or inflammatory passions, Kathās.; *-vidyā,* f. the (esoteric) doctrine of the 5 fires, Śaṃk. (*-prakaraṇa,* n. N. of wk.); *-sādhana,* n. 'doing the 5 fire penance' (a form of self-mortification), Cat. (cf. *pañca-tapas*); °*gny-ādhāna,* n. setting up the 5 sacred fires, TBr., Sch. **Pañcâṅga,** n. (mostly ibc.) 5 members or parts of the body, Kir.; 5 parts of a tree (viz. root, bark, leaf, flower, and fruit), L.; 5 modes of devotion (viz. silent prayer, oblations, libations, bathing idols, and feeding Brāhmans), W.; any aggregate of 5 parts, ib.; mf(*ī*)n. 5-limbed, 5-membered (with *praṇāma*, m. obeisance made with the arms, knees, head, voice, and look, Tantras.); having 5 parts or subdivisions, Kāv. (also °*gika*, Suśr.); m. a tortoise or turtle, L. (cf. *pañcâṅga-gupta*); a horse with 5 spots in various parts of his body, L. (cf. *pañca-bhadra*); (*ī*), f. a bit for horses, KātyŚr.; a kind of bandage, Suśr.; n. a calendar or almanac (treating of 5 things, viz. solar days, lunar days, Nakshatras, Yogas, and Karaṇas), L.; *-kautuka*, n., *-kaumudī*, f., *-gaṇita*, n. N. of wks.; *-gupta*, m. a tortoise or turtle, L. (cf. *pañca-g*°); *-tattva*, n. N. of wk.; *-pattra*, n. a calendar or almanac, L. (see above); *-phala*, n., *-ratnâvalī*, f., *-rudra-nyāsa*, m., *-vinoda*, m. N. of wks.; *-viprahīna* and *-vipratihīna*, m. N. of Buddha, Divyâv.; *-śuddhi*, f. the favourableness of 5 (astrological circumstances, viz. the solar day, lunar day, Nakshatra, Yoga, and Karaṇa), MW.; *-śodhana*, n., *-sarali*, f., *-sādhana*, n. (°*na-grahôddharaṇa*, n., °*na-sāraṇī*, f.), *-sāraṇī*, f. N. of wks.; °*ṅgâdika*, mfn. (a pantomime) dealing with 5 members (cf. above) &c., Mālav. i, ½; °*ṅgânayana*, n. N. of wk. **Pañcâṅguri**, mfn. 5-fingered, AV. **Pañcâṅgula**, mfn. measuring 5 fingers; m. Ricinus Communis (which has 5-lobed leaves), Suśr.; (*ī*), f. a species of shrub, L. **Pañcâṅguli**, mfn. 5 fingers broad, Caṇḍ.; having 5 fingers or finger-like divisions, W. **Pañcâja**, n. the 5 products of the goat, Suśr. (cf. °*ca-gavya*). **Pañcâtapā**, f. doing penance with 5 fires, KālP. (cf. °*ca-tapas*). **Pañcâtmaka**, mfn. consisting of 5 elements (as the body), fivefold (*-tva*, n.), ŚvetUp. **Pañcâdhyāyī**, f. 'consisting of 5 chapters,' N. of sev. wks. **Pañcânana**, mfn. very fierce or passionate (lit. 5-faced), L.; m. N. of Śiva, L. (cf. RTL. 79); a lion, Vcar. (also at the end of names of learned men, e.g. *Jayarāma-p*°, *Viśvanātha-p*°); N. of partic. strong medic. preparations, Rasar.; N. of an author and other men; (*ī*), f. N. of Durgā, Rājat.; *-deśa*, m. N. of a place, Cat. **Pañcânanda-māhātmya**, n. N. of wk. **Pañcânugāna**, n. N. of sev. Sāmans, ĀrshBr. **Pañcā-pañcinā**, f. N. of a partic. brick, MaitrS. **Pañcâpūpa**, mfn. having 5 cakes, AV. **Pañcâpsaras** (R.), °**rasa** (BhP.), n. N. of a lake or pool supposed to have been produced by Manda-karṇi (Śāta-karṇi) through the power of his penance (so called because under it Mandakarṇi formed a secret chamber for 5 Apsaras who had seduced him). **Pañcâbja-maṇḍala**, n. N. of a mystical circle, Tantras. **Pañcâbdâkhya**, mfn. existing for 5 years, Mn. ii, 134. **Pañcâmṛita**, n. sg. and pl. the 5 kinds of divine food (viz. milk, coagulated or sour milk, butter, honey, and sugar), Hcat.; the 5 elements, Mālatīm. v, 2; mfn. consisting of 5 ingredients (as a medicine), L.; n. the aggregate of any 5 drugs of supposed efficacy, W.; N. of a Tantra; °*tâbhisheka-prakāra*, m. N. of wk. **Pañcâmla**, n. sg. the aggregate of 5 acid plants (the jujube, pomegranate, sorrel, spondias, and citron), Bhpr. **Pañcâyatana**, n. N. of a partic. ceremony (at which 5 symbols are used), RTL. 410-416; *-paddhati*, f., *-pratishṭhā-paddhati*, f., and °*nârtha-varṇa-śirshôpanishad*, f. N. of wks. **Pañcâyudha**, m. = °*ca-bāṇa*, in *-prapañca*, m., *-ratna-mālā*, f., *-stava*, m., *-stotra*, n. N. of wks. **Pañcâra**, mfn. (a wheel) having 5 spokes, RV. **Pañcârcis**, m. 'having 5 rays,' the planet Mercury, VP. **Pañcârtha**, n. sg. the 5 things (with Pāśupatas), Sarvad.; *-bhāshya-dīpikā*, f. N. of wk. **Pañcârsheya**, mf(*ī*)n. one who is descended from 5 Ṛishis, ĀpGṛ., Sch. **Pañcā-vaṭa** = *pañca-v*°, q. v. **Pañcâvattá**, mfn. 5 times cut off or taken up, consisting of 5 Avadānas, ŚBr.; n. (MānŚr.), *-tā*, f. and *-tva*, n. (KātyŚr., Sch.) 5 A°s; °*ttin*, mfn. one who offers oblations consisting of A°s, GṛS.; KātyŚr., Sch.; °*ttíya*, mfn. offered in 5 A°s, TBr. **Pañcâvadāna**, n. the offering (of the Havis) in 5 Avadānas, MānGṛ. **Pañcâvayava**, mfn. consisting of 5 members or parts; (with *vākya*) n. a 5-membered argument, a syllogism, Tarkas. **Pañcâvaraṇa-stotra**, n. N. of a Stotra. **Pañcâvarta**, mf(*ā*)n. having 5 whirls, ŚvetUp. **Pañcâvastha**, m. a corpse (resolved into the 5 elements), Gal. **Pañcâvika**, n. the 5 products of the sheep, Suśr. (cf. *pañca-gavya*, °*câja*). **Pañcâśīta** mf(*ī*)n. the 85th (ch. of MBh. and Hariv.) **Pañcâśīti**, f. 85 (ch. of MBh.); N. of wk.; *-tama*, mf(*ī*)n. the 85th (ch. of MBh. and R.) **Pañcâśra**, mfn. 5-cornered, Hcat. **Pañcâśva**, m. 'having 5 horses,' N. of a prince, VP. **Pañcâsu-vandhura**, mfn. whose carriage-seats (?) are the 5 vital airs, BhP. **Pañcâstikāya**, m. N. of wk.; *-bālâvabodha*, m., *-saṃgraha-sūtra*, n. N. of wks. **Pañcâsya**, mfn. 5-faced, 5-headed, MBh.; Hariv.; 5-pointed (as an arrow), MBh.; m. a lion, Kāv.; N. of a partic. strong medicine, Rasar. **Pañcâha**, m. a period of 5 days, Kathās.; (°*há*), mfn. lasting 5 days; m. a Soma oblation with 5 Sutyā days, Br.; ŚrS. **Pañcâhika**, mfn. containing 5 feast days or festivals, KātyŚr., Sch. **Pañcêdhmīya**, n. (?) a nocturnal rite in which 5 torches &c. are used, Āpast. **Pañcêndra**, mfn. one who has the 5 Indrāṇīs as his deity, Pāṇ. i, 2, 49, Sch.; *-kalpa*, mfn. like 5 Indras, MW.; °*drôpâkhyāna* (?), n. N. of wk. **Pañcêndriya**, n. the 5 organs of sense (viz. the eye, ear, nose, tongue, and skin) or the 5 organs of action (viz. hands, feet, larynx, and organs of generation and excretion), W.; pl. N. of a tale; mfn. having the 5 organs of sense, MBh. **Pañcêshu**, m. = °*ca-bāṇa*, Kāv. **Pañcôpacāraka**, mf(*ikā*)n. consisting of 5 oblations, Śāktân. **Pañcôpâkhyāna**, n. N. of the Pañca-tantra; *-saṃgraha*, m. N. of wk. **Pañcâudana**, mfn. prepared with fivefold pulp of mashed grain &c., AV.

Pañcaka, mfn. consisting of 5, relating to 5, made of 5 &c., Mn.; MBh.; Suśr.; Pur.; 5 days old (see below); bought with 5, Pāṇ. v, 1, 22, Sch.; (with *śata*, n.) 5 per cent, Mn.; Yājñ.; taking 5 per cent, Pāṇ. v, 1, 47, Vārtt. 1, Pat.; m. any collection or aggregate of 5, W. (also n.; cf. g. *ardharcâdi*); a partic. caste, VP.; N. of one of the attendants of Skanda, MBh.; of a son of Nahusha, VP.; pl. the 5 first disciples of Gautama Buddha, Jātakam.; (*ikā*), f. a book consisting of 5 Adhyāyas (as those of the AitBr.); N. of a game played with 5 shells, Pāṇ. ii, 1, 10, Sch.; n. an aggregate of 5, a pentad, Hariv.; Var. &c.; a field of battle, L.; *-mālā*, f. a kind of metre, L.; *-māsika*, mfn. one who receives or earns 5 per month, Pāṇ. v, 4, 116, Vārtt. 4, Pat.; *-vidhāna*, n., *-vidhi*, m. N. of wks.; *-śata*, n. 5 per cent, Bījag.; *-śānti*, f., *-śānti-vidhi*, m. N. of wks.; °*kâvalī*, f. a kind of metre, L. (cf. Śiś. iii, 82, Sch.); °*kâshṭaka-cayana-sūtra*, n. N. of wk.

Pañcat, mfn. consisting of five, Pāṇ. v, 1, 60.

Pañcataya, mf(*ī*)n. fivefold, having five parts or limbs, Kap.; Yog. (cf. Pāṇ. v, 2, 42).

Pañcatha, mfn. (cf. Pāṇ. v, 2, 50) the fifth, Kāṭh. [Cf. Zd. *pukhdha*; Gk. πέμπτος; Lat. *quinctus*, *quintus* for *pinctus*; Lith. *pénktas*; Goth. *fimfta*; Germ. *fünfte*; Angl. Sax. *fīfta*; Eng. *fifth*.]

Pañcathu, m. time, L.; the Koil or Indian cuckoo, L.

Páñcan, pl. (said to be fr. √1. *pac*, to spread out the hand with its five fingers; nom. acc. *páñca* [AV. v, 15, 5 *pañcá*]; instr. °*cábhis*; dat. abl. °*cábhyas*; loc. °*cásu* [Class. also °*cabhís*, °*cabhyás*, °*casú*, cf. Pāṇ. vi, 1, 179 &c.]; gen. °*cānám*) five, RV. &c. &c. (cf. under *indriya*, *krishṭi*, *carshaṇi*, *jana*, *bhūta*, *mātra*, *yajña*, *svasṛi* &c.); sg. N. of Kathās. xiv. [Cf. Zd. *pañcan*; Gk. πέντε, Aeol. πέμπε; Lat. *quinque*; Lith. *penkì*; Goth. *fimf*; Germ. *fünf*; Angl. Sax. *fīf*; Eng. *five*.]

Pañcanī, f. a chequered cloth for playing at draughts &c., a chess-board (= *śāri-śriṅkhalā*), L.

Pañcamá, mf(*ī*)n. the fifth, VS.; AV. &c. &c. (cf. Pāṇ. v, 2, 49); forming the 5th part (with or sc. *aṃśa* = ⅕), TBr.; Mn. &c.; = *rucira* or *daksha*, L.; m. (in music) the 5th (later 7th) note of the gamut (supposed to be produced by the air drawn from 5 parts of the body); MBh.; Sāh.; = *-rāga*, Gīt.; the 21st Kalpa (called after the musical note), VāyuP.; the 5th consonant of a Varga (i. e. the nasal), VPrāt.; Pāṇ., Sch.; N. of a Muni, Cat.; (*ī*), f., see below; n. the fifth part, ⅕ (cf. above and Pāṇ. v, 3, 49); copulation (as the 5th of the Tattvas of the Tāntrikas; cf. *pañca-tattva*); (*am*), ind. for the fifth time, fifthly, TBr.; Mn. viii, 125. **-bhāgīya**, mfn. belonging to the fifth part, KātyŚr.; ⅕ (of a Purusha) long, Śulbas. **-rāga**, m. one of the Rāgas or musical modes, Gīt. **-vat**, mfn. having the 5th (note), Pāṇ. v, 2, 130, Sch. **-vilāsa**, m., **-sāra-saṃhitā**, f. N. of wks. **-svara**, n. N. of a metre, Prasann. **Pañcamâra**, m. (with Jainas) the 5th spoke in the wheel of time (also *-ka*), Śatr.; N. of a son of Bala-deva, L. **2. Pañcamâsya**, m. (for 1. see p. 577, col. 1) the Indian cuckoo or Koil (as producing the 5th note of the scale with its mouth or throat), L.

Pañcamaka, mfn. the fifth, Śrut.

Pañcamin, mfn. being in the fifth (month or year) of one's age, Pāṇ. v, 2, 130.

Pañcamī, f. (of °*ma*, q. v.) the fifth day of the half month (sc. *tithi*), ŚrGṛS.; MBh. &c.; the 5th or ablative case (or its terminations), a word in the ablative, Pāṇ. ii, 1, 12 &c.; a termination of the imperative, Kāt.; (in music) a partic. Rāgiṇī or Mūrchanā; a brick having the length of ⅕ (of a Purusha), Śulb.; = *pañcanī*, L.; N. of Draupadī (who was the wife of 5; cf. *pāñcālī*), L.; of a river, MBh.; VP. **-kalpa**, m., **-krama-kalpa-latā**, f., **-varivasyā-rahasya**, n., **-sādhana**, n., **-sudhôdaya**, m., **-stava**, m., **-stava-rāja**, m. N. of wks.

Pañcārī, f. = *pañcanī*, L.

Pañcāśa, mf(*ī*)n. the 50th (ch. of MBh. and R.); + 50 (e. g. °*śaṃ śatam*, 150; cf. Pāṇ. v, 2, 46).

Pañcāśaka, mf(*ikā*)n. 50, Pur.; (*ikā*), f. a collection or aggregate of 50 (cf. *caura-pañcāśikā*, *shaṭ-p*°); N. of sev. wks.

Pañcāśac, in comp. for °*śat*. **-chas**, ind. by fifties, 50 by 50, ĀśvGṛ.

Pañcāśát, f. (*pañcan* + *daśat*; cf. *triṇ-śat*, *catvāriṇ-śat*) fifty, AV. &c. &c. (also mfn. pl., MBh.; Hariv.) [Cf. Zd. *pañcāsata*; Gk. πεντήκοντα; Lat. *quinquāginta*.] **-tama**, mf(*ī*)n. the 50th (ch. of MBh. and Hariv.); *-várshá*, KātyŚr., Sch. **-paṇika**, mfn. (a fine) consisting of 50 Paṇas, Yājñ. **-palika**, mfn. having the weight of 50 Palas, ib.; Hcat. **-sahasrī-mahākāla-saṃhitā**, f. N. of wk.

Pañcāśata, n. (MBh.). °**ti**, f. (Rājat.) fifty.

Pañcāśatka, mf(*ā*)n. consisting of 50, Car.; 50 years old, Kām.

Pañcāśad, in comp. for °*śat*. **-gāthā**, f. N. of a Jaina wk. **-dhā**, ind. in fifty parts, R. **-bhāga**, m. the 50th part, Mn. vii, 130. **-varsha**, mfn. 50 years old (*-tā*, f.), ĀśvŚr.

Pañcāśā, f. fifty, Hcat. (wrongly divided into *pañcan* + *āśā*).

Pañci, m. N. of a man (son of Nahusha), VP.

Pañcika, mfn. having the length of 5, Śulbas.; (*ā*), f., see under *pañcaka*.

Pañcin, mfn. divided into 5, consisting of 5, fivefold, AitBr.; Lāṭy.

Pañcī, in comp. for °*ca* = °*can*. **-karaṇa**, n. (√1. *kṛi*) making into 5, causing anything to contain all the 5 elements, Vedāntas.; N. of sev. wks.; *-tâtparya-candrikā*, f., *-prakriyā*, f., *-mahāvākyârtha*, m. (and °*tha-bodha*, m.), *-vārttika*, n. (and °*kâbharaṇa*, n.), *-vivaraṇa*, n., *-viveka*, m., °*ṇânandâkhyā*, f. N. of wks. **-kṛita**, mfn. made into 5 (cf. above), Vedāntas.; *-ṭīkā*, f. N. of wk.

पञ्चाल *pañcālá*, m. pl. (fr. *pañcan*; cf. *pātāla*) N. of a warrior-tribe and their country in the north of India, ŚBr.; Mn.; MBh. &c. (cf. *apara-*, *pūrva-*); of a Vedic school, ŚBr.; RPrāt.; (sg.) a man belonging to the tribe of the Pañcālas, L.; a king of the P°, MBh. (cf. *pāñc*°); N. of Śiva, ib.; of a man brought by Vishvak-sena to the childless Gaṇḍūsha, Hariv.; of a serpent-demon, L.; a partic. venomous insect, MW.; n. (?) N. of a metre, Col.; (*ī*), f. a doll, puppet, Kād.; a style of singing, L.; a chequered cloth for playing at draughts &c., W. **-caṇḍa**, m. N. of a teacher, AitĀr. **-padavṛitti**, f. (prob.) a kind of hiatus, L. **-rāja** or **-rājan**, m. a king of P°, MW.

Pañcālaka, mfn. relating to the Pañcālas, MBh. (prob. w. r. for *pāñc*°); m. pl. the P°, BhP.; (sg.) a species of venomous insect, Suśr.; (*ikā*), f. a doll, L.; a style of singing, L.

पञ्चि *pañci*, m. N. of a man, VP.

पञ्छीहिल *pañchīhila*, m. N. of a man, Inscr.

पञ्ज् *pañj*, *pañjaka*, *pañjara* &c. See under √*paj*, p. 575, col. 2.

पञ्जल *pañjala*, m. a kind of bulbous plant, L.

पञ्जि *pañji* or *pañjī*, f. the ball of cotton from which thread is spun, L.; (*ī*), f. an almanac, calendar, register, L. **Pañji-kāraka**, m. = *pañjikā-k*°, L. **Pañjī-kara**, m. id., L.

Pañjikā, f. = *pañjī*, L.; a perpetual commentary which explains and analyses every word (also = *kātantra-vṛitti-p*°); a book in which receipts and expenditure are entered, L.; the register or record of human actions kept by Yama, L. **-kāraka**, m. a writer, a man of the Kāyastha tribe; an almanac-maker. **-pradīpa**, m. N. of wk.

पट् *paṭ*, cl. 1. P. *paṭati*, to go, move, Dhātup. ix, 9; to flow (pf. *papāṭa*), Śiś. vi, 72; to split, open, burst asunder (intr.), Hcar.; cl. 10. or Caus. *paṭayati*, to string together, wrap (*granthe* or *veshṭane*; cf. *paṭa*), Dhātup. xxxv, 5; *pāṭayati*, to speak or shine, Dhātup. xxxiii, 79; °*ti* or (MBh.) °*te*, to split, burst (trans.), cleave, tear, pierce, break, pluck out, remove, Up.; Yājñ.; MBh. &c.: Pass. *pāṭyate*, to split, burst, open (intr.), Suśr.

Paṭa, m. (n. L.; ifc. f. *ā*) woven cloth, cloth, a blanket, garment, veil, screen, MBh.; Kāv. &c. (cf. *marut-*, *vāta-*); a painted piece of cloth, a picture, Yājñ.; Kād.; monastic habit, Kāraṇḍ.; a kind of bird, Lalit.; Buchanania Latifolia, L.; = *puras-kṛita*, L.; (*ī*), f. a narrow piece of cloth, the hem or edge of a garment, Bālar.; Hcar.; the curtain of a stage, L. (cf. *apaṭī*); n. a thatch or roof (= *paṭala*), L. **-kāra**, m. a weaver; a painter, L. **-kuṭī**, f. a tent of wool or felt, KātyŚr., Sch. **-gata**, mfn. 'being on cloth,' painted, MBh. **-caura**, m. a cloth-stealer, L. **-bhedana**, n. = *puṭa-bh*°, L. **-maṇḍapa**, m. 'canvas-house,' a tent, Ragh. **-maya**, mf(*ī*)n. made of cloth; n. (scil. *gṛiha*) = prec., Śiś. vi, 24. **-vardhana**, m. N. of a family, Cat. **-vādya**, n. (in music) a kind of cymbal. **-vāpa**, m. w. r. for next. **-1.-vāsa**, m. a tent, L. **-2.-vāsa**, m. a petticoat, L. **-3.-vāsa**, m. perfumed powder (*-tā*, f.), Ratnāv. **-vāsaka**, m. = prec. 3., ib.; N. of a serpent-demon, MBh. **-vāsinī**, f. a kind of woman, L. **-veśman**, n. a tent, Śiś. **-śāṭaka**, m. or n. = *pārīraṇa*, L. **Paṭâkshepa**, m. the not tossing or pushing aside of the stage-curtain (prob. w. r. for *paṭī-kshepa*; cf. also *apaṭī-kshepa*). **Paṭâñcala**, m. the hem or edge of a garment, Mālatīm. **Paṭânta**, m. id., MBh.; Hariv.; Ratnāv. **Paṭântaram** or °**re**, (prob.) w. r. for °*ntam*, Śak. (Pi.) iii, $\frac{26}{27}$ ($\frac{7}{80}$). **Paṭī-kshepa**, m. (dram.) the tossing aside of the stage-curtain; °*peṇa pra-√viś*, to enter in a hurry, Bālar. **Paṭôṭaja**, n. (L.) a mushroom; a tent; sunshine (?). **Paṭôttarīya**, n. an upper garment (of cloth), Mṛicch. **Paṭaṅka**, prob. = next; *-śrī-darpaṇa*, m. N. of wk. **Paṭaṅkas**, n. a tent, L.

Paṭaka, m. cotton-cloth, L.; a camp, encampment, L.; the half of a village, L. (v. l. for *pāṭ*°).

Paṭará, m. or n. a ray (of sunlight), AV.; (*ī*), f., g. *gaurâdi*; (*paṭarā*), m. N. of the third of the 7 suns, TĀr.; VP. (v. l. *paṭala*); N. of Varuṇa, TĀr. ('having a cloth-like skin,' Sāy.)

Paṭaraka, m. a species of plant (= *gundra*), L.

Paṭala, n. (and rarely *ī*, f.) a roof, thatch, Var.; a veil, cover, Kāv.; Pur.; Sāh. (ifc. f. *ā*); a basket, chest, box, Bālar.; a heap, mass, multitude (esp. in comp. with a word denoting 'cloud'), MBh.; Kāv. &c.; n. or m. an enclosing or surrounding skin or membrane (esp. of the eyes), a film over the eyes, cataract &c., Suśr.; Kāraṇḍ.; a chip, piece, portion, Kād.; a section or chapter of a book (esp. of RPrāt.); n. train, retinue, L.; a (sectarian or ornamental) mark on the forehead or other parts of the body with sandal-wood, L.; m. v. l. for *paṭara* (see above); m. f. a tree or a stalk (*vṛiksha*, v. l. *vṛinta*), L. **-prânta**, m. the edge of a roof, L. **Paṭalâṅśuka**, m. the cover of the veil (of darkness), Sāh. **Paṭalânta**, m. = °*la-prânta*, L.

Paṭalaka, m. or n. a cover, screen, veil, Kād.; a little chest or box or basket, ib.; Kathās.; (*ikā*), f. = prec.; Nalac.; heap, mass, multitude, Kāv.

Paṭi, f. a kind of cloth, Pañc. (cf. *paṭī* under *paṭa*); = *vāguli*, L.; a species of plant, L.

Paṭikā, f. woven cloth, Līl. **-vetra-vāna-vikalpa**, m. a partic. art, Cat. (cf. *paṭṭikā-vetra-bāṇa-v*°).

पटच्चर *paṭac-cara*, m. (fr. next + *cara*?) a thief or robber, MBh. (Nīlak. 'a class of Asuras'); pl. N. of a people, MBh.; n. old or ragged clothes, a worn garment, Kād.; Bālar.

पटत् *paṭat*, onomat. (also *paṭat-paṭad-iti*, *paṭat-paṭ-iti* and *paṭat-paṭêti*), L.

पटत्कखन्थ *paṭatka-kantha*, n. N. of a town, g. *cihaṇâdi*.

पटपटा *paṭapaṭā*, onomat. (with √*kṛi*, *bhū* and *as*), L.

Paṭapaṭāya, Nom. P. Ā. °*yati*, °*te*, L.

पटभाक्ष *paṭabhāksha*, m. a kind of optical instrument, Daś. (Sch.)

पटह *paṭaha*, m. (rarely n. or f. *ī*) a kettle-drum, a war-drum, drum, tabor (acc. with √*dā* or Caus. of √*dā* or √*bhram*, to proclaim anything by the sound of a drum), MBh.; Kāv. &c.; m. beginning, L.; hurting, L. **-ghoshaka**, m. a crier who beats a drum before making a proclamation, Kathās. **-ghoshaṇā**, f. a proclamation made by beating a d° (acc. with √*dā* &c. as above), ib. **-tā**, f. the noise or function of a d°, Megh. **-dhvani**, m. the sound of a d°; mfn. sounding like a d°, MW. **-prôdghoshaṇa** and **-bhramaṇa**, n. = *-ghoshaṇā*, Kathās. **-śabda**, m. = *-dhvani*, m., Pañc. **Paṭahânantara**, mfn. (speech) accompanied by the sound of a d°, Kathās. **Paṭahī-vādaka**, m. a drummer, Pañcad.

पटाक *paṭāka*, m. a bird, Uṇ. iv, 14, Sch. (cf. *paiṭ*°); (*ā*), f. a flag, banner, L. (cf. *patākā*).

पटालुका *paṭālukā*, f. a leech, L. (cf. *jalukā*, &c.)

पटि *paṭi*. See under *paṭa*, col. 1.

पटिमन् *paṭiman*, *paṭishṭha*, *paṭīyas*. See under *paṭu* below.

पटिस *paṭisa*, w. r. for *paṭṭiśa*.

पटीर *paṭīra*, m. (√*paṭ*?) the sandal tree, Bhpr.; a ball for playing with or a thorn (*kanduka* or *kaṇṭaka*), L.; the god of love, L.; n. (only L.) Catechu; the belly; a sieve; a radish; a field; a cloud; bamboo manna; height; catarrh; = *haraṇīya*. **-māruta**, m. wind that comes from sandal trees or is produced by fanning with a kind of sieve, Hcar.

पटु *paṭu*, mf(*u* or *vī*)n. (√*paṭ*?) sharp, pungent, acrid, harsh, shrill, keen, strong, intense, violent, MBh.; Kāv. &c.; smart, clever, skilful, crafty, cunning, ib.; great or strong in, fit for, able to; capable of (loc. or comp.), ib.; saline (cf. *tri-*); cruel, hard, L.; healthy, L.; eloquent, L. (cf. *vāk-*); clear, manifest, L.; m. Trichosanthes Dioeca or its leaf, L.; Momordica Charantia, L.; Nigella Indica, L.; a kind of perfume, L.; a species of camphor, L.; N. of a man, Pravar.; of a poet, Cat.; (pl.) of a people, MārkP.; of a caste, VP.; m. n. a mushroom, L.; n. salt, pulverized s°, L. **-karaṇa**, mfn. having sound organs, ML. **-kalpa**, mfn. tolerably clever, Pāṇ. v, 3, 67, Sch. **-ghaṇṭā**, f. a shrill bell, MBh. **-jātīya**, mfn. of a clever sort, Daś. (cf. Pāṇ. v, 3, 69, Sch.) **-tara**, mfn. more or very sharp or clever &c. (*am*, ind.), Kāv.; *-gir*, mfn. having a shriller voice, Vikr.; *-vana-dāha*, m. a raging forest-fire, Ṛit.; *-viveka*, mfn. of keen understanding, Bhartṛ. **-tā**, f., see *vāk-paṭutā*. **-triṇaka**, n. a kind of pungent grass, L. **-tva**, n. sharpness, acuteness, keenness, cleverness, Kāv.; Hit. **-deśīya** or **-deśya**, mfn. = *-kalpa*, Pāṇ. v, 3, 67, Sch. **-pattrikā**, f. a species of shrub, L. **-parṇikā**, f. a species of plant, L. **-parṇī**, f. Bryonia Grandis, L. **-mat**, m. N. of a prince, VP. **-mati**, mfn. clever-minded, Kāv. **-mitra**, m. N. of a prince, VP. **-rūpa**, mfn. very clever, W. (cf. Pāṇ. v, 3, 66).

Paṭiman, m. sharpness, pungency &c., Śṛiṅgār. (cf. g. *pṛithv-ādi*).

Paṭishṭha, mfn. very sharp or clever or skilful (cf. *vacana-*).

Paṭīyas, mfn. sharper, more clever; also = prec.; very able to or fit for (loc. or inf.), Śiś. i, 18; 59.

Paṭuka, m. Trichosanthes Dioeca, L.

Paṭū-√kṛi, to sharpen, stimulate, raise, increase, Jātak.

पटुश *paṭuśa*, m. N. of a Rākshasa, MBh.

पटुस *paṭusa*, m. N. of a prince, Hariv. (v. l. *praghasa*).

पटोल *paṭola*, m. (cf. *paṭu*, *paṭuka*) Trichosanthes Dioeca; n. its fruit, Suśr.; Pañc.; a kind of cloth, L.; (*ī*), f. a species of small cucumber, L.

Paṭolaka, m. an oyster (= *śukti*), L.; (*ikā*), f. = *paṭolī*, L. (cf. *dīrgha-paṭolikā*).

पटौर *paṭaurá*, m. (Padap. *paṭa* + *ūra*?) a partic. member of the body, AV.

पट्ट *paṭṭa*, m. (fr. *pattra*?) a slab, tablet (for painting or writing upon), MBh.; (esp.) a copper plate for inscribing royal grants or orders (cf. *tāmra-*); the flat or level surface of anything (cf. *lalāṭa-*, *śilā-*), MBh.; Kāv. &c.; a bandage, ligature, strip, fillet (of cloth, leather &c.), MBh.; Suśr.; a frontlet, turban (5 kinds, viz. those of kings, queens, princes, generals, and the *prasāda-paṭṭas* or t° of honour; cf. VarBṛS. xlix), tiara, diadem, MBh.; Kāv.; Rājat. (ifc. f. *ā*); cloth (= *paṭa*); coloured or fine cloth, woven silk (= *kauśeya*), Kāv.; Pañc. (cf. *cīna-p*°, *paṭṭâṅśuka* &c.); an upper or outer garment, Bhaṭṭ.; a place where 4 roads meet (= *catush-patha*, L.; Corchorus Olitorius, W.; = *vidūshaka*, Gal.; N. of sev. men, Rājat.; (*ī*), f. a forehead ornament, L.; a horse's food-receptacle (= *tāla-sāraka*), L.; a species of Lodhra, L.; a city, town (cf. *-nivasana*). **-karmaṅ**, n. making cloth, weaving, Pañc.; °*ma-kara*, m. a weaver, ib. **-kila**, m. (for *khila*?) the tenant (by royal edict) of a piece of land, Vet. **-ja**, n. a kind of cloth, MBh. **-talpa**, m. a silken bed, Vet. **-devī**, f. a turbaned queen, the principal wife of a king, Rājat. **-dola**, m. (or °*lā*, f.?) a swing made of cloth, Mṛicch. iv, $\frac{26}{27}$. **-nivasana**, m. a town-dweller, citizen, Daś. **-bandha**, m. or °**dhana**, n. binding or crowning the head with a turban or tiara, L. **-mahādevī** or **-mahishī**, f. = *-devī*, L. **-raṅga**, **-rañjaka**, **-rañjana** and **-rañjanaka**, n. Caesalpina Sappan (a plant used in dyeing), L. **-rāga**, m. sandal, L. **-rājñī**, f. = *-devī*, L. **-lakshaṇa**, n. 'description of various turbans,' N. of VarBṛS. xlix. **-vastra**, n. a kind of cloth (°*trântarī-√kṛi*, to wrap in that cloth), Suśr.; mfn. = next. **-vāsas**, mfn. attired in coloured cloth or wove silk, MBh. **-vāsitā**, f. a kind of head-ornament, L. **-śāka**, n. a species of pot-herb, L. **-śāṭaka** = *paṭa-ś*°, L. **-śālā**, f. 'cloth-house,' a tent, Hcat. **-sūtra**, n. a silk thread; *-kāra*, m. a s°-weaver (N. of a class of Hindūs who are feeders of s°-worms &c.), Col.; *-maya*, mf(*ī*)n. made of s°-thread, Hcat. **-stha**, mfn. 'standing on cloth,' painted, Hariv. **Paṭṭâṅśuka**, n. a kind of garment (prob. made of silk), Ratnāv. (cf. *aṅśu-paṭṭa*). **Paṭṭâbhirāma**, m. N. of an author (also *-śāstrin*), Cat.; *-ṭippaṇī*, f., *-śāstri-pattra*, n., °*rāmīya*, n. N. of wks. **Paṭṭâbhisheka**, m. consecration of a tiara, KātyŚr., Sch. **Paṭṭârohā**, f. = next, W. **Paṭṭârhā**, f. = *paṭṭa-devī*. **Paṭṭâvali**, f. N. of a class of wks. **Paṭṭêśvara-māhātmya**, n. N. of ch. of BhavP. **Paṭṭôpadhāna**, n. a silken pillow or cushion, Kād. **Paṭṭôpâdhyāya**, m. the writer of royal grants or documents &c., Rājat. **Paṭṭôlikā**, f. (for °*ṭṭâval*°?) a title deed, a written legal opinion, L.

Paṭṭaka, m. a board or plate (esp. for writing upon), Rājat.; Kathās.; a bandage, girdle, Hcat.; (*ikā*), f. a tablet, plate, Naish., Sch.; a bandage, ribbon, piece of cloth, fillet, Rājat.; Kathās.; BhP.; cloth, wove silk; a species of Lodhra, L.; N. of a woman, L.; n. a document on a plate, Rājat.; a bandage, piece of cloth, Suśr.

Paṭṭaya, Nom. Ā. °*yate*, to be like a plate of (comp.), Kād.

1. **Paṭṭi** (prob.) = *paṭi*. **-kāra**, m. (*ī*, f.) a silk-weaver (?), L. **-lodhra** and °**dhraka**, m. a species of Lodhra, L.

Paṭṭikā, f. of *paṭṭaka*, q. v. **-°khya** (°*kâkh*°), m. a species of tree, Bhpr. **-lodhra**, m. a species of Lodhra, ib. **-vāpaka**, prob. w. r. for **-vāyaka**, m. a silk-weaver, ribbon-maker, R. **-vetra-bāṇa-vikalpa**, m. N. of a partic. art, BhP., Sch. (cf. *paṭikā-vetra-vāna-v*°).

Paṭṭin, m. a kind of Lodhra, Bhpr.

Paṭṭila, m. Guilandina Bonduc, L.

पट्टन *paṭṭana*, n. a city (cf. *deva-pallī-*, *dharma-*, and *pattana*); (*ī*), f. id., L.

पट्टला *paṭṭalā*, f. a district, a community, Cat. (cf. *pattalā*).

पट्टव *paṭṭava*, m. or n. (?) a kind of cloth, Rājat. v, 161 (w. r. for *paṭṭa-ja*?)

पट्टार *paṭṭāra*, m. or n. (?) N. of a district, g. *dhūmâdi*.

पट्टि 2. *paṭṭi*, m. pl. N. of a people, VP. (cf. *patti*).

पट्टिका *paṭṭikā*. See above.

पट्टिश *paṭṭiśa*, m. a spear with a sharp edge or some other weapon with three points, MBh.; R. &c. (written also *paṭṭisa*, *paṭisa* and *pattisa*).

Paṭṭiśin, mfn. armed with the weapon called Paṭṭiśa, MBh.; Hariv.

पट्टुभट्ट *paṭṭu-bhaṭṭa*, m. N. of an author (1416), Cat.

पट्टेरक *paṭṭeraka*, m. Cyperus Hexastachyus Communis, L.

पठ् *paṭh*, cl. 1. P. (Dhātup. ix, 45) *paṭhati* (°*te*, MBh. &c.; pf. *papāṭha*, ib.; aor. *apāṭhīt*, Gr.; fut. *paṭhishyati*, *paṭhitā*, ib.; ind. p. *paṭhitvā*, Kāv.), to read or repeat aloud, to recite, rehearse, TĀr.; MBh. &c.; to repeat or pronounce the name of a god, to invoke (acc., also with *nāmabhis*), MBh.; Hariv.; to read or repeat or recite to one's self, to peruse, study, Mn.; R.; BhP.; Hit.; to teach, cite, quote, mention, express, declare, Lāṭy.; MBh.; BhP.; Suśr.; to learn from (abl.), BhP.: Pass. *paṭhyate*, to be read or recited or taught or mentioned &c.; MBh.; Hariv.: Caus. *pāṭhayati* (aor. *apīpaṭhat*, Pāṇ. vii, 4, 1, Sch.; fut. *pāṭhayishyati*, Kathās.; Pass. *pāṭhyate*, Hit.), to cause or teach to speak or read, to teach, instruct in (with double acc., Kāś. on Pāṇ. i, 4, 52); to read, recite, Kathās.: Intens. *pāpaṭhīti*, *pāpaṭhyate*, to recite often or repeatedly, Kathās.; to read or study diligently, Var.

Paṭha, m. reading, recitation (?, see comp.); N. of a serpent-demon, MBh. **–mañjarī**, **-samañjarī**, f. (in music) N. of Rāgiṇīs. **–haṅsikā**, f. N. of a Rāga.

Paṭhaka, m. a reader, reciter.

Paṭhana, n. reciting, reading, studying, mentioning, Kāv.; Pur., Sch.; Cat. **Paṭhanâdhinātha**, m. a master in reading or studying, Cat.

Paṭhanīya, mfn. fit to be read or studied, legible, readable, Vop.; Mṛicch., Sch.

Paṭhi, f. = *paṭhana*, L.

Paṭhita, mfn. recited, read, studied, mentioned, MBh.; Kāv.; Suśr. &c. **–tva**, n. the being mentioned, Hcat. **–siddha**, mfn. effective on being (merely) recited, Kathās.; *-sārasvata-stotra*, n. N. of wk. **Paṭhitâṅga**, m. or n. a kind of girdle, BhavP.

Paṭhitavya, mfn. to be studied or read or mentioned, Pat.; MārkP. **–tva**, n. the being to be studied &c., Nyāyam., Sch.

Paṭhiti, f. N. of a partic. figure of speech, Cat.

Paṭhitṛi, mfn. reading, a reader, W.

पठर्वन् *páṭharvan*, m. N. of a man, RV.

पड् *paḍ*, in comp. for *pad* or *paś*, q. v. **–gṛibhi** (*páḍ-*), m. N. of a demon or a man, RV. **–bīśa** (RV.; TS.; AV), **-viśa** (VS.) or **-viṅśa** (*páḍ-*), n. a fetter, (esp.) a f° for the foot of a horse; (*-śaṅku*, m. a post for tying to, ŚBr.); m. a place for fettering, halting-place, TBr. [Lat. *vincio*, *vinculum*?]

पण् *paṇ*, cl. 1. Ā. (Dhātup. xii, 6) *páṇate* (ep. also °*ti*; pf. *pene*, Gr.; aor. *apaṇishṭa*, Bhaṭṭ.; fut. *paṇishyate*, °*ṇitā*, ib.), to honour, praise, Naigh. iii, 14; to barter, purchase, buy, Br.; MBh.; to negotiate, bargain, Āpast.; to bet, stake, lay a wager, play for (with gen. [e. g. *prāṇānām*, Bhaṭṭ.; cf. Pāṇ. ii, 3, 57, Kāś.] or acc. [e. g. *krishṇām*], MBh.); to risk or hazard (as a battle), MBh.; to win anything (instr.) from (acc.), ib.: Caus. *paṇayati* (aor. *apīpaṇat*), to negotiate, bargain, Kāv. (Cf. *paṇāya* and √*pan*.)

Paṇa, m. (ifc. f. *ā*) play, gaming, playing for a stake, a bet or a wager (with gen.; loc. or ifc.; *paṇam* √*kṛi*, to make a bet; *paṇe ni-√as*, to stake at play), Yājñ.; MBh.; R. &c.; a compact, stipulation, agreement, treaty, Kathās.; Vet.; Hit.; the thing staked or the sum played for, wages, hire, reward, MBh.; Mṛicch.; Kathās.; a weight of copper used as a coin (= 20 Māshas = 4 Kākinīs), Mn.; Yājñ.; a partic. measure, Pāṇ. iii, 3, 66 ('a handful,' Sch.); a commodity for sale, L.; price, L.; wealth, property, L.; business, L.; a publican or distiller, L.; a house, dwelling (*gṛiha*, w.r. for *glaha*?), L. **–kāla**, m. time for playing, MBh. **–kriyā**, f. putting in a stake, play or contest for (comp.), Bālar. **–krita**, mfn. received as hire or reward, Hcat. **–granthi**, m. a fair, market, L. **–tā**, f., **-tva**, n. the state or condition of a pledge or stake; price, value, W. **–dhā**, f. Panicum Verticillatum, L. (cf. *paṇyam-dha* and *paṇyândhā*). **–bandha**, m. making a treaty, making peace, Ragh.; a bet or wager (also *-na*, n.), Daś. **–sundarī** (HPariś.), **-strī** (Mṛicch.), f. a venal woman, a prostitute, harlot. **Paṇâṅganā**, f. id., L. **Paṇârdha**, m. or n. (?) half a Paṇa (coin), Kāv. **Paṇârpaṇa**, n. making an agreement, contract, W. **Paṇârha**, mfn. fit to be laid as a wager, MW. **Paṇâsthi** and **sthika**, n. Cypraea Moneta, a cowrie, L.

Páṇana, n. purchasing, buying, ŚBr.; sale, selling, dealing in (comp.), L.; betting, W.

Paṇanīya, mfn. to be laid as a wager, negotiable, MW.

Paṇayitṛi, m. a seller, Mālatīm.

Paṇasa, m. a commodity, an article of sale or commerce, L.; Artocarpus Integrifolia, L.

Paṇasya, Nom. P. °*syati*, to honour, praise, L.

Paṇāya, Nom. P. Ā. °*yati*, id., Pāṇ. iii, 1, 28; Naigh. iii, 14 (v. l. °*te*); to sell (inf. °*yitum*), Kathās.

Paṇāyā, f. business, transaction, L.; a market-place, W.

Paṇāyita, mfn. praised, transacted, W.

Paṇāyitṛi, m. a seller, Mālatīm.

Paṇáyya, mfn. praiseworthy, laudable, ŚBr.

Paṇí, m. a bargainer, miser, niggard (esp. one who is sparing of sacrificial oblations), RV.; AV.; N. of a class of envious demons watching over treasures, RV. (esp. x, 108); AV.; ŚBr.; a thief appearing as a Purohita, BhP.; a market, L.

Paṇika. See *pañcāśat-p*°.

Paṇita, mfn. praised or transacted as business, L.; betted, staked, MBh.; one who has betted or wagered, ib. i, 1225; n. (also *-ka*, L.) a bet, wager, stake, MBh.

Paṇitavya, mfn. vendible, negotiable, Pāṇ. iii, 1, 101; to be praised, W.

Paṇitṛi, m. a trader, seller, Naish.

Paṇin, m. N. of a man, Pāṇ. vi, 4, 165 (cf. *Pāṇina* and °*ni*).

Paṇī-√kṛi, to bet or stake at play (*-kṛita*, mfn., Cat.)

Paṇya, mfn. to be praised or commended, ĀpŚr.; to be bought or sold, vendible (see n. and comp.); to be transacted, L.; (*ā*), f. Cardiospermum Halicacabum, L.; n. (ifc. f. *ā*) an article of trade, a ware, commodity, ŚBr.; Kauś.; Gobh.; MBh. &c.; trade, traffic, business, Kām.; Kāv. (cf. *jñāna-*); a booth, shop, Daś. **–kambala**, m., Pāṇ. vi, 2, 42, Vārtt. 2, Pat. **–jana**, m. a trader, Var. **–tā**, f. the being praiseworthy or (and) an article of trade, Kāv. **–dāsī**, f. a hired female servant, Daś. **–m-dha**, m. (or *-dhā*, f.) Panicum Verticillatum, L. (cf. *paṇyândhā* and *paṇa-dhā*). **–pati**, m. a great merchant, large trader (*-tva*, n.), R. **–pariṇītā**, f. a concubine, Divyâv. **–phala-tva**, n. prosperity or profit in trade, W. **–bhūta**, mfn. being an article of trade, Mṛicch. **–bhūmi**, f. a place where goods are stored, a warehouse (*guṇa-paṇya-bh*°, receptacle of all virtues), Inscr. **–mūlya**, n. the price of a commodity, W. **–yoshit**, f. a venal woman, courtesan, harlot, Mn. **–vat**, mfn. furnished with many goods or commodities, R. **–varcas**, n., Vop. vi, 78. **–vikraya**, m. trade, commerce, Car.; *-śālā*, f. a market-place, bazar, L.; °*yin*, m. a trader, merchant, R. **–vilāsinī**, f. = *-yoshit*, Kathās.; Unguis Odoratus, L. **–vīthikā** (L.), **-vīthī** (Vāsav.), f. a place of sale, market. **–śālā**, f. a bazar or shop, L. **–strī**, f. = *-yoshit*, Var.; Kāv.; Rājat. **–homa**, m. a sacrifice consisting of wares, ĀpGṛ. **Paṇyâṅganā**, f. = *-yoshit*, Bhartṛ.; Kathās. **Paṇyâjira**, n. a market, L. **Paṇyâjīva**, m. 'living by trade,' a tradesman, L.; n. (also *-ka*) a market, W. **Paṇyândhā**, f. Panicum Verticillatum, L. (cf. *paṇa-dhā* and *paṇyam-dha*). **Paṇyârha**, mfn. fit for sale, vendible, W.

पणफर *paṇaphara*, n. (fr. ἐπαναφορά) the astrological house following upon a Kendra (q. v.), Var.

पणव *paṇava*, m. (prob. fr. *pra-ṇava*) a small drum or a kind of cymbal (used to accompany singing), MBh.; Kāv. (also *ā*, f., L.); a kind of metre, Col. (v. l. *pan*°); N. of a prince, VP.

Paṇavin, mfn. possessing a drum (applied to Śiva), MBh.

पण्ड् *paṇḍ* (prob. invented to serve as the root of the words below), cl. 1. Ā. *paṇḍate*, to go, move, Dhātup. viii, 29; cl. 10. P. *paṇḍayati*, to heap together, pile up (v. l. for *piṇḍ*), xxxii, 130, Vop.; cl. 1. or 10. P. *paṇḍati*, °*ḍayati*, to destroy, annihilate, xxxii, 73 (v. l. for *paṅs*).

Paṇḍa, m. a eunuch, weakling, Nār. (cf. *paṇḍra*, *shaṇḍa*); (*ā*), f., see below. **Paṇḍâpūrva**, n. non-occurrence of the results of fate or destiny, L.

Páṇḍaka, m. = *paṇḍa*, MaitrS.; Yājñ.; Kām.; Daśar. (*-tva*, n., Kāṭh.); m. N. of one of the sons of the third Manu Sâvarṇa.

Páṇḍaga, m. (prob.) = *paṇḍa*, °*ḍaka*, AV.

Paṇḍā, f. wisdom, knowledge, learning, L. (cf. g. *tārakâdi*). **–vat**, m. a learned man, L.

Paṇḍitá, mfn. (according to some, for *spandita*) learned, wise, shrewd, clever, skilful in, conversant with (loc. or comp.; cf. Pāṇ. ii, 1, 40); ŚBr.; Up.; MBh. &c.; m. a scholar, a learned man, teacher, philosopher, a Pandit, MBh.; Kāv. &c.; N. of a man (= °*ṭaka*), MBh.; of a Brāhman changed into an antelope, Hariv.; incense, L. **–kara-bhiṇḍipāla**, m. N. of wk. **–jātīya**, mfn. of a clever sort, rather learned, wise, Divyâv. (cf. Pāṇ. v, 3, 69). **–tā**, f. (Bhartṛ.), **-tva**, n. (Mṛicch.) learning, knowledge, wisdom, cleverness, skill. **–paritosha**, m. N. of wk. **–pīḍā-viśārada**, m. N. of a man, Kautukas. **–praśnôttara**, n. N. of wk. **–mānika** (MBh.), **-mānin** (ib.; R.), **-m-manya** (Kād.; Prab.), **-m-manyamāna** (KaṭhUp.), mfn. fancying one's self learned or clever, an ignorant and conceited person. **–rāja**, m. 'prince of learned men,' N. of any great scholar; (esp.) of Jagan-nātha (1600); of another man, BhP.; *-kṛiti*, f., *-śataka*, n. N. of wks. **–vādin**, mfn. pretending to be wise, MW. **–vaidya** and **-śaśin**, m. N. of authors, Cat. **–śiromaṇi**, m. N. of Rāmakṛishṇa-bhaṭṭa, Cat. **–śrī-vara**, m. N. of an author, ib. **–sabhā**, f. an assembly of Pandits or literati, MW. **–sarvasva**, n. N. of wk. **–sūri** and **-svāmin**, m. N. of authors, Cat. **Paṇḍitâhlādinī**, f. N. of wk.

Paṇḍitaka, mfn. wise, learned, pedantic, MBh.; m. N. of a son of Dhṛita-rāshṭra, ib.

Paṇḍitāya, Nom. Ā. °*yate*, to become learned or wise, g. *bhṛiśâdi*.

Paṇḍitiman, m. wisdom, learning, scholarship, g. *dṛiḍhâdi*.

Paṇḍu, m. (prob.) w.r. for next.

Paṇḍra or °**draka**, m. a eunuch, impotent man, Sāh.; MārkP. (cf. *paṇḍa*, *shaṇḍa*).

पण्डालु *paṇḍālu*, m. or f. or n. a kind of pot-herb, Śrikaṇṭh.

पत् 1. *pat*, cl. 4. Ā. (Dhātup. xxvi, 50) *pátyate*, to be master, reign, rule, govern, control, own, possess, dispose of (acc. or instr.), RV.; to partake of, share in (loc.), ib.; to be fit or serve for (dat.), ib. [Prob. Nom. of *páti*; cf. Lat. *potiri*.]

पत् 2. *pat*, cl. 1. P. (Dhātup. xx, 15) *pátati* (ep. also °*te*; pf. *papāta*, *paptimá*, *petátur*, *paptúr*; *paptivás*, RV.; *papatyāt*, AV.; aor. *apaptat*, RV.; Pass. *apāti*, Br.; fut. *patishyáti*, AV.; °*te*, *patitā*, MBh.; Cond. *apatishyat*, Br.; inf. *patitum*, ib. &c. &c.; ind. p. *patitvā́*, AV.; Br.; *-pátya* or *-pā́tam*, Br.), to fly, soar, rush on, RV. &c. &c.; to fall down or off, alight, descend (with acc. or loc.), fall or sink (with or without *adhas* or *narake*, 'to go down to hell;' with *caraṇau* or °*ṇayoḥ*, 'to fall at a person's feet'), Mn.; MBh.; Kāv. &c.; to fall (in a moral sense), lose caste or rank or position, ChUp.; Mn.; Yājñ. &c.; to light or fall upon, fall to a person's share (loc.), MBh.; Kāv. &c.; to fall or get into or among (loc.), Kathās.; Hit.; to occur, come to pass, happen, Pañc.: Caus. *patáyati*, to fly or move rapidly along, RV.; VS.; to speed (trans.; cf. *patayát*); °*te*, to drive away or throw down (?), RV. i, 169, 7; *pātáyati* (ep. also °*te*; aor. *apīpatat*, AV.; Pass. *pātyate*, MBh. &c.), to let fly or cause to fall, to fling, hurl, throw, AV. &c. &c.; to lay low, bring down (lit. and fig.), overthrow, ruin, destroy, MBh.; R. &c. to throw upon or in, lay on (loc.), Kāv.; Suśr.; (with or scil. *ātmānam*) to throw one's self, MBh.; Mṛicch.; to cut off (a head), Hariv.; to knock out (teeth), BhP.; to pour out or shed (water, tears), MBh.; Hariv.; to kindle (fire), Pañc.; to cast (dice), Hariv.; Kathās.; to turn, direct, fix (eyes), R.; to impose or inflict (punishment), Mn.; Yājñ.; to set in motion, set on foot, Rājat. v, 173; to seduce to, betray into (loc.), Kathās.; (with *dvedhā*) to divide in two, ŚBr.; to subtract, Jyot., Sch.; (Ā.) to rush on, hasten, RV. viii, 46, 8: Desid. *pipatishati* (AV.; MaitrS.; ŚBr.) and *pitsati* (Pāṇ. vii, 4, 54), to be about to fly or fall: Intens. *panīpatyate* or °*pātīti*, Pāṇ. vii, 4, 84. [Cf. Zd. *pat*; Gk. πέτομαι, πί-πτω; Lat. *peto*.]

3. **Pat**, mfn. flying, falling (ifc.; cf. *akshi-pát*).

Pata, m. flying, falling (cf. g. *pacâdi* and *jvalâdi*). **–ga**, m. a winged or flying animal, bird, Mn.; MBh. &c.; the sky-flying luminary, i.e. the sun, MBh.; N. of one of the 5 fires in the Svadhākāra, Hariv.; *-pati*, m. 'lord of birds,' N. of Garuḍa,

Mṛicch.; *-pannaga*, m. pl. birds and serpents, R.; *-rāja*, m. 'king of birds,' N. of Garuḍa, BhP.; *-vara*, m. 'chief of b°,' N. of Jaṭāyu, R.; *°gêśvara*, m. 'lord of b°,' N. of Garuḍa (MBh.) or Jaṭāyu (R.); *°gôraga*, m. pl. bird and snake deities, Mn. vii, 23.

Patam, acc. of *pata* in comp. **-gá**, mfn. flying, RV. i, 118, 4; any flying insect, a grasshopper, a bee, a butterfly or moth, ŚBr. (*°táṃga*); Up.; Mn. &c. (*-tā*, f., Prasannar.); a horse, Naigh. i, 14; the sun (cf. *pata-ga*), RV.; AV.; Var. &c.; N. of one of the 7 suns, TĀr.; VP.; a ball for playing with, BhP.; a spark (Sāy.; 'a Piśāca,' Mahidh.), RV. iv, 4, 2; a species of rice, Car.; of tree, L.; 'the Flier,' N. of Kṛishṇa, MBh. xii, 1510 (= *garuḍa*, Nīlak.); BhP.; N. of the author of RV. x, 177 and of this hymn itself, ŚāṅkhBr.; of a mountain, BhP.; = *-grāma*, Rājat.; (pl.) N. of a caste in Plaksha-dvīpa, BhP.; (*ā*), f. N. of a mythical river, Divyâv.; (*ī*), f. N. of one of the wives of Tārksha and mother of the flying animals, BhP.; m. or n. quicksilver, L.; n. a species of sandal wood, Bhpr.; *-kānta*, m. the sun-stone (cf. *sūrya-k°*), Śiś. iv, 16; *-grāma*, m. N. of a village, Rājat.; *-rāja*, m. = *pataga-r°*, Pañc.; *-vat*, ind. like a moth, Kum.; *-vṛitti*, f. the manner of the moth (attracted by a light) i.e. rashness, temerity, Ratnâv.; mfn. behaving like a moth (i.e. very inconsiderately), Pañc.; *°gâśman*, m. the sun-stone (cf. above), Śrikaṇṭh. **-gaka**, m. N. of a mountain, Pur.; (*ikā*), f. a little bird, MBh.; a little bee, L. **-gama**, m. a butterfly or moth, BhP.; a bird, L. **-gará**, mfn. bird-like, RV. iv, 40, 2. **-gin**, m. a bird; (*nī*, f.) a female bird, Hariv.

Pataka, mfn. who or what falls or descends &c.; m. an astronomical table, W.

Patat, mf(*ntī*)n. flying, falling, descending &c.; m. a bird, [1] past.; Kāv. **-pataṃga**, m. the setting sun, Śiś. i, 12. **-prakarsha**, mfn. (in rhet.) 'where preference or superiority sinks or is not observed,' either prosaical or illogical (*-tā*, f.), Kpr.; Sāh. &c.

Pátatra, n. a wing, pinion, feather &c.; RV. &c. &c.; a vehicle, L. (cf. *pattra*).

1. **Patatri**, m. a bird (only gen. pl. *°trīṇām*), MBh.; N. of a partic. fire, PārGṛ.; N. of a warrior on the side of the Kurus, MBh.

2. **Patatri**, in comp. for *°trin*. **-ketana**, mfn. 'characterised by a bird,' (with *deva*) N. of Vishṇu, Hariv. **-rāj** (BhP.), **-rāja** (*pát°*, Suparṇ.), **-vara** (MBh.), m. 'king or best of birds,' N. of Garuḍa.

Patatrín, mfn. winged, feathered, flying (also applied to Agni, the vehicle of the Aśvins &c.), RV.; AV.; VS.; Up. &c.; m. a bird, AV. &c. &c.; a horse, (esp.) the h° in the Aśva-medha sacrifice, R. i, 13, 36; an arrow, MBh. iii, 16430; a partic. fire, TS.; n. du. day and night, RV. i, 158, 4.

Patad, in comp. for *°tat*. **-graha**, m. 'receiving what falls,' a receptacle for alms; a spittoon (also *-grāha*), HPariś.; Sch. (also n.); the rear of an army, L. **-bhīru**, m. 'terrible to birds,' a hawk or falcon, L.

Patana, mfn. who or what flies or falls, Pāṇ. iii, 2, 150; m. N. of a Rākshasa, MBh.; (*pát°*), n. the act of flying or coming down, alighting, descending, throwing one's self down at or into (loc. or comp.), RV. &c. &c.; setting (as the sun), MBh.; going down (to hell), Mn. vi, 61; hanging down, becoming flaccid (said of the breasts), Bhartṛ.; fall, decline, ruin, death, MBh.; Kāv.; loss of caste, apostacy, Pur.; (with *garbhasya*) miscarriage, Var.; (in arithm.) subtraction, Col.; (in astron.) the latitude of a planet, W. **-dharmin**, mfn. what is likely to fall out or off (*°mi-tva*, n.), Suśr. **-śīla**, mfn. accustomed to fall down, Kāv.

Patanīya, mfn. (fr. *patana*) leading to a fall, causing the loss of caste; n. a degrading crime or sin, MBh.; Yājñ.

Patantaka, m. (fr. *patat*) a kind of Aśva-medha performed in a hurried manner, Lāṭy.; Nid.

Patama, m. a bird; L.; a grasshopper, L.; the moon, L. (cf. *patasa*).

Patayālú, mf(*ū*)n. (fr. Caus.) flying, falling, liable to fall, AV. (cf. Pāṇ. iii, 2, 158).

Patayishṇú (RV.), *°ṇuká* (AV.), mfn. id.

Patará or **patáru**, mfn. flying, fugitive, RV.

Patasa, m. = *patama*, L.

Patāka, m. ('flying'), a flag or banner (perhaps incorrect for *°kā*), AdbhBr.; a partic. position of the hand or the fingers in shooting off an arrow, ŚārṅgP. (cf. *tri-p°*); (*ā*), f., see next.

Patākā, f. (ifc. f. *ā*) a flag, pennon, banner, sign, emblem, Br.; MBh.; Kāv. &c. (*°kāṃ* √*labh* or *hṛi*, 'to win the palm,' Daś.; Vcar.); a flag-staff, L.; a partic. high number, MBh. (= *mahā-padma*, Nīlak.); (in dram.) an episode or episodical incident, Daśar.; good fortune, auspiciousness, L.; N. of wk. **-ṃśuka** (*°kâṃś°*), n. a flag, Kathās. **-daṇḍa**, m. a flag-staff, MBh. **-dhvaja-mālin**, mfn. garlanded with flags and banners, ib. **-sthāna** and *°naka*, n. (in dram.) intimation of an episodical incident, Daśar.; Sāh., Sch. **Patākôcchrāya-vat**, mfn. with hoisted banners, MBh.

Patākāya, Nom. *°yate*, to represent a flag or banner, Nalac.

Patākika, mfn. having or carrying a flag or banner, L.

Patākin, mfn. having or bearing a flag, adorned with flags, MBh.; R. &c.; (with *nau*) furnished with sails (?), MBh.; m. an ensign or standard-bearer, ib.; a flag, Hariv.; a chariot, Śiś. xiii, 4; a figure used in divination, L.; N. of a warrior on the side of the Kurus, MBh.; (*inī*), f. an army, Ragh.; Kād. (cf. *dhvajinī*); N. of a partic. divinity, BrahmaP.

Patāpata, mfn. going or inclined to fall, Kauś. (cf. Pāṇ. vi, 1, 12, Vārtt. 6, Pat.; vii, 4, 58, Vārtt. 1, Pat.)

Patitá, mfn. fallen, dropped, descended, alighted, AV. &c. &c.; (ifc.) fallen upon or from (Pāṇ. ii, 1, 24 and 38, Sch.); (with *pādayos* or *pāda-*) having thrown one's self at a person's feet, Kāv.; fallen (morally), wicked, degraded, out-caste (*-tva*, n.), ChUp.; Mn.; MBh. &c.; fallen into, being in (loc. or comp.), Kathās.; happened, occurred, Pañc.; Śukas.; n. flying, MBh. **-garbhā**, f. a woman who miscarries, MW. **-tyāga-vidhi**, m. N. of wk. **-mūrdhaja**, mfn. one whose hair has fallen out, MBh. **-vṛitta**, mfn. leading the life of an out-caste, Hariv. **-sāvitrīka**, m. 'one who is deprived of the Sāvitrī,' a man of the first 3 classes whose investiture (*upa-nayana*, q.v.) has been unduly performed or omitted, GṛS.; Gaut. (cf. *sāvitrī-patita*). **-sthita**, mfn. lying on the ground, Kathās.

Patitânna, n. an out-caste's food, Mn. iv, 213.

Patitêkshita, mfn. looked at by an out-caste, W.

Patitôtthita, mfn. 'fallen and risen,' sunk (in a shipwreck) and saved, Ratnâv.; fallen out and grown again; *-danta*, mfn., ĀpŚr., Sch. **Patitôtpanna**, mfn. sprung from an out-caste, W.

Patitavya, n. the going down to hell, MBh. xii, 3688.

Pátishṭha, mfn. (superl. of 3. *pat*) flying most or best, RV.

Pátīyas, ind. (compar. of 3. *pat*) quickly, speedily, TāṇḍBr.

Patera, m. 'flying, moving,' a bird, Uṇ. i, 59; a bird, L.; a measure of capacity (= *āḍhaka*), L.

Páttra, n. (and m., Śakat.; ifc. f. *ā* and *ī*) the wing of a bird, pinion, feather, VS.; ŚBr. &c.; the feather of an arrow, R.; Ragh.; a bird, L.; any vehicle, a chariot, car, horse, camel &c.; Mn.; MBh.; Kāv.; a leaf, petal (regarded as the plumage of a tree or flower), KātyŚr.; Mn.; MBh. &c.; the leaf of a partic. fragrant plant or a partic. plant with f° leaves, VarBṛS. xvi, 30; Laurus Cassia (L.) and its leaf, Bhpr.; a leaf for writing on, written l°, l° of a book, paper; a letter, document, Kāv.; Rājat.; Pañc. (*pattram āropya*, 'having committed to paper,' Śak.); any thin leaf or plate of metal or gold-leaf, Var.; Suśr. (cf. *patta*); the blade of a sword or knife (cf. *asi-*); a knife, dagger, L.; = *-bhaṅga*, Ragh.; Gīt. [Cf. Gk. πτερόν (for πετερόν); Lat. *penna* (older *pesna* for *pet-na*); Germ. *Feder*; Eng. *feather*.] **-kartarī**, f. shears for cutting off leaves, Kuṭṭanīm. **-kāhalā**, f. the noise made by the flapping of wings or rustling of leaves, L. **-kṛiccbra**, m. a sort of penance (drinking an infusion of the leaves of various plants and Kuśa grass for a given time), L. (cf. *parṇa-k°*). **-kaumudī**, f. N. of wk. **-gupta**, m. a kind of bird, Lalit. (cf. *paksha-g°*); Asteracantha Longifolia, L. **-ghanā**, f. (prob.) a species of cactus, L. **-cārikā**, f. a kind of magic, Divyâv. **-cchaṭā**, f. = *-bhaṅga*, Naish. **-ccheda**, m. leaf-cutting (a kind of sport or art), Kuṭṭanīm.; *-bhakti*, f. a piece cut out of a leaf, Śak. (Pi.) iii, ११ (७४). **-cchedaka**, m. a leaf-cutter (a partic. trade), L. **-cchedya**, n. = *-ccheda*, Kād. (Mṛicch. v, 5, Sch. = *ālekhya*?). **-jhaṃkāra**, m. the current of a river (or the rustling of leaves?), L. **-taṇḍulā**, f. Andrographis Paniculata (also *°lī*, f.), L.; a woman, L. **-taru**, m. a species of tree kindred to Acacia Catechu, L. **-dāraka**, m. 'leaf-divider,' a saw, L. **-devī**, f. N. of a Buddh. deity. **-dhārā**, f. the edge of a leaf, Śak. **-nāḍikā**, f. the fibre or vein of a leaf, L. **-nāmaka**, m. a cinnamon-leaf, Bhpr. **-nyāsa**, m. inserting the feathers (into an arrow), L. **-pati**, m. N. of Garuḍa, Śiś. xx, 73. **-paraśu** or **-parśu**, m. a fine file or saw, L. **-pāka**, m. a medicine which requires cooking, L. **-pāṭha**, m. the perusal of a writing, MW. **-pāla**, m. a long knife or dagger, L.; (*ī*), f. the feathered part of an arrow, L. **-pāśyā**, f. a kind of ornament on the forehead, L. **-piśācikā**, f. a sort of cap or umbrella for the head made of leaves, L. **-puṭa**, m. n. (R.; Ragh.), **-puṭikā**, f. (Cāṇ.) a kind of cup made of a leaf folded or doubled. **-pushpa**, m. a sort of red basil; (*ā*), f. holy basil with small leaves, L. **-pushpaka**, m. Bētula Bhojpatra, L. **-prakāśa**, m. N. of partic. astronomical tables. **-bandha**, m. adorning with leaves or flowers, L. **-bāla**, m. an oar, L. **-bhaṅga**, m. (Kād.), **-bhaṅgi** (Dharmaśarm.) and **-bhaṅgī** (Naish.), f. a decoration consisting in lines or streaks drawn on the face and body with musk and other fragrant substances. **-bhadrā**, f. a species of plant, L. **-mañjarī**, f. = *-bhaṅga*, L. **-māla**, m. Calamus Rotang, L. **-mūlaka**, mfn. resembling leaves and roots, g. *sthūlâdi*. **-yauvana**, n. a young leaf, sprout, W. **-rañjana**, n. embellishing a page, illuminating, gilding, MW. **-ratha**, m. 'using wings as a vehicle,' a bird, MBh.; R. &c.; *-śreshṭha*, m. 'chief of birds,' N. of Garuḍa, Hariv.; *°thêndra*, m. id., BhP.; (*°dra-ketu*, m. 'characterised by Garuḍa,' N. of Vishṇu, Ragh.); *°thêśvara*, m. 'lord of birds,' N. of Jaṭāyu, R. **-rekhā**, f. = *-bhaṅga*, Ragh. **-latā**, f. id., Kād.; a long knife or dagger, L.; N. of a woman, Hcar. **-lavaṇa**, n. 'leaf-salt,' a kind of drug made of partic. leaves mixed with salt, Suśr. **-lekhā**, f. = *-bhaṅga* (ifc. f. *ā*), Hariv.; Kāv.; N. of a woman, Kathās. **-vallarī**, f. = *-bhaṅga*, L. **-valli**, f. id. (also *°lī*, Śiś. viii, 59); N. of 2 kinds of creeper, L. **-vāja**, mfn. feathered (as an arrow), Hariv. **-vāha**, m. 'feather-bearing,' a bird, Śiś. xviii, 73; an arrow, ib. xx, 25; a letter-carrier, postman, L. **-viśeshaka**, m. or n. = *-bhaṅga*, Kum.; Ragh. **-vṛiścika**, m. a species of venomous reptile, Suśr. **-veshṭa**, m. a kind of ear-ring, Ragh. **-śabara**, m. a Śabara (barbarian or mountaineer) who decorates himself with feathers, L. **-śāka**, m. vegetables consisting of leaves, Mn. xii, 65; Yājñ. iii, 213 (or n. 'leaves and pot-herbs'?); *-tṛiṇa*, n. pl. leaves, pot-herbs and grass, Mn. vii, 132. **-śriṅgī** or **-śreṇī**, f. Anthericum Tuberosum, L. **-śreshṭha**, m. Aegle Marmelos, L. **-saṃskāra**, w. r. for *-jhaṃkāra*. **-sirā**, f. the vein or fibre of a leaf, L.; = *-bhaṅga*, L. **-sundara**, m. or n. (?) a species of plant, L. **-sūci**, f. 'leaf-needle,' a thorn, L. **-hasta**, mf(*ā*)n. holding a leaf of paper in the hand, Śak. **-hima**, n. cold, wintry or snowy weather, L. **Pattrâkhya**, n. the leaf of Laurus Cassia or of Flacourtia Cataphracta, L. **Pattrâṅga**, n. (wrongly written *°raṅga*) red sanders; Caesalpinia Sappan; Betula Bhojpatra; = *padmaka*, L. **Pattrâṅgulī**, f. = *°tra-bhaṅga*, L. **Pattrâñjana**, n. 'paper-unguent,' ink, L. **-Pattrâḍhya**, m. 'rich in feathers or leaves &c.,' a peacock, Gal.; n. the root of long pepper, L.; a species of grass, L.; Caesalpinia Sappan, L. **Pattrâmlā**, f. Oxalis Corniculata, L. **Pattrârūḍha**, mfn. committed to paper, written down, Śak. **Pattrâlī**, f. = *°tra-bhaṅga*, L. **Pattrâlu**, m. a species of bulbous plant or reed, L. **Pattrâvalambana**, n. N. of wk. **Pattrâvali**, f. red chalk, L.; (*lī*), a row of leaves, L.; = *°tra-bhaṅga*, Mālatīm.; Caṇḍ.; (*°lī*), a mixture of young Aśvattha leaves with barley and honey, MW. **Pattrâsura**, m. N. of a man, L. **Pattrâhāra**, m. feeding on leaves, MW. **Pattrêśvara-tīrtha**, n. N. of a sacred bathing-place, ŚivaP. **Pattrôpaskara**, m. Cassia Sophora, L. **Pattrôrṇa**, m. Calosanthes Indica, L.; pl. N. of a people, MBh.; wove silk or a s°-garment, (perhaps also) cotton, MBh.; R. &c. (also *°ṇaka*, Var.; or *°ṇā*, f., Hariv.) **Pattrôllāsa**, m. the bud or eye of a plant, L.

Pattraka, ifc. (f. *ā*) = *pattra*, a wing, leaf &c.; m. a leaf (cf. *karṇa-*); Achyranthes Triandra, L.; (*ikā*), f., see below; n. a leaf, (esp.) the leaf of Laurus Cassia, Bhpr.; = *pattra-bhaṅga*, L.

Pattraṇā, f. putting feathers on an arrow, L.

Pattraya, Nom. P. °*yati*, id.; °*trita*, mfn. feathered (as an arrow), Hariv.

Pattrala, mfn. rich in leaves, leafy, HPariś. (cf. g. *sidhmâdi*); n. thin sour milk, L.

Pattrāya, Nom. Ā. °*yate*, to be converted into leaves (for writing), Vāsav.

Pattri, in comp. = °*trin*. **–vāha,** m. a bird, L.

Pattrika, m., g. *purohitâdi*, Kāś.

Pattrikā, f. (of °*traka*), a leaf (for writing upon), a letter, document &c., Śak.; Kād.; Pañc.; a kind of earring (cf. *danta-*), Śiś.; N. of wk. **–°khya** (°*kâkh*°), n. a species of camphor, L. **–praveśa,** m. a festival on the 7th day of the month Āśvina, MW.

Pattrin, mfn. having wings or feathers or leaves, MBh.; Kāv. &c.; m. a bird (esp. a hawk or falcon, L.), Hariv.; Kālid.; an arrow, MBh.; Hariv.; a mountain, L.; possessing a carriage or driving in one, L.; a chariot, L.; a tree, L.; the wine-palm, L.; a species of Achyranthes, L.; a species of creeper and other plants, L.; (*iṇī*), f. a sprout, shoot, L.

Pátman, n. flight, course, path, way, RV.; VS.; Kāṭh.

Patmín, mfn., w.r. for *padmin* (?), Suparṇ.

Patya, n. falling (see *garta-*).

Pátvan, mf(*varī*)n. flying, RV.; VS.; ŚāṅkhBr.; Kauś.; n. flying, flight, RV.; VS. (cf. *āśu-*, *raghu-*, *śyena-*).

Patsala, m. a way, road, Uṇ. iii, 74, Sch.

पत 2. *pata*, mfn. well fed (= *pushṭa*), L.

पतञ्चल *patáñcala* or *patañcalá*, m. N. of a man, ŚBr. (with the patr. *Kāpya*), Pravar.

पतञ्चिका *patañcikā*, f. a bow-string, L.

पतञ्जल *patañjala*, m. N. of a man; pl. his family, g. *upakâdi*.

पतञ्जलि *patañjali*, m. (fr. *pata* + *añj*°?; cf. Pāṇ. vi, 1, 94, Vārtt. 4, Pat., g. *śakandhv-ādi*) N. of a celebrated grammarian (author of the Mahābhāshya); of a philosopher (the propounder of the Yoga philosophy); of a physician &c. **–kāvya,** n., **-carita,** n., **-yoga,** m., **-sūtra,** n. N. of wks.

पति 1. *páti*, m. (cf. √1. *pat*; when uncompounded and meaning 'husband,' instr. *pátyā*; dat. *pátye*; gen. abl. *pátyur*; loc. *pátyau*; but when meaning 'lord, master,' and ifc. regularly inflected with exceptions; cf. Pāṇ. i, 4, 8; 9) a master, owner, possessor, lord, ruler, sovereign, RV. &c. &c.; a husband, ib. (in comp. either with the stem or with the gen., e.g. *duhitṛi-p*° or °*tuḥ-p*°, Pāṇ. vi, 3, 24; when mfn., f. = m., e.g. *-jivat-patyā tvayā*, R. ii, 24, 8, or *patikā*, e.g. *pramīta-patikā*, Mn. ix, 68); one of the 2 entities (with *Pāśupatás*), RTL. 89; a root, L.; f. a female possessor, mistress, Pāṇ. iv, 1, 33, Sch.; a wife (*vṛiddha-p*° = *-patnī*, the w° of an old man, ib. 34, Sch.) [Cf. Gk. πόσις, 'husband'; Lat. *potis*, *pos-sum* for *potis-sum*; Lith. *patis*, 'husband'; Goth. (*bruth-*)*faths*, 'bridegroom'.] **–m-varā,** f. a woman who chooses her husband for herself (cf. *svayam-vara*), Ragh.; Rājat. **–kāma** (*páti-*), mfn. wishing for a h°, AV.; KātyŚr. **–khecara,** m. N. of Śiva, MBh. (Nīlak. 'Garuḍa'). **–gaṇita-ṭīkā,** f. N. of Comm. on Līl. **–ghātinī,** f. the murderess of her husband, Var. **–ghna,** mf(*ī*)n. killing a h°, GṛS.; °*ghnī-pāṇi-lekhā*, f. a line on the hand indicating that a woman will be faithless to her h°, Pāṇ. iii, 2, 53, Sch.; °*ghnī-lakshaṇa*, n. the mark of a h°-killer, W. **–jushṭā** (*páti-*), f. (a woman) liked by her h°, RV. **–tvá** (RV. &c. &c.) and **-tvaná** (RV.), n. matrimony, marriage. **–darśana-lālasa,** mf(*ā*)n. longing to see one's husband, Nal. **–devatā** (MBh.; R. &c.), **-devā** (BhP.), f. regarding a h° as a divinity, honouring a h° above all others. **–dvish,** f. hating one's h°, RV. **–dharma,** m. duty towards a h°, MBh.; *-vatī*, f. fulfilling the duties towards a h°, faithfully devoted to a h°, ib. **–prāṇā,** f. (a wife) whose h° is (as dear to her as) her life, Hit. **–matī,** f. having a h°, married, BhP.; having a lord or master in (instr., e.g. *tvayā*), Pat. **–yāna,** mfn. (a way) leading to a h°, Gobh. **–ríp,** f. deceiving a h°, RV. **–laṅghana,** n. injuring a h° (by marrying another), MW. (cf. Mn. v, 151). **–lālasa,** mf(*ā*)n. longing for a h°, Nal. **–loká,** m. 'h°'s world,' the sphere of a h° in a future life, RV. &c. &c. **–vaṃśya,** mfn. belonging to a h°'s family, L. **–vatī** (*pá*°, RV. x, 85, 21), **-vatnī** (Ragh.; Kathās.; cf. Pāṇ. iv, 1, 32, Sch.), having a h°, a married woman. **–vayas,** f. (regarded as) having the h°'s age, Āpast. **–vidya,** n. finding a h°, RV. x, 102, 11. **–védana,** mfn. procuring a h° (Aryaman), AV. xiv, 1, 17; m. du. a partic. part of the body (attracting a h°?), viii, 6, 1; n. procuring a h° (by means of magical formulas), ii, 36, 2. **–vrata,** n. loyalty or fidelity to a h°, R.; *-guṇa*, m. the virtue of l° or f°, MBh. **–vratā,** f. a devoted and virtuous wife, Mn.; MBh. &c.; *-tva*, n. devotion or loyalty to a h°, MBh.; R.; Kathās.; *-°dhyāya* (°*tâdh*°), m. N. of ch. of SkandaP.; *-maya*, mf(*ī*)n. consisting in a faithful wife, Mcar.; Bālar.; *-māhātmya* and °*tôpâkhyāna*, n. N. of wks. **–śuc,** f. grief for a husband, Hcar. **–śoka,** m. id.; °*kâkula*, mfn. agitated with g° for a h°, Nal. **–sahagamana-nishedha-nirāsa-prakāśa,** m. N. of wk. **–sevā,** f. devotion to a h°, Mn. ii, 67.

1. **Patīya,** Nom. P. °*yati*, to be or become a master, AitĀr.; to become strong, ŚBr.; to wish for a husband, HPariś.; Bhaṭṭ.; to take as h°, Pañcad.

2. **Patīya,** n. being master or mistress, MantraBr.

Pátnī, f. (rarely *patni*) a female possessor, mistress, RV. &c. &c.; a wife (RV. i, 140, 6; iv, 24, 8, even applied to cows), ib. (cf. *pati*, f.); (in astrol.) N. of the 7th mansion, Var. [Cf. Gk. πότνια.] **–karmán,** n. the business of a wife, ŚBr. **–tva,** n. wifehood, matrimony (*-tve √grah*, to take as a w°), MārkP. **–mantra,** m. pl. N. of partic. verses, Vait. **–yūpá,** m. the sacrificial post assigned to the wives of the gods, ŚBr.; KātyŚr. **–vat** (*pát*°), mfn. having a w° or accompanied by wives, RV.; VS.; ŚBr. **–śāla,** n. or **-śālā,** f. a kind of hut or tent for the wives or for the domestic use of the sacrificer, Br.; Lāṭy.; MBh. **–samyājá,** m. pl. the 4 Ājya oblations (offered to Soma, Tvashṭṛi, the wives of the gods, and Agni Gṛiha-pati), Br.; ŚrS. **–samyājana,** n. performing the Patnī-saṃyāja, KātyŚr. **–saṃnahana,** n. girding a w°, ib.; the girdle of a w°, ib., Sch. **Patny-āṭa,** m. the women's apartments, L.

Patnīka, mfn. for *patnī*, ifc. (cf. *a-*, *bahu-*, *sa-*).

पत्काषिन् *pat-kāshin* &c. See p. 583, col. 1.

पत्तङ्ग *pattaṅga*, m. (n., L.; fr. *pattrâṅga*) red sandal, Suśr.; n. Caesalpina Sappan, L.

पत्तन *pattana*, m. pl. N. of a people, VP.; (*ā*), f. N. of a wife of Vikrama, L.; n. (ifc. f. *ā*) a town, city, MBh.; Kāv. &c. (cf. *dharma-* and *paṭṭana*). **–vaṇij,** m. a town-tradesman, L. **Pattanâdhipati,** m. 't°-governor,' N. of a prince, MBh.

पत्तरङ्ग *pattaraṅga*, n. = *paṭṭa-r*°, L.

पत्तलक *pattalaka*, m. N. of a prince, VP.

पत्तला *pattalā*, f. = *paṭṭalā*, Inscr.

पत्तली *pattalī* (for *pattr*°?) *-√kṛi*, to beat into thin leaves, Bhpr.

पत्तवे *pátta.e.* See √2. *pat*, p. 580.

पत्तस् *pat-tas*, *patti*. See p. 583, col. 1.

पत्तूर *pattūra*, m. Achyranthes Triandra, Suśr.; n. red sandal, Bhpr.

पत्तोर्ण *pattorṇa*, v. l. for *pattrôrṇa*, L.

पत्त्र *pattra* &c. See p. 581, col. 2.

पत्त्रङ्ग *pattraṅga*. See *pattrâṅga*, p. 581.

पत्त्राण्य *pattrāṇya*, n. Caesalpina Sappan, L.

पत्नि *patni* for *patnī*. See above.

पथ् *path* (cf. √*panth*), cl. 1. P. *páthati*, to go, move; to fly, Suparṇ.; Dhātup. xx, 17: Caus. *pāthayati*, to throw, send (xxxii, 20, v. l. for *pṛith* and *prath*).

Patha, m. a way, path, road, course, reach, MBh.; Kāv. &c. (generally ifc. for *pathin*; cf. Pāṇ. v, 4, 74). **–kalpanā,** f. juggling tricks, conjuring, L. **–darśaka,** m. 'way-shower,' a guide, conductor, MW. **–sundara,** m. or n. N. of a plant, L. (v. l. *pattra-s*°). **Pathâtithi,** m. 'w°-guest,' a traveller, Rājat. **Pathe-shṭhá,** mfn. standing in the w° or road, RV. **Pathôpadeśaka,** m. = °*tha-darśaka*, Ratnâv. iv, 1/2 (in Prākṛit).

Pathaka, mfn. knowing the way, a guide, L.; m. or n. a district, canton, L.

Pathat, mf(*ntī*)n. going, travelling; m. a road, L.

Páthan-vat, mfn. containing the word *pathin*, ŚBr. (cf. *pathi-mat* below).

1. **Pathi,** for *pathin* in comp. **–kāra,** m. N. of a man, g. *kurv-ādi*. **–kṛit,** mfn. making a way or road, preparing a w°, RV.; AV.; ŚBr.; ŚrS.; m. N. of Agni, TS. **–deya,** n. a toll levied on public roads, L. **–druma,** m. Acacia Catechu, L. **–pá,** mfn. protecting r°s, MaitrS. **–prajña,** mfn. acquainted with roads, W. **–priya,** m. an agreeable fellow-traveller (?), Pāṇ. vi, 1, 199, Sch. **–mat,** mfn. containing the word *pathin*, Br. **–madhye,** ind. in the middle of the road, MW. **–rákshas** (VS.), **-rákshi** (RV.), mfn. = *-pá*.

2. **Pathi,** loc. of *pathin* in comp. **–vāhaka,** mfn. cruel, hard, L.; m. a bird-catcher or a burden-bearer, L. **–shad** (PārGṛ.), **-shádi** (AV.), mfn. sitting in the way. **–shṭhá** (AV.), **-stha** (MBh.), mfn. being in or on the w°, going. **Pathy-aśana,** n., **-odana,** m. provender for a journey, viaticum, Kāv.

Pathika, mf(*ā* or *ī*)n. knowing the way, going on a road, W.; m. a traveller, wayfarer, guide, MBh.; Kāv. &c.; (*ā*), f. red grapes, L. **–jana,** m. a traveller or travellers, Pañc. ii, 1/2. **–saṃhati** and **-saṃtati,** f. (L.), **-sârtha,** m. (Mṛicch.; Mālav.) a company of travellers, a caravan. **Pathikâśraya,** m. an asylum for travellers, an inn, MW.

Pathikāya (only °*yita*, n. impers.), to act as a traveller, Subh.

Pathin, m. (strong stem *pánthan*, older *pánthā*; middle *pathi*; weak *path*; sg. *pánthās* (nom. voc.), *pánthānam* [*pánthām*, RV.; AV.]; *pathā́*, °*thé*, °*thás*, °*thi*; du. *pánthānau*, *pathibhyām*, *pathós*; pl. *pánthānas* [*pánthās*, °*thāsas*, RV.; *patháyas*, Br.]; *pathás* [*pāthás*, RV. ii, 2, 4, perhaps gen. sg.?]; *pathíbhis*, °*bhyas*; *pathām* [°*thīnā́m*, RV.; AV.]; *pathíshu*; cf. Pāṇ. vii, 1, 85 &c.) a way, path, road, course (lit. and fig.; *panthānam √dā*, with gen. to cede the way to; *pathânena*, 'in this w° or manner,' *pathi ni-√as*, see under *ny-as*), RV. &c. &c.; range, reach (cf. *karṇa-*, *darśana-* &c.); sect, doctrine, L.; a division of hell, Mn. iv, 90; N. of a teacher with the patr. Saubhara, BṛĀrUp. [Cf. *patha*; Zd. *panthan*; Gk. πάτος; Lat. *pont-em*; Old Pruss. *pintis*; Slav. *patĭ*.]

Pathila, m. a traveller, Uṇ. i, 58.

Pathī. See *ā-pathī*.

Pathya, mfn. 'belonging to the way,' suitable, fit, proper, wholesome, salutary (lit. and fig.; esp. said of diet in a medical sense), Yājñ.; MBh.; Suśr. &c.; containing elements or leading forms, regular, normal, Lāṭy.; Nid.; m. Terminalia Chebula or Citrina, L.; N. of a teacher of AV.; (*ā*), f. a path, way, road (with *revátī*, 'the auspicious path,' personif. as a deity of happiness and welfare), RV.; TS.; Br.; Terminalia Chebula or Citrina and other plants, L.; N. of sev. metres, Nid.; Col.; N. of a woman, Kathās.; n. a species of salt, L. **–śāka,** m. a species of vegetable, L. **Pathyâpathya,** mfn. wholesome and unwholesome, beneficial or hurtful (esp. in sickness), W.; m. or n. N. of wk.; *-nighaṇṭu*, m., *-nirṇaya*, m., *-vidhāna*, n., *-vidhi*, m., *-viniścaya*, m., *-vibodha*, m. N. of wks. **Pathyâśin,** mfn. eating or an eater of wholesome diet, W.

पद् 1. *pad*, cl. 1. P. *padati*, v.l. for *bad*, to stand fast or fixed, Dhātup. iii, 14, Vop.

पद् 2. *pad*, cl. 4. Ā. (Dhātup. xxvi, 60) *padyate* (°*ti*, AitBr.; MBh.; Pot. *padyām*, R.; Impv. *patsva*, MBh.; pf. *papāda*, RV.; *pede*, Br.; aor. *apadmahi*, °*dran*, RV. [Subj. *padāti*, ib.]; *apatsi*, *patthās*, AV.; Prec. *padīshṭá*, RV.; AV.; fut. *patsyati*, Br.; °*te*, Up.; *pattā*, Gr.; inf. *páttave*, RV; °*tos*, °*tum*, Br.; *-pádas*, RV.; ind. p. *-pádya*, ib.; *-pâdam*, Br.), to fall, fall down or out, perish, RV.; AV.; VS.; Br.; to go, resort or apply to, participate in (acc.), keep, observe, MBh.: Caus. *pādáyati*, °*te*, to cause to fall, AV.; AitBr. (Pass. *pādyate*, Br.; Desid. *pipādayishati*, Br. &c.); *padayate*, to go, Dhātup. xxxv, 44: Desid. *pitsate*, Pāṇ. vii, 4, 54: Intens. *panīpadyate*, Kāv.; *panīpadīti*, Pāṇ. vii, 4, 84.

Pac, in comp. for 3. *pad*. **–chabda** (for *śabda*), m. the noise of feet or footsteps, L. **–chas** (for *śas*), ind. foot by foot, Pāda by Pāda, Br.; PārGṛ.; ChUp.; *-chaḥ-śasya*, n. the recitation by Pādas, Vait. **–chauca** (for *śauca*), n. cleansing or purifying to feet, ĀśvGṛ.

Paj, in comp. for 3. *pad*. **–ja,** m. 'born from the feet (of Brahmā),' a Śūdra, L.

4. **Pat**, in comp. for 3. *pad*. — **kâshin**, mfn. rubbing or galling the feet, walking painfully, Sarvad.; Pâṇ. vi, 3, 54 (W. 'going on foot; m. a footman, foot-soldier'). — **tás**, ind. from or at the feet, RV.; Br.; ŚrS. (also *-tatás*, AV. vi, 131, 1); *-to-dâśa*, mfn. lined with fringes at the f°, ĀpŚr. — **saṅgin**, mfn. sticking or adhering to the f°, AV. — **sukha**, mfn. pleasant to the f°, Hariv.

1. **Patti**, f. (fr. √2. *pad*) going, moving, walking, L.

2. **Patti**, m. (prob. fr. 3. *pad*) a pedestrian, footman, foot-soldier, infantry, VS. &c. &c. (m. c. also °*tī*, R. [B.]); a hero, L.; (pl.) N. of a people, MBh. (v.l. *paśu*); f. the smallest division of an army (1 chariot, 1 elephant, 3 horsemen and 5 foot-soldiers; according to others = 55 foot-soldiers), MBh. — **karman**, n. the business or operations of infantry, MW. — **kâya**, m. (body of) inf°, L. — **kâra**, w. r. for *patti-k*°. — **gaṇaka**, m. (prob.) an officer whose business is to number or muster the inf°, L. — **paṅkti**, f. a line of inf°, W. — **saṃhati**, f. (L.), **-sainya**, n. (MBh.) a body or troop of infantry.

Pattika, mfn. going on foot, pedestrian, Hariv.

Pattin, m. = 2. *patti*, a foot-soldier, footman, ib.

Patsu-tás, ind. (from loc. of 3. *pad* + *tas*) at the feet, RV. viii, 43, 6. °**taḥ-śī**, mfn. lying at the feet, ib. i, 32, 8.

3. **Pád**, m. (in strong cases *pā́d*; ifc. f. *pad* or *padī*) a foot (*padā*, *padbhyām* and °*bhis*, also 'on foot,' RV. &c. &c.; ifc. also 'sticking to the feet of;' cf. *śrī-vishṇu-padī*); a step, R.; a fourth part, a quarter, AV.; ŚBr. [Cf. *pada*; Gk. πούς, ποδ-ός; Lat. *pes*, *ped-is*; Goth. *fôtus*; Angl. Sax. *fôt*; Eng. *foot*; Germ. *Fuss*.] — **anushaṅgá**, m. anything appended to a Pada or quarter of a verse, ŚBr. (cf. *padânush*°). — **âsa**, **-âsana**, see *padâsa*, °*sana* under *pada*. — **ga**, mfn. going on foot, pedestrian; m. a f°-soldier, L. — **ghoshá**, m. the noise of feet or footsteps, AV. — **dhaḍī**, f. (in music) a kind of composition (prob. Prâkr. = *-dhatī*, see next). — **dhati** (for *-hati*), f. 'foot-stroke,' a way, path, course, line, Hariv.; Kâv. &c. (also °*tī*, g. *bahv-ādi*); sign, token, Jâtak.; N. of a class of writings (described as guide-books or manuals for partic. rites and ceremonies and the texts relating to them) and of sev. wks.; a family N. or title (or rather the characteristic word denoting caste or occupation in comps. serving as proper names, e. g. *-gupta*, *-dâsa* at the end of Vaiśya and Śūdra names), L.; *-candrikā*, f., *-cintāmaṇi*, m., *-prakāśa*, m., *-prakāśikā*, f., *-bhūshaṇa*, n., *-ratna*, n., *-sāra*, m. N. of wks. — **dhima** (for *-hima*), n. coldness of the feet, Pâṇ. vi, 3, 54. — **ratha**, m. a footman, foot-soldier, BhP. — **vát**, mfn. having feet, running; n. an animal that uses its feet for locomotion, RV.; AV. **Padâvihâra**, m. paying honour by walking round, Divyâv.

Padá, n. (rarely m.) a step, pace, stride; a footstep, trace, vestige, mark, the foot itself, RV. &c. &c. (*padena*, on foot; *pade pade*, at every step, everywhere, on every occasion; *trīṇi padāni Vishṇoḥ*, the three steps or footprints of Vishṇu [i. e. the earth, the air, and the sky; cf. RV. i, 154, 5; Vikr. i, 19], also N. of a constellation or according to some 'the space between the eyebrows;' sg. *Vishṇoḥ padam*, N. of a locality; *padaṃ* √*dā*, *padāt padam* √*gam* or √*cal*, to make a step, move on; *padaṃ* √*kṛi*, with loc. to set foot in or on, to enter; with *mūrdhni*, to set the foot upon the head of [gen.] i. e. overcome; with *citte* or *hṛidaye*, to take possession of any one's heart or mind; with loc. or *prati*, to have dealings with; *padaṃ ni-*√*dhā* with loc., to set foot in = to make impression upon; with *padavyām*, to set the foot on a person's [gen. or ibc.] track, to emulate or equal; *padam ni-*√*bandh* with loc., to enter or engage in); a sign, token, characteristic, MBh.; Kathās.; Pur.; a footing, standpoint; position, rank, station, site, abode, home, RV. &c. &c. (*padam ā-*√*tan*, to spread or extend one's position; *padāt padam bhrāmayitvā*, having caused to wander from place to place); a business affair, matter, object or cause of (gen. or comp.), Kâv.; Pañc. &c.; a pretext, L.; a part, portion, division (cf. *dvi-*, *tri-*); a square on a chess-board, R.; a plot of ground, Inscr.; the foot as a measure of length (= 12 or 15 fingers' breadth, or ½ or ⅓ or ¾ of a Prakrama), KâtyŚr.; a ray of light (m., L.); a portion of a verse, quarter or line of a stanza, RV. &c. &c.; a word or an inflected word or the stem of a noun in the middle cases and before some Taddhitas, Pâṇ. i, 4, 14 &c.; = *pada-pāṭha*, Prât.; common N. of the P. and Ā., Cat.; any one in a set of numbers the sum of which is required; a period in an arithmetical progression, Col.; a square root, Sūryas.; a quadrant, ib.; protection, L. [Cf. Gk. πέδον; Lat. *peda*; *op-pidum* for *op-pedum*.] — **kamala**, n. a lotus-like foot, L. — **kâra**, m. the author of the Pada-pâṭha, Pâṇ.; Mahîdh. — **kârikâ-ratnamâlâ**, f. N. of wk. — **kâla**, m. = *-pāṭha*, Sāy. — **kṛit**, m. = *-kāra*, L. — **kṛitya**, n. N. of Comm. on Tarkas. — **kaumudî**, f. N. of wk. — **krama**, m. a series of steps, pace, walking, Śiś. i, 52 (cf. *citra-padakramam*); a series of quarters of verses, R.; a partic. method of reciting or writing the Veda (see *krama*); m. pl. (or ibc.) the Pada-pâṭha and the different Krama-pâṭhas, MBh.; *-lakshaṇa*, n. N. of wk.; *-vid*, mfn. familiar with the P°- and K°-pâṭha, Hariv. — **kramaka**, n. the Pada- and Krama-pâṭha, Pâṇ. ii, 4, 5, Sch. — **ga**, mfn. going on foot; m. a footman, foot-soldier, L. — **gata**, mfn. gone on foot; described or recorded in a line or stanza, W. — **gati**, f. going on foot, manner of going, gait, Pañc. — **gâḍha**, m. or n. N. of wk. — **gotra**, n. a family supposed to preside over a partic. class of words, VPrât. (cf. *-devatā*). — **ghâtam**, ind. (with √*han*) to strike with the feet upon (acc.), Pâṇ. iii, 4, 37. — **catur-ûrdhva**, n. a kind of metre (in which every Pada is 4 syllables longer than the preceding), Col. — **candrikâ**, f. 'elucidation of words,' N. of sev. wks. — **cihna**, n. a footmark, footstep, Daś. — **ccheda**, m. separation of words (in speaking), parsing, Śiksh. — **cyuta**, mfn. fallen from a position, dismissed from office, BhP. — **jâta**, n. a class of words, Prât.; a group of (connected) words, a sentence or period, L. — **jñá**, mfn. knowing places or one's own place (i. e. home), RV.; AV. — **jyotis**, n. N. of wk. — **tâ**, f. the original form of a word, RPrât.; = next, Śiś. — **tva**, n. the state of (being) a word, APrât.; Pâṇ. i, 2, 45, Sch. — **tvarâ**, f. 'foot-speeder (?),' a shoe, L. — **dârḍhya**, n. fixedness or security of text, APrât. — **dîpikâ**, f. N. of sev. wks. — **devatâ**, f. a deity supposed to preside over a partic. class of words, VPrât. (cf. *-gotra*). — **dyotinî**, f. N. of Comm. on Gît. — **nidhana**, mfn. having the Nidhana (q. v.) at the end of every quarter of a verse (as a Sâman), TâṇḍBr.; Lâṭy. — **nî**, mfn. following the steps of another, AV. xi, 2, 13. — **nyâsa**, m. putting down the feet, step, footmark, MBh.; R. &c.; position of the feet in a partic. attitude, W.; conduct, procedure (?), id.; writing down (quarters of) verses, Kâv.; Asteracantha Longifolia or Tribulus Lanuginosus, L. — **paṅkaja**, n. = *-kamala*, L. — **paṅkti**, f. a series of footsteps, track, Kâlid.; Pañc.; a series of words, Kir.; a kind of metre (of 5 Padas of 5 syllables each), RPrât.; a sacred brick called after this metre, KâtyŚr. — **pañcaka**, m. or n. N. of wk. — **paddhati**, f. a series or row of footsteps, R. — **padma**, n. = *-kamala*, L. — **pâṭha**, m. the Pada method of recitation or writing (a m° of arranging each word of a Vedic text separately in its original form [cf. *pada*] without regard to the rules of Saṃdhi; cf. *krama-* and *saṃhitā-pāṭha*), VPrât., Sch. — **pâta**, m. footfall, tread, step, W. — **pûraṇa**, mfn. filling out or completing a verse, Nir.; n. the action of completing a verse, L. — **bandha**, m. a footstep, pace, L. — **bhañjana**, n. separation or analysis or explanation of words, L. — **bhañjikâ**, f. a commentary which separates or analyses or explains words, L.; a register, journal, calendar or almanac, W. — **bhâvârtha-candrikâ**, f. N. of wk. — **bhraṇśa**, m. loss of a place, dismissal from an office, Prasannar. — **mañjarî**, f. N. of various wks. — **mâlâ**, f. 'word-wreath,' a magical formula, an incantation, DevîP. — **yojana**, n., °**nâ** and °**nikâ**, f. N. of wks. — **yópana**, mf(*ī*)n. destroying (n. the act of d°) the footsteps, AV. — **racanâ**, f. arrangement of words, literary composition, Vâm. — **ratnâvalî**, f., **-vâkya-ratnâkara** (and °*ra-kārikā-saṃgraha*), m., **-vâkyârtha-pañjikâ**, f. N. of wks. — **vâdya**, n. (in music) a sort of drum. — **vâyá**, m. (√*vī*) a leader, guide, forerunner, AV. — **vi**, f. = *-vī*, a way, path, L. — **vikshepa**, m. a step, pace, walking; a horse's paces, W. — **vigraha** (Hariv.), **-viccheda** (VPrât.), m. separation of words. — **vid**, mfn. conversant or familiar with (gen.), ŚBr. (cf. *-jña*). — **virâma**, m. the pause after a quarter of a verse, TPrât. — **vishṭambha**, m. tread, step, stamp with the foot, W. — **vî́**, m. (nom. *s*) a leader, guide, forerunner, RV.; AV. (cf. *-vāya*); f. (nom. *vī*) a road, path, way, track, reach, range; acc. with √*gam*, *yā* &c., to go the way of (cf. under *artha-padavī*, *ghana-*, *pavana-*, *moksha-*, *yauvana-*, *sādhu-*, *smaraṇa-*, *hāsya-*; *padaṃ* √*dhā* or *ni-*√*dhā padavyām* [comp. or gen.], to tread in the footsteps of a person i. e. imitate or rival him), MBh.; Kâv. &c.; station, situation, place, site, R.; Pañc.; -°*vīya*, n. footsteps, track, RV. x, 71, 3 (if not acc. for *vyàm*). — **vṛitti**, f. the hiatus between two words in a sentence, RPrât.; N. of Comm. on Kpr. — **vedin**, m. 'acquainted with words,' a linguist or philologist, Kuṭṭanîm. — **vyâkhyâna**, n. explanation of words, g. *ṛig-ayanādi*. — **śabda**, m. the noise of footsteps, Mâlatîm. — **śas**, ind. step by step, gradually, R.; word by word, APrât., Sch. — **śâstra**, n. the science of separately written words, APrât., Sch. — **śreṇi**, f. a series of steps, Kathās. — **shṭhîva**, n. sg. the feet and knees, Pâṇ. v, 4, 77. — **saṃhitâ**, f. = *-pāṭha*, TPrât. — **saṃghâṭa**, m. connecting those words together which in the Saṃhitâ are separated by a kind of refrain, Pâṇ. iii, 2, 49, Vârtt. 3, Pat. — **saṃghâta**, m. id., ib.; VPrât.; a writer, an annotator, one who collects or classifies words, W. — **sadhâtu**, n. a manner of singing, Lâṭy. — **saṃdarbha**, m. N. of wk. — **saṃdhi**, m. the euphonic combination of words, R. — **samaya**, m. = *-pāṭha*, TPrât., Sch. — **samûha**, m. a series of words or parts of verses, Gît., Sch.; = *-pāṭha*, VPrât. — **stobha**, m. N. of sev. Sâmans, ÂrshBr.; N. of wk. — **stha**, mfn. standing on one's feet, going on foot, R.; = *-sthita*, MBh.; R. — **sthâna**, n. footprint, footmark, Hariv. — **sthita**, mfn. being in a station or office, Kathās.

Padâkrânta, mfn. following at one's heels, Śak. **Padâghâta**, m. a stroke with the foot, a kick, L. **Padâṅka**, m. footmark; *-dūta*, m. 'the messenger of the f° (Kṛishṇa),' N. of a poem. **Padâṅgî**, f. Cissus Pedata, L. **Padâṅgushṭha**, m. the great toe, MBh. (v. l. *pād*°). **Padâji, Padâti** &c., see sv. **Padâdi**, m. the beginning of a verse or of a word, Prât.; °*dy-avid* (or °*dya-vid*), m. a bad student (lit. who does not know or who knows only the beginning of verses or words), L. **Padâdhyayana**, n. the recitation of the Veda according to the Pada-pâṭha, APrât.; °*dhyāyin*, mfn. reciting the V° in this way, ib. **Padâdhyâhâra-vâda**, m. N. of wk. **Padânuga**, mfn. following at one's (gen.) heels, an attendant or companion, MBh; R. (ifc.); suitable, agreeable to, R. **Padânurâga**, m. a servant; an army, W. **Padânuśâsana**, n. the science of words, grammar, L. **Padânushaṅga**, m. anything added or appended to a Pada, ŚâṅkhŚr. (cf. *pad-anush*°). **Padânusâra**, m. following at one's heels; °*reṇa upa-*√*labh*, to overtake, Mâlatîm. **Padânusvâra**, n. N. of partic. Sâmans, Lâṭy., Sch. **Padânta**, m. the end of a line in a stanza, Lâṭy.; the end of a word, VPrât.; Pâṇ.; mfn. ending with the word *pada*, Pâṇ. vii, 3, 9; *-śuddhâśuddhiya*, n. N. of a Sâman, ÂrshBr.; °*tīya* (R and VPrât.), °*tya* (APrât.), mfn. being at the end of a word, final. **Padântara**, n. an interval of one step (°*re sthitvā*, stopping after taking one step), Śak. (cf. *a-pad*°); another word, Vedântas. **Padânveshin**, mfn. following a footmark, Daś. **Padâbja**, n. = *pada-kamala*, L. **Padâbhilâshin**, mfn. wishing for an office, MW. **Padâbhihoma**, m. pouring out the oblation (*homa*) upon a footprint, Vait. **Padâmnâya-siddhi**, f. N. of wk. **Padâmbhoja**, n. = *pada-kamala*, L. **Padâyata**, mfn. as long as a f°, L.; (*ā*), f. a shoe, L. **Padâravinda**, n. = *pada-kamala*, L. **Padârtha**, m. the meaning of a word, VPrât.; Prab.; BhP. &c. (ifc. also *-ka*, Pat.); that which corresponds to the m° of a w°, a thing, material object, man, person, Var.; Kâv.; Pur.; a head, subject (16 with Naiyâyikas); a category, predicament (7 with Vaiśeshikas, 25 with Sâṃkhyas, 7 with Vedântins); a principle (*-tritaya*, n. a triad of principles, RTL. 119); *-kaumudī*, f. (°*dī-kośa* and *-sāra-kośa*, m.), *-khaṇḍana*, n. (°*na-ṭippaṇa-vyākhyā*, f.), *-guṇa-cintāmaṇi*, m., *-candrikā*, f., *-tattva*, n. (°*tva-nirūpaṇa*, n., *-nirṇaya*, m., *-vivecana*, n.), *-dīpikā*, f., *-dīpinī*, f., *-dharma-saṃgraha*, m., *-nirūpaṇa*, n., *-pārijāta*, m., *-prakāśa*, m., *-prakāśikā*, f., *-pradeśa*, m., *-bodha*, m., *-bhāskara*, m., *-maṇimālā* or *-mālā*, f., *-mālā-vṛitti*, f., *-ratna-mañjūshā*, f., *-ratnamālā*, f., *-vidyā-sāra*, m., *-viveka*, m., *-saṃgraha*, m.,

-sarasī, f., °*thâdarśa*, m. N. of wks.; °*thânusamaya*, m. the performance of one ritual act for all objects in orderly succession before performing another act for all objects in the same order, ĀśvGṛ., Sch. &c. (cf. *kāṇḍânus*°); °*thīya-divya-cakshus*, n., °*thôddeśa*, m. N. of wks. **Padâvagrāham**, ind. making a pause after every quarter of a verse, AitBr.; Vait. **Padâvalī**, f. a series of verses or words, Gīt.; N. of a grammar. **Padâvṛitti**, f. the repetition of a word, VPrāt.; (in rhet.) the repetition of the same word with another meaning, Kāvyâd. **Padâsa** (or °*d-āsa*?), n. N. of 2 Sāmans, ĀrshBr. **Padâsana**, n. a footstool, L. **Padâhata**, mfn. struck by the foot, kicked, MW. **Padâikadeśa**, m. a part of a word, TPrāt., Sch. **Padôccaya**, m. (in dram.) accumulation of words which belong to the subject matter (e.g. Śak. i, 20), Sāh. **Padôpahata**, mfn. (prob.) = *padâhata*, Pāṇ. vi, 3, 52.

Padaka, mfn. versed in the Pada-pāṭha, Divyâv. (g. *kramâdi*); m. a kind of ornament (= *nishka*), L.; N. of a man; pl. his descendants, g. *yaskâdi*; n. a step, pace, MBh.; an office, dignity, Rājat.; a foot, BhP.; (*ikā*), f., see *tri-padikā* and *dvi-p*°.

Padana, mfn. who or what goes or moves, W. (cf. Pāṇ. iii, 2, 150).

Padanīya, mfn. to be investigated, ŚBr. (*-tva*, n., Saṃk.)

Padāji, m. (fr. *pada* + *āji*?, Pāṇ. vi, 3, 52) a footman, foot-soldier, L.

Padāta, w. r. for next and *pādāta*.

Padāti, mfn. (fr. *pada* + *āti*?, Pāṇ. vi, 3, 52) going or being on foot; m. a pedestrian, footman, foot-soldier, MBh.; R. &c.; a peon (in chess), Pañcad.; N. of a son of Janam-ejaya, MBh. **-jana**, m. a footman, pedestrian, MBh.; *-saṃkula*, mfn. mingled with footmen or p°s, ib. **-mātra**, m. only a foot-soldier, MW. **-lava**, m. a most humble (lit. atom) servant, Bālar. (cf. *bhṛitya-paramâṇu*). **Padāty-adhyaksha**, m. a commander of infantry, R.

Padātika, m. (ifc. f. *ā*) a footman, foot-soldier, peon, L. °**tin**, mfn. having foot-soldiers, MBh.; going or being on foot; m. a foot-soldier, MBh.; R. °**tīya**, m. = prec. m., MBh.

Padāra, m. the dust of the feet, L.; a boat, L.

Padālika, m. = *dhundhumāra*, L. (v.l. *pād*°).

Pádi, m. (prob.) a kind of animal, RV. i, 125, 2 (a bird, Mahidh.; = *gantu*, Nir. v, 18).

Padika, mf(*ī*)n. going on foot, pedestrian, g. *parpâdi*; one Pada long, KātyŚr., Sch.; comprising (only) one partition or division, Var.; Hcat.; n. the point of the foot, L.

Padi-baddhá, mf(*ā*)n. (loc. of 3. *pad* + *b*°) tied or bound by the feet, TS.

Padi-√kṛi, to raise to the square root, Āryabh., Sch.; *-kṛita-tva*, n. the being raised &c., ib.

Paduka or °**duma**, m. pl. N. of a people, VP.

Padeka, m. a hawk, falcon, L.

Pádya, mf(*ā*)n. (fr. 3. *pad* and *pada*) relating or belonging to a foot, RV.; Kāṭh.; hurting or coming in contact with the feet, Pāṇ. iv, 4, 83; vi, 3, 53, Sch.; marked with footsteps, ib. iv, 4, 87, Sch.; measuring a Pada in length or breadth, KātyŚr. (also in comp. with numerals; cf. *ardha-*, *daśa-*); consisting of Padas or parts of verses, Br.; ĀśvGṛ.; RPrāt.; consisting of one Pada, KātyŚr., Sch.; forming the end, final, APrāt.; m. a Śūdra, L. (cf. *paj-ja*); a part of a word, verbal element, RPrāt.; (*pádyā*), f. footsteps, paces (pl.), RV.; a way, path, road, L.; a foot as a measure of length, KātyŚr.; n. a verse metre, poetry (opp. to *gadya*, prose), Vām.; Kāvyâd.; Sāh. &c.; N. of sev. hymns. **-kādambarī**, f. N. of a wk. of Kshemêndra. **-trayī-vyākhyāna**, n. N. of a Comm. on the first 3 verses of BhP. (also *bhāgavata-tr*°*-vy*°). **-pañcāśikā**, f., **-prasūnâñjali**, m. N. of wks. **-maya**, mf(*ī*)n. consisting of verses, Sāh. **-mālā**, f., **-muktâvalī**, f., **-racanā**, f., **-veṇī**, f., **-śataka**, n., **-saṃgraha**, m. N. of wks. **Padyâtmikôpanishad**, f. N. of an Up. **Padyâmṛita**, f. (ibc.) nectar of poetry; *-taraṃgiṇī*, *-samudra-ṭīkā*, f., *-saro-vara*, n., *-sôpāna*, n. N. of wks. **Padyâlaya**, m., **Padyâvali**, f. N. of wks.

Padra, padva. See p. 585, col. 2.

Padvan, m. a road, path, way, Un. iv, 112.

1. **Pan**, in comp. before nasals = 3. *pad*. **-naddhā**, f. a shoe, HPariś. **-naddhrī**, id., L. **-nishka**, m. ¼ Nishka, L. **-nejana**, n. washing of the feet, ĀpŚr., Sch.; (*néjanī*), f. pl. (sc. *āpas*) a bath for the f°, TS. **-miśra** = *pāda-m*°, Pāṇ. vi, 3, 56.

Panna, mfn. fallen, fallen down, gone &c.; m. (!) downward motion, fall, creeping on the ground, Uṇ. iii, 10, Sch. **-gá**, m. (ifc. f. *ā*) 'creeping low,' a serpent or serpent-demon, Suparṇ.; MBh. &c.; Cerasus Puddum, L.; (*ī*), f., see below; *-kesara*, m. Mesua Roxburghii, L.; *-nāśana*, m. 's°-killer,' N. of Garuḍa, Hariv.; *-purī*, f. the city of the s°-demons, L.; *-bhojana*, m. 's°-eater,' N. of Garuḍa, MBh.; *-maya*, mf(*ī*)n. formed or consisting of s°s, Hariv.; *-rāja*, m. s°-king, MBh.; *-°gâri*, m. 's-foe,' N. of Garuḍa, Hariv.; of a teacher (v.l. *-gāni*), VP.; *-°gâśana*, m. = *-gabhojana*, L.; *-°gêndra* and *-°gêśvara*, m. 's° king,' MBh. **-gī**, f. a female serpent-demon, a s°-maid, MBh.; R. &c.; a kind of shrub, L.; *-gīrta-kīrti*, mfn. whose praise is sung by s°-maids, Bālar. **-da**, mfn. one whose teeth have fallen out, KātyŚr., Sch. **-rūpa**, mf(*ā*)n. deprived of colour, pale (as a maiden), Car.; °*pīya*, mfn. (chapter) concerning them, ib. **Pannâgāra**, m. N. of a man; pl. his family, Pāṇ. ii, 4, 66, Sch.

पद्म *padma*, m. n. (2. or 3. *pad*?) a lotus (esp. the flower of the lotus-plant Nelumbium Speciosum which closes towards evening; often confounded with the water-lily or Nymphaea Alba), MBh.; Kāv. &c. (ifc. f. *ā*); the form or figure of a lotus, R.; MārkP. (a N. given by the Tāntrikas to the 6 divisions of the upper part of the body called Cakras, q.v.); a partic. mark or mole on the human body, R.; red or coloured marks on the face or trunk of an elephant, L.; a partic. part of a column or pillar, Var.; a kind of temple, ib.; an army arrayed in the form of a lotus, Mn.; MBh.; a partic. posture of the body in religious meditation, Vedânt. (cf. *padmâsana*); a kind of coitus, L.; one of the 9 treasures of Kubera (also personified), R.; one of the 8 treasures connected with the magical art called Padminī, MBh.; Hariv. &c.; a partic. high number (1000 millions or billions), MBh.; R. &c.; a partic. constellation, Var.; N. of a partic. cold hell, Buddh.; a partic. fragrant substance, MBh. (v.l. °*maka*); the root of Nelumbium Speciosum, L.; a species of bdellium, L.; lead, L.; m. a species of plant, L.; an elephant, L.; a species of serpent, Suśr.; N. of Rāma (son of Daśa-ratha), Śatr.; of two serpent-demons, MBh.; R. &c.; of one of the attendants of Skanda, MBh.; of a mythical Buddha, MWB. 136, n. 1.; (with Jainas) N. of the 9th Cakra-vartin in Bhārata and of one of the 9 white Balas; N. of a king, MBh.; of a prince of Kaśmīra (founder of Padma-pura and of a temple; see *padma-svāmin*), Rājat.; of another man, ib.; of a Brāhman, Lalit.; of a mythical elephant, R. (cf. *mahā-padma*); of a monkey, R.; of a mountain, Var.; (*ā*), f. 'the lotus-hued one,' N. of Śrī, Mn.; MBh. &c. (cf. *padma-śrī*); a species of plant, Suśr. (Clerodendrum Siphorantus or Hibiscus Mutabilis, L.); cloves, L.; the flower of Carthamus Tinctoria, L.; N. of the mother of Muni-suvrata (the 20th Arhat of the present Avasarpiṇi), L.; of a female serpent-demon (= the goddess Manasā, wife of the sage Jarat-kāru; cf. *padma-priyā*), L.; of a daughter of king Bṛihad-ratha and wife of Kalki, Pur.; mfn. lotus-hued, being of the colour of a lotus, ShaḍvBr. **-kandâda**, m. a species of bird, Gal. **-kara**, m. a lotus-like hand, BhP.; mf(*ā*)n. l° in h°, Prab.; m. N. of the sun, W.; (*ā*), f. N. of Śrī, BhP. **-karkaṭī**, f. l°-seed, L. **-karṇika**, m. or n. (?) and °**kā**, f. the pericarp of a l° or the central part of an army arrayed in that form, MBh.; (*ā*), f. N. of a Surâṅganā, Siṅhâs. **-kalikā**, f. an unblown l°, MW. **-kalyāṇa-khaṇḍa**, n. N. of ch. of a Pur. **-kāshṭha**, n. the wood of Cerasus Puddum, L. **-kīṭa**, m. a species of venomous insect, Suśr. **-kuṇḍa**, n. a partic. mystical figure, Cat. **-kūṭa**, m. N. of a prince of the Vidyā-dharas, Kathās.; n. N. of the palace of Su-bhīmā, Hariv. **-ketana**, m. N. of a son of Garuḍa, MBh. **-ketu**, m. a partic. comet, Var. **-kesara**, n. the filament of a lotus, L. **-kośa**, m. the calyx of a l°, R.; BhP. (°*śâya*, Nom. Ā. °*yate*, to resemble the c° of a l°, Bālar.; °*śī-√kṛi*, to make into the c° of a l°, HPariś.); a partic. position of the fingers resembling the c° of a l°, Cat.; N. of wk. (also *-jātaka*, n.) **-kshetra**, n. N. of one of 4 districts in Orissa held especially sacred, L. **-khaṇḍa**, n. a quantity of lotuses, Mṛicch.; N. of ch. of the Brahmâṇḍa P.; *-nagara*, n. N. of a city, Siṅhâs. **-gandha**, mf(*ā*)n. smelling like a lotus, L. **-gandhi**, mfn. id., R.; n. Cerasus Puddum, Bhpr. **-garbha**, m. the interior or calyx of a l°, Kāvyâd. ii, 41; 'sprung from a l° or containing lotuses,' N. of Brahmā, RPrāt. (Introd.); of Vishṇu, Hariv.; of Śiva, Śivag.; of the sun, L.; of a lake, Hit.; of a Buddha, Lalit.; of a Bodhisattva, L.; of a Brāhman who was changed into a swan, Hariv. **-giri-purāṇa**, n. N. of a legend. **-gupta**, m. N. of a poet (called also Pari-mala), Cat. **-gṛihā**, f. 'lotus-housed,' N. of Lakshmī, MBh. **-caraṇa**, m. 'l°-foot,' N. of a disciple of Śaṃkarâcārya, Cat. **-cāriṇī**, f. Hibiscus Mutabilis, Bhpr.; a partic. personification, MānGṛ. **-ja**, m. 'lotus-born,' N. of Brahmā, BhP. **-jātaka**, n. N. of wk. **-jāti**, f. = *-bandha*, Kāv. **-tantu**, m. the fibre of a l°-stalk, L. **-tā**, f. the state or condition of a l°, Kāvyâd. **-darśana**, m. 'looking like a l°,' the resin of the Pinus Longifolia, L.; N. of a man, Kathās. **-dalêkshaṇa**, mfn. l°-(leaf-)eyed, Mṛicch. **-dhara**, m. 'l°-bearer,' N. of a prince, Bhadrab. **-nandi** or °**din**, m. N. of an author, Sarvad.; Cat. **-nābha**, m. 'l°-naveled,' N. of Vishṇu (from whose navel sprang the lotus which contained Brahmā, the future creator), MBh.; Hariv.; R.; N. of the 11th month (reckoned from Mārgaśirsha), Var.; a magical formula spoken over weapons, R.; N. of a serpent-demon, MBh.; of a son of Dhṛita-rāshṭra, ib.; of the first Arhat of the future Ut-sarpiṇī, L.; of sev. authors (also *-tīrtha*, *-datta*, *-dīkshita*, *-purī*, *-bhaṭṭa*, *-yājñika*) and other men, Cat.; Inscr.; *-dvādaśī*, f. N. of the 12th day in the light half of the month Āśvayuja, Cat.; *-bīja*, n. the algebra of Padma-nābha, Col. **-nābhi**, m. N. of Vishṇu, L. (cf. *-nābhu*). **-nāla**, m. a lotus stalk, L. **-nidhi**, m. N. of one of the 9 treasures of Kubera (also personified), Pañc. **-nibhêkshaṇa**, mfn. having eyes like lotus-leaves, MW. **-nimīlana**, n. the closing of a l°, Śak. **-netra**, m. 'l°-eyed,' a species of bird, Gal.; N. of a future Buddha, L. **-paṇḍita**, m. N. of an author, Cat. **-pattra**, n. a l°-leaf, MBh. (*-nibhêkshaṇa*, mfn. l°-l°-eyed, MW.); = *-parṇa*, Bhpr. **-pada**, m. = *-pāda*, Cat. **-parṇa**, n. Costus Speciosus or Arabicus, L. **-pāṇi**, m. 'lotus-handed' or 'holding a l° in the hand,' N. of Brahmā, L.; of Vishṇu, Cat.; of the Bodhi-sattva Avalokitêśvara, MWB. 195 &c.; the sun, L. **-pāda**, m. = *-caraṇa*, Cat. (cf. *pāda-padma*); *-rahasya*, n. N. of wk.; °*dâcārya*, m. N. of a teacher, Cat. **-pura**, n. N. of a city, Rājat. **-purāṇa**, n. N. of sev. Purāṇas. **-pushpa**, m. Pterospermum Acerifolium, L.; a species of bird, L.; °*shpâñjali-stotra*, n. N. of a Stotra. **-prabha**, m. N. of a future Buddha; of a Deva-putra, Lalit.; of 6th Arhat of present Avasarpiṇī, L.; (with *sūri*) of an author, Cat.; (*ā*), f. N. of a daughter of Mahā-daṃshṭra, Kathās. **-prabhu**, m. N. of an author, Cat. **-priyā**, f. N. of the goddess Manasā (wife of Jarat-kāru), L. **-bandha**, m. an artificial arrangement of the words of a verse in a figure representing a lotus-flower, Kpr. **-bandhu**, m. 'friend of the l°,' N. of the sun, L.; a bee, L.; *-kula*, n. N. of a family, Cat. **-bīja**, n. l°-seed, L.; °*jâbha*, mfn. 'resembling the l°-s°,' the s° of Euryala Ferox, L. **-bhava**, m. = *-ja*, Hariv.; BhP. **-bhāsa**, m. 'brilliant with (or like) a l°,' N. of Vishṇu, Hariv. (v.l. *-nābha*; cf. *-hāsa*). **-bhū**, m. = *-ja*, Dhūrtan. **-maya**, mf(*ī*)n. made or consisting of l°-flowers, Hariv.; BhP. **-mālin**, mfn. l°-garlanded; m. N. of a Rakshas, R.; (*nī*), f. N. of Śrī, MBh. **-mihira**, m. 'l°-sun,' N. of a writer of the history of Kaśmīra, Rājat. **-mukhī**, f. Alhagi Maurorum, L. **-mūla**, n. l°-root, L. **-yoni**, m. 'l°-born,' N. of Brahmā, Gṛihyās.; MBh. &c. (also °*nin*, Hariv.); of a Buddha, Lalit.; of sev. men, APariś.; Lalit. **-rati**, f. N. of 2 princesses, Kathās. **-ratna**, m. N. of the 23rd Buddh. patriarch, L. **-ratha**, m. N. of sev. princes, Rājat.; HPariś. **-rāga**, m. 'lotus-hued,' a ruby, L. (also *-ka*, Hcat.; °*ga-maya*, mf[*ī*]n. made or consisting of rubies, Kāraṇḍ); (*ī*), f. N. of one of the tongues of Agni, Gṛihyās. **-rāja**, m. 'l°-king,' N. of sev. men, Rājat.; of a poet, Cat. **-rūpa**, mf(*ā*)n. l°-hued; (*ā*), f. N. of Śrī, MBh. **-rekhā**, f. 'l°-line,' a line in the palm of the hand indicating the acquisition of great wealth, L. **-lāñchana**, m. (L.) 'l°-marked,' a king; N. of Brahmā; of Kubera, the sun; (*ā*), f. N. of Śrī; of Sarasvatī; of Tārā. **-līlā-vilāsinī**, f. N. of an astron. wk. **-lekhā**, f. N. of a woman, Rājat. **-locana**, mfn. lotus-eyed, MBh. **-vat**, mfn. full of l°-flowers, Hariv.; (*ī*), f. N. of a wife of Aśoka (cf. *padmā-vatī*); of a town, BhP. **-vana-bāndhava**, m. the sun (cf. *padma-bandhu*); *-vaṉśa*, m. the race of kings descended from the sun (cf. *sūrya-v°*), Prasannar. **-varcas**, mfn. lotus-hued, MBh.; R. **-varṇa**, mfn. id., Hariv.; m. N. of a son of Yadu, ib. **-varṇaka**, n. Costus Speciosus or Arabicus, L. **-vāsā**, f. = *-gṛihā*, L. **-vāhinī**, f. N. of wk. **-vishaya**, m. N. of a country, Kathās. **-vṛiksha**, m. Cerasus Puddum, L. **-vṛishabha-vikrāmin**, m. N. of a future Buddha, L. **-vesha**, m. N. of a king of the Vidyādharas, Kathās. **-vyākośa**, n. a crevice shaped like a l°-bud (made by a thief in a wall), Mṛicch. iii, 13. **-vyūha**, m. N. of a Samādhi, L. **-śas**, ind. by thousands of billions, MBh. **-śāyinī**, f. a species of bird, Gal. **-śekhara**, m. N. of a king of the Gandharvas, Kathās. **-śrī**, 'beautiful as a lotus flower,' N. of Avalokiteśvara, Kāraṇḍ.; of a Bodhi-sattva; f. N. of sev. women, Rājat.; HPariś.; of a lady who wrote on Kāma-śāstra, Cat.; *-garbha*, m. N. of a Bodhi-sattva. **-shaṇḍa**, n. a multitude of lotuses, MBh. (cf. *-khaṇḍa*). **-saṃhitā**, f. N. of wk. **-saṃkāśa**, mfn. resembling a lotus, MW. **-sadman**, m. 'l°-dweller,' N. of Brahmā, Bālar. **-samāsana**, m. id., VP. **-sambhava**, m. = *-ja*, Hariv.; N. of a Buddhist teacher who founded the Red sect in Tibet, MWB. 272 &c. **-saras**, n. l°-lake, N. of sev. lakes, MBh.; Rājat.; Pañc. **-sundara**, m. N. of an author, Cat. **-sūtra**, n. a l°-garland, Hariv. **-sena**, m. N. of sev. men, Kathās.; (*ā*), f. N. of a woman, HPariś. **-saugandhika**, n. pl. the flowers Nelumbium Speciosum and Nymphaea Alba, R.; mfn. (a pond) abounding in these flowers, MBh.; R. &c.; *-vat*, mfn. id., MBh. **-snushā**, f. (L.) N. of Gaṅgā; of Śrī; of Durgā. **-svastika**, n. a Sv° mark consisting of lotus-flowers, MW. **-svāmin**, m. N. of a sacred edifice built by Padma, Rājat. **-hasta**, m. a partic. measure of length, AgP. **-hāsa**, m. 'smiling like or with a lotus,' N. of Vishṇu, L. (cf. *-bhāsa*). **-hema-maṇi**, m. N. of a teacher, Cat. **Padmākara**, m. (ifc. f. *ā*) a lotus-pool or an assemblage of lotuses, Bhartṛ.; Kathās.; *-deva* and *-bhaṭṭa*, m. N. of authors, Cat. **Padmākāra**, mfn. l°-shaped, MW. **Padmāksha**, mf(*ī*)n. l°-eyed, id.; n. l°-seed, W. **Padmāṅka-mudrā**, f. a partic. Mudrā, Kāraṇḍ. **Padmāṅghri**, m. = *°dma-pāda*, Cat. **Padmācala**, m. N. of a mountain, R. **Padmācārya**, m. N. of a teacher, Cat. **Padmāṭa**, m. Cassia Tora, Bhpr. **Padmādi**, a lotus-flower &c.; *-tva*, n., Kāvyād. ii, 95. **Padmādhīśa**, m. N. of Vishṇu, Dhūrtān. **Padmānanda**, m. N. of a poet; *-śataka*, n. his wk. **Padmāntara**, m. a l°-leaf, MW. **Padmālaṃkārā**, f. N. of a Gandharvī, Kāraṇḍ. **Padmālaya**, m. 'dwelling in a l°,' N. of Brahmā, MBh.; (*ā*), f. N. of Śrī, ib.; Hariv.; n. N. of a city, Siṇhās. **Padmā-vatī**, f. (cf. *°dma-v°* and Pāṇ. vi, 3, 119 &c.) Hibiscus Mutabilis, L.; a kind of Prākṛit metre, Col.; N. of Lakshmī, Gīt.; of the goddess Manasā, L.; of one of the Mātṛis attending on Skanda, MBh.; of a Surāṅganā, Siṇhās.; of a Jaina deity, L.; of a wife of king Śṛigāla, Hariv.; of a w° of Yudhi-shṭhira (k° of Kaśmīra), Rājat.; of the w° of Jaya-deva, Gīt.; of a w° of k° Vīra-bāhu, Vet.; of a w° of k° Naya-pāla, ib.; of a poetess, Cat.; of the city of Ujjayinī in the Kṛita-yuga, Kathās.; of another city, VP.; of a river, L.; of Kathās. xvii; *-kalpa*, m., *-pañcāṅga*, n., *-stotra*, n. N. of wks.; *-priya*, m. 'husband of Padmavatī (= Manasā),' N. of Jarat-kāru, L. **Padmāvabhāsa**, m. N. of a kind of philosopher's stone, Kāraṇḍ. **Padmāvali**, f. N. of wk. **Padmāsana**, n. a l° as seat (esp. of an idol), Hariv.; Kum.; a partic. posture in religious meditation, Bhartṛ. (cf. MWB. 240); a kind of coitus, L.; mf(*ā*)n. sitting in a l° or in the position called Padmāsana (*-tā*, f., Cat.); m. N. of Brahmā, VP.; of Śiva, Śivag.; the sun, L.; (*ā*), f. N. of the goddess Manasā, L. **Padmāhvaya**, m. Cerasus Puddum, Bhpr. **Padmāhvā**, f. Hibiscus Mutabilis, L. **Padme-śaya**, m. 'sleeping in a lotus,' N. of Vishṇu, MBh.; Hariv. **Padmottama**, m. N. of a Samādhi, Kāraṇḍ.; of a partic. world, ib.; of a Buddha living in Padmottama and of a future B°, ib. **Padmottara**, m. Carthamus Tinctorius, L.; N. of a Buddha, MWB. 136, n. 1; of the father of Padma, L.; *°rātmaja*, m. patr. of the 9th Cakra-vartin in Bhārata, Jain.; *°rikā-śāka*, n. a species of pot-herb, Car. **Padmotpala-kumud-vat**, mfn. furnished with the lotus flowers called Padma, Utpala and Kumuda, BhP. **Padmodbhava**, mf(*ā*)n. sprung from a l°, MBh.; m. N. of Brahmā, ib.; of a man, Daś.; (*ā*), f. N. of the goddess Manasā, L.; *-prādur-bhāva*, m. N. of ch. of KūrmaP. **Padmopanishad**, f. N. of an Up.; *-dīpikā*, f. N. of Comm. on it.

Padmaka, m. or n. red spots on the skin of an elephant, L.; the wood of Cerasus Puddum, MBh. &c.; m. an army arrayed in the form of a lotus-flower, MBh.; a species of tree, R. (B.); N. of a partic. constellation, Hcat.; of sev. men, Rājat.; n. a partic. posture in sitting, Vedântas.; Costus Speciosus or Arabicus, L.

Padmakin, m. Betula Bhojpatra, L.

Padmāya, Nom. Ā. *°yate*, to resemble the flower of Nelumbium Speciosum, Kāvyād.

Padmāvata, m. N. of a kingdom founded by Padma-varṇa, Hariv.

Padmin, mfn. spotted (as an elephant), MBh.; possessing lotuses, L.; m. an elephant, L.; (*nī*), f., see next.

Padminī, f. (of prec.) Nelumbium Speciosum, a lotus (the whole plant, ifc. *°nīka*, mfn.; cf. *abjinī*, *nalinī* &c.); a multitude of lotuses or a lotus-pond, MBh.; Kāv. &c. (cf. g. *pushkarādi*); a l°-stalk, L.; a female elephant, L.; a partic. magical art, MārkP.; an excellent woman, a woman belonging to the first of the 4 classes into which the sex is divided, RTL. 389; N. of sev. women, Siṇhās. **-kaṇṭaka**, m. a kind of leprosy, Suśr. **-kānta**, m. 'beloved of lotuses,' N. of the sun, L. **-khaṇḍa**, n. a multitude or lake of lotuses, Pañc.; N. of a city, Siṇhās. **-pattra**, n. a l°-leaf, R. **-vallabha** and **-°śa** (*°nīśa*), m. the sun, L. (cf. *-kānta*). **-shaṇḍa** (and *-pura*), n. N. of a city, Siṇhās.

Padmishṭhā, f. N. of a woman, Kathās.

पद्र *padra*, m. (√2. *pad?*) a village or = *saṃveśa*, Uṇ. ii, 13, Sch. (*-vaḍa*, *-saṇḍa* and *-sada* [HPariś.] perhaps w.r. for *-baṭu* or *-baṇḍa*, 'village lad or cripple'); a road in a village, L.; the earth, L.; N. of a district, L.

पद्व *padva*, n. (√2. *pad?*) the earth, L.; a road, L.; a car, L.; mfn., see *nisarga-padva*.

पद्वत् *pad-vat.* See p. 583, col. 1.

पन् 2. *pan*, cl. 1. Ā. *pánate* (pf. *-papana*, *papné*, aor. 3. sg. *panishṭa*), to be worthy of admiration or to admire (acc.), RV.: Pass. *panyáte*, ib.: Caus. *panáyati*, *°te*, to regard with surprise or wonder, to admire, praise, acknowledge, RV.; (Ā.) to rejoice at, be glad of (gen.), ib. (cf. √*paṇ*; *paṇāya*).

Panayáyya, mfn. astonishing, surprising, RV.

Panasya, Nom. Ā. *°syáte* (P. *°syáti*, Naigh. iii, 14), to excite admiration or praise, RV. **°syú**, mfn. showing one's self worthy of admiration, glorious, ib.

Panāya, Nom. P. Ā. *°yáti*, *°te*, to show ostentatiously, boast of (gen.), RV. vi, 75, 6 (cf. Nir. ix, 16). **°náyya**, mfn. admirable, surprising, RV.; AitBr.

Panitá, mfn. admired, praised, RV.

Panitṛí, mfn. praising, acknowledging, ib.

Pánipnat, mfn. (fr. Intens.) showing one's self worthy of admiration or praise, ib.

Panishṭama, (prob.) w.r., SV.

Pánishṭi, f. (prob.) admiration, praise, ib.

Pánishṭha, mfn. (superl.) very wonderful or glorious, RV.

Pánīyas, mfn. (compar.) more or very wonderful, ib.

Panú, f. admiration, ib.

Pánya, mfn. astonishing, glorious, ib. (superl. *-tama*).

Pányas, mfn. = *pánīyas*, ib.

पनक *panaka*, m. a kind of Arum, Śil.

पनस *panasa*, m. (√*pan?*) the bread-fruit or Jaka tree, Artocarpus Integrifolia, MBh.; R. &c.; a thorn, L.; a species of serpent, Suśr.; N. of a monkey, MBh.; R.; (*ī*), f. = *panasikā*, Suśr.; n. the bread-fruit, ib. **-tālikā** or **-nālikā**, f. the bread-fruit tree, L. **Panasâsthi**, n. the kernel of the bread-fruit, Suśr.

Panasikā, f. a kind of disease, pustules on the ears and neck, Suśr. (cf. *pinasa*, *pīnasa*).

पनिष्पद *panishpadá*, mf(*ā*)n. (Intens. of √*spand*) quivering, palpitating, AV.

पन्थ् *panth*, cl. 1. 10. P. *panthati* or *°thayati*, to go, move, Dhātup. xxxii, 39 (cf. √*path*).

Panthaka, mfn. produced in or on the way, Pāṇ. iv, 3, 29; m. N. of a Brāhman, L. **°thalikā**, f. a narrow way or path, Kāraṇḍ.; Divyâv.

पन्थान *panthāna*, m. N. of a partic. magical spell spoken over weapons, R. (v. l. *saṃdhāna*).

पन्दर *pandara*, m. N. of a mountain, VP.

पन्न *panna* &c. See p. 584, col. 2.

पन्नद्धा *pan-naddhā* &c. See p. 584, col. 1.

पपस्य *papasya*, v. l. for *pampasya*.

पपि *papí*, mfn. (√1. *pā*) drinking (with acc.), RV. vi, 23, 4 (cf. Pāṇ. ii, 3, 69, Kāś.); m. the moon, L.

Papí, m. (nom. *s*) the sun or the moon, Uṇ. iii, 159.

Papīti, f. (fr. Intens. of √1. *pā*) mutual or reciprocal drinking, W.

पपु *papu*, m. (√3. *pā*) a protector; f. a nurse, L.

पपुरि *pápuri*, mfn. (√*pṛī*) bountiful, liberal; abundant, RV.

1. **Pápri**, mfn. giving, granting (with gen. or acc.; superl. *-tama*), RV.; VS. (cf. Pāṇ. vii, 1, 103, Sch.)

पपृक्षेण्य *papṛikshéṇya*, mfn. (√*prach*) desirable, RV. v, 33, 6.

पप्रि 2. *pápri*, mfn. (√1. *pṛī*) delivering, saving, RV.; AV.; TS.

पफक *paphaka*, m. N. of a man. **-naraka**, m. pl. the descendants of Paphaka and Naraka, g. *tika-kitavâdi*.

पब्बेक *pabbeka*, m. N. of the father of Kedāra-bhaṭṭa (author of the Vṛitta-ratnâkara), Cat.

पमरा *pamarā*, f. a kind of fragrant substance, L.

पम्पस्य *pampasya*, Nom. P. *°syati*, to feel pain, g. *kaṇḍv-ādi* (v. l. *pap°*).

पम्पा *pampā*, f. (√1. *pā?*; Uṇ. iii, 28, Sch.) N. of a river in the south of India, MBh.; R. &c.; of a lake, Ragh., Sch. **-māhātmya**, n. N. of ch. of SkandaP.

पम्ब् *pamb*, cl. 1. P. *pambati*, to go, move, Dhātup. xi, 35, Vop.

पय् *pay*, cl. 1. Ā. *payate*, to go. move, Dhātup. xiv, 3.

पय 1. *paya*. See *kat-payá*.

पय 2. *paya*, in comp. for *°yas*. **-āhuti**, f. an oblation of milk, ŚBr. **Payôpavasana**, n. a kind of fast when milk is the only food, Pāṇ. vi, 3, 109, Vārtt. 6, P. **Payôshṇī** (MBh.; Var.; Pur.), **°ṇikā** (VP.), f. N. of a river rising in the Vindhya mountain; *°ṇī-jātā*, f. N. of the river Sarasvatī, L.

Payaḥ, in comp. for *°yas*. **-kandā**, f. Batatas Paniculata, L. **-kshīra**, n. a partic. extract from barley, L. **-payôshṇī** = *Payôshṇī*, MBh. **-pāna**, n. drinking milk, a draught of m°, Pāṇ. vi, 2, 150, Kāś. **-pāyikā**, f., id. iii, 3, 111, Kāś. **-pārâvara**, m. the ocean of m°, Kāv. **-pūra**, m. flood of water, Ratnāv. **-pratibimba**, n. the reflected image or fancied appearance of w° (in deserts), Subh. **-pheṇī**, f. a partic. small shrub, L. **-sāman**, n. N. of a Sāman, ĀrshBr. **-sphāti** (*pá°*), f. abundance of milk, AV. xix, 31, 10 (printed *gáyasph°*).

Payaś, in comp. for *°yas*. **-caya**, m. a reservoir, piece of water, lake, L.

Páyas, n. (√1. *pī*) any fluid or juice, (esp.) milk, water, rain; semen virile, (met.) vital spirit, power, strength, RV. &c. &c.; a species of Andropogon, Bhpr.; N. of a Sāman, ŚrS.; of a Virāj, RPrāt.; night, Naigh. i, 7. **-kaṇsa**, m. a cup of milk, L. **-karṇī**, f., Pāṇ. viii, 3, 46, Sch. (cf. *dadhi-karṇa*). **-kāma**, mfn. (prob.) wishing for milk, ib. **-kāmya**, Nom. P. *°yati*, to wish for m°, Pāṇ. viii, 3, 38, Vārtt. 2, Pat. **-kāra** (?), viii, 3, 46, Sch. **-kumbha**, m. a pitcher for holding m°, ib. **-kuśā**, f., ib. **-pa**, m. 'milk-drinker,' a cat, W.; night, MW.

-pati, m. N. of Vishṇu, Vishṇ. **-pá**, mfn. drinking m°, RV. **-pātra**, n. a m°-bowl, L. **-vat** (*pá°*), mfn. full of juice or sap, juicy, succulent, containing water or milk or semen; overflowing, exuberant, copious, powerful, strong, RV.; AV.; TS.; Br.; Gṛ-ŚrS.; (*ī*), f. the night, L.; pl. rivers, Naigh. i, 13. **-vala**, mf(*ā*)n. rich in milk, Hariv. (v. l. °*vin*); m. a goat, L. **-vin**, mfn. abounding in sap or milk, Br.; GṛS.; Mn.; MBh. &c.; (*nī*), f. a milch-cow, MBh.; Var.; Ragh.; a she-goat, L.; a river or N. of a r°, BhP. (cf. g. *pushkarâdi*); the night, L.; N. of sev. plants (Asteracantha Longifolia, Batatas Paniculata, = *kākolī, kshīra-kāk°, jīvantī, dugdha-phenī* &c.), Bhpr.; L.

Payasá, mfn. full of juice or sap, AV. (corrupted fr. *vāyasa*?); n. water, L.

Payasishṭha or **payishṭha**, mfn. superl. of *payas-vin*, Pat.

Payaska, mfn. (ifc.) = *payas*, L.

1. **Payasya**, mfn. made of milk (as butter, cheese &c.), Lāṭy.; m. a cat, L.; N. of a son of Aṅgiras, MBh.; (*ā*), f. coagulated m°, curds (made by mixing sour with hot sweet m°), TS.; Br.; ŚrS.; N. of sev. plants (Gynandropsis Pentaphylla, = *kākolī, kuṭumbinī, dugdhikā* &c.), L.

2. **Payasya**, Nom. P. °*syati*, to flow, become liquid, g. *kaṇḍv-ādi*); Ā. °*syate* = next, Pāṇ. iii, 1, 11, Vārtt. 1, Pat.

Payāya, Nom. Ā. °*yate*, to be fluid, Pāṇ. ib.

Payishṭha. See *payasishṭha* above.

Payo, in comp. for °*yas*. **-gaḍa**, m. (w. r. for *guḍa*?) 'water-drop,' hail, L.; m. n. an island, L. **-grahá**, m. an oblation of milk, ŚBr.; *-samarthana-prakāra*, m. N. of wk. **-ghana**, m. water-lump, hail, L. **-janman**, m. 'w°-birth-place,' a cloud, L. **-da**, mf(*ā*)n. milk-giving (as a cow), Hariv.; yielding water (as a cloud), Subh.; m. a cloud, Kālid.; Var. &c. (*-suhṛid*, m. 'friend of clouds,' a peacock, Sāh.); N. of a son of Yadu, Hariv.; (*ā*), f. N. of one of the Mātṛis attending on Skanda, MBh. **-duh**, mfn. yielding milk or semen, SV. **-dhara**, m. 'containing water or milk,' a cloud, Kāv.; Rājat.; (ifc. f. *ā*) a woman's breast or an udder, MBh.; Kāv. &c.; the root of Scirpus Kysoor, L.; a species of sugar-cane, L.; the cocoa-nut, L.; a species of Cyperus, L.; an amphibrach, Col.; °*rī-√bhū*, to become an udder, Ragh.; °*rônnati*, f. a high breast (and 'rising clouds'), Kāv. **-dhas**, m. (√1. *dhā*) a rainy cloud; the ocean, Uṇ. iv, 229, Sch. **-dhā**, mfn. (√*dhe*) sucking milk, RV. **-dhārā**, f. a stream of water (°*gṛiha*, n. a bath-room with flowing w°), Mṛicch.; N. of a river, Hariv. **-dhi**, m. 'w°-receptacle,' the ocean, Kāv.; *-ja*, n. 'sea-born,' Os Sepiae, L. **-dhika**, n. 'sea-foam,' cuttle-fish bone, L. **-dhra**, m. a woman's breast or an udder, Gal. (cf. *-dhara*). **-nidhana**, n. N. of a Sāman, Lāṭy. **-nidhi**, m. = *-dhi*, Kāv. **-bhaksha**, m. drinking (eating) only milk, SaṃhUp. **-bhṛit**, m. 'water-holder,' a cloud, Śiś. xvi, 61. **-maya**, mf(*ī*)n. consisting of w°, Kathās. **-mānushī**, f. a w°-nymph, Subh. **-mukha**, mfn. having milk on the surface, m°-faced, Hit. **-muc**, mfn. discharging or yielding w° or m°, MBh.; Hcat.; m. a cloud, MBh.; Var.; Kāv. **-'mṛita-tīrtha**, n. N. of a sacred bathing-place, Cat. **-raya**, m. the current of a river, ŚārṅgP. **-rāśi**, m. a piece of water, the ocean, ib.; N. of the number 4, L. **-ruha**, n. 'w°-growing,' a lotus, L. **-latā**, f. Batatas Paniculata, L. **-vāha**, m. 'w°-bearer,' a cloud, Ragh.; Var.; Rājat. **-vidārikā**, f. Batatas Paniculata, L. **-vṛidh**, mfn. full of sap, overflowing, exuberant, vigorous, RV. **-vrata**, n. a vow to subsist on nothing but milk, BhP.; offering m° to Vishṇu and subsisting upon it for 12 days (also for 1 or 3 days as a religious act), W.; (*pá°*), mf(*ā*)n. subsisting on nothing but m°, ŚBr.; °*tá-tā*, f. ib.

Payora, m. Acacia Catechu, L.

पर 1. *pára*, mf(*ā*)n. (√1. *pṛi*; abl. sg. m. n. *párasmāt*, °*rāt*; loc. *párasmin*, °*re*; nom. pl. m. *páre*, °*rās*, °*rāsas*; cf. Pāṇ. i, 1, 34; vii, 1, 16; 50) far, distant, remote (in space), opposite, ulterior, farther than, beyond, on the other or farther side of, extreme; previous (in time), former; ancient, past; later, future, next; following, succeeding, subsequent; final, last; exceeding (in number or degree), more than; better or worse than, superior or inferior to, best or worst, highest, supreme, chief (in the compar. meanings [where also *-tara*], with abl., rarely gen. or ifc.; exceptionally *param śatam*, more than a hundred, lit. 'an excessive h°, a h° with a surplus,' R.; *parāḥ koṭayaḥ*, Prab.; Hcat.), RV. &c. &c.; strange, foreign, alien, adverse, hostile, ib.; other than, different from (abl.), Prab.; left, remaining, Kathās.; concerned or anxious for (loc.), R.; m. another (different from one's self), a foreigner, enemy, foe, adversary, RV. &c. &c.; a following letter or sound (only ifc. mfn., e. g. *ta-para*, having *t* as the f° l°, followed by *t*), RPrāt.; Pāṇ.; (scil. *graha*) a subsidiary Soma-graha, TS.; N. of a king of Kosala with the patr. Āṭṇāra, Br.; of another king, MBh.; of a son of Samara, Hariv.; (sc. *prāsāda*) of the palace of Mitravindā, ib.; m. or n. the Supreme or Absolute Being, the Universal Soul, Up.; R.; Pur.; (*ā*), f. a foreign country, abroad (?), Kathās.; a species of plant, L.; N. of a sound in the first of its 4 stages, L.; a partic. measure of time, Sāy.; N. of a river MBh.; VP. (v. l. *pārā, veṇā, veṇṇā*); of a goddess (cf. s. v.), n. remotest distance, MBh.; highest point or degree, ib.; final beatitude, L. (also *-taram* and *parāt para-taram*); the number 10,000,000,000 (as the full age of Brahmā), VP.; N. of partic. Sāmans, Kāṭh.; any chief matter or paramount object (ifc. [f. *ā*] having as the chief object, given up to, occupied with, engrossed in, intent upon, resting on, consisting of, serving for, synonymous with &c., MBh.; Kāv. &c.); the wider or more extended or remoter meaning of a word, Jaim.; Kull.; (in logic) genus; existence (regarded as the common property of all things), W.; (*am*), ind. afterwards, later; (with abl.) beyond, after (e. g. *param vijñānāt*, beyond human knowledge; *astam-ayāt p°*, after sunset; *mattaḥ p°*, after me; *ataḥ p°* or *param ataḥ*, after this, farther on, hereafter, next; *itaḥ p°*, henceforward, from now; *tataḥ p°* or *tataś ca p°*, after that, thereupon; *nâsmāt p°* [for *nâsm° p°*], no more of this, enough), MBh.; Kāv. &c.; in a high degree, excessively, greatly, completely, ib.; rather, most willingly, by all means, ib.; I will, so be it, Divyāv.; at the most, at the utmost, merely, no more than, nothing but, ib.; but, however, otherwise (*param tu* or *param kiṃ tu*, id.; *yadi p°*, if at all, perhaps, at any rate; *na-p°*, not-but; *na p°-api*, not only-but also; *p° na-api na*, not only not-but not even; *na p°-yāvat*, not only-but even), ib.; (*páreṇa*), ind. farther, beyond, past (with acc.), RV. &c. &c.; thereupon, afterwards, later than, after (with abl. or gen.), Mn.; MBh. &c.; (*paré*), ind. later, farther, in future, afterwards, RV.; MBh.; Kāv. [Cf. Zd. *para*; Gk. *πέρā, πέρāν*; Lat. *peren-die*; Goth. *fairra*; Germ. *fern*; Eng. *far* and *fore*.] **-kathā**, f. pl. talk about another, Bhartṛ. **-kara-gata**, mfn. being in an°'s hands, Pañc. **-karman**, n. service for an°, Kām.; °*nirata*, m. 'engaged in s° for an°,' a servant, Var. **-kalatra**, n. an°'s wife; °*râbhigamana*, n. approaching an°'s w°, adultery, W. **-kāya-praveśana**, n. entering an°'s body (a supernatural art), Cat. **-kārya**, n. an°'s business or affair, Pañc. **-kāla**, mfn. relating to a later time, mentioned later (opp. to *pūrva-*), VPrāt. **-kṛiti**, f. the action or history of another, an example or precedent, Nyāyam., Sch.; Kull. **-kṛitya**, n. an°'s business or affair, Kāv.; mfn. busy for an°, hostile, Mudr.; *-paksha*, m. the h° party, ib. **-krama**, m. doubling the other (i. e. second) letter of a conjunction of consonants, RPrāt. **-krāthin**, m. N. of a Kuru warrior, MBh. **-krānti**, f. the greatest declination, inclination of the ecliptic, Sūryas. **-kshudrā**, f. pl. the very short verses (of Veda), VāyuP. (cf. *kshudra-sûkta*). **-kshetra**, n. another's field or wife (cf. *kshetra*), Mn.; the body in an° life, Pāṇ. v. 2, 92 (cf. *kshetriya*). **-khātaka**, mfn. dug by an°, AVPariś. **-gata**, mfn. being with or relating to an°, MBh. **-gāmin**, mfn. id., Pāṇ. i, 3, 72. **-guṇa**, (ibc.) the virtues of an° (*-grāhin*, mfn. assuming them), Kāv.; mfn. beneficial to an° or to a foe, R. **-gṛiha-vāsa** or **-geha-v°**, m. dwelling in an°'s house, Kāv. **-granthi**, m. 'extreme point of a limb,' an articulation, joint, L. **-glāni**, f. the subjugation of a foe, W. **-cakra**, n. the army of a foe, MBh.; Var. (Sch. 'a hostile prince'); *-sūdana*, m. destroyer of it, BhP. **-citta-jñāna**, n. knowing the thoughts of another, L. **-cintā**, f. thinking of or caring for an°, Kāv. **-cchanda**, m. an°'s will, BhP. (°*dânuvartana*, n. following it, L.); mfn. depending on an°'s will, subservient (also *-vat*), L. **-cchidra**, n. an°'s fault or defect, Kāv. **-ja**, mfn. being behind an°, inferior, Kāṭh.; coming from a foe, MBh. **-jana**, m. an° person, a stranger; (coll.) strangers (opp. to *sva-j°*), Mn. xi, 9. **-janman**, n. a future birth; °*mika*, mfn. relating to it, MW. **-jāta**, m. 'born of another,' a stranger or servant, L. (v. l. *-jita*, 'conquered by an°'). **-jñāna-maya**, mf(*ī*)n. consisting in knowledge of the Supreme Being, VP. **-taṅgaṇa**(?), m. pl. N. of a people, MBh. **-tattva**, in *-nirṇaya*, m., *-prakāśikā*, f., *-vāda*, m. N. of wks. **-tantra**, n. a rule or formula for another rite, KātyŚr.; mf(*ā*)n. dependent on or subject to an°, obedient (opp. to *sva-t°*), MBh.; Kāv.; Suśr. &c.; n. (ibc.) and *-tā*, f. (Sāh.) dependence on an°'s will, Sāh.; *-dṛishṭi*, mfn. one who asserts the dependence of the will, Jātakam.; *-haṅsôpanishad*, f. N. of an Up.; °*trī-kṛita*, mfn. made dependent, brought into another's power, Kull.; ceded, sold, Kathās. **-tama** and **-tara**, mfn. superl. and compar. of *para*. **-tarkaka** or **-tarkuka**, m. a beggar, Var. **-talpa**, m. pl. another's wife, Āpast.; *-gāmin*, m. one who approaches an°'s wife, ib. **-tas**, ind. = abl. of *para*, Kāv.; Pur.; farther, far off, afterwards, behind (*itas-paratas*, here-there; *sapta purushān itaś ca paraś ca*, seven ancestors and seven descendants, Gaut.; *sani parataḥ*, sc. *sati*, when *san* follows, Pāṇ. ii. 4, 48, Sch.), RPrāt.; Hariv.; R. &c.; high above (in rank), Rājat.; (with prec. abl.) after (in time), MBh.; Yājñ. &c.; beyond, above (in rank), Bhag.; Kām.; otherwise, differently, W.; °*taḥ-posha*, mfn. receiving food from another, BhP.; *-°tas-tva*, n. (the state of) being from elsewhere or without, Sarvad. **-tā**, f. highest degree, absoluteness, (ifc.) the being quite devoted to or intent upon, Bhāshāp.; Rājat. **-tāpana**, m. 'paining foes,' N. of a Marut, Hariv. **-tīrthika**, m. the adherent of another sect, L. **-toshayitṛi**, mfn. gratifying others, Śiś. **-tra**, ind. elsewhere, in another place, in a future state or world, hereafter, Mn.; MBh. &c.; below i. e. in the sequel (of a book), Vop., Sch.; *-bhīru*, m. 'one who stands in awe of futurity,' a pious or religious man, W. **-tvá**, n. distance, remoteness, consequence, posteriority, difference, strangeness, superiority to (gen.), Āpast.; MBh.; Pur. &c.; = *-tā*, Kap.; *-ratnâkara*, m. N. of wk. **-dāra**, m. sg. or pl. another's wife or wives, Mn.; MBh. &c.; adultery, Gaut. xxii, 29; *-gamana*, n., °*râbhigamana*, n., °*râbhimarśa*, m., °*rôpasevana*, n. (°*vā*, f.) approaching or touching or courting an°'s wife or wives, adultery, W.; *-parigraha* (R.), *-bhuj* (MārkP.), *-°dārin* (R.), m. one who takes or approaches or enjoys an°'s wife or wives, an adulterer, R. **-duḥkha**, n. an°'s pain or sorrow, W. **-dūshaṇa**, m. (sc. *saṃdhi*) peace purchased by the entire produce of a country, Kām.; Hit. (v. l. *para-bhūshaṇa* and *pari-bh°*). **-devatā**, f. the highest deity, ĀpŚr., Sch.; *-stuti*, f. N. of a hymn. **-deśa**, m. another or a foreign or a hostile country (opp. to *sva-d°*), Var.; Kaṭh.; Pañc.; *-sevin*, mfn. living abroad, a traveller, W.; °*śin*, mfn. foreign, exotic; m. a foreigner or a traveller, ib. **-dosha**, in *-kīrtana*, n. the proclaiming of another's faults, censoriousness, W.; *-jña*, mfn. knowing an°'s faults, Subh. **-dravya**, n. pl. an°'s property, Hit.; °*vyâpahâraka*, mfn. robbing an°'s pr°, Mn. **-droha**, m. injuring an°, ŚārṅgP.; *-karma-dhī*, mfn. inj° an° in deed or thought, Mn.; °*hin*, mfn. tyrannizing over an°, W. **-dveshin**, mfn. hating an°, inimical to an°, W. **-dhana**, n. an°'s wealth, VP.; °*nâsvādana-sukha*, n. feeding luxuriously at an°'s expense, Hit. **-dharma**, m. an°'s duty or business, the duties of an° caste, Mn.; BhP.; an°'s peculiarity (*-tva*, n.), Kap. **-dhyāna**, n. intent meditation, W. **-nindā**, f. reviling others, MW. **-nipāta**, m. the irregular posteriority of a word in a compound (opp. to *pūrva-n°*), Pāṇ., Sch. **-nirmita-vaśa-vartin**, m. 'constantly enjoying pleasures provided by others,' N. of a class of Buddh. deities, Lalit. (cf. MWB. 208). **-nirvāṇa**, n. the highest Nirvāṇa (with Buddhists), Sarvad. **-m-tapa**, mfn. destroying foes (said of heroes), MBh.; R. &c.; m. N. of a son of Manu Tāmasa, Hariv.; of a prince of Magadha, Ragh. **-paksha**, m. the other side, hostile party, enemy, Hit.; N. of a son of Anu, VP. (v. l. *paramêkshu*). **-patnī**, f. the wife of another or of a stranger, Mn.; Kathās. **-pada**, n. the highest position, final emancipation, Mahān. **-parigraha**, m. another's property, Āpast.; an°'s wife, Mn. ix, 42, 43. **-paribhava**, m. humiliation or injury suffered from others, Mṛicch. **-parivāda**, m. = *-nirvāda*, Pañc. **-pāka**, m. another's food or meal, Mn. &c.; *-nivṛitta*, m. one who cooks his own food without observing a partic. ceremony, W.; *-rata*, m. one who lives upon others but observes the due ceremonies, ib.; *-ruci*, m. a constant guest at others' tables, ib.; °*kôpabhojin*, mfn. eating another's or a stranger's food, Suśr. **—pāra-bhūta,** m. N. of Vishṇu, VP. **—piṇḍa,** in *-pushṭaka*, m. 'nourished by an°'s food,' a servant, Mṛicch. viii, $\frac{25}{26}$; °*ddda*, m. 'eating an°'s food,' id., L. **—puraṃjaya,** mfn. conquering an enemy's city (said of heroes), MBh.; R. &c.; m. N. of a king, VP. **—pura-praveśa,** m. entering an enemy's city (as a supernatural art), Sāṃkhyas., Sch. **—purusha,** m. the husband of another woman, Kālid.; 'the Supreme Spirit,' N. of Vishṇu, L. **—pushṭa,** mfn. nourished by an° or a stranger, L.; m. the Kokila or Indian cuckoo (cf. *-bhṛit* below and *anya-p*°), MBh.; Kāv. &c.; (*ā*), f. a female cuckoo, Var.; a harlot, L.; a parasitical plant, L.; N. of a daughter of a king of Kauśāmbī, Kathās.; *-maya*, mf(*ī*)n. being a cuckoo, Hcar.; *-mahôtsava*, m. 'the c°'s great feast,' a mango tree, L. **—pūrusha,** m. the husband of another woman, Kathās. **—pūrva-tva,** n. the state of preceding that which ought to follow, Sāy. on RV. i, 53, 9. **—pūrvā,** f. a woman who has had a former husband, Mn. v, 163; *-pati*, m. her husband, ib. iii, 166. **—paurava-tantava,** m. N. of a son of Viśvāmitra, MBh. **—prakāśaka** and **-praṇava,** m. N. of 2 poets, Cat. **—prayojana,** mf(*ā*)n. useful or beneficial to others, Ragh. **—pravādin,** m. a false teacher, Divyâv. **—prêshya-tva,** n. the service of another, slavery, Mn. xii, 78. **—bala,** n. the foe's army, Mn. vii, 174. **—balīyas,** mfn. each more important than the preceding, Gaut. **—brahman,** n. the Supreme Spirit or Brahman, Bhartṛ.; N. of an Up.; °*ma-prakāśikā*, f., °*ma-stotra*, n., °*mânanda-bodha*, m., °*mâshṭôttara-śata-nāman*, n., °*môpanishad*, f. N. of wks. **—bhāga,** m. superior power or merit, excellence, supremacy, Kālid. (*-tā*, f.); Pañc.; Kathās.; good fortune, prosperity, L.; the last part, remainder, W. **—bhāgya,** n. another's wealth or prosperity, W.; °*gyôpajīvin*, mfn. living upon an°'s fortune, MW. **—1. -bhāva,** mf(*ā*)n. loving another, MBh. **—2. -bhāva,** m. the being subsequent or second member in a compound, Pat. (cf. *-bhūta*). **—bhāshā,** f. a foreign language, L. **—bhū,** in *-jāti-nirṇaya*, m., *-prakaraṇa*, n. N. of wks. **—bhūta,** mfn. following or subsequent (said of words), Kāś. on Pāṇ. viii, 1, 36. **—bhūmi,** f. a foreign or hostile country; *-shṭha*, mfn. being in it, Hit. **—bhūshaṇa,** n. another's ornament, W. (w. r. for *pari-bh*° and *para-dūshaṇa*). **—bhṛit,** mfn. nourishing an°, BhP.; m. a crow, L. (cf. next). **—bhṛita,** m. 'nourished by another,' the Kokila or Indian cuckoo (supposed to leave its eggs to be hatched by the crow), Kāv.; (*ā*), f. the female K°, ib.; *-maya*, mf(*ī*)n. consisting entirely of cuckoos, Kād. **—bhṛitikā,** f. a female cuckoo, Mālav.; N. of a woman, ib. **—bhṛitya,** mfn. to be nourished or supported by another (*-tva*, n.), Hariv.; R. **—bhedaka** (W.), **-bhedana** (Śiś.), mfn. destroying enemies. **—maṇi,** m. 'excellent jewel,' N. of a prince, Kathârṇ. **—mata,** n. a different opinion or doctrine, heterodoxy, W.; *-kālânala*, m. N. of a pupil of Śaṃkara, Cat.; *-khaṇḍana-saṃgraha*, m., *-bhaṅga*, m., *-bhañjana*, n. N. of wks. **—mada,** m. highest degree of intoxication, ŚārṅgS. **—mantra,** v. l. for *mātra*. **—manthu** or **-manyu,** m. N. of a son of Kaksheyu, Hariv. (v. l. °*marksha*). **—marma** (for *-marman*), in *-jña*, mfn. knowing the secret plans or intentions of another, Mn. vii, 154, Kull.; *-bhāshaṇa*, n. telling another's secrets, Siṇhās. **—mātra,** m. or n. (with Buddhists) a partic. high number (v. l. *-mantra*). **—māra,** m. N. of a son of the Ṛishi Śaunaka and ancestor of Bhoja-deva, Inscr.; Cat. (cf. *-mṛityu*). **—mukha-capeṭikā,** f. 'slap in the face of another,' N. of a controversial wk. **—mṛityu,** m. a crow, L. (cf. *-māra*). **—moksha-nirāsa-kārikā,** f. pl. 'memorial rules for preventing another's final beatitude,' N. of wk. **—m-para,** mfn. one following the other, proceeding from one to another (as from father to son), successive, repeated, MBh.; Suśr.; (*am*), ind. successively, uninterruptedly, VPrāt.; m. a great great-grandson or great-grandson with his descendants, L.; a species of deer, L.; *-tas*, ind. successively, continually, mutually, W.; *-bhojana*, n. eating continually, L. **—m-parā,** f. an uninterrupted row or series, order, succession, continuation, mediation, tradition (°*rayā*, ind. by tradition, indirectly), MBh.; Kāv. &c.; lineage, progeny, L.; hurting, killing, L.; *-prâpta* (Bhag.), *-°yāta* (°*râ*y°, Var.), mfn. received by tradition; *-vāhana*, n. an indirect means of conveyance (e. g. the horse which draws a carriage), L.; *-sambandha*, m. an indirect conjunction, Pāṇ. viii, 1, 24, Sch. **—parāka,** m. immolating an animal at a sacrifice, L. **—parita,** mfn. forming an uninterrupted series, continuous, Kpr. **—pariṇa,** mf(*ā*)n. hereditary, traditional, Bhaṭṭ. **—yuvati-ga,** m. = *-dārin*, Var. **—yoshit,** f. another's wife, Gaut. **—ramaṇa,** m. 'a strange lover,' a paramour, Pañc. **—rāshṭra,** n. the country of an enemy, Kull. on Mn. vii, 153. **—rūpa,** n. the following or subsequent sound (*-tva*, n.), Pāṇ.; Sāy. **—loka,** m. the other or future world, ŚBr.; Mn.; MBh. &c.; *-ga*, *-gata*, mfn. going or gone to the f° w°, dying, dead, MBh.; Kāv.; *-gama*, m., *-gamana*, n. dying, death, L.; *-bādha*, m. loss of the f° w°, MW.; *-yāna*, n. = *-gama*, ib.; *-vaha*, mf(*ā*)n. (a river) flowing in or toward the other w°, MBh.; *-vidhi*, m. rites for the o° w°, funeral rites, Kum.; *-sthāna*, n. the state of (being in) the o° w°, SBr.; *-hasta*, mfn. holding in hand (i. e. quite certain of) the o° w°, Mṛicch. viii, $\frac{46}{0}$. **—1. -vat,** ind. like a stranger, Kathās. **—2. -vat,** mfn. subject to or dependent on (instr., gen., loc. or comp.), subservient, obedient, MBh.; Kālid.; helpless, destitute, Mālatīm. viii, $\frac{9}{10}$; *-tā*, f. subjection, obedience to, Vikr.; Rājat. **—varga,** m. the party or side of another, Cāṇ. **—vallabha,** m. pl. N. of a people, VP. **—vaśa,** mfn. subject to another's will, subdued or ruled by (comp.), subservient, obedient, Mn.; Pañc.; Hit.; °*śâkshepa*, m. an objection to anything under the pretext of being dependent on an°, Kāvyâd. ii, 150. **—vaśya,** mfn. = *-vaśa*; *-tā*, f., R. **—vastu,** m. N. of a poet, Cat. **—vācya,** mfn. blamable by others (*-tā*, f.), MBh.; n. another's fault or defect, Śiś. xvi, 30. **—vāṇi,** m. (L.) a judge; a year; N. of Kārttikeya's peacock. **—vāda,** m. the talk of others, popular rumour or report, slander, Pañc.; ŚārṅgP.; objection, controversy, Sāṃkhyak.; °*din*, m. an opponent, controversialist, Śatr. **—vāraṇa,** m. one who averts or drives away enemies, Vikr. iv, 19. **—vitta,** n. another's wealth, R. (w. r. *pari-*). **—vīra-han,** m. killer of hostile heroes, MBh. **—veśman,** n. another's house, Var.; the dwelling of the Supreme, L. **—vyākshepin,** mfn. scattering foes, Mcar. **—vyūha-vināśana,** m. the destroyer of an enemy's ranks, MBh. **—vrata,** m. N. of Dhṛita-rāshṭra, L. **—śakti,** m. N. of an author of Mantras, Cat. **—śarîrâveśa,** m. = *-kāya-praveśana*, ib. **—śāsana,** n. the order of another, MW. **—śiva,** m. N. of an author of Mantras, Cat.; *-mahima-stotra*, n. N. of a Stotra; °*vêndra-sarasvatī*, m. N. of an author. **—śuci,** m. N. of a son of Manu Auttama, MārkP. **—śrī,** f. another's good fortune, Siṇhās. **—śvas,** ind. the day after to-morrow, MBh.; Hariv. &c. (cf. *paraḥ-śvas* under *paras*). **—saṃgata,** mfn. associated or engaged i. e. fighting with another, MBh. **—saṃcāraka,** m. pl. N. of a people, VP. **—saṃjñaka,** m. 'called Supreme,' the soul, L. **—sambandha,** m. relation or connection with another; °*dhin*, mfn. related or belonging to an°, W. **—savarṇa,** mfn. homogeneous with a following letter, Pāṇ.; °*nī-√bhū*, to become h° &c., Pat. **—sasthāna,** mfn. = *-savarṇa*, Prāt. **—sāt-√kṛi,** to give (a woman) into the hands of another i. e. in marriage, Pañc. **—sevā,** f. service of an°, Kathās. **—strī,** f. the wife of an° or an unmarried woman depending on an°, Sāh. **—sthāna,** n. an° place, strange place, Hit. **—sva,** n. sg. or pl. an°'s property, Mn.; MBh. &c.; mfn. = *sarvasva-bhūta*, MantraBr., Sch.; *-graha*, m. seizing an°'s pr°, Prab.; *-tva*, n. an°'s right, W. (*-tvâpâdāna*, n. conferring a r° upon an° as by gift &c., ib.); *-haraṇa*, n. = *-graha*, L.; *-hṛit* (Var.), *-°svâdāyin* (Mn.), mfn. taking or seizing an°'s property; *-°svêhā*, f. desire of an°'s pr°; *-°svôpajīvika* (W.), °*jīvin* (R.), mfn. living upon an°'s pr°, dependent. **—haṇsa,** m. = *parama-h*°, Cat. **—han,** m. 'foe-killer,' N. of a prince, MBh. **—hita,** mfn. friendly, benevolent, W.; n. an°'s welfare, Bhartṛ.; *-grantha*, m. N. of wk.; *-rakshita*, m. N. of an author; *-saṃhitā*, f. N. of wk. **Parâṅkuśa,** in *-nātha*, m. N. of an author, *-pañcaviṇśati*, f., *-pādukā-pañcāśat*, f., *-kuśâshṭaka*, n. N. of Stotras. **Parâgama,** m. the arrival or attack of an enemy, Var. **Parâṅga,** n. the hinder part of the body, Kāv.; a part of that which follows, Pāṇ. ii, 1, 2. **Parâṅga-da,** m. 'giving form to another (sc. to Durgā with whom he forms one body, or to Kāma-deva whose body he restored after reducing it to ashes),' N. of Śiva, L. **Parâcita,** m. 'nourished by an°,' a servant, L. **Parâtman,** m. the Supreme Spirit, BhP.; mfn. one who considers the body as the soul, MBh.; BhP. **Parâdhi,** m. or f. 'the paining of others (?),' hunting, L. **Parâdhīna,** mf(*ā*)n. = °*ra-vaśa*, Mn.; MBh. &c.; (ifc.) entirely engaged in or intent upon or devoted to, Kād.; Rājat.; *-tā*, f. (Kāv.), *-tva*, n. (MW.) dependence upon another, subjection. **Parânanda** (or °*rân*°? cf. under *parā* below), m. N. of an author; *-purāṇa*, n. N. of wk. **Parânīka,** n. a hostile army, Mālatīm. **Parânta,** m. 'the last end,' death (*-kāla*, m. time of d°), MuṇḍUp.; 'living at the remotest distance,' N. of a people, MBh. **Parântaka,** m. a frontier, Divyâv.; pl. N. of a people, L. **Parânna,** n. the food of another, Kāv.; KātyŚr., Sch.; *-paripushṭatā*, f. the living on an°'s food, Yājñ.; *-bhojin*, mfn. eating an°'s food, Hit.; m. a servant, L. **Parâpara,** mfn. remote and proximate, prior and posterior (as cause and effect), earlier and later, higher and lower, better and worse, MBh.; Kāv. &c.; m. = *-guru* below; n. (in logic) a community of properties in a small class under the larger or generic, a species or class between the genus and individual, W.; Grewia Asiatica, Bhpr.; *-guru*, m. a Guru of an intermediate class; N. of the goddess Durgā, W. (cf. *parât-para-g*°); *-jña*, knowing what is remote and proximate &c., MBh.; *-tā*, f., *-tva*, n. higher and lower degree, absolute and relative state, priority and posteriority; the state of being both a genus and a species, Bhāshāp.; *-drishṭârtha*, mfn. knowing the real nature of the remote and proximate &c., Hariv.; °*rêśa*, m. 'lord of the r° and pr°. &c.,' N. of Vishṇu, VP.; °*râtri* (*pârâp*°), mfn. going after another, going in a line (to the next world), AV. 1. **Parâmṛita,** n. (for 2. see p. 590, col. 2) 'the best nectar,' rain, L. 1. **Parâyaṇa,** n. (for 2. see p. 590, col. 3) final end or aim, last resort or refuge, principal object, chief matter, essence, summary (°*naṃ √kṛi*, to do one's utmost), ŚBr.; Up.; MBh. &c.; (in medic.) a universal medicine, panacea, Car.; a religious order or division, W.; (ifc.; f. *ā*) making anything one's chief object, wholly devoted or destined to, engaged in, intent upon, filled or occupied with, affected or possessed by (*-tā*, f., Daś.), Mn.; MBh. &c.; mf(*ā*)n. violent, strong (as pain), MBh. i, 8367 (Nīlak.); principal, being the chief object or final aim, ib.; dependent on (gen.), R.; leading or conducive to (gen.), MBh.; m. N. of a pupil of Yājñavalkya, VāyuP.; *-vat*, mfn. occupying the principal point, most elevated, MBh. **Parâyatta,** mf(*ā*)n. dependent upon another, R.; Pañc.; (ifc.) wholly subdued or overwhelmed by, Kād.; Bālar. **Parâyus,** m. 'one who has reached the highest age or 100 years,' N. of Brahmā, BhP. **Parârtha,** m. the highest advantage or interest, an important object, MBh.; sexual intercourse, Pañc.; an°'s adv° or int° (ibc., °*rtham* or °*rthe*, ind. for another or for others or for something else), Mn.; MBh.; Kāv. &c.; mfn. (also *-ka*) having an° object; designed for an°; dependent on something else (*-tā*, f., *-tva*, n.), ŚrS.; Sāṃkhyak.; Tarka; *-cara*, mfn. intent upon an°'s welfare, Jātakam.; *-caryā*, f. care for an°'s w°, ib.; *-nishṭha*, mfn. fixed on the supreme good, MW.; *-vādin*, mfn. speaking for another, a mediator, a substitute, Yājñ., Sch.; °*rthin*, mfn. striving after the supreme good (emancipation), Cāṇ. **Parârdhá,** m. the more remote or opposite side or half, Br.; KaṭhUp.; MBh.; m. n. the highest number (100,000 billions), VS.; TS.; MBh. &c.; the number of mortal days corresponding to 50 years of Brahmā's life, Pur.; (as mfn. w. r. for °*dhya*.) **Parârdhaka,** m. or n. one half of anything, Kāv. **Parârdhyà,** mf(*ā*)n. being on the more remote or opposite side or half, ŚBr.; most distant in number, of the highest possible number, ib.; highest in rank or quality, most excellent, best, Br.; ChUp.; MBh. &c.; more excellent than (abl.), Ragh. x, 65; n. a maximum (only ifc. 'amounting at the most to'), GṛŚrS. **Parârbuda,** m. a species of fire-fly, L. **Parâvajñā,** f. insulting another, MW. **Parā-vat** (for °*ra-vat*), mfn. offering beatitude, Āpast. **Parâvara,** mf(*ā*)n. distant and near, earlier and later, prior and subsequent, highest and lowest, all-including (*-tva*, n.), MBh.; Pur. &c.; handed down from earlier to later times, traditional, MuṇḍUp.; each successive, BhP.; m. pl. ancestors and descendants, Mn. i, 105; iii, 38; n. the distant and near &c.; cause and effect, motive and consequence, the whole extent of an idea, totality, the universe, MuṇḍUp.; MBh.; Vedântas.; *-jña* (MBh.), *-dṛiś* (MW.), *-vid* (BhP.), mfn. knowing or seeing both distant and near or past and future &c.; *-vibhāga-vid*, mfn. knowing the difference between the d° and n° &c., MBh.; °*rêśa*, m. N. of Vishṇu, VP. (cf. *parâpareśa*). **Parâvasatha-śāyin,** mfn. sleeping in another's house, Hit. **Parâśraya,** m. dependence on others, Hariv.; a refuge to enemies, BhP.; mfn. clinging to others, dependent on others, Śiksh.; (*ā*), f. a parasitical plant, L. **Parâśrita,** mfn. = (and v.l. for) prec. mfn.; a dependent, servant, slave, Hit. **Parâsaṅga,** m. cleaving or adhering to (comp.), Suśr. **Parâskandin,** m. 'assailing another,' a thief, robber, L. **Parâha,** m. the next day, L. **Parâhata,** m. struck by an°, assailed, attacked, W. **Parâhṇa,** m. the afternoon, Var.; Pañc. (w.r. °*hna*). **Parêtara,** mfn. other than hostile, faithful, friendly, Kir. i, 14. **Parêśa,** m. 'the highest lord,' N. of Brahmā or Vishṇu, Pur.; °*śêśa*, m. 'l° of the h° l°,' N. of Vishṇu, MBh. **Parêshṭi,** m. 'having the highest worship,' N. of Brahman, W. **Parêshṭukā,** f. 'highest desire (?),' a cow which has often calved, L. **Parâidhita,** m. 'nourished by another,' the Indian cuckoo (cf. *para-bhṛita*); a servant, L. **Parôkta-khaṇḍana,** n. 'refutation of an°'s words,' N. of wk. **Parôḍhā,** f. an°'s wife, Sāh. **Parôdvaha,** m. 'descendant of an° i.e. of the crow,' the Indian cuckoo, Gal. (cf. *para-bhṛita*). **Parôpakaraṇa,** n. = *-kāra*, Cāṇ.; °*ṇī-√kṛi*, to make one's self an instrument of others, Hit. **Parôpakāra,** m. assisting others, benevolence, charity, Kāv.; °*râi-karasa*, mfn. wholly devoted to the service of others; (*ā*), f. a wife wholly devoted to her husband, MW.; *-dharma-kshānti*, f., Dharmas. 107. **Parôpakārin,** mfn. assisting others, beneficent, charitable, merciful, Kathās. (°*ri-tva*, n., Bhartṛ.); m. N. of a king, Kathās. **Parôpakṛita,** mfn. helped or befriended by another, MW. **Parôpakṛiti,** f. = *-kāra*, ib. **Parôpaga,** mfn. relating to something else (as an adjective), L. **Parôpajāpa,** m. the dissension (or causing d°) of enemies, Daś. **Parôpadeśa,** m. giving advice or instruction to others, Hit. **Parôparuddha,** mfn. besieged by an enemy, blockaded, invested, MW. **Parôpavāsa,** m. dwelling together with another, Āpast. **Parôpasarpaṇa,** n. approaching another, begging, Bhām.

2. **Para,** in comp. for °*ras*. **-uru** (°*rá-*), mf(*vī*)n. broad on the outside or behind, ŚBr. (cf. *paro-varīyas*). **-ushṇih,** f. a kind of metre, Chandaḥs. (also *parôshṇih*, ib.) **-ṛik-śata-gāthā,** mfn. containing 100 verses of the Veda as well as Gāthās, AitBr.

Paraḥ, in comp. for °*ras*. **-kṛishṇa,** mfn. more than black, extremely dark, ChUp. **-puṅsā,** f. (a wife) dissatisfied with her husband, ŚBr. **-purusha,** mfn. higher than a man, ŚāṅkhŚr. **-śatá,** mf(*ā*)n. pl. more than 100, ŚBr.; Kāṭh.; MBh.; containing more than 100 verses, TBr.; *-rg-gātha* (*r* for *ṛi*), mfn. = *para-ṛik-śata-gātha*, ŚāṅkhŚr. **-śvas,** ind. = *para-śv°*, L. **-shashṭá,** mfn. pl. more than 60, ŚBr. **-sahasrá** (AV.; *páraḥ-sahasra*, ŚBr.), mf(*ā*)n. pl. more than 1000. **-sāman** (*pá°*), mfn. having superfluous or surplus Sāmans; m. pl. N. of partic. sacrificial days, TS.; TBr.; Kāṭh.

Paraka, ifc. = *para*, 'the following sound or word,' e.g. *iti-śabda-p°*, followed by the word *iti*, Pāṇ., Sch.

Parakīya, mf(*ā*)n. belonging to another or a stranger, strange, hostile (*-tā*, f.), Mn. (*nipāna*, n. a tank belonging to an°, iv, 201); Śak.; Kām.; (*ā*), f. an°'s wife or a woman dependent on others (*-tva*, n.), Sāh.

Paramá, mf(*ā*)n. (superl. of *pára*) most distant, remotest, extreme, last, RV. &c. &c.; chief, highest, primary, most prominent or conspicuous; best, most excellent, worst (°*meṇa cetasā*, with all the heart; °*ma-kaṇṭhena*, 'with all the throat,' roaring, speaking aloud), ib.; (with abl.) superior or inferior to, better or worse than, MBh.; R.; m. N. of 2 authors, Cat.; n. highest point, extreme limit (*catur-viṅśati-p°*, at the utmost 24), MBh. &c.; chief part or matter or object (ifc., f. *ā* = consisting chiefly of, completely occupied with or devoted to or intent upon), Mn.; MBh.; Kāv. &c.; (*am*), ind. yes, very well; (also *parama-* in comp.; see below) very much, excessively, excellently, in the highest degree, MBh.; Kāv. &c. **-kaṇṭha,** only in °*thena √kruś*, to try with all one's throat i.e. might, Lāṭy. **-kāṇḍa,** m. or n. a very auspicious moment, Vāsav. **-krānti,** f. = *para-kr°*; *-jyā*, f. the sine of the greatest declination, Sūryas., Sch. **-kruddha,** mfn. extremely angry, R. **-krodhin,** m. id., N. of one of the Viśve-devās, MBh. **-gati,** f. any chief resource or refuge (as a god or protector), W.; final beatitude, ib. **-gava,** m. an excellent bull, L. **-gahana,** mfn. very mysterious or profound, W. **-cetas,** n. all the heart, MW. **-jā,** f. = *prakṛiti*, TS., Sch. (prob. corrupted). **-jyā,** mfn. holding supreme power (as Indra), RV. **-tattva,** n. the highest truth; *-prakāśikā*, f., *-rahasyôpanishad*, f. N. of wks. **-tas,** ind. in the highest degree, excessively; worst of all, MW. **-tā** (°*má-*), f. highest position or rank; highest end or aim, ŚBr. **-dāruṇa,** mfn. very dreadful, MBh. **-duḥkhita,** mfn. deeply afflicted, Nal. **-durmedhas,** mfn. exceedingly stupid, MW. **-dru,** m. Amyris Agallocha, ib. **-dharmâtman,** mfn. very dutiful or virtuous, MBh. **-nanda,** m. N. of a teacher, Cat. (w.r. for °*mân°*?; cf. *parân°* under *para*). **-pada,** n. the highest state or position, eminence, final beatitude, W.; *-nirṇāyaka*, m. and *-sopāna*, n. N. of wks.; °*dâtmavat*, mfn. whose essence is the highest of all states (i.e. Brahmā), VP. **-parama,** mfn. highest or most excellent of all, BhP. **-puṅs,** m. the Supreme Spirit, N. of Vishṇu, VP. **-purusha,** m. id.; *-prârthanā-mañjarī*, f., *-mahôtsava-prâyaścitta*, n., *-saṃhitā*, f. N. of wks. **-pūrusha,** m. = *-pur°*, RāmatUp. **-prabha,** m. N. of a man, L. **-prīta,** mfn. exceedingly rejoiced, MBh. **-brahmacāriṇī,** f. N. of Durgā, L. **-brahman,** n. the Supreme Spirit, W. **-bhāsvara,** mfn. excessively radiant, MW. **-manyumat,** mfn. deeply distressed, Nal. **-mahat,** mfn. infinitely great, Yogas. **-moksha,** m. final emancipation, Sāṃkhyapr. **-rasa,** m. 'most excellent beverage,' buttermilk mixed with water, L. **-rahasya,** n. the deepest mystery; *-japa-saṃgraha*, m., *-vāda*, m., *-saṃhitā*, f., °*syôpadeśa-saṃgraha*, m., °*syôpanishad*, f. N. of wks. **-rāja,** m. a supreme monarch, Laghuk. **-ṛksha** (° = *ma-ṛiksha*), m. N. of a king, Hariv. (v.l. *para-manthu* and *-manyu*). **-ṛddhika,** m. (°*ma-ṛiddhika*) excessively fortunate, HPariś. **-ṛshi,** m. (°*ma-ṛishi*) a great or divine sage, MBh.; Pur. &c. **-laghu-mañjūshā,** f. N. of wk. **-vismita,** mfn. greatly surprised or amazed, MW. **-vyomnika,** mfn. dwelling in the highest heaven, L. **-śiva** (with *ācārya* and °*vêndra-sarasvatī*), m. N. of authors. **-śobhana,** mfn. exceedingly brilliant or beautiful, MBh. **-saṃhitā,** f. N. of wk. **-saṃhṛishṭa,** mfn. = *-prīta*, Nal. **-saṃtushṭa,** mfn. highly pleased or satisfied, R. **-samudaya,** mfn. very auspicious or successful, Mṛicch. i, 4. **-saṃmata,** mfn. highly esteemed, much revered, MBh.; R. **-sarvatra,** ind. everywhere, throughout, L. **-svadharman,** mfn. most exact in the observance of the duties of one's own (caste or tribe), W. **-haṅsa,** m. an ascetic of the highest order, a religious man who has subdued all his senses by abstract meditation, MBh.; Pur. &c. (cf. RTL. 87); *-kavaca*, m. or n., *-dharma-nirūpaṇa*, n., *-nirṇaya*, m., *-pañcâṅga*, n., *-paṭala*, m. or n., *-paddhati*, f., *-parivrājaka-dharma-saṃgraha*, m. N. of wks.; *-parivrājakâcārya*, m. N. of Saṃkarâcārya; *-parivrājakôpanishad*, f., *-priyā*, f., *-saṃhitā*, f., *-sahasra-nāman*, n., *-stava-rāja*, m., *-stotra*, n., °*sôpanishad*, f. (°*shad-hṛidaya*, n.), °*sôpâsana-prakāra*, m. N. of wks. **Paramâkshara,** n. the sacred syllable 'Om' or Brahmā, VP., Sch. **Paramâkhya,** mfn. called supreme, considered as the highest, R. **Paramâgama,** in *-cūḍāmaṇi-saṃhitā*, f. and *-sāra*, m. N. of wks. **Paramâṅganā,** f. an excellent or beautiful woman, MBh.; R. **Paramâṭika,** m. N. of a school of the Yajus, AVPariś. (cf. °*mâvaṭ°*). **Paramâṇu,** m. an infinitesimal particle or atom (30 are said to form a mote in a sun-beam), Yājñ.; Yogas.; MBh. &c. (cf. *bhṛitya-p°*); the passing of a sun-beam past an atom of matter, Pur.; n. $\frac{1}{8}$ of a Mātrā, VPrāt.; *-kāraṇa-vāda*, m. the atomistic system of the Vaiśeshikas, Saṃk.; *-tā*, f. infinite minuteness, the state of an atom, Ragh.; BhP.; *-maya*, mf(*ī*)n. consisting merely of atoms, BhP.; °*ṇv-aṅgaka*, m. 'subtle-bodied,' N. of Vishṇu, L. 1. **Paramâtmá,** m. a partic. personification, MaitrS. 2. **Paramâtma,** in comp. = °*tman*; *-gati-prakāśa*, m., *-prakāśa*, m., *-vinoda*, m., *-saṃdarbha*, m., *-stava*, m. N. of wks.; *-maya*, mf(*ī*)n. being entirely the soul of the universe, Hcar. **Paramâtmaka,** mf(*ikā*)n. the highest, greatest, MBh. **Paramâtman,** m. all the heart (only instr. = *parameṇa cetasā*, col. 1), MBh.; the Supreme Spirit, Up.; Mn.; MBh. &c. (cf. RTL. 37). **Paramâdîśvara** (!), m. N. of Sch. on Āryabh. **Paramâdvaita,** m. 'the highest being without a second,' N. of Vishṇu, GaruḍaP.; n. pure, non-duality, W. **Paramânanda,** m. supreme felicity; the Supreme Spirit, soul of the universe, MBh.; Bhartṛ. &c.; N. of sev. authors (also *-cakravartin*, *-dāsa*, *-deva*, *-nātha*, *-pāṭhaka*, *-bhaṭṭâcārya*, *-yogîndra*, *-sarasvatī*, °*dâśrama*), Cat.; *-tantra*, n., *-mādhava-stava*, m., *-laharī-stotra*, n. N. of wks. **Paramânna,** n. 'best food,' rice boiled in milk with sugar (offered to gods or deceased ancestors), Hariv.; Var. &c. **Paramâpakrama,** m. = *para-krānti*, Sūryas. **Paramâpad,** f. the greatest misfortune, MW. **Paramâpama,** m. 'greatest declination,' the inclination of a planet's orbit to the ecliptic, W. **Paramâpsaras,** f. an excellent Apsaras, R. **Paramâmṛita,** n. N. of wk. **Paramâyusha,** m. Terminalia Tomentosa, L. **Paramâyus,** mfn. reaching to a very advanced age, Var. **Paramârâdhya,** m. N. of a man, Cat. **Paramârta,** mfn. much pained or depressed; *-vat*, ind. very piteously, R. **Paramârtha,** m. the highest or whole truth, spiritual knowledge, MBh.; Kāv.; Vedântas. &c. (ibc.; °*ena*, *āt*, in reality); any excellent or important object, W.; the best sense, ib.; the best kind of wealth, ib.; *-tas*, ind. in reality, really, in the true sense of the word, R.; Kālid. &c.; *-tā*, f. the highest truth, reality, Kap., Sch.; *-daridra*, mfn. really poor, Mṛicch.; *-darśana*, m. N. of a Samādhi, Kāraṇḍ.; *-nirṇaya*, m., *-prakāśa*, m., *-pradīpikā*, f., *-prapā*, f., *-bodha*, m. N. of wks.; *-bhāj*, mfn. partaking of the highest truth, Mcar.; *-matsya*, m. a real fish, Ragh.; *-vid*, m. one who knows the highest truth, a philosopher, W.; *-vinda*, mfn. acquiring knowledge of t°, obtaining the best kind of wealth &c., ib.; *-viveka*, m., *-saṃvṛiti-satya-nirdeśa*, m., *-saṃgraha*, m. N. of wks.; *-satya*, n. the real or entire truth, L.; *-saṃdarbha*, m. N. of wk.; *-sarit*, f. really a river, Vikr.; *-sāra*, m. (°*ra-saṃkshepa-vivṛiti*, f., °*ra-saṃgraha*, m.) N. of wks.; *-supta*, mfn. really asleep, Mṛicch.; *-stuti*, f. N. of wk. **Paramârya,** m. a Bodhi-sattva (q.v.), L. **Paramârhata,** m. 'most excellent Arhat,' N. of Kumāra-pāla, L. **Paramâvaṭika,** m. pl. N. of a school of the white Yajus, Āryav. (cf. °*mâṭika*). **Paramâvadhi,** m. utmost term or limit, W. **Paramâsana,** m. (with Śāktas) N. of an author of Mantras, Cat. **Paramâha,** m. an excellent day, L. **Paramêkshu,** m. N. of a son of Anu, VP. (v.l. °*mêshu*). **Paramêśa,** m. the supreme lord, Supreme Being, N. of Vishṇu, MBh.; *-stotrâvalī*, f. N. of wk. **Paramêśvara,** m. the supreme lord, Supreme Being, God; N. of Śiva; of Vishṇu; of Indra; of any eminent prince or illustrious man, MBh.; Kāv. &c. (cf. RTL. 35 &c.); a Jaina, L.; N. of sev. authors (°*rīya*, n. a work of P°), Cat.; (*ī*), f. N. of Durgā, Hariv.; of Sītā, RāmatUp. (°*rī-dāsâbdhi*, m. N. of wk.); n. (sc. *liṅga*) N. of a Liṅga sacred to Śiva, Cat.; *-tantra*, n. N. of wk.; *-tā*, f., *-tva*, n. supremacy, Sarvad.; *-datta*, m. N. of an author; *-pañca-mukha-dhyāna*, n., *-pañca-ratna*, n. N. of wks.; *-praṇidhāna*, n. meditation on God, Sarvad.; *-rakshita*, m. N. of an author; *-varman*, m. N. of a man, L.; *-saṃhitā*, f. N. of wk.; *-sâkshāt-kāra*, m. intuitive perception of God, Sarvad.; *-stuti*, f., *-stotra*, n. N. of wks.; °*râstitva-vādin*, m. one who asserts the existence of God, Sarvad. **Paramêshvāsa,** m. an excellent archer (*-tā*, f.), MBh. **Paramâiśvarya,** n. supremacy, Sāy. **Paramôpâsaka,** m. an excellent 'server' or layman, Buddh.; Hcar.

Paramaka, mf(*ikā*)n. the most excellent, highest, best, greatest, extreme, MBh.; R. &c. (w.r. *pār°* and *paramika*).

Parame, loc. of °*ma* in comp. **-shṭha,** mfn. standing at the top, supreme, superior, Pāṇ. viii, 3, 97; m. N. of Brahma or any supreme deity, W.; (*ā*), f. a kind of metre, L. **-shṭhi,** m. a superior or a chief god of the Jainas, Śatr.; *-tā*, f. supremacy, superiority, TāṇḍBr. **-shṭhin,** mfn. standing at the head, highest, chief, principal, AV. &c. &c.; m. N. of any supreme being, of Agni, AV.; of Prajā-pati, ib. &c.; a son of Pr°, Br.; of Brahmā, MBh.; of Śiva, ib.; of Vishṇu, Ragh.; of Garuḍa, MBh.; of Manu Cakshus, MārkP.; (with Jainas) = *-shṭhi*, L.; the teacher of the t° of any one's t°, L.; a kind of Virāj, RPrāt.; a kind of ammonite, L.; N. of a son of Aja-mīḍha, MBh.; of a son of Indradyumna (Devady°), Pur.; du. Vishṇu and Śrī, BhP.;

(*nī*), f. Ruta Graveolens, L. **-shṭhina** = *-shṭhin*, AV. xix, 9, 4.

Paras, in comp. for °*ras*. **-catvāriṅśá**, mfn. pl. more than forty, ŚBr.

Parás, ind. beyond, further, off, away; in future, afterwards; (as prep. with acc.) on the other side of, beyond, higher or more than; (with instr.) id. (also *pará enā́* or *enā́ paráḥ*); without; (with abl.) beyond, on the other side of (also *enā́ paráḥ*); exclusive of, except, without; (with loc.) over, more than (only *triṅśáti tráyas paráḥ*, three more than thirty, i. e. 33), RV.; VS.; AV.; ŚBr.; (often in comp. with numerals to express a surplus or superiority; cf. prec. and under *paraḥ*). **-tarám** (RV.), **-tarā́m** (AV.), ind. further away, further; *parastarām par*°, f° and f° away, TāṇḍBr. **-tāt** (*pár*°), ind. further away, further on, towards (opp. to *avastāt*, *arvāk*; with gen.) beyond, above, RV. &c. &c.; from afar off, from before or behind, Br.; aside, apart, ib.; hereafter, afterwards, later (opp. to *pūrvam*), RV. &c. &c. **-pa** (°*rás*), mfn. protecting; n. (VS.) = *-tvá*, n. (ŚBr.) protection. **-pā́**, m. a protector, protecting, RV.; TBr.; ŚrS.

Paras-para (fr. nom. sg. m. of *para* + *para*; cf. *anyo'nya*), mf(*ā*)n. mutual, each other's, Bhaṭṭ.; pl. like one another, MBh. xii, 2420; (mostly in the oblique cases of m. sg. °*am*, *eṇa*, *āt*, *asya*), ind. one another, each other, with or from one another, one another's, mutually, reciprocally, Mn.; MBh.; Kāv. &c.; so also ibc. (cf. below); rarely ifc., e. g. *avijñāta-parasparaiḥ*, 'not knowing each other,' Ragh. xvii, 51. **-jña**, m. 'knowing one another,' a friend, an intimate, W. **-prīti**, f. mutual delight or content, Pañc. **-viruddha**, mfn. opposed to o° an°, Mn. **-vivāda**, m. quarrelling with o° an°, Vet. **-vyāvṛitti**, f. mutual exclusion, Saṃk. **-sakhya**, n. m° friendship, Hit. **-samāgama**, m. the meeting one an°, R. **-sukhâishin**, mfn. wishing o° an°'s happiness, Nal. **-sthita**, mfn. standing opposite to o° an°, Ragh. **-hata**, mfn. killed by o° an°, Nal. **-hita**, n. o° an°'s happiness or welfare, R. **Parasparâkrandin**, mfn. calling to o° an°, Kum. **Parasparâdin**, mfn. consuming o° an° or one's own kind, Mn. **Parasparânumati**, f. mutual concurrence or assent, W. **Parasparâmishatā**, f. the being o° an°'s prey, Kām. **Parasparâśraya**, mfn. mutual, reciprocal, Ragh.; m. m° dependence (esp. as a fault in argument), L. **Parasparôtpīḍana**, n. m° pressing or squeezing, Ṛit. **Parasparôpakāra**, m. m° assistance; °*rin*, m. an ally or associate, W.

Parasmai, dat. of *para* in comp. (cf. *ātmane* and Pāṇ. vi, 3, 8). **-pada**, n. 'word for another,' the transitive or active verb and its terminations, Pāṇ. i, 4, 99, &c.; (pl.) iii, 4, 82. **-padin**, mfn. taking those terminations, Pāṇ., Sch. **-bhāsha**, mfn. id., Pat.; (*ā*), f. = *-pada*, Pāṇ., Sch.

1. **Parā** (for 2. see col. 2), f. of *para* in comp. **-cintāmaṇi**, m. N. of wk. **-triṅśikā**, f. N. of wk. **-devī**, f. a partic. form of Devī; *-rahasya-tantra*, n. N. of wk. **-púr**, f. a great body (?), VS., Sch. **-pūjā**, f., **-praveśikā**, f. N. of wks. **-prasāda-mantra**, m. N. of a partic. mystical prayer, L. **-rahasya**, n. N. of wk. **-vedī**, f. = *bṛihatī*, L. **-śakti**, f. (with Śāktas) a partic. form of Śakti, Cat. **-stotra**, n. N. of wk.

Parāt, abl. of *para* in comp. **-para**, mfn. superior to the best, W.; senior to the senior (cf. next); *-guru*, m. the teacher of the t° of the t° of a t°, Cat. (cf. *parâpara-g*° under *para*). **-priya**, m. a species of gourd, L.

Parāri, ind. (*para* + ?) in the year before last, Pāṇ. v, 3, 22. **Parāri-tna**, mfn. belonging to the year before last, iv, 3, 23, Vārtt.

1. **Pare** (for 2. see p. 606, col. 1), loc. of *para* in comp. **-dyavi**, ind. to-morrow, Naish. (cf. Pāṇ. v, 3, 22). **-dyus**, ind. id., W. **-'pa**, mfn. (fr. *ap*) any place whence the water has receded, L. **-prāṇa**, mfn. of higher value or more precious than life, Kathās.

Paro, in comp. for °*ras*. **'mhu** (°*rô*-), mf(*vī*)n. narrow on the outside or at the top, ŚBr. **'ksha** (°*rô*-), mf(*ā*)n. beyond the range of sight, invisible, absent, unknown, unintelligible, AV. &c. &c.; past, completed (in a partic. sense, cf. below and Kās. on Pāṇ. iii, 2, 115); (ibc.) in an invisible or imperceptible manner (cf. below); (*am*), ind. out of sight, behind one's back, in the absence or without the knowledge of (instr.; later gen. or comp.), ŚBr. &c. &c.; (*eṇa*), ind. out of sight, secretly, mysteriously, Br.; Up.; (*āt*), ind. secretly, without the knowledge of (instr.), Br.; (*e*), ind. behind the back of (gen.), Mṛicch.; Pañc. &c.; one's self not being present, Pāṇ. iii, 2, 115; m. an ascetic, L.; N. of a son of Anu, BhP.; (*ā*), f. (sc. *vritti*) a past or completed action, APrāt.; (sc. *vibhakti*) a termination of the perfect tense, Kāt.; N. of a river, VP.; *-kāma* (°*kshá*-), mfn. liking what is secret or mysterious, ŚBr.; *-kṛita*, mfn. (a hymn) in which a deity is not addressed but only spoken of in the 3rd person, Nir. vii, 1; *-jit*, mfn. victorious in an imperceptible manner, BhP.; *-tā*, f. (MBh.), *-tva*, n. (Vedântas.) invisibility, imperceptibility; *-pṛishṭha*, m. a partic. Pṛishṭhya, ŚrS.; *-priya*, mfn. = *-kāma*, AitBr.; *-bandhu* (*parô'ksha*-), mfn. not clear in its relation, MaitrS.; *-buddhi*, mfn. regarding as something distant, indifferent to, Jātak.; *-bhoga*, m. enjoyment or possession of anything in the proprietor's absence, W.; *-manmatha*, mfn. inexperienced in love, Śak.; *-vṛitti*, mfn. living out of sight, Kām.; formed in an obscure or indistinct manner, Nir., Sch.; °*kshârtha*, mfn. having a secret or recondite meaning; n. an absent or invisible object, Hit. **-gavyūti**, ind. beyond the area of pasture-land, RV.; mfn. further than a Gavyūti (q. v.), Kāṭh. **-goshṭhám**, ind. beyond the cowhouse, MaitrS. **-bāhú**, mfn. beyond the arm or reach, ŚBr. **-mātra** (°*rô*-), mfn. immense, huge, vast, RV. **-rajas** (°*rô*-), mfn. being beyond the dust or above the world, ŚBr.; untouched by passion, MW. **-laksha**, mfn. (pl.) more than 100,000, L. **-'varám**, ind. from top to bottom, from hand to hand, in succession, one after another, ŚBr.; ŚāṅkhŚr.; °*rīṇa*, mfn. (fr. prec.) having both superior and inferior, prior and subsequent &c., Pāṇ. v, 2, 10, Sch. **-varīyas** (°*rô*-), mfn. broader on the outside or at the top, TS.; AitBr.; Kāṭh.; better than good, most excellent of all, ChUp. (*-tva*, n., Bālar.); n. the highest happiness, ib. **-viṅśá**, mfn. pl. more than 20, ŚBr. **-'śītá**, mfn. pl. more than 80, ib. **-havis**, n. more than an oblation, Āpast. **-'hu**, w. r. for *'mhu* above.

परण *paraṇa*, mfn. (√1. *pṛi*) crossing (cf. *aritra*-); n. w. r. for *pāraṇa*, reading, Hariv.; N. of a town, Cat.

पररु *pararu*, m. a species of pot-herb, L. (v. l. *pavaru*).

परश *paraśa*, m. a species of gem, BrahmavP.

परशु *paraśú*, m. a hatchet, axe, the axe of a woodcutter; (Naigh. ii, 20) a thunderbolt, RV. &c. &c.; N. of a king, MBh.; w. r. for *parśu*, q. v. [Cf. Gk. πέλεκυς, πέλεκκον &c.] **-cara**, m. 'axe-bearer,' N. of Gaṇêśa; of Paraśu-rāma, L. **-palāśa**, m. the blade of an axe, Kauś. **-phāṇṭa**, m. or n. an infusion warmed by a heated axe, ib. **-mát**, mfn. having an axe, RV. **-rāma**, m. 'Rāma with the axe,' N. of one of the three Rāmas (son of Jamad-agni and sixth Avatāra of Vishṇu, he was a typical Brāhman and his history typifies the contests between the Brāhmans and Kshatriyas), Kāv.; Pur.; MWB. xiii, 1; RTL. 110; 270 (also *-ka*); N. of a prince and of sev. authors (also with *garjara*, *deva*, *miśra*, *muni*), Cat.; *-jayantī*, f. the third day in the light half of Vaiśākha, Cat.; *-prakāśa*, m., *-pratāpa*, m., *-sūtra*, n. N. of wks.; °*mâvatāra*, m. (and °*tāra-kathana*, n.) N. of wks. **-vana**, n., *-prādur-bhāva*, m., *-sahasra-nāman*, n. 'forest of axes,' N. of a hell, MBh. **-hastā**, f. 'axe in hand,' N. of a female attendant on Devī, W.

Paraśava (L.) and °**vya** (Pāṇ. iv, 1, 168), mfn. fr. *paraśu* (cf. *pāraśavya*).

Paraśvadha, m. (ifc. f. *ā*) a hatchet, axe, MBh.; Var.; Kāv. &c. (also written *parasv*°). **Paraśvadhâyudha**, mfn. armed with an axe, L.

Paraśvadhin, mfn. furnished with an axe, MBh.

परश्वत् *paraśvat* or °*śvan*, m. a kind of snake, KaushUp., Sch. (cf. next).

पारस्वत् *pārasvat*, m. (prob.) the wild ass, RV.; AV.; VS.; Nyāyam. (cf. prec. and *pārasvata*).

परा 2. *párā* (for 1. see col. 1), ind. away, off, aside, along, on, (Lat. *per*; it occurs only in *-taram* and *-vat*, and as a prefix to nouns and verbs; it is prob. akin to *para*, *paras*, *pra*.) **-tarám**, ind. further away, RV. **-vát**, f. distance (opp. to *arvā-vat*), ib.; AV.; Br.

पराक् *parāk*, *parāka* &c. See *parāñc*.

पराकाश *parā-kāśa*, m. (√*kāś*) distant view, remote expectation (only in *āśâ-parākāśau*), ŚBr.

पराकृ *parā-√kṛi*, P. *-karoti* (Pāṇ. i, 3, 79; p. *-kurvat*, Bhaṭṭ.), to set aside, reject, disregard. °**karaṇa**, n. setting aside, disdaining, W. **-kṛita**, mfn. set aside, rejected, disdained, ib.

पराकृष् *parā-√kṛish* (only ind. p. *-kṛishya*), to draw away or down, MBh. °**kṛishṭa**, mfn. disparaged, reviled, ib.

पराकॄ *parā-√kṝ* (only ind. p. *-kīrya*), to throw away, lose, forfeit, MBh.

पराक्रम् *parā-√kram*, P. Ā. *-kramati*, °*te* (cf. Pāṇ. i, 3, 39; ind. p. *-kramya*, AV.; ŚāṅkhŚr.; aor. *parâkraṅsta*, Bhaṭṭ.), to march forward, advance; to show courage or zeal, excel, distinguish one's self, AV. &c. &c.; to turn back, MW. °**krama**, m. (sg. and pl.; ifc. f. *ā*) bold advance, attack, heroism, courage, power, strength, energy, exertion, enterprise, MBh.; Kāv. &c.; going out or away, L.; N. of Vishṇu, L.; of a warrior on the side of the Kurus, MBh.; of a chief of the Vidyā-dharas (associated with Ā-krama, Vi-krama and Saṃkrama), Kathās.; *-kesarin*, m. N. of a prince (son of Vikrama-kesarin), Vet.; *-jña*, mfn. knowing the strength (of an enemy), W.; *-vat* (MārkP.), °*min* (MBh.; Hariv.), mfn. showing courage or strength, exerting power. °**krānta** (*párā*-), mfn. advanced, valorous, strong, bold, active, energetic, AV. &c. &c.; eagerly intent upon (with loc., e. g. *palāyane*, on fleeing), MBh.; n. displaying power or energy, Jātak. °**krāntṛi**, mfn. showing courage, exerting power, MBh.

पराक्षिप् *parā-√kship*, P. Ā. *-kshipati*, °*te*, to throw over, upset, carry or tear away, BhP. °**kshipta**, mfn. upset, wrested away; *-manas*, mfn. having the mind carried away or enraptured, ib.

पराख्या *parā-√khyā* (only pf. *-cakhyau*), to see afar off, ŚBr.

पराग *parāga*, m. (prob. for *apa-r*°), the pollen of a flower, Kāv.; Pur. &c.; dust, Ragh. iv, 30; fragrant powder used after bathing, L.; sandal, L.; an eclipse of the sun or moon, L.; fame, celebrity, L.; independence, L.; N. of a mountain, L. **-pushpa**, m. a species of Kadamba, L. **-vat** (W.), °**gin** (Śiś.), mfn. laden or covered with pollen.

परागम् *parā-√gam*, P. *-gacchati*, to go away, depart, die, AV.; ŚBr. °**gata** (*párā*-), mfn. gone, deceased, ib.; come, arrived, Kād.; covered with, full of (comp.), Śiś. °**gantṛi** = *parā-yati*, Sāy. on RV. ix, 71, 7. °**gama**, m. arrival, Nalac.; approach or invasion (of an enemy), Var.

परागा *parā-√1. gā* (only aor. *-gās*, *-gāt*), to go away, fly, escape, RV.; AV.

परागृदृश् *parāg-dṛiś* &c. See p. 590, col. 1.

पराघातन *parā-ghātana*, n. (√*han*, Caus.) place of execution, slaughter-house, Car.

पराङावृत्त *parāṅ-āvṛitta*, *-manas* &c. See p. 590, col. 1.

पराङ्गव *parāṅgava*, m. (fr. ?) the ocean, L.

पराचर् *parā-√car*, P. *-carati*, to go away, depart, RV.

पराजि *parā-√ji*, Ā. *-jayate* (cf. Pāṇ. i, 3, 19; pf. *-jigye*, RV.; p. *-jigyāna*, TS.; aor. *parâjaishṭa*, MBh.; fut. *-jayishye*, ib.; but also P., e.g. Pot. *-jayet* or *-jayyāt*, MBh.; pf. *-jigyathur*, RV.; aor. *parâjaishīt*, MBh.; inf. *-jetum*, R.; ind. p. *-jitya*, ib.), to be deprived of, suffer the loss of (acc.), be conquered, succumb, RV. &c. &c.; to submit to, be overcome by (abl.), Pāṇ. i, 4, 26; to conquer, win, vanquish, overthrow, MBh.; Kāv. &c.; to defeat in a lawsuit, Yājñ. ii, 75. °**jaya**, m. the being deprived of or conquered, loss, defeat (also in a lawsuit), MBh.; Kāv.; Yājñ.; conquest, victory, MBh.; R.; Ragh.; turning away from, desertion, MW. °**jit**, m. N. a son of Rukma-kavaca, Hariv. °**jita** (*párā*-), mfn. conquered, defeated, overthrown, cast (in a lawsuit), condemned by law, RV. &c. &c. °**jishṇu**, mfn. conquered, succumbing (see *á-parāj*°); victorious, triumphant, MBh.

पराञ्च् *parāñc*, mfn. (fr. 2. *añc*; nom. *āṅ*, *ācī*, *āk* or *āñ*) directed or going away or towards some place beyond (opp. to *arvāñc*); turned away, averted, distant, turning from, being beyond or outside of (abl.), not returning, done away with, gone, departed, RV.; AV.; TS.; Br.; Up.; having any one behind; standing or going behind one another, following (abl.), ib.; directed outwards or towards the outer world (as the senses), KaṭhUp.; BhP.; n. the body, BhP. iv, 11, 10; (*k*), ind. away, off, KātyŚr.; AitUp.; (*k* or *ṅ*), outwards, towards the outer world, KaṭhUp.; BhP

Parāk, in comp. for °*rāñc*. **-tva**, n. not turning back, non-recurrence, ŚāṅkhBr.; Lāṭy. **-pushpī**, f. Achyranthes Aspera, L.

Parākā́, distance (only *e* and *āt*, at or from a d°), RV. (cf. Naigh. iii, 26); m. N. of a Tri-rātra, Br.; ŚrS.; of a sort of religious penance (said to consist in fasting for 12 days and nights and keeping the mind attentive and organs subdued), Mn.; Yājñ.; a sacrificial sword, L.; a kind of disease, L.; a species of animal, L.; mfn. small, L. **Parākā́t-tāt**, ind. from a distance, RV. viii, 81, 27.

Parāg, in comp. for °*rāñc*. **-dṛiś**, mfn. having the eye turned towards the outer world, BhP. **-vasu**, mfn. keeping off wealth, Kauś. (opp. to *arvāg-v*°; cf. *parā-v*°).

Parāṅ, in comp. for °*rāñc*. **-āvṛitta**, mfn. turned away, flying, Āpast. **-manas** (*pár*°), mfn. having the mind or thoughts directed backwards, AV. **-mukha**, mf(*ī*)n. having the face turned away or averted, turning the back upon (also *am*, ind.); flying from; averse from, hostile to, regardless of, shunning, avoiding (loc.; gen.; acc. with *prati*, or comp.), Mn.; MBh.; Kāv. &c.; unfavourable, unkind (as fate &c.), MBh.; Kālid.; m. a spell or magical formula pronounced over weapons, R.; n. (ch. of MBh.), *-tā*, f. (Amar.), *-tva*, n. (Var.) turning away, aversion; °*khaya*, Nom. P. °*yati*, to turn back or away, Bhaṭṭ., Sch.; °*khī-√kṛi*, to cause any one to avert the face, put to flight, MBh.; °*khī-√bhū*, to become averted, turn away the face, take to flight, retreat, Kāv.; Vet.; *-bhūta*, mfn. averse from, inauspicious, unfavourable (as fate), Pañc.

Parācī, f. of °*rāñc*, in **-karman**, n. N. of a wk. on funeral rites.

Parācīna, mfn. turned away or downwards or opposite, averted, VS. &c. &c.; being o° or beyond or outside of, BhP.; averse from, indifferent to (abl.), MBh.; unfit, improper, Hcar.; (*am*), ind. away from, beyond (abl.), ŚBr.; more than, Kāṭh.; after, TS.; before the time, L. **-rātra**, n. the second half of the night, ĀpŚr.

Parācais, ind. away, aside, off, RV.; AV.

Parâñcana, n. turning away from, bending aside, Nir. xi, 25. °**cin**, mfn. not returning, non-recurring, Br.

पराञ्ज *parāñja*, m. (only L.) an oil-mill; froth or foam; the blade of a sword or knife (cf. *parañja*).

पराण् 1. *parāṇ* (*parā* with *√an*), P. *parâṇiti* (Desid. *parâṇiniṣhati*), Pāṇ. viii, 4, 19 &c. 2. **Parā́ṇ**, mfn., ib. 20. **Parāṇa**, n. (with *vāyoḥ*) N. of a Sāman, L.

पराणी *parā-ṇī* (*√nī*), P. Ā. *-ṇayati*, °*te*, to lead away or back, AV.

पराणुद् *parā-ṇud* (*√nud*), P. Ā. *-ṇudáti*, °*te* (Ved. inf. *-ṇúde*), to push or drive away, banish, remove, RV. &c. &c. °**ṇutti**, f. driving away, expulsion, removal, TS.

परातंस *parā-taṇsa*, m. (*√taṇs*) the being thrust or pushed aside, Kāṭh.

परातरम् *parā-taram*. See *parā*, p. 589, col. 2.

परात्रस् *parā-√tras*, only Caus. aor. *parâ-titrasat*, to drive away, AV.

परादन *parādana*, m. a horse of Persian breed, L.

परादा *parā-√1. dā*, P. *-dadāti* (pf. *-da-dātha*, aor. *-dās*, *-dāt* [often as Subj.], *-dur*; Ved. inf. *-dai*), to give up or over, deliver, throw away, RV.; AV.; ŚBr.; give in exchange for, barter against (dat.), RV. viii, 1, 5; to exclude from, BhP. **Parā-tta**, mfn. given up &c., Pāṇ. vii, 4, 47, Sch. **Parā-dadi**, mfn. giving up, delivering over, RV. **Parā-dā́na**, n. the act of giving up &c., VS.

परादिश् *parā-√diś* (only pf. *-dideśa*), to order off, remove, AV.

परादृश् *parā-√dṛiś* (pf. *-dadṛiśur*, ind. p. *-dṛiśya*), to perceive, behold, AV.; ŚBr.

परादु *parā-√dru*, P. *-dravati*, to run away, flee, escape, BhP.

पराधाव् *parā-√1. dhāv*, P. *-dhāvati*, to run away, RV.

पराध्मा *parā-√dhmā*, P. *-dhamati*, to blow away, RV.

परानसा *parānasā*, f. (fr. *ī*) administering remedies, medical treatment, L.

पराप *parâpa*, n. (fr. *parā* + *ap*) Pāṇ. vi, 3, 97, Vārtt. 1, Pat.; mfn. (a place &c.) whence water has retired, W.

परापत् *parā-√pat*, P. *-patati*, to fly away or past, escape, depart, RV. &c. &c.; to fall out, fail, be missing, AV.; Br.; GṛS.; Uttarar.; to fly or rush along, Kād.; to fly towards, approach, arrive Hcar.; Kād.: Caus. *-pātayati*, to drive away, AV.; *-pâtam*, ind. p. flying away, MaitrS. °**pātin**, mfn. flying off, getting loose, ĀpŚr. °**pā́tuka**, mfn. miscarrying, abortive, TS.

परापश् *parā-√paś*, P. *-paśyati*, to look far off (or to a distance), AV.; TS.; ŚBr.; to see or perceive (at a distance), ŚBr.; KātyŚr.

परापू *parā-√pū*, P. *-punāti* (ind. p. *-pā-vam*), to purify, cleanse away, VS.; AV.; ĀpŚr. °**pavana**, n. cleansing away, removing by purification, ĀpŚr.

परापृष्ठीभूत्वा *parā-pṛishṭhī-bhūtvā*, ind. having the back turned (?), Divyâv.

पराबब *parābaba*, n. N. of two Sāmans, L. (v.l. °*bava*).

पराभिक्ष *parābhiksha*, w.r. for *parṇa-bh*°.

पराभू *parā-√bhū*, P. *-bhavati* (fut. *-bha-vishyati*; Ved. inf. *-bhúve*), to perish, disappear, be lost, succumb, yield, AV.; Br. &c.; to overcome, conquer, R.; Kām.; (Pass. p. *-bhūyamāna*, BhP.) to harm, hurt, injure, MBh.; Kāv. &c.: Caus. *-bhāvayati*, to overthrow, destroy, AV.; Br. &c.; (Ā.) to vanish, perish, sustain a loss, BhP. °**bhavá**, m. vanishing, disappearance, dissolution, separation, R.; overthrow, defeat, humiliation, mortification, contempt, injury, destruction, ruin, ŚBr.; MBh.; Kāv. &c.; N. of the 40th (or 14th) year in Jupiter's cycle of 60 years, Var. (cf. *parā-vasu*); *-pada*, n. an object of contempt, MW. °**bhāva**, m. defeat, overthrow, MBh.; humiliation, contempt, L. °**bhāvana**, n. suppression, ĀpŚr., Sch. °**bhāvuka**, mfn. about to decline, going to pass away, Kāṭh. °**bhūta** (*párā-*), mfn. vanished, perished, forlorn, ŚBr. (cf. *á-parābh*°); defeated, overcome, harmed, injured, degraded, humbled, MBh.; Kāv. &c. °**bhūti** (*párā-*), f. defeat, overthrow, humiliation, injury, AV.; Kāv.; Pur.

पराभृत *párā-bhṛita*, mfn. (*√bhṛi*) borne or taken off, put aside, hidden, concealed, RV.; AV.

परामि *parā-√mi* or *mī* (only fut. p. *-mesh-yat*), to come back, return, AitBr.

परामृत 2. *parā-mṛita*, mfn. (for 1. see p. 587, col. 3) one who is beyond (i.e. no longer subject to) death, Up.; Śaṃk.

परामृश् *parā-√mṛiś*, P. *-mṛiśati* (inf. *-marshṭum*, ind. p. *-mṛiśya*), to seize or lay hold of, touch, feel, stroke, handle, clutch, ŚāṅkhŚr.; MBh. &c.; to handle roughly, violate (as a woman or a temple), MBh.; R.; to point or refer to (acc.), Śaṃk.; Nīlak.; to consider, deliberate, Bhām.: Pass. *-mṛiśyate*, to be touched, be referred to or meant, Kāś.; Kull. (w.r. *-mṛish*°). °**marśa**, m. seizing, pulling (*keśa-*, by the hair), MBh.; bending or drawing (of a bow), R.; violation, injury, assault, attack, MBh.; R.; Kād.; affection (by disease &c.), MārkP.; remembrance, recollection, Vedântas.; referring or pointing to, Sāh.; reflection, consideration, judgment, MBh.; Bhāshāp.; (in logic) inference, conclusion, drawing conclusions from analogy or experience, knowledge of the minor premiss in its connection with the major; N. of wk.; *-kāraṇa-pakshatā-vāda*, m., *-karya-kāraṇa-bhāva-vi-cāra*, m., *-grantha*, m., *-grantha-rahasya*, n., *-ṭippanī*, f., *-pūrva-paksha-grantha-ṭīkā*, f. (°*tha-kroḍa*, m., °*tha-dīdhiti-ṭīkā*, f., °*tha-prakāśa*, m., °*tha-vivecana*, n., °*thânugama*, m.), *-pūrva-paksha-rahasya*, n., *-rahasya*, n., *-vāda*, m., *-vādârtha*, m., *-vicāra*, m., *-siddhânta-grantha-ṭīkā*, f. (°*tha-kroḍa*, m., °*tha-prakāśa*, m., °*tha-vivecana*, n., °*thâloka*, m.), *-siddhânta-rahasya*, n., *-hetutā-vicāra*, m. N. of wks. °**marśana**, n. taking hold of, touching, seizing, Kauś., Sch.; recollection, consideration, L. °**marśin**, mfn. calling or bringing to mind, pointing or referring to (°*śi-tva*, n.), Sāh. °**mṛishṭa** (*párā-*), mfn. seized or laid hold of, grasped, handled, touched, felt, roughly treated, violated, afflicted (by disease &c.), AV.; MBh. &c.; recollected, considered, referred to, RPrāt.; borne, endured, W.

परायण 2. *parâyaṇa*, n. (*parā* + *√i*) going away, departure or way of departure, final end, last resort, RV.; AV.; ŚBr. (cf. 1. *parâyaṇa*, p. 587).

परायति *parā-yáti*, m. (*√yat*) = *parā-gan-tṛi*, RV. ix, 91, 7 (Sāy.)

परायत्त *parâyatta* &c. See p. 587, col. 3.

पराया *parā-√yā*, P. *-yāti*, to go away, RV.; AV.: Caus. *-yāpáyati*, to bid go away, Kauś.

परारीक *parārīka*, m. (or °*kā*, f.) leek, Āpast. (v.l. *palārīka*).

परारु *parāru*, m. Momordica Charantia, L. (v.l. *pavāru*).

परारुक *parāruka*, m. a stone or rock, L. (v.l. *pavāruka*).

परार्थ *parârtha*, *parârdha* &c. See under *para*, p. 587, col. 3.

परावच् *parā-√vac*, P. *-vakti*, to contradict (opp. to *anu-vac*), ŚBr. °**vāká**, m. contradiction, AV. **Parôkta**, mfn. contradicted, ŚBr. **Parôcya**, mfn. to be contradicted, TS.

परावत् *parā-vat*. See under 2. *parā*, p. 589.

परावत *parāvata*, m. Grewia Asiatica, L.

परावद् *parā-√vad*, P. *-vadati*, to warn off or remove by speaking or reciting, AV.

परावध् *parā√vadh* (only aor. *-avadhīt*, *-vadhīt*), to strike down, crush, tear, RV. i, 38, 6 (*párā-parā vadhīt*); AV.; TS.

परावप् *parā-√2. vap*, P. *-vapati*, to lay aside, remove (as dead bodies, arrows &c.), AV.; VS.; MaitrS.; Br.

परावम् *parā-√vam*, P. *-vamiti* or *-vamati*, to spit or vomit away, Kāṭh.

परावर *parâvara* &c. See p. 587, col. 3.

परावर्त *parā-varta* &c. See *parā-vṛit*.

परावल्ग् *parā√valg*, Ā. *-valgate*, to jump away, TS.

परावसु *parā-vásu*, mfn. keeping off wealth, ŚBr.; ŚāṅkhŚr. (cf. *parāg-v*°); m. N. of the 40th year of Jupiter's cycle of 60 years, Var. (cf. *parā-bhava*); of a Gandharva (associated with Viśvā-vasu), BhP.; of a son of Raibhya (associated with Arvā-vasu), MBh.

परावह् *parā-√vah*, P. *-vahati* (aor. Subj. *-vakshat*), to carry off, take away, bring to (dat.), RV.; AV. °**vaha**, m. N. of one of the 7 winds (the other 6 being called *ā-vaha*, *ud-*, *pari-*, *pra-*, *vi-* and *sam-vaha*), MBh.; Hariv.

परावा *parā-√2. vā*, P. *-vāti*, to blow away, remove by blowing, RV.

परावाक *parā-vāka*. See *parā-vac* above.

परावृज् *parā-√vṛij*, P. *-vṛiṇakti* (impf. *-vṛiṇak*; pf. *-vavṛijur*; aor. *-vark*, *-varktam*), to turn away; (with *śīrshā*) to flee, RV.; to wring off (as a head), ib.; to throw away, remove, reject, abandon, ib. °**vṛikta** (*párā-*), mfn. rejected, cast off, RV. iv 30, 16. °**vṛij**, m. an out-caste, wretch, miserable, RV. (Sāy. 'N. of a person').

परावृत् *parā-√vṛit*, Ā. *-vartate* (ind. p.

-*vṛitya*), to turn back or round (intrans.), return, desist from (abl.), Mn.; MBh.; Kāv. &c.: Caus. -*vartayati*, to turn round (trans.), RV. i, 38, 9; cause to return, MBh. vii, 9201 (B. *pari-vartaya*). °**varta**, m. turning back or round; exchange, barter, HPariś.; reversal of a sentence (in law), W.; restoration, W. °**vartana**, n. turning back or round, MBh. °**vartin**, mfn. turning back, taking to flight, MBh.; R. (*a-parāv*°). °**vartya**, mfn. (fr. Caus.) to be turned back or exchanged or reversed (as a sentence) or restored, W.; -*vyavahāra*, m. appeal (in law), ib. °**vṛit**, m. N. of a son of Rukmakavaca, VP. °**vṛitta**, mfn. turned (also to flight), returned, averted from (abl.), Mn.; MBh.; Kāv. &c.; passed away, disappeared, R.; BhP.; HPariś.; wallowing, rolling (n. as a subst.), L.; exchanged, W.; reversed (as a judgment), ib.; given back, restored, ib. °**vṛitti**, f. turning back or round, returning, revolving, Hariv. (cf. *a-parāv*°); change, interchange, exchange, barter, Kāv.; reversion of a sentence or judgment, W.; restoration of property, ib.; recoiling, rebounding, not taking effect, Cat.

पराव्यध् *parā-√vyadh*, P. -*vidhyati*, to hurl or fling away or out, TS.; MaitrS.; to strike, hit, wound, MBh. °**viddha**, m. N. of Kṛishṇa or Kubera, L. (cf. *pari-viddha* under *pari-vyadh*). °**vyādha**, m. a stone's throw, the range of any missile, ŚBr.

पराशर *parā-śara*. See *parā-śṛī* below.

पराशस् *parā-śás*, f. (√*śaṉs*) calumny, curse, imprecation, TS.; AV.

पराशातयितृ *parā-śātayitṛi*, m. (√*śad*, Caus.) crusher, destroyer, Nir. vi, 30.

पराशॄ *parā-śṛī*, P. -*śṛiṇāti* (Impv. -*śṛiṇīhi*, °*ṇītam*, °*ṇantu*, RV.; aor. -*śarīt* or -*śarait*, AV.), to crush, destroy. °**śará**, m. a crusher, destroyer, RV.; AV.; a partic. wild animal, Bhagavatīg. (w. r. °*sara*); N. of a Nāga, MBh.; N. of a son of Vasishṭha or of a son of Śakti and grandson of V° (according to MBh. the father of Vyāsa; said to be the author of RV. i, 65–73 and part of ix, 97); of a son of Kuthumi, VP.; of the author of a well-known code of laws, RTL. 51 &c.; of sev. writers on medicine and astrology &c. (with *bhaṭṭa*, N. of a poet), Cat.; -*kshetra-māhātmya*, n., -*tantra*, n., -*dharma*, m., -*purāṇa*, n., -*mādhavīya*, n., -*vaṉśa-varṇana*, n., -*vijaya*, m., -*saṃhitā*, f., -*sampāta*, m., -*siddhānta*, m., -*sūtra-vṛitti*, f., -*smṛiti*, f., -*smṛiti-saṃgraha*, m., °*rôpapurāṇa*, n. N. of wks.; °*rin*, m. = *pārāśarin*, L.; °*rêśvara*, m. N. of a Liṅga, SkandaP.; °*vara-tīrtha*, n. N. of a Tīrtha, ŚivaP. °**śīrṇa**, mfn. crushed, destroyed, Nir. vi, 30.

पराश्रय *parâśraya*, *parâśrita*. See under *para*, p. 588, col. 1.

पराश्वस् *parā-√śvas* (only ind. p. -*śvasya*), to confide in (loc.), MBh.

परास् *parâs* (*parā* + √2. *as*), P. *parâsyati* (impf. *parâsyat*; pf. *parâsa*), to throw away or down, cast aside, expose (as a new-born child), abandon, reject, leave, RV. &c. &c. **Parâsa**, m. the range or distance of anything thrown, ŚāṅkhŚr.; n. tin, L. **Parâsana**, n. killing, slaughter, massacre, L. **Parâsin**, mfn. throwing or measuring the distance of anything thrown, TāṇḍBr. **Parâsisishu**, mfn. (fr. Desid.) wishing to drive away, Kir.; desirous to throw or send, W.; wishing to overcome, ib. **Parâsta**, mfn. thrown away, rejected, repudiated, Sāh.; defeated, W. **Parâsya** or **parâsyà**, mfn. to be thrown away, ŚBr.

परासिच् *parā-√sic*, P. -*siñcati* (aor. -*asicat*; Pass. -*sicyate*, aor. -*aseci*), to pour or throw away, cast aside, remove, RV.; TS.; AV.; ŚBr.; ŚrS. °**sikta**, mfn. poured or thrown away, spilled, ŚBr. (cf. *á-parās*°); set aside, rendered useless, MBh.

परासु *parâsu*, mfn. one whose vital spirit is departed or departing; dying or dead, MBh.; Kāv. &c. —**karaṇa**, mfn. causing death, killing, MBh. —**tā**, f., -**tva**, n. exhaustion, death, MBh.

परासू *parā-√sū*, P. -*suvati* (aor. -*sāvīḥ*), to frighten away, RV.; AV.; VS.; TS.

परासृ *parā-√sṛi*, P. -*sarati*, to come near, approach, RV.

परासृज् *parā-√sṛij*, P. -*sṛijati*, to give away, bestow, MBh.

परासेध *parā-sedha*, m. (√1. *sidh*) arrest, imprisonment, Nār.

परास्तम्भ् *parā-√stambh*, P. -*stabhnāti*, to hold back, hinder, ŚBr.

पराहन् *parā-√han*, P. -*hanti* (impf. 2. 3. sg. *párâhan*, pf. 3. pl. *parā-jaghnúr*), to strike down or away, hurl down, overthrow, RV.; MBh.; to touch, feel, grope, VS.; ŚBr. °**hata** (*párā-*), mfn. turned over, tilled (the earth), RV. v, 56, 3; struck down or back, repelled, averted, rejected, MBh.; Kāv.; refuted, contradicted, Nyāyam. °**hati**, f. contradiction, Sarvad.

पराहा *parā-√2. hā*, Ā. -*jihīte*, to give way, let slip, abandon, evade (acc.), TS.

पराहृत *parā-hṛita*, mfn. (√*hṛi*) carried off, removed, ĀpŚr.; BhP.

परि *pári*, ind. round, around, about, round about; fully, abundantly, richly (esp. ibc. [where also *parī*] to express fulness or high degree), RV. &c. &c.; as a prep. (with acc.) about (in space and time), RV.; AV.; against, opposite to, in the direction of, towards, to, ib. (cf. Pāṇ. i, 4, 90; also at the beginning of a comp. mfn.; cf. ib. ii, 2, 18, Vārtt. 4, Pat. and *pary-adhyayana*); beyond, more than, AV.; to the share of (with √*as* or *bhū*, to fall to a person's lot), Pāṇ. i, 4, 90; successively, severally (e.g. *vṛiksham pari siñcati*, he waters tree after tree), ib.; (with abl.) from, away from, out of, RV.; AV.; ŚBr. (cf. Pāṇ. i, 4, 93); outside of, except, Pāṇ. i, 4, 88, Kāś. (often repeated, ib. viii, 1, 5; also at the beginning or the end of an ind. comp., ib. ii, 1, 12); after the lapse of, Mn. iii, 119; MBh. xiii, 4672 (some read *parisaṃvatsarāt*); in consequence or on account or for the sake of, RV.; AV.; according to (esp. *dhármaṇas pári*, according to ordinance or in conformity with law or right), RV. [Cf. Zd. *pairi*; Gk. περί.]

परिंश *pariṉśá*, m. (*pari* + *aṉśa*) the best part of (gen.), RV. i, 187, 8.

परिकथ् *pari-√kath*, P. -*kathayati*, to mention, call, name, Tattvas. °**kathā**, f. a religious tale or narrative, Divyâv.

परिकन्दल *pari-kandala*, mf(*ā*)n. teeming with, full of (comp.), Bhojapr.

परिकम्प् *pari-√kamp*, Caus. -*kampayati*, to cause to tremble, shake, BhP. °**kampa**, m. tremor, great fear or terror, L. °**kampin**, mfn. trembling violently, Uttarar.

परिकर *pari-kara*, *pari-karman* &c. See *pari-kṛi*, col. 3.

परिकर्कश *pari-karkaśa*, mfn. very harsh, Jātakam.

परिकर्त *pari-karta*, °*tana* &c. See *pari-kṛit*.

परिकर्ष *pari-karsha*. See *pari-kṛish*.

परिकल् *pari-√2. kal*, P. -*kālayati*, to drive about, chase, persecute, MBh.; R. °**kālita**, mfn. persecuted, dogged, MBh.

परिकल् *pari-√3. kal*, P. -*kalayati*, to seize, take hold of, Bālar. ix, 18; to swallow, devour, Kād.; Hcar.; to observe, consider as, Śiś. viii, 9. °**kalayitṛi**, mfn. surrounding, encircling, Mcar. v, 10 (read °*yitā*). °**kalitin**, mfn. = °*kalitam yena saḥ*, g. *ishṭâdi*.

परिकल्कन *pari-kalkana*, n. deceit, cheating, Dhātup. (cf. *kalkana*).

परिकल्प *pari-kalpa*, °*pana* &c. See *pari-klṛip*, p. 592, col. 1.

परिकाङ्क्षित *pari-kāṅkshita*, m. (√*kāṅksh*) a devotee, religious ascetic, L. (cf. *pārikāṅkshin*).

परिकातर *pari-kātara*, mfn. very timid or cowardly, Jātakam.

परिकायन *parikāyana*(?), m. pl. N. of a school, L.

परिकासन *pari-kāsana*, n. (√*kās*) frequent coughing, ĀpGṛ.

परिकिरण *pari-kiraṇa*, -*kīrṇa* &c. See *pari-√1. kṛī*, p. 592.

परिकीर्त *pari-√kīrt*, P. -*kīrtayati*, to proclaim on all sides, announce, relate, celebrate, praise, declare, call, name, GṛS.; Mn.; MBh. &c. °**kīrtana**, n. proclaiming, announcing, talking of, boasting, naming, calling, Mn.; MBh. &c. °**kīrtita**, mfn. proclaimed, announced, boasted of, said, called, ib.

परिकुप् *pari-√kup*, P. -*kupyati*, to become greatly moved or excited, to be in a rage, to be very angry, MBh.: Caus. -*kopayati*, to excite violently, to make very angry, ib. °**kupita**, mfn. much excited, very angry, wrathful, ib. °**kopa**, m. violent anger, wrath, Pañc. °**kopita**, mfn. (fr. Caus.) greatly excited, very angry, MBh.

परिकूट *pari-kūṭa*, m. N. of a serpent-demon, L.; a barrier or trench before the gate of a town, L.

परिकूल *pari-kūla*, n. (prob.) the land lying on a shore, Pāṇ. vi, 2, 82, Sch.

परिकृ *pari-√1. kṛi*, P. -*karoti* &c. (cf. *pari-sh-kṛi*), to surround, MBh.; to uphold, Divyâv. °**kara**, mf(*ī*)n. who or what helps or assists, W.; m. (ifc. f. *ā*) attendants, followers, entourage, retinue, train (sg. and pl.), MBh.; Kāv. &c ; multitude, abundance, Bhartṛ.; Bālar.; a girth, zone, waist-band, (esp.) a girdle to keep up a garment (°*ram √bandh* or °*ram √kṛi*, 'to gird up one's loins, make preparations,' and so *pari-kara* = *ārambha*, L.), Hariv.; Kāv.; Rājat. &c.; (in dram.) covert or indirect intimation of coming events in a plot, the germ of the Bīja, Daśar.; (in rhet.) a partic. figure in which many significant epithets or adjectives are employed one after the other to give force to a statement, Kpr.; Sāh. &c.; -*śloka*, Alaṃkārav.; discrimination, judgment, L.; -*bandha*, m. the binding on of a girdle in order to begin any work, MW.; -*bhūta*, mfn. being instrumental, Āryabh., Sch.; -*vijaya*, m. N. of wk.; -*śloka*, m. versus auxiliaris, Alaṃkārav. °**karita**, mfn. accompanied by (instr.), Vcar. °**kartṛi**, m. a priest who performs the marriage ceremony for a younger brother whose elder brother is not yet married, L. °**karman**, m. a servant, assistant, L.; n. attendance, worship, adoration, BhP.; dressing, painting or perfuming the body (esp. after bathing), MBh.; Kālid.; cleansing, purification, Śiś.; preparation, Kathās. (cf. °*kara*); arithmetical computation or operation, W.; °*makathā*, f. prayer (?), Divyâv.; °*māshṭaka*, n. the 8 fundamental rules of arithmetic (viz. addition, subtraction, multiplication, division, finding the square, extracting the square root, finding the cube, extracting the cube root), Col. °**karmaya**, Nom. P. °*yati*, to anoint, decorate, adorn, Gīt.; to make ready, Divyâv.; °*mita*, mfn. arranged, prepared, put in order, Var.; Sarvad. °**karmin**, mfn. adorning, decorating, W.; m. an assistant, servant, slave, ŚrS.; Suśr. °**kṛita**, mfn. surrounded, MBh. °**kriyā**, f. surrounding, inclosing, intrenching, L.; attending to, care of (comp.; cf. *agni-parikriyā*); exercise, practice, enjoyment (cf. *rājya-parik*°); (in dram.) illusion to future action (= *parikara*), Daśar.

परिकृत् *pari-√2. kṛit*, P. -*kṛintati* (ind. p. -*kṛitya*), to cut round, clip, cut off, AV.; R.; to exclude from (abl.), Mn. iv, 219. °**kartana**, mfn. cutting up or to pieces, MBh.; n. cutting, cutting off or out, a circular incision, Suśr.; = next, ib. °**kartikā**, f. sharp shooting pain (esp. in the rectum), Suśr. °**kṛitta**, mfn. cut round, clipped, cut off, ŚBr.

परिकृत् *pari-√3. kṛit* (only p. pres. Ā. -*kṛityamāna*), to wind round, AV.

परिकृश् *pari-√kriś*, only Caus. -*karśayati*, to harass, afflict, BhP.

Pari-kṛiśa, mfn. very thin, emaciate, wasted, Vop.; -*tva*, n. a slender size, Lalit.

परिकृष् *pari-√kṛish*, P. Ā. -*karshati*, °*te*, to draw or drag about (Ā. also 'each other'), MBh.; to lead (an army), R.; to rule, govern, be master of (acc.), MBh.; to harass, afflict, ib.; to ponder, reflect constantly upon (acc.), ib.; (P. -*kṛishati*) to draw or make furrows, to plough, ŚBr.; KātyŚr.; to draw a circle, Śulbas.: Caus. -*karshayati*, to drag to and fro, torment, harass, vex, trouble, R.;

BhP.; to carry (as a nurse), Divyâv. °**karsha**, m. dragging about, MBh. (cf. g. *nirudakâdi*). °**karshaṇa**, n. id., ib.; a circle, Śulbas. °**karshita**, mfn. (fr. Caus.) dragged about, harassed, tortured, R.; BhP. °**karshin**, mfn. dragging away, carrying about (to different places), R. °**kṛishṭa**, m. N. of a teacher, VāyuP.

परिकॄ *pari-√1. kṝ*, P. *-kirati* (ind. p. *-kīrya*), to scatter or strew about, ŚBr.; KātyŚr.; to throw upon, impose, deliver over to (loc.), Ragh. xviii, 32. °**kiraṇa**, n. scattering or strewing about, Kauś., Sch. °**kīrṇa**, mfn. spread, diffused, scattered around, surrounded, crowded, MBh.; Kāv. &c.

परिकॢप् *pari-√klṛip*, Caus. *-kalpayati* (Pass. *-kalpyate*), to fix, settle, determine, destine for (with acc., *artham* ifc., loc. or an inf. with pass. sense), Mn.; MBh.; Kāv. &c.; to choose, VarBṛS. lix, 11; to perform, execute, accomplish, contrive, arrange, make, Yājñ.; Ragh.; Kathās.; to distribute, divide (with an adv. in *dhā*), Mn.; Var.; MBh.; to admit or invite to (loc.), MBh.; to suppose, presuppose, Sarvad. °**kalpa**, m. illusion, Buddh.; w.r. for °*kampa*. °**kalpana**, n. fixing, settling, contriving, making, inventing, providing, dividing, distributing; (*ā*), f. making, forming, assuming (see *rūpa-parik*°); reckoning, calculation, Var. °**kalpita**, mfn. settled, decided; fixed upon, chosen, wished for, expected, made, created, imagined, invented, contrived, arranged, distributed, divided (with *khaṇḍa-śaḥ*, cut or broken in pieces), Mn.; MBh.; Kāv. &c. °**kalpya**, mfn. to be settled &c.; to be calculated, Var. °**klṛipta**, mfn. distributed, scattered, found here and there, MBh.

परिकेश *pari-keśa*, m., g. *nirudakâdi*.

परिक्रन्द् *pari-√krand* (only aor. Caus. *-acikradat*), to cry or make a noise round about (acc.), RV.

परिक्रम् *pari-√kram*, P. *-krămati* (rarely Ā. °*te*; p. *-krămat*; pf. *-cakrāma*, *-cakramur*; aor. *-akramīt*; inf. *-krāntum*; ind. p. *-krāmam* or *-kramya*), to step or walk round or about, circumambulate, roam over, walk through, visit (with acc.), RV. &c. &c.; to go past, escape, AitBr.; to outstrip, overtake, R.: Intens. *-caṅkramati*, to move or walk about perpetually, BhP. °**krama**, m. roaming about, circumambulating, walking through, pervading, MBh.; Pur.; transition, RPrāt. (v.l. *parā-kr*°); following the course of a river down from its source to its mouth and then on the other bank up to its source again, RTL. 348; succession, series, order, Lāṭy.; Kauś.; Mn. iii, 214 (read *āvṛit-parikramam*); a remedy, medicine, Car.; *-saha*, m. 'one who bears running about,' a goat, L. °**kramaṇa**, n. walking or roaming about, ŚāṅkhBr. °**krānta**, mfn. walked round, stepped upon, trod; n. the place stepped upon, foot-steps, traces, R. °**krānti**, f. moving round, revolution, BhP. °**krāmitaka**, n. (fr. Caus.) walking about (only °*kena*, ind., in stage-directions), Bālar.; Viddh.; Pracaṇḍ.

परिक्रिया *pari-kriyā*. See *pari-kṛi*.

परिक्री *pari-√krī*, Ā. *-krīṇīte* (Pāṇ. i, 3, 18; really more frequent in P., e. g. impf. *-akrīṇan*, AV.; Pot. *-krīṇīyāt*, ŚāṅkhŚr.; ind. p. *-krīya*, Gobh.), to purchase, buy, barter, gain, acquire, AV.; ŚBr.; Lāṭy.; Gobh. (with instr. or dat. of the price, e. g. *śatena* or *śatāya*, to buy for a hundred, Pāṇ. i, 4, 44); to hire, engage for stipulated wages, ŚBr.; ŚrS.; to recompense, reward (only p. Ā. *-krīṇāna*), Bhaṭṭ. °**kraya**, m. giving up at the cost of (cf. *prāṇa-parikr*°); hire, wages, KātyŚr., Sch.; redemption, buying off, W.; a peace purchased with money, Kām.; Hit. °**krayaṇa**, n. hiring, engaging, Pāṇ. i, 4, 44. °**krī**, m. N. of an Ekâha, ŚrS. °**krīta**, mfn. purchased, bought, hired, MBh. (applied to a son = *reto-mūlya-dānena tasyām eva* [i. e. *bhāryāyām*] *janitaḥ*, Nilak.)

परिक्रीड् *pari-√krīḍ*, Ā. *-krīḍate* (Pāṇ. i, 3, 21; but P. p. *-krīḍat*, pf. *-cikrīḍuḥ*, ŚBr.), to play about (Impv. Ā. *-krīḍasva*, Bhaṭṭ.)

परिक्रुध् *pari-√krudh*, P. *-krudhyati*, to fly into a rage, become enraged, R.

परिक्रुश् *pari-√kruś*, P. *-krośati* (cf. *-cukruśur*, ind. p. *-kruśya*), to go about crying, to wail, lament, MBh.; R. °**krushṭa**, mfn. lamented; n. lamentation has been made by (instr.), R. °**krośá**, m. 'crier,' prob. N. of a demon, RV. i, 29, 7.

परिक्लम् *pari-√klam*, P. *-klāmati*, °*myati*, to be tired out or exhausted, Kād. °**klānta**, mfn. very tired, tired out, exhausted, MBh.

परिक्लिन्न *pari-klinna*, mfn. (√*klid*) very wet, excessively moist or humid, R. °**kleda**, m. humidity, wetness, MBh. °**kledin**, mfn. wetting or wet, Suśr.

परिक्लिश् *pari-√kliś*, P. Ā. *-kliśyati*, °*te* (p. *-kliśyamāna*, Pāṇ. iii, 4, 55), to suffer, feel pain, be troubled or vexed, MBh.; R.; (only ind. p. *-kliśya*) to pain, torment, vex, harass, R. °**kliśa**, m.(?) vexation, trouble, W. °**klishṭa**, mfn. much vexed or troubled, pained, harassed, afflicted, exhausted, MBh.; R. &c.; n. = °*kleśa*, L.; (*am*), ind. with uneasiness or reluctance, unwillingly. °**kleśa**, m. hardship, pain, trouble, fatigue, MBh.; Kāv. &c. °**kleshṭṛi**, m. a tormentor, torturer, MBh.

परिक्वणन *pari-kvaṇana*, mfn. (√*kvaṇ*) loud-sounding, loud, Nir. vi, 1.

परिक्वथ् *pari-√kvath*, P. *-kvathati*, to become boiling hot, Bālar. v, $\frac{1}{8}$.

परिक्षत *pari-kshata*, mfn. (√*kshan*) wounded, hurt, injured, killed, Mn.; MBh.; Kāv. °**kshati**, f. wounding, injury, lesson, Śiś.

परिक्षय *pari-kshaya*. See *pari-√4. kshi*.

परिक्षर् *pari-√kshar*, P. *-ksharati* (aor. *-akshār*), to cause to flow round (in a stream), RV.; to bestow by pouring forth in a stream, ib.

परिक्षल् *pari-√2. kshal*, P. *-kshālayati* (ind. p. *-kshālya*), to wash out, rinse; wash off, ŚBr. °**kshālana**, n. water for washing, KātyŚr.

परिक्षव *pari-kshavá*, m. (√*kshu*) frequent or ill-omened sneezing, AV.

परिक्षा *pari-kshā*, f. (√*kshai*) clay, mud, dirt, L. °**kshāṇa**, mfn. charred or burnt to a cinder, AitBr. °**kshāma**, mfn. excessively emaciated, dried up, fallen away, Kād.; Rājat.

परिक्षि *pari-√4. kshi*, P. *-kshiṇoti*, to destroy, BhP.: Pass. *-kshīyate*, to waste away, decay, become exhausted, Hit. °**kshaya**, m. disappearing, ceasing, dissolution, decay, destruction, loss, ruin, end, Mn.; MBh.; Kāv. &c. °**kshīṇa**, mfn. vanished, disappeared, wasted, exhausted, diminished, ruined, lost, destroyed; (in law) insolvent, Mn.; Yājñ.; MBh. &c.

परिक्षि *pari-√2. kshi*, P. *-ksheti*, to dwell around (with acc.), AitBr. vi, 32. °**kshi**, m., v.l. for next, VP. °**kshit**, mfn. dwelling or spreading around, surrounding, extending (as Agni, heaven and earth &c.), RV.; AV.; AitBr.; m. N. of an ancient king (son of Abhimanyu and father of Janam-ejaya), MBh.; Hariv.; of a son of Kuru and father of another Jan°, Hariv.; of a son of A-vikshit and brother of Jan°, MBh.; of a king of A-yodhyā, ib. (cf. *parī-kshit* under 1. *parī*, p. 605, col. 1). °**kshita**, w. r. for *pari-cita* or *-kshit*.

परिक्षिप् *pari-√kship*, P. *-kshipati* (pf. *-cikshepa*; ind. p. *-kshipya*), to throw over or beyond, R.; to put or lay or wind round, Suśr.; to throw about, surround, encircle, embrace, ib.; MBh.; R. &c.; to throw or put or fix in (loc.), MBh.; to throw away, squander (as a treasure), Kathās. °**kshipta**, mfn. thrown, thrown about, scattered, surrounded, overspread, MBh.; R. &c.; left, abandoned, W. °**kshepa**, m. throwing about, moving to and fro, Hariv.; surrounding, encircling, being (or that by which anything is) surrounded, MBh.; Kāv. &c.; circumference, extent, Car.; abandoning, leaving, W. °**kshepaka**, mf(*ikā*)n. hung with (ifc.), Karaṇḍ. (cf. Pāṇ. iii, 2, 146). °**kshepin**, mfn. who or what scatters or distributes, W. (cf. Pāṇ. iii, 2, 142).

परिक्षीब *pari-kshība* or °*va*, mfn. drunk, quite intoxicated, W.

परिखचित *pari-khacita*, mfn. (√*khac*) strewn or inlaid with (comp.), Kāraṇḍ.

परिखण्ड *pari-khaṇḍa*, see *pari-shaṇḍa*. °**khaṇḍana**, see *māna-parikh*°. °**khaṇḍaya**, Nom. P. °*yati*, to make small, break, conquer, Bālar.; Bhaṭṭ.

परिखन् *pari-√khan* (only ind. p. *-khāya*), to dig round, dig up, ĀśvGṛ. °**khā**, f. (once ibc. °*kha*, BhP.) a moat, ditch, trench or fosse round a town or fort (also applied to the sea surrounding the earth), Mn.; MBh.; Kāv. &c.; N. of a village in the North country, g. *palady-ādi* (iv, 2, 110); *-sthita*, mfn. impregnable, secure, MBh. xii, 6250; °*khī-kṛita*, mfn. made into a moat or ditch, Ragh. i, 30. °**khāta**, mfn. dug round; m. a furrow, rut, BhP.

परिखिद् *pari-√khid*, P. *-khidyati*, to be depressed or afflicted, feel uneasy, BhP.: Caus. *-khedayati*, to trouble, afflict, destroy, ib. &c. °**khinna**, mfn. depressed, afflicted, exhausted, MBh.; R. &c. °**kheda**, m. (ifc. f. *ā*) lassitude, weariness, exhaustion, MBh.; Kāv. &c. °**khedita**, mfn. (fr. Caus.) afflicted, exhausted, ruined, destroyed, Kāv.; BhP.

परिख्या *pari-√khyā*, P. *-khyāti* (Subj. *-khyatam*, *-khyan*, RV.), to look round, look at, perceive, RV. &c. &c.; to observe, regard, consider, MBh.; R.; to overlook, disregard, RV.: Pass. *-khyāyate*, to be perceived, ChUp. °**khyāta**, mfn. regarded as, passing for (nom.); called, named; celebrated, famous, MBh.; R. °**khyāti**, f. fame, reputation, W.

परिगण् *pari-√gaṇ*, P. *-gaṇayati* (ind. p. *-gaṇya*), to count over, reckon up completely, ascertain by calculation, Suśr.; Hcar.; BhP.; to calculate, reckon, consider, reflect, Megh. (cf. *a-parigaṇayat*). °**gaṇana**, n., °**gaṇanā**, f. complete enumeration, accurate calculation or statement, Megh.; Kull. °**gaṇanīya** (Kull.), °**gaṇya** (see *a-parig*°), mfn. to be enumerated completely or stated accurately. °**gaṇita**, mfn. enumerated, calculated, reckoned, BhP. (cf. *a-parig*°). °**gaṇitin**, mfn. one who has well considered everything, Pāṇ. ii, 3, 36, Kāś.

परिगण *parigaṇa*, m. or n. (?), a house, L.

परिगद् *pari-√gad* (only inf. *-gaditum*), to describe, relate, tell, Bhām. ii, 75. °**gaditin**, mfn. = *parigaditaṃ yena saḥ*, g. *ishṭâdi*.

परिगम् *pari-√gam*, P. *-gacchati* (aor. *-agamat*, AV.; *-gman*, RV.; pf. *-jagmatuḥ*, MBh.; p. *-jaganvas*, RV.; ind. p. *-gátyā*, RV.; ŚBr.; *-gamya*, MBh.; inf. *-gantum*, R.), to go round or about or through, circumambulate, surround, inclose, RV. &c. &c.; to come to any state or condition, get, attain (acc.), MBh.: Pass. *-gamyate*, MBh.: Caus. *-gamayati*, to cause to go round, to pass or spend (time), Ragh. viii, 91. °**ga**, mfn. going round, surrounding, Pāṇ. viii, 4, 38, Sch. °**gata**, mfn. gone round or through, surrounded, encompassed, MBh.; R. &c.; filled, possessed of, visited by, afflicted with (instr. or comp.), ib.; diffused, spread, Kāv.; deceased, dead, Bhartṛ. iii, 49; experienced, known, learnt from (abl.), Kāv.; forgotten, L.; obtained, L.; = *ceshṭita*, L.; °*târtha*, mfn. acquainted or familiar with anything, Kālid. °**gantavya**, mfn. to be got or obtained, L. °**gama**, m. going round, surrounding, Bālar.; knowing, ascertaining, partaking of, occupation with (comp.), ib.; Pracaṇḍ.; spreading, extending, W.; obtaining, ib. °**gamana**, n. id., MW. °**gamita**, mfn. (fr. Caus.) brought, conducted, driven, passed, spent (time), Ragh. °**gamya**, mfn. accessible, to be circumambulated (*a-parig*°), KātyŚr.

परिगर्ज् *pari-√garj*, P. *-garjati*, to roar, cry, scold, R.

परिगर्वित *pari-garvita*, mfn. (√*garv*) very proud or arrogant, Cāṇ.

परिगर्ह् *pari-√garh*, Ā. *-garhate*, to blame greatly, censure, despise, abuse, MBh.: Caus. *-garhayati*, id., ib. °**garhaṇa**, n. excessive blame, censure, ib.

परिगलित *pari-galita*, mfn. (√*gal*) fallen down, MBh.; sunk, Pañc.; flowing, fluid, melted, W.

परिगहन *pari-gahana*, n., g. *kshubhnâdi*.

परिगा *pari-√gā*, P. *-jigāti* (aor. *-agāt*, *-gāt*, *-agur*), to go round or through, circumambulate, permeate, RV.; AV.; to enter (acc.), VS.; ĪśUp.; to come near, approach, reach, visit, afflict, RV.; MBh.; to go out of the way, avoid, shun, RV.; to disregard, neglect, AitBr.; to fail, miss, not to master or understand, BhP.

परिगुणित *pari-guṇita*, mfn. (fr. *-guṇaya*) reiterated, repeated, BhP.; augmented by addition of (comp.), VarBṛS. lxv, 5.

परिगुण्ठित *pari-gunṭhita*, mfn. (√*gunṭh*) veiled in, hidden by (instr.), R.

परिगुण्डित *pari-guṇḍita*, mfn. covered with dust, Śil.

परिगुप् *pari-√gup*, only Desid. *-jugupsate*, to beware of, be on one's guard against (abl.), MBh.

परिगूढक *pari-gūḍhaka*, mfn., g. *ṛiśyâdi*.

परिगृद्ध *pari-griddha*, mfn. very greedy, Divyâv. °**gredha** (!), m. excessive greediness, L.

परिगै *pari-√gai*, P. *-gāyati*, to go about singing, sing or celebrate everywhere, TS.; ŚBr.; ŚrS.; to proclaim aloud (esp. Pass. *-gīyate*), MBh. &c. °**gīta**, mfn. sung, celebrated, proclaimed, declared, MBh.; BhP. °**gīti**, f. a kind of metre, Col.

परिग्रस् *pari-√gras*, P. Ā. *-grasati*, °*te*, to devour, NṛisUp.

परिग्रह् *pari-√grah*, P. Ā. *-gṛihṇāti*, °*ṇīte* (Impv. 2. sg. *-gṛihāṇa*, MBh.; Kālid.; impf. *-agribhṇāḥ*, RV.; 3. sg. *-agṛihṇat*, TS.; 3. pl. *-agṛihṇan*, AV.; Ā. *-agṛihṇanta*, MBh.; pf. 1. sg. *-jagrábha*, RV.; 3. sg. *-jagrāha*, MBh. &c.; ind. p. *-gṛihya*, ŚBr.; MBh.; Kāv. &c.), to take hold of on both sides, embrace, surround, enfold, envelop, VS.; AV.; Br.; MBh. &c.; to fence round, hedge round, TS.; AV.; ŚBr.; KātyŚr.; to occupy on both sides (*sarasvatīm*), MBh.; to seize, clutch, grasp, catch, ib.; to put on, wear (as a dress or ornament), ib.; to take or carry along with one, ib.; Kāv. &c.; to take possession of, master, overpower, RV.; AV.; Br.; Var.; to take (in war), take prisoner, conquer, MBh.; to take (food), ŚBr.; to receive, (also as a guest) accept, ib.; MBh.; Śak.; BhP.; to take, adopt, conform to, follow, Mn.; MBh.; Kāv. &c.; to take by the hand, assist, MBh.; to take (a wife), marry, Śak.; Pañc.; to surpass, excel, Mn.; Prab.; (in Ved. gram.) to enclose (*iti*) between a word twice repeated, RPrāt. (cf. *pari-graha*). °**gṛihīta**, mfn. taken hold of on both sides, AV.; surrounded, embraced, enclosed, enveloped, fenced, TS.; ŚBr.; MBh. &c.; seized, grasped, taken, received, obtained, accepted, adopted, admitted, followed, obeyed, Br.; MBh.; Kāv. &c.; opposed, checked, W.; m., g. *ācitâdi*. °**gṛihīti** (*pári-*), f. grasping, comprehension, TS.; Br. °**gṛihītṛi**, w. r. for °*grah*°. 1. °**gṛihya**, ind. having taken or seized, in company or along with (acc.), MBh.; Kāv. &c.; considering, regarding, W.; *-vat*, (°*gṛíhya-*), mfn. containing the word *parigṛihya*, TS. 2. °**gṛihya**, mfn. to be taken or accepted or regarded, W.; (*ā*), f. designation of a partic. kind of Vedi or sacrificial mound, Kauś.; a married woman, L. °**grahá**, m. (ifc. f. *ā*) laying hold of on all sides, surrounding, enclosing, fencing round (esp. the Vedi or sacrificial altar by means of three lines or furrows), ŚBr.; KātyŚr. &c.; wrapping round, putting on (a dress &c.), assuming (a form &c.), Kāv.; comprehending, summing up, sum, totality, ŚāṅkhBr.; Mn.; taking, accepting, receiving or anything received, a gift or present, MBh.; Kāv. &c.; getting, attaining, acquisition, possession, property (ifc. 'being possessed of or furnished with'), ib.; household, family, attendants, retinue, the seraglio of a prince, ib.; a house, abode, Hariv.; root, origin, foundation, MBh.; admittance (into one's house), hospitable reception, Mn.; MBh.; R.; Kāraṇḍ.; taking (a wife), marrying, marriage, Mn.; MBh. &c.; a wife (also collect.), MBh.; Kāv. &c.; choice, selection, ib.; understanding, conception, Pāṇ., Sch.; undertaking, beginning, commission or performance of, occupation with, Mn.; R.; Hariv.; homage, reverence, grace, favour, help, assistance, MBh.; Kāv. &c.; dominion, control (ifc. 'dependent on, subject to'), R.; Var.; MārkP.; force, constraint, punishment (opp. to *anu-graha*), R.; claim on, relation to, concern with (loc.), Mn.; MBh. &c.; (in Ved. gram.) the double mention of a word both before and after *iti*; the form which precedes *iti*, RPrāt.; a curse, imprecation, oath, L.; an eclipse of the sun, L.; the rear or reserve of an army, L. (v. l. *prati-gr*°); *-tva*, n. state of a wife, marriage, Daś.; *-dvitīya*, mfn. accompanied by one's wife or family, MW.; *-bahu-tva*, n. multitude of wives, Śak.; *-maya*, mf(*ī*)n. consisting of a family, Prab.; *-vat* or °*hin*, mfn. possessed of wealth, having property, MBh.; °*hârthīya*, mfn. having the sense of comprehension i. e. generalization, Nir. i, 7. °**grahaka**, mfn. grasping, taking hold of, undertaking (ifc.), L. °**grahaṇa**, n. wrapping round, putting on, Prab. °**grahītavya**, mfn. to be admitted or supposed, Śaṃk.; to be ruled or controlled, Pat.; to be taken hold of or got into possession, Vajracch. °**grahītṛi**, mfn. taking hold of, seizing; m. assister, helper, VāyuP.; ruler, Pat.; an adoptive father, Pravar.; Kull.; 2 husband, Śak. °**grāhá**, m. the surrounding or fencing round of the Vedi or sacrificial altar with three lines or furrows, TS. °**grāhaka**, mfn. favouring, befriending, Bālar. °**grāhya**, mfn. to be treated or addressed kindly, MBh.

परिग्लान *pari-glāna*, mfn. (√*glai*) wearied out, languid, exhausted, MBh.; R. &c.; averse from (dat.), Pat.

परिघ *pari-gha*, m. (√*han*) an iron bar or beam used for locking or shutting a gate (= *argala*), ChUp.; MBh.; Kāv. &c.; (fig.) a bar, obstacle, hindrance, Ragh.; Kathās.; (once n.) an iron bludgeon or club studded with iron, MBh.; R. &c.; a child which presents a peculiar cross position in birth, Suśr.; a line of clouds crossing the sun at sunrise or sunset, Var.; MBh. &c.; (du.) two birds flying on each side of a traveller (regarded as an omen), Var.; the gate of a palace, any gate, R.; a house, L.; (in astrol.) N. of the 19th Yoga, L.; a pitcher, water-jar, L.; a glass pitcher, L.; killing, striking, a blow, L.; N. of one of the attendants of Skanda, MBh.; of a Cāṇḍāla, ib.; of a virtuous man, Cat. **-guru**, mfn. as heavy as an iron bar, Mālav. **-prâṅśu-bāhu**, m. one whose arm is as long as an i° b°, Śak. **-bāhu**, m. one whose arm resembles an i° b°, MBh. **-saṃkāśa**, mfn. resembling an i° b°, MBh. **-stambha**, m. a door-post, Mālav. **Parighôpama**, mfn. resembling an iron beam, Nal.

Pari-ghāta, m. killing, destroying, removing, Var.; a club, an iron bludgeon, L. °**ghātana**, n. id., L. °**ghātin**, mfn. destroying, setting at nought, transgressing (a command &c.), R.

परिघट् *pari-√ghaṭ*, Caus. P. *-ghāṭayati*, to strike, cause to vibrate (as the strings of a musical instrument), Mṛicch.

परिघट्ट् *pari-√ghaṭṭ*, P. *-ghaṭṭayati*, to press or rub on all sides, stir, excite, affect (as the ear with a tale), Śiś. ix, 64. °**ghaṭṭana**, n. stirring round, stirring up, MBh.; rubbing, Śiś., Sch. °**ghaṭṭita**, mfn. stirred about, touched or rubbed repeatedly, MW.

परिघर्घरम् *pari-ghargharam*, ind. with loud murmuring or grunting, VP. (w. r. °*ghurgharam* or °*ghurghuram*).

परिघर्म्य *pari-gharmya*, m. a vessel for preparing any hot sacrificial beverage, ŚrS.

परिघात *pari-ghāta* &c. See under *pari-gha*.

परिघुष् *pari-√ghush* (only p. *-ghushyat*), to proclaim aloud, Sarvad. °**ghosha**, m. (L.) sound, noise; thunder; improper speech.

परिघूर्ण् *pari-√ghūrṇ*, P. *-ghūrṇati*, to whirl about, flutter, tremble, MBh.

परिघृष् *pari-√ghṛish*, P. *-gharshati*, to rub or pound to pieces, Hariv. °**ghṛishṭika**, w. r. for °*pṛicchika* or °*pṛishṭika*.

परिघ्रा *pari-√ghrā* (only p. Ā. *-jighramāṇa*), to kiss passionately, cover with kisses, MBh.

परिचक्र *pari-cakra*, m. N. of a ch. of the Dvā-viṅśaty-avadānaka; (*ā*), f. N. of a town (v. l. °*vakra*), L.

परिचक्ष् *pari-√caksh*, Ā. *-cashṭe* (3. pl. *-cakshate*; Pot. *-cakshīta*, Pass. *-cakshyate*; Ved. inf. *-cákshi*), to overlook, pass over, despise, reject, Br.; Up.; BhP.; to declare guilty, condemn, ŚBr.; to forbid, Āpast.; to mention, relate, own, acknowledge, MBh.; to call, name, Mn.; MBh. &c.; to address (acc.), answer, BhP. °**cakshā́**, f. rejection, disapprobation, ŚBr. °**cákshya**, mfn. to be despised or disapproved, RV.

परिचतुर्दश *pari-caturdaśa* and °*śan* (nom. acc. °*śa*, instr. °*śais*), fully fourteen, more than fourteen, MBh.; Hariv.

परिचपल *pari-capala*, mfn. always moving about, very volatile, MBh.

परिचय *pari-caya* &c. See under *pari-√1. 2. ci*.

परिचर् *pari-√car*, P. *-carati* (pf. *-cacāra*, ind. p. *-carya*), to move or walk about, go round (acc.), circumambulate, RV. &c. &c.; to attend upon or to (acc., rarely gen.), serve, honour, ib.: Caus. P. *-cārayati* (ind. p. *-cārya*), to surround, Kauś.; to wait on, attend to, Divyâv.; to cohabit, ib.; (Ā. °*te*), to be served or waited upon, ŚBr.; KaṭhUp. °**cará**, mf(*ā́*)n. moving, flowing, VS.; AV.; m. an attendant, servant, follower, ŚBr.; Suśr.; a patrol or body-guard, L.; homage, service, Hariv.; (*ā*), f. N. of partic. verses which may be put at the beginning or middle or end of a hymn, TāṇḍBr.; Lāṭy. °**cáraṇa**, m. an assistant, servant, ŚāṅkhBr.; n. going about, ŚBr.; serving, attending to, waiting upon, Kauś.; GṛS.; MBh. °**caraṇīya**, mfn. to be served or attended to, Kull.; belonging to attendance, Gobh. °**caritavya**, mfn. to be attended on or served or worshipped, Bhartṛ. °**caritṛi**, m. an attendant or servant, ChUp. °**carya**, mfn. = °*caritavya*, ChUp.; MBh.; Hariv.; (*ā*), f. circumambulation, wandering about or through (comp.), Hāsy. i, 9 (w. r. °*carcā*); attendance, service, devotion, worship, MBh.; Kāv. &c.; °*ryā-vat*, mfn. one who attends upon or worships, MBh. °**cāra**, m. attendance, service, homage, MBh.; a place for walking, ib.; an assistant or servant, ib. °**cāraka**, m. an assistant or attendant, Mn.; MBh.; Kāv. &c.; executor (of an order &c.), Hariv.; (*ikā*), f. a female attendant, a waiting maid, MBh.; R. &c. °**cāraṇa**, n. (m. c. for °*caraṇa*) attendance, MBh.; Daśar. °**cāraya**, Nom. P. °*yati*, to take a walk, roam about, SaddhP.; to cohabit, Divyâv.; to attend to, wait on, ib. °**cārika**, m. a servant, assistant, MBh.; pl. fried grain, L. °**cārita**, n. amusement, sport, Divyâv. °**cārin**, mfn. moving about, moveable, MBh.; attending on or to, serving, worshipping, MBh.; Hariv. &c.; m. man-servant (°*cāriṇī*, f. maid), TāṇḍBr.; MBh.; R.; °*ri-tā*, f., Kām. °**cārya**, mfn. to be served or obeyed or worshipped, W. °**cīrṇa**, mfn. attended to, taken care of, MBh.

परिचर्तन *pari-cartana*. See *pari-cṛit*.

परिचर्मण्य *pari-carmaṇya*, n. (*p*° + *carman*) a strip of leather, ŚāṅkhBr.

परिचल् *pari-√cal*, Caus. *-cālayati*, to cause to move round, turn round, MBh.

परिचि *pari-√1. ci*, P. Ā. *-cinoti*, °*nute*, to pile up, ŚBr.; to surround or enclose with (instr.), Śulb.; to heap up, accumulate, augment, increase, RV. &c. &c.: Pass. *-cīyate*, to be increased or augmented, to grow, Ragh. 1. °**caya**, m. heaping up, accumulation, Kauś.; *-vat*, mfn. being at its height, complete, finished, Mālav. iii, 20. 1. °**cayanīya**, mfn. to be collected or accumulated, W. °**cāyya**, m. (sc. *agni*) a sacrificial fire arranged in a circle, ŚBr.; TS.; Kāṭh.; Śulbas.; raising the rent or revenue of a land, W. °**cit**, mfn. piling up or arranging all around, VS. 1. °**cita**, mfn. heaped up, accumulated, gathered, Megh.; Rājat.; BhP.; (with instr.) filled with, containing, BhP. 1. °**cetavya**, mfn. to be collected together, W. 1. °**ceya**, mfn. to be collected all round or from every side, ib.

परिचि *pari-√2. ci* (2. sg. Impv. *-cinu*; p. *-cinvat*; inf. *-cetum*), to examine, investigate, search, MBh.; R.; to find out, know, learn, exercise, practise, become acquainted with (acc.), Kāv.; Rājat.; Pañc.: Pass. *-cīyate*, Kāv.; Hit.: Caus. Ā. *-cāyayate*, to search, seek for, Kāv. 2. °**caya**, m. acquaintance, intimacy, familiarity with, knowledge of (gen., loc., instr. with or sc. *samam*, or comp.), MBh.; Kāv. &c.; trial, practice, frequent repetition, Kāv. (cf. *rati-p*°); meeting with a friend, W.; °*yâvasthā*, f. (with Yogins) a partic. state of ecstasy, Cat. 2. °**cayanīya**, mfn. to be known, W. 2. °**cita**, mfn. known, familiar (°*taṃ* √*kṛi*, to make a person's acquaintance), Hariv.; Kāv.; *-bhū*, mfn. having (its) place well known, MW.; *-vivikta*, mfn. familiarised to seclusion, Śak. v, 10. °**citi**, f. acquaintance, familiarity, intimacy, Śāntiś.

2. **°cetavya** or **°ceya,** mfn. to be known; to be investigated or searched, W.

परिचिन्त् *pari-√cint,* P. *-cintayati* (ind. p. *-cintya*), to think about, meditate on, reflect, consider, MBh.; Kāv. &c.; to call to mind, remember, ib.; to devise, invent, ib. **°cintaka,** mfn. reflecting about, meditating on (gen. or comp.), MBh.; BhP. **°cintanīya,** mfn. to be well considered, Kāv. **°cintita,** mfn. thought of, found out, R.

परिचिह्नित *pari-cihnita,* mfn. marked, signed, subscribed, MBh.; Yājñ.

परिचुद् *pari-√cud,* Caus. *-codayati,* to set in motion, urge, impel, exhort, Mn. iii, 233. **°codita,** mfn. set in motion, brandished, Hariv.; impelled, incited, MBh.

परिचुम्ब् *pari-√cumb,* P. *-cumbati* (ind. p. *-cumbya*), to kiss heartily or passionately, cover with kisses, Kāv.; to touch closely, ib. **°cumbana,** n. the act of kissing heartily &c., Bālar.; Caurap. **°cumbita,** mfn. kissed passionately or touched closely, Caurap.

परिचृत् *pari-√crit,* P. *-critati* (ind. p. *-critya*), to wind round; to tie or fasten together, Kauś. **°cártana,** n. pl. the part of a horse's harness from the girth to the breast and the tail, TS.

परिच्छद् *pari-cchad* (√*chad*), Caus. *-cchādayati* (ind. p. *-cchādya*), to envelop, cover, conceal, MBh.; Pañc. **°cchad,** mfn. furnished or provided or adorned with (comp.), Ragh. i, 19. **°cchada,** m. a cover, covering, garment, dress, ŚāṅkhŚrS.; MBh. &c.; paraphernalia, external appendage, insignia of royalty, R.; goods and chattels, personal property, furniture, Mn.; MBh. &c.; retinue, train, attendants, necessaries for travelling; MBh.; Kāv. &c.; ifc. = *-cchad,* ŚāṅkhŚr.; MBh.; Hariv. &c. **°cchanda,** m. train, retinue, L. **°cchanna,** mfn. covered, clad, veiled, concealed, disguised, MBh.; R.; Hit. &c.

परिच्छिद् *pari-cchid* (√*chid;* inf. *-cchettum,* ind. p. *-cchidya*), to cut on both sides, clip round, cut through or off or to pieces, mutilate, ŚBr.; Lāṭy.; MBh. &c.; to mow or reap (corn), Kāraṇḍ.; to limit on all sides, define or fix accurately, discriminate, decide, determine, Kāv.; Pañc.; Pur.; to separate, divide, part, Siddh.; to avert, obviate, MW. **°cchitti,** f. accurate definition, Kap.; limitation, limit, measure, Pāṇ. iii, 3, 20, Sch.; partition, separation, W. **°cchinna,** mfn. cut off, divided, detached, confined, limited, circumscribed (*-tva,* n.), R.; BhP. &c.; determined, ascertained, Kum.; obviated, remedied, W. **°ccheda,** m. cutting, severing, division, separation, Śaṃk.; Suśr.; accurate definition, exact discrimination (as between false and true, right and wrong &c.), decision, judgment, Kāv.; Śaṃk.; Kull.; resolution, determination, Kād.; a section or chapter of a book, Cat.; limit, boundary, W.; obviating, remedying, ib.; *-kara,* m. N. of a Samādhi, L.; *-vyakti,* f. distinctness of perception, Mālatīm.; *°dākula,* mfn. perplexed (through inability) to decide, Śak.; *°dātīta,* mfn. surpassing all definition, Mālatīm. **°cchedaka,** mfn. ascertaining, defining, Sarvad.; n. limitation, limit, measure, L. **°cchedana,** n. (L.) discriminating, dividing; the division of a book; joyful laughter (?). **°cchedya,** mfn. to be defined or estimated or weighed or measured, Ragh. (*a-paricch°*); Pāṇ.; Sch.; Kull.

परिच्यवन *pari-cyavana,* n. (√*cyu*) descending from heaven (to be born as a man), HPariś.; loss, deprivation of (abl.), Āpast., Sch. **°cyuta,** mfn. fallen or descended from (abl.), MBh.; Kāv.; fallen from heaven (to be born as a man), HPariś.; swerved or deviated from (abl.), R.; deprived or rid of (abl.), Gaut.; MBh.; Pur.; ruined, lost, miserable (opp. to *sam-ṛiddha*), MBh.; streaming with (instr.), ib. **°cyuti,** f. falling down, Kathās.

परिजग्ध *pari-jagdha,* m. (√*jaksh*) a proper name, Pāṇ. vi, 2, 146, Sch.

परिजन *pari-jana,* m. (ifc. f. *ā*) a surrounding company of people, entourage, attendants, servants, followers, suite, train, retinue (esp. of females), MBh.; Kāv. &c.; a single servant, Kālid.; Kathās.; Pañc. **-tā,** f. the condition of a servant, service, Kir. x, 9.

परिजन्मन् *pari-janman,* m. the moon, L.; fire, L. (cf. *pari-jman*).

परिजपित *pari-japita,* mfn. (√*jap*) muttered, whispered, prayed over in a low voice, Gobh. **°japta,** mfn. id., Var.; enchanted, Divyâv.

परिजय्य *pari-jayya.* See *pari-ji.*

परिजल्प् *pari-√jalp,* P. *-jalpati,* to chatter, talk about, speak of (acc.), MBh.; Hariv. **°jalpita,** n. the covert reproaches of a mistress neglected by her lover, W.

परिजा *pari-jā́,* f. (√*jan*) place of origin, source, AV. **°jāta** (*pári-*), mfn. begotten by, descended from (abl.), ib.; fully developed (*a-parij°*), ĀśvGṛ. **°jātaka,** n. N. of a wk. on domestic rites.

परिजि *pari-√ji,* P. *-jayati* (inf. *-jetum*), to conquer, overpower, MBh. **°jayya,** mfn. to be conquered or mastered, Pāṇ. v, 1, 93. **°jetṛi,** m. a victor, conqueror, L.

परिजिहीर्षा *pari-jihīrshā,* f. (√*hṛi,* Desid.) desire of avoiding or removing, Kād. **°jihīrshita,** mfn. kept away, avoided, shunned, Gobh. **°jihīrshu,** mfn. wishing to avoid, L.

परिजृम्भ् *pari-√jṛimbh,* Ā. *-jṛimbhate,* to spread all around, Prasannar.

परिजॄ *pari-√1. jṝ,* P. Ā. *-jīryati,* °*te,* to become worn out or old or withered; to be digested, Suśr. **°jīrṇa,** mfn. worn out, old, withered, faded, decayed, MBh. **°jīryat,** mfn. becoming old, MBh.

परिज्ञा *pari-√jñā,* P. Ā. *-jānāti,* °*nīte* (inf. *-jñātum,* ind. p. *-jñāya*), to notice, observe, perceive, learn, understand, comprehend, ascertain, know or recognise as (2 acc.), RV. &c. &c. **°jñapti,** f. (fr. Caus.) recognition or conversation, Kathās. xxi, 128. **°jñā,** f. knowledge, L. **°jñāta,** mfn. thoroughly known, recognised, ascertained, learned, MBh.; Kāv. &c. **°jñātṛi,** mfn. one who knows or perceives, an observer, knower, Bhag.; wise, intelligent, W. **°jñāna,** n. perception, thorough knowledge, ascertainment, experience, discrimination, MBh.; Hariv.; R. &c.; *-maya,* mf(*ī*)n. consisting in knowledge, BhP.; *°nin,* mfn. having much kn°, wise, Kathās. **°jñeya,** mfn. to be recognised or ascertained, comprehensible, MBh.; Var. &c.

परिज्मन् *pári-jman,* mfn. (√*gam*) running or walking or driving round, surrounding, being everywhere, omnipresent (said of the sun, of the clouds, of sev. gods &c.), RV.; AV. (as loc. or ind. all around, everywhere, RV.); m. the moon, L.; fire, L. (cf. *pari-janman*).

परिज्यानि *pari-jyāni.* See *a-p°.*

परिज्रि *pári-jri,* mfn. (√*jri*) running round, spreading everywhere, RV.

परिज्वन् *pari-jvan,* m. (Uṇ. i, 158) the moon, L.; fire, L. (cf. *pari-jman*); a servant, L.; a sacrificer, L.; Indra, W.

परिज्वल् *pari-√jval,* P. *-jvalati,* to burn brightly, blaze, glare, Kir.

परिडीन *pari-ḍīna* or **°naka,** n. (√*ḍī*) the flight of a bird in circles, flying round, MBh.

परिणति *pari-ṇati.* See *pari-ṇam.*

परिणद् *pari-ṇad* (√*nad*), P. *-ṇadati,* to utter loud cries, Pāṇ. viii, 4, 14 (*-nadya,* MBh. vi, 3256 prob. w. r.)

परिणम् *pari-ṇam* (√*nam*), P. Ā. *-ṇamati,* °*te* (aor. *pary-anaṃsīt,* ind. p. *pari-ṇamya*), to bend or turn aside, AV.; to bend down, stoop, Kāv.; to change or be transformed into (instr.), Vedāntas.; Madhus.; to develop, become ripe or mature, Bālar.; to become old, Kir.; to be digested, MBh.; Pañc.; to be fulfilled (as a word), Pañc.: Caus. *-ṇāmayati* (ind. p. *-ṇāmya;* Pass. *-ṇāmyate,* p. *ṇāmyamāna* or °*myat*), to make ripe, ripen, mature, ŚvetUp.; to bring to an end, pass (as a night), R.; to bend aside or down, stoop, MBh. **°ṇata,** mfn. bent down (as an elephant stooping to strike with its tusks), Megh.; bent down or inclined by (comp.), Bhartṛ.; changed or transformed into (instr. or comp.), Kālid.; Kād.; Sāh.; developed, ripened, mature, full-grown, perfect; full (as the moon); set (as the sun), MBh.; Kāv. &c.; advanced (*vayasā,* in age, R.; also impers. °*taṃ vayasā,* 'life is advanced, old age has come,' Kathās.); digested (as food), Suśr.; elapsed (as time), BhP.; n. capital, wealth accumulated for the sake of profit (?), W.; *-dik-karika,* mfn. containing mythical elephants (see *dik-karin*) stooping to strike with their tusks), Śiś.; *-dvirada,* m. an elephant stooping &c., Kir.; *-prajña,* mfn. of mature understanding, MBh.; *-pratyaya,* mfn. (an action) whose results are matured, Divyâv.; *-vayas,* mfn. advanced in age, Veṇis.; Suśr.; *-śarad,* f. the latter part of the autumn, Megh.; °*tāruṇa,* m. the setting sun, Śak. **°ṇati,** f. bending, bowing, W.; change, transformation, natural development, Sāh.; Pañc.; Sarvad.; ripeness, maturity, Megh.; Mcar.; mature or old age, Vikr.; Śiś.; result, consequence, issue, end, termination (ibc. finally, at last; *śravaṇa-pariṇatim √gam,* to come at last to a person's ears; *pariṇatim √yā,* to attain one's final aim), Kāv.; fulfilment (of a promise), Śāntiś.; digestion, L. **°ṇamana,** n. change, transformation, changing into (instr.), Kap., Sch.; (*ā*), f. (with Buddh.) a kind of worship, Dharmas. xiv. **°ṇamayitṛi,** mfn. causing to bend or to ripen, Megh.; Viddh. **°ṇāma,** m. change, alteration, transformation into (instr.), development, evolution, Sāṃkhyak.; Yogas.; Pur.; Suśr.; ripeness, maturity, Kir.; Uttarar.; Mālatīm.; alteration of food, digestion, Suśr.; Tarkas.; withering, fading, ŚārṅgP.; lapse (of time), MBh.; R.; decline (of age), growing old, ib.; Suśr.; result, consequence, issue, end (ibc and °*me,* ind. finally, at last, in the end), Kāv.; (in rhet.) a figure of speech by which the properties of any object are transferred to that with which it is compared, Kuval.; N. of a holy man, RTL. 269; *-darśin,* mfn. looking forward to the issue or consequences (of any event), prudent, fore-sighted, MBh.; *-dṛishṭi,* f. foresight, providence, MW.; *-nirodha,* m. obstruction (of felicity caused) by human vicissitude (as birth, growth, death &c.), W.; *-pathya,* mfn. suited to a future state or condition, ib.; *-mukha,* mfn. tending or verging towards the end, about to terminate, Śak.; *-ramaṇīya,* mfn. (a day) delightful at its close, ib.; *-vat,* mfn. having a natural development (°*ttva,* n.), Saṃk.; *-vāda,* m. the 'doctrine of evolution,' the Sāṃkhya doctrine, Sarvad.; *-śūla,* n. violent and painful indigestion, Cat. **°ṇāmaka,** mfn. effecting vicissitudes (as time), Hariv. **°ṇāmana,** n. bringing to full development, Jātak.; the turning of things destined for the community to one's own use (Buddh.), L. **°ṇāmika,** mfn. resulting from change, L.; easily digestible, Subh. (w. r. for *pāriṇ°?*). **°ṇāmin,** mfn. changing, altering, subject to transformation, developing, VP.; Saṃk. (°*mi-tva,* n. ib.); ripening, bearing fruits or consequences, BhP.; °*mi-tva,* n. ib.; °*mi-nitya,* mfn. eternal but continually changing, Sāṃkhyak., Sch. **°ṇinaṃsu,** mfn. (fr. Desid.) about to stoop or to make a side thrust (with the tusks, as an elephant), Śiś.

परिणय *pari-ṇaya,* °*yana* &c. See under *pari-ṇī.*

परिणश् *pari-ṇaś* (√*2. naś*), P. *-ṇaśyati,* Pāṇ. viii, 4, 36, Sch. **°ṇashṭa** (!), mfn. ib.

परिणह् *pari-ṇah* (√*nah;* only Pot. *-ṇahet*), to bind round, gird, embrace, surround, MBh. **°ṇaddha,** mfn. bound or wrapped round, Kālid.; Var.; broad, large, Ragh. **°ṇah** = *parīṇah,* q. v. **°ṇahana,** n. binding or girding or wrapping round, veiling, covering, Gobh.; MānGṛ. **°ṇāha,** m. compass, circumference, extent, width, breadth, circumference of a circle, periphery, MBh.; Kāv.; Sūryas.; Suśr.; N. of Śiva, L. (cf. *parī-ṇāha*); *-vat,* mfn. = expensive, large, Vikr.; °*hin,* mfn. id., Hariv.; Kum.; (ifc.) having the extent of, as large as, Pañc.

परिणाय *pari-ṇāya,* °*yaka.* See *pari-ṇī.*

परिणि *pari-ṇi* for *pari-ni,* according to Pāṇ. viii. 4, 17 before a number of roots, viz. *gad, ci, dā, dih, drā, dhā* (see below), *nad, pat, pad, psā, mā, me, yam, yā, vap, vah, viś* (see below), *śam, so, han* (see below).

परिणिंसक *pari-ṇiṃsaka,* mfn. (√*niṃs*) tasting, eating, an eater (with gen.), Bhaṭṭ.; kissing, W. **°ṇiṃsā,** f. eating, kissing, W.

परिणिधा *pari-ṇi-√dhā* (Pāṇ. viii, 4, 17), P. *-dadhāti*, to place or lay round, ŚBr.; ind. p. *-ni-dhāya* (!), KātyŚr.

परिणिविश् *pari-ṇi-√viś* (Pāṇ. ib.), to sit down about, ŚBr.

परिणिष्ठा *pari-ṇishṭhā*. See *pari-nishṭhā*.

परिणिहन् *pari-ṇi-√han* (Pāṇ. viii, 4, 17), P. *-hanti*, to encompass (with stakes &c. fixed in) around, ŚBr.; to strike, smite, MBh. (B. and C. *-nighnantyaḥ* !).

परिणी *pari-ṇī* (√*nī*), P. Ā. *-ṇayati*, °*te* (pf. Ā. *-ṇinye*, Daś.; *-ṇayām āsa*, MBh.; 3. pl. aor. *-aneshata*, RV.; ind. p. *-ṇīya*, Kum.), to lead or bear or carry about or round, RV. &c. &c., (esp.) to lead a bride and bridegroom round the sacrificial fire (with 2 acc.), to marry (said of a bridegroom), MBh.; Kāv. &c.; to lead forward to, put or place anywhere (*agram*, at the head), Bṛ.; to carry away, RV.; to trace out, discover, investigate, Mn.; MBh.; (with *anyathā*) to explain otherwise, Śaṃk.: Caus. *-ṇāyayati*, to pass or spend (time), MBh.; (also *-ṇāpayati*), to cause a man to marry a woman (acc.), Pañcad. °**ṇaya**, m. leading round, (esp.) leading the bride round the fire, marriage, Gṛihyās. (cf. *nava-pariṇayā*); (*ena*), ind. round about, ĀpŚr.; *-vidhi*, m. marriage-ceremony, Vcar. °**ṇayana**, n. the act of leading round (cf. prec.), marrying, marriage, ŚrS. &c. °**ṇāya**, m. leading round; moving or a move (at chess &c.), L. °**ṇāyaka**, m. a leader, guide (in *a-parīṇ*°, being without a g°), R.; a husband, Śiś.; = *-ratna*, Divyâv. °**ṇīta**, mfn. led round, married, MBh.; completed, finished, executed, ib.; n. marriage, Uttarar.; *-pūrvā*, f. a woman married before, Śak.; *-bhartṛi*, m. (prob.) a husband who has married (but not yet led home) his wife, Vet.; *-ratna*, n. (with Buddh.) one of the 7 treasures of a Cakra-vartin, Dharmas. lxxxv. °**ṇetavya**, mfn. to be led round or married, Pañcad.; to be exchanged or bartered against (instr.), Nyāyam., Sch. °**ṇetṛi**, m. 'one who leads round,' a husband, Kālid.; Rājat. °**ṇeya**, mfn. to be led round, ĀśvGṛ.; (*ā*), f. to be led round the fire or married (as a bride), Kathās.; to be investigated or found out, Pat.; to be exchanged for or bartered against (instr.), Sāy.

परिणुत *pari-ṇuta*, mfn. (√4. *nu*) praised, celebrated, BhP.

परिणुद् *pari-ṇud* (√*nud*), P. *-ṇudati*, to pierce, hurt, wound, Suśr.

परितंस् *pari-√taṇs* (only inf. of Caus. *-taṇsayádhyai*), to stir up, RV.

परितकन *pari-takana*, n. (√*tak*) running round or about, L.

Pári-takmya, mfn. wandering, unsteady, uncertain, dangerous, RV.; (*ā*), f. travelling, peregrination, ib.; night (as the wandering, cf. x, 127), ib.

परितड् *pari-√taḍ*, P. *-tāḍayati*, to strike against, touch, Kathās. °**tāḍin**, mfn. striking or hurting everywhere, Bālar.

परितन् *pari-√tan*, P. Ā. *-tanoti*, °*nute* (aor. *-atanat*; ind. p. *-tatya*), to stretch round, embrace, surround, RV.; ŚBr.; KātyŚr. °**tatnú**, mfn. embracing, surrounding, AV.

परितप् *pari-√tap*, P. *-tapati* (fut. *-tapishyati*, MBh.; *-tapsyati*, R.; ind. p. *-tápya*, RV.), to burn all round, set on fire, kindle; to feel or suffer pain; (with *tapas*) to undergo penance, practise austerities, RV. &c. &c.: Pass. *-tapyate* (°*ti*), to be purified (as by fire), Sarvad.; to feel or suffer pain, do penance, practise austerities, MBh.; Kāv. &c.: Caus. *-tāpayati*, to scorch, cause great pain, torment, R.; Pañc.; Hit. °**tapta** (*pári-*), mfn. surrounded with heat, heated, burnt, tormented, afflicted, RV. &c. &c. °**tapti**, f. great pain or torture, anguish, L. °**tāpa**, m. glow, scorching, heat, Kālid.; MārkP.; pain, agony, grief, sorrow, R.; Kathās.; BhP. &c.; repentance, MBh.; Pañc.; N. of a partic. hell, L. °**tāpin**, mfn. burning hot, scorching, Kām.; causing pain or sorrow, tormenting, R.; Śiś.

परितम् *pari-√tam*, P. *-tāmyati*, to gasp for breath, be oppressed, Suśr.

परितर्क् *pari-√tark*, P. *-tarkayati*, to think about, reflect, consider, MBh.; R. °**tarkaṇa**, n. consideration, reflection, MBh. °**tarkita**, mfn. thought about, expected (*a-parit*°), Hariv.; examined (judicially), R.

परितर्ज् *pari-√tarj*, Caus. *-tarjayati*, to threaten, menace, R.; Bhartṛ.

परितस् *pari-tas*, ind. (fr. *pari*) round about, all around, everywhere (*na - paritaḥ*, by no means, not at all), MBh.; Kāv. &c.; as prep. (with acc., once with gen.) round about, round, throughout, AV. &c. &c.

परिताडिन् *pari-tāḍin*, mfn. (√*tāḍ*) striking or hitting everywhere, Bālar.

परितारणीय *pari-tāraṇīya*, mfn. (√*tṛī*, Caus.) to be delivered or saved (?), Cat. (perhaps w. r. for *-cāraṇīya* = *-caraṇīya*).

परितिक्त *pari-tikta*, mfn. extremely bitter, Jātakam.; m. Melia Azedarach, L.

परितीर *pari-tīra*, n. (prob.) = *pari-kūla*, Pāṇ. vi, 2, 182, Sch.

परितुद् *pari-√tud*, P. *-tudati*, to trample down, pound, crush, MBh.

परितुष् *pari-√tush*, P. *-tushyati* (°*te*, BhP.), to be quite satisfied with (gen. or loc. or instr.), to be much pleased or very glad, MBh.; Kāv. &c.: Caus. *-toshayati*, to satisfy completely, to appease, delight, flatter, ib. °**tushṭa**, mfn. completely satisfied, delighted, very glad, Mn.; MBh. &c.; °*ṭâtman*, mfn. contented in mind, MW.; °*ṭârtha*, mfn. completely satisfied, Kathās. °**tushṭi**, f. complete satisfaction, contentment, delight, Tattvas. °**tushya**, ind. being delighted or glad, Kathās. °**tosha**, m. (ifc. f. *ā*) = °*tushṭi*; (with loc. or gen.) delight in, Mn.; MBh. &c.; N. of a man, Cat.; *-vat*, mfn. satisfied, delighted, Kathās. °**toshaka**, mfn. satisfying, pleasing, Siṃhâs. °**toshaṇa**, mfn. id., BhP.; n. satisfaction, gratification, ib. °**toshayitṛi**, mfn. any one or anything that gratifies, pleasing, Śiś. (v. l. *para-t*°). °**toshita**, mfn. satisfied, gratified, delighted, Hariv.; R.; Kathās. °**toshin**, mfn. contented or delighted with (comp.), MBh.; Kathās.

परितृद् *pari-√tṛid*, P. *-tṛiṇatti* (Impv. *-tṛindhi*), to pierce or thrust through, RV.; ŚBr.

परितृप् *pari-√tṛip*, Caus. *-tarpayati*, to satiate or satisfy completely, MBh.; R. °**tarpaṇa**, mfn. satisfying, contenting, BhP.; n. the act of satisfying, Dhātup.; a restorative, Car. °**tṛipta**, mfn. completely satisfied or contented, Śaṃk. °**tṛipti**, f. complete satisfaction, Up.

परितृषित *pari-tṛishita*, mfn. (√*tṛish*) anxiously longing for (comp.), Kāraṇḍ.

परित्यज् *pari-√tyaj*, P. *-tyajati* (°*te*, R.; MārkP.; ind. p. *-tyajya*), to leave, quit, abandon, give up, reject, disregard, not heed, Mn.; MBh. &c.; (with *deham*) to forsake the body i. e. die, BhP.; (with *prâṇān* or *jīvitam*) to resign the breath, give up the ghost, Mn.; MBh.; Daś.; Vet.; (with *nāvam*) to disembark, MW.: Pass. *-tyajyate*, to be deprived or bereft of (instr.), Mn.; Pañc.; Hit. &c.: Caus. *-tyājayati*, to deprive or rob a person of (2 acc.), R. °**tyakta**, mfn. left, quitted &c.; let go, let fly (as an arrow), W.; deprived of, wanting (instr. or comp.), Mn.; MBh. &c.; n. anything to spare, Divyâv.; (*am*), ind. without (comp.), Pañc. °**tyaktṛi**, mfn. one who leaves or abandons, a forsaker, Mn. °**tyaj**, mfn. id., MBh. °**tyajana**, n. abandoning, giving away, distributing, W. °**tyajya**, ind. having left or abandoned &c.; leaving a space, at a distance from (acc.), Var.; with the exception of, excepting, ib. °**tyāga**, m. (ifc. f. *ā*) the act of leaving, abandoning, deserting, quitting, giving up, neglecting, renouncing, Mn.; MBh. &c.; separation from (*sakāśāt*), R.; (pl.) liberality, a sacrifice, Hit.; N. of wk. °**tyāgin**, mfn. leaving, quitting, forsaking, renouncing (mostly ifc.), MBh.; R. °**tyājana**, n. causing to abandon or give up, MW. °**tyājya**, mfn. to be left or abandoned or deserted &c., MBh.; to be given up or renounced, ib.; to be omitted, Sāh.

परित्रस्त *pari-trasta*, mfn. (√*tras*) terrified, frightened, much alarmed, Hariv.; R. &c. °**trāsa**, m. (ifc. f. *ā*) terror, fright, fear, MBh.; Kāv.

परित्रिगर्तम् *pari-trigartam*, ind. round about or outside Tri-garta, Pāṇ. ii, 1, 11; 12, Sch.

परित्रै *pari-√trai*, P. Ā. *-trāti* or *-trāyate* (Impv. *-trāhi*, *-trātu*, *-trāyasva*; fut. *-trāsyate*; inf. *-trātum*), to rescue, save, protect, defend (*-trāyatām* or °*yadhvam*, help! to the rescue!), MBh.; Kāv. &c. °**trāṇa**, n. rescue, preservation, deliverance from (abl.), protection or means of protection, refuge, retreat, Mn.; MBh. &c.; self-defence, L.; the hair of the body, L.; moustaches, Gal. °**trāta**, mfn. protected, saved, rescued, preserved, Kāv.; Pur.; m. N. of a man, L. °**trātavya**, mfn. to be protected or defended or saved from (abl.), Vikr.; Bālar. °**trātṛi**, mfn. protecting, a protector or defender (with gen. or acc.), MBh.; R.; Pañc.

परिदंशित *pari-daṇśita*, mfn. (√*daṇś*) completely armed or covered with mail, MBh. °**dashṭa**, mfn. bitten to pieces, bitten; *-dacchada*, mfn. biting the lips, BhP.

परिदश *pari-daśa*, mf(*ā*)n. pl. full ten, Jātakam.

परिदह् *pari-√dah*, P. *-dahati*, to burn round or through or entirely, consume by fire, dry up, Suśr.: Pass. *-dahyate* (°*ti*, Divyâv.), to be burnt through or wholly consumed, to burn (lit. and fig.), MBh.; Ṛit. &c. °**dagdha**, mfn. burnt, scorched, MBh.; Hariv. &c. °**dahana**, n. burning, W. (cf. *parī-d*°), W. °**dāha**, m. burning hot, Suśr.; mental anguish, pain, sorrow, MBh. °**dāhin**, mfn. burning hot, L.

परिदा *pari-√1. dā*, P. Ā. *-dadāti*, *-datte* (pr. 1. pl. *-dadmasi*, RV.; Impv. *-dehi*; pf. *-dadau*, *-dade*; ind. p. *-dāya*; inf. *-dātum*), to give, grant, bestow, surrender, intrust to or deposit with (dat., loc. or gen.), RV. &c. &c.: Caus. *-dāpayati* (ind. p. *-dāpya*), to cause to be delivered or given up, MBh. °**dá**, f. giving one's self up to the favour or protection of another, devotion, ŚBr.; KātyŚr. °**dāna**, n. id., ĀśvGṛ.; Kauś.; restitution of a deposit, L. (v. l. *prati-d*°). °**dāyin**, m. a father (or another relation) who marries his daughter or ward to a man whose elder brother is not yet married, L. 1. **Pári-tta** (for 2. see p. 605, col. 1), mfn. (Pāṇ. vi, 3, 124) given away, given up, delivered up to (loc.), VS.; MBh. **Parī-tti**, f. delivering, TBr.

परिदिव् *pari-√1. div*, P. *-devati*, °*vayati* (rarely Ā.; pr. p. f. *-devatīm*, MBh.; aor. *pary-adevishṭa*, pf. *pari-didevire*, Bhaṭṭ.; inf. *-devitum*, R.), to wail, lament, cry, bemoan, weep for (acc.), MBh.; Kāv. &c. °**deva**, m. lamentation, MBh.; Lalit. °**devaka**, mf(*ikā*)n. who or what laments or complains, Bhaṭṭ. (Pāṇ. iii, 2, 147). °**devana** (w. r. *-vedana*), n. lamentation, bewailing, complaint, MBh.; Kāv. &c.; (*ā*), f. id., Yājñ.; MBh.; Hit. °**devita** (w. r. *-vedita*), mfn. lamented, bewailed, MBh.; R. &c.; plaintive, miserable (*am*, ind.), ib.; n. wailing, lamentation, ib.; impers. with instr., e.g. °*tam Rāmeṇa*, 'wailing was made by R.' °**devin**, mfn. lamenting, bewailing, Śak. °**dyūna**, mfn. sorrowful, sad, ŚBr.; made miserable by (instr. or comp.), MBh.; R.

परिदिश् *pari-√diś* (pf. *-didesa*), to announce, make known, point out, Br. °**dishṭa**, mfn. made known, pointed out, MBh.

परिदिह् *pari-√dih* (only Subj. *-dehat*), to cover or smear over, RV. °**digdha**, n. meat covered with meal, L.

परिदीन *pari-dīna*, mfn. much dejected or afflicted; *-mānasa* (R.), *-sattva* (MBh.), mfn. distressed in mind.

परिदीप् *pari-√dīp*, Ā. *-dīpyate* (°*ti*), to flare up (lit. and fig.), MBh.

परिदु *pari-√2. du*, Ā. *-dūyate*, to burn (instr.), be consumed by pain or grief, MBh.; R.

परिदुर्बल *pari-durbala*, mfn. extremely weak or decrepit, MBh.; R.; *-tva*, n., Jātakam.

परिदृंहण *pari-dṛiṇhaṇa*, n. (√*dṛiṇh*) making firm, strengthening, ĀpŚr. **-dṛiḍha**, mfn. very firm or strong; m. N. of a man (cf. *pári-dṛiḍha*), L.

परिदृश् *pari-√dṛiś* (pl. Ā. *-dadṛiśrām*, AV.; inf. *-drashṭum*, MBh.), to look at, see, behold, regard, consider, find out, know: Pass. *-dṛiśyate* (pf. *-dadṛiśe*), to be observed or perceived, appear, become visible, KaṭhUp.; R. &c.: Caus. *-darśayati*, to show, explain, MBh.; Bhāshāp. °**drishṭa**, mfn. seen, beheld, perceived, learnt, known, MBh.; *-karman*, mfn. having much practical experience (°*ma-tā*, f.), Car. °**drashṭri**, m. a spectator, perceiver, MBh.

परिदॄ *pari-√dṛi* (only 3. sg. Prec. Ā. *-darshīshṭa*), to break through (the foe), RV. i, 132, 6: Pass. *-dīryate*, to peel or drop off on all sides, to become dropsical, TS.; ŚBr. °**dara**, m. a disease of the gums in which the skin peels off and bleeds, Suśr. °**dīrṇa** (*pári-*), mfn. rent on all sides, swollen, dropsical, ŚBr.

परिद्यून *pari-dyūna*. See *pari-div*.

परिद्रढय *pari-draḍhaya*, Nom. P. °*yati* (fr. *pari-dṛiḍha*), to make firm or strong, Pat.

परिद्रु *pari-√dru*, P. *-dravati*, to run round, RV.

परिद्वीप *pari-dvīpa*, m. N. of a son of Garuḍa, MBh. (v. l. *sarid-dvīpa*).

परिद्वेषस् *pári-dveshas*, m. a hater, RV.

परिधा *pari-√1. dhā*, P. Ā. *-dadhāti*, *-dhatte* (pf. *-dadhur*, *-dadhire*; fut. *-dhāsyati*; aor. *-dhāt*, *-dhīmahi*; ind. p. *-dhāya*; Ved. inf. *pári-dhātavai*), to lay or put or place or set round, RV. &c. &c.; to cast round, turn upon (*dṛishṭim*, with loc., Hariv.); to put on, wear (with or sc. *vāsas*), dress, VS.; AV.; ŚBr. &c.; surround, envelop, enclose, RV. &c. &c.; to conclude or close (the recitation of a hymn), TS.; Br.: Caus. *-dhāpayati* (ind. p. °*yitvā*, Pāṇ. vii, 1, 38, Sch.), to cause a person to wrap round or put on (2 acc.), Br. &c.; to clothe with (instr.), AV.: Desid. *-dhitsate*, to wish to put on, MBh. °**dhāna** (and °*dhānā*), n. putting or laying round (esp. wood), wrapping round, putting on, dressing, clothing, KātyŚr.; R.; Pañc.; a garment, (esp.) an under garment (ifc. f. *ā*), AV.; ŚBr. &c. (also *parī-dh°*); closing or concluding (a recitation), ŚāṅkhBr.; *-vastra*, n. an upper garment, Pañc. iv, §¾; °*nī-√kṛi*, to make into an u° g°, Śiś., Sch.; °*nīya*, n. an under garment; (*ā*), f. (sc. *ṛic*) a concluding or final verse, Br. °**dhāpana**, n. causing to put on (a garment), Kauś.; °*nīya*, mfn. relating to it, ib. °**dhāya**, m. (L.) train, retinue; the hinder parts; a receptacle for water. °**dhāyaka**, m. a fence, enclosure, L. °**dhi**, m. an enclosure, fence, wall, protection, (esp.) the 3 fresh sticks (called *madhyama*, *dakshiṇa*, *uttara*) laid round a sacrificial fire to keep it together, RV. &c. &c.; a cover, garment, BhP.; (fig.) the ocean surrounding the earth, ib.; a halo round the sun or moon, Ragh.; Var.; BhP.; the horizon, MBh.; BhP.; any circumference or circle, Var.; Sūryas.; epicycle, ib.; the branch of the tree to which the sacrificial victim is tied (?), W.; N. of a man, g. *śubhrâdi*; pl. (*shaḍ aindrāḥ*) N. of Sāmans, ĀrshBr.; *-saṃdhi*, m. (prob.) the putting together of the 3 fire-sticks (cf. above), MānŚr.; *-stha*, mfn. being on the horizon (as the sun), MBh.; m. a guard posted in a circle, L.; °*dhī √kṛi*, to hang about, Mcar.; °*dhy-upânta*, mf(*ā*)n. bordered by the ocean (as the earth), BhP. °**dhin**, m. N. of Śiva, MBh. (Nīlak.) °**dheya**, mfn. to be put round &c.; = *paridhi-bhava*, VS. (Mahīdh.; TS. v. l. *barhi-shad*); n. an under garment (?), MW. **Pári-hita**, mfn. put round or on, covered, invested, clothed, RV. &c. &c.

परिधाव् *pari-√dhāv*, P. *-dhā́vati* (ep. also °*te*), to flow or stream round or through, RV.; Suśr.; to run or drive about (with *mṛigayām*, 'to hunt'), MBh.; to run or move round anything (with acc.), AV.; MBh. &c.; to run through or towards or after (with acc.), MBh.; Kāv. &c.: Caus. *-dhāvayati*, to surround, encircle, MBh. °**dhāvana**, n. the running away from, escaping, MBh. °**dhāvin**, m. 'running round,' N. of the 46th (or 20th) of the 60 years' cycle of Jupiter, Var.

परिधीर *pari-dhīra*, mfn. very deep (as a tone or sound), Ghaṭ.

परिधू *pari-√dhū* (only 3. pl. Ā. *-dhunvate*), to shake off, BhP.

परिधूपन *pari-dhūpana*, *pari-dhūmana* and *pari-dhūmāyana*, n. = *dhūmāyana*, Suśr.

परिधूसर *pari-dhūsara*, mfn. quite dust-coloured or grey (*-tva*, n.), Prasannar.

परिधृ *pari-√dhṛi*, P. *-dhārayati*, to carry about, bear, support, AV.; MBh. °**dhāraṇa**, n. bearing, supporting, enduring (with gen.), MBh.; (*ā*), f. patience, perseverance, Mcar. °**dhārya**, mfn. to be preserved or maintained, Hariv. °**dhṛita**, mfn. borne (in the womb), MBh.

परिधृष् *pari-√dhṛish*, P. *-dharshayati*, to attack, rush upon, MBh. °**dharshaṇa**, n. assault, attack, injury, ib.

परिध्वंस *pari-dhvaṇsa*, m. (*√dhvaṇs*) distress, trouble, ruin, MBh.; Hit.; obscuration, eclipse (see *vidhu-*); (also *ā*, f.) loss of caste, mixture of castes, Āpast.; Mn. (also *varṇa-*, Āp., Sch.); an outcaste, Āpast. °**dhvaṇsin**, mfn. falling off, Suśr.; destroying, ruining, Kām.; Hit. v, 118 (v. l.) °**dhvasta**, mfn. covered with (comp.), R.; destroyed, ruined, ib.

परिनन्द् *pari-√nand* (only ind. p. *-nandya*), to rejoice greatly, give great pleasure to (acc.), MBh. xv, 522.

परिनर्तन *pari-nartana*, n. (*√nṛit*), g. *kshubhnâdi*.

परिनाभि *pari-nābhi*, ind. round the navel, Śiś.

परिनिःस्तन् *pari-niḥ-√stan*, P. *-stanati*, to groan loud, R.

परिनिन्द् *pari-√nind*, P. *-nindati* (or *-ṇindati*, Pāṇ. viii, 4, 33), to censure or blame severely, MBh.; BhP. °**nindana**, n., g. *kshubhnâdi*. °**nindā**, f. strong censure, MBh.; censoriousness, Subh.

परिनिम्न *pari-nimna*, mfn. much depressed, deeply hollowed, Suśr.

परिनिर्जित *pari-nir-jita*, mfn. (*√ji*) vanquished, conquered, MBh.; R.

परिनिर्णिज् *pari-nir-ṇij* (*√nij*; only ind. p. *-ṇijya*), to wash, cleanse, MBh.

परिनिर्मित *pari-nir-mita*, mfn. (*√3. mā*) formed, created (said of Vishṇu), Vishṇ.; marked off, limited, R.; settled, determined, MBh. °**vaśavartin**, m. pl. N. of a class of gods in Indra's world, Yogas., Sch. (cf. *paranirmita° v° v°*).

परिनिर्लुठ् *pari-nir-√2. luṭh*, P. *-luṭhati*, to roll down, Rājat.

परिनिर्वपण *pari-nirvapaṇa*, n. (*√2. vap*) distributing, dispensing, giving, W. °**nirvivapsā**, f. (fr. Desid.) desire of giving, liberality. °**nirvivapsu**, mfn. desirous of giving, Bhaṭṭ.

परिनिर्वा *pari-nir-√2. vā*, P. *-vāti*, to be completely extinguished or emancipated (from individual existence), attain absolute rest, Lalit.: Caus. *-vāpayati*, to emancipate completely by causing extinction of all re-births, Vajracch. °**vāṇa**, mfn. completely extinguished or finished (*a-parinirv°*), Śak.; n. complete extinction of individuality, entire cessation of re-births, MWB. 50; 122 &c.; N. of a place where Buddha disappeared, L.; *-vaipulya-sūtra*, n. N. of a Buddh. Sūtra. °**vāpayitavya**, mfn. to be completely extinguished or emancipated, Vajracch. °**vāyin**, mfn. being completely ex° or em°, Divyâv.

परिनिर्विण्ण *pari-nirviṇṇa*, mfn. (*√3. vid*) extremely disgusted with (loc.), MBh. °**cetas**, mfn. faint-hearted, despondent, ib.

परिनिर्वृत *pari-nirvṛita*, mfn. (*√1. vṛi*) completely extinguished, finally liberated, Divyâv. °**nirvṛiti**, f. final liberation, complete emancipation, Rājat.

परिनिर्हन् *pari-nir-√han* (only Impv. *-jahi*), to drive away, expel, AV.

परिनिवृत् *pari-ni-√vṛit*, Ā. *-vartate*, to pass away, MBh.

परिनिश्चय *pari-niścaya*, m. fixed opinion or resolution, MBh.

परिनिश्नथ् *pari-ni-√śnath* (only aor. *-śiśnathaḥ*), to push or strike down, RV.

परिनिषद् *pari-ni-shad* (*√sad*), P. *-shīdati* (3. pl. pf. Ā. *-shedire*, ind. p. *-shadya*), to sit around, RV.

परिनिषिच् *pari-ni-shic* (*√sic*), P. *-shiñcati*, to pour down upon, endow richly, MBh. (cf. next).

परिनिषेव् *pari-ni-shev* (*√sev*), Ā. *-shevate*, MBh. xiii, 3087, prob. w. r. for *-shecyate* (*√sic*).

परिनिष्ठा *pari-ni-shṭhā* (*√sthā*), Caus. *-shṭhāpayati*, to teach thoroughly, Uttarar. °**nishṭhā**, f. extreme limit, highest point, MBh.; Kap.; complete knowledge, familiarity with (loc. or comp.), Śaṃk.; Pur. °**nishṭhāna** (only *a-n°*), n. the being completely fixed, L.; mfn. having a final end or object, Nyāyam., Sch. °**nishṭhāpanīya**, mfn. to be exactly fixed or defined, ĀpŚr. °**nishṭhita**, mfn. quite perfect, accomplished, Śaṃk.; being in (loc.), Hariv.; Pur.; completely skilled in or acquainted with (loc. or comp.), MBh.; Kāv. &c. °**naishṭhika**, mf(*ī*)n. highest, utmost, most perfect, MBh.

परिनिष्पद् *pari-nish-√pad*, Ā. *-padyate*, to change or turn into (nom.), Kāraṇḍ. °**nishpatti**, f. perfection, Vajracch. °**nishpanna**, mfn. developed, perfect, real, existing, Saṃk.; Buddh.; *-tva*, n. real being, reality, Saṃk. °**nishpādita**, mfn. (fr. Caus.) developed, manifested, Kāraṇḍ.

परिनृत् *pari-√nṛit*, P. *-nṛityati*, to dance about or round (acc.), TS.; AV.; MBh.

परिनैष्ठिक *pari-naishṭhika*. See under *pari-ni-shṭhā*.

परिन्यस्त *pari-ny-asta*, mfn. (*√2. as*) stretched out, extended, Kathās. °**nyāsa**, m. completing the sense of a passage, W.; alluding to the development of the seed (*bīja*) or origin of a dramatic plot, Daśar.

परिपच् *pari-√pac*, P. *-pacati*, to bring to maturity, Divyâv.: Pass. *-pacyate*, to be cooked, Pañc.; to be burnt (in hell), Hariv.; to become ripe, (fig.) have results or consequences, Hariv.; Var.; approach one's end or issue, MBh.: Caus. *-pācayati*, to cook, roast, Suśr.; to cause to ripen, bring to maturity or perfection, Kāraṇḍ. °**pakva**, mfn. completely cooked or dressed, W.; completely burnt (as bricks), Var.; quite ripe, mature, accomplished, perfect, MBh.; Kāv.; Suśr.; highly cultivated, very sharp or shrewd, SaddhP.; near death or decay, about to pass away, MBh.; Suśr.; fully digested, W.; *-kashāya*, mfn. = *jitêndriya*, Kull. on Mn. vi, 1; *-tā*, f. being dressed or cooked, maturity; digestion; perfection; shrewdness, W.; *-śāli*, m. ripe rice, Rit. °**pacana**, n. = *tailapācanikā*, Car., Sch. °**pāka**, m. being completely cooked or dressed, Bhpr.; digestion, Vedântas.; ripening, maturity, perfection, Kāv.; Sāṃkhyak.; Suśr.; result, consequence (*āt* and *atas*, in c° of), Mcar.; Rājat.; cleverness, shrewdness, experience, Naish. (cf. *pari-p°*). °**pākin**, mfn. ripening, digesting, W.; (*inī*), f. Ipomoea Turpethum, L. °**pācana**, mfn. cooking, ripening, Suśr.; (fig.) bringing to maturity, Lalit.; n. and *-tā*, f. the act of bringing to m°, Lalit. °**pācayitṛi**, mfn. cooking, ripening, Megh., Sch. °**pācita**, mfn. cooked, roasted, Suśr.

परिपठ् *pari-√paṭh*, P. *-paṭhati*, to discourse, Sarvad.; to enumerate completely, detail, mention, name, MBh.; Suśr.; Pur. °**pāṭha**, m. complete enumeration; (*ena*), ind. in detail, completely, MBh. °**pāṭhaka**, mfn. enumerating completely, detailing, Cat.

परिपण *pari-paṇa*, m. n. (*√paṇ*) = *nīvī* (capital, stock?), L. °**paṇana**, n. playing for, wagering, Mudr. °**paṇita**, mfn. pledged, wagered, promised, W.

परिपण्डिमन् *pari-paṇḍiman*, m. complete whiteness, Śiś.

परिपत् *pari-√pat*, P. *-patati* (3. pl. pf. *-petur*), to fly or run about, wheel or whirl round, rush to and fro, move hither and thither, RV. &c. &c.; to leap down from (abl.), MBh.; to throw one's self upon, attack (with loc.), ib.; Kāv.: Caus. *-pātayati*, to cause to fall down, shoot down or off, MBh.; to throw into (loc.), Mṛicch.; to destroy, Divyâv. °**patana**, n. flying round or about, Śak.

परिपति *pári-pati*, m. the lord of all around, RV.; VS. (Mahīdh. 'flying about').

परिपद् *pari-√pad*, Caus. *-pādayati*, to change (*m* before *r* and the sibilants) into Anu-svāra, RPrāt. °**pád**, f. a trap or snare, RV. °**padin**,

m. an enemy, L. (w.r. for °*parin?*). °**panna**, n. the change of *m* into Anusvāra (cf. above), RPrāt. °**pāda**, m., g. *nirudakâdi*.

परिपन्थक *pari-panthaka*, m. (√*panth*) one who obstructs the way, an antagonist, adversary, enemy, Rājat. °**pantham**, ind. by or in the way, L. °**panthaya**, Nom. P. °*yati*, to obstruct the way, oppose, resist (with acc.), Rājat. °**panthika**, m. an adversary, enemy, MBh. °**panthin**, mfn. standing in the way, hindering; m. = prec., RV. &c. &c. (cf. Pāṇ. v, 2, 89); °*thi-tva*, n., Sāh.; Sarvad. °**panthī-√bhū**, to become the adversary of (gen.), Veṇis.

परिपर *pari-para*. See *a-pari-para*.

Pari-parin, m. (prob. fr. *pari* + *pari*) an antagonist, adversary, VS. (cf. Pāṇ. v, 2, 89).

परिपवन *pari-pavana*. See *pari-pū*, col. 2.

परिपश् *pari-√paś*, P. *-paśyati*, to look over, survey, RV.; AV.; to perceive, behold, see, observe, RV.; TS.; Br.; Up.; to fix the mind or thoughts upon (acc.), MBh.; to learn, know, recognise as (2 acc.), MuṇḍUp.; MBh.; BhP.

परिपशव्य *pári-paśavya*, mfn. (*paśu*) relating to the sacrificial victim, ŚBr.; KātyŚr.

परिपा *pari-√1. pā*, P. *-pibati*, to drink before or after (acc.), AitBr.; to drink or suck out, take away, rob, Kād. °**pắna**, n. a drink, beverage, RV. °**pīta**, mfn. drunk or sucked out, gone through, Kāv.; soaked with (comp.), Suśr.

परिपा *pari-√3. pā*, P. *-pāti* (aor. Subj. *-pāsati*, RV.), to protect or defend on every side, to guard, maintain, RV. &c. &c. °**pắna**, n. protection, defence, covert, RV. °**pālaka**, mf(*ikā*)n. (cf. √*pāl*) guarding, keeping, maintaining, Pur.; taking care of one's property, SaddhP. °**pālana**, n. the act of guarding &c., Vishṇ.; MBh.; Kāv. &c.; fostering, nourishing, Pañc.; (*ā*), f. protection, care, nurture, Bālar. °**pālanīya**, mfn. to be guarded or preserved or kept or maintained, Kād. °**pālayitṛi**, mfn. protecting, defending, Śaṃk. °**pālya**, mfn. = °*pālanīya*, MBh.; R. &c. °**pipālayishā**, f. (fr. Desid. of Caus.) desire of protecting or sustaining or preserving, Śaṃk.

परिपाक *pari-pāka*, °*kin* &c. See *pari-pac*.

परिपाटल *pari-pāṭala*, mfn. of a pale red colour, pale red, Kālid.; Śiś. &c. °**lita**, m. dyed pale red, Hariv.

परिपाटि *pari-pāṭi*, °*ṭī*, f. succession, order, method, arrangement, Var.; Caṇḍ.; Bhām.; Sāh.; arithmetic, Col.

परिपाण्डु *pari-pāṇḍu*, mfn. very light or pale, Kālid.; Ratnâv. °**pāṇḍiman**, m. excessive pallor or whiteness, Śiś. °**pāṇḍura**, mfn. dazzling white, Bālar.; Vcar. °**pāṇḍurita**, mfn. made very pale, ib.

परिपार्श्व *pari-pārśva*, mfn. being at or by one's side, near, at hand, KātyŚr. **—cara**, mfn. going at or by one's side, MBh. **—tas**, ind. at or by the side, on both sides of (gen.), MBh.; Hariv. **—vartin**, mfn. being at the side or near, Kum.; Prab.

परिपिङ्ग *pari-piṅga*, mfn. quite reddish-brown. °**ṅgī-√kṛi**, to dye reddish-brown, Śiś.

परिपिच्छ *pari-piccha*, n. an ornament made of the feathers of a peacock's tail, BhP.

परिपिञ्ज *pari-piñja*, mfn. full of (instr.), Kum.

परिपिञ्जर *pari-piñjara*, mf(*ā*)n. of a brownish red colour, Kād.; Vcar.

परिपिण्डीकृत *pari-piṇḍī-kṛita*, mfn. made up like a ball, Divyâv.

परिपिष् *pari-√pish* (only pf. *-pipesha*), to crush, pound, strike, R. °**pishṭa**, mfn. crushed, trampled down, MBh. °**pishṭaka**, n. lead, L.

परिपीड् *pari-√pīḍ*, P. *-pīḍayati*, to press all round, press together, squeeze, Kāv.; Suśr.; to torment, harass, vex, MBh.; Kāv. &c.; (in augury) to cover, cover up, Var. °**pīḍana**, n. squeezing or pressing out, Suśr.; injuring, prejudicing, Kām. °**pīḍā**, f. pressing, tormenting, R. °**pīḍita**, mfn. pressed; embraced; tormented, Kāv.

परिपीवर *pari-pīvara*, mfn. very fat or plump, Hariv.

परिपुङ्खित *pari-puṅkhita*, mfn. feathered (as an arrow), Bhām.

परिपुच्छय *pari-pucchaya*, Nom. Ā. °*yate*, to wag the tail, Pāṇ. iii, 1, 20, Sch.

परिपुट् *pari-√puṭ*, Pass. *-puṭyate*, to peel off, lose the bark or skin, Suśr. °**puṭana**, n. peeling, losing the bark or skin, ib.; *-vat*, mfn. peeling or dropping off, ib. °**poṭa**, m. peeling off (a partic. disease of the ear), Suśr.; *-ka*, m. id., ib.; *-vat*, mfn. peeling off, losing the skin, ib. °**poṭana**, n. peeling off, desquamation, losing the bark or skin, ib.

परिपुष् *pari-√push*, Caus. *-poshayati* (Pass. pr. p. *-poshyamāṇa*), to nourish, foster. °**pushṭa**, mfn. nourished, cherished (*-tā*, f., Yājñ.); amply provided with, abounding in (comp.), Kull.; augmented, increased, Sāh. °**posha**, m. full growth or development, Sāh. °**poshaka**, mfn. nourishing, confirming, Rājat. °**poshaṇa**, n. the act of cherishing or furthering or promoting, BhP. °**poshaṇīya**, mfn. to be nourished or promoted, Pañc.

परिपुष्करा *pari-pushkarā*, f. Cucumis Maderaspatanus, L.

परिपू *pari-√pū*, P. Ā. *-punāti*, °*nīte*, to purify completely, strain; Ā. (RV. *-pavate*), to flow off clearly. °**pavana**, n. cleaning, winnowing corn, Kull.; a winnowing basket, Nir. °**pūta**, mfn. purified, strained, winnowed, threshed, RV.; Mn. &c. °**pūti**, f. complete cleaning or purification, Bālar.

परिपूज् *pari-√pūj*, P. *-pūjayati*, to honour greatly, adore, worship, MBh.; Kāv. °**pūjana**, n. honouring, adoring, W. °**pūjā**, f. id., MW. °**pūjita**, mfn. honoured, adored, worshipped, ib.

परिपृच्छक *pari-pṛicchaka* &c. See *pari-prach*.

परिपॄ *pari-√pṝi*, Pass. *-pūryate*, to fill (intrans.), become completely full, Rājat.: Caus. *-pūrayati*, to fill (trans.), make full, cover or occupy completely, MBh.; Kāv. &c.; to fulfil, accomplish, go through, Kāraṇḍ. °**pūraka**, mfn. filling, fulfilling, Bhartṛ.; causing fulness or prosperity, Kull. °**pūraṇa**, n. the act of filling, Kāv.; accomplishing, perfecting, rendering complete, Śaṃk.; Kāraṇḍ. °**pūraṇīya**, mfn. to be filled or fulfilled, Hcat. °**pūrayitavya**, mfn. id., Kāraṇḍ. °**pūrita**, mfn. filled or occupied by, furnished with (comp.), MBh.; Kāv. &c.; accomplished, finished, gone through, experienced, Gīt. °**pūrin**, mfn. granting or bestowing richly, Śiś. °**pūrṇa**, mfn. quite full, Kauś.; completely filled or covered with, occupied by (comp.), MBh.; R. &c.; accomplished, perfect, whole, complete, ib.; fully satisfied, content, R.; *-candra-vimala-prabha*, m. N. of a Samādhi, L.; *-tā*, f., *-tva*, n. completion, fulness, satiety, satisfaction, L.; *-bhāshin*, mfn. speaking perfectly i.e. very wisely, R.; *-mānasa*, mfn. satisfied in mind, R.; *-mukha*, mf(*ī*)n. having the face entirely covered or smeared or painted with (comp.), Caurap.; *-sahasra-candra-vatī*, f. 'possessing a thousand full moons,' N. of Indra's wife, L.; *-vyañjanatā*, f. having the sexual organs complete (one of the 80 secondary marks of a Buddha), Dharmas. lxxxiv, 24; °*ṇârtha*, mfn. having attained one's aim, R.; full of meaning, wise (as a speech), MBh.; R.; °*ṇêndu*, m. the full moon, Mṛicch. °**pūrti**, f. fulness, completion, RPrāt., Sch.

परिपेलव *pari-pelava*, mf(*ā*)n. very fine or small, very delicate, Var.; n. (also *-pela*, L.) Cyperus Rotundus or a similar kind of grass, Suśr.

परिपोट *pari-poṭa* &c. See *pari-puṭ*.

परिपोष *pari-posha* &c. See *pari-push*.

परिप्रग्रह् *pari-pra-√grah*, P. *-gṛihṇāti*, to hand or pass round, KātyŚr.

परिप्रछ् *pari-√prach*, P. Ā. *-pṛicchati*, °*te* (pf. *-papraccha*; fut. *-prakshyati*; ind. p. *-pṛicchya*; inf. *-prashṭum*), to interrogate or ask a person about anything, to inquire about (with 2 acc. or with acc. of pers. and acc. with *prati*, loc. or gen. of thing), MBh.; Kāv. &c. °**pṛicchaka**, m. an interrogator, inquirer, GopBr. °**pṛicchanikā**, f. a subject for discussion, Divyâv. °**pṛicchā**, f. question, inquiry, L. °**pṛicchika**, mfn. one who receives anything only when asked for, MBh. (Nilak.) °**pṛishṭika**, mfn. id., ib. °**praśna**, m. question, interrogation, Bhag.; inquiry about (comp.), Pāṇ. ii, 1, 63 &c.

परिप्रणी *pari-pra-ṇī* (√*nī*, only Pass. *-ṇīyáte*), to fetch from (abl.), RV. i, 141, 4.

परिप्रथ् *pari-√prath* (only pf. Ā. *-paprathé*), to stretch round or over (acc.), RV. vi, 7, 7.

परिप्रधन्व् *pari-pra-√dhanv* (only Impv. *dhanva*), to run or stream about, RV.

परिप्रमुच् *pari-pra-√muc* (only Impv. Ā. *-muñcasva*), to free one's self from (abl.), RV. x, 38, 5.

परिप्रया *pari-pra-√yā* (only 2. pl. pr. *-yāthá*), to travel round (acc.), RV. iv, 51, 5.

परिप्रवच् *pari-pra-√vac* (only aor. *-pravocan*), to tell anything earlier than another person (acc.), ChUp. iv, 10, 2.

परिप्रवृत् *pari-pra-√vṛit*, Caus. *-vartayati*, to turn hither, RV. x, 135, 4.

परिप्रश्न *pari-praśna*. See *pari-prach*.

परिप्रस्यन्द् *pari-pra-√syand*, Ā. *-syándate* (aor. P. *-ásishyadat*), to flow forth or round, RV.

परिप्राप् *pari-prâp* (*-pra* + √*āp*), Caus. *-prâpayati*, to get done, bring about, accomplish, Lalit.; Divyâv. °**prâpaṇa**, n. taking place, occurrence, Pat. °**prâpti**, f. obtaining, acquisition, R. °**prâpya**, mfn. to be done, Divyâv. °**prêpsu**, mfn. (fr. Desid.) wishing to gain or obtain, desirous of (acc.), MBh.

परिप्रार्ध *pari-prârdha*, n. proximity, nearness, ŚāṅkhBr.

परिप्री *pari-prí*, mfn. very dear, highly valued, RV. **Pári-prīta**, mfn. id., ib.; much gratified, delighted, MBh.

परिप्रुष् *pari-√prush* (only pr. p. *-prushṇát*), to sprinkle about, TS. °**prúsh**, mfn. sprinkling, splashing, RV.

परिप्रे *pari-prê* (*-pra* + √*i*, only pr. p. *-prayát*), to run through on all sides, RV. ix, 68, 8.

परिप्रेरक *pari-prêraka*, mfn. (√*īr*) exciting, causing, effecting, Sāy.

परिप्रेष् *pari-prêsh* (*-pra* + √*1. ish*), Caus. *prâishayati*, to send forth, despatch, Bhaṭṭ. °**prêshaṇa**, n. sending forth; abandoning, W. °**prêshita**, mfn. sent forth; abandoned, ib. °**prêshya**, m. a servant, MBh. iv, 32 (v.l. *pare pr°*).

परिप्लु *pari-√plu*, Ā. *-plavate* (ind. p. *-plutya*, MBh.; *-plūya*, Pāṇ. vi, 4, 58), to swim or float or hover about or through, Br. &c. &c.; to revolve, move in a circle, ŚBr.; to move restlessly, go astray, Br.; to hasten forward or near, MBh.: Caus. *-plāvayati* (ind. p. *-plāvya*), to bathe, water, MBh. °**plavá**, mfn. swimming, VS.; Kaṭh.; swaying or moving to and fro, ŚāṅkhBr.; running about, unsteady, restless, Śiś.; m. trembling, restlessness, Bhpr.; bathing, inundation, W.; oppression, tyranny, ib.; a ship, boat, R. (v.l. *pāripl°*); N. of a prince (son of Sukhī-bala or Sukhī-vala or Sukhī-nala), Pur.; (*ā*), f. a sort of spoon used at sacrifices, KātyŚr. °**plāvya**, mfn. to be poured over, MBh. °**pluta**, mfn. bathed, one who has bathed in (loc. or comp.), MBh.; flooded, immersed, overwhelmed or visited by (instr. or comp.), MBh.; Kāv. &c.; n. a spring, jump, Var.; (*ā*), f. spirituous liquor, L.

परिप्लुष्ट *pari-plushṭa*, mfn. (√*plush*) burnt, scorched, singed, L. °**plosha**, m. burning, internal heat, Car.

परिफुल्ल *pari-phulla*, mfn. widely opened (as eyes), Śiś.; covered with erected hairs, ib.

परिबन्ध् *pari-√bandh*, Ā. *-badhnīte* (impf. 3. sg. *pary-abandhata*, MBh.; Pass. *pary-abadhyata*, ib.; pf. Ā. *pari-bedhiré*, AV.), to tie to, bind on, put on; to surround, encircle: Caus. *-bandhayati*, to tie round, embrace, span, Cat. °**baddha**, mfn. bound, stopped, obstructed, R. °**bandhana**, n. tying round, L.

परिबाध् *pari-√bādh*, Ā. *-bādhate*, to ward or keep off, exclude from, protect or defend against (abl.), VS.; Br. &c.; to vex, molest, annoy, MBh.; Kāv.: Desid. *-bibādhishate*, to strive to keep or ward off, ŚBr. °**bádh**, f. hindrance or a hinderer, RV. °**bâdha**, m. a noxious or troublesome demon, MantraBr.; (*ā*), f. trouble, toil, hardship, Śak.

परिबुभुक्षित *pari-bubhukshita*, mfn. (Desid. of *pari-√3. bhuj*), very hungry, MBh.

परिबृह् *pari-briṅh* (√2. *briṅh*, also written *vriṅh* in verb. forms and deriv.), P.Ā. *-briṅhati* (or *-brihati*), °*te* (p. pf. Ā. *-babrihāṇa*, prob. solid, strong, RV. v, 41, 12), to embrace, encircle, fasten, make big or strong, Br.: Caus. *-briṅhayati*, to make strong, strengthen, MBh. °**barha**, m. (ifc. f. *ā*) 'surroundings,' retinue, train, furniture, attire, trim, property, wealth, the necessaries of life, MBh.; R. &c.; royal insignia, L.; *-vat*, mfn. (a house) provided with suitable furniture, Ragh. °**barhaṇa**, n. retinue, train, attire, trim, MBh.; worship, adoration, BhP.; (*ā*), f. growth, increase, Nir., Sch. °**briṅhaṇa**, n. prosperity, welfare, BhP.; an additional work, supplement, Mn.; MBh. °**briṅhita** (or °*vriṅhita*; cf. Pāṇ. vii, 2, 21, Sch.), mfn. increased, augmented, strengthened by, connected or furnished with (instr. or comp.), MBh.; BhP.; n. the roar of an elephant, L. °**bṛiḍha** (*pári-*), mfn. firm, strong, solid, ŚBr.; Nir.; m. (only *-vriḍha*) a superior, lord, Rājat. (cf. Pāṇ. vii, 2, 21); comp. *-vraḍhīyas*, Pat.; superl. *-vraḍhishṭha*, ib.; or *-vriḍha-tama* (with *brahma*, n. the supreme spirit), Saṃk.; Nom. P. *-vraḍhaya*, °*yati*, Pat.; *-vraḍhiman*, m. (g. *driḍhâdi*) ability, capability, Śiś. v, 41 (*a-pariv°*).

परिबोध *pari-bodha*, m. (√*budh*) reason (*-vat*, mfn. endowed with reason, Śak. v, 21, v.l.) °**bodhana**, n. exhortation, admonition (also *ā*, f.), Kād. °**bodhanīya**, mfn. to be admonished, ib.

परिब्रू *pari-√brū*, P. *-bravīti* (Pot. *-brūyāt*), to utter a spell or charm, lay under a spell, enchant, AV.; Kaṭh.

परिभक्ष् *pari-√bhaksh*, P. *-bhakshayati*, to drink or eat up (esp. what belongs to another), devour, consume, MBh. °**bhakshaṇa**, n. eating up, consuming, MBh.; being eaten up by (instr.), ib. °**bhakshā**, f. passing over any one at a meal, N. of a partic. observance, ĀpŚr. °**bhakshita**, mfn. drunk or eaten up, devoured, consumed, ŚāṅkhBr.; Lāṭy., Sch.; MBh.

परिभग्न *pari-bhagna*, mfn. (√*bhañj*) broken, interrupted, disturbed, stopped, MBh.; R.; *-krama*, mfn. stopped in one's course, checked in one's progress, MBh. °**bhaṅga**, m. breaking to pieces, shattering, W.

परिभज् *pari-√bhaj* (only ind. p. *-bhajya*), to divide, MBh.

परिभय *pari-bhaya*, m. or n. (√*bhī*) apprehension, fear, Śaṃk.

परिभर्त्स् *pari-√bharts*, P. *-bhartsati* or *-bhartsayati*, to threaten, menace, scold, chide, MBh.; R. °**bhartsana**, n. threatening, menacing, R. °**bhartsita**, mfn. threatened, chided, ib.

परिभव *pari-bhava*, °*vana* &c. See *pari-bhū*.

परिभाण्ड *pari-bhāṇḍa*, n. furniture, utensils, Āpast.

परिभाव *pari-bhāva*, °*vana* &c. See *pari-bhū*.

परिभाष् *pari-√bhāsh*, Ā. *-bhāshate*, to speak to (acc.), address, admonish, MBh.; Hariv.; R.; to declare, teach, explain, define, Gṛihyâs.; Hariv.; Kāś.; to persuade, exhort, encourage, MW.; to abuse, Divyâv. °**bhāshaka**, mfn. abusive, Divyâv. °**bhāshaṇa**, mfn. speaking much (*a-paribh°*), R.; n. speaking, talking, discourse, Subh.; admonition, reprimand, reproof, Mn.; MBh.; Lalit.; rule, precept, W.; agreement (?), ib. °**bhāshaṇīya**, mfn. to be addressed or spoken to; reprehensible, deserving reproof, W. °**bhāshā**, f. speech, discourse, words, MBh.; BhP.; blame, censure, reproof (only pl.), Pat.; Bālar.; any explanatory rule or general definition, (in gram.) a rule or maxim which teaches the proper interpretation or application of other rules, Pāṇ.; (in medic.) prognosis; a table or list of abbreviations or signs used in any work; (also pl.) N. of sev. wks.; *-kroḍa-pattra*, n., *-°ṅka-sūtra* (°*shâṅk°*), n., *-chando-mañjarī*, f., *-ṭīkā*, f., *-prakaraṇa*, n., *-prakāśa*, m., *-prakāśikā*, f., *-pradīpa*, m., *-pradīpârcis*, n., *-bhāshya-sūtra*, n., *-bhāskara*, m., *-mañjarī*, f., *-rahasya*, n., *-°rtha-mañjarī* (°*shârth°*), f., *-°rtha-saṃgraha* (°*shârth°*), m., *-viveka*, m., *-viśesha*, m., *-vṛitti*, f., *-śiromaṇi*, m., *-saṃgraha*, m., *-sāra*, m., *-sāra-saṃgraha*, m., *-sūtra*, n., °*shêndu-bhāskara*, m., °*shêndu-śekhara*, m., °*shêndu-śekhara-saṃgraha*, m., °*shôpaskāra*, m. N. of wks. °**bhāshita**, mfn. explained, said, stated as (nom.), taught, established as a rule, formed or used technically, Hariv.; Bālar.; Bijag.; *-tva*, n., RPrāt., Sch. °**bhāshin**, mfn. speaking, telling (ifc.), R. °**bhāshya**, mfn. to be stated or taught (*a-paribh°*), Pat.

परिभास् *pari-√bhās*, Ā. *-bhāsate*, to appear, ŚBr. °**bhāsita**, mfn. (fr. Caus.) embellished, adorned, Cat.

परिभिद् *pari-√bhid*, Pass. *-bhidyate*, to be broken or destroyed, MBh. °**bhinna** (*pári-*), mfn. broken, split or cleft open, crumbled, ŚBr.; R.; disfigured, deformed, MBh. °**bheda**, m. hurt, injury, R. °**bhedaka**, mfn. breaking through, Cat.

परिभुज् *pari-√1. bhuj*, P. *-bhujati* (*-ábubhojir*, RV. i, 33, 9), to span, encompass, embrace, RV.; VS.; TāṇḍBr. °**bhugna**, mfn. bowed, bent, Bhaṭṭ. (Pāṇ. viii, 4, 31, Sch.)

परिभुज् *pari-√3. bhuj*, P. Ā. *-bhunakti*, *-bhuṅkte* (inf. *-bhoktum*), to eat before another (with acc.), MBh.; to neglect to feed, BhP.; to feed upon, eat, consume, enjoy, Kāv.; Sāh. °**bhukta**, mfn. eaten before another, anticipated in eating, MBh.; eaten, enjoyed, possessed, Kāv.; worn (as a garment), Divyâv. °**bhoktṛi**, mfn. eating, enjoying, SaddhP.; living at another's cost, Mn. ii, 201. °**bhoga**, m. enjoyment, (esp.) sexual intercourse, MBh.; Kāv.; Var.; illegal use of another's goods, W.; means of subsistence or enjoyment, MBh. °**bhogya** (!), n. use, Divyâv.

परिभू *pari-√bhū*, P. Ā. *-bhavati*, °*te* (pf. *-babhūva*, °*bhūtha*, °*bhūvuḥ*, RV.; aor. *-abhūvan*, *-bhuvat*; Subj. *-bhūtas*, *-bhūthas*, ib.; Impv. *-bhūtu*, ib.; Ved. inf. *-bhvé*, ib.; ind. p. *-bhūya*, MBh., Kāv. &c.: Pass. *-bhūyate*, R.; fut. *-bhavishyate*, Bhaṭṭ.), to be round anything, surround, enclose, contain, RV.; AV.; Br.; to go or fly round, accompany, attend to, take care of, guide, govern, RV.; AV.; to be superior, excel, surpass, subdue, conquer, RV. &c. &c.; to pass round or over, not heed, slight, despise, insult, MBh.; Kāv. &c.; to disgrace, MBh.; to disappear, be lost (= *parā-bhū*), ib.: Caus. *-bhāvayati*, °*te* (ind. p. *-bhāvya*), to spread around, divulge, make known, Uttarar.; to surpass, exceed, BhP.; to soak, saturate, sprinkle, Suśr.; ŚārṅgS.; to contain, include, BhP.; to conceive, think, consider, know, recognise as (acc.), Prab.; Rājat.; BhP.; Pañc. °**bhava**, m. insult, injury, humiliation, contempt, disgrace, MBh.; Kāv. &c.; *-pada*, n. an object or occasion of contempt, Kālid.; Hit.; *-vidhi*, m. humiliation, Śṛiṅgār.; °*vâspada*, n. = °*va-pada*, Vikr.; MārkP. °**bhavana**, n. humiliation, degradation, Mālav. °**bhavanīya**, mfn. liable to be insulted or offended or humiliated, Mālav.; Kād.; Kathās. °**bhavin**, mfn. injuring, despising, ridiculing, Inscr.; suffering disrespect, W. (cf. Pāṇ. iii, 2, 157). °**bhāva** (also *pari-bh°*), m. contempt, Pañc. i, $\frac{282}{283}$ (B. °*bhava*). °**bhāvana**, n. cohesion, union, MBh.; (*ā*), f. thought, contemplation, Uttarar.; (in dram.) words exciting curiosity, Sāh. °**bhāvita**, mfn. enclosed, contained, BhP.; (*-tva*, n., RPrāt., Sch., w. r. for *bhāshita-tva*); penetrated, pervaded, ib.; conceived, imagined, ib. °**bhāvin**, mfn. injuring, despising, slighting, mocking, defying (ifc.), Kālid.; Ratnâv. °**bhāvuka**, mf(*ī*)n. who or what shames or humbles or outstrips another (with acc.), Śis. °**bhú**, mfn. surrounding, enclosing, containing, pervading, guiding, governing, RV.; AV.; TS.; TBr.; ĪśUp. °**bhūta**, mfn. overpowered, conquered, slighted, disregarded, despised, Kāv.; Pur.; m. (with *bhaṭṭa*) N. of a poet, Cat.; *-gati-traya*, mfn. surpassing three times the age of man, BhP.; *-tā*, f. humiliation, degradation, Vajracch. °**bhūti** (*pári-*), f. superiority, RV.; contempt, humiliation, disrespect, injury, Kathās.; Pañc.; BhP.

परिभूष् *pari-√bhūsh*, P. *-bhūshati*, to run round, circumambulate, RV.; to wait upon, serve, attend, honour, obey, follow, ib.; to fit out, decorate, ib.; to be superior, surpass in (instr.), ib. ii, 12, 1. °**bhūshaṇa**, m. (sc. *saṃdhi*) peace obtained by the cession of the whole revenue of a land, Kām. (v. l. *para-bh°*). °**bhūshita**, mfn. decorated, adorned, MBh.

परिभृ *pari-√bhṛi*, P. Ā. *-bharati*, °*te* (pf. P. *-babhrima* [1], BhP.; Ā. *-jabhre*, RV.), to bring, RV.; (Ā.) to extend or pass beyond, ib. (also trans. = extend, spread, i, 97, 15); to roam or travel about, BhP. (cf. above).

परिभेद *pari-bheda*, °*dhaka*. See *pari-bhid*.

परिभोग *pari-bhoga* &c. See *pari-√3. bhuj*.

परिभ्रंश् *pari-√bhraṅś*, only pr. p. Ā. in *a-paribhraśyamāna*, mfn. not escaping, Kām. °**bhraṅśa**, m. escape, Hariv. °**bhraṅśana**, n. falling from, loss of (abl.), Pañc. °**bhrashṭa**, mfn. fallen or dropped off; fallen from (often = omitting, neglecting); deprived of (abl. or comp., rarely instr.), Mn.; MBh. &c.; fallen, lost, ruined; sunk, degraded, MBh.; Kāv. &c.; escaped, vanished, MBh.; Kathās.; *-satkarman*, mfn. one whose virtuous acts are lost or in vain, BhP.; *-sukha*, mfn. fallen from happiness, MBh.

परिभ्रज्ज् *pari-√bhrajj*, only pr. p. *-bhrijjyat* (with pass. meaning, MBh. [B.] xi, 97, C. *-bhujyat*) and Caus. *-bharjayati* (Bhpr.), to fry, roast, parch. °**bhṛishṭa**, mfn. fried, roasted, parched, Suśr.

परिभ्रम् *pari-√bhram*, P. *-bhramati*, *-bhrāmyati* (ep. also °*te*; pr. p. *-bhramat*, *-bhrāmyat* and *-bhramamāṇa*; pf. *-babhrāma*, 3. pl. *-babhramuḥ* or *-bhremuḥ*; ind. p. *-bhramya*; inf. *-bhramitum* or *-bhrāntum*), to rove, ramble, wander about or through, MBh.; Kāv. &c.; (also with *maṇḍalam*) to turn or whirl round, move in a circle, describe a c° round, revolve, rotate, MaitrUp.; Hariv.; R.; BhP.: Caus. *-bhrāmayati*, to stir up, shake through, Bhpr. °**bhrama**, mfn. flying round or about (see *khe-paribhr°*); m. wandering, going about, BhP.; circumlocution, rambling discourse, Mṛicch. i, $\frac{2}{3}$; error, W. °**bhramaṇa**, n. turning round, revolving (as of wheels), BhP.; moving to and fro, going about, Prasaṅg.; circumference, Sūryas. °**bhrāmaṇa**, n. (fr. Caus.) turning to and fro, BhP. °**bhrāmin**, mfn. moving hither and thither in (comp.), Bālar.

परिभ्राज् *pari-√bhrāj* (only pf. *-babhrāja*), to shed brilliance all around, R.

परिमण्डल *pari-maṇḍala*, mf(*ā*)n. round, circular, globular, ŚBr.; MBh. &c.; of the measure of an atom, A.; m. (sc. *maśaka*) a species of venomous gnat, Suśr.; n. a globe, sphere, orbit, circumference, MBh.; BhP.; Hcat.; *-kushṭha*, n. a kind of leprosy, Car.; *-tā*, f. whirling about, Kir.; roundness, rotundity, circularity, Kād.; Suśr. (also *-tva*, n., MW.) °**maṇḍalita**, mfn. rounded, made round or circular, Kir.

परिमण्डित *pari-maṇḍita*, mfn. (√*maṇḍ*) adorned or decorated all around, R.

परिमथ् *pari-√math* (only impf. *-ámathnāt*), to pluck (the Soma plant), RV. i, 93, 6. °**mathita**, mfn. (Agni) produced by attrition, ib. iii, 9, 5. °**māthin**, mfn. torturing, Mālatim.

परिमन् *pari-√man* (only Pot. *-mamanyāt*; pf. *-mamnāthe*; aor. Subj. *-máṅsate*), to overlook, neglect, disregard, RV. °**mat**, mfn., Vop. xxvi, 78.

परिमन्त्रित *pari-mantrita*, mfn. (√*mantr*) charmed, consecrated, enchanted, MBh.

परिमन्थर *pari-manthara*, mf(*ā*)n. extremely slow or tardy, Śiś.; Caṇḍ. **-tā**, f. slowness, dullness, Veṇīs.

परिमन्द *pari-manda*, mfn. very dull or faint or weak, Śiś.; (ibc.) a little, ib. **-tā**, f. fatigue, ennui, ib.

परिमन्यु *pari-manyú*, mfn. wrathful, angry, RV.

परिमर *pari-mara*, *pari-marda*, *pari-marśa*. See *pari-mṛi*, *-mṛid*, *-mṛiś*, p. 599.

परिमल *pari-mala*, m. (Prākr. fr. √*mṛid*?) fragrance, or a fragrant substance, perfume (esp. arising from the trituration of fragrant substances), Kāv.; Pañc. &c.; copulation, connubial pleasure,

Kir. (see below); a meeting of learned men, L.; soil, stain, dirt, L.; N. of a poet (also called Padmagupta), Cat.; of sev. wks. and Comms.; *-ja*, mfn. (enjoyment) arising from copulation, Kir. x, 1; *-bhṛit*, mfn. laden with perfumes, Bhartṛ.; *-samā*, f. N. of Comm. on VarBṛS. **°malaya**, Nom. P. *°yati*, to make fragrant, Prasannar. **°malita**, mfn. soiled, deprived of freshness or beauty, W.; perfumed, ib.

परिमा *pari-√mā*, Ā. *-mimīte* (pf. *-mame;* Pass. *-mīyate;* inf. *-mātum*), to measure round or about, mete out, fulfil, embrace, RV. &c. &c.; to measure, estimate, determine, MBh.; Kāv. &c. **°mā**, f. measure, periphery, MaitrS. **°māṇa**, n. measuring, meting out, KātyŚr.; Var.; (also *-ka*, n., Bhāshāp.) measure of any kind, e.g. circumference, length, size, weight, number, value, duration (ifc. 'amounting to'), RV. &c. &c. (cf. *parī-m°*); *-tas*, ind. by measure, in weight, Mn. viii, 133; *-vat* (L.; *°t-tva*, n.); *°ṇin* (Pāṇ.), mfn. having measure, measured, measurable. **°mita** (*pári-*), mfn. measured, meted, limited, regulated, RV. &c. &c.; moderate, sparing, MBh.; Kāv. &c.; *-katha*, mf(*ā*)n. of measured discourse, speaking little, Megh.; *-tva*, n. moderation, limited condition, Kap., Sch.; *-bhuj*, mfn. eating sparingly, abstemious, W.; *-bhojana*, n. moderation in eating, abstemiousness, MW.; *°tâbharaṇa*, mf(*ā*)n. moderately adorned, Mālav.; Pañc.; *°tâyus*, mfn. short-lived, R.; *°tâhāra*, mfn. = *°ta-bhuj*, MBh.; *°têcchatā*, f. moderation in desire, MW. **°miti**, f. measure, quantity, limitation, Bhāshāp.; *-mat*, mfn. limited, Kāv. **°meya**, mfn. measurable, limited, few, MBh. (*a-parim°*), Kāv. &c.; *-tā*, f. measurableness, calculableness, MW.; *-puraḥ-sara*, mfn. having only few attendants, Ragh.

परिमाद *pari-mád*, f., *-māda*, m. (√*mad*) N. of 16 Sāmans which belong to the Mahā-vrata-stotra, Br.; Lāṭy.

परिमार्ग् *pari-√mārg*, P. Ā. *-mārgati*, *°te* (inf. *-mārgitum*), to seek about, search through, strive after, beg for (acc.), MBh.; R. 1. **°mārga**, m. (for 2. see *pari-mṛij*) searching about, Pratāp. **°mārgaṇa**, n. tracing, searching, looking for (gen.), MBh.; R. **°mārgitavya**, mfn. to be sought after, Bhag. **°mārgin**, mfn. tracking, going after, pursuing (comp.), MBh.

परिमि *pari-√1. mi*, P. *-minoti*, to set or place or lay round, TS.; Kāṭh. **°mit**, f. the beam of a roof, joist, rafter &c., AV.

परिमिलन *pari-milana*, n. (√*mil*) touch, contact, Ratnāv. **°milita**, mfn. mixed or filled with, pervaded by (instr.), Śiś.; met from all sides, Prasannar.

परिमीढ *pari-mīḍha*, mfn. (√*mih*) sprinkled with urine, PārGṛ. **°meha**, m. a magical rite in which urine is sprinkled about, ib.

परिमुखम् *pari-mukham*, ind. round or about the face, round, about (any person, &c.), Pāṇ. iv, 4, 29.

परिमुग्ध *pari-mugdha* &c. See *pari-muh.*

परिमुच् *pari-√muc*, P. *-muñcáti* (ind. p. *-mucya;* inf. *-moktum*), to unloose, set free, liberate, deliver from (abl.), AV.; MBh. &c.; to let go, give up, part with (acc.), Kāv.; to discharge, emit, Kathās.: Pass. *-mucyate* (*°ti*, MuṇḍUp.), to loosen or free one's self, get rid of (abl., gen. or instr.), RV. &c. &c.; to be liberated or emancipated (from the ties of the world), Kauś.; Up. **°mukta**, mfn. released, liberated from (comp.); *-bandhana*, mfn. released from bonds, unfettered, Śak. **°mukti**, f. liberation, A. **°mocita**, mfn. (fr. Caus.) liberated, emancipated, Vajracch.

परिमुष् *pari-√mush*, P. *-mushṇāti*, *-mushati* (Pass. pr. p. *-mushyat*, MBh.), to steal, plunder, rob a person of (2 acc.), AV. &c. &c. **°moshá**, m. theft, robbery, TS. &c. &c. **°moshaka**, mfn. stealing, MBh. **°moshaṇa**, n. taking away, Āpast. **°moshin**, mfn. stealing; a thief or robber, ŚBr.

परिमुह् *pari-√muh*, P. Ā. *-muhyati*, *°te*, to be bewildered or perplexed, go astray, fail, ŚvetUp.; MBh.; R.: Caus. *-mohayati* (*°te*, Pāṇ. i, 3, 89), to bewilder, perplex, entice, allure, trouble, disturb, Kauś.; MBh.; Kāv. **°mugdha**, mfn. bewitchingly lovely (*-tā*, f.), Śiś. **°mūḍha**, mfn. disturbed, perplexed (*-tā*, f.), Uttarar.; Śiś. **°mohana**, n. (fr. Caus.) bewildering, fascination, beguiling, Uttarar.; Caurap. **°mohita**, mfn. bewildered, deprived of consciousness or recollection, MBh.; Hariv.; R. **°mohin**, mfn. perplexed, Śiś.; fascinating, bewitching, W.

परिमृ *pari-√mṛi*, Ā. *-mriyate* (pf. 3. pl. *-mamruḥ*, AitBr.), to die (in numbers) round (acc.), Br.; Up. **°mará**, mfn. one round whom people have died, TS.; m. the dying in numbers or round any one; (with *daivaḥ*) the dying of the gods, KaushUp.; (with *brahmaṇaḥ*) N. of a magical rite for the destruction of adversaries, AitBr.; TUp. **°mūrṇa**, mf(*ī*)n. worn out, decrepit, old (as a cow), ŚBr.; KātyŚr. (Sch. = *vṛiddhā*).

परिमृग् *pari-√mṛig*, Ā. *-mṛigayate* (Pass. p. *-mṛigyamāṇa*), to seek, search for, R.

परिमृज् *pari-√mṛij*, P. *-mārshṭi*, *-mṛijati*, *-mārjati*, *-mārjayati* (rarely Ā., e.g. Pot. *-mṛijīta*, Gobh.; ind. p. *-mṛijya;* inf. *-mārshṭum* or *-mārjitum*), to wipe all round, wash, cleanse, purify, RV. &c. &c.; (with *cakshushī*) to wipe tears from the eyes, MBh.; R.; (also Ā.) to cleanse or rinse the mouth, Gaut.; Āpast.; Gobh.; MBh.; to touch lightly, stroke, MBh.; to wipe off or away, remove, efface, get rid of (acc.), R.; Kālid.; BhP.: Pass. *-mṛijyate*, to be rubbed or worn out by use (as teeth), MBh. xii, 5303: Intens. *-marmṛijyate*, to sweep over (acc.), RV. i, 95, 8 (Sāy. 'to cover with radiance'). 2. **°mārga** (for 1. see *pari-mārg*), m. wiping, cleaning; friction, touch, W. **°mārgya**, mfn. to be cleaned or rubbed, Pāṇ. iii, 1, 113 (cf. *°mṛijya*). **°mārja** and **°mārjaka**, see *tunda-pari-mārja*, *°jaka*. **°mārjana**, n. wiping off, cleaning, washing, KātyŚr.; Gaut.; wiping away, removing, Hcat.; a dish of honey and oil, L. **°mārjita**, mfn. cleaned, polished, MBh. **°mṛij**, mfn. washing, cleaning (in *kaṅsa-pari-mṛij*), Pāṇ. viii, 2, 36, Sch. **°mṛija**, see *tunda-parimṛija*. **°mṛijita**, mfn. wiped, rubbed, cleaned, Prab. **°mṛijya**, mfn. to be cleaned or rubbed, Pāṇ. iii, 1, 113 (cf. *°mārgya*). 1. **°mṛishṭa**, mfn. (for 2. see *pari-mṛiś*) wiped off, rubbed, stroked, smoothed, polished, Āpast.; R.; wiped or washed away, removed, BhP.; *paricchada*, mfn. trim, neat, spruce, ib.

परिमृद् *pari-√mṛid*, P. *-mṛidnāti*, *-mardati* (ep. also Ā. *-mardate*), to tread or trample down, crush, grind, wear out, MBh.; Kāv.; to rub, stroke, MBh.; rub off, wipe away (as tears), R.; to excel, surpass, MBh. **°marda**, m. crushing, wearing out, using up, destroying, MBh. **°mardana**, n. id., L.; rubbing in, Car.; a remedy for rubbing in, ib. **°mṛidita**, mfn. trodden or trampled down, crushed, rubbed, ground, Bhavab.

परिमृश् *pari-√mṛiś*, P. Ā. *-mṛiśati*, *°te* (pf. *-mamarśa;* 3. pl. [RV.] *-māmṛiśuḥ;* aor. *-amṛikshat;* ind. p. *-mṛiśya*), to touch, grasp, seize, RV. &c. &c.; to examine, consider, inquire into, ib.; to observe, discover, BhP.: Pass. *-mṛiśyate* (with *pavanais*), to be touched i.e. fanned by the wind, Suśr.; to be considered, MBh.: Intens. *-marmṛiśat*, to encompass, clasp, embrace, RV. **°marśa**, m. touching, contact, Dharmaś.; consideration, reflection, MBh.; **°mārkshṇu**, mfn., Vop. xxvi, 144. 2. **°mṛishṭa**, mfn. (for 1. see *pari-mṛij*) touched, Bhaṭṭ.; seized, caught, found out, Mālav.; considered (see *duḥ-parim°*), Suśr.; spread, pervaded, filled with (instr.), Kir.

परिमृष् *pari-√mṛish*, P. *-mṛishyati* (Pāṇ. i, 3, 82), to be angry with, envy (dat.), Bhaṭṭ. **°marsha**, m. envy, dislike, anger, W.; v.l. for *°marśa*, touching, Hariv.

परिमोक्ष् *pari-√moksh*, P. *-mokshayati* (ind. p. *-mokshya*), to set free, liberate, MBh. **°moksha**, m. setting free, liberation, deliverance, MBh.; R.; removing, relieving, Ragh. ix, 62 (v.l. *pari-mosha*); emptying, evacuation, BhP.; escape from (abl. or gen.), MBh.; final beatitude (= *nir-vāṇa*), A. **°mokshaṇa**, n. unloosing, untying, Suśr.; liberation, deliverance from (gen.), MBh.; Mṛicch.

परिमोटन *pari-moṭana*, n. (√*muṭ*) snapping, cracking, VarBṛS. (= *caṭacaṭā-śabda*, Sch.)

परिम्लै *pari-√mlai*, Ā. *-mlāyate*, to fade or wither away, wane, faint, Mṛicch. **°mlāna**, mfn. faded, withered, Kāv.; BhP.; exhausted, languid, MBh.; become thinner, emaciated, Car.; disappeared, gone, Vām. iv, 3, 8; n. change of countenance by fear or grief, W.; soil, stain, ib. **°mlāyin**, mfn. stained, spotted, Suśr.; m. a kind of disease of the lens or pupil of the eye (*liṅga-nāśa*), ib.; *°yi-tva*, n. falling, sinking, ib.

परियज् *pari-√yaj*, P. *-yajati* (aor. 2. sg. *pary-áyās*), to obtain or procure by sacrificing, RV. ix, 82, 5; to sacrifice or worship before or after another, to perform a secondary or accompanying rite, Br.; ŚrS. **°yajña**, m. a secondary or accompanying rite (which precedes or follows another in any ritual), KātyŚr.; mfn. constituting a secondary rite, ib. **°yashṭṛi**, m. a younger brother performing a Soma sacrifice antecedently to the elder, Āpast. (v.l.) **Parishṭa**, m. an elder brother antecedently to whom the younger performs a S° s°, ib.

परियत् *pari-√yat*, Ā. *-yatate*, to surround, beset, TāṇḍBr. **Pári-yatta**, mfn. surrounded, beset, hemmed in, RV.; TS.; AitBr.

परियम् *pari-√yam*, P. *-yacchati*, to aim, hit, RV.: Caus. *-yamayati*, to serve, assist, Sāy.

परिया *pari-√yā*, P. *-yāti*, to go or travel about, go round or through (acc.), RV. &c. &c.; to run through i.e. assume successively (all shapes), RV. ix, 111, 1; to surround, protect, guard, RV.; to avoid, shun, ib.; to flow off (as Soma), ib.: Caus. *-yāpayati* (ind. p. *-yāpya*), to cause to go round or circumambulate, MBh. **°yāṇa**, n. going about &c., Kāś. on Pāṇ. viii, 4, 29 (cf. *paryāṇa*). **°yāṇi**, see *a-pariyāṇi*. **°yāṇika**, n. a travelling-carriage, Gal. **°yāṇiya**, mfn., Kāś. on Pāṇ. viii, 4, 29. **°yāta**, mfn. come near, arrived from (abl.), R.; one who has travelled about, Hcat.

परियु *pari-√2. yu*, Desid. *-yuyūshati*, to strive to span or embrace, RV. vi, 62, 1. **°yuta**, mfn. clasping, embracing, Nir. ii, 8.

परियोग *pari-yoga*, m. (√*yuj*) = *pali-y°*, Pāṇ. viii, 2, 22, Vārtt. 1. **°yogya**, m. pl. N. of a school, L.

परिरक्ष् *pari-√raksh*, P. *-rákshati* (ep. also *°te;* inf. *-rakshitum*), to guard well or completely, rescue, save, defend from (abl.), RV. &c. &c.; to keep, conceal, keep secret, Mn.; MBh. &c.; to protect, rule, govern (acc.), R.; to avoid, shun, Suśr.; (Ā.) to get out of a person's (gen.) way, R. **°rakshaka**, m. a guardian, protector, L. **°rakshaṇa**, mf(*ī*)n. guarding, protecting, a protector, Hariv.; n. the act of guarding, defending, preserving, keeping, maintaining; protection, rescue, deliverance, Mn.; MBh. &c.; care, caution, Suśr. **°rakshaṇīya**, mfn. to be completely protected or preserved, Pañc.; Prasannar. **°rakshā**, f. keeping, guarding, protection, Mn. v, 94 &c. **°rakshita**, mfn. well guarded or preserved or kept, MBh.; Kāv. &c. **°rakshitavya**, mfn. to be guarded, to be kept secret, MBh. **°rakshitin**, g. *ishṭâdi*. **°rakshitṛi**, mfn. keeping, protecting, a protector, defender, MBh.; R. **°rakshin**, mfn. (ifc.) guarding, protecting, MBh. **°rakshya**, mfn. = *°rakshitavya*, MBh.; R.

परिरटन *pari-raṭana*, n. (√*raṭ*) the act of crying or screaming, W. **°rāṭaka** (Pāṇ. iii, 2, 146). **°rāṭin** (142), mfn. crying aloud, screaming.

परिरथ्य *pári-rathya*, n. a partic. part of a chariot, AV.; (*ā*), f. id., MBh.; a street, road, A.

परिरन्धित *pari-randhita*, mfn. (√*radh*, Caus.) injured, destroyed, BhP.

परिरभ् *pari-√rabh*, Ā. *-rabhate* (pf. 3. pl. *-rebhire;* fut. *-rapsyate;* ind. p. *-rabhya;* inf. *-rabdhum*), to embrace, clasp, MBh.; Kāv. &c.: Desid. *-ripsate*, to wish or try to embrace, Ragh.; Prab. **°rabdha**, mfn. one who has embraced, R.; encircled, embraced, BhP. **°rambha**, m. (cf. *pari-r°*), **°rambhaṇa**, n. embracing, an embrace, Kāv. **°rambhita**, mfn. (fr. Caus.) embraced, quite occupied with or engrossed by (comp.), BhP. **°rambhin**, mfn. (ifc.) clasped, girt by, ib.; embracing, Śiś. **°ripsu**, mfn. (fr. Desid.) wishing to embrace, Hariv.

परिरम् *pari-√ram*, P. *-ramati* (Pāṇ. i, 3, 83), to take pleasure in, be delighted with (abl.), Bhaṭṭ. **°ramita**, mfn. (fr. Caus.) delighted (by amorous sport), Chandom.

परिराज् *pari-√rāj*, P. Ā. *-rājati*, °*te*, to shine on all sides, spread radiance everywhere, R.

परिराप् *pari-rā́p* (Padap. *-rap*), m. pl. (√*rap*) crying or talking all around, N. of a class of demons, RV. °**rāpin**, mfn. whispering to, talking over, persuading, AV.

परिरिप्सु *pari-ripsu*. See *pari-rabh*.

परिरिह् *pari-√rih*, P. *-riháti*, to lick or gnaw on all sides, RV. i, 140, 9 (cf. *pari-lih*).

परिरुच् *pari-√ruc*, Ā. *-rocate*, to shine all around, BhP.

परिरुज् *pari-√ruj*, P. *-rujáti*, to break from all sides, AV. xvi, 1, 2.

परिरुध् *pari-√2. rudh* (only ind. p. *-rodham*, TBr., *-rudhya*, Kpr.), to enclose, obstruct, keep back, hinder. °**ruddha**, mfn. obstructed by, filled with (comp.), R. °**rodha**, m. obstructing, keeping back, resistance, Rājat.

परिल *parila*, m. N. of a man, g. *śivâdi* (cf. *pārila*).

परिलग्न *pari-lagna*, mfn. (√*lag*) stuck, held fast, Śak. i, ३३ (in Prākr.)

परिलघु *pari-laghu*, mfn. very light or small, Uttarar.; easy to digest, Megh.

परिलङ्घ् *pari-√laṅgh*, P. *-laṅghayati*, to overleap, transgress, Pañc. °**laṅghana**, n. leaping to and fro, jumping over, R.

परिलभ् *pari-√labh*, Ā. *-labhate*, to get, obtain, Cat.

परिलम्ब् *pari-√lamb*, Ā. *-lambate*, to remain behind, be slow, stay out, Hariv.; Sūryas. °**lamba**, m., °**lambana**, n. lagging, lingering, Kād. °**lambya**, w.r. for °*rabhya*, Gīt. xi, 25.

परिलष् *pari-√lash*, P. *-lashati*, to desire, long for, BhP.

परिलस् *pari-√las* (only pr. p. *-lasat*), to shine all around, Inscr.

परिलिख् *pari-√likh*, P. *-likhati*, to draw a line or a circle or a furrow round (acc.), ŚBr.; Kauś.; to scrape or smooth round about, R.; to write down, copy, Hcat. °**likhana**, n. smoothing, polishing, MārkP. °**likhita** (*pári-*), mfn. enclosed in a circle, TS. °**lekha**, m. outline, delineation, picture, Kauś.; KātyŚr.; °*khâdhikāra*, m. N. of ch. of Sūryas. °**lekhana**, m. a sacred text beginning with *parilikhitam*, ĀpŚr.; n. drawing lines round about, KātyŚr.

परिलिप् *pari-√lip*, P. *-limpati*, to smear or anoint all round, ŚBr.; Kauś.; MBh.; Suśr.

परिलिह् *pari-√lih*, P. *-ledhi*, to lick all round, lick over, lick, Yājñ.; R.; Pañc.: Intens. (pr. p. *-lelihat*, °*hāna*) to lick all round, lick repeatedly, MBh.; Pañc.; BhP. °**līḍha**, mfn. licked all round, licked over, R. °**lehin**, m. a partic. disease of the ear, Suśr. (cf. *pari-rih*).

परिलुठ् *pari-√2. luṭh*, P. *-luṭhati*, to roll about or up and down, Daś.

परिलुड् *pari-√luḍ*, Caus. *-loḍayati*, to stir up, disturb, MBh.

परिलुप् *pari-√lup*, P. *-lumpati*, to take away, remove, destroy, AitBr.: Pass. *-lupyate*, to be taken away or omitted, RPrāt.; Daś. °**lupta**, mfn. injured, lost, RPrāt., Sch.; *-saṃjña*, mfn. unconscious, senseless, MW. °**lopa**, m. injury, neglect, omission, RPrāt.; Kull.

परिलुभ् *pari-√lubh*, Ā. *-lobhate*, to entice, allure, Mṛicch. viii, 33: Caus. *-lobhayati*, id., R.; Kām.

परिलून *pari-lūna*, mfn. (√*lū*) cut off, severed, Caṇḍ.

परिलेश *pari-leśa*, m. = *pariṇśa*, Sāy. on RV. i, 187, 8.

परिलोक् *pari-√lok*, P. *-lokayati*, to look around, view from all sides, R.

परिलोलित *pari-lolita*, mfn. (√*lul*, Caus.) tossed about, shaken, trembling, Kir.

परिवंश *pari-vaṇśa*, m., °*śaka*, mfn., g. *ṛiśyâdi*.

परिवक्रा *pári-vakrā*, f. a circular pit, ŚBr.; N. of a town, ib., Sch.

परिवञ्च् *pari-√vañc*, P. *-vañcati*, to sneak about, VS.; TS. °**vañcana**, n. or °**nā**, f. taking in, deception, L. °**vañcita**, mfn. (fr. Caus.) deceived, taken in, Hariv.; Hit.

परिवत् *pári-vat*, mfn. containing the word *pari*, Br.

परिवत्स *pari-vatsa*, m. a calf belonging to (a cow), Hariv. (v.l. °*vaṇsa* and *pārivatsa*). °**vatsaka**, m. a son, MBh. (Nīlak.)

परिवत्सर *pari-vatsará*, m. a full year, a year, RV.; TBr.; Mn.; MBh. &c.; the second of a cycle of 5 years, AV.; TS.; Br.; Kauś.; Var. °**vatsarīṇa** (RV.; AV), °**vatsarīya** (MānGṛŚr.), mfn. relating to a full year, lasting a whole year (cf. Pāṇ. v, 1, 92).

परिवद् *pari-√vad*, P. *-vadati*, to speak out, speak of or about (acc.), AV.; Br.; MBh.; (also Ā.) to speak ill of, revile, slander, accuse, MBh.; Kāv. °**vadana**, n. reviling, accusing, clamouring, W. °**vādá**, m. blame, censure, reproach, charge, accusation, AV. &c. &c. (cf. *parī-v°*); an instrument with which the Indian lute is played, L.; *-kathā*, f. abusive language, censure, reproof, MBh.; *-kara*, m. a slanderer, calumniator, Mālav.; *-gir*, f. (pl.) = *-kathā*, Prab. °**vādaka**, m. a complainant, accuser, calumniator, W.; one who plays on the lute, L. °**vādita**, °**tin**, g. *ishṭâdi*. °**vādin**, mfn. speaking ill of, abusing, blaming, MBh.; crying, screaming, W.; censured, abused, ib.; m. an accuser, a plaintiff, complainant, ib.; (*ī*), f. a lute with 7 strings, Kāv. °**vivadishu**, mfn. (fr. Desid.) wishing or trying to accuse others, Śiś.

Pary-udita, mfn. spoken, uttered, ŚBr.

परिवन्द् *pari-vand*, P. *-vandati*, to praise, celebrate, RV.

परिवप् *pari-√1. vap*, P. *-vapati* (ind. p. *a-pary-upya*), to clip or shear round, Kauś.; PārGṛ.; ĀpŚr. °**vapaṇa**, n. clipping, shearing, Pāṇ. viii, 4, 31, Sch. °**vāpaṇa** (Āp. °*na*), n. id., Pāṇ. v, 4, 67. °**vāpita**, mfn. shorn, L.

परिवप् *pari-√2. vap*, P. *-vapati*, to scatter, strew, Lāṭy. °**vāpá**, m. fried grains of rice, Br.; Kāṭh. &c. (= *dadhi*, KātyŚr., Sch.); standpoint, place, MBh. v, 3822 (Nīlak.); a reservoir, piece of water, L.; furniture &c. (= *pari-cchada*), ib.; scattering, sowing, ib. (cf. *parī-v°*). °**vāpika** and °**vāpin**, g. *kumudâdi* and *prêkshâdi*. °**vāpī**, f. a partic. oblation, ŚāṅkhŚr. °**vāpya**, mf(*ā*)n. having or requiring or deserving the Pari-vāpa (see above), KātyŚr. (cf. *parī-v°*).

Pary-upta, mfn. sown; set (as a gem in a ring), W. °**upti**, f. scattering seed, sowing, L.

परिवप्य *pari-vapya*, m. (fr. *vapā*) the Homa which begins and concludes the rites to be performed with the caul or omentum, ĀpŚr. &c. (w.r. *-vāpya*).

परिवर्ग *pari-varga*, *-varjaka* &c. See *pari-vṛij*, p. 601.

परिवर्त *pari-varta*, *-vartaka* &c. See *pari-vṛit*, p. 601.

परिवर्तुल *pari-vartula*, mfn. quite round or circular, Subh.

परिवर्त्मन् *pari-vartman*, mfn. going round about, describing a circle, Kāṭh.; Kauś.

परिवर्धक *pari-vardhaka*, °*dhana* &c. See *pari-vṛidh*, p. 601, col. 3.

परिवर्धित 1. *pari-vardhita*, mfn. (√*vardh*) cut, excavated, MW.

परिवर्मन् *pari-varman*, mfn. wearing a coat of mail, armed, Lāṭy.

परिवर्ह *pari-varha*, °*haṇa*. See *pari-barha* &c. under *pari-bṛiṇh*, p. 598.

परिवलन *pari-valana*, n. winding round or that with which anything is wound round, Hcar.

परिवस् *pari-√4. vas* (only pr. p. Ā. *-vásāna*), to put on, assume, RV. iii, 1, 5; to surround, attend, AV. xiii, 2, 22. °**vastrā**, f. a curtain, Hcar. (v.l. °*tra*, n.) °**vāsas**, n. (an upper garment?), N. of 2 Sāmans, ĀrshBr.

परिवस् *pari-√5. vas*, P. *-vasati* (ind. p. *pary-ushya*), to abide, stay, remain with (instr.), KātyŚr.; R. &c.; (with *saṃsargitayā*) to associate with (acc.), Kull. on Mn. xi, 190: Caus. *vāsayati*, to let stand overnight, ĀśvGṛ. °**vasatha**, m. a village, L. 1. °**vāsa**, m. (2. see s.v.) abode, stay, sojourn, KātyŚr.; Mn.; MBh.; the expulsion of a guilty member, Buddh. °**vāsita**, mfn. respectfully attentive to superiors (?), W.

Pary-ushaṇa, n. (or °*ṇā*, f.) spending the rainy season (Buddh.), HPariś.; Kalpas.; °*ṇā-daśa-śataka-vṛitti*, f., °*ṇâshṭâhnikā* (w.r. *paryūshaṇ°*), f. N. of wks. °**ushita**, mfn. having passed the night, Pañc.; MārkP.; (ifc.) having stood for a time or in some place (e.g. *niśā-p°*, *gomūtra-p°*, Suśr., not fresh, stale, insipid, Mn.; MBh. &c.; (with *vākyam*) a word that has not been strictly kept, MBh.; *-bhojin*, m. the eater of stale food (said to become a maggot or worm in the next birth), W. °**ushitavya**, n. impers. (the rainy season) is to be spent, Kalpas. °**ushṭa**, mfn. old, faded, withered, BhP.

परिवस् *pari-√8. vas*, P. *-vāsayati*, to cut off all around, cut out, Br.; ĀpŚr. °**vāsana**, n. a shred, chip, ĀpŚr.; KātyŚr., Sch.

परिवह् *pari-√vah*, P. *-vahati* (Pāṇ. i, 3, 82, Sch.), to carry about or round, RV. &c. &c.; to drag about, MBh.; to flow around, TS.; Āpast.; to lead home the nuptial train or the bride, take to wife, marry (Pass. *-uhyáte*, p. *-uhyámāna*), RV.; BhP. °**vaha**, m. N. of one of the 7 winds (for the others see *parā-vaha*), MBh.; Hariv.; Śak. vii, 6; of one of the 7 tongues of fire, Col. °**vāha**, m. the overflowing of a tank, a natural or artificial inundation, a watercourse or drain to carry off excess of water, MBh.; Kāv. &c. (cf. *parī-v°*); *-vat*, m. 'having a channel,' a tank, pool, L. °**vāhita**, mfn. drained, W. °**vāhin**, mf(*inī*)n. overflowing, VS.; (ifc.) streaming with, Śak.

परिवार *pari-vāra*, °*raṇa* &c. See *pari-vṛi*.

परिवाश् *pari-√vāś* (only Ā. impf. *pary-avāśanta*), to cry about or together with (acc.), MBh. (B.) xvi, 49 (C. *-arāsanta*).

परिवास 2. *pari-vāsa*, m. (√*vās*) fragrance, odour, Mālatīm. (for 1. see *pari-√5. vas*).

परिविंशत् *pari-viṇśat*, f. quite twenty, twenty at least, MBh.

परिविक्रयिन् *pari-vikrayin*, mfn. (√*krī*) selling, trading in (gen.), MBh.

परिविक्षत *pari-vikshata*, mfn. (√*kshan*) sorely wounded, much hurt, MBh.

परिविक्षोभ *pari-vikshobha*, m. (√*kshubh*) shaking violently, destroying, MBh.

परिविघट्टन *pari-vighaṭṭana*, n. (√*ghaṭṭ*) scattering, destroying, Cat.

परिविचर् *pari-vi-√car*, P. *-carati*, to stream forth in all directions, RV.

परिविण्ण *pari-viṇṇa* = *pari-vinna*, see *pari-√3. vid*.

परिवितर्क *pari-vitarka*, m. thought or anything thought of, Buddh.; examination, Divyâv.

परिविद् *pari-√1. vid* (pf. *-vedă* for pres.; cf. Gk. περίοιδε), to know thoroughly, understand fully, RV.; AV.: Caus. *-vedayate*, Nir. xiv, 22. °**veda**, m. complete or accurate knowledge, MBh. °**vedana**, n. id., ib. (v.l. *pada-v°*). °**vedin**, mfn. knowing, shrewd, W.

परिविद् *pari-√3. vid*, P. *-vindati*, to find out, ascertain, Hariv.; to twine, twist round (see below); to marry before an elder brother (only Pass. *yayā* [Mn. iii, 172] or *yā* [MBh. xii, 6108] *pari-vidyate*, [the woman] with whom such a marriage is contracted). °**vitta** (*pári-*), mfn. twined or twisted round, AV.; m. = *-vitti*, VS.; TS. &c. (*pari-vittá*, TBr.); = °*vinna*, ĀpŚr. °**vitti**, m. an unmarried elder brother whose younger brother is married, Mn.; MBh. &c.; *-tā*, f., Mn.; *-tva*, n., Kull. °**vindaka**, m. a younger b° married before the elder, W. °vindat, m. an unmarried elder b°, ib. °vinna (also written °vinna, m. = °vitti, MBh. xii, 6110; an e° b° whom a y° has anticipated in receiving his share, Āpast., Sch. °vividāná, m. a y° b° who marries before an e°, VS.; Kauś.; a y° b° who has taken his share before an e°, Āpast., Sch. °vettṛi, m. = °vindaka, MBh.; Kāv. &c. (cf. parī-vettṛi). °vedaka, m. id., Yājñ. iii, 238. °vedana, n. the marrying of a younger brother before the elder, Mn.; Yājñ. &c.; gain, acquisition, W.; discussion, ib.; (ā), f. shrewdness, wit, prudence, ib. °vedanīyā or °vedinī, f. the wife of a Parivettṛi (see above), W. °vedya, n. the marrying of a younger brother before the elder, VP.

परिविद्ध pari-viddha. See pari-vyadh.

परिविधाव् pari-vi-√dhāv, P. -dhāvati, to run through on all sides, RV.; to run about, R.

परिविवदिषु pari-vivadishu. See pari-vad.

परिविवस् pari-vi-√2. vas (only pr. p. f. -vyucchántī), to shine forth from i.e. immediately after (abl.), RV. iv, 52, 1.

परिविश् pari-√viś, P. -viśati (fut. -vekshyati), to beset, besiege, TS.; TBr.; R. (often confounded with pari-vish). °veśa, see °vesha under pari-vish. °veśana, n. circumference, the rim of a wheel, MBh. (also written °veshaṇa). °veśas (pári-), m. a neighbour, AV.

परिविश्रान्त pari-viśrānta, mfn. (√śram) quite rested or reposed, MBh.

परिविश्वस् pari-vi-√śvas, Caus. -śvāsayati, to comfort, console, R. °viśvasta, mfn. feeling secure, confident, MBh.

परिविष् pari-√vish, P. -veshati, MBh. (mostly Intens. -veveshṭi, Subj. -vevishati, Pot. -vevishyāt, AV.; Br.; Kāṭh.; -vevishāṇi, -avevishat, Pāṇ. vii, 3, 87, Sch.; Ā. fut. p. -vekshyamāṇa, KātyŚr.; BhP.; ind. p. -vishya, AV.; Ved. inf. -vishe, RV.), to serve, wait on, offer or dress food: Pass. -vishyate, to be served &c., MBh.; to have a halo (said of sun or moon), ShaḍvBr.; Gobh.; Hariv.: Caus. -veshayati (ind. p. -veshya, also written -veś°), to offer food, wait on (acc.), Mn. iii, 228; MBh.; R.; BhP.; to dress food, Campak. °vishṭa (pári-), mfn. surrounded, beset, besieged, RV. i, 116, 20 (fr. pari-viś?); surrounded by a halo (sun or moon), MBh.; Var.; dressed, offered, presented (as food), KātyŚr. °vishṭi (pári-), f. service, attendance, RV. °vishyamāṇa, mfn. being waited on, being at table, ChUp. °veshá, m. (also spelt °veśa) winding round or that with which anything is wound round, Hcar.; dressing or offering of food, AV.; a circle, circumference, the disc of the sun and moon or a halo round them, MBh.; Kāv. &c. (cf. parī-v°); a wreath or crown (of rays), Viddh.; Rājat.; anything surrounding or protecting (e.g. kṛitâṅgaraksha-p°, surrounded by a bodyguard, MW.); putting on, clothing, dressing, L.; °sha-vat or °shin, mfn. surrounded by a halo, MBh. °veshaka, mf(ikā)n. (also °veśaka) one who serves up meals, a waiter, servant, MBh. °véshaṇa, n. (cf. °veśana under pari-viś) attendance, waiting, serving up meals, distributing food, Br.; Gobh.; KātyŚr.; a circle, circumference, MBh.; a halo round the sun or moon, ib.; surrounding, enclosing, W. °veshṭavya (Kull.), °veshya (MW.), mfn. to be served up or offered or presented; n., see paścāt-pariveshya. °veshṭṛi, mf(trī)n. one who serves up meals, a waiter, AV.; Br. &c.; °ṭrī-mat, mfn. having a female servant, KaushUp.

परिविष्णु pari-vishṇu, ind. = sarvato Vishṇum or Vishṇum Vishṇum pari, L.

परिविहार pari-vihāra, m. walking or roaming about, walking for pleasure, BhP.

परिविह्वल pari-vihvala, mfn. extremely agitated, bewildered, R. —tā, f. bewilderment, W.

परिवी pari-vī, -vīta. See pari-vye.

परिवीज् pari-√vīj, Ā. -vījate, to blow upon, fan, MBh.: Caus. -vījayati, id., R.; Pur. °vījita, mfn. fanned, cooled, R.

परिवृ pari-√1. vṛi, P. Ā. -varati, °te (pf. -vavrur, p. -vavrivás; ind. p. -vṛitya), to cover, surround, conceal, keep back, hem in, RV. &c. &c.: Caus. -vārayati, °te (Pāṇ. iii, 1, 87, Vārtt. 16, Pat.; ind. p. -vārya), to cover, surround, encompass, embrace (bāhubhyām), AV. &c. &c. °vāra, m. (also parī-v°) a cover, covering, MBh. (also -ka, KātyŚr., Sch.); surroundings, train, suite, dependants, followers (ifc. [f. ā] surrounded by), MBh.; Kāv. &c.; a sheath, scabbard, Śiś.; a hedge round a village, Gal. (cf. parī-v°); -tā, f. subjection, dependance, Śiś. ii, 90; -pāṭha, m. N. of a Buddh. work, MWB. 62; -vat, mfn. having a great retinue, MBh.; -śobhin, mfn. beautified by a r°, Ragh.; °rī-√kṛi, to use as a r°, surround one's self with (acc.), Kathās. °vāraṇa, n. a cover, covering (ifc. 'covered with' i.e. 'only consisting of'), MBh.; a train, retinue, ib.; keeping or warding off, ib. °vārita, mfn. (fr. Caus.) surrounded by, covered with, veiled in (instr. or comp.), MBh.; Kāv. &c. °vṛita (pári-), mfn. id., Br. &c. &c.; n. a covered place or shed enclosed with walls used as a place of sacrifice, ŚBr.; KātyŚr.; Gobh.; (párī-), mfn. = prec. mfn., RV.; AV.; AitBr.; surrounding, RV.; filled by, full of (comp.), Cat. °vṛiti, f. surrounding, standing round, R.

परिवृ pari-√2. vṛi, Ā. -vṛiṇite, to choose, RV.

परिवृंह् pari-√vṛiṅh or -vṛih. See pari-bṛiṅh, p. 598, col. 1.

परिवृज् pari-√vṛij, P. -vṛiṇakti (Impv. -vṛiṅdhi, -vṛiṇaktu; aor. Subj. -varjati, Pot. -vṛijyāt), to turn out of the way of (acc.), avoid, shun, spare, pass over, RV.; AV.; VS.; Br.; Āpast.; to cast out, expel, AitBr.; (Ā.) to surround, enclose, BhP.: Caus. -varjayati, °te (ind. p. -varjya), to keep off, remove, AV.; to avoid, shun, quit, abandon, not heed, disregard, Mn.; MBh. &c. °vargá, m. avoiding, removing, omitting, RV. (cf. a-parivargam); dependance, VarBṛS. xv, 32. °vargyà, mfn. to be avoided, AV. °varjaka, mfn. (ifc.) shunning, avoiding, giving up, MBh. °varjana, n. the act of avoiding, giving up, escaping, abstaining from (gen. or comp.), Mn.; MBh. &c.; killing, slaughter, L. °varjanīya, mfn. avoidable, to be avoided, Var.; Rājat. °varjita, mfn. (fr. Caus.) shunned, avoided, Kathās.; abandoned or left by, deprived or devoid of (instr. or comp.), MBh.; Kāv. &c. (with saṃkhyayā, countless, innumerable, Pañc.; with ashṭabhis, less by 8, minus 8, Rājat.); wound round, girt, R. °vṛiktá (or pári-vṛikta), mfn. avoided, despised, RV.; AV.; (esp.) párivṛiktā or pari-vṛiktī, f. 'the disliked or despised one,' N. of a wife lightly esteemed in comparison with the favourite wife (mahishī, vāvātā), TS.; AV.; Br.; KātyŚr. °vṛij, f. avoiding, removing, RV.; purification, expiation, MW.

परिवृढ pari-vṛiḍha. See under pari-bṛiṅh.

परिवृत् pari-√vṛit, Ā. -vartate (ep. also °ti; ind. p. -vṛitya or parī-vartam), to turn round, revolve, move in a circle or to and fro, roll or wheel or wander about, circumambulate (acc.), RV. &c. &c.; (with hṛidi or hṛidaye) to run in a person's mind, MBh.; to return, go or come back to (acc.), ib.; to be reborn in (loc.), VP.; (also with anyathā) to change, turn out different, MBh.; Kāv.; to abide, stay, remain, Mn.; MBh. &c.; to act, proceed, behave, R.: Caus. -vartayati, to cause to turn or move round or back or to and fro, MBh.; Kāv. &c.; (Ā.) to roll or bring near (Subj. -vartayāte), RV. v, 37, 3; to overthrow, upset (a carriage), Hariv.; to invert, put in a reverse order, Mṛicch. v, 1/0 (read -vartya for -vṛitya); to change, barter, exchange, MBh.; Hariv. &c.; to renew (an agreement), Mn. viii, 154 &c.; to understand or explain wrongly (words &c.), MBh.; Kāv.; to turn topsyturvy i.e. search thoroughly, R.; to destroy, annihilate, ib.; to straiten, contract, Car.; (Ā.) to cause one's self to be turned round (in having one's head shaved all round), TBr.; ŚBr. (cf. -vartana): Intens. -vávartti, to turn (intrans.) continually, RV. i, 164, 11. °varta, m. revolving, revolution (of a planet &c.), Sūryas.; a period or lapse or expiration of time (esp. of a Yuga, q.v.), MBh.; R. &c.; (with lokānām) the end of the world, R.; a year, L.; moving to and fro, stirring, Prasannar.; turning back, flight, L.; change, exchange, barter (also parī-v°), Yājñ.; MBh.; Kāv. &c.; requital, return, W.; an abode, spot, place, Hariv.; a chapter, section, book &c., Lalit.; N. of a son of Duḥ-saha (son of Mṛityu), MārkP.; of the Kūrma or 2nd incarnation of Vishṇu (also parī-v°), L. °vartaka, mfn. causing to turn round or flow back, Kathās.; MārkP.; bringing to an end, concluding (gen. or comp.), MBh.; m. (in rhet.) the artificial separation of vowels and consonants to get another meaning of a word, Vām. iv, 1, 6; (in dram.) change of occupation, Bhar.; Daśar.; Sāh.; exchange, barter, Vas.; N. of a son of Duḥ-saha (son of Mṛityu), MārkP.; (ikā), f. contraction of the prepuce, phimosis, Suśr. °vártana, mf(ī)n. causing to turn round; (ī), f. (with vidyā) N. of a partic. magical art, Kathās.; n. turning or whirling round, moving to and fro (trans. and intrans.), Kāv.; Suśr.; Pañc.; BhP.; rolling about or wallowing on (comp.), Kālid.; revolution, end of a period of time, MBh.; Hariv.; barter, exchange, Kathās.; Pañc.; Mṛicch.; cutting or clipping the hair, ŚBr.; protecting, defending, Nalac.; = prêraṇa, TBr., Sch.; inverting, taking or putting anything in a wrong direction, W.; requital, return, ib. °vartanīya, mfn. to be exchanged, capable of being exchanged, Kull. on Mn. x, 94. °vartita, mfn. (fr. Caus.) turned round, revolved &c., MBh.; Kāv. &c.; exchanged, bartered, Hariv.; Var.; Kathās.; put aside, removed, destroyed, Mṛicch.; MārkP.; searched thoroughly, R.; taken or put on in a wrong direction, W.; n. the action of turning or wallowing, BhP.; the place where anybody has wallowed on the earth, R. °vartin, mfn. moving round, revolving, ever-recurring, MBh.; Kāv. &c.; (ifc.) changing, passing into, Kathās.; being or remaining or staying in or near or about (loc. or comp.), MBh.; R. &c.; flying, retreating, W.; exchanging, requiting, recompensing, ib.; (ī), f. (sc. vi-shṭuti) a hymn arranged according to the recurring form abc, abc, TāṇḍBr.; Lāṭy. °vṛitta, mfn. (also -ka, g. ṛiśyâdi) turned, turned round, revolved, rolling, moving to and fro, MBh.; Kāv. &c.; lasting, remaining, Śak. vii, 34 (v. l.); passed, elapsed, finished, ended, Hariv.; = pari-vṛita, covered, surrounded, L.; retreated, returned, W.; exchanged, ib.; n. rolling, wallowing, MBh. (v. l. °tti); Mālatim.; an embrace, MW.; -tejas, mfn. spreading brilliance all around, BhP.; -netra, mfn. rolling the eyes, R.; -phalā, f. N. of a plant, Gal.; -bhāgya, mfn. whose fortune has changed or is gone, Mālatim.; °ttârdha-mukha, mf(ī)n. having the face half turned round, Vikr. °vṛitti, f. turning, rolling, revolution, MBh.; Śiś.; return (into this world), Āpast.; exchange, barter (°ttyā, ind. alternately), BhP.; moving to and fro or staying or dwelling in a place, MBh.; end, termination, Kir.; surrounding, encompassing, ib.; (in rhet.) a kind of figure in which one thing is represented as exchanged with another (e.g. Mālav. iii, 16; cf. Vām. iv, 3, 16); substitution of one word for another without affecting the sense (e.g. vṛisha-lāñchana for vṛisha-dhvaja), Kpr.; contraction of the prepuce, phimosis (= °vartikā), Suśr.; m., w.r. for pari-vitti; (ī), f. (pári-v°), prob. w.r. for pari-vṛiktī.

परिवृध् pari-√vṛidh, Ā. -vardhate, to grow, grow up, increase, Kāv.; Rājat.; Suśr.: Caus. -vardhayati, °te, to bring up, rear, increase, augment, MBh.; Kāv.; to rejoice, delight (with gen.), Hariv. °vardhaka, m. 'rearer, sc. of horses,' a groom, hostler, Kād.; Hcar. °vardhana, n. increasing, augmenting, multiplying, MBh.; Kām.; breeding, rearing (as of cattle), Mn. ix, 331. 2. °vardhita (for 1. see p. 600), mfn. increased, augmented, grown, swollen (as the sea), Kālid.; reared, brought up (fam. also -ka), Śak. iv, 15. °vṛiddha, mfn. grown, increased by (comp.), strong, powerful, Hariv.; Kāv. &c.; -tā, f. increase, extension, the swelling and becoming sour of food (in the stomach), Suśr. °vṛiddhi, f. increase, growth, Āpast.; MBh.; Kāv. &c.

परिवृष् pari-√vṛish, Ā. -varshate, to cover with (instr.) as with rain, R.

परिवृस्ति pari-vṛisti, w.r. for -vitti.

परिवे pari-√ve, P. Ā. -vayati, °te, to interweave, BhP.; to fetter, bind, ib.

Páry-uta, mfn. enclosed or set with, ŚBr.

परिवेदन pari-vedana, °dita, w.r. for pari-devana, °vita (see pari-div).

परिवेप् pari-√vep, -vepate, to tremble, R.

परिवेष्ट् pari-√vesht, Caus. -veshṭayati, to wrap up, cover, clothe, surround, embrace, ŚBr. &c.

&c.; to cause to shrink up, contract, MBh. (B. *sam-v*°). °**veshṭana,** n. a cover, covering, MBh.; a ligature, bandage, Mṛicch. iii, 16; surrounding, encompassing, W.; circumference, ib.; (*ā*), f. tying round or up, Sāh. °**veshṭita,** mfn. surrounded, beset, covered, veiled, swathed, Hariv.; R. &c. (*-vat*, mfn. as pf., Kathās.) °**veshṭitṛi,** m. one who surrounds or encloses, ŚvetUp.

परिव्यक्त *pari-vyakta*, mfn. very clear or distinct; (*am*), ind. very clearly or distinctly, MW.

परिव्यथ् *pari-√vyath*, only *-vyathā iti*, PraśnUp. (according to Sch. = Caus. *-vyathayatu*) to disquiet, vex, afflict.

परिव्यध् *pari-√vyadh*, P. *-vidhyati*, to shoot at (acc.), hit, pierce with (instr.), MBh. °**viddha,** m. N. of Kubera, L. (cf. *parā-v*°). °**vyādha,** m. Calamus Fasciculatus or Pterospermum Acerifolium, L.; N. of an ancient sage, MBh. °**vyādhi,** w. r. for prec., Car.

परिव्यय *pari-vyaya*, m. (*pari-vi-√i*) condiment, spices, Mn. vii, 127; expense, cost, Jātakam.

परिव्याकुल *pari-vyākula*, mfn. much confused or disordered; °*lī-√kṛi*, to trouble or confound thoroughly, Jātakam.

परिव्यावृज् *pari-vy-ā-√vṛij* (only Impv. *-vṛiñjantu*), to separate i. e. deliver from (abl.), ŚāṅkhGṛ.

परिव्ये *pari-√vye*, P. Ā. *-vyayati*, °*te* (aor. *-avyata*, *-vyata*, RV.; ind. p. *-vyāya* and *-vīya*, cf. Pāṇ. vi, 1, 44), to wrap or tie round; (Ā.) to wrap one's self up, RV. &c. &c. °**vī,** mfn. wound round, VS. °**vīta** (*pári-*), mfn. veiled, covered, pervaded, overspread, surrounded, encompassed by (instr. or comp.), RV. &c. &c.; n. N. of the bow of Brahmā, L. °**vyáyaṇa,** n. winding round, covering, ŚBr.; ŚrS.; the covered spot, ŚBr. °**vyayaṇīya,** mfn. relating to wrapping round or binding on, ŚrS. °**vyāṇa,** n. winding round, ĀpŚr., Sch.

परिव्रज् *pari-√vraj*, P. *-vrajati* (ind. p. *-vrajya*), to go or wander about, walk round, circumambulate (acc.), ŚBr.; GṛŚrS. &c.; to wander about as a religious mendicant, Up.; Mn.; MBh. &c.; (with Jainas) to become a recluse, HPariś.: Caus. *-vrājayati*, to cause a person to become a recluse, ib. °**vrajya,** mfn. to be gone about (n. impers.), MBh.; (*ā*), f. strolling, wandering from place to place, (esp.) leading the life of a religious mendicant, abandonment of the world, Mn.; Kathās. °**vrāj,** m. (MBh.; R. &c., nom. *ṭ*), °**vrāja** (Āpast.), m. a wandering mendicant, ascetic of the fourth and last religious order (who has renounced the world). °**vrājaka,** m. (*ikā*, f.; ifc. f. *akā*) a wandering religious mendicant, Mālav.; Pañc.; Hit. **vrājī,** f. Sphaeranthus Mollis, L. °**vrājya,** n. religious mendicancy, W.

परिव्रढिमन् *pari-vraḍhiman*, °*ḍhishṭha* &c. See *pari-bṛiṃh*, p. 598.

परिव्रश्च् *pari-√vraśc*, P. *-vṛiścati*, to cut, ŚBr. °**vṛikṇa,** mfn. mutilated, ChUp.

परिशक्तवे *pári-śaktave*, inf. of *pari-√śak*, to overpower, to conquer, RV.

परिशङ्क् *pari-√śaṅk*, Ā. *-śaṅkate* (inf. *-śaṅkitum*), to suspect, doubt, distrust (acc.), MBh.; R. &c.; to believe, fancy to be (2 acc.), ib. °**śaṅkanīya,** mfn. to be doubted or distrusted or feared or apprehended (n. impers. 'distrust must be felt'), Kāv.; Pur. °**śaṅkā,** f. suspicion, distrust, Jātakam.; hope, expectation, R. °**śaṅkita,** mfn. suspicious, distrustful, afraid of (abl. or comp.), MBh.; R.; Pur.; suspected, questionable, MBh.; believed, expected (*a-pariś*°), MBh.; thought to be, taken for (nom.), Gīt. °**śaṅkin,** mfn. fearing, apprehending, Ragh.; afraid on account of (comp.), BhP.

परिशठ *pari-śaṭha*, mfn. thoroughly dishonest or wicked, Car.

परिशन्न *pari-śanna*, mfn. (*√śad*) fallen away or by the side, ĀśvŚr.

परिशप् *pari-śap*, P. Ā. *-śapati*, °*te*, to curse, execrate, TāṇḍBr.; to abuse, revile (aor. *pary-aśāpsīt*), Bhaṭṭ. °**śapta,** n. cursing, reviling, anathema, TāṇḍBr. °**śāpa,** m. id., W.

परिशब्दित *pari-śabdita*, mfn. (*√śabd*) mentioned, communicated, MBh.

परिशमित *pari-śamita*, mfn. (*√śam*, Caus.) allayed, quenched, destroyed, Gīt.

परिशायन *pari-śāyana*. See *pari-śī*.

परिशाश्वत *pari-śāśvata*, mfn. continuing for ever, perpetually the same, MBh.

परिशिञ्जित *pari-śiñjita*, mfn. (*√śiñj*) made to hum or resound from all sides, MBh.

परिशिथिल *pari-śithila*, mfn. very loose or lax, Jātakam.

परिशिष् *pari-√śish*, P. *-śinashṭi* (Pot. *-śiṇshyuḥ*), to leave over, leave as a remainder, Br.; Ā. (pf. *-śiśishe*, °*shire*; fut. *-śekshyate*) and Pass. *-śishyate* (p. *-śishyamāṇa*), to be left as a remainder, to remain behind, AV. &c. &c.: Caus. *-śeshayati*, to leave over, suffer to remain, spare, Ragh.; Rājat.; Pur.; to quit or leave, Bhaṭṭ.; to supply, L. °**śishṭa** (*pári-*), mfn. left, remaining, TS. &c. &c.; n. a supplement, appendix (N. of a class of wks. supplementary to Sūtras); *-kadamba*, m. or n., *-paryāya*, m. pl., *-parvan*, n., *-prakāśa*, m. (and °*śasya-sāra-mañjarī*, f.), *-prabodha*, m., *-saṃgraha*, m., *-siddhānta-ratnākara*, m., *-sūtra-pattra*, n. N. of wks. °**śesha,** mfn. left over, remaining, ŚāṅkhŚr.; Var.; m. n. remnant, remains, rest, MBh.; Var.; supplement, sequel, MBh.; termination, conclusion, L.; (*eṇa*), ind. completely, in full; (*āt*), ind. consequently, therefore, Śaṃk.; *-khaṇḍa*, m. or n. N. of wk.; *-vat*, mfn. having a supplement or appendix, Cat.; *-śāstra*, n. a supplementary work, L. °**śeshaṇa,** n. remainder, residue, BhP. °**śeshita,** mfn. left over, remaining from (comp.), BhP.

परिशी *pari-√śī*, Ā. *-śete* (impf. 3. pl. *aśeran*; 2. du. *-aśāyatam*; 3. sg. *-aśāyata*), to lie round or near or in, surround, remain lying, RV.; TS.; ŚBr. °**śáyana,** n. causing to lie completely in, complete immersion, Baudh.

परिशील् *pari-√śīl*, P. *-śīlayati*, to practise, use frequently, Kāv.; to treat well, cherish, Prasann. °**śīlana,** n. touch, contact (lit. and fig.), intercourse with, application or attachment to, pursuit of (comp.), constant occupation, study, Kāv.; Sāh. °**śīlita,** mfn. practised, used, employed, pursued, studied, Kāv.; inhabited, Pāṇ. iv, 2, 52, Sch.

परिशुच् *pari-√śuc*, P. Ā. *-śocati*, °*te*, to mourn, wail, lament (trans. and intrans.), MBh.: Caus. *-śocayati* (ind. p. *-śocya*), to pain, torment, MBh. (B.) vi, 1902; to lament, bewail, MBh. vii, 10.

परिशुध् *pari-√śudh*, P. Ā. *-śudhyati*, °*te*, to be washed off, become clean or purified, Subh.; (Ā.) to purify or justify one's self, prove one's innocence, Rājat.: Caus. *-śodhayati*, to clear, clean, R.; to clear off, restore, Yājñ. ii, 146; to try, examine, Kathās.; to solve, explain, clear up, Gīt. °**śuddha,** mfn. cleaned, purified, pure; cleared off, paid; acquitted, discharged, MBh.; Kāv.; Pur.; (ifc.) diminished by, that from which a part has been taken away, MBh. °**śuddhi,** f. complete purification or justification, acquittal (°*dhim √kṛi*, to prove one's innocence), Ragh.; Bālar.; Kathās.; rightness, correctness, Kāraṇḍ. °**śodha,** m. = next, W. °**śodhana,** n. cleaning, purification, Uttarar.; discharging, paying off, Kull.

परिशुभ् *pari-√śubh* (*śumbh*), P. *-śúmbhati*, to prepare, AV.; Ā. *-śobhate*, to shine, be bright or beautiful, MBh. °**śobhita,** mfn. adorned or beautified by (instr. or comp.), Hariv.; R.; *-kāyā*, f. N. of an Apsaras and a Gandharvī, Kāraṇḍ.

परिशुश्रूषा *pari-śuśrūshā*. See *pari-śru*.

परिशुष् *pari-√śush*, P. Ā. *-śushyati*, °*te*, to be thoroughly dried up, to shrivel, wither (lit. and fig.), pine, waste away, MBh.; Kāv. &c.: Caus. *-śoshayati* (Pass. *-śoshyate*), to dry up, emaciate, Kāv.; Pañc.; Suśr. °**śushka,** mfn. thoroughly dried or parched up, withered, shrivelled, shrunk (as a vein), hollow (as the cheeks) &c., MBh.; Kāv.; Var.; Suśr.; (with *māṅsa*), n. meat fried in ghee dried and spiced, L.; *-tālu*, mfn. having the palate dried up, Ṛit.; *-palāśa*, mfn. having withered foliage, R. °**śosha,** m. complete dryness, desiccation, evaporation (°*sham √gam*, to become dry or thin), R.; Suśr. °**śoshaṇa,** mfn. drying up, parching, MBh. (v. l. °*shin*); n. drying, parching, emaciating, MBh. °**śoshita,** mfn. dried up, parched, Cat. °**śoshin,** mfn. becoming dry or withered, shrivelling, Rājat.; v. l. for °*śoshaṇa*, MBh.

परिशून्य *pari-śūnya*, mfn. quite empty, (ifc.) totally free from or devoid of, Ragh.

परिशृत *pari-śrita*, m. or n. (*√śrā*?) ardent spirits, liquor, L. (cf. *pari-srut*, *-srutā* under *pari-sru*).

परिशॄ *pari-√śṝi*, Pass. *-śīryate* (ep. also °*ti*), to be cleft or rent asunder, to be split, MBh.

परिश्रम् *pari-√śram* (only ind. p. *-śramya*), to fatigue or exert one's self, R.: Caus. *-śramayati*, to fatigue, tire, Naish. °**śrama,** m. fatigue, exertion, labour, fatiguing occupation, trouble, pain, MBh.; Kāv. &c.; °*māpaha*, mfn. relieving weariness, MW. °**śramaṇa,** mfn. (?) free from fatigue or weariness, BhP., Sch. °**śrānta,** mfn. thoroughly fatigued or worn out, (ifc.) tired of, disgusted with, Mn.; MBh. &c. °**śrānti,** f. fatigue, exhaustion; labour, trouble, W. °**śrāma,** m. fatiguing, occupation, trouble, BhP.

परिश्रि *pari-√śri*, P. *-śrayati* (ind. p. *-śritya*; Ved. inf. *pári-śrayitavai*), to surround, encircle, fence, enclose, TS.; Br.; ŚrS.: Pass. *-śrīyasva*, be surrounded or surround thyself, VS. xxxvii, 13. °**śraya,** m. an enclosure, fence (in *sá-pariś*°), ŚBr.; a refuge, asylum, Pañc. (B.) i, 252; an assembly, meeting, L.; N. of a prince, VP. °**śrayaṇa,** n. encompassing, surrounding with a fence, KātyŚr., Sch. °**śrit,** f. pl. 'enclosers,' N. of certain small stones laid round the hearth and other parts of an altar, ŚBr.; KātyŚr. (ifc. °*śritka*). °**śrita,** mfn. standing round, MBh.; surrounded by (instr. or comp.), Kathās.; BhP.; w. r. for °*śruta*, MBh.; n. (*pári-*) = *pári-vṛita*, n. (see under *pari-√1. vṛi*), TS.; Br.; ŚrGṛS.

परिश्रु *pari-√śru*, P. *-śṛiṇoti* (ind. p. *-śrutya*), to hear, learn, understand, R. °**śuśrūshā,** f. complete or implicit obedience, Śukas. °**śruta,** mfn. heard, learnt, MBh.; R.; Hariv.; known as, passing for (nom.), ib.; famous, celebrated, MBh.; BhP.; w. r. for *prati-ś*°, MBh.; m. N. of an attendant of Skanda, ib.

परिश्रुत् *pari-śrút*, f. = *-srút*, AV. xx, 127, 9.

परिश्लथ *pari-ślatha*, mfn. quite loose or relaxed, Vcar.

परिश्लिष्ट *pari-ślishṭa*, mfn. (*√ślish*) clasped, embraced, W. °**ślesha,** m. an embrace, ib.

परिषञ्ज् *pari-shañj* (*√sañj*), P. *-shajati*, Pāṇ. viii, 3, 63, Sch.; Ā. *-sajjate*, to have one's mind fixed on, be attached or devoted to, MBh.: Desid. *-shishaṅkshati*, Pāṇ. viii, 3, 64, Sch.

परिषण्ड *pari-shaṇḍa*, m. or n. a partic. part of a house, L.; (*ā*), f. a valley (?), Divyâv. (v. l. °*khaṇḍa*). **-vārika,** m. a servant, ib.

परिषद् *pari-shad* (*√sad*), P. *-shadati*, RV.; *-shīdati*, AV.; MBh. (C. also *-sīdati*); to sit round, besiege, beset, RV.; AV.; Kauś.; to suffer damage, be impaired, MBh. °**shád,** mfn. surrounding, besetting, RV.; f. an assembly, meeting, group, circle, audience, council, ŚBr.; Kauś.; Mn. (°*shat-tva*, n. xii, 114); MBh. &c.; N. of a village in the north, g. *palady-ādi*; *-vala*, mfn. surrounded by a council (as a king), Pāṇ. v, 2, 112, Sch.; forming or containing assemblies, Bhaṭṭ.; m. a member of an assembly, assessor, spectator, L. °**shada,** v. l. for *pāri-shada*, *pārshada*. °**shádya,** mfn. to be sought after, RV. vii, 4, 7 (Nir. 'to be avoided;' Sāy. 'sufficient, adequate, competent'); to be worshipped, VS. v, 32 (Mahīdh. 'belonging to an assembly'); m. a member of an assembly, spectator, guest, L. °**shádvan,** mfn. surrounding, besetting, RV. °**shanna** (!), mfn. lost or omitted, AVPariś.

परिषय *pari-shaya*. See *pari-sho*.

परिषह् *pari-shah* (*√sah*), Ā. *-shahate* (impf. *pary-ashahata* or *-asahata*; fut. *pari-soḍhā* [Vop. *-shahitā*]; inf. *-soḍhum*, Pāṇ. viii, 3, 70 &c.; aor. *pary-asahishṭa*, Bhaṭṭ.), to sustain, bear up against (acc.): Caus. aor. *pary-asīshahat*, Pāṇ. viii, 3, 116. °**shahā,** f. forbearance, patience, W. (cf. *parī-sh*°).

परिषिच् *pari-shic* (√*sic*), P. *-shiñcati* (impf. *pary-ashiñcat*, Pāṇ. viii, 3, 63; ind. p. *-siñcitvā* [!], SaddhP.; Pass. pr. p. *-shicyamāna*, R.), to pour out or in (esp. from one vessel into another), to pour or scatter about, sprinkle, diffuse, RV.: Caus. *-secayati* or *-shiñcayati*, to sprinkle, MBh.; to soak, macerate, Suśr.: Desid. *-shishikshati*, Pāṇ. viii, 3, 64, Sch. °**shikta** (*pári-*), mfn. poured out, sprinkled about, diffused, RV.; Lāṭy.; Śiś. °**sheka**, m. sprinkling over, moistening, Suśr.; a bath, bathing apparatus, ib.; MBh.; Var. (cf. *parī-sh*°). °**shecaka**, mfn. pouring over, sprinkling (comp.), g. *yājakâdi* (v.l. °*veshaka*, Kāś.) °**shecana**, n. pouring over, sprinkling, ŚrS.; Var.; Suśr.; water for watering trees, MBh.

परिषिध् *pari-shidh* (√*sidh*), P. *-shedhati* (impf. *pary-ashedhat*), Pāṇ. viii, 3, 63; 65, Sch.: Desid. *-shishedhayishati*, 64, Sch. (cf. *pari-sidh*).

परिषिव् *pari-shiv* (√*siv*), P. *-shīvyati* (impf. *pary-ashīvyat*, Pāṇ. viii, 3, 70), to sew round, wind round, KātyŚr.; Caus. aor. *pary-asishivat*, Pāṇ. viii, 3, 116. °**shīvaṇa**, n. sewing round, winding round, KātyŚr.

परिषु *pari-shu* (√3. *su*), P. *-shuṇoti* (impf. *pary-ashuṇot*, fut. *pari-soshyati*), Pāṇ. viii, 3, 63 &c., Sch.

परिषू *pari-shū* (√1. *sū*), P. *-shuvati* (impf. *pary-ashuvat*), Pāṇ. viii, 3, 63; 65, Sch.; *-shauti*, to grasp, bunch together (?), ĀpŚr. °**shavaṇa**, n. grasping, bunching together, ib. °**shūtá**, mfn. urged, impelled to come forth, elicited (sc. by the gods, said of young grass), TS. °**shūti** (*pári-*), f. urging from all sides, beleaguering, oppression, vexation, RV.

परिषेण *pari-sheṇa*, m. (*p*° + *senā*) N. of a man (see *pārisheṇya*). °**sheṇaya**, Nom. P. °*yati*, (prob.) to surround with an army, Pāṇ. viii, 3, 65, Sch.: Desid. °*shisheṇayishati*, 64, Sch.

परिषेव् *pari-shev* (√*sev*), Ā. *-shevate* (impf. *pary-ashevata*; pf. *pari-shisheva*, Pāṇ. viii, 3, 63 &c.; but there occurs also *-sevate* &c.), to frequent, practise, pursue, enjoy, honour, Kāv.; Pur.; Pañc.

परिषो *pari-sho* (√*so*), P. *-shyati*, Pāṇ. viii, 3, 65, Sch. °**shaya**, m., °**shita**, mfn. ib. 70.

परिषोडश *pari-shoḍaśa*, mfn. pl. full sixteen, MBh.

परिष्कन्द् *pari-shkand* (√*skand*), P. *-shkandati* or *-skandati* (Pāṇ. viii, 3, 74), to leap or spring about, Bhaṭṭ.: Intens. *-canishkadat*, id., RV. viii, 58, 9. °**shkaṇṇa** (Pāṇ. viii, 3, 74) or °**skanna** (MBh.), spilled, scattered; m. = or w. r. for next, L. 1. °**shkandá** (or °*skanda*), m. (Pāṇ. viii, 3, 75, Sch.) a servant (esp. one running by the side of a carriage), VS.; AV.; MBh. &c.; a foster-child, one nourished by a stranger, W. 2. °**shkanda**, m. a temple, Gaut. xix, 14 (v.l. °*shkandha*).

परिष्कृ *pari-sh-√kṛi* (*sh* for *s* inserted, or perhaps original in a √*skṛi* = √1. *kṛi*, cf. *upa-s-kṛi* and *saṃ-s-kṛi*), P. *-kṛiṇoti* (3. pl. *-kṛiṇvánti*, RV. ix, 14, 2; 64, 23; p. *-kṛiṇvát*, ib. 39, 2; impf. *pary-ashkarot* or *-askarot*, Pāṇ. viii, 3, 70; 71), to adorn, fit out, prepare, make ready or perfect, RV. (cf. *pari-kṛi* and Pāṇ. vi, 1, 137). °**sh-kara**, m. ornament, decoration, MBh. viii, 1477 (according to Nilak. = 1. °*shkanda*). °**sh-kāra**, m. = prec. (ifc. f. *ā*), MBh. &c.; cooking, dressing, W.; domestic utensils, furniture, SaddhP.; purification, initiation, ib.; self-discipline, Lalit. (one of the ten powers of a Bodhi-sattva, Dharmas. lxxiv); *-cīvara*, n. a kind of garment, L. °**sh-kṛita** (*pári-*), mfn. prepared, adorned, embellished, furnished with, surrounded or accompanied by (instr. or comp.), RV. &c. &c.; cooked, dressed, W.; purified, initiated, ib. °**sh-kṛiti**, f. finishing, polishing, W.; (in rhet.) a partic. figure of speech = *pari-kara* (see under *pari-kṛi*), Cat. °**sh-kriyā**, f. adorning, decorating, MārkP.; v.l. for *pari-kriyā* in *agni-p*°, q. v.

परिष्टम्भ् *pari-shṭambh* (√*stambh*), P. *-shṭabhnoti* or *-shṭabhnāti* (Caus. aor. *pary-astambhat*), Pāṇ. viii, 3, 67; 116, Sch.

परिष्टि *pari-shṭi*, f. (√1. *as*; cf. *abhi-shṭi*, *upa-sti*) obstruction, impediment, distress, dilemma, RV.

परिष्टु *pari-shṭu* (√*stu*), P. *-shṭauti* (impf. *pary-ashṭaut* or *-astaut*, Pāṇ. viii, 3, 70), to praise, Kām. °**shṭavana**, n. praise, L. °**shṭavanīya**, mfn. intended for a praise (as a hymn), ŚāṅkhŚr. °**shṭuta**, mfn. praised, sung, ib. °**shṭuti** (*pári-*), f. praise, celebration, RV. °**shṭoma**, m. = *pari-stoma*, L.

परिष्टुभ् *pari-shṭubh* (√*stubh*), P. *-shṭobhati* (Pāṇ. viii, 3, 63; 65), to cry or exult on every side, RV.; TāṇḍBr. °**shṭúbh**, mfn. exulting on every side, RV. °**shṭobha**, m. embellishing a Sāman with Stobhas (s. v.), TāṇḍBr.

परिष्ठल *pari-shṭhala*, n. (Pāṇ. viii, 3, 96) surrounding place or site, W.

परिष्ठा *pari-shṭhā* (√*sthā*), P. Ā. *-tishṭhati*, °*te* (pf. *-tashṭhau*; fut. *-shṭhāsyati*, Pāṇ. viii, 3, 64. Sch.; 3. pl. pf. *-tasthuḥ*, RV.; Pañc.; aor. *-shṭhāt*, *-shṭhuḥ*, RV.; *-shṭhāḥ*, Padap.; *-sthāḥ*, AV.), to stand round, be in a person's way, obstruct, hinder, RV. &c. &c.; to crowd from all sides, Pañc.; (Ā.) to remain, survive, MBh.: Caus. *-sthāpayati* (ind. p. *-sthāpya*), to beset, surround, AV.; to place near, cause to stay close by, Kathās. °**shṭhā**, mfn. obstructing, hindering; f. obstruction, impediment, RV.; AV. °**shṭhiti**, f., °**sthāna** (!), n. abode, residence, fixedness, firmness, MW.

परिष्यन्द *pari-shyandá* or *-syanda*, m. (√*syand*; cf. Pāṇ. viii, 3, 72) a river, stream (fig. of words), Bhartṛ.; moisture, L.; (with *sh*) a sandbank, island, ŚBr.; KātyŚr.; keeping or entertaining (a sacred fire), MBh. (v.l. *-spanda*); decoration of the hair, L. (v.l. *-spanda*). °**shyandana** or °**syandana**, n. dropping, oozing, W. °**shyandin** or °**syandin**, mfn. flowing, streaming, L.

परिष्वज् *pari-shvaj* (√*svaj*, *svañj*), Ā. *-shvajate*, rarely P. °*ti* (impf. *pary-ashvajata* or *-asvajata*, Pāṇ. viii, 3, 65; 70; pr. p. *-shvajāna*, R.; pf. *-shasvajé*, AV.; MBh.; *-shasvajire*, R.; *-shasvajaḥ*, BhP.; ind. p. *-shvajya*, MBh.; inf. *-shvaktum*, R.; inf. *-shváje*, RV.), to embrace, clasp, occupy, RV. &c. &c.: Desid. *-shishvaṅkshate*, Pāṇ. viii, 3, 64, Sch. °**shvakta**, mfn. embraced, encircled, surrounded, MBh.; Kāv. &c. °**shvaṅga**, m. embracing, an embrace, MBh.; R. &c.; touch, contact with (comp.), Kām.; Hit.; N. of a son of Devakī, BhP. °**shvaṅgin**, mfn. succumbing, Sāṃkhyas., Sch. °**shvajana**, n. embracing, an embrace, Nir. ii, 27. °**shvajīyas** (*pári-*), mfn. clasping more firmly, AV. °**shvajya**, mfn. to be embraced, MBh. °**shvañjana**, n. embracing, an embrace (*putrasya*, Pāṇ. iii, 116, Sch.) °**shvañjalya** (*pári-*), m. or n. a partic. domestic utensil, AV.

परिष्वन् *pari-shvan* (√*svan*), only Intens. *-sanishvaṇat*, to sound, whiz, RV. viii, 69, 9.

परिष्वष्किन *pari-shvashkita*, n. (√*shvashk*) the act of leaping about, L.

परिसंलिह् *pari-saṃ-√lih*, P. *-leḍhi* (pr. p. *-lihat*), to lick all round, lick over, lick, MBh.

परिसंवत्सर *pari-saṃvatsara*, m. a whole or full year, Mn. iii, 119; MBh.; mfn. a full year old (or older), inveterate, chronic (as a disease), Suśr.; Car.; waiting a full year, Gobh.

परिसंवद् *pari-saṃ-√vad*, P. *-vadati*, to speak together about, agree with regard to (acc.), MBh.

परिसंशुद्ध *pari-saṃ-śuddha*, mfn. (√*śudh*) perfectly clean or pure, BhP.

परिसंसृष्ट *pari-saṃ-sṛishṭa*, mfn. (√*sṛij*) got at from all sides, MBh.

परिसंस्तम्भ् *pari-saṃ-√stambh* (only ind. p. *-stabhya*), to strengthen, comfort, MārkP.

परिसंस्तु *pari-saṃ-stu* (only Pass. pr. p. *-stūyamāna*), to praise, celebrate, MBh.

परिसंस्तॄ *pari-saṃ-√stṛī* (only ind. p. *-stīrya*), to spread i. e. kindle a fire at different places, MBh.

परिसंस्थित *pari-saṃ-sthita*, mfn. (√*sthā*) standing together on every side, MBh.; standing i. e. stopping, remaining (in *a-paris*°), R.

परिसंस्पृश् *pari-saṃ-√spṛiś*, P. *-spṛiśati*, to touch at different places, stroke, MBh.; R.

परिसंहा *pari-saṃ-√2. hā* (only pr. p. *-jíhāna*), to start or spring from (abl.), RV. vii, 33, 10.

परिसंहृष्ट *pari-saṃ-hrishṭa*, mfn. (√*hṛish*) greatly rejoiced, delighted, R.

परिसख्य *pari-sakhya*, n. perfect or true friendship, PārGṛ.

परिसंक्रीड् *pari-saṃ-√krīḍ*, P. *-krīḍati*, to play about, amuse one's self, R.

परिसंक्षिप् *pari-saṃ-√kship*, P. *-kshipati*, to encompass, surround, R.

परिसंख्या *pari-saṃ-√khyā*, P. *-khyāti* (inf. *-khyātum*), to count, enumerate, ŚāṅkhŚr.; Mn.; MBh.; to limit to a certain number, KātyŚr., Sch.; to reckon up, calculate, add together, MBh.; R.; Suśr.; to make good, restore, Car.; Jaim., Sch. °**khyā**, f. enumeration, computation, sum, total, number, ŚāṅkhŚr.; Mn.; MBh. &c.; (in phil.) exhaustive enumeration (implying exclusion of any other), limitation to that which is enumerated, Jaim.; Kull. on Mn. iii, 45; (in rhet.) special mention or exclusive specification, Kpr.; Sāh. °**khyāta**, mfn. reckoned up, enumerated, specified exclusively, W. °**khyāna**, n. enumeration, total, a number, MBh.; exclusive specification, BhP.; a correct judgment, proper estimate, Yājñ. iii, 158.

परिसंघुष्ट *pari-saṃ-ghushṭa*, mfn. (√*ghush*) filled with cries or noise, resonant on all sides, MBh.

परिसंचक्ष् *pari-saṃ-√caksh* (only 3. pl. pr. *-cakshate*), to enumerate, Gobh.; to avoid (see next). °**cakshya**, mfn. to be avoided, Pāṇ. ii, 4, 54, Vārtt. 9, Pat.

परिसंचर *pari-saṃ-cara*, mfn. (√*car*) roving about, vagrant, Bhar.; m. 'a very difficult pass or defile,' a critical period, VāyuP.

परिसंचित *pari-saṃ-cita*, mfn. (√1. *ci*) collected, accumulated, Sāh.

परिसत्य *pari-satya*, n. the full or pure truth, ĀśvŚr.

परिसंतप् *pari-saṃ-√tap* (only ind. p. *-tapya*), to be tormented or afflicted, R. °**tapta**, mfn. scorched, singed, ib.

परिसंतान *pari-saṃtāna*, m. (√*tan*) a string, cord, TS.

परिसभ्य *pari-sabhya*, m. (*sabhā*) a member of an assembly, assessor, L.

परिसमन्त *pari-samanta*, m. (ifc. °*taka*) circumference, circuit, L.

परिसमाप् *pari-sam-√āp*, Pass. *-āpyate*, to be fully completed, arrive at completion, BhP.; to be contained in (loc.), Bhag.; to relate or belong to (loc. or *prati*), Pat. °**sam-āpana**, n. the act of finishing completely, W. °**sam-āpanīya** or °**payitavya**, mfn. to be completely finished, Jaim., Sch. °**sam-āpta**, mfn. finished, complete, Śak.; centred, comprehended, Śiś. °**sam-āpti**, f. entire completion, end, conclusion, Śaṃk.; Sāh.; Pāṇ., Sch.; relating or belonging to (loc. or *prati*), Pat.

परिसमुत्सुक *pari-samutsuka*, mfn. very anxious, greatly agitated or excited, R.

परिसमूह् *pari-sam-√1. ūh*, P. Ā. *-ūhati*, °*te*, to heap or sweep together, ŚBr.; GṛŚrS. °**sam-ūhana**, n. heaping up or sweeping together, GṛŚrS.; BhP. °**sam-ohana** (!), n. id., Kauś., Sch.

परिसमे *pari-samê* (*-sam-ā-√i*), to go back to (acc.), BhP.

परिसम्भू *pari-sam-√bhū* (only 3. pl. pf. *-babhūvúḥ*), to arise, spring, be produced from (abl.), AV.

परिसर *pari-sara*, *pari-sarpa*. See *pari-sṛi*, *pari-sṛip*, p. 604.

परिसहस्र *pari-sahasra*, mfn. pl. a full thousand, ŚāṅkhŚr.

परिसाध् *pari-√sādh*, Caus. *-sādhayati*, to overpower, subject, Hariv.; Kām.; to settle, arrange,

Mn. viii, 187; to prepare (food), Pañcar. °**sādhana**, n. accomplishing, settling, arranging, Mn.; R.; determining, ascertaining, W.

परिसान्त्व् *pari-√sāntv* (also written *śāntv*), Caus. *-sāntvayati*, °*te* (ind. p. *-sāntvya*), to console, comfort, conciliate, MBh.; R.; Kathās. °**sāntvana**, n. the act of consoling &c.; pl. friendly words, flattering speech, Kād. °**sāntvita**, mfn. consoled, conciliated, MBh.; R.; BhP.

परिसामन् *pari-sāman*, n. a Sāman which is occasionally inserted, Lāṭy.

परिसावकीय *pari-sāvakīya*, Nom. P. °*yati* = *sāvakam icchati*, Pāṇ. viii, 3, 65, Vārtt. 5, Pat. (cf. *abhi-sāvakīya* under *abhi-shu*).

परिसिद्धिका *pari-siddhikā*, f. (fr. *-siddhi?*) a kind of rice gruel, L.

परिसिध् *pari-√sidh*, Caus. *-sedhayati*, to drive about (cows), Pāṇ. viii, 3, 113, Kāś. (cf. *pari-shidh*).

परिसीमन् *pari-sīman*, m. a boundary, extreme term or limit, W.

परिसीरम् *pari-sīram*, ind., g. *pari-mukhâdi* (iv, 3, 58).

Pári-sīrya, n. a leather thong on a plough, ŚBr.

परिसृ *pari-√sṛi*, P. *-sarati* (pf. *-sasāra*, *-sasruḥ*; ind. p. *-sṛitya*), to flow or go round, circumambulate (acc.), RV. &c. &c.; to flow or walk about or to and fro, MBh.; BhP. °**sara**, mfn. adjacent, adjoining, contiguous, Sāy. on RV. iii, 33, 2; lying near or on (comp.), Megh.; Uttarar.; m. position, site, Suśr.; verge, border, proximity, neighbourhood, environs, Kāv.; Pañc. (cf. *parī-s°*); a vein or artery, BhP.; death, L.; a rule, precept, L.; a god, L.; *-vishaya*, m. an adjoining place, neighbourhood, Kir. v, 38. °**saraṇa**, n. running or moving about; *-śīla*, mfn. of a restless disposition, Suśr. °**saryā**, f. = *saraṇa*, Pāṇ. iii, 3, 101, Pat.; near approach, W.; service, W. (cf. *parī-s°*). °**sāra**, m. wandering about, perambulation, W. °**sāraka**, m. (g. *vimuktâdi*) N. of a place near the Sarasvatī, AitBr. (cf. *pāris°*). °**sārin**, mfn. wandering or running about, Pāṇ. iii, 2, 142. °**sṛita**, mfn. having roamed or wandered through (acc.), R.; spread everywhere, ib.; m. or n. an enclosed or fenced place, MBh.

परिसृज् *pari-√sṛij*, Caus. *-sarjayati*, to avoid, MBh. °**srishṭa** (*pári-*), mfn. surrounded, covered, AV. °**srashṭṛi**, mfn. being in contact or connected with, MBh.

परिसृप् *pari-√sṛip*, P. Ā. *-sarpati*, °*te* (ind. p. *-sārpam*), to move round about or to and fro, hover, RV.; ŚBr.; MBh. &c.; to creep or crawl upon, Gobh. (see °*sṛipta*); to be near, approach, go to (acc.), MBh.: Caus., see °*sarpita*. °**sarpa**, m. going about in search of, following, pursuing, Daśar.; Pratāp.; walking about, roaming, L.; surrounding, encircling, L.; a species of serpent, Suśr.; N. of a mild form of leprosy (= *vi-sarpa*), Suśr.; Car. (cf. *paris°*). °**sarpaṇa**, n. crawling upon (comp.), Mṛicch.; running to and fro, going or flying about, constantly changing one's place, ĀśvŚr.; R.; Mṛicch.; BhP.; a kind of disease (= °*sarpaṇa*), Suśr. °**sarpita**, mfn. (fr. Caus.) crawled upon by vermin, Car. °**sarpin**, mfn. going or moving or roaming about, MBh. °**sṛipta**, mfn. = °*sarpita*, Gobh.

परिसौवीरम् *pari-sauvīram*, ind. round about (i.e. except) the Sauvīras, Pāṇ. vi, 2, 33, Vārtt. 1, Pat.

परिस्कन्द् *pari-√skand*. See *pari-shkand*.

परिस्खल् *pari-√skhal*, P. *-skhalati*, to reel, stagger, Kathās. °**skhalita**, n. reeling, staggering, ib.

परिस्तॄ *pari-stṛī*, P. Ā. *-stṛiṇoti*, °*ṇute* or *-stṛiṇāti*, °*ṇīte* (perf. 3. pl. *-tastaruḥ*, Bhaṭṭ., *-tastarire*, Śiś.; ind. p. *-stīrya*, GṛS.; Ved. inf. *pári-staritavaí*, MaitrS. [cf. Pāṇ. vi, 2, 51, Sch.]), to strew or lay round, enclose (as fire with grass), AV.; ŚBr. &c.; to envelop, cover (lit. and fig.), Kir.; Śiś.; to spread, extend, GṛS.; R. &c. °**stara**, m. strewing round or heaping together, MBh.; a cover, covering, ib. (v.l. *pari-cchada*). °**stāraṇa**, n. = prec., AV.; GṛŚrS. &c.; (*ī*), f. a partic. sacred text, ĀpŚr. °**staraṇikā**, f. a cow killed at a funeral ceremony (the limbs of the corpse being covered with its limbs), R. (cf. *anu-stáraṇī*). °**staraṇīya**, mfn. fit to be strewed around, serving for a cover, ĀpŚr., Sch. °**staritṛi**, m. one who strews or lays round, ib. °**stīrṇa** (MBh.; R.) and °**stṛita** (Yājñ.; BhP.), spread around, strewed over, covered.

परिस्तोम *pari-stoma*, m. a coverlet, cushion, MBh.; R.

परिस्था *pari-√sthā*, *pari-sthāna*. See *pari-shṭhā*.

परिस्पन्द् *pari-√spand*, Ā. *-spandate* (or °*ti*), to tremble, throb, quiver, MBh.; R. °**spanda**, m. throbbing, stirring, starting, arising, movement, MBh.; Kāv. &c.; keeping, maintaining (a sacred fire), MBh. (v.l. °*shyanda*); train, retinue, L.; decoration of the hair, L.; pressure, crash, MW. °**spandana**, n. throbbing, vibration, motion, L. °**spandita**, n. throbbing, rising, appearing, Mcar.

परिस्पर्धिन् *pari-spardhin*, mfn. (√*spṛidh*) vying with, rivalling, emulating (in comp.), Śak. iv, 4 (v.l.) °**spṛidh**, f. a rival, RV. ix, 53, 1.

परिस्पृश् *pari-√spṛiś*, P. *-spṛiśati* (pf. 3. pl. *-paspṛiśire*), to touch, stroke, MBh.; R.; to pursue, practise, HPariś. °**spṛiś**, mfn. (ifc.) touching, HPariś. °**spṛishṭa**, mfn. smeared or soiled with (blood), MBh.

परिस्फर् *pari-√sphar*, Caus. *-sphārayati*, to spread, divulge, L.

परिस्फीत *pari-sphīta*, mfn. (√*sphāy*) swollen, turgid, Pārśvan.

परिस्फुट् *pari-√sphuṭ*, P. *-sphuṭati* or *-sphoṭati*, to burst open, Suśr.

Pari-sphuṭa, mfn. very clear or manifest, BhP.; fully developed, L.; (*am*), ind. very clearly or distinctly, Kād.

परिस्फुर् *pari-√sphur*, P. *-sphurati*, to throb, quiver, vibrate, Kāv.; to glitter, gleam, BhP.; to burst forth, appear, Kull. °**sphuraṇa**, n. glancing; shooting; budding, W. °**sphurita**, mfn. quivering, palpitating, Uttarar.; dispersed, reflected on all sides, Mālatīm.; opened, expanded, W.; shot, glanced, ib. °**sphūrti**, f. shining forth, appearing, becoming clear or manifest, Kuval.

परिस्मापन *pari-smāpana*, n. (√*smi*, Caus.) causing wonder, surprising; (with *dambhena*) outwitting, L.

परिस्यन्द *pari-syanda*, °*dana* &c. See *pari-shyanda*, p. 603, col. 2.

परिस्रज् *pari-sraj*, f. (√*sṛij*) a garland, ĀpŚr. °**srajin**, mfn. wearing a garland, TBr.; Kāṭh.

परिस्रसा *pari-srasā*, f. (√*srans*) rubbish, lumber, TBr.

परिस्रु *pari-√sru*, P. *-sravati*, to flow round or off, stream, trickle, RV. &c. &c.; (with acc.) cause to flow, RV.; Hariv.; to swim or float about, Sāy.; to glide or pass away (as life), Bhartṛ. °**srava**, m. flowing, streaming, a stream, MBh.; R. &c.; gliding down (*garbha-p°*, the birth of a child), R.; Rottleria Tinctoria, L. °**srāva**, m. flowing, efflux, effluxion, Suśr.; N. of a morbid state ascribed to the overflowing of the moistures of the body, ib.; *-kalpa*, m. a kind of straining or filtering vessel, L. °**srāvaṇa**, n. a straining or filtering vessel, L. °**srāvin**, mfn. flowing; m. (sc. *bhagaṃ-dara*) a form of fistula of the anus, Suśr.; n. (sc. *udara*) an incurable form of swollen or enlarged abdomen, ib.; Bhpr. °**srút**, mfn. flowing round or over, foaming, fermenting, RV.; f. a kind of intoxicating liquor prepared from herbs, AV.; VS.; ŚBr. (°*srún-mat*, mfn. possessing it, ŚBr.); dropping, flowing, W. °**sruta**, mfn. flowed or streamed round, trickled, oozed, R.; Kathās.; (*ā*), f. = °*srut*, f., L.

परिस्वार *pari-svāra*, m. (√*svar*) a partic. mode of singing, Lāṭy.

परिस्विद् *pari-√svid*, Caus. *-svedayati*, to cause to sweat (by applying sudorifics), Suśr.

परिहन् *pari-√han*, P. *-hanti*, to wind round, Kāṭh.; ŚāṅkhŚr.; to extinguish (fire), ŚBr.: Pass. *-hanyate*, to be changed or altered, MBh. (v.l. *prati-h°*); to cease, perish, Pañc. (v.l. *-hīyate*). °**hanana**, n., Pāṇ. viii, 4, 22, Sch. °**hata**, mfn. (Śak. v, 22/23 and Git. v, 13) w. r. for *pari-hṛita*.

परिहर *pari-hara*, °*raṇa* &c. See *pari-hṛi*.

परिहर्षण *pari-harshaṇa*, °*shin*. See *pari-hṛish*, p. 605.

परिहव *pari-havá*, m. (√*hve*) crying or calling upon, invoking (?), AV. °**hūta**, mfn. called together, BhP.

परिहस् *pari-√has*, P. *-hasati* (Pass. aor. *pary-ahāsi*), to laugh, jest or joke with (acc.), laugh at, ridicule, deride, MBh.; Kathās.; Rājat. °**hasita**, mfn. laughed at, ridiculed, MW. °**hāsa**, m. jesting, joking, laughing at, ridiculing, deriding; a jest, joke, mirth, merriment, MBh.; Kāv. &c. (cf. *parī-h°*); *-kathā*, f. an amusing story, Ragh.; *-pura*, n. N. of a town, Rājat.; *-pūrvam*, ind. jokingly, in jest, Ragh.; *-vastu*, n. an object of jest (°*stu-tā*, f.), Pañc.; *-vijalpita*, mfn. uttered in jest, Śak.; *-vedin*, m. a jester, a witty person, W.; *-śīla*, mfn. of a gay or joyous disposition, fond of jesting, Var.; Kāv.; °*la-tā*, f., Ratnâv.; *-hari*, m. N. of a temple of Vishṇu, Rājat. °**hāsya**, mfn. laughable, ridiculous, MW.

परिहस्त *pari-hastá*, m. (g. *nir-udakâdi*) an amulet put round the hand to secure the birth of a child, AV.

परिहा *pari-√3. hā*, P. *-jahāti* (ind. p. *-hāya*; inf. *-hātum*), to leave, abandon, quit, R.; BhP.; to omit, neglect, disregard, Mn.; MBh.; Hariv.: Pass. *-hīyate* (with fut. *-hāsyati*, MBh.), to be avoided or omitted, be destitute or deprived of, desist or be excluded from (abl.), be wanting or deficient, be inferior to (abl. or instr.), wane, fail, decrease, pass away, Mn.; MBh.; Kāv. &c.: Caus. *-hāpayati*, to cause to relinquish or abandon, Naish.; to interrupt, leave unfinished, Mn. viii, 206. °**hāṇa**, n. being deprived of anything, suffering a loss (only *a-parih°*), ŚāṅkhBr. °**hāṇi** or °**hāni**, f. decrease, loss, deficiency, Ragh.; Var.; Suśr. (cf. Uṇ. iv, 51, Sch.) °**hāpaṇīya**, mfn. (fr. Caus.) to be omitted, Kād. °**hāpita**, mfn. robbed or deprived of (instr.), BhP. °**hāpya**, ind. excluding, excepting (acc.), except, ĀpŚr. °**hīṇa** (also written *hīna*), mfn. omitted, lost, disappeared, wanting, MBh.; Kāv.; BhP.; abstaining from, deficient in, deprived or destitute of (abl. or *-tas*, instr., or comp.), ib.

परिहाटक *pari-hāṭaka*, mfn. consisting or made of pure gold, MBh.; a ring worn round the arm or leg, an armlet, anklet, L.

परिहार *pari-hāra* &c. See *pari-√hṛi*.

परिहि *pari-√hi*, P. *-hinóti*, to send or forward to (dat.), RV. vii, 104, 6.

परिहिंसा *pari-hiṇsā*, f. (√*hiṇs*) = *pari-barhaṇā*, Nir., Sch.

परिहिण्ड् *pari-√hiṇḍ*, Ā. *-hiṇḍate*, to fly about, Daś.

परिहित *pari-hita*. See *pari-dhā*, p. 596.

परिहृ *pari-√hṛi*, P. Ā. *-harati*, °*te* (fut. *-harishyati*, MBh.; aor. 3. pl. *-ahṛishata*, RV.; ind. p. *-hṛitya*, R.; Var.; *-hāram*, Br.), to move or carry or take round, TS.; Br.; GṛŚrS.; to put or wrap round (Ā. round one's self), AV. &c. &c.; to put aside, save for (dat.), ŚBr.; to leave, quit, desert, Śiś.; to defend or preserve from (abl.), ChUp.; to spare, VP.; to shun, avoid, leave out, omit, ŚBr.; Gobh.; to save or spare anything (as trouble, care &c.) to (gen.), Ratnâv.; to take away, remove, beware of or abstain from (acc.), MBh.; VP.; (Ā.) to keep away from i.e. neglect, not heed, Āpast.; to answer, refute, Pat.; Śaṃk.; to put twice, repeat (in the Krama-pāṭha), APrāt.; to nourish, foster, cherish, Lalit.: Desid. *-jihīrshati*, to wish to keep away or avoid or shun, remove or conceal, Gobh.; R. (cf. *-jihīrshā*, p. 594). °**hara**, m., v.l. for °*hāra*, reserve, concealment, Śak. (Pi.) i, 22/23. °**haraka**, m., v.l. for °*hāraka*, L. °**haraṇa**, n. moving or taking round, ŚrS.; avoiding, shunning, VP.; leaving, W.; seizing, ib.; refuting, ib. °**haraṇīya**, mfn. to be shunned or avoided, Śak.; Prab.; to be taken away, W.; to be confuted, ib.; *-tā*, f. disdain, rejection, Śiś.; disappearance, unattainableness, ib.; refutation, ib. °**hartavya**, mfn. to be handed over or forwarded,

Nyāyam., Sch.; to be shunned or avoided or abstained from, Nir.; Kāv.; Pañc.; to be kept secret or concealed, Mṛicch.; to be confuted, Śaṃk.; to be repeated (before and after *iti*, cf. next), APrāt. °**hāra** (*pári*-), m. leading round, KātyŚr.; delivering or handing over, Nyāyam., Sch.; shunning, avoiding, excluding, abandoning, giving up, resigning, ŚBr. &c. &c.; seizing, surrounding, W.; concealment, reserve, MBh.; Śak.; leaving out, omission, Sāh.; taking away, removing by arguments, confutation, Śaṃk.; caution, Car.; contempt, disrespect, L.; objection, L.; any objectionable thing or person, W.; (in gram.) the repetition of a word (before and after *iti*, cf. *pari-graha*), APrāt.; (in dram.) remedying or atoning for any improper action, Sāh.; an extraordinary grant, exemption from taxes, immunity, Mn.; R.; MārkP.; Rājat.; = -*sthāna* (below), Mn. viii, 237; bounty, largess, W. (cf. *parī-h*°); 1. -*vat*, mfn. avoidable, MBh. (*a-parih*°); 2. -*vat*, ind. (ifc.) like the omission of, Sāh.; -*viśuddhi*, f. (with Jainas) purification by such mortification and penance as are enjoined by the example of ancient saints or sages, W.; -*sū*, f. (a cow) bearing a calf only after a long time (of barrenness), TS., Sch.; -*sthāna*, n. a space of common land extending round a village or town, Kull. on Mn. viii, 238. °**hāraka**, mf(*ikā*)n. repelling, refuting, MW.; m. or n. an armlet, L. (cf. °*haraka* and *pari-hāṭaka*). °**hārin**, mfn. (ifc.) avoiding, shunning, Daś.; Bālar. °**hārya**, mfn. to be shunned or avoided or omitted or escaped from, MBh.; R. &c.; to be severed or separated, Kathās.; to be taken off or away, W.; to be endowed with a privilege, Yājñ., Sch.; to be repeated (cf. °*hartavya*), APrāt.; m. a bracelet, L. (cf. *pārihārya*). °**hṛita**, mfn. shunned, avoided, Kāv.; abandoned, quitted, W.; taken, seized, ib.; n. what has been wrapped round or put on, BhP. °**hṛiti**, f. shunning, avoiding, AitBr. 1. °**hṛitya**, ind. keeping away, excluding, with the exception of (acc.), R.; at a distance of (acc.), Var. 2. °**hṛitya**, mfn. to be delivered or handed over, AitBr.

परिहृष् *pari-√hṛish*, Caus. -*harshayati*, to delight greatly, cause to rejoice, MBh.; Hariv. °**harshaṇa**, mf(*ī*)n. greatly delighting, MBh. °**harshita**, mfn. greatly delighted, ib. °**harshin**, mfn. delightful, MBh. °**hṛishita**, mfn. delighted, very glad, ib. °**hṛishṭa**, mfn. id. (-*mānasa*, mfn.; R.); blunt, obtuse (teeth), Bhpr.

परिह्नुत *pari-hnuta*, mfn. (√*hnu*) denied, refused, AV.

परिहृत् *pari-hrút*, mfn. (√*hvṛi*) causing to fall, RV. °*hvṛita*, see *á-pari-hvṛita*. °**hvṛiti** (*pári*-), f. deceiving, injuring, harming, RV. viii, 47, 6 (loc. *hṛitā́* !); ix, 79, 2.

परिह्वालम् *pari-hvālam*, ind. (√*hval*) stammering, faltering, ŚBr.

परी 1. *parī*, in comp. for *pari*. -**kshit**, m. (√2. *kshi*) N. of a son of Abhi-manyu and father of Janam ejaya, MBh. &c.; of a son of Kuru, Pur.; of a son of An-aśvan and father of Bhīma-sena, MBh.; of a king of A-yodhyā, ib. (cf. *pari-kshit*). -**kshita** (ŚārṅgP.) and -**kshiti** (Prab., Sch.), m. = prec. -**ṇáśe**, Vedic inf. (√1. *naś*) to attain or to be attained, RV. i, 54, 1. -**ṇáh**, f. (√*nah*; nom. *ṇat*, Pāṇ. vi, 3, 116; viii, 2, 34, Sch.) enclosure or anything enclosed, (esp.) a receptacle or box belonging to a carriage, RV.; AV.; ŚBr.; Kāṭh.; N. of a place on the Saras-vatī, Br.; ŚrS. -**ṇāma**, m. (√*nam*) course or lapse of time, R. (cf. *pari-ṇ*°). -**ṇāya**, m. (√*nī*) = *pari-ṇ*°, L. -**ṇāha**, m. (√*nah*) circumference, width, MBh.; R.; Suśr.; a piece of common land encircling a village, Yājñ.; N. of Śiva, L. (cf. *pari-ṇ*°). -**tat** (√*tan*), Pāṇ. vi, 3, 116, Sch. -**tāpa**, m. = *pari-t*°, MBh. -**tosha**, m. = *pari-t*°, Gīt. - 1. -**tta**, mfn., see *pari-dā* (p. 595). - 2. -**tta**, mfn. (√*do*; cf. Pāṇ. vi, 3, 124) cut round, circumscribed, limited, Buddh.; -*śubha*, m. pl. N. of the gods of the 13th order, MWB. 212; -°*tābha*, m. pl. N. of the gods of the 10th order, ib. 211. -**dāha**, m. burning, cauterizing, Suśr.; Car. -**dhāna**, n. a mantle, garment, MBh. (cf. *pari-dh*°). -**dhāvin**, m. = *pari-dh*°, W. -√**dhyai** (only pf. -*dadhyau*), to meditate, ponder, R. -**pāka**, m. ripening, maturing, full development, Suśr.; Car.; Kāraṇḍ.; the result or consequences of anything, Mcar. (cf. *pari-p*°). -**bhāva**, m. = *pari-bh*°, L. -**māṇa**, n. measure, circumference, size, weight, number, amount, MBh.; Yājñ.; Hcat. (cf. *pari-m*°). -**rambha**, m. = *pari-r*°, Gīt.; Prab.; Bālar. -**varta**, m. exchange, barter, Hit. (v.l.); N. of the Kūrma or 2nd incarnation of Vishṇu, L. (cf. *pari-v*°). -**vartam**, ind. (√*vṛit*) in a circle, recurring, repeatedly, TāṇḍBr. -**vāda**, m. reproof, censure, Mn.; Āpast. -**vāpá**, m. fried grains or sour milk, VS.; furniture, L.; a piece of water, L.; sowing, L. (cf. *pari-v*° under *pari-√2. vap*). -**vāpya**, mfn. = *pari-v*° (under *pari-√2. vap*), KātyŚr. -**vāra**, m. train, retinue, MBh.; Kāv. &c.; a sheath, scabbard, L. (cf. *pari-v*° under *pari-√1. vṛi*). -**vāha**, m. = *pari-v*°, MBh.; the royal insignia, L. -**vettṛi**, m. = *pari-v*°, Mn. iii, 172. -**vesha**, m. a halo round the sun or moon, Hariv. (cf. *pari-v*°). -**śāsa**, m. (√*śas*) anything cut out, an excision, AV.; a kind of tongs used for lifting a kettle from the fire, ŚBr. -**śesha**, m. rest, remainder, AitBr. (cf. *pari-ś*°). -**shahā**, f. = *pari-sh*° (under *pari-shah*), HYog. -**sheka**, m. = *pari-sh*° (under *pari-shic*), Suśr. -**sara**, m. circumference, surroundings, Bālar. (cf. *pari-s*°). -**sarpa**, m. a species of worm causing leprosy, Suśr.; a kind of 1°, Car. (cf. *pari-s*° under *pari-sṛip*). -**saryā**, f. = *pari-s*°, L. -**sāra**, m. going about or round, L. -**hāra**, m. avoiding, shunning, caution, Suśr.; disrespect, L.; (in gram. and dram.) = *pari-h*°. -**hāsa**, m. = *pari-h*°, Cāṇ.; -*keśava*, m. N. of a temple of Vishṇu, Rājat.; -*kshama*, mfn. able to deride or surpass, Bhartṛ.; -*śīla*, mfn. = *pari-hāsa-ś*°, Rājat.

परी 2. *parī* (*pari-√i*), P. *pary-eti* (Impv. *parīhi*, MBh.; Pot. *párīyām*, TS.; impf. *pary-ait*, ŚBr.; pf. *párīyāya*, TS.; fut. *pary-etā*, ChUp.; ind. p. *parītya*, PārGṛ.; *pary-āyam*, Br.; inf. *páry-etave*, RV.), to go about, move in a circle; (trans.) to go or flow round (acc.), circumambulate, surround, include, grasp, span, RV. &c. &c.; to run against or into, reach, attain, AV.; ŚBr.; ChUp.; (with or sc. *manasā*) to perceive, ponder, MBh.; R.: Intens. Ā. *párīyate*, to move round or in a circle, RV. **Parīta**, mfn. standing or moving round, surrounding, MBh.; past, elapsed, expired, R.; surrounded, encompassed, filled, taken possession of, seized (with instr. or in comp.), MBh.; Kāv. &c.; = *viparīta*, inverted, MBh.; w. r. for *parītta*, ib.; m. pl. N. of a people, VP.; °*ta-tā*, f. the being surrounded or filled, L.; °*tin*, mfn. (ifc.) filled with, seized by, Suśr. **Parītya**, mfn. to be circumambulated (*a-par*°), KātyŚr.

Pary-aya, m. revolution, lapse, expiration, waste or loss (of time), Mn.; MBh. &c.; the time of revolution (of a planet), Gaṇit.; change, alteration, ib.; inversion, irregularity, confusion with (comp.), MBh.; Suśr.; contrariety, opposition, W.; deviation from enjoined or customary observances, neglect of duty, ib. °**ayaṇa**, m. going about, walking round, circumambulating (e.g. of a sown field), MānGṛ.; Gobh. (Sch. 'the reaping of corn'); fit to be wound round (an arrow or other object), Kauś.; a horse's saddle or housings (= *paryāṇa*), L.

Pary-āya, m. going or turning or winding round, revolving, revolution, KātyŚr.; course, lapse, expiration of time, MBh.; Hariv.; Vet.; regular recurrence, repetition, succession, turn (ibc. or *eṇa*, ind. in turn, successively, alternately; *caturthe paryāye*, at the fourth time), KātyŚr.; Lāṭy.; Mn. &c.; a regularly recurring series or formula (esp. in the Ati-rātra ceremony), Br.; ŚrS. (-*tva*, n.); = -*sūkta*, Sāy.; a convertible term, synonym (-*tā*, f., -*tva*, n.), Pañc.; Sāh.; Pāṇ., Sch.; way, manner, method of proceeding (*anena pary-āyeṇa*, in this manner), SaddhP.; probability, MBh.; (in rhet.) a partic. figure of speech, Kpr.; Sāh.; (with Jainas) the regular development of a thing and the end of this d°, Sarvad.; opportunity, occasion, L.; formation, creation, L.; point of contact, L.; -*krama*, m. order of succession, regular rotation or turn, MW.; -*cyuta*, mfn. one who has lost his turn, superseded, supplanted, ib.; -*pada-mañjarī*, f., -*muktāvalī*, f., -*ratna-mālā*, f. N. of wks.; -*vacana*, n. a convertible term, synonym, Vārtt. on Pāṇ. i, 1, 68; -*vākya*, n. similar words, Hariv.; -*vācaka*, mfn. expressing a corresponding notion; (with *śabda*), m. a synonym, MBh.; -*vṛitti*, f. alternate course or action, MW.; -*śabda*, m. a synonym, Tattvas.; -*śayana*, n. alternate sleeping and watching, W.; -*śas*, ind. by phrases or sentences, ĀśvŚr.; periodically, Kāṭh.; Suśr.; in succession, by turns, MBh.; -*śastra* (!), n. pl. N. of wk.; -*sūkta*, n. a hymn with regularly recurring phrases or sentences, AVAnukr.; -*sevā*, f. service by rotation, Kum.; °*yâtman*, m. the finite nature, finiteness, Sarvad.; °*yânna*, n. food intended for another, Yājñ.; °*yârṇava*, m. 'ocean of synonyms,' N. of a lexicon; °*yôkta*, n. (in rhet.) a partic. figure of speech (in which the fact to be intimated is expressed by a turn of speech or periphrasis), Sāh.; °*yôkti*, f. id., Vām. °**āyika**, mfn. composed in strophes, AV. °**āyin**, mfn. embracing, including, AitBr.; encompassing (in a hostile manner), AV.; periodical, VS.

Pary-etṛi, m. subduer, conqueror, RV. °**ehi**, m. N. of a man; (*ī*), f. N. of a woman, g. *śārṅgaravâdi*.

परीक्ष् *parīksh* (*pari-√īksh*), Ā. *parīkshate* (pr. p. *parīkshat*, MBh.; impf. *pary-aikshat* [Sāy. -*aicchat*], ŚBr.), to look round, inspect carefully, try, examine, find out, observe, perceive, ŚBr. &c. &c.: Caus. *parīkshayati*, to cause to examine or investigate, Mn. **Parīkshaka**, mfn. trying, examining, W.; m. a prover, examiner, judge, Rājat.; Pañc. **Parīkshaṇa**, n. (rarely °*ṇā*, f.) trying, testing, experiment, investigation, Mn.; MBh. &c. **Parīkshaṇīya**, mfn. to be tried or investigated (-*tva*, n.), Nyāyam., Sch.; to be submitted to ordeal, W. **Parīkshā**, f. inspection, investigation, examination, test, trial by ordeal of various kinds (see 2. *divya*), Mn.; MBh. &c.; N. of wk.; -*kshama*, mfn. standing the test, Sarvad.; -*tattva*, n., -*paddhati*, f. N. of wks.; °*kshârtha*, mfn. wishing to try or test, Āpast. **Parīkshita**, mfn. carefully inspected, tried, examined, Mn.; MBh. &c. **Parīkshitavya**, mfn. to be tried or tested or examined or proved, Var.; Prab. **Parīkshin**, see *nāṇaka-p*°. **Parīkshya**, mfn. = °*kshitavya*, MBh.; Var. **Parīcikshishu**, mfn. (fr. Desid.) wishing to try or examine, L.

परीज्या *parījyā*, f. (*pari* + *ijyā*, √*yaj*) a secondary rite (= *pari-yajña*), ŚāṅkhŚr.

परीणस् *párīṇas*, m. (√*pṛī* ?) plenty, abundance, RV.; (*asā*), ind. richly, abundantly, ib. (cf. Naigh. i, 3). **Parīṇasá**, n. = °*ṇas*, m., RV.

परीत *parīta*. See 2. *parī*, col. 2.

परीति *parīti* = *pushpâñjana*, L.

परीत्त 1. 2. *parī-tta*. See under *pari-dā* and 1. *parī*.

परीध्य *parīdhya* (*pari* + *idhya*, √*indh*), to be kindled, TS.

परीन्दन *parīndana*, n. gratification, present, Vajracch. °**dita**, mfn. gratified, presented, ib.

परीप्स् *parīps*, °*psā*, °*psu*. See *pary-āp*.

परीमन् *párīman* (√*pṛī* ?), bounty, plenty; (°*maṇi*), ind. plentifully, RV. ix, 71, 3.

Parīra, n. a fruit, Uṇ. iv, 30, Sch.

परीरण *parīraṇa*, n. a tortoise, L.; a stick, L.; = *paṭṭa-śāṭaka*, L.

परीश् *parīś* (*pari-√īś*), Ā. *parīshṭe*, to be able to (inf.), Kāśikh.

परीष् *parīsh* (*pari-√3. ish*), P. *pary-eshati* (aor. *pary-aishishat*), to seek or search about for, ChUp.; MBh.; (Ā.) SaddhP.: Caus. *pary-eshayati*, id. SaddhP. **Parīshṭi**, f. investigation, research, inquiry, Jaim.; Pat.; service, attendance, homage, L.; freedom of will, L.

Pary-eshaṇa, n. search, inquiry, investigation, MBh.; striving after, Nyāyas.; (*ā*), f. = *parīshṭi*, Pāṇ. iii, 3, 107, Vārtt. 3, Pat. °**eshṭavya**, mfn. to be sought, MBh.; to be striven after, Car. °**eshṭi**, f. searching for, inquiry, SaddhP.; striving after worldly objects, Jātakam.

परीष्ट *parīshṭa*. See *pari-yaj*, p. 599.

परु *paru*, m. (√*pṛī*; cf. *párus* below) a limb, member (see *yathā-p*°); a mountain, L.; the ocean, L.; the sky, paradise, L. -**śás**, ind. limb by limb, member by member, AV.

Paruc-chepa, m. (prob. fr. *parut* = °*rus* + *śepa*) N. of a Ṛishi (son of Divo-dāsa and author of RV. i, 127), Nir.; TS.; ŚāṅkhBr.

Parut-ka, mfn. (fr. *parut* = °*rus*; cf. prec.) having knots or joints (as grass), ĀpŚr.

Paruś-śas, ind. (fr. *parus*) = *paru-śas* (above), MaitrS.; Kāṭh.

Parushá, mf(*ā*)n. (older, f. *párushṇī*) knotty (as reed), AV.; spotted, variegated, dirty-coloured, RV. &c. &c.; hard, stiff, rugged, rough, uneven, shaggy, MBh.; Kāv. &c.; intertwined with creepers (as a tree), Kathās.; piercing, keen, sharp, violent, harsh, severe, unkind, ib. (*am*, ind.); m. a reed, AV.; an arrow, ŚāṅkhŚr.; Lāṭy.; Grewia Asiatica or Xylocarpus Granatum, L.; (*parúsha*), m. N. of a demon, Suparṇ.; (*ā*), f. a kind of riddle, MW.; (°*shṇī*), f. N. of one of the rivers of the Panjāb now called Rāvī, RV.; n. harsh and contumelious speech, abuse, MBh.; Kāv. &c.; the fruit of Grewia Asiatica or Xylocarpus Granatum, L.; a species of Barleria with blue flowers, L. **–ghana**, m. a dirty-coloured or dark cloud, Pañc. v, 4. **–carman**, n. a rough skin, Pañc. **–tara**, mfn. harsher, sterner, Pañc. **–tva**, n. roughness, harshness, MW. **–vacana**, mfn. speaking harshly or unkindly, Bhartṛ.; n. harsh or contumelious speech, W. **–vāc**, mfn. harsh-spoken, f. = prec. n., W. **–vādin**, mfn. = speaking unkindly, Mcar.; Pañc. **Parushâkshara**, mfn. 'harsh-worded,' harsh (*am*, ind.), Kālid.; Pañc. **Parushâkshepa**, m. (in rhet.) an objection or contradiction containing harsh words, Kāvyâd. ii, 144. **Parushâhva**, m. a species of reed, AV. **Parushêtara**, mfn. other than rough, gentle, mild, Ragh. **Parushôkti**, f. abusive or harsh language, Kāv.; °*ktika*, mfn. using it, L.

Parushita, mfn. addressed or treated harshly, MBh.; R.; Hit.

Parushiman, m. rough or shaggy appearance, AitBr.

Parushī, in comp. for °*sha*. **–kṛita**, mfn. spotted, soiled, stained, Hariv.; treated roughly, Am. **–√bhū**, to be soiled or dirty, Śak. vii, 17 (v.l.)

Parush-mat, mfn. having knots or joints (= *parut-ka*), ĀpŚr., Sch.

Parushya, mfn. variegated, manifold, AitBr.

Párus, n. a joint or knot (esp. of a cane or reed, orig. 'fullness,' i.e. the full or thick part of the stalk), a limb or member of the body, RV.; AV.; VS.; ŚBr.; a part or portion, RV.; TS.; TBr.; Grewia Asiatica, L.

Parūsha, m. Grewia Asiatica (from the berries of which a cooling beverage is prepared) or Xylocarpus Granatum, Suśr. °**shaka**, m. id.; n. the fruit of this tree, ŚāṅkhŚr.; Var.; Suśr.

परुत् *parut*, ind. (Pāṇ. v, 3, 22) last year, L. [Cf. *parāri*; Gk. πέρυτι, πέρυσι; Lith. *pérnay*; Goth. *fairneis*; Angl. Sax. *fyrn*; HGerm. *vërt*, *vërne*.] **Parut-tna**, mfn. belonging to last year, last year's, Pāṇ. iv, 3, 23, Vārtt. 1.

परुद्वार *parudvāra* or *parula*, m. a horse, L.

परुष *parusha*. See under *paru*.

परे 2. *paré* (*parā-√i*; for 1. see p. 589, col. 1), P. *parâiti* (Impv. 2. 3. sg. *párehi*, *parâitu*; pr. p. *parā-yát*; ind. p. *parétya*), to go or run away, go along, go towards (acc.), RV. &c. &c.; to depart, die, RV.; AV.; to reach, attain, partake of (acc.), MBh.; Kir. **Páreta**, mfn. departed, deceased, dead, RV.; AV.; Yājñ.; m. a kind of spectre, a ghost, spirit, L.; *-kalpa*, mfn. almost dead, R.; *-bhartṛi*, m. 'lord of the departed,' N. of Yama, Śiś.; *-bhūmi*, f. 'place of the d°,' a cemetery, Kum.; *-rāj* (L.), *-rāja* (Naish.), m. = *-bhartṛi*, L.; °*tâcarita*, mfn. frequented or inhabited by the d°, Daś.; °*tâvāsa*, m. = *-bhūmi*, ib. **Páreti**, f. departure, RV. **Parêyivás**, mfn. one who has departed or died, RV.

परेक्ष *parêksh* = *parā-√iksh* (Pot. *parékshet*a; ind. p. *parêkshya*), to look at (anything at one's side), TS.; ŚBr.

परेण *pareṇa*. See under 1. *pára*, p. 586, col. 2.

परेद्यवि *pare-dyavi*, *pare-dyus* &c. See p. 589, col. 1.

परेमन् *páreman*, prob. w. r. for *pariman*, SV.

परेष्टु *pareshṭu* and °*ṭukā*, f. a cow which has often calved, L.

परोंहु *paro'ṅhu*, *paro'ksha* &c. See under *paro*, p. 589, col. 1.

परोष्णी *paroshṇī*, f. a cockroach (also written °*shṭī*), L.; N. of a river, Rājat. (Cf. *parushṇī* under *parusha*.)

पर्क *parka*. See *madhu-p°*.

पर्कट *parkaṭa*, m. a heron, L.; (*ī*), f. Ficus Infectoria (*-vriksha*), Hit. (also °*ṭī*, L.); a fresh betel-nut, L.; n. regret, anxiety, L.

पर्जन्य *parjánya*, m. (√*pṛic* or *pṛij*?) a rain-cloud, cloud, RV. &c. &c.; rain, Bhag. iii, 14; rain personified or the god of rain (often identified with Indra), RV. &c. &c.; N. of one of the 12 Ādityas, Hariv.; of a Deva-gandharva or Gandharva, MBh.; Hariv.; of a Ṛishi in several Manv-antaras, Hariv.; MārkP.; of a Prajā-pati (father of Hiraṇya-roman), VP.; (°*nyā* or °*nī*), f. Curcuma Aromatica or Xanthorrhiza, L. [Cf. Goth. *fairguni*; Icel. *fiörgyn*; Lith. *perkúnas*.] **–krandya** (°*ján*°), mfn. muttering like Parjanya or a rain-cloud, RV. **–jinvita** (°*ján*°), mfn. impelled by P°, ib. **–nātha**, m. having P° as protector or patron, MW. **–ninada**, m. 'P°'s sound,' thunder, R. **–patnī** (°*ján*°), f. having P° for husband, AV. **–prayoga**, m. N. of wk. **–retas** (°*ján*°), mfn. sprung from the seed of P°, i.e. nourished by rain (as reed), RV. **–vṛiddha** (°*ján*°), mfn. nourished by P° or the rain-cloud (as Soma), ib. **–śānti**, f. N. of wk. **–sûkta**, n. a hymn to P° (as RV. v, 83), Cat. **Parjányâtman**, mfn. having the nature of P°, TS. **Parjányā-vâta**, m. du. the god of rain and the god of wind, RV.

पर्ण् *parṇ*, cl. 10. P. *parṇayati* (Dhātup. xxxv, 84, a), to be green or verdant (prob. Nom. fr. next or invented to explain it).

Parṇá, n. a pinion, feather (also of an arrow), wing, RV. &c.; Br.; MBh.; a leaf (regarded as the plumage of a tree), RV. &c. &c. (ifc. f. *ā*, but in N. of plants *ī*; cf. Pāṇ. iv, 1, 64); the Pān or betel leaf, L.; m. Butea Frondosa (a large-leaved sacred tree whose wood is used for making sacred vessels, later generally called *palāśa*), RV.; AV.; Br.; Yājñ. (*-tvá*, n., MaitrS.); N. of a teacher, VāyuP. (cf. g. *śivâdi*); (pl.) of a people, VP.; of a place, iv, 2, 145; (*ī*), f. a collect. N. of 4 plants ending with *parṇī*, Car.; Pistia Stratiotes, L.; the leaf of Asa Foetida (?), L. [According to Uṇ. iv, 6 fr. √*pṛī*, but more probably fr. a √*pṛi*, orig. *spṛi*; cf. Lith. *sparna*; HGerm. *varn*, *Farn*; Angl. Sax. *fearn*; Eng. *fern*.] **–kashāyá-nishpakva** (ŚBr.) and **-kashāya-pakva** (KātyŚr.), mfn. boiled with the juice of the bark of the Butea Frondosa or with the juice of any leaves. **–kāra**, m. a vender of betel l°. **–kuṭikā** or **-kuṭī**, f. a hut made of l°, L. **–kṛicchra**, m. 'leaf-penance,' living for a time upon an infusion of leaves and Kuśa grass as a religious observance, Vishṇ.; Yājñ. **–khaṇḍa**, m. a tree without apparent blossoms, any tree, L. **–cara**, m. 'leaf-stalker,' a kind of deer, L. **–cīra-paṭa**, mfn. clad in a garment made of leaves (Śiva), MBh. **–coraka**, m. a gall-nut, L. **–tvá**, n. the state of the Butea Frondosa, MaitrS. **–datta**, m. N. of a man, L. **–dhí**, m. 'feather-holder,' the part of an arrow to which the f°s are fastened, AV. **–dhvas**, mfn. (nom. *t*) causing the falling of leaves, Sch. on Pāṇ. iii, 2, 76 &c. **–nara**, m. 'man of l°,' an effigy stuffed with l° or made of l° and burnt as a substitute for a lost corpse, Cat. **–nāla**, m. a leaf-stalk, petiole, Śaṃk. **–puṭa**, m.n. a leaf rolled into the shape of a funnel, MBh.; R. **–purusha**, m. (prob. = *-nara*) N. of wk. **–prātyika**, m. or n. N. of a place, Rājat. (w. r. for *prāsika*?). **–prâśanin** (Bālar.), **-bhaksha** (Hariv.), mfn. feeding upon leaves. **–bhedinī**, f. the Priyaṅgu tree, L. **–bhojana**, mfn. = *-bhaksha*; m. any animal eating l°, a goat, L. **–maṇi**, m. a kind of magical instrument (made of P° wood?), AV. **–máya**, mf(*ī*)n. made of the wood of the Butea Frondosa, TS.; TBr.; Kāṭh.; °*yī-tva*, n., Nyāyam., Comm. **–mācāla** (?), m. Averrhoa Carambola, L. **–muc**, mfn. (nom. *ṭ*) = *-dhvas*, Uṇ. ii, 22, Sch. **–mṛiga**, m. any animal which frequents the boughs of trees (as a monkey, squirrel &c.), Suśr. **–ruh**, mfn. (nom. *ṭ*) causing leaves to grow, Uṇ. ii, 22, Sch. **–latā**, f. the betel plant, L. **–vat**, mfn. abounding in leaves, leafy, Kāṭh.; MBh. **–valká**, m. the bark of the Butea Frondosa (also pl.), TS.; TBr.; ĀpŚr.; N. of a man, g. *gargâdi*. **–vallī**, f. a species of creeping plant, L. **–vādya**, n. 'leaf-music,' sounds produced by blowing into a folded l°, Hariv. **–vilāsinī**, f. a partic. fragrant substance, Gal. **–ví**, mfn. 'wing-borne,' carried by wings, RV. **–vīṭikā**, f. the Areca nut cut in pieces and sprinkled with spices and rolled up in betel leaves, Rājat. **–śadá**, m. the falling of leaves, AV.; VS.; °*dyà*, mfn. relating to it, TS. **–śabara**, m. pl. N. of a people, MārkP.; (*ī*), f. (prob.) N. of a divine female, Cat. **–śabda**, m. the rustling of leaves, Pañc. **–śayyā**, f. a couch of l°, R. **–śar**, m. a leaf-stalk (esp. of the Butea Frondosa), AitBr. **–śākhā**, f. a bough of the B° Fr°, ŚBr. **–śāda**, m. = *-śada*, Kāṭh. **–śālā**, f. 'leaf-hut,' an arbour, R.; Ragh.; Kād. (esp. as the dwelling of a Buddhist monk, RTL. 81; 430); N. of a great settlement of Brāhmans in Madhya-deśa between the Yamunā and Gaṅgā, MBh.; °*lâgra*, m. N. of a mountain in Bhadrâśva, MārkP.; °*lāya*, Nom. Ā. °*yate*, to be like an arbour, Naish. **–śush**, mfn. (nom. *ṭ*) drying or shrivelling leaves, Uṇ. ii, 22, Sch. **–saṃstara**, m. having l° for a bed, sleeping on l°, MW. **Parṇâdhaka**, m. N. of a man; pl. of his descendants, g. *yaskâdi*. **Parṇâda**, m. 'feeding upon leaves,' N. of an ancient sage, MBh.; of a Brāhman, Nal. **Parṇâsa** (or °*sa*), m. Cedrela Toona or a species of Basilicum, Hariv.; L.; (*ā*), f. N. of sev. rivers, MBh.; Hariv.; Pur. **Parṇâśana**, n. the feeding on l°, SaṃhUp.; m. a cloud, W. **Parṇâśin**, mfn. feeding on l°, Vishṇ. **Parṇâsi**, m. Ocymum Sanctum, W. **Parṇâhāra**, mfn. = °*nâśin*, R. **Parṇôṭaja**, n. 'leaf-hut,' an hermitage, Uttarar. **Parṇôtsa**, m. N. of a village, Rājat.

Párṇaka, m. = *bhilla*, Mahīdh.; N. of a man; pl. of his descendants, g. *upakâdi*; (*ikā*), f. a kind of vegetable, Car.; N. of an Apsaras, Hariv.

1. **Parṇaya**, Nom. P. °*yati*, to be green, Dhātup.

2. **Parṇáya**, m. N. of an enemy ('of an Asura,' Sāy.) slain by Indra, RV. **–ghná**, n. the slaying of Parṇaya, ib.

Parṇala, mfn. full of leaves, leafy, g. *sidhmâdi*; °*lī-bhūta*, mfn. being leafy or green, Bhaṭṭ.

Parṇasa, mfn., g. *tṛiṇâdi*.

Parṇasi, m. (only L.) a house upon or by the water; a lotus; a vegetable; adorning, decoration.

Parṇika, mf(*ī*)n. selling or dealing in Parṇī, g. *kisarâdi*.

Parṇin, mfn. winged, plumed, RV.; leafy, ib.; made of the wood of the Butea Frondosa, R.; m. a tree, MBh.; Butea Frondosa, L.; (°*ṇinī*), f. a species of plant, Suśr.; a collect. N. for 4 partic. plants, Car.; N. of an Apsaras, Hariv. °**ni-latā**, f. Piper Betle, L.

Parṇila, mfn. leafy, Uṇ. iii, 6, Sch.

Parṇīya, mfn. g. *utkarâdi*.

Parṇyà, mfn. relating to leaves, leafy, TS.

पर्णाल *parṇāla*, m. a boat, L.; a spade or hoe, L.; single combat, L.

पर्तृ *partṛi* (√*pṛi*), only instr. pl., with aids, helpfully, RV.

पर्द् *pard*, cl. 1. Ā. (Dhātup. ii, 28) to break wind downwards, Sarasv. i, 25. [Cf. Gk. πέρδω; Lat. *pêdo*, *pôdex*; Lith. *pérdżu*; Germ. *farzen*, *furzen*; Angl. Sax. *feortan*; Eng. *to fart*.]

Parda, m. breaking wind downwards, L.; thick hair, L. °**dana**, n. breaking wind, L.

Pardi, m. or f. N. of a person, L.

पर्प् *parp*, cl. 1. P. *parpati*, to go, Dhātup. xi, 18 (a doubtful root and questionably connected with the following words).

Parpa, n. a wheel-chair (for cripples), Siddh.; young grass; a house, Uṇ. iii, 28, Sch.

Parpaṭa, m. a species of medicinal plant, Suśr. (Hedyotis Burmanniana or Mollugo Pentaphylla, L.); a kind of thin cake made of rice or pease-meal and baked in grease, L.; (*ī*), f. a red-colouring Oldenlandia, Bhpr.; a kind of fragrant earth, L.; a thin crisp cake (prob. = m.), W. **–druma**, m. a kind of tree (= *kumbhī-vriksha*), L. (also °*ṭī-dr*°).

Parpaṭaka, m. a species of medicinal plant (= °*paṭa*), Suśr.; Car.; Bhpr.; (*ī*), f. the same or some other med. plant, Car.

Parpaṭi, m. (with *rāja-putra*) N. of a poet, Cat.

Parpika, m. (and °*kī*, f.) a cripple who moves about by the aid of a chair, Pāṇ. iv, 4, 10, Sch.

पर्परी *parparī*, f. a braid of hair, L.

पर्परीक *parparīka*, m. the sun (√*pṛī*, Uṇ. iv, 19, Sch.); fire, L.; a tank or piece of water, L.

पर्परीण *parparīṇa*, m. (only L.) the vein of a leaf; = *parṇa-cūrṇa-rasa*; = *dyūta-kambala*; n. = *parvan*.

पर्फरीक *parpharīka*, m. one who tears to pieces or fills, RV. x, 106, 6 (Sāy.)

पर्ब् *parb*, cl. 1. P. *parbati*, to go, move, Nalac. (Dhātup. xi, 21; cf. *parp*).

पर्माडि *parmāḍi*, m. N. of a prince of Karṇāṭa (v.l. °*māṇḍi*), Rājat.

पर्यक् *pary-ak*, ind. (orig. n. of an unusual

pary-añc; cf. *praty-añc* &c.) round about, in every direction, BhP.

पर्यगु *paryagu*, mfn. (?) in *pāramahansya-p°*, BhP. iv, 21, 40.

पर्यग्नि *pary-agni*, m. circumambient fire (either a torch carried round the sacrificial animal or = next), Br. — **karaṇa**, n. the ceremony of carrying fire round the s° a°, GṛŚrS.; °*nīya*, mfn. relating to this ceremony, TBr., Sch. — **kartṛi**, m. one who carries fire round the s° a°, MānŚr. — √**kri** (ind. p. -*kṛitvā* or -*kṛitya*), to carry f° round (acc.), Br.; Āpast. — **kṛita** (*pár°*), mfn. encircled with fire, Br. — **kriyamāṇa**, mfn. being encircled with fire; (*e*), ind. during the encircling with fire, AitBr.

पर्यङ्ख् *pary-√aṅkh* (only 3. sg. Subj. Ā. *pary-aṅkháyāte*), to clasp or encircle round, RV. x, 16, 7.

पर्यङ्ग्य *pary-aṅgya*, mfn. (*pari* + *aṅga*) being about or at the side, ŚBr.

पर्यञ्च् *pary-√añc* (only 1. sg. pr. P. *páry-aṇāmi*), to turn about or round, revolve, RV. x, 119, 5.

Pary-aṅka, m. (also *paly°*, Pāṇ. viii, 2, 22) a bed, couch, sofa, litter, palanquin, KaushUp.; MBh.; Kāv. &c. (also °*kikā*, f., Kād.; °*kī-kṛita*, mfn. turned into a couch, Git.); a partic. mode of sitting on the ground (a squatting position assumed by ascetics and Buddhists in meditation), Buddh. (cf. below); a cloth wound round the back and loins and knees while so sitting, L.; N. of a mountain (son of Vindhya), L. — **granthi-bandha**, m. the bending of the legs crossways under the body in sitting, Mṛicch. i, 1. — **paṭṭikā** (Bhpr.), -**pādikā** (L.), f. a species of Lupinus. — **baddha**, mfn. sitting with the legs bent crossways under the body, squatting, Buddh. — **bandhá**, m. (Kum.), -**bandhana**, n. (L.) the act of sitting with the legs bent and binding a cloth round the back and loins and knees. — **bhogin**, m. a kind of serpent, MW. — **stha**, mfn. sitting on a sofa, ib.

पर्यट् *pary-√aṭ*, P. Ā. *pary-aṭati*, °*te* (Impv. *pary-aṭasva*; fut. *pary-aṭishyati*), to roam or wander about, travel over (acc. or loc.), MBh.; Kāv.; Pañc. °**aṭa**, m. pl. N. of a people, R. °**aṭaka**, m. a tramp, vagabond, Mṛicch., Sch. °**aṭana**, n. wandering about, roaming through (gen. or comp.), Pañc.; BhP. °**aṭita**, mfn. one who has roamed or wandered, Pañc.; n. = prec., ib.

पर्यध्ययन *pary-adhyayana*, mfn. averse from study, Pāṇ. ii, 2, 18, Vārtt. 4, Pat.

पर्यन् *pary-√an*, P. *pary-aniti*, Pāṇ. viii, 4, 20, Vārtt. 1, Pat.

पर्यनुबन्ध *pary-anu-bandha*, m. (√*bandh*) binding round, L.

पर्यनुयुज् *pary-anu-√yuj* (ind. p. -*yujya*, Naish.), to ply with questions. °**yukta**, mfn. asked, questioned, Car. °**yoktavya**, mfn. to be questioned, to be urged to answer a question, Saṃk. °**yoga**, m. asking, inquiring, questioning, ĀpŚr., Sch.; an inquiry with the object of refuting a statement, L.; censure, reproach, Yājñ., Sch. °**yojya**, mfn. to be blamed or censured (°*jyôpêkshaṇa*, n. omitting to blame what ought to be blamed), Nyāyas.; Sarvad.

पर्यन्त *pary-antá*, m. circuit, circumference, edge, limit, border; side, flank, extremity, end, TBr.; MBh.; Kāv. &c. (ifc. 'bounded by,' 'extending as far as' [f. *ā*]; or ibc. 'adjoining, neighbouring'); (*am*), ind. entirely, altogether, Sukas; (ifc.) to the end of, as far as, Kap.; *paryantāt paryantam*, from one end to the other, Var.; (*e*), ind. at the end, Kathās.; mf(*ā*)n. coming to an end with, being a match for, Lalit.; extending in all directions, Hariv. (v. l. *pary-asta*). — **deśa**, m. a neighbouring or adjacent district, Hariv. — **parvata**, m. an adjoining hill, L. — **bhū**, f. ground contiguous to the skirts of a river or mountain, W. — **saṃsthita** (Ṛit.), -**stha** (Kathās.), -**sthita** (W.), mfn. limitative, confining, neighbouring.

Paryantikā, f. loss of all good qualities, depravity, L.

Paryantī-√kṛi, to finish; -*kṛita*, mfn. finished, Divyāv.

Paryantīya, mfn. being at the end, ĀpŚr.

पर्यन्य *paryanya*, w. r. for *parjanya*.

पर्यन्विष् *pary-anv-√3. ish*, P. -*icchati*, to seek for, search after, MBh.

पर्यय *pary-aya*, *pary-ayaṇa*, *pary-āya*. See under 2. *pari*.

पर्यर्षण *pary-arshaṇa*. See under *pary-ṛish*.

पर्यवकृ *pary-ava-√kṛī*, P. -*kirati*, to scatter round or about, shed over, MBh.

पर्यवच्छिद् *pary-avacchid* (*ava* + √*chid*), P. -*cchinatti* (-*cchinadāni*), to cut off on both sides or all round, AitBr.

पर्यवदात *pary-ava-dāta*, mfn. (√*dai*) perfectly clean or pure, Kād.; very accomplished, Divyâv.; well acquainted or conversant with (loc.), Car. (-*tva*, n.); well known, very familiar, ib. — **śruta**, mfn. perfectly skilled in art (-*tā*, f.), Car.

पर्यवदो *pary-ava-√do*, P. -*dyati*, to cut off or slice all round, TS. °**dāna**, n. complete destruction or disappearance, Lalit. °**dāpayitṛi**, m. (fr. Caus.) a distributor, Divyâv.

पर्यवधारण *pary-ava-dhāraṇa*, n. (√*dhṛi*) precise determination, careful consideration, refining, subtilizing, Vedântas., Sch.

पर्यवनद्ध *pary-ava-naddha*, mfn. (√*nah*) overgrown, Divyâv.

पर्यवनुद् *pary-ava-√nud*, P. -*nudati*, to push towards (acc.), TāṇḍBr.

पर्यवपन्न *pary-ava-panna*, mfn. (√*pad*) broken down, destroyed, annihilated, frustrated, Pat. °**pāda**, m. transformation, ib.; °*dya*, mfn. effecting transformation, ib.

पर्यवरोध *pary-ava-rodha*, m. (√*rudh*) obstruction, hindrance, L.

पर्यवशिष् *pary-ava-√śish* (only Pot. -*śish-yet*), to border, circumscribe, Vait. °**śesha**, m. end, termination, MW. °**śeshita**, mfn. (fr. Caus.) left remaining, BhP.; regarded as the end of all (i.e. God), MW.

पर्यवष्टम्भ् *pary-ava-shṭambh* (√*stambh*; Pass. -*shṭabhyate*, ind. p. -*shṭabhya*), to surround, invest, Kāv. °**shṭabdha**, mfn. surrounded, invested, Mālatim. °**shṭambhana**, n. surrounding, investing, Uttarar.

पर्यवसृप् *pary-ava-√sṛip*, P. -*sarpati*, to creep up to, approach in a creeping manner, ŚāṅkhBr.

पर्यवसो *pary-ava-√so*, P. -*syati*, to result or end in, amount to (loc. or acc. with *prati*), Kāv.; Sāh.; to finish, complete, conclude, include, MW.; to endeavour, ib.; to perish, be lost, decline, A. °**sāna**, n. end, termination, conclusion, issue (*āt*, ind. in consequence of), Gobh.; Nāg.; Hit.; comprehending, including, amounting to (loc.), Sarvad. °**sānika**, mfn. coming to a close, tending towards an end, MBh. (v. l. *pāryavas°*). °**sāya**, m. = °*sāna*; ifc. = next, Bālar. °**sāyin**, mfn. ending with, amounting to, Uttarar.; Saṃk. (°*yi-tva*, n.) °**sita** (*pary-áva-*), mfn. living farther off (= not quite near), ŚBr., Sch.; (with *lokântaram*) departed to, Uttarar.; finished, concluded, ended, MBh.; Kāv. &c.; amounting to (loc.), Saṃk.; resolved, settled, definitive, Sāh.; -*mati*, mfn. thoroughly acquainted or familiar with (loc.), BhP.

पर्यवस्कन्द *pary-ava-skanda*, m. (√*skand*) the act of jumping down (from a carriage), MBh.

पर्यवस्था *pary-ava-√sthā*, Ā. -*tishṭhate*, to become firm or steady, Bhag.; to fill, pervade (acc.), MBh.: Caus. -*sthāpayati*, to comfort, encourage, ib. °**sthā**, f., °**sthāna**, n. opposition, contradiction, L. °**sthātṛi**, mfn. opposing; an antagonist, adversary, MBh.; Pāṇ. v, 2, 89. °**sthita**, mfn. standing, stationed; (with loc.) contained in, devoted or attached to, intent upon, occupied with, MBh.; R.; Hariv.; merry, content, comfortable, of good cheer, ib.

पर्यवाप् *pary-avâp* (*ava* + √*āp*), P. -*avâp-noti*, to study, Divyâv.

पर्यवे *pary-avê* (*ava*-√*i*), P. -*avâiti* (Pot. -*avêyāt*), to turn round, turn in the right direction, AitBr.; to pass, elapse, ŚBr. °**avêta**, mfn. elapsed, expired, Kauś.; HirGṛ.

पर्यवेक्ष् *pary-avêksh* (*ava*-√*īksh*), Ā. -*avê-kshate*, to regard from every side, MBh.; to look down upon, KaushUp.

पर्यश् *pary-√1. aś*, P. -*aśnoti* (Pot. -*aśyāt*), to arrive at, reach, attain, RV.

पर्यश् *pary-√2. aś*, P. -*aśnāti*, to eat before another (acc.), to pass over a person at a meal (instr.), MBh.

पर्यश्रु *pary-aśru*, mfn. bathed in tears, shedding tears, tearful, MBh.; Kāv.; Rājat.

पर्यस् *pary-√1. as*, P. *pary-asti* (3. du. *pári-shṭaḥ*; 2. pl. *pári-shṭha*; pf. *páry-āsa*), to be in the way of (acc.), RV.; to pass or spend time, ib.

पर्यस् *pary-√2. as*, P. Ā. *pary-asyati*, °*te*, to throw or cast or place round, AV.; AitBr.; to spread round, diffuse, Kir.; to entrap, ensnare (Ā. aor. 3. du. *pary-āsishātām*, Pāṇ. iii, 1, 52, Sch.); to turn round, wallow (ind. p. *pary-asya*), Amar.; to throw down, overturn, upset (aor. *pary-āsthat*), ŚBr.; Mn.; Kathās.: Pass. *pary-asyate* (aor. *pary-āsthata*, Pāṇ. iii, 1, 52, Sch.), to fall down, drop: Caus. *pary-āsayati*, to cause to roll down or shed (as tears), Ragh. °**asana**, n. throwing or tossing about, Car.; casting, sending, W.; putting off or away, ib. °**asta**, mfn. thrown or cast about, spread, diffused, MBh.; Kum.; Amar.; surrounded, encompassed, ensnared, R.; Bhartṛ.; strung, filed on (comp.), Daś.; overturned, upset, inverted, changed, Bhartṛ.; struck, killed, L.; dismissed, laid aside, ib.; -*vat*, mfn. containing the notion expressed by the word *pary-asta*, AitBr.; -*vilocana* (Kum.), -°*astâk-shá* (AV.), mfn. having the eyes cast or directed round, rolling the eyes. °**asti**, f. sitting upon the heels or hams, L. °**astikā**, f. id., Suśr.; a bed, W.; -°*kâkriti*, mfn. one who has sprained both his shoulders, L.

Pary-āsá, m. edging, trimming, ŚBr.; rotation, resolution, BhP.; end, conclusion (N. of partic. concluding strophes in certain hymns), Br.; ŚrS.; inverted order or position, W. °**āsana**, n. (fr. Caus.) revolution, MBh. °**āsita**, see *a-paryāsita*.

पर्यस्तमयम् *pary-astamayam*, ind. about sunset, ŚāṅkhŚr.

पर्यह्न *pary-ahna*, m., APrāt., Comm.

पर्याकुल *pary-ākula*, mf(*ā*)n. full of, filled with (comp.), MBh.; R.; Hariv.; disordered, confused, excited, bewildered, MBh.; Kāv. &c.; turbid (as water), MW. — **tva**, n. confusion, bewilderment, Kum.

Pary-ākulaya, Nom. P. °*yati*, to disturb, excite, bewilder, Śak. (Pi.) i, $\frac{1}{2}$.

Pary-ākulī-√kṛi, id., ib. (v. l.) -√**bhū**, to be confused or bewildered, R.

पर्याकृ *pary-ā-√kṛi* (only Pass. p. -*kri-yamāṇa* and -*kṛita*), to turn round, AV.: Desid. (p. *pary-ā-cikīrshat*) to wish to turn round, TS.

पर्याक्षिप् *pary-ā-√kship*, P. -*kshipati*, to wind round, bind with (instr.), Kum.

पर्याख्यान *pary-ā-khyāna*, n. (√*khyā*), Pāṇ. ii, 4, 54, Vārtt. 7, Pat.

पर्यागम् *pary-ā-√gam*, P. -*gacchati*, to go round, elapse, last, live, MBh. °**āgata**, mfn. revolved, anything that has made its revolution, elapsed, passed (as a year), TS.; finished, done, MBh.; inveterate, ib.; (with *punar*) returned to life, ib.; (ifc.) encircled, ensnared, being in a person's power, ib.

पर्यागल् *pary-ā-√gal*, P. -*galati*, to drop or trickle down on every side, Bhaṭṭ.

पर्यागा *pary-ā-√gā* (only aor. -*āgāt*, 3. pl. -*āgur*), to pursue, be intent upon (acc.), RV. i, 88, 4; to perform a revolution, elapse (as time), MBh.

पर्याचर् *pary-ā-√car*, P. -*carati*, to come near, approach, RV.; AV.

पर्याचान्त *pary-ācānta*, mfn. (√*cam*) sipped prematurely (as water in *ācamana*, q. v.); (with *annam*), n. food left by a person after sipping, Mn. iv, 212.

पर्याचित *pary-ā-cita*, n. (prob.) N. of a place, g. *ācitâdi*.

पर्याण *paryāṇa*, n. (for *pari-yāṇa*; √*yā*) a

circuit (or mfn., forming a c°), AitBr. iv, 17); a saddle, Var.; Kathās. °ṇaya, Nom. P. °yati, to saddle, Nalac. °ṇita, mfn. saddled, Kād.

पर्याणह् *pary-ā-nah* (√nah), P. -ṇahyati, to cover up, cover, ŚBr. °ṇaddha, mfn. covered (?), AV. xiv, 2, 12. °ṇahana, see soma-paryāṇ°.

पर्याणी *pary-ā-ṇī* (√nī), P. -ṇayati (but Impv. pary-ânayata, MBh. i, 5446), to lead round, ŚBr.; GṛS.; MBh.; to lead or bring forward, RV.; MBh.

पर्यातन् *pary-ā-√tan*, P. -tanoti, to spread round, encompass, surround, ŚBr.

पर्यादा *pary-ā-√dā*, Ā. -datte (Pot. -dadīta, ind. p. -dāya), to make one's own, take away from (abl.), RV.; Br.; to take off (any liquid), Suśr.; Car.; to seize, snatch, MBh.; to appropriate, learn, MBh.

पर्यादान *pary-ā-dāna*, n. (√do?) end, exhaustion, Divyâv.

पर्याद्रु *pary-ā-dru*, P. -dravati, to run to and fro, BhP.

पर्याधा *pary-ā-√dhā*, P. -dadhāti (Impv. 2. pl. -dhatta), to lay round, surround (with fire), AV. °âdhātṛi, m. a younger brother who has set up the sacred fire previously to the elder, Gaut.

Pary-āhita, m. an elder brother previously to whom the younger has set up the s° f°, Gaut.; ĀpŚr.

पर्यान्तम् *pary-āntam*, ind. (prob.) w. r. for pary-antam, as far as, up to (comp.), Āpast.

पर्याप् *pary-√āp*, P. -āpnoti (Impv. -āpnuhi; pf. -āpa), to reach, obtain, attain, gain, RV.; TS.; ŚBr.; to make an end of, be content, MBh.: Caus. -āpayati (ind. p. -āpya), to perform, do, Rājat.: Desid. parîpsati, to wish to obtain or reach, desire, Mn.; MBh. &c.; to wish to preserve, guard, MBh.; to wish to get at, lie in wait or ambush, ib.

Parîpsā, f. (fr. Desid.) desire of obtaining or preserving, MBh.; haste, hurry, Pāṇ. iii, 4, 52. **Parîpsu**, mfn. wishing to obtain or preserve, MBh.; desirous of finding out or ascertaining, Kir. iii, 4.

Pary-āpta, mfn. obtained, gained, Uttarar.; finished, completed, full, Up.; Kālid.; extensive, spacious, large, Hariv.; abundant, copious, many, Kāv.; sufficient for (dat. or gen.); adequate, equal to, a match for (gen., dat.; loc. or inf., cf. Pāṇ. iii, 4, 66), MBh.; Kāv. &c.; limited in number, MW.; (am), ind. fully, completely, enough, one's fill, Kāv.; willingly, readily, L.; -kala, mfn. having full digits (as the moon), Ragh.; -kāma, mfn. one whose desires are accomplished or allayed, MuṇḍUp.; -candra, mf(ā)n. adorned by the full moon (as a night), Kum.; -tā, f. copiousness, abundance, Kathās.; satisfaction, gratification, MW.; -dakshiṇa, mfn. accompanied with liberal gifts (as a sacrifice), Ragh.; -nayana, mfn. having a sufficient number of eyes, Hariv.; -bhoga, mfn. possessing or enjoying a sufficiency, Mn.; Yājñ.; -vat, mfn. able, capable, Ragh. (cf. a-pary°). °āpti (páry-), f. end, conclusion, ŚBr.; entireness, fulness, sufficiency, MBh.; Kathās.; Rājat. (cf. Pāṇ. iii, 4, 66); adequacy, competency, fitness for (comp.), Kathās.; Kāś. on Pāṇ. ii, 3, 16; obtaining, acquisition, L.; self-defence, warding off a blow, L.; (in phil.) distinction of objects according to their natural properties, W.

पर्यापत् *pary-ā-√pat*, P. -patati (pf. 3. pl. -petuḥ), to hasten forth, hurry or run away, MBh.; R.; -patat, mf(antī)n. hurrying or rushing about, Śiś. v, 24.

पर्याप्लु *pary-ā-√plu*, Caus. -plāvayati, to make float round, TBr. °plāvá, m. turning round, revolution, TS.; Kāṭh. °pluta, mfn. surrounded, encircled, MBh.

पर्याभू *pary-ā-√bhū* (only aor. pary-ābhūt), to turn upside down (intrans.), ŚBr.

पर्याभृ *pary-ā-√bhṛi*, P. -bharati, to carry near, fetch from (abl.), RV. **Pary-ábhṛita**, mfn. fetched or extracted from (abl.), ib.

पर्यामुच् *pary-ā-√muc*, P. -muñcati, to make loose or take off on all sides, Sāṃkhyak., Sch.

पर्यामृश् *pary-ā-√mṛiś*, P. -mṛiśati, to subdue, conquer, overpower, MW.

पर्याय *pary-āya* &c. See under 2. pari.

पर्यायत *pary-āyata*, mfn. (√yam) extremely long or extended, R.

पर्याया *pary-ā-√yā* (only Impv. -yāhi, -yātam), to approach from (abl.), come near, RV.

पर्यारिन् *pary-ārín*, mfn. (√4. ṛi) toiling a long time without success, attaining one's object in the end (after long effort), TS.; ŚBr.; Kāṭh.

पर्यारुह् *pary-ā-√ruh*, P. -róhati, to rise from (abl.), RV.

पर्याली *paryālī*, ind. (with √kṛi, bhū, and as), g. ūry-ādi.

पर्यालोच् *pary-ā-√loc*, Caus. -locayati (ind. p. -locya), to look after, attend to, consider, ponder, Subh.; Vet. °loca, m. consideration, reflection, HPariś. °locana, n. id., Kull.; (ā), f. id., ib.; ĀpŚr., Sch.; plan, design, Kathās. °locita, mfn. considered, pondered, Kull.; -vat, mfn., Pañc.

पर्यावदान *pary-āvadāna*, n. = pary-avadāna, Kāraṇḍ.

पर्यावप् *pary-ā-√2. vap*, P. -vapati, to add, ŚBr.

पर्यावसथ *pary-āvasatha*, m. = maṭha, Śīl.

पर्याविल *pary-āvila*, mfn. very turbid, much soiled, Ragh.

पर्यावृत् *pary-ā-√vṛit*, Ā. -vártate (ep. also °ti, Pot. -vartet, Hariv.; pf. -vavarta, -vavṛite, MBh.; aor. pary-ā-vart, RV.; ind. p. pari-vṛitya, ĀpŚr.), to turn round (intrans.; trans. only ind. p.), turn away from (abl.), return to (dat.), RV. &c. &c.; to be changed into (instr.), Kād.; to get possessed of (acc.), Hariv.: Caus. -vartayati, to turn or roll round (trans.), TS.; ŚBr.; to change or barter against (Impv. 2. sg. °tāt), ChUp. i, 5, 2: Desid. -vivṛitsati, to wish to roll round, RV. °varta, m. return, exchange, BhP. °vartana, m. N. of a hell, ib.; n. coming back, returning, KātyŚr., Sch. °vartita, mfn. turned round, subverted, reversed, MW.

पर्यावृत *pary-ā-vṛita*, mfn. (√1. vṛi) veiled, covered, Mālatim.

पर्याश्वस् *pary-ā-√śvas*, P. -śvasiti or -śvasati, to breathe out, recover breath, take heart, be at ease, MBh.; R.: Caus. -śvāsayati, °te, to comfort, console, MBh. °śvasta, mfn. comforted, consoled, tranquil, at ease, MBh.

पर्यास् *pary-√ās*, Ā. -āste (3. pl. -āsate; Pot. 3. sg. -āsīta), to sit or assemble round any one (acc.), RV.; ŚBr.; to remain sitting or inactive, RV.; to sue for (acc.), ib. x, 40, 7.

पर्यास *pary-āsa*, °sana. See pary-√2. as.

पर्याहृ *pary-ā-√hṛi*, P. -harati, to hand over to (dat.), ŚBr.; to overturn or turn upside down, ib.; ŚāṅkhŚr. °hāra, m. a yoke worn across the shoulders in carrying a load, L.; conveying, W.; a load, ib.; a pitcher, ib.; storing grain, ib.

पर्याह्वे *pary-ā-√hve*, Ā. -hvayate, to pronounce the Āhāva (s. v.) before and after, AitBr.

Pary-ā-hāva, m. a partic. formula which precedes and follows a verse, ib.; Sāy.

पर्युक *paryuka*, m. N. of a man, Rājat.

पर्युक्त *páry-ukta*, mfn. (√vac) bewitched by words, conjured, AV.

पर्युक्ष् *pary-√uksh*, P. Ā. -ukshati, °te (ind. p. -ukshya), to sprinkle round, ŚrS. °ukshaṇa, n. sprinkling round, sprinkling, GṛŚrS.; (ī), f. a vessel for sprinkling, Kauś.

पर्युत *pary-uta*. See pari-ve, p. 601.

पर्युत्था *pary-ut-thā* (√sthā), P. -ut-tishṭhati, to rise from (abl.), RV.; to appear to (acc.), TāṇḍBr. °utthāna, n. standing up, rising, L.

पर्युत्सुक *pary-utsuka*, mf(ā)n. very restless, much excited, R.; Mālav.; eagerly desirous, longing for (dat.), Ratnāv. -tva, n. an ardent longing, Ragh. °kī-√bhū, to be sorrowful or regretful, Śak.

पर्युत्सृज् *pary-ut-√sṛij*, P. -sṛijati, to give up, leave, abandon, L.

पर्युदञ्चन *pary-ud-añcana*, n. (√añc) debt, L.

पर्युदयम् *pary-udayam*, ind. about sunrise, KātyŚr.

पर्युदस् *pary-ud-√2. as*, P. -asyati, to reject, exclude, MBh. °asana, n. exclusion, Yogas., Sch. °asitavya, mfn. to be excluded or denied, Pat. °asta, mfn. rejected, excluded, Kull. on Mn. iii, 280; -tva, n., ĀpŚr., Sch.; Sāy.

Pary-ud-āsa, m. a prohibitive rule, exception, Pāṇ., Sch.; Kull.

पर्युदित *pary-udita*. See pari-vad, p. 600.

पर्युद्भृत *pary-úd-bhṛita*, mfn. (√bhṛi) brought out, extracted from (abl.), RV.

पर्युद्वस् *pary-ud-√5. vas*, Caus. -vāsayati, to take away, remove, AV.

पर्युद्विज् *pary-ud-√vij* (only fut. -vijishyati), to shrink from, be afraid of (acc.), R.

पर्युपलिप् *pary-upa-√lip*, P. -limpati, to smear all round, Gobh.

पर्युपविश् *pary-upa-√viś*, P. -viśati, to sit down round or near (acc.), ŚBr.; ŚrS. °veśana, n. sitting about, KātyŚr.

पर्युपस्था *pary-upa-√sthā*, P. -tishṭhati, to be or stand round (acc.); to attend, serve, honour with (instr.), MBh.; R.; (Ā.) to join, KātyŚr., Sch. °sthāna, n. waiting upon, serving, R.; rising, elevation, L. °sthāpaka, mfn. leading to or upon, KātyŚr., Sch. °sthita, mfn. standing round, surrounding (acc.), MBh.; R.; drawing nigh, imminent, impending, ib.; slipped, escaped (as a word), R.; intent upon, devoted to (loc.), ib.

पर्युपस्पृश् *pary-upa-√spṛiś* (only ind. p. -spṛiśya), to touch or use (water) for the use of ablution or bathing, MBh.

पर्युपह्वे *pary-upa-√hve*, Ā. -hávate, to call near, invite, RV.

पर्युपागत *pary-upâgata*, mfn. (√gam) standing round, surrounding, BhP.

पर्युपावृत्त *pary-upâ-vṛitta*, mfn. (√vṛit) returned, come back, R.

पर्युपास् *pary-upâs* (-upa-√ās), Ā. -upâste (3. pl. -upâsate, Pot. 3. sg. -upâsīta; impf. 3. sg. -upâsat), to sit round, surround, encompass, MBh.; Kāv. &c.; to be present at, share in, partake of (acc.), MBh.; to approach respectfully, attend upon, worship, Mn.; MBh. &c.: Pass. -upâsyate, to be attended by (instr.), Ragh. x, 63. °upâsaka, mfn. worshipping, a worshipper, MBh.; BhP. °upâsana, n. sitting round, Śak. i, 4/5 (in Prākr.); encamping round, MBh.; friendliness, courtesy, Pratāp.; pardon, excuse, Sāh.; honour, service, worship, Kāraṇḍ. (also ā, f., Divyâv.); joining in or concurrence with any act of reverence, W. °upâsita, mfn. shared in, witnessed, MBh.; worshipped, reverenced; -pūrva-tva, n. the having r° in a former birth, Divyâv. °upâsitṛi, mfn. moving round or about (acc.), MBh.; showing respect or honour, a worshipper, ib. °upâsīna, mfn. sitting upon, Mn. ii, 75; surrounded by (instr.), R. °upâsya, mfn. to be worshipped or served, Jātakam.

पर्युप्त *pary-upta*, °ti. See pari-√2. vap.

पर्युलूखलम् *pary-ulūkhalam*, ind., g. -parimukhâdi.

पर्युषण *pary-ushaṇa*, °shita, °shṭa. See pari-√5. vas, p. 600.

पर्यूर्णु *pary-√ūrṇu*, Ā. -ūrṇute, to cover or conceal one's self, MaitrS.

पर्यूह् *pary-√1. ūh*, P. Ā. -ūhati, °te (impf. -auhat), to heap or pile round, to surround with mounds or embankments, AV.; VS.; TS.; Br. °ūhana, n. sweeping or heaping together, KātyŚr.

पर्यृष् *pary-√1. ṛish*, P. pary-árshati, to flow round, to procure from every side by flowing, RV.

पर्यृष् *pary-√2. ṛish*, P. -ṛishati (3. pl. aor. pary-ārishan = -ārshan), to embrace, clasp round, support, Br.; KātyŚr. **Pary-árshaṇa,** n. clasping round, supporting, making firm, ŚBr.

पर्ये *pary-é* (*-ā-√i*), P. *-áiti* (ind. p. *-étya*), to roam about, AitBr.; to go round, circumambulate (acc.), ŚBr.; to come back, return, ChUp.

पर्येतृ *pary-etṛi, pary-ehi.* See 2. *pari.*

पर्येषण *pary-eshaṇa* &c. See *parísh.*

पर्योग *paryoga,* m. or n. (for *pari-y°; cf. paryāṇa* for *pari-y°*) a kind of vehicle, Car.

पर्योष्ठम् *pary-oshṭham,* ind., g. *pari-mukhâdi.*

पर्व् *parv,* cl. 1. P. *parvati,* to fill, Dhātup. xv, 68 (cf. *√pūrv, pṛī, marv*).

Parva, in comp. for *°van.* — **kāra,** mfn. (prob.) = next, MBh. v, 1227 ('making arrows' or 'putting on a foreign dress,' Nilak.) — **kārin,** mfn. one who for the sake of gain performs on common days such ceremonies as should be performed only on festivals, VP. — **kāla,** m. a periodic change of the moon, R.; MārkP.; the time at which the moon at its conjunction or opposition passes through the node, MBh.; Var.; *-nirṇaya,* m. N. of wk.; *-rāśi,* m. time for festivals, Jyot. — **gāmin,** m. one who approaches his wife on f°, VP. — **gupta,** m. N. of a man, Rājat. — **tantra-vidhi,** m. N. of wk. — **dakshiṇā,** f. the teacher's fee for teaching a partic. portion of the Veda, Gobh. — **divasa,** m. the day of a periodic change of the moon, Hcat. — **dhi,** m. 'period-container,' the moon, L. — **nāḍī,** f. 'moment of the Parvan,' moment of opposition or conjunction, MW. — **nirṇaya,** m. N. of wk. — **pushpikā** (L.), **-pushpī** (Car.), f. Tiaridium Indicum. — **pūrṇatā,** f. preparations for or completion of a festival, L.; joining, uniting, W. — **prakāśa** and **-prabodha,** m. N. of wks. — **bhāga,** m. the wrist, Śak. — **bheda,** m. violent pain in the joints, Suśr. — **mālā,** f. N. of wk. — **mitra,** m. N. of a man, HParis. — **mūla,** n. the time of new moon and full moon, L.; (*ā*), f. a species of plant, L. — **yoni,** mfn. growing from joints or knots; m. a cane or reed, W. — **ratnâvalī,** f. N. of wk. — **ruh,** m. (nom. *ṭ*) the pomegranate tree, L. — **vat,** mfn. containing knots or joints, ĀpŚr., Sch. — **varja,** mfn. except the forbidden days of a month, MW. — **vallī,** f. a species of Dūrvā, L. — **vipad,** m. the moon, Gal. — **śarkaraka,** m. N. of a man, Rājat. — **śás,** ind. limb by limb, l° from l°, piece by piece (*°śaḥ √kṛi,* to cut to pieces), RV. — **śāka,** m. a species of pot-herb, Car. — **saṃgraha,** m. N. of wk. — **saṃdhi,** m. the full and change of the moon, the junction of the 15th and 1st of a lunar fortnight, MBh.; R.; Hariv. — **sambhava,** m. N. of wk. **Parvâṅgula,** n. a partic. measure of length, AmṛitUp. **Parvâvadhi,** m. a joint or knot, L.; a partic. period, the end of a Parvan &c., W. **Parvâsphoṭa,** m. cracking the fingers (regarded as indecorous), Kām. **Parvêśa,** m. the regent of an astronomical node, Var.

Parvaka, n. the knee-joint, L.

Parvaṇa, m. N. of a demon, MBh.; (*ī*), f. the period of a change of the moon, ib.; Hariv.; a species of pot-herb (= *parva-śāka*), Car.; a partic. disease of the so-called juncture or Saṃdhi of the eye, Suśr. (also *°ṇikā*); ifc. = *parvan,* a knot, BhP.

Párvata, mfn. (fr. *parvan,* cf. Pāṇ. v, 2, 122, Vārtt. 10, Pat.) knotty, rugged (said of mountains), RV.; AV. (according to ĀpŚr., Sch. = *parutka, parva-vat*); m. a mountain, mountain-range, height, hill, rock (often personified; ifc. f. *ā*), RV. &c. &c.; an artificial mound or heap (of grain, salt, silver, gold &c. presented to Brāhmans, cf. *-dāna*); the number 7 (from the 7 principal mountain-ranges), Sūryas.; a fragment of rock, a stone (*adrayaḥ parvatāḥ,* the stones for pressing Soma), RV.; a (mountain-like) cloud, ib. (cf. Naigh. i, 10); a tree, L.; a species of pot-herb, L.; a species of fish (Silurus Pabda), L.; N. of a Vasu, Hariv.; of a Ṛishi (associated with Nārada and messenger of the gods, supposed author of RV. viii, 12; ix, 104, 105, where he has the patr. Kāṇva and Kāśyapa), MBh.; Kathās.; of a son of Paurṇamāsa (son of Marīci and Sambhūti), MārkP.; of a minister of king Purū-ravas, Vikr.; of a monkey, R.; of one of the 10 religious orders founded by Saṃkarâcārya's pupils (whose members add the word *parvata* to their names), W.; (*ī*), f. a rock, stone, VS. — **kandara,** n. mountain-cave, Hit. — **kāka,** m. a raven, L. — **kīlā,** f. the earth, Gal. — **cyút,** mfn. shaking mountains (Maruts), RV. — **ja,** mfn. 'm°-born;' (*ā*), f. a river, L. — **jāla,** n. m°-range, Hariv.; R. — **tṛiṇa,** n. 'm°-grass,' a species of grass, L. — **dāna,** n. a gift in shape of a m° (cf. above), Cat.; *-paddhati,* f. N. of wk. — **durga,** n. an inaccessible m°, Bhartṛ. — **dhātu,** m. 'm°-metal,' ore, AmṛitUp. — **nivāsa,** m. 'm°-dweller,' the fabulous animal Śarabha, Gal. — **pati,** m. 'm°-prince,' lord of the m°s, MBh. — **mastaka,** m. n. m°-top, Mn.; MBh. — **mālā,** f. m°-range, Pañcad. — **mocā,** f. a species of Kadalī, L. — **rāj,** m. 'm°-king,' a very high m°, Kāraṇḍ.; N. of the Himâlaya, MBh. — **rāja,** m. id.; *-kanyā* (MW.), *-putrī* (Kum.), f. N. of Pārvatī or Durgā (daughter of H°). — **rodhas,** n. m°-slope, L. — **varṇana-stotra,** n. N. of ch. of ĀdiPur. — **vāsin,** mfn. living in mountains; m. a mountaineer, Var.; (*inī*), f. nard, spikenard, L.; N. of Durgā, L. — **śikhara,** m. n. mountain-top, Hit. — **śreshṭha,** m. the best of m°s, MBh. — **stha,** mfn. situated on a m° or hill, ib. **Parvatâkāra,** mfn. m°-shaped, formed like a m°, MW. **Parvatâgra,** n. m°-top, R. **Parvatâtmajā,** f. m°-daughter, N. of Durgā, Hariv. **Parvatâdhārā,** f. 'm°-holder,' the earth, L. **Parvatâri,** m. 'enemy of the m°s,' N. of Indra (who clipped their wings), L. **Parvatâvṛidh,** mfn. delighting in m°s i.e. in the pressing-stones (said of Soma), RV. **Parvatâśaya,** m. 'resting on m°s,' a cloud, L. **Parvatâśraya,** mfn. = *°ta-vāsin;* m. (also) the fabulous animal Śarabha, L. **Parvatâśrayin,** m. a mountaineer, Var. **Parvatêśvara,** m. lord of the mountains, MBh.; N. of a man, Mudr. **Parvate-shṭhā́,** mfn. dwelling in the heights (said of Indra), RV. **Parvatôpatyakā,** f. a land at the foot of a mountain, Hit.

Parvataka, m. a mountain (see *eka-p°*); N. of a man, Mudr.; of a prince in the Himâlaya, HParis.

Parvatāyana, w. r. for *pārv°,* q. v.

Parvati, f. a rock, stone, TS.

1. **Parvatí,** f. of *parvata,* q. v.

2. **Parvatī,** ind. for *°ta.* — **√kṛi,** to make into a mountain, Bhartṛ.

Parvatíya, mfn. belonging to or produced in mountains, AV.; Hariv. (cf. Pāṇ. iv, 2, 143).

Parvatyà, mfn. = prec., RV.; TS.

Párvan, n. a knot, joint (esp. of a cane or other plant [cf. *parus*], but also of the body), limb, member (lit. and fig.), RV. &c. &c.; a break, pause, division, section (esp. of a book), ŚBr.; MBh. &c.; the step of a staircase, Ragh.; a member of a compound, Prāt.; Nir.; a period or fixed time, RV.; VS.; ŚBr.; GṛŚrS.; (esp.) the Cāturmāsya festival, ŚrS.; the days of the 4 changes of the moon (i.e. the full and change of the m° and the 8th and 14th of each half-month), GṛŚrS.; Mn.; MBh. &c.; a sacrifice performed on the occasion of a change of the moon, R.; the day of the moon's passing the node at its opposition or conjunction, Var.; Sūryas.; MBh. &c.; the moment of the sun's entering a new sign, W.; any partic. period of the year (as the equinox, solstice &c.), ib.; a division of time, e.g. a half-month (24 in a year), MBh.; a day (360), BhP.; a festival, holiday, W.; opportunity, occasion, ib.; a moment, instant, ib.

Parvariṇa, m. (L.) = *parṇa-vṛinta rasa;* = *pattra-cūrṇa-rasa;* = *parṇa-śirā;* = *dyūta-kambala;* = *garva;* = *māruta;* = *mṛitaka* (n.); n. = *parvan.*

Parvasa, m. N. of a son of Paurṇamāsa, VP. (cf. *parvata*); (*ā*), f. N. of the wife of Parvasa, ib.

Parviṇī, f. a holiday, Rājat.

पर्वित *parvita,* m. a species of fish, Silurus Pabda, L.

पर्शान *párśāna,* m. (*√priś* = *spriś* or *prish?*) a precipice, chasm, RV. (Sāy. 'a cloud').

पर्शु 1. *párśu,* m. a rib, AV.; TS.; Br. [cf. Zd. *peresu*]; a curved knife, sickle, AV.; Kauś. [cf. Lat. *falx;* Gr. φάλκης]; N. of a man, RV. viii, 6, 46; pl. N. of a warrior-tribe, Pāṇ. v, 3, 117 (cf. *pārśava*); f. the supporting or side wall of a well, Nir. iv, 6; N. of a woman, RV. x, 86, 23. — **maya,** mf(*ī*)n. shaped like a curved knife, Nir. iv, 3.

Parśukā, f. a rib, Suśr.

पर्शु 2. *parśu,* m. (cf. *paraśu* and Uṇ. i, 34, Sch.) an axe, hatchet, Hariv.; R. — **pāṇi,** m. 'axe in hand,' N. of Gaṇêśa, L.; = next, A. — **rāma,** m. = *Paraśu-r°,* L.

Parśū-mat or **parśū-la,** mfn., g. *sidhmâdi.*

Parśvadha, m. = *paraśvadha,* an axe, hatchet, L.

पर्ष् *parsh* (cf. *prish*), cl. 1. Ā. *parshate,* to grow wet, Dhātup. xvi, 12 (v.l. *varsh* and *sparsh*).

पर्ष 1. *parshá,* m. (*√parsh, prish?*) a bundle, sheaf, RV. x, 48, 7 (Nir. iii, 10).

पर्ष 2. *parsha,* mfn. = *parusha,* rough, violent (as wind), BhP.

पर्षणि 1. *parshaṇi,* mfn. (*√1. pṛi*) carrying over or across (as a ship), RV. i, 131, 2. 2. **Parsháṇi,** Ved. inf. of *√1. pṛi,* ib. x, 126, 3. **Parshika** (?), g. *purohitâdi.* **Parshin,** see *ishu-p°.*

Párshishṭha, mfn. most mighty in delivering or rescuing, RV. x, 126, 3.

पर्षद् *parshad,* f. = *pari-shad,* an assembly, audience, company, society, GṛS.; Yājñ. &c. (4 kinds of society, Divyâv. 299, 14). — **bhīru,** mfn. shy in society, Var. — **vala,** mfn. surrounded by an assembly, Pāṇ. v, 2, 112, Sch.; m. an assistant at an assembly, a spectator, L.

Parshatka, (ifc.) = *pari-shad,* an assembly, Jātakam.

पर्हाण *parhāṇa.* See *a-parhāṇa.*

पल् *pal,* cl. 1. P. *palati,* to go, Dhātup. xx, 9 (perhaps invented to account for *pālayati* or *palāyate*).

पल *pala,* m. (scarcely to be connected with prec.) straw, L.; = *pāla,* g. *jvalâdi;* n. a partic. weight = 4 Karshas = $\frac{1}{100}$ Tulā (rarely m.; ifc. f. *ā*), Mn.; Yājñ.; Suśr. &c.; a partic. fluid measure, Nir. xiv, 7; KātyŚr., Sch.; a partic. measure of time (= $\frac{1}{60}$ Ghaṭī), Gaṇit.; flesh, meat, Yājñ.; Suśr. [Cf. Lat. *palea;* Fr. *paille,* Lith. *pelai.*] — **kshāra,** m. 'flesh-fluid,' blood, L. — **gaṇḍa,** m. a mason (as using straw?), L. — **ṃ-kara,** m. 'f°-maker,' gall, bile, L. — **ṃ-kasha,** m. 'f°-hurter,' a Rākshasa, L.; a lion, L.; the sea, Gal.; bdellium, L.; (*ā*), f. N. of various plants (Asteracantha Longifolia, Butea Frondosa, Dolichos Sinensis &c.), Suśr.; L.; bdellium, L.; red lac, Bhpr.; a fly, L. — **dá,** m. 'straw-giver (?),' a partic. material for building, (prob.) bundles of straw or reeds used for roofing and wainscoting, AV.; ifc. in names of villages (*°dīya,* mfn.), Pāṇ. iv, 2, 142; (*ī*), f. N. of a village, ib. 110. — **pīyūsha-latā,** f. N. of wk. (on the canonical use of various meats). — **priya,** m. 'fond of f°,' a Rākshasa or a raven, L. — **bhā,** f. the equinoctial shadow at midday, Sūryas., Sch.; *-khaṇḍana* and *-sādhana,* n. N. of wks. — **vibhā,** f. = *-bhā,* L. **Palâgni,** m. 'flesh-fire,' the bilious humour, L. **Palâṅga,** (prob.) w. r. for *capal°,* q. v. **Palâda** or *°dana,* m. 'f°-eater,' a Rākshasa, L. **Palânna,** n. rice with meat, Suśr. (v. r. *yavânna*). **Palârdha,** n. a partic. weight (= 2 Karshas), Car. **Palâli,** f. a heap of flesh, A. 1. **Palâśa,** m. a Rākshasa, L.; mfn. cruel (lit. = next), L. 1. **Palâśin,** m. eating flesh, Bhpr.; m. = prec., L.

Palala, m. a Rākshasa, L.; n. ground sesamum, Hariv.; Var.; Suśr. &c.; a kind of sweetmeat made of g° s° and sugar, L.; mud, mire, R.; flesh, L. — **jvara,** m. gall, bile, L. (cf. *palâgni*). — **piṇḍa,** n. a lump of ground sesamum, ŚiraUp. — **priya,** m. 'fond of flesh,' a raven, L. — **Palalâśaya,** m. 'flesh-receptacle,' swelled neck, goitre, L. **Palalâudana,** n. a pap made of ground sesamum seeds, Kāś. on Pāṇ. ii, 3, 45.

Palāla, m. n. a stalk, straw, Mn.; MBh. &c.; the stalk of the Sorghum, Indian millet, Suśr.; m. N. of a demon inimical to children (cf. *anu-p°*), AV.; (*ā*), f. N. of one of the Mātṛis of Skanda, MBh.; (*ī*), f. a stalk, straw, AV. (cf. Pat. on Pāṇ. v, 2, 100). — **dohada,** m. 'longing for straw,' the mango tree (the fruit of which is sometimes ripened in straw), L. — **bhāraka,** m. a load of straw, Mn. xi, 134. **Palālânupalālá,** m. du. P° and Anup° (cf. above), AV. **Palālôccaya,** m. a heap of straw, Kathās.

Palāli. See *pala.*

Palālina, mfn., Pāṇ. v, 2, 100, Vārtt. 1, Pat.

Paláva, m. chaff, husks, AV.; a fish-hook, Vāsav.

Palika, mf(*ā*)n. weighing a Pala, Car.; Hcat.; (ifc. after a numeral) weighing so many P°s, Yājñ.; Suśr. &c.

Palya, n. a sack for corn (prob. containing a certain measure), ŚrS.; a partic. high number, Dharmaśarm. — **kathā-pushpâñjali,** m. N. of wk. — **varcasa,** n., Pat. on Pāṇ. v, 4, 78. **Palyôpama,** m. or n. a partic. high number, W.

Palyalika, m. or n. N. of a place, Cat.

पलक्या *palakyā* (L.), *palaṅkyā* (Bhpr.), f. Beta Bengalensis.

पलक्ष *palaksha*, mf(*ī*)n. white, VS. (cf. *balaksha*).

पलङ्कट *palaṅkaṭa*, mfn. shy, timid, L.

पलव *palava*, m., *plava* (√*plu*), a basket of wicker-work for catching fish, L.; N. of a man, Prav.

पलस *palasa*, w. r. for *panasa*, R.

पलस्तिजमदग्नि *palasti-jamadagni*, m. pl. the grey-haired Jamad-agnis (prob. a branch of this family of Ṛishis), RV. iii, 53, 16 (Sāy.)

पलाक *palāka*, m. n., Siddh.

पलाण्डु *palāṇḍu*, m. (rarely n.) an onion, Mn.; MBh.; Suśr. &c. (cf. Uṇ. i, 38, Sch.) — **bhakshita**, mf(*ā* or *ī*)n. one who has eaten onions, Pāṇ. iv, 1, 53, Sch. — **maṇḍana**, n. N. of a comedy.

पलाप *palāpa*, m. a halter, L.; an elephant's temples, L.

पलापहा *palāpahā*, w. r. for *mal°*.

पलाय् *palây* (fr. *palā* = *parā* and √*ay* = *i*; cf. Pāṇ. viii, 2, 19, Sch.), Ā. *palâyate*, TS.; Br.; MBh. &c. (ep. also P.; pf. *palâyām cakre*, Pañc.; aor. *apalâyishṭa*, Bhaṭṭ.; fut. *palâyishyate*, Hit.; *°ti*, Śatr.; ind. p. *palâyya*, ŚBr. &c.; inf. *palâyitum*, Pañc.); to flee, fly, run away, escape, cease, vanish, TS. &c. &c. °**yaka**, mfn. fleeing, a fugitive, SaddhP. °**yana**, n. fleeing, flight, escape, MBh.; Kāv. &c. (*-kriyām* √*kṛi*, to take to flight, Pañc.); a saddle, TS., Sch. (cf. *paly-ayana*, *paryāṇa*); *-parâyaṇa*, mfn. occupied in flight, fugitive, W.; *-manas*, mfn. thinking of fl°, MW.; *-vishaya*, mfn. having fl° for an object, bent on fl°, ib. **Pálâyita**, mfn. flown, fled, defeated, TS.; Kathās. &c.; n. gallop, L. (v.l. *pul°*). **Palâyin**, mfn. fleeing, flying, taking to flight, MBh.

पलाश 2. *palāśá*, n. (for 1. see under *pala*) a leaf, petal, foliage (ifc. f. *ī*), ŚBr.; GṛŚrS.; MBh.&c.; the blade of a sharp instrument (cf. *paraśu-p°*); the blossom of the tree Butea Frondosa, Pañc.; = *śmaśāna*, L.; = *paribhāshaṇa*, L.; m. (ifc. f. *ā*) the tree B° F° (its older name is *parṇa*, q.v.), Br.; MBh. &c.; Curcuma Zedoaria, L.; N. of Magadha, L.; (ifc. it denotes beauty, g. *vyāghrâdi*); (*ī*), f. a species of climbing plant, L.; cochineal, L.; red lac, L.; mfn. green, L. (w.r. for *pālāśa*). — **tā**, f. the state of foliage, foliation, Kathās. — **nagara**, n. N. of a town, Siṇhâs. — **pattra**, n. a single leaf (esp. of the Butea Frondosa), Hariv.; Pañc.; m. N. of a Nāga, L. — **parṇī**, f. Physalis Flexuosa, L. — **puṭa**, m. n. a receptacle made of a folded leaf, KātyŚr. — **śātana**, m. an instrument for lopping foliage, L **Palâśâkhya**, m. the resin of Gardenia Gummifera, L. **Palâśâṅgā** or °**śântā**, f. a kind of Curcuma, L.

Palâśaka, m. Butea Frondosa or Curcuma Zedoaria, L.; pl. N. of a place, MBh.; (*ikā*), f. a species of climbing plant, L.

Palâśana, n. (?), Nir. xii, 29.

Palâśâmbhā, f. = °*śāṅgā*, L.

2. **Palâśin**, mfn. (for 1. see under *pala*) leafy, covered with foliage, MBh.; m. a tree, Prasannar.; a species of tree (= *kshīra-vṛiksha*), L.; N. of a city or village (said to be the modern Plassey), Kshitîś.; (*inī*), f. N. of sev. rivers, MBh.; MārkP.

Palâśila and °**śiya**, mfn., g. *kāśâdi* and *utkarâdi*.

पलिक्नी *paliknī*. See *palita* below.

पलिघ *pali-gha*, m. a water-pot, pitcher, glass water-vessel, L.; a wall, rampart, L.; the gateway of a building, L.; an iron club or one studded with iron, L. (= *pari-gha*; cf. Pāṇ. viii, 2, 22).

पलिङ्गु *paliṅgu*, m. N. of a man, HirGṛ.

पलित *palitá*, mf(*ā* or *páliknī*, Pāṇ. iv, 1, 39, Vārtt. 1. 2, Pat.) n. grey, hoary, old, aged, RV. &c. &c.; = *pālayitṛi*, Nir. iv, 26; m. N. of a mouse, MBh.; of a prince, Hariv.; VP. (v.l. *pāl°*); (*paliknī*), f. a cow for the first time with calf, L.; n. grey hair (also pl.), AV. &c. &c.; a tuft of hair, Daś.; mud, mire, L.; heat, burning, L.; benzoin, L.; pepper, L. [Cf. Gk. πελιτνός, πολιός &c.; Lat. *palleo, pallidus, pallus*; Lith. *pàlvas*; Slav. *plavŭ*; HGerm. *falo, val, fahl*; Angl. Sax. *fealo*; Eng. *fallow*.] — **m-karaṇa**, mf(*ī*)n. rendering grey, Vāsav. (cf. Pāṇ. iii, 2, 56). — **cchadman**, mfn. (old age) lurking under grey hair, Ragh. xii, 2. — **darśana**, n. the sight or appearance of g° h°, Suśr. — **m-bhavishṇu** or **-m-bhāvuka**, mfn. becoming grey, Pāṇ. iii, 2, 57. — **mlāna**, mfn. grey and withered, Kathās. — **vat**, mfn. grey-haired, HPariś.

Palitin, mfn. grey-haired, MBh.

पलियोग *pali-yoga*, m. = *pari-y°*, Pāṇ. viii, 2, 22, Pat.

पलीजक *palîjaka*, m. (fr. *pali* = *pari* and √*īj* = *ej*) 'stirrer, disturber,' N. of a demon, AV.

पलीश *paliśa*, m. = *palāśa*, Bhpr.

पलेशिनी *paleśinī*, prob. w.r. for *palāśinī*, Inscr.

पल्पूलन *pálpūlana*, n. lye, water impregnated with alkaline salt, TS.; AV.; Kauś.

Palpūlaya, Nom. P. °*láyati*, to wash with alkaline water, to tan, TS.; TBr. °**lita**, mfn. washed, tanned, ŚrS.; Baudh.

पल्य *palya* &c. See under *pala*.

पल्यङ्क *paly-aṅka*, m. = *pary-aṅka* (Pāṇ. viii, 2, 22) a bed, couch, bedstead, Siṇhâs.; Pañcad.; a cloth wound round the loins while sitting on the heels and hams, L.; so sitting, squatting (cf. *pary-aṅka*), L.

पल्यङ्ग् *paly-aṅg* (*pali* = *pari* and √*aṅg*), Ā. *paly-aṅgayate* (ind. p. *-aṅgya*), to cause to go round, stir round, ŚBr.; Pass. *-aṅgyate*, to turn round, revolve, ib.

पल्यय् *paly-√ay* (*paly* = *pari* and √*ay* = √*i*), Ā. *paly-ayate*, ŚBr. (cf. Pāṇ. viii, 2, 19).

Paly-ayana, n. a saddle (= *paryāṇa*), L.; a rein, bridle, Vcar.

पल्याण *palyāṇa*, n. a saddle, L. (also °*na*, Gal.) °**ṇaya**, Nom. °*yati*, to saddle, Bhojacar.

पल्युल *palyula* or °*yūla*, Nom. P. °*layati*, v.l. for *palpūla*, Dhātup. xxxv, 29.

पल्ल् *pall*, cl. 1. *pallati*, to go, move, Dhātup. xv, 34, Vop. (invented after √*pal*, prob. to explain the following words).

Palla, m. a large granary, barn, Suśr.; (*ī*), f., see below. **Pallâraṇya-māhâtmya**, n. N. of wk.

Pallaka. See *dattâraṇḍa-p°* under *datta*.

Palli, f. a small village, (esp.) a settlement of wild tribes, L.; a hut, house, ib. — **pañjaka**, m.pl. N. of a people, VP. — **vāha**, m. a species of wild grass, L.

Pallikā, f. a small village &c. (= *palli*), L.; a small house-lizard, L.

Pallī, f. a small village &c. (= *palli*), Kathās.; a hut, house, L.; a city (esp. ifc., in N. of towns, e.g. *Triśira-p°*, = Trichinopoly); a partic. measure of grain, KātyŚr., Sch.; a small house-lizard, L. — **deśa**, m. N. of a district, Cat. — **patana**, n. (prob.) prognostication by observing the falling of house-lizards; *-kārikā*, f., *-phala*, n., *-vicāra*, m., *-śānti*, f. N. of wks. — **pati**, m. the chief of a village or station, Kathās. — **vicāra**, m., **-vidhāna**, n. N. of wks. — °**śa** (*pallîśa*), m. = *-pati*, L. — **śaraṭa** (?), in °*ṭayoḥ phalâphala-vicāra*, m., °*ṭayoḥ śānti*, f., *-kāka-bhāsâdi-śakuna* and *-vidhāna*, n. N. of wks.

पल्लव 1. *pallava*, m. n. (ifc. f. *ā*) a sprout, shoot, twig, spray, bud, blossom (met. used for the fingers, toes, lips &c.), MBh.; Kāv. &c.; a strip of cloth, scarf, lappet, Kād.; Bālar.; Rājat.; spreading, expansion, L. (cf. below); strength, L. (= *bala*; v.l. = *vana*, a wood); red lac (*alakta*), L.; a bracelet, L.; sexual love, L.; unsteadiness, L.; m. a partic. position of the hands in dancing, Cat.; a libertine, catamite, L.; a species of fish, L.; pl. N. of a people, MBh.; Pur. (v.l. for *pahlava*); of a race of princes, Inscr. — **grâhin**, mfn. putting forth young shoots, sprouting in all directions, diffusive, superficial (as knowledge), Hit.; (with *dosha*), m. the fault of prolixity or diffusiveness, Gīt., Sch.; °*hi-tā*, f. superficial knowledge, sciolism, MW. — **dru**, m. the Aśoka tree, L. — **dhārin**, mfn. bearing blossoms (as a flower), Ragh. — **pūra**, m. N. of a man, L. — **maya**, mf(*ī*)n. consisting of young shoots or twigs (cf. *sulalita-latā-p°*). — **rāga-tāmra**, mfn. red-coloured like a young sh° or t°, Ragh. **Pallavâṅkura**, m. a leaf-bud, L. **Pallavâṅguli**, f. a young shoot like a finger, Mālav. **Pallavâda**, m. 'twig-eater,' a deer, L. **Pallavâdhāra**, m. 't°-holder,' a branch, L. **Pallavâpīḍita**, mfn. bud-laden, MBh. **Pallavâstra**, m. 'having blossoms for missiles,' N. of the god of love, L.

2. **Pallava**, Nom. P. °*vati*, to put forth young shoots, Śatr.

Pallavaka, m. a libertine, gallant, Hcar.; a species of fish (Cyprinus Denticulatus), L.; (*akā*), f. N. of a woman, Mṛicch.; (*ikā*), f. a kind of scarf, L.; N. of a female attendant, Kathās.

Pallavana, n. prolixity, useless speech, Naish.

Pallavaya, Nom. P. °*yati* = 2. *pallava*, Kāv.; to spread, divulge (as news), Vcar.; to make diffuse or prolix (= *vi-stāraya*), Gīt., Sch.

Pallavika, m. = (or v. l. for) *pallavaka*, m., L.

Pallavita, mfn. sprouted, having young shoots (°*taṃ vṛikshaiḥ*, 'young shoots have been put forth by the trees'), Kāv.; spread, extended, Inscr. (*alam* °*tena*, 'enough of further amplification,' A.); (ifc.) filled, full of, Kād.; dyed red with lac, L.; m. the red dye of the lac insect, W.

Pallavin, mfn. sprouting, having young shoots, Kum.; m. a tree, L.

Pallavī-√kṛi (ind. p. *-kṛitya*), to make or change into a very young shoot, Kāvyâd.

पल्लि *palli*, *pallī*. See under √*pall*.

पल्वल *palvala*, n. (m., Siddh.) a pool, small tank, pond. [Cf. Gk. πηλός; Lat. *palus*; Lith. *pùrvas* (?).] — **karshaka**, mfn. ploughing a pool, Hariv. — **tīra**, n. the bank or margin of a p°, Pañc. — **paṅka**, m. the mud of a p°, Kālid.

Palvalâvāsa, m. 'p°-dweller,' a tortoise, L.

Palvalī-√bhū, to become a pool, Jātakam.

Palvalya, mf(*â*)n. marshy, boggy, TS.

पव् *pav*, cl. 1. Ā. *pavate*, to go, Dhātup. xiv, 40 (v.l. for *plav*).

पव *pava*, m. (√*pū*) purification, winnowing corn, Pāṇ. iii, 3, 28, Sch.; air, wind, L.; a marsh, L.; N. of a son of Nahusha, VP.; (*á*), f. purification, RV.; n. cow-dung, L. — **nāla**, (prob.) w.r. for *yava-nāla*.

Pávana, m. 'purifier,' wind or the god of wind, breeze, air (ifc. f. *ā*), MBh.; Kāv. &c.; vital air, breath, Suśr.; Sarvad.; the regent of the Nakshatra Svāti and the north-west region, Var.; N. of the number 5 (from the 5 vital airs), ib.; a householder's sacred fire, Hār.; a species of grass, L.; N. of a son of Manu Uttama, BhP.; of a mountain, ib.; of a country in Bharata-kshetra, W.; (*ī*), f. a broom, L.; the wild citron-tree, L. (v.l. *pacanī*); N. of a river, VP.; n. or m. purification, winnowing of corn, L.; a potter's kiln, Śṛiṅgār.; n. an instrument for purifying grain &c., sieve, strainer, AV.; ĀśvGṛ.; blowing, Kaṇ.; water, L.; mfn. clean, pure, L. — **kshipta**, mfn. tempest-tossed, MW. — **cakra**, n. whirlwind, BhP. (cf. *cakra-vāta*). — **ja**, m. 'son of the wind,' N. of Hanu-mat, Dhūrtan. — **java**, m. 'swift as wind,' N. of a horse, Kathās. — **tanaya**, m. = *-ja*, Ragh.; N. of Bhīma-sena, Megh. — **dūta**, m. or n., **-pañcâśikā**, f. N. of 2 poems. — **padavī**, f. path of the wind, the air, Megh. — **pāvana**, m. or n. N. of wk. — **prabhava**, m. (disease) coming from the wind of the body, Suśr. — **bhū**, m. = *-ja*, MW. — **yoga-saṃgraha**, m. N. of wk. — **raṇhas**, mfn. swift as wind, Pracaṇḍ. — **vāhana**, m. 'having w° as vehicle,' fire, L. — **vijaya**, m. 'victory over the w° or breath,' N. of sev. Tantric wks. — **vyādhi**, m. disease or morbid state of the w° of the body, rheumatism, W.; N. of Uddhava (the friend and counsellor of Kṛishṇa), L. **Pavanâghāta**, m. gust of wind, Rājat. **Pavanâtmaja**, m. = °*na-ja*, L.; N. of Bhīma-sena, Rājat.; fire, MatsyaP. **Pavanâśa**, m. 'feeding on air,' a serpent, snake, L. **Pavanâśana**, m. id., L.; °*śanâśa*, m. 'snake-eater,' a peacock, L.; N. of Garuḍa, L. **Pavanâśin**, m. = °*nâśa*, MārkP. **Pavanâhata**, mfn. struck or shaken by the wind, rheumatic, W. **Pavanêshṭa**, (prob.) w.r. for *yav°*. **Pavanôtkampin**, mfn. trembling in the wind, Śak. **Pavanôdbhrānta**, in *-kārin*, mfn. 'agitating the air,' N. of a partic. mode of fighting, MW.; *-vīci*, f. a wave raised by the winds, ib. **Pavano'mbuja** (!), m. Grewia Asiatica, L.

Pávamāna, mfn. being purified or strained, flowing clear (as Soma), RV.; m. wind or the god of w°, VS.; TS.; Kāv.; Rājat.; N. of a partic. **Agni**

(associated with Pāvaka and Śuci and also regarded as a son of A° by Svāhā or of Antar-dhāna and by Śikhaṇḍinī), TS.; Br.; Pur.; N. of partic. Stotras sung by the Sāma-ga at the Jyotishṭoma sacrifice (they are called successively at the 3 Savanas *bahish-pavamāna, mādhyaṃdina* and *tritīya* or *ārbhava*), TS.; Br.; ŚrS. (cf. RTL. 368); N. of wk.; N. of a prince and the Varsha in Śāka-dvīpa ruled by him, BhP. **-ṭippana,** m. or n., **-pañca-sûkta,** n. pl., **-paddhati,** f., **-sûkta,** n. N. of wks. **-vat,** mfn. accompanied by the Pavamāna-stotra, AitBr. **-sakha,** m. 'friend of the wind,' fire, Śiś. **-soma-yajña,** m. N. of wk. **-havis,** n. offerings to Agni invoked under the title of Pavamāna or Pāvaka or Śuci, TBr., Sch. **-homa,** m. = *-havis;* N. of wk.; *-paddhati,* f., *-prayoga,* m., *-vidhi,* m. N. of wks. **Pavamānâdhyāya,** m. N. of wk. **Pavamānêshṭi,** f. = °*na-havis,* TBr., Sch.; N. of wk. **Pavamānôktha,** n. the series of verses in the mid-day Pavamāna, AitBr.

Pavayitṛí, m. a purifier, TS.

Pavākā, f. a storm, whirlwind, L.

Pavita, mfn. purified, cleansed, W.; n. black pepper, L.

Pavitṛí, m. a purifier, AV.; ŚBr. (cf. *pavītṛí*).

Pavítra, n. a means of purification, filter, strainer, straining-cloth &c. (made of thread or hair or straw, for clarifying fruits, esp. the Soma), RV. &c. &c.; Kuśa grass (esp. two K° leaves for holding offerings or for sprinkling and purifying ghee &c.), ŚBr.; KātyŚr.; Mn. &c. (ifc. also *-ka,* see *sa-pavitraka*), a ring of K° grass worn on the fourth finger on partic. occasions, W.; a purifying prayer or Mantra, Mn.; Yājñ.; MBh.; a means of purifying or clearing the mind, RV. iii, 26, 8; 31, 6 &c.; melted butter, L.; honey, L.; water, L.; rain or rubbing (*varshaṇa* or *gharshaṇa*), L.; copper, L.; the vessel in which the Argha is presented, L. (ifc. *-ka,* MārkP.); the Brāhmanical cord (cf. °*trâropaṇa*); N. of Vishṇu (also *p° pavitrāṇām*), MBh. (cf. RTL. 106); of Śiva, ib.; (with *ādityānām* and *devānām*) N. of Sāmans, ĀrshBr.; a kind of metre, Col.; m. N. of a partic. Soma-sacrifice belonging to the Rājasūya, TāṇḍBr., Sch.; ŚrS.; Sesamum Indicum, L.; Nageia Putranjiva, L.; N. of a man, g. *aśvâdi;* of an Āṅgirasa (the supposed author of RV. ix, 67; 73; 83; 107), RAnukr.; (pl.) N. of a class of deities in the 14th Manv-antara, Pur.; (*ā*), f. N. of sev. plants (basil, saffron, the small Pippala tree &c.), L.; of sev. rivers, MBh.; Pur.; the 12th day of the light half of Śrāvaṇa (a festival in honour of Vishṇu), W.; mf(*ā*)n. purifying, averting evil, pure, holy, sacred, sinless, beneficent, Mn.; MBh. &c. **-kīrti,** mfn. of spotless renown, Dhūrtas. **-giri,** m. N. of a place, Cat. **-tari-√kṛi,** to purify or sanctify in a high degree, Kād. **-tā,** f. purity, cleanness, MārkP.; Rājat. **-tva,** n. id., Uttarar.; Hcat.; the being a means of purification, Kāṭh.; TāṇḍBr. **-darbha,** m. purifying or holy Darbha grass, R. **-dhara,** m. N. of a man, Kathās. **-dhānya,** n. 'pure grain,' barley, L. **-paṭhana,** n. recitation of a purifying prayer or Mantra, MārkP. **-pati,** m. lord of purification or purity, VS. **-pāṇi,** mfn. holding Darbha grass in the hand, Yājñ.; m. N. of an ancient sage, MBh. **-pūta** (°*vítra-*), mfn. clarified with a strainer, ŚBr. **-yoni,** mfn. of spotless origin, Pañc. **-ratha** (°*vítra-*), mfn. having the strainer as a chariot (Soma), RV. **-roga-parihāra-prayoga,** m. N. of wk. **-vat** (°*vítra-*), mfn. having a purifying instrument (as a strainer or Darbha grass), cleansing, purifying, RV.; Br.; GṛŚrS.; N. of Agni, AitBr.; (*ī*), f. N. of a river, BhP. **Pavitrâropaṇa,** n. 'putting on the Pavitra,' investiture with the Brāhmanical cord, (esp.) investing the image of Kṛishṇa or another deity with the sacred thread, N. of a festival on the 12th day of the light half of Śrāvaṇa or Āshāḍha, Pañc.; *-putra-dâikādaśī,* f. and *-vidhāna,* n. N. of wk. **Pavitrârohaṇa,** n. investing with the sacred thread (cf. °*ropaṇa*), N. of a festival in honour of Durgā on the 8th day of the light half of Śrāvaṇa or Āshāḍha, L. **Pavitrêshṭi,** f. N. of a partic. sacrifice (cf. above), Vas.; N. of wk.; *-paddhati,* f., *-prayoga,* m., *-sūtra,* n., *-hautra,* n. N. of wks.

Pavitraka, m. a small sieve or strainer, KātyŚr. (see also under *pavitra*); m. Poa Cynosuroides, L.; Artemisia Indica, L.; Ficus Religiosa or Glomerata, L.

Pavitraya, Nom. P. °*yati,* to cleanse, purify, render happy, Kathās.; Satr.; Pañcad. °**trita,** mfn. purified, sanctified, blessed, happy, Mcar.; Caṇḍak.; BrahmaP.

Pavitrin, mfn. purifying, pure, clean, MBh.

Pavitrī, ind. in comp. for °*tra.* **-karaṇa,** n. purification, means of purifying, W. **-√kṛi,** to purify, cleanse, MBh.; BhP. **-kṛita,** mfn. purified, cleansed, sanctified, Pañc.; Śāntiś. **-√bhū** (ind. p. *-bhūya*), to become pure or clean, L.

Pavītṛí, m. = *pavitṛí,* RV.

Pávyā, f. purification, RV.; = *pavī,* the tire of a wheel (?), ib.

पवरु *pavaru,* m. a species of pot-herb, L. (v. l. *pararu*).

पवष्टुरिक *pavashṭurika,* m. N. of a man, g. *śubhrâdi* (not in Kāś.)

पवस्त *pavásta,* n. (*apa* and √*vas?*) a cover or garment (?), AV. iv, 7, 6; du. heaven and earth, RV. x, 27, 7.

पवारु *pavāru,* °*ruka,* v.l. for *parāru,* °*ruka.*

पवि *paví,* m. (perh. orig. 'brightness, sheen;' cf. *pāvaka* and Uṇ. iv, 138, Sch.) the tire of a wheel (esp. a golden tire on the chariot of the Aśvins and Maruts), RV.; AitĀr.; the metallic point of a spear or arrow, ib.; the iron band on a Soma-stone, ib.; an arrow, Nir. xii, 30; a thunderbolt, Naigh. ii, 20; speech, ib. i, 11; fire, L. **-mat,** mfn. N. of sev. Sāmans, ĀrshBr. **Pavī-nasá,** m. 'having a nose like a spear-head,' N. of a demon, AV.

Pavīra, n. (fr. *pavi*), a weapon with a metallic point, a lance, spear, Nir. xii, 30. **Pávīra-vat** (RV., VS.) or **pavīrá-vat** (AV.), mfn. armed with lance or a goad; = next mfn.

Pávīrava, mfn. having a metallic share (as a plough), TS.; m. a thunderbolt, RV.

Pávīru, m. N. of a man, RV.

पविन्द *pavinda,* m. N. of a man, g. *aśvâdi,* (f. *ā,* Kāś.)

पश् 1. *paś,* only Pres. P. Ā. *páśyati,* °*te* (cf. √*dṛiś* and Pāṇ. vii, 3, 78), to see (with *na,* 'to be blind'), behold, look at, observe, perceive, notice, RV. &c. &c.; to be a spectator, look on (esp. p., e. g. *tasya paśyataḥ,* while he looks on, before his eyes, Mn.; *paśyantī tishṭhati,* she stands and looks on, Śak.); to see a person (either 'visit' or 'receive as a visitor'), MBh.; R. &c.; to live to see, experience, partake of, undergo, incur, Mn.; MBh. &c.; to learn, find out, ib.; to regard or consider as, take for (acc. with acc. or adv. in *vat*), ib.; to see with the spiritual eye, compose, invent (hymns, rites &c.), RV.; Br.; ŚāṅkhŚr.; (also with *sādhu*) to have insight or discernment, Mn.; MBh. &c.; to consider, think over, examine, ib.; to foresee, ib.; (*paśyāmi,* 'I see or I am convinced,' and *paśya,* °*śyata,* 'see, behold, look here!' often employed parenthetically or interjectionally, MBh.; Kāv. &c.). [Orig. identical with √*spaś,* q. v.]

2. **Páś,** f. (only instr. pl. *padbhís*), sight or eye, RV. iv, 2, 12.

1. **Paśu,** ind. see, behold! L.

Paśya, mf(*ā*)n. seeing, beholding, rightly understanding, Up. (cf. Pāṇ. iv, 1, 137).

Paśyat, mf(*antī*)n. seeing, beholding &c.; (*antī*), f. a harlot, L.; N. of a partic. sound, L. **Paśyatohara,** mfn. stealing before a person's eyes, Pāṇ. vi, 3, 21, Vārtt. 1, Pat.

Paśyata, mfn. visible, conspicuous, AV.

Paśyanā, f. See *a-paśyanā.*

पश् 3. *paś,* cl. 10. P. *pāśayati,* to fasten, bind, Dhātup. xxxiii, 45. [Cf. *pash* and *pas;* Zd. *pas;* Lat. *pac-iscor, pax;* Goth. *fahan;* Angl. Sax. *fôn.*]

Paśavyà, mfn. (fr. *paśú*) belonging or relating to cattle, fit or suitable for c°, TS.; Br.; Up.; Yājñ.; MBh.; (with *kāma*), m. sexual love or intercourse, BhP.; n. a herd or drove of cattle, RV. **-tama** (°*vyà-*), mfn. most fit or suitable for c°, TS. **-vāhana,** mfn. = *purīsha-v°,* ŚBr.

2. **Paśú** or **páśu,** m. (instr. *paśúnā* or °*śvā;* dat. *páśve* or *paśáve;* gen. *paśvás* or °*śos;* du. *paśvā;* acc. pl. *paśvás* or °*śūn*) cattle, kine (orig. 'any tethered animal;' singly or collect. 'a herd'), a domestic or sacrificial animal (as opp. to *mṛiga,* 'wild animal;' 5 kinds are enumerated, 'men, kine, horses, goats and sheep' [AV. xi, 2, 9 &c.], to which are sometimes added mules and asses [MBh. vi, 155 &c.] or camels and dogs [AV. iii, 10, 6, Comm.]), RV. &c. &c.; any animal or brute or beast (also applied contemptuously to a man; cf. *nara-p°* and *nṛi-p°*); a mere animal in sacred things i. e. an uninitiated person, Cat.; an animal sacrifice, AitĀr.; BhP.; flesh, RV. i, 166, 6; an ass, L.; a goat, L.; a subordinate deity and one of Śiva's followers, L.; (with Māheśvaras and Pāśupatas) the individual soul as distinct from the divine Soul of the universe, RTL. 89; Ficus Glomerata, L.; (pl.) N. of a people, MBh. (v. l. *patti*); n. cattle (only as acc. before *manyate* [VS. xxiii, 30] and *manyamāna* [RV. iii, 53, 23]; and pl. *paśūni,* R.; Kathās.) [Cf. Zd. *pasu;* Lat. *pecu;* Old Pruss. *pecku;* Goth. *faihu;* Germ. *fihu, vihe, Vieh;* Angl. Sax. *feoh;* Eng. *fee.*] **-karman,** n. the act of offering the victim, sacrifice, ŚrS.; copulation (as a merely animal act), ŚBr., Sch. **-kalpa,** m. the ritual of animal sacrifice, ĀśvGṛ.; *-paddhati,* f. N. of wk. **-kāma** (°*śú-*), mfn. desirous of possessing cattle, TS.; Br. **-kḷipti,** f. = *-kalpa,* TBr., Sch. **-kriyā,** f. = *-karman,* Hariv.; L. **-gaṇa,** m. a group of sacrificial animals, ŚrS. **-gāyatrī,** f. a parody of the sacred Gāyatrī whispered into the ear of a s° an°, L. (*paśu-pāśāya vidmahe śiraś-chedāya dhīmahi tan naḥ paśuḥ pracodayāt;* cf. RV. iii, 62, 10). **-ghāta,** m. slaughter of cattle, Mṛicch. **-ghna,** mfn. slaughtering cattle, Mn. v, 38 (cf. *-han*); *-tva,* n., RāmatUp. **-caryā,** f. acting like animals, copulation, BhP. **-cít,** mfn. piled with animals (as a sacrificial fire), TS. **-jánana,** mfn. producing cattle, MaitrS. **-jāta,** n. a species of animal, MānGṛ.; °*tīya,* mfn. pertaining to the an° kingdom, MW. **-tantra,** n. = *-kalpa,* ŚrS. **-tas,** ind. = abl. of *paśu,* cattle, ShaḍvBr. **-tā,** f. the state of an animal (esp. of a sacrificial an°); bestiality, brutality, Mn.; MBh.; Kāv. **-tṛíp,** mfn. gratifying one's self with cattle i. e. stealing c°, RV. **-tva,** n. = *-tā,* R.; Prab.; Rājat.; (with Māheśvaras and Pāśupatas) the being the individual soul. **-da,** mfn. granting cattle, L.; (*ā*), f. N. of one of the Mātṛis attendant on Skanda, MBh. **-dā** or **-dāvan,** mfn. = prec. mfn., Kauś. **-devata,** mf(*ā*)n. invoking c° as a deity (said of a formula or ceremony), ĀśvGṛ. **-devatā,** f. the deity to whom the victim is offered, ŚrS. **-dharma,** m. the law of animals, manner of beasts (said of the re-marriage of widows), Mn. ix, 66; copulation, L.; the treatment of animals, manner in which animals are treated, Pañc. i, 1⁄186 (°*meṇa vyāpādayāmi*). **-dharman,** m. the manner in which the an° sacrifice is performed, ŚāṅkhŚr. **-dhānya-dhanarddhi-mat** (*r* for *ṛi*), mfn. rich in cattle and corn and money, R. **-nātha,** m. 'lord of cattle,' N. of Śiva, L. (cf. *-pati*). **-pa,** mfn. guarding or keeping c°; m. a herdsman, MBh.; Var. **-pakshiya,** n. N. of wk. **-páti,** m. 'lord of animals' (or 'l° of a servant named Paśu' or 'l° of the soul,' RTL. 89), N. of the later Rudra-Śiva or of a similar deity (often associated in the Veda with Bhava, Śarva, Ugra, Rudra, Mahā-deva, Īśāna and others who together with Bhīma are in later times regarded as manifestations of Rudra), AV. &c. &c.; of Agni, TS.; ŚBr.; of Śiva, MBh. &c. (according to one legend every deity acknowledged himself to be a mere *paśu* or animal when entreating Śiva to destroy the Asura Tri-pura); of a lexicographer; of a Scholiast &c.; *-dhara,* m. N. of a poet, Cat.; *-nagara,* n. 'Śiva's town,' N. of Kāśī or Benares, ib.; *-nātha,* m. N. of a partic. form of Siva, W.; *-purāṇa,* n. (prob.) = ŚivaP.; *-śarman,* m. N. of a man, Cat.; *-śāstra,* n. the sacred book of the Pāśupatas revealed by Śiva, Col.; °*tīśvara-māhātmya* and °*ty-ashṭaka,* n. N. of wks. **-palvala,** n. Cyperus Rotundus, L. **-pā́,** m. a keeper of herds, herdsman, RV.; N. of Pūshan, ib.; du. N. of P° and Revatī, TBr. **-pāla,** m. = *-pa,* Mn.; MBh. &c. (*-vat,* ind. like a herdsman); (pl.) N. of a people to the north-east of Madhya-deśa, R.; Var.; of a king (or perhaps k° of the Paśu-pālas), Pur.; n. the country or kingdom of the Paśu-pālas, Pur. **-pālaka,** m. a herdsman; (*ikā*), f. a h°'s wife, Pāṇ. iv, 1, 48, Pat. **-pālana,** n. the tending or rearing of cattle (the duty of a Vaiśya), Vishṇ. **-pālya,** n. id., MW. **-pāśa,** m. the cord with which the victim is bound, L.; the chains which fetter the individual soul, the world of sense, Prab. **-pāśaka,** m. a kind of coitus, L. **-puroḍāśá,** m. the cake offered at an animal sacrifice, ŚBr.; ŚrS.; *-mīmāṃsā,* f. N. of wk. **-pratiprasthātṛi-prayoga,** m., **-prayoga,** m., **-praśna,** m., **-prāyaścitta,** n. N. of wks. **-preraṇa,** n. the driving of cattle, L. **-bandhá,** m. an animal

sacrifice, AV. &c. &c.; N. of an Ekâha, ŚāṅkhŚr.; N. of wk.; *-kārikā*, f., *-paddhati*, f., *-prayoga*, m., *-prayoga-paddhati*, f. N. of wks.; *-yājin*, mfn. offering an an° s°, ŚBr.; *-yūpá*, m. the post to which the victim is bound, ib. **-bandhaka**, m. a rope for tethering cattle, L. **-bali**, m. N. of wk. **-bhartṛi**, m. = *-nātha*, MBh. **-bheda**, m. a class or species of animal, MW. **-mát**, mfn. connected with or relating to cattle or animals, rich in c° or an°, RV. &c. &c.; connected with an° sacrifices, TāṇḍBr.; containing the word *paśu*, AitBr.; m. an owner of herds or c°, MBh.; n. possession of c°, RV. **-mata**, n. erroneous or false doctrine, Hariv. **-māra**, m. the manner of slaughtering c°, MBh.; (*am* and *eṇa*), ind. according to the m° of sl° c°, ib. **-māraka**, mfn. attended with the sacrifice of animals, BhP. **-medha**, m., *-maitrāvaruṇa-prayoga*, m. N. of wks. **-mohanikā**, f. 'an° stupefier,' a species of plant, L. **-yajña** (VP.), **-yāga** (W.), m. an an° sacrifice. **-yājin**, mfn. offering an an° s°, MaitrS. **-yūka**, m. a louse which infests cattle, Gal. **-rakshaṇa**, n. the tending of c°, W. **-rákshi** (RV.), **-rakshin** (Mn.), m. a herdsman. **-rajju**, f. = *-bandhaka*, L. **-rāja**, m. 'king of beasts,' a lion, L. **-rūpá**, n. anything representing the sacrificial animal, ŚBr. **-vat**, ind. like an an°, Kap.; as in an an°, Gaut.; as in an an° sacrifice, KātyŚr. **-várdhana**, mfn. increasing cattle, RV. ix, 94, 1 (w. r. for *paśur v°* ?). **-vid**, mfn. providing c°, AV. **-vīrya**, n. the strength or power belonging to c°, TāṇḍBr. **-vedi**, f. the Vedi at the animal sacrifice, KātyŚr., Sch. **-vrata** (*paśú-*), mfn. acting or behaving like cattle, MaitrS.; the duty to serve as a sacrificial victim, Jātakam. **-śiras** (L.), **-śīrshá** (TS. &c.), n. the head of an animal. **-śrapaṇá**, n. cooking a sacr° an°, ŚBr.; (*-śrápaṇa*, sc. *agni*), m. the fire on which the flesh of a sacr° an° is cooked, ib. **-śrauta-sūtra**, n. N. of wk. **-shā́**, mfn. (dat. *shé*) bestowing cattle, RV. **-shad** (Hir.), **-shṭha** (TāṇḍBr.), mfn. being or dwelling (lit. sitting and standing) in c° **-sakha**, m. 'friend of c°,' N. of a Śūdra, MBh. **-sáni**, mfn. = *-sha*, VS. **-samāmnāya**, m. 'enumeration of sacrificial animals,' N. of VS. xxix, 48; °*yika*, mfn. mentioned in this ch., Nir. **-sambhava**, mfn. produced by animals (as flesh, honey, butter &c.), Mn. viii, 329. **-sā́dhana**, mf(*ī*)n. leading or guiding cattle, RV. **-sūtra**, n. N. of wk. **-soma**, m. pl. the animal and Soma sacrifices, Mn. xi, 27. **-stoma**, m. N. of the Pañcadaśa-stoma, TāṇḍBr. **-han**, mf(*ghnī*)n. killing c° (see *a-p°*), AV. **-harītakī**, f. the fruit of Spondias Mangifera, L. **-havya**, n. an animal sacrifice, Mn. iv, 28. **-hautra**, n. the office of the Hotṛi at an an° s°, N. of wk.; *-prayoga*, m. N. of wk. **Paśûkhā**, f. the pot in which the sacr° an° is cooked or roasted, KātyŚr. **Paśûdbhavā**, f. = *paśu-yūka*, Gal.

Paśuka = *paśu* in *eka-*; (*ā*), f. any small animal, R.

Paśū-√kṛi, to transform into an animal (esp. into a sacrificial victim), Mṛicch.; Kathās.

Paśv, in comp. for *paśu* before vowels. **-aṅga**, n. a limb or part of a sacrificial animal, anything belonging to it, MānGṛ.; *-tā*, f., Nyāyam. **-ayaná**, n. a festival attended with an° sacrifices, ŚBr. **-áyantra** (?), RV. iv, 1, 14. **-avadāna**, n. sacrifice or offering of animals, W. **-ācāra**, m. N. of a partic. form of the worship of Devī, L. **-ijyā**, f. animal sacrifice, KātyŚr. **-iḍā**, f. the Iḍā (s. v.) part at the an° s°, L. **-ish**, mfn. wishing for cattle, RV. (cf. *gav-ish* and *paśva-ishṭi*). **-ishṭakā́**, f. a brick in the shape of an animal, ŚBr. **-ishṭi**, f. an Ishṭi (q. v.) performed at an an° sacrifice, ĀpŚr. **-èkādaśinī**, f. an aggregate of 11 sacrificial animals, ŚBr.

Pá́śva-ishṭi, mfn. (fr. acc. *paśvas* + *i°*) wishing for herds, RV.

पश्च *paśca*, mfn. hinder, later, western, only ibc. or ind. = *paścā*, °*cāt*; Pāṇ. v, 3, 33. [Cf. *uc-ca*, *nī-ca*; Lat. *pos-t*, *pos-terus*; Lith. *paskui*, *paskutìnis*.] **Paścânutāpa**, m. repentance, regret, Hariv. **Paścânupūrvī**, f. a repeated or recurring series, L. **Paścâpin**, m. a servant, TāṇḍBr., Sch. (w. r. for °*cāyin* ?). **Paścârdhá**, m. the hinder side or part, ŚBr.; GṛŚrS.; MBh.; (*e*, ind. with gen. 'behind'), Śak.; the west side or part, ŚBr.; GṛŚrS.; °*dhyà*, mfn. being on the west side, ŚBr.

Paścā́, ind. (instr. of *paśca*) behind, after, later, westward, in the west (opp. to *purā*), RV.; AV.; Br. (cf. Pāṇ. v, 3, 33). **-já**, mfn. born later, MaitrS.; Kāṭh. **-doshá**, m. the later part of the evening, VS. **-somapa**, mfn. drinking the Soma later or afterwards, Kāṭh.; °*pītha*, m. the act of drinking &c., ib.

Paścāc, in comp. for °*cāt*. **-cará**, mfn. coming or approaching behind, MaitrS.; Kāṭh. **-chramaṇa** (for *śr°*), m. a Buddhist priest who walks behind another B° p° in visiting the laity, L.

Paścā́t, ind. (abl. of *paśca*) from behind, behind, in the rear, backwards, RV. &c. &c.; from or in the west, westwards, AV. &c. &c.; afterwards, hereafter, later, at last (pleonast. after *tatas* or an ind. p.; with *√tap*, to feel pain after, regret, repent), Mn.; MBh. &c.; (as a prep. with abl. or gen.) after, behind, ib.; to the west of, Up.; GṛŚrS. **-karṇám**, ind. behind the ear, ŚBr. **-kāla**, m. subsequent time; (*e*), ind. subsequently, afterwards, L. **-kṛita**, mfn. left behind, surpassed, Ragh.; Kum. **-tara**, mfn. following after (abl.), ĀśvŚr. **-tāpa**, m. 'after-pain,' sorrow, regret, repentance (°*pam √kṛi*, to feel regret, repent), MBh.; Kāv.; (in dram.) repentance at something rejected or omitted from want of judgment, Sāh.; *-samanvita* (R.), *-hata* (Hit.), mfn. smitten by repentance, regretful; °*pin*, mfn. feeling repentance, regretting (with *a* priv.), Yājñ. **-tiryak-pramāṇa**, n. the hinder breadth, KātyŚr., Sch. **-pariveshya**, n. second dish, dessert, Bhpr. **-pāda-dviguṇa**, mfn. (a skin) doubled or folded double by (bending) the hind-foot (inwards), KātyŚr. **-puroḍāśa** (°*cā́t-*), mfn. followed or accompanied by the sacrificial cake, MaitrS. **-puro-māruta**, m. du. east and west wind, Ragh. **-sád**, mfn. sitting behind or towards the west, VS.

Paścá-tāt, ind. from behind, RV.

Paścād, in comp. for °*cāt*. **-akshám**, ind. behind the axle tree, Br.; KātyŚr. **-anavavasāyin**, mfn. following after i.e. adhering to, dependent upon (dat.), TS. **-apavarga**, mfn. closed or completed behind, KātyŚr. **-ahas**, ind. in the afternoon, MBh. **-ukti**, f. repeated mention, repetition, Vop. **-ghāṭa**, m. the neck, Car. **-daghván**, mfn. staying behind, falling short of, MaitrS. **-dvārika**, mfn. favourable to a warlike expedition in the west, L. **-baddha-purusha**, m. (Śak. vi, ½) or **-bāhu-baddha** (ib. [Pi.]; Mṛicch.), (a man) whose hands are bound behind. **-bhāga**, m. hind-part, L.; west side, Var.; mfn. whose conjunction with the moon begins in the afternoon, ib. **-vartin**, mfn. remaining behind, following after, MW. **-vātá**, m. a wind from behind, a west wind, TS.

Paścān, in comp. for °*cāt*. **-nata**, mfn. sunk or depressed behind, MW. **-māruta**, m. a wind blowing from behind (opp. to *puro-m°*), Ragh. **-mukhâśrita**, mfn. turned westwards, R.

Paścāl, in comp. for °*cāt*. **-loka**, mf(*ā*)n. having the world or men behind, TS.

Paścima, mf(*ā*)n. being behind, hinder, later, last, final (f. *ā*, with *kriyā*, the last rite i. e. burning the dead; with *saṃdhyā*, the latter i. e. the evening twilight; with *velā*, evening time, close of day; with *avasthā*, last state i. e. verging on death), GṛŚrS.; Mn.; MBh. &c.; west, western, westerly (*ā*, f. with or sc. *diś*, the west), Mn.; MBh.; Kāv. &c.; (*e*), ind. in the west, Var.; (*ena*), ind. id., ib.; west of (with acc.), Lāṭy. **-jana**, m. pl. the people in the west, Var. **-tantra**, n. N. of a Tantra. **-tas**, ind. from behind, MBh. **-tāna** (sc. *āsana*), n. a partic. manner of sitting, Cat. **-dakshiṇa**, mfn. south-westerly, Hcat. **-darśana**, n. a last look (°*naṃ √dṛiś*, to take one's last look), R.; Daś. **-dik-pati**, m. 'regent of the western region,' N. of Varuṇa, Gal. **-deśa**, m. N. of a district, Romakas. **-dvāra** or **-dvārika**, mfn. = *paścād-dvārika*, L. **-bhāga**, m. the west side, Var. **-raṅga** (cf. *pūrva-r°*) in *-nātha-stotra*, n., *-māhātmya*, n., *-rāja-stava*, m. N. of wks. **Paścimâcala**, m. the western mountain (behind which the sun is supposed to set; opp. to *pūrvâc°*), Vāsav. **Paścimânupāka**, m. N. of a prince, MBh. **Paścimâbhimukha**, mfn. directed towards the west, MW. **Paścimâmbudhi**, m. the western sea, Daś. **Paścimârdha**, m. or n. hind-part or latter half, Var. **Paścimâśā-pati**, m. = °*ma-dik-p°*, Hcat. **Paścimêtara**, mfn. 'opposite of west,' eastern, Kād. **Paścimôttara**, mf(*ā*)n. north-western (°*re*, °*ratas* and °*rasyām* [sc. *diśi*], in the north-west), Var.; Hcat.; *-dik-pati*, m. 'regent of the n°-w°,' N. of the god of wind, L.; *-pūrva*, mfn. (pl.) western, northern, or eastern, Mn. v, 92.

पश्य *paśya*, °*śyat* &c. See 1. *paś*.

पष् *pash*, cl. 1. P. Ā. *pashati*, °*te* (v. l. for *spaś*, Dhātup. xxi, 22); cl. 10. P. *pashayati*, to bind, to hinder, to touch, to go (xxxv, 10); *pāshayati*, to bind (v. l. for *paś*, xxxiii, 45).

पष्ठवह् *pashṭha-váh*, m. (fr. *pashṭha*=*pṛishṭha* [?] + *√vah*; nom. °*vā́ṭ* [VS.] or °*vā́ṭ* [TS]) a bull four years old; N. of an Āṅgirasa, TāṇḍBr.; (*pashṭhauhī́*), f. a heifer four years old, any young cow, VS.; Br.; ŚrS.

पस् *pas*, cl. 1. P. Ā. *pasati*, °*te* (v. l. for *spaś*, Dhātup. xxi, 22); cl. 10. P. *pāsayati*, to bind (v. l. for *paś*, xxxiii, 45).

पसस् *pásas*, n. the membrum virile, AV.; ŚBr. [Cf. Gk. πέος for πέσος; Lat. *pēnis* for *pesnis*; Lit. *pisà*, *pìsti*.]

पस्त्य *pastyà*, n. (fr. *pas* and *tya* [?]; cf. *paś-ca*), a stall, stable (as the back-building?; but cf. also Lat. *postis*), RV.; (*à*), f., see below. **-sád**, m. a member of a family, RV.

Pastyā̀, f. homestead, dwelling, household (also pl.), RV.; du. the 2 halves of the Soma-press, ib. x, 96, 10; sg. the goddess of domestic affairs, ib. iv, 55, 3; viii, 27, 5. **-vat** (°*tyà*), mfn. having (i. e. being kept in) a stall, RV. ix, 97, 18; having a fixed habitation (m. a wealthy man), i, 151, 2; forming or offering a f° h°, ii, 11, 16; iv, 54, 5; belonging to the Soma-press, viii, 7, 29.

पस्पश *paspaśa*, m. (*√spaś*) an introduction, preface, any introductory matter explanatory of the plan of a book, Śiś. ii, 112, Sch.; (*ā*), f. N. of the introduction of the Mahā-bhāshya of Patañjali; mfn. = *niḥ-sāra*, Kpr., Sch.

पहाडी *pahāḍī*, f. (in music) N. of a Rāgiṇī (cf. *pāhāḍikā*).

पह्लव *pahlava*, m. pl. N. of a people (the Parthians or Persians), Mn. x, 44; MBh. &c. (also spelt *pahnava*; in the VP. they are said to be a degraded Kshatriya race conquered by Sagara and sentenced to wear beards).

पह्लिका *pahlikā*, f. Pistia Stratiotes, L.

पा 1. *pā*, cl. 1. P. (Dhātup. xxii, 27) *píbati* (Ved. and ep. also Ā. °*te*; rarely *pipati*, °*te*, Kāṭh.; Br.), cl. 2. *pāti*, *pāthás*, *pānti*, RV.; AV.; p. Ā. *pipāná*, RV., *pípāna*, AV. (pf. P. *papaú*, 2. sg. *papātha*, RV.; *papitha*, Pāṇ. vi, 4, 64, Sch.; *papīyāt*, RV.; p. *papivás*, AV.; Ā. *pape*, *papire*, RV.; p. *papānā*, ib.; aor. or impf. *apāt*, RV. [cf. Pāṇ. ii, 4, 77]; 3. pl. *apuḥ* [?], RV. i, 164, 7; *-pāsta*, AV. xii, 3, 43; Prec. 3. sg. *peyās*, RV.; fut. *pāsyati*, °*te*, Br. &c.; *pātā*, Gr.; ind. p. *pītvā́*, RV. &c. &c., °*tvī*, RV.; *-pāya*, AV. &c. &c.; *-pīya*, MBh.; *pāyam*, Kāvyâd.; inf. *píbadhyai*, RV.; *pātum*, MBh. &c.; *pā́tave*, AV.; Br.; *pā́tavai*, RV.), to drink, quaff, suck, sip, swallow (with acc., rarely gen.), RV. &c. &c.; (met.) to imbibe, draw in, appropriate, enjoy, feast upon (with the eyes, ears &c.), Mn.; MBh.; Kāv. &c.; to drink up, exhaust, absorb, BhP.; Pañc.; to drink intoxicating liquors, Buddh.: Pass. *pīyáte*, AV. &c. &c.; Caus. *pāyayati*, °*te* (pf. *pāyayām āsa*, MBh.; aor. *apīpyat*, Pāṇ. vii, 4, 4; ind. p. *pāyayitvā*, MBh.; inf. *pā́yayitavai*, ŚBr.), to cause to drink, give to drink, water (horses or cattle), RV. &c. &c.: Desid. *pipāsati* (RV. also *pipīshati*), to wish to drink, thirst, ib.: Desid. of Caus. *pipāyayishati*, to wish or intend to give to drink, Kāṭh.: Intens. *pepīyate* (p. °*yamāna* also with pass. meaning), to drink greedily or repeatedly, Up.; Hariv. [Cf. Gk. πέ-πω-κα; Aeol. πώ-νω = πίνω; Lat. *pō-tus*, *pōtum*, *bibo* for *pi-bo*; Slav. *pi-ja*, *pi-ti*.]

2. **Pā**, mfn. drinking, quaffing &c. (cf. *agreṛitu-*, *madhu-*, *soma-* &c.)

1. **Pātavya**, mfn. to be drunk, drinkable, Mn.; MBh. &c.

1. **Pātṛi** (with gen.; *pā́tṛi* with acc.; unaccented with gen. or ifc.), one who drinks, a drinker, RV. &c. &c.

Pā́tra, n. (ifc. f. *ā*) a drinking-vessel, goblet, bowl, cup, dish, pot, plate, utensil &c., any vessel or receptacle, RV. &c. &c.; a meal (as placed on a dish), TS.; AitBr.; the channel of a river, R.;

Kād.; (met.) a capable or competent person, an adept in, master of (gen.), any one worthy of or fit for or abounding in (gen., loc., inf. or comp.), MBh.; Kāv. &c.; an actor or an a°'s part or character in a play, Kālid.; Sāh.; a leaf, L. (cf. *pattra*); propriety, fitness, W.; an order, command, ib.; m. or n. a measure of capacity (= 1 Āḍhaka), AV.; ŚBr.; ŚrS.; a king's counsellor or minister, Rājat.; Pañcar.; (*ī*), f., see 1. *pātrī*. **-kaṭaka**, m. or n. the ring on which an alms-bowl is suspended, L. **-ṭīra** (?), m. (only L.) an ex-minister (W. 'an able or competent m°'); a metal vessel; mucus running from the nose; rust of iron; fire; a heron; a crow. **-tara**, mfn. worthier than (abl.), Hariv. **-tā**, f. the being a vessel or receptacle for (gen. or comp.), Kāv.; Rājat. (with *śītôshṇayoḥ*, endurance of heat and cold, Subh.); = next, Yājñ.; Hit. **-tva**, n. capacity, worthiness, dignity, honour, Hit. **-dhāraṇa**, n. keeping a superfluous alms-bowl longer than is permitted, Buddh. **-nirṇega**, m. a washer or cleaner of vessels, TBr. **-parîshṭi**, f. untimely effort to obtain a new alms-bowl, Buddh. **-pāka**, w. r. for *pattra-p°*. **-pāṇi**, m. 'cup-handed,' N. of a demon inimical to children, PārGṛ. **-pāla**, m. 'vessel-guiding,' a large paddle used as a rudder, L. **-bhūta**, mfn. 'become a recipient,' worthy of receiving from (gen.), MBh.; one who receives respectful treatment from (gen.), Hariv. **-bhṛit**, m. 'taking care of utensils,' a servant, W. **-bheda**, m. breaking a drinking-vessel or cup, MW. **-melana**, n. the bringing together of the characters of a play, ib. **-yojana**, n. arrangement of vessels, KātyŚr. **-vandana**, n. 'adoration of v°s,' N. of wk. **-varga**, m. a company of actors, MW. **-śuddhi**, f. 'cleaning of vessels,' N. of wk. **-śesha**, m. scraps of food, Divyâv. **-saṃskāra**, m. the cleaning of a vessel or dish, L.; the current of a river, L. **-saṃcāra**, m. the handing round of vessels or dishes at a meal, MBh. **-stha**, mfn. being in a receptacle or dish, MW. **-hasta** (*pā́°*), mf(*ā*)n. holding any vessel in the hand, AV.; Śak. **Pātrârtha**, m. any object serving as a v°; *pāṇibhyām °rtham* √*kṛi*, to use the hands as a v°, SāmavBr. **Pātrâvaleham**, ind. licking a v° or dish, Buddh. **Pātrôpakaraṇa**, n. ornaments of a secondary kind (as bells, chowries &c.), KālP.

Pātraka, n. a vessel, bowl, dish (see *ku-* and *carvita-*); (*ikā*), f. a cup, an alms-bowl or alms-dish, BhP.

Pātraya, Nom. P. °*yati*, to use as a drinking-vessel, Bhartṛ.

Pātrasāt-√kṛi, to make a worthy person possessed of anything, Ragh.

Pātrika, mf(*ī*)n. measured or sown or filled by means of any vessel or with the measure Pātra, containing or possessing it &c., Pāṇ. v, 1, 46 &c., Sch.; fit, adequate, appropriate, W.; n. a vessel, cup, dish (in *ku-*, MBh. xii, 8327; B. *-pātraka*).

Pātrin, mfn. possessing a drinking-vessel or a dish, Mn. vi, 52; having fit or worthy persons, W.

Pā́triya, mfn. worthy to partake of a meal, TS. (cf. Pāṇ. v, 1, 68).

1. **Pātrī**, f. (of *pātra*) a vessel, plate, dish, pot, Br.; GṛŚrS.; MBh. &c.; a small or portable furnace, W.; N. of Durgā, MBh. **-tas**, ind. = abl. of *pātrī*, ĀpŚr., Sch. **-nirṇéjana**, n. water for rinsing a vessel, ŚBr.

2. **Pātrī**, ind. in comp. for °*tra*. **-√kṛi**, to make anything a recipient or object of (gen.), Megh.; Bālar.; to dignify, promote to honour (pp. *-kṛita*), Kālid. **-√bhū**, to become a fitting recipient or worthy object (pp. *-bhūta*), MBh.

Pātrīṇa, mf(*ā*)n. measured or sown or filled &c. by means of a Pātra, Pāṇ. v, 1, 53; cf. *pātrika*.

Pātrīya, n. and **pātrīva**, m. n. a kind of sacrificial vessel, L.

Pātre, loc. of *pātra*, in comp. **-bahula**, mfn. (pl.) frequently present at meals, parasitical, g. *pātre-samitâdi* and *yuktârohâdi*. **-samita**, mfn. (pl.) id., ib.; sg. a treacherous or hypocritical person, L.

Pātrya, mfn. = *pātriya*, L.

1. **Pā́na**, n. drinking (esp. d° spirituous liquors), draught, RV. (only ifc.), AV. &c. &c.; drinking the saliva i. e. kissing, Kāv. (cf. *adhara-*); a drink, beverage, ŚBr.; Mn.; MBh. &c.; a drinking-vessel, cup, L.; a canal, L.; m. a distiller or vender of spirituous liquors, an inn-keeper, L. **-kumbha**, m. a drinking-vessel, Hariv. **-goshṭhikā** or **-goshṭhī**, f. a drinking-party; a tavern, L. **-ja**, mfn. caused by d°, Suśr. **-dosha**, m. the vice of d°, drunkenness, Daś. **-pa**, mfn. drinking spirituous liquors, MBh. **-para**, mfn. addicted to drinking, W. **-pātra**, n. a d°-vessel, cup, goblet, Kām.; Kāv.; Pur. **-prasakta**, mfn. = *-para*; *-hṛidaya*, mfn., VarBṛS. **-bhājana** (L.), **-bhāṇḍa** (MBh.), n., id. **-bhū** (Kathās.), **-bhūmī** (Hariv.; Kāv.), f. a d°-place, refreshment-room. **-bhojana**, n. eating and d°, Mālav. **-maṅgala**, n. a d°-party, d°-bout, Kathās. **-matta**, mfn. intoxicated, ib. **-mada**, m. intoxication, ib. **-rata**, mfn. = *-para*, W. **-vaṇij**, m. a vender of spirits, a distiller, L. **-vat**, mfn. abounding in drink, rich in beverages, ChUp. **-vibhrama**, m. 'drink-giddiness,' intoxication, Cat. **-śauṇḍa**, mfn. = *-para*, Pāṇ. vi, 2, 2, Sch. **-sindhu**, **-saindhava**, ib., vii, 3, 119, Sch. **Pānâgāra**, m. or n. a drinking-house, tavern, MBh. **Pānâghāta**, m. 'drink-stroke,' morbid state after d°, Gal. **Pānâjīrṇaka**, n. 'indigestion from d°,' id., ib. **Pānâtyaya**, m. 'end of d°,' id., Suśr.

Pānaka, m. n. (ifc. f. *ā*) a draught, drink, beverage, potion, MBh.; Kathās.; Suśr. **-rasa-rāgâsava-yojana**, n. sg. (BhP., Sch.), or **-rasâsava-rāga-yojana**, n. pl. (Cat.) one of the 64 Kalās or arts.

Pānika, m. a vender of spirituous liquors, R.

Pānila, n. a drinking-vessel, L.

Pānīya, mfn. to be drunk, drinkable, Suśr.; n. a beverage, drink, ib.; Pañc.; water, Mn.; MBh. &c. (cf. Nir. i, 16). **-kākikā**, f. 'sea-crow,' the cormorant, Uṇ. i, 7, Sch. **-kumāra-rasa**, m. a partic. medicinal preparation, Rasar. **-gocara**, see *dūre-pānīya-gocara*. **-cūrṇikā**, f. 'water-dust,' sand, L. **-taṇḍulīya**, n. a partic. herb, Bhpr. **-dūshaka**, mf(*ikā*)n. soiling or troubling w°, R. **-nakula**, m. 'w°-ichneumon,' an otter, L. **-pala**, n. a partic. measure of time (= *pala*), Gaṇit., Sch. **-pṛishṭha-ja**, m. 'w°-surface-born,' Pistia Stratiotes, L. **-phala**, n. 'w°-fruit,' the seed of Euryala Ferox, Bhpr. **-mūlaka**, n. 'w°-root,' Vernonia Anthelmintica. **-varṇikā**, f. sand, L. (prob. w. r. for *-cūrṇikā*). **-varsha**, m. rain, Hit. **-vārika**, m. the attendant of a convent who has the care of drinking-water, Buddh. **-śālā** or **-śālikā**, f. a place (esp. a shed on the road-side) where water is distributed, L. **-śīta**, mfn. too cold to drink, L. **Pānīyâdhyaksha**, m. a water-superintendent, R., Sch. **Pānīyâmalaka**, n. Flacourtia Cataphracta, L. **Pānīyârtham**, ind. for the sake of water, Nal. **Pānīyâlu**, m. a species of bulbous plant, L. **Pānīyâśrā**, f. Eleusine Indica, L.

Pā́nta, m. a drink, beverage (?), RV. (= *pānīya*, Nir. vii, 25).

1. **Pāvan**, mfn. drinking (only ifc.; cf. *asṛik-*, *gharma-*, *ghṛita-* &c.)

पा 3. *pā*, cl. 2. P. (Dhāt. xxiv, 48) *pā́ti* (Impv. *pāhí*; pr. p. P. *pā́t*, Ā. *pānā́*, RV.; pf. *papau*, Gr.; aor. *apāsīt*, Rājat., Subj. *pāsati*, RV.; fut. *pāsyati*, *pātā*, Gr.; Prec. *pāyāt*, Pāṇ. vi, 4, 68, Sch.; inf. *pātum*, MBh.), to watch, keep, preserve; to protect from, defend against (abl.), RV. &c. &c.; to protect (a country) i. e. rule, govern, Rājat.; to observe, notice, attend to, follow, RV.; AitBr.: Caus. *pālayati*, see √*pāl*: Desid. *pipāsati*, Gr.: Intens. *pāpāyate*, *pāpeti*, *pāpāti*, ib. [Cf. Zd. *pā*, *paiti*; Gk. πά-ομαι, πέ-πα-μαι, πῶ-υ, &c.; Lat. *pa-sco*, *pa-bulum*; Lith. *pë-mû*.]

4. **Pā**, mfn. keeping, protecting, guarding &c. (cf. *apâna-*, *ṛitā-*, *go-*, *tanū-* &c.)

1. **Pāta**, mfn. (for 2. see p. 616, col. 3) watched, protected, preserved, L.

2. **Pātavya**, mfn. to be guarded or protected, Hariv.

2. **Pātṛí**, mfn. defending, a defender or protector (with gen., acc. or ifc.), RV. &c. &c.

2. **Pātra**, n. (?), RV. i, 121, 1.

2. **Pāna**, mfn. observing, keeping (see *tanū-*); n. protection, defence (see ib. and *vāta-*).

2. **Pānīya**, mfn. to be cherished or protected or preserved, W.

2. **Pāvan**, mfn. protecting (only ifc.; cf. *abhiśasti-*, *tanū-*).

पांसु *pāṅsu*, °*saka* &c. = *pāṅsu* &c.

पांसक *pāṅsaka*, mfn. (√*pas*, *paṅs*) vitiating, spoiling; contemptible, vile, W.

Pāṅsana, mf(*ī*)n. defiling, vitiating, disgracing, spoiling (ifc.), MBh.; R. &c. (f. *ā*, only in voc. °*sane* [perhaps w. r. for °*sani*] at the end of a Śloka); contemptible, wicked, bad, W.; n. and (*ā*), f. contempt, L.

Pāṅsava, mfn. (fr. *pāṅsu*) formed or consisting of dust, BhP.; (°*vá*), m. patron. of A-sat, ŚBr.; n. a kind of salt, L.

Pāṅsavyà, mfn. (fr. *pāṅsu*), VS. xvi, 45.

Pāṅsin, mfn. = °*sana* (only f. voc. °*tini* in *kula-p°*, R. ii, 73, 5, where B. °*sani*; cf. under *pāṅsana*).

Pāṅsú, m. crumbling soil, dust, sand (mostly pl.), AV. &c. &c.; dung, manure, L.; the pollen of a flower, MW.; (prob.) the menses, Car. (cf. *rajas*); a species of plant, Bhpr.; a kind of camphor, L.; landed property, L. **-kasīsa**, n. sulphate of iron, L. **-kulī**, f. 'quantity of dust,' a high road, L. **-kūla**, n. a dust-heap, (esp.) a collection of rags out of a d°-h° used by Buddhist monks for their clothing, Divyâv.; a legal document not made out in any partic. person's name, L.; *-sīvana*, n. 'the sewing together of rags from a d°-h°,' N. of the place where Gautama Buddha assumed his ascetic's dress, Lalit. (C. *pāṇḍu-s°*); °*lika*, mfn. one who wears clothes made of rags from a d°-h°, Buddh. **-kṛita**, mfn. covered with d°, dusty, Lalit. **-krīḍana**, n. (Vāsav.), **-krīḍā**, f. (HPariś.) playing in the sand. **-kshāra**, n. = *-ja*, L. **-khala**, m. a sand-heap, KātyŚr., Sch. **-guṇṭhita**, mfn. covered with dust, MBh. **-catvara**, n. hail, L. **-candana**, m. N. of Śiva, L. **-cāmara**, m. (only L.) a heap of dust; a tent or perfumed powder (= *paṭa-vāsa*); a bank covered with Dūrvā grass; praise; a small cucumber. **-ja**, n. 'earth-born,' rock or fossil salt, Car. **-jālika**, m. N. of Vishṇu, L. **-dhāna**, m. a heap of sand or dust, Car. **-dhūmra**, mfn. dark red or dark with dust, MW. **-dhvasta-śiroruha**, mfn. having the hair soiled with dust, MBh. **-nipāta**, m. a shower of dust, VarBṛS. **-paṭala**, n. a coating or mass of dust, MW. **-pattra**, n. Chenopodium Album, L. **-parṇī**, f. a species of Cocculus, L. **-piśāca**, m. a class of imps or demons, Lalit. **-bhava**, n. = *-ja*, L. **-mardana**, m. 'dust-destroyer,' an excavation for water round the root of a tree (= *ālavāla*), L. **-rāgiṇī**, f. a species of plant, L. **-rāshṭra**, n. N. of a country; m. pl. its inhabitants (B. *-pāṇḍu-r°*), MBh. **-lavaṇa**, n. a kind of salt, Bhpr. **-lekhana**, n. = *-krīḍana*, Viddh. **-varsha**, m. or n. = *-nipāta*, Mn. iv, 115. **-vikarshaṇa**, n. = *-krīḍana*, MBh. **-saṃcaya**, m. a heap of sand, R. **-samūhana** (Mn.), **-hara** (Gaut.), mfn. raising dust (said of wind). **Pāṅsûtkara**, m. = *-varsha*, VarBṛS.; caustic potash, L.; n. a kind of salt, Bhpr.

Pāṅsuka, n. pl. dust, sand, MBh.; (*ā*), f. a menstruous woman, L.; Pandanus Odoratissimus, L.

Pāṅsurá, mfn. dusty, m. or n. a d° place, RV. i, 22, 7 (cf. Nir. xii, 19); m. a gad-fly, L.; a cripple carried or moving about in a chair, L. (cf. *pāṅsuva*).

Pāṅsulá, mfn. dusty, sandy, ŚBr.; R. &c. (cf. g. *sidhmâdi* and Nir. xii, 19; m. or n. a dusty place, VāyuP.); ifc. sullied, defiled, disgraced by (Śak. v, 28); disgracing, defiling (cf. *kula-p°*); m. (only L.) a wicked or profligate man, a libertine; N. of Śiva and of one of his symbols (a sort of staff crossed at the upper end with transverse pieces representing the breast-bone and adjoining ribs and surmounted by a skull); Guilandina Bonducella; (*ā*), f. the earth; a licentious woman, Vcar.; = *pāṅsukā*, L. **Pāṅsulā-vṛitti-prakāśa**, m. N. of wk.

Pāṅsuva, m. a cripple, L. (cf. *pāṅsura*).

पाक 1. *pā́ka*, mfn. (either fr. √1. *pā* + *ka*, 'drinking, sucking,' or fr. √2. *pac*, 'ripening, growing') very young, GṛS.; simple, ignorant, inartificial, honest, AV.; TS.; ĀśvŚr.; m. the young of an animal (see *ulūka-*, *kapota-*); a child, infant, L.; N. of a Daitya slain by Indra, MBh.; Pur. **-trā́**, ind. in simplicity, in a simple or honest way, RV. **-dūrvā**, f. a species of plant, ib. **-dvish** or **-nishūdana**, m. 'foe or destroyer of the Daitya Pāka,' N. of Indra, L. **-yajña** &c., see under 2. *pāka*. **-vát**, ind. simply, honestly, RV. **-śaṅsá**, mfn. speaking sincerely, ib. **-śāsana**, m. 'punisher of the Daitya Pāka' or 'instructor of the ignorant,' N. of Indra, MBh.; Kāv.; Pur. (cf. RV. i, 31, 14); °*ni*, m. (patr. of prec.) N. of Jayanta, L.; of Arjuna, MBh. **-sútvan**, mfn. offering Soma with a simple or sincere mind, RV. **-sthāman** (*pā́ka-*), m. N. of a man, RV. **-hantṛi**, m. = *-nishūdana*, R.

Pākiman, m., g. *pṛithv-ādi*.

Pākyā̀, ind. in simplicity, in ignorance, RV.

पाक 2. *pāka*, m. (√2. *pac*; ifc. f. *ī*) cooking, baking, roasting, boiling (trans. and intrans.), ŚrS.;

Mn.; MBh. &c.; burning (of bricks, earthenware &c.), ib.; any cooked or dressed food, BhP.; digestion, assimilation of food, Suśr.; ripening, ripeness (of fruit or of a boil), KātyŚr.; Mn.; Var.; Suśr.; inflammation, suppuration, Suśr.; an abscess, ulcer, ib.; ripening of the hair i.e. greyness, old age, L.; maturity, full development (as of the mind &c.), completion, perfection, excellence, Hariv.; Kāv. &c.; development of consequences, result (esp. of an act done in a former life), Var.; Pañc.; MārkP.; any act having consequences, BhP.; the domestic fire, L.; a cooking utensil, L.; general panic or revolution in a country, W. (in comp. 2. *pāka* is not always separable from 1. *pāka*). —**karma-nibandha**, m. N. of wk. —**kuṭī**, f. a potter's kiln, pottery, Gal. —**kṛishṇa**, m. 'black when ripe,' Carissa Carandas; *-phala*, m. id., L. —**kriyā**, f. the act of cooking, Cāṇ. —**ja**, mfn. produced by cooking or roasting, Tarkas.; n. 'obtained by boiling,' black salt, L.; flatulence, L.; *-tva*, n. production by warmth, capability of being affected by contact with fire, Bhāshāp.; *-prakriyā*, f., *-vicāra*, m. N. of wks. —**paṇḍita**, m. a master in the art of cooking, Bhpr. —**pātra**, n. a cooking utensil, a boiler &c., ib. —**puṭī**, f. = *-kuṭī*, L. —**phala**, m. Carissa Carandas, L. (cf. *-kṛishṇa-ph°*). —**bali** (*pā́°*), m. (prob.) = *-yajña*, AV. —**bhāṇḍa**, n. = *-pātra*, Kathās. —**bhedaka**, m. N. of a partic. class of criminals, Hcat. —**matsya**, m. a species of fish, Suśr.; a species of venomous insect, ib.; a kind of fish sauce, L. —**yajñá**, m. (according to some) a cooked (according to others 'a simple or domestic') sacrifice (of 3 [ĀśvGṛ.], 4 [Mn.] or 7 [Āpast.; Baudh.; Gaut.] forms or kinds), TS.; Br.; GṛŚrS. &c. (cf. IW. 188, n. 1); N. of a man, Gobh.; *-nirṇaya*, m., *-paddhati*, f., *-prakāśa*, m., *-prayoga*, m., *-vidhi*, m. N. of wks.; *°ñika*, mfn. relating to the Pāka-yajña, performing it &c., Baudh.; *°ñiya*, mf(*ā*)n. id., ŚBr.; Kauś. —**rañjana**, n. the leaf of the Laurus Cassia, L. —**vatī**, f. a pause of ¾ of an instant between 2 short syllables, MāṇḍŚ. —**śālā**, f. 'cooking-room,' a kitchen, Dhūrtas. —**śāstra**, n. the science of c°, Bhpr. —**śuklā**, f. chalk, L. —**saṃsthā**, f. a form of the Pāka-yajña, ŚāṅkhGṛ. —**sthāna**, n. 'cooking-place,' a kitchen or a potter's kiln, L. —**haṅsa**, m. a kind of aquatic bird, Car. **Pākâgāra**, m. or n. = *°ka-śālā*, Kull. **Pākâtîta**, mfn. over-ripe, Bhpr. **Pākâtīsāra**, m. chronic dysentery, L. **Pākâtyaya**, m. obscuration of the cornea after inflammation, Suśr. **Pākâdi-saṃgraha**, m. N. of wk. **Pākâdhyāya**, m. N. of ch. of wk. **Pākâri**, m. 'digestion's foe (?)' = *śveta-kāñcana*, L. **Pākârú**, m. N. of a partic. disease, VS. **Pākâvalī**, f. N. of wk.

Pākalá, mfn. quite black, TS.; bringing to ripeness (also a boil &c.), causing suppuration, L.; m. a species of fever, Bhpr.; fever in an elephant, L.; fire, L.; wind, L.; = *bodhana-dravya* (w.r. for *rādhana-d°*?), L.; (*ā*), f. Bignonia Suaveolens, L.; (*ī*), f. Cucumis Utilissimus, L.; n. Costus Speciosus or Arabicus, Car. °**kali**, f. a species of plant, L.

Pākin, mfn. becoming mature, ripening, being digested (ifc.; cf. *a-*, *kaṭu-*, *garbha-* &c.); promoting digestion, Car. °**kima**, mfn. cooked, burned (as earthenware), matured, ripened, L.; obtained by cooking or evaporation (as salt), Suśr.; red-hot, L.

Pāku, see *dūre-* and *phale-pāku*. °**kuka**, m. a cook, L.

Pākya, mfn. fit to cook, eatable, KātyŚr.; ChUp. (cf. *bahu-*); obtained by cooking or evaporation, Suśr.; ripening (see *kṛishṭa-*); n. (sc. *lavaṇa*) a kind of salt, Suśr.; m. saltpetre, L.

Pācaka, mf(*ikā*)n. cooking, roasting, baking, MBh.; Kāv. &c.; causing digestion, digestive, Suśr.; bringing to maturity, Tattvas.; m. a cook, Gṛihyās., (*ikā*, f. a female cook; see below); fire, L.; *-tva*, n., Vop.; *-strī*, f. a female cook, Vop.; *°cikā-bhārya*, f. having a cook for a wife, Pāṇ. vi, 3, 37, Sch.

Pācata, mfn. (fr. *pacat*), Pat.

Pācana, mf(*ī*)n. causing to cook or boil, softening, digestive, Suśr.; sour, L.; suppurative, W.; m. fire, L.; red ricinus, L.; acidity, sourness, W.; (*ī*), f. Terminalia Chebula, L.; n. the act of cooking or baking &c.; causing a wound to close, a styptic for closing wounds, Suśr.; extracting extraneous substances from a wound &c. by means of cataplasms, a cataplasm, ib.; a dissolvent, digestive, ib.; Car.; any medicinal preparation or decoction, W.; a sort of drink, ib.; penance, expiation, L. °**canaka**, m. borax, L.; n. a dissolvent, digestive, Car.; a sort of drink, W.; causing a wound to close (by means of styptics &c.), ib. °**canīya**, mfn. to be cooked or digested; dissolving, digestive, Suśr.; Car.

Pācayitṛi, mfn. cooking, digestive, Suśr.

Pācala (only L.), m. a cook; fire; wind; = *rādhana-dravya*, n. dissolving or a dissolvent.

Pācā, °**ci** or °**cikā**, f. cooking, maturing, L. °**cī**, f. a species of plant; *-kaṭu*, m. Plumbago Ceylanica, L.

Pācya, mfn. capable of being cooked or matured, ŚvetUp.

पाक्ष *pāksha*, mf(*ī*)n. (fr. *paksha*) belonging to a half month; relating to a side or party, W.

Pākshapātika, mf(*ī*)n. (fr. *paksha-pāta*) partial, factious, Kām.

Pākshāyaṇa, mf(*ī*)n. belonging to or occurring in a Paksha or fortnight &c., W. (cf. Pāṇ. iv, 2, 80).

1. **Pākshika**, mf(*ī*)n. (fr. *paksha*) favouring a party or faction, Pur.; Gaṇit.; subject to an alternative, that which may or may not take place, possible but not necessary, optional, Śaṃk.; Pāṇ., Sch.; Kull.; m. an alternative, W. —**sūtra-vṛitti**, f. N. of wk.

2. **Pākshika**, m. (fr. *pakshin*) a fowler, bird-catcher, L.

पाखण्ड *pākhaṇḍa*, m. = (and prob. only w.r. for) *pāshaṇḍa*, q.v.

पागल *pāgala*, mfn. (a word used in Bengāli) mad, deranged, demented, BrahmavP.

पाङ्क्त *pāṅkta*, mf(*ī*)n. (fr. *paṅkti*) consisting of five parts, fivefold, Br.; Up.; relating to or composed in the Paṅkti metre, VS.; TS.; AitBr. (cf. Pāṇ. iv, 2, 55, Sch.); m. N. of a kind of Soma, Suśr.; n. (sc. *sāman*) N. of a Sāman, Lāṭy. —**tā**, f. (Śaṃk.), **-tvá**, n. (TS.) fivefoldness.

Pāṅktakākubha, mf(*ī*)n. (fr. *paṅkti-kakubh*) beginning with the Paṅkti and ending with the Kakubh metre, RPrāt.

Pāṅktīhari, m. (prob. patr. fr. *paṅktī-hara*) N. of a man, Rājat.

Pāṅkteya (MBh.), **pāṅktya** (Mn.), mfn. fit to be associated with, admissible into the row of caste-fellows at meals.

पाङ्क्त्र *pāṅktrá*, m. a kind of mouse, VS. (Mahīdh.)

पाङ्गुल्य *pāṅgulya*, n. (fr. *paṅgula*) limping, hobbling, Dhātup. —**hāriṇī**, f. N. of a kind of shrub, L.

पाचक *pācaka*, °*cana* &c. See col. 1.

पाज *pāja*, m. (√*paj*?) N. of a man, Rājat.

Pājaka, m. N. of a man (= prec.), ib.; (with *paṇḍita*) N. of a poet, Cat.; a partic. kitchen utensil, ĀpŚr.

Pā́jas, n. firmness, vigour, strength, RV.; brightness, glitter, sheen (pl. shining colours), ib.; du. heaven and earth (as the two firm or shining surfaces; cf. 'firmament'); food, L. —**vat** (*pā́°*), mfn. firm, strong, brilliant, RV.

Pājasyà, n. the region of the belly (of an animal); the flanks, side, VS.; AV.; ŚBr.

Pājrya, m. patr. fr. *pajra*, ĀrshBr.

पाजिक *pājika*, m. = *prâjika*, a falcon, VarBṛS., Sch.

पाञ्च *pāñca*, Vṛiddhi form of *pañca* (fr. *pañcan*), in comp. —**kapāla**, mf(*ī*)n. relating to or forming part of an oblation offered in 5 cups, Pāṇ. iv, 1, 88, Pat.; °*lika*, n., vii, 3, 17, Kāś. —**karmika**, mfn. relating or applicable to the 5 kinds of treatment, Car. —**kalāpika**, n., Pāṇ. v, 1, 28, Vārtt. 1, Pat. —**gatika**, mf(*ī*)n. consisting of 5 forms of existence, L. —**janī**, f. (fr. *pañca-jana*) patr. of Asiknī, BhP. —**janīna**, mfn., g. *prātijanâdi*. —**janya** (*pā́°*), mf(*ā*)n. relating to the 5 races of men, containing or extending over them &c., RV. &c.; Br.; MBh.; m. N. of Kṛishṇa's conch taken from the demon Pañca-jana, MBh.; Hariv. &c.; fire, L.; fish or a species of f°, L.; N. of one of the 8 Upa-dvīpas in Jambu-dvīpa, BhP.; (*ā*), f. patr. of Asiknī, ib.; *-dhama*, *-dhara* and *-nādin*, m. N. of Kṛishṇa, L. (cf. above); *-vana*, n. N. of a wood, Har.; °*nyāyani*, g. *karṇâdi*. —**daśa**, mf(*ī*)n. (fr. *pañca-daśī*) relating to the 15th day of a month, g. *saṃdhi-velâdi*. —**daśya**, mfn. id., BhP.; n. the aggregate of 15, ŚāṅkhŚr. —**nakha**, mf(*ī*)n. made of the skin of an animal with 5 claws, MBh.; n. (sc. *māṅsa*) the flesh of an an° with 5 claws, Yājñ., Sch. —**nada**, mf(*ī*)n. relating to or prevailing in the Pañjāb, MBh.; m. a prince of the P°, Var.; pl. the inhabitants of the P°, MBh.; Var. —**nāpiti** (fr. *pañca-nāpita*), Pāṇ. ii, 1, 51, Vārtt. 2, Pat. —**prasṛitikī**, f. (fr. *pañca-prasṛita* or °*ti*) a mixture of 4 kinds of grease (a handful of each) with grains of rice, Car. —**bhautika**, mf(*ī*)n. (*-bhūta*) composed of or containing the 5 elements, MBh.; Suśr. &c.; n. (with *ādāna*) the assumption of the 5 el°, Yājñ. —**mūlika**, mf(*ī*)n. coming from the 5 roots, Car. —**yajñika**, mf(*ī*)n. relating to or included in the 5 great religious acts (see *pañca-yajña*), Mn. iii, 83 &c. —**rātra**, m.pl. N. of a Vaishṇava sect following the doctrine of their sacred book called Pañcarātra, Sarvad.; Col.; Cat.; n. the doctrine of the Pāñcarātras, ib. (also °*trya* and °*traka*); N. of sev. wks.; *-prâyaścitta-vidhāna*, n., *-mantra*, m. or n., *-mahôpanishad*, f., *-rakshā*, f., *-rahasya*, n., *-vacana*, n., *-śrī-cūrṇa-paripālana*, n., *-saṃgraha*, m., *-sthāpana*, n.; °*trâgama*, m., °*trârādhana*, n. N. of wks. —**rātrika**, mf(*ī*)n. lasting 5 nights (days), SāmavBr.; m. 'connected with the Pāñcarātra,' N. of Vishṇu, MBh. —**lohitika**, n., Pāṇ. v, 1, 28, Vārtt. 1, Pat. —**lauhitika**, n. ib., Kāś. —**varṇa**, w. r. for *pañca-v°*. —**vārshika**, mf(*ī*)n. 5 years old, Jyot. —**valkika**, mf(*ī*)n. coming from the 5 kinds of bark, Car. —**vāja**, n. N. of 2 Sāmans, ĀrshBr. —**vārshika**, see above. —**vidhya**, n. (fr. *pañca-vidhi*), N. of a Sūtra treating of the 5 Vidhis of a Sāman, L. —**śabdika**, n. the fivefold music, L. —**śara**, mf(*ī*)n. belonging to the (5-arrowed) god of love, Kathās. **Pāñcârthika**, m. a follower or votary of Paśu-pati or Śiva, L. **Pāñcaudanika**, mf(*ī*)n. (fr. *pañcâudana*), Pāṇ. iv, 3, 68; v, 1, 95, Sch.

Pāñcamāhnika, mf(*ī*)n. (fr. *pañcama* + *ahan*) belonging to the fifth day, ŚāṅkhŚr.

Pāñcamika, mf(*ī*)n. (fr. *pañcama*) treated of in the fifth book, Kull.; Cat.

पाञ्चाल *pāñcāla*, mf(*ī*)n. relating or belonging to or ruling over the Pañcālas, MBh.; R. &c.; m. a prince of the P°, ib.; (with *Bābhravya*) N. of an author, Cat.; the country of the P°, L.; pl. the people of the P°, MBh.; Var. &c.; an association of 5 guilds (carpenter, weaver, barber, washerman, and shoe-maker), L.; (*ī*), f., see below; n. the language of the P°, Cat. —**jāti-viveka**, m. N. of wk. —**deśa**, m. the country of the Pañcālas, R. —**nātha** (Var.), **-pati** (BhP.), m. the king of the P°. —**putrikā**, f. N. of Draupadī, Kāvyâd. —**rāja**, m. the king of the P°, MBh. **Pāñcālânuyāna**, n. N. of a partic. play with puppets, Cat. (cf. next, f.)

Pāñcālaka, mf(*ikā*)n. relating or belonging to the people of the Pañcālas, MBh.; m. a king of the P°, ib.; (*ikā*), f. a princess of the P°, ib.; a doll, puppet (also written °*calikā*), L.

Pāñcālāyana and °**cāli**, m. patr. fr. *pañcāla*, Pāṇ. iv, 1, 99; 168, Sch.

Pāñcālika, mf(*ī*)n. = °*laka*; m. N. of a man, Daś.; (*ikā*), f. (with *catuḥ-shashṭi*) the 64 arts collectively, Cat.

Pāñcālī, f. a princess of the Pañcālas, (esp.) N. of Draupadī, MBh.; Hariv. &c.; (with or sc. *rīti*) N. of a partic. poetical style, Dasar.; Vām. &c.; a doll, puppet, L. —**vivāha-kathana**, n., **-svayamvara-varṇana**, n. N. of 2 wks.

Pāñcāleya, m., metron. fr. *pāñcālī*, MBh. (Nīlak.)

Pāñcālya, mfn. = °*cāla*, mfn.; m. = id. m., MBh.

Pā́ñci, m. (fr. *pañcan*) a patronymic, ŚBr. (g. *bahv-ādi*). —**grāma**, m. N. of a village, Rājat.

Pāñcika, m. N. of the leader of the Yakshas, Buddh.; of a man, Hariv.

पाञ्जर *pāñjara* (fr. *pañjara*), mfn. relating or belonging to a cage, Nalac.

Pāñjarya, g. *saṃkāśâdi*.

पाट् *pāṭ*, ind. an interjection used in calling, L. (g. *câdi*).

पाट *pāṭa*, m. (√*paṭ*) breadth, expanse, extension, L.; (in geom.) the intersection of a prolonged side and perpendicular or the figure formed by such an intersection, Col.; = *vādya-tūrôtkara*, Vikr. iv, 12/14, Sch.; (*ā́*), f. a species of plant, AV.; Kauś. (cf. *pāṭhā*); regular order, series, succession, W.; (*ī*), f., see *pāṭī*. **Pāṭâvalī**, f. N. of wk.

Pāṭaka, m. a splitter, divider, Hariv.; (only L.) the half or any part or a kind of village; a shore, bank; a flight of steps leading to the water; a kind of musical instrument; a long span (= *mahā-kish-*

ku); expense or loss of capital or stock; throwing dice; (*ikā*), f., see *dina-pāṭikā*.

Pāṭana, n. splitting, dividing, tearing up, cutting to pieces, destroying, MBh.; Kāv. &c.; (*ā*), f. a cut, incision, Naish. — **kriyā**, f. lancing an abscess or ulcer, Suśr.

Pāṭanīya, mfn. to be split or torn asunder, Kād.

Pāṭita, mfn. split, torn, broken, divided, MBh.; Kāv. &c.; N. of a partic. fracture of the leg, Suśr.

Pāṭin, mfn. splitting, cleaving (ifc.), Hcat.; m. a species of fish, L.

Pāṭī, f. arithmetic, Bījag.; a species of plant, L. — **kaumudī**, f., -**gaṇita**, n., -**līlāvatī**, f., -**sāra**, m. N. of wks.

Pāṭūpaṭa, mfn. (√*paṭ*), Pāṇ. vi, 1, 12, Vārtt. 8, Pat. (*pāṭup*°, Vop.)

Pāṭya, mfn. to be lanced (as an ulcer), Car.; n. a species of pot-herb, L.

पाटच्चर *pāṭaccara*, m. (fr. *paṭaccara*) a thief, robber, Kāv.

पाटल *pāṭala*, mf(*ā*)n. pale red, pink, pallid, Kauś.; Var.; Kāv.; (f. *ī*) made of the Pāṭalī or forming a part of it, g. *bilvâdi*; m. a pale red hue, rose colour, Rājat.; Bignonia Suaveolens (the tree bearing the trumpet-flower), MBh.; Kāv. &c.; a species of rice ripening in the rains, Suśr.; Rottleria Tinctoria, L.; N. of a man, Rājat.; (*ā*), f. Bignonia Suaveolens, Kāv.; red Lodhra, L.; a kind of fresh water fish, Suśr.; a form of Durgā, Tantras.; of Dākshāyaṇī, MatsyaP.; n. the trumpet-flower (also *ā*, f.), MBh.; Kāv. &c.; saffron, L. — **kīṭa**, m. a kind of insect, Vāsav. — **kusuma**, n. the trumpet-flower, Var. — **gaṇḍa-lekha**, mfn. having the complexion of the cheek of a red hue, Ragh. — **cakshus**, mfn. having cataract in the eye, Sāṃkhyas., Sch. (w.r. for *paṭala-c*° ?). — **druma**, m. Rottleria Tinctoria, L. — **pushpa**, n. the trumpet-flower, MBh. **Pāṭalâcala-māhātmya** or **Pāṭalâdri-māhātmya**, n. N. of wk. **Pāṭalā-pushpa-saṃnibha**, n. the wood of Cerasus Puddum, L. **Pāṭalā-vatī**, f. N. of a river, MBh.; VP.; N. of Durgā, Tantras. **Pāṭalôpala**, m. a ruby, Śiś. xvii, 3.

Pāṭalaka, mfn. pale red (N. of the 12th unknown quantity), Col.

Pāṭalaya, Nom. P. °*yati*, to dye pale red, Kād.; Śiś.

Pāṭali, m. f. Bignonia Suaveolens, Suśr.; a species of rice, L. — **putra**, n. N. of the capital of Magadha near the confluence of the Śoṇa and the Ganges (supposed to be the ancient Palibothra and the modern Patnā), Pat.; Kap.; Kathās. (esp. iii, 78) &c.; m. pl. the inhabitants of this city, Pāṇ. ii, 3, 42, Kāś.; -*nāmadheya*, n. (sc. *nagara*) a city called Pāṭaliputra, MW. — **putraka**, mf(*ikā*)n. relating to or coming from P°, Pāṇ. iv, 2, 123, Sch.; n. the city P°, Kathās.

Pāṭalika, mfn. knowing the secrets of others, L.; one who knows time and place, L.; m. a pupil, L.; n. N. of a town (= *Pāṭali-putra*), L.

Pāṭalita, mfn. made red, reddened, W.

Pāṭalin, mfn. possessing trumpet-flowers, Bālar.

Pāṭaliman, m. a pale red or rose colour, Prab.

Pāṭalī, f. Bignonia Suaveolens, Suśr.; = *kaṭabhī* and *mushkaka*, L.; N. of a city, Daś.; of a daughter of king Mahêndra-varman, Kathās. — **putra**, n. = °*li-p*° (above), HPariś.

Pāṭalī-√kṛi, to dye pale red, Kād.

Pāṭalya, n. redness, Kāv.

Pāṭalyā, f. a multitude of trumpet-flowers, L.

पाटव *pāṭava*, m. (fr. *paṭu*) a son or descendant of Paṭu, ŚBr.; Pravar. (cf. Pāṇ. iv, 2, 119, Sch.); mfn. clever, sharp, dexterous, W.; n. sharpness, intensity, Suśr.; Tattvas.; skill, cleverness in (loc.), Kāv.; Rājat.; Hit.; quickness, precipitation in (comp.), Kathās.; health, L.

Pāṭavika, mf(*ī*)n. clever, cunning, fraudulent, Śiś. xix, 56.

पाटहिका *pāṭahikā*, f. Abrus Precatorius (a small shrub), L.

पाटिकावाडि *pāṭikāvāḍi*, N. of a village (prob. Putcabarry), Kshitīś.

पाटीर *pāṭīra*, m. (only L.; cf. *paṭīra*), the sandal tree; a radish; a sieve; a cloud; a field; the pith or manna of the bamboo; tin; catarrh.

पाटूर *pāṭūrá*, m. a partic. part of an animal near the ribs, TS.

पाट्टारक *pāṭṭāraka*, mfn. (fr. *paṭṭāra*), g. *dhūmâdi*.

पाठ *pāṭha*, m. (√*paṭh*) recitation, recital, Kāv.; reading, perusal, study (esp. of sacred texts), Śiksh. &c.; a partic. method of reciting the text of the Veda (of which there are 5, viz. Saṃhitā, Pada, Krama, Jaṭā and Ghana, RTL. 409); the text of a book, ŚrS.; MBh.; the reading (of a text), Naish., Sch.; = *dhātu-pāṭha*, Vop.; (*ā*), f. Clypea Hernandifolia, L. — **ccheda**, m. a break in recitation or in a text; a pause, caesura, L. — **dosha**, m. an error in a t°, false reading, L. — **niścaya**, m., -**niściti**, f. repeated study of a t°, repetition, L. — **praṇālī**, f. recension of a t°, KaushUp., Comm. — **bhū**, f. 'recitation-place,' a place where the Vedas are recited or read, L. — **mañjarī**, f. 'repetition-cluster,' a small talking bird, Graculus Religiosa, L. — **vat**, mfn. well-read, learned, Var. — **viccheda**, m. = -*ccheda*, L. **Pāṭhântara**, n. 'another reading,' a variation of the text in a book or manuscript; °*raya*, P. °*yati*, to have a v. l. for (acc.), L.

Pāṭhaka, m. a reciter, reader (*ikā*, f., Pāṇ. iv, 1, 4, Sch.); a student, pupil, Cat.; a scholar, lecturer, preceptor, teacher (cf. *dharma-*, *nakshatra-*, *smṛiti-*), Mn.; MBh.; Pañc.; a public reciter of the Purāṇas or other sacred works, W.; a Paṇḍit who declares what is the law or custom according to the scriptures, ib.

Pāṭhana, m. (°*nī*, f.), g. *gaurâdi*; n. recitation, teaching, lecturing, Pañcad. **Pāṭhanâśram-bha-pīṭhikā**, f. N. of wk.

Pāṭhika, mfn. conformable to the text, Dāyabh.; (°*kāyana*, m. a patr. [also pl.], Saṃskārak.); (*ā*), f. Clypea Hernandifolia, L.

Pāṭhita, mfn. (fr. Caus.) caused or taught to read, instructed, taught, lectured, Cāṇ.; Pañc.

Pāṭhin, mfn. one who has read or studied any subject; knowing, conversant with (ifc.), MBh.; Pur.; m. a student; a Brāhman (esp. one who has finished his sacred studies), W.; Plumbago Zeylanica (also *pāṭhī-kuṭa*), L.

Pāṭhīna, m. = *pāṭhaka*, L.; Silurus Pelorius or Boalis (a kind of sheat-fish), Mn.; Yājñ.; Kathās. &c.; a species of Moringa with red blossoms, L.

Pāṭheya, mfn., g. *nady-ādi*.

Pāṭhya, mfn. to be recited, R.; Sāh.; to be taught, needing instruction, BhP. — **ratna-kośa**, m. N. of wk.

पाडलीपुर *pāḍalī-pura*, n. = *pāṭali-putra*, Camp.

पाडिनी *pāḍinī*, f. an earthern pot, a boiler, L.

पाण 1. *pāṇa*, m. (√*paṇ*) a stake at play, MBh. (cf. *paṇa*); trade, traffic, W.; praise, W.

1. **Pāṇi**, m. a place of sale, shop, market, W.

पाण 2. *pāṇa*, m. = *pāṇi*, the hand, L.

पाणविक *pāṇavika*, mf(*ī*)n. (fr. *paṇava*) relating to a drum, Kād.; m. a drummer, Pāṇ. ii, 4, 2, Sch.; a species of bird (belonging to the Pra-tuda class), Car.

पाणि 2. *pāṇí*, m. (said to be fr. √*paṇ*) the hand, RV. &c. &c. (often ifc. = holding in the h°, e. g. *asi-p*°, holding a sword in the h°, s° in h°; *pāṇiṃ √grah* or °*ṇau √kṛi*, to take the h° of a bride, marry; °*niṃ √dā*, to give the h° in marriage); a hoof, RV. ii, 31, 2; N. of Sch. on the Daśa-rūpaka, Cat. [Orig *palni*; cf. Gk. παλάμη; Lat. *palma*; Angl. Sax. *folm*; Germ. *fühlen*; Eng. *to feel*.] — **kacchapikā**, f. 'hand-tortoise,' a partic. position of the fingers, KālP. — **karṇa**, m. 'h°-eared,' N. of Śiva, MBh. — **kūrcan** or °**cas**, m. N. of one of the attendants of Skanda, MBh. — **khāta**, n. 'dug with the hand,' N. of a sacred bathing-place, MBh. — **gata**, mfn. being in the hand or at h°, ready, present, Naish. — **gṛihīta**, mfn. taken by the h°, married; (*ā*, HPariś. or *ī*, L.), f. a bride or wife. — **graha**, m. taking (the bride) by the h°, marriage, Var.; Kathās.; -*kara*, m. = -*grahītṛi*, MW.; °*hâdi-kṛitya-viveka*, m. N. of wk. — **grahaṇa**, n. (ifc. f. *ā*) = -*graha*, GṛS.; MBh.; Kāv. &c.; -*mantra*, m. a nuptial verse or hymn, MBh.; Hariv.; -*saṃskāra*, m. the ceremony of h°-taking, Mn. iii, 43. — **grahaṇika**, mfn. relating to marriage, nuptial, Mn.; MBh.; n. a wedding present, MBh. — **grahaṇīya**, mfn. id., Gobh.; (*ā*), f. N. of RV. x, 85, 36 &c., ib. — **grahītṛi**, m. 'h°-taker,' a bridegroom, husband, MBh. — **grāha**, m. id., ib.; Mn.; Gobh.; h°-taking, marriage, W.; (*am*), ind. taking by the h°, Śiś.; -*vat*, m. a bridegroom, Sāy. — **grāhaka**, m. = -*grahītṛi*, Daś. — **gha**, m. 'striking with the hand,' a drummer or one who plays upon any hand-instrument; a workman or handicraftsman, L. (cf. Pāṇ. iii, 2, 55). — **ghāta**, m. a blow with the h°, Siddh.; a boxer, W.; (*am*), ind. striking with the h° upon (acc.), Pāṇ. iii, 4, 37, Sch. — **ghná**, m. one who clasps the h°s, VS. — **candra**, m. N. of a king, Buddh. — **cāpala** (Gaut.), °**lya** (Yājñ.), n. fidgeting with the h°s, snapping the fingers &c. — **ja**, m. 'h°-grown,' a finger-nail, Gīt.; Unguis Odoratus, L. — **tala**, n. the palm of the h°, ĀśvŚr.; Mn.; MBh. &c.; a partic. weight (= 2 Tolakas), L. — **tāla**, m. (in music) a partic. measure, MBh. — **dharma**, m. form of marriage, MBh. — **ṃ-dhama**, mfn. crowded (as a path, where a person blows into his hands to make a noise and attract notice), Kāś. on Pāṇ. iii, 2, 37. — **ṃ-dhaya**, mfn. drinking out of the h°'s, Vop. — **pallava**, m. n. 'h°-twig,' the fingers, MW. — **pātra**, mfn. the h° as a drinking-vessel, ĀruṇUp.; mfn. drinking out of the h°, Bhartṛ. — **pāda**, n. sg. (Āpast.), m. pl. (Suśr.) the h°s and feet; -*capala*, mfn. fidgeting with the h°'s and f°, Mn. iv, 177. — **pīḍana**, n. pressing the h° (of a bride), marriage, Kāv.; Hcat. — **puṭa**, °**ṭaka**, m. or n. the hollow of the h°, Kāv. — **pūra**, mfn. filling the h°; °*rânna*, n. a handful of food, Yājñ. — **praṇayin**, mfn. loved by (i.e. being or resting in) the h° (°*yi-tāṃ sam-upâ-√gam*, to be taken in the h°), Rājat.; (*inī*), f. a wife, ib. — **pradāna**, n. giving the h° (in confirmation of a promise), R. — **bandha**, m. junction of the h°s (in marriage), MBh. — **bhuj**, m. Ficus Glomerata, L. — **mat**, mfn. possessed of h°s, MBh. — **marda**, m. 'rubbing the h° (?),' Carissa Carandas (= *kara-m*°), L.; (*am*), ind. by rubbing with the h°s, Car. — **mānikā**, f. a partic. weight (= -*tala*), ŚārṅgS. — **mita**, mfn. measured or measurable with the h°s, very thin or slender (as a waist), Mālav. — **mukta**, n. (sc. *astra*) a weapon thrown with the h°, a dart, spear, L. — **mukha**, mfn. whose mouth is the h°, ĀśvGṛ. — **mūla**, n. 'h°-root,' the wrist, L. — **ruh** or -**ruha**, m. = -*ja*, L. — **rekhā**, f. a line on the h°, MBh. — **vāda**, m. = -*ghná*, L. (also °*daka*, R.); n. clapping the h°s together, R. — **saṃgraha**, m., °**haṇa**, n. clasping the h° (in confirmation of a promise), R. — **saṃghaṭṭana**, n. = -*pīḍana*, Prasannar. — **sargya**, mfn. twisted with the h°s (as a rope), Pāṇ. iii, 1, 124, Vārtt. 1, Pat. — **stha**, mfn. being or held in the h°, Mn. iv, 74. — **svanika**, m. one who clasps the h°s together, MBh. — **hatā**, f. (sc. *push-kariṇī*) N. of a lake (which the gods created for Gautama Buddha with a stroke of the h°), Lalit.

Pāṇika, ifc. (f. *ā*) = 2. *pāṇi*, the hand, Hcat.; m. N. of one of Skanda's attendants, MBh. (v. l. *kālika*); (*ā*), f. a kind of song or singing, Yājñ.; a kind of spoon, L.

Pāṇin, ifc. = 2. *pāṇi*, the hand, MBh.; R. &c.; m. pl. N. of a family reckoned among the Kauśikas, Hariv.; VP.

Pāṇī, in comp. for 2. *pāṇi*. — **tala**, n. a partic. measure (= *pāṇi-t*°), L.

Pāṇau, loc. of 2. *pāṇi* in comp. — **karaṇa**, n. the taking (of a bride) by the hand, marrying, Naish.

Pāṇy, in comp. for 2. *pāṇi* before vowels. — **āsya**, mfn. = *pāṇi-mukha*, ŚāṅkhGṛ.; Mn. — **upakarsham**, ind. drawing near with the hand, Pāṇ. iii, 4, 49, Kāś. — **upaghātam**, ind. = *pāṇi-ghātam*, Pāṇ. iii, 4, 37, Vārtt. 2, Pat.

1. **Pāṇyà**, mf(*â*)n. (for 2. see p. 616) belonging to the hand, ŚBr.; m. patr. — **kauṇḍinya**, Cat.

पाणिन *pāṇina*, m. patr. fr. *paṇin*, Pāṇ. vi, 4, 165 (prob. = next; cf. iv, 1, 166; Kāś. on ii, 4, 21 and vi, 2, 14).

Pāṇini, m. (according to Pāṇ. iv, 1, 95 patr. fr. *pāṇina*) N. of the most eminent of all native Sanskrit grammarians (he was the author of the *Ashṭâdhyāyī* and supposed author of sev. other works, viz. the Dhātu-pāṭha, Gaṇa-pāṭha, Liṅgânuśāsana and Śikshā; he was a Gāndhāra and a native of Śalātura, situated in the North-West near Attok and Peshawar [see iv, 3, 94 and Śālāturīya]; he lived after Gautama Buddha but B.C. and is regarded as an inspired Muni; his grandfather's name was Devala and his mother's Dākshī [see s. v. and Dāksheya]); of a poet (by some identified with the grammarian). — **kṛiti**, f., Pāṇ. vi, 2, 151, Sch. — **darśana**, n. N. of ch. of Sarvad. — **sūtra-vṛitti**, -**vyākaraṇa-dīpikā**, f., -**sūtra-vṛitty-artha-saṃgraha**, m. N. of wks.

Pāṇinīya, mfn. relating to Pāṇini, written or

composed by P° &c.; m. a disciple or follower of P° (or Pāṇina, iv, 3, 99, Sch.) and his grammar, iv, 2, 64, Sch.; n. (with or sc. *vyākaraṇa*) the system or grammar of P°, iv, 2, 66; 3, 115, Sch.; Śiś.; Kathās.; Hcat. **-mata-darpaṇa**, m., **-liṅgânuśāsana**, n., **-śikshā**, f., **-sūtra**, n. and **-sūtra-sāra-kośa**, m. N. of wks.

पाणीतक *pāṇītaka*, m. N. of one of Skanda's attendants, MBh.; pl. of a people, VP. (v. l. *karīti*).

पाण्ट *pāṇṭa*, (prob.) w. r. for *phāṇṭa*, Vait.

पाण्ड *pāṇḍa*, m. (ī, f.), g. *gaurâdi;* w. r. for *pāṇḍya* and *pāṇḍu*. **-rāja-yaśo-bhūshaṇa**, n. N. of wk.; Cat. (w. r. for *pāṇḍya-r°*?)

पाण्डक *pāṇḍaka*, m. N. of a teacher, VāyuP.

पाण्डर *pāṇḍara, pāṇḍava*. See under *pāṇḍu*.

पाण्डित्य *pāṇḍitya*, n. (fr. *paṇḍita*) n. scholarship, erudition, learning, cleverness, skill, ŚPr.; MBh.; Kāv. &c. **-darpaṇa**, m. N. of wk.

पाण्डु *pāṇḍú*, mf(=m)n. (√*paṇḍ*?) yellowish white, white, pale, ŚBr.; MBh.; Kāv. &c.; jaundiced, Car.; m. jaundice, Car.; pale or yellowish white colour, W.; a white elephant, L.; Trichosanthes Dioeca, L.; a species of shrub, L.; N. of a son of Vyāsa by the wife of Vicitra-vīrya and brother of Dhṛita-rāshṭra and Vidura (he was father of the five Pāṇḍavas), AVPariś.; MBh.; Hariv. &c.; of a son of Janam-ejaya and brother of Dhṛita-rāshṭra, MBh. i, 3745; of a son of Dhātṛi by Āyati, VP. (v.l. *prāṇa*); of an attendant of Śiva, L.; of a Nāga-rāja, L.; pl. of a people in Madhya-deśa, VarBṛS (v.l. *pāṇḍya* and °*dva*); f. Glycine Debilis, L. **-kaṇṭaka**, m. Achyranthes Aspera, L. **-kambala**, m. a white woollen covering or blanket, a warm upper garment, R.; the housings of a royal elephant, W.; a kind of stone, L.; *-śilā*, f. N. of a part of the heavenly Paradise, Divyâv.; *-saṃvṛita* (R.); °*lin* (Pāṇ. iv, 2, 11), mfn. covered or lined with a white woollen blanket. **-karaṇa** or **-karman**, n. (in med.) making or rendering white, Suśr. **-gātra**, mfn. 'pale-bodied,' pale, white; *-tā*, f. paleness, Suśr. **-cchattra**, Nom. P. °*trati*, to resemble a yellow umbrella, Prasannar. **-cchāya**, mfn. white-coloured, Megh. **-taru**, m. Anogeissus Latifolia, L. **-tā**, f., **-tva**, n. whitish-yellow colour, paleness, MBh.; Suśr. &c. **-tīrtha**, n. N. of a sacred bathing-place, ŚivaP. **-dāsa**, m. N. of the patron of Śrī-dhara, Cat. **-dukūla**, n. a white winding-sheet, Lalit.; *-śivana*, n. 'sewing of the wh° w°-sh°,' N. of a place (where Gautama Buddha made a wh° w°-sh°), ib. **-nāga**, m. a wh° elephant, W.; Rottlera Tinctoria, L. **-pattra**, n. a pale leaf (°*trôdara*, n. a calyx of p° leaves), Śak.; mfn. having p° l°s (*-tā*, f.), Var. **-pattrī** or **-patnī**, f. a kind of fragrant substance, L. **-putra**, m. a son of Pāṇḍu, any one of the Pāṇḍava princes, MBh.; (*ī*), f. = *-pattrī*, BhP. **-pṛishṭha**, mfn. 'white-backed,' having no distinguished mark on the body, one from whom nothing great is to be expected, L. **-phala**, m. 'having yellow fruit,' Trichosanthes Dioeca, L.; (*ā*), f. a species of gourd, L.; (*ī*), f. a species of shrub, L. **-bhāva**, m. becoming yellowish-white, Suśr. **-bhūma**, m. a whitish or chalky soil, Yājñ., Sch.; mfn. = *-mṛittika*, mfn., Vop. **-mukha**, mf(*ī*)n. pale-faced, Kathās. **-mṛittika**, mfn. having a whitish or chalky soil, R.; (*ā*), f. = *-bhūma*, m., L. (also °*ka* ibc.) **-mṛid**, f. chalk, a chalky soil, L. **-raṅga**, m. a kind of vegetable, L.; N. of sev. authors, Cat.; (*ā*), f. N. of a goddess(?), ib.; *-māhātmya*, n., *-viṭṭhala stotra*, n., °*gâshṭaka*, n. N. of wks. **-rāga**, m. whiteness, pallor, W.; Artemesia Indica, L. **-rāshṭra**, m. pl. N. of a people, MBh. (v.l. *pāṃsu-r°*). **-roga**, m. 'yellow disease,' jaundice, Var.; Suśr.; *-ghna* and *-nāśana*, mfn. destroying j°, Suśr.; °*gin*, mfn. jaundiced, ib. **-lekha** or °**khya**, n. an outline or sketch made with a style or with chalk, Yājñ., Sch.; L. **-loma-parṇī** (Bhpr.), **-lomaśā** and **-lomā** (L.), f. Glycine Debilis. **-loha**, n. 'white metal,' silver, Daś. **-varṇa**, mfn. white, Nal.; m. whiteness, W. **-varma-deva**, m. N. of a prince, Inscr. **-śarkarā**, f. light-coloured gravel (the disease), GāruḍaP. **-śarmilā**, f. N. of Draupadī (the wife of the sons of Pāṇḍu), L. **-sikata**, mfn. strewn with white sand, Śak. ii, 5. **-sūdana-rasa**, m. a partic. preparation made of quicksilver, Rasêndrac. **-sopāka** or **-saupāka**, m. N. of a partic. mixed caste (the offspring of a Caṇḍāla by a Vaidehī mother), Mn. x, 37 (cf. MBh. xiii, 2588).

Pāṇḍara, mf(*ā*)n. whitish-yellow, pale, white, ŚBr. (cf. *-vāsas*) &c. &c.; m. a species of plant, L.; N. of a mountain, MārkP.; of a Nāga (also °*raka*), MBh.; of a sect (also °*raka*), L.; (*ā*), f. N. of a Buddhist Śakti or female energy, MWB. 216 (cf. *pāṇḍurā*); n. a jasmine blossom, L.; red chalk, L. **-danta**, mfn. having white teeth or tusks (elephant), R. **-dvāra-gopura**, mfn. having white doors and city gates, MBh. **-pushpikā**, f. a species of plant (= *śītalā*), L. **-bhikshu**, m. 'a white-robed mendicant,' N. of a partic. sect, L. **-vāyasa**, m. a wh° crow (= something very rare), Kautukas. **-vāsas** (*pā°*), mfn. wh°-robed, ŚBr. **-vāsin**, mfn. id. (v.l. *pāṇḍura-v°*); (*inī*), f. N. of a Buddh. Tantra deity, L. **Pāṇḍarêtara**, mfn. 'other than white,' black, dark; *-vāsas*, mfn. d°-robed, Suśr.

Pāṇḍala, prob. = °*ḍara* in comp **-meghā**, f. N. of a serpent-maid, Kāraṇḍ.

Pāṇḍava, m. a son or descendant of Pāṇḍu or a partisan of the Pāṇḍavas; (pl.) the 5 reputed sons of Pāṇḍu (Yudhi-shṭhira, Bhīma, Arjuna, Nakula and Saha-deva; cf. Kuntī and Mādrī) or their adherents, MBh.; Kāv. &c.; N. of a mountain, Lalit.; of a country, Cat.; mf(*ī*)n. belonging to or connected with the Pāṇḍavas, MBh. **-kula-prasūta**, mfn. born from the race of the Pāṇḍavas, Lalit. **-gītā**, f., **-carita**, n. N. of 2 poems. **-nakula**, m. N. of a poet, Cat. **-purāṇa**, n. N. of a Pur. **-pratāpa**, m. N. of a poem (in Prākṛit) by Śrī-dhara. **-vahni**, m. pl. 'the Pāṇḍava fires,' N. of the 3 elder sons of Pāṇḍu ('kindled on the Araṇi i.e. Pṛithā or Kuntī;' cf. *Pāṇḍavâraṇi* and *Pṛithâraṇi*), MW. **-śreshṭha**, m. 'best of the sons of Pāṇḍu,' N. of Yudhi-shṭhira, MBh. **Pāṇḍavânanda**, m. N. of a drama. **Pāṇḍavânīka**, n. the army of the Pāṇḍavas, Bhag. **Pāṇḍavâbhīla**, m. N. of Kṛishṇa, L. **Pāṇḍavâraṇi**, f. the Araṇi or mother of the Pāṇḍavas, VP. (cf. °*va-vahni*).

Pāṇḍavāyana, m. (pl.) the children of Pāṇḍu, L.; (sg.) 'friend of the Pāṇḍavas,' N. of Kṛishṇa, L.

Pāṇḍavika, m. a kind of sparrow, L.

Pāṇḍavīya, mfn. = *pāṇḍava*, mfn., MBh.

Pāṇḍaveya, mfn. id., ib.; m. a son of Pāṇḍu or an adherent of the Pāṇḍavas, ib.

Pāṇḍuka, mfn. = *pāṇḍu*, L.; m. a pale or yellowish-white colour, W.; jaundice, L.; a species of rice, Suśr. (cf. °*ḍūka*); (with Jainas) N. of one of the 9 treasures; N. of a son of Janam-ejaya and brother of Dhṛita-rāshṭra, L.; n. N. of a forest, Śatr. °**kin**, mfn. jaundiced, Suśr.

Pāṇḍura, mf(*ā*)n. whitish, white, pale, yellow, R.; Var.; Suśr. &c.; m. a form of jaundice, L.; Anogeissus Latifolia, L.; an Andropogon with white flowers, L.; N. of one of the attendants of Skanda, MBh.; (*ā*), f. Glycine Debilis, L.; of a Buddhist deity, Dharmas. iv (cf. *pāṇḍarā*); n. the white leprosy, vitiligo, L. **-tā**, f. white colour, whiteness, Pañc. **-druma**, m. Wrightia Antidysenterica, Bhpr. **-pṛishṭha**, mfn. = *pāṇḍu-p°*, L. **-phalī**, f. a species of shrub, L. **-vāsin**, mfn. white-robed, MBh. **Pāṇḍurêkshu**, m. a kind of sugar-cane, L.

Pāṇḍuraka, mf(*ikā*)n. whitish, Divyâv.

Pāṇḍuraya, Nom. P. *yati*, to colour white, Vāsav. °*rita*, mfn. white-coloured, Kād.; Bālar.

Pāṇḍuriman, m. white colour, Naish.

Pāṇḍurī-karaṇa, n. colouring white, Vcar. **-√kṛi**, to colour white, Kād.

Pāṇḍūka, m. a species of rice, Var. (cf. *pāṇḍuka*).

Pāṇḍya, m. pl. N. of a people and country in the Dekhan (also v.l. for *pāṇḍu*, m. pl. a people in Madhya-deśa), MBh.; Kāv. &c.; (sg.) a prince of the Pāṇḍyas, ib. (cf. Pāṇ. iv, 1, 168, Vārtt. 3, Pat.); N. of a son of Ākrīḍa, Hariv.; of the mountain range in the country of the P°s, MBh.; R. **-deśa**, m. the country of the P°s, Nilak. **-narêśvara**, **-nātha**, **-rāja**, **-rāshṭrâdhipa**, m. a king or sovereign of the P°s, MBh.; Hariv. &c. **-vāṭa**, m. or n. N. of a district in which pearls are found, Var.; °*ṭaka*, mfn. situated in this district, ib.

Pāṇḍv, in comp. for *pāṇḍu* before vowels. **-ari-rasa**, m. N. of a partic. medicinal preparation, L. **-avabhāsa**, mfn. appearing or looking pale, Suśr. **-āmaya**, m. 'yellow disease,' jaundice, Suśr.; °*yin*, mfn. jaundiced, ib.; Car. **-ārti**, f. = *-āmaya*, Car.

Pāṇḍvà, n. an uncoloured woollen garment, ŚBr.; m. pl. N. of a people in Madhya-deśa (v.r. for *pāṇḍu* and °*ḍya*), Var.

पाण्य 2. *pāṇya*, mfn. (√*paṇ*) praiseworthy, excellent, L. (For 1. see p. 615, col. 3.)

पात् *pāt*, m. (√*pat*) falling; sin, wickedness, W.

2. **Pāta**, m. (for 1. see under √3. *pā*) flying, mode of flying, flight, MBh.; throwing one's self or falling into (loc.) or from (abl.), fall, downfall (also ifc. after what would be a gen. or abl. &c., e.g. *gṛiha-*, fall of a house; *parvata-*, fall from a mountain; *bhū-*, fall on the earth), Mn.; MBh.; Kāv. &c.; alighting, descending or causing to descend, casting or throwing upon, cast, fall (of a thunderbolt), throw, shot, MBh.; R.; Pañcat.; a stroke (of a sword &c.), Kathās.; application (of ointment, of a knife &c.), Kāvyâd.; casting or directing (a look or glance of the eyes), Ragh.; decay of the body (= *deha-pāta*), death, Kathās.; Bādar.; (with *garbhasya*) fall of the fetus, miscarriage, Suśr.; an attack, incursion, Var.; a case, possibility, ŚāṅkhBr.; happening, occurrence, appearance, Prab.; Kathās.; Daśar.; a fault, error, mistake, Sūryas.; the node in a planet's orbit, ib. (cf. IW. 179); a malignant aspect, ib.; N. of Rāhu, L.; pl. N. of a school of the Yajur-veda, ib. **-bheda**, m. = *tāla-kāla-kriyā-viśesha*, L. **-sāriṇī**, f. N. of wk. **Pātâṇḍinīya** (fr. *pāta* + ?) N. of a school of the Yajur-veda, Āryav. **Pātâdhikārôdāharaṇa**, n. N. of wk.

Pātaka, mfn. causing to fall (see *garbha-*); n. (rarely m.; ifc. f. *ā*) 'that which causes to fall or sink,' sin, crime, loss of caste, GṛŚrS.; Mn.; MBh. &c. **-yoga**, m. incurring guilt, acting sinfully, W.

Pātakin, mfn. guilty of a crime, wicked, sinful, a sinner (°*ki-tva*, n.), Hariv.; Kāv.; Pur. &c.

Pātana, mf(*ī*)n. (fr. Caus.) causing to fall, felling, laying low, striking off or down (with gen. or ifc.), MBh.; Hariv.; MārkP.; n. the act of causing to fall &c.; lowering, humbling, W.; the act of casting (as dice or a glance of the eyes), Kathās. (cf. *aksha-*); (with *daṇḍasya*) causing the rod to fall, chastising, punishing, Mn.; (with *garbhasya*) causing the fall of the fetus or abortion, Yājñ.; (with *jalaukasām*) application of leeches, Suśr.; removing, bringing away, ib.; causing to fall asunder, dividing, Saṃk.; N. of a partic. process to which minerals (esp. quicksilver) are subjected, Sarvad.

Pātanikā, f. fitness, correspondence, Bhāmatī.

Pātanīya, mfn. to be caused to fall upon, to be thrown or shot at (loc.), Śak. i, 10 (v.l.)

Pātayitṛi, mfn. one who causes to fall, thrower of (dice &c.), Pāṇ. ii, 1, 10, Sch.

Pātāla, n. (rarely m.; ifc. f. *ā;* perhaps fr. 2. *pāta* as *antarāla* fr. *antar;* cf. Uṇ. i, 116) one of the 7 regions under the earth and the abode of the Nāgas or serpents and demons (cf. RTL. 102, n. 1 &c.; sometimes used as a general N. for the lower regions or hells; in MBh. also N. of a town in the serpent-world), ĀruṇUp.; MBh.; Kāv. &c.; an excavation, hole in the earth, MBh.; the submarine fire, L.; (in astrol.) the fourth house, Var.; N. of a Tīrtha, Cat.; m. = *-yantra* below, L.; (in astron.) N. of Jupiter's year of 361 days; (in music) a kind of measure; N. of the attendant of the 14th Arhat of present Ava-sarpiṇī. **-ketu**, m. N. of a Daitya prince, Prab. **-khaṇḍa**, m. or n. N. of ch. of SkandaP. **-gaṅgā**, f. the Ganges which flows through Pātāla, MW. **-garuḍâhvaya**, m., **-garuḍī**, f. a species of creeper, Bhpr.; L. **-tala**, n. the bottom of P° (°*lam*, ind. down to P°), Hcar. **-nagarī**, f. a town in P°, Kathās. **-nilaya**, m. an inhabitant of P°, an Asura, L.; a serpent, L. **-prastha**, n. N. of a village of the Bāhikas (°*thika*, mfn.), Pat. **-bhogi-varga**, m. N. of ch. of Amara-siṃha. **-yantra**, n. a sort of apparatus for distillation or for calcining and subliming metals, L. **-varṇana**, n. 'description of P°,' N. of ch. of the Pātāla-khaṇḍa. **-vāsin**, m. = *-nilaya*, MW. **-vijaya**, m. 'victory over P°,' N. of a poem.

Pātālâukas, m. an inhabitant of Pātāla, an Asura, L.

Pātika, m. Delphinus Gangeticus, L.

Pātita, mfn. (fr. Caus.) made to fall, felled, struck down, lowered, depressed, overthrown, R.; Kālid. &c.

Pātitya, n. (fr. *patita*) loss of position or caste, degradation, Pur.; Kull.

Pātin, mfn. flying, MBh.; Kāv. &c; falling, sinking, Megh.; Kathās.; rising, appearing, Kathās.; being in (cf. *antaḥ-* and *eka-*); causing to fall, throwing down, emitting (comp.), MBh.; Var.; Rājat.

Pātuka, mfn. falling or apt to fall (=*patana-śīla*, Pāṇ. iii, 2, 154); falling down, Śiś. iii, 3; losing caste or going to the lower regions, MBh. xii, 3444; m. a precipice, L.; an aquatic animal (=*jala-hastin*), L.; N. of a poet, Cat.

1. **Pātya**, mfn. to be felled or caused to fall; to be inflicted or imposed (as a penalty), R.

पातंग *pātaṃga*, mf(*ī*)n. (fr. *pataṃ-ga*) belonging to or peculiar to a grasshopper or moth, Rājat.; brown, MBh. vi, 422.

Pātaṃgi, m. 'the son of the Sun,' N. of the planet Saturn, Var.; Sch.

पातञ्जल *pātañjala*, mf(*ī*)n. composed by Patañjali; m. a follower of the Yoga system of P°, Cat.; n. the Y° s° of P°, ib. (also °*līya*, n.); the Mahā-bhāshya of P°, ib. — **tantra**, n., -**darśana**, n., -**bhāshya**, n. (-*vārttika*, n.), -**rahasya**, n., -**sūtra-bhāshya-vyākhyā**, f., -**sūtra-vṛitti-bhāshya-cchāyā-vyākhyā**, f. N. of wks.

Pātañjali, m., v.l. for *Pat°*.

पातत्रिण *pātatriṇa*, mfn. containing the word *patatrin*, g. *vimuktâdi*.

पातल्य *pātalyà*, n. du. a partic. part of a carriage (=*kīlaka*, Sāy.), RV. iii, 53, 7.

पातसाह *pātasāha*, m.=پادشاہ, a king, Cat.

पाति *pāti*, m.=*pati*, a master, lord, husband, Uṇ. v, 5, Sch.

Pātivratya, n. (fr. *pati-vratā*) devotedness to a husband, conjugal fidelity, BhP.

Pātnī, Vṛiddhi form of *patnī* (f. of *pati*) in comp. — **vatá**, mfn. belonging to Agni *patnī-vat* (s.v.), VS.; TS.; Br.; ŚrS.; containing the word *patnī-vat*, ŚāṅkhBr. — **śāla**, mfn. being in the *patnī-śālā* (s.v.), Lāṭy.

2. **Pātya**, n. (for 1. see above) dominion, MBh.

पातिली *pātilī*, f. (only L.; fr. √*pat*?), a trap or snare for catching deer; a small earthen pot (used by mendicants); a woman of a partic. class.

पातृ 3. *pātṛi*, m. (for 1. 2. see under √1. and 3. *pā*) a species of Ocimum, L.

पात्तिगणक *pāttigaṇaka*, n., fr. *patti-gaṇaka*, g. *udgātr-ādi*.

पात्त्रिक्य *pāttrikya*, n. (fr. *pattrika*), g. *purohitâdi* (Kāś.)

पात्र 1. 2. *pātra*. See √1. and 3. *pā*.

पात्रट *pātraṭa*, mfn. spare, thin, L.; m. a ragged garment (*karpaṭa*) or a cup, pot (*karpara*), L.

पाथ *pātha*, m.=*patha*, g. *jvalâdi*; fire, L.; the sun, L.; n. water, L.; N. of 2 Sāmans, ĀrshBr.

Pā́thas, n. a spot, place, RV.; AV.; Br.; ŚrS.; food, Nir. viii, 17; air, ib. vi, 7; water, Kāv.; Rājat. — **pati**, m. 'lord of the water,' N. of Varuṇa, Kathās.

Pāthika, m., °**kya**, n. (fr. *pathika*), g. *śivâdi* and *purohitâdi*.

Pāthikārya, m. patr. fr. *pathi-kara*, g. *kurv-ādi*.

Pā́this, n.=*pāthas*, KapS. (°*thas*, MaitrS.); =*kīlāla*, L.; n. the sea or the eye, Uṇ. ii, 115, Sch.

Pātheya, n. (fr. *pathin*) provender or provisions &c. for a journey, viaticum, MBh.; Kāv. &c.; =*pāthona*, Jyot. — **vat**, mfn. furnished with provisions for a journey, provisioned, Megh. — **śrāddha**, n. a kind of meal at a Śrāddha, Cat.

Pātheyaka, mfn., g. *dhūmâdi*.

Pātho, in comp. fo °*thas*. — **ja**, n. 'water-born,' a lotus, Kāv.; Rājat.; -°*jinī*, f. the l°-plant, Prasannar. — **da** and -**dhara**, m. 'w°-giver and -holder,' a cloud, Vcar. — **dhi**, m. 'w°-receptacle,' the sea, ib. — **nātha**, m.=*pāthas-pati*, Mcar. — **nidhi**, m. =-*dhi*, L. — **bhāj**, mfn. possessing room or space, ŚāṅkhBr. — **ruha**, n. 'water-grown,' a lotus, L.

Pāthyá, mfn. (prob.) being in the air, heavenly, RV. vi, 16, 15 (N. of a Ṛishi, Sāy.)

पाथोन *pāthona*, m. (fr. Gk. παρθένος) the sign of the zodiac Virgo, Var. (cf. *pārthona*).

पाथ्य *pāthnya*, m. a patr. of Dadhīca, Kāṭh.

पाद् *pād* (√2. *pad*), strong base of 3. *pad*, q.v.; also ifc. (see *tri-p°*, *dvi-p°*, *su-p°*).

Pāda, m. (ifc. f. *ā*, rarely *ī*) the foot (of men and animals), RV. &c. &c. (the pl. sometimes added to proper names or titles in token of respect, e.g. *deva-pādāḥ*, 'the king's majesty,' Pañc.; *Nārāyaṇa-p°*, 'the venerable N°,' Sāh.; *pādaiḥ*, ind. on foot [said of several persons], R.; °*dayoḥ* and °*de* √*pat*, to fall at a person's [gen.] feet, Kāv.; Hit.); the foot or leg of an inanimate object, column, pillar, AV.; ŚBr.; MBh. &c.; a wheel, Śiś. xii, 21; a foot as a measure (=12 Aṅgulas), ŚBr.; ŚrS.; MārkP.; the foot or root of a tree, Var.; the foot or a hill at the f° of a mountain, MBh.; Kāv. &c.; the bottom (*dṛiteḥ pādāt*, 'from the b° of a bag,' v.l. *pātrāt*), MBh. v, 1047; a ray or beam of light (considered as the f° of a heavenly body), ib.; a quarter, a fourth part (the f° of a quadruped being one out of 4), ŚBr.; Mn.; MBh. &c. (pl. the 4 parts i.e. all things required for [gen.], Suśr.); the quadrant (of a circle), Āryabh., Sch.; a verse or line (as the fourth part of a regular stanza), Br.; ŚrS.; Prāt. &c.; the caesura of a verse, AgP.; the chapter of a book (orig. only of a book or section of a b° consisting of 4 parts, as the Adhyāyas of Pāṇini's grammar). — **kaṭaka**, m. n., -**kīlikā**, f. a foot-ring or ornament, anklet. — **kuṭhārikā**, f. a partic. position of the feet, ŚāṅkhGṛ. — **kṛic-chra**, m. 'quarter-penance,' a sort of p° (eating and fasting on alternate nights), Yājñ. — **kshepa**, m. a kick with the foot, Hariv. — **gaṇḍira**, m. swelling of the legs and feet, L. — **gṛihya**, ind. seizing by the foot, RV. — **granthi**, m. 'f°-knot,' the ankle, L. — **grahaṇa**, n. laying hold of or clasping the feet (of a Brāhman or superior, as a mark of respectful salutation), Mn.; Kum. — **ghṛita**, n. melted butter for anointing the f°, MBh. — **catura** or -**catvara**, m. (L.) a slanderer; a goat; a sand-bank; hail; Ficus Religiosa. — **cāpala** (Gaut.), °**lya** (Yājñ.), n. carelessness in placing the feet. — **cāra**, mfn. going on foot, walking, Ragh.; m. a foot-soldier, Uttarar.; walking on foot (*eṇa*, ind. on foot), MBh.; Kālid.; the daily position of the planets, W.; N. of wk. — **cārin**, mfn. going or fighting on foot, having feet, walking, moving, BhP.; Jātakam.; m. a pedestrian, foot-soldier, Kathās. — **cihna**, n. f°-mark, f°-print, MW. — **cchedana**, n. cutting off a f°, Mn. viii, 280. — **ja**, m. 'born from the f° (of Brahmā),' a Śūdra, Hariv. — 1. -**jala**, n. water for (washing) the feet, L. — 2. -**jala**, mfn. containing (i.e. mixed with) one fourth of water, Bhpr. — **jāha**, n.=-*mūla*, L. (g. -*karṇâdi*). — **tala**, n. sole of the foot, MBh.; Suśr.; (*e*), ind. (to fall) at a person's feet, Amar.; °*lâhati*, f. a kick, Kuval. — **tas**, ind. from or at or near the feet (-*taḥ* √*kṛi*, to place at the feet), ŚāṅkhGṛ.; Mn.; Kathās.; by the Pāda (i.e. quarter of a verse), RPrāt.; step by step, by degrees, Kām. — **tra**, m. or n. 'foot-covering,' a shoe, Rājat. (cf. *apa-pādatra*); -*dhāraṇa*, n. wearing shoes, Car. — **trāṇa**, n. = -*tra*, Suśr. — **dārikā** or °**rī**, f. 'feet-chap,' a chilblain, Suśr. — **dāha**, m. a burning sensation in the f°, ib. — **dhāvana**, n. washing the f°, MBh.; R.; °*nikā*, f. sand used for rubbing the f°, L. — **nakha**, m. a toe-nail, Cat. — **namra**, mfn. bowing down to the feet of any one, ML. — **nālikā**, f. an ornament for the feet, an anklet, L. — **niketa**, m. a foot-stool, BhP. — **nivṛit**, mfn. (a metre) wanting one syllable in each Pāda (w. r. -*ni-vṛit*), RPrāt. — **nishka**, m. a quarter of a Nishka (s.v.), Pāṇ. vi, 3, 56, Pat. — **nyāsa**, m. putting down or placing the feet, R.; casting rays (said of the moon), Śak.; a dance or measured step, MW. — 1. 2. -**pa**, see p. 618. — **patana**, n. falling or bowing to another's feet, Ratnāv.; Kathās. — **patita**, mfn. fallen at an°'s f°, Kathās. — **paddhati**, f. a line of footsteps, a track, trail, Pañc. — **padma**, m. 'foot-lotus,' a f° beautiful as a l°, Kāv.; N. of a teacher (=*Padma-pāda*), Cat. — **paricāraka**, m. a humble servant, Mcar. — **pāda-dhāvana**, n. washing one foot with the other, Gaut. — **pālikā**, f. an ornament for the feet, anklet, L. — **pāśa**, m. a foot-rope or an anklet, L.; (*ī*), f. id., ib.; =*khaḍuka*, ib. — **pīṭha**, m. a f°-stool, MBh.; R. &c.; (°*ṭhī*-√*kṛi*), to make into a f°-st°, Kād. — **pīṭhikā**, f. any common or vulgar trade (as that of a barber &c.), L.; white stone, W. — **pūraṇa**, mfn. filling out (a verse &c.), expletive, RPrāt.; n. the filling out a line or the measure of a verse, Pāṇ. vi, 1, 134. — **prakaraṇa-saṃgati**, f. N. of wk. — **prakshālana**, n. washing the feet, Āpast.; Gaut. — **praṇāma**, m. bowing to the feet, prostration, W. — **pratishṭhāna**, n. a foot-stool, MBh. — **pradhāraṇa**, n. 'foot-covering,' a shoe, L. — **prasāraṇa**, n. stretching out the feet, Gaut. — **prasveda**, m. perspiration of the f°, Hcat.; °*din*, mfn. suffering from it, ib. — **prahāra**, m. 'f°-blow,' a kick, Kāv. — **baddha**, mfn. bound or held together by feet, consisting of verses (as a metre), Madhus. — **bandha**, m. a tie or fetter for the feet, MBh. — **bandhana**, n. id., L.; a stock of cattle, L. — **bhaṭa**, m. a foot-soldier, Kathās. — **bhāga**, m. a fourth part, quarter, MBh.; mfn. amounting to a qu°, L. — **bhāj**, mfn. possessing a qu° i.e. being only the fourth part of (gen.) with regard to (loc.), MBh.; dividing into Pādas or verses, L. — **mañjarī**, f. N. of a treatise on RV. — **madhya-yamaka**, n. paronomasia in the middle of the 4 verses of a stanza (as in Bhaṭṭ. x, 5). — **mātra**, n the measure or distance of a foot, ŚrS.; (°*trá*), mf(*ī́*)n. a f° long, ŚBr. — **miśra**=*pan-miśra* (Pāṇ. vi, 3, 56). — **mudrā**, f. the impression of a f°-step, any mark or sign, Rājat.; -*paṅkti*, f. a line of f°-steps, a track, trail, Kathās. — **mūla**, n. 'f°-root,' the sole or heel (also as a polite designation of a person), Kāv.; Pur. (°*le ni*-√*pat*, to fall at a person's feet, R.); the foot of a mountain, Kathās. — **yamaka**, n. paronomasia within the Pādas or single verses, Vām. — **yuddha**, n. 'f°-fight,' fighting on f°, MW. — **raksha**, m. 'f°-guard;' pl. armed men who run by the side of an elephant in battle to protect its feet, MBh.; Hariv. — **rakshaṇa**, n., °**kshikā**, f. 'f°-covering,' a shoe, L. — **rajas**, n. the dust of the feet, MBh.; Mālav. — **rajju**, f. a rope or tether for the foot (of an elephant), L. — **rathī**, f. 'f°-vehicle,' a shoe, L. — **rohaṇa**, m. 'growing from roots,' the Indian fig-tree, L. — **lagna**, mfn. sticking or hanging on the feet, lying at a person's feet, Cāṇ.; Kathās. — **lipta** (and -*sūri*), m. N. of a scholar, L. — **lepa**, m. an unguent for the feet, MārkP.; -*siddhi*, f. its effect, Caṇḍ. — **vat** (*pā́da*-), mfn. having f°, AV. &c. — **vandana**, n. 'saluting the f°,' respectful saluation, Yājñ.; °*nika*, mfn. accompanied by a r° s°, L. — **valmīka**, m. elephantiasis, L. (cf. *valm°*). — **vigraha**, m. pl. (prob.) a mode of reading (cf. *pada-v°*), Hariv. 12030 (v.l. *kāma* [for *krama*?] *v°*); mfn. one-footed (opp. to *catush-pāda*), ib. 11305 &c. — **vidhāna**, n. 'arrangement of verses,' N. of a wk. ascribed to Śaunaka. — **virajas**, f. a shoe (lit. 'keeping the feet dustless'?), L. — **vṛitta**, m. N. a Svarita separated from the preceding Udātta by a hiatus, Prāt.; du. the 2 component elements of a verse, i.e. the long and short syllable, ib. — **veshṭanika**, m. or n. (and *ā*, f.) 'foot-covering,' a stocking, L. — **śabda**, m. the sound of f°-steps, Daś. — **śas**, ind. foot by f°, quarter by qu°, Mn.; MBh.; verse by v°, MānGṛ. — **śākhā**, f. 'f°-branch,' a toe, L. — **śuśrūshā**, f. obedience to (the feet of) any one (gen.), Hariv. — **śesha**, n. a quarter, fourth part (?), Hariv. 16218. — **śaila**, m. a hill at the foot of a mountain, L. — **śotha**, m. 'feet-swelling,' gout, W. — **śauca**, n. cleaning the f°, Yājñ. — **saṃhitā**, f. the junction of words in a quarter of a stanza, VPrāt. — **sevana**, n., °**vā**, f. 'foot-salutation,' service, duty, Kāv. — **stambha**, m. a supporting beam, pillar, post, Yājñ., Sch. — **sphoṭa**, m. a sore or ulcer on the foot, L. — **svedana**, n. causing perspiration in the feet; °*nika*, mfn. produced by it, g. *aksha-dyūtâdi*. — **harsha**, m. numbness of the f°, Suśr. — **hāraka**, mfn. taken away with the f°, Pāṇ., Sch.; m. a stealer with the f° (?), W. — **hīnāt**, ind. without division or transition, Suśr. **Pādâṃśika**, mfn. greater or smaller by a part, Car. **Pādâkulaka**, n. N. of 2 kinds of metre, Col. **Pādâgra**, n. the point or extremity of the foot; -*sthita*, mfn. standing on tip-toe, Ratnāv. **Pādâghāta**, m. 'f°-blow,' a kick, Kathās. **Pādâṅgada**, n., °*dī*, f. 'f°-ring,' an anklet, L. **Pādâṅgulīyaka**, n. a toe-ring, L. **Pādâṅgushṭha**, m. 'f°-thumb,' the great toe, MBh.; -*śritâvani*, mfn. touching the ground with the toes, on tip-toe, MW.; °*thikā*, f. a ring worn on the great toe, W. **Pādâdi** (ibc.), the beginning of a verse; -*madhya-yamaka*, n. paronomasia at the b° and in the middle of a verse (as Bhaṭṭ. x, 15); -*yamaka*, n. p° at the b° of a v° (ib. x, 4); °*dy-anta-yamaka*, n. p° at the b° and end of a v° (ib. x, 11). **Pādâdhishṭhāna**, n. a foot-stool, L. **Pādâdhyāsa**, m. treading upon, kicking, W. **Pādânata**, mfn.=°*da-namra*, ib. **Pādânukramaṇī**, f. N. of wk. **Pādânudhyāta** or °**dhyāna**, mfn. 'thought of by (the feet of) such a one,' the rightful successor of any one (thought of by his predecessor), Inscr. **Pādânuprāsa**, m. alliteration in verses, Vām. **Pādânta**, m. extremity of the feet (°*te*, at a person's f°), Amar.; a claw, Pañc.; the end of a verse; -*yamaka*, n. paronomasia at the end of a verse (as Bhaṭṭ. x, 3). **Pādântara,** n. the interval of a step; °*re,* ind. close by (with gen.), MBh.; after the int° of a step, Śak. (v. l. for *pad°*). **Pādântikam,** ind. near to or towards (the feet of) any one, MārkP. **Pādâbhivandana** or °**vādana,** n. = °*da-vandana,* R. **Pādâmbu,** mfn. containing a fourth part of water, L. **Pādâmbhas,** n. water for washing the feet, Yājñ. **Pādâravinda,** m. 'foot-lotus,' the foot of a deity or a lover &c., Kāv.; *-śataka,* n. N. of a poem. **Pādârghya,** n. 'offering to the feet,' a donation to Brāhmans or other venerable persons, W. **Pādârdha,** n. half a quarter, an eighth, Mn. viii, 404; half a line of a stanza, W. **Pādârpaṇa,** n. putting down or placing the feet, Ragh. **Pādâvanāma,** m. bowing to a person's feet, Śiś. **Pādâvanektṛi,** m. one who washes another's f°, Āpast. **Pādâvaneja** (!), m. washing another's f°, BhP. **Pādâvanejana,** mf(*ī*)n. used for washing the f°, AitBr.; Mn. &c.; (*ī*), f. pl. water for w° the f°, BhP. **Pādâvanejya,** n. = °*ja,* TāṇḍBr. **Pādâvarta,** m. a wheel worked by the f° for raising water from a well, L.; a square foot, KātyŚr., Sch. **Pādâvasecana,** n. water used for washing the feet, Mn. iv, 151. **Pādâshṭhīla,** m. or n. the ankle, MBh. **Pādâsana,** n. a footstool, W. **Pādâsphālana,** n. trampling or shuffling of the feet, floundering, W. **Pādâhata,** mfn. kicked or trodden by the foot, W. **Pādâhati,** f. 'f°-blow,' a kick, treading, trampling &c., Ratnâv.; Kathās. **Pādêshṭakā,** f. the quarter of a brick, Śulbas. **Pādôtphāla,** m. shuffling or moving the feet, MW. **Pādôdaka,** n. 'f°-water,' water used for washing the feet, MBh. &c.; *-tīrtha,* n. N. of a Tīrtha, Cat. **Pādôdara,** m. a serpent ('using the belly in place of feet'), PraśnUp. **Pādôddhūta,** n. stamping the f°, MBh.; VP. **Pādôna,** mfn. less or smaller by a quarter, Āpast. **Pādôpajīvin,** mfn. 'living by a person's mercy (lit. feet),' a servant, messenger &c., Divyâv. **Pādôpadhāna,** n., °**nī,** f. a cushion for the f°, MBh. **Pādôpasaṃgrahaṇa,** n. clasping the f° (of a teacher), Gaut.

Pādaká, m. a small foot, RV. viii, 33, 19; (*ikā*), f. a sandal, shoe, L.; ifc. (f. *ikā*) = foot, R.; Kathās.; mf(*ikā*)n. making a quarter of anything, Var.

1. **Pāda-pa** (√1. *pā*), m. (ifc. f. *ā*) 'drinking at foot or root,' a tree, plant, MBh.; Kāv. &c. (*-ka,* id. ifc., Kathās.) **-khaṇḍa,** m. a grove of trees, L. **-ruhā,** f. Vanda Roxburghii, L. **-vivakshā,** f. N. of wk. **Pādapôpagata,** mfn. abiding under a tree (while expecting death), HPariś. **Pādapôpagamana,** n. the abiding &c. (see prec.), ib.

2. **Pāda-pa** (√3. *pā*), m. a foot-stool or cushion for the feet, L.; (*ā*), f. a shoe, slipper, L.

Pādaya, Nom. P. °*yati,* to stretch out the feet, Dhātup. xxxv, 85.

Pādavika, m. a traveller, L.

Pādāt, m. a foot-soldier, footman, L.

Pādāta, m. id., MBh.; R. &c.; n. infantry, MBh. (g. *bhikshâdi*).

Pādāti and °**tika,** m. = *pādāt,* L. (cf. *padāti*).

Pādāyana, m. patr. fr. *pāda,* g. *aśvâdi.*

Pādāvika, m. = *pādātika,* L.

Pādika, mf(*ī*)n. lasting for a quarter of the time, Mn. iii, 1; amounting to ¼ (n. with *śata,* 25 per cent, MBh.; with or sc. *ahar,* daily wages, Pat.); versed in or studying the Pada-pātha, g. *ukthâdi,* Kāś.

Pādin, mfn. footed, having feet (see m.); having Pādas (as a stanza), W.; claiming or receiving a fourth part, ŚrS.; Mn. viii, 210; m. a footed aquatic or amphibious animal, Suśr.; the heir to a fourth part of an estate, W.

Pādú, m. a foot, RV. (cf. Nir. iv, 15); a place, MānGṛ.

Pāduka, mf(*ā* or *ī*)n. going on foot or with feet, W.; (*ā*), f., see next.

Pādukā, f. a shoe or slipper, MBh.; Kāv. &c. (also °*ka,* m. c. and in °*ka-vat,* mfn. having shoes, Hcat.); impression of the feet of a god or a holy person, MWB. 508; (?) N. of Durgā or another deity (cf. comp. below). **-kāra** or **-kṛit,** m. a shoemaker, L. **-mantra,** m., **-sahasra,** n., **-sahasra-parīkshā,** f. N. of wks.

Pādukin, mfn. having shoes, shoed, Āpast.

Pādū, f. a shoe or slipper, L. **-kṛit,** m. a shoemaker, Rājat.; L. (also spelt °*du-kṛit*).

Pādūna, mfn. less or smaller by a quarter, L. (cf. *pādôna*).

Pādūlaka, m. a broom, ĀpGṛ., Sch.

Pāde-gṛihya, ind. = °*da-gṛihya,* g. *mayūra-vyaṃsakâdi.*

Pádya, mf(*ā*)n. relating or belonging to the foot, Br.; ŚrS. (n. with or sc. *udaka,* water used for washing the feet, ib. &c.); amounting to a quarter of anything, Śulbas.

Pādyaka, mfn. = *pādya-prakāra,* g. *sthūlâdi.*

पादक्रमिक *pādakramika,* mfn. (fr. *pada-krama*) one who recites or knows the Pada-krama, g. *ukthâdi* (Kāś. *pada, krama* for *pada-k°*).

पादव्याख्यान *pāda-vyākhyāna,* mfn. (fr. *pada-v°*), g. *ṛig-ayanâdi.*

पादारक *pādāraka,* m. the masts or ribs of a boat, L.

पादालिक *pādālika,* m. = *dhundhu-māra,* L. (v. l. *pad°*).

पादालिन्द *pādālinda,* m. = *pādāraka,* L.; (*ī*), f. a boat, L.

पाद्धत *pāddhata,* n. (fr. *pad-dhati*), g. *bhikshâdi.*

पाद्म *pādma,* mf(*ī*)n. (fr. *padma*) relating to or treating of the lotus, Pur.; m. N. of a Kalpa or cosmic period, ib.; of Brahmā, ib.; n. = *padma-purāṇa.* **-nitya-pūjā-vidhi,** m. N. of wk. **-purāṇa,** n. = *padma-p°.* **-prayoga,** m., **-maṇḍalârcana,** n., **-mantra,** m., **-vacana,** n., **-veda-mantra,** m., **-saṃhitā,** f. (°*tā-prayoga,* m.) N. of wks. or ch°s of wks. **Pādmôttara,** n. (prob.) = Padma-P° ii.

पान 1. 2. *pāna.* See p. 613, cols. 1 and 2.

पान 3. *pāna,* m. = *apāna,* breathing out, expiration, L.

पानस *pānasa,* mf(*ī*)n. (fr. *panasa*) prepared from the fruit of the Jaka or bread-fruit tree, Kull. on Mn. xi, 95.

पान्थ *pāntha,* m. (fr. *panthan*) a wanderer, traveller, MBh.; Kāv. &c. (ifc. [f. *ā*] = accompanying, not moving from, Naish.); the sun (as the wanderer in the sky), L. **-tva,** n. the life of a wanderer, Kathās. **-devatā,** f. pl. N. of a partic. class of deities, Hcat.

Pānthâyana, mfn., g. *pakshâdi.*

पान्नग *pānnaga,* mf(*ī*)n. (fr. *panna-ga*) formed or consisting of snakes, having serpents, snaky, Hariv.

पान्नागार *pānnāgāra,* mfn., fr. next, Pāṇ. iv, 2, 113, Sch.

Pānnāgāri, m. patr. fr. *pannâgāra,* ib. iv, 2, 60, Sch.

पान्नेजन *pānnéjana,* mf(*ī*)n. (fr. *pan-nejana*) used for washing the feet, KātyŚr.; n. a vessel in which the feet are washed, ŚBr.; KātyŚr.

पाप *pāpá* (ŚBr. xiv, also *pā́pa*), mf(*ī* older than *ā*; cf. Pāṇ. iv, 1, 30)n. bad, vicious, wicked, evil, wretched, vile, low, RV. &c. &c.; (in astrol.) boding evil, inauspicious, Var.; m. a wicked man, wretch, villain, RV. &c. &c.; N. of the profligate in a drama, Cat.; of a hell, VP.; (*ā*), f. a beast of prey or a witch, Hcat.; n. (ifc. f. *ā*) evil, misfortune, ill-luck, trouble, mischief, harm, AV. &c. &c. (often *śāntam pāpam,* 'heaven forefend that evil!' R.; Mṛicch.; Kālid. &c.); sin, vice, crime, guilt, Br.; Mn.; MBh. &c.; (*ám*), ind. badly, miserably, wrongly, AV.; (*áyā*), ind. id., RV.; AV.; *pāpáyāmuyā,* so badly, so vilely, ib. **-kara** and **-kartṛi,** mfn. 'wrong-doing,' wicked, sinful, W. **-karman,** mfn. id.; m. an ill-doer, criminal, sinner, Mn.; MBh. &c.; n. a wicked deed, °*ma-kṛit,* mfn. wicked, an ill-doer, R. **-karmin,** mfn. 'wrong-doing,' wicked, a villain or sinner, MārkP. **-kalpa,** m. a rogue or villain, Mṛicch. **-kāraka** (Kautukas.), **-kārin** (ŚBr. &c.), **-kṛit** (AV. &c., superl. *-tama,* Mn.; Bhag.), mfn. = *-karmin.* **-kṛita,** n. an evil deed, sin, crime, Nal. **-kṛitya,** Nom. P. °*yati* (fr. *-kṛit*), to do wrong, Pat. **-kṛityā,** f. an evil deed, sin, crime, AV. &c. &c. **-kṛitvan,** m. an evil-doer, sinner, villain, AV. **-kshaya,** m. destruction of sin; *-tīrtha,* n. N. of a Tīrtha, SkandaP. **-gati,** m. ill-fated, R. **-gocara,** mfn. evidently involved in (the consequences of) sin, W. **-graha,** m. an inauspicious planet (as Mars, Saturn, Rāhu, Ketu), Var. **-ghna,** mf(*ī*)n. destroying sin or evil, L.; m. a sesamum plant, L.; (*ī*), f., see under *-han.* **-cara,** m. 'walking in sin,' N. of a king in a play, Cat. **-cārin,** mfn. wrong-doing, criminal, MBh. **-cetas,** mfn. evil-minded, wicked, Mn.; MBh. **-celikā** or °**lī,** f. Clypea Hernandifolia, L. **-caila,** n. an inauspicious garment, Kauś. **-ja,** mfn. springing from evil, MW. **-jīva,** mfn. leading an evil life, a villain, BhP. **-tara,** mfn. worse, more or very wicked, MBh. &c. **-tā,** f. inauspiciousness, VarBṛS., Sch. **-timira,** mfn. sin-bedarkened, blinded by sin, MW. **-tvá,** n. evil condition, misery, poverty, RV. **-da,** mfn. bringing misfortune, inauspicious, Var. **-darśana** or °**śin,** mfn. looking at faults, malevolent, R. **-dṛiśvan,** mfn. seeing guilt, knowing an act to be wicked, W. **-deśanā,** f. instruction of the wicked, Dharmas. xix. **-dṛishṭi,** mfn. evil-eyed, MW. **-dhī,** mfn. evil-minded, Nir. **-nakshatra,** n. an inauspicious constellation, Kauś. **-nāpita,** m. a vile or bad barber, W. **-nāman** (*pāpá-*), mfn. having a bad name, ŚBr. **-nāśana,** m. 'destroying the wicked,' N. of Śiva, Śivag.; N. of a temple of Vishṇu; *-māhātmya,* n. N. of wk. **-nāśin,** mfn. sin-destroying, purifying, W. **-nirati,** mfn. 'delighting in sin,' wicked, a wretch, W.; f. attachment to evil, wickedness, ib. **-niścaya,** mfn. having evil designs, malevolent, MBh.; R. **-nishkṛiti,** f. atonement for sin, MW. **-pati,** m. 'sinful master,' a paramour, L. **-parājita** (*pāpá-*), mfn. ignominiously defeated, TBr. **-puṇya,** n. pl. vicious or virtuous (deeds), MW. **-purī,** v. l. for *a-pāpap°* (cf. *pāpā-purī*). **-purusha,** m. a villainous man (a personification of all sin or archetype of a sinner), Tantras. **-pūrusha,** m. a villain, rascal, Mn. **-praśamana-stava,** m. N. of wk. **-priya,** mfn. fond of evil, prone to sin, Veṇīs. **-phala,** mfn. having evil consequences, inauspicious, Var. **-bandha,** m. a continuous series of misdeeds, VP. **-buddhi,** f. evil intent, R.; mfn. evil-minded, wicked, Mn.; MBh.; m. N. of a man, Pañc. **-bhakshaṇa,** m. 'devouring the wicked,' N. of Kāla-bhairava (a son of Śiva), Cat. **-bhañjana,** m. 'breaking the w°,' N. of a Brāhman, Kathās. **-bhāj,** mfn. partaking of sin, guilty, Kum. **-bhāva,** mfn. evil-minded, MW. **-mati,** mfn. id., Nal. **-maya,** mf(*ī*)n. consisting in evil, bad, Jātak. **-mitra,** n. a friend of sin; *-tva,* n. friendship with the wicked, L. **-mukta,** mfn. freed from sin, purified, W. **-mocana,** n. liberating from sin; N. of a Tīrtha, VP.; (*ī*), f. (with *ekādaśī*) N. of wk. **-yakshmá,** m. 'the evil disease,' consumption, TS. (also °*man,* Var.; Hcat.); *-gṛihīta* (°*kshmá-*), mfn. seized by cons°, ib. **-yoni,** f. a bad or low birthplace (lit. 'womb,' as punishment of sin), Mn. iv, 166. **-rahita,** mfn. free from guilt, harmless, Hit. **-rākshasī,** f. an evil female demon, witch, ĀśvGṛ. **-ripu,** m. or n. 'enemy of sin,' N. of a sacred bathing-place, Kathās. **-roga,** m. any bad disease (considered as the penalty of sin in a former life), Gobh.; Mn.; smallpox, L.; hemorrhoids, Gal.; °*gin,* mfn. suffering from a bad d° (cf. above), Mn. **-rddhi** (*r* for *ṛi*), f. 'sin-thriving,' hunting, chase, Vcar.; Pañc.; °*dhika,* m. a hunter, Nalac. **-loká,** m. the evil world, place of suffering or of the wicked, AV.; °*kya,* mf(*ā*)n. belonging to it, hellish, infernal, MBh. **-vasīyas,** mfn. 'bad-better,' inverted, confused, Gobh.; Pañc.; n. = next. **-vasīyasa** (Kāṭh.; TāṇḍBr.), **-vasyasá** (TS.; ŚBr. &c.), n. inversion, confusion. **-vādá,** m. an inauspicious cry (of a bird), AV. **-vināśa,** m. destruction of sin; *-tīrtha,* n. N. of a Tīrtha (also °*śana-t°*), Siṇhās.; Cat. **-vinigraha,** m. restraining wickedness, W. **-viniścaya,** mfn. intending evil, R. **-śamana,** mfn. removing crime, W.; n. a sin-offering, ib.; (*ī*), f. Prosopis Spicigera, L. **-śīla,** mf(*ā*)n. of bad character, wicked (*-tva,* n.), Veṇīs.; Pañc. **-śodhana,** n. 'washing away sins,' N. of a Tīrtha, Kathās. **-saṃśamana,** mfn. removing sin, R. **-saṃkalpa,** mf(*ā*)n. evil-minded, malevolent, ib. **-samā,** n. a bad year, TS.; Vait. **-samācāra,** mf(*ā*)n. of bad conduct, MBh. **-sammita,** mfn. equal in sin or guilt, W. **-sūdana-tīrtha,** n. N. of a Tīrtha, Rājat. (cf. *-vināśana-t°*). **-skandha,** n. pl. accumulation of sin, Kāraṇḍ. **-han,** mf(*ghnī*)n. destroying sin or the wicked, Mn.; (*ghnī*), f. N. of a river; *-ghnī-māhātmya,* n. N. of wk. **-hara,** mfn. removing evil; n. a means of r° e°, Var.; (*ā*), f. N. of a river, MBh. **-hṛidaya,** mf(*ā*)n. bad-hearted, Veṇīs. **Pāpâkhyā,** f. (sc. *gati*) N. of one of the 7 divisions of the planetary courses, Var. **Pāpâṅkuśā,** f. N. of the 11th day in the light half of the month Āśvina, Cat.; (with *ekādaśī*) N. of wk. **Pāpâcāra,** mfn. ill-conducted, vicious, MBh.; m. N. of a king,

Dhūrtan. **Pāpâtman**, mfn. evil-minded, wicked, a wretch, sinner (opp. to *dharmâtman*), Mn.; MBh. &c. **Pāpâdhama**, mfn. the lowest of the wicked, MW. **Pāpânubandha**, m. bad result or consequences, R.; mfn. ill-intentioned, ib. **Pāpânuvasita**, mfn. addicted to sin, sinful, W. **Pāpânta**, n. 'end of sin,' N. of a Tīrtha, VāmP.; °*tikā*, f. a kind of sin, Divyâv. **Pāpâpanutti**, f. 'removal of sins,' expiation, W. **Pāpârambhaka**, mfn. intending evil, Mālatīm. v, 23 (v. l. °*bha-vat*). **Pāpâvahīyam**, ind. leaving sin behind, TS. **Pāpâśaya**, mfn. evil-intentioned, L. **Pāpâhá**, n. an unlucky day, TBr. **Pāpâhi**, m. a snake, serpent, MW. **Pāpôkta**, mfn. addressed in ill-omened words, ŚāṅkhBr.

Pā́paka, mf(*ikā*, once *akī*)n. bad, evil, ŚBr. &c. &c.; m. a villain, rascal, MBh.; an evil or malignant planet, Var.; n. evil, wrong, sin, MBh.

Pāpaya, Nom. Ā. (only *pā́payishṭa*), to suffer a person to fall into misery on account of (abl.), TS.

Pāpala, mfn. imparting or incurring guilt, W.; n. a partic. measure, L.

Pāpāya, Nom. Ā. °*yate*, Vop.

Pāpin, mfn. wicked, sinful, bad; a sinner, criminal, MBh.; Kāv. &c.

Pā́pishṭha, mfn. worst, lowest, most wicked or bad, AV. &c. &c. **-tama** (Daś.) and **-tara** (ChUp.; MBh.), mfn. id.

Pāpīya, mfn. = next, MBh.

Pā́pīyas, mfn. worse, worse off, lower, poorer, more or most wicked or miserable, TS. &c. &c.; m. a villain, rascal, Mn.; R. &c.; (with Buddhists) *māraḥ pāpīyān*, the evil spirit, the devil, Lalit. **-tara**, mfn. worse, more or most bad or wicked, MBh. **-tva**, n. wickedness, depravity, Rājat.

Pāpmán, m. evil, unhappiness, misfortune, calamity, crime, sin, wickedness, AV. &c. &c.; evil demon, devil, Jātakam.; mfn. hurtful, injurious, evil, AV.; AitBr.

पापचक *pāpacaka*, mfn. (fr. √*pac*, Intens.) cooking repeatedly or very much, Pāṇ. i, 1, 4, Vārtt. 6, Pat.

पापठक *pāpaṭhaka*, mfn. (fr. √*paṭh*, Intens.) reading repeatedly or very much, ib.

पापति *pāpati*, mfn. (fr. √*pat*) falling or flying repeatedly, Pāṇ. iii, 2, 171, Vārtt. 4.

पापयल्लव *pāpayallava*, m. (with *sūri*), N. of an author, Cat.

पापाक *pāpāka*, m. N. of a poet, ib.

पापापुरी *pāpāpurī*, f. N. of a town near Rāja-gṛiha, Col. (also written *pāvāpurī*; cf. *pāpa-purī* under *pāpa*).

पामन् *pāmán*, m. (√*pai*?) a kind of skin-disease, cutaneous eruption, scab, AV.; ChUp.

Pāma, in comp. for °*man*. **-ghna**, mf(*ī*)n. destroying skin-disease; m. sulphur, L.; (*ī*), f. a species of plant, L. **-vat**, mfn. having skin-disease, Pāṇ. v, 2, 100. **Pāmâri**, m. 'enemy of skin-disease,' sulphur, L.

Pāmaná, mfn. = *pāma-vat*, ŚBr. (cf. Pāṇ. v, 2, 100). **-m-bhâvuka**, mfn. becoming scabby, TS.

Pāmara, mfn. affected with skin-disease, L. (cf. g. *aśmâdi*); wicked, vile, low, base, W.; m. a man of lowest extraction, Kāv.; Rājat.; a wretch, villain, Hit.; an idiot, fool, Bādar., Sch.; n. bad character, wickedness, MW. **Pāmarôddhārā**, f. 'removing skin-disease,' a species of plant, L.

Pāmā, f. a kind of skin-disease, herpes, scab (a form of mild leprosy), Car. (also pl.); Suśr.

पामार *pāmāra*, m. N. of a family, Cat.

पामावटिक *pāmāvaṭika*, v. l. for *paramâv*°.

पाम्प *pāmpa*, mf(ī)n. belonging to or situated on the river Pampā, Bhaṭṭ. (also °*pana*, MW.).

पाम्पक *pāmpaka*, m. N. of a poet, Cat.

पाम्पाली *pāmpālī* and *pāmpī*, ind. (with √*kṛi*), Gaṇ. 97.

पाय *pāy*, cl. 1. Ā. *pāyayate*, to void excrement, PraśnUp. iv, 2.

1. **Pāyú** (ŚBr. xiv, *pā́yu*), m. the anus, VS. &c. &c. **-kshālana**, n. washing or cleaning the anus; **-bhūmi**, f. (°*mi-tā*, f.) and *-veśman*, n. a water-closet, privy, Rājat. **-bheda**, m. N. of 2 (of the 10) ways in which an eclipse terminates, Var. **Pāyûpastha**, n. the anus and the organs of generation, Mn. ii, 90.

पाय *pāya*, n. (√1. *pā*) water, L. **-guṇḍa**, m. N. of an author, Cat.

Pāyaka, mf(*ikā*)n. drinking (with gen., Kāś. on Pāṇ. ii, 3, 70; cf. *taila-*).

Pāyána, n. causing or giving to drink, RV. i, 116, 9; Kauś.; (*ā*), f. watering, moistening, Suśr.

Pāyam, pāyayitavai. See under √1. *pā*.

Pāyin, mfn. drinking, sucking, sipping at (ifc.; cf. *ambu-*, *kshīra-* &c.); (*inī*), f. (prob.) N. of a town; *-māhātmya*, n. N. of wk.

1. **Pā́yya**, mfn. to be (or being) drunk, L.; to be caused to drink (with acc.), Suśr.; n. drinking (see *pūrva-p*°); water, L.

पायलिसंघ *pāyali-saṃgha*, m. N. of a partic. sect of Jainas, Bhadrab.

पायस *pāyasa*, mf(ī)n. (fr. *payas*) prepared with or made of milk, GṛŚrS.; m. n. food prepared with m°, (esp.) rice boiled in m° or an oblation of m° and rice and sugar, ib.; Mn.; MBh. &c.; the resin of Pinus Longifolia, L. **-dagdha**, mfn. scalded by milk-porridge, MW. **-piṇḍâraka**, m. a rice-eater, Mṛicch. **Pāyasâpūpa**, m. a cake made of milk and rice &c., Mn. v, 7.

Pāyasika, mf(*ī*)n. fond of boiled milk &c., Pāṇ. iv, 2, 47, Vārtt. 17, Pat.

पायिक *pāyika*, m. a foot-soldier, footman (prob. corrupted fr. *pādātika*).

पायीक *pāyīka*, m. N. of a poet, Cat.

पायु 2. *pāyú*, m. (√3. *pā*; for 1. *pāyu* see col. 1) a guard, protector, RV. (esp. instr. pl. 'with protecting powers or actions, helpfully'), AV.; N. of a man, RV. vi, 47, 24 (with *Bhāradvāja*, author of vi, 75; x, 87).

2. **Pāyya**, (prob.) protection (see *nṛi-*, *bahu-*).

पाय्य 3. *pāyya*, n. a measure, Pāṇ. iii, 1, 129 (cf. vi, 2, 122); practice, profession, W.

पाय्य 4. *pāyya*, mfn. low, vile, contemptible, L.

पार 1. *pārá*, mfn. (fr. √*pṛi*; in some meanings also fr. √*pṛī*) bringing across, RV. v, 31, 8; n. (rarely m.) the further bank or shore or boundary, any bank or shore, the opposite side, the end or limit of anything, the utmost reach or fullest extent, RV. &c. &c. (*dūré pāré*, at the farthest ends, RV.; *pāram* √*gam* &c. with gen. or loc., to reach the end, go through, fulfil, carry out [as a promise], study or learn thoroughly [as a science], MBh.; R. &c.; *pāraṃ* √*nī*, to bring to a close, Yājñ.); a kind of Tushṭi (s. v.), Sāṃkhyas., Sch.; m. crossing (see *dush-* and *su-*); quicksilver, L.; a partic. personification, SāmavBr.; Gaut.; N. of a sage, MārkP.; of a son of Pṛithu-shena (Rucirâśva) and father of Nīpa, Hariv.; of a s° of Samara and f° of Pṛithu, ib.; of a s° of Aṅga and f° of Divi-ratha, VP.; (pl.) of a class of deities under the 9th Manu, BhP.; (*ā*), f. N. of a river (said to flow from the Pāriyātra mountains or the central and western portion of the Vindhya chain), MBh.; Pur.; (*ī*), f. a milk-pail, Śiś.; any cup or drinking vessel, Vcar.; Rājat.; pollen, L.; a rope for tying an elephant's feet, L.; a quantity of water or a town (*pūra* or *pura*), L.; a small piece or quantity of anything, Nalac. **-kâṅkshin**, m. = *pāri-k*°, L. **-kāma**, mfn. desirous of reaching the opposite bank, AitBr. **-ga**, mf(*ā*)n. going to the opposite shore, crossing over, MBh.; R.; one who has gone through or accomplished or mastered, knowing thoroughly, fully conversant or familiar with (gen., loc. or comp.), profoundly learned, Mn.; MBh. &c.; n. keeping, fulfilling (of a promise), Hariv. 11565 (w. r. for *pāraṇa*?). **-gata**, mfn. one who has reached the opposite shore of (gen.), passed over in safety, Bhartṛ.; pure, holy, W.; m. (with Jainas) an Arhat or deified saint or teacher. **-gati**, f. going through, reading, studying, L. **-gamana**, n. reaching the opposite shore, crossing, going to the end of (comp.), R. **-gāmin**, mfn. passing over, crossing, landing, Kāraṇḍ.; n. = *para-loka-hitaṃ karma*, MBh. xiii, 2127 (Nīlak.) **-cara**, mf(*ī*)n. arrived at the opposite shore, emancipated for ever, BhP. **-tas** (*pārá-*), ind. on the opp° bank or the further side, beyond (gen.), RV. **-1. -da**, mf(*ā*)n. (for 2. see p. 620) leading across (comp.), Siṃhâs. **-daṇḍaka**, m. N. of a country (part of Orissa), L. **-darśaka**, mfn. showing the opp° shore, BhP. **-darśana**, mfn. beholding the opp° sh°, surveying all things, ib. **-dṛiśvan**, mf(*arī*)n. one who has seen the opp° sh°, far-seeing, wise, completely familiar with or versed in (gen. or comp.), Kām.; Ragh. &c. (cf. Pāṇ. iii, 2, 94). **-dhvaja**, m. pl. 'banners from the further shore,' partic. banners brought from Ceylon and borne in procession by the kings of Kaśmīra, Rājat. **-netṛi**, mfn. leading to the further sh°, making a person (gen.) conversant with (loc.), MBh. **-pāra**, m. N. of Vishṇu, VP.; n. N. of a kind of Tushṭi (s. v.), Sāṃkhyas, Sch. **-m-ita**, mfn. gone to the opposite shore; crossed, traversed; transcendent (as spiritual knowledge), W.; (*ā*), f. (for °*ta-tā*?) coming or leading to the opp° sh°, complete attainment, perfection in (comp.); transcendental virtue (there are 6 or 10, viz. *dāna*, *śīla*, *kshānti*, *vīrya*, *dhyāna*, *prajñā*, to which are sometimes added *satya*, *adhishṭhāna*, *maitra*, *upêkshā*), MWB. 128 (cf. Dharmas. xvii, xviii). **-vinda**, m. 'finding the opposite shore (?),' N. of a partic. personification, SāmavBr. **-skanda**, v. l. for *pari-sk*°. **Pārâpāra**, n. the nearer and the further sh°, both banks (= and v. l. for *pārâvāra*), MatsyaP.; m. the sea, ocean, L. **Pārâyaṇa**, n. going over, reading through, perusing, studying, RPrāt.; Āpast.; (esp.) reading a Purāṇa or causing it to be read, W.; the whole, totality, MBh. xiii, 2701; Pāṇ. iii, 2, 130, Sch.; (esp.) complete text, c° collection of (cf. *dhātu-p*°, *nāma-p*°); N. of a gram. wk. (abridged fr. *dhātu-p*°); (*ī*), f. (L.) action; meditation; light; N. of the goddess Sarasvatī; °*ṇa-krama*, m., °*ṇa-māhātmya*, n., °*ṇa-vidhi*, m. N. of wks.; °*ṇika*, mfn. one who goes through or studies, Pāṇ. v, 1, 72; m. a lecturer, reader of the Purāṇas, W.; a pupil, scholar, W.; pl. N. of a partic. school of grammarians, Cat.; °*ṇīya*, n. N. of a grammar. **Pārâvāra**, n. the further and nearer shore, the two banks (°*rasya nauḥ*, a boat which plies from one side to the other, MBh.; °*re* [ib.] or °*ra-taṭe* [Cat.], on both banks; °*ra-taraṇârtham*, ind. for bringing over from one shore to the other, Kull.); m. the sea, ocean, Prasannar. (cf. *pārâpāra*); °*ra-jālaya*, Nom. to become sea-water, Dharmaś.; °*riṇa*, mfn. on both sides of a river, one who knows both sides or the whole of a subject, W. (cf. Pāṇ. iv, 2, 93, Vārtt. 2, Pat.)

Pāraka, mf(*ī*)n. carrying over, saving, delivering (cf. *ugra-p*°); enabling to cross (a river or the world), W.; satisfying, pleasing, cherishing, ib.; m. pl. N. of a people, R.

Pāraṇa, mfn. bringing over, delivering, Hariv.; m. a cloud (as 'crossing,' sc. the sky), L.; n. carrying through, accomplishing, fulfilling, MBh.; conclusion (esp. of a fast, with or sc. *vrata-*); eating and drinking after a fast, breakfast (also *ā*, f.), Kāv.; Pur.; Rājat.; satisfaction, pleasure, enjoyment (also *ā*, f.), Ragh.; Bālar.; going through, reading, perusal (also *ā*, f. and °*ṇa-karman*, n.), MBh.; Hariv.; completeness, the full text, L.

Pāraṇi, m. a patr., g. *taulvaly-ādi*.

Pāraṇika. See *mahā-p*°.

Pāraṇīya, mfn. having an attainable end, capable of being completed or brought to an end, MBh.; BhP.

1. **Pāraya**, °**yati**. See √*pṛi*, Caus.

2. **Pāraya**, mfn. (fr. prec.) able, adequate, fit for, W.; satisfying, ib. (cf. Pāṇ. iii, 1, 738).

Pārayitṛi, mfn. one who carries or will carry across, ŚBr.

Pārayishṇú, mfn. bringing to the opposite shore or to a happy issue, successful, victorious, RV. &c. &c. (*-tama*, mfn. best in accomplishing, AitBr.); m. N. of a partic. personification, Gobh.

Pāriṇa, mfn. being on or crossing to the other side, W.; (ifc.) well acquainted or completely familiar with (cf. *trivarya-p*°); m., see under *pāriṇa*.

Pārīya, mfn. one who has gone through or studied, completely familiar with (comp.), Hcat.

Pāre, loc. of 1. *pāra* in comp. **-gaṅgam**, ind. on the other side of the Gaṅgā, beyond the Ganges, Pāṇ. ii, 1, 18, Sch. **-jalam**, ind. on the other side of the water, on the opposite bank of a river, Śiś. **-taraṃgiṇi**, ind. beyond the river, Prasannar. **-dhanva**, m. or n. N. of a place; °*vaka*, mfn., Pat. **-baḍavā**, f., Pāṇ. vi, 2, 42. **-viśoka**, ind. on the other side of (the mountain) Viśoka,

Rājat. **-śmaśānam**, ind. beyond or behind the burial-place, Mālatīm. **-sindhu**, ind. on the other side of the Sindhu, beyond the Indus, MBh.

Pārya, mfn. being on the opposite side or bank, TS.; upper, VS.; last, final, decisive, R.; helping through, effective, successful, ib.; n. end, issue, decision, ib.

पार 2. *pāra* (for 1. see p. 619), Vṛiddhi form of *para* in comp. **-kulīna**, mfn. = *para-kule sādhuḥ*, g. *pratijanâdi*. **-kshudra** (with *yajus*), n. N. of a partic. text, ĀpŚr., Sch. **-grāmika**, mf(*ī*)n. (*-grāma*) 'belonging to another village,' hostile, inimical; (with *vidhi*), m. hostile action, hostility, Daś. **-janmika**, mf(*ī*)n. (*-janman*) relating to a future birth, Buddh. **-jāyika** (MBh.), **-jāyin** (Vishṇ.), m. (*-jāyā*) one who intrigues with another's wife, an adulterer. **-tantra**, w. r. for °*trya*. **-tantrika**, mf(*ī*)n. (*-tantra*) belonging to or enjoined by the religious treatises of others, Gṛihyās. **-tantrya**, n. dependence on others, MBh.; Pur.; Rājat. **-talpika**, n. (*-talpa*) adultery, Das. **-trika**, mf(*ī*)n. (*-tra*) relating to or advantageous in another world, MBh. **-trya**, mf(*ā*)n. (*-tra*), id.; Mn.; MBh.; MārkP. **-daṇḍaka**, see under 1. *pāra*. **-dārika**, mf(*ī*)n. (*-dāra*) relating to another's wife, Cat.; m. = *-jāyika*, Yājñ.; MBh.; Kathās. **-dārin**, m. = prec. m., MBh. **-dārya**, n. adultery, Mn.; Yājñ.; MBh. **-deśika** (W.), **-deśya** (Yājñ.), mfn. (*-deśa*) outlandish, foreign, abroad; m. a traveller or a foreigner. **-daurbalya**, n. the inferiority of each following member of a series to the preceding, Jaim. **-dhenu** or °**nuka**, m. N. of a low mixed caste, an Āyogava (q. v.), W. **-bhṛita**, n. a present, offering (prob. w. r. for *prā-bhṛita*), W.; °*tīya*, mfn. relating to a present or offering, sacrificial; belonging to or coming from a cuckoo, Mṛicch. **-m-para**, mfn. further, future (world), Kād. **-m-parī**, f. regular succession, order, Subh. **-m-parīṇa**, mfn. passing from one to another, hereditary, L. **-m-parīya**, mfn. handed down, traditional, Kull. **-m-parya**, n. uninterrupted series or succession, tradition, intermediation, indirect way or manner (*eṇa*, ind. successively, by degrees), Mn.; MBh. &c.; *-kramâgata*, mfn. derived from tradition, Mn. ii, 18; *-prakaraṇa*, n. N. of wk.; °*ryâgata*, mfn. = *-kramâgata*, MBh.; °*ryôpadeśa*, m. traditional instruction, Sūryas. **-yugīṇa**, mfn. (*-yuga*), Gaṇ. 338, Sch. **-lokya**, mfn. (*-loka*) relating to the next world, MBh. **-laukika**, mf(*ī*)n. id., ib. (with *sahāya*, m. a comrade on the way to the next world); N. of a place where pearls are found and the pearls found there, VarBṛS.; n. things or circumstances relating to the next world, MBh.; Hariv. **-vargya**, mfn. (*-varga*) belonging to another party, inimical, MBh. **-vaśya**, n. (*-vaśa*) dependence, Kap. **-straiṇeya**, m. (*-strī*) a son by another's wife, g. *kalyāṇy-ādi*. **-haṅsya**, mfn. (*-haṅsa*) relating to an ascetic who has subdued all his senses, BhP. **Pārârthya**, n. (2. *parârtha*) dependence on or devotedness to another, altruism, disinterestedness, Kathās.; *-nirṇaya*, m. or *-vivecana*, n. N. of wk. **Pārâvarya**, n. (*parâvara*) comprehensiveness, allsidedness, Hariv.; (*eṇa*), ind. on all sides, completely, MBh.

Pārakya, mfn. = *parakīya*, belonging to another or a stranger, alien (opp. to *sva*), hostile, Mn.; MBh. &c.; m. an enemy, Hit.

Pārasyakulīna, mfn. = *parasya kule sādhuḥ*, g. *pratijanâdi*.

पार 3. *pāra*, m. = *pāla*, a guardian, keeper (see *brahma-dvāra-p*°).

पारक *pāraka*. See under 1. *pāra*.

पारकाङ्क्षिन् *pārakāṅkshin*, m. = *pārik*°, L.

पारज् *pāraj* (nom. °*rak*, according to Uṇ. i, 135, Sch. fr. 1. *pāra*), gold.

पारटीट *pāraṭīṭa*, m. (fr. 1. *pāra*?) a stone, rock, L. (cf. *pārāruka*).

पारण *pāraṇa*, °*ṇīya*. See under 1. *pāra*, p. 619, col. 3.

पारत *pārata*, m. (cf. 2. *pārada*) quicksilver, Kathās. xxxvii, 232; pl. N. of a people, Var. (also °*taka*, v. l. in VP.)

पारतस् *pāra-tas*. See p. 619, col. 2.

पारत्रिक *pāratrika*, °*trya*. See under 2. *pāra*.

पारद 2. *pārada*, m. (cf. *pārata*), quicksilver, Var.; Suśr. (*-tva*, n., Sarvad.); m. N. of a partic. personification, SāmavBr.; pl. N. of a people or of a degraded tribe, Mn.; MBh. &c. (cf. IW. 229, n. 1). **-kalpa**, m. N. of wk.

पारबव *pārabava*, n. N. of 2 Sāmans, ĀrshBr.

पारम *pārama*, Vṛiddhi form of *parama* in comp. **-gopucchika**, mfn. = *parama-gopucchena krītam*, Pat. **-rsha** (*p*° + *ṛishi*), mfn. coming from a great Ṛishi, Sarvad. **-sthya**, n. (fr. *parama-stha*), g. *brāhmaṇâdi*. **-haṅsa**, mf(*ī*)n. relating to Parama-haṅsa (s. v.), BhP. **-haṅsya**, mfn. id., ib.; n. the state or condition of a P°-h°, ib.; *-pari*, ind. relating to the most sublime meditation, MW. **Pāramârthika**, mf(*ī*)n. (fr. *paramârtha*) relating to a high or spiritual object or to supreme truth, real, essential, true, Śaṃk.; BhP.; Kull. (cf. IW. 108); one who cares for truth, Pañc.; excellent, best, W.; °*thya*, n. the real or full truth, BhP. **Pārameśvara**, mf(*ī*)n. relating or belonging to or coming from the supreme god (Śiva), Prab.; Kathās.; Pur.; m. or n. N. of wk.; *-puṇyâha-vacana*, n., *-saṃhitā*, f., °*rârādhana-vidhi*, m., °*rīya*, and °*rya*, n. N. of wks. **Pārameśvaraka**, mf(*ikā*)n. composed by Parameśvara (= Paramâdīśvara), Āryabh., Comm. **Pārameshṭha**, m. (fr. *parame-shṭhin*) patr. of Nārada, MBh.; °*shṭhya*, mfn. relating or belonging to or coming from the supreme god (Brahmā), MBh.; Hariv.; Pur.; relating to a king, royal (cf. below); m. patr. of Nārada, MBh. (v. l. °*shṭha*); n. highest position, supremacy, AitBr.; MBh.; Pur.; pl. the royal insignia, BhP. **Pāramaiśvarya**, n. (*paramêśvara*) supremacy, divinity, Sarvad.

Pāramaka, mf(*ikā*)n. = (and v. l. for) *paramaka*, supreme, chief, best, MBh.; R.

Pārami, f. (?) extremity, Divyâv.

पारमित *pāram-ita*, *pāraya* &c. See under 1. *pāra*.

पारवत *pāravata*, m. = *pārāvata*, a pigeon, L

पारवर्ग्य *pāravargya*, °*vaśya*. See under 2. *pāra*, col. 1.

पारशव *pāraśava*, mf(*ī*)n. (fr. *paraśu*; but also written *pārasava*) made of iron (only in *sarva-p*°); N. of a mine in which pearls are found and of the pearls found there, VarBṛS.; m. or n. iron, L.; m. N. of a mixed caste, the son of a Brāhman by a Śūdra woman (f. *ī*), Mn.; MBh. (*-tva*, n.); Var.; a son by another's wife, a bastard, L.; pl. N. of a people in the south-west of Madhya-deśa, Var.; MārkP.

Pāraśavāyana, m. patr. fr. *pāraśava*; g. *bidâdi*.
Pāraśavya, m. patr. of Tirindira, ŚāṅkhŚr.

पारशीक *pāraśīka* = *pārasīka*.

पारश्वध *pāraśvadha* and °*dhika*, mf(*ī*)n. (fr. *paraśvadha*) armed with an axe, L. (cf. Pāṇ. iv, 4, 58).

पारषद *pārashada*, v. l. for *pārishada*, n.

पारस *pārasa*, mf(*ī*)n. Persian; (*ī*), f., see below. °**sika**, mf(*ī*)n. id., Col. (v. l. °*sīka*); m. pl. the P°s, MBh.; VP. °**sī**, f. (with or sc. *bhāshā*) the P° language; *-jātaka*, n. N. of wk.; *-nāma-mālā*, f. a Sanskṛit-P° vocabulary; *-prakāśa* or *-kośa*, m. P° words explain in S°; *-vinoda*, m. P° and Arab terms of astron. and astrol. explained in S°. °**sīka**, mfn. Persian (cf. below), m. (pl.) the Persians, Ragh.; Kathās. &c.; a P° horse, L.; (prob. n.) Persia, Bhpr.; *-taila*, n. 'Persian oil,' Naphtha, Vcar.; *-yamānī*, f. Hyoscyamus Niger, L. °**sīkeya**, mf(*ī*)n. Persian, Bhpr.

पारस्कन्द *pāraskanda*, v. l. for *pari-skanda*.

पारस्कर *pāraskara*, m. (rather fr. *paras* + *kara* than fr. *pāra* + *kara*; but cf. Pāṇ. vi, 1, 157) N. of the author of a Gṛihya-sūtra (forming a supplement to KātyŚrS.) and of a Dharma-śāstra; N. of a district or a town, Gaṇar. 150, Sch.; mf(*ī*)n. composed by Pāraskara. **-gṛihya-sūtra**, n., **-gṛihya-pariśishṭa**, n., **-paddhati**, f., **-gṛihya-mantra**, m., **-smṛiti**, f. N. of wks.

पारस्वत *pārasvata*, mf(*ī*)n. (fr. *parasvat*) relating &c. to the wild ass, AV.

पारापत *pārāpata*, m. = (or v. l. for) *pārāvata*, a pigeon, Kād. **-padī**, f. Cardiospermum Halicacabum or Leea Hirta, L.

Pārāpataka, m. a kind of rice, Suśr.

पारापार *pārâpāra*, *pārâyaṇa*. See under 1. *pāra*, p. 619, col. 3.

पारारुक *pārâruka*, m. a rock, L. (cf. *paraṭīṭa*).

पारावत *pārâvata*, mf(*ī*)n. (fr. *parā-vat*) remote, distant, coming from a distance, foreign, RV. (instr. pl. 'from distant quarters,' AV.); m. N. of a tribe on the Yamunā, RV.; TāṇḍBr.; (ifc. f. *ā*) a turtle-dove, pigeon, MBh.; Kāv. &c.; a kind of snake, Suśr.; N. of a Nāga of the race of Airāvata, MBh.; a monkey, L.; Diospyros Embryopteris, MBh.; Hariv.; Suśr.; a mountain, L.; pl. N. of a class of deities under Manu Svārocisha, Pur.; (*ī*), f. the fruit of the Averrhoa Acida, L.; a form of song peculiar to cowherds, L.; N. of a river, L.; n. the fruit of Diospyros Embryopteris, Hariv.; Suśr. **-ghnī**, f. (of *han*) striking the distant (demon) or at a distance, RV. vi, 61, 2. **-deśa**, m. N. of a country, Cat. **-padī**, f. Cardiospermum Halicacabum, Bhpr.; Car. **-mālāya**, Nom. Ā. °*yate*, to resemble a flock of turtles, Kād. **-savarṇa**, m. pl. 'dove-coloured,' N. of the horses of Dhṛishṭa-dyumna, MBh.; °*ṇâśva*, m. N. of Dh°, ib. **Pārāvatâksha**, m. 'dove-eyed,' N. of a serpent-demon, Kathās. **Pārāvatâṅghri-piccha**, m. a kind of pigeon, L. **Pārāvatâbha**, mfn. pigeon-like, Suśr. **Pārāvatâśva**, m. 'having doves for horses,' N. of Dhṛishṭa-dyumna, MBh. (cf. °*ta-savarṇa*).

Pārāvati, m. patr. of Vasu-rocis, L.

पारावतघ्नी *pārāvata-ghnī*, w. r. for *pārāvata-ghnī*.

पारावर्य *pārāvarya*. See under 2. *pāra*.

पारावार *pārâvāra*. See under 1. *pāra*.

पाराशर *pārāśara*, mf(*ī*)n. proceeding or derived from Parāśara or Pārāśarya, Var.; Pur. (cf. g. *kaṇvâdi*); m. patr. (fr. *parā-śara*, and N. of the poet Vyāsa; pl. N. of a school), Pravar.; Pur.; L.; (*ī*), f., see s. v.; n. the rules of Parāśara for the conduct of the mendicant order, W.; *-kalpika*, mfn. one who studies the P°-kalpa; m. a follower of P°, Pat. on Pāṇ. iv, 2, 60; *-jātaka*, n., *-śikshā*, f., *-sūtra*, n., *-horā*, f. N. of wks. °**śari**, m. patr. of Vyāsa, L. °**śarin**, m. a mendicant of the order of Pārāśarya, L. (cf. Pāṇ. iv, 3, 110); pl. N. of a phil. school, RāmatUp. °**śarī** (*pārâ-*), f. patr. of Parāśara, ŚBr.; a wk. of P°; *-kauṇḍinī-putra* and °*rī-putra* (*pā*°), m. N. of 2 teachers, ŚBr.; *-paddhati*, f., *-mukura*, m., *-mūla*, n., *-vyākhyā*, f., *-horā*, f. N. of wks. °**śarīya**, n. a wk. of Parāśara, Cat. °**śarya** (*pârā-*), m. patr. fr. *parā-śara* (N. of Vyāsa), ŚBr. &c. &c. (cf. Pāṇ. iv. 3, 110); n. a wk. of Parāśara, Cat.; *-vijaya*, m. N. of wk. (= *parāśara-v*°). °**śaryāyaṇa** (*pârā-*), m. patr. fr. *pārāśarya*, ŚBr.

पारि *pāri*, Vṛiddhi form of *pari* in comp. **-kāṅkshaka** and °**kshin**, m. a contemplative Brāhman (in the fourth period of life), L. **-kārmika**, m. (*-karman*) one who takes charge of the lesser vessels or utensils, L. **-kuṭa**, m. an attendant, servant, AitBr. (Sāy.) **-kshi** (I), m. N. of a man, L. **-kshit** (m. c.) and **-kshitá**, m. (*-kshit*) patr. of Janam-ejaya, Br.; MBh.; (°*tī*), f. N. of AV. xx, 127, 7-10; °*tiya*, m. the brother of Pari-kshit, ŚBr.; ŚāṅkhŚr., Sch. **-kshepaka** (or °*pika*), m. or n. (√*kship*) objection (?), Car. **-kha** (fr. *pari-khā*), g. *palady-ādi*. **-khiya**, mfn. (fr. *parikha*), Pāṇ. iv, 2, 141, Sch. **-kheya**, mf(*ī*)n. (fr. *pari-kha*) surrounded by a ditch, ib. v, 1, 17. **-grāmika**, mf(*ī*)n. (*-grāmam*) situated round a village, ib. iv, 3, 61. **-jāta**, m. the coral tree, Erythrina Indica (losing its leaves in June and then covered with large crimson flowers), MBh.; Kāv.; Suśr. &c.; the wood of this tree, R.; N. of one of the 5 trees of paradise produced at the churning of the ocean and taken possession of by Indra from whom it was afterwards taken by Kṛishṇa), MBh.; Kāv. &c. (cf. IW. 519); fragrance, Var.; N. of sev. wks. (esp. ifc.; cf. *dāna-*); of a Nāga, MBh.; of a Ṛishi, ib.; of an author of Mantras (with Śāktas), Cat.; *-ka*, m. the coral tree or its wood, Suśr.; Pur.; N. of a Ṛishi, MBh.; of other men, Hcar. (*-ratnâkara*, m. N. of wk.); m. or n.

N. of a drama (=°*ta-haraṇa*); *-maya*, mf(*ī*)n. made of flowers of the celestial P°, Kathās.; *-ratnâkara*, m. N. of wk. (prob. =°*taka-ratn*°); *-vat*, mfn. possessing the cel° P°, Hariv.; *-vṛitta-khaṇḍa*, n., *-vyākaraṇa*, n. N. of wks.; *-sarasvatī-mantra*, m. pl. N. of partic. magical formulas, Cat.; *-haraṇa*, n. 'robbing the P° tree,' N. of chs. of Hariv. and VP., also of a comedy by Gopāla-dāsa; (°*ṇa-campū*, f. N. of a poem); °*tâcala-māhātmya*, n. N. of wk. **-ṇāmika**, mf(*ī*)n. (*-ṇāma*) digestible, Subh. (w. r. *pari-ṇ*°); subject to development or evolution; (with *bhāva*, m.) natural disposition, Sāṃk.; Sarvad. **-ṇāyya**, n. (*-ṇāya*) property or paraphernalia received by a woman at the time of marriage, Vas.; =(or v. l. for) next, Kathās. **-ṇāhya**, n. (*-ṇāha*) household furniture and utensils, Mn. ix, 11. **-tathyā**, f. (*-tathya*) a string of pearls for binding the hair, L. **-toshika**, mf(*ī*)n. (*-tosha*) gratifying, satisfactory, W.; n. a reward, gratuity, Kāv.; Rājat. **-dṛiḍhi**, m. (*ī*, f.) patr. fr. *pari-dṛiḍhi*, Pat. **-dheya**, m. patr. fr. *pari-dhi*, g. *śubhrâdi*. **-dhvajika**, m. (*-dhvaja*) a standard-bearer, L. **-panthika**, m. (fr. *pari-pantham*) a highwayman, robber, thief, L. (Pāṇ. iv, 4, 36). **-pāṭya**, n. (*-pāṭī*) regularity, methodicalness, W. **-pātra** &c., w. r. for *-yātra* below. **-pāna**, n. drink (?), Divyâv. **-pānthika**, w. r. for *-panthika* above. **-pārśva** (prob. n.), retinue, attendants, bystanders (in a play), Hariv.; °*śvaka*, mf(*ikā*)n. standing at the side, attending on, MBh.; m. (with or sc. *nara*) a servant, attendant, ib.; an assistant of the manager of a play, Bhar.; (*ikā*), f. a chamber-maid, Mālav.; °*śvika*, mfn. =°*śvaka*, R.; Mālav. **-pālya**, n. governorship, Rājat. **-pela**, n. = *pari-pelava*, L. **-plava**, mf(*ā*)n. swimming, MBh.; Kāv.; moving to and fro, agitated, unsteady, tremulous; wavering, irresolute, ib.; (*pári-*), 'moving in a circle,' N. of partic. legends recited at the Aśva-medha and repeated at certain intervals throughout the year, ŚBr.; ŚrS.; Bādar.; m. a boat, R. (v. l. *pari-pl*°); a class of gods in the 5th Manv-antara, Hariv.; (*ā*), f. a small spoon used at sacrifices, Āryav. (cf. *pari-plavā*); n. N. of a Tīrtha, MBh.; *-gata*, mfn. being in a boat, R.; *-tā*, f., *-tva*, n. unsteadiness, inconstancy, Hcar.; Rājat.; *-dṛishṭi* (BhP.) or *-netra* (Ragh.), mfn. having tremulous or swimming eyes; *-prabha*, mfn. spreading tremulous lustre, R.; *-mati*, mfn. fickle-minded, MBh.; °*vīya*, n. an oblation connected with the recitation of a P° legend, ŚāṅkhŚr. **-plāvya**, m. a goose, L.; n. agitation, tremulousness, W. **-barha**, m. sg. and pl. =*pari-b*°, MBh.; N. of a son of Garuḍa, ib. **-bhadra**, m. Erythrina Indica, Bālar.; Suśr.; Azadirachta Indica, L.; Pinus Deodora or Longifolia, L.; N. of a son of Yajña-bāhu, BhP.; n. N. of a Varsha in Śālmala-dvīpa ruled by Pāri-bhadra, ib. **-bhadraka**, m. Erythrina Fulgens, MBh.; Suśr.; Azadirachta Indica, L.; pl. N. of a family, MBh.; n. = next, L. **-bhavya**, n. (*-bhū*) Costus Speciosus or Arabicus, Bhpr. **-bhāvya**, n. id., L.; security, bail (=*prātibh*°), Dāyabh. **-bhāshika**, mf(*ī*)n. (*-bhāshā*) conventional, technical, Suśr.; Sarvad.; *-tva*, n., Kap. **-bhogika**, m. or n. objects possessed or used by Buddha, MWB. 495. **-māṇḍalya**, n. (*-maṇḍala*) globularness, spherical shape, Bādar., Sch. **-māṇya**, n. (*-māṇa*) circumference, compass, MBh. **-mitya**, n. (*-mita*) the being confined, limitation, Sāh. **-mukhika**, mf(*ī*)n. (fr. *pari-mukham*) being before the eyes, near, present, Pāṇ. iv, 4, 29. **-mukhya**, mf(*ā*)n. id.; n. nearness, presence, ib. iv, 3, 58, Vārtt. 1, Pat. **-yātra**, m. (ifc. f. *ā*) N. of the western Vindhya range, MBh.; Var.; Suśr. &c. (also *-ka*, L.); N. of a man (son of Ahīna-gu), Ragh.; Pur. °*trika*, m. an inhabitant of the P° range, Var. **-yānika**, n. (*-yāna*) a travelling carriage, L. **-rakshaka** or **-rakshika**, m. (*-rakshā*) a Brāhman in the fourth period of life, a Bhikshu or Saṃnyāsī, L. **-vatsa**, m. a calf belonging to (cows), Hariv. (v. l. *pari-v*°). **-vittya**, n. (*-vitta*) the being unmarried while a younger brother is married, Yājñ. **-vṛiḍhi**, m. (*ī*, f.) patr. fr. *pari-vṛiḍha*, Pat.; °*ḍhya*, n. (fr. id.), g. *dṛiḍhâdi*. **-vettrya**, n. (*-vettṛi*) the marriage of a younger brother before the elder, VP. **-vedya**, n. id., Yājñ., Sch. **-vrajya**, w. r. for *-vrājya*. **-vrājaka**, mf(*ī*)n. intended for a religious mendicant, Kauś.; n. the life of a r° m°, g. *yuvâdi*; °*jya*, n. id., MBh. (cf. Pāṇ. vii, 3, 60, Sch.) **-śikshā**, f. N. of wk. **-śīla**, m. =*apūpa*, a cake, L. **-śeshya**, n. (*-śesha*) result, consequence, TPrāt., Sch.; (*āt*), ind. consequently, therefore, ergo (also with preceding *atas* or *tasmāt*), ib.; Sāṃk. &c. **-shatka**, mfn. =*parishadam adhīte veda vā*, g. *ukthâdi*. **-shada**, mf(*ī*)n. (*-shad*) fit for an assembly, decent, Car.; relating to a village *parishad*, g. *palady-ādi*; m. a member of an assembly, assessor at a council, auditor, spectator, MBh.; Kāv. &c. (R. [B.] also *-shad*); pl. the retinue or attendants of a god, MBh.; BhP.; n. taking part in an assembly, BhP. **-shadaka**, mf(*ī*)n. done by an assembly, g. *kulālâdi*. **-shadya**, m. a member of an assembly, spectator, councillor, Rājat.; Divyâv. (cf. Pāṇ. iv, 4, 44; 101). **-sheṇya**, m. patr. fr. *pari-sheṇa*, Pat. **-sāraka**, mfn. containing the word *pari-sāraka*, g. *vimuktâdi*. **-sīrya**, mfn. (fr. *pari-sīram*), g. *pari-mukhâdi*. **-hanavya**, mfn. (fr. *pari-hanu*) ib. **-hārika**, mf(*ī*)n. (*-hāra*) having immunity, privileged, Subh.; taking away, seizing, W.; surrounding, ib.; m. a maker of garlands, L.; (*ī*), f. a kind of riddle, Cat. **-hāriṇī** (?), Deśin. **-hārya**, m. a bracelet, MBh.; Kād.; Rājat.; n. taking, seizure, W. **-hāsya**, n. (*-hāsa*) jest, joke, fun; (*ena*), ind. in fun, BhP. **Pārikshit**, m. = next, MBh. xii, 5596. **Pārikshita**, mf(*ī*)n. relating to or treating of or derived from Parī-kshit, Pur.; m. patr. of Janam-ejaya, MBh.; N. of a sovereign to whom the BhP. is supposed to have been addressed and of his successor, W. **Pārīṇahya**, n. (fr. *parī-ṇah*) household furniture or utensils, TS.; v. l. for *pāri-ṇ*°, Mn. ix, 11.

Pāry, in comp. for *pāri* before vowels. **-antika**, mf(*ī*)n. (*-anta*) final, concluding, last, MW. **-avasānika**, mfn. (*-avasāna*) verging to the close, MBh. **-āptika**, mfn. one who has said *pary-āptam*, i. e. 'enough,' Pāṇ. iv, 1, Vārtt. 2. **-ulūkhalya**, mfn. (fr. *pary-ulūkhalam*), g. *pari-mukhâdi*, on Pāṇ. iv, 3, 58, Vārtt. 1. **-oshṭhya**, mfn. (fr. *pary-oshṭhyam*), ib.

पारिण *pāriṇa*, °*ṇaka*, and *pārīṇa*, m. N. of a man, Pravar.

पारितवत् *pārita-vat*, mfn. containing the word *pārita* or other forms of the Caus. of √*pṛī*, ŚāṅkhBr.

पारिन्द्र *pārindra*, m.=*pārīndra*, a lion, L.

पारिल *pārila*, patr. fr. *parila*, g. *śivâdi*.

Pārileya, m. (patr. fr. prec.?), N. of an elephant, Jātakam.

पारिश *pāriśa*, m. Thespesia Populneoides, L. (cf. *pārīsha* and *phalīśa*).

पारी *pārī*, *pārīṇa*. See under 1. *pāra* and *pāriṇa*.

पारीन्द्र *pārīndra*, m. a lion, Kāv. (cf. *pārindra*); a large snake, boa, L.

पारीय *pārīya*. See under 1. *pāra*.

पारीरण *pārīraṇa*, m.=*parīraṇa*, L.

पारीष *pārīsha*, m.=*pāriśa*, Bhpr.

पारु *pāru*, m.=*peru*, the sun, Uṇ. iv, 101, Sch.; fire, L.

पारुच्छेप *pārucchepa*, mf(*ī*)n. derived from Paruc-chepa, Br.; (*ī*), f. pl. N. of partic. verses, Vait.; n. N. of 2 Sāmans, ĀrshBr.

Pārucchepi, m. patr. fr. *paruc-chepa*, RAnukr.

पारुषक *pārushaka*, m. or n. a species of flower, L. (cf. *parūshaka*).

पारुषिक *pārushika*, mfn. (fr. *parusha*) harsh, violent, Divyâv.

Pārusheyá, mf(*ī*)n. spotted, freckled, AV.

Pārushṇá, m. (fr. *parushṇī*, f. of °*rusha*) a kind of bird, VS.

Pā́rushya, n. (fr. *parusha*) roughness, Suśr. (cf. *tvak-p*°); shagginess, dishevelled state (of the hair), Subh.; harshness (esp. of language), reproach, insult (also pl.), AV. &c. &c.; violence (in word or deed; cf. *daṇḍa-p*°, *vāk-p*°); squalor, MW.; the grove of Indra, L. (also *-ka*, Divyâv.); aloe wood, L.; m. N. of Bṛihas-pati, the planet Jupiter, L.

पारेगङ्गम् *pāre-gaṅgam*, *pāre-taraṃgiṇi* &c. See under 1. *pāra*.

पारेरक *pārereka*, m. a sword, scimitar (?), W.

पारेवत *pārevata*, m. a kind of date, L.

पारोक्ष *pāroksha*, mf(*ī*)n. (fr. *paro'ksha*) undiscernible, mysterious (v. l. for next), BhP.

Pārokshya, mf(*ā*)n. undiscernible, invisible, hidden, ib.; n. mysteriousness, mystery, ib.

पारोवर्य *pārovarya*, n. (fr. *paro-'varam*) tradition, Nir. xiii, 12.

पार्घट *pārghaṭa*, n.=*arghaṭa*, ashes, L. (cf. *pārpara*).

पार्जन्य *pārjanyá*, mf(*ā*)n. relating or belonging to Parjanya, VS.; ŚBr.; MBh. &c.

पार्ण *pārṇa*, mf(*ī*)n. (fr. *parṇa*) made or consisting of leaves, raised from leaves (as a tax), L.; made of the wood of the Butea Frondosa, TāṇḍBr.; Gobh.; m. a hut made of leaves, Gal.; patr., g. *śivâdi*. **-valka**, mfn. (fr. *pārṇavalkya*), g *kaṇvâdi*. **-valki**, m. patr. of Nigada, L. **-valkya**, m. patr. fr. *parṇa-valka*, g. *gargâdi*.

पार्थ 1. *pārtha*, m. (fr. *pṛithi*) patr. of Tānva, RAnukr.; n. N. of 12 sacred texts (ascribed to Pṛithi Vainya and repeated during the ceremony of unction in the Rāja-sūya sacrifice), Br.; KātyŚrS.; of sev. Sāmans, Br.; Lāṭy.

Pārthyá, m. a descendant of Pṛithi, RV. x, 93, 15.

पार्थ 2. *pārtha*, m. (fr. *pṛithā*) metron. of Yudhi-shṭhira or Bhīma-sena or Arjuna (esp. of the last; pl. the 5 sons of Pāṇḍu), MBh. (cf. IW. 381, n. 4); N. of a king of Kaśmīra (son of Paṅgu) and of another man, Rājat.; Terminalia Arjuna, L. **-kirāta**, m. N. of the Kirātârjunīya, Cat. **-ja**, m. a son of Pārtha, Rājat. **-parākrama**, m. N. of a drama. **-pura**, n. N. of a city near the confluence of the Go-dāvarī and Vidarbhā, Col. **-maya**, mf(*ī*)n. consisting of sons of Pṛithā, MBh. **-vijaya**, m. N. of wk. **-sārathi**, m. 'Arjuna's charioteer,' N. of Kṛishṇa, RTL. 107; *-miśra*, m. N. of an author or sev. authors, Cat. **-stuti**, f. N. of a Stotra; *-ṭīkā*, f. N. of the Comm. on it.

पार्थ 3. *pārtha*, m.=*pārthiva*, a prince, king, L.

पार्थ 4. *pārtha* or *pārthona*, m. (in astron.)= παρθένος (the Virgo of the zodiac).

पार्थक्य *pārthakya*, n. (fr. *pṛithak*) severalty, difference, variety, Sāh.

Pārthagarthya, n. (fr. *pṛithag-artha*) difference of purpose or meaning &c., Sāṃk.

पार्थव *pārthava*, mf(*ī*)n. belonging or peculiar to Pṛithu, BhP.; m. patr. fr. *pṛithu*, Pravar.; n. width, great extent, ĀpŚr., Sch.

Pārthavī, w. r. for *pārthiva*, n., Hariv.

Pā́rthiva, mf(*ī* or *ā*; cf. Pāṇ. iv, 1, 85, Vārtt. 2)n. (fr. *pṛithivī*, f. of *pṛithu*) earthen, earthy, earthly, being in or relating to or coming from the earth, terrestrial, RV. &c. &c.; (from m. below) fit for kings or princes, royal, princely, MBh.; Hariv.; m. an inhabitant of the earth, RV.; AV.; a lord of the earth, king, prince, warrior, Mn.; MBh. &c.; an earthen vessel, L.; a partic. Agni, Gṛihyās.; the 19th (or 53rd) year in Jupiter's cycle of 60 years, Var.; (pl.) N. of a family belonging to the Kauśikas, Hariv.; (*ī*), f. 'earth-born,' N. of Sītā, Ragh.; of Lakshmī, L.; (with *śānti*) N. of wk.; n. (pl.) the regions of the earth, RV.; an earthy substance, Hariv. (v. l. °*thavi*); Suśr.; Tabernaemontana Coronaria, L. **-tā**, f., **-tva**, n. the dignity or rank of king, royalty, MBh. **-nandinī**, f. the daughter of a k°, MW. **-pūjana**, n. (and *-vidhi*, m.), **-pūjā**, f. N. of wks. **-rshabha** (*r* for *ṛi*), 'k°-bull,' an excellent king, MW. **-liṅga**, n. characteristic or attribute of a king; *-pūjana-vidhi*, m., *-pūjā*, f., *-pūjārādhana*, n., *-māhātmya*, n., *-lakshaṇa*, n., *-vidhāna*, n., °*gôdyāpana*, n. N. of wks. or chs. of wks. **-śreshṭha**, m. best of kings, MBh. **-sutā**, f. a k°'s daughter, MBh. **Pārthivâtmajā**, f. id., ib. **Pārthivâdhama**, m. the lowest or meanest of kings, MW. **Pārthivârcana-vidhi**, m. N. of wk. **Pārthivêndra**, m. the chief or greatest of princes, MW. **Pārthivêśvara**, m. id.; *-cintāmaṇi*, m. (°*ṇi-paddhati*, f.), *-pūjana-vidhi* and *-pūjā-vidhi*, m. N. of wks.

Pārthuraśmá, n. (fr. *pṛithu-raśmi*) N. of sev. Sāmans, Br.; Lāṭy.

पार्द *pārda*, m. a species of tree, Gaṇar. 300, Sch.; (*ā*), f. N. of a woman, ib. **Pārdā-vat**, mfn., ib.

Pārdākī, f. a species of plant, ib.

पार्दायनी *pārdāyanī*, f. (fr. *pardi* or *pardin*), Pāṇ. iv, 2, 99, Pat.

पार्पर *pārpara*, m. (only L.) a handful of rice; consumption or some other disease; a filament of the Nauclea Cadamba; ashes; N. of Yama; =*jaraṭa* (?).

पार्य *pārya*. See under 1. *pāra*, p. 620.

पार्यन्तिक *pāryantika* &c. See under *pāry*, p. 621, col. 2.

पार्वण *pārvaṇa*, mf(ī)n. (fr. *parvan*) belonging or relating to a division of time or to the changes of the moon (such as at new or full moon); increasing, waxing, full (as the moon; *pārvaṇau śaśi-divākarau*, m° and sun at the time of full m°, Ragh. xi, 82), GṛŚrS.; Kāv.; Pur. &c.; m. a half-month (=*paksha*), Jyot.; oblations offered at new and full moon, GṛS. **-caṭa-śrāddha-prayoga**, m. N. of wk. **-candrikā**, m. N. of wk. **-śrāddha**, n. a ceremony in honour of ancestors performed at the conjunction of sun and moon i.e. at new m° and at other periods of the m°'s changes, RTL. 305; N. of wk.; *-paddhati*, f., *-prayoga*, m., *-vidhi*, m. N. of wks.

Pārvāyanāntīya, mf(*ā*)n. belonging to the days of new and full moon and to the solstices, Mn.

पार्वत *pārvata*, mf(ī)n. (fr. *parvata*) being in or growing on or coming from or consisting of mountains; mountainous, hilly, MBh.; Hariv.; Pur. (cf. Pāṇ. iv, 2, 67, Sch.); m. Melia Bukayun, L.; (*ī*), f., see below.

Pārvatāyana, m. patr. of a chamberlain, Śak. vi, 𝑓 (v.l. *Parv°* and *Vātāyana*); cf. Pāṇ. iv, 1, 103.

Pārvati, m. patr. of Daksha, ŚBr.; cf. Pāṇ. ib.

Pārvatika, n. a multitude of mountains, mountain-range, L.

Pārvatī, f. (of °*ta*) a mountain stream, Naigh. i, 13; Boswellia Thurifera, L.; Grislea Tomentosa, L.; a kind of pepper, L.; =*kshudra-pāshāṇa-bhedā* or *jīvanī*, L.; a kind of fragrant earth, L.; a female cowherd or Gopī, L.; N. of the god Śiva's wife (as daughter of Hima-vat, king of the snowy mountains), Up.; MBh.; Kāv. &c. (RTL. 79); of Draupadī, L. (w. r. for *pārshatī*); of sev. other women, Cat.; of a river, VP.; of a cave in mount Meru, Hariv. **-kshetra**, n. 'district of Pārvatī (Durgā),' N. of one of the 4 esp. sacred districts of Orissa, L. **-dharma-putraka**, m. 'adopted son of P°,' N. of Paraśu-rāma, Bālar. **-nandana**, m. 'son of P°,' N. of Kārttikeya, L. **-nātha**, m. 'lord of P°,' N. of sev. men (the father of Tripurāri and the f° of Dharma-siṇha), Cat. **-netra**, m. (in music) a kind of measure. **-pati**, m. 'husband of P°,' N. of Śiva, Bālar. **-pariṇaya**, m. 'marriage of P°,' N. of a poem and a drama. **-paścāttāpa-varṇana**, n., **-pravartana**, n., **-prasādana**, n. N. of wks. **-prāṇa-nātha**, m. 'lord of the life of P°,' N. of Śiva, Bālar. **-mokshaṇa**, n. N. of ch. of GaṇP. **-locana**, m. (in music) a kind of measure. **-°śvara** (°*tīśv°*), m. =°*tī-nātha*; *-liṅga*, n. N. of a Liṅga, SkandaP. **-sakha**, m. 'friend of P°,' N. of Śiva, L. **-sampradāna**, n. N. of ch. of BrahmavP. **-sahasra-nāman**, n., **-stotra**, n. N. of wks. **-svayamvara**, m. N. of a drama.

Pārvatīya, mfn. living or dwelling in the mountains, mountainous; m. a mountaineer, MBh.; R. &c.; Juglans Regia, L.; N. of a sovereign ruling in the mountains, MBh.; (pl.) of a m° tribe, L.

Pārvateya, mf(*ī*)n. belonging or relating to the mountains, m°-born, W.; m. N. of a prince of mountaineers, MBh. (cf. °*tīya*); (*ī*), f. N. of the smaller or upper mill-stone, VS.; n. antimony, L.

पार्शव 1. *pārśava*, m. (fr. 1. *parśu*) a prince of the Parśus, Pāṇ. v, 3, 117.

Pārśukā, f. =*parśukā*, a rib, L.

Pārśvá, n. (rarely m., g. *ardharcâdi*; ifc. f. *ā*; fr. 1. *parśu*) the region of the ribs (pl. the ribs), side, flank (either of animate or inanimate objects), RV. &c. &c.; the side = nearness, proximity (with gen. or ifc.; *ayoḥ*, on both sides; *am*, aside, towards; *e*, at the side, near [opp. to *dūra-tas*]; *āt*, away, from; by means of, through), MBh.; Kāv. &c.; a curved knife, ŚBr.; a side of any square figure, W.; the curve or circumference of a wheel, ib.; (only n.) a multitude of ribs, the thorax, W.; the extremity of the fore-axle nearest the wheel to which the outside horses of a four-horse chariot are attached, L.; a fraudulent or crooked expedient, L.; m. the side horse on a chariot, MBh.; N. of an ancient Buddhist teacher; (with Jainas) N. of the 23rd Arhat of the present Ava-sarpiṇī and of his servant; (du.) heaven and earth, L.; mfn. near, proximate (cf. comp. below). **-ga**, mfn. going at a person's side, accompanying, being in close proximity to (gen. or comp.), an attendant; m. pl. attendants, retinue, Kāv.; Rājat. **-gata**, mfn. being at the s°, attending, accompanying, being close to or beside, Kāv.; Var.; sheltered, screening, MW. **-gamana**, n. the act of going by the s°, accompanying, Kathās. **-candra**, m. N. of an author, Cat. **-cara**, m. an attendant; pl. attendants, retinue, Ragh. **-tás**, ind. by or from the side, at the s°, near, sideways, aside (with gen. or ifc.), VS.; Br. &c. **-da**, m. 'turning the s° towards another,' an attendant; pl. attendants, retinue, MBh. (v.l. *pārshada*). **-dāha**, m. a burning pain in the s°, L. **-deva**, m. N. of an author, Cat. **-deśa**, m. the region of the s°, the ribs, L. **-druma**, m. pl. the trees at the s° or on every s°, MW. **-nātha**, m. N. of a Jaina teacher (predecessor of Mahā-vīra), MWB. 530; *-kāvya*, n., *-gītā*, f., *-caritra*, n., *-daśa-bhāva-visaha*, m., *-namaskāra*, m., *-purāṇa*, n., *-stava*, m., *-stuti*, f. N. of wks. **-parivartana**, n. 'turning round,' N. of a festival on the 11th day of the light half of the month Bhādra (on which Vishṇu is supposed to turn upon the other side in his sleep), Col. **-parivartita**, mfn. turned sidewards, Mālav. **-parivartin**, mfn. being or going by the side of (comp.), Ragh. **-pippala**, n. a species of Haritakī, Bhpr. **-bhaṅga**, m. pain in the s°, Suśr. **-bhāga**, m. 's°-portion,' the side or flank (of an elephant), L. **-maṇḍalin**, m. N. of a partic. posture in dancing, Cat. **-mānī**, f. the longer side of an oblong or the s° of a square, Śulbas. **-ruj**, f. =*-bhaṅga*, Suśr. **-vaktra**, m. 'whose face is in his side,' N. of one of Śiva's attendants, Hariv. **-vartin**, mfn. standing by the s°, an attendant; m. pl. attendants, retinue, Kāv. **-vivartin**, mfn. being by the s° of, living with (gen.), Kathās. **-śaya**, mfn. lying or sleeping on the s°, Pāṇ. iii, 2, 15, Vārtt. 1. **-śāyin**, m. id., N. of a partic. position of the moon, Var. **-śūla**, m. a shooting pain in the side, stitch, pleurisy, Suśr. **-saṃstha**, mfn. lying on the s°, Vet. **-saṃhita**, mfn. laid together (s° by s°), Lāṭy. **-saṃdhāna**, n. laying together (bricks) with their sides, Śulbas. **-sūtraka**, m. or n. a kind of ornament, L. **-stha**, mf(*ā*)n. standing at the side, being near or close to, adjacent, proximate, MBh.; Kāv. &c.; m. an associate, companion; (esp.) a stage manager's assistant (said to serve as a sort of chorus, sometimes an actor in the prelude who explains the plot), L. **-sthita**, mfn. standing at the side, being near or close, Rājat. **Pārśvânucara**, m. 'attending at the s°,' an attendant, body-servant, Ragh. **Pārśvâyāta**, mfn. one who has approached close to, Kathās. **Pārśvârti**, f. pain in the s°, pleurisy, Car. **Pārśvâvamarda**, m. id., ib. **Pārśvâsanna**, mfn. sitting by the s°, standing next, present, Kathās. **Pārśvâsīna**, mfn. sitting by the s°, ib. **Pārśvâsthi**, n. 's°-bone,' a rib, Say. **Pārśvâikādaśī**, f. =°*śva-parivartana*, L. **Pārśvôdara-priya**, m. 'fond of (moving) sideways on the belly,' a crab, L. **Pārśvôpapārśva**, m. du. flank and shoulder-blade, Nal. **Pārśvôpapīḍam**, ind. (to laugh) so as to hold one's sides, Kathās. (cf. Pāṇ. iii, 4, 49, Kāś.)

Pārśvaka, m. a rib, Yājñ.; n. a by-way, dishonest means, Hcat.; mfn. one who seeks wealth or other objects by indirect or side means, Pāṇ. v, 2, 75.

Pārśvatīya, mfn. (fr. *pārśva-tas*) being on or belonging to or situated at the side, g. *gahâdi*.

Pārśvala, mfn., g. *sidhmâdi*.

Pārśvika, mfn. lateral, belonging to the side, W. =°*śvaka*, mfn., L.; m. a sidesman, associate, W.; a juggler, ib.; N. of an ancient teacher, Buddh.; n. =°*śvaka*, n., Vishṇ.; Nār.

Pārśvya, m. du. heaven and earth, Naigh. iii, 30 (v.l. for *pārśvau*). Cf. *antaḥ-pārśvya*.

पार्शव 2. *pārśava*, m. (fr. 2. *parśu*) a warrior armed with an axe, W.

पार्श्व *pārśva*. See col. 1.

पार्षकि *pārshaki*, m. patr., Pravar.

पार्षत *pārshata*, mf(ī)n. (fr. *pṛishata*) belonging to the spotted antelope, made of its skin &c., Kauś.; Mn.; Yājñ.; MBh.; m. patr. of Dru-pada and his son Dhṛishṭa-dyumna, MBh.; (*ī*), f. patr. of Draupadī, ib.; of Durgā (w.r. for *pārvatī*), L.; Boswellia Thurifera, L.; =*jīvanī*, L.

1. **Pārshad**, Vṛiddhi form of *pṛishad* in comp. **-aṇśa**, mfn., g. *utsâdi*. **-aśva**, m. patr., ĀśvGṛ. **-vāṇá**, m. a patron., RV.

पार्षद् 2. *pārshad*, f. (cf. next) an assembly, L.; pl. the attendance or retinue of a god, BhP.

Pārshada, m. (fr. *parshad*) an associate, companion, attendant (esp. of a god), RāmatUp.; MBh.; Suśr. (pl. attendance, retinue, Hariv.; BhP.; Lalit.); a member of an assembly, spectator, Prasannar.; n. a text-book received by any partic. grammatical school (a N. given to the Prātiśākhyas), Nir. i, 17; N. of wk. **-ṭīkā**, f. N. of wk. **-tā**, f. the office of an attendant (esp. of the att° of a god), BhP. **-parišishṭa**, n., **-vṛitti**, f., **-vyākhyā**, f. N. of wks.

Pārshadaka, v.l. for *pārishadaka*, g. *kulālâdi*. °**diya**, mfn. conformable to the received text-book of any partic. grammatical school, RPrāt. °**dya**, m. =*pārishadya*, a member of an assembly, assessor; m. pl. =*pārshada*, pl., L.

पार्षिक *pārshika*, m. metron. of (*ā*), f. N. of a woman, g. *śivâdi*.

Pārshikya, n. (fr. *parshika*), g. *purohitâdi*.

पार्ष्कि *pārshki* (?), f. dung, L.

पार्ष्टिक *pārshṭika*, w. r. for *pārshṭhika*.

पार्ष्टेय *pārshṭeya*, mf(ī)n. (fr. *pṛishṭi*) being within the ribs, AV.

पार्ष्ठिक *pārshṭhika*, mfn. being after the manner of the Pṛishṭhya (Shaḍ-aha), ŚrS.

पार्ष्णि *pārshṇi*, f. (L. also m.; rarely *pārshṇī*, f.; fr. √*pṛish*? cf. Uṇ. iv, 52, Sch.) the heel, RV. &c. &c.; the extremity of the fore-axle to which the outside horses of a four-horse chariot are attached (the two inner horses being harnessed to the *dhur* or chariot-pole), MBh.; the rear of an army (°*ṇiṃ* √*grah* with gen., to attack in the rear), MBh.; Hariv.; Kāv.; the back, W.; a kick; ib.; enquiry, asking, ib.; a foolish or licentious woman, L.; N. of a plant (=*kuntī* or *kumbhī*), L. **-kshemana**, m. N. of a divinity, MBh. **-ga**, mfn. following a person's heels or the rear of an army, L. **-graha**, mfn. seizing or threatening from behind, BhP.; m. a follower, either an ally who supports or an enemy who attacks the rear of a king, MW. **-grahaṇa**, n. attacking or threatening an enemy in the rear, MBh. **-grāha**, mfn. attacking in the rear; m. 'heel-catcher,' an enemy in the rear or a commander in the rear of an army (applied also to hostile planets), Mn.; MBh. &c. **-ghāta**, m. a kick with the heels, Kathās. **-tra**, n. a rear-guard, reserve, L. **-prahāra**, m. =*-ghāta*, Kathās. **-yantṛi**, m. a charioteer who drives a side-horse, MBh. **-vāh** or **-vāha**, m. 'drawing (i. e. harnessed to) the extremities of the axle-tree;' an outside horse, MBh. **-sārathi**, m. du. the two charioteers who drive the outside horses (cf. prec.), MBh. **Pārshṇy-abhighāta**, m. =°*ṇi-ghāta*, Kathās.

Pārshṇila, mfn., g. *sidhmâdi*.

Pārshṇuvi (!), m. a patron., Cat.

पाल् *pāl*, cl. 10. P. (Dhātup. xxxii, 69) *pālayati* (°*te*; also regarded as Caus. of √2. *pā* [Pāṇ. vii, 3, 37, Vārtt. 2, Pat.], but rather Nom. of *pāla* below; p. P. *pālayat*, Ā. °*layāna*; pf. °*layām āsa*; aor. *apīpalat*), to watch, guard, protect, defend, rule, govern; to keep, maintain, observe (a promise or vow), AV.; Mn.; MBh.; Kāv. &c.

Pāla, m. (ifc. f. *ā*) a guard, protector, keeper, R.; Hariv.; a herdsman, Mn.; Gaut.; Yājñ.; MBh.; protector of the earth, king, prince, BhP.; (also n.) a spitting spittoon (as 'recipient'?), L.; N. of a serpent-demon of the race of Vāsuki, MBh.; of a prince, Cat.; (with *bhaṭṭa*) N. of an author, ib.; (*ī*), f. a herdsman's wife, MBh. v, 3608; an oblong pond (as 'receptacle' of water?), Var. (cf. *pālī*). **-kavi-rāja**, m. N. of a poet, Cat. (cf. *śrī-k°-r°*). **-kāvya**, n. N. of a poem, Cat. (w. r. for °*kāpya*? cf. below). **-ghna**, m. a mushroom, L. **-vaṇij**, w. r. for *pāna-v°*.

Pālaka, mf(*ikā*)n. guarding, protecting, nourishing, W.; m. a guardian, protector, MBh. (*ikā*, f.); a foster-father, Rājat.; a prince, ruler, sovereign, ib.; BhP.; a world-protector (=*loka-p°*), Kām.; a horse-keeper, groom, L.; a maintainer, observer, MārkP.; a species of plant with a poisonous bulb, Suśr.; Plumbago Zeylanica, L.; a horse, L.; N. of sev. princes, Mṛicch.; Kathās; Pur.; n. a spittoon, Gal. (cf. *pāla* above). **-gotra**, n. the family or tribe of one's adoptive parents, MW. **Pālakâkhyā**, f. N. of the mother of Pālakāpya (below).

Pālana, mf(*ī*)n. guarding, nourishing (*°nī janani*, f. a foster-mother), MārkP.; n. the act of guarding, protecting, nourishing, defending, Mn.; MBh. &c.; maintaining, keeping, observing, MBh.; Kāv. &c.; the milk of a cow that has recently calved, L. (*-karman*, n. superintendence, Śak.; *-vṛitti*, f. a partic. manner of subsistence, Baudh.) **°laniya**, mfn. to be guarded or protected or maintained or observed, MBh. **°layitṛi**, mfn. protecting, cherishing; a protector or guardian, Kauś.; MBh.; Kāv. &c. **°li**, m. (prob.) a protector, ruler (cf. *go-pāli* and *prajā-p°*). **°lita**, mfn. guarded, protected, cherished, nourished, MBh.; R. &c.; m. Trophis Aspera, L.; N. of a prince (son of Parā-jit or Parā-vṛit), Hariv.; Pur. (v.l. *palita*); of a poet, Cat.; (*ā*), f. N. of one of the Mātṛis attending on Skanda, MBh. **°lin**, mfn. protecting, guarding, keeping, Śukas.; BhP.; m. (ifc.) a ruler, king of, BhP.; N. of a son of Pṛithu, Hariv.; (*inī*), f. Ficus Heterophylla, L. **°lī-vrata**, n. a partic. observance, Cat. **°leya**, mfn. (fr. *pāla*), g. *saṃkāśâdi*. **°lya**, mfn. = *°laniya*, MBh.; Kathās.; being under any one's (gen.) protection or guardianship, Rājat.

पालकाप्य *pālakāpya*, m. N. of an ancient sage or Muni (=*kareṇu-bhū* or =*dhanvan-tari*), L.; of an author, Cat.; n. N. of his wk. (cf. *pālakāvya* above).

पालक्क *pālakka*, m. or n. N. of a country, Inscr.

पालक्या *pālakyā*, f. Beta Bengalensis, Car.

पालङ्क *pālaṅka* (only L.), m. Boswellia Thurifera; a species of bird; m. and (*ī*), f. Beta Bengalensis (also *°kikā*, Bhpr.); (*ī*), f. gum olibanum, incense, L.

Pālaṅkya, n. and (*ā*), f. incense, Suśr.; Beta Bengalensis, Bhpr.

पालङ्गिन् *pālaṅgin*, m. pl N. of a school called after a disciple of Vaiśampāyana, Pāṇ. iv, 3, 104, Sch.

पालद *pālada*, mfn. (fr. *pala-da*), Pāṇ. iv, 2, 110.

पालल *pālala*, mf(i)n. (fr. *palala*) made of powdered sesamum seed, Suśr.

पालवी *pālavī*, f. a kind of vessel, Hariv.

पालहारि *pālahāri*, m. (patr. fr. *palahara?*) N. of a man, Rājat.

पालागल *pālāgalá*, m. a runner, messenger (according to others 'a bearer of false tidings'), ŚBr.; KātyŚr., Sch.; (*ī*), f. the fourth and least respected wife of a prince, ib.

पालाश *pā́lāśa*, mf(i)n. (fr. *palāśa*) coming from or belonging to the tree Butea Frondosa, made of its wood, Br.; GṛŚrS.; MBh. &c.; green, Var.; m. Butea Frondosa, MBh. (m. c. for *palāśa*). **-karman**, n. N. of a partic. ceremony, ĀpGṛ., Sch. **-kalpa** and **-vidhi**, m. N. of wks. **-khaṇḍa**, and **-shaṇḍa**, m. N. of Magadha, L.

Pālāśaka, mfn. (fr. *palāśa*), g. *varāhâdi*.

Pālāśi, m. (patr. fr. *palāśa*), Pravar.

पालि *pāli*, f. (in most meanings and ifc. f. also *ī* [cf. under *pāla*]; according to Uṇ. iv, 129, Sch. fr. √*pal*) the tip or lobe of the ear, the outer ear, Suśr. (cf. *karṇa-* and *śravaṇa-p°*); a boundary, limit, margin, edge, MBh.; Kāv. &c.; a row, line, range, Ratnâv.; Śiś.; Git.; a dam, dike, bridge, Rājat.; a pot, boiler, HPariś.; a partic. measure of capacity (= *prastha*), L.; prescribed food, maintenance of a scholar during the period of his studies by his teacher, L.; the lap, bosom, L.; a circumference, L.; a mark, spot, L.; a louse, L.; a woman with a beard, L. = *praśaṇsā*, L. (*°lī*, ifc. to denote praise, Gaṇ.); = *prabedha*, L. **-m-hira**, m. (w. r. for *-hara*, 'seizing by the tip of the ear'?) a kind of snake, Suśr. **-jvara**, m. a kind of fever, L. **-bhaṅga**, m. bursting of a dike, Rājat. **Pāly-āmaya**, m. a disease of the outer ear, Suśr.

Pālikā, f. (cf. under *pāla*) the tip of the ear, L.; a margin, edge, L.; a pot or boiler, HPariś.; a cheese or butter knife, L.

पालित *pālita*. See under √*pāl*.

पालित्य *pā́litya*, n. (fr. *palita*) greyness (of age), hoariness, AV.; mfn., g. *saṃkāśâdi*.

पालिन्द *pālinda*, m. incense, L.; Jasminum Pubescens, W.; (*ī*), f. Ichnocarpus Frutescens, Suśr. (also *°ndi*); = next, L.

Pālindhī, f. a species of Ipomoea with dark blossoms, L.

पालिशायन *pāliśāyana*, m. patr., Pravar.

पालीवत *pālivata*, m. a species of tree, Var. (prob. = *pārevata*).

पालोहय *pālohaya* (!), m. patr., Pravar.

पाल्लक *pāllaka*, mfn. (fr. *pallī*), g. *dhūmâdi*.

पाल्लवा *pāllavā*, f. (fr. *pallava*, sc. *krīḍā*) a game played with twigs, L.

Pāllavika, mfn. diffusive, digressive, Car.

पाल्वल *pālvala*, mf(ī)n. (fr. *palvala*) coming from a tank or pool, Suśr. **-tīra**, mfn. (fr. *palvala-tīra*), Pāṇ. iv, 2, 106, Sch.

पाव *pāva*, mfn. (√*pū*) only in *hiraṇya-p°*, q. v.; m. (in music) a partic. wind-instrument; (*ā*), f., see col. 3.

Pāvaká, mf(*ā́*)n. pure, clear, bright, shining, RV.; VS.; AV. (said of Agni, Sūrya and other gods, of water, day and night &c.; according to native Comms. it is mostly = *śodhaka*, 'cleansing, purifying'); m. N. of a partic. Agni (in the Purāṇas said to be a son of Agni Abhimānin and Svāhā or of Antardhāna and Śikhaṇḍinī), TS.; TBr.; KātyŚr.; Pur.; (ifc. f. *ā*) fire or the god of fire, Up.; MBh.; Kāv. &c.; N. of the number 3 (like all words for 'fire,' because fire is of three kinds, see *agni*), Sūryas.; a kind of Ṛishi, a saint, a person purified by religious abstraction or one who purifies from sin, MBh.; Premna Spinosa, L.; Plumbago Zeylanica or some other species, L.; Semecarpus Anacardium, L.; Carthamus Tinctoria, L.; Embelia Ribes, L.; (*ikā*), f. (in music) = *pāva*; (*ī*), f. the wife of Agni, L. **-vat**, mfn. containing the word or having the name *pāvaka*; N. of a partic. Agni, AitBr.; ŚrS. **-varcas** (*°ká-*), mfn. brightly resplendent (as Agni), RV. **-varṇa** (*°ká-*), mfn. of pure or brilliant aspect, ib.; VS.; Gaut. **-śocis** (*°ká-*), mfn. (voc. *°ce*) shining brightly, RV. **-suta**, m. patr. of Su-darśana, MBh. **Pāvakâtmaja**, m. patr. of Skanda, ib. **Pāvakâraṇi**, m. Premna Spinosa, L. **Pāvakârcis**, f. a flash of fire, MBh. **Pāvakâstra**, n. a fiery weapon, Uttarar. vi, 𝔰. **Pāvakêśvara**, n. N. of a Tīrtha, ŚivaP.

Pāvaki, m. 'son of Fire,' N. of Skanda, MBh.; Hariv.; R.; of Su-darśana, MBh.; of Vishṇu, Hariv.

Pāvakīya, mfn. coming from the god of fire or relating to him, Cat.; fiery (said of weapons), Bālar. vii, 33 (cf. *pāvakâstra*).

Pāvana, mf(*ī*)n. purifying, purificatory; pure, holy, Mn.; MBh. &c.; living on wind, Nilak.; m. a partic. fire, Kull. on Mn. iii, 185; fire, L.; incense, L.; a species of Verbesina with yellow flowers, L.; a Siddha (s. v.), L.; N. of Vyāsa, L.; of one of the Viśve Devāḥ, MBh.; of a son of Kṛishṇa, BhP.; (*ī*), f. Terminalia Chebula, L.; holy basil, L.; a cow, L.; N. of a river, MBh.; R.; the Ganges or the goddess Gaṅgā, W.; n. the act or a means of cleansing or purifying, purification, sanctification, Mn.; MBh. &c.; penance, atonement, L.; water, L.; cow-dung, L.; the seed of Elaeocarpus Ganitrus (of which rosaries are made), L.; Costus Speciosus, L.; a sectarial mark, L.; = *adhyāsa*, L. **-tva**, n. the property of cleansing or purifying, Sāh. **-dhvani**, m. a conch-shell, L.

Pāvamāná, mf(*ī*)n. (fr. *pavamāna*) relating to Soma juice (while being purified by a strainer) or to Agni Pavamāna, TS.; AV.; TāṇḍBr.; Gobh.; m. pl. the authors of the Pāvamānī hymns or verses, ŚāṅkhGṛ.; (*ī*), f. sg. or pl. N. of partic. hymns (esp. those of RV. ix, AV. xix, 71 &c.), Br.; GṛŚrS.; Mn. &c. (also *°māna*, m.); n. N. of sev. Sāmans, ĀrshBr.

Pāvita, mfn. (fr. √*pū*, Caus.) cleansed, purified, Mn.; MBh. &c.

Pāvitra, n. a kind of metre, Col. (w. r. for *pav°*?).

Pāvitrāyaṇa, m. patr. fr. *pavitra*, g. *aśvâdi*.

Pāvitrya, n. purity, Siṇhās.

Pāvinī, f. (prob.) w. r. for *pāvanī*, MBh. iii, 10543.

Pāvya, mfn. to be cleansed or purified, Bhaṭṭ.

पावन् 1. 2. *pāvan*. See under √1. 3. *pā*.

पावर *pāvara*, m. or n. the die or side of a die which is marked with 2 dots or points (prob. corrupted fr. *dvā-para*), Mṛicch. ii, 8.

पावष्टुरिकेय *pāvashṭurikeya*, m. patr. fr. *pavashṭurika*, g. *śubhrâdi*.

पावा *pāvā*, f. N. of a city near Rāja-gṛiha, Buddh. **-purī**, f. id., ib. (also written *pāpā-p°*).

पाविन्दायन *pāvindāyana*, m. metron. fr. *pavindā*, g. *aśvâdi* (Kāś.)

पावीरव *pā́vīrava*, mf(ī)n. (fr. *pavīru*) proceeding from or relating to the thunderbolt; (*ī*), f. (with or sc. *kanyā*) 'daughter of lightning,' the noise of thunder, RV.

पाश *pā́śa*, m. (once n., ifc. f. *ā*; fr. √3. *paś*) a snare, trap, noose, tie, bond, cord, chain, fetter (lit. and fig.), RV. &c. &c.; (esp.) the noose as attribute of Śiva or Yama, RTL. 81; 290; (with Jainas) anything that binds or fetters the soul, i. e. the outer world, nature, Sarvad. (cf. also RTL. 89); selvage, edge, border (of anything woven), ŚrGṛS.; a die, dice, MBh.; (in astrol.) a partic. constellation; (ifc. it expresses either contempt e. g. *chattra-p°*, 'a shabby umbrella,' or admiration e. g. *karṇa-p°*, 'a beautiful ear;' after a word signifying 'hair' = abundance, quantity e. g. *keśa-p°*, 'a mass of hair'); (*ī*), f. a rope, fetter, Śiś. xviii, 57 (cf. also 2. *pāśī*). **-kaṇṭha**, mfn. having a noose round the neck, Kathās. **-kapālin**, mfn. having a noose and a skull, HPariś. **-krīḍā**, f. 'dice-play,' gambling, Siṇhās. **-jāla**, n. the outer world conceived as a net (cf. above), Sarvad. **-tva**, n. the state or condition of the outer world or nature, ib. **-dyumna** (*pā́śa-*), m. N. of a man, RV. **-dhara**, m. 'holding a noose,' N. of Varuṇa, Hariv. **-pāṇi**, m. 'n° in hand,' id., ShaḍvBr. **-baddha**, mfn. noosed, snared, caught, bound, W. **-bandha**, m. a noose, snare, halter, net, Hit. **-bandhaka**, m. a bird-catcher, Pañc. **-bandhana**, n. a snare, fetter, BhP.; mfn. hanging in a sn°, Kathās. **-bhṛit**, m. = *-dhara*, Var.; Ragh. **-rajju**, f. a fetter, rope, Kathās. **-vat**, mfn. having or possessing a noose (as Varuṇa), MBh. **-hasta**, mfn. n° in hand, VP.; m. N. of Yama, Kathās. **Pāśânta**, m. the back of a garment (opp. to *daśā*), Var. **Pāśâbhidhānā**, f. N. of the 12th day of a half-month, Hcat.

Pāśaka, m. a snare, trap, noose (ifc.; cf. *kaṇṭha-, daṇḍa-*); a die, HPariś.; (*ikā*), f. a strap of leather on a plough, Kṛishis. **-kevalī**, f. N. of wk. (also spelled *pāśākevalī* or *pāśaka-keralī*). **-pīṭha**, m. or n. a gaming-table, Mṛicch.

Pāśaya, Nom. P. *°śayati*, to bind, Nir. iv, 2; Dhātup. xxxiii, 45.

Pāśāya, Nom. Ā. *°yate*, to become a rope, Kāv.

Pāśika, m. one who snares animals, a bird-catcher, Var.; N. of a man, Rājat.; (*ā*), f., see under *pāśaka*.

Pāśita, mfn. tied, fettered, bound, snared, Daś.; AgP.

Pāśin, mfn. having a net or noose, laying snares; m. a bird-catcher, trapper, Āpast.; N. of Varuṇa, MBh.; Hariv.; of Yama, RTL. 290; of a son of Dhṛita-rāshṭra, MBh.

Pāśila, mfn. (fr. *pāśa*), g. *kāśâdi*.

Pāśi-vāṭa, m. pl. N. of a people, MBh.

Pāśyā, f. a multitude of nooses or ropes, a net, Pāṇ. iv, 2, 49.

पाशव *pāśava*, mf(i)n. (fr. *paśu*) derived from or belonging to cattle or animals (with *māṇsa*, n. an° food), Kauś.; Vet.; Suśr.; n. a flock, herd, W. **-pālana**, n. 'nourishing flocks,' pasturage or meadow grass, L. **-mata**, n. an erroneous doctrine, Hariv.

Pāśuka, mf(*ī*)n. relating to cattle (esp. to the sacrificial animal), ŚrS. (cf. Pāṇ. iv, 3, 72). **-cāturmāsya**, n. N. of wk. **Pāśukâdi-prayoga**, m. N. of ch. of Sāyaṇa's Yajña-tantra-sudhā-nidhi.

Pāśupata, mf(*ī*)n. relating or sacred to or coming from Śiva Paśu-pati, MBh.; Kāv. &c.; m. a follower or worshipper of S° P°, Kathās.; Rājat.

(cf. RTL. 59); Agati Grandiflora, L.; Getonia Floribunda, L.; n. = -jñāna, MBh.; N. of a celebrated weapon given by Śiva to Arjuna, MBh. iii, 1650 &c.; of a place sacred to Śiva Paśu-pati, Cat. **-jñāna**, n. the doctrine of the Pāśupatas, Cat. **-brahmôpanishad**, f. N. of an Up. **-yoga**, m. the system of the P°, Sarvad.; *-prakaraṇa*, n., *-vidhi*, m. N. of wks. **-vrata**, n. = *-yoga*, MBh.; N. of the 40th Pariś. of AV.; *-vivaraṇa*, n. N. of a ch. of LiṅgaP. **-vratin**, m. a follower of Śiva Paśu-pati; °*ti-veśa*, mfn. wearing the dress of a f° of Ś° P°, Rājat. **-śāstra**, n. = *-jñāna*, Sarvad. **Pāśupatâstra**, n. Śiva's trident, MBh. **Pāśupatôpanishad**, f. N. of an Up.

Pāśupālya, n. (fr. *paśu-pāla*) the breeding and rearing of cattle, Yājñ.; MBh. &c.

Pāśubandhaka, mf(*ikā*)n. and °**bandhika**, mf(*ī*)n. (fr. *paśu-bandha*) relating to the slaughter of a sacrificial animal.

पाशी 2. *pāśī*, f. (for 1. see under *pāśa*) a stone, Kauś. 83; 85 (v.l. *pāsī*; cf. *pāshāṇa*, *pāsh-*).

पाश्चात्त्य *pāścāttya* or *pāścātya*, mf(*ā*)n. (fr. *paścāt* or *paścā*) hinder, western, posterior, last, MBh.; R.; Pañc. **-nirṇayâmṛita**, n. N. of wk. **-bhāga**, m. the hinder part (of a needle, i.e. its eye), ŚārṅgP. **-rātri** (only *au*, ind.), towards the end of the night, Kathārṇ. **Pāścātyâkara-sambhava**, n. a species of salt coming from the West (= *romaka*), L.

पाषक *pāshaka*, m. an ornament for the feet, BrahmavP.

पाषण्ड *pāshaṇḍa*, mf(*ī*)n. (wrongly spelt *pākhaṇḍa*) heretical, impious, MBh.; Pur.; m. a heretic, hypocrite, impostor, any one who falsely assumes the characteristics of an orthodox Hindū, a Jaina, Buddhist, ib. &c.; m. or n. false doctrine, heresy, Mn.; BhP. **-khaṇḍana**, n. N. of wk. **-capeṭikā**, f. N. of wk. **-tā**, f. heresy, heterodoxy, Inscr. **-dalana**, n., **-mukha-capeṭikā**, f., **-mukha-mardana**, n. N. of wks. **-viḍambana**, n. N. of a comedy. **-stha**, mfn. addicted to heresy, belonging to an heretical sect, Mn. ix, 225. **Pāshaṇḍâsya-capeṭikā**, f. = °*ḍa-mukha-capeṭikā*.

Pāshaṇḍaka or °**ḍika** (L.), °**ḍin** (Mn.; Yājñ. &c.), m. a heretic (cf. IW. 219; 299).

Pāshāṇḍa, °**ḍin**, v.l. for *pāshaṇḍa*, °*ḍin*.

Pāshāṇḍya, n. heresy, Yājñ.

पाषाण *pāshāṇa*, m. (ifc. f. *ā*; according to Uṇ. ii, 90, Sch. fr. √*pash*; cf. *pāsī*) a stone, Br.; MBh. &c.; (*ī*), f. a small stone used as a weight, L.; a spear, A. **-gardabha**, m. a hard swelling on the maxillary joint, Suśr. **-ghāta-dāyin**, mfn. throwing or striking with a stone, Kathās. **-caturdaśī**, f. the 14th day in the light half of the month Mārgaśīrsha (on which a festival of Gaurī is celebrated, when cakes made of rice and shaped like large pebbles are eaten), BhavP. **-caya-nibaddha**, mfn. surrounded with a coping of stone (as a well), Pañc. **-dāraka** or **-dāraṇa**, m. a stone-cutter's chisel, L. **-bheda**, m. Plectranthus Scutellarioides, Car.; *-rasa*, m. its juice, Rasar. **-bhedaka**, m. = *-bheda*, Bhpr. **-bhedana**, m. id. or Lycopodium Imbricatum, L. **-bhedin**, m. id. or Coleus Amboinicus, L. **-maya**, mf(*ī*)n. consisting or made of stone, Kull. **-vajraka-rasa**, m. a partic. medicinal preparation, Rasar. **-śilā**, f. a flat stone, Siṅhās. **-saṃdhi**, m. a cave or chasm in a rock, L. **-setu-bandha**, m. a barrier or dam of stone, Rājat. **-hṛidaya**, mfn. stone-hearted, cruel, MW.

Pāshī, f. = *śilā*, a stone or = *śakti*, a spear, Sāy. on RV. i, 56, 6 (cf. 2. *pāśī*).

Pāshyà, n. pl. stones, a rampart of stones, RV.; du. the two stones for pressing the Soma, ib.

पाष्ठौह *pāshṭhauha*, n. (fr. *pashṭha-vāh*) N. of a Sāman, Br.; Lāṭy.

पास *pāsa*, m. v.l. for *yāsa*; (*ī*), f. v.l. for *pāśī*.

पास्त्य *pāstyá*, mfn. belonging to a house, domestic; n. (?) household, RV. iv, 21, 6.

पाहणपुर *pāhaṇa-pura*, n. N. of a place, Romakas.

पाहाडिका *pāhāḍikā* and *pāhiḍā*, f. (in music) N. of Rāgiṇīs (cf. *pahāḍī*).

पाहात *pāhāta*, m. the Indian mulberry tree, Morus Indica (= *brahma-dāru*), L.

पि 1. *pi*, cl. 6. P. *piyati*, to go, move, Dhātup. xxviii, 112 (cf. √2. *pī*).

पि 2. *pi*. See under *api*.

पिंश् *piṇś* and *piṇsh*. See √*piś* and *pish*.

पिंस् *piṇs*, cl. 1. 10. *piṇsati*, °*sayati*, to speak; to shine, Dhātup. xxxiii, 89.

पिक *piká*, m. the Indian cuckoo, Cuculus Indicus, VS.; Kāv. &c.; (*ī*), f. a female cuckoo, Kathās. **-nikara**, m. a pseudonym of a poet, Cat. **-priyā**, f. 'dear to the cuckoo,' a species of Jambū, L. **-bandhu**, m. 'c°'s friend,' the mango tree, L. **-bāndhava**, m. 'id.,' the spring, L. **-bhakshā**, f. 'c°'s food' = *bhūmi-jambū*, L. **-rāga** and **-vallabha**, m. 'c°'s favourite,' the mango tree, L. **-svarā**, f. 'c°'s note,' N. of a Surâṅganā, Siṅhās. **Pikâksha**, n. 'c°'s eye,' = *rocanī*, L. **Pikâṅga**, m. 'c°-shaped,' a partic. bird, L. **Pikânanda**, m. 'c°'s joy,' the spring, L. **Pikêkshaṇā**, f. 'c°'s eye,' Asteracantha Longifolia, L.

पिक्क *pikka*, m. an elephant 20 years old (= *vikka*), any young el°, L.; (*ā*), f. a collection or string of 13 pearls weighing a Dharaṇa, VarBṛS. lxxxi, 17 (cf. *piccā*).

पिङ्ग *piṅga*, *piṅgara*, *piṅgala*. See under √*piñj*, col. 3.

पिचण्ड *picaṇḍa*, m. n. the belly or abdomen, L.; m. a partic. part or limb of an animal, L. °**ḍaka**, mfn. = °*ḍe kuśalaḥ*, g. *âkarshâdi*; (*ikā*), f. the calf of the leg or the instep, L. °**ḍika**, °**ḍin** (g. *tuṇḍâdi*), °**ḍila** (Kāśīkh.), mfn. big-bellied, corpulent.

Piciṇḍa, m. = *picaṇḍa*, L.; *-vat*, mfn. corpulent, L. °**ḍikā**, f., °**ḍila**, mfn. = *picaṇḍikā*, °*ḍila*.

पिचिल *picila*, m. an elephant, Gal.

पिचु *picu*, m. cotton, Car.; Vangueria Spinosa, Suśr.; a sort of grain, L.; a Karsha or weight of 2 Tolas, Suśr.; a kind of leprosy, L.; N. of Bhairava or of one of his 8 faces, L.; of an Asura, L. **-tūla**, n. cotton, L. **-manda** or **-marda**, m. the Nimb tree, Azadirachta Indica, L. **-vaktrā**, f. N. of a Yoginī, Hcat.

Picavya, m. the cotton plant, L.

Picuka, m. Vangueria Spinosa, Suśr.

Picukīya, mfn., g. *utkarâdi*.

Picula, m. a species of tree (Barringtonia Acutangula or Tamarix Indica), L. (cf. IW. 423, 3); cotton, L.; a kind of cormorant or sea crow, L.

पिच् *picc*, cl. 10. P. *piccayati*, to press flat, squeeze, Dhātup. xxxii, 40 (v.l. for *pich*, q.v.)

Piccaṭa, mfn. pressed flat, squeezed, L.; m. inflammation of the eyes, ophthalmia, L.; n. a substance pressed flat, cake (cf. *tila-p°*); tin or lead, L.

Piccita, mfn. = *piccaṭa*, Suśr.

पिच्चा *piccā*, f. a collection or string of 16 pearls weighing a Dharaṇa, VarBṛS. lxxxi, 17 (v.l. *pivā*; cf. *pikkā*).

पिच्चिट *picciṭa* and °*ṭaka*, m. a species of venomous insect, Suśr.

पिच्छोरा *picchorā*, f. a pipe, flute, ŚrS.

Piccholā, f. id., ib.; = *oshadhi*, L.

पिच्छ् *pich*, cl. 10. P. *picchayati*, to press flat, squeeze, expand, divide, Dhātup. xxxii, 20 (v.l. *picc*; cf. above); cl. 6. P. *picchati*, to inflict pain, hurt, Dhātup. xxviii, 16, Vop.

Piccha, n. a feather of a tail (esp. of a peacock, prob. from its being spread or expanded), MBh.; Kāv. &c.; (pl.) the feathers of an arrow, KātyŚr., Sch.; a tail (also m.), L.; a wing, L.; a crest, L.; (*ā*), f. the scum of boiled rice and of other grain, L.; the gum of Bombax Heptaphyllum, L.; slimy saliva, Car.; the venomous saliva of a snake, L.; a multitude, mass, heap, Car.; the calf of the leg, Var.; a sheath or cover, L.; the areca-nut, L.; a row or line, L.; a diseased affection of a horse's feet, L.; Dalbergia Sissoo, L.; = *mocā* and *picchila*, L.; armour, a sort of cuirass, L. **-bāṇa**, m. 'arrow-feathered,' a hawk, L. **-latikā**, f. a tail-feather, Bālar. **-vat**, mfn. having a tail, tailed, W. **Picchâsrāva**, m. slimy saliva, Car.

Picchaka, m. or n. a tail-feather, Cat. (cf. *citra-p°*); (*ikā*), f. a bunch of peacock's tail-feathers (used by conjurors), Ratnâv.

Picchana, n. pressing flat, squeezing, Car.

Picchala, mfn. slimy, slippery, smeary, MBh.; Kād. (v.l. *picchila*); m. N. of a Nāga of the race of Vāsuki, MBh.; (*ā*), f. N. of sev. plants (Dalbergia Sissoo, Bombax Heptaphyllum &c.), L.; of a river, MBh. (v.l. *picchilā*). **-dalā**, f. Zizyphus Jujuba, L. **Picchalâṅga**, m. Pimelodus Gagora (= *gargara*), Gal.

Picchitikā (!), f. Dalbergia Sissoo, L. (w.r. for *picchilikā*?).

Picchila, mf(*ā*)n. slimy, lubricous, slippery, smeary (opp. to *viśada*), MBh.; Suśr. (*-tva*, n.), &c.; having a tail, W.; m. Cordia Latifolia, L.; Tamarix Indica, L.; (*ā*), f. N. of a river, MBh. (v.l. *picchalā*); of sev. trees and other plants (Dalbergia Sissoo, Bombax Heptaphyllum, Basella Lucida or Rubra, a kind of grass &c.), L. **-cchadā**, f. Basella Cordifolia, L. **-tvac**, m. Grewia Elastica, L.; an orange tree or orange-peel, L. **-bīja**, n. the fruit of Dillenia Indica, L. **-sāra**, m. the gum of Bombax Heptaphyllum, L. **Picchilā-tantra**, n. N. of a Tantra.

Picchilaka, m. Grewia Elastica, L.

Picchilī-√kṛi, to make slippery or smeary, Kād.

Piñcha, n. a wing (= *piccha*), L.

पिजवन *pijavana*, m. N. of a man, Nir. ii, 24 (cf. *paijavana*).

पिजूल *pijūla*, m. N. of a man, g. *aśvâdi*.

पिञ्चदेव *piñca-deva*, m. N. of a man, Rājat.

पिञ्ज् *piñj*, cl. 2. Ā. *piṅkte*, to tinge, dye, paint, Dhātup. xxiv, 18; 20; to join, ib. (cf. √*pṛic*); to sound, ib.; to adore, ib.; Vop.; cl. 10. P. *piñjayati*, to kill; to be strong; to give or to take (?); to dwell, Dhātup. xxxii, 31; to shine; to speak, xxxiii, 84; to emit a sound, Nir. iii, 18. [Cf. Lat. *pingo*?]

Piṅga, mf(*ā*)n. yellow, reddish-brown, tawny, MBh.; Kāv. &c. (cf. g. *kaḍārâdi*); m. yellow (the colour), L.; a buffalo, L.; a mouse, L.; N. of one of the sun's attendants, L.; of a man, ĀśvŚr. (cf. *paiṅgi*, °*gin*); (*piṅgá*, in one place *píṅga*), N. of a kind of divine being (?), AV. viii, 6, 6; 18 &c.; (*piṅgā*), f. a bow-string, RV. viii, 58, 9 (Sāy.; cf. *piṅgala-jya*); a kind of yellow pigment (cf. *go-rocanā*); the stalk of Ferula Asa Foetida, L.; turmeric, Indian saffron, L.; bamboo manna, W.; N. of a woman, MBh.; of Durgā, W.; a tubular vessel of the human body which according to the Yoga system is the channel of respiration and circulation for one side, ib.; (*ī*), f. Mimosa Suma, ib.; n. orpiment, L.; a young animal, MW. **-kapiśā**, f. 'reddish-brown,' a species of cockroach, L. **-cakshus**, m. 'yellow-eyed,' a crab, L. **-jaṭa**, m. 'having y°-braided hair,' N. of Śiva, L. **-tīrtha**, n. N. of a Tīrtha, MBh. **-danta**, m. 'y°-toothed,' N. of a man, Kathās. **-dṛiś**, m. 'y°-eyed,' N. of Śiva, Gal. **-deha**, m. 'y°-bodied,' id., Śivag. **-mūla**, m. 'having a reddish root,' a carrot, L. **-locana**, mfn. having r°-brown eyes, Var. **-varṇavatī**, f. turmeric, L. **-sāra**, m. yellow orpiment, L. **-sphaṭika**, m. 'y°-crystal,' a kind of gem, L. **Piṅgâkshá**, mf(*ī*)n. = °*ga-locana*, VS.; ŚBr. &c.; m. an ape, R.; N. of Agni, MBh.; of Śiva, L.; of a Rakshas, Cat.; of a Daitya, Kathās.; of a wild man, Kāśīkh.; of a bird (one of the 4 sons of Droṇa), MārkP.; (*ī*), f. N. of a deity presiding over families, Cat.; of one of Skanda's attendant Mātṛis, MBh. **Piṅgâsya**, m. 'tawny-faced,' a species of fish, Pilemodius Pangasius, L. **Piṅgêkshaṇa**, mfn. = °*ga-locana*, Var.; N. of Śiva, L. **Piṅgêśa**, m. 'lord of the yellow hue,' N. of Agni, MBh. **Piṅgêśvara**, m. 'id.,' N. of a being attendant on Pārvatī, L.

Piṅgara, m. N. of a man, MW.

Piṅgalá, mf(*â* and *ī*)n. (cf. g. *gaurâdi* and *kaḍārâdi*), reddish-brown, tawny, yellow, gold-coloured, AV. &c. &c.; (in alg. also as N. of the 10th unknown quantity); having r°-b° eyes, KātyŚr., Sch.; m. yellow colour, W.; fire, L.; an ape, L.; an ichneumon, L.; a small kind of owl, L.; a small kind of lizard, L.; a species of snake, Suśr.; a partic. vegetable poison, L.; (with Jainas) N. of a treasure; the 51st (or 25th) year in a 60 years' cycle of Jupiter, Var.; N. of Śiva or a kindred being, GṛS.;

Gaut. &c.; of an attendant of Śiva, Kathās.; of an attendant of the Sun, L.; of a Rudra, VP.; of a Yaksha, MBh.; of a Dānava, Kathās.; of a Nāga or serpent-demon, MBh. i, 1554 (the supposed author of the Chandas or treatise on metre regarded as one of the Vedâṅgas, identified by some with Patañjali, author of the Mahā-bhāshya); of sev. ancient sages, MBh.; R. &c.; pl. N. of a people, MārkP.; (*ā*), f. a species of bird, L.; a kind of owl, Var.; Dalbergia Sissoo, L.; = *karṇikā*, L.; a kind of brass, L.; a partic. vessel of the body (the right of 3 tubular vessels which according to the Yoga philosophy are the chief passages of breath and air; cf. ChUp. viii, 6, 1); a kind of yellow pigment (= *go-rocanā*), L.; N. of Lakshmī, Gal.; of a courtezan who became remarkable for her piety, MBh.; of the female elephant of the South quarter, L.; of an astrological house or period, W.; heart-pea, W.; n. a partic. metal, L.; yellow orpiment, L. — **kāṇva**, m. N. of a teacher, Pat. — **gāndhāra**, m. N. of a Vidyā-dhara, Kathās. — **cchandaḥ-sūtra**, n. N. of Piṅgala's work on metrics; °*do-vṛitti* and °*do-vṛitti-vyākhyā*, f. N. of Comms. on this wk. — **jya**, mfn. having a brown string (Śiva's bow), MBh. vii, 6148 (cf. *piṅgā*). — **tattva-prakāśikā** (and °*śinī*), f. N. of wks. — **tva**, n. a tawny or yellow colour, R. — **nāga**, m. the serpent-demon Piṅgala, IW. 153. — **prakāśa**, m., **-praṇavôpanishad**, f., **-pradīpa**, m., **-bhāvôddyota**, m., **-mata-prakāśa**, m. N. of wks. — **roman**, mfn. tawny-haired (said of a Piśāca), Hariv. — **loha**, n. a kind of metal, L. — **vatsâjīva**, m. N. of a man, Divyâv. — **vārttika**, n., **-vṛitti**, f., **-sāra**, m. (and *-vikāśinī*, f.), **-sūtra**, n. N. of wks. **Piṅgalâksha**, mfn. having reddish-brown eyes, TPrāt., Sch.; m. N. of Śiva, MW. **Piṅgalā-tantra**, n., **Piṅgalā-mata**, n., **Piṅgalâmṛita**, n., **Piṅgalârtha-dīpa**, m., **Piṅgalâryā**, f. N. of wks. **Piṅgalêśvara**, n. N. of a Liṅga, Cat. (*-tīrtha*, n. N. of a Tīrtha, ib.; *-māhātmya*, n. N. of wk., ib.); (*ī*), f. a form of Dākshāyaṇī, ib.

Piṅgalaka, mf(*ikā*)n. reddish-brown, yellow, tawny, AV.; m. N. of a Yaksha, MBh.; of a man (pl. his descendants), g. *upakâdi*; of a lion, Pañc.; (*ikā*), f. a variety of the owl (= *piṅgalā*), Var.; a sort of crane, L.; a kind of bee, Suśr.; N. of a woman, Kathās. °**galita**, mf(*ā*)n. made reddish-brown, become tawny, Kathās. °**galin**, mfn. reddish-brown, R. °**galiman**, m. tawny or yellow colour, Kāv.

Piṅgāśa, m. (only L.) the chief of a community of wild tribes; the head man or proprietor of a village; a kind of fish, Pimelodius Pangasius (= *piṅgâsya*); (*ī*), f. = *nālikā* or *nīlikā*; n. virgin gold.

Piṅgiman, m. tawny or yellow colour, Hariv.

Piñja, mfn. confused, disturbed in mind, L.; full of (cf. *pari-p°*); m. the moon, L.; a species of camphor, L.; (*ā*), f. hurting, injuring, L.; turmeric, L.; cotton, L.; a species of tree resembling the vine-palm, L.; a switch, L.; (*ī*), f., see *tila-piñjī*; n. strength, power, L.

Piñjaṭa, m. the concrete rheum of the eyes, L.

Piñjana, n. a bow or bow-shaped instrument used for cleaning cotton, L.

Piñjara, mf(*ā*)n. reddish-yellow, yellow or tawny, of a golden colour, MBh.; Kāv. &c.; m. a tawny-brown colour, W. (also *-tā*, f., Kathās.; *-tva*, n., Kād.); a horse (prob. bay or chestnut), L.; N. of a mountain, MārkP.; n. (only L.) gold; yellow orpiment; the flower of Mesua Roxburghii; w. r. for *pañjara* ('skeleton' or 'cage'). °**raka**, m. N. of a Nāga, MBh.; n. orpiment, L. °**raya**, Nom. P. °*yati*, to dye reddish-yellow, Ratnâv.; °*rita*, mfn. coloured r°-y°, Daś. °**rika**, n. a kind of musical instrument, Kathās. °**riman**, m. a r°-y° colour, Kād. °**rī-√kṛi**, to dye r°-y°, ib.

Piñjala, mfn. (fr. *piñja*) extremely confused or disordered (cf. *ut-piñjala*); (*ā*), f. N. of a river, MBh.; (*ī*), f. a bunch of stalks or grass, Gobh. (cf. *piñjula*); n. (L.) id.; Curcuma Zerumbet; yellow orpiment. °**laka**, mfn., see *ut-piñjalaka*, *samut-p°*.

Piñjāna, n. gold, L.

Piñjikā, f. a roll of cotton from which threads are spun, L.

Piñjula, n. a bunch of stalks or grass (in *darbha-piñjulā*), MaitrS. °**jūla**, n., °**jūlī**, f. id., Br.; GṛŚrS. °**jūlaka**, m. N. of a man; pl. his descendants, g. *upakâdi*.

Piñjūsha, m. the wax of the ear, L.

Piñjeṭa, n. the excretion or concrete rheum of the eyes, L. (cf. *piñjaṭa*).

Piñjota, f. the rustling of leaves, L.

पिट् *piṭ*, cl. 1. P. *peṭati*, to sound, to assemble or heap together, Dhātup. ix, 24.

Piṭa, m. or n. a basket, box, L.; a roof, L.; a sort of cupboard or granary made of bamboos or canes, W.

Piṭaka, mf(*ā*)n. (usually n.) a basket or box, MBh.; R.; &c. (ifc. f. *ikā*, MānGṛ.); a granary, W.; a collection of writings (cf. *tri-p°*); a boil, blister, Car. (printed *piṭhaka*); Jātak.; a kind of ornament on Indra's banner, MBh.; Var.; m. N. of a man (also *piṭāka*), g. *śivâdi*, L.

Piṭâkyā, f. a multitude of baskets, g. *pāśâdi*.

पिटङ्काकी *piṭaṅkākī* or *piṭaṅkokī*, f. Cucumis Colocynthis, L.

पिटङ्काश *piṭaṅkāśa*, m. Silurus Pabda, L.

पिट्टक *piṭṭaka*, n. the tartar or secretion of the teeth, L. (cf. *kiṭṭa*, *kiṭṭaka*, *pippikā*).

पिट्टय *piṭṭaya*, Nom. P. (fr. *piṭṭa* = *pishṭa*?) °*yati*, to stamp or press into a solid mass, KātyŚr., Sch. **Piṭṭita**, mfn. pressed flat, L.

पिठ् *piṭh*, cl. 1. P. *peṭhati*, to inflict or feel pain, Dhātup. ix, 54.

Piṭha, m. pain, distress, W.

Piṭhaka, w. r. for *piṭaka*.

Piṭhana, n. = *anu-śāsana* (?), Lalit.

Piṭhara, mf(*ī*)n. a pot, pan, MBh.; Var. &c.; m. an addition to a building shaped like a hollow vessel, L.; a kind of hut or store-room, W.; N. of a partic. Agni, Hariv.; of a Dānava, MBh.; Hariv.; n. a churning stick, L.; the root of Cyperus Rotundus, L. — **pāka**, m. the union of cause and effect (i. e. of atoms) by means of heat, Sarvad.

Piṭharaka, m. or n. (*ikā*, f., Divyâv.) a pot, pan (cf. next); m. N. of a Nāga, Hariv. — **kapāla**, n. a fragment of a pot, potsherd, Bhartṛ.

पिठीनस् *piṭhīnas*, m. N. of a man, RV. (cf. *paiṭhīnasi*).

पिडक *piḍaka*, m. (and *ā*, f.) a small boil, pimple, pustule, Rājat.; Suśr. °**kā-vat** and °**kin**, mfn. having boils or pustules, Suśr.

पिण्ड् *piṇḍ*, cl. 1. Ā. 10. P. *piṇḍate*, °*ḍayati*, to roll into a lump or ball, put together, join, unite, gather, assemble, Dhātup. viii, 21; xxxii, 110 (prob. Nom. fr. next).

Piṇḍa, m. (rarely n.) any round or roundish mass or heap, a ball, globe, knob, button, clod, lump, piece (cf. *ayaḥ-*, *māṃsa-* &c.), RV. (only i, 162, 19 and here applied to lumps of flesh), TS.; ŚBr. &c. &c.; a roundish lump of food, a bite, morsel, mouthful; (esp.) a ball of rice or flour &c. offered to the Pitṛis or deceased ancestors, a Śrāddha oblation (RTL. 293; 298–310), GṛŚrS.; Mn.; MBh. &c.; food, daily bread, livelihood, subsistence, MBh.; Kāv. &c.; any solid mass or material object, the body, bodily frame, Ragh.; Saṃk., Vajracch.; the calf of the leg, Mālatīm. v, 16; the flower of a China rose, L.; a portico or partic. part of a house, L.; power, force, an army, L.; m. (du.) the fleshy parts of the shoulder situated above the collar-bone, MBh.; (du.) the two projections of an elephant's frontal sinus, L.; the embryo in an early stage of gestation, L.; a partic. kind of incense, Var. ('myrrh' or 'olibanum,' L.); meat, flesh, L.; alms, Mālatīm. (cf. *-pāta* below); Vangueria Spinosa, L.; quantity, collection, L.; (in arithm.) sum, total amount; (in astron.) a sine expressed in numbers; (in music) a sound, tone; N. of a man, g. *naḍâdi*; n. (L.) iron; steel; fresh butter; (*ā*), f. a kind of musk, L.; (*ī*), f., see 1. *piṇḍī*. — **kanda**, m. a species of bulbous plant (= *piṇḍâlu*), L. — **karaṇa**, n. = *-nirvapaṇa*, PārGṛ. — **kharjūra**, m. (Kād.), °**rikā** and °**rī**, f. (L.) a species of date tree. — **gosa**, m. gum myrrh, W. — **tarkaka**, m. pl. 'inquirers for the Śrāddha oblation (?),' ancestors preceding the great-grandfather (who eat the remnants of the oblation made to the Pitṛis), Gṛihyās.; Baudh. (v. l. *-tarkuka* [also *para-tarkaka* or °*kuka*], *-takshaka*, *-takshuka*, *piṇḍa-tarkya*, *piṇḍôdaka*). — **tas**, ind. from a ball or lump, MW. — **tā**, f. condition of a body, Mcar. — **taila**, n., °**laka**, m. incense, olibanum, L. — **tva**, n. being a lump or ball, density, condensation (*-tvam ā-√gam*, to become thick or intense), Kathās. — **da**, mf(*ā*)n. offering or qualified to offer oblations to deceased ancestors, Yājñ.; MBh.; m. the nearest male relation, W.; a son, Gal.; a patron or master, Bhartṛ.; (*ā*), f. a mother, MBh. (Nīlak.) Cf. *sa-piṇḍa*. — **dātṛi**, mfn. = *-da*, mfn., Yājñ.; Karaṇḍ. — **dāna**, n. the offering of balls of rice &c. (to deceased ancestors), Baudh.; Sāh.; the offering of Śrāddha oblations on the evening of new moon, Nir.; KātyŚr., Sch.; Kull.; giving alms, Kāv. — **nidhāna**, n. = *-nirvapaṇa*, ĀpGṛ. — **niryukti**, f. N. of wk. — **nirvapaṇa**, n. the oblation of balls of rice &c. to deceased ancestors, Mn. iii, 248; 261. — **nivṛitti**, f. cessation of relationship by the Śrāddha oblations (cf. *-sambandha*), Gaut. — **pada**, n. a kind of arithmetical calculation, Jyot. — **pāta**, m. giving alms; *-velā*, f. the hour for g° a°, Mālatīm. iii, $\frac{0}{1}$; °*tika*, m. a receiver of a°, Buddh. — **pātra**, n. the vessel in which Śrāddha oblations are offered, L.; an alms-dish, Karaṇḍ.; alms, ib.; *-nirhāraka*, m. a class of attendants in a monastery, Divyâv. — **pāda** and °**dya**, m. 'thick-footed,' an elephant, L. — **pitṛi-yajña**, m. the oblation to deceased ancestors on the evening of new moon, GṛŚrS.; *-prayoga*, m. N. of wk. — **pushpa**, m. (L.) Jonesia Asoka; the China rose; the pomegranate tree; n. (L.) the flower of J° A°; of the Ch^c r°; of Tabernaemontana Coronaria; of a lotus. — **pushpaka**, m. Chenopodium Album, L. — **prada**, mfn. = *-da*, mfn., Kād. — **phala**, mfn. bearing (long) round fruits, MBh.; (*ā*), f. a kind of bitter gourd, Car. — **bīja**, m. Nerium Odorum, L. — **bījaka**, m. Pterospermum Acerifolium, L. — **bhañjana-śānti**, f. N. of wk. — **bhāj**, mfn. partaking of the Śrāddha oblation; m. pl. deceased ancestors, Śak.; *-bhāk-tva*, n., Saṃk. — **bhṛiti**, f. means of subsistence, livelihood, R. — **maya**, mf(*ī*)n. consisting of a lump of clay, Mṛicch. — **mātrôpajīvin**, mfn. subsisting on a mere morsel, Yājñ. — **mustā**, f. Cyperus Pertenuis, L. — **mūla** and °**laka**, n. Daucus Carota, L. — **yajña**, m. oblation of balls of rice &c. to deceased ancestors, Yājñ. — **rohiṇika**, m. Flacourtia Sapida, L. — **lakshaṇa**, n., **-śikshā**, f. N. of wks. — **lepa**, m. the particles or fragments of the Śrāddha oblations which cling to the hands (they are offered to the three ancestors preceding the great-grandfather), Kull. on Mn. v, 60 (cf. *-tarkaka*). — **lopa**, m. a neglect or cessation of Ś° o°, MW. — **viśuddhi-dīpikā**, f. N. of wk. — **veṇu**, m. a species of bamboo, L. — **śarkarā**, f. sugar prepared from Yavanāla, Gal. — **śīrsha**, mfn. having a (long) round head, MBh. — **sambandha**, m. relationship qualifying a living individual to offer Śrāddha oblations to a dead person, Gaut.; °*dhin*, mfn. qualified to receive the Ś° o° from a living person, MārkP. — **sektṛi**, m. N. of a serpent-demon, MBh. — **stha**, mfn. 'mingled in a lump,' mixed together, Var. — **sveda**, m. a hot poultice, Car. — **haritāla**, n. a partic. kind of orpiment, Bhpr. **Piṇḍâkshara**, mfn. containing a conjunct consonant, Vām. **Piṇḍâgra**, n. a small morsel of a Piṇḍa, Mn. **Piṇḍânvāhārya** or °**yaka**, n. a partic. Śrāddha ceremony in which meat is eaten after offering the balls of rice &c., Mn. iv, 122; 123. **Piṇḍâbhra**, n. hail, L. **Piṇḍâyasa**, n. steel, L. **Piṇḍâlaktaka**, m. a red dye, Mālatīm. **Piṇḍâlu**, m. a species of Cocculus, L.; Dioscorea Globosa, L.; °*luka*, n. a kind of bulbous plant, L.; °*lūka*, m. or n. a batatas, L. **Piṇḍâśa**, °**śaka**, and °**śin**, m. 'eating morsels,' a beggar, L. **Piṇḍâśma**, m., Pāṇ. v, 4, 94, Kāś. **Piṇḍâhvā**, f. the resin of Gardenia Gummifera, L. **Piṇḍôdaka-kriyā**, f. the ceremony of offering balls of rice &c. and water, MW. **Piṇḍôddharaṇa**, n. participating in Śrāddha offerings, presenting them to common ancestors, W. **Piṇḍôpajīvin**, mfn. living on morsels offered by another, nourished by another, Mcar. **Piṇḍôpanishad**, f. N. of an Up.

Piṇḍaka, m. n. a lump, ball, knob, Hariv.; Suśr.; a fragment, morsel, L.; a round protuberance (esp. on an elephant's temples), MBh.; the ball of rice &c. offered at Śrāddhas (cf. *tri-p°*); m. a species of bulbous plant (= *piṇḍâlu*), L.; Daucus Carota, L.; incense, myrrh, L.; a sine expressed in numbers, Sūryas.; a Piśāca, L.; (*ikā*), f. a globular fleshy swelling (in the shoulders, arms, legs, &c.; esp. the calf of the leg), Vishṇ.; Yājñ.; MBh. &c.; a base or pedestal for the image of a deity or for a Liṅga, Var.; Kād.; AgP.; a bench for lying on, Car.; the nave of a wheel, L.; a species of musk, L.

Piṇḍana, n. forming globules or round masses, BhP.; forming balls of rice &c. for a Śrāddha (?), Cat.; m. a mound or bank, W. (cf. *piṇḍala*).

Piṇḍaya, °yati. See √*piṇḍ*.

Piṇḍaraka, m. or n. a bridge, MW. (cf. next).

Piṇḍala, m. a bridge, causeway; a passage over a stream or a raised path across inundated fields, L. (cf. *piṇḍana*, *piṇḍila*).

Piṇḍaśa, m. a beggar, mendicant living on alms (cf. *piṇḍâśa* under *piṇḍa*).

Piṇḍâta, m. incense, L.

Piṇḍâra, m. a beggar, religious mendicant, L.; a buffalo-herdsman or cowherd, L.; Trewia Nudiflora, Var.; an expression of censure, L.; N. of a Nāga, MBh.; n. a kind of vegetable, Bhpr. °**raka**, m. N. of a Nāga, MBh.; of a Vṛishṇi, MBh.; of a son of Vasu-deva and Rohiṇī, Hariv.; n. N. of a sacred bathing-place, MBh.; Hariv.; Pur.

Piṇḍi, f. the nave of a wheel, L. (cf. *piṇḍī*, °*ḍikā*). — **tailika**, m. incense, Gal. (cf. *piṇḍa-tailaka*). — **pāla**, w. r. for *bhindipāla*.

Piṇḍika, n. the penis, LiṅgaP.; (*ā*), f., see *piṇḍaka*.

Piṇḍita, mfn. rolled into a ball or lump, thick, massy, densified, MBh.; Kāv. &c.; mixed, mingled with (comp.), Var.; heaped, collected, united, added, MBh.; R.; (ifc. after a numeral) repeated, counted, numbered, Var.; multiplied, L. — **druma**, mfn. full of trees, R. — **mūlya**, n. a payment in a lump sum, Divyâv. — **sneha**, mfn. containing a thick fatty substance (as the brain), Kull. on Mn. v, 133. **Piṇḍitârtha**, m. the condensed i.e. abridged meaning, the chief point or matter, Mālav. i, 16.

Piṇḍin, mfn. possessing or receiving the Śrāddha oblations, L.; m. an offerer of balls of rice &c. to the Pitṛis, L.; a beggar, L.; a male creature (lit. 'having a body'), JaimBhār.; Vangueria Spinosa, Bhpr.; (*inī*), f. N. of an Apsaras, VP.

Piṇḍila (only L.), mfn. having large calves; skilled in calculations; m. a skilful arithmetician, an astrologer or astronomer; a bridge, causeway, mound; (*ā*), f. Cucumis Maderaspatanus.

1. **Piṇḍī**, f. (g. *gaurâdi*) a ball, lump, lump of food, ĀpŚr.; a pill, L.; the nave of a wheel, L.; a kind of tree, Daś. (Tabernaemontana Coronaria or a species of date tree, L.); Cucurbita Lagenaria, L.; performance of certain gesticulations accompanying the silent repetition of prayers &c. in meditation on real or divine knowledge, W.; N. of a woman, g. *kurv-ādi*. — **khaṇḍa**, m. or n. a small wood of Tabernaemontana Coronaria trees (or 'of Aśoka trees,' W.), Daś. — **jaṅgha**, m. N. of a man; pl. his descendants, g. *yaskâdi*. — **tagara** or °**raka**, m. a species of Tabernaemontana Coronaria, L. — **taru**, m. a thorny Gardenia, L. — **pushpa**, m. Jonesia Asoka, L. — **lepa**, m. a kind of unguent. — **śūra**, m. 'cake-hero,' a cowardly boaster, poltroon, L.

2. **Piṇḍī**, ind. in comp. for *piṇḍa*. — **karaṇa**, n. making into a lump or ball, Kull. on Mn. i, 18. — √**kṛi** (ind. p. -*kṛitya*), to make into a l° or b°, press together, join, unite, concentrate, MBh. &c.; to identify with (*saha*), Saṃk. — **kṛita**, mfn. made into a l° or b°, heaped, collected, joined, united, MBh.; Kāv. &c. — **bhāva**, m. the being rolled together into a b°, Tarkas. — √**bhū**, to be made into a l° or b°, to become a solid body, L. — **bhūta**, mfn. lumped, heaped, joined, united, VPrāt.

Piṇḍītaka, m. Vangueria Spinosa (n. the fruit), Bhpr.; Tabernaemontana Coronaria, L.; a species of basil, L.

Piṇḍīra, mfn. sapless, arid, dry, L.; m. the pomegranate tree, Hariv.; = *hiṇḍīra*, L.

Piṇḍola, m. N. of a man, Buddh.

Piṇḍoli and °**likā**, f. leavings of a meal, L.

पिण्डिपाल *piṇḍipāla*, w. r. for *bhindipāla*, q. v.

पिण्या *piṇyā*, f. Cardiospermum Halicacabum, L.

Piṇyāka, m. n. oil-cake, Mn.; Āpast.; MBh. &c.; Asa Foetida, L.; incense, L.; saffron, L.; (*ā*), f. a species of plant, L.

पित् *pit*. See 1. 2. *a-pit*.

पितरिशूर *pitari-śūra*, *pitā-putra* &c. See under *pitṛi*.

पितु *pitú*, m., once n. (√*pī*, *pyai*) juice, drink, nourishment, food, RV.; AV.; TS.; VS.; AitBr. (cf. Naigh. ii, 7. — **kṛít**, mfn. providing food, RV. — **bhā́j**, mfn. enjoying food, ib. — **bhṛ́it**, mfn. bringing food, ib. — **mát**, mfn. abounding in or accompanied by meat and drink, nourishing, RV.; AitBr.; TBr. — **shā́ṇi** (*sh* for *s*), mfn. bestowing food, RV. — **stoma**, m. 'praise of food,' N. of RV. i, 187.

Pitūya, Nom. P. °*yati* (only p. gen. °*yatás*), to desire food, RV.

पितुःपुत्र *pituḥ-putra* &c. See under *pitṛi*.

पितृ *pitṛí*, m. (irreg. acc. pl. *pitaras*, MBh.; gen. pl. *pitṛiṇām*, BhP.) a father, RV. &c. &c. (in the Veda N. of Bṛihas-pati, Varuṇa, Prajā-pati, and esp. of heaven or the sky; *antarā pitaraṃ mātaraṃ ca*, 'between heaven and earth,' RV. x, 88, 15); m. du. (°*tarau*) father and mother, parents, RV. &c. &c. (in the Veda N. of the Araṇis [q. v.] and of heaven and earth); pl. (°*taras*) the fathers, forefathers, ancestors, (esp.) the Pitṛis or deceased ancestors (they are of 2 classes, viz. the deceased father, grandfathers and great-grandfathers of any partic. person, and the progenitors of mankind generally; in honour of both these classes rites called Śrāddhas are performed and oblations called Piṇḍas [q.v.] are presented; they inhabit a peculiar region, which, according to some, is the Bhuvas or region of the air, according to others, the orbit of the moon, and are considered as the regents of the Nakshatras Maghā and Mūla; cf. RTL. 10 &c.), RV. &c. &c.; a father and his brothers, father and uncles, paternal ancestors, Mn. ii, 151 &c.; R.; Kathās.; a partic. child's-demon, Suśr. [Origin fr. √3. *pā* very doubtful; cf. Zd. *pita*; Gk. πατήρ; Lat. *pater*, *Jup-piter*; Goth. *fadar*; Germ. *Vater*; Eng. *father*.] — **karman**, n. a rite performed in honour of the Pitṛis, obsequial rites, ŚāṅkhŚr.; Mn. — **kalpa**, m. precepts relating to rites in honour of the P°s, Hariv.; N. of a partic. Kalpa (s.v.), Brahmā's day of new moon, L. — **kāṇḍa**, m. or n. N. of wk. — **kānana**, n. 'ancestor-grove,' place frequented by the Pitṛis, place of the departed, R.; Kathās. — **kārya**, n. = -*karman*, Mn.; MBh. &c. — **kilbishá**, n. an offence committed against the P°s, ŚBr. — **kulyā**, f. 'rivulet of the P°s,' N. of a river rising in the Malaya mountains, MārkP. — **kṛita** (°*tṛí*-), mfn. done against or by a father, AV.; committed against the P°s, VS. — **kṛitya**, n. (Hariv.), -**kriyā**, f. (Ragh.) = -*karman*. — **gaṇa**, m. a group or class of P°s, Mn. iii, 194; (*ā*), f. N. of Durgā(?), L. — **gāthā**, f. pl. 'songs of the P°s,' N. of partic. songs, MārkP. — **gāmin**, mfn. belonging or pertaining to a father, W. — **gīta**, n. pl. = -*gāthā*, VP., Sch.; °*tā-kathana*, n. N. of wk. — **gṛiha**, n. house of the fathers, place of the dead, L. — **graha**, m. 'P°-demon,' a partic. demon causing diseases, MBh. — **grāma**, m. 'P°s village,' place of the dead, L. — **ghātaka** (Kathās.), -**ghātin** (Rājat.), -**ghna** (RāmatUp.), m. a parricide. — **ceṭa**(?), m. N. of a man, Buddh. — **tama** (°*tṛí-tama*), m. (with *pitṛīṇām*) the most fatherly of fathers, RV. iv, 17, 17. — **tarpaṇa**, n. the refreshing of the P°s (with water thrown from the right hand), offering water &c. to deceased ancestors, Mn. ii, 171 &c. (cf. RTL. 394, 1; 410); the part of the hand between the thumb and forefinger (sacred to the P°s), L.; sesamum, L. — **tas**, ind. from the father, on the f°'s side, ĀśvGṛ. — **tithi**, f. the day of new moon (sacred to the P°s), L. — **tīrtha**, n. 'Tīrtha (s.v.) of the P°s,' N. of the place called Gayā, L.; a partic. part of the hand (= -*tarpaṇa*), KātyŚr., Sch.; -*māhātmya*, n. N. of ch. of SivaP. — **tva**, n. fatherhood, paternity; the state or condition of a Pitṛi or deified progenitor, MBh.; R. &c. — **datta**, mfn. given by a father (as a woman's peculiar property), MW.; N. of a man (-*ka*, endearing form; cf. *pitṛika*), Pāṇ. v, 3, 83, Vārtt. 1, Pat. — **dayitā**, f. N. of wk. — **dāna** or °**naka**, n. an oblation to the P°s, L. — **dāya**, m. property inherited from a father, patrimony, R. — **dina**, n. the day of new moon (cf. -*tithi*), A. — **deva**, m. pl. the P°s and the gods, Mn. iii, 18; a partic. class of divine beings, R. (= *kavya-vāhanâdayaḥ*, Sch.); mfn. worshipping a father, TĀr.; connected with the P°s and the gods, BhP. — **devata**, mf(*ā*)n. having the P°s for deities, sacred to them, ĀśvGṛ.; (*ā*), f. pl. the P°s and the gods, R. — **devatya**, mfn. = prec. mfn., TS.; Br.; Kauś.; n. = -*daivatya*, Pāṇ. v, 3, 45, Vārtt. 9, Pat. — **daivata**, mf(*ī*)n. relating to the worship of the P°s, ŚāṅkhGṛ.; R.; n. N. of the 10th lunar mansion Maghā (presided over by the P°s), Var.; = next, R. — **daivatya**, n. a sacrifice offered to the P°s on the day called Ashṭakā, R. — **dravya**, n. 'father's substance,' patrimony, Yājñ. ii, 118. — **drohin**, mfn. plotting against one's f°, Daś. — **nāman**, mfn. called after a f°'s name, MW. — **paksha**, m. the half month of the P°s, N. of the dark half in the Gauṇa Āśvina (particularly dedicated to the performance of the Śrāddha ceremonies), RTL. 388; the paternal side or party or relationship, MBh.; pl. the fathers or ancestors, Hariv.; mfn. being on the f°'s side, Kull. on Mn. ii, 32. — **paṅkti-vidhāna**, n. conferring the rights of a Sa-piṇḍa (s.v.), Gal. — **pati**, m. 'lord of the P°s,' N. of Yama, MārkP.; pl. the P°s and the Prajā-patis, BhP. — **pada**, n. the world or state of the P°s, W. — **paddhati**, f. N. of wk. — **pāna**, w.r. for -*yāna*. — **pātra**, n. a cup or vessel used at Śrāddha rites, W. — **pitṛi**, m. a f°'s father, L. — **pīta** (*pitṛí*-), mfn. drunk by the P°s, TS.; TBr. — **pūjana**, n. worship of the P°s, Mn. iii, 262. — **paitāmaha**, mf(*ī*)n. inherited or derived from father and grandfather, ancestral (with *nāman*, n. the names of f° and g°f°), MBh.; R. &c.; m. pl. (and ibc.) f°s and g°f°s, ancestors, ib. (mostly m. c. for -*pitāmaha*). — **paitāmahika**, mfn. = prec. mfn., Pañc. — **prasū**, f. a f°'s mother, W.; 'm° of the P°s,' twilight (the time when the P°s are abroad), L. — **prâpta**, mfn. received from a f°, inherited patrimonially, W. — **priya**, m. 'dear to the P°s,' Eclipta Prostrata, L. — **bandhu**, m. a kinsman by the f°'s side, L.; (*u*), n. relationship by the f°'s s°, AV. — **bāndhava**, m. = prec. m., L. — **bhakta**, mfn. devoted to a f°, A. — **bhakti**, f. filial duty to a f°, W.; N. of wk.; -*taraṃgiṇī*, f. N. of wk. — **bhūti**, m. N. of Sch. on KātyŚr. — **bhogīṇa**, mfn. (fr. -*bhoga*), Pāṇ. v, 1, 9, Sch. — **bhojana**, n. a f°'s food, W.; m. Phaseolus Radiatus, T. — **bhrātṛi**, m. a f°'s brother, W. — **mát** (AV. *pitṛí-mat*), mfn. having a f°, MBh.; R. &c.; having an illustrious f°, VS.; ŚBr.; accompanied by or connected with the P°s, AV.; VS. &c.; mentioning the P°s (as a hymn), AitBr. — **mandira**, n. = -*gṛiha*, MārkP.; W. — **mātṛi-guru-śuśrūshā-dhyānavat**, mfn. only intent on obeying father and mother and teacher, SaṃhUp. — **mātṛi-maya**, mf(*ī*)n. one who thinks only of f° and m°, Subh. — **mātṛi-hīna**, mfn. destitute of f° and m°, orphan, MW. — **mātrartha**, mfn. one who begs for his f° and m°, Mn. xi, 1. — **medha**, m. oblation made to the P°s, ŚrS.; Mn.; MBh. &c.; N. of wk.; -*sāra*, m., -*sūtra*, n. N. of wks. — **yajñá**, m. = -*medha*, RV. &c. &c. — **yā́ṇa** (Ved.) and -**yāna**, mfn. trodden by or leading to the P°s (path), RV.; AV.; ChUp.; m. (with or scil. *pathin*) the path leading to the P°s, RV.; AV.; MBh. &c.; n. (-*yāna*), id.; BhP.; the vehicle of the P°s, a car to convey virtuous persons after their decease to heaven, W. — **rāj**, -**rāja**, or -**rājan**, m. 'king of the P°s,' N. of Yama, MBh. — **rūpa**, mfn. appearing in the shape of an ancestor, ĀpŚr.; m. N. of a Rudra, MBh. — **liṅga**, m. (scil. *mantra*) a verse or formula addressed to the P°s, L. — **loká**, m. a f°'s house, AV. xiv, 2, 52; the world or sphere of the P°s, AV.; ŚBr.; MBh. &c. (cf. RTL. 28). — **vaṃśa**, m. the paternal family, GṛS.; °*śya*, mfn. belonging to it, Kāv. — 1. -**vat**, mfn. having a f° living, W. — 2. -**vát**, ind. like a father, Mn. vii, 80; like the P°s, as if for the P°s &c., RV.; GṛŚrS. — **vadha**, m. murder of a f°, parricide, RāmatUp. — **vana**, n. = -*kānana*, MBh.; Kāv. &c.; °*ne-cara*, m. 'haunting the groves of the dead,' N. of Śiva, W.; a demon, goblin, Vetāla &c., L. — **vartin**, m. 'staying with ancestors,' N. of king Brahma-datta, Hariv. — **vasati**, f. 'abode of P°s,' place of the dead, L. — **vāk-para**, mfn. obedient to (the voice of) parents, W. — **vittá**, mfn. acquired by ancestors, RV.; n. patrimony, Var. — **veśman**, n. a f°'s house, Pañc. — **vrata**, m. a worshipper of the P°s, Bhag.; n. worship of the P°s, W. — **śarman**, m. N. of a Dānava, Kathās. — **śrávaṇa**, mfn. bringing honour to a f°, RV. — **śrāddha**, n. N. of the rites in which the P°s are worshipped, W. — **shád**, mfn. living unmarried with a f°, RV.; 'dwelling with the P°s,' N. of Rudra, PārGṛ. — **shádana**, mfn. inhabited by the P°s, AV.; VS. — **shvasṛi**, f. a f°'s sister, MBh.; °*sā-mātula* (ibc.), paternal aunt and maternal uncle, ib.; °*srīya*, m. a f°'s sister's son, ib. — **saṃyukta**, mfn. connected with (the worship of) the P°s, ĀpGṛ. — **saṃhitā**, f. N. of wk. — **sadman**, n. = -*vasati*, MBh. — **saṃnibha**, mfn. like a f°, fatherly, L. — **sāmānya**, n. the P°s collectively, W. — **sū**, f. = -*prasū*, L. — **sûkta**, n. N. of a Vedic hymn, Cat. — **sthāna**, m. 'one who takes the place of a f°,' a guardian (also °*nīya*), W.; the sphere of the P°s, ib. — **svasṛi**, °**rīya**, incorrect for -*shvasṛi*, °*rīya*. — **hatyā**, f. = -*vadha*, MW. — **han**, m. a parricide,

AV.Paipp. **-hū**, mfn. invoking the P°s; f. (sc. *dvār*) N. of the southern aperture of the human body i.e. the right ear, BhP. (cf. *deva-hū*). **-hūya**, n. invoking or summoning the Pitṛis, ŚBr.

Pitari, loc. of *pitṛi* in comp. **-śūra**, m. 'a hero against his father,' a cowardly boaster, g. *pātre-samitâdi*.

Pitā, nom. of *pitṛi* in comp. **-putrá**, m. du. father and son, AV. &c. &c.; pl. f° and sons, MaitrS.; *-virodha*, m. a contest between f° and s°, Yājñ.; *-samāgama*, m. N. of a Buddh. Sūtra; °*trīya*, mfn. relating to f° and s° (with *sampradāna*, n. transmission of bodily capacities and powers from f° to s°), L.; containing the words *pitṛi* and *putra*, Anup. **-mahá**, m. a paternal grandfather, AV. &c. &c.; N. of Brahmā, Mn.; MBh. &c.; of sev. authors, Cat.; pl. the Pitṛis or ancestors, Yājñ.; MBh.; (*ī*), f. a paternal grandmother, MBh.; Kathās.; Pur.; *-saṃhitā*, f. N. of wk.; *-saras*, n. N. of a place of pilgrimage (also °*hasya saraḥ*), MBh.; *-smṛiti*, f. N. of wk. **-sumati-saṃvāda**, m. N. of ch. of BrahmavP.

Pituḥ, gen. of *pitṛi* in comp. **-putra**, m. the father's son, Pāṇ. vi, 3, 23, Sch. **-shvasṛi** or **-svasṛi**, f. the f°'s sister, Pāṇ. vi, 3, 24; viii, 3, 85.

Pitṛika, ifc. (f. *ā*) = *pitṛi*, father (cf. *jīva-*, *aneka-*, *sa-*); endearing dimin. for *pitṛi-datta*, q.v.

Pitṛivya, m. a father's brother, paternal uncle, Mn.; MBh. &c. (also *-ka*, HPariś.); any elderly male relation, Pañc. [Cf. Gk. πάτρως; Lat. *patruus*.] **-ghātin**, m. the murderer of his father's brother, Pāṇ. iii, 2, 86, Sch. **-putra**, m. a father's brother's son, cousin, Mālav.

Pitr, in comp. for *pitṛi* before vowels. **-arjita**, mfn. acquired by or derived from a father (as property), MW. **-artham**, ind. for a f°'s sake, ib. **-ādy-anta**, mfn. beginning and ending with (a rite to) the Pitṛis (as a Śrāddha), Mn. iii, 205.

Pítrya, mf(*ā*)n. derived from or relating to a father, paternal, patrimonial, ancestral, RV. &c. &c.; relating or consecrated to the Pitṛis, Mn.; MBh. &c. (with *tīrtha*, n. = *pitṛi-t°*, Mn. ii, 59; with *diś*, f. the south, ŚāṅkhGṛ.; with *pra-diś*, id., RV.); m. the eldest brother (who takes the place of a f°), L.; the month Māgha, L.; the ritual for oblations to the P°s, ChUp., Sch.; Phaseolus Radiatus, L.; (*ā*), f. pl. the Nakshatra called Maghā (presided over by the P°s), L.; the day of full moon and the worship of the P°s on that day, L.; n. the nature or character of a father, R.; (with or sc. *karman*) worship of the P°s, obsequial ceremony, ŚBr.; Mn. &c.; the Nakshatra Maghā, Var.; honey, L.; = *pitṛi-tīrtha* (cf. above), W. **-Pítryā-vat**, mfn. (prob.) possessing property inherited from a father, R. **Pitryupavīta**, n. (for °*ryôp°*?) investiture with the thread sacred to the Pitṛis, GopBr.; Vait.; °*tin*, mfn. invested with it, Vait.

पित्त *pittá*, n. (etym. unknown) bile, the bilious humour (one of the three humours [cf. *kapha* and *vāyu*] or that secreted between the stomach and bowels and flowing through the liver and permeating spleen, heart, eyes, and skin; its chief quality is heat), AV. &c. &c. **-kushṭha**, n. a kind of leprosy, Gal. **-kośa** (or °*sha*), m. the gall-bladder, MW. **-kshobha**, m. excess and disturbance of the bilious humour, ib. **-gadin**, mfn. suffering from b° complaints, bilious, Suśr. **-gulma**, m. a swelling of the abdomen caused by (excess of) bile, ib. **-ghna**, mfn. 'bile-destroying,' antibilious; n. an antidote to b° complaints, Suśr. (cf. *-han*). **-jvara** and **-dāha**, m. a bilious fever, L. **-drāvin**, m. 'bile-dispersing,' the sweet citron, L. **-dhara**, mfn. containing b°, bilious, Suśr. **-nibarhaṇa**, mfn. destroying b°, MW. **-prakṛiti**, mfn. being of a b° temperament, Var. **-prakopa**, m. excess and vitiation of the b° humour, MW. **-rakta**, n. plethora, L. (cf. *rakta-pitta*). **-rogin**, mfn. = *-gadin*, Suśr. **-vat**, mfn. having b°, bilious, L. **-vāyu**, m. flatulence arising from excess and vitiation of the b° humour, MW. **-vidagdha**, mfn. burnt or impaired by bile (as sight), Suśr. **-vināśana** and **-śamana**, mfn. 'b°-destroying,' antibilious, ib. **-śoṇita**, n. = *-rakta*, L. **-śopha**, m. a swelling caused by (excess of) b°, Suśr. **-śleshmala**, mfn. producing bile and phlegm, Car. **-sāraka**, m. Azadirachta Indica, L. **-sthāna**, n. = *-kośa*, GarbhUp. **-syanda**, m. a bilious form of ophthalmia, Suśr. **-han**, mf(*ghnī*)n. bile-destroying, ib.; (*ghnī*), f. Cocculus Cordifolius, L. (cf. *-ghna*). **-hara**, mf(*ī*)n. b°-removing, antibilious, Suśr. **Pittâtīsāra**, m. a bilious form of dysentery; °*rin*, mfn. suffering from it, ib. **Pittânta-karasa**, m. a partic. medicinal preparation, L. **Pittâbhishyanda**, m. = *pitta-syanda*, Suśr. **Pittâri**, m. 'bile-enemy,' anything antibilious, N. of sev. plants and vegetable substances (e.g. *parpaṭa*, *takshā* &c.), L. **Pittâsra**, n. = *pitta-rakta*, L. **Pittôdara**, n. = *pitta-gulma*, Bhpr.; °*rin*, mfn. suffering from a bilious swelling of the abdomen, Suśr. **Pittôpasṛishṭa**, mfn. suffering from bile, Yājñ., Sch. **Pittôpahata**, mfn. = *pitta-vidagdha*, Suśr.

Pittala, mf(*ā*)n. bilious, secreting bile, Suśr. (g. *sidhmâdi*); (*ā*) f. Jussiaea Repens, L.; (*ī*), f. Sanseviera Roxburghiana, L.; n. brass, bell-metal, L.; Betula Bhojpatra (its bark is used for writing upon; cf. *bhūrja-pattra*), L.

पित्थ *pittha* and *pitthaka*, m. N. of a man, Rājat.

पित्सत् *pitsat*, mf(*antī*)n. (√*pat*, Desid.) being about to fly or fall &c.; m. a bird, L.

Pitsala, n. a road, path, way, L.

Pitsu, mfn. being about to fly or fall, L.

Pipatishat = *pitsat*, L. °**shā**, f. wish to come down or fall, W. °**shu** = *pitsat*, L.

पित्सरु *pitsaru*. See *soma-p°*.

पिथय *pithaya*, °*yati*, to shut (a door), Lalit. **Pithita**, mfn. shut, covered, ib. (Prob. connected with *pi-dhā*.)

पिदाकु *pídāku*, m. prob. w. r. for *pṛídāku*, MaitrS.

पिदृभ् *pi-√dṛibh* for *api-√dṛibh* (only *-dṛibhmas*), to adhere firmly to or hope in (acc.), ŚāṅkhBr.

पिद्व *pidvá*, m. a species of animal, VS.

पिधा *pi-√dhā* = *api-√dhā* (q. v.)

Pi-dadhat, mfn. covering, veiling, hiding, W.

Pi-dhātavya, mfn. to be covered or shut or closed, Mn. ii, 200. °**dhāna**, n. (m., g. *ardharcâdi*) covering, stopping, shutting, closing, Mālav.; Sāh.; a cover, lid, sheath &c., MBh.; Kāv. &c.; (*-vat*, mfn. covered with a lid, Rājat.); a partic. process to which quicksilver is subjected, Sarvad.; (*ī*), f. a cover, lid, L. °**dhānaka**, n. a cover, sheath (see *khaḍga-pidh°*); (*ikā*), f. a cover, lid, L. °**dhāya**, ind. having covered, Amar. °**dhāyaka**, mf(*ikā*)n. covering, hiding, concealing (*-tā*, f.), Vedântas. °**dhāyin**, mfn. id., Dharmaśarm. °**dhitsu**, mfn. wishing to cover or conceal, Naish.

Pi-hita, mfn. shut, hidden, concealed, covered or filled with (instr.), MBh.; Kāv. &c.; n. a partic. figure of speech which consists in insinuating to a person that one knows his secrets, Kuval. °**hiti**, f. covering, stopping, TāṇḍBr.

पिनस *pinasa*, v.l. for *pīnasa*.

पिनह् *pi-√nah* = *api-√nah* (q. v.)

Pi-naddha, mfn. tied or put on, fastened, wrapped, covered, dressed, armed, MBh.; Kāv. &c. °**naddhaka**, mf(*ikā*)n. dressed, clothed, covered, Hariv. 11164 (m. ornament, Nīlak.)

Pi-nahya, ind. having put on or dressed, MBh.

पिनाक *pínāka*, m. n. a staff or bow, (esp.) the staff or bow of Rudra-Śiva, AV.; VS.; TS.; MBh. &c.; Śiva's trident or three-pronged spear (= *śūla* and *tri-śūla*), L.; falling dust, L.; (*ī*), f. (in music) a kind of stringed instrument; n. a species of talc, Bhpr. (Perhaps fr. *pi* = *api-√nam*; cf. *nāka*.) **-goptṛi**, m. 'preserver of Pināka,' N. of Śiva, MBh. **-dhṛik**, m. 'bearer of P°,' id., ib. **-pāṇi**, m. 'P° in hand,' id., Kum., Sch. **-bhṛit**, m. = *-dhṛik*, L. **-sena**, m. 'armed with P°,' N. of Skanda, AV.Pariś. **-hasta** (*pín°*), m. = *-pāṇi*, N. of Rudra, TS. **Pinākâvasa**, m. N. of Rudra ('concealing P°,' Mahīdh.), VS.

1. **Pināki**, m. (only acc. °*kim*) = *pinākin*, N. of Śiva, MBh.

2. **Pināki**, in comp. for °*kin*. **-diś**, f. 'Śiva's quarter,' the north-east, Var.

Pinākin, m. 'armed with the bow or spear Pināka,' N. of Rudra-Śiva, MBh.; Hariv.; R.; of one of the 11 Rudras, MBh.; Hariv.; (*inī*), f. N. of 2 rivers, L.; °*nī-māhātmya*, n. N. of ch. of BrahmâṇḍaP.

पिनी *pi-√nī*, P. *-nayati*, to put into (acc.), introduce, ĀpGṛ.

पिन्यास *pi-nyāsa*, m. (√2. *as* with *pi-ni*?) Asa Foetida, L. (cf. *piṇyāka*).

पिन्व् *pinv*, cl. 1. P. (Dhātup. xv, 79) *pínvati* (p. *pínvat*, RV.; *pinvát*, AV.; pf. *pipinva*, RV.; Ā. 3. pl. *pinviré*; p. *pinvāná*, ib.; aor. *apinvīt*, Gr.; fut. *pinvishyati*, °*vitā*, ib.), to cause to swell, distend; to cause to overflow or abound, RV.; AV.; Br.; GṛŚrS.; Ā. *pinvate*, to swell, be distended, abound, overflow, ib. (also Ā. = P. and in ŚBr. P. for Ā.): Caus. *pinváyati* = P. *pinvati*, ŚBr.

Pinva, mfn. causing to swell or flow (see *dānu-p°*).

Pinvana, n. a partic. vessel used in religious ceremonies, ŚBr.; KātyŚr.

Pinvantyapīyā, f. (sc. *ṛic*) N. of RV. i, 64, 6 (beginning *pinvanty apo*).

Pínvamāna and **pínvita**, mfn. swollen, swelling, full, ŚBr.

पिपक्ष् *pipaksh*, mfn. (fr. √2. *pac*, Desid.), Vop.

पिपठिष् *pipaṭhish*, mfn. (fr. √*paṭh*, Desid.), ib.

पिपतिषत् *pipatishat*, °*shā*, °*shu*. See *pitsat*.

पिपविषु *pipavishu*, mfn. (fr. √1. *pū*, Desid.) wishing to purify, W.

पिपाठक *pipāṭhaka*, m. N. of a mountain, MārkP.

पिपासत् *pipāsat*, mf(*antī*)n. (fr. √1. *pā*, Desid.) wishing to drink, thirsty, Śak. °**sā**, f. thirst, ŚBr. &c. &c.; *-vat*, mfn. thirsty, Vedântas. °**sāla**, mfn. always thirsty, Car. °**sita** (MBh.; Daś.), °**sin** (MW.), °**su** (MBh.; R.), thirsty, athirst.

पिपिली *pipilī*, f. = *pipīlī*, an ant, L.

पिपिष्वत् *pipishvat* (fr. √*pi* = *pī*, *pyā*), swollen, overfull, abundant, RV.

पिपीतक *pipītaka*, m. N. of a Brāhman who was the first to perform a partic. ceremony in honour of Vishṇu on the day called after him (see f.); (*ī*), f. the 12th day of the light half of the month Vaiśākhā, BhavP. **-dvādaśī-vrata**, n. N. of wk.

पिपील *pipīlá*, m. (√*pīḍ*?) an ant, RV.; MBh.; (*ī*), f. id., L. °**láka**, m. a large black ant, ChUp.; MBh. &c.; (*ikā*), f., see s.v.

Pipīlika, m. an ant, AdbhBr.; MBh. &c.; n. a kind of gold supposed to be collected by ants, MBh. ii, 1860. **-puṭa**, n. an ant-hill, MBh. **-madhya** or **-madhyama**, mf(*ā*)n. thin in the middle like an ant; (*ā*), f. N. of any metre the middle Pāda of which is shorter than the preceding and following, RPrāt.

Pipīlikā, f. the common small red ant or a female ant, AV. &c. &c. **-parisarpaṇa**, n. the running about of ants, Suśr. **-madhya**, mfn. N. of a kind of fast (beginning on the day of full moon with 15 mouthfuls, decreasing by one daily until the day of new moon, and after that increasing by one daily until the next day of full moon), Kull. on Mn. xi, 216. **-vat**, ind. like ants, TāṇḍBr., Sch. **Pipīlikôtkiraṇa**, n. (L.), °**kôdvāpa**, m. (ŚāṅkhŚr.) an ant-hill. **Pipīlikôtsaraṇa**, n. the creeping upwards of ants, L.

पिपीषत् *pipīshat* (ŚāṅkhGṛ.), °*shu* (RV.), mfn. (√1. *pā*, Desid.) wishing to drink, thirsty.

पिपृक्षु *pipṛikshu* (Bhadrab.), *pipṛicchishu* (Saṃk.), mfn. (√*prach*, Desid.) wishing to ask or inquire.

पिप्पका *pippakā*, f. a species of bird, VS. (cf. *pippīka*).

पिप्पटा *pippaṭā*, f. a kind of sweetmeat, W.

पिप्पल *pippala*, m. the sacred fig-tree, Ficus Religiosa (commonly called Peepal), MBh.; Yājñ.; Var. &c. (cf. IW. 39, 3; MWB. 515); a kind of bird, L.; a nipple, L.; = *niranśuka* or °*śula*, L.; the sleeve of a jacket or coat, W.; N. of a son of Mitra and Revatī, BhP.; pl. N. of a school of AV. (prob. w. r. for *pippalâda*); (*ā*), f. N. of a river, VP.; (*ī*), f., see s.v.; (*pippala*), n. a berry (esp. of the Peepal tree), RV. &c. &c.; sensual enjoyment, BhP.; water, L.; the sleeve of a coat, L. **-nātha**, m. N. of a deity, Cat. **-mātra**, mfn.

having the size of a berry, Suśr. **Pippalâda**, mfn. eating the fruit of the Peepal tree, BhP.; given to sensual pleasures, ib.; m. N. of an ancient teacher of the AV.; PraśnUp.; MBh. &c.; pl. his school (also °*daka*); *-tīrtha*, n. N. of a Tīrtha, ŚivaP.; *-śrāddha-kalpa*, m., *-śruti*, f., *-sūtra*, n., °*dôpanishad*, f. N. of wks. **Pippalā-vatī**, f. N. of a river, VP. **— Pippalâśana**, mfn. = *pippalâda*, CūlUp. **Pippalêśa**, m. N. of a man, Siṇhâs.

Pippalaka, m. a pin, Car.; n. a nipple, L.; sewing thread, L.

Pippalâdi, m. N. of a man, Hariv. (v.l. *paipp*°).

Pippalāyana, m. N. of a man, BhP.

Pippalāyani, m. N. of a teacher, ib. (v.l. *paipp*°).

Pippali, f. long pepper, Āpast.; n. (with *Vasishṭhasya*) N. of a Sāman. **— śroṇi**, f. N. of a river, MārkP.

Pippalī, f. a berry, AV.; Piper Longum (both plant and berry), R.; Var.; Suśr. **— mūla**, n. the root of long pepper, Bhpr.; °*līya*, mfn., g. *utkarâdi*. **— lavaṇa**, n. du. pepper and salt, R. **— vardhamāna** and °**naka**, n. N. of a partic. kind of medical treatment in which grains of pepper are given in increasing and decreasing quantity, Suśr.

Pippalikā, f. the small Peepal tree, L.

Pippalīya, mfn., g. *utkarâdi*.

Pippalu, m. N. of a man, g. *gargâdi*.

पिप्पिका *pippikā*, f. the tartar of the teeth, L. (cf. *piṭṭaka*).

पिप्पीका *pippīkā*, f. a species of bird, Var.

पिप्यटा *pipyaṭā*, f. sugar, L.

पिप्रीषा *piprīshā*, f. (√*prī*, Desid.) desire of pleasing or showing kindness, R.; Var., Car. °**shu**, mfn. wishing to give pleasure, MBh.; Hariv.

पिप्रु *pípru*, m. (√*pṛī*) N. of a demon conquered by Indra, RV.

पिप्लु *piplu*, m. (*pi* for *api* + √*plu*?) a freckle, mark, mole, Nal. **— karṇa**, mfn. having a mark on the ear, Kathās. **— pracchādana**, mfn. covering or concealing a mole, Nal.

पिब *piba*, mfn. (√1. *pā*) drinking, who or what drinks, Pāṇ. iii, 1. 137 (cf. *tri-*).

Piba-vat, mfn. containing a form of the verb *pibati*, AitBr.

पिब्द् *pibd* (prob. = *pi-pad*), only pr. p. Ā. *píbdamāna*, becoming or being firm or solid, ŚBr.

Pibdaná, mfn. firm, hard, solid, compact, ŚBr.

पियारु *piyāru*, mfn. (√*pīy*) censuring, mocking, overbearing, mischievous, RV.; AV.

पियाल *piyāla*, m. (for *priyāla*, q. v.) the tree Buchanania Latifolia (in Bengal commonly called Piyal); n. its fruit, MBh.; Hariv.; R. **— bīja**, n. the seed of the Piyal tree, R. **— majjā**, f. the marrow of the Piyal tree, ib.

पिम्परि *pimpari* or °*rī*, f. Ficus Infectoria, L.

पिम्पला *pimpalā*, f. N. of a river, Rājat. (perhaps w.r. for *pippalā*).

पियाक *piyāka*, m. N. of a poet, Cat. (cf. *priyāka*).

पिल् *pil*, cl. 10. P. *pelayati*, to throw, send, impel, incite, Dhātup. xxxii, 65 (cf. *pel*, *vil*).

Pilu or °**luka**, m. a species of tree (= *pīlu*), Suśr. **— parṇī**, f. Sanseviera Roxburghiana, Car.

पिलि *pili*, m. N. of a man, Saṃskārak.

पिलिन्दवत्स *pilinda-vatsa*, m. N. of a disciple of Gautama Buddha, SaddhP.

पिलिपिच्छ *pilipiccha*, °*picchi*, °*picchika* or °*piñja*, m. N. of a demon, Hcat.; AgP.

पिलिप्पिल *pilippilá*, mf(*ā*)n. slippery, VS. (Mahīdh.)

Pilpilá, mf(*ā́*)n. id., MaitrS.; (*ā*), f. N. of Lakshmī, Gal.

पिल्ल *pilla*, mfn. blear-eyed; m. a bleared eye, L. (cf. *paillya*).

Pillakā, f. a female elephant, W.

पिश् 1. *piś* (*piṇś*), cl. 6. P. (Dhātup. xxviii, 143) *piṇśati*, Ved. also Ā. °*te* (pf. *pipéśa*, *pipiśé*, °*śre*, RV.; aor. p. *piśānd*, ib.; *apeśit*, Gr.; fut. *peśishyati*, *peśitā*, Gr.), to hew out, carve, prepare (esp. meat), make ready, adorn (Ā. also 'one's self'); to form, fashion, mould, RV.; TBr.: Pass. *piśyáte*, AV.: Caus. *peśayati*, aor. *apīpiśat*, Gr.: Desid. *pipiśishati* or *pipeśishati*, ib.: Intens., see *pépiśat*, °*śāna*. [Cf. Gk. ποικίλος; Slav. *pisati*; Angl. Sax. *fâh*.]

2. **Piś**, f. ornament, decoration, RV. vii, 18, 2 (cf. *viśva-*, *śukra-*, *su-*).

Piśá, m. = *ruru*, a sort of deer (probably so called from its colour; cf. next), RV. i, 64, 8 (Sāy.); (*ī*), f. Nardostachys Jatamansi, L.

Piśáṅga, mf(*ī*)n. reddish, r°-brown or -yellow, tawny, RV. &c. &c.; m. a r° or tawny colour, W.; N. of a serpent-demon, TāṇḍBr.; MBh. **— jaṭa**, m. 'having a reddish braid of hair,' N. of an ascetic, Kathās. **— tā**, f. (Śiś.), **-tva**, n. (Mcar.), r° or tawny colour. **— bhrishṭi** (*piśáṅga-*), mfn. having r° prongs, RV. i, 133, 5. **— rāti**, mfn. giving r° i.e. golden gifts, RV. **— rūpa** and **-saṃdṛiś** (*piśáṅga-*), of a r° or yellow appearance, RV; AV. **Piśáṅgâśva**, mfn. having r° or tawny horses, RV.

Piśaṅgaka, m. N. of an attendant of Vishṇu, BrahmaP.

Piśaṅgaya, Nom. P. °*yati*, to dye reddish, Kir.

Piśaṅgita, mfn. dyed reddish-yellow, Kād.

Piśaṅgilá, mf(*ā́*)n. reddish, VS.

Piśaṅgī-√kṛi, to dye reddish, Mudr.

Piśācá, m. (ifc. f. *ā*) N. of a class of demons (possibly so called either from their fondness for flesh [*piśa* for *piśita*] or from their yellowish appearance; they were perhaps originally a personification of the ignis fatuus; they are mentioned in the Veda along with Asuras and Rākshasas, see also Mn. xii, 44; in later times they are the children of Krodhā, cf. IW. 276); a fiend, ogre, demon, imp, malevolent or devilish being, AV. &c. &c. (ifc. 'a devil of a –,' Kād.); N. of a Rakshas, R.; (*ā*), f. N. of a daughter of Daksha and mother of the Piśācas, VP.; (*ī*), f. a female P°, a she-devil, AV. &c. &c. (also ifc. = m.); excessive fondness for (ifc.; e.g. *āyudha-p*°, e° f° for fighting), Bālar.; Anarghar.; a species of Valerian, L.; N. of a Yoginī, Hcat. **— kāla-cakra-yuddha-varṇana**, n. N. of wk. **— kshāyaṇa**, mfn. destroying Piśācas, AV. **— gṛihītaka**, m. one possessed of P°s or demons, Kād. **— caryā**, f. the practice of P°s, BhP. **— cātana**, mfn. driving away P°s, AV. **— jámbhana**, mfn. crushing P°s, ib. **— tā**, f., **-tva**, n. the state or condition of a P°, demoniacal nature, Kāv.; Kathās. **— dakshiṇā**, f. a gift (such as given) among P°s, MBh. **— dīpikā**, f. 'lamp of the P°s,' an ignis fatuus, MW. **— dru**, m. Trophis Aspera (the favourite haunt of P°s), L. **— pati**, m. 'lord of P°s,' N. of Śiva, Kāv. **— bādhā**, f. demoniacal possession, MW. **— bhāshā**, f. 'P° language,' a corrupt dialect or gibberish (mostly used in plays), Kathās. **— bhāshya**, n. N. of Comm. on Bhag. (cf. *paiśāca-bh*°). **— bhikshā**, f. alms (such as given) among P°s, Āpast. (cf. *-dakshiṇā*). **— mocana**, n. 'deliverance of the P°s,' N. of ch. of SkandaP.; = *-tīrtha*, ib.; *-kathana*, n. N. of ch. of KūrmaP.; *-tīrtha*, n. N. of a sacred bathing-place, SkandaP. **— vadana**, mfn. having the face of a P°, Mcar. **— vidyā-veda**, m. the Veda of the P°s, ĀśvŚr. **— vṛiksha**, m. = *-dru*, L. **— veda**, m. = *-vidyā-veda*, GopBr. **— śvan**, m. 'dog-P°s,' N. of a demon malevolently disposed towards children, ĀpGṛ., Sch. **— saṃcāra**, m. = *-bādhā*, MW. **— sabha**, n. assemblage of P°s or fiends, pandemonium, L. **— han**, mfn. 'slaying P°s,' Kāṭh. **Piśācâṅganā**, f. a female P°, a she-devil, Prab. **Piśācâlaya**, m. 'abode of P°s,' phosphorescence, Var. **Piśācôdumbara**, m. a species of tree, ĀpGṛ., Sch. **Piśācôraga-rākshasa**, m. pl. P°s, serpents, and Rākshasas, Nal.

Piśācaka, mf(*ikā*)n. = *piśāce kuśalaḥ*, g. *ākarshâdi*; m. a Piśāca, MBh.; Var. &c.; (*ikā*), f. = *piśācī* (esp. ifc.; cf. *āśā-*, *āyudha-*, *gandha-* &c.); N. of a river, MārkP.; (sc. *bhāshā*) f. = *piśāca-bh*°, L. °**ka-pura**, n. N. of a village, Rājat.

Piśācakin, m. N. of Kubera (Vaiśravaṇa), Pat. on Pāṇ. v, 2, 129.

Piśāci, m. = *piśāca* or N. of a demon, RV. i, 133, 5.

Piśācikī, f. N. of a river (= *daśârṇā*), Gal. (cf. under *piśācaka*).

Piśācī-karaṇa, n. transforming into a Piśāca, Cat.

Piśitá, mfn. made ready, prepared, dressed, adorned, AV.; (*ā*), f. Nardostachys Jatamansi, L.; n. (also pl.) flesh which has been cut up or prepared, any flesh or meat, AV. &c. &c.; a small piece, AV. vi, 127, 1. **— nibha**, mfn. resembling flesh, Suśr. **— paṅkâvanaddhâsthi-pañjara-maya**, mf(*ī*)n. consisting of a skeleton of bones covered with flaccid flesh, Prab. **— piṇḍa**, m. a piece of f°, ib. **— praroha**, m. a fleshy excrescence, Suśr. **— bhuj**, mfn. eating flesh, a f°-eater, Var. **— locana**, mfn. having fleshy eyes, Sarvad. **— vasā-maya**, mf(*ī*)n. consisting of f° and fat, Prab. **Piśitâkāṅkshin**, mfn. greedy for f°, MBh. **Piśitâma**, (prob.) n. raw f°, ŚāṅkhGṛ. **Piśitâśa**, m. a f°-eating demon, a Piśāca or Rakshas, Hariv.; Rājat; (*ā*), f. N. of a Yoginī, Hcat. **Piśitâśana**, mfn. f°-eating, MBh.; Suśr.; m. a wolf, MBh.; = prec. m., R. **Piśitâśin**, mfn. = prec. mfn., MBh.; m. a f°-eating demon, R.; N. of a demon, Hariv. **Piśitêpsu**, mfn. eager for f° or meat, MW. **Piśitâudana**, m. or n. boiled rice with meat, Bhpr.

Piśi, f. of *piśa*, q. v.

Piśuna, mfn. backbiting, slanderous, calumnious, treacherous, malignant, base, wicked; a backbiter, informer, betrayer, RV. &c. &c.; (ifc.) showing, betraying, manifesting, telling of, memorable for, Kālid.; Kathās.; Pur.; m. cotton, L.; a crow, L.; N. of Nārada; of a goblin dangerous to pregnant women, MārkP.; of a Brāhman, Hariv.; of a minister of Dushyanta, Śak.; (*ā*), f. Medicago Esculenta, L.; n. informing against, betraying, MBh.; saffron, L.; (*ī*), f. N. of a river (described as the Mandākinī), R. (cf. IW. 351, 2). **— tā**, f. slander, scandal, detraction, Bhartṛ. **— vacana**, **-vākya**, n. (W.); **-vāda**, m. (Hit.) evil speech, detraction, slander.

Piśunaya, Nom. P. °*yati*, to betray, manifest, show, indicate, Śak.; Ratnâv.

Piśunita, mfn. betrayed, shown, Ratnâv.; Bālar.

1. **Pishṭá**, mfn. (for 2. see √*pish*) fashioned, prepared, decorated (superl. *-tama*), RV.; AV.; VS.; n. = *rūpa*, Naigh. iii, 7.

पिशिक *piśika*, m. pl. N. of a people in the south, Var.; MārkP.

पिशील *piśīla*, n. a wooden vessel or dish, ŚBr. (also *-ka*, KātyŚr., Sch.); (*ī*), f. = *piśīla-vīṇā*, Lāṭy. **— mātra**, n. = *bāhvor antarālam*, ĀpŚr., Sch. **— vīṇā**, f. a kind of stringed instrument, Lāṭy.

पिष् *pish*, cl. 7. P. (Dhātup. xxix, 15) *pinashṭi* (rarely Ā.; Subj. 2. 3. sg. *pinak*, RV.; Impv. *pinshá*, AV.; *pinshe*; *apinshat*; *pisheyam*, MBh.; pf. *pipésha*, *pipishe*, RV.; aor. *apikshan*, ŚBr.; fut. *pekshyati*, Up.; *peshṭā*, Gr.; ind. p. *pishṭvā*, *-pésham*, Br.; *pishya*, MBh.; inf. *péshṭum*, *péshṭavai*, Br.), to crush, bruise, grind, pound, hurt, injure, destroy (fig. also with gen., Pāṇ. ii, 3, 56), RV. &c. &c.: Caus. *peshayati* (aor. *apīpishat*, Gr.), to crush, bruise, grind &c., GṛS.; MBh.; Car. (Gr. also 'to give; to be strong; to dwell'). [Cf. Zd. *pish*; Gk. πτίσσω [?]; Lat. *pinsere*, *pīsere*.]

2. **Pishṭá**, mfn. (for 1. see above) crushed, ground &c., RV. &c. &c.; clasped, squeezed, rubbed together (as the hands), W.; kneaded, ib.; m. a cake, pastry, L.; N. of a man, g. *śivâdi*; pl. his descendants, g. *upakâdi*; (*ī*), f., see s. v.; n. flour, meal, anything ground (*na pinashṭi pishṭám*, 'he does not grind flour' i.e. he does no useless work), BhP.; lead, L. **— ja**, mfn. made of flour, Hcat. **— pacana**, n. a pan for baking f°, Suśr. **— paśu**, m. an effigy of a sacrificial animal made with f° or dough, Mn. v, 37; *-khaṇḍana-mīmāṃsā*, f., *-tiraskariṇī*, f., *-nirṇaya*, m., *-saraṇi*, f., *-sādhaka-grantha*, m. N. of wks. **— pāka**, m. a quantity of baked flour; *-bhṛit*, mfn. containing b° f°, L.; m. a boiler, A. **— pācaka**, n. = *-pacana*, L. **— pātrī**, f. a pastry-dish, L. **— piṇḍa**, m. a cake of flour, TBr., Sch. **— pūra**, m. a sort of cake (made of f° and butter), L. (cf. *ghṛita-p*°). **— pesha**, m. 'grinding f° or what is already ground,' useless labour, BhP. **— peshaṇa**, n., id.; *-nyāya*, m. the rule of g° f° (°*yena*, on the principle of 'grinding the ground' i.e. labouring uselessly), ĀpGṛ., Sch. **— bhājana**, mfn. receiving meal, GopBr. **— bhuj**, mfn. eating m°, BhP. **— maya**, mf(*ī*)n. made of or mixed with flour, SāmavBr.; MBh. &c.; (with *jala*), n. water sprinkled with f°, MBh. **— meha**, m. f°-like diabetes; °*hin*, mfn. suffering from it, Suśr. **— rasa**, m. water mixed with f°, MBh.; Suśr. **— rātrī**, f. an effigy made of f° symbolizing an inauspicious night, AV.Pariś.; °*tryāḥ kalpa*, m. N. of 5th Pariś. of AV. **— lepa**, m. f°-blot, impurity from meal or f° sticking to clothes &c., MānGṛ. **— varti**, f. a sort of cake made of f°, L. **— saurabha**, n. pulverized sandal-wood, L. **— svedam**, ind. (with

√*svid*, Caus., to foment) until the dough swells, Sāmav-Br. **Pishṭâda,** mfn. eating flour, BhP. **Pishṭânna,** n. food prepared from flour, Suśr.; *-dāna,* n. N. of wk. **Pishṭôdaka,** n. water mixed with f°, MBh. **Pishṭôdvapanī,** f. a partic. sacrificial vessel, L.

Pishṭaka, m. a cake or anything made of flour, pastry, L.; a disease of the eyes, opacity of the cornea, Suśr.; (*ikā*), f. a sort of grit, Bhpr.; Tamarindus Indica, L.; n. flour or meal, Subh.; pounded sesamum-seeds, L. **— saṃkrānti,** f. N. of a partic. festival, W.

Pishṭāta and °**taka,** m. perfumed powder or dust (which the Hindus sprinkle over each other at the Holī or spring festival), Ratnâv.; Kād.; Rājat. (cf. RTL. 430).

Pishṭi, f. powder, Rasêndrac.

Pishṭika, n. a cake made of rice flour, L.

Pishṭī, f. flour, meal, Bhpr. **— rasa,** m. a partic. medicinal preparation, Rasêndrac.

Pishṭi-√kṛi, to grind down, Nīlak.

Pishṭauṇḍī, f. Tamarindus Indica, L. (cf. under *pishṭaka*).

पिष्टप *pishṭapa,* v. l. for *vishṭapa,* q. v.

पिष्यल *pishyala,* w. r. for *pippala,* q. v.

पिस् *pis,* cl. 4. P. (Naigh. ii, 14) *písyati* (pf. 3. pl. *pipisuḥ*), to stretch, expand, ŚBr.; cl. 1. *pesati,* to go, move, Dhātup. xvii, 69; cl. 10. *pesayati,* id.; to hurt; to be strong; to give or to take; to dwell, xxxii, 32 (cf. *pish,* Caus.)

पिस्पृक्षु *pispṛikshu,* mfn. (√*spṛiś*) wishing or being about to touch; (with *jalam* or *salilam*) being about to rinse the mouth or to perform ablutions, MBh.; R.

पिहित *pi-hita, pi-hiti.* See *pi-√dhā.*

पिहुलि *pihuli,* m. N. of a serpent-demon, L.

पी 1. *pī* (connected with √1. *pā,* to which belong pass. *pīyáte,* pp. *pīta, pitvā* &c.), cl. 4. Ā. *pīyate,* to drink, MBh.; Dhātup. xxvi, 32.

पी 2. *pī* or *pi* (connected with √*pyai*), cl. 1. Ā. *páyate* (cl. 2. Ā. pr. p. *píyāna,* cl. 3. P. Impv. *pīpihí*; impf. *ápipet, ápīpayat*; Subj. *pipyatam,* °*tām*; *pīpayat,* Ā. °*yanta*; p. Ā. *pīpyāna*; pf. P. *pīpāya,* 2. sg. *pīpetha,* 3. pl. *pipyur*; p. Ā. *pipyāná*), to swell, overflow, be exuberant, abound, increase, grow; (trans.) to fatten, cause to swell or be exuberant, surfeit, RV.

पीठ *pīṭha,* n. (rarely *ī,* f.; possibly corrupted fr. *pi-sad,* to sit upon) a stool, seat, chair, bench, GṛS.; MBh. &c.; a religious student's seat (made properly of Kuśa grass), W.; case, pedestal (esp. of an idol), Rājat.; Var., Sch.; royal seat, throne, RāmatUp.; place, office (cf. *pīṭhâdhikāra*); N. of various temples (erected on the 51 spots where the limbs of Pārvatī fell after she had been cut to pieces by the discus of Vishṇu), L.; a district, province, Pañc.; a partic. posture in sitting, Cat.; (in geom.) the complement of a segment, Col.; m. a kind of fish, L.; the sun, Gal.; N. of an Asura, MBh.; of a minister of Kaṅsa, Hariv. **— keli,** m. a male confidant, parasite, L. **— ga,** m. moving about in a wheel-chair, lame, crippled, MBh. **— garbha,** m. the cavity in the pedestal of an idol, Var., Sch. **— cakra,** n. a chariot with a seat, ĀśvGṛ. **— cintāmaṇi,** m. N. of wk. **— nāyikā,** f. a girl of fourteen (before menstruation) who impersonates Durgā at the festival of that goddess, L. **— nirūpaṇa,** n., **-nirṇaya,** m. N. of wks. **— nyāsa,** m. N. of a partic. mystical ceremony, Tantras. **— bhū,** f. a basis, basement, L. **— marda,** mfn. very impudent, L.; m. a companion, parasite, MBh. iv, 674 (= *rāja-priya,* Nīlak.); the companion of the hero of a drama in any great enterprise, Daśar.; Sāh.; a dancing master who teaches courtezans, L.; (*ikā*), f. a lady who assists the heroine of a drama in securing her lover, Mālav. i, 1½. **— lakshaṇa,** n. N. of wk. **— vivara,** m. = *-garbha,* Var., Sch. **— śakti-nirṇaya,** m. N. of wk. **— sarpa** (MBh.; Nīlak. 'a boa'), **-sarpin** (VS.), mfn. = *-ga.* **— sūtra,** n. N. of wk. **— sthāna,** n. N. of a city (= *prati-shṭhāna*), Siṇhās. **Pīṭhâdhikāra,** m. appointment to a place or office, Rājat. **Pīṭhôpapāli,** mfn. one whose ear-lobes have been entirely cut off, Suśr.

Pīṭhaka, m. or n. a stool, chair, bench, BhP.; a kind of palanquin, Kāraṇḍ.; (*ikā*), f. a stool, bench, R.; Mālav.; Kathās.; a base, pedestal (esp. of an idol, Kathās.), Kāraṇḍ.; Var., Sch. (cf. *pūrva-pīṭhikā*).

Pīṭhāya, Nom. Ā. °*yate,* to become a stool, L.

पीड् *pīḍ* (prob. fr. *pisd* = *pi-√sad*), pf. *pipīḍé,* to be squeezed or pressed out (as Soma), RV. iv, 22, 8; cl. 10. P. or Caus. *pīḍayati* (ep. also °*te*; aor. *apīpīḍat* or *apipīḍat,* Pāṇ. vii, 4, 3), Dhātup. xxxii, 11; to press, squeeze (*kālaṃ kālena pīḍayan,* 'pressing time against time,' i. e. 'leaving everything to time,' Mn. i, 51), AV. &c. &c.; to hurt, harm, injure, oppress, pain, vex, Mn.; MBh. &c.; to beleaguer (a city), R.; to break (a vow), Yājñ.; to neglect (one's family), MBh.; (in astrol.) to cover (esp. with something inauspicious), to eclipse, obscure, Var.: Pass. *pīḍyate,* to be pressed or pained or afflicted, MBh.; Kāv. &c.; to cause pain, hurt, Pañcad.

Pīḍa, m. n., in *tila-p°, triṇa-p°.*

Pīḍaka, m. an oppressor (cf. *tālu-p°*).

Pīḍana, mfn. pressing, afflicting, molesting, paining (cf. *cakshu-p°*); n. the act of pressing or squeezing, R.; Kathās.; Gīt.; an instrument for pressing, press (= *pīḍana-dravya*), Suśr.; the act of oppressing or suppressing, paining, harassing, afflicting, R.; Kām.; Rājat; devastation, laying a country waste, W.; misfortune, calamity, Mn. ix, 299; obscuration, eclipse (of a planet, cf. *graha-p°*), Suśr.; suppression (of sounds, a fault in pronunciation), RPrāt.

Pīḍanīya, mfn. used for pressing, serving for a press, Suśr.; = next, MBh.

Pīḍayitavya, mfn. to be oppressed or harassed or molested or pained, MBh.

Pīḍā, f. pain, suffering, annoyance, harm, injury, violation, damage (*ayā,* ind. with pain, i. e. unwillingly), Mn.; MBh. &c.; devastation (cf. *pīḍana*), W.; restriction, limitation, KātyŚr., Sch.; obscuration, eclipse (of a planet, cf. *graha-p°*), Var.; pity, compassion, L.; a chaplet or garland for the head, L. (cf. *āpīḍa*); Pinus Longifolia, L.; a basket, L.; w. r. for *pīṭha.* **— kara,** mfn. pain-causing, afflicting, tormenting, Yājñ. **— karaṇa,** n. the causing of pain, torturing, W. **— kṛit,** mfn. = *-kara,* Var. **— kṛita,** n. the infliction of pain or disadvantage, Gaut. **— gṛiha,** n. torture-chamber, house of correction, Sāy. **— bhāj,** mfn. showing wavy marks of pressure or indentations, Kir. **— yantra-gṛiha,** n. = *pīḍā-gṛiha,* Sāy. **— sthāna,** n. (in astrol.) an unlucky position, inauspicious distance (of a planet), Var.

Pīḍāya, Nom. Ā. °*yate,* to feel pain, be uneasy, Sāṃkhyak., Sch.

Pīḍita, mfn. squeezed, pressed, Mn.; MBh. &c.; hurt, injured, afflicted, distressed, troubled, badly off, ib.; covered, eclipsed, obscured, Var.; laid waste, W.; bound, tied, ib.; suppressed; badly pronounced, APrāt.; (*am*), ind. closely, R.; n. damage, Gaut.; harassment, annoyance, MBh. (v. l. *pīḍana*); a kind of coitus, L. **— tā,** f., **-tva,** n. the being pressed or afflicted or distressed, Suśr.

Pīḍin, mfn. annoying, distressing (ifc.), Naish.

पीत 1. *pītá,* mfn. (√1. *pā*) drunk, sucked, sipped, quaffed, imbibed, RV. &c. &c.; ifc. having drunk, soaked, steeped, saturated, filled with (also with instr.), Mn.; MBh. (cf. g. *āhitâgny-ādi*); n. drinking, L. **— kośa,** mfn. one who has ratified a treaty by drinking from a cup, Rājat. (cf. under *kośa*). **— taila,** mfn. one who has drunk oil, filled with oil (cf. *taila-pīta*); (*ā*), f. Cardiospermum Halicacabum and some other species, L. **— dugdhā,** f. a cow whose milk has been pledged (lit. already drunk), L.; a cow tied up to be milked, any milch cow, W.; a kind of shrub (= *kshīriṇī*), L. **— nidra,** mfn. immersed in slumber, BhP. **— pratibaddha-vatsā,** f. a cow whose calf has drunk milk and been tied up, Ragh. **— madya,** mfn. one who has d° wine or any other intoxicating liquor, MW. **— māruta,** m. a kind of snake, Car. **— rasa,** m. whose juice is d°, ib. **— vat,** mfn. one who has d°, Suśr.; containing √1. *pā,* AitBr. **— vipīta,** mfn., g. *śāka-pārthivâdi* (cf. *bhukta-vibhukta*). **— śesha,** mfn. left from drinking; m. remainder of anything drunk, Gobh.; R. **— śoṇita,** mfn. (a sword) that has d° blood, bloody, Kathās. **— soma-pūrva,** mfn. (a Brāhman) who has d° before the Soma-juice (at a sacrifice), Mn. xi, 8. **Pītâbdhi,** m. 'by whom the ocean was d°,' N. of the Muni Agastya (s. v.), L. **Pītâvaśesha,** mfn. drunk up with the exception of a small remainder, Kām. **Pītôdaka,** mfn. one who has d° water or whose w° has been d°, KaṭhUp.

1. **Pīti,** f. drinking (with acc. or gen.), a draught, RV.; a tavern, L.; m. a horse, L.

1. **Pītin,** mfn. drinking, one who has drunk (see *soma-p°*); m. a horse, L.

Pītu, m. 'who drinks or dries up,' the sun or fire, Up. i, 71, Sch.; the chief elephant of a herd, L. **— dāru** (*pītu-*), m. a kind of tree (= *deva-dāru* or = *khadira*), ŚBr.; Kāṭh. (cf. *pīta-dāru*).

Pītvá, ind. having drunk or quaffed, RV. &c. &c. **— sthiraka,** mfn. somewhat refreshed by a draught, g. *mayūra-vyaṅsakâdi.*

Pītví (RV.) and **pītvīnam** (Kāś. on Pāṇ. vii, 1, 48), ind. having drunk or quaffed.

1. **Pītha,** m. a drink, draught (cf. *go-p°, surā-p°, soma-p°*); n. water, L.; melted butter, L.

Pīthi, m. a horse, L. (cf. *pīti*).

Pīthin, mfn. drinking up, exhausting (cf. *kośa-p°*).

पीत 2. *pīta,* mf(*ā*)n. (possibly fr. √2. *pī* or √*pyai,* the colour of butter and oil being yellowish) yellow (the colour of the Vaiśyas, white being that of the Brāhmans, red that of the Kshatriyas, and black that of the Śūdras), GṛS.; Up.; MBh. &c.; m. yellow colour, W.; a y° gem, topaz, L.; a y° pigment prepared from the urine of kine, L.; N. of sev. plants (Alangium Hexapetalum, Carthamus Tinctorius, Trophis Aspera), L.; of the Vaiśyas in Śālmala-dvīpa, VP.; (*ā*), f. N. of sev. plants (Curcuma Longa and Aromatica, a species of Dalbergia Sissoo, a species of Musa, Aconitum Ferox, Panicum Italicum, = *mahā-jyotishmatī*), L.; a kind of y° pigment (= *go-rocanā*), L.; a mystical N. of the letter *sh,* Up.; n. a y° substance, ChUp.; gold, L.; y° orpiment, L. **— kadalī,** f. a species of banana, L. **— kanda,** m. Daucus Carota, L. **— karavīraka,** m. oleander with y° flowers, L. **— kāvera,** n. saffron, L.; bell-metal, L. **— kāshṭha,** n. y° sanders, L.; Chloroxylon Swietenia, L. **— kīlā,** f. a species of plant (= *āvartakī*), L. **— kushṭha,** n. y° leprosy, L. **— kedāra,** m. a species of rice, Gal. **— kauśeya-vāsas,** mfn. dressed in y° silk; m. N. of Kṛishṇa, MW. **— gandha,** n. y° sandal, L. **— ghoshā,** f. a species of creeper with y° flowers, L. **— cañcu,** m. 'y°-beak,' a kind of parrot, Gal. **— candana,** n. y° sandal, L.; saffron, L.; turmeric, L. **— campaka,** m. 'y° as the Campa,' a lamp, L.; a looking-glass, Gal. **— taṇḍula,** m. Panicum Italicum, Gal.; (*ā*), f. id. (also °*likā*), L.; a species of Solanum, L. **— tā,** f. yellowness, MBh. **— tuṇḍa,** m. 'y°-beak,' Sylvia Sutoria, L. **— tva,** n. = *-tā,* MW. **— dāru,** m. Pinus Deodora and Longifolia, L.; Curcuma Aromatica, L.; Chloroxylon Swietenia, L. **— dīptā,** f. N. of a Buddh. deity, Kālac. **— dru,** m. Pinus Longifolia or Curcuma Aromatica, L. **— nīla,** mfn. 'yellow-blue,' green, L. **— parṇī,** f. 'y°-leaved,' Tragia Involucrata, L. **— pādaka,** m. a tree similar to the Bignonia, L. **— pādā,** f. 'y°-footed,' Turdus Salica, L. **— pura,** n. 'y°-town,' N. of a town, Siṇhās. **— pushpa,** m. 'y°-flowered,' N. of sev. plants (Pterospermum Acerifolium or some other species, Michelia Champaka, Tabernaemontana Coronaria, a species of y° Barleria), L.; (*ā*), f. the colocynth, L.; a kind of shrub, L.; Cajanus Indicus, L., (*ī*), f. Andropogon Acicularis, L.; the colocynth and other kinds of gourd, L.; a Barleria with y° flowers, L.; n. Tabernaemontana Coronaria, L. **— prasava,** m. = *-karavīraka,* L. **— phala,** m. 'having y° fruits,' Trophis Aspera, L. (also °*laka*); Averrhoa Carambola, L. **— bījā,** f. 'having y° seed,' Trigonella Foenum Graecum, L. **— bhasman,** m. a partic. preparation of quicksilver, L. **— bhṛiṅga-rāja,** m. an Eclipta with y° flowers, L. **— maṇi,** m. 'y° gem,' a topaz, L. **— maṇḍūka,** m. a kind of y° frog, L. **— mastaka,** m. 'y°-head,' Loxia Philippensis, L. **— mākshika,** n. y° pyrites, L. **— māñjishṭha,** mfn. yellowish-red, MW. **— muṇḍa,** m. = *-mastaka,* L. **— mudga,** m. a y° variety of the Phaseolus Mungo, W. **— mustā,** f. a species of Cyperus, L. **— mūlaka,** n. Daucus Carota, L. **— yūthī,** f. y° jasmine, L. **— rakta,** mfn. yellowish-red, orange (*-cchāya,* mfn. orange-coloured), L.; m. = next, L. **— ratna,** m. = *-maṇi,* L. **— ratnaka,** m. a species of y° gem (= *go-meda*), Bhpr. **— rambhā,** f. a kind of Musa, L. **— rāga,** mfn. of a y° colour; m. yellowness, W.; m. or n. the fibres of the lotus &c., L.; n. wax, L. **— rohiṇī,** f. Gmelina Arborea, L. **— loha,** m. y° metal, queen's m° or a mixed m° resembling gold, W. **— varṇa,** m. 'y°-coloured,' a species of parrot, Gal. **— varṇaka,** m. Pimelodus Gagora, L. (cf. *gargara*).

—**vālukā**, f. turmeric, L. —**vāsas**, mfn. dressed in y°, m. N. of Vishṇu, MBh.; R. —**vṛiksha**, m. 'y° tree,' Pinus Longifolia, Bhpr.; a species of Śyonāka, L. —**śāla** or -**śālaka**, m. Terminalia Tomentosa, L. —**sāra**, m. a y° gem (= *go-medaka*), L.; the sandal tree, L.; Alangium Hexapetalum, L.; Citrus Medica, L.; olibanum, L.; n. y° sanders, L. —**sāraka**, m. Alangium Hexapetalum, L.; Azadirachta Indica, L. —**sāri**, n. antimony, L. —**skandha**, m. 'y°-shouldered,' a hog, L. —**sphaṭika**, m. 'y° crystal,' a topaz, L. —**sphoṭa**, m. 'y° pustules,' the itch or scab, L. —**harita**, mfn. 'yellowish-green;' *-cchāya*, mfn. of a y°-g° colour, L. **Pītâṅga**, m. a kind of frog, L.; a species of Śyonāka, L. **Pītâmbara**, mfn. dressed in y° clothes; m. N. of Vishṇu-Kṛishṇa, Gīt.; a dancer or actor, L.; a religious mendicant wearing y° garments, W.; N. of sev. men and authors (also with *śarman* and *bhaṭṭa*); °*rāpaddhati*, f. N. of wk. **Pītâmlāna**, m. y° amaranth, L. **Pītâruṇa**, mfn. yellowish-red; m. N. applied to mid-dawn, L. (cf. *nīlâruṇa*). **Pītâvabhāsa**, mfn. of y° appearance (*-tā*, f.), Suśr. **Pītâśman**, m. 'y° stone,' a topaz, L.

Pītaka, mf(*ikā*)n. yellow, MBh.; R.; Suśr. (also applied to the 4th unknown quantity, Col.); m. y° amaranth, L.; Odina Pennata, L.; (*ikā*), f. saffron, L.; turmeric, L.; y° jasmine, L.; n. (only L.) orpiment; brass; honey; saffron; y° sanders; aloe wood; Curcuma Aromatica; Terminalia Tomentosa, a species of Śyonāka. —**druma**, m. Curcuma Aromatica, L. —**mākshika**, n. y° pyrites, MBh. (cf. *pīta-m°*).

Pītana, m. a species of tree (Spondias Mangifera, Pentaptera Tomentosa or Ficus Infectoria), L.; n. orpiment, L.; saffron, L.; Pinus Deodora, L.

Pītanaka, m. Spondias Mangifera, L.

Pītala, mfn. yellow, L.; m. y° colour, W.; n. brass, ib.

Pītalaka, n. brass, L.

Pītiman, m. a yellow colour, Vām.

पीति 2. *pīti*, f. (√3. *pā*; for 1. see p. 629) protection (see *nṛi-p°*).

2. **Pītha**, m. id. (see *go-p°*).

Pīthya, n. id. (see *go-p°*).

पीतु *pītu*. See p. 629, col. 3.

पीथी *pīthī*, f. (prob.) = *vīthī*, Divyâv. (others 'market-place').

पीथे *pīthe*, m. N. of a chief builder, Inscr.

पीदारी *pīdārī*, f. N. of a mother or female deity, RTL. 228.

पीन *pīna*, mf(*ā*)n. (√2. *pī*) swelling, swollen, full, round, thick, large, fat, fleshy, corpulent, muscular, MBh.; Kāv. &c.; (with *sveda*), m. profuse perspiration, Suśr. —**kakud-mat**, mfn. having a fat hump, Pañc. —**tarala**, mfn. having a large central gem, Hariv. —**tā**, f., -**tva**, n. fatness, corpulency, compactness, denseness, Kāv. —**nitambā**, f. 'having full hips,' N. of a metre, Col. —**vakshas**, mfn. full-breasted, large-chested, MW. —**śroṇi-payodhara**, mfn. having swelling hips and breasts, Nal. —**stana**, m. the full breast (of a woman), Vikr. v, 15. **Pīnâṅsa**, m. a high shoulder, MBh.; mfn. fat-shouldered, ib. **Pīnâyata-kakudmat**, mfn. having a full and prominent hump, Pañc. **Pīnôttuṅga-stanī**, f. (a woman) having a large and prominent breast, MW. **Pīnôdhas** (MBh.), °**dhnī** (L.), f. (a cow) with full or swelling udders.

Pīnara, mfn., g. *aśmâdi*.

Pīpivás, mf(*pipyúshī*)n. swelling, overflowing, exuberant, flowing with (gen. or acc.), RV.

1. **Pīyūsha**, m. n. the milk of a cow during the first seven days after calving, biestings; (met.) any thick fluid, cream, juice, RV.; AV.; Kauś.; Suśr.; nectar (the drink of immortality produced at the churning of the ocean of milk), Kāv. &c. —**kaṇikā**, f. 'nectar-drop,' N. of Comm. —**tā**, f. condition or quality of n°, Kāv. —**garala**, n. n° and poison, Hit. —**dyuti** and -**dhāman**, m. 'n°-rayed,' the moon, Kāv. —**dhārā**, f. stream of n°, N. of sev. works; *-kir*, m. 'pouring out streams of n°,' the moon (whose rays are said to be filled with n°), Viddh. —**pūrṇa**, mfn. full of n°, n°-like, Kāv. —**bhānu**, m. = *-dyuti*, ib. —**bhuj**, m. 'n°-quaffer,' a god, ib. —**mayūkha** (Kāv.), -**mahas** and -**ruci** (L.), m. = *-dyuti*. —**laharī**, f. 'stream of n°,' N. of a poem. —**varṇa**, mfn. milk-white, white, L.; m. a wh° horse, Gal. —**varsha**, m. a shower of n°; °*shāya*, Nom. Ā. °*yate*, to become or turn into a sh° of n°, Bhartṛ. —**sāgara**, m. 'sea of n°,' N. of sev. wks.

2. **Pīyūsha**, Nom. P. °*shati*, to become or turn into nectar, MW.

1. **Pīva**, mfn. fat, RV.; AitBr.; (*ā*), f. water, L.

2. **Pīva**, Nom. P. °*vati*, to be fat or corpulent, Dhātup. xv, 55.

3. **Pīva**, in comp. = *pīvas*. **Pīvôpavasana**, mfn. covered with fat, VS. (cf. *payôpavasana* and Pāṇ. vi, 3, 109, Vārtt. 6, Pat.)

Pīvan, mf(*arī*)n. swelling, full, fat, strong, robust, RV. &c. &c.; m. wind, L.; (*arī*), f. a young woman, L.; a cow, L.; Asparagus Racemosus, L.; Desmodium Gangeticum, Bhpr.; N. of a spiritual daughter of the Barhi-shad Pitṛis and wife of Veda-śiras, Hariv.; of a princess of Vidarbha, MārkP. [Cf. Gk. πίων for πίϝων, πίειρα.]

Pīvara, mfn. fat, stout, large, plump, thick, dense, full of or abounding with (comp.), MBh.; Kāv. &c.; m. a tortoise, L.; N. of one of the Saptarshis under Manu Tāmasa, MārkP.; of a son of Dyuti-mat, VP.; (*ā*), f. Physalis Flexuosus, L.; Asparagus Racemosus, Bhpr.; N. of a daughter of the Gandharva Huhu, Kathās.; n. N. of a Varsha in Krauñca-dvīpa, VP. —**tva**, n. thickness, density, Dhūrtas. —**stanī**, f. a woman with large breasts or a cow with a large udder, L.

1. **Pīvarī**, f. of *pīvan*, q.v.

2. **Pīvarī**, ind. for *pīvara*. —**kṛita**, mfn. fattened, MBh.

Pīvas, n. fat, RV.; AV. [Cf. Gk. πῖαρ.] **Pīvaḥ-sphāká**, mfn. swelling with fat, AV. **Pīvas-vat**, mfn. abundant, exuberant, RV.

Pīvasá, mf(*ā*)n. swelling, swollen, abounding with fat, fat, abundant, RV.; TBr.

Pīvishṭha, mfn. extremely fat, ŚBr.

Pīvo, in comp. = *pīvas*. —**anna** (*pī°*), mfn. having rich or abundant food, RV. —**aśva** (*pī°*), mfn. having fat horses. —**rūpa**, mfn. having a fat appearance, AitBr.

पीनस *pī-nasa*, m. (prob. fr. *pī* = *api* + *nas*; cf. *apī-nasa*) cold (affecting the nose), catarrh, Suśr. —**nāśana**, mfn. destroying catarrh, ib.; (*ā*), f. Cucumis Utilissimus.

Pīnasita (Var.), °**sin** (Suśr.), mfn. having a cold, Suśr.

पीपरि *pīpari*, m. a tree kindred to Ficus Infectoria, L.

पीबस *pības*. See *pīvas*.

पीय् *pīy*, cl. 1. P. *pīyati*, to blame, abuse, revile, scoff, deride, RV.; AV.; Nir. iv, 25; to gladden (cf. Uṇ. iv, 76).

Pīyaka, m. 'abuser,' (prob.) N. of a class of demons, AV.

Pīyatnú, mfn. scornful, RV.

Pīyú, m. scornful, injurious, RV.; m. (L.) an owl; a crow; fire; gold; time.

पीयूक्षा *pīyūkshā*, f. a species of tree; (*-vana* = *-vana*, Pāṇ. viii, 4, 5).

Pīyūkshila, mfn., g. *kāśâdi*.

पील् *pīl*, cl. 1. *pīlati*, to check or stop, to become stupid, Dhātup. xv, 14.

Pīlu, m. (cf. Uṇ. i, 38, Sch.) a species of tree (Careya Arborea or Salvadora Persica, L.), MBh.; R. &c.; a group of palm trees or the stem of the palm, L.; a flower, L.; the blossoms of Saccharum Sara, L.; a piece of bone (*asthi-khaṇḍa*), L.; an arrow, L.; a worm, L.; an atom, Sarvad.; an elephant (cf. Arabic فيل, Persian پيل), L.; (*ú*), n. the fruit of the Pīlu tree, AV. —**kuṇa**, m. the season of the ripening of the P° fruit, Pāṇ. v, 2, 24 (cf. *pailukuṇa*). —**pati**, m. a keeper of elephants, L. —**pattra**, m. Sanseviera Roxburghiana, L. —**parṇī**, f. id., L.; Momordica Monadelpha, L.; a kind of drug, L. —**pāka**, m. the junction of atoms caused by heat, Sarvad. —**matī** (*pīlú-*), f. (with *dyaus*) the central or middle region of the sky (between Udan-vatī and Pra-dyaus), AV. —**vana**, n. a forest consisting of Pīlu trees, Buddh. —**vaha**, n. N. of a district, Pāṇ. vi, 3, 121 (cf. *pailuvahaka*). —**vādin**, m. one who asserts the eternity of atoms, Saṃkar. —**sāra**, m. N. of a mountain (also called *pīlu-giri*), Buddh.; *-stūpa*, m. N. of a Stūpa, ib.

Pīluka, m. N. of a tree, L. (cf. *kāka-pīluka*, *kāla-p°*); an ant, L. (cf. *pīlaka*).

Pīlunī, f. Sanseviera Roxburghiana, L.

पीलक *pīlaka*, m. an ant, L. (cf. *pipīla* and *pīluka*).

पीला *pīlā*, f. N. of an Apsaras, AV.; of a woman, L.

पीष् *pīsh* = √*pish* in *apīshan*, AV. iv, 6, 7.

पु *pu*, mfn. cleaning, purifying (see *su-pú*).

पुंयान *pum-yāna*, &c. See under 2. *puṅs*.

पुंस् 1. *puṅs*, cl. 10. *puṅsayati*, to crush, grind, Dhātup. xxxii, 94 (Nom. fr. next?).

पुंस् 2. *púṅs*, m. (the strong cases from *pumāṅs* [cf. Pāṇ. vii, 1, 89]; sg. nom. *púmān*; voc. *púmas* or *púman*; acc. *púmāṅsam*; du. nom. *púmāṅsau*; pl. nom. *púmāṅsas* [irreg. *puṅsas*, MBh. iii, 13825]; the weak from *puṅs* [e.g. sg. instr. *puṅsā*; loc. *puṅsi*, acc. pl. *puṅsás*], which loses its *s* before consonants [e.g. instr. pl. *pum-bhis*; loc. plur. *puṅsú*]; for *puṅs*, ibc. see Pāṇ. viii, 3, 6) a man, a male being, RV. &c. &c.; (in gram.) a masculine (word), ŚBr.; Pāṇ.; Vop.; a human being, MBh.; Kāv. &c.; a servant, attendant, BhP.; the soul, spirit, spirit of man (= *purusha*; with *para* or *parama*, the Supreme Spirit, Soul of the Universe, Vishṇu), KapS.; Tattvas.; Sāṃkhyak.; MBh.; Pur.; Kathās. —**kaṭī**, f. a man's hip, L. —**karmâśaya**, m. the qualities of man as dependant on the acts done in a previous existence, Sarvad. —**kāmā**, f. a woman desirous of a lover or husband, Pāṇ. viii, 3, 6, Kāś. —**kṛityā**, ind. by applying masculine forms, ŚBr. —**kokila**, m. the male of the Indian cuckoo (*-tva*, n.), MBh.; Kāv. &c. —**traya**, n. three generations, Hcat. —**tva**, n. the being a man (opp. to *strī-bhāva*), Pur.; manhood, virility, Yājñ.; Suśr.; semen virile, Hariv.; (in gram.) masculineness, the masculine gender, L.; Pāṇ., Sch.; *-dosha*, m. 'want of manhood,' impotence, Gal.; *-vigraha*, m. Andropogon Schoenanthus, L. —**putra**, m. a male child, boy, Pāṇ. viii, 3, 6, Kāś. —**prajanana**, n. the male organ of generation, Nir. —**pravāda**, m. any grammatical or case form in the masculine gender, RPrāt. —**vat** (*púṅs-*), mfn. containing a male being, TS.

1. **Pum**, in comp. for 2. *puṅs*. —**yāna**, n. (prob.) = *nara-y°*, a palanquin, APrāt., Sch. —**yuj** (L.), and -**yoga**, m. (Pāṇ. iv, 1, 48) connection with or relation to a man. —**ratna**, n. a jewel of a man, an excellent man, Rājat. —**rāśi**, m. a male sign of the zodiac (as Aries &c.), Var. —**rūpa**, n. the form or shape of a man (°*paṃ* √*kṛi*, to assume the f° of a man), MW.; (*púm-*), mf(*ā*)n. having the f° of a man, MaitrS. —**lakshman**, n. the mark of a man, manliness, Rājat. —**liṅga**, n. id., MBh.; the male organ, W.; the masculine gender, Kum., Sch.; mf(*ā*)n. having the mark of a man, AgP.; (in gram.) being masculine; *-tā*, f., Kum., Sch. —**vat**, ind. like a man, like or in or with a man &c., MBh.; Kāv.; like or in or with the masculine gender, ŚrS.; Pāṇ.; Vop. (*-vad-vidhāna*, n. ceremonies as on the birth of a male, MW.) —**vatsa** (*púm-*), m. a bull-calf, ŚBr.; mf(*ā*)n. having (or surrounded by) bull-calves, BrahmaP. —**vṛisha**, m. the musk rat, L. —**vesha**, mf(*ā*)n. wearing male attire, dressed like a man, Kathās. —**vyañjana**, n. the mark or attribute of a man, ĀpŚr. —**śabda**, m. a masculine word, L. —**savana**, mfn. bringing forth a male, producing a m° child, BhP.; Car.; n. (with or sc. *vrata*) 'male-production rite,' N. of the 2nd of the 12 Saṃskāras performed in the third month of gestation and before the period of quickening, GṛS.; MBh. &c. (cf. RTL. 353; 355); a fetus, BhP.; milk, L.; *-prayoga* and °*nâḍi-prayoga*, m. N. of wks. —**súvana**, n. bringing forth a male child, AV. —**sū**, f. bringing forth only m° children, ĀpGṛ. —**strī**, du. a m° and a female child, Mn. iii, 49.

2. **Pum**, in comp. before *k*, *j*, &c. —**kandā**, f. a species of plant, L. —**kshīra**, n., -**kshura**, m., Pāṇ. viii, 3, 9, Kāś. —**khe'ṭa**, m. a male planet, L. —**khyāna**, n., Siddh. on Pāṇ. viii, 3, 6. —**gava**, m. (ifc. f. *ā*) a bull, Lāṭy.; Hariv.; a hero, eminent person, chief of (ifc. cf. *kuru-p°*, *gaja-p°* &c.); a kind of drug, L.; *-ketu*, m. 'marked by a bull,' N. of Śiva, Kum. —**guṇa-jantu-jīva**, m. the living or animal soul combined with the qualities of man, Tattvas. —**janman**, n. the birth of a male child; °*ma-kara* and °*ma-da*, mfn. causing or granting it, Var.; °*ma-yoga*, m. a constellation under which m° children are born, ib. —**dāna**, n., APrāt., Sch. —**dāsa**, m. a m° slave, Pāṇ. viii, 3, 6, Kāś. —**devata**, mfn. addressed to a m° deity (as a hymn),

Cat. **—dhvaja**, m. 'm°-marked,' a m° animal, L. **—nakshatra**, n. a m° Nakshatra, Kauś.; any constellation under which males are procreated, W. **—napuṇsaka**, n. masculine and neuter, L. **—nāga**, m. 'elephant among men,' any distinguished man, L.; a white elephant, L.; N. of a plant (Rottleria Tinctoria or Calophyllum Inophyllum), L.; a white lotus, L.; a nutmeg, L. **—nāṭa**, m. Cassia Tora, Bhpr. **—nāḍa**, m. id., ib.; N. of a prince, Inscr. **—nāmadheya**, mfn. 'that which is called man,' a male, Kauś.; R. **—nāman** (*púm-*), mfn. having a masculine name, ŚBr.; MBh. &c.; m. Rottleria Tinctoria, L.

Puṇś, in comp. for 2. *puṇs* (cf. Pāṇ. viii, 3, 6). **—calī**, f. 'running after men,' a harlot, courtezan, AV. &c. &c. (*-cala*, m. a fornicator, VarBṛS. xxiii, 5); °*lī-putra*, m. a harlot's son, Mṛicch.; °*līya*, m. id., Rājat. **—calū**, f. a harlot, VS.; m. a whoremonger, KātyŚr. **—cihna**, n. 'male-mark,' membrum virile, L. **—cora**, m. a male thief, L. **—chagalā**, f. having a kid (as its young), ĀpŚr.

Puṇsa, in comp. for 2. *puṇs*. **—1. -vat**, mfn. having a son, ŚāṅkhGṛ. (cf. *puṇs-vat*). **—2. -vat**, ind. like (with) a man, HPariś.

Puṇsaka. See *na-p°*.

Puṇsânuja, m. (instr. of *puṇs* + *an°*) having an elder brother (?), Pāṇ. vi, 3, 3, Vārtt. 2 (cf. *pum-anuja*).

Puṇsī, f. a cow which has a bull-calf, Kauś.

Puṇska (ifc., f. *ā*) = *puṇs*, g. *ura-ādi* (cf. *ukta-p°*, *bhāshita-p°*).

Pum, in comp. for 2. *puṇs*. **—anujā**, f. 'born after a male child,' having an elder brother, Pāṇ. iii, 2, 100, Kāś. (cf. *puṇsânuja*). **—apatya**, n. male offspring, L. **—artha**, m. the aim of man (*-tā*, f.), TBr., Sch.; (*am*), ind. for the sake of the soul, KapS. **—ākhya**, mfn. designated as male or masculine, Pāṇ. viii, 3, 6, Sch.; (*ā*), f. a name or designation for male beings, L.; Pāṇ. iv, 1, 48, Sch. **—ācāra**, m. the custom or usage of men, Pāṇ. viii, 3, 6, Sch. **—paśu**, m. a man as sacrificial victim, Kathās. **—prakṛiti**, f. the nature or character of a man, Var. **—bhāva**, m. the being a man, manhood, masculine gender, Daś. **—bhūman**, m. a word of the masc° gender in the plural number, L. **—mantra**, m. a magical formula regarded as male, Sarvad. **—mṛiga**, m. a male antelope, Mahīdh.

पुंसोक *puṇsoka*, m. N. of a poet, Cat.

पुंस्ति *puṇsti*, n. N. of a Sāman, ĀrshBr.

पुक *puka*, m. = *dāna*, Gaṇar. 299.

Pukin, mfn., g. *prekshâdi*.

पुक्कश *pukkaśa*, *pukkasha*, m., w.r. for *pulkasa*, q.v.

Pukkasa, m. id.; (*ī*), f. the indigo plant, L.; = *kalikā* or *kālikā*, L.

पुल्कक *púlkaka* or *púlkaka*, m. = *pulkasa*, MaitrS.

पुङ्ख *puṅkha*, m. the shaft or feathered part of an arrow (which comes in contact with the bowstring), MBh.; Kāv. &c.; a hawk, falcon, L.; = *maṅgalâcāra*, L.

Puṅkhita, mfn. shafted or feathered (as an arrow); *-śara*, mfn. having or armed with shafted or feathered arrows (as the god of love), Amar.

पुङ्खिलतीर्थ *puṅkhila-tīrtha*, n. N. of a place of pilgrimage (= *Rāma-t°*), ŚivaP.

पुङ्ग *puṅga*, m. n. a heap, collection, quantity (cf. *puñja*), L.; (*ī*), f. N. of a partic. kind of woman, BrahmavP.

पुङ्गल *puṅgala*, w. r. for *pudgala*.

पुङ्गव *puṅgava*. See p. 630, col. 3.

पुच्छ *púccha*, m. n. (ifc. f. *ā* or *ī*; cf. Pāṇ. iv, 1, 55, Vārtt. 1-3) a tail, the hinder part, AV. &c. &c.; last or extreme end (as of a year), ŚāṅkhBr. **—kaṇṭaka**, m. 'whose sting is in its tail,' a scorpion, A. **—jāha**, n. = *-dhi*, MW. **—dā**, f. a bulbous plant used as a remedy for sterility, L. (cf. *putra-dā*). **—dhi**, m. the root of the tail, AV. **—bandha**, m. a (horse's) tail-band or crupper, Gal. **—brahmavāda**, m. N. of a Vedânta wk.; *-khaṇḍana*, n., *-nirākaraṇa*, n. N. of wks. **—mūla**, n. = *-dhi*, L. **—lakshaṇa**, n. N. of a Nyāya wk.; *-kroḍa*, m., *-ṭīkā*, f., *-dīdhiti-ṭīkā*, f., *-prakāśa*, m., *-vivecana*, n., °*ṇânugama*, m. N. of wks. **—vat**, mfn. having a tail, tailed, Kathās. **Pucchâgra**, n. tip of the tail, Hit.; (prob. m.) N. of a mountain, W. **Pucchâṇḍaka**, m. N. of a Nāga of the race of Takshaka, MBh. **Pucchâsya-cārin**, mfn. moving along with tail and mouth, Suśr. **Pucchêśvara**, m. or n. (?) N. of a place, Inscr. **Pucchôṭikā**, f. (*p°* + ?) = *puccha-bandha*, Gal.

Pucchaka (ifc., f. *ikā*; cf. *kroshṭu-pucchikā*); = *puccha*, L.; m. N. of a man, Cat.

Pucchaya. See *ut-pucchaya*.

Pucchala. See *kapucchala*.

Pucchin, mfn. = *puccha-vat*; m. a cock, L.; Calotropis Gigantea, L.

पुच्छटि *pucchaṭi*, n. or °*ṭī*, f. snapping or cracking the fingers, L. (cf. *mucuṭī*).

पुछ् *puch*, cl. 1. P. *pucchati*, to be careless, Dhātup. vii, 35 (v. l. for *yuch*, *much*).

पुञ्ज *puñja*, m. (mostly ifc.; f. *ā*) a heap, mass, quantity, multitude, MBh.; Kāv. &c. **—rāja**, m. N. of a grammarian, Cat. **—śas**, ind. in heaps or numbers, MBh.

Puñjaya, Nom. P. °*yati*, to heap, press together, Kād.; Bālar.

Puñjātuka, n. = *phalelāṅku* (?), L.

Puñji, f. = *puñja*, L. **—shṭha**, mfn. heaped, accumulated; (*puñjí-*), m. a fisherman or a bird-catcher, VS.; ĀśvŚr. (cf. Pāṇ. viii, 3, 97).

Puñjika, m. hail, L. **—sthalā** (VS. &c.), **-sthalī** (BhP.), °**kā-stanā** (MārkP.) and °**kā-sthalā** (L.), N. of an Apsaras.

Puñjita, mfn. heaped, made up into a ball, pressed or put together, Kāv.; Rājat.

Puñjishṭha. See *puñji*.

Puñjī, in comp. for *puñja*. **—kartavya**, mfn. to be heaped or collected, Bhaṭṭ., Sch. **—kṛita**, mfn. heaped, collected, Mahīdh. **—kṛitya**, ind. by heaping or collecting, KātyŚr., Sch. **—bhū**, mfn. to be heaped or gathered or pressed or collected together, Kād.; Hcar.

पुञ्जील *puñjīla*. See *darbha-p°*.

पुट् *puṭ*, cl. 6. P. (Dhātup. xxviii, 74) *puṭati*, to clasp, fold, envelop in (instr.), Bhpr.; to rub together with (instr., ib.); cl. 1. P. *poṭati*, to grind, pound, Dhātup. ix, 38 (v. l. for *muṭ*); cl. 10. P. *puṭayati*, to be in contact with, xxxv, 58; *poṭayati*, to speak or to shine (*bhāshârthe* or *bhāsârthe*), xxxiii, 80; to grind or pound, xxxii, 72, Vop.; to be small, xxxii, 24 (v. l. for *puṭṭ*).

Puṭa, m. n. a fold, pocket, hollow space, slit, concavity (ifc. f. *ā*), Mn.; MBh. &c. (also *ī*, f., Śāntiś.); a cloth worn to cover the privities (also *ī*, f.), W.; a horse's hoof, L.; an eyelid (cf. *-bheda*); m. a cup or basket or vessel made of leaves, SBr. (cf. *ūsha-*), Mn.; MBh. &c.; a casket (= *sampuṭa*), L.; the enveloping or wrapping of any substance (esp. for baking or heating it; cf. *puṭa-pāka*), Bhpr.; any cake or pastry filled with seasoning or stuffing of any kind, ib.; N. of a metre (= *śrī-puṭa*), L.; of a man, g. *aśvâdi*; n. a nutmeg, L.; two vessels joined together (for the sublimation of medicinal substances), W. **—kanda**, m. a species of bulbous plant, L. **—grīva**, m. 'hollow-necked,' a churn, L.; a copper vessel, L. **—dhenu**, f. a not yet full-grown cow with a calf, Hcat. **—pāka**, m. a partic. method of preparing drugs (the various substances being wrapped up in leaves, covered with clay, and heated in fire), Car.; Bhpr.; digesting, subliming, W.; *-yukti*, f. the application of the method called *puṭa-pāka*, Suśr. **—bhid**, mfn. burst or cleft asunder, Var. **—bheda**, m. a bend or the mouth of a river, L.; 'parting of the eye-lids,' opening, Uttarar. vi, 3; a town, L.; a kind of musical instrument, L. **—bhedaka**, mfn. = *-bhid*, Var. **—bhedana**, n. a town, city, MBh. **Puṭâñjali**, m. the two hollowed hands put together (cf. *añjali*), Hcat. **Puṭâpuṭikā**, f., g. *śākapârthivâdi*. **Puṭâlu**, m. a species of bulbous plant, L. **Puṭâhvaya**, m. = *puṭa-pāka*, Susr. **Puṭôṭaja**, n. a white umbrella or parasol, L. **Puṭôdaka**, n. 'having water in its hollow or interior,' a cocoa-nut, L.

Puṭaka, m. a fold, pocket, slit, cavity, Kāv.; Pur.; a partic. position of the hands, Cat.; a bag or vessel made of a leaf doubled over in a funnel-shape, Rājat.; (*ikā*), f. a bag or vessel (cf. m.), Pañc.; a bi-valved shell, L.; cardamoms, L.; n. a nutmeg, L.; a water-lily, L. **Puṭakânuvāsana**, n. a funnel-like enema, Kauś., Sch.

Puṭakinī, f. (fr. *puṭaka*, g. *pushkarâdi*) a lotus or group of lotuses, Vāsav. **—pattra**, n. a lotus-leaf, Śak. (in Prākṛit).

Puṭana, n. enveloping, wrapping up, Bhpr.

Puṭan-naṭa, m. Cyperus Rotundus, L. (cf. *kuṭan-naṭa*).

Puṭita, mfn. split, torn up (= *pāṭita*), L.; sewn, stitched (= *syūta*), L.; rubbed, ground, W.; contracted, W.; n. the hollow of the hands (= *hasta-puṭa*), L.; = *ahi-puṭa* (?), L.

1. **Puṭī**, f., see *puṭa*.

2. **Puṭī**, ind. (with √*kṛi*) to make into a funnel-shaped vessel, Bālar.

पुट्ट् *puṭṭ*, cl. 10. P. *puṭṭayati*, to be or become small, diminish, Dhātup. xxxii, 24 (v. l. *puṭ*).

पुड् *puḍ*, cl. 6. P. *puḍati*, to leave, quit, Dhātup. xxviii, 90; cl. 1. P. *poḍati*, to grind, pound, ix, 38 (v. l. for *muṭ*).

पुण् *puṇ*, cl. 6. P. *puṇati*, to act piously or virtuously, Dhātup. xxviii, 43 (invented to serve as base for *puṇya*, *ni-puṇa* &c.?); cl. 10. P. *poṇayati*, to collect, accumulate (v. l. for *pūl*, *pūlyati*).

Puṇaka, m. N. of a man, Hcar., Sch.

Puṇika, m. N. of a man, Kāś.; (*ā*), f. N. of a woman, L.

पुणतामकर *puṇatāmakara*, m. N. of Mahādeva (the author of the Ātmatva-jāti-vicāra &c.), Cat.

पुण्ट् *puṇṭ*, cl. 10. P. *puṇṭayati*, to speak or to shine, Dhātup. xxxiii, 118.

पुण्ड् *puṇḍ*, cl. 1. P. *puṇḍati*, to rub, grind, reduce to powder, Dhātup. ix, 38 (v. l. for *muṭ*).

पुण्ड *puṇḍa*, m. = *puṇḍra*, a mark, sign, L. **—kaksha** and **-vardhana**, w. r. for *puṇḍra-k°* and *-v°*.

पुण्डरिन् *puṇḍarin*, m. Hibiscus Mutabilis, L.

पुण्डरिस्रजा *puṇḍari-srajā́*, f. either 'a lotus-wreath' (if *puṇḍari* is substituted for *puṇḍarīka*) or 'a wreath of Hibiscus Mutabilis' (see above), TS.; TBr.

पुण्डरीक *puṇḍárīka*, n. (√*puṇ* [?]; cf. Uṇ. iv, 20, Sch.) a lotus-flower (esp. a white lotus; ifc. expressive of beauty, cf. g. *vyāghrâdi*), RV. &c. &c. (it is sacred to Śikhin, one of the Buddhas, MWB. 515); a white umbrella, L.; a kind of drug, L.; (m. or n.?) a mark on the forehead, Śatr.; N. of a Tīrtha, MBh.; m. a kind of sacrifice, MBh.; a species of rice, Suśr.; a kind of fragrant mango, L.; Artemisia Indica, L.; a variety of the sugar-cane, L.; a tiger, L.; a kind of bird, L.; a kind of serpent, L.; a kind of leprosy, L.; fever in an elephant, L.; white (the colour), L.; N. of a Nāga, MBh.; of the elephant of the south-east quarter, Ragh.; of an ancient king, MBh.; of a son of Nabha or Nabhas, Hariv.; of a Brāhman renowned for filial piety, and afterwards worshipped as the god Viṭhobā, RTL. 263; (with Jainas) of a Gaṇa-dhara, Śatr.; of a hermit (son of Sveta-ketu and Lakshmī), Kād.; of a poet, Cat.; of a mountain, Śatr.; (*ā*), f. N. of an Apsaras, MBh.; of a daughter of Vasishṭha (wife of Prāṇa or Pāṇḍu), VP.; of a river in Krauñca-dvīpa, ib. **—kavi**, m. N. of a poet, Cat. **—dalôpama**, mfn. resembling a l°-leaf, L. **—nayana**, mfn. lotus-eyed; m. N. of Vishṇu or Kṛishṇa, VP.; a species of bird, Gal. **—palāśâksha**, mfn. l°-(leaf-) eyed, R. **—pura**, n. N. of a town; *-māhātmya*, n. N. of wk. **—purāṇa**, n. N. of a Pur. **—plava**, m. a species of bird, L. **—mukha**, mf(*ī*)n. l°-faced, Mālatīm.; (*ī*), f. a kind of leech, Suśr. **—locana**, mfn. = *-nayana*, mfn. **—vat** (°*ká-*), mfn. abounding with l°-flowers, AV.; m. N. of a mountain in Krauñca-dvīpa, VP. **—vana-māhātmya**, n. N. of wk. **—viṭṭhala**, m. N. of an author who lived under Akbar, Cat. **Puṇḍarīkâksha**, m. 'l°-eyed,' N. of Vishṇu or Kṛishṇa, MBh.; Kāv. &c.; of an author, Cat.; a species of aquatic bird, Car.; n. N. of a partic. drug, L.; *-stotra*, n., °*kôpanishad*, f. N. of wks. **Puṇḍarīkâtapatra**, n. having the l° for an umbrella (said of the autumn), Ragh. **Puṇḍarīkânvaya**, m. an elephant of P°'s (see above) race, an el° with peculiar marks, Gal. **Puṇḍarīkêkshaṇa**, m. 'l°-eyed,' N. of Vishṇu or Kṛishṇa, MBh. **Puṇḍarīkôdara-prabha**, mfn. resplendent as the interior of a white lotus, MW.

Puṇḍarīkiṇī, f. N. of a town in Videha, HPariś.

Puṇḍarīyaka, m. N. of one of the Viśve Devāḥ,

MBh.; n. the flower of Hibiscus Mutabilis, L.; a kind of drug (prob. = next), Bhpr.

Puṇḍarya, n. a medicinal plant used as a remedy for diseased eyes, L.

पुण्ड्र *puṇḍra*, m. N. of a son of the Daitya Bali (ancestor of the Puṇḍras), MBh.; (pl.) of a people and their country (the modern Bengal and Behar), AitBr.; MBh. &c.; of a son of Vasu-deva, VP.; sugar-cane (or a red variety of it), L.; Gaertnera Racemosa, L.; Ficus Infectoria, L.; Clerodendrum Phlomoides, L.; a white lotus-flower, L.; a worm, L.; m. or n. a mark or line made on the forehead with ashes or colouring substances to distinguish Vaishṇavas fr. Śaivas &c., a sectarian mark, KātyŚr., Sch.; RTL. 66; 67 (cf. *ūrdhva-p°*, *tri-p°*); n. N. of a mythical city between the mountains Hima-vat and Hema-kūṭa, VāyuP. **-kaksha**, m. N. of a mountain, Divyâv. (w. r. *puṇḍa-k°*). **-keli**, m. an elephant, L. **-nagara**, n. 'city of the Puṇḍras,' N. of a town (cf. *pauṇḍranāgara*). **-vardhana**, n. N. of a town in Gauḍa, Pañc. (w. r. *puṇḍa-v°*). **-vidhi**, m., **-stotra**, n. N. of wks. **Puṇḍrêkshu**, m. sugar-cane, L.

Puṇḍraka, m. (pl.) the Puṇḍras (s. v.), Mn. x, 44 (v. l. *pauṇḍ°*); MBh.; (sg.) a prince of the P°, MBh.; N. of sev. plants (= *puṇḍra*), L.; a frontal sectarian mark (see *ūrdhva-p°*, *tri-p°*); a man who lives by breeding silk-worms, Col.; N. of a poet (also *Puṇḍroka*), Cat.

Puṇḍhra, w. r. for *puṇḍra*, a sectarian mark.

पुण्य *púṇya*, mf(*ā*)n. (perhaps fr. √2. *push*, according to Uṇ. v, 15 from √*pū*; see also √*puṇ*) auspicious, propitious, fair, pleasant, good, right, virtuous, meritorious, pure, holy, sacred, RV. &c. &c.; m. N. of a poet, Cat.; of another man, Buddh.; m. or n. N. of a lake, MBh.; (*ā*), f. holy basil, L.; Physalis Flexuosa, L.; N. of a daughter of Kratu and Saṃnati, VP.; n. (ifc. f. *ā*) the good or right, virtue, purity, good work, meritorious act, moral or religious merit, MBh.; Kāv. &c.; a religious ceremony (esp. one performed by a wife in order to retain her husband's affections and to obtain a son; also *-ka*), MBh.; Hariv.; a brick trough for watering cattle, W. **-kartṛi** (MBh.), **-karman** (ib.; R. &c.), mfn. acting right, virtuous, pious. **-kāla**, m. an auspicious time, Hcat.; *-tā*, f. auspiciousness of time, Sūryas.; *-vidhi*, m. N. of wk. **-kīrti**, mfn. bearing a good name, famous, celebrated, MBh.; m. N. of a man (whose shape was assumed by Vishṇu), SkandaP. **-kūṭa**, m. a great multitude of meritorious acts, Kāraṇḍ. **-kṛit**, mfn. = *-kartṛi*, ŚBr.; MBh. &c.; m. N. of one of the Viśve Devāḥ, MBh. **-kṛityā́** (ŚBr.), **-kriyā** (Āpast.), f. a good or meritorious action. **-kshetra**, n. a holy place, a place of pilgrimage, VarBṛS., Sch.; N. of Buddha, Divyâv. **-gandha** (*pú°*), mfn. sweet-scented, fragrant, RV.; MBh.; Ragh.; m. Michelia Champaka, L. **-gandhi** (*pú°*, AV.), **-gandhin** (MBh.), mfn. sweet-scented, fragrant. **-gṛiha**, n. a house of charity, an alms-house or a temple, R. **-geha**, n. a house i.e. a place or seat of virtue, Daś. **-janá**, m. a good or honest man, L.; (pl.) good people (N. of a class of supernatural beings, AV. &c. &c.; in later times N. of the Yakshas and of a partic. class of Rākshasas, Kāv.; Pur.); *°nêśvara*, m. 'lord of Y°s,' N. of Kubera, Ragh. **-janman** (*pú°*), mfn. of pure or holy origin, MaitrS. **-jala**, mfn. having pure water, ML. **-jita**, mfn. gained or attained by good works, ChUp.; Kāv. **-tara**, mfn. purer, holier, *°rī-√kṛi*, to make p° or h°, Ragh. **-tā**, f. (MBh.), **-tva**, n. (Kum.) purity, holiness. **-tīrtha**, n. a sacred shrine or place of pilgrimage, Hit.; N. of a Tīrtha, W.; mf(*ā*)n. abounding with Tīrthas, R. **-tṛiṇa**, n. a sacred grass (N. of the white variety of Kuśa grass), L. **-darśana**, mf(*ā*)n. of beautiful appearance, Ragh.; m. Coracias Indica, L. **-duh**, mfn. yielding or granting happiness or beatitude, MBh. **-nātha**, m. (with *upādhyāya*) N. of a man, Cat. **-nāman**, m. N. of one of the attendants of Skanda, MBh.; *°ma-ślokâvalī*, f. N. of wk. **-nivaha**, mfn. conferring religious merit, meritorious, BhP. **-pāpêkshitṛi**, mfn. seeing good and bad deeds, Mn. viii, 91. **-pāla-rāja-kathā**, f. N. of wk. **-pāvana**, m. or n. a proper N., Cat. **-puṇyatā**, f. perfect holiness, Rājat. **-purusha**, m. a man rich in religious merit, a pious man, MW. **-pratāpa**, m. the efficacy of virtue or of religious merit, ib. **-prada**, mfn. = *-nivaha*, Hariv. **-prasava**, m. pl. (with Buddhists) N. of one of the 18 classes of gods of the world of form, Dharmas. **-phala**, n. the fruit or reward of good works, Mn. iii, 95 &c.; mfn. having or receiving good fruit, R.; m. N. of the garden of Lakshmī, L. **-bala**, m. N. of a king of Puṇya-vatī, Avadānas.; N. of one of the 10 forces of a Bodhi-sattva, Dharmas. **-bharita**, mfn. abounding in holiness or bliss, Śatr. **-bhaj** (Kād.), **-bhājin** (Śatr.), mfn. partaking of bliss, happy. **-bhū**, f. 'the holy land,' N. of Āryâvarta (s. v.), L. **-bhūmi**, f. id., L.; the mother of a male child, W. **-manyá**, mfn. thinking one's self good, MaitrS. **-maya**, mf(*ī*)n. consisting of good or of merit, Prab. **-mahas**, mfn. of pure glory, Mcar. i, 18. **-mahêśâkhya**, mfn. named 'holy and great lord,' Divyâv. **-mitra**, m. N. of a Buddhist patriarch. **-yoga**, m. the effect of virtuous actions in a former life, W. **-rāja**, m. N. of an author, Cat. **-rātra**, m. an auspicious night, L. **-rāśi**, m. N. of a man, L.; of a mountain, Śatr. **-lakshmīka** (*pú°*), mfn. auspicious, prosperous, ŚBr. **-labdha**, mfn. attained by good works, MBh. **-loka** (*pú°*), mfn. belonging to or sharing in a better world, ŚBr. **-vat**, mfn. righteous, virtuous, honest, MBh.; auspicious, happy, Kathās.; Hit.; (*ī*), f. N. of a country, Avadānaś. **-varjita**, m. 'destitute of virtue,' N. of a fictitious country, Kautukas. **-vardhana**, mfn. 'increasing merit,' Hariv.; n. N. of a city, Vet. (cf. *puṇḍra-v°*). **-varman**, m. N. of a prince of Vidarbha, Daś. **-vallabha**, m. N. of a man, L. **-vāg-buddhi-karmin**, mfn. pure in word and thought and deed, MBh. **-vijita**, mfn. acquired by merit, merited, MW. **-śakuna**, m. a bird of good omen, MBh. **-śālā**, f. a house of charity, alms-house, L. **-śīla**, mfn. of a virtuous disposition, virtuous, pious, righteous, MBh. **-śesha**, m. N. of a prince, L. **-śrīka**, mfn. = *-lakshmīka*, Mcar. **-śrī-garbha**, m. N. of a Bodhi-sattva, L. **-śloka**, mf(*ā*)n. 'well spoken of,' of good fame or reputation, BhP. (*°kêdya-karman*, mfn. one whose actions must be praised in auspicious verses, ib.); m. N. of Nala or Yudhi-shṭhira or Kṛishṇa, MBh.; Pur.; (*ā*), f. N. of Sītā or Draupadī, Pur. **-saṃcaya**, m. a store of virtue or religious merit, MW. **-sáma**, n. a good year, TS.; Vait.; (*am*), ind., g. *tishṭhadgv-ādi*. **-sambhāra**, m. = *-saṃcaya*, Kāraṇḍ.; (with Buddhists) the equipment of meritorious acts, Dharmas. **-sāra**, m. N. of a prince, Kathārṇ. **-sundara** (or *-gaṇi*), m. N. of a grammarian, Cat. **-sena**, m. N. of a prince, Kathās.; of another man, Buddh. **-skandha**, m. = *-saṃcaya*, Kāraṇḍ. **-stambha-kara** (?), m. N. of a man, Cat. **-sthāna**, n. a sacred place, consecrated ground, Yājñ. **Puṇyâkara**, m. N. of the father of Śaṃkara, Cat. **Puṇyâgni**, m. the public fire kept burning in a city square for the use of all, Subh. **Puṇyâtman**, mfn. 'pure-souled,' virtuous, pious, Kāv.; Hit. **Puṇyā-nagara**, n. N. of a town, Cat. **Puṇyânanda-nātha**, m. N. of an author, Cat. **Puṇyânubhāva**, m. pleasing majesty or dignity, Uttarar. iv, 22. **Puṇyâlaṃkṛita**, m. 'adorned by virtue,' N. of a demon, Lalit. **Puṇyâśaya**, mfn. = *°ṇya-śīla*, Hcar. **Puṇyâhá**, n. a happy or auspicious day; wishing a person a h° or a° day (*°haṃ* with √*vac*, Caus. 'to wish a person [acc.] a h° or a° day'), Br.; GṛŚrS.; MBh. &c.; *-prayoga*, m., *-mantra*, m. N. of wks.; *-vācana*, n. proclaiming or wishing an auspicious day, MBh.; N. of wk. (also *°na-prayoga*, m.); mfn., Pāṇ. v, 1, 111, Vārtt. 3, Pat.; *-śabda* (BhavP.) and *-svana* (MBh.), m. = *-vācana*, n. **Puṇyâika-karman**, mfn. doing only virtuous actions, Hit. **Puṇyôdaka**, mfn. having sacred waters, Megh.; (*ā*), f. N. of a river in the next world, MBh. **Puṇyôdaya**, m. the occurrence of good fortune (resulting from virtuous acts done in a former life), Hit. **Puṇyôdyāna**, mfn. having beautiful gardens, MW.

Puṇyaka, n. N. of a partic. ceremony performed by a woman (= *puṇya*, n., q. v.), MBh.; Hariv.; the present made to a wife on the occasion of the P° ceremony, Hariv. **-vrata**, n. the worship of Kṛishṇa for a year with daily presents (to be performed by a woman desirous of a son), BrahmavP.

Puṇyī-√kṛi, to sanctify, consecrate, HPariś.

पुत् *put* or *pud* (a word invented to explain *putra* or *put-tra*, see Mn. ix, 138, and cf. Nir. ii, 11), hell or a partic. hell (to which the childless are condemned), MBh.; Kāv. &c. **Pun-nāman**, mfn. having the name Put, called Put, Mn. ix, 138.

पुत *puta*, m. (du.) the buttocks, L.; a kind of metre, Col. (prob. w. r. for *puṭa*, cf. *śrī-puṭa*).

पुत्तल *puttala*, m. (prob. fr. *putra*) a puppet, doll, small statue, effigy, image (*-dahana*, n., *-vidhāna*, n., and *-vidhi*, m. burning an effigy in place of the body of one who has died abroad), Cat.; (*ī*), f. = m.; an idol; *°lī-cālana*, n. a partic. game with dolls, Gal.; *°lī-pūjā*, f. idol-worship, idolatry, MW.

Puttalaka, m. (and *ikā*, f.) = *puttala*, *°lī*; *°liko vidhiḥ* = *puttala-v°* above.

Puttikā, f. a doll, puppet, BhP.; the white ant or termit (so called from its doll-like form), Mn.; MBh.; Pañc.; = *pataṃgikā*, a small kind of bee, Bhpr.; a gnat, Nīlak. = *plushi*, Śaṃk.; Sāy.

पुत्र *putrá*, m. (etym. doubtful, perhaps fr. √2. *push*; traditionally said to be a comp. *put-tra*, 'preserving from the hell called Put,' Mn. ix, 138) a son, child, RV. &c. &c. (also the young of an animal; cf. Pāṇ. viii, 1, 15, Sch.; ifc. it forms diminutives, cf. *dṛishat-p°* and *śilā-p°*; voc. sg. du. pl. often used to address young persons 'my son, my children &c.'; du. 'two sons' or 'a son and a daughter'; cf. Pāṇ. i, 2, 68); a species of small venomous animal (= *putraka*), Cat.; (in astrol.) N. of the fifth house, Var.; N. of a son of Brahmishṭha, Ragh.; of a son of Priya-vrata, VP. &c. &c.; (*ī*), f. a daughter, MBh.; Hariv. &c.; a doll or puppet (see *dāru-putrī*); ifc. used to form diminutives (see *asi-putrī*); a species of plant, L.; N. of Pārvatī, L. [Cf. Zd. *puthra*; Gk. παῖς and Lat. *puer* (?).] **-kandā**, f. a bulbous plant (supposed to cause fecundity), L. **-karman**, n. a ceremony relating to a son, MBh. **-kalatra-nāśa-bhīta**, mfn. fearful of the destruction of wife and children, MW. **-kāma** (*putrá-*), mfn. desirous of sons or children; *-kṛishṇa-pañcamī-vrata*, n. N. of a partic. observance, Cat.; *°mêshṭi*, f. an oblation made by one desirous of offspring, ĀśvŚr. **-kāmika**, mf(*ī*)n. (a sacrifice) aiming at the birth of a son, MBh. **-kāmya**, Nom. P. *°yati*, to wish for a son, Śāntiś. (cf. Pāṇ. iii, 1, 9, Sch.) **-kāmyā́**, f. wish for sons or children, AV.; R. &c.; *°myêshṭi*, f. N. of wk. **-kārya**, n. = *-karman*, MBh. **-kṛit**, m. f. an adopted child, MW. **-kṛitaka**, mfn. adopted as a child, Śak. **-kṛitya**, n. the duty of a son, ib. **-kṛithá**, m. or n. the bringing forth or procreation of children, RV. **-krama-dīpikā**, f. N. of wk. **-ghnī**, see *-han*. **-jagdhī**, f. 'one who has devoured her children,' an unnatural mother, Pāṇ. viii, 8, 48, Vārtt. 2, Pat. **-jananī**, f. a species of plant, L. **-jāta**, mfn. one to whom a son is born, having a son, g. *āhitâgny-ādi*. **-jīva**, w. r. for **-m-jīva**, *°vaka*, m. 'giving life to children,' Putranjiva Roxburghii (from its seeds are made necklaces which are supposed to keep children in good health), L. **-tā**, f. (AitBr.), **-tva**, n. (MBh. &c.) sonship, filial relationship. **-tīrtha**, n. N. of a sacred bathing-place (also of 2 chs. of PadmaP.), Cat. **-da**, mfn. giving sons or offspring, W.; (*ā*), f. N. of a kind of shrub, L.: of a species of bulbous plant, L.; = *vandhyā-karkoṭakī*, L. **-dātrī**, f. 'child-giver,' N. of a creeping plant (growing in Mālava and supposed to promote fecundity), L. **-dāra**, n. son (child) and wife, Mn. iv, 239 &c. **-dharma**, m. filial duty; *-tas*, ind. according to the ceremonies usual on the birth of a son, MW. **-nāman**, mfn. having the name son, called son, MānGṛŚrS. **-niveśana**, n. the habitation or abode of a son, MW. **-piṇḍa-pālana**, m. (with *upavāsa*) 'cherishing the body of a son,' N. of a ceremony, Śak. ii, 14/17 (MW. p. 51, n. 1; v. l. *-pāraṇa*). **-pitṛi**, m. du. son and father, Kathās. **-putra**, m. a son's son, a grandson, Gal.; *°trâdinī*, f. an unnatural mother (see *putra-jagdhī* and Pāṇ. viii, 8, 48, Vārtt. 2, Pat.) **-pura**, n. N. of a town, Kathās. **-pautra**, n. sg. and m. pl. sons and grandsons, Mn.; MBh. &c.; *°traka*, n. sg. id., Subh.; *°trin*, mfn. having s°s and g°s, MBh.; *°triṇa*, mfn. transmitted to s°s and g°s, hereditary, Pāṇ. v, 2, 10 (*°ṇa-tā*, f., Bhaṭṭ.) **-pratigraha-vidhi**, m. N. of wk. **-prati-nidhi**, m. a substitute for a son (as an adopted son &c.), W. **-prada**, mfn. giving sons or children (in *-śiva-stotra*, n. N. of a Stotra); (*ā*), f. N. of a species of Solanum, L. **-pravara**, m. the eldest son, MBh.; BhP. **-priya**, mfn. dear to a son, Veṇis.; m. 'fond of offspring,' N. of a kind of bird, R. **-phala-bhaktṛi**, mfn. enjoying the advantage of having a son, MW. **-bhadrā**, f. a species of plant, L. **-bhāga**, m. a son's share or portion, Mn. ix, 215. **-bhāṇḍa**, n. a substitute for a son, one who is to be regarded as a son, Mcar.; Bālar. **-bhāva**, m. sonship, filial relation, Nir. iii, 4; 5. **-bhūya**, n. id., HPariś. **-máya**, mf(*ī*)n. consisting or formed of a son, ŚBr. **-martyā**, f. the dying of sons, ĀpŚr. **-moṭikāputra** (?), Divyâv. **-rodam**, ind. (with √*rud*) to weep over a son, ChUp. **-lābha**, m. obtaining a son or sons, MW. **-1. -vat**, ind. like a son or sons, as with a son &c., Mn.; MBh. **-2. -vat** (*putrá-*), mfn. having a son or sons or children, VS.; Mn.; MBh. &c. **-vadhū**, f. a son's wife, daughter-in-law, L. **-vala**, mfn. = 2. *-vat*, L. **-vidya**, n. = *-lābha*, AV. **-śṛiṅgī**, f. Odina Pinnata, L. **-śreṇī**, f. Salvinia Cucullata, Suśr.; Odina Pinnata, L.; Anthericum Tuberosum, L. **-sakha**, m. fond or a friend of children, Hariv. **-saṃkarin**, mfn. mixing or confusing children (through mixed marriages), MBh. **-saṃgraha**, m. N. of wk. **-saptamī**, f. the 7th day in the light half of the month Aśvina, Cat.; *-vrata-kathā*, f. N. of wk. **-sahasraka**, mf(*ikā*)n. having 1000 sons, MBh. **-sahasrin**, mfn. id., ib. **-sāma-prayoga**, m. N. of wk. **-sū**, f. the mother of a son, W. **-sena** (*putrá-*), m. N. of a man, MaitrS. **-sneha**, m. love of or for a son, MBh.; *-maya*, mf(*ī*)n. consisting in the love for a son, BhP. **-svīkāra**, m. making one's own i.e. adopting a son; *-nirūpaṇa*, n., *-nirṇaya*, m., *-vidhi*, m. N. of wks. **-hata**, mfn. 'whose sons have been killed,' N. of Vasishṭha, TāṇḍBr.; (*ī*), f. = *-jagdhī*, Pāṇ. viii, 4, 48, Vārtt. 2, Pat. **-han**, mf(*ghnī*)n. killing a child, Car.; Suśr. **-hīna**, mfn. sonless, childless (*-tva*, n.), MW. **Putrâcārya**, m. (a father) having his son for his teacher, Mn. iii, 160. **Putrâdinī**, f. = *putra-jagdhī*, Pāṇ. viii, 4, 48 (when used literally spelt with two *t*'s, e.g. *puttrâdinī vyāghrī*, 'a tigress eating her young,' ib., Sch.) **Putrânnâda**, mfn. eating the food of a son, living at a son's expense, L. **Putrârthin**, mf(*inī*)n. wishing for a son, MBh. **Putrêjyā**, f. (prob.) = *putrêshṭi*; *-prayoga*, m. N. of wk. **Putrêpsu**, mfn. wishing for a son, W. **Putrêshṭi**, f. a sacrifice performed to obtain male children or one performed at the time of adoption, L.; *-prayoga*, m. N. of wk. **Putrêshṭikā**, f. = *putrêshṭi*. **Putrâiśvarya**, n. 'son's proprietorship,' a resignation of property or power by a father to his son, W. **Putrâishaṇā**, f. desire or longing for a son, ŚBr. **Putrôtpatti-paddhati**, f. N. of wk. **Putrôtsaṅgā**, f. pregnant with a son, MBh.

Putraká, m. a little son, boy, child (often used as a term of endearment; ifc. f. *ikā*), RV. &c. &c.; a puppet, doll, figure of stone or wood or lac &c. (cf. *kṛitrima-*, *jatu-*, *śilā-*; g. *yāvâdi*); a rogue, cheat, L.; a species of small venomous animal (enumerated among the Mūshikas), Suśr.; a grasshopper, L.; a fabulous animal with 8 legs (= *śarabha*), W.; hair, L.; a species of tree, L.; a grinding-stone, Gobh., Sch.; N. of the supposed founder of Pāṭaliputra, Kathās.; of a mountain, L.; (*akā*), f. = next, Pāṇ. vii, 3, 45, Vārtt. 10, Pat.

Putrikā, f. a daughter (esp. a d° appointed to raise male issue to be adopted by a father who has no sons), Mn.; MBh. &c.; a puppet, doll, small statue, Bhartṛ.; Kathās.; (ifc. = a diminutive; cf. *asi-*, *khaḍga-*); the cotton or down of the tamarisk, W. **-putra**, m. a daughter's son who by agreement or adoption becomes the son of her father, ŚāṅkhŚr., Sch. **-pūrva-putra**, m. the son of a d° adopted before (cf. above), MBh. **-prasū**, f. the mother of a d°, L. **-bhartṛi**, m. a d°'s husband, MW. **-suta**, m. a d°'s son, a grandson, W.

Putrín, mf(*iṇī*)n. having a son or sons, possessing children (m. and f. the father or the mother of a son or of children generally), RV. &c. &c.; (*iṇī*), f. Siphonantus Indica and another plant, L.; (with *piḍakā*) a pustule which has small p°s round it, Suśr.; °*ṇy-āpta*, mfn. born of one who is already mother of a son, Mn. ix, 143.

1. **Putriya**, mf(*ā*)n. relating to a son (cf. *a-p°*).

2. **Putriya**, Nom. P. °*yáti*, to wish for a son or children, AV.

1. **Putrī**, f. of *putra*, q.v.

2. **Putrī**, in comp. for *putra*. **-karaṇa**, n. the adoption of sons; *-mimāṇsā*, f. N. of wk. **-kṛita**, mfn. adopted as a son, Ragh.; Rājat. **-√bhū**, to become a son, BhP.

1. **Putrīya**, mf(*ā*)n. relating to a son, procuring a son, MBh.; Kāv.; Suśr.; m. a disciple, Divyâv. **-varga-prayoga**, m., **-sthālīpāka-prayoga**, m. N. of wks.

2. **Putrīya**, Nom. P. °*yáti*, to wish for a son or children, RV. vii, 96, 4 (pr. p. °*yát*); to treat like a son, Pāṇ. iii, 1, 10, Sch. (Desid. *puputrīyishati*, *putitrīyishati* or *putrīyiyishati*, Pāṇ. vi, 1, 3, Vārtt. 4, Pat.; *puputitrīyiyishishati*, Vop.)

Putrīyā, f. the desire of or wish for a son, Pāṇ. iii, 3, 102, Sch.

Putrīyitṛi, mfn. one who wishes for a son, Pāṇ. iii, 2, 170, Sch.

Putrya, mf(*ā*)n. = *putriya* or °*trīya*, ShaḍvBr.; GṛS. **-paśavya**, mf(*ā*)n. fit for sons and cattle, SaṃhUp.

पुथ् *puth*, cl. 4. P. *puthyati*, to hurt, Dhātup. xxvi, 12: Caus. *pothayati* (Ā. p. *pothayāna*, fut. *pothayishye*), to crush, kill, destroy, MBh.; Hariv.; to overpower or drown (one sound by another), Kathās.; to speak or to shine (*bhāshârthe* or *bhāsârthe*), Dhātup. xxxiii, 102.

Pothita, mfn. hurt, injured, killed, destroyed, MBh.; R.

पुदक *pudaka*, m. pl. N. of a people, VP.

पुद्गल *pudgala*, mf(*ā*)n. beautiful, lovely, handsome, MārkP.; m. the body, Hit. i, 41, v. l.; (with Jainas) material object (including atoms), Ṣaṃk.; MWB. 535; the soul, personal entity, Lalit.; man, Var.; the Ego or individual (in a disparaging sense), SaddhP.; N. of Śiva, MBh. (= *deha*, Nīlak.); a horse of the colour of rock-crystal, Gal. **-pati**, m. a prince, king, Var.

Puddala, w.r. for prec.

पुन *puna*, mfn. (√1. *pū*) purifying, cleansing (only ifc., cf. *kim-p°*, *kulam-p°* &c.)

पुनर् *púnar*, ind. back, home, in an opposite direction, RV. &c. &c. (with √*i*, *gam*, *yā*, to go back or away; with √*dā*, to give back, restore; with √*bhū*, to turn round; with √*as* and dat., to fall back upon); again, once more (also with *bhūyas*), ib. (with √*bhū*, to exist again, be renewed, become a wife again, re-marry); again and again, repeatedly, ib. (mostly *púnaḥ p°*, which with *na* = nevermore); further, moreover, besides, ib. (also *punar aparam*; *ādau-punar-paścāt*, at first-then-later); however, still, nevertheless, MBh.; Kāv. &c. (at the end of a verse it lays stress on a preceding *atha vā*, *api vā* or *vā* alone; *punar api*, even again, on the other hand, also; *kadā p°*, at any time, ever; *kim p°*, how much more or less? however; *p°-p°*, now-now; at one time-at another time). **-apagama**, m. going away again (*a-punar-ap°*), Kām. **-abhidhāna**, n. mentioning ag°, Kull. **-abhisheka**, m. anointing ag°, AitBr. **-abhyākāram**, ind. drawing near repeatedly to one's self, ib. **-abhyāghāram**, ind. (prob.) w.r. for prec., GopBr. **-abhyāvartam**, ind. while repeating, under repetition, TāṇḍBr. **-abhyunnīta**, mfn. poured upon again, Jaim. **-arthin**, mfn. requesting ag°; °*thi-tā*, f. repeated request, BhP. **-asú**, mfn. breathing or coming to life ag°, ŚBr. **-āgata**, mfn. come back ag°, returned, Mn.; Hit. **-āgama**, m. coming back, return, ŚāṅkhGṛ. **-āgamana**, n. id., MBh.; R. &c.; being born ag°, re-birth, Sarvad. **-āgāmin**, mfn. coming back, returning, Nir. iv, 16. **-āgrantham**, ind. by repeatedly twining round, AitBr. **-ājāti**, f. re-birth, GopBr. **-ādāyam**, ind. repeatedly, Br.; GṛŚrS. **-ādi**, mfn. beginning afresh, repeated, TāṇḍBr. **-ādhāna**, n. renewing or replacing a consecrated fire, Mn. v, 168; N. of wk.; *-dhāryâgnihotra-prayoga* (?), m., *-prayoga*, m., *-śrauta-sūtra*, n., °*nâgnihotra*, n. N. of wks. **-ādheya**, mfn. to be renewed or replaced (on the altar, said of fire), TBr.; ĀśvŚr.; n. renewing or replacing the consecrated fire, TS.; Br.; ŚrS.; m. N. of a Soma festival, KātyŚr.; *-prayoga*, m. N. of wk. **-ādheyaka**, n. = *-ādheya*, n., TBr., Sch. **-ādheyika**, mf(*ī*)n. relating to the act of replacing the consecrated fire, KātyŚr., Sch. **-ānayana**, n. leading back, MBh. **-ābhāva**, m. re-appearing (*á-punar-ābh°*), MaitrS. **-āmnāna**, n. mentioning again, Lāṭy. **-āyana**, n. coming back, return, ĀśvŚr. **-ālambhá**, m. seizing or taking hold of again, TS. **-āvarta**, m. return, re-birth; *-nandā*, f. N. of a sacred bathing-place, MBh. **-āvartaka**, mfn. recurring (fever), Car. **-āvartana**, see *a-punar-āv°*. **-āvartin**, mfn. returning (to mundane existence), Yājñ.; leading back (to m° ex°), Bhag.; Hariv.; subject to successive births, W. **-āvṛitta**, mfn. repeated, AitBr. **-āvṛitti**, f. return, re-appearance, re-birth, Yājñ.; repetition, ĀśvŚr. **-āśrita**, mfn. run hither again (as a chariot), MaitrS. (*-āsritá* ?). **-āhāra**, m. taking up ag°, KātyŚr.; (*am*), ind. bringing hither repeatedly, ĀpGṛ. **-ukta**, mf(*ā*)n. said ag°, reiterated, repeated, MBh.; R. &c. (ibc. and *am*, ind. repeatedly); superfluous, useless, Vikr. iii, $\frac{7}{8}$; Hcar.; n. repetition, useless repetition, tautology, ŚrS.; MBh.; Kāv. &c.; *-janman*, m. 'whose birth is repeated,' a Brāhman, L.; *-tā*, f., *-tva*, n. repetition, (esp.) useless r°, tautology, Sāh.; *-bhukta-vishaya*, mfn. (an occupation) in which the objects of sense are repeatedly enjoyed, Bhartṛ.; *-vad-ābhāsa*, m. seeming tautology (a figure of speech), Sāh.; *-vādin*, mfn. repeating the same things, talking idly, Śak. **-uktāya**, Nom. Ā. °*yate*, to occur repeatedly, Bālar. **-ukti**, f. = *-ukta*, n., Prāt.; a mere empty word, Vcar.; *-mat*, mfn. tautological, Prāt. **-uktī-√kṛi**, to render superfluous or useless, Kathās. **-utthāna**, n. rising again, resurrection, MW. **-utpatti**, f. re-appearance, re-birth, Col. **-utpādana**, n. reproduction, ChUp. **-ut-sṛishṭa**, mfn. let loose again (as a bull, goat &c.), TS.; KātyŚr. **-utsyūtá**, mfn. sewed or mended again, patched up, TS.; Lāṭy. &c. **-upagamana**, n. coming back, returning, Kathās. **-upanayana**, n. a second initiation of a Brāhman (when the first has been vitiated by partaking of forbidden food; cf. *punaḥ-saṃskāra*), Cat.; *-prayoga*, m., *-vidhāna*, n., *-vidhi*, m. N. of wks. **-upalabdhi**, f. obtaining again, Vikr. **-upasadana**, n. repeated performance, Gaut. **-upâkaraṇa**, n. repeated beginning of study, Gobh. **-upâgama**, m. coming back, return, Kathās. **-upôḍhā**, f. married again, re-married, MW. **-gamana**, n. going or setting out ag°, Pañc. **-garbha-vatī**, f. pregnant ag°, Hit. **-gava**, m., Pāṇ. ii, 2, 18, Vārtt. 4, Pat. **-geya**, mfn. to be sung ag° (*a-punar-g°*), L. **-grahaṇa**, n. repeatedly taking up (with a ladle &c.), KātyŚr.; repetition, ib. **-janman**, n. re-birth, metempsychosis, Bhag.; Hit.; mfn. born ag°, regenerated (*a-punar-j°*), Kathās.; °*ma-jaya*, m. 'victory over re-birth,' liberation, final emancipation, W.; °*mâkshepa*, m. N. of wk. **-jāta**, mf(*ā*)n. born ag°, regenerated, MBh. &c. **-jīvātu**, f. re-birth, TāṇḍBr. **-ḍīna**, n. a partic. manner of flying, MBh. **-ṇava** (*púnar-*), mf(*ā*)n. renewed, restored to life or youth, MaitrS.; MānŚr. (also *punar-ṇavá*; cf. *-nava*). **-tta**, mf(*ā*)n. = *punar-datta*, given back, restored, TāṇḍBr. **-darśana**, n. seeing ag°, Kāv.; (*āya*), ind. 'au revoir,' Mṛicch. **-dātṛi**, m. giving ag°, a rewarder, recompenser, ĀśvŚr. **-dāya**, ind. giving ag°, restoring, RV. **-dāra-kriyā**, f. taking a second wife (after the death of the first), Mn. v, 168. **-dīyamāna**, see *á-p°-d°*. **-dyūta**, n. repeated gambling, MBh. **-dhenu**, f. a cow that ag° gives milk, Lāṭy. **-nava** (*púnar-*), mf(*ā*)n. becoming new or young ag°, renewed, AV.; Br. &c. (also *punar-navá*; cf. *punar-ṇ°*); m. a finger-nail (cf. *-bhava*), L.; (*ā*), f. hog-weed, Boerhavia Procumbens, Suśr.; °*vā-maṇḍūra*, n. a partic. medicinal preparation, Rasar. **-nigrantham**, ind. intertwining ag°, AitBr. **-nitunna**, mfn. thrust in or pierced ag°, Kaṭh.; = next, ib. **-niṛitta**, mfn. ag° repeated in detail, AitBr. **-nivartam**, ind. returning (*a-p°-n°*), TāṇḍBr. **-nishkṛitá**, mfn. repaired or mended ag°, TS.; Kaṭh. **-bandha-yoga**, m. tying or fettering ag°, Kap. **-bāla**, mfn. become a child ag°, R. (cf. παλίμπαις); °*lya*, n. second childhood, weakness from old age, ib. **-bhakshya**, mfn. to be enjoyed ag° (*a°-p°-bh°*), TBr. **-bhava**, mfn. born ag°, BhP.; m. new birth, transmigration, MBh.; Kāv. &c.; a finger-nail, L. (cf. *-nava*); a species of Punar-navā with red flowers, L. **-bhavin** (?), m. the sentient soul (existing ag° after the dissolution of one body in another form), W. **-bhāryā**, f. a second wife = re-marriage, Kāv. **-bhāva**, m. new birth (*a°-p°-bh°*), Prab. **-bhāvin**, mfn. being born ag° (*a°-p°-bh°*), Hariv. **-bhū**, mfn. being renewed, restored to life or youth, RV.; AV.; f. a virgin widow re-married, AV. &c. &c.; re-existence, W. **-bhoga**, m. repeated enjoyment or fruition, perception of pleasure or pain as a reward of former actions, Col. **-magha** (*púnar-*), mfn. 'having repeated gifts,' avaricious, covetous, AV.; repeatedly offering oblations or granting gifts, ib.; TS.; TBr. **-manyá**, mfn. (prob.) again thinking of, remembering, RV. **-māra**, m. repeated dying (*a-p°-m°*), VP. **-mṛita**, n. (*a-p°-m°*), id., BhP. **-mṛityú**, m. id., GopBr. **-yajñá**, m. a repeated sacrifice, ŚBr. **-yātrā**, f. a repeated procession, L. **-yāman**, mfn. useful again (cf. *yāta-y°*), ŚāṅkhBr. **-yuddha**, n. renewal of war, Cat. **-yuvan** (*púnar-*), mfn. ag° young, ŚBr.; *°va-tva*, n., Car. **-lābha**, m. obtaining ag°, recovery, MBh. **-lekhana**, n. writing down ag°, Yājñ., Sch. **-vaktavya**, mfn. to be repeated; *-tā*, f., Kull. **-vacana**, n. saying ag°, repetition, ŚāṅkhBr. **-vaṇya**, see *ajīta-p°-v°*. **-vat**, mfn. containing the word *punar*, AitBr. **-vatsa**, m. a weaned calf that begins to suck ag°, Lāṭy.; (with *Kāṇva*) N. of the author of RV. viii, 7, Anukr. **-varaṇa**, n. choosing ag°, KātyŚr. **-vasu** (*púnar-*), m. 'restoring goods,' N. of the 5th or 7th lunar mansion, RV. &c. &c. (mostly du., cf. Pāṇ. i, 2, 61; *-tvá*, n., MaitrS.); N. of Vishṇu or Kṛishṇa, MBh.; of Śiva, L.; of Kātyāyana or Vararuci, L.; of a son of Taittiri (son of Abhijit and father of Āhuka), Hariv.; of a son of Abhijit (Ari-dyota) and father of Āhuka, Pur.; of other men, Pāṇ. i, 2, 61, Sch.; of a partic. world, L.; commencement of wealth, L. **-vāda**, m. repetition, tautology, Kap. **-viroha**, m. sprouting again (of plants), Car. **-vivāha**, m. second marriage, Sāy.; *-vidhi*, m. N. of wk. **-hán**, mfn. destroying in return, RV. **-havis** (*púnar-*), n. repeated sacrificial oblation, ŚBr.

Punaḥ, in comp. for *punar*. **-karaṇa**, n. making again, re-making, transforming, Baudh.; Vait. **-karman**, n. a repeated action, ŚāṅkhBr. **-kāma**, m. a repeated wish, ĀpŚr. **-kriyā**, f. = *-karman*, KātyŚr. **-pada**, n. 'repeated verse or line,' a refrain, Br.; mf(*ā*)n. containing a r°, ib. **-parājaya**, m. losing again (*a-punaḥ-p°*), AitBr. **-paridhāna**, n. putting on (a garment) again, KātyŚr. **-pāka**, m. repeated cooking or baking, Mn.; Yājñ. **-punā**, f. N. of a river (the Punpun in S. Behar, perhaps so called from its windings), VāyuP. **-pratinivartana**, n. coming back again, return, R. **-pratyupakāra**, m. retribution, retaliation, Pañc. **-pramāda**, m. repeated negligence, Āpast. **-prayoga**, m. repetition, Vait.; *°gá-rūpa*, mfn., ŚBr. **-pravṛiddha**, mfn. grown again (n. impers.), Pāṇ. ii, 2, 18, Vārtt. 4, Pat. **-prâdhyeshaṇa**, n. repeated invitation to study, ŚāṅkhGṛ. **-prâpya**, mfn. to be obtained again, recoverable, MW. **-prâyaṇīya**, mfn. (a ceremony &c.) at which the Prâyaṇīya (s.v.) is repeated, ŚāṅkhGṛ. **-prêpsā**, f. desire of obtaining again, Kathās. **-śramaṇa**, w. r. for *puraḥ-śr°* (?), Divyâv. **-saṃskāra**, m. renewed investiture, repetition of any Saṃskāra, Mn.; R.; N. of wk. (cf. *punar-upanayana*). **-saṃskṛita**, mfn. fitted up again, repaired, mended, ŚāṅkhBr.; KātyŚr. **-saṃgama**, m. meeting ag°, reunion, Kathās. **-saṃdarśana**, n. seeing one another ag°, R. **-saṃdhāna**, n. uniting ag°, re-uniting, Sāh.; re-kindling of the household fire, Saṃskārak.; *-prayoga*, m. N. of wk. **-sambhava**, mfn. coming into existence ag° (*a-p°-s°*), Rājat. **-sará**, mf(*ā*)n. running back, RV.; N. of the Achyranthes Aspera (the flowers of which are turned back), AV. **-siddha**, mfn. prepared or cooked again, Gaut. **-sukha**, mfn. ag° agreeable or pleasant, Pāṇ. ii, 2, 18, Vārtt. 4, Pat. **-stuti**, f. repeated praise, a r° ceremony, ŚāṅkhBr. **-stoma**, m. N. of an Ekâha, Br.; Gaut.; Vait.

Punaś, in comp. for *punar*. **-candrā**, f. N. of a river, MBh. **-cara**, mfn. running back, returning, AV. Paipp. **-carvaṇa**, n. chewing the cud, ruminating, Siddh. **-citi**, f. piling up again, TS.; ŚBr. &c.

Punas, in comp. for *punar*. **-tati**, f. a repeated sacrificial performance, ŚāṅkhBr. **-tarām**, ind. over and over again, Śiś. xvii, 6.

Punā, in comp. for *punar*. **-rāja**, m. a new king, Pat.; *°jâbhisheka*, m. the consecration of a new king, Vas.

पुनान *punāna, punita.* See √*pū*.

पुन्थ् *punth*, cl. 1. P. *punthati*, to give or suffer pain, Dhātup. iii, 7 (v. l. *yunth*).

पुंदान *puṃ-dāna* &c. See p. 630, col. 3.

पुन्द्र *pundra*, w. r. for *puṇḍra*.

पुंनक्षत्र *puṃ-nakshatra* &c. See under *pum*, p. 631, col. 1.

पुपूतनि *pupūtáni* (?), RV. x, 132, 6.

पुपूषत् *pupūshat*, mf(*antī*)n. (√*pū*, Desid.) wishing to cleanse or purify, W.

Pupūshā, f. the wish or desire to cleanse or purify, ib.

पुप्पुट *puppuṭa*, m. N. of a partic. disease (swelling of the palate and gums), Suśr. (also *-ka*).

पुप्फुल *pupphula*, m. flatulency, wind in the stomach, L.

पुप्फुस *pupphusa*, m. the lungs, L. (cf. *phupphusa*); the pericarp or seed-pod of a lotus, L.

पुम् *pum, pum-anujā* &c. See p. 631.

पुर् 1. *púr*, f. (√*pṛī*) only instr. pl. *pūrbhís*, in abundance, abundantly, RV. v, 66, 4.

पुर् 2. *pur*, cl. 6. P. *purati*, to precede, go before, lead, Dhātup. xxviii, 56 (prob. invented to furnish an etymology for *puras* and *purā* below).

1. **Pura** (for 2. see p. 635), in comp. for *puras*. **-ushṇih**, f. N. of a metre, RPrāt. **-etṛí**, m. one who goes before, a guide, leader, RV.; AV.; VS.; Br. **-ga**, mfn. (for *puro-ga*) inclined or disposed towards (comp.), MārkP.; *°gā-vaṇa*, n. N. of a forest, Pāṇ. viii, 4, 4. **-jyotis**, n. N. of the region or the world of Agni, L. (w. r. for *puro-j°*?). **-tas**, ind. before (in place or time), in front or in presence of (gen. or comp.), KaṭhUp.; MBh. &c.; *-taḥ-√kṛi*, to place in front, cause to precede, honour, R.; Kathās.

Puraḥ, in comp. for *puras*. **-pāka**, mf(*ā*)n. whose fulfilment approaches near (as a hope or prayer), Kum. **-prasravaṇa** (*puráḥ-*), mfn. pouring or streaming forth, RV. viii, 100, 9. **-prahartṛi**, m. one who fights in the front (of the battle), Ragh. **-phala**, mfn. having fruit well advanced, promising fruit, ib. **-śukram**, ind. while Śukra (the planet Venus) is before one's eyes, Kum. iii, 43. **-sád**, mfn. sitting in front, presiding, RV. i, 73, 3; sitting towards the east, VS.; TS. **-sará**, mf(*ī*)n. going before or in advance; m. a forerunner, precursor, harbinger, attendant, AV. &c. &c.; ifc. (f. *ā*) attended or preceded by, connected with, MBh.; Kāv. &c.; (*am*), ind. along with, among, after, by means of (comp.), Kathās.; Pañc.; Pur. **-stha**, mfn. standing before one's eyes, clearly visible, Mālatīm. **-sthātṛi**, mfn. standing at the head, a leader, RV. **-sthāyin**, mfn. = *-stha*, MW. **-sthita**, mfn. impending, imminent, Śak. (v. l.) **-sphurat**, mfn. opening or becoming manifest before any one, W.

Puraś, in comp. for *puras*. **-cakram**, ind. before the wheel, ĀpŚr. **-caraṇa**, mfn. making preparations, preparatory to (comp.; *-tā*, f.), MBh.; n. a preparatory or introductory rite, preparation, ŚBr.; *-karman*, n. id., ib.; *-kaumudī*, f., *-kaustubha*, m. or n., *-candrikā*, f., *-dīpikā*, f., *-paddhati* (and *°ti-mālā*), f., *-prapañca*, m., *-rasôllāsa*, m., *-vidhi*, m., *-viveka*, m. N. of wks. **-caryā**, f. = *-caraṇa*, Kāv.; *-rasâmbudhi*, m. N. of wk. **-chada**, m. a nipple, L.; Imperata Cylindrica, L.

Purás, ind. in front, in advance, forward; (as prepos.) before (of place and time), in the presence or before the eyes of (gen., abl., acc. or comp.), RV. &c. &c.; in comparison with (gen.), Vcar.; in or from or towards the east, eastward, VS.; Br. &c. (*dakshiṇataḥ puraḥ*, towards the south-east, MBh.); previously, first, first of all, Ratnâv. iii, 7. [Cf. *pra, purā, pūrva*; Gk. πάρος, 'before.'] **-karaṇa**, n. the act of placing in front &c.; making perfect (?), W. **-karaṇīya** (W.), **-kartavya** (Hit.), mfn. to be placed in front or honoured or prepared or fitted out or made complete. **-kāra**, m. placing in front, honouring, preference, distinction, Kāv.; Hit.; accompanying, attending (ifc. 'preceded or accompanied by, joined or connected with, including'), MBh.; arranging, putting in array, making complete, W.; attacking, assailing &c., ib. **-kārya**, mfn. = *-kartavya*; to be appointed to, to be charged or commissioned with (loc. or inf.), MBh.; Kāv. **-√kṛi** (P. Ā. *-karoti, -kurute*), to place before or in front, cause to precede, RV. &c. &c.; to make one's leader, place in office, appoint, MBh.; to respect, honour, MBh.; Kāv. &c.; to place above all, prefer, choose, attend to, ib.; to show, display, R.; Rājat. **-kṛita**, mfn. placed in front &c.; honoured, esteemed, attended, accompanied by, possessed of, occupied with (comp.), MBh.; Kāv. &c.; attacked, assailed, accused &c., L.; (*am*), ind. among, amidst, with (comp.), MBh.; *-madhyama-krama*, mfn. taking or adopting a middle course, MW. **-kṛitya**, ind. having placed in front or honoured &c.; often = regarding, concerning, on account of, about, MBh.; Kāv. &c. **-kriyā**, f. a preceding action, preparatory rite, Cat.; showing honour, demonstration of respect, Ragh.; *-caryā*, f. N. of wk.

Purastāj, in comp. for *°tāt*. **-japa**, m. a prayer murmured before, Siṃhâs. **-jyotishmatī** (Col.), f., **-jyotis** (RPrāt.), n. N. of a metre.

Purástāt, ind. before, forward, in or from the front, in the first place, in the beginning, RV. &c. &c.; in or from the east, eastward, ib.; in the preceding part (of a book), above, RPrāt.; (but also) further on i.e. below, Suśr.; (as prepos.) before (of place or time), in front or in presence or before the eyes of (gen., abl., acc. or comp.), RV. &c. &c.; in comparison with (gen.), Vcar. **-kratú**, m. a sacrifice which begins immediately, ŚBr. **-tiryak-pramāṇa**, n. the width in front, KātyŚr. **-tna**, mfn. preceding, going before, Shaḍguruś. **-puroḍāśa** (*°rást°*), mfn. preceded or accompanied by a Puroḍāśa (s.v.), MaitrS. **-prishṭhya**, n. N. of a partic. Sattra, TāṇḍBr. **-pravaṇa** (*°rást°*), mfn. bent forward, TS. **-stobha**, m. a preceding Stobha (s. v.), Lāṭy.; mfn. preceded by a St°, ib. **-svāhā-kāra**, m. (ĀpŚr., Sch.), **-svāhā-kṛiti**, f. (*°rást°*; TS.; ŚBr.) preceded by the exclamation Svāhā.

Purastād, in comp. for *°tāt*. **-agni-shṭoma**, mfn. beginning with an Agni-shṭoma (s. v.), Vait. **-anūka**, n. the longitudinal streaks on the back part of an altar, KātyŚr., Sch. (cf. *prāg-an°*). **-apakarsha**, m. anticipation, Kāś. on Pāṇ. ii, 3, 29. **-apavāda**, m. an anticipatory exception, VPrāt., Sch. **-ucca**, mfn. high in the east, KātyŚr. **-udarka**, mfn. beginning with the refrain, AitBr. **-uddhāra** (*°rást°*), m. a part given in advance, ŚBr. **-upacāra**, mfn. accessible from the east, KātyŚr. **-upayāma** (*°rást°*), mfn. preceded by the Upayāma verses (s. v.), TS. **-granthi** (*°rást°*), mfn. having the knot turned towards the east, ŚBr. **-daṇḍa**, mfn. having the handle towards the east, Lāṭy. **-dhoma** (for *homa*), m. an introductory sacrifice, Vait.; Gobh.; *-bhāj* (ĀpŚr., Sch.) and *-vat* (Kauś.), mfn. having an i° s°. **-bṛihatī**, f. a species of the Bṛihatī metre, RPrāt. **-bhāga** (*°rást°*), mfn. one who receives his share before another, TS. **-vadaná**, n. preface, introduction, ŚBr.

Purastān, in comp. for *°tāt*. **-mukha**, mfn. standing before a person's face, Mṛicch.

Purastāl, in comp. for *°tāt*. **-lakshaṇa** (*°rást°*), mf(*ā*)n. having one's characteristic in front or at the beginning, ŚBr. **-lakshman** (*°rást°*), mfn. marked in front or at the beginning, TS.

Purā́, ind. (cf. *pra, puras, pūrva*) before, formerly, of old (with *na*, 'never'), RV. &c. &c.; in a previous existence, VarYog.; (with pres. = pf.) from of old, hitherto, up to the present time (also with *sma*, cf. Pāṇ. iii, 2, 122; with *na*, 'never yet'), RV. &c. &c.; at first, in the beginning, Bhartṛ. (opp. to *paścā, paścāt*, Pāṇ. v, 3, 33, Kāś.); soon, shortly (with pres. = fut.), Kālid.; Naish.; (as prep., mostly in earlier language, with abl., rarely with dat. or gen.) before; securely from; except, beside; (with pres. = fut. [cf. Pāṇ. iii, 3, 4], once with Pot.) ere, before (sometimes with *na* or *na* and *yāvat* [followed by *tāvat*], with *mā* or *yadi*, MBh.; Kāv. &c.) **-kathā**, f. a story of the past, an old legend, BhP. **-kalpa**, m. a former creation, former age (loc. sg. or pl. in the olden time), Up.; MBh. &c.; = prec., MBh.; the performance of sacrificial acts in former times, AitBr. (pref.); *-vid*, mfn. knowing former times, familiar with the past, MBh. **-kṛita**, mfn. done formerly or long ago, MBh.; begun, commenced, W.; n. an action performed long ago; *-phala*, n. the result of it, Var. **-kṛiti**, f. a former mode of action, Hariv. **-ga**, g. *kṛiśâśvâdi* (cf. *pura-ga*). **-jā́**, mfn. former, existing from old, primeval, RV. **-mathana-vallabha**, n. a kind of Agallochum used as a perfume, L. **-yoni**, mfn. of ancient origin or lineage (said of kings), MBh. **-vasu**, m. N. of Bhīshma, L. **-vid**, m. knowing the events of former times, GopBr.; Mn.; MBh. &c. **-vṛitta**, mf(*ā*)n. that which has occurred or one who has lived in former times, long past, ancient, MBh.; Pur.; n. former mode of action, any event or account or history of the past, ib.; *-kathā*, f. an old story or legend, Hit. (also °*ttâkhyāna*, n., W.; °-*na-kathana*, n. telling old stories, MW.); -*sáh* or -*sā́h*, mfn. (nom. -*shā́ṭ*; cf. Pāṇ. viii, 3, 56) superior from ancient times, RV. (Sāy. 'conqueror of cities'). **—hitá** (°*rā́h*°?), mfn. set before first, ŚBr. **1. Purôdbhava**, mfn. (for 2. see under 2. *pura*) of prior origin, W. **Purôpanīta**, mfn. formerly obtained or possessed, W.

Purāṇá, mf(*ī* or *ā*)n. belonging to ancient or olden times, ancient, old (also = withered, worn out, opp. to *nūtana*, *nava*), RV. &c. &c.; m. a Karsha or measure of silver (= 16 Paṇas of cowries), Mn. viii, 136 (also n., L.); N. of a Ṛishi, Kāṭh.; pl. the ancients, MW.; n. a thing or event of the past, an ancient tale or legend, old traditional history, AV. &c. &c.; N. of a class of sacred works (supposed to have been compiled by the poet Vyāsa and to treat of 5 topics [cf. *pañca-lakshaṇa*]; the chief Purāṇas are 18, grouped in 3 divisions: viz. 1. Rājasa exalting Brahmā [e. g. the Brahma, Brahmâṇḍa, Brahma-vaivarta, Mārkaṇḍeya, Bhavishya, Vāmana]; 2. Sāttvika exalting Vishṇu [e. g. the Vishṇu, Bhāgavata, Nāradīya, Garuḍa, Padma, Varāha]; 3. Tāmasa exalting Śiva [e. g. the Śiva, Liṅga, Skanda, Agni or in place of it the Vāyu, Matsya, Kūrma]; by some the P°s are divided into 4, and by others into 6 groups; cf. IW. 509 &c.); N. of a wk. (containing an index of the contents of a number of P°s and some other wks.) **—kalpa**, m. = *purā-k*°, BhP. **—ga**, m. 'singing of the past,' N. of Brahmā, L.; a reciter of the Purāṇas, W. **—gir**, m. 'praising the p°,' N. of Brahmā, Gal. **—gīta**, m. 'sung by the ancients,' id., Gal. **—dāna-māhātmya**, n. N. of ch. of BrahmâṇḍaP. **—dṛishṭa**, mfn. seen or approved by ancient sages, Vas.; °*tânta-śataka*, n. N. of a poem. **—dvitīyā**, f. the former wife, L. **—pañca-lakshaṇa**, n., **—pañjī**, f., **—padârtha-saṃgraha**, m. N. of wks. **—purusha**, m. 'primeval male,' N. of Vishṇu, Siṉhâs. **—prôkta**, mfn. proclaimed by ancient sages, Pāṇ. iv, 3, 105. **—mahimôpavarṇana**, n. N. of ch. of PadmaP. ii. **—māhātmya**, n. N. of ch. of LiṅgaP. **—ratna**, n. N. of wk. **—vát**, ind. as of old, RV. **—víd**, mfn. knowing the things or events of the past, AV.; knowing the P°s, Prab. **—vidyā**, f., **-veda**, m. knowledge of the things or events of the past, ŚrS. **—śravaṇa**, n. hearing or studying the P°s; -*mahiman*, m., -*māhātmya*, n., -*vidhi*, m. N. of wks. **—saṃhitā**, f. a collection of the P°s, BhP. **—saṃgraha**, m., **—samuccaya**, m., **—sarvasva**, n., **—sāra** and **—sāra-saṃgraha**, m. N. of wks. **—siṉha**, m. N. of Vishṇu as man-lion, R. **Purāṇânta**, m. N. of Yama, L. **Purāṇârka-prabhā**, f., **Purāṇârṇava**, m., **Purāṇârtha-prakāśaka**, m. N. of wks. **Purāṇâvatāra**, m. N. of ch. of PadmaP. **Purāṇôkta**, mfn. enjoined by or written in the P°s, MW.

Purāṇaka, ifc. (f. *ikā*) = *purāṇa*, a partic. coin (cf. *tri-p*°).

Purāṇīya, mfn., see *tri-p*° and *pañca-p*°.

Purāṇya, Nom. P. °*ṇyati*, to talk of the past, relate past events, g. *kaṇḍv-ādi*.

Purā-tana, mf(*ī*)n. belonging to the past, former, old, ancient (*e*, ind. formerly, in olden times), Mn.; MBh. &c.; used-up, worn out, Suśr.; m. pl. the ancients, Rājat.; n. an ancient story, old legend, R.; a Purāṇa, Hcat. **—yoga-saṃgraha**, m. N. of wk.

Puro, in comp. for *puras*. **—agni** (*puró-*), m. the foremost Agni, fire in front, VS. **—'kshám**, ind. before the axle-tree, ŚBr. **—ga**, mf(*ā*)n. going before, leading, a leader, chief, principal (ifc. preceded or accompanied by), MBh.; Kāv. &c. **—gata**, mfn. standing or being in front or before a person's eyes, Ragh.; preceded, gone before, W. **—gati**, m. a dog, L. **—gantṛi**, m. a messenger who goes before, Pāṇ., Sch. **—gama**, mfn. = -*ga*, MBh.; Kāv. &c. **—gamana**, n. going before, preceding, W. **—gavá**, m. one who precedes, a leader (f. °*vī́*), RV.; AV. **—gā́**, m. a leader, RV.; VS. &c. **—gāmin**, mfn. going before, preceding; m. a leader or a dog, L. **—guru**, mfn. heavy before or in front, TāṇḍBr. **—granthi**, mfn. = *purastād-g*°, ĀpŚr. **—janman**, mfn. born before; °*ma-tā*, f. priority of birth, Ragh. **—java**, mfn. excelling in speed, swifter than (comp.), BhP.; m. one who goes before, a servant, attendant (ifc. accompanied by, furnished with), Divyâv.; N. of a son of Medhâtithi and the Varsha ruled by him, BhP.; of Prāṇa, ib. **—jiti** (*puró-*), f. previous possession or acquisition, RV. **—jyotis**, mfn. preceded by light or radiance, AitBr. **—ḍāś** (or -*ḷāś*, nom. -*ḷā́s*), m. a mass of ground rice rounded into a kind of cake (usually divided into pieces, placed on receptacles; cf. *kapāla*) and offered as an oblation in fire, RV. &c. &c. **—ḍāśá**, m. id., AV. &c. &c. (RTL. 367); any oblation, Mn. v, 23; the leavings of an offering, L.; Soma juice, L.; a prayer recited while offering oblations in fire, Pāṇ., Sch.; -*tā*, f. state or condition of an oblation; acc. with √*nī*, to offer in fire, burn, Pārvat.; -*bṛigalá*, n. a piece of the sacrificial cake, ŚBr.; -*bhuj*, m. eater of the s° c°, a god, Śiś.; -*vatsā* (*ḍāśá-*), f. having a s° c° for a calf, AV.; -*svishṭa-kṛit*, m. the Sv° connected with the s° c°, AitBr.; -*hara*, m. 'receiver of the s° c°,' N. of Vishṇu, Vishṇ.; °*śika*, mf(*ī*)n., Pāṇ. iv, 3, 70; °*śin*, mfn. connected with the s° c°, TS.; °*śīya*, mfn. relating to or destined for the s° c°, ĀpŚr.; °*śeḍā́*, f. the Iḍā portion of the s° c°, ŚBr.; °*śyà*, mfn. = °*śīya*, MaitrS. **—dha** (m.c.) or **-dhas**, m. 'placed at the head,' chief priest of a king, domestic chaplain, MBh.; Kāv. &c.; N. of a man, Saṃskārak. **—√dhā**, P. Ā. -*dadhāti*, -*dhatte*, (Ā.) to place before or at the head, to appoint (esp. to priestly functions), charge, commission, RV. &c. &c.; to propose (as a prize), RV. v, 86, 5; (P.) to place foremost, value highly, esteem, honour, be intent upon or zealous for, take to heart, RV. &c. &c. **—dhā**, f. charge, commission, (esp.) the rank and office of a Purohita, TS.; AV.; Br.; -*kāma* (-*dhā́-*), mfn. desirous of the rank of a P°, TBr. **—dhātṛi**, m. the giver of a commission, the appointer of a P°, AitBr. **—dhāna**, n. priestly ministration, Sāy. **—dhānīya**, m. = *puro-hita*, TāṇḍBr. **—dhikā**, f. preferred to other women, a favourite wife, Hariv. **—niḥsaraṇa**, n. going out first, Kāv. **—'nuvākyā̀**, f. (sc. *ṛic*) an introductory or invitatory verse, AV.; TS.; Br.; °*kyà-vat*, mfn. having an int° v°, ŚBr. **—balāka**, mfn. 'having (only) cranes in front of one's self,' overtaking all others (said of Parjanya), ShaḍvBr. **—bhaktakā**, f. breakfast, Divyâv. **—bhāga**, m. the front or forepart (*mama* °*ge*, before me), Daś.; officiousness, obtrusiveness (°*gam* √*muc*, to quit the field, retire discomfited), Hariv.; Kād.; malevolence, envy, Mālav.; mf(*ā*)n. standing before a person's eyes, R.; obtrusive, meddlesome, MW. **—bhāgin**, mfn. taking the first share, obtrusive, forward, Kālid.; grudging, censorious, malevolent, Rājat. **—bhāvin**, mfn. impending, imminent, Kathās. **—bhū́**, mfn. being in front or at the head of, excelling, superior to (acc.), RV. **—māruta**, m. a wind blowing from before or in f°, east wind (opp. to *paścān-m*°), Ragh. **—mukha**, mfn. having its face or aperture directed towards the east, Kauś. **—yā́van**, mfn. going in front, leading, RV. **—yúdh** or **-yodhá**, mfn. fighting before or in front, RV. **—rathá**, mfn. 'one whose chariot is foremost,' leaving all behind, pre-eminent, superior, RV. **—rukka**, see *a-puror*°. **—rúc**, mfn. shining in front or in the east, RV.; f. N. of partic. Nivid formularies recited at the morning oblation in the Ājya ceremony before the principal hymn or any part of it, TS.; Br.; -*rug-adhyāya*, m. N. of wk.; -*ruṅ-mat*, mfn. furnished with P°, ŚBr. **—vat**, ind. as before, BhP. **—vatsa**, m. N. of a man, L. **—vartin**, mfn. being before a person's eyes, Mallin.; forward, obtrusive, Nīlak. on Hariv. **—vasu**, mfn. preceded or accompanied by wealth, TBr. **—vātá**, m. = -*māruta* (ifc. f. *ā*), TS. &c.; the wind preceding a thunderstorm, ChUp.; -*sáni*, mfn. bringing east wind, TS. **—vāda**, m. a former mention, Nyāyam. **—vṛitta**, mf(*ā*)n. being or going before, preceding, Hariv. **—vṛishêndra**, mfn. preceded or accompanied by an excellent bull, BhP. **—havis** (*puró-*), mfn. having the sacrifice in front or towards the east, TS. **—hita** (*puró-*), mfn. placed foremost or in front, charged, commissioned, appointed; m. one holding a charge or commission, an agent; (esp.) a family priest, a domestic chaplain, RV. &c. &c. (RTL. 352 &c.); -*karman*, n. N. of 3rd Pariś. of AV.; -*tva*, n. the rank of a Purohita, MBh. **—hiti**, f. priestly ministration (= *puro-dhāna*, Sāy.), RV. **—hitikā**, f. a favourite wife (cf. *puro-dhikā*) or N. of a woman, g. *śivâdi*.

पुर् 3. *púr*, f. (in nom. sg. and before consonants *pūr*) a rampart, wall, stronghold, fortress, castle, city, town (also of demons), RV. &c. &c.; the body (considered as the stronghold of the *purusha*, q. v.), BhP.; the intellect (= *mahat*), VP.; N. of a Daśa-rātra, KātyŚr. [Perhaps fr. √*pṛī* and orig. identical with 1. *pur*; cf. Gk. πόλις.]

2. **Pura** (for 1. see p. 634, col. 2), n. (ifc. f. *ā*) a fortress, castle, city, town (a place containing large buildings surrounded by a ditch and extending not less than one Kos in length; if it extends for half that distance it is called a *kheṭa*, if less than that, a *karvaṭa* or small market town; any smaller cluster of houses is called a *grāma* or village, W.), Mn.; MBh. &c.; the female apartments, gynaeceum, MBh. (cf. *antaḥ-p*°, *nārī-p*° &c.); a house, abode, residence, receptacle, BhP.; Tattvas.; an upper story, L.; a brothel, L.; 'the city' κατ' ἐξοχήν i.e. Pāṭali-putra or Patnā, L.; = *tri-pura*, the 3 strong holds of the Asuras, Kathās.; the body (cf. 3. *pur*), BhP.; the skin, L.; a species of Cyperus, L.; N. of a constellation, Var.; a leaf rolled into the shape of a funnel, L. (prob. w. r. for *puṭa*); N. of the subdivisions of the Vedânta wk. *tri-purī* or *tri-puṭī* (perhaps also w. r. for *puṭa*), Cat.; mf(*ā*)n. a kind of resin, bdellium, Suśr.; L.; m. N. of an Asura = *tri-pura* (cf. *pura-jit*), of another man, g. *kurv-ādi*; (*ā*), f. a stronghold, fortress (cf. *agni-purā* and *aśma-p*°); a kind of perfume, L.; (*ī*), f. a fortress, castle, town, TĀr.; MBh. &c.; N. of a town (the capital of Kaliṅga, noted for the worship of Jagan-nātha or Kṛishṇa, IW. 244, n. 1); the sanctuary or adytum of a temple, Inscr.; the body, BhP.; N. of one of the 10 orders of mendicants (said to be founded by disciples of Śaṃkara, the members of which add the word *purī* to their names), W. **—koṭṭa**, n. 'city-stronghold,' a citadel; -*pāla*, m. the governor of a citadel, Pañc. **—jana**, m. sg. town-folk, citizens, Ratnâv. **—jānu**, v. l. for *puru-j*°, VP. **—jit**, m. 'conqueror of fortresses or of Pura,' N. of Śiva, Kathās.; of a prince (son of Aja and father of Arishṭa-nemi), BhP. **—taṭī**, f. a small market-town, L. **—toraṇa**, n. 'city-arch,' the outer gate of a c°, MW. **—dāha**, m. burning of the 3 fortresses (= *tripura-d*°), Kathās. **—devatā**, f. the tutelary deity of a town, W. **—dvāra**, n. (ifc. f. *ā*), a city gate, Mn.; R. **—dvish**, m. 'foe of Pura,' N. of Śiva, BhP. **—nārī**, f. 'town-woman,' a courtezan, Dhūrtan. **—niveśa**, m. the founding of a city, MW. **—pakshin**, m. 'town-bird,' a b° living in a city, tame b° (opp. to *vanya-p*°), Var. **—pāla**, °**laka**, m. the governor of a c°, BhP. **—bhid** (Prasannar.), **-mathana** (Bālar.), **-mathitṛi** (Ānand.), m. 'destroyer of fortresses or of Pura,' N. of Śiva. **—mārga**, m. the street of a town, Ragh. **—mālinī**, f. 'crowned with castles,' N. of a river, MBh. **—raksha** (Daś.), **-rakshin** (Kathās.), m. a watchman of a town, constable. **—rāshṭra**, n. pl. cities and kingdoms, MW. **—rodha**, m. the siege of a fortress or city, ib. **—loka**, m. sg. = -*jana*, Pañcad. **—vadhū**, f. = -*nārī*, Siṉhâs. **—vara**, n. 'chief town,' a king's residence, Jātakam. **—vāsin**, mfn. dwelling in a town, a citizen, MBh. **—vāstu**, n. ground suitable for the foundation of a city, Hariv. **—vairin** (Prasann.), **-śāsana** (Kum.), m. 'foe or chastiser of Pura,' N. of Śiva. **—han**, m. 'slayer of Pura,' N. of Vishṇu, BhP. **—hita**, n. the welfare of a city, MW. **Purâṭṭa**, m. a watch-tower on a c° wall, R. **Purâdhipa** (Kathās.), °**dhyaksha** (MBh.), m. the governor of a c° or fortress, prefect of police. **Purârāti**, m. = *pura-dvish*, Kathās. **Purâri**, m. id., ib.; Kum.; N. of Vishṇu (-*tva*, n.), BhP. **Purârdha-vistara**, mfn. being of the extent of half a town, L.; m. part of a t°, a suburb, ward, division, W. **Purā-vatī**, f. 'rich in castles,' N. of a river, MBh. (cf. *pura-mālinī*). **Purâsuhṛid**, m. = *pura-dvish*, L. **Purôtsava**, m. 'town-festival,' a f° solemnized in a city, Kathās. 2. **Purôdbhava** (for 1. see under *purā*), m. (or *ā*, f.) 'growing in towns,' N. of a plant, L. **Purôdyāna**, n. 'city garden,' a pleasure-garden belonging to a town, park, MBh.; R. &c. **Pur'oka**, m. 'town-dweller (?),' N. of a poet, Cat. **Purâhkas**, m. an inhabitant of a town or of Tripura, L.

Puram, acc. of 3. *púr* or 2. *pura*, in comp. **—jana**, m. the living principle, life, soul (personif. as a king), BhP.; N. of Varuṇa, Gal.; (*ī*), f. understanding, intelligence (personif. as the wife of a king), ib.; -*carita* and -*nāṭaka*, n. N. of dramas. **—jaya**, m. 'city-conqueror,' N. of a hero on the side of the Kurus, MBh.; of a son of Sṛiñjaya and father of Janam-ejaya, Hariv.; of a son of Bhajamāna and Sṛiñjarī (or Sṛiñjayā), ib.; (= *Kakut-stha*) N. of a son of Śaśāda, VP.; of a son of Vindhya-śakti, ib.; of Medhâvin, MatsyaP.; of an elephant (son of Airāvaṇa), Hariv. **—da**, m. = -*dara*, N. of Indra, L. **—dará**, m. 'destroyer of strongholds,' N. of Indra, RV. &c. &c. (also of the I° of the 7th Manv-antara, Pur.); of Agni, RV.; of Śiva, Śivag.; a thief, house-breaker, L.; of a man, Siṇhâs.; (*ā*), f. N. of Gaṅgā or another river, L.; n. Piper Chaba, L.; *-cāpa*, m. Indra's bow, the rainbow, Var.; *-pura*, n. I°'s city (°*rātithi*, m. 'guest of I°'s c°' i.e. dead), Daś.; N. of another city, L.; (*ī*), f. N. of a town in Mālava, Vcar.; *-harit*, f. Indra's quarter of the sky, the east, Prasannar.

Púraya, m. N. of a man, RV.; (n.?) a castle, town, Gal.

1. **Puri**, loc. of 3. *pur*, in comp. **-śayá**, mfn. (invented to explain *purusha*) reposing in the fortress or fastness (i.e. the body), ŚBr.; GopBr.

2. **Puri**, f. a town or a river, Uṇ. iv, 142, Sch. **-kāya**, m. N. of a prince, VP.; (*ā*), f. N. of a town, ib.

Purikā, f. N. of a town, MBh.; Hariv.

Purī, f., see under 2. *pura*. **-kāya**, m. N. of a king, VP. (cf. *puri-k°*). **-dāsa**, m. N. of the author of Caitanya-candrôdaya (also called *Kavi-karṇa-pūra*), Cat. **-°ndra-sena** (*purīnd°*), m. N. of a prince, VP. **-mat**, m. N. of a king, BhP. **-moha**, m. the thorn-apple, Datura, L. **-loka**, m. pl. town's-folk, citizens, Siṇhâs. **-śreshṭhā**, f. 'best of towns,' N. of Kāśī or Benares, Gal. **Pury-ashṭa** or °**ṭaka**, n. the eight constituent parts of the body, Kull. on Mn. i, 56.

Puró-han, mfn. (acc. pl. of 3. *pur* + *h°*) destroying strongholds, RV.

Púrya, mfn. being in a stronghold or fastness, RV.

Pūḥ-kāmya, Nom. (fr. 3. *pur* + *kāma*), P. °*yati*, to wish for a castle or town, L.

Pūr, in comp. for 3. *pur* before cons. **-jáyana**, n. 'conquest of a fortress,' N. of a partic. ceremony, MaitrS. **-devī**, f. the tutelary goddess of a town, BhP. **-dvār**, f., **-dvāra**, n. the gate of a city, L. **-pati** (*pū́r-*), m. the lord of a castle or city, RV. **-bhíd**, mfn. one who breaks down strongholds or fortresses, ib. **-bhídya**, n. the breaking down strongholds or fortresses, ib. **-mārga**, m. a road leading to a town, Siṇhâs. **-yā́ṇa**, mfn. leading to the fortress (i.e. to the celestial world), AV.

पुरञ्जर *purañjara*, m. the armpit, L.

पुरट *puraṭa*, n. gold, L.

पुरण *puraṇa*, m. (√*prī*) the sea, ocean, Uṇ. ii, 81, Sch.

पुरण्ड *puraṇḍa*, m. pl. N. of a dynasty, VP. (cf. *puruṇḍa*).

पुरतस् *pura-tas*. See p. 634, col. 2.

पुरंधि *púraṃdhi*, mfn. (etym. much contested; prob. fr. acc. of 1. or 3. *pur* and √*dhā*, 'bearing fulness' or 'bearing a body') prolific, not barren (lit. and fig.), bountiful, munificent, liberal, RV.; VS.; TS.; f. a woman, wife, RV. i, 116, 7; 13; 117, 19 &c.; liberality, munificence, kindness (shown by gods to man, e.g. RV. i, 5, 3; 158, 2 &c.; or by man to gods in offering oblations, e.g. i, 123, 6; 134, 3 &c.; also personif. as goddess of abundance and liberality, e.g. vii, 36, 8 &c.) **-vat** (*púr°*), mfn. abundant, copious, RV. ix, 72, 4.

Puraṃdhri or °**dhrī**, f. (perhaps at first identical with prec. and later connected with √*dhṛi*) a wife, woman (esp. a married woman having or able to bear children), Kālid.; Kathās.; Rājat.

पुरला *puralā* (?), f. N. of Durgā, L.

पुरवी *puravī*, f. (in music) N. of a Rāgiṇī (cf. *puruvī*).

पुरस् *puras*, *purastāt*. See p. 634.

पुरा *purā*. See p. 634, col. 3.

पुराटङ्क *purāṭaṅka*, m. N. of a man, Cat. (cf. *pauranṭaka*).

पुराण *purāṇa*, *purātana*. See p. 635.

पुरातल *purātala*, n. the region below the seven worlds, L. (cf. *talâtala*).

पुराधस् *purādhas*, m. N. of an Āṅgirasa, ĀrshBr. (v.l. *pra-rādhas*).

पुरासणी *purāsaṇī* or °*sinī*, f. a species of creeper, L.

पुरि 1. and 2. *puri*; *purī*. See above.

पुरितत् *puritat*, w. r. for *purītat*, L.

पुरीकय *purīkáya*, m. a species of aquatic animal, AV.

पुरीकषेण *purīkasheṇa*, m. N. of a king, VP.

पुरीतत् *purītát*, m. n. (fr. 3. *pur* or *purī* + √*tan*?) the pericardium or some other organ near the heart; the intestines, VS.; AV.; ŚBr.; Kaush-Up. (cf. *parī-tat* and *pulītat*).

पुरीष *púrīsha*, n. (√*pṛī*) earth, land, RV.; (esp.) crumbling or loose earth, rubbish (perhaps 'that which fills up,' as opp. to that which flows off, the 'solid' opp. to the fluid), rubble, anything used to fill up interstices in a wall, VS.; TS.; ŚBr.; GṛŚrS.; feces, excrement, ordure, ŚBr. &c. &c. (ifc. f. *ī*, BhP.); a disk, orb (e.g. *sūryasya*, i.e. 'fulness of the sun'?), RV. x, 27, 21; (with *Ātharvaṇa*) N. of a Sāman, ĀrshBr.; (*ī*), f. N. of a partic. religious observance, BhP. (= *cayana*, Sch.) **-nigrahaṇa**, mfn. stopping or obstructing the bowels, Suśr. **-pada**, n. N. of partic. passages inserted (to fill up) in the recitation of the Mahānāmnī verses, Br.; ŚrS. **-bhīru**, m. N. of a prince, BhP. **-bheda**, m. diarrhoea, Car. **-bhedin**, mfn. 'loosening the feces,' relaxing the bowels, MW. **-mūtra-pratighāta**, m. obstruction of the solid and liquid excretions, Cat. **-vat** (*púr°*), mfn. furnished with rubbish or loose earth (used for filling interstices), TS.; (*ī*), f. N. of a kind of brick, ŚBr. **-vā́hana** or **-vāhaná**, mf(*ī*)n. removing rubbish or refuse, VS.; TS.; Kāṭh. (cf. Pāṇ. iii, 2, 65). **-virañjanīya**, mfn. changing the colour of the feces, L. **-saṃgrahaṇīya**, mfn. making the feces more solid, ib. **Purīshâdhāna**, n. 'receptacle of excrement,' the rectum, Yājñ. **Purīshôtsarga**, m. the voiding of excrement, Pañc.; Hit.

Purīshaṇa, n. the voiding of excrement, Var.; m. excrement, feces, L.; the rectum or anus, Gal.

Purīshama, m. Phaseolus Radiatus, L.

Purīshaya, Nom. P. °*yati*, to void excrement, L.

Purīshita, mfn. voided, evacuated (as excrement); voided upon, g. *tārakâdi*.

Purīshín, mfn. possessing land or inhabiting it or extending over it, RV.; 'bearing or carrying rubbish,' N. of the Sarayū or of another river, v, 53, 9.

Purīshyà, mfn. being in the earth (said of fire), RV.; TS.; VS.; rich in land, ŚBr.; excremental, AitBr. **-vāhana**, mf(*ī*)n. (prob.) = *purīsha-v°*, Pāṇ. iii, 2, 65.

पुरु *purú*, mf(*pūrvī́*)n. (√*pṛī*) much, many, abundant (only *purū́*, °*rū́ṇi*, °*rūṇām* and sev. cases of f. *pūrvī*; in later language only ibc.), RV. &c. &c. (°*rū́*, ind. much, often, very [also with a compar. or superl.]; with *simā́*, everywhere; with *tirás*, far off, from afar; *purūrú*, far and wide; *purú víśva*, one and all, every, RV.); m. the pollen of a flower, L.; heaven, paradise, L.; (cf. *Pūru*) N. of a prince (the son of Yayāti and Śarmishṭhā and sixth monarch of the lunar race), MBh.; Śak.; of a son of Vasu-deva and Saha-devā, BhP.; of a son of Madhu, VP.; of a son of Manu Cākshusha and Naḍvalā, Pur. [Cf. Old Pers. *paru*; Gk. πολύ; Goth. *filu*; Angl. Sax. *feolu*; Germ. *viel*.] **-kāraka-vat**, mfn. having many agents or factors, BhP. **-kútsa**, m. N. of a man, RV.; of a descendant of Ikshvāku, ŚBr.; of a son of Māndhātṛi, Hariv.; of another man, VP. **-kutsava**, m. N. of an enemy of Indra, GāruḍaP. **-kútsānī**, f. N. of a woman (prob. wife of Puru-kutsa), RV. **-kṛit**, mfn. = *-kṛitvan*, ib.; increasing (with gen.), ib. **-kṛitvan**, mfn. achieving great deeds, efficacious, ib. **-kṛipā**, f. abundant mercy or compassion, BhP. **-kshú**, mfn. rich in food, ib.; liberally granting (with gen.), ib. **-gūrtá**, mfn. welcome to many, RV. **-cétana**, mfn. visible to many, very conspicuous, ib.; TBr. **-ja**, mfn. much, L. (cf. *puruha*); m. N. of a prince (the son of Su-śānti), BhP. **-jātá**, mfn. variously manifested or appearing, RV. **-jāti**, m. = *-ja*, m., Hariv.; Pur. **-jit**, m. 'conquering many,' N. of a hero on the side of the Pāṇḍus and brother of Kunti-bhoja, MBh.; of a prince the son of Rucaka, BhP.; of a son of Ānaka, ib. **-nāman** (*purú-*), mfn. having many names (said of Indra), RV. **-nīthá**, n. a song for many voices, choral song, ib. **-táma** (*purū́-*), mfn. very much or many, abundant, frequent, ever-recurring, ib. **-tmán**, mfn. existing variously, ib. **-trā́**, ind. variously, in many ways or places or directions; many times, often, RV.; VS.; AV. **-da**, n. gold, L. (cf. *puraṭa*). **-daṇśaka**, m. 'many-teethed,' a goose (so called from its serrated beak), L. **-dáṇsa**, mfn. abounding in mighty or wonderful deeds, RV. **-dáṇsas**, mfn. id., ib.; m. N. of Indra, L. **-datra**, mfn. rich in gifts, RV. **-dáma**, mfn. possessed of or belonging to many houses, AV. **-daya**, mfn. abounding in compassion, BhP. **-dasmá**, mfn. = *-daṇsa*, RV.; VS. **-dasyu**, mfn. (people), consisting chiefly in robbers, BhP. **-dína**, n. pl. many days, RV. **-deva-campū**, f. N. of a poem. **-drapsá**, mfn. abounding in drops of water (said of the Maruts), ib. **-drúh**, mfn. injuring greatly, ib. **-dhá** (before 2 consonants) or **-dhā́**, ind. variously, frequently, RV.; AV.; *-pratīka* (*-dhā́-*), mfn. appearing variously, RV. **-niḥshídh** or °**shídhvan**, mfn. repelling many (foes), ib. **-nishṭhā́**, mfn. excelling among many, ib. **-nṛimṇá**, mfn. displaying great valour, ib. **-pánthā**, m. (nom. °*thās*) N. of a man, ib. **-paśu**, mfn. rich in cattle, ŚāṅkhGṛ. **-putrá**, mf(*ā́*)n. having many sons or children, RV. **-péśa** or **-péśas**, mfn. multiform, ib. **-prajātá**, mfn. variously propagated, ib. **-praśastá**, mfn. praised by many, ib. **-priyá**, mf(*ā́*)n. dear to many, RV.; VS. **-práisha** or **-práishá**, mfn. inciting many, RV. **-prauḍha**, mfn. possessing much self-confidence, BhP. **-bhuj**, mfn. enjoying much, RV. **-bhū́**, mfn. being or appearing in many places (superl. *-tama*), ib. **-bhūta**, w. r. for *-hūta*, Hariv. **-bhójas**, mfn. containing many means of enjoyments, greatly nourishing, RV.; m. a cloud, L. **-madga** (?), m. N. of a man, ĀrshBr. (w. r. *-mahna*). **-manas**, mfn. (formed for the explanation of 2. *puṇs*), Nir. ix, 15. **-mántu**, mfn. full of wisdom, intelligent, RV. **-mandrá**, mfn. delighting many, ib. **-māyá** (RV.), **-māyin** (BhP.), mfn. possessing various arts or virtues, wonderful. **-mā́yya**, m. N. of a man, RV. **-mitrá**, m. N. of a man, RV.; of a warrior on the side of the Kurus, MBh.; Hariv. **-mīḍhá** (AV. &c.), **-mīḷhá** (RV.), m. N. of a man (with the patr. Āṅgirasa or Sauhotra; the supposed author of RV. iv, 43; 44); of a son of Su-hotra, MBh.; of a grandson of Su-hotra and son of Hastin (Bṛihat), Hariv.; Pur.; of a man with the patr. Vaidadaśvi, TāṇḍBr. **-médha** (RV.) or °**dhas** (SV.), mfn. endowed with wisdom; N. of a man with the patr. Āṅgirasa (author of RV. viii, 89; 90). **-rátha**, mfn. having many chariots, RV. **-ravasa**, w. r. for *purū-r°* below, MārkP. **-rāja-vaṇśa-krama**, m. N. of a poem. **-rā́van**, mfn. 'much-howling,' N. of a demon, VS. **-rúc**, mfn. shining brightly, RV. **-ruj**, mfn. subject to many diseases, BhP. **-rū́pa**, mf(*ā*)n. multiform, variegated, RV.; forming various shapes, VS.; AV. **-lampaṭa**, mfn. very lascivious, BhP. **-vártman**, mfn. having many ways or paths, AV. **-várpas**, mfn. multiform, variegated, RV. **-vaśa**, m. N. of a prince, VP. **-vā́ja**, mf(*ā*)n. powerful, very strong, RV. **-1. -vā́ra**, mfn. having an ample tail or mane (as a horse or ox), ib. **-2. -vā́ra**, mfn. rich in gifts, ib.; *-push-ṭi*, mfn. granting treasured riches, ib. **-viśruta**, m. 'much renowned,' N. of a son of Vasu-deva, BhP. **-vī́ra**, mf(*ā*)n. possessed of many men or male offspring, RV. **-vépas**, mfn. much excited or exciting, ib. **-vratá**, mfn. having many ordinances (said of Soma), ib. **-śakti**, mfn. possessing various powers, BhP. **-śā́ka**, m. helpful (superl. *-tama*), RV.; AV. **-śishṭa**, m. N. of a man (cf. *pauruśishṭi*). **-ścandrá**, mfn. much-shining, resplendent, RV. **-shánti** (Padap. *-sánti*), m. N. of a man, RV.; TāṇḍBr. **-shṭutá**, mfn. highly lauded, praised by many, RV.; MBh.; Hariv.; m. N. of Śiva, Śivag. **-sambhṛitá**, mfn. accumulated by many, RV. **-sena**, m. N. of a poet, Cat. **-spārhá** (TBr.) and **-spṛíh** (RV.), mfn. much desired. **-hanman**, m. N. of a man (author of RV. viii, 59, 2) with the patr. Āṅgirasa (RAnukr.) or Vaikhānasa (TaṇḍBr.) **-hāni**, f. a great loss, Kāv. **-huta**, m. N. of a prince, AgP. **-hūtá**, mfn. much invoked or invoked by many, RV. &c. &c.; m. N. of Indra, Mn.; MBh. &c. (*-kāshṭhā*, f. I°'s quarter i.e. the east, Dhūrtan.; *-dvish*, m. I°'s foe, N. of Indra-jit, MW.); (*ā*), f. N. of a form of Dākshāyaṇī, MatsyaP. **-hūti**, f. manifold invocation, BhP. **-hotra**, m. N. of a son of Anu, ib. **Purûdvaha**, m. N. of a son of the 11th Manu, MārkP. **Purûrúṇā**, ind. far and wide, RV.

Puruha or °**hu**, mfn. much, many, L.

Purū, in comp. for °*ru*. — **táma**, mfn., see under *puru*. — **rávas**, mfn. crying much or loudly, RV. i, 31, 4; m. N. of an ancient king of the lunar race (the lover of Urvaśī [cf. RV. x, 95; ŚBr. xi, 5, 1 and Kālidāsa's drama Vikramôrvaśī], son of Budha and Iḷā, father of Āyus and ancestor of Puru, Dushyanta, Bharata, Kuru, Dhṛita-rāshṭra and Pāṇḍu, supposed to have instituted the 3 sacrificial fires [VS. v, 2]; according to Nir. x, 46 he is one of the beings belonging to the middle region of the universe, and is possibly to be connected with the Sun as Urvaśī is with the Dawn; according to others a Viśva-deva or a Pārvaṇa-śrāddha-deva), RV. &c. &c. — **ravasa**, m. = prec. m., MārkP. — **rúc**, mfn. much shining, SV. (cf. *puru-ruc*). — **vásu**, mfn. abounding in goods or riches, RV.; AitBr. — **vṛít**, mfn. moving in various ways, AV.

Purūcí, f. (of an unused *purv-añc*) abounding, abundant, full, comprehensive, RV.; AV.

Purv-aṇīka, mfn. variously manifested or appearing, RV.

पुरुञ्ज *puruñja* or *puruṇḍa*, m. pl. N. of a dynasty, VP.

पुरुद्वत् *purudvat*, m. N. of a prince, Hariv.; Pur.

पुरुवी *puruvī*, f. (in music) N. of a Rāgiṇī.

पुरुष *púrusha*, m. (m. c. also *pū́r*°; prob. fr. √*pṛī* and connected with *puru*, *pūru*; ifc. f. *ā*, rarely *ī*; cf. Pāṇ. iv, 1, 24) a man, male, human being (pl. people, mankind), RV. &c. &c.; a person, (*pumān purushaḥ*, a male person, ŚāṅkhGṛ.; Mn.; *daṇḍaḥ p*°, punishment personified, Mn.; esp. grammatical pers.; with *prathama*, *madhyama*, *uttama* = the 3rd, 2nd, 1st pers., Nir.; Pāṇ.), an officer, functionary, attendant, servant, Mn.; MBh. &c. (cf. *tat-p*°); a friend, L.; a follower of the Sāṃkhya philosophy (?), L.; a member or representative of a race or generation, TS.; Br.; Mn. &c.; the height or measure of a man (= 5 Aratnis = 120 Aṅgulas), ŚBr.; Śulbas.; Var.; the pupil of the eye, ŚBr.; (also with *Nārāyaṇa*) the primaeval man as the soul and original source of the universe (described in the Purusha-sûkta, q.v.), RV.; ŚBr. &c.; the personal and animating principle in men and other beings, the soul or spirit, AV. &c. &c.; the Supreme Being or Soul of the universe (sometimes with *para*, *parama* or *uttama*; also identified with Brahmā, Vishṇu, Śiva and Durgā), VS.; ŚBr. &c. &c.; (in Sāṃkhya) the Spirit as passive and a spectator of the Prakṛiti or creative force, IW. 82 &c.; the 'spirit' or fragrant exhalation of plants, RV. x, 51, 8; (with *sapta*) N. of the divine or active principles from the minute portions of which the universe was formed, Mn. i, 19; N. of a Pāda in the Mahānāmnī verses, Lāṭy.; of the 1st, 3rd, 5th, 7th, 9th and 11th signs of the zodiac, Jyot.; of a son of Manu Cākshusha, BhP.; of one of the 18 attendants of the sun, L.; pl. men, people (cf. above); N. of the Brāhmans of Krauñca-dvīpa, BhP.; (with *pañca*) N. of 5 princely personages or miraculous persons born under partic. constellations, Var.; Rottleria Tinctoria, L.; Clerodendrum Phlomoides, L.; (*ī*), f. a woman, female, RV. &c. &c.; m. or n. = *purushaka*, m. n., Śiś. v, 56, Sch.; n. (!) N. of mount Meru, L. — **kāma**, mfn. desirous of men, TāṇḍBr. — **kāra**, m. human effort (opp. to *daiva*, fate), Mn.; Yājñ.; manly act, virility, heroism, MBh.; Kāv. &c.; haughtiness, pride, Pat.; N. of a grammarian, Cat.; *-phala*, n. the fruit or result of human effort, L.; *-mīmāṃsā*, f. N. of wk. — **kuṇapá**, n. a human corpse, TS. — **kesarin**, m. 'man-lion,' N. of Vishṇu in his 4th appearance on earth, Sak. (cf. *nara-siṃha*). — **kshīrá**, n. human milk, MaitrS. — **kshetra**, n. a male or uneven zodiacal sign or astrological house, Var. — **gati**, f. N. of a Sāman, Gaut. — **gandhi** (*pú*°), mfn. smelling of men, AV. — **gātra**, mfn. endowed with human or manly limbs, Kauś. — **ghnī**, f. (with *strī*) a woman who kills her husband, Yājñ. (cf. *pūrusha-han*). — **cchandasá**, n. 'man's metre,' the metre suited for men, i.e. the Dvi-padā, ŚBr. — **jana**, m. sg. men, people, Pañcad. — **jātaka**, n. N. of wk. — **jīvana**, mf(*ī*)n. enlivening or animating men, AV. — **jñāna**, n. knowledge of men or mankind, Mn. vii, 211. — **tantra**, mfn. dependent on the subject, subjective (*-tva*, n.), Sāṃk. — **tā** (°*shá*-), f. manhood, manliness; ind. (as instr.) after the manner of men, among men, RV. — **tejas** (*pú*°), mfn. having a man's energy or manly vigour, AV. — **trā́**, ind. = *-tā*, ind., RV. (cf. Pāṇ. v, 4, 56). — **tva**, n. manhood, manliness, MBh.; Pur.; *-tvá-tā*, ind. after the manner of men, RV. — **daghna**, mfn. of the height or measure of a man, W. — **datta**, m. N. of a man, Mudr. — **dantikā**, f. N. of a medicinal root, L. — **damya-sārathi**, m. a driver or guide of men (compared with young draught-oxen), Divyâv. — **dravya-sampad**, f. abundance of men and material, MW. — **dvayasa**, mf(*ī*)n. = *-daghna*, L. — **dvish**, m. an enemy of Vishṇu, MW. — **dveshin**, mfn. man-hating, misanthropic, W.; (*iṇī*), f. an ill-tempered or fractious woman, ib. — **dharma**, m. personal rule or precept, KātyŚr. — **dhaureyaka**, m. a man superior to other people, Hcat. — **nāya**, m. 'man-leader,' a prince, ChUp. — **niyama**, m. (in gram.) a restriction as to person. — **nishkráyaṇa**, mfn. one who redeems a person, TS. — **pati**, m. 'lord of men,' N. of Rāma, MW. — **parīkshā**, f. 'trial of man,' N. of a collection of moral tales. — **paśu**, m. a beast of man, a brutal man, Pañc.; VP.; a man as a sacrificial victim, BhP.; the soul compared with an animal, IW. 85; a human animal, man, W. — **puṃgava**, m. 'man-bull,' an eminent or excellent man, W. — **puṇḍarīka**, m. 'man-lotus,' = prec., ib.; (with Jainas) N. of the 6th black Vāsudeva. — **pura**, n. N. of the capital of Gāndhāra, the modern Peshāwar (پيشاور), L. — **prabhu**, m. N. of a prince, VP. — **bahumāna**, m. the respect or esteem of mankind, Bhartṛ. — **mātrá**, mf(*ī*)n. of the height or measure of a man, ŚBr.; KātyŚr.; n. the size of a man, TS. — **mānin**, mfn. fancying one's self a man or hero (°*ni-tva*, n.), MBh. — **mukha**, mf(*ī*)n. having the face of a man, Kauś. — **mṛigá**, m. a male antelope, VS.; TS., Sch. — **medhá**, m. the sacrifice of a man, Br.; MBh. &c.; N. of the supposed author of VS. xx, 30 (perhaps w.r. for *puru-medha*, q.v.) — **yogin**, mfn. relating to a person or subject, KātyŚr. — **yoni** (*pú*°), mfn. descended from or begotten by a man (male), MaitrS. — **rakshas**, n. a demon in the form of a man, Kauś. — **rājá**, m. a human king, TS. — **rūpa**, n. the shape of a man, AitBr.; (*pú*°), mfn. = next, ŚBr. — **rūpaka**, mfn. shaped like a man, AitBr. — **réshaṇa** (AV.), **-reshin** (Kauś.), mfn. hurting men. — **rshabha** (*r* for *ṛi*), m. = *-puṃgava*, MBh.; R. — **vacas**, mfn. called Purusha, ChUp. — **vat**, mfn. accompanied by men, ŚBr. — **vadhá**, m. manslaughter, murder, AV.; slaughter of a husband, Vet. — **vara**, m. the best of men, VP.; N. of Vishṇu, MBh.; of a prince, VP. — **varjita**, mfn. destitute of human beings, desolate, MW. — **vāc**, mfn. having a human voice, VS.; ŚBr. — **vāha**, m. 'Vishṇu's vehicle,' N. of Garuḍa, BhP. — **vāham**, ind. (with *vahati*, he moves in such a way as to be) borne or drawn along by men, Pāṇ. iii, 4, 43. — **vidha** (*pú*°), mfn. man-like, having a human form (*-tā*, f.), ŚBr.; TUp. — **vyāghrá**, m. 'man-tiger,' N. of a demon, ŚBr.; = *-śārdūla*, MBh.; R.; a vulture, L. — **vrata**, n. N. of 2 Sāmans, ĀrshBr. — **śārdūla**, m. 'man-tiger,' an eminent man, W. — **śiras**, n. a human head, KātyŚr. — **śīrshá**, n. id., ŚBr.; °*shaka*, m. or n. N. of an instrument used by thieves, Daś. — **saṃskāra**, m. a ceremony performed on a (dead) person, Āpast. — **samavâya**, m. a number of men, W. — **sammita** (*pú*°), mfn. man-like, TBr. — **sāman**, n. N. of a Sāman, ĀpŚr. — **sāmudrika-lakshaṇa**, n. 'divination from bodily signs,' N. of wk. — **siṇha**, m. 'man-lion,' an eminent man or hero, Kāv.; (with Jainas) N. of the 5th of the black Vāsudevas, L. — **sûkta**, n. 'the Purusha hymn,' N. of RV. x, 90 (describing the Supreme Soul of the universe and supposed to be comparatively modern), RTL. 17; 23 &c.; *-bhāshya*, n., *-vidhāna*, n., *-vyākhyā*, f., *-vyākhyāna*, n., *-shoḍaśôpacāra-vidhi*, m., °*ktôpanishad*, f. N. of wks. — **han**, mfn., only f. *-ghnī*, q.v. **Purushâṇsaka**, m. N. of a teacher, g. *śaunakâdi* (Kāś. °*shāsaka*). **Purushâkāra**, mfn. of human form or shape (*-tā*, f.), Hcat. **Purushâkṛiti**, f. the figure of a man, ŚrS. **Purushâṅga**, m. n. the male organ of generation, MW. (cf. *narâṅga*). **Púrushâjāna**, mfn. of human descent or origin, ŚBr. **Purushâd**, mfn. eating or destroying men, RV.; AV. **Purushâda**, mf(*ī*)n. id.; m. a cannibal, a Rakshas (*-tva*, n.), MBh.; R.; BhP.; (pl.) N. of a race of cannibals in the east of Madhya-deśa, Var. **Purushâdaka**, mfn. men-devouring, MBh.; R.; (pl.) N. of certain cannibals, MārkP. **Purushâdya**, m. 'first of men,' N. of Vishṇu, L.; (with Jainas) N. of Ādi-nātha or of Ṛishabha (the first Arhat of present Avasarpiṇī). **Purushâdhama**, m. 'lowest or vilest of men,' an outcast, the worst of servants, W. **Purushâdhikāra**, m. manly office or duty, Kir. **Purushânṛita**, n. falsehood respecting men, Mn. ix, 71. **Purushântara**, n. another man or person, a mediator, interposer, R. (*am*, ind. by a mediator, indirectly, Vikr. ii, 16); another or a succeeding generation, MārkP.; (*-vedin*, mfn. knowing the heart of mankind, MW.; °*rátman*, m. 'man's inner self,' the soul, L.); m. (sc. *saṃdhi*) an alliance negotiated by warriors chosen by both parties, Kām.; Hit. **Purushâyaṇa**, mf(*ā*)n. going to or uniting with the soul, PraśnUp. **Purushâyata**, mfn. of the length of a man, Hcat. **Purushâyusha**, n. the duration of a man's life, age of man, Ragh. (cf. Pāṇ. v, 4, 77); *-ka*, n. id., Gal. **Purushârtha**, m. any object of human pursuit; any one of the four objects or aims of existence (viz. *kāma*, the gratification of desire; *artha*, acquirement of wealth; *dharma*, discharge of duty; *moksha*, final emancipation), Mn.; Prab.; Kap. (*-tva*, n.); Sāṃkhyak. &c.; human effort or exertion, MBh.; R. &c.; (*am*), ind. for the sake of the soul, Kap.; for or on account of man, W.; *-kāra*, m., *-kaumudī*, f., *-cintāmaṇi*, m. N. of wks.; *-trayīmaya*, mf(*ī*)n. intent only upon the 3 objects of man (*kāma*, *artha* and *dharma*), Siṇhâs.; *-prabodha*, m., *-prabodhinī*, f., *-ratnâkara*, m., *-siddhy-upâya*, m., *-sudhā-nidhi*, m., *-sūtra-vṛitti*, f., °*rthânuśāsana*, n. N. of wks. **Purushâvatāra**, m. human incarnation, Siṇhâs. **Purushâsin**, m. 'man-eater,' a Rākshasa, W. **Purushâsthá**, n. a human bone, AV.; °*sthimālin*, m. 'wearing a necklace of human skulls,' N. of Śiva, L. **Purushâhuti**, f. an invocation addressed to men, TS. **Purushêndra**, m. 'lord of men,' a king; *-tā*, f. sovereignty, MBh. **Purushêshita** (*pú*°), mfn. caused or instigated by men, AV. **Purushôkti**, f. the name or title of man, W.; °*ktika*, mfn. having only the name of man, destitute, friendless, ib. **Purushôttama**, see below. **Purushôpahāra**, m. the sacrifice of a man, Hcar.

Purushaka, ifc. = *purusha*, a man, male, Pat.; m. n. standing on two feet like a man, the rearing of a horse, prancing, Śiś. v, 56.

Purushāya, Nom. Ā. °*yate*, to behave or act like a man, play the man, Hariv. °**shāyita**, mfn. acting like a man, playing the man (esp. in sexual intercourse), Amar., Sch. (*-tva*, n.); n. a kind of coitus, Kpr.; Kuval.

Purushī-√bhū, to become a man, R.; Kathās.

Purushôttama, m. the best of men, an excellent or superior man, Hariv.; Sāh.; the best of servants, a good attendant, Kāv.; the highest being, Supreme Spirit, N. of Vishṇu or Kṛishṇa, MBh.; Kāv. &c. (IW. 91, n. 3 &c.); = *-kshetra*, Cat.; (with Jainas) an Arhat; N. of the fourth black Vāsudeva; a Jina (one of the generic terms for a deified teacher of the Jaina sect); N. of sev. authors and various men (also *-dāsa*, *-dīkshita*, *-deva*, *-deva-śarman*, *-paṇḍita*, *-prasāda*, *-bhaṭṭa*, *-bhaṭṭâtmaja*, *-bhāraty-ācārya*, *-miśra*, *-manu-sudhîndra*, *-sarasvatī*, °*mâcārya*, °*mânanda-tīrtha*, °*mânanda-yati*, °*mâśrama*). — **kshetra**, n. 'district of the Supreme Being,' N. of a district in Orissa sacred to Vishṇu, BrahmaP.; *-tattva* and *-māhātmya*, n. N. of wks. — **khaṇḍa**, m. or n., **-caritra**, n. N. of wks. — **tīrtha**, n. N. of a Tīrtha; *-prayoga-tattva*, n. N. of wk. — **pattra**, n., **-purāṇa**, n., **-purī-māhātmya**, n., **-prakāśa-kshetra-vidhi**, m., **-mantra**, m., **-māhātmya**, n., **-vāda**, m., **-śāstrīya**, n., **-sahasra-nāman**, n. N. of wks.

Purushyà, mfn. pertaining to man, human, RV.

पुरूरवस् *purū-ravas*. See col. 1.

पुरोग *puro-ga* &c. See p. 635, col. 1.

पुरोचन *purocana*, m. N. of a man, MBh.

पुरोटि *puroṭi*, m. = *pattra-jhaṃkāra* or *pura-saṃskārā*, L. ('the current of a river,' W.)

पुरोडाश् *puro-ḍāś*, °*śa* &c. See p. 635.

पुर्य *purya*, *pury-ashṭa*. See p. 636.

पुर्व् *purv* (cf. *prī*), cl. 1. P. *pūrvati*, to fill, Dhātup. xv, 67; cl. 10. *pūrvayati*, to dwell, xxxii, 126.

पुर्वणीक *purv-aṇīka*. See p. 637, col. 1.

पुल् *pul*, cl. 1. 6. 10. P. *polati, pulati, polayati*, to be great or large or high, to be piled or heaped up, Dhātup. xx, 11; xxxii, 61.

Pula, mfn. extended, wide, L.; m. horripilation (see under *pulaka*), L.; N. of an attendant of Śiva, L.; (*ā*), f. the soft palate or uvula, L.; N. of a partic. pace of horses, Śiś. v, 60, Sch.; (*ī*), f. a bunch (see *triṇa-pulī*); n. size, extent, L. **-keśin** and **-keśi-vallabha**, m. N. of princes, L.

Pulaka, m. a species of edible plant, MBh.; a species of tree, L.; (pl.) erection or bristling of the hairs of the body (considered to be occasioned by delight or rapture rather than by fear), Kāv.; Pur. (also n., but mostly occurring ibc. and ifc. with f. *ā*); a bunch (see *triṇa-p°*); a kind of stone or gem, Var.; flaw or defect in a gem, L.; a kind of insect or vermin, L.; a cake of meal with which elephants are fed, L.; orpiment, L.; a Gandharva, L.; = *asurājī* (?), L.; N. of a prince, VP.; of a Nāga, L.; n. a species of earth, L.; horripilation (cf. above); °*kâkulâkṛiti*, mfn. 'having the frame excited by bristling hair,' thrilled with joy, MW.; °*kâṅkita-sarvâṅga*, mf(*ī*)n. having the whole body covered with bristling hair, Pañc.; °*kâṅkura*, m. (sprout of) b° h°, Git.; °*kâṅga*, m. the noose or cord of Varuṇa, L.; °*kâcita*, mfn. covered with b° h°, Śak. (Pi.) iii, 12 (v.l. °*kâñcita*); °*kâlaya*, m. N. of Kubera, L.; °*kôtkampa*, mfn. trembling with a thrill of delight, Kathās.; °*kôdgama*, m. erection of the hair, Bhartṛ.; °*kôddhūshita-śarīra* (B. °*dhṛishita-ś°*), mfn. having the body covered with erected hairs, Pañc.; °*kôdbheda*, m. = °*kôdgama*, Bhartṛ. °**kaya**, Nom. P. °*yati*, to have or feel the hair of the body erect (with rapture or delight), Git. °**kita**, mfn. having the h° of the b° erect, thrilled with joy, Kāv.; Pañc.; Hit.; *-sarvâṅga*, mf(*ī*)n. having the whole b° covered with bristling hair, Pañc. °**kin**, mfn. = °*kita*, W.; m. Nauclea Cordifolia, L. °**kī-kṛita**, mfn. = °*kita*, BhP.

Pulasa, mfn., g. *triṇâdi*.

Pulasti, mfn. (perhaps fr. *pulas* for *puras*; but according to Uṇ. iv, 179, Sch. fr. *pula* and √3. *as*) wearing the hair straight or smooth, VS.; m. N. of a man, g. *gargâdi*. °**tya**, m. N. of an ancient Ṛishi (one of the mind-born sons of Brahmā; also enumerated among the Prajā-patis and seven sages, and described as a lawgiver), AV. Pariś.; Pravar.; Mn.; MBh. &c. (IW. 517, n. 1); N. of Śiva, Śivag.; *-siddhânta*, m., *-smṛiti*, f., °*tyâshṭaka*, n. N. of wks.

Pulaha, m. (*pula* + √2. *hā*?) N. of an ancient Ṛishi (one of the mind-born sons of Brahmā enumerated among the Prajā-patis and seven sages), AV. Pariś.; Pravar.; Mn.; MBh. &c. (IW. 517, n. 1); N. of a star, Hariv.; N. of Śiva, Śivag.; °*hâśrama*, m. N. of a hermitage, BhP. (= *harikshetra*, Sch.)

Pulāka, m. n. shrivelled or blighted or empty or bad grain, Mn.; MBh. &c.; a partic. species of grain, L.; a lump of boiled rice, L. (°*kôdaka*, n. rice-water, Suśr.); brevity, abbreviation, compendium, L.; celerity, dispatch (*-kārin*, mfn. making haste, hastening), L. °**kin**, m. a tree, L.

Pulānikā, f. (prob.) induration of the skin, Suśr.

Pulāyita, n. a horse's gallop, L. (cf. *ardha-p°*).

Pulina, m. n. (g. *ardharcâdi*) a sandbank, a small island or bank in the middle of a river, an islet, a sandy beach (ifc. f. *ā*), MBh.; Kāv. &c.; the bank of a river (= *tīra*), Ragh., Sch.; m. N. of a mythical being conquered by Garuḍa, MBh.; of a poet, Cat. **-jaghanā**, f. having sandbanks for hips (said of the Gambhīrā river personified as a female), Megh. **-dvīpa-śobhita**, mfn. beautified by shoals and islets, MW. **-pradeśa**, m. situation or place of an island, Kathās. **-maṇḍita**, mfn. adorned with sandbanks or islets, R. **-vati**, f. (prob.) N. of a river, g. *ajirâdi*.

Pulinda, m. pl. (Uṇ. iv, 85) N. of a barbarous tribe, AitBr.; MBh. &c.; (sg.) a man or the king of this tribe; a barbarian, mountaineer, MBh.; Kathās.; N. of a king, BhP.; the mast or rib of a ship (= *polinda*), L.; (*ā*), f. N. of a serpent-maid, Kāraṇḍ.; (*ī*), f. a Pulinda woman, BhP.; (in music), N. of a Rāga. °**duka**, m. pl. N. of a barbarous tribe (= *pulinda*), MBh.; (sg.) N. of a king of the Pulinda and Śabara and Bhilla, Kathās.; of a son of Ārdraka, VP.; (*ikā*), f. (in music) = *pulindī*.

पुलिक *pulika*, m. N. of a man, VP.; (*ā*), f. yellowish alum, L.

Pulikeśin, m. = *pula-keśin*, Inscr.

पुलिमत् *pulimat*, m. N. of a man, VP. (cf. *pulomat*).

पुलिरिक *pulirika*, m. a snake, L.

पुलिश *puliśa*, m. = Paulus (Alexandrinus), N. of the author of a Siddhânta (also °*śâcārya*), VarBṛS., Sch.

पुलीकय *pulīkaya*, m. a partic. aquatic animal, MaitrS. (cf. *kulīkaya*, *kulīpaya* and *purīkaya*).

Pulīkā, f. a species of bird, MaitrS. (cf. *kulīkā*).

पुलीतत् *pulītát*, n. = *purītat*, MaitrS.

पुलु *pulu*, mfn. = *puru* in comp. **-kāma**, mfn. having many desires, covetous, RV. i, 179, 5. **Pulv-aghá**, mfn. doing much evil, ib. x, 86, 21.

पुलुष *pulusha*, m. N. of a man (cf. *paulushi*).

पुलोम 1. *puloma*, m. (m. c.) = *puloman*, R.; (*ā*), f. N. of a daughter of the demon Vaiśvānara (she was loved by the demon Puloman, but became the wife of Bhṛigu or Kaśyapa), MBh.; Hariv.; Pur.; Acorus Calamus (= *vacā*), L.

2. **Puloma**, in comp. for °*man*. **-jā**, f. 'daughter of Puloman,' N. of Indrāṇī, Prasannar. **-jit**, m. 'conqueror of P°,' N. of Indra, Cat. **-tanayā**, f. = *-jā*, Gal. **-dvish**, m. 'enemy of P°,' N. of Indra, L. **-nishūdana** (Gal.), **-bhid** (L.), m. 'destroyer of P°,' N. of Indra (who destroyed his father-in-law P° in order to avert his imprecation consequent on the violation of his daughter). **Pulomâri**, m. = °*ma-dvish*, Kāvyâd. **Pulomârcis**, m. 'having the lustre of P°,' N. of a prince, VP. **Pulomâvi**, m. (prob.) w.r. for °*mâri*, ib.

Puloman, m. N. of a demon (the father-in-law of Indra by whom he was destroyed), MBh.; Hariv.; Pur.; of a prince, VP.

पुलोमत् *pulomat*, m. N. of two princes, VP. (cf. *pulimat*).

पुलोमही *pulomahī*, f. opium, L.

पुल्कक *púlkaka*. See *púklaka* and next, MaitrS.

पुल्कस *pulkasa*, m. (*ī*, f.) N. of a despised mixed tribe, Gaut.; MBh. (also °*kaka*, BhP.; cf. *paulkasá* and *pukkaśa*).

पुल्य *pulya*, mfn., g. *balâdi*.

पुल्ल *pulla*, mfn. expanded, blown, L.; n. a flower, L. (prob. w.r. for *phulla*).

पुल्वघ *pulvaghá*, mfn. See *pulu*.

पुष् 1. *push*, cl. 4. P. *pushyati*, to divide, distribute, Dhātup. xxvi, 106 (v.l. for *vyush*, q.v.)

पुष् 2. *push*, cl. 1. P. (Dhātup. xvii, 50) *poshati* (trans.), only Nir. x, 34; cl. 4. P. (Dhātup. xxvi, 73) *púshyati* (trans. and intrans.; m.c. also Ā. °*te*), RV. &c. &c.; cl. 9. P. (Dhātup. xxxi, 57) *pushṇāti* (trans.), MBh.; Kāv. &c. (pf. *pupósha*, *pupushyās*, RV.; aor. *apushat* or *aposhīt*, Gr.; Pot. *pusheyam*, RV.; Prec. *pushyāsam*, °*sma*, Br.; fut. *poshishyati*, *pokshyati*; *poshitā*, *poshṭā*, Gr.; Pass. *pushyate*, Kāv.; aor. *aposhi*, Gr.; inf. *pushyáse*, RV.), to be nourished (with instr., e.g. *bhāryayā*, MBh. xiii, 4569), to thrive, flourish, prosper (also with *pósham*, *pushṭim* or *vṛiddhim*), RV.; AV.; VS.; ŚBr. (rarely in later language, e.g. MBh. [see above], and sometimes in Bhaṭṭ., where also 3 sg. *pushyati-tarām*); to cause to thrive or prosper, nourish, foster, augment, increase, further, promote, fulfil (e.g. a wish), develop, unfold, display, gain, obtain, enjoy, possess, RV. &c. &c.: Caus. *poshá-yati* (aor. *apūpushat*, Gr.), to rear, nourish, feed, cause to thrive or prosper, RV. &c. &c.; to cause to be reared or fed by (instr.), Śak.: Desid. *pupo-shishati*, *pupushishati*, *pupukshati*, Gr.: Intens. *popushyate*, *poposhṭi*, ib.

3. **Push**, mfn. (ifc.) nourishing, causing to thrive (cf. *viśva-p°*); showing, displaying, Śiś. x, 32.

Pusha, mfn. (ifc.) nourishing, cherishing (cf. *graha-p°*); m. N. of a teacher, Cat.; (*ā*), f. Methonica Superba, L.

Pushita, mfn. nourished, nurtured (= *pushṭa*), W.

Pushka, a word formed for the explanation of *pushkala*, g. *sidhmâdi* (perhaps also underlying the formation of *pushkara*, *pushpa* and *pushka-jit*; cf. *paushka-jiti*).

Púshkara, n. (rather fr. *pushka* + *ra* than fr. *push* + *kara*; but cf. Uṇ. iv, 4) a blue lotus-flower, a lotus, Nelumbium Speciosum or Nymphaea Nelumbo (ifc. f. *ā*), AV. &c. &c. (met. 'the heart,' MBh. v, 1790); the bowl of a spoon (ifc. f. *ā*), RV.; Br.; GṛŚrS.; the skin of a drum, Kālid.; the tip of an elephant's trunk, Var.; water, ŚBr.; the sky, heaven, Prab. (cf. Naigh. i, 3); a night of new moon falling on a Monday or Tuesday or Saturday, Hcat.; an arrow, L.; the blade or the sheath of a sword, L.; a cage, L.; Costus Speciosus or Arabicus, L.; a part, L.; the art of dancing, L.; union, L.; war, battle, L.; intoxication, L.; N. of a celebrated place of pilgrimage (now called Pokhar in the district of Ajmere, cf. RTL. 558), MBh.; Hariv.; Pur. &c. (also pl.; according to Vishṇ., Sch. there are three, viz. *jyeshṭha*, *madhyama* and *kanishṭha*); m. n. = *-dvīpa*, MBh.; Pur.; = *brahmâṇḍa*, Nīlak.; (with Jainas) one of the 5 Bhārata, L.; m. Ardea Sibirica, Pañc.; (in astrol.) an inauspicious Yoga, an ill-omened combination of a lucky lunation with an unlucky day, ¾ of a lunar mansion, W.; a kind of drum, MBh.; a kind of serpent, L.; the sun, L.; a pond, lake, L.; a kind of disease, L.; the regent of P°-dvīpa (below), MārkP.; N. of Kṛishṇa, MBh.; of Śiva, Śivag.; of a son of Varuṇa, MBh.; Pur.; of a general of the sons and grandsons of Varuṇa, L.; of an Asura, Hariv.; of a son of Kṛishṇa, BhP.; of a Buddha, Lalit.; of a prince (the brother of Nala), Nal.; of a son of Bharata, VP.; of Su-nakshatra, BhP.; of a son of Vṛika and Dūrvâkshī, ib.; of an author, Cat.; of a mountain in P°-dvīpa, MBh.; m. pl. N. of a class of clouds said to occasion dearth and famine, L. (cf. *pushkarâvartaka*); of the inhabitants of Kuśa-dvīpa corresponding to Brāhmans, VP.; of the lunar mansions Punar-vasu, Uttarâshāḍhā, Kṛittikā, Uttara-phalgunī, Pūrva-bhādrapadā and Viśākhā collectively, L.; (*ī*), f. (g. *gaurâdi*) N. of one of the 8 wives of Śiva, Cat. (perhaps w.r. for *pushkasī* i.e. *pulkasī*). **-karṇikā**, f. the finger on the tip of an elephant's trunk, Gal. **-kalpa**, m. N. of wk. **-cūḍa**, m. 'lotus-crested,' N. of one of the 4 elephants that support the earth, BhP. **-ja**, n. 'l°-born,' N. of the root of Costus Speciosus, L. **-tīrtha**, n. N. of a sacred bathing-place, L. **-dvīpa**, m. N. of a Dvīpa or great division of the earth, L. **-nāḍī**, f. Hibiscus Mutabilis, L. **-nābha**, m. 'l°-naveled,' N. of Vishṇu, BhP. **-pattra**, n. a l°-leaf, Bhartṛ.; *-netra*, mfn. having eyes like l°-leaves, Ragh. **-parṇá**, n. a l°-petal and a kind of brick named after it, AV.; ŚBr. &c.; °*ṇikā* or °*ṇī*, f. Hibiscus Mutabilis, L. **-palāśa**, n. = *-parṇa*, Lāṭy. **-purāṇa**, n. N. of a Purāṇa. **-prādur-bhāva**, m. N. of wk. **-priya**, m. or n. wax, L. **-bīja**, n. l°-seed, Mṛicch.; Suśr.; Costus Speciosus or Arabicus, L. **-mālin**, m. 'wearing a l°-wreath,' N. of a man, MārkP. **-māhātmya**, n. N. of wk. **-mukha**, n. the aperture of the tip of an elephant's trunk, Śiś.; mf(*ī*)n. (a vessel) having a mouth like the tip of an el°'s tr°, Āryav. **-mūla** (Bhpr.), °**laka** (L.), n. the root of Costus Speciosus or Arabicus. **-vana**, n. the forest in the Tīrtha Pushkara, TBr., Sch.; *-prādur-bhāva*, m., *-māhātmya*, n. N. of wks. **-vyāghra**, m. 'water-tiger,' an alligator, L. **-śāyikā**, f. a species of aquatic bird, Suśr. **-śikā**, (prob.) w.r. for next. **-śikhā** or **-śiphā**, f. Costus Speciosus or Arabicus, L. **-sad**, m. N. of a man; pl. his descendants, g. *yaskâdi*. **-sāgara**, m. or n. Costus Speciosus or Arabicus, L. **-sādá**, m. a species of bird (according to TS., Sch. = *pushkara-sarpa* or *bhramara*). **-sādi**, m. N. of a teacher, Āpast. (prob. w.r. for *paushkarasādi*). **-sādin**, m. = *-sāda*, Mahīdh. **-sārin**, m., w.r. for *paushkarasādi*. **-sārī**, f. 'having the essence of the lotus,' a kind of writing, Lalit. **-sthapati**, m. N. of Śiva, MBh. (= *brahmâṇḍasya svāmī*, Nīlak.) **-sraj**, f. a lotus-wreath, TāṇḍBr.; (*pú°*), mfn. wearing a l°-wr°, RV.; AV.; ŚBr.; m. du. N. of the two Aśvins, L. **Pushkarâksha**, mf(*ī*)n. l°-eyed, MBh.; m. N. of Vishṇu, L.; of a man,

BrahmavP.; of a prince, Ratnâv.; of a poet, Cat. **Pushkarâkhya,** m. Ardea Sibirica, L. **Pushkarâgra,** n. the tip or extremity of an elephant's trunk, Pañc. **Pushkarâṅghrija,** m. or n. Costus Speciosus or Arabicus, L. **Pushkarâcchādikā,** f. a species of bird, Gal. **Pushkarâraṇya,** n. =*pushkara-vana*, MBh. **Pushkarâruṇi,** m. N. of a prince, BhP. **Pushkarā-vatī,** f. 'abounding in lotuses,' N. of a town (=the Πευκελαῶτις of the ancients and the Pousekielofati of Hiouen-Thsang), R.; Kathās.; Pur. (cf. Pāṇ. vi, 3, 119, Sch.); a form of Dākshāyaṇī, MatsyaP. **Pushkarâvartaka,** m. N. of a partic. class of clouds, Kālid. (cf. *pushkalâv°*). **Pushkarâshṭaka,** n. N. of wk. **Pushkarâhva** (Car.), °**hvaya** (L.), m. Ardea Sibirica; n. Costus Speciosus or Arabicus. 1. **Pushkarêkshaṇa,** mfn. lotus-eyed; m. (with *purusha*), N. of Vishṇu, R. 2. **Pushkare-kshaṇa,** mfn. being for a moment in the sky, MW. **Pushkarôddhṛita,** mfn. raised with the extremity of the trunk, ib.

Pushkarāya, Nom. Ā. °*yate*, to act as or represent a drum, Daśar.

Pushkarikā, f. a kind of disease (formation of abscesses on the penis), Suśr.; N. of a woman, Daś.

Pushkarin, mfn. abounding in lotuses, R.; m. an elephant, Dhūrtan.; a sword, Gal.; N. of a prince (=*pushkarâruṇi*), VP.; (*iṇī*), f. a lotus pool, any pool or pond, RV. &c. &c.; Costus Speciosus or Arabicus, L.; Hibiscus Mutabilis, L.; a female elephant, L.; N. of a river, ŚivaP.; of the wife of Bhumanyu, MBh.; of the w° of Cākshusha and mother of Manu, Hariv.; of the m° of Manu Cākshusha, VP.; of the w° of Vyushṭa and m° of Cakshus and grandm° of Manu, BhP.; of the w° of Ulmuka, ib.; of a temple in Maru or Marwar, Buddh.

Pushkalá, mf(*ā*)n. (cf. *pushka*) much, many, numerous, copious, abundant, MBh.; Kāv. &c.; rich, magnificent, full, complete, strong, powerful, excellent, best, AV. &c. &c.; loud, resonant, resounding, MBh.; Hariv.; Pur.; purified, L.; m. (v.l. °*kara*) a kind of drum, MBh.; (in music) a partic. stringed instrument; N. of Śiva, Śivag.; of a son of Varuṇa, L.; of an Asura, Hariv.; of a Ṛishi, Cat.; of a son of Bharata, R.; of a Buddha, Lalit.; of a Tīrtha (rather n.), L.; pl. N. of a people, MārkP.; of the military caste in Kuśa-dvīpa, VP.; (*ī*), f., g. *gaurâdi;* n. (ifc. f. *ā*) the bowl of a spoon, Gṛihyās. (v.l. °*kara*); a partic. measure of capacity (=8 Kuñcis=64 handfuls), ĀpŚr., Sch.; a partic. weight of gold, KātyŚr., Sch.; alms to the extent of 4 mouthfuls of food, W.; (rather m.) N. of mount Meru, L. **–mocana,** n., **-vijaya,** m. N. of chs. of PadmaP. **Pushkalā-vata,** m. an inhabitant of Pushkalā-vatī, Var. (also °*taka*); N. of an ancient physician (v.l. *paushk°*), Cat.; n. N. of the residence of Pushkala (son of Bharata), R.; (*ī*), f. N. of a city (=*pushkarā-vatī*). **Pushkalâvarta,** m. (prob.) = next; *-māhātmya*, n. N. of wk. **Pushkalâvartaka,** m. N. of a partic. class of clouds (=*pushkarâv°*), Mallin. on Śiś. xv, 107.

Pushkalaka, m. the musk-deer, L.; a post, wedge, pin, bolt, L.; a Buddhist or Jaina mendicant, L. (w.r. *pushyalaka*).

Pushṭá, mfn. nourished, cherished, well-fed, thriving, strong, fat, full, complete, perfect, abundant, rich, great, ample, Mn.; MBh. &c.; rich in, blessed with (instr.), Daś.; full-sounding, loud, Hariv.; burnt, W. (w.r. for *plushṭa*?); incubated, brooded over, MW.; n. growth, increase, gain, acquisition, wealth, property (esp. of children or cattle), RV.; VS.; AV. **–tā,** f., **-tva,** n. the being well-fed, a prosperous or thriving condition, MW. **–páti,** m. the lord of prosperity or welfare, AV. **–vipushṭa,** m. du. the well-fed and the ill-fed, Pañc. **Pushṭâṅga,** mf(*ī*)n. fat-limbed, well-fed, fat, Hit. **Pushṭârtha,** mfn. having a complete sense, fully intelligible (*a-p°*), Sāh. **Pushṭá-vat,** mfn. breeding or rearing cattle, RV.

Púshṭi (or *pushṭí*, esp. RV.), f. well-nourished condition, fatness, plumpness, growth, increase, thriving, prosperity, wealth, opulence, comfort, RV. &c. &c.; breeding, rearing (esp. of cattle; also with *paśoḥ*), RV.; TS.; ŚBr.; development, fulness, completeness, Sāh.; N. of a partic. ceremony performed for the attainment of welfare or prosperity, Cat.; N. of a daughter of Daksha and wife of Dharma, MBh.; Hariv.; Pur.; of the mother of Lobha, MārkP.; of a d° of Dhruva, VP.; of a d° of Paurṇamāsa, ib.; of a Śakti, Hcat.; one of the 16 Mātṛikās or divine mothers, L.; of a Kalā of the moon, BrahmaP.; of a Kalā of Prakṛiti and w° of Gaṇêśa, BrahmavP.; of a form of Dākshāyaṇī, MatsyaP.; of a form of Sarasvatī, W.; Physalis Flexuosa, L. **–kara,** mf(*ī*)n. nourishing, causing to thrive or grow, Var.; Suśr.; MārkP. **–karman,** n. a religious ceremony performed for the attainment of prosperity, GṛŚrS.; MBh.; n. a verse or formula relating to this cer°, Kauś. **–kānta,** m. 'beloved of Pushṭi,' N. of Gaṇêśa, L. **–kāma** (*pú°*), mfn. wishing for pr°, AV. &c. &c. **–gu** (*pú°*), m. N. of a man (said to be a Kāṇva and author of RV. viii, 51, 1). **–da,** mfn. yielding or causing pr°, nourishing, cherishing, Hariv.; Var.; Suśr.; m. pl. N. of a class of Pitṛis, MārkP.; (*ā*), f. N. of a drug (=*vṛiddhi*), L.; Physalis Flexuosa, L. **–dāvan,** mf(*arī*)n. = *-da*, mfn., Kauś. **–páti,** m. the lord of pr° or welfare, TS.; Br.; GṛŚrS. **–pravāha-maryādā-bheda,** m. N. of wk.; *-vivaraṇa*, n. N. of Comm. on it. **–mát,** mfn. thriving, abundant, prosperous, well off, RV. &c. &c.; containing the word *pushṭi* or any other derivative of √2. *push*, ŚBr.; ŚrS.; m. N. of a prince, VP. **–mati,** m. N. of an Agni, MBh. **–mārga,** m. 'the way of well-being,' N. of the doctrine of a Vaishṇava sect founded by Vallabhâcārya, RTL. 134. **–m-bharā,** mfn. bringing prosperity (said of Pūshan), RV. **–līlā-ṭīkā,** f. N. of wk. **–várdhana,** mfn. increasing pr° or welfare, RV. &c. &c.; m. a cock, L. **–śrāddha,** n. N. of a partic. Śrāddha, VP. **Pushṭicchu,** mfn. desirous of pr° or w°, KātyŚr.

Pushṭika, m. N. of a poet, Cat.; (*ā*), f. a bivalve shell, an oyster (prob. w.r. for *puṭikā*).

Pushṭy-artha, n. N. of a Śrāddha ('for health and well-being of body'), RTL. 305.

Púshpa, n. (for *pushka*?) a flower, blossom (ifc. f. *ā*, in names of plants oftener *ī;* cf. Pāṇ. iv, 1, 64, Vārtt. 1), AV. &c. &c.; the menstrual flux, Suśr.; a partic. disease of the eye, albugo, Suśr.; a spot on the nails and teeth, Car.; (in dram.) gallantry, politeness, declaration of love, Daśar.; Sāh.; Pratāp.; N. of a Sāman, TāṇḍBr.; Lāṭy.; of a book, Divyâv.; a kind of perfume, L.; the vehicle of Kubera, L.; blooming, expanding, L.; m. a topaz, R.; N. of a serpent-demon, MBh.; of a son of Ślishṭi, Hariv.; of a son of Śaṅkha, ib. (C. *pushya*); of a Bodhi-sattva (?), Lalit.; of a mountain, MārkP.; of a book (prob. =*pushpa-sūtra*), Divyâv.; (*ā*), f. N. of the town Campā, L. **–karaṇḍa** or °**ḍaka,** n. 'flower-basket,' N. of a grove near Avantī or Oujein (also °*dôdyāna*, n., Mṛicch.) **–karaṇḍinī,** f. N. of Oujein (cf. prec.), L. **–kárṇa,** mfn. having a f° (-shaped mole) in the ear, TS. **–kāra,** m. N. of the author of the Pushpa-sūtra, L. **–kāla,** m. 'f°-time,' the spring, Var.; the time of the menses, Suśr. **–kāsīsa** (Suśr.), °**saka** (L.), n. green or black sulphate of iron. **–kīṭa,** m. 'f°-insect,' a large bee, L. **–ketana,** m. 'characterized by f°s,' the god of love, L. **–ketu,** m. id., MBh.; vitriol used as a collyrium, Caurap.; calx of brass, W.; N. of a Buddha, L.; of a prince of Pushpa-bhadra, HPariś. **–gaṇḍikā,** f. N. of a kind of farce in which men act as women and women as men, Bhar.; Sāh. ('contrary purpose or effort of man and woman,' W.) **–giri,** m. 'flower-mountain,' N. of a mythical m° (the favourite resort of Varuṇa), W. **–gṛiha,** n. 'f°-house,' a conservatory, R. **–granthana,** n. wearing a wreath or garland of f°s, Vet. **–ghātaka,** m. 'f°-destroyer,' the bamboo (whose stem is said to decay after the plant has flowered), L. **–caya,** m. a quantity of f°s, W.; gathering f°s, ib. **–cāpa,** m. a bow of f°s, the bow of the god of love, Kālid.; the g° of l°, Kathās. **–cāmara,** m. 'having f°s for a chowrie,' Artemisia Indica or Pandanus Odoratissimus, L. **–cintāmaṇi,** m. N. of wk. **–cūla,** m. 'f°-crested,' N. of a man, HPariś.; (*ā*), f. N. of a woman, ib. **–ja,** mfn. 'f°-born,' derived or coming from f°s (*-jaṃ rajaḥ*, pollen, Sāh.); m. the juice of f°s, L.; (*ā*), f. N. of a river rising in the Vindhya mountains, MārkP. **–jāti,** f. 'f°-born,' N. of a river rising in the Malaya mountains, VP. **–da,** m. 'f°-giving,' a tree, L. **–daṇshṭra,** m. 'having f°s for fangs,' N. of a serpent-demon, MBh. **–danta,** m. 'f°-toothed,' N. of Śiva, R.; of an attendant of Śiva, MBh.; of an attendant of Vishṇu, BhP.; (also *-ka*) of a Gandharva (author of the Mahimnaḥ Stavaḥ), Cat.; of a Vidyā-dhara, L.; of a serpent-demon, L.; (with Jainas) of the 9th Arhat of present Avasarpiṇī; of a partic. being, Hcat.; of the elephant of the north-west quarter, ib.; of the mountain Śatruṃ-jaya, Śatr.; (du.) sun and moon, ib.; (*ī*), f. N. of a Rākshasī, Buddh.; n. N. of a temple, Kathās.; of a palace, Buddh.; of a gate, Hariv.; *-tīrtha*, n. N. of a Tīrtha, SkandaP.; *-bhid*, m. N. of Śiva, L. (prob. w. r. for *pūsha-danta-bhid*); *-vat*, mfn. one who has flowered teeth, Hcat.; °*tânvaya*, m. an elephant with partic. marks (descended from the race of Pushpa-danta), Gal. **–dāman,** n. a garland of f°s, Śṛiṅgār.; a kind of metre, Col. **–drava,** m. the juice of f°s, L.; an infusion of f°s (as rose-water &c.), L. **–druma,** m. a tree which bears f°s; *-kusumita-mukuṭa*, m. 'having a flowery diadem like a tree in bloom,' N. of a Gandharva-rāja, L. **–dha,** m. the offspring of an out-caste Brāhman, Mn. x, 21. **–dhanus** and **-dhanvan,** m. 'armed with a bow of f°s,' N. of the god of love, Kāv. **–dhāraṇa,** m. 'f°-bearer,' N. of Kṛishṇa, MBh. **–dhvaja,** m. = *-ketana*, L. **–nāṭaka,** m., v.l. for *-baṭuka*. **–nikara,** m. throwing f°s, W.; a multitude of f°s, MW. **–niksha,** m. 'f°-kissing,' a bee, L. **–niryāsa** and °**saka,** m. exudation or juice of f°s, L. **–netra,** n. 'f°-tube,' a kind of catheter, Suśr. **–ṃ-dhaya,** m. 'f°-sucking,' a bee, L. **–nyāsa,** m. an offering of f°s, W. **–paṭa,** m. flowered cloth, Mṛicch., Sch. **–pattra,** m. 'f°-feathered,' a kind of arrow, L. **–pattrin,** mfn. having f°s for arrows (said of the bow of Kāma-deva), W. **–patha,** m. (L.), **-padavī,** f. (Hāsy.) 'course of the menses,' the vulva. **–pāṇḍu,** m. a species of serpent, Suśr. **–puṭa,** m. a cup or bag filled with f°s, L.; the hands arranged in the shape of the calyx of a f°, Cat.; (in music) a partic. position in dancing. **–pura,** n. (Ragh. &c.), **-purī,** f. (Daś.) N. of the city Pāṭali-putra or Palibothra. **–peśala,** mfn. as delicate as a f°, Kathās. **–pracaya,** m. plucking f°s (to steal them), Pāṇ. iii, 3, 60. **–pracāya,** m. plucking or gathering f°s, ib.; °*yikā*, f. id., Uṇ. ii, 32, Sch. (*tava pushpa-pracāyikā*, it is thy turn to gather f°s, Pāṇ. vi, 2, 74, Sch.) **–1.-phala,** m. Feronia Elephantum, L.; Benincasa Cerifera, L. **–2.-phala,** n. f°s and fruits, MBh.; *-druma*, m. pl. trees bearing f°s and fr°s, Ragh.; *-vat*, mfn. bearing f°s and fr°s, Suśr. **–baṭuka,** m. a courtier, gallant, Cat. (v.l. *-nāṭaka*). **–bali,** m. an oblation of f°s, MārkP. **–bāṇa,** m. 'f°-arrowed,' the god of love; *-vilāsa*, m. N. of a poem (attributed to a certain Kālidāsa). **–bhaṅga,** m. a festoon of f°s ('treading on f°s,' Sch.), MW. **–bhadra,** m. 'beautiful with f°s,' a kind of pavilion with 62 columns, Vāstuv.; N. of a man, Mṛicch.; n. N. of a city, HPariś.; (*ā*), f. N. of a river, BhP. **–bhadraka,** n. N. of a partic. wood, BhP. **–bhava,** mfn. being or contained in f°s; m. the nectar of f°s, W. **–bhājana,** n. a f°-basket, Śak. **–bhūti,** m. 'essence of f°s,' N. of a prince, Hcar. **–bhūshaṇa,** n. 'ornament of f°s,' N. of a Nāṭaka, Sāh. **–bhūshita,** n. 'adorned with f°s,' N. of a Prakaraṇa, ib. **–bherôtsa** (?), m. N. of a man, Buddh. **–mañjarikā,** f. a species of creeper, L. ('blue lotus,' W.) **–maya,** mf(*ī*)n. made or consisting of f°s, flowery, MBh.; Kāv. **–māṭham,** ind. (with √*math*) to crush like a f°, Bālar. **–mālā,** f. a garland of f°s, R.; N. of a Dik-kanyā (s.v.), Pārśvan.; N. of a poem and of another wk. (on f°s to be used or avoided in the worship of deities); °*la-kathā*, f. N. of wk., Pañcad.; °*lā-maya*, mf(*ī*)n. consisting of f°-garlands, Hcat.; °*lin*, mfn. wearing a f°-g°, Jātak. **–māsa** or **-māsa,** m. 'f°-month,' the spring, R. **–mitra,** m. (v.l. *pushya-m°*) N. of a king (according to the Brāhmanical account, a general of the last Maurya dynasty and father of prince Agni-mitra, or according to Buddhists, a king, the successor of Pushya-dharman), Mālav.; Pur.; Buddh. (cf IW. 167, n. 2); of another king, VP.; *-sabhā*, f. the court of king P°, Pāṇ. i, 1, 68, Vārtt. 7, Pat. **–megha,** m. a cloud raining f°s; °*ghī-√kṛi*, to turn into a cl° r° f°s, Megh. **–yamaka,** n. a Yamaka (s.v.) of the final syllables of all lines of a stanza, e.g. Bhaṭṭ. x, 14. **–rakta,** mfn. red as a f°, Megh.; dyed red with vegetable colour, W.; m. Hibiscus Phoeniceus, L. **–racana,** n. making f°s into a garland (one of the 64 arts or Kalās), Gal. **–rajas,** n. 'f°-dust,' pollen; (esp.) saffron, L. **–ratha,** m.

'f°-chariot,' a car for travelling or for pleasure, R.; Hcat. — **rasa** (or °*sâhvaya*), m. (having the name) f°-juice, the nectar or honey of f°s, L. — **rāga**, m. 'f°-hued,' a topaz, Var. — **rāja**, m. 'f°-king (?),' id., L. — **reṇu**, m. 'f°-dust,' pollen, Ragh. — **rocana**, m. Mesua Roxburghii, L. — **lāva**, m. a f°-gatherer or garland-maker (also °*vin*), L.; (*ī*), f. a female f°-gatherer, Megh. — **liksha**, m. 'f°-licker,' a bee, W. (cf. *-niksha*). — **lipi**, f. 'f°-writing,' N. of a partic. style of writing, Lalit. — **lih**, m. (nom. *ṭ*) a large black bee, W. — **līlā**, f. 'f°-sport,' N. (of a woman?), Cat. — 1. -**vat** (*púshpa-*), mfn. having f°s or decorated with f°s, flowery, blooming, RV. &c. &c.; m. N. of a Daitya, MBh.; of a man, Saṃskārak.; of a prince, Hariv.; Pur.; of a mountain in Kuśa-dvīpa, MBh.; (du.) sun and moon, Bālar.; Gaṇit. (perhaps fr. *-vanta*); (*ī*), f. (a woman) having the menses, L.; (a cow) longing for the bull, BhP., Sch.; N. of a sacred bathing-place, MBh. — 2. -**vat**, ind. like a f°, Bhartṛ. — **vana**, n. N. of a mountain; *-māhātmya*, n. N. of wk. — **vartman**, m. 'f°-path,' N. of Dru-pada, Hcar. — **varsha**, n. 'f°-rain,' f°s showered upon a hero on any great occasion, Ragh. (also °*shaṇa*, MW.); m. N. of a mountain, BhP. — **vahā**, f. 'carrying f°s,' N. of a river, ib. — **vāṭikā** (Kuval.), -**vāṭī** (Pañc.), f. a f°-garden. — **vāhana**, m. 'having a flowery car,' N. of a king of Pushkara, AgP. — **vāhinī**, f. (= *-vahā*) N. of a river, Hariv. — **vicitrā**, f. N. of a metre, L. — **viśikha**, m. = *-bāṇa*, Alaṃkārav. — **vṛiksha**, m. a tree bearing blossoms, L. — **vṛishṭi**, f. = *-varsha*, n., Ratnâv. — **veṇī**, f. a chaplet or garland of f°s, R.; N. of a river, MBh. — **śakaṭikā**, f. a voice coming from heaven; *-nimitta-jñāna*, n. knowledge of the omens which result from heavenly voices (one of the 64 arts or Kalās), BhP., Sch. — **śakaṭī**, f. (L.) and *-jñāna*, n. (Gal.) = prec. — **śakalin**, m. 'having f°-like scales,' a kind of serpent, Suśr. — **śakuna**, m. 'f°-bird,' Phasianus Gallus, MBh. (v. l.) — **śayyā**, f. a couch of f°s, Śak. — **śara**, m. = *-bāṇa*, L.; °*râsana*, m. = *-dhanus*, Vcar. — **śilī-mukha**, m. = *-bāṇa*, Prasannar. — **śūnya**, m. 'f°less,' Ficus Glomerata, L. — **śekhara**, m. a garland of f°s, Kathās. — **śrī-garbha**, m. 'filled with the beauty of f°s,' N. of a Bodhi-sattva, L. — **samaya**, m. 'f°-season,' the spring, L. — **sādhāraṇa**, m. 'common time for f°s,' id., L. — **sāyaka**, m. = *-bāṇa*, Dhūrtas. — **sāra**, m. the nectar or honey of f°s, L. (*-sudhā-nidhi*, m. N. of wk.); (*ā*), f. holy basil, BrahmavP. — **sitā**, f. 'white like f°s,' a kind of sugar, Bhpr. — **sūtra**, n. N. of a Sūtra work (ascribed to Gobhila or to Vara-ruci) on the change of Ṛiks into Sāmans; *-bhāshya*, n. N. of Comm. on it. — **saurabhā**, f. 'smelling like f°s,' Methonica Superba, L. — **snāna**, n., v.l. for *pushya-sn°*. — **sraj**, f. a garland of f°s, Kāv. — **sveda**, m. = *-sāra*, L. — **hārin**, mfn. stealing or taking away f°s, Pāṇ. vi, 2, 79, Sch. — **hāsa**, m. 'smiling with f°s,' a f°-garden, Hariv.; N. of Vishṇu, ib.; of a man, L.; (*ā*), f. a woman during menstruation, L. — **hīna**, mfn. f°less, not flowering, L.; (*ā*), f. a woman past child-bearing, L.; Ficus Glomerata, L. **Pushpâkara**, mfn. rich in f°s, flowery; m. (with *māsa*) the flowery month, spring, Vikr.; *-deva*, m. N. of a poet, Cat. **Pushpâgama**, m. 'f°-advent,' the spring, Ṛitus. **Pushpâgra**, n. 'f°-point,' a pistil, Vām. **Pushpâjīva** and °**vin**, m. 'living by f°s,' a gardener, florist, garland-maker, L. **Pushpâñjana**, n. calx of brass employed as a collyrium, L. **Pushpâñjali**, m. two handfuls of f°s, L.; N. of sev. wks. (also *-stotra* and °*lyashṭaka*, n.); mfn. presenting f°s or a nosegay in both hands opened and hollowed, W. **Pushpâṇḍa** and °**ḍaka**, m. a kind of rice, Gal. **Pushpânana**, m. 'f°-faced,' N. of a Yaksha, MBh. **Pushpânuga**, n. a powder promoting menstruation, Car. **Pushpânta**, mfn. perishing after the blossom (?), SāmavBr. **Pushpâpaṇa**, m. a flower-market, Pañcad. **Pushpâpīḍa**, m. 'chaplet of f°s,' N. of a Gandharva, Śukas. **Pushpâbhikīrṇa**, mfn. strewed with f°s, Lalit.; m. a kind of spotted snake, Suśr. **Pushpâbhisheka**, m. = °*pa-snāna*, Var. **Pushpâmbu**, n. the honey or nectar of f°s, L. **Pushpâmbhas**, n. f°-water, N. of a sacred bathing-place, MBh. **Pushpâyudha**, m. 'f°-armed,' the god of love, Kāv. **Pushpârāma**, m. a f°-garden, Kathās. **Pushpârṇa**, m. 'f°-stream,' N. of a son of Vatsara and Svar-vīthi, BhP. **Pushpârpaṇa**, n. N. of wk. **Pushpâvakīrṇa**, m. 'strewed with f°s,' N. of a prince of the Kiṃnaras, Kāraṇḍ. **Pushpâvacaya**, m. gathering f°s, W. (cf. Vām. v, 2, 42); °*cāyikā*, f. the g° of f°s (a kind of play or sport), Cat.; °*cāyin*, m. g° f°s, a f°-gatherer, W. **Púshpā-vat**, mfn. = 1. *púshpa-vat*, TS.; (*ī*), f. N. of a town, Cat. **Pushpâvali-vanarāji-kusumitâbhijña**, m. 'knowing the season of the flowering of the rows of f°s and of the forest-trees,' N. of a Buddha, Lalit. (v.l. *pushpa-bali-v°*). **Pushpâśin**, mfn. eating f°s, Vishṇ. **Pushpâsava**, m. a decoction of f°s, R.; Ṛitus.; honey, L. **Pushpâsāra**, m. = °*pa-vṛishṭi*, Megh. **Pushpâstaraka**, m. (Cat.), °*raṇa*, n. (BhP., Sch.) the art of strewing f°s (one of the 64 Kalās). **Pushpâstra**, m. = °*pâyudha*, L. **Pushpâhara**, mfn. one who takes or plucks f°s, W. **Pushpâhvā**, f. Anethum Sowa, L. **Pushpêshu**, m. = °*pa-bāṇa*, Kathās. **Pushpôtkaṭā**, f. N. of a Rākshasī (the mother of Rāvaṇa and Kumbha-karṇa), MBh. **Pushpôttara**, m. or n. (with Jainas) N. of a partic. heaven, W. **Pushpôdakā**, f. 'having f°s for water,' N. of a river in the lower world, MBh. **Pushpôdbhava**, m. 'sprung from f°s,' N. of a man, Daś. **Pushpôdyāna**, n. a f°-garden, MW. **Pushpôpagama**, mfn. bearing f°s, Vishṇ. **Pushpôpajīvin**, m. = *pushpâjīvin*, R.

Pushpaka, m. a kind of serpent, Suśr.; N. of a mountain, MārkP.; (*ikā*), f. the tartar of the teeth, L.; the mucus of the tongue, Gal.; the mucus of the glans penis or urethra, L.; the last words of a chapter (which state the subject treated therein), L.; n. (rarely m.) N. of the self-moving aerial car of Kubera (also *-vimāna*, n.; it was carried off by the demon Rāvaṇa and constantly used by him till he was slain by Rāma-candra, who then employed the car to transport himself and Sītā back to Ayodhyā), MBh.; R. &c.; N. of a forest, Hariv.; calx of brass or green vitriol used as a collyrium, L.; a bracelet (esp. one of jewels), L.; a small earthen fire-place or furnace on wheels, L.; a cup or vessel of iron, L.; a partic. disease of the eyes (albugo), L.

Pushpāya, Nom. Ā. °*yate*, to become a flower, Kulârṇ.

Pushpita, mf(*ā*)n. flowered, bearing flowers, blooming, in bloom, MBh.; Kāv. &c.; having marks like flowers, variegated, spotted, (said of bad teeth), Car.; exhaling an odour indicative of approaching death, ib.; completely manifested, fully developed, Kathās.; florid, flowery (as speech), Bhag.; m. N. of a Buddha, Lalit.; (*ā*), f. a menstruous woman, L. — **palāśa-pratima**, mfn. resembling a Butea Frondosa in flower, MW. **Pushpitâksha**, mfn. having spots (albugo) on the eye, VarBṛS., Sch.; °*kshi-tva* (!), n. ib. **Pushpitâgra**, mfn. covered at the extremities with flowers or blossoms, MBh.; Gīt.; (*ā*), f. N. of a metre.

Pushpitaka, m. N. of a mountain, Hariv.

Pushpin, mfn. bearing flowers, flowering, blossoming, RV. &c. &c.; florid, flowery (as speech), BhP.; (*iṇī*), f. (a woman) in menstruation or desirous of sexual intercourse, Kāv.; BhP.

Pushpya, Nom. P. °*yati* (p. Ā. °*yamāṇa*) to bear flowers, flower, blossom, bloom, MBh.; Kāv. &c. (cf. √*pushp*, °*pyati* in Dhātup. xxvi, 15).

Púshya, n. nourishment (pl.), Car.; the blossom or flower i.e. the uppermost or best of anything (cf. Gk. ἄνθος; Lat. *flos*), RV.; (*pushyà*), m. N. of the 6th (or 8th, but see *nakshatra*) lunar asterism (also called Sidhya and Tishya), AV. &c. &c.; (= *-yoga*), the conjunction of the moon with Pushya, Mn.; MBh. &c.; N. of the month Pausha, VP.; of the Kali-yuga or fourth age, W.; of one of the 24 mythical Buddhas, MWB. 136, n. 1; of various princes, VP.; n. N. of a Sāman, ĀrshBr.; (*pushyā́*), f. a species of plant, AV.; the asterism Pushya, L. — **dharman**, m. N. of a prince, Buddh. — **netra**, mfn. having the asterism Pushya for a guide, Pāṇ. v, 4, 116, Vārtt. 2, Pat. — **mitra**, m. N. of a prince, VP.; pl. his dynasty, ib. (cf. *pushpa-m°*). — **yaśas**, m. N. of a man with the patr. Audavraji, L. — **ratha**, m. the asterism P° as a car, Śiś.; a carriage for pleasure, ib. (cf. *pushpa-r°*). — **lipi**, v.l. for *pushpa-l°*. — **snāna**, n. a partic. ceremony of purification performed while the moon is passing through the asterism P°, Var. (v.l. *pushpa-s°*). **Pushyâbhisheka**, m. id., ib. (v.l. *pushpâbh°*).

पुष्कर *pushkara*, °*kala*. See pp. 638, 639.

पुष्कलेत्र *pushkaletra*, m. N. of a village, Rājat.

पुष्कश *pushkaśa*, °*kasa*, v.l. for *pukkaśa*, *pulkasa*, q.v.

पुष्किरिणी *pushkiriṇī*, f. often for *pushkariṇī*, Divyâv.

पुष्पलक *pushpalaka*, m. a post, pin, stake, peg, wedge, L. (cf. *pushkalaka*).

पुप्फस *pushpasa*, m. the lungs, L. (cf. *pupphusa*, *phupphusa*).

पुष्पाणनाड *pushpāṇanāḍa*, m. N. of a Grāma, Rājat.

पुष्यलक *pushyalaka*, w. r. for *pushkalaka*.

पुस् *pus*, cl. 10. P. *posayati*, to discharge, emit, Dhātup. xxxii, 92.

पुस्त् *pust*, cl. 10. P. *pustayati*, to respect or disrespect (?), Dhātup. xxxii, 52; to bind, Vop. (cf. √*bust*).

पुस्त *pusta*, m. n. (g. *ardharcâdi*) working in clay, modelling, Kathās.; (also *ā*, f.) a manuscript, book, Var. (cf. below); Hcat.; mfn. covered, filled, W. — **karman**, n. plastering, painting, W. — **maya**, mf(*ī*)n. formed of metal or wood, wrought in clay, modelled, Suśr. — **vārtta**, m. one who lives by books or makes books, VarBṛS.

Pustaka, m. or n. a protuberant ornament, boss (see below); mf(*ikā*)n. a manuscript, book, booklet, Hariv.; Kāv.; Var. &c. — **kara**, m. an embosser, VarBṛS., Sch. **Pustakâgāra**, n. 'book-room,' a library, MW. **Pustakâstaraṇa**, n. the wrapper of a manuscript, Hcat.

पू 1. *pū*, cl. 9. P. Ā. (Dhātup. xxxi, 12) *punā́ti*, *punītè* (3. pl. Ā. *punáte*, AV., *punatè*, RV.; 2. sg. Impv. P. *punīhí*, RV. &c., *punāhí*, SV.); cl. 1. Ā. (xxii, 70) *pávate* (of P. only Impv. *-pava*, RV. ix, 19, 3, and p. gen. pl. *pavatām*, Bhag. x, 31; p. Ā. *punāná* below, *pávamāna*, see p. 610, col. 3; 1. sg. Ā. *punīshe*, RV. vii, 85, 1; pf. *pupuvuḥ*, °*ve*, Br.; *ápupot*, RV. iii, 26, 8; aor. *apāvishuḥ*, Subj. *apavishṭa*, RV.; fut. *pavishyati*, *pavitā*, Gr.; ind. p. *pūtvā́*, AV.; *pūtvī́*, RV.; *pavitvā*, Gr.; *-pūya* and *-pāvam*, Br. &c.; inf. *pavitum*, Br.), to make clean or clear or pure or bright, cleanse, purify, purge, clarify, illustrate, illume (with *sáktum* 'to cleanse from chaff, winnow;' with *krátum* or *manīshā́m* 'to enlighten the understanding;' with *hiraṇyam* 'to wash gold'), RV. &c. &c.; (met.) to sift, discriminate, discern; to think of or out, invent, compose (as a hymn), RV.; AV.; (Ā. *pávate*) to purify one's self, be or become clear or bright; (esp.) to flow off clearly (said of the Soma), RV.; to expiate, atone for, ib. vii, 28, 4; to pass so as to purify; to purify in passing or pervading, ventilate, RV. &c. (cf. √*pav*): Pass. *pūyáte*, to be cleaned or washed or purified; to be freed or delivered from (abl.), Mn.; MBh. &c.: Caus. *paváyati* or *pāvayati* (ep. also °*te*; aor. *apīpavat*, Gr.; Pass. *pāvyate*, Kāv.), to cleanse, purify, TS.; Br. &c.: Desid. *pupūshati*, *pipavishate*, Gr.: Desid. of Caus. *pipāvayishati*, Gr. [Cf. Gk. πῦρ; Umbr. *pir*; Germ. *Feuer*; Eng. *fire*.]

Punāná, mfn. being clear or bright or purified, RV. (also with *tanvàm* or *tanvā̀*); washing off, destroying (sin), RV. vi, 66, 4; pouring forth i.e. showing (brightness); ii, 3, 5.

Punitá, mfn. cleaned, purified, MBh.

2. **Pū**, mfn. cleansing, purifying (ifc.; cf. *anna-*, *uda-*, *ghṛita-* &c.)

1. **Pūtá**, mfn. (for 2. see √*pūy*, p. 641) cleaned, purified, pure, clear, bright, RV. &c. &c.; m. (L.) a conch-shell; white Kuśa grass; Flacourtia Sapida; du. the buttocks (cf. *puta*); (*ā*), f. a species of Dūrvā grass, L; N. of Durgā, L. [Cf. Lat. *pūtus*, *pūrus*.] — **kratā** (*pūtá-*), f. N. of a woman, RV. (cf. next). — **kratāyī**, f. the wife of Pūta-kratu, Pāṇ. iv, 1, 36; the wife of Indra, Uṇ. i, 78, Sch. — **kratu** (*pūtá-*), m. 'pure-minded,' N. of a man, RV. (cf. Pāṇ. iv, 1, 36); N. of Indra, Uṇ. i, 78, Sch. — **gandha**, m. a species of plant (= *varvara*), L. — **tṛiṇa**, n. white Kuśa grass, L. — **daksha** (*pūtá-*), mfn. pure-minded (also °*kshas*), RV.; m. N. of an Āṅgirasa (author of RV. viii, 83). — **dru**,

m. 'pure tree,' Butea Frondosa, L. — **dhānya**, n. 'winnowed grain,' sesamum, L.; mf(*ā*)n. containing w° g°, AVPaipp. — **pattrī**, f. holy basil, L. — **pāpa** or -**pāpman**, mfn. purified or freed from sin, MBh. — **phala**, m. 'pure-fruited,' the bread-fruit tree, L. — **bándhana**, mf(*ī*)n. attached to that which is p°, RV. — **bandhu** (*pūtá*-), mfn. of p° descent or noble race, RV. — **bhṛit**, m. a kind of vessel which receives the Soma juice after it has been strained, VS.; TS.; Br. — **mati**, m. 'pure-minded,' N. of Śiva, Śivag. — **mūrti**, mfn. having one's form or body cleansed, pure, purified, Rājat. — **yavam**, ind. at the time of winnowing barley, g. *tishṭhadgv-ādi* (cf. *pūyamāna-y*°). **Pūtâtman**, mfn. pure-minded (°*ma-tā*, f.), Hariv.; m. N. of Vishṇu, RTL. 106; a saint, ascetic; a man purified by ablution, W.

1. **Pūti**, f. (for 2. see col. 3) purity, purification, ŚBr.; MBh. — **dhānya**, w.r. for *pūta-dh*° (above).

Pūtríma, mfn. purified, pure, clean, AV.

Pūna, mfn. destroyed (= *vi-nashṭa*), Pāṇ. viii, 2, 44, Vārtt. 3, Pat. **Pūnā-devī**, f. N. of a woman, Cat.

Pūni, f. purifying, cleansing (?), Pāṇ. viii, 2, 44, Vārtt. 1, Pat. (v.l. *dhūni*).

Pūyámāna, mfn. being cleansed or purified &c., RV.; m. N. of a man, L. — **yavam**, ind. at the time of winnowing barley, g. *tishṭhadgv-ādi* (cf. *pūta-y*°).

पू 3. *pū*, mfn. (√1. *pā*) drinking (see *agre-pū*).

पुःकाम्य *puḥ-kāmya*. See p. 636, col. 1.

पूग *pūga*, m. (ifc. f. *ā*; cf. *puñja*) any assemblage or combination or body of persons, a multitude, number, mass, quantity (in one place n.), ŚāṅkhBr.; Mn.; MBh. &c.; a country court or an assembly of townsmen, IW. 296, n. 1; disposition, property, nature, W.; the Areca Catechu, called betel-nut tree (n. its nut), Var.; Kāv.; Suśr.; = *kaṇṭaki-vṛiksha*, L.; = *chanda* or *chandas*, L.; = *bhāva*, L. — **kṛita**, mfn. made into a heap, gathered, collected, Pāṇ. vi, 2, 46, Sch. — **khaṇḍa**, m. or n. a piece of Areca-nut, Rājat. — **pātra**, n. a betel-box or = next, L. — **pīṭha**, n. 'betel-receptacle,' spitting-pot, spittoon (the Areca-nut, when chewed with betel, producing saliva), L. — **pushpikā**, f. Areca-nut and flowers (presented to the principal guests at a marriage festival), L. — **pota**, m. a young Areca-tree, BhP. — **phala**, n. 'fruit of the Areca tree,' commonly called 'betel-nut,' Var.; Suśr. — **yajña**, m. a sacrifice offered for a number of persons; °*ñiya*, mfn. relating to it, MBh. — **roṭa** or -**voṭa** (?), m. Phoenix Paludosa, L. — **vaira**, n. enmity against a number of persons, MBh.

Pūgatitha, mfn. numerous, manifold, Pāṇ. v, 2, 52 (cf. *gaṇat*°, *bahut*°).

Pūgī, f. the Areca Catechu (producing a nut chewed with betel-leaf). — **phala**, n. the Areca-nut, Subh. — **latā**, f. the Areca-palm, Kād.

Pūgya, mfn. belonging to a multitude; (ifc.) belonging to the troop or band of, g. *vargyâdi*.

पूज् *pūj*, cl. 10. P. (Dhātup. xxxii, 100) *pūjayati* (ep. also Ā. °*te* and cl. 1. P. *pūjati*; pf. *pupūjire*, MBh.; aor. *apūpujat*, Gr.; ind. p. *pūjayitvā*, Mn. &c.; *pūjya*, MBh.), to honour, worship, revere, respect, regard, ĀśvGṛ.; Mn.; MBh. &c.; to honour or present with (instr.), Mn. vii, 203; to initiate, consecrate, Vet.

Pūjaka, mf(*ikā*)n. honouring, respecting, worshipping, a worshipper (with gen. or ifc.), Mn.; MBh. &c. **Pūjana**, n. reverencing, honouring, worship, respect, attention, hospitable reception, ib. (-*mālikā*, f. N. of wk.); an object of reverence, Pāṇ. viii, 1, 67; (*ī*), f. = °*janīyā*, f., MBh.; Hariv.; a hen-sparrow, L. **Pūjanīya**, mfn. to be revered or worshipped, venerable, honourable (compar. -*tara*; superl. -*tama*), MBh.; R. &c.; (*ā*), f. N. of a female bird (a friend of king Brahma-datta), Hariv. **Pūjayāna**, mfn. honouring, reverencing, MW. **Pūjayitavya**, mfn. = °*janīya*, Nir.; Hit. **Pūjayitṛi**, mfn. honouring, worshipping, a worshipper, MBh.

Pūjā, f. honour, worship, respect, reverence, veneration, homage to superiors or adoration of the gods, GṛS.; Mn.; MBh. &c. — **kara**, mfn. paying respect or showing homage to (comp.), Pañc. — **karman**, mfn. denoting the action of honouring, meaning 'to honour,' Nir. — **kāṇḍa**, n., -**krama**, m., -**khaṇḍa**, m. or n. N. of wks. — **gṛiha**, n. 'house of worship,' a temple, Dhūrtan. — **nyāsa-vidhi**, m. N. of wk. — **paṭṭaka**, n. a deed or document of honour, Lokapr. — **pathya-mālā**, f., -**paddhati**, f., -**prakāśa**, m., -**pradīpa**, m., -**ratna**, n., -**ratnâkara**, m. N. of wks. — °**rha** (°*jârha*), mfn. worthy of reverence or honour, venerable, respectable, Kathās. — **vat**, mfn. enjoying honour or distinction, Śaṃk. — **vidhi**, m. paying respect, showing homage, L.; N. of wk. — **vaikalya-prâyaścitta**, n. N. of wk. — **satkāra**, m. = -*vidhi*, Ratnâv. — **sambhāra**, m. (Mālatīm.), °**jôpakaraṇa**, n. (Ratnâv.) the requisites for the worship or adoration of a god. °**jôpayogi-sāman**, n. pl. N. of wk.

Pūjita, mfn. honoured, received or treated respectfully, worshipped, adored, Mn.; MBh. &c.; honoured by (gen. or comp.; Pāṇ. ii, 2, 12) or on account of (comp.), Mn.; MBh. &c.; acknowledged, recommended, MBh.; Suśr.; frequented, inhabited, MBh.; consecrated, Kathās.; supplied with (comp.), MBh.; R.; m. a god, L.; n. N. of a place, Divyâv. — **pattra-phalā**, f. N. of a plant, L. — **pūjaka**, mfn. honouring the honoured, MBh.

Pūjila, mfn. = °*janīya*; m. a god, Uṇ. i, 57.

Pūjya, mfn. = °*janīya* (superl. -*tama*), Mn.; MBh. &c.; m. an honourable man, Car.; a father-in-law, L. — **tā**, f. (MBh.), or -**tva**, n. (MārkP.) venerableness, honourableness, the being entitled to honour. — **pāda**, m. N. of Deva-nandin, Cat. (°*da-caritra*, n. N. of wk.) — **pūjā**, f. honouring those worthy of honour (°*jā-vyatikrama*, m. neglecting to do so), Ragh.

पूण् *pūṇ*, cl. 10. P. *pūṇayati*, to collect or heap together, Dhātup. xxxii, 92 (v.l.); cf. *puṇ*, *pūl*.

पूत् *pūt*, ind. an onomat. expressive of blowing or hard breathing (prob. w.r. for *phūt*, *phut*, q.v.) — **kārī**, f. N. of Sarasvatī, L.; of the capital of the Nāgas or serpent race, W.

पूतन *pūtana*, m. a partic. class of demons or spirits (also = *vetāla*), Mālatīm.; Bālar.; SaddhP.; (*ā*), f., see next.

Pūtanā, f. N. of a female demon (said to cause a partic. disease in children, and to have offered her poisoned breast to the infant Kṛishṇa who seized it and sucked away her life; regarded also as one of the Mātṛis attending upon Skanda, and as a Yoginī), MBh.; Hariv.; Kāv.; Pur.; a kind of disease in a child (ascribed to the demon P°), W.; Terminalia Chebula, L.; a species of Valeriana, L.; w.r. for *pṛitanā*. — **keśa**, m., °**śī**, f. a species of plant, Car. — **tva**, n. the state or condition of Pūtanā, Kāraṇḍ. — **dūshaṇa**, m. 'P°-destroyer,' N. of Kṛishṇa, L. — **mokshaṇa-prastāva**, m. N. of ch. of BrahmavP. — **vidhāna**, n. N. of wk. — °**ri** (°*nâri*), -**sūdana** and -**han**, m. 'enemy, destroyer, slayer of P°,' N. of Kṛishṇa, L.

Pūtanāya, Nom. P. °*yati*, to represent Pūtanā, BhP.

Pūtanikā, f. the demon Pūtanā, Git.

पूतर *pūtara*, m. a partic. aquatic animal, Gaṇar. iv, 291 (applied to an insignificant or mean person = *adhama* and opp. to *kuñjara*), HPariś.

पूतुदारु *pūtu-dāru*, m. = *pūta-dru*, the tree Butea Frondosa, Kauś.

Pūtú-dru (AV.), **pūtu-dru** (TS.), m. the tree Acacia Catechu or Pinus Deodora; n. its fruit.

पूथिका *pūthikā* (?), f. a species of culinary plant, Suśr. (v.l. *pṛithukā* and *yūthikā*).

पूप *pūpa*, m. a cake, a sort of bread, MBh.; R. &c. (cf. *apūpa*). — **śālā**, f. a cake room, baker's shop, Mn. ix, 264 (prob. *apūpa-ś*°). **Pūpâshṭakā**, f. the 8th day of the wane of the moon after the day Āgrahāyaṇī, L.

Pūpalā (L.), °**likā** (Car.), or °**lī** (L.), f. a kind of sweet cake fried with ghee or oil, L.

Pūpālika, m. (Suśr.), °**likā** (ib.) and °**lī** (L.), f. id.

Pūnikā, f. id., L.

Pūpīya or **pūpya**, mfn., g. *apūpâdi*.

पूय् *pūy*, cl. 1. P. *pūyati* (TS.; ŚBr. &c.), Ā. *pūyate* (Dhātup. xiv, 13), to become foul or putrid, stink. [Cf. Zd. *pū*, *puiti*; Gk. πύον, πύθω; Lat. *pūs*, *pūteo*; Lith. *púti*; Goth. *fūls*; Germ. *faul*; Eng. *foul*.]

2. **Pūta**, mfn. (for 1. see √*pū*, p. 640) putrid, foul-smelling, stinking, L.

2. **Pūti**, mfn. (for 1. see col. 1) putrid, foul-smelling, stinking, fetid, ill-smelling, AV. &c. &c. (after a finite verb expressive of blame or censure, e.g. *pacati pūti* or *pūtiḥ*, Pāṇ. viii, 1, 69, Pat.); m. purulent matter, pus, MBh. ix, 2259; Guilandina Bonduc, Bhpr.; civet, L.; f. a stench, stink, W.; n. a species of grass, L. — **karaja** (!) and -**karañja**, m. Guilandina Bonduc, L. — **karṇa**, m. a disease of the ear with discharge of putrid matter, Suśr.; -*tā*, id., ib. — **karṇaka**, m. id., Suśr.; Guilandina Bonduc, L. (v.l. °*ṇika*). — **kāshṭha** and °**ṭhaka**, n. Pinus Deodora and Longifolia, L. — **kīṭa**, m. 'stinking insect,' a kind of insect, Suśr. — **kushmāṇḍāya**, Nom. (fr. *p°-kushmāṇḍa*) Ā. °*yate*, to resemble a rotten gourd i. e. be quite worthless, Sarvad.; °*dāyamāna-tva*, n. complete worthlessness, ib. — **khasha**, m. a kind of animal, Āpast. (cf. -*ghāsa*). — 1. -**gandhá**, m. fetid odour, stench, TS.; Mn.; Yājñ. — 2. -**gandha**, mfn. foul-smelling, stinking, L.; m. sulphur, L.; Terminalia Catappa, L.; (*ā*), f. Vernonia Anthelminthica, L.; tin, L. — **gandhi**, mfn. ill-smelling, fetid, MBh. (cf. Pāṇ. v, 4, 135). — **gandhika**, mfn. id., L.; (*ā*), f. Serratula Anthelminthica, L. — **ghāsa**, m. 'eating putrid food,' a species of animal living in trees, Suśr. — **tailā**, f. 'containing ill-smelling oil,' Cardiospermum Halicacabum, L. — **tva**, n. putrid state, stinking, Suśr. — **nasya**, n. a disease of the nose causing offensive breath, Suśr. (w.r. *pūta-n*°). — **nāsā-gada**, m. id., L. — **nāsika**, mfn. having a fetid nose, Yājñ. — **pattra**, m. 'having ill-smelling leaves,' a variety of Śyonāka, L. — **parṇa**, m. 'id.,' Pongamia Glabra, L. — **pushpikā**, f. 'having ill-smelling blossoms,' Citrus Medica, L. — **phalā** or °**lī**, f. 'bearing ill-smelling fruit,' Serratula Anthelminthica, L. — **bhāva**, m. putrid state, stench, Kap. — **mayūrikā**, f. Ocimum Villosum, L. — **māṇsa**, n. dead or decayed flesh, W. — **māsha**, m. N. of a man, ĀśvŚr. — **mukta**, m. or n. voiding excrement, L. — **mṛittika**, m. or n. 'having fetid soil,' N. of a hell, Mn.; Yājñ. — **meda**, m. Vachellia Farnesiana, L. — **rajjú**, f. a rotten cord, AV.; Kauś. — **vaktra**, mfn. 'fetid-mouthed,' one who has offensive breath, Yājñ.; -*tā*, f., Mn. — **vaya**, v.l. for -*ghāsa*, Suśr. — **vāta**, m. foul wind expelled from the bowels, BhP.; Aegle Marmelos, L. — **vṛiksha**, m. 'ill-smelling tree,' Calosanthes Indica, L. — **vraṇa**, n. a foul ulcer, MW. — **śapharī**, f. rotten fish, Kauś. — **śārijā** (?), f. a polecat, civet-cat, L. — **śṛiñjaya**, m. pl. N. of a people, VP. **Pūty-aṇḍa**, m. a partic. ill-smelling insect, MBh. (v.l.); a musk-deer, L.

Pūtika, mfn. foul, stinking, putrid, MBh.; m. = *pūtīka*, ĀśvŚr.; MBh.; Suśr.; Guilandina Bonduc, Bhpr.; (*ā*), f. Basella Cordifolia, L.; a white ant (w.r. for *puttikā*?), MBh.; Pañc.; n. ordure, excrement, W. **Pūtikā-mukha**, m. a bivalve shell, L. **Pūtikêśvara-tīrtha**, n. N. of a Tīrtha on the banks of the Revā or Narma-dā, ŚivaP.

Pūtīka, m. a species of plant serving as a substitute for the Soma plant (often explained by *rohisha*, perhaps Guilandina Bonduc), TS.; Br.; ŚrS; Suśr.; the polecat, civet-cat, L. (cf. *pūtika*).

Pūtī-karañja, v.l. for *pūti-k*°.

Pūya, m. n. purulent matter, pus, suppuration, discharge from an ulcer or wound, ŚBr. &c. &c. — **bhuj**, mfn. eating purulent carcasses, Mn. xii, 72. — **rakta**, m. (sc. *roga*) 'having purulent blood,' a kind of disease of the nose with discharge of p° blood, Suśr. — **vaha**, m. 'filthy-streamed,' N. of a partic. hell, VP. — **śoṇita**, n. purulent blood, ichor, Mn. iii, 180. **Pūyâbha**, n. 'resembling pus,' a kind of bloody-flux, L. **Pūyâri**, m. 'hostile to suppuration,' the Nimb tree, Azadirachta Indica (the leaves of which are used to produce dispersion or absorption of p° matter), L. **Pūyâlasa**, m. a partic. disease of the place of junction (*saṃdhi*) of the eye; suppuration at the joints, white swelling, Suśr. **Pūyôda**, m. 'having fetid water,' N. of a partic. hell (cf. *pūya-vaha*).

Pūyana, n. pus, discharge from a wound or sore, L.

पूर *pūra*, mfn. (√*pṛī*, Caus.) filling, making full (cf. *pāṇi*-); fulfilling, satisfying (cf. *kāma*-); m. the act of filling, fulfilling &c., Kāv.; Pur.; the swelling or rising of a river or of the sea, a large quantity of water, flood, stream (also met. = abundance, high degree, esp. ifc.), Kāv.; Suśr. &c.; a cake, R. (cf. *ghṛita-*); a kind of breath-exercise = *pūraka* below, BhP.; the cleansing of a wound, L. (cf. *pūraṇa*); the citron tree (= *bīja-pūra*), L.; (*ī*), f. N. of a woman, Cat.; n. a kind of incense, L.; bdellium, L.; mf(*ā*)n. a sort of unleavened cake fried with ghee or oil, W. (cf. *pūrikā* below). **Pūrâmla**, n. the fruit of Spondias Mangifera, L. **Pūrôtpīḍa**, m. excess or superabundance of water, Kathās.

Pūraka, mfn. filling, completing, fulfilling, satisfying (ifc. or with gen.; cf. Pāṇ. ii, 3, 70, Kāś.), Mn.; MBh. &c.; m. flood, stream, effusion, BhP.; (in arithm.) the multiplier; a ball of meal offered at the conclusion of the oblations to the Pitṛis, L. (also *-piṇḍa*, m., Kull. on Mn. v, 85); closing the right nostril with the forefinger and then drawing up air through the left and then closing the left nostril and drawing up air through the right (as a religious exercise), RTL. 402; the citron tree, L.; (*ikā*), f. a sort of cake, MBh.; Yājñ. (°*kâpūpa*); Bhpr. &c. — **kumbhaka-recaka**, m. pl. or n. pl. (?) inhaling and then retaining and then exhaling air, MW.

Pūraṇa, mf(*ī*)n. filling, completing, satisfying, causing, effecting, KātyŚr.; Saṃk.; Hariv.; drawing (a bow), MW.; m. 'completer,' N. of the masculine ordinal numbers from *dvitīya* upwards, Pāṇ. ii, 2, 11 &c.; a dam, bridge, L.; the sea, L.; a medicinal oil or embrocation, L.; N. of a man, ĀśvŚr.; (with the patr. *Vaiśvāmitra*) N. of the author of RV. x, 160; (*ī*), f. an ordinal number in the feminine gender, Pāṇ. v, 4, 116 &c.; Bombax Heptaphyllum, L.; (du.) the cross threads in weaving cloth, warp, Rājat.; N. of Durgā, MW.; of one of the two wives of the popular deity Ayenār, RTL. 219; (*pūr*°), n. the act or filling or filling up, puffing or swelling up, AV. &c. &c.; fulfilling, satisfying, Mālav.; furnishing, equipping, Var.; (with *dhanushaḥ*) drawing or bending a bow to the full, MBh.; R.; (in medic.) injection of fluids or supplying with food; (in astron.) the revolution of a heavenly body through its orbit, Sūryas.; (in arithm.) multiplication; rain, L.; a sort of cake, Bhpr.; Cyperus Rotundus, L.; the cross threads in weaving cloth, warp, L. — **kāśyapa**, m. N. of a man, Buddh. — **pariśishṭa**, n. N. of wk. — **pratyaya**, m. an affix forming an ordinal, Pāṇ., Sch. — **vyākhyā**, f. N. of Comm. on MānGṛ.

Pūraṇīya, mfn. to be filled up, to be supplied, Jaim., Sch.

Pūram, pūrayitvā. See √*prī*.

Pūrayitavya, mfn. to be filled or filled up, Pāṇ. vi, 3, 59; to be satisfied, Nir. vii, 23.

Pūrayitṛi, mfn. one who fills or fulfils or satisfies, Kāv.; m. N. of Vishṇu, MBh.; of Śiva, Śivag.

Pūrikā. See under *pūraka*.

Pūrita, mfn. filled, completed &c.; made full or strong, intensified (as a sound), MBh.; filled with wind, blown (as a conch), BhP.; multiplied, overspread, W.

Pūrin, mfn. filling, making full (ifc.), MBh.

Pūrṇá, mfn. filled, full, filled with or full of (instr. or gen. or comp.), RV. &c. &c.; abundant, rich, Kāv.; fulfilled, finished, accomplished, ended, past, ŚāṅkhGṛ.; MBh.; R. &c.; concluded (as a treaty), Rājat.; complete, all, entire, ŚāṅkhBr.; Mn.; MBh. &c.; satisfied, contented, R.; (ifc.) perfectly familiar with, Hcat.; drawn, bent to the full (as a bow), MBh.; Hariv.; (in augury) full-sounding, sonorous and auspicious (said of the cry of birds and beasts, opp. to *dīpta*, q.v.); uttering this cry, VarBṛS.; strong, capable, able, L.; selfish, self-indulgent, W.; m. a partic. form of the sun, Cat.; a kind of tree, R.; (in music) a partic. measure; N. of a Nāga, MBh.; of a Deva-gandharva, ib.; of a Buddhist ascetic, Lalit.; (*ā*), f. N. of the 15th Kalā of the month, BrahmaP.; of the 5th, 10th and 15th Tithis, Var.; N. of a woman, Vet.; (with Śāktas) of an authoress of Mantras, Cat.; of 2 rivers, VP.; n. fulness, plenty, abundance, AV.; TS.; water, Naigh. i, 12; the cipher or figure 0, Gaṇit. — **kaṇsa**, m. a full cup, L. — **kakud**, mfn. 'full-humped,' humpbacked, Pāṇ. v, 4, 146, Sch. — **kākud** or °**da**, mfn., Pāṇ. v, 4, 149. — **kāma**, mfn. one whose wishes are fulfilled, satisfied, Mcar.; *-tā*, f., MārkP. — **kāraṇa**, mfn. (ifc.) fulfilling, satisfying, BrahmavP. — **kūṭa**, m. a partic. class of birds, Var. — **kumbha**, m. (ifc. f. *ā*) a full cup or jar, (esp.) a cup full of water (also with *apām*), Mn.; Ragh.; a cup filled with holy water and used at the consecration of a king, W.; a partic. mode of fighting, MBh.; N. of a Dānava, Hariv. (v.l. *kumbha-karṇa*); m. or n. a hole (in a wall) of the shape of a water-jar, Mṛicch.; mf(*ā*)n. having a full pitcher, ŚāṅkhŚr. — **kośā**, f. 'having a full pod,' a species of plant, Var. — **koshṭhā**, f. a species of Cyperus, L. — **kha**, mfn. (prob.) having its axle-hole well greased (said of a waggon), SaṃhitUp. — **gabhasti** (*pūrṇá-*), mfn. one whose arms or hands are full (of wealth), RV. — **garbha**, mf(*ā*)n. one whose interior is well-filled, Bhpr.; (*ā*), f. pregnant, ready to bring forth, MW. — **giri**, m. N. of a place, Cat. — **candra**, m. the full moon, MBh.; R.; N. of a Bodhi-sattva, Buddh.; of an author, Cat.; *-nibhânana*, mf(*ā*)n. having a face like the full moon, Nal.; *-prâyaścitta-prakaraṇa*, n. N. of wk.; *-prabhā*, f. the lustre of the full moon, MW. — **cāttra**, n. a spindle wound round with yarn, Gobh. — **tā**, f. (Hariv.) and **-tva**, n. (Kathās.) fulness. — **tūṇa**, mfn. full-quivered, having the quiver full, MW. — **darvá**, n. a ceremony with a full ladle, ŚBr.; ŚāṅkhŚr. (v.l. °*vya*). — **deva**, m. N. of an author, Cat. — **dharma**, m., w.r. for *pūrta-dh*° (below). — **parvêndu**, f. the day of full moon, A. — **pātrá**, m. n. a full vessel or cup, as much as will fill a vessel, a cupful (as a measure of capacity properly 256 handfuls of rice), ŚBr.; TBr.; GṛŚrS. (also *ī*, f., ŚāṅkhGṛ.); n. a vessel full of rice presented at a sacrifice to the superintending and officiating priests, W.; a v° filled with valuable things to be distributed as presents (esp. a present made to any one who brings good news), Mālatīm.; Kād.; Hcar.; *-pratibhaṭa*, mfn. emulating the fullness or a full v° i.e. overflowing, supreme (as glory), Rājat.; *-maya*, mf(*ī*)n. consisting of a full v°, amounting to a f° v° or to only so much (as a speech), MBh.; Kathās.; *-vṛittyā*, ind. after the manner of a full v°, plentifully, abundantly, Mālatīm. — **purī**, m. N. of a scholar, Cat. — **purushârtha-candra**, m. or n. N. of a drama. — **prakāśa**, m. N. of an author, Cat. — **prajña**, m. N. of Madhva (also called Madhya-mandira), and of his adherents, Sarvad. (cf. IW. 118; 119); *-darśana*, n. N. of ch. of Sarvad. — **bandhura**, for *-vandhura*, VS. — **bīja**, m. a citron, L. — **bhadra**, m. N. of a serpent-demon, MBh.; of the father of the Yaksha Hari-keśa, SkandaP.; of several men, Hariv.; Daś.; of a scholar (who revised the Pañcatantra in 1514), Cat. — **bhedinī**, f. a species of plant, L. — **maṇḍala**, n. a full circle, Cat. — **mā**, f. full-moon (day), L. — **mānasa**, mfn. having a satisfied mind, contented, R. — **mās** (*pūrṇá-*), m. full moon, ŚBr. — **māsa** (*pūrṇá-*), m. full moon; a ceremony on the day of f° m°, TS.; Br.; MBh. &c.; f° m° personified as son of Dhātṛi and Anumati, BhP.; N. of a son of Kṛishṇa, BhP.; (*ī*), f. = *pūrṇa-mā*, ĀpŚr., Comm. — **mukta**, mfn. shot from a bow completely bent (as an arrow), R. — **mukha**, n. a full mouth; instr. (blowing) with full cheeks, MānŚr.; m. a species of bird, R.; N. of a serpent-demon, MBh. — **mushṭi**, m. f. a handful, ŚāṅkhGṛ. — **maitrāyaṇī-putra**, m. N. of a man, Buddh. — **yoga**, m. a partic. mode of fighting, MBh. — **yauvana**, mfn. one whose youth is in full vigour, Daś. — **ratha**, m. a complete warrior, Kathās. — **lakshmīka**, mfn. full of magnificence or wealth, Kathās. — **vandhura** (*pūrṇá-*), mfn. having the chariot-seat filled, RV. — **vapus**, mfn. 'full-bodied,' full (the moon), MBh. — **varman**, m. N. of a man, Buddh. — **viṇśati-varsha**, mfn. full 20 years old, Mn. — **vighana**, mfn. full but not hard (?), ŚāṅkhGṛ. — **vaināśika**, mfn. maintaining the doctrine of absolute annihilation; m. pl. N. of Buddhists (= *sarva-vaināśika*), Col. — **śakti**, f. 'Full energy,' N. of a partic. form of Rādhā, W. (cf. RTL. 187); *-mat*, mfn. possessing that Energy (Kṛishṇa), ib. — **śrī**, mfn. having fullness of fortune, Subh. — **śruti**, mfn. having the ears filled, MW. — **samaya**, m. N. of a Kshapaṇaka, Cat. — **sena**, m. N. of an author, Cat. — **saugandha**, m. N. of a man, L. — **sruva**, m. a full ladle called *sruva*, MānŚr. — **homa**, m. = *pūrṇâhuti*, Gobh.; Kauś.; Vait. **Pūrṇâksha** and °**kshya** (!), m. N. of a Maudgalya, Car. **Pūrṇâṅka**, m. 'a full figure or number,' an integer, MW.; *-gaṇita*, n. arithmetic of integers, MW. **Pūrṇâṅgada**, m. N. of a serpent-demon, MBh. **Pūrṇâñjali**, m. 'full Añjali' two handfuls, Kauś. **Pūrṇânaka**, n. 'full drum,' a partic. drum, L.; the sound of a drum, L.; clothes and garlands presented to friends at a feast (v.l. *pūrṇālaka*; cf. *pūrṇa-pātra*), L.; a vessel, L.; a moon-beam, L. **Pūrṇā-nadī**, f. N. of a sacred river, MW. **Pūrṇânanda**, m. full delight, RāmatUp.; N. of the Supreme Being, A.; of sev. authors (also *-tīrtha*, *-nātha*, *-sarasvatī* &c.), Cat.; *-prabandha*, m. N. of wk. **Pūrṇâpūrṇa**, mfn. full and not full, Pañcat. **Pūrṇâbhilāsha**, mfn. one whose wishes are fulfilled, satisfied, contented, MW. **Pūrṇâbhishikta**, m. pl. a partic. sect of the Śāktas, W. **Pūrṇâbhisheka**, m. a partic. ceremony among the Śāktas, W.; *-paddhati*, f. N. of wk. **Pūrṇâbhra-rasa**, m. a partic. medicament, Rasêndrac. **Pūrṇâmṛita**, mfn. full of nectar; (*ā*), f. N. of the 16th Kalā of the moon, BrahmaP.; °*tâṇśu-vadana*, mfn. having a face like the full moon, Kathās. **Pūrṇâyata**, n. a completely bent bow, Hariv. **Pūrṇâyus**, m. N. of a Gandharva, MBh.; Hariv. (v.l. *ūrṇâyu*). **Pūrṇârtha**, mfn. one who has attained his object, whose wishes have been realized, BhP. **Pūrṇâvatāra**, m. N. of the 4th, 7th and 8th incarnations of Vishṇu, A. **Pūrṇâśā**, f. N. of a river, MBh. (v.l. *parṇâśā*). **Pūrṇâśrama**, m. N. of an author, °*mīya*, n. his wk. **Pūrṇâhutí**, f. 'complete oblation,' an offering made with a full ladle, Br.; GṛŚrS.; MBh.; Rājat. (°*tika*, mfn. relating to it, KātyŚr., Sch.); *-prayoga*, m., *-mantra*, m. pl. N. of wks. **Pūrṇêccha**, mfn. one whose wishes have been realized, Kathās. **Pūrṇêndu**, m. the full moon, Kāv.; Kathās. &c.; *-bimbânana*, mfn. having a face like a full moon, MW.; *-rasa*, m. a partic. medicament, Rasar.; *-vadana*, mfn. having a face like a full moon, MW. **Pūrṇêśa**, m. N. of an author (°*ī*, f. of an authoress) of Mantras among Śāktas, Cat. **Pūrṇôtkaṭa**, m. N. of a mountain, MārkP. **Pūrṇôtsaṅga**, mf(*ā*)n. far advanced in pregnancy, MBh. (v.l. *putrôtsaṅgā*); m. N. of a prince, VP. **Pūrṇôda**, mf(*ā*)n. having a full bed (as a river), R. **Pūrṇôdarā**, f. N. of a deity, Cat. **Pūrṇôpamā**, f. a complete comparison (containing the four requisites *upamāna*, *upameya*, *sādhāraṇa-dharma*, and *upamā-vācaka* or *sādṛiśya-pratipādaka*; opp. to *luptôpamā*), Kpr.; Kuval.; Pratāp.

Pūrṇaka, m. a species of tree, R.; the blue jay (= *svarṇa-cūḍa*), MBh. (Nīlak.); a cock, MW.; a partic. vessel or utensil (used by the Magas), VP.; = *dhānya-jvara*, Gal.; (*ikā*), f. a species of bird described as having a double or cleft beak (also called *nāsā-chinnī*), Mālatīm. °**ṇālaka**, n., v.l. for *pūrṇânaka*. °**ṇiman**, m. N. of a brother of Kaśyapa and son of Marīci and Kalā, BhP.

Pūrṇimā, f. the night or day of full moon, Rājat.; Sūryas.; *-dina*, n. the day of f° m°, Pañcat. (°*nimânta*, m. the end of the day of f° m°, MW.); *-manoratha-vrata*, n. N. of a partic. observance, Cat. — **rātri**, f. the night of f° m°, Hemac.; *-śarvarī*, f. the night of f° m°, Kpr. °**ṇimāsī**, f. (according to some) = *paurṇamāsī*, q.v., L.

Pūrṇī-√kṛi, to make complete, Kathās.

Pūrtá, mfn. filled, full, complete, completed, perfected, Pur.; (*ishṭaś ca pūrtaś ca dharmau*, = *ishṭâpūrta*, q.v., MārkP.); covered, concealed, L.; n. fulfilling, fulfilment; granting, rewarding, a reward, merit, a meritorious work, an act of pious liberality (such as feeding a Brāhman, digging a well &c.), RV. &c. &c.; keeping, guarding, L.; N. of wk. (also *-kamalâkara*); *-dharma* (w.r. *pūrṇa-dh*°), m. a meritorious work (cf. *pūrta*), MārkP.; *-prakāśa*, m., *-mālā*, f., °*tôddyota*, m. N. of wks. **Pūrtaya**, Nom. P. °*yati* (with *dharmam*) to perform the meritorious works called *pūrta* (see above), BhP. **Pūrtí**, f. filling, completion, Pāṇ., Sch. (cf. *pāda-p*°); ending, coming to an end, Naish.; granting, rewarding, reward, RV.; TS.; satiety, satisfaction, MW.; *-kāma* (*pūrti-*), mfn. (ifc.) desirous of completing or supplying, BhP.; desirous of a grant or reward, AV. **Pūrtin**, mfn. possessing the merit of pious liberality (cf. *pūrta*), TS.; Kāṭh.; Pāṇ., Sch.; filling, completing, effective, W. **Pūrtvan**, mfn. one who has eaten his fill, Kāṭh.

Pūrya, mfn. to be filled or satisfied, Br.; MBh.

पूरु **pūrú**, m. (orig. = *puru*, and connected with *purusha*, *pūrusha*) a man, people, RV.; N. of a tribe (associated with the Yadus, Turvaśas, Druhyus), ib.; of a class of demons, ŚBr.; of an ancient prince (the son of Yayāti and Śarmishṭhā), MBh.; Śak.; Pur. (cf. Pāṇ. iv, 1, 168, Vārtt. 3,

Pat.); of a descendant of Atri and author of RV. v, 16; 17, RAnukr.; of a son of Manu and Naḍvalā, Hariv.; of a son of Jahnu, BhP.

Pūrusha, m. (m. c.) = *pu̍rusha*, RV. &c. &c. **-ghná**, mfn. slaying men, RV. **-tvá-tā**, ind. = *purusha-tvá-tā*, ib. **Pūrushâd**, mfn. devouring men, RV.; AV. **Pūrushâda**, m. N. of a tribe of cannibals, VarBṛS.

Pūrv-āyus. See *pūrvâyus* under *pūrva.*

पूर्जयन *pūr-jáyana*, *pūr-dvār* &c. See p. 636, col. 1.

पूर्व *pū́rva*, mf(ā)n. (connected with *purā, puras, pra*, and declined like a pron. when implying relative position whether in place or time, but not necessarily in abl. loc. sg. m. n., and nom. pl. m.; see Pāṇ. i, 1, 27; 34; vii, 1, 16) being before or in front, fore, first, RV. &c. &c.; eastern, to the east of (abl.), ib.; former, prior, preceding, previous to, earlier than (abl. or comp.), ib. (*gaja-pūrva*, preceding the number 'eight,' i.e. seven, the seventh, Śrutab.; *māsena p°* or *māsa-p°*, earlier by a month, Pāṇ. ii, 1, 31; ifc. often = formerly or before, e.g. *strī-p°*, f° a wife; *āḍhya-p°*, f° wealthy; esp. after a pp., e.g. *kṛita-p°*, done before, *dṛishṭa-p°*, seen b°; ifc. also preceded or accompanied by, attended with, e.g. *smita-pūrvā vāk*, speech accompanied by smiles; sometimes not translatable, e.g. *mṛidu-pūrvā vāk*, kind speech); ancient, old, customary, traditional, RV. &c. &c.; first (in a series), initial, lowest (opp. to *uttara*; with *dama* or *sāhasa* 'the lowest fine'), Mn. viii, 120 &c.; (with *vayas*) 'first age,' youth, MBh.; foregoing, aforesaid, mentioned before (abl.), Mn.; MBh.; Pāṇ.; m. an ancestor, forefather (pl. the ancients, ancestors), RV. &c. &c.; an elder brother, R.; N. of a prince, BhP.; (*ā*), f. (with or sc. *diś*) the east, MBh.; R.; N. of a country to the east of Madhya-deśa, L.; of the Nakshatras Pūrva-phalgunī, Pūrvâshāḍhā and Pūrva-bhadrapadā collectively, Var.; n. the fore part, Śak. ii, 4 (cf. Pāṇ. ii, 2, 1); a partic. high number (applied to a period of years), Buddh.; N. of the most ancient of Jaina writings (of which 14 are enumerated), L.; N. of a Tantra, Cat.; an ancient tradition, W.; (*am*), ind. before (also as a prep. with abl.), formerly, hitherto, previously (sometimes with pres.), RV. &c. &c. (often ibc., e.g. *pūrva-kārin*, active before, *pūrvôkta*, said b°; also ifc. in the sense of 'with,' e.g. *prīti-pūrvam*, with love; *mati-pūrvam*, with intention, intentionally; *mṛidu-p° √bhāsh*, to speak kindly; cf. above; also with an ind. p., e.g. *p°-bhojam* or *-bhuktvā*, having eaten b°, Pāṇ. iii, 4, 24; *adya-p°*, until now, hitherto; *p°-tataḥ*, first-then; *p°-paścāt*, previously-afterwards; *p°-upari*, previously-subsequently; *p°-adhunā* or *adya*, formerly-now); (*eṇa*), ind. in front, before; eastward, to the east of (opp. to *apareṇa*, with gen. or acc.; cf. Pāṇ. v, 3, 35, Sch.), ŚBr. &c. &c.; (with *tataḥ*) to the east of that, MBh. **-karman**, n. a former work or action, Śaṃk.; Kathās.; preparation, Suśr.; °*ma-kṛita-vādin*, m. one who asserts that only preceding actions determine the following, Jātak. **-kalpa**, m. the preceding or aforesaid manner, PārGṛ.; MBh.; (*e* or *eshu*), ind. in former times, MBh.; Kull. **-kāma-kṛitvan**, mfn. fulfilling former wishes, AV. **-kāya**, m. the fore (part of the) body (of animals) or the upper (part of the) body (of men), KātyŚr.; MBh. &c. **-kārin**, mfn. active at first, ŚāṅkhŚr. **-kārya**, mfn. to be done before or first, R. **-kāla**, m. a former or previous time, L.; mfn. belonging to a f° t°, previously mentioned (*-tā*, f.), VPrāt. **-kālika** (MBh.), **-kālīna** (Nyāyak. *-tva*, n.), mfn. belonging to former times, ancient. **-kāshṭhā**, f. the eastern quarter, A. **-kṛit**, mfn. active from ancient times, VS. **-kṛita**, mfn. done formerly or in a prior existence, previous; n. (with or sc. *karman*) an action done in former times or in a former birth, Mn.; MBh. **-kṛitvarī**, f. acting beforehand, AV. **-kṛishṇīya**, n. N. of wk. **-koṭi**, f. anticipation, L.; the starting point of a discussion, the first statement = *pūrva-paksha* (q.v.), A. **-kramâgata**, mfn. descended from ancestors, Yājñ. **-kriyā**, f. preparation, Siṇhâs. **-ga**, mfn. going before, preceding, MBh.; Rājat.; belonging to what precedes, Hemac. **-gaṅgā**, f. 'eastern Gaṅgā,' N. of the Narmadā or Revā river, Kathās. **-gata**, mfn. gone before, Śak.; n. N. of a Jaina wk. belonging to the Dṛishṭi-vāda. **-gátvan**, mfn. going to meet, RV. **-gama**, m. (ifc.) a predecessor, Kāraṇḍ. **-grāmin**, m. N. of a family, Cat. **-ghaṭa-karpara**, m. or n. N. of wk. (prob. the first part of the poem Ghaṭa-karpara). **-ṃ-gata**, mfn. going before, Dhūrtan. **-ṃ-gama**, mfn. id., L.; serving zealously, obedient, Divyâv.; ifc. attended by, furnished with, L. **-cit**, mfn. piling up first, preceding in piling up, VS. **-citī**, f., w. r. for *-citti*, MBh. **-citta** (*pū́rva-*), mfn., w. r. for *-cit*, AV. **-citti** (*pūrvá-*), f. foreboding, presentiment (only dat. 'at the first notice, forthwith'), RV.; (prob.) first notion or conception, VS.; N. of an Apsaras, VS.; MBh.; Hariv.; Pur.; (prob.) w. r. for *-cita*, VS. **-cittikā** (Gal.) and **-cittī** (MBh.), f. N. of an Apsaras = *-citti*. **-cintana**, n. former cares or trouble, Rājat. **-codita**, mfn. formerly stated or prescribed, Mn.; *-tva*, n., PārGṛ. **-já**, mfn. born or produced before or formerly, former; ancient, primaeval, RV. &c. &c.; first-born, elder, the eldest (son, brother &c.), MBh.; Kāv. &c.; produced by something antecedent, caused, MW.; born in the east, eastern, W.; antecedent (to what precedes in comp.), L.; m. an elder brother, the eldest b°, Mn.; MBh. &c.; an ancestor, forefather, R.; Ragh.; Kathās. &c.; the eldest son, Gaut.; the son of the elder wife, A.; (pl.) the deified progenitors of mankind, W.; the Pitṛis living in the world of the moon, A.; (*ā*), f. an elder sister, ib.; *-deva*, m. N. of Brahmā, MBh. **-janá**, m. pl. men of former times, AV. **-janman**, n. a former birth, f° state of existence or life, Ragh.; Hit.; Kathās.; m. an elder brother, Ragh.; °*ma-kṛita*, mfn. done in a former birth or previous state of existence, Hit.; °*mārjita*, mfn. acquired in some former state of existence (as merit &c.), MW. **-jā́**, mfn. born or produced before, RV. **-jāti**, f. = *-janman*, Kathās. **-jāvan**, mfn. born or produced before, RV. **-jina**, m. 'ancient sage,' N. of Mañju-śrī, L. **-jñāna**, n. knowledge of a former life, Yājñ. **-tana**, mfn. former, earlier, MBh. **-tantra**, n. N. of a Tantra. **-tara** (*pū́rva-*), mfn. earlier, previous, prior, anterior, RV. &c.; (*am*), ind. before, first, previously, Bhag.; R. **-tas**, ind. before, in front, towards or in the east, Gobh.; MBh.; Kāv. &c.; first, in the first place, BhP. **-taskara**, m. a former thief, Mn. **-tā**, f. the being preceded or accompanied by (comp.), Daś. **-tāpanīya**, n. (and °*yôpanishad*, f.) N. of the first half of the Nṛisiṇha-tāpanīyôpanishad, Col. (cf. *uttara-tāpanīya*). **-tāpinī**, f. = *-tāpanīya*; *-dīpikā*, f., Cat. **-tra**, ind. previously, in the preceding part, above (opp. to *uttara-tra*), Pāṇ. viii, 2, 1; = loc. of *pūrva*, e.g. *pūrvatra janmani*, 'in a former life,' Kathās.; *p° dine*, on the day before, L. **-traigartaka**, mfn. (fr. *-trigarta*), L. **-traiyalinda**, mfn. (fr. next), Pat. **-tryalinda**, N. of a village, Pat. **-tva**, n. precedence, priority, former state or condition, Jaim.; Pāṇ., Sch. **-thā** (*pūrvá-*), ind. formerly or as formerly, previously, first, RV.; TBr. **-dakshiṇa**, mf(ā)n. south-eastern, KātyŚr.; MārkP. **-datta**, mfn. given before, Hcat. **-darśana**, m. N. of a man, BhP. **-dāvika**, mfn. (fr. *-devikā*), Pāṇ. vii, 3, 1, Sch. **-dik-pati** or **-dig-īśa**, m. 'regent of the eastern quarter,' N. of Indra, L. **-dina**, n. the earlier part of the day, forenoon, MW. **-diś**, f. the eastern region, east quarter, Pañcad. **-diśya**, mfn. situated towards the east, bearing east; eastern, MW. **-dishṭa**, mfn. determined by former actions, BhP.; n. the award of destiny, A. **-dīkshā́**, f. the former consecration, ŚBr.; °*kshin*, mfn. taking the f° c°, AitBr. **-dugdha**, mfn. sucked out or plundered before, Daś. **-dushkṛita-bhoga**, m. the pain or penalty consequent on sins committed in a former birth, MW. **-dṛishṭa**, mfn. seen before, Kathās.; appeared in former times, primaeval, MBh.; declared by the ancients, Mn. ix, 87. **-dṛishṭi**, f. a former view or sight, MW. **-deva**, m. a primaeval deity, MBh. (applied also to the Pitṛis = *-devatā*, Mn. iii, 192); an Asura or demon (offspring of Kaśyapa, the parent of both gods and demons), Siṇhâs. **-devikā**, f. N. of a village in the eastern part of India, Pāṇ., Sch. **-deśa**, m. the eastern direction; (*e*, to the east of [abl.], Pāṇ., Sch.); the eastern country, MBh. **-deha**, m. a former body; (*e*), ind. in a f° birth or existence, Hariv. **-dehika** and **-daihika** (also *paurva-d°*), mfn. done in a former existence, MBh. **-dvāra**, mfn. favourable in the eastern region, Sūryapr. **-dvārika**, mfn. favourable to an expedition towards the east, Var. **-nagarī**, f., g. *nady-ādi*. **-nadaka**, n. a hollow bone in the upper part (of the thigh), KātyŚr. **-nipāta**, m. (in gram.) the irregular priority of a word in a comp. **-nimitta**, n. an omen, Lalit. **-nivāsa**, m. 'former habitation,' a former existence, Divyâv.; *-jñāna*, n. (with Buddhists) knowledge of the past lives of all beings, MW.; °*sânusmṛiti*, f. 'recollection of former habitations,' reminiscence of f° existence (one of the 10 powers of a Buddha), Dharmas. 20; 76. **-nivishṭa**, mfn. made formerly or in ancient times (as a pond), Mn. ix, 281. **-nyāya**, m. a previous judgment, Yājñ., Sch. **-nyāsa**, m. N. of wk. **-pakshá**, m. the fore part or side, TBr.; the first half of a lunar month, the fortnight of the waxing moon, TS.; Br.; Lāṭy. &c. (°*kshâha*, a day in the first half &c., ĀpGṛ.); the first half of a year, KātyŚr.; an action at law, the first statement of the plaintiff, first step in a law-suit, Yājñ.; Vishṇ.; Nār.; the first objection to an assertion in any discussion, the primâ facie view or argument in any question, Śaṃk.; Suśr.; MārkP. (cf. IW. 99); *-grantha*, m., °*tha-ṭīkā*, f., °*tha-prakāśa*, m., °*tha-rahasya*, n., °*thânu-gama*, m., *-nirukti*, f. N. of wks.; *-pāda*, m. the first step of a legal process or law-suit, the plaint of the plaintiff, W.; *-rahasya*, n., *-lakshaṇa*, n., *-vyāpti*, f., °*ti-kroḍa*, m., °*ti-lakshaṇa*, n., *-vyutpatti-lakshaṇa*, n., *-vyutpatti-vāda*, m., °*kshâvalī*, f. N. of wks. **-pakshaya**, Nom. P. °*yati*, to make the first objection to an assertion in any discussion, Bādar., Sch. **-pakshin**, mfn. one who makes the first obj° to an ass°, ib. **-pakshī-√kṛi** = *-pakshaya*. **-pakshīya**, mfn. situated on the front side, Pāṇ. iv, 2, 138. **-pañcāla** (*pūrvá-*), m. pl. the eastern Pañcālas, Pāṇ. vi, 2, 103, Sch.; sg. — *pūrvaḥ pañcālānām*, Pāṇ. vii, 3, 13, Sch. **-patha**, m. a former way, w° gone before, Kathās. **-pada**, n. the first member of a comp., Prāt.; Pāṇ. &c.; *-prakṛiti-svara*, mfn. having the original accent of the first member of a comp.; *-tva*, n., Pāṇ. ii, 1, 4, Vārtt. 2. **-padika**, mfn. relating to the first member of a comp. W.; = *pūrva-padam adhīte veda vā*, Pāṇ. iv, 2, 60, Kāś. **-padya**, mfn. belonging to the first member of a comp., RPrāt. **-parigraha**, m. first claim, prerogative, precedence, MBh.; mf(ā)n. claimed as first privilege by (gen.), R. **-pariccheda**, m. and **-paribhedya** (?), n. N. of wks. **-parvata**, m. the eastern mountain (from behind which the sun is supposed to rise), L. **-paścāt**, adv. from the east to the west, Hcat.; °*cān-mukha*, mf(*ī*)n. flowing to the east and west, R. **-paścâyata**, mfn. spreading or running from the east to the west, Hcat.; MārkP. **-paścima**, mf(ā)n. directed from the east to the west, Sūryas.; *-tas*, adv. from the east to the west, Hcat. **-pā́**, mfn. drinking first or before others, RV. **-pāñcālaka**, mfn. belonging to the eastern Pañcālas, Pāṇ. vi, 2, 105, Sch. **-pāṭali-putra**, n. N. of a city; °*traka*, mfn. being in Pūrva-p° (?), Pāṇ. vii, 3, 14, Sch. **-pāṇinīya**, m. pl. the disciples of Pāṇini living in the east; mfn. relating to them, Pāṇ. vi, 2, 104, Sch. **-pāda**, m. a forefoot, KātyŚr.; ŚāṅkhŚr.; N. of a man (v. l. *pūjya-p°*), Cat. **-pāna** (Nir.), **-pā́yya** (RV.), n. = *-pīti*. **-pālin**, m. N. of a prince, MBh.; of Indra, A. **-pitāmaha**, m. a forefather, ancestor, MBh.; Kathās. **-pīṭhikā**, f. introduction, Daś.; N. of wk. (?) **-pīti** (*pūrvá-*), f. precedence in drinking, RV. **-purusha**, m. a forefather, ancestor, Kauś.; Bālar.; Pañcat.; (pl. forefathers, ancestors, Kād.); 'the primaeval Soul,' N. of Brahmā, Hariv. **-pūjita**, mfn. consecrated before, Kathās. **-pūrṇa-māsī**, f. the first or real day of full moon, Jyot. **-pūrva**, mf(ā)n. each previous or preceding one, each one mentioned previously (also *-tama*), MBh.; m. pl. forefathers, ancestors, MBh.; °*vânugaṇḍikā*, f. N. of a range of hills (cf. *apara-gaṇḍikā*), MBh.; °*vôkta*, mfn. each one mentioned previously, Vedântas. **-péya**, n. precedence in drinking, RV.; AitBr.; precedence, AV. **-prajñā́**, f. knowledge of the past, remembrance, memory, ŚBr. **-pratipanna**, mfn. one who has promised before, Kathās. **-prayoga**, m. N. of wk. **-pravṛitta**, mf(ā)n. formerly happened or done or fixed &c., R. **-prasthita**, mfn. gone before, set out in advance, Vikr. **-prāyaś-citta**, n. N. of wk. **-prêta**, mfn. gone or flown away before, TāṇḍyaBr.; deceased, dead, Divyâv.; m. pl. the Pitṛis; *-pūjaka*, mfn. worshipping the P°, Lalit. **-phalgunī**, f. 'the first Phalgunī,' N. of the 11th Nakshatra (cf. *uttara-phalgunī*), VP.; Uṇ., Sch.; *-bhava*, m. N. of Bṛihas-pati or the planet Jupiter, L. **-bandhu**, m. first i.e. best friend, Mṛicch. **-bādha**, m. suspension or annulment of something preceding, Siṇhâs. **-brāhmaṇa**, n. N. of wk.

-bhakshikā, f. (prob.) w.r. for *-bhikshikā*. **-bhadra-pada**, m. (and *ā*, f.pl.) = *-bhādrap°*, L. **-bhava**, m. a former life, Hemac. **-bhāga**, m. the fore part, L.; the upper part (opp. to *adho-bhāga*), Suśr.; *dina-p°*, the earlier part of the day, forenoon, morning, Ragh.; mfn. whose conjunction with the moon begins in the forenoon, Sūryapr. **-bhấj**, mfn. receiving the first share, the first sharer, preferred, privileged, excellent, RV.; belonging to the preceding, Prāt. **-bhādrapada**, m. (and *ā*, f.pl.) the 25th Nakshatra, the former of the two called Bhādrapadā (containing two stars), MBh.; VP.; Col. **-bhāva**, m. prior or antecedent existence, priority, KapS.; Bhāshāp.; (in rhet.) disclosing an intention, Daśar.; Pratāp. **-bhāvin**, mfn. being anterior, preceding, TBr., Comm.; *°vi-tva*, n. priority, Kap. **-bhāshin**, mfn. speaking first, polite, complaisant, R. **-bhikshikā**, f. a breakfast, Divyâv. **-bhukti**, f. prior or long-continued possession, Mn.viii, 252. **-bhūta**, mfn. existing previously, preceding, Pāṇ., Sch. **-bhū-bhṛit**, m. the eastern mountain (from behind which the sun is supposed to rise); a former prince, Subh. **-magadha**, m.pl. the eastern Magadhas. **-madra**, m.pl. the eastern Madras (cf. *paurvam°*), L. **-madhyâhna**, m. the forenoon, Kathās. **-māgadhaka**, mfn. relating or belonging to the eastern Magadhas, L. **-mārin**, mfn. dying before, GṛŚrS.; Mn. &c. **-mīmāṅsā**, f. 'inquiry into or interpretation of the first or Mantra portion of the Veda,' N. of the system of philosophy attributed to Jaimini (as opp. to *uttara-m°*, which is an inquiry into the later or Upanishad portion; the *pūrva-m°* is generally called *the* M°, and in interpreting the Vedic text discusses the doctrine of the eternity of sound identified with Brahma, IW. 98 &c.); N. of a wk. of Soma-nātha; *-kārikā*, f.pl. and *°sârtha-saṃgraha*, m. N. of wks. **-mukha**, mfn. having the face turned towards the east, Hcat. **-yaksha**, m. 'the first Yaksha,' N. of Maṇi-bhadra (one of the Jinas or Jaina teachers), L. **-yāmya**, mfn. south-eastern; (*e*), ind. in the south-east, Hcat. **-yāyāta**, n. the more ancient form of the legend of Yayāti or that current in the east, Siddh. **-yāyin**, mfn. moving towards the east, Sūryas. **-yấvan**, m. 'going before,' a leader, RV. **-yoga**, m. olden time, history of o° t°, SaddhP. **-raṅga**, m. the commencement or prelude of a drama, a prologue, an overture, Śiś. ii, 8; Daśar.; Sāh. &c. **-rāga**, m. earliest or incipient affection, love between two persons which springs from some previous cause, Sāh. **-rāja**, m. an ex-king, Mudr. **-rātrá**, m. the first part of the night, the time from dusk to midnight, AitBr.; Kauś.; KātyŚr.; MBh. &c.; *-krita*, mfn. done during the f° p° of the n° (= *tre kṛ°*, Pāṇ. ii, 1, 45, Sch.) **-rūpá**, n. indication of something approaching, an omen, AV.; something prior or antecedent to, (esp.) the symptom of occurring disease, Car.; Suśr.; the first of two concurrent vowels or consonants (*-tā*, f.), TUp.; Prāt. &c.; (in rhet.) a figure of speech which describes the unexpected return of anything to its former state, Kuval.; mf(*ā*)n. having the previous form or shape, being as before, Dhūrtas. **-lakshaṇa**, n. indication of anything about to occur, Car. **-1. -vat**, mfn. having (or relating to) something preceding or antecedent, VPrāt.; (an argument) in which a conclusion is drawn from a previous cause to an effect, Nyāyad.; f. one who has been previously married, Āp.; *°vat-tara*, mfn. antecedent, former, R. **-2. -vát**, ind. as before, as hitherto, as heretofore, as aforesaid; according to something previous (applied in the Nyāya to a kind of inference such as inferring from the previous appearance of a cloud that rain will fall), RV. &c. &c. **-vayas**, mfn. or **-vayaska**, mfn. being in the first period or stage of life, young, MBh. **-vayasá**, n. the first period or stage of life, youth, Br. **-vayasín**, mfn. being in the first period of life, young, TBr. **-vartin**, mfn. existing before, preceding, prior, previous; *°ti-tā*, f. (Bhāshāp.), *°ti-tva*, n. (Mṛicch., Sch.) former existence, precedence, priority. **-váh** (*vấh*), mfn. drawing in front, being the first horse or leader, or harnessed for the first time (applied to a horse), Br.; Kāṭh.; ĀpŚr. **-vākya**, n. (in dram.) an allusion to a former utterance, Sāh. **-vāda**, m. the first plea or plaint in an action at law, Vishṇ.; Yājñ., Sch. **-vādin**, m. 'speaking first,' 'making the first statement of a case,' a complainant, plaintiff, Yājñ. **-vāyu**, m. the east wind, Var. **-vārshika**, mfn. relating to the first half of the rainy season, Pāṇ. vii, 3, 11, Sch. **-vid**, mfn. knowing the things or events of the past, Mn. ix, 44. **-videha**, m. the country of the eastern Videhas (with Buddhists 'one of the 4 continents,' Dharmas. 120); *-lipi*, f. a partic. mode of writing, L. **-vidhi**, m. a preceding rule, Kāś. on Pāṇ. i. 4, 51; N. of wk. **-vipratishedha**, m. the conflict of two statements or rules the first of which is opposed to the second, ĀpŚr., Comm. **-vihita**, mfn. deposited or buried before (as a treasure), Mṛicch. **-vṛita**, mfn. chosen before, Kum. **-vṛitta**, mfn. formerly happened; relating to a previous occurrence, Hariv.; n. a former event, previous occurrence, Kālid.; Śaṃk.; former conduct, MārkP. **-vairin**, mfn. one who is the first to begin hostilities, MBh. **-śāṅsapa**, mfn. (fr. *-śiṅśapā*), Pāṇ. vii, 3, 1, Sch. **-śānti**, f. N. of wk. **-śārada**, mfn. relating to the first half of the autumn, Pat. on Pāṇ. i, 1, 72. **-śāstra**, n. N. of wk. **-śishya**, m. (and *ā*, f.) a former or ancient pupil, Mālatim. **-śīrsha**, mf(*ā*)n. having the head or top turned towards the east, MBh. **-śaila**, m. = *-parvata*, L.; pl. N. of a Buddhist school; *-saṃghârāma*, m. N. of a Buddhist monastery. **-śaiva-dīkshā-vidhi**, m. and **-shaṭka** (?), n. N. of wks. **-saṃhitā**, f. N. of wk. **-sakthá**, n. (prob.) the upper part of the thigh, Pāṇ. v, 4, 98. **-saṃcita**, mfn. gathered before, Mn. vi, 15. **-saṃjalpa**, m. an introduction in the form of a dialogue, Car. **-sád**, mfn. sitting in front, SV. **-saṃdhyā**, f. 'earlier twilight,' dawn, day-break, W. **-sabhika**, m. the chief of a gambling house, Mṛicch. **-samudra**, m. the eastern sea, Var. **-sara**, mf(*ī*)n. going before, preceding, Pāṇ. iii, 2, 19; Bhaṭṭ. **-sasya**, n. earliest-sown grain, Var. **-sāgara**, m. the eastern sea, Ragh.; VarBṛS. **-sāra**, mfn. going eastwards, Pāṇ. iii, 2, 19, Sch.; *-sārasvādinī*, f. N. of wk. **-sārin**, mfn. preceding, taking precedence of all others, MBh. **-sāhasa**, n. the first or heaviest fine or punishment, Mn. **-siddha**, mfn. previously settled or determined or proved, KapS. **-siddhânta**, m., and *-pakshatā*, f. N. of wks. **-supta**, mfn. formerly or already fallen asleep, Pañcat. **-sū́**, mfn. first bringing forth, RV.; firstborn, ancient, primaeval, ŚāṅkhŚr. **-sūri**, m. an ancient master (of music), Saṃgīt. **-sevā**, f. first use or practice of (gen.), Baudh. **-stha**, mfn. standing first, most excellent, MBh. **-sthiti**, f. first or former state, MW. **-svara**, m. (in gram.) having the accent of the preceding, MW. **-hūti** (*pūrvá-*), f. first or earliest invocation, morning prayer, RV.; VS. **-homá**, m. an introductory sacrifice, TBr. **Pūrvâgni**, m. 'original or primaeval fire,' the householder's sacred f° (= *āvasathya*), AV.; ŚBr.; KātyŚr.; *-vahana*, n. a vehicle for carrying the s° f°, KātyŚr.; *-vấh*, n. a bull carrying the s° f°, ŚBr.; KātyŚr. **Pūrvâṅga**, n. the former body, Kathās.; a constituent part of the preceding, VPrāt., Sch.; m. the first day in the civil month, Sūryapr. **Pūrvâcarita**, mfn. formerly done or followed, W. **Pūrvâcala**, m. = *°va-parvata*, VarP.; Śatr. **Pūrvâcārya-vṛittânta-dīpikā**, f. N. of a comm. on wks. of the Rāmânuja school. **Pūrvâtitha**, n. (= *paurv°*) N. of sev. Sāmans, ĀrshBr. **Pūrvâtithi**, m. N. of a man, Cat. **Pūrvâdi**, mfn. beginning with the word *pūrva*, Var. **Pūrvâditas**, ind. beginning from the east, ib. **Pūrvâdya**, mfn. beginning with the east, ib. **Pūrvâdri**, m. = *°va-parvata*, Kathās. **Pūrvâdhika**, mfn. greater than before; *-dyuti*, mfn. more brilliant than b°, Kathās. **Pūrvâdhikārin**, m. a prior owner, former proprietor, MW. **Pūrvâdhirāma**, n. the more ancient form of the story of Rāma or the form current in the east, Pāṇ., Sch. **Pūrvâdhyushita**, mfn. formerly inhabited, R. **Pūrvânubhūta**, mfn. formerly felt or enjoyed, Caurap. **Pūrvânuyoga**, m. N. of a Jaina wk. belonging to the Dṛishṭi-vāda. **Pūrvânushṭhita**, mfn. observed or performed before; *-tva*, n., Baudh. **Pūrvânta**, m. (in gram.) the end of a preceding word; anticipation (= *pūrva-koṭi*), L.; *-tas*, ind. in advance, Lalit. **Pūrvâpakārin**, mfn. one who has injured another before, R. **Pūrvâpara**, mfn. being before and behind; directed forward and backward, eastern and western, KātyŚr.; Kālid. &c. (*-tva*, n., Śaṃk.); prior and subsequent, first and last; preceding and following, following one another, connected with one another, KātyŚr.; MBh. &c.; (*ám*), ind. one after another, RV.; ĀpŚr., Sch.; n. that which is before and behind, east and west, Sūryas.; connection, Mn. viii, 56; the proof and thing to be proved, W.; *-grantha*, m. N. of wk.; *-dakshiṇa*, mf(*ā*)n. eastern, western and southern, MBh.; *-dina*, n. forenoon and afternoon, Cat; *-rātri*, f. the former and latter half of the night, ŚāṅkhGṛ.; *-prayoga*, m. N. of wk.; *-virodha*, m. opposition of prior and subsequent, inconsistency, incongruity, MW.; *-smārta-prayoga*, m. N. of wk.; *°parâyata*, mf(*ā*)n. running from east to west, KātyŚr., Sch.; *°parī-bhāva*, m. the following one another, succession, Sarvad.; *°parī-√bhū*, to follow one another, be connected with one another, Nir.; Sāh.; *°parya*, n. = *paurvāparya*; (*eṇa*), ind. one after another, KātyŚr., Sch.; VarBṛ., Sch. **Pūrvâpaharaṇā**, f., g. *ajâdi*, Kāś. (v.l. *°pahāṇā*). **Pūrvâpúsh** (?), RV. viii, 22, 2 (Sāy. = *pūrveshām poshakaḥ*; v.l. *pūrvâyus*, q.v.) **Pūrvā-bhādrapadā**, f. the 25th Nakshatra, MBh. (v.l. *pūrva-bh°*). **Pūrvâbhibhāshin**, mfn. = *-pūrva-bhāshin*, q.v., Rājat. **Pūrvâbhimukha**, mf(*ā*)n. turned or flowing towards the east (as rivers), Suśr. **Pūrvâbhirāmā**, f. N. of a river, MBh. **Pūrvâbhisheká**, m. previous anointing; (Sāy. 'a partic. Mantra'), ŚBr. **Pūrvâbhyāsa**, m. the repetition of what precedes; (*ena*), ind. afresh, anew, ŚārṅgP. **Pūrvâmbudhi**, m. the eastern ocean, Kathās. **Pūrvâyús**, mfn. (prob.) 'of an early age,' young, RV. (v. l. for *pūrvâpúsh*, q.v.; others *pūrv-āyus*, 'having or granting vital power'). **Pūrvârāma**, m. 'eastern garden,' N. of a Buddhist monastery. **Pūrvârcika**, n. N. of the first half of the Sāma-veda (the second half of which is called *uttarârcika*). **Pūrvârjita**, mfn. attained or gained formerly or by former works, Kathās. **Pūrvârdhá**, m. (later n.) the front or upper part; eastern side; (opp. to *jaghanârdha*, *uttarârdha* &c.), TS.; ŚBr.; GṛŚrS. &c.; the fore or first half (of a hemistich), Śrutab.; (with *dinasya*) forenoon, Bhartṛ. &c.; *-kāya*, m. the front or upper part of the body, MBh.; *-bhāga*, m. the upper part, top, Ragh.; *-lambin*, mfn. having the foremost half inclined, leaning forward, MW. **Pūrvârdhya**, mfn. being on the eastern side, Lāṭy.; KātyŚr.; Pāṇ., Sch. **Pūrvâvadhīrita**, mfn. formerly disdained, Śak. **Pūrvâvedaka**, m. 'making the first statement,' a plaintiff, Yājñ. **Pūrvâśā**, f. the east, Hcat. **Pūrvâśin**, mfn. eating before another (abl. or loc.), MBh. **Pūrvâshāḍhā**, f. the first of two constellations called Ashāḍhā (the 18th or 20th Nakshatra or lunar asterism), Var.; Pur.; *°ḍha-janana-śānti*, f. N. of wk. **Pūrvâsin**, mfn. shooting before (another), AV. **Pūrvâhṇá**, m. the earlier part of the day, forenoon (mostly loc.; sometimes incorrectly *pūrvâhna*), RV. &c. &c.; (*°hṇa-kāle* or *°hṇe-k°*, *°hṇa-tare* or *°hṇe-t°*, *°hṇa-tame* or *°hṇe-t°* [Pāṇ. vi, 3, 17, Sch.], *°hṇe-tarām* or *-tamām* [v, 4, 11, Sch.], ind. in the forenoon; *-hṇa-krita*, mfn. = *°hṇe-kṛ°* [ii, 1, 45, Sch.], to be done in the f°; *°hṇâparâhṇayoḥ*, ind. in the f° and afternoon, Lāṭy.; Gobh.; *°hṇe-geya*, mfn. [ii, 1, 43, Sch.] to be sung in the f°); *°hṇaka*, m. 'born in the forenoon,' N. of a man, Pāṇ. iv, 3, 28; *°hṇa-tana* or *°hṇe-tana* (vi, 3, 17, Sch.), mfn. belonging or relating to the forenoon; *°hṇika*, mf(*ī*)n. id., MBh.; n. a matutinal ceremony or sacrifice = *p°-kriyā* (or *-vidhi*), MBh. **Pūrvêtara**, mf(*ā*)n. 'other than eastern,' western, L. **Pūrvedyús**, ind. on the day before, yesterday (opp. to *uttare-dyus*, *apare-dyus* &c.), TS.; Br.; GṛŚrS. &c.; Mn. &c.; early, betimes, in the morning, L.; during that portion of a day on which religious ceremonies are to be performed = *dharmâhe*, *dharma-vāsare*, L.; *°dyur-āhṛitá*, mfn. fetched on the day before, ŚBr.; *°dyur-dugdhá*, mfn. milked on the day before, ŚBr. **Pūrvêndra**, m. a former Indra, MBh. **Pūrvêshukāmaśamī**, N. of a village, Pāṇ. ii, 1, 50 &c., Sch.; *°vaishukāmaśama*, mfn. (fr. prec.), iv, 2, 107 &c., Sch. **Pūrvôkta**, mfn. said before, formerly stated, aforesaid, before mentioned, Mn.; Kathās. &c.; *-parāmarśaka*, mfn. referring to something before mentioned, MW. **Pūrvôcita**, mfn. before accustomed, known from former days, former, R. **Pūrvôttara**, mf(*ā*)n. north-eastern, MBh.; MārkP.; Hcat. &c.; (*e*), ind. in the north-east, Hcat.; du. or (ibc.) the antecedent and subsequent, the preceding and following, VPrāt.; Pāṇ., Sch.; *-śānti*, f. N. of wk. **Pūrvôtthāyin**, mfn. rising the first (in the morning), Gaut.; MBh. **Pūrvôtthita**, mfn. risen before (as smoke), Ragh. **Pūrvôtpatti**, mfn. arising before, KapS. **Pūrvôtpanna**, mfn. produced or arisen or existent before; *-tva*, n. = *pūrva-bhāva*, Bhāshāp. **Pūr-**

vôdak-plava, mfn. inclined towards the north-east, Var. **Pūrvôdita**, mfn. aforesaid, before mentioned, W. **Pūrvôpakārin**, mfn. one who has formerly done a service to another, MBh. **Pūrvôpakrama**, mf(*ā*)n. beginning from the east, Gobh. **Pūrvô-panihita**, mfn. previously hidden away (as a treasure), Mn. viii, 37. **Pūrvôpapanna**, mfn. (prob.) having prior claims, MBh. **Pūrvôpa-sṛitá**, mfn. approached or arrived first, TBr. **Pūrvôpârjita**, mfn. formerly occupied or acquired, Pañc.

Pūrvaka, mf(*ikā*)n. earlier, former, previous, prior, first, MBh.; Kāv. &c. (*strī-p°*, 'one who was formerly a woman,' *bhūta-p°*, 'having been before;' ifc. also = preceded or accompanied by, connected with, consisting in; *am*, ind. = after, with, amid, according to); m. a forefather, ancestor, Hariv.; R.; MārkP. **Pūrvaya**, only in *upâdhāyya-p°*, mfn. 'having an edge or border' (of braid), trimmed, edged, TS. **Pūrvika**, mfn. former, ancient, Kāraṇḍ.; formerly invited, L.; w. r. for *pūrvaka*, MBh.

Pūrviṇa, mfn. derived from ancestors or forefathers, ancestral, ĀśvŚr. **Pūrvin**, mfn. id. (cf. Pāṇ. iv, 4, 133, and see *a-, daśa-, strī-p°*). **Pūrvineshṭhá**, mfn. (prob.) w. r., SV. **Pūrví**, f., see *purú*. **Pūrviṇa**, mfn. = *pūrviṇa*, Pāṇ. iv, 4, 133.

Pūrveṇa, ind. See under *pūrva*.

Pūrvyá (rarely *pū́rvya*), mf(*ā*)n. former, previous, ancient, old (opp. to *navīyas, nū-tana* &c.), RV.; AV.; ŚāṅkhŚr.; ŚvetUp.; precedent, first, RV.; RPrāt.; next, nearest, RV.; most excellent, ib.; ŚBr. (Sch. 'young'); (*ám*), ind. before, formerly, at first, long since, hitherto, RV.; *-stuti* (*pūrvyá-*), f. first or principal praise, RV.

पूल् *pūl*, cl. 1. 10. P. *pūlati, pūlayati*, to collect, gather, Dhātup. xv, 21; xxxii, 93.

Pūla, m. a bunch, bundle, MānGṛ.; KātyŚr., Sch. (also *-ka*); pl. straw, ĀśvŚr., Sch.

पूलाक *pūlāka*, g. *palāśâdi*.

पूलास *pūlāsa*, n., g. *saṃkalâdi*, Gaṇar. 81. **-kuraṇḍa**, g. *rāja-dantâdi*.

Pūlāsaka, in *-karaṇḍa*, Kāś.; *-kuraṇḍa*, n., g. *rāja-dantâdi*, Gaṇar. 83.

पूल्य *pūlya*, n. an empty or shrivelled grain of corn, AV.

पूष् *pūsh* (= √2. *push*), cl. 1. P. *pūshati*, to nourish, increase, Dhātup. xvii, 24.

1. **Pūsha**, m. a kind of mulberry tree, L.; (*ā*), f. N. of the third Kalā of the moon, BrahmaP.

2. **Pūsha**, in comp. for *°shan*. **-danta-hara**, m. 'taking away Pūshan's teeth,' N. of Śiva, L. **-dhra**, (prob.) w. r. for *pṛisha-dhra*. **-bhāsā**, f. 'sun-splendour,' N. of the capital of Indra, L. (w. r. *-bhā-shā*). **-mitra**, m. 'friend of P°,' N. of a man, L. **-rāti**, mfn. (prob.) giving growth or increase, RV. **Pūshâtmaja** or **Pūshânuja**, m. 'son or younger brother of P°,' N. of Parjanya, MBh. (Nīlak.) **Pūshâshṭóttara**, n. N. of a Stotra. **Pūshâsuhṛid**, m. 'enemy of P°,' N. of Śiva, L.

Pūshaṇ, in comp. for *°shan*. **-vát**, mfn. accompanied by Pūshan, RV.; VS.; AitBr.

Pūsháṇa, m. N. of a god (= Pūshan), RV.; (*ā*), f. N. of one of the Mātṛis attending on Skanda, MBh.

Pūshán, m. (the *a* not lengthened in the strong cases, but acc. *°shāṇam*, in MārkP.) N. of a Vedic deity (originally connected with the sun, and therefore the surveyor of all things, and the conductor on journeys and on the way to the next world, often associated with Soma or the Moon as protector of the universe; he is, moreover, regarded as the keeper of flocks and herds and bringer of prosperity; in the Brāhmaṇas he is represented as having lost his teeth and feeding on a kind of gruel, whence he is called *karambhâd*; in later times he is one of the 12 Ādityas and regent of the Nakshatra Revatī or Paushṇa; du. 'Pūshan and Aryaman,' VP., Sch.); the sun, Kād.; Bālar.; (?) growth, increase (cf. *pūsha-rāti*); the earth, L.

Pūshkara, n. a word formed for the explanation of *pushkara*, ŚBr.

पृ 1. *pṛi*, cl. 3. P. (Dhātup. xxv, 4) *pí-parti* (3. pl. *píprati*, RV.; Impv. *pipṛihi*, BhP.; *para*, VS.; cl. 9. P. *pṛiṇāti*, 'to protect,' Dhātup. xxxi, 19; pf. 3. pl. *pipruḥ*, BhP. [= *pūr-ṇāḥ*, Sch.]; aor. Subj. *parshi, parshati, parsha, pārishat*, RV.; *apārīt*, Bhaṭṭ.; inf. *parsháṇi*, RV.), to bring over or to (acc.), bring out of, deliver from (abl.), rescue, save, protect, escort, further, promote, RV.; AV.; VS.; ŚāṅkhGṛ.; BhP.; Bhaṭṭ.; to surpass, excel (acc.), RV. viii, 50, 8; AV. xi, 5, 1; 2; to be able (with inf.), BhP.: Caus. *pāráyati* (ep. and m. c. also *°te*; aor. *apīparat*; Pass. *pāryate*), to bring over or out, rescue, protect, save, preserve, keep alive, RV. &c. &c.; to get over, overcome, bring to an end, ib.; to resist, withstand, be a match for (acc.), Mn.; MBh. &c.; to be capable of or able to (with an inf. which after *pāryate* has a pass. sense; cf. √*śak* and Pāṇ. iii, 4, 66, Sch.), Kāv.; Pur. &c. [Cf. Gk. περάω, πόρος, πορεύεσθαι; Lat. *porta, peritus*; Slav. *pirati*; Germ. *fahren*; Eng. *to fare*.]

पृ 2. *pṛi*, cl. 5. P., 6. Ā. *pṛiṇoti* or *priyate* (Dhātup. xxvii, 12; xxviii, 109), to be busy or active (only in *ā-√pṛi* and *vy-ā-√pṛi*, q. v.)

पृक्का *pṛikkā*, f. Trigonella Corniculata, L. (cf. *spṛikkā*).

पृक्त *pṛikta, pṛikti.* See under √1. *pṛic*.

पृक्थ *pṛiktha*, n. possession, property, wealth, L. (cf. *riktha*).

पृक्ष् *pṛiksh*, f. (nom. wanting; prob. fr. √1. *pṛic*) refreshment, satiation, nourishment, food, RV.

पृक्ष *pṛikshá*, mfn. (either connected with *pṛiśni, pṛishat* or fr. √1. *pṛic*) spotted, dappled (others 'fleet, swift;' others 'having or bringing food'); m. a spotted (or a swift &c.) horse (others 'beast of burden;' others 'food, nourishment, abundance'), RV.; N. of a man, ib. ii, 13, 8; = *saṃgrāma*, Naigh. ii, 17. **-prayaj** (*°kshá-*), mfn. in which oblations of food begin to be offered (said of the dawn), RV. iii, 7, 10 (Sāy.; according to others 'hastening with swift horses'). **-yāma** (*°kshá-*), mfn. 'driving swift horses' (prob. N. of a family), RV. i, 122, 7.

पृक्षु *pṛikshú*, (prob.) w. r. for *pṛitsú*, SV.

पृक्षुध *pṛikshúdh*, mfn. (?), RV. i, 141, 4.

पृच् 1. *pṛic*, cl. 7. P. (Dhātup. xxix, 25) *pṛiṇákti*, Ā. *pṛiṅkté* (or cl. 2. *pṛikte*, Dhātup. xxiv, 20; cl. 1. P. *pṛiñcati*, AV.; cl. 3. P. *pipṛigdhi, pipṛikta*, RV.; pf. *papricuḥ*, AitBr.; *papṛicāsi*, *°cyāt*, *°cānā*, RV.; aor. *párcas* [p. *pṛi-cāná*, ib.; Prec. *pṛicīmahi*], ib.; *aprāk*, AV.; *apṛi-kshi*, *°kta*, ib.; *aparcīt*, *°cishṭa*, Gr.; fut. *parcish-yati*, *°te*, *parcitā*, ib.; inf. *-pṛice*, *-pṛicas*, RV.), to mix, mingle, put together with (instr., rarely loc.; *dhanushā śaram*, 'to fix the arrow upon the bow,' Bhaṭṭ.), unite, join, RV. &c. &c.; to fill (Ā. one's self?), sate, satiate, RV.; MBh.; to give lavishly, grant bountifully, bestow anything (acc. or gen.) richly upon (dat.), RV.; to increase, augment, ib. (Prob. connected with √*pṛī*, to fill; cf. also √*pṛij*.)

Pṛiktá, mfn. mixed or mingled with, full of; brought into contact with, touching (instr. or comp.), RV. &c. &c.; n., w. r. for *pṛiktha*, L.

Pṛikti, f. touch, contact, L.

2. **Pṛic**, f. food, nourishment, refreshment, RV. v, 74, 10 (cf. *ghṛita-, madhu-*).

पृच्छक *pṛicchaka*, mf(*ikā*)n. (√*prach*) one who asks or inquires about (gen.), Yājñ.; Śak.; Pañc.; inquiring into the future, VarBṛS.; m. an inquirer, inquisitive person, W.

Pṛicchana, n. asking, inquiring, W.

Pṛicchā, f. asking, questioning (acc.), question about (comp.), Kāv.; an inquiry into the future, VarBṛS.

Pṛicchya, mfn. to be asked or inquired after, BhP.

पृज् *pṛij, pṛiñj*, cl. 2. Ā. *pṛikte, pṛiṅkte*, Dhātup. xxiv, 20 (v. l. for *pṛic*); 15 (v. l. for *pij*). Cf. *an-ava-pṛigṇa, ava-prajjana*; *parjanya*.

पृड् *pṛiḍ*, cl. 6. P. *pṛiḍati*, to gladden, delight, Dhātup. xxviii, 39.

पृण् *pṛiṇ*, cl. 6. P. *pṛiṇati* (p. *pṛiṇát*, Ved. inf. *pṛiṇádhyai*), see √*prī*.

पृणाका *pṛiṇākā*, f. the female young of an animal (see *hariṇa-p°*).

पृत् *pṛit*, f. (only in loc. pl. *pṛitsú*, in one place [i, 129, 4] *pṛitsúshu*, RV.; but according to Vop. also in other cases; viz. *pṛitas, pṛitā, pṛidbhyām*) battle, contest, strife. **-sutí**, m. or f. hostile attack (Sāy. 'a host'), RV.

Pṛitana, n. an army or a hostile encounter, TBr.; (*ā*), f., see next.

Pṛitanā, f. battle, contest, strife, RV.; VS.; Br.; a hostile armament, army, RV. &c. &c. (in later times esp. a small army or division consisting of 243 elephants, as many chariots, 729 horse, and 1215 foot = 3 Vāhinīs); pl. men, mankind, Naigh. ii, 3. **-°j** (*°nâj*), mfn. rushing to or in battle, RV. (AV. v. l. *°nâjí*). **-°ja** (*°nâja*), m. = *śūra*, a hero, SāṅkhŚr. **-jaya**, m. victory in b° or over armies, PārGṛ. **-jít**, mfn. victorious in b°, AV.; ŚāṅkhBr.; m. N. of an Ekāha, ŚāṅkhŚr. **-°jya** (*°nâjya*), n. 'rushing together in b°,' close combat, fight, RV. **-ni** or **-pati**, m. a leader in b°, commander, general, MBh. **-shāh**, mfn. victorious in b°s, RV.; AV.; m. N. of Indra, L. **-sháhya** (RV.) and **-sáhya** (TBr.), n. = *-jaya*. **-°háva** (*°nâh°*), m. challenge to battle, fight, RV.

Pṛitanāya, Nom. P., only p. *°yát*, fighting together, engaged in combat, RV.; AV.; VS. *°yú*, mfn. hostile; m. an enemy, RV.

Pṛitanya, Nom. P. *°yáti*, to attack, assail, fight against (acc.), RV.; AV. *°nyā*, f. an army, BhP. *°nyú*, mfn. attacking, hostile; m. an enemy, RV.; VS.

Pṛitsu, loc. of *pṛit* in comp. **-túr**, mfn. victorious in battle, RV.

Pṛitsudha (?), m. = *saṃgrāma* (v. l. for *pṛitsu*, Naigh. ii, 17).

Pṛitsúshu. See *pṛit*.

पृथ् 1. *pṛith*, cl. 10. P. *parthayati*, to extend, Dhātup. xxxii, 10 (cf. √*prath*, of which it is only the weak form).

2. **Pṛith**, f. = *Pṛithā* below, L.

Pṛithá, m. the flat or palm of the hand, ŚBr.; a partic. measure (the length of the h° from the tip of the fingers to the knuckles, or = 13 Aṅgulis), KātyŚr.; (*ā*), f., see below. **-mātrá**, n. the breadth of a hand, TBr.; mfn. a h° broad, KātyŚr. **-vāna** (*pṛitha-*), m. N. of a man, RV. **-hara**, m., w. r. for *pṛithu-h°*, MBh. **Pṛithâśva**, m. N. of a king, MBh.

Pṛithā, f. N. of a daughter of Śūra and adopted d° of Kuntī and one of the wives of Pāṇḍu (mother of Karṇa before her marriage, and of Yudhi-shṭhira, Bhīma, and Arjuna after her m°; see Kuntī), MBh.; Hariv. &c. **-ja**, m. 'son of P°,' N. of Arjuna, L.; Pentaptera Arjuna, L. **-janman**, m. 'id.,' N. of Yudhi-shṭhira, Pracaṇḍ. **-tmaja** (*°thâtm°*), m. = prec., Veṇīs. **-pati**, m. 'husband of P°,' N. of Pāṇḍu, L. **-bhū**, m. 'son of P°,' N. of Yudhi-shṭhira, Pracaṇḍ. **-raṇi** (*°thâr°*), f. 'the Araṇi P°,' N. of Kuntī the wife of Pāṇḍu (as the mystical wood from which the Pāṇḍavas were struck out or generated; cf. *Pāṇḍava-vahni* and *Pāṇḍavâraṇi*). **-suta**, m. 'son of P°,' N. of Arjuna, Kir. **-sūnu**, m. 'id.,' N. of Yudhi-shṭhira, Veṇīs.

Pṛithak, ind. (√*pṛith* or *prath* + *añc*) widely apart, separately, differently, singly, severally, one by one (often repeated), RV. &c. &c.; (as a prep. with gen. or instr.; cf. Pāṇ. ii, 3, 32) apart or separately or differently from, L.; (with abl.) without, Prab.; except, save, Bhaṭṭ. **-karaṇa**, n. separating, setting apart, ĀpŚr., Sch.; Pāṇ., Sch. **-kāma**, mfn. (pl.) having different wishes, KātyŚr. **-kārya**, n. a separate or private affair, Mn. vii, 120. **-kula**, mfn. (pl.) belonging to different families, L. **-√kṛi**, to make separate, sunder, KātyŚr.; to keep off, avert, Sāy. **-kṛita**, mfn. separated, sundered, cut off, MārkP. **-kṛiti**, f. an individual, BhP. **-kriyā**, f. separation, disunion, Mn.; Yājñ. **-kshetra**, m. pl. children of one father by different wives or by wives of d° classes, Yājñ., Sch. **-cara**, mf(*ī*)n. going separately or alone, MW. **-ceshṭā**, f. pl. d° activities, Bhag. **-tā**, f. separateness, severalty, singleness, individuality, Nyāyam., Sch. **-tva**, n. id., ŚāṅkhŚr.; Nir.; MBh. &c. (cf. IW. 68); (*ena*), ind. singly, one by one, MBh.; *-tas* (ŚāṅkhŚr.) and *-śas* (Nyāyam., Sch.), separately, singly. **-tvacā**, f. 'diverse-barked,' Sanseviera Zeylanica, L. **-pada**, mfn. consisting of single i. e. uncompounded words (*-tva*, n.), Vām. **-parṇikā**, f. 'diverse-leaved,' =

-**tvacā**, L. -**parṇī**, f. id., L.; Hemionitis Cordifolia, Car.; Suśr. -**piṇḍa**, m. a distant kinsman who offers the Śrāddha oblation (see *piṇḍa*) by himself and not together with the other relations, Mn. v, 78 (Kull. = '*samānôdaka*'). -**śabda**, m. a separate or distinct or independent word, Vop. -**śayyā**, f. sleeping apart, Hit. -**śāyin**, mfn. (pl.) sleeping alone or apart, Vishṇ. -**śruti**, mfn. uttering a distinct sound, distinctly heard, RPrāt. -**sukha**, mfn. (pl.) having different joys, MBh. -**sthita**, mfn. existing separately, separate, MW. -**sthiti**, f. separate existence, separation, Vikr.

Pṛithakat, ind. = *pṛithak*, Pāṇ. v, 3, 72, Sch.

Pṛithag, in comp. for °*thak*. -**abhimati**, mfn. regarding the world as separate (from God), MW. -**artha**, mfn. (pl.) having separate or distinct advantages, MBh.; having s° or d° meanings (-*tā*, f.), Kir. -**ātman**, mfn. 'having a s° nature or essence,' separate, distinct, individual, W.; m. individualized spirit, the individual soul (as distinct from universal spirit or the soul of the universe), ib.; °*ma-tā*, f. separateness, severalty, L.; discrimination, judgment, W.; °*mikā*, f. separate or individual existence, individuality, L. -**ālaya**, mfn. (pl.) having s° dwellings, Kathās. -**īśa-mānin**, mfn. regarding God as s° from the universe, MW. -**upâdāna**, n. s° mention, Pāṇ. iv, 2, 113, Sch. -**gaṇa**, m. a s° company or class, Mn. i, 37. -**guṇa**, mfn. having distinct properties, W. -**gotra**, mfn. (pl.) belonging to different families, MārkP. -**jana**, m. a man of lower caste or character or profession, Mn.; MBh. &c. (-*vat*, ind., Ragh. viii, 89); an ordinary professing Buddhist, MWB. 132; a fool, blockhead, Śiś.; a villain, L.; pl. common people, the multitude (also sg.), Mn.; MBh. &c.; = *pṛithak-kshetra*, W.; -*kalyāṇaka*, m. a man wishing for conversion, Divyâv. -**jana-pada**, n. each single country or people, Lāṭy. -**jaya**, m. victory in a separate combat or duel (*a-pṛith*°), Gaut. -**dṛiś**, mfn. seeing something different from (abl.), BhP. -**devata**, mfn. having a separate or special deity, Sāy. -**dvāra**, n. pl. special doors i.e. means of attainment, MBh. -**dharma-vid**, m. pl. each knowing different laws, Gaut. -**bīja**, m. Semecarpus Anacardium, L. -**bhāva**, m. separate state or condition, difference, distinctness, individuality, KaṭhUp.; MBh. &c. -√**bhū**, to be peculiar to, Divyâv.; -*bhūta*, mfn. become separate, separated, different, MW. -**yoga**, mfn. (prob.) w.r. for -*bhāga* (having different lots) or -*bhoga* (h° d° enjoyments), Kathās. -**yoga-karaṇa**, n. the separation of a grammatical rule into two, Pāṇ., Sch. (cf. *yoga-vibhāga*). -**rasa-maya**, mf(*ī*)n. made of a distinct or special sap or essence, BhP. -**rūpa**, mfn. variously shaped, diverse, different, manifold, L. -**lakshaṇa**, mf(*ā*)n. having d° characteristics, KātyŚr. -**vartman** (*pṛithag*-), mfn. having d° courses, ŚBr.; ChUp. -**varsha**, n. pl. a year in each case, each and every year, Gaut. -**vādin**, mfn. each saying something different, ŚBr. -**vidha**, mfn. of d° kinds, manifold, various, Mn.; MBh. &c.; d° from (abl.), BhP.

Pṛithaṅ, in comp. for °*thak*. -**nishṭha**, mfn. existing by itself, being something different or distinct in each case, MBh.

Pṛithavī, f. = *pṛithivī*, L.

Pṛithi, m. N. of a man (protected by the Aśvins, according to Sāy. a Rājarshi), RV. (Cf. *pṛithī*, *pṛithu*; *pārtha*, °*thya*.) -**sava**, m. N. of a partic. ceremony, TBr., Sch.

Pṛithikā, f. a centipede, L.

Pṛithivi, f. = °*vī*. -**tvá**, n. the state or condition of the earth, TS.; TBr. -**dā**, mfn. earth-giving, Kāṭh.; ĀpŚr. -**bhāga** (°*ví*-), mfn. having the e° as a share, entitled to it, TS. -**mūla**, m. 'e-rooted,' N. of a man, L. -**loká**, m. the e° regarded as a world, ŚBr. -**shád**, mfn. = -*sad*, AV.; -*shṭha* or -*shṭhā́*, mfn. standing on the e°, stepping firmly (as a horse), RV. -**sád**, mfn. sitting on the earth, VPrāt.

Pṛithiví, f. (= *pṛithvī*, f. of *pṛithu*) the earth or wide world ('the broad and extended One,' personified as *devī* and often invoked together with the sky [cf. 3. *div* and *dyāvā-pṛithivī*; RTL. 182]; according to VP. daughter of *Pṛithu*; the Veda makes 3 earths, one called *bhūmi*, inhabited by men, and 2 under it; there is also an earth between the world of men and the circumambient ocean [ŚBr.] and one extending through the 3 worlds [Naigh.]), RV. &c. &c.; land, ground, soil, ib.; earth regarded as one of the elements, Prab.; Suśr.; = *antariksha*, Naigh. i, 3; °*vyā vrata* and *saṃsarpa*, n. N. of Sāmans, ĀrshBr. -**kampa**, m. an earthquake, MBh. -**kṛitsna**, n. one of the 10 mystical exercises called Kṛitsna, L. -**kshit**, mfn. dwelling on or ruling over the e°, m. a prince, king, KātyŚr.; ChUp. &c. -**grantha**, m. N. of wk. -**candra**, m. 'e°-moon,' N. of a prince of the Tri-gartas, Rājat. -**jaya**, v.l. for next, Hariv. -**m-jaya**, mfn. e°-conquering; m. N. of a Dānava, MBh.; of a son of Virāṭa, ib. -**tala**, n. 'e°-surface,' ground, the terrestrial or infernal regions, MBh.; Kāv. &c. -**tīrtha**, n. N. of a Tīrtha, MBh. -**tva**, n. state or condition of the e°, earthiness, Sarvad. -**daṇḍapāla**, m. the police-magistrate of a country (-*tā*, f.), Mṛicch. -**devī**, f. N. of a woman, Kathās. -**dyā́vā** (°*ví*-), nom. du. e° and heaven, RV. (cf. *dyāvā-pṛithivī*). -**dhara**, m. (with *miśrâcārya*) N. of an author, Cat. -**dharaṇa**, n. a prop or support of the e°, Hariv. -**m-dadā**, f. 'e°-giving,' N. of a Gandharvī, Kāraṇḍ. (cf. *pṛithivi-dā*). -°**ndra** (°*vîndra*), m. 'the Indra of the e°,' a prince, king, A. -**pati**, m. 'e°-lord,' a prince, king, TBr.; Mn. &c.; N. of Yama, L.; (with *sūri*) N. of an author, Cat.; a species of bulbous plant growing on the Himālaya, L. -**paripālaka**, m. 'e°-guardian,' a prince, king, MārkP. -**pārvataka**, m. or n. rock-oil, petroleum (?), L. -**pāla** (MBh.; Kāv.), °**laka** (MārkP.), m. = -*paripālaka*. -**prá**, mfn. e°-filling, AV. -**plava**, m. 'e°-flood,' the sea, Gal. -**bhuj**, m. 'e°-enjoyer,' a king, Vikr.; Rājat. -**bhujaṃga**, m. 'e°-lover,' a king, MārkP. -**bhṛit**, m. 'e°-bearer,' a mountain, Śiś. -**maṇḍa**, m. or n. e°-scum, L. -**maṇḍala**, m. or n. the circuit of the e°, MW. -**máya**, mf(*ī*)n. formed of e°, earthen, ŚBr. -**rasa**, m. e°-sap, L. -**rājya**, n. 'e°-dominion,' sovereignty, Kathās. -**ruha**, m. 'e°-grower,' a plant, tree, Hariv. -**loka**, m., v.l. for °*vi-loká*, q.v. -**vara-locana**, m. N. of a Bodhi-sattva, Kāraṇḍ. -°**śa** (*vîśa*), m. 'e°-lord,' a king, MārkP. -**śakra**, m. 'the Indra of the e°,' id., L. -°**śvara** (°*vîśv*°), m. = °*vîśa*°, R.; MārkP. -**shad**, mfn. abiding on e°, MānŚr. (v.l. -*sad*). -**saṃśita** (°*ví*-), mfn. impelled by the e°, AV. -**sava**, m. N. of a partic. ceremony, ĀpŚr.

Pṛithivy, in comp. for °*vī* before vowels. -**āpīḍa**, m. N. of 2 princes of Kaśmīra, Rājat. -**upasaṃkramaṇā**, f. N. of a Kiṃ-narī, Kāraṇḍ.

Pṛithī, m. (nom. °*thī*, dat. °*thyai* or °*thaye*, gen. °*thyās*) N. of a mythical personage with the patr. Vainya (said to have been the first anointed sovereign of men, to have ruled also the lower animals, and to have introduced the arts of husbandry into the world; he is enumerated among the Ṛishis and said to be the author of RV. x, 148), RV.; AV.; Br. (cf. *pṛithi*, *pṛithu*; *pārtha*).

Pṛithú, mf(*vī́* or *u*)n. broad, wide, expansive, extensive, spacious, large; great, important; ample, abundant; copious, numerous, manifold, RV. &c. &c. (*u*, ind.); prolix, detailed, Var.; smart, clever, dexterous, L.; m. a partic. measure of length (= *pṛitha*), L.; fire, L.; N. of Śiva, MBh.; of one of the Viśve Devās, VP.; of a Dānava, Hariv.; of a son of An-enas, MBh.; Hariv.; of a Vṛishṇi and son of Citraka, ib.; of a son of Citra-ratha, BhP.; of a descendant of Ikshvāku (son of An-araṇya and father of Tri-śaṅku), R.; of a son of Pāra, Hariv.; of a son of Prastāra, VP.; of a son of Rucaka, BhP.; of a son of one of the Manus, Hariv.; of one of the Saptarshis, ib.; of a son of Vaṭêśvara (father of Viśākha-datta), Cat.; of a son of Veṇa, MWB. 423; of a monkey, R.; (*u*), f. Nigella Indica, L.; = *hiṅgu-pattrī*, L.; opium, L.; (*vī*), f. see below. [Cf. Gk. πλατύς; Germ. *platt*; Eng. *plate*.] -**karman**, m. N. of a son of Śaśa-bindu and grandson of Citra-ratha, VP. -**kalpiṇī**, f., v.l. for *patha-kalpanā*. -**kīrti**, mfn. far-famed, R.; N. of a son of Śaśa-bindu, VP.; f. N. of a daughter of Surā, Hariv. -**kucôtpīḍam**, ind. pressing a full bosom, Prab. -**kṛishṇā**, f. a species of cumin, Bhpr. -**kola**, m. a species of jujube, L. -**ga**, m. pl. 'far-moving,' N. of a class of deities under Manu Cākshusha, VP. -**gmán**, mfn. (prob.) = -*jman*, RV. -**grīva**, m. 'broad-necked,' N. of a Rākshasa, RV. -**cārv-añcitêkshaṇa**, mf(*ā*)n. having large and beautiful and curved eyes, Nal. -**cchada**, m. 'broad-leaved,' a species of plant, L. -**jaghana**, mf(*ā*)n. large-hipped, Bhartṛ. -**jaya**, m. 'victorious far and wide,' N. of a son of Śaśa-bindu, VP. -**jman**, mfn. broad-pathed, AV. (cf. -*gman*). -**jráya** (f. *ī*) and -**jráyas**, mfn. widely extended, RV. -**ṃ-jaya**, v.l. for °*thu-j*°. -**tama**, mfn. broadest, widest, largest, greatest, MW. -**tara**, mfn. broader, wider, larger, greater; °*rī*√*kṛi*, to open (the eyes) wider, Ratnâv. -**tā**, f., -**tva**, n. breadth, width, largeness, greatness, Suśr.; Var. -**daṃshṭra**, mfn. large-tusked, MBh. -**datta**, m. N. of a frog, Pañcat. -**darśin**, mfn. far-seeing, far-sighted (met.), Suśr. -**dātṛi**, m., v.l. for -*dāna*. -**dāna**, m. N. of a son of Śaśa-bindu, VP. -**dīrgha-bāhu**, mfn. having broad and long arms, MW. -**dharaṇi-dhara**, m. N. of Vishṇu, MBh. -**dharma**, m., v.l. for -*karman*. -**dhāra**, mfn. broad-edged, MBh.; R. -**nitamba**, mfn. large-hipped, MW. -**pákshas**, mfn. br°-flanked (said of a horse), RV. -**pattra**, m. a kind of garlic (= *rakta-laśuna*), L. -**párśu**, mfn. armed with large sickles, RV. -**palāśikā**, f. Curcuma Cedoaria (= *śaṭī*, *palāśaka*), L. -**pāja-vat**, mfn. containing the word *pṛithu-pā́jas*, ĀpŚr. -**pā́jas**, mfn. far-shining, resplendent, RV. -**pāṇi** (*pṛithú*-), mfn. br°-handed, RV. -**pīna-vakshas**, mfn. having a br° and fleshy breast, Var. -**pragāṇa** (*pṛithú*-), mfn. having a wide approach or access, approached by w° avenues, RV. -**pragāman** (*pṛithú*-), mfn. w°-striding, taking w° strides, RV. -**prajña**, mfn. having a w° understanding, L. -**pratha**, mfn. far-famed, having a wide reputation, Rājat. -**protha**, mfn. having broad or w° nostrils (said of a horse), MBh. -**bāhu**, mfn. broad-armed, having brawny arms, MBh. -**bījaka**, m. lentils, L. -**budhna** (or *pṛithú-b*°), mfn. br°-based, having a br° basis or foot, having a br° sole or under-part, RV.; AV.; VS.; ShaḍvBr.; Lāṭy.; br° in the hinder part (as a worm), Car. -**bhuvana**, n. the wide world, Bhartṛ. -**mat**, m. N. of a prince, VP. -**mukha**, mfn. wide-mouthed, Pāṇ. vi, 2, 168; having a thick point, KātyŚr. -**mṛidvīkā**, f. 'w° grape,' (prob.) a raisin, MBh. -**yaśas**, mfn. far-famed, of w° renown, MBh.; Hariv.; VarBṛ.; m. N. of a son of Śaśa-bindu, VP.; of a son of Varāha-mihira, Cat.; of an author, ib. -**yāman**, mfn. having a broad path (said of Ushas), RV. -**raśmi**, m. N. of a Yati, PañcavBr.; Kāṭh. -**rukma** or °**man**, m. N. of a son of Parā-jit (or Parā-vṛit), Hariv.; VP. -**roman**, m. 'having br° hairs or scales,' a fish, VarBṛS.; *mayugma*, n. the zodiacal sign Pisces, VarBṛ. -**lalāṭatā**, f. having a wide forehead (one of the 80 minor marks of a Buddha), Dharmas. lxxxiv, 72. -**locana**, mf(*ā*)n. having large eyes, MBh. -**vaktrā**, f. 'wide-mouthed,' N. of one of the Mātṛis attending on Skanda, MBh. -**vakshas**, mfn. having a broad breast, R. -**vega**, m. 'having excessive force or impetus,' N. of a prince, MBh. -**vyaṇsa**, mfn. br°-shouldered, MBh. -**śimba**, m. a species of Śyonāka, L. -**śiras** (*pṛithú*-), mfn. br°-headed, flat-headed, AV.; Suśr.; f. N. of a daughter of Puloman, Hariv. -**śṛiṅga**, m. a br°-horned species of sheep, Bhpr. -**śekhara**, m. 'broad-crested,' a mountain, L. -**śrava**, m., w.r. for next. -**śrávas**, mfn. far-famed, of wide renown; m. N. of a man, RV.; MBh.; of a son of Śaśa-bindu, Hariv.; VP.; BhP.; of a son of Raghu, BhP.; of a son of the 9th Manu, MārkP.; of a serpent-demon, PañcavBr.; MBh.; of a being attendant upon Skanda, MBh. (w.r. -*śrava*); of the elephant of the north quarter, Var. -**śrī**, mfn. having great fortune, highly prosperous, MBh. -**śroṇi** (*pṛithú*-) and -**śroṇī**, f. broad-hipped, having large hips or buttocks, ŚBr.; MBh. -**sheṇa** (*sh* for *s*), m. 'having an extensive army,' N. of a son of Rucira (or Rucirâśva), Hariv.; VP. (v.l. -*sena*); of a son of Vibhu, BhP. -**shṭu** or -**shṭuka**, mfn. having a br° tuft of hair, RV. (= -*jaghana*, Nir.) -**sattama**, m. N. of a prince, VP. -**sattva-vat**, mfn. abounding in great living creatures, MW. -**sampad**, mfn. possessing large property, rich, wealthy, Rājat. -**sena**, m., v.l. for -*sheṇa*, q.v. -**skandha**, m. 'b°-shouldered,' a boar, L. -**hara**, m. N. of Śiva, MBh. **Pṛithûdaka**, n. 'having extensive waters,' N. of a sacred bathing-place on the northern bank of the Sarasvatī, MBh.; m. and -*svāmin*, m. N. of the author of a Comm. on the Brahma-gupta, BhP.; Col. **Pṛithûdara**, m. 'br°-bellied,' a ram, L.; N. of a Yaksha, Kathās. **Pṛithûpâkhyāna**, n. 'episode of Pṛithu,' N. of the 29th and 30th ch. of Part II of PadmaP.

Pṛithuka, m. n. rice or grain flattened; rice scalded with hot water and then dried over a fire and ground in a mortar, TBr.; BhP.; Suśr. (also -*taṇḍula*, Āp.; BhP.); m. a boy, the young of any animal, Hariv.; Śiś. &c.; pl. a species of grain, Car.; v.l. for *pṛithu-ga*, VP.; (*ā*), f. a girl, L.; a species of plant (= *hiṅgu-pattrī*), L.

Pṛithukīya and **pṛithukya**, mfn. (fr. *pṛithuka*), g. *apūpâdi*.

Pṛithula, mf(*ā*)n. broad, large, great, MBh.; Śiś.; Kathās.; m., v.l. for *pṛithulâksha*, VP.; (*ā*), f. a species of plant (= *hiṅgu-pattrī*), L. **-locana**, mf(*ā*)n. large-eyed, MBh. **-vakshas**, mfn. broad-breasted, MBh. **-vikrama**, mfn. of great heroism, BhP. **Pṛithulâksha**, m. 'large-eyed,' N. of a prince (son of Catur-aṅga), MBh.; Hariv.; VP.; BhP. **Pṛithulâñjas**, mfn. of great energy, MārkP.

Pṛithū-√kṛi, to extend, expand, enlarge, spread out, MW.

Pṛithvikā, f. = *pṛithvīkā*.

Pṛithvī́, f. (cf. *pṛithivī*) the earth (also as an element), RV. &c. &c.; Nigella Indica, L.; Boerhavia Procumbens, L.; = *hiṅgu-pattrī*, L.; great cardamoms, L.; N. of 2 kinds of metre, Col.; N. of the mother of the 7th Arhat of present Avasarpiṇī, L. **-kurabaka**, m. a species of tree, L. **-khāta**, n. a hole or pit in the earth, cavern, MW. **-garbha**, m. N. of Gaṇêśa, L.; of a Bodhi-sattva, W. **-gṛiha**, n. a dwelling in the e°, a cave, Hariv. **-candrôdaya**, m. N. of wk. **-ja**, m. 'e°-born,' a tree, A.; N. of the planet Mars, A.; n. a species of salt (= *gaḍa-lavaṇa*), L. **-tala**, n. the ground, dry land, Pañcad. **-daṇḍapāla-tā**, f., v.l. for *pṛithivī-a°*. **-dāna-vidhi**, m. N. of wk. **-dhara**, m. 'e-supporter,' a mountain, Naish.; N. of a demon, Var.; Vāstuv.; Hcat.; (also -*bhaṭṭa* and °*rācārya*) N. of sev. authors, Cat.; of the author of Comm. on Mṛicch., Cat. **-pati**, m. 'e°-lord,' a prince, king, sovereign, Prab.; Kathās.; -*tva*, n. princedom, kingdom, Kathās. **-pāla**, m. N. of a man, Rājat. **-pura**, n. N. of a town in Magadha, Śatr. **-premôdaya**, m. N. of wk. **-bhara**, m. (?) a species of the Aty-ashṭi metre, W. **-bhuj**, m. 'e°-enjoyer,' a prince, king, Bālar.; Inscr. **-bhṛit**, m. 'earth-bearer,' a prince, king, Subh. **-malla** and **-malla-rāja**, m. N. of authors, Cat. **-rāja**, m. N. of a prince and poet, Cat.; -*vijaya*, m. N. of a poem. **-rājya**, n. e°-dominion, kingdom, Kathās. **-rūpa**, m. N. of a prince, Kathās. **-varāha-saṃvāda**, m. N. of ch. of VarP. **-°śa** (°*vīśa*), m. 'lord of the earth,' a prince, king, sovereign, MBh.; -*tā*, f. princedom, kingdom, Hcat. **-sāra-taila**, n. a partic. med. preparation, L. **-hara**, m. N. of a man, Rājat.

Pṛithvīkā, f. large or small cardamoms, L.; Nigella Indica, Suśr. (also *pṛithvikā*); L.

पृदाकु *pṛídāku*, m. an adder, viper, snake, VS.; TS.; AV.; MBh. (also *pṛidākū́*, f.); a tiger or panther, L. [cf. Lat. *pardus*, *pardalis* &c.]; an elephant, L.; a tree, L. **-sānu** (*pṛid°*), mfn. having a surface like that of a serpent, smooth or shining like a serpent, RV.

पृशन *pṛíśana*, n. (√*spṛiś*) clinging to; (*ī́*), f. tender, gentle, RV. °**nāyú**, f. = °*nī*, ib.

पृश्नि *pṛíśni*, mfn. (Uṇ. iv, 52) variegated, dappled, piebald, speckled, spotted (said esp. of cows, serpents, frogs &c.), RV.; AV.; Br.; ŚrS.; MBh.; (pl.) manifold, different (as desires), TS.; dwarfish, thin, small, L.; m. N. of a prince (the father of Śvaphalka), Hariv.; VP.; (pl.) N. of a family of Ṛishis, MBh. (°*nayo 'jāh*, the supposed authors of RV. ix, 86, 31-40, Anukr.); (*i*), f. a dappled cow (fig. = milk, the earth, a cloud, the starry sky), RV.; MBh.; a ray of light, L.; N. of the mother of the Maruts, RV.; of the wife of Savitṛi, BhP.; of the wife of king Su-tapas (who in a former birth under the name of Devakī was mother of Kṛishṇa), ib.; (*ī*), f. Pistia Stratiotes, L.; n. (with *Bharadvājasya*) N. of 2 Sāmans, ĀrshBr. [Cf. √*prish*; Gk. περκνός.] **-garbha** (*pṛí°*), mf(*ā*)n. being in the variegated bosom or in the b° of the v° one, RV.; m. N. of Vishṇu-Kṛishṇa, Vishṇ.; MBh. &c. **-gu** (*pṛí°*), mfn. = next; m. N. of a man, RV. i, 112, 7. **-go** (*pṛí°*), mfn. driving with dappled cows, ib. vii, 18, 10. **-tvá**, n. the being variegated &c., TS. **-dhara**, m. 'earth-bearer,' N. of Kṛishṇa, W. **-niprêshita**, mfn. sent or hastening down to Pṛiśni i.e. the earth, RV. vii, 18, 10 (Sāy. 'sent by P°'). **-parṇikā**, f. Hemionitis Cordifolia or Uraria Lagopodioides, L. **-parṇī́**, f. id., ŚBr.; KātyŚr.; Suśr. **-bāhu** (*pṛí°*), mfn. having speckled arms i.e. front legs (said of a frog), AV.; m. N. of a mythical being, ib. **-bhadra**, m. 'propitious to Devakī or to the earth,' N. of Kṛishṇa, L. **-mat**, mfn. containing the word *pṛiśni*, AitBr. **-mantha**, m. a drink made by stirring and mixing ingredients coming from a speckled cow, Kauś. **-mātṛi** (*pṛí°*), mfn. having the earth for a mother (said of herbs), AV.; h° P° for a m° (said of the Maruts), RV.; AV. **-vat** (*pṛí°*), mfn. = -*mat*, TBr. **-vāla**, mf(*ā*)n. having a spotted tail, ĀpŚr. **-śapha**, mf(*ā*)n. having spotted hoofs, ib. **-śṛiṅga**, m. 'having a small or a variegated crest,' N. of Vishṇu or of Gaṇêśa, L. **-sakthá**, mfn. having spotted thighs, TS.; Kāṭh. **-hán**, mfn. slaying the speckled (snake), AV.

Pṛiśnikā, f. Pistia Stratiotes, L.

Pṛiśnī, f. See *pṛiśni*.

Pṛiśny-āhvayā, f. = *pṛiśni-parṇī*, Suśr.

पृष् *prish*, cl. 1. P. *parshati*, to sprinkle; to weary; to vex or hurt; to give, Dhātup. xvii, 55; cl. 1. Ā. *parshate* (xvi, 12, v.l. for *varsh*), to become wet. (Perhaps akin to √*prush*; cf. also *pṛiśni*.)

Pṛisha, in comp. for °*shat*. **-dhra**, m. N. of a man, RV. viii, 52, 4 (supposed author of RV. viii, 56); of a son of one of the Manus, MBh.; of a warrior on the side of the Pāṇḍavas, ib. (w.r. -*dhru*; cf. *pṛiśni-dhara*). **Pṛishôkta**, m. N. of a prince, VP. **Pṛishôtthāna**, mfn., g. *pṛishôdarâdi* (v.l. °*shôdvāni*). **Pṛishôdará**, mf(*ā*)n. having a spotted belly, TS. (cf. Pāṇ. vi, 3, 109). **Pṛishôdyāna**, n. a small garden or grove, L. **Pṛishôdvāni**, see °*shôtthāna*.

Pṛishat, mf(*atī*)n. spotted, speckled, piebald, variegated, AV.; VS.; Br.; GṛŚrS.; sprinkling, W.; m. the spotted antelope, R. (cf. g. *vyāghrâdi*, where Kāś. *pṛishata*); a drop of water (only pl.; °*tām pati*, m. 'lord of the drops of w°,' the wind), Śiś. vi, 55; (*atī*), f. a dappled cow or mare (applied to the animals ridden by the Maruts), RV.; VS.; ŚBr.; ŚrS.; a spotted doe, MBh.; R. &c.; = *pārshatī*, the daughter of Pṛishata, MBh. i, 6390; n. a drop of water or any other liquid, Hariv.; BhP. **-tā**, f., **-tva**, n. the being spotted or variegated, KātyŚr., Sch.

Pṛishata, mfn. having white spots, speckled, variegated, L.; (°*tá*), m. the spotted antelope, VS. &c. &c. (*ī*, f., see under *pṛishat*); a drop of water, MBh.; Hariv.; Kāv.; a spot, mark, Var.; N. of the father of Dru-pada, MBh.; Hariv.; Pur. **Pṛishatâśva**, m. air, wind (= *pṛishad-aśva*), L.

Pṛishatka, m. a round spot, Harav.; an arrow (as being variegated or as being as swift as an antelope), L. (cf. IW. 405, n. 1); the versed sine of an arc, Gaṇit.

Pṛishad, in comp. for °*shat*. **-aṅsa**, g. *utsâdi* (Kāś. *pṛisha*, *daṅse*). **-aśva** (*pṛí°*), mfn. having piebald horses or having antelopes for horses (said of the Maruts), RV.; m. wind or the god of w°, Hcar.; N. of Śiva, Śivag.; N. of a man (pl. his descendants), Pravar.; MBh.; of a son of An-araṇya and father of Hary-aśva, VP.; of a son of Virūpa, BhP. **-ājyá**, n. curdled or clotted butter, ghee mixed with coagulated milk (forming an oblation), RV.; TS.; Br.; GṛŚrS.; -*dhānī*, f. a vessel for an oblation of ghee and curds, ĀpŚr.; -*praṇutta* (°*jyá-*), mfn. driven away from the obl° of ghee and c°, AV. **-dhra**, w.r. for *pṛisha-dhra*. **-yoni** (*pṛí°*), mfn. (prob.) = *pṛiśni-garbha*, RV. **-vat** (*pṛí°*), mfn. party-coloured, variegated, RV. **-vatsa**, mfn. having a spotted calf, Kāṭh. **-varā**, f. 'best among spotted antelopes,' N. of a wife of Ruru and daughter of a Vidyā-dhara by Menakā (a sort of antelope), Kathās. **-vala**, m. 'Piebald,' N. of a horse of Vāyu or the wind (cf. -*aśva*), L. **-vāṇa**, m. 'having variegated arrows,' N. of a man (cf. *pārshadvāṇa*).

Pṛishanti, m. a drop of water, L.

Pṛishāta, mfn. spotted, variegated, Gal.

Pṛishâtaka, m. n. a mixture of ghee and coagulated milk or some similar compound (cf. *pṛishad-ājya*), AV.; GṛŚrS.; m. (pl.) a kind of ceremony, PārGṛ.; N. of Rudra, MānGṛ.; (*ī*), f. a kind of disease or N. of a female demon causing it, AV.

Pṛishita, n. rain, Gobh.

पृषभाषा *pṛishabhāshā*, f. = *pūsha-bhāsā*, L.

पृषाकर *pṛishākara* (?), f. a small stone used as a weight, L.

पृष्ट *pṛishṭá*, mfn. (√*prach*) asked, inquired, questioned, interrogated, demanded, wished for, desired, welcome, RV. &c. &c.; n. a question, inquiry, ĀpGṛ.; Pāṇ. **-prativacana**, n. the act of answering a question or inquiry, Pāṇ. iii, 2, 120. **-bandhu**, mfn. one by whom adherents or praisers are wished for (Agni), RV. iii, 20, 3 **-hāyana**, m. an elephant ('whose years are inquired about,' sc. in buying or selling?), L. **Pṛishṭâbhidhāyin**, mfn. answering when asked, i. e. not puzzled how to answer an inquiry, Var.

Pṛishṭvā, ind. See √*prach*.

पृष्टपर्णी *pṛishṭa-parṇī*, f. Hemionitis Cordifolia, L. (cf. *pṛiśni-p°*).

पृष्टि 1. *pṛishṭí*, f. a rib (cf. *parśu*), RV.; AV. (°*ṭī*, xi, 1, 34); VS.; ŚBr. **-tás**, ind. on the ribs, TS. **-vā́h**, mfn. carrying on the sides (or on the back), AV. **-sācayá**, mfn. joined with the ribs, ŚBr. **Pṛishṭy-āmayá**, m. a pain in the side, AV.; °*yín*, mfn. suffering from it, RV.

Pṛishṭyā́, f. a side-horse (mare), AV. vi, 102, 2 (cf. *prashṭi*).

पृष्टि 2. *pṛishṭi*, f. touch, L. (cf. *spṛishṭi*); a ray of light, L. (cf. *pṛiśni*).

पृष्टि 3. *pṛishṭi* = *pṛishṭha*, Pañcad.; Kauś., Sch.

पृष्ठ *pṛishṭhá*, n. (prob. fr. *pra-stha*, 'standing forth prominently;' ifc. f. *ā*) the back (as the prominent part of an animal), the hinder part or rear of anything, RV. &c. &c. (*pṛishṭhena* √*yā*, with gen., to ride on; °*ṭhena* √*vah*, to carry on the back; °*ṭhaṃ* √*dā*, to give the back, make a low obeisance; °*ṭhe*, ind. behind or from behind); the upper side, surface, top, height, ib. (with *diváh* or *nā́kasya*, the surface of the sky, vault of heaven; cf. *ghṛita-p°*); the flat roof of a house (cf. *gṛiha-p°*, *harmya-p°*); a page of a book, MW.; N. of a partic. arrangement of Sāmans (employed at the midday libation and formed from the Rathaṃtara, Bṛihat, Vairūpa, Vairāja, Śākvara, and Raivata S°s), TS.; Br.; ŚrS.; N. of various Sāmans, ĀrshBr. **-ga**, mfn. mounted or riding on, Kathās. **-gāmin**, mfn. going behind, following, devoted or faithful, Pañcat. (B.) **-gālana** (?), HYogas. **-gopa**, m. one who guards or protects the rear of a fighting warrior, MBh. **-granthi**, m. 'back-knot,' a hump on the back, L.; a kind of swelling, L.; mfn. hump-backed, A. **-ghna**, m. 'killing from behind' (?); N. of a man, Cat. **-cakshus**, m. 'having eyes in the back,' a crab, L.; a bear, V. **-ja**, m. 'back-born,' N. of a form (or a son) of Skanda, MBh. (v.l. *pṛishṭha-taḥ*). **-jāha**, n. 'back-root,' (prob.) os coccygis, L. **-tap**, mfn. having one's back burned (by the sun), Āpast. **-talpana**, n. the exterior muscles of an elephant's back, L. **-tás**, ind. from or on or behind the back, behind (with gen. or ifc.); to the back, backwards; secretly, covertly, ŚBr. &c. &c. (with √*kṛi*, to place on the back, R.; to neglect, abandon, forsake, give up, renounce, MBh.; R. &c.; with √*gam*, to go behind, follow, pursue, Pañc.; with √*bhū*, to be behind, be disregarded or of no account, MBh.); -°*to-bhāvam*, ind., Pāṇ. iii, 4, 61, Sch.; -°*to-mukha*, mfn. with back turned, Divyâv. **-tāpa**, m. 'back-burning,' noon, midday, MBh. **-dṛishṭi**, m. 'looking backwards,' a bear, L. **-deśa**, m. the back part, rear; (*e*), ind. behind (with gen.), Pañcat. **-dhāraka**, mfn. bearing on the back, bearing (a weight as burden), ĀpŚr., Sch. **-pātin**, mfn. being behind a person's back, following, watching, observing, controlling, Rājat. **-pīṭhī**, f. a broad back Bālar. **-phala**, n. (in alg.) the superficial contents of a figure, Col. **-bhaṅga**, m. 'breaking or bending the back,' N. of a mode of fighting, MBh. **-bhāga**, m. the hinder part, back, rear, Kāv. **-bhūmi**, f. the upper story or roof-terrace of a house, Kathās. **-madhya**, m. the middle of the back, MW. **-māṅsa**, n. the flesh on the back (°*saṃ* √*khād* or *bhaksh*, 'to eat the flesh of a person's back,' backbite), MBh.; Kāv.; °*sâda* or °*sâdana*, mfn. a backbiter, slanderer, L.; backbiting, slandering, A. **-yájvan**, m. one who sacrifices on high places, RV. **-yāna**, n. 'going on the back (of a horse &c.),' riding, Suśr.; mfn. = next,

Kām. **-yâyin,** mfn. riding on the back of (comp.), Kām., Sch. **-raksha,** m. = -*gopa*, MBh. **-rakshaṇa,** n. protection or defence of the back, MārkP. **-lagna,** mfn. hanging about a person's (gen.) back, following, Pañc. **-vaṇśa,** m. the back-bone, Suśr. **-vāstu,** n. the upper story of a house, Mn. iii, 91. **-vâh,** mfn. 'borne on the back,' riding, Hariv.; carrying a load on the back, MaitrS.; w. r. for *pashṭha-v°* and *prashṭha-v°*, q. v. **-vāha,** m. a beast of burden, draught-ox, Nīlak. **-vāhya,** m. id., L. **-śamanīya,** m. N. of a partic. Agni-shṭoma, Nyāyam., Sch. **-śaya,** mfn. lying on the back, g. *pārśvâdi*. **-śṛiṅga,** m. 'having horns over the back,' a wild goat, L.; *°gin*, m. (L.) 'id.,' a ram; a buffalo; a eunuch; N. of Bhīma. **-śveta,** m. 'white on the back or on the other side,' N. of a kind of rice, Gal. **-stotra,** n. N. of a partic. arrangement of Sāmans (= *prishṭha*, q. v.), Br.; ŚrS. **Prishṭhâkshepa,** m. acute and violent pain in the back, Car. **Prishṭhânuga** (R.), **°gāmin** (Pañcat.), mfn. going behind, following. **Prishṭhânuprishṭhaka,** mf(*ikā*)n. being behind a person's back, pursuing, following. **Prishṭhâvaguṇṭhana-paṭa,** m. a horse-cloth (covering the back), Kād. **Prishṭhâshṭhīla,** m. or n. the back of a tortoise, Bālar. **Prishṭhâsthi,** n. the back bone, L. **Prishṭhôdaya,** mfn. rising from behind (applied to the zodiacal signs Aries, Taurus, Gemini, Sagittarius, and Capricorn), Var. **Prishṭhôpatāpa,** m. the shining of the sun upon the back, SāmavBr.

Prishṭhaka, n. the back, R.; *°ke* √*kṛi*, to place behind, postpone, neglect, resign, Caurap.; Pañc.

Prishṭhī-√bhū, to become depressed or dejected, L. (prob. w. r. for *pishṭī-√bhū*).

Prishṭhe, loc. of *prishṭha* in comp. **-mukha,** mf(*ī*)n. having the face in the back, MBh.

Prishṭhyà, mfn. belonging to or coming from the heights (with *payas* or *andhas*, n. the milk or the plant from the heights, i. e. the Soma), RV.; carrying on the back; m. (with or sc. *aśva*) a horse for riding or for draught, Lāṭy.; MBh.; (*ā*), f. the edge which runs along the back of a Vedi, KātyŚr.; Sulbas.; (*pṛi°*), mfn. forming the Stotras called Prishṭha, TāṇḍBr.; having these Stotras (said of a partic. period of 6 sacrificial days [as subst. m.], viz. *prishṭhyâhan*, *prishṭhya-tryaha*, *-pañcâha*, *-stotriya*, *-caturtha*, *-shashṭha*, Vait.); m. = *prishṭhānām samūhaḥ*, Pāṇ. iv, 2, 42, Vārtt. 1, Pat. **-stoma,** m. N. of 6 Ekāhas or of a period of 6 sacrificial days (cf. above), ŚrS. **Prishṭhyâvalamba,** m. (sc. *pañcâha*), a period of 5 sacrificial days, ib.

पृष्णि **prishṇi,** (L.) mfn. = *priśni*; f. = *pārshṇi* or = *priśni* (ray of light).

पृष्णिपर्णी *prishṇi-parṇī*, w. r. for *priśni-p°*.

पृष्व *prishva*, mf(*ā*)n. produced by rime or hoar-frost, TS. (Sch.)

पृ 1. *prī*, cl. 9. P. (Dhātup. xxxi, 19) *priṇāti*, RV.; cl. 6. P. (√*priṇ*, xxviii, 40) *priṇāti*, ib.; cl. 3. P. (xxv, 4) *piparti*, ib. (also Ā.; Impv. *pipṛiprihi*, BhP. iv, 19, 38; pf. *papāra*, 3. pl. *paparuḥ* or *papruḥ*, Pāṇ. vii, 4, 12; *pupūre*, *°rire*, Bhaṭṭ.; *-pupūryās*, RV.; *papṛivás* [?], MaitrS.; aor. *apārīt*, Gr., *pūrishṭhās*, TĀr.; Impv. *pūrdhi*, RV.; Prec. *priyāsam*, AV., *pūryāt*, Gr.; fut. *parīshyati*, *parītā*, Gr.; ind. p. *pūrtvā*, Gr., *-pūrya*, MBh.; *-pūram* [in comp. with its object; cf. *udara-p°*, *goshpada-p°*, *carma-p°*, and Pāṇ. iii, 4, 31; 32]; inf. *priṇádhyai*, RV.; *-puras*, Kāṭh.; *pūritum*, R.), to fill (Ā. 'one's self'), RV.; AV.; to fill with air, blow into (acc.), Bhaṭṭ.; to sate, cherish, nourish, bring up, RV.; AV.; to refresh (as the Pitṛis), Bhaṭṭ. (aor. *apārīt*, v. l. *atārpsīt*); to grant abundantly, bestow on (dat.), present with (instr.), RV.; AV. (often p. *priṇát* = bounteous, liberal, ungrudging); to fulfil, satisfy (as a wish), BhP.: Pass. *pūryáte* (ep. also *°ti*, and RV. Ā. *pūryate*, p. *pūryamāṇa*), to be filled with, become full of (instr.), be sated, RV.; VS.; ŚBr.; MBh. &c.; to become complete (as a number), Lāṭy.: Caus. *pārayati*, to fill, Dhātup. xxxii, 15; to fulfil (only aor. *pīparat*), RV.; *pūráyati* (Dhātup. xxxiii, 126), *°te* (Pass. *pūryate* [cf. above]; aor. *apūri*, *apūrishṭa*), to fill, fill up with (instr.), ŚBr.; GṛŚrS.; MBh. &c.; to fill (with a noise, said also of the noise itself), MBh.; R.; to fill with wind, blow (a conch), ib.; to draw (a bow or an arrow to the ear), R.; to make full, complete, supplement (a sentence), Kuval.; to cover completely, overspread, bestrew, surround, MBh.; Kāv. &c.; to load or enrich or present with (instr.), ib.; to fulfil (a wish or hope), AV. &c. &c.; to spend completely (a period of time), R.: Desid. *piparīshati*, *pupūrshati*, Gr.: Intens. *pāparti*, *popūrti*, *popūryate*, ib. [Cf. Gk. πίμπλημι; Lat. *plere*, *plenus*; Lit. *pìlti*, *pìlnas*; Slav. *plŭnŭ*; Goth. *fulls*; Germ. *voll*; Eng. *full*.]

पेकि *peki*, m. or f. a species of bird, Svapnac.

पेचक *pecaka*, m. (√1. *pac*?) an owl (cf. *krishṇa-p°*); the tip or the root of an elephant's tail, Var.; a couch, bed (= *paryaṅka*), L.; a louse, L.; a cloud, L.; (*ikā*), f. a kind of owl, Hariv. (v. l. *picaka* and *pecuka*).

Pecakin, m. an elephant, L. (v. l. *picakin*).

Pecila, m. id., L. (v. l. *picila*).

पेचु *pecu*, n. Colocasia Antiquorum, L.

Pecuka, n., **°culi,** f. id., L.

पेज *peja*, m., see *tila-p°*; (*ā*), f. = *peyā*, L.

पेञ्जूषा *peñjūshā*, f. the wax of the ear, L.

पेट *peṭa*, mf(*ā* or *ī*)n. (√*piṭ*?) a basket, bag, L.; a multitude, L.; a retinue, L.; m. the open hand with the fingers expanded (= *pra-hasta*), L. **-kandaka,** m. a species of bulbous plant, Gal. **Peṭâlu,** n. id., ib.

Peṭaka, mf(*ikā*)n. a little basket, casket, box, Daś.; Sāy.; Kull. (cf. *kośa-peṭaka*, *bhūshaṇa-peṭikā*); m. n. = *dvaṃdva*, L.; n. a multitude, company, quantity, number, Rājat.; Kathās. (*°kam* √*kṛi*, with instr. 'to join or consort with'); (*ikā*), f. a species of plant, L.

Peṭāka, m. a basket, L.

Peṭṭāla, m. or n. id., Mālatim. vi, 18 (v. l. *°laka*).

Peḍā, f. id. (?), Divyâv.

पेट्टिभट्ट *peṭṭi-bhaṭṭa*, m. N. of the father of Viśvêśvara-bhaṭṭa, Cat.

पेड्डनाचार्य *peḍḍanâcārya*, m. N. of an author, Cat.

पेड्डुभट्ट *peḍḍa-bhaṭṭa*, m. N. of the commentator Mallinātha, Cat.

पेढाल *peḍhāla*, m. N. of the eighth Arhat of the future Utsarpiṇī, L.

पेण् *peṇ*, cl. 1. P. *peṇati*, to go; to grind; to embrace, Dhātup. xiii, 15 (cf. *paiṇ*, *praiṇ*, *laiṇ*).

पेण्ड *peṇḍa*, m. a way, road, Gal.

पेत्व *pétva*, m. (√1. *pā*?) a ram, wether, RV.; AV.; VS.; TBr.; a small part, W; n. nectar, Amṛita, Uṇ. iv, 115, Sch.; ghee or clarified butter, L.

पेदु *pedú*, m. (√*pad*?) N. of a man (under the especial protection of the Aśvins, by whom he was presented with a white horse that killed serpents), RV.

पेपीयमान *pepīyamāna*, mfn. (√1. *pā*, Intens.) drinking separately or greedily, ChUp.; Hariv.

Peya, mfn. to be drunk or quaffed, drinkable, MBh.; Kāv. &c.; to be tasted, tastable, MBh. (opp. to *ghreya*, *spṛiśya* &c.); to be taken (as medicine), Car.; to be drunk in or enjoyed by (cf. *śrotra-p°*); m. (sc. *yajña-kratu*) a drink offering, libation, ŚāṅkhŚr.; (*ā*), f. rice gruel or any drink mixed with a small quantity of boiled rice, MBh.; Car.; Suśr.; a species of anise (= *miśreyā*), L.; n. a drink, beverage, MBh.; R.; Suśr.

1. **Perú,** mfn. drinking, VS. (Mahīdh.; perhaps rather = 3. *péru*); (*péru*), thirsty (?), TS.; m. (only L.) the sun; fire; the ocean; the golden mountain (cf. *meru*).

पेब् *peb*, cl. 1. Ā. *pebate*, Dhātup. x, 11 (v. l. for *sev*, q. v.)

पेयालम् *peyālam* (?), ind. once more, repeatedly, L.

पेयूष *peyūsha*, m. or n. (= and v. l. for *pīyūsha*, q. v.) biestings; fresh butter; nectar, L.

पेरज *peraja* or *peroja*, n. a turquoise, L. (cf. Pers. فيروزه).

पेरणि *peraṇi* or *°ṇī*, f. (in music) a kind of dance.

पेरमभट्ट *perama-bhaṭṭa*, m. N. of the father of Jagan-nātha Paṇḍita-rāja, Cat.

पेरलस्थलमाहात्म्य *perala-sthala-māhātmya*, n. N. of ch. of SkandaP.

पेरा *perā*, f. a kind of musical instrument, Bhaṭṭ.

पेरु 2. *perú*, mfn. (√1. *pṛi*) carrying across, rescuing, delivering, RV. (For 1. see col. 2.)

पेरु 3. *péru*, mfn. (√*pī*, *pyai*) swelling or causing to swell, RV.; TĀr.; m. seed, germ, offspring (with *apâm* = Soma), ib., VS.; TS.; MaitrS.

पेरुक *perukâ*, m. N. of a man, RV.

पेरुभट्ट *peru-bhaṭṭa*, m. (with *lakshmīkānta*) N. of the Guru of Jagan-nātha Paṇḍita-rāja, Cat. (cf. *perama-bh°*).

पेल् *pel*, cl. 1. 10. P. *pelati* (Dhātup. xv, 34), *pelāyati* (Naigh. ii, 14), to go.

Pela, m. a small part, W.; going, W.; n. = next, L.

Pelaka, m. a testicle, L.

Pelava, mf(*ā*)n. delicate, fine, soft, tender, Kālid.; Kathās. (ifc. 'delicate like' or 'too d° for'); thin, slim, slender, Śiś.; Suśr. (opp. to *bahala*). **-kshauma,** n. fine linen, Suśr. **-pushpa-pattrin,** mfn. having tender flowers for arrows, Kum.

Peli, g. *chāttry-ādi*. **-śālā,** f., ib.

Pelin, m. a horse, W.

Pelu-vāsa (?), m. a chameleon, L.

पेव् *pev*, cl. 1. Ā. *pevate*, = *sev*, Dhātup. xiv, 33.

पेश *péśa*, m. (√*piś*) an architect, carpenter (?), RV. i, 92, 5; vii, 34, 11; ornament, decoration, AitBr.; BhP. (cf. *puru-* and *su-*; g. *gaurâdi* and *sidhmâdi*); (*ī*), f., see below.

Péśana, mf(*ī*)n. well formed, beautiful, RV.; AV.

Peśalá, mf(*ā*)n. (g. *sidhmâdi*) artificially formed, adorned, decorated, VS.; TBr.; beautiful, charming, lovely, pleasant, MBh.; Kāv. &c.; soft, tender, delicate, Kālid.; expert, skilful, clever, Bhartṛ.; fraudulent, crafty, L.; (*am*), ind. tenderly, delicately, Kathās.; m. N. of Vishṇu, V.; n. charm, grace, beauty, loveliness, BhP. **-tva,** n. dexterity, skill, VarBṛS., Sch. **-madhya,** mfn. slender-waisted, Ragh. **Peśalâksha,** mfn. having beautiful eyes; *-tā*, f., Rājat.

Peśalī-√kṛi, to render beautiful, R.

Péśas, n. shape, form, colour, RV.; an artificial figure, ornament, embroidery, an embroidered garment, ib.; VS.; AitBr. **-karī,** f. a bee (conceived of as a female), Gal. **-kārin,** m. a wasp, BhP. **-kārī,** f. a female embroiderer, VS.; ŚBr. **-kṛit,** m. the hand (as 'the artist'), BhP.; a wasp, ib. **-vat** (*péśas-*), mfn. decorated, adorned, VS.

Peśi, m., w. r. for *peshi*; f. an egg or = next, L.

Peśikā, f. rind, shell (of fruit), Suśr.

Peśitṛi, m. one who cuts in pieces or carves, a carver, VS.

1. **Peśī,** f. (g. *gaurâdi*) a piece of flesh or meat (also *māṇsa-p°* or *peśī māṇsa-mayī*), ShaḍvBr.; Gobh.; MBh. (cf. *piśita*); the fetus shortly after conception (*-tva*, n.), Nir.; MBh.; Suśr.; a muscle (of which there are said to be 500 in the human body), Yājñ.; Suśr.; the peel or rind (of fruit), Suśr. (cf. *peśikā*); a kind of drum, MBh.; a sheath, scabbard, L.; a shoe, L.; the egg of a bird, L.; spikenard, L.; a blown bud, L.; N. of a Piśācī and a Rākshasī, L.; of a river, L. **-kośa,** m. a bird's egg, L.

2. **Peśī,** ind. for *°śa*. **-kṛita,** mfn. cut into pieces, carved, R. (cf. 1. *peshī*).

Peśy-aṇḍa, n. a piece of flesh (esp. the fetus soon after conception), BhP.; a bird's egg, L.

Peśvara, mfn. (prob.) who or what grinds, Vop.

पेष् *pesh*, cl. 1. Ā. *peshate*, to exert one's self, strive diligently, Dhātup. xvi, 14.

पेष *pesha*, mf(*ī*)n. (√*pish*) pounding, grinding (ifc.), Baudh. (cf. *śilā-p°*); m. the act of pounding or grinding or crushing, Śiś. (cf. *pishṭa-p°*).

Peshaka, mf(*ikā*)n. one who pounds or grinds (cf. *gandhaka-peshikā*).

Peshaṇa, n. pounding, grinding (of grain), KātyŚr.; Hcat.; crushing (°ṇam-√yā, to be crushed), MārkP.; a threshing floor, L.; a hand-mill, L.; Euphorbia Antiquorum, L.; (ī), f., see below. **-vat**, mfn. a word formed for the explanation of *pipishvat*, Sāy.

Peshaṇi, f. = next, L.

Peshaṇī, f. a grind-stone, Mn. iii, 68. **-putraka**, m. a small grind-stone, L.

Peshaṇīya, mfn. to be ground or pounded or pulverized, MW.

Peshāka, m. a small grind-stone, L.

Peshi, m. a thunderbolt, L.

1. **Peshī**, ind. for *pesha*. **-√kṛi** (ind. p. *-kṛitya* or *-kṛitvā*), to crush, pound, MBh. (cf. 2. *peśī*).

Peshṭṛi, mfn. who or what pounds or grinds, Kull.

Peshya, mfn. = *peshaṇīya*; (ifc.) to be ground into, Suśr.

पेषी 2. *péshī*, f. swaddling-clothes, RV. v, 2, 2 (others 'churning-stick;' others 'nurse;' Sāy. = *hiṇsikā, piśācikā*).

पेष्ट्र *peshṭra*, n. (√*piś*) a bone, AV.

पेस् *pes*, cl. 1. P. *pesati*, to go (= *pis*), Dhātup. xvii, 69.

Pésuka, mfn. (√*pis*) spreading, extending, ŚBr.

Pesvara, mfn. (Pāṇ. iii, 2, 175) going, moving, W.; destructive, ib.; splendid, ib.

पै *pai*, cl. 1. P. *pāyati*, to dry, wither, Dhātup. xxii, 23.

पैङ्ग *paiṅga*, mfn. (fr. *piṅga*) relating to a rat or mouse, Kauś.; m. N. of a teacher (prob. w.r. for °*gya*); n. N. of wk. **-rājá**, m. a kind of bird, VS.

Paiṅgākshī-putra, m. and °**trīya**, mfn. (fr. *piṅgākshī-putra*), Pāṇ. iv, 2, 28, Vārtt. 1; 2, Pat.

Paiṅgāyani-brāhmaṇa, n. N. of wk., ĀpŚr.

Paiṅgi, m. patr. of Yāska, L.

Paiṅgin, mfn. derived from Paiṅgya, Pāṇ., Sch.; m. a follower of P°, Anup. **-Paiṅgi-rahasya-brāhmaṇa**, n. N. of wk.

Paiṅgī, f. of °*gya*. **Paiṅgī-pútra**, m. N. of a teacher, ŚBr.

Paiṅgya, m. patr. of a teacher, Br.; MBh.; n. the doctrine of P°, Br. **-smṛiti**, f. N. of wk.

Paiṅgyāyana-brāhmaṇa, n. N. of wk. (cf. *Paiṅgāyani-br°*).

पैङ्गरायण *paiṅgarāyaṇa*, m. patr. fr. *piṅgara*, g. *naḍādi*.

पैङ्गल *paiṅgala*, m. (sg. and pl.) patr. fr. *piṅgala*, g. *kaṇvādi*; n. the manual of Piṅgala. **-kāṇva**, m.pl. the followers of Piṅgala-kāṇva, Pāṇ. i, 1, 173, Vārtt. 8, Pat. **Paiṅgalôpanishad**, f. N. of wk.

Paiṅgalāyana (g. *naḍādi*), °**yani** (Saṃskārak.; cf. next), m. patr. fr. *piṅgala*.

Paiṅgalaudāyani, m., g. *pailādi* (Kāś. *paiṅgalāyani*).

Paiṅgalya, m. patr. fr. *piṅgala*, g. *gargādi*; n. brown or tawny colour, Suśr.

पैच्छिल्य *paicchilya*, n. (fr. *picchila*) sliminess, mucilaginousness, Suśr.

पैज *paija*, m. N. of a teacher, BhP.

पैजवन *paijavaná*, m. (fr. *pijavana*) patr. of Su-dās and of several men, RV. &c. &c.

पैजूलायन *paijūlāyana*, patr. fr. *pijūla*, g. *aśvādi*.

पैञ्जूष *paiñjūsha*, m. the ear, L. (cf. *piñjūsha, peñjūsha*).

पैटक *paiṭaka* or *paiṭāka*, m. patr. fr. *piṭāka*, g. *śivādi*.

Paiṭākika, mfn. = *piṭākena harati*, g. *utsaṅgādi*.

पैटकलायन *paiṭakalāyana*, m. sg. and pl. patron., Saṃskārak.

पैठर *paiṭhara*, mf(ī)n. (fr. *piṭhara*) cooked in a saucepan, R.

Paiṭharika, m. (prob.) one who uses a saucepan for making musical sounds, Pat.

पैठसर्प *paiṭhasarpa*, mfn. (fr. *pīṭha-sarpin*), Pāṇ. vi, 4, 144, Vārtt. 1, Pat.

Paiṭhika, m. (prob.) patr. fr. *pīṭha*, Hariv.

पैठीन *paiṭhīna*, m. = next, Cat.

Paiṭhīnasi, m. patr. of an ancient teacher (a Muni and author of a system of laws), AVPariś.; Pravar. &c. **-smṛiti**, f. N. of wk.

Paiṭhīnasya, m. patr., Saṃskārak.

पैडिक *paiḍika*, mf(ī)n. (fr. *piḍakā*) relating to boils or pustules, Suśr.

पैड्व *paiḍva*, w. r. for *paidva*.

पैण् *paiṇ*, cl. 1. P. *paiṇati*, to go; to send; to embrace, Dhātup. xiii, 15 (cf. *peṇ*).

पैण्डपातिक *paiṇḍapātika*, mf(ī)n. (fr. *piṇḍa-pāta*) living on alms, Buddh.

Paiṇḍāyana, m. patr. fr. *piṇḍa*, g. *naḍādi*.

Paiṇḍikya, n. (fr. *piṇḍika*), g. *purohitādi*.

Paiṇḍinya, n. (fr. *piṇḍin*), L. °**dya**, n. metron. (fr. *piṇḍī*), Pāṇ. iv, 1, 151.

पैतदारव *paitadārava*, mfn. (fr. *pīta-dāru*), g. *rajatādi*.

पैतरावण *paitarāvaṇa*, m. patr. (fr. *pīta-rāvaṇa?*), Pravar.

पैता *paitā*, Vṛiddhi form of *pitā* in comp. **-putrīya**, mfn. relating to father and son, KātyŚr. **-maha**, mf(ī)n. relating to or derived from a grandfather, AitBr.; MBh.; relating to or derived from or presided over by Brahmā, MBh.; Kāv. &c.; m. B°'s son (patr. of Manu), MBh; (pl.) forefathers, ancestors, MW.; n. the lunar mansion called Rohiṇī, Var.; *-tīrtha*, n. N. of a Tīrtha, ŚivaP.; *-siddhânta*, m., °*hī-bhāshya*, n. N. of wks. **-mahaka**, mfn. belonging or relating to a grandfather, Pāṇ. iii, 4, 77, Sch.

Paitri, Vṛiddhi form of *pitṛi* in comp. **-kriyā**, f. N. of wk. **-matyá**, mfn. sprung from one who has an illustrious father, ĀpŚr., Sch.; m. the grandson of an illustrious man, VS.; Pravar. (g. *kurv-ādi*). **-medhika**, mfn. relating to a sacrifice to the Pitṛis; m. or n. N. of wk.; *-vidhāna*, n., *-vidhāna-prayoga*, m., *-vidhi*, m., *-sūtra*, n. N. of wks. **-yajñika** (Lāṭy.), **-yajñīya** (Mn.), mfn. = *-medhika*. **-shvaseya**, mf(ī)n. sprung from a father's sister or paternal aunt, Mn.; MBh. (cf. Pāṇ. iv, 1, 133); m. a f°'s s°'s son, BhP.; (ī), f. a f°'s s°'s daughter, Mn. xi, 171. **-shvasrīya**, mfn. = prec., Pāṇ. iv, 1, 132.

Paitṛika, mf(ī)n. belonging to a father, paternal, ancestral, Mn.; MBh. &c.; relating or sacred to the Pitṛis, Rājat.; n. a sacred rite or Śrāddha in honour of deceased ancestors, MBh. **-tithi-nirṇaya**, m. N. of wk. **-dhana**, n. ancestral property, patrimony, MW. **-bhūmi**, f. the country of one's ancestors; a paternal estate, W. **-vidhāna**, n. N. of wk. **-shvaseya**, m., °**yī**, f. = *paitṛi-sh°* above.

Paitra, mf(ī)n. = *paitṛika*, ŚāṅkhŚr.; MBh.; n. a partic. part of the hand (cf. *pitṛi-tīrtha*), W.

Paitrâhorātra, m. a day and night of the Pitṛis (= one month), W.

Paitrika, (prob.) w. r. for *paitṛika*.

Paitrya, mf(ī)n. relating or belonging to the Pitṛis, MārkP.; Suśr.

पैतुदारव *paitudārava*, mfn. relating to or derived from the tree Pītu-dāru, Br.; ŚrS.

Paitudrava, mfn. = *daivadārava*, ŚāṅkhŚr., Sch.

पैत्त *paitta*, mf(ī)n. (fr. *pitta*) relating to the bilious humour, bilious, Suśr.

Paittika, mf(ī)n. id., ib.; of a bilious temperament, Var.

पैत्तल *paittala*, mf(ī)n. (fr. *pittala*) made of brass, brazen, L.

पैद्व *paidvá*, m. (scil. *aśva*) the serpent-killing horse of Pedu, RV.

पैनद्धक *painaddhaka*, mfn. (fr. *pi-naddha*), g. *varāhādi*.

पैनाक *paināka*, mf(ī)n. (fr. *pinākin*) belonging to or coming from Rudra-Śiva, R.; m. patr. fr. *pināka*, Pravar.

पैन्य *painya*, n. (fr. *pina*) fatness, thickness, Dhātup. ix, 46.

पैप्पल *paippala*, mf(ī)n. (fr. *pippala*) made of the wood of the holy fig-tree, Mcar. °**lava**, mfn., g. *kaṇvādi*. °**lavya**, m. (fr. *pippalu*), g. *gargādi*.

Paippalāda, mf(ī)n. derived from Pippalâda, GarbhUp.; m. patr. fr. *pippalāda*; pl. N. of a school of the AV.; °*dôpanishad*, f. N. of an Up. °**daka**, mf(ī)n. peculiar to or taught by Pippalâda or Paippalāda; n. the treatise or text of Pippalâda, Pāṇ. iv, 2, 104, Vārtt. 23, Pat. °**di**, m. patr. of a teacher, Pravar.; MBh.; Hariv.; (pl.) N. of a school of the AV., Col.

Paippalāyani, m. patr. of a teacher, VP. (cf. *pippalāyani*).

Paippali-kacchapa, mfn., Kāś. on Pāṇ. iv, 2, 126.

पैयवन *paiyavana*, w. r. for *paijavana*.

पैयूक्ष *paiyūksha*, mfn. (fr. *piyūksha*), g. *tālādi*.

पैयूष *paiyūsha*, n. = *piyūsha*, L.

पैल *paila*, m. (metron. fr. *pīlā*, Pāṇ. iv, 1, 118) N. of a teacher (a sage and promulgator of the Ṛig-veda), GṛS.; MBh. &c. **-garga**, m. N. of a man, MBh. **-garbha**, m. 'offspring of P°,' N. of a man, MW. **-meli**, m. patr., Saṃskārak. **-śyāparṇeya**, m. pl., g. *kārta-kaujapādi*. **-sūtra-bhāshya**, n. N. of wk.

Pailīya, m.pl. the disciples of Paila, Pat.

Paileya, m. metron. fr. *pīlā*, Pāṇ. iv, 1, 118.

पैलव *pailava*, mf(ī)n. made of the wood of the Pīlu tree (as the staff borne by a Vaiśya), Mn.; Gaut.

Pailu, Vṛiddhi form of *pīlu* in comp. **-kuṇa**, mfn., g. *utsādi*. **-mūla**, mfn. = *pīlu-mūle dīyate kāryaṃ vā*, g. *vyushṭādi*. **-vaha**, °**haka**, Pāṇ. iv, 2, 122, Sch. **-śīrshi**, m., **-śīrshyā**, f., Pāṇ. vi, 1, 61, Vārtt. 3, Pat.

पैल्य *pailya*, m., v. l. for *paila*, ĀrshBr.

पैल्ल्य *paillya*, n. (fr. *pilla*) blear-eyedness, Car.

पैल्व *pailva*, m., v. l. for *paila*, ĀrshBr.

Pailvakāyana, m. sg. and pl. patr., Saṃskārak.

पैशल्य *paiśalya*, n. (fr. *peśala*) graciousness, affability, MBh.

पैशाच *paiśāca*, mf(ī)n. relating or belonging to the Piśācas, demon-like, infernal, GṛS.; Mn.; MBh. &c. (with *graha*, m. demoniacal possession, MBh.); m. a Piśāca or kind of demon (also as N. of a tribe), MBh. (cf. g. *parśv-ādi*); the eighth or lowest form of marriage (when a lover secretly embraces a damsel either sleeping or intoxicated or disordered in her intellect), Mn. iii, 34; (ī), f. a present made at a religious ceremony to secure friendly regard, W.; (in dram.) a sort of jargon spoken by demons on the stage (cf. *piśāca-bhāshā*); night, L.; n. N. of wk. **-bhāshya**, n. N. of Comm. on Bhag.

Paiśācika, mf(ī)n. relating to the Piśācas, demoniacal (cf. *eūlikā-p°*).

Paiśācya, n. demoniacal nature, BhP.

पैशुन *paiśuna*, n. (fr. *piśuna*) tale-bearing, backbiting, calumny, malignity, wickedness, Mn.; MBh. &c.

Paiśunika, mfn. slanderous, Divyâv.

Paiśunya, n. = *paiśuna*, n., Mn.; MBh. &c. (*-vādin*, mfn. slanderous, Daś.); = *bhikshâśitva*, L. (prob. w. r. for *paiṇḍinya*).

पैष्ट *paishṭa*, mf(ī)n. (fr. *pishṭa*) made of flour, ground or made up into a cake, Gṛihyās.; Hcat.; m. patr. fr. *pishṭa*, g. *śivādi*; (ī), f. spirituous liquor distilled from rice or other grain, L. (cf. RTL. 193).

Paishṭika, mf(ī)n. made of meal or flour, Suśr.; (ā), f. = *paishṭī*; n. a quantity of cakes, L.

पैसुकायन *paisukāyana*, m. patr., Pravar.

पो *po* (nom. *pauḥ*), fr. Nom. *pāvaya*, Pāṇ. i, 1, 58, Vārtt. 2, Pat.

पोगण्ड *pogaṇḍa*, mfn. not full-grown or adult, young, Pur.; deformed, having a redundant or defective member, L.; m. a boy, one from his 5th to his 16th year, W. (cf. *a-p°*).

Paugaṇḍa, mf(ī)n. relating to a boy, oyish, Pur.; n. (also °*ḍaka*) boyhood, a period lasting from the 5th to the 16th year, BhP., Sch.

पोञ्च् *poñch*, cl. 1. Ā. *poñchate*, to clean (shoes), Divyâv. (prob. for *prôñch*, q.v.)

पोट *poṭa*, m. (√*puṭ* ?) the foundation of a house, L. (cf. *pota*); putting together, uniting, mixing, L.; = *śakala* (?), Hcar., Sch.; (*ā*), f. a hermaphrodite or a woman with a beard, Hcar.; a female servant or slave, L.; (*ī*), f. the rectum, PārGṛ., Sch.; a large alligator, L. **-gala**, m. (only L.) a species of reed; Saccharum Spontaneum; a fish; = *pañcajanya*.

Poṭaka, m. a servant, KātyŚr., Sch.; (*ikā*), f. a species of plant, L.

Poṭāya, Nom. Ā. °*yate* = *poṭām karoti*, Pāṇ. iii, 1, 17, Vārtt. 1.

पोटल *poṭala* (Car.) and °*laka* (KātyŚr., Sch.), m., °*likā* (L.), f. a bundle or packet.

Poṭṭala, n., °**lī**, f. id., L.

Poṭṭalaka, m. or n. id., Car.

Poṭṭalī-√kṛi, to put together into a bundle or packet, Car.

पोटिक *poṭika*, m. a pustule, boil, L.

पोट्टिल *poṭṭila*, m. (with Jainas) N. of the ninth Arhat of the future Utsarpiṇī, L.

पोडु *poḍu*, m. the parietal bone, the bone forming the upper part of the skull, L.

पोत *pota*, m. (hardly fr. √*pū*; but cf. Uṇ. iii, 86) a young animal or plant (mostly ifc., e.g. *mṛiga-p*° 'a y° deer,' *cūta-p*° 'a y° mango tree'), MBh.; Kāv. &c.; a fetus which has no enveloping membrane, L.; cloth, a garment, L.; the foundation of a house, L. (cf. *poṭa*); m. n. a vessel, ship, boat, MBh.; Hariv.; Var.; Kāv. [Cf. Lat. *putus*; Lit. *pautas*.] **-ja**, mfn. produced from a fetus which has no enveloping membrane (opp. to *jarāyu-ja*), L. **-tva**, n. the state or condition of (being) a ship, Mcar. **-dhāra** (Gal.), °**rin** (Śatr.), m. a ship-owner, master of a vessel. **-plava**, m. 'floating in a ship,' a seaman, mariner, Var. **-baṇij**, see *-vaṇij*. **-bhaṅga**, m. shipwreck, Kathās.; Pañc. **-raksha**, m. 'ship-governing,' the rudder of a boat, L. **-vaṇij**, m. 'ship-merchant,' a voyaging merchant, Hit. **-vāha** (L.), °**haka** (Pañcad.), m. 'boat-conductor,' a boatman, steersman. **-śāli**, m. small or young rice, L. **Potâcchādana**, n. 'cloth-covering,' a tent, L. **Potâdhāna**, n. small fry, a shoal of young fish, Vāsav. **Potâbha**, m. a species of camphor, Gal. (cf. *potāsa*).

Potaka, m. a young animal or plant (mostly ifc.; cf. *pota*), MBh.; Kāv. &c.; N. of a serpent-demon, MBh.; the site or foundation of a house, L. (cf. *gṛiha-p*°); (*ikā*), f. (only L.) cloth, a garment; Basella Lucida or Rubra; Anethum Sowa; = *mūla-potī*; (*ī*), f. Turdus Macrourus or Basella Lucida, L.

Potāya, Nom. Ā. °*yate*, to be a ship, Siṅhās.

Potyā, f. = *potānām samūhaḥ*, g. *pāśâdi*.

पोतन *potana*, n. N. of a town, HParis.

पोतरक *potaraka*, m. or n. = next, Buddh.

Potala, m. or n. N. of a seaport on the Indus (= Πατάλα; later applied to the residence of the Dalai Lama in Lhassa), Buddh. (cf. MWB. 292 &c.)

Potalaka, m. or n. N. of a mountain (= *potala*?), L.; (*ikā*), f., see *go-potalikā*. **-priya**, m. 'fond of the mountain P°,' N. of a Buddha or of a Jina, L.

पोताल *potāla*, m. N. of a Brāhman, L.; w. r. for *potala*.

पोतास *potāsa*, m. a species of camphor, L. (Eng. *potash*?).

पोतिमत्सक *potimatsaka*, m. N. of a prince, MBh. (v. l. *pautimatsyaka* and *yotimatsaka*).

पोतु *potu*, m. (√1. *pū*) = *mānabhāṇḍa-śodhaka*, L.

Pótṛi or **potṛi**, m. 'Purifier,' N. of one of the 16 officiating priests at a sacrifice (the assistant of the Brahman; = *yajñasya śodhayitṛi*, Sāy.), RV.; Br.; ŚrS.; Hariv.; N. of Vishṇu, L.; (*trī*), f. N. of Durgā, Gal. (cf. *pautrī*). **-tva-prayoga** or °**tṛi-prayoga**, m. N. of wk.

Potrá, n. the Soma vessel of the Potṛi, RV.; the office of the P°, ib.; KātyŚr.; the snout of a hog, Ṛit.; Hcar.; a ploughshare, L.; a garment or a thunderbolt (= *vastra*, v. l. *vajra*, L.); a ship or boat, L. (cf. *pota*). **-maṇḍala**, n. 'snout-orb,' the round snout (of a hog &c.), Ṛit. **Potrâyudha**, m. armed with a snout, a hog, boar, L.

Potri, in comp. for °*trin*. **-daṇshṭrā-ja**, m. a kind of gem (supposed to be produced in the tusk of a boar), L. **-rathā**, f. 'hog-vehicled,' (with Buddhists) N. of Māyā; (with Jainas) N. of a Śakti or female divinity.

Potrin, m. 'snouted,' a wild boar, Vcar.

Potrī, f. a garment (?), Divyâv.

Potrīya, mfn. relating or belonging to the Potṛi, AitBr.; KātyŚr.

Ponaka. See *śata-p*°.

Popuva, mfn. (fr. Intens.) purifying much or repeatedly, Pāṇ. i, 1, 4, Sch.

पोथ *potha*, m. (√*puth*) a blow, stroke, R.

Pothakī, f. a kind of ulcer on the eyelids, Suśr. (cf. *poṭika*).

Pothikā. See *ava-p*°.

पोन्नूरुस्थलमाहात्म्य *ponnūru-sthala-māhātmya*, n. N. of wk.

पोया *poyā*, f. a kind of wind instrument, Kalpas.

पोयालदह *poyāladaha*, m. or n. N. of a tank or pool, Kshitîś.

पोर *pora* = *parvan*, in *nīla-p*° and *śata-p*°, q.v.

Poraka, id. in *śata-p*°.

पोल *pola*, m. (√*pul*) magnitude, bulk, heap, L. (g. *jvalâdi*); (*ī*), f., see next.

Polikā (Bhpr.), °**lī** (L.), a kind of cake (cf. *pūlikā*, *paulī*, *pūpālī*).

पोलिन्द *polinda*, m. the mast or the ribs of a ship or boat, L. (cf. *padāra*, °*raka*, *pādālinda*).

पोविय *poviya*, m. N. of the father of Gaṅga-dāsa, Cat.

पोष *pósha*, m. (√*push*) thriving, prosperity, abundance, wealth, growth, increase, RV.; AV.; Br.; GṛŚrS.; nourishing, nurture, rearing, maintaining, supporting, Kāv.; Pur. &c. °**shaka**, mf(*ikā*)n. nourishing, feeding, a nourisher, supporter, breeder, keeper, Mn.; MBh. &c.; (ifc.) subsisting on or by, Hariv. °**shaṇa**, mfn. nourishing, cherishing (cf. *paksha-p*°); n. the act of nourishing, fostering, keeping, supporting, MBh.; Kāv. &c. °**shaṇīya**, mfn. to be nourished or kept or protected, MārkP. °**sham**, ind. (with √*push*) to thrive or prosper in (comp.), Pat.

Poshayitṛi, mfn. (fr. Caus.) one who nourishes or cherishes or rears, L. °**shayitnú**, mfn. causing to grow or thrive, nourishing, fostering, RV.; m. the Indian cuckoo, L. °**shayishṇú**, mfn. causing to thrive, advantageous, beneficial, AV.

Poshas. See *viśvâyu-poshas*.

Poshita, mfn. nourished, cherished, supported, MW. °**shitavya**, mfn. to be cherished or protected, W. °**shitṛi**, mfn. one who breeds or rears, Kull.

Poshin, mfn. nourishing, rearing, Kathās.

Poshuka, mfn. prospering, growing, ShaḍvBr.

Poshṭṛi, mfn. = °*shitṛi*, MBh.; Var.; m. grey bonduc, W.; *-vara*, mfn. the best of nourishers, nourishing best, W.

Póshya, mfn. thriving, well fed, RV.; abundant, copious, ib.; causing wealth or prosperity, AV.; to be nourished or fed or brought up or taken care of, MBh.; Kāv.; Pur.; *-putra* (W.), *-putraka* (Pur.), m. an adopted son; *-putra-karaṇa*, n. adoption, MW.; *-varga*, m. a class of persons or objects to be cherished (as parents, children, guests, and the sacred fire), W. °**shyá-vat**, mfn. causing prosperity, beneficial, RV.

पोषध *poshadha*, m. (with Buddhists) fasting, a fasting day, Lalit.; sacred day, Jātak.; °*dhôtsava*, m. sacred festival, Jātak.; °*dhôshita*, mfn. keeping the fast, Divyâv. **Poshadhika**, mfn. relating to fasting or a f° day (?), L. **Poshadheya**, n. fasting must be observed, Lalit.

पौंश्चलीय *pauṇścalīya*, mfn. (fr. *puṇś-calī*) belonging or relating to harlots, meretricious; *-vidyā*, f. knowledge concerning h°s, Rājat. °**caleyá**, m. the son of a h°, TBr. °**calya**, n. female incontinency, harlotry, Mn.; Hariv.

पौंसवन *pauṇsavana*, n. fr. and = *puṃsavana*, L. (See p. 630, col. 3.)

पौंसायन *pauṇsāyaná*, m. patr. fr. 2. *puṇs*, ŚBr.

Pauṇsna, mf(*ī*)n. worthy of or fit for or relating to a man, manly, human, BhP.; n. manhood, virility, ib.

Paúṇsya, mfn. belonging to men, manly, Śaṃk.; n. manhood, virility, manly strength or a manly deed, RV.

पौक्कस *paukkasa*, v. l. for *paulkasa*, Brahm-Up.

पौगण्ड *paugaṇḍa*, °*ḍaka*. See *pogaṇḍa*.

पौच्छ *pauccha*, mfn. (fr. *puccha*) being on the tail, caudal, Kathās.

पौञ्जिष्ठ *pauñjishṭhá*, m. (fr. *puñjishṭha*) a fisherman (v. l. °*shṭa*), AV.; TBr.; patr. (v. l. *pauj*°), Saṃskārak.

पौटलि *pauṭali*, m. a patr., Saṃskārak.

पौटायन *pauṭāyana*, m. a patr. fr. *puṭa*, g. *aśvâdi*.

पौड *pauḍa*. See *pakta-p*°.

पौणकि *pauṇaki*, m. patr. fr. *puṇaka*, Hcar.

पौणिकि *pauṇiki*, m., °*kyā*, f. patr. fr. *puṇika*, Pāṇ. iv, 1, 79, Sch.

पौणिकेर *pauṇikera*, m. metron. (fr.?), Pat.

पौण्डरीक *pauṇḍarīka*, mf(*ī*)n. (fr. *puṇḍarīka*) made or consisting of lotus-flowers (as a garland), Mālatīm.; m. a kind of Soma sacrifice lasting 11 days, ShaḍvBr.; ŚrS. &c.; patr. of Kshema-dhṛitvan, TāṇḍBr.; n. (sc. *kushṭha*) a kind of leprosy, Suśr. **-kārikā**, f., **-klṛipti-prayoga**, m., **-daśa-divasa-paddhati**, f., **-paddhati**, f., **-prayoga**, m., **-ratnâkara**, m., **-sāman**, n. pl., **-hotṛi-saptaka**, n., **-hautra-prayoga**, m. N. of wks.

पौण्डरीय *pauṇḍarīya*, °*rīyaka* and °*rya*, n. a kind of drug used as a remedy for diseased eyes (= *puṇḍarya*), L.

पौण्ड्र 1. *pauṇḍra*, m. (fr. *puṇḍra*) a species of sugar-cane of a pale straw colour, Suśr.; (pl.) N. of a people and of a country (said to include part of South Behar and Bengal), MBh.; Hariv.; Pur.; (sg.) a king of this country (regarded as a son of Vasudeva), ib.; N. of the conch-shell of Bhīma, MBh.; n. a sectarian mark, KātyŚr., Sch. **-rāja**, m. a king of the Pauṇḍras, Kathās. **-vishaya**, m. the country of the P°s, ib.

2. **Pauṇḍra**, Vṛiddhi form of *puṇḍra* in comp. **-nāgara**, mfn., Pāṇ. vii, 3, 24, Sch. **-matsyaka**, m. N. of a prince, MBh. **-vatsa**, m. N. of a Vedic school, L. (v. l. *-vaccha*). **-vardhana**, n. N. of a city (= *puṇḍra-v*°), R.; Kathās. (also *-vivardhana*, Uṇ. ii, 13, Sch.); m. N. of a country (Behar), L.

Pauṇḍraka, m. the pale straw-coloured species of sugar-cane, Bhpr.; a prince or (pl.) the people of the Pauṇḍras, Mn.; MBh.; Hariv.; Pur.; N. of a partic. mixed caste of hereditary sugar-boilers (the son of a Vaiśya by a woman of the distiller class, regarded as one of the degraded races of Kshatriyas), Mn. x, 44; n. (as mfn. ifc.) a sectarian mark, BhP.

Pauṇḍrika, m. a species of sugar-cane, L.; pl. N. of a people, MBh.

पौण्ढ्र *pauṇḍhra*, w. r. for *pauṇḍra*.

पौण्य *pauṇya*, mfn. (fr. *puṇya*) acting rightly, virtuous, worthy, TāṇḍBr.; KātyŚr.

पौतक्रत *pautakratá*, m. metron. fr. *pūtakratā*, RV.

पौतन *pautana*, m. (fr. *pūtanā*?) N. of a country or people, Suśr. (Sch. = *mathurā-pradeśa*).

Pautanya, n. (fr. *pūtanā*), Pat.

पौतरीय *pautarīya*, mfn. (fr. *pūtara*), Gaṇ.

पौतव *pautava*, n. a kind of measure, L. (cf. *potu*).

पौति *pauti*, Vṛiddhi form of *pūti* in comp. **-nāsikya**, n. fetor of the nostrils, Mn. xi, 50. **-māsha**, mfn. (fr. *-māshya*), g. *kaṇvâdi*. **-māshya**, m. (g. *gargâdi*) patr. or metron. of a teacher, BṛĀrUp. (also °*shī-putra*); (*ā*), f., Pāṇ. iv, 1, 74, Vārtt. 1, Pat. **-māshyāyaṇa** (*pauti-*), m. patr. fr. prec., ŚBr.; (*ī*), f., Pat.

पौतिक *pautika*, mfn. (fr. *pūtika* or °*kā*), g. *saṃkalâdi*; (*ī*), f. a kind of pot-herb, L.
Pautikya, n., g. *purohitâdi*, Kāś.

पौतुद्रव *paútudruva*, mfn. relating to the tree Pūtu-dru, ĀpŚr.

पौतृक *pautṛika*, mfn. (fr. *potṛi*), Pāṇ. iv, 3, 78, Sch.

पौत्तिक *pauttika*, n. (fr. *puttikā*) a kind of honey, Bhpr.

पौत्र 1. *paútra*, mf(*i*)n. (fr. *putra*) derived from or relating to a son or children, AV.; MBh. &c. (with *ishṭi*, f. 'a sacrifice performed to obtain a son,' R.); m. a son's son, grandson, AV.; Br. &c. (also *-ka*, Kāv.); (*ī*), f. a granddaughter, MBh.; Hariv.; Kathās.; N. of Durgā, L. **-jīvika**, n. an amulet made of the seeds of Putranjiva Roxburghii, Suśr. **-martya**, n. the dying of children, MantraBr. **-mṛityu**, m. id., HirGṛ. **Pautrâgha**, n. any injury or evil happening to children, AV. **Pautrâdya**, (prob.) w. r. for prec.
Pautrāyaṇa, m. patr. fr. *pautra*, ChUp.
Pautrika, m. patr. fr. *putrika* or = next.
Pautrikeya, m. (fr. *putrikā*) the son of a daughter adopted to raise issue for her father, Kull. **-vat**, mfn. having a grandson by an adopted daughter, ib.
Pautrikya, n. (fr. *putrika*), g. *purohitâdi*.
Pautrin, mfn. (fr. *pautra*) having a grandson, Mn. ix, 136.

पौत्र 2. *pautra*, n. the office of the Potṛi, g. *udgātrâdi*.

पौदन्य *paudanya*, n. N. of a city, MBh. (v. l. *vaidanya*).

पौद्गलिक *paudgalika*, mfn. (fr. *pudgala*) substantial, material, Śīl.; selfish, Divyâv.

पौनः *paunaḥ*, Vṛiddhi form of *punaḥ* in comp. **-punika**, mfn. frequently reiterated, repeated again and again, Vop. **-punya**, n. frequent repetition; (*ena*), ind. again and again, repeatedly, Vedântas.; Kāś.; Vop.
Paunar, Vṛiddhi form of *punar* in comp. **-ādheyika**, mf(*ī*)n. relating to the rite of replacing or renewing the sacrificial fire, ŚrS. **-ukta**, n. repetition, tautology, Kād. **-uktika**, mfn. = *punaruktam adhīte veda vā*, g. *ukthâdi*. **-uktya**, n. = *-ukta*, Ragh.; Śaṃk.; Sāh. **-nava**, mfn. belonging to the Punar-navā (Boerhavia Procumbens), Suśr. **-bhava**, mf(*ā*)n. relating or belonging to a widow who has married a second husband; m. the son of a widow remarried, Mn.; Gaut.; MBh. &c.; m. (with *bhartṛi*) a woman's second husband, Mn. ix, 176. **-bhavika**, mf(*ī*)n. relating to regeneration, L. **-vasava**, mfn. relating to the physician Punar-vasu; m. (with *yuvan*) a student of medicine, Hcar. **-vācanika** or **-vācika**, mfn. pleonastic, superfluous, ĀśvGṛ., Sch.

पौपिक *paupika*, m. pl. (fr. *pūpa*?) patron., Saṃskārak.

पौम्पा *paumpā*, f. N. of a sacred lake; *-māhātmya*, n. N. of wk.

पौयमानि *pauyamāni*, m. patr. fr. *pūyamāna*, Pat.

पौर 1. *paurá*, m. (√*prī*) 'filler, increaser,' N. of Soma (Sāy. = *udara-pūraka*); of Indra (Sāy. = *pūrayitṛi*); of the Aśvins &c., RV.; of a Ṛishi (author of RV. v, 73; 74); (pl.) of a dynasty, VP.

पौर 2. *paura*, mf(*ī*)n. (fr. *pura*) belonging to a town or city, urban, civic; m. a townsman, citizen (opp. to *jānapada*), Gaut.; MBh.; Kāv. &c.; a prince engaged in war under certain circumstances (= *nāgara*, q.v., applied also to planets opposed to each other), Var.; (pl.) N. of a dynasty, VP.; (*ī*), f. the language of the servants in a palace, L.; n. a species of fragrant grass, L. **-kanyā**, f. a maiden of the city, Ragh. **-kārya**, n. public business, Śak. **-jana**, m. townsfolk, citizens, MBh.; R. &c. **-jānapada**, mf(*ī*)n. belonging to town and country; m. pl. townsmen and country-people, MBh.; R. **-mukhya**, m. chief man of the city, Daś. **-yoshit**, f. a woman living in a city, townswoman, MW. **-ruci-deva**, m. N. of a man, Kathās. **-loka**, m. sg. and pl. = *-jana*, Kathās.; Pañc. **-vṛiddha**, m. = *-mukhya*, MBh.; Daś. **-sakhya**, n. fellow-citizenship, Mn. ii, 134. **-strī**, f. = *-yoshit*, W. **Paurâgragaṇya**, m. = *paura-mukhya*, Daś. **Paurâṅganā**, f. = °*rayoshit*, Megh.
Pauraka, m. a garden in the neighbourhood of a city or round a house, L.
Pauraṃjana, mf(*ī*)n. sprung or descended from Puraṃ-jana and Puraṃ-janī, BhP.
Pauraṃdara, mf(*ī*)n. (fr. *puraṃ-dara*) relating to or derived from or sacred to Indra, MBh.; Kāv. &c.; n. the Nakshatra Jyeshṭhā, Var.
Paurika, m. a townsman, citizen, MārkP.; a governor of a city, L.; N. of a prince of the city of Purikā, MBh.; pl. N. of a people, MārkP.

पौरकुत्सी *paurakutsī*, f., w. r. for *pauru-k*°, Hariv.

पौरगीय *pauragīya*, mfn. (fr. *pura-ga*), g. *kṛiśâśvâdi*.

पौरण *pauraṇa*, m. patr. fr. *pūraṇa*, ĀśvŚr.; (*ī*), f., w. r. for *paurāṇī*, Hariv.

पौरण्टक *pauraṇṭaka* and °*ṭhaka*, m. N. of a teacher, Cat. (w. r. *paurandaka*).

पौरंध्र *pauraṃdhra*, mfn. (fr. *puraṃdhri*) belonging to a woman, feminine, Viddh.

पौरव *paurava*, mf(*ī*)n. (fr. *pūru*) belonging to or descended from Pūru, MBh. (cf. Pāṇ. iv, 1, 168, Vārtt. 3, Pat.); m. a descendant of P°, ib. &c.; pl. the race of P°, Śak.; Pur.; N. of a people in the north or north-east of India, MBh.; R.; Var. (v. l. *paulava*); (*ī*), f. N. of the wife of Vasu-deva or of Yudhi-shṭhira, Pur.; (in music) N. of a Mūrchanā or a Rāga. **-tantava**, see *para-p*°*-t*° (p. 587, col. 1).
Pauravaka, m. pl. N. of a people, MBh.
Pauravīya, mfn. devoted to Pūru, Pāṇ. iv, 3, 100, Sch.

पौरश्चरणिक *pauraścaraṇika*, mfn. (fr. *puraś-caraṇa*), Pāṇ. iv, 3, 72.
Paurastya, mf(*ā*)n. (fr. *puras*) situated in front, foremost, Ragh.; BhP.; eastern (*-pavana*, m. east wind, Kathās.); pl. the people in the east (= *gauḍa*), Kāvyâd.

पौराण *paurāṇa*, mf(*ī*)n. (fr. *purāṇa*) relating to the past or to former times, previous, ancient, primeval, Paurānic, MBh.; Hariv.; R. °*ṇika*, mf(*ī*)n. id., Kāv.; Pur.; Suśr.; versed in ancient legends and stories, MBh. (cf. Pat. on Pāṇ. iv, 2, 60); of the value of one Purāṇa (coin), Saṃskārak.; m. a Brāhman well read in the Purāṇas, a mythologist, W.

पौरिक *paurika*. See above.

पौरिण *pauriṇa*, w. r. for *pauraṇa*.

पौरु *pauru*, Vṛiddhi form of *puru* in comp. **-kutsa**, m. patr. of Trasa-dasyu, Br.; MBh. &c. (*ī*, f., Hariv.) **-kutsi** (*paúru-*), **-kutsyá**, m. id., RV. **-madga**, n. N. of 2 Sāmans, ĀrshBr. (w. r. *-mahna*). **-mīḍha** or **-mīḷha**, n. N. of a Sāman, ŚrS. **-śishṭi**, m. N. of a teacher, TĀr. **-hanmana**, n. N. of sev. Sāmans, Br.; Lāṭy. **-hūta**, mfn. belonging to Puru hūta i.e. Indra, Śak. **Paurūravasa**, mfn. belonging or relating to Purū-ravas, MBh.; m. patr. fr. *purūravas*, ĀśvŚr. (w. r. *pauroravasa*).

पौरुष 1. *paurushá*, mf(*ī*)n. (fr. *purusha*) manly, human, ŚBr.; MBh. &c.; belonging or sacred to Purusha, RPrāt.; Mn.; MBh. &c.; = *purusha-dvayasa*, *-daghna* or *-mātra*, Pāṇ. v, 2, 37; 38; m. a weight or load which can be carried by one man, Mn. viii, 404 (Kull.); N. of a Rākshasa, VP. (v. l. *paurusheya*); (*ī*), f. a woman, ŚāṅkhŚr.; a period of 3 hours (= *yāma*), HPariś.; n. manhood, virility (opp. to *strītva*), R.; manliness, manly strength or courage or deed, valour, heroism, MBh.; Kāv. &c.; force (opp. to *buddhi*, 'intellect'), Kathās.; a man's length, VarBṛS.; a generation, ĀśvŚr.; MārkP.; semen virile, L.; the penis, Suśr.; a sun-dial, L. **-tā**, f., and **-tva**, n. manhood, manly strength or spirit, W.
2. **Paurusha**, Vṛiddhi form of *purusha* in comp. **-medhika** (*paúr*°), mfn. relating or belonging to a human sacrifice, ŚrS. **-vidhika**, mfn. man-like, human, Nir. **Paurushâda**, mfn. relating or peculiar to man-eaters or cannibals, Hariv. **Paurushâsakin**, m. pl. the school of Purushâsaka, g. *śaunakâdi* (Kāś. v. l. °*shāṅsakin*).
Paurushika, m. a worshipper of Purusha, BhP.
Paúrusheya, mf(*ī*)n. relating to or derived from or made by man, human, RV.; VS.; AV.; Br.; MBh.; coming from the soul, spiritual, Kap., Sch.; m. a hireling, day-labourer, SaddhP.; = *samūha*, *vadha* or *purushasya padântaram* (?), L.; N. of a Rākshasa, BhP.; n. human action, the work of man, AV. **-tva**, n. human nature or origin, Jaim., Sch. **-veda-vādin**, m. one who asserts the human origin of the Veda, Sarvad.
Paurushya, mfn. relating to Purusha, VPrāt.; n. manliness, manly strength or courage, heroism, MārkP.

पौरेय *paureya*, mfn. (fr. *pūra*), g. *sakhy-ādi*.

पौरो *pauro*, Vṛiddhi form of *puro* = *puras* in comp. **-gava**, m. an overseer or superintendent of a royal household, (esp.) the inspector of the royal kitchen, MBh.; Hariv.; Rājat. **-ḍāśa**, m. relating to the Puroḍāśa (s.v.), ŚBr.; m. a Mantra recited upon making the P° oblation, Siddh.; °*śika*, mf(*ī*)n. fr. prec., KātyŚr., Sch. (cf. Pāṇ. iv, 3, 70, Sch.); °*śiya*, mfn., ĀpGṛ., Sch. **-dhasa**, m. patr. fr. *puro-dhas*, Saṃskārak.; the office of the Purohita, BhP. **-bhāgya**, n. envy, malice, Kālid. **-hita**, mf(*ī*)n. belonging to or proceeding from a Purohita, MārkP. **-hitika**, m. metron. fr. *puro-hitikā*, g. *śivâdi*. **-hitya**, mfn. belonging to the family of a Purohita, ĀśvŚr.; n. the office of a P°, Kauś.; MBh.; Kāv. &c.

पौर्ण *paurṇa*, Vṛiddhi form of *pūrṇa* in comp. **-darva**, n. = *pūrṇa-d*°, ĀśvŚr. **-māsá**, mf(*ī*)n. relating to the full moon, usual or customary at f° m°, having the f° m°, ŚBr. &c. &c.; m. n. f° m° sacrifice, AV. &c. &c. (*-dharma*, m. the duty or rule of the f° m° sacr°, KātyŚr.; *-vat*, ind. like (at) the f° m° sacr°, ib.; *-sthālī-pāka-prayoga*, m., °*sêshṭi*, f. and °*sêshṭi-prayoga*, m. N. of wks.); m. patr. of a man, Saṃskārak.; of a son of Marīci and Sambhūti, Pur.; of a prince of the Āndhra dynasty, ib.; n. a day of f° m°, GṛŚrS., MBh.; (*ī*), f. a day or night of f° m°; (°*sy-adhikaraṇa*, n. N. of wk.); °*saka*, m. f° m° sacrifice, AgP.; °*sāyana*, n. a kind of f° m° sacr°, ŚāṅkhŚr.; °*sika*, mf(*ī*)n. used for the f° m° sacr°, KātyŚr., Sch.; °*sya*, n. a f° m° sacr°, ib.; MBh. **-vatsa**, m. pl. N. of a school of the Yajur-veda, AVPariś. **-saugandhi**, m. patr. fr. *pūrṇa-saugandha*, Saṃskārak.
Paurṇamī, f. a day of full moon (= *pūrṇimā*), L.
Paurṇima, m. (fr. *pūrṇimā*) an ascetic; (*ā*), f. = prec., W.

पौर्त *paurta*, mfn. (fr. *pūrta*) with *karman*, n. a meritorious or charitable work (such as feeding Brāhmans, digging wells &c.), MBh.; MārkP.
Paurti, m. patr. fr. *pūrta*, Pat.
Paurtika, mfn. relating to a charitable or meritorious work, Mn.; Hcat.

पौर्य *paurya*, patr. fr. *pura*, g. *kurv-ādi*.

पौर्व 1. *paurva*, mf(*ī*)n. (fr. *pūrva*) relating or belonging to the past; relating to the east, eastern, W.
2. **Paurva**, Vṛiddhi form of *pūrva* in comp. **-kālya**, n. priority of time, Pat. **-janmika**, mfn. done in a former life, Vajracch. **-dehika** or **-daihika**, mfn. belonging to or derived from a former body or a f° existence, done in a f° life, Yājñ.; MBh.; Hariv. **-nagareya**, mfn., fr. *pūrva-nagarī*, g. *nady-ādi*. **-pañcālaka**, mfn. = *pūrvaḥ pañcālānām*, Pāṇ. vii, 3, 13, Sch. **-padika**, mfn. seizing by the fore-foot (?), Kāś. on Pāṇ. iv, 4, 39; relating to the first member of a compound, Pat. (cf. *auttarap*°). **-bhaktika**, mf(*ī*)n. taken before eating, Car. **-madrika**, mfn., fr. *pūrva-madra*, Pāṇ. iv, 2, 108, Kāś. **-varshika**, mfn. = *pūrvāsu varshāsu bhavaḥ*, ib. vii, 3, 11, Sch. **-śāla**, mfn. = *pūrvasyāṃ śālāyāṃ bhavaḥ*, ib. iv, 2, 107, Kāś. **Paurvâtitha**, m. patr. fr. *pūrvâtithi*, Prav.; n. N. of a Sāman, Br. **Paurvāparya**, n. priority and posteriority, the relation of prior and posterior, succession, continuity, Lāṭy.; Śaṃk. &c. **Paurvārdhaka** or °*dhika*, mfn. living or situated on the eastern side of (gen.), Pāṇ., Sch. **Paurvâhṇika**, mfn. (w. r. °*hnika*) relating to the morning, produced in the forenoon, matutinal, KātyŚr.; MBh. &c.
Paurvika, mf(*ī*)n. former, prior, ancient, old, ancestral, Mn.; MBh. &c.; (*ī*), f. an ancestress, MBh.

पौल *paula*, m. sg. and pl. patr., Saṃskārak. **-hasti**, m. patr., ib.

पौलव *paulava*, v. l. for *paurava*, q. v.

पौलस्त्य *paulastya*, mfn. relating to or descended from Pulasti or Pulastya, R.; m. patr. of Kubera or Rāvaṇa, MBh.; Hariv.; R.; of Vibhīshaṇa, L.; (pl.) the brothers of Dur-yodhana, MBh.; (pl.) a race of Rākshasas, L.; the moon, L.; N. of an author; (*-smṛiti*, f. N. of wk.); w. r. for *paurastya*, Kathās.; (°*stī*), f. patr. of Sūrpa-ṇakhā (the sister of Rāvaṇa), L.

पौलाक *paulāka*, mfn. (fr. *pūlāka*), g. *palāśâdi*.

पौलास *paulāsa*, mfn. (fr. *pūlāsa*), g. *saṃkalâdi*.

पौलि *pauli*, m. grain half dressed or scorched or fried with ghee and made into a sort of cake, L.; patr. (also pl.), Saṃskārak.

Paulikā, f. a kind of cake, L. (v. l. *polikā*).

पौलिन्य *paulinya*, mfn. (fr. *pulina*), g. *saṃkāśâdi*.

पौलिश *pauliśa*, mfn. derived from or composed by Puliśa; *-mata*, n., *-siddhânta*, m. N. of astron. wks.

पौलुषि *paúlushi*, m. (fr. *pulusha*) patr. of Satya-yajña, ŚBr.

पौलोम *pauloma*, mfn. relating to or treating of Pulomā (N. of the 4th–12th Adhyāyas of MBh. i; cf. IW. 371, n. 1); relating to Puloman or Pulomā or Pulomī, MBh.; Hariv.; m. N. of a Ṛishi, Hariv.; (pl.) of a class of demons, KaushUp.; MBh. &c.; (*ī*), f., see next.

Paulomī, f. 'daughter of Puloman,' N. of the wife of Indra, Kāv.; Pur.; of the wife of Bhṛigu (cf. *pulomā*), VāyuP. **-pati**, m. 'lord or husband of Paulomī,' N. of Indra, Bhām. **-vallabha**, m. 'lover of P°,' N. of Indra, Bālar. **Paulomīśa**, m. = °*mī-pati*, L.

पौल्कस *paulkasá*, m. (= *pulkasa*) the son of a Nishāda or of a Śūdra father and of a Kshatriyā mother, VS.; ŚBr. &c.

पौष *pausha*, mf(*ī*)n. relating to or occurring at the time when the moon is in the asterism Pushya, Ragh.; Var.; m. the month Pausha (December–January, when the full moon is in the asterism Pushya), GṛŚrS.; MBh. &c.; N. of the 3rd year in the 12 years' cycle of Jupiter, VarBṛS.; (*ī*), f. the night or day of full moon in the month Pausha, Kauś.; n. a festival or a partic. festival, L.; a fight, combat, L.; N. of sev. Sāmans, Br. **-māhātmya**, n. N. of wk.

Paushya, mfn. relating to the asterism Pushya, MBh.; relating to king Paushya (°*shyôpâkhyāna*, n. N. of MBh. i, 3; cf. IW. 371, n. 1); m. N. of a prince (the son of Pūshan and king of Karavīra-pura), MBh.

पौषध *paushadha*, m. (cf. *poshadha*) a fasting day, Kalpas.; HPariś. (also *-dina*, n.)

पौष्कजिति *paushkajiti*, m. patr. (fr. *pushkajit*?), Saṃskārak.

पौष्कर *paushkara*, mf(*ī*)n. relating to or made of or connected with the blue lotus, MBh.; Hariv.; Pur.; (m. with or scil. *prādur-bhāva*, 'the appearance of Vishṇu in the form of a lotus flower,' Hariv.); relating to or derived from Costus Speciosus or C° Arabicus; n. the root (with or sc. *mūla*) or fruit of C° Sp° or Ar°, Suśr.; L.; N. of wk. **-tantra**, n., **-saṃhitā**, f. N. of wks.

Paushkaraka, mfn. = *paushkara* (also with *prādur-bhāva*), Hariv.

Paushkarasādi, m. (fr. *pushkara-sad*) N. of a grammarian, TPrāt.

Paushkariṇī, f. = *pushkariṇī*, a lotus pool, L.

Paushkareyaka, mfn., g. *kattry-ādi*.

पौष्कल *paushkula*, m. (fr. *pushkala*) a species of grain, MārkP.; n. N. of sev. Sāmans, Br.

Paushkalāvata, m. (fr. *pushkalā-vatī*) N. of a physician, Suśr.; mfn. derived from or composed by Paushk°, ib.

Paushkaleyaka, mfn., g. *kattry-ādi*.

Paushkalya, n. full growth, maturity, complete development, BhP.

पौष्कि *paushki*, m. patron. (Kāś., v. l. in g. *taulvaly-ādi*).

पौष्टिक *paushṭika*, mf(*ī*)n. (fr. *pushṭi*) relating to growth or welfare, nourishing, invigorating, furthering, promoting (with gen.), Gṛihyās.; Mn.; MBh. &c.; n. a cloth worn during the ceremony of tonsure, L.

Paushṭī, f. (fr. *pushṭa*?) N. of the wife of Pūru, MBh.

पौष्ठिमेर *paushṭhimera*, m. patron., Saṃskārak.

पौष्ण *paushṇa*, mf(*ī*)n. (fr. *pūshan*) belonging or relating or sacred to Pūshan, VS.; TS.; Br.; ŚrS.; relating to the sun, Jyot.; n. the Nakshatra Revatī, Var. (w. r. °*nya*).

Paushṇāvata, m. pl. patron, Saṃskārak. (prob. w. r. for *paushṭāvata* fr. *pushṭā-vat*).

पौष्प *paushpa*, mf(*ī*)n. (fr. *pushpa*) relating to or coming from or made of flowers, flowery, floral, Kāv.; Pur. (often w. r. for *paushya*, MBh.); (*ī*), f. N. of the city of Pāṭali-putra (= *pushpa-purī*), L.

Paushpaka, mfn. = *paushpa*, Hcat.; n. oxide of brass considered as a collyrium, green vitriol, L.

Paushpaketava, mfn. (fr. *pushpa-ketu*) relating to the god of love, Bālar.

Paushpāyaṇa, m. patr. fr. *paushpi*, g. *taulvaly-ādi*.

Paushpi, m. patr. fr. *pushpa*, ib.

Paushpiya, mfn., fr. *paushpi*, Pāṇ. iv, 2, 113, Sch.

पौष्पञ्जि *paushpañji* or °*piñji*, m. patr. of a teacher, VāyuP.; °*piñjin*, m. pl. his disciples, ib.

पौष्पिण्डि *paushpiṇḍi* or °*piṇḍya* or °*pidya*(?), m. N. of an ancient teacher, Cat.

पौष्य *paushya*. See under *pausha*.

पौष्यञ्जि *paushyañji*, °*yiñji*, v. l. or w. r. for *paushpañji*, °*piñji*.

पौस्कर *pauskara*, w. r. for *paushkara*.

प्ना *pnā*, f. the braided hair of Śiva, L.

प्याट् *pyāṭ*, ind. a particle used in calling, ho! hallo! L. (cf. g. *câdi*).

प्याय् *pyāy*. See *pyai* below.

प्युक्ष्ण *pyukshṇa*, m. or n. a covering for a bow (made of sinews or of the skin of a serpent; only *-veshṭitam dhanuḥ*), ŚBr.; KātyŚr.

प्युष् *pyush*, cl. 4. 10. P. *pyushyati*, *pyoshayati*, v. l. for *vyush*, Dhātup. xxvi, 7.

प्युस् *pyus*, cl. 4. P. *pyusyati*, v. l. for *vyush*, Dhātup. xxvi, 106.

प्यै *pyai* or *pyāy*, cl. 1. Ā. (Dhātup. xxii, 68; xiv, 17) *pyāyate* (pf. *papye*, Gr.; aor. *apyāyi*, ib.; *apyāsam*, AitĀr.; Prec. *pyāyishīmahi* or *pyāsishīmahi*, AV.; VS.; Br.; fut. *pyāsyate* or *pyāyishyate*, Gr.; *pyātā*, *pyāyitā*, ib.), to swell, be exuberant, overflow: Caus. *pyāyáyati*, °*te*, AV. &c.; (Pass. *pyāyyáte*, Br.) to make overflow, fill up (mostly in comp. with *ā*, see *ā-pyai*; cf. √*pi*, *pī*).

Pyāta (TS.) or **pyāna** (Gr.), mfn. fat, swollen (= *pīna*).

Pyāyana, mfn. causing to thrive, promoting growth or increase, invigorating, Nir.; n. growth, increase, Vop.

Pyāyita, mfn. fat; grown fat; increased; strengthened, refreshed (= *pīna*), MW.

प्र 1. *prá*, ind. before; forward, in front, on, forth (mostly in connection with a verb, esp. with a verb of motion which is often to be supplied; sometimes repeated before the verb, cf. Pāṇ. viii, 1, 6; rarely as a separate word, e.g. AitBr. ii, 40); as a prefix to subst. = forth, away, cf. *pra-vṛitti*, *pra-sthāna*; as pref. to adj. = excessively, very, much, cf. *pra-caṇḍa*, *pra-matta*; in nouns of relationship = great-, cf. *pra-pitāmaha*, *pra-pautra*; (according to native lexicographers it may be used in the senses of *gati*, *ā-rambha*, *ut-karsha*, *sarvato-bhāva*, *prāthamya*, *khyāti*, *ut-patti*, *vyavahāra*), RV. &c. &c. [Cf. *puras*, *purā*, *pūrva*; Zd. *fra*; Gk. πρό; Lat. *pro*; Slav. *pra-*, *pro-*; Lith. *pra-*; Goth. *faúr*, *faúra*; Germ. *vor*; Eng. *fore*.]

प्र 2. *pra*, mfn. (√*prī* or *prā*) filling, fulfilling; (n. fulfilment, ifc.; cf. *ākūti-*, *kakshya-*, *kāma-*); like, resembling (ifc.; cf. *ikshu-*, *kshura-*).

प्रउग *prá-üga*, n. (prob. fr. *pra-yuga*) the forepart of the shafts of a chariot, RV. (cf. *hiraṇya-p*°); TS.; ŚBr.; KātyŚr.; a triangle, MānGṛ.; Śulbas.; m. n. = *-śastra*, RV.; VS.; Br.; ŚrS. **-cit**, mfn. piled up or arranged in the form of a triangle, ŚBr. **-citi**, f. arrangement in the f° of a tr°, MaitrS. **-śastra**, n. N. of the second Śastra or hymn at the morning libation, Vait.; N. of wk. **-stotra**, n. N. of a partic. Stotra, ib. **Praügâdhyāya**, m. N. of wk.

Pra-ügyà, mfn. being at or on the forepart of the shafts of a chariot, ŚBr.

प्रकङ्कत *pra-kaṅkatá*, m. a partic. venomous worm or reptile, RV.

प्रकच *pra-kaca*, mfn. (prob.) having the hair erect, L. (cf. *ut-k*°, *vi-k*°).

प्रकट 1. *pra-kaṭa*, mf(*ā*)n. (according to Pāṇ. v, 2, 29 fr. *pra* + affix *kaṭa*; but prob. Prākr. = *pra-kṛita*, cf. *ava-k*°, *ut-k*°, *ni-k*°, *vi-k*°, *sam-k*°), evident, clear, manifest, open, plain, public, Sūryas.; Kāv.; Kathās. (*prakaṭaḥ so 'stu*, 'let him show himself'); Pur. &c.; m. N. of a Śaiva philosopher, Cat.; ibc. and (*am*), ind. evidently, visibly, openly, in public, Var.; Kathās.; Pañc.; *-prīti-vardhana*, m. 'evidently increaser of joy,' N. of Śiva, Śivag.; *-raktânta-nayana*, mfn. having the eye-corners visibly red, Pañc.; *-vaikṛita*, mf(*ā*)n. openly inimical, Rājat.; *-śīrsha*, mfn. bearing the head uplifted, Mṛicch.; °*ṭâprakaṭa*, mf(*ā*)n. open and not open, L.

2. **Pra-kaṭa**, Nom. P. °*ṭati* (pr. p. °*ṭat*), to appear, become manifest, Hariv. °**kaṭana**, n. manifesting, bringing to light, ŚārṅgP. °**kaṭaya**, Nom. P. °*yati*, to manifest, disclose, evince, display, Kāv.; Pur. °**kaṭāya**, Nom. P. °*yati*, to manifest, reveal, proclaim, VarP. °**kaṭita**, mfn. manifested, unfolded, proclaimed, public, evident, clear, Kāv.; Pur.; *-hatâśesha-tamas*, mfn. having openly destroyed utter darkness, Kāv. °**kaṭī**, ind. (= °*kaṭa*) in *-karaṇa*, n. making visible, manifesting, proclaiming, Cat.; *-√kṛi* (ind. p. *-kṛitya*), to manifest, unfold, display, Kāv.; Pañc. &c.; *-kṛita*, mfn. manifested, shown, displayed, Kāv.; Pur.; *-√bhū* (ind. p. *-bhūya*), to become manifest, appear, Kāv.; Kathās.; *-bhūta*, mfn. manifest, open, plain, Kāv.; Pur.; Pañc.

प्रकण्व *pra-kaṇva*, m. 'freed from evil' (?), N. of a place, Pāṇ. vi, 1, 153, Kāś.

प्रकथ् *pra-√kath*, P. *-kathayati* (ind. p. *kathayya*, Pāṇ. vi, 4, 56, Sch.), to announce, proclaim, R. °**kathana**, n. announcing, proclaiming, Pāṇ. i, 3, 32 (*am*, ind. enclit. after a finite word, g. *gotrâdi*).

प्रकमन *pra-kamana*, n. (√2. *kam*), Pāṇ. viii, 4, 34, Sch. °**kamanīya**, mfn. ib.

प्रकम्प् *pra-√kamp*, Ā. *-kampate*, to tremble, shake, quiver, MBh.; R.; to become lax, be loosened, Suśr.; to vibrate (said of sound), RPrāt.: Caus. *-kampayati*, to cause to tremble, R.; BhP.; to swing, wave, brandish, shake, Br.; KātyŚr. °**kampa**, mfn. trembling, R.; m. (ifc. f. *ā*) trembling or violent motion, quaking, staggering &c., MBh.; Kāv. &c. °**kampana**, mf(*ā* or *ī*)n. trembling violently, W.; m. wind, air, Śiś.; N. of a hell, L.; of an Asura, Kathās.; n. great trembling, violent or excessive motion, MBh.; Hariv. (cf. Pāṇ. viii, 4, 32, Sch.) °**kampanīya**, mfn. to be made to tremble, Vop. °**kámpita** (!), mfn. trembling, quaking, Suparṇ.; R.; (fr. Caus.) made to tremble, shaken, Bhaṭṭ.; n. trembling or violent motion, Var. °**kampin**, mfn. trembling, moving to and fro, MārkP. °**kampya**, mfn. to be caused to tremble or shake, R. (cf. *dush-prak*°).

प्रकर 1. *pra-kara* &c. See *pra-√kṛi*.

प्रकर 2. *pra-kara*. See *pra-√kṝi*, p. 654.

प्रकर्ष *pra-karsha* &c. See *pra-√kṛish*.

प्रकल् *pra-√2. kal*, P. *-kālayati*, to drive onwards, chase, pursue, MBh.; to drive out (cattle for grazing), Gobh.; to urge on, incite, Kāṭh. °**kālana**, mfn. driving on, chasing, pursuing, MBh.; Hariv.; m. N. of a Nāga of the race of Vāsuki, MBh.

प्रकला *pra-kalā*, f. part of a part, a minute portion, L. **Prakala-víd**, mfn. knowing very little, ignorant, RV. vii, 18, 15 (Sāy.; = *vaṇij*, Nir.)

प्रकल्पक *pra-kalpaka*, °*pana* &c. See *pra-√klṛip*.

प्रकल्याण *pra-kalyāṇa*, mfn. very excellent, Śivag.

प्रकश *pra-kaśá*, m. the thong or lash of a whip, AV.; the urethra (cf. *niruddha-p°*), Suśr.; hurting, killing, W.

प्रकस् *pra-√kas*, Caus. *-kāsayati*, to drive away, Dhūrtas. (in Prākr.); to cause to bloom, Ghaṭ.

प्रकाङ्क्ष् *pra-√kāṅksh*, P. *-kāṅkshati*, to wish for, desire, Suśr.; to watch, lie in wait, waylay, MBh. °**kāṅkshā**, f. desire of food, appetite, Car.

प्रकाण्ड *pra-kāṇḍa*, m. n. the stem or trunk of a tree from the root to the branches, Śiś. ix, 45; a branch, shoot, W.; (ifc.) anything excellent of its kind, Mcar.; Bālar.; Naish. (cf. *go-*, *-mantri-*; also °*ḍaka*, Bhaṭṭ.); m. the upper part of the arm, L. (cf. *pra-gaṇḍa*). **Prakāṇḍara**, m. a tree, L.

प्रकाम *pra-kāmá*, m. joy, delight, VS.; pl. objects of desire, R.; ibc. and *am* or *-tas*, ind. with delight, willingly, according to desire, sufficiently, very much, indeed, MBh.; Kāv. &c. **—bhuj**, mfn. eating till satisfied, eating enough, Ragh. **—vikasat**, mfn. expanding or blooming abundantly, Amar. **—vinata**, mfn. quite drooping, Śak. **—vistāra**, m. great expansiveness, Ragh. **Prakāmântas-tapta**, mfn. internally consumed by heat, Mṛicch. **Prakāmâlokanīyatā**, f. the being an object that may be viewed at pleasure, Kum. **Prakāmôdya**, n. talking to the heart's content, talkativeness, VS.; ŚBr.

प्रकार *pra-kāra* &c. See *pra-√kṛi*.

प्रकाश् *pra-√kāś*, Ā. *-kāśate* (ep. also P. °*ti*), to become visible, appear, shine, become evident or manifest, Up.; MBh.; Kāv. &c.: Caus. *-kāśayati* (rarely °*te*), to make visible, cause to appear or shine, illumine, irradiate, show, display, manifest, reveal, impart, proclaim, ib.: Intens. (only pr.p. *-cākaśat*) to illumine (and) to survey, RV. iv, 53, 4. °**kāśa**, mfn. visible, shining, bright, ŚāṅkhBr.; MBh. &c.; clear, manifest, open, public, Mn.; MBh. &c. (*nāmadheyam prakāśaṃ kritvā*, 'pronouncing a name out loud,' ŚāṅkhGṛ.); expanded, W.; universally noted, famous, celebrated for (instr. or comp.), MBh.; Kālid.; renowned throughout (comp.), Ragh.; (ifc.) having the appearance of, looking like, resembling, MBh.; R. &c.; ibc. and (*am*), ind. openly, publicly, before the eyes of all, Mn.; MBh. &c. (°*śam nâbhyudaikshata*, 'he did not look up openly,' R.); aloud, audibly (esp. in dram., opp. to *ātma-gatam*, *sva-gatam* &c.); m. clearness, brightness, splendour, lustre, light, RV. &c. &c.; (fig.) light, elucidation, explanation (esp. at the end of titles of explanatory works, e.g. *kāvya-*, *tarka-* &c.); appearance, display, manifestation, expansion, diffusion, MBh.; Kāv.; Sāh.; publicity, fame, renown, glory, Hariv.; sunshine, open spot or air, MBh.; Śak.; MārkP. (*e*, ind. openly, publicly, before the world, ifc. in the presence of, MBh.; Prab.); the gloss on the upper part of a (horse's) body, VS. (Mahīdh.); w.r. for *prak°*, TBr.; a chapter, section, Cat.; N. of sev. wks., ib.; laughter, L.; N. of a Brāhman (son of Tamas), MBh.; of Manu Raivata, Hariv.; (pl.) the messengers of Vishṇu, L.; n. bell-metal, brass, L.; *-kartṛi*, m. 'light-maker,' N. of the sun, MBh.; *-karman*, m. 'whose work is to give light,' N. of the sun, MBh.; *-kāma*, mfn. wishing for renown, ĀśvŚr.; *-kraya*, m. a purchase made publicly, MW.; *-tā*, f. brightness, brilliance, splendour, Yājñ.; Pañcat.; publicity (°*tāṃ √gam*, to become known or public, Mudr.); renown, MBh.; *-tva*, n. clearness, brightness, Naish., Sch.; appearance, manifestation (*sva-*, 'of one's self'), Sāh.; celebrity, renown, MBh.; *-datta*, m. N. of a poet, Cat.; *-devī*, f. N. of a princess, Rājat.; *-dhara*, m. N. of an author, Cat.; *-nārī*, f. 'public woman,' a prostitute, Mṛicch.; *-vañcaka*, m. 'open rogue,' a public deceiver or cheat, MW.; *-vat*, mfn. (*-vat-tva*, n.) bright, brilliant, shining, ChUp.; Ragh., Sch.; Śaṃk.; m. N. of one of the feet of Brahmā, ChUp.; *-varsha*, m. N. of a poet, Cat.; *-vāda*, m., *-saṃhitā*, f., *-saptati*, f., *-sūtra*, n. N. of wks.; °*śâkāśa-kānti*, mfn. bright as a clear sky, MW.; °*śâtmaka*, mfn. = °*śâtman* (°*ka-tva*, n. the possession of a brilliant nature or character, brilliancy), Śaṃk.; °*śâtman*, mfn. brilliant in character or nature, brilliant, shining, Sūryas.; m. N. of Śiva, Śivag.; the sun, L.; N. of sev. men and authors (also with *yati* and *svāmin*), Cat.; °*śâditya*, m. and °*śânanda*, m. N. of authors, Cat.; °*śi-karaṇa*, n. giving light, illuminating, R.; °*śi-√kṛi*, P. Ā. to give light, illumine, Var.; to publish, make known, Hariv.; °*śi-bhāva*, m. the becoming light, morning twilight, Nir.; °*śêtara*, mfn. 'other than visible,' invisible, Śak.; °*śêndra*, m. N. of a man (the father of Kshemêndra), Cat.; °*śôdaya*, m. N. of wk. °**kāśaka**, mf(*ikā*)n. clear, bright, shining, brilliant, Sāṃkhyak.; Tattvas.; MBh.; universally known, renowned, Rājat.; irradiating, illuminating, giving light, BhP.; Sāṃkhyak., Sch.; MBh. &c.; making clear, illustrating, explaining, Sarvad.; Śaṃk.; making apparent or manifest, disclosing, discovering, publishing, evincing, betraying, Sāh.; MārkP.; indicating, expressing, L.; m. 'light-giver,' the sun, Kathās.; (*ikā*), f. N. of sev. Comms.; n. bell-metal, brass, L.; °*ka-jñātṛi* and *-prajñātṛi*, m. 'knowing the giver of light, i.e. the sun,' a cock, L.; °*ka-tva*, n. illustration, explanation, Vedântas. °**kāśana**, mfn. illuminating, giving light, RāmatUp.; MBh.; (*ā*), f. teaching, L.; n. illuminating, giving light; causing to appear, displaying, bringing to light, publicly showing or manifesting, Nir.; MBh.; Suśr. &c.; *-vat*, mfn. irradiating, illuminating, Nir. °**kāśanīya**, mfn. to be displayed, to be shown or manifested, MW. °**kāśita**, mfn. become visible, brought to light, clear, manifest, apparent, evident; displayed, unfolded, discovered; illumined, enlightened, irradiated; published, promulgated, MBh.; R.; Suśr. &c.; *-viruddha-tā*, f. and °*ddha-tva*, n. (in rhet.) a partic. awkwardness in expression (saying something at variance with what ought to be said), Sāh. °**kāśin**, mfn. visible, clear, bright, shining, MBh.; Hariv.; making visible or manifest, Pañcat.; °*śi-tā*, f. and *-tva*, n. clearness, brightness, brilliance, light, MBh. °**kāśya**, mfn. to be brought to light or made manifest, Sāṃkhyak.; Śaṃk.; Sāh.; n., w.r. for *prāk°*, q.v., MBh.; R.; MārkP.; *-tā*, f. the being manifest, publicity, Rājat.

प्रकिरण *pra-kiraṇa*, *-kīrṇa* &c. See *pra-√kṛī*.

प्रकीर्त् *pra-√kīrt*, P. *-kīrtayati*, to announce, proclaim, declare, call, name, state, approve, Mn.; Yājñ.; MBh. &c. °**kīrtana**, n. announcing, proclaiming, extolling, praising, MBh.; MārkP.; (*ā*), f. mentioning, naming, Nir. °**kīrti**, f. celebration, declaration, Bhag. °**kīrtita**, mfn. announced, proclaimed, revealed, stated, said, mentioned, Mn.; Yājñ.; named, called, Mn.; Pañc.; approved, praised, celebrated, Yājñ.; Pañc.

प्रकुञ्च *pra-kuñca*, m. (cf. *kuñci*) a partic. measure of capacity (somewhat more or less than a handful), Suśr.; = *pala*, Car.

प्रकुट् *pra-√kuṭ* (only ind. p. *-kuṭya*), to cut or carve (meat) into small pieces, MBh.

प्रकुथित *pra-kuthita*, mfn. (√*kuth*) putrid, putrescent, Suśr. °**kotha**, m. putrefaction, putridity, ib.; mfn. in °*thôdaka*, n. filthy water, ib.

प्रकुप् *pra-√kup*, P. *-kupyati*, to be moved or agitated; to become enraged, fly into a passion, MBh.; R. &c.: Caus. *-kopayati*, to set in motion, agitate, excite, provoke to anger, Mn.; MBh. &c. °**kupita** (*prá-*), mfn. moved, agitated, shaken, RV. ii, 12, 2; very angry, incensed, enraged, Mn.; Yājñ. &c. °**kupta**, mfn. enraged, incensed, Vikr. iv, 57. °**kopa**, m. effervescence, excitement, raging (of diseases, war &c.), Var.; Rājat.; tumult, insurrection, Hit.; violent anger, rage, fury, wrath, ire, Mn.; MBh. &c.; (in med.) excess, superabundance, vitiation, Suśr. °**kopaṇa** or °**kopana**, mf(*ī*)n. (fr. Caus.; cf. Pāṇ. viii, 4, 31, Sch.) exciting, irritating, provoking, Suśr.; n. anything irritating, irritation, ib.; provoking, exasperating, incensing, MBh.; Hit. °**kopaṇīya** or °**kopanīya**, mfn. to be irritated or provoked, Pāṇ. viii, 4, 31, Sch. °**kopita**, mfn. (fr. Caus.) irritated, provoked, enraged, R. °**kopitṛi**, mfn. exciting, disquieting, disturbing (ifc.), MBh. °**kopin**, mfn. irritated, Car.; (ifc.) irritating, stimulating, ib.

प्रकुब्रता *prakubrátā*, f. (of unknown etym. and meaning), ŚBr.

प्रकुल *pra-kula*, n. a handsome or excellent body, L. (v.l. *pra-hvala*).

प्रकूज् *pra-√kūj*, P. *-kūjati*, to utter groans, Car. °**kūjana**, n. groaning, ib.

प्रकूटा *pra-kūṭā*, f. See *paca-prak°* under 2. *paca*, p. 575, col. 2.

प्रकूर्द् *pra-√kūrd*, P. *-kūrdati*, to jump forward, leap about, Pañc.

प्रकूष्माण्डी *pra-kūshmāṇḍī*, f. N. of Durgā, L.

प्रकृ *pra-√1. kṛi*, P. Ā. *-karoti*, *-kurute*, *-kriṇoti*, °*ṇute* &c., to make, produce, accomplish, perform, achieve, effect, RV. &c. &c.; to make into, render (with double acc.), Mn.; MBh. &c.; (with *dārān*) to take to wife, marry, MBh.; to appoint, charge with (loc.), PārGṛ.; Mn.; Yājñ.; to enable to, make fit for (inf.), RV.; to remove, destroy, kill, AV.; Hariv.; (only Ā. by Pāṇ. i, 3, 32) to violate, pollute (a girl), Mn. viii, 370; (Ā.) to induce, move, incline, RV.; to make a person perform anything, PārGṛ.; (with *manas* or *buddhim*) to set the heart upon, make up the mind to (dat. or loc.), resolve, determine, Mn.; MBh.; R.; to gain, win, conquer, RV.; to lay out, expend, Pāṇ. i, 3, 32; to put forward, mention first, make the subject of discussion, ib.; to serve, honour, worship, Bhaṭṭ.: Caus. *-kārayati*, to cause to be made or prepared, Gaut.

1. **Pra-kara**, mf(*ī*)n. (for 2. see *pra-kṛī*) doing much or well, W.; m. aid, friendship, ib.; usage, custom, ib.; respect, ib.; seduction, ib.; (*ī*), f. a kind of song, Yājñ.; an episodical interlude inserted in a drama to explain what follows, Daśar. (also °*rikā*, Pratāp.); theatrical dress or disguise, W. °**karaṇa**, n. production, creation, Hariv.; treatment, discussion, explanation; treatise, monograph, book, chapter (esp. introduction or prologue), GṛŚrS.; MBh.; Sarvad.; a subject, topic, question, matter, occasion, opportunity, MBh.; Kāv. &c.; (*asminn eva °raṇe*, 'on this occasion' or 'in this connection,' MBh.; *na ca °raṇam vetsi*, 'nor do you know what is the matter,' Kathās.); a kind of drama with a fictitious plot (such as Mṛicch., Mālatīm. &c.), Sāh. (IW. 471); treating with respect, W.; doing much or well, ib.; N. of wk. (cf. *nyāyapr°*); *-tas*, ind. occasionally, Suśr.; *-tva*, n., Vedântas.; *-pañcikā*, f., *-pāda*, m., *-vādârtha*, m. N. of wks.; *-śas*, ind. according to species or kind (opp. to *pṛithak-tvena*), Nir.; *-sama*, m. a kind of sophism, an assertion by two opponents of some argument which has the same force of argument pro and con, Nyāyas.; Car.; °*ṇī* (or °*ṇikā*), f. a drama of the same character as the Prakaraṇa but of less extent, Sāh. °**karaṇikā** and °**karikā**, see above. °**kartavya**, mfn. to be prepared, MBh.; to be disclosed or brought to light, Pañcat.; to be appointed to (loc.), MBh. °**kartṛi**, mfn. one who causes, MBh.

Pra-kāra, m. sort, kind, nature, class, species, way, mode, manner, APrāt.; Kauś.; Mn.; MBh. &c.; *kena °reṇa*, in what way? how? Pañc.; °*raiḥ*, in one way or another, R.; *Rāmāyaṇasya Bhāratasya vā °raḥ*, a kind of R. or MBh., Rājat. (mostly ifc. mfn.; cf. *tri-* 'of three kinds,' *nānā-*, *bahu-*); similitude or difference, L.; *-ka*, mfn. = *kāra*, ifc. (cf. *tat-*, *nish-*); *-tā*, f. speciality, Bhāshāp.; *-vat*, mfn. belonging to a species, Pāṇ. v, 3, 69, Sch. °**kārya**, mfn. to be evinced or manifested, Pañc. °**kṛita**, mfn. made, done, produced, accomplished, prepared, RV. &c. &c.; appointed, charged, KātyŚr.; (ifc.) made or consisting of (*tat-p°*), Pāṇ. v, 4, 21; commenced, begun or one who has c° or b°, iii, 4, 71; put forward, mentioned, under discussion or in question, KātyŚr.; Kathās.; Sāh.; (in rhet.) = *upa-meya*, Kpr.; wished, expected, MW.; genuine, real, MW.; m. N. of a man, g. *aśvâdi*; n. something begun, L.; original subject, present case, MW.; *-tā* (*pra-kṛitá-*), f. the being begun or in process of execution, ŚBr.; *-tva*, n. the being the subject of discussion, Śaṃk.; the being offended, Jātakam.; °*târtha*, mfn. having the original sense; real, true, Kathās.; °*tôkta*, mfn. being spoken of as the original subject of discussion, Sāh. °**kṛiti**, f., see next p. °**kriyā**, f. producing, production, Sarvad.; procedure, way, manner, MBh.; a ceremony, observance, formality, Hariv.; Kathās.; Rājat.; precedence, high position, elevation, privilege, MBh.; Rājat.; Kathās.; the insignia of high rank, Rājat.; characterisation, Nyāyas.; a chapter (esp. the introductory ch° of a work), Śaṃk.; Cat.; (in med.) a prescription, Bhpr.; (in gram.) etymological formation; rules for the f° and inflection of words, MW.; *-kaumudī* (and °*dī-vṛitti*), f., -°*ñjana-ṭīkā* (°*kriyâñj°*), f., *-pradīpa*, m., *-bhūshaṇa*, n., *-mañjarī*, f., *-ratna*, n., *-rūpâvalī*, f., -°*rṇava* (°*kriyârṇ°*), m., *-saṃgraha*, m., *-sarvasva*, n., *-sāra*, m. N. of gram. wks.

Pra-kṛiti, f. 'making or placing before or at first,' the original or natural form or condition of anything, original or primary substance (opp. to *vi-kṛiti,* q. v.), Prāt.; Nir.; Jaim.; MBh.; cause, original source, Mn.; MBh.; Śak. &c.; origin, extraction, Mṛicch.; nature, character, constitution, temper, disposition, MBh.; Kāv.; Suśr. &c. (ibc. and °*tyā,* ind. by nature, naturally, unalterably, properly, Prāt.; ŚrS.; Mn. &c.); fundamental form, pattern, standard, model, rule (esp. in ritual), ŚrS.; (in the Sāṃkhya phil.) the original producer of (or rather passive power of creating) the material world (consisting of 3 constituent essences or Guṇas called *sattva, rajas* and *tamas*), Nature (distinguished from *purusha,* Spirit as Māyā is d° from Brahman in the Vedânta); pl. the 8 producers or primary essences which evolve the whole visible world (viz. *a-vyakta, buddhi* or *mahat, ahaṃ-kāra,* and the 5 *tan-mātras* or subtle elements; rarely the 5 elements alone), IW. 80 &c.; (in mythol.) a goddess, the personified will of the Supreme in the creation (hence the same with the Śakti or personified energy or wife of a deity, as Lakshmī, Durgā &c.; also considered as identical with the Supreme Being), W.; IW. 140; RTL. 223; (pl.) N. of a class of deities under Manu Raibhya, Hariv.; (in polit.) pl. a king's ministers, the body of ministers or counsellors, ministry, Mn.; MBh. &c.; the subjects of a king, citizens, artisans &c., ib.; the constituent elements or powers of the state (of which 7 are usually enumerated, viz. king, minister, allies, treasure, army, territory, fortresses, Mn. ix, 294; 295); the various sovereigns to be considered in case of war (viz. the *madhyama, vijigīshu, udāsīna* and *śatru;* to which should be added 8 remoter princes, viz. the *mitra, ari-mitra, mitra-mitra, arimitra-mitra, pārshṇi-grāha, ākranda, pārshṇigrāhâsāra, ākrandâsāsa;* each of these 12 kings has 5 Prakṛitis in the form of minister, territory, fortresses, treasure and army, so that the total number of Prakṛitis may be 72), Mn. vii, 155; 157, Kull.; (in gram.) the crude or elementary form of a word, base, root, an uninflected word, Sāh.; Pāṇ., Sch.; Vop.; N. of 2 classes of metres, Col.; (in arithm.) a co-efficient, multiplier, ib.; (in anat.) temperament, the predominance of one of the humours at the time of generation, W.; (with *tṛitīyā*) the third nature, a eunuch, MBh.; matter, affair, Lalit.; the male or female organ of generation, L.; a woman or womankind, L.; a mother, L.; an animal, L.; N. of a woman, Buddh.; N. of wk. — **kalyāṇa,** mf(*ī*)n. beautiful by nature, MārkP. — **kṛipaṇa,** mfn. naturally plaintive; n° feeble (in discriminating), MW. — **khaṇḍa,** n. N. of BrahmavP. ii. — **gāna,** n. N. of wk. — **guṇa,** m. one of the 3 constituent essences of P° (see *guṇa*), MW. — **ja,** mfn. springing from nature, inborn, innate, Bhag. — **tattva-nirūpaṇa,** n. N. of wk. — **tarala,** mfn. naturally changeful, volatile, fickle, dissolute, W. — **tva,** n. the state or condition of being the original or natural or fundamental form of anything, Kap.; Śulbas. — **nishṭhura,** mfn. naturally hard or cruel, R. — **pāṭha,** m. = *dhātup°,* list of verbal roots, Pat. — **purusha,** m. a minister, servant, Megh.; a standard or model of a man, Siṇhâs.; (du.) nature and spirit, L. — **pralaya,** m. = *-laya,* MW. — **bhava,** mfn. natural, usual, common, Var. — **bhāva,** m. the natural state or unaltered condition of anything, ĀśvŚr.; mfn. = *-bhava,* Var. — **bhūta,** mfn. being in the original state or condition, original; °*tĕkāra,* m. the original sound or letter *i,* MW. — **bhūman,** n. pl. plurality of original form or nature, Nir. vii, 4. — **bhojana,** n. usual food, Car. — **mañjarī,** f. N. of wk. — **maṇḍala,** n. the aggregate of the Prakṛitis or of a king's subjects, the whole kingdom, Ragh. — **mat,** mfn. having the original or natural form or shape, natural, usual, common, MBh.; in a natural or usual frame of mind, R. — **maya,** mf(*ī*)n. being in the natural state or condition, RāmatUp. — **laya,** m. absorption into Prakṛiti, the dissolution of the universe, Sāṃkhyak.; N. of a class of Yogins, Yogas. — **vat,** ind. as in the original form, Upal. — **vikṛiti,** f. mutation of the original form or state, Rājat.; *-yāga-kāla-viveka,* m. N. of wk.; *-sva-bhāva,* m. the relation of (a word in its) radical form to (itself under the) mutations (of inflection &c.), MW. — **vishama,** mfn. naturally rough, Bhartṛ. — **vihāra-kārikā,** f. pl. N. of wk. — **śraishṭhya,** n. superiority of origin, Mn. x, 3. — **shṭha,** mfn. = *-stha,* Car. — **sampanna,** mfn. endowed with a noble nature, R. — **siddha,** mfn. effected by nature, natural; n. true or real nature, Bhartṛ. — **subhaga,** mfn. naturally pleasant or agreeable, Megh. — **stha,** mfn. being in the original or natural state, genuine, unaltered, unimpaired, normal, well, healthy, Yājñ.; Kāv.; Var.; Suśr. (also *-sthita,* Var.); inherent, innate, incidental to nature, Ragh.; bare, stripped of everything, MW.; *-darśana,* mfn. one who has recovered the faculty of sight, Śak. (Pi.) iii, $\frac{3}{1}\frac{0}{7}$. — **sthita,** mfn., see *-stha.* — **hautra,** n. N. of wk. **Prakṛitī-jana,** m. sgl. the subjects of a king, R. **Prakṛitīśa,** m. 'lord of subjects,' a magistrate, Hariv. **Prakṛitishṭi-nirṇaya,** m., **Prakṛityṛic,** f. N. of wks.

प्रकृत् *pra-√2. kṛit,* P. *-kṛintati* (ep. also *-kartati*), to cut off; to cut up, cut to pieces, AV.; MBh. °**kṛintá,** m. one who cuts to pieces, TS. (v.l. *vi-kṛintá*).

प्रकृशित *pra-kṛiśita* (√*kṛiś*), mfn. attenuated, thin, emaciate, W.

प्रकृष् *pra-√kṛish,* P. *-karshati,* to draw or stretch forth, drag along or away, Kauś.; MBh. &c.; to push off, remove from (abl.), R.; to lead (an army), MBh.; R.; to draw or bend (a bow), MBh.; to distract, trouble, disturb, R.: Caus. *-karshayati,* to cause (a field) to be ploughed, ĀśvGṛ. °**karsha,** m. pre-eminence, excellence, superiority, excess, intensity, high degree, MBh.; Kāv. &c. (often ifc., e.g. *adhva-pr°,* a great distance, R.; *kāla-pr°,* a long time, Suśr.; *guṇa-pr°,* extraordinary qualities, Mṛicch.; *phala-pr°,* mfn. consisting chiefly in fruit, Suśr.; *śakti-pr°,* possessing extraordinary power, Inscr.); length of time, duration, Car.; absoluteness, definitiveness, W.; (in gram.) the effect of the prefix *pra* upon roots, ib.; ibc. and (*āt* or *eṇa*), ind. eminently, intensely, thoroughly, in a high degree, MBh.; Kāv. &c.; *-gamana,* n. going absolutely or finally, departure, W.; *-tantra,* mfn. dependent on excellence or superior strength, MW.; *-vat,* mfn. pre-eminent, excelling by or in (comp.), Śaṃk. °**karshaka,** m. 'harasser, disquieter,' N. of the god of love, L. °**karshaṇa,** m. one who distracts or troubles, MBh.; n. drawing away, ib.; pushing forth, advancing, RPrāt.; drawing furrows, ploughing, W.; extension, length, duration (*kāla-*), Suśr.; a bridle or whip, MBh. vii, 6446; the act of harassing or disquieting, MW.; excellence, superiority, W.; realizing by the use of a pledge more than the interest of the money lent upon it, ib. °**karshaṇīya,** mfn. to be dragged away or moved along, KātyŚr., Sch. °**karshita,** mfn. (fr. Caus.) drawn forth or out &c.; exceeded in profit (as the interest of a loan), W.; n. profit on a pledge beyond the interest of the money lent upon it, W. °**karshin,** mfn. drawing forth, causing to move, leading (an army), Hariv.; excellent, pre-eminent, distinguished, Jātak. °**kṛishṭa,** mfn. drawn forth, protracted, long (in space and time), MBh.; R.; superior, distinguished, eminent, Mn.; MBh. &c. (*-tara,* mfn., Pañcat.; *-tama,* mfn., Daś.); violent, strong, Ratnâv.; distracted, harassed, disquieted, MW.; *-keśâkhya,* m. coral (lit. having the name 'beautiful hair;' cf. *pra-vāla*), Kāvyâd.; *-tā,* f. (MW.), *-tva,* n. (Hit.) transcendent excellence, pre-eminence, superiority. °**kṛishya,** mfn. = °*karshaṇīya,* KātyŚr.; excessive, much; *-kutsita,* mfn. strongly censured, Pāṇ. ii, 3, 17, Vārtt. 1, (*prakṛishṭa-k°,* Bhaṭṭ. ii, 36, Sch.)

प्रकॄ *pra-√1. kṝi,* P. *-kirati,* to scatter forth, strew, throw about, ŚBr.; MBh. &c.; to issue forth, spring up, R.; Suśr.: Pass. (and P. Pot. *-kīryāt*) to disappear, vanish, MBh.

2. **Prakara,** m. (for 1. see *pra-kṛi*) a scattered heap, heap, multitude, quantity, plenty, MBh.; Kāv. &c.; a nosegay, W.; (*ī*), f. a place where four roads meet, L.; n. aloe wood, Agallochum, L. °**karitṛí,** m. one who sprinkles (or seasons?), VS. °**kiraṇa,** n. scattering, throwing about, MārkP. °**kīrṇa,** mfn. scattered, thrown about, dispersed, Nir.; MBh.; Kāv.; squandered, Dhūrtas.; disordered, dishevelled, MBh.; R.; Suśr.; waved, waving, Śiś. xii, 17; mixed, containing various subjects, miscellaneous, Kām.; standing alone, nowhere mentioned, Vishṇ.; confused, incoherent (as speech), Śiś. ii, 63; expanded, opened, W.; spread abroad, published, ib.; m. Guilandina Bonduc, L.; a horse (?), Gal.; n. a miscellany, any miscellaneous collection, L.; a chapter or section of a book, L.; extent, L.; N. of a class of Jaina works, MWB. 533; scattering or throwing about, A.; *-keśa,* mf(*ī*)n. having dishevelled hair, MBh.; Suśr.; (*ī*), f. N. of Durgā, L.; *-pūjā,* f., *-mantra,* m. pl. N. of wks.; *-maithuna,* mfn. living in mixed (connubial) intercourse, MBh.; *-saṃgraha,* m. N. of wk.; °*ṇâdhyāya,* m. a chapter containing miscellaneous subjects (N. of VarBṛS. xxii); °*ṇâmbara-mūrdhaja,* mfn. with disordered garments and dishevelled hair, MBh. °**kīrṇaka,** mfn. scattered, dispersed, occurring singly or in single instances, VarBṛS.; mixed, containing various things, ib., Sch.; m. a horse, L.; m. (L. n.) a tuft of hair used as an ornament for horses, MBh.; R.; a chowrie (the tail of the Bos Grunniens used as a fan or fly-flap and as an orn° for h°), L.; n. a miscellany, any collection of heterogeneous objects, Vām. i, 3, 12; a section or division of a book, L.; N. of the 3rd part of the Vākyapadīya and of another wk., Cat.; (in law) a case not provided for by the Śāstras and to be decided by the judge or king, W.; extent, length, L.; *-dāna,* n. pl. N. of wk. °**kirya,** mfn. to be scattered or strewed &c., L.; m. (and *ā,* f.) N. of some medic. plant or plants, Car.; Suśr. (Guilandina Bonduc and a species of Karañja, L.)

प्रकृत् *pra-√kṛit.* See *pra-√kīrt.*

प्रक्लृप् *pra-√klṛip,* Ā. *-kalpate* (rarely P. °*ti*), to prosper, succeed, AV.; to be fit or suitable (with inf.), KātyŚr., Sch.: Caus. *-kalpayati,* to place in front, put at the head, honour, AV.; ŚBr.; to put down on (loc.), MBh.; to appoint or elect to, select for (loc.), ib.; BhP.; to put in the place of (gen.), Pat.; to contrive, invent, devise, prepare, provide, Mn.; MBh. &c.; to fix, settle, determine, Mn.; Yājñ.; to prescribe, Car.; to make out, ascertain, calculate, Var.; to make into, choose for (2 acc. or acc. and loc.), BhP.; to suppose, imagine (with acc. and loc.), MBh. °**kalpaka,** mf(*ikā*)n. being in the right place, Pat. °**kalpana,** n. placing in, raising to (comp.), Sāh.; (*ā*), f. fixing, settlement, allotment, Mn. viii, 211; n. or f. supplying or mixing with (*saha*), Car. °**kalpayitṛi,** m. one who prepares or arranges, ŚBr. °**kalpita,** mfn. made, done, prepared, arranged, appointed, MBh.; Kāv. &c.; shed (as a tear), Amar.; (*ā*), f. a kind of riddle, Cat. °**kalpya,** mfn. to be appointed or settled or fixed or determined, Mn.; Yājñ. °**klṛipta,** mfn. done, made, prepared, arranged, ready, R.; Kathās.; being in the right place, being right, Pat.; (*am*), ind. readily, easily, ŚBr.; *-tva,* n. progress, success KātyŚr.; *-snāna-maṇḍana,* mfn. one whose ablutions and toilet have been arranged, R. °**klṛipti,** f. the being there, existing, KātyŚr. (w. r. °*kṛiti*); the being in the right place, being right or correct, Pat.

प्रकेत *pra-ketá,* m. (√4. *cit*) appearance, apparition, sight, RV.; perception, intelligence, knowledge (concr. = a knower, vii, 11, 1; x, 104, 6), ib. °**ketana,** n. appearance, apparition (used to explain prec.), Nir. ii, 19.

प्रकोष्ठ *pra-koshṭha,* m. the fore-arm, Kālid.; BhP.; Suśr.; a room near the gate of a palace, Mudr.; (also n., L.) a court in a house, a quadrangle or square surrounded by buildings, Mṛicch.; a part of a door-frame, W. °**koshṭhaka,** m. a room near the gate of a palace, Kum.

प्रकोष्णा *prakoshṇā* (!), f. N. of an Apsaras, VP.

प्रक्खर *prakkhara,* m. iron armour for the defence of a horse or elephant, L. (cf. *pra-kshara, pra-khara*).

प्रक्रन्द् *pra-√krand* (only aor. 3. sg. *-akran*), to call or invoke loudly, RV. v, 59, 1: Caus. (only aor. *-acikradat*) to roar, move with a rushing sound, ib. ix, 77, 1.

प्रक्रम् *pra-√kram,* P. Ā. *-krāmati, -kramate,* (P.) to step or stride forwards, set out, walk on, advance, proceed, resort to (acc.; aor. Ā. *-cákramanta,* RV. ii, 19, 2; *prâkraṃsta,* Bhaṭṭ.), march, pass, go, RV. &c. &c.; (with *pradakshiṇam*) to walk around from left to right, BhP.; to cross, traverse, R.; (Ā.) to undertake, commence, begin (with acc., *artham* ifc., or inf.), MBh. (also P., e.g. *varayām pra-cakramuḥ* = °*yām-cakruḥ,* i, 1809); Kāv. &c. (cf. Pāṇ. i, 3, 42); to act or behave towards (loc.), MBh.: Caus. *-krāmayati,* to cause to step forwards, PārGṛ.: Desid. *cikraṇsishyate*, Pāṇ. vii, 2, 36, Vārtt. 2, Pat. °**krantṛi**, m. (L.) one who proceeds or begins; conquering, overpowering, surpassing. °**kramá**, m. (ifc. f. *ā*) stepping, proceeding, L.; a step, stride, pace (also as a measure of distance, the length of which is variously stated at 2 or 3 or 3½ Padas, also at more or less), Br.; GṛŚrS.; commencement, beginning, procedure, course, KātyŚr.; Mālatīm.; Prab.; Kathās.; leisure, opportunity, L.; relation, proportion, degree, measure, Vedântas.; method, order, regularity (esp. in the position of words and in gram. construction; cf. *-bhaṅga*); the reading of the Krama (= *krama-pāṭha*, q.v.), Pat.; discussing any point in question; the case in qu°, MW.; (pl.) a series of oblations corresponding to the movements of a sacrificial horse, ŚBr.; KātyŚr.; *-tritīya*, n. the third of a square pace, KātyŚr.; *-bhaṅga*, m. (in rhet.) want of order or method, the breaking of symmetry in composition or the violation of gram. construction (= *bhagna-prakramatā*), Kāvyâd., Sch.; °*ga-vat*, mfn. wanting method or symmetry, irregular, unsymmetrical, Pratāp.; *-viruddha*, mfn. stopped in the beginning, Prab. °**kramaṇa**, n. stepping forwards, proceeding, advancing towards (comp.), KātyŚr.; Kālid.; issuing forth, Tattvas. °**kramaṇīya** (W.), and °**kramitavya** (Pat.), mfn. to be gone or proceeded. °**kramitṛi**, m. = °*krantṛi*, Pat. °**kramya**, mfn. = °*kramaṇīya*, W. °**krānta**, mfn. proceeded, gone &c., Kāv.; commenced, begun, L.; previously mentioned or stated, MW.; n. the setting out on a journey, Yājñ.; the point in question, MW.; *-tva*, n. commencement, beginning, Kull.; the being meant or understood by anything, Hcat. °**krāmaṇī**, f. a kind of magic, Divyâv.

प्रक्रय *pra-kraya*, m. (√1. *krī*) = *klṛiptika* (?), L. °**krí**, mfn. to be bought, purchasable, AV.

प्रक्रीड् *pra-√krīḍ*, P. Ā. *-krī́ḍati* (*krī́ḷati*), °*te*, to play, sport, disport one's self, frolic, amuse one's self (with anything, instr.; with a person, instr. or *saha*), RV.; AV.; MBh. &c. °**krīḍá**, m. play, pastime, VS.; Hariv.; (with *marutām*) N. of a Sāman, ĀrshBr.; a place of sports, playground, ĀśvGṛ. °**krīḍita**, mfn. playing, sporting, MBh. °**krīḍín**, mfn. playing, sporting, RV. vii, 56, 16.

प्रक्रुश् *pra-√kruś*, P. *-krόśati*, to raise a cry, cry out, MBh.; R.; to utter (cries, acc.), call, R.; to invoke, call upon, cry out to (acc.), MBh. °**krośa**, m. a shriek, scream, Lāṭy.

प्रक्लिद् *pra-√klid*, Ā. *-klidyate*, to become moist or humid, to become wet, MBh.; Suśr.: Caus. *-kledayati*, to moisten, wet, make wet, Suśr.; w.r. for *-kleśayati*, Car. °**klinna**, mfn. moist, humid, wet, R.; Suśr.; putrefied, Car.; moved with compassion or sympathy, BhP.; *-tva*, n. being m° or h°, Suśr.; *-vartman*, n. a kind of disease of the eyelids (cf. *klinna-v*°), Suśr.; *-hṛidayêkshaṇa*, mfn. having the heart and eyes moist (with affection), MW. °**kleda**, m. moistness, wetness, humidity, MBh.; *-vat*, mfn. becoming moist or wet, Suśr. °**kledana**, mfn. moistening, wetting, ib. °**kledin**, mfn. id., ib.; fusing, liquefying, resolving (*-ditva*, n.), Car.

प्रक्लिश् *pra-√kliś*, Caus. *-kleśayati*, to put in a morbid state, Car. (w.r. *-kled*°).

प्रक्वण् *pra-√kvaṇ*, P. *-kvaṇati*, to sound, HPariś. °**kvaṇa**, m. (f. ifc. *ā*) the sound of a Vīṇā or lute, Pāṇ., Sch. °**kvāṇa**, m. the sound of a Vīṇā, L.; w.r. for *prahvāṇa*, TāṇḍBr.

प्रक्वाथ *pra-kvātha*, m. (√*kvath*) seething, boiling, Jātak.

प्रक्ष 1. *prakshá*, m. (for *plakshá*, to explain an etymology), TS.

प्रक्ष 2. *praksha*, mfn. in *vana-prakshá*, v.l. for *-krakshá*, ŚV.; in *nāgarājasama-pr*°, w.r. for *nāgarādiva dush-prêkshyaḥ*, MBh.

प्रक्षपण *pra-kshapaṇa*, *-kshaya* &c. See *pra-√kshi*.

प्रक्षर् *pra-√kshar*, P. *-ksharati*, to stream forth, stream, ooze, RV.; ŚāṅkhŚr.; Pañcad.; to drop down, Bhaṭṭ. °**kshara**, m. iron armour for the defence of a horse or elephant (cf. *pra-khara*, *prakkhara*), Hemac. °**ksharaṇa**, n. flowing forth, oozing, GopBr.; Mn., Sch.

प्रक्षल् *pra-√kshal*, P. *-kshālayati*, to wash off, wash away, rinse, ŚBr.; ŚrS.; Mn.; MBh. &c.; to cleanse, purify, MBh.: Caus. Ā. *-kshālāpayate* (Pot. °*yīta*), to have anything (as one's feet) washed, ĀśvGṛ. °**kshālaka**, mfn. washing, one who washes, Mn.; MBh.; R. (cf. *sadyaḥ-p*°). °**kshālana**, mfn. performing frequent ablutions, one who performs f° a°, R.; n. washing, w° off, cleaning, cleansing, purifying, KātyŚr.; Pur.; Mn.; MBh. &c.; bathing, MW.; a means of cleaning, anything used for purifying, water for washing, KātyŚr.; Lāṭy.; Yājñ.; Suśr.; °*nârthāya*, ind. for the sake of washing, MW. °**kshālanīya**, mfn. to be washed away or cleansed; to be purified, ib. °**kshālayitṛi**, m. one who washes (the feet of his guest), ĀpGṛ. °**kshālita**, mfn. washed, cleansed; expiated, ib.; *-pāṇi*, mfn. having one's hands washed, MānGṛ.; *-pāda*, mfn. having one's feet w°, Pāṇ. vi, 2, 110, Sch. 1. °**kshālya**, mfn. to be w° or purified, MārkP. 2. °**kshālya**, ind. having w° or rinsed, ŚBr.; MBh.

प्रक्षाम *pra-kshāma*, mfn. (prob.) burnt, singed (said of a sacrifice); ĀpŚr.

प्रक्षि *pra-√kshi*, P. *-kshiṇāti*, to spoil, destroy, wear out, exhaust, RV.; AV.; ŚBr.: Pass. *-kshīyate*, to be destroyed, perish, MBh.; to be worn out or exhausted or diminished, MW. °**kshapaṇa**, n. (fr. Caus.) destroying, Rājat. °**kshaya**, m. destruction, ruin, vanishing, end, MBh.; Hariv.; Sarvad. °**kshayaṇa**, mfn. causing to perish, destroying (in *ghaṭa-p*°, q.v.) °**kshīṇa** (*prá-*), mfn. destroyed, perished; vanished, disappeared; decayed, wasted, diminished (*-candra*, m. the waning moon, Var.), AV.; BhP.; Hit. &c.; atoned, MW.; n. the spot where any one has perished (e.g. *prakshīṇam idam Deva-dattasya*, this is the spot where D° perished), Pāṇ. vi, 4, 60, Sch.

प्रक्षिन् *prakshin*. See *upala-p*°.

प्रक्षिप् *pra-√kship*, P. Ā. *-kshipáti*, *-kshipate*, to cast, hurl, throw or fling at or into (loc.), place in, put before, Mn.; MBh.; Kāv. &c.; to let down, Kathās.; to launch a ship, Divyâv.; to add, Sūryas.; to insert, interpolate, Pāṇ., Sch.; R., Sch.: Caus. *-kshepayati*, to cause or order to cast or put into (loc.), MBh. °**kshipta**, mfn. thrown or cast at, hurled, flung; thrown forth, projected, Hit.; inserted, interpolated, Pāṇ. vi, 3, 83, Sch.; *-vat*, mfn. one who has thrown at, one who has thrown, W. °**kshipya**, ind. having thrown at, h° hurled, Pañc. °**kshepa**, m. throwing, casting, projecting; throwing into or upon, scattering upon, Mn.; Kull.; BhP.; putting, placing (*pāda-p*°, pl. steps, Kād.); adding to, increasing (e.g. a dose), Car.; anything added or thrown into drugs while in course of decoction, an ingredient, L.; insertion, interpolation, TBr., Sch.; ĀpŚr., Sch.; Śaṃk.; (also °*paka*, m.) the sum deposited by each member of a commercial company, Līl.; the box of a carriage, BhP.; *-lipi*, f. a partic. style of handwriting, Lalit. °**kshepaka**, m., see °*kshepa*. °**kshepaṇa**, n. pouring upon, Suśr.; (ifc.) throwing on or into, Śaṃk.; Yājñ., Sch.; fixing (as a price), Yājñ. °**kshepaṇīya**, mfn. to be thrown or cast forth, to be th° away, MW. °**kshepin**, mfn. (ifc.) throwing upon, placing upon, Nir. °**kshepṭavya**, mfn. to be thrown into or upon (loc.), to be scattered upon, Yājñ.; Hariv.; Hcat.; Kathās. °**kshepya**, mfn. to be thrown or put on (as an ornament), Śak., Sch.

प्रक्षीबित *pra-kshībita* or *-kshīvita* (fr. √*kshīb* or √*kshīv*), drunken, intoxicated, Pāṇ. viii, 2, 55, Sch.

प्रक्षुद् *pra-√kshud*, P. *-kshuṇatti*, to pound, crush, Bhaṭṭ. °**kshuṇṇa**, mfn. crushed, Bhaṭṭ.; pierced through, lacerated, Pañcat.

प्रक्षुभ् *pra-√kshubh*, Ā. P. *-kshobhate*, *-kshubhyati*, to be moved or shaken or agitated or confused; to totter, stagger, MBh.; Kāv. &c.: Caus. *-kshobhayati*, to agitate, excite, Suśr. °**kshobhana**, n. agitating, exciting, Prab.

प्रक्षै *pra-√kshai*, P. *-kshāyati*, to be consumed, burn (intr.), TBr.

प्रक्ष्णु *pra-√kshṇu* (only pf. *-cukshṇuvuḥ*), to sharpen, whet, point, Bhaṭṭ.

प्रक्ष्वेडन *pra-kshveḍana* (Pañc.) or °*ḍanā*, f., °*dana*, m., °*danā*, f. (L.; √*kshviḍ* or *kshviḍ*) an iron arrow (as humming or whizzing); calling aloud, clamour, W. °**kshveḍā**, f. humming, grumbling, MBh. °**kshveḍita** (or °*dita*), mfn. clamorous, shouting, noisy, MBh.; R.; unctuous, W.; n. shout, hum, R.; *-vat*, mfn. noisy; unctuous, W.

प्रखन् *pra-√khan* (only aor. *-khān*), to dig up, uproot, eradicate, Kathās.

प्रखर *pra-khara*, mfn. very hard or rough, Prasannar.; very hot or acrid, Bhām.; m. iron armour for the defence of a horse or elephant, L. (cf. *prakkhara*, *pra-kshara*); a mule, L.; a dog, L.

प्रखल *pra-khala*, m. a great scoundrel or villain, Mṛicch.

प्रखाद् *pra-√khād*, P. *-khādati*, to eat up, devour, RV. °**khādá**, mfn. swallowing, devouring, ib.

प्रखिद् *pra-√khid* (only pr. p. *-khidát*), to thrust away, VS.

प्रखुद् *pra-√khud*, P. *khudáti*, futuere, AV.; ŚāṅkhGṛ.

प्रख्या *pra-√khyā*, P. *-khyāti*, to see, RV. (Subj. *-khyat*; inf. *-khyai*); ŚBr. (ind. p. *-khyāya*); to announce, proclaim, extol, BhP. (Impv. *-khyāhi*): Pass. *-khyāyate*, to be seen or known; to be visible or public or acknowledged or celebrated, Mn.; MBh. &c.: Caus. *-khyāpayati*, to make generally known, proclaim, announce, publish, Mālatīm.; Rājat. °**khyá**, mfn. visible, clear, bright, ŚBr.; MBh.; (*ā*), f. look, appearance (only ifc. = resembling, like), MBh.; R. &c.; brightness, splendour (only ifc.), R.; perceptibility, visibility, Jaim.; making manifest, disclosure, Daśar. °**khyas**, m. = *Prajā-pati*, Uṇ. iv, 232, Sch.; the planet Jupiter, L. °**khyāta**, mfn. known, celebrated, acknowledged, recognised, MBh.; Kāv. &c.; forestalled, claimed by right of pre-emption, Mn. (see below); pleased, happy, W.; *-bala-vīrya*, mfn. of celebrated strength and valour, R.; *-bhāṇḍa*, n. (with *rājñaḥ*) a commodity the pre-emption of which is claimed by a king, Mn. viii, 399; *-vaptṛika*, mfn. having a celebrated father, L.; *-sad-bhartṛi*, m. known as a good husband, Kathās. °**khyāti**, f. visibility, perceptibility, celebrity (only *a-prakh*°), MBh.; praise, eulogium, W. °**khyāna**, n. the being perceived or known, Pāṇ. i, 2, 54; = °*khyāpana*, R. °**khyānīya**, mfn. to be celebrated or made known, Vop. °**khyāpana**, n. making known, report, information, R.; Daś. °**khyāpanīya**, mfn. to be made known or published, Vop. °**khyāpita**, mfn. known as, named (with nom.), Caṇḍ. °**khyāyamāna**, mfn. being celebrated or spoken about, Nal.

प्रग *pra-ga*. See under *pra-√gam* below.

प्रगट *pragaṭa*, w.r. for *pra-kaṭa*, HYog.

प्रगण् *pra-√gaṇ*, P. *-gaṇayati*, to reckon up, calculate, MBh. (ind. p. *-gaṇayya*, Pāṇ. vi, 4, 56, Sch.)

प्रगण्ड *pra-gaṇḍa*, m. the upper part of the arm (also *-°ḍaka*), L. (cf. *pra-kāṇḍa*); (*ī*), f. an outer wall or rampart, MBh.

प्रगदित *pra-gadita*, mfn. (√*gad*) spoken, speaking, beginning to speak, W. °**gādya**, mfn. Pāṇ. iii, 1, 100, Sch.

प्रगम् *pra-√gam*, P. *-gacchati* (ep. also Ā. °*te*), to go forwards, set out, advance, proceed, go to, reach, attain, RV. &c. &c. °**ga**, mfn. going before, preceding, Pāṇ. viii, 4, 38, Sch.; (*e*), ind., see below. °**gata**, mfn. gone forward, started, MBh.; Kāv. &c.; separate, apart (see below); gone with difficulty, W.; *-jānu* or °*nuka*, mfn. having the knees far apart, bandy-legged, bow-legged, L. °**gama**, m. the first manifestation of love, first advance in courtship, Pratāp. °**gamana**, n. = prec., Pāṇ. viii, 4, 34, Sch.; a speech containing an excellent answer, Sāh.; progress, advance, W.; difficult progress (?), ib.; disputing (?), ib. °**gamanīya**, mfn., Pāṇ. viii, 4, 34, Sch. °**gāman**, n. walk, gait, step (see *pṛithu-g*°). °**gāmin**, mfn. setting out, being about to depart, R. (v.l. *prāg-g*°).

Pra-ge, ind. early in the morning, at dawn, at day-break ('when the sun goes forth'?), Lāṭy.; Mn. &c.; to-morrow morning, Siṃhâs.; *-tana*, mfn. (Pāṇ.

iv, 3, 23) matutinal, early, Bālar.; relating to the next day, future, L.; *-niśa*, mfn. one who (sleeps) in the early morning as (if it were) night, MBh.; *-śaya*, mfn. asleep early in the morning, ib.

प्रगयण *pra-gayaṇa*, n. an excellent answer, Daś. (w.r. for *-gāmana*?)

प्रगर्ज् *pra-√garj*, P. *-garjati*, to begin to thunder, MBh. °**garjana**, n. roaring, roar (cf. *siṇha-*). °**garjita**, n. a roar, noise, din, L.

प्रगर्धिन् *pra-gardhín*, mfn. (√*gṛidh*) pressing or hastening onwards, eager, RV.

प्रगल् *pra-√gal*, Caus. *-gālayati*, to cause to fall off, Car. °**galita**, mfn. dripped down, Megh.

प्रगल्भ् *pra-√galbh*, Ā. *-galbhate*, to be bold or confident, behave resolutely, Śiś.; to be capable of or ready to (loc. or inf.), Bālar.; Vcar.; to be equal to or fit to pass for (nom.), Sarvad.; to be arrogant or proud, W. °**galbha**, mf(*ā*)n. bold, confident, resolute, brave, strong, able, MBh.; Kāv. &c.; proud, arrogant, impudent, Ragh.; skilful, Kād.; illustrious, eminent, W.; mature (as age), MW.; m. N. of the fire employed at the Jātakarman, Gṛihyās.; (with *ācārya*) N. of an author (called also Śubhaṃ-kara), Cat.; (*ā*), f. a bold and confident woman (esp. one of the classes of heroines in dram. composition), Sāh.; N. of Durgā, L.; (*am*), ind. courageously, resolutely, Mṛicch.; *-kulāla*, m. a skilful potter, Bhartṛ.; *-tā*, f. (Kum.), *-tva*, n. (W.) boldness, wilfulness, resolution, energy, strength, power; *-manas*, mfn. resolute-minded (*a-*), Amar.; *-lakshaṇa*, n. and °*ṇa-prakāśa*, m. N. of wks.; *-vāc*, mfn. speaking confidently or proudly, Kum. °**galbhita**, mfn. proud, arrogant, MW.; eminent, conspicuous, ib.; shining or resplendent with (instr.), Cat.

प्रगा *pra-√gā*, P. *-jigāti*, to go forwards, proceed, advance, move, go, RV.; MBh. 1. °**gāṇa**, n. (for 2. see under *pra-√gai*) access, approach, see *pṛithu-prag°*.

प्रगाढ *pra-gāḍha* &c. See *pra-√gāh* below.

प्रगाथ *pra-gātha*. See *pra-√gai*, col. 2.

प्रगाह् *pra-√gāh*, Ā. *-gāhate*, to dive into, penetrate, pervade, RV. °**gāḍha**, mfn. dipped or steeped in, mixed with, soaked, impregnated (ifc.), Suśr.; much, excessive, MBh.; rich in, full of (ifc.), Kām.; advanced, late (hour), Daś.; hard, difficult, L.; (*am*), ind. much, exceedingly, greatly, Kāv.; Suśr.; tightly, firmly, W.; n. a crowd, MBh. iv, 1977 (= *saṃ-kaṭa*, Nilak.); pain, privation, penance, W.; *-tā*, f., *-tva*, n. abundance, excessiveness, MW.; hardness, ib. °**gāhana**, n. dipping or plunging into (gen.), ĀpŚr.

प्रगीत *pra-gīta*, °*ti*. See *pra-√gai*.

प्रगुण *pra-guṇa*, mf(*ā*)n. straight (lit. and fig.), right, correct, honest, upright, Mālatīm.; Hcar.; being in a good state or condition, excellent, Ragh.; Mālatīm.; *-racanā*, f. = next, Daśar. °**guṇana**, n. putting straight, arranging, Mālatīm. °**guṇaya**, Nom. P. °*yati*, to put straight, set right, Dhanaṃj.; to develop, exhibit, manifest, Nyāyam. °**guṇita**, mfn. made even or smooth or straight, put in order, properly arranged, Bālar.; Pañc. °**guṇin**, mfn. smooth or even i.e. friendly towards (loc.), MBh.

Pra-guṇī, in comp. for °*guṇa*. **-karaṇa**, n. putting straight, arranging properly, KātyŚr., Sch. **-√kṛi**, to put straight or in order, make smooth or even, Car.; Pañc.; to make amenable to (loc.), Mudr.; to nourish, bring up, A. **-√bhū**, to make one's self fit or ready for (dat.), Kuv.

Praguṇya, mfn. more exceeding, excellent, W.

प्रगुप् *pra-√gup*, Caus. *-gopayati*, to protect, guard, Pañc.; Bhaṭṭ.; to conceal, keep secret, Hcat. °**gopana**, n. protection, preservation, salvation, W.

प्रगुर् *pra-√gur* (only aor. *-gūrta*), to cry aloud, RV. i, 173, 2 (Sāy. 'to make great efforts').

प्रगृ *pra-√1. gṛi*, P. *-gṛiṇāti*, to proclaim, announce to (loc.), RV. i, 152, 5; to extol, praise, BhP.

प्रगे *pra-ge*. See under *pra-√gam*.

प्रगै *pra-√gai*, P. *-gāyati* (ep. also Ā. °*te*), to begin to sing, sing, celebrate, praise, extol; to sound, resound, RV.; MBh.; BhP. 2. °**gāṇa**, n. (for 1. see *pra-gā*) singing, song, L. °**gātṛi**, m. a singer, MBh. ('excellent singer,' L.) °**gāthá**, m. a kind of stanza (the combination of a Bṛihatī or Kakubh with a Sato-bṛihatī so as to form a triplet), VS.; RPrāt. &c.; N. of a Ṛishi with the patr. Kāṇva and Ghaura, the author of RV. viii, 1, 2; 10; 48; 51-54; (pl.) N. of RV. viii (which contains a great many Pr° stanzas); *-kāram*, ind. combining into a Pr° stanza, Lāṭy. °**gāyin**, mfn. beginning to sing, singing, Hariv. °**gīta**, mfn. recited in a singing tone, sung, Sarvad.; resonant with singing, vocal, MBh.; R.; singing, one who has begun to sing, Kathās.; n. song, Ṛitus.; Caur.; a sing-song or drawling recitation (regarded as a fault), Śiksh. °**gīti**, f. a kind of metre, Col.

प्रग्रथ् *pra-√grath*, P. *-grathnāti* or *-grathati*, to string together, join, connect, Nyāyam., Sch. °**grathana**, n. connecting or stringing together, intertwining, Sāy.

प्रग्रस् *pra-√gras*, P. *-grasati*, to eat up, devour, swallow, MBh.

प्रग्रह् *pra-√grah*, P. Ā. *-gṛihṇāti* °*ṇīte*, to hold or stretch forth, hold, AV. &c. &c.; to offer, present, ŚBr.; ŚāṅkhŚr.; to seize, grasp, take hold of, take, ŚrS.; MBh. &c.; to accept, receive, Śak.; Var.; to draw up, tighten (reins), stop (horses), Śak.; to befriend, favour, further, promote, MBh.; Hariv.; R.; to keep separated or isolated (cf. below): Caus. (inf. *-grāhitum*) to receive, accept, MBh. °**gṛihīta**, mfn. held forth or out, taken, accepted &c., R.; Hariv. &c.; lofty, Divyâv.; joined, united with (ibc.), BhP.; kept separate, pronounced without observing the rules of Saṃdhi; *-pada*, mf(*ā*)n. having the words pronounced separately, RPrāt. 1. °**gṛihya**, mfn. to be seized or taken or accepted, MBh.; Kāv. &c.; (in gram.) to be taken or pronounced separately, not subject to the rules of Saṃdhi (as the final *ī*, *ū*, and *e* of the dual terminations, e.g. *kavī etau*, 'these two poets'), Prāt.; Pāṇ. &c. 2. °**gṛihya**, ind. having taken or grasped, carrying away with, with, MBh.; Kāv. &c. °**graha**, m. (ifc. f. *ā*) holding in front, stretching forth, MBh.; seizing, clutching, taking hold of (°*haṃ gataḥ*, seized, taken), ib.; Hariv.; a partic. manner of fighting, MBh. (= *śatror uttānapātanârtham pādâkarshaṇam* or = *gala-hastakaḥ*, Nīlak.); the seizure of the sun or moon, beginning of an eclipse (cf. *graha*), Sūryas.; friendly reception, kindness, favour, MBh.; Hariv.; obstinacy, stubbornness (°*haṃ gataḥ*, obstinate, stubborn), MBh.; a rein, bridle, KaṭhUp.; MBh. &c.; a ray of light (like all words meaning 'rein' or 'bridle'), L.; a rope, halter, cord, string, thong, MBh.; the cord or string suspending a balance, L.; a guide, leader, ruler (also as N. of Vishṇu-Kṛishṇa), MBh.; a companion, satellite, ib.; binding, L.; taming, breaking (a horse), L.; the arm, L.; a species of plant, Car. (Cassia Fistula, L.); a vowel not subject to the rules of Saṃdhi, TPrāt. (*-tva*, n., Sch.; cf. 1. *pra-gṛihya*); N. of a partic. sacrificial rite (also *-homa*, KātyŚr., Sch.); mf(*ā*)n. receiving, kind, hospitable (with *sabhā*, f. a hall of reception, an audience hall), R. (B.); = *ūrdhva-bāhu* (?), R., Sch. (cf. *prâñjali-pragr°*); *-vat*, mfn. (ifc.) one who has seized, holding, MBh.; receiving kindly, obliging, R. (Sch. 'keeping down the wicked' or 'controlling the organs of sense'); °*hâdi-darpaṇa*, m. N. of wk.; °*hin*, mfn. guiding the reins, BhP. °**grahaṇa**, m. a leader, guide (only ifc. [f. *ā*] 'led by'), MBh.; stretching forth, offering, ŚāṅkhŚr.; taking, seizing, holding, ib.; the seizure of the sun and moon, commencement of an eclipse, VarBṛS.; Sūryas.; a means for taming or breaking in, MBh.; the being a leader or guide, authority, dignity, ib.; a rein, bridle, MW.; a check, restraint, ib. °**grahītavya**, mfn. to be checked or controlled, Vajracch. °**grāha**, m. (only L.) seizing, taking, bearing, carrying (cf. Pāṇ. iii, 3, 46); a rein, bridle (cf. ib. 53); the string of a balance (cf. ib. 52); *-vat*, mfn. having the string of a balance, MW. °**grāham**, ind. taking the words separately, not pronouncing them according to the rules of Saṃdhi, AitBr.

प्रग्रीव *pra-grīva*, m. n. (g. *ardharcâdi*; also *-ka*, ifc., Hcar.) a wooden balustrade or fence round a building, Rājat. viii, 328; a window, lattice, balcony (projecting like a neck; cf. *grīvā*), L.; a summer-house, pleasure-house, L.; a painted turret, L.; a stable, L.; the top of a tree, L.

प्रग्लै *pra-√glai*, P. *-glāyati*, to fade, wither away, Bhaṭṭ. (Sch. *-mlāyati*): Caus. *-glāpayati*, Vop. °**gla**, mfn. wearied, fatigued, exhausted, W.

प्रघट् *pra-√ghaṭ*, Ā. *-ghaṭate*, to exert one's self, devote one's self to (loc.), Bhaṭṭ.; to commence, begin, ib. °**ghaṭaka**, (ifc.) a precept, rule, doctrine, Cat. °**ghaṭā**, f. the rudiments or first elements of a science; *-vid*, m. = *śāstra-gaṇḍa*, L.; a general reader (but not a profound one), W. (cf. *chāttra-g°*).

प्रघट्टक *pra-ghaṭṭaka*, m. (√*ghaṭṭ*) a precept, rule, doctrine, Kap., Sch. (cf. *pra-ghaṭaka*).

प्रघण *pra-ghaṇa*, m. n. (√*han*) a place or a terrace before a house, Hcar. (also °*ghāṇa*), L.; an iron mace or crowbar, L.; a copper pot, L. °**ghana**, m. = prec.; also v.l. for *prathana*, Phaseolus Mungo, L. °**ghāṇa**, m. n. = or v.l. for °*ghaṇa*, Hcar.; L.; the trunk of a tree, L. °**ghātá**, m. a blow, stroke, TS., Sch.; a battle, fight, L.; the edging of a garment, ŚBr. °**ghāna**, see °*ghāṇa*.

प्रघस *pra-ghasa*, m. (√*ghas*) a devourer (pl. N. of false gods), L. (cf. Pāṇ. ii, 4, 37; 38); N. of a Rākshasa, MBh.; of a monkey follower of Rāma, R.; (*ā*), f. N. of one of the Mātṛis attending on Skanda, MBh. °**ghāsa**, see *Varuṇa-praghāsá*. °**ghāsín** (VS.), °**ghāsyà** (TS.), mfn. voracious.

प्रघातय *pra-ghātaya*, P. °*yati* (Caus. of *pra-√han*), to strike, kill, Divyâv.

प्रघुण *praghuṇa*, m. a guest, visitor, L. (prob. w.r. for *prāghuṇa*).

प्रघुष् *pra-√ghush*, Caus. *-ghoshayati*, to cause to announce aloud, proclaim, MBh. °**ghushṭa**, mfn. sounding forth, Var. °**ghosha**, m. sound, noise, BhP. (also *-ka*, L.); N. of a son of Kṛishṇa, BhP. °**ghoshin**, m. 'roaring,' N. of the 9 classes of the Maruts, MW.

प्रघूर्ण *pra-ghūrṇa*, mfn. (√*ghūrṇ*) turning round or rolling violently, W.; wandering, roaming, ib.; m. a guest, visitor, L. (prob. w.r. for *prāgh°*).

प्रघृ *pra-√ghṛi*, P. *-gharati*, to ooze out, Divyâv.

प्रघृष् *pra-√ghṛish*, P. *-gharshati*, to rub to pieces, Kauś.; to rub into, anoint, Suśr. °**gharsha**, m. rubbing, anointing, Car. °**gharshaṇa**, m. grinding, crushing, destroying, Kāv.; n. rubbing, a remedy for rubbing in or anointing, Car. °**ghṛishṭa**, mfn. rubbed in, embrocated, anointed, Suśr.

प्रच *praca*. See *acyuta-pr°* and *nakha-pr°*.

प्रचकित *pra-cakita*, mfn. (√*cak*) trembling, shuddering, terrified, Pañc.

प्रचक्र *pra-cakra*, n. an army in motion, L.

प्रचक्ष् *pra-√caksh*, Ā. *-cashṭe*, to tell, relate, declare, MBh.; Ragh.; to suppose, regard or consider as (acc.), Mn.; MBh. &c.; to name, call, Mn.; BhP.: Caus. *-cakshayati*, to irradiate, illumine, RV. °**cakshaṇam**, ind. (after a fin. verb), g. *gotrâdi*. °**cakshas**, m. N. of the regent of the planet Jupiter, Bṛihas-pati, W.

प्रचङ्कश *pra-caṅkaśa*. See *a-pr°*.

प्रचण्ड *pra-caṇḍa*, mf(*ā*)n. excessively violent, impetuous, furious, fierce, passionate, terrible, direful, formidable, MBh.; Kāv. &c.; great, large, hot, burning, sharp (see comp. below); m. a species of oleander with white flowers, L.; N. of a Dānava, Kathās.; of a goblin, MārkP.; of a son of Vatsa-prī and Su-nandā, ib.; (*ā*), f. a species of Dūrvā with white flowers, L.; a form or Śakti of Durgā, Cat. **-ghoṇa**, mfn. large-nosed, having a long or prominent nose, MBh. **-caṇḍikā**, f. a form of Durgā; *-sahasra-nāma-stotra*, n. N. of a Stotra. **-tarī-√bhū**, to become fiercer or more passionate, Kād. **-tā**, f. great violence or passion, Uttarar. **-deva**, m. N. of a prince, W. **-pāṇḍava**, n. 'the wrathful sons of Pāṇḍu,' N. of a drama by Rāja-śekhara (= *Bāla-bhārata*). **-bhairava**, (prob.) m. N. of a Vyāyoga (kind of drama). **-bhairava-rasa**, m. N. of a partic. medicinal preparation, L. **-mādhava**, m. (with *Kāśmīra*) N. of a poet, Cat. **-mūrti**, m. Crataeva Roxburghii, L. **-vadana**, mf(*ā*)n. having a terrible face, Dhūrtas. **-varman,** m. N. of a prince, Daś. **-śakti,** m. N. of a man, Kathās. **-śara-kārmuka,** mfn. having sharp arrows and a terrible bow (said of the god of love), MBh. **-śephas,** m. N. of a man, Kautukar. **-sūrya,** mfn. having a hot or burning sun, Ṛitus. **-sena,** m. N. of a prince, of Tāmra-liptikā, Vet. **Pracaṇḍâtapa,** m. fierce or stifling heat, Ṛit. **Pracaṇḍôgrā,** f. N. of a Yoginī, Hcat.

प्रचत् *pra-√cat,* Caus. Ā. *-cātayate,* to drive or scare away, remove, destroy, RV. °**cátā,** ind. secretly, in secret, ib.

प्रचपल *pra-capala,* mfn. very unsteady or restless, Hariv.

प्रचय *pra-caya* &c. See *pra-√1. ci.*

प्रचर् *pra-√car,* P. *-carati* (ep. also Ā. °*te*), to proceed towards, go or come to, arrive at (acc.), RV. &c. &c.; to come forth, appear, MBh.; R. &c.; to roam, wander, Prab.; BhP.; to circulate, be or become current (as a story), R.; Var.; to set about, perform, discharge (esp. sacred functions, with instr. of the object or of the means employed), AV.; Br.; KātyŚr.; to be active or busy, be occupied or engaged in (loc.), MBh.; BhP.; to proceed, behave, act in peculiar manner, Mn.; MBh. &c.; to come off, take place, BhP.: Caus. *-cārayati,* to allow to roam, turn out to graze, Hariv.; to make public, W. °**cara,** m. a road, way, path, L.; usage, custom, currency, W.; going well or widely, ib.; pl. N. of a people, R. (v. l. *praccara* and *pra-stara*). °**caraṇa,** n. going to graze, Cat.; proceeding with, beginning, undertaking, ŚrS.; Bālar.; circulating, being current, W.; employing, using, MW.; (*ī*), f. (sc. *sruc*) a wooden ladle employed for want of a better at a sacrifice, ŚBr.; KātyŚr. °**caraṇīya,** mfn. being in actual use, ŚBr. °**carita,** mfn. followed, practised, Mn. x, 100; arrived at, visited, R.; current, publicly known, Car., Sch. °**caritavya,** mfn. to be proceeded with or undertaken, to be performed, AitBr. °**caritos,** inf. (with *purā*) before he (the Adhvaryu) sets to work, GopBr.; Vait. °**caryā,** f. an action, process, ĀśvŚr. °**cāra,** m. roaming, wandering, Hariv. (cf. *bhikshā-*); coming forth, showing one's self, manifestation, appearance, occurrence, existence, MBh.; Kāv. &c.; application, employment, use, ib.; conduct, behaviour, Mn.; MBh. &c.; prevalence, currency, custom, usage, W.; a playground, place of exercise, Hariv.; pasture-ground, pasturage, Mn. ix, 219 (= Vishṇ. xviii, 44, where Sch. 'a way or road leading from or to a house'); Yājñ.; MBh.; Hariv.; R. °**cāraṇa,** n. (prob.) scattering, strewing, Kād. °**cārita,** mfn. allowed to wander or roam about, MW.; made public or manifest, ib. (cf. g. *tārakâdi*). °**cārin,** mfn. coming forth, appearing, MBh.; following, adhering or sticking to (loc. or comp.), ib.; proceeding with, acting, behaving, ib.; going about, wandering, MW.

प्रचल् *pra-√cal,* P. *-calati* (rarely Ā. °*te*), to be set in motion, tremble, quake, TBr.; MBh. &c.; to stir, move on, advance, set out, depart, MBh.; BhP.; Pañcat.; to start, spring up from (a seat), R.; to swerve, deviate from (abl.), MBh.; to become troubled or confused, be perplexed or bewildered or excited, ib.; BhP.: Caus. *-calayati,* to set in motion, move, jog, wag, Kāv.; to remove from (abl.), Suśr.; *-cālayati,* to cause to shake or tremble, R.; to stir up, stir round, Pañcat. °**cala,** mfn. moving, tremulous, shaking, MBh.; Kāv.; Suśr.; what goes well or widely, W.; current, circulating, customary, ib.; *-kāñcana-kuṇḍala,* mfn. (an ear) adorned with golden rings, Ṛitus.; *-dāsa,* m. N. of a poet, Cat.; *-latā-bhuja,* mfn. having tremulous arm-creepers (= slender arms that tremble), Prab.; *-siṇha,* m. N. of a poet, Cat.; *-°calâṅga,* mfn. having tremulous limbs, MBh. °**calaka,** m. a species of venomous reptile, Suśr. (cf. °*calāka*). °**calakin,** w. r. for °*calākin.* °**calat,** mfn. moving, trembling, shaking, MBh.; Kāv. &c.; going, proceeding far or much, W.; circulating, being current or customary, W.; prevailing, being recognized (as authority or law), ib. °**calana,** n. trembling, shaking, rocking, swaying, MaitrUp.; Pañcat.; retiring, flight, Pañcat.; going well or widely, W.; circulating, being current or customary, ib. °**calāka,** m. shooting with arrows, L.; a peacock's tail or crest, L.; a chameleon, Āpast.; a snake or other venomous animal (cf. °*calaka*), Suśr.; (°*calākā*), f. springing up, TS., Sch. °**calākin,** m. a peacock, L.; a snake, L. °**calāya,** Nom. P. °*yati,* to nod the head (while asleep), Jātak. °**calāyana,** n. nodding the head (on first becoming intoxicated), Car. °**calāyita,** mfn. nodding the head (while asleep and in a sitting posture), L.; rolling about, tumbling, tossed about (as a ship), MW.; n., see under *āsina.* °**calita,** mfn. set in motion, moved, shaken, tremulous, rolling (as the eye), MBh.; R. &c.; one who has set out, proceeded, departed, Pañcat.; Hit.; Vet.; confused, bewildered, perplexed, MBh.; BhP.; current, customary, circulating, W.; prevailing, recognized, received (as authority or law), ib.; n. going away, departure, BhP. °**cālaka,** mf(*ikā*)n. causing to tremble, trembling with (comp.), L. °**cālana,** n. stirring, stir, noise (?), Pañcat.

प्रचषाल *pra-cashāla,* n. a partic. ornament on a sacrificial post, MBh.

प्रचाय *pra-cāya* &c. See below.

प्रचाल *pracāla,* m. the neck of the Vīṇā or Indian lute, L. (w. r. for *pravāla*).

प्रचि *pra-√1. ci,* P. Ā. *-cinoti, -cinute,* to collect, gather, pluck, Gobh.; MBh. &c.; to mow or cut down (enemies), MBh.; to increase, augment, enhance, Var.: Pass. *-cīyate,* to be gathered or collected, to grow, thrive, multiply, MBh.; Kāv.

Pra-caya, m. (ifc. f. *ā*) collecting, gathering, Pāṇ. iii, 3, 40 (cf. *pushpa-*); accumulation, heap, mass, quantity, multitude, Ṛitus.; Rājat.; Suśr.; growth, increase, A.; slight aggregation, W.; = *-svara,* TPrāt.; (in alg.) the common increase or difference of the terms in a progression; *-kāsh-ṭhâgata,* mfn. one who has attained the highest degree of intensity, Nyāyam., Sch.; *-svara,* m. 'accumulated tone,' the tone occurring in a series of unaccented syllables following a Svarita, RPrāt.; Śiksh. °**cayana,** n. gathering, collecting (see *phala-*). °**cāya,** m., °**cāyikā,** f. gathering, plucking, collecting (with the hand or in turn, cf. *pushpa-*; the latter also 'a female who gathers,' A.) °**cita,** mfn. gathered, collected, heaped, accumulated; covered or filled with (instr. or comp.), MBh.; Suśr.; pronounced with the Pracaya tone, accentless, VPrāt.; m. (also *-ka*) N. of a metre, Col.; *-svara,* m. = *pracaya-svara.* °**cinvat,** mfn. gathering, collecting, plucking, MBh.; Hariv.; m. N. of a son of Janam-ejaya, Hariv.; Pur. °**ceya,** mfn. to be collected or gathered; to be increased, MW.; spreading everywhere, Jātak.

प्रचिक *pracika,* g. *purohitâdi* (Kāś.)

प्रचिकीर्षु *pra-cikirshu,* mfn (√1. *kṛi,* Desid.) wishing or intending to requite, BhP.

प्रचित् *pra-√cit,* P. Ā. *-ciketti, -cikitte,* to know or make known, RV.; to become visible or manifest, appear, ib.; TS.: Caus. *-cetayati,* to make known, cause to appear, RV.; (Ā.) to appear, ib.: Desid. *-cikitsati,* to show, point out, ib. °**cikita** (*prá-*), mfn. knowing, familiar or conversant with, VS. (Mahīdh.) °**cetana,** mfn. illumining, illustrating, SV. °**cetas** (*prá-*), mfn. attentive, observant, mindful, clever, wise (said of the gods, esp. of Agni and the Ādityas), RV.; AV.; VS.; TS.; happy, delighted, L.; m. N. of Varuṇa, Hariv.; Kālid.; BhP.; of a Prajā-pati (an ancient sage and law-giver), Mn. i, 35 (*-smṛiti,* f. N. of wk.); of a prince (son of Duduha), Hariv.; of a son of Duryāman, VP.; of a son of Dur-mada, BhP.; pl. (w. r. *prāc*°) N. of the 10 sons of Prācīna-barhis by a daughter of Varuṇa (they are the progenitors of Daksha), MBh.; Hariv.; Pur. °**cetasa,** w. r. for *prāc*°; (*ī*), f. Myrica Sapida, L. °**cetita,** mfn. (see *a-prac*°) noticed, observed. °**cetúna,** mfn. affording a wide view or prospect, RV.

प्रचिति *pra-citi,* f. (√2. *ci*) investigation, examination (= *vi-citi*), Kuṭṭanim.

प्रचिन्त् *pra-√cint,* P. *-cintayati,* to think upon, reflect, consider, find out, devise, contrive, MBh.; Kāv. &c. 1. °**cintya,** ind. having reflected or considered, MBh. 2. °**cintya,** mfn. to be r° or c°, ib.

प्रचीबल *pracībala,* m. or n. a species of plant, Suśr.

प्रचीर *pra-cīra,* m. N. of a son of Vatsa-prī and Su-nandā, MārkP.

प्रचीर्ण *pra-cīrṇa,* mfn. (√*car*) come forth, appeared, MBh.

प्रचुद् *pra-√cud,* P. *-codati,* to set in motion, drive on, urge, impel, RV.: Caus. *-codayati,* id., RV. (Ā. to hasten, make haste, viii, 24, 13); MBh.; Kāv. &c.; to excite, inspire, RV.; to command, summon, request, demand, Mn.; MBh. &c.; to announce, make known, proclaim, Mn. iii, 228. °**cudita,** mfn. (m. c. for °*codita*) hurled, shot off, MBh. °**coda,** m. instigation, Buddh. °**codaka,** mf(*ikā*)n. instigating; (*ikā*), f. 'inflamer,' N. of the 4 daughters of Niyojikā (daughter of the demon Duḥ-saha), MārkP. °**codana,** n. instigating, exciting, MBh.; direction, order, command, R.; a rule or law, W.; saying, ib.; sending, ib.; (*ī*), f. Solanum Jacquini, L. °**codita,** mfn. (fr. Caus.) driven on, urged, impelled, MBh.; Ragh.; asked, requested, ordered, directed, Mn. (cf. *a-prac*°); R.; decreed, determined, BhP.; announced, proclaimed, ŚvetUp.; sent, dispatched, W. °**codin,** mfn. driving forward, urging, Kathās.; (*inī*), f. Solanum Jacquini, L.

प्रचुपित *pra-cupita.* See *upasthita-p*°.

प्रचुर *pracura,* mf(*ā*)n. much, many, abundant (opp. to *alpa*); plenteous, plentiful, frequent; (ifc.) abounding in, filled with, MBh.; Kāv. &c.; m. a thief, A. **-candana,** n. much sandal, Ṛitus. **-cchala,** mfn. hidden in manifold disguises, MBh. **-tā,** f. (Var.), **-tva,** n. (Hariv. &c.) abundance, multitude. **-nitya-dhanâgama,** mfn. receiving many and constant supplies of money, Bhartṛ. **-paribhava,** m. frequent humiliation, ib. **-pādapa,** mfn. abounding with trees, R. **-purusha,** mfn. abounding with men, populous, W.; m. a thief, L. **-ratna-dhanâgama,** mfn. having a large income of gems and money, MW. **-loma,** mfn. having too much hair, Kull.

Pracurī, in comp. for °*ra.* **-karaṇa,** n. making abundant, augmenting, increasing, W. **-kṛita,** mfn. augmented, increased, ib. **-√bhū,** to become abundant, increase, Śiś.

प्रचूर्ण् *pra-√cūrṇ,* P. *-cūrṇayati* (only aor. *prâcucūrṇat*), to crush, grind to dust, Bhaṭṭ.

प्रचृत् *pra-√cṛit,* P. *-cṛitati,* to loose, loosen, untie, AV.; ĀśvŚr. °**cṛitta,** mfn. loose, dishevelled; *-śikha,* mfn. with dish° hair, ĀśvGṛ.

प्रचेतन *pra-cetana* &c. See *pra-√cit.*

प्रचेतृ *pracetṛi,* m. a charioteer, L. (w. r. for *pra-vetṛi*).

प्रचेल *pra-cela,* n. (√*cel* ?) yellow sandal-wood, L. °**celaka,** m. a horse, L.

प्रचेलुक *praceluka,* m. a cook, L. (w. r. for *paceluka*).

प्रचोद *pra-coda* &c. See *pra-√cud.*

प्रच्छद् *pra-cchad* (√*chad*), P. Ā. *-cchādayati,* °*te,* to cover, envelop, wrap up (Ā. with instr. 'to cover one's self with, put on'), ŚBr.; GṛŚrS.; MBh. &c.; to be in the way, be an obstacle to (acc.), R.; to hide, conceal, disguise, keep secret, Mn.; MBh. &c. °**chád,** f. a cover, covering, VS.; MaitrS. °**cchada,** m. a cover, coverlet, wrapper, blanket, L.; *-paṭa,* m. (L.), *-vāsas,* n. (Kathās.) id. °**cchanna,** mfn. covered, enveloped, shut up, ŚBr.; MBh. &c.; hidden, concealed, unobserved, private, secret, disguised (ibc. and *am,* ind. 'secretly, covertly'), Mn.; MBh. &c.; n. a private door; a lattice, loop-hole, L.; *-gupta,* mfn. secretly hidden, Bhartṛ.; *-cāraka* and *-cārin,* mfn. acting secretly or fraudulently, R.; *-taskara,* m. a secret thief, Mn.; *-pāpa,* m. a s° sinner, ib.; *-vañcaka,* m. a s° rogue or rascal, ib.; *-vritti,* f. a s° manner or way, Śukas.; °*cchannī-√bhū,* to hide or conceal one's self, L. °**cchādaka,** mf(*ikā*)n. concealing, covering (ifc.), MārkP.; Suśr.; m. the song of a wife deserted by her husband (sung with the accompaniment of a lute and containing a covert description of her sorrows), L. °**cchādana,** mfn. concealing, hiding (cf. *piplu-*); n. covering, concealing, concealment, MBh.; Pañcat.; an upper or outer garment, L.; *-paṭa,* m. a cover, coverlet, wrapper, Pañcat. °**cchādita,** mfn. covered, wrapped up, clothed, hidden, concealed, R.; Suśr. 1. °**cchādya,** ind. having covered or hidden, MBh. 2. °**cchādya,** mfn. to be covered or hidden, Kāv.

प्रच्छन *pracchana.* See under √*prach.*

प्रच्छान *pra-cchāna, pra-cchita.* See under *pra-ccho* below.

प्रच्छाय *pra-cchāya,* (prob.) n. a shadowy place, dense shade, Hariv.; Śak.; Kathās.

प्रच्छिद् *pra-cchid* (√*chid*), P. Ā. *-cchinatti, -cchintte,* to cut off or through, pierce, split, cleave, AV. &c. &c.; to rend or take away, withdraw, MBh.: Caus. *-cchedayati,* to cause to cut off &c.; MBh.: Caus. of Intens. *-cecchidayya,* Pat. °**cchid,** mfn. cutting off or to pieces, VS. (cf. Pāṇ. iii, 2, 61, Sch.). °**cchindyā-karṇa,** mf(*ī*)n. whose ear is to be cleft, MaitrS. (cf. Pāṇ. vi, 3, 115). °**ccheda,** m. a cutting, slip, strip, KātyŚr.; a musical division, bar (?), Divyâv. °**cchedaka,** m. a song sung by a wife who thinks her husband false to her, Sāh. (cf. *pra-cchādaka*). °**cchedana,** n. dividing into small pieces, ShaḍvBr. °**cchedya,** see *a-pracchedya.*

प्रच्छुड् *pra-cchuḍ* (√*chuḍ*), Caus. *-cchoḍayati,* to stretch out, Kāraṇḍ.

प्रच्छृद् *pra-cchṛid* (√*chṛid*), Caus. *-cchardayati,* to vomit, Suśr. °**cchardana,** n. emitting, exhaling, Yogas.; vomiting, an emetic, Suśr. °**cchardi** (Gal.), °**cchardikā** (Pāṇ. iii, 3, 108, Sch.), f. vomiting, sickness.

प्रच्छो *pra-ccho* (√*cho; only* ind. p. *-cchayitvā*), to bleed by making incisions in the skin, cup, lance, scarify, Suśr. °**cchāna,** n. scarifying, making sore, ib. °**cchita,** mfn. cut, lanced, scarified, ib.

प्रच्यु *pra-cyu,* Ā. *-cyavate* (ep. also P. °*ti*), to move, proceed, depart, TS.; AV.; ŚBr.; to swerve or deviate from (abl.), MBh.; to be deprived of, lose (abl.), ib.; Kāv.; Pañcat.; to come or stream forth, ib.; to fall down, drop, stumble, ŚBr.; MBh.; R.; to fall (scil. from heaven i. e. be born again), HPariś.: Caus. *-cyāvayati,* to move, shake, RV.; to eject, remove or dispel or divert from (abl.), ib. &c. &c.; to cause to fall (lit. and fig.), MBh.; Daś.; BhP.; Suśr. °**cyava,** m. fall, ruin, Kāṭh.; withdrawal, Kap., Sch.; advancement, improvement, MW. °**cyavana,** mfn. removing, destroying, Car. (w. r. for °*cyāvana*?); n. falling down (esp. from heaven i. e. being born again), HPariś.; departure, withdrawal, Suśr.; loss, deprivation (with abl.), MBh.; oozing, dropping, A. °**cyāvana,** n. means of removing or diminishing, a sedative, Suśr.; causing to give up, diverting from (abl.), Pāṇ., Sch. °**cyāvuka,** mfn. transitory, fragile, ŚāṅkhBr. °**cyuta** (*prá-*), mfn routed, put to flight, expelled, banished, retreated, AV.; streamed forth or issued from (abl.), ib.; MBh. &c.; fallen from (lit. and fig.), swerved from, deprived of (abl. or comp.), Mn.; MBh. &c.; subtracted, Bījag.; *-tva,* n. deviation, retreat, MW. °**cyuti,** f. going away, withdrawing, departing, Saṃk.; loss, deprivation (with abl.), ib.; falling from, giving up (ifc.), Var., Sch.; decay, fall, ruin (*a-pr°*), ŚBr.; ŚāṅkhŚr.

प्रछ् *prach,* cl. 6. P. (Dhātup. xxviii, 120), *pṛiccháti* (Ved. and ep. also Ā. *pṛicchate;* pf. *papraccha,* Br. &c., *papṛikshé* [?], RV. iv, 43, 7; aor. *áprākshīt,* AV. &c., *áprāṭ,* RV., *aprashṭa,* Kāv.; fut. *prakshyati,* Br. &c., *prashṭā,* Gr.; ind. p. *pṛishṭvā, -pṛicchya,* MBh.; inf. *práshṭum,* AV. &c., *-pṛiccham, °cche,* RV.), to ask, question, interrogate (acc.); to ask after, inquire about (acc.); to ask or interrogate any one (acc.) about anything (acc., dat., loc., *prati* or *adhikṛitya* with acc.; *arthe* or *hetoḥ* ifc.), RV. (pr. p. Ā. *pṛicchamāna,* 'asking one's self,' x, 34, 6) &c. &c.; (in astrol.) to consult the future, Var.; (with *nāmato mātaram*) to inquire about one's (gen.) mother's name, Śak.; (with *na*) not to trouble one's self with, ĀśvŚr.; to seek, wish, long for; to ask, demand, beg, entreat (acc.), RV.: Pass. *pṛicchyáte,* to be asked or questioned about (act., dat. &c., as above), RV. &c. &c.: Caus. *pracchayati* (aor. *apapraċchat*), Gr.: Desid. *pipṛicchishati,* Pāṇ. i, 2, 8: Intens. *parīpṛicchyate,* Pāṇ. vii, 4, 90, Pat. [Orig. *prik;* cf. Lat. *preces, procus; poscere* for *porscere;* Slav. *prositi;* Lith. *praszýti;* Germ. *frâhên, fragen; forskôn, forschen.*]

Pracchana, n. (and °*nā,* f.) asking, inquiring, a question, inquiry, L.

प्रज *pra-ja.* See under *pra-*√*jan.*

प्रजङ्घ *pra-jaṅgha,* m. N. of a monkey and of a Rākshasa, R.; (*ā*), f. a partic. portion of the lower part of the thigh, Jātak.

प्रजन् *pra-*√*jan,* Ā. *-jāyate* (ep. also P. °*ti*), to be born or produced, spring up from (abl.) be begotten (by [instr. or abl.]; from [abl.]; or with [loc.]; in [loc. or *adhi*]), RV. &c. &c.; to become an embryo, ŚBr.; to be born again, MBh.; to propagate offspring with or by (instr.), RV.; ŚBr.; Mn.; to bring forth, generate, bear, procreate (acc.); beget on (loc. or instr.), MBh.; to cause to be reproduced, ŚBr.: Caus. *-janayati,* to cause any one (acc.) to propagate offspring (instr.), RV.; to beget, procreate, MaitrS. (aor. *prajanayām akaḥ;* cf. Pāṇ. iii, 1, 42); AV.; ŚBr.; to cause to be reproduced, ŚBr.: Desid. *-jijanishate,* to wish to be born, ŚBr.: Desid. of Caus. *-jijanayishati,* to wish to cause to be conceived or born, ib. °**ja,** mf(*ā*)n. bringing forth, bearing (see *a-praja*); m. a husband, L.; (*ā*), f., see below. 1. °**jajñi,** mfn. (for 2. see under *pra-jñā*) able to beget (see 1. *a-prajajñi*). °**jana,** m. begetting, impregnation, generation, bearing, bringing forth (rarely n.), Mn.; MBh.; one who begets, generator, progenitor, BhP.; °*nártham,* ind. for the sake of procreation, Mn. ix, 96. °**jánana,** mfn. begetting, generating, generative, vigorous, VS.; ŚBr.; n. the act of begetting or bringing forth, generation, procreation, birth, production (lit. and fig.), AV. &c. &c.; generative energy, semen, TS.; TBr.; ŚrS.; the male (RV.; Br.) or female (L.) generative organ; offspring, children, BhP.; = *pra-gama* or *pra-gata,* L.; *-kāma,* mfn. desirous of begetting or bringing forth, Kauś.; *-kuśala,* mfn. skilled in midwifery, Suśr.; *-vat* (°*jánana-*), possessing generative power, AV. °**janayitṛi,** m. a generator, begetter, progenitor, TS.; Br. °**janikā,** f. a mother, L. °**janishṇú,** mfn. generative, procreative, producing, ŚBr.; Kāṭh. (cf. Pāṇ. iii, 2, 136); being born or produced, W.; growing, standing (as corn), ib. °**janishyamāṇā,** f. about to bring forth, being near the time of delivery, Suśr. °**janú,** m. f. the organ of generation (of females), TBr. °**januka** (?), m. the body, L. °**jas** (ifc.) = °*jā* (cf. *dush-, bahu-*); m. N. of a son of Manu Auttami, VP. °**jāta** (*prá-*), mfn. born, produced, RV. &c. &c.; (*ā*), f. a woman who has borne a child, ŚrS.; MBh. &c. (cf. *ṛita-*). °**jāti** (*prá-*), f. generating or generative power, generation, production, bringing forth, delivery, Br.; ŚrS.; BhP.; = *upa-nayana,* initiation with the sacred thread (as causing second birth), BhP., Sch.; m. N. of a prince, MārkP. (v. l. *pra-jāni*); *-kāma,* mfn. desirous of propagation, AitBr.; *-mat,* mfn. containing words relating to generation, ib.; °*tyānanda,* m. the joy of propagation, BhP.

Prajā́, f. (ifc. f. *ā;* cf. *pra-ja* above) procreation, propagation, birth, RV.; AV.; offspring, children, family, race, posterity, descendants, after-growth (of plants), RV. &c. &c.; a creature, animal, man, mankind; people, subjects (of a prince), ib.; seed, semen, VS. (cf. *-nisheka*); an era, Divyâv. **—kara,** m. a symbol. N. for 'a sword' (!), L. **—kalpa,** m. the time of creation, Hariv. (perhaps w. r. for *purā-k°*). **—kāma** (°*jā́-*), mfn. desirous of offspring, AV. &c. &c.; m. desire of o°, ML. **—kāra,** m. the author of creation, Hariv. **—gupti,** f. protection of subjects, Āpast. **—ghnī,** see *-han.* **—candra,** m. 'people's moon,' honorific N. of a prince, Rājat. **—tantu,** m. a line of descendants, a race, TUp.; BhP. **—tīrtha,** n. the auspicious moment of birth, BhP. **—dā,** f. 'granting offspring,' N. of a species of shrub, L. **—dāna,** n. procreation of children, Āpast.; 'people's gift,' silver, L. **—dvāra,** n. 'gate or means of obtaining progeny,' N. of the sun, MBh. **—dhara,** mfn. supporting creatures (said of Vishṇu), Vishṇ. **—°dhyaksha** (°*jādh°*), m. 'surveyor of c°s,' N. of the sun, MBh.; of Kardama and Daksha, BhP. **—nātha,** m. 'lord of c°s,' N. of Brahmā or Manu, Prab.; of Daksha, Bh.; = *-pa,* Ragh.; Rājat. **—nisheka,** m. infusion of semen, impregnation, offspring, Ragh. xiv, 60. **—°ntaka** (°*jānt°*), m. 'destroyer of creatures,' Yama, god of death, L. **—** 1. **pa,** mfn. (for 2. see *pra-*√*jap*) protecting subjects, Nalac.; m. a prince, king, L. **—pati** (°*jā́-*), m. 'lord of creatures,' N. of Savitṛi, Soma, Agni, Indra &c., RV.; AV.; a divinity presiding over procreation, protector of life, ib.; VS.; Mn.; Suśr.; BhP.; lord of creatures, creator, RV. &c. &c. (N. of a supreme god above or among the Vedic deities [RV. (only x, 21, 10), AV.; VS.; Br.] but in later times also applied to Vishṇu, Śiva, Time personified, the sun, fire, &c., and to various progenitors, esp. to the 10 lords of created beings first created by Brahmā, viz. Marīci, Atri, Aṅgiras, Pulastya, Pulaka, Kratu, Vasishṭha, Pracetas or Daksha, Bhṛigu, Nārada [Mn. i, 34; cf. IW. 206, n. 1], of whom some authorities count only the first 7, others the last 3); a father, L.; a king, prince, L.; a son-in-law, L.; N. of the 5th (39th) year in a 60 years' cycle of Jupiter, Var.; the planet Mars, a partic. star, δ Aurigae, Sūryas.; (in astrol.) = 2. *kāla-nara,* q.v.; a species of insect, L.; N. of sev. men and authors, Cat.; (*ī*), f. a matron, lady, Divyâv.; N. of Gautama Buddha's aunt and nurse (with the patr. Gautamī, the first woman who assented to his doctrines), Lalit.; *-gṛihīta* (°*jā́-p°*), mfn. seized by Prajā-pati, VS.; *-carita,* n. N. of wk.; *-citi,* f. P°'s layer, ŚBr.; *-datta,* m. N. of a man, Pat.; *-nivāsinī,* f. N. of a Gandharvī, Kāraṇḍ.; *-pati,* m. 'lord of the P°s,' N. of Brahmā, BhP.; of Daksha, ib.; *-bhakshita* (°*jā́-p°*), mfn. eaten by P°, VS.; *-mukha* (°*jā́-p°*), mfn. having P° as head or chief, ŚBr.; *-yajña,* m. 'sacrifice to P°,' the procreation of children enjoined by law, VP.; *-loká,* m. P°'s world (situated between the sphere of Brahmā and that of the Gandharvas), ŚBr.; *-śarman,* m. N. of a man, L.; *-sṛishṭa* (°*jā́-p°*), mfn. created by P°, AV.; ŚBr.; *-smṛiti,* f. N. of wk.; *-hṛidaya,* n. 'P°'s heart,' N. of a Sāman, ŚrS. (also *Prajā́pater-hṛid°,* ŚBr.; TS.) **—patika,** m. endearing form of *Prajāpati-datta,* Pat. **—patya,** w. r. for *prājāpatya.* **—paddhati,** f. N. of wk. **—paripālana,** n. the protection of subjects, Vishṇ. **—pāla,** m. 'protector of creatures,' N. of Kṛishṇa, MBh.; a prince, king, ib.; Rājat.; N. of a king, VarP. **—pālana,** n. = *-paripālana,* Mn. ix, 253 &c.; N. of wk. **—pāli,** m. 'protector of creatures,' N. of Śiva, Śivag. (cf. *go-pāli*). **—pālya,** n. the office of protector of the people, royal office, R. **—°mṛitatva** (°*jāmṛ°*), n. perpetuity of posterity, AV. **—°rtham** and °**rthe** (°*jā́rth°*), ind. for the sake of offspring, MBh. **—vat** (°*jā́-*), mfn. having or granting offspring or children, prolific, fruitful, RV. &c. &c.; m. N. of a Ṛishi and his hymn, ĀśvGṛ.; (with the patr. *Prājāpatya*) supposed author of RV. x, 183, Anukr.; (*atī*), f. pregnant, BhP.; (ifc.) bringing forth, mother of, MārkP. (cf. *vīra-*); a brother's wife, Ragh.; the wife of an elder brother, L.; N. of a tutelary deity of the Su-mantus, VarP.; of a Surāṅganā, Siṃhâs.; of the wife of Priya-vrata, MārkP. **—varī,** f., v. l. for *-vatī* (f. of prec.), MānGṛ. **—vid,** mfn. bestowing or granting progeny, AV. **—vṛiddhi,** f. increase or abundance of offspring, Āpast. **—vyāpāra,** m. care for or anxiety about the people, Siṃhâs. **—vyṛiddha-paśu-vyṛiddha,** mfn. one who has ill luck with his children and cattle, ĀpŚr. **—śānti,** f. N. of wk. **—sáni,** mfn. = *-vid,* VS. **—sṛij,** m. creator of beings, N. of Brahmā and Kaśyapa, Rājat.; father or king, Śiś. i, 28, Sch. **—han,** mf(*ghnī*)n. killing offspring, destroying progeny, PārGṛ. **—hita,** mfn. favourable to or good for offspring or subjects; n. water, W. **Prajêpsu,** mfn. desirous to obtain offspring, MW. **Prajêśa,** m. 'lord of creatures,' N. of the god presiding over the procreation of offspring, BhP.; 'lord of the people,' a prince, king, Ragh.; BhP. **Prajêśvara,** m. 'lord of creatures,' creator (cf. *prājeśvara*); a prince, king, Hariv.; Ragh. **Prajêhā,** f. desire of offspring, MBh. **Prajôtpatti,** f. the raising up of progeny, MW. **Prajôtpādana,** n. id., Suśr.

Pra-jānā, f. the place of bringing forth, AitĀr. °**jāni,** m. N. of a prince, Pur. (cf. *-jāti*). °**jāyinī,** f. about to bring forth, Suśr.; (ifc.) bearing, bringing forth, a mother of (cf. *vīra-*). °**jijanayishitavyā,** mfn. (fr. Desid. of Caus.) wished to be born, ŚBr. °**jijanishamāṇa,** mfn. (fr. Desid.) wishing to be born or produced, ŚBr.

प्रजप् *pra-*√*jap,* P. *-japati,* to recite in a low tone, whisper, mutter, MBh. 2. °**jāpa,** mfn. (for 1. see under *pra-jā*) muttering prayers, praying, Nalac.

प्रजय *pra-jaya.* See under *pra-*√*ji.*

प्रजल्प् *pra-*√*jalp,* P. *-jalpati,* to talk, speak, tell, communicate, announce, proclaim, Yājñ.; MBh. &c. °**jalpa,** m. prattle, gossip, heedless or frivolous words (esp. words used in greeting a lover), L.

°**jalpana**, n. talking, speaking, Pañcat. °**jalpita**, mfn. talked, spoken, ib.; one who has begun to talk, Kum.; n. spoken words, talk, MBh.

प्रजव *pra-java*. See *pra-√jū* below.

प्रजहित *pra-jahita*. See *pra-√3. hā*.

प्रजागृ *pra-√jāgṛi*, P. *-jāgarti*, to watch, watch over (loc.), Bhaṭṭ.; to lie in wait for (gen.), MBh.: Caus. *-jāgarayati* (aor. *-ajīgaḥ*), to wake (trans.), RV. °**jāgara**, mfn. one who wakes, waking, MBh. &c.; m. a watchman, guardian, BhP.; N. of Vishṇu, MBh.; waking, watching, attention, care (also pl.), MBh.; Kāv. &c; waking up (intr.), Kām.; (*ā*), f. N. of an Apsaras, MBh. °**jāgaraṇa**, n. being awake, Suśr. °**jāgarūka**, mfn. wide awake, Śrikaṇṭh.

प्रजापयितृ *prajāpayitṛí*, m., w.r. for *pra-dāpayitṛí*, TBr.

प्रजि *pra-√ji*, P. *-jayati*, to win, conquer, AV. &c. &c. °**jayá**, m. victory, conquest, ŚBr. °**jit**, mfn. conquering, defeating, Pāṇ. iii, 2, 61, Sch.

प्रजित *prajita*, mfn. driven, impelled, urged on (prob. w.r. for *prâjita*; see *tottra-, daṇḍa-*).

प्रजिन *prajina*, m. wind, air (also spelt *prajīna*), L.

प्रजिन्व् *pra-√jinv*, P. *-jinvati* or *-jinoti*, to refresh, animate, promote, further, RV.

प्रजिहीर्षु *pra-jihīrshu*, mfn. (Desid. of √*hṛi*) being about to strike or hit, Rājat.

प्रजीवन *pra-jīvana*, n. (√*jīv*) livelihood, subsistence, Mn. ix, 163. °**jīvin**, m. N. of a minister of Megha-varṇa (the king of the crows), Pañcat.

प्रजुष्ट *pra-jushṭa*, mfn. (√*jush*) strongly attached to or intent on (loc.), Mn. ii, 96.

प्रजू *pra-√jū*, Ā. *-javate*, to hasten forwards, RV. iii, 33, 1 (?): Caus. *-jāvayati*, to set in rapid motion, dart, shoot (arrows), Nir. ix, 17. °**javá**, m. haste, rapidity, RV.; mfn. rapid, swift, Gal.; (°*jávam*), ind. hastily, rapidly, TS. °**javana**, mfn. running very quickly, Uttarar. °**javita**, mfn. driven on, impelled, MBh.; Hariv.; R.; (ifc.) urged on, incited, summoned by (= *pra-codita*), Hariv. °**javin**, mfn. hastening, rapid, swift, Kād.; Kathās. (Pāṇ. iii, 2, 156); m. a runner, courier, express.

प्रजृम्भ् *pra-√jṛimbh*, Ā. *-jṛimbhate*, to begin to yawn, open the mouth, MBh.

प्रजॄ *pra-√jṝī*, P. *-jīryati*, to be digested, Suśr. °**jīrṇa**, mfn. digested, Car.

प्रज्जटिका *prajjaṭikā*, f. a kind of Prākṛit metre, Col.

प्रज्जि *prajji*, m. N. of a man, Rājat.

प्रज्ञ 1. *pra-jña*, mfn. = *pra-jñu*, L.

प्रज्ञा *pra-√jñā*, P. *-jānāti*, to know, understand (esp. a way or mode of action), discern, distinguish, know about, be acquainted with (acc.), RV. &c. &c.; to find out, discover, perceive, learn, MBh.; Kāv. &c.: Caus. *-jñāpayati*, to show or point out (the way), ŚBr.; to summon, invite, Lalit. 2. °**já-jñi**, mfn. (for 1. see *pra-√jan*) knowing, conversant with, ŚBr.

2. **Pra-jña**, mf(*ā*)n. (for 1. see above) wise, prudent, MāṇḍUp.; (ifc.) knowing, conversant with (cf. *nikṛiti-, pathi-*); (*ā*), f., see col. 2; *-tā* (°*jñá-*), f. knowledge, ŚBr. °**jñaka**, see *akṛita-prajñaka*. °**jñapta**, mfn. (fr. Caus.) ordered, prescribed (cf. *vaidya-*); arranged (as a seat), Divyâv. °**jñapti**, f. teaching, information, instruction, BhP.; an appointment, agreement, engagement, W.; arrangement (of a seat), Divyâv.; (with Jainas) a partic. magical art personified as one of the Vidyā-devīs, Kathās. (L. also °*tī*); *-kauśika*, m. N. of a teacher acquainted with the magical art called Prajñapti, Kathās.; *-vādin*, m. pl. N. of a Buddhist school, SaddhP.; *-śāstra*, n. N. of wk. °**jñāta**, mfn. known, understood, found out, discerned, known as (nom.), well-known, public, common, notorious, Mn.; MBh. &c. °**jñātavya**, mfn. to be known, discernible, KaushUp. °**jñāti** (*prá-*), f. knowing the way to (gen.) or the right way, ŚBr.; TāṇḍBr. °**jñātṛi**, m. one who knows the way, guide, conductor, RV. °**jñātra**, see *a-prajñātrá*. °**jñāna**, mf(*ī*)n. prudent, wise, L.; easily known, AV.; n. knowledge, wisdom, intelligence, discrimination, AV. &c. &c.; a distinctive mark, token of recognition, any mark or sign or characteristic, AV.; MBh.; R. &c.; a monument, memorial, ŚBr.; *-kumuda-candrikā*, f. N. of wk.; *-ghaná*, m. nothing but knowledge, ŚBr. (cf. under *ghaná*); *-tṛipta*, mfn. satiated with, i.e. full of knᵒ, MBh.; *-saṃtati*, f. a train of thought, Tattvas.; °*nâ-nanda*, °*nâśrama*, and °*nêndra*, m. N. of authors, Cat. °**jñāpana**, n. (fr. Caus.) statement, assertion, Nyāyas., Sch.; *-pradeśa-vyākhyā*, f.; °*nôpâṅga*, n. N. of wks. °**jñāpanīya** or °**jñāpayitavya**, mfn. to be asserted, Nyāyas., Sch. °**jñāpita**, mfn. betrayed, disclosed, Śak. i, $\frac{2}{2}\frac{3}{4}$ (v.l.)

Pra-jñā́, f. wisdom, intelligence, knowledge, discrimination, judgment, ŚBr. &c. &c.; device, design, ŚBr.; ŚāṅkhŚr.; a clever or sensible woman, W.; Wisdom personified as the goddess of arts and eloquence, Sarasvatī, L.; a partic. Śakti or energy, Hcat.; (with Buddh.) true or transcendental wisdom (which is threefold, Dharmas. 110), MWB. 126; 128; the energy of Ādi-buddha (through the union with whom the latter produced all things), MWB. 204. **-kara**, m. N. of a Buddh. scholar and of Sch. on Nalôd. **-kāya**, m. N. of Mañju-śrī, Buddh. **-kūṭa**, m. N. of a Bodhi-sattva, SaddhP. **-kośa**, m. N. of a man, Kathās. **-gupta**, mfn. protected by understanding (*-śarīra*), ŚārṅgP.; N. of a Buddh. scholar. **-ghana**, m. nothing but intelligence, BhP. **-cakshus**, n. the eye of understanding, Mālav.; Vajracch.; mfn. 'mind-eyed,' wise, intelligent, MBh. iii, 13891; blind, ib. i, 147 &c.; m. N. of the blind king Dhṛita-rāshṭra, L. **-candra**, m. 'moon of wisdom,' N. of a scholar, Buddh. **-°ḍhya** (°*jñā-ḍhya*), m. 'rich in wᵒ,' N. of a man, Kathās. **-°tman** (°*jñât°*), mfn. 'one whose nature is wᵒ,' being all wᵒ, AitĀr. **-°ditya** (°*jñâd°*), m. 'sun of wᵒ,' N. applied to a very clever man, Rājat. **-deva**, m. 'god of wᵒ,' N. of a scholar, Buddh. **-°ntaka** (°*jñânt°*), m. 'destroyer of wᵒ,' (with Buddh.) one of the 10 gods of anger, Dharmas. 11. **-pāramitā**, f. perfection in wᵒ, Kathās.; Kāraṇḍ.; (with Buddh.) one of the 6 or 10 transcendent virtues, Dharmas. 17; 18; MWB. 128; *-sūtra*, n. N. of wk. **-°pêta** (°*jñâp°*), mfn. destitute of wᵒ or knowledge, KaushUp. **-prakāśa**, m. N. of wk. **-pratibhāsita**, m. 'illumined by wᵒ,' a partic. Samādhi, Kāraṇḍ. **-bhadra**, m. 'excelling in wᵒ,' N. of a scholar, Buddh. **-maya**, mf(*ī*)n. made or consisting of wᵒ or understanding, MBh. **-mātrā**, f. an element of cognition, organ of sense, KaushUp. **-vat**, mfn. wise, knowing, shrewd, intelligent, Kathās.; Pañcat. &c. **-vardhana-stotra**, n. N. of a Stotra. **-varman**, m. 'having wᵒ for armour,' N. of a man, Buddh. **-vāda**, m. a word of wᵒ, Bhag. **-vṛiddha**, mfn. old in wᵒ or knowledge, MBh. **-sahāya**, mfn. 'having wᵒ for a companion,' wise, intelligent, Kathās. **-sāgara**, m. 'sea of wᵒ,' N. of a king's minister, Kathās. **-sûkta-muktâvalī**, f. N. of wk. **-hīna**, mfn. destitute of wᵒ, ignorant, silly, unwise, W.

Prajñāla, mfn. wise, prudent, g. *sidhmâdi*.

Prajñin, mfn. id., L.

Prajñila, mfn. id., g. *picchâdi*.

प्रज्ञु *pra-jñu*, mfn. having the knees far apart, bandy-legged, bow-legged, L. (cf. Pāṇ. v, 4, 129).

प्रज्वल् *pra-√jval*, P. *-jvalati* (ep. also Ā. °*te*), to begin to burn or blaze, be kindled (lit. and fig.), flame or flash up, shine, gleam, TBr.; ChUp.; MBh. &c.: Caus. *-jvālayati*, to set on fire, light, kindle, inflame, GṛŚrS.; ChUp.; MBh. &c.; (with Buddh.) to illustrate, explain, Divyâv. **-°jvalana**, n. blazing up, flaming, burning, Var.; Pratāp. °**jvalanīya**, mfn. to be set on fire, inflammable, MW. °**jvalita**, mfn. flaming, blazing, burning, shining, Lāṭy.; MBh.; Kāv. &c.; n. flaming up, blazing, burning, Hariv. °**jvālana**, n. kindling, setting on fire, Vishṇ. °**jvālā**, f. a flame, light, R. °**jvālita**, mfn. lighted, kindled, MW.

प्रज्वार *pra-jvāra*, m. (√*jvar*) the heat of fever (sometimes personified), BhP.

प्रडीन *pra-ḍīna*, mfn. (√*ḍī*) flown up or forward, taking flight, R.; Mṛicch.; n. the act of flying, flying forward, MBh.

प्रण *praṇa*, mfn. (fr. 1. *pra*) ancient, old, Pāṇ. v, 4, 30, Vārtt. 7, Pat.

प्रणख *pra-ṇakha*, m. or n.(?) the point of the nails, ChUp.

प्रणद् *pra-ṇad* (√*nad*), P. *-ṇadati*, to resound, begin to sound or roar or cry, MBh.; R. °**ṇadana**, n. = °*ṇāda*, L. °**ṇadita**, mfn. sounding, buzzing, humming (as a bee), Śiś. °**ṇāda**, m. a loud sound or noise (esp. expressive of approbation or delight), shout, cry, roar, yell, neigh &c., MBh.; R.; a murmur or sigh of rapture, W.; noise or buzzing in the ear (from thickening of the membranes &c.), Suśr.; N. of a Cakra-vartin, Divyâv. °**ṇādaka**, mfn. sounding &c., Pāṇ. viii, 4, 14, Sch.

प्रणपात् *pra-ṇapāt*, m. a great-grandson, RV. [Cf. Lat. *pro-nepos*.]

प्रणभ् *pra-ṇabh* (√*nabh*), Ā. *-ṇabhate*, to burst, split, cleave, RV.

प्रणम् *pra-ṇam* (√*nam*), P. Ā. *-ṇamati*, °*te* (ind. p. *-ṇamya*), to bend or bow down before (often with *murdhna, sirasa* &c.), make obeisance to (dat., gen., loc. or acc.), Mn.; MBh. &c.: Caus. *-nāmayati* (ind. p. *-namayya*), to cause a person (acc.) to bow before (dat.), Kālid.; to bow, incline, ib. °**ṇata**, mfn. bent forwards, bowed, inclined, ŚāṅkhBr.; Mn. &c.; bowed to, saluted reverentially, BhP.; bent towards, offered respectfully, Mālav. (cf. below); humble, submissive to (gen. or acc.), MBh.; R.; BhP.; skilful, clever, W.; a partic. kind of accentuation, Sāy.; of a Pariś. of SV.; *-kāya*, mfn. having the body bent down, SaddhP.; *-bahu-phala*, mfn. one to whom various fruits or good things are offered, Mālav. i, 1; *-vat*, mfn. bowing, bent, bowed, W.; *-śiras*, mfn. having the head bowed, inclined, stooping, W.; °*tâtmavat*, mfn. 'having one's person bowed,' inclined, stooping, R. (B.); °*tâśesha-sā-manta*, mfn. one to whom all his neighbours bow or are submissive, L. °**ṇati**, f. bending, bowing, inclination, salutation, reverence, obeisance, MBh.; Kāv. &c. °**ṇamana**, n. bowing before, salutation, reverence (gen. or comp.), Bhartṛ.; Kathās. **-ṇamayya**, ind. bowing, Divyâv. °**ṇamita**, mfn. bent, bowed, inclined (*-śiras* = *praṇata-ś°*), Mālav.; offered or given respectfully, Amar.; a partic. kind of accentuation, SaṃhUp. °**ṇamra**, mfn. bowing, inclined; °*rī-√bhū*, to bow down, Kāv. °**ṇāma**, m. (ifc. f. *ā*) bending, bowing, a bow, respectful salutation, prostration, obeisance (esp. to a Brāhman or to a deity), MBh.; Kāv. &c.; *-kṛiti*, f. making an obeisance, Pañcat.; *-mitra*, m. N. of a man, HPariś.; °*mâñjali*, m. reverential salutation with the hands opened and hollowed, Daś.; °*mâdara*, m. reverential salutation, Kum. °**ṇāmin**, mfn. bending, bowing before, honouring (comp.), MBh.

प्रणय *pra-ṇaya*, °*yana* &c. See *pra-ṇī*.

प्रणव *pra-ṇáva*. See *pra-ṇu*.

प्रणश् *pra-ṇaś* (√1. *naś*), P. *-ṇaśati*, to reach, attain (only aor. *-ṇak* and *-naśīmahi*), RV.

प्रणश् *pra-ṇaś* (√2. *naś*), P. *-ṇaśati* or *-naśyati* (ep. also Ā. °*te*; fut. *-naṅkshyati*; inf. *-nashṭum*, Pāṇ. viii, 4, 36, Sch.), to be lost, disappear, vanish, RV. &c. &c.; to flee, escape, Bhaṭṭ.: Caus. *-nāśayati*, to cause to disappear or perish, AV.; ŚBr.; MBh. &c.; to allow to be lost i.e. leave unrewarded, Hit. °**ṇāśa**, m. vanishing, disappearance, cessation, loss, destruction, death, R.; Var.; Suśr. &c. °**ṇāśana**, mf(*ī*)n. (fr. Caus.) causing to disappear, removing, destroying (ifc.), MBh.; Hariv.; Suśr. &c.; n. destruction, annihilation, Ragh. °**ṇāśin**, mfn. = °*ṇāśana*, mfn. (only f. *inī* at the end of a verse), MBh.; Hariv.; R.

Pra-nashṭa, mfn. (wrongly written *pra-ṇashṭa*, Pāṇ. viii, 4, 36, Sch.) lost, disappeared, vanished, ceased, gone, perished, destroyed, annihilated, Mn.; MBh. &c. **-jñānika**, mfn. one whose knowledge or memory is destroyed, Suśr. **-vinaya**, mfn. uncivil, rude, MW. **-svāmika**, mfn. (property) the owner of which has disappeared, Mn. viii, 30. **Pranashṭâdhigata**, mfn. lost and found again, ib., 33.

प्रणस *pra-ṇasa*, mfn. having a prominent nose, Pāṇ. v, 4, 119, Sch.

प्रणाडिका *pra-ṇāḍikā* or °*ḍī*, f. a channel, water-course, drain (met. = intervention, interposition); °*dikayā* (Sarvad.), or °*dyā* (ŚBr., Sch.), ind. mediately, indirectly.

Pra-ṇāla, m. a channel from a pond, water-course, drain, L.; (prob.) a row, series, Kād.; (*ī*), f. a channel &c., R.; Mṛicch.; Śiś.; Bhpr.; recension (of a text; cf. *pātha-*); intervention, interposition, Naish. °**ṇālikā**, f. a channel &c. (cf. *sruk-praṇ°*); intervention, medium, L.; (*ayā*), ind. indirectly, Mahidh.

प्रणि *pra-ṇi* for *pra-ni*, according to Pāṇ. viii, 4, 17 before a number of roots, viz. *gad* (see below), *ci*, 1. *dā*, *dih*, *de*, *do*, *drā*, *dhā* (see below), *dhe*, *nad* (see below), *pat* (see below), *pad*, *psā*, *mā*, *me*, *yam*, *yā*, *vap*, *vah*, *vā*, *śam*, *so*, *han* (see below); according to Vop. xii, 1 also before 1. *mi*.

प्रणिंसित *pra-ṇinsita*, mfn. (√*nins*) kissed, W. °**ṇinsitavya** or °**ninsitavya**, mfn. to be kissed, Pāṇ. viii, 4, 33.

प्रणिक्ष् *pra-ṇiksh* (√*niksh*; only fut. *-ṇikshishyati*), to devour, Bhaṭṭ. °**nikshaṇa** or °**nikshaṇa**, n., Pāṇ. viii, 4, 33, Sch.

प्रणिगद् *pra-ṇi-√gad* (Pāṇ. viii, 4, 17), P. *-ṇigadati*, to speak, say, declare, Śiś. vi, 44.

प्रणिज् *pra-ṇij* (√*nij*; aor. *prāṇaikshīt*), to wash away, cleanse, AV.; TS.; ŚBr. °**ṇéjana**, mf(*ī*)n. washing or wiping away, Lāṭy.; n. the act of washing or bathing, AV.; water for washing, ŚBr.

प्रणिज्ञा *pra-ṇi-√jñā*, P. *-jānāti*, to reflect, consider, Bhaṭṭ.

प्रणिधा *pra-ṇi-√dhā* (Pāṇ. viii, 4, 17), P. Ā. *-dadhāti*, *-dhatte*, to place in front, cause to precede, MBh.; to put down, deposit, ib.; to place in, bring into (loc.), ib.; to set (a gem) in (loc.), Hit.; to put on, apply, Suśr.; to touch, MBh.; to turn or direct (the eyes or thoughts) upon (loc.), MBh.; Hariv. &c. (with *manas* and inf. 'to resolve upon,' Bhaṭṭ.; scil. *manas*, 'to give the whole attention to, reflect, consider,' MBh.; *ātmā praṇidhīyatām*, 'one must think,' ib.); to send out or employ (a spy or emissary), to spy, MBh.; R.; to find out or ascertain anything (acc.) to be (acc.), MBh. °**ṇidhātavya**, mfn. to be turned upon (loc.), Car. °**ṇidhāna**, n. laying on, fixing, applying (also pl.), Car.; Suśr.; access, entrance, L.; exertion, endeavour, SaddhP.; respectful conduct, attention paid to (loc.), MBh.; profound religious meditation, abstract contemplation of (comp.), Ragh.; Kathās.; Vedāntas.; vehement desire, Lalit.; vow, ib.; prayer (threefold), Dharmas. 112. °**ṇidhāyin**, mfn. employing, sending out (spies), Prasannar. °**ṇidhi**, m. watching, observing, spying, MBh.; sending out (spies or emissaries), R.; a spy, secret agent, emissary, Mn.; MBh. &c. (°*dhī-√bhū*, to become a spy, Pañcat.); an attendant, follower, L.; care, attention, L.; asking, solicitation, request, SaddhP.; prayer, Divyâv.; N. of a son of Bṛihad-ratha, MBh. °**ṇidheya**, mfn. to be applied or injected (as a clyster), Suśr.; to be sent out (as a spy), MBh.; n. employing, sending out (of emissaries), MW. °**ṇihita**, mfn. laid on, imposed, applied, Suśr.; put down, deposited, Bālar.; BhP.; outstretched, stretched forth, Megh.; Sāh.; directed towards, fixed upon (loc.), Hariv.; Bhartṛ.; BhP.; delivered, committed, entrusted to (dat.), Bālar.; contained in (comp.), BhP.; sent out (as a spy), MBh.; found out, discovered, ib.; ascertained or stated, Mn. viii, 54; one who has his thoughts concentrated on one point, intent upon (loc.), R.; Bhaṭṭ.; obtained, acquired, W.; prudent, cautious, wary, ib.; resolved, determined, ib.; agreed to or admitted, ib.; *-dhī* (Bhartṛ.), °*tâtman* (Āpast.), mfn. having the mind fixed upon (loc. or comp.); °*têkshaṇa*, mfn. having the eyes directed towards or fixed upon (comp.), Hariv.

प्रणिध्यै *pra-ṇi-√dhyai* (only pf. *-dadhyau*), to attend to (acc.), BhP.

प्रणिनद् *pra-ṇi-√nad* (only pr. p. *-nadat*; cf. Pāṇ. viii, 4, 17), sounding deep or like thunder, W. °**ṇinâda**, m. a deep sound, ib.

प्रणिन्द् *pra-ṇind* (√*nind*; only ind. p. *-ṇindya*; cf. Pāṇ. viii, 4, 33), to blame, censure, upbraid, Bhaṭṭ. °**ṇindana** or °**nindana**, n. censuring, upbraiding, Pāṇ. ib., Sch.

प्रणिपत् *pra-ṇi-√pat* (Pāṇ. viii, 4, 17), P. *-patati* (esp. ind. p. *-patya*), to throw one's self down before, bow respectfully to (acc., rarely dat. or loc.), Mn.; MBh. &c.: Caus. *-pātayati*, to cause a person (acc.) to bow down or fall prostrate, Mālav. °**ṇipatana**, n. throwing one's self down before, falling at a person's feet, Amar. °**ṇipatita**, mfn. bowed down in reverence, saluting, MBh.; R. °**ṇipāta**, m. (ifc. f. *ā*) falling at a person's feet, prostration, humble submission to (gen.), salutation, reverence, obeisance, MBh.; Kāv. &c.; *-gata*, mfn. resorting to a respectful salutation, MBh.; *-puraḥ-saram*, ind. preceded by prostration, with an obeisance, MārkP.; *-pratīkāra*, mfn. having submission for a remedy, counteracted by submission, Ragh.; *-rasa*, m. 'taking pleasure in submission,' N. of a magical formula pronounced over weapons, R. °**ṇipātin**, mfn. falling at a person's feet, submissive, humble, MBh.

प्रणिहन् *pra-ṇi-√han* (Pāṇ. viii, 4, 17), P. *-hanti*, to slay, kill, destroy, extirpate, MBh.; Kāv. (with acc. or gen.; cf. Pāṇ. ii, 3, 56, Sch.); to bend down lower (the hand), VPrāt.; to pronounce lower (than Anudātta), ib. °**ṇihata**, mfn. = *dvishṭa*, *prati-skhalita* or *baddha*, L.

प्रणिहित *pra-ṇihita*. See *pra-ṇi-√dhā*.

प्रणी *pra-ṇī* (√*nī*), P. Ā. *-ṇayati*, °*te*, to lead forwards, conduct, advance, promote, further, RV. &c. &c.; to bring or lead to, convey (esp. the sacrificial fire or water or Soma to its place at the altar), ib.; to offer, present, Bhaṭṭ.; to produce, perform, execute, finish, Up.; MBh.; Kāv. &c.; to do away with, remove, dispel, MBh.; to manifest affection, love, desire, MBh.; to show, represent (a drama), Bālar.; Prasannar.; to inflict (as punishment), Mn.; MBh. &c.; to apply (as a clyster), Car.; to establish, fix, institute, promulgate, teach, MBh.; Kāv. &c.; to write, compose, Sarvad.; (Ā.) to draw in (the breath), ŚBr.: Desid. *-ninīshati* (!), to wish to lead or conduct, RV.

Pra-ṇaya, m. a leader, Pāṇ. iii, 1, 142 (*jyotishām*, Nir. ii, 14); guidance, conduct, MBh.; manifestation, display, Mṛicch.; setting forth (an argument), Jātakam.; affection, confidence in (loc.), love, attachment, friendship, favour (ibc.; *āt*, *ena* and °*yôpêtam*, ind. confidentially, affectionately, openly, frankly), MBh.; Kāv. &c.; desire, longing for (loc.; *anyathā*, 'for something else'), ib.; an entreaty, request, solicitation, R.; Vikr.; reverence, obeisance, L.; final beatitude, L.; *-kalaha*, m. a quarrel of lovers, mere wanton quarrelsomeness, Megh.; Kād.; Pañcat.; *-kupita*, mfn. angry through love, feigning anger, Megh.; *-kopa*, m. the (feigned) anger of a coquette towards her lover, MW.; *-peśala*, mfn. soft through affection, R.; *-prakarsha*, m. excess of aff°, extraordinary attachment, Kathās.; *-bhaṅga*, m. breach of confidence, faithlessness, Vikr.; Pur.; *-madhura*, mfn. sweet through affection, Bhartṛ.; *-maya*, mf(*ī*)n. full of confidence, Jātakam.; *-māna*, m. 'love-pride,' the jealousy of l°, W.; *-vacana*, n. a declaration of l° or affection, Megh.; *-vat*, mfn. possessing candour, unceremonious, frank, open, confident, Kālid.; attached or devoted to, loving (loc. or comp.), ib.; desirous of, longing for (loc.), Śiś.; (ifc.) familiar with, used to, Bālar.; *-vighāta* = *-vihata*, A.; *-vimukha*, mf(*ī*)n. averse from love or friendship, Megh.; *-vihati*, f. refusal of a request, non-compliance, W.; *-spṛiś*, mfn. exciting love, affectionate, Mālatīm.; °*yâparâdha*, m. an offence against (mutual) affection or confidence, Amar.; °*yâpahārin*, mfn. taking with c° or without shyness, MW.; °*yâmṛita-pañcāśaka*, n. N. of wk.; °*yī-√kṛi*, to attach closely, Vcar.; °*yī-√bhū*, to become attached or affectionate, Suśr.; °*yônmukha*, mf(*ī*)n. expectant through love, Mālav.; °*yôpêta*, mfn. possessing candour, frank, open, MārkP. °**ṇayana**, n. bringing forwards, conducting, conveying, fetching, ŚrS.; MBh. &c.; means or vessel for bringing or fetching (cf. *agni-*); showing, betraying (cf. *śraddhā-*); (with *daṇḍasya* or *daṇḍa-*), applying (the rod), infliction of (punishment), Mn.; Yājñ.; establishing, founding (of a school), BhP.; execution, performance, practice, MBh.; Kāv.; bringing forward, adducing, L.; composing, writing, L.; satisfying, satiating, R. °**ṇayanīya**, mfn. used in bringing or fetching (as wood employed in carrying the sacred fire), ŚrS. °**ṇayin**, mfn. having affection for (gen.), attached to, beloved, dear, intimate, familiar, MBh.; Kāv. &c.; feeling attracted towards, longing for, desirous of (instr. or comp.), affectionate, loving, kind, ib.; (ifc.) clinging to, dwelling or being in; turned towards, aiming at; combined or provided with, Kāv.; m. a friend, favourite, Kum. v, 11; a husband, lover; (*inī*, f.) a beloved female, wife, Kālid.; Bhartṛ.; Kathās. &c.; a worshipper, devotee, Kum. iii, 66; a suppliant, suitor, Vikr.; °*yi-kriyā*, f. the business or affair of a lover or friend, Vikr. iv, 31; °*yi-jana*, m. a friend or lover (also collect.), Kālid.; °*yi-tā*, f. attachment or devotion to, desire or longing for (gen., loc. or comp.), Kāv.; °*yi-bhava*, mfn. being attached to, being in (comp.), Bālar. i, 49; °*yi-mādhava-campū*, f. N. of a poem. °**ṇāyaka**, m. a leader, chief or commander (of an army), MBh. °**ṇāyya**, mfn. (only L.) dear, beloved, fit, worthy; blameless, desireless; disapproved, rejected. °**ṇinīshenya**, mfn. (fr. Desid.) forming the entrance or beginning (as a day), TāṇḍBr.

Pra-ṇí, m. a leader or guide, TBr.; f. guidance, furtherance, devotion (?), RV. iii, 38, 2. °**ṇīta** (*prá-*), mfn. led forwards, advanced, brought, offered, conveyed (esp. to the altar, as fire or water or Soma), RV. &c. &c.; brought into, reduced to (e.g. *tamas*, to blindness, RV.; *vaśam*, to submission, BhP.); directed towards (loc.), Sāh.; hurled, cast, shot, MBh.; led towards i.e. delivered, given (as a son; others 'exposed'), MBh. i, 4672; performed, executed, finished, made, done, prepared, Up.; MBh. &c.; inflicted, sentenced, awarded, Mn.; MBh. &c.; established, instituted, taught, said, written, MBh.; Kāv. &c.; (*-tva*, n., Sarvad.) wished, desired (cf. *manaḥ-*); good (as food), Divyâv.; entered, approached, L.; m. (scil. *agni*) fire consecrated by prayers or mystical formulas, W.; (*ā*), f. a partic. vessel used at sacrifices, a sort of cup, L.; N. of a river, L.; pl. (scil. *āpas*) water fetched on the morning of a festival for sacrificial uses, holy water, ŚBr.; ŚrS. &c.; n. anything cooked or dressed (such as a condiment), A.; °*ta-vijñāpana*, n. begging for dainties, L.; °*tā-kāle*, ind. = *praṇītānām praṇayana-kāle*, ŚāṅkhŚr.; °*tā-caru*, m. the vessel for the holy water, ŚāṅkhGṛ.; °*tā-praṇáyana*, n. the vessel in which holy water is fetched, ŚBr.; GṛŚrS. °**ṇīti** (*prá-*), f. conduct, leading, guidance, RV.; AV.; leading away, AV.; favour, MW. °**ṇīya**, mfn. to be led on, Pāṇ. iii, 1, 123. °**ṇetavya**, mfn. to be led or guided, MBh.; to be accomplished or executed or used or applied, ib. °**ṇetṛí**, m. a leader, guide, RV. &c. &c. (Ved. with gen. or acc.; Class. gen. or comp.); a maker, creator, MBh.; Hariv.; an author, promulgator of a doctrine, MBh.; Pur.; a performer or one who plays a musical instrument, L.; one who applies (a clyster), Car.; *-mat*, mfn. containing the notion of leading, AitBr. °**ṇetra**, see *vāyú-praṇetra*. °**ṇenī**, mfn. (fr. Intens.) leading or guiding constantly or repeatedly, RV. °**ṇeya**, mfn. to be guided or led, docile, obedient, MBh.; Hariv.; Śaṃk.; to be (or being) used or applied, Bālar.; Car.; to be executed or accomplished, MBh.; to be fixed or settled, ib.

प्रणु *pra-ṇu* (√*nu*), P. Ā. *-ṇavati*, °*te*, to roar, bellow, sound, reverberate, RV.; AV.; P. *-ṇauti*, to make a humming or droning sound; (esp.) to utter the syllable *Om*, Br.; ChUp.; ŚrS. °**ṇáva** (or *prá-ṇ°*), m. (ifc. f. *ā*) the mystical or sacred syllable *Om*, VS.; TS.; ŚBr.; Mn. (ifc. also *-ka*) &c. (*-tva*, n., RāmatUp.); a kind of small drum or tabor = (and prob. w. r. for) *paṇana*, L.; *-kalpa*, m., *-darpaṇa*, m., *-pariśishṭa*, n., *-vyākhyā*, f., °*vârcana-candrikā*, f., °*vârtha-nirṇaya*, m., °*vârtha-prakāśikā-vyākhyāna*, n., °*vôpanishad*, f. N. of wks. °**ṇuta**, mfn. praised, celebrated, lauded, BhP.

प्रणुद् *pra-ṇud* (√*nud*), P. *-ṇudati*, °*te*, (inf. *-ṇódam*, RV.), to push on, propel, set in motion, drive or scare away, RV. &c. &c.: Caus. *-ṇodayati*, to push or thrust away, KaṭhUp.; to move, excite, Pañcat.; to press a person to do anything (2 acc.), Var. °**ṇutta** (*prá-*), mfn. pushed away, repelled, set in motion, AV. °**ṇud**, mfn. (ifc.) = next, MBh.; Suśr.; who or what enjoins or commands, W. °**ṇuda**, mfn. (ifc.) driving or scaring or forcing away, Hariv. °**ṇudita**, mfn. beaten, struck, MBh. (Nilak.) °**ṇunna**, mfn. = °*ṇutta*, MBh.; R.; Śiś.; sent, dispatched, MW.; shaken, trembling, ib. °**ṇottavya**, mfn. to be propelled, AitBr. °**ṇoda**, m. driving, guiding (horses &c.), W.; directing, ordering, ib. °**ṇodita**, mfn. (fr. Caus.) set in motion, agitated,

Pañcat.; driven, guided; directed, ordered, W. °**ṇodya**, mfn. to be driven or turned away, to be removed, MW.

प्रण्यस्त *pra-ṇy-asta*, mfn. (√2. *as*) beat down or depressed in front, TPrāt.

प्रतक्वन् *pra-tákvan*, mfn. (√*tak*) rushing on; steep, precipitous, TS.

Pra-táṅkam, ind. gliding, creeping, AV.

प्रतक्ष् *pra-√taksh* (only pf. Ā. *-tatakshire*), to build, make, produce, RV.

प्रतट *pra-taṭa*, n.(?) a high bank, Ml.

प्रतड् *pra-√taḍ*, P. *-tāḍayati*, to strike down, knock down, MBh.; Pañcat.

प्रतत *pra-tata*. See *pra-√tan*.

प्रततामह *pra-tatāmaha*, m. a great-grand-father, AV.

प्रतद्वसु *pratád-vasu*, mfn. (for *prathad-v°* or *pra-tata-v°*?) increasing wealth, RV. viii, 13, 27 (= *prâpta-vasu*, Nir.; = *vistīrṇa-dhanu*, Sāy.)

प्रतन् *pra-√tan*, P. Ā. *-tanoti*, *-tanute*, to spread (intr.) or extend over, cover, fill, AV. &c. &c.; to spread (trans.), disperse, diffuse, continue, propagate, VS. &c. &c.; to show, display, reveal, Śiś.; to undertake, begin, perform, execute, effect, cause, do, make (also with 2 acc.), MBh.; Kāv.; Rājat.: Pass. *-tāyate*, to spread or extend from, proceed from (abl.), ChUp.; *-tanyate*, to be continued or extended or particularized, Sarvad. °**tata** (*prá-*), mfn. spread over, diffused, covered, filled, RV.; R.; Suśr.; (*am*), ind. continuously, unintermittingly, MW. °**tati**, f. spreading, extension, L.; (also *ī*), a creeping plant, L. °**tāná**, m. a shoot, tendril, AV. &c. &c.; a plant with tendrils, Mn.; Var.; (met.) branching out, ramification, Kathās.; Suśr.; N. of a section of a wk. whose name ends in *kalpa-latā*, Cat.; diffuseness, prolixity, Sarvad.; a kind of disease, tetanus, epilepsy, L.; N. of a man (pl., his descendants), g. *upakâdi*; (*ā* or *ī*), f. N. of a plant (= *go-jihvā*), L.; °*na-vat*, mfn. having shoots or tendrils, Suśr.; ramified, ib. °**tānita**, mfn. treated diffusely or in a prolix manner, Sarvad. °**tānin**, mfn. having shoots or tendrils, L.; spreading, extending, W.; (*inī*), f. a spreading creeper, climbing plant, L.

प्रतन *pra-tana*, mf(ī)n. (fr. 1. *pra*) ancient, old, Pāṇ. v, 4, 30, Vārtt. 7, Pat. (cf. *pra-tna*).

प्रतनु *pra-tanu*, mfn. very thin or fine, delicate, minute, slender, small, insignificant, Kāv.; Suśr. (also *-ka*; ind. *-kam*); °*nū-√kṛi*, to render thin, emaciate, diminish, weaken, MBh.; Jātakam.

प्रतप् *pra-√tap*, P. *-tapati*, to give forth heat, burn, glow, shine (lit. and fig.), MBh.; Kāv. &c.; to feel pain, suffer, R.; to warm, heat, shine upon, ŚBr. &c. &c.; to roast, bake, R.; Suśr.; to kindle, light, illumine, RV.; to pain with heat, torment, harass, MBh.; Kāv.: Pass. *-tapyate*, to suffer pain, BhP.: Caus. *-tāpayati* (fut. *-tāpitā*, MBh. viii, 1971), to make warm, heat, GṛŚrS.; MBh. &c.; to set on fire, irradiate, illuminate, R.; to destroy or pain with heat, torment, harass, MBh.; R. &c. °**tapa**, m. the heat of the sun; *-tra*, n. a parasol, BhP. °**tapat**, mf(*antī*)n. burning, glowing, shining (lit. and fig.), feeling pain, doing penance, MBh.; m. the sun, MW. (cf. MBh. iv, 42); an ascetic, R. °**tapana**, n. warming, heating, KātyŚr.; MBh.; Suśr.; °*ne-√kṛi*, (prob.) to put near the fire, make warm (ind. p. *-kṛitya* or *-kṛitvā*), g. *sâkshād-ādi*. °**tapta**, mfn. hot, glowing, shining, MBh.; subjected to great heat, annealed, BhavP.; pained (esp. by heat), tortured, harassed, MBh.; Kāv. &c.; (prob.) n. annealed gold, R. °**taptṛi**, m. one who burns or singes, Śaṃk. °**tāpa**, m. glowing heat, heat, warmth, Kāv.; Var.; Suśr.; splendour, brilliancy, glory, majesty, dignity, power, strength, energy, Mn.; MBh. &c.; Calotropis Gigantea (= *arka*), L.; N. of a man, MBh.; Rājat.; *-candra*, m. N. of a king, Kathās.; of a Jaina author, Sarvad.; *-deva* (Cat.), *-dhavala* (Inscr.), m. N. of princes; *-nārasiṇha* or *-nṛisiṇha*, m. N. of wks.; *-pāla*, m. N. of a man, Rājat.; *-pura*, n. N. of a town, ib.; *-mārtaṇḍa*, m. N. of sev. wks.; *-mukuṭa*, m. N. of a prince, Vet.; *-rāja*, m. N. of a king, Dharmaś.; *-rāma-pūjā*, f. N. of wk.; *-rudra*, m. N. of a king of the Kākatiyas (or according to others of Vijayanagara or of Eka-śilā; sev. wks. are attributed to him, though in reality composed by different authors), Cat.; °*dra-kalyāṇa*, n. N. of a drama; °*dra-yaśo-bhūshaṇa*, or = °*drīya*, n. N. of a wk. by Vidyā-nātha on rhetoric (in which king Pratāpa-rudra is eulogized); *-vat*, mfn. full of splendour, majestic, glorious, powerful, MBh.; R. &c.; m. N. of Śiva, Śivag.; of an attendant of Skanda, MBh.; *-velâvalī*, f. (in music) N. of a Rāga; *-śīla*, m. N. of a king (= *Śīlāditya*), Rājat.; *-śekhara*, m. (in music) a kind of measure; *-siṇha* and *-siṇha-rāja*, m. N. of authors, Cat.; °*pâditya*, m. N. of sev. princes (*-tā*, f.), Rājat.; °*pâlaṃkāra*, m. N. of wk. (prob. = °*pa-rudrīya*); °*pêndra*, m. N. of the sun, Hcar. °**tāpana**, mfn. making hot, paining, tormenting, MBh.; R.; Suśr.; m. N. of Śiva, Śivag.; a partic. hell, BhP.; n. warming, heating, turning, paining, distressing, MBh.; Suśr. °**tāpasa**, m. Calotropis Gigantea Alba, Bhpr. °**tāpin**, mfn. burning, scorching, paining (ifc.); glowing, shining, splendid, majestic, powerful, MBh.; Hariv.; Rājat.

प्रतम् *pra-√tam*, P. *-tāmyati*, to become exhausted or breathless, faint away, lose self-consciousness, perish, AitBr.; MBh.; Suśr. °**tamaka**, m. a partic. form of asthma, Suśr. °**tām**, mfn. (nom. °*tān*), Pāṇ. vi, 4, 15; viii, 2, 64, Kāś. (also ind.; cf. g. *svar-ādi*). °**tāmaka**, m. = °*tamaka*, Car.

प्रतमाम् *pra-tamām*, ind. (fr. 1. *prá*) especially, particularly, ŚBr.; AitBr. **Pra-tarám** (RV.; AV.), °**rām** (VS.; ĀśvŚr.), ind. further, more particularly, in future.

प्रतर *pra-tara*, °*raṇa* &c. See *pra-√tṛī*.

प्रतर्क् *pra-√tark*, P. *-tarkayati*, to form a clear view or notion of (acc.), to gather, conclude, MBh.; Suśr.; to regard as, take for (2. acc.), Bhaṭṭ. °**tarka**, m. conclusion, supposition, conjecture, MBh.; Śak. °**tarkaṇa**, n. judging, reasoning, discussion, logic, L. °**tarkya**, see *a-pratarkya*.

प्रतर्दन *pra-tardana*. See under *pra-√tṛid*.

प्रतल *pra-tala*, m. the open hand with the fingers extended, L.; m. n. one of the divisions of the lower regions, L. (cf. *pātāla*).

प्रतवस् *prá-tavas*, mfn. mighty, powerful, active (said of the Maruts), RV.

प्रताम्र *pra-tāmra*, mfn. excessively red, very red, Śak.

प्रतार *pra-tāra*, °*raka* &c. See under *pra-√tṛī*.

प्रति 1. *práti*, ind. (as a prefix to roots and their derivative nouns and other n°, sometimes *pratī*; for 2. see p. 664) towards, near to; against, in opposition to; back, again, in return; down upon, upon, on; before nouns it expresses also likeness or comparison (cf. *prati-candra*); or it forms Avyayībhāvas of different kinds (cf. *prati-kshaṇam*, *prati-graham*, *praty-agni* &c.; rarely ifc. e.g. *sūpa-prati*, a little broth, Pāṇ. ii, 1, 9); or as a prep. with usually preceding acc., in the sense of towards, against, to, upon, in the direction of (e.g. *śabdam p°*, in the dir° of the sound, R.; *agnim pr°*, against the fire, Mn.; also *praty-agni*, ind., Pāṇ. vi, 2, 33, Sch.; *ripum pr°*, ag° the enemy, Mn.; *ātmānam pr°*, to one's self, Ratnâv.); opposite, before, in the presence of (e.g. *rodasī pr°*, bef° heaven and earth, RV.); in comparison, on a par with, in proportion to (e.g. *Indram pr°*, in compar° with I°, RV.; *sahasrāṇi pr°*, on a par with i.e. equivalent to thousands, ib.; also with abl. or *-tas*; cf. Pāṇ. i, 4, 92; ii, 3, 11); in the vicinity of, near, beside, at, on (e.g. *yūpam pr°*, near the sacrificial post, AitBr.; *Gaṅgām pr°*, at or on the Ganges, R.; *etat pr°*, at this point, TS.; *āyodhanam pr°*, on the field of battle, MBh.); at the time of, about, through, for (e.g. *Phālgunam pr°*, about the month Ph°, Mn.; *ciram pr°*, for a long time, MBh.; *bhṛiśam pr°*, often, repeatedly, Car.); or used distributively (cf. Pāṇ. i, 4, 90) to express at every, in or on every, severally (e.g. *yajñam pr°*, at every sacrifice, Yājñ.; *yajñam yajñam pr°*, TS.; *varsham pr°*, every year, annually, Pañcat.; in this sense often comp.; cf. above); in favour of, for (Pāṇ. i, 4, 90; e.g. *Pāṇḍavān pr°*, in favour of the P°s, MBh.); on account of, with regard to, concerning (Pāṇ. ib., e.g. *sīmām pr°*, conc° a boundary, Mn.; *Gautamam pr°*, with reg° to G°, R.); conformably or according to (e.g. *mām pr°*, acc° to me, i.e. in my opinion, Mālav.; cf. *mām praty araṇyavat pratibhāti*, 'it seems to me like a forest,' Hit.; *na bubhukshitam prati bhāti kiṃ cit*, 'to a hungry man nothing is of any account,' Kāś. on Pāṇ. ii, 3, 2); as, for (after a verb meaning 'to regard or consider;' cf. Vikr. iv, 69); or as prep. with abl. in return or as compensation for, instead or in the place of (Pāṇ. i, 4, 92, Sch.); with abl. or *-tas* see above; with abl. or gen. (?) to express 'about,' 'at the time of' (only *pr° vastoḥ*, 'at daybreak,' RV.); as prep. with gen. = with reference to, Hariv. 10967. [Cf. Zd. *paiti*; Gk. προτί, ποτί, πρός.]

Prati, in comp. with nouns not immediately connected with roots. — **kañcuka**, m. (prob.) a critic, a critical work, Āryabh. — **kaṇṭham**, ind. 'throat by throat,' singly, severally, one by one (so that each is reckoned), RPrāt. — **kaṇṭhukayā**, (prob.) w.r. for °**ṭhikayā**, ind. id., Divyâv. — **kapālam**, ind. in every cup, KātyŚr., Sch. — **karkaśa**, mf(*ā*)n. equally hard, of the same hardness as (comp.), Mṛicch. — **kalam**, ind. at every moment, constantly, perpetually, Vcar. — **kalpa**, m. counter-part (cf. *a-pr°* and see also *prati-√klṛip*). — **kalpam**, ind. in each cosmic period, Nīlak. — **kaśa**, mfn. (prob.) not obeying the whip, Pāṇ. vi, 1, 152, Sch. — **kashṭa**, mfn. comparatively (i.e. beyond expectation) bad, Suśr. — **kāṇḍam**, ind. for every section or chapter, Baudh. — **kāmá**, mfn. being according to wish or desire, desired, beloved, AV.; (*ám*), ind. according to wish, at will, RV.; ŚrS. — **kāmin**, mfn. contrary to desire, disagreeable, ŚāṅkhBr.; (*inī*), f. a female rival, Śiś. — **kāmyà**, mfn. being according to wish or liking, AV. — **kāya**, m. 'counter-body,' an adversary, Kir.; a target, butt, mark, ib.; an effigy, likeness, picture, L.; a bow, Gal. — **kitava**, m. an adversary at play, Daś. — **kīla**, m. an opposite post or peg, Pat. — **kuñjara**, m. a hostile elephant, MBh. — **kuṇḍam**, ind. in every fire-pit, Hcat. — **kūpa**, m. a moat, ditch, L. — **kūla**, mf(*ā*)n. 'against the bank' (opp. to *anu-kūla*, q.v.), contrary, adverse, opposite, inverted, wrong, refractory, inimical, disagreeable, unpleasant, Mn.; MBh. &c.; (*kūlam*), ind. contrarily, against, in inverted order, AV. &c. &c.; n. inverted order, opposition; (*ena*, in inv° o°, BhP.; °*leshu sthitaḥ*, offering opposition, Mn. ix, 275); *-kārin* (Mālav.), *-kṛit* (R.), mfn. acting adversely, inimical; *-tas*, ind. in contradiction to (*-to √vṛit*, to be in c° to), MBh.; *-tā*, f. (Kāv. &c.), *-tva*, n. (MW.) adverseness, opposition, hostility; perverseness, contumacy; *-darśana*, mfn. looking cross or awry, having an ungracious aspect, MW.; *-daiva*, mfn. opposed by fate (*-tā*, f. hostility of fate), Pañcat.; *-pravartin*, mfn. (a ship) taking an adverse course or (tongue) causing unpleasantness, ŚārṅgP. (v.l.); *-bhāshin*, mfn. speaking against, contradicting, R.; *-vacana*, n. refractory speech, contradiction, Pañcat.; *-vat*, mfn. refractory, contumacious, MBh.; *-vartin*, mfn. being adverse to, disturbing, troubling, Kum.; *-vāda*, m. = *-vacana*, MBh.; *-vādin*, mfn. = *-bhāshin*, ib.; *-visarpin*, mfn. (a ship) moving against the wind or stream, (a tongue) moving unpleasantly, ŚārṅgP. (cf. *-pravartin*); *-vṛitti*, mfn. resisting, opposing (with gen.), BhP.; *-vedanīya*, mfn. causing an unpleasant effect, Tarkas.; *-śabda*, mfn. sounding unpleasantly, Kum.; °*lâcarita*, n. an offensive action, injurious conduct, Ragh.; °*lôkta*, n. pl. contradiction, Kathās. — **kūlaya**, Nom. P. °*yati*, to resist, oppose, R.; Kād. — **kūlika**, mfn. hostile, inimical, Mcar. (prob. w.r. for *prāt°*). — **kṛittikā**, f., g. *aśvâdi*. — **koṇam**, ind. for or in every quarter of the sky, Hcat. — **kriyam**, ind. for each action, Kap. (see also under *prati-√kṛi*). — **krūra**, mfn. cruel in return, returning harshness, MBh. (*a-pratikr°*). — **kshaṇam**, ind. at every moment, continually, Kālid.; Rājat. &c. — **kshatra**, m. N. of a descendant of Atri (author of RV. v, 46, Anukr.; of a son of An-enas, Hariv.; of a son of Kshatra-vṛiddha, VP.; of a son of Śamin, Hariv. — **kshapam**, ind. every night, Śiś. — **kshaya**, m. a guard, L. — **kshetra**, n. place, stead; (*e*), ind. instead of (gen.), Gṛihyās. — **kshepa**, °**paṇa**, see *pra-√kship*. — **kshoṇi-bhṛit**, m. opposition king, Vcar. — **khura**, m. a partic. wrong position of a child at birth, Suśr. — **kheṭaka**, g. *aśvâdi*. — **gaja**, m. = *-kuñjara*, MBh.; Hariv.

— **gātram**, ind. in every limb (only ibc.), Dhūrtas. — **giri**, m. an opposite mountain, BhP. — **gu**, ind. against a cow, Mn. iv, 52. — **gṛiham** (KātyŚr.), **-geham** (Rājat.), ind. in every house. — **grāmam**, ind. in every village, Rājat.; °*ma-samīpam*, ind. near every v°, Dharmaś. — **cakra**, n. a discus which is a match for any other, MBh.; a hostile army, Nīlak. — **candra**, m. a mock moon, paraselene, R. — **caraṇam**, ind. in every school or branch, L. — **citi**, ind. in every layer or pile, KātyŚr. — **codanam**, ind. on every order or injunction, ĀśvŚr. — **cchanda**, m. a reflected image; any image, likeness, substitute, Hariv.; Rājat.; *-kalyāṇa*, mfn. obliging, complaisant, L. — **cchandaka**, m. = *-cchanda*, Kull.; mfn. versed in, familiar with, Nalac. — **cchāyā**, f. reflection, likeness, image, shadow, phantom, Hariv.; Sāṃk.; the distorted image of a sick man (indicative of approaching death), Car.; *-maya*, mf(*ī*)n. consisting of the dist° im° of a sick man, ib. — **cchāyikā**, f. an image, phantom, Naish. — **jaṅghā**, f. the shin-bone, L. — **janá**, m. an adversary, AV.; °*nya* (*práti-*), mfn. adverse, hostile, RV. — **janam**, ind. in every one, Śiś. — **janman**, see *prati-√jan*. — **jihvā** and **-jihvikā**, f. the uvula, L. — **jūti-varpas** (*práti-*), mfn. assuming any form according to impulse, RV. iii, 60, 1. — **tad-vid**, f. recognition of the contrary, KaushUp. — **tantram**, ind. according to each Tantra or opinion, W.; °*tra-darpaṇa*, m. N. of wk.; °*tra-siddhânta*, m. a doctrine adopted in various systems (but not in all), Nyāyas.; Car. — **tarām**, ind. (with √*bhū*) to retire or shrink more and more, ŚBr. — **taru**, ind. at each tree, Gīt. — **tāla**, m. (in music) a kind of measure; (*ī*), f. the key of a door, L. — **tālaka**, m. = prec. (m. and f.), L. — **tūṇī**, f. a modification of the nervous disease called Tūṇī, Suśr. (cf. *pra-tūṇī*). — **try-aham**, ind. for three days at a time, Gaut. — **daṇḍa**, mfn. refractory under the rod, disobedient, obstinate, TāṇḍBr. — **dantin**, m. = *-kuñjara*, Kir.; °*ty-anīkam*, ind. against the army of elephants, ib. — **dinam** and **-divasam**, ind. day by day, daily, every day, Kāv.; Var.; Pañcat. — **diśam**, ind. in every direction or quarter, all around, GṛŚrS.; Megh. &c. — **dūta**, m. a messenger sent in return, Rājat.; Kathās. — **dṛiś**, mfn. similar, like, TS. — **dṛiśam**, ind. in or for every eye, BhP. — **dṛishṭânta**, m. a counter example, Nyāyas.; *-sama*, m. an irrelevant objection by adducing a c° ex° which ignores the opponent's example, ib. — **devatā**, f. a corresponding deity, MuṇḍUp.; °*tam*, ind. = *-daivatam*, KātyŚr. — **deśam**, ind. = *-diśam*, Var.; Rājat. — **deham**, ind. in each body, Sāṃk. — **daivatam**, ind. for each deity, ib. — **doshám**, ind. in the evening, in the dark, RV. — **dvaṃdva**, m. an adversary, rival, foe (in *a-pratidv°*), MBh.; R. &c.; n. opposition, hostility, W.; °*dvaya*, Nom. P. °*yati*, to rival, Divyâv.; °*dvin*, m. = °*dva*, m. (ifc. vying with), MBh.; Kāv.; °*dvī-bhūta*, mfn. being an adv°, Sāṃk. — **dvādaśan**, mfn. pl. twelve in each case, Gaut. — **dvāram** (Kathās.), **-dvāri** (BhP.), ind. at every gate or door. — **dvipa**, m. = *-kuñjara*, Kir. — **dvirada**, m. id., MBh.; Hariv. — **dvīpam**, ind. in every part of the world, Hcar. — **dhī**, mfn. (ifc.) as intelligent as, Pracaṇḍ. — **dhura**, m. a horse harnessed by the side of another, VS., Sch. (cf. *a-pratidh°*). — **nagaram**, ind. in every town, Hcar. — **nadi**, ind. at every river, Bālar. — **naptṛi**, m. a great grandson, a son's grandson, L. (cf. *pra-ṇapāt*). — **namaskāra**, mfn. one who returns a salutation, ŚāṅkhŚr. — **nayana** (ibc.), into the eye, Mālatīm. — **nava**, mfn. new, young, fresh; *-javā-pushpa*, n. a newly opened China rose, Megh. — **nāga**, m. = *-kuñjara*, MBh. — **nāḍī**, f. a branch vein, L. — **nāman** (*práti-*), mf(*mnī*)n. having corresponding names, related by name, ŚBr.; °*ma*, ind. by n°, mentioning the n°, Veṇis.; °*ma-grahaṇam*, ind. mentioning each individual n°, Kād. — **nāyaka**, m. 'counter hero,' the adversary of the hero (in a play), Sāh.; an image, likeness, counterfeit, Śrīkaṇṭh. — **nārī**, f. a female rival, Śiś. — **niśam**, ind. every night, Kathās. — **niścaya**, m. a contrary opinion, MBh. — **nishka**, m. or n. (?) a Nishka (s.v.) in each case, Hcat. — **nishṭha**, mfn. standing on the opposite side, Car. — **nṛipati**, m. = *-kshoṇibhṛit*, Dhanaṃj. — **nyāyám**, ind. in inverted order, ŚBr. — **nyāsa**, a counter deposit, Nār. — **nyūṅkha**, m. a corresponding insertion of the vowel *o*, ŚāṅkhŚr.; °*khaya*, Nom. °*yati*, to insert the vowel *o* in the corresponding stanza or verse, ib. — **paksha**, m. the opposite side, hostile party, opposition, MBh.; Kāv. &c.; an obstacle, Divyâv.; an adversary, opponent, foe, ib. (ifc. = a rival in, match for, equal, similar, Kāvyâd.); a respondent, defendant (in law), W.; m. N. of a king, VāyuP.; *-graha*, m. the taking of the opposite side (°*haṃ cakruḥ*, they took the opp° side), MBh.; *-caṇḍa-bhairava*, m. N. of the chief of a partic. sect, Cat.; *-janman*, mfn. caused by the enemy, Śiś.; *-tā*, f. (BhP.), *-tva*, n. (Sāṃk.) opposition, hostility; °*kshita*, mfn. containing a contradiction, contradictory, Bhāshāp.; nullified by a contradictory premiss (one of the 5 kinds of fallacious middle terms), MW. — **pakshin**, m. an opponent, adversary, Sāṃk.; °*kshi-tā*, f. self-contradiction, the being self-contradictory, MW. — **pacanam**, ind. at each cooking, Gobh., Sch. — 1. **-paṇa**, m. (for 2. see p. 667) the stake of an adversary at play, Kathās. — **paṇya**, n. merchandise in exchange, Divyâv. — **pattra-phalā**, f. a kind of gourd, L. — **patnī**, f. (m. c. for °*tnī*) a female rival (*-vat*, BhP.); ind. for each wife, ĀpŚr., Sch. — **patha**, m. way back, Harav.; (*am*), ind. along the road, Kathās. (cf. Pāṇ. iv, 4, 42); backwards, Rājat.; °*tha-gati*, mfn. going along the road, Kum. iii, 76; °*thika*, mfn. id., Pāṇ. iv, 4, 42. — 1. **-pad**, ind. (cf. *prati-√pad*, p. 667) = *-padam*; *-darśinī*, f. 'looking at every step,' a woman, L. — **pada**, n. N. of an Upâṅga; (*am*), ind. (also °*da*, ibc.) at every step, on every occasion, at every place, everywhere, Kāv.; at every word, word by word, Sarvad.; literally, expressly (Pāṇ. ii, 2, 10, Vārtt. 1; vi, 2, 26, Sch.); each, singly, R. (= *pratyekam*, Sch.); °*da-tva*, n. walking step by step, Kāṭh. — **padmam**, ind. at every lotus flower, Hcat. — **parṇa-śiphā**, f. Anthericum Tuberosum, L. — **paryāyam**, ind. at every turn, GṛŚrS. — **parva**, ind. at every change of the moon, Vcar. — **palam**, ind. every moment, Bhām. — **pallava**, m. an opposite or outstretched branch, Ragh. — **paśu**, ind. at every sacrificial victim, TBr., Sch. — 1. **-pāṇa**, m. (for 2. see s.v.) a counter-pledge, anything staked against another thing, MBh.; a counter-stake, counter-game, revenge at play, Nal. (cf. *-paṇa*, above). — **pātram**, ind. (in dram.) in each part, in e° character, by every actor, Śak. — **pādapam**, ind. in every tree, Vikr. — **pādam**, ind. in e° Pāda, in e° quarter of a verse, Piṅg. — **pāpa**, mfn. wicked or evil in return, recompensing evil for evil, MBh. — **pāpin**, mfn. id., Nīlak. — **piṇḍam**, ind. in each Piṇḍa (s.v.), MānŚr. — **puṃ-niyata**, mfn. settled for every soul singly, Sarvad. — **púr**, f. a hostile castle, MaitrS. — **pura**, g. *aṅśv-ādi*, Kāś. — **purusha** or **-pūr°**, m. 'a counter-person,' a similar man; a companion, assistant; a deputy, substitute, KātyŚr., Sch.; (*a-pratip°*, unmatched, BhP.); the effigy of a man (which thieves push into the interior of a house before entering it themselves), Mṛicch.; (ibc. and *ám*, ind.) man by man, every m°, for each m°, Br.; GṛŚrS.; Hcar.; Āp.; for each soul, Sāṃkhyak. — **pushyam**, ind. at each time of the moon's entrance into the constellation Pushya, Var. — **pustaka**, n. a copy of an original manuscript, a c° in general, Sāy. on ŚBr. — **pūrusha**, see *-purusha* above. — **pūrvâhṇam**, ind. every forenoon, Pāṇ. vi, 2, 33, Sch. — **pṛishṭhā**, f. each page of a leaf, Cat. — **praṇavam**, ind. at every repetition of the syllable *Om*, KātyŚr.; °*va-saṃyukta*, mfn. accompanied each time with the s° *Om*, Yājñ. — **praṇāma**, m. a bow or obeisance in return, saluting in turn, Rājat.; Kād. — **pratí**, mf(*tínī*)n. being a counter-part, counter-balancing; being a match for, equal to (acc.), Br.; Nir. — **pratīka** (ibc.) and °**kam**, ind. at each initial word, ĀśvŚr.; on or at every part of the body, Naish. — **prabhātam**, ind. every morning, Kathās.; Inscr. — **prayāṇakam**, ind. with each day's journey, Kād. — **prayoga**, m. counter-application or parallel setting forth of a proposition, Sarvad. — **praśna**, m. a question asked in return, ĀpŚr.; an answer, Var.; (*ám*), ind with regard to the controversy, ŚBr. (Sāy.) — **prasava**, see under *prati-pra-√1. sū*. — **prasavam**, ind. in each birth, Sarvad. — **prākāra**, m. an outer rampart, L. — **prâṇi**, ind. in or for every living creature, Bādar., Sch. — **prāś** (*práti-*), m. an opponent in controversy, adversary in a lawsuit (see *prati-√prach*), AV. — **prāśita**, mfn. opposed in debate, Kauś. — **priya**, mfn. agreeable to (gen.), ĀpŚr.; n. kindness or service in return, MBh.; Ragh. — **prêkshaṇa**, n. looking at in return, Āp. — **prâisha**, m. a cry or call in return, direction given in r°, KātyŚr. — **phalī-karaṇam**, ind. at each cleaning of the corn, KātyŚr., Comm. — **phullaka**, see p. 668. — **bandhu**, m. an equal in rank or station, MBh. — 1. **-bala**, n. a hostile army, Vcar.; Daś. — 2. **-bala**, mfn. having equal strength or power, equally matched, a match for (with gen. or ifc., e.g. *astra-p°*, equal in arms), being able to (dat. or inf.), MBh.; R.; (cf. *a-p°*). — **bāṇi**, see *-vāṇi* below. — **bāhu**, m. fore-arm, Var.; an opposite side (in a square or polygon), Col.; N. of sev. men, BhP. — 1. **bimba**, n. (rarely m.) the disc of the sun or moon reflected (in water); a reflection, reflected image, mirrored form, MBh.; Pañcat.; Kāv. &c. (also °*baka*); a resemblance or counterpart of real forms, a picture, image, shadow, W.; (among the synonyms of 'equal,' Kāvyâd.); N. of the chapters of the Kāvya-prakāśâdarśa, Cat.; *-vartin*, mfn. being reflected or mirrored, MW.; *-bimbâta* (?), m. a mirror, W. — 2. **bimba**, Nom. P. °*bati*, to be reflected or mirrored, Kap., Sch.; °*bita*, mfn. reflected, mirrored (*-tva*, n.), ib. &c.; °*bī-√kṛi*, to reflect, represent, equal, Daś. — **bimbana**, n. the being reflected, Sāṃkhyaprav., Sch.; Nīlak.; reflection; comparing together, comparison, Sāh. — **bimbaya**, Nom. P. °*yati*, to reflect, mirror, L. (cf. °*bita* above). — **bīja**, n. bad seed, L. — **bījam**, ind. for every sort of grain, ĀpŚr. — **bhaṭa**, mfn. a match for, vying with (gen. or comp.), rivalling, Vcar.; Caṇḍ.; Rājat.; (°*ṭī-√kṛi*, to equalize to, Naish.; m. an adversary, Rājat.); *-tā*, f. emulousness, emulation, Rājat. — **bhaya**, mf(*ā*)n. exciting fear, formidable, terrible, dangerous, ĀśvGṛ.; Gobh.; MBh. &c.; n. fear (with abl. or ifc.), MBh.; Rājat.; danger, ĀśvGṛ.; Rājat.; (*am*), ind. formidably, frightfully, Ragh.; *-kara* and °*yaṃ-k°*, mfn. causing fear, R.; Kathās.; *-bhayâkāra*, mfn. having a formidable aspect, MW. — **bhavam**, ind. for this and all future births, L. — 1. **-bhāga** (ibc.), for every degree, Siddhântaś. (for 2. see under *prati-√bhaj*). — **bhī**, f. fear, Bhojapr. — **bhuja**, m. = *-bāhu*, Col. — **bhūpāla**, m. = next, Vcar.; (pl.) each single prince, all the princes together, Naish. — **bhūbhṛit**, m. a hostile prince, Vcar. — **bhairava**, mf(*ā*)n. dreadful, Var. — **maṅgala-vāra**, m. pl. (prob.) every Tuesday, Cat. — **mañca** and °**caka**, m. (in music) a kind of measure, Saṃgīt. — **maṇṭhaka**, (prob.) m. id., Cat. (cf. *manthaka*). — **maṇḍala**, n. a secondary disk (of the sun &c.), Hariv.; an eccentric orbit, Col. — **matsya**, m. pl. N. of a people, MBh.; VP. (v.l. *-māsya*). — **mantram**, ind. with or at every formula or verse, KātyŚr.; Gaut. — **mandiram**, ind. in every house, Rājat. — **manv-antara**, n. every Manv-antara; *am* (Mcar.), *e* (Hcat.), ind. in e° M°. — **malla**, m. an opponent in wrestling or boxing, an antagonist or rival, Hariv.; Kathās.; Vcar.; *-tā*, f. rivalry, Harav. — **mahânasa**, n. every kitchen, Gobh., Comm. — **mahā-vyāhṛiti**, ind. at each Mahā-vyāhṛiti, KātyŚr. — **mahisha**, m. a hostile buffalo, Kāv. — **māṅsa**, n. new or restored flesh, Kathās. — **mātṛi**, ind. mother by mother, every mother, Gaut. — **mātrā**, f. pl. every measure (of time), NṛisUp. — **māyā**, f. counter-spell, c°-charm, MBh.; Kathās. — **mārga**, m. the way back, MBh.; (*e*), ind. on the way, Divyâv. — **mārgaka**, m. the city of Hari-ścandra (said to hover in the air), L. — **mālā**, f. an exercise analogous to capping verses, reciting verse for v° as a trial of memory or skill (one of the 64 Kalās, Cat.), W. — **māsa** (ibc.) and °**sam**, ind. every month, monthly, L. — **māsya**, m. pl. N. of a people (v.l. for *-matsya*, q.v.) — **mitra**, w.r. for *praty-amitra*, q. v., MBh. — **mukula** (ibc.), in or upon every bud, Prab. — **mukha**, n. the reflected image of the face, Harav.; (in dram.) a secondary plot or incident which hastens or retards the catastrophe, the Epitasis (also °*kha-saṃdhi*), Daśar.; Pratāp.; Sāh., Sch.; an answer, Sāh.; mf(*ā* or *ī*)n. standing before the face, facing, R.; BhP.; Vajracch.; being near, present, R.; (ibc. or *am*, ind.) towards, in front, before, GṛS.; Mn.; MBh.; (*ī*), w.r. for *-mukharī*, q.v., Saṃgīt.; °*khâṅga*, n. (in dram.) progressive narration of events, W. — **mukharī**, f. a partic. mode of drumming, Saṃgīt. — **mudrā**, f. a counter-seal, Mn.; Kull.; the impression of a seal, Lalit. — **muhus**, ind. again and ag°, repeatedly, Prab.; Caurap.; Śāntiś. — **muhūrta** (ibc.) and °**tam**, ind. every moment, constantly, Caurap. — **mūrti**, f. a corresponding form, image, L. — **mūshikā**, f. a species of rat, W. — **yāmini**, ind. every night, Kathās. **–yuvati,** f. a concubine, female rival, Vcar. **–yuvam,** ind. towards the young man, Śiś. viii, 35. **–yūthapa,** m. the leader of a hostile herd (of elephants), MBh. **–yūpam,** ind. post by post, ĀpŚr. **–yogam,** ind. rule by rule, Pat. **–yoní,** ind. according to source or origin, ŚBr. **–rajani,** ind. every night, Naish. **–ratha,** m. an opposite fighter in a war-chariot, an adversary in war, equal a°, Kathās. (cf. *a-p°*); N. of a descendant of Atri (author of the hymn RV. v, 47), RAnukr.; of a son of Mati-nāra and father of Kaṇva, Hariv.; of a son of Vajra and father of Sucāru, ib. **–rathyam,** ind. in every road, Kāv. **–rāja** (Kull.) or **°jan** (R.), m. a hostile king, royal adversary. **–rājam,** ind. king by king, for every k°, Pat. **–rātram** (Hit.) or **°tri** (Vcar.), ind. each night, nightly. **–ripu,** ind. against the enemy or the enemies, Śiś. **–rūpa,** n. the counterpart of any real form, an image, likeness, representation, MBh.; Var.; BhP. (also *ā*, f., KaushUp.); a pattern, model for imitation (cf. *-dhṛik* below); anything falsified, a counterfeit of (gen.), Vishṇ.; mf(*ā*)n. like, similar, corresponding, suitable, proper, fit, RV. &c. &c. (*°pam akurvan,* not requiting, MārkP.); agreeable, beautiful, MBh.; m. N. of a Dānava, ib.; (*ā*), f. N. of a daughter of Meru, BhP.; *-carya,* mfn. exemplary in conduct, worthy of imitation, MW.; *-caryā́,* f. suitable or exemplary conduct, ŚBr.; *-tā,* f. resemblance, Harav.; *-dhṛik,* mfn. offering (i.e. being) a model or pattern, BhP. **–rūpaka,** n. an image, a picture, L.; forgery, Nār.; (prob.) a forged edict, MBh.; mf(*ikā*)n. similar, corresponding, having the appearance of anything (generally ifc.), MBh.; Mn.; Śak. &c.; m. a quack, charlatan, Car. **–rūpya,** in *a-p°*, w.r. for *a-prātirūpya,* see *prātir°*. **–raudra-karman,** mfn. acting cruelly against others, R. **–lakshaṇa,** n. 'a counter-mark,' mark, sign, MBh.; R. **–liṅgam,** ind. at every Liṅga, Rājat. **–lipi,** f. a copy, transcript, written reply, L. **–loka,** m. every world, Hcat. **–lomá,** mf(*ā*)n. against the hair or grain (opp. to *anu-l°*), contrary to the natural course or order, reverse, inverted; adverse, hostile, disagreeable, unpleasant; low, vile, ŚBr.; RPrāt.; ŚrS. &c.; left, not right, W.; contrary to caste (where the mother is of a higher caste than the father), ib.; (ibc. and *ám,* ind.) against the hair, ag° the grain, in reversed or inverted order, TS.; Br.; ĀśvŚr. &c.; m. N. of a man; pl. his descendants, g. *upakâdi;* (*ā*), f. a partic. incantation (to be recited from the end to the beginning), Kathās.; n. any disagreeable or injurious act; (*ena*), ind. in an unfriendly manner, unpleasantly, Cāṇ.; *-ja,* mfn. born in the inverse order of the classes (as of a Kshatriya father and Brāhmaṇī mother, or of a Vaiśya f° and Kshatriyā m° or B° m°, in which cases the wife is of a higher caste than the husband; cf. Mn. x, 16), W.; *-tas,* ind. in consequence of the inverted order or course, Mn. x, 68; invertedly, in inverted order or series, Yājñ.; MBh.; Pañcat.; *-rūpa,* mfn. inverted, KaushUp.; *°mânuloma,* mfn. speaking against or for anything; (ibc. and *am,* ind.) in inverted order or course and in the natural o° or c°, Mn.; Yājñ.; *°ma-tas,* ind. in an unfriendly and friendly manner, R. **–lomaka,** mfn. against the hair or grain, reverse, inverted, BhP.; n. inverted order, perversion, Pañcat. **–vaktram,** ind. on every face, Hcat. **–vat,** mfn. containing the word *prati,* AitBr. **–vatsara,** m. a year, MBh.; (*am*), ind. every y°, yearly, Rājat.; Kathās. **–vanam,** ind. in every wood or forest, Bhartṛ. **–vanitā,** f. a female rival, Śiś. **–vargam,** ind. group by gr°, KātyŚr. **–varṇa,** m. every caste, Hcat.; (*am*), ind. c° by c°, Gaut. **–varṇika,** mfn. having a corresponding colour, similar, L. **–vartmán,** mfn. taking an opposite road or course, AV. **–varman,** see *su-prati-v°*. **–varsha** (ibc.) or **°sham** (ind.), every year, yearly, MārkP.; Pañcat. **–vallabhā,** f. = *-yuvati,* Vcar. **–vashaṭkāram,** ind. at each exclamation Vashaṭ, ĀśvŚr. **–vasati,** ind. in every habitation or house, Kathās. **–vastu,** n. a counterpart, equivalent; anything given in return, anything contrasted with another, Kathās.; Pratāp.; *-vastûpamā,* f. (rhet.) a simile or parallel (in which a p° is drawn between two different objects by stating some common characteristic belonging to both), Kāvyâd.; Sāh.; Kuval. &c. **–vahni-pradakshiṇam,** ind. at each perambulation from left to right of the sacred fire, Kathās. **–vākyam,** ind. in every sentence, L. **–1. -vāṇi,** mfn. unseemly, unsuitable, L. **–2. -vāṇi,** f. n. an answer, L.; opposition, L. (w.r. *°vāni*); f. = *paribhāshā, prajñapti* &c., Gal. **–vāta,** m. a contrary wind, Mn; Suśr.; (*am*), ind. against the wind, KātyŚr.; Śak.; Pañcat.; (*e*), ind. on the lee side, MW. **–1. -vāraṇa,** m. (for 2. see under *prati-√1. vṛi*) a hostile elephant, Hariv.; a sham or mock el°; (with *daitya*), a Daitya in the form of an el°, BhP. **–vārttā,** f. account, information, Śak. **–vāsaram,** ind. every day, daily, Rājat.; Kathās.; Hcat.; (*e*), ind. = *tad-dinam,* L. **–vāsarika,** mfn. daily, Hcat. **–vāsudeva,** m. 'opponent of a Vāsudeva,' (with Jainas) N. of nine beings at enmity with V° (= *Vishṇu-dvish*), Col. **–viṭapam,** ind. to every branch, Śāntiś. **–vidyam,** ind. in every doctrine, Gaut. **–vindhya,** m. N. of a king who ruled over a particular part of the Vindhya mountains, MBh.; of a son of Yudhi-shṭhira; pl. N. of his descendants, MBh.; Pur. **–vipāśam,** ind. along the Vipāś river, Laghuk. **–vimba** &c. = *-bimba* &c. **–1. -virati,** ind. (for 2. see *prati-vi-√ram*) at every pause, at each cessation or disappearance, Śāntiś. **–viśva,** mfn. pl. one and all; (*eshu*), ind. in all cases, Cat. **–visha,** n. 'counter-poison,' an antidote, L.; mf(*ā*)n. containing an ant°, Rājat.; (*ā*), f. Aconitum Heterophyllum, Car.; Bhpr. **–vishaya,** m. pl. the various objects of sense, L.; (ibc. and *am,* ind.) in relation to each single object of s°, Sāṃkhyak. **–vishṇu,** ind. at every (image of) Vishṇu, Vop.; towards V°, in place of V°, W. **–vishṇuka,** m. Pterospermum Suberifolium, L. **–vīra,** m. an antagonist, a well-matched opponent, MBh.; Vcar.; BhP.; *-tā,* f. the being a w°-m° o°, antagonism, Prab. **–vīrya,** n. (the being a match for in valour) in *a-p°*, mfn. unequalled, matchless, irresistible, MBh.; R.; *a-prativīryârambha,* not having sufficient strength to undertake anything, SaddhP. **–vṛitta,** n. an eccentric circle, Gol. **–vṛittântam,** ind. according to the saying, as they say, Rājat. **–vṛitti,** ind. according to the modulation (of the voice), RPrāt. **–vṛisha,** m. a hostile bull, Hariv. **–vedam,** ind. at or for every Veda, Yājñ.; Bādar.; *°da-śākham,* ind. for every branch or school of the V°, Madhus. **–vedântam,** ind. in every Upanishad, Bādar., Sch. **–velam,** ind. on every occasion, MBh. **–veśa** (*práti-* or *pratī-;* cf. Pāṇ. vi, 3, 122, Vārtt. 3), mf(*ā*)n. neighbouring, a neighbour, RV.; TS.; ŚBr. &c.; auxiliary, Br.; TBr., Comm.; m. a neighbouring house, L.; *-tás,* ind. from the neighbourhood, ŚBr.; *-vāsin,* mf(*inī*)n. living in the neighbourhood; m. f. a neighbour, Alaṃkārak. **–veśin** (or *pratī-v°*), mfn. neighbouring; m. and (*nī*), f. a neighbour, Dhūrtas.; Mṛicch.; Sāh. **–veśma,** ind. in every house, Śiś. **–veśman,** n. a neighbour's house, Pañcat. **–veśya,** m. a neighbour, MBh. **–vaira,** n. requital of hostilities, revenge, MBh. **–vyoma** or **°man,** m. N. of a prince, Pur. **–śatru** (*práti-*), m. an adversary, opponent, enemy, AV.; Kuval., Sch. **–śabda** (or *°daka,* Kād.; Hcar.), m. echo, reverberation, MBh.; R.; Ragh. &c.; *-ga,* mfn. going after a sound or in the direction of a s°, MBh.; *-vat,* mfn. re-echoing, resounding, Kathās. **–1. śaraṇa,** n. (for 2. see under *prati-√śrī*) confidence in (ifc.), Divyâv.; *-bhūta,* mfn. resorted to (acc.), ib. (cf. *-saraṇa* under *prati-√sṛi*). **–śarâsana,** n. an adversary's bow, Vās. **–śarīram,** ind. concerning one's own body or person, Pat. **–śaśin,** m. a mock moon, paraselene, Var. **–śākham,** ind. for every branch or school (of the Veda), Bādar., Sch. **–śākha-vat,** see *-śākhā*. **–śākhā,** f. a side branch, s° shoot (pl. all the schools of the Veda, BhP.); *-nāḍī,* f. a branch vein, PraśnUp.; *°khavat,* mfn. having anything as side branches, MBh. **–1. -śāsana,** n. (for 2. see *prati-√śās*) a rival command or authority (cf. *a-p°*), Ragh. **–śilpa,** n. a counter-Śilpa, ŚāṅkhŚr. **–śishya,** m. under-disciple (?), Divyâv. **–śukra-budha** (ibc.), towards the planets Venus or Mercury, Var. **–śukram** (perhaps two words), ind. towards the planet Venus, R. **–śulka,** w.r. for *-śrutkā* (see under *prati-√śru*), Lalit. **–śṛiṅgeṇa,** ind. horn by h°, Hcat. **–śrotas,** ind. w.r. for *-srotas,* q.v. **–śloka,** m. a counter-Śloka, Siṇhās.; L.; (*am*), ind. at every Śl°, BhP. **–shka** &c., see *prati-shkaśa,* p. 671. **–saṃyoddhṛi,** m. an adversary in war, MBh. **–saṃvatsaram,** ind. every year, yearly, Yājñ.; ĀpSr., Comm. **–saṃskāram,** ind. at every ceremony, ĀpŚr. **–saṅgakshikā,** f. a cloak to keep off the dust (worn by Buddhist mendicants), L. (prob. w.r. for *-saṃkakshikā*). **–sadanam,** ind. every one to his dwelling, Mcar. **–sadṛiksha** or **-sadṛiś** (*práti-*), mfn. similar, VS. **–sadma,** ind. at or in every house, BhP. **–sama,** mfn. equal to, a match for, MBh.; Nāg. **–samantam** (*práti-*), ind. on every side, everywhere, ŚBr. **–sambandhi,** ind. according to the respective connection, Sāh. **–sarga,** see under *prati-√sṛij*. **–sargam,** ind. in every creation, Mn., Kull. **–savya,** mfn. in inverted order, inverted, reverse, L. **–sāma,** mfn. (prob.) unkind, unfriendly, Pāṇ. v, 4, 75. **–sāmanta,** m. 'a hostile neighbour,' enemy, adversary, Kuval.; Hcar. **–sāmarthya,** n. relative suitableness, R. **–sāyam,** ind. towards evening, Gobh. **–siṇha,** m. a hostile lion, Kathās. **–sīrā,** f. a curtain, L.; a screen or wall of cloth, an outer tent, W. **–sundarī,** f. = *-yuvati,* q.v., Vcar. **–sūrya** (or *°yaka*), m. a mock sun, parhelion, Var.; a kind of lizard, a chameleon (which lies or basks in the sun), Uttarar.; Suśr.; (*am*), ind. opposite to the sun, Mn.; *-matsya,* m. a partic. appearance in the sun; (accord. to Comm.) a mock sun and a comet, Ap.; *-śayânaka,* m. 'lying or basking in the sun,' a kind of lizard, a chameleon, L. **–senā,** f. an opposing or hostile army, Hariv. **–somā,** f. a kind of plant (= *mahisha-vallī*), L. **–somôdaka-dvijam,** ind. against the moon or water or a Brāhman, Mn. iv, 52. **–skandha,** m. every shoulder (instr. 'each on his sh°'), Hit.; N. of an attendant of Skanda (v.l. *kapi-sk°*), MBh.; (*am*), ind. upon the shoulders, W.; in every section of a book, Pratāp. **–strī,** mfn. lying on a woman, ChUp. **–sthānam,** ind. in every place, everywhere, Prab., Sch. **–sneha,** m. (prob.) w.r. for *pati-s°*, Kathās. **–srota,** mf(*ā*)n. = next (*Mandakinīm °tām anuvraja,* go up the M° i.e. up or against the stream), R. **–srotam** (BhP.) or **-srotas** (Mn.; MBh.; Hariv. &c.), ind. against the stream, up the s°; (w.r. *śrotas*). **–svam,** ind. 'each for itself,' one by one, singly, ĀśvŚr.; RPrāt., Comm. **–svāhākāram,** ind. at every exclamation Svāhā, ĀpGṛ. **–hasta** (*-tva,* n., Vcar.), **-hastaka** (Hit.), m. a deputy, substitute, proxy. **–hasti,** ind. towards elephants, MBh. **–hastin,** m. the keeper of a brothel, Daś. (Sch. 'a neighbour'). **–hṛidayam,** ind. in every heart, BhP., Sch.

Praty, in comp. before vowels for *prati* above. **–aṅśa,** m. a portion, share, Buddh. **–aṅśu,** m. = *pratigato 'ṇśuḥ,* Pāṇ. vi, 2, 193; mfn. = *pratigatā aṇśavo 'sya,* ib., Sch. **–aṇsa,** m. = *-aṅśa,* q.v. **–aṇsam,** ind. on the shoulders, Śiś. **–ák,** see *pratyáñc*. **–aksha,** see s.v. **–akshara,** (ibc.) in each syllable, Vās.; *-ślesha-maya,* mf(*ī*)n. containing a Ślesha in each s°, ib. **–agam,** ind. on every mountain, Dharmaśarm. **–agni,** ind. towards the fire, Kauś.; at or near or in every fire, KātyŚr.; MBh. **–agra,** mf(*ā*)n. fresh, recent, new, young, MBh.; R.; Kāv. &c.; repeated, reiterated, Hariv.; Kathās.; pure, W.; (ibc. and *am,* ind.) recently, Mṛicch.; Kathās.; m. N. of a son of Vasu Upari-cara and prince of the Cedis, BhP. (cf. *-agraha* below); *-ksharat,* mfn. fresh-flowing, flowing freshly, Prab.; *-gandhā,* f. a species of shrub, Rhinacanthus Communis, L.; *-tā,* f. or *-tva,* n. newness, freshness, W.; *-prasavā,* f. recently delivered, having lately brought forth, Pāṇ. ii, 1, 65, Sch.; *-yauvana,* mf(*ā*)n. being in the bloom of youth, Kathās.; *-rūpa,* mf(*ā*)n. juvenile, young, MBh.; *-vayas,* mfn. young in age, youthful, MBh.; R.; n. youth, W.; *-śodhita,* mfn. recently purified, pure, L. **–agraha,** m. N. of a son of Vasu and king of the Cedis, MBh.; Hariv.; (= *-agra;* prob. a contracted form for *pratyaggraha*). **–aṅka,** mf(*ā*)n. recently marked (as cattle), Pāṇ. ii, 1, 14, Kāś. **–aṅkam,** ind. in every act (of a drama), Sāh. **–aṅga,** n. a minor or secondary member of the body (as the forehead, nose, chin, fingers, ears &c.; the 6 Aṅgas or chief members being the trunk, head, arms and legs), MBh.; R.; Suśr. &c.; a division, section, part, Suśr.; Nir.; a subdivision (of a science &c.), W.; a weapon, BhP.; m. a kind of measure, Saṃgīt.; N. of a prince, MBh.; (ibc. or *am,* ind.) on every part or member of the body, on the limbs severally, Pañcat.; Hit.; Gīt.; Kathās.; for one's own person, Pat. (cf. *-vartin*); for every part or subdivision (of a sacrifice &c.), Mn.; (in gram.) in each base, Pāṇ. i, 1, 29, Pat.; *-tva,* n. the belonging to, TPrāt.; *-dakshiṇā,* f. a fee for each part (of a sacrifice),

Mn.; *-vartin,* mfn. occupying one's self with one's own person, Pat. **—aṅgiras,** m. N. of a mythical personage (who like Aṅgiras married several of the daughters of Daksha), R. **—aṅgirasa,** m. N. of a mythical personage regarded as the father of certain Ṛicas, Hariv.; VP. **—aṅgirā,** f. Acacia Sirissa, Rasar.; a form of Durgā, one of the goddesses of the Tāntrikas, Cat.; *-kalpa,* m., *-tattva,* n., *-pañcâṅga,* n., *-prayoga,* m., *-mantra,* m., *-mantra-ṛik-samudāya,* m., *-sahasra-nāman* and °*ma-stotra,* n., *-siddha-mantrôddhāra,* m., *-sûkta,* n., *-stotra,* n., *-stotrôpâsanâdi,* m. or n. N. of wks. **—ajira,** n., g. *aṅsv-ādi,* Pāṇ. vi, 2, 193. **—añc,** see p. 674. **—adhikaraṇam,** ind. at each paragraph, Nyāyam. **—adhidevatā,** f. a tutelary deity who stays in front or near one, Hcat. **—anantara,** mfn. being in the immediate neighbourhood of (gen.), R.; standing nearest (as an heir), Mn. viii, 185; closely connected with, immediately following, MBh.; R.; (*am*), ind. immediately after (abl.), MBh.; next in succession, W.; °*rī-√bhū,* to betake one's self close to (gen.), Prasannar. **—anilam,** ind. against the wind, MW. **—anīka,** mfn. hostile, opposed, injuring (with gen.); withstanding, resisting, MBh.; BhP.; Sarvad.; opposite, Suśr.; Sarvad.; equal, vying with, Kāvyâd.; m. an adversary, enemy, BhP.; n. a hostile army, MBh.; Hariv.; hostility, enmity, a hostile relation, h° position, rivalry (sg. and pl.), MBh.; R.; injuring the relatives of an enemy who cannot be injured himself, Pratāp.; Kpr.; Kuval.; injuring one who cannot retaliate (?), W.; *-tva,* n. =*-bhāva,* Suśr.; the state of an enemy, hostility, MW.; *-bhāva,* m. being the contrary, Nyāyad. **—anuprâsa,** m. a kind of alliteration, Śiś., Comm. **—anumāna,** n. a contrary deduction, opposite conclusion, KapS. **—anuyoga,** m. a counter-question, qu° in return, Car. **—anûkântam,** ind. at the end of each back part of the altar, KātyŚr., Comm. **—anta,** mfn. bordering on, adjacent or contiguous to, skirting, W.; m. a border, frontier, Ragh.; Lalit.; a bordering country i.e. a c° occupied by barbarians, L.; (pl.) barbarous tribes, Var.; *-janapada,* n. a bordering country; °*dôpapatti,* f. birth in a bord° or barbarous c° (with Buddhists one of the eight inauspicious ways of being born), Dharmas. 134; *-deśa,* m. a country bordering upon another, Śāṅkh., Sch.; *-parvata,* m. an adjacent (small) hill, L.; *-vāsa,* n. (!) a frontier-place, Lalit. **—antarī-√bhū** = *-anantarī-√bhū,* Uttarar. **—antāt,** ind. in each case to the end, Lāṭy. **—antika,** mfn. being or situated at the border, Kāraṇḍ. **—antima,** mfn. = *-antika,* Divyâv. **—andhakāra,** mfn. spreading shadow, Buddh. **—apara,** mfn. = *-avara,* q.v., Vajras. **—apāya,** m. perishing again, Śīl. **—abdam,** ind. every year, yearly, Kathās. **—abhyāsam,** ind. at each repetition, ĀpŚr., Comm. **—amitra,** mfn. opposed as an enemy, hostile; m. an enemy, opponent, adversary, MBh. **—ayanam,** ind. every half year, Yājñ. **—ayanastvá,** n. obtaining again, recovery, TBr. **—ara,** m. (ŚvetUp., Comm.) or **—arā,** f. (Śvet Up.) an intermediate spoke of a wheel. **—araṇya** (ibc.), near or in a forest, Buddh. **—ari,** m. a well-matched opponent, equally powerful enemy, MBh. **—arka,** m. a mock sun, parhelion, Var. **—argala,** n. the rope by which a churning-stick is moved, Gal. **—arṇam,** ind. at each syllable, Sarvad. **—artham,** ind. in relation to anything, Jaim.; at every object, in every case, Pāṇ. ii, 1, 6, Sch.; w.r. for *aty-a°,* MBh. **—ardha,** g. *aṅsv-ādi,* Kāś. **—ardhi** (*práty-*), mfn. (prob.) possessing or claiming half of, having equal claims, equal to (gen.), RV. **—arham,** ind. in *yathā-p°,* q.v. **—ava-bhāsha** or °**shā,** w.r. for *-bhāsa,* q.v., Uttarar. **—ava-marsha,** °**sha-vat,** w.r. for *ava-marśa,* °*śa-vat,* q.v. **—avayava** (ibc.) or °**vam** (ind.), on or at every part of the body, Naish., Comm.; in e° p° or particular, in detail, Bādar., Sch.; *-varṇanā,* f. a detailed or minute description, Vikr. **—avara,** mfn. lower, more insignificant, less honoured than, (abl.), Mn.; MBh.; R. &c.; *-kālam,* ind. after, later than (with abl. or ifc.), Car. **—aśman,** m. red chalk, L. **—ashṭhīlā,** f. a kind of nervous disease, Suśr.; Bhpr. **—asta-gamana,** n. the setting (of the sun), ChUp., Sch. **—astam,** ind. (with √*gam*) to go down, cease, Sarvad.; *-aya,* m. the setting (of the sun); cessation, disappearance, end, destruction, Bādar., Sch. **—astra,** n. missile hurled in return, BhP.; Kathās. **—aha,** mfn. daily, Rājat.; (*am*), ind. day by d°, every d°, KātyŚr.; Mn.; Kāv. &c.; in the morning, W. **—ākāra,** m. a scabbard, sword-sheath, L. **—āgāra** (?), m. former place or state, W. **—ācāra,** m. suitable behaviour, conformable conduct, MBh. **—ātapá,** m. a sunny place, ŚBr.; KātyŚr. **—ātma** (ibc.), or °**mam,** ind. for every soul, in ev° s°, Sarvad.; singly, Pat.; °*ma-viniyata,* mfn. individual, Car. **—ātmaka,** mfn. belonging to one's self, SaddhP. **—ātmika,** mfn. = *-ātmaka,* ŚāṅkhGṛ.; peculiar, original, Car. **—ātmya,** n. similarity with or resemblance to one's self; (*ena*), ind. after one's own image, BhP. **—ādarśa,** m., w.r. for *-ādeśa,* q.v., Pañcat. **—āditya,** m. a mock sun, parhelion, AVPariś.; MBh.; (ibc.) towards the sun (e.g. *p°-guda,* one whose hinder parts are t° the s°, Suśr.) **—ānīka,** m. (with *rājan*) a partic. personification, ŚāṅkhGṛ. **—āpīḍa,** m. a kind of metre, Col. **—āmnāyam,** ind. for every single text-book, ĀśvŚr., Comm. **—ārdra,** mfn. fresh; *-tara,* mfn., Buddh. **—ārdrā,** f., g. *aṅsv-ādi* to Pāṇ. vi, 2, 193. **—ārdrī-√kṛi,** to moisten again, refresh ag°, Kād.; to wipe out, efface, Kir. **—ārdhapura,** g. *aṅsv-ādi* (Kāś. *praty-ardha, prati-pura*). **—ālayam,** ind. in every house, Dharmaśarm. **—āvāsakam,** ind. to every station, to e° tent, Kād. **—āvāsam,** ind. in every house, Vcar. **—āśam,** ind. in all directions, Veṇīs. **—āśā,** f. confidence, trust, hope, expectation, Prab.; Kathās. &c. (°*śa-tva,* n. ifc., Mālatīm.) **—āśin,** mfn. hoping, expecting, W.; trusting, relying upon, MW. **—āha,** mfn., w.r. for *-aha,* q.v., Rājat. **—āhuti,** ind. at each oblation, ĀpŚr.; Kauś. **—uta,** see p. 677. **—uttara,** n. a reply to an answer, rejoinder, answer, Pañcat.; Hit.; Prab. &c.; °*rī-karaṇa,* n. replying, an answer, Mcar.; °*rī-√kṛi,* to answer, Kād. **—udadhi,** ind. at the sea, Bālar. **—upamāna,** n. a counter comparison, the ideal of an ideal, Vikr. **—upasadam,** ind. at each celebration of an Upasad, KātyŚr. **—upâsanam,** ind. for every kind of worship, Bādar., Sch. **—urasa,** n. = *pratigatam uraḥ,* Vop.; (*am*), ind. against the breast, upon the b°, Śiś.; Kir. (cf. Pāṇ. v, 4, 82). **—ulūka,** m. a bird resembling an owl; (according to the Sch.) a hostile owl or a crow regarded as an owl's enemy, BhP. **—ulūkaka,** m. a bird resembling an owl, Hariv. **—ushṭra,** m., g. *aṅsv-ādi* to Pāṇ. vi, 2, 193. **—ūrdhvam,** ind. on the upper side of (acc.), above, Suśr. **—ṛicam,** ind. at or in each verse, GṛŚrS. **—ṛitu,** ind. in each season, Vait. **—eka,** mfn. each one, e° single o°, every o°, Jaim., Sch.; n. a partic. sin, Buddh.; (ibc. or *am,* ind.) one by one, one at a time, singly, for every single one, ŚāṅkhŚr.; Mn.; Kāv. &c.; *-naraka,* m. a partic. hell, Divyâv.; *-buddha,* m. a Buddha who lives in seclusion and obtains emancipation for himself only (as opp. to those Buddhas who liberate others also), Buddh. (cf. MWB. 134 &c.); (*-kathā,* f., *-catushṭaya,* n. N. of wks.; *-tva,* n. the state of a Pratyeka Buddha, Buddh.); *-bodhi,* f. = *-buddha-tva,* Kāraṇḍ.; *-śas,* ind. one by o°, singly, severally, MBh. **—enas** (*práty-*), m. an officer of justice, punisher of criminals, ŚBr.; a surety, the heir nearest of kin who is responsible for the debts of a deceased person, Kāṭh.; ŚāṅkhŚr.; MaitrS. **—enasya,** n. the nearest heirship to (gen.), Kāṭh.

प्रति 2. *prati,* m. N. of a son of Kuśa, BhP.

प्रतिक *pratika,* mf(ī)n. (fr. 1. *prati*) worth a Kārshāpaṇa or 16 Paṇas of cowries, Pāṇ. v, 1, 25, Vārtt. 2.

प्रतिकम्प् *prati-√kamp,* Caus. *-kampayati,* to shake, cause to tremble, MBh.

प्रतिकर *prati-kara* &c. See *prati-√1. kṛi.*

प्रतिकर्ष *prati-karsha,* m. (√*kṛish*) aggregation, combination, KātyŚr., Sch.; anticipating that which occurs afterwards, W. °**kṛishṭa,** mfn. ploughed back again, L.; thrust back, KātyŚr.; rejected, despised, L.

प्रतिकाङ्क्ष् *prati-√kāṅksh,* Ā. *-kāṅkshate,* to wish or long for, R. °**kāṅkshitavya,** mfn. to be expected, Vajracch. °**kāṅkshin,** mfn. wishing for, desirous of (gen. or comp.), MBh.; Hariv.

प्रतिकाश *prati-kāśa,* m. = *prati-k°,* L.

प्रतिकुञ्चित *prati-kuñcita,* mfn. (√*kuñc*) bent, curved, W.

प्रतिकूज् *prati-√kūj,* P. *-kūjati,* to coo or warble in return (with acc.), R.

प्रतिकृ *prati-√1. kṛi,* P. Ā. *-karoti, -kurute,* (inf. *pratī-kartum,* BhP.), to do or make an opposition, AitBr.; to return, repay, requite (good or evil [acc.], with gen. dat. or loc. of pers.), MBh.; R. &c.; to counteract, resist (acc. or gen.), ib.; to treat, attend to, cure (a disease), Suśr.; to repair, mend, restore, Mn.; to pay back (a debt), Gaut.: Caus. Ā. *-kārayate,* to cause to be repeated, ŚBr.: Desid. *-cikīrshati,* to wish to take revenge on (acc. or loc.) for (acc.), MBh.; R. °**kara,** mf(*ī*)n. acting against, counteracting (ifc.), Suśr.; m. requital, compensation, R.; Rājat. °**karaṇīya,** mfn. to be counteracted or prevented, remediable, MW. °**kartavya,** mfn. to be requited or returned, to be repaid (lit. and fig.), MBh.; Hariv.; Ṣaṃk.; to be counteracted or resisted, R.; Prab.; to be treated or cured, Suśr. °**kartṛi,** m. a requiter, recompenser, MBh.; an opponent, adversary, Kull. °**karman,** n. requital, retaliation, corresponding action, MBh.; R.; counteraction, cure, medical treatment, Car.; decoration, toilet, personal adornment, MBh.; R. &c.; (*a*), ind. in every work, at each performance or celebration, KātyŚr.; MBh. °**kāra,** m. (cf. *pratī-k°*) requital, retaliation, reward, retribution, revenge, R.; Kathās.; Rājat.; opposition, counteraction, prevention, remedy, MBh.; Suśr.; = *sama* and *bhaṭa,* L.; *-karman,* n. opposition, resistance, Rājat.; *-jña,* mfn. knowing what remedy should be applied, MBh.; *-vidhāna,* n. medical treatment, Ragh. °**kārin,** see *a-pratikārin.* °**kārya,** mfn. (cf. *pratī-k°*) to be revenged; n. retribution, MBh. i, 6259 (Nilak., m. 'an enemy'). °**kṛita,** mfn. returned, repaid, requited &c., R.; n. recompense, requital, MBh.; resistance, opposition, Ragh. °**kṛiti,** f. resistance, opposition, prevention, Hariv.; retaliation, return, revenge, W.; an image, likeness, model; counterpart, substitute, MBh.; Kāv. &c. °**kriyā,** f. requital (of good or evil), retaliation, compensation, retribution, MBh.; Kāv. &c.; opposition, counteraction, prevention, remedy, help, ib. (ifc. = removing, destroying); *-tva,* n., MBh.; venting (of anger), Kathās.; embellishment, decoration (of the person), MBh.; *-śūlinī-stotra,* n. N. of a Stotra.

Prati-cikīrsh, mfn. (fr. Desid.; nom. °*cikīr* before *b*) wishing to requite (loc.), HPariś. °**cikīrshā,** f. wish to requite, desire to be revenged upon (acc. or loc.), MBh.; BhP. °**cikīrshu,** mfn. wishing to return or requite, MBh. (v.l. *-jihīrshu*).

प्रतिकॄ *prati-√kṝi,* P. *-kirati,* to scatter towards (cf. *prati-s-√kṝi* and Pāṇ. vi, 1, 141). °**kīrṇa,** mfn. scattered towards, MW.

प्रतिकॢप् *prati-√kḷip,* Ā. *-kalpate* (pf. *-cāklṛipe*), to be at the service of (acc.), receive hospitably, ŚBr.; to regulate, arrange, AV. °**kalpya,** mfn. to be arranged or prepared, MBh. (for *prati-kalpa,* see p. 661, col. 3).

प्रतिकोप *prati-kopa* (√*kup*), m. anger against (any one), wrath, MBh.

प्रतिक्रम् *prati-√kram,* P. *-krāmati* (pf. *-cakrāma* and *-cakrame*), to come back, return, ŚBr.; ChUp.; MBh.; to descend, decrease (in number, opp. to *abhi-√kram*), Nid.; to confess, Śatr. °**krama,** m. reversed or inverted order, Pratāp. °**krámaṇa,** n. stepping to and fro, ŚBr.; going to confession, Kalpas.; *-vidhi,* m., *-sūtra,* n. N. of wks.

प्रतिक्रुध् *prati-√krudh,* P. *-krudhyati,* to be angry with (acc.) in return, Mn.; MBh. °**krodha,** m. anger in return, Kull.

प्रतिक्रुष्ट *prati-krushṭa,* mfn. (√*kruś*) miserable, poor, Divyâv. °**krośá,** m. crying out to, halloing, AV.

प्रतिक्षि *prati-√2. kshi* (only pr. p. *-kshiyát,* RV., *-kshyát,* TS.), to settle near (acc.)

प्रतिक्षिप् *prati-√kship,* P. *-kshipati* (cf. Pāṇ. i, 3, 80), to throw into (loc.), MBh. (v.l. *pari-*); to push against, hurt, Suśr.; to reject, despise, oppose, contradict, ridicule, confute, Kathās.; Sarvad.; Lalit. °**kshipta,** mfn. thrown into &c. (cf. prec.; *-tva,* n., Sarvad.); sent, dispatched, L.; n. medicine, L. °**kshepa,** m. contest, MBh. (v.l. *vyati-*); objection, contradiction, repudiation, ib.;

Sarvad. °kshepaṇa, n. contradiction, opposing, contesting, Prab.

प्रतिक्षुत prati-kshuta, n. (√kshu) sneezing, wheezing, W.

प्रतिख्या prati-√khyā, P. -khyāti (impf. -akhyat), to see, behold, RV.; AV.; Br. °khyāti, f. renown (v. l. for pra-vikh°), L.

प्रतिगद् prati-√gad, P. -gadati, to speak in return, answer, MBh.

प्रतिगम् prati-√gam, P. -gacchati, to go towards, go to meet, RV.; MBh. &c.; to go back, return, go home, MBh.; Kāv. &c. °gata, mfn. gone towards or back, MBh.; flying backwards and forwards, wheeling in flight, W.; lost from the memory, R. °gati, f. (L.), °gamana, n. (R.) return.

प्रतिगर्ज् prati-√garj, P. -garjati, to roar against or in return, answer with roars, MBh.; to resist, oppose, Hariv.; Ragh.; to vie with (instr. or gen.), Kāvyâd. °garjana, n. (AVPariś.), °garjanā, f. (MBh.) thundering or roaring against or in return, an answering roar.

प्रतिगा prati-√gā (only aor. -agāt), to go back, return.

प्रतिगाह् prati-√gāh, Ā. -gāhate, to penetrate, enter, R.

प्रतिगु prati-√3. gu (only Intens. -jóguve), to proclaim, RV.

प्रतिगुप्त prati-gupta, mfn. (√gup) guarded, protected, Inscr. °gúpya, mfn. to be guarded; (am), ind. one must guard against (abl.), ŚBr.

प्रतिगृध् prati-√gṛidh, P. -gṛidhyati, to be greedy or eager for (acc.), MBh.

प्रतिगृभाय prati-gṛibhāya, Nom. P. °yati, to take, receive; (esp.) to take into the mouth, eat, RV.

प्रतिगॄ prati-√gṝī, P. Ā. -gṛiṇāti, -gṛiṇīte, to invoke, salute (acc.), RV.; (with dat.; cf. Pāṇ. i, 4, 41, Sch.) to respond in recitation or chanting (also with prati-garam), ib.; TS.; Br.; ŚrS.; to agree with (dat.), Vop. °gará, m. the responsive call of the Adhvaryu to the address of the Hotṛi, TS.; Br.; ĀśvŚr. °garitṛi, m. one who makes a responsive cry or chant, AitBr.; ŚāṅkhŚr. °gīrya, mfn. to be answered in recitation or chanting, AitBr.

प्रतिग्रह् prati-√grah, P. Ā. -gṛihṇāti, -gṛihṇīte (irreg. 2. sg. Impv. -gṛihṇa, R.; aor. -ajagrabhat, AitBr.), to take hold of, grasp, seize (in astrol. = to eclipse, obscure), AV. &c. &c.; to take (as a present or into possession), appropriate, receive, accept, RV. &c. &c. (śirasā, 'with the head' i.e. 'humbly, obediently,' R.); to gain, win over, R.; to take as a wife, marry, Mn.; MBh. &c.; to take = eat, drink, RV.; VS.; TBr.; to receive (a friend or guest), RV. &c. &c.; to receive (anything agreeable as a good word or omen), R.; Kālid.; to assent to, acquiesce in, approve, MBh.; R.; (rarely) to receive (an enemy), oppose, encounter, MBh.; Ragh.: Caus. -grāhayati, to cause to accept, present with (2 acc.), MBh.; R.; Kālid.; to answer, reply, BhP.: Desid. -jighṛikshati, to wish to accept, Gaut. °gṛihīta, mfn. taken, received, accepted, married, MBh.; Kāv. &c. °gṛihītavya, °gṛihītṛi, w. r. for °grahītavya, °grahītṛi. °gṛihya, mfn. to be accepted, acceptable, TS. ('from,' gen., Pāṇ. iii, 1, 118, Vārtt. 1, Pat.); one from whom anything may be accepted (see a-pratigṛihyá). °grahá, m. receiving, accepting, acceptance of gifts (as the peculiar prerogative of Brāhmans; cf. IW. 237; 262), ŚBr.; ŚrS.; Mn.; MBh. &c. (°grahaṃ √kṛi, to receive presents, Mn.); friendly reception, MBh.; favour, grace, MBh.; taking a wife, marrying, R.; receiving with the ear i. e. hearing, Kathās.; a grasper, seizer (keśa-, a hair-cutter, barber), Gobh.; a receiver, KātyŚr.; R.; a chamber-vessel or any similar convenience for sick persons, Car.; a spittoon, L.; a gift, present (esp. a donation to a Brāhman at suitable periods), Yājñ.; MBh. &c. (instr. 'as a present,' Kathās.); N. of the objects or functions corresponding to the 8 Grahas, L.; = kriyā-kāra, L.; the reserve of an army (a detachment posted with the general 400 yards in the rear of a line), W.; the sun near the moon's node, ib.; -kalpa, m. N. of Pariś. of MānGṛS.; -dhana, n. money received as a present, Kathās.; mfn. one whose wealth consists only in presents, Pañcat.; -prâpta, mfn. received as a present, Kathās.; -prāyaścitta-prakāra, m. N. of wk. °grahaṇa, mfn. accepting, ŚāṅkhGṛ. (perhaps w. r.); n. receipt, acceptance, ib.; Lāṭy.; taking a wife, marrying, R. (cf. á-pratig°); a vessel, ŚāṅkhGṛ. °grahaṇīya, mfn. to be taken or accepted, acceptable, W. °grahin, mfn. one who receives, a receiver (opp. to dātṛi), MBh. °grahītavya, mfn. to be received, Kull. °grahītṛi, mfn. id., AV. &c. &c.; m. one who takes a wife, one who marries (nom. °tā, also as 3. sg. fut.), MBh.; R. °grāha, m. a spittoon, L.; accepting gifts, W. °grāhaka, mfn. one who receives or accepts (see á-pratig°). °grāhín, mfn. id., TS. °grāhya, mfn. to be taken or accepted, acceptable, MBh.; R. (cf. a-pratig°); one from whom anything may be received, MBh. (cf. °gṛihya and Pāṇ. ib.); m. N. of partic. Grahas, TBr., Sch.

प्रतिघ prati-gha, m. (√han) hindrance, obstruction, resistance, opposition (cf. a-p°); struggling against (comp.), Car.; anger, wrath, enmity, Mcar.; Lalit. (one of the 6 evil passions, Dharmas. 67); = mūrchā, L.; combat, fighting, W.; an enemy, ib.; opposition, contradiction, L. °ghāta, m. (cf. pratī-gh°) warding off, keeping back, repulse, prevention, resistance, opposition, MBh.; Kāv. &c.; rebound, Kum.; -kṛit, mfn. depriving any one (gen.) of (gen.), Yājñ.; -vid, mfn. knowing how to resist, apt to resist, MBh. °ghātaka, mf(ikā)n. disturbing, MBh.; (ifc.) = °ghāta, ib. °ghātana, n. warding off, repulsing, ib.; killing, slaughter, L. °ghātaya (Caus. of prati-√han), °yati, to ward off, MBh. °ghātin, mfn. keeping off, repulsing, disturbing, injuring, Daś.; Kām.; dazzling (netra-), Kum. °ghna, n. the body, L.

प्रतिघोषिन् prati-ghoshin, mfn. (√ghush) roaring or crying out against; (iṇī), f. N. of a class of demons, ŚāṅkhŚr.

प्रतिङ्गिरा pratiṅgirā, f. N. of a Buddh. deity, W.

प्रतिचक्ष् prati-√caksh, Ā. -cashṭe, to see, perceive, RV.; BhP.; to expect, BhP.; to cause to see, let appear, show, RV. °caksha, see su-praticakshá. °cákshaṇa, n. looking at, viewing, RV.; BhP. (showing, displaying, Sch.); appearance, look, aspect, AV. °cakshin, mfn. regarding, observing, AVPaipp. °cákshya, mf(ā)n. visible, conspicuous, RV.

प्रतिचर् prati-√car, P. -carati, to advance towards, approach, RV.; TS.: Caus. -cārayati, see below. °cāra, m. personal adornment, toilet, Śil. °cārita, mfn. (fr. Caus.) circulated, proclaimed, published, MBh. °cārin, mfn. exercising, practising, L.

प्रतिचिकीर्ष् prati-cikīrsh. See prati-√1. kṛi.

प्रतिचिन्त् prati-√cint, P. Ā. -cintayati, °te, to consider again, reflect upon, remember, R.; Caur. °cintana, n. thinking repeatedly, considering, W. °cintanīya, mfn. to be thought over again, Kāv.

प्रतिचुद् prati-√cud, Caus. -codayati, to drive or urge on, impel, R. °codanam, see p. 662, col. 1. °codanā, f. prevention, prohibition, BhP. (= nishedha, opp. to vidhi, or = smṛiti, opp. to śruti, Sch.) °codita, mfn. impelled or excited against (acc.), R.

प्रतिच्छद् prati-cchad (√chad), P. -cchādayati, to cover, envelop, hide, conceal, Kauś.; MBh. &c. °cchadana, n. a cover, covering, L. °cchanna, mfn. covered, enveloped, hidden, concealed, disguised, MBh.; Kāv. &c.; endowed or furnished with (ifc.), MBh. iii, 1268.

प्रतिच्छिद् prati-cchid (√chid), P. -cchinatti, to cut or tear off, ŚāṅkhŚr. (v. l. pra-cch°); to retaliate by cutting to pieces, MBh. °ccheda, m. cutting off; resistance, opposition, W.

प्रतिच्यवीयस् práti-cyavīyas, mfn. (√cyu) pressing closer against or towards, RV. x, 86, 6.

प्रतिजग्ध práti-jagdha, mfn. (√2. jaksh) eaten, consumed, MaitrS.

प्रतिजन् prati-√jan, Ā. -jāyate, to be born or produced again, PraśnUp. °janman, n. re-birth, Kathās. °jāta, mfn. born again, renewed; -kopa, mfn. once more angry, MBh.

प्रतिजप् prati-√jap, P. -japati, to mutter in response, Gobh. °jāpa, m. the act of muttering against, Kauś.

प्रतिजल्प् prati-√jalp, P. -jalpati, to answer, reply, MBh.; R. °jalpa, m. an answer, reply, L. °jalpaka, m. a polite but evasive answer, L.

प्रतिजागृ prati-√jāgṛi, P. -jāgarti, to watch beside (acc.), RV.; VS.; AV.; to keep (?), Divyâv. °jāgara, m. watchfulness, attention, L. °jāgaraṇa, n. watching, guarding, attending to, MārkP. °jāgaraṇaka, m. or n. (?) a district, Inscr. °jāgṛivi, mfn. watchful, attentive, Cat.

प्रतिजि prati-√ji, P. -jayati, to conquer, defeat (in battle or at play), TS.; MBh.: Desid. -jigīshati, to wish to conquer or defeat, attack, assail, MBh.

प्रतिजिहीर्षु prati-jihīrshu, mfn. (√hṛi Desid.) wishing to return or requite, MBh. (v. l. °cikīrshu; cf. p. 664, col. 3).

प्रतिजीवन prati-jīvana, n. (√jīv) returning to life, resuscitation, R. °jīvita, n. id., Bālar.

प्रतिजुष् prati-√jush, Ā. -jushate, to be kind or tender towards (acc.), honour, serve, RV.; to be gratified by, delight in (acc.), ib.

प्रतिजॄ prati-√2. jṛī, Ā. -jarate (inf. -jarádhyai), to roar (as fire) in the direction of, to call out to, salute (acc.), RV.

प्रतिज्ञा prati-√jñā, P. Ā. -jānāti, -jānīte, to admit, own, acknowledge, acquiesce in, consent to, approve, RV.; AV.; MBh.; to promise (with gen., dat. or loc. of pers., and acc. with or without prati or dat. of thing, also with inf., MBh.; Kāv. &c.; with vākyam and gen. 'to promise fulfilment of a person's word,' MBh.; with satyam 'to promise verily or truly,' ib.); (Ā.) to confirm, assert, answer in the affirmative, ŚBr.; ĀśvGṛ.; MBh. &c.; to maintain, assert, allege, state, MBh.; R. &c. (śabdaṃ nityatvena, 'to assert the eternity of sound,' Pāṇ. i, 3, 22, Sch.); (Ā.) to bring forward or introduce (a topic), Nyāyam., Sch.; to perceive, notice, learn, become aware of, MBh.; Hariv.; to remember sorrowfully (only in this sense P. by Pāṇ. i, 3, 46; but really Ā., MBh. xii, 8438). °jña, mfn. acknowledging (ifc.), Vajracch.; (ā), f., see below.

Pratijñā, f. admission, acknowledgment, assent, agreement, promise, vow, MBh.; Kāv. &c.; a statement, assertion, declaration, affirmation, ib.; (in logic) a proposition, the assertion or proposition to be proved, the first member or avayaya of the five-membered Nyāya syllogism, IW. 61; (in law) a plaint, complaint, indictment, prosecution, Yājñ. — kara, m. N. of Sch. on Nalôd. (usually called Prajñā-k°). — ntara (°jñânt°), n. (in logic) a subsequent proposition on failure of the first, Nyāyas. — pattra or °traka, n. a promissory note, a written contract, bond, W. — paripālana, n. adherence to a promise, keeping one's word, VP. — pariśishṭa, n. N. of Pariś. of the white Yajur-veda. — pāraga, mfn. one who keeps his word, R. — pāraṇa, n. fulfilment of a vow, MBh. — pālana, n. = -paripālana, MBh. — pūrvakam, ind. so as to begin with the plaint, Yājñ., Sch. — bhaṅga, m. breach of a promise; -bhīru, mfn. apprehensive of breaking a promise, MW. — lakshaṇa, n. (prob.) 'the characteristic of a proposition;' -kroḍa, m., -ṭīkā, f., -dīdhiti-ṭīkā, f., -rahasya, n., -vivecana, n., °ṇânugama, m., °ṇâloka, m. N. of wks. — vāda and -vādârtha, m. N. of wks. — virodha, m. contradiction between a logical proposition and the argument, Nyāyas.; acting contrary to a promise or agreement, W. — vivāhita, mfn. promised in marriage, betrothed, ib. — saṃnyāsa, m. abandonment of one's own proposition (after hearing the argument of the opponent), Nyāyas.; breaking a promise, W. — sūtra, n. N. of Pariś. on the white Yajur-veda. — hāni, f. giving up a proposition or argument, Nyāyas.

Prati-jñāta (práti-), mfn. admitted, acknowledged, KātyŚr.; Mn.; promised, agreed, MBh.; Kāv. &c.; declared, stated, asserted, proposed, alleged, ib.; agreeable, desirable, ŚBr.; °târtha, m. a statement, averment, Yājñ. °jñātavya, mfn. to be promised or assented to, W. °**jñāti,** (prob.) w. r. for *prati-prajñāti.* °**jñāna,** n. admission, assertion, assent, agreement, promise, APrāt.; Yājñ., Sch.; bringing forward or introducing (a topic), Kull.; *-vākya,* n. N. of Pariś. of the white Yajur-veda. °**jñāpita,** mfn. betrayed, Śak. i, $\frac{2}{3}\frac{3}{4}$ (v.l.; cf. *pra-jñāpita*). °**jñeya,** mfn. to be promised or assented to, W.; m. a panegyrist, herald, bard, L.

प्रतिज्वल् *prati-√jval,* P. *-jvalati,* to flame, blaze, shine, MBh.

प्रतितड् *prati-√taḍ,* P. *-tāḍayati,* to strike in return, MBh. °**tāḍitavya,** n. (impers.) a blow must be returned, L.

प्रतितप् *prati-√tap,* P. *-tapati,* to throw out or emit heat towards or against (acc.), AV.; TāṇḍBr.; to heat, warm, foment, GṛŚrS.

प्रतितर *prati-tara,* m. (√*tṛī*) a sailor, oarsman, ferryman, Suśr.

प्रतितर्कित *prati-tarkita,* mfn. (√*tark*) expected, comprehensible (*a-pr°*), R. (B.)

प्रतितर्ज् *prati-√tarj* (only ind. p. *-tarjya*), to menace, threaten, terrify, Kir. xiv, 26.

प्रतितिज् *prati-√tij,* to emit heat or fire against or towards, MaitrS. (only Impv. *práti-tigdhi* and *-titigdhi,* for which Kāṭh. *prati-tityagdhi* [!], and ĀpŚr. *prati-tindhi* [!]).

प्रतिथि *pra-tithi,* m. N. of a Ṛishi and teacher (with the epithet Deva-taratha), VBr.; Bālar.

प्रतिदह् *prati-√dah,* P. *-dahati* (fut. *-dhakshyati*), to burn towards, encounter with flames, consume, RV.; AV.; ŚBr.; ChUp.: Pass. *-dahyate* (°*ti*), to be burnt or consumed by fire, MBh.

प्रतिदा *prati-√1. dā,* P. Ā. *-dadāti, -datte,* to give back, restore, return, AV. &c. &c.; to give, offer, present, MBh.; R.: Caus. *-dāpayati,* to cause to be given back or restored, Yājñ. °**dātavya,** mfn. to be given back or restored, Yājñ. °**dāna,** n. restitution (of a desposit), restoration, L.; giving or a gift in return, Daś.; Pāṇ. i, 4, 92; exchange, barter, L. (v. l. for *pari-d°*). °**dāpya,** mfn. to be caused to be restored, Āpast. °**deya,** mfn. to be given back or returned, Yājñ.; MBh.; n. a pledge, pawn; an article purchased and given back, W.

Prati-tta. See *á-pr°*.

प्रतिदारण *prati-dāraṇa,* n. (√*dṛī*) battle, fighting, fierce conflict, L.

प्रतिदिव् *prati-√2. div,* P. *-dīvyati,* to throw or cast against, Pāṇ. ii, 3, 59, Sch.; to play at dice with (acc.), to stake anything (gen. or acc.) at dice against, AV.; MBh. °**divan,** m. the sun, L.; a day, Uṇ. i, 156, Sch. °**dívan,** m. an adversary at play, RV.; AV.; the sun, L.

प्रतिदिश् *prati-√diś,* Caus. *-deśayati,* to point towards, point out, MBh.; to confess, L. °**diśam** and °**deśam,** see p. 662, col. 1. °**deśanīya,** mfn. to be reported or related, L.

प्रतिदीप्त *prati-dīpta,* mfn. (√*dīp*) flaming against, MBh.

प्रतिदुह् *prati-√duh* (P. impf. *-aduhat,* aor. *-adhukshat*), to add by milking, TS.; (P. Pot. *-duhīyat,* Ā. Subj. *-dohate*) to yield (like milk), grant, RV. (cf. Nir. i, 7). °**dúh,** n. (nom. *dhuk*; gen. instr. also *dhushas,* °*shā*) fresh milk, milk still warm, AV.; TS.; MaitrS.; Br.; ŚrS.; °*dhuk-tva,* n., TS.

प्रतिदूषित *prati-dūshita,* mfn. (√*2. dush,* Caus.) defiled, rendered unclean, contaminated, Mn. iv, 65.

प्रतिदृश् *prati-√dṛiś* (ind. p. *-dṛiśya*), to look at, behold, perceive, notice, ŚBr.; Ā. and Pass. *-dṛiśyate,* to become visible, appear, appear as, be, RV. &c. &c.: Caus. *-darśayati,* to cause to see, show, teach, MBh. °**darśa,** m. (cf. *pratī-d°*) looking at, viewing, ŚāṅkhŚr. °**darśana,** n. id., R.; (ifc. f. *ā*) sight, look, appearance, MBh. °**dṛiś,** °**dṛiśam,** see p. 662, col. 1. °**dṛishṭa,** mfn. beheld, visible, conspicuous, famous, celebrated, BhP. (=*pra-khyāta,* Sch.); °*ṭānta,* see p. 662, col. 1.

प्रतिद्रु *prati-√dru* (only aor. *-adudruvat*), to run towards (acc.), Bhaṭṭ.

प्रतिद्रुह् *prati-druh,* m. (√*druh*) one who seeks to injure in return (*a-p°*), BhP.

प्रतिधा *prati-√1. dhā,* P. Ā. *-dadhāti, -dhatte* (Ved. inf. *práti-dhātave*), to put on or in or near or back, return, restore (loc. or dat.), RV.; AV.; Br.; to adjust (an arrow), aim, ib.; to put to the lips (for drinking), RV. iv, 27, 5; to put down (the feet), step out, Br.; to offer, present, AitBr.; to use, employ, Śatr.; to restrain, BhP.; (Ā.) to commence, begin, approach, RV.; AV. °**dhā,** f. putting to the lips, a draught, RV. °**dhāna,** n. (ifc.) putting to or on, Gobh.; adopting precautions, Kull. °**dhí,** m. a cross-piece on the pole of a carriage, RV.; VS.

Práti-hita, mfn. put on or in &c.; (*ā*), f. an arrow fitted to the bow-string, RV.; AV.; °*têshu,* mfn. = °*hitāyin,* Kauś. °**hitāyin,** mfn. one who has adjusted the arrow, ŚBr. °**hiti,** f. adjusting an arrow, Kāṭh.

प्रतिधाव् *prati-√1. dhāv,* P. Ā. *-dhāvati,* °*te,* to run back, AV.; to rush upon (acc.), attack, MBh.; R. °**dhāvana,** n. rushing upon, onset, attack, MBh. (v. l. *-bādhana*).

प्रतिधी *prati-√dhī* (only pf. *-dīdhima*), to expect, hope, RV. °**dhī,** mfn., see p. 662, col. 1.

प्रतिधृ *prati-√dhṛi,* P. Ā. *-dhārayati,* °*te,* to keep back, stop, check, ŚBr.; to keep erect, support, AitBr. °**dhartṛi,** m. one who keeps back or stops, VS.

प्रतिधृष् *prati-√dhṛish* (only pf. *-dadharsha* and Ved. inf. *-dhṛishe*), to be bold against, brave, defy, RV.; Kāṭh. (cf. *a-pratidhṛishṭa* and °*dhṛishya*).

प्रतिध्यात *prati-dhyāta,* mfn. (√*dhyai*) thought upon, meditated, MBh. (v. l. *pra-dhyāta*).

प्रतिध्वनि *prati-dhvani,* m. (√*2. dhvan*) echo, reverberated sound, Hcar. °**dhvāna,** m. (n., L.) id., Hit. °**dhvānita** (Nāg.), °**dhvānin** (Sāh.), mfn. sounding, resounding.

प्रतिध्वस्त *prati-dhvasta,* mfn. (√*dhvaṇs*) sunk, hanging down, MBh.

प्रतिनद् *prati-√nad,* P. *-nadati,* to sound back, answer with a cry or shout, MBh.; R. &c.: Caus. *-nādayati,* to cause to resound, make resonant, fill with cries, ib. °**nāda,** m. echo, reverberation, Kād. °**nādita,** mfn. (fr. Caus.) filled with sounds, resonant, echoing or echoed, Hariv.; R. °**ninada,** m. = °*nāda,* Kir.

प्रतिनन्द् *prati-√nand,* P. *-nandati,* to greet cheerfully, salute (also in return), bid welcome or farewell, address kindly, favour, befriend, AV. &c. &c.; to receive joyfully or thankfully, to accept willingly (with *na,* to decline, refuse, reject), Mn.; MBh. &c.: Caus. *-nandayati,* to gladden, delight, gratify, MBh.; Kām. °**nanda,** m. N. of a poet, Cat. °**nándana,** n. greeting, salutation, friendly acceptance, AV.; thanksgiving, MW. °**nandita,** mfn. saluted or accepted kindly or cheerfully, MBh.; Kāv. &c.

प्रतिनम् *prati-√nam* (only pf. *-nānāma*), to bow or incline towards (acc.), RV.

प्रतिनर्द् *prati-√nard,* P. Ā. *-nardati,* °*te,* to roar or cry against or after (food), greet or hail with cries, MBh.; Hariv.

प्रतिनाह *prati-nāha* (√*nah*), see *karṇa-pr°* and cf. *pratī-nāha* under 1. *pratī,* p. 673.

प्रतिनिःसृज् *prati-niḥ-√sṛij,* P. *-sṛijati,* to drive towards, give up to (dat.), ŚBr. °**niḥsarga,** m. giving back, abandonment, Lalit. (w. r. *niḥ-saṅga*). °**niḥsṛijya,** mfn. to be given up or abandoned, L. °**niḥsṛishṭa,** mfn. driven away, Divyâv.

प्रतिनिक्षिप् *prati-ni-√kship,* P. *-kshipati,* to put down or deposit again, MBh.

प्रतिनिगद् *prati-ni-√gad,* P. *-gadati,* to speak to, address, KātyŚr.; to recite or repeat singly, TBr., Sch.

प्रतिनिग्रह् *prati-ni-√grah,* Ā. *-gṛihṇīte,* to take up (liquids), ladle out, ŚBr. °**nigrāhya,** mfn. to be ladled out, ĀpŚr. (cf. °*nirgr°*).

प्रतिनिधा *prati-ni-√dhā,* P. *-dadhāti,* to put in the place of another, substitute, ŚrS.; Śaṃk.; to order, command, MBh.; to slight, disregard, MW. °**nidhātavya,** mfn. to be substituted, Nyāyam., Sch. °**nidhāpayitavya,** mfn. to be caused to be substituted, ib. °**nidhi,** m. substitution; a substitute, representative, proxy, surety, ŚrS.; Mn.; MBh. &c.; a resemblance of a real form, an image, likeness, statue, picture, Kāv.; (ifc.) an image of i. e. similar, like, Kāvyâd. (°*dhī-√kṛi,* to substitute anything [acc.] for [comp.], MBh.; Ragh.) °**nidheya,** mfn. to be substituted, Nyāyam.

प्रतिनिन्द् *prati-√nind,* P. *-nindati,* to abuse, blame, censure, MBh.

प्रतिनिपात *prati-ni-pāta,* m. (√*pat*) falling down, alighting, MBh.

प्रतिनियत *prati-ni-yata,* mfn. (√*yam*) fixed or adopted for each single case, particular or different for each case, Kap.; Saṃk. °**niyama,** m. a strict rule as to applying an example to particular persons or things only, Kap.

प्रतिनिरस् *prati-nir-√2. as,* P. *-asyati,* to throw back, ĀpŚr.

प्रतिनिर्ग्राह्य *prati-nir-grāhya,* mfn. (√*grah*) to be taken up with a ladle, ĀpŚr. (cf. *prati-nigr°*).

प्रतिनिर्जित *prati-nir-jita,* mfn. (√*ji*) appropriated, turned to one's own advantage, MBh.

प्रतिनिर्दिश् *prati-nir-√diś* (only Pass. *-diśyate*), to point or refer back, Kāś. on Pāṇ. i, 2, 53. °**nirdishṭa,** mfn. referred to again, KātyŚr., Sch. °**nirdeśa,** m. a reference back to (with gen.), renewed mention, Śaṃk. °**nirdeśaka,** mfn. pointing or referring back (ifc.), KātyŚr., Sch. °**nirdeśya,** mfn. referred to or mentioned again, Sāh.

प्रतिनिर्यत् *prati-nir-√yat,* Caus. *-yātayati,* to give back, return, MBh. °**niryātana,** n. giving back, returning, Pāṇ. ii, 3, 11, Sch.; rewarding, retaliation, L.

प्रतिनिर्या *prati-nir-√yā,* P. *-yāti,* to come forth again, MBh.; MārkP.

प्रतिनिर्वप् *prati-nir-√2. vap,* P. *-vapati,* to distribute in return, TS.; TBr.; Kauś.

प्रतिनिवारण *prati-ni-vāraṇa,* n. (√*1. vṛi*) keeping off, warding off, BhP.

प्रतिनिवासन *prati-ni-vāsana,* n. (√*4. vas*) a kind of garment, Buddh.

प्रतिनिविष्ट *prati-ni-vishṭa,* mfn. (√*viś*) quite prepossessed with (loc.), R.; obstinate, obdurate; *-mūrkha,* m. an obstinate fool, Bhartṛ. °**niveśa,** m. obstinacy, obdurateness, Baudh.

प्रतिनिवृत् *prati-ni-√vṛit,* Ā. *-vartate* (P. 2. pl. fut. *-vartsyatha,* MBh.), to turn back or round, return, MBh.; Kāv. &c.; to turn away from (abl.), escape, run away, take flight, MBh.; to cease, be allayed or abated, BhP.: Caus. *-vartayati,* to cause to go back, turn back, avert, R.; BhP. °**nivartana,** n. returning, coming back (see *punaḥ-pr°*). °**nivartita,** mfn. (fr. Caus.) caused to return, led back, R. °**nivṛitta,** mfn. turned back or from (abl.), come back, return, MBh.; Kāv. &c. °**nivṛitti,** f. coming back, return, ĀpŚr., Sch.

प्रतिनिष्क्रय *prati-nish-kraya,* m. (√*krī*) retaliation, retribution, L.

प्रतिनिष्पू *prati-nish-√pū,* P. *-punāti,* to cleanse or winnow again, purify, KātyŚr.; Kauś.; Suśr. °**pūta,** mfn. cleansed, winnowed, Suśr.

प्रतिनिस्तॄ *prati-nis-√tṛī,* P. *-tarati,* to accomplish, Divyâv.

प्रतिनिहन् *prati-ni-√han* (only 2. pers. pf. *-jaghántha*), to aim a blow at (acc.), RV. i, 52, 15. °**nihata,** mfn. hit, slain, killed, MBh.

प्रतिनी *prati-√nī,* P. *-nayati,* to lead towards or back, AV. &c. &c.; to put into, mix, Kauś. °**nāyaka,** see p. 662, col. 1.

प्रतिनु *prati-√nu,* P. *-nauti,* to commend, approve, Pat.

प्रतिनुद् *prati-√nud,* P. Ā. *-nudati,* °*te,* to thrust back, repulse, ward off, RV.; VS.; Br. °**noda,** m. thrusting back, repulse, TāṇḍBr. (cf. *á-pr°*).

प्रतिनृत् *prati-√nṛit,* P. *-nṛityati,* to dance before (in token of contempt), mock in turn by dancing before (acc.), MBh.: Intens. *-narnṛitīti*, to dance before (in token of love), delight or gladden by dancing before (acc.), Pat.

प्रतिन्यस् *prati-ny-√2. as* (only ind. p. *-nyasya*), to place apart or lay down separately (for different persons), deposit, R. (v.l. *pra-vi-n°*). °**nyāsa,** see p. 662, col. 1.

प्रतिन्यागम् *prati-ny-ā-√gam*, P. *-gacchati*, to come back, return, Kāṭh.

प्रतिप *pratipa*, m. N. of a prince, L. (prob. w.r. for *pratīpa*, q. v.)

प्रतिपण 2. *prati-paṇá*, m. (√*paṇ*) barter, exchange, AV. (for 1. see p. 662, col. 1).

प्रतिपत् *prati-√pat*, P. *-patati*, to hasten towards, run to meet (acc.), MBh.

प्रतिपद् *prati-√pad*, Ā. *-padyate* (ep. fut. also *-patsyati*), to set foot upon, enter, go or resort to, arrive at, reach, attain, VS. &c. &c.; to walk, wander, roam, ChUp.; to come back to (acc.), return, MBh.; to happen, occur, take place, PārGṛ.; MBh.; to get into (acc.), meet with, find, obtain, receive, take in or upon one's self, ŚBr. &c. &c.; to receive back, recover, AitBr.; Śak.; to restore to favour, Ragh.; to undertake, begin (acc., dat. or inf.), practise, perform, accomplish, Nir.; MBh.; Kāv. &c.; to do anything to any person, act or proceed or behave towards or against (loc., gen. or acc.), MBh.; Hariv.; R.; to make, render, MBh.; to fall to a person's (acc.) lot or share, PārGṛ.; to let a person (dat.) have anything, Āpast.; to give back, restore, Mn. viii, 183; to perceive, find out, discover, become aware of or acquainted with, understand, learn, MBh.; R. &c.; to deem, consider, regard, Saṃk.; Sāh.; to answer affirmatively, say yes (with or scil. *tathā* or *tathêti*), acknowledge, assent, agree, promise, MBh.; Kāv. &c.; to begin to speak, commence (with acc. or instr.), RV.; Br.; to answer, ChUp. (also with *uttaram*, R.): Caus. *-pādayati*, to convey or lead to, procure, cause to partake of (2 acc.), give a present to, bestow on (loc., dat. or gen.), Kauś.; Mn.; MBh. &c.; to give in marriage, Āpast.; to spend, ib.; to present with (instr.), Kāraṇḍ.; to put in, appoint to (loc.), R.; to produce, cause, effect, MBh.; R. &c.; to establish, substantiate, prove, set forth, explain, teach, impart, MBh.; R. &c.; to deem, consider, regard as (2 acc.), Pañcat. (v.l. *-vadasi* for *-pādayasi*): Desid. *-pitsate* (Pāṇ. vii, 4, 54), to wish to attain, Saṃk.; to wish to know, Bhām.: Desid. of Caus. *-pipādayishati*, to wish or intend to explain or analyze, Saṃk. °**pattavya,** mfn. to be obtained or received, MBh.; to be given (as an answer), R.; to be conceived or understood, Car.; Saṃk.; to be done or begun, MBh.; n. (impers.) it is to be assumed or stated, Saṃk.; one should act or proceed or behave, MBh.; Daś.; Pañcat. °**patti,** f. gaining, obtaining, acquiring, Gaut.; Saṃk.; perception, observation, ascertainment, knowledge, intellect, MBh.; Kāv. &c.; supposition, assertion, statement, Bhartṛ.; Tattvas.; admission, acknowledgment, Yājñ.; giving, granting, bestowing on (loc. or comp.), MBh.; Kām.; causing, effecting, Kām.; beginning, action, procedure in or with (loc., gen. or comp.), MBh.; Kāv. &c. (*tatra kā pratipattiḥ syāt*, what is to be done there? MBh.; *kā tasya pratipattiḥ*, what is to be done with it? Kull.); respectful reception or behaviour, homage, welcome, ib. (°*ttiṃ √dā*, to show honour, Śak.); confidence, assurance, determination, R. (cf. *a-pratip°*); resource, means for (loc.), expedient against (gen.), Jaim.; high rank or dignity, rule, reign, Cat.; conclusion, ĀśvŚr.; *-karman*, n. a concluding rite or ceremony, ĀpŚr., Sch.; *-daksha*, mfn. knowing how to act or what is to be done, Pañcat.; *-darśin*, mfn. showing what ought to be done, SaddhP.; *-nishṭhura*, mfn. difficult to be understood, Ragh.; *-paṭaha*, m. a kind of kettle-drum (allowed only to chiefs of a certain rank), L.; *-parāṅmukha*, mf(*ī*)n. averse from compliance, obstinate, unyielding, Bhaṭṭ.; *-pradāna*, n. the giving of preferment, conferring promotion, Hit.; *-bheda*, m. diversity of views, difference of opinions, RPrāt.; *-mat*, mfn. possessing appropriate knowledge, knowing what is to be done, active, prompt, R.; Kām.; Suśr.; celebrated, high in rank, W.; *-viśārada*, mfn. = *-daksha*, MBh. °**pattṛi,** mfn. one who perceives or hears, Sāh.; one who comprehends or understands, Saṃk.; one who maintains or asserts, ĀpŚr., Sch. °**pád,** f. access, ingress, entrance, VS.; ŚBr.; the path to be walked, the right path, L.; beginning, commencement, TS.; TBr.; an introductory verse or stanza, Br.; ŚrS.; (also °*padā* or °*padī*) the first day of a lunar fortnight (esp. of the moon's wane), AgP.; L.; understanding, intelligence, L.; taste for anything, Jātak.; rank, consequence, W.; a kettle-drum, ib.; °*paccandra*, m. the moon on the first day, the new moon (esp. revered and saluted), Ragh.; °*pat-tūrya*, n. a kind of kettle-drum (cf. °*patti-paṭaha*), L.; °*pan-maya*, mfn. obedient, willing, Jātak. °**padā** or °**padī,** f., see under °*pad*. °**panna,** mfn. come up or resorted to, got into (acc.), approached, arrived, MBh.; Kālid.; met with, obtained, found, gained, won, Kād.; overcome, conquered, subdued, W.; undertaken, begun, done, ib.; ascertained, known, understood, Kum.; familiar with (loc.), MBh.; convinced, sure of anything, Saṃk.; one who has consented or agreed to or promised, Kathās. (also *-vat*); Pañcat.; agreed upon, promised, consented to, R.; Pañcat. (*-tva*, Śukas.); avowed, acknowledged (as a brother), admitted (as a debt), Yājñ.; Pañcat.; answered, replied, Kathās.; offered, given, presented to (loc.), Āpast.; acting or behaving towards (loc.), MBh.; *-prayojana*, mfn. one who has attained his object, R. °**pannaka,** m. 'arrived at an aim,' (with Buddh.) N. of the 4 orders of Āryas (viz. the Śrota-āpanna, Sakṛid-āgāmin, An-āgāmin, and Arhat), L. °**pādaka,** mf(*ikā*)n. causing to obtain, giving, presenting to (loc.), MBh. (*a-pratip°*); stating, demonstrating, explaining, teaching (*-tva*, n.), MBh.; Kāś.; Vedântas.; effective, accomplishing, promoting, MW.; m. or n.(?) a receptacle for hair, L. °**pādana,** n. causing to attain, giving, granting, bestowing on, presenting to (loc. or comp.), MBh.; Kāv. &c.; giving back, restoring, returning, MBh. (*a-pratip°*, Kull.); bringing back, R.; putting in, appointing to (loc.), inauguration, ib.; producing, causing, effecting, accomplishing, W.; stating, setting forth, explaining, teaching, propounding, illustrating, Var.; Saṃk.; Sāh.; beginning, commencement, MBh.; action, worldly conduct, W. °**pādanīya,** mfn. to be given, to be married, Śak.; to be propounded or discussed or treated of, Kap., Sch.; to be accomplished, MW. °**pādayitavya,** mfn. to be offered or given, Kād. °**pādayitṛi,** m. a giver, bestower on (loc.), Āpast.; a teacher, propounder, instructor, Kāś. °**pādita,** mfn. caused to attain, given (also in marriage), delivered, presented, MBh.; Hariv.; R.; stated, proved, set forth, explained, taught, MBh.; Kathās.; BhP.; (*-tva*, n.), Sāh.; caused, effected, produced, MBh.; R. °**pāduka,** mf(*ī*)n. recovering, Śiś.; determining, ascertaining, W.; causing, effecting, ib. °**pādya,** mfn. to be treated of or discussed, to be explained or propounded (*-tva*, n.), Saṃk.; Vedântas.; Kāś.

Prati-pitsā, f. (fr. Desid.) desire of obtaining, striving after (comp.), Saṃk. °**pitsu,** mfn. desirous of obtaining, longing for (acc. or comp.), ib.; desirous of hearing or learning (acc.), Gobh., Sch. °**pipādayishā,** f. desire of setting forth or discussing or treating of (acc.), Kāvyâd., Sch. °**pipādayishu,** mfn. wishing to explain, about to treat of, Kull.

प्रतिपराणी *prati-parā-ṇī* (√*nī*), P. Ā. *-ṇayati*, °*te*, to lead back, ŚBr.

प्रतिपराहृ *prati-parā-√hṛi*, P. *-harati*, to hand over, ŚBr.

प्रतिपरिगमन *prati-pari-gamana*, n. (√*gam*) walking round backwards or again, ĀpŚr., Sch.

प्रतिपरी *prati-parí* (*pari* + √*i*), P. *-paryeti*, to go round in a reverse direction, KātyŚr.

प्रतिपरे *prati-parê* (*parā* + √*i*), ind. p. *-parêtya*, to return again, ŚBr.

प्रतिपर्यावृत् *prati-pary-ā-√vṛit*, Ā. *-vartate*, to turn round in an opposite direction, ŚāṅkhŚr.; Kauś.

प्रतिपर्याहृ *prati-pary-ā-√hṛi*, P. *-harati*, to turn round again, ŚāṅkhŚr.

प्रतिपश् *prati-√paś*, only pr. P. *-paśyati*, to look at, perceive, see, behold, RV.; AV.; Br.; MBh.; to live to see, experience, MBh.; (Ā. °*te*) to see in one's own possession, AV.

प्रतिपाण 2. *prati-pāṇá* (√*paṇ*), m. (for 1. see p. 662, col. 2) ready to exchange, bartering, AV.

प्रतिपान *prati-pāna*, n. (√1. *pā*) drinking, Āpast. (cf. *pratī-p°*); water for drinking, R.

प्रतिपाल् *prati-√pāl*, P. *-pālayati* (ep. also °*te*), to protect, defend, guard, keep, MBh.; R.; to observe, maintain, ib.; to wait, wait for, expect, ChUp.; MBh.; Kāv. &c. °**pālaka,** mf(*ikā*)n. protecting, preserving; a protector, W. °**pālana,** n. guarding, protecting, keeping, cherishing, MBh.; Kāv. &c.; maintaining, observing, MBh.; R.; waiting, expecting, Ratnâv. °**pālanīya** (Śak.), °**pālayitavya** (MBh.), mfn. to be guarded or watched or waited for. °**pālita,** mfn. cherished, protected; practised, followed, W. °**pālin,** mfn. guarding, MBh. °**pālya,** mfn. = °*pālanīya*, MBh.; Śak.

प्रतिपित्सा *prati-pitsā*, *-pitsu*, *-pipādayishā*, *-pipādayishu*. See col. 2.

प्रतिपिष् *prati-√pish*, P. *-pinashṭi* (ep. impf. *-apiṇshat*), to rub one thing against another, rub together, MBh. (*karaṃ kare* or *hastair hastâgram*, the hands); to bruise, grind, crush, destroy, Nir.; ChUp.; MBh. °**pishṭa,** mfn. rubbed or rubbing against each other (as horses), struck against each other, crossed (as swords); bruised, crushed, MBh.; Suśr. °**pesham,** ind. rubbing or pressing against each other (*uraḥ-pratipeshaṃ yudhyante*, they fight breast to breast), Pāṇ. iii, 4, 55, Sch.

प्रतिपीड् *prati-√pīḍ*, P. *-pīḍayati*, to press, oppress, harass, afflict, MBh.; R. °**pīḍana,** n. oppressing, harassing, molesting, Kām.

प्रतिपीय् *prati-√pīy*, P. *-pīyati*, to abuse, revile, RV.

प्रतिपूज् *prati-√pūj*, P. *-pūjayati*, to return a salutation, reverence, salute respectfully, honour, praise, commend, approve, Mn.; MBh. &c. °**pūjaka,** mfn. honouring, revering, a reverer (ifc.), R. °**pūjana,** n. doing homage, honouring, revering (with gen.), R. °**pūjā,** f. id (with gen. or loc.), MBh. °**pūjita,** mfn. honoured, revered, presented with (instr.), Mn.; MBh. &c.; exchanged as civilities, W. °**pūjya,** mfn. to be honoured, Mn.

प्रतिपॄ *prati-√pṝ*, P. *-pṛiṇāti* (only 2. du. Impv. *-pṛiṇītám*), to bestow in return, RV. vii, 65, 5: Caus. *-pūrayati*, to fill up, make full, ĀśvGṛ.; Suśr.; to fill (said of a noise), MBh.; to sate, satiate, satisfy, ib.; to fulfil, accomplish, R.

Prati-pūraṇa, n. filling up, filling, R.; injecting a fluid or other substance, pouring a fluid over, Suśr.; the being filled with (instr.), Gaut.; obstruction, congestion (of the head), Car. °**pūrita,** mfn. filled with, full of, Hariv.; satisfied, contented, BhP. °**pūrṇa,** mfn. id., ChUp.; MBh. &c.; *-bimba*, mfn. 'having its disc filled,' full (the moon), MBh.; *mānasa*, mfn. (having one's heart) satisfied, Hariv. °**pūrti,** f. fulfilment, perfection, Lalit.

प्रतिप्रग्रह् *prati-pra-√grah*, P. *-gṛihṇāti*, to take up or receive again, MBh.

प्रतिप्रच्छ् *prati-√prach*, P. *-pṛicchati*, to ask, question, inquire of (2 acc.), R.; Kathās. °**praśna,** m. a question in return, ĀpŚr.; Vait.; an answer, Var. °**prāś,** °**prāśita,** see p. 662, col. 2.

प्रतिप्रज्ञा *prati-pra-√jñā*, P. *-jānāti*, to seek out or find again, ŚBr. °**prajñāti,** f. discrimination, ascertainment, statement, AitBr.; Kāṭh.

प्रतिप्रदा *prati-pra-√dā*, P. *-dadāti*, to give back again, MBh. °**pratta,** mfn. given up, delivered, ŚBr. °**pradāna,** n. giving back, returning, R.; giving in marriage, ib.

प्रतिप्रब्रू *prati-pra-√brū*, P. *-bravīti*, to speak in return, reply, answer, ŚBr.

प्रतिप्रभ *prati-prabha*, m. N. of an Ātreya (author of RV. v, 49), Anukr.; (*ā*), f. reflection (of fire), MBh.

प्रतिप्रमुच् *prati-pra-√muc*, P. *-muñcati*, to admit (a calf to the cow), ŚBr.

प्रतिप्रयम् *prati-pra-√yam*, P. *-yacchati*, to give back, return, restore, TS.; GṛŚrS.; Daś.

प्रतिप्रयवण *prati-pra-yavaṇa*, n. (√2. *yu*) repeated mixture, Suśr.

प्रतिप्रया *prati-pra-√yā*, P. *-yāti*, to go back, return, RV. &c. &c. °**prayāṇa,** n. going back, return, R. (°ṇakam, see p. 662, col. 2). °**prayāta,** mfn. gone back, returned, MBh.; Kāv. &c.

प्रतिप्रयुज् *prati-pra-√yuj,* P. Ā. *-yunakti, -yuṅkte,* to add instead of something else, substitute, TāṇḍBr.; (Ā.) to pay back, restore (a debt), MBh. (B.)

प्रतिप्रवच् *prati-pra-√vac* (only pf. *-prô-vāca* and ind. p. *-prôcya*), to report, relate, tell, TS.; Br. °**prôkta,** mfn. returned, answered, AitBr.; BhP.

प्रतिप्रविद् *prati-pra-√1. vid,* Caus. *-vedayati,* to proclaim, announce, TS.

प्रतिप्रविश् *prati-pra-√viś,* P. *-viśati,* to go back, return, R.

प्रतिप्रवृत् *prati-pra-√vṛit,* Caus. *-vartayati,* to lead towards, Kauś.

प्रतिप्रश्न *prati-praśna.* See *prati-√prach.*

प्रतिप्रश्रब्धि *prati-pra-śrabdhi,* f. (√*śrambh*) omission, removal, L.

प्रतिप्रसू *prati-pra-√1. sū,* Ā. *-suvate,* to allow or enjoin again, ĀpŚr., Sch. °**prasava,** m. counter-order, suspension of a general prohibition in a particular case, Śaṃk.; KātyŚr., Sch.; Kull.; an exception to an exception, TPrāt., Sch.; return to the original state, Yogas. °**prasavam,** ind., see p. 662, col. 2. °**prasūta,** mfn. re-enjoined after having been forbidden, KātyŚr., Sch.

प्रतिप्रसृप् *prati-pra-√srip,* P. *-sarpati,* to creep near again, ĀśvŚr.

प्रतिप्रस्थातृ *prati-pra-sthātṛi,* m. (√*sthā*) N. of a priest who assists the Adhvaryu, TS.; Br.; ŚrS. °**prasthāna,** m. N. of a partic. Soma-Graha, VS.; n. the office of the Prati-prasthātṛi (see °*prāsthānika*); the milk-vessel of the Pr°, ĀpŚr. °**prāsthānika,** mfn. relating to the office of the Pr°; (with *karman*), n. the office of the Pr°, MBh.

प्रतिप्रहार *prati-pra-hāra,* m. (√*hṛi*) a counter-blow, returning a blow, Hariv.; Ragh.

प्रतिप्रहि *prati-pra-√hi,* P. *-hiṇoti,* to drive or chase back, AV.; ŚBr.

प्रतिप्रह्वे *prati-pra-√hve* (only Pass. *-hūyate*), to call near, invite to (acc.), RV.

प्रतिप्राया *prati-prâ-√yā,* P. *-yāti,* to come near, approach, RV.

प्रतिप्राश् *prati-prāś, -prāśita.* See *prati-√prach* and p. 662, col. 2.

प्रतिप्रास् *prati-prâs* (*pra* + √2. *as*), P. *-prâsyati,* to throw or cast upon, KātyŚr.

प्रतिप्लवन *prati-plavana,* n. (√*plu*) jumping or leaping back, R.

प्रतिफल् *prati-√phal,* P. *-phalati,* to bound against, rebound, be reflected, Kāv.; to requite, MW. °**phala,** m. (L.), °**phalana,** n. (Kāv.) reflection, image, shadow; (W.) return, requital, retaliation.

प्रतिफुल्लक *prati-phullaka,* mfn. flowering, in blossom, L.

प्रतिबन्ध् *prati-√bandh,* P. Ā. *-badhnāti, -badhnīte* (ep. impf. also *-abandhat*), to tie to, fasten, fix, moor (Ā., anything of one's own), ŚBr.; Hariv. &c.; to set, enchase, MBh.; to exclude, cut off, Ragh.; Kull.; to keep back or off, keep at a distance, Daś.; Naish.; to stop, interrupt, Śak. °**baddha,** mfn. tied or bound to, fastened, fixed, Kām.; Ragh.; Suśr.; twisted, wreathed (as a garland), Mālatīm. ii, ⅟; dependent on, subject to (comp.), Kād.; Śaṃk.; attached to, joined or connected or provided with (instr.), Kap.; MBh.; Hit.; harmonizing with (loc.), Kum.; fixed, directed (*upari* or comp.), Śaṃk.; Pañcat.; hindered, excluded, cut off, Mallin.; kept at a distance, MBh.; entangled, complicated, Var.; disappointed, thwarted, crossed, vexed, L.; (in phil.) that which is always connected or implied (as fire in smoke), MW.; *-citta,* mfn. one whose mind is turned to or fixed on (comp.), Pañcat.; *-tā,* f. the being connected with (comp.), L.; *-prasara,* mfn. hindered or blunted in its course (as a thunderbolt), Mallin. on Kum. iii, 12; *-rāga,* mfn. having passion in harmonious connection with (loc.), Kum. vii, 91. °**badhya,** mfn. to be obstructed or hindered, L. °**banddhṛi,** m. a hinderer, preventer, obstructor; *-tā,* f., Naish. °**bandha,** m. connection, uninterruptedness, Kap.; Kāś.; a prop, support, Kād.; investment, siege, Hariv.; obstacle, hindrance, impediment, Kālid.; Śaṃk.; opposition, resistance, Śak. (*ena,* by all kinds of res°, Nal.); a logical impediment, obstructive argument, Sarvad.; stoppage, suspension, cessation, Pāṇ. iii, 3, 51 (cf. *varsha-pr°*); vii, 1, 45; *-kārin,* mfn. creating obstacles, hindering, preventing, W.; *-mukta,* mfn. freed from obst°, Śatr.; *-vat,* mfn. beset with obst°, difficult to attain, Mālav. °**bandhaka,** (ifc.) = °*bandha,* impediment, obstacle, MBh.; mf(*ikā*)n. obstructing, preventing, resisting, MBh.; Rājat.; TPrāt., Sch.; m. a branch, L.; N. of a prince, VP. °**bandhana,** n. binding, confinement, obstruction, W. °**bandhi,** m. contradiction, objection, L.; *-kalpanā,* f. (in logic) an assumption liable to a legitimate contradiction, Sarvad. °**bandhin,** mfn. meeting with an obstacle, being impeded or prevented, Pāṇ. vi, 2, 6; (ifc.) impeding, obstructing; *-tā,* f., Vikr.

प्रतिबाध् *prati-√bādh,* Ā. *-bādhate* (ep. also P. °*ti*), to beat back, ward off, repel, MBh.; R.; to check, restrain, ŚBr.; to pain, torment, vex, Hariv.; R. °**bādhaka,** mf(*ikā*)n. thrusting back, repelling (ifc.), R.; preventing, obstructing, MW. °**bādhana,** n. beating back, repulsion (gen., acc., or comp.), MBh.; BhP. °**bādhita,** mfn. beaten back, repelled, MBh. °**bādhin,** mfn. obstructing; m. an opponent, MW.

प्रतिबुध् *prati-√budh,* Ā. *-budhyate* (ep. also P. °*ti*), to awaken (intr.), awake, wake, Mn.; MBh. &c.; to perceive, observe, learn, RV. (2. pf. Subj. *-búbodhatha*; p. Ā. *-búdhyamāna,* 'attentive'); AV.; Br.; BhP.; to awaken (trans.), RV.: Pass. (only aor. *-abodhi*) to expand, BhP.: Caus. *-bodhayati,* to awaken (trans.), Kāv.; Kathās.; BhP.; to instruct, inform, admonish, MBh.; Kāv. &c.; to commission, charge, order, MW. °**buddha** (*práti-*), mfn. awakened, awake (also said of the Dawn), RV. &c. &c.; one who has attained to perfect knowledge, ŚBr. (cf. MWB. 98, n.); illuminated, enlightened, BhP.; observed, recognized, ib.; known, celebrated, W.; made prosperous or great, ib.; *-vastu,* mfn. understanding the real nature of things, BhP.; °*ddhâtman,* mfn. having the mind roused or awakened, awake, MW. °**buddhaka,** mfn. known, recognized (*a-pratib°*), MBh. °**buddhi,** f. awakening, Cat.; hostile disposition or purpose (= *śatru-b°*), MW.; *-vat,* mfn. having hostile intentions, ib. °**bodha,** m. (cf. *pratī-b°*) awaking, waking, Ragh.; BhP.; perception, knowledge, KenUp.; BhP.; instruction, admonition, Śukas.; N. of a man, g. *bidâdi*; *-vat,* mfn. endowed with knowledge or reason, Śak. °**bodhaka,** mfn. awakening (with acc.), R.; m. a teacher, instructor, Siṅhâs. °**bodhana,** mfn. awakening, enlivening, refreshing (ifc.), BhP.; Suśr.; (*ā*), f. awaking, recovering consciousness, Kād.; n. awaking, expanding, spreading, MBh.; Suśr.; awakening (trans.), R.; instruction, explanation, BhP. °**bodhanīya,** mfn. to be awakened, Ratnâv. °**bodhita,** mfn. awakened, R.; instructed, taught, admonished, W. °**bodhin,** mfn. awaking, about to awake, Kathās. (cf. g. *gamy-ādi*).

प्रतिब्रू *prati-√brū,* P. Ā. *-braviti, -brūte,* to speak in reply, answer, RV. &c. &c. (also with 2 acc., R.); (Ā.) to answer i.e. return (an attack &c.), RV.; to refuse, deny, BhP.

प्रतिभक्ष् *prati-√bhaksh,* P. *-bhakshayati,* to eat separately or alone, ĀśvŚr.

प्रतिभज् *prati-√bhaj,* P. *-bhajati,* to fall again to one's share, return to (acc.), Daś. 2. °**bhāga,** m. (for 1. see p. 662, col. 3) division, VāyuP. (w.r. for *pra-vibh°*?); a share, portion, daily present (consisting of fruit, flowers &c. and offered to a king), Mn. viii, 307; *-śas,* ind. in divisions or classes, Suśr.

प्रतिभञ्ज् *prati-√bhañj,* P. *-bhanakti,* to fracture, break in pieces, RV.; AV.; TBr.

प्रतिभण् *prati-√bhaṇ,* P. *-bhaṇati,* to speak in reply, answer, Bhaṭṭ. °**bhaṇita,** mfn. answered, replied, W.

प्रतिभण्डितव्य *prati-bhaṇḍitavya,* mfn. (√*bhaṇḍ*) to be derided or scoffed in return, L.

प्रतिभा *prati-√bhā,* P. *-bhāti,* to shine upon (acc.), Lāṭy.; to come in sight, present or offer one's self to (gen. or acc.), MBh.; R. &c.; to appear to the mind (also with *manasi*), flash upon the thoughts, become clear or manifest, occur to (acc. or gen.), Up.; MBh. &c. (*nôttaram pratibhāti me,* 'no answer occurs to me,' Hariv.); to seem or appear to (gen., acc. with or without *prati*) as or like (nom. with or without *iva* or *yathā*, or *-vat,* ind.), MBh.; Kāv. &c. (*iti pratibhāti me manaḥ,* 'so it seems to my mind,' MBh.); to seem fit, appear good, please to (gen. or acc.), Vikr.; Pañcat. &c. (*sā bhāryā pratibhāti me,* 'this one would please me as a wife,' Kathās.) °**bha,** mfn. wise, intelligent, Ragh. viii, 79 (v.l.) °**bhā,** f. an image, Nir.; light, splendour (see *nish-pr°*); appearance (*a-pr°*), Gaut.; fitness, suitableness (*a-pr°*), ŚrS.; intelligence, understanding, MBh.; Kāv.; Sāh.; presence of mind, genius, wit, Kām.; audacity, boldness (*a-pr°*), Nyāyad.; a thought, idea, Daś.; Kathās.; a founded supposition, Naish.; fancy, imagination, MBh.; Kathās.; Sāh.; *-kshaya,* m. loss or absence of knowledge, want of sense, Kull.; *-tas,* ind. by fancy or imagination, Kathās.; *-°nvita* (°*bhânv°*), mfn. intelligent, wise, L.; confident, bold, L.; *-balāt,* ind. by force of reason or intelligence, wisely, Rājat.; *-mukha,* mfn. at once hitting the right, quick-witted, L. (confident, arrogant, W.); *-vat,* mfn. endowed with presence of mind, shrewd, intelligent, Kathās.; confident, bold, L.; m. (L.) the sun, the moon, fire; *-vaśāt,* ind. = *-tas,* Kathās.; *-vilāsa,* m. N. of sev. wks.; *-hāni,* f. privation of light, dulness, darkness, W.; = *-kshaya,* ib. °**bhāta,** n. (prob.) a symbolical offering, Hariv. (v.l. °*bhāna* and °*bhāva*). °**bhāna,** n. becoming clear or visible, obviousness, TS., Sch.; intelligence, Hariv.; eloquence, Lalit.; brilliancy, W.; boldness, audacity, ib.; v.l. for °*bhāta,* Hariv.; *-kūṭa,* m. N. of a Bodhi-sattva, L.; *-vat,* mfn. endowed with presence of mind, quick-witted, shrewd, intelligent, MBh.; Kāv. &c. (*-tva,* n., Mālatīm.); bright, brilliant, W.; bold, audacious, ib.

प्रतिभाष् *prati-√bhāsh,* Ā. *-bhāshate* (ep. also P. °*ti*), to speak in return or to (acc.), answer, relate, tell, MBh.; Kāv. &c.; to call, name (2 acc.), Śrut. °**bhāshā,** f. an answer, rejoinder, L. °**bhāshya,** n. N. of ch. of BhavP.

प्रतिभास् *prati-√bhās,* Ā. *-bhāsate,* to manifest one's self, appear as or look like or as (nom.), Rājat. (*nānā-tvena,* 'to appear different,' Vedântas.); to shine, be brilliant, have a bright appearance, Kathās. °**bhāsa,** m. appearance, look, similitude, Vedântas.; Sāh.; appearing or occurring to the mind, Kpr.; R., Sch.; illusion, Lalit. °**bhāsana,** n. appearing, appearance, Kap., Sch.; Sāy.; look, semblance, Sāh.

प्रतिभिद् *prati-√bhid,* P. *-bhinatti,* to pierce, penetrate, MBh.; to disclose, betray, Daś.; to reproach, censure, be indignant with (acc.), Ragh.; Śiś. °**bhinna,** mfn. pierced, divided, W.; distinguished by (instr. or comp.), Kum. vii, 7; 35. °**bhinnaka,** mfn. undecided (?), Divyâv. °**bheda,** m. (ifc. f. *ā*) splitting, dividing (?), MBh.; discovery, betrayal, Rājat.; Kathās. °**bhedana,** n. piercing, cutting, dividing, W.; putting out (as the eyes), Yājñ.

प्रतिभुज् *prati-√bhuj,* P. *-bhunakti,* to enjoy, MBh.; to eat food besides the prescribed diet, Car. °**bhukta,** mfn. one who has eaten food reserved for him, Car.; one who has eaten food other than the prescribed diet, ib. °**bhoga,** m. enjoyment, MBh.; = next, Car.; v.l. for *-bhāga,* Mn. viii, 307. °**bhojana,** n. prescribed diet, Car. °**bhojita,** mfn. one who has been allowed to eat food besides the pr° d°, ib. °**bhojin,** mfn. eating the pr° d°, ib.

प्रतिभू *prati-√bhū,* P. *-bhavati,* to be equal to or on a par with (acc.), ŚBr.: Caus. *-bhāvayati,* to observe, become acquainted with (acc.), MBh.: Pass. *-bhāvyate,* to be considered as, pass for (nom.), Rājat. °**bhāva,** m. counterpart (*-tā,* f.), Prasannar.; corresponding character or disposition, W.; *-vat,* mfn. having corresponding characters, social, ib. °**bhū,** m. a surety, security, bail, Mn.; MBh.; Kāv. &c.

प्रतिभूष् *prati-√bhūsh,* P. *-bhūshati,* to make ready, prepare, fit out, RV.; to serve, wait upon, honour, worship, ib.; TS.; to concede, acquiesce in, agree to (acc.), RV.

प्रतिभृ *prati-√bhṛi,* P. *-bharati,* to carry towards, offer, present, RV.; (*-bibharti*), to support (a parent), Divyâv. °**bhṛita,** mfn. offered, prevented, ib.

प्रतिमण्डित *prati-maṇḍita*, mfn. (√*maṇḍ*) decorated, adorned, SaddhP.

प्रतिमन् *prati-√man*, Ā. *-manute*, to render back in return or in reply, contrast with (also with 2 acc.), VS.; ChUp.: Caus. *-mānayati*, to honour, esteem, approve, consider, regard, MBh.; R. &c. °**mānanā**, f. homage, reverence, Śiś. °**mānayitavya**, mfn. to be regarded or considered, Mudr.

प्रतिमन्त्र् *prati-√mantr*, P. *-mantrayati*, to call out or reply to, ŚrS.; to consecrate with sacred texts, MBh. °**mantraṇa**, n. an answer, reply, Kauś. °**mantrayitavya**, mfn. to be answered, L. °**mantrita**, mfn. consecrated with sacred texts, MBh.

प्रतिमन्यूय *prati-manyūya*, Nom. Ā. °*yate*, see *á-pratimanyūyamāna*.

प्रतिमर्श *prati-marśa*, m. (√*mṛiś*) a kind of powder used as a sternutatory, Car.; Suśr. (w.r. *-marsha*).

प्रतिमा *prati-√mā*, Ā. *-mimite* (Ved. inf. *prati-mai*), to imitate, copy, RV.; VS.; Kauś.

Prati-mā, m. a creator, maker, framer, AV.; VS.; (*á*), f. an image, likeness, symbol, RV. &c. &c.; a picture, statue, figure, idol, Mn.; Hariv.; Ragh. (IW. 218, 1; 241); reflection (in comp. after a word meaning 'moon,' cf. below); measure, extent (cf. below); N. of a metre, RPrāt.; the part of an elephant's head between the tusks (also °*ma*, m.), L. (ifc. like, similar, resembling, equal to, TBr.; MBh. &c.; having the measure of, as long or wide &c. as, e.g. *tri-nalva-pr*°, 3 Nalvas long, Hariv.; °*ma-tā*, f., *-tva*, n. reflection, image, shadow, W.); *-gata*, mfn. present in an idol (as a deity), Ragh.; *-candra*, m. 'reflection-moon,' image of the m°, Ragh.; *-dāna*, n., *-dravyâdi-vacana*, n. N. of wks.; *-paricāraka*, m. an attendant upon an idol (= *devala*), Kull. (cf. IW. 218, 1); *-pūjā*, f. worship of images, MWB. 464; *-pratishṭhā*, f. (and °*thā-vidhi*, m.), *-rodanâdi-prâyaścitta-vidhi*, m., *-lakshaṇa*, n. N. of wks.; *-viśesha*, m. a sort of image, a kind of figure, MW.; *-śaśâṅka*, m. = *-candra*, Ragh.; *-samprôkshaṇa*, n. N. of wk.; °*mêndu*, m. = °*mā-candra*, Rājat. °**mātavya**, mfn. comparable, MW. °**mā́na**, n. a counterpart, well-matched opponent, adversary, RV.; a model, pattern, MBh.; BhP.; an image, picture, idol, L.; comparison, likeness, similarity, resemblance, MBh.; Mālatīm.; a weight, Vishṇ.; Yājñ. (cf. *pratī-m*°); = *-bhāga*, MBh.; *-pratimāna-kalpa*, mfn. like, similar, MBh.; *-bhāga*, m. the part of an elephant's head between the tusks, L. °**mita**, mfn. imitated, reflected, mirrored, Kathās.; Rājat. **-miti**, f. reflected image, Śrīkaṇṭh. **-meya**, mfn. comparable (see *a-pratim*°).

प्रतिमित् *prati-mít*, f. (√*mi*) a prop, stay, support, AV.

प्रतिमिह् *prati-√mih*, P. *-mehati*, to make water in the direction of (acc.), MBh.; R.

प्रतिमीव् *prati-√mīv*, P. *-mīvati*, to push or press back, TS.; to close by pressing, shut, ŚBr.

प्रतिमुच् *prati-√muc*, P. Ā. *-muñcati*, °*te*, to put (clothes, a garland &c.) on (dat., gen., loc.), to fix or fasten on, append, AV. &c. &c.; (Ā., later also P.) to put on one's self, dress one's self, assume (a shape or form), RV. &c. &c.; to attach or fasten to (loc.), KātyŚr.; BhP.; to inflict on (loc.), TBr.; to set at liberty, release, let go, send away, Ragh.; Rājat.; Kathās.; to give up, resign, Mṛicch.; Pañcat.; to return, restore, pay back (as a debt), MBh.; to fling, hurl, RV.; MBh.; R.: Pass. *-mucyate*, to be freed or released from (abl.), Mn.; MBh. &c.: Caus. *-mocayati*, to set free, rescue, save, MBh. °**mukta**, mfn. put on, applied, Ragh.; fastened, tied, bound, BhP.; released, liberated, freed from (abl.), Ragh.; Rājat.; MārkP.; given up, relinquished, Mṛicch.; flung, hurled, MBh. °**moka**, m. (ifc.) putting or hanging round, ŚBr. °**mocana**, n. liberation, release from (comp.), MBh.; Ragh. °**mocita**, mfn. released, saved, delivered, Mṛicch.

प्रतिमुट् *prati-√muṭ*, Caus. *-moṭayati*, to put an end to, kill, Chandom.

प्रतिमुद् *prati-√mud*, Ā. *-modate* (rarely P. °*ti*), to rejoice at, welcome with joy, be glad to see (with acc., rarely gen.), RV. &c. &c.: Caus. *-modayate*, to gladden, cheer, ŚBr.: Desid. of Caus. *-mumodayishati*, to wish to make cheerful, ib.

प्रतिमुह् *prati-√muh*, Caus. *-mohayati*, to bewilder, confound, AV.

प्रतिमोक्ष *prati-moksha*, m. (√*moksh*) liberation, deliverance; (with Buddh.) emancipation, L.; the formulary for releasing monks by penances, Kāraṇḍ.; *-sūtra*, n. N. of Buddh. Sūtras, MWB. 268. °**mokshaṇa**, n. remission (of taxes), Kām.

प्रतियज् *prati-√yaj*, P. *-yajati*, to sacrifice in return or with an aim towards anything (acc.), ŚBr.; ĀpŚr. °**yāga**, a sacrifice offered with an aim towards anything, ĀpŚr., Sch.

प्रतियत् *prati-√yat*, Ā. *-yatate*, to guard against, counteract, ŚBr.; Śak. i, ३३ (v.l.): Caus. *-yātayati*, to retaliate, requite (with *vairam* or °*rāṇi*, 'to take revenge'), MBh. °**yatna**, m. care bestowed upon anything, effort, endeavour, exertion, Pāṇ. i, 3, 32; ii. 3, 53 &c.; preparation, elaboration, manufacture, Śiś. iii, 54 (cf. *a-pr*°*-pūrva*); imparting a new quality or virtue, Kāś. on Pāṇ. ii, 3, 53; retaliation, requital, W.; (also = *lipsa*, *upagraha* or °*hana*, *nigrahâdi*, *grahaṇâdi*, *pratigraha*, L.); mfn. exerting one's self, taking care or trouble, L.; cautious, heedful, Jātak. °**yātana**, n. requital, retaliation (*vaira-pr*°, 'taking revenge'), MBh.; (*ā*), f. an image, model, counterpart, a picture, statue (of a god &c.), Ragh.; Śiś.; Hcar.; (ifc.) appearing in the shape of, Hcar.

प्रतियभ् *prati-√yabh* (only inf. *-yabdhum*), to have intercourse with a female, TBr., Sch.

प्रतियम् *prati-√yam*, P. *-yacchati*, to be equivalent to, be worth as much as (acc.), TBr.; to grant or bestow perpetually (Impv. *-yaṃsi*), RV.; to return, restore, BhP.

प्रतिया *prati-√yā*, P. *-yāti*, to come or go to (acc., also with *prati*), RV.; MBh.; to go against (acc.), Hariv.; to go or come back, return to or into (acc.), MBh.; Kāv. &c.; to comply with, oblige, please (acc.), R.; to equal, be a match for (acc.), BhP.; to be returned or requited, ib.: Caus. *-yāpayati*, to cause to return to (acc.), BhP. °**yāta**, mfn. gone towards or against or back or away, turned, returned, opposed, MBh.; R.; *-nidra*, mfn. 'one whose sleep is gone,' awakened, wake, BhP.; *-buddhi*, mfn. one whose mind is turned towards (dat.), R.

प्रतियु *prati-√2. yu*, P. *-yauti*, to tie to, bind, fetter, TS. °**yuta**, mfn. tied to, bound, fettered, ib. °**yuvana**, n. repeated mixture, Hcat.

प्रतियुज् *prati-√yuj*, P. Ā. *-yunakti*, *-yuṅkte*, to fasten on, tie to (acc.), RV.; (Ā.) to pay back (a debt), MBh. (C. *prati-pray*°): Caus. *-yojayati*, to fix on, adjust (the arrow on the bow), MBh. °**yoga**, m. resistance, opposition, contradiction, controversy, BhP.; an antidote, remedy, Kathās.; co-operation, association, W.; the being a counterpart of anything, ib. °**yogi**, in comp. = °*yogin*; *-jñāna-kāraṇatā*, f., *-jñāna-kāraṇatā-vāda*, m.; *-jñānasya hetutva-khaṇḍana*, n. N. of wks.; *-tā*, f. correlation, dependent existence, Bhāshāp., Sch.; mutual co-operation, partnership, W.; *-tā-vāda*, m. N. of wk.; *-tva*, n. = *-tā*, Tarkas.; *-nirūpaṇa*, n., °*gyanadhikaraṇe nāśasyôtpatti-nirāsa*, m. N. of wks. °**yogika**, mfn. antithetical, relative, correlative (*-tva*, n.), Tarkas.; Vedântap. °**yogin**, mfn. id., Tarkas.; Saṃk.; TS., Sch. &c. (cf. *a-pratiy*°); m. an adversary, rival, Mcar.; any object dependent upon another and not existing without it, W.; a partner, associate, ib.; a counterpart, match, ib. °**yojayitavya**, mfn. to be fitted with strings, Ragh.

प्रतियुध् *prati-√yudh*, Ā. P. *-yudhyate*, °*ti*, to fight against, be a match for (acc.), fight, MBh.; Hariv.; R.: Caus. *-yodhayati*, id., MBh.; Var. °**yuddha**, mfn. fought against, fought, R.; n. fighting against, battle in return, Hariv. °**yoddhavya**, mfn. to be attacked in return, MBh. °**yoddhṛi**, m. an antagonist, adversary, well-matched opponent, ib.; R.; one who begins a battle, Mn. xi, 81 (v.l.) °**yodha**, m. an opponent, adversary, MBh.; Ragh. °**yodhana**, n. fighting against, assailing in turn, MBh. °**yodhin**, m. an antagonist, well-matched opponent, g. *gamy-ādi* (cf. *a-pratiy*°).

प्रतिर *pra-tira*, °*ram*. See under *pra-√tṛī*.

प्रतिरक्ष् *prati-√raksh*, P. *-rakshati*, to preserve, guard, protect, AV.; MBh.; to keep (a promise), MBh.; to be afraid of, fear (acc.), VS. °**rakshaṇa**, n. preserving, protecting, W. °**rakshā**, f. safety, preservation; °*shârtham*, ind. for the sake of saving, MW.

प्रतिरञ्जित *prati-rañjita*, mfn. (√*rañj*) coloured, reddened, MBh.; R.

प्रतिरप् *prati-√rap*, P. *-rapati*, to whisper to, tell something (acc.) in a whisper to (dat.), RV.

प्रतिरम् *prati-√ram*, P. *-ramati*, to look towards with joy, long for, expect (acc.), Kāraṇḍ. °**rata**, mfn. delighting in, zealous for (loc.), R.

प्रतिरम्भ *prati-rambha*, m. (√*rabh*) = *prati-lambha*, L.; passion, rage, violent or passionate abuse, W.

प्रतिरस् *prati-√ras*, P. *-rasati*, to echo, resound, Caṇḍ. °**rasita**, n. echo, resonance, Veṇīs.

प्रतिराज् *prati-√rāj*, Ā. *-rājate*, to shine like (*iva*), equal in splendour, Hariv.

प्रतिराध् *prati-√rādh* (only ind. p. *-rādhya*), to counteract, oppose (acc.), Gaut.: Desid. *-ritsati*, Pāṇ. vii, 4. 54, Vārtt. 1, Pat. °**rāddha**, mfn. counteracted, Gaut. °**rādha**, m. 'obstacle, hindrance,' N. of partic. verses of the AV., AitBr.; Vait. (cf. *pratī-r*°, p. 673).

प्रतिरिह् *prati-√rih*, P. *-rihati*, to lick, AV.

प्रतिरु *prati-√ru*, P. *-rauti*, to cry or call to (acc.), Var. °**ravá**, m. crying or calling out to, quarrelling, Pañcat.; (also pl.) echo, ib.; Kathās.; Rājat.; (prob.) = *upa-rava*, VS.; ŚBr. °**ruta**, mfn. answered by crying or calling, Var. °**rurūshu**, mfn. wishing to speak or tell, W.

प्रतिरुच् *prati-√ruc*, Ā. *-rocate*, to please (with acc.), RV.: Caus. *-rocayati*, to be pleased to (acc.), resolve, decide upon, MBh.

प्रतिरुध् *prati-√rudh*, P. Ā. *-ruṇaddhi*, *-runddhe* or *-rundhati*, °*te*, to check, hinder, prevent, oppose, resist, TS.; Br. &c.; to confine, keep back, shut off, MBh.; BhP.; to cover, conceal, MBh.; Hariv. °**ruddha**, mfn. checked, prevented, stopped, disturbed, interrupted, Mn.; MBh. &c.; shut off, kept away, withdrawn, MBh.; BhP.; rendered imperfect, impaired, MW. °**roddhṛi**, m. an opposer (with gen.), Mn.; MBh. °**rodha**, m. opposition, impediment, obstruction (*-kara*, mfn. obstructing, Suśr.); = *tiraskāra*, *vyutthāna*, *caurya*, L. °**rodhaka**, m. an opposer, preventer, Kād.; a robber, thief, Mālav.; an obstacle, W. °**rodhana**, n. obstruction, prevention, MBh.; allowing anything (gen.) to pass by fruitlessly, Mn. ix, 93. °**rodhin**, mfn. obstructing, hindering &c.; m. a robber, thief, Mālatīm.

प्रतिरुह् *prati-√ruh*, P. *-rohati*, to sprout or grow again, MBh.: Caus. *-ropayati*, to plant anything in its proper place, Var.; to plant again (lit. and fig.), re-establish, Ragh. °**rūḍha**, mfn. imitated, BhP. °**ropita**, mfn. (fr. Caus.) planted again, Ragh.

प्रतिरोषितव्य *prati-roshitavya*, n. impers. (√*rush*) anger is to be returned, L.

प्रतिल् *pra-√1. til*, P. *-tilati*, to be desirous of sexual intercourse, VS. (= *snihyati*, Mahīdh.)

प्रतिलङ्घ् *prati-√laṅgh*, Caus. *-laṅghayati*, to mount, sit down upon (acc.), Sarvad.; to transgress, violate, MBh.

प्रतिलभ् *prati-√labh*, Ā. *-labhate*, to receive back, recover, MBh.; Kāv. &c.; to obtain, gain, partake of (acc.), MBh.; BhP.; to get back i. e. get punished, MBh.; to learn, understand, MBh.; R.; to expect, R.: Pass. *-labhyate*, to be obtained or met with, appear, Saṃk.: Caus. *-lambhayati*, to provide or present with (instr.), HPariś. °**labhya**, mfn. to be received or obtained, obtainable, BhP. °**lambha**, m. receiving, obtaining, finding, getting, Nir.; Kāv.; recovering, regaining (ifc.), Kād.; conceiving, understanding, Sarvad.; censure, abuse, W. °**lambhita** (fr. Caus.), n. obtaining, getting, MW.; censure, reviling, ib. °**lābha**, m. recovering, receiving, obtaining, Saṃk.

प्रतिलम्ब् *prati-√lamb* (only ind. p. *-lambya*), to hang up, suspend, Pañcat. i, $\frac{453}{454}$ (v. l.)

प्रतिलिख् *prati-√likh*, P. *-likhati*, to write back, answer by letter, Mālav.; to wipe off, cleanse, purify, HPariś. °**likhita,** mfn. written back, answered, Mālav. °**lekhana,** n. or °**nā,** f. the regular cleaning of all implements or objects for daily use, HPariś.

प्रतिलिह् *prati-√lih*, Caus. *-lehayati*, to cause to lick at (2 acc.), ŚBr. (cf. *prati-√rih*).

प्रतिली *prati-√lī*, Pass. *-līyate*, to disappear, BhP. °**līna,** mfn. unmoved or retired, ŚāṅkhGṛ.

प्रतिलुभ् *prati-√lubh*, Caus. *-lobhayati*, to illude, infatuate, RV.; to attract, allure, MBh.

प्रतिवच् *prati-√vac*, P. *-vakti*, to announce, indicate, recommend, RV. i, 41, 4 (Ā. Subj. aor. *-voce*); to speak back, answer, reply (also with 2 acc.), VS. &c. &c.; to refute, Śaṃk. °**vaktavya,** mfn. to be answered or replied to, to be given (as an answer), R.; to be opposed or contradicted, ib.; to be contested or disputed, Śaṃk. °**vaktṛi,** mfn. answering to (gen.), explaining (the law), Baudh. °**vacana,** m. a verse or formula serving as an answer, ĀpŚr.; n. a dependent or final clause in a sentence, Nir.; an answer, Mṛicch.; Prab. &c.; an echo, W.; °*nī-kṛita*, mfn. answered, Śak. °**vacas,** n. (also with *uttara*) an answer, reply, MBh.; Kathās.; an echo, W. °**vākya,** n. an answer, Nal.; mfn. answerable, W. °**vāc,** f. an answer, Śiś.; (pl.) yelling at (acc.), MBh. °**vācika,** n. an answer, Naish. °**vācya,** mfn. to be contradicted (*a-prativ°*), GobhGṛ. **Práty-ukta,** mfn. answered (pers. and thing), Br.; MBh. &c.; n. = next, Megh. **Praty-ukti,** f. an answer, Satr.

प्रतिवद् *prati-√vad*, P. *-vadati*, to speak to (acc.), RV.; Kauś.; to speak back, answer, reply to (acc.), MBh.; Kāv. &c.; to repeat, KaṭhUp.; MBh.: Intens. p. *-vāvadat*, mfn. contradicting, AitBr. °**vaditavya,** mfn. to be contested or disputed, Śaṃk. °**vāda,** m. contradiction, rejection, refusal, AitĀr. (*a-prativ°*); MBh.; BhP.; an answer, reply, rejoinder, MW. °**vādin,** mfn. contradicting, disobedient (see *á-prativ°*); answering, rejoining, MW.; m. an opponent, adversary, Mālav.; VarYog.; a defendant, respondent (°*di-tā*, f.), Yājñ.; Kull.; °*di-bhayam-kara*, m. N. of an author, Cat. **Praty-udita,** mfn. rejected, repelled, BhP., Sch.

प्रतिवध् *prati-√vadh* (only aor. *-avadhīt*), to beat back, ward off, MBh.

प्रतिवन्द् *prati-√vand* (only ind. p. *-vandya*), to receive deferentially, Kum.

प्रतिवप् *prati-√2. vap*, P. *-vapati*, to insert (jewels &c.), set or stud with (instr.), Ragh.; to fill up, ĀśvŚr.; to add, TBr. °**vāpa,** m. (cf. *pratī-v°*) admixture of substances to medicines either during or after decoction, Car. **Praty-upta,** mfn. fixed into (loc.), Uttarar.; (ifc.) set with, Daś.

प्रतिवस् *prati-√4. vas*, Ā. *-vaste*, to put on, clothe one's self in (acc.), RV. °**vāsita,** mfn. (fr. Caus.) dressed or clothed in (instr.), MBh.

प्रतिवस् *prati-√5. vas*, P. *-vasati* (ep. also Ā. °*te*), to live, dwell, MBh.; Kāv. &c.: Caus. *-vāsayati*, to cause to dwell, settle, RV.; to lodge, receive as a guest, MBh. °**vasatha,** m. a settlement, village, L. °**vāsita,** mfn. (fr. Caus.) inhabited, Divyâv. °**vāsin,** mfn. neighbouring, a neighbour, MBh.

प्रतिवह् *prati-√vah*, P. *-vahati*, to lead or draw towards, RV.; Hariv.; to oppose, Divyâv.: Caus. *-vāhayati*, to carry along, MBh. °**vahana,** n. leading back, L.; beating back, warding off, L. °**vāha,** m. (cf. *pratī-v°*) N. of a son of Śvaphalka, Hariv. °**vodhavya,** mfn. to be carried home, R.

प्रतिवाश् *prati-√vāś*, Ā. *-vāśyate*, to bellow or cry out against or in return, RV.; TāṇḍBr.; Lāṭy.; Var. °**vāśa,** mfn. to be contradicted or opposed (v. l. °*śya* in *a-prativ°*), PārGṛ.

प्रतिविघात *prati-vi-ghāta*, m. (√*han*) striking back, warding off, defence, MBh.

प्रतिविज्ञा *prati-vi-√jñā*, P. *-jānāti*, to acknowledge gratefully, MBh.

प्रतिविद् *prati-√1. vid*, P. *-vetti*, to perceive, understand, RV.: Caus. *-vedayati*, to make known, report, announce (also with 2 acc.), MBh.; R. &c.; to offer, present, RV.; AV.; MBh. &c. °**vedita,** mfn. (fr. Caus.) apprised or informed of (acc.), R. °**vedin,** mfn. experiencing, knowing, (ifc.), Lalit.

प्रतिविद् *prati-√3. vid*, P. Ā. *-vindati*, °*te*, to find in addition, Br.; (Ā. p. *-vidāna*) to be opposite to (acc.), ŚBr.; to become acquainted with (acc.), MBh. °**vedin,** see *prati-√1. vid*.

प्रतिविधा *prati-vi-√1. dhā*, P. Ā. *-dadhāti*, *-dhatte*, to dispose, arrange, prepare, make ready, R.; to despatch (spies), ib.; to counteract, act against (gen.), Kād.; to contradict a conclusion, Śaṃk. °**vidhātavya,** mfn. to be used or employed, MBh.; to be provided against, Prasannar.; n. (impers.) care should be taken, R. °**vidhāna,** n. arrangement against, prevention, precaution (gen. or comp.), R.; Pañcat.; care or provision for (comp.), Prasannar.; Kull.; a subsidiary or substituted ceremony, W. °**vidhi,** m. a means or remedy against, BhP.; retaliation, MW. °**vidhitsā,** f. (fr. Desid.) desire or intention to counteract, Kathās. °**vidheya,** mfn. to be counteracted or to be done in any special case, Kālid.; to be rejected, Vām.; n. (impers.) measures should be taken, Kād.; Pat. °**vihita,** mfn. counteracted, guarded against, Mudr.

प्रतिविनुद् *prati-vi-√nud*, P. *-nudati*, to get rid of, Divyâv.

प्रतिविपरी *prati-vi-parī* (*pari-√i*), P. *-pary-eti*, to turn back again, KātyŚr. °**viparīta,** mfn. exactly opposite, Car.

प्रतिविबुध् *prati-vi-√budh*, Ā. *-budhyate*, to be awakened, Divyâv.

प्रतिविभज् *prati-vi-√bhaj* (only ind. p. *-bhajya*), to distribute severally, apportion, KātyŚr. °**vibhāga,** m. distribution, apportionment, ib.

प्रतिविरम् *prati-vi-√ram*, P. *-ramati*, to abstain, Divyâv. 2. °**virati,** f. (for 1. see p. 663, col. 2) desisting from (abl.), leaving off, L.

प्रतिविरुद्ध *prati-vi-ruddha*, mfn. (√*rudh*) rebellious, Divyâv.

प्रतिविशिष्ट *prati-vi-śishṭa*, mfn. (√*śish*) more distinguished or peculiar, better or worse, MBh. °**viśesha,** m. peculiarity, singularity, a peculiar circumstance, ib. °**viśeshaṇa,** n. detailed specification, TPrāt., Sch.

प्रतिविश्रब्ध *prati-vi-śrabdha*, mfn. (√*śrambh*) full of confidence or trust, MBh.

प्रतिविसृज् *prati-vi-√sṛij*, P. *-sṛijati*, to send out, despatch, RV.

प्रतिविहा *prati-vi-√3. hā*, P. *-jahāti*, to quit, abandon, MBh.

प्रतिवी *prati-√vī*, P. *-veti*, to receive, accept, RV.

प्रतिवीक्ष् *prati-vīksh* (*vi-√īksh*), only ind. p. *-vīkshya*, to look upon, observe, perceive, R. °**vīkshaṇa,** n. looking upon, returning a look, MW. °**vīkshaṇīya** and °**vīkshya,** see *dush-prativ°*.

प्रतिवीत *prati-vīta*, mfn. (√*vye*) covered, GopBr.; *-tama*, mfn. totally covered, muffled, suppressed, low (as a voice), Vait.

प्रतिवृ *prati-√1. vṛi*, Caus. *-vārayati*, to keep back, ward off, restrain, prevent, prohibit, MBh.; R. &c.; to contradict, refute, R. °**vāra,** m. warding off, resisting (*a-prativ°*), Suśr. 2. °**vāraṇa,** mfn. (for 1. see p. 663, col. 2) keeping or warding off, opposing, preventing, MBh.; n. the act of keeping off &c., ib.; R. (cf. *dush-prativ°*). °**vārita,** mfn. kept off, prohibited, prevented, Mn.; MBh. &c.; n. prohibition, R. °**vārya,** mfn. to be warded off or restrained or prevented (*a-prativ°*), MBh.; R.

प्रतिवॄ *prati-√2. vṛi* (only Ā. aor. *-avṛishata*), to choose, elect, AV.

प्रतिवृज् *prati-√vṛij*, P. *-varjati* &c., to throw against, Kāṭh.

प्रतिवृत् *prati-√vṛit*, Ā. *-vartate*, to accrue to (acc.), Mn. i, 81 (v. l. for *upa-v°*): Caus. *-vartayati*, to fling, hurl, RV. °**vartana,** n. return, reappearance (*a-prativ°*), MBh. °**vartman,** °**vārttā** and °**vṛitta,** see under *prati*.

प्रतिवृष् *prati-√vṛish*, P. *-varshati*, to rain or pour down upon, cover with (instr.), MBh. °**varshaṇa,** n. pouring out or emitting again, Śrīkaṇṭh.

प्रतिवेश *prati-veśa*, °*śin* &c. See p. 663.

प्रतिवेष्ट् *prati-√vesht*, Ā. *-veshṭate*, to shrink back, TS.: Caus. *-veshṭayati*, to strike or drive or turn or bend back, ib., Prāt.

प्रतिवोढव्य *prati-vodhavya*. See under *prati-√vah*, col. 1.

प्रतिव्यध् *prati-√vyadh*, P. *-vidhyati* (ep. also Ā. °*te*), to shoot against, hit, wound, RV. &c. &c.: Pass. *-vidhyate*, to be aimed at or hit, to be touched upon or discussed, AV. °**viddha,** mfn. pierced, wounded, MBh.

प्रतिव्याहार *prati-vyāhāra*, m. an answer, reply, Kāraṇḍ.

प्रतिव्यूह् *prati-√vyūh*, Ā. *-vyūhate* (rarely P. °*ti*), to array one's self against (acc.), draw up (an army) against, MBh. °**vyūḍha,** mfn. drawn out in array against; broad, R. °**vyūha,** m. drawing out an army in opposite battle-array, MBh.; echo, reverberation, Hariv. 3605 (Nilak.; others 'multitude'); N. of a prince, VP. (v. l. °*vyoman*).

प्रतिव्रज् *prati-√vraj*, P. *-vrajati*, to return home, Bhaṭṭ.

प्रतिशंस् *prati-√śaṅs*, P. *-śaṅsati*, to call or shout to, praise, ŚBr. (cf. *á-pratiśaṅsat* and °*śasta*).

प्रतिशक् *prati-√śak* (only pf. *-śekuḥ*), to keep one's ground against, be a match for (acc.), MBh.: Desid. *-śikshati*, to allure, invite, RV.

प्रतिशङ्क् *prati-√śaṅk*, Ā. *-śaṅkate*, to be doubtful or anxious, hesitate, MBh.; to trouble one's self about, care for (acc.), BhP. °**śaṅkanīya,** mfn. to be doubted about or feared, W. °**śaṅkā,** f. (ifc.) doubt, supposition, Kām.; constant fear or doubt, W.

प्रतिशप् *prati-√śap*, P. *-śapati*, to curse in return (with acc. or gen.), R.; BhP. °**śāpa,** m. a curse in return, retorted imprecation, MBh.; Kād.; Pur.

प्रतिशम् *prati-√śam*, Caus. *-śāmayati* (ind. p. *-śāmya* or *-śāmayitvā* or *-śamayya*), to re-establish, restore, put to rights, Vajracch.; Divyâv. °**śama,** m. (ifc.) deliverance from, cessation of, MBh. °**śānta,** mfn. extinguished, allayed; *-kopa*, mfn. one whose anger is past, ib.

प्रतिशरण 1. 2. *prati-śaraṇa*. See p. 663 and *prati-√śṛī*.

प्रतिशासन 2. *prati-śāsana* (for 1. see p. 663, col. 2), n. giving orders, commissioning, sending a servant on a message, L. °**śāsti,** f. id., MW. °**śishṭa,** mfn. sent on a message, despatched, Śiś.; refused, L.; celebrated, famous, W.

प्रतिशिक्ष् *prati-√śiksh*. See *prati-√śak*.

प्रतिशी *prati-√śī* (only pf. *-śiśye* and fut. *-śeshyāmi*), to lie or press against, i. e. urge, importune, MBh. °**śayita,** mfn. pressing, importuning, importuned, Kād.; Hcar.; n. the act of importuning, molestation, Kād. °**śīvan,** mf(*arī*)n. serving as a couch or resting-place, AV.; TS.

प्रतिशीत *prati-śīta* (Pāṇ. vi, 1, 25, Sch.), °**śīna** and °**śīna-vat** (Kāś., ib.), mfn. melted, fluid, dropping. °**śyā,** f., °**śyāya,** m. a cold, catarrh, Suśr.; Car. °**śyāyin,** mfn. having a cold, Suśr.

प्रतिशुच् *prati-√śuc*, P. *-śocati*, to burn towards or against (acc.), MaitrS.

प्रतिशुष् *prati-√śush*, P. *-śushyati*, to be dried up, wither, perish, RV.

प्रतिशॄ *prati-√śṛī*, P. *-śṛiṇāti*, to break off or in pieces, RV.; TS.; TBr. °**śara,** m. breaking, going in pieces (*a-pratiś°*), AitBr. 2. °**śaraṇa,** n. (for 1. see p. 663, col. 2) breaking off, blunting (a point or edge), TBr., Sch.

प्रतिशोभित *prati-śobhita*, mfn. (√*śubh*, Caus.) beautified with (instr.), Hariv. (v. l. for *pari-ś°*).

प्रतिश्रम *prati-śrama*, m. (√*śram*) toil, trouble, Divyâv.

प्रतिश्रय *prati-śraya*, m. (√*śri*) refuge, help, assistance, MBh.; a place of refuge, shelter, asylum, house, dwelling, Mn.; MBh. &c.; a receptacle, recipient (*tvam tasya pratiśrayaḥ*, 'you know all this'), MBh.; a Jaina-monastery, HPariś.; an alms-house, a place where food &c. is given away, L.; a place of sacrifice, L.; an assembly, L. °**śrita**, n. a place of refuge, MBh.

प्रतिश्रु *prati-√śru*, P. *-śriṇoti*, to hear, listen, RV. i, 25, 20 (Ā. 3. sg. *śriṇve*, 'to be heard' or 'audible,' i, 169, 7); to listen, give ear to (gen.), Vajracch.; to assure, agree, promise anything (acc.) to any one (gen. or dat.), RV. &c. &c.: Desid. *-śuśrūshati*, to wish to promise, Pāṇ. i, 3, 59. °**śravá**, mfn. answering, VS. xvi, 34 (Mahīdh. 'echo, reverberation'); m. (ifc. f. *ā*) promise, assurance, R.; Rājat.; MārkP.; °*vânte*, ind. after the expiration of a promise i.e. the lapse of a promised period, R. °**śravaṇa**, n. hearkening to, listening (cf. below); answering, Gaut.; assenting to, agreeing, promising, Mn. ii, 195 (others 'hearkening' or 'answering'); MBh. (*-pūrva*, mfn. promised, assured); Pāṇ. viii, 2, 99 (Kāś. 'hearkening'); (prob.) a partic. part of the ear, ShaḍvBr. °**śravas**, m. N. of a son of Bhīma-sena, MBh. °**śrut**, f. an echo, resonance, Ragh.; a promise, assurance, Siṇhâs. °**śruta**, mfn. heard, R.; promised (also in marriage), assented, agreed, accepted (°*te*, 'the promise having been made'), GṛS.; Yājñ.; MBh. &c.; echoing, resounding, R.; m. N. of a son of Ānaka-dundubhi, BhP.; n. a promise, engagement (see above). °**śruti**, f. an answer, Hariv.; Śatr.; a promise, assent, Vait.; = next, Śiś. °**śrutkā**, f. an echo, reverberation, VS.; ChUp. °**śrotas**, w.r. for °*srotas*. °**śrotṛi**, mfn. one who promises or assents, MW.

प्रतिश्वस् *prati-√śvas* (only pr. p. *-śvasat*), to breathe fiercely or with a snorting sound towards or against, RV.

प्रतिषञ्ज् *prati-shañj* (√*sañj*), P. Ā. *-shajati*, °*te*, to attach something to (loc.; Ā. 'to one's self'), TS.; Lāṭy. (cf. *prati-saṅgin*).

प्रतिषिच् *prati-shic* (√*sic*), P. *-shiñcati*, to pour upon, mix together, TS.; ŚrS.; (*-siñcati*), to besprinkle or moisten in return, BhP. °**shicya**, mfn. to be besprinkled or moistened, TBr. °**sheka**, m. besprinkling, moistening, TBr., Sch. °**shekyà**, mfn. accompanied by the act of bespr° or m°, MaitrS.

प्रतिषिध् *prati-shidh* (√2. *sidh*), P. *-shedhati* (ep. also Ā. °*te*), to drive away, RV.; to keep back, ward off, prevent, restrain from (abl.), Mn.; MBh. &c.; to forbid, prohibit, disallow, Nir.; MBh.; R. &c.: Caus. *-shedhayati*, to keep back, prevent, restrain, ĀśvGṛ.; MBh. &c.; to prohibit, interdict, Āpast.; MBh.; Hariv.; to deny, Sarvad. °**shiddha**, mfn. driven back, kept off, prevented, omitted, MBh.; Kāv. &c.; forbidden, prohibited, disallowed, refused, denied, Mn.; MBh. &c.; *-vat*, mfn. one who has forbidden or interdicted something, Rājat.; *-vāma*, mfn. refractory when driven back, Śak. vi, 1/8 (v.l.); *-sevana*, n. doing what is prohibited, W.; *-sevin*, mfn. following or doing what is forbidden, ib. °**sheddhavya**, mfn. to be warded off or kept back or prohibited or forbidden, MBh.; R.; to be denied, Nyāyas. °**sheddhṛi**, mfn. one who wards off or keeps back &c., MBh.; R.; resisting (with acc.), BhP. °**shedha**, m. keeping back, warding off, prevention, repulsion (of a disease), Mn.; MBh.; Suśr.; prohibition, refusal, denial, ŚrS.; Nir.; Kālid.; contradiction, exception, W.; (in (gram.) negation, a negative particle, VPrāt.; Pāṇ.; Vām.; (in rhet.) enforcing or reminding of a prohibition, Kuval.; (in dram.) an obstacle to obtaining the desired object, Sāh.; °*dhâkshara*, n. 'words of denial,' a negative answer, Śak. iii, 22 (v.l.); °*dhâtmaka*, mfn. having a n° form or character, Yājñ., Sch.; °*dhâpavāda*, m. annulment of a prohibition, Kāś. on Pāṇ. ii, 3, 68; °*dhârthīya*, mfn. having the meaning of a negation, Nir.; °*dhôkti*, f. expression of denial or refusal, Kāvyâd.; °*dhôpamā*, f. a comparison expressed in a negative form, ib. °**shedhaka**, mf(*ikā*)n. keeping off, prohibiting, preventive, MBh.; denying, negative, TPrāt. °**shedhana**, mfn. keeping or warding off, MBh.; n. the act of k° or w° off, restraining from (abl.), prevention, repulsion (of a disease), Mn.; MBh.; Suśr.; rejection, refutation, Suśr. °**shedhanīya**, mfn. to be kept back or restrained or prevented, Ragh.; Pañcat. °**shedhayitṛi**, mfn. denying, negative, Śaṃk. °**shedhya**, mfn. to be prevented or rejected or prohibited, Pat.; to be denied or negatived, Nyāyas., Sch.

प्रतिषिव् *prati-shiv* (√*siv*), P. *-shīvyati*, to sew on, Kāṭh. °**shevaṇa**, n. sewing on, ĀpŚr., Sch.

प्रतिष्कभ् *prati-shkabh* (√*skabh*), only inf. *-shkábhe*, for leaning or pressing one's self against, RV. i, 39, 2.

प्रतिष्कश *prati-sh-kaśa*, m. (according to Pāṇ. vi, 1, 152 fr. √*kaś*) a messenger or guide or spy, L.; a whip or leather thong, W. (cf. *kaśā*). °**shka**, m. (abridged fr. prec.) a messenger or spy, L. °**shkasha**, m. a leather thong, L. °**shkasa**, m. = °*shka*, L.

प्रतिष्कु *prati-shku* (√*sku*), only impf. *pratyaskunot*, to cover in return (with arrows &c.), Bhaṭṭ. °**shkuta**, see *á-prati-shkuta*.

प्रतिष्टब्ध *prati-shṭabdha*, mfn. (√*stambh*) obstructed, impeded, stopped, withstood, W. °**shṭambha**, m. obstruction, impediment, hindrance, Ragh. °**shṭambhin**, mfn. impeding (ifc.), R. (cf. *prati-stambh*).

प्रतिष्टुति *práti-shṭuti*, f. (√*stu*) praise or a song of praise, RV.; TāṇḍBr. °**shṭotṛi**, m. one who rivals in praising, ĀśvŚr.

प्रतिष्टुभ् *prati-shṭubh* (√*stubh*), P. *-shṭobhati*, to shout in return, answer with a shout, RV.

प्रतिष्ठा *prati-shṭhā* (√*sthā*), P. Ā. *-tishṭhati*, °*te*, to stand, stay, abide, dwell, RV. &c. &c.; to stand still, set (as the sun), cease, MBh.; BhP.; to stand firm, be based or rest on (loc.), be established, thrive, prosper, RV. &c. &c.; to depend or rely on (loc.), Vajracch.; to withstand, resist (acc.), MBh.; Hariv.; to spread or extend over (acc.), MBh.: Caus. *-shṭhāpayati*, to put down, place upon, introduce into (loc.), Br.; GṛŚrS.; to set up, erect (as an image), Ratnâv.; to bring or lead into (loc.), MBh.; to establish in, appoint to (loc.), ib.; R. &c.; to transfer or offer or present to, bestow or confer upon (dat. or loc.), ĀśvGṛ.; Mn.; MBh. &c.; to fix, found, prop, support, maintain, TS.; Br.; MBh.; Hariv.; to hold against or opposite, R. °**shṭhá**, mf(*ā*)n. standing firmly, steadfast, ŚBr.; MBh.; resisting, Kauś.; (ifc.) ending with, leading to, Jātak.; famous, W.; m. N. of the father of Su-pārśva (who was 7th Arhat of present Avasarpiṇi), L.; (*ā*), f., see next; n. point of support, centre or base of anything, RV. x, 73, 6 (*pratishṭhā hṛidyā jaghantha*, 'thou hast stricken to the quick;' *pratishṭhā* may also be acc. pl. of next).

Prati-shṭhā́, f. (ifc. f. *ā*) standing still, resting, remaining, steadfastness, stability, perseverance in (comp.), VS. &c. &c.; a standpoint, resting-place, ground, base, foundation, prop, stay, support, RV. &c. &c.; a receptacle, homestead, dwelling, house, AV. &c. &c. (ifc. abiding or dwelling in, Ragh.; Pur.); a pedestal, the foot (of men or animals), AV.; Br.; ŚāṅkhŚr.; limit, boundary, W.; state of rest, quiet, tranquillity, comfort, ease, MBh.; Kāv.; setting up (as of an idol &c., RTL. 70); pre-eminence, superiority, high rank or position, fame, celebrity, Kāv.; Kathās.; Rājat.; establishment on or accession to (the throne &c.), Hariv.; Śak.; Var.; Rājat.; the performance of any ceremony or of any solemn act, consecration or dedication (of a monument or of an idol or of a temple &c.; cf. *prâṇa-pr°*), settling or endowment of a daughter, completion of a vow, any ceremony for obtaining supernatural and magical powers, Var.; Kathās.; Rājat.; Pur.; a mystical N. of the letter *ā*, L.; N. of one of the Mātṛis attending on Skanda, MBh.; of sev. metres, RPrāt.; (with *Prajā-pateḥ*) N. of a Sāman, ĀrshBr.; = *hrasva*, Naigh. iii, 2; = *yoga-siddhi* or *-nishpatti*, L.; *-kamalâkara*, m., *-kalpalatā*, f., *-kalpâdi*, m. pl. N. of wks.; *-kāma* (°*shṭhā́-*), mfn. desirous of a firm basis or a fixed abode or a high position, TS.; TāṇḍBr.; GṛŚrS.; BhP.; *-kaumudī*, f., *-kaustubha*, m. or n., *-cintāmaṇi*, m., *-tattva*, n., *-tantra*, n., *-tilaka*, n. N. of wks.; *-tva*, n. the being a basis or foundation, Śaṃk.; *-darpaṇa*, m., *-darśa*, m., *-dīdhiti*, f., *-dyota*, m., *-nirṇaya*, m. N. of wks.; *-°nvita* (°*shṭhânv°*), mfn. possessed of fame, celebrated, MW.; *-paddhati*, f., *-mayūkha*, m., *-ratna*, n., *-rahasya*, n., *-lakshaṇa*, n. N. of wks.; *-vat*, mfn. having a foundation or support, TUp.; *-vidhi*, m., *-viveka*, m., *-saṃgraha*, m., *-samuccaya*, m., *-sāra*, m., *-sāra-saṃgraha*, m., *-hemâdri*, m., °*shṭhôddyota*, m. N. of wks. °**shṭhātṛi**, m. N. of a partic. priest (= *prati-prasthātṛi*), Hariv. °**shṭhāna**, n. a firm standing-place, ground, foundation, PārGṛ.; MBh. &c.; a pedestal, foot, TBr.; MBh.; R.; the foundation (others 'consecration') of a city, SkandaP.; N. of a town at the confluence of the Gaṅgā and Yamunā (on the left bank of the G° opposite to Allāhābad, the capital of the early kings of the lunar dynasty), MBh.; Hariv.; Kathās. &c. (IW. 511, n. 1); m. N. of a locality on the Go-dāvarī, Kathās.; (du.) of the constellation Proshṭha-pada, L. °**shṭhāpana**, n. fixing, placing, locating; (esp.) the erection or consecration of the image of a deity, Var. (*-paddhati*, f. N. of wk.); establishment, corroboration, Sarvad.; (*ā*), f. counter-assertion, statement of an antithesis, Car. °**shṭhâpam**, ind. p. (of Caus.) placing, locating, ŚBr.; (as inf.) for founding or establishing, TāṇḍBr. °**shṭhāpayitavya**, mfn. to be placed or fixed or established, Kāraṇḍ. (w. r. °*sthâp°*). °**shṭhāpayitṛi**, m. a founder, establisher, VPrāt. °**shṭhāpita**, mfn. set up, fixed, erected, Kathās. °**shṭhā́pya**, mfn. to be placed or located or fixed, TS.; AitBr.; to be consigned or transferred or entrusted to (loc.), MBh. °**shṭhí**, f. resistance, RV. vi, 18, 12 (Sāy. '*āśraya*'). °**shṭhikā**, f. a basis, foundation, Hcat. °**shṭhita** (*práti-*), mfn. standing, stationed, placed, situated in or on (loc. or comp.), MBh.; R. &c.; abiding or contained in (loc.), ŚBr. &c. &c.; fixed, firm, rooted, founded, resting or dependent on (loc. or comp.), AV. &c. &c.; established, proved, Mn. viii, 164; ordained for, applicable to (loc.), ib., 226; secure, thriving, well off, ChUp.; Hariv. &c.; familiar or conversant with (loc.), MBh.; transferred to (loc.), Hariv.; undertaken, Pañcat. (B. *anu-shṭhita*); ascended into, having reached (comp.), Śak. vii, 8/9 (v.l.); complete, finished, W.; consecrated, ib.; endowed, portioned, ib.; established in life, married, ib.; prized, valued, ib.; famous, celebrated, ib.; m. N. of Vishṇu, A.; *-pada*, mfn. containing verses of a fixed or constant number of syllables, AitBr.; *-mātra*, mfn. having just got a firm footing, Mṛicch.; *-yaśas*, mfn. one whose renown is well founded, Ratnâv. (*su-pr°*); *-saṃtāna*, mfn. one who has progeny or offspring secured, MW. °**shṭhiti** (*práti-*), f. standing firmly, a firm stand or footing, VS.; Br.

प्रतिष्ठासु *pra-tishṭhāsu*, mfn. (√*sthā*, Desid.) wishing to start, Śiś.; wishing to stay or remain, W.

प्रतिष्ठिव् *prati-√shṭhiv*, P. *-shṭhīvati*, to spit upon (acc.), AV.

प्रतिष्णा *prati-shṇā* and °*shṇikā*, f. (√*snā*), g. *sushāmâdi*, Kāś. °**shṇāta** (with *sūtra*) and °**snāta**, mfn., Pāṇ. viii, 3, 90, Kāś.

प्रतिष्वद् *prati-shvad* (√*svad*), Caus. *-shvadayati*, to taste, relish, Kām., Sch.

प्रतिसंयत् *prati-sam-√yat*, Ā. *-yatate*, to fight against, ŚBr. °**saṃyatta**, mfn. completely prepared or armed, MBh.

प्रतिसंयात *prati-saṃ-yāta*, mfn. (√*yā*) going against, assailing (with acc.), MBh.

प्रतिसंयुक्त *prati-saṃ-yukta*, mfn. (√*yuj*) bound or attached to something else, MBh. (B.)

प्रतिसंयुध् *prati-saṃ-√yudh* (only pf. *-yuyudhuḥ*), to resist an attack together, BhP. °**saṃyoddhṛi**, m. an adversary in war, MBh.

प्रतिसंरभ् *prati-saṃ-√rabh*, Ā. *-rabhate*, to seize, take hold of, MBh. vii, 3169 (B. *-saṃ-carate*). °**saṃrabdha**, mfn. (pl.) holding one another by the hands, MBh.; excited, furious, ib.; R.

प्रतिसंरुद्ध *prati-saṃ-ruddha*, mfn. (√*rudh*) contracted into itself, shrunk, BhP.

प्रतिसंलयन *prati-saṃ-layana*, n. (√*lī*) retirement into a lonely place, privacy, Lalit.; Divyâv.; complete absorption, SaddhP. °**saṃlīna**, mfn. retired, in privacy, Divyâv.; complete retirement for the sake of meditation, Lalit.

प्रतिसंवद् *prati-saṃ-√vad*, Ā. *-vadate*, to agree with any one (acc.), AitBr.

प्रतिसंविद् *prati-saṃ-√1. vid*, Caus. *-vedayati*, to recognize (?), Divyâv. (Ā. p. *-vedayamāna*, 'feeling,' ib.) °**saṃvid**, f. analytical science (4 with Buddhists), Dharmas. 51; Lalit.; °*vit-prâpta*, m. N. of a Bodhi-sattva, ib.; °*vin-niścayâvatārā*, f. N. of a partic. Dhāraṇī, L. °**saṃvedaka**, mfn. giving detailed information, L. °**saṃvedana**, n. experiment, enjoyment, Nyāyas., Sch. °**saṃvedin**, mfn. feeling, experiencing, being conscious of anything, ib.

प्रतिसंविधान *prati-saṃ-vi-dhāna*, n. (√1. *dhā*) a counter action, stroke in return, Mcar.

प्रतिसंवेष्ट् *prati-saṃ-√vesht*, Ā. *-veshṭate*, to shrivel, shrink up, contract, MBh.

प्रतिसंश्रि *prati-saṃ-√śri*, P. *-śrayati*, to seek refuge or protection in reply, MBh.

प्रतिसंश्रु *prati-saṃ-√śru* (only ind. p. *-śrutya*), to promise, MBh.

प्रतिसंसृज् *prati-saṃ-√sṛij*, P. *-sṛijati*, to mingle with (instr.), Suśr. °**saṃsarga**, m. = *pratisarga*, VāyuP. °**saṃsṛishṭa**, mfn. mingled with (instr.), ib.; *-bhakta*, mfn. one who is temperate in eating, ib.

प्रतिसंस्कृ *prati-saṃ-skṛi* (√*skṛi* = *kṛi*; only Pot. *-kuryāt*), to repair, restore, Mn. ix, 279. °**saṃskāra**, m. restoration (°*ram* √*kṛi*, to restore), Kāraṇḍ. °**saṃskāraṇā**, f. id., L. °**saṃskṛita**, mfn. joined or united with (comp.), Suśr.

प्रतिसंस्तम्भ् *prati-saṃ-√stambh* (only ind. p. *-stabhya*), to strengthen, encourage, MārkP.

प्रतिसंस्तर *prati-saṃ-stara*, n. (√*stṛi*) friendly reception, L.

प्रतिसंस्थान *prati-saṃ-sthāna*, n. (√*sthā*) settling in, entering into (comp.), Lalit.

प्रतिसंस्मृ *prati-saṃ-√smṛi*, P. *-smarati*, to remember, R.

प्रतिसंहित *prati-saṃhita*. See col. 2.

प्रतिसंहृ *prati-saṃ-√hṛi*, P. Ā. *-harati*, °*te*, to draw together, contract (with *ātmānam*, 'one's self' i. e. to shrink, return to its usual bed, said of the sea), Hariv.; to draw or keep back, withdraw (as a weapon, the eye &c.), MBh.; Kāv.; to take away, put off, Āpast.; to absorb, annihilate, destroy, MBh.; Pur.; Jātak.; to check, stop, repress, MBh.; R. &c.; to change, MW.: Caus. *-hārayati*, to retract, R. °**saṃharaṇīya**, n. (sc. *karman*) a partic. punishment, L. °**saṃhāra**, m. drawing in, withdrawing, MBh.; giving up, resigning, ib.; keeping away, abstention from (abl.), ib.; compression, diminution, W.; comprehension, ib. °**saṃhṛita**, mfn. kept back, checked, restrained, R.; comprehended, included, W.; compressed, reduced in bulk, ib. °**saṃjihīrshu**, mfn. (fr. Desid.) wishing to withdraw or to be freed from (abl.), BhP.

प्रतिसंहृष् *prati-saṃ-√hṛish*, P. *-harshati*, to rejoice again, be glad, MBh. °**saṃhṛishṭa**, mfn. glad, merry, R.

प्रतिसंकाश *prati-saṃ-kāśa*, m. (√*kāś*) a similar appearance, resemblance, MBh.

प्रतिसंक्रम् *prati-saṃ-√kram*, Ā. *-kramate*, to go back again, come to an end, BhP.: Caus. *-krāmayati*, to cause to go back or return, ib. °**saṃkrama**, m. re-absorption, dissolution (m.c. also °*krāma*), ib.; (ifc. f. *ā*) impression, Sarvad.

प्रतिसंक्रुद्ध *prati-saṃ-kruddha*, mfn. (√*krudh*) angry with, wroth against (acc.), MBh.: R.

प्रतिसंख्या *prati-saṃ-√khyā* (only ind. p. *-khyāya*), to count or reckon up, number, ŚBr.; KātyŚr. °**saṃkhyā**, f. consciousness; *-nirodha*, m. (with Buddh.) the conscious annihilation of an object (?), Dharmas. 32 (cf. *a-pr°-n°*). °**saṃkhyāna**, n. the tranquil consideration of a matter, Jātak.

प्रतिसङ्गिन् *prati-saṅgin*, mfn. (√*sañj*) cleaving or clinging to, adhering; (*a-pr°*) not meeting with any obstacle, irresistible, Hariv.

प्रतिसंग्रह् *prati-saṃ-√grah*, P. Ā. *-gṛihṇāti*, °*ṇīte*, to receive, accept, MBh.; R.; to meet with, find, MBh.

प्रतिसच् *prati-√sac*, Ā. *-sacate*, to pursue with vengeance, ŚBr.

प्रतिसंचर् *prati-saṃ-√car*, P. *-carati*, to meet, come together, MBh. °**saṃcara**, m. going or moving backwards (*a-pr°*), Suśr.; re-absorption or resolution (back again into Prakṛiti), Sāṃk.; MārkP.; that into which anything is re-absorbed or resolved, MBh.; a place of resort, haunt, ib.

प्रतिसंजात *prati-saṃ-jāta*, mfn. (√*jan*) born, sprung up, arisen, R.

प्रतिसंज्ञा *prati-saṃ-√jñā*, Ā. *-jānīte*, to be kindly disposed, ŚBr.

प्रतिसद् *prati-√sad*, P. *-sīdati* (Pāṇ. viii, 3, 66), to start back, abhor, MBh.

प्रतिसंदिश् *prati-saṃ-√diś*, P. *-diśati*, to give a person (acc. or *haste* with gen.) a message or commission in return, R.; Kād.; to send back a message to (gen.), MBh.; to order, command, ib. °**saṃdeśa**, m. a message in return, answer to a m°, R.; Mṛicch.; Kathās. °**saṃdeshṭavya**, mfn. (an answer) to be given in reply to a m°, Kād.

प्रतिसंधा *prati-saṃ-√1. dhā*, P. Ā. *-dadhāti*, *-dhatte*, (P.) to put together again, re-arrange, ŚBr.; (Ā.) to put on, adjust (an arrow), MBh.; (Ā.) to return, reply, Hariv.; BhP.; (P. Ā.) to remember, recollect, Nyāyas.; (Ā.) to comprehend, understand, Prab. vi, $\frac{3}{4}$. °**saṃhita**, mfn. aimed at, directed against, MBh. °**saṃdhātṛi**, m. one who recollects or remembers, Nyāyas. °**saṃdhāna**, n. putting together again, joining together, MBh.; Kāv. &c.; a juncture, the period of transition between two ages, VāyuP.; memory, recollection, Nyāyas., Sch.; praise, panegyric, L.; self-command, suppression of feeling for a time, W.; a remedy, MW. °**saṃdhi**, m. reunion, MBh.; re-entry into (comp.) or into the womb, L.; re-birth, Divyâv.; the period of transition between two ages, VāyuP.; resistance, adverseness (of fate), MBh.; *-jñāna*, n. recognition, Nyāyas., Sch. °**saṃdhita**, mfn. (cf. *saṃdhaya*) fastened, strengthened, confirmed, BhP. °**saṃdheya**, mfn. to be opposed (*a-pr°*, 'irresistible'), MBh. °**sāṃdhānika**, m. (fr. °*saṃdhāna*) a bard, panegyrist, L.

प्रतिसमय्य *prati-samayya*, ind. having arranged, Divyâv. (prob. w. r. for *-śamayya*; see *prati-√śam*).

प्रतिसमस् *prati-sam-√2. as*, P. *-asyati* (ind. p. *-āsam*), to put back again to its place, ĀpŚr.

प्रतिसमादिश् *prati-sam-ā-√diś*, P. *-diśati*, to answer, reply, Daś.; to order, command, R. °**samādishṭa**, mfn. bidden, directed, ordered, commanded, R.; MārkP.

प्रतिसमाधा *prati-sam-ā-√1. dhā*, P. *-dadhāti*, to put back again, replace, re-arrange, restore, Daś.; to redress, correct (an error), Śaṃk. °**samādhāna**, n. collecting one's self again, composure, Kād.; cure, remedy, W. °**samāhita**, mfn. fitted to the bowstring (as an arrow), MBh.

प्रतिसमापन *prati-sam-āpana*, n. (√*āp*) the going against, attacking (with gen.), R.

प्रतिसमाश्रित *prati-sam-ā-śrita*, mfn. (√*śri*) depending on (acc.), MBh.

प्रतिसमास् *prati-sam-√ās*, Ā. *-āste*, to be a match for, cope with, resist (acc.), MBh.; R. °**samāsana**, n. the being a match for, withstanding, resisting (with gen.), MBh. °**samāsita**, mfn. equalled, opposed, fought, ib.

प्रतिसमिन्ध् *prati-sam-√indh*, Ā. *-inddhe*, to kindle again, rekindle, ŚBr.

प्रतिसमीक्ष् *prati-sam-√īksh*, Ā. *-īkshate*, to hold out, persevere (Sch. = √*jīv*), BhP. °**samīkshaṇa**, n. looking at again, returning a glance, ib.

प्रतिसम्बुद्ध *prati-sam-buddha*, mfn. (√*budh*) restored to consciousness, recovered, MBh.

प्रतिसम्भू *prati-sam-√bhū*, P. *-bhavati*, to apply or give one's self to (acc.), MBh.

प्रतिसम्मुद् *prati-sam-√mud*, Caus. *-modayati*, to give friendly greeting, Divyâv. °**sammodana**, n. greeting, salutation (also *ā*, f.); *-kathā*, f. friendly address as a salutation, Jātak.

प्रतिसह् *prati-√sah*, Ā. *-sahate*, to be a match for, overcome (acc.), R.

प्रतिसुप्त *prati-supta*, mfn. (√*svap*) fallen asleep, sleeping, MBh.

प्रतिसृ *prati-√sṛi*, P. *-sarati* (ind. p. *-sāram*, ŚāṅkhBr.), to go against, rush upon, attack, assail (acc.), Hariv.; to return, go home, BhP.; to go round or from place to place (not only on the main road), TS.: Caus. *-sārayati*, to cause to go back, Car.; to put back again, restore to its place, Kālid.; to spread over, tip or touch with (instr.), Suśr.; to put asunder, sever, separate, SaddhP.: Pass. to void or emit per anum (?), Suśr. °**sará**, m. (ifc. f. *ā*) a cord or ribbon used as an amulet worn round the neck or wrist at nuptials &c., AV. &c. &c. (also *ā*, f. [Var.; Dharmas. 5]; and n. [g. *ardharcâdi*]); a bracelet, Kir.; a line returning into itself, circle, ŚBr.; assailing, an attack (*a-pr°*), Hariv.; a wreath, garland, L.; a follower, servant, L.; the rear of an army, L.; dressing or anointing a wound, L.; day-break, L.; *-bandha*, m. a partic. nuptial ceremony, ĀpGṛ., Sch.; pl. N. of partic. magical verses or formulas protecting from demons, ŚBr.; m. n. a watch, guard, L.; (*ā*), f. (cf. above) a female servant, L.; (with Buddh.) one of the 5 protectors, Dharmas. 5. °**saraṇa**, mfn. leaning or resting upon (ifc.; *-tā*, f.), Lalit.; n. streaming back (of rivers), Car.; leaning or resting on (comp.), L. °**sarya**, mfn. present in an amulet or at an incantation, VS. (Mahīdh.) °**sāraṇa**, n. (fr. Caus.) dressing and anointing the edges of a wound (or an instrument for doing so), Suśr.; N. of a partic. process to which minerals (esp. quicksilver) are subjected, Cat. °**sāraṇīya**, mfn. to be dressed or anointed (as a wound), Car.; to be applied for dressing a wound, Suśr. °**sārita**, mfn. (fr. Caus.) repelled, removed, Vikr.; dressed (as a wound), Suśr. °**sārin**, mfn. going round or from one to the other, MBh. °**sṛita**, mfn. met, encountered, pushed back, removed, Suśr.

प्रतिसृज् *prati-√sṛij*, P. *-sṛijati*, to hurl or utter in reply (a curse), BhP.; to send away, despatch, Śak. iv, $\frac{2}{2}\frac{1}{2}$ (v. l.) °**sarga**, m. secondary or continued creation out of primitive matter, Pur.; dissolution, destruction, ib.; the portion of a Purāṇa which treats of the destruction and renovation of the world, IW. 511; 517. °**sṛishṭa**, mfn. (v. l. °*śishṭa*, only L.) despatched, despised, celebrated, given.

प्रतिसृप् *prati-√sṛip*, P. *-sarpati*, to creep back, ChUp.; to creep into, enter, MBh.

प्रतिसेव् *prati-√sev*, Ā. *-sevate*, to pursue, follow (pleasure), Divyâv.; to be kind towards (acc.), serve, honour (= *prati-√jush*), Sāy. on RV. iii, 33, 8.

प्रतिस्कृ *prati-s-√kṛi*, P. *-kirati* (pf. *-caskare*), to hurt, injure, to tear to pieces, Śiś. i, 47; Pāṇ. vi, 1, 141. °**s-kīrṇa**, n. the being hurt or injured, Pāṇ. ib., Sch. (cf. *prati-√kṛī*).

प्रतिस्खलित *prati-skhalita*, mfn. (√*skhal*) warded off, Śiś. (= *prati-shkuta*, Nir. vi, 16).

प्रतिस्तम्भ् *prati-√stambh*, P. Ā. *-stabhnāti*, *-stabhate*, to lean or press (Ā. 'one's self') against, Hariv.; Pañcat. °**stabdha**, mfn. leaned against, pressed, MBh.; stopped, checked, Bhaṭṭ.; obstructed, constipated, Suśr. (cf. *prati-shṭabdha*).

प्रतिस्नात *prati-snāta*, mfn. (√*snā*) bathed, washed, Pāṇ. viii, 3, 90, Kāś. (cf. *prati-shṇāta*).

प्रतिस्पन्दन *prati-spandana*, n. (√*spand*) throbbing, vibration, W.

प्रतिस्पर्ध् *prati-spardh*, Ā. *-spardhate*, to emulate, compete, rival, BhP. °**spardhā**, f. emulation, rivalry, L. °**spardhin**, mfn. emulous, coping with (gen.), a rival, MBh.; Rājat.; Kāraṇḍ.; (ifc.) resembling, like, Kāvyâd.

प्रतिस्पश *prati-spaśá* (TS.), *-spāśana* (AV.), mfn. (√*spaś*) spying, watching, lying in wait.

प्रतिस्फुर् *prati-√sphur*, P. *-sphurati*, to push away, remove, RV.

प्रतिस्मृ *prati-√smṛi*, P. Ā. *-smarati*, °*te*, to remember, recollect (acc.), RV.; MBh.; Hariv.: Caus. *-smārayati*, to remind, MBh. °**smṛiti**, f. 'recollection,' N. of a partic. kind of magic, MBh.

प्रतिस्वन् *prati-√svan*, P. *-svanati*, to resound, MBh.: Caus. *-svānayati*, to make resound, BhP. °**svana**, m. (also pl.) echo, reverberation, Vcar.; BhP.

प्रतिस्वर *prati-svara*, m. (√*svar*) a reverberated sound, echo, MBh.; Ragh.; a focus, Nir. vii, 23.

प्रतिहन् *prati-√han*, P. *-hanti* (ep. also Ā. pf. *-jaghne*), to beat against (gen.), TāṇḍBr.; to attack, assail, MBh.; to strike down, ib.; to crush, break, RV.; to put on a spit, ib. i, 32, 12; to strike in return, strike back, ward off, remove, dispel, check, prevent, frustrate, MBh.; Kāv. &c.; (with *ājñām*), to disregard a command, Śiś.: Pass. *-hanyate*, to be beaten back &c., MBh.; Kāv. &c.; to be kept away from or deprived of (abl.), Śaṃk.: Caus. *-ghātayati*, see under *prati-gha*. °**hata**, mfn. struck or striking against, R.; Śak.; Rājat.; repelled, warded off, checked, impeded, obstructed, prevented, omitted, MBh.; Kāv. &c.; dazzled (as eyes, i.e. impeded in their functions), BhP.; dulled, blunted (as teeth by acids, = *hṛishita*), L. (cf. Pat. on Pāṇ. vii, 2, 29); hostile (cf. below); disappointed, L.; hated, disliked, L.; tied, bound, L.; sent, despatched, L. (prob. w. r. for *pra-hita*); *-dhī*, mfn. hostile-minded, having hostile intentions, Bhartṛ.; *-mati*, mfn. id., W.; *-raya*, mfn. whose current is impeded, Megh. °**hati**, f. a stroke, blow, Bālar.; beating back, recoil, rebound, Śiś.; disappointment, W. °**hatya**, ind. in inverse direction, Kauś. °**hanana**, n. impeding, suppressing, Yogas., Sch.; striking again, returning a blow, W. °**hantavya**, mfn. to be opposed or resisted, MBh.; Hariv. °**hantṛi**, m. one who wards off, preventer, Ragh. (v. l. °*hartṛi*).

प्रतिहर्य् *prati-√hary*, P. Ā. *-háryati*, °*te*, to desire, love, accept gladly, long for, RV.; AV.; to despise, reject, AV.

प्रतिहा *prati-√3. hā*, P. *-jahāti*, to leave unheeded, neglect, Hariv.: Pass. *-hīyate*, to stay behind (abl.), be defeated, MBh. °**hāna** (?), cf. next.

Pratihāna-kūṭa, m. a partic. Samādhi, Kāraṇḍ. (prob. w. r. for *pratihāra-k°*).

प्रतिहास *prati-hāsa*, m. (√*has*) returning a laugh, laughing with or at, W.; fragrant oleander, Nerium Odorum, L.

प्रतिहिंसा *prati-hiṅsā*, f. (√*hiṅs*) retaliation, revenge, W. °**hiṅsita**, mfn. injured in return; n. = prec., Pañcat.

प्रतिहित *prati-hita* &c. See *prati-√dhā*.

प्रतिहु *prati-√hu*, P. *-juhoti*, to offer a supplementary sacrifice, Gobh. °**hotavya**, mfn. to be offered as a suppl° s°, ib., Sch. °**homa**, m. a supplementary sacrifice, Jaim.; Nyāyam.

प्रतिहृ *prati-√hṛi*, P. Ā. *-harati*, °*te* (ind. p. *pratī-hāram*, Kauś.; inf. *prati-hartave*, BhP.), to throw back, AV.; to strike or pound, Kauś.; to keep shut, close by pressure (an udder), TāṇḍBr.; to bring back, Lāṭy.; to deliver, offer, present, BhP.; to procure, ib.; (Ā.) to take i.e. eat, ChUp.; to join in the Sāman hymns as Pratihartṛi (see below), Lāṭy.: Caus. *-hārayati*, to have one's self announced to (gen.), Jātakam.: Desid. *-jihīrshati*, to wish to requite or revenge, MBh. (cf. *prati-jihīrshu*).

Prati-háraṇa, n. throwing back, repelling, rejecting, AV.; avoiding, shunning, L. °**hartṛí**, m. (cf. *pratī-h°*) one who draws back or absorbs, a destroyer, MBh.; one who keeps or wards off, an averter, Ragh.; N. of one of the 16 priests (the assistant of the Udgātṛi), Br.; ŚrS. &c.; N. of a king (son of Pratihāra or of Pratīha), Pur.

Prati-hāra, m. striking against, touch, contact (esp. of the tongue with the teeth in the pronunciation of the dentals), RPrāt.; shutting, closing, stopping (*a-pr°*), TāṇḍBr.; N. of partic. syllables in the Sāman hymns (with which the Pratihartṛi begins to join in singing, generally at the beginning of the last Pada of a stanza; also *pratī-h°*, AV.; ŚāṅkhBr.), Br.; ŚrS. &c.; N. of a partic. magical formula spoken over weapons, R. (v. l. °*ra-tara*); (that which keeps back), a door, gate (also *pratī-h°*, L.; cf. comp. below); a door-keeper, porter, Hariv.; Kāv.; Pur. &c. (also *pratī-h°*; du. two d°-k°s i.e. two statues at the entrance of a temple, VarBṛS.; *ī*, f. a female d°-k°, portress, Priyad.); a juggler, L.; juggling, trick, disguise, L.; *-goptrī*, f. a female door-keeper, Vcar.; *-tara*, m., see above; *-pa*, m. a door-keeper, BhP.; *-bhūmi*, f. 'd°-place,' a threshold, Kum.; the office of a porter or a portress, Ragh.; *-rakshī*, f. = *-goptrī*, Vcar.; *-vat*, mfn. containing the P° syllables (above), Lāṭy.; *-sūtra*, n. N. of wk. °**hāraka**, m. a juggler, L. °**hārāya**, Nom. to act as door-keeper (°*yitam*, impers.), Prasannar. °**hārya**, mfn. to be pushed back or repelled, resistible, R. (cf. *a-pr°*); n. jugglery, L.; N. of an Avadāna.

Prati-hṛita, mfn. held back, ŚBr.; fastened, KātyŚr.

प्रतिहृष् *prati-√hṛish*, Ā. *-hṛishyate*, to show joy in return for anything, MBh.: Caus. *-harshayati*, to gladden, rejoice, ib. °**harsha**, m. expression of joy, Dhātup. °**harshaṇa**, mfn. (fr. Caus.) causing joy in return, R.

प्रतिहेष् *prati-√hesh*, Ā. *-heshate*, to neigh towards (acc.), Var.

प्रतिह्रास *prati-hrāsa*, m. (√*hras*) abbreviation, abridgment, ŚrS.

प्रतिह्वर *prati-hvará*, m. (√*hvṛi*) a slope, the rising vault (of the sky), RV.

प्रतिह्वे *prati-√hve*, Ā. *-huváte*, to call, RV.

प्रती 1. *pratī*, in comp. for *prati* (cf. Pāṇ. vi, 3, 122; Vārtt. 3, Pat.) **-kāra**, m. = *prati-k°* (see under *prati-√kṛi*), MBh.; Kāv. &c.; an alliance resting on the requital of former services, Kām. **-kārya**, mfn. (cf. *prati-k°*) one on whom vengeance might be taken, punishable (*a-pr°*), Rājat. **-kāśá**, m. reflexion, resemblance, appearance, AV.; Kauś.; (ifc.) similar, resembling, like, MBh.; R. &c. **-ghāta**, m. (cf. *prati-gh°*) warding off (ifc.), MBh.; m. prevention, obstruction, repression, hindrance, resistance, Mn.; MBh. &c. **-ghātin**, mfn., in *a-pratīghāti-tā*, q. v. **-toda**, m. N. of partic. initial forms of Padas in hymns, Nid. **-darśá**, m. (cf. *prati-d°*) N. of a man, ŚBr. **-nāha**, m. (cf. *prati-n°*, p. 666, col. 2) obstruction, constipation, Car.; Suśr.; a flag, banner, ŚBr.; *-bhājana*, n. that which represents a b°, ib. **-pāna**, n. (cf. *prati-p°*) drinking, Āpast. **-bodhá**, m. (cf. under *prati-√budh*) vigilance, AV. **-māna**, n. (cf. *prati-m°*) a weight (measure), Mn. viii, 403. **-rādha**, m. = *prati-r°*, Śāṅkh. **-vartá**, mfn. returning into itself (= *pari-sara*), AV. **-vāpa**, m. = *prati-v°*, Suśr.; a disease, pestilence, L. **-vāha**, m. (cf. *prati-v°*) fee, reward, GopBr.; Kauś. **-ví**, mfn. (cf. *prati-√vī*) receiving gladly, accepting, RV.; m. or f. acceptance, ib. **-veśa**, **'śin** = *prati-v°* (p. 663, col. 2). **-sāram**, see *prati-√sṛi*. **-hartṛi**, m. (cf. *prati-h°*) a door-keeper, porter, Rājat. **-hārá**, m. (in most meanings) = *prati-hāra*, q. v.; a partic. alliance, L. (w. r. for *prati-kāra* above); N. of a family of kings, Cat.; *-tā*, f. (Rājat.), *-tva*, n. (Pañcat.) the office of a door keeper or chamberlain; *-dhuraṃ-dharā*, f. a female door-keeper, Vcar. **-hāram**, see *prati-√hṛi*. **-hāsa**, m. (cf. *prati-h°*) Nerium Odorum, L.

प्रती 2. *pratī* (*prati-√i*), P. *praty-eti*, to go towards or against, go to meet (as friend or foe), RV. &c. &c.; to come back, return, ib.; to resort or apply to, RV.; AV.; ŚBr.; to fall to a person's (dat.) lot or share, AitBr.; to receive, accept, MBh.; (also Pass.) to admit, recognize, be certain of, be convinced that (2 acc.), GṛŚrS.; Nir.; R. &c.; to trust, believe (with gen.), Kathās.: Pass. *pratīyate*, to be admitted or recognized, follow, result, Kāv.; Śaṃk.; Hit. (p. °*yamāna*, known, understood, implicit, Pāṇ.; Sāh.): Caus. *praty-āyayati* (Pass. *praty-āyyate*), to lead towards i.e. cause to recognize or acknowledge, convince (any one of the truth of anything), Kālid.; to make clear, prove, Śaṃk.; Sāh.: Desid. *pratīshishati*, to wish or try to understand, Pāṇ. ii, 4, 47, Sch. **Pratīta**, mfn. acknowledged, recognized, known (*Śyāma iti*, 'by the name of S°'), Nir.; Mn.; MBh. &c.; convinced of anything, trusting in, firmly resolved upon (comp.), KaṭhUp.; MBh.; Hit.; satisfied, cheerful, glad, pleased, AitBr.; MBh. &c.; respectful, L.; past, gone, L.; clever, wise, L.; m. N. of a divinity enumerated among the Viśve Devās, MBh.; *-sena*, m. N. of a prince, Buddh.; °*tâksharā*, f. N. of a Comm. on the Mitâksharā; °*tâtman*, mfn. confident, resolute, MBh.; °*târtha*, mfn. having a recognized or acknowledged meaning, Nir.; °*tâśva*, m. N. of a prince, VP. **Prátīti**, f. going towards, approaching, RV.; the following from anything (as a necessary result), being clear or intelligible by itself, Vedāntas.; clear apprehension or insight into anything, complete understanding or ascertainment, conviction, Śak.; Śaṃk.; Kathās. &c.; confidence, faith, belief, Daś.; trust, credit, Inscr.; fame, notoriety, W.; respect, ib.; delight, ib.; *-mat*, mfn. known, understood, Harav. **Pratītya**, n. confirmation, experiment, RV. vii, 68, 6; comfort, consolation, ib. iv, 5, 14 (others 'mfn. to be acknowledged or recognized'); *-samutpāda*, m. (Buddh.) the chain of causation, Lalit. (twelvefold; cf. Dharmas. 42).

Pratyaya, m. belief, firm conviction, trust, faith, assurance or certainty of (gen., loc. or comp.); proof, ascertainment, Mn.; MBh. &c. (*pratyayaṃ √gam*, to acquire confidence, repose c° in, MBh.; *asty atra pratyayo mama*, that is my conviction, Kathās.; *kaḥ pratyayo 'tra*, what assurance is there of that? ib.); conception, assumption, notion, idea, KātyŚr.; Nir.; Śaṃk. &c.; (with Buddhists and Jainas) fundamental notion or idea (*-tva*, n.), Sarvad.; consciousness, understanding, intelligence, intellect (in Sāṃkhya = *buddhi*); analysis, solution, explanation, definition, L.; ground, basis, motive or cause of anything, MBh.; Kāv. &c.; (in med.) = *nimitta*, *hetu* &c., Cat.; (with Buddhists) a co-operating cause; the concurrent occasion of an event as distinguished from its approximate cause; an ordeal, Kāty.; want, need, Kāraṇḍ.; fame, notoriety, Pāṇ. viii, 2, 58; a subsequent sound or letter, Prāt.; an affix or suffix to roots (forming verbs, substantives, adjectives and all derivatives), Prāt.; Pāṇ.; an oath, L.; usage, custom, L.; religious meditation, L.; a dependant or subject, L.; a householder who keeps a sacred fire, L.; *-kara* (R.), *-kāraka* (Pañcat.), *-kāraṇa* (Śak.), mfn. one who awakens confidence, trustworthy; *-kārin*, mfn. id., L.; (*iṇī*), f. a seal, signet, L.; *-tattva-prakāśikā*, f. N. of wk.; *-tva*, n. (cf. above) the being a cause, causality, Sarvad.; *-dhātu*, m. the stem of a nominal verb, Pat.; *-prativacana*, n. a certain or distinct answer, Śak.; *-mauktika-mālā*, f. N. of wk.; *-lopa*, m. (in gram.) elision of an affix; *-sarga*, m. (in Sāṃkhya) the creation which proceeds from Buddha; *-svara*, m. (in gram.) an accent on an affix; °*ayâtma*, mfn. causing confidence, R. (v. l. *pratyag-ātma*); °*ayâdhi*, m. a pledge which causes confidence in regard to a debt, L.; °*ayânta-śabda-kṛid-anta-vyūha*, m. N. of wk. °**tyayāya**, Nom. P. °*yati*, to convince, HPariś. (prob. w. r. for Caus. *praty-āyayati*). °**tyayika**, mfn. (in *ātma-pr°*) that of which everybody can convince himself, MBh. °**tyayita**, mfn. proved, trustworthy (compar. *-tara*), Jaim.; w. r. for °*tyāyita*, Pañcat. °**tyayitavya**, mfn. credible, Śaṃk. °**tyayin**, mfn. deserving confidence, trustworthy, R.; trusting, believing, W.

Praty-āya, m. toll, tribute, L. °**āyaka**, mfn. (fr. Caus.) causing to know or understand (*-tva*, n.), Sarvad.; convincing, credible, MBh. 1. °**āyana**, mfn. (for 2. see *praty-√i*) convincing, credible, MBh. (v. l. °*āyaka*); (*ā*), f. convincing, persuasion, Kathās.; consolation, comfort, Ratnâv.; n. elucidation, explanation, demonstration, Kathās.; Sāh.; (*am*), ind. (after a finite verb), Siddh. °**āyayitavya**, mfn. to be explained or demonstrated, Mālav. °**āyita**, mfn. convinced of, trusting (ifc.), Pañcat. (w. r. °*ayita*); m. a trustworthy person, confidential agent, commissioner, ŚāṅkhBr. °**āyitavya**, w. r. for °*āyayitavya*, Mālav. °**āyya**, mfn. to be encouraged or comforted, Subh.

Praty-etavya, mfn. to be acknowledged or admitted, to be understood as (nom.), RPrāt.; Śaṃk. °**etṛi**, mfn. believing, trusting, a believer, W.

प्रतीक *pratīka*. See p. 675, col. 1.

प्रतीक्ष् *pratīksh* (*prati-√īksh*), Ā. *pratīkshate* (ep. also P. °*ti*), to look at, behold, perceive, AV.; KātyŚr.; to look forward to, wait for, expect, TS. &c. &c.; to look at with indifference, bear with, tolerate (acc.), Mn. ix, 77.

Pratīksha, mf(*ā*)n. looking backward (see *a-pr°*); (also °*kshaka*, R.) looking forward to, waiting for, expectant of (ifc.), MBh.; Kāv. &c.; having regard to (ifc.), Hariv.; (*ā́*), f. expectation, TBr.; KaṭhUp.; consideration, attention, respect, veneration, Āpast.; MBh.; R. **Pratīkshaṇa**, n. looking to or at, considering, regard, attention, BhP.; observance, fulfilment, Prab. **Pratīkshaṇīya**, mfn. to be waited for or expected, Kull.; to be looked at or considered or regarded, W. **Pratīksham**, ind. having expected (ifc., e. g. *śarat-pr°*), R. **Prati-**

kshita, mfn. contemplated, considered; respected, honoured; expected, hoped, W. **Pratîkshin**, mfn. looking or waiting for, expecting, MBh.; Rājat. 1. **Pratîkshya**, mfn. to be expected or waited for, Mn.; MBh. &c.; to be observed or fulfilled, Śiś.; to be considered or regarded, respectable, worthy, Ragh.; Rājat. 2. **Pratîkshya**, ind. 'while expecting or waiting,' gradually, slowly, Mṛicch. iii, 1⅛.

प्रतीच्छक pr..îcchaka. See pratish.

प्रतीड् pratî.. (prati-√îḍ), only 3. pl. *pratî-ḷate*, to praise, RV. vii, 76, 7.

प्रतीत pratî.. &c. See under 2. prati.

प्रतीत्त pratî-tta. See á-pratîtta.

प्रतीन्धक pratîndhaka, m. (√indh) N. of a prince of Videha, R.

प्रतीन्व् pratînv (prati-√inv), P. *pratînvati*, to urge, promote, advance, RV. i, 54, 7.

प्रतीप pratîpa, mf(ā)n. (fr. *prati + ap*; cf. *anūpa*, *dvîpa*, *samîpa*) 'against the stream,' 'ag° the grain,' going in an opposite direction, meeting, encountering, adverse, contrary, opposite, reverse, MBh.; R.; Ragh. &c.; inverted, out of order, Suśr.; Var.; displeasing, disagreeable, Mn.; MBh.; R.; Hariv.; resisting, refractory, cross, obstinate; impeding, hindering, BhP.; MBh.; R. &c.; backward, retrograde; turned away, averted, W.; m. an adversary, opponent, BhP.; N. of a prince, the father of Śaṃtanu and grandfather of Bhishma, AV.; MBh.; Hariv. &c.; n. (in rhet.) inverse comparison (e. g. 'the lotus resembles thine eyes,' instead of the usual comparison 'thine e° resemble the l°;' 5 forms are enumerated), Kuval.; Pratāp.; Sāh.; Kpr.; N. of a gram. wk.; (*ám*), ind. against the stream, backwards; against, RV. &c. &c.; in return, Bālar.; in inverted order, Mn.; refractorily (with √*gam*, to resist, Śak.; with *abhy-upa-√gam*, to go against, oppose, R.) **-ga**, mf(ā)n. going against, flowing ag°, f° backwards, Ragh.; Var. **-gati**, f. (VarBṛS., Sch.) or **-gamana**, n. (ib.; Kum.) a retrograde movement. **-gāmin**, mfn. (ifc.) going against, acting in contravention to, Daś. **-taraṇa**, n. sailing ag° the stream, Vikr. **-darśanî** or **-°rśinî**, f. 'turning away the face,' a woman, L. **-dîpaka**, n. a partic. figure of speech, Bhaṭṭ., Sch. **-vacana**, n. contradiction, Amar. **Pratîpâśva**, m. N. of a prince, VP. (v. l. *Pratîkâśva*). **Pratîpôkti**, f. contradiction, Naish.

Pratîpaka, mfn. opposed to, hindering, hostile, BhP.; m. N. of a prince, ib.

Pratîpaya, Nom. P. °*yati*, to oppose one's self to, be hostile to (loc.), BhP.; to cause to turn back, bring back, reverse, Kum.

Pratîpāya, Nom. Ā. °*yate*, to oppose one's self to, be hostile to, be against (gen.), Bhaṭṭ. (g. *sukhâdi*).

Pratîpin, mfn. unfavourable, unkind, g. *sukhâdi*.

प्रतीप्स् pratîps, Desid. of *praty-√āp*, q.v.

प्रतीर् pratîr (*prati-√îr*), only Caus. 2. du. impf. *praty-airayatam*, to put on, fix on, RV. i, 117, 22.

प्रतीर pra-tîra, m. N. of a son of Manu Bhautya, MārkP.; n. = *tîra*, a shore, bank, L.

प्रतीष् pratîsh (*prati-√3. ish*), P. *pratîcchati* (ind. p. *pratîshya*), to strive after, seek, RV. x, 129, 4; to receive, accept from, MBh.; Kāv. &c.; to regard, mind, attend to, obey, ib. **Pratîcchaka**, m. one who receives, a receiver, Mn. iv, 194.

प्रतीषित pra-îshita, mfn. (√*ish*) stretched out towards, Kāṭh.

प्रतुद् pra-√tud, P. -*tudati*, to strike at, cut through, pierce, MBh.; Hariv.; BhP.; Caus. -*todayati*, to push on, urge, instigate, MBh.; Mṛicch. °**tud**, m. 'pecker,' N. of a class of birds (including the falcon, hawk, owl, parrot, crow, raven, peacock &c.), Āpast. °**tuda**, m. id., Gaut.; Mn.; Yājñ.; Suśr.; an instrument for piercing, Suśr. °**todá**, m. a goad or long whip, AV. &c. &c. (also -*yashṭi*, f., Divyâv.); sg. (with *Aṅgirasām*) and du. (with *Kaśyapasya*), N. of Sāmans, ĀrshBr.; -*yantra*, n. N. of wk. °**todin**, see *śroṇi-pratodín*.

प्रतुर् pra-tur. See *su-pratúr*.

प्रतुर्व् pra-√turv (only pr. p. -*túrvat*), to be victorious, RV. v, 65, 4.

प्रतुष् pra-√tush, P. -*tushya'i*, to delight in (instr.), Bhaṭṭ.: Caus. -*toshayati*, to give pleasure, gratify, BhP. °**tushṭi**, f. satisfaction (-*da*, mfn. giving s°), Pañcat. °**tosha**, m. 'gratification,' N. of one of the 12 sons of Manu Svāyambhuva, BhP.

प्रतुस्तुषु pra-tustushu. See *pra-√stu*.

प्रतूणी pra-tūṇî, f. a kind of disease (causing pain of the nerves extending from the rectum and generative organs to the bowels; w. r. for *prati-tūṇî*?), Suśr.

प्रतूर्ण pra-tūrṇa, °*tūrta* &c. See *pra-√tvar*.

प्रतृद् pra-√tṛid (only ind. p. -*tṛidya*), to thrust through with a spit, ŚBr. °**tardana**, mfn. piercing, destroying (said of Vishṇu), Vishṇ.; m. N. of a king of Kāśi (son of Divo-dāsa and author of RV. ix, 96), Br.; MBh. &c.; of a Rākshasa, R.; of a class of divinities under Manu Auttama, MārkP. °**tṛiṇṇa**, n. (piercing i.e. splitting, scil. the words) recitation of the Pada-pāṭha, AitĀr. °**tṛid**, mfn. cleaving, piercing (applied to the Tṛitsus), RV. vii, 33, 14.

प्रतृप् pra-√tṛip, Caus. -*tarpayati*, to satiate, refresh, strengthen, satisfy, Pañcat.; Suśr.

प्रतॄ pra-√tṝî, P. Ā. -*tarati*, °*te* (Ved. also -*tirati*, °*te*; inf. -*tíram*), to go to sea, pass over, cross, ŚBr. &c. &c.; to set out, start, RV.; ŚBr.; (Ā.) to rise, thrive, prosper, RV.; to raise, elevate, augment, increase, further, promote, ib.; AV.; ŚBr.; MBh.; to extend, prolong (esp. with *āyus*, 'to promote long life;' Ā. 'to live on, live longer'), RV.: Caus. -*tārayati* (aor. *prâtîtarat*), to extend, widen, MBh.; to prolong (life), AV.; to mislead, take in, deceive, Mṛicch.; Kathās.; to lead astray, seduce, persuade to (dat. or loc.), Ragh.; Kathās. °**tara**, m. passing over, crossing (cf. *dush-* and *su-pr°*); N. of the joints (*saṃdhi*) on the neck and of the spinal vertebrae, Suśr. °**táraṇa**, mf(î)n. furthering, promoting, increasing (with *āyushaḥ*, 'prolonging life'), RV.; AV.; VS.; PārGṛ.; n. going to sea, passing over, crossing, MBh.; Kāv. &c °**tarîtṛi** (RV.), °**tárîtṛi** (AV.), m. a furtherer, promoter (esp. of long life). °**tāra**, m. passing over, crossing (with gen.), MBh.; R.; deception, fraud, L. °**tāraka**, mfn. cheating, deceitful, a deceiver, Bhartṛ.; Vcar. °**tāraṇa**, n. (fr. Caus.) ferrying over, carrying across, ŚārṅgP.; passing over, crossing (m. c. for °*taraṇa*), R.; Rājat.; deceiving, cheating (also *ā*, f.), ŚārṅgP.; L. °**tāraṇîya**, mfn. to be deceived, deceivable, KātyŚr., Sch. °**tārayitṛi**, m. a furtherer, promoter, AitBr. °**tārita**, mfn. misled, deceived, imposed upon, MBh.; Kāv. &c.; persuaded or seduced to (dat.), Ragh. (v. l. *pra-codita*). 1. °**tirá**, mfn. furthering, granting success or victory, AitĀr. 2. °**tîra**, mfn. (?) carrying across, furthering, helping, TS. (Sch.) °**tîrṇa** (*prá-*), mfn. having put to sea, ŚBr.; having spread over (acc.), Ragh.

प्रतोली pra-tolî, f. a broad way, principal road through a town or village (ifc. °*lika*), MBh.; Kāv. &c.; a kind of bandage applied to the neck or to the penis, Suśr.

प्रत्त prá-tta, prá-tti. See *pra-√1. dā*.

प्रत्न pra-tná, mf(ā)n. former, preceding; ancient, old; traditional, customary, RV.; AV.; TS.; Br.; BhP.; n. a kind of metre, RPrāt. **Pratnáthā**, ind. as formerly, as of old, in the usual manner, RV. 1. **Pratna-vát**, ind., id., ib. 2. **Pratnávat**, mfn. containing the word *pratna*, ŚBr.

प्रत्यंश praty-aṇśa &c. See p. 663, col. 3.

प्रत्यक् pratyak. See p. 675, col. 1.

प्रत्यक्ष praty-aksha, mf(ā)n. present before the eyes, visible, perceptible (opp. to *paro'ksha*, q.v.), Up.; MBh. &c.; clear, distinct, manifest, direct, immediate, actual, real, ŚBr. &c. &c.; keeping in view, discerning (with gen.), MBh.; n. ocular evidence, direct perception, apprehension by the senses (in Nyāya one of the 4 Pramāṇas or modes of proof, cf. *pramāṇa*); superintendence of, care for (gen.), Mn. ix, 27; (in rhet.) a kind of style descriptive of impressions derived from the senses, Kuval.; (*pratyáksham*), ind. (also °*ksha* ibc.) before the eyes, in the sight or presence of (gen. or comp.), clearly, explicitly, directly, personally, AV. &c. &c.; (*āt*), ind. explicitly, actually, really, Br.; (*ena*), ind. before the eyes, visibly, publicly, expressly, directly, Lāṭy.; MBh.; MārkP.; (*e*), ind. before one's face, publicly, Pañcat. **-karaṇa**, n. one's own perception, Car. **-kṛita**, mfn. addressed directly or personally, containing a personal address, Nir.; (*ā*), f. (scil. *ṛic*) a hymn or verse in which a deity is addressed directly or in the 2nd person, MW. **-khaṇḍa**, m. n. N. of part I of the Tattva-cintāmaṇi.; -*cintāmaṇi*, m. and -*vyākhyā*, f. N. of wks. **-cārin**, mfn. walking personally before the eyes of (gen.), Kāvyâd. **-jñāna**, n. immediate perception, Tarkas. **-tamāt** or **-tamām**, ind. most perceptibly or directly or really &c., Br. **-tas**, ind. before the eyes, visibly, perceptibly (°*taḥ śrutam*, heard p° or with the ears), MBh.; Pāṇ., Sch.; Kathās.; evidently, clearly, plainly, MW. **-tā**, f. the being before the eyes, b° visible, visibility, MBh.; Kathās.; MārkP. &c.; addressing in the 2nd person, MW.; (*ayā*), ind. before the eyes of any one, Pañcat. **-tva**, n. ocular evidence, explicitness, KātyŚr.; the being ocular evidence or immediate perception, Sarvad.; addressing in the 2nd person, MW. **-darśana**, n. seeing with one's own eyes; the power of discerning (the presence of a god), MBh.; m. an eye-witness, L. **-darśin**, mfn. seeing anything (gen.) with one's own eyes, one who has seen with his own e°, MBh. **-darśivas**, mfn. one who has seen anything with his own e°; seeing anything (acc.) clearly as if before the e°, MBh.; Hariv.; Sūryas. **-dîpikā**, f. N. of wk. **-dṛiś**, mfn. seeing distinctly, one who sees anything (acc.) clearly as if before the e°, MārkP. **-dṛiśya**, mfn. to be seen with the e°, visible, perceptible, Nir.; Kathās. **-dṛishṭa**, mfn. seen with the e°, Ratnâv.; Kathās. **-dvish** (*pratyák-sha-*), mfn. not liking that which is clear, ŚBr. **-dharman**, mfn. keeping in view the merits (of men), MBh. **-para**, mfn. setting the highest value on the visible, Car. **-pariccheda**, m. N. of wk. (also °*da-mañjūshā*, f. and °*da-rahasya*, n.) **-parikshaṇa**, n. real observation, Var. **-pṛishṭha**, m. a partic. Pṛishṭhya, ĀśvŚr. **-pramā**, f. a correct notion obtained through the senses, Vedântap. **-pramāṇa**, n. ocular or visible proof, the evidence of the senses; an organ or faculty of perception, W.; N. of wk. (also °*nyâloka-ṭippaṇî*, f.) **-phala**, mfn. having visible consequences (-*tva*, n.), Āp.; n. a visible consequence, MW. **-bandhu** (*pratyáksha-*), mfn. with evident relation, MaitrS. **-bṛihatî**, f. an original Bṛihatî, ŚāṅkhŚr. **-bhaksha**, m. real eating, ŚrS. **-bhūta**, mfn. become visible, appeared personally, Hit. **-bhoga**, m. enjoyment or use of anything in the presence or with the knowledge of the owner, W. **-maṇi**, m., **-maṇi-raśmi-cakra**, n. N. of wks. **-rucidattîya**, n. N. of wk. (= -*vāda*). **-vat**, ind. as if it were evident, Āp. **-vāda**, m. N. of wk. by Ruci-datta. **-vādin**, mfn. 'asserting perception by the senses,' one who admits of no other evidence than p° by the s°; m. a Buddhist, L. **-vidhāna**, n. an express injunction, Gaut. **-vishayî-√bhū**, P. -*bhavati*, to move only within range of the sight, Naish., Comm. **-vihita**, mfn. expressly enjoined, ŚāṅkhŚr. **-vṛitti**, mfn. having a form visible to the eye; composed clearly or intelligibly (as a word), Nir., Sch. **-siddha**, mfn. determined by evidence of the senses, MW. **Pratyakshâgamana**, n. approaching in person, Siṇhās. **Pratyakshânumāna**, n. (-*ṭîkā*, f. and -*śabda-khaṇḍana*, n.) N. of wks. **Pratyakshâvagama**, mfn. plainly intelligible, Bhag.

Pratyakshaya, Nom. P. °*yati*, to make visible or perceptible, Mālav.; to see with one's own eyes, Kād.

Pratyakshāya, Nom. Ā. °*yate*, to come clearly before the eyes, be visible; °*yamāṇa-tva*, n. coming clearly before the eyes, Sāh.

Pratyakshin, mfn. seeing with one's own eyes; m. an eye-witness, Jātak.

Pratyakshî, in comp. for °*ksha*. **-karaṇa**, n. looking at, viewing, Mn., Kull.; making manifest or apparent, W. **-√kṛi**, to make visible or evident, MW.; to inspect, look at or see with one's own eyes, MBh.; Mṛicch.; Kād. &c. **-kṛita**, mfn. seen with the e°, Śak.; Hit.; made present or visible, manifested, displayed, W. **-√bhū**, to come before the e°, be visible, appear in person, Kathās.; Siṇhās.

प्रत्यञ्च् praty-áñc, mfn. (nom. *pratyáṅ*;

praticī, pratīcī [and *pratyañcī*, Vop.]; *pratyák*) turned towards, facing (acc.), RV.; AV.; VS.; coming (opp. to *arvāñc*, 'going'), RV.; being or coming from behind, turning the back, averted, moving in an opposite direction, ib.; Br.; KātyŚr.; westward, western, occidental, to the west of (abl.), VS.; AV.; Br.; Mn. &c.; turned back or inward, inner, interior, Prab.; BhP.; Vedântas.; equal to, a match for (acc.), AV.; past, gone, L.; m. the individual soul, Prab. vi, $\frac{1}{2}$; (*pratīcī*), f. (with or scil. *diś*) the west, AV. &c. &c.; N. of a river, BhP.; (*pratyák*), ind. backwards, in an opposite direction, RV.; AV.; behind (abl.), KātyŚr.; down (opp. to *ūrdhvam*), KaṭhUp.; westward, to the west of (abl.), ŚrS.; MBh.; BhP.; inwardly, within, BhP.; Vedântas.; in former times, L.

Prátīka, mf(*ā*)n. (for *praty-aka*; cf. *anūka*, *apāka*, *abhīka*) turned or directed towards; (ifc.) looking at, BhP.; (prob.) going uphill, MBh.; adverse, contrary, inverted, reversed, L.; n. exterior, surface, RV.; outward form or shape, look, appearance, face (cf. *ghṛita-p°*, *cāru-p°*, *tvesha-p°*), ib.; Nir.; the face (esp. the mouth), RV.; ŚBr.; PārGṛ.; the front, MW.; an image, symbol, ChUp., Sch.; a copy, Vām.; (also m.) the first part (of a verse), first word, Br. &c. &c.; m. a part, portion, limb, member, L. (cf. *prati-pr°*, p. 662, col. 2); N. of a son of Vasu and father of Ogha-vat, BhP.; of a son of Maru, VP. **–tva**, n. the being an image or symbol, ChUp., Sch. **–darśana**, n. a symbolic conception, Bādar., Sch. **–vat** (*prátīka-*), mfn. having an outward form or face or mouth; m. N. of Agni, TS. **Pratīkâśva**, m. N. of a prince, BhP. **Pratīkôpâsana**, n. image-worship, the service of idols, Mn., Kull.

Pratīcī, f. of *pratyáñc*. **–pati**, m. 'lord of the west,' N. of Varuṇa, the ocean, Prasannar. **–'śa** (*°cīśa*), m. id., L.

Pratīcīná, mfn. turned towards, going or coming t°, RV.; (*°cīna*), mfn. turned away from, turning the back, RV.; being behind, coming from b°, AV.; turning westward, western, TS.; Br.; subsequent, future (with abl.), RV.; TBr.; (*am*), ind. back to one's self, TBr.; backwards, behind, TS.; TBr.; Kāṭh.; BhP. **–grīva** (*pratīcīna-*), mfn. having the neck turned westward, Br. **–prajanana** (*pratīcīna-*), mfn., ŚBr. **–phala** (*pratīcīna-*), mfn. having fruit turned or bending backwards, ib.; AV. **–mukha**, mf(*ī*)n. having the face turned westward, ŚBr. **–śiras** (*pratīcīna-*), mfn. having the head turned westward, ib. **–stoma**, m. a partic. Ekâha, Vait. **Pratīcīnêḍa**, mfn.; n. (with *Kāśīta*) N. of a Sāman, ĀrshBr.

Pratīcya, mfn. being or living in the west, MBh.; R.; (ibc.) the west, western country, MBh.; (*ā*), f. N. of the wife of Pulastya, ib.; (*pratīcya*), n. a designation of anything remote or concealed, Naigh. iii, 25 (perhaps w. r. for *pratītya*).

Pratyak, in comp. for *°tyañc*. **–cintāmaṇi**, m. N. of wk. **–cetana**, mfn. one whose thoughts are turned inwards or upon himself, Yogas.; (*ā*), f. thoughts t° i° or u° one's self, ib. **–tattva-dīpikā** (or *-pradīpikā*), f., **-tattva-viveka**, m. N. of philos. wks. **–tva**, n. backward direction, d° towards one's self, BhP., Sch. **–parṇī**, f. Achyranthes Aspera (= *apâmārga*), L.; Anthericum Tuberosum (= *dravantī*), ib. **–pushkara**, mf(*ā*)n. having the bowl turned westward (as a ladle), AitBr. **–pushpī**, f. Achyranthes Aspera, L.; (accord. to Pāṇ. iv, 1, 64, Vārtt. 1 the correct form would be *-pushpā*). **–prakāśa**, m. N. of a teacher, Cat. **–pravaṇa**, mfn. devoted to the individual soul; (*-tā*, f.), Prab. **–śiras**, mfn. (ĀpŚr. &c.) and **-śīrshī**, f. (Kauś.) having the head turned towards the west. **–śreṇī**, f. N. of various plants (Anthericum Tuberosum, Croton Polyandrum or C° Tiglium, Salvinia Cucullata &c.), Car.; L. **–śrotas**, mfn. w. r. for *-srotas*. **–sarasvatī**, f. the western Sarasvatī, BhP. **–sthalī**, f. N. of a Vedi, R. **–srotas**, mfn. flowing towards the west, MBh.; R.; Śiś., Sch. **–svarūpa**, m. N. of an author, Cat.

Pratyag, in comp. for *°tyañc*. **–aksha**, n. an inner organ, BhP.; mfn. having inner organs, ib.; *-ja*, mfn. discerned by the internal faculties, visible to the eye of the soul, MW. **–ātma**, mfn. concerning the personal soul or self, R. **–ātman**, m. the individual soul, KaṭhUp.; Vedântas.; BhP. &c.; an individual, Bādar., Sch.; *°ma-tā*, f. being an individual soul, RāmatUp.; *°ma-tva*, n. universal permeation of spirit, MW. **–ānanda**, mfn. inwardly rejoicing, appearing as inward delight, Vedântas. **–āśā-pati**, m. 'lord of the western quarter,' N. of Varuṇa, L. **–āśis**, f. a personal wish, KātyŚr., Sch.; mfn. containing a p° w°, ĀpŚr. **–udak**, ind. towards the north-west, ĀśvŚr. **–ekarasa**, mfn. having taste or pleasure only for the interior, delighting only in one's own soul, RāmatUp. **–jyotis**, n. the inward light, Mcar. **–dakshiṇatas**, ind. towards the south-west, KātyŚr. **–dakshiṇā**, ind. towards the south-west, ĀśvŚr.; *-pravaṇa*, mfn. sloping t° the s°-w°, ĀśvGṛ. **–diś**, f. the western quarter, AV.; AitBr.; MBh. &c. **–dṛiś**, f. a glance directed inwards, BhP.; mfn. one whose glance is d° i°, RāmatUp. **–dhāman**, mfn. radiant within, internally illuminated, BhP. **–ratha**, m. N. of a prince, VP.; pl. N. of a warrior-tribe (also called *Ahi-cchattra*; cf. *prātyagrathi*), Pāṇ. iv, 1, 173. **–vahana-prayoga**, m. N. of wk.

Pratyaṅ, in comp. for *°tyañc*. **–mukha**, mf(*ī*)n. having the face turned away or westward, GṛŚrS. &c.; *-tva*, n. facing the west, Hcat.

प्रत्यञ्ज् *praty-√añj*, P. *-anakti* or *-añjati*, to smear over, besmear, ŚBr.; to decorate, adorn, RV. **°añjana**, n. smearing, anointing, Suśr.; Bhpr.

प्रत्यद् *praty-√ad*, P. *-atti*, to eat in return or in compensation for anything, ŚBr. **°adana**, n. eating, food, L.

प्रत्यधिश्रि *praty-adhi-√śri*, P. *-śrayati*, to put down beside (the fire), KātyŚr.

प्रत्यधी *praty-adhī* (*adhi-√i*), Ā. *-adhīyate*, to read through or study severally, MBh.

प्रत्यनुज्ञा *praty-anu-√jñā*, P. *-jānāti*, to refuse, reject, spurn, R.

प्रत्यनुतप् *praty-anu-√tap*, Pass. *-tapyate*, to feel subsequent remorse, repent, regret, R.

प्रत्यनुनी *praty-anu-√nī*, P. Ā. *-nayati*, *°te*, to speak friendly words, induce to yield, persuade, MBh.; (Ā.) to beg a person's (acc.) pardon for (acc.), ib.

प्रत्यनुभू *praty-anu-√bhū*, P. *-bhavati*, to enjoy singly or severally, PraśnUp.; Divyâv.

प्रत्यनुयाच् *praty-anu-√yāc*, P. *-yācati*, to beseech, implore (with acc.), R.

प्रत्यनुवाशित *praty-anu-vāśita*, mfn. (√*vāś*) roared against, answered by roaring, Var.

प्रत्यनुस्मृ *praty-anu-√smṛi*, P. *-smarati*, to remember, R.

प्रत्यपकृ *praty-apa-√kṛi* (only ind. p. *-kṛitya*), to take vengeance on (acc.), Daś. **°apakāra**, m. offending or injuring in return, retaliation, Kum.

प्रत्यपया *praty-apa-√yā*, P. *-yāti*, to go back, withdraw, retreat, flee into (acc.), MBh.

प्रत्यपवह् *praty-apa-√vah*, P. *-vahati*, to drive back, repel, BhP.

प्रत्यपसृप् *praty-apa-√sṛip*, Caus. *-sarpayati*, to cause to go back, put to flight, MBh.

प्रत्यपोर्णु *praty-apôrṇu* (*-apa-√ūrṇu*), Ā. *-apôrṇute*, to uncover one's self in the presence of (acc.), TS.

प्रत्यभिघृ *praty-abhi-√ghṛi*, Caus. *-ghārayati*, to sprinkle over repeatedly, GṛS. **°abhighāraṇa**, n. sprinkling over afresh, GṛŚrS.

प्रत्यभिचर् *praty-abhi-√car*, P. *-carati*, to use spells or charms against, AV.; ŚāṅkhŚr. **°abhicaraṇa**, mfn. using spells or charms against, AV.

प्रत्यभिचित *praty-abhi-cita*, mfn. (√1. *ci*) built up in defence, GopBr. (w. r. *-jita*).

प्रत्यभिज्ञा *praty-abhi-√jñā*, P. Ā. *-jānāti*, *-jānīte*, to recognize, remember, know, understand, MBh.; Kāv. &c.; to come to one's self, recover consciousness, Kathās.: Caus. *-jñāpayati*, to recall to mind, Saṃk. **°abhijñā**, f. recognition, Kap.; Bhāshāp. &c. (ifc. *°jña*, mfn., Daś.; Rājat.); regaining knowledge or recognition (of the identity of the Supreme and individual soul), Sarvad.; *-darśana*, n. N. of a philos. system, IW. 118; *-vimarśinī*, f. N. of Comm. on *-hṛidaya*; *-śāstra*, n. N. of a philos. manual; *-sūtra*, n., *-hṛidaya*, n. N. of wks. **°abhijñāta**, mfn. recognized, known, MBh.; Śak. &c.; *-vat*, mfn., Kathās. **°abhijñāna**, n. recognition, MBh.; Kāv. &c.; a token of rec° (brought by a messenger to prove that he has accomplished his mission), R.; reciprocity, ĀśvŚr., Sch.; *-ratna*, n. a jewel (given as token) of recognition, MW. **°abhijñāpana**, n. causing to recognize, Saṃk. **°abhijñāyamāna-tva**, n. the being recognized, Kap., Sch.

प्रत्यभिधा *praty-abhi-√1. dhā*, P. Ā. *-dadhāti*, *-dhatte*, to take or draw back, re-absorb, BhP.; (Ā.) to reply, answer, ib. **°abhihita**, mfn. answered, having received an answer from (instr.), Śak.; approved, MBh.

प्रत्यभिधाव् *praty-abhi-√1. dhāv*, P. *-dhāvati*, to run or hasten towards, R.

प्रत्यभिनन्द् *praty-abhi-√nand*, P. *-nandati*, to greet in return, return a salutation, MBh.; to bid welcome, Śak. (v. l. for *abhi-n°*). **°abhinandita**, mfn. saluted, welcomed, MBh. **°abhinandin**, mfn. receiving thankfully (ifc.), Ragh.

प्रत्यभिप्रस्था *praty-abhi-pra-√sthā*, Ā. *-tishṭhate*, to set out for, depart, MBh.

प्रत्यभिभाषिन् *praty-abhi-bhāshin*, mfn. (√*bhāsh*) speaking to, addressing (acc.), R.

प्रत्यभिभूत *praty-abhi-bhūta*, mfn. (√*bhū*) overcome, conquered, Prab. v, 8 (v. l. *aty-abhibh°*).

प्रत्यभिमिथ् *praty-abhi-√mith*, P. *-methati*, to answer scornfully or abusively, ŚBr. **°abhimethana**, n. a scornful reply, ŚāṅkhŚr.

प्रत्यभिमृश् *praty-abhi-√mṛiś*, P. *-mṛiśati*, to stroke or rub over, touch, lay hold of, Gobh.; Vait. **°abhimarśa**, m. (AitBr.), **°śana**, n. (Lāṭy.) stroking or rubbing over, rubbing, touching. **°abhimṛishṭa**, mfn. touched (*a-praty-abh°*), AitBr.

प्रत्यभिया *praty-abhi-√yā*, P. *-yāti*, to go against (acc.), BhP.

प्रत्यभियुज् *praty-abhi-√yuj*, Ā. *-yuṅkte*, to make a counter attack against (acc.), Bālar.: Caus. *-yojayati*, to make a counter plaint or charge against (acc.), Yājñ. **°abhiyukta**, mfn. attacked by (instr.), Prab. (*-vat*, mfn., Kathās.); accused in return or by a counter plaint, MW. **°abhiyoga**, m. a counter plaint or charge, recrimination, Yājñ.

प्रत्यभिलेख्य *praty-abhi-lekhya*, n. (√*likh*) a counter document, a document brought forward by the opposing party, Vas.

प्रत्यभिवद् *praty-abhi-√vad*, P. *-vadati*, to return a salute, greet in return, Āpast.: Caus. Ā. *-vādayate*, id., Mṛicch. **°abhivāda**, m. return salutation, Pāṇ. viii, 2, 83. **°abhivādaka**, mfn. returning a s°, Kull. **°abhivādana**, n. the act of ret° a s°, Mn. ii, 126. **°abhivādayitṛi**, mfn. one who returns a salutation, Kull.

प्रत्यभिस्कन्दन *praty-abhi-skandana*, n. (√*skand*) a counter plaint or charge, an accusation brought against the accuser or plaintiff, Yājñ., Sch. (cf. *praty-abhiyoga*).

प्रत्यभिहृ *praty-abhi-√hṛi*, Caus. *-hārayati*, to offer, present, Gobh. (v. l.)

प्रत्यभ्यनुज्ञा *praty-abhy-anu-jñā*, f. (√*jñā*) leave, permission, ĀśvGṛ. **°anujñāta**, mfn. dismissed on taking leave, allowed to depart, MBh.

प्रत्यभ्युत्थान *praty-abhy-utthāna*, n. (√*sthā*) rising from a seat through politeness (ifc. f. *ā*), Kād.

प्रत्यय *pratyaya* &c. See p. 673, col. 3.

प्रत्यर्च् *praty-√arc*, P. *-arcati*, to shine upon (acc.), RV.; Caus. *-arcayati*, to greet in return or one by one, MBh.; R. **°arcana**, n. returning a salutation or obeisance, MBh. **°arcita**, mfn. saluted in return, MBh.

प्रत्यर्थ् *praty-√arth*, P. *-arthayati*, to challenge (to combat), Bhaṭṭ. **°arthaka**, m. an opponent, adversary, L. **°arthika** (ifc.), id., MBh. **°arthin**, mfn. hostile, inimical; (ifc.) opposing, rivalling, emulating, MBh.; Kāv. &c.; m. an adversary, opponent, rival, ib.; (in law) a defendant, Mn.; Yājñ. &c.; *°thi-tā*, f. and *°thi-tva*, n. the state of a defendant at law, MW.; *°thi-bhūta*, mfn. become an obstacle, Kum.; °thy-āvedana, n. (in law) the verbal information or deposition of the defendant which is written down by the officers of the court, MW.

प्रत्यर्द् praty-√ard, Caus. -ardayati, °te, to oppress or assault in return, R.

प्रत्यर्पण praty-arpaṇa &c. See praty-√ṛi.

प्रत्यवकर्शन praty-ava-karśana, mfn. (√kriś) bringing down, baffling, annihilating, BhP.

प्रत्यवगम् praty-ava-√gam, P. -gacchati, to know singly or exactly, MBh.

प्रत्यवग्रह् praty-ava-√grah, P. -gṛihṇāti, to draw or put back, MaitrS.; to retract, revoke, recall, R.

प्रत्यवतॄ praty-ava-√tṛī, P. -tarati, to disembark, Divyâv.

प्रत्यवदो praty-ava-√do, P. -dāti or -dyati, to divide again, TBr.

प्रत्यवधा praty-ava-√1. dhā, P. -dadhāti, to put in again, ŚBr.

प्रत्यवनेजन praty-ava-nejana, n. (√nij) washing off again, PārGṛ.

प्रत्यवभाष् praty-ava-√bhāsh, Ā. -bhāshate, to call to, Divyâv.

प्रत्यवभास praty-ava-bhāsa, m. (√bhās) becoming visible, appearance (ifc. f. ā), Uttarar. (w. r. °bhāshā).

प्रत्यवभुज् praty-ava-√1. bhuj, P. -bhujati, to bend back, Kauś.

प्रत्यवमृश् praty-ava-√mṛiś, P. -mṛiśati, to touch, Kauś.; to reflect, meditate, Daś.; BhP. °**avamarśa**, m. (wrongly spelt °sha) inner contemplation, profound meditation, BhP.; counter conclusion, Kull.; recollection, Hariv.; consciousness, Jātakam.; -vat, mfn. absorbed in thought, meditative, MBh. °**avamarśana**, n. contemplation, meditation, BhP.

प्रत्यवमृष् praty-ava-√mṛish, P. Ā. -mṛishyati, °te, or -marshati, °te, to endure reluctantly, suffer beyond endurance, MW.

प्रत्यवरुध् praty-ava-√2. rudh (only ind. p. -rudhya), to recover, BhP. °**avaruddha**, mfn. stopped, suppressed, ib. °**avarodhana**, n. obstruction, interruption, MBh.

प्रत्यवरुह् praty-ava-√ruh, P. -rohati, to come down again, descend from (abl.), alight upon (acc.), TS.; Br.; ĀśvŚr.; to descend (from a seat, chariot &c.) in honour of (acc.), TS.; ŚBr.; MBh.; to celebrate the festival called Pratyavarohaṇa, Śāṅkh-Gṛ.: Caus. -ropayati, to bring down from, deprive of (abl. or instr.), MBh. °**ávarūḍhi**, f. descending towards, TS. °**avarohá**, m. id.; a descending ser. Br.; ŚrS. °**avarohaṇa**, n. = °avarūḍhi, ŚrS.; N. of a partic. Gṛihya festival in the month Mārgaśirsha, GṛS. °**avarohaṇīya**, m. a partic. Ekâha sacrifice forming part of the Vājapeya, ŚrS. °**avaroham**, ind. descending, AitBr. °**avarohin**, mfn. descending, moving downwards, Br.; Lāṭy.; moving or rising from a seat (a-pratyav°), KātyŚr.; (iṇī), f. N. of a partic. litany, TāṇḍBr.

प्रत्यवसद् praty-ava-√sad, P. -sīdati, to sink down, perish, MBh.

प्रत्यवसृज् praty-ava-√sṛij, P. -sṛijati, to throw on (loc.), Hariv.; to relinquish, leave, ŚBr.

प्रत्यवसृत praty-ava-sṛita, mfn. (√sṛi) gone away, Divyâv.

प्रत्यवसृप् praty-ava-√sṛip, P. -sarpati, to creep towards, ŚBr.

प्रत्यवसो praty-ava-√so, P. -syati, to come back, return to (loc.), ŚBr. °**avasāna**, n. consuming, eating, Pāṇ. i, 4, 52. °**avasita**, mfn. relapsed into the old (bad) way of life, MBh.; Nār. (Sch. 'one who has given up the life of a religious mendicant'); consumed, eaten, L. (cf. Pāṇ. vi, 2, 195, Kāś.)

प्रत्यवस्कन्द praty-ava-skanda, m. (√skand) an attack, surprise, Kathās.; = next, L. °**avaskandana**, n. a special plea at law (admitting a fact, but qualifying or explaining it so as not to allow it to be a matter of accusation), Bṛihasp.

प्रत्यवस्था praty-ava-√sthā, Ā. -tishṭhate, to return, re-appear (with punar), BhP.; to resist, oppose, object to, Kap., Sch.; to stand alone or separately, MW.; to re-attain, recover, Bhaṭṭ.: Caus. -sthāpayati, to cause to stand firm, encourage (with ātmānam, 'to collect one's self, recover'), Vikr. °**avasthā**, f. = pary-avasthā, L. °**avasthātṛi**, m. an opponent, adversary, L. °**avasthāna**, n. objection, Nyāyas.; removal, setting aside, L.; former state or place, status quo, W.; opposition, hostility, ib. °**avasthāpana**, n. (fr. Caus.) refreshing, strengthening, Car.

Praty-avasthita, mfn. standing separately or opposite, R.; being in a partic. condition, MBh.

प्रत्यवहन् praty-ava-√han, P. -hanti, to strike back, repel, RV. v, 29, 4.

प्रत्यवहृ praty-ava-√hṛi (only Ved. inf. -hartos), to lessen, shorten, diminish, AitBr.: Caus. -hārayati, to suspend, interrupt, finish, MBh. °**avahāra**, m. drawing back, withdrawal, MBh.; dissolution, re-absorption, Ragh.

प्रत्यवाप् praty-avâp (ava-√āp), only pf. -avâpuḥ, to re-obtain, recover, Śiś.

प्रत्यवे praty-avê (-ava-√i), P. avâiti, to come down again, reach in descending, Br.; to offend, sin, Śaṃk. °**avâya**, m. decrease, diminution, Kāty-Śr.; MBh.; reverse, contrary course, opposite conduct, Mn. iv, 245; annoyance, disappointment, Śak.; Prab.; offence, sin, sinfulness, Āpast.; Vedântas.; disappearance of what exists or non-production of what does not exist, W.

प्रत्यवेक्ष् praty-avêksh (-ava-√īksh), Ā. -avêkshate (ep. also P. °ti), to look at, ŚBr.; to inspect, examine, look or inquire after, MBh.; R. &c.; to consider, have regard for (acc.), R. °**avêkshaṇa**, n. looking after, care, attention, Kām.; Kull.; (ā), f. (with Buddhists) one of the 5 kinds of knowledge, Dharmas. 94. °**avêkshā**, f. = prec. n., Rājat. °**avêkshya**, mfn. to be regarded or paid attention to, MBh.

प्रत्यष्ट praty-ashṭa, mfn. (√1. aś) fallen to a person's (loc.) lot or share, Kauś.

प्रत्यस् praty-√1. as, P. -asti, to be equal to or a match for (acc.), RV.; ŚBr.

प्रत्यस् praty-√2. as, P. -asyati, to throw to or down, AV.; to turn over or round, ŚBr. °**asta** (práty-), mfn. thrown down, laid low, VS.; ŚBr.; thrown off, given up, Bhartṛ. °**astra**, n. a missile hurled in return, Kathās.

प्रत्यह् praty-√ah (only pf. -āha), to say anything in the presence of (acc.), AV.; to tell, relate (with acc. of pers. and thing), Hit.; to answer, reply to (acc.), ŚBr.

प्रत्याकलित praty-ā-kalita, mfn. (√3. kal) enumerated, held forth, reproached, Daś.; interposed, introduced (as a step in legal process), W.; n. judicial decision as to which of the litigants is to prove his case after the defendant has pleaded, Yājñ., Sch.; (defendant's) supplement to the written deposition of two litigants, Nār.

प्रत्याकाङ्क्ष् praty-ā-√kāṅksh, Ā. -kāṅkshate, to be desirous of, long for, expect, MBh.

प्रत्याकृष् praty-ā-√kṛish, P. -kṛishati, to withdraw, BhP.

प्रत्याक्रम् praty-ā-√kram, P. Ā. -krāmati, -kramate, to step back, ĀpŚr.

प्रत्याक्रुश् praty-ā-√kruś, P. -krośati, to challenge or revile in return, MBh. °**ākroshṭavya**, mfn. to be reviled in return, L.

प्रत्याक्षेपक praty-ā-kshepaka, mf(ikā)n. (√kship) reviling in turn, deriding (-tva, n.), Kuval.

प्रत्याख्या praty-ā-√khyā, P. -khyāti, to proclaim one by one, ŚBr.; to refuse, repudiate, reject, ib. &c. &c.; to deny, Daś.; to refute, Śaṃk.; to counteract (by remedies), Suśr.: Desid. -cikhyāsati, to wish to refute, Śaṃk. °**ākhyāta**, mfn. rejected, refused, disallowed, denied (-tva, n.), MBh.; Kāv. &c.; prohibited, interdicted, Śak.; set aside, outvied, surpassed, Mālav.; informed, apprised, W.; celebrated, notorious, ib. °**ākhyātavya**, mfn. to be opposed or refuted, Śaṃk. °**ākhyātṛi**, m. a refuser, BhP. °**ākhyāna**, mfn. conquered, overcome (as a passion), HYog.; n. rejection, refusal, denial, disallowance, repulse, MBh.; Kāv. &c.; counteracting, combating (of feelings &c.), HYog.; non-admittance, refutation, Śaṃk.; N. of a Jaina wk.; -saṃgraha, m. N. of wk. °**ākhyāyam**, ind. enumerating one by one, TS.; ŚBr. °**ākhyāyin**, mfn. rejecting, refuting (a-pr°), GṛS. °**ākhyeya**, mfn. to be declined or refused, MBh.; Yājñ.; to be refuted or denied, W.; to be cured, curable (as a disease), Car.

प्रत्यागम् praty-ā-√gam, P. -gacchati, to come back again, return, TBr.; MBh.; Kāv. &c.; to come to one's self, recover consciousness, revive, Kālid. °**āgata**, mfn. come back again, returned, arrived, MBh.; Kāv. &c.; -prâṇa, mfn. one who has recovered his breath or life, MBh.; -smṛiti, mfn. one who has rec° his memory, R.; °tâsu, mfn. = -prâṇa, Ragh. °**āgati**, f. coming back, return, arrival, Hariv. °**āgama**, m. id., ib.; R. &c.; °mâvadhi, ind. till (my) return, MW. °**āgamana**, n. coming back, return to (acc.), coming home again, MBh.; Kāv. &c.; (nirūha-pr°) the coming back of a clyster, Suśr.

प्रत्यागॄ praty-ā-√gṝi, P. -gṛiṇāti, to speak to in return, answer, respond, ŚāṅkhŚr.

प्रत्याचक्ष् praty-ā-√caksh, Ā. -cashṭe, to refuse, decline, reject, repulse (with acc. of pers. or thing), ŚrS.; MBh.; Kāv. &c.; to answer, refute, oppose in argument, MW. °**ācakshāṇaka**, mfn. desirous of refuting or objecting to (acc.), Nyāyas., Sch.

प्रत्याजन् praty-ā-√jan, Ā. -jāyate, to be born again, Kāraṇḍ. (Pot. -jāyeyam, SāmavBr.)

प्रत्यातन् praty-ā-√tan, P. Ā. -tanoti, -tanute, to extend in the direction of, shine upon or against, irradiate, RV.; AV.; to bend (a bow) against (acc.), RV.

प्रत्यादा praty-ā-√dā, Ā. -datte, to receive back, MBh.; to take back, revoke, ib.; to draw forth from (abl.), BhP.; to repeat, return, AV.; ŚāṅkhŚr. °**ādāna**, n. re-obtaining, recovery, MBh.; repetition, reiteration, RPrāt.; ĀśvŚr. °**āditsu**, mfn. (fr. Desid.) desirous of recovering or obtaining, BhP. °**ādeya**, mfn. to be received back, to be (or being) received, Inscr.

प्रत्यादिश् praty-ā-√diś, P. -diśati, to enjoin, direct, advise, R.; BhP.; to report, relate (with 2 acc.), MBh.; to summon, Hit.; to decline, reject, repel, MBh.; Kāv. °**ādishṭa**, mfn. enjoined, directed, &c.; overcome, surpassed, MBh.; Śak.; Ragh.; informed, apprised, W.; warned, cautioned, ib.; declared (as from heaven), ib. °**ādeśa**, m. order, command, Vet.; an offer, Jātakam.; rejection, refusal, Kālid.; warning, determent, prevention, Mn. viii, 334; obscuring, eclipsing, Daś.; putting to shame, Kād.; who or what puts to shame, shamer of, reproach to (gen.), Vikr. °**ādeshṭṛi**, m. one who warns or cautions, MW.

प्रत्यादृ praty-ā-√dṛi, Ā. -driyate, to show respect to (acc.), ŚBr.

प्रत्याद्रु praty-ā-√dru, P. -dravati, to run against, rush upon (acc.), MBh.

प्रत्याधान praty-ā-dhāna, n. (√dhā) a place where anything is deposited or laid up, repository, ŚBr.

प्रत्याध्मान praty-ā-dhmāna, n. (√dhmā) a partic. nervous disease, a kind of tympanites or wind-dropsy, Suśr.

प्रत्यानह् praty-ā-√nah, P. -nahyati, to put upon, cover with, ŚBr. °**ānāha**, m. inflammation in the chest, pleuritis, Gal.

प्रत्यानी praty-ā-√nī, P. Ā. -nayati, °te (inf. -nayitum, R.), to lead or bring back, restore, Kauś.; R.; BhP.; to recover, regain, Hariv.; BhP.; to pour or fill up again, ŚBr.; Kauś.: Desid. Ā. -ninīshate, to wish to bring back, try to rearrange or restore, MBh. °**ānayana**, n. leading or bringing back, recovery, restoration, Hariv.; Vikr.; Kād. °**āninīshu**, mfn. (fr. Desid.) desirous of bringing back, W. °**ānīta**, mfn. led or brought back, BhP. °**āneya**, mfn. to be repaired or made good, MBh.

प्रत्याप् praty-√āp, only Desid. pratīpsati, to ask (a girl) in marriage, Kathās.

प्रत्यापत्ति *praty-ā-patti*, f. (√*pad*) return, BhP.; turning back (from evil), conversion, MBh. (= *vairāgya*, Nilak.); restoration, restitution, Pāṇ. iii, 1, 26, Vārtt. 6; viii, 4, 68, Vārtt. 1; expiation, Āpast. (= *śuddhi*, Sch.) °**āpanna,** mfn. returned, regained, restored, Daś.; BhP.

प्रत्याप्लवन *praty-ā-plavana*, n. (√*plu*) springing or leaping back, R.

प्रत्याब्रू *praty-ā-√brū*, P. *-bravīti*, to reply to, answer (acc.), MBh.

प्रत्याभू *praty-ā-√bhū*, P. *-bhavati*, to be at hand or at a person's (acc.) command, TS.

प्रत्याम्ना *praty-ā-√mnā* (only *-mnāyus*), to repeat or recite again, RPrāt. °**āmnātavya,** mfn. to be rejected (*a-pr*°), BhP. °**āmnāna,** n. contrary determination, altered purpose, Lāṭy.; KātyŚr., Sch. °**āmnāya,** m. id., ĀpŚr.; (in log.) the proposition re-stated, conclusion (= *nigamana*).

प्रत्याय *praty-āya* &c. See p. 673, col. 3.

प्रत्याया *praty-ā-√yā*, P. *-yāti*, to come back, return to (acc.), MBh.; Kāv. &c.

प्रत्यारम्भ *praty-ā-rambha*, m. (√*rabh*) beginning again, recommencement, Kauś.; prohibition, Pāṇ. viii, 1, 31; annulment, Pat.

प्रत्यारुह् *praty-ā-√ruh*, Caus. *-ropayati*, to cause to mount again, R.; Uttarar.

प्रत्यालभ् *praty-ā-√labh*, Ā. *-labhate*, to seize by the opposite side, ĀśvŚr.; to take up an attitude of resistance (see *a-pratyālabhamāna*).

प्रत्यालिङ्ग् *praty-ā-√liṅg*, P. *-liṅgati*, to embrace in return, Mṛicch.

प्रत्याली *praty-ā-√lī* (only Ā. pf. *-lilye*), to cling to (acc.), L.

प्रत्यालीढ *praty-ā-līḍha*, mfn. (√*lih*) eaten, L.; extended towards the left, L.; n. a partic. attitude in shooting (the left foot advanced and right drawn back), L.

प्रत्यावप् *praty-ā-√2. vap*, P. *-vapati*, to cast or throw upon once more, Kauś.; MānGṛ.

प्रत्यावृत् *praty-ā-√vṛit*, Ā. *-vartate*, to turn against (acc.), RV.; to return, come back, Kathās.; Hit. &c.: Caus. *-vartayati*, to drive back, repel, RV.; ŚBr. °**āvartana,** n. coming back, returning, R. °**āvṛitta,** mfn. turned back (as a face), Amar.; returned, come back, ib.; Megh. &c.; repeated, Var. °**āvṛitti,** f. coming back, return, Mālatīm.

प्रत्याव्रज् *praty-ā-√vraj*, P. *-vrajati*, to go back, return, Lāṭy.; ĀśvGṛ.

प्रत्याशंस् *praty-ā-√śaṇs*, Ā. *-śaṇsate*, to expect, presuppose, R.

प्रत्याशी *praty-ā-√śī*, Ā. *-śete*, to lie before (acc.), RV.

प्रत्याश्रय *praty-ā-śraya*, m. (√*śri*) a shelter, refuge, dwelling, Sāṃkhyak., Sch.

प्रत्याश्रु *praty-ā-√śru*, Caus. *-śrāvayati*, to pronounce the ejaculatory response, AV.; Br. &c. °**āśrāvá,** m. (VS.), °**āśrāvaṇa,** n. (ŚBr.; ŚrS.) the ej° r° (a partic. sacrificial formula). °**áśrāvita** (Br.), °**áśruta** (TS.), n. id.

प्रत्याश्वस् *praty-ā-√śvas*, P. *-śvasiti*, to breathe again, respire, revive, take heart again, MBh.; Kāv. &c.: Caus. *-śvāsayati*, to comfort, console, encourage, R. °**āśvasta,** mfn. refreshed, revived, recollected, MBh.; Hariv.; R. °**āśvāsa,** m. breathing again, respiration, recovery, MBh. °**āśvāsana,** n. (fr. Caus.) consolation, R.

प्रत्यास् *praty-√ās*, Ā. *-āste*, to sit down opposite or in the direction of (acc.), ŚBr.

प्रत्यासंकलित *praty-ā-sam-kalita*, n. (√3. *kal*) the putting together or combining of various evidence, consideration pro and con, Smṛitit.

प्रत्यासङ्ग *praty-ā-saṅga*, m. (√*sañj*) combination, connection, VPrāt.

प्रत्यासद् *praty-ā-√sad*, P. *-sīdati*, to be near or close at hand, Nyāyas., Sch.; to wait for, expect, Kir. °**āsatti,** f. immediate proximity (in space, time &c.), close contact, Lāṭy.; Śak. &c.; good humour, cheerfulness, Ratnâv.; (in gram.) analogy. °**āsanna,** mfn. near at hand, close to (gen. or comp.), proximate, neighbouring, MBh.; Kāv. &c.; imminent, Megh.; Kathās. &c.; closely connected or related, Āpast.; MBh.; feeling repentance, MBh. (Nīlak.); n. = *-tā*, f. proximity, neighbourhood, MBh.; *-mṛityu*, mfn. one whose death is imminent, at the point of death, MW.

प्रत्यासेव् *praty-ā-√sev*, Ā. *-sevate* = *prati-√jush*, Caus., Nir. viii, 15.

प्रत्यास्था *praty-ā-√sthā*, P. *-tishṭhati*, to keep firm, stand fast, AV.

प्रत्यास्वर *praty-ā-svara*, mfn. (√*svṛi*) shining back, reflecting, ChUp.

प्रत्यास्वादक *praty-ā-svādaka*, m. (√*svad*) a fore-taster (?), Nalac.

प्रत्याहन् *praty-ā-√han*, P. *-hanti* (pf. Ā. *-jaghne*), to drive back, keep away, ward off, AV.; MBh. °**āhata,** mfn. driven back, repelled, repulsed, rejected, MBh.; Kāv. &c.

प्रत्याहृ *praty-ā-√hṛi*, P. *-harati*, to draw in or back, ŚāṅkhŚr.; MBh. &c.; to withdraw (the senses from worldly objects), Pur.; to replace, fetch or bring back, recover, ŚrS.; MBh.; Kāv. &c.; to rearrange, restore, R.; to take up again, continue (a business, sacrifice &c.), MBh.; Hariv.; to report, relate, MBh.; to utter (a speech), cry, MW.; to withdraw (what has been created), destroy, Hariv.; Pur.; w.r. for *pra-vyā-hṛi*, MBh. &c. °**āharaṇa,** n. drawing hither and thither, Gobh., Sch.; bringing back, recovery, Vikr.; drawing back, withdrawing (esp. the senses from external objects), Vedântas. °**āharaṇīya** or °**āhartavya,** mfn. to be taken back or withheld or restrained or controlled, W.

Praty-āhāra, m. drawing back (troops from a battle), retreat, MBh.; withdrawal (esp. of the senses from external objects), abstraction, MBh.; Mn.; Pur.; Vedântas. (cf. IW. 93); withdrawing (of created things), re-absorption or dissolution of the world, MBh.; (in gram.) the comprehension of a series of letters or roots &c. into one syllable by combining for shortness the first member with the Anubandha (s. v.) of the last member; a group of letters &c. so combined (as *ac* or *hal* in the Śiva-Sūtras), Pāṇ. i, 1, 1 &c.; (in dram.) N. of a partic. part of the Pūrva-raṅga (s. v.), Sāh.; speaking to, address (°*ram-√kṛi*, with gen., to speak to a person), Kāraṇḍ. (prob. w. r. for *pravyāh*°); sound, ib. (prob. w. r. for id.) °**āhārya,** mfn. to be taken back or withheld &c.; to be heard or learnt from (abl.), MBh. °**āhṛita,** mfn. resumed, restrained, withheld, W.

प्रत्याह्वे *praty-ā-√hve*, Ā. *-hvayate* (ind. P. *-hūya*), to answer a call, BhP.; to respond to the Āhāva (s. v.), TS. °**āhvaya,** m. echo, resonance, BhP. °**āhvāna,** n. answering a call, ĀśvŚr., Sch.

प्रत्युक्त *praty-ukta*. See *prati-√vac*, p. 670.

प्रत्युक्ष् *praty-√uksh*, P. *-ukshati*, to sprinkle, ĀpŚr.

प्रत्युच्चर् *praty-uc-car* (*-ud-√car*), Caus. *-cārayati*, to rouse up, excite, urge, MBh.; to repeat, RPrāt. °**uccāra,** m. repetition, L. °**uccāraṇa,** n. speaking in return, answering (*a-pratyuc*°), Nyāyas., Sch.

प्रत्युच्छ्रि *praty-ucchri* (*-ud-√śri*), P. Ā. *-chrayati*, °*te*, (P.) to erect against, ŚBr.; (Ā.) to rise against, revolt, ib. °**úcchrita,** mfn. rising, ib.

प्रत्युज्जीव् *praty-ujjīv* (*-ud-√jīv*), P. *-jīvati*, to return to life, revive, Ratnâv.; Kathās.: Caus. *-jīvayati*, to restore to life, revivify, resuscitate, Pañcat. °**ujjīvana,** n. returning to life, reviving, MBh.; Kād.; Bālar.; (fr. Caus.) restoring to life, revivifying, MBh.; Kād.

प्रत्युत *praty-uta*, ind. on the contrary, rather, even, Kāv.; Kathās.; Pur. &c. (cf. 2. *utá*).

प्रत्युत्कर्ष *praty-ut-karsha*, m. (√*kṛish*) outdoing, surpassing, Pratāp.

प्रत्युत्क्रम *praty-ut-krama*, m. (√*kram*) undertaking, the first step or measure in any business, L.; setting out to assail an enemy, W.; declaration of war, W. °**utkramaṇa,** n. id., W. °**utkrānta,** mfn. about to pass away; *-jīvita*, mfn. one whose life is about to pass away, almost dead, Daś. °**utkrānti,** f. = *-utkrama*, L.

प्रत्युत्तम्भ् *praty-ut-tambh* (√*stambh*), P. *-tabhnāti* or *-tabhnoti*, to prop up, support, AitBr. °**úttabdhi,** f. upholding, propping up, supporting, fixing, Br. °**uttambha,** m. (TāṇḍBr.), °**uttambhana,** n. (Sāy.) id.

प्रत्युत्तर *praty-uttara* &c. See p. 664.

प्रत्युत्तॄ *praty-ut-√tṝ* (only ind. p *-uttīrya*), to come home, return, R.; to betake one's self to (acc.), id.

प्रत्युत्था *praty-ut-thā* (√*sthā*), P. *-tishṭhati*, to rise up before (acc.), rise to salute, go to meet, Br.; Mn.; MBh. &c. °**utthāna,** n. rising from a seat to welcome a visitor, respectful salutation or reception, Mn.; Gaut.; MBh. &c.; rising up against, hostility, Hariv. (v. l. *abhy-utth*°). °**utthāyika,** v. l. or w. r. for °*yuka*. °**utthāyin,** mfn. rising again, ŚBr. °**utthāyuka,** mfn. rising respectfully (*a-pratyutth*°), GopBr.; ŚrS. (v. l. °*yika*). °**utthita,** mfn. risen to meet (acc.), MBh.; R. °**uttheya,** mfn. to be honoured or saluted by rising from the seat, AitBr.

प्रत्युत्पन्न *praty-ut-panna*, mfn. (√*pad*) existing at the present moment, present, prompt, ready, MBh.; Kāv. &c.; reproduced, regenerated, W.; (in arithm.) produced by multiplication, multiplied, Col.; n. multiplication or the product of a sum in m°, ib. **—jāti,** f. (in arithm.) assimilation consisting in m°, or reduction to homogeneousness by m°, ib. **—mati,** mfn. ready-minded, sharp, confident, bold, MBh.; Suśr.; Śak. v, 1/8 (*-tva*, n. presence of mind, ib., v. l.); m. 'Ready-wit,' N. of a fish, Kathās.; Hit.

प्रत्युत्पा *praty-ut-√5. pā*, Ā. *-pipīte*, to rise against (acc.), TS.

प्रत्युत्सद् *praty-ut-√sad*, P. *-sīdati*, to resort to (acc.), ŚBr.

प्रत्युदाव्रज् *praty-ud-ā-√vraj*, P. *-vrajati*, to go in a contrary direction, Kauś.

प्रत्युदाहृ *praty-ud-ā-√hṛi*, P. *-harati*, to speak in return, reply, answer, R.; (in gram.) to adduce a contrary example, Pāṇ., Sch. °**udāharaṇa,** n. a counter example or illustration, ib.; Vām.; VPrāt., Sch. °**udāhārya,** mfn. to be adduced as a c° ex°, Pat. °**udāhṛita,** mfn. named, answered, BhP.

प्रत्युदि *praty-ud-√i*, P. *-eti*, to ascend to (acc.), AV.; to rise and go towards (acc.), ib. &c.

प्रत्युदित *praty-udita*. See *prati-√vad*.

प्रत्युदीक्ष् *praty-ud-√īksh*, Ā. *-īkshate*, to look up at, perceive, behold, R.; Bhaṭṭ.

प्रत्युदीर् *praty-ud-√īr* (only ind. p. *-īrya*), to utter in return, reply, BhP.

प्रत्युद्गम् *praty-ud-√gam*, P. *-gacchati* (ep. also Ā. °*te*), to go out towards, advance to meet (a friend or an enemy), Mn.; MBh. &c.; to come forth again, Prasannar.; to set out for (acc. or loc.), Kāraṇḍ. °**udgata,** mfn. gone to meet (a friend or an enemy), MBh.; met, encountered, R.; Ragh.; risen as from a seat, W. °**udgati,** f. (Kād. &c.), °**udgama,** m. (Ragh. &c.), °**udgamana,** n. (Prab.) going forth towards, rising from a seat (as a mark of respect) and going out to meet (esp. a guest). °**udgamanīya,** mfn. to be met or treated respectfully, L.; fit or suitable for the respectful salutation of a guest, Kum.; n. a clean suit of clothes, the upper and lower garments as worn at meals &c., L.

प्रत्युद्गा *praty-ud-√1. gā* (only aor. *-údgāḥ*), to rise before or over (acc.), RV.

प्रत्युद्गार *praty-ud-gāra*, m. (√*gṝ*) a kind of nervous disease, L.

प्रत्युद्गीत *praty-ud-gīta*, mfn. (√*gai*) answered in singing or in chanting, Lāṭy.

प्रत्युद्ग्रह् *praty-ud-√grah*, P. *-gṛihṇāti*, to set aside, dismiss, Lāṭy. °**udgraha,** m., °**udgrahaṇa,** n. setting aside, dismissing, ib., Sch.

प्रत्युद्घात *praty-udghāta*, prob. w. r. for *praty-udyāta*.

प्रत्युद्दीप् *praty-ud-√dīp*, Ā. *-dīpyate*, to flame against, ŚBr.

प्रत्युद्धरण *praty-uddharaṇa*, n. (√*hṛi*) recovering, re-obtaining, W. °**uddhāra**, m. offering, tendering, L. °**uddhṛita**, mfn. re-obtained; rescued, delivered from (abl.), Ragh.

प्रत्युद्धा *praty-uddhā* (*-ud-*√1. *hā*), only aor. *-ahāsata*, to ascend towards (acc.), RV.

प्रत्युद्यम् *praty-ud-√yam*, P. *-yacchati*, to counterbalance (acc.), TāṇḍBr. °**udyata**, mfn. presented, offered, BhP.; w. r. for °*udgata*. °**udyama**, m. (TāṇḍBr.), *ā*, f. (ŚāṅkhBr.) counterbalance, equipoise. °**udyamin**, mfn. maintaining an equipoise, counterbalancing, ŚāṅkhBr. °**udyāmin**, mfn. id., resisting, refractory, AitBr.; ŚBr.

प्रत्युद्या *praty-ud-√yā*, P. *-yāti*, to rise and go towards or against, go to meet (a friend or an enemy), MBh.; Kāv. &c. °**udyāta**, mfn. met, encountered, received, Kālid. °**udyātṛi**, mfn. going forth against, attacking an assailant, MBh. °**udyāna**, n. the act of going forth against &c., L.

प्रत्युद्वद् *praty-ud-√vad*, Caus. *-vādayati*, to cause to resound, ŚBr.

प्रत्युद्व्रज् *praty-ud-√vraj*, P. *-vrajati*, to go forth to meet, Ragh.

प्रत्युन्नमन *praty-un-namana*, n. (√*nam*) rising or springing up again, rebounding, Suśr.

प्रत्युन्मिष् *praty-un-mish* (*-ud-*√1. *mish*), P. *-mishati*, to rise or shine forth (as the sun), Daś.

प्रत्युपकृ *praty-upa-√kṛi*, Ā. *-kurute*, to do a service in return, requite a favour, Pañcat. °**upakāra**, m. returning a service or favour, gratitude, MBh.; Kāv. &c. °**upakārin**, mfn. requiting a favour, grateful, R. °**upakriyā**, f. = °*upakāra*, Kād.; Rājat.; Kathās.

प्रत्युपक्रम् *praty-upa-√kram*, Ā. *-kramate*, to go or march forth against (acc.), GopBr.

प्रत्युपगम् *praty-upa-√gam*, P. *-gacchati*, to come near, approach, MW. °**upagata**, mfn. come near, approached, ib.

प्रत्युपदिश् *praty-upa-√diś*, P. *-diśati*, to explain singly or severally, Suśr.; to teach anything (acc.) in return to (dat.), Mālav. °**upadishṭa**, mfn. advised or cautioned in return, MW. °**upadeśa**, m. instruction or advice in return, Kum.

प्रत्युपद्रु *praty-upa-√dru*, P. *-dravati*, to rush against, fall upon, assail (acc.), MBh.; Pañcat.

प्रत्युपधा *praty-upa-√1. dhā*, P. *-dadhāti*, to put or place upon, cover, SBr.

प्रत्युपपन्न *praty-upa-panna*, v. l. for *praty-utpanna*, in *-mati*, °*ti-tva*, Sak. v, $\frac{1}{2}\frac{1}{0}$.

प्रत्युपभुज् *praty-upa-√2. bhuj*, Ā. *-bhuṅkte*, to eat, enjoy, R. °**upabhoga**, m. enjoyment, MārkP.

प्रत्युपया *praty-upa-√yā*, P. *-yāti*, to go again towards, return, MBh.

प्रत्युपरुद्ध *praty-upa-ruddha*, mfn. (√2. *rudh*) obstructed, choked, BhP.

प्रत्युपलब्ध *praty-upa-labdha*, mfn. (√*labh*) gained back, recovered, Vikr.; BhP. **-cetas**, mfn. one who has recovered his senses, MW.

प्रत्युपविश् *praty-upa-√viś*, P. *-viśati*, to sit down opposite to or before (acc.); to beset or besiege a person (to make him yield), MBh.; R.: Caus. *-veśayate*, to cause a person to beset or besiege another, Āpast.; to oppose, resist, R. °**upavishṭa**, mfn. one who besets or besieges another, Āpast. °**upaveśa**, m., °**śana**, n. besetting or besieging a person (to make him yield), R.

प्रत्युपव्रज् *praty-upa-√vraj*, P. *-vrajati*, to go against, attack (acc.), MBh.

प्रत्युपसृ *praty-upa-√sṛi*, P. *-sarati*, to return, BhP.

प्रत्युपस्था *praty-upa-√sthā*, P. Ā. *tishṭhati*, °*te*, (Ā.) to stand opposite to, ŚBr.; (Ā.) to wait on, MBh.; (P.) to insist on (loc.), Vajracch.: Caus. *-sthāpayati*, to call forth, manifest, Śaṃk. °**upasthāna**, n. proximity, imminence, Śaṃk. °**upasthāpana**, n. mental realization, ib.

Praty-upasthita, mfn. come near to (acc.), approached, arrived, MBh.; Hariv. &c.; standing or being in (loc. or comp.), Hariv.; Var.; present, assisting at (loc.), SaddhP.; gone against, standing opposite to (acc.), MBh.; assembled, ib.; happened, occurred (or about to happen, imminent), MBh.; Kāv. &c.; collecting, pressing (as urine), Suśr.

प्रत्युपस्पृश् *praty-upa-√spriś*, P. *-spriśati*, to touch or sip again (water for internal ablution), Gobh. °**upasparśana**, n. touching or sipping (water) again, ib.

प्रत्युपहार *praty-upa-hāra*, m. (√*hṛi*) handing back, restitution, Ragh.

प्रत्युपह्वे *praty-upa-√hve*, Ā. *-havate*, to call, invite, Br. °**upahavá**, m. a response to an invitatory formula or the repetition of it, ib.; ĀśvŚr.

प्रत्युपाकरण *praty-upâ-karaṇa*, n. (√1. *kṛi*) recommencement of Vedic study, Gobh.

प्रत्युपाधा *praty-upâ-√1. dhā*, Ā. *-dhatte*, to regain, recover, BhP.

प्रत्युपाहृ *praty-upâ-√hṛi*, P. *-harati*, to give up, desist, MBh.

प्रत्युपे *praty-upé* (*-upa-√i*), P. *-upâiti*, to approach again, recommence, AitBr.; Kauś. °**upeya**, mfn. to be met or dealt with, MBh.

प्रत्युपेक्षित *praty-upêkshita*, mfn. (√*īksh*) disregarded, neglected, R.

प्रत्युपोदित *praty-upôdita*, mfn. (√*vad*) addressed with offensive words, TāṇḍBr.

प्रत्युप्त *praty-upta*. See *prati-√vap*, p. 670.

प्रत्युष् *praty-√ush*, P. *-oshati*, to singe, scorch, RV. °**ushṭa** (*práty-*), mfn. burnt or consumed one by one, VS. °**ushyá**, mfn. to be singed or scorched, ŚBr.

प्रत्यूह् *praty-√ūh*, P. Ā. *-uhati*, °*te* (ind. p. *-uhya*, Naish.), to push back, strip off, RV.; ŚBr.; ŚrS.; to bring back, recover, BhP.; to ward off, keep away, AV.; ŚBr.; ChUp.; to interrupt, Mn.; Naish.; to offer, present, ŚBr. °**ūḍha**, mfn. rejected, refused, R.; neglected, Divyâv.; surpassed, excelled, BhP.; covered, enveloped, Sarvad. °**ūha**, m. an obstacle, impediment, MBh.; Kāv. &c. °**ūhana**, n. interruption, discontinuance, ŚāṅkhŚr.

प्रत्यृ *praty-√ṛi*, Caus. *-arpayati*, to cause to go towards, throw towards, AV.; to fasten, fix, put on, ŚBr.; Ragh.; to render up, deliver back, restore, return, Mṛicch.; Kālid.; to give again or anew, Kathās. °**ṛita**, mfn. fixed, inserted, Nir.

Praty-arpaṇa, n. giving back, restoring, returning, Ragh.; Kull. °**arpaṇīya**, mfn. to be given back, Kull. °**arpita**, mfn. restored, Yājñ.

प्रत्ये *praty-ê* (*-ā-√i*; P. pr. 3. pl. *-ā-yanti*, p. *-ā-yat*; Pot. *-êyāt*; pf. *-êyāya*; ind. p. *-êtya*), to come back, return to (acc.), ŚBr.; KātyŚr.; ChUp.; MBh. 2. °**āyana**, n. (for 1. °*āy*° see p. 673, col. 3) setting (of the sun), ChUp.

प्रत्येतव्य *praty-etavya*. See p. 673, col. 3.

प्रत्येष *praty-êsh* (*ā-√ish*), Ā. *-êshate*, to attach one's self to, enter into (loc.), RV. v, 86, 3.

प्रत्रस् *pra-√tras*, P. *-trasati*, to flee in terror, AV.; ŚBr.: Caus. *-trāsayati*, to frighten or scare away, AV. °**trāsá**, m. trembling, fear, ib.

प्रत्वक्ष् *pra-√tvaksh*, only in Ā. pr. p. *-tvakshāṇá*, eminent, superior, RV. °**tvakshas** (*prá-*), mfn. energetic, vigorous, strong (Maruts and Indra), ib.

प्रत्वर् *pra-√tvar*, Ā. *-tvarate*, to hasten forwards, speed, MBh. °**tūrṇa**, mfn. quick, fleet, Hcar. (cf. Pāṇ. viii, 2, 61). °**tūrta** (*prá-*), mfn. id., ŚBr. °**tūrtaka**, mfn. containing the word *pratūrta*, g. *goshad-ādi*. °**tūrti** (*prá-*), f. rapid or violent motion, haste, speed, RV.; mfn. hastening, rapid, violent, ib.; VS.

प्रथ् 1. *prath*, cl. 1. Ā. (Dhātup. xix, 3) *práthate* (rarely P. °*ti*, e. g. impf. 2. du. *áprathatam*, RV.; Impv. *prathantu*, VS.; pf. *paprathatuḥ*, BhP.; mostly Ā., pf. *paprathé*, p. *paprathāná*, RV.; aor. *prathishṭa*, p. *prathāná*, ib.; fut. *prathishyate*, *prathitā*, Gr.), to spread, extend (intrans.; P. trans. and intrans.), become larger or wider, increase, RV. &c. &c.; to spread abroad (as a name, rumour &c.), become known or celebrated, MBh.; Kāv. &c.; to come to light, appear, arise, Kir.; Rājat.; to occur (to the mind), Rājat.: Caus. *pratháyati* (rarely °*te*; aor. *apaprathat*, Pāṇ. vii, 4, 95; Subj. *papráthat*, RV.; *paprathanta*, ib.; *práthayi*, TS.), to spread, extend, increase, RV. &c. &c. (*prathayati-tarām*, Ratnâv. iv, 3; Ā. intr., RV.; AV.); to spread abroad, proclaim, celebrate, R.; Hariv.; BhP.; to unfold, disclose, reveal, show, Kāv.; Pur.; to extend over i. e. shine upon, give light to (acc.), RV. iii, 14, 4.

Pratha, m. N. of a Vāsishṭha (supposed author of RV. x, 181, 1), Anukr.; (*ā*), f. spreading out, extending, flattening, scattering, Nyāyam.; KātyŚr., Sch.; fame, celebrity, Śiś.; Kathās.; Rājat. (°*thāṃ* √*gam* or *gā*, to become famous or celebrated, Rājat.; °*thāpaha*, mfn. destroying fame, ib.); growing, becoming (in *anyathā-pr*°, 'the becoming different'), Vedântas.

Práthana, n. spreading out, extending, flattening, Nir.; RPrāt.; the place for spreading &c., TBr.; unfolding, displaying, showing, Rājat.; throwing, projecting, W.; celebrating, ib.; m. Phaseolus Mungo, L. (cf. *pra-ghana*).

Prathaya, Nom. P. °*yati* = *prithum ācashṭe*, Pat. (cf. Caus. of √*prath*).

Pratháyat, mfn. spreading out, extending &c., AV. &c. &c.; seeing, beholding, W.

Prathayitṛi, mfn. one who spreads or expands or divulges or proclaims, BhP.

Práthas, n. width, extension, RV. **-vat** (*práthas-*), mfn. wide, spacious, VS.

Prathita, mfn. spread, extended, increased; divulged, displayed, published, known, celebrated, MBh.; Kāv. &c.; cast, thrown, W.; intent upon, engaged in, ib.; m. N. of Manu Svārocisha, Hariv.; of Vishṇu, A. **-tithi-nirṇaya**, m. N. of wk. **-tva**, n. fame, celebrity, L. **-yaśas**, mfn. of wide renown, Mālav. **-vidiśā-lakshaṇa**, mfn. renowned under the title of Vidiśā, Megh. **Prathitânurāga**, mfn. manifesting or showing affection, MW.

Prathiti, f. extension of fame, celebrity, notoriety, L.

Prathimán, m. extension, width, greatness, RV. &c. &c. (instr. *prathinā́*, RV.)

Prathimin, mfn. having size or magnitude, W.; (*inī*), f., Pāṇ. v, 2, 137, Sch.

Prathivī, w. r. for *prithivī*, the earth.

Práthishṭha, mfn. broadest, widest, very large or great, RV.; ŚBr. (Pāṇ. vi, 4, 161, Sch.)

Práthīyas, mfn. broader, wider; also = prec., ŚBr.; Prab. (Pāṇ. vi, 4, 161, Sch.)

Prathu, mfn. (= *prithu*) wide, reaching farther than (abl.), Rājat.; m. N. of Vishṇu, MBh.

Prathuka, m. (= *prithuka*) the young of any animal, L.

प्रथ् 2. *prath* or *prith*, cl. 10. P. *prāthayati* or *parthayati*, to throw, cast; to extend, Dhātup. xxxii, 19.

प्रथम *prathamá*, mf(*ā*)n. (for *pra-tama*, superl. of 1. *pra*; rarely declined as a pron., e. g. °*másyāḥ*, AV. vi, 18, 1; °*me*, PañcavBr. xxv, 18, 5; R. iv, 37, 11; Kir. ii, 44; cf. Pāṇ. i, 1, 33) foremost, first (in time or in a series or in rank); earliest, primary, original, prior, former; preceding, initial, chief, principal, most excellent, RV. &c. &c.; often translateable adverbially = ibc. (cf. below) and (*ám*), ind. firstly, at first, for the first time; just, newly, at once, forthwith (also *āt*, Hariv.); formerly, previously (*am* also as prep. with gen. = before, e. g. Mn. ii, 194; *prathamam-anantaram* or *paścāt*, first–afterwards; *pr*°*-tatas*, first–next); m. (in gram., scil. *varṇa*), the first consonant of a Varga, a surd unaspirate letter; (scil. *purusha*), the first (= our 3rd) person or its terminations; (scil. *svara*), the first tone; (in math.) the sum of the products divided by the difference between the squares of the cosine of the azimuth and the sine of the amplitude; (*ā*), f. (in gram.) the first or nominative case and its terminations; du. the first two cases and their t°s. **—kathita**, mfn. aforesaid, before-mentioned, Megh. **—kalpa**, m. a primary or principal rule, Mn. **—kalpika**, m. a term applied to a Yogī just commencing his course (cf. *prāthama-k°*), Yogas., Comm. **—kalpita**, mfn. placed first, first in rank or importance, Mn.; MBh. **—kusuma**, m. or n. (?) white marjoram, L. **—garbha**, m. first pregnancy, first litter, GṛS.; VS.; Mahidh.; (*-gárbhā*), f. pregnant for the first time, ŚBr. **—grantha**, m. N. of a poem by Jagaj-jīvana-dāsa. **—cittôtpādika**, mfn. one who first thinks (of doing anything), Kāraṇḍ. **—cchád**, mfn. typical, figurative, RV. (accord. to Sāy. *=prathamam ācchādayitṛi*, covering first). **—já** or **-jā́**, mfn. firstborn, a firstling; original, primary, RV. &c. &c.; (*-ja*), being the issue of the first (i.e. f°-mentioned) marriage, Yājñ. **—jāta**, mfn. firstborn, AitBr.; Gobh. **—taram**, ind. first of all, Divyâv. **—tas**, ind. first, at first, firstly, Lāṭy.; Mn.; MBh. &c.; forthwith, immediately, Hariv.; before, in preference to (with gen.), Caurap., (ifc.) before, sooner than, ŚārṅgP. **—tri-sauparṇa**, m. N. of Vishṇu, MBh. **—darśana**, n. first sight; (*e*), ind. at f° s°, MW.; *-dina*, n. the first day of seeing any one (gen.), Hit. **—divasa**, m. a first day, principal d°, MW. **—dugdhá**, mfn. just milked, ŚBr. **—dhāra**, m. a first drop, Kauś. **—nirdishṭa**, mfn. first mentioned, f° named; *-tā*, f., Hcat. **—parāpātin**, mfn. flying off first, ĀpŚr. **—parigṛihīta**, mfn. formerly married, Śak. **—purusha**, m. the first (= our 3rd) person in the verb or its terminations, L. (see above); N. of an author, Cat. **—pravada**, mfn. uttering the first sound (as a child), Kauś. **—prasūtā**, f. (a cow) that has calved for the first time, Hcat. **—pluta**, mfn. leapt off first, ĀpŚr. **—bhakshá**, m. (ŚBr.), **-bhakshaṇa**, n. (ĀpŚr., Comm.) the first enjoyment of (gen.), ŚBr. **—bhā́j**, mfn. one to whom the first share is due, RV. **—bhāvin**, mfn. becoming or being like the first, RPrāt. **—maṅgala**, mfn. highly auspicious, MW. **—mañjarī**, f. a partic. Rāga, Saṃgīt. (cf. *patha-m°*). **—yajñá**, m. the first sacrifice, Br.; ĀśvŚr. **—yauvana**, n. early youth, Var. **—rātra**, m. the beginning of night, Br.; Car. **—vayas**, n. earliest age, youth, Vcar. **—vayasin**, mfn. young, ŚBr. **—vashaṭ-kārá**, m. making the first exclamation Vashaṭ over (gen.), ib. **—vasati**, f. the original home, Vcar. **—vāsyá**, mfn. worn formerly (as a garment), AV. **—vittā́**, f. a first wife, KātyŚr. **—viraha**, m. first separation; (*e*), ind. immediately after s°, MW. **—vṛittânta**, m. former circumstances, earlier history, Śak. **—vaiyākaraṇa**, m. a beginner in grammar, Pāṇ. vi, 2, 56, Sch.; a distinguished or first-rate grammarian, ib. **—śravas** (*°má-śr°*; superl. *-śravas-tama*), mfn. having a distinguished reputation, RV. **—śrī**, mfn. one who has just become rich or fortunate, Mṛicch. **—saṃgama**, m. N. of a man, Kathās. **—samāvṛitta**, mfn. just turned towards (loc.), Nir. **—sāhasa**, m. the first or lowest degree of punishment or fine, MW. **—su-kṛita**, n. a former service or kindness, ib. **—soma**, m. the first oblation of Soma; *-tā*, f., KātyŚr., Comm. **—sthāna**, n. the first or lowest scale (in pronunciation, low but audible), KātyŚr. **—svara**, m. the first sound, SaṃhUp.; mfn. supplied with the f° s°, Lāṭy.; n. N. of a Sāman, ĀrshBr. **Prathamâgāmin**, mfn. occurring first, first mentioned, Nir. **Prathamâdeśa**, m. placing (a word) at the beginning of a sentence, ib. **Prathamâbhitapta**, mfn. first scorched or scalded (with tears), Ragh. **Prathamâbhidheya**, n. original meaning; *-tā*, f., Śiś. **Prathamârdha**, m. n. the first half, Śrutab. **Prathamâvara-tva**, n. the being the first and the last, Kum. **Prathamâstam-ita**, n. the having just set (said of the sun), KātyŚr. iv, 15, 12. **Prathamâhám**, ind. on the first day, ŚBr. **Prathamâhāra**, m. the first application, KātyŚr. **Prathamêtara**, mfn. 'other than first,' the second, Piṅg., Sch. **Prathamôtpatita**, mfn. leapt off first, MānŚr. **Prathamôtpanna**, mfn. produced first, firstborn, MW. **Prathamôdita**, mfn. first uttered, uttered previously, Ragh.

Prathamaka, mfn. first, foremost, Śrutab.

प्रदक्षिण *pra-dakshiṇa*, mf(*ā*)n. moving to the right, ŚāṅkhGṛ.; standing or placed on the right (with √*kṛi* or *pra-√kṛi*, 'to turn towards persons or things so as to place them on one's right,' 'turn the right side towards' as a token of respect), Mn.; MBh. &c.; auspicious, favourable, MBh.; R.; respectful, reverential, MBh.; (*ám*), ind. from left to right, so that the r° side is turned towards a person or object, AV. &c. &c. (also ibc.; cf. comp. below; with √*kṛi* and *pra-√kṛi* as above); towards the south, Mn.; Var. (*eṇa*, ind. = *ám* in both meanings, BhP.; Var.); m., (*ā*) f., and n. turning the right side towards, circumambulation from left to right of a person or object (gen. or comp.; with √*kṛi* or √1. *dā*, dat., gen. or loc.) as a kind of worship, R.; Kathās.; Pañcat.; RTL. 68, 2; 145 &c. **—kriyā**, f. going round from left to right (as a mark of respect), Ragh. **—gāmi-tā**, f. the state of one who walks towards the right (one of the 80 minor marks of Buddhists), Dharmas. 84, 15. **—paṭṭikā**, f. a yard, court-yard, L. **Pradakshiṇânuloma**, mfn. respectful and obedient (said of a slave), MBh. **Pradakshiṇârcis**, mfn. shooting out flames towards the right, Ragh. **Pradakshiṇâvarta**, mfn. turned towards the r°, MBh.; R.; Var.; *-nābhitā*, f. having a navel which turns to the r°, Dharmas. 84, 40 (cf. *°ṇa-gāmitā*); *-śikha*, mfn. = *°ṇârcis*, MBh.; *°taka-romatā*, f. having single hairs on the body and all turning to the r°, Dharmas. 83. **Pradakshiṇâvṛitka**, mfn. turned towards the right, having (any one or anything) on the right, Yājñ.

Pradakshiṇaya, Nom. P. *°yati*, to go round from left to right, Śāntiś.; Rājat.

Pradakshiṇit, ind. from left to right, so as to turn one's right side towards any one or anything, RV.

Pradakshiṇī-√kṛi, P. Ā. *-karoti, -kurute*, to turn the right side towards (acc.), go round from left to right, MBh.; Kāv. &c.

प्रदग्ध *pra-dagdha* &c. See *pra-√dah*.

प्रदघस् *pra-dághas* (Ved. inf. of √*dagh*), to cause to fall, throw down, ŚBr. (w. r. *-dághos*).

प्रदण्डवत् *pra-daṇḍa-vat*, mfn. inflicting severe punishment, Parāś.

प्रदत्त *pra-datta* &c. See *pra-√1. dā*.

प्रदम् *pra-dam*, Caus. *-damayate*, to subdue, conquer, Bhaṭṭ. **°dānta**, m. pl. N. of a school, L. **°dām**, m. (nom. *dān*), Pāṇ. viii, 2, 64, Sch.

प्रदर *pra-dara*. See *pra-√dṛī*.

प्रदर्प *pra-darpa*, m. (√*dṛip*) pride, arrogance, MW. **°dṛipita**, see *á-pradṛipita*. **°dṛipta**, mfn. proud, haughty, conceited, MW. **°dṛipti** (*prá-*), f. haughtiness, arrogance, madness, RV.

प्रदर्विदा *pra-darvidā* (?), Kāś. on Pāṇ. vi, 3, 63 (cf. *pra-pharvidā*).

प्रदर्श *pra-darśa* &c. See *pra-√dṛiś*.

प्रदल *pra-dala*, m. an arrow (= *pra-dara*), L.

प्रदव *pra-dava*, *°vya* &c. See *pra-√2. du*.

प्रदस् *pra-√das*, P. *-dasyati*, to dry up, become dry, Kāṭh.

प्रदह् *pra-√dah*, P. *-dahati* (ep. also Ā. *°te*), to burn, consume, destroy, AV. &c. &c.: Pass. *-dahyate* (ep. also *°ti*), to take fire, be burnt, burn, MBh.; Kāv. &c.: Caus. *-dāhayati*, to cause to be burnt, Vcar. **°dagdha** (*prá-*), mfn. burnt, destroyed, ŚBr.; R.; Var.; *°dhâhuti* (*prá-*), mfn. one who has burnt the sacrificial oblation, ŚBr. **°dagdhavya**, mfn. to be burnt, MBh. **°dāha**, m. burning, heating, consuming by fire, Br.; Gaut.; destruction, annihilation, Śaṃk.

प्रदा *pra-√1. dā*, P. *-dadāti*, rarely Ā. *-datte* (Ved. inf. *prá-dātos*, TS.; irreg. Pot. P. *-dadet*, Hcat.), to give away, give, offer, present, grant, bestow, RV. &c. &c. (with or scil. *bhāryām*, to give in marriage; with *prativacas*, to g° an answer; with *pravṛittim*, to g° information about an event; with *yuddham*, to g° battle; with *dvandva-yuddham*, to engage in single combat; with *vidyām*, to communicate or impart knowledge; with *hutāśanam*, to set fire to); to give up, abolish, TS.; to sell (with instr. of price), Pañcat.; to restore (anything lost &c.), Mn.; to pay, discharge (a debt), Yājñ.; to put or place in (loc.), ib.; MBh.: Pass. *-dīyate*, to be given away, be given, Mn.; MBh. &c.: Caus. *-dāpayati*, to cause to give, TS. &c. &c.; to compel to give back or to repay, Yājñ.; Kull.; to cause to put in or to, MBh.; Bhpr.; to put or place in (loc.), Car.; (with *vastim*), to apply a clyster, ib.: Desid. *-ditsate*, to wish to give in marriage, Daś.

Prá-tta, mfn. (for *pra-datta*) given away (also in marriage), offered, presented, granted, bestowed, TS. &c. &c.; *-vat*, mfn. one who has given or presented, W. **Prá-tti**, f. giving away, giving, gift, TS.; AitBr.

Pra-da, mf(*ā*)n. giving, yielding, offering, granting, bestowing, causing, effecting, uttering, speaking (cf. *anna-*, *jaya-*, *bahu-*, *sukha-*, *-śāpa* &c.); (*ā*), f. a gift, L. **°datta**, mfn. = *pratta*, R.; Kathās.; Pañcat. (*-nayanôtsava*, mfn. affording a feast to the eyes i.e. beautiful to behold, Kathās.); m. N. of a Gandharva, R. **°dadi**, see *á-pradadi*.

Pra-dātavya, mfn. to be given (also in marriage) or offered or presented or restored or imparted &c. (*teshām saṃskṛitam pradātavyam*, to these Sanskṛit is to be imparted i.e. these are to be taught Sanskṛit, Sāh.), Mn.; MBh. &c.; to be placed or put into, Var. **°dātṛi**, m. a giver, bestower (mostly in comp. with the object, rarely with the receiver), AV. &c. &c.; an offerer, presenter (*visha-*, of poison), Car.; one who gives a daughter in marriage, Mn.; MBh.; an imparter (of knowledge), Pañcat.; a granter (of a wish), BrahmavP. (f. *trī*); N. of Indra, TS.; ŚBr.; of one of the Viśve Devāḥ, MBh. **°dātrikā**, f. a female giver, MaitrS.

1. **Pra-dā́na**, n. (for 2. see below) giving, bestowal, presentation (esp. of an offering in the fire; also N. of the sacred text recited on this occasion), TS. &c. &c.; a gift, donation, Mn.; MBh. &c.; giving away in marriage, Mn.; Yājñ. &c.; applying (of a clyster), Suśr.; turning (the eyes), Kum.; making (an attack), Pañcat.; uttering (a curse), VP.; granting (a boon), MBh.; teaching, imparting, announcing, declaring, Mn.; R.; Kathās.; *-kṛipaṇa*, mfn. mean or niggardly in making presents, MBh.; *-pūrvam*, ind. with a present, Kathās.; *-ruci*, m. 'delighting in giving,' N. of a man, Buddh.; *-vat*, mfn. giving, liberal, MBh.; *-śūra*, m. 'a hero in giving,' an excessively liberal man, Lalit.; N. of a Bodhi-sattva, SaddhP. **°dānaka**, n. an offering, donation, Cat. **°dānika**, see *go-pr°*, *jala-pr°* and *dattâpradānika*. **°dāpayitṛi**, m. a giver, TS. **°dāpya**, mfn. to be caused to give or compelled to pay, Yājñ. **°dāya**, n. a present, MBh. **°dāyaka**, mfn. giving, granting, presenting, bestowing (gen. or comp.), MBh.; R. &c.; *-tva*, n., Kull. **°dāyin**, mfn. id., Mn.; MBh. &c.; *°yi-tva*, n., Kum. **°di**, m. a gift, present, Pāṇ. iii, 3, 92, Sch. **°ditsā**, f. (fr. Desid.) desire to give, Jātakam. **°ditsu**, mfn. (fr. Desid.) wishing to give (with acc.), MBh.

Pra-deya, mf(*ā*)n. to be given or presented or granted or offered or communicated or imparted or taught (with dat., sometimes in comp. with the recipient), Mn.; MBh. &c.; to be instructed or initiated in (loc.), MBh.; (*ā*), f. to be given in marriage, marriageable, MBh.; R.; Kathās.; m. a present, gift, MBh.; R.

प्रदान 2. *pra-dāna*, n. (√*do*) a goad, L. (for 1. see under *pra-√1. dā*).

प्रदान्त *pra-dānta*. See *pra-√dam*.

प्रदास *pra-dāsa*, m. (?), Divyâv.

प्रदिग्ध *pra-digdha*. See *pra-√dih*.

प्रदिव् *pra-dív*, f. (fr. 3. *div*, 'heaven;' nom. *-dyaus*) the third or highest heaven (in which the Pitṛis are said to dwell), AV.; the fifth of seven heavens, ŚāṅkhBr.; mfn. (fr. 3. *div*, 'day' [cf. Lat. *diu*]) existing from olden times, ancient, RV.; (*-dívas*, ind. from of old, long since, always, ever (*ánu prad°*, as of old, as formerly), ib.; AV.; (*-dívi*), ind. at all times, always, ever, RV.

प्रदिश् *pra-√diś*, P. Ā. *-diśati*, *°te*, to point out, show, indicate, declare, appoint, fix, ordain, RV. &c. &c.; to direct, bid, urge, R.; to assign, apportion, grant, Mn.; MBh. (*-diśyati*, i, 6472); Kāv. &c.: Caus. *-deśayati*, to urge on, incite, MBh.; R.: Intens. (pr. p. *-dédiśat*), to animate, RV.

Pra-diś, f. pointing to or out, indication, direction, order, command, dominion, RV.; AV.; VS.; a direction, quarter, region of the sky, ib.; MBh.; Hariv. (acc. pl. 'in all directions, everywhere,' MBh.; with *pitryā*, 'the region of the Pitṛis' i.e. the south, AV.); an intermediate point or half-quarter (as north-east), AV. &c. &c. **°dishṭa** (*prá-*), mfn. pointed out, indicated, fixed, ordained, RV. &c. &c.

Pra-deśa, m. (ifc. f. *ā*) pointing out, showing, indication, direction, decision, determination, Nir.; ŚrS.; appeal to a precedent, Suśr.; an example (in grammar, law &c.), RPrāt.; MBh.; Yājñ., Sch.; a spot, region, place, country, district (often in comp. with a part of the body, e.g. *kaṇṭha-*, *hṛidaya-*), MBh.; Kāv. &c. (n., Pañcad.); a short while (see comp. below); a wall, L.; a short span (measured from the tip of the thumb to that of the forefinger), L.; (with Jainas) one of the obstacles to liberation, Sarvad. ('atomic individuality,' W.); *-kārin*, m. N. of a kind of ascetic, L.; *-bhāj*, mfn. of short duration, Daśar.; *-vat*, mfn. possessing or occupying a place, Brahmas., Sch.; *-vartin*, mfn. = *-bhāj* (°*ti-tvā*, f.), Hcar.; *-śāstra*, n. a book containing examples, MBh.; *-stha*, mfn. = *-bhāj*, Sāh.; being or situated in a district, MW. °**deśana,** n. a gift, present, offering, L.; (*ī*), f. = °*śini*, L. °**deśita,** mfn. urged, directed, MBh. °**deśinī,** f. the forefinger (or the corresponding toe), ŚrS.; MBh. &c. °**deshṭṛi,** m. one who pronounces judgment, chief justice, Pañcat.

प्रदिह् *pra-√dih*, P. *-degdhi*, to smear over, besmear, anoint, Suśr. °**digdha,** mfn. smeared over, anointed, stained or covered with (instr. or comp.), ib.; MBh.; R. &c.; n. (scil. *māṃsa*) a kind of dish prepared with meat, L.; m. a kind of sauce or gravy, W. °**deha,** m. a plaster, a thick or viscid ointment, poultice, Suśr.; applying a plaster, unction, ib.; solid food (perhaps inspissated juice &c.), ib. °**dehana,** n. smearing, anointing, Kauś.

प्रदी *pra-√2. dī* (only pr. Subj. *-dīdayat* and pf. *-dīdiyuḥ*), to shine forth, RV.

प्रदीप् *pra-√dīp*, Ā. *-dīpyate*, to flame forth, blaze, burst into flames, ŚBr.; MBh.; Var.: Caus. *-dīpayati*, to set on fire, light, kindle, inflame, KātyŚr.; MBh. &c. °**dīpa,** m. a light, lamp, lantern, MBh.; Kāv. &c. (often ifc. 'the light i.e. the glory or ornament of,' e.g. *kula-pr°*, q.v.; also in titles of explanatory wks. = elucidation, explanation, e.g. *mahābhāshya-pr°*); N. of wk.; *-mañjarī*, f. N. of Comm. on the Amara-kośa; *-śaraṇa-dhvaja*, m. N. of a Mahoraga-rāja, L.; *-sāha*, m. N. of a prince, Cat. (*sāha* = شاه); *-siṃha*, m. N. of an author, Cat. °**dīpaka,** m. (*ikā*), f. and n. a small lamp, a lamp, MBh.; (ifc.) explanation, commentary, Cat. °**dīpana,** mfn. inflaming, exciting, Suśr.; m. a sort of poison, L.; n. the act of kindling or inflaming, R. °**dīpāya,** Nom. Ā. °*yate*, to act as a lamp, Mṛicch. °**dīpiya** or °**dīpya,** mfn., g. *apūpâdi*. °**dīpta,** mfn. kindled, inflamed, burning, shining, ŚBr. &c. &c.; excited, stimulated, MBh.; Kāv. &c.; (in augury) clear, shrill (opp. to *pūrṇa*), VarBṛS.; *-bhās*, mfn. shining bright, Ṛit.; *-śiras*, mfn. one whose head is hot or burning, Vedântas.; °*tâksha*, m. 'having lustrous eyes,' N. of a Yaksha, Kathās. °**dīpti,** f. light, lustre, brilliancy, L.; *-mat*, mfn. bright, radiant, luminous, MBh.

प्रदीर्घ *pra-dīrgha*, mfn. exceedingly long, Var.; Suśr.

प्रदु *pra-√2. du*, Ā. *-dūyate*, to be consumed by fire, ChUp.; P. *-dunoti*, to distress, pain, press hard, Suśr.; Bhaṭṭ. °**dava,** mfn. burning, inflaming, Pāṇ. iii, 1, 142, Kāś. °**davyà,** m. (with *agni*) a forest fire, ŚBr. °**dāvá,** m. id., MaitrS. °**dāvyà,** m. (with *agni*) id., TS.; ŚāṅkhBr.; ŚrS.

प्रदुग्ध *pra-dugdha*. See *á-* and *savya-pra-dugdha*.

प्रदुष् *pra-√dush*, P. *-dushyati*, to become worse, deteriorate, Suśr.; to be defiled or polluted, fall (morally), Mn.; Yājñ.; to commit an offence against (acc.), MBh.; to become faithless, fall off, ib.: Caus. *-dūshayati*, to spoil, deprave, corrupt, pollute, defile, MBh.; Kāv. &c.; to abuse, blame, censure, R.; (with *cittam*) to be angry, Divyâv. °**dushṭa,** mfn. corrupt, wicked, bad, sinful, MBh.; Kāv. &c.; wanton, licentious (woman), Ṛit. °**dūshaka,** mfn. polluting, defiling, MBh. °**dūshaṇa,** mfn. corrupting, defiling, impairing, MBh.; Suśr. °**dūshita,** mfn. corrupted, spoilt, made worse, MBh.; R.; Var.; Suśr. 1. °**dosha,** mfn. (for 2. see col. 2) corrupt, bad, wicked, Śiś.; m. defect, fault, disordered condition (of the body or of a country), mutiny, rebellion, Pañcat.; *-nirṇaya*, m., *-śānti*, f., °*shôdyāpana*, n. N. of wks.

प्रदुह् *pra-duh*, mfn. (nom. *-dhuk*) milking, Pāṇ. iii, 2, 61, Sch. °**doha,** see *su-pradoha*. °**dohana,** m. N. of a man (see *prādohani*).

प्रदृश् *pra-√dṛiś*, Pass. *-dṛiśyate* (cf. *pra-√paś*), to become visible, be seen, appear, RV. &c. &c.: Caus. *-darśayati*, to make visible, show, indicate, explain, teach, describe, Mn.; MBh. &c.: Desid. *-didṛikshate*, to wish to see, Bhaṭṭ.

Pra-darśa, m. look, appearance (see *su-prad°*); direction, injunction, Suśr. °**darśaka,** mfn. showing, indicating, RPrāt.; proclaiming, foretelling, MārkP.; teaching, expounding, Cat.; m. a teacher, MBh.; n. (?) a doctrine, principle, Kap., Sch. (v.l. *pra-ghaṭṭaka*). °**darśana,** n. look, appearance (often ifc., with f. *ā*), MBh.; R.; pointing out, showing, propounding, teaching, explaining, RPrāt.; MBh.; Saṃk.; an example, Yājñ.; prophesying, W.; (*ā*), f. indication, Kāvyâd., Sch.; m.pl. N. of a class of deities under Manu Auttami, VP. °**darśita,** mfn. shown, pointed out, indicated; taught, mentioned, specified, Mn.; MBh. &c.; prophesied, W. °**darśin,** mfn. (ifc.) seeing, viewing, MBh.; Suśr.; pointing out, showing, indicating, MBh.; Hariv.; Kathās.

प्रदृ *pra-√dṛī* (of P. only Ved. Impv. *-dárshi*), to break or tear to pieces, RV. vi, 26, 5: Pass. *-dīryate*, to cleave asunder, split open (intr.), AitBr.; KātyŚr.; to be dispersed or scattered (as an army), MBh.: Caus. *-dārayati*, to split, cleave, tear asunder, ib. °**dará,** m. dispersion, rout (of an army), MBh.; a crevice, cleft (in the earth), VS.; Br. &c.; moenorrhagia (a disease of women), Car.; a kind of arrow, MBh.; rending, tearing, W.; pl. N. of a people, MBh.

प्रदेश *pra-deśa* &c. See *pra-√diś*.

प्रदोष 2. *pra-dosha*, m. (for 1. see under *pra-dush*) the first part of the night, evening (also personified as a son of Doshā and associated with Niśītha and Vyushṭa), MBh.; Kāv.; Pur. &c.; (*ám*), ind. in the evening, in the dark, RV.; GṛŚrS. **-kāla,** m. evening tide, Hit. **-timira,** n. ev° darkness, the dusk of early night, Mṛicch. **-pūjā-vidhi,** m., **-mahiman,** m., **-māhātmya,** n. N. of wks. **-ramaṇīya,** mfn. pleasant or delightful in the ev°, MW. **-velā,** f. = *-kāla*, A. **-śiva-pūjā,** f. N. of wk. **-samaya,** m. = *-kāla*, A. **-stotra,** n. N. of ch. of SkandaP. **Pradoshâgama,** m. the coming on of ev°, nightfall, Amar. **Pradoshânila,** m. the evening wind, Mṛicch.

Pradoshaka, m. evening, Mṛicch. v, 35 (v.l.); born in the evening (?), Pāṇ. iv, 3, 28.

प्रद्यु *pra-dyu*, n. merit (of good works) leading to heaven or securing heaven, L.

प्रद्युत् *pra-√1. dyut*, Ā. *-dyotate*, to begin to shine, ŚBr.: Caus. *-dyotayati*, to irradiate, illumine, Prab.; BhP. °**dyutita,** mfn. beginning to shine, illuminated, Pāṇ. i, 2, 21, Sch.

Pra-dyotá, m. radiance, light, ŚBr.; a ray of l°, L.; N. of a Yaksha, MBh.; of a king of Magadha and founder of a dynasty, VP.; Kathās.; of a king of Ujjayinī and other princes, Lalit.; Priyad.; BhP. °**dyotana,** m. the sun, L.; N. of a prince of Ujjayinī, Lalit.; (with *bhaṭṭâcārya*) N. of an author, Cat.; (pl.) of a dynasty, BhP.; n. blazing, shining, light, L. °**dyotita,** mfn. = *dyutita*, Pāṇ. i, 2, 21, Sch. °**dyotin,** mfn. (ifc.) illustrating, explaining, Cat.

प्रद्युम्न *pra-dyumna*, m. 'the pre-eminently mighty one,' N. of the god of love (re-born as a son of Kṛishṇa and Rukmiṇī, or as a son of Saṃkarshaṇa and then identified with Sanat-kumāra), MBh.; Kāv. &c.; the pleasant (= *kāma*), Subh.; the intellect (= *manas*), Śaṃk.; N. of a son of Manu and Naḍvalā, BhP.; of a king, Kathās.; of sev. authors and teachers, Cat.; of a mountain, Rājat.; of a river, ib. **-pura,** n. 'Pradyumna's city,' N. of a town on the Candra-bhāgā or Chenab, Kathārṇ. **-rahasya,** n. 'P°'s secret,' N. of wk. **-vijaya,** m. 'P°'s victory,' N. of a drama. **-śikhara,** n. 'P°'s peak,' N. of a mountain, Kathās.; *-pīṭhâshṭaka*, n. N. of wk. **Pradyumnâgamana,** n. P°'s arrival; °*manīya*, mfn. treating of it, Pāṇ. iv, 3, 88, Sch. **Pradyumnâcārya,** m. former N. of Veda-nidhi-tīrtha (died in 1576), Cat. **Pradyumnânanda,** m. 'P°'s joy,' N. of a Bhāṇa (also °*dīya*, n.) **Pradyumnâbhyudaya,** m. 'P°'s rise,' N. of a Nāṭaka. **Pradyumnâstra,** n. P°'s weapon, Kathās. **Pradyumnôttara-carita,** n. 'P°'s further deeds,' N. of a poem. **Pradyumnôpâkhyāna,** n. 'the story of P°,' N. of a tale.

Pradyumnaka, m. N. of the god of love, BhP.

प्रद्राणक *pra-drāṇaka*, mfn. (√2. *drā*) sorely distressed, very needy or poor, ChUp.

प्रद्रु *pra-√dru*, P. *-dravati* (ep. also Ā. °*te*), to run forwards, run away, flee, RV. &c. &c.; to hasten towards, rush upon or against (acc.), MBh.; R.; to escape safely to (acc.), MBh. (v.l. *prâd°*): Caus. *-drāvayati*, to cause to run away, put to flight, MBh. °**drava,** mfn. fluid, liquid, Suśr. °**drāva,** m. running away, flight, Bhaṭṭ. (Pāṇ. iii, 3, 27); going quick or well, W. °**drāvin,** mfn. fleeing, runaway, fugitive, Kauś. (Pāṇ. iii, 2, 145).

Prá-druta, mfn. run away, fled, departed, TBr.; MBh.

प्रद्रुह् *pra-druh*, mfn. (nom. *-dhruk*) one who hurts or injures, Pāṇ. iii, 2, 61, Sch.

प्रद्रेक् *pra-√drek*, Ā. *-drekate*, to begin to neigh or roar or bellow &c., Bhaṭṭ.

प्रद्वार् *pra-dvār*, f. a place before a door or gate, MBh. (v.l. *a-dvār*). °**dvāra,** n. id., R.; Kathās.

प्रद्विष् *pra-√dvish*, P. Ā. *-dveshṭi*, *-dvishṭe*, to feel dislike or repugnance for, hate, show one's hatred against (acc.), MBh.; R.

Pra-dvish, mfn. (nom. *ṭ*) disliking, hating, Pāṇ. iii, 2, 61, Sch. °**dvesha,** m. dislike, repugnance, aversion, hatred, hostility to (loc., gen. or comp.), MBh.; Kāv. &c.; (*ī*), f. N. of the wife of Dīrghatamas, MBh. °**dveshaṇa,** n. hatred, dislike of (comp.), MBh. °**dveshṭṛi,** mfn. one who dislikes or hates; a disliker, hater, W.

प्रधन *pra-dhána*, n. (cf. *dhána*) spoil taken in battle, a prize gained by a victor, the battle or contest itself, RV. &c. &c.; the best of one's goods, valuables, Nār.; tearing, bursting &c. (= *dāraṇa*), L.; m. N. of a man; pl. his descendants, BrahmaP. **Pradhanâghātaka,** mfn. bringing about a contest, Hcar. **Pradhanâṅgaṇa,** n. a battle-field, Vcar. **Pradhanôttama,** n. 'best of battles,' a great battle or contest, MW.

Pradhanyà, mf(*ā*)n. forming the spoil or booty (as cattle), RV.

प्रधमन *pra-dhamana*. See *pra-√dhmā*.

प्रधर्ष *pra-dharsha* &c. See *pra-√dhṛish*.

प्रधा *pra-√1. dhā*, Ā. *-dhatte*, to place or set before, offer, RV.; to send out (spies), ib. vii, 61, 3; to give up, deliver, TS.; Kāṭh.; to devote one's self to (acc.), Lalit.

Pra-dha, m., Pāṇ. iii, 1, 139, Sch.; (*ā*), f., ib. vi, 4, 64, Sch.; N. of a daughter of Daksha, MBh.; MārkP. (prob. w. r. for *prādhā*).

Pradhāna, n. a chief thing or person, the most important or essential part of anything, KātyŚr.; Mn.; MBh. &c.; (ibc.) the principal or first, chief, head of; [often also ifc. (f. *ā*), e.g. *Indra-pradhāna*, (a hymn) having Indra as the chief object or person addressed, Nir.; *prayoga-p°*, (the art of dancing) having practice as its essential part, chiefly practical, Mālav.]; 'the Originator,' primary germ, original source of the visible or material universe (in Sāṃkhya = *prakṛiti*, q. v.), IW. 53, 1 &c.; primary or unevolved matter or nature, Sarvad.; supreme or universal soul, L.; intellect, understanding, L.; the first companion or attendant of a king, a courtier, a noble (also m.), L.; an elephant-driver (also m.), L.; (in gram.) the principal member of a compound (opp. to *upasarjana*, q. v.); mf(*ā*)n. chief, main, principal, most important; pre-eminent in (instr.); better than or superior to (abl.), MBh.; Kāv. &c.; m. N. of an ancient king, MBh.; (*ā*), f. N. of a Śakti, Tantr. (cf. IW. 522). **-karman** or **-kārya,** n. chief or principal action; principal mode of treatment (in med.), Suśr.; Madhus. **-kāraṇa-vāda,** m. the doctrine that Pradhāna is the original cause (according to the Sāṃkhya), Bādar., Sch. **-tama,** mfn. most excellent or distinguished, most important, chiefest, MBh.; Suśr. **-tara,** mfn. more excellent, better, MārkP. **-tas,** ind. according to eminence or superiority, Mn.; MBh.; Hariv. **-tā,** f. pre-eminence, excellence, superiority, prevalence, R.; Hariv.; Hit.; Vedāntas.; the being Pradhāna, q.v.; (in MBh. iii, 173=*jagat-kāraṇatā*; cf. *śarīra-p°*). **-tva,** n. pre-eminence, superiority, excellence, ĀśvŚr.; MBh.; (in Sāṃkhya) the being Pradhāna, Sāṃkhyak., Sch. **-dhātu,** m. 'chief element of the body,' semen virile, L. **-purusha,** m. a chief person, most distinguished personage, an authority, Mn.; Mālav.; 'the supreme soul,' N. of Śiva, MBh.; °*shâtīta,* m. transcending Pradhāna and Purusha (matter and spirit); N. of Śiva, MW. **-bhāj,** mfn. 'receiving the chief share,' most excellent or distinguished, MBh. **-bhūta,** mfn. one who is the chief person, Kāś. on Pāṇ. i, 4, 54. **-mantrin,** m. a prime minister, R.; Hit.; Vet. **-mitra,** n. a chief friend, R. **-vādin,** m. one who asserts the Sāṃkhya doctrine (of Pradhāna), Bādar., Sch. **-vāsas,** n. the best clothes, full-dress, Mṛicch. **-vṛishṭi,** f. copious rain, heaviest rain, Var. **-śishṭa,** mfn. taught or laid down as of primary importance, MW. (cf. *anvācaya-ś°*). **-sabhika,** m. the chief of a gambling-house, Mṛicch. **-sevā,** f. chief or principal service, Pañcat. **Pradhānâṅga,** n. a chief member, the ch° m° of the body; most eminent person in a state; principal branch of a science &c., W. **Pradhānâtman,** m. supreme or universal soul, N. of Vishṇu, VP.; (identified with the original cause of the universe or Viśva-bhāvana, W.) **Pradhānâdhyaksha,** m. a chief superintendent; *-tā,* f. the office of ch° s°, Kathās. **Pradhānâmātya,** m. a prime minister, W. **Pradhānôttama,** mfn. best of the eminent, illustrious; warlike, brave, W.

Pradhānaka, n. (in Sāṃkhya) the original germ out of which the material universe is evolved (= *pradhāna, a-vyakta,* q.v.), Tattvas.

Pradhānya, w.r. for *prādh°,* q.v., MBh.

Pra-dhí, m. the felly of a wheel (also pl.), RV. &c. &c.; orb, disc (of the moon), RV. x, 138, 6; a segment, Śulbas.; *-maṇḍala,* n. the circumference of (the felly of) a wheel, MW.; °*dhy-anika,* n. the centre of a segment, Śulbas.; a well, L.

प्रधा *pra-√2. dhā.* See *pra-√dhe,* col. 2.

प्रधाव् *pra-√1. dhāv,* P. Ā. *-dhāvati,* °*te,* to run forwards, r° forth, r° away, set out, start, RV.; ŚāṅkhŚr.; MBh. &c.; to rush upon, Kathās.; to run or go to (acc.), Mn.; MBh. &c.; to pervade, permeate, Suśr.; to become diffused, spread, MBh.: Caus. P. *-dhāvayati,* to put to flight, Kathās.; to drive away, dr°, Br. 1. °**dhāvana,** m. a runner, L. °**dhāvita,** mfn. run away, set out, started, MBh.; R.; Pañcat. &c.

प्रधाव् *pra-√2. dhāv,* P. Ā. *-dhāvati,* °*te,* to wash or rub off, ŚBr.: Caus. P. Ā. *-dhāvayati,* °*te,* to wash or cause to w° off, MBh. 2. °**dhāvana,** m. air, wind, L. (regarded as a 'purifier,' cf. *pavana;* or perhaps fr. √1. *dhāv,* reg° as a 'runner'); n. rubbing or washing off, Suśr.; Gaut.

प्रधि *pra-dhi.* See above.

प्रधी 1. *pra-√dhī* (or *-dīdhī,* only p. pr. *-dīdhyat* and *-dīdhyāna*), to long for, strive after, RV. i, 113, 10; to look out, be on the watch, AV. x, 4, 11.

प्रधी 2. *pra-dhī,* f. great intelligence, Vop.; mfn. of superior i°, pre-eminently intelligent, ib.

प्रधुर *pra-dhura,* n. the tip of a pole, ĀpŚr.

प्रधू *pra-√dhū,* P. Ā. *-dhūnoti,* °*nute,* to move forward, PañcavBr.; to blow away, ChUp.; MBh.; to blow or shake out (the beard after drinking), RV.: Intens. *-dodhuvat, -dūdhot,* to blow (the beard, acc.); to blow into (loc.), RV.

Pra-dhūpita, mfn. fumigated, perfumed, MBh.; heated, burnt; lighted, inflamed; afflicted; excited, W.; (*ā*), f. (with or scil. *diś*) the quarter to which the sun is proceeding, L.; a woman in trouble or affliction, ib.

Pra-dhūmita, mfn. smothered with smoke, giving out smoke, smouldering, Ragh.

प्रधृ *pra-√dhṛi* (only pf. Ā. *-dadhre,* with *manas*), to set the mind upon anything (dat.), resolve, determine, MBh.: Caus. P. *-dhārayati,* to chastise, inflict a punishment on any one (loc.; cf. *daṇḍam √dhṛi*), MBh.; to keep in remembrance, ib.; to reflect, consider, ib.; Pat.; (*pradhārayantu,* w.r. for *pra dhārā yantu,* ĀśvGṛ. iii, 12, 14). °**dhāraṇa,** mfn. keeping, preserving, protecting (see *pāda-pr°*); (*ā*), f. constantly fixing one's mind on a certain object, MBh.

प्रधृष् *pra-√dhṛish,* P. *-dharshati, -dhṛishṇoti,* to be bold against, assail with courage or daring, lay hands on, hurt, injure, harass, overpower, overcome, R.: Caus. P. *-dharshayati,* id., ib.; Kaush-Ār.; MBh. &c.; to violate (a woman), MBh.; to destroy, devastate, R. °**dharsha,** m. attacking, assaulting, assailing (see *dush-p°*). °**dharshaka,** mfn. (ifc.), molesting, hurting, violating (the wife of another), MBh.; R.; Hariv. °**dharshaṇa,** mfn. (ifc.) attacking, molesting, harassing, MBh.; n. or (*ā*), f. attacking, assailing, an attack, assault, ill-treatment, molestation (*keśa-p°,* dragging by the hair), MBh.; R. °**dharshaṇīya,** mfn. to be assailed, assailable, open to attack, exposed to injury or ill-treatment, MBh. °**dharshita,** mfn. (fr. Caus.) attacked, hurt, injured, MBh.; R.; BhP.; haughty, arrogant, W.; *-vat,* mfn. arrogant, proud, W. °**dharshin,** mfn.=°*dharshaṇa,* mfn., Dharmaśarm. °**dhṛishṭa,** mfn. treated with contumely, W.; proud, arrogant, ib. °**dhṛishṭi,** f. overpowering, subjugation, ŚāṅkhŚr. °**dhṛishya,** mfn. to be hurt or injured, violable (see *a-p°, dush-p°, su-p°*).

प्रधे *pra-√dhe,* Caus. *-dhāpayati,* to cause to suck, MānGṛ.

प्रध्मा *pra-√dhmā* (or *dham*), P. (Ā. Pot. *-dhmāyīta,* ChUp.) *-dhamati,* to blow before or in front, blow away, AV.; to scare, Car.; to destroy, MBh.; to blow into (esp. into a conch shell, acc.), ib.; Suśr.; Hariv. &c.; (Ā.) to cry out, ChUp. vi, 14, 1; Śaṃk.; (others, 'to be tossed about,' 'wander about'): Caus. P. Ā. *-dhmāpayati,* °*te,* to blow into, bl° (a conch shell), MBh.; R.; Hariv. °**dhamana,** n. blowing into (the nose, as powder); a sternutatory, Suśr. °**dhmā,** mfn. blowing violently, MW. °**dhmāpana,** n. (fr. Caus.) a remedy for difficult respiration (in med.), Suśr. °**dhmāpita,** mfn. blown into, blown (as a conch shell), MBh.

प्रध्यै *pra-√dhyai,* P. Ā. *-dhyāyati,* °*te,* to meditate upon, think of (acc. with or without *prati*), Gobh.; MBh.; Hariv.; to reflect, consider, MBh.; R.; Kir.; to excogitate, devise, hit upon, MBh. °**dhyāna,** n. meditating upon, reflection, thinking, deep thought, subtle speculation, MBh.; R.; Suśr.; Car.

प्रध्रज् *pra-√dhraj,* P. *-dhrajati,* to run forward, RV. i, 166, 4.

प्रध्वंस् *pra-√dhvaṇs,* Ā. *-dhvaṇsate,* to flow off (as water), ĀśvGṛ.; to fall to pieces, perish, ChUp.: Caus. *-dhvaṇsayati,* to scatter, sprinkle, ŚBr.; to cause to fall, destroy, cause to perish, MBh.; Śiś. °**dhvaṇsa,** m. utter destruction, annihilation, perishing, disappearance, Var.; Bhartṛ.; =°*dhvaṇsâbhāva* (below), Sarvad.; *-tva,* n. state of destruction, desolation, ruin, KapS., Sch.; °*dhvaṇsâbhāva,* m. non-existence in consequence of annihilation, ceasing to exist, Tarkas.; Sarvad. &c. °**dhváṇsana,** mfn. destroying, annihilating, MBh.; m. one who destroys, a destroyer (as a partic. personification), ŚBr. (cf. *prādhvaṇsana*). °**dhvaṇsita,** mfn. (fr. Caus.) destroyed, annihilated, dispelled, MW. °**dhvaṇsin,** mfn. passing away, transitory, perishable (*utpanna-p°,* arisen and passing away again, i.e. having no further consequences, TPrāt., Comm.), MBh.; (ifc.) destroying, annihilating, R. °**dhvasta,** mfn. destroyed, perished, disappeared, MBh.; R.; Bhartṛ.; BhP.

प्रध्वन् *pra-√dhvan,* P. *-dhvanati,* to sound, resound, Śiś.: Caus. *-dhvanayati,* to cause to sound, Car. °**dhvāna,** m. a loud sound, Dharmaśarm.

प्रनक्ष् *pra-√naksh,* P. Ā. *-nakshati,* °*te,* to draw near, approach, RV. vii, 42, 1.

प्रनप्तृ *pra-naptṛi,* m. a great grandson, Uṇ., Sch.

प्रनभ् *pra-√nabh,* Ā. *-nabhate,* to burst asunder, open, AV.

प्रनर्द् *pra-√nard,* P. *-nardati,* Pāṇ. viii, 4, 14, Sch. °**nardaka,** mfn., ib.

प्रनष्ट *pra-nashṭa.* See *pra-ṇaś,* p. 659.

प्रनायक *pra-nāyaka,* mfn. one whose leader is away, whose rulers are abroad; destitute of a guide, Pāṇ. i, 4, 59; viii, 4, 14, Sch.

प्रनाल *pra-nāla, -nālī*=*-ṇāla, -ṇālī,* q.v.

प्रनाशिन् *pra-nāśin,* w.r. for *-ṇāśin,* q.v.

प्रनिंसित *pra-niṇsita,-niṇsitavya*=*-ṇiṇsita, -ṇiṇsitavya,* q.v.

प्रनिक्षण *pra-nikshaṇa*=*-ṇikshaṇa,* Pāṇ. viii, 4, 33, Sch.

प्रनिघातन *pra-nighātana,* n. (fr. *pra-ni-√han*) killing, slaughter, murder, L.

प्रनिन्दन *pra-nindana*=*-ṇindana,* Pāṇ. viii, 4, 33, Sch.

प्रनिभिद् *pra-ni-√bhid,* P. *-bhinatti,* Pāṇ. viii, 4, 18, Sch.

प्रनिरक्ष् *pra-ni-√raksh,* P. *-rakshati,* Vop.

प्रनीड *pra-nīḍa,* mfn. w.r. for *pra-ḍīna,* (q.v.), MBh. xii, 9314.

प्रनुद् *pra-nud,* mfn. w.r. for *-ṇud* (q.v.), Suśr.

प्रनृत् *pra-√nṛit,* P. Ā. *-nṛityati,* °*te,* to dance forwards, begin to d°, d°, AV.; MBh.; R. &c.; to gesticulate as in dancing (in token of derision) before any one (acc.), MBh.: Caus. *-nartayati,* to cause to dance, Kathās.; id. (met.), Kād. °**nartita,** mfn. caused to d° forwards, set in motion, shaken, agitated; dandled, MW. °**nṛitta,** mfn. one who has begun to d°, dancing, MBh.; R.; Kathās.; n. a dance, MārkP.; *-vat,* mfn. having begun to d°, MBh.; Kathās. °**nṛitya,** mfn. or n. w.r. for °*nṛitta.* °**nṛitya-vat,** w.r. for °*nṛitta-vat.*

प्रपक्ष *pra-paksha,* m. the extremity of a wing (of an army drawn out in the form of a bird), MBh.; R.; mfn. forming the ex° of a w° (in an army so arranged), MBh.; m. N. of a son of Kṛishṇa, VP.

प्रपच् *pra-√1. pac* (or *pañc*). See *pra-pañcaya* under *pra-pañca.*

प्रपच् *pra-√2. pac,* P. Ā. *-pacati,* °*te,* to begin to cook, Pāṇ. viii, 1, 44, Sch.; to be accustomed to cook, R. °**pakva,** mfn. (in med.) inflamed, Suśr. °**pāka,** m. ripening (of a boil &c.), Suśr.; digestion, Car.; (prob.) a partic. part of the flesh of a victim, Kauś.

प्रपञ्च *pra-pañca,* m. (√1. *pac* or *pañc*) expansion, development, manifestation, MāṇḍUp.; Kāv.; Kathās.; manifoldness, diversity, Kāv.; Śaṃk.; Pañcat.; amplification, prolixity, diffuseness, copiousness (in style; °*cena* and °*ca-tas,* ind. diffusely, in detail), Hariv.; Hit.; manifestation of or form of (gen.), Hit.; Bhāshāp.; appearance, phenomenon, Vcar.; (in phil.) the expansion of the universe, the visible world, Up.; Kap.; Sarvad.; (in rhet.) mutual false praise, Pratāp.; (in dram.) ludicrous dialogue, Sāh.; (in gram.) the repetition of an obscure rule in a clearer form, Pāṇ., Sch.; (said to be encl. after a finite verb, g. *gotrâdi*); deceit, trick, fraud, error, L.; opposition, reversion, L.; *-catura,* mfn. skilful in assuming different forms, Amar.; *-tva,* n.=*maraṇa,* death, Sāṃkhyas. (v.l.); *-nirmāṇa,* n. the creation of the visible world, BhP.; *-buddhi,* mfn. having a cunning mind, artful; m. N. of a man, Kathās.; *-mithyā-tva,* n. the unreality of the visible world; °*tvânumāna,* n., (°*māna-khaṇḍana,* n. and °*ḍana-paraśu,* m.) N. of wks.; *-vacana,* n. diffuse or prolix discourse, Hit.; *-viveka,* m., *-sāra,* m., *-sāra-viveka,* m. and *-sāra-sāra-saṃgraha,* m. N. of wks.; °*câmṛita-sāra,* m. N. of wk.; °*câsya,* mf(*ā*)n. (prob.) having various faces, Hcat. °**pañcaka,** mf(*ikā*)n. multiplying, Hcat.; amplifying, explaining in detail, L.; (*ikā*), f. N. of a Yoginī, Hcat. °**pañcana,** n. development, diffusion, copiousness, prolixity, MBh.; Pur.; Sarvad.

Pra-pañcaya, Nom. P. °*yati,* to develop, amplify, explain in detail, Śaṃk.; Sāh.; to dwell upon a note (acc.) in music, Gīt. °**pañcita,** mfn. amplified, extended, treated at length, Hariv.; Rājat.; represented in a false light, BhP.; erring, mistaken, W.; deceived, beguiled, W.

प्रपठ् *pra-√paṭh,* P. *-paṭhati,* to recite aloud, Hariv. °**pāṭha** or °**pāṭhaka,** m. a lecture (i.e. chapter or subdivision of a book), TS.; Br. &c. °**pāṭhita,** mfn. (fr. Caus.) taught, expounded, L.

प्रपण *pra-paṇá,* m. (√*paṇ*) exchange, barter, AV.

प्रपत् *pra-√pat*, P. *-patati*, to fly away or along, hasten towards (loc.), fly or fall down upon (loc.), fall, RV. &c. &c.; to fall from, be deprived of, lose (abl.), MBh.: Caus. *-pātayati*, to cause to fly away, AV.; ŚBr.; to chase, pursue, MBh.; to throw down, ib.: Desid. *-pipatishati*, to wish to hurry away, AV.: Intens. *-pāpatīti*, to shoot forth, RV. °**patana**, n. flying forth or away, MBh. (cf. *haṅsa-*); flying or falling down, falling from (abl. or comp.) or into (loc. or comp.), Gaut.; MBh. &c.; a steep rock, precipice, L.; death, destruction, W. °**patita**, mfn. flown away or along, fallen, come down, fallen or got into (acc.), MBh.; Kāv. &c.

Pra-pāta, m. a partic. mode of flying, Pañcat.; springing forth, Var.; an attack, L.; starting off, setting out, departure, Kathās.; falling down, falling from (abl. or comp.) or into (loc. or comp.), MBh.; Kāv. &c.; falling out (of teeth, hair &c.), Suśr.; discharge, emission, flow (of semen), VP.; letting fall (a glance on anything), Kum.; a steep rock, cliff, precipice, MBh.; Hariv. &c.; a steep bank or shore, L.; a cascade, waterfall, L.; °*tâbhimukha*, mf(*ī*)n. inclined to precipitate one's self from a rock, Kathās.; °*tâmbu*, n. water falling from a rock, Rājat. °**pātana**, n. (fr. Caus.) causing to fall, throwing down, R.; throwing, casting (*aksha-p*°, 'c°-dice'), Hariv. °**pātam**, ind. falling down, MBh. °**pātin**, m. a rock, cliff, mountain, L. °**pitvá**, see col. 2. °**pitsu**, mfn. (fr. Desid.) wishing to fall or throw one's self down, Śiś.

प्रपथ *prá-patha*, m. a way, journey (esp. to a distant place), RV.; AitBr.; (ifc. f. *ā*) a broad road or street, Kāṭh.; BhP.; mfn. 'about to go off'(?), loose, relaxed, L. °**pathin**, mfn. roaming on distant paths (superl. *-tama*), RV.; m. N. of a man, ib. °**pathyà**, mfn. being on the road, wandering (also applied to Pūshan, the protector of travellers), VS.; (*ā*), f. = *pathyā*, Terminalia Chebula or Citrina, L. °**pātha**, m. a road, way, L.

प्रपद् 1. *pra-√2. pad*, Ā. *-padyate* (ep. also P.), to fall or drop down from (abl.), throw one's self down (at a person's feet), MBh.; to go forwards, set out for, resort to, arrive at, attain, enter (with acc., rarely loc.), AV. &c. &c.; to fly to for succour, take refuge with (acc.), TS. &c. &c.; to fall upon, attack, assail, RV.; AV.; to come to a partic. state or condition, incur, undergo (acc.), MBh.; Kāv. &c.; (with an adv. in *sāt*), to become, e.g. *sarpasāt pra-√pad*, to bec° a serpent, Bhaṭṭ.; to obtain, gain (*patim*, 'as husband'), partake of, share in (acc.), ib.; to adopt or embrace (a doctrine), Rājat.; to undertake, commence, begin, do, MBh.; Kāv.; to form (a judgment), MBh.; to assume (a form), Kathās.; to enjoy (pleasure), R.; to take to (dat.), Hariv.; to come on, approach, appear, AV.; R.; Hariv.; to take effect, succeed, MBh.; to turn out (*anyathā*, 'differently' i.e. without any effect or consequence), Hariv.; to admit (a claim), R.: Caus. *-pādayati*, °*te*, to cause to enter, introduce into (acc. or loc.), Br.: Desid. P. *-pitsati*, to wish to enter, ŚBr.; Ā. *-pitsate* (cf. Pāṇ. vii, 4, 54), to be going to incur or undertake, Daś.

Pra-patti, f. pious resignation or devotion, Śāṇḍ.; *-pariśīlana*, n., °*tty-upâdhitva-nishedha*, m. N. of wks.

2. **Pra-pad**, f. a way, AitBr.; N. of partic. sacred texts, Br.; GṛŚrS. °**padana**, n. entering, entrance into (comp.), ĀśvGṛ.; Vait.; access, approach, ŚBr.; ChUp. °**padam**, ind. a term applied to a partic. mode of recitation (in which the Vedic verses are divided, without reference to the sense and construction, into parts of an equal number of syllables and between these parts partic. formulas inserted containing the word *pa-padye*), AitBr.

Pra-panna, mfn. arrived at, come to (*śaraṇam*, for protection), got into (any condition), ChUp.; MBh.; Kāv. &c.; (with *pādau*) fallen at a person's feet, R.; suppliant (cf. comp.); approached, appeared, happened, occurred, R.; acknowledged (as a claim), Yājñ.; provided with (instr.), Śak. I, I; effecting, producing, W.; poor, distressed, ib.; *-gati-dīpikā*, f., *-dina-caryā*, f., *-dushṭârishṭa-śānti*, f., *-pārijāta*, m. N. of wks.; *-pāla*, m. 'protector of suppliants,' N. of Kṛishṇa, MBh.; *-mālikā*, f., *-lakshaṇa*, n. N. of wks.; °*nnâmṛita*, n. 'nectar for suppliants,' N. of a legendary biography of Rāmānuja (cf. RTL. 119 &c.); °*nnârti-hara*, mf(*ī*)n. relieving the distress of suppliants, MW. °**pāda**, see *á-prapāda*. °**pâduka**, mfn. falling away prematurely (as a fetus), TS.; Kāṭh. °**pitsu**, mfn. desirous of plunging into (loc.), Śiś.; d° of entering upon (acc.), Kir.

प्रपद् 3. *prá-pad*, f. (fr. 3. *pad*) the fore part of the foot, AV.

Prá-pada, n. id. the point of the foot, tip of the toes (*ais*, ind. on tiptoe), RV. &c. &c.

Prapadīna, w.r. for *ā-prapadīna*, q.v.

प्रपन्न *pra-panna* &c. See col. 1.

प्रपन्नाड *prapannāḍa*, m. Cassia Tora, L. (cf. *prapunāṭa* &c.)

प्रपर्ण *pra-parṇa*, mfn. whose leaves are fallen, Pat.

प्रपलाय् *pra-palāy* (*palā* = *parā* and *√ay* = *i*), Ā. *-palāyate* (ind. p. *-palāyya*), to run away, flee, escape, MBh.; Hariv.; R. °**palâyana**, n. running away, flight, rout, Pañcat. °**palâyita**, mfn. run away; routed, defeated, Kathās.; Pañcat. °**palâyin**, mfn. running away, flying, a fugitive, MBh.

प्रपलाश *pra-palāśa*, mfn. = *pra-parṇa*, Pat.

प्रपवण *pra-pavaṇa* or *pra-pavana*, n. (√1. *pū*) purifying, straining (Soma juice), Pāṇ. viii, 4, 34, Sch. °**pavaṇīya** or °**pavanīya**, mfn. to be cleansed or purified, ib.

प्रपश् *pra-√paś*, P. *-paśyati* (ep. also Ā. °*te*), to see before one's eyes, look at, observe, behold, RV. &c. &c.; to judge, discern, MBh.; to know, understand, R.; to regard as, take for (two acc.), MBh. °**paśyat** or °**paśyamāna**, mfn. well-discerning, judicious, sensible, intelligent, MBh.

प्रपा *pra-√1. pā*, P. *-pibati* (ind. p. *-pāya*, Pāṇ. vi, 4, 69), to begin to drink, drink, RV. &c. &c.; to imbibe (*cakshushā*, with the eye i.e. feast the eyes upon), MBh.

Pra-pā́, f. a place for supplying water, a place for watering cattle or a shed on the road-side containing a reservoir of water for travellers, fountain, cistern, well, AV. &c. &c. (cf. Pāṇ. iii, 3, 58, Vārtt. 4, Pat.); a supply of water, affluent (of a tank &c.), L.; *-pālikā* or °*lī*, f. a woman who distributes water to travellers, Vcar.; *-pūraṇa*, n. filling a cistern with water; °*ṇīya*, mfn. serving to fill a c° with w°, Pāṇ. v, I, III, Vārtt. I, Pat.; *-maṇḍapa*, m. a shed with water for travellers, Vcar.; *-vana*, n. 'fountain-grove,' a cool grove, L. °**pāṇa**, n. drinking, a drink or beverage (in *a-prap*° and *su-prap*°; cf. also *pra-pāna*). °**pāṇīya**, mfn. to be drunk, drinkable, W. °**pāna**, n. drinking, sipping, R.; the under part of a horse's upper lip (which he uses in drinking), Var. (v.l. °*pāṇa*). °**pānaka**, n. sherbet, Bhpr.; Sāh. °**pāyin**, mfn. drinking, one who drinks, W. °**pīti**, f. the act of drinking, Kauś., Sch.

प्रपा *pra-√3. pā*, P. *-pāti*, to protect, defend from (abl.), BhP. °**pāyin**, mfn. who or what protects, W. °**pālaka**, m. (cf. √*pāl*) a guardian, protector, Kāv. °**pālana**, n. guarding, protecting, protection, Cat. °**pālin**, m. 'protector,' N. of Baladeva, L.

प्रपाक *pra-pāka*. See *pra-√2. pac*.

प्रपाटिका *pra-pāṭikā*, f. a young shoot or sprout, L.

प्रपाठक *pra-pāṭhaka*. See *pra-√paṭh*.

प्रपाणि *pra-pāṇi* or °*ṇika*, m. the fore-arm, Car.

प्रपाण्डु *pra-pāṇḍu* or °*ḍura*, mfn. very white, of a dazzling white colour, Suśr.

प्रपात *pra-pāta* &c. See *pra-√pat*.

प्रपादिक *prapādika* or °*dika*, m. a peacock, L.

प्रपादुक *pra-pāduka* &c. See above.

प्रपितामह *prá-pitāmaha*, m. a paternal great-grandfather, VS.; TS.; (°*mahá*) AV. &c. &c.; N. of Kṛishṇa and Brahmā, MBh.; (*ī*), f. a paternal great-grandmother, ib.; m. pl. great-grandfathers, ancestors, R.; Kathās.

Pra-pitṛivya, m. a paternal grand-uncle, L.

प्रपित्व *pra-pitvá*, n. (perhaps for *pra-pit-tva* fr. √*pat*; cf. *apa-pitva*) start, flight, haste, RV.; the advanced day i.e. evening, ib.

Pra-pitsu. See col. 2.

प्रपिन्व् *pra-√pinv*, P. Ā. *-pinvati*, °*te*, to swell, be full of, be rich, flow over, RV.

प्रपिष् *pra-√pish*, P. *-pinashṭi*, to crush to pieces, pound, Pañcat.: Caus. *-peshayati*, to pound, grind or crush to pieces, Suśr. °**pishṭa** (*prá-*), mfn. crushed or ground down, ŚBr.; KātyŚr.; *-bhāga* (°*ṭá-*), mfn. whose share has been ground down, TS.

प्रपी *pra-√pī* &c. See *pra-√pyai*.

प्रपीड् *pra-√pīḍ*, P. *-pīḍayati*, to press, squeeze, ŚBr.; MBh.; Suśr.; to suppress (the breath), ChUp.; to afflict, torment, harass, MBh.; Kāv. &c. °**pīḍana**, n. pressing, squeezing, Suśr.; an astringent, ib. °**pīḍita**, mfn. pressed, afflicted, tortured, MBh.; Kāv. &c.

प्रपीति *pra-pīti*. See *pra-√1. pā*.

प्रपुट *pra-puṭa*, m. 'a large cornucopia,' Kauś. (*dṛiḍhaḥ puṭaḥ*, Sch.)

प्रपुण्डरीक *pra-puṇḍarīka*, v.l. for *pra-pauṇḍ*°, q.v.

प्रपुत्र *pra-putra*, m. a grandson, descendant, Inscr.

प्रपुथ् *pra-√puth*, Caus. *-pothayati*, to push away (*anyo'nyam*, 'each other'), R.

प्रपुनाट *prapunāṭa* (L.), °*nāḍa* (Suśr.), *prapuṁnaḍa* or °*nāṭa* (L.), °*nāḍa* (Suśr.), °*nāla* (L.), m. Cassia Tora or Cavia Alata.

प्रपुराण *pra-purāṇa*, mfn. very old, kept a long time, Car.

प्रपुष् *pra-√push*, P. *-pushyati* (RV.), *push-ṇāti* (BhP.), to nourish, feed, support.

प्रपुष्पित *pra-pushpita*, mfn. flowering, in blossom, blooming, MBh.; R.

प्रपूज् *pra-√pūj*, P. *-pūjayati*, to respect, honour, esteem, MBh.; Kāv.; Śaṃk.; to honour i.e. present with (instr.), Hcat. °**pūjita**, mfn. honoured, respected, MBh.

प्रपृ *pra-√1. pṛi* (only aor. Subj. *-parshi*), to carry across, bring over (*ati*), RV. i, 174, 9.

प्रपृच् *pra-√pṛic*, P. *-pṛiṇakti* or *-pṛiñcati*, to come in contact with (acc.), RV.; TBr.

प्रपृथक् *pra-pṛithák*, ind. singly, one by one, AV.

प्रपृष्ठ *pra-pṛishṭha*, mfn. having a prominent or protuberant back, Pāṇ. vi, 2, 177, Sch.

प्रपॄ *pra-√pṝ*, P. *-pṛiṇāti* (see *pra-pra-√pṝ*), Pass. *-pūryate*, to be filled, become full or satiated, be completed or fulfilled or accomplished, MBh.; Kāv. &c.: Caus. *-pūrayati*, to fill up, complete, MBh.; R.; to make rich, enrich, Mṛicch. °**pūraka**, mf(*ikā*)n. filling up, fulfilling, satisfying, Kāvyâd., Sch.; (*ikā*), f. Solanum Jacquini, L. °**pūraṇa**, mf(*ī*)n. filling up (oil, and) increasing (love), Cat.; the act of filling up, filling, putting in, inserting, injecting (with loc. or comp.), Suśr.; satiating, satisfying, Cat.; bending (of a bow), R.; adorning, embellishing (of Indra's banner), Var. °**pūrita**, mfn. filled up, completed, MBh.

प्रपौण्डरीक *pra-pauṇḍarīka*, n. the root of Nymphaea Lotus, Car. (v.l. *prapuṇḍ*°); Hibiscus Mutabilis, Suśr.

प्रपौत्र *pra-pautra*, m. the son of a son's son, a great-grandson, Kathās.; Rājat. (also °*traka*, Yājñ.); (*ī*), f. a great-granddaughter, Hcat.

प्रप्यस *pra-pyasá*, mfn. swelling, AV. (cf. next).

प्रप्यै *pra-√pyai*, Ā. *-pyāyate*, to swell out, swell up, be distended or exuberant, RV.; VS.; TS.: Caus. *-pyāyayati*, to cause to swell out, distend, RV.; ŚBr.

Prá-pīta, mfn. swollen out, swollen up, distended, RV. **Prá-pīna**, mfn. id., VS.

Prá-pyāta, mfn. id., TS. °**pyāna**, mfn. id., Pāṇ. vi, 1, 28, Sch.

Pra-pyāyana, n., **-pyāyanīya**, mfn., Pāṇ. viii, 4, 34, Sch.

Pra-pyāyayitṛi, mfn. (fr. Caus.) causing to swell out, distending, ŚBr.

प्रप्रजन् *pra-pra-√jan*, Ā. *-jāyate*, to be born again and again, RV. v, 58, 5.

प्रप्रपृ *pra-pra-√pṛī*, P. *-priṇāti*, to fill up, complete, RV. v, 5, 5.

प्रप्रर्ष् *pra-prarsh* (*-pra-√ṛish*), P. *-arshati*, to stream forth towards (dat.), RV. ix, 9, 2.

प्रप्रवी *pra-pra-√vī*, P. *-veti*, to advance against, attack, RV. vii, 6, 3.

प्रप्रशंस् *pra-pra-√śaṇs*, Pass. *-śasyate*, to be praised, RV. i, 138, 1 (cf. vi, 48, 1).

प्रप्रश्रु *pra-pra-√śru*, Pass. (3. sg.) *-śriṇve*, to be celebrated, RV. vii, 8, 4.

प्रप्रस्था *pra-pra-√sthā*, Ā. *-tishṭhate*, to rise, advance, RV. i, 40, 7.

प्रप्रास् *pra-prâs* (*-pra-√1. as*), P. *-asti*, to be in a high degree or prominently, RV. i, 150, 3.

प्रप्री *pra-√prī*, Caus. *-prīṇayati*, to make pleasant, Divyâv.

प्रप्रुथ् *pra-√pruth*, P. *-prothati*, to snort (as a horse), RV.; TS.; to blow or puff out (the cheeks), RV. iii, 32, 1; to shake the limbs noisily, TāṇḍBr., Sch. °**prothá**, m. snorting, blowing, puffing, MaitrS.; the nostrils of a horse, Āpast.; N. of a partic. plant (sometimes used as a substitute for the Soma), TāṇḍBr.

प्रप्रे *prá-pré* (*-pra-√i*), P. 3. pl. *-yanti*, to go forth, move on, advance, RV. iii, 9, 3.

प्रप्लु *pra-√plu*, Ā. *-plavate*, to go to sea (*samudram*), float or sail away, TS.; AitBr.: Caus. *-plāvayati*, to cause to float or sail away, ShaḍvBr.; to wash or flood with water, ŚBr.; GṛŚrS. °**plāvana**, n. flooding with water, extinguishing (a fire), AitBr. °**pluta** (*prá-*), mfn. dipped in water, VS.

प्रफर्वी *prapharví*, f. a wanton or lascivious girl, RV.; AV.; VS.; °*vi-dā* (ĀpŚr.), °*vī-dā* (Kāṭh.), f. bestowing a wanton girl.

प्रफुल्त *pra-phulta*, mfn. = *pra-phulla*, Pāṇ. vii, 4, 89, Sch. °**phulti**, f. blooming, blossoming, ib.

Praphulla, mfn. (see √*phull, phal*) blooming forth, blooming, blown, MBh.; Kāv. &c.; covered with blossoms or flowers, R.; Hariv.; expanded, opened wide (like a full-blown flower), shining, smiling, cheerful, pleased (see comp.) **-naga-vat**, mfn. rich in blooming trees, R. **-nayana** (W.), **-netra** (Śatr.), mfn. having fully opened or sparkling eyes, having eyes expanded with joy. **-vadana**, mfn. having the face expanded with joy, looking gay or happy, W.

प्रबन्ध् *pra-√bandh*, P. *-badhnāti*, to bind on, fasten, fetter, check, hinder, ŚBr. &c &c. °**baddha**, mfn. bound, tied, fettered, ChUp. &c. &c.; dependent on (comp.), MBh.; checked, stopped, suppressed; *-mūtra*, mfn. suffering from retention of urine, Suśr. °**banddhṛi**, m. 'one who connects together,' a composer, author, Pratāp.; an interpreter (°*ddhṛi-tā*, f.), Naish. °**bandha**, m. a connection, band, tie (*garbha-nāḍī-prab*°, the umbilical cord), Suśr.; an uninterrupted connection, continuous series, uninterruptedness, continuance, Hariv.; Kāv. &c.; a composition, (esp.) any literary production, Kāv.; Rājat.; Pratāp.; a commentary, Naish., Sch.; *-kalpanā*, f. a feigned story, a work of fiction, L.; *-kośa*, m., *-cintāmaṇi*, m. N. of wks.; *-varsha*, m. incessant rain, Var.; °*dhâdhyāya*, m. N. of the 4th ch. of the Saṃgīta-darpaṇa and of the Saṃgīta-ratnākara; °*dhârtha*, m. the subject-matter of a composition or treatise, A. °**bandhana**, n. binding, fettering, Kir.; connection, bond, tie, Suśr.

प्रबभ्र *prababhra*, m. N. of Indra, Kāṭh. (cf. *pravabhrá*).

प्रबर्ह *pra-barha*, m. (√1. *bṛih*) the best, most excellent, MBh.; R. (cf. *pra-varha*).

प्रबर्हण *pra-barhaṇa*, n. (√2. *bṛih, bṛiṇh*) tearing off or out, ĀpŚr., Sch. °**barham**, see *pra-varham*.

प्रबल 1. *pra-bala*, mf(*ā*)n. strong, powerful, mighty, great, important (as a word), violent (as pain), MBh.; Kāv. &c.; dangerous, pernicious, MārkP.; (ifc.) abounding in, Suśr.; (*ám*), ind. greatly, much, ŚBr.; m. N. of a son of Kṛishṇa, BhP.; of an attendant of Vishṇu, ib.; of a Daitya, Kathās.; w.r. for *pra-vāla*, L.; (*ā*), f. Paederia Foetida, L.; (*ī*), f., see s.v. **-tara**, mfn. stronger, very strong or mighty, Prab. **-tā**, f. (Rājat.), **-tva**, n. (Kull.) strength, power, might, validity. **-toya**, mfn. abounding in water, Rājat. **-nirṇaya-vyākhyā**, f. N. of wk. **-rudita**, n. strong crying, excessive weeping, Megh. **-vat**, mfn. strong, mighty, MBh. **-virasā**, f. decay, Divyâv.

2. **Pra-bala**, Nom. P. °*lati*, to become strong or powerful, L. °**balana-tā**, f. strengthening, Kāv.

Prabalaya, Nom. P. °*yati*, to strengthen, increase, Mcar.

1. **Prabalī**, in comp. for °*bala*. **-√bhū**, P. *-bhavati*, to become strong or mighty, Kathās.

प्रबली 2. *prabalī*, f. a class, division of a community (?), Inscr.

प्रबह्लिका *pra-bahlikā*. See *pra-vahlikā*.

प्रबाध् *pra-√bādh*, Ā. *-bādhate* (ep. also P. °*ti*), to press forward, drive, urge, promote, RV.; Nir.; to repel, drive away, keep off, MBh.; Kāv. &c.; to torment, vex, hurt, injure, annoy, ib.; to set aside, annul, Pāṇ. vii, 2, 90, Sch.: Intens., see below. °**bādhaka**, mfn. (ifc.) pressing back, keeping away, Suśr.; refusing, MW. °**bādhana**, n. keeping off, keeping at a distance, MBh; MārkP.; pressing hard upon, tormenting, paining, MBh. (also *ā*, f., Jātakam.); refusing, denying, MW. °**bādhita** (*prá-*), mfn. driven, urged on, RV. x, 108, 9; oppressed, MW. °**bādhin**, mfn. (ifc.) harassing, paining, tormenting, Bālar. °**bábadhāna**, mfn. (fr. Intens.) hastening on before, overtaking, RV.

प्रबाल *pra-bāla*. See *pra-vāla*.

प्रबालक *pra-bālaka*, m. N. of a Yaksha, MBh.; (*ikā*), f. N. of a woman, Vāsav. introd. (printed °*vālikā*).

प्रबालिक *pra-bālika* (or *-vālika*?), m. a kind of purslain, L.

प्रबाहु *pra-bāhu*, m. the fore-arm, Var.; VP.; 'long-armed,' N. of a man, MBh. (also °*huka*, VP.)

प्रबाहुक् *pra-bâhuk*, ind. in an even line, on a level, TS.; Br. (= *bāhulyena*, TBr., Sch.) °**hukam**, ind. at the same time or on high, L. (g. *svar-ādi*).

प्रबुध् *pra-√budh*, Ā. *-budhyate* (Ved. inf. *-búdhe*), to wake up, wake, awake (intrans.), RV. &c. &c.; to expand, open, bloom, blossom, MBh.; Kāv. &c.; P. *-bodhati*, to become conscious or aware of, know, understand, recognise as (2. acc.), MBh.: Caus. *-bodhayati*, to wake up, awaken (trans.), MBh.; Kāv. &c.; to cause to expand or bloom, Kum.; to stimulate (by gentle friction), ŚārṅgS.; to make sensible, cause to know, inform, admonish, persuade, convince, MBh.; Kāv. &c.; to instruct, teach (two acc.), Cāṇ. °**buddha**, mfn. awakened, awake, roused, expanded, developed, opened, blown, Up.; MBh. &c.; come forth, appeared, Vcar.; (anything) that has begun to take effect (as a spell), Cat.; known, understood, recognised, Kap.; enlightened, clear-sighted, clever, wise, Kathās.; Hcar.; m. N. of a teacher, BhP.; *-tā*, f. intelligence, wisdom, MārkP.

Pra-budh, mfn. watchful, attentive, RV.; f. awaking, ib. °**budha**, m. a great sage, BhP.

Pra-bodha, m. awaking (from sleep or ignorance), becoming conscious, consciousness, Kāv.; Kathās.; Pañcat.; opening, blowing (of flowers), Kālid.; manifestation, appearance (of intelligence), Pañcat. (v. l.); waking, wakefulness, Śak.; knowledge, understanding, intelligence, Ragh.; BhP.; Śāntiś.; awakening (trans.), R.; friendly admonition, good words (pl.), Naish.; reviving of an evaporated scent, VarBṛS.; N. of wk.; *-candra*, m. 'the moon of knowledge,' kn° personified and compared with the moon, Prab.; *-candrikā*, f. 'moonlight of kn°,' N. of sev. wks.; *-candrôdaya*, m. 'rise of the moon of kn°,' N. of a celebrated philosophical drama and of sev. other wks.; °*daya-saṃgraha*, m., °*dayâmalaka*, m. or n. (?) N. of wks.; *-cintāmaṇi*, m., *-dīpikā*, f., *-prakāśa*, m., *-mañjarī*, f., *-mānasôllāsa*, m., *-ratnâkara*, m. N. of wks.; *-vatī*, f. N. of a Surâṅganā, Siṇhās.; *-siddhi*, f., *-sudhâkara*, m., *-sūkti-vyākhyā*, f. N. of wks.; °*dhânanda*, m. (with *sarasvatī*), N. of an author, Cat.; °*dhôtsava*, m. = °*dhinī* (below); N. of wk. (cf. *Nārāyaṇa-prabodh*°); °*dhôdaya*, m. rise of knowledge, Prab.; N. of wk. °**bodhaka**, mfn. awakening, causing to open or blossom, Subh.; m. a minstrel whose duty is to wake the king, L.; (ifc.) = °*bodha*, understanding, intelligence (e.g. *sukha-prabodhaka*, f. *ikā*, of easy intelligence i.e. easily intelligible, Cat.) °**bodhana**, mfn. awaking, arousing, Ṛit.; Pañcat.; m. N. of a Buddha, Buddh.; (*ī*), f. the 11th day in the light half of the month Kārttika, celebrated as a festival in commemoration of the waking of Vishṇu, Pur.; Alhagi Maurorum, L.; n. waking, awaking, MBh.; Kāv. &c.; awakening, arousing, MBh.; Hariv.; knowledge, understanding, comprehension, Pañcat.; enlightening, instructing, ib.; Prab.; reviving of an evaporated scent, L. °**bodhita**, mfn. (fr. Caus.) awakened, aroused &c., MBh.; Kāv. &c. (also *-vat*, Sāh.); (*ā*), f. N. of a metre, Chandom. °**bodhin**, mfn. awaking, Ragh.; coming forth from (abl.), R.; (*inī*), f. the 11th day in the light half of Kārttika (= °*bodhanī*), Cat.; °*dhi-tā*, f. awaking, wakefulness (*a-prab*°), MBh. °**bodhya**, mfn. (fr. Caus.) to be awakened, MBh.; Kathās.; Suśr.

प्रब्रू *pra-√brū*, P. Ā. *-bravīti*, *-brūte*, to exclaim, proclaim, announce, declare, teach, indicate, betray, RV.; AV.; TS.; Br.; GṛŚrS.; to praise, celebrate, RV.; to speak kindly to (dat.), ib.; to say, tell, relate, MBh.; Kāv. &c. (with two acc., Bhaṭṭ.; with *satyam*, to speak the truth, speak sincerely, VarBṛS.); to read before (gen. or dat.), MW.; to call, name, BhP.; to describe as (two acc.), MBh.; to announce i.e. recommend anything to (dat.), offer, present, Āpast. (cf. *ni-√1. vid*, Caus.)

प्रभज् *pra-√bhaj*, P. Ā. *-bhajati*, °*te*, to execute, accomplish, Pañcar.; to honour, Buddh.; to divide, MW. °**bhāga**, m. division, KātyŚr.; (fr. *pra + bhāga*) the fraction of a fraction, a sub-fraction, Col.; *-jāti*, f. reduction of sub-fractions to a common denominator, ib. °**bhāj**, mfn., Pāṇ. iii, 2, 62, Sch.

प्रभञ्ज् *pra-√bhañj*, P. *-bhanákti*, to break up, crush, destroy, rout, defeat, RV. &c. &c.: Pass. pr. p. *-bhajyamāna*, being broken to pieces or broken up, BhP. °**bhagna**, mfn. crushed to pieces, defeated, MBh.; R. °**bhaṅgá**, m. a breaker, crusher, RV.; breaking, crushing, destruction, R. °**bhaṅgin**, mfn. breaking, crushing, destroying, RV. °**bhaṅgura**, mfn. breaking (perishable?), L. °**bhañjana**, mfn. = °*bhaṅgin*, Kauś.; MBh.; Hariv.; m. wind or the god of wind, storm, tempest, hurricane, MBh.; R. &c.; a nervous disease, Suśr.; a partic. Samādhi, Kāraṇḍ.; N. of a prince, MBh.; n. the act of breaking to pieces, AdbhBr.

प्रभद्र *pra-bhadra*, n. Azadirachta Indica, L.; (*ā*), f. Paederia Foetida, L. °**bhadraka**, mfn. exceedingly handsome or beautiful, MBh.; R.; n. a kind of metre, Col.; a combination of 4 Ślokas containing one sentence, Kāvyâd., Sch.

प्रभर्तव्य *pra-bhartavya* &c. See *pra-√bhṛi*.

प्रभव *pra-bhava* &c. See under *pra-√bhū*.

प्रभा *pra-√1. bhā*, P. *-bhāti*, to shine forth, begin to become light, shine, gleam, RV. &c. &c.; to appear, seem, look like (nom. with or without *iva*), MBh.; Kāv. &c.; to illuminate, enlighten, TUp.

Prabhā, f. light, splendour, radiance, beautiful appearance (ifc. often mfn., with f. *ā*), Mn.; MBh. &c.; the shadow of the gnomon on a sun-dial, Sūryas.; light variously personified (as wife of the sun, or as wife of Kalpa and mother of Prātar, Madhyaṃ-dina and Sāya i.e. morning, midday and evening, or as a form of Durgā in the disc of the sun), Hariv.; Pur.; N. of a Śakti, Hcat.; of an Apsaras, MBh.; of a daughter of Svar-bhānu and mother of Nahusha, Hariv.; of the city of Kubera, L.; of a kind of metre, Col.; of sev. wks. **-kara**, m. 'light-maker,' the sun (du. sun and moon), MBh.; Kāv.; Kathās.; the moon, L.; fire, L.; a partic. Samādhi, Kāraṇḍ.; N. of Śiva, Śivag.; of a class of deities under the 8th Manu, MārkP.; of a serpent-demon, MBh.; of a sage of the race of Atri, Hariv.; Pur.; of a son of Jyotish-mat, VP.; of a teacher of the Mīmāṇsā philosophy (associated with Kumārila-bhaṭṭa), Col.; of sev. other teachers and authors (also *Prabhākara-guru, -candra, -datta, -deva, -nandana, -mitra*), Cat.; *-paricceda*, m. N. of wk.; *-vardhana*, m. N. of a king, Hcar.; *-varman*, m. N. of a minister, Rājat.; *-siddhi*, m. N. of a scholar, Buddh.; *-svāmin*, m. N. of the statue of the tutelary deity of Prabhākara-varman, Rājat.; °*râhnika*, n. N. of wk.; (*ī*), f. (with Buddhists) one of the 10 stages of perfection, Dharmas. 64; n. N. of a Varsha, MBh. **-kīṭa**, m. 'light-insect,' a fire-fly, L. **-°ñjana** (°*bhâñj*°), m. Hyperanthera Moringa, L. **-tarala**, mfn. tremulously radiant, flashing, Śak. **-tīrtha**, n. N. of a Tīrtha, ŚivaP. **-°nanā** (°*bhân*°), f. N. of a Surâṅganā, Siṇhâs. **-pada-śakti**, f. N. of wk. **-pallavita**, mfn. overspread with lustre, Vikr. **-pāla**, m. N. of a Bodhisattva, Buddh. **-praroha**, m. a shoot i.e. flash or ray of light, Ragh. **-maṇḍala**, n. (also °*la-ka*, n., Kathās.) a circle or crown of rays, ib.; *-śobhin*, mfn. shining with a circle of rays, Ragh.; N. of wk.; m. a partic. Samādhi, Kāraṇḍ. **-maya**, mf(*ī*)n. consisting of light, shining, MBh.; Hariv.; m. a partic. Gaṇa of Śiva, Harav. **-lepin**, mfn. covered with splendour, Hcar. **-°locana** (°*bhâl*°), n. N. of wk. **-vat**, mfn. luminous, radiant, splendid, MBh.; Kāv. &c.; (*ī*), f. the lute of one of the Gaṇas or demigods attendant on Śiva, L.; a kind of metre, Śrutab.; (in music) a partic. Śruti, Saṃgit.; N. of a Buddh. deity, Lalit.; of the wife of the sun, MBh.; of one of the Mātṛis attendant on Skanda, ib.; of an Apsaras, VP.; of a Surâṅganā, Siṇhâs.; of a sister of the Asura Indra-damana, L.; of a daughter of king Vajra-nābha and wife of Pradyumna, Hariv.; of the wife of Citra-ratha king of Aṅga, MBh.; of the daughter of Suvira and wife of Marutta, MārkP.; of a Tāpasī, MBh.; of the mother of Malli (the 19th Arhat of present Avasarpiṇī), L.; of the daughter of the Śreshṭhin Soma-datta and wife of Madana the son of Vikrama-sena, Śukas.; of a river, W.; (*-pariṇaya*, m. 'the marriage of Prabhāvatī,' N. of a drama by Viśva-nātha). **-°valī** (°*bhâv*°), f. N. of wk. **-vyūha**, m. N. of a Buddh. deity, Lalit. **Prabhêśvara-tīrtha**, n. N. of a Tīrtha, ŚivaP.

Prabhāta, mfn. shone forth, begun to become clear or light, MBh.; Kāv. &c.; m. N. of a son of the sun and Prabhā, VP.; (*ā*), f. N. of the mother of the Vasus Pratyūsha and Prabhāsa, MBh.; n. daybreak, dawn, morning, Gaut.; MBh. &c. **-karaṇīya**, n. a morning rite or ceremony, Śak. **-kalpa**, mf(*ā*)n. nearly become light, approaching dawn (as night), R. **-kāla**, m. time of daybreak, early morning, Suśr. **-prâya**, mfn. = *-kalpa*, Kād. **-samaya**, m. = *-kāla*, MBh.

Pra-bhāna, n. light, radiance, shining, Pāṇ. viii, 4, 34, Sch. °**bhāṇīya**, mfn. to be irradiated or lighted, ib. °**bhānu**, m. N. of a son of Kṛishṇa, BhP. °**bhāpana**, n. (from Caus.) causing to shine, Pāṇ. viii, 4, 34, Vārtt. 2, Pat. °**bhāpanīya**, mfn. to be caused to shine, Pāṇ. ib., Sch.

प्रभाग *prabhāgá*. See *pra-√bhaj*.

प्रभारक *prabhāraka*, w.r. for *prabhā-kara*, MBh.

प्रभाव *pra-bhāva* &c. See *pra-√bhū*.

प्रभाष् *pra-√bhāsh*, Ā. *-bhāshate* (ep. also P. °*ti*), to speak, tell, declare, disclose, manifest, explain, call, name, MBh.; Kāv. &c.; to talk to, converse with (acc.), MBh. °**bhāsha**, m. declaration, doctrine, Hariv. (Nilak.); w.r. for *-bhāsa*. °**bhāshaṇa**, n. explanation, Suśr.; °*ṇīya*, mfn. relating to an expl°, ib. °**bhāshita**, mfn. spoken, uttered, declared, MBh.; Kāv. &c.; n. speech, talk, Var. °**bhāshin**, mfn. saying, speaking, MBh.; BhP.

प्रभास् *pra-√bhās*, Ā. *-bhāsate* (ep. also P. °*ti*), to shine, glitter, be brilliant, MBh.; Hariv.; to appear like (*iva*), MBh.: Caus. *-bhāsayati*, to irradiate, illuminate, enlighten, MBh.; R. °**bhāsa**, m. 'splendour,' 'beauty,' N. of a Vasu, MBh.; of a being attendant on Skanda, ib.; of a deity under the 8th Manu, MārkP.; (with Jainas) of one of the 11 Gaṇâdhipas, L.; of a son of a minister of Candra-prabha king of Madra, Kathās.; (pl.) N. of a race of Ṛishis, MBh.; m. or n. N. of a celebrated place of pilgrimage on the west coast of the Dekhan near Dvārakā, MBh.; Kāv.&c. (also *-kshetra*, n., *-kshetra-tīrtha*, n., *-deśa*, m.); *-kshetra-tīrtha-yātrânukrama*, m., *-kshetra-māhātmya*, n., *-khaṇḍa*, m. or n., and °*śeśvara-māhātmya*, n. N. of wks. °**bhāsana**, n. irradiating, illumining, MBh. °**bhāsura** (R.), °**bhāsvat** (Hariv.), mfn. shining forth, shining brightly, brilliant. °**bhāsvara**, mfn. id., R.; Kathās.; clear, shrill (as a voice), L.; (*ā*), f. a partic. mythical plant, Divyâv.

प्रभिद् *pra-√bhid*, P. *-bhinatti*, to cleave, split asunder, break, pierce, open, RV. &c. &c.: Pass. *-bhidyate*, to be broken in pieces, crumble, ŚBr.; to be dissolved, open, KaṭhUp.; to split, divide (intr.), MBh.: Caus. of Intens. *-bebhidayya*, Pat. °**bhid**, mfn., Pāṇ. iii, 2, 61, Sch. °**bhinna**, mfn. split asunder, cleft, broken, pierced, opened, MBh.; Kāv. &c.; blown (as a flower), Sāh.; exuding (as blood), Suśr.; flowing with juice (cf. *-karaṭa*; m. an elephant in rut), MBh.; R.; broken through, interrupted, R.; disfigured, altered, depressed, MBh.; *-karaṭa*, mfn. having the temples cleft and flowing with juice (as a rutting elephant), MBh.; R. (°*ṭā-mukha*, mfn. having the fissure in the temples flowing with juice, MBh.); *-vish*, mfn. secreting or relaxing the feces, aperient, Suśr.; °*bhinnâñjana*, n. mixed collyrium, an eye-salve mixed with oil, Ṛitus.; Pañcat. °**bheda**, m. splitting, piercing, cutting through, Yājñ.; MBh.; Ragh.; the flowing of juice from the temples of an elephant, Megh.; division, subdivision, variety, species, kind, sort, MBh.; Kap.; Hcat.; Suśr. °**bhedaka**, mf(*ikā*)n. tearing asunder, cleaving, piercing (cf. *carma-prabhedikā*). °**bhedana**, mfn. id., MBh.

प्रभी *pra-√bhī* (only pf. *-bibhayām-cakāra*), to be terrified at (abl.), Bhaṭṭ. °**bhīta**, mfn. terrified, afraid, MBh.

प्रभु *pra-bhu*. See under *pra-√bhū* below.

प्रभुज् *pra-√1. bhuj* (only ind. p. *-bhujya*), to bend, incline, Br.; Kauś. °**bhugna**, mfn., Pāṇ. viii, 4, 29, Sch.

प्रभुज् *pra-√3. bhuj* (only pr. p. *-bhuñjatī*), to befriend, protect (?), RV. i, 48, 5. °**bhukta**, mfn. begun to be eaten (as rice), Pāṇ. i, 2, 21, Sch.

प्रभू *pra-√bhū*, P. *-bhavati* (rarely Ā. °*te*; Ved. inf. *-bhūshâṇi*), to come forth, spring up, arise or originate from (abl.), appear, become visible, happen, occur, ŚBr. &c. &c.; to be before, surpass (with *prishṭham*, 'to be greater or more than the back can carry,' applied to wealth, RV. ii, 13, 4); to become or be numerous, increase, prevail, be powerful, RV. &c. &c. (3. sg. *prabhavati-tarām*, 'has more power,' Vikr. v, 18); to rule, control, have power over, be master of (gen., loc. or dat.), Mn.; MBh. &c.; to be equal to or capable of (dat. or loc.), ib.; to be a match for (dat.), Pāṇ. ii, 3, 16, Vārtt. 2, Pat.; to be able to (inf.), Kālid.; Kathās. &c.; to profit, avail, be of use to (dat.), RV.; Br.; to implore, beseech (?), Hariv.: Caus. *-bhāvayati*, to increase, spread out, extend, augment, multiply (esp. the Soma by placing it in a greater number of vessels), Br.; to provide more amply, endow more richly; cause to thrive or prosper, cherish, nurture, ib.; MBh. &c.; (as Nom. fr. *-bhāva* below) to gain or possess power or strength, rule over (acc.), MBh.; R.; to recognise, R.: Desid. of Caus. *-bibhāvayishati*, to wish to increase or extend, AitBr.

Pra-bhavá, mfn. prominent, excelling, distinguished, RV.; m. production, source, origin, cause of existence (as father or mother, also 'the Creator'), birthplace (often ifc., with f. *ā*, springing or rising or derived from, belonging to), Up.; Mn.; MBh. &c.; might, power (= *pra-bhāva*), L.; N. of a Sādhya, Hariv.; of Vishṇu, A.; of sev. men, HPariś.; N. of the first or 35th year in a 60 years' cycle of Jupiter, Var.; *-prabhu* and *-svāmin*, m. (with Jainas) N. of one of the 6 Śruta-kevalins, L. °**bhavat**, mf(*antī*)n. coming forth, arising &c.; mighty, powerful, potent, MBh.; Kāv. °**bhavana**, n. production, source, origin (ifc. 'springing from;' cf. *meru-prabh*° and Pāṇ. viii, 4, 34, Sch.); ruling, presiding (?), W. °**bhavanīya**, mfn., Pāṇ. ib. °**bhavitṛi**, mfn. powerful, potent; m. a great lord or ruler, Bhartṛ. °**bhavishṇu**, mfn. = prec. (also m.; with gen. or loc. 'lord over'), MBh.; Kāv. &c.; *-tā*, f. lordship, supremacy, dominion, tyranny, Var.; power to (inf.), Rājat. °**bhavya**, mfn. (fr. *pra-√bhū*), Pāṇ. iii, 1, 107, Sch.; (fr. *pra-bhava*) being at the source or origin, original, Lāṭy.; fit for rule (?), W. °**bhāva**, m. (ifc. f. *ā*) might, power, majesty, dignity, strength, efficacy, Mn.; MBh. &c. (°*veṇa*, °*vāt* and °*vatas*, ind. by means or in consequence of, through, by); supernatural power, Kālid.; splendour, beauty, MBh.; R.; tranquillizing, conciliation (?), L.; N. of the chapters of the Rasika-priyā, Cat.; N. of a son of Manu Sva-rocis, MārkP.; *-ja*, mfn. proceeding from conscious majesty or power, W.; *-tva*, n. power, strength, Kām.; *-vat*, mfn. powerful, strong, mighty, MBh.; Kathās. °**bhāvaka**, mfn. prominent, having power or influence, Śatr.; Siṇhâs. °**bhāvana**, mf(*ī*)n. (fr. Caus.) creating, creative, MBh.; explaining, disclosing (= *prakāśaka*), R. (B.); m. creator, MBh.; R.; Hariv.; (*ā*), f. disclosing, revealing, promulgation (of a doctrine), HYog. °**bhāvaya**, Nom. °*yati*, see under Caus. above. °**bhāvayitṛi**, mfn. making powerful or mighty, Daś. °**bhāvita** (Kām.), °**bhāvin** (Śiś.), mfn. powerful, mighty.

Pra-bhú, mfn. (Ved. also *ū*, f. *vī*) excelling, mighty, powerful, rich, abundant, RV. &c. &c.; more powerful than (abl.), MBh.; having power over (gen.), VP.; able, capable, having power to (loc., inf. or comp.), Kāv.; a match for (dat.), Pāṇ. ii, 3, 16, Vārtt. 2, Pat.; constant, eternal, L.; m. a master, lord, king (also applied to gods, e. g. to Sūrya and Agni, RV.; to Prajā-pati, Mn.; to Brahmā, ChUp.; to Indra, R.; to Śiva, MBh.; to Vishṇu, L.); the chief or leader of a sect, RTL. 142; a sound, word, L.; quicksilver, L.; N. of a deity under the 8th Manu, MārkP.; of a son of Kardama, Hariv.; of a son of Śuka and Pīvarī, ib.; of a son of Bhaga and Siddhi, BhP.; of a poet, Cat.; of sev. other men, HPariś.; (°*bhvī*, f. N. of a Śakti, Pañcar.); *-kathā*, f. N. of wk.; *-tā*, f. lordship, dominion, supremacy, Yājñ. (v. l.); Kathās.; power over (loc.), Śak.; possession of (comp.), Ragh.; prevalence (instr. 'for the most part'), Ratnâv.; *-tva*, n. lordship, sovereignty, high rank, might, power over (gen., loc. or comp.), MBh.; Kāv. &c.; prevalence (instr. 'for the most part'), Suśr.; *-tva-bodhi*, f. knowledge joined with supreme power, Kāraṇḍ.; *-tvâkshepa*, m. (in rhet.) an objection based on power (i.e. on a word of command), Kāvyâd. ii, 138; *-deva*, m. N. of a Yoga teacher, Cat.; (*ī*), f. (with *lāṭī*) N. of a poetess, ib.; *-bhakta*, mfn. devoted to his master (as a dog), Cāṇ.; m. a good horse, L.; *-bhakti*, f. loyalty, faithfulness, MW.; *-liṅga-caritra*, n., *-liṅga-līlā*, f., *-vaṇśa*, m. N. of wks.; *-śabda-śesha*, mfn. having only the title of lord remaining, Ragh. °**bhū** = °*bhu* (cf. above); *-tva*, n. sufficiency, KātyŚr. (cf. *prabhu-tva*); *-vasu* (°*bhū-*, Padap. °*bhú-*), mfn. abundantly wealthy (said of Indra and Soma), RV.; m. N. of a descendant of Aṅgiras, author of RV. v, 35, 36; ix, 35, 36.

Prá-bhūta, mfn. come forth, risen, appeared &c.; (ifc.) become, transformed into, Daś.; abundant, much, numerous, considerable, high, great, ŚBr. &c. &c. (compar. *-tara*, Pañcat.; superl. *-tama*, Daś.); abounding in (comp.), R.; able to (inf.), Sāh.; governed, presided over, W.; mature, perfect, ib.; m. a class of deities in the 6th Manvantara, Hariv. (v.l. *pra-sūta*); n. (in phil.) a great or primary element (= *mahā-bhūta*), Sāṃkhyak.; *-jihvatā*, f. having a long tongue (one of the 32 signs of perfection of a Buddha), Dharmas. 83 (also *-tanu-jihv*°, 'having a long and thin t°, ib.); *-tā*, f. quantity, plenty, multitude, large number, Śiś.; *-tva*, n. id., Pañcat.; sufficiency, KātyŚr. (v.l. for *prabhū-tva*); *-dhana-dhānya-vat*, mfn. rich in money and corn, R.; *-nāgâśva-ratha*, mfn. having many elephants and horses and chariots, MBh.; *-bhrānta*, n. much roaming, Pañcat.; *-yavasêndhana*, mfn. abounding in fresh grass and fuel, ib.; *-ratna*, m. N. of a Buddha, SaddhP.; *-rūpa*, n. great beauty, MW.; *-vayas*, mfn. advanced in years, old, Kāv.; *-varsha*, n. pl. many years, Pañcat.; *-śas*, ind. many times, often, Car.; °*tôtka*, m. ardently desirous of or longing for, Kāvyâd. iii, 118. °**bhūtaka**, mfn. containing the word *prabhūtā*, g. *goshad-ādi*; m. pl. a partic. class of deceased relatives, KāṭhAnukr. °**bhūti** (*prá-*), f. source, origin, TāṇḍBr.; imperious demeanour, violence, RV. iv, 54, 3; sufficiency, RV.; TBr.; a ruler, lord (?), RV. viii, 41, 1. °**bhūvarī**, f. reaching or extending beyond (acc.), VS. °**bhūshṇu**, mfn. powerful, strong, able, L. (cf. °*bhavishṇu*).

प्रभूष् *pra-√bhūsh*, P. *-bhūshati*, to offer, present, RV. i, 159, 1.

प्रभृ *pra-√bhṛi*, P. Ā. *-bharati*, °*te*, to bring forward, place before, offer, present, RV.; AV.;

ŚāṅkhŚr.; to stretch forth, extend, RV.; to hurl, cast, ib.; (Ā.) to quiver, ib.; to be borne along, rush on, ib.; to praise, ib. °**bhartavya**, mfn. to be supported or nourished, Yājñ. °**bhartṛi** (*prá-*), m. bringer, procurer (with acc.), RV. °**bharman** (*prá-*), n. placing before, presenting, RV.; reciting, recitation, ib.

Prá-bhṛita, mfn. brought forward &c.; placed in (loc.), introduced, RV.; filled with (instr.), R. (B.) °**bhṛiti** (*prá-*), f. bringing forward, offering (of sacrifice or praise), RV.; AV.; a throw or stroke, RV.; beginning, commencement, ŚBr. &c. &c. (ifc. = 'commencing with' or 'et caetera,' e.g. *munayaḥ Somaśravaḥ-prabhṛitayaḥ*, 'the Munis beginning with S°' i.e. 'the Munis, S° &c.'; in this sense also °*tika*); ind. (after an abl., adv. or ifc.) beginning with, from—forward or upward, since, GṛŚrS.; Mn.; MBh. &c. (e.g. *bālyāt prabhṛiti*, 'from boyhood upwards;' *janma-pr°*, 'from birth;' *adya pr°*, 'beginning from to-day, henceforth;' *tataḥ* or *tadā pr°*, 'thenceforth' &c.)

Pra-bhṛithá, m. an offering, oblation, RV.

प्रभेद *pra-bheda.* See *pra-√bhid.*

प्रभ्रंश् *pra-√bhraṅś*, Ā. *-bhraśyate*, to fall away, slip off, drop down, disappear, vanish, R.; Suśr.; to escape from (abl.), TBr.; KātyŚr.; to be deprived of (abl.), Mṛicch.: Caus. *-bhraṅśayati*, to cause to fall down, cast down, Suśr.; to cause to fall from, deprive of (abl.), MBh.; Ragh. °**bhraṅśa**, see *á-prabhraṅśa*. °**bhraṅśathu**, m. a disease of the nose accompanied with discharge of mucus, Suśr. °**bhraṅśana**, see *nāva-prabh°* under 2. *nāva*. °**bhraṅśita**, mfn. (fr. Caus.) caused to fall down, deprived of, expelled from (abl.), MBh. °**bhraṅśin**, mfn. falling off, falling down, Ragh. °**bhraṅśuka**, mf(*ā*)n. falling off, vanishing, disappearing, ŚBr.; TBr. °**bhrashṭa**, mfn. fallen down, Ratnâv.; strayed, run away, escaped from (abl.), ib.; Mṛicch.; broken, W.; *-śīla*, mf(*ā*)n. of fallen character, immoral, Var. °**bhrashṭaka**, n. a chaplet or wreath of flowers suspended from the lock on the crown of the head, L.

प्रभ्रम् *pra-√bhram*, P. *-bhramati* or *-bhrāmyati*, to roam about, wander through (acc.), Kathās.

प्रभ्राज् *pra-√bhrāj*, Ā. *-bhrājate*, to shine forth, gleam, AV. °**bhrāj**, mfn. (nom. *ṭ*) shining forth, Āpast.

प्रम् *pram*, ind. (√1. *prā*). See *goshpada-pram.*

प्रमंहिष्ठीय *pramaṇhishṭhīya*, n. N. of the hymn RV. i, 57 (beginning with *prá máṇhishṭhāya*), AitBr.; N. of sev. Sāmans, ĀrshBr.

प्रमगन्द *prá-maganda*, m. the son of a usurer, RV. iii, 53, 14 (Sāy.; others 'N. of a king').

प्रमग्न *pra-magna.* See *pra-√majj* below.

प्रमङ्कन *pra-maṅkana*, n., Pat. on Pāṇ. viii, 4, 32.

प्रमङ्गन *pra-maṅgana*, n., Kāś. on Pāṇ. ib.

प्रमज्ज् *pra-√majj*, P. *-majjati*, to immerse one's self in, dip into, Kāṭh. °**magna**, mfn. immersed, dipped, drowned, Pāṇ. viii, 4, 29, Sch.

प्रमणस् *pra-maṇas*, mfn. careful, attentive, kind, AV.; good-natured, cheerful, Hariv. (cf. *pra-manas*).

प्रमण्डल *pra-maṇḍala*, n. (prob.) the felly of a wheel, MBh.

प्रमत *pra-mata.* See *pra-√man.*

प्रमत्त *pra-matta.* See *pra-√mad.*

प्रमथ् *pra-√math* (or *manth*), P. *-mathati* or *-mathnāti*, to stir up violently, churn (the ocean), Ragh.; to tear or strike off, drag away, ŚBr.; MBh.; R.; to handle roughly, harass, distress, annoy, MBh.; Kāv. &c. (ind. p. *-mathya*, violently, forcibly); to destroy, lay waste, MBh.: Caus. *-māthayati*, to assault violently, harass, annoy, MBh. °**matha**, m. 'Tormentor,' N. of a class of demons attending on Śiva, MBh.; Kāv. &c. (cf. RTL. 238); of a son of Dhṛita-rāshṭra, MBh.; a horse, L.; (*ā*), f. Terminalia Chebula or Citrina, L.; N. of the wife of Kshupa and mother of Vira, MārkP.; pain, affliction, W.; *-nātha* (Kād.), *-pati* (L.), m. 'lord of the Pramathas,' N. of Śiva; *-prathama*, m. 'first of the P°s,' N. of Bhṛiṅgiriṭi, Bālar.; °*thâdhipa*, m. 'ruler of the P°s,' N. of Siva, VarBṛS.; of Gaṇêśa, L.; °*thâlaya*, m. 'abode of torment,' hell, L. °**mathana**, mf(*ī*)n. harassing, tormenting, hurting, injuring, MBh.; Hariv.; R.; destroying, Subh.; m. N. of a magical formula pronounced over weapons, R.; N. of a Dānava, Kathās.; hurting, destroying, killing, R.; agitating, churning, W. °**mathita**, mfn. well churned, W.; torn off, dragged away, harassed, annoyed, injured, killed, MBh.; Kāv. &c.; *-puraḥ-sara*, mfn. having the leader killed, Kām. °**mathin**, mfn. harassing, annoying, tormenting, Mudr. °**mathyā**, f. a kind of paste or dough prepared by boiling any medicinal substance in water, Car.; Bhpr. °**mantha**, m. a stick used for rubbing wood to produce fire, KātyŚr. °**manthu**, m. N. of a son of Vīra-vrata and younger brother of Manthu, BhP. [cf. Προμηθεύς].

Pra-mātha, m. stirring about, racking, paining, tormenting, MBh.; Hariv.; rape (cf. *Draupadī-pr°*); subjugation, destruction (of enemies), Uttarar.; N. of a son of Dhṛita-rāshṭra, MBh.; of one of the attendants of Skanda, ib.; of a Dānava, Kathās.; pl. N. of a class of fiends attending on Śiva, Hariv. (cf. *pramatha*). °**māthita**, mfn. (fr. Caus.) roughly handled, violated, ravished, forcibly carried off, MBh. °**māthin**, mfn. stirring about, tearing, rending, troubling, harassing, destroying, MBh.; Kāv. &c.; striking off, used for striking off, MBh.; (in med.) throwing out i.e. producing secretion of the vessels, Car.; Bhpr.; m. N. of the 13th (47th) year of a 60 years' cycle of Jupiter, Var. (also w.r. for *pra-mādin*); of a Rākshasa, MBh.; of a son of Dhṛita-rāshṭra, ib.; of a monkey, R.; (*inī*), f. N. of an Apsaras, MBh.; Hariv.

प्रमद् *pra-√mad* (or *mand*), P. (rarely Ā.) *-madati*, *-mandati*, *-mādyati* (°*te*), to enjoy one's self, be joyous, sport, play, RV.; to be careless or negligent, to be indifferent to or heedless about (abl. or loc.), RV. &c. &c.; to neglect duty for, idle away time in (loc.), Mn.; MBh. &c.; to be thrown into confusion, MBh.: Caus. P. *-mădayati*, to gladden, delight, Bālar.; Ā. *-mādayate*, to enjoy, indulge in, RV.

Pra-matta, mfn. excited, wanton, lascivious, rutting, Mn.; Pañcat.; drunken, intoxicated, Śak.; mad, insane, W.; inattentive, careless, heedless, negligent, forgetful of (abl. or comp.), Mn.; MBh. &c.; indulging in (loc.), MBh.; R.; blundering, a blunderer, W.; *-gīta*, mfn. sung or recited by an intoxicated person, Pat.; *-citta*, mfn. careless-minded, heedless, negligent, Kām.; *-tā*, f. inattentiveness, sleepiness, mental inactivity (*a-pram°*), Rājat.; *-rajju*, f. (?), Kauś.; 1. *-vat*, mfn. inattentive, careless (*a-pram°*), MBh.; 2. *-vat*, ind. as if drunk, like one intoxicated, MW.; *-śramaṇa*, n. (with Jainas) N. of the 6th among the 14 stages which lead to liberation, Cat. °**mád** (or **prá-mad**), f. lust, desire, VS.; AV.

Pra-mada, m. joy, pleasure, delight, MBh.; Kathās.; mfn. wanton, dissolute, Ragh. (also °*daka*, Nir.); mad, intoxicated, L.; m. the thorn-apple, L.; the ankle, L.; N. of a Dānava, Hariv.; of a son of Vasishṭha and one of the sages under Manu Uttama, BhP.; (*ā*, f., see below); *-kaṇṭha*, m. N. of a man, Rājat.; *-kānana*, n. = °*dā-k°*, L.; *-ropya*, n. N. of a city in the Dekhan, Pañcat.; *-vana*, n. = °*dā-v°*, Kālid. °**madana**, n. amorous desire, Kauś.; a pleasure-grove, MānGṛ. °**madā**, f. (of °*da*) a young and wanton woman, any woman, Mn.; MBh. &c.; the sign of the zodiac Virgo, L.; N. of 2 kinds of metre, Col.; *-kānana*, n. the royal garden or pleasure-ground attached to the gynaeceum, L.; *-jana*, m. womankind, the female sex, R.; Var.; *-°nana* (°*dân°*), n. a kind of metre, Col.; *-vana*, n. = *-kānana*, R.; (°*na-pālikā*, f. a woman who has the inspection of a royal pleasure-garden, Mālav.); *-°spada* (°*dâsp°*), n. the gynaeceum of a prince, Kathās. °**madāya**, Nom. P. °*yati*, to behave like a wanton woman, BhP. °**maditavya**, mfn. to be neglected or disregarded; n. (impers.) one should be negligent regarding (abl.), TaittUp. °**madvara**, mf(*ā*)n. inattentive, careless, HPariś.; (*ā*), f. N. of the wife of Ruru and mother of Śunaka, MBh.; Kathās. °**manda**, m. a species of fragrant plant, Kauś. °**mandanī**, f. N. of an Apsaras, AV.

Pra-māda, m. intoxication, RV.; MBh.; madness, insanity, L.; negligence, carelessness about (abl. or comp.), Kauś.; Mn.; MBh. &c.; an error, mistake, W.; a partic. high number, L.; *-cārin*, mfn. acting in a careless manner, Kāraṇḍ.; *-pāṭha*, m. a wrong reading, Śaṃk.; *-vat*, mfn. = °*mādin*, L. °**mādikā**, f. a deflowered girl, L.; an imprudent or careless woman, W. °**mādita**, mfn. (fr. Caus.) trifled away, forfeited, lost, R. °**mādin**, mfn. negligent, careless, incautious, indifferent, MBh.; Kāv. &c.; drunken, intoxicated, W.; insane, ib.; (°*di-tā*, f., Jātak.); n. N. of the 47th (21st) year of a 60 years' cycle of Jupiter, L. (cf. *pra-nāthin*).

प्रमन् *pra-√man* (only Ā. 1. pl. pr. *-manmahe*), to think upon, excogitate, RV. i, 62, 1. °**mata**, mfn. thought out, excogitated, wise, MW. °**mataka**, m. N. of an ancient sage, MBh. °**mati** (*prá-*), f. care, providence, protection; provider, protector, RV.; AV.; m. N. of a Ṛishi in the 10th Manv-antara, Hariv. (v.l. *prām°*); of a son of Cyavana and father of Ruru, MBh.; of a prince (son of Janam-ejaya), R.; of a son of Prāṇśu, BhP.

Pra-mánas, mfn. careful, tender, AV.; pleased, cheerful, willing, MBh.; Kāv. (cf. *pra-maṇas*).

Pra-mantra, m. or n. (?) a partic. high number, Buddh. (cf. *pra-mātra*).

Pra-manyu, mfn. incensed or enraged against (loc.), MBh.; very sad, Daś.

प्रमन्थ *pra-manth.* See *pra-√math.*

प्रमन्द *pra-manda*, °*danī.* See under *pra-√mad.*

प्रमय 1. 2. *pra-maya.* See under *pra-√mā* and *pra-√mī.*

प्रमर *pra-mará.* See under *pra-√mṛi.*

प्रमर्द *pra-marda*, °*daka* &c. See under *pra-√mṛid.*

प्रमहस् *prá-mahas*, mfn. of great might or splendour (said of Mitra-Varuṇa), RV.

प्रमा *pra-√mā*, Ā. *-mimīte* (Ved. inf. *pramé*; Pass. *-mīyate*), to measure, mete out, estimate, AV.; ŚrS.; MBh.; to form, create, make ready, arrange, RV.; MBh.; to form a correct notion of (acc.), understand, know, MaitrUp.; Hariv.; Hit.: Caus. *-māpayati*, to cause correct knowledge, afford proof or authority, MW. 1. °**maya**, m. (for 2. see under *pra-√mī*) measuring, measure, L.

Pra-má, f. basis, foundation, AV.; measure, scale, RV.; right measure, true knowledge, correct notion, Prab.; Kap.; Tarkas.; IW. 59 &c.; a kind of metre, RPrāt.; *-tva*, n. accuracy of perception, Bhāshāp.; *-tva-cihna*, n. N. of wk.

Pramāṇa, n. (ifc. f. *ā*) measure, scale, standard; measure of any kind (as size, extent, circumference, length, distance, weight, multitude, quantity, duration), KātyŚr.; KaṭhUp.; Mn. &c. (instr. 'on an average,' Jyot.); prosodical length (of a vowel), Pāṇ. i, 1, 50, Sch.; measure in music, MBh. (Nilak.); accordance of the movements in dancing with music and song, Saṃgīt.; measure of physical strength, Śak. (cf. comp. below); the first term in a rule of three sum, Col.; the measure of a square i.e. a side of it, Śulbas.; principal, capital (opp. to interest), Col.; right measure, standard, authority, GṛŚrS.; Mn.; MBh. &c. (*pramāṇam bhavatī*, 'your ladyship is the authority or must judge,' Nal.; in this sense also m. and f. sg. and pl., e.g. *vedāḥ pramāṇāḥ*, 'the Vedas are authorities,' MBh.; *strī pramāṇī yeshām*, 'they whose authority is a woman,' Pāṇ., Sch.); a means of acquiring Pramā or certain knowledge (6 in the Vedānta, viz. *pratyaksha*, perception by the senses; *anumāna*, inference; *upamāna*, analogy or comparison; *śabda* or *āpta-vacana*, verbal authority, revelation; *an-upalabdhi* or *abhāva-pratyaksha*, non-perception or negative proof; *arthâpatti*, inference from circumstances; the Nyāya admits only 4, excluding the last two; the Sāṃkhya only 3, viz. *pratyaksha*, *anumāna* and *śabda*; other schools increase the number to 9 by adding *sambhava*, equivalence; *aitihya*, tradition or fallible testimony; and *ceshṭā*, gesture, IW. 60 &c. &c.); any proof or testimony or evidence, Yājñ.; MBh.; Kāv. &c.; a correct notion, right perception (= *pramā*), Tarkas.; oneness, unity, L.; = *nitya*, L.; m. (cf. n.) N. of a large fig-tree on the bank of the Ganges, MBh.; (*ī*), f. (cf. n.) N. of a metre, Col. **-kuśala**, mfn. skilful in arguing, Kap. **-koṭi**, f. the point in an argument which is regarded as actual proof, Sarvad. **-khaṇḍana**, n., **-jāla**, n. N. of wks. **-jña**, mfn. knowing the modes of proof, A.; m. N. of Śiva, Śivag. **-ṭīkā**, f., **-tattva**, n. N. of wks. **-tara**, n. a greater authority than (abl.; *-tva*, n.), L. **–tas,** ind. according to measure or weight, Mn. viii, 137; according to proof or authority, W. **–tā,** f., *-tva*, n. authority, warranty, MBh. (the latter also 'correctness,' Nilak.) **–darpaṇa,** m. N. of wk. **–dṛishṭa,** mfn. sanctioned by authority, Kap.; demonstrable, Ml. **–nāma-mālā,** f., **-nirṇaya,** m. N. of wks. **–pattra,** n. a written warrant, MW. **–patha,** m. the way of proof (acc. with *na* and *ava-√tṝ*, 'not to admit of proof'), Sarvad. **–padârtha,** m. N. of wk. **–paddhati,** f. = *-patha* (°*tiṃ na adhy-√ās* = °*thaṃ na ava-√tṝ*), Sarvad.; N. of wk. **–pallava,** m. or n., **-pārâyaṇa,** n. N. of wks. **–purusha,** m. an umpire, arbitrator, judge, Hit. **–pramoda,** m. N. of wk. **–pravīṇa,** mfn. skilful in arguing, Prasannar. **–bhakti,** f., **-bhāshya-ṭīkā,** f. N. of wks. **–bhūta,** m. 'authoritative,' N. of Śiva, Śivag. (cf. *-jña*). **–mañjarī,** f., **-mālā,** f. N. of wks. **–yukta,** mfn. having the right measure, Var. **–ratna-mālā,** f. N. of wk. **–rāśi,** m. the quantity of the first term in a rule of three sum, Āryabh. **–lakshaṇa,** n., **-lakshaṇa-parîkshā,** f. N. of wks. **–vat,** mfn. established by proofs, well-founded, Prab. **–vākya,** n. authoritative statement, authority, Madhus. **–vārttika,** n., **-viniścaya,** m., N. of wks. **–śāstra,** n. any wk. of sacred authority, scripture, MW. **–saṃgraha,** m., **-samuccaya,** m., **-sāra,** m. (and °*ra-prakāśikā*, f.) N. of wks. **–siddhi,** m. N. of a man, Kathās. **–sūtra,** n. a measuring cord, Mṛicch. **–stha,** mfn. of normal size, Hcat.; being in a normal state or condition, imperturbed, Hariv. **Pramāṇâdarśa,** m. N. of a drama. **Pramāṇâdi-nirūpaṇa,** n. and **Pramāṇâdi-prakāśikā,** f. N. of wks. **Pramāṇâdhika,** mfn. being beyond measure, excessive, unnaturally strong, Śak.; longer than (comp.), Mṛicch. **Pramāṇânurūpa,** mfn. corresponding to (a person's) physical strength, Śak. **Pramāṇântara,** n. another means of proof (*-tā*, f.), Bhāshāp. **Pramāṇâbhāva,** m. absence of proof, want of authority, W. **Pramāṇâbhyadhika,** mfn. exceeding in size, bigger, Pañcat. **Pramāṇâyāma-tas,** ind. according to size and length, MBh.

Pramāṇaka (ifc.) = *pramāṇa*, measure, quantity, extent, MBh.; argument, proof, Kull.; (*ikā*), f. a kind of metre, Chandom.

Pramāṇaya, Nom. P. °*yati*, to regard or set up a person (acc.) as an authority in (loc.), Hit.; to use as evidence, Sarvad. °**māṇita,** mfn. adjusted, Car.; proved, demonstrated, shown clearly, Rājat.

Pramāṇī, in comp. for °*ṇa*. **–karaṇa,** n. setting up or quoting as an authority, Pat. **–kṛita,** mfn. meted out for or apportioned to (gen.); regarded as authority, conformed to, Kālid.; Kathās.; Rājat.; regarded as evidence, R. **–bhūta,** mfn. become or regarded as an authority or proof, W.

Pra-mātṛi, mfn. (for 2. see col. 2) one who has a correct notion or idea, authority, performer of (the mental operation resulting in a) true conception, Kap., Sch.; Vedântas.; Sarvad.; (*-tā*, f., Sarvad.; *-tva*, n., Saṃk.); a partic. class of officials, Inscr. °**māpaka,** mfn. proving, Sarvad.; m. an authority, MW. 1. °**māpaṇa,** n. (for 2. see col. 2) form, shape, MBh.

Pra-mita, mfn. meted out, measured, KātyŚr. (ifc. measuring, of such and such measure or extent or size, Var.; cf. *māsa-pram*°); limited, moderate, little, few, Var.; Kathās.; that about which a correct notion has been formed, Saṃk.; known, understood, established, proved, W.; m. N. of a teacher, VP.; °*tâkshara*, n. pl. 'measured syllables,' few words, Kathās.; (*ā*), f. N. of a metre, Śrutab.; °*tâbha*, m. pl. 'of limited splendour,' N. of a class of gods in the 5th Manv-antara, VP. °**miti,** f. a correct notion, right conception, knowledge gained or established by Pramāṇa or proof, Nyāyas., Sch.; Sarvad.; manifestation, BhP.; inference or analogy, W.; measuring, ib. °**meya,** mfn. to be measured, measurable (also = limited, small, insignificant, Naish.), to be ascertained or proved, provable, MBh.; Kāv. &c.; that of which a correct notion should be formed, Vedântas.; n. (ifc. f. *ā*) an object of certain knowledge, the thing to be proved or the topic to be discussed, Kap., Sch.; Vedântas.; MBh.; R. (cf. IW. 63); *-kamala-mārtaṇḍa*, m., *-ṭīkā*, f., *-tattva-bodha*, m. N. of wks.; *-tva*, n. provableness, demonstrability, Tarkas.; *-dīpikā*, f., *-nava-mālikā*, f., *-pariccheda*, m., *-mālā*, f., *-muktâvalī*, f., *-ratnâvalī*, f., *-saṃgraha*, m., *-saṃgraha-vivaraṇa*, n., *-sāra*, m., *-sāra-saṃgraha*, m. N. of wks.

प्रमातव्य *pra-mātavya.* See *pra-√mī* below.

प्रमातृ 2. *pra-mātṛi*, f. (for 1. see col. 1) the mother's mother, VP.

Pra-mātāmaha, m. a maternal great-grandfather, GobhŚrāddh.; AgP. (v. l. °*mātṛi-kāmaha*); (*ī*), f. a maternal great-grandmother, W.

प्रमात्र *pra-mātra*, m. or n. (?) a partic. high number, Buddh.

प्रमाथ *pra-mātha* &c. See *pra-√math.*

प्रमाद *pra-māda* &c. See *pra-√mad.*

प्रमापण 1. *pra-māpaṇa.* See *pra-√mā.*

प्रमापण 2. *pra-māpaṇa* &c. See *pra-√mī.*

प्रमार *pra-mārá.* See *pra-√mṛi.*

प्रमार्जक *pra-mārjaka* &c. See *pra-√mṛij.*

प्रमि *pra-√1. mi*, P. Ā. *-minoti, -minute*, to erect, build, KaushUp.; to judge, observe, perceive, Sāh.; Nyāyad., Comm.; Suśr. (ind. p. *pra-māya*). 2. °**mita,** n. (for 1. see col. 1) a hall, KaushUp.

प्रमिद् *pra-√mid*, P. Ā. *-medyati, -medate*, to begin to become fat, L. °**minna,** mfn. one who has begun to become fat, Pāṇ. vii, 2, 17. °**medita,** mfn. id., ib.; one who has begun to show affection, Bhaṭṭ. (*-vat*, mfn. id., Pāṇ. i, 2, 19); being or made unctuous, unctuous, greasy, MW.

प्रमिह् *pra-√mih*, P. *-mehati*, to make water, pass urine, MBh. °**mīḍha,** mfn. passed as urine; thick, compact, L. °**meha,** m. urinary disease (N. applied to all u° d°, of which there are 21 varieties including diabetes, gleet, gonorrhoea &c.), Suśr.; Var. &c. °**mehaṇa,** mfn. causing flow of urine, Kauś. (others °*mehana*, n. 'the penis'). °**mehin,** mfn. suffering from urinary disease, Suśr.

प्रमी *pra-√mī*, P. *-mināti* (*-mīṇāti*, Pāṇ. viii, 4, 15; *-minoti*, BhP.; Ved. inf. *-míyam, -míye* and *-metos*, cf. below), to frustrate, annul, destroy, annihilate, RV.; AV.; BhP.; to change, alter, RV.; to neglect, transgress, infringe, ib.; to miss, lose (one's way or time), forget, ib.; ŚBr.; to cause to disappear, put out of sight, RV.; to leave behind, outstrip, surmount, surpass, ib.; Bhaṭṭ.: (Ā. or Pass. *-mīyate*, aor. Subj. *-meshṭhāḥ*) to come to naught, perish, die, AV. &c. &c.: Caus. *-māpayati*, to destroy, annihilate, kill, slay, Nir.; Mn.; Yājñ. &c.; to cause to kill, Yājñ.

2. **Pra-maya,** m. (for 1. see *pra-√mā*) or °**mayā,** f. (only L.) ruin, downfall, death, Kāṭh.; Rājat.; Kathās.; killing, slaughter, W. °**mayú,** mfn. liable to be lost or destroyed, perishable, AV.

Pra-mātavya, mfn. to be slain, MBh.

2. **Pra-māpaṇa,** mf(*ī*)n. (fr. Caus.; for 1. see col. 1) murdering, a murderer, Yājñ.; n. (also °*māpana*, L.) slaughter, Mn.; Yājñ.; MBh. &c. °**māpayitṛi,** mfn. causing to perish; *-tva*, n. destructiveness, murderousness, Śaṃk. on ChUp. °**māpita,** mfn. destroyed, killed, slain, Rājat. °**māpin,** mfn. destroying, killing, W.

Pra-māyu (ShaḍvBr.) or °**māyuka** (TS.; Br.; ĀśvGṛ.), mfn. liable to destruction, perishable, dying away.

Pra-míyam (Ved. inf.), to miss, lose, RV. iv, 55, 7. °**míye** (Ved. inf.), to frustrate, annihilate, ib. iv, 54, 4.

Pra-mī, mfn., in *vāta-p*°, q. v. °**mīnat,** mfn. injuring, killing; overcoming, subduing, W. °**mīta,** mfn. deceased, dead, Kāṭh.; TS.; Mn.; MBh.; immolated, L.; m. an animal immolated, A.; *-patikā*, f. (a wife) whose husband is dead, a widow, Mn. °**mīti,** f. ruin, destruction, Nir. °**mīya,** mfn., see *a-p*°. °**metos** (Ved. inf.), to perish, TBr.

प्रमीढ *pra-mīḍha.* See *pra-√mih* above.

प्रमील् *pra-√mīl*, P. *-mīlati*, to close or shut the eyes, Git. °**mīlaka,** m. (Bhpr.; Car.), °**mīlikā,** f. (Car.) shutting the eyes, sleepiness. °**mīlā,** f. (ifc. f. *ā*) id., Naish.; lassitude, enervation, exhaustion from indolence or fatigue, W.; N. of a woman (sovereign of a kingdom of women), A. °**mīlita,** mfn. one who has the eyes closed, with closed eyes, MBh. °**mīlin,** m. N. of a demon (who causes closed eyes or faintness), AV.

प्रमीव् *pra-√mīv*, P. *-mīvati*, to push towards, press; to instigate, incite, TS.; ŚBr.

प्रमुक्ति *pra-mukti.* See *pra-√muc* below.

प्रमुख *pra-mukha*, mfn. turning the face towards, facing (acc.), R.; first, foremost, chief, principal, most excellent, Hit.; (generally ifc.; f. *ā*) having as foremost or chief, headed or preceded by, accompanied by or with [cf. *prīti-p*°; *Vasishṭha-p*°], MBh.; Kāv.; honourable, respectable, L.; m. a chief, respectable man, sage, W.; a heap, multitude, L.; Rottleria Tinctoria, L.; n. the mouth, MW.; commencement (of a chapter), BṛĀrUp.; Śaṃk.; time being, the present, the same time, Pratāp.; (ibc. or *e*, ind.) before the face of, in front of, before, opposite to (with gen. or comp.), MBh.; Kāv.; (with *√kṛi*) to cause to go before or precede, R. **–tas,** ind. at the head of, in front of, before the face of, before, opposite to (with gen. or ifc.), MBh.; Hariv.; before all others, first, in the first place, BhP. **–tā,** f. or **-tva,** n. superiority, predominance, W.

प्रमुग्ध *pra-mugdha.* See *pra-√muh.*

प्रमुच् *pra-√muc*, P. Ā. *-muñcati*, °*te*, to set free, let go, liberate, release from (abl.), RV.; AitBr.; MBh.; Yājñ.; to loosen, loose, untie, unbind, undo, RV.; ŚBr.; KātyŚr.; ChUp.; to rid one's self of (gen.), escape, R.; (ind. p. *-mucya*, having liberated one's self from [abl.], ChUp.); to drive away, banish, shake off, RV.; VS.; TBr.; MBh.; to give up, resign, renounce, MBh.; R.; to discharge, emit, throw out, shed, AV.; MBh.; R. &c.; to hurl, fling, throw, shoot, MBh.; Kathās.; to utter, MW.; to throw or put on (as a garland &c.), ib.; to lend, bestow, MBh.; R.: Pass. *-mucyate*, to free one's self from (abl. or instr.), Mn.; MBh.; BhP. &c.; to be loosened, become loose or detached, fall off (as fruits), ŚBr.; MBh.; to leave off, cease, ŚBr.; KaṭhUp.: Caus. *-mocayati*, to liberate from (abl.), MBh.; to loosen, untie, Ragh., Sch.: Desid. *-mumukshati*, to be about to give up or resign, MBh.

Pra-mukta, mfn. loosened, untied, released, liberated from (abl. or instr.), MBh.; R.; free from (abl.), L.; forsaken, abandoned, R.; given up, renounced, ib.; discharged, thrown out, shed, Var.; Kāraṇḍ.; hurled, shot, R. °**mukti** (*prá-*), f. liberation; pl. N. of partic. sacred texts, TBr. iii, 8, 18, 4.

Pra-muca (MBh.; MārkP.) or °**ci** (R.) or °**cu** (MBh.; Hariv.), m. N. of a Ṛishi. °**mucyamāna-homa,** m. pl. N. of partic. oblations accompanied with prayers beginning with *pramucyamānaḥ*, Vait.

Pra-moka, m. liberation, Śiś. °**moktavya,** mfn. to be liberated, to be set free, MBh. °**mocana,** mf(*ī*)n. liberating from (comp.), MBh.; Hariv.; MārkP.; (*ī*), f. a species of cucumber, L.; n. setting free, the act of liberating from (comp.), Kathās.; Kull.; discharging, emitting, shedding, MBh. (Cf. *unmocana-pramocanā.*)

प्रमुद् *pra-√mud*, Ā. *-modate*, to become joyful, rejoice greatly, exult, be delighted, AV. &c. &c.: Caus. *-modayati*, to make glad, delight, Mn.; MBh.; Hariv.; Sāh. °**mud,** mfn. pleased, happy, L.; (°*múd*), f. gladness, delight, pleasure (esp. sensual pl°), RV.; VS.; ŚBr.; MBh.; Pañcat. (°*mude √bhū*, to become a cause of delight). °**mudita,** mfn. delighted, pleased, glad, VS.; MBh.; R. &c.; gladsome (said of the autumn), MBh.; w. r. for *pracudita* (which m. c. for *pra-codita*), MBh.; (*ā*), f. (with Buddhists) N. of one of the 10 Bhūmis, Dharmas. 64; n. gladness, gaiety, Var.; Kathās.; N. of one of the 8 Sāṃkhya perfections, Sāṃkhyak., Sch.; *-pralamba-sunayana*, m. N. of a Gandharva prince, L.; *-vat*, mfn. pleased, Kathās.; *-vadanā*, f. N. of a metre, Col.; *-hṛidaya*, mfn. delighted in heart, Git.

Pra-modá, m. (also pl.; ifc. f. *ā*) excessive joy, delight, gladness, VS.; Up.; MBh. &c.; (also n.) one of the 8 Sāṃkhya perfections, Tattvas.; Sāṃkhyak., Sch.; (with Jainas) joy as exhibited in the virtuous, HYog.; Pleasure personified, Hariv. (as a child of Brahmā, VP.); the 4th year in a 60 years' cycle of Jupiter, VarBṛS. viii, 29; a strong perfume, BhP.; a kind of rice, Gal.; N. of a being attendant upon Skanda, MBh.; of a Nāga, ib.; of an author, Cat.; of sev. men, VP.; Rājat.; *-cārin*, w. r. for *pramāda-c*°, q. v.; *-tīrtha*, n. N. of a Tirtha, W.; *-nṛitya*, n. joyous dancing, a joyful dance, MW.; °*modâḍhyā*, f. a partic. plant, = *aja-modā*, Gal. °**modaka,** m. a kind of rice (= *shashṭikā*), Suśr.; Car.; N. of a man, Mudr. °**modana,**

mfn. making glad, exhilarating, MBh.; m. N. of a Ṛishi, R.; n. making glad, ib.; gladness, joyousness, ib. (cf. *sa-p°*). °**modam**, ind., in *uccaiḥ-p°*, with loud expressions of joy, Prab. °**modamāna**, n. (Sāṃkhyak., Sch.) or °**nā**, f. (Tattvas.) 'rejoicing,' N. of one of the 8 Sāṃkhya perfections (cf. *sadā-pramudita*). °**modita**, mfn. delighted, rejoiced, MW.; m. N. of Kubera, L.; (*ā*), f. N. of one of the 8 Sāṃkhya perfections, Tattvas. °**modín**, mfn. causing excessive joy, delighting, AV.; delighted, happy, W; m. a kind of rice (= °*modaka*), Vāgbh.; (*inī*), f. Odina Wodier (= *jiṅginī*), Bhpr.

प्रमुर्छ् *pra-√murch*, P. *-mūrchati*, to become thick or solid, congeal, ŚBr.

प्रमुष् *pra-√mush*, P. *-mushṇāti*, to steal away, rob, carry off, take away, RV.; ŚBr.; PārGṛ. &c. °**mushita**, mfn. stolen or taken away (also °*mushṭa*), BhP.; distracted, beside one's self, ib.; Kathās.; (*ā*), f. a kind of riddle, Cat.

Pra-mosha, m. stealing or taking away, BhP.

प्रमुह् *pra √muh*, P. *-muhyati*, to become bewildered or infatuated, MBh.; to faint, swoon, ib.; Suśr.: Caus. *-mohayati*, to bewilder, infatuate, MBh. °**mugdha**, mfn. unconscious, fainting, Uttarar.; Mālatīm.; very charming, Pañcar. °**mūḍha**, mfn. bewildered, unconscious, MBh.; Hariv.; Uttarar.; infatuated, foolish, MuṇḍUp.; ŚārṅgP.; disjointed, MBh.; *-saṃjña*, mfn. having the mind perplexed, bewildered, infatuated, R. °**moha**, m. bewilderment, infatuation, MBh.; Suśr.; Uttarar.; insensibility, fainting, W.; *-citta*, mf(*ā*)n. bewildered in mind, MBh. °**mohana**, mf(*ī*)n. bewildering the mind, MBh.; Hariv. °**mohita**, mfn. bewildered, infatuated, MBh. °**mohin**, mfn. (ifc.) bewildering, infatuating, ib.

प्रमूत्रित *pra-mūtrita*, mfn. begun to be urined (n. impers.), Subh., Sch.

प्रमूर *pra-mūra*, in *á-p°*, q. v.

प्रमूर्छ् *pra-√mūrch*. See *pra-√murch*.

प्रमूषिका *pra-mūshikā*, f. the external corner of the eye, VarBṛS. lviii, 7, Comm.

प्रमृ *pra-√mṛi*, Caus. P. *-mārayati*, to put to death, ŚBr. °**mará**, m. death, RV. °**maraṇa**, n. dying, death, BṛĀrUp., Śaṃk. °**mārá**, m. dying, AV. °**mṛita**, mfn. deceased, dead, MBh.; withdrawn or gone out of sight; covered, concealed, W.; n. death, MBh.; MārkP.; tillage, cultivation (as causing the death of many beings), Mn. iv, 4, 5 (cf. x, 83). °**mṛitaka**, mfn. dead, BhP.

प्रमृगम् *pra-mṛigam*, ind. (√*mṛig*), g. *tishṭhadgv-ādi*. °**mṛigya**, mfn. to be sought or searched after; peculiarly adapted to or fitted for (dat.), Kām.

प्रमृज् *pra-√mṛij*, P. *-mārshṭi* (*-mārjati*, °*te*, MBh.; *-mārjayati*, Suśr.), to wipe, wipe off, wash off, clean, cleanse, Kāṭh.; ŚBr.; GṛŚrS. &c.; to rub, pass the hand over, rub gently, stroke, MBh.; R.; to wipe out, wash out, remove, expel, rid one's self of, ib.; GopBr.; Kāv. &c.; to render unavailing, frustrate (as a wish), Rājat.; to destroy, AitBr.; to make ready, prepare, MW. °**mārjaka**, mfn. wiping off, causing to disappear, removing, MBh. °**mārjana**, n. the act of rubbing off, wiping off, Suśr.; (*aśru-p°*, the wiping away or drying of tears, consoling, MBh.; R.; Hariv.; Kām.; weeping, MBh.); causing to disappear, removing, Kāvyâd.

Pra-mṛishṭa, mfn. rubbed off, cleaned, polished, MBh.; Mālav. &c.; rubbed with (instr.), R.; wiped away, removed, expelled, Ragh.; given up, left, Hariv. (v. l. *prasṛishṭa*).

प्रमृड *pra-mṛiḍa*, mfn. gracious, making glad or happy, BhP.

प्रमृण् *pra-√mṛiṇ*, P. *-mṛiṇati*, to crush, destroy, RV. °**mṛiṇá**, mf(*ā*)n. destroying, crushing, RV.; TBr.

प्रमृत *pra-mṛita* &c. See *pra-√mṛi*.

प्रमृद् *pra-√mṛid*, P. *-mṛidnāti*, to crush down, bruise, destroy, ravage, devastate, MBh.; R.; Hariv. &c. °**marda**, m. N. of a partic. position of the moon in the Nakshatras, Sūryapr. °**mardaka**, mfn. crushing down, crushing, destroying, Lalit.; m. N. of a demon, ib. °**mardana**, mfn. crushing down, crushing, destroying, MBh.; R.; Hariv.; expelling, Suśr.; m. N. of Vishṇu, MBh.; of an attendant of Śiva, L.; of a demon causing disease, Hariv.; of a Vidyā-dhara, Kathās.; of a general-officer of Śambara, Hariv.; n. crushing, destroying, ib. °**mardita**, mfn. (fr. Caus.) crushed, bruised, R. °**marditṛi**, mfn. one who crushes, a destroyer, MBh. °**mardin**, mfn. (ifc.) crushing, destroying, Hariv.

प्रमृश् *pra-√mṛiś*, P. *-mṛiśati*, to lay hold of, touch, handle, AV.; ŚBr.; Kathās. (to reflect, consider, deliberate, Mahīdh.) °**mṛiśá**, mfn. laying hold of, handling, VS. (= *paṇḍita*, Mahīdh.) °**mṛishṭi**, f. rubbing over with (comp.), Hcar.

प्रमृष् *pra-√mṛish* (only pf. *-mamarsha*, aor. *-marshishṭhāḥ*, and inf. *-mṛishe*), to forget, neglect (with acc. or dat.), RV. (to destroy, Sāy.) °**mṛishya**, mfn., in *a-pramṛishyá*, q. v.

प्रमॄ *pra-√mṝi*, P. *-mṛiṇāti* (cf. *pra-mṛiṇ*), to crush, destroy, RV.; AV.

Prá-mūrṇa, mfn. crushed, destroyed, AV.

प्रमे *pra-mé*, ind. See under *pra-√mā*.

प्रमेतोस् *pra-metos*. See under *pra-√mī*.

प्रमेदित *pra-medita*. See *pra-√mid*.

प्रमेय *pra-meya*. See p. 686, col. 1.

प्रमेह *pra-meha* &c. See under *pra-√mih*.

प्रमोक *pra-moka* &c. See *pra-√muc*.

प्रमोक्ष *pra-moksha*, m. (√*moksh*) letting fall, dropping, losing, R.; discharging, dismissing, liberation, I° from (comp.); final deliverance, MBh.; R. °**mokshaka**, m. N. of a mountain, Divyâv.; of a serpent demon, L. °**mokshaṇa**, n. the end of an eclipse, Var.

प्रमोत *pra-móta* (perhaps fr. √*mīv*), a partic. kind of disease (others, 'mfn. mute'), AV. ix, 8, 4.

प्रमोद *pra-moda* &c. See *pra-√mud*.

प्रमोष *pra-mosha*. See *pra-√mush*.

प्रमोह *pra-moha* &c. See *pra-√muh*.

प्रम्रद् *pra-√mrad* (only Ved. inf. *-mradé*), to destroy, kill, ŚBr. (cf. *pra-mrid*).

प्रम्लुच् *pra-√mluc*, P. *-mlocati*, to go down, sink d°, ŚBr. °**mlócantī** (VS.) or °**mlocā** (MBh.; Hariv.; Pur.), f. N. of an Apsaras.

प्रम्लै *pra-√mlai*, P. *-mlāyati*, to fade or wither away, Bhaṭṭ.; Kuval.; to be sad or dejected or languid, A.

Pramlāna, mfn. faded, withered, MBh.; R.; Kām.; Ragh.; soiled, dirty, Prab. **-vadana**, mfn. having a sickly-looking face, MBh. **-śarīra**, mfn. withered in body, having an exhausted frame, Var.

Pramlānī-√bhū, P. *-bhavati*, to fade away, Pañcar.

प्रयक्ष् *pra-√yaksh*, P. Ā. *-yakshati*, °*te* (inf. *-yákshe*), to hasten forward, press onward, be eager; (with acc.) to strive after, pursue, attain, RV. °**yaksha** (*prá-*), mfn. eager, strenuous (?), RV. i, 62, 6 (= *pūjya*, Sāy.)

प्रयज् *pra-√yaj*, P. Ā. *-yajati*, °*te* (inf. *-yájadhyai*), to worship, sacrifice to (acc.), RV.; to offer the Prayāja sacrifice (cf. below), TS. °**yáj**, f. an offering, oblation, AV. °**yajyu** (*prá-*), mfn. worshipful, adorable, RV. (= *prakarsheṇa pūjya*, Sāy.; others 'pressing onwards, rushing on').

Prayāga, m. 'place of sacrifice,' N. of a celebrated place of pilgrimage (now called Allāhābād) at the confluence of the Gaṅgā and Yamunā with the supposed subterranean Sarasvatī (also *-ka*, AgP.; cf. *tri-veṇī*; ifc. also in Deva-p°, Rudra-p°, Karṇa-p° and Nanda-p°), Mn.; MBh. &c. (cf. RTL. 375; as N. of a country, Priy. i, ½; pl. the inhabitants of P°, MBh.); a sacrifice, L.; a horse, L. (cf. *pra-yoga*); N. of Indra, L.; N. of a man (also *-ka*), Rājat. **-kṛitya**, n. N. of ch. of the Tristhalī-setu (q.v.) **-tīrtha**, n. N. of a Tīrtha, SkandaP. **-dāsa**, m. N. of 2 men, Cat. **-prakaraṇa**, n., **-praghaṭṭaka**, m. or n. (?) N. of chs. of the Tristhalī-setu. **-bhaya**, m. 'fearing sacrifice,' N. of Indra, L. **-māhātmya**, n., **-ratna-kroḍa**, m., **-rājâshṭaka**, n. N. of wks. **-vana**, n. N. of a forest, R. **-setu**, m. N. of wk.

Prayājá, m. 'pre-sacrifice,' preliminary offering (cf. *anu-yāja*, q.v.), N. of partic. texts or invocations, and of the Ājya libations at which they are employed (they form part of the Prâyaṇīya or introductory ceremony in a Soma sacrifice and are generally 5, but also 9 and 11 in number), RV.; TS.; VS.; Br.; GṛŚrS.; a principal ceremony or sacrifice, W. **-tva**, n. the state or condition of a Prayāja, Kapishṭh. **-vat** (°*yājá-*), mfn. accompanied by a P°, TS.

Prayājânuyājá, m. pl. preliminary offering and after-sacrifice, AitBr. **Prayājâhuti**, f. the offering of a P°, ib.

Prayājyā, f. (also pl.) the words spoken at the moment of offering the P°, TBr., Sch.

प्रयत् *pra-√yat*, Ā. *-yatate*, to be active or effective, TBr. (ep. also P. °*ti*); to strive, endeavour, exert one's self, devote or apply one's self to (loc., dat., acc., *arthe*, *artham*, *hetos*, or inf.), ŚrS.; Mn.; MBh. &c. °**yatana**, n. effort, endeavour (used to explain *pra-yatna*), Pat. °**yatita**, n. (impers.) pains have been taken with (loc.), MBh. °**yatitavya**, n. (impers.) pains have to be taken with (loc.), R.; Bālar.; Car. °**yatta**, mfn. intent, eager, Bhartṛ. °**yattavya**, n. (impers.) = °*yatitavya*, Nal. °**yatna**, m. persevering effort, continued exertion or endeavour, exertion bestowed on (loc. or comp.), activity, action, act, Mn.; MBh. &c. (instr. sg. and pl. abl. and *-tas*, ind. with special effort, zealously, diligently, carefully; °*tna*, ibc. and °*tnāt*, ind. also = hardly, scarcely); great care, caution, Pañcat.; (in phil.) active efforts (of 3 kinds, viz. engaging in any act, prosecuting it, and completing it); pl. volitions (one of the 17 qualities of the Vaiśeshikas), IW. 68; (in gram.) effort in uttering, mode of articulation (also *āsya-pray°*, distinguished into *ābhyantara-p°* and *bāhya-p°*, internal and external effort), Prāt.; Pāṇ. i, 1, 9, Sch.; (*ā*), f. N. of a partic. Śruti, Saṃgīt.; *-cchid*, mfn. frustrating a person's (gen.) efforts, Mudr.; *-prêkshaṇīya*, mfn. hardly visible, Śak.; *-muktâsana*, mfn. rising with difficulty from a seat, Ragh.; *-vat*, mfn. assiduous, diligent, persevering, Kām.; °*tnânanda*, m. N. of wk.

प्रयभ् *pra-√yabh*, P. *-yabhati*, futuere, TBr.

प्रयम् *pra-√yam*, P. Ā. *-yacchati*, °*te*, to hold out towards, stretch forth, extend, RV.; AV.; to place upon (loc.), MBh.; to offer, present, give, grant, bestow, deliver, despatch, send, effect, produce, cause (with dat., gen. or loc. of pers. and acc. of thing), RV. &c. &c. (with *vikrayeṇa*, to sell; with *uttaram*, to answer; with *śāpam*, to pronounce a curse; with *yuddham*, to give battle, fight; with *visham*, to administer poison; with *buddhau*, to set forth or present to the mind); to restore, pay (a debt), requite (a benefit), Mn.; MBh. &c.; to give (a daughter) in marriage, AitBr.; ĀśvGṛ.; Mn. &c.

Prá-yata, mfn. outstretched, far-extended, RV.; AV.; placed upon (loc.), RV.; offered, presented, given, granted, bestowed, RV. &c. &c.; piously disposed, intent on devotion, well prepared for a solemn rite (with loc. or ifc.), ritually pure (also applied to a vessel and a place, Āpast.; R.), self-subdued, dutiful, careful, prudent, KaṭhUp.; Mn.; MBh. &c.; m. a holy or pious person, W.; *-tā*, f., *-tva*, n. purity, holiness, MBh.; *-dakshiṇa* (*práy°*), mfn. one who has made presents (to the priests at a sacrifice), a giver, donor, RV.; *-parigraha-dvitīya*, mfn. accompanied by a pious or chaste wife, MW.; *-mānasa*, mfn. pious-minded, devout, ascetic, MBh.; °*tâtman* or °*tâtma-vat*, mfn. id., Mn.; R. °**yati** (*prá-*), f. offering, gift, donation, RV.; intention, will, effort, exertion, ib.; VS. °**yantṛi**, mfn. one who offers or presents, a giver, bringer (with gen. or acc.), RV.; a guide, driver (*gaja-*, of elephants), MBh. °**yamaṇa**, n. purification, Āpast. °**yāma**, m. dearth, scarcity (= *nīvāka*), L.; checking, restraining, W.; extension, length (in space or time), Jātakam.; progress, ib. °**yāmya**, mfn. to be checked or controlled, ib.

प्रयस् 1. *pra-√yas*, P. *-yásyati* (cf. Pāṇ. iii, 1, 71), to begin to bubble, AV.; to endeavour, labour, strive after (dat.), Naish. °**yasta** (*prá-*), mfn. bubbling over, RV.; AV.; striving, eager, Śak.; well cooked or prepared, L. (cf. 2. *práyas*). °**yāsá**, m. exertion, effort, pains, trouble (ibc., with loc. or gen., *-arthāya* or *-nimittena*), VS.; TS.; Kāv. &c.

(cf. *a-prayāsena*); high degree, Jātakam.; *-bhāj*, mfn. capable of exertion, active, energetic, W. °**yāsita**, n. (fr. Caus.) effort, exertion, Mālatīm. (v.l. *ā-yāsita*).

प्रयस् 2. *práyas*, n. (√*prī*) pleasure, enjoyment, delight, RV. (*práyase*, iv, 21, 7 = *práyase*); object of delight, pleasant food or drink, dainties, libations (*práyāṅsi nadīnām*, 'refreshing waters'), ib.; mfn. valuable, precious (?), W. **–vat** (*práyas-*), mfn. having or bestowing pleasant food, offering libations, RV. (°*svanto 'trayaḥ*, N. of the authors of v, 20); n. N. of a Sāman, ĀrshBr.

1. **Prayo-gá** (Padap. *pra-yóga*), mfn. (for 2. see under *pra-√yuj*) coming to a meal, RV. x, 7, 5 (Sāy. = *pra-yoktavya*); m. N. of a Ṛishi, TS.; (with *Bhārgava*) author of RV. viii, 91, Anukr.

प्रया *pra-√yā*, P. *-yāti*, to go forth, set out, progress, advance towards or against, go or repair to (acc., also with *acchā* or *prati*, or loc.), RV. &c. &c.; to walk, roam, wander, MBh.; Kāv. &c.; to part, go asunder, be dispersed, pass away, vanish, die, ib.; to get into a partic. state or condition, enter, undergo, incur (acc.), ib.; to proceed i.e. behave, Bhartṛ. (v.l.); to cause to go i.e. to lead into (acc.), Hcat.: Caus. *-yāpayati*, to cause to set out, ŚBr. (cf. Pāṇ. viii, 4, 29; 30, Sch.): Desid. *-yiyāsati*, to wish to set out, ib.: Caus. of Desid. *-yiyāsayati*, to cause a person to wish to set out, Bhaṭṭ.

Pra-yá, f. onset, RV.

Pra-yáṇa, n. (Kāś. on Pāṇ. viii, 4, 29) setting out, starting, advancing, motion onwards, progress, journey, march, invasion, RV. &c. &c. (with *garda-bhena*, 'riding on an ass,' Pañcat.); departure, death (cf. *prāṇa-pray°*); onset, beginning, commencement, Kāṭh.; ŚBr.; *-kāla*, m. time of departure, death, Bhag.; *-paṭaha*, m. a drum beaten while marching, Hcar.; *-purī*, f. N. of a town (°*rī-māhātmya*, n. N. of wk.); *-bhaṅga*, m. the breaking or suspending of a journey, a halt, Pañcat.; *-vicāra*, m. N. of wk.; °*nârha*, mfn. deserving death, W. °**yāṇaka**, n. a journey, march, Kāv.; Pañcat. &c. (cf. *a-pray°*). °**yāṇi**, see *a-prayāṇi*. °**yāṇīya** or °**yānīya**, mfn., Pāṇ. viii, 4, 30, Sch. °**yāta**, mfn. set out, gone, advanced, MaitrUp.; R. &c.; arrived at, come to (acc.), MBh.; Kāv. &c.; gone or passed away, vanished, deceased, dead, Kathās. °**yātavya**, mfn. to be attacked or assailed, MBh.; n. (impers.) one should set out, ib.; R.; Kathās. °**yātṛi**, m. one who goes or can go or fly, Kathās.; setting out on a march or journey, Var. °**yātrā**, f., see *prāyātrika*. °**yāpaṇa** or °**yāpana**, n. (fr. Caus.), Pāṇ. viii, 4, 30, Sch. °**yāpaṇi**, see *a-prayāpaṇi*. °**yāpaṇīya** or °**yāpanīya**, mfn., Pāṇ. viii, 4, 30, Sch. °**yāpita**, mfn. driven or sent away, made to go or pass away, W. °**yāpin**, mfn. (du. °*piṇau* or °*pinau*), Pāṇ. viii, 4, 30, Sch. °**yāpya**, mfn. to be caused to go, to be sent away, AitBr. °**yāpyamāṇa** or °**yāpyamāna**, mfn., Pāṇ. viii. 4, 30, Sch. °**yāman** (*prá-*), n. setting out, start, RV. °**yāyin**, mfn. (du. °*yiṇau*, Kāś. on Pāṇ. viii, 4, 29) going forwards, marching, driving, riding, MBh.; R. °**yāvan**, see *vṛisha-* and *supra-yāvan*. °**yiyu**, mfn. (fr. Desid.) used for driving (as a horse), RV. (Nir. iv, 15).

प्रयाग *pra-yāga*, °*yāja*. See *pra-√yaj*.

प्रयाच् *pra-√yāc*, P. Ā. *-yācati*, °*te*, to ask for, beg, solicit, request (with acc. of pers. and thing), MBh.; Hariv.; R. °**yācaka**, mfn. asking, requesting, imploring (with *artham* ifc.), MBh. °**yācana**, n. asking, begging, imploring, ib.

प्रयाण *pra-yāṇa* &c. See under *pra-√yā*.

प्रयास *pra-yāsa*. See under *pra-√yas*.

प्रयु *pra-√1. yu* (only aor. Subj. *-yoshat*), to remove, keep away, RV. viii, 31, 17. 1. °**yuta** (*prá-*), mfn. absent in mind, inattentive, heedless, careless (cf. *a-pray°*), RV.; VS.; (*pra-yúta*), n. (also m., Siddh.) a million, VS. &c. &c. (cf. 2. *a-yúta*). °**yuti** (*prá-*), f. absence (with *manasaḥ* = thoughtlessness), RV. °**yutvan**, see *á-prayutvan*. °**yotṛi**, m. a remover, expeller, RV.

प्रयु *pra-√2. yu*, P. *-yauti*, to stir, mingle, TS.; MaitrS.; to disturb, destroy, Nir. °**yút**, mfn. stirring, mingling, TBr. 2. °**yuta** (*prá-*), mfn. mingled with (instr.), MānŚr.; confused (as a dream), MānGṛ.; destroyed, annihilated, MaitrS.; m. N. of a Deva-gandharva, MBh.; °*teśvara-tīrtha*, n. N. of a place of pilgrimage, SkandaP. °**yuvana**, n. stirring, mingling, Hcat.

प्रयुछ् *pra-√yuch*, P. *-yucchati*, to be absent; (with or scil. *manasā*) to be absent in mind, be careless or heedless, RV.

प्रयुज् *pra-√yuj*, Ā. *-yuṅkte* (rarely P. *-yunakti*; cf. Pāṇ. i, 3, 64), to yoke or join or harness to (loc.), RV.; to unite with (instr.), AV.; to turn (the mind) to (loc.), RV.; to prepare for (dat.), ib.; to set in motion, throw, cast (also dice), discharge, hurl at (loc. or dat.), MBh.; Kāv. &c.; to utter, pronounce, speak, recite, ib.; to fix, place in or on (loc.), BhP.; to direct, order, urge to (dat. or loc.), MBh.; Kāv. &c.; to choose for (two acc.), Kum.; to lead towards, bring into (acc.), BhP.; to use, employ, practise, display, exhibit, perform, accomplish, contrive, do, Br. &c. &c.; to undertake, commence, begin, Vait.; R.; to cause, effect, produce, Kum.; BhP.; Sarvad.; to represent on the stage, act, Mṛicch.; Kālid.; to lend (for use or interest), Mn.; Yājñ.: Pass. *-yujyate*, to be fit or suitable, conduce to (dat.), Kāv.; Pañcat.: Caus. *-yojayati*, to throw, discharge, hurl at or against (loc.), MBh.; to utter, pronounce, R.; to show, display, exhibit, BhP.; (with *manas*) to concentrate the mind, ŚvetUp.; to urge, direct, appoint to (loc.), MBh.; BhP.; to transfer or entrust to (dat.), MBh.; to undertake, begin, Kām.; to represent on the stage, Hariv.; Sāh.; to cause to be represented by (instr.), Uttarar.; to use, employ, MBh.; Kām.; Suśr. &c.; to perform, practise, Mn. iii, 112; (with *vṛiddhim*) to take interest, ib. x, 117; (with *prayogam*) to invest capital, SaddhP.; to be applicable, g. *kshubhnâdi*; to aim at, have in view, Pāṇ. vi, 3, 62, Sch.: Desid. *-yuyukshate*, to wish to use, want, require, Pat.

Pra-yukta, mfn. yoked, harnessed, MBh.; R. &c.; stirred (by wind), Ragh.; directed, thrown, hurled, MBh.; Kāv. &c.; drawn (as a sword), BhP.; vented (as anger), MBh.; uttered, pronounced, recited, Up.; Siksh. &c.; urged, ordered, bidden, Gobh.; Bhag. &c.; used, employed, practised, performed, done, Br.; Kauś.; MBh. &c.; undertaken, begun, contrived, R.; Mālav.; Prab.; made, prepared, Kum.; (n. impers.) behaved or acted towards (loc. or acc. with *prati*), Śak.; lent (on interest), Yājñ.; suitable, appropriate, Pañcat. (see *a-pray°*); resulting from (comp.), ib.; n. a cause, W.; *-tama*, mfn. most used, AitBr.; *-saṃskāra*, mfn. to which polish has been applied, polished (as a gem), Ragh. °**yukti** (*prá-*), f. impulse, motive, RV.; setting in motion, employment, TBr.; Śaṃk.; Rājat. °**yuga**, n., orig. form of *praüga* (q. v.), VPrāt.

Pra-yúj, (prob.) f. a team, RV.; impulse, motive, VS.; AV.; acquisition, RV.; (°*yujām havīṅshi* or °*yug-ghav°*, N. of 12 oblations, one of which is offered each month, ŚBr.); mfn. joining, connected with (lit. or fig., as a cause, motive &c.), W. °**yoktavya**, mfn. to be thrown or discharged, MBh.; to be used or employed, applicable, suitable, ib.; R. &c.; to be exhibited or represented, Mālav.; to be uttered or pronounced or recited, Śiksh.; Śaṃk. °**yoktṛi**, m. a hurler, shooter (of missiles), MBh.; R.; an executor, agent (of an action), MBh.; Ragh. &c.; an undertaker (of a sacrifice), KātyŚr., Sch.; a procurer, MBh.; an employer, ib.; Kām.; an actor, mime, Ragh.; a speaker, reciter, RPrāt.; Kāvyâd.; a performer (of music), R.; a composer, author, poet, Uttarar.; a money-lender, Yājñ., Sch.; *-tā*, f., *-tva*, n. the state or condition of an employer, Sarvad. °**yoktra**, n. harness, Divyâv.

2. **Prayoga**, m. (for 1. see under 2. *práyas*, col. 1) joining together, connection, Var.; position, addition (of a word), VPrāt.; Pāṇ. (loc. often = in the case of, Kāś. on Pāṇ. i, 4, 25; 26 &c.); hurling, casting (of missiles), MBh.; R. &c.; offering, presenting, Hariv.; undertaking, beginning, commencement, ŚBr.; ŚrS.; a design, contrivance, device, plan, Mālav.; Rājat.; application, employment (esp. of drugs or magic; cf. IW. 402, 1), use, GṛŚrS.; MBh. &c. (*ena*, *āt* and °*ga-tas*, ifc. = by means of); practice, experiment (opp. to 'theory'), Mālav.; a means (only *ais*, by use of means), MBh.; Suśr.; (in gram.) an applicable or usual form, Siddh.; Vop.; exhibition (of a dance), representation (of a drama), Mṛicch.; Kālid. (°*ga-to √ dṛiś*, to see actually represented, see on the stage, Ratnâv.); a piece to be represented, Kālid.; Prab.; utterance, pronunciation, recitation, delivery, ŚrS.; RPrāt.; Pāṇ., Sch.; a formula to be recited, sacred text, Śiksh.; lending at interest or on usury, investment, Mn.; MBh.; principal, loan bearing interest, Gaut.; an example, L.; cause, motive, affair, object, W.; consequence, result, ib.; ceremonial form, course of proceeding, ib.; a horse (cf. *pra-yāga*), L. **–kārikā**, f., **-kaustubha**, m. or n. N. of wks. **–grahaṇa**, n. acquirement of practice, Daś. **–candrikā**, f., **-cintāmaṇi**, m., **-cūḍāmaṇi**, m. N. of wks. **–jña**, mfn. skilful in practice, Suśr. **–tattva**, n., **-darpaṇa**, m., **-dīpa**, m., **-dīpikā** and °**kā-vṛitti**, f. N. of wks. **–nipuṇa**, mfn. = *-jña*, Bhartṛ. **–pañcaratna**, n., **-paddhati**, f. N. of wks. **–pāda**, n. smoking for the sake of one's health, Car. **–pārijāta**, m., **-pustaka**, m. or n. N. of wks. **–pradhāna**, mfn. consisting chiefly in practice (not in theory), Mālav. **–mañjarī**, f., **-maṇi-mālikā**, f., **-mantra**, m., **-mayūkha**, m., **-muktâvalī**, f., **-mukha-vyākaraṇa**, n., **-ratna**, n., **-ratna-kroḍa**, m., **-ratna-mālā** or °**likā**, f., **-ratna-saṃskāra**, m., **-ratnâkara**, m., **-ratnâvalī**, f., **-vidhi**, m., **-viveka** and °**ka-saṃgraha**, m. N. of wks. **–vīrya**, n. (with Buddhists) energy in practice (one of the 3 energies), Dharmas. 108. **–vṛitti**, f., **-vaijayantī**, f., **-śikhāmaṇi**, m., **-saṃgraha** and °**ha-viveka**, m., **-saraṇi**, f., **-sāra**, m., **-sāraṇī**, f., **-sāra-samuccaya**, m. N. of wks. **Prayogâṇḍabilā**, f. N. of wk. **Prayogâtiśaya**, m. (in dram.) 'excess in representation,' pronouncing the name of a character the moment that he enters the stage, Pratāp.; the useless appearance of a character on the stage during the prelude, Sāh. **Prayogâmṛita**, n. N. of wk. **Prayogârtha**, mfn. having the sense of *prayoga*, L.

Prayogin, mfn. being employed or used, applicable, usual (°*gi-tva*, n.), KātyŚr.; having some object in view, W.; performing (on the stage); m. an actor, Bhar. °**yogīya**, mfn. treating of the application (of medicines &c.), Cat. °**yogya**, m. any animal harnessed to a carriage, draught animal, ChUp. °**yojaka**, mf(*ikā*)n. causing, effecting, leading to (gen. or comp.), MBh.; Rājat.; Sarvad.; (ifc.) prompting, instigating, instigator, promoter, Pāṇ. i, 4, 55; effective, essential, Sāh.; deputing, anointing, W.; m. an author, composer, Yājñ.; a money-lender, creditor, ib.; a founder or institutor of any ceremony, W.; an employer, A.; *-kartṛi-tva*, n. the acting as instigator or promoter, W.; *-tā*, f. (Nyāyam., Sch.), *-tva*, n. (Kāś.) agency; °*kâdhyāya-bhāshya*, n. N. of wk.

Pra-yojana, n. (ifc. f. *ā*) occasion, object, cause, motive, opportunity, purpose, design, aim, end, Prāt.; MBh.; Kāv. &c.; *prayojanena*, with a particular intention, on purpose, MBh.; °*na-vaśāt*, id., Pañcat.; *kena* °*nena*, from what cause or motive? Prab.; *kasmai* °*nāya*, *kasmāt* °*nāt*, *kasya* °*nasya* and *kasmin* °*ne*, id., Kāś. on Pāṇ. ii, 3, 27; °*nam ati-√ kram*, to neglect an opportunity, MBh.; profit, use or need of, necessity for, Kāv.; Pañcat. &c. (with instr., *taruṇā kim prayojanam*, what is the use of the tree? Kuval.; *bhavatv etaiḥ kusumaiḥ prayojanam*, let these flowers be used, Śak.; with gen. or dat., Kāś. on Pāṇ. ii, 3, 27; ii, 3, 72); means of attaining, Mn. vii, 100; (in phil.) a motive for discussing the point in question, IW. 64; *-vat*, mfn. having or connected with or serving any purpose or interest, interested, R.; serviceable, useful, Suśr. (°*t-tva*, n., Sarvad.); having a cause, caused, produced, W. °**yojayitṛi**, m. (fr. Caus.) a causer, occasioner, Āpast. °**yojya**, mfn. to be cast or shot (missile), MBh.; Hariv.; to be used or employed or practised (*-tva*, n.), Mn.; MBh. &c.; to be appointed or commissioned, dependent, a servant or slave, Sarvad.; to be represented (on the stage), Sāh.; n. capital (to be lent on interest); *-tva*, n. the state of being used or employed (*a-pray°*), Vām.; the state of being appointed or commissioned, dependence (*a-pray°*), Sarvad.

प्रयुध् *pra-√yudh*, Ā. *-yudhyate* (rarely P. °*ti*), to begin to fight, attack, fight with (acc.), RV.; MBh.; R.; Hariv.: Caus. *-yodhayati*, to cause to begin to fight, ĀśvGṛ.; to attack, combat, Hariv.: Desid. Ā. *-yuyutsate*, to wish to fight with (instr.), MBh. °**yutsu**, m. (only W.) a warrior; a ram; an ascetic; air, wind; N. of Indra (for °*yuyutsu*). °**yuddha**, mfn. fighting, one who has fought, MBh.; Hariv.; R.; Kathās.; n. fight, battle, Kathās.; °*yuddhârtha*, mfn. having the sense of *pra-yuddha* (accord. to others, m. = *pratyutkrama*, war, battle, going to w° or b°; accord. to others v.l. for *prayogârtha*), L. °**yúdh**, mfn. attacking, assailing, RV. v, 59, 5. °**yoddhṛi**, mfn. one who fights, a combatant, Sāy.

प्रयुवन *pra-yuvana.* See under *pra-√2. yu.*

प्रयै *pra-yaí.* See under *pra-√yā.*

प्रयोक्तव्य *pra-yoktavya, pra-yoga, pra-yojaka.* See *pra-√yuj°.*

प्रयोतृ *pra-yotṛí.* See under *pra-√1. yu.*

प्रय्यमेध *prayyamedha=praiyyamedha* (w.r. for *praiyamedha*, q.v.), AitBr.

प्ररक्ष् *pra-√raksh*, P. *-rakshati*, to protect against, save from (abl.; see *-rakshita* below). °**raksha**, mfn. one from whom any one is protected, Siddh. °**rakshaṇa**, n. protecting, protection, Pañcat. °**rakshita**, mfn. protected against, saved from (abl.), Pañcat. (v.l.)

प्ररथम् *pra-ratham*, ind., g. *tishṭhadgv-ādi.*

प्ररद् *pra-√rad*, P. *-radati*, to scratch or cut in, dig out (as a channel), mark out (as a path), RV.

प्ररप् *pra-√rap*, P. *-rapati*, to prate, talk, RV.

प्ररश् *pra-√rapś* (only Ā. pf. *-rarapśe*), to reach beyond (abl.), RV.

प्ररम् *pra-√ram*, Caus. P. *-ramayati*, to delight or gladden greatly, exhilarate, Nir. ii, 18.

प्रराधस् *pra-rādhas*, m. (√*rādh*) N. of a descendant of Aṅgiras, SV. (v.l. *purādhas*). °**rā́dhya**, mfn. to be satisfied or made content, RV. v, 39, 3.

प्ररिच् *pra-√ric*, Ā. *-ricyate*, to excel, surpass, be superior to (abl.), RV.; TS.; to empty excessively, become ex° empty, TĀr.: Caus. *-recayati*, to leave remaining, RV.; to quit, abandon, ib. °**ríkvan**, mfn. reaching beyond, surpassing (with abl.), RV. i, 100, 15. °**reká**, m. (iii, 30, 19) and °**récana**, n. (i, 17, 6) abundance, plenty, RV.

प्ररी *pra-√ri*, P. *-riṇāti*, to sever, detach, take away, RV. ii, 22, 4; Ā. *-rīyate*, to penetrate, enter (?), v, 7, 8.

प्ररु *pra-√ru*, P. *-rauti*, to roar or cry out loudly, RV.

प्ररुच् *pra-√ruc*, Ā. *-rocate*, to shine forth, RV.; to be liked, please, ŚBr.: Caus. *-rocayati*, to enlighten, illuminate, RV.; to cause to shine, ib.; to make apparent or specious, make pleasing, AV.; TS.; Br. °**rocana**, mf(*ī*)n. exciting or inciting to love (as a spell), seductive, Kathās.; (*ā*), f. highest praise, Bālar.; (in dram.) exciting interest by praising an author in the prologue of a drama, Daśar.; Sāh.; Pratāp. (also n.); favourable description of that which is to follow in a play, ib.; n. stimulating, exciting, Mālatīm.; seduction, Prab.; praising, ChUp.; Śaṃk.; Kap., Sch.; Mālatīm.; illustration, explanation, PañcavBr. °**rocita**, mfn. (fr. Caus.) commended, praised, approved, liked, MBh.

प्ररुज् *pra-√ruj*, P. *-rujati*, to break down, break, RV.; MBh.; BhP. °**ruja**, m. N. of a mythical being conquered by Garuḍa, MBh.; of a Rākshasa, ib.

प्ररुद् *pra-√rud*, P. *-roditi*, to begin to mourn or cry or weep, lament or cry aloud, ŚāṅkhGṛ.; MBh.; R. &c.; to weep with any one (acc.), MBh. °**rudita**, mfn. one who has begun to weep, weeping, MBh.; R.; Vikr.; Kathās.

प्ररुध् *pra-rudh*, P. Ā. *-ruṇaddhi, -runddhe*, to keep or hold back, check, stop, Br.; MBh.

प्ररुह् *pra-√ruh*, P. *-rohati*, to grow up, shoot forth, shoot up, VS.; Br.; ChUp. &c.; to heal up (as a wound), MBh. (v.l.); to grow, increase, MBh.; Rājat.; ŚārṅgP.: Caus. *-ropayati*, to fasten to, put into or on (loc.), Var. °**rúh**, mfn. shooting forth, growing up (like a plant); (with *giri*), m. a mountain which rises in the foreground, Hariv. 5327; f. a shoot, a new branch, AV. °**rūḍha**, mfn. grown up, full-grown, R.; Kāv.; Var.; (ifc.) overgrown with, Hariv.; filled up, healed up, R.; grown, widely spread, become great or strong, Sāh.; BhP.; Kathās. &c.; old, L.; growing or proceeding from a root, rooted, fastened, L.; arisen or proceeded from (comp.), Hariv.; R.; Śak.; BhP.; *-kaksha*, mfn. a place where shrubs have grown, ĀpŚr.; *-keśa*, mfn. one whose hair has grown long, having l° h°, Pañcat.; *-mūla*, mfn. having roots gone deep, A.; *-śāli*, m. full-grown rice, MW. °**rūḍhi**, f. the having shot up, Hcar.; growth, increase, Rājat. °**ródhana**, n. rising, ascending, TS. °**ropita**, mfn. (fr. Caus.) sown, planted, R.; Sāh.; shown or done (as a kindness), Rājat. °**roha**, m. germinating, sprouting, growing or shooting forth (lit. and fig.; cf. *dṛiḍha-p°*); Kum.; Kull. &c.; a bud, shoot, sprout, sprig, Hariv.; Kāv.; Suśr. &c.; an excrescence, Suśr.; a new leaf or branch, MW.; (fig.) a shoot = ray (of light; see *prabhā-p°*), Kum.; Ragh.; BhP.; *-vat*, mfn. possessing vegetation, covered with v°, Suśr. °**rohaka**, mfn. causing to grow, Nalac. °**rohaṇa**, n. germinating, sprouting, growing or shooting forth, growth (lit. and fig.), MBh.; Sāṃkhyak., Sch.; Siṅhās.; a bud, shoot, sprig, MBh.; Hariv. °**rohin**, mfn. growing or shooting up, sh° up from (comp.), Mn. i, 46; (ifc.) causing to grow, propagating, MBh.; Hariv.; Hcat.; °*hi-śakhin*, mfn. (a tree) whose branches grow again, Yājñ. ii, 227.

प्ररूप् *pra-√rūp*, P. *-rūpayati*, to expound, expose, explain (esp. in the Jaina system), Sarvad. °**rūpaṇa**, n. (or °*ṇā*, f.) exposing, teaching, Siṅhās.

प्ररेक *pra-reká*, °*récana.* See *pra-√ric.*

प्ररेज् *pra-√rej*, Ā. *-rejate*, to tremble at (acc.), RV. i, 38, 10: Caus. *-rejayati*, to cause to tremble, ib. iv, 22, 3.

प्रर्क्षीय *pra-rkshīya*, Nom. P. °*yati* (fr. *pra-rksha=pra+ṛiksha*), Vop. ii, 4; (also *prārkshīya.*)

प्रर्च्छक *prarcchaka*, mfn. (fr. *pra+ṛicchaka*), Pat.

प्रर्षभीय *prarshabhīya*, Nom. P. °*yati* (fr. *prarshabha = pra + ṛishabha*), Pāṇ. vi, 1, 22, Sch.; (also *prārshabhīya.*)

प्रलघु *pra-laghu*, mfn. very inconsiderable, very small (as an attendance), Kād.; *-tā*, f., Mudr.

प्रलप् *pra-√lap*, P. *-lapati*, to speak forth (inconsiderately or at random), prattle, talk idly or incoherently, trifle, TBr.; MBh.; Kāv. &c.; to talk, converse, BhP.; to speak forth, speak, MBh.; Pañcat.; to exclaim, Bhartṛ.; to lament, bewail, Pañcat.; to speak or tell in a doleful manner, MBh.; R.; to call upon or invoke in piteous tones, MBh.: Caus. *-lāpayati*, to cause or incite to speak, Mṛicch. °**lapana**, n. prattling, talking, Pañcat.; Sāh.; lamentation, Uttarar. °**lapita**, mfn. spoken forth, spoken, said, W.; spoken dolefully, invoked piteously, Sāh.; n. prattling, talk, Pañcat.; Nītis.; lamentation, Pañcat.; Sāh. °**lāpá**, m. talk, discourse, prattling, chattering, AV. &c. &c.; (also n.) lamentation (*ārta-p°*, l° of one in pain), MBh.; R.; Pañcat. &c.; incoherent or delirious speech, raving, Cat.; *-vat*, mfn. one who speaks confusedly or incoherently, Suśr.; *-han*, m. a kind of medic. preparation, L.; °*pâika-maya*, mf(*ī*)n. 'consisting only of lamentation,' doing nothing but lament, MW. °**lāpaka**, m. speaking incoherently, Bhpr. °**lāpana**, n. (fr. Caus.) causing or teaching to speak, Cat. °**lāpin**, mfn. (generally ifc.; °*pi-tva*, n.) chattering, talking much or unmeaningly, talking, speaking, MBh.; R.; Yājñ. &c.; lamenting, wailing, R.; (fever) attended with delirium, Bhpr.; °*pi-tā*, f. amorous conversation or prattle, Pratāp.

प्रलभ् *pra-√labh*, Ā. *-labhate*, to lay hold of, seize, MBh.; to get, obtain, Kathās.; to overreach, cheat, deceive, befool, MBh.; BhP.: Caus. *-lambhayati*, to cheat, deceive, BhP. °**labdha**, mfn. seized, MBh.; overreached, cheated, deceived, MW. °**labdhavya**, mfn. to be cheated or fooled, MBh. °**labdhṛi**, mfn. a cheat, deceiver, MBh. °**lambha**, m. obtaining, gaining, R.; (also pl.) overreaching, deceiving, MBh. °**lambhana**, n. overreaching, deceiving, BhP.; that by which any one is deceived, Jātakam.

प्रलम्फन *pra-lamphana*, n. a jump, L.

प्रलम्ब् *pra-√lamb*, Ā. *-lambate*, to hang down, Daś.; Suśr.

Pralamba, mf(*ā*)n. hanging down, depending, pendent, pendulous (generally ibc.), KātyŚr., Sch.; MBh.; Hariv.; R.; bending the upper part of the body forward, MBh.; prominent, MW.; slow, dilatory, W.; m. hanging on or from, depending, L.; a branch, L.; a shoot of the vine-palm, L.; a cucumber, Bhpr.; a garland of flowers worn round the neck, W.; a kind of necklace of pearls, L.; the female breast, L.; tin (?), W.; N. of a Daitya slain by Bala-rāma or Kṛishṇa, MBh.; Hariv.; Kathās. &c.; of a mountain, R.; (*ā*, f. N. of a Rākshasī, Buddh.); *-keśa*, mfn. one whose hair hangs down, VP.; *-ghna*, m. 'slayer of Pralamba,' N. of Bala-rāma and of Kṛishṇa, L.; *-tā*, f. the hanging down, being pendulous, Kād.; *-nāsika*, mfn. one who has a prominent nose, A.; *-bāhu*, mfn. one whose arms hang down, MBh.; Hariv.; BhP.; Buddh. (*-tā*, f. one of the 32 signs of perfection, Dharmas. 83); m. N. of a man, Kathās.; *-bhid*, m. 'crusher of Pralamba,' N. of Bala-rāma, L.; *-bhuja*, mfn. one whose arms hang down, L.; m. N. of a Vidyā-dhara, Kathās.; *-mathana* (Hariv.), *-han* (MBh.), *-hantṛi* (L.), m. 'slayer of Pralamba,' N. of Bala-rāma and of Kṛishṇa; °*bâṇḍa*, m. a man with pendent testicles, Vet.; °*bôjjvala-cāru-ghoṇa*, mfn. having a prominent and bright and handsome nose, MBh.; °*bôdara*, m. 'having a pendent belly,' N. of a prince of the Kiṃ-naras, Kāraṇḍ.; of a fabulous mountain, ib. °**lambaka**, m. fragrant Rohisha grass, L. °**lambana**, n. hanging down, depending, L. °**lambita**, mfn. hanging down, pendulous, Kathās.; (*alam-kāra-p°* for *pralambitâlaṃ-k°*, having pendent ornaments, Lalit.) °**lambin**, mfn. hanging down, depending, Suśr.; Hariv. (cf. *tri-pr°*).

Pralambī-√kṛi, to make to hang down, R.

प्रलम्भ *pra-lambha*, °*lambhana.* See *pra-√labh.*

प्रलय *pra-laya* &c. See under *pra-√lī.*

प्रललाट *pra-lalāṭa*, mfn. having a prominent forehead, MBh.

प्रलव *pra-lavá* &c. See under *pra-√lū.*

प्रलाप *pra-lāpa* &c. See under *pra-√lap.*

प्रलिख् *pra-√likh*, P. Ā. *-likhati*, °*te*, (P.) to scratch, draw lines in (acc.), Mn. iv, 55; to draw lines, write, Hcat.; (P. Ā.) to scrape together, PārGṛ.; (Ā.) to comb one's head (Sch. 'to draw lines'), Kauś.; PārGṛ.

प्रलिप् *pra-√lip*, P. Ā. *-limpati*, °*te*, to smear, besmear, stain (Ā. to smear &c. one's self), ŚBr.; GṛŚrS.; Kauś. &c.: Caus. *-lepayati*, to smear, besmear, MBh.; Var. °**lipa**, mfn. one who smears or plasters, W. °**lipta**, mfn. cleaving or sticking to (loc.), MBh. °**lepa**, m. cleaving to (comp.), Bhpr.; an unguent, ointment, salve, plaster, Suśr.; MārkP.; Var.; a hectic or slow fever, Car. °**lepaka**, mfn. anointing, smearing, plastering, W.; m. a plasterer, an anointer, W.; a partic. marine substance, lime made of calcined shells (?), L.; a hectic or slow fever, Suśr.; Bhpr.; (*ikā*), f., g. *mahishy-ādi.* °**lepana**, n. the act of anointing or smearing, MW.; an unguent, salve, plaster, Car. °**lepya**, m. clean or well-trimmed hair (perhaps correctly for a form *pralebhya*), L.

प्रलिश *prá-liśa*, m. N. of a mystic being, Suparṇ.

प्रलिह् *pra-√lih*, P. Ā. *-leḍhi, -līḍhe*, to lick up, cause to melt on the tongue, Suśr. °**leha**, m. a kind of broth, L. °**lehana**, n. the act of licking, Gobh.

प्रली *pra-√lī*, Ā. *-līyate* (ind. p. *-līya* or *-lāya*), to become dissolved or reabsorbed into (loc.), disappear, perish, die, Br.; Mn.; MBh. &c.

Pra-laya, m. dissolution, reabsorption, destruction, annihilation; death; (esp.) the destruction of the whole world at the end of a Kalpa (s. v.), ShaḍvBr.; ChUp.; Śaṃk.; MBh.; Kāv. &c.; setting (of the stars), Subh.; end (*saṃjāta-nidrā-p°*, mfn. having done sleeping, Pañcat.); cause of dissolution, Bhag.; Bṛih.; fainting, loss of sense or consciousness, Pratāp.; Sāh.; Suśr.; sleepiness, Gal.; N. of the syllable *Om*, AtharvaśUp.; *-kāla*, m. the time of universal dissolution, MW.; *-kevala*, mfn. = °*layâkala* (q. v.), Sarvad.; *-ghana*, m. the cloud which causes the destruction of the world, Hit.; *-ṃ-kara*, mf(*ī*)n. causing destruction or ruin, Up.; Kāv.; *-jaladhara-dhvāna*, m. the rumbling or muttering of clouds at the dissolution of the world, MW.; *-tā*, f. dissolution (*-tāṃ √gam*, to perish, be annihilated), Hariv.; *-tva*, n. id. (*-tvāya √klṛip = -tāṃ √gam*), MBh.; BhP.; *-dahana*, m.

the fire causing the destruction of the world, Ratnâv.; Amar.; *-sthiti-sarga,* m. pl. destruction, preservation and creation (of the world), Kum.; °*layâkala,* mfn. (an individual soul) to which *mala* and *karman* still adhere (with Śaivas), Sarvad.; °*layânta-ga,* mfn. perishing only at the destruction of the world (the sun), MārkP.; °*layôdaya,* m. du. dissolution and creation, Bhag.; Suśr.; Kathās. °**láyana,** n. a place of repose, a bed, AV. °**láyam,** ind. (with √*i* or *car*) to hide one's self, be hidden, Br.; Kāṭh.

Pralīna, mfn. dissolved, reabsorbed into (loc.), disappeared, lost, died, MBh.; R.; Suśr. &c.; slacked, tired, wearied, AitBr.; unconscious, insensible, W.; flown away, MBh. (v. l. *pra-ḍīna*). **—tā,** f. or **-tva,** n. dissolution, destruction, annihilation, the end of the universe, L.; unconsciousness, fainting, L. **—bhū-pāla,** mfn. whose monarchs have been destroyed, MW. **Pralînêndriya,** mfn. one whose senses have slacked or languished (°*ya-tva,* n., Sāy.)

प्रलुठ् *pra-√luṭh,* P. *-luṭhati,* to roll forwards, roll, r° along the ground, r° round, Pañcat.; to be agitated, heave, toss, wallow, MW. °**luṭhita,** mfn. rolling about, Bhaṭṭ. °**loṭhana,** n. the act of rolling; heaving, tossing (as of the ocean), W. °**loṭhita,** mfn. (anything) that has begun to roll, Bhaṭṭ.; rolling; heaving, tossing, W.

प्रलुप् *pra-√lup,* P. *-lumpati,* to pluck or pull out, Hariv.: Pass. *-lupyate,* to be robbed, MBh.; to be interrupted or disturbed or violated or destroyed, MW. °**lupta,** mfn. robbed, Uttarar.; Rājat.; having lost (with abl.), MārkP. °**lopa,** m. destruction, annihilation, Lalit.

प्रलुभ् *pra-√lubh,* P. Ā. *-lubhyati,* °*te,* (Ā.) to lust after, be lustful, follow one's lusts, go astray sexually (said of a wife), ŚāṅkhGṛ.; Mn.; to allure, entice, seduce, pollute, MBh.: Caus. *-lobhayati,* to cause to lust after, allure, entice, attempt to seduce, MBh.; R.; Pur. &c.; to divert the attention of any one by (instr.), Suśr. °**lubdha,** mfn. seduced, MBh.; (*ā*), f. (a woman) who has conceived an illicit affection for (*saha*), Pañcat.

Pra-lobha, m. allurement, seduction, Pañcat.; BhP.; desire, cupidity, W. °**lobhaka,** m. 'allurer,' N. of a jackal, Pañcat. °**lobhana,** mfn. causing to lust after, alluring, seducing, BhP.; (*ī*), f. gravel, sand, L.; n. allurement, inducement, MBh.; R.; Kathās.; Rājat.; that which allures, a lure, bait, MW.; (also w. r. for *pralambhana,* Bhag.) °**lobhita,** mfn. allured, enticed, BhP. °**lobhin,** mfn. alluring, seducing, MārkP.; lusting after, MW. °**lobhya,** mfn. to be lusted after, alluring, Subh.

प्रलू *pra-√lū,* P. Ā. *-lunāti, -lunīte,* to cut off, HPariś.

Pra-lavá, m. a part cut off, chip, fragment (as of a reed &c.; others 'the sheath of a leaf;' others 'a dead leaf'), ŚBr.; KātyŚr. °**lavana,** n. the reaping of corn, GṛS. °**lavitṛi,** mf(*trī*)n. one who cuts off, Pāṇ. vi, 1, 174, Sch. °**lavitra,** n. an instrument for cutting off, Pāṇ. vi, 2, 144, Sch. °**lūna,** mfn. cut off, MW.; m. a kind of insect, Suśr.

प्रलेप *pra-lepa* &c. See under *pra-√lip.*

प्रलेह *pra-leha,* °*lehana.* See *pra-√lih.*

प्रलोल *pra-lola,* mfn. being in violent motion, agitated, R.

प्रलोलुप *pra-lolupa,* m. N. of a Kunti (a descendant of Garuḍa), MārkP.

प्रल्कारीय *pralkārīya,* Nom. (fr. *pra* + *lṛi-kāra*) P. °*yati,* Pāṇ. vi, 1, 92, Sch. (also *prālkārīya*).

प्रव *pravá,* mfn. (fr. √*pru*) fluttering, hovering, RV. **-ga,** m. = *plava-ga,* a monkey, L. **—ṃ-ga,** m. = *plavaṃ-ga,* id., L. **—ṃ-gama,** m. = *plavaṃ-g°,* id., L.

Pravaka, mfn. one who goes, W.

प्रवङ्ग *pra-vaṅga,* m. pl. N. of a people, MārkP.

प्रवच् *pra-√vac,* P. *-vakti* (inf. *-vâce,* RV. ix, 95, 2), to proclaim, announce, praise, commend, mention, teach, impart, explain (with acc. of thing and dat. or gen. of person), RV. &c. &c.; to tell of, betray, TS.; to give, deliver (with acc. and dat.), RV.; Br.; to speak, say, tell (with acc., rarely dat. of person, and acc. of thing), PraśnUp.; MBh.; Hariv. &c.; to declare to be, call (2 acc.), Śrutab.: Caus. *-vācayati,* to cause to announce, Gobh.: Desid. *-vivakshati,* MBh. xii, 3767 (w. r. *-vivakshataḥ* for *-vivikshataḥ*). °**vaktavya,** mfn. to be announced or imparted or taught or explained, Mn.; MBh. °**vaktṛi,** mfn. one who tells or imparts or relates, Yājñ.; a good speaker, MBh.; an announcer, expounder, teacher (*-tva,* n.), ĀśvŚr.; Mn.; R. &c.; the first relater of a legend (ifc. *-ka*), L.

Pra-vacana, m. one who exposes, propounds, BhP.; n. speaking, talking, Pañcat.; recitation, oral instruction, teaching, expounding, exposition, interpretation (cf. *Sāṃkhya-pravacana-bhāshya*), ŚBr.; Up.; PārGṛ.; RPrāt. &c.; announcement, proclamation, Lāṭy.; excellent speech or language, eloquence, W.; an expression, term, Nir.; a system of doctrines propounded in a treatise or dissertation; sacred writings (esp. the Brāhmaṇas or the Vedâṅgas), Mn.; MBh.; Hariv. &c. (cf. IW. 145); the s° w° of Buddhists (ninefold), Dharmas. 62; the s° w° of the Jainas, Hemac., Sch.; (*am,* enclitic after a finite verb, g. *gotrâdi*); *-paṭu,* mfn. skilled in speaking, eloquent, Bhartṛ.; *-sāra-gāthā,* f. and *-sārôddhāra,* m. N. of wks. °**vacanīya,** mfn. to be taught or propounded, ŚāṅkhGṛ.; to be well or elegantly spoken, W.; m. a propounder, teacher, Pāṇ.; L.; a good speaker, W.

Pra-vāka, m. a proclaimer (see *soma-p°*). °**vāc,** mfn. eloquent, L.; talkative, Mudr.; boastful, bragging, Bālar. °**vācaka,** mfn. declaratory, explanatory, MW.; speaking well, eloquent, W. °**vácana,** n. a proclamation, promulgation, RV. x, 35, 8; fame, renown, RV. iv, 36, 1; a designation, name (see *dvi-p°*). °**vácya,** mfn. to be proclaimed aloud, praiseworthy, glorious, RV.; to be spoken to, Hariv.; n. a literary production, Pāṇ. vii, 3, 66, Sch.

Prôkta, mfn. announced, told, taught, mentioned, Mn.; BhP.; Var.; Pāṇ.; said, spoken, spoken to, addressed, MBh.; Prab.; Var.; Hit.; called, declared, said, Mn.; Bhag.; Hariv.; Pañcat. &c.; meaning, signifying (with loc.), L.; (*e*), ind. it having been announced, KātyŚr. **—kārin,** mfn. doing what one has been told, BhP. **—vat,** mfn. one who has said or declared, W.

प्रवट *pra-vaṭa,* m. (√*vaṭ?*) wheat, L.

प्रवण *pra-vaṇá* (prob. fr. 1. *pra* and suffix *vana,* cf. *vag-vaná, sat-vaná, śushuk-vaná;* but according to Pāṇ. viii, 4, 5 fr. *pra* and *vana,* 'wood'; according to others from √*pru*), m. or n. (?) the side of a hill, slope, declivity, abyss, depth, RV.; Kāṭh.; MBh. (in RV. only loc. sg. and once pl.; in MBh. viii, 2369 also abl. sg.); m. a place where four roads meet, L.; a moment, L.; a whirlpool, L.; n. an access to (loc.), MBh.; (*e*), ind. in a precipitous course, hurriedly, hastily, MBh.; mf(*ā*)n. declining, bent, sloping down, steep, abrupt, TS.; Br.; GṛŚrS.; Mn. &c.; (ifc.) directed towards (cf. *udak-, dakshiṇā-, nimna-* &c.); inclined or disposed or devoted to, intent upon, full of (loc., dat., gen., inf. or comp.), MBh.; Kāv. &c.; wasted, decayed, disappeared, R.; generous, L.; humble, modest, L. [Cf. Gk. πρηνής; Lat. *prōnus.*] **—tā,** f. inclination, propensity, proneness to (comp.), Prab.; Kuval. **—praharsha,** mfn. one whose joy or happiness has disappeared, R. (v. l. in B. *pravinashṭa-harsha*). **—vat,** mfn. having a steep descent or declivity, Nir. **—vidheyī-√bhū,** to obey gladly, Inscr. **Pravaṇe-ja,** mfn. = *pravāte-já,* Nir. viii, 9.

Pravaṇaya, Nom. P. °*yati,* to become inclined or attached to, Dharmaś.; to make ready, prepare, accomplish, effect, produce, ib.

Pravaṇāyita, n. (fr. Nom. °*ṇāya*) inclination, propensity, bias, Sāh.

Pravaṇī-√kṛi, to dispose favourably, Kum. **-√bhū,** to become favourably disposed, GopBr.

Pravát, f. the side or slope of a mountain, elevation, height, RV.; AV.; heavenly height (7 or 3 in number), ib.; (*pravato napāt,* 'son of the heavenly height' i.e. Agni, AV.); a sloping path, smooth or swift course (instr. sg. or pl. 'downhill, precipitately, swiftly'), RV.; TUp.; (*prá-vat*), mfn. directed forwards or towards, blazing forth (said of Agni), TS.; AitBr.; containing the syllable *pra* or *pṛi,* Br. **—vat** (°*vát-v°*), mfn. abounding in heights, hilly, RV.; sloping downwards, affording a swift motion, ib.

Pravad, in comp. for °*vat.* **—bhārgava,** n. N. of a Sāman, ĀrshBr. **—yāman** (°*vád-*), mfn. having a downward path, rapid in its course (as a chariot), RV.

प्रवणि *pra-vaṇi.* See *nish-pravaṇi.*

प्रवत्स्यत् *pra-vatsyat.* See *pra-√5. vas.*

प्रवद् *pra-√vad,* P. Ā. *-vadati,* °*te* (Ved. inf. *prá-vaditos*), to speak out, pronounce, proclaim, declare, utter, say, tell, RV. &c. &c.; to speak to (acc.), Bhaṭṭ.; to raise the voice (said of birds and animals), R.; Var.; to roar, splash (said of water), ĀśvGṛ.; (cf. *a-pravadat*) to assert, affirm, state, ŚvetUp.; Var.; to pronounce to be, call, name (2 acc.), Mn.; MBh. &c.; to offer for sale (with instr. of price), Pañcat. (v. l.): Caus. *-vādayati,* to cause to sound, play (with acc. of the instrument), ŚāṅkhŚr.; MBh. &c.; (without an object) to play, make music, Hariv. (also *-vādyati,* with act. meaning, MBh. xii, 1899). °**vadá,** mfn. sounding forth, sounding (as a drum), Kauś.; m. a herald, bard (?), AV. v, 20, 9. °**vadana,** n. a proclamation, announcement, ŚāṅkhŚr. °**vaditṛi,** mfn. one who speaks out, uttering (gen. or acc.), TS.; MBh. °**vadishu,** see *vāk-pravadishu.*

Pra-vāda, m. speaking forth, uttering, ĀśvŚr.; MBh.; expressing, mentioning, Nir.; talk, report, rumour, popular saying or belief, MBh.; Kāv. &c. (°*dāya,* in order to spread the rumour, Kathās.; °*dena,* according to r°, as the saying goes, MBh.); ill rumour about (gen.), slander, calumny (pl.), Kāv.; mutual defiance, words of challenge (prior to combat), Bhaṭṭ.; (ifc.) passing one's self off as, R.; (in gram.) any form or case of (gen. or comp.; opp. to a specified f° or c°), Prāt.; (*ā*), f. anything belonging to (comp.), Vait. °**vādaka,** mfn. causing to sound, playing (a musical instrument), Hariv. °**vādin,** mfn. giving forth a sound, uttering a cry, MBh.; (ifc.) stating, declaring, reporting, speaking of, Lāṭy.; MBh.; (fr. °*vāda*), being in some grammatical form or case, RPrāt. °**vādya,** mfn., Pāṇ. ii, 4, 56, Sch.

Prôdita, mfn. spoken out, uttered, Hariv.

प्रवध् *pra-√vadh* (only Pass. pr. 3. pl. *-vadhyante* and ind. p. *-vadhya*), to kill or slay, Pañcat.

प्रवन् *pra-√van,* Ā. *-vanute* (Ved. inf. *prá-vantave*), to vanquish, conquer, gain, procure, RV.

प्रवप् *pra-√1. vap,* P. Ā. *-vapati,* °*te,* to shave off (the beard &c.), RV.: TS.; GṛS. 1. °**vapana,** n. shaving off, GṛS.

प्रवप् *pra-√2. vap,* P. *-vapati,* to scatter, strew, throw, RV. &c. &c.: Caus. *-vāpayati,* to scatter, strew, TS.; Kāṭh. 2. °**vapaṇa,** n. scattering, sowing, GṛS. °**vāpayitṛi,** mfn. (fr. Caus.) one who scatters forth or pours out, Kāṭh. °**vāpin,** mfn. scattering, sowing in (comp.), Mn. ix, 51.

प्रवप *pra-vapa,* mfn. (*pra* + *vapā*) having a thick membrane or omentum, Pāṇ. viii, 4, 16, Sch.

प्रवभ्र *pravabhrá,* m. N. of Indra, MaitrS. (cf. *prababhra*).

प्रवयण 1. 2. *pra-vayaṇa.* See *pra-√vi* and *pra-√ve.*

प्रवयस् *prá-vayas,* mfn. strong, vigorous, in the prime of life, RV.; TS.; Kāṭh.; advanced in age, aged, old, ancient, ĀśvGṛ.; Ragh.; Car.

प्रवय्या *pra-vayyā.* See under *pra-√vī.*

प्रवर 1. *pra-vara,* mf(*ā*)n. (fr. *pra* + *vara* or fr. *pra* √2. *vṛi;* for 2. and 3. see p. 693) most excellent, chief, principal, best, Mn.; MBh. &c.; eldest (son), MBh.; better than (abl.), BhP.; greater (opp. to *sama,* 'equal,' and *nyūna,* 'smaller'), Var.; (ifc.) eminent, distinguished by, Hariv.; m. a black variety of Phaseolus Mungo, L.; Opuntia Dillenii, L.; N. of a messenger of the gods and friend of Indra, Hariv.; of a Dānava, ib.; (*ā*), f. N. of a river (which falls into the Godāvarī and is celebrated for the sweetness of its water), MBh.; VP.; n. aloe wood, Bhpr.; a partic. high number, Buddh. **—kalyāṇa,** mfn. eminently beautiful, Hariv. **—jana,** m. a person of quality, Mṛicch. **—dhātu,** m. precious metal, Var. **—nṛipati,** m. N. of a prince (= *-sena*), Var. **—pura,** n. N. of a town in Kaśmīra, ib. **—bhūpati,** m. = *-sena,* Rājat. **—mūrdhaja,** mfn. having beautiful hair, R. **—rūpa,** mf(*ā*)n. having a b° form, MBh. **—lalita,** n. N. of a metre, Chandom. **—vaṃśa-ja,** mfn. descended from a noble family, Hariv. **—vāhana,** m. du. 'having the best horses,' N. of the Aśvins, L. **—sena**, m. N. of 2 princes of Kaśmīra (cf. *-nṛipati* and *-bhūpati*), Rājat. (cf. IW. 494, 2). **Pravarêśa**, m. a noble lord (?), Rājat.; N. of a prince (=°*ra-sena*), ib. **Pravarêśvara**, m. N. of a temple built by Pravara-sena, ib.

प्रवर्ग *pra-varga. pra-vargya, pra-varjana.* See under *pra-√vṛij.*

प्रवर्ण् *pra-√varṇ*, P. *-varṇayati*, to communicate, MBh.

प्रवर्त *pra-varta* &c. See under *pra-√vṛit.*

प्रवर्धक *pra-vardhaka* &c. See *pra-√vṛidh.*

प्रवर्ष *pra-varsha* &c. See under *pra-√vṛish.*

प्रवर्हम् *pra-várham.* See under *pra-√vṛih.*

प्रवलाकिन् *pravalākin*, m. a peacock, L.; a snake, L. (prob. w.r. for *pra-calākin*).

प्रवल्ग् *pra-√valg*, P. Ā. *-valgati*, °*te*, to move the limbs quickly, bound, leap, MBh.; Hariv. °**valgita**, mfn. bounding, leaping, fluttering, Hariv.

प्रवल्ह् *pra-√valh*, Ā. *-valhate*, to test with a question or a riddle, puzzle (with acc.), AitBr. °**valha**, m. a riddle, enigma, ŚrS. °**valhikā**, f. id. (N. of AV. xx, 133), Br.; ŚrS. °**valhita**, mfn. enigmatical, Nir.

प्रवस् *pra-√4. vas*, Ā. *-vaste*, to put on (clothes), to dress, R.

प्रवस् *pra-√5. vas*, P. *-vasati* (rarely Ā., e.g. pf. *-vāsām cakre*, ChUp.; fut. *-vatsyati*, ĀśvŚr.; ind. p. *prôshya*, ŚBr.), to go or sojourn abroad, leave home, depart, RV. &c. &c.; to disappear, vanish, cease, Hariv.; to stop at a place, abide, dwell, MBh.; R.; (=Caus.) to banish to (loc.), R.: Caus. *-vāsayati*, to make to dwell in, Divyāv.; to order to live abroad, turn out, expel, banish, Mn.; MBh. &c.: Desid. *-vivatsati*, to intend to set out on a journey, Śiś.; to be about to depart from (abl.), Car. °**vatsyat**, mfn. about to dwell abroad; *-patikā*, f. the wife of a man who intends to make a journey, L. °**vasathá**, n. departure, separation from (abl.), RV.; TBr.; ĀpŚr. °**vasana**, n. setting out on a journey, departing, Amar.; dying, decease, Hcar. °**vastavyà**, n. (impers.) it is to be set out on a journey, TS.

Pra-vāsa, m. dwelling abroad, foreign residence, absence from home, RV. &c. &c. (acc. with *√gam* or *yā*, *pra-√vas* or *ā-√pad*, to go abroad; abl. with *ā-√i*, *upâ-* or *parā-√vṛit*, to return from abroad); (in astron.) heliacal setting of the planets, Var.; *-kṛitya*, n. N. of wk.; *-gata*, mfn. gone abroad, being away from home, MW.; *-gamana-vidhi*, m. N. of wk.; *-para*, mfn. addicted to living abroad, MW.; *-pariśishṭa*, n., *-vidhi*, m. N. of wks.; *-stha* (Ragh.), *-sthita* (Kathās.), mfn. being absent from home; °*sôpasthāna*, n.; °*sôpasthāna-prayoga*, m., °*sôpasthāna-vidhi*, m.; °*sôpasthāna-haviryajña-prâyaścitta*, n. N. of wks. °**vāsana**, n. (fr. Caus.) sending away from home, exile, banishment from (abl.), Mn.; MBh. &c.; killing, slaying, L. °**vāsanīya**, n. (scil. *karman*) the punishment of exile, L. °**vāsita**, mfn. sent abroad, exiled, banished, MBh. °**vāsin**, mfn. dwelling abroad, absent from home, Kāṭh.; MBh. &c. °**vāsya**, mfn. (fr. Caus.) to be sent abroad, to be banished, Mn. viii, 284.

Prôshita, mfn. one who has set out on a journey, absent from home, abroad, KātyŚr.; Mn.; MBh. &c.; effaced, Ragh.; set (as the sun), Var.; deceased, dead, Hcar.; *-trāsa*, m. fear of one who is absent, MW.; *-bhartṛikā*, f. (a wife) whose husband is abroad; *-maraṇa*, n. dying abroad or in a foreign country, W.; *-vat*, mfn. sojourning away from home, strange, a stranger, ib. **Prôshúsha**, mfn. one who has been absent or abroad, ŚBr.

1. **Prôshya**, ind. having set out on a journey, abroad, absent, ŚBr.; *-pāpīyas*, mfn. one who has become worse by living abroad, Bhaṭṭ.

2. **Prôshyà**, mfn. roaming, wandering, TBr.

प्रवसु *pra-vasu*, m. N. of a son of Ilina, MBh.

प्रवह् *pra-√vah*, P. *-vahati* (Pāṇ. i, 3, 81), to carry forwards, draw or drag onwards, RV.; AitBr.; ŚrS.; R.; to carry off in flowing, wash away, RV.; ĀśvGṛ.; R.; to lead or bring to (acc.), MBh.; Bhaṭṭ.; to bear, Bhaṭṭ.; to exhibit, show, utter, BhP.; (Ā.) to drive onwards, RV.; to flow along, Kathās.; Rājat.; to rush, blow (as wind), MBh.: Caus. *-vāhayati*, to cause to go away, send off, dismiss, ĀśvŚr.; to cause to swim away (Pass., to be washed away), MārkP.; HPariś.; to set in motion or on foot, Hariv.; R. °**vaha**, mf(*ā*)n. bearing along, carrying (ifc.), MBh.; R.; m. N. of one of the 7 winds said to cause the motion of the planets, MBh.; Hariv. &c. (cf. IW. 179); wind, air, L.; N. of one of the 7 tongues of fire, Col.; a reservoir into which water is carried, Yājñ.; flowing or streaming forth, L. (cf. *-vāha*); going forth, g° from a town, W. °**vahaṇa**, n. sending away i.e. giving (a girl) in marriage, SāmavBr.; creation, Hariv. (v.l.); a carriage (for women), Mṛicch.; a kind of litter, L.; (also n. and *ī*, f.; ifc. f. *ā*) a ship, R.; Kathās.; °*ṇa-bhaṅga*, m. shipwreck, Ratnâv.

Pra-vāhá, m. (ifc. f. *ā*) a stream, river, current, running water (°*he-mūtrita*, n. 'making water in a river,' doing a useless action, Pāṇ. ii, 1, 47, Sch.); met. = continuous flow or passage, unbroken series or succession, continuity, ŚBr. &c. &c.; continuous use or employment, Śaṃk.; c° train of thought, Sarvad.; N. of ch. in Sad-ukti-karṇâmṛita; flowing or streaming forth, L. (cf. *-vaha*); course of action, activity, L.; course or direction towards, W.; a pond, lake, ib.; a beautiful horse, L.; N. of one of the attendants of Skanda, MBh.; (pl.) N. of a people, VP.; (*ī*), f. sand, L. (also °*hôtthā*, f., Gal.) °**vāhaka**, mfn. carrying forwards, bearing or carrying well, W.; m. a Rākshasa, imp, goblin (also *ika*), L.; (*ikā*), f. a sudden desire to evacuate, diarrhœa, Suśr. (*ikā*, ind., g. *svar-ādi*). °**vāhaṇa**, mfn. carrying off or away, VS.; m. N. of a man, ŚBr.; ChUp.; (*ī*), f. the sphincter muscle (which contracts the orifice of the rectum), Suśr.; n. driving forth, protrusion, ib.; evacuation (esp. if from sudden desire), ib.; Car. °**vāhaṇeya** or °**vāhaṇeyi**, m. (*ī*, f., Pat.) patr. fr. °*vāhaṇa*, Pāṇ. vii, 3, 28; 29, Sch. (cf. g. *śubhrâdi*). °**vāhaṇeyaka**, mfn. (fr. °*vāhaṇeya*), Pāṇ. vii, 3, 29, Sch. °**vāhayitṛi**, m. (fr. Caus.) one who bears or carries away (*-tva*, n.), VS., Sch. °**vāhita**, m. (fr. Caus.) N. of a Ṛishi in the third Manv-antara, VP.; n. the 'bearing down' (of a woman in labour), Car. °**vāhin**, mfn. drawing, carrying, bearing along or away, AV. &c. &c.; (ifc.) streaming, MBh.; R.; (fr. °*vāha*) abounding in streams, g. *pushkarâdi*; m. a draught animal, ŚāṅkhŚr. °**vāhyà**, mfn. (fr. °*vāha*) fluviatic, VS.

Pra-voḍhṛi or °**voḷhṛi**, m. one who carries off (with gen. or ifc.), RV.; MBh. **Prâuḍha**, see s.v.

प्रवह्लि *pra-vahli*, °*likā* or °*lī*, f. a riddle, enigma, L. (cf. *pravalha*, °*hikā*).

प्रवा *pra-√vā*, P. *-vāti*, to blow forth, blow, RV. &c. &c.; to smell, yield a scent, MBh.; R. &c.

Pra-vā́, f. blowing forth, blowing, AV.; VS.; TS.; N. of a daughter of Daksha, VāyuP. °**vātá**, mfn. blown forward, agitated by the wind (see below); n. a current or draught of air, windy weather or a windy place, TS. &c. &c.; *-dīpa-capala*, mfn. flickering or unsteady like a lamp agitated by the wind, Kathās.; *-nīlôtpala*, n. a lotus flower ag° by the wind, Kum.; *-śayana*, n. a bed placed in the middle of a current of air, Mālav.; *-sāra*, m. N. of a Buddha, Lalit. (v.l. *pravāṭa-sāgara* i.e. *pravāḍa-s°*); *-subhaga*, mfn. (a spot) delightful by (reason of) a fresh breeze, Śak.; °*te-jā*, mfn. growing in an airy place, RV. °**vāyyà**, n. (prob.) flight, fleetness, AV.

प्रवाक *pra-vāka, pra-vāc* &c. See under *pra-√vac.*

प्रवाड *pra-vāḍa*, m. or n. (?) = *pra-vāla*, coral, SaddhP. **—sāgara**, m. N. of a Buddha, Lalit. (v.l. for *pravāta-sāra*).

प्रवाण *pra-vāṇa*, °*ṇi*. See under *pra-√ve.*

प्रवाद *pra-vāda* &c. See under *pra-√vad.*

प्रवापयितृ *pra-vāpayitṛi*, °*pin*. See under *pra-√2. vap.*

प्रवायक *pra-vāyaka.* See under *pra-√vī.*

प्रवाय्य *pra-vāyya.* See under *pra-√vā.*

प्रवार *pra-vāra*, °*raṇa* &c. See under *pra-√1. 2. vṛi.*

प्रवाल *pra-vāla*, m. n. (prob. fr. *√val*, but also written *pra-bāla*; ifc. f. *ā*) a young shoot, sprout, new leaf or branch (to which feet and lips are often compared), MBh.; Kāv. &c.; coral, Mn.; MBh. &c. (in this sense also written *pra-vāḍa*); the neck of the Indian lute, L.; m. an animal, L.; a pupil, L.; mfn. having shoots or sprouts, Dharmaś.; having long or beautiful hair (=*prakṛishṭa-keśa-yukta*), ib. **—padma**, n. a red lotus-flower, Suśr. **—phala**, n. red sandal-wood, Bhpr. **—bhasman**, n. calx of coral, MW. **—maṇi-śṛiṅga**, mfn. having horns of coral and gems, ib. **—vat**, mfn. having new leaves or shoots, W. (cf. *bahu-pushpa-pravāla-vat*). **—varṇa**, mfn. coral-coloured, red, Suśr. **Pravālâśmantaka**, m. or n. (prob.) coral, ib.

Pravālaka, n. coral, Hcat. (see also *prabālaka*).

प्रवाश् *pra-√vāś*, P. *-vāśati*, to begin to croak or make a croaking noise, Var.

प्रवास *pra-vāsa* &c. See col. 1.

प्रवाह् *pra-√vāh*, Ā. *-vāhate*, to bear down (said of a woman in labour), Suśr.: Caus. *-vāhayati*, id., ib. 2. °**vāhita**, n. (for 1. see *pra-√vah*) bearing down, Car.

प्रवाह *pra-vāha* &c. See *pra-√vah.*

प्रविक *pravika*, g. *purohitâdi* (Kāś.)

प्रविकट *pra-vikaṭa*, mfn. very large, huge, Harav.

प्रविकर्ष *pra-vikarsha*, m. drawing (the bow-string), Kir. °**vikarshaṇa**, n. drawing, dragging, Jātakam.

प्रविकस् *pra-vi-√kas*, P. *-kasati*, to open, expand (intr.), Śiś.; to appear, become manifest, Prasannar.

प्रविकॄ *pra-vi-√kṝī*, P. *-kirati* (ind. p. *-kīrya*), to scatter about, disperse, diffuse, MBh. °**vikīrṇa**, mfn. scattered, dispersed, diffused, R.; Suśr.; *-kāmā*, f. a woman who has various lovers, Var.

प्रविख्यात *pra-vi-khyāta*, mfn. (*√khyā*) universally known, renowned, MBh.; known as, named, called (nom.), MārkP. °**vikhyāti**, f. renown, celebrity, L.

प्रविगत *pra-vi-gata*, mfn. (*√gam*) passed away, disappeared, Var.

प्रविगल् *pra-vi-√gal*, P. *-galati*, to stream forth, Mālatim.; to cease, disappear, ib. °**vigalita**, mfn. oozing, Divyâv.

प्रविगाह् *pra-vi-√gāh*, Ā. *-gāhate*, to dive into, enter (acc.), R.

प्रविग्रह *pra-vi-graha*, m. (*√grah*) separation of words by dividing or breaking up the Saṃdhi, RPrāt.

प्रविघट् *pra-vi-√ghaṭ*, P. *-ghāṭayati*, to divide, disunite, Kir. °**vighaṭana**, n. hewing off or asunder, Mcar. °**vighaṭita**, mfn. hewn off, severed, Mcar.

प्रविचक्ष् *pra-vi-√caksh*, Ā. *-cashṭe*, to declare, mention, name, MBh.

प्रविचय *pra-vicaya.* See below.

प्रविचर् *pra-vi-√car*, P. *-carati*, to go forwards, advance, MBh.; Hit.; to roam about, Mṛicch.; to walk or wander through (acc.), MBh.: Caus. *-cārayati*, see below. °**vicāra**, m. distinction, division, species, kind, Suśr.; *-mārga*, m. pl. springing from side to side (an artifice in fighting), Kir. °**vicāraṇā**, f. id., Car. °**vicārita**, mfn. (fr. Caus.) examined or investigated accurately, Pañcat.

प्रविचल् *pra-vi-√cal*, P. *-calati*, to become agitated, tremble, quake, MBh.; to become confused or disturbed, Hariv.; to deviate or swerve from (abl.), MBh.; Bhartṛ.: Caus. *-cālayati*, to cause to tremble, shake, Hariv. °**calita**, mfn. moved, shaken, MBh.

प्रविचि *pra-vi-√2. ci*, P. *-cinoti*, to search through, investigate, examine, MBh.; R.

Pra-vicaya, m. investigation, examination, Lalit. °**vicita**, mfn. tried, proved, tasted, MBh.

प्रविचिन्त् *pra-vi-√cint*, P. *-cintayati*, to think about, reflect upon (acc.), MBh.; R. °**vicintaka**, mfn. reflecting beforehand, foreseeing, Hariv.

प्रविचेतन *pra-vicetana*, n. (√4. *cit*) comprehending, understanding, Hariv.

प्रविचेष्ट् *pra-vi-√cesht*, Ā. *-ceshṭate*, to rove about, Veṇīs.

प्रविज् *pra-√vij* (only Ā. 3. pl. pf. *-vivijre*), to rush forth, RV. x, 111, 9: Caus. *-vejayati*, to drive away, MBh. °**vikta** (*prá-*), mfn. trembling, quaking, RV. °**vejita**, mfn. (fr. Caus.) hurled, thrown, shot off, MBh.

प्रविजय *pra-vijaya*, m. pl. N. of a people, MārkP.

प्रविजह्य *pra-vi-jahya*, mfn. (fr. √*jah*; cf. *pra-vi-*√3. *hā*) to be given up or abandoned, L.

प्रविजृम्भ् *pra-vi-√jṛimbh*, Ā. *-jṛimbhate*, to open or expand (intr.), appear in full vigour or splendour, Bālar.

प्रविज्ञा *pra-vi-√jñā*, P. *-jānāti*, to know in detail or accurately, Suśr.

प्रवितत *pra-vi-tata*, mfn. (√*tan*) spread out, expanded, wide, Hariv.; Kāv. &c.; undertaken, begun, MBh.; arranged, Kathās.; dishevelled, W.

प्रवितप्त *pra-vi-tapta*, mfn. (√*tap*) scorched up, pained with heat, Kām.

प्रविद् *pra-√1. vid*, P. *-vetti*, to know, understand, RV.; AV.; MBh.: Caus. *-vedayati*, °*te*, to make known, communicate, relate, TUp.; MBh.; (P.) to know or understand right, MuṇḍUp. °**vid**, f. knowledge, science, RV. (cf. Pāṇ. iii, 2, 61). °**vidvás**, mfn. knowing, wise, RV.; AV.; TBr. °**vettṛi**, m. a knower, R. °**veda**, m. (see *á-pra-veda*); *-kṛit*, mfn. (prob.) making known, AV. °**vedana**, n. making known, proclaiming, Pāṇ. iii, 3, 153. °**vedin**, mfn. knowing well or accurately, Mn. ix, 267. °**vedya**, mfn. to be made known, MBh.

प्रविद् *pra-√3. vid*, P. Ā. *-vindati*, °*te*, to find, find out, invent, RV.; to anticipate, ŚBr.: Intens. *-vevidīti*, to attain, partake of (acc.), RV.

प्रविदलन *pra-vidalana*, n. pounding, crushing, Mcar.

प्रविदार *pra-vi-dāra*, m. (√*dṛī*) bursting asunder, Var. °**vidāraṇa**, n. (fr. Caus.) causing to burst asunder, L.; war, battle, L.; tumult, crowd, L.

प्रविदित्सु *pra-vi-ditsu*, mfn. (fr. Desid. of √1. *dā*) wishing to perform, Harav. (w. r. for *-dhitsu*?).

प्रविदुह् *pra-vi-√duh* (only P. 3. pl. pr. *-duhanti*), to milk or drain out completely (fig.), RV.

प्रविद्ध *pra-viddha*. See *pra-√vyadh*.

प्रविद्रुत *pra-vi-druta*, mfn. (√*dru*) running or flowing asunder, scattered, dispersed, MBh.

प्रविधा *pra-vi-√1. dhā*, P. Ā. *-dadhāti*, *-dhatte*, to place apart, divide, Suśr.; (Ā.) to meditate, think upon, R.; Rājat.; to place in front, put at the head, pay attention to, Śukas. °**vidhāna**, n. a means employed, Vishṇ.

प्रविध्वस्त *pra-vi-dhvasta*, mfn. (√*dhvaṇs*) thrown away, R.; tossed about, agitated, Hariv.

प्रविनश् *pra-vi-√2. naś* (only Ā. 2. sg. fut. *-naṅkshyase*), to perish utterly, be destroyed, R. °**nashṭa**, mfn. utterly destroyed, ib.

प्रविनिर्धूत *pra-vi-nir-dhūta*, mfn. (√*dhū*) thrown or flung away or towards or at, MBh.

प्रविपल *pra-vipala*, m. or n. (?) a partic. minute division of time, a small part of a Vipala, Siddhāntaś.

प्रविभज् *pra-vi-√bhaj*, P. *-bhajati*, to separate, divide, distribute, apportion, PraśnUp.; Mn.; MBh. &c. °**vibhakta**, mfn. separated, divided, distributed &c., Mn.; MBh. &c.; one who has received his share, Mn. viii, 166; (ifc.) divided into or consisting of, Kull.; divided or distinguished by (instr. or comp.), Bhag.; Śaṃk.; variously situated, scattered, R.; *-raśmi*, mfn. having the rays distributed, distributing rays, Śak.

Pravibhāga, m. separation, division, distribution, classification, Mn.; MBh. &c.; a part, portion, Uttarar. **-vat**, mfn. having subdivisions, subdivided, MBh. **-śas**, ind. separately, singly, MBh.; Hcat.

प्रविभावक *pra-vibhāvaka*, mfn. (√*bhū*) causing to appear, representing, Bhar.

प्रविभिन्न *pra-vi-bhinna*, mfn. (√*bhid*) broken or torn off, wounded, R.

प्रविभुज् *pra-vi-√1. bhuj*, P. *-bhujati*, to bend back, Suśr.

प्रविमुच् *pra-vi-√muc*, P. Ā. *-muñcati*, °*te*, to set free, liberate, R.; to give up, relinquish, abandon, MBh.; Kathās. &c.: Pass. *-mucyate*, to be freed from or rid of (abl.), Suśr.

प्रविमृश् *pra-vi-√mṛiś* (only ind. p. *-mṛiśya*, w. r. *-mṛishya*), to think upon, ponder, reflect, deliberate, MBh.; R.

प्रवियुत *pra-vi-yuta*, mfn. (√2. *yu*) completely filled, crammed, Nir. ix. 26.

प्रविर *pravira*, m. yellow sandal, L.

प्रविरत *pra-vi-rata*, mfn. (√*ram*) one who has desisted from (abl.), Rājat.

प्रविरल *pra-virala*, mf(*ā*)n. separated by a considerable interval, isolated, few, very rare or scanty, Var.; Ragh.; Kathās. &c.

प्रविरूढ *pra-vi-rūḍha*, mfn. (√*ruh*) sprouted, grown, Divyâv.

प्रविलभ् *pra-vi-√labh*, Ā. *-labhate*, to regain, recover, MBh. xiv, 1732 (prob. w. r. for *prati-l*°; B. *vi-pra-l*°).

प्रविलम्ब् *pra-vi-√lamb*, only pr. p. Ā. *-lambamāna*, hanging, suspended, Divyâv.: Caus. (ind. p. *-lambya*) to hang up, Pañcat. (v. l. *prati-l*°). °**vilambita**, mfn. hanging forwards, projecting (*ati-pra-vil*°), Suśr.; n. loitering, delaying, ŚārṅgP. °**vilambin**, mfn. projecting, prominent, Var.

प्रविलय *pra-vilaya*. See *pra-vi-√lī*.

प्रविलस् *pra-vi-√las*, P. *-lasati*, to shine forth brightly, BhP.; to appear in full strength or vigour, Gīt., Sch.

प्रविलसेन *pravila-sena* or *pravilla-sena*, m. N. of a prince, VP.

प्रविलापन *pra-vilāpana* &c. See *pra-vi-√lī*.

प्रविलापिन् *pra-vilāpin*, mfn. (√*lap*) grieving, lamenting, Kathās.

प्रविली *pra-vi-√lī*, Ā. or Pass. *-līyate* (°*ti*), to become dissolved, melt or vanish away, MuṇḍUp.; MBh. &c.: Caus. *-lāpayati*, to cause to disappear or dissolve itself into (loc.), Śaṃk.; BhP., Sch.; to dissolve, melt (trans.), Suśr. °**vilaya**, m. melting, Suśr.; = next, Śaṃk. °**vilayana**, n. complete dissolution or absorption, Car. °**vilāpana** or °**vilāpitatva**, n. (fr. Caus.) complete absorption or annihilation, Śaṃk. °**vilāpayitavya** or °**vilāpya**, mfn. to be completely annihilated, ib.

प्रविलुप् *pra-vi-√lup*, Caus. *-lopayati*, to give up, abandon, Kāv. °**vilupta**, mfn. cut away, removed, destroyed, vanished, gone, Kum.; Kathās.

प्रविलोक् *pra-vi-√lok*, P. *-lokayati*, to look forwards or about, R.; to perceive, notice, consider, Kathās.; (in astron.) to observe, Gol.

प्रविलोल *pra-vilola*, mfn. very unsteady, Caurap.

प्रविवर्धित *pra-vi-vardhita*, mfn. (√*vṛidh*) very much increased, Rājat.

प्रविवाद *pra-vivāda*, m. altercation, quarrel, dispute, Vet.

प्रविविक्षु *pra-vivikshu*. See under *pra-√viś*.

प्रविविच् *pra-vi-√vic* (only Pass. *-vicyate*), to test, examine, Cat. °**vivikta**, mfn. separate, solitary, lonely (loc. pl. 'in a solitude'), MBh.; R.; fine, delicate, ŚBr. &c. &c.; sharp, keen, MBh.; *-cakshus*, mfn. sharp-sighted, MBh.; *-tā*, f. keeping away from worldly objects or desires, Jātakam; *-bhuj*, mfn. eating delicate food, MāṇḍUp.; °*tâhāra*, mfn. id., ŚBr. °**viveka**, m. complete solitude, L.

प्रविवेपित *pra-vi-vepita*, mfn. (√*vep*, Caus.) caused to tremble, R.

प्रविव्रजिषु *pra-vivrajishu* and *pra-vivrājayishu*. See under *pra-√vraj*.

प्रविश् *pra-√viś*, P. Ā. *-viśati*, °*te*, to enter, go into, resort to (acc. or loc.), RV. &c. &c. (with *agnim*, *agnau*, *madhyam agneḥ*, *vahnau*, or *citāyām*, 'to ascend the funeral pyre;' with *karṇayoḥ*, 'to come into the ears i.e. be heard;' with *ātmani* or *cittam*, 'to take possession of the heart;' in dram. 'to enter the stage'); to reach, attain, Sarvad.; to have sexual intercourse with (acc., applied to both sexes), MBh.; Suśr.; to enter upon, undertake, commence, begin, devote one's self to (acc., rarely loc.), MBh.; Hariv.; R. &c. (with *piṇḍīm* or *tarpaṇam*, 'to accept or enjoy an oblation'); to enter into i.e. be absorbed or thrown into the shade by (acc.), Hariv. (with [*svāni*] *aṅgāni* or *gātrāṇi*, 'to shrink, shrivel,' R.; Kathās.): Caus. *-veśayati*, °*te*, to cause or allow to enter, bring or lead or introduce to, usher into (acc. or loc.), AV. &c. &c. (without an object, 'to bring into one's house &c.,' esp. 'to bring on the stage'); to lead home as a wife, i.e. marry, MBh.; to lay or store up, deposit in, put or throw into (loc. or acc.), Mn.; MBh. &c.; to enter i.e. commit to paper, write down, Yājñ., Sch.; to initiate into (acc.), Prab.; to instil into (loc.) = teach, impart, Kathās.; to spend (money), Pañcat.; to enter, come or be brought into (acc.), Var.; BhP.: Desid. *-vivikshati*, to wish to enter into (acc.), MBh.; R. °**vivikshu**, mfn. (fr. Desid.) wishing or being about to enter (acc.), MBh.; Kām.

Prá-vishṭa, mfn. entered, R.; Ragh.; one who has entered or gone or come into, being in or among (loc., acc. or comp.; cf. *madhya-prav*°), RV. &c. &c. (in dram. 'one who has entered the stage'); sunk (as an eye), Suśr.; appeared or begun (as an age), Vet.; one who has entered upon or undertaken, occupied with, intent upon, engaged in (loc. or comp.) BhP.; Rājat.; initiated into (acc.), Prab.; agreeing with (loc.), MBh.; made use of, invested (as money), Yājñ.; Rājat.; (*ā*), f. N. of the mother of Paippalādi and Kauśika, Hariv. (prob. w. r. for *śravishṭhā*). °**vishṭaka**, n. entering the stage (only °*kena*, ind. in stage directions), Mṛicch.; Śak.; Pracaṇḍ. &c. °**vishṭakāya**, Nom. Ā. °*yate*, to appear in person, Kād.

Pra-veśa, m. (ifc. f. *ā*) entering, entrance, penetration or intrusion into (loc., gen. with or without *antar*, or comp.), MBh.; Kāv. &c. (acc. with √*kṛi*, to make one's entrance, enter); entrance on the stage, Hariv.; Mālav.; the entrance of the sun into a sign of the zodiac, Var.; coming or setting in (of night), L.; the placing (e. g. of any deposit) in a person's house or hand, Pañcat.; interfering with another's business, obtrusiveness, Kathās.; the entering into i.e. being contained in (loc.), Pāṇ. ii, 1, 72, Sch.; Sāh.; employment, use, utilisation of (comp.), Kull.; Inscr.; income, revenue, tax, toll (cf. *-bhāgika*); intentness on an object, engaging closely in a pursuit or purpose, W.; manner, method, Lalit.; a place of entrance, door, MBh.; Kāv. &c.; the syringe of an injection pipe, Suśr.; *-bhāgika*, m. (prob.) a receiver or gatherer of taxes, Rājat. °**veśaka**, ifc. = *veśa*, entering, entrance, Kathās.; m. a kind of interlude (acted by some of the subordinate characters for the making known of what is supposed to have occurred between the acts or the introducing of what is about to follow), Kālid.; Ratnâv.; Daśar.; Sāh. &c. (cf. *vishkambhaka* and IW. 473); N. of wk. °**veśana**, n. entering, entrance or penetration into (loc., gen. or comp.), KātyŚr.; Yājñ.; MBh. &c.; sexual intercourse, PārGṛ.; a principal door or gate, L.; conducting or leading into (loc.), introduction, KātyŚr.; MBh. &c.; driving home (cattle), Gobh. °**veśanīya**, mfn. (fr. prec.), g. *anupravacanâdi*. °**veśayitavya**, mfn. (fr. Caus.) to be introduced, Śak. (v. l.) °**veśita**, mfn. (fr. Caus.) caused to enter, brought or sent in, introduced, MBh.; Kāv. &c.; thrown into (any condition, as sleep &c.), Ragh.; appointed, installed, BhP.; (*ā*), f. impregnated, pregnant (*dārakam*, 'with a boy'), Divyâv.; n. causing to appear on the stage, BhP. °**veśin**, mfn. (ifc.) entering into, MBh.; having sexual intercourse with, Car.; (fr. °*veśa*), having an entrance accessible over or through (comp.), Hariv. °**veśya**, mfn. to be entered, accessible, open, MBh.; Hariv.; Śak.; to be played (as a musical instrument), Ragh.; to be let or conducted into, be introduced, MBh.; R.; to be put back or re-introduced (said of the intestines), Suśr. °**veshṭavya,** mfn. to be entered or penetrated or pervaded, accessible, open, Kāv.; Kathās.; to be caused or allowed to enter, to be admitted, Hariv.; n. (impers.) one should enter or penetrate into (loc.), Mn.; MBh. &c. °**veshṭṛi,** mfn. one who enters or goes into, Vedāntas. (*-tva,* n.)

प्रविशम् *pra-vi-√śam,* Caus. *-śāmayati,* to extinguish, destroy, annihilate (?) Divyâv.

प्रविशिष् *pra-vi-√śish,* P. *-śinashṭi,* to magnify, increase, augment, Uttarar.

प्रविशीर्ण *pra-vi-śīrṇa,* mfn. (√*śṛī*) fallen off (as flesh), Suśr.

प्रविशुध् *pra-vi-√śudh,* Caus. *-śodhayati,* to clean perfectly, MBh.; Suśr. °**viśuddha,** mfn. perfectly clean, R.

प्रविश्लेष *pra-viślesha,* m. separation, parting, L.

प्रविषण्ण *pra-vi-shaṇṇa,* mfn. (√*sad*) dejected, sad, spiritless, R.

प्रविषय *pra-vishaya,* m. scope, range, reach (of the eye &c.; °*yaṃ dṛishter √gam,* 'to become visible'), Kum. xvii, 21.

प्रविषा *pra-vishā,* f. a birch tree, L. (cf. *upa-vishā, prati-vishā*).

प्रविष्ट *pra-vishṭa,* °*ṭaka* &c. See under *pra-√viś.*

प्रविसर्पिन् *pra-visarpin,* mfn. spreading or diffusing (intr.) slowly, Jātakam.

प्रविसृत *pra-vi-sṛita,* mfn. (√*sṛi*) pouring forth, Kathās.; spread, divulged, Vāgbh.; run away, fled, MBh.; violent, intensive, Mṛicch.; Pañcar.

प्रविस्तृ *pra-vi-√stṛi,* P. *-stṛiṇāti* &c., to spread, expand, Hcat. °**vistara,** m. circumference, compass, extent, ib.; Pur. (°*reṇa,* ind. 'in great detail'). °**vistāra,** m. id., Cat.

प्रविस्पष्ट *pra-vi-spashṭa,* mfn. (√*spaś*) perfectly visible or evident, Kum. xii, 42.

प्रविहत *pra-vi-hata,* mfn. (√*han*) beaten back, put to flight, MBh.

प्रविहा *pra-vi-√3. hā,* P. *-jahāti,* to relinquish, give up, abandon, R. (ind. p. *-hāya,* 'disregarding, passing over').

प्रविहार *pra-vihāra,* m. moving onwards, Pārvat.

प्रवी *pra-√vī,* P. *-veti,* to go forth, RV.; to strive after, make for, enter into, ib.; to attack, assail, ib.; to enter, fertilize, impregnate ib.; TS.; AV.; Kāṭh.; to urge on, inspirit, animate, RV.

1. **Pra-vayaṇa,** mfn. (for 2. see under *pra-√ve*) fit for driving forwards (as a stick), Pāṇ. ii, 4, 57, Sch.; n. a goad, ib.; L. °**vayaṇīya,** mfn. to be driven forwards, Pāṇ. ii, 4, 56, Sch. °**vayyā,** f. to be impregnated (as a cow), Pāṇ. vi, 1, 83. °**vāyaka,** mfn. driving forwards, Pāṇ. ii, 4, 56, Sch.

Prá-vīta, mfn. impregnated, AV. (cf. *a-prav°, ṛita-prav°*). °**vetṛi,** m. a charioteer, Pāṇ. ii, 4, 56, Vārtt. 1, Pat. °**veya,** mfn., Pāṇ. vi, 1, 83, Sch.

प्रवीण *pra-vīṇa,* mf(*ā*)n. (*pra + vīṇā*) skilful, clever, conversant with or versed in (loc. or comp.), Kāv.; Kām. (cf. g. *śauṇḍādi*); m. N. of a son of the 14th Manu, Hariv. (v.l. *Pra-vīra*). **–tā,** f., **-tva,** n. skill, proficiency, Kāv.

Pravīṇī-√kṛi, to render skilful, Siṇhâs.

प्रवीतिन् *pra-vītin,* mfn. (√*vye*) having the sacred thread hanging down the back, Gal. (cf. *upa-vītin, ni-vītin*).

प्रवीर *prá-vīra,* mfn. preceding or surpassing heroes, RV. x, 103, 5 (cf. *abhí-vīra*); m. a hero, prince, chief among (gen. or comp.), a person excellent or distinguished by (comp.), MBh.; Kāv. &c. (ifc. f. *ā*); N. of a son of Pūru, MBh.; of a son of Pracinvat (grandson of Pūru), Hariv.; Pur.; of a son of Dharmanetra, Hariv.; of a son of Hary-aśva, VP.; of a son of the 14th Manu, Hariv. (v.l. *pra-vīṇa*); of a Caṇḍāla, MārkP.; pl. N. of the descendants of Pravīra (son of Pūru), MBh. **–bāhu,** m. 'strong-armed,' N. of a Rākshasa, R. **–vara,** m. 'best of heroes,' N. of an Asura, Kathās.

Pravīraka, m. N. of sev. men, Mudr.

प्रवीविविक्षु *pra-vī-vivikshu,* mfn. (Desid. of √*vish*) being about to embrace or inundate (said of the ocean), R.

प्रवृ *pra-√1. vṛi,* P. *-vṛiṇoti,* to ward off, keep away, RV.: Caus. *-vārayati,* id., MBh.

2. **Pra-vará,** m. (for 1. see p. 690) a cover, ŚBr. (Sāy. *pra-vāra;* cf. Pāṇ. iii, 3, 54); an upper garment, Var. 1. °**varaṇa,** n. (for 2. see under *pra-√2. vṛi*) the festivities at the end of the rainy season, Buddh. °**vāra,** m. a covering, cover, woollen cloth, BṛĀrUp. (cf. 2. *pra-vara*). °**vāraka,** m. = 1. *pravaraṇa,* L.; woollen cloth, L. 1. °**vāraṇa,** n. (for 2. see under *pra-√2. vṛi*) prohibition, L.; = 1. *pravaraṇa,* L. (also *ā,* f.; cf. MWB. 84). 1. °**vārita,** mfn. (for 2. see under *pra-√2. vṛi*) clothed with (instr.), Kāraṇḍ.

प्रवृ *pra-√2. vṛi,* P. Ā. *-vṛiṇāti,* (Ved.) *-vṛiṇīte; -vṛiṇoti, -vṛiṇute* (3. sg. aor. Subj. *-vṛita,* RV.), to choose out, choose as (acc.) or for (dat.), RV.; Br.; MBh.; BhP.; to accept gladly, RV. ix, 101, 13: Caus. *-varayati,* to choose, select, MBh.; *-vārayati,* to please, gratify, R. (For 1. **Pravara,** mfn. best, &c., see p. 690, col. 3.)

3. **Pra-vara,** m. a call, summons (esp. of a Brāhman to priestly functions), AitBr.; an invocation of Agni at the beginning of a sacrifice, a series of ancestors (so called because Agni is invited to bear the oblations to the gods as he did for the sacrificer's progenitors, the names of the 4 or 5 most nearly connected with the ancient Ṛishis being then added), Br.; ŚrS.; a family, race, L.; an ancestor, KātyŚr., Sch. (*ī,* f., Pat.); *-kāṇḍa,* m. or n. a chapter about a series of ancestors, Cat.; *-khaṇḍa,* m. or n., *-darpaṇa,* m., *-dīpikā,* f., *-nirṇaya,* m., *-mañjarī,* f., *-ratna,* n. N. of wks.; *-vat,* mfn. having a series of ancestors, L.; °*râdhyāya,* m., °*re-kṛita-śānti,* f. N. of wks. 2. °**varaṇa,** n. (for 1. see above) a call, summons, invocation (*ati-prav°*), ĀśvŚr.; any religious ceremony or observance (= *anu-shṭhāna*), Hcat.; °*ṇīya,* mfn. fit for religious observances, ib. 2. °**vāraṇa,** n. (for 1. see above) satisfying, fulfilment of a wish, MBh. v, 146. 2. °**vārita,** mfn. (for 1. see above) offered, set out for sale, MBh. v, 6006 (B. *pra-codita*). °**vārya,** mfn. to be satisfied, MBh. v, 149. °**vṛita,** mfn. chosen, selected, adopted (as a son), BhP.; *-homa,* m. an oblation offered on the appointment of a priest, ŚrS.; °*mīya,* mfn. relating to it, ŚāṅkhBr.; °*tâhuti,* f. = °*tahoma,* ib.; Vait.

प्रवृक्ण *pra-vṛikṇa.* See *pra-√vraśc.*

प्रवृज् *pra-√vṛij,* P. Ā. *-vṛiṇakti, -vṛiṅkte* (Ved. inf. *-vṛíje*), to strew (the sacrificial grass), RV.; Br.; to place in or on the fire, heat, ib.; to perform the Pravargya ceremony, Br.; KātyŚr.

Pra-varga, m. a large earthenware pot (used in the Pravargya ceremony), Sāy. on RV. vii, 103, 8; w.r. for next; °*gâvarta-bhūshaṇa,* m. N. of Vishṇu, Hariv. °**vargyà,** m. a ceremony introductory to the Soma sacrifice (at which fresh milk is poured into a heated vessel called *mahā-vīra* or *gharma,* or into boiling ghee), Br.; ŚrS.; MBh. &c.; n. N. of a Sāman, ĀrshBr.; *-kāṇḍa,* m. N. of ŚBr. xvi (in the *Kāṇva-śākhā*); *-prayoga,* m. N. of wk.; *-vat* (°*gyá-*), mfn. connected with the Pravargya ceremony, ŚBr.; ŚrS.; *-sāman,* n. N. of a Sāman, ĀrshBr. °**várjana,** n. performance of the Prav° ceremony, placing in or near the fire, ŚBr. °**vṛikta** (*prá-*), mfn. placed in or near the fire, ŚBr. °**vṛijya,** mfn. to be placed in or near the fire, ĀpŚr.

Pra-vṛiñjana, n. = °*várjana,* ib. °**vṛiñjanīya,** mfn. used at the Pravargya ceremony, KātyŚr.

प्रवृत् *pra-√vṛit,* Ā. *-vartate* (ep. also P. °*ti*), to roll or go onwards (as a carriage), be set in motion or going, ChUp.; MBh. &c.; to set out, depart, betake one's self, MBh.; R. &c.; to proceed (*vartmanā* or °*ni,* on a path; *apathena,* on a wrong path), Kāv.; Kathās.; to come forth, issue, originate, arise, be produced, result, occur, happen, take place, VS.; Br.; MBh. &c.; to commence, begin to (inf.), set about, engage in, be intent upon or occupied with (dat., loc., or *artham* ifc.), MBh.; Kāv. &c.; to proceed against, do injury to (loc.), MBh.; R.; Ragh.; to debauch (*anyo 'nyam,* 'one another'), MBh.; to act or proceed according to or with (instr. or abl.), MBh.; Kāv. &c.; to behave or conduct one's self towards, deal with (loc.), ib.; to hold good, prevail, ib.; to continue, keep on (pr. p.), Hariv.; Sarvad.; to be, exist, MārkP.; to serve for, conduce to (dat., or *artham* ifc.), Sarvad.; to mean, be used in the sense of (loc.), ib.; to let any one (gen.) have anything (acc.), MBh.: Caus. *-vartayati,* to cause to turn or roll, set in motion, RV. &c. &c.; to throw, hurl, pour forth, RV.; MaitrS.; to send, Prab.; to set on foot, circulate, diffuse, divulge, MBh.; Kāv. &c.; to introduce, appoint, instal, ib.; to produce, create, accomplish, devise, invent, perform, do, make, ib. (with *setum,* to erect a dam; with *vyaya-karma,* to effect expenditure; with *loka-yātrām,* to transact the business of life; with *kathām,* to relate a story); to exhibit, show, display, R.; BhP.; to undertake, begin, KātyŚr.; MBh. &c.; to use, employ, Bhaṭṭ.; to induce any one to do anything, betray into (loc.), Kathās.; to proceed against (loc.), MBh.

Pra-vartá, m. a round ornament, AV. (TS., Sch. 'an ear ring;' cf. *pra-vṛitta*); engaging in, undertaking, W.; excitement, stimulus, ib. °**vartaka,** mf(*ikā*)n. acting, proceeding, L.; setting in motion or action, setting on foot, advancing, promoting, forwarding, Up.; Mn.; MBh. &c.; producing, causing, effecting, MBh.; Kāv. &c.; m. a founder, author, originator of anything, ib.; an arbiter, judge, W.; n. (in dram.) the entrance of a previously announced person on the stage (at the end of the introduction), Sāh.; Pratāp. (cf. *pra-vṛittaka* and *prā-varta*); *-jñāna* and °*kīya,* n. N. of wks. °**vartana,** mf(*ī*)n. being in motion, flowing, Ragh. x, 38 (C. °*vartin*); (*ā*), f. incitement to activity, Gaut.; (in gram.) order, permission, the sense of the precative or qualified imperative tense (?), W.; n. advance, forward movement, rolling or flowing forth, R.; Var.; Yājñ., Sch.; walking, roaming, wandering, R.; activity, procedure, engaging in, dealing with (instr. or loc.), MBh.; Kāv. &c.; going on, coming off, happening, occurrence, MBh.; Hariv. &c.; conduct, behaviour, MBh.; bringing near, fetching, ŚāṅkhŚr.; erection, construction, Mn.; Yājñ., Sch.; causing to appear, bringing about, advancing, promoting, introducing, employing, using, MBh.; R. &c.; informing, W. °**vartanīya,** mfn. to be set in motion or employed, Kull.; to be begun, Yājñ., Sch. °**vartamānaká,** mfn. (dimin. of the pr. p. °*vartamāna*) coming slowly forth from (abl.), RV. i, 191, 16. °**vartayitṛi,** m. (fr. Caus.) one who sets in motion or action, instigator of (gen.) or to (loc.), Kād.; Saṃk. (*-tva,* n.); an erector, builder, founder, introducer, VP.; Yājñ., Sch.; an employer, Kull. °**vartita,** mfn. (fr. Caus.) caused to roll on or forwards, set in motion, set on foot, MBh.; Kāv. &c.; set up, established, introduced, appointed, ib.; built, erected, made, performed, accomplished, ib.; related, told, Sāh.; made pure, hallowed, Mn. xi, 196; informed, apprized, W.; stimulated, incited, ib.; lighted, kindled, MW.; dispensed, administered, Ml.; allowed to take its course, ib.; enforced, ib. °**vartitavya,** n. (impers.) one should act or proceed, Prab.; Sāh. °**vartitṛi,** m. one who causes or effects, producer, bringer, MBh.; one who settles or determines, Yājñ. °**vartin,** mfn. issuing, streaming forth, moving onwards, flowing, Kālid.; Śatr.; active, restless, unsteady (*a-prativ°*), ŚBr.; Up.; causing to flow, MBh.; Hariv.; causing, effecting, producing, ib.; using, employing, Hariv.; introducing, propagating, Cat.; (*ī*), f. N. of a Jaina nun, HPariś. °**vartya,** mfn. to be (or being) excited to activity, Saṃk.

Pra-vṛít, f. (?), VS. xv, 9. °**vṛitta,** mfn. round, globular, ŚāṅkhBr.; driven up (as a carriage), ChUp.; circulated (as a book), Pañcat.; set out from (*-tas*), going to, bound for (acc., loc., inf., or *artham* ifc.; *dakshiṇena,* 'southwards;' with *pathā,* 'proceeding on a path'), MBh.; Kāv. &c.; issued from (abl.), come forth, resulted, arisen, produced, brought about, happened, occurred, VS. &c. &c.; come back, returned, MBh.; commenced, begun, MBh.; Kāv. &c.; (also *-vat,* mfn.) having set about or commenced to (inf.), Kathās.; purposing or going to, bent upon (dat., loc., or comp.), Kāv.; Kathās.; Rājat.; engaged in, occupied with, devoted to (loc. or comp.), Mn.; MBh. &c.; hurting, injuring, offending, MBh.; acting, proceeding, dealing with (loc.), Mn.; MBh. &c.; existing, Āpast.; who or what has become (with nom.), R.; (with *karman,* n. action) causing a continuation of mundane existence, Mn. xii, 88; w.r. for *pra-citta* and *pra-nṛitta*; (°*vṛittá*), m. =°*varta*, a round ornament, ŚBr.; (*ā*, f. N. of a female demon, MārkP.); *-karman*, n. any act leading to a future birth, W.; *-cakra*, mfn. 'whose chariot wheels run on unimpeded,' having universal power (°*kra-tā*, f.), Yājñ.; *-tva*, n. the having happened or occurred, Jaim.; *-pānīya*, mfn. (a well) with abundant water, MBh.; *-pāraṇa*, n. a partic. religious observance or ceremony, Śak. (v.l.); *-vāc*, mfn. of fluent speech, eloquent, MBh.; *-samprahāra*, mfn. one who has begun the fight (°*ra-tva*, n.), Kathās.; °*ttâśin*, m. N. of a partic. class of ascetics, Baudh. °**vṛittaka**, n. =°*vartaka*, n., Pratāp.; N. of a metre, Col. °**vṛitti**, f. moving onwards, advance, progress, GṛŚrS.; MBh.; Suśr.; coming forth, appearance, manifestation, ŚvetUp.; Kālid.; Rājat.; rise, source, origin, MBh.; activity, exertion, efficacy, function, Kap.; Sāṃkhyak.; MBh. &c. (in the Nyāya one of the 82 Prameyas, IW. 63); active life (as opp. to *ni-vṛitti* [q.v.] and to contemplative devotion, and defined as consisting of the wish to act, knowledge of the means, and accomplishment of the object), W.; giving or devoting one's self to, prosecution of, course or tendency towards, inclination or predilection for (loc. or comp.), Rājat.; Hit.; Sāh.; application, use, employment, Mn.; MBh.; MārkP.; conduct, behaviour, practice, Mn.; MBh. &c.; the applicability or validity of a rule, KātyŚr.; Pāṇ., Sch.; currency, continuance, prevalence, ib.; fate, lot, destiny, R.; news, tidings, intelligence of (gen. or comp.), MBh.; Kāv. &c.; cognition (with *vishaya-vatī*, 'a sensuous c°'), Yogas.; the exudation from the temples of a rutting elephant, L. (cf. Vikr. iv, 47); N. of Avanti or Oujein or any holy place, L.; (in arithm.) the multiplier, W. (w.r. for *pra-kṛiti*?); *-jña*, m. 'knowing the news,' an emissary, agent, spy, L.; *-jñāna*, n. = *-vijñāna*, Sarvad.; *-nimitta*, n. the reason for the use of any term in the particular significations which it bears, MW.; *-nivṛitti-mat*, mfn. connected with activity and inactivity, BhP.; *-parāṅmukha*, mf(*ī*)n. disinclined to give tidings, Vikr.; *-pratyaya*, m. a belief in or conception of the things relating to the external world, Buddh.; *-mat*, mfn. devoted to anything, Kaiy.; *-mārga*, m. active or worldly life, occupancy about the business and pleasures of the world or with the rites and works of religion, MW.; *-vacana*, mfn. (a word) expressing activity, Kāś. on Pāṇ. ii, 3, 51; *-vijñāna*, n. cognition of the things belonging to the external world, Buddh.; °*tty-aṅga*, n. N. of wk.

प्रवृध् *pra-√vṛidh*, P. *-vardhati*, to exalt, magnify, RV. viii, 8, 22; Ā. *-vardhate* (rarely P. °*ti*), to grow up, grow, increase, gain in strength, prosper, thrive, RV. &c. &c.: Caus. *-vardhayati*, °*te*, to strengthen, increase, augment, extend, RV. &c. &c.; to raise, exalt, cause to thrive, Hariv.; to rear, cherish, bring up, Kathās.

Pra-vardhaka, mf(*ikā*)n. augmenting, increasing, enhancing, Inscr. °**vardhana**, mfn. id., Hariv.; Suśr.; n. augmenting, increase, W.

Prá-vṛiddha, mfn. grown up, fully developed, increased, augmented, intense, vehement, great, numerous, RV. &c. &c.; swollen, heaving, R.; Kālid.; risen to wealth or power, prosperous, mighty, strong, MBh.; Var.; (also with *vayasā*) advanced in age, grown old, MBh.; Kathās.; expanded, diffused, W.; full, deep (as a sigh), ib.; haughty, arrogant, MW.; w.r. for *pra-vṛitta*, *-viddha*, *-buddha*. °**vṛiddhi**, f. growth, increase, Var.; Kālid.; Rājat.; rising, rise (*arghasya*, 'of price'), Var.; prosperity, increasing welfare, rising in rank or reputation, ib.; Rājat.

Pra-vṛídh, f. growth, RV. iii, 31, 3.

प्रवृश्च्य *pra-vṛiścya*. See *pra-√vraśc*.

प्रवृष् *pra-√vṛish*, P. *-varshati*, to begin to rain, rain, shed or shower abundantly with (instr.), MBh.; Kāv. &c.: Caus. *-varshayati*, to cause to rain, TS.; ŚBr. °**varsha**, m. (also pl.) rain, MBh.; Pañcat. °**varshaṇa**, m. N. of a mountain, BhP.; n. beginning to rain, raining, causing to rain, MBh.; Var. (Sch. 'first rain'). °**varshin**, mfn. raining, causing to rain, showering, discharging, MBh.; R. &c. (cf. *ūrdhva-prav*°). °**vṛishṭa**, mfn. begun to rain or to pour down (instr.), MBh.; R.; Kathās.; (*e*), ind. when it rains, Var.

प्रवृह् *pra-√vṛih*, P. Ā. *-vṛihati*, °*te*, to tear out or off or asunder, destroy, RV.; TS.; Br.; Up.; (Ā.) to draw towards one's self, attract, ŚBr. °**várham**, ind. plucking off, ŚBr. °**vṛiḍha**, mfn. torn off, Kāṭh. (Cf. *pra-√1. bṛih*.)

प्रवे *pra-√ve*, P. *-vayati*, to weave on, attach to, RV.; TS.; ŚBr.; Up.

2. **Pra-vayaṇa**, n. (for 1. see under *pra-√vī*) the upper part of a piece of woven cloth, AitBr. °**vāṇa**, n. the edging or trimming of a piece of woven cloth, Lāṭy. °**vāṇi** or °**vāṇī**, f. a weaver's shuttle, L. **Prôta**, see s.v.

प्रवेक *pra-veka*, mfn. (√*vic*) choicest, most excellent, principal, chief (always ifc.), MBh.; R. &c.

प्रवेग *pra-vega*, m. (√*vij*) great speed, rapidity, MBh.; R. (cf. *śara-pr*°). °**vegita**, mfn. moving swiftly, rapid, R.

प्रवेट *pra-veṭa*, m. barley, L. (cf. *pra-vaṭa*, *prāvaṭa*).

प्रवेणी *pra-veṇī*, f. a braid of hair worn by widows and by wives in the absence of their husbands, R. (°*ṇi*, L.); a piece of coloured woollen cloth (used instead of a saddle), MBh. (°*ṇi*, L., also 'the housings of an elephant'); N. of a river, MBh.

प्रवेतृ *pra-vetṛi*, *pra-veya*. See *pra-√vī*.

प्रवेत्तृ *pra-vettṛi*, *pra-veda* &c. See *pra-√1. vid*.

प्रवेध *pra-vedha*. See *pra-√vyadh*.

प्रवेप् *pra-√vep*, Ā. *-vepate* (m. c. also P. °*ti*), to tremble, shiver, quake, MBh.; Kāv. &c.: Caus. *-vepayati* (aor. *prâvīvipat*), to cause to tremble, shake, RV. &c. &c. °**vepa**, m. trembling, quivering, R. °**vepaka**, m. trembling, shivering, shuddering, Suśr. °**vepathu**, m. id., ib. °**vepana**, m. N. of a serpent-demon, MBh.; n. trembling, shuddering, tremulous motion, agitation, Car.; Pāṇ., Sch.; Vop. (w.r. °*vepaṇa*). °**vepanin**, mfn. causing (enemies) to tremble (said of Indra), RV. °**vepanīya**, mfn. to be caused to tremble, Pāṇ. viii, 4, 34, Sch. °**vepita**, n. the act of trembling, Kir. °**vepin**, mfn. trembling, shaking, tottering, Nir. ix, 8.

प्रवेरय *pra-veraya*, Nom. P. °*yati* (cf. √*vel*, *vell*), to cast, hurl, MBh. °**verita**, mfn. cast, hurled, ib. (v.l.)

प्रवेल *pravela*, m. a yellow variety of Phaseolus Mungo, L.

प्रवेश *pra-veśa* &c. See *pra-√viś*.

प्रवेष्ट् *pra-√vesht*, Caus. *-veshṭayati*, to cover, enclose, surround, TS.; to twine or fasten round, ĀpŚr.; MānGṛ.

Pra-veshṭa, m. (only L.) an arm; the fore-arm or wrist (cf. *pra-koshṭha*); the fleshy part of the back of an elephant on which the rider sits; an e°'s housings; an e°'s gums (see also *danta-pr*°). °**veshṭita**, mfn. covered with (instr.), MBh.

प्रवेष्टक *praveshṭaka*, w.r. for *pra-vishṭaka* (see *pra-√viś*).

प्रवेष्टव्य *pra-veshṭavya*, °*ṭṛi*. See *pra-√viś*.

प्रवोढृ *pra-vodhṛi*. See *pra-√vah*.

प्रव्यक्त *pra-vy-akta*, mfn. (√*añj*) evident, apparent, manifest (compar. *-tara*), Suśr. °**vyakti**, f. appearance, manifestation, ib.

प्रव्यथ् *pra-√vyath*, Ā. *-vyathate* (ep. also P. °*ti*), to tremble, be afraid of (gen.), be disquieted or distressed, MBh.; R. &c.; = Caus., R.: Caus. *-vyathayati*, to frighten, disquiet, distress, MBh.; R.; Hariv. °**vyathita**, mfn. affrighted, distressed, pained, MBh.; Hariv.; R. &c.

प्रव्यध् *pra-√vyadh*, P. *-vidhyati*, to hurl, cast, throw away or down, RV. &c. &c.; to hurl missiles, shoot, AV.; ŚBr.; to pierce, transfix, wound, MBh.; Suśr.

Prá-viddha, mfn. hurled, cast, thrown into (loc.), RV. &c. &c.; thrown asunder, spilt (as water), R.; crammed, filled, MBh.; abandoned, given up, R. °**vedha**, m. a bow-shot, ĀpŚr., Sch.; a partic. measure of length, Divyâv. °**vyādha**, m. id., the distance of the flight of an arrow, ŚBr.; TBr.; ŚrS.

प्रव्यस् *pra-vy-√2. as*, P. *-asyati*, to lay down, place upon (loc.), R.

प्रव्याहृ *pra-vy-ā-√hṛi*, P. *-harati*, to utter forth, speak, MBh.; R.; to utter inarticulate sounds, howl, yell, roar, ib. (v.l. *pratyāhṛi*); to declare beforehand, foretell, predict, MW.: Caus. *-hārayati*, to speak, MBh. °**vyāharaṇa**, n. the uttering of sounds, faculty of speech, Divyâv. °**vyāhāra**, m. (v.l. or w.r. *pratyāh*°) prolongation or continuation of discourse, MBh. (= *prakṛishṭôkti*, Nilak.); speaking to, address (°*raṃ √kṛi*, with gen., 'to address a person'), Kāraṇḍ.; sound, ib. °**vyāhṛita**, mfn. speaking, MBh.; spoken, foretold, predicted, ib.

प्रव्रज् *pra-√vraj*, P. *-vrajati*, to go forth, proceed, depart from (abl.), set out for, go to (acc., loc. or dat.), ŚBr.; Up.; GṛŚrS.; MBh. &c.; to leave home and wander forth as an ascetic mendicant, ŚrS.; Mn.; MBh. &c.; (with Jainas) to become a monk, HPariś.: Caus. *-vrājayati* (w.r. *-vraj*°), to send into exile, banish from (abl.), MBh.; R. &c.; to compel any one to wander forth as an ascetic mendicant or to become a monk, MBh.; HPariś.

Pra-vivrajishu, mfn. (from Desid.) wishing to take the vow of a monk, HPariś. °**vivrājayishu**, mfn. (from Desid. of Caus.) wishing to send into exile, desirous of banishing, Bhaṭṭ.

Pra-vrajana, n. going abroad, MBh. °**vrajikā**, w.r. for °*vrajitā* and °*vrājikā*. °**vrajita**, mfn. gone astray or abroad, R.; Kāś. on Pāṇ. ii, 3, 38; run away (said of horses), MBh.; (also with *vanam*) one who has left home to become a religious mendicant or (with Jainas) to become a monk, Mn.; MBh.; HPariś.; m. a religious mendicant or a monk, MBh.; Var.; Suśr.; (*ā*), f. a female ascetic or a nun, Yājñ.; Var.; Kād.; Sāh.; Nardostachys Jatamansi, L.; another plant (*muṇḍīrī*), L.; n. the life of a religious mendicant, MBh. °**vrajya**, n. going abroad, migration, MBh.; (*ā*), f. id., ib.; going forth from home (first rite of a layman wishing to become a Buddh. monk), MWB. 77; roaming, wandering about (esp. as a religious mendicant, in a dress not authorized by the Veda), Mn.; MBh.; Kāv. &c.; the order of a rel° m°, MBh.; Var.; °*jyā-yoga*, m. a constellation under which future rel° m°s are born, Var.; °*jyâvasita*, m. a rel° m° who has renounced his order, Yājñ.

Pra-vrāj, m. a religious mendicant, Var.; Kathās. °**vrājá**, m. the bed of a river, RV. °**vrājaka**, m. a rel° m°, R.; Kathās.; (*ikā*), f. a female ascetic (also °*jaka-strī*), Kathās. °**vrājana**, n. banishment, exile, MBh.; R. °**vrājita**, mfn. become a monk, Divyâv. °**vrājin**, m. = °*vrāj*, ŚBr.; mfn. running after (see *dvi-pravrājinī*).

प्रव्रश्च् *pra-√vraśc*, P. *-vṛiścati* (ind. p. *-vṛiścya*), to cut or hew off, cut or tear to pieces, lacerate, wound, AV.; Br.; Bhaṭṭ. °**vṛikṇa**, mfn. cut or hewn off, BhP. °**vraścana**, m. an instrument for cutting fuel, a knife for cutting wood, Pāṇ., Sch. (cf. *idhma-pr*°). °**vraska**, m. a cut, Kauś.

प्रव्ली *pra-√vlī*, P. *-vlīnāti*, to overwhelm by pressure, crush, ĀpŚr. °**vlaya**, m. sinking down, collapse, AitBr. °**vlīna** (*prá-*), mfn. overwhelmed by pressure, crushed, sunk down, AV.; Br.

प्रशंयुवाक *pra-śaṃyuvāka*, w.r. for *śaṃy*°.

प्रशंस् *pra-√śaṇs*, P. Ā. *-śaṇsati*, °*te* (irreg. Pot. *-śaṇsīyāt*, Cāṇ.), to proclaim, declare, praise, laud, extol, RV. &c. &c.; to urge on, stimulate, RV. i, 84, 19; to approve, esteem, value (with *na*, to disapprove, blame), MBh.; Kāv. &c.; to foretell, prophesy, Cāṇ. °**śaṇsaka**, mfn. (ifc.) praising, commending, MBh.; R.; HYog. °**śaṇsana**, n. praising, commending, Vedântas.; Pāṇ., Sch. (w.r. °*śaṇśana*). °**śaṇsanīya**, mfn. to be praised, laudable, Kād. °**śaṇsā**, f. praise, commendation, fame, glory (with Buddhists one of the 8 worldly conditions, Dharmas. 61), ŚBr. &c. &c. (cf. *aprastuta-p*°, *strī-p*°; w.r. °*śaṇśā*); *-nāman*, n. an expression of praise, Nir.; *-mukhara*, mfn. loud with praise, praising loudly (°*rânana*, mfn. 'one whose mouth is l° w° pr°,' speaking loudly in praise of anything), Rājat.; *-°lāpa* (°*sâl*°), m. applause, acclamation, Daś.; *-vacana*, n. pl. a laudatory speech, MBh.; *-°vali* (°*sâv*°), f. a poem of praise, panegyric, Bālar.;

°*śaṇsôpamā*, f. (in rhet.) laudatory comparison, comparing to anything superior, Kāvyâd. °**śaṇsita,** mfn. praised, commended, Pañcar. °**śaṇsitavya,** mfn. to be praised, praiseworthy, W. °**śaṇsin,** mfn. (ifc.) praising, commending, eulogizing, MBh.; R. °**śaṇstavya,** mfn. to be praised, praiseworthy, R. (cf. °*śastavya*). °**śaṇsya,** mfn. to be pr°, praisew°, RV.; MBh.; R.; Uttarar. (v.l.); preferable to, better than (abl.), Mn. ii, 95, Kull.; (cf. 1. °*śasya.*)

Praśastá, mfn. praised, commended, considered fit or good, happy, auspicious (as stars, days &c.), RV.; ĀśvGṛ.; Mn.; MBh. &c.; better, more excellent, Gaut.; best, Āpast.; consecrated (as water), Var.; m. N. of a man, Kathās.; of a poet, Cat.; (*ā*), f. N. of a river, MBh.; *-kara*, m. N. of an author (perhaps the writer of a wk. entitled Praśasta), Cat.; *-kalaśa*, m. N. of a man, Rājat.; *-tā*, f. (MW.) or *-tva*, n. (Mcar.) excellence, goodness; *-paribhāshā*, f. N. of wk.; *-pāda*, m. N. of an author, Sarvad.; Cat.; *-bhāshya*, n. N. of wk., Cat.; *-vacana*, n. pl. laudatory words, praises, Mṛicch.; °*śastâdri*, m. N. of a mountain to the west of Madhya-deśa, Var. °**śastavya,** mfn. to be praised, praiseworthy, R. (cf. *-śaṇstavya*). °**śasti** (*prá-*), f. praise, fame, glorification, RV.; Uttarar.; Daśar. &c. (°*tim* √*dhā*, to bestow pr° upon, value highly [with loc.], RV.); liking, desire (as of food), RV.; (in dram.) a benediction (praying for peace &c. in the reign of a prince), Sāh.; instruction, guidance, warning, RV.; an edict, Vcar.; Bālar.; (metrical) eulogistic inscription, Ml.; excellence, eminence, W.; N. of a guide to letter-writing, Cat. (also °*tikā*); *-kāśikā*, f. N. of wk.; *-kṛit*, mfn. bestowing praise, praising, RV.; *-gāthā*, f. a song of praise, Caṇḍ.; *-taraṃga*, m. N. of wk.; *-paṭṭa*, m. a written edict, Rājat.; *-prakāśikā*, f. N. of wk. (= *-kāśikā*); *-ratnâkara*, m. N. of wk.; *-ratnâvalī*, f. N. of a poem by Viśva-nātha, Sāh. 1. °**śasya,** mfn. to be praised, praiseworthy, excellent, eminent, RV.; Nir.; MBh. &c.; to be called happy, to be congratulated, MBh. (cf. °*śaṇsya*); *-tā*, f. excellence, eminence, Hemac. 2. °**śasya,** ind. having praised or commended, MBh.; R.; Pañcat.; BhP.

प्रशक् *pra-√śak*, P. *-śaknoti* (fut. also Ā. *-śakshye*, MBh.), to be able to (inf.), MBh.; Hariv. °**śakta,** mfn., w. r. for °*sakta*, MBh. °**śakya,** mfn. one who does his utmost, Kauś., Sch.

प्रशक *praśaka*, w. r. for *pra-śākha*, col. 2.

प्रशठ *pra-śaṭha*, mfn. very false or wicked (*-tā*, f.), L.

प्रशद् *pra-√śad*, only Caus. *-śātayati*, to cause to fall down, break off, pluck, Vcar. °**śattvan,** m. the ocean, Uṇ. iv, 116, Sch.; (*arī*), f. a river, ib.

प्रशम् *pra-√śam*, P. *-śāmyati*, to become calm or tranquil, be pacified or soothed, settle down (as dust), Mn.; MBh. &c.; to be allayed or extinguished, cease, disappear, fade away, ib.: Caus. *-śamayati* (rarely *śām°*), to appease, calm, quench, allay, extinguish, terminate, ib.; to make subject, subdue, conquer, MBh. °**śama,** m. calmness, tranquillity (esp. of mind), quiet, rest, cessation, extinction, abatement, MBh.; Kāv. &c.; m. N. of a son of Ānaka-dundubhi and Śānti-deva, BhP.; (*ī*), f. N. of an Apsaras, MBh.; *-ṃ-kara*, mfn. causing the cessation of (gen.), disturbing, interrupting, R.; *-rati-sūtra*, n. N. of wk.; *-sthita*, mfn. being in a state of quiescence, Ragh.; °*mâyana*, mfn. walking in tranquillity, BhP. °**śamaka,** mfn. one who brings to rest, quenching, allaying, Kāraṇḍ. °**śamana,** mfn. tranquillizing, pacifying, curing, healing, MBh.; Hariv.; Suśr.; n. the act of tranquillizing &c., MBh.; Kām.; Daś.; Pur.; Suśr.; securing, keeping safe (of what has been acquired), Mn. vii, 56 (others 'bestowing aptly;' others 'sanctification;' cf. Ragh. iv, 14); killing, slaughter, L.; (scil. *astra*) N. of a weapon, R. °**śamita,** mfn. (fr. Caus.) tranquillized, relieved, quelled, quenched, allayed, MBh.; Hariv. &c.; atoned for, expiated, Uttarar.; *-ripu*, mfn. one who has all enemies pacified, Mṛicch.; °*târi*, mfn. id., Ragh.; °*tôpadrava*, mfn. one who has all calamities quelled, MW.

Pra-śān, ind., g. *svar-ādi* (cf. °*śām*). °**śānta,** mfn. tranquillized, calm, quiet, composed, indifferent, Up.; Mn.; MBh. &c.; (in augury) auspicious, boni ominis, Var.; extinguished, ceased, allayed, removed, destroyed, dead, MBh.; Kāv. &c.; *-kāma*, mfn. one whose desires are calmed, content, BhP.; *-cāritra-mati*, m. N. of a Bodhi-sattva, Lalit.; *-cārin*, m. pl. 'walking tranquilly,' (prob.) N. of a class of deities, ib.; *-citta*, mfn. 'tranquil-minded,' calm, Vedântas.; *-ceshṭa*, mfn. one whose efforts have ceased, resting, MW.; *-tā*, f. tranquillity of mind, MBh.; *-dhī*, mfn. = *-citta*, BhP.; *-bādha*, mfn. one who has all calamities or hindrances quelled, MW.; *-bhūmipāla*, mfn. 'having the kings extinguished,' without a king (said of the earth), Rājat.; *-mūrti*, mfn. of tranquil appearance, Var.; *-rāga*, m. N. of a man, Cat.; *-viniścaya-pratihārya-nirdeśa*, m. N. of a Buddh. Sūtra; *-vinitêśvara*, m. N. of a divine being, Lalit.; °*tâtman*, mfn. 'tranquil-souled,' composed in mind, peaceful, calm, Bhag.; BhP.; °*târāti*, mfn. one whose enemies have been pacified or destroyed, Prab.; °*tôrja*, mfn. one whose strength has ceased, weakened, prostrated, W.; °*tôlmuka*, mfn. extinguished, W.; °*tâujas*, mfn. = °*tôrja*, MW. °**śāntaka,** mfn. tranquil, calm, Bhar. °**śānti,** f. sinking to rest, rest, tranquillity (esp. of mind), calm, quiet, pacification, abatement, extinction, destruction, MBh.; Kāv. &c.; *-dūtī*, f. 'messenger of rest,' N. of old age, Kathās. °**śám,** mfn. (nom. °*śān*) painless, unhurt, ŚBr. (cf. °*śān* above). °**śāma,** m. tranquillity, pacification, suppression, W. °**śāmita,** mfn. (fr. Caus.) pacified i. e. subdued, conquered, Hariv.

प्रशर्ध *pra-śardha*, mfn. (√*śṛidh*) bold, daring, RV.

प्रशल *praśala*, w. r. for *prasala*.

प्रशस् *pra-śas*, f. (√1. *śas*) a hatchet, axe, knife, AitBr. (Nir., Sch.; others = *pra-śasta*, *pra-kṛishṭa-cchedana* &c.)

प्रशस्त *pra-śasta* &c. See *pra-√śaṇs*.

प्रशाख *pra-śākha*, mfn. having great branches (as a tree), Pāṇ. vi, 2, 177, Sch.; (also °*śaka*) N. of the 5th stage in the formation of an embryo (in which the hands and feet are formed), Buddh.; (*ā*), f. a branch or twig, MBh.; R.; (prob.) extremity of the body, Suśr.; °*kha-vat*, mfn. (m. c. for °*khā-v°*) having numerous branches, R. °**khikā,** f. a small branch, twig, MBh.

प्रशातिका *praśātikā*. See *prasātikā*.

प्रशान्त *pra-śānta* &c. See under *pra-√śam*.

प्रशास् *pra-√śās*, P. *-śāsti* (ep. also Ā.), to teach, instruct, direct, RV.; ŚBr.; R.; to give instructions to, order, command (acc.), MBh.; R.; MārkP.; to chastise, punish, MBh.; Kathās.; to govern, rule, reign (also with *rājyam*), be lord of (acc. with or without *adhi*), ŚBr.; Mn.; MBh. &c.; to decide upon (loc.), MBh. °**śāsaka,** m. = °*śāstṛi*, Pañcat. (B.) °**śâsana,** n. guidance, government, rule, dominion, RV.; ŚBr.; ChUp.; MBh.; enjoining, enacting, W. °**śāsita,** mfn. governed, administered, R.; enjoined, enacted, W. °**śāsitṛi,** m. a governor, ruler, master, dictator, Mn.; MBh.; Saṃk. °**śāsta,** w. r. for °*śasta*, ĀpŚr. °**śāstṛí,** m. 'director,' N. of a priest (commonly called Maitrāvaruṇa, the first assistant of the Hotṛi), RV. &c. &c.; a king, Uṇ. ii, 94, Sch. °**śāstrá,** n. the office of the Praśāstṛi, RV. ii, 2, 1; ĀpŚr.; his Soma vessel, ib. ii, 36, 6. 1. °**śāsya,** ind. having ruled or commanded, MBh. 2. °**śāsya,** mfn. one who has to receive orders from (gen.), Bālar.

Praśishṭa, mfn. ruled over, reigned, governed, commanded, MW. °**śishṭi** (*prá-*), f. injunction, command, order, TBr.; ĀśvŚr. °**śis,** f. order, direction, precept, RV.; AV.; TBr.; ĀśvŚr.

प्रशिथिल *pra-śithila*, mf(*ā*)n. very loose, relaxed, lax, Hariv.; Kāv.; Suśr.; very feeble, hardly perceptible, Śaṃk. **— bhuja-granthi,** mfn. one who loosens the clasp of the arms, Sāh.

Praśithilī, in comp. for °*la*. **— kṛita,** mfn. rendered very loose, greatly loosened, Ṛitus. **— bhūta,** mfn. become loose or lax, Suśr.

प्रशिष *praśisha*, m. N. of a man; pl. N. of his descendants, Cat.

प्रशिष्य *pra-śishya*, m. the pupil of a pupil, BhP. **— tva,** n. the condition of a pupil's pupil, L.

प्रशी *pra-√śī*, Ā. *-śete*, to lie down upon (acc.), RV.

प्रशीत *prá-śīta*, mfn. (√*śyai*) congealed, frozen, ŚBr.

प्रशीर्ण *pra-śīrṇa*. See *pra-√śṛī*.

प्रशुक्रीय *praśukrīya*, mfn. beginning with *pra śukrā* (said of RV. vii, 34, 1), ŚāṅkhBr.

प्रशुच् *pra-√śuc*, Ā. *-śocate*, to glow, beam, radiate, RV. °**śócana,** mfn. burning on, continuing to burn, AV.

प्रशुचि *pra-śuci*, mfn. perfectly pure, R.

प्रशुद्धि *pra-śuddhi*, f. (√*śudh*) purity, clearness, MBh.

प्रशुभ् *pra-√śubh* (only Ā. 3. sg. pr. *-śobhe* = *śobhate*), to be bright, sparkle, RV. i, 120, 5.

प्रशुम्भ् *pra-√śumbh* (only 3. pl. *-śumbhante*), to glide onwards, fly along, RV. i, 85, 1 (Sāy. 'to adorn one's self highly').

प्रशुश्रुक *praśuśruka*, m. N. of a prince (a son of Maru), R. (B. *praśuśruva*; cf. *pra-suśruta*).

प्रशुष् *pra-√śush*, P. *-śushyati*, to dry up, become dry, Kām. °**śosha,** m. dryness, aridity, Suśr. °**śoshaṇa,** m. 'drying up,' N. of a demon producing illness, Hariv.

प्रशून *pra-śūna*, mfn. (√*śvi*) swollen, Suśr.

प्रशॄ *pra-√śṛī*, P. *-śṛiṇāti*, to break in pieces, break off, crush, RV.; ŚBr.; KātyŚr. °**śīrṇa,** mfn. broken, smashed, ŚBr.; KātyŚr.; MBh.

प्रश्चुत् *pra-√ścut* (or *-ścyut*), P. *-ścotati* (*-ścyotati*), to trickle forth, drip down, Mālatīm.; to pour forth, shed, spill, Bhaṭṭ. °**ścutita,** mfn. dripped down, Gobh. °**ścotana,** n. trickling, dripping, Uttarar.

प्रश्न 1. *praśna*, m. basket-work, a plaited basket, Kauś. (Sch. 'a turban').

प्रश्न 2. *praśná*, m. (√*prach*) a question, demand, interrogation, query, inquiry after (comp.; cf. *kuśala-p°*), ŚBr. &c. &c.; judicial inquiry or examination (cf. *sâkshi-p°*); astrological inquiry into the future (cf. *divya-*, *deva-*, *daiva-p°*); a subject of inquiry, point at issue, controversy, problem, ŚBr. &c. &c. (*praśnam pra-√brū*, 'to decide a controverted point;' °*nam* √*i*, with acc. or °*nam ā-√gam*, with loc. of pers., 'to lay a question before any one for decision;' *praśnas tava pitari*, 'the point at issue is before thy father'); a task or lesson (in Vedic recitation), RPrāt.; a short section or paragraph (in books), Col. &c. **— kathā,** f. a story containing a question, Kathās. **— kalpalatā,** f., **-krishṇīya,** n., **-koshṭhī,** f., **-kaumudī,** f., **-grantha,** m., **-caṇḍêśvara,** m., **-candrikā,** f., **-cintāmaṇi,** m., **-cūḍāmaṇi,** m., **-jñāna,** n., **-tantra,** n., **-tilaka,** n., **-dīpikā,** f. N. of wks. **— dūtī,** f. a riddle, enigma, perplexing question, L. **— nidhi,** m., **-nirvācana,** n., **-nīlakaṇṭha,** m., **-pañjikā,** f. N. of wks. **— pūrvaka,** mfn. preceded by a question, Kāś. on Pāṇ. iii, 2, 120; (°*kam* or *-pūrvam*), ind. with a preceding question, after examination, Hcat. **— prakaraṇa,** n., **-prakāśa,** m., **-pradīpa,** m., **-brahmârka,** m., **-bhāga,** m., **-bhārgava-kerala,** m., **-bhairava,** m., **-mañjūshā,** f., **-manoramā,** f., **-māṇikya-mālā,** f., **-mārga,** m., **-mārtaṇḍa,** m., **-ratna,** n., **-ratna-sāgara,** m., **-ratnâṅkura,** m., **-ratnâvalī,** f., **-rahasya,** n., **-lakshaṇa,** n. N. of wks. **— vādin,** m. a fortune-teller, astrologer, Gal. **— vidyā,** f., **-vinoda,** m. N. of wks. **— vivāká,** m. one who decides controversies, an arbitrator, VS. **— vivāda,** m. a controverted question, controversy, MBh. **— viveka,** m., **-vaishṇava,** m., **-vyākaraṇa,** n., **-śataka,** n., **-śāstra,** n., **-śiromaṇi,** m., **-śekhara,** m., **-ślokâvalī,** f., **-saṃgraha,** m., **-saptati,** f., **-sāra,** m., **-sāra-samuccaya,** m. **-sāra-samudra,** m., **-sārâmnāya,** m., **-sârôddhāra,** m., **-sudhâkara,** m. N. of wks. **— Praśnâkhyāna,** n. du. question and answer, Kāś. on Pāṇ. ii, 3, 28. **Praśnâdika,** m. or n., °**nânushṭhāna-paddhati,** f., °**nârṇava,** m. (= °*na-vaishṇava* or *vaishnava-śāstra*), °**nâryā,** f., °**nâvalī,** f. N. of wks. **Praśnôttara,** n. question and answer, a verse consisting of q° and a°, Cat.; *-tantra*, n., *-maṇi-mālā*, f., *-mālā*, f., *-mālikā*, f., *-ratna-mālā*, f., *-ratnâvalī*, f. N. of wks. **Praśnôpadeśa,** m., **Praśnôpanishad,** f. N. of wks.

Praśnaya, Nom. P. °*yati*, to question, interrogate, inquire after (2 acc.), Kāvyâd.

Praśnin, m. a questioner, interrogator, VS.

Prashṭavya, mfn. to be asked or questioned about (acc. with or without *prati*), Mn.; Yājñ.; MBh.&c.; to be consulted about (loc.), MBh.; MārkP.; to be inquired into, Śak.; MārkP.; n. (impers.) one should ask or inquire about, Mālav.

Prashṭṛi, m. one who asks or inquires, interrogator, querist, KaṭhUp.; MBh.; MārkP.

प्रश्नि *praśni*, °*nī*, w. r. for *priśni*, °*nī*.

प्रश्रथ *pra-śratha*, m. or *pra-śranthana*, n. (√*śranth*) laxity, relaxation, flaccidity, Pāṇ.; Vop.

प्रश्रब्धि *pra-śrabdhi*, f. (√*śrambh*) trust, confidence, L.

प्रश्रय *pra-śraya* &c. See *pra-√śri*.

प्रश्रवण *praśravaṇa*, w. r. for *pra-sravaṇa*.

प्रश्रवस् *prá-śravas*, mfn. loud-sounding (said of the Maruts), RV. (Sāy. = *prakṛishṭânna*).

प्रश्रि 1. *praśri*, w. r. for *priśni*.

प्रश्रि 2. *pra-√śri*, P. -*śrayati*, to lean against, fix, Kāṭh.; to join or add to (loc.), RV.

Pra-śraya, m. leaning or resting on, resting-place, ŚārṅgP.; inclining forward i.e. respectful demeanour, modesty, humbleness, affection, respect, civility (personified as a son of Dharma and Hrī), MBh. &c. &c.; -*vat*, mfn. deferential, respectful, civil, modest, BhP. °*yâvanata*, mfn. bent down deferentially, MBh.; °*yôttara*, mfn. (words) full of modesty or humbleness, ib. °**śrayaṇa**, n. respectful demeanour, modesty, BhP. °**śrayin**, mfn. behaving respectfully, courteous, modest (°*yitā*, f.), Kām.

Pra-śrita, mfn. bending forward deferentially, humble, modest, courteous, well-behaved (*am*, ind. humbly, deferentially), MBh.; Kāv. &c. (often w. r. °*sṛita*); hidden, obscure (as a meaning), MBh.; m. N. of a son of Ānaka-dundubhi and Śānti-deva, BhP.

प्रश्रु *pra-√śru*, Ā. 3. sg.-*śriṇve*, to be heard, be audible, RV. v, 87, 3; to become known or celebrated, ib. iv, 41, 2 &c. °**śravaṇa** and °**śravas**, see above.

प्रश्लथ *pra-ślatha*, mfn. very loose, greatly relaxed, languid, flaccid, Daś. (cf. *pra-śratha*).

प्रश्लित *pra-ślita*, mfn. (for *pra-śrita*) bent, inclined (N. of the rule of Saṃdhi that changes *as* to *o* before sonant letters), RPrāt.

प्रश्लिष्ट *pra-ślishṭa*, mfn. (√*ślish*) twisted, entwined, coalescent (applied to the Saṃdhi of *a* or *ā* with a following vowel and of other vowels with homogeneous ones, also to the vowel resulting from this Saṃdhi and its accent), Prāt.; ŚāṅkhŚr.; Pat.

Pra-ślesha, m. close contact or pressure, Amar.; coalescence (of vowels), Prāt.; Siddh.

प्रश्वस् *pra-√śvas*, P. -*śvasiti*, to breathe in, inhale, MBh.: Caus. -*śvāsayati*, to cause to breathe, ŚBr.; to comfort, console, Hariv. °**śvasitavya**, n. (impers.) recovery of breath i.e. recreation should be procured for (gen.) or by (instr.) or through or by means of (instr.), TaittUp. °**śvāsa**, m. breathing in, inhaling, Suśr.

प्रष्टव्य *prashṭavya*, °*ṭri*. See under *praśna*.

प्रष्टि *prá-shṭi*, m. (√1. *as*; cf. *abhi-shṭi*, *upa-sti*, *pari-shṭi*) 'being beyond or in front,' a horse harnessed by the side of other yoke-horses or in front of them, a side-horse or leader, RV.; AV.; Br.; a man at one's side, bystander, companion, RV.; Lāṭy.; a tripod (supporting a dish), TS., Sch. — **mat** (*prá°*), mfn. having side-horses (as a chariot), RV. — **vāhana** (*prá°*), mfn. (a chariot) drawn (also) by side-horses, yoked (at least) with 3 horses, ŚBr.; AitĀr. — **vāhin**, mfn. id., TBr.; TāṇḍBr.

प्रष्ठ *pra-shṭha*, mf(ī)n. (√*sthā*; cf. Pāṇ. viii, 3, 92) standing in front, foremost, principal, best, chief, Ragh.; Rājat.; m. a leader, conductor, Kuval.; a species of plant, L.; (*ī*), f. the wife of a leader or chief, L. — **tva**, n. the being in front, pre-eminence, superiority, Rājat. — **vah**, m. (strong -*vāh*, weak *prashṭhâuh*; nom. -*vāṭ*, Pāṇ. viii, 2, 31, Sch.) a side-horse, L.; a young bull or steer training for the plough, W.; (*prashṭhâuhī*), f. a cow for the first time with calf, L. (cf. *pashṭhavah*, °*thauhī*).

प्रष्ठिव् *pra-√shṭhiv*, P. -*shṭhīvati*, to spit out, ĀśvŚr.

प्रष्ठिवाहिन् *prashṭhi-vāhin*, w.r. for *prashṭi-v°*.

प्रष्णवैष्णव *prashṇa-vaishṇava*, w. r. for *praśna-v°*.

प्रस् *pras*, cl. 1. Ā. *prasate*, to extend, spread, diffuse, Dhātup. xix, 4; to bring forth young, Vop.

प्रसकल *pra-sakala*, mfn. very full (as a bosom), Śiś.

प्रसक्त *pra-sakta*, °*ti*. See under *pra-√sañj*.

प्रसक्षिन् *pra-sakshin*. See under *pra-√sah*.

प्रसङ्क्तव्य *pra-saṅktavya*. See under *pra-√sañj*.

प्रसंख्या *pra-saṃ-√khyā*, P. -*khyāti*, to count, enumerate, MBh.; to add up, calculate, ĀśvŚr.; MBh. °**saṃkhyā**, f. total number, sum, MBh.; reflection, consideration, KātyŚr. °**saṃkhyāna**, mfn. collecting or gathering (only for present needs), MBh. xiv, 2852, v.l. (Nīlak.); m. payment, liquidation, a sum of money, ib. iii, 10298 (Nīlak. 'a measure to mete out anything'); n. counting, enumeration, BhP.; reflection, meditation, MBh.; Tattvas.; reputation, renown, MBh. iii, 1382 (Nīlak.); -*para*, mfn. engrossed or absorbed in meditation, Kum.

प्रसङ्ग *pra-saṅga*. See under *pra-√sañj*.

प्रसंघ *pra-saṃgha*, m. a great multitude or number, MBh. vii, 8128 (v.l. *pra-varsha*).

प्रसच् *pra-√sac*, P. -*sishakti*, to pursue, RV. x, 27, 19.

प्रसंचक्ष् *pra-saṃ-√caksh*, Ā. -*cashṭe* (Pot. -*cakshīt*), to reckon up, recount, enumerate, Lāṭy.; to penetrate, investigate, Nyāyas., Sch.

प्रसञ्ज् *pra-√sañj*, P. Ā. -*sajati*, °*te*, (P.) to hang on, attach to (loc.), Lāṭy.; to hang with i.e. to provide or supply with (instr.), ŚBr.; to cling to (loc.), Daś.; to engage with any one (loc.) in a quarrel or dispute, ChUp.; (only ind. p. -*sajya*) to be attached to the world, BhP.; to result, follow, be the consequence of anything, Sarvad.; to cause to take place, Pat.; (Ā.) to attach one's self to (acc.), MBh.: Pass. -*sajyate* or -*sajjate* (°*ti*), to attach one's self, cling to, be devoted to or intent upon or occupied with (loc.), Mn.; MBh. &c.; to be in love (pr. p. -*sajjantī*), Hariv.; (-*sajjate*), to be the consequence of something else, result, follow, be applicable, Pat.; Bhāshāp.; Sarvad.: Caus. P. -*sañjayati*, to cause to take place, Naish.; Ā. -*sajjayate*, to attach to, stick in (loc.; with *na*, 'to fly through,' said of an arrow), R.

Pra-sakta, mfn. attached, cleaving or adhering or devoted to, fixed or intent upon, engaged in, occupied with (loc. or comp.), Mn.; MBh. &c.; clinging to the world, mundane, BhP.; being in love, enamoured, MBh.; Kāv.; (ifc.) supplied or provided with, R. (v.l. *pra-yukta*); resulting, following, applicable, Kāś.; Kathās.; Sarvad.; continual, lasting, constant, eternal, MBh.; Kāv. &c.; used, employed, W.; got, obtained, ib.; opened, expanded, ib.; contiguous, near, A.; (°*saktá*), w.r. for °*sattá*, AV.; ibc. and (*am*), ind. continually, incessantly, eternally, ever, Kāv.; -*dhī* or -*hṛidaya*, mfn. with heart or mind intent upon or occupied with (comp.), Var.; °*tâśru-mukha*, mf(ī)n. having the face wet with tears, R. °**saktavya**, mfn. to be attached to (loc.), Kathās. °**sakti**, f. adherence, attachment, devotion or addiction to, indulgence or perseverance in, occupation with (loc. or comp.), Mn.; Kir.; Kathās. (cf. *a-pras°* and *ati-pras°*); occurrence, practicability (°*tim pra-√yā*, 'to be practicable'), Rājat.; (in gram.) bearing upon, applicability (of a rule), RPrāt., Sch.; connection, association, W.; inference, conclusion, ib.; a topic of conversation, ib.; acquisition, ib. °**saṅktavya**, mfn. to be caused to take place, Pat.

Pra-saṅga, m. adherence, attachment, inclination or devotion to, indulgence in, fondness for, gratification of, occupation or intercourse with (loc., gen. or comp.), Mn.; MBh. &c. (*ena*, ind. assiduously, zealously, eagerly; cf. also below); evil inclination or illicit pursuit, Mn. ix, 5; union, connection (ifc. 'connected with,' e.g. *madhu-prasaṅga-madhu*, 'honey connected with or coming in the spring season'), Ratnâv. i, 17; (pl.) all that is connected with or results from anything, Kām.; occurrence of a possibility, contingency, case, event, ŚrS.; Mn.; Saṃk.; Pāṇ., Sch. (e.g. *ecaḥ pluta-prasaṅge*, 'in the event of a diphthong being prolated'); applicability, Vajras.; an occasion, incident, conjuncture, time, opportunity, MBh.; Kāv. &c. (ibc.; *ena*, *āt* and *atas*, ind. when the occasion presents itself, occasionally, incidentally; *prasaṅge kutrâpi*, 'on a certain occasion;' *amunā prasaṅgena*, *tat-prasaṅgena* or *etat-prasaṅge*, 'on that occasion'); mention of parents (?, = *guru-kīrtita*), Sāh.; (in dram.) a second or subsidiary incident or plot, W.; N. of a man, Kathās.; (pl.) of a Buddhistic school; -*nivāraṇa*, n. the prevention of (similar) cases, obviation of (like future) contingencies, Kull. on Mn. viii, 334; -*prôshita*, mfn. happening to be departed or absent, Daś.; -*ratnâkara*, m., -*ratnâvalī*, f. N. of wks.; -*vat*, mfn. occasional, incidental, Daś.; -*vaśāt*, ind. according to the time, as occasion may demand, MW.; -*vinivṛitti*, f. the non-recurrence of a case, Mn. viii, 368; -*sama*, m. (in Nyāya) the sophism that the proof too must be proved, Nyāyas.; Sarvad.; °*gânusaṅgena*, ind. by the way, by the by, Sāṃkhyas., Sch.; °*gâbharaṇa*, n. N. of a modern poetical anthology. °**saṅgin**, mfn. attached or devoted to (comp.), Ṛitus.; Śaṃk.; connected with, dependent on, belonging to, contingent, additional, MBh.; Suśr.; occurring, appearing, occasional, incidental, MBh.; Pat.; secondary, subordinate, non-essential, MBh.; °*gi-tā*, f. attachment, addiction to, intercourse with (comp.), MBh.; Tattvas. °**sajya**, mfn. to be attached to or connected with; applicable; -*tā*, f. applicability, Śaṃkar.; -*pratishedha*, m. the negative form of an applicable (positive) statement, Pat. (also °*sajyāyām pr°*, ib.; °*dha-tva*, n., Sāh.) °**sañjana**, n. attaching, uniting, combining, connecting, W.; applying, bringing into use, bringing to bear, giving scope or opportunity, introduction, ib. °**sañjayitavya**, mfn. = °*saṅktavya*, ĀpŚr., Sch.

प्रसद् *pra-√sad*, P. -*sīdati* (ep. also Ā. °*te*), to fall into the power of (acc.), MaitrS.; AitBr.; to settle down, grow clear and bright, become placid or tranquil (as the sea or sky; met. applied to the mind), MBh.; Kāv.&c.; to become clear or distinct, KaṭhUp.; Kām.; to become satisfied or pleased or glad, be gracious or kind (with gen. 'to favour;' with inf. 'to deign to;' Impv. often 'be so gracious, please'), Mn.; MBh.&c.; to be successful (as an action), Ragh.: Caus. -*sādayati* (m.c. also °*te*; Pass. -*sādyate*), to make clear, purify, Kāvyâd.; Kathās.; to make serene, gladden (the heart), Bhartṛ.; to render calm, soothe, appease, propitiate, ask a person (acc.) to or for (inf., dat., loc., *arthe* with gen., or *artham* ifc.), Mn.; MBh. &c. °**sattá**, mfn. satisfied, pleased, RV. v, 60, 1. °**satti**, f. clearness, brightness, purity, W.; graciousness, favour, Bālar.; Siṇhâs. °**sadman**, in *dīrghá-p°*, q. v. °**sanna**, mfn. clear, bright, pure (lit. and fig.), MBh.; Kāv. &c.; distinct, perspicuous, MBh.; Kām.; true, right, plain, correct, just, Mālav.; Mālatim.; placid, tranquil, R.; Var.; Āp.; soothed, pleased; gracious, kind, kindly disposed towards (with loc., gen., or acc. and *prati*), favourable (as stars &c.); gracious, showing favour (as a speech), MaitrUp.; MBh.; Kāv. &c.; m. N. of a prince, Hemac.; (*ā*), f. propitiating, pleasing, W.; spirituous liquor made of rice, Car.; Pat.; -*kalpa*, mfn. almost quiet, tolerably calm, Pañcat.; -*gātra-tā*, f. having tranquil limbs (one of the 80 minor marks of a Buddha), Dharmas. 84; -*caṇḍikā*, f. N. of a drama; -*candra*, m. N. of a prince, HPariś.; -*jala*, mfn. containing clear water, R.; -*tarka*, mfn. conjecturing right, Mālav.; -*tā*, f. brightness, clearness, purity, Suśr.; clearness of expression, perspicuity, Cat.; complacence, good humour, Kāv.; Rājat.; VP.; -*tva*, n. clearness, purity, MBh.; Ragh.; -*pāda*, m. or n. (?) N. of wk. by Dharma-kīrti; -*prāya*, mfn. rather plain or correct, Mālatim.; -*mukha*, mfn. 'placid-countenanced,' looking pleased, smiling, W.; -*rasa*, mfn. clear-juiced, Kpr.; -*rāghava*, n. N. of a drama by Jaya-deva; -*veṅkaṭêśvara-māhâtmya*, n. N. of a legend in the Bhavishyôttara-Purāṇa; -*salila*, mfn. = -*jala*, MBh.; °*sannâtman*, mfn. gracious-minded, propitious, MaitrUp.; °*sannêrā*, f. spirituous liquor made of rice, L.

Pra-sāda, m. (ifc. f. *ā*) clearness, brightness, pellucidness, purity (cf. *ambu-p°*), Up.; Kālid. &c.

(Nom. P. °sādati, to be clear or bright, Śatr.); clearness of style, perspicuity, Pratāp.; Kāvyâd.; Sāh.; brightness (of the face), Ragh.; calmness, tranquillity, absence of excitement, KaṭhUp.; Suśr.; Yogas.; serenity of disposition, good humour, MBh.; Suśr.; Ragh. &c.; graciousness, kindness, kind behaviour, favour, aid, mediation (°dāt, ind. through the kindness or by the favour of; °daṃ-√kṛi, to be gracious; cf. dush-p°, dṛik-p°), Gobh.; MBh.; Kāv. &c.; Kindness personified as a son of Dharma and Maitrī, BhP.; clarified liquor, a decoction, Car.; settlings, a residuum, ib.; free gift, gratuity, Ratnâv.; a propitiatory offering or gift (of food, = p°-dravya, prasādânna), L.; the food presented to an idol, or the remnants of food left by a spiritual teacher (which any one may freely appropriate to his own use), RTL. 69; 145 &c.; approbation, W.; well-being, welfare, W.; N. of a Comm. on the Prakriyā-kaumudī; -cintaka, w.r. for -vittaka, Bālar.; -dāna, n. a propitiatory gift, a gift in token of favour, gift of food by a superior, MW.; -paṭṭa, m. a turban of honour (worn as a token of royal favour), Var.; -paṭṭaka, n. a written edict of favour, Lokapr.; -parāṅmukha, mf(ī)n. not caring for any one's favour, Amar.; withdrawing f° from any one (gen.), Pañcat.; -pātra, n. an object of f°, Daś.; -puraga, mfn. inclined to f°, favourably inclined, MārkP.; -pratilabdha, m. N. of a son of Māra, Lalit.; -bhāj, mfn. being in favour, Sāṃkhyas., Sch.; -bhūmi, f. an object of f°, favourite, Hcar.; -mālā, f. N. of wk.; -vat, mfn. pleased, delighted; gracious, favourable, L. (-vatī-samādhi, m. a partic. Samādhi, Buddh.); -vitta, mf(ā)n. (Kād.; Kathās.; Rājat.; Bālar.) or -vittaka, mfn. (Kathās.) rich in favour, being in high f° with any one (gen. or comp.); m. a favourite, darling; -shaṭ-ślokī, f., -stava, m. N. of 2 Stotras; -su-mukha, mf(ī)n. inclined to favour (others 'having a clear or serene face'), Mālav.; Ragh.; -stha, mfn. abiding in serenity, kind, propitious; happy, W.; °sādântara, n. another (mark of) favour, MW.; °sādânna, n., see °sāda above; °sādī-√kṛi, to bestow as a mark of favour, bestow graciously, present (with gen. of person), Pañcat.; Kād.; Rājat. &c. **°sādaka**, mfn. clearing, rendering clear or pellucid, Mn.; gladdening, exhilarating, R.; propitiating, wishing to win any one's favour, ib. (cf. su-p°). **°sādana**, mf(ī)n. clearing, rendering clear (cf. ambu-p°, toya-p° &c.); calming, soothing, cheering, R.; Suśr.; BhP.; m. a royal tent, L.; (ā), f. service, worship, L.; n. clearing, rendering clear (netra-p°, 'administering soothing remedies to the eyes'), Suśr.; calming, soothing, cheering, gratifying (cf. śruti-p°), rendering gracious, propitiating (tvat-prasādanāt, 'for the sake of propitiating thee'), MBh.; Kāv. &c.; boiled rice, L.; w.r. for pra-sādhana, Hariv.; Mālav. **°sādanīya**, mfn. cheering, pleasing (cf. guru-p°), Lalit.; to be rendered gracious. **°sādayitavya**, mfn. to be rendered gracious towards (upari), Pañcat. **°sādita**, mfn. cleared, rendered clear (a-p°), Kāvyâd.; pleased, conciliated &c., MBh.; worshipped, W.; n. pl. kind words, Hariv. **°sādin**, mfn. clear, serene, bright (as nectar, the eyes, face &c.) Mālatīm.; Bālar.; clear, perspicuous (as a poem), Bālar.; (ifc.) calming, soothing, gladdening, pleasing, MBh.; showing favour, treating with kindness, MW. **°sādya**, mfn. to be rendered gracious, be propitiated, MBh.; R.; Sāh.; Bālar. **°sedivas**, mfn. one who has become pleased or propitiated, favourable, W.

प्रसन् pra-√san (only Ā. aor. 3. pl. -sishanta), to win, be successful, RV. x, 142, 2.

प्रसंधा pra-saṃ-√dhā, P. Ā. -dadhāti, -dhatte, to fix or fit (an arrow) to (a bow-string), MBh. **°saṃdhāna**, n. combination (e.g. of words in the Krama, q.v.), APrāt.; ib., Sch. **°saṃdhi**, m. N. of a son of Manu, MBh.

प्रसन्न pra-sanna &c. See p. 696, col. 3.

प्रसन्नतेयु prasannateyu(?) and prasanneyu (?), m. N. of two sons of Raudrāśva, VP.

प्रसभ pra-sabha, n. (prob. fr. √sabh = sah) N. of a variety of the Trishṭubh metre, Var.; ibc. = (am), ind. forcibly, violently, Mn.; MBh. &c. (cf. pra-sahya); exceedingly, very much, Ṛitus.; Śiś.; importunately, Bhag. **-damana**, n. forcible taming (of wild animals), Śak. **-haraṇa**, n. carrying off by force, violent seizure, Yājñ. **Prasabhôddhṛita**, mfn. torn up by force; °târi, mfn. one who has forcibly uprooted his enemies, Ragh.

प्रसमीक्ष् pra-sam-√īksh, Ā. -īkshate, to look at or upon, observe, perceive, see, Mn.; MBh. &c.; to wait for, BhP.; to reflect upon, consider, deliberate, ib.; to acknowledge, regard as (acc.), MBh. **°samīkshaṇa**, n. considering, deliberating, discussing, W. **°samīkshā**, f. deliberation, judgment, ib. **°samīkshita**, mfn. looked at or upon, observed, considered, MBh.; Suśr; regarded, declared, MBh. 1. **°samīkshya**, mfn. to be considered or weighed or discussed, W. 2. **°samīkshya**, ind. having looked at or considered, ŚvetUp.; -parîkshaka, mfn. one who investigates or examines deliberately, Car.

प्रसमीड् pra-sam-√īḍ (only inf. -īḍitum), to praise, celebrate, BhP.

प्रसयन pra-sayana. See pra-√1. si.

प्रसर pra-sara, pra-saraṇa. See pra-√sṛi.

प्रसर्ग pra-sarga, pra-sarjana. See pra-√sṛij.

प्रसर्प pra-sarpa &c. See pra-√sṛip.

प्रसल prasala, m. the cold season, winter, L. (v.l. praśala).

प्रसलवि pra-salavi, ind. towards the right side, ŚBr.; ŚāṅkhŚr. (opp. to apa-salavi; w.r. prasavi, ŚāṅkhBr.)

प्रसव 1. 2. 3. pra-sava. See pra-√3. su and pra-√1. 2. sū.

प्रसव्य 1. pra-savya. See vāja-pr°.

प्रसव्य 2. pra-savya, mfn. turned towards the left, to the left side (am, ind.; opp. to pra-dakshiṇa, q.v.), GṛŚrS.; R.; contrary, reverse, L.; favourable, L.

प्रसह् pra-√sah, Ā. -sahate (rarely P. °ti; ind. p. -sahya see below), to conquer, be victorious, RV.; AV.; to bear up against, be a match for or able to withstand, sustain, endure (acc.), MBh.; Kāv. &c.; to check, restrain, R.; to be able to (inf.), MBh. **°sakshin**, mfn. overpowering, victorious, RV. **°sáh** (°sâh), mfn. id., RV. **°saha**, mfn. (ifc.) enduring, withstanding, Kām.; m. endurance, resistance (see dush-pr°); a beast or bird of prey, Car.; Suśr.; (ā), f. Solanum Indicum, L. **°sahana**, m. a beast of prey, L.; n. resisting, overcoming, Pāṇ. i, 3, 33 (°ne √kṛi, g. sâkshād-ādi, where Kāś. pra-hasane); embracing, Kāvyâd., Sch. **°sahishṇu**, see a-pras°. 1. **°sahya**, mfn. to be conquered or resisted &c.; capable of being c° or r° (inf. with pass. sense), MBh. 2. **°sahya**, ind. having conquered or won, Mālav. i, 2; using force, forcibly, violently, Mn.; Gaut. &c.; exceedingly, very much, MBh.; R.; Mṛicch.; at once, without more ado, Kathās.; necessarily, absolutely, by all means (with na, 'by no means'), Mn.; Var.; BhP.; Kathās.; -kārin, mfn. acting with violence, MārkP.; -caura, m. 'violent thief,' a robber, plunderer, L.; -haraṇa, n. forcible abduction, robbing, plundering, MBh.; °hyôḍhā, f. married by force, ib. **°sahvan**, mfn. overpowering, defeating, Br.; ŚrS. **°sāha**, m. overpowering, defeating, force, violence (see a- and dush-pr°); controlling one's self, MW.

प्रसातिका prasātikā, f. pl. a kind of rice with small grains, MārkP. (praśāt°, Car.; cf. pra-śādhikā).

प्रसाद pra-sāda &c. See pra-√sad.

प्रसाध् pra-√sādh, Caus. -sādhayati, to reduce to obedience or subjection, subdue, TS.; Mn. &c.; to reduce to order, arrange, settle, AV.; Kām.; Ragh.; Suśr.; to adorn, decorate, Kāv.; Kathās.; to manage, perform, execute, accomplish, RV. &c. &c.; to gain, acquire, Vcar.; Pañcat.; to find out by calculation, Gaṇit.; to prove, demonstrate, Nīlak. **°sādhaka**, mf(ikā)n. (ifc.) adorning, beautifying, Vāsav.; MārkP.; accomplishing, perfecting, W.; cleansing, purifying, ib.; m. an attendant who dresses his master, valet de chambre, Kām.; Ragh.; (ikā), f. a lady's maid, Ragh.; wild rice, Bhpr. (cf. prasātikā). **°sādhana**, mf(ī)n. accomplishing, effecting, RV.; m. a comb, L.; (ī), f. id. (keśa-pr°), Suśr.; a partic. drug (= siddhi), L.; n. (ifc. f. ā) bringing about, perfecting, Nir.; arranging, preparing, Suśr.; embellishment, decoration, toilet and its requisites, Mn.; MBh. &c.; w.r. for °sādana; -vidhi, m. mode of decoration or embellishment, Kathās.; -viśesha, m. the highest decoration, most excellent ornament, Kālid. **°sādhita**, mfn. accomplished, arranged, prepared (a-pras°, su-pr°), Kathās.; Suśr.; proved, MW.; ornamented, decorated, W.; °dhitâṅga, mf(ī)n. having the limbs ornamented or decorated, MW. **°sādhya**, mfn. to be mastered or conquered, R.; accomplishable, practicable, W.; to be destroyed or defeated, ib.

प्रसामि pra-sāmí, ind. incompletely, partially, half, ŚBr.

प्रसार pra-sāra &c. See pra-√sṛi.

प्रसाह pra-sāha. See pra-√sah.

प्रसि pra-√1. si (only Ā. pf. -sishye, with pass. meaning), to bind = render harmless, Rājat. **°sayana**, n. used to explain pra-siti, Nir. vi, 12. 1. **°sita**, mfn. (for 2. see below) bound, fastened, W.; diligent, attentive, attached or devoted to, engrossed by, engaged in, occupied with (loc. or instr.; cf. Pāṇ. ii, 3, 44), Ragh.; Siddh.; lasting, continuous, SaddhP. 1. **°siti** (prá-), f. (for 2. see below) a net for catching birds, RV. iv, 4, 1 &c. (Nir.; Sāy.); a ligament, binding, fetter, L.

प्रसिच् pra-√sic, P. -siñcati, to pour out, shed, emit, AV. &c. &c.; to sprinkle, water, MBh.; Hariv.; to fill (a vessel), KaushUp.: Pass. -sicyate, to be poured out or flow forth, MBh.; Suśr.; to be watered i.e. refreshed, MBh.: Caus. -secayati, to pour into (loc.), Yājñ. **°sikta**, mfn. poured out, Uttarar.; Suśr.; (ifc.) sprinkled with, MBh. **°seka**, m. flowing forth, dropping, oozing, effusion, MBh.; Kāv.; Suśr.; emission, discharge, Ṛitus.; sprinkling, wetting, L.; exudation, resin, R.; running or watering of the mouth or nose, vomiting, nausea, Suśr.; (-tā, f. id., ŚārṅgS.); the bowl of a spoon or ladle, KātyŚr. **°sekin**, mfn. discharging a fluid, Suśr.; suffering from morbid flow of saliva, ib. **°secana**, n. (ifc. f. ā) the bowl of a spoon or ladle, ĀpŚr., Sch.; -vat, mfn. having a bowl or spout (for pouring out fluids), ĀpŚr.

प्रसित 2. prá-sita, mfn. (√2. si; cf. pra-√1. si above) darting along, RV.; n. pus, matter, L. 2. **°siti** (prá-), f. (for 1. see above) onward rush, onset, attack, assault, RV.; a throw, cast, shot, missile, VS.; TBr.; stretch, reach, extension, sphere, RV.; succession, duration, VS.; dominion, power, authority, influence, RV.

प्रसिध् pra-√2. sidh, P. Ā. -sedhati, °te, to drive on, RV.; TāṇḍBr.; Lāṭy.

प्रसिध् pra-√3. sidh, P. -sidhyati (rarely Ā. °te), to be accomplished or effected, succeed, Mn.; MBh. &c.; to result from (abl.), Mn. xii, 97; to be explained or made clear, Kāś. on Pāṇ. iii, 1, 122. **°siddha** (prá-), mfn. brought about, accomplished, Kum. (a-pras°); arranged, adorned (as hair), ib.; well known, notorious, celebrated, TS. &c. &c.; (ā), f. (in music) a partic. measure, Saṃgīt.; -kshatriya-prâya, mfn. consisting for the most part of renowned Kshatriyas, MW.; -tā, f. (Nīlak.), -tva, n. (Sarvad.) celebrity, notoriety. **°siddhaka**, m. N. of a prince descended from Janaka (son of Maru and father of Kṛitti-ratha), R. **°siddhi**, f. accomplishment, success, attainment, Mn.; Yājñ.; Kām.; BhP.; proof, argument, Kathās.; general opinion, publicity, celebrity, renown, fame, rumour, Var.; Kāv.; Kathās.; -mat, mfn. universally known, famous, Kathās.; -viruddha-tā, f. the state of being opposed to general opinion, Sāh. (= khyāti-v°); -hata, mfn. having no value, very trivial, Kpr.

प्रसिव् pra-√siv, P. -sīvyati, to sew up, ŚBr.

प्रसीदिका prasīdikā, f. a small garden, L. (v.l. prasedikā).

प्रसु pra-√3. su, Caus. -sāvayati, to cause continuous pressing (of Soma), Nidānas.

1. **Pra-savá**, m. (for 2. and 3. see p. 698, col. 1) the pressing out (Soma juice), RV.; ŚrS. **°savitra**, n. (prob.) a Soma press, Pāṇ. vi, 2, 144, Sch. **°sút**, mfn. streaming forth (as Soma from the press), SV.; f. (continued) pressing (of Soma), TāṇḍBr. **°suta** (prá-), mfn. pressed or pressing continuously, TS.; ŚBr.; ŚrS.; m. the S° so pressed; n. continued pressing of Soma, ChUp.; m. or n. a partic. high number (see mahā-pr°). **°suti**, f. a S° sacrifice, Hcat. **°suva**, m. = °sava above, ŚāṅkhBr.

प्रसुप् *pra-sup, pra-supta* &c. See under *pra-√svap.*

प्रसुश्रुत *pra-suśruta*, m. N. of a prince (son of Maru), Pur. (cf. *pra-śuśruka*).

प्रसुह्म *pra-suhma*, m. pl. N. of a people, MBh.

प्रसु *pra-√1. su*, P. *-suvati, -sauti* (Impv. *-suhi* with v.l. *-sūhi*, KātyŚr.), to set in motion, rouse to activity, urge, incite, impel, bid, command, RV.; AV.; Br.; to allow, give up to, deliver, AV.; Br.; ŚrS.; to hurl, throw, Bhaṭṭ., Sch.

2. **Prá-sava**, m. (for 1. *pra-√3. su*) setting or being set in motion, impulse, course, rush, flight, RV.; AitBr.; stimulation, furtherance, aid, RV.; AV.; Br. &c.; pursuit, acquisition, VS.; = next, TBr. 1. °**savitrí**, m. (for 2. see below) an impeller, exciter, vivifier, VS.; Br. 2. °**savin**, mfn. (for 2. see below) impelling, exciting, Pāṇ. iii, 2, 157. °**savītri**, m. = °*savitri*, RV. 1. °**sūti** (*prá-*), f. (for 2. see below) instigation, order, permission, TS.; TBr.; Kāṭh.

प्रसू *pra-√2. sū*, Ā. *-sūte, -sūyate* (rarely P. *-savati, -sauti*; once Pot. *-sunuyāt*, Vajracch.), to procreate, beget, bring forth, obtain offspring or bear fruit, produce, Br.; Mn.; MBh. &c.; (mostly Ā. *-sūyate*, rarely °*ti*) to be born or produced, originate, arise, Mn.; MBh. &c.

3. **Pra-savá**, m. (ifc. f. *ā*; for 1. 2. see above) begetting, procreation, generation, conception, parturition, delivery, birth, origin, VS. &c. &c.; augmentation, increase, MBh.; birthplace, ib.; Śaṃk.; (also pl.) offspring, posterity, Mn.; MBh. &c. (*kisalaya-pr°*, 'a young shoot,' Ragh.); a flower, MBh.; Kāv.; Suśr. (also n., R.); fruit, L.; *-karma-kṛit*, m. one who performs the act of begetting, begetter, MBh.; *-kāla*, m. the time of delivery or bringing forth, Var.; *-gṛiha*, n. a lying-in chamber, MW.; *-dharmin*, mfn. characterized by production, productive, prolific, ib.; *-bandhana*, n. the footstalk of a leaf or flower, L.; *-māsa*, m. the last month of pregnancy, MW.; *-vikāra*, m. a prodigy happening at the birth of a child, Var.; *-vedanā*, f. the pangs of childbirth, throes of labour, Pañcat.; *-samaya*, m. = *-kāla*, Var.; *-sthalī*, f. 'birthplace,' a mother, Mahān.; *-sthāna*, n. a receptacle for young, a nest, MW.; °*vôtthāna*, n. N. of the 17th Pariś. of the Yajur-veda; °*vônmukha*, mf(*ī*)n. expecting childbirth, about to be delivered, Ragh. °**savaka**, m. Buchanania Latifolia, L. °**savat**, mf(*antī*)n. bringing forth, bearing; (*antī*), f. a woman in labour, Mn. iv, 44. °**savana**, n. bringing forth, bearing children, fecundity, Hit. (v.l.) °**savāpitā**, f. delivered, Divyâv. 2. °**savitṛi**, m. (for 1. see *pra-√1. sū*) a begetter, father, Bālar.; Prasannar.; (*trī*), f. a mother, L.; bestowing progeny, MBh. 2. °**savin**, mfn. (for 1. see *pra-√1. sū*) bringing forth, bearing children, Megh.; MārkP.; Car.

Pra-sū, mfn. bringing forth, bearing, fruitful, productive, RV. &c. &c.; (ifc.) giving birth to (cf. *pitṛi-pr°*, *putrikā-pr°*, *strī-pr°*); f. a mother, Inscr.; L.; a mare, L.; a young shoot, tender grass or herbs, sacrificial grass, RV.; Br.; KātyŚr.; a spreading creeper, the plantain, L.; *-sū-mat* (AV.), *-sū-maya* (ĀpŚr.), *-sū-vara* (f. *varī*, RV.), mfn. furnished with flowers. °**sūkā**, f. a mare, L. °**sūta** (*prá-*), mf(*ā*)n. procreated, begotten, born, produced, sprung ('by' or 'from,' abl. or gen.; 'in,' loc. or comp.; cf. Pāṇ. ii, 3, 39), Up.; Mn.; MBh. &c.; m. pl. (or sg. with *gaṇa*) N. of a class of gods under Manu Cākshusha, Hariv.; MārkP.; n. a flower, L.; any productive source, MW.; (in Sāṃkhya) the primordial essence or matter, Tattvas.; (*ā*), f. a woman who has brought forth a child, recently delivered (also = finite verb), AV. &c. &c. 2. °**sūti**, f. (for 1. see *pra-√1. sū*) procreation, generation, bringing forth (children or young), laying (eggs), parturition, birth, Mn. iv, 84 (*-tas*); MBh.; Kāv. &c.; coming forth, appearance, growth (of fruit, flowers &c.), Kālid.; Prab.; a production, product (of plants or animals), MBh.; a procreator, father or mother, Hariv.; Var.; Ragh.; a child, offspring, progeny, Mn.; MBh. &c.; N. of a daughter of Maru and wife of Daksha, Pur.; *-ja*, n. 'birth-produced,' pain (resulting as a necessary consequence of birth), L.; *-vāyu*, m. air generated in the womb during the pangs of childbirth, MW. °**sūtikā**, f. recently delivered, Yājñ., Sch.; (ifc.) giving birth to (cf. *naśyat-pr°*); (a cow) that has calved, Cāṇ. (cf. *sakṛit-pr°*). °**sūna**, mfn. born, produced (= *-sūta* or *jāta*), L.; n. (ifc. *ā*) a flower, blossom, MBh.; Kāv. &c.; fruit, L.; *-bāṇa*, m. 'having f°s for arrows,' the god of love, Kām.; *-mālā*, f. a garland of f°s, Mālatīm.; *-varsha*, m. a shower of f°s (rained from heaven), BhP.; *-stabaka*, m. a bunch of blossoms or f°s, BhP.; °*nâñjali*, mfn. presenting a nosegay held in both hands opened and hollowed (= *pushpâñjali*), Cat.; °*nâśuga* (Naish.), °*nêshu* (L.), m. = °*na-bāṇa*. °**sūnaka**, m. a kind of Kadamba, L.; n. a flower, L. °**sūyat**, mf(*antī*)n. being born, MBh. xiii, 5687.

प्रसूका *pra-sūkā*. See col. 1.

प्रसूच् *pra-√sūc*, P. *-sūcayati*, to indicate, manifest, MBh.

प्रसृ *pra-√sṛi*, P. *-sisarti* (only Ved.) and *-sarati* (sometimes also Ā. °*te*), to move forwards, advance ('for' or 'against,' acc.), proceed (lit. and fig.), spring up, come forth, issue from (abl.), appear, rise, spread, extend, RV. &c. &c.; to break out (as fire, a disease &c.), MBh.; Pañcat. (v.l.); to be displaced (as the humours of the body), Suśr.; to be diffused (as odour), Kathās.; to pass, elapse (as night), Vikr.; to commence, begin, Bhartṛ.; Kathās. (also Pass., e.g. *prâsāri yajñah*, 'the sacrifice began,' ŚBr.); to prevail, hold good, take place, Sarvad.; to stretch out (hands), RV.; to agree, promise, Inscr.: Caus. *-sārayati*, to stretch out, extend, VS. &c. &c.; to spread out, expose (wares &c. for sale), Mn.; R. &c.; to open wide (eyes, mouth, &c.), Mṛicch.; BhP.; to diffuse, circulate, exhibit, Var.; Śaṃk.; to prosecute, transact, Kād.; (in gram.) to change a semivowel into the corresponding vowel, Pat.: Intens. (*-sasre*, °*rāte*, °*rāṇa*) to extend, be protracted, last, RV.

Pra-sara, m. (ifc. f. *ā*) going forwards, advance, progress, free course, coming forth, rising, appearing, spreading, extension, diffusion, Kālid.; Kād.; Śaṃk. &c.; range (of the eye), Amar.; prevalence, influence, Śak.; boldness, courage, Mṛicch.; a stream, torrent, flood, Gīt.; BhP.; (in med.) morbid displacement of the humours of the body, Suśr.; multitude, great quantity, Śiś.; a fight, war, L.; an iron arrow, L.; speed, L.; affectionate solicitation, L.; (*ā*), f. Paederia Foetida, L.; n. (in music) a kind of dance, Saṃgīt.; *-yuta*, mfn. possessing extension, extensive (as a forest), R. °**saraṇa**, n. going forth, running away, escaping, Mṛicch.; (in med.) = °*sara*, Suśr.; holding good, prevailing, TPrāt., Sch.; complaisance, amiability, BhP.; spreading over the country to forage, L.; = next, L. °**saraṇi** (or °*ṇī*), f. surrounding an enemy, L. °**sāra**, m. spreading or stretching out, extension, Suśr.; Kull.; a trader's shop, Nalac.; opening (the mouth), Vop.; raising (dust), Bālar.; = prec., L. °**sāraṇa**, n. (fr. Caus.) stretching or spreading out, extending, diffusing, displaying, developing, Br.; Bhāshāp.; Suśr.; augmentation, increase, Kām.; changing a semivowel into a vowel, APrāt., Sch. (cf. *sam-pras°*); = °*saraṇi*, L.; spreading over the country for collecting forage, L.; (*ī*), f. = °*saraṇi*, L.; Paederia Foetida, L. °**sāraṇin**, mfn. containing a semivowel liable to be changed into a vowel, Pāṇ., Vārtt. °**sārita**, mfn. (fr. Caus.) held forth, stretched out, expanded, spread, diffused, Mn.; MBh.; Kāv. &c.; laid out, exhibited, exposed (for sale), R.; published, promulgated, Var.; Śaṃk.; *-gātra*, mfn. with outstretched limbs (*su-pr°*), Sāh.; *-bhoga*, mfn. (a serpent) with expanded coils, Pañcat.; °*tâgra*, mfn. (fingers) with extended tips, Cat.; °*tâṅguli*, mfn. (a hand) with extended fingers, L. °**sārin**, mfn. coming forth, issuing from (comp.), Śak.; spreading, extending (trans. and intrans.; esp. stretching one's self out in singing), PārGṛ. (cf. *vāk-pras°*); Saṃgīt.; extending over (comp.), Sāh. (°*ri-tva*, n.); going along gently, gliding, flowing, creeping, W.; (*iṇī*), f. (in music) N. of a Śruti, Saṃgīt.; Paederia Foetida, Bhpr.; Mimosa Pudica, L.; N. of wk. 1. °**sārya**, ind. (fr. Caus.) having stretched out or put forth &c., MBh. 2. °**sārya**, mfn. (fr. Caus.) to be changed into a vowel, Pat.

Prá-sṛita, mfn. come forth, issued from (abl. or comp.), ŚvetUp.; MBh.; Kāv. &c.; displaced (as the humours of the body), Suśr.; resounding (as tones), Kathās. (n. impers. with instr. 'a sound rose from,' ib.); held or stretched out, TBr.; Bhartṛ.; Kathās.; wide-spreading, MuṇḍUp.; Bhag.; extending over or to (loc.), Kathās.; intent upon, devoted to (comp.), R.; Vajracch.; prevailing, ordinary, ŚBr.; Kāṭh.; intense, mighty, strong, Uttarar.; Daś.; Kathās.; set out, departed, fled, Daś.; Kathās.; w.r. for *pra-śrita*, humble, modest, quiet, MBh.; R. &c.; m. the palm of the hand stretched out and hollowed as if to hold liquids, GṛŚrS.; (also n., L.) a handful (as a measure = 2 Palas), ŚBr. (also *-mātra*, n.); ŚrS.; Suśr.; pl. N. of a class of deities under the 6th Manu, VP.; (*ā*), f. the leg, L.; n. what has sprung up or sprouted, grass, plants, vegetables, MBh.; Pañcar.; agriculture (prob. w.r. for *pra-mṛita*), L.; *-ja*, m. N. of a partic. class of sons, MBh.; *-mātra*, n., see above; °*tâgra-pradāyin*, mfn. offering the best of all that has grown, MBh.; °*tâgra-bhuj*, mfn. eating the best &c., ib. °**sṛiti** (*prá-*), f. streaming, flowing, Śak.; (successful) progress, TĀr.; extension, diffusion, MBh.; swiftness, haste, Nīlak.; the palm of the hollowed hand, Kauś.; a handful as measure (= 2 Palas), Yājñ.; BhP.; *-m-paca*, see *nīvāra-pr°*; *-yāvaka*, m. eating groats made of not more than a handful of barley, Gaut. °**sṛitvara**, mfn. breaking forth, Bhām. °**sṛimara**, mfn. streaming forth, Bhartṛ.; being at the head of (gen.), Hcar.

प्रसृज् *pra-√sṛij*, P. *-sṛijati* (aor. P. *-asrāk*, Ā. *-asṛikshata*), to let loose, dismiss, send off to (acc.), RV. &c. &c.; to give free course to (anger &c., with acc.), MBh.; to stretch out (the arms), RV.; to scatter, sow, MārkP.; to engage in a quarrel with (loc.), MBh. (prob. w.r. for *pra-sajati*): Pass. *-sṛijyate*, to go forth or out, leave home, Gobh.; Lāṭy.: Desid. *-sisṛikshati*, to wish to dismiss or send off, ŚāṅkhBr.

Pra-sargá (or °*sárga*), m. pouring or flowing forth, RV.; dismissal, ŚāṅkhŚr. °**sarjana**, mf(*ī*)n. darting forth, Kauś.

Pra-sṛishṭa, mfn. let loose, dismissed, set free, MBh.; having free course, uncontrolled, ib.; Car.; given up, renounced, Hariv. (*-vaira*, mfn. 'one who has given up enmity,' ib.); hurt, injured, MW.; w.r. for *pra-mṛishṭa*, R.; (*ā*), f. pl. (prob.) a partic. movement in fighting, MBh. (= *sarvâṅga-saṃśleshaṇa*, VP., Sch.)

प्रसृप् *pra-√sṛip*, P. *-sarpati*, to creep up to, glide into (acc.), RV.; VS.; Br.; ŚrS.; to advance, proceed, move towards (acc.), Vait.; MBh. &c.; to stream or break forth, MBh.; Śiś.: to set in (as darkness), Kathās.; to spread, extend, be diffused, Śatr.; Uttarar.; to set to work, act, proceed in a certain way, Kām.; Kathās.; to advance, progress, Bhaṭṭ.

Pra-sarpa, m. going to the part of the sacrificial enclosure called the Sadas, MBh. (= *agni-visarjana*, Nīlak.); n. N. of a Sāman, ĀrshBr. °**sarpaka**, m. an assistant who is under the superintendence of the Ṛitvij or a mere spectator at a sacrifice (so designated from entering the Sadas; cf. prec.), ŚrS. °**sárpaṇa**, n. going forwards, entering (loc.), MBh.; = °*sarpa*, ĀśvŚr.; a place of refuge, shelter, RV. °**sarpita**, mfn. (fr. Caus.) crawling along, Ṛitus. °**sarpin**, mfn. coming forth, issuing from (comp.), Śak. (v.l.); creeping along, crawling away, Var.; going to the Sadas (cf. °*sarpaka*), ĀśvŚr. °**sṛipta**, mfn. spread, diffused, Uttarar.; = °*sarpaka*, KātyŚr.

प्रसृमर *pra-sṛimara*. See *pra-√sṛi*.

प्रसृष्ट *pra-sṛishṭa*. See *pra-√sṛij*.

प्रसेक *pra-seka, pra-secana* &c. See under *pra-√sic*, p. 697.

प्रसेदिका *prasedikā*, v.l. for *prasīdikā*, q.v.

प्रसेदिवस् *pra-sedivas*. See *pra-√sad*, p. 696.

प्रसेन 1. *pra-sena*, m. or n. (?), °*nā*, f. a kind of jugglery, VarBṛS., Sch.

प्रसेन 2. *pra-sena*, m. N. of a prince (son of Nighna or Nimna), Hariv.; Pur.; of a king of Ujjayinī (succeeded by Vikramârka or Vikramâditya), Inscr.

Prasena-jit, m. N. of sev. princes (esp. of a sovereign of Śrāvastī contemporary with Gautama Buddha, MWB. 407), MBh.; R.; Hariv.; Pur. &c.

प्रसेव *pra-seva*, m. (√*siv*) a sack or a leather bottle, L.; the damper on the neck of a lute, L.

Pra-sevaka, m. a sack, bag, Suśr.; Nalac.; a damper (= prec.), L.; (*ikā*), f., see *carma-prasevikā*.

प्रस्कण्व *prá-s-kaṇva*, m. N. of a Vedic Ṛishi with the patr. Kāṇva (author of RV. i, 44–50; viii, 49; ix, 95; according to BhP. grandson of Kaṇva), RV.; Pāṇ.; Nir. &c.; pl. the descendants of Praskaṇva, BrahmaP.

प्रस्कन्द् *pra-√skand*, P. *-skandati* (ind. p. *-skandya* or *-skadya*), to leap forth or out or up or down, TS.; Br.; MBh. &c.; to gush forth (as tears), Gaut.; to fall into (acc.), R.; to fall upon, attack, MBh.; to shed, spill, Br.; Up.: Caus. *-skandayati*, to cause to flow (a river; others 'to cross'), MBh.; Hariv.; to pour out (as an oblation), MBh. °**skanda**, m. a kind of root, MBh. (v.l.) °**skandana**, mfn. leaping forward, attacking (said of Śiva), MBh.; one who has diarrhoea, Car.; n. leaping over or across (comp.), ĀpŚr., Sch.; voiding excrement, L.; a purgative, Car. °**skandikā**, f. diarrhoea, Car. °**skandin**, mfn. leaping into (comp.), GopBr.; attacking, daring, bold, Jātakam.; m. N. of a man, L. °**skanna**, mfn. shed, spilt, MBh.; R.; lost, gone, BhP.; having attacked or assailed, MBh.; m. a transgressor, sinner, one who has violated the rules of his caste or order, W.

प्रस्कुन्द् *pra-skunda*, m. a support (?), MBh. v, 2700 ('an altar or elevated floor of a circular shape,' Nīlak.)

प्रस्खल् *pra-√skhal*, P. *-skhalati*, to stagger forwards, reel, totter, stumble, tumble, MBh.; Kāv. &c. °**skhalat**, mfn. reeling, tottering, Kathās.; °*lad-gati*, mfn. with a tottering step, ib. °**skhalana**, n. the act of stumbling, reeling, falling, BhP.; Suśr. °**skhalita**, mfn. staggering, stumbling, MBh.; one who has failed, Kām.

प्रस्तन् *pra-√stan*, only Caus. *-stanayati*, to thunder forth, RV.

प्रस्तब्ध *prá-stabdha*, mfn. (√*stambh*) stiff, rigid, ŚBr.; Suśr.; *-gātra*, mfn. having stiff or rigid limbs, Suśr. °**stambha**, m. becoming stiff or rigid, ib.

प्रस्तर *pra-stara* &c. See *pra-√stṛi*.

प्रस्तव *pra-stava* &c. See *pra-√stu*.

प्रस्तीत *pra-stīta* or *pra-stīma*, mfn. (√*styai*; see Pāṇ. viii, 2, 54) crowded together, swarming, clustering, W.; sounded, making a noise, ib.

प्रस्तु *pra-√stu*, P. *-stauti* (in RV. also Ā. *-stavate*, with act. and pass. sense, and 1. sg. *-stushe*), to praise before (anything else) or aloud, RV. &c. &c.; to sing, chant (in general, esp. said of the Prastotṛi), Br.; Lāṭy.; ChUp.; to come to speak of, introduce as a topic, Prab.; Hit.; BhP.; to undertake, commence, begin, Mālav.; Dhūrtas.; Bhaṭṭ.; to place at the head or at the beginning, Sarvad.: Caus. *-stāvayati*, to introduce as a topic, suggest, MBh.; Mālatīm.

Pra-tushṭushu, mfn. (fr. Desid.) wishing to praise, W.; wishing to begin, MW.

Pra-stava, m. a hymn of praise, chant, song, MārkP.; a favourable moment (cf. *a-pr°*), R.

Pra-stāva, m. introductory eulogy, the introduction or prelude of a Sāman (sung by the Pra-stotṛi), Br.; Lāṭy.; ChUp.; the prologue of a drama (= *prastāvanā*), Hariv.; introducing a topic, preliminary mention, allusion, reference, Kāv.; Pañcat.; the occasion or subject of a conversation, topic, ib.; occasion, opportunity, time, season, turn, convenience, ib.; Kathās.; Hit. (*e* or *eshu*, on a suitable occasion, opportunity; *ena*, incidentally, occasionally, suitably; with *tava*, at your convenience); beginning, commencement, Pañcat.; Hit.; sport, ease (= *helā*), L.; N. of a prince (son of Udgītha), BhP.; *-krameṇa*, ind. by way of introduction, Hit.; *-cintāmaṇi*, m., *-taraṃgiṇī*, f. N. of wks.; *-tas*, ind. on the occasion of (*kathā-pr°*, in course of conversation), Kathās.; *-pāṭhaka*, m. = *vaitālika*, the herald or bard of a king, Nalac.; *-muktâvalī*, f. N. of wk.; *-yajña*, m. a topic of conversation to which each person present offers a contribution (as at a sacrifice), MW.; *-ratnâkara*, m., *-śloka*, m. pl. N. of wks.; *-sadṛiśa*, mf(*ī*)n. suited to the occasion, appropriate, seasonable, Hit.; *-sūtra*, n. N. of wk.; °*vânugatam*, ind. on a suitable occasion, Pañcat.; °*vântara-gata*, mfn. occupied with something else, Jātakam. °**stāvanā**, f. sounding forth, blazing abroad, Daś.; introduction, commencement, beginning, preface, exordium, MBh.; Mālav.; Mcar.; a dramatic prologue, an introductory dialogue spoken by the manager and one of the actors (of which several varieties are enumerated, viz. the Udghāṭyaka, Kathôdghāta, Prayogâtiśaya, Pravartaka, and Avalagita), Kālid.; Ratnâv.; Sāh.; Pratāp. &c. °**stāvita**, mfn. (fr. Caus.) caused to be told or related, mentioned, Mālatīm. °**stāvya**, mfn. (fr. Caus.) to be preluded or introduced with a Prastāva (as a Sāman), Lāṭy.

Prá-stuta, mfn. praised, TS.; Br.; proposed, propounded, mentioned, introduced as a topic or subject under discussion, in question, MBh.; Kāv. &c.; commenced, begun, R.; Mālav.; Hit.; (with inf., one who has c° or b°, Kathās.); Rājat.; ready, prepared, W.; happened, ib.; made or consisting of, ib.; approached, proximate, ib.; done with effort or energy, ib.; n. beginning, undertaking, Mālatīm.; (in rhet.) the chief subject-matter, that which is the subject of any statement or comparison (= *upameya*; cf. IW. 109, 457, and °*tâṅkura*); *-tva*, n. the being a topic under discussion, Kull.; *-yajña*, mfn. prepared for a sacrifice, MW.; °*tâṅkura*, m. a figure of speech, allusion by the mention of any passing circumstance to something latent in the hearer's mind, Kuval. °**stuti** (*prá-*), f. praise, eulogium, RV.; ChUp.

Pra-stotṛi, m. N. of the assistant of the Udgātṛi (who chants the Prastāva), Br.; ŚrS.; MBh. &c.; *-prayoga*, m., *-sāman*, n. N. of wks. °**stotrīya**, mfn. relating to the Prastotṛi, Lāṭy., Sch.

प्रस्तुभ् *pra-√stubh* (only pr. p. Ā. *-stubhānā*, with pass. sense), to urge on with shouts, RV.: Caus. *-stobhayati*, to greet with shouts, BhP.; to scoff, deride, insult, ib. °**stobha**, m. allusion or reference to (gen.), BhP.; du. (with *Rajer Āṅgirasasya*) N. of 2 Sāmans, ĀrshBr.

प्रस्तुम्प् *pra-s-√tump*, P. *-tumpati*, g. *pāraskarâdi*.

प्रस्तृ *pra-√stṛi*, P. Ā. *-stṛiṇoti*, *-stṛiṇute* or *-stṛiṇāti*, *-stṛiṇīte*, to spread, extend (trans. and intrans.), AV.; ŚBr.; Kauś.; (with *giraḥ*) to pour out i. e. utter words, speak, Naish.

Pra-stará, m. (ifc. f. *ā*) anything strewed forth or about, a couch of leaves and flowers, (esp.) a sacrificial seat, RV. &c. &c.; (ifc.) a couch of any material, MBh.; a flat surface, flat top, level, a plain, Mn.; MBh.; R.; a rock, stone, Kāv.; Hit.; a gem, jewel, L.; a leather bag, Mṛicch., Sch.; a paragraph, section, Cat.; a tabular representation of the long and short vowels of a metre, W.; musical notation, ib.; pl. N. of a people, R. (v. l. for *pra-cara*); *-ghaṭanôpakaraṇa*, n. an instrument for breaking or splitting stones, Hit.; *-bhājanā*, n. a substitute for sacrificial grass, ŚBr.; *-sveda*, m. and *-svedana*, n. inducing perspiration by lying on a straw-bed, Car.; °*re-shṭhá* (or *-shṭhā́*), mfn. being on a couch or bed, VS. °**staraṇa**, m. (or *ā*, f.) a couch, seat, Hariv. (cf. *rukma-pr°*). °**stariṇī**, f. Elephantopus Scaber, L.

Pra-stāra, m. (ifc. f. *ā*) strewing, spreading out, extension (also fig. = abundance, high degree), MBh.; Kāv.; a litter, bed of straw, Hariv.; a layer, Śulbas.; a flight of steps (leading down to water), MBh.; a flat surface, plain, Hariv. (v. l. °*stara*); a jungle or wood overgrown with grass, L.; a process in preparing minerals, Cat.; a representation or enumeration of all the possible combinations of certain given numbers or of short and long syllables in a metre, Col.; (in music) a kind of measure, Saṃgīt.; N. of a prince (son of Udgītha), VP. (prob. w. r. for *prastāva*); *-cintāmaṇi*, m. N. of wk.; *-paṅkti*, f. a kind of metre, RPrāt.; *-pattana*, n. N. of wk. °**stārin**, mfn. spreading out, extending to (comp.); n. a partic. disease of the white of the eye, Suśr.

Pra-stira, m. a bed or couch made of flowers and leaves, L. °**stīrṇa** (*prá-*), mfn. spread out, extended, ŚBr.; flat (as the tip of the tongue), AV. °**stṛita**, w. r. for °*mṛita*, L.

प्रस्था *pra-√sthā*, P. *-tishṭhati* (rarely Ā. °*te*), to stand or rise up (esp. before the gods, an altar &c.), RV.; TS.; VS.; to advance towards (acc.), ŚBr.; ŚāṅkhŚr.; (Ā.; cf. Pāṇ. i, 3, 22) to be awake, MBh.; (Ā., m. c. also P.) to set out, depart from (abl.), proceed or march to (acc. with or without *prati*) or with a view to or in order to (dat. or inf.), ĀśvGṛ.; MBh.; Kāv. &c.; (with *ākāśe*) to move or abide in the open air, R.: Caus. *-sthāpayati*, to put aside, AV.; to send out, send to (acc. with or without *prati*) or for the purpose of (dat. or loc.), send away or home, dispatch messengers &c., dismiss, banish, MBh.; Kāv. &c.; drive, urge on (horses), Kum.: Desid. Ā. *-tishṭhāsate*, to wish to set out, Śaṃk.; Bhaṭṭ.

Pra-stha, mfn. going on a march or journey, going to or abiding in (cf. *vana-pr°*); stable, firm, solid, W.; expanding, spread, ib.; m. n. table-land on the top of a mountain, MBh.; Kāv. &c.; a level expanse, plain (esp. at the end of names of towns and villages; cf. *indra-*, *oshadhi-*, *karīra-pr°*, and see Pāṇ. iv, 2, 110); a partic. weight and measure of capacity (= 32 Palas or = ¼ of an Āḍhaka; or = 16 Palas = 4 Kuḍavas = ¼ of an Āḍhaka; or = 2 Śarāvas; or = 6 Palas; or = $\frac{1}{16}$ of a Droṇa), MBh.; Kāv.; Suśr. &c.; m. N. of a monkey, R.; *-kusuma* or *-pushpa*, m. 'flowering on mountain-tops,' a species of plant, a variety of Tulasī or basil, L.; *-m-paca*, mf(*ā*)n. cooking the amount of a Prastha (said of a cooking utensil capable of containing one P°), Pāṇ. iii, 2, 33, Sch.; *-vat*, m. a mountain, L. °**sthā́**, = °*stha* in *-vat*, mfn. having a platform, AV.; (*vatī*), f. N. of a river, Hariv.

Pra-sthāna, n. setting out, departure, procession, march (esp. of an army or assailant), MBh.; Kāv. &c.; walking, moving, journey, advent, ib.; sending away, dispatching, Yājñ.; departing this life, dying (cf. *mahā-pr°*); religious mendicancy, MBh.; a way to attain (any object), course, method, system, Madhus.; KātyŚr., Sch.; a sect, Sarvad.; an inferior kind of drama (the character of which are slaves and outcasts), Sāh.; starting-point, place of origin, source, cause (in *jñāna-pr°*, N. of wk.); *-trayabhāshya*, n. N. of wk.; *-dundubhi*, m. a drum giving the signal for marching, Kād.; *-bheda*, m., *-ratnâkara*, m. N. of wks.; *-vat*, ind. as in setting forth, as on a departure, Var.; *-viklava-gati*, mfn. one whose step falters in walking, Śak.; *-vighna*, m. an obstacle to proceeding or to sending anything (*-kṛit*, mfn. causing an obst° &c.), Yājñ.; non-attendance at a festival, impeding its taking place, W.; °*naka*, n. setting out, departure, Nalac.; °*nâvalī*, f. N. of wk.; °*nika*, mfn., see *cátush-pr°*; also w. r. for *prâsthānika*; °*nīya*, mfn. belonging or relating to a departure, Lāṭy. °**sthāpana**, n. (fr. Caus.) causing to depart, sending away, dismissing, dispatching, MBh. (also *ā*, f.); Kāv. &c. (with *diśaḥ*, 'sending into all quarters of the world,' R.); *dhvani-pr°*, 'giving currency to an expression,' Sāh. °**sthāpanīya**, mfn. (fr. Caus.) to be sent or dispatched, W.; to be carried or driven off, ib. °**sthāpita**, mfn. (fr. Caus.) sent away, dismissed, dispatched, Kum.; held, celebrated (as a feast), Divyâv. °**sthāpya**, mfn. (fr. Caus.) to be sent away or dispatched, MBh. °**sthāyin**, mfn. setting forth, departing, marching, going, Kathās. (cf. g. *gamy-ādi*). °**sthāyīya** and **-sthāyya**, in *sākam-sth°*, q. v. °**sthā́vat**, see above under *pra-stha*. °**sthāvan**, mfn. swift, rapid, RV.

Prasthika, mfn. (fr. *pra-stha*), see *ardha-pr°*; (*ā*), f. the sounding-board of a lute, Harav., Sch.; (prob.) Hibiscus Cannabhinus, Bhpr.

Prá-sthita, mfn. set forth, prepared, ready (as sacrifice), RV.; Br.; ŚrS.; rising, upright, RV.; standing forth, prominent, AV.; appointed, installed, R.; set out, departed, gone to (acc. with or without *prati*, dat. or loc.) or for the purpose of (dat.), MBh.; Kāv. &c.; (*-vat*, mfn. = *pra-tasthe*, 'he has set out,' Kathās.); (ifc.) reaching to, Śak. vii, $\frac{4}{5}$ (v. l. *prati-shṭhita*); (*am*), impers. a person (instr.) has set out, BhP.; n. setting out, going away, departure, Bhartṛ.; N. of partic. Soma vessels (see next); *-yājyā*, f. a verse pronounced on offering the Prasthita vessels, ŚrS. (*-homa*, m. the oblation connected with it, Vait.); °**sthiti**, f. setting out, departure, march, journey, Kād. °**stheya**, n. (impers.) it ought to be set out, MBh.

प्रस्नव *pra-snava*, *pra-snāvin*. See under *pra-√snu*.

प्रस्ना *pra-√snā*, P. *-snāti*, to enter the water (with or without an acc.), RV.; MaitrS.; Br.: Caus. *-snāpayati*, to bathe (intrans.) in (acc.), RV.; AV. °**sna**, m. a bath, vessel for bathing, L. °**snapita**, mfn. (fr. Caus.) bathed, AV. °**snātṛi**, m. one who bathes, a bather, Nir. °**snéya**, mfn. suitable for bathing, ŚBr.; Nir.

प्रस्निग्ध *pra-snigdha*, mfn. (√*snih*) very oily or greasy, Śak.; very soft or tender, Ragh.

प्रस्नु *pra-√snu*, P. Ā. *-snauti*, *-snute*, to emit fluid, pour forth, flow, drip, distil, TS.; Kathās.; (Ā.) to yield milk (aor. *prâsnoshṭa*), Pāṇ. iii, 1, 89, Sch.: Desid. *-susnūshishyate*, vii, 2, 36, Vārtt. 2, Pat.

Pra-snava, m. (often v. l. °*srava*) a stream or flow (of water, milk &c.), MBh.; Hariv.; pl. tears, MBh.; urine, ib.; *-saṃyukta*, mfn. flowing in streams, gushing forth (tears), MBh. °**snavana**, n. emitting fluid, ĀpŚr., Sch. °**snavitrīya**, Nom. P. °*yati* = *prasnavitṝvâcarati*, Pat. °**snāvin**, mfn. (ifc.) dropping, pouring forth, Nir.

Pra-snuta, mfn. yielding milk, MBh.; R. &c.; *-stanī*, f. having breasts that distil milk (through excess of maternal love), MW.

प्रस्नुषा *pra-snushā*, f. the wife of a grandson, MBh.

प्रस्पन्द् *pra-√spand*, Ā. *-spandate* (ep. also P. °*ti*), to quiver, throb, palpitate, MBh.; Ragh.; Suśr. °**spandana**, n. quivering, trembling, throbbing, Suśr.

प्रस्पर्ध् *pra-√spardh*, Ā. *-spardhate*, to emulate, compete, vie with (instr. or loc.) or in (loc.), R.; Hariv. °**spardhin**, mfn. (ifc.) rivalling with, equalling, Mcar.

प्रस्फार *pra-sphāra*, mfn. (√*sphar*) swollen, puffed up, self-conceited, Nalac.

प्रस्फिज् *pra-sphij*, mfn. large-hipped, Pat.

प्रस्फुट् *pra-√sphuṭ*, P. *-sphuṭati*, to burst open, be split or rent, MBh.; R.: Caus. *-sphoṭayati*, to cleave through, split, pierce, Hariv.; Kathās.; to slap or clap the arms, MBh. °**sphuṭa**, mfn. cleft open, burst, expanded, blown, L.; divulged, published, known, open, evident, clear, plain, Kāv.; Pur.; Kathās. &c.; °**sphoṭaka**, m. N. of a Nāga, L. °**sphoṭana**, n. splitting, bursting (intrans.), Var.; opening, expanding, causing to blow or bloom, L.; making evident or manifest, L.; striking, beating, L.; winnowing corn, a winnowing basket, L.; wiping away, rubbing out, L.

प्रस्फुर् *pra-√sphur*, P. *-sphurati* (pr. p. Ā. *-sphuramāṇa*, MBh.), to spurn or push away, AV.; to become tremulous, throb, quiver, palpitate, RV. &c. &c.; to glitter, sparkle, flash, shine forth (lit. and fig.), Hariv.; Kāv.; Kathās.; to be displayed, become clear or visible, appear, Kāv.; Var. °**sphurita**, mfn. become tremulous, quivering, vibrating, MBh.; Kāv. &c. (°*tâdhara*, mfn. one whose lower lip quivers, MBh.); clear, evident, L.

प्रस्फुलिङ्ग *pra-sphuliṅga*, m. or n. (?) a glittering spark, Mcar.

प्रस्मि *pra-√smi*, Ā. *-smayate* (ep. P. pr. p. *-smayat*), to burst into laughter, Nir.; MBh.; Hariv.

प्रस्मृ *pra-√smṛi*, P. *-smarati*, to remember, MBh.; to forget (Pass. *-smaryate*), Bālar. °**smartavya**, mfn. to be forgotten, ib. °**smṛita**, mfn. forgotten, Naish. °**smṛiti**, f. forgetting, forgetfulness, W.

प्रस्यन्द् *pra-√syand*, P. Ā. *-syandati*, °*te* (often w. r. for *-spand*), to flow forth, run away, dart, fly, RV.; GṛS.; MBh.; to drive off (in a carriage), ŚBr.: Caus. *-syandayati*, to make flow, MBh. °**syanda**, m. flowing forth, trickling out, L. °**syandana**, n. id., MBh.; exudation, Rājat. °**syándin**, mfn. oozing forth, ŚBr.; ĀpŚr.; MBh.; shedding (tears), Ratnâv.; m. a shower of rain, Gaut.

प्रस्रंस् *pra-√sraṇs*, Ā. *-sraṇsate*, to fall down, miscarry (said of the fetus), Suśr. °**sraṇsa**, m. falling down or asunder, Br. °**sraṇsana**, n. a dissolvent, Car. °**sraṇsin**, mfn. letting fall, dropping, miscarrying, Suśr.

प्रस्रु *pra-√sru*, P. *-sravati* (rarely Ā. °*te*), to flow forth, flow from (abl.), AV. &c. &c.; to flow with, let flow, pour out (acc.), MBh.; Kāv. &c.: Caus. Ā. *-srāvayate*, to make water, ŚBr.

Pra-srava, m. (often v. l. °*snava*) flowing forth, MBh.; Kāv. &c.; a stream, flow, gush (lit. and fig.), ib.; a flow of milk (loc. 'when the m° flows from the udder'), Mn. (esp. v, 130); MBh. &c.; (pl.) gushing tears, MBh.; (pl.) urine, ib. (v. l.); (pl.) morbid matter in the body, Car.; the overflow of boiling rice, L.; n. a waterfall, R. (B.); *-yukta*, mfn. flowing with milk (breasts), Hariv.; *-saṃyukta*, mfn. id., ib.; flowing in a stream (as tears), MBh. °**srávaṇa**, n. (sometimes w. r. °*śravaṇa*) streaming or gushing forth, trickling, oozing, effusion, discharge, RV. &c. &c. (often ifc., with f. *ā*); the flowing of milk from the udder, Yājñ.; MārkP.; milk, Gal.; sweat, perspiration, L.; voiding urine, L.; a well or spring, Mn.; Yājñ.; Ṛitus.; a cascade, cataract, L.; a spout, the projecting mouth of a vessel (out of which any fluid is poured), RV.; (also with *plāksha*, n.) N. of a place where the Sarasvatī takes its rise, ŚrS.; MBh.; Rājat.; m. N. of a man, L.; of a range of mountains on the confines of Malaya, R.; *-jala*, n. spring-water, L. °**sravin**, mfn. (ifc.) streaming forth, discharging, Nir.; Rājat.; (a cow) yielding milk, Ragh. °**srāva**, m. flowing, dropping, W.; urine, Car. (w. r. °*śrāva*); the overflowing scum of boiling rice, L.; *-karaṇa*, n. the urethra, L.

Pra-sruta, mfn. flowed forth, oozed out, issued, MBh.; Hariv.; discharging fluid, humid, moist, wet, MBh.; Kāv.; Suśr. °**sruti**, f. flowing forth, oozing out, L.

प्रस्वन *pra-svana*, m. (√*svan*) sound, noise, MBh. °**svanita** (*prá-*, fr. Caus.), sounding, roaring, RV. °**svāna**, m. a loud noise, L.

प्रस्वप् *pra-√svap*, P. *-svapiti* or °*pati* (Pot. Ā. *-svapīta* or °*peta*, MBh.), to fall asleep, go to sleep, sleep, Br.; MBh.; Hariv.

Pra-súp, mfn. asleep, RV.

Pra-supta, mfn. fallen into sleep, fast asleep, sleeping, slumbering, Mn.; MBh. &c.; closed (said of flowers), Kālid.; having slept, Hit.; asleep i. e. insensible, Suśr.; quiet, inactive, latent, BhP.; *-tā*, f. = next, Suśr. °**supti**, f. sleepiness, ŚārṅgS. (paralysis, W.)

Pra-svāpa, mfn. causing sleep, soporific, MBh.; m. falling asleep, sleep, BhP.; a dream, ib. °**svāpaka**, mf(*ikā*)n. causing to fall asleep, MW.; causing to die, slaying, ib. °**svāpana**, mf(*ī*)n. causing sleep, MBh.; Kāv. &c. (°*nī daśā*, f. condition of s°, MārkP.); n. the act of sending to s°, R. °**svāpinī**, f. 'sending to sleep,' N. of a daughter of Sattra-jit and wife of Kṛishṇa, Hariv.

प्रस्वादस् *prá-svādas*, mfn. (√*svad*) very pleasant or agreeable, RV.

प्रस्वार *pra-√svāra*. See *pra-√svṛi*.

प्रस्विद् *pra-√svid*, Ā. *-svedate*, to begin to sweat, get into perspiration, Suśr.; to become wet or moist, L. °**svinna**, mfn. covered with perspiration, sweated, perspired, R.

Pra-sveda, m. great or excessive perspiration, sweat, MBh.; Vet.; Sāh.; m. an elephant, Gal.; *-kaṇikā*, f. a drop of sw°, Prab.; *-jala*, n. sw°-water, MārkP.; *-bindu*, m. = *-kaṇikā*, Caur. °**svedita**, mfn. sweated, perspired, W.; hot, causing perspiration, ib.; *-vat*, mfn. suffering or producing persp°, ib. (cf. Pāṇ. i, 2, 19, Sch.) °**svedin**, mfn. sweating, covered with perspiration, Hit.

प्रस्वृ *pra-√svṛi*, P. *-svarati*, to lengthen or prolate a tone in uttering it, RPrāt.

Pra-svāra, m. the prolated syllable Om (repeated by a religious teacher at the beginning of a lesson), ib.

प्रहण *prahaṇa*, w. r. for *pra-haraṇa*, Hariv.

प्रहणेमि *prahu-ṇemi* or *praha-nemi*, m. the moon, L. (prob. w. r. for *graha-nemi*, q. v.)

प्रहन् *pra-√han*, P. *-hanti* (pf. Ā. *-jaghnire*, MBh.), to strike, beat, slay, kill, destroy, RV. &c. &c. (with acc.; according to Pāṇ. ii, 3, 56 also with gen.) °**haṇana**, n. striking &c., Pāṇ. viii, 4, 22, Sch.; a kind of amorous sport (= *jaghana-dvaya-tāḍana*), L.

Pra-hata, mfn. struck, beaten (as a drum), killed, slain, MBh.; Kāv. &c.; cut to pieces, BhP.; hewn down, Subh.; repelled, defeated, W.; spread, expanded, ib.; contiguous, ib.; learned, accomplished (= *śâstra-vid*, Gal.), ib.; (ifc.) a blow or stroke with, g. *aksha-dyūtâdi*; *-muraja*, mfn. having drums beaten, resounding with the beating of drums, Megh. °**hati**, f. a stroke, blow, Kād.; Bālar.

Pra-han, see *a-prahan*. °**hantavya**, mfn. to be killed or slain, Hariv. °**hantṛi**, mfn. striking (or 'he will strike') down, killing, slaying, RV.; MBh.

प्रहर *pra-hara* &c. See *pra-√hṛi*.

प्रहरित *pra-harita*, mfn. of a beautiful greenish colour, Car.

प्रहर्ष *pra-harsha* &c. See *pra-√hṛish*.

प्रहस् *pra-√has*, P. *-hasati* (ep. also Ā. °*te*), to burst into laughter (also with *hāsam*), MBh.; Kāv. &c.; to laugh with (acc.), MBh.; Pañcat.; to laugh at, mock, deride, ridicule, MBh.; R. &c. °**hasa**, m. N. of Śiva, Gal.; of a Rakshas, R. °**hasat**, mf(*antī*)n. laughing, smiling, MBh.; (*antī*), f. a species of jasmine, L.; another plant, L.; a large chafing-dish or fire-pan, L. °**hasana**, n. laughter, mirth, mockery, derision, Uttarar.; Hit. (°*nam*, enclit. after a finite verb, g. *gotrâdi*; °*ne √kṛi*, to mock, deride, g. *sâkshād-ādi*, Kāś.); (in rhet.) satire, sarcasm; (esp.) a kind of comedy or farce, Daśar.; Sāh. &c. °**hasita**, mfn. laughing, cheerful, Hariv.; Kāv.; Pur.; m. N. of a Buddha, Lalit.; of a prince of the Kiṃ-naras, Kāraṇḍ.; n. bursting into laughter, BhP.; displaying bright gaudy colours, Jātakam.; *-netra*, m. 'laughing-eyed,' N. of a Buddha, Lalit.; *-vadana* (Pañcat.), °*tânana* (Hariv.), mfn. with laughing face. °**hāsa**, m. loud laughter, laughter, Hariv.; Kāv.; derision, irony, Pāṇ. i, 4, 106 &c.; appearance, display, Veṇīs.; splendour of colours, Jātakam.; an actor, dancer, L.; N. of Śiva, L. (cf. °*hasa*); of an attendant of Ś°, MBh.; of a Nāga, ib.; of a minister of Varuṇa, R.; of a Tīrtha (w. r. for °*bhāsa*?), L.; n. (with *Bharad-vājasya*) N. of a Sāman (w. r. for *prāsāha*), L. °**hāsaka**, m. one who causes laughter, a jester, L. °**hāsita**, mfn. (fr. Caus.) caused to laugh, MW. °**hāsin**, mfn. laughing, derisive, satirical, AV.; shining bright, Jātakam.; m. the buffoon of a drama (= *vidūshaka*), L.

प्रहस्त *pra-hasta*, mfn. long-handed, Inscr.; m. (n., Pāṇ. vi, 2, 183, Sch.) the open hand with the fingers extended, KātyŚr., Sch.; N. of a Rākshasa, MBh.; R.; of a companion of Sūrya-prabha (son of Candra-prabha, king of Śākala; he had been an Asura before), Kathās.; *-vāda*, m. N. of work. °**hastaka**, m. the extended hand, L.; m. or n. (scil. *tṛica*) N. of RV. viii, 95, 13-15.

प्रहा *pra-√2. hā*, Ā. *-jihīte*, to drive off, haste away, RV.; to spring up, ŚBr.

प्रहा *pra-√3. hā*, P. *-jahāti* (3. pl. pr. irreg. *-jahanti*, MBh.; fut. 3. du. Ā. *-hāsyete*, R.), to leave, ŚBr. &c. &c.; to desert, quit, abandon, give up, renounce, violate (a duty), break (a promise), MBh.; Kāv. &c.; to send off, throw, hurl, Bhaṭṭ.; (incorrectly for Pass.) to cease, disappear, MBh.: Pass. *-hīyate*, to be relinquished or neglected, be lost, fail, cease, perish, Mn.; MBh.; to be vanquished, succumb, MBh.: Caus. *-hāpayati*, to drive away, remove, destroy, BhP.

Pra-jahitá, mfn. (irreg. fr. the pres. stem) quitted, abandoned, RV. viii, 1, 13 (applied to a fire that has been abandoned, TāṇḍBr.; ŚrS.)

Pra-há, f. a good throw at dice, any gain or advantage, RV.; AV.; TāṇḍBr. (= *pra-hantṛi*, Sāy.); *-vat*, mfn. acquiring gain, gaining, RV. (= *prahara-ṇa-vat*, Sāy.) °**hāṇa**, n. relinquishing, abandoning, avoiding, Śiś.; Śaṃk.; Lalit.; abstraction, speculation, meditation, Lalit.; Vajracch.; exertion, Dharmas. 45. °**hāṇi**, f. cessation, disappearance, ŚvetUp.; Pur.; want, deficiency, MW. °**hātavya**, mfn. to be relinquished or abandoned, Vajracch. °**hāna** and °**hāni**, w. r. for °*hāṇa* and °*hāṇi*. °**hāpaṇa**, n. (fr. Caus.) driving away, forced abandonment or departure, W.

Prahīṇa, mfn. (cf. Kāś. on Pāṇ. viii, 4, 29) left, remaining, BhP.; standing alone i. e. having no relatives, Vas.; cast off, worn out (as a garment), Gaut.; failing in (instr.), MBh.; ceased, vanished, Jātakam.; (ifc.) wanting, destitute of, MBh.; m. removal, loss, waste, destruction, W. **—jīvita**, mfn. one who has abandoned life, dead, slain, W. **—dosha**, mfn. one whose sins have vanished, sinless, Vedāntas.

प्रहाय्य *pra-hāyyà*. See 1. *pra-√hi*.

प्रहार *pra-hāra*. See *pra-√hṛi*.

प्रहि 1. *pra-√hi*, P. Ā. *-hiṇoti*, *-hiṇute*; *-hiṇvati*, *-hiṇvate* (cf. Pāṇ. viii, 4, 15; pf. *-jighāya*, KaushUp.; 1. sg. pr. Ā. *-hishe*, RV.; Aor. P. *prâhait*, AV.; Impv. *prá-heta*, RV.; inf. *pra-hyè*, ib.), to urge on, incite, RV.; to direct, command,

Lāṭy.; KaushUp.; to convey or send to, furnish, procure, bestow on (dat.), RV. &c. &c.; to hurl, cast, throw upon, discharge at (dat. or loc.), Kāv.; Pur.; to turn the eyes towards (acc.), Kād.; to dispatch (messengers), drive away, dismiss, send to (acc. with or without *prati*, dat., gen. with or without *antikam* or *pārśvam*) or in order to (dat. or inf.), RV. &c. &c.; (Ā.) to rush on, RV.; to forsake (=*pra-√3. hā*), BhP.: Caus. aor. *prâjīhayat*, Pat.: Desid. of Caus. *pra-jighāyayishati*, ib.

Pra-hāyyà, m. one who is to be sent, a messenger, AV. (v.l. °*hārya*; cf. °*heya*).

Práhita, mfn. urged on, incited, stirred up, RV.; BhP.; hurled, discharged at, Hariv.; R.; Pur.; thrown forward i.e. stretched out (as an arm), MBh.; imbedded (as nails), Sāh.; (ifc.) directed or turned towards, cast upon (as eyes, the mind &c.), Kālid.; BhP.; conveyed, sent, procured, Daś.; Kathās.; Pañcat.; sent out, dispatched (as messengers), RV. &c. &c.; sent away, expelled, banished to (dat.), R.; Kathās.; sent to or towards or against (loc., gen. with or without *pārśve*, or dat.), appointed, commissioned, MBh.; Kāv. &c.; m. du. (with *Gaurīviteḥ* and *Śyāvâśvasya*) N. of 2 Sāmans, ĀrshBr.; n. sauce, gravy, condiment, L. **–m-gama**, mfn. going on an errand or mission to (gen.), PārGṛ.; *-vat*, mfn. one who has sent out, (=fin. verb) he sent out, R.; Kathās. **Prahitâtman**, mfn. resolute, Divyâv.

Prá-hetavya, mfn. to be sent out or dismissed, Campak. °**heti**, m. a missile, weapon, VS.; N. of a king of the Rākshasas, Pur.; of an Asura, ib. °**hetṛi**, m. one who sends forth or impels, RV. °**héya**, mfn. to be sent away or dispatched, serving as a messenger, AV.; ŚBr.

प्रहि 2. *pra-hi*, m. (according to Uṇ. iv, 134 fr. *pra-√hṛi*, but cf. *pra-dhi*) a well.

प्रहितु *prahitu* (only °*toḥ saṃyojane*), N. of 2 Sāmans, ĀrshBr. (cf. *pra-hita* above).

प्रहिम *pra-hima*, mfn. having severe winters (?), Pāṇ. viii, 4, 16, Pat.

प्रहीण *pra-hīṇa*. See *pra-√3. hā*.

प्रहु *pra-√hu*, P. Ā. *-juhoti*, *-juhute*, to sacrifice continually, offer up, RV.: Caus. *-hāvayati*, to pour out or down, ĀpŚr.

Prá-huta, mfn. offered up, RV.; Br.; GṛS. &c.; m. (scil. *yajña*) sacrificial food offered to all created beings, Mn. iii, 73 &c. (n., L.) °**huti** (*prá-*), f. an oblation, sacrifice, RV.

Pra-hoshá, m. id., ib. °**hoshin**, mfn. offering oblations or sacrifices, ib.

प्रहृ *pra-√hṛi*, P. Ā. *-harati*, °*te*, to offer (esp. praise, 1. sg. pr. *-harmi*), RV. i, 61, 1; to thrust or move forward, stretch out, RV.; TS.; ŚBr.; to put into, fix in (loc.), RV.; to hurl, throw, discharge at (loc.), AV. &c. &c.; to throw or turn out, ŚāṅkhŚr.; to throw (into the fire), Br.; KātyŚr.; to strike, hit, hurt, attack, assail (with acc., loc., dat. or gen.; Ā. also 'to fight with each other'), AV.; Mn.; MBh. &c.: Caus. Ā. *-harayate*, to stir up, excite, rouse, RV. iv, 37, 2: Desid. *-jihīrshati*, to wish to take away, MBh.; to wish to throw, ŚBr.; to wish to strike or assail, MBh.; Daś. (cf. *-jihīrshu*, p. 659).

Pra-hara, m. (ifc. f. *ā*) a division of time (about 3 hours = 6 or 7 Nāḍikās; lit. 'stroke,' scil. on a gong), Var.; Kathās.; Pañcat.; the 8th part of a day, a watch, Kathās.; N. of the subdivisions in a Śakuna (q.v.); *-kuṭumbī*, f. a species of plant, L.; *-virati*, f. the end of a watch (at 9 o'clock in the forenoon), Amar. °**haraka**, m. striking the hours, Vet.; a period of about 3 hours, watch, Śiś. (cf. *ardha-praharikā*). °**haraṇa**, n. striking, beating, pecking, Pañcat.; attack, combat, MBh.; throwing (of grass into the fire), TS., Sch.; removing, dispelling, Śaṃk.; a weapon (ifc. f. *ā*), MBh.; Kāv. &c. (cf. *kṛita-pr°*); a carriage-box, BhP.; w. r. for *pra-vahaṇa*, L.; m. the verse spoken in throwing grass into the fire, ĀpŚr.; N. of a son of Kṛishṇa, BhP.; *-kalikā* or *-kalitā*, f. a kind of metre, Chandom.; Col.; *-vat*, mfn. fighting, Sāy. °**haraṇīya**, mfn. to be attacked or fought, MBh.; to be removed or dispelled or destroyed, Prab.; n. a weapon, MBh.; Hariv. °**harin**, m. one who announces the hours by beating a gong &c., a watchman, bellman, L. °**hartavya**, mfn. to be attacked or fought, MBh.; Hariv.; n. (impers.) one should strike or attack (dat. or loc.), ib.; Kāv.; Kathās. °**hartṛi**, m. a sender, dispatcher, Śiś.; an assailant, combatant, warrior, MBh.; Kāv. &c.

Pra-hāra, m. striking, hitting, fighting, Vcar.; a stroke, blow, thump, knock, kick &c. ('with,' comp.; 'on,' loc. or comp.), Mn.; Yājñ.; MBh. &c.; m. a necklace, Dharmaś.; *-karaṇa*, n. dealing blows, beating, MW.; *-da*, mfn. (ifc.) giving a blow to, striking, Yājñ.; *-varman*, m. N. of a prince of Mithilā, Daś.; *-vallī*, f. a kind of perfume, Bhpr.; °*rârta*, mfn. hurt by a blow, wounded, Yājñ.; n. chronic and acute pain from a wound or hurt, W. °**hāraṇa**, n. a desirable gift, L. (v.l. for 2. *pra-vāraṇa*). °**hārin**, mfn. striking, smiting, beating with (comp.), attacking, fighting against (gen. or comp.), MBh.; Kāv. &c.; m. a good fighter, champion, hero, Nir. v, 12; °*ri-tā*, f. striking, hitting, Divyâv. °**hāruka**, mfn. carrying off, tearing away, Kāṭh. °**hárya** (or °*hāryà*), mfn. to be taken away or removed, ŚBr. (cf. *pra-hāyyà* under *pra-√hi*); to be beaten, MW.

Prá-hṛita, mfn. thrown (as a stone), AV.; stretched out or lifted up (as a stick), ŚBr.; struck, beaten, hurt, wounded, hit, smitten, MBh.; Kāv. &c.; m. N. of a man, g. *aśvâdi*, n. a stroke, blow; (impers. 'a blow has been struck,' Hariv.; Ragh.; Sah.; °*te sati*, 'when a blow has been struck,' Mn. viii, 286); a fight with (comp.), Ragh. xvi, 16 (cf. g. *aksha-dyūtâdi*).

प्रहृष् *pra-√hṛish*, P. *-hṛishyati* (m. c. also Ā. °*te*), to rejoice, be glad or cheerful, exult, MBh.; Kāv. &c.: Caus. *-harshayati*, to set (the teeth) on edge, Car.; to cause to rejoice, gladden, inspirit, encourage, ŚāṅkhBr.; MBh.; R. &c.

Pra-harsha, m. erection (or greater er°) of the male organ, Car.; erection of the hair, extreme joy, thrill of delight, rapture (°*shaṃ √kṛi*, with loc. 'to delight in'), MBh.; Kāv. &c.; *-vat*, mfn. delighted, glad, MBh.; R. °**harshaṇa**, mf(*ī*)n. causing erection of the hair of the body, enrapturing, delighting, MBh.; Hariv.; m. the planet Mercury or its ruler, L. (cf. °*shula*); (*ī*), f. (cf. °*shiṇī*) turmeric, L.; a kind of metre, Chandom.; n. erection (of the hair of the body), Car.; rapture, joy, delight, MBh.; gladdening, delighting, ib.; the attainment of a desired object, Kuval.; *-kara*, mf(*ī*)n. causing great joy, enrapturing, MBh. °**harshita**, mfn. (fr. Caus.) stiffened (as reed), Suśr.; made desirous of sexual intercourse, Car.; greatly delighted, enraptured, very happy, MBh.; R. °**harshin**, mf(*iṇī*)n. gladdening (with gen.), MBh.; (*iṇī*), f. (cf. °*shaṇī*) turmeric, L.; a kind of metre, Śrutab. °**harshula**, m. the planet Mercury, L. (cf. °*shaṇa*).

Pra-hṛishṭa, mfn. erect, bristling (as the hair of the body), MBh.; R.; BhP.; thrilled with delight, exceedingly pleased, delighted, ib.; Var.; Kathās.; Pañcat. &c.; *-citta*, mfn. delighted at heart, exceedingly glad, A.; *-manas*, mfn. id., MBh.; *-mukha*, mfn. having a cheerful face, looking pleased (*a-pr°*), MārkP.; *-mudita*, mfn. exceedingly pleased and cheerful, R.; *-rūpa*, mfn. of pleasing form, MBh.; erect in form, MW.; *-roman*, mfn. one who has erected hair, R.; m. N. of an Asura, Kathās.; *-vadana*, mfn. = *-mukha*, MārkP.; °*ṭâtman*, mfn. = °*ṭa-citta*, MBh.; R. °**hṛishṭaka**, m. a crow, W.

प्रहेणक *pra-heṇaka*, n. a kind of pastry, Divyâv. (cf. *pra-helaka*).

प्रहेति *pra-heti* &c. See *pra-√hi*.

प्रहेलक *pra-helaka*, n. (√*hil?*) a kind of pastry, sweetmeat &c. distributed at a festival, L. (cf. *pra-heṇaka*). °**helā**, f. playfulness, free or unrestrained behaviour; (*ayā*), ind. freely, without constraint, Pañcat. °**heli** (L.), °**helikā** (Kāvyâd., 6 kinds), f. an enigma, riddle, puzzling question. °**heli**, f. id.; *-jñāna*, n. the art or science of proposing riddles, L.

प्रहोष *pra-hosha*, °*shin*. See under *pra-√hu*.

प्रह्ये *pra-hye*. See under *pra-√hi*.

प्रह्राद *pra-hrāda*, m. (√*hrād*) N. of the chief of the Asuras (with the patr. Kāyādhava, and father of Virocana), TBr.; of a son of Hiraṇya-kaśipu (he was an enemy of Indra and friend of Vishṇu), MBh.; Hariv.; BhP. (cf. *pra-hlāda*). °**hrādi**, m. pl., v.l. for *pra-hlādīya*, KaushUp.

प्रह्रास *pra-hrāsa*, m. (√*hras*) shortening, diminution, wane, MBh.

प्रह्लाद् *pra-√hlād*, Ā. *-hlādate*, to be refreshed or comforted, to rejoice, Kir.: Caus. *-hlādayati*, °*te*, to refresh, comfort, delight, MBh.; R. &c.

Pra-hla, mfn. pleased, glad, Gal. °**hlatti**, f. pleasure, delight, Pāṇ. vi, 4, 95, Sch. °**hlanna**, mfn. pleased, glad, happy, Pāṇ. vi, 4, 95, Sch. °**hlanni**, f. = °*hlatti*, Siddh.

Pra-hlāda, m. joyful excitement, delight, joy, happiness, MBh.; R.; Suśr.; sound, noise, L.; a species of rice, Gal.; N. of a pious Daitya (son of Hiraṇya-kaśipu; he was made king of the D°s by Vishṇu, and was regent of one of the divisions of Pātāla; cf. *pra-hrāda*), MBh.; VP. (RTL. 109); of a Nāga, MBh.; of a Prajā-pati, ib.; pl. N. of a people, ib.; *-campū*, f., *-carita*, n., *-vijaya*, m., *-stuti*, f., *-stotra*, n. N. of wks. °**hlādaka**, mf(*ikā*)n. causing joy or pleasure, refreshing, Ṛitus. °**hlādana**, mf(*ī*)n. id., MBh.; Kāv.; Suśr.; m. (with *yuva-rāja*) N. of a poet (brother of king Dhārā-varsha, 1208), Cat.; n. (Hariv.; Suśr.) and (*ā*), f. (Bālar.) the act of causing joy or pleasure, refreshment. °**hlādanīya**, mfn. refreshing, comforting, Lalit. °**hlādita**, mfn. (fr. Caus.) rejoiced, delighted, MBh.; R. °**hlādin**, mfn. delighting, refreshing, MBh. °**hlādīya**, m. pl. the attendants of the Asura Prahlāda, KaushUp. (cf. *pra-hrādi*).

प्रह्व *pra-hva*, mf(*ā*)n. (√*hvṛi*) inclined forwards, sloping, slanting, bent, GṛŚrS.; MBh. &c. (*-tva*, n., VP., Sch.); bowed, stooping, bowing before (gen.), MBh. (°*vâñjali*, mfn. bowing with hands joined in token of respect, R.); humble, modest, MBh.; Kāv. &c.; inclined towards i.e. intent upon, devoted to, engaged in, L.; (*ī*), f. N. of a Śakti, RāmatUp. °**hvaṇa**, n. bowing down in reverence, BhP. °**hvaya**, Nom. P. °*yati*, to render humble, Uttarar. °**hvāna**, mfn. bent, bowing, TāṇḍBr.

Prahvī, in comp. for *pra-hva*. **–kṛita**, mfn. bent forwards, bowed, W.; conquered, won, ib. **–bhūta**, mfn. bowing, humble, modest, Bālar.

प्रह्वल् *pra-√hval*, P. *-hvalati*, to begin to reel, quake, tremble, Bhaṭṭ.

Pra-hvala, n. a beautiful body, L. (cf. *prakula*).

प्रह्वलीका *pra-hvalīkā*, w.r. for *pra-valhikā*.

प्रह्वे *pra-√hve* (Ā. *-havate* &c.; 1. sg. impf. *-ahve*), to invoke, RV. **Pra-hvāya**, m. call, invocation, Pāṇ. iii, 3, 72.

प्रा 1. *prā*, cl. 2. P. (Dhātup. xxiv, 53) *prāti* (pf. P. *paprau* or *paprā*, 2. sg. *paprātha*, p. *paprivás*, f. °*prushī*, RV.; Ā. *papre*, 2. sg. °*prishe*, ib.; AV.; *papre* as Pass., Bhaṭṭ.; aor. 3. sg. *aprāt* or *aprās*, RV.; Subj. *prās* or *prâsi*, ib.; aor. Pass. *aprāyi*, AV.), to fill, RV.; AV.; Br.; Bhaṭṭ. [Cf. Gk. πλή-ρης; Lat. *plē-nus*.]

2. **Prá**, mfn. filling (ifc. = 2. *pra*; cf. *antariksha-*, *kāma-*, *kratu-* &c.)

1. **Prāṇa**, mfn. (for 2. see p. 705, col. 1) filled, full, L.

Prātá, mfn. id., RV.

Prāti, f. filling (= *pūrti*), L.; the span of the thumb and forefinger, L.

प्रा 3. *prā*, Vṛiddhi or lengthened form of 1. *pra* in comp. (cf. Pāṇ. vi, 3, 122).

Observe in the following derivatives, only the second member of the simple compound from which they come is given in the parentheses, leaving the preposition *pra* (lengthened to *prā* in the derivatives) to be supplied. **–kaṭya**, n. (fr. *-kaṭa*) publicity, manifestation, Nilak. **–karaṇika**, mfn. (fr. *-karaṇa*) belonging to the matter in question or to a chapter or to a class or genus, MānGṛ.; KātyŚr.; being the subject of any statement, MW. **–karsha**, n. N. of Sāmans, ĀrshBr. **–karshika**, mfn. deserving preference, g. *chedâdi*. **–kashika**, m. (fr. *-kasha*; see Uṇ. ii, 41, Sch.) a dancer employed by a woman or one supported by another's wives, L. **–kāmya**, n. (fr. *-kāma*) freedom of will, wilfulness, MBh.; Kum.; MārkP.; irresistible will or fiat (one of the 8 supernatural powers), MWB. 245. **–kāra**, see s.v. **–kāśá**, m. a metallic mirror (others 'a kind of ornament'), Br.; ŚrS. **–kāśya**, n. (fr. *-kāśa*) the being evident, manifestness, celebrity, renown, MBh.; Kāv.;

Suśr. **-kṛita**, see s.v. **-kramika**, mfn. (fr. *-krama*) one who undertakes much (without finishing anything), Gaut., Sch. **-kshālana**, w.r. for *pra-ksh°*. **-kharya**, n. (fr. *-khara*) sharpness (of an arrow), Naish., Sch.; wickedness, W. **-gadya**, mfn. (fr. *-gadin*), Pāṇ. iv, 2, 80. **-galbhī**, f. (fr. *-galbha*) boldness, confidence, resoluteness, determination, Bālar. **-galbhya**, n. id., MBh.; Kāv. &c.; importance, rank, W.; manifestation, appearance, Kpr.; proficiency, MW.; *-buddhi*, f. boldness of judgment, Pañcat.; *-vat*, mfn. possessed of confidence, bold, arrogant, Kathās. **-gāṅgam**, w.r. for *prāg-gaṅgam*, Pat. **-gātha**, mf(*ī*)n. belonging to the Pragāthas (i.e. to RV. viii), ĀśvŚr.; m. patr. of Kali and Bharga and Haryata, RAnukr. **-gāthaka**, mf(*ikā*)n. = prec. mfn., ŚāṅkhŚr. **-gāthika**, mfn. derived from Pragātha, ŚrS. **-gītya**, n. (fr. *-gīta*) notoriety, celebrity, excellence, Nalac. **-guṇya**, n. (fr. *-guṇa*) right position or direction, Car. **-gharma-sád**, mfn. sitting in a region of fire or light, RV. vi, 73, 1 (Sāy.) **-ghāta**, w.r. for *pra-gh°*, L. **-ghāra**, m. sprinkling, aspersion, L. **-caṇḍya**, n. (fr. *-caṇḍa*) violence, passion, Mālatīm. **-cinvat**, m. N. of a son of Janam-ejaya (= *pra-cinvat*), MBh. **-curya**, n. (fr. *-cura*) multitude, abundance, plenty, Bādar.; Rājat.; Pañcat.; amplitude, prolixity, TPrāt., Sch.; prevalence, currency, Śaṃk.; Rājat.; (*eṇa*), ind. in a mass, fully, mostly, MārkP.; in detail, BhP. **-cetas**, m. pl. N. of the 10 sons of Prācīna-barhis (= *pra-cetas*), MBh. **-cetasa**, mfn. relating to Varuṇa (= *pra-cetas*; with *āśā*, f. the west), Hcar.; descended from Pracetas (m. patr. of Manu, Daksha, and Vālmīki), MBh.; Hariv.; Pur.; pl. = *-cetas*, pl., L.; *-stava*, m. N. of VP. xiv. **-jahita**, m. = *pra-j°*; m. a Gārhapatya fire maintained during a longer period of time, ŚrS. **-jāpata**, °**tya**, **-jāvata**, **-jeśa**, °**śvara**, see s.v. **-jñá**, mf(*ā* and *ī*)n. (fr. *-jñā*) intellectual (opp. to *śārīra*, *taijasa*), ŚBr.; Nir.; MāṇḍUp.; intelligent, wise, clever, KaṭhUp.; Mn.; MBh. &c.; m. a wise or learned man, MBh.; Kāv. &c.; intelligence dependent on individuality, Vedāntas.; a kind of parrot with red stripes on the neck and wings, L.; (*ā*), f. intelligence, understanding, L.; (*ī*), f. the wife of a learned man, L.; *-kathā*, f. a story about a wise man, MW.; *-tā*, f. (Mn.), *-tva*, n. (Vedāntas.) wisdom, learning, intelligence; *-bhūta-nātha*, m. N. of a poet, Cat.; *-māna*, m. respect for learned men, W.; *-mānin* (Śaṃk.), *-m-mānin* (Kathās.), *-vādika* (MBh.), mfn. thinking one's self wise. **-ṇāyya**, mfn. proper, fit, suited, ChUp. iii, 11, 5 (v.l. *pra-n°*). **-ṇāhá**, m. cement (used in building), AV. **-ṇītya**, n. prob. w.r. for *-mītya*, q.v. **-tardana**, mf(*ī*)n. belonging to or derived from Pratardana, L. **-titheyī**, f. (fr. *-tithi*) N. of a female sage, GṛS. (v.l. *-tītheyī*). **-tuda**, mfn. derived from the Pratudas or peckers (a kind of bird), Car. **-tṛidá**, m. patr. fr. *pra-tṛid*, ŚBr. (Sāy.) **-dakshiṇya**, n. (fr. *-dakshiṇa*) circumambulation while keeping one's right side towards an object, MBh.; respectful behaviour, Car. **-dānika**, mfn. (fr. *-dāna*) relating to an oblation, KātyŚr., Sch. **-dúr**, see s.v. **-deśá**, m. (ifc. f. *ā*) the span of the thumb and forefinger (also a measure = 12 Aṅgulas), ŚBr.; GṛŚrS.; MBh. &c.; place, country, L. (v.l. for *pra-d°*); *-pāda*, mf(*ī*)n. (a seat) whose legs are a span long, KātyŚr.; *-mātrá*, n. the measure of a span, ŚBr. (with *bhūmeḥ*, 'a mere span of land,' MBh.); mf(*ī*)n. a span long, Br.; GṛŚrS. &c.; *-sama*, mf(*ā*)n. id., KātyŚr.; °*śâyāma*, mf(*ā*)n. id., Gobh. **-deśana**, n. = *pra-deśana*, a gift &c., L. **-deśika**, mfn. having precedents, Nir. (with *guṇa*, m. the authorized function or meaning of a word); local, limited, Rājat.; m. (also °*keśvara*) a small land-owner, chief of a district, Kauś. **-deśin**, mfn. a span long, Gṛihyās.; (*inī*), f. the forefinger, KātyŚr., Sch. (prob. w.r. for *pra-deśinī*). **-dosha**, mfn. belonging or relating to the evening, vespertine, Bhpr.; °*shika*, mfn. id., Pañcat. (cf. Pāṇ. iv, 3, 14). **-dohani**, m. patr. fr. *pra-dohana*, g. *taulvaly-ādi*. **-dyumni**, m. patr. fr. *pra-dyumna*, MBh.; Hariv. (cf. g. *bahv-ādi*). **-dyoti**, m. patr. fr. *pra-dyota*, Cat. **-dhanika**, n. (fr. *-dhana*) an implement of war, weapon, BhP. **-dhā**, f. (cf. *pra-dhā*) N. of a daughter of Daksha and mother of sev. Apsaras and Gandharvas, MBh.; Hariv. **-dhānika**, mfn. (fr. *-dhāna*) pre-eminent, distinguished, superior, BhP.; (in Sāṃkhya) derived from or relating to Pradhāna or primary matter, MBh.; BhP. **-dhānya**, n. predominance, prevalence, ascendency, supremacy, KātyŚr.; Śaṃk.; Suśr. &c.; ibc.; °*nyena*, °*nyāt*, and *-tas*, ind. in regard to the highest object or chief matter, chiefly, mainly, summarily, Nir.; MBh.; Hariv. &c. (*-stuti*, mfn. chiefly praised); m. a chief or most distinguished person, Vet. **-dheya**, mfn. descended from Prādhā, MBh. (cf. *karṇa-prādheya*). **-dhváṅsana**, m. patr. fr. *pra-dhvaṅsana*, ŚBr. **-nāḍī**, f. = (or w.r. for) *pra-ṇāḍī* = *pra-ṇālī*, MBh. **-paṇika**, m. (fr. *-paṇa*; but cf. Uṇ. ii, 42) a trader, dealer, MBh.; Śiś. **-prābandha**, see *kesara-prābandhā*. **-balya**, n. (fr. *-bala*) superiority of power, predominance, ascendency, Vedāntas.; Suśr.; force, validity (of a rule), TPrāt., Sch. **-bālika**, see *-vālika*. **-bodhaka**, m. = (and v.l. for) *pra-b°*, a minstrel employed to wake the king in the morning, R.; = next, L. **-bodhika**, m. (fr. *-bodha*) dawn, daybreak, L. **-bhañjana**, n. the Nakshatra Svāti (presided over by Pra-bh°, the god of wind), Var.; °*ni*, m. patr. of Hanūmat (son of Pra-bh°), Mcar. **-bhava**, n. (fr. *-bhu*) superiority, L. **-bhavatya**, n. (fr. *-bhavat*), id., Mn. viii, 412. **-bhākara**, mf(*ī*)n. derived from Prabhā-kara, Dharmaś.; m. a follower of Pr°, Vedāntas.; n. the work of Pr°, Pratāp., Sch.; *-khaṇḍana*, n. N. of wk.; °*kari*, m. patr. of the planet Saturn, Var. **-bhātika**, mf(*ī*)n. (fr. *-bhāta*) relating to morning, matutinal, Pañcat.; Suśr. **-bhāsika** (with *kshetra*), n. = *pra-bhāsa-ksh°*, Cat. **-bhūtika**, mf(*ī*)n. = *pra-bhūtam āha*, Pāṇ. iv, 4, 1, Vārtt. 2, Pat. **-bhṛita**, n., once in Divyâv. m. (fr. *-bhṛiti*) a present, gift, offering (esp. to a deity or a sovereign), Kathās.; Rājat. (*cikitsā-prābhṛita*, m. a man whose gift is the art of medicine, a skilful physician, Car.); N. of the chapters of the Sūrya-prajñapti (the subdivisions are called *prābhṛita-prābhṛita*); °*ta-ka*, n. a present, gift, Mālav.; °*tī-√kṛi*, to make a present of, offer, Kathās. **-mati**, m. N. of one of the 7 sages in the 10th Manv-antara, Hariv. (v.l. *pra-mati* and *prāptati*). **-māṇika**, mf(*ī*)n. (fr. *-māṇa*) forming or being a measure, Hcat. (cf. *pra-māṇika*); founded on evidence or authority, admitting of proof, authentic, credible, Dāyabh.; one who accepts proof or rests his arguments on authority, Sarvad.; a president, the chief or head of a trade, W.; *-tva*, n. authoritativeness, cogency, Mallin.; *-vārttika*, n. N. of wk. **-māṇya**, n. (fr. *-māṇa*) the being established by proof, resting upon authority, authoritativeness, authenticity, evidence, credibility, Nir.; Mn.; MBh. &c.; *-vāda*, m. N. of sev. wks. (also °*da-kroḍa*, m., *-ṭīkā*, f., *-rahasya*, n., *-vicāra*, m., *-śiromaṇi*, m., *-saṃgraha*, m., °*dârtha*, m.); *-vādin*, mfn. one who affirms or believes in proof, Sarvad. **-mādika**, mf(*ī*)n. (fr. *-māda*) arising from carelessness, erroneous, faulty, wrong (with *pāṭha*, m. a w° reading), Mallin.; Siddh.; Cat.; *-tva*, n. erroneousness, incorrectness, Sāṃkhyak., Sch. **-mādya**, m. (fr. *-māda*) Adhatoda Vasica or Gendarussa Vulgaris, L.; n. madness, fury, intoxication, W. **-mītya**, n. (fr. *-mīta*) debt (lit. 'death'?), L. **-modika**, mf(*ī*)n. (fr. *-moda*) charming, enchanting, Mcar.; °*dya*, n. rapture, delight, Lalit.; Divyâv. **-yatya**, n. (fr. *-yata*) purity, pious disposition or preparation for any rite, ĀpŚr.; Śaṃk.; BhP. (*a-prāy°*). **-yāṇika**, mf(*ī*)n. (fr. *-yāṇa*) fit for a march or journey, MBh. **-yātrika**, mf(*ī*)n. (fr. *-yātrā*) id., ib.; Hariv. **-yāsá**, m. = *pra-y°*, VS. **-yu**, **-yus**, see *a-prāyu*, °*yus*. **-yudh**, f. (?) fight, battle; *-yud-dheshin* (for *-heshin*) or *-yudh-eshin*, m. a horse, L. (lit. 'neighing in or longing for the battle'). **-yoktra**, mf(*ī*)n. (fr. *-yoktṛi*) relating to an employer, Pat. **-yogi** (*prā-*), m. patr. fr. *pra-yoga*, MaitrS. **-yogika**, mf(*ī*)n. (fr. *-yoga*) applied, used, applicable, Kām. (cf. g. *cheddâdi*); (with *dhūma*, m.) a kind of sternutatory, Suśr. **-yojya**, mfn. belonging to things requisite or necessary, Dhāyabh. **-roha**, m. a shoot, sprout (= *pra-r°*), Cat.; mf(*ī*)n. accustomed to rise or ascend, g. *chattrâdi*. **-lamba**, mf(*ī*)n. hanging down, R.; m. a kind of pearl ornament, L.; the female breast, L.; a species of gourd, L.; n. (?) a garland hanging down to the breast, Ragh. (also °*baka*, n. and °*bikā*, f., L.) **-lepika**, mfn. = *pralepikā-yā dharmyam*, g. *mahishy-ādi*. **-leya**, mf(*ī*)n. (fr. *-laya*, Pāṇ. vii, 2, 3) produced by melting, ib., Sch.; m. fever in goat or sheep, Gal.; n. (?) hail, snow, frost, dew, Megh.; Var.; Rājat. &c. (also as Nom. P. °*yati*, to resemble hail &c., Dhūrtas.); *-bhū-dhara*, m. 'snow-mountain,' Hima-vat, Vcar.; *-raśmi* (Var.) or *-rocis* (Prasannar.), m. 'frosty-rayed,' the moon; *-varsha*, m. falling (lit. 'raining') of snow, Venis.; *-śaila*, m. = *-bhūdhara*, Kathās.; °*yâṅśu*, m. = °*ya-raśmi*, Var.; °*yâdri*, m. = °*ya-bhū-dhara*, Vcar.

-vacana (VPrāt.) and **-vacanika** (TS., Sch.), usual while reciting Vedic texts. **-vaṭa**, m. barley, L. (cf. *pra-vaṭa* and *pra-veṭa*). **-vaṇá**, mfn. being among the crags (fire), RV. iii, 22, 4; °*ṇi* (?), Uṇ. ii, 103, Sch. **-1. -vara**, mf(*ī*)n. (fr. 3. *pra-vará*, p. 693; for 2. see *prā-√1. vṛi*), Pat. **-vareya**, m. patr. fr. *pra-vara*, Kāṭh. **-vargá**, mf(*ī*)n. distinguished, eminent, RV. **-vartaka**, see under *prā-√vṛit*, p. 709. **-varshin**, mfn. raining, ŚāṅkhGṛ. **-vahaṇi**, w.r. for *-vāhaṇi*. **-vāduka**, m. an opponent in philosophical discussion, Nyāyas., Sch. **-vālika**, m. (fr. *-vāla*) a vendor of coral, R. **-vāsa**, mf(*ī*)n., g. *vyushṭâdi*; °*sika*, mf(*ī*)n., g. *guḍâdi* and *saṃtâpâdi*. **-vāhaṇi** (*prā-*), m. patr. fr. *pra-vāhaṇa*, TS.; ĀpŚr., Sch. &c. (w.r. *prā-vahaṇi* and *prāhaṇi*; cf. g. *taulvaly-ādi*, Kāś.); °*ṇeya*, m. patr. fr. °*ṇi*, Pravar. (cf. g. *śubhrâdi*; also *pravāhaṇeya*, Pāṇ. vii, 3, 28); °*ṇeyaka* (also *prav°*), m. patr. fr. °*ṇeya*, Pāṇ. vii, 3, 29, Kāś.; °*ṇeyi* (also *prav°*), m. id., ib. **-vīṇya**, n. (fr. *-vīṇa*) cleverness, dexterity, skill, proficiency in (loc. or comp.), Ragh.; Kathās. **-vṛittika**, mf(*ī*)n. (fr. *-vṛitti*) corresponding to a former mode of action, KātyŚr., Sch.; (ifc.) well acquainted with, Hariv. **-vṛish** &c., see s.v. **-veṇya**, n. (fr. *-veṇī*) a fine woollen covering, R. (v.l. °*ṇī*). **-vepá**, m. the swaying of pendent fruit (on a tree), RV. **-veśana**, mf(*ī*)n., g. *vyushṭâdi*, n. a workshop, L. **-veśika**, mf(*ī*)n. (fr. *-veśa*) relating to entrance (into a house or on the stage), Vikr.; Bālar.; Pracaṇḍ. (with *ākshiptikā* and *dhruvā*, f. N. of partic. airs sung by a person on entering the stage, ib.); auspicious for entrance, Var.; °*śya*, n. the being accessible, accessibility (only *a-prāv°*), L. **-vrājya**, n. (fr. *-vrāj*) the life of a religious mendicant, vagrancy, MBh. (w.r. *-vrajya*); MārkP. **-śastya**, n. (fr. *-śasta*) the being praised, celebrity, excellence, Mālatīm.; Kathās. **-śāstra**, n. the office of Praśāstṛi, KātyŚr. (cf. g. *udgātṛ-ādi*); government, rule, dominion, MW. **-śṛiṅga**, mfn. having the horns bent forwards, VS.; TS. **-śravaṇa**, v.l. for *-sravaṇa*, m. **-ślishṭa**, mf(*ī*)n. N. of a kind of Svarita produced by the combination of 2 short *i*'s, APrāt. (w.r. *prāk-śl°*). **-shṭha**, mf(*ī*)n., Pat. **-saṅga**, m. a kind of yoke for cattle, MBh.; *-vāhīvāh*, mfn. = *ushṭri*, ĀpŚr., Sch. **-saṅgika**, mf(*ī*)n. (fr. *-saṅga*) resulting from attachment or close connection, BhP.; incidental, casual, occasional, Uttarar.; Kathās.; Rājat.; Sāh. (opp. to *ādhikārika*); inherent, innate, W.; relevant, ib.; opportune, seasonable, MW. **-saṅgya**, mfn. (fr. *-saṅga*) harnessed with a yoke, Pāṇ. iv, 4, 76; m. a draught beast, W. **-sacá**, mf(*ī*)n. congealed (water), TBr. (Sch.); m. congealing, freezing, TS. (Sch.) **-sarpaka**, m. = *pra-s°*, KātyŚr., Sch. **-sáh**, mfn. mighty, strong, RV. i, 129, 4; f. force; (°*hā*), ind. by force, violently, mightily, RV.; TS.; Br. **-saha**, m. force, power, ŚBr. (*āt*, ind. by force, MānGṛ.); (*ā*), f. N. of the wife of Indra, AitBr. **-sāda**, see s.v. **-sāha**, mfn., see *jagat-prās°*; n. (with *Bharad-vājasya*) N. of a Sāman, ĀrshBr. **-sūtika**, mf(*ī*)n. (fr. *-sūti*) relating to childbirth, MW. **-senajitī**, f., patr. fr. *prasena-jit*, MBh. **-seva**, m. a rope (as part of a horse's harness), TBr. (cf. *pra-s°*). **-skaṇva**, mf(*ī*)n. derived from Praskaṇva, ŚāṅkhŚr.; n. N. of a Sāman, ĀrshBr. **-stārika**, mf(*ī*)n. (fr. *-stāra*) Pāṇ. iv, 4, 72, Kāś. **-stāvi**, m. patr. fr. (and v.l. for) *-stāva*, VP. **-stāvika**, mf(*ī*)n. (fr. *-stāva*) introductory, L.; having a prelude (as a hymn), Lāṭy.; opportune (*a-pr°*), Mālatīm. **-stutya**, n. (fr. *-stuta*) the being propounded or discussed, MW. **-sthānika**, mf(*ī*)n. (fr. *-sthāna*) relating or favourable to departure, MBh.; R. &c.; n. preparations for d°, MBh. (cf. *mahā-pr°*). **-sthika**, mf(*ī*)n. containing or weighing or bought for a Prastha, KātyŚr., Sch.; Suśr.; n. (with *kshetra*) a field sown with a Pr° of grain, Pāṇ. v, 1, 45, Sch. **-sravaṇa**, mf(*ī*)n. coming from a spring (as water), Suśr.; m. (with *plaksha*) the source of the Sarasvatī or the place where the S° reappears, TāṇḍBr.; ŚrS.; patr. fr. *pra-sravaṇa*, ŚāṅkhBr. (v.l. *prā-śr°*). **-haṇi**, w.r. for *-vāhaṇi*. **-harika** (Dharmaś.; Kād.; cf. *câtush-prâh°*), **-hārika** (Cat.), m. (fr. *-hāra*) a police officer, watchman. **-hṛitāyana**, m. patr. fr. *pra-hṛita*, g. *aśvâdi*. **-hrādi** (*prā-*), m. patr. fr. *pra-hrāda* (N. of Virocana and Bali), AV.; MBh. &c. **-hlādanīya**, w.r. for *pra-hl°*, Lalit.

प्रांशु **prâṅśu**, mfn. (said to be fr. *pra* + *aṅśu*) high, tall, long, MBh.; Kāv. &c.; strong, intense,

Naish.; m. N. of a son of Manu Vaivasvata, Hariv.; Pur.; of a son of Vatsa-prī (or -prīti), Pur. **-tā,** f. height, loftiness, R. **-prākāra,** mfn. having long walls, Kathās. **-labhya,** mfn. to be obtained or reached (only) by a tall person, Ragh.

Prâṅśuka, mfn. large, big (said of an animal), HYog.

प्राक् *prāk.* See under *prāñc*, col. 3.

प्राकट्य *prākaṭya* &c. See under 3. *prā.*

प्राकर *prākara*, m. N. of a son of Dyutimat, MārkP.; n. N. of a Varsha called after Prākara, ib. (v.l. *pīvara*, VP.)

प्राकार *prā-kāra*, m. (fr. *prā* for *pra* and √1. *kṛi*; cf. Pāṇ. vi, 3, 122, Vārtt. 1, Pat.) a wall, enclosure, fence, rampart (esp. a surrounding wall elevated on a mound of earth; ifc. f. *ā*), ŚrS.; Mn.; MBh. &c. **-karṇa,** m. 'Wall-Ear,' N. of a minister of the owl-king Ari-mardana, Pañcat. **-khaṇḍa,** m. the fragments of a wall, Mṛicch. **-dharaṇī,** f. the platform upon a wall, R. **-bhañjana,** mfn. breaking down walls, Kathās. **-mardi,** m. patr. fr. next, g. *bāhv-ādi.* **-mardin,** m. 'wall-crusher,' N. of a man, ib. **-śesha,** mfn. having only ramparts left, Ml. **-stha,** mfn. one who stands or is stationed upon a rampart, Mn. vii, 74 &c. **Prākārâgra,** n. the top of a wall, L.

Prākārīya, mfn. fit for a wall, Pāṇ. v, 1, 12, Sch.

Prākāruka, mfn. (prob.) scattering about, Kāṭh.

प्राकृ *prâ-√kṛi*, P. Ā. *-karoti, -kurute* &c., to drive away, Kāṭh.

प्राकृत *prākṛita*, mf(*ā* or *ī*)n. (fr. *pra-kṛiti*) original, natural, artless, normal, ordinary, usual, ŚBr. &c. &c.; low, vulgar, unrefined, Mn.; MBh. &c.; provincial, vernacular, Prākritic, Vcar.; (in Sāṃkhya) belonging to or derived from Prakṛiti or the original element; (in astron.) N. of one of the 7 divisions of the planetary courses (according to Parāśara comprising the Nakshatras Svāti, Bharaṇī, Rohiṇī and Kṛittikā); m. a low or vulgar man, Mn. (viii, 338); MBh. &c.; (with or scil. *laya, pralaya* &c.) resolution or reabsorption into Prakṛiti, the dissolution of the universe, Pur.; n. any provincial or vernacular dialect cognate with Sanskrit (esp. the language spoken by women and inferior characters in the plays, but also occurring in other kinds of literature and usually divided into 4 dialects, viz. Śaurasenī, Māhārāshṭrī, Apabhraṅśa and Paiśācī), Kāv.; Kathās.; Kāvyâd. &c. **-kalpataru,** m., **-kāmadhenu,** f., **-kośa,** m., **-candrikā,** f., **-cchandaḥ-kośa,** m., **-cchandaḥ-sūtra,** n., **-cchandash-ṭīkā,** f. N. of wks. **-jvara,** m. common fever (occurring from affections of the wind in the rainy season, of the bile in the autumn, and of the phlegm in the spring), W. **-tva,** n. original or natural state or condition, KātyŚr.; vulgarity (of speech), L. **-dīpikā,** f., **-nāma-liṅgânuśāsana,** n., **-pañcī-karaṇa,** n., **-pāda,** m., **-piṅgala,** m., **-prakāśa,** m. (and *-bhāshya*, n.), **-prakriyā-vṛitti,** f., **-pradīpikā,** f., **-prabodha,** m. N. of wks. **-pralaya,** m. the total dissolution of the world, W. **-bhāshā-kāvya,** n., **-bhāshântara-vidhāna,** n. N. of wks. **-bhāshin,** mfn. speaking Prākrit, Mṛicch. **-mañjarī,** f., **-maṇi-dīpikā,** f., **-manoramā,** f. N. of wks. **-mānusha,** m. a common or ordinary man, W. **-mitra,** n. a natural friend or ally, a sovereign whose kingdom is separated by that of another from the country with which he is allied, W. (cf. *prākṛitâri* and °*tôdāsīna*). **-rahasya,** n., **-lakshaṇa,** n., **-laṅkêśvara,** m., **-vyākaraṇa,** n. (and °*ṇa-vṛitti*, f.) N. of wks. **-śāsana,** n. a manual of the Prākrit dialects, Gr. **-saṃskāra,** m., **-saṃjīvanī,** f., **-saptati,** f., **-sarvasva,** n., **-sāhitya-ratnâkara,** m., **-subhāshitâvalī,** f., **-sūtra,** n., **-setu,** m. N. of wks. **Prākṛitâdhyāya,** m. and °**tânanda,** m. N. of wks. **Prākṛitâri,** m. a natural enemy, a sovereign of an adjacent country, Mallin. **Prākṛitâshṭâdhyāyī,** f. N. of wk. **Prākṛitôdāsīna,** m. a natural neutral, a sovereign whose dominions are situated beyond those of the natural ally, W.

Prākṛitāyana, m. patr. fr. *pra-kṛita*, g. *aśvâdi.*

Prākṛitika, mf(*ī*)n. relating to Pra-kṛiti or the original element, material, natural, common, vulgar, Sāṃkhyak.; Pur.; Tattvas.

प्राकोटक *prākoṭaka*, m. pl. N. of a people, MBh.; mfn. relating to the Prākoṭakas, ib. (v.l. *prāk-kośala*).

प्राक्कर्मन् *prāk-karman, prāg-agra* &c. See under *prāñc*, col. 3, and p. 704, col. 1.

प्रागहि *prāgahi*, m. N. of a teacher, ŚāṅkhŚr. °**hīya,** mfn. relating to Prāgahi, ib.

प्रागार *prâgāra*, m. or n.(?) a principal building, Inscr.

प्राग्र *prâgra* (*pra-agra*), n. the highest point, summit, Nir. **-sara,** mfn. going in the forefront, foremost in (comp.), Hcar.; chief among (gen.), Śak. v, 15 (v.l. *-hara*). **-hara,** mfn. taking the best share, chief, principal among (gen. or comp.), Kālid., Hcar.

Prâgrya, mfn. chief, principal, most excellent, MBh.; Hariv.

प्राग्राट *prāgrāṭa*, n. thin coagulated milk, L.

प्राघुण *prāghuṇa*, m. (Prākṛit for *prâ-ghūrṇa*; cf. *prāhuṇa*) a visitor, guest, Kathās. °**ghuṇaka** (Pañcat.), °**ghuṇika** (Bhām.), m. id. (°*ṇiki* √*kṛi*, to make a visitor of, cause to reach; *kathā mama śravana-prāghuṇikī-kṛitā*, 'the tale was made to reach my ears' i.e. 'was communicated to me,' Naish.)

Prâghūrṇa, m. (lit. 'one who goes forth deviously') a wanderer, guest, Pañcat. °**ghūrṇaka,** m. id. (v.l.) °**ghūrṇika,** m. id., L. (v.l.); (*ā*), f. hospitable reception, Vet.

प्राङ् *prāṅ* &c. See p. 704, col. 3.

प्राङ्ग *prâṅga* (*pra-aṅga*), n. a kind of drum (=*paṇava*), L. (cf. next).

प्राङ्गण *prâṅgaṇa* (*pra-aṅgaṇa*), n. a court, yard, court-yard, Ratnâv.; Kathās.; Pur. &c. (also written °*gana*); a kind of drum, L. (cf. prec.)

प्राचण्ड्य *prācaṇḍya, prācurya* &c. See under 3. *prā*, p. 702, col. 1.

प्राचार *prâcāra* (*pra-ācāra*), mfn. contrary to or deviating from ordinary institutes and observances, W.; m. a winged ant, Hariv. (v.l.)

Prâcārya, m. the teacher of a teacher or a former teacher, Āpast. (=*pragata ācārya*, Pat.)

प्राचिका *prācikā*, f. (cf. *prājika*) a musquito, L.; a female falcon, L.

प्राचिक्य *prācikya*, n., fr. *pracika*, g. *purohitâdi* (Kāś.)

प्राचीन *prācīna* &c. See p. 704, col. 3.

प्राचीर *prācīra*, m. or n. (fr. *pra-cīra*?) an enclosure, hedge, fence, wall, Kull.; L.

प्राच्य *prācya.* See p. 705, col. 1.

प्राछ् *prāch*, incorrect for *prāś.* See 3. *prāś.*

प्राजक *prâjaka*, m. (fr. *pra-√aj*) a driver, coachman, Mn. viii, 293 &c. **Prâjana,** m. a whip, goad, Gobh.; KātyŚr., Sch. (also *prâja*, Gṛihyās.); °*nin*, m. one who bears a whip, Gṛihyās. **Prâjika,** m. a hawk, VarBṛS., Sch. (cf. *prācikā*). **Prâjitṛi,** m. =*prâjaka*, L. **Prâjin,** m. (prob.) =*prâjaka*; °*ji-dhara*, m. N. of a man, Rājat.; °*ji-pakshin*, m. a partic. bird (cf. *vāji-p*°); °*ji-mathikā*, f. N. of a place, Rājat.

प्राजरुहा *prājaruhā* and *prājaryā*, ind., with √*kṛi*, g. *sâkshād-ādi* (Kāś.)

प्राजल *prājala*, m. pl. N. of a Vedic school, L. (v.l. *prājvalana* and *prâñjali*).

प्राजापत *prājāpata*, mf(*ī*)n. = next, mfn., g. *mahishy-ādi*; (*ī*), f. N. of AV. v, 2, 7, Kauś.

Prājāpatyá, mf(*ā́*)n. coming or derived from Prajā-pati, relating or sacred to him, AV. &c. &c.; m. a descendant of Pr° (patr. of Patam-ga, of Prajāvat, of Yakshma-nāśana, of Yajña, of Vimada, of Vishṇu, of Saṃvaraṇa, of Hiraṇya-garbha), RAnukr.; (with or scil. *vivāha* or *vidhi*) a form of marriage (in which the father gives his daughter to the bridegroom without receiving a present from him), ĀśvGṛ. i, 6; Mn. iii, 30 &c.; (with or scil. *kṛicchra* or *upavāsa*) a kind of fast or penance (lasting 12 days, food being eaten during the first 3 once in the morning, during the next 3 once in the evening, in the next 3 only if given as alms, and a plenary fast being observed during the 3 remaining days, Mn. xi, 105; Yājñ. &c.; (with *śakaṭa*, also n.) the chariot of Rohiṇī, N. of an asterism, Var.; Pañcat.; (with or scil. *tithi*) the 8th day in the dark half of the month Pausha, Col. (°*tyāś catvāraḥ prastobhāḥ*, N. of Sāmans, ĀrshBr.; superl. °*tya-tama*, Kapishṭh.); a son born in the Pr° form of marriage, Vishṇ.; a Kshatriya and a Vaiśya, GopBr.; Vait.; N. of the confluence of the Gaṅgā and Yamunā, L. (cf. MBh. i, 2097); (with Jainas) N. of the first black Vāsudeva, L.; (*ā*), f. patr. of Dakshiṇā, RAnukr.; giving away the whole of one's property before entering upon the life of an ascetic or mendicant, W.; N. of a verse addressed to Prajā-pati, ĀpGṛ.; (with *śakaṭī*) = m. n. with *śakaṭa*, MW.; n. generative energy, procreative power, AV.; TS.; (with or scil. *karman*) a partic. kind of generation in the manner of Prajā-pati, MBh.; Hariv.; a partic. sacrifice performed before appointing a daughter to raise issue in default of male heirs, W.; the world of Prajā-pati, MārkP.; (with or scil. *nakshatra* or *bha*) the asterism Rohiṇī, MBh.; Var.; (also with *aksharya, prayas-vat* and *mādhucchandasa*) N. of Sāmans, ĀrshBr. **-tva,** n. the state or condition of belonging or referring to Prajā-pati, Saṃk. **-pradāyin** (or *-sthāna-pr*°), mfn. (prob.) procuring the place or world of Pr°, MārkP. **-vrata,** n. N. of a partic. observance, ĀpGṛ., Sch. **-sthalī-pāka-prayoga,** m. N. of wk. **Prājāpatyêshṭi,** f. N. of wk.

Prājāpatyaka, mfn. belonging or referring or sacred to Prajā-pati, MBh.

Prājāvata, mf(*ī*)n. (fr. *prajā-vat*), g. *mahishy-ādi.*

Prājesa, mf(*ī*)n. (fr. *prajêśa*) sacred to Prajā-pati; n. the Nakshatra Rohiṇī, VarBṛS.

Prājeśvara, mf(*ī*)n. (fr. *prajêśvara*) id., ib.

प्राजिधर *prâji-dhara* &c. See *prâjaka.*

प्राज्ञ *prājña* &c. See p. 702, col. 1.

प्राज्य *prâjya*, mfn. (? fr. *pra*+*ājya*, 'having much ghee') copious, abundant, large, great, important, MBh.; Kāv. &c.; lasting, long, Rājat.; high, lofty, A. **-kāma,** mfn. rich in enjoyments, R. **-dakshiṇa,** mfn. abounding in sacrificial fees, MBh. **-bhaṭṭa,** m. N. of an author, Cat. **-bhuja,** mfn. long-armed, Ml. **-bhojya,** mfn. (prob.) = *-kāma*, ib. **-vikrama,** mfn. possessing great power, Kum. **-vṛishṭi,** mfn. sending rain in abundance (said of Indra), Śak. **Prâjyêndhana-tṛiṇa,** mfn. (a place) abounding in fuel and grass, Hariv.

प्राञ्च् *prāñc*, mfn. (fr. *pra* + 2. *añc*; nom. *prā́ṅ, prā́cī, prā́k*; cf. Pāṇ. vi, 1, 182) directed forwards or towards, being in front, facing, opposite, RV.; VS.; AV.; Mn. (acc. with √*kṛi*, to bring, procure, offer, RV.; to stretch forth [the fingers], ib.; to make straight, prepare or clear [a path], ib.; [also with *pra-√tir* or *-√nī*] to advance, promote, further, ib.; with Caus. of √*klṛip*, to face, turn opposite to, Mn. vii, 189); turned eastward, eastern, easterly (opp. to *ápāc*, western), RV. &c. &c.; being to the east of (abl.), Mn. ii, 21; running from west to east, taken lengthwise, KātyŚr.; (with *viśvataḥ*) turned to all directions, RV.; inclined, willing, ib.; lasting, long (as life), AV.; (esp. ibc.; cf. below) previous, prior, former; (*prā́ñcas*), m. pl. the people of the east, eastern people or grammarians, Pāṇ. i, 1, 75 &c.; (*prā́cī*), f. (with or scil. *diś*) the east, ŚBr. &c.; MBh. &c.; the post to which an elephant is tied, L.; (*prā́k*; *prāṅ*, Lāṭy.; KātyŚr.), ind. before (in place or in order or time; as prep. with abl. [cf. Pāṇ. ii, 1, 11; 12], rarely with gen.; also in comp. with its subst., Pāṇ. ib.), ŚrS.; Up.; MBh. &c.; in the east, to the east of (abl.), RV.; Lāṭy.; before the eyes, Hit. i, 76; at first, formerly, previously, already, Mn.; MBh. &c.; (with *eva*), a short while ago, recently, just, Śak.; still more so, how much more (=*kim-uta*), Buddh.; above, in the former part (of a book), Mn.; Pāṇ.; first, in the first place, above all, Kathās.; MārkP.; from now, henceforth, Var.; up to, as far as (with abl.; esp. in gram., e.g. *prāk kaḍārāt*, up to the word *kaḍāra*, Pāṇ. ii, 1, 3); between (=*avântare*), L.; early in the morning, L.; w.r. for *drāk*, MBh.; (*prācā́*), ind. forwards, onwards, RV.; eastwards, ib.; (*prācā́s*), ind. from the front, ib.

Prāk, in comp. for *prāñc.* **-karman,** n. preparatory medical treatment, Suśr.; an action done in a former life, Kathās. **-kalpa,** m. a former age or era, MārkP. **-kāla,** m. a former age or time, W. **-kālīna,** mfn. belonging to former or ancient times, ancient, previous, former, W. **-kūla**, mfn., *-tā*, f., w. r. for *-tūla* &c., q. v. **-kṛita**, mfn. done before, done in a former life, MBh.; n. an action done in a f° l°, Siṇhâs. **-kevala**, mfn. manifested from the first in a distinct form (without preliminary symptoms, as a disease), Suśr. **-kośala** (or *-kosala*), mfn. belonging to the eastern Kośalas (as a prince), MBh. (v. l. *prākoṭaka*). **-caraṇa**, mfn. previously excited (said of the female generative organs previous to coitus), Car.; ŚārṅgS. **-ciram**, ind. before it is too late, in good time, MBh. **-chāya**, n. the falling eastward of a shadow, Mn. **-tanaya**, m. a former pupil, BhP. (v. l. *prâpta-naya*). **-tarām**, ind. somewhat more eastward, MānŚr. **-tiryak-pramāṇa**, n. the breadth in front, KātyŚr., Comm. **-tūla**, mfn. having panicles (of Kuśa grass) turned towards the east, GṛS.; Mn.; BhP.; n. a panicle of Kuśa grass turned eastward, W.; *-tā*, f. the being turned towards the e° (of sacrificial vessels), Prayogar.; (w. r. *-kūla*, °*tā*). **-pada**, n. the first member of a compound, Piṅg., Sch. **-paścimâyata**, mf(*ā*)n. running from east to west, Hcat. **-puṇya-prabhava**, mfn. caused by merit accumulated in former existences, MW. **-pushpā**, f. N. of plant, Pāṇ. iv, 1, 64, Vārtt. 1. **-pravaṇa** (*prā́k-*), mf(*ā*)n. sloping eastward, ŚBr. **-prastuta**, mfn. mentioned before, Mālatīm. **-prahāṇa**, m. the first blow, A. **-prātarāśika**, mfn. to be studied before breakfast, SaṃhUp. **-phala**, m. the bread-fruit tree (= *panasa*), L. **-phalgunī**, f. = *pūrva-ph°* (q. v.), Var.; *-bhava*, m. Bṛihaspati or the planet Jupiter (born when the moon was in the mansion Prāk-phalgunī), L. **-phālguna**, m. the planet Jupiter, L. (cf. prec.); (*ī*), f. = *pūrva-ph°* (q. v.), Var. (v. l. *-phalgunī*). **-phālguneya**, m. the planet Jupiter (cf. prec.), L. **-śas**, ind. eastwards, towards the east, Gobh. **-śiras** (*prā́k-*), mfn. having the head turned to the east, ŚBr.; GṛŚrS.; MBh.; MārkP. **-śirasa** (W.) or **-śiraska** (Suśr.), mfn. id. **-śṛiṅga-vat**, m. N. of a Ṛishi, MBh. **-śrotas**, w. r. for *-srotas*, q. v. **-ślishṭa**, mfn. v. l. for *prāślishṭa*, q. v. **-saṃstha**, mfn. (*-tva*, n.) ending in the east, KātyŚr. **-saṃdhyā**, f. morning twilight, Hariv.; Var. **-samāsa**, mfn. having the joint (?) or tie turned eastward, Lāṭy. **-soma**, mfn. (MānGṛ.) or **-saumika**, mf(*ī*)n. (Yājñ.) preceding the Soma sacrifice. **-srotas**, mfn. flowing eastward (w. r. *-śrotas*), R.

Prāktana, mf(*ī*)n. former, prior, previous, preceding, old, ancient (opp. to *idānīntana*), Hariv.; Ragh.; BhP. &c. **-karman**, n. any act formerly done or done in a former state of existence; fate, destiny, Pañcat. **-janman**, n. a former birth, Kum.

Prāktás (AV.) or **prā́ktāt** (RV.), ind. from the front, from the east.

Prāg, in comp. for *prāñc*. **-agra**, mf(*ā*)n. having the tip or point turned forward or eastward (*-tā*, f), GṛŚrS.; BhP. **-anurāga**, m. former affection, Mālatīm. **-anūka**, n. the stripes stretching lengthways on the back part of an altar, KātyŚr., Comm. **-apaccheda**, m. a division made lengthwise, ib. **-apám**, ind. (fr. *-apāk*) from the front towards the back, in a backward direction, ŚBr. **-aparâyata**, mf(*ā*)n. extending from east to west, Var. **-apavargam**, ind. with its end to the east, Āp. **-abhāva**, m. the not yet existing, non-existence of anything which may yet be, Bhāshāp.; Sāṃkhyak., Comm. &c.; (in law) the non-possession of property that may be possessed, W.; *-vāda*, m., *-vicāra*, m., *-vicāra-rahasya*, n., *-vijñāna*, n., °*vôjjīvana*, n., N. of wks. **-abhihita**, mfn. before mentioned; *-tva*, n., Hcat. **-avasthā**, f. a former state, a former condition of life, Rājat.; Sāy. **-āṅgam**, ind. prob. w. r. for *-gaṅgam*, 'east of the Ganges,' MBh. **-āyata**, mf(*ā*)n. extending eastward, ĀśvŚr.; MBh. **-āhuti**, f. morning libation, ŚāṅkhGṛ., Comm. **-āhnika**, mfn. relating to the forenoon (= *paurvāhṇika*), MBh. **-ukti**, f. previous utterance, VPrāt., Sch. **-uttara**, mf(*ā*)n. north-eastern, MBh.; Hariv.; R.; (*ā*), f. (with or scil. *diś*) the north-east, MBh.; R.; (*eṇa* [MBh.] or *-tas* [Var.]), ind. n°-eastwards, to the n°-east of (with abl. or gen.); *-dig-bhāga* (Pañcat.) or *-dig-vibhāga* (MBh.), m. the n°-eastern side of (gen.) **-utpatti**, f. first appearance, f° manifestation (of a disease), Car. **-udañc**, mf(*īcī*)n. north-eastern, GṛŚrS.; Yājñ.; MBh.; Pur.; (*īcī*), f. (with or scil. *diś*) the north-east, ib.; (*ak*), ind. to the n°-e°, ĀśvŚr.; *-udak-pravaṇa*, mfn. sloping n°-eastward or sloping towards the east or north, ShaḍvBr.; Lāṭy.; Kauś.; °*ak-plava* (Hariv.) or °*ak-plavana* (MBh.; MārkP.), mfn. inclining towards the north-east; °*ag-agra*, mfn. having the tips turned somewhat east and somewhat north, ĀpGṛ. (Sch.); °*aṅ-mukha*, mfn. having the face turned to the n°-e° (or to the e° or n°), Mn.; BhP. **-uddhāra-saṃgraha**, m. N. of wk. **-ūḍhā**, f. (a woman) formerly married, Viddh. **-gaṅgam**, ind., see *prāg-āṅgam*. **-gamana-vat**, mfn. having a forward motion, going forwards, Vedântas. **-gāmin**, mfn. going before, preceding, intending to go before, R. **-guṇa**, mfn. possessing any previously mentioned quality, RāmatUp. **-granthi**, mfn. having the knots turned eastward, KātyŚr. **-grāmam**, ind. before the village or to the east of the v°, Pāṇ. ii, 1, 12, Sch. **-grīva**, mfn. having the neck turned eastward, GṛŚrS.; Kauś. **-ghuta**, n. (KātyŚr.) or **-ghoma**, m. (*prāg-homa*, TBr., Comm.) a previous oblation. **-janmaka**, mf(*ikā*)n. belonging to a former life, HPariś. (*ikā*, f. = *devâṅganā*). **-janman**, n. a former birth, f° life, BhP.; Kathās.; Rājat. **-jāta**, n. (Bhartṛ.) or **-jāti**, f. (Kathās.) id. **-jyotisha**, mfn. lighted from the east, ŚāṅkhGṛ.; relating to the city of Prāg-jy°, MBh.; m. N. of a country (= *kāma-rūpa*), L.; the king of the city of Prāg-jy° (N. of Bhaga-datta), MBh.; (pl.) N. of a people living in that city or its environs, MārkP.; Var.; n. N. of a city, the dwelling-place of the demon Naraka, MBh.; Hariv.; R.; Rājat.; Ragh.; N. of a Sāman, MBh. (Nīlak.); *-jyeshṭha*, m. N. of Vishṇu, ib. **-dakshiṇa**, mf(*ā*)n. south-eastern, Kauś.; MārkP.; (*ā*), f. the south-east; ind. to the south-east, KātyŚr.: °*ṇāñc*, mf(*ācī*)n. directed or turned to the south-east, ŚāṅkhŚr.; °*ṇā-pravaṇa*, mfn. sloping south-eastward, ĀśvGṛ. **-daṇḍa**, mf(*ā*)n. having the stem or stalk turned eastward, Kauś.; AitBr.; ŚāṅkhŚr.; (*am*), ind., ĀpŚr.; Vait. **-daśa** (*prā́g-*), mfn. having the border turned eastward, ŚBr. **-1. -diś**, f. 'the eastern quarter,' the east, Hariv. **-2. -diś**, mfn. one who has been pointed to or mentioned before, Hariv. **-deśa**, m. the eastern country, country of the eastern people, Pāṇ. i, 1, 75, Sch. (°*śam*, w. r. for *-diśaḥ* [see prec.], Hariv. 444). **-daihika**, mfn. belonging to life in a former body, Car. **-dvār**, f. a door on the east side, BhP. **-dvāra**, mfn. having doors towards the east, Kauś.; ŚāṅkhGṛ.; KātyŚr.; (also *-dvārika*, Var., Comm.); N. of the 7 lunar mansions beginning with Kṛittikā, Var.; n. the place before a door, R.; Ragh.; a door on the east side, MānGṛ. **-dvārika**, mfn., see prec. **-bodhi**, m. N. of a mountain, MWB. 399. **-bhakta**, n. taking medicine before a meal, Suśr.; medicine to be taken before a meal, Car. **-bhava**, m. a previous life, Siṇhâs. **-bhāga**, m. the fore or upper part, Śiś. iv, 49 (v. l. *-bhāra*); the eastern side, Var. **-bhāra**, m. (prob. fr. Prākr. *pabbhāra* = *pra-hvāra*, √*hvṛi*) the slope of a mountain, Mālatīm.; Kathās.; Bālar.; bending, inclining (cf. *prācīna-p°*; *purataḥ-p°*, bent to the front, Lalit.); inclination, propensity, Lalit. (ifc. = inclined to, Divyâv.); the being not far from, Yogas.; a (subsiding) mass, multitude, heap, quantity, Bhartṛ.; Prab. &c.; a shelter-roof, L. (v. l. for *-bhāga*, q. v.) **-bhāva**, m. prior existence, L.; superiority, excellence, W.; w. r. for *-bhāra* in the sense of 'slope of a mountain' (L.) and 'being not far from' (Yogas.); *-tas*, ind. from a prior state of existence, W. **-bhāvīya**, mfn. belonging to a pr° ex°, Śaṃk., Sch. **-rūpa**, n. previous symptom (of disease), Cat. **-lagna**, n. horoscope, VarYogay. **-lajja**, mf(*ā*)n. being ashamed at first, Rājat. **-1. -vaṇśa**, m. a former or previous generation, Hariv.; N. of Vishṇu, ib. **-2. -vaṇśa**, mfn. having the supporting beams turned eastward, KātyŚr.; Āp.; m. the space before the Vedi (perhaps a kind of sacrificial chamber having columns or beams towards the east and situated opposite to the Vedi; accord. to others, a room in which the family and friends of the person performing the sacrifice assemble), ĀpŚr.; Hariv.; Ragh.; BhP. **-vaṇśika**, mfn. relating to the space before the Vedi, ĀpŚr., Comm. **-vacana**, n. a former decision, VPrāt., Sch.; anything formerly decided or decreed, MBh. **-vaṭa**, m. or n. (?) N. of a city, R. **-vat**, ind. as before, as previously, as formerly, Kathās.; as in the preceding part (of a book), Pāṇ. i, 2, 37, Vārtt. 2, Sch. **-vāṭa-kula**, n. N. of a family, Bhadrab. **-vāta**, m. east-wind, Car. **-vṛitta**, n. former behaviour, Kathās.; (in law) = 1. *prāṅ-nyāya* (q. v.), Bṛihasp.; °*ttânta*, m. a former event, previous adventure, Vet. **-vṛitti**, f. conduct or life in a former existence, Kathās. **-vesha**, m. a f° dress, Rājat. **-hāra**, m. w. r. for *-bhāra*, q. v. **-homa**, see *-ghoma*, col. 2.

Prāgivīya, mfn., fr. *prāg iva*, Pāṇ. v, 3, 70.

Prāgghitīya, mfn., fr. *prāgghitāt*, ib. iv, 4, 75.

Prāgdiśīya, mfn., fr. *prāg diśaḥ*, ib. v, 3, 1.

Prāgdīvyatīya, mfn., fr. *prāg dīvyataḥ*, ib. iv, 1, 83.

Prāgdhitīya, mfn., w. r. for °*gghitīya*.

Prāṅ, in comp. for *prāñc*. **-āyata**, mfn. = *prāg-āy°* (q. v.), Kauś. **-īkshaṇa**, n. looking eastward, KātyŚr., Comm. **-īsha**, mfn. having the pole turned eastward, ib. **-nayana**, n. moving eastward, ib. **-nāsikā** or °**kī**, f., Pāṇ. iv, 1, 60, Sch. **-1. -nyāya**, m. (in law) a former trial of a cause, special plea, W.; °*yôttara*, n. a defendant's plea that the charge against him has already been tried, Yājñ., Sch. **-2. -nyāya**, mfn. turned eastward according to rule, ŚāṅkhŚr. **-mukha**, mf(*ā* or *ī*)n. having the tip or the face turned forward or eastward, facing e°, GṛŚrS.; Mn.; MBh. &c. (also °*khâñcana*, Sāy. on RV. x, 18, 3; °*kha-karaṇa*, n., Lāṭy.; °*kha-tva*, n., Hcat.); inclined towards, desirous of, wishing (ifc.), Kathās.; (*am*), ind. eastwards, Sūryas. **-śāyin**, mfn., see *adhaḥ-p°*.

Prācā, ind., see *prāñc*. **-jihva** (*prā́cā-*), mfn. moving the tongue forwards (said of Agni), RV. i, 140, 3. **-manyu**, mfn. striving to move forwards (said of Indra), ib. viii, 50, 9.

Prācī, f. of *prāñc*. **-pati**, m. 'lord of the east,' N. of Indra, L. **-pratīci-tas**, ind. from the east or fr° the west, Uttamac. **-pramāṇa**, n. length (opp. to breadth), KātyŚr., Sch. **-mūla**, n. the eastern horizon, Megh. **-sarasvatī-māhātmya**, n. N. of wk.

Prācīna, mf(*ā*)n. turned towards the front or eastward, eastern, easterly, RV.; TS.; Br. &c.; former, prior, preceding, ancient, old, Mn., Kull.; Hāyan.; m. n. a hedge (= *prācīra*), L.; (*ā*), f. Clypea Hernandifolia, L.; the Ichneumon plant, L.; n. N. of a Sāman, ĀrshBr.; (*am*), ind. in front, forwards, before (in space and time; with abl.), eastwards, to the east of (abl.), RV.; AV.; TS.; Br. &c.; subsequently (*átaḥ-p°*, 'further on from that point'), ŚBr. **-āvītin**, mfn. = °*nâvītin* (q. v.), Mn. **-karṇa**, mf(*ā*)n. having the wood-knots turned eastward (said of a branch of the Udumbara tree), ĀpŚr. **-kalpa**, m. a former Kalpa or period of the world's duration, Sāṃkhyak., Sch. **-kūla** (BhP.) = *prāk-k°* = *prāk-tūla*, q. v. (v. l. *prācīna-mūla*). **-garbha**, m. N. of an ancient Ṛishi also called Apântara-tamas, MBh. **-gāthā**, f. an ancient story or tradition, MW. **-gauḍa**, m. N. of the author of the Saṃvatsara-pradīpa, Cat. **-grīva** (*prācīna-*), mfn. having the neck turned eastward, Br. **-tā**, f. antiquity, oldness, MW. **-tāná**, m. the warp or longitudinal threads of a web, TS. **-tilaka**, m. 'having a mark towards the east (?),' the moon, L. **-tva**, n. = *-tā*, MW. **-paksha** (*prācīna-*), mf(*ā*)n. having the feathers turned forward (as an arrow), AV. **-panasa**, m. 'the eastern Jaka tree,' Aegle Marmelos, L. **-prakriyā**, f. N. of a gramm. wk. (= *prakriyā-kaumudī*), Cat. **-prajanana** (*prācīna-*), mfn., ŚBr. vii, 4, 2, 40. **-pravaṇa**, mfn. sloping eastward, ĀpŚr. **-prāg-bhāra**, mfn. bending or inclining e°, Buddh. **-barhis**, m. (nom. °*hi* before *ṛi*) 'eastern light (?),' N. of Indra, Ragh.; of a Prajā-pati of the race of Atri, MBh.; of a son of Havir-dhāman (or Havir-dhāna) and father of the 10 Pracetas, MBh.; Hariv.; Pur.; of a son of Manu, BhP. **-mata**, n. an ancient belief, a belief sanctioned by antiquity, MW. **-mātrā-vāsas**, n. a partic. article of women's clothing, ĀpŚr. **-mūla**, mfn. having roots turned eastward, BhP. **-yoga**, m. 'ancient Yoga,' N. of a man, g. *gargâdi*; of an ancient teacher, father of Patañjali, VāyuP. **-yogi-pútra** (*prā́cīna-*), m. N. of a teacher, ŚBr. **-yogya** (*prā́cīna-*), m. patr. fr. *-yoga*, ŚBr.; Up. &c.; (pl.) N. of a school of the Sāma-veda, Āryav., Caraṇ. **-raśmi** (*prā́cīna-*), mfn. having reins directed forward, RV. x, 36, 6. **-vaṇśa** (*prā́cīna-*), mf(*ā*)n. having the supporting beams turned eastward, TS.; ŚBr.; Kāṭh. (cf. *prāg-v°*); n. a hut which has the s° b° t° e°, TS. **-vṛitti**, f. N. of Comm. on the Uṇādi-sūtras. **-śāla**, m. N. of a man, ChUp. **-śiva-stuti**, f. N. of an ancient hymn in praise of Śiva. **-shaḍ-aśīti**, f. N. of wk. **-haraṇa**, n. carrying towards the east, c° to the eastern fire, ĀśvŚr. **Prācīnâgra**, mfn. having its points turned eastward (said of sacred grass), ŚBr. **Prācīnâtāna**, m. pl. (AitBr.) or n. sg. (KaushUp.; v. l. pl.) = *prācīna-tānā*, q. v. **Prācīnâpavītin**, mfn. = °*nâvītin* (q. v.), ŚāṅkhŚr. **Prācīnâmalaka**, m. Flacourtia Cataphracta; n. its fruit, MBh.; Hariv.; Suśr. **Prācīnâvavītin**, mfn. = °*nâvītin* (q. v.), ŚBr. **Prācīnâvītá**, mfn. = °*nâvītin*, Gal.; n. the wearing of the sacred cord over the right shoulder (as at a Śrāddha), TS.; Lāṭy.; ŚāṅkhGṛ. **Prācīnâvītin**, mfn. (Br.; GṛŚrS.; Gobh.; Mn.) or °**nôpavītá**, mfn. (AV.) wearing the sacred cord over the right shoulder.

Prācais, ind. forwards, RV. i, 83, 2 (cf. *uccais, nīcais, parācais*).

Prācyà or **prācyá**, mf(*ā*)n. being in front or in the east, living in the east, belonging to the east, eastern, easterly, AV.; RPrāt., Sch.; MBh.; R. &c.; preceding (also in a work), prior, ancient, old (opp. to *ādhunika*), Bālar.; Sāh.; N. of partic. hymns belonging to the Sāma-veda, Hariv.; BhP.; m. N. of a man, Buddh.; (pl.) the inhabitants of the east, the eastern country, Br.; KātyŚr.; MBh. &c.; the ancients, ŚārṅgP.; (*ā*), f. (with or scil. *bhāshā*) the dialect spoken in the east of India, Sāh. **–kaṭha**, m. pl. the eastern Kaṭhas (a school of the black Yajur-veda), Caraṇ.; Āryav. **–pada-vṛitti**, f. a term applied to the rule according to which *e* remains in partic. cases unchanged before *a*, RPrāt. **–pāñcālī**, f. pl., SaṃhUp. xvi, 3. **–bhāshā**, f. the dialect of the east of India, MW. **–ratha**, m. a car used in the eastern country, Lāṭy. **–vṛitti**, f. a kind of metre, Piṅg.; Col. **–sapta-sama**, mfn., Pāṇ. vi, 2, 12, Sch. **–sāman**, m. pl. N. of partic. chanters of the Sāma-veda, BhP. **Prācyâdhvaryu**, m., Pāṇ. vi, 2, 10, Sch. **Prācyâvantya**, m. pl. N. of a people, Suśr. **Prācyôdañc**, mf(*īcī*)n. running from east to north, Hcat.

Prācyaka, mfn. situated in the east, BhP.

Prācyāyana, m. patr. fr. *prācya*, g. *aśvâdi*.

प्राञ्जन *prāñjana* (*pra-añj*°), n. paint or cement (on an arrow), AV.

प्राञ्जल *prāñjala*, mfn. (prob. fr. *pra*+*añjali*, and = *prāñjali*) straight, Suśr.; upright, honest, sincere, ĀpŚr., Sch.; level (as a road), Kād. **–tā**, f. straightness, plainness (of meaning), Pañcat.

Prāñjali, mf(*ī*)n. joining and holding out the hollowed open hands (as a mark of respect and humility or to receive alms; cf. *añjali, kṛitâñj*°), Mn.; MBh. &c.; m. pl. N. of a school of the Sāma-veda, Āryav. (also *-dvaita-bhṛit*; v. l. *prājvalanā dvaita-bhṛitaḥ* and *prājalā dvaita-bhṛityāḥ*). **–pragraha**, mfn. holding the hands joined and outstretched, R. (v. l. °*liḥ pragr*°). **–sthita**, mfn. standing with joined and outstretched hands, ib.

Prāñjalika (MBh.), °**lin** (Hariv.) = *prâñjali*.

Prāñjali-√bhū, to stand holding out the joined and hollowed open hands, Kāraṇḍ.

प्राडाहति *prādāhati*, m. patr., g. *taulvaly-ādi* (v. l. *prāṇāhoti*, Kāś.)

प्राड्विवाक *prāḍ-vivāka*. See under 3. *prāś*, p. 709, col. 2.

प्राण् *prāṇ* or *prān* (*pra-√an*), P. *prāṇiti* (Pāṇ. viii, 4, 19, Sch.; impf. *prâṇat*, vii, 3, 99, Sch.) or *prâniti* (Vop.), to breathe in, inhale, KenUp.; to breathe, RV.; AV.; ŚBr.; Up.; to blow (as the wind), AitBr.; to live, AV.; Bhaṭṭ.; to smell, Saṃk.: Caus. *prâṇayati* (aor. *prâṇiṇat*, Pāṇ. viii, 4, 21, Sch.), to cause to breathe, animate, AV.; Bhaṭṭ.: Desid. *prâṇiṇishati*, Pāṇ. viii, 4, 21, Sch.

Prâṇ, mfn. breathing, Pāṇ. viii, 4, 20, Sch.

2. **Prâṇá**, m. (ifc. f. *ā*; for 1. see under √*prā*, p. 701) the breath of life, breath, respiration, spirit, vitality; pl. life, RV. &c. &c. (*prâṇān* with √*muc* or √*hā* or *pari-√tyaj*, 'to resign or quit life;' with √*raksh*, 'to save l°;' with *ni-√han*, 'to destroy l°;' *tvam me prâṇaḥ*, 'thou art to me as dear as l°;' often ifc.; cf. *pati-, māna-pr*°); a vital organ, vital air (3 in number, viz. *prâṇa, apâna* and *vyāna*, AitBr.; TUp.; Suśr.; usually 5, viz. the preceding 3 with *sam-āna* and *ud-āna*, ŚBr.; MBh.; Suśr. &c.; cf. MWB. 242; or with the other vital organs 6, ŚBr.; or 7, AV.; Br.; MuṇḍUp.; or 9, AV.; TS.; Br.; or 10, ŚBr.; pl. the 5 organs of vitality or sensation, viz. *prâṇa, vāc, cakshus, śrotra, manas*, collectively, ChUp. ii, 7, 1; or = nose, mouth, eyes and ears, GopBr.; ŚrS.; Mn. iv, 143); air inhaled, wind, AV.; ŚBr.; breath (as a sign of strength), vigour, energy, power, MBh.; R. &c. (*sarva-prâṇena* or *-prâṇaiḥ*, 'with all one's strength' or 'all one's heart;' cf. *yathā-prâṇam*); a breath (as a measure of time, or the t° requisite for the pronunciation of 10 long syllables = ⅙ Vināḍikā), Var.; Āryabh.; VP.; N. of a Kalpa (the 6th day in the light half of Brahmā's month), Pur.; (in Sāṃkhya) the spirit (= *purusha*), Tattvas.; (in Vedânta) the spirit identified with the totality of dreaming spirits, Vedântas.; RTL. 35 (cf. *prâṇâtman*); poetical inspiration, W.; myrrh, L.; a N. of the letter *y*, Up.; of a Sāman, TāṇḍBr. (*Vasishṭhasya prâṇâpânau*, ĀrshBr.); of Brahmā, L.; of Vishṇu, RTL. 106; of a Vasu, BhP.; of a son of the Vasu Dhara, Hariv.; of a Marut, Yājñ., Sch.; of a son of Dhātṛi, Pur.; of a son of Vidhātṛi, BhP.; of a Ṛishi in the 2nd Manv-antara, Hariv. **–kara**, mf(*ī*)n. 'life-causing,' invigorating, refreshing, Cāṇ.; m. N. of a man, L. **–karman**, n. vital function, Bhag. **–kṛicchra**, n. peril of life, MBh.; BhP. **–kṛishṇa**, m. (also with *viśvāsa*) N. of 2 authors, Cat. **–grahá**, m. 'breath-catcher,' the nose, A.; pl. N. of partic. Soma vessels, TS. **–ghātaka** (MW.), **-ghna** (Suśr.), mf(*ī*)n. life-destroying, killing, mortal. **–caya**, m. increase of vitality or strength, Var. **–cit**, mfn. forming a deposit of breath, ŚBr. **–cití**, f. a mass or deposit of breath, ib. **–cchid**, mfn. cutting life short, deadly, fatal, Var. **–ccheda**, m. destruction of life, murder; *-kara*, mfn. causing d° of l°, murderous, Hit. **–tejas** (°*ṇá-*), mfn. whose splendour or glory is life or breath, ŚBr. **–toshiṇī**, f. N. of a wk. on Tantric rites (1821). **–tyāga**, m. abandonment of life, suicide, death, Kāv.; Kathās. **–trāṇa**, n. saving of l°, Mālatīm.; *-rasa*, m. N. of a partic. mixture, L. **–tvá**, n. the state of breath or life, ŚBr.; Kap. **–dá**, mf(*ā*)n. life-giving, saving or preserving life, AV. &c. &c.; m. Terminalia Tomentosa or Coccinia Grandis, L.; N. of Brahmā, L.; of Vishṇu, A.; (*ā*), f. Terminalia Chebula, L.; a species of bulbous plant, L.; Commelina Salicifolia, L.; (with *guḍikā*) a kind of pill used as a remedy for hemorrhoids, L.; n. water, L.; blood, L. **–dakshiṇā**, f. the gift of life, Kathās.; Pañcat. **–daṇḍa**, m. the punishment of death, MW. **–dayita**, m. 'dear as l°,' a husband, Amar. **–dávat**, see *-dāvat*. **–dā́**, mfn. giving breath, VS. **–dātṛi**, mfn. one who saves another's life, MBh. **–dāna**, n. gift of (i. e. saving a person's) life, Kathās.; resigning l°, Pañcat.; anointing the Havis with Ghṛita during the recitation of sacred texts supposed to restore l°, KātyŚr. **–dāvat**, mfn. l°-giving, AV. (*-dávat* prob. w. r.) **–durodara**, n. playing for l°, staking l°, MBh. **–dṛih**, mfn. (nom. *-dhṛik*) sustaining or prolonging the breath, Kāṭh. **–dyūta**, n. play or contest for l°, MBh.; °*tâbhidevana*, mfn. (a battle) played or fought with l° as a stake, ib. **–droha**, m. attempt on another's l°, Pañcat.; °*hin*, mfn. (ifc.) seeking another's l°, Daś. **–dhara**, m. N. of a man, Kathās.; *-miśra*, m. N. of an author, Cat. **–dhāra**, mfn. possessing l°, living, animate; m. a living being, MW. **–dhāraṇa**, n. support or maintenance or prolongation of life (°*ṇam* √*kṛi* [P.], to support another's l°; [Ā., also with °*ṇāṃ*], to support one's own l°, take food), MBh.; R. &c.; means of supporting l°, livelihood, MBh.; R. **–dhārin**, mfn. saving a person's (gen.) life, Hariv. **–dhṛik**, see *-dṛih*. **–nātha**, m. (ifc. f. *ā*) 'lord of life,' a husband, lover, Amar.; N. of Yama, L.; N. of a heresiarch (who had a controversy with Śaṃkara at Prayāga), Cat.; (with *vaidya*) N. of an author of sev. medic. wks. **–nārāyaṇa**, m. N. of a king of Kāma-rūpa, Cat. **–nāśa**, m. 'loss of l°,' death, Veṇīs. **–nigraha**, m. restraint of breath, Vedântas. **–m-dada**, m. 'l°-giver,' N. of Avalokiteśvara, Kāraṇḍ. **–pata**, mfn. (fr. next), g. *aśvapaty-ādi*. **–pati**, m. 'l°-lord,' the soul, MBh.; a physician, Car.; a husband, MW. **–patnī**, f. 'breath-wife,' the voice, ShaḍvBr. **–parikraya**, m. the price of l°, L. **–parikshīṇa**, mfn. one whose l° is drawing to a close, Pañcat. **–parigraha**, m. possession of breath or l°, existence, Amar. **–parityāga**, m. abandonment of l°, Mṛicch. **–paripsā**, f. desire of saving l°, MW. **–pā́**, mfn. protecting breath or l°, VS. **–pratishṭhā**, f. N. of wk.; *-paddhati*, f., *-mantra*, m. N. of wks. **–prada**, mfn. restoring or saving another's l°, Kathās. (*-phala*, n. N. of wk.); (*ā*), f. a species of medic. plant, L. **–pradāyaka**, mf(*ikā*)n. = *-prada*, mfn., Kathās. **–pradāyin**, mfn. id., ib. **–prayāṇa**, n. departure or end of l°, Rājat. **–prahāṇa**, n. loss of l°, Siṇhâs. **–prâśanin**, mfn. feeding only on breath (i. e. on the mere smell of food or drink), Pracaṇḍ. **–priya**, mfn. dear as l°, Vet.; m. a husband, lover, Naish., Sch. **–prêpsu**, mfn. wishing to preserve his l°, being in mortal fright, MBh. **–bādha**, m. danger to l°, extreme peril, Mn. iv, 31 (v. l.), Kām.; BhP. (also *ā*, f., A.) **–buddhi**, f. sg. l° and intelligence, R. (v. l.) **–bhaksha**, m. feeding only on breath or air (cf. *-prâśanin*), ŚrS.; (*am*), ind. while feeding only on breath or air, KātyŚr. **–bhaya**, n. fear for l°, peril of death, R.; Kathās.; Pañcat. **–bhāj**, mfn. possessing l°; m. a living being, creature, man, Śiś. **–bhāsvat**, m. 'l°-light' (?), the ocean, L. **–bhūta**, mfn. being the breath of l°, Ṛitus. **–bhṛit**, mfn. supporting l°, TS.; ŚBr.; = *-bhāj*, ŚBr. &c. &c.; N. of partic. bricks used in erecting an altar, TS.; ŚBr.; N. of Vishṇu, A. **–mát**, mfn. full of vital power, vigorous, strong, MaitrS. **–máya**, mf(*ī*)n. consisting of v° air or breath, ŚBr.; *-kośa*, m. the vital case (one of the cases or investitures of the soul), Vedântas. **–mokshaṇa**, n. = *-tyāga*, Pañcat. **–yama**, m. = *prâṇâyāma*, L. **–yātrā**, f. support of life, subsistence, MBh.; Kāv. &c.; °*trika*, mfn. requisite for subs° (°*ka-mātra*, mfn. possessing only the necessaries of l°), Mn.; MBh. **–yuta**, mfn. endowed with l°, living, alive, Cāṇ. **–yoni**, f. the source or spring of l°, Hariv. **–rakshaṇa**, n. or °**ksha**, f. preservation of l°; °*kshaṇârtham* or °*kshârtham*, ind. for the pr° of l°, Mn., MBh. **–randhra**, n. 'breath-aperture,' the mouth or a nostril, BhP. **–rājya-da**, mfn. one who has saved (another's) life and throne, Kathās. **–rodha**, m. suppression of breath, BhP.; N. of a partic. hell, ib. **–lābha**, m. saving of l°, Gaut.; Mn. xi, 80 (w. r. °*ṇâlābha*). **–lipsu**, mfn. desirous of saving l°, MBh. **–vat**, mfn. = *-yuta*, KātyŚr.; Śak.; vigorous, strong, powerful, Suśr.; Hariv. (compar. *-vat-tara*). **–vallabhā**, f. a mistress or wife as dear as l°, Pañcat. **–vidyā**, f. the science of breath or vital airs, Col. **–vināśa**, m. loss of l°, death, Śāntiś. **–viprayoga**, m. separation from l°, death, Āpast. **–vīrya**, n. strength of breath, TāṇḍBr. **–vṛitti**, f. vital activity or function, Rājat.; support of life, Āpast. **–vyaya**, m. renunciation or sacrifice of l°, Kathās. **–vyāyacchana**, n. peril or risk of l°, Gaut. **–śakti**, f. a partic. Śakti of Vishṇu, Cat. **–śarīra**, mfn. whose (only) body is vital air, ChUp. **–saṃyama**, m. suppression or suspension of breath (as a religious exercise), Yājñ. **–saṃrodha**, m. id., Cat. **–saṃvāda**, m. an (imaginary) dispute (for precedence) between the vital airs or the organs of sense, Col. **–saṃśaya**, m. danger to life, Gaut.; Āpast. (also pl.) **–saṃśita** (°*ṇá-*), mfn. animated by the vital airs, AV. **–saṃhitā**, f. a manner of reciting the Vedic texts, pronouncing as many sounds as possible during one breath, VPrāt., Sch. **–saṃkaṭa**, n. danger to l°, BhP. **–sadman**, n. 'abode of vital airs,' the body, L. **–saṃtyāga**, m. abandonment of l°, MārkP. **–saṃdeha**, m. danger to l°, Pañcat. **–saṃdhāraṇa**, n. support of l° (°*ṇaṃ* √*kṛi*, with instr., to feed or live on), Hcat. **–saṃnyāsa**, m. giving up the spirit, R. **–sama**, mf(*ā*)n. equal to or as dear as l°, MBh.; m. a husband or lover, L.; (*ā*), f. a wife or mistress, Gīt. **–sambhṛita**, m. wind, air (w. r. for *-sambhūta*?). **–sammita**, mfn. = *-sama*, mfn., MārkP.; reaching to the nose, GṛS. **–sāra**, n. vital energy, Rājat.; mfn. full of strength, vigorous, Śak. **–sūtra**, n. the thread of life, MantrBr. **–hara**, mf(*ī*)n. taking away or threatening l°, destructive, fatal, dangerous to (comp.), Yājñ.; R.; Cāṇ.; capital punishment, R. **–hāni**, f. loss of l°, death, Siṇhâs. **–hāraka**, mf(*ikā*)n. taking away l°, destructive, killing, Kāv.; m. a kind of poison, L. **–hārin**, mfn. = prec. mfn., R. **–hitā**, f., see s. v. **–hīna**, mfn. bereft of l°, dead, Kāv. **Prâṇâkarshin**, mf(*iṇī*)n. attracting the vital spirit (said of a partic. magical formula), Cat. **Prâṇâgnihotra**, n. N. of wk. (also *-vidhi*, m. and °*trôpanishad*, f.) **Prâṇâghâta**, m. destruction of life, killing of a living being, Bhartṛ. **Prâṇâcārya**, m. a physician to a king, Vāgbh. **Prâṇâtipāta**, m. destruction of life, killing, slaughter, MBh.; R. &c. (with Buddhists one of the 10 sins, Dharmas.) **Prâṇâtilobha**, m. excessive attachment to l°, HYog. (printed °*ṇital*°). **Prâṇâtman**, m. the spirit which connects the totality of subtle bodies like a thread = *sūtrâtman* (sometimes called *Hiraṇya-garbha*), vital or animal soul (the lowest of

the 3 souls of a human being; the other 2 being *jîvâtman* and *paramâtman*), Tarkas. (cf. IW. 114). **Prâṇâtyaya**, m. danger to life, Yājñ.; Hariv.; Daś. **Prâṇada**, mfn. 'l°-devouring,' deadly, murderous, Bhaṭṭ. **Prâṇâdhika**, mf(*ā*)n. dearer than l° (also *-priya*), Kathās.; superior in vigour, stronger, BhP. **Prâṇâdhinâtha**, m. 'life-lord,' a husband, L. **Prâṇâdhipa**, m. 'id.,' the soul, ŚvetUp. **Prâṇânuga**, mfn. following a person's breath i. e. following him (acc.) unto death, Hit. **Prâṇânta**, m. 'l°-end,' death, Ragh.; mfn. capital punishment, Mn. viii, 359. **Prâṇântika**, mf(*ī*)n. destructive or dangerous to l°, fatal, mortal, capital (as punishment), Mn.; MBh. &c.; l°-long, Gaut.; Pañcat. (B.; *am*, ind.); desperate, vehement (as love, desire &c.), Kathās.; n. danger to l°, MBh. **Prâṇâpahârin**, mfn. taking away l°, fatal, deadly, W. **Prâṇâpâná**, m. du. air inhaled and exhaled, AV.; inspiration and expiration (personified and identified with the Aśvins), Pur.; (with Vasishṭhasya) N. of 2 Sāmans, ĀrshBr. **Prâṇâbâdha**, m. injury or danger to l°, Mn. iv, 51; 54. **Prâṇâbharaṇa**, n. N. of a poem. **Prâṇâbhisara**, m. a saver of life, Car. 1. **Prâṇâyana**, n. (for 2. see below) an organ of sense, BhP. **Prâṇâyâma**, m. (also pl.) N. of the three 'breath-exercises' performed during Saṃdhyā (see *pūraka, recaka, kumbhaka*, IW. 93; RTL. 402; MWB. 239), Kauś.; Yājñ.; Pur.; *-śas*, ind. with frequent b°-exercises, Āpast.; °*min*, mfn. exercising the b° (in 3 ways), Yājñ. **Prâṇârtha-vat**, mfn. possessed of life and riches, Kāv. **Prâṇârthin**, mfn. eager for l°, ib. **Prâṇâlâbha**, w. r. for °*ṇa-lābha*, q. v. **Prâṇâvarodha**, m. suppression of breath, Mṛicch. **Prâṇâvâya**, n. N. of the 12th of the 14 Pūrvas or ancient writings of the Jainas. **Prâṇâhuti**, f. an oblation to the 5 Prāṇas, A. **Prâṇeśa**, m. 'lord of l°,' a husband, Sāh.; 'lord of breath,' N. of a Marut, Yājñ., Sch.; (*ā*), f. a mistress, wife, Kathās. **Prâṇeśvara**, m. 'lord of l°,' a husband, lover, MBh.; Kāv.; Hit.; a partic. drug, Cat.; pl. the vital spirits personified, Hariv.; (*ī*), f. a mistress, wife, Inscr. **Prâṇâikaśata-vidha**, mfn. having 101 variations of the vital airs, ŚBr. **Prâṇôtkramaṇa**, n. (MW.) or °*ṇôtkrānti*, f. (Kathās.) 'breath-departure,' death. **Prâṇôtsarga**, m. giving up the ghost, dying, MBh. **Prâṇôpasparśana**, n. touching the organs of sense, Gaut. **Prâṇôpahâra**, m. 'oblation to life,' food, BhP. **Prâṇôpêta**, mfn. living, alive, Divyâv.

Prâṇaka, m. a living being, animal, worm, Kāraṇḍ.; Terminalia Tomentosa or Coccinia Grandis, L.; myrrh (*bola*) or a jacket (*cola*), L.

Prâṇatha, m. breathing, respiration, VS.; air, wind, L.; the lord of all living beings (= *prajā-pati*), L.; a sacred bathing-place, L.; mfn. strong, L.

Prâṇana, mfn. vivifying, animating, BhP.; m. the throat, L.; n. breathing, respiration, RV.; MBh.; Śaṃk.; the act of vivifying or animating, BhP. **Prâṇanânta**, m. end of life, death, MBh.

Prâṇanta, m. (Uṇ. iii, 127) air, wind, L.; a kind of collyrium, L.; (*ī*), f. sneezing, sobbing, L.

Prâṇayita, mfn. (fr. Caus.) caused to breathe, kept alive, Daś.; animated, longing to (inf.), Rājat.

2. **Prâṇâyana**, m. (for 1. see under *prâṇa*) the offspring of the vital airs, VS. (cf. g. *naḍâdi*).

Prâṇi, in comp. for *prâṇin*. — **ghâtin**, mfn. killing living beings, Kathās. — **jâta**, n. a class or species of animals, Mahīdh. — **tva**, n. the state of a living being, life, Śāṇḍ. — **dyûta**, n. gambling with fighting animals (such as cocks or rams &c.), Yājñ. — **pîḍâ**, f. giving pain to living beings, cruelty to animals, W. — **bhava**, mfn. (a sound) coming from a l° b°, Saṃgīt. — **mat**, mfn. possessed or peopled with l° b°s, Sāh. — **mâtṛi**, f. the mother of a l° b°, W.; a kind of shrub, L. — **yodhana**, n. setting animals to fight (= *-dyūta* above), MW. — **vadha**, m. slaughter of l° b°s; *-prâyaścitta*, n. N. of wk. — **svana**, m. sound of animals, L. — **hiṅsâ**, f. injuring or killing an an°, Rājat. — **hita**, mfn. favourable or good for l° b°s; (*ā*), f. a shoe, W. (cf. *prâṇahitā*). **Prâṇy-aṅga**, n. a part or limb of an animal or man, L.

Prâṇika, mfn. speaking without making a noise, L.

Prâṇinishu, mfn. (fr. Desid.) wishing to breathe or live, Bhaṭṭ. (cf. Pāṇ. viii, 4, 21).

Prâṇin, mfn. breathing, living, alive; m. a living or sentient being, living creature, animal or man, ŚBr. &c. &c. (also n., ĀpŚr.)

प्राणतज *prāṇataja*, m. pl. (with Jainas) N. of a subdivision of the Kalpa-bhavas, L.

प्राणहिता *prāṇahitā*, f. a shoe, L. (perhaps w. r. for *prāṇāhikā*; cf. *prāṇāha* and *prâṇi-hitā*).

प्राणाह *prāṇāha*. See p. 702, col. 1.

प्राणाहति *prāṇāhati*, m. patr., g. *taulvaly-âdi* (Kāś.)

प्रात *prātá*. See √*prā*, p. 701, col. 3.

प्रातर् *prātár*, ind. (fr. 1. *pra*; *prâtar*, Uṇ. v, 59) in the early morning, at daybreak, at dawn, RV. &c. &c. (*prātaḥ prātaḥ*, every morning, Daś.); next morning, to-morrow, AV. &c. &c.; Morning personified as a son of Pushpārṇa and Prabhā, BhP. [Cf. Gk. πρωΐ; Germ. *fruo, früh*.] — **agnihotra-kâlâtikrama-prâyaścitta**, n. N. of wk. — **adhyeya**, mfn. to be recited every morning, Pat. — **anuvâká**, m. 'morning recitation,' the hymn with which the Prātaḥ-savana begins, Br.; ŚrS. — **anta** and **-apavarga**, mfn. ending in the m°, KātyŚr., Sch. — **abhivâda**, m. m° salutation, Gobh. — **avanegá**, m. m° ablution, MaitrS. (ĀpŚr., Sch., w. r. °*neka*). — **aśaná**, n. = *-āśa*, MaitrS. — **ahna**, m. = *-dina*, Gobh.; N. of a man, Cat. — **âśa**, m. m° meal, breakfast, GṛŚrS.; MBh. &c.; °*śita*, mfn. one who has breakfasted, Mn. iv, 62. — **âhuti**, f. m° oblation (the second half of the daily Agni-hotra sacrifice), Br.; ŚrS. — **itvan**, mfn. going out early; m. a m° guest, RV. (voc. °*tvas*). — **upasthâna**, n., **-aupâsana-prayoga**, m. N. of wks. — **geya**, mfn. to be sung in the m°; m. a minstrel who wakes the king in the m°, L. — **japa**, m. m° prayer, Kauś. — **jit**, mfn. winning or conquering early, RV. — **nâdin**, m. 'crowing in m°,' a cock, Bhpr. — **dina**, n. the early part of the day, forenoon, L. — **dugdhá**, n. morning milk, ŚBr. — **doha**, m. id. or m° milking, ŚrS. — **bhoktṛi**, m. 'early eater,' a crow, L. — **bhojana**, n. = *-āśa*, L. — **mantra**, m. the hymn or verse to be recited in the morning, Baudh. — **mâdhyaṃdina-savana**, n. N. of wk. — **yajña**, m. m° sacrifice, AitBr. — **yâvan**, mfn. = *-itvan*, RV.; Br. — **yuktá**, mfn. yoked early (as a car), TBr. — **yúj**, mfn. id.; yoking e°, ib. — **vastṛi**, mfn. shining e°, GṛŚrS. — **vikasvara**, mfn. rising e°, L. — **veshá**, mfn. active e°, TBr. — **huta**, n. e° sacrifice, BhP. — **homa**, m. id.; *-prayoga*, m., *-vidhi*, m. N. of wks.

Prâtaḥ, in comp. for *prâtar*. — **kalpa**, mf(*ā*)n. (night) almost morning, early dawn, Pañcad. — **kârya**, n. m° business or ceremony, MBh. — **kâla**, m. morning time, early m°, daybreak, Hit.; *-vaktavya*, n. N. of a Stotra. — **kṛitya**, n. N. of wk. — **kshaṇa**, m. = *-kāla*, Pañcad. — **paddhati**, f. N. of wk. — **prahara**, m. m° watch (from 6 to 9 o'clock), Kathās. (cf. *prahara*). — **saṃdhyâ**, f. m° twilight, dawn, Pur. (cf. RTL. 401); *-prayoga*, m., *-vandana*, n. and °*na-vidhi*, m. N. of wks. — **sava**, m., **-savaná**, n. the m° libation of Soma (accompanied with 10 ceremonial observances, viz. the *prâtar-anuvāka, abhi-shava, bahish-pâvamāna-stotra, savanīyāḥ paśavaḥ, dhishṇyôpasthāna, savanīyāḥ puroḍāśāḥ, dvi-devatya-grahāḥ, dvi-devatya-bhaksha, ṛitu-yājāḥ, ājya* or *praüga-śastra*), AV.; VS.; Br. &c.; °*vanika* and °*vanīya*, mfn. relating to the m° libation of Soma, ŚrS.; °*nika-darśa-pūrṇamāsa-prayoga*, m. N. of wk. — **sâvá**, m. m° preparation or libation of Soma, RV. — **snâna**, n. m° ablution, Pur.; *-vidhi*, m. N. of wk. — **snâyin**, mfn. one who bathes in the early m°, Pur. — **smaraṇa**, n. 'early remembrance or tradition,' N. of wk.; *-śloka*, m. pl., *-stotra*, n., °*ṇâshṭaka*, n., °*ṇīya*, n. N. of wks.

Prâtaś, in comp. for *prâtar*. — **candra**, m. the moon in the morning; *-dyuti*, mfn. having the colour of the moon in the m° i. e. pale, Mālatīm.

Prâtas, in comp. for *prâtar*. — **tarâm**, ind. very early in the morning, Bhaṭṭ. — **tri-vargâ**, f. N. of the river Gaṅgā, MBh. xiii, 1446 (Nīlak.)

Prâtastána, mf(*ī*)n. relating to the morning, matutinal, TS.; Priyad.; n. early morning (one of the 5 parts of the day; the other 4 being *saṃgava* or morning, midday, afternoon, and evening), TBr.

Prâtastya, mfn. matutinal, Amar., Sch.

प्रातर *prātara*, m. N. of a Nāga, MBh.; v.l. for *pra-tāra*, g. *kṛiśâśvâdi*. **Prâtarîya**, mfn., g. *kṛiśâśvâdi*.

प्राति 2. *prāti* (for 1. see under √*prā*), Vṛiddhi or lengthened form of 1. *prati* in comp. In the following derivatives formed with 2. *prāti* only the second member of the simple compound from which they come is given in the parentheses (leaving the preposition *prati*, which is lengthened to *prāti* in the derivatives, to be supplied). — **kaṇṭhika**, mf(*ī*)n. (fr. *-kaṇṭham*) seizing by the throat, Pāṇ. iv, 4, 40. — **kâmin**, mfn. (fr. *-kāmam*; acc. m. c. °*mīm*) a servant or messenger, MBh. — **kûlika**, mf(*ī*)n. (fr. *-kūla*) opposed to, contrary, Mcar. (w. r. *prati-k°*); Bhaṭṭ.; *-tā*, f. opposition, hostility, Śiś. — **kûlya**, n. (fr. *-kūla*) contrariety, adverseness, opposition, MBh.; disagreeableness, unpleasantness, ib.; (ifc.) disagreement with, TPrāt., Sch. — **kshepika**, mf(*ī*)n. (fr. *-kshepa*), L. — **janîna**, mf(*ī*)n. (fr. *-jana*) suitable for an adversary, Pāṇ. iv, 4, 99, Sch.; (fr. *-janam*) suitable for everybody, popular, Harav. — **jña**, n. (fr. *-jñā*) the subject under discussion, APrāt. — **daivasika**, mf(*ī*)n. (fr. *-divasam*) happening or occurring daily, Āryabh. — **nidhika**, m. (fr. *-nidhi*) a substitute, KātyŚr. — **paksha**, mf(*ī*)n. belonging to the enemy, hostile, adverse, contrary, Śiś. — **pakshya**, n. (fr. *-paksha*) hostility, enmity against (gen.), Kathās. — **pathika**, mf(*ī*)n. going along a road or path, Pāṇ. iv, 4, 42; m. a wayfarer, Divyâv. — **pada**, mf(*ī*)n. (fr. *-pad*) forming the commencement, ŚāṅkhŚr.; m. N. of a man, Śatr. — **padika**, mf(*ī*)n. (fr. *-padam*) express, explicit (°*kânurodhāt*, ind. in conformity with express terms, expressly), Nīlak.; n. the crude form or base of a noun, a n° in its uninflected state, Pāṇ. i, 2, 45 &c.; APrāt.; Sāh. (*-tva*, n., Pāṇ. i, 2, 45, Sch.); m. fire, L.; *-saṃjñā-vāda*, m. N. of wk. — **pîyá**, m. patr. of Balhika, ŚBr. — **peya**, m. id. (also pl.), Pravar.; MBh. — **paurushika**, mf(*ī*)n. (fr. *-paurusha*) relating to manliness or valour, MBh. — **bodha**, m. patr. fr. *prati-b°*, g. *bidâdi*; °*dhāyana*, m. patr. fr. *prātibodha*, g. *haritâdi*; °*dhī-putra*, m., see *pratī-bodhī-p°*. — **bha**, mf(*ī*)n. (fr. *-bhā*) intuitive, divinatory; n. (with or scil. *jñāna*) intuitive knowledge, intuition, divination, Śiś.; Kathās.; Pur. (*-vat*, ind. Nyāyas.); (*ā*), f. presence of mind, MBh. — **bhaṭya**, n. (fr. *-bhaṭa*) rivalry, Mcar. — **bhâvya**, n. (fr. *-bhū*) the act of becoming bail or surety, surety for (gen.), Mn.; MBh. &c.; certainty of or about (gen.), Rājat. — **bhâsika**, mf(*ī*)n. (fr. *-bhāsa*) having only the appearance of anything, existing only in appearance, Bādar.; Gov. — **moksha**, m. = *prati-m°*, q. v., Buddh. — **rûpika**, mfn. (fr. *-rūpa*) counterfeit, spurious, Car.; using false weight or measure, Gaut.; °*pya*, n. similarity of form (*a-prātir°*), MBh. — **lambhika**, mfn. (fr. *-lambha*) ready to receive, expecting, L. — **lomika**, mf(*ī*)n. (fr. *-lomam*) against the hair or grain, adverse, disagreeable, Pāṇ. iv, 4, 28. — **lomya**, n. (fr. *-loma*) contrary direction, inverse order, Nir.; Mn. &c.; opposition, MBh.; Rājat. (*a-prâtil°*). — **veśika**, m. (fr. *-veśa*) a neighbour, Kathās. — **veśmaka**, w. r. for next. — **veśmika**, m. (fr. *-veśman*) a neighbour, Rājat.; HPariś.; (*ī*), f. a female n°, HPariś. — **veśya**, mfn. (fr. *-veśa*) neighbouring, Hcar. (also ifc., Yājñ.); m. an opposite neighbour, Mn. viii, 392 (cf. *ānuveśya*); any n°, MBh.; Daś.; °*śyaka*, m. id., Pañcat. — **śâkhya**, n. (fr. *-śākham*) a treatise on the peculiar euphonic combination and pronunciation of letters which prevails in different Śākhās of the Vedas (there are 4 P°s, one for the Śākala-śākhā of the RV.; two for particular Śākhās of the black and white Yajur-vedas, and one for a Śākhā of the AV.; cf. IW. 149, 150); *-kṛit*, m. the author of a P°, Pāṇ. viii, 3, 61, Sch.; *-bhāshya*, n. N. of Uvaṭa's Comm. on RPrāt. — **śravasa**, m. patr. fr. *prati-śravas*, Pravar. (w. r. *prati-śravasa*). — **śrutká**, mf(*ī*)n. (fr. *-śrut*) existing in the echo, ŚBr. — **shṭhita**, w. r. for *-svika*. — **satvanam**, ind. in the direction of the Satvan (s. v.), AitBr. (*-sutvanám*, AV.; ŚāṅkhŚr.) — **sîma**, m. (fr. *-sīman*) a neighbour, Divyâv. — **svika**, mf(*ī*)n. (fr. *-sva*) own, not common to others, KātyŚr., Sch.; granting to every one his own due, MW. — **hata**, m. a kind of Svarita accent, TPrāt. — **hantra**, n. (fr. *-hantṛi*) the state or condition of a revenger, vengeance, MW. — **hartra**, n. the office or duty of the Pratihartṛi, KātyŚr. — **hâra**, m. a juggler, L.; °*raka*, m. id., L.; °*rika*, mf(*ī*)n. containing Pratihāras (as a Vedic hymn), Lāṭy.; m. a door-keeper, Gaut.; a juggler, conjurer, L. — **hârya**, n. (fr. *-hāra*) the office of a door-keeper, Nalac.; jugglery, working miracles, a miracle, Lalit.; Kāraṇḍ.; Divyâv.; *-saṃdarśana*, m. a partic. Samādhi, Kāraṇḍ.

Prâtîtika, mf(*ī*)n. (fr. *pratīti*) existing only in the mind, mental, subjective, Sarvad.

Prātīpa, m. (fr. *pratīpa*) patr. of Śam-tanu, MBh. °**pika**, mf(*ī*)n. contrary, adverse, hostile, Pāṇ. iv, 4, 28. °**pya**, n. hostility, HPariś.

Prātībodhī-putra, m. N. of a teacher, AitĀr. (cf. under *prāti-bodha* above).

Praty, in comp. for *prāti* before vowels. **–aksha** (g. *prajñâdi*), **-akshika** (Sarvad.), mf(*ī*)n. perceptible to the eyes, capable of direct perception. **–antika**, m. (fr. *-anta*) a neighbouring chief, VarBṛS. **–ayika**, mf(*ī*)n. (fr. *-aya*) relating to confidence, confidential; m. (with *pratibhû*) a surety for the trustworthiness of a debtor, Yājñ. **–avêkshā**, w. r. for *praty-av°*. **–ahika**, mf(*ī*)n. (fr. *-aham*) occurring or happening every day, daily, Kap.; Sūryas., Sch.; Kull.

प्रातिका *prātikā*, f. the China rose, Hibiscus Rosa Sinensis, L.

प्रातिक्य *prātikya*, n. (fr. *pratika*), g. *purohitâdi*.

प्रातीथेयी *prātītheyī*, (prob.) w.r. for *prātitheyī* (see p. 702, col. 1).

प्रातुद *prātuda*, *prātṛida* &c. See under 3. *prā*, p. 702, col. 1.

प्रात्यग्रथि *prātyagrathi*, m. patr. fr. *pratyagratha*, Pāṇ. iv, 1, 173.

प्राथमकल्पिक *prāthamakalpika*, mf(*ī*)n. (fr. *prathama-kalpa*) being (anything) first of all or in the strictest sense of the word (v. l. for *prathama-kalpita*, q.v., Mn. ix, 166); m. a student who is a beginner, L.; a Yogī just commencing his course, Sarvad. (cf. *prathama-kalpika*).

Prāthamika, mf(*ī*)n. (fr. *prathama*) belonging or relating to the first, occurring or happening for the first time, primary, initial, previous &c., TPrāt.; Vedântas.; Kull.

Prāthamya, n. priority, ĀpŚr., Sch.; Kull.

प्राद् *prâd* (*pra-√ad*; only 3. pl. impf. *prâdan*), to eat up, devour, ŚBr.

प्रादक्षिण्य *prādakshiṇya*, *prādānika* &c. See under 3. *prā*, p. 702.

प्रादा *prâ-dā* (*pra-ā-√1. dā*), P. *-dadāti* (inf. *prâ-dātum*, ind. p. *prâ-dāya*), to give, bestow, MBh.

प्रादित्य *prâditya* (*pra-ād°*), m. N. of two princes, Buddh.

प्रादुर् *prādúr*, ind. (prob. fr. *prā* = *pra* + *dur*, 'out of doors;' *prā-dús*, g. *svar-ādi*; °*dush* before *k* and *p*, Pāṇ. viii, 3, 41; °*duḥ shyāt*, *shanti* for *syāt*, *santi*, 87) forth, to view or light, in sight, AV. &c. &c. (with √*as* or *bhū*, to become manifest, be visible or audible, appear, arise, exist; with √*kṛi*, to make visible or manifest, cause to appear, reveal, disclose). **–bhāva**, m. becoming visible or audible, manifestation, appearance (also of a deity on earth), GṛŚrS.; MBh. &c. **–bhūta**, mfn. come to light, become manifest or evident, appeared, revealed, MBh.; Kāv. &c.

Prādush, in comp. for *prādur* (cf. above). **–karaṇa**, n. bringing to light, manifestation, production, GṛŚrS. **–kṛita**, mfn. made visible, brought to light, manifested, displayed, made to blaze (as fire), Mn.; MBh. &c.; *-vapus*, mfn. one whose form is manifested, appearing in a visible form (as a deity), Rājat. **–pīta**, mfn., Pāṇ. viii, 3, 41, Sch.

Prādushya, n. = *prādur-bhāva*, Uṇ. ii, 118, Sch.

प्रादुराक्षि *prādurākshi*, m. patr., Pravar. (w. r. for *prādur-akshi?*)

प्राद्रु *prâ-dru* (*pra-ā-√dru*), P. *-dravati*, to run away, flee, escape, MBh.

प्राधा *prādhā*, *prādhānika* &c. See under 3. *prā*, p. 702.

प्राधी *prâdhī* (*pra-adhi-√i*), P. Ā. *prâdhyeti*, °*dhīte*, to continue to study, advance in studies, ŚāṅkhGṛ. **Prâdhīta**, mfn. one who has begun his studies, R.; advanced in study, well-read, learned (said of Brāhmans), Gaut. **Prâdhyayana**, n. commencement of recitation or study, ŚāṅkhGṛ.

प्राध्येषण *prâdhy-eshaṇa*, n. (fr. *pra-adhi-√1. ish*) incitement, exhortation (to study), ŚāṅkhGṛ.; Kathās.

प्राध्व *prâdhva*, mfn. (fr. *pra* + *adhvan*; but accord. to some fr. *pra* and √*dhvṛi* = *hvṛi*) being on a journey, Pāṇ. v, 4, 85; inclined, L.; humble, L.; distant, long, W.; m. start, precedence, first place (°*dhve* √*kṛi*, with acc. and gen. 'to place a person at the head of'), Kāṭh.; a long way or journey, L.; a bond, tie, L.; a joke, sport, L.; (*am*), ind. far away (with √*kṛi*, 'to put aside'), MBh.; after the precedent of (gen.), Āpast.; favourably, kindly, Ragh.; humbly, Hcar.; conformably, L. **Prâdhvaná**, n. the bed of a river or stream, RV.

प्राध्वर *prâdhvara*, mf(*ī*)n. (only °*rī-śākhā?*), Cat.

प्रान् *prân*. See *prâṇ*, p. 705, col. 1.

प्रानाडी *prānāḍī*. See under 3. *prā*, p. 702.

प्रानून *prānūna*, m. pl. N. of a people, Baudh.

प्रान्त *prânta* (*pra-anta*), m. n. (ifc. f. *ā*) edge, border, margin, verge, extremity, end, MBh.; Kāv. &c. (*yauvana-pr°*, the end of youth, Pañcat.; *oshṭha-prântau*, the corners of the mouth, L.); a point, tip (of a blade of grass), Kauś.; back part (of a carriage), Vikr. (ibc., finally, eventually, Kāv.; Pañcat.); m. thread end of a cloth, L.; N. of a man, *g. aśvâdi*; mfn. dwelling near the boundaries, Divyâv. **–ga**, mfn. living close by, L. **–cara**, mfn. id. (ifc.), MārkP. **–tas**, ind. along the edge or border (of anything), marginally, L. **–durga**, n. 'border-stronghold,' a suburb or collection of houses outside the walls of a town, L. **–nivāsin**, mfn. dwelling near the boundaries, MBh. **–pushpā**, f. a kind of plant, L. **–bhūmi**, f. final place or term; (*au*), ind. finally, at last (others 'up to the verge of the border'), Yogas. **–virasa**, mfn. tasteless in the end, Pañcat. **–vṛiti**, f. 'end-circle,' the horizon, Mālatīm. **–śayanâsana-bhakta**, mfn. living in the country (also *-śayana-bhakta* and *-śayanâsanâsevin*), Divyâv. **–stha**, mfn. inhabiting the borders, MW.

Prāntāyana, mfn. patr. fr. *prânta*, g. *aśvâdi*.

प्रान्तर *prântara* (*pra-an°*), n. a long desolate road, MārkP.; Hit.; the country intervening between two villages, L.; a forest, L.; the hollow of a tree, L. **–śūnya**, n. a long dreary road, W.

प्राप् *prâp* (*pra-√āp*), P. Ā. *prâpnoti* (irreg. Pot. *prâpeyam*), to attain to, reach, arrive at, meet with, find, AV. &c. &c.; to obtain, receive (also as a husband or wife), MBh.; Kāv. &c.; to incur (a fine), Mn. viii, 225; to suffer (capital punishment), ib. 364; (with *diśaḥ*) to flee in all directions, Bhaṭṭ.; to extend, stretch, reach to (*ā*), Pāṇ. v, 2, 8; to be present or at hand, AV.; (in gram.) to pass or be changed into (acc.), Siddh.; to result (from a rule), be in force, obtain (also Pass.), Kāś.: Caus. *prâpayati*, °*te* (ind. p. *prâpayya* or *prâpya*, Pāṇ. vi, 4, 57, Sch.), to cause to reach or attain (2 acc.), advance, promote, further (P., ChUp.; MBh. &c.; Ā., TBr.; MBh.); to lead or bring to (dat.), VP.; to impart, communicate, announce, relate, Mn.; MBh. &c.; to meet with, obtain, R.: Desid. *prêpsati*, to try to attain, strive to reach, ŚBr.

1. **Prâpa**, m. (for 2. p. 708, col. 1) reaching, obtaining (cf. *dush-prâpa*). **Prâpaka**, mf(*ikā*)n. causing to arrive at, leading or bringing to (gen. or comp.); Kathās.; KātyŚr., Sch.; procuring, Kull.; establishing, making valid, L.; m. a bringer, procurer, Kathās. **Prâpaṇa**, mf(*ī*)n. leading to (comp.), Saṃk.; n. occurrence, appearance, Jaim.; reach, extension (*bāhvoḥ prâpaṇânte*, 'as far as the arms reach'), KātyŚr.; arriving at (loc.), Kathās.; attainment, acquisition, Mn.; Āpast.; MBh.; bringing to, conveying, Dhātup.; establishing, making valid, TPrāt., Sch.; reference to (loc.), ĀśvŚr.; elucidation, explanation, Pat.; = *ātañcana*, L. **Prâpaṇīya**, mfn. to be reached, attainable, MBh.; to be caused to attain, to be brought or conveyed to (acc.), Megh.; Kathās. **Prâpayitṛi**, mfn. one who causes to attain, procurer, Sāy. **Prâpita**, mfn. (fr. Caus.) caused to attain to or arrive at, led, conveyed or conducted to or into, possessed of (acc.), MBh.; Kāv. &c.; got, procured, ib.; brought before (the king), commenced (as a lawsuit), Mn. viii, 43; occurred, obtained (*-tva*, n.), Nyāyam. **Prâpin**, mf(*iṇī*)n. attaining to, reaching (comp.), Kālid. **Prâpipayishu**, mfn. (fr. Desid.) wishing to cause to reach; (with *adhaḥ*) wishing to press down, Śiś. v, 69.

Prâpta, mfn. attained to, reached, arrived at, met with, found, incurred, got, acquired, gained, Mn.; MBh. &c.; one who has attained to or reached &c. (acc. or comp.), AV. &c. &c.; come to (acc.), arrived, present (*prâpteshu kāleshu*, at certain periods), Mn.; MBh. &c.; accomplished, complete, mature, full-grown (see *a-pr°*); (in med.) indicated, serving the purpose, Suśr.; (in gram.) obtained or following from a rule, valid (*iti prâpte*, 'while this follows from a preceding rule'), Pāṇ. i, 1, 34, Sch. &c.; fixed, placed, L.; proper, right, L.; m. pl. N. of a people, MārkP. **–karman**, n. that which results or follows (as direct object of an action) from a preceding rule (°*ma-tva*, n.), Pāṇ. ii, 3, 12, Sch. **–kārin**, mfn. one who does what is right or proper, Suśr. **–kāla**, m. the time or moment arrived, a fit time, proper season, MBh.; Kāv. &c. (*-tva*, n., KātyŚr.); mf(*ā*)n. one whose time has come, seasonable, suitable, opportune, ib.; (with *dehin*), m. a mortal whose time i.e. last hour has come, Hariv.; (with *kumārī*), f. a marriageable girl, Śak.; (*am*), ind. at the right time, opportunely, MBh. **–krama**, mfn. fit, proper, suitable, Jātakam. **–jīvana**, mfn. restored to life, Hit. **–tva**, n. the state of resulting (from a grammatical rule), TPrāt. **–dosha**, mfn. one who has incurred guilt, R. **–pañca-tva**, mfn. 'arrived at (dissolution into) 5 elements,' dead, L. **–prakāśaka**, mfn. advanced in intelligence, Sāṃkhyak., Sch. **–prabhāva**, m. one who has attained power, Kāv. **–prasavā**, f. a woman who is near parturition, Uttarar. **–bīja**, mfn. sown, R. **–buddhi**, mfn. instructed, intelligent, W.; becoming conscious (after fainting), ib. **–bhāra**, m. a beast of burden, L. **–bhāva**, mfn. wise, W.; handsome, ib.; one who has attained to any state or condition, of good disposition, MW.; m. a young bullock, L. (w. r. for *-bhāra?*) **–mano-ratha**, mfn. one who has obtained his wish, R. **–yauvana**, mf(*ā*)n. one who has obtained puberty, being in the bloom of youth, Nal. **–rūpa**, mfn. fit, proper, suitable, Daś.; pleasant, beautiful, L.; learned, wise, L. **–rtu** (*ta-ṛitu*), f. a girl who has attained puberty, L. **–vat**, mfn. one who has attained to or gained, MW. **–vara**, mfn. fraught with blessings, ib. **–vikalpa**, m. an alternative or option between two operations one of which results from a grammatical rule (*-tva*, n.), Kāś. on Pāṇ. i, 4, 53. **–vibhāshā**, f. id., ib. i, 3, 50. **–vyavahāra**, m. a young man come of age, an adult, one able to conduct his own affairs (opp. to 'a minor'), MW. **–śrī**, mfn. possessed of fortune, Kum.; Pañcat. **–sūrya**, mf(*ā*)n. having the sun (vertical), Var. **Prâptânujña**, mfn. allowed to withdraw or depart, R. **Prâptâparādha**, mfn. guilty of an offence, Mn. viii, 299. **Prâptârtha**, mfn. one who has attained an object or advantage, Kathās.; m. an object attained, Kap.; °*thâgrahaṇa*, n. the not securing an advantage gained, MW. **Prâptâvasara**, m. a suitable occasion or opportunity; mfn. suitable, fit, proper, Mālatīm. **Prâptôdaka**, mfn. (a village) that has obtained water, Pāṇ. ii, 3, 1, Sch. **Prâptôdaya**, mfn. one who has attained exaltation, MW.

Prâptavya, mfn. to be reached or attained or gained or procured, MBh.; Kāv. &c.; to be met with or found, Hit. **–m-artha**, m. N. given to a man (who whenever asked his name replied *prâptavyam artham labhate manushyaḥ*, 'a man takes anything that is to be got'), Pañcat.; n. (when used with *nāman*), a name, ib.

Prâpti, f. advent, occurrence, AV.; Yājñ.; Pañcat.; reach, range, extent, Sūryas.; reaching, arrival at (comp.), R.; the power (of the wind) to enter or penetrate everywhere, BhP.; the power of obtaining everything (one of the 8 superhuman faculties), MārkP.; Vet.; MWB. 245; saving, rescue or deliverance from (abl.), Ratnâv.; attaining to, obtaining, meeting with, finding, acquisition, gain, Mn.; MBh. &c.; the being met with or found, Nyāyas., Sch.; discovery, determination, Sūryas.; obtainment, validity, holding good (of a rule), KātyŚr.; Pāṇ.; APrāt.; (in dram.) a joyful event, successful termination of a plot (Daśar.); a conjecture based on the observation of a particular thing, Sāh.; lot, fortune, luck, ŚvetUp.; MBh.; (in astrol.) N. of the 11th lunar mansion, Var.; a collection (= *saṃhati*), L.; N. of the wife of Śama (son of Dharma), MBh.; of a daughter of Jarā-saṃdha, Hariv.; Pur. **–mat**, mfn. met with, found, Nyāyas., Sch.; (ifc.) one who has attained to or reached, Sarvad. **–śaithilya**, n. diminution of probability, slight p°, MBh. **–sama**, m. a partic. Jāti (q. v.) in logic, Nyāyas. **Prâptyāśā**, f. the hope of obtaining (an object), Sāh.

Prâpya, mfn. to be reached, attainable, acquirable, procurable, MBh.; Kāv. &c.; fit, proper, suitable, MBh. **-kārin**, mfn. effective (only) when touched (°ri-tva, n.), Nyāyas., Sch. **-rūpa**, mfn. rather easy to attain, Jātakam.

प्राप 2. *prâpa*, n. (fr. *pra* + 2. *áp*), Pāṇ. vi, 3, 97, Vārtt. 1, P. (for 1. *prâpa* see p. 707, col. 2) abounding with water?

प्रापणिक *prāpaṇika* &c. See under 3. *prā*, p. 702, col. 2.

प्रापय *prāpaya*, Nom. °*yati* (artificially formed fr. *priya*) = *priyam ā-cashṭe*, Pat. (cf. *prâp*, Caus.)

प्राबल्य *prābalya* &c. See under 3. *prā*, p. 702, col. 2.

प्राभव *prābhava* &c. See under 3. *prā*, ib.

प्राभिणी *prâbhi-ṇī* (*pra-abhi-√nī*; only 2. sg. Subj. aor. *-ṇeshi*), to lead to (acc.), RV. i, 31, 18.

प्रामति *prāmati*, *prāmāṇika* &c. See under 3. *prā*, p. 702.

प्राय *prâyá*, m. (fr. *pra* + *aya*; √5. *i*) going forth, starting (for a battle), RV. ii, 18, 8; course, race, AV. iv, 25, 2; departure from life, seeking death by fasting (as a religious or penitentiary act, or to enforce compliance with a demand; acc. with *√ās*, *upa-√ās*, *upa-√viś*, *upa-√i*, *ā-√sthā*, *sam-ā-√sthā* or *√kṛi*, to renounce life, sit down and fast to death; with Caus. of *√kṛi*, to force any one [acc.] to seek death through starvation), MBh.; Kāv. &c.; anything prominent, chief part, largest portion, plenty, majority, general rule (often ifc., with f. *ā* = chiefly consisting of or destined for or furnished with, rich or abounding in, frequently practising or applying or using; near, like, resembling; mostly, well-nigh, almost, as it were; cf. *ārya-*, *jita-*, *jñāti-*, *triṇa-*, *daṇḍa-*, *duḥkha-*, *siddhi-pr°* &c.; also *-tā*, f.), ŚBr.; Lāṭy.; Mn.; MBh. &c.; a stage of life, age, L.; (*am*), ind., g. *go-trâdi*. **-gata**, mfn. approaching departure from life, nigh unto death, MBh. **-citta**, n., *-citti*, f. = *prâyaś-c°*, Pāṇ. vi, 1, 157, Sch. **-darśana**, n. a common or ordinary phenomenon, Pāṇ. ii, 3, 23, Vārtt. **-bhava**, mfn. being commonly the case, usually met with, Pāṇ. iv, 3, 39. **-vidhāyin**, mfn. resolved to die of starvation, Rājat. **-śas**, ind. for the most part, mostly, generally, as a rule, MBh.; Kāv. &c.; in all probability, Kathās. **Prâyôpagamana**, n. going to meet death, seeking death (by abstaining from food), R. **Prâyôpayogika**, mfn. most common or usual, Car. **Prâyôpavishṭa**, mfn. one who sits down and calmly awaits the approach of death (cf. *prâya*), MBh.; Rājat.; BhP. **Prâyôpaveśa**, m., °*śana*, n. abstaining from food and awaiting in a sitting posture the approach of death, MBh.; R. &c. **Prâyôpaveśanikā**, f. id., W. **Prâyôpaveśin**, mfn. = *prâyôpavishṭa*, MBh.; Rājat. **Prâyôpêta**, mfn. id., MBh.

Prâyaṇa, mfn. going forth, going, VS.; n. entrance, beginning, commencement, TS.; Br.; Up.; the course or path of life, MBh.; BhP.; going for protection, taking refuge, BhP.; departure from life, death, voluntary d° (°*ṇam √kṛi*, to court d°), Mn. ix, 323; a kind of food prepared with milk, Pur. **-tas**, ind. in the beginning, TāṇḍBr. **Prâyaṇânta**, m. the end of life; (*am*), ind. unto death, PraśnUp.

Prâyaṇīya, mfn. relating to the entrance or beginning, introductory, Br.; ĀśvŚr.; m. (scil. *yāga* or *karma-viśesha* or *atirātra*) the introductory libation or the first day of a Soma sacrifice, Br.; ŚrS.; (*ā*), f. (scil. *ishṭi*) an introductory sacrifice; ib. (*-vat*, ind., Vait.); n. = m., ib. (*-tva*, n., Kapishṭh.)

Prâyaś, in comp. for 1. *prâyas*. **-citta**, n. (*prâyaś-*; 'predominant thought' or 'thought of death,' cf. Pāṇ. vi, 1, 157, Sch.) atonement, expiation, amends, satisfaction, ŚBr.; GṛŚrS.; Mn.; MBh. (v, 1086 as m.) &c.; N. of sev. wks.; mfn. relating to atonement or expiation, expiatory, ShaḍvBr.; *-kadamba*, m. or n., *-kamalâkara*, m., *-kalpataru*, m., *-kāṇḍa*, m. or n., *-kārikā*, f., *-kautūhala*, n., *-kaumudī*, f., *-krama*, m., *-khaṇḍa*, m. or n., *-grantha*, m., *-candrikā*, f., *-cintāmaṇi*, m., *-tattva*, n., *-taraṃga* (?), m., *-dīpikā*, f., *-nirūpaṇa*, n., *-nirṇaya*, m., *-paddhati*, f., *-parāśara*, m. or n., *-pārijāta*, m., *-prakaraṇa*, n., *-prakāśa*, m., *-pratyâmnâya*, m., *-pradīpa*, m., *-pradīpikā*, f., *-prayoga*, m., *-bhāshya*, n., *-mañjarī*, f., *-manohara*, m., *-mayūkha*, m., *-mādhavīya*, n., *-mārtaṇḍa*, m., *-muktâvalī*, f., *-muktâvalī-prakāśa*, m., *-ratna*, n., *-ratna-mālā*, f., *-rahasya*, n., *-vāridhi*, n., *-vidhāna*, n., *-vidhi*, m., *-vinirṇaya*, m., *-viveka*, m., *-vivekôddyota*, m., *-vyavasthā-saṃkshepa*, m., *-śakti*, f., *-śata-dvayī*, f. (or *-śata-dvayī-prâyaścitta*, n.), *-śekhara*, m., *-śrauta-sūtra*, n., *-saṃkalpa*, m., *-saṃgraha*, m., *-samuccaya*, m., *-sāra*, m., *-sāra-kaumudī*, f., *-sāra-saṃgraha*, m., *-sârâvali*, f., *-sudhānidhi*, m., *-subodhinī*, f., *-sūtra*, n., *-setu*, m., *-sthāna*, n., *-hemâdri*, m., °*ttâṇḍa-bilā*, f., °*ttâdi-godāna*, n., °*ttâdi-saṃgraha*, m., °*ttâdhikāra*, m., °*ttâdhyāya*, m., °*ttâdhyāya-bhāshya*, n., °*ttâparârka*, m. N. of wks.; °*ttâhuti*, f. an expiatory sacrifice, Br.; ĀśvŚr.; °*ttêndu-śekhara*, m. and °*ra-sāra-saṃgraha*, m. N. of wks.; °*ttêshṭi*, f. = °*ttâhuti*, GṛŚrS.; °*ttêshṭi-candrikā*, f., °*ttôddyota*, m., °*ttâugha-sāra*, m. N. of wks. **-citti** (*prâyaś-*), f. atonement, expiation, AV.; VS.; Br.; N. of a plant, Kauś.; mfn. expiating (said of Agni), GṛS.; *-mat*, mfn. one who makes atonement or performs penance, TāṇḍBr. **-cittika**, mf(*ī*)n. expiatory, ĀśvŚr.; expiable, Buddh.; requiring an expiation, L. **-cittin**, mfn. one who does penance or has to make expiation, MBh. **-cittīya**, mfn. serving as an atonement, expiatory, Kauś.; Pat.; Sarvad.; bound to perform penance (*-tā*, f.), Mn. xi, 47 (*-cittīya*, Nom. Ā. °*yate*, to be obliged to perform penance, Mn.; MBh.) **-cetana**, n. atonement, expiation, Mcar.

1. **Prâyas**, ind. (for 2. see below) for the most part, mostly, commonly, as a general rule, MBh.; Kāv. &c.; in all probability, likely, perhaps, MBh.; abundantly, largely, W.

Prâyasya, mfn. prevalent, predominant, RPrāt., Sch.

Prâyika, mfn. common, usual, ĀpŚr., Sch.; Kull.; excessive, redundant, MW.; containing the greater part (but not everything), Vām. v, 2, 24. **-tva**, n. usage, custom, ĀpŚr., Sch.; redundance, superfluity, MW.; the containing &c., Vām. v, 2, 24.

Prâyeṇa, ind. mostly, generally, as a rule, ŚrS.; Mn.; R. &c.; most probably, likely, Hit. (cf. *prâyaśas* and 1. *prâyas*).

Prâyo, in comp. for 1. *prâyas*. **-devatā**, f. the prevalent or predominant deity, Nir. vii, 4. **-bhāvin**, mfn. being commonly found or met with, Bhpr. (cf. *prâya-bhava*). **-vāda**, m. a current saying, proverb, Bālar.

प्रायत्य *prāyatya* &c. See under 3. *prā*, p. 702, col. 2.

प्रायस 2. *prâyas*, n. (for 1. see above) = 2. *prâyas*, RV. iv, 21, 7. **Prâyo-gá**, mfn. (prob.) = 1. *prayo-gá*, RV. x, 106, 2.

प्राया *prâ-yā* (*pra-ā-√yā*), P. *-yāti*, to come near, approach, RV.

प्रायु *prā-yu*, *prā-yus*. See *a-pr°*.

प्रायुध् *prâ-yudh* (*pra-ā-√yudh*), Ā. *-yudhyate*, to fight, Śiś. xviii, 32.

Prâyuddheshin &c. See *prā-yudh* under 3. *prā*, p. 702.

प्रायुस् *prâyus* (*pra-āyus*), n. increased vitality, longer life, MaitrS.

प्रायेण *prâyeṇa*. See under *prâya* above.

प्रार् *prâr* (*pra-√ṛi*), P. *prêyarti* (aor. 3. pl. *prâran*, Ā. *prârata*; pf. *prâruḥ*), to set in motion, arouse, RV. v, 42, 14; to send or procure to (dat.), x, 116, 9; to arise, stir, come forth, appear, i, 39, 5 &c.: Caus. *prârpayati* (ind. p. *prârpyā*), to set in motion, stir up, animate, RV.; VS. **Prârpaṇa**, m. an arouser, RV.

प्रारभ् *prâ-rabh* (*pra-ā-√rabh*), Ā. *-rabhate*, to seize, lay hold on (acc.), RV. vi, 37, 5; to begin, commence, undertake (with acc. or inf.), MBh.; Kāv. &c. °**rabdha**, mfn. commenced, begun, undertaken, MBh.; Kāv. &c.; one who has c° or b° (also *-vat*, mfn.), Amar.; Rājat.; Kathās.; n. an undertaking, enterprise, Kāv.; Pañcat.; *-karman* (Nīlak.), *-kārya* (Kull.), mfn. one who has commenced or undertaken a work. °**rabdhi**, f. beginning, commencement, W.; the post to which an elephant is tied, L.

Prârambha, m. commencement, beginning, undertaking, enterprise, Kāv.; Var.; Pur. &c. °**rambhaṇa**, n. beginning, commencing, L.; °*ṇīya*, mfn., g. *anuvacanâdi*. °**ripsita**, mfn. (fr. Desid.) intended or meant to be begun, Sāh.; Sarvad.

प्रारुह् *prâ-ruh* (*pra-ā-√ruh*), P. *-rohati*, to ascend, rise, MBh. °**roha**, see *prā-r°* under 3. *prā*, p. 702.

प्रार्क्षीय *prārkshīya*, Nom. P. °*yati* = *prarkshīya*, Vop.

प्रार्च् *prârc* (*pra-√arc*), P. *prârcati*, to shine forth, RV.; to sing, praise, celebrate, commend, ib.; BhP.: Caus. (aor. *prârcicat*) to honour, worship, Bhaṭṭ.

प्रार्छ् *prârch* (*pra-√ṛich*), P. *prârcchati*, to move on, Pāṇ. vi, 1, 91, Sch.

Prârcchaka, mfn. (fr. *pra* + *ṛicchaka*), Pat.

प्रार्ज् *prârj* (*pra-√ṛij*), Caus. *prârjayati*, to grant, bestow, Nir. iii, 5.

Prârjayitṛi, mfn. one who grants or bestows (used to explain *parjanya*), Nir. x, 10.

प्रार्जुन *prârjuna*, m. pl. N. of a people, Inscr.

प्रार्ञ्ज् *prârñj* (*pra-√ṛiñj*), P. *-ṛiñjati*, to run through (acc.), RV. iii, 43, 6.

प्रार्ण *prârṇa* (*pra-ṛiṇa*), n. a chief or principal debt, Pāṇ. vi, 1, 89, Vārtt. 7, Pat.

प्रार्थ् *prârth* (*pra-√arth*), Ā. *prârthayate* (ep. also P. °*ti* and pr. p. °*yāna*), to wish or long for, desire (acc.), KaṭhUp.; MBh. &c.; to ask a person (acc.) for (acc. or loc.) or ask anything (acc.) from (abl.), MBh.; Kāv. &c.; to wish to or ask a person to (inf.), ib.; to demand in marriage, woo, Ratnâv.; to look for, search, Bhaṭṭ.; to have recourse to (acc.), Kathās.; to seize or fall upon, attack, assail, Ragh.; Kir.

Prârtha, mfn. (prob.) eager or ready to set out on a journey, AV.; Br. **Prârthaka**, mf(*ikā*)n. wishing for, soliciting, courting; m. a wooer, suitor, Hit. (v. l.); Kull. (see *a-pr°*). **Prârthana**, n. wish, desire, request, entreaty, solicitation, petition or suit for (loc. or comp.), MBh.; Kāv. &c.; °*nâbhāva*, m. absence of solicitation, Hit. **Prârthanā**, f. = °*na*, MBh.; Kāv. &c. (°*nayā*, ind. at the request or petition of any one); prayer (as forming part of the worship of the gods), RTL. 16; *-duḥkha-bhāj*, mfn. one who feels the pain of begging, Bhartṛ.; *-pañcaka*, n. N. of a wk. (containing prayers to Rāmānuja); *-bhaṅga*, m. refusal of a request, asking in vain, MārkP.; *-śataka*, n. N. of a Stotra (in praise of Durgā); *-siddhi*, f. accomplishment of a desire, Ragh. **Prârthanīya**, mfn. to be desired or wished for, desirable, MBh.; Śaṃk.; Pañcat.; to be asked or begged, Kād.; n. the third or Dvāpara age of the world, L. **Prârthayitavya**, mfn. worthy of desire, desirable, Kālid. **Prârthayitṛi**, mfn. one who wishes for or asks; m. a solicitor, suitor, wooer, Śak.; Hit. **Prârthita**, mfn. wished for, desired, wanted, MBh.; Kāv. &c.; requested, solicited, ib.; attacked, assailed, Ragh.; obstructed, besieged, L.; killed, hurt, L.; n. wish, desire, R.; Ragh.; *-durlabha*, mfn. desired but hard to obtain, Kum.; *-vat*, mfn. one who has asked or asks, W. **Prârthin**, mfn. (ifc.) wishing for, desirous of, Ragh.; Rājat.; Kathās.; attacking, assailing, Ragh. **Prârthya**, mfn. to be desired or wished for by (instr., gen. or comp.), desirable, Hariv.; Kāvyâd.; BhP.; n. (impers.) one should request, BhP.

प्रार्द् *prârd* (*pra-√ard*), Caus. *prârdayati*, to cause to flow away, RV. vi, 17, 12; to exert beyond measure, overwork, Nir. vi, 32. **Prârdaka**, mfn. one who exerts beyond measure, Nir. ib.

प्रार्ध् *prârdh* (*pra-√ṛidh*), Ā. *prârdhate*, to attain, Divyâv.

प्रार्ध *prârdha*. See *pari-prârdha*.

प्रार्पण *prârpaṇa*. See under *prâr*, col. 2.

प्रार्ष् *prârsh* (*pra-√ṛish*), P. *prârshati*, to flow forth, RV.

प्रार्षभीय *prārshabhīya*, Nom. P. °*yati* = *prarshabhīya*, Vop.

प्राहँ *prârh* (*pra-√arh*), only 3. pl. pf. Ā. *pra-arhire*, to distinguish or signalize one's self, RV. x, 92, 11.

प्रालम्ब *prālamba, prāleya* &c. See under 3. *prā*, p. 702, col. 2.

प्राल्कारीय *prālkārīya*, Nom. °*yati*=*pralkārīya*, Pāṇ. vi, 1, 92, Sch.

प्राव् *prâv* (*pra-√av*), P. *prâvati*, to favour, befriend, help, protect, promote, comfort, sate, satisfy, content, RV.; VS.; AV. **Prâvitṛí**, m. a protector, patron, friend, RV.; ŚBr.; KātyŚr. **Prâvitrá**, n. protection, guardianship, Br.; ŚāṅkhŚr. **Prâví**, mfn. attentive, mindful, RV.

प्रावचन *prāvacana*, °*nika* &c. See under 3. *prā*, p. 702, col. 3.

प्रावन् *prāvan*. See *kratu-pr*°.

प्रावनिज् *prâva-nij* (*pra-ava-√nij*), P. *-nenekti*, to wash off, AV.

प्रावर *prāvara, prāvarshin*. See under 3. *prā*, p. 702, col. 3.

प्रावसो *prâva-so* (*pra-ava-√so*), P. *-syati*, to settle among (acc.), ŚBr.

प्राविश् *prâ-viś* (*pra-ā-√viś*), P. *-viśati*, to come or resort to (acc.), ŚāṅkhŚr.: Caus. *-veśayati*, to let or lead in (loc.), MBh.; Daś.

प्राविष्क्रियमाण *prâvish-kriyamāṇa*, mfn. (√*kṛi*) shown, Divyâv. (w. r. for *āvish-kṛ*°?)

प्रावृ *prâ-*1. √*vṛi* (*prā* prob. for *pra*; cf. *apā-√vṛi*), P. Ā. *-vṛiṇoti, -vṛiṇute* (inf. *-varitum*, Mṛicch.), to cover, veil, conceal, AV.; Gaut.; Āpast.; to put on, dress one's self in (acc., rarely instr.), MBh.; Kāv. &c.; to fill, MBh. — 2. °**vara**, m. (for 1. see under 3. *prā*, p. 702, col. 3) an enclosure, fence (cf. *mahi-pr*°), L. °**varaka**, m. N. of a district (=°*vāra*), MBh. °**váraṇa**, n. (ifc. f. *ā*) covering, veiling, Āpast.; a cover, upper garment, cloak, mantle, ŚBr. &c. &c. °**varaṇīya**, n. an outer garment, cloak, mantle, L. °**vāra**, m. id., MBh.; Kām.; Mṛicch. (also *-ka*); N. of a district (=°*varaka*), MBh.; mfn. found in outer garments or cloaks, Kāv.; *-karṇa*, m. 'Cloak-Ear,' N. of an owl, MBh.; *-kīṭa*, m. 'clothes-insect,' = *kuṇa*, L.; a louse, W.; °*rika*, m. a maker of cloaks, R.; °*rīya*, P. °*yati*, to use as a cl°, Pāṇ. iii, 1, 10, Sch. °**vuvūrshu**, mfn. (fr. Desid.) wishing or intending to wear, W.

Prá-vṛita, mfn. covered, enclosed, screened, hid in (instr. or comp.), RV. &c. &c.; put on (as a garment), Hcar.; Kathās.; Hit.; filled with (instr.), R.; m. n. a veil, mantle, wrapper, L.; n. covering, concealing, Gaut.; (*ā*), f. a veil, mantle, ShaḍvBr. °**vṛiti**, f. an enclosure, fence, hedge, L.; (with Śaivas) spiritual darkness (one of the 4 consequences of Māyā), Sarvad.

प्रावृत् *prā-√vṛit* (*prā* m. c. for *pra*), Caus. *-vartayati*, to produce, create, MBh.; Hariv. °**vartaka**, mf(*ikā*)n. producing, founding (a race), Hariv.

प्रावृष् *prā-vṛísh*, f. (fr. *pra-√vṛish*) the rainy season, wet season, rains (the months Āshāḍha and Śrāvaṇa, comprising the first half of the rainy season which lasts in some parts from the middle of June till the middle of October), RV. &c. &c. (°*shi-ja*, mfn. produced in the rainy seasons, Śiś.)

Prāvṛiṭ, in comp. for *prāvṛish*. — **kāla**, m. the rainy season, Var.; Pañcat.; *-vaha*, mf(*ā*)n. (a river) flowing only in the rainy season, MārkP.

Prāvṛiḍ, in comp. for *prāvṛish*. — **atyaya**, m. the time following the rainy season, autumn, L.

Prāvṛiṇ, in comp. for *prāvṛish*. — **maya**, mf(*ī*)n. resembling the rainy season, Hcar.

Prāvṛisha, m. the rainy season, the rains, Hariv.; (*ā*), f. id., L.

Prāvṛishāyaṇī, f. 'produced by rains,' Boerhavia Procumbens, L.; Mucuna Pruritus, Bhpr.

Prāvṛishika, mfn. relating to or born in the rainy season, BhP. (cf. Pāṇ. iv, 3, 26); m. a peacock, L. °**shíṇa**, mfn. (day) beginning the rainy season, RV. °**sheṇya**, mfn. relating to the r° s°, Kālid.; Bālar. (cf. Pāṇ. iv, 3, 17); coming in showers, abundant, much, L.; m. Nauclea Cadamba or Cordifolia, L.; Wrightia Antidysenterica, L.; (*ā*), f. Mucuna Pruritus, L.; a species of Punar-navā with red flowers, L. °**sheya**, m. pl. N. of a people, MBh. °**shya**, m. Nauclea Cordifolia, L.; Wrightia Antidysenterica, L.; Asteracantha Longifolia, L.; n. a cat's eye (gem), L.

प्राश् 1. *prâś* (*pra-√*1. *aś*), P. *prâśnoti* (aor. *prâṇaṭ*), to reach, attain, RV.; to fall to the lot or share of (acc.), ib.: Caus. *prâśāpayati*, to cause to reach or attain, MānGṛ.

Prâshṭa, mfn. arrived at, gained (=*prâpta*), Nir. (Sch.); *-varṇa*, mfn. = *pṛiśni*, ib.

प्राश् 2. *prâś* (*pra-√*2. *aś*), P. *prâśnāti* (rarely Ā. °*nīte*), to eat, consume, devour, taste, enjoy, RV. &c. &c.: Caus. *prâśayati*, to cause to eat, feed, ĀśvGṛ.; Mn.; Kathās. **Prâśa**, m. eating, feeding upon (cf. *ghṛita-, dhūma-pr*°); food, victuals, Kauś.; MBh.; Suśr. **Prâśaka**, m. eating, enjoying, Sāy. on RV. i, 40, 1. **Prâśana**, n. eating, feeding upon, tasting, GṛŚrS. &c. &c.; (fr. Caus.) causing to eat, feeding (esp. the first feeding of a child; cf. *anna-pr*°), Mn.; Yājñ.; food, victuals (cf. *amṛita-pr*°), MBh.; R.; Hariv.; (*ī*), f. enjoyment, (cf. *rasa-pr*°), Vait.; °*nārthīya*, mfn. meant for food, ŚāṅkhGṛ.; °*nin*, see *parṇa-* and *prâṇa-prâśanin*. **Prâśanīya**, mfn. to be eaten, eatable, serving as food; n. food, MBh.; R. **Prâśavyà**, n. (fr. *prâś* or *prâśa*) food, provisions, RV. **Prâśita**, mfn. eaten, tasted, devoured, TS. &c. &c.; n. the daily oblation to deceased progenitors, Mn. iii, 74. **Prâśitavyà**, mfn. to be eaten, eatable, esculent, ŚBr.; MBh. **Prâśitṛí**, mfn. one who eats, an eater, AV.; MBh. **Prâśitrá**, n. the portion of Havis eaten by the Brahman at a sacrifice, TS.; ŚBr.; ŚrS. (*-vat*, ind., Vait.); = *-haraṇa*, BhP.; anything edible, W.; *-háraṇa*, n. a vessel in which the Brahman's portion of Havis is placed, ŚBr.; GṛŚrS.; °*triya*, see *a-prâśitriya*. **Prâśin**, see *amṛita-pr*°. 1. **Prâśū**, m. (for 2. see below) an eater, guest (?), RV. i, 40, 5 (Mahīdh. 'very swift' = *śīghra*, cf. *prâśú*). **Prâśya**, mfn. to be eaten, eatable, TBr.; KātyŚr.; R.

प्राश् 3. *prâś*, m. (√*prach*) asking, inquiring, a questioner, Yājñ., Sch. (cf. *śabda-pr*° and Uṇ. ii, 57); f. (?) statement or assertion in a debate or lawsuit, AV. ii, 27, 1; 5 (cf. *prati-prâś*).

Prâḍ-vivāka, m. 'one who interrogates and discriminates,' a judge (esp. the chief j° of a stationary court), Mn.; Gaut.; Bhar. (cf. IW. 296, 1).

प्राशस्त्य *prāśastya* &c. See under 3. *prā*, p. 702, col. 3.

प्राशा *prâśā* (*pra-āśā*), f. ardent desire or longing for, TāṇḍBr.; Mālatīm.

प्राशातिक *prāśātika*, n. a leguminous plant, ĀpŚr.

प्राशु *prâśú* (*pra-āśú*), mfn. very quick or speedy, RV. (= *kshipra*, Naigh. i, 15); (*u*), ind. quickly, swiftly, ĀpŚr. — **sháh** (*-sháṭ*), mfn. (prob.) swiftly finishing (a meal), RV. iv, 25, 6 ('rapidly victorious,' Sāy.)

प्राशू 2. *prāśū*, m. (for 1. see under 2. *prâś*) = *parā-krama*, TBr., Sch. (cf. *satya-pr*°).

प्राश्निक *prāśnika*, mf(*ī*)n. (fr. *praśna*) containing questions (cf. *bahu-pr*°); m. an inquirer, arbitrator, umpire, MBh.; R.; Mālav.; a witness, L.; an assistant at a spectacle or assembly (?), W.

Práśni-putrá, m. N. of a teacher, ŚBr.

प्राश्वमेध *prâśvamedha* (*pra-aśv*°), m. a preliminary horse sacrifice, Kathās.

प्राश्वस् *prâ-śvas* (*pra-ā-√śvas*), Caus. *-śvāsayate*, to comfort, console, R.

प्राष्ट *prâshṭa*. See above under 1. *prâś*.

प्रास् *prâs* (*pra-√*1. *as*), P. *prâsti*, to be in front of or in an extraordinary degree, excel, preponderate, RV.

प्रास् *prâs* (*pra-√*2. *as*), P. *prâsyati*, to throw or hurl forth, throw into (loc.), cast, discharge (a missile), RV. &c. &c.; to upset, Mn. xi, 176; (with *anṣam*) to cast lots, lay a wager, TāṇḍBr.

Prâsa, m. casting, throwing, Br.; ŚrS.; scattering, sprinkling, Pratāp.; a barbed missile or dart, MBh.; Kathās.; a partic. constellation or position of a planet, Var.; N. of a man, Rājat.; *-bhārata*, n. N. of a poem; °*saka*, m. a die, dice, L.; °*sika*, mfn. armed with a dart or javelin, Pāṇ. iv, 4, 57, Sch.; m. a spearman, L. **Prâsana**, n. throwing forth or away or down, throwing, casting, ŚrS.; Jaim. **Prâsta**, mfn. thrown away or off, cast, hurled, discharged, BṛĀrUp.; Mn.; expelled, turned out, banished, W.

प्रासङ्ग *prāsaṅga*, °*gika* &c. See under 3. *prā*, p. 702, col. 3.

प्रासाद *prāsāda*, m. (for *pra-s*°, lit. 'sitting forward,' sitting on a seat in a conspicuous place; cf. Pāṇ. vi, 3, 122) a lofty seat or platform for spectators, terrace, ŚāṅkhŚr.; Mn.; the top-story of a lofty building, Kād.; a lofty palatial mansion (approached by steps), palace, temple, AdbhBr.; MBh.; Kāv. &c.; (with Buddhists) the monks' hall for assembly and confession, MWB. 426. — **kalpa**, m. N. of wk. — **kukkuṭa**, m. a domestic pigeon, L. — **gata**, mfn. gone to (the roof of) a palace, Nal. — **garbha**, m. an inner apartment or sleeping chamber in a palace, Hit. — **tala**, n. the flat roof of a house or palace, MBh. — **dīpikā**, f. N. of wk. — **parā-mantra**, m. N. of a partic. magical formula (a combination of the letters *ha* and *sa* = *parā-prāsāda-mantra*), W. — **pṛishṭha**, n. a terrace or balcony on the top of a palace, Hit. — **pratishṭhā**, f. the consecration of a temple; *-dīdhiti*, f. N. of wk. — **prastara**, m. = *-tala*, Mn. ii, 204. — **maṇḍanā**, f. a kind of orpiment, L. — **lakshaṇa**, n. N. of wk. — **vāsin**, mfn. dwelling in a palace, Pat. — **śāyin**, mfn. accustomed to sleep in a p°, MBh. — **śṛiṅga**, n. the spire or pinnacle of a p° or temple, a turret, ib. — **stha**, mfn. standing on (the roof of) a p°, Nal. **Prāsādâgra**, n. = °*da-tala*, R. **Prāsādâgrya**, n. pl. most excellent palaces, MW. **Prāsādâṅgana**, n. (or °*nā*, f.) the courtyard of a p° or temple, Rājat.; Pañcat. **Prāsādânukīrtana**, n. N. of wk. **Prāsādârohaṇa**, n. going up into or entering a palace; °*ṇīya*, mfn., Pāṇ. v, 1, 111, Vārtt. 1, Pat. **Prāsādâlaṃkāra-lakshaṇa**, n. N. of wk.

Prāsādika, mf(*ā*)n. (fr. *pra-sāda*) kind, amiable, Lalit.; given by way of blessing or as a favour, MW.; (fr. *prā-sāda*) pleasant, beautiful, ib.; Kāraṇḍ.; (*ā*), f. a chamber on the top of a palace, Hcar.

Prāsādivārika, m. a kind of attendant in a monastery, Buddh.

1. **Prāsādīya**, Nom. P. °*yati*, to imagine one's self to be in a palace, Pāṇ. iii, 1, 10, Vārtt. 1, Pat.

2. **Prāsādīya**, mfn. belonging to a palace, palatial, splendid, W.

Prāsādya, mfn. id., Śil.

प्रास्थिक *prāsthika*. See p. 702, col. 3.

प्राह् *prâh* (*pra-√ah*), only pf. *prâha*, to announce, declare, utter, express, say, tell (with dat. or acc. of pers. and acc. of thing), ŚBr.; Mn.; MBh. &c.; to record, hand down by tradition, ŚBr.; (with 2 acc.) to call, name, regard or consider as, Mn.; MBh. &c.

प्राह *prâha*, m. instruction in the art of dancing, L.

प्राहणि *prāhaṇi, prāharika* &c. See under 3. *prā*, p. 702, col. 3.

प्राह्वनीय *prâhavanīya*, mfn. (*prā* or *prâ* + √*hve*?) worthy to be received as a guest, Buddh.

प्राहुण *prāhuṇa*, m. (fr. *prâghuṇa*, q. v.) a guest, Kathās.; (*ī*), f., ib. **Prāhuṇaka**, m., °**ṇikā**, f. = prec. m., f., Kathās.

प्राह्ण *prâhṇa*, m. (fr. *pra* + *ahna*) the early part of the day, forenoon, morning, ShaḍvBr.; BhP.; Suśr.; (*am*), ind. in the morning, g. *tishṭhadgv-ādi*.

Prâhṇe, ind. early, in the morning, MBh. xiv, 1277. — **tarām** and **-tamām**, ind. earlier or very early in the morning.

Prâhṇetana, mfn. relating to the forenoon, happening in the morning, matutinal, Pāṇ. iv, 3, 23.

प्रिय *priya, priyāla*. See under √1. *prī* below.

प्री 1. *prī*, cl. 9. P. Ā. (Dhātup. xxxi, 2) *prīṇāti, prīṇīte*; cl. 4. Ā. (xxvi, 35) *prīyate* (rather Pass.; ep. and m. c. also °*ti* and *priyate*, °*ti*; pf. *pipriyé*, p. °*yāná*, Subj. *piprâyat*; Impv. *piprâyasva* or °*prīhi*, RV.; aor. *apraishīt*,

Br., Subj. *préshat*, RV.; *apreshṭa*, Gr.; fut. *preshyati*, °*te*, *pretā*, ib.), P. to please, gladden, delight, gratify, cheer, comfort, soothe, propitiate, RV. &c. &c.; (mostly Ā. *prīyate*) to be pleased or satisfied with, delight in, enjoy (gen., instr., loc. or abl.), ib.; (Ā.; ep. and m.c. also P. and *prī*°) to like, love, be kind to (acc.), MBh.; R.: Caus. *prīṇayati* (*prāpayati*, Siddh., *prāyayati*, Vop.), to please, delight, gratify, propitiate, ĀśvGṛ.; Yājñ.; MBh. &c.; to refresh, comfort, Car.: Desid. *piprīshati*, to wish to please or propitiate, RV.: Intens. *peprīyate*, *peprayīti*, *pepreti*, Gr. [Cf. Goth. *frijôn*, *frijônds*; Germ. *friunt*, *freund*; Angl.Sax. *freónd*; Eng. *friend*; Slav. *prijati*; Lith. *prëtelius* &c.]

Priyá, mf(*ā*)n. beloved, dear to (gen., loc., dat. or comp.), liked, favourite, wonted, own, RV. &c. &c. (with abl. 'dearer than,' R.; Kathās.; Pañcat.; *priyam* √*kṛi*, Ā. *kurute*, either 'to gain the affection of, win as a friend,' RV.; or 'to feel affection for, love more and more,' MBh.); dear, expensive, high in price (cf. *priya-dhānyaka*, *priyânna-tva*); fond of, attached or devoted to (loc.), RV. (id. in comp., either ibc., e.g. *priya-devana*, 'fond of playing,' or ifc., e.g. *aksha-priya*, 'fond of dice,' cf. Pāṇ. ii, 2, 35, Vārtt. 2; ifc. also = pleasant, agreeable, e.g. *gamana-priya*, 'pleasant to go,' vi, 2, 15, Sch.); m. a friend, Gaut.; a lover, husband, MBh.; Kāv. &c.; a son-in-law, Mn. iii, 119 (Kull.); a kind of deer, L.; N. of 2 medicinal plants, L.; (*ā*), f. a mistress, wife, MBh.; Kāv. &c. [cf. Old Sax. *frī*, Angl.Sax. *freó*, 'a wife']; the female of an animal, Var.; news, L.; small cardamoms, L.; Arabian jasmine, L.; spirituous liquor, L.; N. of a daughter of Daksha, VP.; of various metres, Col.; n. love, kindness, favour, pleasure, MBh.; Kāv. &c.; (*am*), ind. agreeably, kindly, in a pleasant way, Kāv.; (*eṇa*), id.; willingly, Hit. (v.l., also *priya-priyeṇa*, Pāṇ. viii, 1, 13). **–ṃ-vada**, mf(*ā*)n. speaking kindly, agreeable, affable to (gen. or comp.), MBh.; Kāv. &c.; m. a kind of bird, R.; N. of a Gandharva, Ragh.; of a poet, Cat.; (*ā*), f. a kind of metre, Col.; N. of a woman, Śak.; Daśak.; °*da-ka*, m. N. of a man, Mudr. **–kara**, mfn. causing or giving pleasure, R. **–karman**, mfn. doing kind actions, kind, Kām.; n. the action of a lover, BhP. **–kalatra**, m. fond of one's wife, MW. **–kalaha**, mfn. quarrelsome, VarBṛS. **–kāma**, mf(*ā*)n. desirous of showing kindness to (gen.), friendly disposed, MBh. **–kāmya**, m. Terminalia Tomentosa, L.; (*ā*), f. the desire of showing kindness to (gen.), MBh. **–kāra**, mfn. doing a k° or a favour to (gen.), MBh.; congenial, suiting, W. **–kāraka**, mfn. causing pleasure or gladness, agreeable, Mn. **–kāraṇa**, n. the cause of any favour; (*āt*), ind. for the sake of doing a f°, MBh.; R. **–kārin**, mfn. showing kindness to; °*ri-tva*, n. the act of sh° k°, Kathās. **–kṛit**, mfn. doing a kindness, MBh.; R.; m. a friend, benefactor, W.; *-tama*, mfn. doing that which pleases most, MW. **–kshatra**, mfn. ruling benevolently (said of the gods), RV. viii, 27, 19. **–guḍa**, mfn. one who likes sugar, fond of s°, Pāṇ., Sch. **–ṃ-kara**, mf(*ī* or *ā*)n. acting kindly towards, showing kindness to (gen.), VS.; MBh.; Hariv. &c.; causing pleasure, agreeable, Hariv.; exciting or attracting regard, amiable, W.; m. N. of a Dānava, Kathās.; of sev. men, ib.; Kshitîś.; (*ī*), f. Physalis Flexuosa, L.; a white-blooming Kaṇṭakārī, L.; = *bṛihaj-jīvantī*, L. **–ṃ-karaṇa**, mf(*ī*)n. acting kindly to, Pāṇ. iii, 2, 56; exciting or attracting regard, amiable, MW. **–ṃ-kāra**, mfn. = *priya-kāra* (q.v.), MW. **–catura**, mfn., Vop. iii, 110. **–cikīrshā**, f. the desire of doing a kindness to (gen.), MBh. **–cikīrshu**, mfn. wishing to do a k° to (gen.), Bhag. **–jana**, m. a dear person, the beloved one, Amar. **–jāta**, mfn. dear when born, born beloved or desired (said of Agni), RV. viii, 60, 2. **–jāni**, m. a gallant, Hcar. **–jīva**, m. Calosanthes Indica, L. **–jīvita**, mfn. loving life; *-tā*, f. love of life, Sāh. **–tanaya**, mfn. loving a son, Jātakam. **–tanu** (*priyá-*), mfn. loving the body, l° life, AV. v, 18, 6. **–tama** (*priyá-*), mfn. most beloved, dearest, RV.; AV.; ŚBr. (once = *-tara*, R.); m. a lover, husband, Kāv.; Celosia Cristata, L.; (*ā*), f. a mistress, wife, Kāv. **–tara**, mfn. dearer &c., R.; Pañcat.; *-tva*, n. the being dearer to any one (loc.) than (abl.), MBh. **–tā** (*priyá-*), f. the being dear, ŚBr.; Mn.; MBh. &c.; the being fond of (comp.), love, Kathās.; Rājat. **–toshaṇa**, m. a kind of coitus, L. **–tva**, n. the being dear, b° beloved, MBh.; R.; the being fond of (comp.), Kum.; Suśr. **–da**, mfn. giving desired objects, L.; (*ā*), f. Rhinacanthus Communis, L. **–dattā**, f. a mystical N. of the earth, MBh.; N. of a woman, Kathās. **–darśa**, mfn. pleasant or agreeable to look at (opp. to *dur-darśa*), MBh. **–darśana**, mfn. pleasant or grateful to the sight of (gen.), MBh.; Kāv.; m. a parrot, L.; a kind of date tree, L.; Terminalia Tomentosa, L.; Mimusops Kauki, L.; a plant growing in wet weather on trees and stones (in Marāṭhī called *dagaḍaphūla*, in Hindūstānī پتهر کي پهول), L.; a partic. Kalpa, Buddh.; N. of a prince of the Gandharvas, Ragh.; of a son of Vāsuki, Kathās.; (*a*), f. N. of a Surâṅganā, Siṅhâs.; of sev. women, Vās.; Priy.; (*ī*), f. Gracula Religiosa, L.; n. the look of a friend, Pañcat. **–darśikā**, f. N. of a princess, Priy.; of a drama. **–darśin**, m. 'looking with kindness (upon everything,' N. of Aśoka, Inscr. **–dāsa**, m. N. of the author of a Comm. on the Bhakta-mālā, MW. **–devana**, mfn. fond of play or gambling, MBh. **–dhanva**, m. 'fond of the bow,' N. of Śiva, MBh. **–dhā́**, ind. lovingly, kindly, TS. **–dhānya-kara**, mfn. causing dearness of corn (opp. to *su-bhiksha-kārin*), VarBṛS. iv, 20. **–dhāma** (*priyá-*), mfn. fond of home, loving the sacrificial enclosure (said of Agni), RV. i, 140, 1. **–dhāman** (*priyá-*), mfn. = prec. (said of Indra), AV.; (s° of the Ādityas), ŚBr.; ŚrS. **–ṃ-dada**, mfn. giving what is pleasant, Kāraṇḍ.; (*ā*), f. N. of a Gandharvī, ib. **–nivedana**, n. good tidings, Mṛicch. **–nivedayitṛi** (or °*ditṛi*), m. a messenger of g° t°, Śak. **–nivedikā**, f. a female m° of g° t°, Mālatīm. **–pati** (*priyá-*), m. lord of the beloved or desired, VS. **–putra**, m. a kind of bird, BrahmaP. **–prada**, m. N. of an author of Śākta Mantras, Cat. **–praśna**, m. a kind inquiry (as after any one's welfare &c.), Hcar. **–prasādana**, n. the conciliation of a husband, reconciliation with any object of affection, MW.; *-vrata*, n. a vow for the c° of a h°, ib. **–prâṇa**, mfn. fond of life, ib. **–prâya**, mfn. exceedingly kind or amiable (as speech), L.; of pleasing speech, well-spoken, eloquent, W.; n. eloquence in language, W. **–priyeṇa**, ind. with pleasure, willingly, Pāṇ. viii, 1, 13. **–prêpsu**, mfn. desirous of obtaining a beloved object, lamenting the loss or absence of any b° o°, grieving for an o° of affection, W. **–bhāva**, m. feeling of love, A. **–bhāshaṇa**, n. speaking kindly, kind or friendly speech, Hit. **–bhāshin**, mfn. speaking kindly or agreeably, R.; (*iṇī*), f. Gracula Religiosa, L. **–bhojana**, mfn. fond of good food, Bhpr. **–maṅgalā**, f. N. of a Surâṅganā, Siṅhâs. **–maṇḍana**, mfn. fond of trinkets or ornaments, Śak. **–madhu**, m. 'fond of wine,' N. of Bala-rāma (the half-brother of Kṛishṇa), L. **–mānasa**, mfn. fond of the lake Mānasa (the Rāja-haṅsa or Royal-goose), MW. **–mālyânulepana**, m. 'fond of garlands and ornaments,' N. of an attendant of Skanda, MBh. **–mitra**, m. N. of a mythical Cakra-vartin, W. **–mukhā**, f. N. of a Gandharvī, Kāraṇḍ. **–mukhyā**, f. N. of an Apsaras, VP. **–medha** (*priyá-*), m. N. of a Ṛishi (a descendant of Aṅgiras and author of the hymns RV. viii, 1–40, 57, 58, 76; ix, 28) and (pl.) of his descendants, RV.; Nir.; of a descendant of Aja-mīḍha, BhP.; *-vát*, ind. as Priya-medha, RV.; *-stuta* (*priyá-m*°), mfn. praised by P°, ib. (accord. to Sāy. = *priya-yajñair ṛishibhiḥ stutaḥ*). **–ṃ-bhavishṇu**, mfn. becoming dear or agreeable, Bhaṭṭ. (Pāṇ. iii, 2, 57); *-tā*, f. (W.) or *-tva*, n. (MW.) the b° d°. **–bhāvuka**, mfn. becoming dear, Git. (Pāṇ. iii, 2, 57); *-tā*, f. (Bhaṭṭ.) or *-tva*, n. (MW.) the b° d°. **–yajña**, mfn. fond of sacrifices, Sāy. **–raṇa**, mfn. delighting in war, warlike, MW. **–ratha** (*priyá-*), m. (prob.) N. of a man, RV. i, 122, 7 (accord. to Sāy. mfn. = *prīyamāṇa-ratha-yukta*). **–rūpa**, mfn. having an agreeable form, g. *manojñâdi* to Pāṇ. v, 1, 133. **–vaktṛi**, mfn. one who speaks kindly or agreeably, flattering, a flatterer, Pañcat.; *-tva*, n. speaking kindly, Cāṇ. **–vacana**, mfn. one whose words are kind or friendly, speaking kindly, Sāy. on RV. i, 13, 8; m. = *bhakti-mān rogī*, L.; n. kind or friendly speech, Vikr. **–vacas**, mfn. speaking kindly, not out of tune, L.; n. kind or friendly speech, Sāh. **–vat** (*priyá-*), mfn. possessing friends, Bhar.; containing the word *priya*, TS.; Kāṭh. **–vadya**, n. = *-vāda* (q.v.), ĀpŚr. **–vayasya**, m. a dear friend, MW. **–varṇī**, f. = *priyaṅgu*, L.; Echites Frutescens, W. **–vallī**, f. = *priyaṅgu* or *phalinī*, L. **–vasantaka**, m. 'the desired spring' and 'the dear Vasantaka,' Ratnâv. i, 8. **–vastu**, n. a favourite object or topic, MW. **–vāc**, mfn. one whose words are kind, kind in speech, Kām.; Var.; f. kind speech, gentle words, (*-vāk-sahita*, mfn. accompanied by k° w°), Hit. **–vāda**, m. k° or agreeable speech, MBh.; R. **–vādikā**, f. a kind of musical instrument, L. **–vādin**, mfn. speaking kindly or agreeably, flattering, a flatterer, VS.; MBh.; R. &c. (°*di-tā*, f., MBh.; R.); m. (Car.) or (*inī*), f. (L.) a kind of bird, Gracula Religiosa. **–vinā-kṛita**, mfn. abandoned by a lover, deserted by a husband, MW. **–viśva**, mfn., Pāṇ. i, 1, 29, Sch. **–vrata** (*priyá-*), mfn. having desirable ordinances or fond of obedience (said of the gods), RV.; ŚBr.; KātyŚr.; m. N. of a king (a son of Manu and Śata-rūpā), Hariv.; Pur.; of a man, Br. **–śālaka**, m. Terminalia Tomentosa, L. (also spelt *-sālaka*). **–śishyā**, f. N. of an Apsaras, VP. **–śravas**, mfn. loving glory (said of Kṛishṇa), BhP. **–sá**, mfn. granting desired objects, RV. ix, 97, 38. **–saṃvāsa**, m. living together with loved persons, MBh. **–sakha**, mfn. loving one's friends, Laghuj.; m. a dear friend, MBh.; Bhartṛ.; Megh.; the tree Acacia Catechu (= *khadira*), L.; (*ī*), f. a dear female friend, Daś. **–saṃgamana**, n. 'meeting of friends,' N. of a place (in which Indra and Vishṇu are said to have met with their parents Aditi and Kaśyapa), Hariv. 7647. **–satya**, mfn. pleasant and true (as speech), L.; a lover of truth, A.; n. speech at once pleasing and true, W. **–saṃtati**, mfn. having a beloved son, MW. **–saṃdeśa**, m. a friendly message, A.; Michelia Champaca, L. **–samāgama**, m. re-union with a beloved object, MW. **–samucita**, mfn. befitting a lover, ib. **–samudra**, m. N. of a merchant, HPariś. **–samprahāra**, mfn. fond of litigation, Bālar. **–sarpishka**, mfn. fond of melted butter, Laghuk. **–sahacarī**, f. a dear female companion, beloved wife, MW. **–sālaka**, m. = *-śālaka*, q.v. **–sāhasa**, mfn. addicted to rashness; *-tva*, n., VarBṛS. **–sukha**, m. N. of an author, Cat. **–suhṛid**, m. a dear friend, kind or good f°, Hit. **–sena**, m. N. of a man, Divyâv. **–sevaka**, mfn. loving servants, kind towards s°, Rājat. **–stotra**, mfn. fond of praise, RV. i, 91, 6. **–svapna**, mfn. fond of sleep, sluggish, Ragh. **–svāmin**, m. N. of an author, Cat. **–hita**, mfn. at once agreeable and salutary, VP.; n. things which are a° and s°, MBh.; Mn.; R.; Gaut. (du.) **Priyâkhya**, mfn. announcing good tidings, R.; Pat.; called 'dear,' Prab. **Priyâkhyāna**, n. agreeable news, pleasant tidings, MW.; *-dāna*, n. a gift in return for pl° t°, Jātak.; *-puraḥsara*, mfn. preceded by pl° t°, MW. **Priyâkhyāyin**, m. a teller announcing good news, Divyâv. **Priyā-jana**, m. pl. mistresses, dear ones &c. (collectively), Śiś. **Priyâtithi**, mfn. fond of guests, hospitable, MBh. **Priyâtmaka**, m. a kind of bird classed with the Pratudas, Car. (v.l. °*tma-ja*). **Priyâtman**, mfn. of a pleasant nature, pl°, agreeable, R.; °*tma-ja*, m. = °*tmaka*, q.v. **Priyā-dāsa**, m. N. of an author, Cat. **Priyâdhāna**, n. a friendly office, MW. **Priyânna**, n. expensive food, MW.; *-tva*, n. dearth, scarcity, VarBṛS. **Priyâpatya**, m. a kind of vulture, L. **Priyâpāya**, m. the absence of a beloved object, MW. **Priyâpriyá**, n. sg. du. or pl. pleasant and unpleasant things, AV.; ChUp.; Mn. &c. **Priyā-mukhī-√bhū**, P. *-bhavati*, to be changed into the face of a loved woman, Naish. **Priyâmbu**, mfn. fond of water; m. the mango tree, L. **Priyârtham**, ind. for the sake of a beloved object, as a favour, MBh.; Megh.; Rājat. **Priyârha**, mfn. deserving love, amiable, MW.; m. N. of Vishṇu, A. **Priyâlâpa**, m. N. of a man, Vṛishabhān. **Priyâlâpin**, mfn. speaking kindly or agreeably, Bhartṛ. **Priyá-vat**, mfn. having a mistress, enamoured, AV. iv, 18, 4. **Priyā-viraha**, m. N. of an author, Cat. **Priyâsu**, mfn. fond of life, W. **Priyâsūyamatī**, f. N. of a woman, Rājat. **Priyâlikā**, f. a kind of bean, L. **Priyâishin**, mfn. friendly disposed to (comp.), Hariv. **Priyôkti**, f. friendly speech, Sāh. **Priyôdita**, mfn. kindly spoken, W.; n. kind speech, L. **Priyôpapatti**, f. a happy event or circumstance, pleasant occurrence, MW. **Priyôpabhoga**, m. the enjoyment of a lover or of a mistress, ib.; *-vandhya*, mfn. barren or destitute of the e° of a l°, ib. **Priyôsriya**, mfn. loving cows, amorous (said of a bull), RV. x, 40, 11.

Priyaka, m. a kind of deer with a very soft skin, Śiś.; Suśr.; a chameleon, L.; a kind of bird, MBh.;

a bee, L.; N. of sev. plants (Nauclea Cadamba, Terminalia Tomentosa &c.), L.; a kind of tree, R.; Hariv.; Var.; N. of a being attending on Skanda, MBh.; of a man, g. *bidâdi*; (*ī*), f. the skin of the Priyaka, R.; n. N. of a flower, Śiś.

Priyáṅgu, m. f. panic seed, Panicum Italicum, VS.; TS.; Br.; Kauś.; Aglaia Odorata, L.; Sinapis Ramosa, MBh.; Kathās.; long pepper, L.; a medicinal plant and perfume (commonly called Priyaṅgu and described in some places as a fragrant seed), L.; a partic. creeper (said to put forth blossoms at the touch of women), MBh.; Kāv. &c.; Italian millet, MW.; n. (prob.) panic seed or mustard seed, Suśr.; Bhpr.; saffron, L. **-dvīpa**, n. N. of a country, Buddh. **-śyāmā**, f. N. of the wife of Nara-vāhana-datta, Vās. **Priyaṅgv-ākhyā**, f. panic seed, L.

Priyaṅgukā, f. Panicum Italicum, SāmavBr.

Priyāka, m. N. of an author, Cat.

Priyā-√kṛi, P. *-karoti*, to act kindly towards, do a favour to (acc.), Pāṇ.; Vop.; Bhaṭṭ.

Priyāya, Nom. Ā. °*yáte*, to treat kindly, AV.; MBh. (v. l. *priyam ivâcarate*, Nīlak.; cf. *prīyāya*); to make friends with (instr.), RV.

Priyāla, m. the tree Buchanania Latifolia (commonly called Piyāl), MBh.; R.; Suśr. &c.; (*ā*), f. a vine, a bunch of grapes (= *drākshā*), L. **-tāla-kharjūra-harītakī-vibhītaka**, m. pl. Piyāl, palm, date and yellow and beleric myrobalan trees, MW.

Priyīya, Nom. P. °*yati*, to think a person to be another's mistress, HYog.

2. **Prī**, mfn. (ifc.) kind, delighted (see *adha-prī*, *kadha-prī*, *ghṛita-prī* &c.)

1. **Prīṇa**, mfn. (for 2. see col. 3) pleased, satisfied, W.

Prīṇana, mfn. pleasing, gratifying, appeasing, soothing, Suśr.; n. the act of pleasing or delighting or satisfying, MBh.; BhP.; Ratnâv.; a means of pleasing or delighting or satisfying, MBh.; BhP.

Prīṇayitṛi, mfn. one who gladdens or delights; (*trī*), f., Sāy. on RV. iv, 42, 10 (w. r. *prīṇāyitrī*).

Prīṇayitvā, ind. having pleased or propitiated, W.

Prīṇita, mfn. pleased, gratified, delighted, MBh.; Pañcat.; Bhaṭṭ.

Prītá, mfn. pleased, delighted, satisfied, joyful, glad; pl° or d° or s° with, j° at, g° of (with instr., loc., gen., or ifc.), RV. &c. &c.; beloved, dear to (gen. or comp.), Cāṇ.; Hit.; kind (as speech), Hit.; (*ā*), f. a symbolical expression for the sound *sh*, RāmatUp. (v. l. *pītā*); n. jest, mirth, L.; pleasure, delight, W. **-citta**, mfn. delighted at heart, A. **-tara**, mfn. more highly pleased, Ragh. **-manas** (R.), **-mānasa** (MBh.), or °**tâtman** (ib.; Mn.), mfn. pleased or gratified in mind.

Prīti, f. any pleasurable sensation, pleasure, joy, gladness, satisfaction (with loc. or ifc.; with ind. p., 'joy at having done anything'), GṛŚrS. &c. &c.; friendly disposition, kindness, favour, grace, amity (with *samam* or ifc.), affection, love (with gen., loc., or ifc.), MBh.; Kāv. &c.; joy or gratification personified (esp. as a daughter of Daksha or as one of the two wives of Kāma-deva), Hariv.; Pur.; Kathās.; N. of a Śruti, Saṃgīt.; the 2nd of the 27 astrological Yogas, L.; N. of the 13th Kalā of the moon, Cat.; a symbolical expression for the sound *dh*, RāmatUp.; (*yā*), ind. in a state of joyful excitement, gladly, with joy, MBh.; R.; Ragh.; Kathās.; in a friendly way, amicably, Mn.; R.; Ragh. &c. **-kara**, mfn. causing pleasure to (comp.), MārkP.; Pāṇ. vi, 2, 15, Sch. (cf. *a-p*°); inspiring love or affection, MW.; m. N. of two authors, Cat. **-karaṇa**, n. the act of causing pleasure, gratifying, MW. **-karman**, n. an act of friendship or love, kind action, Mn. **-kūṭa**, N. of a village, Vāsav., introd. **-candra**, m. N. of a preceptor, MW. **-ccheda**, m. destruction of joy, Mṛicch. **-jushā**, f. N. of the wife of A-niruddha, L. **-tṛish**, m. N. of the god of love, L. **-da**, mfn. giving pleasure, L.; inspiring love or regard, affectionate, W.; m. a jester or buffoon in a play, L. **-datta**, mfn. given through love or affection, L.; n. (?) property or valuables presented to a female by her relations and friends at the time of her marriage, and constituting part of her peculiar property, MW. **-dāna**, n. (Ragh.) or **-dāya**, m. (MBh.; R.; Rājat.) 'gift of love,' a present made from love or affection. **-dhana**, n. money given from love or friendship, R. **-pātra**, n. an object of affection, a beloved person or thing, MW. **-puroga**, mfn. preceded by aff°, affectionate, loving, MBh. **-pūrvakam** (Mn.; Bhag.) or **-pūrvam** (MBh.), ind. with the accompaniment of kindness, kindly, affectionately. **-pramukha**, mfn. preceded by kindness, kind, friendly; *-vacana*, n. a speech p° by k°, kind sp°, affectionate words, Megh. **-bhāj**, mfn. enjoying friendship, receiving friendly offices, Kathās. **-bhojya**, mfn. to be eaten joyfully or cheerfully, MW. **-mat**, mfn. having pleasurable sensations, pleased, gratified, glad, satisfied, MBh.; Kāv.; MārkP.; having love or affection for (loc., gen. or acc.), affectionate, favourable, loving, MBh.; R.; Hariv.; MārkP.; kind (as words), R.; (*atī*), f. a kind of metre, Col. **-manas**, mfn. joyous-minded, pleased in mind, content; kind, W. **-maya**, mf(*ī*)n. made up of joy, arisen from joy (as tears), R. **-yuj**, mfn. beloved, dear, Kir. **-rasâyana**, n. 'an elixir of joy,' any nectar-like beverage causing joy, Hit. **-vacana** (A.) or **-vacas** (Hit.), n. kind or friendly words. **-vardhana**, mfn. increasing love or joy, A.; m. the 4th month, Sūryapr.; N. of Vishṇu, A. **-vāda**, m. a friendly discussion, MW. **-vivāha**, m. a love-marriage, love-match, ib. **-viśrambha-bhājana**, n. a repository of affection and confidence, ib. **-śrāddha**, n. a funeral offering to the Pitṛis of both parents (performed by some one in place of the eldest surviving son, and to be re-performed at some other period by this son in person), ib. **-saṃyoga**, m. relation of friendship, R. **-saṃgati**, f. a covenant of fr°, friendly alliance with (instr.), ŚārṅgP. **-saṃdarbha**, m. N. of wk. **-sambodhy-aṅga**, n. (with Buddhists) joyfulness (one of the 7 requisites for attaining supreme knowledge), Dharmas. 49. **-snigdha**, mfn. moist through love or charming through affection (said of the eyes), Megh.

Prīyati, m. an expression for √*prī*, MBh.

Prīyāya, Nom. Ā. °*yate*, to rejoice at (acc.), MBh. (cf. *priyāya*).

Preṇā, instr. for *premṇā*, see *premán*.

Preṇí, mfn. = *pretṛí*, RV. i, 112, 10 (of obscure meaning, AV. vi, 89, 1).

Pretṛí, mfn. a lover, cherisher, benefactor, RV.; ŚāṅkhŚr.

Predhā́, ind. = *priya-dhā́* (q. v.), MaitrS.

1. **Prema** (ifc. f. *ā*) = *premán*, love, affection (cf. *sa-p*°); (*ā*), f., see below.

2. **Prema**, in comp. for *premán*. **-tattva-nirūpaṇa**, n. N. of a Bengālī poem by Kṛishṇa-dāsa. **-dhara**, m. N. of an author, Cat. **-nārāyaṇa**, m. N. of a king, Inscr. **-nidhi**, m. N. of sev. authors, Cat. **-pattanikā**, f. N. of wk. **-para**, mfn. intent on love, filled with affection, affectionate, loving, constant, W. **-pātana**, n. rheum, L.; tears (of joy), W. **-pātra**, n. an object of affection, a beloved person or thing, MW. **-pīyūsha-latā-kartarī**, f. N. of wk. **-bandha**, m. (ŚārṅgP.; Rājat.) or **-bandhana**, n. (BhP.) the ties of love, love, affection. **-bhakti-candrikā**, f., **-bhakti-stotra**, n. N. of wks. **-bhāva**, m. state of affection, love, R. **-rasâyana**, n., °**yanânurāga**, m., **-rāja**, m. N. of wks. **-rāśī-√bhū**, P. *-bhavati*, to become one mass of affection, Megh. **-ṛddhi** (°*ma-ṛid*°), f. increase of aff°, ardent love, MW. **-latikā**, f. the small creeping plant 'love,' Kpr. **-vat**, mfn. full of love, affectionate, Subh.; (*atī*), f. a mistress, L. **-viśvāsa-bhūmi**, f. an object of l° and confidence, MW. **-sāgara**, m. an ocean of l°, ib. **-sāhi** (*sāhi* = شاه), m. = *-nārāyaṇa*, Inscr. **-sena**, m. N. of a prince, Siṃhâs. **Premâkara**, m. abundance of love, Daś. **Premâmṛita**, n. 'love-ambrosia,' N. of a metrical list of 112 names of Kṛishṇa and of sev. other wks. **Premârdra**, mfn. overflowing with love, Mālatīm. **Premâśru**, n. a tear of affection, MW. **Premêndu-sāgara**, m., **Premôkty-udaya**, m. N. of wks.

Premaṇīya, mfn. fit for exciting love &c., Buddh.

Premán, m. n. love, affection, kindness, tender regard, favour, predilection, fondness, l° &c. towards (loc. or comp.), TS.; Br.; Kāv. &c. (also pl.); joy, L.; m. sport, a jest, joke, Sāh.; wind, L.; N. of Indra, L.; of various men, Rājat.; (*premṇā*, Ved. *preṇā́*), ind. through love or affection, RV.; TS.; MBh.

Premā, in comp. for *premán*. **-bandha**, m. = *prema-b*° (above), Amar.; Ratnâv.; Veṇis. **-vatī**, f. N. of a Surâṅganā, Siṃhâs.

Premin, mfn. loving, affectionate, L.

Préyas, mfn. (compar. fr. *priya*) dearer, more agreeable, m° desired, RV.; AV.; ŚBr. &c.; m. a lover, Amar.; Kathās.; a dear friend, Mālatīm.; (*asī*), f. a mistress, Bhartṛ.; Dhūrtas.; n. (in rhet.) flattery, Pratāp.; Kuval.; Sāh. **-kara**, m. the hand of a lover, BhP. **-tā**, f. (Rājat.) or **-tva**, n. (BhP.) the being dearer or very dear. **-vin**, mfn. containing flattery, Kāv. **Preyo-'patya** (fr. °*yas* + *ap*°), m. 'very fond of offspring,' a heron, L.

Préshṭha, mfn. (superl. fr. *priya*) dearest, most beloved or desired, RV.; (in address) KaṭhUp.; BhP.; very fond of (loc.), RV. vi, 63, 1; m. a lover, husband, BhP.; (*ā*), f. a mistress, wife, L.; a leg, L. **-tama**, mfn. dearest, most beloved, BhP.

प्रीण 2. *prīṇa* (for 1. see under √*prī*), mfn. (fr. 1. *pra*) old, ancient, former, Pāṇ. v, 4, 30, Vārtt. 7, Pat. (cf. *pra-ṇa*, *pra-tna*, *pra-tana*).

प्रीतु *prītu*, m. a bird (?), W.

प्रु *pru*, cl. 1. Ā. (Dhātup. xxii, 61) *pravate* (pf. *pupruve*, ŚBr.; aor. *proshṭhāḥ*, ĀśvŚr.), to spring up, Bhaṭṭ.: Caus. *prāvayati* (aor. *apupravat* or *apipravat*), to reach to (acc.), ib. (cf. Pāṇ. i, 3, 86): Desid. of Caus. *puprāvayishati* or *piprāvayishati*, Pāṇ. vii, 4, 81, Sch. (cf. *ati-√pru*, *apa-√pru* &c.; and √*plu*).

Prut (ifc.), see *antariksha-*, *udu-*, *upari-* and *kṛishṇa-prút*.

प्रुथ *pruth*, cl. 1. P. Ā. *próthati*, °*te*, to pant, neigh, snort (as a horse), RV.; ĀśvŚr.: Caus. *prothayati*, to employ force, Āpast.: Intens. (only p. *pópruthat*) to snort aloud, RV. i, 30, 16 (cf. √*proth*).

Protha, m. n. (g. *ardharcâdi*) the nostrils of a horse, MBh.; Var. (cf. *prithu-p*°); the snout of a hog, MBh.; m. the loins or hip (of a man), Bhpr.; the womb, L.; a cave, L.; a petticoat, L.; terror, fright, L.; a traveller (?), L.; mfn. notorious, famous (?), W.; placed, fixed (?), ib. **Prothátha**, m. panting, snorting, RV. **Prothin**, m. a horse, L.

प्रुष 1. *prush*, cl. 5. P. Ā. *prushṇóti*, °*nuté* (fut. *proshishyate*, TS.; pf. *puprosha*, aor. *aproshīt*, Gr.), to sprinkle, shower, wet, moisten, RV.; VS.; TS.; cl. 10. P. Ā. (or Nom.) *prushāyáti*, °*te*, id., RV.; cl. 9. P. (Dhātup. xxxi, 55) *prushṇāti* (p. *prushṇát*, Br.), id.; to become wet, fill, L.; cl. 4. P. *prushyati*, see *vi-√prush*. [Cf. Lat. *pruīna* for *prusvīna*; Goth. *frius*; Germ. *friosan*, *frieren*; Eng. *freeze*.]

2. **Prush** (ifc.), see *abhra-* and *ghṛita-prúsh*.

Prushitá, mfn. sprinkled, wet, RV. **-psu** (°*tá-*), mfn. dappled, piebald (as horses), ib.

Prushṭa, °*ṭāyate*, Pāṇ. iii, 1, 17, Vārtt. 1.

Prushva, m. the rainy season, Uṇ. i, 151, Sch.; (*prushvā́* or *prúshvā*), f. a drop of water, rime, ice, AV.; VS.; ŚBr.

Prushvāya, Nom. Ā. °*yate*, to fall in drops, trickle, Uṇ. i, 151.

Proshaka, m. pl. N. of a people, MBh.

प्रुष 3. *prush*, cl. 1. P. (Dhātup. xvii, 53) to burn.

Prushṭa, mfn. burnt, L.

Prushva, m. heat, L.; mfn. hot, L.

Prosha, m. burning, combustion, L.

प्रू *prū*. See *kaṭa-prū*.

प्रूष *prūsh* (for *prush*). See *ashṭā-prush*.

प्रे *prê* (*pra-√5. i*), cl. 2. P. *prâiti* (Ved. inf. *prâitos*, AitBr.), to come forth, appear, begin, RV.; BṛĀrUp.; MBh.; to go on, proceed, advance (esp. as a sacrifice), RV.; VS.; to go forwards or farther, come to, arrive at, enter (acc.), ib.; ŚBr.; Up.; MBh.; to go out or away, depart (this life, with or without *asmāl lokāt* or *itas*), die, Br.; Up.; Mn.; MBh. &c.: Intens. Ā. *prêyate*, to drive or go forth (said of Ushas), RV.

Preta, mfn. departed, deceased, dead, a dead person, ŚBr.; GṛŚrS.; MBh.; m. the spirit of a dead person (esp. before obsequial rites are performed), a ghost, an evil being, Mn.; MBh. &c. (cf. RTL. 241, 271; MWB. 219). **-karman**, n. an obsequial rite, MBh. **-kalpa**, m. 'obs° ordinance,' N. of GaruḍaP. ii. **-kāya**, m. a dead body, corpse, Kathās. **-kārya**, n. = *-karman*, MBh.; R.; BhP. **-kṛitya**, n. id., MBh. (*ā*, f., Mn. iii, 127); *-nirṇaya* and °*tyâdi-nirṇaya*, m. N. of wks. **-gata**, mfn. gone to the departed, dead, MBh. **-gati**, f. the way of the dep° (with √*gam*, 'to die'), ib. **-gṛiha**, n. 'dead-house,' a burning-place, L. **-gopa**,

m. guardian of the dead (in Yama's house), R. **–cārin,** m. 'roaming among the d°,' N. of Śiva, Śivag. **–tva,** n. being d°, Hariv.; the state of a ghost, Hcat.; Kāraṇḍ. **–dāha,** m. burning of the d°, MW.; °*hâgni,* m. corpse-fire, L. **–dīpikā,** f. N. of wk. **–dhūma,** m. smoke of the dead i. e. of a funeral pile, Mn.; Yājñ. **–nadī,** f. river of the d° (= *vaitaraṇī,* q. v.), L. **–nara,** m. a d° man, a ghost, W. **–nātha,** m. 'lord of the d°,' N. of Yama, Bālar. **–niryātaka,** m. a carrier of d° bodies, Mn. iii, 166. **–nirhāraka,** m. id., ib. (v. l.) **–paksha** or °**shaka,** m. = *pitṛi-p°* (q. v.), L. **–paṭaha,** m. a drum beaten at the burning of the dead, L. **–patākā,** f. a flag used at the b° of the d°, Hcar. **–pati,** m. = *-nātha,* MārkP.; *-paṭaha,* m. 'Yama's drum,' drum beaten at the b° of the d°, Kād. **–pātra,** n. a vessel used at a Śrāddha ceremony, W. **–piṇḍa-bhuj,** mfn. one who partakes of the Piṇḍa (q. v.) at a Śrāddha, Hcar. **–pitṛi,** mfn. one whose father is d°, MānGṛ. **–pura,** n. (L.), **-purī,** f. (Daś.), city of the d°, Yama's abode. **–pradīpa,** m. N. of wk. **–prasādhana,** n. adornment of a corpse, Kathās. **–bhakshiṇī,** f. N. of a goddess, Cat. **–bhāva,** m. the being d°, death (°*vāya saṃsiddhaḥ,* 'ready to die'), R.; *-stha,* mfn. dead, ib. **–bhūmi,** f. 'place of the d°,' a burning-ground, MW. **–mañjarī,** f. N. of ch. of GaruḍaP. **–mukti-dā,** f. N. of wk. **–medha,** m. a funeral sacrifice, R. **–moksha,** m. N. of ch. of the Māgha-māhātmya. **–rākshasī,** f. Ocimum Sanctum, L. (v. l. *apêta-* and *a-prêta-r°*). **–rāja,** m. = *-nātha,* R.; *-niveśana,* n., *-pura,* n. Yama's abode or city, MBh. **–loka,** m. the world of the dead (in which they remain for one year or until the Śrāddha ceremonies are completed), MBh. **–vat,** ind. as if dead, MW. **–vana,** n. 'grove of the dead,' a burning-ground, L. **–vaśa,** m. power of the dead (°*śaṃ* √*nī,* to put to death), MBh. **–vāhita,** mfn. possessed by an evil spirit, L. **–śarīra,** n. the body with which a departed spirit is invested, RTL. 28. **–śilā,** f. 'stone of the dead,' N. of a stone near Gayā on which Piṇḍas are offered (see *piṇḍa*), GaruḍaP. **–śuddhi,** f. (Mn.), **-śauca,** n. (GaruḍaP.) purification after the death of a kinsman. **–śrāddha,** n. the obsequial ceremonies performed for a relative at death and every month for a year and at every anniversary after death. **–saṃklṛipta,** mfn. (food) prepared in honour of the dead, Āpast. **–sparśin** (ŚāṅkhGṛ.), **-hāra** (Mn.), m. = *-niryātaka.* **Prêtâdhipa,** m. = °*ta-nātha,* Hariv.; *-nagarī,* f. Yama's residence, Kād. **Prêtâdhipati,** m. the lord of the dead or of departed spirits, ShaḍvBr. **Prêtânna,** n. food offered to a dead person, Mn.; Āpast. **Prêtâyana,** m. 'way of the dead,' N. of a partic. hell, Kād. (w. r. °*tāpana*). **Prêtâlaya,** m. a kind of thorn-apple, L. **Prêtâvāsa,** m. = °*ta-gṛiha,* BhP. **Prêtâsthi,** n. a bone of a dead man; *-dhārin,* m. 'wearing dead men's bones,' N. of Śiva, Kāv. **Prêtêśa** (Yājñ., Sch.), °**śvara** (R.), m. = °*ta-nātha.* **Prêtôddeśa,** m. an offering to deceased ancestors, W.

Prêti, f. departure, flight, RV.; VS.; approach, arrival, TāṇḍBr. **–vat** (*prê°*), mfn. containing the word *prêti* or any form of *prê,* TS. **Prêti-shaṇi** (Padap. °*ti-sh°*), mfn. striving to move forwards (said of Agni), RV.

Prêtika, m. the soul of a dead man, a ghost, L.

Prêtya, ind. having died, after death, in the next world, in the life to come, hereafter (opp. to *iha*), ŚBr.; Mn.; MBh. &c. **–jāti,** f. rank or position in the next world, MBh. **–bhāj,** mfn. enjoying (the fruits of anything) in the n° w°, Hariv. **–bhāva,** m. the state after death, future life, Gaut.; MBh.; R. (cf. IW. 63); °*vika,* mfn. relating to it (opp. to *aihalaukika*), MBh.

Prêtvan, mf(*arī*)n. moving along, straying about (as cattle), Br.; m. wind, air, L.; N. of Indra, L.

Prêhi, 2. sg. Impv. in comp. (cf. 1. *prôha* under *prôh*). **–kaṭā,** f. a rite in which no mats are allowed, g. *mayūra-vyaṇsakâdi.* **–kardamā,** f. a rite in which no impurity of any kind is all°, ib. **–dvitīyā,** f. a rite at which no second person is all° to be present, ib. **–vaṇijā,** f. a rite at which no merchants are allowed to be present, ib.

प्रेकीय *pr'ekīya,* Nom. P. °*yati* (fr. *pra* + *eka*), Vop. (cf. *praîkīya*).

प्रेक्ष् *prêksh* (*pra-*√*īksh*), Ā. *prêkshate* (ep. also P. °*ti*), to look at, view, behold, observe, TS. &c. &c.; to look on (without interfering), suffer, say nothing, Mn.; MBh.

Prêkshaka, mf(*ikā*)n. looking at, viewing or intending to view, MBh.; R.; Hariv.; considering, judging, Yājñ., Sch.; m. a spectator, member of an audience, MānGṛ.; °*kêrita,* mfn. (a word) uttered by a spectator, MBh. **Prêkshaṇa,** n. viewing, looking at or on (at a performance), GṛS.; Mn.; BhP.; (ifc. *ā*) a view, look, sight, Megh.; the eye, Suśr.; any public show or spectacle, Mn.; Pañcat.; Kathās.; a place where public exhibitions are held, W.; *-kūṭa,* n. the pupil of the eye, Suśr.; °*ṇâlambha,* n. sg. looking at and touching (women), Mn. ii, 179. **Prêkshaṇaka,** mfn. looking at, a spectator, Yājñ.; n. a spectacle, show (as opp. to reality), Bālar.; Hcat. **Prêkshaṇika,** mfn. = prec. mfn., W.; m. an actor (?), Vet.; (*ā*), f. a woman fond of seeing shows, W. **Prêkshaṇīya,** mfn. to be seen, visible, Śak.; (ifc.) looking like, resembling, Megh.; worth seeing, sightly, beautiful to the view, MBh.; Kālid.; n. a show, spectacle, Vet.; *-ka,* n. = prec. n., Kathās.; *-tama* and *-tara,* mfn. most and more sightly or beautiful, MBh.; *-tā,* f. sightliness, beautifulness, Rājat.

Prêkshā, f. seeing, viewing, beholding, regarding, looking on (at a performance), MBh.; R.; BhP. (often ifc., cf. *dharma-prêksha, mukha-pr°*); a sight or view (esp. a beautiful s° or v°), BhP.; a public show or entertainment, Mn.; Hariv.; Kathās.; (ifc.) the being understood or meant as, Nir. i, 17; circumspection, consideration, reflection, MBh.; Hariv.; Rājat.; the branch of a tree, L. **–kārin,** mfn. one who acts with deliberation, Kir. **–**°**gāra** (°*kshâg°*), m. n. a play-house, theatre, MBh.; Hariv.; VP. **–gṛiha,** n. id., Hariv. **–pūrva** (ibc.) or °**vam,** ind. with deliberation, Hariv.; Rājat. **–prapañca,** m. a stage-play, Bālar. **–vat,** mfn. circumspect, deliberate, prudent, Sāṃkhyak., Sch.; Nīlak. **–vidhi,** m. a stage-play, Bālar. **–samāja,** n. sg. public shows and assemblies, Mn. ix, 84 (v. l. °*jau,* m. du.)

Prêkshita, mfn. looked at &c.; n. a look, glance, MBh.; R. &c. **Prêkshitavya,** mfn. to be seen or beheld, Ratnâv. **Prêkshitṛi,** mfn. one who looks on, spectator, Hariv.

Prêkshin, mfn. looking at, viewing, regarding (°*kshi-tva,* n.), MBh.; R. &c.; (ifc.) having the eyes or glance of (cf. *mṛiga-pr°*).

Prêkshya, mfn. to be seen, visible, MBh.; to be looked at or regarded, Kathās.; worth seeing, sightly, Kālid.; Rājat.

प्रेङ्ख् *prêṅkh* (*pra-*√*iṅkh*), P. Ā. *prêṅkhati,* °*te,* to tremble, shake, vibrate, AitĀr.; Kāv.: Caus. P *prêṅkhayati,* to swing (trans.), Ragh.; Ā. °*te,* to swing one's self, RV. vii, 88, 3.

Prêṅkhá, mfn. trembling, rocking, swaying, pitching, RV.; AV.; m., n. and (*ā*), f. a swing, a sort of hammock or swinging-cot, Br.; ŚrS.; BhP.; Suśr. (m. du. the two posts between which a swing moves, Āpast.; id. [with *Nakulasya Vāma-devasya*] and sg. [with *Marutām*] N. of Sāmans, ĀrshBr.; °*kha-phalaka,* n. the board or seat in a swing, ŚāṅkhŚr.; °*khêṅkhana,* n. swinging, BhP.); (*ā*), f. dancing, L.; a partic. pace of a horse, L.; wandering, roaming, L.

Prêṅkhaṇa, mfn. (ifc.) moving towards, Bhaṭṭ.; n. swinging, Bhar.; a swing, L.; a kind of minor drama (having no Sūtra-dhāra, hero &c.), Sāh.; IW. 472; *-kārikā,* f. a female swinger or dancer, Bhar. °**khaṇīya,** mfn. to be swung or made to oscillate, Vop.

Prêṅkhita, mfn. swung, shaken, set in motion, L.; joined to, being in contact with (?), W.

Prêṅkhola, mfn. swinging, dancing, moving to and fro, Vcar.; m. a swing hammock, ib.; blowing (of the wind), Mālatīm.; Nom. °*lati,* to swing, oscillate, Mālatīm.; Pracaṇḍ.

Prêṅkholana, n. swinging, rocking, Kād.; Suśr. °**laya,** Nom. °*yati,* to swing, rock, Dhātup. °**lita,** mfn. swung, rocked, oscillating, Kād.

प्रेङ्गण *prêṅgaṇa,* n. (fr. *pra* + √*iṅg*), Pāṇ. viii, 4, 32, Sch.

प्रेड् *prêḍ* (*pra-*√*iḍ*), Ā. *prêṭṭe,* to implore, praise, celebrate, RV.

प्रेडक *preḍaka,* mfn. = *prêraka,* Sāṃkhyak., Sch. (*-tva,* n.)

प्रेणा *preṇā, preṇi.* See p. 711, col. 2.

प्रेत *prêta* &c. See p. 711, col. 3.

प्रेदि *predi,* m. N. of a man, GopBr. (v. l. *proti,* p. 713, col. 2).

प्रेद्ध *prêddha* (*pra-iddha*), mfn. kindled, lighted, aflame, RV.

प्रेन्व् *prênv* (*pra-*√*inv*), P. *prênoti,* to send forth, impel forwards or upwards, RV.

Prênvana, n., °**vaniya,** mfn., Pāṇ. viii, 4, 2, Vārtt. 6, Pat.

प्रेप *prepa,* mfn. (*pra* + *ap,* water), Pat.

प्रेप्सा *prêpsā,* f. (fr. Desid. of *pra-*√*āp*) wish to obtain, desire, longing for, Nir. vii, 17; supposition, assumption, ib. vi, 32.

Prêpsu, mfn. wishing to attain, desirous of obtaining, seeking, longing for, aiming at (acc. or comp.), Mn.; MBh. &c.; anxious to rescue or save (see *prâṇa-pr°*); supposing, assuming, Nir. vi, 32.

प्रेमन् *preman, preyas* &c. See p. 711, col. 2.

प्रेर् *prêr* (*pra-*√*īr*), Ā. *prêrte,* to move (intrans.), come forth, arise, appear, RV.; AV.; TS.; ŚBr.: Caus. *prêrayati,* to set in motion, push on, drive forwards, urge, stimulate, excite, RV. &c. &c.; to send, dispatch, MBh.; R.; to turn, direct (the eyes), R.; Śak. (v. l.); to raise (the voice), utter, pronounce (words, prayers &c.), RV. &c. &c.

Prêraka, mfn. setting in motion, urging, dispatching, sending (*-tva,* n.), Hariv.; Rājat. **Prêraṇa,** n. driving out; see *paśu-pr°*; (also *ā,* f.) setting in motion, urging, inciting, direction, command, impelling to (*prati* or comp.), Naish.; Kathās.; Rājat.; Hit.; activity, action, Yājñ.; Megh.; the sense of the causal verb, Vop. **Prêraṇīya,** mfn. to be urged on or incited, Rājat. **Prêrayitṛi,** mfn. one who urges or incites or sends, MW.; a ruler, ib. **Prêrita,** mfn. urged, impelled, dispatched, sent, Kālid.; Kathās.; Suśr.; turned, directed (as the eye), Śak. (v. l.); incited to speak, Daś.; passed, spent (as time), Bhartṛ. **Prêritṛi,** mfn. one who urges or incites, an inciter, ŚvetUp. **Prêrtvan,** m. the sea, ocean, Uṇ. iv, 116, Sch.; (*arī*), f. a river, ib.

प्रेष् 1. *presh,* cl. 1. Ā. *preshate,* to go, move, Dhātup. xvi, 18 (v. l. *hresh*).

प्रेष् 2. *prêsh* (*pra-*√*ish*), P. Ā. *prêshyati,* °*te* (Ved. inf. *prêshe,* Pāṇ. iii, 4, 9, Sch.; ind. p. *praîsham* s. v.), to drive on, urge, impel, send forth, RV.; MBh.; to invite, summon, call upon (another priest to commence a recitation or a ceremony [acc.], e. g. *sāma prêshyati,* 'he calls upon to commence the recitation of a Sāman;' esp. Impv. *prêshya,* 'call upon to recite or offer [acc. or gen.] to [dat.]'), ŚBr.; KātyŚr. (cf. Pāṇ. ii, 3, 61; viii, 2, 91): Caus. *prêshayati,* to hurl, fling, cast, throw, MBh.; R.; Bhaṭṭ.; to turn or direct the eyes, Śak. ii, 2 (v. l. *prêrayantyā*); to send forth, dismiss, dispatch, MBh.; Kāv. &c.; to send into exile, banish, R.; Kathās.; to send word, send a message to a person (gen.), R.

3. **Prêsh,** f. pressing, pressure (with *hemán,* 'urging pressure'), RV. ix, 97, 1. **Prêsha,** m. urging on, impelling, impulse, ib. i, 68, 5; sending, dispatching, L.; pain, affliction, L. **Prêshaka,** mfn. sending, directing, commanding, MBh.

Prêshaṇa, n. the act of sending &c., charge, commission, Gaut.; MBh.; R.; BhP.; rendering a service, MBh.; Ratnâv. (pl.); *-kṛit,* mfn. one who executes a commission, MBh.; °*ṇâdhyaksha,* m. a superintendent of the commands (of a king), chief of the administration, Cāṇ. **Prêshaṇīya,** mfn. to be sent or dispatched, MW. **Prêshayitṛi,** mfn. = *prêshaka,* R. **Prêshita,** mfn. set in motion, urged on, impelled, RV.; hurled, flung, thrown, ŚBr.; sent, dispatched on an errand, MBh.; Kāv. &c. (*-vat,* mfn., Hit.); sent into exile, banished, R.; turned, directed (as the eyes), Śak. i, 23 (v. l. *prêrita*); ordered, commanded, Vop. **Prêshitavya,** mfn. to be invited (to commence a ceremony), AitBr.

Prêshya, mfn. to be sent or dispatched, fit for a messenger, Kathās.; m. a servant, menial, slave (*ā,* f. a female servant, handmaid), MBh.; Kāv. &c.; n. servitude, Yājñ. (in *śūdra-pr°,* v. l. for *-praishya*); behest, command (see next); *-kara,* mfn. executing the orders of (gen.), MBh.; *-jana,* m. servants (collectively), household, Mn.; Nal.; a servant, Prab.; *-tā*, f. (Mn.), *-tva*, n. (ib., MBh.), *-bhāva*, m. (Mālav.) the state or condition of a servant, servitude; *-vadhū*, f. a female servant, handmaid, MBh.; the wife of a slave, MW.; *-varga*, m. a train of servants, retinue, R.; °*shyā-tva*, n. the state of a female servant, being a handmaid, Rājat.

Praíshá, m. sending, direction, invitation, summons, order, call (esp. upon the assistant priest to commence a ceremony), AV.; Br.; MBh. &c.; pain, affliction, frenzy, madness (?), L.; *-kara*, mfn. executing orders, a servant, Āpast.; *-kṛit*, mfn. id., Vait.; giving orders, commanding, Kauś. (Sch.); *-pratīka-yājyā*, f. a Yājyā beginning with a Praisha, ĀpŚr.; °*shâdhyāya*, m. N. of wk. °**shika**, mfn. belonging to or connected with the Praishas, Nir.

Praishaṇika, mfn. (fr. *praísha*) executing orders (as a means of livelihood), g. *vetanâdi*; fitted for the execution of commands, g. *chedâdi*.

Praísham, ind., in the formula *praíshaiḥ* or *ishṭibhiḥ praísham icchati*, 'he strives to start (the sacrifice compared to a hunted animal) with invocations or exclamations,' AitBr.; ŚBr.

Praíshyá, mfn. (with *jana*, AV.) = m. a servant, slave, Mn.; R.; (*ā*), f. a female servant, ib.; n. servitude, ib.; Var. **-jana**, m. servants, train, retinue, R. **-bhāva**, m. the state or condition of a slave, servitude, Kum.

प्रेष्ठ *preshṭha*. See p. 711, col. 3.

प्रेहण *prêhaṇa*, n. (fr. *pra-√īh*), Pāṇ. viii, 4, 31, Sch.

प्रेहि *prêhi* &c. See p. 712, col. 2.

प्रैकीय *praîkīya*, Nom. P. °*yati* = *pr'ekīya*, Vop.

प्रैण् *praiṇ*, cl. 1. P. *praiṇati*, v. l. for *paiṇ*.

प्रैणान *praiṇāná*, mfn. = *prīṇāná* (√*prī*), propitiated, gratified, AV.

प्रैतोस् *praîtos*. See *pré* (*pra-√i*), p. 711.

प्रैध् *praîdh* (*pra-√edh*), cl. 1. Ā. *praîdhate*, Pāṇ. vi, 1, 89, Sch.

प्रैय 1. *praiya*, n. (fr. *priya*), g. *pṛithv-ādi*.

2. **Praiya**, Vṛiddhi form of *priya* in comp. **-medha**, m. patr. fr. Priya-m°, AitBr. (w. r. *praiyyam°*); N. of Sindhu-kshit, RAnukr.; n. N. of various Sāmans, ĀrshBr. **-rūpaka**, n. (fr. *priya-rūpa*), Naish. **-vrata**, mf(*ī*)n. relating to Priya-vrata, BhP.; m. patr. fr. Priy°, ib.; n. P°'s life or adventures, ib.

Praiyaka, m. patr. fr. *priyaka*, g. *bidâdi*.

Praiyaṅgava, mf(*ī*)n. (fr. *priyaṅgu*) relating to or prepared from panic grass, Maitr.; TS. (w. r. *praiyyaṅ°*, Kāṭh.) °**vika**, mf(*ī*)n. knowing the tale of Priyaṅgu, Pat.

Praiyyamedha, w. r. for *praiyam°*; see above.

प्रोक्त *prôkta* &c. See *pra-√vac*.

प्रोक्ष् *prôksh* (*pra-√uksh*), P. *prôkshati*, to sprinkle upon, besprinkle, consecrate (for sacrifice), RV.; VS.; ŚBr.; GṛŚrS.; to sacrifice, kill, slaughter (a sacrificial victim), MBh.; R.: Caus. *prôkshayati*, to sprinkle, besprinkle, Suśr.

Prôksha, m. the act of sprinkling upon, ĀpŚr. **Prôkshaṇa**, n. id., consecration by sprinkling (of a sacrificial animal or of a dead body before burial), TS. &c. &c.; a vessel for holy water, Hariv. (v. l. °*ṇī*); immolation of victims, L. (*-vidhi*, m. N. of wk.); (*ī*), f., see below. **Prôkshaṇī**, f. pl. = °*ṇī*, pl., VS.; ŚBr. &c. **Prôkshaṇī**, f. a vessel for holy water, Hariv. (v. l. °*ṇa*); pl. water for sprinkling or consecrating (mixed with rice and barley), AV.; VS.; Br.; GṛŚrS.; *-dhānī*, f. (ĀpŚr.), *-pātra*, n. (Nilak.) a vessel for sprinkling water; °*nyāsādana*, n. placing of the Prôkshaṇī vessel, L. **Prôkshaṇīya**, mfn. to be sprinkled; n. (sg. and pl.) water used for consecrating, Hariv.; MārkP. **Prôkshita**, mfn. sprinkled, purified or consecrated by sprinkling, ŚBr.; Mn.; Yājñ.; immolated, killed, L. **Prôkshitavya**, mfn. to be sprinkled or consecrated, MārkP.

प्रोघीय *pr'oghīya*, Nom. P. °*yati* (fr. *pra* + *ogha*), Vop. (cf. *praûghīya*).

प्रोच्चण्ड *prôccaṇḍa* (*pra-ucc°*), mfn. exceedingly terrible, very violent, Uttarar.; Mcar.

प्रोच्चर् *prôc-car* (*pra-ud-√car*), P. *-carati*, to utter a sound, utter, pronounce, Hariv.: Caus. *-cārayati*, to cause to sound, Pañcat. °**cārita**, mfn. (fr. Caus.) caused to sound, sounding, ib.

प्रोच्चल् *prôc-cal* (*pra-ud-√cal*), P. °*lati*, to start, set out on a journey, Kathās.

प्रोच्चाटना *prôccāṭanā* (*pra-ucc°*), f. driving away, removal, destruction, Prasannar.

प्रोच्चैस् *prôccais* (*pra-ucc°*), ind. very loudly, Kathās.; Pañcat.; exceedingly high, in a very high degree, Prab.

प्रोच्छल् *prôc-chal* (*pra-ud-√śal*), P. °*lati*, to spurt out, gush or flow forth, Śiś.

प्रोच्छून *prôcchūna* (*pra-ucch°*), mfn. swelled, swollen up, W.

प्रोच्छ्रित *prôcchrita* (*pra-ucch°*), mfn. lifted up, raised, Hariv.; high, lofty, Mṛicch.

प्रोच्छ्वस् *prôc-chvas* (*pra-ud-√śvas*), P. *prôcchvasiti*, to breathe strongly or loudly, Pañcat.

प्रोज्जासन *prôjjāsana* (*pra-ujj°*), n. killing, slaughter, L.

प्रोज्ज्वल् *prôj-jval* (*pra-ud-√jval*), P. °*lati*, to shine brightly, flash, glitter, Hariv.

प्रोज्झ् *prôjjh* (*pra-√ujjh*), P. *prôjjhati*, to abandon, leave, quit, forsake, avoid, efface, Pañcat.; Hit.; to subtract, deduct, Sūryas.

Prôjjhana, n. abandoning, forsaking, quitting, letting go, W.

Prôjjhita, mfn. abandoned, forsaken, shunned, avoided, Prab.; Pañcat.; (ifc.) free from, wanting, Var.

Prôjjhya, ind. having left or abandoned, Kirāt.; leaving aside, with exception of, Var.

प्रोञ्छ् *prôñch* (*pra-√uñch*), P. *prôñchati*, to wipe out, efface, Mṛicch.

Prôñchana, n. wiping out, effacing (lit. and fig.), Naish. (*ucchishṭa-pr°*, gathering up the remnants, Kull. on Mn. ii, 241).

प्रोड्डी *prôḍ-ḍī* (*pra-ud-√ḍī*, only ind. p. *-ḍīya*), to fly up, fly away, Mṛicch. (v. l.) °**ḍīna**, mfn. having flown up or away, MBh.; R.; Rājat.

प्रोढम् *proḍham*, ind., g. *tishṭhadgv-ādi*.

प्रोण्ठ *proṇṭha*, m. a spitting-pot, spittoon, L.

प्रोत *prôta*, mfn. (fr. *pra* + *uta* or *ūta*; √*ve*) sewed (esp. with the threads lengthwise, and opp. to *ôta*, cf. under *ā-√ve*, p. 156); strung on, fixed on or in, put or sticking in (loc. or comp.), ChUp.; MBh. &c.; set, inlaid, MBh.; contained in (loc.), pervaded by (instr.), ŚBr.; Up.; fixed, pierced, put on (a spit), MBh.; Kāv. &c.; m. n. woven cloth, clothes, L. **-ghana**, mfn. immersed in clouds (said of the horns of Śiva's bull), Kum. **-śūla**, mfn. put on a spit, impaled, Rājat. (cf. *śūla-prôta*). **Prôtôtsādana**, n. a parasol, umbrella, L.

Prôtaya, Nom. P. °*yati*, to infix, insert, inlay, KātyŚr., Sch.

Prôti (or *Prôti*?), m. N. of a man, ŚBr.

प्रोत्कट *prôtkaṭa* (*pra-utk°*), mfn. very great, Kathās. **-bhṛitya**, m. a high official, Pañcat.

प्रोत्कण्ठ *prôtkaṇṭha* (*pra-utk°*), mfn. stretching out or lifting up the neck, BhP.; Nom. P. °*ṭhayati*, to awaken longings, excite desires in (acc.), Ṛitus.

प्रोत्कूज् *prôt-kūj* (*pra-ud-√kūj*), P. *-kūjati*, to hum, buzz, Dhanaṃj.

प्रोत्क्रुष्ट *prôt-krushṭa* (*pra-utk°*), n. a loud cry or uproar, loud sound, Hariv.

प्रोत्क्षिप्त *prôtkshipta* (*pra-utk°*), mfn. threshed, winnowed, Bhpr.

प्रोत्खन् *prôt-khan* (*pra-ud-√khan*), P. Ā. *-khanati*, °*te*, to dig up or through or out, R. °**khāta**, mfn. dug up, dug out, Mṛicch.

प्रोत्खै *prôt-khai* (*pra-ud-√khai*), P. *-khāyati*, to dig up, dig out, Bhaṭṭ.

प्रोत्तान *prôttāna* (*pra-utt°*), mfn. stretched out widely, Var.

प्रोत्ताल *prôttāla* (*pra-utt°*), mfn. very loud, Prasannar.

प्रोत्तुङ्ग *prôttuṅga* (*pra-utt°*), mfn. very high or lofty, elevated, prominent, Kāv.; Kathās.; MārkP.

प्रोत्तॄ *prôt-tṝ* (*pra-ud-√tṝ*), P. *-tarati*, to cross over, emerge, Rājat.

प्रोत्था *prôt-thā* (*pra-ud-√sthā*), P. *prôttishṭhati*, to rise, spring up, start, MBh.; Mṛicch.; Kathās. **Prôtthita**, mfn. come forth, sprouted, Ṛitus.; sprung from (comp.), issued, Prab.

प्रोत्पत् *prôt-pat* (*pra-ud-√pat*), P. *-patati*, to fly upwards, soar aloft, Bhaṭṭ.

प्रोत्पद् *prôt-pad* (*pra-ud-√pad*), Caus. *-pādayati*, to bring forth, produce, cause, effect, MBh. °**panna**, mfn. produced, originated, developed, BhP.

प्रोत्फल *prôtphala* (*pra-ut-ph°*), m. a species of tree resembling the fan-palm, L.

Prôtphulla (*pra-utphulla*), mfn. (√*phal*) widely expanded, full blown, MBh.; Kāv. **-nayana**, mfn. having the eyes wide open, MBh.

प्रोत्सद् *prôt-sad* (*pra-ud-√sad*), Caus. *-sādayati*, to drive away, remove, destroy, MBh.; R. (Mn. ix, 261 w. r. for *-sāh°*). °**sādana**, n. causing to perish, destroying, MW.; contriving, device (?), W.

प्रोत्सह् *prôt-sah* (*pra-ud-√sah*), P. *-sahati*, to take courage or heart, boldly prepare to (inf.), Bhaṭṭ.: Caus. *-sāhayati* (irreg. *-sāhati*, MBh. i, 2233), to exhort, urge on, inspirit, instigate, Mn. ix, 261 (w. r. *-sād°*); MBh. (vi, 4437 w. r. for *-sād°*), R.; Kathās. &c. °**sāha**, m. great exertion, zeal, ardour, Kathās.; stimulus, incitement, W. °**sāhaka**, m. an inciter, instigator (esp. of any crime), W. °**sāhana**, n. (fr. Caus.) the act of inspiriting or inciting, instigation, invitation to (comp.), MBh.; R. &c. °**sāhita**, mfn. (fr. Caus.) incited, instigated, stimulated, encouraged, R.; Kathās.; Prab.

प्रोत्सिक्त *prôtsikta* (*pra-uts°*), mfn. exceedingly proud or arrogant, Sāh.

प्रोत्सृ *prôt-sṛi* (*pra-ud-√sṛi*), P. *-sarati*, to pass away, disappear, be gone, Caṇḍ.: Caus. *-sārayati*, °*te*, to drive away, disperse, dispel, destroy, MBh.; Hariv.; Mṛicch.; to urge on, exhort, incite, MW.; to grant, offer (see below).

Prot-sāraṇa, n. (fr. Caus.) sending away, removing, expelling, W. °**sārita**, mfn. (fr. Caus.) offered, granted, given, Hit.; ejected, expelled, W.; urged forwards, incited, MW.

प्रोत्सृज् *prôt-sṛij* (*pra-ud-√sṛij*), P. *-sṛijati*, to cast out, Divyâv.

प्रोत्सृप् *prôt-sṛip* (*pra-ud-√sṛip*), Ā. *-sarpate*, to fall out of joint, BhP.

प्रोथ् *proth*, cl. 1. P. Ā. (Dhātup. xxi, 6) *prothati*, °*te*, to be equal to or a match for, be able to withstand (gen. or dat.), Bhaṭṭ.; (P.) to be full, L.; to destroy, subdue, overpower, W. (cf. √*pruth*).

Protha &c. See under √*pruth*.

प्रोदक *prôdaka* (*pra-ud°*), mfn. dripping, wet, moist, Āpast.; that from which the water has run off, Gobh.; °*kī-bhāva*, m. dripping off of water, Āpast.

प्रोदर *prôdara* (*pra-ud°*), mfn. big-bellied, Pat.

प्रोदि *prôd-i* (*pra-ud-√5. i*), P. *-eti*, to go up, rise, Bhartṛ.; to come forth, appear, Sāh.; Subh.

प्रोदित *prôdita*, *prôdyamāna*. See *pra-√vad*.

प्रोद्गत *prôdgata* (*pra-udg°*), mfn. projecting, prominent, Kathās.

प्रोद्गारिन् *prôdgārin* (*pra-udg°*), mfn. (ifc.) giving out from, emitting, Dhanaṃj. °**gīrṇa**, mfn. cast out, Divyâv.

प्रोद्गीत *prôdgīta* (*pra-udg°*), mfn. begun to be sung, Prab.

प्रोद्ग्रीवम् *prôdgrîvam* (*pra-udg°*), ind. while stretching out the neck, Kāv.

प्रोद्घुष् *prôd-√ghush* (*pra-ud-√ghush*), Caus. *-ghoshayati*, to cause to resound, proclaim, MBh. °**ghushṭa**, mfn. filled with noise, resonant, resounding, ib. °**ghoshaṇā**, f. sounding aloud, proclaiming, proclamation, Kathās. (also °*ṇa*, n., W.)

प्रोद्दण्ड *prôddaṇḍa* (*pra-udd°*), mfn. prominent, swollen, Cat.

प्रोद्दाम *prôddāma* (*pra-udd°*), mfn. immense, extraordinary, prodigious, Inscr.; Prasannar.

प्रोद्दीप्त *prôddîpta* (*pra-udd°*), mfn. blazing up, blazing, Ml.

प्रोद्धा *prôd-dhā* (*pra-ud-√2. hā*, only Ā. pr. p. *prôjjihāna*), to flash up, rise to the sky, RV.

प्रोद्धूषित *prôddhūshita*. See *prôddhṛishita*.

प्रोद्धृ *prôd-dhṛi* (*pra-ud-√hṛi*), P. Ā. *-dharati*, °*te*, to lift up, draw up (as water from a well), MBh.; Hariv.; R.; to extract from (abl.), extricate, save, deliver, Kathās.; Prasannar. °**dhāra**, m. lifting up, bearing, Dharmaś.

प्रोद्धृषित *prôddhṛishita* (*pra-uddhṛish°*), mfn. bristling (as the hair of the body), thrilling, shuddering, Pañcat. 13 (w. r. °*dhūshita*).

प्रोद्बुद्ध *prôdbuddha* (*pra-udb°*), mfn. awakened (met.), Cat. °**bodha**, m. awaking, appearing, Gīt.; awakening, rousing, Prasannar.

प्रोद्भिन्न *prôdbhinna* (*pra-udbh°*), mfn. broken or burst forth, germinated, Kāv.

प्रोद्भूत *prôdbhūta* (*pra-udbh°*), mfn. come forth, sprung up, arisen, Hariv.; Kāv.; MārkP.

प्रोद्यम् *prôd-yam* (*pra-ud-√yam*), P. *-yacchati*, to lift up, raise, Bhaṭṭ. °**yata**, mfn. uplifted (*-yashṭi*, mfn. having an upl° stick), Pañcat.; raised (voice), RV.; being about to (inf.), Hariv.

प्रोद्वह् *prôd-vah* (*pra-ud-√vah*), P. *-vahati*, to utter, manifest, Pañcar. °**vāha**, m. marriage, BhP.

प्रोद्विज् *prôd-vij* (*pra-ud-√vij*), Caus. *-vejayati*, to frighten, terrify, MBh.; BhP. °**vigna**, mfn. terrified, alarmed, BhP.

प्रोद्वीचि *prôd-vîci* (*pra-udv°*), mfn. waving, fluctuating, Nalac.

प्रोन्नद् *prôn-nad* (*pra-ud-√nad*), P. *-nadati*, to roar out, roar, Hariv.

प्रोन्नम् *prôn-nam* (*pra-ud-√nam*), Caus. *-namayati*, to raise up, erect, Suśr. °**nata**, mfn. raised up, elevated, lofty, high, Var.; Pañcat.; superior, Pañcat. °**namita**, mfn. (fr. Caus.) raised up, erected, Suśr.

प्रोन्नी *prôn-nî* (*pra-ud-√nî*), P. *-nayati*, to lead or bring up, raise, elevate, Kām.; BhP.

प्रोन्मथ् *prôn-math* (*pra-ud-√math*), Pass. *-mathyate*, to be disturbed, Divyâv. °**māthin**, mfn. destroying, annihilating, Prab.

प्रोन्मद् *prôn-mad* (*pra-ud-mad*), P. *-mādyati*, to begin to grow furious, begin to rut (as an elephant), Inscr.

प्रोन्मील् *prôn-√mîl* (*pra-ud-√mîl*), P. *-mîlati*, to open the eyes, Bhaṭṭ.; to open (as a flower), blossom, Prab.; to come to light, appear, Cat.: Caus. *-mîlayati*, to open (the eyes), Kathās.; to unfold, reveal, manifest, Cat.

प्रोन्मूलित *prôn-mūlita*, mfn. (*pra-ud-√mūl*) uprooted, disturbed (?), Divyâv.

प्रोभ् *prôbh* (*pra-√ubh*, only ind. p. *prôbhya*), to bind, ŚBr.

Prômbhaṇa, n. filling, W. (cf. Pāṇ. viii, 4, 32, Sch.) **Prômbhita**, mfn. filled, W.

प्रोरक *proraka*, m. fever in an ass, Gal.

प्रोर्णु *prôrṇu* (*pra-√ūrṇu*), P. Ā. *prôrṇoti* or °*nauti*; °*ṇute*, to cover, veil, envelop, AV.; TS.; KātyŚr.; Bhaṭṭ.; (Ā.) to be covered or veiled, VS.; TS.; Br.; Kauś.: Intens. *prôrṇonūyate*, to cover completely, Bhaṭṭ. (cf. Pāṇ. iii, 1, 23, Vārtt. 3, Pat.)

Prôrṇunavishu, mfn. (fr. Desid.) wishing to cover or conceal, Bhaṭṭ. °**ṇunāva** (!), mfn.; (with *jvara*), m. a kind of fever, Bhpr. °**ṇunūshu**, mfn. (fr. Desid.) wishing to cover, W. °**ṇuvitṛi**, mfn. one who covers or envelops, W.

प्रोल्लङ्घ् *prôl-laṅgh* (*pra-ud-√laṅgh*), Caus. °*ghayati*, to go beyond, transgress, violate, Dharmaś.; Divyâv.

प्रोल्लस् *prôl-las* (*pra-ud-√las*; only P. pr. p. *prôllasat*), to shine brightly, glitter, Śiś.; to sound, be heard, Kathās.; to move to and fro, Kathās.

Prôllāsita, mfn. (fr. Caus.) gladdened, delighted, Kathās.

Prôllāsin (*pra-ull°*), mfn. shining, resplendent, Nalac.

प्रोल्लाघित *prôllāghita* (*pra-ull°*; cf. Pāṇ. viii, 2, 55, Sch.), mfn. recovered from sickness, convalescent, strong, robust, W.

प्रोल्लिख् *prôl-likh* (*pra-ud-√likh*), P. *-likhati*, to draw lines on (acc.), Amar.; to scratch in, Gṛihyas. °**lekhana**, n. drawing marks or lines, scratching, marking, W.

प्रोल्लोल *prôllola* (*pra-ull°*), mfn. moving to and fro, unsteady, Nalac.

प्रोष *prosha*, *proshaka*. See under √1. 3. *prush*, p. 711.

प्रोषध *proshadha*, m. fasting (=*poshadha*), Bhadrab.

प्रोषित *prôshita* &c. See under *pra-√5. vas*.

प्रोष्टिल *proshṭila*, m. (with Jainas) N. of a Daśa-pūrvin (for *prôshṭh°*?).

प्रोष्ठ *próshṭha*, m. (prob. fr. *pra+oshṭha*=*ava-stha*, 'standing out below') a bench, stool, TBr.; m. a bull, Pāṇ. v, 4, 120, Sch.; N. of a man, g. *śivâdi*; pl. N. of a people, MBh. (°*shṭa*, VP.); (*î*), f. Cyprinus Pausius, Bhpr. (also m., L.) **-padá**, m. (and *ā*, f.), sg. du. and pl. 'the foot of a stool,' N. of a double Nakshatra of the 3rd and 4th lunar mansions, AV. (*próshṭhap°*); Br.; GṛŚrS.; MBh. &c. **-pāda**, mf(*ī*)n. born under the Nakshatra Proshṭha-pada, Pāṇ. vii, 3, 18. **Proshṭhe-śayá**, mfn. lying on a bench, RV.

Proshṭhika, m. N. of a man, g. *śivâdi*; (*ā*), f. Cyprinus Sophore, Rasar.

Praushṭha, m. patr. fr. *proshṭha*, g. *śivâdi*.

Praushṭhapada, mf(*ī*)n. relating to the Nakshatra Proshṭha-pada, Pāṇ. vii, 3, 18; m. (with or scil. *māsa*), the month Bhādra or August–September (also called *pūrva-bhādrapadā* and *uttara-bh°*), MBh.; R.; BhP.; N. of one of Kubera's treasure-keepers, R.; (*ā*), f. pl. = *proshṭha-padā*, PārGṛ.; (*ī*), f. full moon in the month Bhādra, GṛŚrS.; n. N. of a Pariś. of SV.

Praushṭhapadika, mf(*ī*)n., fr. *proshṭha-padā*, Pāṇ. iv, 2, 35.

Praushṭhika, m. patr. fr. *proshṭhika*, g. *śivâdi*.

प्रोष्ण *prôshṇa* (*pra-ushṇa*), mfn. burning hot, scorching, Pañcat.

प्रोष्य *prôshya* &c. See under *pra-√5. vas*.

प्रोह् *prôh* (*pra-√1. ūh*), P. *prôhati*, to push forward or away, VS.; KātyŚr.; Nir.; to throw down, KātyŚr.; to effect or bring about by transposition, TāṇḍBr.

1. **Prôha**, m. an elephant's foot or the ankle of an el°, L.; in *prôha-kaṭā* and *-kardamā*, v.l. for *prêhi-kaṭā* and *-kard°*, g. *mayūra-vyaṅsakâdi*, Kāś.

Prôhaṇa, n. the act of pushing away (?), Pāṇ. viii, 4, 31, Sch.

Prôhya-padi or **-pādi** (Kāś.), ind. (prob.) by or in pushing away the foot, g. *dvidaṇḍy-ādi*.

1. **Prauha**, m. = 1. *prôha*, L.

प्रोह 2. *prôha*, mfn. (fr. *pra-√2. ūh*) skilful, clever, L.; m. logical reasoning, ib.

2. **Prauha**, mfn. and m. id., L.

प्रौक्त *praukta*, mf(*ī*)n. having the sense of '*tena-prôktam*,' proclaimed by that (said of a suffix), Pāṇ. iv, 3, 101.

प्रौग *prauga*, w. r. for *praüga*, MānGṛŚrS.

प्रौघीय *praughîya*, Nom. °*yati*=*pr'oghîya*, Vop.

प्रौढ *prauḍha*, mfn. (fr. *pra+ūḍha*, √*vah*) raised or lifted up (see *-pāda*); grown up, full-grown, Hariv.; Kāv.; Rājat.; mature, middle-aged (as a woman; in Subh. *bālā*, *taruṇī*, *prauḍha* and *vṛiddhā* are distinguished; cf. f. below); married, W.; luxuriant (as a plant), Bhartṛ.; Kāvyâd.; large, great, mighty, strong, Kāv.; Kathās.; Pañcat.; violent, impetuous (as love), Prab.; Rājat.; thick, dense (as darkness), Mālatīm.; full (as the moon), W.; (ifc.) filled with, full of (see *mṛidu-pr°*); proud, arrogant, confident, bold, audacious, impudent (esp. said of a woman), Kāv.; BhP.; controverted, W.; m. (in music) N. of one of the 7 Rūpakas; (with Śāktas) N. of one of the 7 Ullāsas; n. (with *brāhmaṇa*) = *tāṇḍya-brāhmaṇa*, Sāy.; (*ā*), f. a married woman from 30 to 55 years of age, W.; a violent or impetuous woman (described as a Nāyikā who stands in no awe of her lover or husband), W. **-carita-nāman**, n. pl. N. of a wk. by Vallabhâcārya on the titles of Kṛishṇa derived from 128 of his exploits during adolescence. **-jalada**, m. a dense cloud, Bhartṛ. **-tātparya-saṃgraha**, m. N. of wk. **-tva**, n. confidence, arrogance, Kathās. **-dor-daṇḍa**, m. a strong and long arm, Prab. **-pāda**, mfn. one whose feet are raised (on a bench or in some partic. position), Mn.; Gaut.; Hcat. **-pushpa**, mfn. having blossoms full-grown (as a tree), Megh. **-prakāśikā**, f. N. of a Comm. on Prab. **-pratāpa**, mfn. of mighty prowess, renowned in arms, MW.; *-mārtaṇḍa*, m. N. of a wk. on the appropriate seasons for the worship of Vishṇu. **-priyā**, f. a bold or confident mistress, Ragh. **-manoramā**, f. N. of a Comm. on Siddh. and other wks.; *-kuca-mardana*, n., *-khaṇḍana*, n. N. of wks **-yauvana**, mfn. being in the prime or bloom of youth (*ati-* and *an-ati-pr°*), Megh.; Hit. **-vatsā**, f. having a full-grown calf, L. **-vāda**, m. a bold or arrogant assertion, Hcar. **-vyañjaka**, m. N. of wk. **-svaram**, ind. with a strong or loud voice, Pañcad. **Prauḍhâkṛishṭa**, mfn. impetuously or furiously dragged along, Śak. i, 32 (v. l. for *pādâkṛ°*). **Prauḍhâṅganā**, f. a bold woman, Bhartṛ. **Prauḍhâcāra**, m. pl. bold or confident behaviour, Kathās. **Prauḍhânta**, m. (with Śāktas) one of the 7 Ullāsas. **Prauḍhôkti**, f. a bold expression or speech, Kuval.

Prauḍhi, f. full growth, increase, Kathās.; full development, maturity, perfection, high degree, ib.; BhP.; greatness, dignity, Vcar.; self-confidence, boldness, assurance, Kāv.; Kathās.; zeal, exertion, W.; controversy, discussion, ib. **-vāda**, m. a bold assertion, pompous speech, L. (cf. *prauḍha-v°*).

Prauḍhiman, m. the state of full growth, Vām. v, 2, 56.

Prauḍhi-√bhū, P. *-bhavati*, to grow up, increase, come to maturity, Ragh.; Rājat.

प्रौण *prauṇa*, mfn. clever, learned, skilful, L. (cf. 2. *prauha*, *proha*).

प्रौष्ठ *praushṭha* &c. See under *proshṭha*.

प्रौह 1. 2. *prauha*. See col. 2.

प्लक *plaka*. See *kaśa-plaká*.

प्लक्ष् *plaksh*, cl. 1. P. Ā. *plakshati*, °*te*, to eat, consume, Dhātup. xxi, 27 (v. l. for *blaksh*).

प्लक्ष *plakshá*, m. the waved-leaf fig-tree, Ficus Infectoria (a large and beautiful tree with small white fruit), AV. &c. &c.; the holy fig-tree, Ficus Religiosa, L.; Thespesia Populneoides, L.; a side door or the space at the s° of a d°, L.; = *dvîpa*, Pur.; N. of a man, TBr.; (with *prāsravaṇa*) = *-prasravaṇa*, TāṇḍBr.; ŚrS.; (*ā*), f. N. of the river Sarasvatī, MBh.; Hariv. **-gā**, f. N. of a river, VP. **-jātā**, f. 'rising near the fig-tree,' N. of the Sarasvatī, MBh. **-tîrtha**, n. N. of a place of pilgrimage, Hariv. **-tvá**, n. the state or condition of being a fig-tree, MaitrS. **-dvîpa**, m. n. N. of a Dvîpa, VP. (cf. IW. 420). **-nyagrodha**, m. du. Ficus Infectoria and F° Indica, Pāṇ. ii, 2, 29, Sch. **-praroha**, m. the shoot or sprout of a fig-tree, Ragh. **-prasravaṇa**, n. (ŚrS.), **-rāj**, m. (A.), **-rāja**, m. (MBh.), 'source and king of the fig-tree,' N. of the place where the Sarasvatī rises. **-vat**, mfn. surrounded by fig-trees; (*ī*), f. N. of a river (prob. the Sarasvatī), MBh. **-śākhā**, f. a branch of the fig-tree, MaitrS.; *-vat*, mfn. furnished with it, Gobh. **-samudbhavā**, f. = *-jātā*, L. **-samudra-vācakā**, f. N. of the river Sarasvatī, L. **-sravaṇa**, n. = *-prasr°*, Kull. **Plakshâvataraṇa**, n. N. of a place of pilgrimage, MBh.; MārkP. **Plakshôdumbara**, m. a species of tree, Kauś.

Plakshakīya, mfn., fr. *plaksha*, g. *naḍâdi*.

Plāksha, mf(*ī*)n. belonging or relating to or coming from the Ficus Infectoria, TS.; AitBr.; m. pl. the school of Plākshi, Pāṇ. iv, 2, 112, Sch.; n. the fruit of the fig-tree, L.; (with *prasravaṇa*) n. N. of the place where the Sarasvatī rises, ŚrS.

Plākshaki, m. patr. fr. *plaksha*, Pravar.

Plākshāyaṇa, m. patr. fr. *plākshi*, TPrāt.

Plākshí, m. patr. fr. *plaksha*, TĀr.; TBr.; (*ī*), f., Pāṇ. iv, 1, 65, Sch.

प्लक्षर् *pla-√kshar* (for *pra-kshar*, formed to explain *plaksha*), Caus. *-kshārayati*, to cause to stream forth, pour out, MaitrS.

प्लति *platí*, m. N. of a man, RV.

Plāta, m. patr. fr. *plati*, AitBr.

प्लब् *plab* or *plav*, cl. 1. Ā. *plabate, plavate*, to go, Dhātup. x, 10 (v.l.) and xiv, 10 (cf. *√plu*).

प्लयोग *pla-yoga*, m. (prob. = *pra-y°*) N. of a man, Sāy.

Plâyogi, m. patr. of Āsaṅga, RV.; ŚāṅkhŚr.

प्लव *plava, plavaka* &c. See col. 2.

प्लाक्ष *plāksha* &c. See above.

प्लाय् *plây* (*pla* = *pra* and *√ay* = *i*; cf. *pla-√kshar* and *pla-yoga*), Ā. *plâyate*, to go away, go along, MaitrS.

Plâya, m. = *prâya*, abundance; (ifc.) having plenty of (*vyādhi-*), ŚāṅkhŚr.

प्लाव *plāva* &c. See col. 2.

प्लाशि *plāśí*, m. sg. and pl. a partic. part of the intestines (= *śiśna* or *śiśna-mūla-nāḍyaḥ*, Mahīdh.), RV.; AV.; VS.; ŚBr.

प्लाशुक *plâśuka*, mfn. (fr. *pla* = *pra* and *āśu-ka*) rapidly growing up again, ŚBr.; KātyŚr.

Plâśu-cit, mfn. quick, speedy (= *kshipra*), Naigh. ii, 15.

प्लिह् *plih*, cl. 1. Ā. *plehate*, to go, move, Dhātup. xvi, 41 (formed to explain the next words?).

Plihan, m. = *plīhan*, the spleen, Yājñ. iii, 94.

Plīha, in comp. for *plīhan*. **-ghna**, m. 'destroying the spleen,' Andersonia Rohitaka, L. **-pushā**, f. Adelia Nereifolia, L. **-śatru**, m. 'enemy of the spleen,' Andersonia Rohitaka, L. **Plīhā-kárṇa** (for *°ha-k°*), mfn. suffering from a partic. disease of the ear called *plīhan*, VS. (Mahīdh.) **Plīhâri**, m. 'id.,' Ficus Religiosa, L. **Plihôdara**, n. disease of the spleen, Suśr.; *°rin*, mfn. splenetic, ib.

Plīhán, m. the spleen (from which and from the liver the Hindūs suppose the blood to flow), AV.; VS.; ŚBr.; Suśr.; disease of the spleen (said to be equally applied to enlargement of the mesenteric glands &c.), Suśr. [Orig. *splīhan*; cf. Gk. σπλήν, σπλάγχνον; Lat. *lien* for *splihen*; Slav. *slezena* for *splezena*; Eng. spleen.]

Plīhā, f. = *plīhan*, L. **-śatru**, m. Adelia Nereifolia, L. (cf. *°ha-s°*). **-hantrī**, f. id., Bhpr.

प्ली *plī*, cl. 9. P. *plināti*, to go, move, Dhātup. xxxi, 82 (v.l.)

प्लीथा *plīthā*, f. pl. N. of a partic. class of Apsaras, MaitrS. (v.l. *plīyā*).

प्लु *plu*, cl. 1. Ā. (Dhātup. xxii, 62; cf. xiv, 40) *plávate* (rarely P. *°ti*; pf. *pupluve*, Br. &c., 3. pl. *°vuḥ*, Hariv.; aor. *aploshṭa*, Br. &c., 2. pl. *aploḍhvam*, Pāṇ. viii, 3, 78, Sch.; Prec. *ploshīshṭa*, vii, 2, 43, Sch.; fut. *ploshyati*, *°te*, Br. &c.; ind. p. *-plūya*, ŚBr.; *-plutya*, MBh. &c.), to float, swim, RV. &c. &c.; to bathe, MBh.; Ragh.; to go or cross in a boat, sail, navigate, MBh.; Hariv.; to sway to and fro, hover, soar, fly, Br.; MBh.; Hariv.; to blow (as the wind), MBh.; Var.; to pass away, vanish by degrees, ŚBr.; R. (v.l.); to be lengthened or prolated (as a vowel, see *pluta*), RPrāt.; ĀpŚr., Sch.; (older form *pru*, q.v.) to hop, skip, leap, jump, spring from (abl.) or to or into or over or upon (acc.), MBh.; R. &c.: Caus. *plāvayati* (rarely *°te* or *plavayati*; aor. *apiplavat*, Bhaṭṭ., *apupl°*, Gr.), to cause to float or swim, bathe, wash, inundate, submerge, KātyŚr.; MBh. &c.; to overwhelm i.e. supply abundantly with (instr.), MBh.; to wash away, remove (guilt, sin &c.), MBh.; BhP.; to purify, MBh.; to prolate (a vowel), ŚrS.; to cause to jump or stagger, Bhaṭṭ.: Desid. of Caus. *piplāvayishati* or *puplāvayishati*, Pāṇ. vii, 4, 81: Desid. *puplūshate*, Gr.: Intens. *poplūyate*, to swim about or rapidly, R.; Var. [Cf. Gk. πλέω for πλεϝω, πλύνω; Old Lat. *per-plovere*; Lat. *pluit, pluvius*; Lith. *plauti*; Angl.Sax. *flovan*; Germ. *flawjan, flawên, vlouwen* &c.]

Plavá, mf(*ā*)n. swimming, floating, ŚāṅkhGṛ.; Suśr.; sloping towards, inclined, Hariv.; Var.; Hcat. (in astrol. applied to a constellation situated in the quarter ruled by its planetary regent, Var., Sch.); transient, MuṇḍUp.; m. n. (ifc. f. *ā*) a float, raft, boat, small ship, RV. &c. &c.; m. a kind of aquatic bird (= *gātra-samplava, kāraṇḍava, jala-vāyasa, jala-kāka* or *jala-kukkuṭa*, L.), VS. &c. &c.; a frog, L.; a monkey, L.; a sheep, L.; an arm, L.; a Caṇḍāla, L.; an enemy, L.; Ficus Infectoria, L.; a snare or basket of wicker-work for catching fish, L.; the 35th (or 9th) year in a cycle of Jupiter, VarBṛS.; swimming, bathing (ifc. f. *ā*), MBh.; R.; Kathās.; flooding, a flood, the swelling of a river, MBh.; MārkP.; the prolated utterance of a vowel (= *pluti*), L.; protraction of a sentence through 3 or more Ślokas (= *kulaka*), L.; sloping down or towards, proclivity, inclination, L.; (in astrol.) = *plava-tva*, VarBṛS., Sch.; a kind of metre, Col.; N. of a Sāman (also with *Vasishṭhasya*), ĀrshBr.; jumping, leaping, plunging, going by leaps or plunges, R. (cf. comp. below); returning, L.; urging on, L.; n. Cyperus Rotundus or a species of fragrant grass, Suśr. [Cf. Gk. πλόος for πλοϝος, πλοῖον.] **-ga**, mfn. = *plava*, mfn. (in astrol.), VarBṛS., Sch.; m. 'going by leaps or plunges,' a frog, Hariv.; R.; a monkey, R.; Ragh.; Kathās.; a sort of aquatic bird, the diver, L.; Acacia Sirissa, L.; N. of the charioteer of the Sun, L.; of a son of the Sun, L.; (*ā*), f. the sign of the zodiac Virgo, Var.; *°gêndra*, m. 'monkey chief,' N. of Hanumat, BhP. **-gati**, m. 'moving by jumps,' a frog, L. **-m-ga**, mfn. 'moving by jumps,' flickering (said of fire), MBh.; m. a monkey, ib.; Ṛitus.; a deer, L.; Ficus Infectoria, L.; N. of the 41st (15th) year in a sixty years' cycle of Jupiter, Var. **-m-gama**, m. (cf. prec.) a frog, R.; Hariv.; a monkey, Mn.; R.; Kathās.; (*ā*), f. a kind of metre, Col.; *°mêndu*, m. 'monkey-moon,' N. of Hanumat, MW. **-tva**, n. (in astrol.) the position of a constellation in the quarter ruled by its planetary regent, VarBṛS. **-1. -vat**, ind. as with a boat, MBh. **-2. -vat**, mfn. possessing a ship or a boat, ib.

Plavaka, m. a leaper (by profession), a rope-dancer &c., MBh.; a frog, L.; a Caṇḍāla, L.; Ficus Infectoria, L.

Plavana, mf(*ā*)n. inclined, stooping down towards (cf. *prāg-udak-pl°*); m. a monkey, L.; n. swimming, plunging into or bathing in (comp.), MBh.; Gīt.; Rājat.; Suśr.; flying, MBh.; R.; leaping, jumping over (comp.), R.; capering (one of a horse's paces), Sāṃkhyak., Sch.; a kind of water Cyperus, L.

Plavākā, f. a boat, L. *°vika*, m. a ferry-man, L.

Plavita, n. swimming or springing, Lalit. *°vitṛi*, m. a leaper (with gen. of distance), R.

Plāva, m. flowing over, filling a vessel till it overflows, Yājñ.; MārkP.; leaping, BhP.

Plāvana, n. (fr. Caus.) bathing, immersion, ablution, MBh.; filling a vessel to overflowing (for the purification of fluids), L.; inundation, flood, deluge (cf. *jala-pl°*); prolation (of a vowel), Āpast. *°vayitṛi*, mfn. one who causes to swim, causing to cross or go in a boat, MBh. *°vita*, mfn. made to swim or overflow, deluged, soaked, moistened or covered with (comp.), MBh.; Kāv. &c.; washed away, removed, destroyed, BhP.; lengthened, prolated (as a vowel, see *pluta*), ŚrS.; BhP.; n. inundation, flood, deluge, Kād.; a song in which the vowels are prolated, BhP. *°vin*, mfn. (ifc.) spreading, promulgating, Yājñ.; flowing from, Śiś.; m. a bird or a deer, L. *°vya*, mfn. to be bathed or steeped in (instr.), Var.; to be jumped or leaped, W.

Pluta, mfn. floated, floating or swimming in (loc.), bathed, overflowed, submerged, covered or filled with (instr. or comp.), Yājñ.; MBh.; R. &c.; protracted, prolated or lengthened (as a vowel) to 3 Mātrās (q.v.), Prāt.; Pāṇ. (esp. i, 2, 27); ŚrS. &c. (also said of a kind of measure, Cat.); flown, R.; leaped, leaping, MBh.; Hariv.; n. a flood, deluge (pl.), Hariv.; leaping, moving by leaps, MBh.; R.; Vcar.; capering (one of a horse's paces), L. **-gati**, f. moving by leaps, Dhātup.; m. a hare, L. **-tva**, n., see *udagra-pluta-tva*. **-meru**, m. (in music) a kind of measure, Saṃgīt. **-vat**, mfn. one who has leaped or jumped, R.; Hariv.

Pluti, f. overflowing, a flood, Var.; prolation (of a vowel, cf. *pluta*), Prāt.; Pāṇ., Sch.; ŚrS.; a leap, jump, Śak. i, 7, v.l. (also met.; cf. *maṇḍūka-pl°*); capering, curvet (one of a horse's paces), L.

प्लुष् *plush*, cl. 1. 4. P. (Dhātup. xvii, 54; xxvi, 107) *ploshati* and *plushyati* (pf. *puplosha*, Gr.; aor. *aploshīt*, ib.; fut. *ploshishyati, ploshitā*, ib.), to burn, scorch, singe, Suśr. (only Pass. *plushyate*); cl. 9. P. *plushṇāti* (Impv. *plushāṇa*), id., Bhaṭṭ.; to sprinkle; to anoint; to fill, Dhātup. xxxi, 56 (cf. *√prush*).

Plukshi, m. fire, Uṇ. iii, 155, Sch.; the burning of a house (?), L.; oil, L.

Plúshi, m. a species of noxious insect, RV.; VS.; ŚBr. (a flying white-ant, L.)

Plushṭa, mfn. burned, scorched, singed, Ṛitus.; Var.; Suśr.; frozen, Vcar.

Plushṭāya, Nom. Ā. *°yate*, Pat. on Pāṇ. iii, 1, 17.

Plosha, m. burning, combustion, Ratnâv.; Rājat.; a burning pain, Car.

Ploshaṇa (Mālatim.), *°shin* (Bālar.), mfn. burning, scorching, singeing.

Ploshṭṛi, m. one who burns or consumes by fire, Pur.

प्लुस् *plus*, cl. 4. P. *plusyati*, to burn, Dhātup. xxvi, 107 (v.l. for *plush*); to share, Vop.

प्लेङ्ख *plêṅkhá* (*pla-īṅkha*; cf. *prêṅkha*), m. a swing, TS.; TBr.

प्लेव् *plev*, cl. 1. Ā. *plevate*, to serve, wait upon, Dhātup. iv, 38 (cf. *√peb, pev, sev*).

प्लोत *plota*, m. or n. (?) cloth, stuff; a bandage, Suśr. (cf. *prôta*).

Ploti, f. thread, connection (in *karma-p°*), Divyâv.

प्लोष *plosha* &c. See under *√plush*.

प्सा 1. *psā*, cl. 2. P. (Dhātup. xxiv, 47) *psâti* (Impv. *psāhi, psātu*, AV.; pf. *papsau*, Gr.; aor. *apsāsīt*, Bhaṭṭ.; Prec. *psāyāt*, ŚBr.; or *pseyāt*, Gr.; fut. *psāsyati, psātā*, ib.; ind. p. *-psâya*, Br.; Pass. impf. *apsīyata*, ib.), to chew, swallow, devour, eat, consume; to go, Naigh. ii, 14. (For *bhsā* = *bhasā* = *√bhas* + *ā*; cf. *√mnā* and *man*, *√yā* and *i* &c.)

Psáras, n. a feast, enjoyment, delight, RV. (cf. *devá-psaras*).

2. **Psā**, f. eating, food, L.; hunger, L.

Psātá, mfn. chewed, eaten, devoured, ŚBr.; hungry, L.

Psāna, n. eating, food, L.

1. **Psu**. See 1. *á-psu*.

Psúras, n. food, victuals, RV. x, 26, 3. [Cf. Zd. *fshu*.]

Psnya. See *viśvá-psnya*.

प्सात्कार *psāt-kāra*, m. a partic. sound, L.

प्सु 2. *psu* (prob. = *bhsu* fr. *bhāsu*, *√bhās*), aspect, appearance, form, shape (only ifc.; cf. *aruṇá-*, *ṛita-psu*, &c.)

फ PHA.

फ 1. *pha*, aspirate of *pa*. **-kāra**, m. the letter or sound *pha*.

फ 2. *pha* (only L.), mfn. manifest; m. a gale; swelling; gaping; gain; = *vardhaka*; = *yaksha-sādhana*; n. flowing; bursting with a popping noise; bubbling, boiling; angry or idle speech.

फकीरचन्द्र *phakira-candra*, m. N. of an author, Cat.

फक्क् *phakk*, cl. 1. P. (Dhātup. v, 1) to swell (?), Pratāp.; to creep, steal along, L.; to have a preconceived opinion (cf. *phakkikā*); to act wrongly, behave ill, L.

Phakka, m. a cripple, L.

Phakkikā, f. a previous statement or thesis to be maintained (= *pūrva-paksha, codya, deśya*), L.; logical exposition, W.; a sophism, trick, fraud, ib.; a collection of 32 letters, a Grantha, L. — **prakāśa**, m., **-vyākhyāna**, n. N. of wks.

फगुल *phagula* (?), m. N. of a man, Pravar.

फञ्जी *phañjī*, f. Clerodendrum Siphonantus, L.

Phañjikā, f. id., L.; Lipeocercis Serrata, L.; Alhagi Maurorum, L. **Phañji-pattrikā** or **-puttrikā**, f. Salvinia Cucullata, L.

फट् *phaṭ*, ind. (onom.) crack! VS.; AV.; TĀr. (also a mystical syllable used in incantation).

फट *phaṭa*, m. the expanded hood or neck of a serpent, L.; (*ā*), f. id., MBh.; a tooth, L.; a cheat (!), L. **Phaṭâṭopa**, m. the expanding of a serpent's hood, Pañcat. **Phaṭâṭopin**, m. a serpent, ŚārṅgP.

फडिङ्गा *phaḍiṅgā*, f. a grasshopper, L.

फण् *phaṇ*, cl. 1. P. (Dhātup. xix, 73) *pháṇati* (Naigh. ii, 14; pf. *paphāṇa*, 2. sg. *paphaṇitha* or *pheṇitha*, Pāṇ. vi, 4, 125; aor. *aphāṇīt*, vii, 2, 27; fut. *phaṇishyati*, °*ṇitā*, Gr.), to go, move, Bhaṭṭ. (with *samāptim*, 'to be accomplished,' Bhojapr.): Caus. *phāṇḍayati* (or *phaṇ*°, Vop.), to cause to bound, RV. viii, 58, 13; to draw off (the surface of a fluid), skim, Lāṭy.: Desid. *piphaṇishati*, Gr.: Intens. pr. p. *-panīphaṇat* (RV.), *pamphaṇat* (ŚāṅkhŚr.), bounding, leaping.

Phaṇá, m. scum, froth, TBr. (cf. *phena*); (also *ā*, f.) the expanded side of the nose, a nostril, Suśr.; (also *ā*, f.) the expanded hood or neck of a serpent (esp. of the Coluber Nāga), MBh.; Kāv. &c.; a stick shaped like a serpent's hood, ŚāṅkhGṛ.; mfn. having the fingers shaped like a serpent's hood, L. — **kara**, m. a serpent, snake (esp. the Coluber Nāga), L. — **dhara**, m. id., L.; N. of Śiva, L. — **bhṛit**, m. = *-kara*, Kir.; Rājat.; N. of the number 9 (or 8), Śrutab. — **maṇi**, m. 'hood-gem,' a jewel in the h° of a s°, W. — **maṇḍala**, n. 'h°-orb,' the rounded h° of a s°, Ragh. — **vat**, mfn. having a h°, hooded (as a s°), MBh.; Pañcat.; m. = *-kara*, L. — **śreṇī**, f. a line or row of serpents' hoods, Gīt. — **stha**, mfn. being in a s°'s h° (as a gem), Ragh. **Phaṇâṭopa**, °**pin**, v. l. for *phaṭâṭ*° (q. v.), L. **Phaṇâtapatra**, mfn. having a hood for a parasol (said of a s°), Rājat.

Phaṇā, f. of *phaṇa*, in comp. — **kara**, m. = °*ṇa-kara*, L. **Phaṇā-dhara**, m. = °*ṇa-dhara*, L. — **phalaka**, n. the flat surface of a s°'s hood, Bhartṛ. — **bhara**, m. = *-dhara*, L. — **bhṛit**, mfn. having a hood (as a serpent). — **maṇi-sahasraruc**, f. the splendour of the thousand jewels on the hood (of the s°-king), Śiś. — **vat**, m. 'possessing a h°,' Coluber Nāga, Bālar.; a kind of supernatural being, Hcat.

1. **Phaṇí**, m. a serpent (only gen. pl. *phaṇīnām*), Suparṇ.

2. **Phaṇi**, in comp. for *phaṇin*. — **kanyā**, f. the daughter of a serpent-demon, Rājat. — **kesara**, m. Mesua Roxburghii, L. — **khela**, m. a quail, L. (prob. w. r. for *phāla-kh*°). — **jā**, f. a species of plant, L. — **jihvā**, f. 's°'s tongue,' N. of 2 plants (*mahā-śatāvarī* and *mahā-samaṅga*), L. — **jihvikā**, f. id. and Emblica Officinalis, L. — **talpa-ga**, m. 'resorting to a serpent as a couch,' N. of Vishṇu, L. — **nāyaka**, m. 's°-chief,' N. of Vāsuki, Siṅhâs. — **pati**, m. a huge s°, Bhartṛ.; N. of Śesha, ib., Prasannar.; of Patañjali, Vcar.; Sarvad. — **priya**, m. 's°'s friend,' the wind, L. — **phena**, m. 's°'s saliva,' opium, L. — **bhārikā**, f. Ficus Oppositifolia, L. — **bhāshita-bhāshyâbdhi**, m., **-bhāshya**, n., **-bhāshyâbdhi**, m. N. of Patañjali's Mahā-bhāshya, Cat. — **bhuj**, m. 'serpent-eater,' a peacock, L. — **mukha**, n. 's°'s mouth,' a kind of spade used by housebreakers, Daś. — **latā** (Bālar.), **-vallī** (L.; ifc. °*līka*), **-vīrudh** (Bālar.), f. betel-pepper. — **hantrī**, f. Piper Chaba (?), L. — **hṛit**, f. a species of Alhagi, L. **Phaṇîndra**, m. 'serpent-king,' N. of Śesha, MBh.; of Patañjali, Cat.; °*drêśvara*, m. N. of one of the 8 Vīta-rāgas of the Buddhists, W. **Phaṇîśa**, m. N. of Patañjali, Cat. (cf. °*ṇîndra*). **Phaṇîśvara**, m. = °*ṇîndra*, L.; Cat.

Phaṇikā, f. Ficus Oppositifolia, L. **Phaṇikêśvara**, m. = *phaṇîndrêśvara*, W.

Phaṇita, mfn. gone or diluted (?), W.; n. and °*ti*, f., w. r. for *bhaṇita*, °*ti*, Bhojapr.

Phaṇin, m. 'hooded,' a serpent (esp. Coluber Nāga), Kāv.; Kathās.; Pur.; N. of Rāhu and Patañjali, L.; Cat.; a species of shrub, L.; (prob.) n. tin or lead, Kālac.

Phaṇīya, n. the wood of Cerasus Puddum, L.

फणिकार *phaṇikāra*, m. pl. N. of a people, Var. (v. l. *karṇikāra*).

फणिज्झ *phaṇijjha* and °*aka*, m. marjoram and another similar plant, Suśr.; Bhpr.; (*akā*), f. a species of basil with small leaves (commonly called *rāma-dūtī*), W.

फणी *phaṇī*, f. N. of a river, Cat. — **cakra**, n. N. of wk.

फण्ड *phaṇḍa*, m. the belly (√*phāṇḍa*), Uṇ. i, 113, Sch.

फत् *phat*, ind., an interjection (in *phat*-√*kṛi*, prob. w. r. for *phut*-√*kṛi*). — **kārin**, m. a bird, L.

फतिहभूपति *phatiha-bhūpati* and *phatiha-śāha*, m. N. of a king of Kaśmīra, Cat. (= فتح شاه).

फतेपुर *phate-pura*, n. N. of a city, Kshitîś.

फत्तेसाहप्रकाश *phattesāha-prakāśa*, m. N. of wk.

फर् *phar* (= *sphar*), only Intens. Subj. *pharpharat*, to scatter, RV. x, 106, 7 (Sāy. 'to fill').

Phárvara, m. (prob.) a scatterer, sower, ib. x, 106, 2 (Sāy. 'filling').

Phárīva, mfn. (prob.) scattering, distributing, liberal, ib. 8.

फर *phara*, n. a shield (= *phalaka*), L.

फरञ्ज *pharañja*, N. of a place, Cat.

फरुण्ड *pharuṇḍa*, m. green onion, L.

फरुवक *pharuvaka*, n. a betel-box or a spittoon, L.

फरेन्द्र *pharendra*, m. Pandanus Odoratissimus, L.

फर्फराय *pharpharāya*, Nom. Ā. °*yate*, to dart to and fro, Kāv.

फर्फरीक *pharpharīka*, m. (√*sphar, sphur*) the palm of the hand with the fingers extended, Uṇ. iv, 20; (*ā*), f. a shoe, L.; = *madana*, L.; n. softness, L.; a young shoot or branch, L. (cf. *parpharīka*).

फर्व् *pharv*, cl. 1. P. *pharvati*, to go, Mahīdh. on VS. xii, 71.

फर्वर *pharvara*. See √*phar*.

फर्वी *pharvī*. See *prapharvī*.

फल् *phal*, cl. 1. P. (Dhātup. xv, 9) *phalati* (ep. also Ā. °*te*; pf. *paphāla*, MBh., 3. pl. *pheluḥ*, Bhaṭṭ.; cf. Pāṇ. vi, 4, 122; aor. *aphālīt*, Gr.; fut. *phalishyati*, MBh.; *phalitā*, Gr.), to burst, cleave open or asunder, split (intrans.), MBh.; R. &c.; to rebound, be reflected, Kir.; BhP.; (Dhātup. xv, 23; but rather Nom. fr. *phala* below) to bear or produce fruit, ripen (lit. and fig.), be fruitful, have results or consequences, be fulfilled, result, succeed, Mn.; MBh.; Kāv. &c.; to fall to the share of (loc.), Hit.; to obtain (fruit or reward), MBh.; to bring to maturity, fulfil, yield, grant, bestow (with acc., rarely instr.), MBh.; Kāv. &c.; to give out, emit (heat), Kir.; (Dhātup. xx, 9) to go (cf. √*pal*): Caus. *phālayati*, aor. *apīphalat*, Gr. (cf. *phālita*): Desid. *piphalishati*, Gr.: Intens. *pamphulyate, pamphulīti, pamphulti*, ib. [Cf. √*sphaṭ, sphuṭ*; Germ. *spalten*; Eng. *split*.]

Phála, n. (ifc. f. *ā* or *ī*) fruit (esp. of trees), RV. &c. &c.; the kernel or seed of a fruit, Amar.; a nutmeg, Suśr.; the 3 myrobalans (= *tri-phalā*, q. v.), L.; the menstrual discharge, L. (cf. *pushpa*); fruit (met.), consequence, effect, result, retribution (good or bad), gain or loss, reward or punishment, advantage or disadvantage, KātyŚr.; MBh.; Kāv. &c.; benefit, enjoyment, Pañcat. ii, 70; compensation, Yājñ. ii, 161; (in rhet.) the issue or end of an action, Daś.; Sāh.; (in math.) the result of a calculation, product or quotient &c., Sūryas.; corrective equation, ib.; Gol.; area or superficial contents of a figure, Āryabh.; interest on capital, ib.; the third term in a rule of three sum, ib., Sch.; a gift, donation, L.; a gaming board, MBh. [cf. Goth. *spilda*; Icel. *spjald*]; a blade (of a sword or knife), MBh.; R.; Kum.; the point of an arrow, Kauś.; a shield, L.; a ploughshare (= *phāla*), L.; a point or spot on a die, MBh. iv, 24; m. Wrightia Antidysenterica, L., (*ā*), f. a species of plant, Car.; w. r. for *tulā*, Hcat.; (*ī*), f. Aglaia Odorata, L.; a kind of fish (= *phali*), L. — **kaksha**, m. N. of a Yaksha, MBh. — **kaṇṭakā**, f. Asclepias Echinata, L. — **kalpalatā**, f. N. of wk. — **kāṅkshin**, mfn. desirous of reward, Kum. — **kāma**, m. desire of reward, Jaim. — **kāmanā**, f. desire of a result or consequence, W. — **kāla**, m. the time of fruits, MW. — **krishṇa**, m. Carissa Carandas, L.; *-pāka*, m. id., L. — **kesara**, m. 'having hairy fruit,' the cocoa-nut tree (the f° of which is covered with a fibrous coat resembling hair), L. — **kośa** (Suśr.) or °**śaka** (L.), m. sg. and du. 'seed receptacle,' the scrotum. — **khaṇḍana**, n. fruit destruction, frustration of results, MW. — **khaṇḍava**, m. the pomegranate tree, L. — **khelā**, f. a quail (= *phāla-kh*°), L. — **grantha**, m. a work describing the effects (of celestial phenomena on the destiny of men), VarBṛS., Sch.; N. of wks. — **graha**, mfn. 'receiving fruits,' deriving profit or advantage, BhP.; m. the act of doing so, Śatr. — **grāhi** (TS.; AitBr.; Kāṭh.) or **-grahishṇu** (ŚāṅkhŚr.), mfn. fruit-bearing, fruitful. — **grāhin**, m. a fruit tree, L. — **ghṛita**, n. 'fruit-ghee,' a partic. aphrodisiac, ŚārṅgS.; a medicament used in diseases of the uterus, ib. — **candrikā**, f. N. of sev. wks. — **camasa**, m. a cup containing pounded figs (with young leaves and sour milk instead of Soma), KātyŚr., Sch.; Jaim.; (others 'ground bark of the Indian fig-tree with sour milk'). — **cāraka**, m. 'fruit-distribution,' a partic. official in Buddhist monasteries, L. — **coraka**, m. a kind of perfume, L. — **cchadana**, n. a house built of wooden boards, L. — **tantra**, mfn. aiming only at one's own advantage, Kum., Comm. — **tas**, ind. in relation to the reward or result, Āpast.; consequently, accordingly, virtually, MW. — **tā**, f. the being fruit, the state of f°, Kathās. — **traya**, n. 'f°-triad,' the 3 myrobalans, L.; 3 sorts of f° collectively (the f° of the vine, of Grewia Asiatica or Xylacarpus Granatum and Gmelina Arborea), ib. — **trika**, n. 'f°-triad,' the 3 myrobalans, ib. — **tva**, n. = *-tā*, Kathās. — **da**, mf(*ā*)n. 'f°-giving,' yielding or bearing f°, Mn.; bringing profit or gain, giving a reward, rewarding, giving anything (gen. or comp.) as a reward, BhP.; Bhartṛ.; Kathās. &c.; a f° tree, tree, L. — **danta-vat**, mfn. having fruit-teeth or fruit for teeth, Hcat. — **dātṛi** or **-dāyin**, mfn. 'f°-giving,' yielding f°, giving a result, MW. — **dīpikā**, f. N. of wk. — **dharman**, mfn. 'having the nature of fruit,' ripening soon and then falling to the ground or perishing, MBh. — **nirvṛitti**, f. = *-nishpatti*, KātyŚr.; Jaim.; final consequence or result, W. — **nivṛitti**, f. cessation of consequences, W. — **nishpatti**, f. production of fruit, fulfilment of consequences, attainment of reward, Kap. — **ṃ-dadā**, f. N. of a female Gandharva, Kāraṇḍ. — **pañcâmla**, n. a collection of 5 kinds of acid vegetables and fruits, L. (cf. *phalâmla-pañcaka*). — **pariṇati**, f. the ripeness of fruit, Megh. — **pariṇāma**, m. id., A. — **parivṛitti**, f. a fruitful harvest, Āp. — **pāka**, m. the ripening of fruit (see below); the fulfilment of consequences, VarBṛS.; Carissa Carandas, L. (cf. *pāka-phala* and *krishṇa-p°-ph°*); *-nishṭhā* (Suśr.), °*kāntā* (Mn.), °*kâvasānā* (L.), °*kâvasānikā* (L.), f. a plant ending or perishing with the ripening of f°, an annual plant. — **pākin**, m. Thespesia Populneoides, L. — **pātana**, n. knocking down or gathering f°, Mn. — **pādapa**, m. a f° tree, R. — **puccha**, m. a partic. species of esculent root or bulb, L. — **pura**, n. N. of a city (= *phalaka-p*°), Rājat. — **pushpa**, (ibc.) fruits and flowers; *-vat*, mfn. adorned with fr° and fl°, Hcat.; *-vṛiddhi*, f. increase or growth of fr° & fl°, MW.; °*pôpaśobhita*, mfn. adorned with fr° and fl°, MW. — **pushpā**, f. a species of date tree, L.; Ipomoea Turpethum, L. — **pushpita**, mfn. covered with fr° and fl°, BrahmaP. — **pushpī**, f. Ipomoea Turpethum, L. — **pūra**, m. 'full of kernels,' the citron tree, L. — **pūraka**, m. id., Bhpr.; (prob.) n. the citron, Car. — **pracayana**, n. gathering fruits,

PārGṛ. — **prajanana**, n. the production of f°, Rājat. — **prada**, mfn. bringing profit or a reward, BhP. — **pradāna**, n. the giving of f° (a marriage-ceremony), BṛĀrUp., Śaṃk. — **pradīpa**, m. N. of wk. — **prayukta**, mfn. connected with or producing consequences, yielding fruit, W. — **prasūti**, f. a growth of f°, crop of f°, Ragh. — **prâpti**, f. obtaining (the desired) f° or result, success, Ratnâv.; Kāś. — **priyā**, f. Aglaia Odorata, L.; a species of crow, L. — **prêpsu**, mfn. wishing to obtain f°, desirous of attaining results, R. — **bandhin**, mfn. forming or developing f°, Ragh. — **bhaksha**, mfn. feeding on f°; *-tā*, f., Gaut. — **bhāga**, m. a share in any product, sh° of advantage or profit, BhP.; N. of wk. — **bhāgin**, mfn. sharing in profit or advantage, partaking of a reward, Mn. iii, 143. — **bhāj**, mfn. receiving fruit, sharing in a rew°, MBh. — **bhuj**, mfn. enjoying fruit, MW.; m. a monkey, Prasannar. — **bhūti**, m. N. of a Brāhman, Kathās. — **bhūmi**, f. 'retribution-land,' place of reward or punishment (i. e. heaven or hell), Kathās. — **bhūyas-tva**, n. a greater reward, ĀśvGṛ. — **bhṛit**, mfn. fruit-bearing, fruitful, Kāv. — **bhoga**, m. enjoyment of consequences; possession of rent or profit, usufruct, W. — **bhogin**, mfn. enjoying fruits or cons°, receiving profits, ib. — **bhogya**, mfn. that of which one has the usufruct (a pledge), Yājñ. — **matsyā**, f. the aloe plant, L. — **maya**, mf(*ī*)n. consisting of fruits, Hcat. — **mukhyā**, f. a species of plant (= *aja-modā*), L. — **mudgarikā**, f. a kind of date tree, L. — **mūla**, n. sg. or du. or pl. fruits and roots, Mn.; MBh.; R.; Kathās.; *-maya*, mf(*ī*)n. formed of f° and r°, Hcat.; *-vat*, mfn. supplied with f° and r°, R. — **mūlin**, mfn. having (edible) f° and r°, MārkP. — **yukta**, mfn. connected with a reward, KātyŚr. — **yoga**, m. the attainment of an object, Mudr.; Sāh.; remuneration, reward, MBh.; R.; (*āt*), ind. because the reward falls to (his) share, KātyŚr. — **rājan**, m. 'king of fruits,' a water-melon, L. — **rāśi**, m. the 3rd term in rule of three, Āryabh. — **vat** (*phála-*), mfn. fruit-bearing, fructiferous, covered or laden with fruits, AV.; VS.; GṛS. &c.; yielding results, successful, profitable, advantageous, AV.; Āpast.; Hit. (*-tā*, f., Jaim.; Mcar.; *-tva*, n., ChUp., Śaṃk.; Sāh.); having profit or advantage, Vop.; (in dram.) containing the result or end of a plot, Sāh.; (*atī*), f. a twig of a partic. thorn tree; (others 'the plant *priyaṅgu*;' cf. *phalinī*), ShaḍvBr.; Gobh.; N. of wk. — **vandhya**, mfn. barren or destitute of fruits, not bearing f°, L. (cf. *phalâv°*). — **varti**, f. (in med.) a suppository, SārṅgS. — **vartula**, m. Gardenia Latifolia, L.; n. a water-melon, ib. — **vallī**, f. a series of quotients, Āryabh., Comm.; Col. — **vākya**, n. promise of reward, KātyŚr., Comm. — **vikrayiṇī**, f. a female fruit-seller, BhP. — **vṛiksha**, m. a fruit tree, L. — **vṛikshaka**, m. the bread-fruit tree, L. — **śāḍava**, see *-shāḍava*. — **śālin**, mfn. yielding wages, Kir.; experiencing consequences, sharing in results (°*li-tva*, n.), L. — **śaiśira**, m. Zizyphus Jujuba, L. — **śreshṭha**, m. 'best of fruits,' the mango tree, L. — **shāḍava**, m. the pomegranate tree, L. (written *śāḍ°*). — **saṃyukta**, mfn. connected with a reward, KātyŚr. — **saṃyoga**, m. the being conn° with a r°, Jaim. — **saṃstha**, mfn. bearing fruit, MW. — **sampad**, f. abundance of f°, good result, success, prosperity, W. — **sambaddha**, m. 'f°-endowed,' the tree Ficus Glomerata, L. — **sambhava** or **-sambhū**, mfn. produced in or by f°, W. — **sambhārā**, f. 'having abundance of f°,' the tree Ficus Oppositifolia, L. — **sahasra**, n. a thousand fruits; du. two thousand f°, MW. — **sāṃkarya-khaṇḍana**, n. N. of wk. — **sādhana**, n. effecting any result, Kāś. on Pāṇ.; a means of eff° any r°, W. — **siddhi**, f. realising an object, success, a prosperous issue, Sāh.; Kāś. on Pāṇ. — **stana-vatī**, f. (a female) having fruits for breasts, Hcat. — **sthāna**, n. the stage in which fruits or results are enjoyed, Buddh. — **sneha**, m. 'having oil in its f°,' a walnut tree, L. — **hāni**, f. loss of f° or profit, W. — **hārin**, mfn. f°-seizing, stealing f°, Pāṇ. vi, 2, 79, Sch. — **hārī**, f. N. of Kālī (a form of Durgā), L. — **hīna**, mfn. 'yielding no fruits' and 'giving no wages,' Pañcat. — **hetu**, mfn. one who has results for a motive, acting with a view to r°, Bhag. **Phalâkāṅkshā**, f. hope or expectation of favourable consequences, ib. **Phalâkāṅkshin**, mfn. desirous of results, wishing for fav° cons°, ib. **Phalâgama**, m. 'access of fruits,' production of f°, load of f°, Śak.; the fruit season, autumn, R. **Phalâgra**, n. 'f°-beginning,' f°-time, Hariv.; *-śākhin*, mfn. having fruits at the ends of its branches, ib. **Phalâḍhya**, mf(*ā*)n. 'rich in f°,' covered with f°, Mṛicch.; Ragh.; (*ā*), f. the wild plantain, L. **Phalâdana**, m. 'f°-eater,' a parrot, L. (cf. *phalâśana*). **Phalâdhikāra**, m. a claim for wages, KātyŚr. **Phalâdhyaksha**, m. 'superintendent of f°,' Mimusops Kauki, L. **Phalânubandha**, m. sequence of results, the consequences or results of (comp.), Śāntiś. **Phalânumeya**, mfn. inferable from c° or r°, Ragh. **Phalânusaraṇa**, n. rate or aggregate of profits, MW. **Phalânta**, m. 'ending with fruit,' a bamboo, L. **Phalânveshin**, mfn. seeking f° or results, looking for a reward, MW. **Phalâpūrva**, n. the mystic power which produces the consequences of a sacrificial act, Nyāyam., Comm. **Phalâpêkshā**, f. regard to results, expectation of cons°, W. **Phalâpêta**, mfn. deprived of fruit, unproductive, unfertile, ib. **Phalâphalikā**, f., g. *śāka-pārthivâdi*. **Phalâbdhi**, m. N. of wk. **Phalâbhisheka**, m. N. of wk. **Phalâbhoga**, m. non-enjoyment of profits &c., MW. **Phalâmla**, m. Rumex Vericarius, L.; n. a tamarind, L.; *-pañcaka*, n. the 5 acid or sour fruits, viz. bergamot, orange, sorrel, tamarind and citron, L. (cf. *amla-pañca* and *phala-pañcâmla*). **Phalâmlika**, mfn. having anything made with sour fruit, Hariv. **Phalârāma**, m. a fruit-garden, orchard, L. **Phalârthin**, mfn. one who aims at fruits or reward, Pañcat.; °*thi-tva*, n., Jaim. **Phalâvandhya**, mfn. not barren of f°, bearing f°, L. **Phalâśana**, m. 'f°-eater,' a parrot, L. (cf. *phalâdana*). **Phalâśin**, mfn. feeding or living on f°, Vishṇ.; Suśr. **Phalâsakta**, mfn. attached to f° or results, acting for the sake of reward; fond of f°, seeking to pluck f°, W. **Phalâsava**, m. a decoction of f°, Kathās. **Phalâsthi**, n. 'having f° with a hard rind,' a cocoa-nut, L. **Phalâhāra**, m. feeding or living on f°, Suśr. **Phale-grahi**, mfn. bearing f°, fruitful, successful (=*phala-g°*), Mālatīm.; Naish. (cf. Pāṇ. iii, 2, 26). **Phale-grāhi** or °**hin**, mfn. b° f°, L. **Phalêtara-tā**, f. the being other than f°, Daś. **Phalêndrā**, f. a species of Jambū, Bhpr. **Phale-pāka**, **-pākā**, **-pāku**, g. *nyaṅkv-ādi*. **Phale-pākin**, m. Hibiscus Populneoides, L. **Phale-pushpā**, f. Phlomis Zeylanica, Bhpr. **Phale-ruhā**, f. Bignonia Suaveolens, ib. **Phalôccaya**, m. collecting or a collection of fruits, W. **Phalôttamā**, f. 'best of f°,' a kind of grape without stones, L.; the 3 myrobalans, L.; the benefit arising from sacred study (?), W.; a small sort of rope (?), W. **Phalôtpati** (!), m. the mango tree, L. **Phalôtpatti**, f. production of fruit, profit, gain, advantage, Pāṇ., Sch. **Phalôtprêkshā**, f. a kind of comparison, Kuval. **Phalôdaka**, m. N. of a Yaksha, MBh. **Phalôdaya**, m. arising or appearance of consequences or results, recompense, reward, punishment (with gen. or loc. or comp.), Mn.; Yājñ.; R. &c.; joy, L.; heaven, L. **Phalôdgama**, m. pl. development of fruits, Bhartṛ. **Phalôddeśa**, m. regard to results, W. **Phalôdbhava**, mfn. obtained or derived from f°, Suśr. **Phalônmukha**, mfn. being about to give f°, Mcar. **Phalôpagama**, mfn. bearing f°, Vishṇ. **Phalôpajīvin**, mfn. living by the cultivation or sale of f°, R. **Phalôpabhoga**, m. enjoyment of f°, partaking of reward or of the consequences of anything, Kap. **Phalôpêta**, mfn. possessing fruit, yielding fruit, MW.

Phalaka (ifc., f. *ikā*) = *phala*, fruit, result, gain (*-tva*, n.), Kull. on Mn. ii, 146; menstruation (cf. *nava-phalikā*); (*phálaka*), n. (m., g. *ardharcâdi*; ifc. f. *ā*) a board, lath, plank, leaf, bench, Br.; GṛŚrS., &c.; a slab or tablet (for writing or painting on; also = page, leaf), Kāv.; Yājñ., Sch.; Lalit.; a picture (= *citra-ph°*), Mṛicch. iv, $\frac{3}{4}$; a gaming-board (cf. *śāri-ph°*); a wooden bench, MBh.; a slab at the base (of a pedestal; cf. *sphaṭika-ph°*); any flat surface (often in comp. with parts of the body, applied to broad flat bones, cf. *aṃsa-*, *phaṇā-*, *lalāṭa-ph°* &c.); the palm of the hand, ŚBr.; the buttocks, L.; the top or head of an arrow, Kull. on Mn. vii, 90; a shield, MBh.; bark (as a material for clothes), MBh.; Hariv.; the pericarp of a lotus, Śiś.; = *-yantra*, Gol.; a layer, W.; the stand on which a monk keeps his turban, Buddh.; m. Mesua Roxburghii, L.; (*ā* or *ikā*), f., see below. — **paridhāna**, n. putting on a bark garment, MBh. — **pāṇi**, m. a soldier armed with a shield, L. — **pura**, n. N. of a town in the east of India, Pāṇ. vi, 2, 101 (cf. *phala-pura*). — **yantra**, n. an astronomical instrument invented by Bhās-kara, Gol. — **saktha**, n. a thigh like a board, Pāṇ. v, 4, 98, Sch. **Phalakâkhya-yantra**, n. = °*ka-yantra*, Gol. **Phalakā-vana**, n. N. of a forest sacred to Sarasvatī, Cat. (°*kī-vana*, MBh.) **Phalakâsâdana**, n. the obtaining or reaching a plank (said of a drowning person), Ratnâv.

Phalakā, f., v.l. for *halakā*, g. *prêkshâdi*.

Phalakin, mfn. having a board or a shield, L.; v.l. for *halakin*, g. *prêkshâdi*; m. a wooden bench (v.l. *phalaka*), MBh.; a kind of fish, L.; (prob. n.) sandal-wood, L.; (*inī*), f. a plank, Divyâv.

Phalana, n. bearing fruit or producing consequences, W.

Phalasa, mfn. (fr. *phala*), g. *tṛiṇâdi*; m. the bread-fruit or Jaka tree (= *panasa*), L.

Phalahaka, m. a plank, board (= *phalaka*), Kathās.; Rājat. (others 'N. of a place').

Phalahī, f. the cotton tree, cotton plant, L.

Phalāya, Nom. Ā. °*yate*, to be the fruit or result of, Daś. (*phálāyetām*, w.r. for *pál°*, MaitrS.)

Phali, m. a kind of fish (= *phalakin*), L.; a bowl or cup, Śil.

Phalika, mfn. (ifc.) enjoying the reward for, MBh.; m. a mountain, L.

Phalikā, f. Dolichos Lablab or Thespesia Populneoides, L.

Phaliṭa, mfn. bearing or yielding fruit, producing consequences, fruitful, successful, fulfilled, developed, accomplished, MBh.; Kāv. &c. (n. impers. with instr. 'fruit was borne by,' Rājat.; Hit.); resulting as a consequence, Pat.; m. a tree (esp. a fruit t°), L.; (*ā*), f. a menstruous woman, L.; n. a fragrant resin (= *śaileya*), L. (prob. w.r. for *palita*).

Phalitavya, n. (impers.) fruit should be borne by (instr.), MBh.

Phalin, mfn. bearing or yielding fruit, fruitful (met. = productive of results or consequences), RV. &c. &c.; reaping advantage, successful, AV.; having an iron point (as an arrow), Ragh.; m. a fruit tree, MBh.; (*inī*), f. a species of plant (= *agni-śikhā* or *priyaṅgu*), L.; (with *yoni*) the vagina injured by too violent sexual intercourse, Suśr. **Phalîśa**, m. Thespesia Populneoides, L.

Phalina, mfn. bearing fruit, Mālatīm. (cf. Pāṇ. v, 2, 122, Vārtt. 4, Pat.); m. the bread-fruit tree, L.

Phalī, in comp. for *phala*. — **káraṇa**, n. separating the grain from the husks, cleansing of grain, KātyŚr., Sch.; m. pl. chaff (of rice) or smallest grains, Br.; GṛŚrS.; (sg.) BhP.; *-homá*, m. an oblation of chaff or smallest grains, TBr.; ĀpŚr. — **kāra**, m. pl. = prec. m. pl., BhP. — **√kṛi**, P. *-karoti* (Ved. inf. *phalī-kartavaí*), to separate the fruit or grain from the husks, thresh, winnow, Br.; GṛŚrS.; — **kṛita**, mfn. threshed, winnowed, ŚBr. — **√bhū**, P. *-bhavati*, to obtain fruit or reward, Mṛicch., Sch.

Phalīya, mfn. (fr. *phala*), g. *utkarâdi*.

Phalya, n. a flower, bud, L.

Phāla, m. (or n., L.) a ploughshare, RV.; Kāṭh.; Kauś.; Yājñ.; a kind of hoe or shovel, R.; a bunch or bundle, Naish.; a nosegay, Bālar.; a jump, Vcar.; HPariś.; the core of a citron, L.; N. of Śiva, L.; of Bala-rāma, L.; n. a garment of cotton, A.; a ploughed field, ib.; = (or w.r. for) *bhāla*, the forehead, Cat.; mf(*ī*)n. made of cotton, L. — **kuddāla-lāṅgalin**, mfn. furnished with a hoe and a spade and a plough, R. — **kṛishṭa**, mfn. tilled with the plough, MBh.; growing on arable land, produced by cultivation (opp. to *āraṇya*), Kāṭh.; m. or n. a ploughed or cultivated soil, Mn.; Gaut.; m. fruit grown on a c° s°, ŚāṅkhBr.; Mn.; Yājñ. — **khelā**, f. a quail, L. (cf. *phaṇi-* and *phala-khela*). — **gupta**, m. 'ploughshare-defended,' N. of Bala-rāma, L. (cf. *halâyudha*). — **camasa**, n. (?) a partic. part of the ploughshare, Kauś. — **datī**, f. 'pl°-toothed,' N. of a female demon, Pāṇ. v, 4, 143, Sch. **Phālâhata**, mfn. 'pl°-struck,' ploughed, Yājñ. ii, 158.

Phālita, mfn. expanded, blown, MBh. (Nīlak.)

Phālīkaraṇa, mfn. (fr. *phalī-k°*) made of husks or the smallest grains, ŚāṅkhBr.

Phulti, f. full expansion or perfection (?), Pāṇ. vii, 4, 89, Sch.

Phulla, mf(*ā*)n. (Pāṇ. vii, 4, 89; viii, 2, 55) split or cleft open, expanded, blown (as a flower), MBh.; Kāv. &c.; abounding in flowers, flowery, ib.; opened wide, dilated (as eyes), Pañcat.; puffed inflated (as cheeks), Bālar.; loose (as a garment), Mṛicch.; beaming, smiling (as a face), Kāvyâd.; m. N. of a saint, Cat.; (prob.) n. a full-blown flower, KālP.; Nom. P. *phullati* (cf. Dhātup. xv, 24) to open, expand, blow (as a flower), MBh. **-tubarī**, f. alum, L. **-dāman**, n. a kind of metre, Chandom. **-drishṭi, -nayana** and **-netra**, mfn. having eyes dilated (with joy), smiling, happy, W. **-nalinī**, f. a lotus plant in full bloom, Mṛicch. **-padmôtpala-vat**, mfn. abounding in full-blown lotus flowers of various kinds, R. **-pura**, n. N. of a town, Rājat. **-phāla**, m. the wind raised in winnowing corn, L. (cf. *phalla, phala*). **-locana**, mfn. = *-drishṭi*; m. 'full-eyed,' a kind of antelope, L.; n. a large full eye, W. **-vat**, mfn. expanded, blossoming, blowing, Pāṇ. viii, 2, 35, Sch. **-vadana**, mfn. 'smiling-faced,' looking pleased or happy, W. **-sūtra**, n. N. of wk. **Phullâmbikā**, f. N. of a woman, Cat. **Phullâraṇya-māhātmya**, n. N. of ch. of AgP. **Phullôtpala**, n. 'having blooming lotus flowers,' N. of a lake, Hit.

Phullaka, m. a worm or a snake, L.

Phullana, mfn. (ifc.) puffing up, inflating, Vcar.

Phulli, f. expanding, blossoming, W.

Phullita, mfn. expanded, blown, L.

फलय *phalaya*, m. N. of a mountain, Cat.

फलसतीण *phalasatīṇa*, m. or n. (?) N. of a country (Palestine ?), Cat.

फलायोषित् *phalāyoshit*, f. a cricket, L. (cf. *phaḍiṅgā*).

फलिग *phaligá* (Padap. °*li-gá*), m. (prob.) a cask or leather-bag or anything to hold fluids (applied to clouds or water-receptacles in mountains), RV.

फलूष *phalūsha*, m. a species of creeper, L.

फलेलाङ्कु *phalelāṅku*, n. = *puñjātuka* (?), L.

फलोनि *phaloni* (!), f. pudenda muliebria, L.

फल्क *phalka*, mfn. one who has an expanded or extended body (= *visāritâṅga*), L.; = *viśodhitâṅka* (?), L.

फल्गु *phalgú*, mf(*ū* or *vī*)n. reddish, red, TS.; small, minute, feeble, weak, pithless, unsubstantial, insignificant, worthless, unprofitable, useless, VS. &c. &c.; f. Ficus Oppositifolia, L.; a red powder usually of the root of wild ginger (coloured with sappan wood and thrown over one another by the Hindūs at the Holī festival; cf. *phalgûtsava*), W.; the spring season, L.; (scil. *vāc*) a falsehood, lie, L.; N. of a river flowing past Gayā, MBh.; Hariv.; du. (in astrol.) N. of a Nakshatra. **-tā**, f. (MBh.), **-tva**, n. (Mn.) worthlessness, vanity, insignificance. **-tīrtha**, n. N. of a sacred bathing-place near Gayā, Vishṇ. **-da**, mfn. 'giving little,' avaricious, BhP.; (*ā*), f. N. of a river (= *phalgu*), Pur. **-prāsaha** (°*gú-*), m. of little strength, ŚBr. **-rakshita**, m. N. of a man, HPariś. **-vāṭikā**, f. Ficus Oppositifolia, L. **-vṛinta**, m. a species of Symplocos, L. **-vṛintāka**, m. a species of Calosanthes, L. **-śrāddha**, n. a kind of Śrāddha, RTL. 312. **-hastinī**, f. N. of a poetess, Cat. **Phalgûtsava**, m. the vernal festival commonly called Holī (cf. RTL. 430), W.

Phalguṇa, °*ṇaka*, °*ṇī*, w.r. for *phalguna*, °*naka*, °*nī*.

Phálguna, mf(*ī*)n. reddish, red, VS.; TS.; born under the Nakshatra Phalgunī, Pāṇ. iv, 3, 34; m. N. of a man (*-svāmin*, m. a temple built by Ph°), Rājat.; the month Phālguna, L.; N. of Arjuna, L.; (*ī*), f., see below. °**naka**, m. N. of a man, Rājat.; pl. N. of a people, MārkP. °**nāla**, m. the month Phālguna (= *phālgunāla*), L.

Phálgunī, f. (sg. du. and pl.) N. of a double lunar mansion (*pūrvā* and *uttarā*), AV. &c. &c.; Ficus Oppositifolia, L.; N. of a woman, Pravar. **-pūrṇa-māsá**, m. the full moon in the Nakshatra Uttara-Phalgunī, TS. **-pūrva-samaya**, m. the time when the moon is in the N° Pūrva-Ph°, MBh. **-bhava**, m. N. of the planet Jupiter, L.

Phalguluka, m. pl. N. of a people, Var.; MārkP.

Phalgvà, mfn. weak, feeble, RV. iv, 5, 14.

Phālguṇa, °*ṇī*, w.r. for *phālguna*, °*nī*.

Phālguná, mf(*ī*)n. relating to the Nakshatra Phalgunī, ŚBr.; ŚrS.; born under the N° Ph°, Pāṇ. iv, 3, 34 (v.l.); m. (with or scil. *māsa*) the month during which the full moon stands in the N° Ph° (February–March), Mn.; MBh.; N. of Arjuna (= *phalguna*), MBh.; Hariv.; Terminalia Arjuna (= *nadī-ja*), L.; (*ī*), f., see below; n. a species of grass used as a substitute for the Soma plant (and also called *arjunānī*), ŚBr.; TBr.; ĀśvŚr.; N. of a place of pilgrimage, BhP. **-māhātmya**, n. N. of wk. **Phālgunânuja**, m. 'younger brother of the month Phālguna,' the vernal month Caitra, L.

Phālgunāla, m. the month Phālguna (= *phalgunāla*), L.

Phālgunī, m. patr. fr. *phālguna* (= *arjuna*), MBh.

Phālgunika, mfn. relating to the Nakshatra Phalgunī or to the day of full moon in the month Phālguna, Pāṇ. iv, 2, 23; m. (scil. *māsa*) the month Phālguna, L.

Phālgunī, f. the lunar mansion Phalgunī (q. v.), Hariv.; R.; MārkP.; = *-paurṇamāsī*, GṛŚrS. **-paksha**, m. the dark half in the month Phālguna, Lāṭy. **-paurṇamāsī**, f. the day of full moon in the month Phālguna (on which the Holī or great vernal festival is celebrated), Pāṇ. vi, 3, 63, Sch. **-bhava**, m. N. of the planet Jupiter, L. (cf. *phalgunī-bh°*).

Phālgunya, m. N. of the planet Jupiter, L.

फल्फ् *phalph*, to grow, increase (*vṛiddhau*), KātyŚr., Sch.

Phalpha. See *vi-phalpha*.

फल्लकिन् *phallakin*, m. a kind of fish (= *phalakin*), L.

फल्लफल *phalla-phala*, m. the wind raised in winnowing grain (= *phulla-phāla*), L.

फषाजिग *phashājiga* and *phashājima*, m. or n. (?) N. of two places, Cat.

फा *phā*, m. (nom. *phās*) heat, L.; idle talk, L.; increase or increaser, L.

फाट् *phāṭ*, ind. an interjection of calling, W.

फाटकी *phāṭakī*, f. alum (= *sphāṭī*), L.

फाणि *phāṇi*, f. (√*phaṇ* ?) unrefined sugar, molasses, L.; flour or meal mixed with curds (= *karambha*), L.

Phāṇita, m. (Nīlak.) n. (fr. Caus. of √*phaṇ*; cf. Pāṇ. vii, 2, 18, Sch.) the inspissated juice of the sugar cane and other plants, Āpast.; MBh.; Hariv. [Cf. Arab. فانيذ; Pers. پانيد; medieval Lat. *penidium*.] **Phāṇitī-bhūta**, mfn. inspissated, Suśr.

Phāṇṭa, mf(*ā*)n. (contracted from *phāṇita*; cf. Pāṇ. vii, 2, 18) obtained by straining or filtering, Ṛigvidh.; made or won by an easy process, readily or easily prepared, L.; one who does not exert himself or takes things easy, L.; m. an infusion, decoction, pounded medicinal substances mixed with four parts of hot water and then filtered, ŚārṅgS. (also °*ṭaka*, m.); Bhaṭṭ.; n. the first particles of butter that are produced by churning, ŚBr.; Kauś. **Phāṇṭâhṛita**, m. N. of a man, Pāṇ. iv, 1, 90, Sch.; patr. fr. *phāṇṭâhṛiti*; pl. the disciples of Phāṇṭâhṛiti, iv, 1, 150, Sch. **Phāṇṭâhṛitāyani**, m. patr. fr. *phāṇṭâhṛiti*, Pāṇ. iv, 1, 150. **Phāṇṭâhṛiti**, m. N. of a man (a Sauvīra), ib., Sch.; patr. fr. °*hṛita*, 90, Sch.

Phāṇṭaya, Nom. fr. *phāṇṭa* (ind. p. °*yitvā*), Kauś., Sch.

Phāṇḍa, n. the belly (= *phaṇḍa*), L.

Phāṇḍin, m. N. of a serpent-demon, L.

फारिव *phāriva*. See under √*phar*.

फारी *phārī*, f. black cumin, L.

फाल *phāla* &c. See p. 717, col. 3.

फाल्गुन *phālguna* &c. See col. 1.

फि *phi*, m. a wicked man, L.; idle talk, L.; anger, L.

फिङ्गक *phiṅgaka*, m. the fork-tailed shrike (= *kaliṅga, kuliṅga*), L.

फिट्सूत्र *phiṭ-sūtra*, n. N. of a grammat. wk. by Śāṃtanavâcārya. **-vṛitti**, f. the same with comm.

फिरङ्ग *phiraṅga*, mfn. Frankish, European (with *vyādhi*, m. = °*gâmaya*), Bhpr.; m. the country of the Franks i. e. Europe, or = °*gâmaya*, L. **-roṭi**, f. European bread, L. **Phiraṅgâmaya**, m. the disease of the Franks i. e. syphilis, Bhpr.

Phiraṅgin, m. a Frank, a European (f. *iṇī*), L.

फिराल *phirāla*, m. or n. (?) N. of a place, Cat.

फिरिण्ड *phiriṇḍa*, m. N. of a prince, Cat.

फु *phu*, m. a magical formula, L.; useless or idle talk, L.

फुक *phuka*, m. a bird, L.

फुट *phuṭa*, m. n. (or °*ṭā*, f.) the hood or expanded neck of a snake (= *phaṭa, phaṇa*), L. **Phuṭâṭopa**, m. the swelling of a serpent's hood, Pañcat.

फुट्टक *phuṭṭaka*, n. a kind of cloth (also °*ka-vastra*, n.), Divyâv.; (*ikā*), f. a sort of woven texture, Kathās.

फुडुत् *phuḍut*, ind. an interjection, Kāśīkh., Sch.

फुत् *phut* or *phūt*, ind. an onomat. word (used only with √°*kṛi*, and its derivatives; sometimes expressive of contempt). **-kara**, m. 'making a crackling noise,' fire, L. **-kartu-manas**, mfn. wishing to make a derisory noise, intending to cry aloud, MW. **-kāra**, m. puffing, blowing, hissing, the hiss of a serpent (also *phūt-k°*), Kathās.; Kuval.; shrieking, screaming, Bhartṛ.; Kathās.; *-randhra*, n. the hole to which the mouth is applied in playing a flute, Saṃgīt.; *-vat*, mfn. hissing, shrieking, L. **-kārya**, mfn. in *a-phūt-k°*, requiring no blowing, Kathās. **-√kṛi**, P. Ā. *-karoti, -kurute*, to puff, blow, make a bubbling noise, blow into, Pañcat.; Hit.; to shriek, yell, Kathās.; Pañcat.; to be insolent or defiant, Ratnâv. iv, 12. **-kṛita**, mfn. puffed, blown &c.; n. the sound of a wind instrument, L.; a loud scream, shriek, Rājat. **-kṛiti**, f. the blowing of a wind instrument, Saṃgīt.; blowing, hissing, Naish.; crying aloud, R.

फुप्फु *phupphu*, ind. an onomat. word. **-kāraka**, mf(*ikā*)n. panting, [illegible]ping, L.

Phupphusa, m. (Suśr.) and **phuphusa**, n. (ŚārṅgS.) the lungs.

फुम्फुआ *phumphuā*, ind. imitation of the sound made by the crackling of a fire, L.

फुराफुराय *phurāphurāya*, Nom. Ā. °*yate*, to tremble, flicker, Mṛicch.

फुलिङ्ग *phuliṅga*, m. syphilis, Cat. (cf. *phiraṅga*).

फुल्ल् *phull*, cl. 1. P. *phullati* (Dhātup. xv, 24), see under *phulla*, p. 717, col. 3.

फुल्लरीक *phullarīka*, m. a district, place, L.; a serpent, L. (cf. *phullaka*, col. 1).

फूत् *phūt*, *phūt-kāra* &c. See *phut* above.

फेञ्चक *pheñcaka*, m. a kind of bird, Cat.

फेट् *pheṭ*, ind. an onomat. word. **-kāra**, m. howling, a howl, Śatr. (cf. *phet* &c.)

फेण *pheṇa* &c. See *phena*.

फेण्ट *pheṇṭa*, m. a kind of bird, Cat.

फेत् *phet*, ind. an onomat. word. **-kāra**, m. howling (of the wind or of animals), BhP.; Prab., Sch. **-kārin**, mfn. howling, yelling (as a jackal), Prab.; °*riṇī-tantra* or °*rīya-tantra*, n. N. of wk. **-kṛita**, n. howling, a howl, Śatr.

फेन *phéna*, m., once n. (often written *pheṇa* and prob. connected with √*phaṇ*; but see Uṇ. iii, 3) foam, froth, scum, RV. &c. &c.; moisture of the lips, saliva, Mn. iii, 19; n. (m., L.) Os Sepiae (white cuttle-fish bone, supposed to be indurated foam of the sea); Car.; m. N. of a man (son of Ushad-ratha and father of Su-tapas), Hariv.; (*ā*), f. a kind of shrub (= *sātalā*), L.; (*ī*), f. a kind of food, L. [Cf. Slav. *pěna*; Angl.Sax. *fam*; Eng. *foam*; Germ. *Feim*.] **-giri**, m. N. of a mountain near the mouth of the Indus, R.; Var. (v.l. *pheṇa-g°*). **-tā**, f. frothiness, vapour, W. **-dugdhā**, f. a kind of small shrub (= *dugdha-phenī*), L. **-dharman**, mfn. 'having the nature of foam,' transient, MBh. **-pa**, mfn. 'foam-drinking,' feeding on foam, MBh.; BhP.; (feeding on fruits fallen from the trees, BhP., Sch.) **-piṇḍa**, m. 'mass of foam,' a mere bubble, nonsense, L. **-prakhya**, mfn. f°-like, resembling foam, Yājñ. **-mehin**, mfn. discharging frothy urine, Suśr. **-1. -vat**, mfn. frothy, foaming, MBh. **-2. -vat**, ind. like foam, Śāntiś. **-vāhin**, mfn. 'carrying off the scum;' (with *vastra*), n. a filtering cloth,

L.; m. Indra's thunderbolt, L. (rather 'N. of Indra;' cf. *phenâśani*). **Phenâgra,** n. 'point of foam,' a bubble on the water, L. **Phenâśani,** m. 'having foam for a thunderbolt,' N. of Indra, L. (cf. *phena-vāhin*). **Phenâhāra,** mfn. feeding on foam, MBh. (cf. *phena-pa*). **Phenôpama,** mfn. resembling foam (said of life), Hit.

Phenaka, m. Os Sepiae, L.; ground rice boiled in water (also *ā*, f.), L.; a kind of pastry, L. (also *ikā*, f., Bhpr.) °**nala,** mfn. frothy, foamy, L. (cf. *phenila*). °**nāya,** Nom. Ā. °*yate* (also P. °*yati*, g. *lohitâdi*), to foam, froth, MBh.; Hcar.

Phenila, mf(*ā*)n. foamy, frothy, spumous, MBh.; Kāv. &c.; m. a kind of tree, Vāsav.; Zizyphus Jujuba, Bhpr.; Sapindus Detergens, L.; (*ā*), f. Sap° D°, Car.; Hingcha Repens, L.; = *sarpâkshī*, L.; n. the fruit of Sap° D° or of Ziz° J° or of Madana, L.

Phénya, mfn. existing in foam, VS.

फेर *phera*, m. (onomat.) a jackal, L.

Pheraṇḍa, m. a jackal, L. (also °*ruṇḍa*, L.)

फेरल *pherala*, m. or n. N. of a place, Cat. (perhaps w. r. for *kerala*).

फेरव *phe-rava*, m. (from onomat. *phe* + *rava*) a jackal, Mālatīm.; Prab.; Pracaṇḍ.; a Rākshasa, Kathās.; mfn. fraudulent, malicious, injurious, L. **Pheravī-tantra,** n. N. of wk.

Pheru, m. a jackal, BhP. **-vinnā,** f. a species of plant, L.

फेल् *phel*, cl. 1. P. *phelati*, to go, move, Dhātup. xv, 35.

फेल *phela*, n. remnants of food, refuse, orts (also °*lā*, °*li*, °*likā*, °*lī*), L.; a partic. high number, Buddh.; (*ā*), f. (prob.) w. r. for *pelā* = *peṭā*, a small box, Divyâv.

फेलुक *pheluka*, m. the scrotum, L.

फौल्लि *phaulli*, f. (fr. *phulla*), Pāṇ. viii, 2, 42, Vārtt. 4, Pat.

ब BA.

ब 1. *ba*, the third letter of the labial class (often confounded with *va*). **-kāra,** m. the sound or letter *ba*, the soft form of *pa*.

ब 2. *ba*, m. = *varuṇa*; *sindhu*; *bhaga*; *gandhana*; *vapana* &c., L.

बंह् *baṇh*, cl. 1. Ā. (Dhātup. xvi, 32) *baṇhate*, to grow, increase; Caus. *baṇhayate*, to cause to grow, Br. (cf. *bahala*, *bahu*, *bahula*).

Baṇhiman, m. muchness, abundance, multitude, Pāṇ. vi, 4, 157.

Báṇhishṭha, mfn. (superl. of *bahula*, Pāṇ. vi, 4, 157) strongest, most abundant, most, RV.; MBh.; very low or deep, Bālar.; = next, Śāntiś., Sch.

Báṇhīyas, mfn. (compar. of *bahula*, Pāṇ. vi, 4, 157) very stout or fat, MaitrS.

बक *baka*, m. (also written *vaka*) a kind of heron or crane, Ardea Nivea (often fig. = a hypocrite, cheat, rogue, the crane being regarded as a bird of great cunning and deceit as well as circumspection), Mn.; MBh. &c.; Sesbana Grandiflora, L.; an apparatus for calcining or subliming metals or minerals, L.; N. of Kubera, L.; of a demon, MānGṛ.; of an Asura (said to have assumed the form of a crane and to have been conquered by Kṛishṇa), BhP.; of a Rākshasa killed by Bhīma-sena, MBh.; of a Ṛishi (with the patr. Dālbhi or Dālbhya), Kāṭh.; ChUp.; MBh.; of a peasant, HPariś.; of a king, Rājat.; (pl.) of a people, MBh.; (*ī*), f. a female crane, Vās., Sch.; a female demon = *Pūtanā*, BhP., Sch. **-kaccha,** m. N. of a place, Kathās. **-kalpa,** m. N. of a partic. Kalpa or period of the world, Cat. **-cara,** m. = *-vratin*, MW. **-ciñcikā,** f. a sort of fish (= *bakâcī*), L. **-jit,** m. 'conqueror of Baka,' N. of Bhīma-sena, L. **-tva,** n. the state or condition of a crane, MārkP. **-dvīpa,** m. N. of a Dvīpa, Pañcar. **-dhūpa,** m. a kind of perfume, L. **-nakha,** m. N. of a son of Viśvā-mitra, MBh.; *-guda-pariṇaddha*, m. pl. the descendants of Baka-nakha and Guda-pariṇaddha, g. *tikakitavâdi*. **-nishūdana,** m. 'destroyer of Baka,' N. of Bhīma-sena, L. **-pañcaka,** n. the 5 days during which even the heron eats no fish (N. of the last 5 Tithis of the bright half of the month Kārttika), Cat. **-pushpa,** m. Agati Grandiflora, L. **-yantra,** n. 'crane-instrument,' N. of a partic. form of retort, L. **-rāja,** m. the king of the cranes (called Rāja-dharman, son of Kaśyapa; see MBh. xii, 6336). **-ripu,** m. 'enemy of Baka,' N. of Bhīma-sena, Veṇīs. **-vat,** ind. like a crane or heron, Mn.; Cāṇ. **-vatī,** f. N. of a river, Rājat. **-vadha,** m. 'the killing of Baka,' N. of MBh. i, 6103-6315 (cf. IW. 386). **-vṛiksha,** m. a kind of tree, MW. **-vṛitti,** mfn. one who acts like a heron, a hypocrite, Mn.; Yājñ. **-vairin,** m. = *-ripu*, L. **-vrata,** n. 'crane-like conduct,' hypocrisy, ŚārṅgP.; *-cara*, m. = next, Mn. **-vratika,** or °**tin,** m. a hypocrite (esp. a false devotee), Mn. **-saktha,** m. N. of a man; pl. his descendants, g. *yaskâdi*. **-sahavāsin,** m. 'fellow-lodger of the heron,' a lotus flower, Kuval. **Bakâri,** m. 'enemy of Baka,' N. of Kṛishṇa, BhP. **Bakâlīna,** mfn. lurking like a heron, MBh. **Bakêśa,** m. N. of a temple founded by Baka, Rājat.

Bakabakāya, Nom. Ā. °*yate*, to croak, Subh. (v. l. for *bhakabh*° and *makam*°).

Bakâcī, f. a kind of fish (= *baka-ciñcikā*), L.

Bakāya, Nom. P. °*yati*, to represent or act like the Asura Baka, BhP.

Bakerukā, f. a small crane, L.; the branch of a tree bent by the wind, L.

Bakoṭa, m. a kind of crane, L.

बकुर *bákura*, m. (prob.) a horn, trumpet (or other wind instrument used in battle; cf. *bākura*, *bekurā*), RV. i, 117, 21 (Naigh. 'a thunderbolt, lightning').

बकुल *bakula*, m. (also written *vakula*) a kind of tree, Mimusops Elengi (said to put forth blossoms when sprinkled with nectar from the mouth of lovely women), MBh.; Kāv. &c.; N. of Śiva, MBh. xiii, 1223; of a country, Buddh.; (*ā*), f. Helleborus Niger, L.; (*ī*), f. a kind of drug, L.; n. the fragrant flower of Mimusops Elengi, MBh.; Kāv. &c. **-dāman,** n. a garland of Bakula flowers, Mālatīm. **-mālā,** f. id., ib.; N. of a woman, Vāsav. **-mālinī-pariṇaya,** m. N. of a drama. **-medhī,** f. N. of a temple, Divyâv. **Bakulâbharaṇa-câṭu,** n. N. of a poem. **Bakulâbharaṇa-muni,** m. N. of a sage, Cat. **Bakulâraṇya-māhātmya,** n. N. of ch. of BrahmavP. **Bakulâvali,** f. = °*la-dāman*, Mālatīm.; °*likā*, f. N. of a woman, Mālav.

Bakulita, mfn. furnished with Bakula trees or flowers, g. *tārakâdi*.

Bakūla, m. the Bakula tree, L.

बगदाद *bagadāda*, N. of a city, Bagdad, Cat.

Bagadāru, N. of a place, ib.

Bagadāha, N. of a place, ib.

बज *bajá*, m. (prob.) N. of a herb used as a charm against evil spirits, AV.

बट् *báṭ*, ind. in truth, certainly (Sāy. = *satyam*), RV.

बटरक *baṭaraka*, n. pl. circular lines of light which appear before the closed eye, AitĀr.

बटु *baṭu*, m. (also written *vaṭu*) a boy, lad, stripling, youth (esp. a young Brāhman, but also contemptuously applied to adult persons), MBh.; Kāv. &c.; N. of a class of priests, Cat.; a form of Śiva (so called from being represented by boys in the rites of the Śāktas), ib.; Calosanthes Indica, L. **-carita-nāṭaka,** n. N. of a drama. **-dāsa,** m. N. of a man, Cat. **-mātra,** m. a mere stripling, MW. **-rūpin,** mfn. having the form of a lad or stripling, ib.

Baṭuka, m. a boy, lad &c. = *baṭu*, Kathās.; BhP.; a stupid fellow, blockhead, W.; N. of a class of priests, Cat.; a form of Śiva (among the Śāktas), ib. **-kavaca,** m. or n. N. of ch. of wk. **-nātha,** m. N. of a pupil of Śaṃkarâcārya, Cat. **-pañcâṅga,** n. (and °*ga-prayoga-paddhati*, f.), **-pañjara,** n., **-pūjā-paddhati,** f. N. of wks. **-bhairava,** m. a form of Bhairava, Cat.; *-kavaca*, m. or n., *-tantra*, n., *-dīpa-dāna*, n., *-pañcâṅga*, n., *-pūjā*, f. (and °*jā-paddhati*, f.), *-sahasra-nāman*, n. (and °*ma-stotra*, n.), *-stava-rāja*, m., *-stotra*, n., °*vâpad-uddharaṇa-paṭala*, n. N. of wks. **Baṭukârcana,** n. the worship of B°; *-candrikā*, f., *-dīpikā*, f., *-vidhi*, m. N. of wks. **Baṭukâshṭaśata-nāman,** n. N. of wk.

Baṭū-karaṇa, n. the act of making into a youth, initiation of a boy by *upa-nayana*, q. v., L.

बट्टलोहक *baṭṭa-lohaka*, n. damasked steel, L.

बट्टीशीव्रत *baṭṭīśī-vrata*, n. '32 observances,' N. of ch. of BhavP. ii.

बडपिला *baḍapilā*, f. N. of a village, Inscr.

बडबा *baḍabā* &c. See *vaḍabā*.

बडा *baḍā* or *balā*, ind. = *báṭ*, RV. viii, 69, 1.

बडाह *baḍāha*, m. N. of a prince, Vāsav., introd.

बडिश *baḍiśa*, m., f. (*ā* or *ī*) and n. (also written *vaḍiśa* and *valiśa*; cf. also *bariśī*) a hook, fish-hook, MBh.; R.; Pur.; Suśr.; a partic. surgical instrument in the form of a hook, Suśr.; N. of a man with the patr. Dhāmārgava, Car. **-yuta,** mfn. joined to or fastened on a hook, MW.

बणिज् *baṇij* &c. See *vaṇij*.

बण्ड *baṇḍá*, mf(*ā*)n. (also written *vaṇḍa*) maimed, defective, crippled (esp. in the hands or feet or tail), AV.; ŚrS. (Sch. also = impotent, emasculated; cf. *paṇḍa*); w. r. for *caṇḍa*, *vaṇṭha*, *raṇḍa*, L.; (*ā*), f. an unchaste woman, L. (prob. w. r. for *raṇḍā*).

बत 1. *bata*, ind. (later usually *vata*; g. *svar-ādi*) an interjection expressing astonishment or regret, generally = ah! oh! alas! (originally placed immediately after the leading word at the beginning of a sentence, or only separated from it by *iva*; rarely itself in the first place, e. g. Mālav. iii, $\frac{2\frac{1}{2}}{}$; in later language often in the middle of a sentence), RV. &c. &c.

बत 2. *batá*, m. a weakling, RV. x, 10, 13.

बद् *bad* or *band*, cl. 1. P. *badati* or *bandati*, to be firm or steady; Dhātup. iii, 14 (cf. √3. *pad*).

बदक्सान *badaksāna*, the country Badakshān, Bhpr. (v. l. *bād*°).

बदर *badara*, m. the jujube tree, Zizyphus Jujuba, L.; another tree (= *deva-sarshapa*), L.; the kernel of the fruit of the cotton plant, L.; dried ginger, L.; N. of a man, g. *naḍâdi*; (*ā*), f. the cotton shrub, L.; a species of Dioscorea, L.; Mimosa Octandra, L.; Clitoria Ternatea, L.; (*ī*), f., see below; (*bád*°) n. the edible fruit of the jujube (also used as a weight), VS. &c. &c.; the berry or fruit of the cotton shrub, L. **-kuṇa,** m. the time when the fruit of the jujube becomes ripe, g. *pīlv-ādi*. **-dvīpa,** m. N. of a place, Divyâv. **-pācana,** n. 'j°-ripening,' N. of a sacred bathing-place, MBh. **-phalī,** f. a species of j° tree, L. **-yūsha,** m. a decoction of the fruit of the jujube, Suśr. **-vallī,** f. a species of j° tree, L. **-saktú,** m. pl. meal of the fruit of the j°, ŚBr.; MaitrBr. **Badarâmalaka,** n. Flacourtia Cataphracta (rather its fruit), L.

Badarikā, f. the fruit or berry of the jujube, Hit.; N. of one of the sources of the Ganges and the neighbouring hermitage of Nara and Nārāyana (= *badarī*), Hariv.; Kathās. &c. **-khaṇḍa,** m. or n. N. of ch. of SkandaP. **-tīrtha,** n. N. of a sacred bathing-place, MBh. **-māhātmya-saṃgraha,** m., **-vana-māhātmya,** n. N. of wks. **Badarikâśrama,** m. N. of a hermitage (cf. above); *-māhātmya*, n., *-yātrā-vidhi*, m. N. of wks.

Badarī, f. the jujube tree (also wrongly for its berry), ŚāṅkhŚr.; MBh. &c.; the cotton shrub, L.; Mucuna Pruritus, L.; N. of one of the sources of the Ganges &c. (= *badarikā*), MBh.; Kāv. &c. **-kedāra-māhātmya,** n. N. of wk. **-cchada,** m., °**dā,** f. Unguis Odoratus, L.; (*ā*), f. a kind of jujube, L. **-tapovana,** n. the penance grove or hermitage at Badarī, Kir. **-nātha,** m. N. of a temple at B°, W.; of sev. authors, Cat. **-nārāyaṇa,** m. N. of a place, Cat. **-pattra,** m., °**aka,** n. Unguis Odoratus, L. **-pācana,** n. = °*ra-pācana*, MBh. **-prastha,** m. N. of a city, g. *karky-ādi*. **-phalā,** f. a Vitex with blue flowers, L. **-māhātmya,** n. N. of ch. of SkandaP. **-vaṇa,** n. N. of a wood, Pāṇ. viii, 4, 6, Sch. **-vana,** n. id., ib.; *-māhātmya*, n. N. of wk. **-vāsā,** f. 'dwelling at B°,' N. of Durgā, L. **-śaila,** m. 'rock of B°,' N. of a place of pilgrimage (the Bhadrināth of modern travellers), Pur.

बद्ध *baddha* &c. See p. 720, col. 2.

बद्धप्पि *baddhappi* (?), n. the clasped hand, fist, L. (v. l. *baddhāppi*).

बद्धृ *báddhṛi*, wrongly for *vadhṛi*, ŚBr.

बद्बधाना *badbadhānā́*. See √*bādh*.

बड्व *badva*, n. (once m.) a large number, multitude (Sāy. '100 Koṭis;' others '10,000 millions;' BhP., Sch. 'the number 13,084'), Br.; MBh.; BhP. — **śas**, ind. in large numbers, AitBr.

बड्वन् *badvan*, m. a causeway, highway, PañcavBr.; Lāṭy.

बध् *badh*, *bádhya*, even in Vedic texts sometimes = *vadh*, *vádhya*.

Badhya-tás, ind. (freedom) from the crowd, AV. xii, 1, 2 (v.l. *madhya-tás*).

बधिर *badhirá* &c. See col. 3.

बधू *badhū́*, f., wrongly for *vadhū́*, AV. viii, 6, 14.

बध्योग *badhyoga*, m. N. of a man, g. *bidâdi* (cf. *bādhyoga*).

बध्व *badhva*, m. N. of a man, AitĀr. (cf. *bādhva*).

बन्द् *band*. See √*bad*, p. 719, col. 3.

बन्दि 1. *bandi*(?), m. a Buddhist pupil, MWB. 263 (cf. n. 1).

1. **Bandī-kṛita**, mfn. (for 2. see *bandī*) turned Buddhist, Nalac. (Sch. 'fr. *banda*, a Buddhist').

बन्दिआरयु *bandiārayu*, N. of a place mentioned in the Romakas., Cat.

बन्दिन् 1. *bandin*, m. (also written *vandin*, q.v., and m.c. °*di*) a praiser, bard, herald (who sings the praises of a prince in his presence or accompanies an army to chant martial songs; these bards are regarded as the descendants of a Kshatriya by a Śūdra female), Mn.; MBh. &c.

2. **Bandi**, in comp. for °*din*. — **tā**, f. (Rājat.), -**tva**, n. (Bhām.) the state or condition of a bard. — **pāṭha**, m. the panegyric of a bard, L. — **putra**, m. = *bandin*, Ragh. — **strī**, f. a female bard, Kull. on Mn. x, 48.

बन्दिन् 2. *bandin*, m. (also written *vandin*) a prisoner, captive, slave, BhP.; plunder, spoil (see *-grāha*).

3. **Bandi**, in comp. for °*din*. — **graha**, m. taking prisoner, capture, Mcar. — **grāha** (Yājñ.), -**caura** (L.), m. 'plunder-seizer,' a housebreaker (esp. one breaking into a temple or place where sacred fire is preserved), burglar, robber. — **śālikā**, f. a prison, Gal. — **śūlā**, f. a harlot, prostitute, ib. — **sthita**, mfn. sitting in prison, imprisoned, Kum.

Bandī, f. (cf. Pers. بندی) a male or female prisoner, Kālid.; Bhaṭṭ.; prey, booty, spoil, BhP. — **kāra**, m. 'booty-maker,' a robber, thief, L. — 2. -**kṛita**, mfn. made prisoner, taken captive, Kālid.; Kathās. (m. a prisoner, Bālar.; Hcat.); seized i.e. overwhelmed, Bālar. — **gṛihīta**, mfn. robbed, Kād. — **graha**, m. plunder, spoil, BhP., Sch. — **pāla**, m. 'keeper of prisoners,' a jailor, MW.

बन्ध् *bandh*, cl. 9. P. (Dhātup. xxxi, 37) *badhnā́ti* (rarely Ā. *badhnīté*; cl. 1. P.Ā. *bandhati*, °*te*, MBh.; cl. 4. P. *badhyati*, Hariv.; Impv. *badhāna*, AV., *bandhāna*, MBh., *-badhnīhi*, BhP., *bandha*, R.; pf. P. *babándha*, 3. pl. *bedhús*, AV., *babandhus*, MBh.; Ā. *bedhé*, °*dhiré*, AV., *babandhe*, Gr.; fut. *bhantsyati*, Br. &c., *bandhishyati*, °*te*, MBh.; *banddhā*, Gr.; aor. *abhāntsīt*, Gr.; Prec. *badhyāt*, ib.; inf. *banddhum* or *bandhitum*, R., *bádhe*, AV., ind. p. *baddhvā́*, AV., °*dhvā́ya*, Br., *-badhya*, ib.; *-bandham*, Pāṇ. iii, 4, 41, Sch.), to bind, tie, fix, fasten, chain, fetter, RV. &c. &c.; to bind round, put on (Ā.; later also P. 'on one's self') AV.; ŚBr.; MBh. &c.; to catch, take or hold captive, met. = to attach to world or to sin, Mn.; MBh.; Kap.; to fix, direct, fasten, rivet (eyes, ears or mind) on (loc. or inf.), MBh.; Kāv.; Kathās.; to arrest, hold back, restrain, suppress, stop, shut, close, Yājñ.; MBh.; Kathās.; to bind a sacrificial victim, offer, sacrifice (with dat. of the deity to whom it is presented), RV.; Br.; KātyŚr.; to punish, chastise, Hit.; to join, unite, put together or produce anything in this way, e.g. fold (the hands), clench (the fist), knit or bend (the eyebrows), arrange, assume (a posture), set up (a limit), construct (a dam or a bridge), span, bridge over (a river), conceive or contract (friendship or enmity), compose, construct (a poem or verse), MBh.; Kāv. &c.; to form or produce in any way, cause, effect, do, make, bear (fruit), strike (roots), take up (one's abode), ib.; to entertain, cherish, show, exhibit, betray (joy, resolution &c.), ib.: Pass. *badhyáte* (°*ti*, Hariv.), to be bound &c. &c.; (esp.) to be bound by the fetters of existence or evil, sin again, Mn.; BhP.; to be affected by i.e. experience, suffer (instr.), Pañcat.: Caus. *bandhayati* (aor. *ababandhat*), to cause to bind or catch or capture, imprison, ŚBr. &c. &c.; to cause to be built or constructed, Ragh.; Rājat.; to cause to be embanked or dammed up, Rājat.; to bind together (also *bādhayati*), Dhātup. xxxii, 14: Desid. *bibhantsati*, Gr.: Intens. *bābanddhi*, *bābadhyate*, ib. [Cf. Zd. *band*; Gr. πενθερός, πεῖσμα; Lat. *foedus*, *fides*; Lit. *bèndras*; Goth. Angl. Sax. *bindan*; Germ. *binden*; Eng. *bind*.]

Baddhá, mfn. bound, tied, fixed, fastened, chained, fettered, RV. &c. &c.; captured, imprisoned, caught, confined, ib. (*śatāt*, 'for a debt of a hundred,' Pāṇ. ii, 3, 24, Sch.); bound by the fetters of existence or evil, Kap.; hanged, hung, R.; tied up (as a braid of hair), Megh.; (ifc.) stopped, checked, obstructed, impeded, restrained, suppressed, MBh.; Kāv. &c.; girt with, ŚāṅkhŚr.; (with instr. or ifc.) inlaid or studded with, set in, MBh.; Kāv. &c.; attached to, riveted or fixed on (loc.), ib.; joined, united, combined, formed, produced, ib.; composed (as verses), R.; (esp. ibc.; cf. below) conceived, formed, entertained, manifested, shown, betrayed, visible, apparent (cf. *jāta*, ibc.), MBh. Kāv. &c.; clenched (as the fist), Hariv.; R.; folded (as the hands), Mṛicch.; contracted (as friendship or enmity), R.; Śak.; taken up (as an abode), Rājat.; built, constructed (as a bridge), R.; Ragh.; embanked (as a river), Rājat.; congealed, clotted (as blood; opp. to *drava*), Suśr.; alloyed (as quicksilver), L.; m. or n.? (with Jainas) that which binds or fetters the embodied spirit (viz. the connection of the soul with deeds), MW. — **kakshya**, mfn. = *-parikara*, Baudh. — **kadambaka**, mfn. forming groups, Śak. — **kalāpin**, mfn. one who has his quiver tied on, MBh. — **kesara**, mfn. having the filaments formed, Suśr. — **guda**, n. a kind of obstruction of the bowels, Suśr.; °*din*, mfn. suffering from it, ib. — **godhâṅgulitra-vat**, mfn. having the (finger-protectors called) Godhā and Aṅguli-tra fastened on, MBh. — **graha**, mfn. insisting on something, Kathās. — **citta**, mfn. having the thoughts fixed upon (loc.), MBh. — **jihva**, mfn. tongue-tied, Śiksh. — **tūṇīra**, mfn. equipped with a quiver, MBh. — **tṛishṇa**, mfn. (ifc.) desirous of, longing for, Ragh. — **darbha**, m. a stick bound with Darbha grass, L. — **dṛishṭi**, mfn. having one's gaze fixed on (loc.), Śak. — **dvesha**, mfn. entertaining hatred, Rājat. — **niścaya**, mf(*ā*)n. firmly resolved, resolute, MBh.; Kathās. — **nishyanda** or -**nisyanda**, mfn. having the flow or discharge of anything impeded, Suśr.; impeding it, ib. — **netra**, mf(*ā*)n. having the eyes fixed on anything, gazing steadfastly, MBh. — **nepathya**, mfn. attired in a theatrical dress, R. — **paṅka-vat**, mfn. having the mud hardened, Hariv. — **parikara**, mfn. having the girdle girded on, i.e. ready, prepared for anything, Ratnâv. — **purīsha**, mfn. having constipated bowels (*-tva*, n.), Suśr. — **pṛishṇa** or -**pṛishṭha**, m. N. of a man, L. — **pratijña**, mf(*ā*)n. one who has made a promise or vow, Kathās. — **pratiśrut**, mfn. echoing, resonant with echoes, Ragh. — **phala**, m. Pongamia Glabra, L. — **bhāva**, mf(*ā*)n. one who has fixed his affection upon, enamoured of (loc.), Vikr.; Kathās. — **bhīmândhakāra**, mf(*ā*)n. wrapped in terrible darkness, Śṛiṅgār. — **bhū** or **bhūmi**, f. prepared ground, pavement, L.; °*mika*, mfn. having a pavement, L. — **maṇḍala**, mfn. having circles formed, ranged in circles, Ragh. — **mushṭi**, mfn. having a closed hand, L.; close-fisted, covetous, Naish.; *-tva*, n., Kathās. — **mūtra**, mfn. obstructing the urine, Suśr. — **mūla**, mf(*ā*)n. firmly rooted, one who has gained a firm footing, Kāv.; Rājat.; *-tā*, f., Kathās. — **mauna**, mfn. observing silence, silent, R.; Hariv. — **rabhasa**, mf(*ā*)n. impetuous, passionate, Rājat. — **rasāla**, m. a highly prized species of Mango, L. — **rāga**, mfn. one who has formed an affection for, fond of (loc.), Pañcat. — **rājya**, mfn. one who has gained sovereignty, succeeded to the throne, Rājat. — **laksha**, mfn. (ifc.) = *-dṛishṭi*, Vikr. — **vatsa** (*baddhá-*), mfn. (a cow) whose calf has been tied up (in the stable), ŚBr. — **varcas**, mfn. obstructing the bowels, Suśr. — **vasati**, mfn. having one's abode fixed, dwelling in (loc.), Rājat. — **vāc**, mfn. obstructing speech, BhP. — **viṭka**, mfn. having one's bowels obstructed (*-tā*, f.), Suśr. — **viṇ-mūtra**, mfn. obstructing the feces and urine, Suśr. — **vīra** (*baddhá-*), mfn. one whose heroes or retainers have been bound, TS. — **vepathu**, mfn. seized with tremor, trembling, Daś. — **vaira**, mf(*ā*)n. one who has contracted hostility with (instr. or comp.), R.; Śak. — **śas**, w.r. for *badva-śas* (col. 1). — **śikha**, mfn. having the hair bound up (into a knot on the crown of the head), L.; not yet tonsured i.e. young, L.; (*ā*), f. a species of plant, L. — **śrotra-manaś-cakshus**, mfn. having ears and mind and eyes fixed on (loc.), MBh. — **sūta**, m. a partic. preparation of quicksilver, Sarvad. — **sneha**, mfn. conceiving affection for (loc.), Kathās. — **spṛiha**, mfn. (ifc.) feeling a longing for, Bhartṛ. **Baddhâṅguli-tra** or °**li-trāṇa**, mfn. having the finger-guard fastened on, MBh. **Baddhâñjali**, mfn. one who has joined the hollowed palms of the hands (cf. *añjali*), Mṛicch.; *-puṭa*, mfn. forming a cup with the hollowed h°, R. **Baddhâdara**, mfn. (ifc.) attaching great value to, Subh. **Baddhânanda**, mfn. having pleasure attached, joyful (as a day), Kathās. **Baddhânurāga**, mf(*ā*)n. feeling affection, enamoured, ib. **Baddhânuśaya**, mfn. conceiving an intense hatred, R. **Baddhândhakāra**, mfn. wrapped in darkness, Kathās. **Baddhâmbu**, n. water derived from a current, L. **Baddhâyudha**, mfn. accoutred with arms, MBh. **Baddhâvasthiti**, mfn. constant, Rājat. **Baddhâśa**, mfn. (ifc.) entertaining hope of, Kathās. **Baddhâśaṅka**, mfn. filled with anxiety or suspicion, Kathās. **Baddhôtsava**, mfn. enjoying a festival or holiday, ib. **Baddhôdyama**, mfn. making united efforts, Rājat.

Báddhaka, m. one who is bound, a captive, prisoner, AV. — **mócana**, n. setting free a prisoner, ib.

Badhirá, mf(*ā*)n. (sometimes written *vadhira*) deaf, RV. &c. &c.; m. N. of a serpent-demon (son of Kaśyapa), MBh. — **tama**, mfn. quite deaf, Kāv. — **tā**, f., -**tva**, n. deafness, ib. **Badhirândha**, m. 'deaf and blind,' N. of a serpent-demon, MBh. (cf. above).

Badhiraka, m. N. of a man (pl. 'his descendants'), g. *upakâdi*; (*ikā*), f. N. of a woman, g. *śivâdi*.

Badhiraya, Nom. P. °*yati*, to make deaf, deafen. Daś.; Mcar.

Badhirita, mfn. made deaf, deafened, Daś.; Kād.; Prab.

Badhiriman, m. deafness, g. *dṛiḍhâdi*.

Badhirī-√kṛi, P. *-karoti*, to make deaf, deafen, Prab. — **kṛita**, mfn. deafened, MBh.; Kathās.

Bandhá, m. binding, tying, a bond, tie, chain, fetter, RV. &c. &c.; a ligature, bandage, Suśr.; damming up (a river), MārkP.; capture, arrest, imprisonment, custody, Mn.; MBh. &c.; connection or intercourse with (comp.), Pañcat.; BhP. (ifc. = connected with, conducive to, MBh.); putting together, uniting, contracting, combining, forming, producing, MBh.; Kāv. &c.; joining (the hollowed hands), Ragh.; anything deposited (°*dhe* √*sthā* = to remain deposited), Campak.; a deposit, pledge, Rājat.; any configuration or position of the body (esp. of the hands and feet), Ragh.; Kum.; a partic. mode of sexual union (there are said to be 16, 18, 36, or even 84, L.), Caur.; constructing, building (of a bridge &c.), MBh.; Rājat.; bridging over (the sea), Vcar.; knitting (the brows), Rājat.; fixing, directing (mind, eyes, &c.), Cat.; assumption, obtainment (of a body), Ragh.; (ifc.) conceiving, cherishing, feeling, betraying, Hariv.; Kālid.; a border, framework, inclosure, receptacle, L.; a sinew, tendon, L.; the body, L.; (in phil.) mundane bondage, attachment to this world, ŚvetUp.; Bhag. &c. (opp. to *mukti*, *moksha*, 'final emancipation,' and regarded in the Sāṃkhya as threefold, viz. *prakṛiti-*, *vaikārika-*, and *dakshiṇā-b°*); combination of sounds (in rhet.), construction or arrangement of words, Kāvyâd.; Pratāp.; arrangement of a stanza in a partic. shape, Kpr.; arrangement of musical sounds, composition, Śatr.; a disease which prevents the eyelids from quite closing, Suśr.; (ifc. with numerals) a part (cf. *pañca-*, *daśa-b°*). — **kampa**, m. N. of a poet, Cat. — **karaṇa**, n. binding, fettering, holding back (also by magic), Kathās. — **kartṛi**, m. a binder, fetterer, restrainer (said of Śiva), MBh. — **kaumudī**, f. N. of a poem and a wk. on metrics. — **tantra**, n. a complete army (possessing the 4 divisions of chariots, elephants, horse, and foot), W. — **traya-vidhāna**, n. N. of wk. — **deśa**, m. N. of a country, Cat. — **nṛit-

ya, n. (in music) a kind of dance, Saṃgīt. **—pārushya**, n. forced construction of words, Pratāp. **—pāśá**, m. a bond, fetter, AV. **—maya**, mf(ī)n. consisting of bonds, serving for or being like a bond, MW. **—mudrā**, f. the impression or mark of fetters, ib. **—mocanikā** or **-mocinī**, f. 'releasing from bonds,' N. of a Yoginī, Kathās. **—vimocana-stotra**, n. N. of a Stotra. **—stambha**, m. 'binding-post,' the post to which an elephant is tied, L.

Bandhaka, m. a binder, one who is employed in binding (esp. animals), MBh.; a catcher (see *nāga-* and *pāśa-b°*); a violator, ravisher, L.; a band, tie (see *paśu-b°*); a dam, dike (see *jala-b°*); a promise, vow, L.; exchanging, barter, W.; a city, L.; (ifc. with numerals) a part (see *sa-daśa-b°*); m. or n. (?) pledging or a pledge (see *sa-b°*); (ī), f. ('connected,' scil. with many men), an unchaste woman, harlot, courtezan, MBh.; Kāv. &c.; a barren woman, L. (cf. *bandhyā*); a female elephant, L.; n. binding, confinement, W. **—tva**, n. the being a fetter, Sāṃkhyak., Sch.

Bándhana, mf(ī)n. binding, tying, fettering, RV. &c. &c.; captivating (with gen. or ifc.; cf. *bhava-b°* and Pāṇ. iv, 4, 96, Sch.); holding fast, stopping, MW.; (ifc.) dependent on, ib.; n. the act of binding, tying, fastening, fettering, Mn.; MBh. &c.; (also ī, f., L.) a bond, tie (also fig.), rope, cord, tether, ŚBr. &c. &c. (ifc. with f. *ā* = bound to or fettered by); binding on or round, clasping, Kāv.; Pañcat.; binding up, bandaging, a bandage, Suśr.; catching, capturing, confining, detention, custody, imprisonment or a prison, Mn.; Kathās.; Pur.; building, construction, MBh.; R. &c.; embanking or an embankment, ib.; bridging over, Hit.; alloying (of metals), Bhpr.; joining, junction, connection, coherence, RV.; MBh.; fixing upon, directing towards (loc.), L.; checking, suppressing, Amar.; (in phil.) mundane bondage (opp. to final liberation); hurting, killing, L.; a stalk, stem, peduncle (of a flower), RV. &c. &c.; a sinew, muscle, L. **—kārin**, mfn. (ifc.) fettering, i. e. clasping, embracing (°*ri-tā*, f.), Daś. **—granthi**, m. a noose, rope for tying cattle, L. **—pālaka**, m. a gaol-keeper, L. **—rajju**, f. a rope or string for tying, MW. **—veśman**, n. 'house of bondage,' a prison, L. **—stha**, mfn. being in prison or captivity, a captive, prisoner, Kālid.; ŚārṅgP. **—sthāna**, n. 'place for fastening,' a stall, stable, L. **Bandhanâgāra**, n. = °*na-veśman*, Mṛicch. **Bandhanâdhikāra**, m. N. of 3rd ch. of 1st part of the Rasêndra-kalpa-druma (q. v.) **Bandhanâlaya**, m. = °*na-veśman*, L.

Bandhanika, m. a gaoler, turnkey, Gaut.; Vishṇ.

Bandhanīya, mfn. to be (or being) bound or tied, Kathās.; Śak., Sch.; to be captured or taken prisoner, Inscr.; to be embanked, R. (Sch. 'm. = *setu*, embankment').

Bandhayitṛi, m. (fr. Caus.) one who binds or ties up, a binder, Kull. on Mn. viii, 342.

Bandhi, m. N. of an Asura, L.

Bandhita, mfn. (fr. Caus.) caused to be bound (*śatena*, 'imprisoned for a hundred pieces of money'), Pāṇ. ii, 3, 24, Sch.

Bandhitra, n. (!) the god of love, love, L. (cf. *vadhitra*); a spot, mole, L.

Bandhin, mfn. binding, clasping (cf. *dṛiḍha-bandhinī*); catching (cf. *matsya-bandhin*); causing, effecting, producing (cf. *phala-b°*, *rāga-b°*); showing, evincing, betraying (cf. *vātsalya-b°*).

Bándhu, m. connection, relation, association, RV. &c. &c. (ifc. with f. *ū* = belonging to, coming under the head of, i. e. 'being only in name;' cf. *kshatra-*, *dvija-b°* &c.; 'resembling' Bālar. v, 66, 'frequented by' ib. iii, 20, 'favourable for' ib. iv, 87; cf. Pāṇ. vi, 1, 14); respect, reference (*kena bandhunā*, 'in what respect?'), ŚBr.; kinship, kindred, Mn. ii, 136; a kinsman (esp. on the mother's side), relative, kindred, RV. &c. &c. (in law, a cognate kinsman in a remote degree, one subsequent in right of inheritance to the Sa-gotra; three kinds are enumerated, personal, paternal and maternal); a friend (opp. to *ripu*), MBh.; Kāv.; BhP.; a husband, Ragh.; a brother, L.; Pentapetes Phoenicea, L. (= *bandhūka*); N. of a metre, Col.; (in astrol.) of the fourth mansion, Var.; of a Ṛishi with the patr. Gaupāyana or Laupāyana (author of RV. v, 24 and x, 56-60), RAnukr.; of Manmatha, L. **—kāma**, mfn. loving relations or friends, MBh. **—kṛit**, see *á-bandhukṛit*. **—kṛitya**, n. the duty of a kinsman, friendly service, MBh.; Kāv.; Pur. **—kshít**, mfn. dwelling among relations, RV. **—jana**, m. a kinsman, friend, Bhartṛ.; kinsfolk, relations, MBh.; R. **—jīva**, m. 'living in groups,' Pentapetes Phoenicea (a plant with a red flower which opens at midday and withers away the next morning); n. its flower, Kāv.; Suśr.; °*vâbhitāmra*, mfn. deep-red like the blossom of P° Ph°, Hariv. **—jīvaka**, m. = prec. m., Suśr.; N. of a Cakra-vartin, Kathās. **—jīvin**, m. a kind of ruby, L. **—tā** (°*dhú-*), f. connection, relation, kinship, RV.; TS.; Br.; relations, kinsfolk, Mālatīm. **—tva**, n. relationship, affinity, R. **—dagdha**, mfn. 'cursed by relations,' an abandoned wretch (= *hataka*), L. **—datta**, mfn. 'given by r°,' Yājñ.; m. N. of a man, W.; (*ā*), f. N. of a woman, Kathās. **—dāyāda**, m. kinsman and heir, Mn. ix, 158; mfn. entitled to inheritance by relationship, MBh. **—pati**, m. lord of kindred or relations, g. *aśvapaty-ādi*. **—pāla**, m. 'kindred-protector,' N. of a man, Daś. **—pālita**, m. 'k°-protected,' N. of a prince, VP. **—pushpamāla**, mfn. wearing a chaplet of Bandhu flowers, MW. **—pṛich**, mfn. seeking or caring for relations, RV. iii, 54, 16 (cf. *pṛishṭa-bandhu*). **—prabha**, m. N. of a Vidyā-dhara, Kathās. **—priya**, mfn. dear to friends or relations, MBh. **—prīti**, f. love of f° or r°, Megh. **—bhāva**, m. relationship, friendship, Kathās. **—bhāshita**, n. the talk or speech of relations, MW. **—mat** (*bándhu-*), mfn. having relations, RV. &c. &c.; surrounded by r°, Ragh.; m. N. of a king, Pur.; of another man, Cat.; (*atī*), f. N. of sev. women, Daś.; Kathās.; of a town, Divyâv.; °*tīyaka*, mfn. belonging to this town, ib. **—mitra**, m. 'friend of relations,' N. of a man, Kathās. **—vañcaka**, m. 'deceiver of r°,' N. of a Vidūshaka, Dhūrtas. **—1. -vat**, mfn. having r°, MW. **—2. -vat**, ind. like a r°, Mn. **—varga**, m. the whole body of r°, kindred, MW. **—hīna**, mfn. destitute of r°, friendless, W. **Bandhv-eshá**, m. inquiring after kindred, RV.

Bandhuka, m. Pentapetes Phoenicea, L.; a bastard, L. (cf. *bandhula*); (*ā*), f., g. *prêkshâdi*; (ī), f. an unchaste woman, L. (cf. *bandhakī*). °**kin**, mfn., g. *prêkshâdi*.

1. **Bandhura**, mf(*ā*)n. (Uṇ. i, 42, Sch.; cf. Vām. v, 2, 42) bent, inclined, Kāv.; Pañcat.; curved, rounded, pleasant, beautiful, charming, Inscr.; Kālid.; Caur.; (ifc.) adorned with, Kād.; undulating, uneven, L.; deaf, L. (cf. *badhira*); injurious, mischievous, W.; m. (only L.) a bird; a goose; Ardea Nivea; Pentapetes Phoenicea; Embelia Ribes; a partic. bulbous plant growing on the Hima-vat mountain, L.; oil-cake; the vulva, L.; (*ā*), f. a harlot, L.; N. of a procuress, Hāsy.; (pl.) the meal of parched corn, L.; n. a diadem, crest, L. **—komalâṅguli**, mfn. (a hand) that has rounded or delicate fingers, Śak. **—gātrī**, f. (a woman) who has lovely or rounded limbs, Ragh.

Bandhurita, mfn. inclined, bent, Sāh.; curved, Bālar.

Bandhurīya, w. r. for *bandhur esha*, MBh. vi, 2659.

Bandhula, mfn. inclined, bent, depressed, L.; lovely, charming, L.; m. a bastard, Mṛicch.; Pentapetes Phoenicea, L.; N. of a Ṛishi, Pravar. **Bandhulânvaya**, m. the posterity of Bandhula, MW.

Bandhū, in comp. for °*dhu*. **—√kṛi**, to make a friend of, bring into connection with (comp.), Bālar. **—kṛita**, mfn. made a friend, Sāh. **—√bhū**, to become a relative of, become like, resemble, Naish.

Bandhūka, m. Pentapetes Phoenicea (n. its flower), Kāv.; Kathās.; Suśr.; Terminalia Tomentosa, L. **—pushpa**, n. the flower of P° Ph° (*-rajas*, n. its pollen), Ṛitus.; Terminalia Tomentosa, L.

Bandhūra, mfn. (Uṇ. i, 42, Sch.) bent, wavy, uneven, L.; lovely, charming, L.; m. a hole, chasm, L.

Bandhūli, m. Pentapetes Phoenicea, L.

Bandhya, mfn. to be bound or fettered or imprisoned, Yājñ.; to be constructed, ib., Sch. (cf. *vandhya*). **Bandhyâśva**, prob. w. r. for *vadhryaśva*, q. v.

बन्धाकि *bandhāki*, m. a mountain, L.

बन्धुर 2. *bándhura*, n. (for 1. see above) = *vandhura*, VS.; AV.; MBh. (B.)

बप्प *bappa* and *bappaka*, m. N. of a prince, Inscr.

बप्यनील *bapyanīla*, N. of a country, Rājat.

बप्स् *baps*. See √*bhas*.

बफार *baphāra* and *babakāṇa*, m. or n. (?) N. of places, Cat.

बबबा *bababā*, ind. an onomat. word; with √*kṛi*, to crackle (as fire), AitBr.

बबर *babará*, m. N. of a man, TS.; of a place, Cat.

बबाड *babāḍa*, m. N. of a village, Inscr.

बबूआण *babūāṇa*, m. or n. (?) N. of a place, Cat.

बबृहाणा *babṛihāṇá*. See √2. *bṛih*.

बब्बुल *babbula* (Subh.) and *babbūla* (ŚārṅgP.), m. Acacia Arabica (cf. *varvūra*).

बभस *babhasa*, m. (√*bhas*) a devourer, ChUp.

बभूक *babhūka*, w. r. for *babhruka*, VarBṛS.

बभ्र *babhra* (√*bhṛi*), in *pra-babhra*, q. v.

Babhrí, mfn. bearing, carrying (with acc.), RV. vi, 23, 4; being carried, ib. iii, 1, 12 (others 'carrying away' i. e. victorious); nourishing (?), AV. xi, 1, 31.

बभ्रवी *babhravī*, prob. w. r. for *bābhravī*, q. v.

बभ्रु *babhrú*, mf(*u* or *ū*)n. (according to Uṇ. i, 23 fr. √*bhṛi*) deep-brown, reddish-brown, tawny, RV. &c. &c.; bald-headed, L.; m. a kind of large ichneumon, L.; any ichneumon, MBh.; Hariv.; a man with deep-brown hair, Mn. iv, 30 (others 'a reddish-brown animal' or 'the Soma creeper'); Cuculus Melanoleucus (= *cātaka*), L.; a species of vegetable, L.; N. of Kṛishṇa-Vishṇu or of Śiva, MBh.; a king, prince, ib.; a partic. constellation (= *babhruka*), VarBṛS., Sch.; N. of sev. men (cf. g. *gargâdi*); of a descendant of Atri (author of RV. v, 30), Anukr. (also with the patr. Daivāvṛidha and Kaumbhya, Br.; MBh.; Pur.); of a disciple of Śaunaka, VP.; of a son of Viśva-mitra, MBh. (also pl., Hariv.); of a son of Viśva-garbha, Hariv.; of a Vṛishṇi, MBh.; Hariv.; of a son of Druhyu, Hariv.; of a son of Roma-pāda or Loma-pāda, ib.; of a Gandharva, R.; of a country (= *-deśa*), L.; (*u*), f. a reddish-brown cow, BhP.; n. a dark-brown colour or any object of that c°, W. [Cf. Gk. φρύνη, φρῦνος; Lith. *béras, brúnas;* Germ. *brūn, braun;* Eng. *brown.*] **—karṇa** (°*bhrú-*), mf(ī)n. brown-eared, AV.; TS. **—keśa**, mf(ī)n. brown-haired, ĀpGṛ., Sch. **—deśa**, m. N. of a country, Cat. **—dhātu**, m. red ochre, L. **—dhūta** (°*bhrú-*), mfn. pressed out by Babhru (as Soma), RV. **—nīkāśa** (°*bhrú-*), mfn. appearing or looking brownish, VS. **—piṅgala**, mfn. reddish-brown, MBh. **—mālin**, m. 'brown-garlanded,' N. of a Muni, ib. **—loman** (°*bhrú-*), mf(*mnī*)n. brown-haired, MaitrS.; ĀpŚr. **—vaktra**, mfn. 'ichneumon-faced,' having the face of an i°, MW. **—vāha**, m. = next, Cat. **—vāhana**, m. N. of a son of Arjuna, king of Mahôdaya, MBh.; Pur. **—smṛiti**, f. N. of wk.

Babhruká, mfn. brownish, ŚBr.; (*bábhr°*), m. (prob.) a kind of ichneumon, VS.; GopBr.; N. of a constellation (near which all planets pass when in the 7th and 10th houses), VarBṛS., Sch.

Babhruśa, mfn., g. *lomâdi*.

Babhluśá, mfn. brownish, VS.; MaitrS.

बम्ब् *bamb*, cl. 1. P. *bambati*, to go, Dhātup. xi, 24, 25.

बम्बगैरव *bambagairava*, m. or n. (?) N. of a place, Cat.

बम्बविश्ववयस् *bamba-viśvavayas* (MaitrS.) and *bambā-viśvavayas* (TS.; cf. g. *vanaspaty-ādi*, Kāś.), m. du. N. of 2 men (also *bambhār-viśvavayas*, Kāṭh.)

बम्बुरेवण *bamburevaṇa*, m. or n. (?) N. of a place, Cat.

बम्भर *bambhara*, m. a bee, L.

Bambharâlī or °**lī**, f. a fly, L.

बम्भारव *bambhā-rava*, m. lowing (of cows), Var. (cf. *bhambhārava*).

बम्भारि *bambhāri*, m. N. of one of the 7 tutelary deities of the Soma plant, VS.

बर *bara*, m. N. of Bala-rāma (= *bala*), L.

बरट *baraṭa*, m. a species of grain, Gṛihyās. (cf. *barbaṭa*).

बरासी *barāsī*, f. a partic. article of clothing or kind of woven cloth, MaitrS.; Br.; ŚrS. (also spelt *varāsi* and *varāsī*).

बरिशी *bariśī*, f. (also written *var°*) a fish-hook, L.

बरीवर्द *barīvarda*, m. (also written *var°*) = *balīvarda*, a bull, L.

बरु *baru*, m. N. of a descendant of Aṅgiras (author of RV. x, 96), Br.; ŚrS.

बरोदा *barodā*, f. N. of a country and city in Gujarāt, Cat.

बर्कर *barkara*, mfn. deaf, Gal.; m. (also written *varkara*) a kid, lamb, ĀpŚr.; a goat, L.; any young animal, L.; sport, joke, L. **—karkara**, mfn. (?) of all kinds, Amar.

बर्कु *bárku*, m. N. of a man with the patr. Vārshṇa, ŚBr.

बर्जर *barjara*, m. or n. (?) N. of a place, Cat.

बर्जह *bárjaha*, m. an udder, RV.

Barjahyà, n. a nipple, AV.

बर्ब् *barb*, cl. 1. P. *barbati*, to go, move, Dhātup. xi, 24.

बर्बट *barbaṭa*, m. Dolichos Catjang, L. (cf. *baraṭa*); (*ī*), f. id., L.; a harlot, L.

बर्बर *barbara*, mfn. (also written *varvara*) stammering (see *-tā*); curly, Kāṭh.; m. (pl.) the non-Āryans, barbarians, MBh.; R. &c.; the country of the barbarians, W.; a low fellow, blockhead, fool, loon (used mostly in the voc.), Hit.; (only L.) curly hair; Clerodendrum Siphonantus; Cleome Pentaphylla; a partic. fragrant plant; Unguis Odoratus; a kind of worm; two kinds of fish; the noise of weapons; a kind of dance; (*ā*), f. a kind of fly, L.; a species of Ocimum, L.; a kind of vegetable, L.; a partic. flower, L.; N. of a river, VP.; (*ī*), f., see below; n. vermilion, L.; gum-myrrh, L.; yellow sandal-wood, L.; = *barbarī*, f. and *°rīka*, n. **—tā**, f. a partic. stammering pronunciation of the letter *r*, RPrāt. **—sthāna**, n. N. of a district, MW. **Barbarôttha**, n. white sandal-wood, L.

Barbari, m. N. of a man, Cat. (cf. *varvara*).

Barbarita, mfn., g. *kāśâdi*.

Barbarin, mfn. curly-haired, Pañcad.

Barbarī, f. a species of Ocimum, Bhpr.; = *barbara*, n. and *°rīka*, n.; N. of a river, VP. **—gandha**, m. a partic. plant (= *aja-modā*), L.

Barbarīka, n. (only L.) curly hair or a partic. mode of wearing the hair; a kind of vegetable; Ocimum Villosum; Clerodendrum Siphonantus; m. a form of Śiva. **Barbarīkôpâkhyāna**, n. N. of ch. of the SkandaP.

बर्बा *barbā*, f. a species of Ocimum, L.

बर्बुर *barburá*, n. (or m.) water, Naigh. i, 12; m. = *babbula*, Subh.

बर्स *barsá*, m. n. tip, point, thin end, TS.; Br. **—naddhi**, f. the tying of a knot, AitBr.

बर्स्व *bársva*, m. (prob.) the socket of a tooth, VS.; Kāṭh.

बर्ह् *barh* or *varh* (cf. √*bṛih*, *vṛih*), cl. 1. Ā. *barhate* (only Dhātup. xvi, 39), to speak; to hurt; to give or cover (*dāna*, v.l. *chādana*); cl. 10. P. (xxxiii, 96) to speak; to shine.

बर्ह *barha*, m. n. (also written *varha*; √1. *bṛih*, 'to pluck out') a tail-feather, the tail of a bird (esp. of a peacock), MBh.; Kāv. &c.; a leaf (*ketaka-b°*), Ragh.; n. a kind of perfume, L. **—ketu**, m. N. of a son of Sagara, Hariv.; of a son of the ninth Manu, MārkP. **—candraka**, m. and **-netra**, n. the eye in a peacock's tail, L. **—pushpa**, n. Acacia Sirissa, L. **—bhāra**, m. 'burden of feathers,' a peacock's tail, Hariv.; Megh.; a tuft of p°'s feathers on the shaft of a lance or on the handle of a club, W. **—vat**, mfn., g. *vimuktâdi*. **Barhâpīḍa** (Hariv.), **°ḍaka** (Hcat.), m. a wreath of peacock's feathers (worn on the crown of the head).

1. **Barhaṇa**, mf(*ī*)n. tearing or pulling out (see *mūla-b°*); dazzling (the eyes), Bālar.; n. pulling out (see *mūla-b°*); a leaf, L.; Tabernaemontana Coronaria, L.

Barhāyita, mfn. (fr. Nom. *barhāya*) resembling the eyes on a peacock's tail, BhP.

1. **Barhi**, in comp. for *°hin*. **—kusuma**, n. = *-pushpa*, L. **—citraka**, n. N. of VarBṛS. xliv. **—cūḍā**, f. Celosia Cristata, L. **—cchada**, m. the feather of a peacock, Śṛiṅgār.; n. the plumage of a peacock, ib. **—dhvaja**, m. 'symbolised by a peacock,' N. of Skanda, Bālar.; (*ā*), f. N. of Durgā, L. **—pushpa**, n. (L.), **-barha**, n. (Bhpr.) a kind of perfume. **—yāna**, m. 'having a peacock for vehicle,' N. of Skanda, Kāśīkh. **—vāhana**, m. 'id.,' N. of Gaṇeśa, Kathās. **—śikha**, n. = *pushpa*, L.

2. **Barhi**, m. N. of a descendant of Aṅgiras, GopBr.

3. **Barhi**, in comp. for *°his* (m. c. also n. = *barhis*, BhP.) **—shád**, mfn. seated or placed on the sacrificial grass, RV.; TS.; m. (pl.) the Pitṛis or deceased ancestors (also a partic. class of Pitṛis), Mn. (esp. iii, 196; 199); MBh. &c.; N. of a son of Havirdhāna and Havir-dhānī, BhP. **—shada**, m. N. of a Ṛishi, MBh.

Barhiḥ, in comp. for *°his*. **—śushman**, m. fire, the god of fire, L. **—shad**, m. N. of a Ṛishi (v.l. for *Barhi-shad*), BhP. **—shṭha**, mfn. standing or placed on the sacrificial grass; m. (prob.) a sacrificial gift, BhP. **—shṭhá**, mfn. = prec. mfn., RV.

Barhiṇa, mfn. adorned with peacock's feathers, MBh.; m. a peacock, Mn.; Āpast.; MBh. &c.; n. Tabernaemontana Coronaria, L.; N. of one of the 1000 small islands of Bharata-varsha, L. **—lakshaṇa**, mf(*ā*)n. = *barhiṇa*, mfn., R. **—vāja**, m. an arrow feathered with peacock's plumes, MBh. **—vāsas**, mfn. (an arrow) provided with peacock's feathers, R. (B.) **—vāhana**, m. N. of Skanda, L.

Barhin, m. a peacock, MBh.; Kāv. &c.; N. of a Deva-gandharva, MBh.; of a Ṛishi (= *Barhi-shada*), ib.; n. a kind of perfume, L.

Barhir, in comp. for *°his*. **—uttha**, m. 'arising from grass,' fire, Bālar. **—jyotis**, m. fire or the god of fire, L. **—mukha**, m. 'fire-mouthed,' a deity (so called because sacrifices are mostly offered to the gods in fire), L. **—homa**, m. an oblation (prepared) for the sacrificial grass, Vait.

Barhish, in comp. for *°his*. **—keśa**, m. 'grass-haired,' fire or the god of fire, L. **—pala** or **-pūla** (Kāś.), n., g. *kaskâdi*. **—mat** (*°hísh-*), mfn. accompanied or provided with sacrificial grass, RV.; Br.; Mn.; having fire or light, blazing, shining, W.; m. one who has or spreads s° gr°, a worshipper, sacrificer, RV.; N. of Prācīna-barhis, BhP.; (*atī*), f. N. of a wife of Priya-vrata and daughter of Viśvakarman, BhP.; N. of a city in Brahmâvarta, ib.

Barhishka, mfn. formed of or covered with sacrificial grass, MBh.; n. sacrificial grass, ib.

Barhishya, mfn. belonging to or fitted for sacrificial grass, RV.; Br.; n. (with *Kaśyapasya*) N. of a Sāman, ĀrshBr.

Barhís, n. (rarely m.) 'that which is plucked up,' sacrificial grass, a bed or layer of Kuśa grass (usually strewed over the sacrificial ground and esp. over the Vedi, to serve as a sacred surface on which to present the oblations, and as a seat for the gods and for the sacrificers), RV. &c. &c.; n. Sacrificial Grass personified (and enumerated among the Prayāja and Anuyāja deities), RV.; Br.; sacrifice, RV.; BhP.; ether, L.; water, L.; a kind of perfume, L.; m. fire, light, splendour, L.; Plumbago Zeylanica, L.; N. of a man, MaitrUp.; of a son of Bṛihad-rāja, BhP.; pl. the descendants of Barhis, Saṃskārak. **—tṛiṇa**, n. a blade of the sacrificial grass, KātyŚr.

बर्हण 2. *barháṇa*, mfn. (√2. *bṛih*) strong, vigorous; only (*°ṇā*), ind. strongly, firmly, really, certainly, RV. **Barhaṇa-cakra**, n. N. of a mountain village, Rājat. **Barháṇā-vat**, mfn. energetic, vigorous, mighty; ind. with might, RV. **Barhaṇâśva**, m. N. of a prince (son of Nikumbha), BhP.

Barhas. See *ádri-b°* and *dvi-bárhas*.

Bárhishṭha, mfn. (superl.) mightiest, strongest, highest, Br.; (*am*), ind. strongest, loudest, RV.; n. Andropogon Muricatus, Suśr.; the resin of Pinus Longifolia, L.

बल् 1. *bal*, only Intens. *balbalīti*, to whirl round in a circle, ŚBr.

बल् 2. *bal*, cl. 1. P. *balati*, to breathe, live, Dhātup. xx, 10; 'to hoard grain' or 'to prevent wealth' (*dhānyâvarodha*), ib.; to be distressed (?), Git.; Ā. *balate* (v.l. for *bhalate*), to mention; to hurt; to give, xiv, 24; cl. 10. P. *balayati*, to live, xxxii, 84; *bālayati*, aor. *abībalat*, to nourish, rear, xxxii, 68; Ā. *bālayate* (v.l. for *bhāl°*), to explain, describe, xxxiii, 27.

Bala, n. (or m., g. *ardharcâdi*) power, strength, might, vigour, force, validity, RV. &c. &c. (*balāt*, 'forcibly, against one's will, without being able to help it;' also = *bala* ibc., or *balena*, *bala-tas*, with gen. or ifc., 'by force, by the power or on the strength or in virtue or by means of, by'); force or power of articulation, TUp.; force considered as sixth organ of action (cf. *karmêndriya*), MBh.; (the Buddhists reckon 10 forces, the ascetic Śaivas four, which according to Sch. on R. [B.] are *sāman*, *dāna*, *bheda*, and *nigraha*); Force personified as one of the Viśve Devāḥ, MBh.; power of, expertness in (loc.), Nal.; stoutness, bulkiness, L.; (also pl.; ifc. f. *ā*) military force, troops, an army, Mn.; MBh. &c.; (L. also shape; body; semen virile; gum; blood; a young shoot; bone); m. a crow, MBh.; Crataeva Roxburghii, L.; half-ripe barley, L.; N. of a demon conquered by Indra (the brother of Vṛitra, in older texts *Vala*), RV. &c. &c.; of an elder brother of Kṛishṇa (also called Bala-deva, Bala-bhadra, Bala-rāma &c.), MBh.; Pur.; cf. IW. 332 &c.; (with Jainas) a white Bala or elder brother of Vāsudeva (9 in number, viz. Acala, Vijaya, Bhadra, Su-prabha, Su-darśana, Ānanda, Nandana, Padma, and Rāma); N. of a son of Varuṇa and brother of Surā, MBh.; of an attendant on Skanda, ib.; of a son of Aṅgiras, ib.; of a son of Parikshit, ib.; of a son of Parijātra, BhP.; of a son of Kṛishṇa, ib.; of a lexicographer (also written *Vala*), Naish., Sch.; of a horse of the Moon, VP.; (*ā*), f. Sida Cordifolia, Suśr. (du. the plants Balā and Ati-balā, ib.); N. of a partic. charm, R.; Ragh. (cf. *ati-b°*); the youngest sister in a drama, L.; N. of a daughter of Daksha, R.; of a daughter of Raudrāśva, Hariv.; of a female divinity who executes the orders of the 17th Arhat of the present Avasarpiṇī, L.; of a peasant girl, Lalit.; (*balá*), n. = *valá*, a cavern, AV.; mfn. strong, robust, L.; sick (= *amin*), L. [Cf. Lat. *valere*, *valor* &c.] **—kara**, mfn. inspiring strength, strengthening, R.; Suśr. **—kāma**, mfn. desiring strength, ŚrS. **—kāya**, m. 'armed body,' an army, Divyāv. **—kṛit**, mfn. strengthening, Suśr. **—kṛita**, mfn. done by force or against free consent, Mn. viii, 168 &c. **—kṛiti**, f. a mighty deed, Nir. **—krama**, m. N. of a mountain, VP. **—kshobha**, m. commotion in the forces, mutiny in an army, Var. **—gupta**, m. N. of a man, Mudr.; (*ā*), f. N. of a peasant girl, Lalit. **—cakra**, n. 'circle of power,' dominion, sovereignty (*-vartin*, m. a powerful sovereign), Buddh.; an army, host, MBh. **—ja**, mfn. produced by strength or power, W.; m. n. a heap of corn, grain, L.; (*ā*), f. id., ĀpŚr.; a pretty woman, L.; the earth, L.; Arabian jasmine, L.; a rope, ĀpŚr., Sch.; N. of a river, BrahmaP.; n. (only L.) a city-gate, any gate; a field; war; a pretty figure; pith, marrow. **—jyeshṭha**, mfn. one whose superiority is dependent on his strength or power, MBh. **—da**, m. 'strength-giving,' a partic. form of Agni, Gṛihyās.; MBh.; an ox, bullock, Kathās. (*°dī-bhūta*, mfn. become an ox, ib.); a partic. medicinal plant (= *jīvaka*), L.; (*ā*), f. Physalis Flexuosa, L.; N. of a daughter of Raudrāśva, Hariv. (v.l. *balā*). **—darpa**, m. pride of strength, MW. **—dā́** (RV.; Kauś.), **-dā́van** (AV.), mfn. conferring or imparting power. **—déya**, n. bestowal of strength, RV. **—deva**, m. wind, L.; N. of the elder brother of Kṛishṇa (said to have been produced from a white hair of Vishṇu, and regarded as a Nāga), MBh.; Kāv. &c.; of a Nāga-rāja, L.; of a Brāhman, Kathās.; of sev. authors (also with *vidyā-bhūshaṇa*), Cat.; *-pattana*, n. N. of a town, Var.; *-svasṛi*, f. N. of Śiva's wife, L.; *°vâhnika*, n. N. of wk.; (*ā*), f. Ficus Heterophylla, L. **—dvish**, m. 'Bala's foe,' N. of Indra, L. **—dhara**, m. 'might-bearer,' N. of a Brāhman, Kathās.; of a warrior, ib. **—nagara**, n. N. of a town, Buddh. **—nāśana**, m. 'destroyer of Bala,' N. of Indra, MBh. **—nigraha**, m. reducing strength, weakening, W. **—nisūdana**, m. = *-nāśana*, Hariv. &c. **—m-dharā**, f. N. of Bhīma-sena's wife, MBh. **—pati** (*bála-*), m. lord of strength, ŚBr.; a general, commander, Var. **—pura**, n. Bala's stronghold, RAnukr. **—pūrṇa**, w. r. for next. **—pūrva**, mf(*ā*)n. preceded by the word *bala*, Hcat. **—prada**, mfn. giving strength, Suśr. **—pramathanī**, f. N. of a form of Durgā, Hcat. **—prasū**, f. Bala's (i. e. Baladeva's) mother, Rohiṇī, L. **—prāṇa**, n. strength and spirit. **—bandhu**, m. N. of a son of Manu Raivata, MārkP.; of a son of Bhṛigu in the 10th Dvāpara, VāyuP. **— bali,** f. strong(?), Divyâv. **—bhadra,** mfn. strong, powerful, L.; Bos Gavaeus, L.; Symplocos Racemosa, L.; a species of Kadamba, L.; N. of Bala-rāma or of An-anta (the great serpent identified with him), Pur.; W.; of a descendant of Bharata, of various men (esp. teachers and authors, also with *ācārya, kāyastha, pañcânana, bhaṭṭa, miśra, śukla, sūri*), Cat.; of a mountain in Śāka-dvīpa, BhP.; (*ā*), f. a young girl, maiden, L.; Ficus Heterophylla, L. **— bhadrikā,** f. Ficus Heterophylla, L.; a kind of cake made of bean-flour, L. **— bhid,** mfn. breaking or routing an army, W.; m. 'slayer of Bala,' N. of Indra, MBh.; Kāv. &c. (*-bhit-sakhi,* m. a friend of I°, MW.); a partic. Ekâha, PañcavBr.; ŚrS. **— bhṛit,** mfn. 'might-bearing,' powerful, strong, MBh. **— mada,** m. pride in power, MBh. **— mukhya,** m. the chief of an army, R. **— yukta** or **-yuta,** mfn. endowed with strength, powerful, Var. **— rāma,** m. N. of the elder brother of Kṛishṇa and third of the Rāmas (regarded as the 8th Avatāra of Vishṇu, sometimes as an incarnation of the great serpent Śesha or An-anta; he is also called Bala, Bala-deva, Bala-bhadra, and Halâyudha, cf. IW. 332 &c.), MBh.; Pur.; *-pañcânana,* m. N. of a grammarian, Cat. **— vat** (*bála-*), mfn. possessing power, powerful, mighty, strong, intense, VS. &c. &c.; vehement (as love, desire &c.), MBh.; dense (as darkness), Mṛicch.; preponderating, prevailing (also with abl., 'over'), VPrāt.; accompanied by an army, Inscr.; ind. powerfully, strongly, vehemently, much, well, ŚBr. &c. &c.; m. N. of the 8th Muhūrta, Var.; (*atī*), f. small cardamoms, L.; *-tama* (*bál°*), mfn. most powerful, strongest, mightiest, RV.; AV. &c.; *-tara,* mfn. more powerful, stronger, Mn.; MBh. &c.; *-tā,* f. (MBh.; Rājat.), *-tva,* n. (Kap.) powerfulness, superiority, preponderance. **— varjita,** mfn. destitute of strength, weak, infirm, Var. **— varṇin,** mfn. strong and looking well, Suśr. **— vardhana,** mfn. increasing power, strengthening, W.; m. N. of a son of Dhṛita-rāshṭra, MBh. **— vardhin,** mfn. = prec. mfn., W.; (*inī*), f. a species of medicinal plant (= *jīvaka*), L. **— varman,** m. N. of a king, Inscr.; *°ma-deva,* m. id., ib.; N. of a merchant, Kathās. **— vikarṇikā,** f. N. of a form of Durgā, Hcat. **— vijñāyá,** mfn. recognisable by strength, RV. **— vinyāsa,** m. arrangement of forces, array of troops, L. **— vipula-hetu-mati,** n. N. of an Asura, Buddh. **— vīrya,** n. strength and heroism, MBh.; m. 'possessing st° and h°,' N. of a descendant of Bharata, Śatr.; *-parākrama,* mfn. strong and heroic and valorous, MW. **— vṛitra,** (ibc.) Bala and Vṛitra; *-ghna, -nishūdana,* and *-han,* m. 'destroyer of B° and V°,' N. of Indra, MBh. **— vyasana,** n. the defeat or rout of an army, Kām.; Hit.; *-saṃkula,* mfn. (a king) embarrassed by disorder in (his) army, ib. **— vyāpad,** f. decrease of strength, Suśr.; Bhpr. **— vyūha,** m. a partic. Samādhi, L. **— śarman,** m. N. of a lexicographer, Cat. **— śālin,** mfn. having or possessing strength, strong, vigorous (*°li-tā,* f.), MBh.; possessing a great army, Var. **— samūha,** m. assemblage of forces, army, Ratnâv. **— sūdana,** mfn. destroying armies, MBh.; m. 'destroyer of Bala,' N. of Indra, MBh. **— sena,** m. N. of a warrior, Kathās.; (*ā*), f. a strong army, an army, host, MBh. **— stha,** mfn. 'being in strength or power,' strong, powerful, vigorous, MBh. (cf. *balâvastha*); m. 'being or belonging to an army,' a warrior, soldier, ib.; R. **— sthala,** m. N. of a son of Parijātra, BhP. (v. l. *balaḥ sthalaḥ*). **— sthiti,** f. 'army-station,' a camp, encampment, L.; a royal residence, royal camp or quarters, W. **— han,** mf(*ghnī*)n. one who slays or destroys armies, Hariv. (v. l. *-vat*); m. 'destroyer of strength,' phlegm, the phlegmatic humour, L. **— hantṛi,** m. 'slayer of Bala,' N. of Indra, MBh. **— hara,** m. 'taking away strength,' N. of a man, Rājat. **— hīna,** mfn. destitute of strength, weak (*-tā,* f.), R. **Balâksha,** m. N. of a prince, MBh. **Balâgra,** n. the utmost strength, extreme force, Hariv.; the head of an army, ib.; R. **Balâṅgaka,** m. 'strong-limbed (?),' the spring season, L. **Balâñcitā,** f. 'strongly stretched (?),' N. of Rāma's lute, L. **Balâḍhya,** m. 'rich in strength, strengthening (?),' a bean, L. **Balâtmikā,** f. Tiaridium Indicum, L. **Balâdhika,** mfn. superior in strength, surpassing in power, MBh.; Kathās. **Balâdhikaraṇa,** n. pl. the business or affairs of an army, MBh. **Balâdhyaksha,** m. the superintendent or commander of an army, a general, minister of war, Mn.; R.; Hariv. **Balânīka,** m. N. of a man, MBh. (cf. *bala-sena*). **Balânuja,** m. the younger brother of Baladeva, i.e. Kṛishṇa, L. **Balânvita,** mfn. possessed of power, powerful, strong, W.; suggestive of power, Ml.; leading an army, W. **Balâpakarsham,** ind. by force, W. **Balâbala,** mfn. at one time strong at another weak, MārkP.; n. strength and weakness, relative strength or power or weight or highness or dignity or importance, Mn.; Yājñ.; Kāv. &c.; *-bīja-bhaṅga,* m., *-sūtra-bṛihad-vṛitti,* f., *°lâkshepa-parihāra,* m. N. of wks. **Balâbhra,** n. 'army-cloud,' an army in the form of a cloud, MBh. **Balârāti,** m. = *bala-dvish,* L. **Balâri,** m. id.; Mṛicch. (v. l.); Bhām. **Balârthin,** mfn. desirous of power, Mn. ii, 37. **Balâvalepa,** m. pride of strength or prowess, MārkP. **Balâvastha,** mfn. powerful, strong, ib. (cf. *bala-stha*). **Balâśva,** m. N. of a king (called also Karam-dhama), ib. **Balâsura,** m. N. of a washerman, Kathās. **Balâhvā,** f. Sida Cordifolia, L.; *°hva-kanda,* m. a kind of esculent root, L. **Balêśa,** m. the chief or commander of an army, Var. **Balôtkaṭā,** f. N. of one of the Mātṛis attending on Skanda, MBh. **Balôtsāha,** m. ardour of troops or forces, R. **Balônmatta,** mfn. intoxicated with power, R. **Balôpapanna,** mfn. endowed with power or strength, MW. **Balôpavishṭa,** mfn. id., W. **Balôpêta,** mfn. id., ib. **Balâugha,** m. a multitude of troops, numerous force, Śiś.

Balaka, m. N. of a demon, Hariv. (cf. *valaka*); a dream at nightfall, L.; n. a mixture of treacle and milk, L.

Balana, mfn. strengthening, L.; n. the act of strengthening, Dhātup.

Balaya, Nom. P. *°yati,* see *upôd-balaya.*

Balala, m. = *bala-rāma,* L.

Balāt, ind. (abl. of *bala,* q. v.) in comp. **— kāra,** m. employment of force, violence, oppression, injustice (ibc.; *am* and *eṇa,* ind. = forcibly, violently), Kāv.; Kathās.; (in law) the detention of the person of a debtor by his creditor to recover his debt, W.; *°râbhilāshin,* mfn. wishing to use force, intending to violate, Kathās. **— kārita,** mfn. = next, Cat. **— kṛita,** mfn. treated violently, forced, overpowered, MBh.; Kāv.; Pur.

1. **Balāya,** Nom. Ā. *°yate* (for 2. see col. 3), to put forth strength, Nir. x, 3.

Balin, mfn. powerful, strong, mighty, stout, robust, RV. &c. &c.; m. a soldier, Inscr. (cf. *bala-stha*); N. of Vatsa-prī, MārkP.; (only L.) a hog, bull, buffalo, camel, kind of sheep, serpent, Phaseolus Radiatus, a sort of jasmine, the phlegmatic humour, N. of a Bala-rāma; (*inī*), f. Sida Cordifolia, L.

Baliman, m. power, strength (in *a-b°*), ChUp.

Bálishṭha, mfn. (superl. fr. *balín*) most powerful, very strong or mighty, ŚBr. &c. &c.; stronger or mightier than (abl.), Ragh.; m. a camel, L. **— tama,** mfn. most powerful, mightiest, AitBr.

Báliyas, mfn. (compar. fr. *balín*) more or most powerful or mighty or strong or important or efficacious, ŚBr. &c. &c.; ind. more powerfully or strongly &c., GopBr. **— tara,** mfn. more powerful, stronger, mightier, Kām. **— tva,** n. pre-eminence in strength, superior power, predominance, Kām.

Balīyasa, mfn. = *balīyas,* MBh.

Balūla, mfn. powerful, strong, g. *sidhmâdi;* = *balaṃ na sahate,* Pāṇ. v, 2, 122, Vārtt. 8, Pat.

Balya, mf(*ā*)n. (cf. Pāṇ. iv, 2, 80) strengthening, giving strength, Suśr.; powerful, strong, vigorous, W.; m. a Buddhist mendicant, L.; (*ā*), f. N. of various plants (Sida Cordifolia or Rhombifolia, Physalis Flexuosa, Paederia Foetida &c.), L.

बलक्ष *baláksha,* mf(*ī*)n. (also written *valaksha*) white, TS. &c. &c.; m. white (the colour), W.; (with *paksha*) the light half of a month, L. **— gu,** m. 'white-rayed,' the moon, Kāvyâd. **— taṇḍulā,** f. Sida Cordifolia, L.

बलखिन् *balakhin,* mfn. coming from Balkh, Kshitîś.

बलङ्ग *balaṅga, balasha* and *balahasha,* m. or n. (?), N. of places, Cat.

बलभ *balabha,* m. a partic. venomous insect, Suśr.

बलाक *balāka,* m. (also written *valāka*) a kind of crane (the flesh of which is eaten), Gaut.; Hariv.; N. of a pupil of Śākapūṇi, VP.; of a pupil of Jātūkarṇya, BhP.; of a hunter, MBh.; of a son of Pūru and grandson of Jahnu, BhP.; of a son of Vatsa-prī, MārkP.; of a Rākshasa, ib.; (*ā*), f., see below. **Balākâśva,** m. N. of a descendant of Jahnu, MBh.; Hariv.

Balā́kā, f. a crane (more usual than *°ka,* m., q. v.), VS. &c. &c.; a mistress, loved woman, L. (Megh. 9?); N. of a woman, g. *bahv-ādi.* **— kauśiká,** m. N. of a preceptor, ŚBr. **— paṅkti-hāsin,** mfn. smiling with rows of cranes, MBh.

Balākikā, f. a species of small crane, L.

Balākin, mfn. abounding in cranes, Kālid. (cf. g. *vrīhy-ādi*); m. N. of a son of Dhṛita-rāshṭra, MBh.

बलात्कार *balāt-kāra* &c. See col. 2.

बलाद्या *balādyā,* f. Sida Cordifolia, L. (prob. w. r. for *balâhvā*).

बलामोटा *balāmoṭā,* f. Artemisia Vulgaris or Alpinia Nutans, L.

बलाय 2. *balāya,* m. (for 1. see col. 2) Crataeva Roxburghii, L.

बलालक *balālaka,* m. Flacourtia Cataphracta, L.

बलास *balása,* m. (also written *balāsa*) a partic. disease, consumption or phthisis, VS.; AV.; the phlegmatic humour, Suśr. **— kshaya-kara,** mfn. destroying the phlegmatic humour, Suśr. **— grathita,** n. a kind of ophthalmia, ib. **— ghna,** mfn. = *-kshaya-kara,* Suśr. **— nāśana,** mf(*ī*)n. destroying consumption, AV. **— basta,** m. a partic. disease of the eye, L. **— vardhana,** mfn. increasing the phlegmatic humour, Suśr.

Balāsaka, m. a yellow spot in the white of the eye (caused by disease), Suśr.

Balāsin, mfn. consumptive, phthisical, AV.

बलाहक *balāhaká* or *valāhaká,* m. (Naigh. i, 10) a rain or thunder-cloud, any cloud, MBh.; Kāv. &c. (ifc. f. *ā*); one of the 7 clouds appearing at the destruction of the world, Cat.; a mountain, L.; Cyperus Rotundus, L.; a kind of crane (= *balāka*), L.; a kind of snake, Suśr.; a kind of metre, Col.; N. of a serpent-demon, MBh.; Hariv.; Pur.; of a commander, Kād.; of one of the 4 horses of Vishṇu, ib.; of a brother of Jayad-ratha, MBh.; of a Daitya, L.; of a mountain, Kathās.

बलि *balí,* m. (perhaps fr. √*bhṛi*) tribute, offering, gift, oblation (in later language always with √*hṛi*), RV. &c. &c.; tax, impost, royal revenue, Br.; Mn.; MBh. &c.; any offering or propitiatory oblation (esp. an offering of portions of food, such as grain, rice &c., to certain gods, semi-divine beings, household divinities, spirits, men, birds, other animals and all creatures including even lifeless objects; it is made before the daily meal by arranging portions of food in a circle or by throwing them into the air outside the house or into the sacred fire; it is also called *bhūta-yajña* and was one of the 5 *mahā-yajñas* or great devotional acts; cf. RTL. 411, 421), GṛŚrS.; Mn. (esp. iii, 69, 71); MBh. &c. (often ifc. with the object, the receiver, the time, or the place of the offering); fragments of food at a meal, W.; a victim (often a goat or buffalo) offered to Durgā, MW.; the handle of a chowrie or fly-flapper, Megh.; N. of a Daitya (son of Virocana; priding himself on his empire over the three worlds, he was humiliated by Vishṇu, who appeared before him in the form of a Vāmana or dwarf, son of Kaśyapa and Aditi and younger brother of Indra, and obtained from him the promise of as much land as he could pace in three steps, whereupon the dwarf expanding himself deprived him of heaven and earth in two steps, but left him the sovereignty of Pātāla or the lower regions), MBh.; Pur. &c. (cf. IW. 328); N. of Indra in the 8th Manv-antara, Pur.; of a Muni, MBh.; of a king, ib.; Pañcat.; of a son of Su-tapas, Hariv.; Pur. (cf. *vali*). **— kara,** m. pl. taxes and duties, MBh.; mfn. offering propitiatory sacrifices, W. (cf. Pāṇ. iii, 2, 21). **— karambha,** m. sacrificial cake, W. **— karman,** n. offering oblations to all creatures, GṛS.; Mn. &c.; presentation or payment of tribute, MW. **— kṛit,** mfn. paying taxes, tributary, AitBr. **— gāyatrī,** f. N. of a Mantra employed by the Śāktas, RTL. 201. **— ceshṭitavarṇana,** n. N. of ch. of GaṇP. ii. **— tantra,** n. the regular form of an oblation to all creatures, Gobh. **— dāna,** n. the presentation of an offering to a deity (consisting of rice, milk, fruits &c. when presented to Vishṇu, or of living victims when offered to Śiva or Durgā), Pur.; presentation of grain &c. to all creatures, Cat.; *-paddhati*, f., *-vidhi*, m. N. of wks. **–dvish,** m. 'hater of Bali,' N. of Vishṇu, L. **–dhvaṇsin,** m. 'destroyer of B°,' id., L. **–nandana,** m. 'son of B°,' N. of the Asura Bāṇa, L. **–niyamanôdyuta,** mfn. prepared to subdue Bali, MW. **–m-dama,** m. 'tamer of Bali,' N. of Vishṇu, L.; *-prakhya*, mfn. equal to V°, MW **–pīṭha-lakshaṇa,** n. N. of wk. **–putra,** m. = *-nandana*; *-mokshaṇa*, n. N. of ch. of BrahmavP. iv. **–pushṭa,** m. 'nourished by food-offerings,' a crow, Śiś. **–podakī,** f. Basella Cordifolia, L. **–pratigrāhaka,** mf(*ikā*)n. receiving oblations, Divyâv. **–priya,** mf(*ā*)n. fond of offering oblations, Vishṇ.; m. Symplocos Racemosa (fabled to grow faster if presented with obl° consisting of incense, lights &c.), L. **–bandhana,** m. 'binder or killer of Bali,' N. of Vishṇu, L. **–bhadra,** w. r. for *bala-bh°*. **–bhuj,** mfn. devouring oblations, Kāv.; enjoying offerings (said of gods), MW.; m. a crow, Kathās.; BhP.; a sparrow, L.; a crane, W. **–bhṛit,** mfn. paying tribute, tributary, MBh. (cf. *-hṛit*). **–bhoja** or **-bhojana,** m. a crow, R. (cf. *-bhuj*). **–mát,** mfn. receiving taxes or tribute (said of Agni), TBr.; provided with food-oblations (said of a house), Ragh. **–mandira,** n. 'Bali's abode,' the infernal regions, W. **–mahānarêndrâkhyāna,** n. N. of wk. **–mātra,** n. a mere offering (to all beings), as much in quantity as an oblation to all creatures, MW. **–vāka,** m. N. of a Muni, MBh. (v. l. *balīv°*). **–vidhāna,** n. the offering of an oblation, Siṇhâs. **–vindhya,** m. N. of a son of Manu Raivata, BhP. **–vṛisha-han,** m. N. of a prince, VP. **–veśman,** n. = *-mandira*, L. **–vyākula,** mfn. busied in offering oblations, MW. **–shaḍ-bhāga,** m. the sixth part as tribute, MBh.; *-hārin*, mfn. taking the s° p° as t°, Mn. viii, 308. **–sadman,** n. = *-mandira*, L. **–sūdana,** w. r. for *bala-s°*. **–han,** m. 'slayer of Bali,' N. of Vishṇu, L. **–haraṇa,** mf(*ī*)n. adapted for the presentation of oblations, ĀśvGṛ.; n. the pr° of obl°, GṛS.; Suśr. (cf. RTL. 329 &c.); *-vidhi*, m. N. of wk. **–hārá,** mfn. paying taxes or tribute, AV.; m. = *-haraṇa*, n., MānGṛ. **–hṛit,** mfn. = *-hāra*, mfn., RV.; AV.; TS. **–homa,** m. the offering of oblations, Hariv. **Balîndra-sahasra-nāman,** n. N. of wk. **Baly-upakhyāna,** n. N. of ch. of the Vāsishṭha-rāmāyaṇa.

Balika, m. (cf. *valika*) N. of a serpent-demon, L.; (*ā*), f. Sida Cordifolia and Rhombifolia, L.; mfn. one who takes his food every 6th day, L.

Balī-kṛita, mfn. presented as an offering, Kathās.

बलिवर्द *balivárda*, m. a bull or ox, TBr. &c. &c. (also *balīv°*; w. r. *°vardha*); (*balīvardī*), f. N. of a woman, g. *kalyāṇy-ādi* (Kāś.)

Balivardin, m. N. of a man, g. *śubhrâdi* (Kāś. *baliv°*).

Balīvardineya, m. metron. fr. *balīvardī*, Vop.

बलिश *baliśa*, n., °*śi* or °*śī*, f. (also written *val°*) a hook, fish-hook, L. (cf. *baḍiśa*).

बलिष्ठ *bálishṭha, báliyas.* See p. 723, col. 2.

बलिष्णु *balishṇu*, mfn. disregarded, despised, L. (arrogant, disrespectful, W.)

बलीन *balīna*, m. a scorpion, W.; N. of an Asura, MBh. (v. l. *balīvīra*).

बलीवाक *balīvāka.* See *bali-v°* under *bali.*

बलीह *balīha*, m. pl. N. of a people, MBh. (cf. *balhika*).

बलूक *balūka*, wrongly for *valūka*, KātyŚr.

बल्कस *bálkasa*, n. dregs or sediment left in the distillation of ardent spirits, ŚBr.

बल्बज *bálbaja*, m. (later *balvaja* or *valvaja*) Eleusine Indica (a species of coarse grass not liked by cattle), TS. &c. &c. **–maya,** mf(*ī*)n. made of Balbaja grass, g. *śarâdi.* **–stukā́,** f. a bunch or tuft of Balbaja grass, RV.

Balbajika, mfn., g. *kumudâdi.*

बल्बला *balbalā*, onomat. (with √*kṛi*) to stammer, stutter, PañcavBr. **–kāra,** m. stammering, stuttering, SaṃhUp.; (*am*), ind., ib.

बल्बूथ *balbūthá*, m. N. of a man, RV.

बल्बूल *balbūlá*, m. N. of a serpent-demon, Suparṇ.

बल्य *balya.* See p. 723, col. 2.

बल्ल *balla*, w. r. for *valgā*, MBh. vii, 1217.

बल्लव *ballava*, m. (also written *vallava*) a cowherd, MBh.; Hariv.; Kāv. (cf. *go-b°*); N. assumed by Bhīma-sena when cook to king Virāṭa, MBh.; a cook, L.; pl. N. of a people, MBh.; (*ī*), f. a cowherdess, L. **–tā,** f. (Bālar.), **-tva,** n. (Hariv.) the business or duty of a cowherd. **–yuvati,** f. (°*tī*, L.), a young cowherdess, Gīt.

बल्लाल *ballāla*, m. N. of various men, Col.; of a king, Kuval.; of the father of Śaṃkara, Cat. **–deva** (with *daiva-jña*), m. N. of the author of the Bhoja-prabandha, Cat. **–miśra,** m. N. of a king, Vāsav., Introd. **–sena-deva,** m. N. of an author, Cat.

बल्व *balva*, n. (also written *valva* or *valava*) N. of the second Karaṇa or astrological division of the day, L.; (*ī*), f., w. r. for *vallī.*

बल्वज *balvaja.* See *balbaja.*

बल्श *balśa* = *valśa* in *śatá-balśa*, q. v.

बल्हि *balhi*, m. N. of a country, Balkh, Uṇ. iv, 117, Sch. (written *vahli*).

Balhika, n. = *bālhika*, Asa Foetida, L.

बव *bava*, n. (also written *vava*) N. of the first Karaṇa or astrological division of the day, Sūryas.

बष्कय *bashkáya*, mfn. (prob.) one year old, a yearling, RV. i, 164, 5 (cf. g. *utsâdi*).

Bashkayaṇī or °**yiṇī,** f. a cow with a young calf, L. (cf. Pāṇ. ii, 1, 65).

Báshkiha, mfn. old, decrepit, VS.; MaitrS. (*vashk°*).

बष्ट *bashṭa*, m. (Prākṛ.) = *mūrkha*, a fool, L.

बस्त *bastá*, m. (also written *vasta*) a goat, RV. &c. &c. **–karṇa,** m. Shorea Robusta, L. **–gandhā,** f. Ocimum Villosum, L. **–gandhâkṛiti,** f. a partic. plant growing in Mālava (= *lakshmaṇā*), Bhpr. **–māram,** ind. after the manner of the dying of a goat, Suśr. **–mukha,** mf(*ī*)n. goat-faced, MW. **–mūtra,** n. the urine of a goat, MW. **–modā,** f. N. of a plant (= *aja-modā*), L. **–vāśin,** mfn. bleating like a g°, AV. (w. r. °*sin*). **–śṛiṅgī,** f. Odina Pinnata, L. **Bastâjina,** n. a goat-skin, MaitrS. **Bastântrī,** f. Argyreia Speciosa or Argentea, L. **Bastâbhivāśin,** mfn. (w. r. °*sin*) = *basta-vāśín*, AV. **Bastâmbu,** n. = *basta-mūtra*, Bhpr.

बस्ति *basti* &c. See *vasti.*

बस्त्य *bastya.* See *vāja-bastya.*

बस्रि *básri*, ind. quickly, RV. i, 120, 12 (= *kshipram*, Sāy.)

बह् *bah*, short form of √*baṇh*, q. v.

Bahaya, Nom. P. °*yati* (fr. *bahu*), Pat.

Bahala, mfn. thick, dense, compact, firm, solid, Kāv.; Rājat.; Suśr.; bushy, shaggy (as a tail), Ml.; wide, extensive, Suśr.; deep, intense (as a colour), Śiś.; harsh (as a tone), Prab.; manifold, copious, abundant (ibc. = in a high degree; ifc. = filled with, chiefly consisting of), Kāv. (often v. l. *bahula*); m. a kind of sugar-cane, L.; (*ā*), f. large cardamoms, L. (cf. *bahulā*); Anethum Sowa, L. **–gandha,** n. a species of sandal, L.; (*ā*), f. large cardamoms, L. **–cakshus,** m. Odina Pinnata, L. **–tā,** f. thickness, Suśr. **–tvaca,** m. the white flowering Lodhra, L. **–vartman,** m. n. a partic. disease of the eyes, a swollen eyelid, Suśr. **Bahalâṅga,** m. Odina Pinnata, L. **Bahalânurāga,** mfn. deep red, Śiś.

Bahalita, mfn. grown thick or compact or strong, Kāv.

Bahalī-√**bhū,** P. *-bhavati*, to become a thick or compact mass, Car.

Bahú, mf(*vī* or *u*)n. much, many, frequent, abundant, numerous, great or considerable in quantity (n. also as subst. with gen.), RV. (rarely in Maṇḍ. i–ix); AV. &c. &c. (*tad bahu-yad*, 'it is a great matter–that,' MBh.; *tvayā me bahu kṛitaṃ-yad*, 'you have done me a great service by–or that–,' Nal.; *kim bahunā*, 'what occasion is there for much talk?' i. e. 'in short,' Śak.; Hit.); abounding or rich in (instr.), ŚBr.; large, great, mighty, AV. &c. &c.; (*ú*), ind. much, very, abundantly, greatly, in a high degree, frequently, often, mostly, RV. &c. &c. (often ibc., where also = nearly, almost, rather, somewhat; cf. *bahu-tṛiṇa, bahu-trivarsha* and Pāṇ. v, 3, 68; *bahu-*√*man* = to think much of, esteem highly, prize, value); n. the plural number, AitBr. **–kaṇṭaka,** mfn. 'many-thorned,' N. of sev. plants (a species of Asteracantha; Alhagi Maurorum; Phoenix Paludosa), L.; (*ā*), f. = next, L. **–kaṇṭā,** f. 'many-thorned,' Solanum Jacquini, L. **–kanda,** m. 'having bulbous roots,' Amorphophallus Campanulatus, L.; (*ī*), f. Cucumis Utilissimus or a kind of gourd, L. **–kara,** mf(*ī*)n. doing much, busy, useful in many ways to (gen.), Bhaṭṭ. (cf. Pāṇ. iii, 2, 21); one who sweeps, a sweeper, L. (√*kṝi*?); m. a camel, L.; a species of jujube, L.; (*ā* or *ī*), f. a broom, L. (√*kṝi*?). **–karaṇīya,** mfn. one who has (or complains of having) much to do, who never has time for anything, L. **–karṇikā,** f. Salvinia Cucullata, L. **–kalka,** m. Buchanania Latifolia, L. **–kalpa,** mfn. manifold, multifarious, MBh. **–kalyāṇa,** mf(*ā* or *ī*)n. very illustrious, most noble, Nal. **–kāma,** mfn. having many wishes or desires, ŚāṅkhŚr. **–kāra,** mfn. doing or effecting much, VS. **–kāraṇīya,** mfn. = *-karaṇīya*, L. **–kālam,** ind. for a long time, MW. **–kālīna,** mfn. of long standing, old, ancient, ib. **–kīṭa,** m. N. of a Grāma in the north, g. *palady-ādi.* **–kulīna** or **-kulya,** Sch. on Pāṇ. iv, 1, 140 (cf. *bāhukuleyaka*). **–kusumita,** mfn. full of blossoms. **–kūrca,** m. a species of cocoa-nut, L. **–kṛita,** mf(*ā*)n., Pāṇ. iv, 1, 52, Vārtt. 5, Pat. **–kṛitya,** mfn. = *-karaṇīya*, L. **–ketu,** m. N. of a mountain, R. **–krama,** m. a Krama (q. v.) of more than three words, RPrāt. **–kshama,** mfn. enduring much, Kum.; m. a Jaina saint or a Buddha, L. **–kshāra,** m. a kind of alkali, L. **–kshīrā,** f. a cow which gives much milk, L. **–gandha,** mfn. strong-scented; m. the resin of Boswellia Thurifera, L.; (*ā*), f. a bud of Michelia Champaka, L.; Jasminum Auriculatum, L.; Nigella Indica, L.; n. cinnamon, L.; a kind of sandal, L.; *-dā*, f. musk, L. **–garhya-vāc,** mfn. saying much that is to be censured, too talkative, loquacious, L. **–gava,** m. 'having much cattle,' N. of a prince, Hariv.; Pur. **–giri,** m. N. of a district, Var. **–gú,** mf(*ū*)n. rich in cattle, ĀpŚr. **–guḍā,** f. Solanum Jacquini, L. **–guṇa,** mfn. many-threaded (as a rope), Pāṇ. vi, 2, 176, Sch.; manifold, multifarious, much, MBh.; R.; having many good qualities or virtues, Pāṇ. vi, 2, 176, Sch.; m. N. of a Deva-gandharva, MBh. **–guru,** m. one who has read much but superficially, a sciolist (= *cumbaka*), L. **–guhā,** f. = *-guḍā*, L. **–go,** mfn. having much cattle, MW. **–gotra-ja,** mfn. having many blood relations, Kathās. **–granthi,** m. 'many-knotted,' Tamarix Indica, L. **–graha,** mfn. receiving or holding much (said of a minister and a water-jar), Hit. **–carmaka,** mf(*ikā*)n., Pat. **–cārin,** mfn. roaming much or widely, AV. **–citra,** mfn. very various or manifold, Pañcat. **–cchada,** m. Alstonia Scholaris, L. **–cchala,** mf(*ā*)n. deceitful, Kir.; *-tva*, n., Veṇis. **–cchinnā,** f. a species of Cocculus, L. **–jana,** m. a great multitude of people (*-parivāra*, m. a partic. Samādhi; *-hita*, n. the common weal), Buddh.; mf(*ā*)n. surrounded by many people, ĀpŚr. **–janma-bhāj,** mfn. subject to many births, Sāy. on RV. i, 164, 3. **–janya** (*bāhu-j°*?), prob. n. a multitude of people, L. **–jalpa,** mfn. very talkative, loquacious, ŚārṅgP. **–jalpitṛi,** m. a talker, prattler, R. **–java,** mfn. very swift, Nir. **–jāta,** mfn. grown mighty, ib. **–jālī,** f. a kind of cucumber, L. **–jña,** mfn. possessed of great knowledge; *-tā*, f. great knowledge, MW. **–tanaya,** mfn. one who has many sons, Daś. **–tantrī,** mfn. (nom. *īs*) many-fibred (said only of the body, Pāṇ. v, 4, 159). **–tantrīka,** mf(*ā*)n. (fr. *bahu + tantrī*) having many strings (as a musical instrument), L. **–tama,** mfn. very many, most, most numerous &c.; farthest, remotest (e. g. *ā bahutamāt purushāt*, as far as the remotest descendant), ShaḍvBr. **–tara,** mf(*ā* or *ī*)n. more (or most) abundant or numerous &c.; greater or very great, MBh.; Kāv. &c.; (*am*), ind. more, very or too much, for the greater part, chiefly, Vet.; SaddhP.; *-ka*, mfn. very much or numerous, Pat.; *-kaṇiśa*, m. a kind of corn or grain (cf. *guccha-kaṇiśa*). **–tarām,** ind. in a high degree, exceedingly, much, Caur. **–tas,** ind. from or by much or many; from many sides, Pāṇ. v, 3, 7, 8, Sch. **–tā,** f. numerousness, muchness, abundance, plenty, multiplicity, plurality, Vet. (cf. *-tva*). **–tiktā,** f. Solanum Indicum, L. **–titha,** see p. 626, col. 1. **–tṛiṇa,** mfn.

abounding in grass, Kathās.; n. much like g°, almost g°, a mere blade of g°, Bhartṛ.; Śiś.; m. Saccharum Munjia, L. **—tṛishṇa,** mfn. having great thirst, Kāv. **—tra,** ind. in many ways or places, amongst many, Pāṇ. v, 3, 10, Sch. **—trā,** ind. amongst many, to many, RV. (cf. Pāṇ. v, 4, 56, Sch.) **—trivarsha,** mfn. well-nigh three years old, Lāṭy. **—tva,** n. muchness, abundance, multitude, MBh.; Kāv. &c.; plurality, majority, Mn. viii, 73; (in gram.) the plural number (cf. *bahu-tā*). **—tvakka,** m. (fr. *bahu + tvac*), 'having much bark,' Betula Bhojpatra, L. **—tvac,** m. id., L.; Astonia Scholaris, L. **—thā,** ind. in numerous ways, in various manners, Pāṇ. v, 3, 23, Sch. **—da,** mfn. 'much-giving,' liberal, munificent, W. **—dakshiṇá,** mfn. marked by many fees or donations (as a religious ceremony), liberal, lavish, bountiful, ŚBr. **—daṇḍika,** or **—daṇḍin,** mfn. having many staff-bearers, W. **—dantī,** f. N. of a woman; *-suta,* m. 'the son of Bahu-dantī,' N. of an author, Kām. (v. l. *valgudantī-sukha*). **—darśaka,** mf(*ikā*)n. or **—darśin,** mfn. seeing much, prudent, circumspect, L.; °*śi-tā,* f. circumspection, ib. **—dala-kaniśa,** m. a partic. species of grain, L. **—dāna,** n. a rich gift, Kāv.; (*á*), mfn. = *-dāyin,* ŚBr. **—dāman** or **—dāmā,** f. N. of one of the Mātṛis attending on Skanda, MBh. **—dāyin,** mfn. 'much-giving,' liberal, munificent, ChUp. **—dāsa-purusha,** mfn. having many slaves and servants, ĀpŚr. **—dāsa-pūrushá,** mf(*á*)n., id., TBr. **—duḥkha-vāsam,** ind. (with √*vas*) to have a very painful abode, BhP. **—dugdha,** mfn. having much milk, L.; (*ā*), f. (a cow) giving much milk, L. (also *-vatī,* Hcat.); m. wheat, L. **—dugdhikā,** f. 'having much milk,' Tithymalus Antiquorum (which yields a caustic milky juice), L. **—dṛiśvan,** m. one who has seen much, a great observer, very experienced, L. **—dṛishṭa,** mfn. = prec., W. **—deya,** n. munificence, liberality, GopBr. **—devata,** mfn. (a hymn) addressed to many deities (*-tva,* n.), Nir.; ŚrS. **—devatya,** mfn. belonging to many deities, TS.; ŚBr. **—deśa-darśin,** mfn. one who has seen many countries, a great traveller, W. **—daivata,** mfn. relating to many deities, Nir. **—daivatya,** mfn. = prec., Cat.; n. N. of wk. **—dosha,** m. great harm or disadvantage, Mṛicch.; mf(*ā*)n. having many faults or drawbacks, very wicked or bad, R.; Mṛicch. **—dohanā,** f. yielding much milk, MBh. **—dhana,** mfn. possessing much wealth, wealthy, rich (*-tva,* n.), Śak.; m. N. of a man, L.; °*nêśvara,* m. a very rich man, Kathās. **—dhanya,** w. r. for *dhānya.* **—dhanvin,** mfn. having many bows (said of Śiva), MBh. **—dhā,** see p. 726, col. 2. **—dhānya,** m. 'abounding in corn,' N. of the 12th or 46th year in a 60 years' cycle of Jupiter, Var. **—dhānyaka,** m. or n. (?) N. of a place, MBh. **—dhāra,** n. 'many-edged,' a diamond or the thunderbolt of Indra, L. **—dhīvan,** mf(= m. or *arī*)n. rather skilful, Vop. iv, 10. **—dhenuka,** n. a great multitude of milch cows, MBh. **—dheya** (!), m. pl. N. of a school, L. **—dhmātá,** mfn. often annealed or cast (as iron), ŚBr. **—nāda,** m. 'loud-sounding,' a conch shell, L. **—nāman,** mfn. having many names, BhP. **—niḥsrita,** w. r. for *bāhu-n*°, q. v. **—nishka** or **—naishkika,** mfn. worth many Nishkas, Pāṇ. v, 1, 30, Sch. **—paṭu,** mfn. rather clever, Pāṇ. v, 3, 68, Sch. **—pattra,** mfn. many-leaved; m. an onion, L.; (*ā*), f. a partic. fragrant flower, L.; (*ī*), f. N. of various plants (Aloe Perfoliata, L.; basil; a species of Solanum &c.), L.; n. talc, L. **—pattrikā,** f. Flacourtia Cataphracta, L.; Trigonella Foenum Graecum, Bhpr.; = *mahā-śatāvarī,* L. **—patnīka,** mfn. having many wives, Śak.; performed by m° w°, KātyŚr., Sch.; *-tā,* f. polygamy, MBh. **—patnī-kṛit,** m. one who takes many wives, MW. **—patnī-tā,** f. polygamy, ib. **—pad** (strong form *-pād*), m. 'many-rooted,' the Indian fig-tree, L. **—pada,** mfn. many-footed, BhP. **—pannaga,** m. N. of a Marut, Hariv. (v. l. *brahma-p*°). **—parṇá,** mf(*á*)n. many-leaved, TS.; TBr.; m. Alstonia Scholaris, L.; (*ā*), f. Trigonella Foenum Graecum, L. **—parṇikā,** f. Salvinia Cucullata, L. **—paśu,** mfn. rich in cattle, Br.; GṛS. **—pākya,** mfn. one at whose house much is cooked (for the poor), ChUp. **—pād,** see *-pad.* **—pāda,** mf(*ā*)n. many-footed, MBh.; composed of several Pādas (q. v.), RPrāt.; m. the Indian fig-tree, L. **—pāyya,** mfn. protecting many; n. a large hall, RV. (cf. *nṛi-pāyya*). **—putra,** mf(*ā*)n. one who has many sons or children, MānGṛ. (*-tā,* f., *-tva,* n., MW.); m. Alstonia Scholaris; N. of a Prajā-pati, R.; Pur.; (*ī*), f. Asparagus Racemosus, Bhpr.; Flacourtia Cataphracta, L.; N. of Durgā, L. **—putrikā,** f. N. of one of the Mātṛis attending on Skanda, MBh.; w. r. for *-pattrikā.* **—pushṭá,** mfn. being in great prosperity, MaitrS. **—pushpa,** m. 'many-blossomed,' Erythrina Indica, L. (*ī* or *ikā,* f. Grislea Tomentosa, Bhpr.); *-prabāla-vat,* mfn. having many flowers and young shoots, R.; *-phalôpêta,* mfn. having many flowers and fruits, MW. **—prakāra,** mfn. of many kinds, manifold, MārkP.; n. ind. in many ways, manifoldly, R. **—prakṛiti,** mfn. consisting of many primary parts or verbal elements (as a compound), VPrāt. **—praja,** mf(*ā*)n. having a numerous progeny, R. (also °*jás,* RV.); cf. Pāṇ. v, 4, 123; m. (only L.) a hog; a mouse; Saccharum Munjia. **—prajña,** mfn. very wise, Ml. **—prajñāna-śālin,** mfn. possessed of much knowledge, Kathās. **—pratijña,** mfn. containing more than one proposition, complicated, W.; (in law) comprising many counts (as a plaint), Yājñ., Sch. **—pratyarthika,** mfn. having many adversaries or opponents, MW. **—pratyavâya,** mfn. connected with many difficulties, Nāg. **—prada,** mfn. 'much-bestowing,' liberal, munificent, bountiful, L. **—prapañca,** mfn. very diffuse or prolix, Hit. **—pralāpin,** mfn. (Var.); °*pi-tā,* f. (Prasannar.) = *-bhāshin,* °*shi-tā.* **—pravāha,** mfn. 'many-streamed,' flowing in m° streams, W. **—prasū,** f. a mother of m° children, L. **—prāśnika,** mfn. containing m° questions, MW. **—priyá,** mfn. dear to many (= *puru-priyá*), ŚBr. **—preyasī,** mfn. having many loved ones, Vop. **—phala,** mfn. 'm°-fruited,' fertile, W.; m. a partic. fruit tree, L.; Nauclea Cadamba, L.; (*ā*), f. N. of various plants (Solanum Indicum or another variety of Solanum; Glycine Debilis; a species of Convolvulus Turpethum; various kinds of cucurbitaceous plants, Flacourtia Cataphracta), L.; (*ī*), f. N. of various plants (Emblica Officinalis; Ficus Oppositifolia &c.), L. **—phalikā,** f. a species of jujube, L. **—phenā,** f. a species of plant (= *sātalā*); °*na-rasā,* f. = *saptalā,* Car. **—bala,** mfn. possessing great strength; m. a lion, L. **—bāhu,** mfn. many-armed; m. N. of a prince, Hariv. **—bīja,** mfn. having much seed, VarYog.; n. the fruit of Anona Reticulata or Squamosa, L.; (*ā*), f. Trigonella Foenum Graecum, Bhpr.; a kind of Musa, L. **—bollaka,** m. a great talker, Divyâv. **—bhaksha,** mfn. eating much, a great eater, MW. **—bhadra,** m. pl. N. of a people, MārkP. **—bhastraka,** mf(*ā* or *ikā*)n. (fr. *bahu + bhastrā*), Pāṇ. vii, 3, 47, Sch. **—bhāgya,** mfn. of great good fortune, fortunate, W. **—bhāshin,** mfn. talking much, garrulous, ĀśvŚr. (*a-b*°); °*shi-tā,* f. (MBh.) and °*shya,* n. talkativeness, garrulity. **—bhuj,** mfn. = *-bhaksha,* MBh. **—bhuja,** mfn. having many arms; (*ā*), f. N. of Durgā, L. **—bhūmi,** m. N. of a prince, VP. **—bhūmika,** mfn. having many floors or stories, Hcat. **—bhṛijj,** mfn. (nom. *-bhṛiṭ*) roasting or frying much, Vop. **—bhoktṛi,** m. a great eater, Gobh., Sch. **—bhogyā,** f. 'to be enjoyed by many,' a courtesan, prostitute, Daś. **—bhojaka,** mfn. eating much, Subh. **—bhojana,** w. r. for *-bhojaka.* **—bhojin,** mfn. eating much, voracious (°*ji-tā,* f.), Kull. on Mn. ii, 57. **—bhauma,** mf(*ī*)n. = *-bhūmika,* R. **—mañjarī,** f. basil, Bhpr. **—mata,** mfn. much thought of, highly esteemed, valued, MBh.; Kāv. &c.; having many different opinions, W. **—mati,** f. high opinion or esteem, Kir. **—matsya,** mfn. having many fish; n. a place abounding in fish, Kauś. **—madhya-ga,** mfn. going among or belonging to many, Mn. ix, 199. **—mantavya,** mfn. to be thought much of or esteemed highly, estimable, MBh. **—mala,** m. 'having much dross,' lead, L. **—māna,** m. high esteem or estimation, great respect or regard for (with loc. of pers. or thing, rarely with gen. of pers.), MBh.; Kāv. &c.; n. a gift made by a superior to an inferior, MW. **—mānin,** mfn. thought much of, highly esteemed, MBh. **—mānusha-saṃkīrṇa,** n. 'crowded with many people,' an arbour, bower, Gal. **—mānya,** mfn. to be thought much of, to be highly esteemed, estimable, Kull. on Mn. ii, 117. **—māya,** mfn. artful, deceitful, treacherous, MBh.; Pañcat. **—mārgī,** f. a place where many roads meet; (v. l. °*ga,* n.), L. **—māla** or **—mālaka,** mfn. possessing many necklaces, MW. **—mālya-phala,** mfn. rich in garlands and fruits, Pat. **—māsha-tilá,** mf(*á*)n. rich in beans and sesamum, TS.; ĀpŚr. **—mitra,** mfn. having many friends, Āpast.; m. N. of a man (see *bāhumitrāyaṇa*). **—mukha,** mf(*ī*)n. 'many-mouthed,' speaking variously, BhP. **—mūtra,** mfn. making water in excess; *-tā,* f. diabetes, L. **—mūtraka,** m. a kind of chameleon, L. **—mūrti,** mfn. multiform; f. the wild cotton shrub, L. **—mūrdhan,** mfn. many-headed, W.; m. N. of Vishṇu, L. **—mūla,** mfn. many-rooted, W.; m. a sort of reed or grass, L.; Hyperanthera Moringa, L.; (*ā*), f. Asparagus Racemosus, L.; (*ī*), f. Emblica Officinalis, L.; °*la-phalânvita,* mfn. provided or furnished with many roots and fruits, MW. **—mūlaka,** m. a species of reed, L.; N. of a Nāga, MBh.; n. the sweet-scented root of Andropogon Muricatus, Bhpr. **—mūlya,** mfn. high-priced, precious (*-tā,* f.), Pañcat.; n. a large sum of money, Rājat. **—mṛiga,** mfn. abounding in deer, MW. **—maulya,** w. r. for *-mūlya,* MBh. **—yajvan,** mfn. or **—yajvā,** f., Vop. iv, 5. **—yājin,** mfn. one who has offered many sacrifices, TS.; AitBr.; GṛS. **—yājya,** mfn. one who has many institutors of a sacrifice, one who sacrifices on behalf of many, Kull. on Mn. iii, 151. **—yojanā,** f. N. of one of the Mātṛis attending on Skanda, MBh. **—rajas,** mfn. very dusty or containing much pollen, Kāvyâd. **—ratna,** mf(*ā*)n. rich in gems or jewels, Siṇhâs.; °*tnāya,* Nom. Ā. °*yate,* to contain many j°, ib. **—ratha,** m. N. of a king, Hariv.; Pur. **—randhrikā,** f. 'much perforated,' N. of a particular medicinal root, L. **—ramya,** mfn. very delightful, MW. **—rasá,** mfn. having much juice, juicy, ŚBr.; (*ā*), f. Cardiospermum Halicacabum, L. **—rājan,** mfn., **—rājā,** f., Vop. iv, 5. **—rāyas-poshá,** mf(*á*)n. possessing much wealth, TS.; ĀpŚr. **—rāśi,** mfn. (in arithm.) composed of numerous terms; (with *paksha*), m. a series of many terms, Col. **—ripu,** mfn. one who has many foes, MW. **—ruhā,** f. a species of Cocculus, L. **—rūpá,** mf(*á*)n. multiform, variegated, checkered; manifold, VS. &c. &c.; m. N. of Śiva, MBh.; of Rudra, ib.; Pur.; of a son of Medhâtithi, BhP.; (only L.) a chameleon; hair; the resin of Shorea Robusta; the sun; N. of Brahmā; of Vishṇu; of the god of love; of a Buddha; (*ā*), f. N. of one of the seven tongues of fire, L.; n. N. of a Varsha, BhP.; *-kalpa,* m. N. of wk.; *-garbha-stotra,* n. N. of a Stotra; °*pâshṭaka-tantra,* n. a collective N. for eight Tantras (viz. the *Brāhmī-tantra, Māheśvarī-t*°, *Kaumārika-t*°, *Vaishṇavī-t*°, *Vārāhī-t*°, *Indrāṇī-t*°, *Cāmuṇḍā-t*°, *Śiva-dūtī-t*°), Cat. **—rūpaka,** mf(*ikā*)n. multiform, manifold, MBh.; m. a kind of animal, L.; *-śobhita,* adorned in many ways, variously decorated, MBh. (v. l. °*pâṅgas*°). **—rūpin,** mfn. = *-rūpaka,* mfn., BhP. **—rekha,** m. pl. many lines or wrinkles, marks of care or pain, W. **—retas,** m. 'having much seed,' N. of Brahmā, L. **—rai,** mfn. having great riches, very rich, MW. **—roman,** m. 'having much hair or wool;' a sheep, L. **—lavaṇa,** n. 'containing much salt;' a soil impregnated with salt, L. **—vaktavya,** mfn. to be said much about, Rājat. **—vacana,** n. the plural number, the case-endings and personal terminations in the plural number, ŚBr. &c. **—vat,** ind. plurally, in the plural number (e. g. *api dvi-vad api bahu-vat,* both in the dual and plural), Nir. **—varṇa,** mfn. many-coloured (*-tā,* f.), Suśr. **—varta,** N. of a place (see *bāhuvartaka*). **—varsha-sahasrika,** mfn. lasting many thousand years, MBh. **—varsha-sahasrin,** mfn. id., many thousand years old, ib. **—valka,** m. 'having much bark,' Buchanania Latifolia, L. **—valkala,** m. id., Bhpr. **—vallī,** f. Hoya Viridiflora, L. **—vādin,** mfn. talking much, garrulous, babbling, VS. **—vāra** or **—vāraka,** m. Cordia Myxa, Bhpr. (°*ka-phala,* n. its fruit, Kull.) **—vāram,** ind. many times, often, Caur. **—vārshika,** mf(*ī*)n. lasting many years, m° y° old, R.; Hcat. **—vi,** mfn. containing many birds, Uṇ. iv, 133, Sch. **—vikrama,** mfn. very powerful, MW. **—vighna,** mfn. presenting many obstacles or difficulties (*-tā,* f.), Cāṇ. **—vid,** mfn. much-knowing, very learned, TBr.; ChUp. **—vidya,** mfn. id. (*-tā,* f.), Kāv. **—vidha,** mf(*ā*)n. of many sorts or kinds, manifold, various, MBh.; Kāv. &c.; (*am,* ind. diversely, in several directions, up and down, R.; Mṛicch.; Pañcat.); m. N. of a prince, VP. **—vistara,** m. great extension, Subh.; (*-yuktam,* ind. in all directions, everywhere, R.); mf(*ā*)n. of wide extent, widely spread, ib. (also °*tāra,* Ml.); manifold, various, MBh.; Hariv.; very detailed (*am,* ind.), R. **—vistīrṇa,** mfn. wide-spread, widely diffused (*-tā,* f.), Vcar.; (*ā*), f. Abrus Precatorius (a shrub bearing a small red and black berry and commonly called Kucai), L. **—vīja,** see *-bīja.* **—vīrya,** mf(*ā*)n. very powerful or efficacious, MBh.; m. N. of various plants (Terminalia Bellerica; Bombax Heptaphyllum &c.), L.; (*ā*), f.

Flacourtia Cataphracta, L. **-vyaya** or **-vyayin**, mfn. spending much, prodigal, L. **-vyāpin**, mfn. far-spreading, extending wide, Sāh. **-vyāla-nishevita**, mfn. infested or inhabited by many snakes or wild beasts, MBh. **-vrīhi**, mfn. possessing much rice; m. a relative or adjective compound (in which, as in the word *bahu-vrīhi* itself [cf. *tat-purusha*], the last member loses its character of a substantive and together with the first member serves to qualify a noun), Pāṇ. ii, 2, 23; 35 &c.; *-vat*, ind. like a Bahu-vrīhi or relative compound, Pāṇ. viii, 1, 9. **-śakti**, mfn. possessing great power; m. N. of a prince, Pañcat. **-śatru**, mfn. having many enemies, Kām.; Hit.; m. a sparrow, L. **-śabda**, m. the plural number, Lāṭy. **-śalya**, m. a variety of Khadira with red blossoms, L. **-śas**, see col. 2. **-śasta**, mfn. very excellent; very right or good or happy, MW. **-śākha**, mf(*ā*)n. 'many-branched,' having many branches or ramifications, multifarious, manifold, TS.; TBr.; m. Euphorbia Antiquorum, L. (*-tva*, n.) **-śākhin**, mfn. = prec. mfn., MBh. **-śāla**, m. Euphorbia Antiquorum. **-śāstra-jña**, mfn. acquainted with many books or sciences, MW. **-śikha**, mfn. 'many-pointed;' (*ā*), f. Commelina Salicifolia and another species, L. (v. l. *vahni-ś°*). **-śubhāya**, Nom. Ā. *°yate*, to be or become a great blessing, Śatr. **-śūnya**, mfn. very empty or void, MW. **-śṛiṅga**, mfn. many-horned, L.; m. N. of Vishṇu. **-śruta**, mfn. one who has studied much, very learned, well versed in the Vedas, Mn.; MBh. &c.; m. N. of a minister, Siṇhās. **-śruti**, f. the occurrence of the plural in a text, ŚrS. **-śrutīya**, m. pl. 'having deep erudition,' N. of a Buddhist school. **-śreyasī**, mfn., Pāṇ. i, 2, 48, Vārtt. 3, Pat. **-saṃvatsara**, n. a Soma sacrifice that lasts many years, ŚāṅkhŚr. **-saṃkhyāka**, mfn. numerous, Sāy. **-sattva**, mfn. abounding in animals, MBh. **-satya**, m. N. of the tenth Muhūrta, Var. **-sadācāra**, mfn., Siddh. (cf. *-samudācāra*). **-sadṛiśa**, mfn. very similar, very fit or right, Pañcat. **-saṃtati**, mfn. having a numerous posterity or after-growth; m. Bambusa Spinosa, L. **-samudācāra**, mfn., Pāṇ. vi, 2, 176, Sch. **-sampuṭa**, m. a species of bulbous root, L. **-sarpishka**, mfn. prepared with much ghee, Vishṇ. **-sava**, mfn. offering many sacrifices or doing anything for many years, BhP., Sch.; containing many sacrifices or years, ib. **-sasya**, mfn. rich in grain; m. N. of a village, Kathās. **-sādhana**, mfn. possessing many resources (*-tā*, f.), Śiś. **-sâdhāra**, mfn. having many supports, Kathās. (cf. *niḥ-sâdh°*). **-sādhāraṇa**, mfn. common to many, MW. **-sāmi**, N. of wk. **-sārá**, mfn. containing much pith, pithy, substantial, ŚBr.; m. Acacia Catechu, L. **-sāhasra**, mf(*ā* or *ī*)n. amounting to many thousands, MBh.; R.; (a sacrifice) of which m° th° partake, R.; (*ī*), f. m° thousands, R. (B.) **-su**, mfn. much-bearing, fertile; m. a hog, boar; (*ū*), f. a sow, L. **-suta**, mfn. having a large progeny or after-growth; (*ā*), f. Asparagus Racemosus, L. **-suvarṇa**, mfn. rich in gold (*-tā*, f.), Rājat. **-suvarṇaka**, mfn. costing or possessing much gold, R.; m. N. of an Agrahāra on the Ganges, Kathās.; of a prince, ib. **-sū**, see *-su*. **-sûkta**, mfn. consisting of many hymns, g. *guṇâdi*. **-sūti**, f. a female who has borne many children (also *°tikā*), L.; *-go*, f. a cow that calves often, L. **-sūvarī**, f. bearing many children, RV. ii, 32, 7. **-stavâvali**, f. N. of a collection of hymns. **-spṛiś**, mfn. reaching to many, generally spread or diffused, Śiś. **-svana**, mfn. 'much-sounding,' making many sounds; m. an owl, L. **-svara**, mfn. many-syllabled, containing more than two syllables (*-tva*, n.), TPrāt. **-svarṇa-laksha-mūlya**, mfn. worth many hundred thousand pieces of gold, Kathās. **-svāmika**, mfn. having m° owners or proprietors, MW. **-hastika**, mf(*ā*)n. rich in elephants, TBr. **-hiraṇyá**, mf(*ā*)n. rich in gold, ĀpŚr.; m. N. of an Ekāha commonly called Dū-ṇāśa, KātyŚr. **Bahûdaka** (*°hu-ud°*), mfn. having much water, R.; m. a kind of mendicant who begs his food at bathing-places, MBh. **Bahûdana** (*°hu-od°*?), n. collection of various kinds of food (?), BhP. **Bahûdita** (*°hu-ud°*), n. loquacity, L. **Bahûrj**, mfn. possessing much strength, Pāṇ. vii, 1, 72, Vārtt. 4, Pat.

Bahuka, mf(*ā*)n. bought at a high price, dear-bought, L.; m. Calotropis Gigantea, L.; a crab, L.; a kind of gallinule, L.; the digger of a tank, L.

Bahútaya, mfn. manifold, various, TS.

Bahutitha, mfn. manifold, various, many, much, MBh.; Kāv.; Pur. (cf. Pāṇ. v, 2, 52); *bahutithe 'hani*, on the 'manieth' day, during many days, Nal. ix, 12; (*am*), ind. much, greatly, MBh.

Bahudhā́, ind. in many ways or parts or forms or directions, variously, manifoldly, much, repeatedly, RV. &c. &c. (with √*kṛi*, to make manifold, multiply, MBh.; to make public, divulge, ib.) **-gata**, mfn. gone in various directions, dispersed, scattered, MW. **-°tmaka** (*°dhâtm°*), mf(*ikā*)n. existing in various forms, manifold in essence, R.

Bahura-madhya, mfn. (*bahura* = *bahula* + *m°*) thick in the middle (said of the Soma juice during the process of fermentation), AitBr. (Sāy.)

Bahulá, mf(*ā́*)n. thick, dense, broad, wide, spacious, ample, large, RV. &c. &c.; abundant, numerous, many, much, ib. (*am*, ind. often, frequently, Nir.; Prāt.; Pāṇ.); accompanied by, attended with, ChUp.; Mn.; MBh. &c.; (in gram.) variously applicable, comprehensive (as a rule); born under the Pleiades, Pāṇ. iv, 3, 33; black, L.; m. (or n.?) the dark half of a month, MBh.; Kāv. &c.; m. Agni or fire, L.; N. of a Prajā-pati, VP.; of a king of the Tāla-jaṅghas, MBh.; m. pl. N. of a people, MārkP.; (*ā*), f. a cow, L.; cardamoms, Bhpr.; the indigo plant, L.; N. of the twelfth Kalā of the moon, Cat.; of a goddess, Pur.; of one of the Mātṛis attending on Skanda, MBh.; of the wife of Uttama who was son of Uttāna-pāda, MārkP.; of the mother of a Samudra, HPariś.; of a mythical cow, Col.; of a river, MBh.; f. pl. = *kṛittikās*, the Pleiades, Var.; L.; n. the sky, L.; factitious black salt, L.; white pepper, L.; a partic. high number, Buddh. **-gandha**, n. 'richly-scented,' a kind of sandal wood, Gal.; (*ā*), f. cardamoms. **-cchada**, m. a red-flowering Hyperanthera, L. **-tara**, mfn. thicker, denser (*dvi-guṇo bahula-taraḥ*, twice as thick), ŚBr. **-tā**, f. (Suśr.) or **-tva**, n. (MBh. &c.) muchness, multiplicity, abundance, numerousness; the being rich in, abounding in (comp.); comprehensiveness. **-tṛiṇa**, mfn. rich in grass, KātyŚr. **-parṇa**, mfn. many-leaved, ib. **-palāśa**, mf(*ā*)n. id., ib. **-varman**, mfn. enveloped in a thick covering, ŚāṅkhŚr. **Bahulânta**, mfn. 'thick at the end,' having a thick sediment (as Soma juice; cf. *bahura-madhya*), RV. **Bahulâbhimāna**, mfn. much-threatening, menacing (said of Indra), ib. **Bahulâyāsa**, mfn. involving much trouble, Bhag. **Bahulâlāpa**, 'm°-talking,' talkative, garrulous, loquacious, ŚārṅgP. **Bahulâvishṭa**, mfn. thickly peopled, densely populated, AitBr. **Bahulâśva**, m. 'having many horses,' N. of a king, Pur. **Bahulêtara-paksha**, m. du. the dark and the other (i. e. light) half of a month, Var. **Bahulâushadika**, mfn. overgrown with herbs, ĀśvGṛ.

Bahulaka, incorrect for *bāhulaka*, q. v.

Bahulikā, f. pl. the Pleiades (= *bahulās*), L.

Bahulita, mfn. augmented, increased, Śiś.

Bahulī, in comp. for *bahula*. **-karaṇa**, n. multiplying, magnifying, W.; winnowing (for *phalī-karaṇa*?), ib. **-karishṇu**, mfn. striving or endeavouring to increase, BhP. **-kāra**, m. great zeal or care for, Lalit. **-kṛita**, mfn. made much or manifold or wide, extended, increased, augmented, aggrandized, MBh.; Hariv.; Pur.; made much of, much practised or cared for, Prab.; made public, promulgated, Śak.; MBh.; Prab.; distracted, MBh.; Hariv.; threshed, winnowed (for *phalī-kṛita*?), L. **-bhāva**, m. the becoming wide-spread, public, general notoriety, Kathās. **-bhū**, P. *-bhavati*, to become widespread, spread, increase (intrans.), Kāv.; Pañcat.; to become public or known, Ragh. **-bhūta**, mfn. become spread or public or known, Śak.

Bahuśás, ind. manifoldly, repeatedly, much, often, TS. &c. &c.

Bahv, in comp. for *bahu*. **-akshara**, mfn. many-syllabled, polysyllabic, RPrāt.; *-tva*, n. polysyllableness, ĀpŚr., Sch.; *°rântya*, mfn. being at the end of a polysyllabic word, MW. **-agni**, mf(*ī*)n. N. of partic. verses in which various Agnis are mentioned, ŚāṅkhBr. **-ac** or **-ac-ka**, mfn. (in gram.) having several vowels, polysyllabic. **-ajavikā́**, mf(*ā́*)n. having many goats and sheep, TBr. **-adhyayana** (Siddh.), **-adhyāya**, mfn. consisting of many chapters, g. *guṇâdi*. **-anartha**, mfn. attended with many evils, MW. **-anná**, mfn. rich in food, RV.; ŚBr. **-ap** or **-apa**, mfn. containing much water, watery, Uṇ. ii, 58, Sch. **-apatya**, mfn. having a numerous progeny; (in astrol.) promising or foretelling a n° pr°; m. a hog or a mouse, L.; (*ā*), f. a cow that has often calved, W. **-apâya**, mfn. attended with many dangers, Pañcat. **-abaddha-pralāpin**, mfn. talking much that is unmeaning, MW. **-abhidhāna**, n. the plural number, RPrāt. **-amitra**, mfn. having many enemies, Kām. **-artha**, mfn. having much meaning or import, important, L.; having many meanings or objects, L. **-árha**, mfn. extremely precious, MaitrS. **-avarodha**, mfn. having many wives, Daś. **-aśvá**, mf(*ā*)n. having many horses, TBr.; m. N. of a son of Mudgala, VP. **-ājya**, mfn. abounding in ghee, ĀpŚr. **-ādin**, mfn. eating much, a great eater, Nir. **-āśin**, mfn. id. (*-tva*, n.), Cāṇ.; m. N. of one of the sons of Dhṛitarāshṭra, MBh. **-āścarya**, mfn. containing many wonderful objects, MBh.; *-maya*, mf(*ī*)n. id., Kathās. **-āśrayā**, f. N. of a Kiṃ-narī, Kāraṇḍ. **-īśvara**, N. of a sacred place on the bank of the Revā or Narmadā river; *-māhātmya*, n. N. of wk. **-ṛic**, mfn. 'many-versed,' containing many verses, Siddh.; f. a N. of the Ṛig-veda or of a Śākhā of the RV., Col. **-ṛica**, mf(*ā*)n. id., BhP.; m. (*ī*, f.) one conversant with the Ṛig-veda, a priest of it or the Hotṛi priest who represents it in the sacrificial ceremonies, Br. &c. &c.; *-kārikā*, f. pl., *-gṛihya-kārikā*, f. pl., *-gṛihya-pariśishṭa*, n., *-paddhati*, f., *-brāhmaṇa* (= *aitareya-br°*), n., *-śrāddha-prayoga*, m., *-shoḍaśa-karma-mantra-vivaraṇa*, n., *-saṃdhyā-bhāshya*, n., *°câhnika*, n., *°kôpanishad* (= *aitareyôp°*), f. N. of wks. **-enas**, mfn. very sinful, Mn. xi, 234. **-aushadhika**, mfn. abounding in herbs, ŚāṅkhGṛ. (prob. w. r. for *-osh°*).

बहनक *bahanaka*, m. pl. N. of a people, VP.

बहादुर *bahādura*. See *bāhādura*.

बहिष्क *bahishka*, w. r. for *barhishka*.

बहिस् *bahís*, ind. (the final *s* is changed before *k* and *p* into *sh*; cf. Pāṇ. viii, 3, 41) out, forth, outwards, outside (a house, village, city, kingdom &c.; also with abl. or ifc. = out of, apart from, except, beside), Br. &c. &c. (with √*kṛi*, to place outside, expel, banish, exclude; with √*bhū*, to come forth; with √*gam* or *yā*, to go out &c.; cf. comp.) **-tanva**, mfn. one whose limbs extend over the body (of the fire-altar), Śulbas. **-tapas**, n. outward penance, Yogaś.

Bahiḥ, in comp. for *bahís*. **-śālā**, f. an outer hall, GṛS. **-śīta**, mfn. cool or cooling on the outside, Suśr. **-śri** (*°hiḥ-*), ind. said of a partic. pronunciation, ŚBr. **-saṃstha**, mfn. lying or situated outside (the town), Kathās. **-sád**, mfn. one who sits outside (said of a person held in low esteem), TBr. **-sadas** or **-sadasam**, ind. outside the Sadas, ŚrS. **-saṃdhya**, mfn. one who performs his morning and evening prayers outside (the village), Gaut. (*-tva*, n.) **-stoma-bhāgám**, ind. outside the bricks called Stoma-bhāgā, ŚBr. **-stha**, **-sthāyin**, **-sthita**, mfn. being outside, external, outer, MW.

Bahir, in comp. for *bahís*. **-aṅga**, mfn. relating to the exterior, external, unessential (opp. to *antar-aṅga*), Śaṃk.; Pāṇ., Sch. (*-tā*, f.; *tva*, n.); m. an external part, outer limb or member, property, &c., W; a stranger, indifferent person, ib.; the preliminary part of a religious ceremony, MW. **-ante**, ind. externally and internally, ib. **-argala** (only ifc., f. *ī*), an outer bolt or bar, Kathās. **-artha**, m. an external object, BhP. **-ātmám**, ind. outside one's own person, away from one's self, MaitrS. **-indriya**, n. an outer organ, organ of sense or perception (as the eye) or of action (as the hand), W. **-gata**, mfn. gone out or forth, externally manifested, R.; Kathās.; *-tva*, n., Mṛicch., Sch. **-gamana**, n. the act of going out or forth, W. **-gāmin**, mfn. going out or forth, MW. **-gira**, m. pl. N. of a people, MārkP. (cf. next). **-giri**, m. a country situated on the other side of a mountain, MBh.; pl. the inhabitants of that c°, ib. (also *°girya*, pl., ib.) **-gīta**, n. a song accompanied by a stringed instrument, L. **-geham**, ind. outside the house, abroad, ib. **-grāmam**, ind. o° the village, Pāṇ. ii, 1, 12, Sch.; *°ma-pratiśraya*, mfn. living o° the v°, Mn. x, 36. **-jānu**, ind. so that the hands are outside (not between) the knees, Hcat. **-nidhana**, w. r. for *-nidh°*, q. v. **-dṛiś**, mfn. seeing only what is outside, superficial (in judgment), Śak., Sch. **-deśa**, m. a foreign country, W.; a place without a town or village, ib. **-dvāra**, n. an outer gate or the space outside a door or gate, MBh.; Kathās.; *-prakoshṭhaka*, n. a portico, a covered terrace in front of the door of a house, W. **-dvārin**, mfn. being out-of-doors, Nār. **-dhā́**, ind. out, outward, outside of or away from (abl.), VS.; Br.; ChUp.; *-bhāva*, m. the being outward or external, KātyŚr. **-dhvajā**, f. N. of Durgā, L. **-niḥsāraṇa**, n. taking out, removal, Pāṇ. v, 4, 62, Sch. **-nidhana**, n. the singing of a finale outside or apart, TāṇḍBr. **-nirgamana**, n. going out of (abl.), Cat. **-nyāsa-sūtra**, n. N. of wk. **-bhava**, mfn. being outside, external (opp. to *antar-ja*), L. **-bhavana**, n. the being outside, coming forth, emanation, MW. **-bhāga**, m. the outer side or part, exterior, KātyŚr., Sch. **-bhāva**, m. the being outside (abl.), ib. **-bhūta**, mfn. being out, expelled or excluded from (ifc.), Pāṇ. iii, 1, 119, Sch.; expired (as a period of time), MW.; inattentive, careless, ib. **-maṇḍala-stha**, mf(*ā*)n. standing outside a circle, ŚāṅkhGṛ. **-manas**, mfn. being outside the mind, external, Sarvad. **-manaska**, mfn. out of mind, Divyâv. **-mātṛikā**, f. N. of wk. **-mukha**, mf(*ī*)n. coming out of the mouth (opp. to *antar-m°*), L.; (ifc.) one who turns his face away, indifferent to (°*khī-√bhū*, to turn away from), Śaṃk. (also with loc., Divyâv.); one who has his mind directed to external things, Śaṃk.; m. a deity (prob. w. r. for *barhir-m°*), L. **-mudra**, m. (?) N. of a form of devotion (opp. to *antar-m°*), Cat. **-yāga-pūjā**, f., **-yāga-ratna**, n. N. of wks. **-yātrā**, f. (R.), **-yāna**, n. (Mṛicch.) going or driving out, excursion. **-yūti**, mfn. placed or fastened outside, Bhaṭṭ. **-yoga**, m. relation to 'outside,' sense or meaning of '*bahis*, outside,' Pāṇ. i, 1, 36; external meditation (cf. *antar-y°*), Cat.; N. of a man (pl. his descendants), g. *yaskâdi*. **-yoní**, ind. outside the fire-place, ŚBr. **-lamba**, mfn. obtuse-angular (*ā*), f. an obtuse-angular triangle, Col. **-lāpikā**, f. a kind of enigma (not containing a solution; opp. to *antar-l°*), L. **-loma** (°*hír-*), mfn. having the hair turned outwards, MaitrS. **-loman**, mfn. id., Āpast. **-vartin**, mfn. being on the outside, L. **-vāsas**, n. an outer or upper garment (cf. *a-bahirv°*). **-vikāra**, m. 'outward change or disfigurement,' syphilis, L.; mfn. (in Sāṃkhya) external to the Vikāras, free from change, MW. (cf. IW. 83); (*am*), ind., Śiś. i, 33. **-vṛitti**, f. occupation with external objects, Kathās. **-vedi**, f. the space outside the Vedi or sacrificial altar, MBh.; MārkP.; (*i*), ind. outside the sacrificial altar, MaitrS.; Br.; MBh. &c. **-vedika**, mfn. being or taking place outside the Vedi (see prec.), Kull. **-vyasana**, n. external vice, licentiousness, immorality, L.; °*nin*, mfn. immoral, dissolute, L.

Bahiś, in comp. for *bahis*. **-cara**, mfn. going out, moving or appearing outside, external, MBh.; (with *prāṇa*, m. or *hṛidaya*, n. 'another life or heart outside one's self, dear as one's own life or heart,' ib.; Hariv.; Kathās. &c.); m. 'crawling out of its shell,' a crab, L.; an external spy, MBh.

Bahish, in comp. for *bahis*. **-karaṇa**, n. expulsion, exclusion from (abl.), Kāś. on Pāṇ. ii, 4, 10; an external organ (opp. to *antaḥ-k°*), Kām. **-karman**, n. a sacred rite performed outside the sacrificial place, ŚāṅkhŚr. **-kāra**, m. expulsion, removal, L. **-kārya**, mfn. to be removed or excluded from (abl.), Mn. ii, 11; 103. **-kuṭī-cara**, m. a crab (cf. *bahiś-cara*). **-kṛita**, mfn. turned out, expelled or excluded from, rejected or abandoned by (abl. or comp.), Mn.; MBh. &c.; shut off by = dwelling beyond (instr.), MBh.; restraining or free from, deprived or destitute of (comp.), MBh.; Kathās.; Rājat.; become apparent, embodied, manifest, Kathās. **-kṛiti**, f. = *-kāra*, L. **-kratu**, ind. outside or apart from the sacrifice, ĀpŚr., Sch. **-kriya**, mfn. excluded from sacred rites, MārkP. **-kriyā**, f. an outer act, external rite or ceremony, MBh. **-tva**, n. outwardness, the being external, Pat. **-paṭa**, m. = *-vāsas*, Cat. **-patnī-saṃyāja**, n. being outside the Patnī-saṃyāja (s. v.), Lāṭy. (*-tva*, n.) **-pathám**, ind. outside the road, MaitrS. **-paridhí**, ind. outside the enclosure, TS.; ŚBr.; KātyŚr. **-pavamāná**, m. N. of a Stoma or Stotra (generally consisting of 3 Tricas and sung outside the Vedi during the morning libation), TS.; Br.; ŚrS.; ChUp.; (*ī*), f. (scil. *stotriyā*, i. e. *ṛic*) its single verses, PañcavBr.; °*nâstāva*, m. the place where the B°-Stotra is sung, ĀpŚr. **-pavitrá**, mfn. destitute of or wanting the Pavitra (s. v.), ŚBr. **-piṇḍa**, mfn. having the knots outside, KātyŚr. **-prajña**, mfn. one whose knowledge is directed towards external objects, Up. **-prākāra**, m. an outer wall or rampart, MBh. **-prāṇa**, m. external breath or life, anything near the heart or as dear as life, R.; money, BhP.; (°*hísh-*), mfn. one whose breath or life is outside, TS.

Bahíshṭāt, ind. outside, TS.; Br. °**ṭāj-jyotis**, n. N. of a Trishṭubh the last Pāda of which contains 8 syllables, RPrāt. °**ṭād-viśasana**, n. (a hide) the flesh-side of which is turned outwards, ĀpŚr.

Bahī, in comp. before *r* for *bahis*. **-rajju**, ind. outside a rope, KātyŚr.

बहीनर *bahīnara*, m. (also written *vah°*) N. of a man, MBh.; BhP.

बहु *bahu* &c. See p. 724.

बहुतलवशा *bahutalavaśā*, f. Iris Pseudacorus, L.

बहुरद *bahurada*, m. pl. N. of a people (v. l. for *bāhubādha*), VP.

बहेटक *baheṭaka*, m. Terminalia Belerica, L.

बह्रामखान *bahrāmakhāna*, m. = بہرام خان.

बह्लि *bahli*, *bahlika*, *bahlīka*, v. l. for *balhi* &c., q. v.

बाक *bāka*, n. (fr. *baka*) a multitude of cranes, Pāṇ. iv, 2, 37, Sch.

Bākarukā, f. a kind of crane, L.

Bākāyana, m. patr. fr. *baka* (also pl.), Saṃskārak. (cf. g. *naḍâdi*).

बाकुर *bākurá*, m. (fr. *bákura*), with *dṛiti* (perhaps) a kind of bag-pipe, RV. ix, 1, 8.

बाकुल *bākula*, mfn. relating to or coming from the Bakula tree, Suśr.; n. the fruit of the Bakula tree, L.

बाजबहादुरचन्द्र *bāja-bahādura-candra*, m. N. of a son of Nīla-candra and patron of Ananta-deva, Cat. (cf. *bāhādura*).

बाड् *bāḍ* (*vāḍ*, Vop.), cl. 1. Ā. *bāḍate*, to bathe, dive, Dhātup. viii, 34.

Bāḍita, mfn. sunk, Divyâv.

बाडब *bāḍaba*. See *vāḍaba*.

बाडभीकर *bāḍabhīkara*, m. N. of a grammarian, TPrāt.

बाडीर *bāḍīra*, m. a hired labourer, L.

बाडेयीपुत्र *bāḍeyī-pútra*, m. N. of a teacher, ŚBr.

बाढ *bāḍhá* or *bāḷhá*, mfn. (√*baṇh*; cf. Pāṇ. v, 63) strong, mighty (only ibc. and in *bāḷhé*, ind.), loudly, strongly, mightily, RV.; (*bāḍham* or *vāḍham*), ind. assuredly, certainly, indeed, really, by all means, so be it, yes (generally used as a particle of consent, affirmation or confirmation), MBh.; Kāv. &c. **-vikrama**, mfn. of excessive prowess, very powerful or strong, W. **-sṛitvan**, mfn. striding mightily along, RV. i, 122, 10.

बाण *bāṇá* or *vāṇá* (RV.), *bāṇa* (AV.; later more usually *vāṇa*, q. v.), m. a reed-shaft, shaft made of a reed, an arrow, RV. &c. &c.; N. of the number five (from the 5 arrows of Kāma-deva; cf. *pañca-b°*), Sūryas.; Sāh.; the versed sine of an arc, Gaṇit.; a mark for arrows, aim, BhP.; a partic. part of an arrow, L.; Saccharum Sara or a similar species of reed, Bhpr.; the udder of a cow (*vāṇá*, RV. iv, 24, 9), L.; music (for *vāṇá*), AV. x, 2, 17; = *kevala*, L.; N. of an Asura (a son of Bali, an enemy of Vishṇu and favourite of Śiva), MBh.; Pur.; of one of Skanda's attendants, MBh.; of a king, Hariv.; (also *-bhaṭṭa*) of a poet (the author of the Kādambarī, of the Harsha-carita, and perhaps of the Ratnâvalī), Cat.; of a man of low origin, Rājat.; m. (Śiś.) or (*ā*), f. (L.) a blue-flowering Barleria; (*ā*), f. the hind part or feathered end of an arrow, L.; n. the flower of Barleria, Kir.; Śiś.; the body, PraśnUp. **-gaṅgā**, f. 'arrow Ganges,' N. of a river flowing past Someśa (and said to have been produced by Rāvaṇa by cleaving a mountain with an a°), VarP. **-gocara**, m. the range of an a°, MBh.; Mālatīm. **-jit**, m. 'conqueror of the Asura Bāṇa,' N. of Vishṇu, L. **-tā**, f. the being an a°, Kum. **-tūṇa**, m. 'a°-quiver,' a quiver; °*ṇī-kṛita*, mfn. made into a quiver, Kathās. **-dhi**, m. 'a°-receptacle,' a quiver, MBh. **-nāśā**, f. N. of a river, Cat. **-nikṛita**, mfn. pierced or wounded by an a°, W. **-pañcânana**, m. N. of a poet, Cat. **-patha**, m. a°-path, a bow-shot; *-vartin*, v. l. for *-pāta-v°* below; °*thâtīta*, mfn. passed beyond the range of an arrow, Vikr. **-parṇī**, f. N. of a plant, Kauś. **-pāṇi**, mfn. 'arrow-handed,' armed with arrows, W. **-pāta**, m. 'arrow-fall,' the range of an arrow; *-vartin*, mfn. being within the range of an a°, Śak. (v. l. *-patha-v°*). **-puṅkhā**, f. the feathered end of an a°, MW.; N. of a plant resembling the Indigo plant, L. **-pur**, f. or **-pura**, n. the capital of the Asura Bāṇa, L. **-bhaṭṭa**, m. N. of the author Bāṇa, Cat. **-maya**, mf(*ī*)n. consisting of arrows, arrowy, MBh. **-mukti**, f. or **-mokshaṇa**, n. discharge of an a°, L. **-mukha** (*bā́ṇa-*), mfn. having a°s in the mouth, Suparṇ. **-yojana**, n. 'a°-union,' a quiver, Pañcat. **-rekhā**, f. 'a°-line,' a long wound made by an a°, R. **-liṅga**, n. a white stone found in the Narmadā river and worshipped as the Liṅga of Śiva, RTL. 69. **-vat** (*bā́ṇa-*), mfn. 'made of or containing reed,' an arrow, ŚBr.; ŚrS.; a quiver, VS.; ŚBr. **-varshaṇa**, n., **-vṛishṭi**, f. a shower of arrows or darts, MW. **-varshin**, mfn. showering a°s, Ragh. **-vāra**, m. a multitude of a°s, L.; n. a breastplate, armour, ib. **-saṃdhāna**, n. the fitting of an arrow to the bow-string, Śak. **-siddhi**, f. the hitting of a mark by an a°, Kām. **-sutā**, f. 'daughter of Bāṇa,' N. of Ushā (the wife of Aniruddha), L. **-han**, m. 'slayer of B°,' name of Vishṇu, L. **Bāṇaparṇī**, w. r. for °*ṇa-p°*, q. v. **Bāṇâbhyāsa**, m. 'arrow-throwing,' archery, L. **Bāṇâri**, m. 'enemy of B°,' id., L. **Bāṇavalī**, f. a series of 5 Ślokas (containing only one sentence), Kāvyâd., Sch. **Bāṇâśraya**, m. 'arrow-receptacle,' a quiver, L. **Bāṇâsana**, n. 'a°-discharger,' a bow, Śak.; a bow-string, L.; °*nī-√kṛi*, to make into a bow, Hariv. **Bāṇâsura**, m. the Asura Bāṇa; *-vadha* and *-vijaya*, m. 'the killing and conquering of the A° B°,' N. of wks. **Bāṇêśvara**, m. N. of a Liṅga (prob. = *bāṇa-l°*), Cat.; N. of sev. authors, ib.

Bāṇin, mfn. having an arrow or arrows, MBh.; R.

Bāṇeya, m. an adherent of the Asura Bāṇa, Hariv.

बाणि *bāṇi*, °*ṇī*. See *vāṇi*, °*ṇī*.

बाणिज *bāṇija*, °*jya*. See *vāṇija*, °*jya*.

बादक्सान *bādaksāna* = Bādakshān, Bhpr. (v. l. *bad°*).

बादर *bādara*, mf(*ī*)n. (fr. *badara*) belonging to or derived from the jujube tree, Suśr.; made of cotton, L.; coarse (opp. to *sūkshma*), Śil.; m. or (*ā*), f. the cotton shrub, L.; m. pl. N. of a people, Var.; n. the jujube (= *badara*), Suśr.; the berry of Abrus Precatorius or the plant itself, L.; silk, L.; water, L.; a conch shell which winds from left to right, L. = *vāra* (N. of a plant or w. r. for *vāri*?), L.

Bādarāyaṇa, m. (patr. fr. *badara*; cf. g. *naḍâdi*) N. of sev. teachers and authors (esp. of a sage identified with Vyāsa, said to be the author of the Vedânta-sūtras; of an astronomer; of the author of a Dharma-śāstra &c.), IW. 106 &c.; mfn. written or composed by Bād°, Cat. **-praśna**, m. N. of an astrol. wk. **-sūtra**, n. N. of the Vedânta-s°.

Bādarāyaṇi, m. (patr. fr. prec.) N. of Śuka, Cat.; = *Bādarāyaṇa*, ib.

Bādari, m. (patr. fr. *badara*) N. of a philosopher, Bādar.

Bādarika, mfn. one who gathers the fruit of the jujube tree, Pāṇ. iv, 4, 32, Sch.

बादाम *bādāma*, m. an almond-tree, Pers.

बाध् *bādh*, cl. 1. Ā. (Dhātup. ii, 4) *bādhate*, ep. and m. c. also P. °*ti* (pf. *babādhé*, RV.; aor. *bādhishṭa*, ib., *bādhishṭām*, TĀr.; fut. *bādhishyate*, °*ti*, MBh. &c., *bādhitā*, Gr.; inf. *bādhe*, RV., *bādhitum*, MBh.; ind. p. *bādhitvā*, see s. v., *bādhya*, RV.), to press, force, drive away, repel, remove, RV. &c. &c.; (with *várīyas*) to force asunder, RV. x, 113, 5; to harass, pain, trouble, grieve, vex, RV. &c. &c.; to resist, oppose, check, stop, prevent, MBh.; Kāv. &c.; to set aside (as a rule), annul, invalidate, Pāṇ., Sch.; Nilak. &c.; to suffer annoyance or oppression, TS.: Pass. *bādhyate*, to be pressed &c.; to be acted upon, suffer, Pañcat.: Caus. *bādhayati* (aor. *ababādhat*, Pāṇ. vii, 4, 2), to oppress, harass, attack, trouble, vex, R.; Bhaṭṭ.: Desid. *bibādhishate*, to wish to remove or chase away, ĀpŚr., Sch.; *bībhatsate*, to feel an aversion for, loathe, shrink from (abl.), Br.; ŚrS. &c. (cf. Pāṇ. iii, 1, 6): Intens. *bābadhe* (see *pra-√bādh*); *badbadhé*, to press hard, hem in, confine, RV.; pr. p. *badbadhāná*, striking, knocking against (acc.),

RV. vii, 69, 1; hemmed in, pent up, i, 52, 10 &c. [Cf. √vadh, also for kindred words.]

1. **Bādhá**, m. a harasser, tormentor, Hariv.; annoyance, molestation, affliction, obstacle, distress, pain, trouble, RV. &c. &c.; (also *ā*, f.; cf. Vām. v, 2, 44) injury, detriment, hurt, damage, MBh.; Kāv. &c.; danger, jeopardy (see *prâṇa-*); exclusion from (comp.), Pañcat.; suspension, annulment (of a rule &c.), Sāh.; Pāṇ., Sch. &c.; a contradiction, objection, absurdity, the being excluded by superior proof (in log., one of the 5 forms of fallacious middle term), Kap.; Bhāshāp. &c. **-cintāmaṇi**, m., **-tā**, f., **-pūrva-paksha-grantha-kroḍa**, m., °**tha-ṭīkā**, f., °**tha-prakāśa**, m., °**tha-vivecana**, n., °**thânugama**, m.; **-buddhi-pratibadhyatâ-vāda**, m., **-buddhi-pratibadhya-pratibandhaka-bhāva-vāda**, m., **-buddhi-pratibandhakatā-vicāra**, m., **-buddhi-vāda**, m., **-buddhi-vādârtha**, m., **-buddhi-vicāra**, m., **-rahasya**, n., **-vāda**, m., **-vicāra**, m., **-vibhājaka**, m. or n., **-siddhânta-grantha-ṭīkā**, f., °**tha-kroḍa**, m., °**tha-prakāśa**, m., °**tha-vivecana**, n., °**thānugama**, m. N. of wks. **Bādhânta**, m. N. of wk.

2. **Bā́dha**, m. (prob.) urging, impulse (Naigh. ii, 9 = *bala*; Sāy. = *bādhaka*, *bādhana*), RV. vi, 11, 5; i, 61, 2; 132, 5 (?).

Bādhaka, mf(*ikā*)n. oppressing, harassing, paining (see *śatru-b°*); opposing, hindering, injuring, prejudicing, MBh.; Pur. (*-tā*, f.); setting aside, suspending, annulling, Śaṃk.; Sarvad. (*-tva*, n.); m. a partic. disease of women, L.; a kind of tree, Gobh.; mf(*ī*)n. belonging to or derived from the Bādhaka tree, ShaḍvBr.; ŚrS. **-maya**, mf(*ī*)n. = prec. mfn., SāmavBr.

Bādhana, mfn. oppressing, harassing (see *śatru-b°*); opposing, refuting, L.; (*ā*), f. uneasiness, trouble, pain, Nyāyas.; n. opposition, resistance, oppression, molestation, affliction (also pl.), R.; Śak.; removing, suspending, annulment (of a rule &c.), Vedântas.; Pāṇ., Sch.

Bādhanīya, mfn. to be removed, Nyāyam., Sch.

Bādhayitṛi, m. an injurer, opposer (°*trī*, f.), Sāy.

Bādhitá, mfn. pressed, oppressed &c., RV. &c. &c.; (in gram.) set aside, annulled; (in logic) contradictory, absurd, false, incompatible (cf. *a-bādhita*). **-tva**, n. the being suspended or refuted or contradicted, Vedântas.

Bādhitavya, mfn. to be pressed hard or harassed or pained, MBh.; to be suspended or annulled, KātyŚr., Sch.

Bādhitṛi, m. an oppressor, harasser, annoyer, MBh.; Bālar.; Prab.

Bādhitvā, ind. having pressed hard or harassed, MW.; (in gram.) destroying or neutralizing the effect of a previous rule.

Bādhin, mfn. (ifc.) injuring, impeding, Jātakam.

Bādhya, mfn. to be (or being) pressed hard or harassed or distressed or pained or checked or suppressed, Kāv.; Kathās.; Pur. &c.; to be (or being) set aside or suspended or annulled, Vop. **-tva**, n. the state of being set aside, suspension, annulment, Kap. **-bādhakatā**, f. the condition of oppressed and oppressor, BhP.; the c° of one who pains such as deserve to be pained, ib. **-retas**, m. one whose generative fluid is obstructed, impotent, Kull. on Mn. ix, 79.

Bādhyamāna-tva, n. the condition of being suspended or set aside, suspension, annulment, Nilak.

बाधिरक *bādhiraka*, mfn. (fr. *badhira*), g. *arīhaṇâdi*.

Bādhirika, m. metron. fr. *badhirikā*, g. *śivâdi*.

Bādhirya, n. deafness, MBh.; Suśr.

बाधूल *bādhūla*, m. N. of a family, Cat. **-śishya**, m. N. of an author, ib. **-smṛiti**, f. N. of wk.

बाध्योग *bā́dhyoga* (ŚBr.), *bādhyauga* (Kāś. on Pāṇ. vii, 3, 20), patr. fr. *badhyoga*.

Bādhyaugāyana, m. patr. fr. *badhyoga*, g. *haritâdi*.

बाध्व *bādhva*, m. patr., N. of a Ṛishi, AitĀr. (w. r. *bādhya*).

बान्धकि *bāndhaki*, m. patr. or metron., g. *taulvaly-ādi*.

Bāndhakineya, m. (fr. *bandhakī*) the son of an unmarried woman, a bastard, L. (g. *kalyāṇy-ādi*).

Bāndhakeya, m. id., g. *śubhrâdi*.

बान्धव *bāndhava*, m. (fr. *bandhu*) a kinsman, relation (esp. maternal r°), friend (ifc. f. *ā*), Mn.; MBh. &c.; a brother, A.; (*ī*), f. a female relative, Kathās. **-jana**, m. relatives, kinsmen (collectively), Mṛicch.; Pañcat. **-tā**, f. relationship, Caṇḍ. **-dhurā**, f. a friendly turn, kindness, Mālatīm. vii, 4 (= *mitra-kṛitya*, Sch.)

Bāndhavaka, mfn. belonging or relating to kinsmen, kindred, Hariv.

Bāndhavya, n. connection by blood, relationship, Kathās.

बान्धुक *bāndhuka*, mf(*ī*)n. belonging to or derived from the Bandhuka tree, Kāṭh. (ĀpŚr. *māndhuka*).

बान्धुकिनेय *bāndhukineya*, m. metron. fr. *bandhukī*, g. *kalyāṇy-ādi*.

Bāndhukya, n. marriage, Gal.

Bāndhupata, mf(*ī*)n., fr. *bandhu-pati*, g. *aś-vapaty-ādi*.

बापण्णभट्ट *bāpaṇṇa-bhaṭṭa*, m. N. of an author, Cat.

बापय *bāpaya*, m. N. of Kāśī-nātha-bhaṭṭa, q. v.

बापुभट्ट *bāpu-bhaṭṭa*, m. N. of an author (also called Ananta-bhaṭṭa), Cat.

बापूदेव *bāpū-deva*, m. N. of an author, Cat.

बाप्यदेव *bāpya-deva*, m. N. of the writer of a partic. inscription, Inscr.

बाबखानचरित्र *bābakhāna-caritra*, n. N. of wk.

बाबर *bābara*, n. (fr. *babara*) N. of a Pañcarātra, ĀśvŚr.; of a place, Cat.

बाबुजीव्यास *bābujī-vyāsa*, m. N. of an author, Cat.

बाबेरी *bāberī*, f. N. of a city, Cat.

बाभ्रव *bā́bhrava*, mf(*ī*)n. belonging or relating to Babhru, PañcavBr.; m. patr. fr. *bábhru*, ŚBr. (cf. Pāṇ. iv, 1, 106); (*ī*), f. N. of Durgā, L.; n. N. of various Sāmans, ĀrshBr. **-dāna-cyuta** and **-śālaṅkāyana** (*bā́bhr°*), m. pl., g. *kārta-kaujapa*.

Bābhravāyaṇi, m. (patr. fr. *babhru*) N. of a son of Viśvā-mitra, MBh.

Bābhravīya, mfn. relating or belonging to Bābhravya, Cat.; m. pl. his disciples, ib.

Bābhravya, m. N. of various authors and teachers (also with *kauśika* and *pañcāla*, and *śāṇḍilā*, pl.), GṛS.; Hariv.; Cat. (cf. Pāṇ. iv, 1, 106); of other men, Ratnâv.; MārkP.; (*ā*), f. N. of a woman, L.

Bābhravyaka, mfn. inhabited by Bābhravyas, g. *rājanyâdi*.

Bābhravyāyaṇī, f. of *bābhravya*, g. *lohitâdi*.

Bābhruka, mfn. (fr. *babhru*) like an ichneumon i.e. (prob.) brown, brownish, g. *aṅguly-ādi*.

बायभट्ट *bāya-bhaṭṭa*, m. N. of a son of Kṛishṇa and father of Advaita, Cat.

बार *bāra*, m. or n. (?) an opening, aperture (see *jihmá-* and *nīcīna-b°*).

बारहट *bārahaṭa*, m. N. of Nara-hara-dāsa (the author of the Hindī work Avatāra-caritra or Caturviṇśaty-avatāra-caritra), Cat.

बारेज्य *bārejya*, N. of a town, Cat.

बार्ढ्य *bārḍhya* or *vārḍhya*, n., fr. *bṛiḍha* (*vṛiḍha*), g. *dṛiḍhâdi*.

बार्बर *bārbara*, mfn. born in the country of the barbarians, g. *takshaśilâdi*.

Bārbaraka, mfn. (fr. *barbara*), g. *dhūmâdi*.

बार्बरीट *bārbarīṭa*, m. (only L.) the kernel of the mango fruit; a young shoot; tin; the son of a harlot.

बार्ह *bārha*, mfn. (fr. *barha*) made of the feathers of a peacock's tail, BhP.

Bārhiṇa-lakshmaṇa, mfn., (prob.) w. r. for *barhiṇa-l°*, q. v.

बार्हत् *bārhat*, Vriddhi form of *bṛihat* in comp. **-sāmā**, f. (*-sāman*) N. of a woman, AV.

Bārhata, mf(*ī*)n. relating to the Sāman Bṛihat, VS.; TS.; Br.; ŚrS.; relating to the metre Bṛihatī, TS.; RPrāt. &c.; m. pl. the Soma keepers, RV. x, 85, 4 (Sāy.); n. the fruit of the Bṛihatī (a variety of the Solanum).

Bārhataka, m. N. of a man, Mālav. i, $\frac{6}{7}$ (w. r. *vāhataka*).

Bārhatānushṭubha, mfn. consisting of a Bṛihatī and an Anushṭubh, RPrāt.

Bārhad, in comp. for *bārhat*. **-agna**, m. pl. the descendants of Bṛihad-agni, g. *kaṇvâdi*. **-isha-va** (m. c.), m. patr. fr. Bṛihad-ishu (also pl.), BhP. **-ukthá**, m. patr. fr. Bṛihad-uktha, Br.; n. N. of various Sāmans, ĀrshBr. **-gira**, mf(*ī*)n. relating to Bṛihad-giri; n. N. of various Sāmans, ĀrshBr. **-daivata**, n. N. of a wk. (= *bṛihad-devatā* and ascribed to Śaunaka), Shaḍguruś. **-bala**, mf(*ī*)n. relating to Bṛihad-bala, BhP. **-ratha**, mf(*ī*)n. relating to Bṛihad-ratha, MBh.; m. patr. of Jarā-saṃdha, ib.; Hariv.; pl. (with *bhū-pālāḥ*), Pur. **-rathi**, m. pl. patr. of Jarā-saṃdha, L.

Bārhas, Vriddhi form of *bṛihas* in comp. **-pata**, mf(*ī*)n. relating to or descended from Bṛihas-pati, MBh.; R. **-patyá**, mfn. id., AV. &c. &c. (with *bha* or *nakshatra*, n. the constellation Pushya, Sūryas.; with *māna*, n. 'Jupiter's measure,' a method of reckoning time, ib.); m. patr. fr. Bṛihas-pati (N. of Śaṃyu, Agni, Tapur-mūrdhan, Bharad-vāja), TS.; ŚBr.; Nir. &c.; a pupil of B°, BhP.; an infidel, materialist, ib.; Hariv.; n. the Artha-śāstra of B°, ethics, morality, Lalit.; N. of various Sāmans, ĀrshBr.; *-jyotiḥ-śāstra*, n., or °*tir-grantha*, m., *-tantra*, n., *-mahiman*, m., *-muhūrta-vidhāna*, n., *-saṃhitā*, f., *-sūtra-ṭīkā*, f., *-smṛiti*, f. N. of works.

बार्हवत *bārhavata*, mf(*ī*)n. containing the word *barha-vat*, g. *vimuktâdi*.

बार्हिषद *bārhishada* or *bārhiḥshada*, m. patr. fr. *barhi-shad* or *barhiḥ-shad* (also pl.), BhP.

बाल् *bāl*, ind. onomat. an interjection imitating the sound of a falling body, AV.

बाल *bāla*, mf(*ā*)n. (cf. *vāla*) young, childish, infantine, not full-grown or developed (of persons and things), GṛS.; Up.; Mn.; MBh. &c.; newly risen, early (as the sun or its rays), Ragh.; new or waxing (as the moon), ib.; Kum.; puerile, ignorant, simple, foolish, Mn.; Hariv.; Kāv.; pure (as an animal fit for sacrifice), L.; m. a child, boy (esp. one under 5 years), Mn.; MBh. &c.; (in law) a minor (minors are classified as *kumāra* or boys under 5 years of age, *śiśu* under 8, *pogaṇḍa* from the 5th to the end of the 9th or till the 16th year, and *kiśora* from the 10th to the 16th year); a fool, simpleton, Mn.; Pañcat.; any young animal, L.; a colt, foal, L.; a five years old elephant, L.; Cyprinus Denticulatus or Rohita, L.; N. of a Rakshas, VP.; of a prince, Rājat.; (*ā*), f. a female child, girl, young woman (esp. one under 16 years), Mn.; MBh. &c.; a one year old cow, L.; small cardamoms, L.; Aloe Indica, L.; a kind of metre, L.; a partic. mystical prayer, Cat.; N. of the mother of Vālin and Su-grīva (said to have been formed by Prajā-pati out of some dust which had fallen into his eyes), R.; n. Andropogon Muricatus, L.; heat, L. **-kadalī**, f. a young plantain tree, Musa Sapientum, Mṛicch. **-kamalinī**, f. a y° lotus plant, Mālatīm. **-kavi**, m. N. of an author, Cat. **-kāṇḍa**, m. 'the boy (Rāma) section,' N. of the first book of the Rāmāyaṇa (*ādi-k°* in B.) and of the Adhyātma-rāmāyaṇa (s. v.) **-kāvya**, n. N. of a poem. **-kunda**, m. a young jasmine; °*dânuviddha*, mfn. adorned with y° jasmine blossoms, Megh. **-kṛishṇa**, m. the boy Kṛishṇa or K° as a boy, RTL. 136; N. of a man also called Gaṅgā-dhara, W.; of various authors (also *-dāsa*, *-dīkshita*, *-bhaṭṭa* and *-miśra-*), Cat.; *-krīḍā-kāvya*, n. and *-campū*, f. N. of 2 poems; °*nânanda*, m. N. of an author, Cat.; °*nâshṭaka*, n. N. of a Stotra. **-keli** or **-kelī**, f. child's play or amusement, Daś. **-kriyā**, f. doings or conduct of children, MārkP. **-krīḍana**, n. = *-keli*, Kāv.; °*naka*, n. id., Hariv.; (pl.) N. of ch. of Vātsyāyana's Kāmasūtra; m. a child's toy or plaything, MBh.; a ball, L.; N. of Śiva, MBh.; Cypraea Moneta, L. **-krīḍā**, f. = *-keli*, Cat.; *-kāvya* and *-varṇana*, n. N. of wks. **-khilya**, see *vāla-kh°*. **-gaja**, m. a young elephant, BhP. **-gaṇapati-pūjā**, f. N. of work. **-garbhiṇī**, f. a cow with calf for the first time, L. **-gādā-dharī**, f. N. of wk. (= *tarka-saṃgraha-*

dīpikā). **-gopāla**, m. Kṛishṇa as a youthful herdsman, Pañcar.; N. of an author (also °*lêndra*, Cat.); *-tīrtha*, m. N. of the teacher of Dhana-pati, ib.; *-yatîndra*, m. N. of an author, ib. **-govinda**, m. N. of an author, Cat. **-gaurī-tīrtha**, n. N. of a sacred bathing-place in Śrī-māla, Cat. **-graha**, m. 'seizer of children,' a kind of demon (said to cause 9 kinds of possession), MBh.; AgP.; Suśr.; *-pratishedha*, m., *-yoga-śānti*, f., °*hôpaśamana*, n. N. of wks. **-ghna**, m. a child-murderer, Mn. xi, 190. **-candra**, m. the young or waxing moon (also °*dra-mas*), Kāv.; n. a cavity of a partic. shape (made in a wall), Mṛicch. **-candrikā**, f. N. of a woman, Daś. **-carita** or °**tva**, n. 'childish doings,' N. of wks. or chs. of wks. treating of the youthful adventures of a deity, (esp.) of ch. of GaṇP.; °*ta-nāman*, n. N. of wk. **-carya**, m. 'behaving like a child,' N. of Skanda, L.; (*ā*), f. the behaviour of a child, R. **-cāturbhadrikā**, f. a partic. mixture for children, L. **-cikitsā**, f. 'treatment of ch°,' N. of sev. medic. wks. **-cūta**, m. a young mango tree, Ragh. **-jātaka**, n. 'child's nativity,' N. of wk. **-jātīya**, mfn. childish, foolish, simple, L. **-tanaya**, m. a young son, W.; Acacia Catechu, L. **-tantra**, n. midwifery, L.; N. of a wk. on m°. **-taru**, m. a young tree, Śak. **-tā**, f. (MBh.), **-tva**, n. (Kāv.; Pur.) childhood, boyhood. **-tṛiṇa**, n. young grass, Kuval. **-darśam**, ind. at the sight of a boy, Kathās. **-dalaka**, m. 'small-leafed,' Acacia Catechu, L. **-deva**, m. N. of a man, Cat.; patr. fr. *bala-d°*, Pat. **-dhana**, n. the property of a minor or infant, Mn. viii, 147. **-netra**, mf(*ā*)n. guided or steered by a fool (as a ship), MBh. **-paṇḍita**, m. N. of an author, Cat. **-pattra**, m. 'small-leafed,' N. of a tree, Kāv. (Hedysarum Alhagi or = next, L.) **-pattraka**, m. Acacia Catechu, L. **-pāṭha**, m. N. of wk. **-pādapa**, m. = *-taru*, Śak. **-pāśyā**, f. a string of pearls or other ornament for the hair, W. **-putra**, mf(*ā*)n. having children or young, MBh.; R. **-putraka**, m. a little son, Kathās. **-pushpikā** or **-pushpī**, f Jasminum Auriculatum, L. **-prakāśa**, m., **-prabodhikā** and °**dhinī**, f. N. of wks. **-pramathanī**, f. a partic. Sakti, Hcat. **-bandhana**, m. 'child-binder,' N. of a demon, PārGṛ. **-buddhi-prakāśinī**, f. N. of wk. **-bodha** (and *-saṃgraha*), m. N. of wks. **-bodhaka**, m. instructing the young, Cat.; (*ikā*), f. N. of wk. **-bodhanī**, f. N. of wk.; *-nyāsa*, m. and *-bhāva-prakāśa*, m. N. of wks. **-bhañjaka**, m. N. of a man, Rājat. **-bhadraka**, n. a kind of mineral poison (?), L. **-bhārata**, n. 'the little Bharata' (opp. to the Mahā-bh° or great Bh°), N. of a Kāvya, a Campū, and a drama (= *pracaṇḍa-pāṇḍava*). **-bhāva**, m. state of a child, childhood, minority, infancy, youth, Mn. viii, 118 (Kull. 'inattention'); MBh. &c.; children collectively, Mālatīm.; recent rise (of a planet), Kāv. **-bhāshā-vyākaraṇa-sūtra-vṛitti**, f., **-bhūshā**, f. (and °*shā-sāra*, m.), N. of wks. **-bhṛitya**, m. a servant from childhood, Kathās. **-bhairavī-dīpa-dāna**, n. N. of wk. **-bhaishajya**, n. a kind of collyrium (= *rasâñjana*), L. **-bhojya**, n. 'children's food,' pease, L. **-mati**, mfn. of childish intellect, MBh. **-manoramā**, f. 'pleasant to children,' N. of sev. grammars. **-mandāra-vṛiksha**, m. a young coral tree, Megh. **-maraṇa**, n. (with Jainas) a fool's manner of dying (12 in number, among which is suicide); *-vidhi-kartavyatā*, f. N. of wk. **-mallavena-siddhânta**, m. N. of wk. **-mitra**, n. a friend from boyhood, Mṛicch. **-mukundâcārya**, m. N. of an author, Cat. **-mūla**, m. a young radish, L. **-mūlaka**, m. a species of plant, Suśr.; (*ikā*), f. Hibiscus Cannabinus, Bhpr. **-mūshikā**, f. a small rat, mouse, L. **-mṛiga**, m. a young deer, fawn, R. **-mṛiṇāla**, m. n. a tender filament or fibre of the lotus, Bhartṛ. **-m-bhaṭṭa**, m. N. of sev. men and authors, Cat.; mf(*ī*)n. written or composed by Bālam-bhaṭṭa, ib.; °*ṭṭīya*, n. N. of wk. **-yajñôpavītaka**, n. the sacred thread worn across the breast, L.; a sort of substitute for the s° th° worn by children (?), W. (cf. *bālôpavīta*). **-rakshaṇa**, n. 'guarding children;' *-vidhāna*, n. N. of wk. **-rakshā**, f. = *-rakshaṇa*; *-stava*, m., *-stotra*, n. N. of wks. **-rañjinī**, f. 'pleasing children,' N. of an elementary grammar by Bāla-śāstrin. **-rāghavīya**, n. N. of a poem. **-rāja**, n. (?) lapis lazuli, W. (cf. *bāla-sūrya*). **-rāma-bharata**, n. N. of a poem. **-rāmāyaṇa**, n. 'the little Rāmāyaṇa,' N. of a Nāṭaka by Rāja-śekhara (cf. *mahārām°* and *bāla-bhārata*). **-rūpa**, m. or n. (?) N. of an author or of a wk.; *-dhara*, m. 'bearing a boy's form,' N. of Śiva, MW.; *-dhṛik*, mfn. having a boy's form, assuming the f° of a dwarf, ib. **-roga**, m. disease of children, Cat. **-latā**, f. a young creeper, Ragh. **-līlā**, f. = *-keli*, BhP. **-vatsa**, mf(*ā*)n. one whose child is still a boy, MBh.; R.; m. a young calf, Ragh.; 'child's favourite,' a dove, pigeon, W. **-vanitā**, f. a y° woman, Hit. **-vāhya**, m. 'ridden by children,' a y° goat, L. **-vinashṭa** or °**ṭaka**, m. N. of a man, Kathās. **-vinodinī**, f., **-vivekinī**, f. N. of wks. **-vṛiksha**, m. = *-taru*, Ragh. **-vaidhavya**, n. child-widowhood, ŚārṅgP. **-vyākaraṇa**, n. 'a child's gr°,' N. of a grammar. **-vrata**, m. N. of the Buddhist saint Mañjuśrī, L. **-śarman**, m. N. of a man, Cat. **-śāstrin**, m. N. of a grammarian and of a living writer, Cat. **-śṛiṅga**, mfn. having young (i. e. not yet full-grown) horns, Hariv. **-sakhi**, m. = *-mitra*, Kathās.; the friend of a fool (*-tva*, n.), Subh. **-saṃjīvana**, n. N. of ch. of GaṇP. ii. **-saṃdhyā**, f. early twilight, dawn, L.; °*dhyâbha*, mfn. 'dawn-like,' of a purple colour, MW. **-sarasvatī**, m. N. of an author, Cat.; °*tīya*, n. (with or scil. *kāvya*) N. of wk. **-sâtmya**, n. 'suitable for children,' milk, L. **-sāra-yantra**, n. N. of wk. **-siṇha**, m. N. of a man, Inscr. **-suhṛid**, m. = *-mitra*, Kathās. **-sūrya** and °**yaka**, n. lapis lazuli, L. **-sthāna**, n. condition of a child, childhood, youth, inexperience, MW. **-hatyā**, f. child-murder, ib. **-han**, mf(*ghnī*)n. ch°-murdering, BhP. **Bālā-kalpa**, m., **Bālā-kavaca**, m. or n. N. of wks. **Bālâgra**, n. (*vāl°*?) a dove-cot, Mṛicch. i, 50/1 (Sch.) **Bālâcārya**, m. N. of a teacher, Cat. **Bālā-tantra**, n. N. of wk. **Bālâtapa**, m. early heat of the sun, heat of the morning sun, Mn.; Kālid. (also pl.); *-rakta*, mfn. red with the morning sunbeams, Ragh. **Bālā-tripura-sundarī-pūjana-prayoga**, m. N. of wk. **Bālâditya**, m. the newly risen sun, morning sun, MBh.; N. of princes, Rājat.; *-vrata*, n. N. of wk. **Bālā-dīkshita**, m. N. of an author, Cat. (cf. *bāla-d°*). **Bālâdhyāpaka**, m. a teacher of boys (*-tā*, f.), Rājat. **Bālânucara-gupta** or °**gopta**, m. N. of Śiva, MBh. **Bālā-pañcaratna**, n. N. of wk. **Bālâpatya**, n. youthful progeny, W. **Bālā-paddhati**, f. N. of wk. **Bālâbhyāsa**, m. early application, study during childhood, MW. **Bālâmaya**, m. a child's disease; *-pratishedha*, m. N. of wk. **Bālârishṭa**, n. and °**ṭādhyāya**, m. N. of wks. **Bālâruṇa**, m. early dawn, Kum.; mfn. red like e° d°, Ragh. **Bālârka**, m. the newly risen sun, MBh.; *-komala*, mfn. soft as the orient sun, MW.; *-pratimā*, f. the image or reflection of the orient sun, Ragh.; *-varṇa*, mfn. coloured like the o° s° (said of Śiva), MBh.; °*kāya*, Nom. (°*yita*, mfn.) to resemble the orient sun, Subh. **Bālârcā-paddhati**, f., **Bālâloka-saṃkshepa**, m. N. of wks. **Bālâvabodha**, m. instruction of the young (also °*dhana*, n., Pañcat.); N. of 2 wks.; *-paddhati*, f. N. of a Comm. on ŚāṅkhGṛ. **Bālāvarṇana**, n. N. of ŚārṅgP. xx. **Bālâvastha**, mfn. being in childhood, still young, Vikr.; (*ā*), f. childhood, youth, MW. **Bālâśoka**, m. a young Aśoka tree, Vikr. **Bālâshṭaka** and **Bālâshṭôttara-śatanāma-stotra**, n. N. of Stotras. **Bālâsura**, m. N. of an Asura; *-vadha*, m. N. of ch. of GaṇP. ii. **Bālā-hatyā**, f. the murdering of female children, MW. **Bālêndu**, m. the new or waxing moon, Kum. **Bālêśvara**, m. N. of an author, Cat. **Bālêshṭa**, m. 'liked by children,' a jujube tree, L. **Bālôpacaraṇa**, n. medical treatment of children (also °*cāra*), Cat.; °*ṇīya*, mfn. relating to it; n. N. of ch. of wk., ib. **Bālôpanishad**, f. N. of an Upanishad. **Bālôpavīta**, n. = *bāla-yajñôpavītaka*, a cloth covering the privities, W.

Bālaka, mf(*ikā*)n. young, childish, not yet full-grown, MBh.; Kāv. &c.; m. a child, boy, youth (in law 'a minor'), the young of an animal, ib. (*ikā*, f. a girl, Kāv.; Pur.); a young elephant five years old, Śiś. v, 47; a fool, simpleton, L.; a kind of fish, L.; N. of a prince (v. l. *pālaka*), Pur. **-tva**, n. childhood, childishness, W. **-pralapita**, n. childish talk, foolish prattle, MW. **-priya**, mfn. fond of children; (*ā*), f. colocynth, L.; Musa Sapientum, L. **-hatyā**, f. infanticide, MW.

Bālakīya, mfn. childish, infantine, W.

Bālāyani, m. metron. of a teacher, BhP. (cf. g. *tikâdi*).

Bāli, °**lin**. See *vāli*, °*lin*.

Bāliman, m. childhood, youth, immaturity, g. *pṛithv-ādi*.

1. **Bāliśa**, mf(*ā*)n. young, childish, puerile, ignorant, simple, foolish, MBh.; Kāv. &c.; m. a fool, simpleton, blockhead, ib. **-tā**, f. (Uttarar.), **-tva**, n. (Hariv.) childishness, simplicity, folly. **-mati**, mfn. childish-minded, foolish, MBh.

Bāliśya, n. (g. *brāhmaṇâdi*) childishness, youth, thoughtlessness, folly, Mn.; MBh. &c.

1. **Bāleya**, mfn. fit or proper for children, L.; tender, soft, L. (for 2. see below).

Bâlya or **bālyâ**, n. boyhood, childhood, infancy, ŚBr.; Mn.; MBh. &c.; crescent state (of the moon), Kum. vii, 35; = *bāliśya*, ŚBr.; MBh.; Kāv. &c. **-kāla**, m. the period or age of childhood, MW. **-tā**, f. boyhood, infancy, R.

बालन्दन *bālandana*, m. patr. of Vatsa-prī (cf. *bhālandana*).

बालाकि *bâlāki*, m. metron. fr. *balākā*, ŚBr. (cf. g. *bāhv-ādi*).

Bālâkyā. See *kâśyapī-bālâkyā-māṭharī-putra*.

बालाह *bālāha* (or *vāl°*), m. N. of a mythical horse, Buddh.

Bālāhaka, m. id., ib.; N. of a serpent-demon, Hariv.; *yuddhe bālāhaka-jambu-māle*, 'in the contest between Bālāhaka and Jambu-māla,' Nīlak.

बालिश 2. *bāliśa*, n. (for 1. see above) = Pers. بالش, a pillow, cushion, L.

बालीवर्दिनेय *bālīvardineya*, m. patr. fr. *balīvardin*, g. *śubhrâdi*; metron. fr. *balīvardī*, g. *kalyāṇy-ādi* (cf. *balīvardineya*).

बालीश *bālīśa*, m. retention of urine, L.

बालु *bālu*, *bāluka* &c. See *vālu* &c.

बालेय 2. *bāleya*, mfn. (fr. *bali*) fit for an offering or oblation, Ragh.; descended from Bali, Hariv.; m. an ass, Var.; a species of Cyperus, Bhpr.; = *-śāka*, L.; a kind of radish, L. (prob. w. r. for *śāleya*); patr. fr. *bali*, KātyŚr.; (pl.), VP.; N. of a Daitya, L. **-śāka**, m. a kind of vegetable (= *aṅgāra-vallī*), L. **Bāleyârdhika**, mfn., Pāt.

बालोक *bāloka*, m. N. of an author, Cat.

बाल्बज *bālbaja*, mf(*ī*)n. (fr. *balbaja*) made of the grass Eleusine Indica, ŚBr.; MBh. (B. *bālvaja*).

Bālbajabhārika, mfn. (fr. *balbaja* + *bhāra*) laden or burdened with Balbaja grass, g. *vaṇśâdi*.

Bālbajika, mfn. bearing Balbaja grass, ib. (cf. *balbajika*).

बाल्हव *bālhava*, m. an inhabitant of Balkh (*ī*, f.), Bālar.

Bālhāyana, mf(*ī*)n., fr. *bālhi*, Pāṇ. iv, 2, 99, Pat.

Bālhi, **bāhli** or **vāhli**, N. of a country, Balkh, ib. **-ja** or **-jāta**, mfn. born or bred in Balkh (as a horse), MBh.; R. **Bālhîśvara**, m. pl. N. of a dynasty, VP.

Bālhika or **bāhlika**, m. (pl.) N. of a people, MBh.; a king of the Bālhikas, ib.; Hariv.; Pur.; N. of a son of Pratīpa, Hariv.; (pl.) of a dynasty, BhP.; mfn. of the Balkh breed (as horses), MBh.; R.; n. (w. r. *bālhaka*) saffron, L.; Asa Foetida, L.

Bālhikeya-miśra, m. N. of an author, Cat.

Bālhīka, **bāhlīka** or **vāhlīka**, m. (pl.) N. of a people, MBh.; R. &c.; a prince of the Bālhīkas, MBh.; N. of a son of Janam-ejaya, ib.; of a son of Pratīpa, ib.; Pur.; of the father of Rohiṇī (wife of Vasu-deva), Hariv.; of a Gandharva, L.; of a poet, Cat.; (*ī*), f. a princess or any woman of the Bālhīkas (also N. of *Mādrī*, q. v.), MBh.; Bālar.; mf(*ī*)n. belonging to or derived from the B°s, L.; n. = *bālhika*, L. **-bhāshā**, f. the language of the Bālhīkas (enumerated among the Prākṛit dialects), Sāh. **Bālhīkêśa**, m. lord of the Bālhīkas, R.

बावादेव *bāvā-deva* and *bāvā-śāstrin*, m. N. of authors, Cat.

बावेरुजातक *bāveru-jātaka*, n. N. of wk.

बाष्कय *bāshkaya*, mfn., fr. *bashkaya*, g. *utsâdi*.

बाष्कल *bāshkala*, m. N. of a teacher (a pupil of Paila), GṛS.; of a Daitya, Hariv.; of a son of Anuhrāda, BhP.; (pl.) N. of a family regarded as belonging to the Kauśikas, Hariv. (v. l. *vāskala*); a warrior (*vāshk°*), L.; mfn. belonging to or derived from Bāshkala, ĀśvŚr., Sch.; large, great (*vāshk°*), W.; m. pl. the pupils of B° (a school of the Ṛig-

veda), Cat. — **śākhā**, f. the B° recension (of the RV.), ib. **Bāshkalôpanishad**, f. N. of an Upanishad.
Bāshkalaka, mf(*ikā*)n. belonging to or derived from the Bāshkalas, L.; (*ikā*), f. the Ṛig-veda text of the B°, ŚāṅkhŚr., Sch.
Bāshkali, m. patr. of a teacher, VP.

बाष्किह *bāshkiha*, m. patr. fr. *bashkiha*, PañcavBr.

बाष्प *bāshpa*, m. (also written *vāshpa*, cf. Uṇ. iii, 28) a tear, tears, MBh.; Kāv. &c.; steam, vapour, R.; Ragh.; Pañcat.; a kind of pot-herb, Vāgbh.; iron, L.; N. of a disciple of Gautama Buddha; (*ī*), f. a kind of plant (= *hiṅgu-pattrī*), L. — **kaṇṭha**, mf(*ī*)n. 'having tears in the throat,' almost choked with t°, Śak. — **kala**, mfn. inarticulate through t°, MBh. — **candra**, m. N. of an author, Cat. — **durdina**, mfn. clouded by tears; °*nâksha*, mf(*ā* or *ī*)n. having eyes clouded by t°, Daś. — **paryâkulêkshaṇa** (R.), **-pihita-locana** (Pañcat.), mfn. having eyes suffused with t°. — **pūra**, m. a flood of t°, Mālatīm. — **prakara**, m. a flow or gush of t°, Śiś. — **pramocana**, n. the shedding of tears, MBh. — **bindu**, m. a tear-drop, tear, R. — **mukha**, mfn. having the face bedewed with t°, R. — **moksha**, m., **-mocana**, n. = *-pramocana*, Kāv. — **viklaba**, mfn. overcome with t°, confused with weeping, R.; *-bhāshin*, mf(*inī*)n. speaking (with a voice) interrupted with w°, ib. — **vṛishṭi**, f. a shower of tears, Ragh. — **saṃdigdha**, mfn. (a voice) indistinct by suppressed t°, Nal. — **salila**, n. water of tears, Ratnâv. **Bāshpâkula**, mfn. dimmed or interrupted by t°, MBh. **Bāshpâpluta**, mfn. id., A. **Bāshpâmbu**, n. = °*pa-salila*, Ratnâv.; *-pūra*, m. a flood of t°, MW.; *-śīkara*, m. pl. t°-drops, Kathās. **Bāshpâvilêkshaṇa**, mfn. having eyes dimmed by t°, MBh. **Bāshpâsāra**, m. = °*pa-vṛishṭi*, Mālav. **Bāshpôtpīḍa**, m. a gush or torrent of t°, Kād.; Hcar. **Bāshpôdbhava**, m. the rising or starting of t°, MW.
Bāshpaka (ifc. f. *ā*), steam, vapour, Suśr.; m. a kind of vegetable (= *mārisha*), Bhpr.; (*ā*), f. = *hiṅgu-pattrī*, L.; (*ikā*), f. a kind of vegetable, Vāgbh.
Bāshpāya, Nom. Ā. °*yate*, to shed tears, weep, Kāv.; to emit vapour or steam, L.
Bāshpin, mf(*inī*)n. (ifc.) shedding tears or any liquid like tears, R.
Bāshpīkā, f. a kind of plant (= *bāshpī*), L.

बास *bāsa*, *bāskala*, w. r. for *bhāsa*, *bāshkala*.

बास्त *bāsta*, mf(ī)n. (fr. *basta*) coming from a goat (°*taṃ carma*, a goat-skin), Mn. ii, 41.
Bāstāyana, m. patr. fr. *basta*, g. *aśvâdi*.
Bāstika, n. a multitude of goats, R.

बास्प *bāspa*, w. r. for *bāshpa*.

बाह् *bāh*. See √*vāh*.

बाह *bāha*, m. the arm = 1. *bāhu*, L. (also *ā*, f., Uṇ. i, 28); a horse, L. (see *vāha*); mfn. firm, strong, L.
1. **Bāháva**, m. (Pāṇ. vii, 1, 39, Vārtt. 1, Pat.) = 1. *bāhu*, the arm (also n., ŚBr.)
Bāhavi, m. patr. fr. 1. *bāhu*, Pāṇ. iv, 1, 96; N. of a teacher, ĀśvGṛ.
Bāhā-bāhavi, ind. arm against arm, in close combat (= *bāhū-bāhavi*), Vop.

बाहट *bāhaṭa*, m. N. of an author, Cat. — **nighaṇṭu**, m. N. of wk.
Bāhaṭīya, mfn. written or composed by Bāhaṭa; n. a work of B°, Cat.

बाहड *bāhaḍa*, m. N. of a man, Śatr.

बाहदुर *bāhadura*, (prob.) w.r. for *bāhādura*.

बाहन्नोपनिषद् *bāhannôpanishad* (?), f. N. of an Upanishad.

बाहल्य *bāhalya*, n. (fr. *bahala*) thickness, Suśr.

बाहव 2. *bāhava*, n. (fr. *bahu*), g. *pṛithv-ādi*.

बाहादुर *bāhādura*, m. a modern title of honour conferred by Muhammadan kings (= Pers. بهادر).

बाहिर्वेदिक *bāhirvedika*, mf(ī)n. (fr. *bahir-vedi*) situated or taking place outside the Vedi, KātyŚr., Sch. (cf. *bahir-vedika*).

बाहीक *bāhīká*, mfn. (fr. *bahis*; but also written *vāhīka*) being outside, external, exterior, Pāṇ. iv, 1, 85, Vārtt. 5, Pat.; relating to the Bāhīkas, g. *palady-ādi*; m. (pl.) N. of a despised people of the Pañjāb, ŚBr. &c. &c. (often confounded with the Bālhīkas); a man of the Bāhīkas, MBh.; N. of a priest, Cat.; = *upa-śama*, Buddh.; = *kāshṭhaka*, *pālaka*, or *go-rakshaka*, Hcar., Sch.; an ox, L.; n. N. of a lake or piece of water in the country of the Bāhīkas, MBh.

बाहु 1. *bāhú*, m. and (L.) f. (fr. √*bah*, *baṇh*; for 2. *bāhu*, see col. 3) the arm, (esp.) the fore-arm, the arm between the elbow and the wrist (opp. to *pra-gaṇḍa*, q. v.; in medic. the whole upper extremity of the body, as opp. to *sakthi*, the lower ext°), RV. &c. &c.; the arm as a measure of length (= 12 Aṅgulas), Śulbas.; the fore-foot of an animal (esp. its upper part), RV.; AV.; Br.; ĀśvGṛ.; the limb of a bow, ŚBr.; the bar of a chariot-pole, Gobh.; the post (of a door; see *dvāra-b°*); the side of an angular figure (esp. the base of a right-angled triangle), Sūryas.; the shadow of the gnomon on a sun-dial, ib.; (also du.) the constellation Ārdrā, L.; m. N. of a Daitya, MBh.; of a prince (who brought ruin upon his family by his illegal actions), ib.; of a son of Vṛika, Hariv.; of a son of Vajra, VP. [Cf. Gk. πᾶχυς, πῆχυς; Germ. *buog*, *Bug*; Angl. Sax. *bōg*; Eng. *bough*.] — **kara**, mfn. active with the arms, Pāṇ. iii, 2, 21. — **kuṇṭha**, mfn. crippled in the arms, L. — **kuntha** (?), m. a wing, L. — **kubja**, mfn. = *-kuṇṭha*, W. — **kshád**, mfn. offering the fore-legs (i. e. the inferior parts of an animal, said of a parsimonious sacrificer), RV. x, 27, 6. — **cāpa**, m. 'arm-bow,' a fathom (as a measure), L. — **cchinna**, mfn. having a broken a°, KaushUp. — **cyút** (?), AV. xviii, 3, 25. — **cyuta** (*bāhú-*), mfn. fallen from the arm, dropped out of the hand, RV.; TS. — **ja**, m. 'arm-born,' a Kshatriya (as sprung from the arm of Brahmā), L. (cf. Mn. i, 31); a parrot, L.; sesamum growing wild, L. — **jūta** (*bāhú-*), mfn. quick with the a°, RV. — **jyā**, f. the cord of an arc, sine, Sūryas. — **taraṇa**, n. crossing a river (with the a°, i. e. by swimming), Gaut. — **tā́** (*bāhú-*), ind. in the arms, RV. (cf. *devá-tā*, *purushá-tā*). — **trāṇa**, n. 'arm-fence,' armour for the arms, L. — **daṇḍa**, m. 'arm-staff,' a long arm, R.; Daś.; a blow or punishment inflicted with the arm or fist, MW. (cf. *bhuja-d°*). — **dā**, f. 'arm-giver,' N. of Su-yaśā (a wife of Parīkshit), MBh.; of a river (into which Gaurī the wife of Prasena-jit is said to have been transformed; prob. identical with the Vitastā or Hydaspes and modern Jhelum), ib.; R. &c.; of another river, VP.; *-nadī-māhātmya*, n. N. of wk. — **niḥsṛita**, n. a partic. method of fighting (by which a sword is twisted out of a person's hands), Hariv. — **pāśa**, m. = *-bandhana*, Ratnâv.; a partic. attitude in fighting, MBh. — **pracālakam**, ind. shaking the arms, L. — **pratibāhu**, m. du. (in geom.) the opposite sides of a figure, Col. — **prasāra**, m. stretching out the arms, BhP. — **praharaṇa**, m. striking with the arms, a striker, boxer, W.; n. boxing, wrestling, ib. — **phala**, n. (in geom.) the result from the base sine, Sūryas.; the sine of an arc of a circle of position contained between the sun and the prime vertical, Siddhântaś. — **bandhana**, n. (ifc. f. *ā*) 'a°-fetter,' encircling arms, Kalid.; m. the shoulder-blade, R. — **bala**, n. power or strength of a°, Mn.; MBh. &c.; m. 'strong in a°,' N. of a prince, Kathās. — **balín**, mfn. strong in a°, ŚBr.; MBh.; N. of a man, L. — **bādha**, m. pl. N. of a people, MBh. (v. l. *bāhu-bādhya*, *bahurada*). — **bhaṅgi**, f. bending or twisting the arms, MW. — **bhūshaṇa**, n., **-bhūshā**, f. 'a°-ornament,' armlet, L. — **bhedin**, m. 'a°-breaker,' N. of Vishṇu, L. — **mát**, mfn. having (strong) a° (said of Indra), AV.; (*atī*), f. N. of a river, L. — **madhya**, mfn. occupying a middle position with the a°, MBh. (cf. *jaṅghā-jaghanya*). — **maya**, mf(*ī*)n. made or done with the a°, W. — **mātrá**, n. = *-cāpa*, TS.; mf(*ī*)n. as long as an a°, ib. — **mūla**, n. 'a°-root,' the a°-pit, Nir.; *-vibhūshaṇa*, n. an ornament worn on the upper arm, L. — **yuddha**, n. 'a°-fight,' a close fight, MBh.; Kathās. — **yodha** or **-yodhin**, m. a wrestler, boxer, Hariv. — **rakshā**, f. armour for the upper arm, L. — **latā**, f. an arm (lithe as a) creeper, Rājat. (also °*tikā*, f., Śṛiṅgār.); °*tântara*, n. the space between the arms, the breast, bosom, Kāvyâd. — **vat**, m. 'having (strong) a°,' N. of a man, VP. — **vikshepa**, m. moving the a°, swimming, MBh.; Kathās. — **vighaṭṭana** or **-vighaṭṭita**, n. a partic. attitude in wrestling, VP. — **vimarda**, m. = *-yuddha*, Ragh. — **vīrya**, mfn. strength of a°, AV. &c. &c.; mfn. strong of a°, TāṇḍBr. — **vṛiktá**, m. N. of a descendant of Atri (author of RV. v, 71; 72), Anukr. — **vyāyāma**, m. 'arm-exercise,' gymnastic, MBh. — **śakti**, m. 'strong of a°,' N. of a king, Kathās. — **śardhin**, mfn. relying on his a° (said of Indra), RV. x, 103, 3. — **śālin**, mfn. possessing strong a°, MBh.; Hariv.; Kathās.; m. N. of Śiva, MBh.; of a Dānava, Kathās.; of a warrior, ib.; of a son of Dhṛita-rāshṭra, MBh.; of Bhīma, ib.; of a prince, ib. — **śikhara**, n. 'the upper part of the a°,' the shoulder, Hariv. — **sambhava**, m. 'a°-born,' a Kshatriya, L. (cf. *bāhu-ja*). — **sahasra-bhṛit**, m. 'having a thousand a°,' N. of Arjuna Kārtavīrya (killed by Paraśu-rāma), L. — **sahasrin**, mfn. having a thousand a°, MBh.; Hariv.; VP. — **svastika**, m. or n. 'a°-cross,' the arms crossed, MBh. (Nīlak.) **Bāhûtkshepam**, ind. so as to lift up the arms or hands, Śak. **Bāhûpapīḍam**, ind. pressing with the arms, Bhaṭṭ.
Bāhuka, ifc. = 1. *bāhu*, the arm (cf. *hrasva-bāhuka*); mf(*ā*)n. servile, dependent, L.; swimming with the arms, Baudh. (cf. Pāṇ. iv, 4, 7, Sch.); dwarfish, BhP.; m. a monkey, L.; N. of a Nāga, MBh.; of a prince, ib.; of a son of Vṛika (= *bāhu*), Pur.; (also written *vāh°*) N. assumed by Nala upon his becoming charioteer to king Ṛitu-parṇa, Nal.; (*ā*), f. N. of a river, L.
1. **Bāhula**, n. (for 2. see below) armour for the arms, L.; N. of a place in Dakshiṇā-patha, Cat.
Bāhū-bāhavi, ind. arm to arm, hand to hand (in close combat), Śiś. xviii, 12 (cf. *bāhā-bāhavi*).
Bāhv, in comp. for 1. *bāhu*. — **aṅká**, m. the bend of the arm, ἀγκών, AV. — **ojas**, n. strength of arm, RV. viii, 82, 2; strong in a°, viii, [illegible], 6 &c.; strong in the fore-legs (said of a horse), i, 135, 9.

बाहु 2. *bāhu* (for 1. see col. 2), Vṛiddhi form of *bahu* in comp. — **kīṭa**, mfn., g. *palady-ādi*. — **kuleyaka**, m. patr. fr. *bahu-kula*, Pāṇ. iv, 1, 140, Sch. — **garta**, mfn., ib. iv, 2, 137, Sch. (°*taka*, Kāś. on iv, 2, 126). — **guṇya**, n. possession of many excellences, Mn. vii, 71. — **janya**, mfn. spread among many people, L.; n. a great multitude of people, crowd, L. — **dantaka**, n. (with *śāstra*) N. of a treatise on morals abridged by Indra, MBh. (cf. next). — **dantin**, m. N. of Indra, L. (cf. *bahudantī-suta*); °*ti-putra*, m. a son of Indra (N. of Jaya-datta, author of a Tantra), Daś. — **danteya**, m. = *-dantin*, L. — **bali**, m. (fr. *bahu-bala*?) N. of a mountain, Śatr. — **bhāshya**, n. (fr. *bahu-bhāshin*) talkativeness, g. *brāhmaṇâdi*. — **mitrāyaṇa**, m. patr. fr. *bahu-mitra*, Saṃskārak. — **rūpya**, n. (fr. *bahu-rūpa*) manifoldness, g. *brāhmaṇâdi* (Kāś.) — **vartaka**, mfn. (fr. *bahu-varta*), Pāṇ. iv, 2, 126, Sch. (Kāś. *-gartaka*). — **vāra**, m. = *bahu-v°*, L. — **vidha**, m. patr. (fr. *bahu-v°*?), Pravar. — **śāla**, mfn. prepared from Euphorbia Antiquorum; *-guḍa*, m. pills so prepared, ŚārṅgS. — **śrutya**, n. great learning, erudition, MBh. **Bāhvṛicya**, n. the sacred tradition of the Bahv-ṛicas, the Ṛig-veda, ŚāṅkhŚr. (cf. Pāṇ. iv, 3, 129).
2. **Bāhula**, mfn. (fr. *bahula*; for 1. see above) manifold, g. *saṃkalâdi*; m. the month Kārttika (when the moon is near the Pleiades; see *bahulā*), L.; fire, L.; a Jina, Gal.; N. of a prince, VP.; n. manifoldness, g. *pṛithv-ādi*; *-grīva*, m. 'having a variegated neck,' a peacock, L. °**laka**, n. manifoldness, diversity, Kār. on Pāṇ. ii, 1, 32; Pat.; (*āt*), ind. from giving too wide applicability (to a rule), Uṇ. i, 36; 37, Sch. °**li**, m. N. of a son of Viśvā-mitra, MBh. °**leya**, m. metron. of Skanda (fr. *bahulā*, the Pleiades), L. °**lya**, n. abundance, plenty, multitude, variety, MBh.; Kāv. &c.; the usual course or common order of things, Hariv.; (*ena*), ind. usually, ordinarily, as a rule, Śaṃk.; Pāṇ., Sch.; Jātakam.; (*āt*), ind. id., Śaṇḍ.; in all probability, Hit.

बाहुक् *bāhuk*. See *pra-bāhuk*.

बाह्य *bāhya*, mf(*ā*)n. (fr. *bahis*; in later language also written *vāhya*, q. v.; m. nom. pl. *bāhye*, ŚBr.) being outside (a door, house, &c.), situated without (abl. or comp.), outer, exterior (acc. with √*kṛi*, to turn out, expel), AV. &c. &c.; not belonging to the family or country, strange, foreign, MBh.; Kāv. &c.; excluded from caste or the community, an out-caste, Mn.; MBh. &c.; diverging from, conflicting with, opposed to, having nothing to do with (abl. or comp.), ib.; (with *artha*), a meaning external to (i.e. not resulting from) the sounds or letters forming a word, Pāṇ. i, 1, 68, Sch.; m. a corpse (for *vāhya*?), Kāv.; N. of a man (pl. his family), Saṃskārak.; (pl.) N. of a people, VP.; (*ā*), f. (scil. *tvac*) the outer bark of a tree, ŚBr.; (ifc. f. *ā*) the outer part, exterior, Rājat.; ibc. and (*am, ena, e*), ind. outside, without, out, ŚBr. &c. &c.; (*āt*), ind. from without, Pañcat. **–kaksha**, m. the outer side (of a house), Rājat. **–karaṇa**, n. an external organ of sense, MārkP.; Śaṃk. **–karṇa** and **-kuṇḍa**, m. N. of two Nāgas, MBh. **–taddhita**, n. (in gram.) an external or secondary Taddhita suffix (added after another one), Pāṇ. vii, 3, 29, Sch. **–tara**, mfn. being outside, outer, external, Śaṃk.; turned out (of caste or society), an out-caste, Mn. x, 30. **–tás**, ind. outside, externally, on the outside of (with gen. or abl.), VS. &c. &c.; *-to-nara*, m. pl. 'external men,' N. of a people, MārkP. **–tā**, f., **-tva**, n. the state of being outside, exclusion, deviation or divergence from (abl.), Hariv.; Rājat. &c. **–druti**, f. 'external solution,' a process in the preparation of quicksilver, Sarvad. **–prakṛiti**, f. pl. the constituents of a foreign state exclusive of the king (cf. *prakṛiti*), Pañcat. **–prayatna**, m. (in gram.) the external effort in the production of articulate sounds, Pāṇ. i, 1, 9, Sch. **–rata**, n. = *-sambhoga*, Cat.; w.r. for *-tara*, Kathās. **–liṅgin**, m. a heretic, L. **–vastu**, n. external wealth or riches, Kum. **–vāsin**, mfn. dwelling outside a village or town (said of Caṇḍālas), MBh. **–sambhoga**, m. 'external coition,' (prob.) gratification of sexual passion outside the vulva, Cat. **–sparśa**, m. contact with external objects, Bhag.; MārkP. **Bāhyâṅsa**, mfn. holding the hands outside (not between) the knees, Gobh. (cf. *bahir-jānu*). **Bāhyânta**, m. the outer end or corner (of the eye), L. **Bāhyântar**, ind. from without and within, Prab. **Bāhyâbhyantara**, mfn. external and internal (as diseases), Suśr. **Bāhyâyāma**, m. a partic. disease of the nerves, ib. **Bāhyârtha**, m. an external meaning (cf. *bāhya artha* above), Madhus.; external objects or matter or reality; *-bhaṅga-nirākaraṇa*, n. N. of wk.; *-vāda*, m. the doctrine that the ext° world has a real existence, Śaṃk.; *-vādin*, mfn. maintaining the reality of the ext° w°, ib. **Bāhyâlaya**, m. the abode of out-castes i.e. the country of the Bāhīkas, MBh. (v.l. *vāhyanaya*). **Bāhyā-śakalá**, m. a fragment from a tree's outer bark, ŚBr. **Bāhyâśva**, m. N. of a man, Hariv. (v.l. *vāh*°). **Bāhyêndriya**, n. an outer organ of sense, Vedântas. **Bāhyôpavana**, n. a grove situated outside (a town, *puryāḥ*), BhP.

Bāhyaka-sṛiñjarī and **bāhyakā**, f. N. of Sṛiñjarī and one of the two wives of Bhajamāna (an older sister of Upa-bāhyakā), Hariv.

बाह्लक *bāhlaka, bāhlava, bāhli* &c. See *bālhava* &c., p. 729, col. 3.

बाह्वट *bāhvaṭa*, m. N. of a poet, Cat.

बिट् *biṭ* (or *viṭ*), cl. 1. P. *beṭati*, to swear, shout, address harshly, Dhātup. ix, 30.

बिटक *biṭaka*, m.n., (*ā*), f.= *piṭaka*, a boil, L.

बिठक *biṭhaka*, n.= *antariksha*, the sky, Nir. vi, 30.

बिड् *biḍ* (or *viḍ*) = *biṭ*, Dhātup. ix, 30 (v.l.)

बिडारक *biḍāraka*, m. a cat, L. (cf. next).

बिडाल *biḍāla*, m. (also written *viḍāla*, of doubtful origin; cf. Uṇ. i, 117) a cat, Mn.; MBh. &c.; a partic. remedy for the eye, Bhpr. (cf. °*laka*); the eye-ball, L.; (*ā*), f. a female cat, R. (also *ī*, Uṇ. i, 117, Sch.); (*ī*), f. a partic. disease and the female demon presiding over it (reckoned among the Yoginīs), Hcat.; a species of plant, L. **–pada** or **-padaka**, n. a partic. measure of weight (= *karsha*), ŚārṅgS.; Suśr. **–putra**, m. 'cat's son,' N. of a man, Rājat. **–vaṇij**, m. 'cat-dealer,' nickname of a man, ib. **–vratika**, mfn. 'acting like a cat,' false, hypocritical, L. (cf. *baiḍāla-vr*°). **Biḍālâksha**, mf(*ī*)n. cat-eyed, Hcat.; (*ī*), f. N. of a Rākshasī, R.

Biḍālaka, m. a cat, Cat.; the eyeball, L.; application of ointment to the eye, Car.; Bhpr.; (*ikā*), f. a little cat, kitten, Subh.; n. yellow orpiment, L.

बिद् *bid* or *bind* (cf. *bhid*), cl. 1. P. *bindati*, to cleave, split, Dhātup. iii, 27 (perhaps invented on account of the following words of more or less questionable origin).

Bida, m. (also written *vida*) N. of a man, Pāṇ. iv, 1, 104; pl. his family, ĀśvŚr. **–kula** (*vida-*), n. = *vaidasya* and *vaidayoḥ kulam*, Pāṇ. ii, 4, 64, Vārtt. 1, Pat. **Bidā-puṭa**, m. N. of a man, g. *aśvâdi*, Kāś. (v.l. *bida, puṭa*).

Bidala, n. (cf. *vi-dala*) anything split off or produced by splitting (cf. comp.) **–kārī**, f. a woman employed in splitting bamboos, VS. **–saṃhita**, mfn. composed or made up of halves, AitBr.

Bidura, v.l. for *bhidura*, q.v.

Binda. See *kusuru-binda*.

Bindavi, g. *gahâdi* (cf. *baindavi*).

Bindavīya, mfn., ib.; m. a prince of the Bindus, g. *dāmany-ādi*.

Bindú, m. (once n., MBh.; in later language mostly written *vindu*) a detached particle, drop, globule, dot, spot, AV. &c. &c.; (with *hiranyaya*) a pearl, AV. xix, 30, 5 (cf. *-phala*); a drop of water taken as a measure, L.; a spot or mark of coloured paint on the body of an elephant, Kum.; (ifc. also *-ka*) the dot over a letter representing the Anusvāra (supposed to be connected with Śiva and of great mystical importance), MBh.; Kathās.; BhP.; a zero or cypher, R. (in manuscripts put over an erased word to show that it ought not to be erased = 'stet,' Naish.); a partic. mark like a dot made in cauterizing, Suśr.; a mark made by the teeth of a lover on the lips of his mistress, L.; a coloured mark made on the forehead between the eyebrows, L.; (in dram.) the sudden development of a secondary incident (which, like a drop of oil in water, expands and furnishes an important element in the plot), Sāh. (ifc. also *-ka*); m. N. of a man, g. *bidâdi*; of an Āṅgirasa (author of RV. viii, 83; ix, 30), Anukr.; of the author of a Rasa-paddhati, Cat.; pl. N. of a warrior tribe, g. *dāmany-ādi*. **–ghṛita**, n. a partic. medic. compound taken in small quantities, ŚārṅgP. **–citra** and **-citraka**, m. the spotted antelope, L. **–jāla** and **-jālaka**, n. collection or mass of dots or spots (esp. on an elephant's face and trunk), L. **–tantra**, m. a die, dice, L.; m. n. a kind of chess-board, L.; a playing-ball, L. **–tīrtha**, n. N. of a sacred bathing-place, Cat.; *-māhātmya*, n. N. of wk. **–deva**, m. = *ṇa*, a Buddhist deity, L.; N. of Śiva, W. **–nātha**, m. N. of a teacher, Cat. **–pattra**, m. Betula Bhojpattra, L. **–pattraka**, m. a species of Amaranthus, L. **–pratishṭhāmaya**, mf(*ī*)n. founded or based upon the Anusvāra, L. **–phala**, n. a pearl, L. **–brahmānandīya**, n. N. of wk. **–bheda**, m. N. of a partic. Yoga posture, L. **–mat**, mfn. having drops or bubbles or clots, formed into balls or globules, AitBr.; KātyŚr.; m. N. of a son of Marīci by Bindu-matī, BhP.; (*atī*), f. N. of a kind of verse, Kād.; of a drama, Sāh.; of the wife of Marīci (cf. above), BhP.; of a daughter of Śaśa-bindu and wife of Māndhātṛi, Hariv.; of the murderess of Vidūratha, Vāsav., Introd.; of a fisherman's daughter, Kathās. **–mādhava**, m. a form of Vishṇu, Cat. **–mālin**, m. (in music) a kind of measure, Saṃgīt. **–rāji**, m. 'row of spots,' N. of a kind of serpent, Suśr. **–rekhaka**, m. a kind of bird, L. (cf. prec. and next). **–rekhā**, f. a row or line of points or dots, Rājat.; N. of a daughter of Caṇḍavarman, Kathās. **–vāsara**, m. the day of fecundation, L. **–śarman**, m. N. of a poet, Cat. **–saṃgraha**, m., **-saṃdīpana**, n. N. of wks. **–saras**, n. N. of a sacred lake, MBh.; R.; (m. c. also *-sara*), BhP.; *-tīrtha*, n. N. of a sacred bathing-place, Cat. **–sāra**, m. N. of a king (son of Candra-gupta), VP.; HPariś. **–sena**, m. N. of a king (son of Kshatraujas), VP. **–hrada**, m. N. of a lake (said to have been formed by the drops of the Ganges shaken from Śiva's hair), Cat. **Bindûpanishad**, f. N. of an Upanishad.

Binduka, m. a drop, R.; N. of a Tīrtha, Vishṇ. (see also under *bindu*).

Bindukita, mfn. dotted over, Śak., Sch.

Binduraka, m. Ximenia Aegyptiaca, L.

Bindula, m. a partic. venomous insect, Suśr. (written *vi*°).

Bindūya, Nom. Ā. °*yate*, to form drops, drip down (p. °*yamāna*, dripping, wet), Mālatīm.

बिबिबाभवत् *bibibā-bhávat*, mfn. (onomat. *bibibā* + pr. p. of √*bhū*) crackling, MaitrS.

बिबोधयिषु *bibodhayishu*, mfn. (fr. Desid. of Caus. of √*budh*) wishing to rouse, intending to wake, R. (cf. *bubodhayishu*).

बिब्बोक *bibboka*, m. (also written *vivvoka* or *vibboka*) haughty indifference, L.; (in erotic poetry) affectation of indifference towards a beloved object through pride and conceit, Śiś. viii, 29; Sāh.

बिभक्षयिषा *bibhakshayishā*, f. (fr. Desid. of √*bhaj*) a desire of eating or enjoying, Nyāyam. °**yishu**, mfn. desirous of eating, MBh.; MārkP.; *-daṇshṭrin*, mfn. 'having teeth d° of e°,' hungry-mouthed, VarBṛS.

बिभणिषु *bibhaṇishu*, mfn. (fr. Desid. of √*bhaṇ*) desirous of speaking, Śil.

बिभित्सा *bibhitsā*, f. (fr. Desid. of √*bhid*) a desire to break through or destroy or pierce or penetrate (with acc. or gen.), MBh.; Kād. (cf. Siddh. on Pāṇ. ii, 3, 66). °**tsu**, mfn. desirous of breaking through &c. (with acc.), MBh.; BhP.

Bibhedayishu, mfn. (fr. Desid. of Caus.) desirous of dividing or disuniting, MBh.

बिभीषिका *bibhīshikā*, w.r. for *vibh*°.

बिभ्रक्षु *bibhrakshu*, mfn. (fr. Desid. of √*bhrajj*) wishing to parch or destroy, Bhaṭṭ.; m. fire, W.

Bibhrajjishu, m. 'that which wishes to destroy,' fire, Bhaṭṭ.; *-prakhya*, mfn. resembling fire, ib. (= *agni-tulya*, Sch.)

बिभ्रत् *bibhrat*, mfn. (pr.p. of √*bhṛi*) bearing, carrying, RV. &c. &c. **Bibhrad-vāja**, m. = *bharad-v*°, AitĀr.

बिम्ब *bimba*, m. n. (also written *vimba* or *vimva*, of doubtful origin, but cf. Uṇ. iv, 95, Sch.; ifc. f. *ā*) the disk of the sun or moon, Kāv.; Pur. &c.; any disk, sphere, orb (often applied to the rounded parts of the body), Kālid.; Pañcat.; a mirror, ŚvetUp.; Kum.; an image, shadow, reflected or represented form, picture, type, R.; BhP.; Rājat.; (in rhet.) the object compared (as opp. to *prati-bimba*, 'the counterpart' to which it is compared), Sāh.; Pratāp.; m. a lizard, chameleon, Gaut.; N. of a man, Rājat.; (*ā*), f. Momordica Monadelpha (a plant bearing a bright-red gourd), L.; N. of 2 metres, Col.; N. of the wife of Bālâditya (king of Kaśmīra), Rājat.; (*ī*), f. Momordica Monadelpha, Suśr. (cf. g. *gaurâdi*); N. of the mother of king Bimbi-sāra (below), Buddh.; n. the fruit of the Momordica Monadelpha (to which the lips of women are often compared), MBh.; Kāv. &c. **–jā**, f. Momordica Monadelpha, L. **–tattva-prakāśikā**, f. N. of wk. **–pratibimba**, (ibc.) original and counterfeit, object of comparison and that with which it is compared; *-tā*, f., *-tva*, n. (Sāh.); *-bhāva*, m. (Pratāp.) condition of or° and c° &c.; *-vāda*, m. N. of wk. **–pratishṭhā**, f., **-pratishṭhā-vidhi**, m. N. of wks. **–phala**, n. the Bimba fruit, Bhartṛ.; °*lâdhar'oshṭha*, mfn. having lips as red as the B° fr°, Kum. **–lakshaṇa**, n. N. of wk. **–sāra**, v.l. for *bimbi-sāra*, Lalit. **Bimbâgata**, mfn. 'gone to an image,' reflected, W. **Bimbâdhara**, m. a nether lip (red like the B° fruit), Śak. **Bimbânubimbatva**, n. = *bimba-pratibimba-tva*, Sāh. **Bimbêśvara**, m. N. of a temple founded by the princess Bimbā, Rājat. **Bimbôpadhāna**, n. a cushion, pillow, Divyāv. **Bimb'-oshṭha**, mf(*ī*)n. having lips like the B° fruit, red-lipped, MBh.; Kāv. &c. (f. also °*baushṭhā*, Uṇ. ii, 4, Sch.)

Bimbaka, n. the disk of the sun or moon (also *ikā*, f.), L.; the fruit of Momordica Monadelpha, L. (also *ikā*, f.); a round form, roundness (of a face), Divyâv. °**baki**, m. N. of a prince, Kathās. °**baṭa**, m. the mustard plant, L. °**bara**, m. n. a partic. high number, Buddh. °**bāva**, n., Pāṇ. v, 2, 109, Vārtt. 3, Pat.

Bimbita, mfn. mirrored back, reflected, Rājat. °**binī**, f. the pupil of the eye, L. °**biya**, m. N. of a man, Rājat.

Bimbi-sāra, m. (from *bimbin* or *bimbī* + *s*°?) N. of a king of Magadha (contemporary and patron of Gautama Buddha), MWB. 48 &c. (v.l. *vidhi-sāra, vidmi-sāra, vindu-sena, vindhya-sena*).

Bimbu, m. the betel-nut tree, L.

Bimboka, m. N. of a poet, Cat.

बिरद *birada, biruda*, w.r. for *vi-ruda*.

बिराल *birāla*, m. = *biḍāla*, a cat, L.

बिल् *bil* (or *vil*, connected with *bid*, q.v.), cl. 6. 10. P. *bilati*, *belayati*, to split, cleave, break, Dhātup. xxviii, 67; xxxii, 66.

Bila, n. (also written *vila*; ifc. f. *ā*) a cave, hole, pit, opening, aperture, RV. &c. &c.; the hollow (of a dish), bowl (of a spoon or ladle) &c., AV.; VS.; ŚBr.; ŚrS.; m. Calamus Rotang, L.; Indra's horse Uccaiḥ-śravas, L.; N. of two kinds of fish, L. **-kārin**, m. 'hole-maker,' a mouse, L. **-m-gama**, m. 'hole-goer,' a snake, MW. **-dhā́vana**, mfn. (sensu obsceno) rimam tergens, TS. **-yoni**, mfn. of the breed of Uccaiḥ-śravas, Kir. **-vāsa**, mfn. living in holes, burrowing; m. an animal that lives in holes, Suśr.; a pole-cat, L. **-vāsin**, mfn. = prec., MBh.; m. an animal that lives in holes, ib.; a snake, L. **-śaya**, mfn. and m. = prec., MBh. **-śāyin**, mfn. = *-vāsa*, mfn., Suśr.; m. any animal that lives in holes, ib. **-svarga**, m. 'subterranean heaven,' the lower regions, hell, BhP. **Bilâyana**, n. a subterranean cave or cavern, BhP. **Bilāsin**, m. (for *bila-vāsin*?) a serpent, Kuṭṭanīm. **Bile-vāsin**, mfn. and m. = *bila-v°*, L. **Bile-śaya**, mfn. and m. = *bila-ś°*, MBh.; BhP.; Suśr.; m. also N. of a teacher of the Haṭha-vidyā, Cat. **Bilêśvara**, m. N. of a place of pilgrimage, Cat. (perhaps w.r. for *bilvêśvara*). **Bilâukas**, mfn. and m. = *bila-vāsa*, Mn.; MBh.

Bilasa, mfn., g. *triṇâdi*.

Bilma, n. a slip, bit, chip, RV. ii, 35, 12; a broken helmet, ŚatarUp., Sch.; an ash-pit, L. **-grahaṇa**, n. grasping or understanding by bits i.e. by degrees, Nir. i, 20.

Bilmin, mfn. having a helmet, VS. (Mahīdh.)

Billa, n. (also written *villa*) a pit, hole, reservoir (= *talla* or *ālavāla*), L.; Asa Foetida, L. **-mūlā**, f. a species of esculent bulbous plant, L. **-sū**, f. a mother of ten children, L.

Bilvà, m. (in later language also *vilva*) Aegle Marmelos, the wood-apple tree (commonly called Bel; its delicious fruit when unripe is used medicinally; its leaves are employed in the ceremonial of the worship of Śiva; cf. RTL. 336), AV. &c. &c.; (*ā*), f. a kind of plant (= *hiṅgu-pattrī*), L.; n. the Bilva fruit, MBh.; Kathās.; a partic. weight (= 1 Pala, = 4 Akshas, = ¼ Kuḍava), Suśr.; ŚārṅgS.; a kind of vegetable, Suśr.; a small pond, pool, L. (cf. *billa*). **-ja**, see *bailvaja*. **-tejas**, m. N. of a serpent-demon, MBh. **-daṇḍa** or **-daṇḍin**, m. 'having a staff of B° wood,' N. of Śiva, ib. **-nātha**, m. N. of a teacher of the Haṭha-vidyā, Cat. **-pattra**, m. N. of a serpent-demon, MBh.; *-maya*, mf(*ī*)n. made or consisting of B° leaves, Kathās. **-pattrikā**, f. N. of Dākshāyaṇī (under which she was worshipped at Bilvaka), Cat. **-parṇī**, f. a kind of vegetable, Car. **-pāṇḍara** or **-pāṇḍura**, m. N. of a serpent-demon, MBh. **-peśikā** or **-peśī**, f. the dried shell of the B° fruit, Suśr. **-maṅgala**, m. N. of a poet (also called Līlā-śuka), Cat.; *-ṭīkā*, f., *-stotra*, n. N. of wks. **-madhya**, n. the flesh of the B° fruit, Var.; Car. **-mātra**, n. the weight of a B° fruit, Suśr.; mfn. having the weight or size of a B° f°, ib.; ŚārṅgP. **-vana**, n. a wood of B° trees; *-māhātmya*, n. N. of wk. (also *bilva-vṛiksha-*, *bilvâṭavī-*, and *bilvâdri-m°*). **Bilvântara**, m. a species of tree, Bhpr. **Bilvâmraka**, m. or n. (?) N. of a place on the Revā or Narmadā river; *-māhātmya*, n. N. of wk. **Bilvâraṇya-māhātmya**, n., **Bilvâshṭaka**, n. and **Bilvêśvara-māhātmya**, n. N. of wks. **Bilvôda-kêśvara**, m. N. of a temple of Śiva, Hariv. **Bilvôpanishad**, f. N. of an Upanishad.

Bilvaka, m. N. of a serpent-demon, MBh.; N. of a place of pilgrimage, ib. (cf. *bailvaki*); a crab, L.

Bilvakīyā, f. a place planted with Bilva trees, g. *naḍâdi* (cf. *bailvaka*).

Bilvala, n. N. of a town, L.

बिलाल *bilāla*, m. = *birāla*, a cat, L.

बिलिन्थ *bilinthá*(?), Suparṇ. xv, 2.

बिलिश *biliśa*, m. or n. (?) = *baḍiśa*, a fish-hook or the bait on it, Suparṇ. xvii, 2.

बिल्हण *bilhaṇa*, m. N. of a minister and poet, Vcar.; Rājat.; of other authors (also *-deva*), Cat. **-kāvya**, n., **-caritra**, n., **-pañcāśikā**, f., **-śataka**, n., **°ṇīya**, n. N. of wks.

बिश् *biś* (or *viś*), cl. 1. P. *beśati*, to go, Dhātup. xvii, 71 (= √*piś*, q.v.)

बिश *biśa*, *bisha*, w.r. for *bisa*.

बिशायक *biśāyaka* (or *viś°*), m. a species of Euphorbia, L. (cf. *biśâkara*).

बिष्कल *bishkala*, m. a tame hog (noted for its fecundity), L.; (*ā*), f. parturient, a woman in travail, AV.

बिस् *bis* (or *vis*), cl. 4. *bisyati*, to go, move, Naigh. ii, 14; to split or grow, Nir. ii, 24; to urge on, incite, Dhātup. xxvi, 108; to cast, throw, Vop.

Bisa, n. (m. only Hariv. 15445; also written *visa*; ifc. f. *ā*) a shoot or sucker, the film or fibre of the water-lily or lotus, also the stalk itself or that part of it which is underground (eaten as a delicacy), RV. &c. &c.; the whole lotus plant, MBh. xii, 7974. **-kaṇṭhikā**, f. and **-kaṇṭhin**, m. a kind of small crane, L. **-kisalaya-ccheda-pātheya-vat**, mfn. having pieces of fibres of young lotus as provisions for a journey, Megh. **-kusuma**, n. a lotus-flower, L. **-khá**, mfn. one who digs up fibres of lotus-roots, RV. **-khādikā**, f. 'eating l°-fibres,' N. of a play or sport, L. **-granthi**, m. a knot on a l°-stalk, MBh. (used for filtering or clearing water, Suśr.); a partic. disease of the eyes, Suśr. **-ja**, n. a l°-flower, L. **-tantu**, m. a l°-fibre, MBh.; *-maya*, mf(*ī*)n. made of l°-f°s, Daś.; Kād. **-nābhi**, f. the l°-plant (*padminī*), L. **-nāsikā**, f. a kind of crane, L. (cf. *-kaṇṭhikā*). **-pushpa** (W.), **-prasūna** (Śiś.), n. a l°-flower. **-mṛiṇāla**, n. a l°-fibre, MBh.; Suśr. **-latā**, f. the l°-plant, Śṛiṅgār. **-vatī** (*bísa-*), f. a place abounding in l°-fibres, ŚBr. **-vartman**, n. a partic. disease of the eyes, Suśr. (cf. *-granthi*). **-śālūka**, m. (!) a l°-root, L. **Bisâkara** or **°kāra**, m. a species of Euphorbia, L. **Bisâbharaṇa**, n. an ornament made of l°-fibres, Śak. **Bisôrṇā**, f. = *bisa-mṛiṇāla*, Āpast.

Bisala, n. a sprout, bud, young shoot, L.

Bisinī, f. a lotus (the whole plant) or an assemblage of lotus-flowers, Kāv.; Kathās. **-pattra**, n. a lotus-leaf, ML.

Bisila, mfn. (fr. *bisa*), g. *kāśâdi*.

बिह्लण *bihlaṇa*, incorrect for *bilhaṇa*.

बीज *bīja*, n. (also written *vīja*, of doubtful origin; ifc. f. *ā*) seed (of plants), semen (of men and animals), seed-corn, grain, RV. &c. &c.; a runner (of the Indian fig-tree), Vcar.; any germ, element, primary cause or principle, source, origin (ifc. = caused or produced by, sprung from), ChUp.; MBh.; Kāv. &c.; the germ or origin of any composition (as of a poem, of the plot of a drama, of a magical formula &c.), R.; BhP.; Daśar.; Pratāp.; calculation of original or primary germs, analysis, algebra, Col.; truth (as the seed or cause of being), L.; anything serving as a receptacle or support (= *ālambana*), Yogaś.; the mystical letter or syllable which forms the essential part of the Mantra of any deity, RTL. 197 &c.; the position of the arms of a child at birth, BhPr.; quicksilver (?), Sūryas.; marrow, L.; m. = *bījaka*, the citron tree, Āryabh. **-kartṛi**, m. 'producer of seed,' N. of Śiva, Śivag. **-kāṇḍa-prarohin** (Mn. i, 46) and **-kāṇḍa-ruha** (i, 48), mfn. springing from a seed or from the (slip or portion taken from a) stalk. **-kṛit**, n. 'producing semen,' an aphrodisiac, L. **-kośa**, m. N. of a Tantra; = (*ī*), f. a seed-vessel (esp. of the lotus), L.; a pod, L.; *°śôddhāra*, m. N. of wk. **-kriyā**, f. the operation of analysis, algebraic solution, Col. **-gaṇita**, n. calculation of primary causes, analysis, algebra; N. of the 2nd part of Bhās-kara's Siddhânta-śiromaṇi; *-prabodha*, m., *°tôddharaṇa*, n. N. of Comms. on it. **-garbha**, m. Trichosanthes Dioeca, L. **-gupti**, f. 'seed-protector,' a pod, L. **-cintā-maṇi-tantra**, n. N. of a Tantra. **-tas**, ind. from or according to seed, W. **-tva**, n. the being an origin or cause, causality, Nīlak. **-darśaka**, m. 'explainer of the germ or plot of a play,' a stage-manager, L. **-dravya**, n. primary or original matter, Bhpr. **-dhānī**, f. N. of a river, R. **-dhānya**, n. coriander, L. **-nātha**, see *baijanātha*. **-nighaṇṭu**, m. N. of wk. **-nirvāpaṇa**, n. scattering or sowing seed, Pañcat. **-nyāsa**, m. (in dram.) the laying down or making known the germ of a plot, Daśar. **-pallava**, m. or n. (?) N. of Comm. on Bījag. **-pādapa**, m. Semecarpus Anacardium, L. **-pura**, w.r. for *-pūra*. **-purusha**, m. the progenitor of a tribe or family, MW. **-pushpa**, n. N. of various plants (= *madana* and *maruvaka*), L. **-pushpikā**, f. Andropogon Saccharatus, L. **-pūra**, m. (Suśr.), **-pūraka**, m. (MBh.; R. &c.), **-pūrī**, f. (Pañcad.), **-pūrṇa**, m. (Suśr.) 'seed-filled,' a citron, Citrus Medica; (*°ra* or *°raka*), n. a citron, Kathās.; *°ra-rasa*, m. citron-juice, Suśr. **-peśikā**, f. 'semen-receptacle,' the scrotum, L. **-prada**, m. 'yielding or sowing seed,' a generator, Bhag. **-prabhāva**, m. the power of the seed, Mn. x, 72. **-praroha** (Kap.), **°hin** (Mn.), mfn. growing from seed. **-phalaka**, m. Citrus Medica, L. **-bhūta**, mfn. being or forming the s°, Mn.; MBh. **-mati**, f. (in alg.) a mind capable of analysis or of comprehending causes, Col. **-mantra**, n. N. of a mystical syllable of a Mantra (cf. above), W. **-mātṛikā**, f. the seed-vessel of the lotus, L. **-mātra**, n. only as much as is required for seed i.e. for the procreation of offspring or for the preservation of a family, MBh.; R.; Pañcat.; N. of RV. ix, Bṛih. **-muktâvalī**, f. N. of wk. **-mushṭi**, m. or f. a handful of seed, R. **-yajña**, m. 'seed-offering,' N. of a partic. allegorical sacrifice, MBh. **-ratna**, m. 'having gems of seed, a kind of bean, MW. **-ruha**, mfn. growing from s°, Mn.; m. grain, corn, W.; *°hā-√kṛi*, Gaṇar. ii, 98. **-recana**, n. Croton Jamalgota, L. **-līlāvatī**, f. N. of wk. **-1. -vat**, ind. like seed, MBh. **-2. -vat**, mfn. possessing seed, provided with s° or grain, Mn.; ĀśvGṛ. **-vapana**, n. sowing seed, PārGṛ. **-vara**, m. 'best of grains,' Phaseolus Radiatus, L. **-vāpa**, m. a sower, L.; sowing; *-gṛihya*, n. N. of wk. **-vāpin**, m. 'sowing seed,' a sower, L. **-vāhana**, m. 'seed-bearer,' N. of Śiva, Śivag. **-vivṛiti**, f. N. of Comm. on Bījag. (also *°ti-kalpalatâvatāra*, m.) **-vṛiksha**, m. Terminalia Tomentosa, L. **-śesha-mātra**, n. nothing but seed as a remainder. **-saṃhṛiti-mat**, mfn. containing the germ and catastrophe (of a play), Sāh. **-saṃcaya**, m. a heap or collection of seed or grain, MW. **-sū**, f. 'bringing forth s°,' the earth, L. **-sektṛi**, m. 'sprinkler of s°,' a generator, Kull. on Mn. ix, 51. **-harā** or **-hāriṇī**, f. 'taking away seed,' N. of a witch (daughter of Duḥsaha), MārkP. **Bījâkshara**, n. the first syllable of a Mantra or spell, L. **Bījâṅkura**, m. a seed-shoot, seedling, Kum.; Pañcat.; N. of Comms. on Bījag. and Līl.; du. seed and sprout, BhP.; *-nyāya*, m. the rule of s° and sp° (where two things stand to each other in the relation of cause and effect), A.; *-vat*, ind. (in phil.) like the continuous succession of s° and sp°, MW. **Bījâñjali**, m. a handful of s° or grain, Mṛicch. **Bījâḍhya**, m. 'abounding in s°,' Citrus Medica, Suśr. **Bījâdhyaksha**, m. 'presiding over s°,' N. of Śiva, Śivag. **Bījâpahāriṇī**, f. = *bīja-harā*, MārkP. **Bījâbhidhāna**, n. N. of a Tantra wk. **Bījâmla**, n. the fruit of Spondias Mangifera, L. **Bījârṇava-tantra**, n. N. of a Tantra wk. **Bījârtha**, mfn. desirous of seed i.e. of procreation, Āpast. **Bījâśva**, m. 'seed-horse,' a stallion, Rājat. **Bījôt-krishṭa**, w.r. for next. **Bījôtkrashṭṛi**, m. one who picks out (a few good) grains (to make a person think the rest is equally good), Mn. ix, 291. **Bījôdaka**, n. 'grain-(like) water,' hail, L. **Bījôdā-haraṇa-bāla-bodhinī**, f. and **Bījôpanayana**, n. N. of wks. on alg. **Bījôpti**, f. sowing seed; *-cakra*, n. a kind of astrol. diagram for indicating good or bad luck following on the sowing of seed, MW.; *-vidhi*, m. the manner of sowing seed, ib.

Bījaka, n. seed, Suśr.; a list, HPariś.; m. Citrus Medica, R.; Hariv. &c.; a citron or lemon, Suśr.; Terminalia Tomentosa, L.; the position of the arms of a child at birth, Suśr.; Bhpr.; N. of a poet.

Bījaryā, ind. (with √*kṛi*), Gaṇar. ii, 98 (cf. *bīja-ruhā-√kṛi*).

Bījala, mfn. furnished with seed or grain, seedy, L. (cf. *baijala*).

Bījā, ind. by or with seed, sowing with seed, W. **-kara** (or *°jâk°*?), m. N. of a poet, Cat. **-√kṛi**, P. *-karoti*, to sow with seed, sow, Pāṇ. v, 4, 58 (others 'to harrow after sowing'). **-kṛita**, mfn. (a field) ploughed or harrowed after sowing (cf. prec.), W.

Bījika, mfn. seedy, abounding in seeds, g. *kumudâdi*.

Bījita, mfn. sown with seed, having for seed, W.

Bījin, mfn. bearing seed, seedy (as a plant), Suśr.; (ifc.) being of the race or blood of (e.g. *rāja-b°*, q.v.), Rājat.; m. the owner or giver of seed, the real progenitor (as opp. to *kshetrin*, the nominal father or merely the husband of a woman), Mn. ix, 51 &c.; Gaut.; any begetter, father, L.; the sun, L.

Bījya, mfn. sprung or produced from seed, W.; descended from a good family, Gal.; (ifc.) sprung from or belonging to the family of, L. (cf. *mahā-b°* and g. *gav-ādi*).

बीभ् *bībh*, cl. 1. Ā. *bībhate*, to boast, Dhātup. x, 21 (Vop. *cībh*).

बीभत्स *bībhatsa*, mf(*ā*)n. (fr. Desid. of √*bādh*) loathsome, disgusting, revolting, hideous, ŚāṅkhBr.; ŚrS.; MBh. &c.; loathing, detesting, L.; envious, cruel, wicked, L.; changed or estranged in mind, L.; m. disgust, abhorrence; (with *rasa*) the sentiment of disgust (one of the 8 Rasas, q. v.), Daśar.; Sāh.; N. of Arjuna, L.; (*ā́*), f. loathing, abhorrence, VS. (cf. *á-b°*); n. anything loathsome or hideous, a h° sight, Mālatīm.; *-karman*, mfn. doing loathsome or wicked things (as an abusive word), Mcar.; *-tā*, f. loathsomeness, detestableness, MBh.; Prab. **°tsaka**, m. N. of a man, Mudr. **°tsú**, mfn. loathing, detesting, feeling disgust or repugnance, RV.; AV.; Kauś.; reserved, coy (said of a woman), RV. i, 164, 8; m. N. of Arjuna, MBh.

बीरिट *bīriṭa*, m. a crowd, multitude, RV. vii, 39, 2 ('air,' Nir. v, 27).

बीरिण *bīriṇa*. See *dúr-bīriṇa* and cf. *vīriṇa*.

बीश *bīsa*. See *páḍ-bīsa*.

बुक् *buk*, ind. an onomat. word. **–kāra**, m. the roaring of a lion, cry of any animal, L.

बुक *buka*, m. = *hāsya*, laughter, Gaṇar.; (also written *vuka*) Agati Grandiflora, Bhpr.

Bukin, mfn., g. *prekshâdi*.

बुक्क् *bukk*, cl. 1. 10. P. *bukkati*, *bukkayati*, to bark, yelp, sound, talk, Dhātup. v, 4; xxxiii, 39 (Kāś. also 'to give pain').

Bukka, mf(*ā* or *ī*)n. the heart, L. (*ā*, f., Mcar.); m. a goat, L.; the Ricinus plant, L.; N. of a prince (who reigned at Vidyā-nagara 1359–79 and was the patron of Sāyaṇa; he is also called *Bukka-bhūpati*, *-mahīpati*, *-rāja*, *-rāya*, and *Bukkaṇa*), Nyāyam.; Col.; Cat.; m. and f. = *samaya* (w. r. for *hṛidaya*?), L. **Bukkâgramāṅsa**, n. the heart, L. (prob. a wrong blending of *bukkā* and *agramāṅsa*).

Bukkan, m. the heart, L.

Bukkana, n. the bark of a dog or any noise made by animals, L.

बुक्कस *bukkasa*, m. a Caṇḍāla, L. (cf. *pukkasa*); (*ī*), f. the indigo plant, L.; = *kālī* (black colour?), L.

बुङ्ग् *buṅg* (or *vuṅg*), cl. 1. P. *buṅgati*, to forsake, abandon, Dhātup. v, 52.

बुट् *buṭ*, cl. 1. 10. P. *boṭati*, *boṭayati*, to hurt, kill, Dhātup. xxxii, 116 (Vop.)

बुड् *buḍ*, cl. 6. P. *buḍati*, to cover, conceal, Dhātup. xxviii, 101 (v.l. for *cuḍ*); to emit, discharge, ib. 90 (v.l. for *puḍ*).

बुडबुड *buḍabuḍa*, ind. an onomat. word imitative of the bubbling sound made by the sinking of an object in water, HPariś. (cf. *budbuda*).

बुडिल *buḍila*, m. N. of a man, GopBr.

बुद् *bud*, cl. 1. P. Ā. *bodati*, °*te*, to perceive, learn, Dhātup. xxi, 12 (cf. *bund* and *budh*).

बुद्ध *buddha*, *buddhi*. See cols. 2 and 3.

बुद्बुद *budbuda*, m. (onomat.; cf. *buḍabuḍa*) a bubble (often as a symbol of anything transitory), RV. (cf. comp.); MBh.; Kāv. &c. (ifc. f. *ā*); an ornament or decoration resembling a bubble, L.; an embryo five days old, Nir.; BhP. (n.); Suśr.; (*ā*), f. N. of an Apsaras, MBh.; n. a partic. disease of the eye, Suśr. **–tva**, n. the being a (mere) bubble (as an embryo), MārkP. **–yāśu** (°*dá-*), mfn. one whose semen is a (mere) bubble, impotent, RV. x, 155, 4. **Budbudâkāratā**, f. the form or nature of a (mere) bubble, A. **Budbudâksha**, mfn. one who has a partic. disease of the eyes, L.

बुध् 1. *budh*, cl. 1. P. Ā. (Dhātup. xxi, 11) *bódhati*, °*te*; cl. 4. Ā. (xxvi, 63) *búdhyate* (ep. also P. °*ti*; pf. P. *bubodha*, MBh.; Subj. *búbodhati*, RV.; Ā. *bubudhé*, p. *bubudhāná*, ib.; aor. P. Subj. *bodhishat*, ib.; Impv. *bodhi*, ib.; Ā. 3 pl. *abudhram*, °*ran*; p. *budhāná*, ib., Subj. *budhánta*, ib.; °*abhutsi*, ib.; Prec. Ā. *bhutsīshṭa*, Pāṇ. i, 2, 11, Sch.; fut. *bhotsyati*, °*te*, Br. &c.; *boddhā*, Gr.; ind. p. *buddhvā*, Yājñ.; MBh.; *-budhya*, Br. &c.; inf. *búdhe*, Br.; *budhí*, RV.; *boddhum*, MBh. &c.), to wake, wake up, be awake, RV. &c. &c.; to recover consciousness (after a swoon), Kāvyâd.; Bhaṭṭ. (aor. Pass. *abodhi*); to observe, heed, attend to (with acc. or gen.), RV.; to perceive, notice, learn, understand, become or be aware of or acquainted with, RV. &c. &c.; to think of i. e. present a person ('with,' instr.), RV. iv, 15, 7; vii, 21, 1; to know to be, recognize as (with two acc.), MBh.; R. &c.; to deem, consider or regard as (with two acc.), R.; Kathās.: Pass. *budhyate* (aor. *abodhi*), to be awakened or restored to consciousness; see above: Caus. *bodhayati*, °*te* (aor. *abūbudhat*; Pass. *bodhyate*), to wake up, arouse, restore to life or consciousness, RV. &c. &c.; to revive the scent (of a perfume), VarBṛS.; to cause (a flower) to expand, Kāv.; to cause to observe or attend, admonish, advise, RV. &c. &c.; to make a person acquainted with, remind or inform of, impart or communicate anything to (with two acc.), MBh.; Kāv. &c.: Desid. *bubhutsati*, °*te* (Gr. also *bubodhishati*, °*te*, and *bubudhishati*, °*te*), to wish to observe, desire to become acquainted with, Nyāyas.; BhP.: Desid. of Caus., see *bibodhayishu* and *bubodhayishu*: Intens. *bobudhīti* (Gr. also *bobudhyate*, *boboddhi*), to have an insight into, understand thoroughly (with acc.), Subh. [Cf. Zd. *bud*; Gk. πυθ for (φυθ) in πυνθάνομαι, πυθέσθαι; Slav. *bŭdĕti*, *bŭdrŭ*; Lith. *budĕti*, *budrùs*; Goth. *biudan*; Germ. *biotan*, *bieten*; Angl. Sax. *bēodan*; Eng. *bid*.]

Buddha, mfn. awakened, awake, MBh.; expanded, blown, SāmavBr.; conscious, intelligent, clever, wise (opp. to *mūḍha*), MBh.; Kāv. &c.; learnt, known, understood, Āpast.; MBh. ('by,' usually instr., but also gen. according to Pāṇ. ii, 2, 12; 3, 67, Sch.); m. a wise or learned man, sage, W.; (with Buddhists) a fully enlightened man who has achieved perfect knowledge of the truth and thereby is liberated from all existence and before his own attainment of Nirvāṇa reveals the method of obtaining it, (esp.) the principal Buddha of the present age (born at Kapila-vastu about the year 500 B.C., his father, Śuddhodana, of the Śākya tribe or family, being the Rāja of that district, and his mother, Māyā-devī, being the daughter of Rāja Su-prabuddha, MWB. 19 &c.; hence he belonged to the Kshatriya caste and his original name Śākya-muni or Śākya-siṇha was really his family name, while that of Gautama was taken from the race to which his family belonged; for his other names see ib. 23; he is said to have died when he was 80 years of age, prob. about 420 B.C., ib. 49, n. 1; he was preceded by 3 mythical Buddhas of the present Kalpa, or by 24, reckoning previous Kalpas, or according to others by 6 principal Buddhas, ib. 136; sometimes he is regarded as the 9th incarnation of Vishṇu, Hariv.; Kāv.; Var. &c.); n. knowledge, BhP. (B. *buddhi*). **–kapālinī**, f. N. of one of the 6 goddesses of magic, Dharmas. 13, n. **–kalpa**, m. N. of the present Buddha era (which has already had 4 Buddhas, Gautama being the fourth). **–kāya-varṇa-parinishpatty-abhinirhārā**, f. a partic. Dhāraṇī, L. **–kshetra**, n. B°'s district, the country in which a B° appears, Kāraṇḍ.; *-pariśodhaka*, n. N. of one of the 3 kinds of Praṇidhāna, Dharmas. 112; *-varalocana*, n. a partic. Samādhi, Kāraṇḍ. **–gayā**, f. B°'s Gayā, N. of a sacred place near Gayā (in Behār), where Gautama B° and all the other B°s are said to have attained to true wisdom, MWB. 31 &c. **–gupta**, m. (prob.) w. r. for *budha-g°*. **–guru**, m. a Buddhist spiritual teacher, MW. **–ghosha**, m. N. of a Buddhist scholar (who lived at the beginning of the 5th century A.D.; the name is not found in Sanskṛit works), MWB. 65 &c. **–cakshus**, n. 'B°'s eye,' N. of one of the 5 sorts of vision, Dharmas. 66. **–carita**, n. 'the acts of Buddha,' N. of a Kāvya by Aśva-ghosha. **–caritra**, n. B°'s history, narrative of B°'s life, N. of wk. **–carya**, n. B°'s acts or life, Buddh. **–cchāyā**, f. B°'s shadow, ib. **–jñāna**, n. B°'s knowledge, ib.; *-śrī*, m. N. of a Buddhist scholar, ib. **–tva**, n. the condition or rank of a Buddha, Kathās. **–datta**, m. 'given by B°,' N. of a minister of king Caṇḍa-mahāsena, ib. **–dāsa**, m. N. of a scholar, Buddh. **–diś** (?), m. N. of a prince, ib. **–deva**, m. N. of a man, ib. **–dravya**, n. 'B°'s property,' (prob.) the relics deposited in a Stūpa (= *staupika*), L.; avarice, miserly accumulation of wealth (?), W. **–dvādaśī-vrata**, n. a partic. observance; N. of ch. of VarP. **–dharma**, m. B°'s law, Buddh.; B°'s marks or peculiarities, ib.; *-saṃgha*, m. pl. Buddha, the law, and the monkhood, MW. **–nandi** (?), m. N. of the 8th Buddhist patriarch, Buddh. **–nirmāṇa**, m. a magic figure of Buddha, Divyâv. **–paksha** (?), m. N. of a king, Buddh. **–pāla**, m. N. of a man, ib. **–pālita**, m. N. of a disciple of Nāgārjuna, ib. **–piṇḍī**, f. a mass of Buddhas, Divyâv. **–purāṇa**, n. B°'s Purāṇa, N. of Parāśara's Laghu-lalita-vistara. **–bhaṭṭa** and **-bhadra**, m. N. of 2 men, Buddh. **–bhūmi**, m. N. of a Buddhist Sūtra wk. (also *-sūtra*, n.) **–mantra**, n. a Buddhist prayer or charm (= *dhāraṇī*), L. **–mārga**, m. B°'s way or doctrine, Buddh. **–mitra**, m. N. of the 9th Buddhist patriarch (who was a disciple of Vasu-bandhu), ib. **–rakshita**, m. 'guarded by B°,' N. of a man, ib.; (*ā*), f. N. of a woman, Mālatīm. **–rāja**, m. N. of a king, Buddh. **–vacana**, n. 'B°'s word,' the Buddhist Sūtras, ib. **–vat** (*buddhá-*), mfn. containing a form of √*budh*, ŚBr. **–vana-giri**, m. N. of a mountain, Buddh. **–vapur-dhārin**, mfn. bearing the body or form of B°, Cat. **–vishaya**, m. = *-kshetra*; °*yâvatāra*, m. N. of wk. **–saṃgīti**, f. N. of wk. **–siṇha**, m. N. of a man, Buddh. **–sena**, m. N. of a king, ib. **Buddhâgama**, m. B°'s doctrine (personified), Prab. **Buddhâṇḍaka**, w. r. for *buddhâiḍūka*, q. v. **Buddhânusmṛiti**, f. continual meditation on B°, Lalit.; N. of a Buddhist Sūtra. **Buddhânta**, m. waking condition, the being awake, ŚBr. **Buddhâlaṃkārâdhishṭhitā**, f. a partic. Dhāraṇī, L. **Buddhâvataṇsaka**, m. or n. (?) N. of wk. **Buddhâvatāra**, m. 'B°'s descent,' N. of ch. of the Khaṇḍa-praśasti (q. v.) **Buddhâiḍūka**, m. a temple in which relics of Buddha are preserved (= *caitya*), L. **Buddhôkta-saṃsārâmaya**, m. N. of wk. **Buddhôpâsaka**, m. (*ikā*, f.) a worshipper of Buddha, Mṛicch.

Buddhaka, m. N. of a poet, Cat.

Buddhi, f. the power of forming and retaining conceptions and general notions, intelligence, reason, intellect, mind, discernment, judgment, Mn.; MBh. &c.; perception (of which 5 kinds are enumerated, or with *manas* 6; cf. *indriya*, *buddhîndriya*); comprehension, apprehension, understanding, Sāh.; (with *ātmanaḥ*, or *buddhir brāhmī*) knowledge of one's self, psychology, Car.; (in Sāṃkhya phil.) Intellect (= *adhy-avasāya*, the intellectual faculty or faculty of mental perception, the second of the 25 Tattvas; cf. *buddhi-tattva*), IW. 80 &c.; presence of mind, ready wit, Pañcat.; Hit.; an opinion, view, notion, idea, conjecture, MBh.; Kāv. &c.; thought about or meditation on (loc. or comp.), intention, purpose, design, ib. (*buddhyā*, with the intention of, designedly, deliberately; *anugraha-b°*, with a view to i. e. in order to show favour; *buddhiṃ* √*kṛi* or *pra-*√*kṛi*, to make up one's mind, resolve, decide, with loc., dat., acc. with *prati*, or inf.); impression, belief, notion (often ifc. = considering as, taking for), Kāv.; Kathās.; Pur.; Hit.; right opinion, correct or reasonable view, R.; Ragh.; a kind of metre, L.; N of the 5th astrol. mansion, VarBṛS., Sch.; Intelligence personified (as a daughter of Daksha and wife of Dharma and mother of Bodha), MBh.; Pur.; N. of a woman, HPariś. **–kara**, m. (with *śukla*) N. of an author, Cat. **–kāmā**, f. N. of one of the Mātṛis attendant on Skanda, MBh. **–kārī**, f. N. of a princess, Kathās. **–kṛit**, mfn. (ifc.) one who forms the notion of, supposing, conjecturing, Kathās. **–kṛita**, mfn. acted wisely, MBh. **–gamya** or **-grāhya**, mfn. to be apprehended by the intellect, intelligible, MBh. **–cintaka**, mfn. one who thinks wisely, R. **–cchāyā**, f. reflex action of the understanding on the soul, Sarvad. **–cyuta**, mfn. one who has lost his intellect, MW. **–jīvin**, mfn. subsisting by intelligence, rational, intelligent, Mn. i, 96. **–tattva**, n. the intellectual faculty or principle (the 2nd of the 8 Prakṛitayaḥ or 'producers' in the Sāṃkhya, coming next to and proceeding from Mūla-prakṛiti or A-vyakta), Siddhāntaś. (cf. IW. 83). **–tas**, ind. from or by the mind, MW. **–devī**, f. N. of a princess, L. **–dyūta**, n. 'intellect-game,' game at chess, Pañcad. **–pura**, n. city of the intellect; *-māhātmya*, n. N. of ch. of BrahmâṇḍaP. **–puraḥ-sara**, mfn. = next, MW. **–pūrva**, mf(*ā*)n. preceded by design, premeditated, intentional, wilful, R.; Kād.; (*am*), ind. intentionally, purposely, Āpast.; MBh. **-pūrvaka,** mfn. (and °*kam,* ind.) = prec., MBh.; Pañcat. (*-tva,* n., Nīlak.) **-pradāna,** n. the giving a commission, TBr., Sch. **-pradīpa,** m. N. of wk. **-prabha,** m. N. of a king, Kathās. **-prāgalbhī,** f. soundness of judgment, Pañcat. **-bala,** n. a partic. kind of play, Siṇhâs. **-bhṛit,** mfn. possessing intelligence, wise, W. **-bheda** (Bhag.), **-bhrama** (MW.), m. disturbance or aberration of mind. **-mat,** mfn. endowed with understanding, intelligent, learned, wise, GṛŚrS.; MBh. &c.; humble, docile, W.; famed, known (?), ib.; m. a rational being, man, ib.; the large shrike, L.; *-tara,* mfn. more or very intelligent, R.; *-tā,* f. (MW.), *-tva,* n. (Kām.) intelligence, wisdom. **-matikā,** f. N. of a woman, Veṇis. **-maya,** mf(*ī*)n. consisting in intellect, MBh. **-moha,** m. confusion of mind, R. **-yukta,** mfn. endowed with understanding, intelligent, MW. **-yoga,** m. devotion of the intellect, intellectual union with the Supreme Spirit, ib.; *-maya,* mf(*ī*)n. consisting in or sprung from it, MBh. **-rāja,** m. (with *samrāj*) N. of an author, Cat. **-lakshaṇa,** n. a sign of intellect or wisdom, A. **-lāghava,** n. lightness or levity of judgment, R. **-vara,** m. N. of a minister of Vikramâditya, Kathās. **-varjita,** mfn. destitute of understanding, foolish, ignorant, ib. **-vāda,** m. N. of wk. **-vidhvaṇsaka,** mfn. destroying consciousness or reason, Bhpr. **-vināśa,** m. loss of understanding, deficiency of intellect, Hit. **-virodhin,** m. N. of a man, Dhūrtan. **-vilāsa,** m. play of the mind or fancy, MW.; N. of wk. **-vilāsinī,** f. N. of Comm. on Līlāv. **-vivardhana,** mfn. increasing the understanding, Mn. **-vishaya,** m. a matter apprehensible by reason, MW. **-visphuraṇa,** m. a partic. Samādhi, Kāraṇḍ. **-vṛiddhi,** f. growth or development of intellect, growth of understanding or wisdom (*-kara,* mfn. producing it), Mn. iv, 19; m. N. of a disciple of Śaṃkara, Cat. **-vaibhava,** n. strength or force of understanding, MW. **-śakti,** f. an intellectual faculty, L. **-śarīra,** m. N. of a man, Kathās. **-śastra,** mfn. armed with understanding, Śiś. **-śālin,** mfn. = *-yukta,* MBh. **-śuddha,** mfn. pure of purpose, Kām. **-śuddhi,** f. purification of the mind, Vedântas. **-śrī-garbha,** m. N. of a Bodhi-sattva, Buddh. **-śreshṭha,** mfn. best (when effected) by the intellect, MBh. **-saṃkīrṇa,** m. a kind of pavilion, Vāstuv. **-sampanna,** mfn. = *-yukta,* ĀśvGṛ. **-sahāya,** m. a counsellor, minister, L. **-sāgara,** m. 'ocean of wisdom,' N. of a man, Vet. **-skandha-maya,** mf(*ī*)n. one whose trunk or stem is the intellect, MBh. **-stha,** mfn. fixed in or present to the mind (*-tva,* n.), Hit. **-hīna,** mfn. = *-varjita; -tva,* n., Hit. **Buddhîndriya,** n. an organ of sense or perception (5 in number, viz. eye, ear, nose, tongue, and skin, opp. to *karmêndriyāṇi,* q.v.; *manas,* 'the mind' belonging to both; cf. *indriya*), Mn.; Kap.; Suśr. &c. (cf. IW. 84, n. 1). **Buddhy-atīta,** mfn. beyond the reach of the understanding, MW. **Buddhy-adhika,** mfn. superior in intellect, R. **Buddhy-avajñāna,** n. disregard or contempt of any one's understanding, W.

2. **Budh,** mfn. (nom. *bhut*) awaking (cf. *ushar-búdh*); intelligent, wise (cf. *a-budh*).

Budha, mfn. awaking (cf. *ushar-budha*); intelligent, clever, wise, Mn.; MBh. &c.; m. a wise or learned man, sage, ib.; a god, L.; a dog, L.; N. of a descendant of Soma (and hence also called *Saumya, Saumāyana,* author of RV. x, 1, and father of Purū-ravas; identified with the planet Mercury); Mercury (regarded as a son of Soma or the moon), PañcavBr.; MBh.; R. &c.; of a descendant of Atri and author of RV. v, 1, Anukr.; of a son of Vega-vat and father of Tṛiṇa-bindu, Pur.; of various authors, Cat.; (*e*), ind. on a Wednesday (= *budha-vāre*), L.; (*ā*), f. Nardostachys Jatamansi, L. **-kauśika,** m. N. of an author, Cat. **-gupta,** m. N. of a prince (also written *buddha-g°*), Buddh. **-cāra,** m. N. of a ch. of Bhaṭṭôtpala's Comm. on VarBṛS. and of a ch. of Yavanêśvara's Mīna-rāja-jātaka. **-jana,** m. a wise man, W. **-tāta,** m. B°'s (or the planet Mercury's) father, the moon, L. **-darśana-cāra,** m. N. of ch. of Yavanêśvara's Mīna-rāja-jātaka. **-dina,** n. B°'s (or the planet Mercury's) day, Wednesday, Cat. **-deśa,** m. N. of a place, MW. **-nāḍī,** f., **-pūjā,** f., **-prakāśa,** m., **-manohara,** m. or n., **-rañjinī,** f. N. of wks. **-ratna,** n. 'B°'s gem,' an emerald, L. **-vāra,** m. = *-dina,* L. **-śānti,** f. N. of wk. **-sānu,** m. = *parṇa* or = *yajña-purusha,* L. **-suta,** m. 'B°'s son,' N. of Purū-ravas (the first king of the lunar dynasty), Pur. **-sūkta,** n. N. of wk. **-smṛiti,** f. N. of wk. **Budhâshṭamī,** f. 'the 8th (day) of B°,' N. of a festival, Cat.; *-vrata,* n., *-vrata-kāla-nirṇaya,* m. N. of wks.

Budhaka, m. N. of a man, Veṇis.

Búdhan-vat, mfn. containing the root *budh,* TBr.

Budhāná, mfn. awaking, rousing, RV. iv, 51, 8, vii, 68, 9; being heeded (?), ib. iv, 23, 8; knowing, wise, prudent, L.; one who speaks kindly, L.; m. a sage, spiritual guide, holy teacher, L.

Budhita, mfn. known, understood, W.

Budhila, mfn. wise, learned, L.

Budheya, m. pl. N. of a school of the white Yajur-veda, Āryav.

Budhya, mfn. See *a-budhyá.*

Bubodhayishu, mfn. (fr. Desid. of Caus.) wishing to excite the attention, desirous of admonishing, MārkP. (cf. *bibodhayishu*).

Bubhutsā, f. (fr. Desid.) desire to know, curiosity about (acc. or comp.), BhP.; Yājñ., Sch. °**tsita,** n. id., BhP. **-°tsu,** mfn. wishing to know (acc. or comp.), MBh.; Daś. &c.; curious, inquisitive, Naish.; desirous to know everything (said of the gods), MBh.

Boddhavya, mfn. (√*budh*) to be attended to or noticed, MBh.; Kathās.; to be known or perceived or observed or recognized, perceptible, intelligible, Up.; MBh. &c.; to be enlightened or admonished or instructed or informed, one who is informed, Pañcat.; Sāh.; to be awakened or aroused, MW.; n. (impers.) it is to be watched or be awaked, Pañcat. (v. l. *pra-b°*).

Boddhṛi, m. one who perceives or comprehends, Sāh.; one who knows or is versed in (loc. or comp.), ChUp.; Yājñ.; MBh. &c. (*-tva,* n., Kap.)

Bodhá, mfn. knowing, understanding, AshṭāvS. (cf. g. *jvalâdi*); m. waking, becoming or being awake, consciousness, AV.; MBh. &c.; the opening of blossom, bloom, Cat.; the taking effect (of spells; acc. with *pra-√yā,* 'to begin to take effect'), ib.; exciting (a perfume), Var.; perception, apprehension, thought, knowledge, understanding, intelligence, Kāv.; Rājat.; Pur.; designation, Sāh.; Pāṇ., Sch.; awakening, arousing, W.; making known, informing, instructing, MW.; Knowledge personified as a son of Buddhi, Pur.; N. of a man, MārkP. (cf. Pāṇ. iv, 1, 107); pl. N. of a people, MBh. **-kara,** mf(*ī*)n. one who wakens or rouses or teaches or informs, W.; m. 'awakener,' a minstrel who wakes a prince in the morning with music, L. **-gamya,** mfn. attainable by the intellect, intelligible, MW. **-ghanâcārya,** m. N. of a teacher, Cat. **-citta-vivaraṇa,** w. r. for *bodhi-c°.* **-tas,** ind. through wisdom or understanding, MW. **-dhishaṇa,** m. one whose intellect is knowledge, BhP. **-pañcadaśikā,** f. N. of wk. **-pūrvam,** ind. knowingly, consciously (*a-bodhap°*), Śak. **-pṛithvīdhara,** m. N. of a teacher, Cat. **-prakriyā,** f. N. of wk. **-maya,** mf(*ī*)n. consisting of (pure) knowledge, Subh. **-rāyâcārya,** m. (later *Satya-vīra-tīrtha*) a modern (1864) high priest of the Mādhva sect, Cat. **-vatī,** f. N. of a Surâṅganā, Siṇhâs. **-vāsara,** m. 'waking-day,' the 11th day in the light half of the month Kārttika (in which Vishṇu awakes from his sleep; cf. *bodhanī*), SkandaP. **-vilāsa,** m., **-sāra,** m., **-siddhi,** f., **-sudhâkara,** m. N. of wks. **Bodhâtman,** m. (with Jainas) the intelligent and sentient soul, Col. **Bodhânanda-ghana,** m. N. of a teacher, Cat. (cf. *Bodha-ghanâcārya*). **Bodhâraṇya-yati,** m. N. of the Guru of *Bhāratī-yati,* Cat. **Bodhâryā,** f. N. of wk. **Bodhêndra,** m. N. of an author, Cat. **Bodhâika-siddhi,** f. N. of wk.

Bodhaka, mf(*ikā*)n. awakening, arousing, R.; causing to know, explaining, teaching, instructing, a teacher, instructor, Kāv.; Vedântas.; Sarvad.; (ifc.) denoting, indicating, signifying (*-tva,* n.), Pāṇ., Sch.; Vedântas.; m. a spy, informer, W.; N. of a man (pl. his descendants), Pravar.; of a poet, Cat.

Bodhana, mf(*ī*)n. causing to awake or expand (a flower), arousing, exciting, R.; Hariv.; Suśr.; enlightening, teaching, instructing (cf. *bāla-bodhinī*); m. the planet Mercury, W.; N. of a mountain, VP.; (*ī*), f. intellect, knowledge, L.; long pepper, L.; = *bodha-vāsara,* PadmaP.; a partic. Śakti, Hcat.; n. waking, being awake, KātyŚr.; Suśr.; perceiving, understanding, Ragh.; causing to wake, awakening, arousing, MBh.; R. &c.; causing (a spell) to take effect, Cat.; calling forth a perfume, burning incense, L.; causing to perceive or understand, Sāh.; instructing, teaching, informing, Hariv.; Kāv.; denoting, indicating, signifying, Sāh.; Pāṇ., Sch.; 'the awaking of Durgā,' N. of a festival on the 9th day of the dark half of the month Bhādra, Col. **-mantra,** m. N. of ch. of PSarv.

Bodhanīya, mfn. to be admonished, Yājñ., Sch.; to be known or understood, MBh.; to be made known or explained, W.

Bodhán-manas, v. l. for *bodhín-m°.*

Bodhayitavya, mfn. (fr. Caus.) to be made acquainted with, to be informed of (acc.), Prab.

Bodhayitṛí, m. (fr. Caus.) an awakener, RV. i, 161, 13; a teacher, preceptor, MW.

Bodhayishṇu, mfn. (fr. Caus.) wishing to awaken or to arouse, R.

Bodhāna, mfn. prudent, clever, wise, L.; m. a wise man; N. of Bṛihas-pati, L.

Bodhāyana, m. N. of a teacher and author of the Brahma-sūtra-vṛitti (said to have commented also on the Bhagavad-gītā and 10 Upanishads), Cat. **-kalpa-vivaraṇa,** n., **-prayoga,** m., **-śrauta,** n., **-sūtra,** n. N. of wks. (cf. *Baudhāyana*).

Bodhāyanīya, n. (and *-gṛihya-mālā,* f.) N. of wks.; (*ā*), f. a partic. drug, L.

Bodhi, m. f. (with Buddhists or Jainas) perfect knowledge or wisdom (by which a man becomes a Buddha or Jina), the illuminated or enlightened intellect (of a B° or J°), Kathās.; Rājat.; Śatr.; Lalit. (cf. MWB. 97, 188 &c.); m. the tree of wisdom under which perfect w° is attained or under which a man becomes a Buddha, the sacred fig-tree, (Ficus Religiosa), Hcat. (MWB. 35, 181 &c.); 'wakener,' a cock, L.; N. of a man (= Buddha in a former birth), Jātakam.; of a mythical elephant, Lalit.; of a place, L.; pl. N. of a people, R.; mfn. learned, wise, Uṇ. iv, 117. **-citta-vivaraṇa,** n., **-cittôtpādana-śāstra,** n. N. of wks. **-taru,** m. 'tree of wisdom,' Ficus Religiosa, L. (cf. above). **-da,** m. (with Jainas) an Arhat, L. **-druma,** m. = *-taru,* L. **-dharma,** m. N. of a Buddhist patriarch (whose original name was Bodhi-dhana), L. **-nyāsa,** m. N. of wk. **-paksha-dharma,** m. a quality belonging to (or a constituent of) perfect intelligence, Lalit.; *-nirdeśa,* m. N. of wk. **-pakshika,** mfn. belonging to perfect intelligence (with *dharma,* m. = *paksha-dh°,* Dharmas. 43). **-bhadra,** m. N. of a teacher, Buddh. **-maṇḍa,** m. or n. (?) seat of wisdom (N. of the seats which were said to have risen out of the earth under 4 successive trees where Gautama Buddha attained to perfect wisdom), MWB. 232 (cf. next). **-maṇḍala,** n. N. of the place where Gautama Buddha attained to perfect wisdom, Lalit. **-ruci,** m. N. of a scholar, Buddh. **-vṛiksha,** m. = *-taru,* L. **-saṃghârāma,** m. N. of a monastery, Buddh. **-sattva,** m. 'one whose essence is perfect knowledge,' one who is on the way to the attainment of p° k° (i. e. a Buddhist saint when he has only one birth to undergo before obtaining the state of a supreme Buddha and then Nirvāṇa), Śiś.; Kathās.; Rājat.; Buddh. (the early doctrine had only one Bodhi-sattva, viz. Maitreya; the later reckoned many more, MWB. 134, 188, 189); N. of the principal Buddha of the present era (before he became a Buddha), Śiś., Sch.; L.; of a poet, Cat.; *-caryā,* f. the actions or condition of a Bodhi-sattva, Lalit.; *-caryâvatāra,* f. N. of wk.; *-tā,* f. the state of a B°-s°, Bodhi-sattvaship, Kathās.; *-paksha-nirdeśa,* m., *-piṭaka,* m. or n., *-buddhânusmṛiti-samādhi,* m., *-bhūmi,* f. N. of wks.; *-saṃcodinī,* f. N. of a partic. ray of light, Lalit.; *-samuccayā,* f. N. of a Buddh. deity; °*tvâṅśa,* m. part of a B°-s°; °*tvâvadāna-kalpa-latā,* f. N. of wks. **-siddhi,** f. N. of wk. **Bodhy-aṅga,** n. a requisite for attaining perfect knowledge, Lalit. (7 in number, Divyâv.; Dharmas. 49); *-vatī,* f. a partic. Samādhi, L.

Bodhita, mfn. (fr. Caus.) made known, apprised, explained; informed, instructed; admonished, reminded, MBh.; R.

Bodhitavya, mfn. to be made known, to be imparted or communicated, L. (cf. *bodhayitavya*).

Bodhin, mfn. (ifc.) intent upon, careful of, MārkP.; knowing, familiar with, Cat.; causing to know or perceive, Sāh.; awakening, enlightening (cf. *jñāna-, tattva-, bāla-bodhinī*).

Bodhín-manas, mfn. (according to Padap. fr. *bodhít-m°*) one whose mind is awake, watchful, attentive, RV.

Bodhila, m. (fr. *bodhi*) N. of a teacher, Buddh.

Bodheya, m. pl. N. of a Vedic school (cf. *addhā-b°* and *baudheya*).

Bodhya, mfn. to be known or understood, to be regarded or recognized as (nom.), Vedântas.; BhP.; Sāh. &c.; to be made known, Vedântas.; to be enlightened or instructed, Kathās.; m. N. of a Ṛishi, MBh. **-gītā**, f. N. of MBh. xii, 178.

Bauddha, mf(*ī*)n. (fr. *buddhi*) being in the mind, mental (=not uttered), Vām. v, 2, 62; relating to intellect or understanding, Sāh.; (fr. *buddha*), relating or belonging to Buddha, Buddhist, Prab.; Rājat.; Vedântas. &c. (cf. MWB. 529, 1). **-darśana**, n. Buddhist doctrine, N. of Sarvad. ii. **-dūshaṇa**, n. N. of wk. **-dhik-kāra**, m. N. of wk. (= *ātma-tattva-viveka*); *-gādā-dharī*, f., *-guṇânandī*, f., *-dīdhiti*, f., *-rahasya*, n. N. of Comms. on it. **-mata**, n. B° doctrine, N. of wk.; *-dūshaṇa*, n., *-nivarhaṇa*, n. N. of wks. **-śāstra**, n. B° doctrine, N. of wk. **-saṃgati**, f. N. of a work on Alam-kāra (quoted in Vās.)

Baudha, mf(*ī*)n. relating to Budha or the planet Mercury, Sūryas. (with *ahan*, n. day of M°, Wednesday, Vishṇ.); m. patr. of Purū-ravas, L.

Baudhāyana, m. patr. of an ancient teacher (author of Gṛihya-, Dharma- and Śrauta-sūtras); N. of a Vidūshaka, Caṇḍ.; mf(*ī*)n. relating to or composed by B°, AgP.; pl. his race or school, Saṃskārak. **-caraka-sautrāmaṇī**, f., **-tati**, f., **-prayoga**, m., **-vidhi**, m., **-śikshā**, f., **-śrauta-prayoga-sāra**, m., **-saṃgraha**, m., **-smṛiti**, f., **°nī-pariśishṭa**, n. N. of wks.

Baudhāyanīya, mfn. relating or belonging to Baudhāyana; m. pl. N. of a school of the black Yajur-veda. **-prayoga-sāra**, m. N. of wk.

Baudhi, m. patr. fr. *bodha*, Pāṇ. iv, 1, 107, Sch.; fr. *baudhi*, ii, 4, 58, Vārtt. 1, Pat.

Baúdhī-pútra, m. N. of a teacher, ŚBr.

Baudheya, m. pl. N. of a school (cf. *bodheya*).

Baudhya, mfn. born in Bodha, g. *śaṇḍikâdi*; m. patr. fr. *bodha* (Pāṇ. iv, 1, 107), N. of a teacher, VP.

बुध्न *budhná*, m. n. (probably not connected with √*budh*; but cf. Uṇ. iii, 5) bottom, ground, base, depth, lowest part of anything (as the root of a tree &c.), RV.; AV.; ŚBr. (*búdhna*); ŚrS.; ChUp.; the sky, Nir.; the body, ib.; N. of a son of the 14th Manu, VP.; often w. r. for *budhnya*. [Cf. Gk. πυθμήν; Lat. *fundus*; Germ. *bodam*, *bodem*, *Boden*; Angl. Sax. *botm*; Eng. *bottom*.] **-roga**, m. a partic. disease, Car. (cf. *bradhna* and *bradhma*). **-vat** (*budhná-*), mfn. having a foot or basis, TS.

Budhníya, mfn. = next, TBr.

Budhnyà, mfn. being on the ground or at the base, coming from or belonging to the depths, RV. &c. &c. (very often in connexion with *áhi*, q. v.); N. of a son of the 14th Manu, VP.

बुन्द् *bund*, cl. 1. P. Ā. (Dhātup. xxi, 12; v. l. *cund* and *bundh*) to perceive, learn, understand, Bhaṭṭ..

बुन्द *bundá*, m. an arrow, RV. (= *ishu*, Nir.)

बुन्दिर *bundira*, n. a house, L.

बुन्ध् *bundh*, cl. 10. P. *bundhayati*, to bind, Dhātup. xxxii, 14 (cf. *bund*).

बुबुर *bubura*, m. water (= *udaka*, Naigh. i, 12).

बुबोधयिषु *bubodhayishu*. See p. 734, col. 2.

बुभुक्षा *bubhukshā*, f. (fr. Desid. of √3. *bhuj*) desire of enjoying anything, MBh.; wish to eat, appetite, hunger, R.; Var. &c.; *-°panaya* (*°kshâp°*), m. 'that which takes away hunger,' food, R.; *-pīḍita*, mfn. pained by h°, hungry, MW. **°kshita**, mfn. hungry, starving, ravenous, Mn.; MBh. &c. **°kshu**, mfn. wishing to eat, hungry, MārkP.; desirous of worldly enjoyment (opp. to *mumukshu*), Kull. on Mn. ii, 224.

बुभुत्सा *bubhutsā* &c. See p. 734, col. 2.

बुभूर्षा *bubhūrshā*, f. (fr. Desid. of √*bhṛi*) desire of supporting (gen.), Āpast. **°shu**, mfn. (ifc.) wishing to nourish or support, Śaṃk.

बुभूषक *bubhūshaka*, mfn. (fr. Desid. of √*bhū*) wishing the welfare of, wishing to be of service to (gen. or comp.), MBh. **°shā**, f. desire of being or living, ŚāṅkhBr.; BhP. **°shu**, mfn. wishing to be or become anything (nom.), Śiś.; HPariś.; wishing to become powerful or prevail, KātyŚr.; MBh.; BhP.; wishing the welfare of (gen.), MBh.

बुम्भी *bumbhī*, f. coarse ground meal, L.

Bumbhikā, f. id., ib.

बुरि *buri*, f. the female organ of generation (= *buli*), Gal.

बुरुड *buruḍa*, m. a basket-maker, mat-maker, BhP., Sch.

बुल् *bul*, cl. 10. P. *bolayati*, to cause to sink, submerge, Dhātup. xxxii, 62; to sink, dive, plunge into and emerge again, W.

Buli, f. = *buri* or the anus, L.

बुल *bula*, g. *balâdi*, Kāś.

Bulya, mfn., ib.

बुलिल *bulilá*, m. N. of a man (= *budila*), ŚBr.

बुल्व *bulbá*, mfn. (prob.) oblique, ŚBr.

बुल्ल *bulla*, m. N. of a man, Rājat.

बुवम् *buvam*, ind. an onomat. word, TBr., Sch. (cf. *sa-buva*).

बुश *buśa*, *busha*, w. r. for *busa*.

बुस् *bus*, cl. 4. P. *busyati*, to discharge, pour forth, emit, Dhātup. xxvi, 110; to divide, distribute (v. l. for √*vyush*).

Busá, n. (prob.) vapour, mist, fog, RV. x, 27, 4; chaff and other refuse of grain, any refuse or rubbish, Kauś.; Suśr.; water, Naigh.; Nir.; dry cow-dung, W.; the thick part of sour curds, ib.; wealth, ib.; (*ā*), f. (in dram.) a younger sister, ib. **-plāvī**, f. a beetle (?), Divyâv.

Busasa, mfn. (fr. *busá*), g. *tṛiṇâdi*.

बुस्त् *bust*, cl. 10. P. *bustayati*, to honour, respect &c. (= or v. l. for √*pust*, q. v.)

बुस्त *busta*, m. n. (g. *ardharcâdi*) the burnt exterior of roast meat, L.; the husk or shell of fruit, L.

बुह्ना *buhnā*. See *śveta-b°*.

बूक्क *būkka*, mfn. = *bukka*, the heart, L.

Būkhan, n. id., Col.

बूत्कार *būt-kāra*, m. the screaming of monkeys, Kāv.

बूबशर्मन् *būba-śarman*, m. N. of a man (the father of Viṭṭhala Dīkshita, about 1620), Cat.

बूष *būsha*, w. r. for *busa*.

बृंह् *bṛiṅh*, *bṛiṅhaṇa* &c. See √2. 4. *bṛih*.

बृगल *bṛigala*, n. a fragment, piece, morsel (see *ardha-* and *puroḍāśa-b°*).

बृन्दारण्य *bṛindâraṇya*, *bṛindā-vana*. See *vṛindâr°*, *vṛindā-v°*.

बृबदुक्थ *bṛibád-uktha*, m. N. of Indra, RV. viii, 32, 10 (either *mahad-uktha*, 'highly lauded,' or *vaktavyam asmā uktham*, 'one to whom praise is to be ascribed,' Nir. vi, 4).

बृबु *bṛibú*, m. N. of a man (according to Sāy. 'the carpenter of the Paṇis'), RV. vi, 45, 31; Mn. x, 107.

बृबूक *bṛibūka*, n. water, RV. x, 27, 33 (cf. Naigh. i, 12; others 'mfn. dense, thick').

बृषी *bṛishī*. See *bṛisī* below.

बृसय *bṛisaya*, m. N. of a demon (Sāy.= *tvashṭṛi*), RV. i, 93, 4; (prob.) a sorcerer, conjuror, vi, 61, 3.

बृसी *bṛisī*, f. (also written *bṛishī*, *vṛisī* or *vṛishī*) a roll of twisted grass, pad, cushion, (esp.) the seat of a religious student or of an ascetic, ŚrS.; MBh. &c. **Bṛisikā**, f. id., L.

बृह् 1. *bṛih* or *vṛih*, cl. 6. P. (Dhātup. xxviii, 57) *bṛiháti*, *vṛiháti* (pf. *babarha*, *vavárha*; fut. *varkshyati*, *varhishyati*; *varḍhā*, *varhitā*; aor. *barhīt*, *avṛikshat*; ind. p. *vṛiḍhvā*, *varhitvā*, *vṛihya*, *barham*, *várham*; Ved. inf. *vṛihas*: Pass. *vṛihyate*; aor. *varhi*), to tear, pluck, root up (without a prep. only with *mūlam*, TS.; Āpast.): Caus. *barháyati* (see *ni-*√2. *bṛih*): Desid. *vivṛikshati*, *vivarhishati*, Gr.: Intens. *varīvarḍhi*, *varīvṛihyate*, ib.

1. **Bṛiḍha** or **vṛiḍhá**, mfn. pulled up, eradicated, Br. (cf. Pāṇ. vi, 3, 111, Sch.)

बृह् 2. *bṛih* or *bṛiṅh*, cl. 1. P. (Dhātup. xvii, 85) *bṛiṅhati* (also *°te*, ŚBr. and *bṛihati*, AV.; pf. *babarha*, AV.; Ā. p. *babṛihāṇá*, RV.), to be thick, grow great or strong, increase (the finite verb only with a prep.): Caus. *bṛiṅhayati*, *°te* (also written *vṛ°*), to make big or fat or strong, increase, expand, further, promote, MBh; Kathās.; Pur.; Suśr.; *barhayati*, see *sam-*√2. *bṛih*: Intens. *barbṛihat*, *barbṛihi*, see *upa-*√*bṛih*.

Bṛiṅhaṇa, mfn. (fr. Caus.) making big or fat or strong, nourishing, Suśr.; m. a kind of sweetmeat, W.; n. the act of making big &c., ib.; a means for making strong or firm, RPrāt. **-tva**, n. the quality of making fat or strong, Suśr.; the quality of making solid or firm, Hariv.

Bṛiṅhaṇīya, mfn. to be fattened or nourished, Pāṇ. viii, 4, 2, Sch.; fattening, nutritious, Suśr.

Bṛiṅhayitavya, mfn. to be nourished or strengthened, Suśr.

Bṛiṅhayitṛi, mfn. strengthening, increasing, L.

1. **Bṛiṅhita**, mfn. (for 2. see under √4. *bṛih*) strengthened, nourished, cherished, grown, increased, MBh.; Hariv. &c.; (*ā*), f. N. of one of the Mātṛis attendant on Skanda, MBh. (v. l. *bṛiṅhila*).

2. **Bṛiḍha** or **vṛiḍha**. See *pari-*√2. *bṛih*.

3. **Bṛih**, prayer. See *bṛihas-pati*.

Bṛihaka, m. N. of a Deva-gandharva, MBh.

Bṛihác, in comp. for **bṛihát**. **-cañcu**, f. a kind of vegetable, L. **-cāṇakya**, n. the larger collection of precepts by Cāṇakya (q. v.) **-citta**, m. Citrus Medica, L. **-cintāmaṇi**, m. N. of wk.; *-ṭīkā*, f. N. of a Comm. on it. **-chattrā**, f. a species of plant, KātyŚr., Sch. **-chada**, m. a walnut, L. **-chandas** (*°hác-*), mfn. high-roofed, having a lofty ceiling, AV. **-chandêndu-śekhara**, m. N. of wk. **-charīra** (*°hác + śar°*), mfn. having a vast body, RV.; Suśr. **-chalka** (*°hac + śa°*), m. 'large-scaled,' a kind of prawn, L. **-chātâtapa** (*°hac + śā°*), m. 'the larger Śātâtapa,' N. of a partic. recension of Ś°'s law-book, Cat. **-chānti-stava** (*°hac + śā°*), m. the larger Śānti-stava, W. **-chāla** (*°hac + śā°*), m. a large or lofty Vatica Robusta, MBh. **-chimbī** (*°hac + śi°*), f. a kind of cucumber, L. **-chuka** (*°hac + śu°*), m. a kind of peak, Bhpr. **-chṛiṅgāra-tilaka** (*°hac + śṛi°*), n. the larger Śṛiṅgāra-tilaka, Cat. **-choka** (*°hac + śo°*), mfn. being in great sorrow, Prab. **-chravas** (*°hác + śra°*), mfn. loud-sounding, RV.; loudly praised, far-famed, ib.; BhP. **-chrī-krama** (*°hac + śrī°*) m. N. of wk. **-chloka** (*°hac + ślo°*), mfn. loudly praised, BhP.; m. N. of a son of Uru-krama by Kīrtti, ib.

Bṛiháj, in comp. for *bṛihát*. **-jaghana**, mfn. having large hips, MW. **-jana**, m. a great or illustrious man, ib. **-jātaka**, n. N. of Varāha-mihira's larger wk. on nativities (cf. *svalpa-jātaka*); of another wk.; *-śloka-vyākhyāna*, n. of a metrical Comm. by Bhaṭṭôtpala on the former wk. **-jābālôpanishad**, f. N. of an Upanishad on the divinity of Kālâgni-rudra. **-jālá**, n. a large net or snare, AV. **-jīraka**, m. large cumin, Bhpr. **-jīvantikā** (MW.), *-jīvantī* or *-jīvā* (L.), f. a kind of plant (= *priyaṃ-karī*). **-jyotis** (*°háj-*), mfn. bright-shining, TS.; m. N. of a grandson of Brahmā, MBh.

Bṛihaṭ, in comp. for *bṛihát*. **-ṭika**, m. N. of a man, Rājat. **-ṭīkā**, f. 'large commentary,' N. of wk. by Kumārila.

Bṛihaḍ, in comp. for *bṛihát*. **-ḍhakkā**, f. a large drum, L.

Bṛihát, mf(*atī*)n. (in later language usually written *vṛihat*) lofty, high, tall, great, large, wide, vast, abundant, compact, solid, massy, strong, mighty, RV. &c. &c.; full-grown, old, RV.; extended or bright (as a luminous body), ib.; clear, loud (said of sounds), ib.; m. N. of a Marut, Hariv.; of a prince, MBh.; of a son of Su-hotra and father of Aja-mīḍha, Hariv.; m. or n.(?) speech (*°tām pati* = *bṛihas-pati*), Śiś. ii, 26; (*tī*), f., see s. v.; n. height (also = heaven, sky), RV.; N. of various Sāmans composed in the metrical form Bṛihatī (also with *Āgneyam*,

Bharad-vājasya, Bhāradvājam, Vāmadevyam, Sauram), ĀrshBr.; N. of Brahman, BhP.; of the Veda, ib.; (*át*), ind. far and wide, on high, RV.; firmly, compactly, ib.; brightly, ib.; greatly, much, ib.; aloud, ib. (also *atā́*, AV.) **-kathā**, f. 'great narrative,' N. of a collection of tales ascribed to Guṇāḍhya (from which the Kathā-sarit-sāgara of Somadeva is said to have been abridged), Kāvyâd.; Kathās.; of another wk.; *-mañjarī*, f. N. of a collection of tales ascribed to Kshemêndra; *-vivaraṇa* and *-sāra-saṃgraha*, m. N. of wks. **-kanda**, m. a kind of onion or garlic or another bulbous plant, L. **-kapola**, mfn. having fat puffy cheeks, TPrāt., Comm. **-karman**, m. 'doing mighty acts,' N. of sev. kings, Hariv.; Pur. **-kalpa**, m. N. of a Kalpa, the 7th day in the bright half of the moon in Brahmā's month (see 1. *kalpa*), L.; the last day in the dark half of the month, Cat.; *-latā*, f. N. of wk. **-kāya**, m. 'large-bodied,' N. of a son of Bṛihad-dhanus, BhP. **-kāla-jñāna**, n. 'the large K° -jñ° or knowledge of times,' N. of wk. **-kāla-śāka**, m. a partic. shrub, L. (w. r.) **-kāśa**, m. a partic. kind of reed (= *khaḍgaṭa*), L. **-kīrti**, mfn. far-famed, MBh.; VarBṛS.; m. N. of a grandson of Brahmā, MBh.; of an Asura, Hariv. **-kukshi**, mfn. having a large or prominent belly, L.; f. N. of a Yoginī, Hcat. **-kuśaṇḍikā**, f. N. of a part of the Ājya-tantra, Kauś., Comm. **-kṛishṇa-gaṇôddeśa-dīpikā**, f. N. of wk. **-ketu** (°*hát-*), mfn. having great clearness or brightness (said of Agni), RV.; m. N. of a king, MBh. **-kośala-khaṇḍa**, m. n.(?) N. of wk. **-kośātakī**, f. a kind of gourd, L. **-kaustubhâlaṃkāra**, m. N. of wk. **-kshaṇa**, m. N. of a king, VP. (v. l. *-kshaya, -kshetra* and *bṛihad-raṇa*). **-kshata**, m. N. of a partic. mythical being, VarBṛS. **-kshatra**, m. N. of sev. kings, MBh.; Hariv.; Pur. **-kshaya** and **-kshetra**, m., see *-kshaṇa*. **-tantra-pati**, m. a partic. functionary, Cat.; = *dharmâdhikārin*, Śrikaṇṭh.; *-tva*, n., ib. **-tapas**, n. great self-mortification, a partic. severe penance, MW.; mfn. practising great self-mortification or austerity, ib.; °*po-vrata*, n. a partic. penitential observance, Cat. **-tarka-taraṃgiṇī**, f. N. of wk. **-tāla**, m. Phoenix Paludosa (= *hintāla*), L. **-tiktā**, f. Clypea Hernandifolia, L. **-tīrtha-māhātmya**, n. N. of wk. **-tuhina-śarkara**, mfn. full of great lumps of ice, MW. **-tṛiṇa**, n. strong grass, Gobh.; the bamboo cane, L. **-tejas**, mfn. having great energy, MW.; m. the planet Jupiter, VP. **-toḍala-tantra**, n. N. of a Tantra wk. **-tva**, n. greatness, largeness, large extent, MBh.; Hariv.; Kathās. **-tvac**, m. Alstonia Scholaris, L. **-tvan** (?), m. N. of a Deva-gandharva, MBh. (v. l. °*had-dhan*). **-pattra**, m. 'having large leaves,' Symplocos Racemosa, Car.; a species of bulbous plant, L.; (*ā*), f. id., ib. **-parāśara**, m. 'the larger Parāśara,' N. of a partic. recension of P°'s law-book. **-paribhāshā-saṃgraha**, m. N. of wk. **-parva-mālā**, f. N. of wk. **-palāśa**, mf(*ā*)n. having great leaves, AV. **-pāṭali**, m. the thorn-apple, L. **-pāda**, mf(*ā*)n. large-footed, Kathās.; m. the Indian fig-tree, L. **-pārevata**, m. a kind of fruit tree (= *mahā-p°*), L. **-pālin**, m. wild cumin, L. **-pīlu**, m. a kind of Pīlu tree (= *mahā-p°*), L. **-pushpa**, mfn. having large flowers, MW.; (*ī*), f. a kind of Crotolaria (= *ghaṇṭā-ravā*), L. **-pṛishṭha**, mfn. having the Bṛihat-sāman as the basis of the Pṛishṭha-stotra, AitBr.; ŚrS. **-pracetas**, m. 'the larger Pracetas,' N. of a partic. recension of a law-book by P°. **-prayoga**, m. N. of wk. **-phala**, mfn. having large fruit, bringing great profit or reward, L.; m. a species of plant (= *caceṇḍā*), L.; pl. N. of a class of Buddhist gods, Buddh.; (*ā*), f. N. of various plants (a species of wild cucumber; Beninkasa Cerifera; = *mahā-jambū*; = *mahêndra-vāruṇī*), L. **-shoḍaśa-kāraṇa-pūjā**, f. N. of wk. **-saṃvarta**, m. 'the great Saṃvarta,' N. of a legal wk. **-saṃhitā**, f. 'the great composition,' N. of an astrological wk. by Varāha-mihira; of a philos. wk.; of a Dharma. **-saṃketa**, m. N. of wk. **-sarvânukramaṇī**, f. N. of an Anukramaṇī. **-sahāya**, mfn. having a powerful companion, Śiś. **-sāman** (°*hát-*), mfn. having the Bṛihat-sāman for a Sāman, ĀpŚr.; PañcavBr.; m. N. of an Āṅgirasa, AV.; (*-sāmā*, w. r. for *bṛihat-sāma*, Bhag.) **-sumna** (°*hát-*), mfn. of great benevolence or kindness, RV. **-sūrya-siddhânta**, m. the larger Sūrya-siddhânta, Col. **-sena**, m. N. of various kings, MBh.; VP.; of a son of Kṛishṇa, BhP.; of a son of Su-nakshatra, ib.; (*ā*), f. N. of Damayantī's nurse, Nal. **-soma**, w. r. for *-sāma*, TBr., Comm. **-sphij**, m. 'having large buttocks,' N. of a man, Pañcat.

Bṛihata, m. N. of a son of the 9th Manu, Hariv.

Bṛihatikā, f. an upper garment, mantle, wrapper, Pāṇ.; L.; Solanum Indicum, L.

Bṛihatī, f. fr. *bṛihát*, N. of a partic. metre of 36 (orig. 8 + 8 + 12 + 8) syllables or (later) any metre containing 36 syllables (ifc. °*tīka*, mfn.), RV.; RPrāt.; AV.; Br. &c.; a symbolical expression for the number 36, ŚrS.; (pl.) N. of partic. bricks forming part of the sacrificial fire-altar, ŚBr.; Śulbas.; a partic. Solanum (*-dvaya*, n. two species of it), ŚāṅkhGṛ.; Suśr.; a part of the body between the breast and backbone, Suśr.; (du.) heaven and earth, Gal.; speech (a sense inferred from certain passages); a mantle, wrapper, L.; a place containing water, reservoir, L.; the lute of Nārada or Viśvā-vasu, L.; N. of two wks.; N. of sev. women, Hariv.; BhP. **-kalpa**, m. N. of wk. **-kāram**, ind. having converted (or with conversion) into Bṛihatī-strophes, ĀśvŚr. **-pati**, m. the planet Jupiter, L. **-śastra**, n., **-shashṭhī**, f. N. of wks. **-sahasrá**, n. a thousand Bṛihatīs, ŚBr.; ŚāṅkhŚr.; N. of wk.

Bṛihatīka, mfn. See *bṛihatī*.

Bṛihatka, mfn. = *bṛihát*, large, great, W.; n. N. of a Sāman.

Bṛihád, in comp. for *bṛihát*. **-agni**, m. N. of a Ṛishi, Hariv.; *-mukha*, n. a partic. medicinal powder, Bhpr. **-aṅga**, mfn. having large limbs, large-bodied, L.; having many parts, MW.; m. an elephant, L.; a large el° (or one that is usually the leader of a wild herd), W. **-aṅgiras**, m. 'the larger Aṅgiras,' N. of a partic. recension of a law-book by A°. **-atri**, m. 'the larger Atri,' N. of a wk. on med. **-anīka** (°*hád-*), mfn. powerful-looking, SV. **-abhidhāna-cintāmaṇi**, m. the larger Abhidhāna-cintāmaṇi by Hema-candra. **-amara** or **-amara-kośa**, m. 'the larger Amara-kośa,' N. of a partic. recension of the Am° with interpolations. **-ambālikā**, f. N. of one of the Mātṛis attending on Skanda, MBh. **-ambā-śataka**, n. N. of wk. **-amla**, m. Averrhoa Carambola, L. **-arka**, mf(*ī*)n.(?), AV. viii, 9, 14. **-aśva**, m. N. of a Gandharva, Cat.; of various men, MBh.; R.; Hariv.; Pur. **-ashṭa-varga**, m. N. of wk. **-asṛiṅ-mati**, m. 'having a great inclination for blood,' a partic. demon, W. **-ātreya**, m. 'the larger Ātreya,' N. of a wk. on med. **-āra**, m. N. of an Asura, L. **-āraṇyaka** (also *-āraṇya*, n., °*kôpanishad*, f.), n. N. of a celebrated Upanishad forming the last 5 Prapāṭhakas or last 6 Adhyāyas of the Śatapatha-Brāhmaṇa; *-bhāshya*, n., *-bhāshya-ṭīkā*, f., *-bhāshya-vārttika*, n., *-vārttika-sāra*, m. n.(?), *-viveka*, m., *-vishaya-nirṇaya*, m., *-vyākhyā*, f., °*kôpanishat-khaṇḍârtha*, m., °*kôpanishad-vārttika*, n. N. of wks. **-ishu**, m. N. of various men, Hariv.; Pur. **-īśvara-dīkshitīya** and °**ra-purāṇa**, n. N. of wks. **-uktha** (*bṛihád-*), mfn. having loud hymns of praise, loudly praised, RV.; VS.; m. N. of an Agni (son of Tapas), MBh.; (with *Vāmadevya*) N. of a man (author of RV. x, 54–56), Anukr.; (with *Vāmneya*) of another man, PañcavBr.; of a son of Deva-rāta, VP. **-ukthi** (!), m. N. of a Ṛishi, Cat. **-úksh** (RV.) and **-uksha** (*bṛihád-*, VS.), mfn. sprinkling abundantly, shedding copiously. **-ukshan** (*bṛihád-*), mfn. one who has great oxen, RV. **-uttara-tāpinī**, f. N. of an Upanishad. **-elā**, f. large cardamoms, L. **-opaśā**, f. (with *hrasvā*) N. of a Sāman, ĀrshBr. **-garbha**, w. r. for *vṛisha-darbha*, MBh. **-gala**, mfn. thick-necked, TPrāt., Comm. **-giri**, mfn. (prob.) calling or shouting loudly (the Maruts), RV.; m. N. of a Yati, PañcavBr. **-gītā-vyākhyā**, f. N. of wk. **-guru**, m. N. of a man, MBh.; *-gurv-āvali-pūjā-śānti-vidhāna*, n. N. of wk. **-guha** ('having large caves') or **-gṛiha**, m. pl. 'large-housed,' N. of a people (dwelling in a country lying behind the Vindhya mountains near Malwa, and perhaps comprising Bandelkhand), L. **-gola**, n. a water-melon, L. **-gaurī-vrata**, n. N. of a partic. religious observance, Cat.; N. of wk. (also °*ta-kathā*, f.) **-grāvan** (*bṛihád-*), mfn. like a huge stone, VS. **-dantī**, f. N. of a plant, Bhpr. **-darbha**, m. N. of a king (v. l. *-bhānu*), Hariv.; VP. **-dala**, m. a species of Lodhra, L.; Phoenix Paludosa, L. **-diva** (*bṛihád-*), mfn. 'belonging to the lofty sky,' heavenly, celestial, RV. (also *-divā́*); m. (with *Ātharvaṇa*) N. of the author of RV. x, 120, Anukr.; N. of that hymn, AitBr.; (*eshu*), ind. in heavenly heights, ib.; (*ā́*), f. N. of a goddess (associated with Iḷā, Sarasvatī and others), ib. **-durga**, m. N. of a man, Hariv. **-devatā**, f. N. of a large wk. (enumerating and explaining the deities to which each hymn of the RV. is addressed). **-deva-sthāna**, n. N. of a Sāman, ĀrshBr. **-dyuti**, f. a great light, radiance, splendour, MW.; mfn. intensely brilliant, Kir. **-dyumna**, m. N. of a king, MBh. **-dhan** (*han*), see *bṛihat-tvan*. **-dhanus** (Hariv.; BhP.) and **-dharman** (Hariv.), m. N. of kings. **-dharma-purāṇa**, n. 'the large Dharma-purāṇa,' N. of wk. **-dharma-prakāśa**, m. 'the large Dharma-prakāśa,' N. of wk. **-dhala** (°*d-ha°*), n.(?) a large plough, L. **-dhātrī**, f. a partic. medicament, L. **-dhārâvalī** (°*d-hā°*), f. 'the larger Hārâvalī,' N. of a dictionary. **-dhārīta** (°*d-hā°*), m. the larger Hārīta. **-dhustūra**, m. a large thorn-apple, MW. **-dhemâdri** (°*d-he°*), m. the larger Hemâdri. **-dhoma-paddhati** (°*d-ho°*), f. N. of wk. **-dhvaja**, m. N. of a king, VP. **-dhvanī**, f. 'loud-sounding,' N. of a river, MBh. **-bala**, m. 'having great strength,' N. of two kings, MBh.; Hariv.; Pur. **-bīja**, m. 'having large seeds,' or 'abounding in seed,' Spondias Mangifera, L. **-bṛihaspati**, m. N. of the larger recension of Bṛihas-pati's law-book. **-brahman**, m. N. of a grandson of Brahmā, MBh.; °*ma-saṃhitā*, f. N. of wk.; °*môttara-khaṇḍa*, m. N. of a part of the Skanda-Purāṇa. **-bhaṭṭa**, m. N. of an author, Cat. **-bhaṭṭārikā**, f. N. of Durgā, L. **-bhaya**, m. N. of one of the sons of the 9th Manu, MārkP. **-bhāgavatâmṛita**, n. N. of Comm. **-bhānu** (*bṛihád-*), mfn. shining brightly, RV.; Lāṭy.; m. fire or the god of fire, L.; N. of a partic. Agni, MBh.; of a son of Sattrâyaṇa and a manifestation of Vishṇu, BhP.; of a son of Kṛishṇa, ib.; of a king, Pur. **-bhās**, mfn. shining brightly, ĀpŚr. **-bhāsa**, m. 'having great splendour,' N. of a grandson of Brahmā, MBh.; (*ā*), f. N. of a daughter of the god of the sun and wife of Agni Bhānu, MBh. **-bhuja**, mfn. long-armed, L. **-yama**, m. N. of the larger recension of Y°'s law-book. **-yājñavalkya**, m. N. of the larger recension of Y°'s law-book. **-yātrā**, f. N. of a wk. by Varāha-mihira. **-yogi-yājñavalkya-smṛiti**, f. N. of work. **-raṇa**, m. N. of a king, BhP. (c. *bṛihat-kshaṇa*). **-ratna-kārikā**, f., **-ratnâkara**, m. N. of wks. **-rathá**, m. a powerful hero, RV.; (*bṛihád-*) N. of sev. men, RV.; MBh.; R. &c.; of Indra, L.; a sacrificial vessel, L.; a partic. Mantra, L.; a part of the Sāma-veda, L.; (*ā*), f. N. of a river, Hariv. **-rathaṃtara**, n. du. the Sāmans Bṛihat and Rathaṃtara, AitBr.; KaushUp.; Gaut.; *-sāman*, mfn. having the Bṛihat and Rath° Sāman for a Sāman, ĀpŚr. **-rayi** (*bṛihád-*), mfn. having abundant possessions, RV. **-ravas** (*bṛihád-*), mfn. loud-sounding, VS. **-rāja**, m. N. of a king, Pur.; *-mārtaṇḍa*, m. N. of wk. **-rāvan**, mfn. sounding or crying loud, KapS. **-rāvin**, m. 'crying loud,' a species of small owl, L. **-ri** (*bṛihád-*), mfn. = *-rayi*, q. v., RV. **-rūpa**, m. a species of owl, L.; N. of a Marut, Hariv. **-reṇu** (*bṛihád-*), mfn. stirring up thick dust, RV. **-roma** and °**ma-paṭṭana**, N. of places, Cat. **-vat** (*bṛihád-*), mfn. one to whom the Bṛihat-sāman is addressed, VS.; (*atī*), f. N. of a river, MBh. **-vadha**, m. manifold murder, BhP.; murder of a Brāhman, ib. **-vayas** (*bṛihád-*), mfn. grown strong, very powerful, very vigorous, TS.; Lāṭy. **-valka**, m. a species of Lodhra, L. **-vasishṭha**, m. the larger Vasishṭha. **-vasu**, m. N. of two men, VBr.; VP. **-vāta**, m. a kind of grain, L. **-vādin**, mfn. boasting, a boaster, MBh. **-vārāha-yantra-māhātmya**, n. N. of wk. **-vāruṇī**, f. a kind of plant, L. **-vāsishṭha**, m. the larger Vāsishṭha. **-vivāha-paṭala**, N. of wk. **-vishṇu**, m. N. of the larger recension of V°'s law-book. **-vṛitti**, f., **-vaiyākaraṇa-bhūshaṇa** and **-vyāk°-bh°**, n. N. of wks. **-vyāsa**, m. the larger Vyāsa. **-vrata**, n. the great vow (of chastity), BhP.; mfn. observing the great vow, ib.

Bṛihan, in comp. for *bṛihát*. **-nakhī**, f. a partic. perfume, L. **-naṭa**, m. N. of Arjuna, L. **-naḍa**, m. reed-grass, Amphidonax Karka, L.; N. of Arjuna, L. **-nala**, m. a kind of large reed, Vās.; the arm, W.; (also *ā*, f.) the name assumed by Arjuna when living in the family of king Virāṭa as a eunuch in female attire, MBh.; Vās. **-nāṭa**, m. (in music) a partic. Rāga, Saṃgīt. **-nāṭaka**, n. N. of a play (prob. the *mahā-n°*). **-nāyakī-**

daṇḍaka, m. or n. (?), N. of wk. **-nārada-purāṇa, -nāradīya** or **-nāradīya-p°,** n. N. of a Purāṇa. **-nāradīya-tantra,** n. N. of a Tantra. **-nārāyaṇa,** n., **-nārāyaṇī,** f. or **-nārāyaṇôpanishad,** f. the large or Nārāyaṇa Upanishad (treating of Vedāntic doctrine and forming the last Prapāṭhaka of the Taittirīya Āraṇyaka of the black Yajur-veda). **-nālika,** n. a cannon, L. **-nighaṇṭi,** m. 'the large glossary,' N. of a dictionary. **-nirvāṇa-tantra,** n. N. of a Tantra. **-niveśa,** mfn. having large dimensions, large, protuberant, MW. **-nīla-tantra,** n. N. of wk. **-nīlī,** f. N. of plant (= *mahā-n°*), L. **-netra,** mfn. 'large-eyed,' (perhaps) far-sighted (fig.), Cat. **-naukā,** f. N. of a favourable position in the game of Catur-aṅga, L. **-mati,** mfn. high-minded, RV.; m. N. of the author of RV. ix, 39, 40, Anukr. **-madhya,** mf(*ā*)n. large in the middle, Kām. **-manas.** m. N. of a grandson of Brahmā, MBh.; of a king, Hariv.; BhP. **-manu,** m. 'the larger Manu,' N. of a law-book (prob. the precursor of the present version, mentioned by Mādhava and other commentators). **-mantra,** m. N. of a grandson of Brahman, MBh.

Brihanta, mfn. = *brihát,* large, great, ŚvetUp.; m. N. of a king, MBh.

Brihal, in comp. for *brihát.* **-laksha-homa,** m. a partic. oblation, Cat. **-lohita,** N. of a mythical tank or pond, KālP.

Brihas-páti, m. (also written *vrih°-p°;* fr. 3. *brih + pati;* cf. *brahmaṇas-pati*) 'lord of prayer or devotion,' N. of a deity (in whom Piety and Religion are personified; he is the chief offerer of prayers and sacrifices, and therefore represented as the type of the priestly order, and the Purohita of the gods with whom he intercedes for men; in later times he is the god of wisdom and eloquence, to whom various works are ascribed; he is also regarded as son of Aṅgiras, husband of Tārā and father of Kaca, and sometimes identified with Vyāsa; in astronomy he is the regent of Jupiter and often identified with that planet), RV. &c. &c. (cf. RTL. 215); N. of a prince (great-grandson of Aśoka), Buddh.; of a king of Kaśmīra, Rājat.; of the author of a law-book, IW. 203; 302; of a philosopher, ib. 120; of other authors (also with *miśra* and *ācārya,* cf. above), Cat.; (with *Āṅgirasa,* cf. above) N. of the author of RV. x, 71; 72, Anukr. **-karaṇa,** n. N. of wk. **-gupta,** m. N. of man, VBr. **-cakra,** n. 'cycle of Brihas-pati,' the Hindū cycle of 60 years; a partic. astrological diagram, MW. **-cāra,** m. N. of VarBṛS. viii. **-tantra,** n. N. of wk. **-datta,** m. N. of a man, Pāṇ. v, 3, 83, Sch. **-pakshatā,** f. N. of wk. **-purohita** (*bṛihas-páti-*), mfn. having Brihas-pati for a Purohita, VS.; m. N. of Indra, A. **-praṇutta** (*bṛihas-páti-*), mfn. expelled by Bṛ°, AV. **-prasūta** (*bṛihas-páti-*), mfn. enjoined by Bṛ°, RV. **-mat,** mfn. accompanied by Bṛ°, ŚrS. **-mata,** n. N. of wk. **-miśra,** m. N. of a Sch. on Ragh. **-vat,** mfn. = *-mat,* AitBr. **-vāra,** m. Jupiter's day, Thursday. **-śānti,** f., **-śānti-karman,** n. N. of wks. **-śiras,** mfn. 'Brihaspati-headed,' (prob.) having the head shaved like Bṛ°, Kauś. **-saṃhitā,** f. N. of two wks. **-sama,** mfn. equal to Bṛ°, like Bṛ°, MW. **-savá,** m. N. of a festival lasting one day (said to confer the rank of a Purohita on those observing it), Br.; Kāṭh.; ŚrS.; BhP.; *-klṛipti,* f., *-prayoga,* m., *-hautra-prayoga,* m. N. of wks. **-siddhânta,** m. N. of wk. **-suta** (*bṛihas-páti-*), mfn. pressed out (as Soma juice) by Brihas-pati, TS. **-suratā,** f. a proper N., MW. **-sūtra,** n., **-stotra,** n. N. of wks. **-stoma,** m. N. of an Ekâha, PañcavBr. **-smṛiti,** f. Brihaspati's law-book.

Brihaspatika, °tiya or **°tila,** m. (fr. *°ti-datta*) familiar diminutives, Pat. on Pāṇ. v, 3, 83.

बृह् 4. *brih* or *briṅh* (also written *vrih* or *vriṅh*), cl. 1. P. (Dhātup. xvii, 85) *briṅhati* (or *barhati;* 3. pl. pf. Ā. *babriṅhire,* Śiś. xvii, 31), to roar, bellow, trumpet (said of an elephant), MBh.; Hariv. &c.; also cl. 10. P. (Dhātup. xxxiii, 95) to speak; to shine.

2. **Briṅhita,** n. (for 1. see under √2. *brih*) the roar or noise made by elephants, MBh.; Kāv. &c.

बृह्मण *brihmaṇa* (?), m. or n. N. of wk.

बॄ *brī.* See √*vrī.*

बेकनाट *bekanāṭa,* m. a usurer, RV. viii, 55, 10 (Nir.)

बेकुरा *bekurā,* f. (cf. *bakura*) a voice, sound, PañcavBr.; Lāṭy. (cf. Naigh. i, 11).

Bekúri, f. (prob.) playing a musical instrument (said of Apsaras), TS.; Lāṭy. (*vek°,* Kāth.; *bhek°,* VS.; *bhāk°,* ŚBr.)

बेटी *beṭī,* f. (prob.) a courtezan, Kāv. (cf. Hind. *beṭī*).

बेडा *beḍā,* f. a boat, A. (cf. *veḍā*).

बेदरकर *bedarakara,* m. (prob.) an inhabitant of the city Bedar or Bidar, L. (also proper N.)

बेभिदितव्य *bebhiditavya,* mfn. (√*bhid,* Intens.) to be repeatedly split, Pāṇ. vi, 4, 49, Sch.

बेम्ब *bemba,* m. N. of a man.

Bembā-rava, m. a partic. sound (cf. *bambhā-r°*).

बेश् *beś,* cl. 1. P. *beśati,* to go (= √*pis, pes*), Dhātup. xvii, 71.

बैकि *baiki,* m. patr., g. *taulvaly-ādi,* Kāś.

बैजनाथ *baijanātha,* m. (prob. patr. fr. *bīja-nātha*) N. of an author, Cat.

Baijala-deva, m. N. of a prince and author, ib. (cf. *bījala* under *bīja*).

Baijavāpa, m. (also written *vaij°*) patr. fr. *bīja-vāpa,* ŚBr. **-grihya,** n., **-smṛiti,** f. N. of wks.

Baijavāpāyana, m. patr. fr. prec., ib.; N. of an author, Cat.

Baijavāpi, m. patr. fr. *bīja-vāpa* or *°pin,* MaitrS.; Car. (cf. g. *raivatikâdi*); pl. N. of a warrior tribe, g. *dāmany-ādi.* **°pīya,** mfn. (fr. prec.), g. *raivatikâdi;* m. a prince of the Baijavāpis, g. *dāmany-ādi.*

Baiji (fr. *bīja*), g. *gahâdi* (Kāś. *vaidaji*).

बैजिक *baijika,* mfn. (fr. *bīja*) relating to seed, seminal, paternal (opp. to *gārbhika,* relating to the womb, maternal), Mn. ii, 27; sexual, v, 63; belonging to any primary cause or source or principle, original, MW.; m. a young shoot, sprout, L.; n. oil prepared from Moringa Pterygosperma, L.; cause, source, L.; the spiritual cause of existence, soul, spirit, L. **°jīya,** mfn. (fr. *baiji*), g. *gahâdi.* **°jeya,** m. patr. fr. *bīja,* g. *śubhrâdi.*

बैट्संख्या *baiṭ-saṃkhyā* (?), f. a kind of Anukramaṇī to the three Vedas, Cat.

बैडाल *baiḍāla,* mf(*ī*)n. (fr. *biḍāla*) belonging to a cat, peculiar to cats, feline, MBh. **-vrata,** n. 'cat-like observance,' putting on a show of virtue or piety to conceal malice and evil designs, MW. **-vrati,** m. one who leads a chaste or continent life merely from the absence of women or temptation, L. **-vratika** (Mn.; Kāv.; Pur.), **-vratin** (Pur.), mfn. acting like a cat, hypocritical, a religious impostor (= *bhaṇḍa-tapasvin*).

Baiḍāli-karṇaka-kantha and **-karṇi-kantha,** n. (prob.) N. of a city, g. *cihaṇâdi.*

बैद 1. *baida,* m. (also *vaida*) patr. fr. *bida,* AitBr.; ĀśvŚr. (*ī,* f., Pat.) **-kula,** n. (prob.) the family of the Baidas, Pāṇ. ii, 4, 64, Vārtt., Pat.

2. **Baida,** mfn. (fr. 1. *baida*), Pāṇ. iv, 3, 127, Sch.; m. a partic. Try-aha, KātyŚr. **-tri-rātra,** m. a partic. Tri-rātra, ŚrS.

Baidāputāyana, m. patr. fr. *bidā-puta,* g. *aśvâdi,* Kāś.

Baidāyana, m. patr. fr. *bida,* g. *aśvâdi.*

Baidi, m. id., Pāṇ. iv, 1, 104, Sch.

बैदल *baidala.* See *vaidala.*

बैन्द *baindá,* m. N. of a degraded tribe, VS. (= *nishādha,* Mahīdh.)

बैन्दव *baindava,* m. (also written *vai°*) patr. fr. *bindu,* g. *bidâdi.*

Baindavi, m. pl. N. of a warrior tribe, g. *dāmany-ādi.* **°vīya,** m. a prince of the Baindavis, ib.

बैम्बकि *baimbaki,* m. (also written *vai°*) patr. fr. *bimba,* Pāṇ. iv, 1, 97, Vārtt., Pat.

बैल *baila,* mf(*ī*)n. (fr. *bila,* also written *vaila,* q.v.) living in holes (m. an animal l° in h°), Car.; relating to or derived from animals l° in h°, MBh.

Bailāyana, mfn., g. *pakshâdi.*

Bailya, mfn. N. of a man, g. *aśvâdi* (v.l. for *bailva*).

Bailyāyana, m. patr. fr. *bailya,* ib.

बैल्मवेगरुद्र *bailma-vega-rudra,* m. pl. N. of a partic. class of Śaiva ascetics, Kāraṇḍ.

बैल्व *bailvá,* mf(*ī*)n. (fr. *bilva*) relating to or coming from the Bilva tree, made of Bilva wood, ŚBr. &c. &c.; covered with B° trees, Pāṇ. iv, 2, 67, Sch.; m. N. of a man, g. *aśvâdi;* n. the fruit of the B° tree, L. **-maya,** mf(*ī*)n., Pāṇ. iv, 3, 155, Sch.

Bailvaka, mfn., g. *arīhaṇâdi.* **°kīya,** mfn. (fr. prec.), Pat.

Bailvaja (fr. *bilva-ja*), g. *rājanyâdi* (v.l. *bailvala*). **°jaka,** mfn. (with *deśa*) inhabited by Bailvajas, ib.

Bailvayata, m. patr., g. *kraudy-ādi* (f. *°tyā,* ib.)

Bailvala, g. *rājanyâdi,* Kāś. **°laka,** mfn. inhabited by Bailvalas, ib.

Bailvavana, m. (prob.) an inhabitant of Bilvavana or a wood of Bilva trees, g. *rājanyâdi.* **°naka,** mfn. (with *deśa*) inhabited by Bailvavanas, ib.

Bailvāyana, m. patr. fr. *bailva,* g. *aśvâdi.*

बैष्क *baishka* (prob. n., cf. *veshka, bleshka, meshka*), flesh from an animal killed by a beast of prey or in a trap, Gaut.

बैहीनरि *baihīnari,* m. (also written *vaih°*) patr. fr. *bahīnara,* Pāṇ. vii, 3, 1, Vārtt. 6, Pat. (others 'fr. *vih°*'); N. of a chamberlain, Mudr.

बोकडी *bokaḍī,* f. Argyrela Speciosa or Argentea, L.

बोकण *bokaṇa,* m. or n. (?) N. of a place, Cat.

बोक्काण *bokkāṇa,* m. a horse's nose-bag (which contains his food), L.

बोद्धव्य *boddhavya, boddhṛi, bodha, bauddha* &c. See p. 734, col. 2.

बोपण्णभट्टीय *bopaṇṇa-bhaṭṭīya,* n. N. of wk. (cf. *bāpaṇṇa*).

बोपदेव *bopadeva.* See *vopadeva.*

बोरसिद्धि *borasiddhi,* f. N. of a place, Cat.

बोल्लक *bollaka,* m. (*bahu-b°*) a great talker, Divyāv. (cf. Hind. *bolnā,* to speak).

बोहित्थ *bohittha,* m. n. a boat, ship, L. (cf. *vahitra*).

बौध्न्य *baudhnya,* m. pl. (fr. *budhna*) N. of a school (cf. *baudheya, bodheya*).

बौभुक्ष *baubhuksha,* mf(*ī*)n. one who is always hungry, a starveling, g. *chattrâdi.*

ब्युस् *byus.* See √*vyush.*

ब्रण् *braṇ.* See √1. *vraṇ.*

ब्रध्न *bradhná,* mfn. (of doubtful origin; Uṇ. iii, 5) pale red, ruddy, yellowish, bay (esp. as the colour of a horse, but also applied to Soma and the Puroḍāśa), RV.; TS.; great, mighty, Naigh. iii, 3; m. the sun, RV.; AV.; Mn. iv, 231 (cf. *vishṭap*); the world of the sun, TBr. (Sch.); a horse, Naigh. i, 14; the point or some other part of an arrow (in *śatá-b°,* q.v.); a partic. disease (cf. *bradhma* and *budhna-roga*), L.; N. of a son of Manu Bhautya, MārkP.; n. lead, Bhpr. (often w.r. for *budhna* and *budhnya*). **-cakra,** n. the zodiac, Gaṇit. **-tva,** n. greatness, mightiness, Sāy. **-bimba** (Hcar.), **-maṇḍala** (Kād.), n. the disc of the sun. **-loka** (*bradhná-*), mfn. being in the world of the sun, AV.

Bradhnaśva, m. N. of a prince, MBh. (w.r. for *bradhnâśva* or *vadhry-aśva*?)

ब्रध्म *bradhma,* m. a partic. disease, Car. (written *vr°;* cf. *bradhna* and *budhna-roga*).

ब्रह् *brah,* cl. 1. P. *brahmati,* to go, move, Naigh. ii, 14.

ब्रह्मन् *bráhman,* n. (lit. 'growth,' 'expansion,' 'evolution,' 'development,' 'swelling of the spirit or soul,' fr. √2. *brih*) pious effusion or utterance, outpouring of the heart in worshipping the gods, prayer, RV.; AV.; VS.; TS.; the sacred word (as opp. to *vāc,* the word of man), the Veda, a sacred text, a text or Mantra used as a spell (forming a distinct class from the *ṛicas, sāmāni* and *yajūṅshi;* cf. *brahma-veda*), RV.; AV.; Br.; Mn.; Pur.; the Brāhmaṇa portion of the Veda, Mn. iv, 100; the sacred syllable Om, Prab., Sch. (cf. Mn. ii, 83); religious or spiritual knowledge (opp. to religious observances and bodily mortification such as *tapas* &c.), AV.; Br.; Mn.; R.; holy life (esp. continence, chastity; cf. *brahma-carya*), Śak. i, 24/25; Śaṃk.; Sarvad.;

(exceptionally treated as m.) the Brahmă or one self-existent impersonal Spirit, the one universal Soul (or one divine essence and source from which all created things emanate or with which they are identified and to which they return), the Self-existent, the Absolute, the Eternal (not generally an object of worship, but rather of meditation and knowledge; also with *jyéshṭha, prathama-jā́, svayám-bhu, a-mūrta, para, paratara, parama, mahat, sanātana, śāś-vata*; and = *paramâtman, ātman, adhyātma, pradhāna, kshetra-jña, tattva*), AV.; ŚBr.; Mn.; MBh. &c. (IW. 9, 83 &c.); n. the class of men who are the repositories and communicators of sacred knowledge, the Brāhmanical caste as a body (rarely an individual Brāhman), AV.; TS.; VS.; ŚBr.; Mn.; BhP.; food, Naigh. ii, 7; wealth, ib. 10; final emancipation, L.; m. (*brahmán*), one who prays, a devout or religious man, a Brāhman who is a knower of Vedic texts or spells, one versed in sacred knowledge, RV. &c. &c. [cf. Lat. *flāmen*]; N. of Bṛihas-pati (as the priest of the gods), RV. x, 141, 3; one of the 4 principal priests or Ṛitvijas (the other three being the Hotṛi, Adhvaryu, and Udgātṛi; the Brahman was the most learned of them and was required to know the 3 Vedas, to supervise the sacrifice and to set right mistakes; at a later period his functions were based especially on the Atharva-veda), RV. &c. &c.; Brahmā or the one impersonal universal Spirit manifested as a personal Creator and as the first of the triad of personal gods (= *prajā-pati*, q. v.; he never appears to have become an object of general worship, though he has two temples in India, see RTL. 555 &c.; his wife is Sarasvatī, ib. 48), TBr. &c. &c.; = *brahmaṇa āyuḥ*, a lifetime of Brahmā, Pañcar.; an inhabitant of Brahmā's heaven, Jātakam.; the sun, L.; N. of Śiva, Prab., Sch.; the Veda (?), PārGṛ.; the intellect (= *buddhi*), Tattvas.; N. of a star, δ Aurigae, Sūryas.; a partic. astron. Yoga, L.; N. of the 9th Muhūrta, L.; (with Jainas) a partic. Kalpa, Dharmaś.; N. of the servant of the 10th Arhat of the present Avasarpiṇī, L.; of a magician, Rājat.

1. **Brahma,** m. a priest (see *asura-, ku-, mahā-br°*); n. the one self-existent Spirit, the Absolute, R.

2. **Brahma,** in comp. for *brahman.*—Observe that in the following derivatives the nom. n. (Brahmă) is used for the impersonal Spirit and the nom. m. (Brahmā) for the personal god. **-ṛishi,** see *brahma-rshi.* **-kanya,** (prob.) m. Clerodendrum Siphonantus, L. **-kanyaka,** (prob.) m. id., L.; (*ā*), f. Ruta Graveolens, L.; N. of Sarasvatī, L. **-kara,** m. an impost paid to the Brāhmanical class, Inscr. **-karman,** n. the office of the Brahman (i. e. presiding priest) or of the Brāhmans, ŚāṅkhŚr.; MBh.; °*ma-pustaka,* n. N. of a manual on ceremonies, RTL. 401, n. 2; °*ma-prakāśaka* or °*ma-pradāyaka,* m. N. of Krishṇa, Pañcar.; °*ma-samādhi,* mfn. occupied with or meditating upon the one self-existent Spirit, Bhag. **-kalā,** f. N. of Dākshāyaṇī who dwells in the heart of men, Cat. **-kalpa,** mfn. like Brahmā, R.; m. the cosmic period of Brahmā, MBh.; N. of wk. **-kāṇḍa,** n. the inner portion of the Veda which relates to sacred knowledge or the kn° of Brahmă (= *jñāna-k°*, and opp. to *karma-k°*, q. v.), Śaṇḍ.; N. of a wk. (or ch. of a wk.) of Bhartṛi-hari, Sarvad. **-kāya,** m. pl. N. of a partic. class of deities, MBh.; °*yika,* mfn. belonging to the Brahma-kāyas, Lalit. (Dharmas. 128; MWB. 210). **-kārá,** mfn. making or offering prayers, RV. **-kāraṇa-vāda,** m. N. of wk. **-kāshṭha,** m. Thespesia Populneoides, L. **-kileya** (?), m. N. of a man, Pravar. **-kilbishá,** n. an offence against Brāhmans, RV. **-kuṇḍa,** n. N. of a sacred pool, KālP. **-kuśā,** f. a species of cumin, Bhpr.; = *aja-modā,* L. **-kūṭa,** m. a thoroughly learned Brāhman, MBh.; N. of a mountain, KālP. **-kūrca,** n. a partic. kind of penance (in which the 5 products of the cow are eaten; cf. *pañca-gavya*), Cat.; *-vidhi,* m. N. of the 38th Pariś. of the AV. **-kṛit,** mfn. making or offering prayers (also applied to Indra, Vishṇu, the Maruts &c.), RV.; MBh.; Pañcar. **-kṛita,** m. N. of a man, g. *śubhrâdi.* **-kṛiti** (*bráhma-*), f. prayer, devotion, RV. **-ketu,** m. N. of a man, Cat. **-kaivarta-purāṇa,** n. N. of a Purāṇa. **-kośá,** m. the treasury of the Brahmă i. e. of the sacred word or text, the entire collection of the Vedas, TĀr.; PārGṛ.; MaitrUp.; N. of Atri, VP.; (*ī*), f. a species of plant (= *aja-modā*), L. **-kshatra,** n. sg. and du. Brāhmans and Kshatriyas, AitBr.; VP.; *-sava,* m. pl. N. of partic. rites, Mn. v, 23. **-kshetra,** n. N. of a sacred district, MBh.; Hariv. **-khaṇḍa,** n. N. of BrahmavP. i. **-gandha,** m. the fragrance of Brahmă, KaushUp. **-garbha,** m. the embryo of a Brāhman (?), Cat.; N. of a law-giver (*-smṛiti,* f. his wk.); (*ā*), f. Ocimum Villosum, L. **-gavī,** f. a Brāhman's cow, AV.; ŚBr.; du. N. of 2 classes of verses or formulas, Kauś. **-gāthā-stuti,** f. N. of wk. **-gāyatrī,** f. N. of a magical Mantra composed after the model of the Gāyatrī, Pañcar.; RTL. 201. **-gārgya,** m. N. of a man, Hariv. **-giri,** m. N. of a mountain, KālP.; (?) of Comms. on various Upanishads, Cat. **-gītā,** f. pl. N. of partic. verses (MBh. xiii, 2146-2152) ascribed to Brahmā; N. of wk.; *-parâtmânusaṃdhāna,* n., *-vyākhyā,* f. N. of wks. **-gītikā,** f. 'the song of Brahmā,' N. of partic. verses, Yājñ. **-gupta,** m. N. of a son of Brahmā (by the wife of the Vidyā-dhara Bhīma), Kathās.; of an astronomer (son of Jishṇu and author of the Brahma-sphuṭa-siddhânta, born A.D. 598), IW. 176; of a chief of the Bhakta sect, Cat.; of a Trigarta-shashṭha, Kār. on Pāṇ. v, 3, 116 (v. l. *brāhma-g°*); pl. N. of a race, ib.; °*tīya,* m. a prince of the Brahma-guptas, ib. **-gola,** m. 'Brahmā's globe,' the universe, L. **-gaurava,** n. the potency (of the weapon given) by Brahmā, Bhaṭṭ. **-granthi,** m. N. of the knot which ties together the 3 threads forming the sacred cord, Gobh., Sch. (RTL. 361); of a partic. joint of the body, Cat. **-graha,** m. = *-rākshasa,* L. **-grāhin,** mfn. worthy to receive that which is holy, KaushUp. (v. l. °*mârgha*). **-ghātaka,** m. a Brāhman-killer, Pañcat. **-ghātin,** m. id., Śak., Sch.; (*inī*), f. a woman on the second day of the menses, Vet.; Bhpr. **-ghosha,** m. murmur (arising from the recital) of prayers (also pl.), MBh.; R. (also °*sha-rava,* m., Hcat.); the sacred word or text, the Veda, Uttarar. **-ghna,** m. = *-ghātaka,* R.; (*ī*), f., see *-han.* **-cakra,** n. 'Brahmă's wheel,' the circle of the universe, ŚvetUp.; N. of a partic. magical circle, Cat. **-candrikā,** f. N. of wk. **-cárya,** n. study of the Veda, the state of an unmarried religious student, a state of continence and chastity (also *ā,* f., Hariv.), AV. &c. &c. (acc. with √*grah, car, vas, ā-*√*gam, upa-*√*i,* to practise ch°; cf. *-cārin*); *-tva,* n. the unmarried state, continence, chastity, Hariv.; *-vat,* mfn. leading the life of an unmarried religious student, practising ch°, Āpast.; MBh.; *-vrata,* n. a vow of ch°, BrahmaP.; *-skhalana,* n. deviating from ch°, MW.; °*ryâśrama,* m. the period of unmarried religious studentship, MBh. **-cāraṇī,** f. Clerodendrum Siphonantus, L. (prob. w. r. for *-cāriṇī*). **-cārika,** n. religious studentship, MBh. **-cārín,** mf(*iṇī*)n. practising sacred study as an unmarried student, observing chastity, RV. &c. &c.; m. a young Brāhman who is a student of the Veda (under a preceptor) or who practises chastity, a young Br° before marriage (in the first period of his life), AV.; Mn.; MBh. &c. (cf. *āśrama* and IW. 192 &c.; RTL. 84 &c.; the N. Brahma-cārin is also given to older unmarried Brāhmans, esp. if versed in the Veda, and by the Tantras to any person whose chief virtue is continence); N. of a Gandharva, MBh.; of Skanda, L.; of Śiva, Śivag.; (*iṇī*), f. N. of Durgā, DevīP.; a woman who observes the vow of chastity, W.; Clerodendrum Siphonantus, L. (v. l. °*raṇī*); Thespesia Populneoides, L.; = *karuṇī,* L.; °*ri-vāsa,* m. the living of a Brahma-cārin (in the house of his religious teacher), Āpast.; °*ri-vāsin,* mfn. living as a Brahma-c° &c.; TS. **-cití,** f. Brahmă's layer in the fire-altar, ŚBr. **-cintana-nirākaraṇa,** n. N. of wk. **-caitanya-yati,** m. N. of an author, Cat. **-códana,** mf(*ī*)n. inciting or urging Brahmā or Brahmă, VS. (Mahīdh.) **-ja,** mfn. sprung from that which is holy (said of Kārttikeya), MBh.; m. pl. N. of partic. clouds, VP.; (with Jainas) N. of a class of divinities, L.; *-jña,* mfn. 'born from and knowing Brahmă' or 'knowing what is Br°-born' i. e. 'knowing all things,' KaṭhUp. **-jaṭā,** f. or **-jaṭin,** m. Artemisia Indica, L. **-janman,** n. 'spiritual birth,' investiture with the sacred thread, Mn. ii, 146; 170; mfn. 'Brahmā-born' (said of Prajā-pati), Hariv. **-japa,** m. a partic. formula of prayer, MānGṛ. **-jātaka,** n. N. of wk. **-jāmala,** w. r. for *-yāmala.* **-jāyā́,** f. the wife of a Brāhman, RV. x, 109; (with *Juhū*) N. of the supposed authoress of this hymn, Anukr. **-jāra,** m. the paramour of a Brāhman's wife, RāmatUp. **-jāla-sūtra,** n. N. of a Buddh. Sūtra (cf. MWB. 106). **-jijñāsā,** f. the desire of knowing Brahmă, Bādar. (cf. IW. 104). **-jīva-nirṇaya,** m. N. of wk. **-jīvin,** mfn. subsisting by sacred learning, L.; m. a mercenary Brāhman (who converts his religious duties into a trade), W. **-jushṭa** (*bráhma-*), mfn. gratified by prayer or devotion, AV. **-jūta** (*bráhma-*), mfn. incited by p° or d°, RV.; AV. **-jña,** mfn. possessing sacred knowledge, knowing the sacred text, spiritually wise, holy (said also of gods e. g. of Vishṇu, Kārttikeya), MBh.; Bhartṛ. **-jñāna,** n. divine or sacred knowledge (esp. kn° of the universal permeation of the one Spirit as taught by the Vedânta), spiritual wisdom, Hariv.; Bhartṛ.; *-tantra,* n., *-mahātantra-rāja,* m., *-vipratipatti,* f., °*nôpadeśa,* m. N. of wks. **-jñānin,** mfn. = *-jña,* L. **-jyá,** mfn. molesting or oppressing Brāhmans, AV.; TBr. (cf. Pāṇ. iii, 2, 3, Vārtt. 1, Pat.) **-jyéya,** n. the act of oppressing Brāhmans, AV. **-jyeshṭha,** m. (printed °*ṭhya*) the elder brother of Brahmā, Pañcar.; (*bráhma-*), mfn. having Brahmă as first or chief, AV.; TBr. **-jyotis,** n. the splendour of Brahmă or of the Supreme Being, Pañcar. (also written *brahma-jy°*); (*bráhma-*), mfn. having the splendour of Br° (Sch. 'of the presiding priest'), TS.; m. N. of Śiva, Śivag. **-tattva,** n. the true knowledge of Brahmă, W.; *-praśnôttara-ratnâvalī,* f., *-vivaraṇa,* n., *-saṃhitôddīpanī,* f., *-subodhinī,* f. N. of wks. **-tantra,** n. all that is taught in the Veda, MBh.; Hariv.; °*tre gāyatrī-pañjara,* n. N. of wk. **-tarka-stava,** m. N. of a Vedânta wk.; *-vivaraṇa,* n. N. of a Comm. on it. **-tas,** ind. from the Brāhmans, MW. **-tā,** f. the state or condition of a Brāhman, 'Brāhmanhood,' Pāṇ. v, 1, 136, Sch.; the state or nature of Brahmă, divine nature, BhP. **-tāla,** m. (in music) a kind of measure, Saṃgīt. **-tīrtha,** n. N. of a place of pilgrimage on the Revā or Narmadā river, MBh.; Costus Speciosus or Arabicus, L. **-tuṅga,** m. N. of a mountain, MBh. **-tulya,** n. N. of a Jyotisha; *-gaṇita,* n., *-ṭīkā,* f., *-siddhânta,* m. N. of wks. **-tejas,** n. the power and glory of Brahmā, KaushUp.; Hariv. &c. (°*jo-maya,* mf[*ī*]n. formed of B°'s glory, Mn.; Pañcar.); the glory or lustre supposed to surround a Brāhman; (*bráhma-*) having the glory or power of Brahmă (AV.) or of a Brāhman (MW.); m. N. of a Buddha, Lalit. **-tvá,** n. the office of the Brahman or chief priest, ŚBr.; GṛŚrS.; Hariv.; Brāhmanhood, R.; Ratnâv.; the state of or identification with Brahmă, MBh.; Pur.; *-paddhati,* f., *-prayoga,* m. N. of wks. **-tvac,** m. or f. (?) Alstonia Scholaris, L. **-da,** mfn. imparting religious knowledge, Mn. **-daṇḍa,** m. 'Brahmā's staff,' N. of a mythical weapon, MBh.; Hariv.; R.; the curse of a Brāhman, Pur.; Rājat. (v. l. *brāhma-d°*); N. of Śiva, MBh.; Clerodendrum Siphonantus, L.; N. of a partic. Ketu, Var.; of a prince, VP.; (*ī*), f. a species of plant, L. (= *adhyaṇḍā,* KātyŚr., Sch.) **-daṇḍin,** m. N. of a sage, Kathās. **-dattá,** mfn. given by Brahmā, TĀr.; g° by Brahmă, MBh.; R.; m. N. of various men (cf. g. *naḍâdi*); of a man with the patr. Caikitāneya, ŚBr.; of a king (pl. his descendants), MBh.; of a prince of the Pañcālas in Kāmpilya, ib.; R. &c.; of a king of the Śālvas, Hariv.; of a prince in Vārāṇasī, Kathās.; of a prince in Śrāvastī, Buddh.; (cf. MWB. 420, 1) of a prince in Campā, ib.; of a prince in Kusuma-pura, ib.; of the 12th Cakra-vartin in Bhārata, L.; of a Brāhman, Hariv.; Pañcat.; of a merchant, Kathās.; of the father of Krishṇa-datta, Cat.; of sev. authors, ib. **-darbhā,** f. Ptychotis Ajowan, Bhpr. **-dātṛi,** mfn. = *-da,* Mn. ii, 146. **-dāna,** n. the gift of the Veda or of sacred knowledge, ib. iv, 232. **-1. -dāya,** m. (fr. 1. *dāya*) = prec., MW.; mfn. imparting or teaching s° k°, BhP. **-2. -dāya,** m. (fr. 2. *dāya*) s° k° as an inheritance (*-hara,* mfn. receiving it from [gen.], Mn. iii, 3; °*yâda,* mfn. [according to Sch.] either 'enjoying s° k° as an i°' or 'Brahmā's son,' BhP.); m. the earthly possession of a Brāhman, BhP.; °*yâpahārin,* mfn. robbing it, ib. **-dāru,** m. n. Morus Indica, L. **-dāsa,** m. N. of the father of Nārāyaṇa-dāsa (author of the Praśnârṇava), Cat.; of a king (about 1600), ib. **-dina,** n. a day of Brahmā, MW. **-dūshaka,** mfn. falsifying the Vedic texts, Hcat. **-deya,** mfn. given in marriage after the manner of Brāhmans (cf. Mn. iii, 27), MānGṛ.; MBh.; (with *vidhi*), m. marriage of this kind, Hariv.; n. instruction in the Veda or sacred knowledge (°*yânusaṃtāna,* mfn. one in whose family Vedic teaching is hereditary, Gaut.; Vishṇ.; Mn. [v, 183, v. l. °*yâtma-saṃtāna,* 'the son of a woman married according to the Brāhma

rite;' cf. *ātma-s°*]); gift to Brāhmans, Divyâv. **-deva**, m. (also with *paṇḍita*) N. of various authors, Cat. **-daitya**, m. a Brāhman changed into a Daitya, L. **-dvāra**, n. entrance into Brahmă, MaitrUp.; *-pāra*, m. (= *pāla*) the guardian of it, ib. **-dvish**, mfn. hostile to sacred knowledge or religion, impious (said of men and demons), RV.; hating Brāhmans, Mn. iii, 154, Kull. **-dvesha**, m. hatred of sacred knowledge or of Brāhmans, Siṇhâs. **-dveshin**, mfn. = *-dvish*, MW. **-dhara**, mfn. possessing s° k°, MBh. **-dharma-dvish**, mfn. hostile to s° k° and the law, Mn. iii, 41. **-dhātu**, m. an essential portion of Brahmă, Cat. **-dhāman**, n. Brahmă's place or abode, BrahmUp. **-dhvaja**, m. N. of a Buddha, Lalit.; *°jôpanishad*, f. N. of an Upanishad. **-nadī**, f. 'Brahmă's river,' N. of the Sarasvatī, BhP. **-nandin** and **-nāga**, m. N. of two authors, Cat. **-nābha**, m. 'having Brahmă (proceeding out of a lotus on his) navel,' N. of Vishṇu, L. **-nāmâvali**, f. N. of wk. **-nāla**, n. N. of a sacred bathing-place in Benares, KāśīKh. **-nirukta**, n., **-nirūpaṇa**, n., **-nirṇaya**, m. N. of wks. **-nirvāṇa**, n. extinction in Brahmă, absorption into the one self-existent Spirit, Bhag.; BhP. **-nishṭha**, mfn. absorbed in contemplating Brahmă or the one s° Sp°, MuṇḍUp.; m. the mulberry tree, L. **-nīḍa**, n. the resting-place of Brahmă or of 'the holy,' MaitrUp. **-nutta** (*bráhma-*), mfn. driven away by a sacred text or spell, AV. **-pati** (*bráhma-*), m. = *brahmaṇas-pati*, ŚBr. **-pattra**, n. 'Brahmă's leaf,' the leaf of Butea Frondosa, L. (cf. *-pādapa*). **-patha**, m. the way to Brahmă or to Brahmă, Up.; BhP.; *-kovida*, mfn. knowing the way to Br°, L. **-pada**, n. the place of Brahmă, MaitrUp.; the station or rank of Brahmă or of a Brāhman, W. **-pannaga**, m. N. of a Marut, Hariv. (v. l. *bahu-p°*). **-parishad**, f. an assembly of Brāhmans, A. **-parishadya**, m. pl. = *-pārshadya*, Buddh. **-parṇī**, f. Hemionitis Cordifolia, L. **-parvata**, m. 'Brahmă's mountain,' N. of a place, Cat. **-palāśa**, m. pl. N. of a school of the Atharva-veda, Āryav. (v. l. *brāhma-p°*). **-pavitra**, n. Kuśa grass, L. **-pāda** (ibc.) Brahmă's feet; *-stotra*, n. N. of a Stotra. **-pādapa**, m. 'Brahmă's tree,' Butea Frondosa, L. (cf. *-pattra*). **-pāra**, m. the final object of all sacred knowledge, VP.; = next, ib.; *-maya*, mf(*ī*)n. (with *japa*, m.) a partic. prayer, ib.; *-stotra*, n. N. of a Stotra; *°râyaṇa*, n. a complete study of the Veda, Uttarar.; Mcar. **-pārshadya**, m. pl. (with Buddhists) Brahmă's retinue, N. of a class of deities, Lalit. (cf. Dharmas. 128). **-pāśa**, m. 'Brahmă's noose,' N. of a mythical weapon, Bhaṭṭ. **-pitṛi**, m. Brahmă's father,' N. of Vishṇu, Pañcar. (cf. *-nābha*). **-piśāca**, m. = *-rākshasa*, L. **-putrá**, m. the son of a priest or Brāhman, RV.; ŚBr.; ĀśvŚr.; a son of Brahmă (as Sanat-kumāra, Vasishṭha &c.), Hariv.; R.; Pur. (*-tā*, f.); a kind of vegetable poison, Bhpr.; N. of a river (rising on the Tibet side of the Himālaya and falling with the Ganges into the Bay of Bengal), Cat.; of a lake, ib.; of a place of pilgrimage (prob. the source of the Brahma-putra river), W.; of a sacred district, L.; (*ī*), f. a kind of esculent root (= *vārāhī*), L.; 'Brahmă's daughter,' N. of the river Sarasvatī, L. (cf. *-nadī*). **-pura**, n. 'Brahmă's town,' N. of a city in heaven, MBh. (*-māhātmya*, n. N. of wk.); of a city on earth, Var.; Hit.; of a kingdom, Buddh.; the heart, MāṇḍUp.; the body, ChUp. (cf. IW. 116, 2); (*ī*), f. Brahmă's citadel in heaven or his capital on the mountain Kailāsa, L. (*-māhātmya*, n. N. of wk.); N. of a city on earth, Rājat.; of the city Benares, Prab.; of any city the inhabitants of which are mostly Brāhmans, MW.; of a peak in the Himâlaya range, L.; *°râkhya*, mfn. named Brahma-pura, Hit.; *°râbhidheya*, mfn. (with *nāma*) to be called by the name B°-p°, Cat. **-puraka**, m. pl. N. of a people, MārkP. **-purastāt**, ind. when or where the Brāhmans have the first place, AitBr. **-purāṇa**, n. N. of one of the 18 Purāṇas (also called *Ādi-p°*; it is supposed to have been revealed by Brahmă to Daksha, and its main object appears to be the promotion of the worship of Kṛishṇa), IW. 514. **-purusha**, m. an assistant of the Brahman or chief priest, KātyŚr., Sch.; a minister of Brahmă (also said of the 5 vital airs), ChUp.; GṛS.; = *-rākshasa*, L. **-purogava** (*bráhma-*), mfn. preceded by Brahmă or 'the holy,' ŚBr. **-purohita** (*bráhma-*), mfn. having the sacerdotal class for a Purohita, ŚBr.; Kāṭh.; m. pl. 'the high priests of Brahmă,' (with Buddhists) N. of a class of divinities, Lalit. (cf. Dharmas. 128). **-pushpa**, m. N. of a man (cf. *brāhmapushpi*). **-pūta** (*bráhma-*), mfn. purified by devotion, AV.; p° by Brahmă, L. **-pṛishṭa** or **-pṛishṭha**, m. N. of a man, Vcar. **-prakṛitika**, mfn. emanating from or originating in Brahmă (*-tva*, n.), Saṃk. **-prajāpati**, m. du. Brahmă and Prajāpati, Lāṭy. **-pratishṭhā-prayoga**, m. N. of wk. **-prabha**, m. N. of a man, Divyâv. **-pralaya**, m. 'Brahmă's destruction,' the universal d° that takes place at the end of every 100 years of Br° (and in which even Br° himself is swallowed up), MW. **-prasūta** (*bráhma-*), mfn. impelled by Brahmă, ŚBr. **-prâpta**, mfn. one who has obtained Brahmă, KaṭhUp. **-prâpti**, f. obtainment of or absoption into Brahmă, MW. **-prâyaścitta**, n. pl. N. of wk. **-priya**, mfn. fond of devotion or of sacred knowledge, Vishṇ.; MBh. **-prí**, mfn. delighting in prayer or devotion, RV. **-bandhava**, n. (prob.) the office or occupation of a nominal Brāhman (cf. next), AitBr. **-bandhu**, m. an unworthy or merely nominal Brāhman (Sāy. 'a Brāhman who omits his Saṃdhyā devotions'), AitBr.; ChUp.; GṛŚrS. &c. (*°dhū*, f., Gaut.; Gobh.; *°dhu tā*, f., MBh.; compar. and superl. *°dhū-tara*, *°dhū-tama*, Pāṇ. vi, 3, 44, Sch.) **-balá**, n. Brāhmanical power, MaitrS.; m. N. of a man, Cat. **-bali**, m. N. of a teacher, Cat. **-bindu**, m. a drop of saliva sputtered while reciting the Veda, L.; *°dûpanishad*, f. N. of an Upanishad. **-bileya** (?), m. N. of a man, Cat. **-bīja**, n. 'seed of the Veda,' the sacred syllable *Om*, BhP.; m. the mulberry tree, L. **-bodha**, m., **-bodhinī**, f. N. of wks. **-bodhyā**, f. N. of a river, MBh. (B. *-vedhyā*). **-bruva**, m. = next, A. **-bruvāṇa**, mfn. calling one's self or pretending to be a Brāhman, MBh. **-bhaṭṭa**, m. N. of a poet, Cat. **-bhadrā**, f. Ficus Heterophylla, L. **-bhavana**, n. Brahmă's abode, MBh. **-bhāgá**, m. the share of a Brahman or chief priest, AV.; Br.; ŚrS.; the mulberry tree, L. **-bhāva**, m. absorption in the one self-existent Being or Brahmă, MBh., Sch.; *-stotra*, n. N. of a Stotra by Śaṃkarâcārya. **-bhāvana**, mfn. revealing or imparting religious knowledge, BhP. **-bhid**, mfn. dividing the one Brahmă into many, Prab. **-bhuvana**, n. Brahmă's world, Bhag. **-bhūta**, mfn. become i. e. absorbed in Brahmă, Mn.; MBh.; VP. n. identification with Brahmă, VP. **-bhūti**, f. twilight, L. **-bhūmi-jā**, f. 'growing in Brahmă's land,' a kind of pepper, L. **-bhūya**, n. identification with or absorption into Brahmă, Mn.; MBh. &c. (*-tva*, n.); Brāhmanhood, BhP. **-bhūyas**, mfn. becoming one with Brahmă, MBh.; n. absorption into Br°, ib. **-bhrashṭa**, mfn. one who has fallen from (i. e. who has forfeited) sacred knowledge, Hcat. **-maṅgala-devatā**, f. N. of Lakshmī, Cat. **-maṭha**, m. 'Brahmă's college,' N. of a theological college in Kaśmīra, Rājat. **-maṇḍūkī**, f. Clerodendrum Siphonantus, L. **-mati**, m. N. of a demon, Buddh. **-mantra**, m. or n. N. of wk. **-maya**, mf(*ī*)n. formed or consisting of or identified with Brahmă, AitBr.; KaushUp.; MBh. &c.; belonging to or fit for a Brāhman, W. **-maha**, m. a feast in honour of the Brāhmans, MBh. **-māṇḍūkī**, f. = *-maṇḍ°*, KātyŚr., Sch. **-māla**, m. pl. N. of a forest, R. (B.) **-mitra**, m. 'having Brahmă or the Brāhmans for friends,' N. of a Muni, MārkP. (cf. Pāṇ. vi, 2, 165, Sch.) **-mīmāṇsā**, f. 'investigation into Brahmă or the spiritual doctrine of the Veda,' N. of the Vedânta philosophy treating of the one self-existent Spirit, IW. 98 &c. (cf. *-sūtra*). **-mukha** (*bráhma-*), mf(*ā*)n. preceded by the priests, following or inferior to them, TS.; R. **-muhūrta**, m. a partic. hour of the day, Siṇhâs. **-mūrti**, mfn. having the figure or form of Brahmă, MW. **-mūrdha-bhṛit**, m. 'carrying Brahmă's head,' N. of Śiva (as having in a dispute cut off one of Br°'s heads), W. **-mekhala**, m. Saccharum Munjia (of which the sacred thread of a Brāhman is made), L. **-medhyā**, f. N. of a river, MBh. (cf. *-bodhyā*). **-yajñá**, m. 'Vedic offering,' recitation of portions of the Veda and sacred books at the Saṃdhyā, ŚBr.; ĀśvGṛ. &c. (one of the 5 Mahā-yajñas or great devotional acts, Mn. iii, 69; 70; cf. IW. 194; RTL. 393); N. of the sacred texts for daily recitation; *-tarpaṇa*, n., *-devarshi-pitṛi-tarpaṇa*, n., *°prayoga*, m., *-saṃhitā*, f., *°jñâdi-vidhi*, m., *°jñôpanishad*, f. N. of wks. **-yaśas**, n. Brahmă's glory, KaushUp.; *°śaḥ-svāmin*, m. N. of a poet, Cat.; *°śasa*, n. = *°yaśas*, AitBr.; *°śasin*, mfn. renowned for sanctity, Br. **-yashṭi**, f. Clerodendrum Siphonantus or Ligusticum Ajowan, L. **-yāga**, m. = *-yajña*, Cat. **-yātu**, m. N. of a partic. class of demons, Kāṭh. **-yāmala** or **-yāmila**, n. N. of a Tantra. **-yuga**, n. the age of the Brāhmans (opp. to *kshatrasya yugam*), Hariv. **-yúj**, mfn. harnessed by prayer (i. e. bringing Indra in answer to p°, said of his horses), RV. **-yūpa**, m. 'Brahmă's sacrificial post,' N. of a place, L. **-yogá**, m. employment of devotion, binding power of devotion, AV.; cultivation of spiritual knowledge, W. **-yogin**, m. N. of an author, Cat. **-yoni**, f. original source or home in Brahmă, TĀr. (*-stha*, mfn. 'abiding in Br°' or 'intent on the means of union with Br°,' Mn. x, 74); N. of a place of pilgrimage (also *°nī*), MBh.; Pur.; of a mountain (= *-giri*), L.; mfn. having one's source or home in Brahmă, ŚāṅkhGṛ.; descended or sprung from Brahmă, Ragh.; MārkP. **-rakshas**, n. a class of evil demons, Kathās. (cf. *-rākshasa*). **-ratna**, n. any valuable present made to Brāhmans, R. **-ratha**, m. the chariot or carriage of a Brāhman, ib. **-randhra**, n. 'Brahmă's crevice,' a suture or aperture in the crown of the head (through which the soul is said to escape on death), Pur.; Siṇhâs (RTL. 291). **-rava**, m. muttering of prayers, Hcat. **-rasa**, m. the savour of Brahmă, KaushUp.; *°sâsava*, m. Br°'s nectar, BhP. **-rahasya-saṃhitā**, f. N. of wk. **-rākshasa**, m. a kind of evil demon, the ghost of a Brāhman who led an unholy life, Mn.; MBh. &c.; a species of plant, L.; (*ī*), f. N. of one of the 9 Samidhs, Gṛihyas. **-rāja**, m. N. of a man, Rājat.; of a prince, Inscr. **-rājanyà**, m. du. a Brāhman and a Kshatriya, AV. **-rāta**, m. 'given by Brahmă,' N. of Śuka, BhP.; N. of the father of Yājñavalkya, VP. **-rāti** or **-rātri**, w. r. for *brāhma-rāti*. **-rātra**, m. 'Brahmă's night,' N. of a partic. hour of night, BhP. **-rāśi**, m. the whole mass of sacred texts or knowledge, VPrāt.; R.; a partic. constellation, MBh.; N. of Paraśu-rāma, MW. **-rīti**, f. a kind of brass, L. **-rūpa**, m. N. of Vishṇu, Vishṇ. **-rūpiṇī**, f. a species of parasitical plant, L. **-rekhā**, f. 'Brahmă's line,' the lines of a man's destiny supposed to be written by Br° on the forehead of a child on the 6th day after its birth, RTL. 370, 373. **-ṛshi** (= and for *-ṛishi*), m. 'Brāhmanical sage,' N. of a partic. class of sages supposed to belong to the Br° caste (as Vasishṭha &c.), MBh.; R. &c. (cf. *deva-ṛshi*, *maha-ṛshi*, *rāja-ṛshi*); *-tā*, f., *-tva*, n. the state or rank of a Brahmarshi, ib.; *-deśa*, m. the country of the Brahmarshis (including Kuru-kshetra and the country of the Matsyas, Pañcālas, and Śūra-senakas), Mn. ii, 19. **-lakshaṇa-vākyârtha**, m. N. of an abridgment of the Vedânta-sudhā-rahasya. **-likhita**, n., **-lekha**, m. 'Brahmă's writing,' = *-rekhā*, RTL. 370. **-loká**, m. (also pl.) the world or heaven of Brahmā (a division of the universe and one of the supposed residences of pious spirits), AV. &c. &c. **-laukika**, mfn. inhabiting Brahmă's world, Yājñ.; MBh. **-vaktṛi**, m. a proclaimer or teacher of sacred knowledge, Hariv. **-1. -vat**, ind. according to the sacred text or the Veda, R.; like the Veda, Āpast. **-2. -vat**, mfn. possessing Brahmă or sacred knowledge, TUp.; MBh. **-vada** (or *-vala*), m. pl. N. of a Vedic school, L. (prob. w. r.) **-vadya**, n. recitation of sacred texts, ŚāṅkhBr.; = *brahmôdya*, ib.; mf(*ā*)n. (in *°dyā-kathā*), Vop. **-vadha**, m. the murder of a Brāhman, Cat. **-vadhyā**, f. id., MBh.; *-kṛita*, n. act of murdering a Br°, ib. **-váni**, mfn. devoted to Brāhmans, VS. (Mahīdh.) **-varaṇa**, n. election of a chief priest, KātyŚr. **-varcas** = *°casa*, in *°cas-vin*, mfn. = *°casin*, ĀśvGṛ.; Mn.; MBh. &c. **-varcasá**, n. divine glory or splendour, pre-eminence in holiness or sacred knowledge, sanctity, superhuman power, AV. &c. &c.; *-kāma*, mfn. desirous of holiness or sacred knowledge, Mn. ii, 37; *°sín*, mfn. eminent in sacred knowledge, holy (compar. *°si-tara*), VS.; AS.; Br.; MBh.; *°sya*, mf(*ā*)n. conferring sanctity or sacred knowledge, Br.; BhP. **-varta**, m. = *°mâvarta*, L. **-vardhana**, n. copper (as peculiarly suitable for sacrificial utensils), L. **-varman**, n. 'Brahmă's armour,' N. of partic. oblations, ĀpŚr. **-vala**, see **-vada**. **-vallī**, f. 'Brahmă's tendril or creeper,' N. of an Upanishad (= *brahmânanda-vally-upanishad*); *-lipi*, f. a partic. mode of writing, Buddh. **-vāc**, f. 'Brahmă's word,' the sacred text, ĀrshBr. **-vātīya**, m. N. of a class of Munis, Hariv. **-vādá**, m. discourse on or explanation of sacred texts, TBr.; BhP.; N. of a Nyāya wk. (also *°dârtha*, m.); mfn. (m. c.) = next, Hariv. **-vādin**, mfn. discoursing on sacred texts, a defender or expounder of the Veda, AV. &c. &c. (*inī*, f., Var.; °*di-tva*, n., MBh.); one who asserts that all things are to be identified with Brahmă, a Vedântin, Saṃk. **—vā́dya**, n. rivalry in sacred knowledge or in magical power, TS. **—vā-luka**, n. N. of a Tīrtha, MBh. **—vāsa**, m. the abode or heaven of Brahmā, Hariv. **—vāhas** (*bráhma-*), mfn. one to whom prayers are offered, RV. **—vit-tva**, n. (fr. next) knowledge of Brahmă (the one self-existent Spirit of the Universe), Vedântas. **—vid**, mfn. knowing the one Brahmă, a Vedic philosopher, AV. &c. &c. (also *-vida*); skilled in sacred spells or magic, MBh.; m. N. of Śiva, RTL. 84; *-āśīrvāda-paddhati*, f. N. of wk. **—vidyā́**, f. knowledge of 'the one self-existent Being,' kn° of Brahmă, sacred knowledge, ŚBr. &c. &c. (cf. IW. 219); N. of an Upanishad (cf. below); *-tīrtha*, m. N. of an author; *-paddhati*, f., *-°bhāraṇa* (°*dyâbh°*), n., *-mahôdadhi*, m., *-vijaya*, m., *-vilāsa*, m., °*dyôpanishad*, f. N. of wks. **—vidvas**, mfn. one who knows Brahmă or the one universal Spirit, KaushUp. **—vidvish**, mfn. = *-dvish*, Cat. **—vi-vardhana**, mfn. 'increasing sacred knowledge,' N. of Vishṇu, MBh. **—viśesha-citta-paripṛic-chā**, f. N. of a Buddhist Sūtra wk. **—vishṇu-mahêśvara-dāna**, n. N. of wk. **—vishṇv-arka-vat**, mfn. accompanied by Brahmā and Vishṇu and the Sun, Hcat. **—vihāra**, m. pious conduct, perfect state (4 with Buddhists), Lalit.; Divyâv.; Dharmas. 16. **—vīṇā**, f. a partic. stringed instrument, Saṃgīt. **—vṛiksha**, m. the divine tree, Brahmă regarded as a tree, Bhag., Sch.; Butea Frondosa or Ficus Glomerata, L. **—vṛitti**, f. the livelihood or subsistence of a Brāhman, BhP. **—vṛiddha** (*bráhma-*), mfn. grown or increased by prayer, AV. **—vṛiddhi**, f. increase of Brāhmanical power, Āpast.; m. N. of a man, L. **—vṛinda**, n. a company or assemblage of Brāhmans, MW.; (*ā*), f. N. of the city of Brahmă, W. **—veda**, m. 'the Veda of sacred spells or charms,' the Atharva-veda, AV. Anukr.; ŚāṅkhGṛ. &c.; the V° of the Brāhmans (as opp. to *kshatra-veda*, q.v.), R.; knowledge of Brahmă, W.; kn° of the Vedas, ib.; *-pariśishṭa*, n. N. of wk.; *-maya*, mf(*ī*)n. consisting of the Brahma-veda, L. **—vedi**, f. 'Brahmā's altar,' N. of the country between the 5 lakes of Rāma in Kuru-kshetra, L. **—vedin**, mfn. = *-vid*, acquainted with the Veda or spiritual knowledge, Mn. i, 97. **—vedhyā**, see *-bodhyā*. **—vaivarta** or °**taka**, n. 'metamorphoses of Brahmă' (who is identified with Kṛishṇa), N. of a Purāṇa (one of the most modern of the 18, containing prayers and invocations addressed to Kṛishṇa with narratives about his loves for the Gopīs and Rādhā &c.), VP.; Pañcar. (IW. 514 &c.); °*ta-rahasya*, n., °*ta-sāra*, m. N. of wks. **—vyavahāra**, m. N. of wk. **—vrata**, n. N. of a religious observance, MBh.; a vow of chastity (*-dhara*, mfn. practising the vow of chastity), Pañcat. **—śabda** (ibc.), B°'s word; *-vāda*, m., *-śakti-vāda*, m., °*dârtha-vāda*, m., °*dârtha-vicāra*, m. N. of wks. **—śambhu**, m. N. of an astronomer, Cat. **—śalya**, m. Acacia Arabica, L. **—śāyin**, mfn. resting in Brahmă, L. **—śālā**, f. Brahmā's hall, MaitrUp.; N. of a place, MBh. **—śāsana**, m. N. of a Grāma, L.; n. a command of Brahmă or of a Brāhman, L.; an edict addressed to the Brāhmans (= *dharma-kīlaka*), L. **—śiras**, n. 'Brahmā's head,' N. of a mythical weapon, MBh; R.; Hariv. (also *-śīrshan*, BhP.); °*raḥ-khaṇḍana*, n. N. of ch. of KūrmaP. **—śumbhita** (*bráhma-*), mfn. purified or adorned by devotion, AV. **—śrī**, f. N. of a Sāman, Br. **—saṃśita** (*bráhma-*), mfn. sharpened by prayer or by a sacred text, RV.; AV.; Br.; ĀśvŚr. **—saṃsad**, f. Brahmā's hall of assembly, Pañcar.; an assembly of Brāhmans, KathUp. **—saṃstha**, mfn. wholly devoted to Brahmă or sacred knowledge, ChUp. **—saṃhitā**, f. a collection of prayers, Hariv.; N. of sev. wks. (also *-vyākhyā*, f.) **—satī**, f. N. of the river Sarasvatī, L. **—sattra**, n. sacrifice of devotion or meditation, constant repetition of Vedic texts, Mn. ii, 106; BhP.; °*ttrin*, mfn. offering the sacr° of d°; absorbed in the self-existent One, MBh. **—sadana**, n. the seat of the chief priest, ŚrS.; = *-sadas*, BhP.; N. of a Tīrtha, Cat. **—sadas**, n. the residence or court of Brahmă, MBh. **—sabhā**, f. the hall or court of Brahmā, Ragh.; Pañcar.; N. of a lotus pond, Divyâv. **—sambandha**, m. union with the Supreme Spirit, RTL. 136; = *-rāk-shasa*, L. **—sambhava**, mfn. sprung from Brahmă, Hariv.; m. (with Jainas) N. of the second black Vāsudeva, L.; N. of the author of a law-book, Cat.; *-smṛiti*, f. N. of his wk. **—saras**, n. 'Brahmā's lake,' N. of a very sacred bathing-place, MBh. **—sarpa**, m. 'Brahmā's serpent,' a kind of snake, L. **—savá**, m. purification of prayer, RV. ix, 17, 24; N. of a partic. libation, Mn. v, 23 (= *brahma-kshatra-s°*). **—sāgara**, m. N. of a place, Cat. **—sāt-kṛita**, mfn. brought into union with Brahmā, BhP. **—sāmá** or **-sāmán**, n. N. of a Sāman (sung to a text recited by the chief priest or by the Brāhmaṇâc-chaṅsin), TS.; Br.; ŚrS.; °*mika*, mfn. relating to it, PañcavBr., Sch. **—sāyujya**, n. intimate union or identification with Brahmā, L. **—sārshṭi-tā**, f. union or equality with Brahmā, Mn. iv, 232. **—sāvarṇa**, m. N. of the 10th Manu, Pur. (also °*ṇi*, ib.); n. his Manv-antara, ib. **—siddhânta**, m. N. of various astron. wks. (also *-paddhati*, f.) **—siddhi**, m. N. of a Muni, Kathās.; of a Vedânta wk.; *-vyākhyā-ratna*, n. N. of a Comm. on it. **—suta**, m. 'Brahmā's son,' N. of the Ketu Brahma-daṇḍa, Var.; (*ā*), f. Br°'s daughter, Hcat. **—suvar-calā**, f. a species of plant, Suśr. (Helianthus or Clerodendrum Siphonantus, L.); an infusion of it (drunk as a penance), Mn. xi, 160. **—sū**, m. 'Brahmā's son,' N. of Kāma-deva or of Aniruddha (K°'s son), L. **—sûkta**, n. N. of wk. **—sūtra**, n. the sacred thread worn over the shoulder, Yājñ.; MBh. &c.; a Sūtra work treating of the knowledge of Brahmă (esp. the aphorisms of the Vedânta philosophy ascribed to Bādarāyaṇa or Vyāsa, also called *bādarāyaṇa-* or *vedânta-* or *vyāsa-* or *śārī-raka-sūtra*, and *uttara-* or *brahma-mīmānsā*); *-ṛiju-vyākhyā*, f., *-kārikā*, f., *-candrikā*, f., *-tan-tra-dīpikā*, f., *-tātparya*, n. N. of wks.; *-pada*, n. the word or statement of a Brahma-sūtra, Bhag.; Hariv.; mf(*ā* or *ī*)n. consisting of such a word or st°, Hariv.; *-pradīpa*, m., *-bhāshya*, n. (°*shya-dīpikā*, f., *-vārttika*, n., *-sāra*, m.), *-laghu-vārttika*, n., *-vṛitti*, f. (and °*ti-vārttika*, n.), *-saṃgati*, f., °*trâdvaita-vṛitti*, f., °*trânubhāshya*, n. (and °*shya-pradīpa*, m., *-vivaraṇa*, n.), °*trânuvyākhyāna*, n., °*trârtha-prakāśikā*, f., °*trârtha-maṇi-māla*, f., °*trôpanyāsa*, m. (and °*sa-vṛitti*, f.) N. of various Comms. on the Br°-sūtra, and Comms. on them. **—sū-trin**, mfn. invested with the Brāhmanical cord, Yājñ. **—sūnu**, m. (with Jainas) N. of the 12th king of Bhārata, L. **—sṛij**, m. 'Brahmā's creator,' N. of Śiva, Śivag. **—soma**, m. N. of a sage, Kathās. **—stamba**, m. N. of a man, Cat. (cf. *brāhmastambi*). **—stuti**, f. N. of a hymn of praise (also °*ti-stotra*), Cat. **—stena**, m. a thief of that which is sacred, one who obtains a knowledge of the Veda by illicit means, MBh. **—steya**, n. unlawful acquisition of the Veda (cf. prec.), Mn. ii, 116. **—sthala**, n. N. of a city, Cat. (cf. *-pura*); of a village, Kathās. **—sthāna**, n. 'Brahmā's place,' N. of a Tīrtha, MBh.; m. the mulberry tree, L. **—sphuṭa-siddhânta**, m. N. of an astron. wk. by Brahma-gupta (also called *brahma-siddhânta*). **—sva**, n. the property i.e. lands or money of Brāhmans, Caṇḍ.; Pañcar. **—svarūpa**, mfn. of the nature or essence of the one self-existing Spirit, W. **—svāmin**, m. N. of a man, Cat. **—haṅ-sôpanishad**, f. N. of an Upanishad. **—hatyā́**, f. murder of a Brāhman (or any crime equally heinous), VS. &c. &c. **—hán**, mf(*ghnī*)n. 'Brāhman-slaying,' the murderer of a Brāhman, TS. &c. &c.; (*ghnī*), f. Aloe Perfoliata, L. **—hari**, m. N. of a poet, Cat. **—huta**, n. 'offering to Brahmā or the Brāhmans,' hospitality, L. (cf. *brāhmya-huta*). **—hṛidaya**, m. n. the star Capella, Sūryas. **—hrada**, m. N. of a lake, Cat. **Brahmâkshara**, n. the sacred syllable *Om*, BhP.; *-maya*, mf(*ī*)n. consisting of sacred syllables Hariv. **Brahmâgāra**, n. the house of the chief priest, KātyŚr. **Brahmâgra-bhū**, m. a horse, L. (cf. next and *brahmâtma-bhū*). **Brahmâṅga-bhū**, mfn. one who has touched the several parts of his body during the repetition of Mantras, Kum. iii, 15 (Mall.); m. = prec., A. **Brahmâñjali**, m. joining the hollowed hands while repeating the Veda, Mn. ii, 71; *-kṛita*, mfn. one who has joined the h° h° in token of homage to the V°, ib., 70; ĀśvGṛ. &c. **Brahmâṇḍa**, n. 'Brahmā's egg,' the universe, world (also pl.), Hariv.; Sūryas.; Pur. (also *-kaṭāha*, m., Āryabh., Sch.); N. of a Purāṇa and an Upa-purāṇa; *-kapāla*, m. the skull or hemisphere of the world, the inhabited earth, Hcar.; *-kalpa*, m., *-jñāna-mahārāja-tantra*, n., and *-tantra*, n. N. of Tāntric wks.; *-purāṇa*, n. N. of one of the 18 Purāṇas (so called as revealed by Brahmā and containing an account of the egg of Brahmā and the future Kalpas; cf. IW. 514; 521); *-bhāṇḍôdara*, n. the interior of the vessel-like egg of Brahmā, MW.; *-yāmale pañcamī-sādhana*, n. N. of wk. **Brahmâtithi**, m. 'Br°'s guest,' N. of a Kāṇva (author of RV. viii, 5). **Brahmâtma-bhū**, m. a horse (cf. *brahmâṅga-* and °*mâgra-bhū*). **Brahmâdanī**, f. a species of plant (= *haṅsa-padī*), L. **Brahmâdarśa**, m. 'Brahmā's mirror,' N. of wk. **Brahmâdi-jātā**, f. the river Go-dāvarī, L. (v.l. °*mâdri-j°*). **Brahmâ-ditya**, m. N. of an author (also called *Brahmârka*), Cat. **Brahmâdi-śīrsha**, m. or n.(?) N. of a place, Cat. 1. **Brahmâdya**, mfn. (fr. 1. *ādya*) beginning with Brahmā, Mn. i, 50. 2. **Brahmâdya**, mfn. (fr. 2. *ādya*) to be eaten by priests or Brāhmans, Br. **Brahmâdri-jātā**, f., see °*mâdi-jātā*. **Brah-mâdhigama**, m. devotion to sacred study or the Veda (also °*mana*, n., W); °*mika*, mfn. relating to it, Mn. ii, 64. **Brahmânanda**, m. 'joy in Brahmă,' the rapture of absorption into the one self-existent Spirit, RāmatUp.; N. of various men and authors (also *-giri*, *-parama-haṅsa*, *-bhāratī*, *-yogin*, *-yogîndra*, *-sārasvatī*, and °*din*, m.); of various wks. (also *-vallī*, f., *-vilāsa*, m., *-sūtra-muktâvali*, f., *-stava*, m., °*dīya* and °*dīya-khan-ḍana*, n.) **Brahmâpêta**, m. N. of one of the 7 Rākshasas said to dwell in the sun during the month Māgha, VP. **Brahmâbhyāsa**, m. study and repetition of the Veda, Mn. iv, 149. **Brahmâmṛita**, n. N. of a Vedânta wk.; *-varshiṇī*, f. N. of a Comm. on the Brahma-sūtras. **Brahmâmbhas**, n. 'holy water,' the urine of a cow, L. **Brahmâyaṇa** or °**na**, m. N. of Nārāyaṇa, Hariv. **Brahmâyatana**, n. a temple of Brahmā, Var.; °*tanīya*, mf(*ā*)n. leaning on or supported by Brāhmans, Lāṭy. **Brah-mâyus**, n. Brahmā's life-time, Vishṇ.; mfn. living as long as Br°, Siṅhâs.; m. N. of a Brāhman, Buddh. **Brahmâraṇya**, n. 'holy forest,' a grove in which the Veda is studied, L.; N. of a forest, Hit.; *-māhātmya*, n. N. of wk. **Brahmârambha**, m. beginning to repeat the Veda, Mn. ii, 71. **Brah-mârka**, m., see °*mâditya*. **Brahmârgha**, mfn. worthy of Brahmā or of sacred knowledge, KaushUp. (v.l. for °*ma-grāhin*). **Brahmârpaṇa**, n. the offering of sacred texts, Pañcar.; N. of a magical spell, ib. **Brahmâlaṃkāra**, m. the ornament of Brahmă, KaushUp. **Brahmā-vatī**, f. N. of a woman, Divyâv.; of a lotus pond, ib. **Brahmâva-bodha**, m. N. of wk. (also *-viveka-sindhu*, m.) **Brahmâvarta**, m. 'the holy land,' N. of the country situated between the rivers Sarasvatī and Dṛishadvatī to the N.W. of Hastinā-pura, Mn. ii, 17; 19; AVPariś. &c. (IW. 209); of a Tīrtha, MBh. (also *-tīrtha*, n., Cat.); of a son of Ṛishabha, BhP. **Brahmâvalī-bhāshya**, n. N. of wk. **Brahmā-vāda-nagara**, n. N. of a city, Siṅhâs. **Brahmâvāsa**, m. 'home of or in Brahmă,' N. of a wk. (on salvation to be attained in Benares). **Brahmâsana**, n. the seat of the chief priest, ŚrS.; (ifc. f. *ā*) a partic. posture suited to devout religious meditation, Kād.; *-nivishṭa*, mfn. seated in that posture, Rājat. **Brahmâstra**, n. 'Brahmā's missile,' N. of a mythical weapon (which deals infallible destruction), MBh.; R.; Kathās.; of a partic. kind of incantation, Cat. (cf. IW. 402, 1); *-kalpa*, m., *-kavaca*, m. or n., *-kārya-sādhana*, n., *-paddhati*, f., *-vidyā-pūjā-paddhati*, f., *-vidhāna-paddhati*, f. N. of wks. **Brahmâsya**, n. the mouth of Brahmā, MBh.; the m° of a Brāhman, Cat. **Bráh-mâhuta**, mfn. one to whom oblations of prayer and devotion have been made, AV. **Brahmâhuti**, f. the offering of pr° or d°, Mn. ii, 106. **Bráh-mêddha**, mfn. lighted or kindled with prayers, AV. **Brahmêndra**, m. (with *sarasvatī* or °*dra-svāmin*) N. of authors, Cat. **Brahme-śaya** (for °*maṇi-ś°*), m. 'resting in Brahmă,' N. of Kārttikeya, MBh.; of Vishṇu, ib. **Brahmêśa-vaishṇava**, mfn. descended from Brahmā and Śiva and Vishṇu, MārkP. **Brahmêśvara**, m. N. of an author, Cat.; *-tīrtha*, n. N. of a Tīrtha on the Revā or Narmadā river, Cat. **Brahmâikya-prakaraṇa**, n. N. of wk. **Brahmôjjha**, mfn. one who has neglected or forgotten the Veda, Gaut.; n. (Āpast.) = *-tā*, f. (Mn.), *-tva*, n. (Yājñ., Sch.) neglecting or forgetting the V°, (cf. IW. 270). **Brahmoḍumbara**, w.r. for °*môdumbara*. **Brahmôttara**, mfn. treating principally of Brahmā or consisting chiefly of Brāhmans; m. N. of a superhuman being, Lalit.; (with Jainas) of a partic. Kalpa, Dharmaś.; pl. N. of a people, MārkP.; n. N. of a town, Divyâv.; of ch. of SkandaP. (also called *-khaṇḍa*, n. or *laghu-śiva-purāṇa*, n.) **Brahmôda-tīrtha**, n. (Cat.) and **Brahmôdum-**

bara, m. or n. (MBh.; C. °*môd*°) N. of Tīrthas. **Brahmôdya,** n. rivalry in sacred knowledge, playful discussion of theological questions or problems, Br.; ŚrS.; mf(*ā*)n. relating to sacred questions or problems, Vop.; (*ā*), f. (with *kathā*) a story or riddle from the Veda, Mn. iii, 231 (cf. *brahma-vadya*). **Brahmôpadeśa,** m. instruction in sacred knowledge, A.; *-netṛi,* m. Butea Frondosa, ib. (cf. *-môpanetṛi*). **Brahmôpanishad,** f. mystical teaching concerning Brahmā (ChUp.) or the Brāhmans (MBh. xv, 940); N. of 2 Upanishads. **Brahmôpanetṛi,** m. Butea Frondosa, L. (cf. °*padeśa-netṛi*). **Brahmôpāsanā,** f. worship of Brahmā, RTL. 493. **Brahmôpêta,** m. N. of a Rakshas, VP. (cf. *Brahmâpêta*). **Brahmâudana,** m. boiled rice distributed to Brāhmans and esp. to the chief priest at a sacrifice, AV.; TS.; Br.; ŚrS. **Brahmâupagava,** m., Pāṇ. vi, 1, 88, Sch.

Bráhmaṇas-páti, m. (fr. *brahmaṇas,* gen. of *brahman* + *p*°) = *bṛihas-páti,* RV. &c. &c. (*-sûkta,* n. N. of wk.); °*ṇas pátnī,* f. the wife of the priest called Brahman, TS.

1. **Brahmaṇya,** Nom. P. °*yáti* (only pr. p. °*yát*) to pray, be devout or religious, RV.

2. **Brahmaṇyá,** mfn. relating to Brahmā or Brahma, devoted to sacred knowledge or friendly to Brāhmans, religious, pious, MBh.; Kāv. &c.; m. N. of Kārttikeya, MBh.; of the planet Saturn, W.; the mulberry tree, L.; Saccharum Munjia, L.; (*ā*), f. N. of Durgā, L.; (°*ṇyá*), n. (pl.) 'praise' or 'sacrificial food' (?), RV. viii, 6, 33 (Sāy.) **-tā,** f. friendliness towards Brāhmans, piety, MBh.; BhP. **-tīrtha,** m. N. of a teacher, Cat. **-deva,** m. N. of Vishṇu, Hariv. (= *brahmaṇyānāṃ śreshṭhaḥ,* Sch.) **-bhāskara,** m. N. of a man, Cat.

1. **Bráhmaṇ-vat** (°*vát,* TBr.), mfn. accompanied by prayer, devout, AV.; Br.; practising a sacred work (and 'having a Brāhman'), TS.; Kāṭh.; including or representing the Brāhmans (as Agni), Br.; ŚrS.; containing the word *brahman,* AitBr.; (*ī*), f. N. of an Ishṭakā, TS.

2. **Brahmaṇ-vát,** ind. like Brahmā or Brahma or a Brāhman, ŚBr.; KātyŚr.

Brahmāṇī, f. the Śakti or personified female energy of Brahmā, the wife of Br°, Pur. (cf. IW. 522); N. of Durgā, Hariv.; DevīP. (w.r. *brāhmāṇī* or *brāhmaṇī*); a kind of perfume, L.; a kind of brass, L.; N. of a river, MBh. (v.l. *brāhmaṇī*). **-mantra,** m. a partic. verse or formula, MārkP.

Brahmāya, Nom. Ā. °*yate,* to become Brahmā, Vās.

Brahmin, mfn. belonging or relating to Brahmā or Brahma, TĀr.; 'possessing sacred knowledge,' N. of Vishṇu, MBh.

Bráhmishṭha, mfn. (superl. fr. *brahmán*) a Brāhman in the highest degree (as a N. of Bṛihaspati or Prajā-pati and of very learned and pious Brāhmans or princes), TS. &c. &c.; m. N. of a prince, Ragh.; (*ā*), f. N. of Durgā, DevīP.

1. **Bráhmī,** f. holy, devout (?), RV. ix, 33, 5 (Sāy. = *brāhmaṇa-prêrita*); a kind of fish, Macrognathus Pancalus (commonly called Pancal), L.; a kind of vegetable, L.; Clerodendrum Siphonantus, L.

2. **Brahmī,** in comp. for °*ma* or °*man.* **-bhūta,** m. N. of Śaṃkarâcārya, Gal.

Bráhmīyas, mfn. (compar. fr. *brahmán*) more or most devout or skilled in sacred knowledge; m. a pious or learned Brāhman, Br.

Brāhmá, mf(*ī*)n. (fr. *brahman,* for which it is also the Vṛiddhi form in comp.) relating to Brahmā or Brahma, holy, sacred, divine, AV. &c. &c.; relating to sacred knowledge, prescribed by the Veda, scriptural, Mn. ii, 150 &c.; sacred to the Veda (with or scil. *tīrtha,* n. the part of the hand situated at the root of the thumb), ii, 59 &c.; relating or belonging to the Brāhmans or the sacerdotal class, peculiar or favourable to or consisting of Brāhmans, Brāhmanical, Mn.; MBh. &c. (with *nidhi,* m. money bestowed on the sacerdotal class, Mn. vii, 89); belonging to an inhabitant of Brahmā's world, Jātakam.; m. (with or scil. *vivāha*) N. of a form of marriage (in which the bride is bestowed on the bridegroom without requiring anything from him), Mn. iii, 21 &c.; N. of a man (son of Kṛishṇa and father of Mahêśvara), Cat.; patr. of Nārada, L.; of Kavi, MBh.; of Ūrdhva-nābhan and Raksho-han, RAnukr.; (*ī*), f., see *brāhmī*; n. sacred study, study of the Veda, BhP.; (with or scil. *tīrtha*), see above. **-kārikā,** f. pl. N. of partic. Kārikās, Cat. **-kṛiteya,** m. patr. fr. *brahma-kṛita,* g. *śubhrâdi.* **-gupta,** m. pl. (fr. *brahma-gupta*) N. of a race, Kār. on Pāṇ. v, 3, 116 (v.l. *brahma-g*°); °*ptīya,* m. a prince of the Brāhmaguptas, ib. (v.l. *brahma-g*°). **-daṇḍa,** m. (prob.) w.r. for *brahma-d*°, Rājat. **-dattāyana,** m. patr. fr. *brahma-datta,* g. *śubhrâdi.* **-deya,** mfn. = *brahma-d*°, mfn., MBh. iii, 12729 (B.); Kull. on Mn. iii, 185. **-parvan,** n. N. of wk. **-palāśa,** m. pl. N. of a school (also read *brahma-p*°, q.v.) **-piṅgā** (?), f. silver, W. **-purāṇa,** n. = *brahma-p*°, VP. **-pushpi,** m. patr. fr. *brahma-pushpa,* Cat. (w.r. *brahma-pushpi*). **-prajāpatya,** mfn. (fr. *brahma-prajāpati*), L. **-muhūrta,** m. n. a partic. period of the day (that included between the 4th Ghaṭikā and the 2nd before sunrise), dawn, L. (cf. Mn. iv, 92). **-rāti,** m. (fr. *brahma-rāta*) patr. of Yājñavalkya, VāyuP. **-laukika,** mfn. (fr. *brahma-loka*) possessing claims to Brahmā's world, R. **-vivāha,** m. = °*mo viv*° above. **-siddhânta,** m. N. of wk. **Brāhmâho-rātra,** m. a day and night of Brahmā (a period of 2000 ages of the gods or 2 Kalpas of mortals), L. (cf. Mn. i, 72). **Brāhmêshṭi,** f. a partic. Ishṭi, Up. **Brāhmôḍhā,** f. a woman married according to the Brāhma rite, Vishṇ., Sch. **Brāhmôtsava,** m. a class of periodical religious festivals, RTL. 510. **Brāhmaudanika,** m. (fr. *brahmâudana*; with or scil. *agni*) the fire on which the rice for the priests is boiled, ĀpŚr.

Brāhmaka, n. = *-brahmaṇā kṛitam* (*saṃjñāyām*), g. *kulâlâdi*; (*ikā*), f. Clerodendrum Siphonantus, L.

Brāhmaṇa, mfn. relating to or given by a Brāhman, befitting or becoming a Br°, Brāhmanical, AV.; TBr.; MBh.; (°*ṇá*), m. one who has divine knowledge (sometimes applied to Agni), a Brāhman, a man belonging to the 1st of the 3 twice-born classes and of the 4 original divisions of the Hindū body (generally a priest, but often in the present day a layman engaged in non-priestly occupations although the name is strictly only applicable to one who knows and repeats the Veda), RV. &c. &c.; = *brāhmaṇâc-chaṅsin,* KātyŚr.; a Brāhman in the second stage (between Mātra and Śrotriya), Hcat.; N. of the 28th lunar mansion, L.; (*ī*), f., see *brāhmaṇī*; n. that which is divine, the divine, AV.; sacred or d° power, ib.; ĀśvGṛ.; Brāhmanical explanation, explanations of sacred knowledge or doctrine (esp. for the use of the Brāhmans in their sacrifices), Br.; the Brāhmaṇa portion of the Veda (as distinct from its Mantra and Upanishad portion) and consisting of a class of works called Brāhmaṇas (they contain rules for the employment of the Mantras or hymns at various sacrifices, with detailed explanations of their origin and meaning and numerous old legends; they are said by Sāyaṇa to contain two parts: 1. *vidhi,* rules or directions for rites; 2. *artha-vāda,* explanatory remarks; each Veda has its own Brāhmaṇa, that of the RV. is preserved in 2 works, viz. the Aitareya, sometimes called Āśvalāyana, and the Kaushītaki or Śāṅkhāyana-Br°; the white Yajur-veda has the Śata-patha Br°; the black Yajur-veda has the Taittirīya-Br° which differs little from the text of its Saṃhitā; the SV. has 8 Br°s, the best known of which are the Prauḍha or Pañca-viṅśa and the Shaḍviṅśa; the AV. has one Br° called Go-patha), Nir.; GṛŚrS. &c.; the Soma vessel of the Brahman priest, RV.; AV.; a society or assemblage of Brāhmans, a conclave, W. **-kalpa,** m. pl. the Brāhmaṇas and Kalpas (two kinds of Vedic texts), Pāṇ. iv, 3, 105; mfn. like a Brāhman, AitBr. **-kāmyā,** f. love for Br°s, Mṛicch. **-kāraka,** mfn. making a person a Br°, Pat. on Pāṇ. ii, 2, 6. **-kumāra,** m. a Br° boy, TāṇḍBr. **-kula,** n. the house of a Br°, Gobh. **-kṛita,** m. N. of a man; °*teya,* m. patr. fr. prec. (*ī,* f.), g. *śārṅgaravâdi.* **-gṛiha,** n. = *-kula,* KātyŚr., Sch. **-ghna,** m. the killer of a Brāhman, Mn. ix, 232. **-caṇḍāla,** m. 'Caṇḍāla among Br°s,' a degraded or out-caste Br°, Mn. ix, 87; the son of a Sūdra father by a Brāhmanī mother, W. **-ja,** mf(*ā*)n., said of an Ishṭi, ĀpŚr., Sch. (cf. Pāṇ. iii, 2, 101, Sch.); n. = next, MW. **-jātá,** n. (ŚBr.), **-jāti,** f. (W.) the Brāhmanical caste or race; °*tīya,* mfn. belonging to it, W. **-jīvikā,** f. the occupation or subsistence of a Brāhman, ib. **-jushṭa,** mfn. pleasing to Br°s, ŚāṅkhGṛ. **-ḍimbha,** m. a Br° lad, young Br°, Mālatīm. **-tarpaṇa,** n. the feeding or satisfying of Br°s, SāmavBr. **-tā,** f. the rank or condition of a Br°, AitBr.; Mn. **-trā,** ind. among the Br°s, Pāṇ. v, 4, 55, Sch. **-tva,** n. = *-tā,* Lāṭy., Sch.; Mallin.; *-vicāra,* m. N. of wk. **-dārikā,** f. a Br° girl, Buddh. **-dravya,** n. the property of a Br°, Mn. ix, 198. **-dveshin,** mfn. hating Br°s, R. **-dhana,** n. the fee bestowed on Br°s, Vait. **-nindaka,** mfn. reviling Br°s, MBh. **-pañcikā,** f., **-paddhati,** f. N. of wks. **-patha,** m. a Brāhmaṇa text, RPrāt., Sch. **-pāla,** m. N. of a prince, L. **-putraka,** m. a Brāhman boy, Kathās. **-prasaṅga,** m. the applicability of the term Brāhmaṇa, the idea of Brāhman, Vajras. **-prātiveśya,** m. a neighbouring Brāhman, Yājñ. ii, 263. **-priya,** m. a friend of Br°s (said of Vishṇu), Vishṇ. **-bruva,** m. 'calling one's self a Brāhman,' a Br° only by name or a Br° who disgraces his caste, Mn.; MBh. &c. (cf. *dvija-bruva* and *brahma-bruvāṇa*). **-bhāva,** m. the rank or condition of a Br°, L. **-bhāshya,** n. N. of wk. **-bhūyishṭha,** mfn. principally consisting of (or containing) Br°s, R. **-bhojana,** n. the feeding of Br°s (as a religious act), ShaḍvBr.; GṛS.; *-vidhi,* m. N. of wk. **-mahimâdarśa,** m. N. of wk. **-mukhīna,** m. pl. N. of partic. verses or formulas, TĀr., Sch. **-yajñá,** m. a sacrifice intended for Br°s, ŚBr.; a s° offered by Br°s, MBh. **-yashṭikā** or **-yashṭī,** f. Clerodendrum Siphonantus, L. **-rūpa-bhṛit,** mfn. bearing the form of a Br°, MW. **-lakshaṇa,** n. N. of wk. **-liṅga,** mfn. resembling the texts called Brāhmaṇas (said of verses or formulas), Kauś. **-vacana,** n. the statement of a Brāhmaṇa text, Āpast. **-vát,** mfn. connected with a Br°, TS.; (*brāh*°), possessed of or in accordance with a Brāhmaṇa, correct, TBr.; (*atī*), f. N. of partic. Ishṭakās, Nyāyam., Sch. **-vadha,** m. the murder of a Brāhman, Mn. xi, 89. **-vara,** m. N. of a prince, Kathās. **-varcasá,** n. the excellence or dignity of a Brāhman, AV. (cf. *brahma-v*°). **-vākya,** n. = *-vacana,* KātyŚr., Sch. **-vācana,** n. the recitation of benedictions (as becomes Br°s), Hcat. (w.r. *brāhmaṇa-v*°). **-vidhi,** m. any injunction (contained) in a Brāhmaṇa work, Kauś. **-vilāpa,** m. 'the Brāhman's lament,' N. of an episode of the MBh. (i, 6104 &c., more usually called Baka-vadha-parva). **-vihita,** mfn. prescribed in a Brāhmaṇa, Lāṭy. **-vedam,** ind. (to feed &c.) as many Brāhmans as one knows, Pāṇ. iv, 3, 29, Sch. **-śramaṇa-nyāya,** m. the rule or phrase of the Brāhman Śramaṇa; (*āt*), ind. according to the phrase 'a Br° Śr°' (which involves a contradiction as it expresses a Br° Buddhist; cf. *śramaṇa*), Sāh. **-saṃstha,** mfn. belonging to or abiding with a Br°, W. **-sattama,** m. the best of Br°s, MW. **-saṃtarpaṇa,** n. = *-tarpaṇa,* ib. **-sarvasva,** n. N. of wk. **-sava,** m. N. of a partic. sacrifice, TBr., Sch. **-sāt,** ind. to the Brāhmans (with √*kṛi,* to present to or bestow on the Br°s, MBh.; Hariv.; Kathās.; with √*as,* to belong to the Br°s), MBh. **-stuti,** f. 'praise of the Br°s,' N. of ch. of PurS. **-sva,** n. the property of Br°s, Āpast. **-svara,** m. the accent usual in a Brāhmaṇa, KātyŚr., Sch. **-hita,** mfn. suitable to or fit for a Brahman, W. **Brāhmaṇâkriya,** m. an initiated Br° who is not familiar with sacrifices, Hcat. **Brāhmaṇâc-chaṅsín,** m. (fr. °*ṇāt-śaṅ*°) 'reciting after the Brāhmaṇa or the Brahman,' a priest who assists the Brahman or chief priest at a Soma sacrifice, Br.; ŚrS.; °*sina ukthya,* n., °*si-prayoga,* m., °*si-śastra,* n. N. of wks.; °*sīya,* n. (KātyŚr.), °*sīyā,* f. the office of the Br°-ch°; °*syà,* mfn. relating to the Br°-ch°, ŚBr.; n. his office, ib. **Brāhmaṇâtikrama,** m. disrespect towards Brāhmans, Mn. iii, 63. **Brāhmaṇâtmaka,** mfn. belonging to Br°s, W.; containing an account of the Br°s, ib. **Brāhmaṇâda,** mfn. devouring Br°s (said of a Rākshasa), MBh. **Brāhmaṇâdarśana,** n. absence of Brāhmanical instruction or guidance, Mn. x, 43 (others 'not seeing or consulting Brāhmans'). **-Brāhmaṇâpaśraya,** mfn. seeking refuge in Br°s, MW. **Brāhmaṇâbhāshaṇa,** n. N. of a kind of artificial composition (contained in the Kavi-kalpa-latā, q.v.) **Brāhmaṇâbhyupapatti,** f. protection or preservation of a Brāhman, Mn. viii, 112. **Brāhmaṇêshṭa,** m. the mulberry tree, L. **Brāhmaṇôkta,** mfn. prescribed in a Brāhmaṇa, ŚrS.

Brāhmaṇaka, m. a bad Brāhman, a Br° only by name, MBh.; a country inhabited by warlike Br°s, Pāṇ. v, 2, 71 (°*kīya,* mfn. iv, 2, 104, Vārtt. 30, Pat.); (*ikā*), f. (prob.) a species of lizard, Cat. (cf. *brāhmaṇī*); Trigonella Corniculata, L.

Brāhmaṇāyaná, m. a mere descendant of a Brāhman, ŚBr.; Kauś. (Sch. 'a Br° whose father or elder brother or any elder relative is still alive'); a Brāhman sprung from learned and holy progenitors, W.

Brāhmaṇi, in comp. for °*ṇī*. **-kalpā, -gotrā, -celī, -tamā, -tarā, -bruvā, -matā, -rūpā,** and **-hatā**, f., Pāṇ. vi, 3, 43, Sch.

Brāhmaṇika, mfn. derived from or relating to the Brāhmaṇas, Pāṇ. iv, 3, 72.

Brāhmaṇī, f. (of °*ṇa*) a Brāhmaṇī woman or a Brāhman's wife, Kāṭh.; GṛŚrS.; MBh. &c. (ifc. °*ṇīka*, cf. *sa-brāhmaṇikā*); a kind of lizard with a red tail, R., Sch. (cf. *brāhmaṇikā*); a kind of large-headed ant, L.; a kind of wasp, L.; Clerodendrum Siphonantus, L.; Trigonella Corniculata, L.; Ruta Graveolens, L.; a kind of brass, L.; = *buddhi*, Nilak.; N. of a river, MBh.; w. r. for *brahmāṇī*. **-gāmin**, m. the paramour of a Brāhmaṇī woman or of a Brāhman's wife, W. **-tva**, n. the state or condition of a Brāhmaṇī woman, Vop. **-sattamā**, f. the best of Brāhmaṇī women, MW.

Brāhmaṇī-√bhū, P. *-bhavati* (ind. p. *-bhūya*), to become a Brāhman, ŚBr.

Brā́hmaṇya, mfn. (fr. *brā́hmaṇa*) fit for Brāhmans, MBh.; m. the planet Saturn, L. (cf. 2. *brahmaṇya*); n. the state or rank of a Brāhman, Brāhmanhood, priestly rank or character, ŚBr. &c. &c. (cf. *a-br*°); a multitude or assembly of Brāhmans, R. (cf. Pāṇ. iv, 2, 42).

Brāhmāṇī, w. r. for *brahmāṇī*, q. v.

Brā́hmi, mfn. (fr. *bráhman*) holy, divine, VS.

Brāhmī, f. (of *brāhmá*, q. v.) the Śakti or personified energy of Brahmā (regarded as one of the 8 Mātṛis or divine mothers of created beings; in MBh. ix, 2655 they are said to attend Skanda), L.; speech or the goddess of speech (= Sarasvatī); MBh. i, 19; N. of Durgā, DevīP.; the wife of a Brāhman, W.; (in music) N. of a Mūrchanā, Saṃgīt.; a religious practice, pious usage (°*myā*, ind. according to pious usage), R.; a woman married according to the Brāhma rite, Gaut.; Vishṇ. (cf. *-putra*); the constellation Rohiṇī, L.; a female fish or frog, W.; a species of ant, L.; N. of various plants (Clerodendrum Siphonantus, Ruta Graveolens, Enhydra Hingcha &c.), L.; a kind of brass, L.; N. of a river, Śatr.; (with *saṃhitā*) N. of wk. **-kanda**, m. a species of bulbous plant, L. **-kuṇḍa**, n. N. of a sacred cavity in the ground, Cat. **-tantra**, n. N. of a Tantra. **-putra**, m. the son of a woman married according to the Brāhma rite, Mn. iii, 37. **-śānti-saṃkalpa**, m., **-śānty-avadhāna-krama**, m. N. of wks.

Brāhmya, mfn. relating to Brahmā or Brahmā or to the Brāhmans, Mn.; MBh. &c. (often v. l. *brāhma*); m. (with *muhūrta* or °*taka*) dawn, the hour preceding sunrise, HYog.; Pañcar.; n. (with or scil. *huta*) worship or veneration paid to Brāhmans (considered as one of the 5 great sacraments = *dvijāgryârcā* or *manushya-yajña*), Mn. iii, 73, 74; = *dṛiśya* or *vismaya*, L. **-tīrtha**, n. a partic. part of the hand (cf. under *brāhma*), MārkP. **-muhūrta**, m. = °*myo muhūrtaḥ*, MW. **-huta**, n. = °*myaṃ hutam*, W.

ब्राध्नायन्य *brādhnāyanya*, m. patr. fr. *bradhna*, g. *kuñjâdi* (f. °*yanī*; m. pl. °*yanāḥ*, Pāṇ. v, 3, 113, Sch.)

ब्राह्म *brāhma*, *brāhmaṇa* &c. See p. 741.

ब्रुव *bruva*. See col. 2.

ब्रू *brū*, cl. 2. P. Ā. (Dhātup. xxiv, 35) *bravīti*, *brūte* (only pr. stem; the other forms are supplied by √*vac*, cf. Pāṇ. ii, 4, 53; *brūmi* for *bravīmi*, R.; Subj. *brávas*, °*vat*, RV.; Impv. *brūhi*, ep. also *bravīhi*, *bruvadhvam*; *brūtāt*, Pāṇ. vii, 1, 35, Sch.; impf. *abruvam* for *abravam*, Up.; MBh.; pr. p. Ā. ep. *bruvamāṇa* for *bruvāṇa*; Prec. 2. pl. *brūyāsta*, Nal. xvii, 36, prob. w. r. for *brūyās tat*), to speak, say, tell (either intrans.; or with acc. of pers. or thing; or with acc. of thing and acc., dat., gen. or loc. of person = to tell or relate anything to; with two acc. also = declare or pronounce to be, call), RV. &c. &c.; to speak about any person or thing (acc. with or without *prati* or *adhikṛitya*), Mn.; MBh.; Kāv. &c.; to proclaim, predict, Var.; to answer (either intrans. with *punar* or trans. with *praśnam*, 'a question'), Mn.; MBh.; (with *anyathā*) to speak or decide or judge wrongly, Mn.; Pañcat.; (Ā., rarely P.) to call or profess one's self to be (nom., rarely with *iti*), RV.; Br.; MBh.; (Ā.) to designate for one's self, choose, AitBr.; (Ā.) to be told by itself, tell itself (tell its tale), Pāṇ. iii, 1, 89, Vārtt. 1, Pat. [Cf. Zd. *mrū*.]

Bruva, mf(*ā*)n. calling one's self by a name without any real title to it; being merely nominally (ifc.; cf. *kshatriya-*, *dvija-*, *brāhmaṇa-bruva*).

Bruvāṇa, mfn. speaking, telling, saying; ifc. = prec. (cf. *brahma-br*°).

ब्ली *blī*. See √*vlī*.

ब्लेष्क *bleshka*, m. a snare, noose for catching, Kāṭh.

भ BHA.

भ 1. *bha*, aspirate of *ba*. **-kāra**, m. the letter or sound *bha*.

भ 2. *bha*, (in gram.) N. of the weakest base of nouns (as opp. to *pada* and *aṅga*, q. v.) i. e. of the base before the vowel terminations except in strong cases, before feminine suffixes, and before Taddhitas beginning with vowels or *y*, Pāṇ. i, 4, 18 &c.

भ 3. *bha*, (in prosody) a dactyl. **-vipulā**, f. N. of a metre, Piṅg., Sch.

भ 4. *bha* (√1. *bhā*), m. N. of the planet Venus or its regent (= *śukra*), L.; semblance, delusion, error, L.; (*ā́*), f. light or a beam of l°, lustre, splendour, MBh.; Hariv.; Var. &c. (cf. 2. *bhā*); the shadow of a gnomon, Sūryas.; appearance, resemblance, likeness (ifc.; cf. *agni-bha*, *guḍa-bhā*, *tantu-bha*); n. a star, planet, asterism, lunar a° or mansion (and so also the number 27; cf. *nakshatra*), sign of the zodiac, GṛS.; Sūryas.; Var.; Śatr. &c. **-kakshā**, f. the path of the asterisms, Sūryas. **-gaṇa**, m. = *-cakra*, ib.; Var.; BhP.; = next, Sūryas.; Var. **-gama**, m. the revolution of a planet, Hcat. **-gola**, m. the starry sphere, vault of heaven, Sūryas. **-cakra**, n. the whole multitude of stars or asterisms, ib.; Var.; *-nābhi*, f. the centre of the zodiac, MW. **-datta**, m. N. of an astronomer, VarBṛS. (v. l. *badanta*, q. v.) **-pa**, mfn. the regent of an asterism, ib. **-pañjara**, m. 'cage of a°s,' the firmament, Āryabh. **-pati**, m. lord of a°s, the moon, L. **-praśasta**, mfn. favourable in regard to the a°, ŚāṅkhGṛ. **-bhrama**, m. 'star-revolution,' a sidereal day, Gaṇit. **-maṇḍala**, n. = *-cakra*, Sūryas. **-yuj**, mfn. connected with or present in a lunar mansion, Jyot. **-latā**, f. Paederia Foetida, L. **-varga**, m. = *-cakra*, L. **-vāsara**, m. a sidereal day, Gaṇit. **-vicārin**, mfn. passing through or present in an asterism, Var. **-saṃdhi**, m. 'point of junction of the a°s,' N. of the last quarters of the a°s Āślesha, Jyeshṭhā, and Revatī. **-samūha**, m. 'aggregate of the lunar a°s,' N. of the number 27, Jyot. **-sūcaka**, m. 'indicator of asterisms,' an astrologer, L. **Bhâṅśa**, m. portion of an asterism, Jyot. **Bhêna**, m. 'lord of stars,' the sun or the moon, L. **Bhêśa**, m. the regent of an asterism &c., L.

भ 5. *bha*, m. (prob. onomat.) a bee, L.

भंसस् *bhaṅsas*, n. a partic. part of the intestine or abdomen, RV.; AV. (cf. *bhasád*).

भकभकाय *bhakabhakāya* (onomat.; cf. *bheka*, a frog, and Gk. βρεκεκεκέξ), Nom. Ā. °*yate*, to croak, Subh. (cf. *bakabakāya*, *makamakāya*).

भक्किका *bhakkikā*, f. a cricket, L. (cf. *phaḍiṅgā*).

भक्कुड *bhakkuḍa* or *bhakkura*, m. a species of fish, Bhpr.

भक्त *bhakta*, *bhakti* &c. See p. 743.

भक्ष् *bhaksh* (prob. a secondary form fr. √*bhaj* or Nom. fr. *bhakshá*; cf. also √*bhiksh* and *bhañj*), cl. 10. P. (Dhātup. xxxii, 22) *bhakshấyati* (rarely Ā. °*te*), and in later language also cl. 1. P. Ā. (Dhātup. xxi, 27) *bhakshati*, °*te* (pf. *bhakshayām āsa*, MBh. &c.; fut. *bhakshayishyati*, °*te*, ib.; aor. *ababhakshat*, ŚBr.; Pass. *abhakshi*, BhP.; inf. *bhakshayitum*, MBh., °*kshitum*, Pañcat.; ind. p. *bhakshayitvā*, MBh.; *-bhakshya*, ib.; *-bhaksham*, ŚāṅkhŚr.), to eat or drink, devour, partake of (with acc., in Ved. also with gen.; in the older language usually of fluids, in the later only exceptionally so), RV. &c. &c.; to sting, bite, Kathās.; to consume, use up, waste, destroy, Mn.; MBh. &c.; to drain the resources of, impoverish, Kām.: Caus. *bhakshấyati*, see above; to cause anything (acc.) to be eaten by (acc. or instr.), Pāṇ. i, 4, 52, Vārtt. 7, Pat.: Desid. *bibhakshishati* or °*kshayishati*, to wish to eat or devour, MBh.; ĀpŚr., Sch. (cf. *bibhakshayishu*).

Bhakshá, m. drinking or eating, drink or (in later language) food, RV. &c. &c. (often ifc., with f. *ā*, having anything for food or beverage, eating, drinking, living upon); *-kāra*, m. 'food-maker,' a cook, baker, L.; *-ṃ-kārá*, mfn. furnishing food, MaitrS. (cf. Pāṇ. vi, 3, 72, Vārtt. 2, Pat.); *-ṃ-kṛita* (°*kshám-*), mfn. drunk or eaten, enjoyed, TS.; ĀśvŚr.; *-japa*, m. the prayer muttered while drinking Soma, ĀśvŚr.; *-pattrī*, f. betel-pepper (the leaf of which serves for food), L.; *-bīja*, w. r. for *bhakshya-b*°; *-mantra*, m. a verse spoken while drinking Soma, ŚāṅkhŚr. °**kshaka**, mfn. one who eats, an eater, enjoyer, one who feeds or lives upon (often ifc.), Hariv.; Kāv.; Hit.; voracious, gluttonous, a gourmand, W.; m. food, Hcat.; (*ikā*), f. eating, chewing (cf. *ikshu-bh*°); a meal, food (cf. *ushṭra-bh*°). °**kshaṇa**, mfn. eating, one who eats (cf. *dāḍima-*, *pāpa-bh*°); n. the act of eating, drinking, feeding, ŚrS.; Nir.; MBh. &c.; eating what excites thirst, L.; chewing, L.; the being eaten by (instr.), Mn.; R.; (*bhấ*°) a drinking vessel, RV. °**kshaṇīya**, mfn. to be (or being) eaten, Pañcat.; *-tā*, f. eatableness, ŚārṅgP. °**kshayitavya**, mfn. to be eaten or devoured, edible, MBh.; Pañcat. °**kshayitṛi**, m. an eater, enjoyer, MBh. °**kshitá**, mfn. eaten or drunk, chewed, masticated, devoured, enjoyed, partaken of, ŚBr. &c. &c.; eaten (said of a partic. bad pronunciation of words), L.; n. the being eaten by (instr.), R.; *-śesha*, m. remnants of food, leavings, MW.; °*shâhāra*, m. a meal of leavings, ib. °**kshitṛi**, m. = °*kshayitṛi*, MBh. °**kshin**, mfn. (mostly ifc.; °*shi-tva*, n.) eating, devouring, MBh.; Hariv.; R. °**kshiván**, mfn. eating, enjoying, TBr. (cf. *bhakti-ván*, *-vás*). °**kshya**, mfn. to be eaten, eatable, fit for food, Mn.; MBh. &c.; n. anything eaten, food (esp. such as requires mastication), ib.; m. food, dish, ib. (prob. w. r. for *bhaksha*); *-kāra*, *-kāraka* and *-ṃ-kāra*, m. a baker, L.; *-bīja*, m. Buchanania Latifolia, L.; *-bhakshaka*, m. du. food and the eater, Hit.; *-bhojya-maya*, mf(*ī*)n. consisting of food of all kinds, MBh.; *-bhojya-vihāravat*, mfn. furnished with various kinds of food and places of refection, ib.; *-mālyâpaṇa*, m. a market where victuals and garlands are sold, ib.; *-vastu*, n. edible matter, victuals, viands, MW.; °*kshyâbhakshya*, n. what may and may not be eaten, food allowed and prohibited, Mn. v, 26; °*kshyâlābu*, f. a variety of cucumber (= *rājâlābu*), L.

भक्षटक *bhakshaṭaka*, m. a variety of Asteracantha Longifolia, L.

भक्षाली *bhakshālī*, f. N. of a place, g. *dhūmâdi* (not in Kāś.)

भक्षिणी *bhakshiṇī*, f. Coix Barbata, L.

भग *bhága*. See p. 743, col. 2.

भगन *bhagana*, w. r. for *bha-gaṇa* (see under 4. *bha*, col. 2).

भगनराय *bhaganarāya*, m. N. of a man, Cat.

भगल *bhagala*, m. N. of a man, Pravar. (cf. g. *arīhaṇâdi*); (*ā*), f. N. of a woman, g. *bāhvâdi* (cf. *bhāgala*, °*laka* &c.)

भगवत् *bhágavat* &c. See p. 743, col. 3.

भगाल *bhagāla*, n. = *kapāla*, a skull, PārGṛ. (cf. Uṇ. iii, 76, Sch.)

Bhagālin, m. 'bedecked with skulls,' N. of Śiva, L.

भगिन् *bhagín*, *bhagīratha*. See p. 744.

भगेश *bhagêsa*. See p. 743, col. 3.

भग्न *bhagna* &c. See under √*bhañj*.

भग्नी *bhagnī*. See p. 744, col. 2.

भंकारी *bham-kārī*, f. 'uttering the sound *bham*, humming,' a gad-fly, L.

भङ्ग *bhaṅgá* &c. See p. 744, col. 3.

भङ्गान *bhaṅgāna*, m. Cyprinus Bangana, L.

भङ्गारी *bhaṅgārī*, f. = *bham-kārī*, a gad-fly, L.

भङ्गि *bhaṅgi*, °*gu*, °*gura* &c. See p. 744.

भज् *bhaj*, cl. 1. P. Ā. (Dhātup. xxxiii, 29) *bhájati*, °*te* (2. sg. as Impv. *bhakshi*, RV.; pf. P. *babhája*, Ā. *bheje*, RV. &c.; 2. sg. *babhaktha*, ŚBr.; *bhejitha*, Pāṇ. vi, 4, 122; aor. P. 2. 3. sg. *abhāk*, RV.; Br.; *abhākshīt*, °*kshus*, BhP.; Subj. *bhakshat*, RV.; Ā. *ábhakshi*, °*kta*, RV. &c.; Prec. Ā. *bhakshīyá*, RV.; 3. sg. °*kshīshṭa*, Br.; °*kshīta*, SV.; fut. *bhakshyati*, °*te*, Br. &c.; *bhajishyati*, °*te*, MBh. &c.; *bhaktā*, Gr.; inf. *bhaktum*, Br. &c.; *bhajitum*, MBh.; ind. p. *bhaktvā*, AV. &c., °*tvāya*, RV.; *-bhajya* and *-bhājam*, Br.), to divide, distribute, allot or apportion to (dat. or gen.), share with (instr.), RV. &c. &c.; (Ā.) to grant, bestow, furnish, supply, ib.; Ā. (rarely P.) to obtain as one's share, receive as (two acc.), partake of, enjoy (also carnally), possess, have (acc., Ved. also gen.), ib.; (Ā., rarely P.) to turn or resort to, engage in, assume (as a form), put on (garments), experience, incur, undergo, feel, go or fall into (with acc., esp. of abstract noun, e.g. *bhītim*, to feel terror; *nidrām*, to fall asleep; *maunam*, to become silent), MBh.; Kāv. &c.; to pursue, practise, cultivate, Mn.; R.; Suśr.; to fall to the lot or share of (acc.), MBh.; R. &c.; to declare for, prefer, choose (e.g. as a servant), MBh.; to serve, honour, revere, love, adore, MBh.; Kāv. &c.: Caus. *bhājáyate*, °*te* (aor. *abībhajuḥ*, ŚBr., *ababhājat*, Gr.), to divide, Sūryas.; to deal out, distribute, Gaut.; to cause any one (acc.) to partake of or enjoy (acc. or gen.), RV.; ŚBr.; to put to flight, pursue, chase, drive into (acc.), Bhaṭṭ.; to cook, dress (food), Vop.: Desid. *bibhakshati*, °*te*, MBh. (cf. √*bhiksh*): Intens. *bābhajyate*, *bābhakti*, Gr. [Cf. Gk. φαγεῖν; φᾱγός, φηγός; Lat. *fāgus*; Goth. Old S. *bōk*; Germ. *Buch*, *Buchstabe*; Eng. *buck-*, *beech*.]

Bhaktá, mfn. distributed, assigned, allotted, RV. &c. &c.; divided, Sūryas.; (ifc.) forming part of, belonging to, Pāṇ., Sch.; (ifc.) loved, liked, Pāṇ. iv, 2, 54; served, worshipped, W.; dressed, cooked, ib.; engaged in, occupied with, attached or devoted to, loyal, faithful, honouring, worshipping, serving (loc., gen., acc. or comp.), MBh.; Kāv. &c.; m. a worshipper, votary (esp. as N. of a division of the Śāktas), IW. 523, n. 1; n. food or a meal, Mn.; MBh. &c.; boiled rice, Uttarar.; any eatable grain boiled with water; a vessel, L.; a share, portion, MW. **–kaṅsa**, m. a dish of food, Pāṇ. vi, 2, 71, Sch. **–kara**, m. = *-kāra*, Pat.; artificially prepared incense, L. **–kāra**, m. 'food-preparer,' a cook, L. **–kṛitya**, n. preparations for a meal, Divyâv. (*kṛita-bh*°, one who has made a meal, ib.) **–gītāṭikā**, f. N. of wk. **–cchanda**, m. desire of food, hunger, appetite, Suśr. **–jayantī**, f. N. of wk. **–jā**, f. nectar, W. **–tā**, f. devotedness, attachment, inclination, W. **–tūrya**, n. music played during a meal, L. **–tva**, n. (ifc.) the forming part of, belonging to, Pāṇ. vii, 4, 30, Vārtt. 2, Sch. **–da** (Mn.), **-dātṛi** (W.), **-dāyaka** (Mn.), **-dāyin** (MW.), mfn. giving food, supporter, maintainer. **–dāsa**, m. 'food slave,' a slave who serves for his daily food, Mn. viii, 415. **–dvesha**, m. aversion from food, loss of appetite, Suśr.; °*shin*, mfn. one who has lost his appetite, ib. **–pātra**, n. = *-kaṅsa*, Rājat. **–pulāka**, m. or n. (?) a mouthful of rice kneaded into a ball, L. **–pratishṭhā**, f. N. of wk. **–maṇḍa** or °**ḍaka**, m. n. the scum of boiled rice, L. **–mayastotra**, n., **-mālā**, f. (and °*lāgra-grantha*, m. cf. RTL. 117), **-mīmāṅsā**, f., **-moda-taraṃgiṇī**, f. N. of wks. **–ruci**, f. = *-cchanda*, Suśr. **–rocana**, mfn. exciting appetite, ib. **–vatsala**, mfn. kind to worshippers or to faithful attendants, MW.; *-māhātmya*, n. N. of ch. of PadmaP. **–vilāsa**, m., **-vaibhava**, n., **-vrāta-saṃtoshika**, m. or n. N. of wks. **–śaraṇa**, n. 'food-receptacle,' a store-room or kitchen, ĀśvGṛ. **–śālā**, f. 'f°-hall,' (prob.) = prec. (others 'audience-chamber'), Rājat. **–siktha** or °**thaka**, m. = *-pulāka*, L. **Bhaktākāṅkshā**, f. = °*ta-cchanda*, Suśr. **Bhaktâgra**, m. or n. a refectory, Divyâv. **Bhaktâbhilāsha**, m. = °*ta-cchanda*, Suśr. **Bhaktâbhisāra**, m. an eating room (others 'giving of food'), Divyâv. **Bhaktâmṛita**, n. and **Bhaktârādhana-prayoga-maṇi-mālikā**, f. N. of wks. **Bhaktâruci**, f. = °*ta-dvesha*, Suśr. **Bhaktôddeśaka**, m. 'food-prescriber,' a partic. official in a Buddhist monastery, L. **Bhaktôpasādhaka**, m. 'food-dresser,' a cook, R.

Bhaktí, f. distribution, partition, separation, RV.; TāṇḍBr. &c. (cf. *kshetra-*, *bhaṅgi-bh*°); a division, portion, share, AitBr.; a division of a Sāman (also called *vidhi*, of which 7 or 5 are enumerated), Lāṭy.; Śaṃk.; division by streaks or lines, Ragh.; a streak, line, variegated decoration, Hariv.; Kāv.; a row, series, succession, order (°*tyā* and °*ti-tas*, ind. in succession), RPrāt.; (ifc.) the being a part of (*aj-bhakteḥ*, 'on the part of the vowels'), belonging to, Siddh. &c.; that which belongs to or is contained in anything else, an attribute, Nir.; Prāt.; predisposition (of body to any disease), Car.; attachment, devotion, fondness for, devotion to (with loc., gen. or ifc.), trust, homage, worship, piety, faith or love or devotion (as a religious principle or means of salvation, together with *karman*, 'works,' and *jñāna*, 'spiritual knowledge;' cf. IW. 326, RTL. 97), ŚvetUp.; Bhag.; Kāv.; Pur. &c.; (ifc.) assumption of the form of, Megh. 61; often w.r. for *bhaṅgi* or *bhukti*; (°*tyā*), ind. not in the regular sense, figuratively, Śaṃk. **–kara**, mf(*ī*)n., Pāṇ. iii, 2, 21. **–kalpataru**, m., **-kalpalatā**, f., N. of wks. **–gamya**, mfn. accessible by devotion (Śiva), Śivag. **–candrikā**, f., **-candrikôllāsa**, m., **-candrôdaya**, m. N. of wks. **–ccheda**, m. pl. divided lines or streaks of painting or decoration (esp. the separating or distinguishing marks on the forehead, nose, cheeks, breast and arms, which denote devotion to Vishṇu, Kṛishṇa &c.), Hariv.; Megh.; VP. **–jña**, mfn. knowing faith or devotion, faithfully attached; *-tā*, f. (Jātak.), *-tva*, n. (Kām.) devotion, faithfulness, loyalty. **–tattva-rasāyana**, n., **-taraṃgiṇī**, f., **-dīpikā**, f., **-dūtī**, f. N. of wks. **–namra**, mfn. bent down in devotion, making a humble obeisance, Megh.; VP. **–pūrvakam** (Pañcat.), **-pūrvam** (Cat.), ind. preceded by devotion, devoutly, reverentially. **–pūrva-paksha**, m., **-prakaraṇa**, n., **-pratipādaka**, m. or n., **-prabhā**, f. N. of wks. **–pravaṇa**, mfn. faithfully devoted, Vṛishabhân. **–praśaṅsā-varṇana**, n., **-prârthanā**, f., **-bindu**, m., **-bhava**, m. N. of wks. **–bhāj**, mfn. possessing true devotion, firmly attached or devoted to (loc. or comp.), Pañcat.; Śatr. **–bhāva-pradīpa**, m., **-bhūshaṇa-saṃdarbha**, m., **-mañjarī**, f. N. of wks. **–mat**, mfn. = *-bhāj*, MBh.; Kāv. &c.; accompanied by devotion or loyalty, BhP. **–mahat**, mfn. truly devoted, Divyâv. **–mahôdaya**, m. N. of wk. **–mārga**, m. 'the way of devotion' (regarded as a means of salvation and opp. to *karma-* and *jñāna-m*°; cf. above), RTL. 63; *-nirūpaṇa*, n., °*gôpadeśa-dīkshā*, f. N. of wks. **–mīmāṅsā-sūtra**, n., **-muktâvalī**, f. N. of wks. **–yoga**, m. devoted attachment, loving devotion, BhP.; N. of 1st ch. of Śiva-gītā. **–ratna**, n., **-ratnâkara**, m., **-ratnâvalī**, f. N. of wks. **–rasa**, m. a sense of devotion, feeling of loving faith, Kathās.; °*sâbdhi-kaṇikā*, f., °*sâmṛita*, n., °*sâmṛita-bindu*, m., °*sâmṛita-sindhu*, m., °*sâyana*, n. N. of wks. **–rāga**, m. affection or predilection for (loc.), MBh. **–laharī**, f., **-vardhinī**, f. N. of wks. **–vāda**, m. declaration of devotion or attachment, MBh. **–vijaya**, m., **-vilāsa**, m. (and °*sa-tattva-dīpikā*, f.), **-vivṛiddhy-upâya-grantha**, m., **-śata**, n., **-śataka**, n., **-śāstra**, n., **-saṃvardhana-śataka**, n., **-saṃdarbha**, m. (and °*bha-padyâvalī*, f.), **-saṃnyāsa-nirṇaya-vivaraṇa**, n., **-sāgara**, m., **-sāmānya-nirūpaṇa**, n., **-sāra**, m. (and °*ra-saṃgraha*, m.), **-siddhânta**, m., **-sudhôdaya**, m., **-sūtra**, n. (RTL. 97), **-haṅsa**, m. N. of wks. **–hīna**, mfn. destitute of devotion, Mudr. **–hetu-nirṇaya**, m. N. of wk. **Bhaktī-dyāvāpṛithivī**, f. du. N. of the deities to whom the Garbha-puroḍāśa is offered, ĀpŚr., Sch.; °*vya*, mfn. sacred to these deities, ĀpŚr. **Bhakty-adhikaraṇa-mālā**, f., **Bhakty-upakrama**, m., **Bhakty-ullāsa-mañjarī**, f. N. of wks.

Bhaktika, only ifc.; see *uttara-*, *eka-*, and *paurva-bhaktika*.

Bhaktila, mfn. attached, faithful, trusty (said of horses), L.

Bhaktiván (MaitrS.), °**vás** (AV.), mfn. partaking of (with gen.; cf. *bhakshi-ván*).

Bhaktṛi, mfn. devotedly attached, an adorer, worshipper, MW. **–tva**, n. adoration, worship, ib.

Bhága, m. (ifc. f. *ā* and *ī*, g. *bahv-ādi*) 'dispenser,' gracious lord, patron (applied to gods, esp. to Savitṛi), RV.; AV.; N. of an Āditya (bestowing wealth and presiding over love and marriage, brother of the Dawn, regent of the Nakshatra Uttara-Phalgunī; Yāska enumerates him among the divinities of the highest sphere; according to a later legend his eyes were destroyed by Rudra), ib. &c. &c.; the Nakshatra U°-Ph°, MBh. vi, 81; the sun, ib. iii, 146; the moon, L.; N. of a Rudra, MBh.; good fortune, happiness, welfare, prosperity, RV.; AV.; Br.; Yājñ.; BhP.; (ifc. f. *ā*) dignity, majesty, distinction, excellence, beauty, loveliness, RV.; AV.; Br.; GṛS.; BhP.; (also n., L.) love, affection, sexual passion, amorous pleasure, dalliance, RV.; AV.; Br.; KātyŚr.; BhP.; (n., L.; ifc. f. *ā*) the female organ, pudendum muliebre, vulva, Mn.; MBh. &c.; (*ā*), f. in *bhagā-nāmnī* below; n. a partic. Muhūrta, Cat.; the perinaeum of males, L.; m. n. = *yatna*, *prayatna*, *kīrti*, *yaśas*, *vairāgya*, *icchā*, *jñāna*, *mukti*, *moksha*, *dharma*, *śrī*, L. [Cf. Zd. *bagha* = Old Pers. *baga*; Gk. Ζεὺς βαγαῖος; Slav. *bogŭ*, *bogatŭ*; Lith. *bagótas*, *na-bágas*.] **–kāma**, mf(*ā*)n. desirous of sexual pleasure, KātyŚr. **–ghna**, m. 'slayer of Bhaga,' N. of Śiva, MBh. **–tti** (*bhága-*), f. (for *bh*° + *datti*) a gift of fortune, RV. ix, 63, 17. **–datta**, m. 'given by Bhaga,' N. of a prince of Prāg-jyotisha, MBh.; of a king of Kāmrūp, MW. **–dā**, f. 'giving welfare,' N. of one of the Mātṛis attending on Skanda, MBh. **–dāraṇa**, n. a partic. disease, Hcat. (cf. *bhagaṃ-dara*). **–deva**, mfn. 'whose god is the female organ,' lustful, a libertine, MBh. **–devata**, mf(*ā*)n. having Bhaga for a deity, R.; (*ā*), f. a hymeneal divinity, W. **–daivata**, mfn. = prec. mfn. (with *nakshatra*), MBh.; conferring conjugal felicity, ib.; n. the Nakshatra Uttara Phalgunī, ib.; *-māsa*, m. the month Phālguna, ib. **–dheya**, m. N. of a man, VP. **–nandā**, f. N. of one of the Mātṛis attending on Skanda, MBh. **–netra** (ibc.), Bhaga's eyes; *-ghna*, *-nipātana*, *-han*, *-hara* (MBh.); *-hṛit* (Suśr.); °*trântaka* (L.), °*trâpahârin* (Hariv.), m. 'destroyer of Bhaga's eyes,' N. of Śiva. **–m-dara**, m. 'lacerating the vulva,' a fistula in the pudendum muliebre or in the anus &c. (5 to 8 forms enumerated; cf. *bhaga-dāraṇa*), Suśr.; ŚārṅgS. (cf. Kāś. on Pāṇ. iii, 2, 41); N. of an ancient sage, Var. **–pura**, n. N. of the city of Multān, L. **–bhakta** (*bhága-*), mfn. fortune-favoured, endowed with prosperity, RV. i, 24, 5. **–bhakshaka**, m. 'living by the vulva,' a procurer, pander, L. **–1. -vat**, ind. like a vulva, Vishṇ., Sch. **–2. -vat**, mfn., see below. **–vitta**, m. N. of a man, Pāṇ. iv, 1, 90, Sch. **–vṛitti**, mfn. subsisting by the vulva, Nār. **–vedana**, mfn. proclaiming connubial felicity, MBh. (v.l. for *-daivata*). **–han**, m. 'slayer of Bhaga,' N. of Śiva (transferred to Vishṇu), MBh. xiii, 7009. **–hārin**, m. = *-ghna*, MBh. **Bhagâkshi-han**, m. = *bhaga-netra-han*, MBh. **Bhagâṅka**, m. the mark of the vulva (as a brand), ib.; mf(*ā*)n. marked or branded with a v°, ib. **Bhagâṅkita**, mfn. = prec. mfn., ib. **Bhagâṅkura**, m. the clitoris, L. **Bhagâdhāna**, mfn. bestowing matrimonial felicity, Hariv. **Bhagā-nāmnī**, f. having the name 'Bhagā,' Kāṭh. **Bhagâsya**, mfn. whose mouth is used as a vulva, Vishṇ. **Bhage-'vita** (= *bhage* + *avita*, Padap.), satisfied with good fortune or prosperity, RV. x, 106, 8. **Bhageśa**, m. the lord of fortune or prosperity, ŚvetUp.

Bhagavac, in comp. for °*vat*. **–caraṇâravinda-dhyāna**, n. N. of wk. **–chāstra** (for °*vat-śā*°), n. N. of ch. of VarP.

2. **Bhágavat**, mfn. (for 1. see under *bhága*) possessing fortune, fortunate, prosperous, happy, RV.; AV.; GṛS.; BhP.; glorious, illustrious, divine, adorable, venerable, AV. &c. &c.; holy (applied to gods, demigods, and saints as a term of address, either in voc. *bhagavan*, *bhagavas*, *bhagos* [cf. Pāṇ. viii, 3, 1, Vārtt. 2, Pat., and viii, 3, 17], f. *bhagavatī*, m. pl. *bhagavantaḥ*; or in nom. with 3. sg. of the verb; with Buddhists often prefixed to the titles of their sacred writings); m. 'the divine or adorable one,' N. of Vishṇu-Kṛishṇa, Bhag.; BhP.; of Śiva, Kathās.; of a Buddha or a Bodhi-sattva or a Jina, Buddh. (cf. MWB. 23); (*ī*), f., see below. **–tattva-dīpikā**, f. and **tattva-mañjarī**, f. N. of wks. **–tama** and **-tara**, mfn. more or most holy or adorable, GṛS. **–tva**, n. the condition or rank of Vishṇu, BhP. **–padī**, f. N. of the source of the Gaṅgā (said to have sprung from Vishṇu's foot or from an aperture made in the mundane egg by the toe-nail of Vishṇu), ib. RTL. 347. **–pādâcārya**, m. N. of an author, Cat. **–pādâbhāshaṇa**, n., **-pūjā-vidhi**, m., **-pratishṭhā-vidhi**, m., **-prasāda-mālā**, f., **-samārādhana-vidhi**, m., **-siddhânta-saṃgraha**, m., **-smṛiti**, f., **-sva-**

tantratā, f., **-svarūpa,** n., **-svarūpa-vishaya-śaṅkā-nirāsa,** m. N. of wks.

Bhagavatī, f. (of °*vat*) N. of Lakshmī, Pañcar.; of Durgā, ib.; = °*ty-aṅga* (below). **-kīlaka,** m., **-keśâdi-pāda-stava,** m., **-gītā,** f. N. of wks. **-dāsa,** m. N. of a man, Cat. **-padya-pushpâñjali,** m., **-purāṇa,** n., **-bhāgavata-purāṇa,** n., **-sūtra,** n., **-stuti,** f. N. of wks. **Bhagavaty-aṅga,** n. N. of the 5th Aṅga of the Jainas.

Bhagavad, in comp. for °*vat.* **-arcana,** n. 'worship of Bhagavat i.e. Kṛishṇa;' *-prastāva,* m. and *-māhātmya,* n. N. of chs. of PadmaP. **-ānanda,** m. N. of an author, Cat. **-ārādhana,** n. 'propitiation of Bh°;' *-krama,* m., *-samarthana,* n. N. of wks. **-āśraya-bhūta,** mfn. being the seat or resting-place of Bh°, Ml. **-udyama-nāṭaka,** n. N. of a play. **-upanayana,** n. 'initiation of Bh°,' N. of wk. **-gītā,** f. pl. (sometimes with *upanishad;* once °*ta,* n., BhP.) 'Kṛishṇa's song,' N. of a celebrated mystical poem (interpolated in the MBh. where it forms an episode of 18 chapters from vi, 830–1532, containing a dialogue between Kṛishṇa and Arjuna, in which the Pantheism of the Vedânta is combined with a tinge of the Sāṃkhya and the later principle of *bhakti* or devotion to Kṛishṇa as the Supreme Being; cf. IW. 122 &c.); *-gūḍhârtha-dīpikā,* f., *-ṭīkā,* f., *-tātparya,* n. (°*rya-candrikā,* f., °*rya-dīpikā,* f., °*rya-nirṇaya,* m., °*rya-bodhikā,* f., °*rya-bodhinī,* f.), *-pratipada,* n., *-prasthāna,* n., *-bodhaka,* n., *-bhāva-prakāśa,* m., *-bhāshya,* n. (and °*shya-vivaraṇa,* n.), *-māhātmya,* n., *-rahasya,* n., -°*rtha* (°*târ°*) *-saṃgraha,* m. (°*ha-rakshā,* f.), -°*rtha-sāra,* m., °*rtha-stotra,* n., *-lakshâbharaṇa,* n., *-laghu-vyākhyā,* f., *-vivaraṇa,* n., *-vyākhyā,* f., -°*śaya* (°*tâś°*), n., *-samaṅgalâcāra-śloka-paddhati,* f., *-sāra,* m., *-sāra-saṃgraha,* m., *-hetu-nirṇaya,* m. N. of wks. **-guṇa** (ibc.), 'the qualities or virtues of Bh°;' *-darpaṇa,* m., *-sāra-saṃgraha,* m. N. of wks. **-govinda,** m. N. of a poet, Cat. **-dāsa,** m. N. of the author of a Comm. on Gīt. **-dṛiśa,** mf(*ī*)n. resembling the Supreme, ChUp. **-druma,** m. 'Bh°'s (i.e. Buddha's) tree,' (prob.) the sacred fig-tree, L. **-dharma-varṇana,** n., **-dhyāna-muktâvalī,** f., **-dhyāna-sopāna,** n. N. of wks. **-bhakti** (ibc.), 'devotion to Bh° or Kṛishṇa;' *-candrikā,* f., *-candrikôllāsa,* m., *-taraṃgiṇī,* f., *-nirṇaya,* m., *-māhātmya,* n., *-ratnâvalī,* f., *-rasâyana,* n., *-vilāsa,* m., *-viveka,* m., *-sādhana,* n., *-sāra-saṃgraha,* m., *-stotra,* n. N. of wks. **-bhaṭṭa,** m. N. of the author of a Comm. on the Rasa-taraṃgiṇī, Cat. **-bhāvaka,** m. N. of the author of a Comm. on ChUp., ib. **-bhāskara,** m. N. of wk. (= *bhagavanta-bh°*). **-yauvanôdgama,** m. N. of ch. of the Kṛishṇa-krīḍita. **-rāta,** m. N. of a man, BhP. **-vilāsa-ratnâvalī,** f. N. of wk. **-viśesha,** m. N. of a man, Buddh.

Bhagavadīya, m. a worshipper of Bhagavat i.e. Vishṇu or Kṛishṇa (*-tva,* n.), BhP.

Bhagavan, in comp. for °*vat.* **-nanda-saṃvāda,** m. N. of BrahmavP. iv, ch. 74–79. **-nāma** (ibc. for °*man*), 'the name or names of Bhagavat i.e. Vishṇu;' *-kaumudī,* f., *-māhātmya,* n. (°*tmya-saṃgraha,* m.), *-smaraṇa-stuti,* f., °*mâmṛita-rasôdaya,* m., °*mavalī,* f. N. of wks. **-maya,** mf(*ī*)n. wholly devoted to Vishṇu or Kṛishṇa, Kathās. **-māna-pūjā,** f. N. of a hymn by Śaṃkarâcārya.

Bhagavanta, m. N. of the author of the Mukunda-vilāsa. **-deva,** m. N. of a prince (king of Bhareha, son of Sāhi-deva and a patron of Nīla-kaṇṭha, cf. next), Cat. **-bhāskara,** m. N. of a law-book by Nīla-kaṇṭha (17th cent.)

Bhagaval, in comp. for °*vat.* **-lāñchana-dhāraṇa-pramāṇa-śata-pradarśana,** n., **-līlā-cintāmaṇi,** m. N. of wks.

Bhagas, n. = *bhaga,* ĀśvGṛ. i, 23, 15.

Bhagín, mfn. prosperous, happy, fortunate, perfect, splendid, glorious, AV.; ŚBr. (superl. °*gí-tama*); TBr.; ŚrS.; m. N. of Sch. on Amara-kosa (abridged fr. *bhagī-ratha,* q.v.), L.; (*inī*), f., see below.

Bhaginikā, f. a little sister, Kāthas. (cf. next).

Bhaginī, f. a sister ('the happy or fortunate one,' as having a brother), Mn.; MBh. &c. (in familiar speech, also for *-bhrātṛi,* 'brother,' Pañcat.); any woman or wife, L. **-pati** (Kathās.), **-bhartṛi** (g. *yuktârohy-ādi*), m. a sister's husband. **-bhrātṛi,** m. du. sister and brother, L. **-suta,** m. a sister's son, Pañcat.

Bhaginīya, m. (prob.) a sister's son.

Bhagīna. See *viśo-* and *veśa-bhagīna.*

Bhagīratha, m. (prob. fr. *bhagin + ratha,* 'having a glorious chariot'), N. of an ancient king (son of Dilipa and great-grandfather of Sagara, king of Ayodhyā; he brought down the sacred Gaṅgā from heaven to earth and then conducted this river to the ocean in order to purify the ashes of his ancestors, the 60,000 sons of Sagara; cf. IW. 322), MBh.; R.; Pur. &c.; N. of sev. authors (also with *ṭhakkura* and *megha;* cf. *bhagin*), Cat.; of an architect of recent date, Inscr.; of a mountain, Śatr. **-kanyā,** f. 'daughter of Bhagī-ratha,' N. of Gaṅgā, Prasannar. **-datta,** m. N. of a poet, Cat. **-patha** (A.), **-prayatna** (MW.), m. 'Bh°'s path or labour,' N. of any Herculean effort or exertion. **-yaśas,** f. N. of a daughter of Prasena-jit, Kathās. **-sutā,** f. = *-kanyā,* MBh. **Bhagīrathôpâkhyāna,** n. N. of ch. xxxv of the Vāsishṭha-rāmāyaṇa.

Bhagos. See *bhagavat.*

Bhagnī, f. = *bhaginī,* a sister, L.

Bhajaka, m. a distributer, apportioner (see *cīvara-bh°*); a worshipper, MW. °**jana,** m. N. of a prince, VP.; n. the act of sharing, W.; possession, ib.; (ifc.) reverence, worship, adoration, Prab., Sch. (also *-tā,* f., with loc., Cāṇ.); *-vārika,* m. a partic. official in a Buddhist monastery, L.; °*nâ-nanda,* m. N. of an author, Cat.; °*nâmṛita,* n. N. of wk. °**janīya,** mfn. to be loved or revered or waited upon, venerable, MBh.; BhP. °**jamāna,** mfn. apportioning &c., MBh.; fitting, meet, appropriate, L.; N. of various princes, Hariv.; Pur. °**ji,** m. N. of a prince (also °*jin* and °*jina*), ib. °**jitavya** (MBh.), °**jenya** (BhP.), °**jya** (Vop.), mfn. = °*janīya.*

Bhaja-govinda-stotra, n. N. of wk. (cf. *bhagavad-govinda*).

भजेरथ *bhajératha,* RV. x, 60, 2 (Padap. *bhaje + aratha*), prob. *bhajé* (inf.) or *bháje* (1. sg. fr. √*bhaj*) + *ráthasya.*

भञ्ज् 1. *bhañj,* cl. 7. P. (Dhātup. xxix, 16) *bhanakti* (pf. *babháñja,* RV. &c., 3. pl. Ā. *babhañjire,* Hariv.; aor. *abhāṅkshīt,* MBh.; fut. *bhaṅkshyati,* °*ktā,* ib.; ind. p. *bhaṅktvā, bhaktvā* or *-bhajya,* ib.), to break, shatter, split, RV. &c. &c.; to break into, make a breach in (a fortress, with acc.), Hit.; to rout, put to flight, defeat (an army), MBh.; Hariv.; Rājat.; to dissolve (an assembly), Hcar.; to break up i.e. divide (a Sūtra), Siddh.; to bend, R.; to check, arrest, suspend, frustrate, disappoint, MBh.; Kāv. &c.: Pass. *bhajyáte* (ep. also °*ti;* aor. *abhāji* or *abhañji,* Pāṇ. vi, 4, 33), to be broken or break (intr.) &c., AV. &c. &c.: Caus. *bhañjayati* (aor. *ababhañjat*), Gr.: Desid. *bibhaṅkshati,* ib.: Intens. *bambhajyate* or °*jīti,* ib. [Perhaps for orig. *bhrañj;* cf. *bhraj;* Lat. *frangere, nau-fraga;* Germ. *brechen;* Eng. *break.*]

Bhagna, mfn. broken (lit. and fig.), shattered, split, torn, defeated, checked, frustrated, disturbed, disappointed, Mn.; MBh. &c. (sometimes forming the first instead of the second part of a comp., e.g. *grīvā-bhagna, dharma-bh°* for *bhagna-grīva, -dharma;* also 'one who has broken a limb,' BhP.); bent, curved, R.; lost, Mn. viii, 148; n. the fracture of a leg, Suśr. **-kāma,** see *a-bhagnak°.* **-krama,** n. the breaking i.e. violating of grammatical order or construction, Pratāp. **-ceshṭa,** mfn. broken in effort, disappointed, MW. **-jānu,** m. having a broken knee or leg, W. **-tā,** f. the condition of being broken; (with *pravahaṇasya*) shipwreck, Daś. **-tāla,** m. (in music) a kind of measure, Saṃgīt. **-daṇshṭra,** mfn. having the tusks or fangs broken, R. **-danta-nakha,** mfn. having the teeth and claws br°, Kām. **-darpa,** mfn. one whose pride is br°, humiliated, MW. **-nidra,** mfn. one whose sleep is br° or interrupted, ib. **-netra,** mfn. affecting the eyes (said of a kind of fever), L. **-pariṇāma,** mfn. prevented from finishing (anything), Siṇhâs. **-pādarksha** (°*da-ṛik°*), n. N. of 6 Nakshatras collectively (viz. Punar-vasū, Uttarâshāḍhā, Kṛittikā, Uttara-Phalgunī, Pūrva-Bhādrapadā, and Viśākhā; cf. *push-kara*), L. **-pārśva,** mfn. suffering from pain in the side, Suśr. **-pṛishṭha,** mfn. 'broken-backed,' coming before or in front of (?), L. **-prakrama,** n. 'broken arrangement,' (in rhet.) the use of a word which does not correspond to one used before, Kpr. (also *-tā,* f., Sāh.) **-pratijña,** mfn. one who has br° a promise, faithless, Hariv. **-bāhu,** mfn. br°-armed, BhP. **-bhāṇḍa,** mfn. one who has br° his pots, MW. **-manas,** mfn. 'broken-hearted,' discouraged, disappointed, BhP. **-manoratha,** mf(*ā*)n. one whose wishes are disappointed, R. **-māna,** mfn. = *-darpa,* BhP. **-yācña,** mf(*ā*)n. one whose request has been refused, ib. **-yuge,** ind. when the yoke is broken, Mn. viii, 291. **-vishāṇaka,** mfn. having br° horns or tusks, L. **-vrata,** mfn. one who has br° a vow, Rājat. **-śakti,** mfn. one whose strength is br°, Rājat. **-śṛiṅga,** mfn. = *-vishāṇaka,* Śak. i, 32 (v.l.) **-saṃdhi,** mfn. one whose joints are br°, GāruḍaP. **-saṃdhika,** n. buttermilk (= *ghola*), L. **Bhagnâtman,** m. 'broken-bodied,' N. of the Moon (cut in two by the trident of Śiva), L. **Bhagnâpad,** mfn. one who has conquered adversity, ŚārṅgP. **Bhagnâśa,** mfn. one whose hopes are broken, disappointed in expectation, Hit. **Bhagnâsthi,** mfn. one whose bones are broken, Śak.; *-bandha,* m. a splint, L. **Bhagnôtsāha-kriyâtman,** mfn. one whose energy and labour have been frustrated, MBh. **Bhagnôdyama,** mfn. one whose efforts have been frustrated, Pañcar. **Bhagnôru-daṇḍa,** mfn. 'broken-thighed,' having the bone of the thigh fractured, BhP.

Bhaṅktṛi, mfn. one who breaks, breaker, crusher, destroyer, Mn.; Bālar.

Bhaṅgá, mfn. breaking, bursting (said of the Soma), RV. ix, 61, 13; m. breaking, splitting, dividing, shattering, breaking down or up, VS. &c. &c.; a break or breach (lit. and fig.), disturbance, interruption, frustration, humiliation, abatement, downfall, decay, ruin, destruction, Mn.; MBh. &c.; fracture (see *asthi-bh°*); paralysis, palsy, L.; bending, bowing, stretching out (see *karṇa-, gātra-, -grīvā-bh°*); knitting, contraction (see *bhrū-bh°*); separation, analysis (of words), Sāh.; overthrow, rout, defeat (also in a lawsuit), Hit.; Kām.; Yājñ., Sch.; rejection, refusal, Kālid.; refutation, Sarvad.; panic, fear, Rājat.; pain (see *pārśva-bh°*); a piece broken off, morsel, fragment, Kālid.; Kād.; a bend, fold, Sāh. (cf. *vastra-bh°*); a wave, Ragh.; Gīt. [cf. Lith. *bangà*]; a water-course, channel, L.; fraud, deceit, L.; a tortuous course, roundabout way of speaking (= or w.r. for *bhaṅgi*), Sarvad.; toilet, fashion (for *bhaṅgi?*), Var.; = *gamana,* L.; N. of a serpent-demon, MBh.; (with Buddhists) the constant decay taking place in the universe, constant flux or change; (with Jainas) a dialectical formula beginning with *syāt,* q.v.; (*bhaṅgā*), m. hemp, AV.; (*ā*), f., see below. **-kara,** m. N. of two men (sons of Avikshit and Sattrā-jit), MBh. **-naya,** m. removal of obstacles, Col. **-bhāj,** mfn. being broken, W. **-vat,** mfn. 'having folds' and 'having waves,' Nāg. **-vāsā,** f. turmeric, L. **-śravas,** m. N. of a man, L. **-sârtha,** mfn. deceitful, fraudulent, L. **Bhaṅgâsura,** m. N. of a man (cf. *bhāṅgâsuri*).

Bhaṅgā, f. hemp (Cannabis Sativa); an intoxicating beverage (or narcotic drug commonly called 'Bhang') prepared from the hemp plant, ŚārṅgS.; Convolvulus Turpethum, L. **-kaṭa,** m. the pollen of hemp, L. **-svana,** m. N. of a Rājarshi, MBh.

Bhaṅgi or **bhaṅgī,** f. breaking, Inscr.; a bend, curve, Dhūrtas.; a roundabout mode of acting or speaking, circumlocution (°*gyā,* ind. 'in an indirect manner'), Kāvyâd.; Daś.; Kathās. &c.; explaining, L.; mode, manner, way, Vcar.; way of dressing, fashion, toilet, Bālar.; Rājat.; (ifc.) mere appearance or semblance of, Kathās.; Rājat.; fraud, deception, L.; irony, wit, repartee, W.; modesty, MW.; = *bhaṅga* (with Jainas), Sarvad.; figure, shape, Siddhāntaś.; a step (see *bhakti*); a wave, Naish. **-bhāva,** m. (fr. °*gin + bh°?*) the state of being bent or contracted; (*drig-bhaṅgi-bh°*) a frowning aspect, Sāh. **-bhūta,** mfn. (ifc.) having the appearance of, resembling, Bālar. **-mat,** mfn. possessing undulations, curled (as hair), MBh. **-vikāra,** m. distortion of the features (*mukha-bhaṅgi-v°*) a wry face, grimace, Kād. **Bhaṅgī-bhakti,** f. division or separation into (a series of) waves or wave-like steps, Megh. **Bhaṅgy-antareṇa,** ind. in an indirect manner, Sāh.; in another manner, Sarvad.

Bhaṅgin, mfn. fragile, transient, perishable (see *kshaṇa-* and *tat-kshaṇa-bh°*); (in law) defeated or cast in a suit, L.

Bhaṅgīka. See *vividha-bh°.*

Bhaṅgīla, n. defect in the organs of sense, W.

Bhaṅgu, m. N. of a demon, Vcar. **-giri,** m. N. of a mountain, ib.

Bhaṅgura, mf(*ā*)n. apt to break, fragile, transitory, perishable, Kāv.; Pur. &c.; changeable, variable, Kathās.; Rājat.; bent, curled, crisped, wrinkled, Kāv.; Kathās.; fraudulent, dishonest, W.; m. a bend or reach of a river, L.; (*ā*), f. N. of two plants (= *ati-vishā* or *priyaṅgu*), L. **-tā,** f.

fragility, transitoriness, Cat. **—niścaya,** mfn. forming changeable resolutions, inconstant, Rājat.

Bhaṅgurá-vat, mfn. having crooked ways, crafty, treacherous, RV.

Bhaṅguraka. See *mṛityu-bh°*.

Bhaṅguraya, Nom. P. °*yati*, to break to pieces, destroy, Inscr.; to crisp, curl (trans.), Sāh.

Bhaṅgurī-karaṇa, n. making fragile, ib.

Bhaṅgya, mfn. fit to be broken, breakable, g. *daṇḍâdi*; mf(*ā*)n. a field of hemp, L. (cf. Pāṇ. v, 2, 4). **—śravas,** m. N. of a man (cf. *bhaṅga-śravas*).

Bhañjaka, mf(*ikā*)n. who or what breaks or divides or destroys, W.; m. a breaker (of doors), Kull.; (*ikā*), f. breaking, plucking (ifc. after the names of plants to denote partic. games; cf. *uddālaka-pushpa-bh°* and *śāla-bhañjikā*); Rubia Munjista, L. °**jana,** mfn. breaking, a breaker, destroyer, dispeller, R.; Kathās. &c.; causing violent pain, Suśr.; m. falling to pieces or decay of the teeth (also °*naka*), Suśr.; (*ā*), f. explanation, L.; n. breaking, shattering, crushing, destroying, annihilating, frustrating, MBh.; R. &c.; violent pain (*aṅga-bh°*), Suśr.; disturbing, interrupting, dispelling, removing, Pañcar.; Mallin. &c.; smoothing (of hair), Viddh.; °*nā-giri*, m. N. of a mountain, g. *kiṃśulakâdi*. °**jam,** see *mṛiṇāla-bhañjam*. °**jaru,** m. a tree growing near a temple, L. °**jā,** f. N. of Durgā, L. °**jin,** mfn. breaking, dispelling (see *mada-bhañjin*). °**jī,** f., see *śāla-bhañjī*.

भञ्जिपत्त्रिका *bhañjipattrikā*, f. Salvinia Cucullata, L. (cf. *phañji-pattrikā*).

भट् *bhaṭ*, cl. 1. P. *bhaṭati*, to hire, nourish, maintain, Dhātup. ix, 20; cl. 10. P. *bhāṭayati*, to speak, converse, xix, 18: Caus. *bhāṭayati*, to hire, L. (prob. Nom. fr. next).

Bhaṭa, m. (fr. *bhṛita*) a mercenary, hired soldier, warrior, combatant, MBh.; Kāv. &c.; a servant, slave, Kāvyâd.; VP.; a humpback, Gal.; N. of a serpent-demon, Buddh.; = *Ārya-bhaṭa* (cf. below); pl. N. of a degraded tribe, L. (cf. *bhaṭṭa*, *bhaḍa*, *bhaṇḍa*; according to some 'a person whose father is a Brāhman and whose mother is a Naṭī'); (*ā*), f. coloquintida. **—dīpikā,** f. N. of a Comm. on Ārya-bhaṭa. **—peṭaka,** n. a troop of soldiers, Vcar. **—prakāśa,** m., **-prakāśikā,** f. N. of wks. **—balâgra,** m. a hero, Divyâv.; n. an army, ib. **—bhaṭa-mātṛi-tīrtha,** n. N. of a Tīrtha, Cat.

Bhaṭârka, m. N. of the founder of the Valabhī dynasty, Inscr. (cf. *bhaṭṭârka*). **Bhaṭôdyoga,** m. exertion of soldiers, L.

Bhaṭīya, mfn. relating to Ārya-bhaṭa, Cat. **—dīpikā,** f. = *bhaṭa-d°*, ib.

भटभटाय *bhaṭabhaṭāya* (onomat.), Nom. P. °*yate*, to make a gurgling sound, gurgle, Cat.

भटित्र *bhaṭitra*, mfn. roasted on a spit, Bhpr.

भट्कला *bhaṭkalā*, f. N. of a Tīrtha, Cat.

भट्ट *bhaṭṭa*, m. (fr. *bhartṛi*) lord, my lord (also pl. and *-pāda*, m. pl.; according to Daśar. ii, 64, a title of respect used by humble persons addressing a prince; but also affixed or prefixed to the names of learned Brāhmans, e. g. *Kedāra-*, *Govinda-bh°* &c., or *Bhaṭṭa-kedāra* &c., below, the proper name being sometimes omitted, e. g. *Bhaṭṭa* = *Kumārila-bh°*; also any learned man = doctor or philosopher), Rājat.; Vet. &c.; N. of a partic. mixed caste of hereditary panegyrists, a bard, encomiast, L.; an enemy (?), W.; often w. r. for *bhaṭa*; (*ā*), f. N. of an enchantress, Rājat.; mf(*ā*)n. venerable, L. **—kārikā,** f. pl. N. of partic. Kārikās. **—kedāra,** m. = *Kedāra-bh°*, q. v. **—gopāla,** m. N. of an author, Pratāp., Sch.; of another man, Mālatīm. **—divākara,** m. N. of a man, Cat. **—dīpikā,** f. N. of wk. (cf. *bhaṭa-d°*). **—nāyaka,** m. N. of a poet and a rhetorician, Cat. **—nārāyaṇa,** m. N. of the author of the Veṇī-saṃhāra and of other writers, Kshitîś.; Cat. **—paddhati,** f. N. of wk. **—pāda,** m. pl., see above. **—prakāśa,** m. N. of wk. (cf. *bhaṭa-pr°*). **—prayāga,** m. 'the chief place of sacrifice,' the spot where the Yamunā falls into the Gaṅgā, L. **—phalguna,** m. N. of a man, Rājat. **—bala-bhadra** and **-bījaka,** m. N. of authors, Cat. **—bhāshya,** n. N. of wk. **—bhāskara,** m. N. of an author (also *-miśra*); °*rīya*, n. N. of his wk. **—madana, -malla, -yaśas** and **-rāma,** m. N. of authors, Cat. **—vārttika,** n. N. of wk. **—viśvêśvara, -śaṃkara, -śālīya-pītâmbara, -śiva, -śrī-śaṃkara, -sarvajña, -somêśvara** and **-svāmin** (cf. *bhaṭṭi*), m. N. of various scholars and authors, Cat. **Bhaṭṭâcārya,** m. a title given to a learned Brāhman or any great teacher or doctor (esp. to Kumārila-bhaṭṭa, but also to various other scholars and authors); *-cūḍāmaṇi*, m. N. of Jānakīnātha; *-śatâvadhāna*, m. N. of Rāghavêndra; *-śiromaṇi*, m. N. of Raghu-nātha. **Bhaṭṭâlaṃkāra,** m. N. of wk. **Bhaṭṭôtpala,** m. N. of a Sch. on Var. **Bhaṭṭôpama,** m. N. of a learned Buddhist.

Bhaṭṭaraka, mf(*ikā*)n. venerable, L.

Bhaṭṭāra, m. a noble lord (= *pūjya*), L.; 'honourable,' N. of various men, Rājat. **—svāmin** and **-hari-candra,** m. N. of authors, Cat.

Bhaṭṭāraka, m. a great lord, venerable or worshipful person (used of gods and of great or learned men, esp. of Buddhist teachers and of a partic. class of Śaiva monks), Inscr.; Vet.; Hit. &c.; (in dram.) a king, W.; the sun, ib.; Ardea Nivea, L.; (*ikā*), f. 'noble lady' or 'tutelary deity,' N. of Durgā, Vet. (cf. *jayā-* and *mahā-bhaṭṭārikā*); a king's mother (in the plays), L.; mf(*ikā*)n. venerable, L. **—maṭha,** m. N. of a college, Rājat. **—vāra,** m. 'day of the great lord i. e. the sun,' Sunday, Hit. **Bhaṭṭārakâyatana,** n. a temple, Pañcat.

Bhaṭṭi, m. N. of a poet (also called Bhartṛi-svāmin or -hari, or Bhaṭṭa-svāmin or Svāmi-bhaṭṭa). **—kāvya,** n. 'the poem of Bhaṭṭi,' N. of an artificial poem by Bh° (originally called Rāvaṇa-vadha; celebrating the exploits of Rāma and illustrating Sanskṛit grammar by the systematic application of all possible forms and constructions). **—candrikā** and **-bodhinī,** f. N. of Comms. on Bhaṭṭ.

Bhaṭṭika, m. N. of the mythical progenitor of copyists (son of Citra-gupta and grandson of Brahmā), Cat.

Bhaṭṭinī, f. (fr. *bhartṛi*, Prākr. *bhaṭṭā*; formed in analogy to *patnī*) a noble lady (applied to queens not crowned or consecrated like the Devī, to the wife of a Brāhman and any woman of high rank), L.

Bhaṭṭīya, w. r. for *bhaṭīya*.

Bhaṭṭoji, m. N. of a grammarian (son of Lakshmī-dhara, author of the Siddhânta-kaumudī and other wks.) **—dīkshita** or **-bhaṭṭa,** m. id. **Bhaṭṭojīya,** n. a work of Bhaṭṭoji, Cat.

भड *bhaḍa*, m. N. of a partic. mixed caste, Cat. (cf. *bhaṭa*). **—harī-mātṛi-tīrtha,** n. N. of a Tīrtha, Cat. (cf. *bhaṭabhaṭa-m°*).

भडित *bhaḍita*, m. N. of a man, g. *gargâdi*; pl. his descendants, g. *yaskâdi*.

भडिल *bhaḍila*, m. a servant or a hero, Uṇ. i, 55, Sch.; N. of a man, g. *aśvâdi*; pl. his descendants, g. *yaskâdi*.

भण *bhaṇ*, cl. 1. P. (Dhātup. xiii, 4) *bhaṇati* (pf. *babhāṇa*, 2. sg. *babhaṇitha*, Pāṇ. vi, 4, 121 Sch.; aor. *abhāṇīt*, Bhaṭṭ.; fut. *bhaṇishyati*, °*ṇitā*, Gr.; ind. p. *bhaṇitvā*, Pañcat.; inf. *bhaṇitum*, Gr.: Pass. *bhaṇyate*, BhP.; aor. *abhāṇi*, Bhaṭṭ.), to speak, say to (acc. with or without *prati*), Var.; Daś.; Pañcat.; to call, name (two acc.), Vet.: Caus. *bhāṇayati*; aor. *abībhaṇat* or *ababhāṇat*, Siddh.; Vop. (Prob. a later form of √*bhan*.)

Bhaṇa, see *dur-bhaṇa*. °**ṇati,** w. r. for °*ṇiti*. °**ṇana,** mfn. (ifc.) speaking, proclaiming, Gīt. °**ṇanīya,** mfn. to be told or said, Sarvad. °**ṇita,** mfn. uttered, spoken, said, related, Pañcat.; Vet.; Gīt.; n. (also pl.) speech, talk, relation, description, Vet.; Gīt. °**ṇiti,** f. speech, talk, discourse, Kāv.; Rājat.; Pratāp. (w. r. °*ṇati*); *-maya*, mf(*ī*)n. consisting in eloquence, Śrīkaṇṭh. °**ṇitṛi,** mfn. a speaker, speaking, talking, MW.

भण्ट् *bhaṇṭ*, cl. 10. P. *bhaṇṭayati*, to deceive, Dhātup. xxxii, 50, Vop.

भण्टाकी *bhaṇṭākī*, f. Solanum Melongena, L. (v. l. *bhaṇḍākī*).

भण्टुक *bhaṇṭuka*, m. Calosanthes Indica, L. (v. l. *bhaṇḍuka*).

भण्ड् *bhaṇḍ*, cl. 1. Ā. *bhaṇḍate*, to reprove; to deride; to jest; to speak, Dhātup. viii, 20; cl. 1. 10. P. *bhaṇḍati*, °*ḍayati*, to be or render fortunate; to do an auspicious act (*kalyāṇe* or *śive*), xxxii, 50. (Prob. a later form of √*bhand*.)

Bhaṇḍa, m. a jester, buffoon, mime (also as N. of a partic. mixed caste), Pur.; Kathās.; Sarvad; (*ā*), f., see *śveta-bh°*; (*ī*), f., see below; n. = *bhāṇḍa*; pl. utensils, implements, Āpast.; *-tapasvin*, m. a hypocritical ascetic, MW.; *-tva*, n. buffoonery, Subh.; *-dhūrta-niśācara*, m. pl. (prob.) jesters and rogues and night-revellers, BhP., Introd.; *-hāsinī*, f. a harlot, prostitute, L. °**ḍaka,** m. a water wagtail, L.; N. of a poet, Cat.; (*ikā*), f. Rubia Munjista, L. °**ḍana,** n. mischief, L.; war, L.; armour, L. (cf. *bhāṇḍana*). °**ḍanīya,** mfn. to be derided, Kautukas. °**ḍara,** m. a partic. kind of combat, L. °**ḍākī,** see *bhaṇṭākī*. °**ḍi,** m. N. of a minister of Śrī-harsha, Hcar.; f. a wave, L. (cf. *bhriṇḍi*); *-jaṅgha*, m. N. of a man, Sch. on Pāṇ. ii, 4, 58. °**ḍita,** mfn. derided, L.; m. N. of a man, g. *gargâdi*; pl. his descendants, g. *yaskâdi*. °**ḍin,** w. r. for °*ḍi*. °**ḍiman,** m. deceit, L. °**ḍira,** m. Acacia Sirissa, L.; (*ī*), f. Rubia Munjista, L. °**ḍila,** m. fortune, welfare, Uṇ. i, 55, Sch.; a messenger, ib.; an artisan, L.; Acacia or Mimosa Sirissa, L.; N. of a man, g. *aśvâdi*; pl. his descendants, g. *yaskâdi*. °**ḍī,** f. Rubia Munjista, Car.; *-pushpa-nikāśa*, mfn. resembling the flowers of R° M°, MBh.; *-ratha*, m. N. of a man, g. *tika-kitavâdi*. °**ḍītakī,** f. = °*ḍī*, Bhpr. °**ḍīra,** m. Ficus Indica, R. (B.), Sch.; Amaranthus Polygonoides or Acacia Sirissa, L.; N. of a lofty Nyagrodha tree upon the Go-vardhana mountain, Hariv. (v.l. *bāṇḍ°*); (*ī*), f. = *bhaṇḍī*, L.; Hydrocotyle Asiatica, L.; °*ra-latikā*, f. = next, L. °**ḍīla,** m. Rubia Munjista, L. °**ḍu,** g. *suvāstv-ādi*. °**ḍuka,** m. Calosanthes Indica, L. °**ḍūka,** m. id., L.; a kind of fish, Bhpr.

भदन्त *bhadanta*, °*dāka*, °*dra*. See under √*bhand* below.

भद्दालिन् *bhaddālin*, m. N. of a man, Divyâv.

भन् *bhan*, cl. 1. P. *bhánati* (prob. connected with √*bhā*; cf. the later form *bhaṇ*), to sound, resound, call aloud, speak, declare, RV. (= *arcati*, Naigh. iii, 14).

भनन्दन *bhanandana*, m. N. of a man, MārkP. (prob. w. r. for *bhalandana*).

भन्द् *bhand*, cl. 1. Ā. (Dhātup. ii, 11) *bhándate*, to be greeted with praise, receive applause, RV. (L. also = to be or make fortunate or excellent; to be or make glad; to shine; to honour or worship): Caus. *bhandayati*, to cause to prosper, Dhātup. xxxii, 50, Vop.

Bhadanta, m. (Uṇ. iii, 130, Sch.) a term of respect applied to a Buddhist, a Buddhist mendicant, Var.; Hcar.; Kathās.; v.l. for *bha-datta*, q.v. **—gopadatta** and **-ghoshaka,** m. N. of 2 Buddhist teachers. **—jñāna-varman,** m. N. of a poet, Cat. **—dharma-trāta** and **-rāma,** m. N. of 2 Buddhist teachers. **—varman,** m. N. of a poet, Cat. **—śrī-lābha,** m. N. of a Buddhist teacher.

Bhadāka, m. fortune, prosperity (or mfn., auspicious, fortunate), Uṇ. iv, 15, Sch. (*kalyāṇe*).

Bhadrá, mf(*ā́*)n. blessed, auspicious, fortunate, prosperous, happy, RV. &c. &c.; good, gracious, friendly, kind, ib.; excellent, fair, beautiful, lovely, pleasant, dear, ib.; good i. e. skilful in (loc.), MBh. iv, 305; great, L.; (with *nṛipati*, m. a good or gracious king, Yājñ.; with *kānta*, m. a beautiful lover or husband, Pañcat.; with *diś*, f. the auspicious quarter i.e. the south, MBh.; with *vāc*, f. kind or friendly speech, BhP.; voc. m. and f. sg. and pl. *bhadra*, °*dre*, °*drāḥ* often in familiar address = my good sir or lady, my dear or my dears, good people, Mn.; MBh. &c.; *ám* and *áyā*, ind. happily, fortunately, joyfully, RV.; AV.; °*am* with √*kṛi* or *ā*-√*car*, to do well, Hit.); m. (prob.) a sanctimonious hypocrite, Mn. ix, 259 (v.l. °*dra-prêkshaṇikaiḥ*); a partic. kind of elephant, R. (also N. of a world-elephant, ib.) a bullock, L.; a water wagtail, Var. (cf. *-nāman*); Nauclea Cadamba or Tithymalus Antiquorum, L.; N. of Śiva, L.; of mount Meru, L.; of a class of gods (pl.) under the third Manu, BhP.; of a people (pl.), AVPariś.; of one of the 12 sons of Vishṇu and one of the Tushita deities in the Svāyambhava Manv-antara, BhP.; (with Jainas) of the third of the 9 white Balas, L.; of a son of Vasu-deva and Devakī (or Pauravī), BhP.; Kathās.; of a son of Kṛishṇa, BhP.; of a son of Upacārumat, Buddh.; of an actor, Hariv.; of a friend of Bāṇa, Vās., Introd.; (with Buddhists) N. of a partic. world; (*ā*), f. a cow, L.; N. of various plants (=

anantā, aparijātā, krishṇā, jīvantī, nīlī, rāsnā &c.), L.; N. of a metre, Col.; of the 2nd, 7th and 12th days of the lunar fortnight, W.; of the 7th movable Karaṇa (s. v.; cf. also 2. *bhadrā-karaṇa*); of a form of Durgā, VP.; of a goddess, Pañcar.; of a Buddhist deity, L.; of a Śakti, Hcat.; of Dākshāyaṇī in Bhadrêśvara, Cat.; of a Vidyā-dharī, R.; of a Surâṅganā, Siṇhâs.; of a daughter of Surabhi, R.; of a wife of Vasu-deva, Hariv.; Pur.; of the wife of Vaiśravaṇa, MBh.; of a daughter of Soma and wife of Utathya, ib.; of a daughter of Raudrāśva and the Apsaras Ghṛitācī, Hariv.; of a Kākshīvatī and wife of Vyushitâśva, MBh.; of a daughter of Meru and wife of Bhadrâśva, BhP.; of a daughter of Śruta-kīrti and wife of Kṛishṇa, BhP.; of various rivers (esp. of one described as rising on the northern summit of Meru and flowing through Uttara-kuru into the northern ocean), Pur.; the celestial Ganges, L.; of a lake, Hcat.; n. prosperity, happiness, health, welfare, good fortune (also pl.), RV. &c. &c. (*bhadram tasya* or *tasmai*, prosperity to him! Pāṇ. ii, 3, 73; *bhadraṃ te* or *vaḥ* often used parenthetically in a sentence = 'if you please,' or to fill up a verse; *bhadram upalāḥ*, happiness to you, O stones! Śāntiś.; *bhadram* with √*kṛi* and dat., to grant welfare to, bless, RV.); gold, L.; iron or steel, L.; a kind of Cyperus (= *-musta*), L.; a partic. posture in sitting, Cat.; a partic. Karaṇa, L. (cf. f.); a partic. mystic sign, AgP.; a partic. part of a house, Nalac.; N. of various Sāmans, ĀrshBr. **-kaṇṭa**, m. Asteracantha Longifolia, L. **-kanyā**, f. N. of the mother of Maudgalyāyana, Buddh. **-kapila**, m. N. of Śiva, L. **-karṇikā**, f. N. of Dākshāyaṇī in Go-karṇa, Cat. **-karṇêśvara**, m. N. of a Tīrtha, MBh. **-kalpa**, m. 'the good or beautiful Kalpa,' N. of the present age, Divyâv. (cf. MWB. 135); n. of a Buddh. Sūtra wk.; °*pika*, mfn. living in the Bhadra-kalpa, Divyâv. **-kāpya**, m. N. of a man, Car. **-kāra**, m. N. of a son of Kṛishṇa, Hariv.; (pl.) of a people, MBh. **-kāraka**, mfn. causing prosperity, prosperous, auspicious, Var. **-kālī**, f. N. of a goddess (later a form of Durgā), ŚāṅkhGṛ.; Mn.; MBh. &c.; of one of the Mātṛis attending on Skanda, MBh.; of a village on the right bank of the Ganges, L.; of a plant (= *gandholī*), L.; *-kavaca*, n. N. of ch. of BrahmavP. iii; *-cintāmaṇi*, m.; *-purāṇa*, n. N. of wks.; *-pūjā-yantra*, n. N. of a mystical diagram, Cat.; *-pūjā-vidhi*, m., *-manu*, m., *-mantra*, m. pl., *-māhātmya*, n. N. of wks. or chs. of wks. **-kāśī**, f. a kind of Cyperus, L. **-kāshṭha**, n. the wood of Pinus Deodora, L. **-kumbha**, m. 'auspicious jar,' a golden jar filled with water from a holy place or from the Ganges (used esp. at the consecration of a king), L. **-kṛit**, mfn. causing prosperity or welfare, RV.; TS.; (with Jainas) N. of the 24th Arhat of the future Utsarpiṇī, L. **-gaṇita**, n. the construction of magical squares or diagrams, Col. **-gandhikā**, f. Cyperus Rotundus, L.; Asclepias Pseudosarsa, W. **-gupta**, m. N. of a Jaina saint, HPariś. **-gaura**, m. N. of a mountain, MārkP. **-ghaṭa** (Hcat.), **-ghaṭaka** (Kathās.), m. 'vase of fortune,' a lottery vase. **-ṃ-kara**, mfn. = °*drā-kāraka*, L.; m. N. of a man, Kathās.; (pl.) of a country, Divyâv.; n. N. of a town in Vidarbha, Buddh. **-ṃ-karaṇa**, mfn. = prec. mfn., Pāṇ. vi, 3, 70, Vārtt. 8, Pat. **-cāru**, m. N. of a son of Kṛishṇa, MārkP. **-cūḍa**, m. Euphorbia Tirucalli, L. **-ja**, m. Wrightia Antidysenterica, L. **-jaya**, m. N. of a man, Buddh. **-jātika**, mfn. 'of noble birth' and 'descended from the elephant called Bhadra,' Siṇhâs. **-jāni**, mfn. having a beautiful wife, RV. **-tara**, mfn. more prosperous, happier, better, MBh.; Hit. **-taruṇī**, f. Rosa Moschata, L. **-tás**, ind. fortunately, happily, AV. **-tā**, f. honesty, probity, Kām.; prosperity, good fortune (also *-tva*, n.), MW. **-tuṅga**, m. N. of a Tīrtha, MBh. **-turaga**, n. N. of a Varsha, Gol. **-tva**, n., see *-tā*. **-datta**, m. (in dram.) a name given to Śakas, Sāh. **-danta**, m. N. of an elephant, Kathās. **-dantikā**, f. a species of Croton, L. **-dāru**, m. n. Pinus Deodora, Hariv.; Var.; Suśr.; P° Longifolia, L. **-dīpa**, m. N. of wk. **-deva**, v. l. for next. **-deha**, m. N. of a son of Vasu-deva, VP. **-dos**, m. 'auspicious-armed,' N. of a man, Bhadrab. **-dvīpa**, m. N. of an island, MārkP. **-nāman**, m. N. of a bird (the water wagtail or the woodpecker), L. **-nāmikā**, f. Ficus Heterophylla, L. **-nidhi**, m. 'treasure of fortune,' N. of a costly vessel offered to Vishṇu, Pur. **-pada**, n. N. of a metre, Col.; (*ā*), f. N. of the 3rd and 4th lunar asterisms, Var. &c. (also n.; °*dā-yoga*, m. N. of ch. of Bhaṭṭôtpala's Comm. on VarBṛS.) **-parṇā**, f. Paederia Foetida, L. **-parṇī**, f. Gmelina Arborea, Sāy. on ŚBr.; = prec., L. **-pāda**, mfn. born under the Nakshatra Bhadra-padā, Pāṇ. vii, 3, 18, Sch. **-pāpá**, n. sg. good and evil, AV. xii, 1, 48; m. pl. the g° and the e°, ib. 47. **-pāla**, m. N. of a Bodhi-sattva, Buddh. **-pīṭha**, n. a splendid seat, throne, PārGṛ.; R. &c.; (prob. m.) a kind of winged insect, Mṛicch. **-pura**, n. N. of a city, Cat. (cf. *bhadrā-nagara*). **-balana**, m. = *bala-bhadra*, N. of the elder brother of Kṛishṇa, Bālar. **-balā**, f. Paederia Foetida or Sida Cordifolia, L. **-bāhu**, m. N. of a partic. four-footed animal, L.; 'auspicious-armed,' N. of a son of Vasu-deva and Rohiṇī (Pauravī), Pur.; of a king of Magadha, Kathās.; (also *-svāmin*) of a celebrated Jaina author (one of the 6 Śruta-kevalins; *-caritra*, n., *-śāstra*, n., *-saṃhitā*, f. N. of wks.); (*ū*), f. N. of a woman, Pāṇ. iv, 1, 67, Sch. **-bhaṭa**, m. N. of a man, Mudr. **-bhuja**, m. whose arms confer prosperity (said of princes), MārkP.; N. of a man, Bhadrab. **-bhūshaṇā**, f. N. of a goddess, Pañcar. **-manas**, f. N. of the mother of the elephant Airāvata, MBh. **-manda**, m. a partic. kind of elephant (also °*dra* and °*dra-mṛiga*), R. (B.); N. of a son of Kṛishṇa, VP. **-mallikā**, f. N. of a partic. plant (= *gavâkshī*), L. **-mātṛi**, see *bhādramātura*). **-mukha**, mfn. one whose face (or whose look) confers prosperity, Kālid.; Daś.; Kād. &c. (only used in the voc. or in the nom. with the meaning of a 2nd pers. = 'good or gentle sir,' pl. 'good people;' accord. to Sāh. a prince is so to be addressed by the inferior characters in plays; in the Divyâv. it is a term of address to inferior persons). **-muñja**, m. a species of plant akin to Saccharum Sara, Bhpr. **-musta**, m. (Ṛitus.), **-mustaka**, m. and **-mustā**, f. (L.) a kind of Cyperus (only ifc.) **-mṛiga**, m. a kind of elephant, R. **-yava**, n. the seed of Wrightia Antidysenterica, L. **-yāna**, m. N. of a man; °*nīya*, m. pl. his school, Buddh. (*bhadrā-yana*, prob. w. r.) **-yoga**, m. a partic. astrological Yoga, Cat. **-ratha** and **-rāja**, m. N. of 2 men, Hariv. **-rāma**, m. N. of an author, Cat. **-ruci**, m. N. of a man, Buddh. **-rūpā**, f. N. of a woman, Kathās. **-reṇu**, m. N. of Indra's elephant, L. (v. l. *-veṇu*). **-rohiṇī**, f. a species of plant (= *kaṭukā*), Suśr. **-lakshaṇa**, n. the mark of a Bhadra elephant (whose chief and inferior limbs are in good proportion), L. **-latā**, f. Gaertnera Racemosa, L. **-vaṭa**, n. N. of a Tīrtha, Hariv. **-vat**, mfn. fraught with good, auspicious, MBh.; (*ī*), f. a wanton woman, courtezan, TBr.; Gmelina Arborea, L.; N. of a daughter of Kṛishṇa, Hariv.; of a wife of Madhu, ib.; of a female elephant, Kathās.; n. Pinus Deodora, L. **-vadana**, m. 'auspicious-faced,' N. of Bala-rāma, L. **-vargīya**, m. pl. N. of the first 5 disciples of Gautama Buddha, Lalit. **-varman**, m. Arabian jasmine, L.; N. of a man (cf. *bhādravarmaṇa*). **-vallikā**, f. Hemidesmus Indicus, L. **-vallī**, f. Jasminum Sambac, L.; Gaertnera Racemosa, L.; Vallaris Dichotomus, L. **-vasana**, n. splendid apparel, Hariv. **-vāc**, mfn. speaking auspiciously, RV. **-vācya**, n. wishing well, congratulation, VS.; Br. **-vādín**, mfn. uttering auspicious cries (said of a bird), RV. **-vinda**, m. N. of a son of Kṛishṇa, Hariv. **-virāj**, f. N. of a metre, Col. **-vihāra**, m. N. of a Buddhist monastery. **-veṇu**, m., see *-reṇu*. **-vrāta** (*bhadrá-*), mfn. having or forming a happy assemblage, RV. **-śarman**, m. N. of a man, VBr. (cf. g. *bāhv-ādi*). **-śākha**, m. N. of a form of Skanda, MBh. **-śāla-vana**, v. l. for *sāla-v°*, q. v. **-śilā**, f. N. of a town, Divyâv. **-śila**, m. N. of a man, Cat. **-śoci**, mfn. beautifully shining, glittering, RV. **-śaunaka**, m. N. of an ancient physician, Car. **-śraya**, n. sandal-wood, L. **-śravas**, m. N. of a son of Dharma, BhP. **-śriya**, n. sandal-wood, Suśr. **-śrī**, f. id., L.; m. the sandal tree, L. **-śrút**, mfn. hearing good or pleasant things, AV. **-śreṇya**, m. N. of a king, Hariv. **-shashṭhī**, f. N. of a form of Durgā, Hariv. **-saras**, n. N. of a lake, Hcat. **-sāman**, m. N. of a man (cf. *bhādrasāma*). **-sāra**, m. N. of a king, VāyuP. **-sāla-vana**, n. N. of a forest, MBh. (B.; C. *śāla-v°*). **-suta**, m. = *bhadrâtmaja*, L. **-sená**, m. N. of a man with the patr. Ājātaśatrava, ŚBr.; of a son of Vasu-deva and Devakī, Pur.; of a son of Ṛishabha, ib.; of a son of Mahishmat, ib. (also °*naka*); of a king of Kaśmīra, Cat.; (with Buddhists) N. of the leader of the host of the evil spirit Māra-pāpīyas, Lalit. **-somā**, f. N. of a river in Uttara-kuru, MārkP.; of the Ganges, L. **-svapna** (*bhadrá-*), m. a good dream, AV. **-hasta**, mfn. having beautiful or auspicious hands (said of the Aśvins), RV. **-hrada**, m. (prob.) = *-saras*, Pat. **Bhadrâkāra** and °**kṛiti**, mfn. of auspicious features, A. **Bhadrâksha**, m. 'auspicious-eyed,' N. of a king, Kathās. (cf. *bhallâksha*). **Bhadrâṅga**, m. 'beauteous-framed,' N. of Bala-bhadra, L. **Bhadrâtmaja**, m. 'son of iron (?),' a sword, L. **Bhadrânanda**, m. N. of an author, Cat. **Bhadrâbhadra**, mfn. good and bad; n. good and evil, MW. **Bhadrâyudha**, m. 'handsome-weaponed,' N. of a warrior, Kathās.; of a giant, Buddh. **Bhadrâyus**, m. N. of a man, Cat. **Bhadrâvakāśā**, f. N. of a river, Col. **Bhadrā-vatī** (for *dra-v°*?), f. a species of tree (= *kaṭphala*), Kauś. **Bhadrâvaha**, mfn. causing prosperity; (with *ghrita*), n. a partic. medic. preparation, Bhpr. **Bhadrâśrama** (or °*drâśr°*?), m. N. of a hermitage, SkandaP. **Bhadrā-śraya**, n. = °*dra-śraya*, L. **Bhadrâśva**, m. N. of a son of Vasu-deva and Rohiṇī, VP.; of a son of Dhundhu-māra, BhP.; of a king also called Śveta-vāhana, Cat.; of a son of Āgnīdhra and (also n.) a Dvīpa or Varsha called after him (the eastern division), MBh. &c.; n. N. of a country lying east of the Ilâvṛita country, L. **Bhadrâsana**, n. a splendid seat, throne, Yājñ.; MBh. &c.; a partic. posture of a devotee during meditation, Sarvad. **Bhadrâhá**, n. an auspicious day, favourable season, AV. **Bhadrêndra**, m. N. of a man, Cat. **Bhadrêśa**, °**śvara**, see *Bhadrêśa* &c. 1. *bhadrā* below. **Bhadrâilā**, f. large cardamoms, L. **Bhadrôdaya**, n. a partic. medic. compound, Suśr. **Bhadrôpavāsa-vrata**, n. a partic. religious observance, Cat. **Bhadrâudanī**, f. Sida Cordifolia and Rhombifolia, Car.

Bhadramyā and °**yikā**, f., Pat.

Bhadraka, mf(*ikā*)n. good, brave, Mn.; MBh.; Kathās. (m. voc. pl. °*kāḥ* in address, Daś.); fine, handsome, beautiful, L.; m. a kind of bean, R. (Sch.); Cyperus Pertenuis (?), Saṃskārak.; Pinus Deodora, L.; (pl.) N. of a people, R.; N. of a prince, BhP.; v. l. for *bhadrika*, q. v.; (*ikā*), f. an amulet, MBh.; Myrica Sapida, L.; N. of 2 metres, Col.; (*akā*), f. N. of a woman, Kathās.; n. Cyperus Rotundus, L.; a partic. posture in sitting (= *bhadrâsana*), Cat.; a kind of metre, Col.; a partic. mystic sign, AgP.; a harem, Gal.

1. **Bhadrā**, f. of *bhadra*, in comp. **-1. -karaṇa**, n. the Karaṇa (s. v.) called *bhadrā*, Hcat. **-nagara**, n. N. of a city, Cat. (cf. *bhadra-pura*). **-°nanda**, see °*drânanda* under *bhadra*. **-mahiman**, m. N. of wk. **-vrata**, n. a partic. religious ceremony (also called *vishṭi-vrata*), Cat. **-°śrama** (°*drâś°*), see *bhadrâśr°* under *bhadra*. **Bhadrêśa**, m. 'husband of Bhadrā i.e. Durgā,' N. of Śiva, Pañcar. (cf. *Umêśa*). **Bhadrêśvara**, m. N. of various statues and Liṅgas of Śiva (cf. prec.), Pur.; of a place, Cat.; of a Kāyastha, Rājat.; of an author, Cat. (also *-sūri* and °*rācārya*).

2. **Bhadrā**, ind. (g. *sâkshād-ādi*), in comp. **-2. -karaṇa**, n. 'making beautiful,' the act of shaving, L. **-√kṛi**, P. *-karoti*, to shave, Daś. (cf. *madrā* and Pāṇ. v, 4, 67, Pat.)

Bhadrāraka, m. N. of one of the 18 lesser Dvīpas, L.

Bhadrāla-pattrikā and **bhadrālī**, f. Paederia Foetida (= *gandhālī*), L.

Bhadrika, m. N. of a prince of the Śākyas, Buddh. (v. l. *bhadraka*).

Bhadriṇa, m. N. of a man, Pravar.

Bhandád-ishṭi, mfn. (prob.) hastening along with shouts and yells (said of the Maruts), RV. v, 87, 1 (cf. *krandád-ishṭi*).

Bhandána, mf(*ā*)n. shouting, yelling (Mahīd. 'gladdening' or 'beautifying'), VS.; TS.; (*ā*), f. (also pl.) acclamation, applause, praise, RV.; pl. rain-making sunrays, L.

Bhandanāya (Nom. fr. prec.), only pr. p. °*yát*, to shout loudly, yell, RV.

Bhandanīya, mfn. a word formed in Nir. xi, 19, to explain *bhadra*, q. v.

Bhandila, n. fortune, L.; tremulous motion, L.; a messenger (?), L.

Bhándishṭha, mfn. (superl.) shouting most loudly, praising most highly, RV.

भन्धुक *bhandhuka* or °*dhruka*, m. N. of a place, SkandaP.

भप *bha-pa, bha-pañjara* &c. See 4. *bha.*

भप्पट *bhappaṭa*, m. N. of a man (who built a temple named after him *bhappaṭêśvara*), Rājat.

भम्भ *bhambha*, m. or n. the mouth or aperture of an oven or stove, Car.; m. smoke, L.; a fly, L.; (*ā*), f. a kettledrum, HPariś.

Bhambharālikā (or °*râl*°?), f. a gnat, mosquito, L.

Bhambharālī, f. a fly, L.

Bhambhā-rava, m. the lowing of cows (v. l. for *bambhā-rava*), VarBṛS.

भम्भासार *bhambhāsāra*, m. N. of a king (v. l. *bimbisāra*), L.

भय *bhayá*, n. (√*bhī*) fear, alarm, dread, apprehension; fear of (abl., gen. or comp.) or for (comp.), RV. &c. &c. (*bhayāt*, ind. 'from fear;' *bhayam* √*kṛi* with abl. 'to have fear of;' *bhayaṃ* √*dā*, 'to cause fear, terrify'); sg. and pl. terror, dismay, danger, peril, distress; danger from (abl. or comp.) or to (comp.), ib.; the blossom of Trapa Bispinosa, L.; m. sickness, disease, L.; Fear personified (as a Vasu, a son of Nir-ṛiti or Ni-kṛiti, a prince of the Yavanas and husband of the daughter of Time), Pur. (also n.; and *ā*, f., as a daughter of Kāla or Vaivasvata, and wife of the Rākshasa Heti). **–kampa**, m. tremor from fear, MW. **–kara** and **-kartṛi**, mfn. causing f°, terrible, dangerous, MBh. **–kṛit**, mfn. id.; m. N. of Vishṇu, A. **–ṃ-kara**, mf(*ī*)n. terrible (*am*, ind.), MBh.; Kāv. &c.; m. a kind of small owl, L.; a kind of falcon, L.; N. of one of the Viśve Devāḥ, MBh.; of various persons, ib.; Kathās.; Lalit.; (*ī*), f. N. of one of the Mātṛis attending on Skanda, MBh. **–ṃ-kartṛi**, mfn. = *bhaya-kartṛi*, MBh. **–caurya**, n. a theft committed with fear or danger, L. **–jāta**, m. N. of a man, L. **–ḍiṇḍima**, m. 'terror-drum,' a drum used in battle, L. **–trasta**, mfn. trembling with fear, frightened, Pañcat. **–trātṛi**, m. a saver from fear or danger, Cāṇ. **–da**, mfn. inspiring f°, causing danger (gen. comp.), Har.; Var.; m. N. of a prince, VP. **–darśin**, mfn. apprehensive of danger, fearful, W. **–dāna**, n. a gift offered from fear, Hcat. **–dāya** (W.), **-dāyin** (Ragh.), mfn. = *-da*, mfn. **–druta**, mfn. fled or fleeing through f°, L. **–dhana**, mfn. fearful, terrible, Priy. **–nāśana**, mfn. removing fear; m. N. of Vishṇu, A. **–nāśin**, mfn. = prec. mfn.; (*inī*), f. Ficus Heterophylla, L. **–nimīlitâksha**, mfn. having the eyes closed from fear, MW. **–pratīkāra**, m. removal of fear, L. **–prada** (MBh.), **-pradāyin** (Var.), mfn. = *-da*, mfn. **–prastāva**, m. season of fear or alarm, W. **–brāhmaṇa**, m. a timid Brāhman, L. **–bhañjana**, m. N. of an author, Cat. **–bhrashṭa**, mfn. = *-druta*, L. **–vidhāyin**, mfn. = *-kara*, W. **–vipluta**, mfn. panic-struck, W. **–vihvala**, mfn. disturbed or agitated with fear, MW. **–vyūha**, m. 'fear-array,' N. of a partic. mode of marshalling an army, Kām. **–śīla**, mfn. of a timorous disposition, timid, MW. **–śoka-samāvishṭa**, mfn. filled with fear and sorrow, Mn.; MBh. **–saṃhṛishṭa-roman**, mfn. having the hair erect with terror, horrified, Bhaṭṭ. **–saṃtrasta-mānasa**, mfn. having the mind scared with t°, Pañcat. **–stha** (*bhayá-*), m or n. (?) a perilous situation, RV. ii, 30, 6. **–sthāna**, n. occasion of danger or alarm, MBh.; *-śata*, n. pl. hundreds of occasions of d°, ib. **–hartṛi** (MBh.), **-hāraka** (Pañcar.), **-hārin** (A.), mfn. removing or dispelling fear. **–hetu**, m. cause for fear, danger, W. **Bhayâkrānta**, mfn. overcome with f°, A. **Bhayâtīsāra**, m. diarrhoea (caused) by f°, Bhpr. **Bhayâtura**, mfn. distressed with fear, afraid, W. **Bhayânanā**, f. N. of a Yoginī, Hcat. **Bhayânvita**, mfn. filled with fear, alarmed, MW. **Bhayâpaha**, mfn. warding off f° or danger, MBh.; m. a prince, king, L. **Bhayâbādha**, mfn. undisturbed by fear, Nal. **Bhayâbhaya**, n. danger and security, Bhag. **Bhayârta**, mfn. distressed with f°, frightened, MānGṛ. **Bhayâvadīrṇa**, mfn. bewildered with f°, MBh. **Bhayâvaha**, mfn. bringing fear or danger, formidable, fearful, ŚvetUp.; MBh. &c. **Bhay-'éḍaka**, m. a wild ram, TĀr.; ĀpŚr. **Bhayâika-pravaṇa**, mfn. wholly inclined to fear, engrossed by fear, W. **Bhayôttara**, mfn. attended with fear, Hit. **Bhayôpaśama**, m. soothing or allaying fear, encouraging, ib.

Bhayana, n. fear, alarm, L.

Bháyamāna, m. N. of a man, RV. i, 100, 17 (Sāy.; accord. to Anukr. the author of RV. i, 100).

Bhayānaka, mf(*ā*)n. (prob. fr. *bhayāna* for *bhayamāna*) fearful, terrible, dreadful, formidable, MBh.; Kāv. &c.; n. terror(?), W.; m. the sentiment of terror (as one of the 9 Rasas in poetical or dramatic composition), Sāh.; Pratāp. &c.; a tiger, L.; Rāhu or the ascending node personified, L. **–tā**, f., **-tva**, n. fearfulness, formidableness. **–rasa-nirdeśa**, m. N. of ch. of ŚārṅgP.

Bhayālu, mfn. timid, afraid (°*luka* in Prākr.), Ratnāv.

Bhayya, mfn. to be feared, Pāṇ. vi, 1, 83; n. (impers.) one should be afraid of (abl.), PañcavBr.

भर *bhára*, mf(*ā*)n. (√*bhṛi*) bearing, carrying, bringing; bestowing, granting; maintaining, supporting (mostly ifc.; cf. *ṛitam-, kulam-, deham-, vājam-bh*° &c.); m. (ifc. f. *ā*) the act of bearing or carrying &c.; carrying away or what is carried away, gain, prize, booty, RV.; AV.; war, battle, contest, ib.; a burden, load, weight (also a partic. measure of weight = *bhāra*, q. v., L.), Hariv.; Kāv. &c. (acc. with √*kṛi*, to place one's weight, support one's self, Hit.); a large quantity, great number, mass, bulk, multitude, abundance, excess, Kāv.; Kathās. &c. (*bhareṇa* and °*rāt*, ind. in full measure, with all one's might, Kād.); raising the voice, shout or song of praise, RV.; n. du. (with *Indrasya* or *Vasishṭhasya*) N. of 2 Sāmans, ĀrshBr. **–hūti** (*bhára-*), m. a war-cry, RV. viii, 52, 15; mfn. raising a war-cry, ib. v, 48, 4. **Bhareshu-jā́**, mfn. existing in i. e. fit for wars and battles (said of Soma), RV. i, 91, 21.

Bharaṭa, m. a potter or a servant, L. (cf. Uṇ. i, 104, Sch.)

Bharaṭaka, m. a partic. class of mendicants (also °*ḍaka*); *-dvātriṃśikā*, f. N. of a collection of 32 popular tales. °**ṭika**, mf(*ī*)n. = *bharaṭena harati*, g. *bhastrâdi.*

Bharaṇa, mf(*ī*)n. bearing, maintaining, L.; m. N. of a Nakshatra (= *bharaṇī*), L.; (*ī*), f., see below; n. the act of bearing (also in the womb), carrying, bringing, procuring, RV. &c. &c.; wearing, putting on, Gīt.; maintaining, supporting, nourishing, MBh.; Kāv. &c.; wages, hire, MBh.

Bharaṇi, m. f. (prob.) N. of a Nakshatra (= *bharaṇī*), Siddh. **–sheṇa** or **-sena**, m. N. of a man, Pāṇ. viii, 3, 100, Sch.

Bharaṇika, mf(*ī*)n. = *bharaṇena harati*, g. *bhastrâdi.*

Bharaṇī, f. (of °*ṇa*) Luffa Foetida or a similar plant, L.; (also pl.) N. of the 7th Nakshatra (containing 3 stars and figured by the pudendum muliebre), AV. &c. &c. **–bhū**, m. 'born from Bharaṇī,' N. of Rāhu, L. **Bharaṇy-āhvā**, f. Tiaridium Indicum, L.

Bharaṇīya, mfn. to be borne or supported or maintained, MBh.; Śaṃk.; Kull.; m. a dependant, W.

Bharaṇḍa, m. a master, lord, Uṇ. i, 128, Sch.; a bull, L.; a worm, L.; the earth (?), L.

1. **Bharaṇya** (fr. *bharaṇa*), Nom. P. °*yati* = *sam-√bhṛi*, g. *kaṇḍv-ādi* (Gaṇar.)

2. **Bharaṇya**, mfn. (for *bharaṇīya*) to be maintained or cherished or protected, W.; m. N. of a son of Muni, Hariv. (v. l. *āraṇya*); n. wages, hire (also *ā*, f.), L.: cherishing, maintaining, L.; the asterism Bharaṇī, L. **–bhuj**, m. 'receiving wages,' a hireling, servant, labourer, L.

Bharaṇyu, m. a protector or master, L.; a friend, L.; fire, L.; the moon, L.; the sun, L.

Bhárat, mfn. bearing, carrying &c., RV. &c. &c.; m. pl. N. of the military caste, TāṇḍBr.

Bharatá, m. 'to be or being maintained,' N. of Agni (kept alive by the care of men), RV.; Br.; Kauś.; of a partic. Agni (father of Bharata and Bharatī), MBh.; a priest (= *ṛitvij*), Naigh. iii, 18; an actor, dancer, tumbler, Yājñ.; Mālatīm.; Prab.; a weaver, L.; a hireling, mercenary, L.; a barbarian, mountaineer (= *śabara*), L.; the fire in which the rice for Brāhmans is boiled, L.; N. of Rudra (the Maruts are called his sons), RV. ii, 36, 8; of an Āditya, Nir. viii, 13; of a son of Agni Bharata, MBh.; of a celebrated hero and monarch of India (son of Dushyanta and Śakuntalā, the first of 12 Cakra-vartins or Sārvabhaumas i. e. universal emperors), RV.; Br.; MBh. &c.; of a son of Dhruva-saṃdhi and father of Asita, R.; of a son of Daśaratha and Kaikeyī (and younger brother of Rāma, to whom he was very much devoted), MBh.; R. &c.; of a son of Ṛishabha, Pur.; of a son of Vītihotra, VP.; of a Manu (who gave the name to the country Bhārata), ib.; of a son of Manu Bhautya, MārkP.; of a king of Aśmaka, Vāś., Introd.; of various teachers and authors (esp. of an ancient Muni supposed author of a manual of the dramatic art called Nāṭya-śāstra or Bharata-śāstra); = Jaḍa-bharata (q. v.), A.; = Bharata-mallika (below); pl. 'the descendants of Bharata,' N. of a tribe, RV. &c. &c.; (*ā*), f. N. of an Apsaras, VP.; (*ī*), f. N. of a daughter of Agni Bharata, MBh.; of a river, VP.; n. pl. N. of a partic. Varsha, L. **–ṛishabha**, m. = *bharatarshabha*, N. of Viśvā-mitra, AitBr. (cf. RV. iii, 53, 24). **–khaṇḍa**, n. N. of a part of Bharata-varsha (= *kumārikā*), L. **–jña**, mfn. 'knowing the science of Bh°,' conversant with dramatic writings and rules, Śiś. **–tva**, n. the name of Bh°, MBh. **–dvādaśâha**, m. N. of a partic. festival, ŚrS. **–dvirūpa-kośa**, m. N. of wk. **–pāla**, m. N. of a man. **–putra** (Ratnāv.; Bālar.) and **-putraka** (L.), m. 'son of Bh°,' an actor, mime. **–pura**, n. N. of a town, Cat. **–prasū**, f. 'mother of Bh°,' N. of Kaikeyī (wife of Daśaratha), L. **–malla**, m. N. of a grammarian, Col. **–mallika** (or *-mallikā*), m. N. of an author (= *-sena*), Cat. **–roha**, m. N. of a man, Kathās. **–rshabha** (°*ta-ṛi*°), m. the best or a prince (lit. 'bull') of the Bh°s, MBh. **–varsha**, n. 'country of Bh°,' a N. of India (= *bhārata-v*°), L. **–vākya**, n. 'speech of Bh°,' N. of the last verse or verses of a play (preceded almost always by the words *tathâpīdam astu bharata-vākyam*); N. of ch. of R. vii, and PadmaP. iv. **–śārdūla**, m. the noblest (lit. 'tiger') of the Bh°s, MBh. **–śāstra**, n. Bh°'s manual (of the dramatic art, = *nāṭya-ś*°), Cat.; another manual of music (by Raghu-nātha), ib. **–śreshṭha** and **-sattama**, m. the best of the Bh°s, ib. **–sūtra**, n. N. of a rhet. wk. by Śārṅgadhara (also *-vṛitti*, f., by Vidyā-bhūshaṇa). **–sena**, m. N. of Sch. on various poems (lived about 100 years ago), Cat. **–svāmin**, m. N. of Sch. on SV. &c., ib. **Bharatâgraja**, m. 'elder brother of Bh°,' N. of Rāma, Vop. **Bharatârṇava**, m. N. of wk. **Bharatâvāsa**, m. 'abode of Bh°,' N. of PadmaP. iv. **Bharatâśrama**, m. 'hermitage of Bh°,' N. of a hermitage, Cat. **Bharatêśvara-tīrtha**, n. N. of a Tīrtha, ib.

Bharatha, m. a world-protector (= *loka-pāla*), Uṇ. iii, 115, Sch.; a king, W.; fire (cf. *bharata*), L.

Bharad, in comp. for °*rat*. **–vāja** (*bharád-*), m. 'bearing speed or strength (of flight),' a skylark, R.; N. of a Ṛishi (with the patr. Bārhaspatya, supposed author of RV. vi, 1–30; 37–43; 53–74; ix, 67, 1–3; x, 137, 1, and Purohita of Diva-dāsa, with whom he is perhaps identical; Bh° is also considered as one of the 7 sages and the author of a law-book), RV. &c. &c. (°*jasya a-dāra-sṛit* and *a-dāra-sṛitau, arkau, upahavau, gādham, nakāni, pṛiśninī, prāsāham, bṛihat, maukshe, yajñâyajñīyam, lomanī, vāja-karmīyam, vāja-bhṛit, vishamāṇi, vratam, sundhyuḥ* and *saindhukshitāni*, N. of Sāmans, ArshBr.); of an Arhat, Buddh.; of a district, Pāṇ. iv, 2, 145; of an Agni, MBh.; of various authors, Cat.; pl. the race or family of Bharad-vāja, RV.; *-gārga-pariṇaya-pratishedha-vādârtha*, m. N. of wk.; *-dhanvantari*, m. N. of a divine being, ŚāṅkhGṛ.; *-pravraska*, n. N. of AV. ii, 12; *-prâdur-bhāva*, m. N. of ch. of Bhpr.; *-śikshā*, f., *-saṃhitā*, f., *-sūtra*, n., *-smṛiti*, f. N. of wks. **–vājaka**, m. a skylark. **–vājin**, m., in °*nāṃ vratam*, N. of a Sāman, ĀrshBr.

Bháradhyai. See √*bhṛi.*

Bharama, m. N. of a man, g. *śubhrâdi.*

Bháras, n. bearing, holding, cherishing, RV.; AV.; PañcavBr. (cf. *viśva-* and *sa-bh*°).

Bhari, mfn. bearing, possessing, nourishing (cf. *ātmam-, udaram-, kukshim-*, and *saho-bh*°).

Bhariṇī, f. of 2. *bharita* below.

1. **Bharita**, mfn. (fr. *bhara*) nourished, full (opp. to *rikta*, 'empty'), filled with (gen. or comp.), MBh.; Kāv. &c.

2. **Bharita**, mf(*ā* or °*riṇī*)n. = *harita*, green, L.

Bharítra, n. the arm, RV. iii, 36, 7 (Naigh.; rather 'a kind of hammer').

Bhariman, m. supporting, nourishing, L.; a household, family, Uṇ. iv, 147, Sch.

Bharishá, mfn. rapacious, avaricious, greedy, RV.

Bhárīman, m. supporting, nourishing, nourishment, RV.; a household, family, Uṇ. iv, 1, 147, Sch.

Bharu, m. a lord, master, Uṇ. i, 7, Sch.; a husband, Gal.; N. of Vishṇu or Śiva (du. V° and Ś°), Kād.; gold, L.; the sea, L.

Bharṇas. See *sahásra-bh°*.

Bhartavyà, mfn. to be borne or carried, R.; to be supported or maintained or nourished, ŚBr. &c. &c.; to be hired or kept, VarBṛS.

Bhartṛi, m. (once in ŚBr. *bhártṛi*) a bearer [cf. Lat. *fertor*], one who bears or carries or maintains (with gen. or ifc.), RV.; ŚBr.; MBh.; a preserver, protector, maintainer, chief, lord, master, RV. &c. &c. (*trī́*, f. a female supporter or nourisher, a mother, AV.; Kauś.; TBr.); (*bhártṛi*), m. a husband, RV. v, 58, 7; Mn.; MBh. &c. **-guṇa**, m. the excellence or virtue of a husband, Mn. ix, 24. **-ghna**, mfn. murdering a master or supporter (*-tva*, n.), MBh.; (*ī*), f. a woman who murders her h°, Yājñ. **-cittā**, f. thinking of a h°, Kathās. **-jaya**, m. ruling a h°, Rājat. **-tā**, f. (W.), **-tva**, n. (MBh. &c.) masterhood, husbandship; *°tām-gata*, mfn. subject, married, W. **-darśana**, n. the sight of a husband; *-kāṅkshā*, f. desire of seeing a h°, Ml.; *-lālasa*, mfn. longing to see a h°, MBh. **-dāraka**, m. a king's son, crown prince (esp. in dram.), Sāh.; (*ikā*), f. princess, Mālav.; Kād. **-duhitṛi**, f. = prec. f., Kād. **-dṛiḍha-vratā**, f. strictly faithful to a husband, MW. **-devatā** or **-daivatā**, f. idolizing a h°, Hariv. **-prâpti-vrata**, n. a partic. observance performed to obtain a h°, Cat. **-priya**, mfn. devoted to one's master, Mālav. **-bhakta**, mfn. id., Kāvyâd. **-matī**, f. possessing a h°, a married woman, Śak. **-menṭha**, m. N. of a poet (*-tā*, f.), Pracaṇḍ. **-yajña**, m. N. of an author, Cat. **-rājyâpaharaṇa**, n. seizure of a h°'s kingdom, Pañcat. **-rūpa**, mfn. having the form of a h°, Kathās. **-loka**, m. the h°'s world (in a future life), Mn. v, 165. **-vatsalā**, f. tender to a h°, Mālav. **-vallabha-tā**, f. the being loved by a h°, Kālid. **-vyatikrama**, m. transgression against a h°, Āpast. **-vyasana-pīḍita**, mfn. afflicted by a h°'s or master's calamity, MBh. **-vrata**, n. devotion to a h°, Hariv. (*-cāriṇī*, f. faithful to a h°, R.); (*°tā*), f. = *°ta-cāriṇī*, MBh.; *°tā-tva*, n. fidelity to a h°, R. **-śoka**, m. grief for a h° or lord; *-para*, mfn. absorbed in it, MBh.; *-parītâṅgin*, mfn. whose limbs are affected by it, ib.; *°kâbhipīḍita*, mfn. afflicted by it, ib. **-sāt**, ind. to a h°; *-kṛitā*, f. a married woman, Yājñ. **-sārasvata**, m. N. of a poet, Cat. **-sthāna**, n. N. of a place of pilgrimage, MBh. **-sneha**, m. love of a h°; *-parīta*, mfn. filled with love to a h°, R. **-svāmin**, m. N. of the poet Bhaṭṭi, Cat. **-hari**, m. N. of a well-known poet and grammarian (of the 7th century A.D.; author of 300 moral, political, and religious maxims comprised in 3 Śatakas, and of the Vākyapadīya and other gram. wks., and according to some also of the Bhaṭṭi-kāvya); *-śataka*, n. N. of Bh°'s collection of couplets (cf. above and IW. 533). **-hārya-dhana**, mfn. (a slave) whose possessions may be taken by his master, Mn. viii, 417. **-hīna**, mfn. abandoned by a husband or lord, MBh. **-hema**, m. = *-hari*, Cat. **Bhartrīśvara** (*°tṛi + īśv°*), m. N. of an author, Gaṇar.

Bhartṛika, ifc. (f. *ā*) = *bhartṛi*, a husband (cf. *prôshita-*, *mṛita-*, *svâdhīna-bh°*).

Bhartrima (?), mfn. maintained, nourished, supported, W.

Bharma, n. wages, hire, L.; gold, L.; the navel, L.; a partic. coin, W.

Bharmaṇyā, f. wages, hire, L.

Bhárman, n. support, maintenance, nourishment, care, RV. (cf. *arishṭa-*, *garbha-*, *jātū-bh°*); a load, burden, L.; = *bharma*, L.

Bharmin, m. a person whose father is a Brāhman and whose mother is a Pulkasī, L.

Bharvara, m. = *jagad-bhartṛi* or *prajā-pati*, Sāy. on RV. iv, 21, 7 (cf. *bhārvara*).

भरग *bha-ra-ga*, a word invented to explain *bharga* (*-tva*, n.), MaitrUp.

भरट *bharaṭa*, *°raṇa*, *°ratá* &c. See p. 747.

भरहपाल *bharaha-pāla*, m. N. of a man, Cat.

Bharahêśvara-vṛitti, f. N. of wk. (cf. *bhareha-nagarī*).

भरुक *bharuka*, m. N. of a prince, BhP. (v.l. *kuruka* or *ruruka*).

भरुकच्छ *bharu-kaccha*, m. N. of country or (pl.) a people, MBh.; Var. (v.l. *°kacchapa* or *marukaccha*; cf. Βαρύγαζα); of a Nāga, L. **-nivāsin**, m. an inhabitant of Bharu-kaccha, Var.

भरुज *bharuja*, m. (√*bhrajj*?) a jackal, L. (cf. g. *aṅguly-ādi*; v.l. *bharūjā*); roasted barley, Āpast.; (*ā* and *ī*), f. rice boiled and fried in ghee, Gaṇar. (cf. next).

Bharūja, mf(*ā*)n. (√*bhrajj*, Nir. ii, 2) of a partic. colour (?); (*ī*), f. (prob.) N. of some wild animal, AV.

भरुटा *bharuṭā*, f., *°ruṭaka* and *°rūṭaka*, n. (√*bhrī*?) fried meat, L.

भरेषुजा *bhareshu-jā*. See p. 747, col. 2.

भरेहनगरी *bhareha-nagarī*, f. N. of a town, Cat. (cf. *bharaha-pāla*).

भर्ग *bhárga*, m. (√*bhrij*) radiance, splendour, effulgence, ŚBr.; ŚāṅkhŚr.; N. of Rudra-Śiva, Kathās.; Prab. (as N. of the number 11, Gaṇit.); of Brahmā, L.; of a man with the patr. Prāgātha (author of RV. viii, 49; 50), Anukr.; of a king, the son of Veṇu-hotra, Hariv.; of a son of Vīti-hotra, BhP.; of a son of Vahni, ib.; (pl.) N. of a people, MBh.; n. N. of a Sāman, ĀrshBr. **-bhūmi**, m. N. of a king, VP. **-śikhā**, f. N. of wk. **Bhargâṅghri-bhūshaṇa**, n., **Bhargôpanishad**, f. N. of wks.

Bhárgas, n. radiance, lustre, splendour, glory, RV.; Br.; GṛŚrS.; Up. [cf. Gk. φλέγος; Lat. *fulgur*]; N. of a Brahmā, L.; of a Sāman, Lāṭy. **-vat** (*bhá°*), mfn. clear, shrill (said of the voice), AV.

Bhargāyaṇa, (prob.) w.r. for *bhārg°*.

Bhargya, m. N. of Śiva, L.

भर्छु *bharchu*, m. N. of a poet, Cat. (prob. w.r. for *bharvu*).

भर्जन *bharjana*, mfn. (√*bhrij*) roasting, i.e. burning, destroying (with gen.), BhP.; n. the act of roasting or frying, KātyŚr.; a frying-pan, ib., Sch.

भर्णस् *bharṇas*. See col. 1.

भर्तव्य *bhartavya*, *bhartṛi*. See col. 1.

भर्त्स् *bharts*, cl. 10. Ā. (Dhātup. xxxiii, 9) *bhartsayate* (really P. *bhartsayati* and once Ā. p. *°sayamāna*, Pañc. [B]; rarely cl. 1. *bhartsati*; fut. *bhartsyāmi* [AV.], prob. w.r.; Pass. *bhartsyate*, MBh.), to menace, threaten, abuse, revile, deride, AV.; MBh.; Kāv. &c.

Bhartsaka, mfn. (ifc.) threatening, reviling, L. *°sana*, n. (or *ā*, f.) threatening, a threat, menace, curse, Kathās.; Sāh. *°sita*, mfn. threatened, menaced, Kāv.; Pañc.; n. = prec., Daś.

भर्त्सपत्त्रिका *bhartsa-pattrikā*, (prob.) w.r. for *bhṛiśa-p°*.

भर्ब् *bharb* or *bharbh*, cl. 1. P. *bharbati*, *bharbhati*, to hurt, injure, Dhātup. xv, 71.

भर्भरा *bharbharā*, ind. (with √*bhū*) to become entangled or confounded, MaitrS.

भर्म *bharma* &c. See col. 1.

भर्म्याश्व *bharmyáśva* (?), m. N. of a prince (father of Mudgala), BhP. (cf. *hary-aśva* and *bhārmyaśva*).

भर्व् *bharv*, cl. 1. P. *bhárvati*, to chew, devour, eat, RV.; to hurt, injure, Dhātup. xv, 71 (cf. *bharb*).

Bharva. See *sú-bharva*.

Bharvu, m. N. of a poet, Cat. (cf. *bharchu*).

भर्वर *bharvara*. See col. 1.

भर्ष्टव्य *bharshṭavya*, mfn. (√*bhrajj*) to be fried or roasted, Pāṇ. vi, 4, 47.

भल् *bhal* (or *bal*), cl. 1. Ā. *bhalate*, to describe or expound or hurt or give, Dhātup. xiv, 24; cl. 10. Ā. *bhālayate*, to describe or behold; to throw up (?), xxxiii, 27 (cf. *ni-*, *nir-*, *śam-*√*bhal*).

भल 1. *bhala*, ind. certainly, indeed, RV.; AV. (cf. *bal*, *baṭ*, and Marāṭhī *bhalla*, 'well!')

भल 2. *bhala*, m. (only dat. *bhalāya*) a term used in addressing the Sun, MantraBr.; Gobh. (cf. *bhalla*).

भलता *bha-latā*. See under 4. *bha*, p. 742.

भलत्र *bhalatra* (?), n., Siddh.

भलन्दन *bhalandana*, m. N. of a man (father of Vatsa-prī or Vatsa-prīti), Pur.; pl. his descendants, g. *yaskâdi* (*bhanandana*, *bhalanda* and *°dava* prob. w.r.)

भलानस् *bhalānás*, m. pl. N. of a partic. race or tribe, RV. vii, 18, 7.

भलुह *bhaluha*, m. a dog, L.

भलूट *bhalūṭa*, m. N. of an author, Gaṇar.

भल्ल् *bhall*, cl. 1. Ā. *bhallate* = *bhal*, *bhalate*, Dhātup. xiv, 25.

Bhalla, mfn. auspicious, favourable (= *bhadra* or *śiva*), L.; m. a bear, Hit. (cf. *accha-bhalla*, *bhalluka*, *bhallūka*); a term used in addressing the Sun (only dat.; cf. 2. *bhala*), MantraBr.; Gobh.; (pl.) N. of a people, Pāṇ. v, 3, 114, Sch. (v.l. *malla*); N. of Śiva (cf. above); a kind of arrow or missile with a point of a partic. shape, MBh.; Kāv. &c. (also *ī*, f., and n.); a partic. part of an arrow, MBh.; (*ī*), f. Semecarpus Anacardium, Bhpr.; n. an arrow-head of a partic. shape, ŚārṅgP. **-pāla**, g. *sakhy-ādi* (v.l. for *bhalla*, *pāla*). **-pucchī**, f. 'bear's tail,' Hedysarum Lagopodioides, L. **Bhallâksha**, m. a term used in addressing a flamingo (= *bhadrâksha*), ChUp.

Bhallaka, m. a bear, Pancar.; (*ikā*), f. Semecarpus Anacardium, L. *°kīya*, g. *utsâdi*.

Bhallāka. See *bhallāṭa* below.

Bhallāta, m. the marking-nut plant, Semecarpus Anacardium, ŚārṅgS. (n. = next, n.)

Bhallātaka, m. id., Bhpr. (also *°kī*, f., L.); n. the Acajou or cashew-nut, the marking-nut (from which is extracted an acid juice used for medicinal purposes, and a black liquid used for marking linen), MBh.; Suśr.; Pur. **-taila**, n. the oil of the cashew-nut, Suśr.

Bhalli, f. a kind of arrow (= *bhallī*), Dharmaś.

Bhallika, m. N. of a man, Buddh.

Bhalluka, m. a bear, L. (Uṇ. iv, 41); a monkey, L.

Bhallūka, m. id., MBh.; BhP.; a dog, L.; a kind of shell, Suśr.; a partic. plant, Suśr. (a species of Śyonāka or Bignonia Indica, L.) **-yuvan**, m. the cub of a bear, a young bear, Mālatīm.

भल्लट *bhallaṭa*, m. N. of a poet, Rājat. **-śataka**, n. the 100 couplets of Bhallaṭa.

भल्लवि *bhallavi*, m. N. of a man, Śaṃk.

भल्लाट *bhallāṭa*, m. a bear, L. (cf. *bhalla*, *bhalluka*); N. of a partic. supernatural being, Hcat. (w.r. *bhalvāṭa*); of a king, Hariv.; Pur. (v.l. *°lāka* and *°lāda*); of a mountain, MBh.; of a gate, Hariv.; of a poet (prob. w.r. for *bhallaṭa* or *bhallāla*, q.v.) **-nagara**, n. N. of the capital of king Śaśi-dhvaja, Pur.

भल्लात *bhallāta*, *°taka*. See above.

भल्लाल *bhallāla*, m. N. of an author, Cat. **-saṃgraha**, m. N. of Bhallāla's work.

भल्लिक *bhallika*, m., see above; (*ā*), f., see under *bhallaka*.

भल्लु *bhallu*, mfn. applied to a species of fever, Bhpr. (others *phalgu*); m. N. of a teacher, L.

भल्लुक *bhalluka*, *bhallūka*. See above.

भल्वाचि *bhalvāci* (?), m. N. of a man, VāyuP.

भल्वाट *bhalvāṭa*, w.r. for *bhallāṭa* above.

भव *bhavá*, m. (√*bhū*) coming into existence, birth, production, origin (= *bhāva*, Vop.; ifc., with f. *ā* = arising or produced from, being in, relating to), Yājñ.; MBh.; Kāv. &c.; becoming, turning into (comp.), Kāṭh.; being, state of being, existence, life (= *sat-tā*, L.), ŚārṅgP. (cf. *bhavântara*);

worldly existence, the world (=*saṃsāra*, L.), Kāv.; Pur.; (with Buddhists) continuity of becoming (a link in the twelvefold chain of causation), Dharmas. 42 (MWB. 102); well-being, prosperity, welfare, excellence (=*śreyas*, L.), MBh.; Kāv. &c.; obtaining, acquisition (=*āpti*, *prâpti*), L.; a god, deity, W.; N. of Agni, ŚBr.; of a deity attending on Rudra and frequently connected with Śarva (later N. of Śiva or a form of Śiva; or N. of a Rudra, and as such of the number 11 or of the 11th lunar mansion, Gol.; Var., Sch.; du. *bhavau*=Bhava i. e. Śiva and his wife Bhavānī, BhP.; cf. Vām. v, 2, 1), AV. &c. &c.; of the 1st and 4th Kalpa, Cat.; of a Sādhya, VP.; of a king, MBh.; of a son of Pratihartṛi, VP.; of Viloman, ib.; of a rich man, Buddh.; of an author, Cat.; n. the fruit of Dillenia Speciosa, L.; =*bhavya*, *bhavishya*, *bhāvana*, L. **-kalpa**, m. N. of a partic. Kalpa, VāyuP. **-kāntāra**, m. or n. (?) the wilderness of worldly existence, L. **-ketu**, m. N. of a partic. phenomenon in the sky, Var. **-kshiti**, f. the place of birth, BhP. **-khāmi** (?), m. N. of a man, Rājat. (prob. w. r. for *-svāmin*, q. v.) **-grāmiṇa-vādvôkta**, m. N. of a poet, Cat. **-ghasmara**, m. a forest conflagration, L. **-candra**, m. N. of a man, Cat. **-cchid**, mfn. preventing births or transmigration, Kāv.; BhP. **-ccheda**, m. prevention of births or tr°, Śiś.; N. of a Grāma, Rājat. **-jala**, n. the water (or ocean) of worldly existence, Kāv. **-trāta**, m. N. of an ancient teacher, VBr.; of a son of Bhava, Buddh. **-datta**, m. N. of a man, HPariś.; of the author of Comms. on Naish. and Śiś. **-dā**, f. N. of one of the Mātṛis attending on Skanda, MBh. **-dāru**, n.=*devadāru*, Pinus Deodora, L. **-deva**, m. N. of various authors (also with *paṇḍita kavi*, *bāla-valabhī-bhujaṃga*, *bhaṭṭa* and *miśra*), Cat. **-nanda**, m. N. of an actor, Kathās. **-nandana**, m. patr. of Skanda, Vās. **-nandin**, m. N. of a man, Buddh. **-nāga**, m. N. of an author, Cat. **-nātha**, m. N. of an author (also with *ṭhakkura*, *mahā-mahôpâdhyāya* and *miśra*), Cat. **-nāśinī**, f. 'destroying worldly existence,' N. of the river Sarayū, Pur. **-nigaḍa-nibandha-cchedana**, mf(*ī*)n. (Pañcar.) or **°dha-vināśin** (MW.), mfn. destroying the chains and fetters of worldly existence. **-nibandha-vināśin**, mfn. destroying the fetters of worldly ex°, RāmatUp. **-pratisaṃdhi**, m. entering into ex°, L. **-bandhêśa**, m. 'lord of the fetters of w° ex°,' N. of Śiva, Pañcar. **-bhaṅga**, m. annihilation of w° ex°, delivery from births or transmigration, Hcat. **-bhāj**, mfn. partaking of worldly ex°, living, W. **-bhāva**, m. love of w° ex°, NīlarUp. (cf. *-manyu*). **-bhāvana**, mfn. conferring welfare, BhP.; m. 'author of ex°,' N. of Vishṇu, MW.; (*ā*), f. (ifc.) regarding anything as good fortune, Śāntiś. **-bhīta**, m. N. of a poet, Cat. (lit. = next). **-bhīru**, mfn. afraid of worldly ex° or re-birth, Siṇhâs. **-bhūta**, mfn. being the origin or the source of all being, ŚvetUp. **-bhūti**, f. welfare, prosperity, AgP.; Hcat.; m. N. of a celebrated poet (who lived in the 8th century A. D., author of the 3 dramas Mālatīmādhava, Mahā-vīra-carita or Vīra-carita, and Uttara-rāma-carita; cf. IW. 499). **-bhoga**, (ibc.) the pleasures or enjoyments of the world, Śāntiś. **-manyu**, m. resentment against the world, NīlarUp. (cf. *-bhāva*). **-maya**, mf(*ī*)n. consisting of or produced from Śiva, MBh. **-mocana**, m. 'releasing from worldly existence,' N. of Kṛishṇa, Gīt. **-rasa**, m. delight in w° ex°, Siṇhâs. **-rud**, a drum played at funeral ceremonies, L. **-lābha-lobha-satkāra-parāṅmukha**, mfn. averse to the benefit (and) to the longing for attainment of w° ex° (said of a Buddhist convert), Divyâv. **-vāri-nidhi**, m.=*bhava-jala*, Vcar. **-viti**, f. liberation from the world, cessation of worldly acts, Kir. **-vyaya**, m. du. birth and dissolution, Bhag. **-vrata-dhara**, mfn. devoted to Śiva, a worshipper of Ś°, BhP. **-śarman**, m. N. of a man, Kathās.; of an author (and minister of king Nṛi-siṇha of Mithilā), Cat. **-śekhara**, m. 'Śiva's crest,' the moon, Pracaṇḍ. **-saṃśodhana**, m. a partic. Samādhi, Kāraṇḍ. **-saṃkrānti**, f. N. of a Buddhist Sūtra. **-saṅgin**, mfn. attached to worldly existence, Hcat. **-saṃtati**, f. an uninterrupted series of births and transmigrations, Vcar. **-samudra** (A.), **-sāgara** (Siṇhâs.), m. the ocean of w° ex°. **-sāyujya**, n. union with Śiva (after death), MBh. **-sāra** (Ml.), **-sindhu** (BhP.), m. =*-jala*. **-svāmin**, m. N. of a man, VBr.; of various authors, Cat. **Bhavâgra**, n. the farthest end of the world, Buddh. **Bhavâṅgaṇa**, n. the court of a Śiva temple, Hcat. **Bhavâcala**, m. N. of a mountain, MārkP. **Bhavâtiga**, mfn. one who has overcome worldly existence, Pañcar. **Bhavâtmaja**, m. 'Bhava's i. e. Śiva's son,' N. of Gaṇeśa or Kārttikeya, A.; (*ā*), f. N. of the goddess Manasā, L. **Bhavânanda**, m. N. of various authors (also with *śarman* and *siddhânta-vāg-īśa*), Cat.; (*ī*), f. N. of Bh°'s Comm. on the Tattva-cintāmaṇi-dīdhiti; °*dī-prakāśa* and *-pradīpa*, m. N. of Comms. on it; °*dīya*, n., °*dīya-khaṇḍana*, n., *-vyākhyā*, f. and *-saṃgraha*, m. N. of wks. **Bhavânta-kṛit**, m. 'destroying worldly existence,' N. of Brahmā or of a Buddha, L. **Bhavântara**, n. another existence (a former ex°, KātyŚr.; a later ex°, Pañcar.); *-prâpti-mat*, mfn. one who has obtained an° ex°, Sarvad. **Bhavâbdhi**, m. the ocean of worldly ex°, Śāntiś.; *-nāvi-navika*, m. a pilot on the boat (which crosses) the ocean of w° ex°, Pañcar. **Bhavâbhava**, m. du. ex° and non-ex°; prosperity and adversity, MW. **Bhavâbhāva**, m. non-ex° of the world, W. **Bhavâbhibhāvin**, mfn. overcoming the w°, ib. **Bhavâbhishṭa**, m. 'dear to Śiva,' bdellium, L. **Bhavâmbudhi** (A.), °**bu-rāśi** (Bhartṛ.), m. = *bhavâbdhi*. **Bhavâyanā** (or °*nī*), f. 'coming from Śiva,' N. of the Ganges, L. **Bhavâraṇya**, n. = °*va-kāntāra*, Śāntiś. **Bhavâri**, m. an enemy of worldly existence, RāmatUp.; an enemy of Śiva, Nalac. **Bhavā-rudrá**, m. du. Bhava and Rudra, AV. **Bhavârṇava**, m. = *bhavâbdhi*, Pañcar. **Bhavârta**, m. sick of w° ex°, MW. **Bhavā-śarvá**, m. du. Bhava and Śarva, AV.; °*rvīya*, mfn. relating to them, AVPariś. **Bhavêśa**, m. 'lord of w° ex°,' N. of Śiva, Pañcar.; of a king (father of Hara-siṇha), Cat.; of two authors, ib. **Bhavôccheda**, m. = °*va-ccheda*, R. **Bhavôttāraka**, m. a partic. Samādhi, Kāraṇḍ. **Bhavôdadhi**, m. = *bhavâbdhi*, Vcar. **Bhavôdbhava**, m. N. of Śiva, Kir.

Bhavaka (ifc.) = *bhava*, being, existence (e. g. *parârtha-bh°*, existing for others), BhP.; (*ā*), f. = *bhavatāt*, Pāṇ. vii, 3, 45, Vārtt. 3, Pat.

Bhávat, mf(*antī*)n. being, present, RV. &c. &c.; m. f. (nom. *bhávān*, °*vatī*; voc. *bhavan* or *bhos*, q. v.; f. °*vati*; cf. Mn. ii, 49) your honour, your worship, your lordship or ladyship, you (lit. 'the gentleman or lady present;' cf. *atra-* and *tatra-bh°*; used respectfully for the 2nd pers. pron., but properly with the 3rd and only exceptionally with the 2nd pers. of the verb, e. g. *bhavān dadātu*, 'let your highness give;' sometimes in plur. to express greater courtesy, e. g. *bhavantaḥ pramāṇam*, 'your honour is an authority'), ŚBr. &c.; (*antī*), f. the present tense, Pat.; (*atī*), f. a partic. kind of poisoned arrow, L. **-putra**, m. your honour's son, your son, MW. **-pūrva**, mf(*ā*)n. preceded by *bhavat*, GṛS.; (*am*), ind. with *bhavat* at the beginning, Mn. ii, 49. **-sneha**, m. the love for your ladyship or for you, R.

Bhavad, in comp. for *bhavat*. **-antya**, mf(*ā*)n. having *bhavat* at the end, PārGṛ. **-anya**, mfn. other than you, Ml. **-ahârârtham**, ind. for your food, ib. **-uttaram**, ind. with *bhavat* at the end, Mn. ii, 49. **-deva**, m. N. of a man, Cat. (for *bhava-deva*?). **-bhī**, mfn. having fear present, i. e. afraid, W. **-bhūta-bhavye**, ind. in present, past, and future, Vop. **-vacana**, n. your honour's speech, MW. **-vasu** (*bhávad-*), mfn. having wealth present, i. e. wealthy, opulent, AV. **-vidha**, mfn. any one like your honour or like you, R.; Pañcat. **-vidhi**, m. your honour's manner (i. e. the way in which you are treated), MW. **-viraha-nāma**, n. the mere mention of separation from you, Ml.

Bhavadīya, mfn. your honour's, your, MBh.; BhP.; Pañcat.

Bhavan, in comp. for *bhavat*. **-madhya**, mf(*ā*)n. having *bhavat* in the middle, GṛS.; (*am*), ind. with *bhavat* in the m°, Mn. ii, 79. **-manyu**, m. N. of a prince, VP.

Bhavana, n. (m., g. *ardharcâdi*) a place of abode, mansion, home, house, palace, dwelling (ifc. f. *ā*), Mn.; Mbh. &c.; horoscope, natal star (see *bhavanêśa*); m. N. of a Ṛishi in the 2nd Manvantara, VP.; a dog, L.; n. coming into existence, birth, production, Kap., Sch.; Kāś. on Pāṇ. i, 4, 31; a site, receptacle (ifc.), Pañcat.; the place where anything grows (ifc. = field, cf. *śāli-bh°*); = *bhuvana*, water, L. **-dvāra**, n. a palace-gate, Ratnâv. **-pati**, m. = *-svāmin*, A.; pl. (with Jainas) a partic. class of gods, L. **-sthāna**, n. the place or room for a house, Hcat. **-svāmin**, m. the lord of a house, paterfamilias, ib. **Bhavanâdhīśa**, m. pl. = prec., L. **Bhavanêśa**, m. the regent of a horoscope or natal star, Var. **Bhavanôdara**, n. the interior apartments of a house, W. **Bhavanôdyāna**, n. a garden belonging to a house or palace, Mālatīm.

Bhavanīya, mfn. to be about to become or be or happen (*yushmābhir etad bhavanīyaṃ ca nânyathā*, 'and you must not let this be otherwise'), Kathās.; n. (impers.) it is to be about to become; (with instr.) one should be, Vop.

Bhavanta, m. time, Uṇ. iii, 128; present time, L.; (*ī*), f. a virtuous wife (cf. *satī*), W.

Bhavanti, m. (?) time being, present time, Uṇ. iii, 50 (cf. *bhavantī* under *bhavat*).

Bhavā, in comp. before *d* for *bhavat*. **-dṛiksha**, mf(*ī*)n. any one like your honour or like you, Vop. **-dṛiś** and **-dṛiśa**, mf(*ī*)n. id., Kāv.; Kathās.; Rājat.

Bhavānī, f. (fr. *bhava*; cf. *indrāṇī*, *rudrāṇī*, *śarvāṇī* and Pāṇ. iv, 1, 49) N. of a goddess identified in later times with Pārvatī (she is the wife of Śiva in her pacific and amiable form; cf. RTL. 79), GṛŚrS.; Hariv. &c.; of various women, Cat.; of a river, L. **-kavaca**, n. 'Bh°'s armour,' N. of wk. **-kānta**, m. 'Bh°'s husband,' N. of Śiva, Siṇhâs. **-guru** (L.), **-tāta** (Bhām.), m. 'Bh°'s father,' N. of Hima-vat. **-dāsa**, m. N. of a king (also with *cakra-vartin*), Inscr.; Cat.; of various authors (also with *kavi-rāja*), Cat. **-nandana**, m. N. of a poet, Cat. **-pañcâṅga**, n. N. of wk. **-pati**, m. = *-kānta*, Inscr.; Kāv. **-para**, m. or n. N. of a Stotra, **-pūjā-paddhati**, f. N. of wk. **-prasāda**, m. N. of an author, Cat. **-bhujaṃga**, N. of a Stotra. **-vallabha**, m. = *-kānta*, Bālar. **-vilāsa** (?), N. of a poem. **-śaṃkara**, m. N. of various authors, Cat. **-sakha**, m. 'Bh°'s friend,' N. of Śiva, Bālar. **-sahasra-nāman**, n. N. of ch. of BhavishôttaraP.; °*ma-bījâksharī*, f., °*ma-yantra*, n. and °*ma-stotra*, n. N. of wks. **-sahāya**, m. N. of an author, Cat. **-stava-rāja**, m., **-stava-śataka**, n., **-stotra**, n. N. of work. **Bhavāny-ashṭaka**, n. N. of work.

Bhavāyya, m. N. of an author, Cat.

Bhavika, mfn. well-meaning, righteous, pious, HPariś.; happy, well, right, prosperous, L.; n. a salutary state, prosperity, happiness, L.

Bhavita, mfn. = *bhūta*, become, been, L.

Bhavitavyà, mfn. = *bhavanīya*; n. = °*vya-tā*; impers. also with two instr., e. g. *mayā tavânucareṇa bhavitavyam*, 'I must become thy companion,' MBh.; Kāv. &c. **-tā**, f. the being about to be, inevitable consequence, necessity, fate, destiny, Kāv.; Kathās.

Bhavitṛi, mf(*trī*)n. becoming, being (cf. *tiro-bh°*); what is or ought to become or be, future, imminent (°*tā*, also used as future tense with or without √*as*, ŚBr.; with *bhūta* and *bhavyam*, MBh. vii, 9468), Br. &c. &c.; being or faring well, L.

Bhávitos. See under √*bhū*.

Bhavitra, n. (prob.) the earth or the world, RV. vii, 35, 9 (*bhuvanam antariksham udakaṃ vā*, Sāy.; cf. *bhāvitra*).

Bhavin, mfn. living, being, L.; m. a living being, man, Vcar.

Bhavinin, m. a poet, L. (°*vina*, prob. w. r.)

Bhavila, mfn. = *bhavya*, future, Uṇ. i, 55, Sch.; good, L.; m. = *viṭa*, L.; N. of a man (son of Bhava), Buddh.; n. a house, L.

Bhavishṭha. See *sam-bh°*.

Bhavishṇú, mfn. what is or ought to become or be, imminent, future, L.; faring well, thriving, MaitrS.; (ifc. after an adv. in *am*) becoming (cf. *andham-*, *āḍhyam-*, *dūram-bh°* &c., and Pāṇ. iii, 2, 57).

Bhavishya, mfn. to be about to become or come to pass, future, imminent, impending, MBh.; Kāv. &c.; n. the future, Hariv.; Pur.; = *-purāṇa* (below). **-kāla**, m. the future tense, MW. **-jñāna**, n. knowledge of futurity, MW. **-gaṅgā**, f. N. of a river, Cat. **-purāṇa**, n. N. of one of the 18 Purāṇas (the original of which is said to have been a revelation of religious rites and observances, IW. 512, n. 1); °*ṇīya*, mfn. relating to the BhavP.

Bhavishyôttara or °**ra-purāṇa,** n. N. of the 2nd part of the BhavP. (which is of the same character as the first).

Bhavishyát, mfn. about to become or be, future, AV. &c. &c.; (*antī*), f. the first future tense, Pāṇ. iii, 3, 15, Vārtt. 1; n. the future, f° time, AV. &c. &c.; the future tense, AitBr.; water, L.; the fruit of Dillenia Indica, L. **-kāla,** m. future time, MW.; mf(*ā*)n. relating to a f° t°, Pat. on Pāṇ. iii, 3, 132. **-tā,** f., **-tva,** n. futurity, Śaṃk. **-purāṇa,** n. = °*shya-purāṇa*, Cat.

Bhavishyad, in comp. for °*shyat*. **-anadyatana,** m. not the same day in the future, Kāś. on Pāṇ. iii, 2, 135. **-ākshepa,** m. an objection with regard to the f°, Kāvyâd. 125 and 126. **-vaktṛi** or **-vādin,** mfn. predicting future events, prophesying, MW.

Bhávītva, mfn. future, RV. ii, 24, 5.

Bháviyas, mfn. (compar.; cf. *bhavishṭha*) more abundant or plentiful, RV. i, 83, 1.

Bhávya, mfn. being, existing, present, RV. &c. &c.; to be about to be or become, future (= *bhāvin*), MārkP.; Pañcar. (also for the future tense of √*bhū*, MBh. iv, 928, v.l. *bhāvya*); likely to be, on the point of becoming (see *dhenu-* and *dhenum-bhavyā*); what ought to be, suitable, fit, proper, right, good, excellent, Kāv.; Pur.; Kathās.; handsome, beautiful, pleasant, MBh.; Kāv. &c.; gracious, favourable (= *prasanna*), R.; auspicious, fortunate, Ragh.; BhP.; righteous, pious, Vcar.; true, L.; m. Averrhoa Carambola, MBh. &c.; N. of a Ṛishi in the 9th Manv-antara, VP.; of a son of Dhruva (the polar star), Hariv.; of a son of Priya-vrata, Pur.; of a teacher, Buddh.; of a poet, Cat.; (pl.) a partic. class of gods under Manu Cākshusha, Pur.; (*ā*), f. N. of Umā (Pārvatī), L.; Piper Chaba (prob. w.r. for *cavyā*); n. that which is or exists (= *yad bhavati*), RV. &c. &c.; being, existing, the being present, AV. &c. &c.; future time (see *bhavad-bhūta-bhavya*); fruit, result, reward, (esp.) good result, prosperity, Ragh.; Dhūrtan.; a bone, L.; the fruit of Averrhoa Carambola or of Dillenia Indica, L.; m. or n. one division of the poetical Rasas or sentiments, W. **-jīvana,** m. N. of an author, Cat. **-tā,** f. suitableness, excellence, beauty, Rājat.; futurity, MW. **-manas,** mfn. well-meaning, benevolent, Pracaṇḍ. **-rūpa,** n. good figure or form, MBh.; R.; mf(*ā*)n. handsome, beautiful, R. **Bhavyâkṛiti,** mfn. of good form or appearance, lovely, beautiful, Kathās.

भवर्ग *bha-varga* &c. See under 4. *bha*.

भवीयस् *bháviyas*. See above.

भशिरा *bhaśirā* (?), f. Beta Bengalensis, W.

भश्रु *bhaścu*, m. N. of a poet, Cat. (prob. w.r. for *bharvu*).

भष् *bhash*, cl. 1. P. (Dhātup. xvii, 44) *bhashati* (ep. also Ā. °*te*; inf. *bhashitum*), to bark, growl (also fig. = rail against, reproach, revile, with acc.), MBh.; Rājat.

Bhashá, mf(*ī*)n. barking, yelping, chiding, VS. (cf. g. *pacâdi*); m. a dog, L.; (*ā*), f. a species of plant, L.; (*ī*), f. a bitch, L.

Bhashaka, m. a barker, dog, L.

Bhashaṇa, m. id., L.; N. of a dog, Vcar.; n. barking, L.

Bhashita, n. barking, L.

भषत् *bhashat* (?), m. the heart, W.; the thigh, ib.; wood, ib.

भस् 1. *bhas*, cl. 3. P. (Dhātup. xxv, 18) *bábhasti* or (3. sg. and pl.) *bápsati* (2. du. *bhasathas*, RV.; Subj. *babhasat* or *bhásat*, ib.; *babdhām*, Pāṇ. vi, 4, 100; fut. *bhasitā*, vii, 2, 8, Vārtt. 1, Pat.; inf. *bhasitum*, ib.), to chew, masticate, devour, consume, RV.; AV.; ŚBr. (cf. √*psā*); to blame, abuse, Dhātup. xxv, 18 (cf. √*bharts*); to shine, ib.

2. **Bhas** = *bhasman*, ashes (only loc. *bhasi*), BhP.

Bhasat, m. a bird, L.

Bhasád, f. (Uṇ. i, 129) the hinder or secret parts, (esp.) pudendum muliebre, RV.; AV.; VS.; Br.; GṛŚrS. (°*sat-tás*, ind. on or from the posteriors; down to the p°); glans penis (= *liṅgâgra*), Mahīdh.; Mons Veneris, W.; the region of the hips (= *kaṭi-pradeśa*), ĀpŚr., Sch.; (with *ā*), down the region of the hips (L. also 'flesh; a piece of wood; a float, raft; a sort of duck; the sun; a month; time').

Bhasadyà, mfn. being or situated on the hinder parts, AV.

Bhasana, m. a bee, L.

Bhasanta, m. time, L.

Bhasala, m. a large black bee, L.

Bhasita, mfn. reduced to ashes, BhP.; n. ashes, Bhām.

Bhastrakā, f. dimin. fr. *bhastrā*, Vop. (cf. *bhastrākā* and *bhastrikā*, Pāṇ. vii, 3, 47).

Bhastra-phalā, prob. w. r. for *bhastrā-phalā*.

Bhástrā, f. a leathern bottle or vessel (used for carrying or holding water), ŚBr. &c. &c.; a skin, pouch, leathern bag (cf. *mātrā-* and *hema-bh°*); a bellows or a large hide with valves and a clay nozzle so used, Kāv.; Pur.; a partic. manner of recitation, TāṇḍBr. **-phalā,** f. a species of plant, Pāṇ. iv, 1, 64, Vārtt. 2, Pat. **-vat,** mfn. furnished with a bellows or sack, L.

Bhastrākā, f. dimin. fr. *bhastrā*, L. (cf. Pāṇ. vii, 3, 47).

Bhastrika, mf(*ī*)n. = *bhastrayā harati*, Pāṇ. iv, 4, 16; (*ikā*), f. a little bag, Daś. (cf. Pāṇ. vii, 3, 47).

Bhastrī, f. = *bhastrā*, L.

Bhastrīya, mfn. (fr. *bhastrā*), g. *utkarâdi*.

Bhasma, in comp. for *bhasman*. **-kāra,** m. 'making i. e. using ashes,' a washerman, L. **-kūṭa,** m. a heap of a°, MBh.; N. of a mountain in Kāma-rūpa, KālP. (cf. *bhasmâcala*). **-kṛit,** mfn. (ifc.) reducing to a°, Pañcar. **-kṛita,** mfn. reduced to a°, R. **-kaumudī,** f. N. of wk. **-gandhā, -gandhikā,** and **-gandhinī,** f. 'having the smell of a°,' a kind of perfume, L. **-garbha,** m. Dalbergia Ougeinensis, L.; (*ā*), f. a species of plant, L.; a kind of perfume, L. **-gātra,** m. 'whose limbs are (reduced to) ashes,' N. of the god of love, Pracaṇḍ. **-guṇṭhana,** n. covering with a°, Prab. **-graha,** m. 'taking ashes,' a partic. part of a Brāhman's education, Divyâv. **-caya,** m. a heap of a°, MW. **-cchanna,** mfn. covered with a°, ib. **-jābâlôpanishad,** f. N. of an Up. **-tas,** ind. out of the a°, i. e. from death, Kathās. **-tā,** f. the state or condition of a° (acc. with √*yā*, to become a°), Hariv. **-tūla,** n. frost, snow, L.; a shower of dust, L.; a number of villages, L. **-dhāraṇa,** n. application of ashes (on the head and other parts of the body), RTL. 400; *-vidhi*, m. N. of wk. **-puñja,** m. a heap or quantity of ashes, MārkP. **-praharaṇa,** mfn. having ashes for a weapon (said of a fever), Pañcar. (cf. *-bāṇa*). **-priya,** m. 'friend of a°,' N. of Śiva, Śivag. **-bāṇa,** m. 'having a° for arrows,' fever, Gal. **-bhūta,** mfn. become ashes, dead, R. **-māhātmya,** n. N. of ch. of PadmaP. **-meha,** m. a sort of gravel, Suśr. **-rājī,** f. a row or stripe of ashes, ĀśvŚr. **-rāśi,** m. a heap of a°, L.; °*śī-kṛita*, mfn. turned or changed into a heap of a°, R. **-rudrâksha-dhāraṇa-vidhi,** m., **-rudrâksha-māhātmya,** n. N. of wks. **-reṇu,** m. the dust of a°, R. **-roga,** m. a kind of disease (= *bhasmâgni*), MW.; °*gin*, mfn. suffering from it, ib. **-rohā,** f. a species of plant, L. **-lalāṭikā,** f. a mark made with a° on the forehead, Kād. **-lepana,** n. smearing with a°, Cāṇ. **-vādâvalī,** f. N. of wk. **-vidhi,** m. any rite or ceremony performed with a°, MW. **-vedhaka,** m. camphor, L. **-śayyā-śayāna,** m. 'lying on a couch of a°,' N. of Śiva, MW. **-śarkarā,** f. (prob.) potash, Suśr. **-śāyin,** mfn. lying on a°, R.; m. N. of Śiva, Śivag. **-śuddhi-kara,** m. 'performing purification with a°,' N. of Śiva, Śivag. **-samīpa,** n. nearness of a°, BhP., Sch. **-sāt,** ind. to or into ashes (with √*kṛi* or *-sād-√nī*, to reduce to a°; (*-sād*), with √*as*, *bhū*, *gam* and *yā*, to be reduced to a°, become a°), MBh.; Hariv. &c. **-sūta-karaṇa,** n. the calcining of quicksilver, Cat. **-snāna,** n. purification by a°; *-vidhi*, m. N. of wk. **Bhasmâkhya,** mfn. called a°, nothing but a°, MBh. **Bhasmâgni,** m. (in medic.) N. of a disease in which the food is over-digested or as it were reduced to ashes. **Bhasmâṅga,** mfn. ash-coloured, L. **Bhasmâcala,** m. N. of a mountain in Kāma-rūpa, KālP. (cf. *bhasma-kūṭa*). **Bhasmâdi-lakshaṇa,** n. N. of wk. 1. **Bhasmânta,** n. nearness of ashes; (*e*), ind. near ashes, ŚāṅkhBr.; ŚrS. 2. **Bhásmânta,** mfn. ending in ashes, finally burnt (as the body), ŚBr. **Bhasmânti,** ind. near a°, BhP. **Bhasmâp,** f. pl. (°*mâpah*) water with a°, Yājñ. **Bhasmâlābuka,** n. (ifc.) a gourd or vessel for preserving a°, Kād. **Bhasmâvaśesha,** mfn. of whom nothing remains but ashes, Kālid. **Bhasmâvṛitâṅga,** mfn. having the body covered with ashes, MW. **Bhasmâsura,** m. N. of an Asura, Vcar. **Bhasmâhvaya,** m. camphor, L. **Bhasmêśvara,** m. a partic. medicinal preparation, Bhpr.; N. of Śiva as a future Tathā-gata, Karaṇḍ. **Bhasmôddhūlana,** n. smearing the body with ashes, Kpr.; °*lita-vigraha*, m. 'whose body is smeared with a°,' N. of Śiva, Śivag. **Bhasmôdvapana,** n. pouring out a°, KātyŚr. **Bhasmôpanishad,** f. N. of wk.

Bhasmaka, mfn. (with *agni*) = *bhasmâgni*, ŚārṅgS.; n. a partic. disease of the eyes or morbid appetite from over-digestion (cf. *bhasmâgni*), L.; gold, L.; the fruit of Embelia Ribes, L.

Bhásman, mfn. chewing, devouring, consuming, pulverizing, RV. v, 19, 5; x, 115, 2; n. (also pl.) 'what is pulverized or calcined by fire,' ashes, AV. &c. &c. (*yushmābhir bhasma bhakshayitavyam*, 'you shall have ashes to eat,' i. e. 'you shall get nothing,' Hit.; *bhasmani-huta*, mfn. 'sacrificed in a°,' i. e. 'useless,' Pāṇ. ii, 1, 47, Sch.); sacred ashes (smeared on the body; cf. *bhasma-dhāraṇa*).

Bhasmasaya, Nom. P. °*yati*, to burn to ashes, Harav.

Bhasmasā́, ind. to ashes = *bhasma-sāt* (?), prob. w. r. for *masmasā́*.

Bhasma-sāt, with √*kṛi* &c., see col. 2.

Bhasmā-√kṛi, P. Ā. *-karoti*, *-kurute*, to reduce to ashes, MW.

Bhasmī, in comp. for *bhasman*. **-karaṇa,** n. reducing to ashes, burning, Dhātup.; calcining, W. **-√kṛi,** P. Ā. *-karoti*, *-kurute*, to make into a°, reduce to a°, MBh.; R. &c. **-kṛita,** mfn. reduced to a°, burnt, ib.; calcined, W. **-bhāva,** m. the state or condition of becoming ashes (°*vaṃ gataḥ*, 'reduced to a°'), Kathās. **-√bhū,** P. *-bhavati*, to become a°, MBh.; Kāv. &c. **-bhūta,** mfn. become ashes, reduced to ashes, Sarvad.; being mere ashes, i. e. wholly worthless, Mn. iii, 97; iv, 188.

भसद् *bhasad*, &c. See col. 1.

भस्त्रा *bhastrā*, *bhastrika* &c. See col. 2.

भस्मन् *bhasman* &c. See above.

भा 1. *bhā*, cl. 2. P. (Dhātup. xxiv, 43) *bhāti* (pr. p. *bhāt*, f. *bhāntī* or *bhātī*, Vop.; Pot. *bhāyāt*, TBr.; pl. *babhau*, Mn.; MBh. &c.; aor. *abhāsīt*, Gr.; Bhaṭṭ.; fut. *bhāsyáti*, Br. &c.), to shine, be bright or luminous, RV. &c. &c.; to shine forth, appear, show one's self, ib.; to be splendid or beautiful or eminent, MBh.; Kāv. &c. (with *na*, to cut a poor figure, Kathās.); to appear as, seem, look like, pass for (nom. with or without *iva* or adv. in *vat*), MBh.; Kāv. &c.; to be, exist, W.; to show, exhibit, manifest, Bhaṭṭ. (v. l.): Pass. *bhāyate*, impers. radiance is put forth by (instr.), Bhaṭṭ.: Caus. *bhāpayate*; aor. *abībhapat*, Gr.: Desid. *bibhāsati*, ib.: Intens. *bābhāyate*, *bābheti*, *bābhāti*, ib. [Cf. √*bhan*, *bhāsh*, *bhās*; Gk. φημί, φάσκω; Lat. *fāri* &c.; Germ. *Bann*; Eng. *ban*.]

2. **Bhā́,** f. (nom. prob. *bhā́s*) light, brightness, splendour &c. (cf. f. of 4. *bha*), VS.; ŚBr.; m. the sun, L. (cf. 2. *bhās*). **-kūṭa,** m. 'having a bright point,' a species of fish, Vās. (also *bhā-kuṭa*, L.); N. of a mountain (prob. the part of the Himālaya called Bhākūr), ib., Sch. **-kośa,** m. 'light-repository,' the sun, L. **-gaṇa,** m. = *bha-gaṇa* (under 4. *bha*), BhP. **-tvakshas** (*bhā́-*), mfn. producing l°, RV. i, 143, 3. **-nikara,** m. a mass of light or rays, MārkP. **-nemi,** m. 'l°-circle,' the sun, L. **-maṇḍala,** n. a circle of l°, garland of rays, L. **-mati,** f. (fr. *bhā-mat*) N. of a Comm. by Vācaspati-miśra on Śaṃkarâcārya's Comm. on the Brahma-sūtras (also °*tī-nibandha*); *-kāra*, m. N. of Vācaspati-miśra; *-tilaka*, n., *-vilāsa*, m. N. of Comms. on the Bhāmatī. **-ravi,** m. N. of the author of the Kirātârjunīya (first mentioned in an Inscr. of 634 A.D.) **-ruci,** m. N. of an author on Dharma and Vedânta, Cat. **-rūpa** (*bhā́-*), mfn. shining, brilliant, ŚBr., Up. **-** 1. **-vana,** n. (for 2. *bhāvana*, see p. 755, col. 1) a forest of rays, Ghaṭ. **-sarva-jña,** m. N. of an author, Cat.

Bhāta, mfn. shining, appearing &c.; = *prabhāta*, L.; n. (impers.) appearance has been made by (instr.), BhP.

Bhāti, f. light, splendour, BhP.; evidence, perception, knowledge, ib.

Bhātu, m. the sun, L.; = *dīpta*, L. (cf. *bhānu*).

Bhāna, n. appearance, evidence, perception, Vedāntas.; Bhāshāp. &c.; light, lustre, L. **-tas**, ind. in consequence of the appearance, MW. **-vat**, mfn. having the appearance, ib.

Bhānava, mfn. peculiar to the sun, L.; (*ī*), f. a kind of pace, Saṃgīt.

Bhānavīya, mfn. coming from or belonging to the sun, MaitrUp.; Naish.; n. the right eye, L.

Bhānú, m. appearance, brightness, light or a ray of light, lustre, splendour, RV. &c. &c.; the sun, MBh.; Kāv. &c.; a king, prince, master, lord, L.; N. of the chapters of the dictionary of an anonymous author, Cat.; N. of Śiva, L.; of an Āditya, RāmatUp.; of a Deva-gandharva, MBh.; of a son of Kṛishṇa, ib.; of a Yādava, Hariv.; of the father of the 15th Arhat of the present Avasarpiṇī, L.; of a prince (son of Prati-vyoma), BhP.; of a son of Viśva-dhara and father of Hari-nātha, Cat.; of a pupil of Śaṃkarâcārya, Cat.; of various authors (also with *dīkshita*, *paṇḍita*, *bhaṭṭa* &c.), ib.; pl. the Ādityas (children of Bhānu), Hariv.; Pur.; the gods of the 3rd Manv-antara, Hariv.; f. a handsome wife (= *bhānu-matī*), L.; N. of a daughter of Daksha (wife of Dharma or Manu and mother of Bhānu and Āditya), Hariv.; VP.; of the mother of Devarshabha, BhP.; of a daughter of Kṛishṇa, Hariv.; of the mother of the Dānava Śakuni &c., BhP. **-kara**, m. N. of a poet, Cat. **-kesara**, m. 'ray-maned,' the sun, L. **-candra**, m. 'ray-moon,' N. of a prince, VP.; of an author, Cat.; *-gaṇi*, m. N. of Sch. on Vasanta-rāja's Śakunârṇava. **-caritra**, n. N. of a poem. **-ja**, m. 'son of the sun,' the planet Saturn, Cat. **-ji** (also with *dīkshita*) and **-jit**, m. N. of authors, Cat. **-tā**, f. the state or condition of being the sun, Naish. **-datta**, m. N. of various authors (also with *miśra*), Cat. (cf. IW. 457); °*ttaka*, m. endearing form fr. *Deva-datta*, Pat. **-dina**, n. Sunday, Cat. (cf. *-vāra*). **-deva**, m. N. of a king, Sāh. **-nātha**, m. (with *daiva-jña*) N. of an author, Cat. **-paṇḍita**, m. (with *vaidya*) N. of a poet, ib. **-prabandha**, m. N. of a Prahasana by Veṅkaṭêśa. **-phalā**, f. Musa Sapientum, L. **-mát**, mfn. luminous, splendid, beautiful, RV. &c. &c.; containing the word *bhānu*, ŚāṅkhŚr.; m. the sun, MBh.; Kāv.; Var.; N. of a man with the patr. Aupamanyava, VBr.; of a warrior on the side of the Kurus (son of Kaliṅga, Sch.), MBh.; of a son of Kuśa-dhvaja or Keśi-dhvaja, Pur.; of a son of Bṛihad-aśva, BhP.; of a son of Bharga, ib.; of a son of Kṛishṇa, ib.; (*atī*), f. N. of a daughter of Aṅgiras, MBh.; of a d° of Kṛita-vīrya (wife of Ahaṃ-yāti), ib.; of a d° of the Yādava Bhānu, Hariv.; of a d° of Vikramâditya, L.; of the mother of Śaṃkara (Sch. on Śak.), Cat.; °*tī-pariṇaya*, m. N. of a poem. **-mata-liṅga-śāstra** and **-mata-śilpa-śāstra**, n. N. of wks. **-matin**, m. (fr. *bhānu-mat* or *-matī*) N. of a man, ŚāṅkhŚr. **-maya**, mf(*ī*)n. consisting of rays, MBh. **-mitra**, m. N. of a prince (son of Candra-giri), VP. (cf. next); of a son of Udaya-siṃha, Inscr. **-ratha**, m. N. of a prince (son of Candra-giri), VP. (cf. prec.); of a son of Bṛihad-aśva, ib. (cf. *-mat*). **-vana**, n. 'sun-wood,' N. of a forest, Hariv. **-varman**, m. 'sun-armoured,' N. of a man, Daś. **-vāra**, m. Sunday, L. (cf. *-dina*). **-śakti-rāja**, m. N. of a king, Inscr. **-sheṇa**, m. N. of a poet, Cat. **-sena**, m. N. of a man, MBh.

Bhānula, m. (endearing form fr. *Bhānu-datta*, Pat. on Pāṇ. v, 3, 83) N. of a prince, VP.

1. **Bhāma**, m. (for 2. see p. 752, col. 3) light, brightness, splendour, RV. **-nī**, mfn. bringing light (said of the Purusha in the eye), ChUp.

1. **Bhāmín**, mfn. (for 2. see p. 752, col. 3) shining, radiant, splendid, beautiful, RV. &c. &c.; (*inī*), f. a beautiful woman, MBh.; Kāv. &c.; N. of the daughter of a Gandharva, MārkP.

Bhāminī-vilāsa, m. N. of a poem by Jagannātha Paṇḍita-rāja (the 1st ch. contains allegorical precepts, the 2nd amatory subjects, the 3rd an elegy on a wife's death, the 4th teaches that consolation is only attainable through worshipping Kṛishṇa).

भाउलाचार्य *bhāulâcārya*, m. N. of an author (also written *bhāḍalâcārya*), Cat.

भाऋजीक *bhā-ṛijīka* (2. *bhās* + *ṛijīka*), mfn. radiant with light, light-shedding (said of Agni), RV.

भांश *bhāṅśa*. See under 4. *bha*.

भाःकर *bhāḥ-kara*, *-karaṇa*, *-khara*, *-pati*, *-pheru* = *bhās-kara* &c.; see 2. *bhās*, p. 756.

भाःकूट *bhāḥ-kūṭa* = *bhā-k°*; see 2. *bhā*, p. 750.

भाःसत्य *bhāḥ-satya* (2. *bhās* + *satya*), mfn. one whose real essence is light, ŚBr.

भाकुरि *bhākúri*, a word invented to explain *bhekúri*, ŚBr.; patr., Pravar. (cf. *bākurá*).

भाक्त 1. *bhākta*, mf(*ī*)n. (fr. *bhakta*) regularly fed by another, a dependent, retainer, Pāṇ. iv, 4, 68; fit for food, ib. iv, 4, 100.

2. **Bhākta**, mf(*ī*)n. (fr. *bhakti*) inferior, secondary (opp. to *mukhya*), Saṃk.; ĀpŚr., Sch.; m. pl. 'the faithful ones,' N. of a Vaishṇava and Śaiva sect, W.

Bhāktika, mfn. = 1. *bhākta*, regularly fed by another, a dependent, retainer, Pāṇ. iv, 4, 68 (also *nitya-bh°*, Āpast.)

भाक्त्व *bhāk-tva*, n. (fr. *bhāj*, ifc.) the partaking of or belonging to, Pat.

भाक्ष *bhāksha*, mf(*ī*)n. (√*bhaksh*) habitually eating, gluttonous (= *bhakshā śīlam asya*), g. *chattrâdi*.

भाक्षालक *bhākshālaka*, mfn. relating to or coming from the place Bhakshālī, g. *dhūmâdi*.

भाग 1. *bhāgá*, m. (√*bhaj*) a part, portion, share, allotment, inheritance (in Ved. also = lot, esp. fortunate lot, good fortune, luck, destiny), RV. &c. &c.; a part (as opp. to any whole; *bhāgam bhāgam* with Caus. of √*klṛip* or *bhāgān* with √*kṛi*, to divide in parts); a fraction (often with an ordinal number, e.g. *ashṭamo bhāgaḥ*, the eighth part, or in comp. with a cardinal, e.g. *śata-bh°* = $\frac{1}{100}$; *aśīti-bh°* = $\frac{1}{80}$), Up.; Mn.; MBh. &c.; a quarter (see *eka-bh°*, *tri-bh°*); part i.e. place, spot, region, side (ifc. taking the place of, representing), Lāṭy.; MBh. &c. (in this sense also n.; see *bhūmi-bh°*); part of anything given as interest, W.; a half rupee, L.; the numerator of a fraction, Col.; a quotient, MW.; a degree or 360th part of the circumference of a great circle, Sūryas.; a division of time, the 30th part of a Rāśi or zodiacal sign, W.; N. of a king (also *bhāgavata*), Pur.; of a river (one of the branches of the Candra-bhāgā), L.; mfn. relating to Bhaga (as a hymn), Nir.; n. N. of a Sāman, ĀrshBr. **-kalpanā**, f. the allotment of shares, Yājñ. **-jāti**, f. reduction of fractions to a common denominator, Col.; *-catushṭaya*, n. four modes of red° of fr° &c., ib. **-ṃ-jaya**, m. N. of a man, Saṃskārak. **-dá**, mfn. granting a share, VS.; f. N. of a town, Kālac. **-dughá**, m. one who deals out portions, distributer, VS.; TS.; Br. **-dhá**, mf(*ā́*)n. paying what is due, TS.; (*ā*), f. a share, portion, ĀpŚr. **-dhāna**, n. a treasury, Kauś. **-dhéya**, n. a share, portion, property, lot, fate, destiny, RV. &c. &c.; happiness, prosperity, Bhartṛ.; (also m. and (*ī*) f.) the share of a king, tax, impost, Śak. ii, $\frac{12}{13}$; m. one to whom a share is due, heir, co-heir, L.; mf(*ī*)n. due as a share or part, VS. (cf. Pāṇ. iv, 1, 30). **-pāṭha**, m. 'partial quotation' the qu° of a verse by the Pratika (s.v.), Kauś., Sch. **-bhāj**, mfn. having a share (in anything), interested, a partner, MBh.; Pur. **-bhuj**, m. 'tax-enjoyer,' a king, MārkP. **-mātṛi**, f. (in alg.) a partic. rule of division. **-mukha**, m. N. of a man, Rājat. **-lakshaṇā**, f. insinuation or intimation of a part, Vedântas. **-vijñeya**, m. N. of a man, Saṃskārak. **-viveka**, m. N. of a wk. on inheritance. **-vṛitti**, f. N. of a gram. wk. (also °*ttikā*); *-kāra*, m. N. of its author, Cat. **-śas**, ind. in parts or portions (with Caus. of √*klṛip*, 'to divide in parts'), MBh.; Hariv.; one part after another, by turns, by and by, Mn.; MBh. &c. **-hara**, mfn. taking a part, sharing, a co-heir, MBh. **-hāra**, m. division, Col. **-hārin**, mfn. = *-hara*, Yājñ. **Bhāgânubandha-jāti**, f. assimilation of quantities by fractional increase, reduction of quantities to uniformity by the addition of a fraction, Col. **Bhāgânubhāgena**, ind. with a greater or smaller share, at a different rate, MBh. **Bhāgâpavāha-jāti**, f. assimilation of quantities by fractional decrease, reduction of quantities to uniformity by the subtraction of a fraction, Col. **Bhāgâpavāhana**, n. id., Lil. **Bhāgâpahārin**, mfn. receiving a share, Vishṇ. **Bhāgârthin**, mfn. desirous of a share (as of a sacrifice), R. **Bhāgârha**, mfn. entitled to a portion or inheritance, L.; to be divided according to shares, L. **Bhāgâsura**, m. N. of an Asura, Cat.

2. **Bhāga**, Vṛiddhi form of *bhaga* in comp. **-vata**, see s.v. **-vati**, m. (prob.) patr. fr. *bhaga-vat*, Saṃskārak. **-vitta**, m. pl. the pupils of Bhāgavittika, Pāṇ. iv, 1, 90, Sch. **-vittāyana**, m. patr. fr. next, ib. iv, 1, 148, Sch. **-vitti** (*bhā́ga-*), m. patr. fr. *bhaga-vitta*, ŚBr. (cf. Pāṇ. iv, 1, 90; 148, Sch.); N. of a son of Kuthumi, Cat. **-vittika**, m. patr. fr. prec., Pāṇ. ib.; °*kīya*, mfn., ib.

Bhāgaka (ifc.) = *bhāga*, a part, portion, share, Kathās.; m. (in arithm.) a divisor, W.

Bhāgavata, mf(*ī*)n. (fr. *bhaga-vat*) relating to or coming from Bhagavat i.e. Vishṇu or Kṛishṇa, holy, sacred, divine, MBh.; Hariv.; Pur.; m. a follower or worshipper of Bh° or Vishṇu, ib. (cf. IW. 321, 1); N. of a king, VP.; n. N. of a Purāṇa (cf. *Bhāgavata-p°*). **-kathā-saṃgraha**, m. N. of wk. **-kaumudī**, f. an explanation of some difficult passages in the BhP. **-krama-saṃdarbha**, m., **-candra-candrikā**, f., **-campū**, f., **-cūrṇikā**, f., **-tattva-dīpa**, m., **-tattva-dīpa-prakāśâvaraṇa-bhaṅga**, m., **-tattva-bhāskara**, m., **-tattva sāra**, m., **tātparya**, n., **-tātparya-nirṇaya**, m., **-nibandha-yojanā**, f., **-padya-trayī-vyākhyāna**, n. N. of wks. **-purāṇa**, n. N. of the most celebrated and popular of the 18 Purāṇas (especially dedicated to the glorification of Vishṇu-Kṛishṇa, whose history is in the 10th book; and narrated by Śuka, son of Vyāsa, to king Parī-kshit, grandson of Arjuna), IW. 331; 315 &c.; *-kroḍa-pattra*, n. pl., *-tattva-saṃgraha*, m., *-prakāśa*, m., *prathama-śloka-trayī-ṭīkā*, f., *-prasaṅga-dṛishṭântâvalī*, f., *-prāmāṇya*, n., *-bandhana*, n., *-bṛihat-saṃgraha*, m., *-bhāvârtha-dīpikā-prakaraṇa-krama-saṃgraha*, m., *-bhāvârtha-dīpikā-saṃgraha*, m., *-bhūshaṇa*, n., *-mañjarī*, f., *-mahā-vivaraṇa*, n., *-sārârtha-darśinī*, f., *-sūcikā*, f., *-svarūpa-vishayaka-śaṅkā-nirāsa*, m., °*nâdya-śloka-trayī-ṭīkā*, f., °*ṇârka-prabhā*, f. N. of wks. connected with the BhP. **-māhātmya**, n., **-muktā-phala**, n., **-rahasya**, n., **-vādi-toshiṇī**, f., **-śruti-gītā**, f., **-saṃkshepa-vyākhyā**, f., **-saṃgraha**, m., **-saṃdarbha**, m., **-saptâhânukramaṇikā**, f., **-samuccaye sahasra-nāma-stotra**, n., **-sāra**, m., **-sāra-saṃgraha**, m., **-sāra-samuccaya**, m., **-siddhânta-saṃgraha**, m., **-stotra**, n. N. of wks. **Bhāgavatâmṛita**, n., °**tâmṛita-kaṇikā**, f., °**tâshṭaka**, n., °**tôtpala**, n. N. of wks.

Bhāgavatī, f. of °*vata*, in comp. **-mata-paddhati**, f., **-māhātmya**, n., **-saṃhitā**, f. N. of wks.

Bhāgika, mf(*ā*)n. relating to a part, forming one part, Suśr. (with *śata*, n. one part in a hundred i.e. one per cent.; with *viṅśati*, f. five per cent., Pāṇ. v, 1, 49, Sch.); m. N. of a man, Rājat.

Bhāgin, mfn. entitled to or receiving or possessing a share, partaking of, blessed with, concerned in, responsible for (loc., gen. or comp.); inferior, secondary, A.; m. a partner, owner, possessor, fortunate man, TS. &c. &c.; 'the whole' as consisting of parts, Kap.; a co-heir, W.; (*inī*), f. a co-heiress, ib.

Bhāgineya or °**yaka**, m. (fr. *bhaginī*) a sister's son, PārGṛ.; MBh.; Kāv. &c. (also in friendly address to any younger person, Divyâv.); (°*yī*), f. a sister's daughter, MW.

Bhāgī-√kṛi, P. Ā. *-karoti*, *-kurute*, to divide, share, MBh.; Bhartṛ.

Bhāgīya, mfn. (ifc.) belonging to, connected with, Divyâv.

Bhāgīyas, mfn. (compar. of *bhāgin*) entitled to a larger share, Hariv.

Bhāgīratha, mf(*ī*)n. (fr. *bhagīr°*) relating to Bhagīratha; (*ī*), f. N. of the Ganges (or of one of the 3 main streams or branches of it, viz. the great western branch; cf. *nava-dvīpa*), MBh.; Kāv. &c. **-tīrtha**, n. N. of a sacred bathing-place, Cat.; mfn. coming from Bh°-t° (as water), L.

Bhāgīrathī, f. of °*ratha*, in comp. **-campū**, f. N. of a poem. **-nātha**, m. 'lord or husband of Bhāgīrathī i.e. of Gaṅgā,' N. of the ocean, Bālar. **-prârthana**, n. N. of a Stotra. **-vallabha**, m. = *-nātha*, Bālar.

1. **Bhāgya**, mfn. (fr. *bhaga*) relating to Bhaga; n. (with *yuga*) the 12th or last lustrum in Jupiter's cycle of 60 years, VarBṛS.; (scil. *bha* or *nakshatra*) the asterism of Bhaga i.e. Uttara-Phalgunī, ib.

2. **Bhāgya**, mfn. (√*bhaj*) to be shared or divided, divisible (=*bhajya*), Vop.

3. **Bhāgya**, mfn. (fr. *bhāga*) entitled to a share, g. *daṇḍâdi*; (with *śata, viṇśati* &c.) = *bhāgika*, Pāṇ. v, 1, 42, Sch.; lucky, fortunate (compar. *-tara*), MBh.; R.; n. sg. or pl. (ifc. f. *ā*) fate, destiny (resulting from merit or demerit in former existences), fortune, (esp.) good fortune, luck, happiness, welfare, MBh.; Kāv. &c. (*ena*, ind. luckily, fortunately, Hit.); reward, BhP. **–krameṇa**, ind. in course of fortune, Mṛicch. **–pañca**, m. a kind of pavilion, Vāstuv. **–bhāva**, m. state of fortune, MW. **–yoga**, m. a lucky or fortunate juncture, A. **–rahita**, mfn. deserted by fortune, miserable, Bhartṛ. **–ṛksha** (°*gya-ṛi*°), n. the asterism Pūrva-Phalgunī, Hcat. **–vat**, mfn. having good qualities or fortune, happy, prosperous, Kāv.; Pañcat.; *-tā*, f. happiness, prosperity, Sāh. **–vaśāt**, ind. from the force or influence of destiny, through fate, Pañcat. **–viparyaya** (Rājat.), **-viplava** (Ragh.), m. ill-luck, misfortune. **–vṛitti**, f. course or state of fortune, destiny, MW. **–vaishamya**, n. (R.), **-saṃkshaya**, m. (MBh.) bad fortune, calamity. **–samṛiddhi** (Inscr.), **-sampad** (Ragh.), f. good fortune, prosperity. **Bhāgyâyatta**, mfn. dependent on fate, Śak. **Bhāgyôdaya**, m. rise of fortune, rising prosperity, Amar.

Bhāj, mfn. (mostly ifc.; exceptionally with gen.) sharing or participating in, entitled to, possessing, enjoying, perceiving, feeling, sensible of, devoted to, intent upon, Br. &c. &c.; forming a part of, belonging to, RPrāt.; joined or connected with, liable to, MBh.; Kāv. &c.; occupying, inhabiting, frequenting, dwelling or living in or on, Kāv.; MārkP.; going or resorting to, falling into, seeking, Ragh.; Kir.; revering, worshipping, Bhag.; Ragh.; what is due, duty, concern (=*kartavya*), Bhaṭṭ.

Bhājaka, m. (fr. Caus.) a divisor (in arithm.), Col.

Bhā́jana, n. (fr. Caus.) sharing, division (in arithm.), Col.; mf(*ā*)n. (ifc.) sharing or participating in, entitled or relating or belonging to, Br. &c. &c.; n. 'partaker of,' a recipient, receptacle, (esp.) a vessel, pot, plate, cup, &c. MBh.; Kāv. &c.; (with gen. or ifc. with f. *ā*), a place or person in which anything is collected or in whom any quality is conspicuous, any fit object or clever or deserving person, ib. (cf. *pātra*); the act of representing, representation (*ena*, ind. with gen. in the place of; ifc. a representative, deputy, substitute, serving for, equivalent to), Br.; GṛS.; a partic. measure (=an Āḍhaka=14 Palas), ŚārṅgS.; m. N. of a man; pl. his descendants, g. *bidâdi*. **–tā**, f. (ifc.) the being a vessel for, possession of, BhP. **–cārika**, v.l. (or w.r.) for *-vārika*, q.v. **–tva**, n. the being a fit vessel for (gen.), merit, worthiness, Mālav. **–loka**, m. (with Buddhists) the world of inanimate things (opp. to *sattva-l*°, q.v.), Dharmas. 89. **–vat**, mfn. a word used to explain *bhadra*, Nir. iv, 10 &c. **–vārika**, m. a vessel-keeper, Divyâv. (cf. *-cārikā*).

Bhājanī-bhūta, mfn. (ifc.) one who has become a vessel for or who has obtained, Kathās.; Lalit.

Bhājayu, mfn. (fr. Caus.) sharing with others, generous, liberal, RV.

Bhājā, f. = *vakra-yashṭi*, Gaṇar. (cf. Pāṇ. iv, 1, 42).

Bhājita, mfn. (fr. Caus.) shared, divided, Sūryas.; distributed, portioned, W.; n. a share, portion, ib.

Bhājin, mfn. (ifc.) sharing, participating in, ChUp.; Kum.; connected with, Kām.

Bhājī, f. rice-gruel (=*śrāṇā*), Pāṇ. iv, 1, 42 (=*paṅka-vyañjana-viśesha*, Vop., Sch.)

Bhājya, mfn. to be shared or distributed &c.; (in arithm.) to be divided, as subst. = a dividend, Siddhântaś.

भागल *bhāgala*, m. patr. fr. *bhagala* (also pl.), Saṃskārak. °**laka**, mfn., g. *arīhaṇâdi*. °**li**, m. patr. or metron. of a teacher, Kauś.; Vait. °**leya**, m. patr. fr. *bhāgali*, Saṃskārak.

भागीरथ *bhāgīratha*. See p. 751, col. 3.

भागुणिमिश्र *bhāguṇi-miśra*, m. N. of an author, Cat.

भागुरायण *bhāgurāyaṇa*, m. N. of a minister, Viddh.

Bhāguri, m. N. of a man, Bṛih.; of an astronomer, VarBṛS.; of a lexicographer and grammarian, Cat.; of a lawyer, ib.; (*ī*), f. N. of wk.

भांकार *bhāṃ-kāra*, m. = *jhaṃ-kāra*, HPariś. (cf. *bherī-bh*°).

Bhāṃ-kṛita, n. id., ib.

भाङ्ग *bhāṅga*, mf(*ī*)n. (fr. *bhaṅgā*) hempen, made or consisting of hemp, Kauś.; n. (scil. *kshetra*) a field of hemp, Gal.

Bhāṅgaka, n. (fr. *bhaṅga*) a tattered or ragged cloth, L.

Bhāṅgāsuri, m. (fr. *bhaṅgâsura*) patr. of Ṛitu-parṇa, MBh. **–nṛipâjñā**, f. the command of king Bhāṅgāsuri, MW.

Bhāṅgīna, mf(*ī*)n. = *bhāṅga* (also n.), L.

भाङ्गिल *bhāṅgila*, m. or n. (?), N. of a place, Rājat.

Bhāṅgileya, m. N. of a man (or mfn. 'coming from Bhāṅgila'?) ib.

भाज् *bhāj, bhājana*. See col. 1.

भाजक् *bhājak*, ind. (g. *câdi*) quickly, swiftly, L.

भाट *bhāṭa*, m. or n. (√*bhaṭ*) wages, hire, rent, L.

Bhāṭaka, m. = prec., Āryav. **–jīvikā**, f. subsistence by wages &c., HYogaś.

Bhāṭi, f. wages, (esp.) earnings of prostitution, Kathās.

भाट्ट *bhāṭṭa*, m. a follower of Bhaṭṭa (i.e. Kumārila-bh°), Vedântas.; pl. N. of a people, Rājat.; n. the work of Bh°, Pratāp., Sch. **–kaustubha**, m. or n., **-cintāmaṇi**, m., **-tantra**, n., **-dinakara**, m. (and °*rīya*, n.), **-dīpikā**, f. (and °*kā-nyakkāra*, m., °*kā-saṃgraha*, m.) N. of wks. **–deśa**, m. the country of the Bhāṭṭas, L. **–nayôddyota**, m., **-paribhāshā**, f. (and °*shā-prakāśikā*, f.), **-bhāskara**, m., **-rahasya**, n., **-śabda-pariccheda**, **-śabdêndusekhara**, m., **-saṃgraha**, m., **-sāra**, m. (and °*ra-kārikā*, f.) N. of wks. **Bhāṭṭâlaṃkāra**, m., **Bhāṭṭôtpāṭana**, n. N. of wks.

भाडित *bhāḍita*, mfn. relating to Bhāḍitya, g. *kaṇvâdi*.

Bhāḍitāyana, m. patr. fr. *bhaḍita*, VBr. (cf. g. *aśvâdi*). °**ḍitya**, id., g. *gargâdi*.

भाडिलायन *bhāḍilāyana*, m. patr. fr. *bhaḍila*, g. *aśvâdi*.

भाण् *bhāṇ*, onomat., imitation of the noise of breathing or hissing, ŚBr.

भाण *bhāṇa*, m. (√*bhaṇ*) recitation (esp. of the Buddhist law), MWB. 44; N. of a sort of dramatic entertainment (in which only one of the interlocutors appears on the scene, or a narrative of some intrigue told either by the hero or a third person), Daśar.; Sāh.; Pratāp. (cf. IW. 471). **–sthāna**, n. N. of a place, Cat.

Bhāṇaka, m. (cf. *dharma-bh*°) a proclaimer, declarer, reciter, MWB. 70; (*ikā*), f. a kind of dramatic performance, Sāh. (cf. *bhāṇa* and IW. 472).

भाण्ड *bhāṇḍa*, m. (√*bhaṇḍ*?) Thespesia Populneoides (=*gardabhâṇḍa*), L.; (*ī*), f. a species of plant, Suśr. (perhaps = *bhaṇḍī*, Rubia Munjista, or Hydrocotyle Asiatica, L.); n. (ifc. f. *ā*) any vessel, pot, dish, pail, vat, box, case, Mn.; MBh. &c.; any implement, tool, instrument, ib.; horse-trappings, harness, MBh.; R.; any ornament, ib.; a musical instrument (cf. *-vādana*); goods, wares, merchandise (also m. pl.), Mn.; Yājñ.; MBh. &c.; capital, Kathās.; treasure, L.; the bed of a river, L.; (fr. *bhaṇḍa*) mimicry, buffoonery, L. (cf. *putra-* and *bhrātṛi-bh*°). **–gopaka**, m. the keeper of vessels or utensils (in a temple), Buddh. **–pati**, m. a possessor of wares, merchant, Rājat.; Pañcat. **–puṭa**, m. 'sharpener of instruments i.e. razors,' a barber, L.; a partic. contrivance for calcining metals, Bhpr. **–pushpa**, m. a sort of snake, L. **–pūrṇa**, mfn. (a cart) laden with vessels or with merchandise, Mn. viii, 405. **–pratibhāṇḍaka**, n. 'commodity for commodity,' computation of the exchange of goods, barter, Col. **–bhajaka**, m. the distributer of vessels or utensils (in a temple), Buddh. **–bharaka**, m. the contents of any vessel, W. **–mūlya**, n. capital consisting in wares, Kathās. **–rañjaka-mṛittikā**, f. a partic. colouring earth used by potters, Bhpr. **–vādana**, n. playing on a musical instrument, Mn. x, 49. **–vādya**, n. a musical instrument, Bhar. **–śālā**, f. a storehouse, magazine, Śatr. **Bhāṇḍâgāra**, n. id.: a treasury, Yājñ.; MBh. &c.; a treasure, Kathās.; °*rika*, m. a treasurer, ib. **Bhāṇḍânusārin**, mfn. hanging to a pot or vessel, MW. **Bhāṇḍā-pura**, n. N. of a city, Rājat. **Bhāṇḍâvakāśa-da**, m. one who grants (thieves) room for (concealing their) implements, Mn. ix, 271. **Bhāṇḍôdara**, n. the cavity or interior of a vessel, MW. **Bhāṇḍôpapurāṇa**, n. N. of an Upa-purāṇa.

Bhāṇḍaka, m. (Siddh.) or n. a small vessel, cup, plate, box, chest, Kathās.; (ifc.) goods, merchandise, ib.; (*ikā*), f. an implement, tool, L.; a kind of plant (see *kāla-bh*°).

Bhāṇḍana, (prob.) n. a quarrel, Divyâv.

Bhāṇḍāyana (Uttarar.), °**ni** (MBh.), m. patr. fr. *bhāṇḍa*.

Bhāṇḍāra, m. = (and fr.) *bhāṇḍâgāra*, a storehouse, Cat. (cf. RTL. 248). **–gṛiha**, n. id., Kuval., Sch.

Bhāṇḍārika (Bhojapr.), °**rin** (Cāṇ.), m. = *bhāṇḍâgārika*.

Bhāṇḍi, a razor-case, g. *chāttry-ādi*. **–vāha**, m. a barber, L. **–śālā**, f. (prob.) a barber's shop, Pāṇ. vi, 2, 86.

Bhāṇḍika, m. a barber, L.; (*ā*), f. an instrument (?), Divyâv.

Bhāṇḍijaṅghi, m. patr. fr. *bhaṇḍi-jaṅgha*, Pat. on Pāṇ. ii, 4, 58.

Bhāṇḍita, mfn. relating to Bhāṇḍitya, g. *kaṇvâdi*. °**tāyana** (Lāṭy.), °**tya** (g. *gargâdi*), m. patr. fr. *bhaṇḍita*.

Bhāṇḍinī, f. a chest, basket, MBh.

Bhāṇḍila, m. a barber, L. °**lāyana**, m. patr. fr. *bhaṇḍila*, g. *aśvâdi*.

Bhāṇḍīka, m. a kind of bird, VarBṛS.

Bhāṇḍīra, m. N. of a lofty Nyag-rodha tree on Go-vardhana in Vṛindā-vana, Hariv.; Gīt.; of a Dānava, Kathās. **–bhāshā-vyākaraṇa**, n. N. of wk. **–vana-nandana** and **-vana-vāsin**, m. N. of Kṛishṇa, Pañcar.

भाति *bhāti, bhātu*. See p. 750 &c.

भादिग *bhādiga*, m. N. of a man, Cat.

भाद्र *bhādra*, m. (fr. *bhadra*, of which it is also the Vṛiddhi form in comp.) the month Bhādra (=*-pada* below), Rājat.; (*ī*), f. (scil. *tithi*) the day of full moon in the month Bh°, Col. **–dārava**, mfn. relating to or coming from Bhadra-dāru, Pāṇ. iv, 3, 139, Sch. **–pada**, m. (fr. *bhadra-padā*) the month Bhādra (a rainy month corresponding to the period from about the middle of August to the middle of September), Var.; Rājat.; Suśr.; (*ā*), f. du. and pl. = *bhadra-padā*, N. common to the 3rd and 4th Nakshatras (q.v.), Sūryas.; VP.; (*ī*), f. the day of full moon in the month Bh°, KātyŚr., Sch. **–bāhavī**, f. (with *saṃhitā*) N. of wk. **–bāheya**, m. metron. fr. *bhadra-bāhu*, Pat. **–mātura**, m. (fr. *bhadra-mātṛi*) the son of a virtuous or handsome mother, Pāṇ. iv, 1, 115. **–mauñja**, mf(*ī*)n. made from the plants Bhadra and Muñja (as a girdle), Kauś. **–varmaṇa**, m. patr. fr. *bhadra-varman*, Vop. **–śarmi**, m. patr. fr. *bhadra-śarman*, g. *bāhv-ādi*. **–sāma**, m. patr. fr. *bhadra-sāman*, Pāṇ. vi, 4, 170, Sch.

भान *bhāna, bhānu* &c. See p. 751, col. 1.

भान्त *bhāntá*, mfn. (√*bhām*?) = *vajra-rūpa*, having the shape of a thunderbolt, or = *candra*, the moon, VS. (Mahīdh.) &c.

भान्द *bhānda*, n. N. of an Upa-purāṇa, Cat. (prob. w.r. for *skānda*).

भाम् *bhām*, cl. 1. Ā. (Dhātup. xii, 8) *bhāmate*, cl. 10. P. (xxxv, 20) *bhāmayati* (occurs only in derivatives, but the grammarians give also pf. *babhāme*, aor. *abhāmishṭa*, fut. *bhāmishyate*, °*mitā*; Caus. *bhāmayati*; Intens. *bābhāmyate*), to be angry or impatient.

2. **Bhāma**, m. (for 1. see p. 751, col. 1; for 3. below) passion, wrath, anger, RV.; AV.; VS.; ŚBr.; BhP.; (with *kavi*), N. of a poet, Cat.; (*ā*), f. a passionate woman, L.; N. of one of the wives of Kṛishṇa (=*satya-bhāmā*), Kathās.

Bhāmitá, mfn. enraged, angry, RV.; TS.

2. **Bhāmin**, mfn. (for 1. see p. 751, col. 1) passionate, angry; (*ī*), f. an angry or passionate woman, vixen (often used as a term of endearment = *caṇḍī*, *māninī*, and not always separable from 1. *bhāminī*), BhP.

भाम 3. bhāma or °maka, m. a sister's husband, BhP.; L.

भामह bhāmaha, m. N. of the author of the Alaṃkāra-śāstra and of the Prākṛita-manoramā (Comm. on the Prākṛita-prakāśa), Cat.

भायजात्य bhāyajātya, m. (patr. fr. bhaya-jāta) N. of Kapi-vana, Nid.; of Nikothaka (q.v.)

भायवशान्ति bhāyavaśānti(?), f. N. of wk.

भार bhārá, m. (√bhṛi) a burden, load, weight, RV. &c. &c.; heavy work, labour, toil, trouble, task imposed on any one (gen. or comp.), MBh.; Kāv. &c.; a large quantity, mass, bulk (often in comp. with words meaning 'hair'), Hariv.; Kāv. &c.; a partic. weight (= 20 Tulās = 2000 Palas of gold), Hariv.; Pañcat.; Suśr.; = bhāra-yashṭi, Kāraṇḍ.; a partic. manner of beating a drum, Saṃgīt.; N. of Vishṇu, L.; of a prince, VP. **–kshama**, mfn. able to bear loads (as a ship), Suśr. **–ga**, m. 'going under a yoke' or 'undergoing loads,' a mule, L. **–jīvin**, m. 'subsisting by carrying loads,' a porter, Kathās. **–tara**, mfn. heavy, ponderous (?), Divyâv. **–daṇḍa**, n. pl. N. of partic. Sāmans, Vas. **–pratyavara**, mfn. (actions) lowest by reason of the bearing of loads, MBh. **–bhārin**, mfn. bearing l° (superl. °ri-tama), TS. **–bhūti-tīrtha**, n. N. of a Tīrtha, Cat. **–bhṛit**, mfn. = -bhārin, RV. **–yashṭi**, f. a pole or yoke for carrying loads, L. **–vat**, mfn. loaded, weighty; -tva, n. weightiness, MBh. **–vah** (strong form -vāh), mf(bhārâuhī)n. carrying a l°, Vop. **–vaha**, m. a horse's canter (also n. and -ā, f.), L. **–vāha**, mfn. = -vah; a porter, carrier, MBh.; m. an ass, L.; (ī), f. indigo, L. **–vāhaka**, m. a load-bearer, porter, VarBṛS., Sch. **–vāhana**, m. id., L.; a beast of burden, L.; an arm, Pañcad.; n. a vehicle for loads, cart, waggon, W. **–vāhika**, mfn. carrying l°, a porter, W. **–vāhin**, mfn. id., Hit.; Suśr. **–vṛiksha**, m. Cytisus Cajan, L. **–śriṅga**, m. a kind of antelope, L. **–saha**, mf(ā)n. able to carry a great load, very strong or powerful, MBh.; Hariv.; m. an ass, L. **–sādhana**, mfn. accomplishing great things (said of weapons), very efficacious, ib.; R. **–sādhin**, mfn. id., Hariv. **–hara**, mfn. = -vāhika, L. **–hārika**, mfn. id.; relating to the carrying of loads, W. **–hārin**, mfn. l°-bearing (said of Kṛishṇa), Pañcar. **Bhārâkrānta**, mf(ā)n. overloaded (as a ship), R.; (ā), f. N. of a metre, Chandom. **Bhārâvataraṇa** (MBh.), °tāraṇa (SkandaP.), n. the taking down or removal of a load from (abl.) **Bhārôḍhi**, f. the bearing of a load, Rājat. **Bhārôddharaṇa**, n. the lifting of a l°, MW. **Bhārôdvaha**, m. a l°-carrier, porter, Var. **Bhārôpajīvana**, n. subsistence by carrying loads, Pañcat. **Bhārâuhī**, see bhāra-vah.

Bhāraka, (prob.) m. a burden, load, weight (ifc., f. ikā, loaded with; cf. phaṇi-bhārikā), Mn.; Kathās.; a partic. weight (= bhāra), Hcat.; (ikā), f. a heap, multitude, Śiś.

Bhārāya, Nom. Ā. °yate, to form a load, be a load for (gen.), Kuval.; BhP.

Bhārika, mfn. forming a load, heavy, swollen (said of a partic. form of elephantiasis), Suśr.; m. a carrier, porter, Rājat.; Kathās.

Bhārin, mfn. bearing a load, heavily laden, a bearer, porter, Mn.; Yājñ.; Kathās.; Śiś.; (ifc.) bearing, carrying, Kāvyâd.; heavy, ponderous (°ri-tva, n.), MW.; deep, low (said of a tone), Śiś.

भारङ्गी bhāraṅgī, f. = bhārgī, Clerodendrum Siphonantus, L.

Bhāraṅgika, mf(ā or ī)n. (fr. prec.), g. kāśy-ādi.

भारडसामन् bhāraḍa-sāman, n. (prob.) v.l. for bhāruṇḍa-s°, Cat.

भारण्ड bhāraṇḍa, m. N. of a fabulous bird, Śatr.; Pañcat.; (ī), f. the female of this bird, Pañcat.

भारत bhārata, mf(ī)n. descended from Bharata or the Bharatas (applied to Agni either 'sprung from the priests called Bh°' or 'bearer of the oblation'), RV. &c. &c.; belonging or relating to the Bharatas (with yuddha, n., saṃgrāma, m., samara, m., samiti, f. the war or battle of the Bh°; with or scil. ākhyāna, n., with itihāsa, m. and kathā, f. the story of the Bh°, the history or narrative of their war; with or scil. maṇḍala, n. or varsha, n. 'king Bh°'s realm' i.e. India), MBh.; Kāv. &c.; inhabiting Bh°-varsha i.e. India, BhP.; m. a descendant of Bharata (also in pl. for bharatās), RV. &c. &c.; (with aśva-medha), N. of the author of RV. v, 27; (with deva-vāta and deva-śravas), N. of the authors of RV. iii, 23; fire, L.; an actor, L. (cf. bharata); N. of the sun shining on the south of Meru, L.; (ī), f., see below; n. the land of Bh° i.e. India (cf. above); the story of the Bh° and their wars (sometimes identified with the Mahā-bhārata, and sometimes distinguished from it), MBh.; Rājat.; IW. 371, n. 1 and 2; (with saras), N. of a lake, Śatr. **–karṇa**, m. N. of an author, Cat. **–campū**, f. N. of a poem by Ananta-kavi. **–tātparya-nirṇaya**, m., **-tātparya-saṃgraha**, m., **-nirvacana**, n., **-pada-prakāśa**, m., **-bhāva-dīpa**, m., **-mañjarī**, f., **-mālā-kośa**, m. N. of wks. **–varsha**, n. = tam varsham above. **–vyākhyā**, f., **-śravaṇa-vidhi**, m., **-saṃgraha-dīpikā**, f. N. of wks. **–sattama**, m. the best of the descendants of Bharata, MBh. **–sāvitrī**, f., **-sāvitrī-stotra**, n., **-sūci**, f. N. of wks. **–sūtra**, n. 'short sketch of the Mahābhārata,' N. of MBh. i, 61. **Bhāratâcārya**, m. N. of a preceptor, Cat.; of Arjuna-miśra (Sch. on MBh.) **Bhāratârtha-dīpikā**, f. and **Bhāratârtha-prakāśa**, m. N. of two Commentaries on MBh.

Bhāratī, f. of °rata; a female descendant of Bharata, L.; N. of a deity (in RV. often invoked among the Āprī deities and esp. together with Ilā and Sarasvatī, accord. to Nir. viii, 13 a daughter of Āditya; later identified with Sarasvatī, the goddess of speech), RV. &c. &c.; speech, voice, word, eloquence, literary composition, dramatic art or recitation, MBh.; Kāv. &c.; (with vṛitti), a partic. kind of style, Daśar.; Sāh. (cf. IW. 503, n. 1); the Sanskṛit speech of an actor, L.; a quail, L.; Ocymum Sacrum, L.; N. of a river, MBh.; one of the 10 orders of religious mendicants traced back to pupils of Śaṃkarâcārya (the members of which add the word bhāratī to their names), W.; Cat. **–kavi**, m. N. of a poet, ŚārṅgP. **–kṛishṇâcārya**, m. N. of a preceptor, W. **–candra**, m. N. of a king, Inscr. **–tīrtha**, m. N. of an author (the Guru of Sāyaṇa), Cat. (°thīya, n. his wk.); n. N. of a sacred bathing-place, Cat. **–nīrājana**, n. N. of a poem (containing the praise of Sarasvatī) by Lakshmī-nārāyaṇa. **–yati**, m. N. of an author, Cat. **–vat**, mfn. accompanied by Bhāratī (said of Indra), AitBr. **–śrī-nṛisiṉha**, m. N. of a teacher, Cat.

Bhāratīya, n. N. of wk.

Bhārateya, m. patr. fr. bhārata (or bharata), g. śubhrâdi.

भारद्वाज bhāradvāja, mf(ī)n. coming from or relating to Bharad-vāja, ŚBr. &c. &c.; m. patr. fr. bharad-vāja, g. bidâdi; N. of various men (esp. of supposed authors of hymns, viz. of Ṛijiśvan, Garga, Nara, Pāyu, Vasu, Śāsa, Śirimbitha, Śunahotra, Sapratha, Su-hotra, q.v.; but also of others, e.g. of Droṇa, of Agastya, of Śaunya, of Sukeśan, of Satya-vāha, of Śūsha Vāhneya, of one of the 7 Ṛishis, of a son of Bṛihas-pati &c., and of many writers and teachers, pl. of a Vedic school), RAnukr.; MBh.; Cat.; IW. 146, 161 &c.; the planet Mars, L.; a skylark, Pañcat.; pl. N. of a people, VP.; (ī), f. a female descendant of Bharad-vāja (with rātri, N. of the author of RV. x, 127; cf. also bhāradvājī-putra below); a skylark, PārGṛ.; the wild cotton shrub, L.; N. of a river, MBh.; VP.; n. a bone, L.; N. of various Sāmans, ĀrshBr.; of a place, Pāṇ. iv, 2, 145 (v. l. for bhar°). **–gārgya-pariṇaya-pratishedha-vādârtha**, m., **-prayoga**, m., **-śikshā**, f., **-śrāddha-kāṇḍa-vyākhyā**, f., **-saṃhitā**, f. N. of wks. **Bhāradvājâgni-saṃdhânâdi-smārta-prayoga**, m. N. of wk.

Bhāradvājaka, mf(ikā)n. belonging or relating to Bharad-vāja; (ī), f. a skylark, SāmavBr.

Bhāradvājāyana, m. patr. fr. Bharad-vāja, PañcavBr.

Bhāradvājin, m. pl. N. of a school, L. (cf. °jīya).

Bhāradvājī-pútra, m. N. of a teacher, ŚBr.

Bhāradvājīya, mfn. coming from or relating to Bhāradvāja; pl. N. of a grammatical school, Cat.

भारम bhārama, m. N. of a man, g. śubhrâdi, Kāś. (v.l. for bharama).

Bhārameya, m. patr. fr. bharama or bhārama, ib.

भारय bhāraya, m. = bhāradvāja, a skylark, ib.

भारव bhārava, m. a bow-string, L.; (ī), f. sacred basil, L.

भारवि bhā-ravi. See under 2. bhā.

भाराय bhārāya. See col. 1.

भारि bhāri, m. a lion, L. (prob. w. r. for ibhâri, q.v.)

भारिक bhārika, bhārin. See col. 1.

भारीट bhārīṭa, m. a partic. bird, L.

भारु bhāru, m. N. of a son of Kṛishṇa, VP.

भारुजिक bhārujika, mfn. (fr. bharuja), g. aṅguly-ādi.

भारुण्ड bhāruṇḍa, m. a partic. bird, MBh. (cf. bhāraṇḍa, bhuruṇḍa); n. N. of various Sāmans, Vishṇ.; MBh. &c.; of a forest, R.

भारुष bhārusha, m. the son of a Vaiśya Vrātya and an unmarried Vaiśyā, L.; a person who worships the mothers or Śaktis on a burning-ground or at cross-roads &c., L.

भारूजिक bhārūjika, mfn. (fr. bharūjā), v.l. in g. aṅguly-ādi.

भार्ग bhārga, m. a king of the Bhargas, Pāṇ. iv, 1, 178; N. of a son of Pratardana, Hariv. (v.l. bhārgava); of a king also called Bharga, VP.; pl. N. of a people, MBh. (B. bhargāḥ); (ī), f. a queen of the Bhargas, Pāṇ. iv, 1, 178; Clerodendrum Siphonantus, Suśr. (prob. w.r. for bhārṅgī); Piper Chaba, L. **–bhūmi**, m. N. of a king, Hariv.; BhP. **–vana**, n. N. of a forest, Hariv. (v.l. bhānu-v°). **–śrī-kānta-miśra**, m. N. of an author, Cat.

Bhārgāyaṇa, m. (fr. bharga) patr. of Sutvan, AitBr.

Bhārgi, m. patr. fr. bharga, Pāṇ. iv, 1, 111, Sch.

भार्गलेश्वरतीर्थ bhārgaleśvara-tīrtha, n. N. of a Tīrtha, Cat.

भार्गव bhārgavá, mf(ī)n. relating to or coming from Bhṛigu, Up.; MBh. &c.; belonging to Śukra (cf. below), R.; patr. fr. bhṛigu (pl. bhṛigavaḥ), Pāṇ. ii, 4, 65; N. of Śukra (regent of the planet Venus and preceptor of the Daityas), R.; Var. &c.; of Śiva, MBh.; of Paraśu-rāma, ib.; of various men (esp. supposed authors of hymns, viz. of Iṭa, Kali, Kṛitnu, Gṛitsamada, Cyavana, Jamad-agni, Nema, Prayoga, Vena, Somâhuti and Syūma-raśmi, q.v.; but also of many other writers or mythological personages, e.g. of Itala, of Ṛicika, of Dvi-gat, of Driśāna, of Mārkaṇḍeya, of Pramati &c.), Br.; ŚrS.; MBh.; RAnukr.; a potter, MBh. (Nīlak.); an astrologer, L.; an archer, a good bowman (like Paraśu-rāma), L.; an elephant, L.; pl. the descendants of Bhṛigu (properly called bhṛigavaḥ; cf. above), MBh.; Hariv.; N. of a people, MBh.; Pur.; (ī), f. a female descendant of Bhṛigu, Pāṇ. ii, 4, 65; Bhārgava's i.e. Śukra's daughter, R.; N. of Deva-yānī, f., MBh.; BhP.; of Lakshmī, L.; of Pārvatī, L.; Panicum Dactylon and another species, L.; n. N. of various Sāmans, ĀrshBr. **–kalpa-vallī-cakra-vidyā-rahasya**, n., **-campū**, f., **-dīpikā**, f., **-nāma-sahasra**, n., **-pañcâṅga**, n., **-purāṇa**, n. N. of wks. **–priya**, n. 'dear to Śukra or the planet Venus,' a diamond, L. **–bhūmi**, prob. w. r. for bhārga-bhūmi, VP. **–muhūrta**, m. or n. N. of wk. **–rāghavīya**, mfn. relating to Paraśu-rāma and Rāma-candra, Bālar. **–rāma**, m. N. of an author, Cat. **–śreshṭha**, m. the best of the descendants of Bhṛigu, MBh. **–sarvasva**, n., **-sūtra**, n. N. of wks. **Bhārgavârcana-candrikā**, f., °na-dīpikā, f. N. of wks. **Bhārgavôpapurāṇa**, n. N. of an Upapurāṇa. **Bhārgavôpâkhyāna**, n. N. of the 13th ch. of the Vāsishṭha-rāmāyaṇa.

Bhārgavaka, n. a diamond, L.

Bhārgavāya, Nom. Ā. °yate, to resemble Śukra, L.

Bhārgavīya, mfn. relating to Bhṛigu; n. N. of wk. (°yāny-adbhutāni, N. of the 70th Pariś. of the AV.)

भार्ङ्गी bhārṅgī, f. (fr. bhṛiṅga) Clerodendrum Siphonantus, VarBṛS. (cf. bhārgī).

भार्णिकार्दमि bhārṇikārdami, m. patr., Cat.

भार्द्वाजी bhārdvājī, f. = bhāradvājī, the wild cotton shrub, L.

भार्मन् *bhárman*, m. or n. (√*bhṛi*) a board for bearing or holding, a table, RV. viii, 2, 8.

भार्म्य *bhārmya*, m. patr. of Mudgala, BhP. (cf. next); N. of a prince, VP. (also pl.)

Bhārmyaśva, m. (fr. *bhṛimy-aśva*) patr. of Mudgala, Nir.; ĀśvŚr.

भार्य *bhāryà*, mfn. (√*bhṛi*) to be borne or supported or cherished or nourished or maintained, TS.; Br.; Hariv.; m. one supported by or dependent on another, a servant, ib.; a mercenary, soldier, Pāṇ. iii, 1, 112, Sch.; (*ā̀*), f., see below.

Bhāryaka (ifc.) = *bhāryā*, a wife; see *sa-bhāryaka*.

Bhāryā̀, f. (f. of *bhāryà*) a wife (or the female of an animal), Br. &c. &c. **-jita**, mfn. ruled by one's w°, Hariv. **-°ṭa** (°*ryāṭa*), mfn. living by the prostitution of a w°, L. **-°ṭika** (°*ryāṭ*°), m. a husband ruled by his w°, a hen-pecked h°, L.; a kind of deer, L.; N. of a Muni, L. **-tva**, n. the condition of a w°, wifehood, Mn.; Kathās. **-drohin**, mfn. acting maliciously towards a wife, Kathās. **-°dhikārika** (°*ryâdh*°), mfn. relating to the chapter on wives, Cat. **-pati**, m. du. man and wife, g. *rāja-dantâdi*; *-tva*, n. wedlock, matrimony Kathās. **-°rthin** (°*ryârth*°), mfn. seeking or desiring a w°, MW. **-vat**, mfn. having a w°, MBh. **-vṛiksha**, m. Caesalpina Sappan, L. **-sama**, mfn. equal to a wife, Ml. **-sauśruta**, m. a Sauśruta (s. v.) ruled by his wife, Pāṇ. vi, 2, 69, Sch. **Bhāryôḍha**, m. = *ūḍha-bhārya*, married (said of a man), Bhaṭṭ. (g. *āhitâgny-ādi*).

Bhāryāru, m. (fr. *bhāryā*) the father of a child by another man's wife, L.; a kind of deer or antelope, L.; N. of a mountain, L.

भार्वर *bhārvarà*, m. 'son of Bharvara, i.e. Prajā-pati,' N. of Indra, RV. iv, 21, 7 (Sāy.)

भार्श्य *bhārśya*, n. (fr. *bhṛiśa*) vehemence, excessiveness, g. *dṛiḍhâdi*.

भाल *bhāla*, n. (L. also m.; fr. √*bhā* ?) the forehead, brow, Kāv.; Rājat. &c.; splendour, lustre, Inscr. **-kṛit**, m. N. of a man, Pravar. **-candra**, m. 'having the moon on his forehead,' N. of Gaṇeśa, Pur.; °*drâcārya*, m. N. of a teacher, Cat. **-darśana**, n. 'appearing on the f°,' red lead, L. **-darśin**, mfn. watching the f° or brow (scil. of his master), attentive (as a servant), MW. **-dṛiś**, **-nayana** or **-locana**, m. 'having an eye in the f°,' N. of Śiva, L. **-vibhūshaṇa**, m. Clerodendrum Phlomoides, L. **Bhālâṅka**, mfn. having auspicious marks on the f°, L.; m. a tortoise, L.; Cyprinus Rohita, L.; a species of potherb, L.; N. of Śiva, L.

Bhālu, m. the sun, Uṇ. i, 5, Sch.

भालन्दन *bhālandaná*, m. patr. fr. *bhalandana*, g. *śivâdi*; N. of Vatsa-prī, TS.; PañcavBr.

Bhālandanaka, mfn. (fr. *bhālandana*), g. *arīhaṇâdi*.

भालयानन्दाचार्य *bhālayânandâcārya*, m. N. of a teacher, Cat.

भालु *bhālu*. See above under *bhāla*.

भालुक *bhāluka*, m. a bear, L. (cf. *bhalla* and *bhālluka*).

Bhālūka, m. id., L.

भालुकि *bhāluki*, m. (prob. patr.) N. of a Muni, MBh.; of various authors, Cat.

Bhālukin, m. (also written *vālukin*) N. of a teacher, Cat.

भाल्ल *bhālla*, mfn. (fr. *bhalla*), g. *saṃkalâdi*. **-pāleya**, mfn. (fr. *bhalla-pāla*), g. *sakhy-ādi*, v. l.

Bhāllakīya, mfn. (fr. *bhallakīya*), g. *utsâdi*.

Bhālluka or **bhāllūka**, m. a bear, L.

Bhālleya, mfn. (fr. *bhalla*), g. *sakhy-ādi*.

भाल्लवि *bhāllavi*, m. patr. fr. *bhallavi*, ChUp.; Śaṃk.; pl. N. of a school, TāṇḍBr. (also °*vin*, pl., ĀpŚr., Sch.) **-brāhmaṇa**, n., **-śākhā**, f., **-śruti**, f. N. of wks. **Bhāllavy-upanishad**, f. N. of an Upanishad.

Bhāllaveyá, m. patr. fr. *bhāllavi*, Śaṃk. on ChUp.; N. of Indra-dyumna, ŚBr.; of a teacher, ib. **-śruti**, f. N. of wk. **Bhāllaveyôpanishad**, f. N. of an Upanishad.

भाव *bhāvá*, m. (√*bhū*) becoming, being, existing, occurring, appearance, ŚvetUp.; KātyŚr. &c.; turning or transition into (loc. or comp.), MBh.; RPrāt.; continuance (opp. to cessation; *ekôti-bhāva*, continuity of the thread of existence through successive births, Buddh., wrongly translated under *ekôti-bh*°), MBh.; state, condition, rank (with *sthāvira*, old age; *anyam bhāvam āpadyate*, euphem. = he dies; state of being anything, esp. ifc., e.g. *bāla-bhāva*, the state of being a child, childhood = *bāla-tā* or *-tva*; sometimes added pleonastically to an abstract noun, e.g. *tanutā-bhāva*, the state of thinness), Up.; ŚrS.; MBh. &c.; true condition or state, truth, reality (ibc. and *bhāvena*, ind. really, truly), MBh.; Hariv.; manner of being, nature, temperament, character (*eko bhāvaḥ* or *eka-bh*°, a simple or artless nature; *bhāvo bhāvaṃ nigacchati* = birds of a feather flock together), MBh.; Kāv. &c.; manner of acting, conduct, behaviour, Kāv.; Sāh.; any state of mind or body, way of thinking or feeling, sentiment, opinion, disposition, intention (*yādṛiśena bhāvena*, with whatever disposition of mind; *bhāvam amaṅgalaṃ* √*kṛi*, with loc., to be ill disposed against; *bhāvaṃ dṛiḍhaṃ* √*kṛi*, to make a firm resolution), Mn.; MBh. &c.; (in rhet.) passion, emotion (2 kinds of Bhāvas are enumerated, the *sthāyin* or primary, and *vyabhicārin* or subordinate; the former are 8 or 9 according as the Rasas or sentiments are taken to be 8 or 9; the latter 33 or 34), Kāv.; Sāh.; Pratāp. &c.; conjecture, supposition, Mn.; Pañcat.; purport, meaning, sense (*iti bhāvaḥ*, 'such is the sense' = *ity arthaḥ* or *ity abhiprâyaḥ*, constantly used by commentators at the end of their explanations); love, affection, attachment (*bhāvaṃ* √*kṛi*, with loc., to feel an affection for), MBh.; Kāv. &c.; the seat of the feelings or affections, heart, soul, mind (*paritushṭena bhāvena*, with a pleased mind), ŚvetUp.; Mn.; MBh. &c.; that which is or exists, thing or substance, being or living creature (*sarva-bhāvāḥ*, all earthly objects; *bhāvāḥ sthāvara-jaṅgamāḥ*, plants and animals), MuṇḍUp.; MBh. &c.; (in dram.) a discreet or learned man (as a term of address = respected sir), Mṛicch.; Mālav.; Mālatīm.; (in astron.) the state or condition of a planet, L.; an astrological house or lunar mansion, ib.; N. of the 27th Kalpa (s. v.), ib.; of the 8th (42nd) year in Jupiter's cycle of 60 years, VarBṛS.; (in gram.) the fundamental notion of the verb, the sense conveyed by the abstract noun (esp. as a term for an impersonal passive or neuter verb having neither agent nor object expressed, e.g. *pacyate*, 'there is cooking' or 'cooking is going on'), Pāṇ. iii, 1, 66; 107 &c.; N. of the author of the Bhāva-prakāśa (= *miśra-bhāva*), Cat.; wanton sport, dalliance, L.; birth, L.; place of birth, the womb, L.; the world, universe, L.; an organ of sense, L.; superhuman power, L.; the Supreme Being, L.; advice, instruction, L.; contemplation, meditation, L. (cf. *-samanvita*). **-kartṛika**, mfn. (a verb) having for its agent the state implied by it, an impersonal verb, Kāś. on Pāṇ. ii, 3, 54. **-karman**, n. du. the neuter and passive state (e.g. *aśāyi*, it was slept, fr. √2. *śī*), Pāṇ. iii, 1, 66. **-kalpa**, m., **-kalpalatā**, f., **-keralīya**, n., **-kaumudī**, f. N. of works. **-gambhīram**, ind. (to laugh) from the bottom of the heart i. e. heartily, BhP.; deeply, gravely, ib. **-gamya**, mfn. to be (or being) conceived by the mind, Megh. **-garhā**, f. censure implied in the notion of a verb, Pāṇ. iii, 1, 24. **-gupti-śataka**, n., **-grantha**, m. N. of wks. **-grāhin**, mfn. understanding the sense, appreciating the sentiment, Pañcar. **-grāhya**, mfn. to be conceived with the heart, ŚvetUp. **-m-gama**, mfn. touching the heart, charming, lovely, Caurap. **-candrikā**, f., **-cintā**, f., **-cintāmaṇi**, m., **-cūḍā-maṇi**, m. N. of wks. **-ceshṭita**, n. amorous gesture, wanton sport, BrahmaP. **-ja**, m. 'heart-born,' love or the god of love, W. **-jña**, mfn. knowing the heart, MW.; (*ā*), f. Panicum Italicum, L. **-taraṃgiṇī**, f. N. of wk. **-tas**, ind. (ifc.) in consequence of being anything, Hit. **-tri-bhaṅgī**, f. N. of wk. **-tva**, n. the state of becoming or being &c., L. **-darśin**, w. r. for *bhāla-d*°. **-dāsa**, m. N. of a man, Cat. **-dīpa**, m., **-dīpikā**, f. N. of wks. **-devī**, f. N. of a poetess, Cat. **-dyotanikā**, f. N. of 2 wks. **-dharma-gaṇi** and **-nātha**, m. N. of men, Cat. **-nārāyaṇa-māhātmya**, n. N. of wk. **-neri**, m. a kind of dance, Saṃgīt. **-padârtha**, m. a thing which has a real or positive existence, MW. **-pāda** (?), m. N. of a lexicographer, Cat. **-pushpa**, n. the heart compared to a flower, VP. **-prakāśa**, m. N. of various wks. (esp. of a medical wk. by Bhāva-miśra); *-kośa*, m., *-nighaṇṭu*, m. N. of wks. **-prakāśaka**, m., **-prakāśikā**, f., **-pratyaya-vādârtha**, m., **-pratyaya-śakti-vicāra**, m., **-pradīpa**, m. (and °*pôddyota*, m.), **-pradīpikā**, f., **-prabodhinī**, f., **-phala**, n. (and °*lâdhyāya*, m.) N. of wks. **-bandhana**, mfn. fettering or joining hearts (as love), Ragh. **-bala**, m. (prob.) the force of sentiment (one of the 10 forces of a Bodhi-sattva), Dharmas. 75. **-bodha**, m. N. of wk. **-bodhaka**, mf(*ikā*)n. revealing any sentiment or feeling, L. **-bhaṭṭa**, m. (with *saṃgīta-rāya*) N. of an author, Cat. **-madhura**, mfn. sweet by (imitating or following) nature (as a picture), Śak. **-miśra**, m. (in dram.) a gentleman, person of dignity or consequence, ib. (only in Prākṛit); N. of various authors (cf. *bhāva-prakāśa*), Cat. **-yatin**, m. an ascetic by life or conduct, HPariś.; °*tī-*√*bhū*, P. *-bhavati*, to begin to live as a real ascetic, ib. **-ratna**, m. N. of an author; *-kośa*, m., *-samuccaya*, m. N. of wks. **-rahasya-sāmānya**, n. N. of wk. **-rāma-kṛishṇa**, m. N. of a man, Cat. **-rūpa**, mfn. really existing, real, actual, Śaṃk.; n. (?) N. of wk. **-lava-vyākhyā**, f., **-leśa-prakāśikā**, f. N. of wks. **-vacana**, mfn. signifying a state or action, denoting the abstract notion of a verb, Pāṇ. ii, 3, 15; iii, 3, 11; = *bhāva-kartṛika*, ii, 3, 54. **-vat**, mfn. being in any state or condition, Pāṇ. ii, 3, 37, Sch. (cf. g. *rasâdi*). **-vācaka**, n. (?) an abstract noun, MW. **-vikāra**, m. a modification of the notion 'to be' or 'to become,' Nir. i, 2. **-vidyêśvara**, m. N. of an author, Cat. **-vibhāvinī**, f. N. of a Comm. on Gīt. **-vilāsa**, m. N. of a poem in honour of king Bhāva-siṇha. **-viveka**, m. N. of a teacher, Buddh.; N. of various wks. **-viśodhinī**, f. N. of wk. **-vṛitta**, mfn. relating to creation or cosmogony (as a hymn; also °*ttīya*); m. N. of Brahmā, L.; (*ī*), f. N. of a goddess, Naigh. **-śataka**, n. N. of a poem. **-śabalatā**, f., **-śabala-tva**, n., **-śabalā**, f. (in rhet.) mixture or union of various emotions, Kuval.; Pratāp. &c. **-śabda**, m. a verb, Jaim., Sch. **-śarman**, m. N. of an author, Cat. **-śānti**, f. the allaying of any (transitory) emotion, W. **-śuddhi**, f. purity of mind, ŚārṅgP. **-śūnya**, mfn. void of affection or attachment, Mālav. **-saṃśuddhi**, f. = *-śuddhi*, Bhag. **-saṃdhi**, m. the union or co-existence of two emotions, Kuval. **-samanvita**, mfn. endowed with existence, existing, living (others 'endowed with the faculty of meditation'), Bhag. x, 8. **-samāhita**, mfn. fixed or collected in mind (others 'concentrating the mind on Brahmā' or 'on the heart'), Mn. vi, 43. **-sarga**, m. the intellectual creation (opp. to *bhautika s*°, the material cr°), MW. **-sāra**, m. or n. (?) a girdle (with Magas), VP. **-sāra-viveka**, m. N. of wk. **-siṇha**, m. N. of a king (also *-deva*; cf. *-vilāsa*), Cat.; *-prakriyā*, f. N. of an elementary grammar. **-sena**, m. N. of a grammarian, Cat. **-skhalita**, n. an offence (committed only) in the mind, Vikr. **-stha**, mfn. being in love, enamoured, Kum. **-sthira**, mfn. fixed or rooted in the heart, Śak. **-snigdha**, mfn. heartily attached, affectionately disposed, Pañcat. **-svabhāva**, m. N. of wk. **Bhāvâkūta**, n. the first emotions of love, Amar. **Bhāvā-gaṇeśa-dīkshita**, m. N. of a man, Cat. **Bhāvâcārya**, m. N. of a Sch. on Gīt. **Bhāvâṭa**, m. (only L.) = *bhāvaka*, affection, emotion; the external expression of amatory feeling; a pious or holy man; an amorous man; an actor; dress, decoration. **Bhāvâtmaka**, mfn. 'consisting of reality,' real, actual (*-tā*, f.), Śaṃk. **Bhāvâdi-prābhṛita**, n. N. of wk. **Bhāvâdvaita**, n. natural or material cause (as thread of cloth), MW. **Bhāvâdhyāya**, m. N. of wk. **Bhāvânandī**, see *bhav*° &c. **Bhāvânuga**, mfn. 'following the object,' natural, simple, W.; (*ā*), f. a shadow, L. (cf. *bhāvâlīnā*). **Bhāvântara**, n. another state or condition, MW. **Bhāvâbhāsa**, m. simulation of feeling or emotion, W. **Bhāvârtha**, m. the simple or obvious meaning (of a word, phrase &c.), W.; the subject-matter, ib. (cf. comp.); mfn. having a verbal meaning (*-tva*, n.), Jaim., Sch.; *-kaustubha*, n., *-caraṇa* (and °*ṇa-bāshya*), n., *-cintāmaṇi*, m., *-dīpikā*, f., *-prakāśikā*, f., °*thâdhikaraṇa*, n. N. of wks. **Bhāvâlīnā**, f. 'cleaving to an object,' a shadow, L. (cf. *bhāvânugā*). **Bhāvâva**, mfn. kind to creatures, tender, passionate, Śiś. (= *bhāvān* or *jantūn avati*, Sch.) **Bhāvā-viśva-nātha-dīkshita**, m. N. of a man, Cat. **Bhāvêśa-phala**, n. N. of wk. **Bhāvâika-rasa**, mfn. influenced solely by the sentiment of love, Kum.

Bhāvôdaya, m. the rising of emotion or passion, Pratāp.; Kuval.

Bhāvaka, mfn. (fr. Caus.) causing to be, effecting (comp.), MBh.; promoting any one's (gen.) welfare, ib.; imagining, fancying (gen. or comp.), AshṭāvS.; having a taste for the beautiful or poetical, Daś.; singing with expression, Saṃgīt.; m. sentiment, affection, L.; the external expression of amatory sentiments, W.; (*ā*), f. N. of a female demon (prob. w. r. for *bhāvukā*), Vcar.

2. **Bhāvana**, mf(*ī*)n. (fr. Caus.; for 1. see 2. *bhā*, p. 750) causing to be, effecting, producing, displaying, manifesting, MBh.; Kāv.; BhP.; promoting or effecting any one's (gen. or comp.) welfare, MBh.; R. &c.; imagining, fancying, AshṭāvS.; teaching, MBh.; m. a creator, producer, efficient, MBh.; Kāv.; N. of Śiva (= *dhyātṛi*), MBh.; of Vishṇu, A.; of the 22nd Kalpa (q.v.); (*ā*), f., and n. the act of producing or effecting, Nir.; Sāh.; BhP.; forming in the mind, conception, apprehension, imagination, supposition, fancy, thought, meditation (*bhāvanayā*, ind. in thought, in imagination; °*nām* √*bandh*, with loc., to occupy one's imagination with, direct one's thoughts to), MBh.; Kāv.; Saṃk.; Vedāntas. &c.; (in logic) that cause of memory which arises from direct perception, Tarkas.; application of perfumes &c. (= *adhivāsana*), L.; (*ā*), f. demonstration, argument, ascertainment, Yājñ.; feeling of devotion, faith in (loc.), Pañcat.; reflection, contemplation (5 kinds with Buddhists, MWB. 128); saturating any powder with fluid, steeping, infusion, ŚārṅgS.; (in arithm.) finding by combination or composition; (with Jainas) right conception or notion; the moral of a fable, HPariś.; N. of an Upanishad; a crow, L.; water, L.; n. furthering, promoting, MBh.; the fruit of Dillenia Speciosa, L.; (ifc.) nature, essence, RāmatUp.

Bhāvanā, f. of prec., in comp. **-purushôttama-nāṭaka**, n. N. of a drama. **-maya**, mf(*ī*)n. produced by imagination or meditation; (*ī*), f. (with *vidyā*) wisdom obtained by med°, Dharmas. **-mārga**, m. a spiritual state, Divyāv. **-yukta**, mfn. thoughtful, anxious, MW. **-vicāra**, m., **-viveka**, m. N. of wks. **-°śraya** (°*nāśr*°), m. 'refuge of thought,' N. of Śiva, Pañcar. **-sāra-saṃgraha**, m. N. of wk. **Bhāvanôpanishad**, f. N. of an Upanishad.

Bhāvanikā, f. N. of a woman, Kathās.

Bhāvanīya, mfn. (fr. Caus.) to be manifested or effected or accomplished, Nīlak.; to be suffered or endured (as pain), Kād.; to be cherished or nourished, MBh.; to be conceived or imagined or fancied or supposed (n. impers.), Kāv.; Sarvad.; to be proved or taught, MW.

Bhāvayavya, m. (fr. *bhāvayu*), patr. of Svanaja, ŚāṅkhŚr.; N. of the author of RV. i, 126, 6.

Bhāvayitavya, mfn. (fr. Caus.) to be cherished or protected or taken care of, AitUp. °**yitṛi**, mfn. causing to be, cherishing, protecting, a protector or promoter, AitUp.; MBh.; (as fut.) one who will cause to be or call to life, BhP.

Bhāvayu, mfn. cherishing, taking care of, protecting, RV. x, 86, 15.

Bhāvi, in comp. for *bhāvin*. **-cakra-vartin**, m. a future king, hereditary prince, Daś. **-tā**, f. the state of being or becoming &c., Daś.; futurity, predestination, ib.; (ifc.) conforming one's self to, Kām. **-tva**, n. the state of being or becoming (in *anya-bh*°), Suśr.; the being obliged to take place, inevitableness, necessity, MBh.; BhP. **-prāyaścitta**, n. N. of wk. **Bhāvy-upadha**, m. (scil. *visarjanīya*) the Visarjanīya following in the Padapāṭha after any vowel except *a* or *ā*, MW.

Bhāvika, mf(*ī*)n. actually being or existing, real, natural, Sāṃkhyak.; full of feeling or sentiment, expressive, Mālav.; future, W.; n. language full of feeling or passion (= *bhāvuka*), Pratāp.; a figure of speech which consists in describing the past or future so vividly that it appears to be present, Sāh.; Kpr. &c.

Bhāvita, mfn. (fr. Caus.) caused to be, created, produced, obtained, got, MBh.; Kāv. &c.; (ifc.) made to become, transformed into, Bhag.; Saṃk.; Sāh.; manifested, displayed, exhibited, Daś.; cherished, protected, fostered, furthered, promoted, MBh.; Kāv. &c.; cultivated, purified (see comp. below); well-disposed, good-humoured, Kād.; elated, in high spirits, MBh.; thought about, imagined, fancied, conceived, known, recognised, MBh.; Kāv. &c.; proved, established, Yājñ.; meant or destined for (loc.), ŚārṅgP.; convicted, Yājñ.; MBh.; soaked in, steeped, infused, Suśr.; ŚārṅgS.; perfumed with, scented, L.; pervaded or inspired by, occupied or engrossed with, devoted to, intent upon (instr. or comp.), MBh.; Saṃk.; Pur.; directed towards, fixed upon, BhP.; (in arithm.) involving a product of unknown quantities; n. a result or product obtained by multiplication (often expressed by the first syllable *bhā*), Col. (cf. IW. 133). **-buddhi**, mfn. one who has cultivated or purified his mind, Sāh. **-bhāvana**, mfn. being one's self furthered and furthering others, MBh. **-vat**, mfn. one who has imagined or conceived or infused &c., W. **Bhāvitâtman**, mfn. 'one whose soul is purified by meditating on the universal soul' or 'whose thoughts are fixed on the Supreme Spirit,' meditative, devout, holy, a sage, saint, MBh.; Kāv. &c.; (ifc.) engaged in, intent upon, Śiś. xii, 38; m. N. of the 13th Muhūrta, L.

Bhāvitaka, n. = *bhāvita*, n., Col.

Bhāvitra, n. the three worlds (viz. earth, heaven, and the lower regions or the atmosphere), the universe, Uṇ. iv, 1, 170, Sch. (cf. *bhavitra*).

Bhāvin, mfn. becoming, being, existing, wont to be (often ifc.), RPrāt.; Hariv.; Ragh.; about to be, future, imminent, predestined, inevitable (often used as fut. tense of √*bhū*), MBh.; Kāv. &c.; as one ought to be, good, able, capable (in *a-bh*°), Hariv.; (ifc.) being possessed of, MBh.; attached to (e.g. *hari-bh*°), Vop.; manifesting, showing, Mallin.; furthering, blessing, Hcat. (cf. *loka-bh*°); worshipping, ib.; beautiful, illustrious, MW.; m. N. of every vowel except *a* and *ā* (prob. as 'liable to become the corresponding semivowel'), VPrāt.; N. of the Śūdras in Plaksha-dvīpa, VP.; (*inī*), f. a noble or beautiful woman, MBh.; Kāv. &c.; a wanton woman, W.; a partic. musical composition, Saṃgīt.; N. of one of the Mātṛis attending on Skanda, MBh.; of the daughter of a Gandharva, MārkP.

Bhāvuka, mfn. being, becoming, disposed or about to be (often ifc. after an adv. in *am*; cf. *andhambh*°, *āḍhyam-bh*° &c., and Pāṇ. iii, 2, 57), TS. &c. &c.; having a taste for the beautiful or poetical, BhP.; producing, productive, L.; happy, well. auspicious, prosperous, W.; m. a sister's husband, HPariś.; (*ā*), f. N. of a female demon, Vcar. (cf. *bhāvakā*); n. happiness, welfare, L.; language full of feeling or passion, Pratāp. (cf. *bhāvika*).

Bhāvyà, mfn. (fr. √*bhū* or its Caus.) future, about to be or what ought to be or become, RV. &c. &c. (in later language often used as fut. tense of √*bhū*; cf. *bhāvin*); to be effected or accomplished or performed, Kum.; BhP.; to be apprehended or perceived, Kathās.; to be (or being) imagined or conceived, AshṭāvS. (cf. *dur-bh*°); easy to guess or understand, Vām.; to be (or being) argued or demonstrated or admitted or approved, Yājñ.; Kāv.; to be convicted, Mn. viii, 60; m. N. of a man (= *bhāvayavya*, Nir.), RV. i, 126, 1 (others 'to be worshipped,' others 'future'); of a king (= *bhāvya-ratha* or *bhānu-ratha*), VP.; n. (impers.) it is to be by (instr.), Mn. v, 150; it should be understood, Mṛicch., Sch. **-tā**, f., **-tva**, n. the state of being about to happen, futurity, KātyŚr. **-ratha**, m. N. of a king, VP. (cf. *bhāvya*).

भावड *bhāvaḍa*, m. N. of a man, Śatr.

भावत *bhāvata*, mfn. (fr. *bhavat*), Pāṇ. iv, 2, 115, Sch.

Bhāvatka, mfn. your honour's, your, Kathās. (cf. Pāṇ. ib.)

भावला *bhāvalā*, f. N. of the wife of Bhāvaḍa, Śatr.

भावाट *bhāvâṭa*, *bhāvâva*. See under *bhāva*.

भाष् 1. *bhāsh*, cl. 1. Ā. (Dhātup. xvi, 11) *bhā́shate* (ep. also P. °*ti*; pf. *babhāshe*, Br. &c.; fut. *bhāshishyate* or *bhāshitā*, Gr.; aor. *abhāshishi*, °*shṭhāḥ*, °*shata*, Bhaṭṭ.; inf. *bhāshitum*, Up.; *bhāshṭum*, MBh.; ind. p. *bhāshitvā*, *-bhāshya*, ib.), to speak, talk, say, tell (with acc. of thing or person, sometimes also with acc. of thing and person), Br. &c. &c.; to speak of or about or on (acc.), Kām.; to announce, declare, Gobh.; to call, name, describe as (with two acc.), Mn.; Śrutab.; to use or employ in speaking, Nir.; Suśr.; Pass. *bhāshyate* (aor. *abhāshi*), to be spoken, be addressed or spoken to, MBh.; Kāv. &c.: Caus. *bhāshayati*, °*te* (aor. *ababhāshat* or *abībhashat*, Pāṇ. vii, 4, 3), to cause to speak or talk, MārkP.; to cause to speak, i. e. to think, agitate, disquiet, R.; to say, speak, MBh.: Desid. *bibhāshishate*, Gr.: Intens. *babhāshyate*, *bābhāshṭi*, ib. (sometimes confounded with *bhash*; cf. √*bhaṇ* and *bhās*).

Bhāshaka, mfn. (ifc.) speaking, talking about, Kāv.

Bhāshaṇa, n. (ifc. f. *ā*) the act of speaking, talking, speech, talk, Nir.; Mn.; MBh. &c.; kind words, kindness (= *sāma-dānâdi*), Sāh.; (in dram.) expression of satisfaction after the attainment of an object, Pratāp.; (*ī*), f. resembling, L. (°*ṇī-kshaulema* (?), m. N. of a family, Saṃskārak.)

Bhāshā, f. speech, language (esp. common or vernacular speech, as opp. to Vedic or in later times to Sanskṛit), Nir.; Pāṇ.; Mn.; MBh.; any Prākṛit dialect or a partic. group of 5 of them (viz. Māhārāshṭrī, Śaurasenī, Māgadhī, Prācyā, and Avantī, also called Pañca-vidhā Bhāshā; cf. under *prākṛita*, p. 703), Cat.; description, definition, Bhag.; (in law) accusation, charge, complaint, plaint, Dhūrtas.; Yājñ., Sch.; N. of Sarasvatī, L.; (in music) of a Rāgiṇī. **-kumuda-mañjarī**, f., **-kaumudī**, f. N. of wks. **-citraka**, n. a play on words, conundrum, Bālar. **-jña**, m. 'versed in languages,' N. of a man, Kathās. **-°nuśāsana** (°*shânuś*°), n. N. of a Prākṛit grammar. **-°ntara** (°*shânt*°), n. another dialect or version, translation, MW. **-pariccheda**, m. 'definition of (the categories of) speech,' N. of a compendium of the Nyāya system by Viśva-nātha, IW. 60, n. 1. **-pāda**, m. the plaint or charge (the first of the 4 stages of a lawsuit; also N. of wk.) **-prakāśikā**, f., **-mañjarī**, f., **-ratna**, n., **-°rṇava** (°*shârṇ*°), n., **-līlāvatī**, f., **-vivṛiti-gītā**, f., **-vṛitti**, f., **-vṛitty-artha-vṛitti**, f. N. of wks. **-sama**, m. 'Prākṛit-like,' a sentence so arranged that it may be either Sanskṛit or Prākṛit, Sāh. **-samiti**, f. (with Jainas) moderation in speech, Sarvad.

Bhāshika, mfn. belonging to common or vernacular speech, Nir.; (*ā*), f. speech, language, Cat.; n. general rule, ŚāṅkhGṛ. **-sūtra**, n. N. of a Sūtra (on the manner of marking the accent in the ŚBr.) attributed to Kātyāyana. **-svara**, m. = *brāhmaṇa-svara*, KātyŚr.

Bhāshita, mfn. spoken, uttered, said; spoken to, addressed, Mn.; MBh. &c.; n. speech, language, talk, ib. **-puṇska**, mfn. = *ukta-puṇska* (q. v.), Pāṇ. vi, 3, 34 &c. (*-tva*, n., vii, 3, 48, Sch.)

Bhāshitavya, mfn. to be spoken to or addressed, R. (v. l. for *bhajitavya*).

Bhā́shitṛi, mfn. speaking, a speaker, talker (with acc. or ifc.), ŚBr.; MBh. &c.

Bhāshin, mfn. saying, speaking, loquacious (mostly ifc.), MBh.; Kāv. &c. **Bhāshi-pakshin**, m. a talking bird, Subh.

Bhāshya, n. speaking, talking, Suśr.; any work in the common or vernacular speech, VPrāt.; GṛS.; Hariv.; an explanatory work, exposition, explanation, commentary (esp. on technical Sūtras), MBh.; Var. &c.; N. of Patañjali's Comm. on the Sūtras of Pāṇini (cf. *mahā-bhāshya*); of the 4th ch. of the BhavP.; a sort of house or building, L. **-kāra**, m. N. of various commentators (of Patañjali, Śaṃkarâcārya, a poet &c.), Pāṇ.; Vārtt.; VPrāt., Sch.; Cat.; *prapatti*, f., *-stotra*, n. N. of wks. **-kṛit**, m. the writer of any Comm., (esp.) N. of Patañjali, Pāṇ. viii, 1, 73, Sch. **-kaiyaṭīya**, n. Kaiyaṭa's Comm. on P°'s Bhāshya. **-candrikā**, f., **-ṭīkā**, f., **-dīpikā**, f., **-navâhnika**, n., **-pratyaya**, m., **-pratyayôdbodha**, m., **-pradīpa**, m. (°*pa-vivaraṇa*, n. and °*pôddyotana*, n., IW. 168), **-bhānu-prabhā**, f. N. of wks. **-bhūta**, mfn. being an explanation, serving as a commentary, Śiś. ii, 24. **-ratna-prakāśikā**, f., **-ratna-prabhā**, f., **-ratnâvalī**, f., **-rāja**, m., **-vārttika**, n., **-vishaya-vākya-dīpikā**, f., **-vyākhyā**, f. N. of wks. **Bhāshyârtha-saṃgraha**, m., **Bhāshyâvatārikā**, f. N. of wks.

भाष् 2. *bhāsh* (√*bhash*), occurring only in *raksho-bhāsh*, q. v.

भाष *bhāsha* w.r. for *bhāsa*, q.v.

भास् 1. *bhās*, cl. 1. Ā. (Dhātup. xvi, 23) *bhāsate* (in older language also P. *bhā́sati*, AV. &c.; p. *bhā́sat*, RV.; pf. *babhāse*, MBh.; aor. *abhāsishṭa*, Gr.; fut. *bhāsishyate*, *bhāsitā*, ib.), to shine, be bright, RV. &c. &c.; to appear ('as' or 'like,' nom. or instr. of an abstract noun), occur to the mind, be conceived or imagined, become clear or evident, Sāh.; Vedântas. &c.: Caus. *bhāsayati*, °*te* (aor. *ababhāsat* and *abībhasat*, Pāṇ. vii, 4, 3), to make shine, illuminate, Up.; MBh. &c.; to show, make evident, cause to appear ('by way of,' instr. of an abstract noun), Bhaṭṭ.; Cat.: Desid. *bibhāsishate*, Gr.: Intens. *bābhāsyate*, *bābhāsti*, ib. (cf. √*bhā*, of which √*bhās* is a secondary form).

2. **Bhā́s**, n. f. (cf. 2. *bhā*) light or ray of light, lustre, brightness, RV. &c. &c. (*bhāsām nidhi* [Prasaṅg.] and *bhāsām pati* [Hcat.], m. 'receptacle or lord of rays of light,' the sun); an image, reflection, shadow, MW.; glory, splendour, majesty, L.; wish, desire, L. **-kara**, mfn. (also *bhāḥ-kara*, Pāṇ. viii, 3, 46, Sch.) 'making light,' shining, glittering, bright, MBh.; Bhartṛ. (v. l. *bhāsura* and °*svara*); m. (ifc. f. *ā*) the sun, TĀr. &c. &c.; N. of Śiva, MBh.; fire, L.; a hero, L.; Calotropis Gigantea, L.; (also with *dīkshita*, *paṇḍita*, *bhaṭṭa*, *miśra*, *śāstrin*, *ācārya* &c.) N. of various authors (esp. of a celebrated astronomer, commonly called Bhāskarâcārya, q. v.); often found at the end of names (e. g. *jñāna-bh*°, *brahmanya-bh*° &c.); n. gold, L.; a kind of breach (made by thieves in a wall), Mṛicch.; N. of a Tīrtha, Cat.; *-kaṇṭha*, m. N. of an author, Cat.; *-caritra*, n. N. of wk.; *-deva*, m. N. of a poet; *-nandin*, m. the son of the god of the sun, Mṛicch.; *-nṛisiṇha*, m. N. of a Sch. on Vātsyāyana's Kāma-sūtra (he wrote in 1788); *-priya*, m. 'fond of the sun,' a ruby, L.; *-bhāshya*, n. N. of wk.; *-rāya*, m. N. of various authors, Cat.; *-lavaṇa*, n. a partic. mixture, Bhpr.; *-vat*, mfn. possessing a sun, Hcat.; *-varman*, m. N. of a man, Daś.; of various princes, Hcar.; Vās., Introd.; *-vrata*, n. N. of a partic. religious observance, Cat.; *-śarman* and *-śishya*, m. N. of authors, Cat.; *-saptamī*, f. N. of the 7th day in the light half of the month Māgha, W.; *-sena*, m. N. of a poet, Cat.; *-stotra*, n. N. of a hymn to the sun; °*râcārya*, m. N. of various authors (esp. of a celebrated astronomer who lived in the 12th century and wrote the Siddhânta-śiromaṇi, IW. 176 &c.); °*râvarta*, m. a partic. kind of headache, L.; °*râhnika*, n. N. of wk.: °*rêshṭā*, f. Polanisia Icosandra, L. **-karaṇa**, Vop. ii, 44; Pāṇ. viii, 3, 46, Sch. **-kari**, m. (patr. fr. *bhās-kara*) N. of the planet Saturn, L.; of the monkey king Su-grīva, Bālar.; of a Muni, MBh. **-karīya**, mfn. belonging to or coming from Bhās-kara; m. a pupil of Bh°, Sāy.; n. N. of wk. **-khara, -pati, -pheru**, Vop. ii, 45; Pāṇ. viii, 3, 46, Sch. **-vat** (*bhā́s-*), mfn. luminous, splendid, shining, RV. &c. &c.; m. the sun, light, brightness, Kāv.; Kathās. &c.; a hero, L.; (*atī*), f. the city of the sun, W.; N. of the dawn or of a river, Naigh. i, 8; 13; N. of a wk.; °*tīkaraṇa*, n., °*tī-vivaraṇa*, n. N. of wks.

Bhā́-ṛijīka. See p. 751, col. 1.

Bhā́ḥ-satya. See p. 751, col. 2.

Bhāsá, m. light, lustre, brightness (often ifc.), MBh.; Hariv.; Kathās.; impression made on the mind, fancy, MW.; a bird of prey, vulture (L. = *śakunta*, *kukkuṭa*, *gridhra* &c.), AdbhBr.; Āpast.; MBh.; Hariv. &c. (w. r. *bhāsha*); a cow-shed, L.; N. of a man, Rājat.; of a dramatic poet (also called Bhāsaka), Mālav.; Hcar. &c.; of a son of a minister of king Candra-prabha, Kathās.; of a Dānava, ib.; of a mountain, MBh.; (*ī*), f. N. of the mother of the vultures (a daughter of Tāmrā), MBh.; Hariv.; Pur.; of a daughter of Pradhā, MBh.; n. (m., TBr.) N. of a Sāman, Br.; ŚrS. **-karṇa**, m. N. of a Rākshasa, R. **-tā**, f. the being a vulture or bird of prey, Mn. xi, 25. **-vilāsa-saṃvāda**, m. N. of ch. of the Vasishṭha-rāmāyaṇa.

Bhāsaka, mfn. (fr. Caus.) causing to appear, enlightening, making evident or intelligible (ifc.), Vedântas.; Sarvad. (*-tva*, n.); N. of a dramatic poet (see *bhāsa*).

Bhāsana, n. shining, glittering, brilliance, splendour, Pāṇ.; Nir.

Bhāsanta, mfn. splendid, beautiful, L.; m. the sun or the moon or a star, L.; the bird Bhāsa, L.; (*ī*), f. an asterism, Nakshatra, L.

1. **Bhā́sas**, n. (for 2. see col. 2) brightness, light, lustre, RV. vi, 4, 3; 12, 5.

Bhāsá-ketu, mfn. (fr. instr. of 2. *bhās* + *k*°) perceivable by or appearing through light, RV. x, 20, 3.

Bhāsāya, Nom. Ā. °*yate*, to resemble the bird Bhāsa, Kāv.

Bhāsin, mfn. shining, brilliant (see *ūrdhva-* and *jyotir-bh*°).

Bhāsu, m. the sun, L.

Bhāsura, mfn. shining, radiant, bright, splendid, Kāv.; Rājat. &c.; (ifc.) excellent in, distinguished by, Cat.; terrible (?), L.; m. a crystal, L.; a hero, L.; n. Costus Speciosus or Arabicus, L. **-tva**, n. splendour, Mālav. **-deha**, mfn. having a splendid body or form, MBh. **-pushpā**, f. Tragia Involucrata, L. **-mūrti**, mfn. = *-deha*, MBh. **-hemarāśi**, m. a glittering heap of gold, Ragh. **Bhāsurânanda-nātha**, m. N. of Bhāskarâcārya after his initiation, Cat.

Bhāsuraka, m. N. of a man, Mudr.; (also *-siṇha*), N. of a lion, Pañcat.

Bhā́sya, mfn. (fr. Caus.) to be made visible, to be brought to light (*-tva*, n.), Vedântas. **-sūtra**, n. N. of a ch. in the Kātantra treating of the meaning of grammatical forms.

Bhāsvará, mf(*ā*)n. shining, brilliant, bright, resplendent, ŚBr. &c. &c.; m. the sun, L.; a day, L.; N. of a satellite of the god of the sun, MBh.; of a Buddhist deity (?), L.; n. Costus Arabicus or Speciosus, L. **-varṇa** (*bhā́sv*°), mfn. light-coloured, having the colour of light, ŚBr.

भासद *bhāsada*, m. (fr. *bhasad*) a buttock, RV. (du., VS.)

भासस् 2. *bhā́sas*, n. (√*bhas*) food, prey, RV. iv, 33, 4 (cf. 1. *bhāsas*, col. 1).

भासिन् *bhāsin*, *bhāsura*. See above.

भासोक *bhāsoka*, m. N. of a poet, Cat.

भास्कर *bhās-kara* &c. See 2. *bhās*, col. 1.

भास्त्रायण *bhāstrāyaṇa*, n. (fr. *bhastrā*), g. *arīhaṇâdi*.

Bhāstrāyaṇaka, mfn. (fr. prec.), ib.

भास्मन *bhāsmana*, mf(*ī*)n. (fr. *bhasman*) made or consisting of ashes, ashy, Śiś.

Bhāsmāyana. See next.

Bhāsmāyanya, m. patr. fr. *bhasman*, g. *kuñjâdi*; pl. *bhāsmāyanāḥ*, ib.

भिःखराज *bhiḥkha-rāja*, m. N. of a king, Rājat.

भिक्ष् *bhiksh* (fr. Desid. of √*bhaj*, lit. 'to wish to share or partake'), cl. 1. Ā. (Dhātup. xvi, 5) *bhikshate* (ep. also P. °*ti*; pf. *bibhikshe*, Br. &c.; aor. *abhikshishṭa*, Gr.; fut. *bhikshishyate*, MBh.; inf. *bhikshitum*, ib.), to wish for, desire (acc. or gen.), RV. &c. &c.; to beg anything (esp. alms) from (two acc. or acc. of thing and abl. of pers.), VS. &c. &c.; to be weary or distressed (?), L.: Caus. *bhikshayati*, to cause to beg, Rājat.

Bhikshaṇa, n. (and *ā*, f., L.) the act of begging, asking alms, Āpast.; MBh.

Bhikshā́, f. the act of begging or asking (with √*kṛi*, to beg; with √*aṭ*, *car*, *bhram* and *yā*, to go about begging), ŚBr. &c. &c.; any boon obtained by begging (alms, food &c.), AV. &c. &c. (also ifc., e.g. *putra-bhikshām dehi*, 'grant the boon of a son,' R.); hire, wages, L.; service, L. **-kara-gupta**, m. N. of a poet, Cat. **-karaṇa**, n. asking alms, mendicancy, Dhūrtas. **-cara**, mf(*ī*)n. going about begging, a mendicant, R.; m. N. of a son of Bhoja (also called *bhikshu*), Rājat. **-caraṇa**, n. (GṛS.), **-cárya**, n. (ŚBr.; *ā*, f., PārGṛ.; °*rya-caraṇa*, n. ib.) going about for alms, mendicancy. **-cāra**, mfn. = *-cara*, mfn., ŚārṅgP. **-°ṭana** (°*kshâṭ*°), mfn. id., L.; m. N. of a poet, Cat.; n. wandering about for alms, mendicancy, Kāv.; Pur. &c. (acc. with √*kṛi*, to go about begging, Pañcat.; with Caus. of √*kṛi*, to cause to go about begging, ib.); N. of ch. of BrahmâṇḍaP.; *-kāvya*, n. N. of a poem; *-nāṭaka*, n. N. of a drama. **-°nna** (°*kshânna*), n. food obtained as alms, Hit. **-pātra**, n. a mendicant's bowl, alms-dish, Pañcat. **-biḍāla**, m. = *bhikshā biḍāla iva*, Pāṇ. vi, 2, 72, Sch. **-bhāṇḍa**, n. = *-pātra*, Kathās. **-bhuj**, mfn. living on alms, Rājat. **-māṇava**, m. a beggar boy (as a term of contempt), Pāṇ. vi, 2, 69, Sch. **-°yaṇa** (°*shây*°), n. = (and v. l. for) *bhikshâṭana*, Bhartṛ. **-°rthin** (°*kshârthin*), mfn. asking for alms, a beggar or mendicant, Mn. viii, 23. **-°rha** (°*kshârha*), mfn. worthy of alms, MW. **-vat**, mfn. receiving alms, begging, MBh. **-vāsas**, n. a beggar's dress, Pāṇ. vi, 2, 71, Sch. **-vṛitti**, mfn. living on alms, begging, Pañcar. **-°śin** (°*kshâśin*), mfn. eating begged food, dishonest, Bhartṛ.; Kathās.; °*śi-tva*, n. mendicancy, roguery, Hit. **-°hāra** (°*kshâh*°), m. begged food, Bhartṛ.; mfn. = *bhikshā-bhuj*, ŚārṅgP. **Bhikshôtkara**, m. scattering alms, W. **Bhikshôpajīvin**, mfn. = *bhikshā-vṛitti*, MW.

Bhikshāka, m. a beggar, mendicant, Rājat.; (*ī*), f. a female beggar, Pāṇ. iii, 2, 155.

Bhikshita, mfn. begged, solicited or obtained as alms (cf. *śūdra-bh*°), Yājñ.; MBh.

Bhikshitavyà, mfn. to be begged or asked for, ŚBr.

Bhikshin, mfn. begging, asking for alms, R.

Bhikshu, m. a beggar, mendicant, religious m° (esp. a Brāhman in the fourth Āśrama or period of his life, when he subsists entirely on alms), Mn.; MBh. &c. (cf. RTL. 55, n. 1); a Buddhist mendicant or monk, Kathās.; Lalit. (cf. MWB. 55); a partic. Buddha, L.; Asteracantha Longifolia, L.; Sphaerantus Mollis, L.; N. of an Āṅgirasa (author of RV. x, 117), RAnukr.; of a son of Bhoja, Rājat.; of a poet, Cat.; n. N. of an Upanishad (cf. *bhikshukôpanishad*). **-caryā**, f. 'a mendicant's course of life,' begging, BhP. **-tattva**, n. N. of wk. **-bhāva**, m. monkhood, priesthood, Divyâv. **-rākshasa**, m. a Rākshasa in the shape of a religious mendicant, Jātakam. **-saṃgha**, m. the association of Buddhist monks, Lalit. **-saṃghāṭī**, f. mendicant's clothes, old or ragged raiment, Suśr. **-sūtra**, n. a collection of rules or precepts for mendicants, Pāṇ. iv, 3, 110; *-bhāshya-vārttika*, n. N. of a Comm. on prec. **-hala**, m. or n. (?) N. of a partic. square-measure, Inscr.

Bhikshuka, m. a beggar, mendicant, a Brāhman of the m° order (cf. *bhikshu*), GṛS.; Mn.; MBh. &c. (RTL. 386); (*ī*), f., see below. **-satī**, f. a virtuous female mendicant, L. **Bhikshukôpanishad**, f. N. of an Upanishad.

Bhikshukī, f. (of prec.) a female mendicant, MBh.; R. &c. **-parāka**, m. or n. (?) N. of a building, Rājat.

Bhikshuṇī, f. a Buddhist female mendicant or nun, Lalit.; Divyâv. (MWB. 86).

Bhikshya, Nom. P. °*yati*, to beg or ask for alms, g. *kaṇḍv-ādi* (not in Kāś.)

भिण्ड *bhiṇḍa*, m. (or *ā*, f., Pañcat.), *bhiṇḍaka*, or °*ḍitaka*, m. (L.) Abelmoschus Esculentus.

भिण्डिमाल *bhiṇḍimāla*, m. (or *ā*, f.) = *bhindipāla*, L.

भित्त *bhitta*, *bhitti*. See p. 757, col. 1.

भिद् 1. *bhid*, cl. 7. P. Ā. (Dhātup. xix, 2) *bhinátti*, *bhintte* (impf. 2. 3. sg. *ábhinat*, RV.; Subj. *bhinádaḥ*, ib.; Impv. *bindhí*, ib.; *binddhi*, Var. [cf. *binddhi-lavaṇā*]; cl. 1. P. *bhédati*, RV.; Pot. *bhideyam*, AV.; pf. *bibhéda*, RV.; aor. 2. 3. sg. *bhét*, RV.; *abhaitsīt*, R.; *bhitthās*, TS.; Prec. *bhitsīshṭa*, Gr.; fut. *bhetsyáti*, °*te*, Br. &c.; Cond. *abhetsyat*, Up.; fut. *bhettā*, Gr.; inf. *bhéttavai*, ŚBr.; *bhettum*, ib. &c.; ind. p. *bhittvā́*, *-bhidya*, RV. &c.), to split, cleave, break, cut or rend asunder, pierce, destroy, RV. &c. &c.; to pass through (as a planet or comet), Hariv.; Var.; to disperse (darkness), R.; Śak.; to transgress, violate, (a compact or alliance), MBh.; Kāv. &c.; to open, expand, MaitrUp.; Megh.; to loosen, disentangle, dissolve, MBh.; Kāv. &c.; to disturb, interrupt, stop, ib.; to disclose, betray, Mn.; MBh. &c.; to disunite, set at variance, ib.; to distinguish, discriminate, L.: Pass. *bhidyáte* (ep. also °*ti*, aor. *abhedi*, Br.; MBh. &c.; pf. *bibhide*, Kālid.), to be split or broken, burst (intrans.), Br. &c. &c.; to be opened (as a closed hand, eyes &c.), Kāv.; Pur.; to overflow (as water), R.; Hariv.; to be loosened, become loose, MuṇḍUp.; Kāv.; to be stopped or interrupted, MBh.; to be disclosed or betrayed, Kāv.; to be changed or altered (in mind), be won over, Kāv.; Pur.; to be disunited, MBh.; to keep aloof from (instr.), ib.; to be distinguished, differ from (abl.), Sāṃkhyak.; Kāv. &c.: Caus. *bhedayati*, °*te* (aor. *abībhidat*; cf. also *bhidāpana*), to cause to split or break &c.; to split, break, shatter, crush, destroy, MBh.; Hariv.; Hit.; to separate, divide (see *bhedita*); to disunite, set at variance, perplex, unsettle (in opinion), seduce, win over, MBh.; R.: Desid. *bibhitsati*, °*te*, to wish to break through or disperse or defeat, RV.; MBh. (cf. *bibhitsā*): Desid. of Caus., see *bibhedayishu*: Intens. *bebhiditi* or *bebhetti*, to cleave repeatedly, Bhaṭṭ. [Cf. Lat. *findo*; Germ. *beissen*; Eng. *bite*.]

Bhitta, n. a fragment, section, ŚāṅkhGṛ.; = *bhitti*, a partition, wall, Inscr.

Bhitti, f. breaking, splitting, Kāṭh.; a mat (made of split reeds), ŚBr.; a wall (of earth or masonry), partition, panel, MaitrUp.; Inscr. &c.; (ifc. with parts of the body) a wall-like surface (cf. *kapola-*, *gaṇḍa-bh°*); a fragment, bit, portion, L.; a place, spot, Mudr.; a rent, fissure, L.; a flaw, deficiency, W.; an opportunity, occasion, L. **–khātana**, m. 'wall-digger,' a rat, L. **–caura**, m. 'wall-burglar,' a house-breaker, L. **–pātana**, m. 'wall-destroyer,' a kind of rat, L.

Bhittika, mf(*ā*)n. (ifc.) = *bhitti*, breaking, splitting, Hcat.; a wall, ib.; (*ā*), f. a partition, wall, L.; a small house-lizard, L.; Asparagus Racemosus, L.

Bhitra, n. (for *bhit-tra?*) a kind of dance, Saṃgīt.

2. **Bhid**, mfn. (ifc.) breaking, splitting, piercing, destroying, Kāv.; Kathās.; Pur. (cf. *aśma-*, *giri-*, *tamo-*, *pura-bhid* &c.); f. a wall (= *bhitti*), RV. i, 174, 8; separation, distinction, BhP.; a sort, kind, species, L.

Bhidaka, m. 'cutter' or 'wounder,' a sword, L.; Indra's thunderbolt, L.

Bhidā, f. splitting, bursting, destroying, destruction, Kāv. (cf. *dur-bhida*); separation (see *-bhṛit*); distinction, difference, Kāv.; BhP.; a kind or species, Sāh.; coriander, L. **–bhṛit**, mfn. 'broken' or 'enduring separation,' Śiś. vi, 5.

Bhidāpana, n. (from an irreg. Caus. *bhidāpaya*) causing to break or pound or trample on, BhP.

Bhidi, m. a thunderbolt, Uṇ. iv, 142, Sch.

Bhidira, n. id., ib. i, 52, Sch.

Bhidu, m. id., ib. i, 24, Sch.

Bhidura, mfn. (ifc.) breaking, splitting, piercing, destroying, Hcar.; easily split or broken, fragile, brittle, Mālatim. (cf. Vām. v, 2, 60); divided, variegated, mingled or mingling with, Śiś.; m. a chain for an elephant's feet, L.; n. a thunderbolt, Uṇ. i, 52, Sch. **–svana**, m. 'making a piercing noise,' N. of an Asura, Hariv.

Bhidelima, mfn. easily broken, brittle, fragile, Sadukt. (cf. Pāṇ. iii, 1, 96, Vārtt. 1, Pat.)

Bhidya, m. a rushing river or N. of a r°, Ragh.; Bhaṭṭ. (cf. Pāṇ. iii, 1, 115); n. splitting, breaking, destroying (cf. *pūr-bhidya* and *śīrsha-bhidya*).

Bhidra, n. a thunderbolt, Uṇ. ii, 13, Sch.

Bhid-vat, mfn. containing the √*bhid*, Kāṭh.

Bhindú, m. a breaker, destroyer, RV. i, 11, 4; a bubble on liquids, TS.; ĀpŚr. (cf. *bindu*); f. a woman who brings forth a still-born child, L. (cf. *nindu*).

Bhindura, m. Ficus Infectoria, L.

Bhinddhi-lavaṇā, f. (fr. 2. sg. Impv. + *l°*) constant sprinkling of salt, g. *mayūra-vyaṅsakâdi* (cf. *paca-lavaṇā*).

Bhinná, mfn. split, broken, shattered, pierced, destroyed, RV. &c. &c.; leaky (as a ship), MBh.; broken through, transgressed, violated, Mn.; MBh. &c.; divided into parts, anything less than a whole, Yājñ.; Kāv. &c.; opened, expanded, blown, MBh.; Kāv. &c.; detached, disjoined, loosened, ib.; interrupted, disturbed, Bhartṛ.; disclosed, betrayed, R.; disunited, set at variance, MBh.; seduced, bribed, Kām.; Hit.; changed, altered, Yājñ.; Suśr.; distinct, different from or other than (abl. or comp.), GṛŚrS.; Kāv. &c.; deviating, abnormal, irregular, Kāv.; mixed or mingled with (instr. or comp.), ib.; cleaving to (loc. or comp.), ib.; = *bhinna-karaṭa*, MBh. i, 7006; m. (in arithm.) a fraction, Līlāv.; (*ā*), f. Sanseviera Roxburghiana, L.; n. a fragment, bit, portion, W.; a wound from a pointed weapon, a stab, Suśr.; a partic. mode of fighting, Hariv. **–kaṭa** (Ragh.), **-karaṭa** (MBh.), mfn. a rutting elephant having a fissure in the temples (from which fluid exudes). **–karîndra-kumbha-muktā-maya**, mf(*ī*)n. consisting of pearls fallen from the crack in the frontal protuberances of a chief elephant, ŚārṅgP. **–karṇa**, mfn. having divided ears (said of partic. animals), Pāṇ. vi, 3, 115. **–kalpa**, mfn. having different rites, ŚrS. **–kāla**, mfn. one who does not keep to the right time, ŚāṅkhGṛ. **–kumbha**, m. a person who has regained his liberty by redeeming his pledge, L. **–kūṭa**, mfn. each employing a different stratagem, Kām. (Sch.); n. an army whose inferior officers have perished, L. **–krama**, mfn. out of order or place, displaced, Kuval.; TāṇḍyaBr., Comm. &c. **–kleśa**, mfn. one in whom the (Buddhistic) Kleśas (s. v.) are destroyed, L.; *-tva*, n., ib. **–gaṇḍa-karaṭa**, mfn. = *-karaṭa*, Bhartṛ. **–gati**, mfn. going with great strides or quickly, Śak. **–garbha**, mfn. disunited in the centre, disorganised (said of an army), Kām. **–gātrikā**, f. Cucumis Usitatissimus, L. **–guṇana**, n. multiplication of fractions, Col. **–ghana**, m. the cube of a fraction, ib. **–jāti**, mfn. pl. of different rank, Yājñ., Comm.; *-mat*, mfn. id., MārkP. **–jātīya**, mfn. of a different kind, ĀpŚr., Comm.; of a d° tribe or caste, MW. **–tantra**, mfn. occurring or happening in different actions, KātyŚr. **–tva**, n. the state of being different from (comp.), Sāh. **–darśin**, mfn. seeing diff° things, s° a difference, making a d° (opp. to *sama-d°*), partial, BhP. **–dalā**, f. Sanseviera Roxburghiana, L. **–dṛiś**, mfn. = *-darśin*, BhP. **–deśa**, mfn. occurring or happening in various places; *-tva*, n., Śak. **–deha**, mfn. 'whose body is pierced,' wounded, MW. **–nau** or **-nauka**, mfn. 'whose ship is broken,' shipwrecked, ib. **–parikarman**, n. an arithmetical operation with fractions, Col. **–prakāra**, mfn. of a different kind or sort, MW. **–bhāga-hara** (prob. w. r. for *-hāra*), m. division of fractions, Līl. **–bhājana** or **-bhāṇḍa**, n. a broken pot or vessel, potsherd, MW. **–bhinnâtman**, m. chick-pea, Cicer Arietinum, L. **–mantra**, mfn. one who has betrayed a plan, R. **–marman**, mfn. pierced in the vital organs, mortally wounded, MW. **–maryāda** (Cāṇ.; Uttarar.) or **-maryādin** (MārkP.), mfn. whose course is broken, separated from the right way, uncontrolled, unrestrained, regardless, disrespectful. **–mastaka-piṇḍaka** or **°ḍika**, mfn. whose skull and forehead are cloven, (an elephant) whose frontal prominences have fissures, MW. **–yojanī**, f. Plectranthus Scutellarioides, Bhpr. (w. r. *-yājanī*). **–ruci**, mfn. having a different taste, Ragh.; Mālav. **–liṅga**, n. incongruity of gender in a comparison, Pratāp. **–liṅgaka**, mf(*ikā*)n. containing words of different gender, ib. **–vacana**, mf(*ā*)n. containing words of d° number, ib.; n. incongruity of number in a comparison, ib. **–vat**, mfn. one who has divided, MW. **–varga**, m. the square of a fraction, Col. **–varcas**, mfn. voiding excrement, Suśr.; Car. (also °*ska*); having thin evacuations (*-tva*, n.), Car. **–varṇa**, mfn. changed in colour, discoloured, pale, Megh.; of a different caste or tribe, MW. **–vartman**, mfn. separated from the right way, Kām. **–viṭka**, mfn. (fr. 3. *vish*) = *-varcas*, Suśr.; Bhpr.; *-tva*, n. = *-varcas-tva*, ŚārṅgS. (Sch. 'change of colour in the faeces'). **–vṛitta**, mfn. one who has abandoned the path of duty, leading a bad life, MBh.; Yājñ.; containing a metrical fault, Cat. **–vṛitti**, mfn. having different occupations, Bhaṭṭ.; h° a d° profession, Yājñ., Comm.; leading a bad life, following evil courses (= *-vṛitta*; *-tā*, f.), Mn.; MBh.; w. r. for *-vṛitta*, Cat. **–vyavakalita**, n. subtraction of fractions, Col. **–śakṛit**, mfn. = *-varcas*, Car. **–saṃhati**, mfn. whose union is broken, disunited, MW. **–saṃkalana** (MW.) or **°kalita** (Col.), n. addition of fractions. **–svara**, mfn. having a broken or changed voice, Suśr.; discordant, MW.; *-mukha-varṇa*, mfn. h° a br° or ch° voice and complexion, Pañcat. **–hṛiti**, f. division of fractions, Līl. **–hṛidaya**, mfn. pierced through the heart, Ragh. **Bhinnâñjana**, n. divided antimony or collyrium mixed (with oil &c.), eye-ointment, Kāv.; Suśr.; *-cayôpama*, mfn. like a quantity of pounded antimony, Hariv.; *-varṇa*, mfn. having the colour of p° a° (*-tā*, f.), Śiś.; *-saṃnibha*, mfn. similar to p° a°, Ṛitus.; °*nâkāra* (Hariv.) or °*nâbha* (MW.), mfn. appearing like p° a°. **Bhinnâbhinna**, mfn. distinct and not d°, separate and not s°, MW. **Bhinnârtha**, mfn. having different aims, ĀpŚr., Comm.; having a clear or distinct meaning, clear, perspicuous, Śak.; *-tā*, f. clearness, intelligibleness, ib. **Bhinnôdara**, m. 'born from a different womb,' a brother by a different mother, a half brother, MW.

Bhinnaka, mfn. broken, MantraBr.; m. 'a seceder,' a Buddhistic mendicant, L.; N. of a musical mode or Rāga, Vikr.; (*ī*), ind. with √*kṛi*, to divide, separate, Śiś.

Bhettavya, mfn. to be broken or split, R.; to be betrayed or divulged, Hariv.

Bhettṛí, mfn. breaking, splitting, bursting through, piercing; a breaker &c., RV. &c. &c.; a conqueror, Cat.; an interrupter, disturber, frustrator, Kām.; a divulger, betrayer, MBh.; Yājñ.; a factious or seditious man, MW.; m. N. of Skanda, Mṛicch.; N. of a partic. magical spell recited over weapons, R.

Bheda, °*dana* &c. See p. 766.

भिन्द् *bhind*, v. l. for √*bind*, q. v.

भिन्दिपाल *bhindipāla* or °*laka*, m. a short javelin or arrow thrown from the hand or shot through a tube (others 'a stone fastened to a string' or 'a kind of sling for throwing stones'), MBh.; R. &c. (v. l. *bhindapāla*, *bhiṇḍimālā*, *bhindomāla*, *bhindimālā* or °*laka*, *bhindumāla*).

भिन्दु *bhindu*, *bhinna* &c. See col. 1.

भियस् *bhiyás* &c. See p. 758, col. 1.

भिरिण्टिका *bhiriṇṭikā*, f. a species of plant (= *śveta-guñjā*), L. (v. l. *bhṛiṇṭikā*).

भिरु *bhiru*, m. N. of a man (also °*ruka*), Divyâv. **–kaccha**, n. N. of a town, ib.

भिल् *bhil* = √*bil*, q. v.

भिल्म *bhilma*, n. a word used to explain *bilma*, Nir. i, 20.

भिल्ल *bhilla*, m. N. of a wild mountain race, (prob.) the 'Bheels' (who live in the Vindhya hills, in the forests of Malwa, Mewar, Kandesh, the Dakhin), Kāv.; Kathās. &c. (ifc. f. *ā*); a king of the Bhillas, Kathās.; the son of a Śabara and an Andhrī (who was previously married to a Nishṭhya), L.; a species of Lodhra, L.; (*ī*), f. a Bhilla woman, ŚārṅgP.; Symplocos Racemosa, L. **–gavī**, f. = *gavayī*, the female of the Bos Gavaeus, L. **–taru**, m. Symplocos Racemosa, L. **–bhūshaṇā**, f. the seed of Abrus Precatorius, L.

Bhillin, m. Symplocos Racemosa, L.

Bhillī, f. of *bhilla*, in comp. **–cakrêśvara**, m. N. of Vishṇu, Pañcar. **–nātha**, m. N. of an author, Cat.

Bhilloṭa or °*ṭaka*, m. a species of plant (prob. = *bhilla-taru*), Suśr.

भिश्चा *bhiścā*, f. N. of a woman, Rājat.

भिषज् 1. *bhishaj* (prob. = *abhi* + √*saj*, 'to attach, plaster'), only 3. sg. pr. *bhishákti*, to heal, cure, RV. viii, 68, 2.

Bhishak, in comp. for 2. *bhishaj*. **–cakra-cittôtsava**, m., **-cakra-nidāna**, n. N. of wks. **–tama** (°*shák-*), mfn. most healing; m. du. 'the best physicians,' the Aśvins, RV.; AV.; BhP. **–tara** (°*shák-*), mfn. more healing, AV. **–tva**, n. the state or condition of a phys°, Sāy. **–pāśa**, m. an inferior phys°, quack doctor, Vop. (cf. under *pāśa*). **–priyā**, f. 'dear to a phys°,' Cocculus Cordifolius, L.

Bhishag, in comp. for 2. *bhishaj*. **–jita**, n. 'subdued by physicians' any drug or medicine, Car. **–bhadrā**, f. a species of Croton, L. (v. l. *visha-bh°*). **–rāja-miśra**, m. N. of an author, Cat. **–vatī**, f. pl. N. of partic. verses containing the word *bhishaj*, ĀpŚr. **–vara**, m. du. 'best of physicians,' the Aśvins, Var. **–vid**, m. 'knowing remedies,' a physician, Car.

Bhishaṅ, in comp. for 2. *bhishaj*. **–mātṛi**, f. Gendarussa Vulgaris, L.

2. **Bhisháj**, mfn. curing, healing, sanative, RV. &c. &c.; m. a healer, physician, ib.; a remedy, medicine, RV.; AV.; Car.; N. of a man with the patr. Ātharvaṇa, L.; of a son of Śata-dhanvan, Hariv. **–āvarta**, m. N. of Kṛishṇa, MBh.

Bhishaja, m. N. of a man, g. *gargâdi* (Kāś.)

1. **Bhishajya**, Nom. P. °*jyáti* (g. *kaṇḍv-ādi*) to heal, cure, possess healing power, RV. &c. &c.; to be physician to any one (dat.), Bālar.; to be a physician or remedy for, i. e. to gain the mastery over anything (loc.), ib.

2. **Bhishajya**, mf(*ā*)n. sanative, healing, healthful, Kāṭh.; (*ā*), f. healing, cure, remedy, ŚāṅkhBr.

Bhishajyitá, mfn. healed, cured, ŚBr. (w. r. *bhishajyayitá* &c.)

Bhishṇaja, m. N. of a man, g. *gargâdi* (cf. *bhishaja*).

Bhishṇajya, Nom. P. °*yati* (g. *kaṇḍv-ādi*), 3. sg. impf. *abhishṇak*, to heal, refresh, RV. x, 131, 5.

भिषय *bhishaya*, °*yati*. See √*bhī*.

भिषायक *bhishāyaka*, m. a Yaksha, Rājat. **–pura**, n. N. of a town, ib.

भिष्मा *bhishmā*, v. l. for *bhissā*.

Bhishmikā, °*mitā*, °*mishṭā*, v. l. for *bhissaṭā* or *bhissitā*.

भिस्सटा *bhissaṭā* or *bhissitā*, f. cooked rice, L.

Bhissā, f. boiled rice, L.

भिहु *bhihu* (?), m N. of a mountain, Buddh.

भी 1. *bhī*, cl. 3. P. (Dhātup. xxv, 2) *bibhéti* (du. *bibhītas* or *bibhitas*, Pot. *bibhīyāt* or *bibhiyāt*, Pāṇ. vi, 4, 115; Pot. 3. pl. *bibhyeyuḥ*, MBh. xii, 459; impf. 3. pl. *abibhayuḥ*, Pāṇ. vii, 3, 83, Sch.; ep. also Ā. 1. sg. *bibhye* and and P. 3. sg. *bibhyati*, pl. *bibhyanti*; Ved. also cl. 1. Ā. *bháyate*, and accord. to Dhātup. xxxiv, 15, cl. 10. P. *bhāyayati*; pf. *bibhāya*, 3. pl. *bibhyuḥ*, RV. &c. &c.; *bibhāya*, AitBr.; *bibhayām cakāra*, ŚBr., cf. Pāṇ. iii, 1, 39; aor. *abhaishīt*, °*shma*, °*shuḥ*, RV.; AV. &c., 2. sg. *bhaishīs*, AV., *bhais*, Br. &c., esp. in *mā bhais*, 'do not be afraid;' once for plural = *mā bhaishṭa*, R. i, 55, 25; *bhes*, Br.; *bhema*, RV., p. Ā. *bhiyānā*, ib.; fut. *bhetā*, Gr.; cond. *abheshyat*, ŚBr.; inf. *bhiyáse*, RV.; *bhetum*, MBh. &c.), to fear, be afraid of (abl. or gen., rarely instr. or acc.), RV. &c. &c.; to fear for, be anxious about (abl.), R.: Pass. *bhīyate*, aor. *abhāyi*, Gr.: Caus. *bhīshayate* (ŚBr. &c.; cf. Pāṇ. i, 3, 68), *bhīshayati* (MBh.; once m.c. *bhish*°, BhP.; p. *bhīshayāṇa*, MBh.; aor. *bībhishaḥ*, TS., °*shathāḥ*, RV.), *bhāyayati*, °*te* (Pāṇ. i, 3, 68, Sch.; Pot. *bhāyayes*, Megh. 61; v.l. *bhīshayes*; aor. *bībhayat*, *abībhayanta*, RV.; ind. p. -*bhāyya*, Br.), *bhāpayate* (Pāṇ. vi, 1, 56, Sch.), to terrify, put in a fright, intimidate, RV. &c. &c.: Desid. *bibhīshati*, Gr.: Intens. *bebhīyate*, *bebhayīti*, *bebheti*, ib. [Cf. √*bhyas*; Lith. *bijótis*; Slav. *bojati*; Germ. *biben*, *beben*.]

Bhiyás, m. fear, apprehension (only acc. and instr.), RV. (cf. *bhiyáse* under √1. *bhī*).

Bhiyásāna, mfn. fearful, timid, AV.

Bhiyā, f. fear, dread, L.

Bhiyānā. See √1. *bhī*.

2. **Bhī**, f. fear, apprehension, fright, alarm, dread of (abl., loc., acc. with *prati*, or comp.), RV. &c. &c. — **kara**, mfn. causing fear, R. — **mat**, mfn. fearful, Nalôd.

Bhītá, mfn. frightened, alarmed, terrified, timid, afraid of or imperilled by (abl. or comp.), RV. &c. &c.; anxious about (comp.), Pañcar.; (*am*), ind. timidly, Śiksh.; n. fear, danger, L.; (impers.) fear has been shown, Śriṅgār. — **gāyana**, m. a timid or shy singer, Saṃgīt. — **m-kāram**, ind. (with *ā*-√*kruś*) to call any one a coward, Bhaṭṭ. — **cārin**, mfn. acting timidly (*a-bhītac*°), R. — **citta**, mfn. afraid in mind, Daś. — **paritrāṇa-vastûpâlambha-paṇḍita**, mfn. clever in finding fault with the means of rescuing the terrified, Hit. — **bhīta**, mfn. very much frightened, exceedingly afraid, Bhag. — 1. -**vat**, mfn. one who is afraid, W. — 2. -**vat**, ind. like a frightened person, timidly, MBh.

Bhīti, f. fear, alarm, dread, danger (often ifc.), Yājñ.; Kāv. &c. — **krit**, mfn. causing or exciting fear, Rājat. — **cchid**, mfn. keeping away fear or danger, Bhartṛ. — **tas**, ind. (ifc.) through fear of, Kathās. — **nāṭitaka**, n. mimic representation of fear, Śak. — **mat**, mfn. timid, shy, Hāsy.

Bhīti, f. N. of one of the Mātṛis attending on Skanda, MBh. (B.)

Bhīmá, mf(*ā*)n. fearful, terrific, terrible, awful, formidable, tremendous, RV. &c. &c. (ibc., fearfully &c.); m. Rumex Vesicarius, L.; N. of Rudra-Śiva, ĀśvGṛ.; Uṇ., Sch.; of one of the 8 forms of Śiva, Pur.; of one of the 11 Rudras, Pur.; of a Deva-gandharva, MBh.; of one of the Devas called Yajña-mush, ib.; of a Dānava, ib.; Kathās.; of a Vidyādhara, Kathās.; of a son of the Rākshasa Kumbhakarṇa, Cat.; of the second son of Pāṇḍu (also called Bhīma-sena and Vṛikôdara; he was only the reputed son of P°, being really the son of his wife Pṛithā or Kuntī by the wind-god Vāyu, and was noted for his size, strength and appetite), MBh.; Kāv.; Pur. &c.; of sev. other men, AitBr.; MBh.; Hariv. &c.; pl. the race of Bhīma, MBh.; (*ā*), f. a whip, L.; a bullock's gall-stone, L.; N. of a form of Durgā, Hariv.; of an Apsaras, R.; of sev. rivers, MBh.; of a district, Rājat.; of a town, Buddh. — **karman**, mfn. terrible in act, dreadful, Bhag. — **kārmuka**, mfn. having formidable bows, MW. — **kāvya**, n. N. of wk. — **khaṇḍa**, n. N. of ch. in MBh. and SkandaP. — **gava** or -**gu**, m. (*gava* or *gu* = *go*) N. of man (cf. *bhaimagava*). — **gupta**, m. N. of a king, Rājat. — **grāha-vat**, mfn. having formidable crocodiles, MBh. — **candra**, m. N. of a king, Buddh. — **jananī**, f. 'Bhīma's mother,' N. of the Ganges, L. — **jā**, f. patr. of Damayantī, Naish. — **jānu**, m. N. of a king, MBh. — **tā**, f. terribleness, R. — **tithi**, f. = *bhīmâikādaśī*, MatsyaP. — **darśana**, mfn. frightful in appearance, MBh. — **dāsa-bhūpāla**, m., -**deva**, m. N. of authors, Cat. — **dvādaśī**, f. N. of the 12th day of the light half of the month Māgha (cf. *bhīmâikādaśī*), W.; -*vrata*, n. a partic. observance; N. of ch. of BhavP. — **dhanvan**, m. 'having a formidable bow,' N. of a prince, Daś. — **dhanvāyana**, mf(*ī*)n. bearing f° bows, MBh. — **nagara**, n. 'Bhīma's city,' N. of a town (cf. -*pura*), L. — **nātha**, m. N. of an author, Cat. — **nāda**, m. a terrific sound, Kāv.; 'sending forth a t° s°,' a lion, L.; N. of one of the 7 clouds at the destruction of the world, Cat. — **nāyaka**, m. N. of a man, Rājat. — **parākrama**, mfn. possessing formidable power or prowess, MBh.; m. N. of a man, Kathās.; of Śiva, MW.; of wk. — **pāla**, m. N. of a king, Cat. — **putrikā**, f. Bhīma's daughter, Ml. — **pura**, n. N. of a town situated on the Ganges, Kathās. — **pūrva-ja**, m. N. of Yudhi-shṭhira, Śiś. — **bala**, m. 'possessing terrible strength,' N. of one of the Devas called Yajña-mush, MBh.; of one of the sons of Dhṛita-rāshṭra, ib. — **bhaṭa**, m. N. of a man, Kathās. — **bhaṭṭa**, m. N. of an author, Cat. — **bhavā**, f. patr. of Damayantī; °*vī*-√*bhū*, P. -*bhavati*, to assume the shape of D°, Naish. — **bhuja**, m. 'having formidable arms,' N. of a man, Kathās. — **mukha**, m. 'of fearful aspect or appearance,' N. of a monkey, R. — **ratha**, m. N. of a Rākshasa, GāruḍaP.; of sev. men, MBh.; Hariv.; Pur.; (*ā* or *ī*), f. N. of a river in the Himālaya mountains, MBh.; Hariv.; Pur.; Var.; (*ī*), f. (prob. for -*rātrī* or Prākṛit -*ratti*) 'the fearful night,' N. of the 7th night in the 7th month of the 77th year of life (supposed to be the ordinary period of life after which a person is in his dotage and exempt from religious duties; cf. *kāla-rātrī*), L. — **rūpa**, mfn. of terrible form, of fearful aspect, MW. — **rūpi-stotra**, n. N. of wk. — **vikrama**, mfn. of terrific prowess; m. N. of one of the sons of Dhṛita-rāshṭra, MBh.; of wk. — **vikrānta**, mfn. terribly powerful or courageous; m. a lion, L. — **vigraha**, mfn. of fearful form, terrific in appearance, MW. — **vinoda**, m. N. of wk. — **vega**, mfn. of fearful speed; m. N. of a Dānava, Hariv.; of one of the sons of Dhṛita-rāshṭra, MBh.; -*rava*, mfn. possessing terrific velocity and giving a t° sound, Hariv.; m. N. of one of the sons of Dhṛita-rāshṭra, MBh. — **śaṃkara**, n. (scil. *liṅga*) N. of one of the 12 most sacred Liṅgas, Cat.; W. — **śara**, m. 'having terrible arrows,' N. of a son of Dhṛita-rāshṭra, MBh. — **śāsana**, m. 'terrible in punishing,' N. of Yama, L. — **śāha**, m. (*śāha* = شاه) 'the t° king,' N. of a king, Cat. — **śukla**, m. N. of a king, Buddh. — **sāhi**, m. N. of a poet, Kshem. — **siṅha**, m. (ŚārṅgP.), °*ha-paṇḍita*, m. (Cat.) N. of poets. — **sutā**, f. = -*jā*, Ml. — **sena** (*bhīmá*-), m. 'having a formidable army,' N. of a Deva-gandharva, MBh.; of a Yaksha, Cat.; of the second son of Pāṇḍu (cf. *bhīmá*), MBh.; Hariv.; Lalit.; of various other men, ŚBr.; ŚāṅkhŚr.; MBh. &c.; a kind of camphor, L.; -*maya*, mfn. consisting of Bhīma-sena, MBh. — **svāmin**, m. N. of a Brāhman, Inscr. — **hāsa**, n. the flocculent seeds or down &c. blown about in the air in summer, L. (v. l. for *grīshma-hāsa*). **Bhīmâkāra**, m. and °**mā-deva**, m. N. of two men, Rājat. **Bhīmâṅgada**, m. N. of a man, Mṛicch. **Bhīmâdy-upâkhyāna**, n. N. of ch. of the Vāsishṭha-rāmāyaṇa. **Bhīmā-māhātmya**, n. N. of wk. **Bhīmêśa**, n. N. of a place sacred to Śiva, Cat. **Bhīmêśvara**, n. id., ib.; -*tīrtha*, n. N. of a Tīrtha, ib.; -*bhaṭṭa*, m. N. of an author, ib.; -*māhātmya*, n. N. of wk. **Bhīmâikādaśī**, f. N. of the 11th day in the light half of the month Māgha, L. (cf. *bhīma-dvādaśī*). **Bhīmôttara**, m. N. of a Kumbhâṇḍa, L. **Bhīmôdarī**, f. N. of Umā, L. **Bhīmâñjas**, mfn. having terrible strength, Mcar.

Bhīmaka, m. N. of a demon, Hariv.; -*lambaka*, m. N. of an author, Cat.

Bhīmayú, mfn. fearful, dreadful, RV. v, 56, 3.

Bhīmara, m. a spy, L.; n. war, battle, L.

Bhīmalá, mfn. fearful, dreadful, VS. 30, 6.

1. **Bhīra**, mfn. (for 2. see p. 759) intimidating, Śiś.

Bhīrú, mf(*ū*)n. fearful, timid, cowardly, afraid of (abl. or comp.), RV. &c. &c.; (with *paratra*) dreading the beyond or the hereafter, Yājñ., Sch. (ifc. expressive of blame, Gaṇar. on Pāṇ. ii, 1, 53); m. a jackal, L. (cf. *pheru*); a tiger, L.; various kinds of fish, L.; a centipede, L.; a kind of sugar-cane, L.; Asparagus Racemosus, L.; f. a timid woman (esp. voc. *bhīru*, 'O timid one!'), Kāv.; a shadow, L.; a she-goat, L.; Solanum Jacquini, L.; n. a species of plant, L.; silver, L. — **kaccha**, m. pl. N. of a people, MārkP. (prob. w. r. for *bharu-k*°). — **cetas**, m. 'timid-hearted,' a deer, L. — **jana**, m. one whose servants are cowards, MW. — **tā**, f., -**tva**, n. fearfulness, timidity, cowardice, dread of (comp.), Kāv.; Rājat.; Suśr. — **pattrī** or -**parṇī**, f. Asparagus Racemosus, L. — **bāla**, m. a kind of water ratan, L. — **bhīru**, mfn. very timid or shy, Hariv. — **yodha**, mfn. having cowardly soldiers, MW. — **randhra**, m. 'having a formidable cavity,' a furnace, oven, L. — **shṭhāna**, n. (prob.) a dreadful place, Pāṇ. viii, 3, 81. — **sattva**, mfn. fearful by nature, timorous, Śukas. — **hṛidaya**, mfn. id.; m. a deer, L.

Bhīruka, mfn. fearful, timorous, shy, afraid of (comp.), MBh.; Kāv.; formidable, W.; m. an owl, L.; a bear, L.; a kind of sugar-cane, Suśr.; Bhpr. &c. (v. l. °*raka*); N. of a man, Buddh.; n. a wood, forest, L. — **jana**, m. one whose servants are cowards, MW.

Bhīlu, mfn. = *bhīru*, timid, L.

Bhīluka, mfn. id.; (ifc.) afraid of, Kathās.; m. a bear, L. (cf. *bhallūka*).

Bhīshaka, m. (fr. Caus.) N. of one of Śiva's attendants, L. (cf. *bhīmaka*); (*ikā*), f. N. of a goddess, Cat.

Bhīshaṇa, mf(*ā* or *ī*)n. (fr. Caus.) terrifying, frightening, formidable, horrible (with gen. or ifc.), MBh.; Kāv. &c.; = *gāḍha*, L.; m. (scil. *rasa*) the sentiment of horror (in poet. composition), W. (cf. *bhayānaka*); N. of Śiva, L.; a form of Bhairava (= Yama), Cat.; Boswellia Thurifera, L.; Phoenix Paludosa, L.; a pigeon, dove, L.; N. of a Rākshasa, Cat.; (*ā*), f. N. of a goddess (= Nirṛiti), VarYogay.; n. the act of terrifying or frightening, MBh. — **tva**, n. terribleness, horribleness, MBh.

Bhīshaṇaka, mfn. terrifying, horrible, MBh.; Hariv.; R.

Bhīshaṇīya, mfn., id., Kāraṇḍ.

Bhīshaya, °**yati**. See √*bhī*.

1. **Bhīshā**, f. the act of frightening, intimidation, Mn. viii, 264.

2. **Bhīshā**, ind. through fear of (abl.), RV.; Br.; Up.

Bhīshita, mfn. terrified, frightened, MBh.

Bhīshi-dāsa, m. N. of the patron of Nārāyaṇa (author of a Comm. on Gīt.), Cat.

Bhīshu-gati (?), mfn. intimidating, Bhpr.

Bhīshmá, mfn. terrible, dreadful, ŚBr. &c. &c.; m. (scil. *rasa*) = *bhīshaṇa*, MW.; death, Nyāyas., Sch.; N. of Śiva, L.; a Rākshasa, L.; N. of a son of Śāṃtanu and Gaṅgā (in the great war of the Bharatas he took the side of the sons of Dhṛita-rāshṭra against the sons of Pāṇḍu, and was renowned for his continence, wisdom, bravery, and fidelity to his word, cf. IW. 375 and RTL. 561–564), MBh.; Hariv.; Pur.; pl. the race or followers of Bhīshma, MBh.; n horror, horribleness, W. — **garjita-ghosha-svara-rāja**, m. N. of a number of Buddhas, Buddh. — **jananī**, f. 'Bhīshma's mother,' N. of Gaṅgā, L. — **pañcaka**, n. 'five days sacred to Bh°,' the 5 days from the 11th to the 15th in the light half of the month Kārttika, AgP.; -*vrata*, n. N. of a partic. observance performed during this period, ib. — **pañjara-stotra**, n. N. of a Stotra. — **parvan**, n. N. of the 6th book of the MBh. — **miśra**, m. N. of two authors, Cat. — **mukti-pradāyaka**, m. 'giving release to Bh°,' N. of Vishṇu, Pañcar. — **ratna-parikshā**, f. 'trial of the jewel of Bh°,' N. of wk. (?), Cat. — **sū**, f. = -*jananī*, L. — **stava-rāja**, m. 'Bh°'s hymn to Kṛishṇa,' N. of MBh. xii, 47. — **stuti**, f. N. of a Stotra from the MBh. and from the BhP. — **svara-rāja**, m. 'king of terrible sounds,' N. of a Buddha, Buddh. **Bhīshmâshṭamī**, f. the 8th day in the light half of the month Māgha (when there is a festival sacred to Bhīshma), W.

Bhīshmaka, m. Bhīshma the son of Śāṃtanu (used contemptuously), MBh. v, 5981; N. of another king (the father of Rukmiṇī who was carried off by Kṛishṇa), MBh.; Hariv.; Pur. **Bhīshmakâtmajā**, f. 'Bh°'s daughter,' patr. of Rukmiṇī, Śiś.

Bhetavya, mfn. to be feared or dreaded (n. often impers., esp. *na bhetavyam*, with abl. or gen., 'one need not be afraid of'), MBh.; Kāv. &c.

Bheya, mfn. = prec. (n. impers. with abl., e. g. *arer bheyam*, 'one must fear an enemy'), MBh.

भीणी *bhīṇī*, f. N. of one of the Mātṛis attending on Skanda, MBh. (B. *bhīti*).

भीमरिका *bhīmarikā*, f. N. of a daughter of Kṛishṇa by Satya-bhāmā (v. l. *bhīmanikā*).

भीर 2. *bhīra*, m. pl. (for 1. see p. 758, col. 2) N. of a people, VP. (prob. w.r. for *ābhīra*).

Bhīraka. See under *bhīruka*.

भीलभूषणा *bhīla-bhūshaṇā*, w. r. for *bhilla-bh°*, q. v.

भीलु *bhīlu, bhīluka.* See p. 758, col. 3.

भीषक *bhīshaka*, °*shaṇa* &c. See p. 758.

भीषटाचार्य *bhīshaṭâcārya* (?), m. N. of a medical author, Cat.

भु *bhu*, mfn. (ifc.) = 2. *bhū*, becoming, being, existing, produced (cf. *agni-*, *pra-bhu* &c.)

भुःखार *bhuḥkhāra*, m. a country in Tartary, Bokhāra, Rājat. (cf. *bhūḥkhāra*).

भुक् *bhúk*, ind. an exclamation of surprise, AV.

भुक्क *bhukka*, m. N. of a king, Cat. **-bhū-pāla**, m. king Bhukka, ib.

भुक्त *bhukta, bhukti.* See √2. *bhuj*.

भुग्न *bhugna.* See √1. *bhuj*.

भुङ् *bhuṅ*, a syllable inserted in partic. Sāmans, PañcavBr., Sch.

भुज् 1. *bhuj*, cl. 6. P. (Dhātup. xxviii, 124) *bhujáti* (pf. *bubhoja*, aor. *abhaukshīt*, fut. *bhokshyati* and °*ktā*, Gr.; really only pr. stem, aor. *-dubhojīs* and ind. p. *-bhujya* after *nir* and *pari*; cf. also *bhujam* in *bhujaṃ-ga* and *bhujaṃ-gama*), to bend, curve; (?) to sweep (cf. 1. *bhují*), RV.: Pass. *bhujyate*, to be bent down or disheartened, Hit. iv, 28. [Cf. Gk. φεύγω; Lat. *fugio*; Goth. *biugan, baugjan* (?); Germ. *biogan, biegen*; Angl. Sax. *búgan*; Eng. *bow*.]

Bhugna, mfn. bent, curved, crooked, distorted, ĀśvGṛ.; MBh. &c.; furrowed (as the brows), Kāvyâd.; forced aside, Prab.; bent down, cowed, disheartened, Kathās.; N. of the Saṃdhi of *o* and *au* before non-labial vowels, RPrāt. **-dṛiś** or **-netra**, mfn. accompanied by distortion of the eyes (as a fever), Bhpr.

2. **Bhuj.** See *tri-bhúj*.

Bhuja, m. (ifc. f. *ā*) the arm, MBh.; Kāv. &c. (*bhujayor antaram*, the breast, Bhartṛ.; cf. *bhujântara*); the hand, Pāṇ. vii, 3, 61; the trunk of an elephant, MBh. iii, 15736; a branch, bough, BhP.; a bending, curve, coil (of a serpent; see comp. below); the side of any geometrical figure, KātyŚr., Sch.; the base of a triangle, Sūryas.; the base of a shadow, ib.; the supplement of 2 or 4 right angles or the complement of 3 right angles, MW.; (*ā*), f., see col. 2. **-koṭara**, m. the armpit, L. **-ga**, see *bhujaga*. **-m-ga** and **-m-gama**, see *bhujaṃga* and *bhujaṃgama*. **-cchāyā**, f. shadow of the arms, secure shelter, Hit. **-jyā**, f. (in astron.) the base sine, Sūryas. **-taru-vana**, n. a forest the trees of which are its arms, Rājat. **-daṇḍa** (Gīt.), °**daka** (L.), m. 'arm-staff,' a long arm. **-dala**, m. 'arm-leaf,' the hand, L. **-nagara**, n. N. of a town, Cat. **-pratibhuja**, n. opposite sides in a plane figure, Col. **-phala**, n. = *bāhu-phala*, the result from the base sine, Sūryas. **-bandhana**, n. clasping in the arms, an embrace, Gīt. **-bala-bhīma**, m. N. of an author, Cat. **-balin**, m. 'strong in the arm,' N. of a Jaina teacher. **-madhya**, n. 'space between the arms,' the breast, Ragh. **-mūla**, n. 'arm-root,' the shoulder, MBh. **-yashṭi**, f. = *-daṇḍa*, Ragh. **-yoktra**, n. clasping or embracing arms, MBh. **-rāma**, m. N. of an author (= *bhajanânanda*), Cat. **-latā**, f. 'arm-creeper,' a long slender arm, Megh.; Ratnâv. **-vīrya**, mfn. strong in the arm, Pracaṇḍ.; n. vigour of arm, MW. **-śālin**, mfn. possessing strong arms, Kathās. **-śikhara** (Kād.), **-śiras** (L.), n. 'arm-head,' the shoulder, L. **-saṃśraya**, m. going to or taking refuge in the arms (of another), MBh. **-sambhoga**, m. 'union of arms,' an embrace, R. **-sūtra**, n. the base sine, MW. **-stambha**, m. paralysis of the arms, Bhpr. **Bhujâghāta**, m. a blow with the arm, MBh. **Bhujâṅka**, m. an embrace, R. **Bhujântara**, n. 'between the arms,' the breast, MBh.; Kālid.; Kathās. (*am*, ind. between the arms, in the embrace); a partic. astron. correction, Siddhântaś. **Bhujântarāla**, n. = *bhujântara*, the breast, chest, Mālav. **Bhujâpīḍa**, m. clasping or embracing in the arms, W. **Bhujā-bhuji**, ind. arm to arm, in close fight, Naish. (cf. *keśā-keśi*). **Bhujôpapīḍam**, ind. by or while clasping in the arms, Daś.

Bhujaga (fr. *bhuja* + *ga*), m. 'going in curves,' a snake, serpent, serpent-demon (ifc. f. *ā*), MBh.; Kāv. &c. (*-tva*, n., MBh.); (*ī*), f. a female snake, a serpent-maid, MBh.; Kāv.; Kathās.; a species of shrub, L.; N. of a river, Dharmaś.; (prob. n.) tin or lead, Kālac. **-dāraṇa**, m. 'serpent-destroyer,' N. of Garuḍa, L. **-pati**, m. the king of serpents, Vās. **-pushpa**, m. a species of plant, Suśr. **-bhojin**, m. 's°-eater,' a peacock, W. **-rāja**, m. 's°-king,' N. of Śesha, Kir.; °*jāya*, Nom. P. °*yate*, to become a s°-king, Vās. **-latā**, f. betel-pepper, L. **-valaya**, m. a bracelet consisting of a snake, MW. **-śiśu-sṛita**, mf(*ā*)n. going like a young s°; (*ā*), f. N. of a metre, Piṅg. **Bhujagâtmajā**, f. 's°-daughter,' a young female s°, MBh. **Bhujagântaka**, m. 's°-destroyer,' N. of Garuḍa, L. **Bhujagâbhojin**, m. = °*gâśana*, L. **Bhujagâri**, m. 'serpent-foe,' a peacock, Harav. **Bhujagâśana**, m. 'serpent-eater,' N. of Garuḍa, L. **Bhujagâhvaya**, n. lead, L. **Bhujagêndra**, m. 'serpent-king,' a large serpent, MBh. **Bhujagêśvara**, m. 'serpent lord,' N. of Śesha, Hariv.

Bhujaṃga, m. (fr. *bhujam*, ind. p. of √*bhuj* + *ga*) a serpent, snake, serpent-demon, Kāv.; Suśr.; N. of the number eight, Sūryas.; the paramour of a prostitute, Kāvyâd.; Sāh.; the dissolute friend of a prince, Kāvyâd.; any constant companion of a prince, Hcar.; a lover (see *pṛithivī-bh°*), the keeper of a prostitute, L.; a species of Daṇḍaka metre, VarBṛS., Sch.; N. of a man, Rājat.; (*ī*), f. a serpent-nymph, MBh.; Kathās.; a species of shrub, L.; (prob. n.) tin or lead, L. **-kanyā**, f. a young female snake or a serpent-nymph, Mṛicch. **-ghātinī**, f. 'killing snakes,' a species of plant (used as an antidote), L. **-jihvā**, f. 'serpent's-tongue,' a sp° of pl° similar to Sita Cordifolia, L. **-damanī**, f., **-parṇinī**, f. two species of plants, L. **-pihita**, mfn. covered with s°'s, MW. **-pushpa**, m. a sp° of pl°, L. **-prayāta**, n. 's°-like course,' N. of a metre, Śrutab.; *-stotra*, n. N. of a hymn addressed to Śiva; °*tâshṭaka*, n. N. of wk. **-bha**, n. 'serpent-asterism,' N. of the Nakshatra Āślesha, Var. **-bhuj**, m. 's°-eater,' a peacock, L.; N. of Garuḍa, L. **-bhogin**, m. 'id.,' a peacock, L. (v.l. *-bhojin*). **-bhojin**, m. id., L.; a kind of snake, L.; N. of Garuḍa, L. **-latā**, f. betel-pepper, L. **-vijṛimbhita**, n. a species of the Utkriti metre, Col. **-śatru**, m. 's°-foe,' N. of Garuḍa, Mālatīm. **-śiśu**, m. a kind of Bṛihatī metre, W. **-saṃgatā**, f. N. of a metre, Chandom. **-stotra**, n. N. of a Stotra. **-han**, m. 'serpent-killer,' N. of Garuḍa, L. **Bhujaṃgâkshī**, f. N. of 2 plants (= *nakulêshṭā* and *rāsnā*), L. **Bhujaṃgâkhya**, m. Mesua Roxburghii, L. **Bhujaṃgêndra**, m. the king of snakes, R. **Bhujaṃgêrita**, n. a kind of metre, Ked. **Bhujaṃgêśa**, m. 's°-lord,' N. of Piṅgala.

Bhujaṃgama (*bhujaṃ-gama*), m. a serpent, serpent-demon, Kāv.; Suśr.; N. of the number eight, Sūryas.; of Rāhu, L.; of a Nāga, L.; (*ā*), f. a female serpent, a serpent-maid, MBh.; n. lead, L. **-maya**, mf(*ī*)n. consisting of snakes, L.

Bhujaṃgikā, f. N. of a village, Inscr.

Bhujā, f. a winding, curve, coil (of a snake), BhP.; the arm or hand, Pracaṇḍ. (cf. comp.); the side of any geometrical figure, Āryabh.; Hcat. **-kaṇṭa**, m. 'hand-thorn,' a finger-nail, L. **-dala**, m. = *bhuja-d°*, L. **-madhya**, n. 'the middle of the arm,' the elbow, L. (cf. *bhuja-m°*). **-mūla**, n. = *bhuja-m°*, Sāh. **-latā**, f. (ifc. f. *ā*) = *bhuja-l°*, Śiś.

1. **Bhují**, f. (for 2. see col. 3) clasping, enfolding (others 'sweeping'), RV. x, 106, 4 (cf. *dáśa-* and *śatá-bhuji*).

Bhuj-mán, mfn. abounding in windings or valleys, fertile, RV. viii, 50, 2 (prob. also i, 65, 5; read *bhujmā*).

1. **Bhujyú**, f. (for 2. see col. 3) a snake or viper (cf. *bhujaṃ-ga*, 1. *bhoga* &c.), RV. x, 95, 8 (others 'a doe'), VS. xviii, 42.

भुज् 3. *bhuj*, cl. 7. P. Ā. (Dhātup. xxix, 17) *bhunákti, bhuṅkté* (rarely cl. 6. P. Ā. *bhuñjati*, °*te*, Up.; MBh.; 3. pl. Ā. *bhuñjaté*, RV.; Pot. P. *bhuñjīyāt*, Gobh.; pf. Ā. *bubhujé*, °*jmahe*, °*jriré*, RV.; 3. pl. P. °*juḥ*, MBh.; aor. *abhaukshīt, abhukta*, Gr.; *bhójam, bhójate, bhujema*, RV.; *bhukshishīya*, Br.; fut. *bhokshyati*, °*te*, MBh. &c.; *bhoktā*, R.; inf. *bhójase, bhújam, bhujé*, RV.; *bhoktum*, MBh. &c.; ind. p. *bhuktvā* or *bhuṅktvā*, ib.), to enjoy, use, possess, (esp.) enjoy a meal, eat, eat and drink, consume (mostly Ā.; in Ved. generally with instr., later with acc.), RV. &c. &c.; to enjoy (carnally), Gṛihyas.; MBh.; Kāv.; to make use of, utilize, exploit, Mn.; MBh. &c.; (with *pṛithivīm, mahīm* &c.) to take possession of, rule, govern, MBh.; Kāv. &c.; to suffer, experience, undergo, be requited or rewarded for (acc.) or at the hands of (gen.), RV. &c. &c.; (P.) to be of use or service to (acc.), RV.; TS.; Br.; Up.; to pass, live through, last (a time), Rājat.; BhP.; (in astron.) to pass through, fulfil, Sūryas.: Pass. *bhujyate* (aor. *abhoji*), to be enjoyed or eaten or possessed or made use of, Br.; MBh. &c.: Caus. *bhojayati* (*te*°, m.c.; cf. Pāṇ. i, 3, 87; once *bhuñjāpayati*, Pañcat. ii, 49, v.l.; aor. *abūbhujat*, °*jata*, Gr.), to cause to enjoy or eat, feed with (two acc. or acc. of pers. and instr. of thing; cf. Pāṇ. i, 4, 52), AV. &c. &c.; to use as food, Car.: Desid. *bubhukshati* (once), °*te*, to wish to eat, be hungry, MBh.; BhP.; to wish to enjoy or partake of, Naish. (cf. *bubhukshā*, °*kshita*, °*kshu*): Intens. *bobhujyate*, to be eaten frequently, VarBṛS.; *bobhokti* and *bobhujīti*, to eat or enjoy frequently, Gr. [Cf. Lat. *fungor*.]

Bhukta, mfn. enjoyed, eaten, made use of, possessed &c., MBh.; Kāv. &c.; one who has eaten a meal (= *bhukta-vat*, Siddh.), Kauś.; Suśr. (cf. *bhukta-pīta*); n. the act of eating, L.; the thing eaten or enjoyed, food, MBh. (ifc. feeding or living on, Pañcat.); the place where any person has eaten, R. (cf. Pāṇ. ii, 2, 13, Sch.) **-pīta**, mfn. one who has eaten and drunk, Kathās. **-pūrvin**, mfn. one who has eaten before, Pāṇ. v, 2, 87, Sch. **-bhoga**, mf(*ā*)n. made use of, used, enjoyed, R.; one who has enjoyed an enjoyment or suffered a suffering, MW. **-bhogya**, mf(*ā*)n. of which that which is to be enjoyed has been enjoyed, ŚvetUp. (v.l. *-bhoga*). **-mātre**, ind. immediately on having eaten, Mn. iv, 121. **-vat**, mfn. one who has eaten (as finite verb), ĀśvGṛ.; Mn.; Kathās.; *-vaj-jane*, ind. when people have eaten their meal, Mn. vi, 56. **-vibhukta**, mfn., g. *śāka-pārthivâdi*. **-vriddhi**, f. the swelling of food (in the stomach), Suśr. **-śesha**, n. the remnants of a meal, leavings, Mn.; R. (also °*shaka*, L.); left from a meal, R.; Pañcat. **-samujjhita**, n. = prec. n., L. **-supta**, mfn. sleeping after a meal, Kathās. **Bhuktâsava**, m. (in astron.) the equivalent in respirations of the part of the sign traversed, MW. **Bhuktôcchishṭa**, n. the rejected leavings or remnants of food, L.

Bhukti, f. enjoyment, eating, consuming, ĀśvGṛ.; Pañcat.; fruition, possession, usufruct, Mn.; Yājñ.; Kāv.; food, victuals, Kāv.; Rājat.; (in astron.) the daily motion of a planet, Sūryas. (cf. *paksha-bh°*); a limit, MW. **-dāna**, n. giving for fruition, Pañcad. **-pātra**, n. a food-dish, Rājat. **-prakaraṇa**, n. N. of wk. **-prada**, m. Phaseolus Mungo, L. **-matī**, f. N. of a river, MBh. (v. l. *mukti-m°*). **-varjita**, mfn. not allowed to be enjoyed, Pañcat. **-sapta-śatī**, f. N. of a poem.

Bhuktvā, ind. having enjoyed or eaten or possessed, MBh. (cf. under √3. *bhuj*) **-suhita**, mfn. satisfied after eating, g. *mayūra-vyaṇsakâdi*.

4. **Bhúj**, f. enjoyment, profit, advantage, possession or use of (gen.), RV.; AV. (*bhujé*, also as infin.); m. an enjoyer, eater (said of Agni), RV. x, 20, 2; mfn. (ifc.) enjoying (also carnally), eating, consuming, partaking of, possessing, ruling, Mn.; MBh. &c. (with words meaning 'earth' = 'king'; cf. *kshiti-bh°* &c.); enjoying the reward of, suffering for (*kilbisha-bh°*), MārkP.; passing, through, fulfilling (*vyakta-bh°*), BhP.

2. **Bhují**, f. (for 1. see col. 2) the granting of enjoyment, favour, RV.; one who grants favours, a protector, patron (said of the Aśvins), ib.; m. N. of Agni, Uṇ. iv, 141, Sch.

Bhujishya, mfn. granting food, useful, AV. (cf. *a-bh°*); free, independent, L.; m. a slave, servant (*-tā*, f.), Caṇḍ.; Divyâv. (cf. Uṇ. iv, 178, Sch.); a comrade, companion, L.; a person who has regained his liberty by redeeming his pledge, L.; a cord wound round the wrist of a girl before her marriage (= *hasta-sūtraka*), L.; the hand, L.; a string, L.; (*ā*), f. any woman dependent on or working for others, a slave-girl, maid-servant, Yājñ.; MBh.; Kāv. &c.; a harlot, courtezan, L.

2. **Bhujyú**, mfn. (for 1. see col. 2) wealthy, rich, RV. viii, 22, 1; 46, 20 (Sāy. = *rakshaka*; others 'easily guided,' fr. √1. *bhuj*); N. of a son of Tugra (protected by the Aśvins), ib. i, 112, 6; 116, 3 &c.; of a man with the patr. Lāhyāyani, ŚBr.; a pot, vessel, L.; food, L.; fire, L.

Bhuñjāpaya, °yati. See √3. bhuj, Caus.

Bhoktavya, mfn. to be enjoyed or eaten, Yājñ.; Kāv. &c.; to be used or employed, Mn. viii, 144; to be possessed or governed or ruled, MārkP.; to be utilized or exploited, MBh.; to be fed (n. impers. 'a meal is to be eaten'), MBh.; Hariv.

Bhoktṛi, m. (*trī*, f.) one who enjoys or eats, enjoyer, eater, experiencer, feeler, sufferer, MaitrUp.; MBh. &c. (also as fut. of √3. *bhuj*, R.); a possessor, ruler of a land, king, prince, Inscr.; a husband, lover, L. **-tva**, n. the state of being an enjoyer &c., enjoyment, possession, perception, MaitrUp.; Bhag.; BhP. **-śakti**, f. the faculty of the soul as the enjoyer and possessor of nature, Sarvad.

Bhokshyaka, m. N. of a people, VP.

Bhogya, bhojanīya, bhojya. See p. 767.

भुजिङ्ग *bhujiṅga*, m. pl. N. of a people, MBh. (B. *kaliṅga*).

भुट्ट *bhuṭṭa*, m. N. of a man, Rājat. **-pura**, n. N. of a town built by Bhuṭṭa, ib. **Bhuṭṭêśvara**, m. N. of a temple built by Bhuṭṭa, ib.

भुट्व *bhuṭva*, v.l. for *bhuṭṭa*.

भुड्ड *bhuḍḍa*, m. N. of a poet (contemporary of Maṅkha), L.

भुणिक *bhuṇika*, m. N. of a man, Kāś. on Pāṇ. iv, 1, 79 (cf. *bhauṇikyā*).

भुण्ड् *bhuṇḍ*, cl. 1. Ā. *bhuṇḍate*, to support, Dhātup. viii, 24; to select, Vop. (cf. √*huṇḍ*).

भुमन्यु *bhumanyu*, m. N. of a son of Bharata, MBh.; of a son of Dhṛita-rāshṭra, ib. (cf. *bhavan-manyu*).

भुय्य *bhuyya*, m. N. of a man, Rājat.

भुर् *bhur* (prob. a secondary form of √*bhṛi*, not in Dhātup.), P. Ā. *bhuráti*, °*te*, to move rapidly or convulsively, stir, palpitate, quiver, struggle (in swimming), RV.: Intens. *járbhurīti* (p. *járbhurat*, °*rāṇa*), to flicker (as fire), ib. [Cf. Gk. φύρω, πορφύρω; Lat. *furere*.]

Bhuraṇa, mfn. quick, active (said of the Aśvins), RV.

Bhuraṇya, Nom. P. °*yáti*, to be active or restless, stir, RV.; to stir (trans.), agitate (a liquid), ib.

Bhuraṇyú, mfn. quivering, stirring, quick, eager, restless, active, ib.; the sun, L.; N. of Vishṇu, L.

Bhurij, f. du. the arms or hands (as 'quick in moving'), RV. iv, 2, 14 &c.; AV. xx, 127, 4 (this meaning, given Naigh. ii, 4, seems to suit all passages; others translate 'scissors' or 'a carpenter's vice'); heaven and earth, Sāy.; sg. the earth, Uṇ. ii, 72, Sch.; a metre with one or two superfluous syllables, hypermeter, RPrāt.; ŚāṅkhŚr. &c. (opp. to *ni-cṛit*, q.v.); N. of partic. insertions in liturgical formularies, PañcavBr.

Bhurváṇi, mfn. restless, impatient, RV. i, 56, 1.

Bhurván, restless motion (of water), ib. i, 134, 5.

भुरज् *bhuraj* (prob. connected with √*bhṛijj* and *bhrajj*), only 3. pl. impf. Ā. *bhurájanta*, to boil, bubble, RV. iv, 43, 5.

भुरिषह् *bhuri-shah* (strong form *-shāh*; = *bhūrisah*), mfn. bearing much, RV. ix, 88, 2.

भुरुण्ड *bhuruṇḍa*, m. a species of animal, MBh. (cf. *bhāraṇḍa*, *bhāruṇḍa*, *bheruṇḍa*); N. of a man, Pravar.

भुर्भुरिका *bhurbhurikā* and *bhurbhurī*, f. a sort of sweetmeat, L.

भुव *bhuva*, °*vat*, °*vana* &c. See cols. 2. 3.

भुशुण्ड *bhuśuṇḍa*, m. N. of a man, Cat.

भुशुण्डि *bhuśuṇḍi* or °*ḍī*, f. a kind of weapon (perhaps fire-arms; also written *bhushuṇḍi*, °*ḍī*, and *bhūśuṇḍi*, °*ḍī*), MBh.; R. &c.

भुसुक *bhusuka*, *bhusukha*, or *bhusura*, m. N. of a Yogin, Vcar.

भू 1. *bhū*, cl. 1. P. (Dhātup. i, 1) *bhávati* (rarely Ā. °*te*; pf. *babhū́va*, 2. pers. °*ūtha* or °*ūvitha*, cf. Pāṇ. vii, 2, 64; *babhūyās*, °*yāt*, *babhūtu*, RV.; Ā. *babhūve* or *bubhūve*, Vop.; cf. below; aor. *ábhūt*, °*ūvan*; Impv. *bodhi* [cf. √*budh*], *bhūtu*, RV.; aor. or impf. *ábhuvat*, *bhúvat*, *bhuvāni*, ib.; Prec. *bhūyāsam*, 2. 3. sg. °*yās*, ib.; *bhūyāt*, AV.; *bhūyishthās*, BhP.; *bhavishāt* [?], AitBr.; *abhavishṭa*, *bhavishīshṭa*, Gr.; fut. *bhavishyáti*, ep. also °*te* and 2. pl. °*shyadhvam*; *bhavitā*, Br. &c.; inf. *bhuvé*, *-bhvè*, *bhūshaṇi*, RV.; *bhavitum*, °*tos*, Br.; ind. p. *bhūtvā́*; *bhūtvī́*, RV.; *-bhū́ya*, RV. &c.; *-bhūyam*, *-bhávam*, Br.), to become, be (with nom. or adv. or indecl. words ending in *ī* or *ū*, cf. *kṛishṇī-√bhū* &c.), arise, come into being, exist, be found, live, stay, abide, happen, occur, RV. &c. &c. (often used with participles and other verbal nouns to make periphrastical verbal forms; with a fut. p. = to be going or about to, e.g. *anuvakshyan bhavati*, he is going to recite, ŚBr.; the fut. of √*bhū* with a pf. p. = a fut. pf., e.g. *kṛitavān bhavishyasi*, you will have done, MBh.; the pf. P. *babhūva* after the syllable *ām* is put for the pf. of verbs of the 10. cl. &c. [cf. √1. *as* and √1. *kṛi*]; the Ā. appears in this meaning, Śiś. ix, 84; Kum. xiv. 46; observe also *bhavati* with a fut. tense, it is possible that, e.g. *bhavati bhavān yājayishyati*, it is possible that you will cause a sacrifice to be performed, Pāṇ. iii, 3, 146, Sch.; *bhavet*, may be, granted, admitted, Kāś. on P. iii, 2, 114; *bhavatu*, id., well, good, enough of this, Kāv.; Hit.; *iti ced bhavet*, if this question should be asked, Mn. x, 66; *kva tad bhavati*, what is to become of this, it is quite useless, TBr.; with *na* = to cease to exist, perish, die, MBh.; Kāv. &c.; with *iha na*, not to be born on earth, MBh.; with *śata-dhā*, to fall into a hundred pieces, MBh.; with *dūrataḥ*, to keep aloof, ŚārṅgP.; with *manasi* or *cetasi* and gen., to occur to the mind of any one, Kād.; id. with gen. alone, Lalit.); to fall to the share or become the property of, belong to (cf. 'esse alicujus;' with gen., rarely dat. or loc., accord. to Vop. also with *pari* or *prati* and preceding acc.), RV. &c. &c.; to be on the side of, assist (with gen. or *-taś*), MBh. v, 1301 (cf. Pāṇ. v, 4, 48, Sch.); to serve for, tend or conduce to (with dat. of thing), RV. &c. &c. (with *phalāya*, to bear fruit, Kām.); to be occupied with or engaged in, devote one's self to (with loc.), MBh.; Kāv.; to thrive or prosper in (instr.), turn out well, succeed, RV.; TS.; Br.; to be of consequence or useful, Mn. iii, 181; (also Ā., Dhātup. xxxiv, 37) to fall or get into, attain to, obtain, Br.; MBh.; (with *idám*) to obtain it, i.e. be successful or fortunate, TS.: Pass. *bhūyate* (or °*ti*, Up.: aor. *abhāvi*) sometimes used impers., e.g. *yair bhavishyate*, by whom it will be existed, i.e. who will be, Rājat.: Caus. *bhāvayati* (rarely °*te*; aor. *abībhavat*, Gr.; inf. *bhāvitum*, R.; Pass. *bhāvyate* &c., MBh.), to cause to be or become, call into existence or life, originate, produce, cause, create, Pur.; Sāh.; to cherish, foster, animate, enliven, refresh, encourage, promote, further, AitUp.; MBh. &c.; to addict or devote one's self to, practise (acc.), MBh.; HYog.; to subdue, control, R.; (also Ā.; Dhātup. xxxiv, 37) to obtain, Jaim., Sch.; to manifest, exhibit, show, betray, MBh.; Kām.; Daś.; to purify, BhP.; to present to the mind, think about, consider, know, recognize as or take for (two acc.), MBh.; Kāv. &c.; to mingle, mix, saturate, soak, perfume, Kauś.; Suśr. (cf. *bhāvita*, p. 755, col. 1): Desid. of Caus. *bibhāvayishati* (Pāṇ. vii, 4, 80, Sch.), to wish to cause to be &c., Br.: Desid. *búbhūshati* (°*te*), to wish or strive to become or be, RV. &c. &c.; (with *kshipram*), to strive to be quickly possessed, MBh.; to want to get on, strive to prosper or succeed, TS.; Br.; MBh.; to want to have, care for, strive after, esteem, honour, MBh.; Hariv.; to want to take revenge, BhP.: Intens. *bóbhavīti*, *bobhavati*, *bobhoti*, *bobhūyate*, to be frequently, to be in the habit of, BhP.; Bhaṭṭ.; to be transformed into (acc.), RV.; AV.; (with *tiraḥ*), to keep anything (instr.) secret, ŚBr. [Cf. Zd. *bū*; Gk. φύω, ἔφυν; Lat. *fuit*, *fuat* &c.; Slav. *byti*; Lith. *búti*; Germ. *bim*, *bin*; Angl. Sax. *beó*; Eng. *be*.]

Bhava, °*vat*, °*vita* &c. See p. 748 &c.

Bhāva, °*vanīya* &c. See p. 754 &c.

Bhúva, m. N. of Agni, VS. (Mahīdh.); Kauś.; of a son of Pratihartṛi, VP.; a mushroom, L.; (prob. n.) = *bhuvas*, the atmosphere. **-pati** (*bhúva-*), m. the lord of the atmosphere. **-bhartṛi**, m. id., MBh. **Bhuvâdi-varṇana**, n. N. of wk.

Bhuvad, in comp. for °*vat* (prob. an old pr. p. of √*bhū*). **-vat** (*bhúvad-*), mfn. giving prosperity (said of the Ādityas), TS.; Kāṭh.; Āśv.; ĀśvŚr. **-vásu**, mfn. giving wealth, Nir. iv, 15, Sch. (prob. a mistake of RV. viii, 19, 37, where read *bhuvad* [for *abhuvat*] *vásuḥ*).

Bhúvana, n. a being, living creature, man, mankind, RV. &c. &c.; (rarely m.) the world, earth, ib. (generally 3 worlds are reckoned [see *tri-bhuvana* and *bhuvana-traya*], but also 2 [see *bhuvana-dvaya*], or 7 [MBh. xii, 6924] or 14 [Bhartṛ.]; cf. RTL. 102, n. 1); place of being, abode, residence, AV.; ŚBr.; a house (v. l. for *bhavana*), L.; (?) causing to exist (= *bhāvana*), Nir. vii, 25; water, Naigh. i, 15; m. N. of a partic. month, TS.; of a Rudra, VP.; of an Āptya (author of RV. x, 157), RAnukr.; of a teacher of Yoga, Cat.; of another man, MBh. **-kośa**, m. the globe or sphere of the earth, Kād.; N. of sev. wks. **-candra**, m. 'moon of the world,' N. of a man, Rājat. **-carita**, n. the doings of the w°, Kāv. **-cyavá**, mfn. shaking the w°, RV. **-jñāna**, n. knowledge of the w°, Cat. **-tala**, n. the surface of the earth, Caurap.; Introd. **-traya**, n. the three w°s (heaven, atmosphere, and earth), Śak. **-dīpa**, m., **-dīpaka**, m. (and °*kaśāstra*, n.), **-dīpikā**, f. N. of wks. **-dvaya**, n. the two w°s (heaven and earth), Ragh. **-dvish**, m. an enemy of the w° or earth, Śiś. **-pati** (*bhúv°*), m. the lord of beings or of the w°, VS.; Br.; ŚrS. (also w. r. for *bhavana-p°*). **-pāla**, m. N. of a Sch. on Hāla's Gāthā-kośa, Cat. **-pāvana**, mf(*ī*)n. w°-purifying; (*ī*), f. N. of Ganges, BhP. **-praṇetṛi**, m. 'leader of beings,' Time (personified as the Creator), VarBṛS., Sch. **-pratishṭhā-dāna-vidhi**, m. N. of a ch. of BhavP. **-pradīpikā**, f. N. of wk. **-bhartṛi**, m. = *-pati*, MBh. **-bhāvana**, m. the creator of the world, Mālatīm. **-matī**, f. N. of a princess, Rājat. **-malla-vīra**, m. N. of a man, Col. **-mātṛi**, f. 'w°-mother,' N. of Durgā, Vāstuv. **-rāja**, m. N. of a king, Rājat. **-vidita**, mfn. known in the w°, Megh. **-vinyāsa**, m. N. of ch. of KūrmaP. **-vṛittānta**, m. = *-carita*, Daś. **-śāsin**, m. 'world-ruler,' a king, prince, Rājat. **-sád**, mfn. reposing or situated in the w°, TS. **-hita**, n. the welfare of the w°, MW. **Bhuvanâṇḍaka**, n. the w°-egg, Kād. **Bhuvanâdbhuta**, mfn. astonishing the world, Rājat. **Bhuvanâdhīśa** (RāmatUp.), °**śvara** (Hcat.), m. 'lord of the w°,' N. of a Rudra. **Bhuvanânanda**, m. 'joy of the w°,' N. of an author, Cat. **Bhuvanâbhyudaya**, m. 'prosperity of the world,' N. of a poem, &c. **Bhuvanâlokana**, n. the sight of the w°, MW. **Bhuvanêśa**, m. lord of the w°, ŚvetUp.; N. of a Rudra, RāmatUp.; of a place, Cat.; (*ī*), f. N. of a goddess, Cat.; °*śī-pārijāta*, m. N. of work; °*śī-yantra*, n. N. of a mystical diagram, Tantras. **Bhuvanêśānī**, f. the mistress of the w°, Pañcar. **Bhuvanêśvara**, m. 'lord of the w°,' a prince, king, Rājat.; N. of Śiva, MBh.; of an author, Cat.; (*ī*), f., see below; n. N. of a temple and city sacred to Ś°, RTL. 68, 3; 93; *-māhātmya*, n. N. of wk. **Bhuvanêśvarī**, f. 'mistress of the w°,' N. of various goddesses, Pañcar.; RTL. 188; *-kaksha-puṭa-tantra*, n., *-kalpa*, m., *-kavaca*, n., *-daṇḍaka*, m. or n., *-dīpa-dāna*, n., *-pañcâṅga*, n., *-paṭala*, n., *-paddhati*, f. N. of wks.; *-pūjā-yantra*, n. N. of a mystical diagram, Tantras.; *-rahasya*, n., *-varivasyā-rahasya*, n., *-śānti-prayoga*, m., *-sahasra-nāman*, n. (and °*ma-stotra*, n.), *-stotra*, n., °*śvary-arcana-paddhati*, f. N. of wks. **Bhuvane-shṭhā́**, mfn. being in the world or in all existing things, AV.; ĀśvŚr. **Bhuvanâukas**, m. 'inhabitant of heaven,' a god, MBh.

Bhuvanti, m. = *bhuvaṃ tanoti*, *bhū-maṇḍala-vistāraka*, VS. xvi, 19 (Mahīdh.)

Bhúvas, ind. (orig. nom. or voc. pl. of 2. *bhū*) the air, atmosphere (one of the 3 sacred utterances or Vyāhṛitis [q. v.] uttered between *bhūr*, earth, and *svar* [qq. vv.], heaven; it comes 2nd of the series when 7 or 14 worlds are enumerated, RTL. 403, 102, n. 1), VS.; Br. &c. (it becomes *bhuvar* in *bhuvar-loka*, 'the world of the air,' VP.); one of the mind-born sons of Brahmā, Hariv. 11506; N. of the 2nd and 11th Kalpa (q. v.), VāyuP.

Bhuvi, loc. of 2. *bhū*, in comp. **-shṭha** (for *stha*), mfn. standing on the earth (not in a chariot), BhP.; dwelling on earth (not in heaven), MBh. **-spṛiś**, mfn. touching the ground, BhP.

Bhuvis, m. (?) the sea, ocean, Uṇ. ii, 113, Sch.; f. heaven, L.

2. **Bhū́**, mfn. becoming, being, existing, springing, arising (ifc.; cf. *akshi-*, *giri-*, *citta-*, *padma-bhū* &c.); m. N. of Vishṇu, MBh. xii, 1509 (Nīlak.); of an Ekāha, ŚrS.; f. the act of becoming or arising, Pāṇ. i, 4, 31; the place of being, space, world or

universe (also pl.), RV.; AV.; the earth (as constituting one of the 3 worlds, and therefore a symbolical N. for the number 'one'), Mn.; MBh. &c.; one of the three Vyāhṛitis (see *bhúvas*, *bhūr*, pp. 760 and 763); earth (as a substance), ground, soil, land, landed property, ib.; floor, pavement, Megh.; a place, spot, piece of ground, RV. &c. &c.; the base of any geometrical figure, Āryabh.; object, matter (see *vivāda-saṃvāda-bhū*); a term for the letter *l*, RāmatUp.; a sacrificial fire, L. **–kadamba**, m. (and *ā*, f.) N. of plants, L. **–kadambaka**, m. Ptychotis Ajowan, L.; (*ikā*), f. a species of plant, L. **–kanda**, m. a partic. medicinal plant, Vāgbh. **–kapittha**, m. Feronia Elephantum; n. the fruit of it, L. **–kampa**, m. an earthquake, AdbhBr.; Yājñ.; Var.; N. of a man, Vās., Introd.; *-lakshaṇa*, m. N. of the 33rd ch. of Bhaṭṭôtpala's Comm. on VarBṛS.; *-vicāra*, m. N. of wk. **–karṇa**, m. the diameter of the earth, Sūryas. **–karṇi**, m. N. of a man, Cat. **–karbudāraka**, m. Cordia Myxa, L. **–kaśyapa**, m. N. of Vasu-deva (the father of Kṛishṇa), L. **–kāka**, m. 'earth-crow,' N. of sev. birds (a species of heron; the curlew; a species of pigeon), L. **–kāṇḍa**, m. 'earth-chapter,' N. of a ch. of the Bhūri-prayoga. **–kāśyapa**, m. a king, Bālar. **–kumbhī**, f. N. of a plant, L. **–kushmāṇḍī**, f. Batatas Paniculata, L. **–keśa** (only L.), m. 'earth-hair,' the Indian fig-tree; Blyxa Octandra; (*ā*), f. a Rākshasī; (*ī*), f. Vernonia Anthelminthica. **–kshit**, m. 'earth-destroyer,' a hog, L. **–kshīra-vāṭikā**, f. N. of a place, Rājat. **–khaṇḍa**, m. n. 'earth-section,' N. of a section of the SkandaP. and of the PadmaP. (=*bhūmi-kh*°). **–kharjūrī**, f. a species of date, L. **–gata**, mfn. being or existing on the earth, MārkP. **–gandha-pati**, m. N. of Śiva, Hcat. **–gara**, n. 'earth-poison,' mineral p°, L. **–garbha**, m. N. of the poet Bhava-bhūti, L. **–gṛiha**, n. an underground room or chamber, Car.; Kathās.; a partic. part of a diagram, Pañcar.; RāmatUp. **–geha**, n. an underground room, Kathās. **–gola**, m. 'earth-ball,' the terrestrial globe, earth, Kāv.; Pañcar.; BhP.; N. of wk.; *-kha-gola-virodha-parihāra*, m., *-varṇana*, n. N. of wks.; *-vidyā*, f. knowledge of the terrestrial globe, geography, MW.; *-vistāra*, m., *-vṛittânta*, m., *-vyavasthā-tantrôktā*, f., *-saṃgraha*, m., *-sāra*, m. n. (?), *-hastâmalaka*, n. N. of wks. **–golaka**, m. the terrestrial globe, BhP. **–ghana**, m. the body, L. **–ghnī**, f. aluminous slate, L. **–cakra**, n. 'earth-circle,' the equator or equinoctial line, W. **–cara**, mf(*ā*)n. going on the earth, inhabiting the earth (also m.), MBh.; Hariv.; Pañcat. &c.; moving or living on land, MW. **–caryā**, f. = next, A. **–chāya**, n. or **-chāyā**, f. 'earth-shadow,' darkness, L. **–jantu**, m. 'e°-animal,' a kind of snail, L. **–jambu** or °**bū**, f. wheat, L.; Flacourtia Sapida or its fruit, L. **–tala**, n. the surface of the ground, the earth, MBh.; Pañcat.; Ragh.; Kathās.; *-stha*, mfn. standing or being on the face of the earth, MW.; *-sthāna*, m. a man, Gal.; °*lônmathana*, m. 'earth-shaker,' N. of a Dānava, Hariv. **–talikā**, f. Trigonella Corniculata, L. **–tumbī**, f. a kind of cucumber, L. **–tṛiṇa**, m. (cf. *bhū-s-tṛiṇa*) 'earth-grass,' Andropogon Schoenanthus, L.; a kind of fragrant grass, L. **–**°**ttama** (*bhūtt*°), n. 'best of minerals,' gold, L. **–darī-bhavā**, f. Salvinia Cucullata, L. **–dāra**, m. 'rooting up the earth' and 'a hog,' KāśīKh. **–dina**, n. (Gaṇit.) or **–divasa**, m. (Āryabh.) a civil day. **–deva**, m. a divinity upon earth, a Brāhman (cf. *-sura*), Cat.; L.; N. of Śiva, Śivag.; of various men, Cat.; *-śukla*, m. N. of a poet, Cat. **–dhana**, m. 'whose property is the earth,' a king, prince, L. **–dhara**, mfn. 'e°-bearing,' dwelling in the e°, R.; m. 'earth-supporting,' N. of Kṛishṇa, BhP.; of Baṭuka-bhairava, L.; a mountain (ifc. f. *ā*), MBh.; Hariv.; Pur. &c.; 'mountain' and 'king,' Harav.; a term for the number seven, Sūryas.; N. of Śiva or of the serpent-demon Śesha, MBh.; a kind of chemical or medical apparatus, L.; N. of sev. men, Cat.; *-guhântara-tas*, ind. from within the caves of the mountains, MW.; *-ja*, m. 'mountain-born,' a tree, MBh. (Nilak.); *-tā*, f. the state or act of supporting the earth, Kum.; *-yantra*, n. a partic. apparatus for boiling, Bhpr.; *-rāja*, m. = *-dharêśvara*, A.; *-dharâtmaka* or *-dharâdhīśa*, m. N. of Baṭuka-bhairava, L.; *-dharâraṇya*, n. a mountain-forest, Mālatīm.; *-dharêśvara*, m. 'mountain-lord,' N. of Hima-vat, Kum. **–dhātrī**, f. 'earth-mother,' N. of Baṭuka-bhairava, L.; Flacourtia Cataphracta, L. **–dhra**, m. = *-dhara*, a mountain, Śatr. **–nandana**, m. N. of a king, Kathās. **–nāga**, m. 'earth-snake,' a kind of snail or snail-shell, Rasêndrac. **–nāman**, f. a kind of fragrant earth, L. **–nāyaka**, m. a prince or king, Daś. **–nimba**, m. Gentiana Chirata, Suśr.; ŚārṅgS. **–nīpa**, m. = *-kadamba*, L. **–nīlā-pañca-sūkta** (?), n. N. of wk. **–netṛi**, m. 'earth-leader,' a king, prince, L. **–pa**, m. 'earth-protector,' a king, prince, Var.; Pañcat.; Kathās. &c.; a term for the number sixteen, Gaṇit.; *-tā*, f. sovereignty, kingship, Rājat.; *-putra*, m. a king's son, prince, MārkP.; *-samuccaya-tantra*, n. N. of wk.; *-siṃha*, m. N. of a man, Cat.; *-suta*, m. = *-putra*, MārkP.; °*pâdi-skandha-lakshaṇa*, n. N. of wk.; °*pêshṭa*, m. 'liked by kings,' a kind of tree, L. **–pati** (*bhū́*-), m. 'lord of the earth,' N. of Rudra, TS.; TBr.; ĀśvŚr.; of Indra, ŚrS.; of Baṭuka-bhairava, L.; of one of the Viśve-Devāḥ, MBh.; a king, monarch, prince, MBh.; R.; Ragh. &c.; a partic. bulbous plant existing on the Himavat, L.; a partic. Rāga, Saṃgīt.; N. of a poet (perhaps Bhoja; cf. *bhū-pāla*), Cat.; of an author, Cat.; of a priest of the gods, L.; pl. N. of a partic. class of gods under Manu Raivata, MārkP.; *-veśman*, n. a king's palace, L.; *-stuti*, f. N. of a hymn. **–patita**, mfn. fallen to the earth, VP. **–pada**, m. 'earth-fixed, earth-rooted,' a tree, L.; (*ī*), f. Arabian jasmine, Jasminum Zambac, L. **–paridhi**, m. the circumference of the earth, Sūryas. **–pala**, m. a kind of rat, L. (cf. *-phala*). **–palāśa**, m. a kind of plant, L. **–pavitra**, n. 'earth-purifying,' cowdung, L. **–pāṭalī**, f. a kind of plant, L. **–pāta**, m. falling on the ground, f° down, Sāh. **–pāla**, m. 'earth-guardian,' a king, prince, Kāv.; Hit.; Kathās. &c.; N. of Bhoja-rāja, Cat.; of a son of Soma-pāla, Rājat.; of a country, Inscr.; (*ī*), f. N. of a partic. scale in the Hindū musical system, Col.; *-bhūshaṇa*, n. N. of wk.; *-loka*, m. a multitude of princes, Hcar.; *-vallabha*, m. a king's favourite (said of horses), Kād.; N. of an encyclopaedia (of Dharma, Alaṃkāra, Jyotis &c.), Cat.; *-śrī*, f. 'king's fortune,' N. of a temple of Śiva, Cat.; *-sāhi*, m. (*s*° = شاه) N. of a king, Inscr.; *-stotra*, n. N. of a hymn. **–pālana**, n. 'earth-protection,' sovereignty, dominion, A. **–piṭharī**, f. a partic. plant, Bhpr. (v.l. *bhūmi-valli*). **–putra**, m. 'son of the earth,' the planet Mars, Sūryas.; (*ī*), f. 'daughter of the earth,' N. of Sītā, R. **–pura**, n. a partic. part of a diagram, RāmatUp. (cf. *-gṛiha*). **–pūga**, m. a kind of Areca plant growing on the ground, L. **–prakampa**, m. (ifc. f. *ā*) an earthquake, Var. **–pratimā-dāna**, n. N. of wk. **–pradāna**, n. a gift of land, MW. **–phala**, m. Phaseolus Mungo, L.; a kind of rat, L. (cf. *-pala*). **–badarī**, f. a species of jujube, L. **–bala**, (prob.) n. N. of wk. **–bimba**, m. n. 'earth-ball,' the globe, Pañcar. **–bhaṭa**, m. N. of a man, Rājat. **–bhaṭṭa**, m. N. of an author, Cat. **–bhartṛi**, m. 'earth-supporter, earth-lord,' a king, prince, Rājat. **–bhāga**, m. a portion of ground, a place, spot, station, Kām.; Kathās.; (*krośa-mātro-bh*°), a way of not more than a Krośa, Pañcat. **–bhuj**, m. 'earth-possessor,' a king, prince, MBh.; Kām.; Kathās. &c. **–bhū**, m. metron. of the planet Mars, Gaṇit. **–bhṛit**, m. 'earth-supporter,' a mountain, MBh.; Var.; Kum. &c.; a term for the number 'seven,' Gaṇit.; N. of Vishṇu, Cat.; a king, prince, Var.; Kathās.; MārkP. &c.; *-sabha*, n. a king's palace or a meeting of kings, L. **–bhramaṇa-vicāra**, **-bhrama-vāda-khaṇḍana-nirāsa**, m. N. of wks. **–maṇḍala**, n. 'earth-circle,' orbis terrarum, the terrestrial globe, Cāṇ.; Pur.; Kathās. &c.; the circumference or circuit of the earth, Sūryas. **–mat**, m. 'possessing the e°,' a king, prince, L. **–1. -maya**, mf(*ī*)n. (for 2. see p. 763, col. 1) formed or produced from the e°; (*ī*), f. N. of Chāyā or Shadow (personified as wife of the Sun), L. **–mahêndra**, m. a prince, king, L. **–mitra**, m. 'earth-friend,' N. of a king, BhP. **–yuktā**, f. a kind of palm, L. **–rati**, m. 'earth-joy,' N. of a magical spell recited over weapons, R. **–ratna**, n. N. of wk. **–ramaṇa**, m. a prince, king, Daś. **–ruṇḍī**, f. Heliotropium Indicum, L. **–ruh**, m. 'earth-grower,' a plant, tree, Prab.; Caṇḍ. &c. **–ruha**, m. id., Suśr.; BhP.; Terminalia Arjuna and Glabra, L.; n. a pearl, L. **–lakshaṇa-paṭala**, m. n. N. of a Mantra. **–lagnā**, f. 'clinging to the ground,' Andropogon Aciculatus, L. **–latā**, f. an earth-worm, L. **–lavaṇa**, n. factitious salt, L. **–liṅga**, n. N. of a district of Śālva (cf. *bhauliṅgi*); (*ā*), f. N. of a town, R.; *-śakuna* or °*ni*, m. a species of bird (said to make a sound like *mā sāhasam*, 'no rashness!'), MBh. **–loka**, m. (ifc. f. *ā*) the terrestrial world, earth, Kathās.; MārkP. (cf. *bhūr-l*°); *-kailāsa-māhātmya*, n. N. of a ch. of the BrahmôttKh.; *-sura-nāyaka*, m. an Indra of the earth, Rājat. **–valaya**, m. n. the circumference of the earth, BhP.; the terrestrial globe, MW. **–vallabha**, m. 'earth's favourite,' a king, prince, Inscr. **–vallūra**, n. 'earth's flesh,' a mushroom, L. **–vah** (strong form *-vāh*, weak *bhūh*), mfn., Vop. **–vāka**, m. N. of an author, Cat. **–vārāha-prayoga-vidhi**, m. N. of wk. **–vṛitta**, n. 'earth-circle,' the equator, MW. **–śakra**, m. 'earth-Indra,' a king, prince, L. **–śamī**, f. a kind of Acacia, L. **–śaya**, m. 'lying or dwelling on the earth,' N. of Vishṇu, MBh.; any animal living in the e°, Car. **–śayyā**, f. a couch on the bare ground, Kām.; Pañcat. **–śarkarā**, f. a species of bulbous plant, L. **–śuddhi**, f. purification of the ground, MW.; *-lakshaṇa*, n. N. of wk. **–śelu**, m. the plant Cordia Myxa, L. **–śravas**, m. an ant or mole hill, W. **–śvabhra**, n. a hole in the ground, hollow, L. **–saṃskāra**, m. 'ground-preparation,' a term for five methods of preparing and consecrating the Khara (q.v.) at a sacrifice (viz. *pari-sam-ūh*, *upa-lip*, *lekhāḥ kṛi*, *pāṅsūn ud-dhṛi*, *adbhir abhy-uksh*; some enumerate seven), KātyŚr., Sch. **–suta**, m. 'earth-son,' the planet Mars, Sūryas.; Var.; (*ā*), f. 'daughter of the e°,' N. of Sītā, L. **–sura**, m. 'earth-god,' a Brāhman, BhP.; Daś. (cf. *-deva*). **–sūkta** and °**ta-bhāshya**, n., **-stuti**, f. N. of hymns. **–s-tṛiṇa**, m. Andropogon Schoenanthus, Mn.; Hariv.; Suśr.; Vāgbh. (cf. *bhū-tṛiṇa*). **–stha**, mfn. living on the e°, MBh.; m. a man, L. **–spṛiś**, m. 'touching the ground,' a man, L.; a Vaiśya, L. **–sphoṭa**, m. 'e°-blister,' a mushroom, L. **–svarga**, m. 'heaven on e°,' N. of the mountain Sumeru, L. **–svargāya**, Nom. Ā. °*yate*, to become a heaven on earth, Daś. **–svāmin**, m. a landlord, landholder, MW.

Bhūtá, mf(*ā*)n. become, been, gone, past (n. the past), RV. &c. &c.; actually happened, true, real (n. an actual occurrence, fact, matter of fact, reality), Yājñ.; R. &c.; existing, present, Kaṇ.; (ifc.) being or being like anything, consisting of, mixed or joined with, Prāt.; Up.; Mn. &c. (also to form adj. out of adv., e. g. *ittham-*, *evam-*, *tathā-bh*°); purified, L.; obtained, L.; fit, proper, L.; often w.r. for *bhṛita*; m. a son, child, L.; a great devotee or ascetic, L.; (pl.) N. of an heretical sect (with Jainas, a class of the Vyantaras), L.; N. of Śiva, L.; of a priest of the gods, L.; of a son of Vasu-deva and Pauravī, BhP.; of a son-in-law of Daksha and father of numerous Rudras, ib.; of a Yaksha, Cat.; (*ā*, f.) the 14th day of the dark half of the lunar month, SkandaP. (L. also m.); N. of a woman, HParis.; n. (cf. above) that which is or exists, any living being (divine, human, animal, and even vegetable), the world (in these senses also m.), RV. &c. &c.; a spirit (good or evil), the ghost of a deceased person, a demon, imp, goblin (also m.), GṛS.; Up.; Mn. &c. (cf. RTL. 241); an element, one of the 5 elements (esp. a gross el° = *mahā-bh*°, q.v.; but also a subtle el° = *tan-mātra*, q.v.; with Buddhists there are only 4 el°), Up.; Sāṃkhyak.; Vedântas. &c.; N. of the number 'five' (cf. *mahā-bh*° and *pāñcabhautika*); well-being, welfare, prosperity, VS.; TS.; AitBr. **–karaṇa**, n. 'causing a word to have a past meaning,' N. of the augment, APrāt.; *-vatī*, f. (scil. *vibhakti*) the character and personal endings of the augmented verbal forms (i. e. of impf., aor. and Cond.), Kāt. **–kartṛi**, m. 'maker of beings,' Brahmā, the creator, R. **–karman**, m. N. of a man, MBh. **–kāla**, m. past time or the preterite tense, VPrāt.; Pāṇ., Sch.; °*lika*, mfn. relating to it, Pāṇ. iii, 2, 84, Sch. **–kṛit**, mfn. forming beings, creative, AV.; m. the creator, ib. &c.; pl. a class of gods, ŚāṅkhŚr. **–ketu**, m. N. of a son of Manu Daksha-sāvarṇi, BhP.; of a Vetāla, Kathās. **–keśa**, m. Corydalis Goveniana, L. (also n. and *ī*, f.); (*ī*), f. a species of plant, Bhpr. (L Nardostachys Jatamansi, Vitex Negundo and white basil). **–kesarā**, f. Trigonella Foenum Graecum, L. **–koṭi**, f. 'the highest culminating point for all beings,' absolute non-entity (= *śūnya-tā*), Buddh. **–krānti**, f. (for °*tâkr*°?) possession by spirits, L. **–gaṇa**, m. the host of living beings, MaitrUp.; a multitude of spirits or ghosts, R.; Kathās.; °*ṇâdhipa*, m. N. of Nandin (q.v.), Kathās. **–gandhā**, f. a species of fragrant plant or a partic. perfume, L. **–gṛihya**, m. pl. a class of domestic spirits, PārGṛ. **–grasta**, mfn. possessed by an evil spirit, MW. **–grāma**, m. = *-gaṇa* (in both meanings), MBh.; Pur.; a multitude of plants, L.; any aggregate or elementary matter, the body, W. **-ghna**, m. 'destroying spirits or demons,' a camel, L.; garlic, L.; Betula Bhojpatra, L.; (*ī*), f. the sacred basil or = *muṇḍitikā*, L. **-caturdaśī**, f. the 14th day in the dark half of the month Kārttika (consecrated to Yama), L. **-cārin**, m. 'moving among demons,' N. of Śiva, Śivag. **-cintā**, f. investigation into the elements, Suśr. **-caitanika**, m. an adherent of the doctrine that the mind or intellect is produced from material elements, Nyāyas., Sch. **-caitanya**, n. intellectuality of matter, ib. **-jaṭā**, f. Nardostachys Jatamansi, L.; another species of Valeriana, Bhpr. **-jananī**, f. the mother of all beings, Mālatim. **-jaya**, m. victory over the elements, Cat. **-jyotis**, m. 'light of living beings,' N. of a king, BhP. **-ḍāmara**, m. or n. N. of 2 Tantras; (*ī*), f. N. of a deity, Pañcad. **-tantra**, n. the doctrine of spirits (as contained in the 6th ch. of the Ashṭâṅga-hṛidaya). **-tanmātra**, n. a subtle element, Sāṃkhyas., Sch. **-tā**, f. reality, truth, Vās. **-tṛiṇa**, n. a species of grass, L. **-tva**, n. the state of being an element, MBh. **-dattā**, f. N. of a woman, HPariś. **-damanī**, f. one of the 9 Śaktis of Śiva, L. **-dayā**, f. compassion towards all creatures, universal benevolence, W. **-dāhīya**, mfn. apt to burn or destroy all creatures, Āpast. **-drāvin**, m. red oleander, L.; a partic. tree (= *bhūtâṅkuśa*), L. **-druma**, m. Cordia Latifolia, L. **-druh**, mfn. injuring beings, injurious, BhP. **-dhara**, mfn. retaining (in the mind) or remembering the past, R.; (*ā*), f. 'supporting beings,' the earth, L. **-dhātrī**, f. 'supporter of beings,' sleep, Car.; the earth, Kād. **-dhāman**, m. N. of a son of Indra, MBh. **-dhāriṇī**, f. = *-dharā*, Mālav. **-nanda**, m. N. of a king, Kathās. **-nātha**, m. 'lord of beings or spirits,' N. of Śiva, Ragh.; Caṇḍ.; N. of a poet, Cat. **-nāyikā**, f. 'leader of the Bhūtas,' N. of Durgā, L. **-nāśana**, mfn. destroying evil beings; m. Semecarpus Anacardium, L.; pepper, L.; black mustard, L.; n. Asa Foetida, L.; the berry or seed of Elaeocarpus Ganitrus, L. **-nicaya**, m. 'aggregation of elements,' the body, Śāntiś. **-páti**, m. 'lord of beings' (esp. of evil beings, N. of Rudra-Śiva, Bhava, Śarva and Agni), AV.; MBh. &c.; Ocimum Sanctum, L. **-pattrī**, f. sacred basil, L. **-pāla**, m. the guardian of living beings, BṛĀrUp. **-pura**, m. pl. N. of a people, Var.; (*ī*), f. N. of a town; °*rī-māhātmya*, n. N. of wk. **-pushpa**, m. Calosanthes Indica, L. **-pūrṇimā**, f. the day of full moon in the month Āśvina (when the Bhūtas are worshipped), L. **-pūrva**, mf(*ā*)n. who or what has been before, prior, former, ancient, old (also °*vaka*), MBh.; Kāv. &c. (°*vam*, ind. formerly); deceased, MBh.; *-tā*, f. former circumstances, Kām. **-prakṛiti**, f. the origin of all beings, Nir. xiv, 3. **-pratishedha**, m. the warding off evil spirits or demons, Cat. **-prâya**, w.r. for *bhauta-p*°. **-prêta-piśâcâdya**, m. pl. the Bhūtas, Prêtas, Piśācas &c., RāmatUp. (cf. RTL. 241). **-bali**, m. = *-yajña*, Gal.; N. of a grammarian, Cat. **-bāla-grahônmāda**, m. madness produced by the action of Bhūtas or demons inimical to children, Pañcar. **-brahman**, m. = *devalaka*, L. **-bhartṛi**, m. 'lord of beings or spirits,' N. of Śiva, Rājat. **-bhava**, mfn. existing in all beings, Hariv. **-bhavyá**, n. past and future, AV.; °*vyêśa*, m. the lord of past and future, MBh. **-bhāvana**, mfn. creating or causing the welfare of living beings, MBh.; N. of Śiva or Vishṇu or Brahmā, ib. (*-bhāvana*, mfn. causing the welfare of those who cause the w° of l° b°, Hariv.); n. = *sva-rūpa*, BhP., Sch. **-bhāvin**, mfn. creating living beings, Up.; past and future, Kpr. **-bhāshā**, f. the (so called) language of demons or Piśācas (a Prākrit dialect), Kathās.; *-maya*, mf(*ī*)n. composed in the Piś° d° (as the Bṛihat-kathā), Kāvyâd. **-bhāshita**, n. = *-bhāshā*, Cat. **-bhṛit**, mfn. sustaining the elements or creatures, Bhag. **-bhairava**, m. N. of a partic. medical compound, Bhpr.; *-tantra*, n. N. of a Tantra. **-bhautika**, mfn. consisting of the elements or of anything formed from them, L. **-maya**, mf(*ī*)n. containing all beings, Hariv.; consisting of the five elements, Naish.; as anything is in reality, true, genuine, BhP. **-mahêśvara**, m. = *-bhartṛi*, R. **-mātṛi**, f. = *-jananī* (N. of Gaurī, Brahmī &c.), MBh.; *-tôtsava* (!), n. a partic. festival, Cat. **-mātṛikā**, f. 'mother of beings,' the earth, Gal. **-mātra**, n. the rudiment of an element, W.; (*ā*), f. pl. the subtle elements (see *tan-mātra*), Mn. xii, 17; the coarse and subtle el°, BhP. (in this sense a Dvandva comp.), Sch.; the 10 primary objects (viz. *vāc*, *gandha*, *rūpa*, *śabda*, *anna-rasa*, *karman*, *sukha-duḥkhe*, *ānanda* or *rati* or *prajāti*, *ityā*, *manas*), KaushUp. **-mārī**, f. a partic. resin, L. **-yajña**, m. the offering of food &c. to all created beings (see *mahā-yajña* and *bali*, and cf. RTL. 421), ŚBr.; ĀśvGṛ. **-yoni**, f. the origin or source of all beings, KaivUp. **-raya**, m. pl. a class of gods under the 5th Manu, BhP. **-rāj**, m. = *-bhartṛi*, ib. **-rūpa**, mfn. having the form of a Bhūta, implike, Pañcar. **-lakshaṇa**, n. N. of wk. **-lipi**, f. 'demon-writing,' N. of a partic. magical formula, Cat. **-1. -vat**, ind. as if it were past, Pāṇ. iii, 3, 132. **-2. -vat**, mfn. having been, W.; containing the word *bhūta*, AitBr.; surrounded by demons, Hcat. **-varga**, m. the host of demons or spirits, MārkP. **-vādin**, mfn. telling the real fact or truth, MW. **-vāsa**, m. the abode of beings, Hariv. (v. l. °*tâv*°); Terminalia Bellerica, Bhpr. **-vāhana**, mfn. 'having the Bhūtas for his vehicle,' N. of Śiva, Śivag.; *-sārathi*, m. Śiva's charioteer, ib.; n. a chariot drawn by Bhūtas, L. **-vikriyā**, f. possession by evil spirits, epilepsy, L. **-vijñāna**, n. the knowledge of evil beings, demonology, Cat. **-víd**, mfn. knowing all beings, ŚBr.; knowing (how to ward off) evil sp°, Subh. **-vidyā**, f. = *-vijñāna*, ChUp.; Suśr. **-vināyaka**, m. a leader of evil beings, BhP. **-viveka**, m. N. of wk. **-vishṇu**, m. N. of an author, Cat. **-vīra**, m. pl. N. of a race, AitBr. **-vṛiksha**, m. 'demon-tree,' Trophis Aspera, L.; Calosanthes Indica, L.; Terminalia Bellerica, L. **-veshī**, f. a white-flowering Vitex Negundo, L. **-śarman**, m. N. of a man, MBh. **-śuddhi**, f. 'removal of evil demons,' N. of a ceremony, RTL. 197; N. of a Tantra. **-saṃsāra**, m. the course or circuit of existence (through continuous states of being), Mn. i, 50. **-saṃkrāmin**, mfn. dependent on beings that have existed before, TS. **-saṃgha**, m. the totality of beings or of the elements, MārkP. **-saṃcāra**, m. possession by evil spirits, L. **-saṃcārin**, m. 'moving among creatures,' a forest conflagration, L. **-saṃtāpa**, m. 'torture of beings,' N. of an Asura, BhP. **-saṃtāpana**, m. 'torturer of beings,' N. of a Daitya (son of Hiraṇyâksha), Hariv. **-samāgama**, m. the meeting of mortals, MBh. **-sampṛikta**, mfn. combined with elementary matter, W. **-samplava**, m. the flooding or drowning of all creatures, universal deluge, Āpast.; MBh. &c. **-sammohana**, mfn. bewildering all beings, Up. **-sarga**, m. a creation of beings (e. g. of Deva-yonis or divine beings in 8 classes, of men, and of Tiryag-yonis in 5 classes, viz. cattle, birds, wild animals, creeping things, and plants), MBh.; Pur.; creation of the elements, Pur. **-sâkshin**, m. an eye-witness of created beings (who sees all they do), MBh. **-sâdhana**, mf(*ī*)n. leading all creatures towards their end (Mahīdh. 'producing cr°'), VS.; (*ī*), f. the earth, A. **-sāra**, m. a species of Calosanthes Indica, L.; (*ī*), f. collective N. of the 3 myrobolans (Terminalia Chebula, T° Bellerica, and Phyllanthus Emblica), L. **-sūkshma**, n. = *-tanmātra*, Sāṃkhyas., Sch. **-sṛishṭi**, f. the creation of Bhūtas, MW.; the illusion effected by the power of the Bh° ib.; the whole class of Bh° collectively, ib. **-stha**, mfn. being in living creatures, residing in the elements, BhP. **-sthāna**, n. the abode of living creatures, MBh. **-hatyā**, f. the killing of a living creature, BhP. **-hantrī**, f. 'destroying evil spirits,' a species of Dūrvā grass, L.; = *vandhyā karkoṭakī*, L. **-hara**, m. bdellium, L. **-hārin**, m. Pinus Devadāru, L. **-hāsa**, m. 'demoniacal laughter,' a kind of fever, Bhpr. **Bhūtâṇśa**, m. N. of the author of RV. x, 106 (a descendant of Kaśyapa), Nir. xii, 41. **Bhūtâṅkuśa**, m. a kind of tree, L. **Bhūtâtmaka**, mfn. possessing the essence of the elements, Cat. **Bhūtâtman**, m. 'soul of all beings,' N. of Brahmā, R.; of Mahā-purusha, i. e. Vishṇu, Hariv.; of Śiva, L.; the individual soul, Mn. v, 109; Yājñ. iii, 34 &c.; 'nature of all beings,' war, conflict, L.; mfn. one whose soul is subdued or purified, MBh. (cf. *bhāvitâtman*); m. 'the self consisting of the elements,' the body, MaitrUp.; Mn. xii, 12 (opp. to *kshetra-jña*). **Bhūtâdi**, m. 'original or originator of all beings,' N. of Mahā-purusha or the Supreme Spirit, Hariv.; m. n. (in Sāṃkhya) N. of Aham-kāra (as the principle from which the elements are evolved). **Bhūtâdika**, mfn. beginning with the elements, the el° &c., RāmatUp.; (with *ahaṃ-kāra*) = *bhūtâdi*, m. n. **Bhūtâdhipati**, m. the lord of all beings, ŚBr. **Bhūtânadyatana**, m. not the current day in past time, Kāś. on Pāṇ. iii, 3, 135. **Bhūtânukampā**, f. compassion towards all beings, Ragh. **Bhūtântaka**, m. 'destroyer of beings,' the god of death, MBh. **Bhūtâbhishaṅga**, m. possession by evil spirits, Bhpr. **Bhūtârabdha**, mfn. formed from the elements; pl. (? n.) all organic matter, Kull. **Bhūtâri**, m. 'enemy of evil beings,' Asa Foetida, L. **Bhūtârta**, mfn. tormented by demons, L. **Bhūtârtha**, m. anything that has really happened or really exists, real fact, Kāv.; Var. &c.; an element of life, MW.; *-kathana*, n. (Rājat.), *-varṇana*, n. (ib.), *-vyāhṛiti*, f. (Ragh.) statement of facts; °*thânubhava*, m. the apprehension of any matter of fact, Śaṃk. **Bhūtârma**, n., Pāṇ. vi, 2, 91. **Bhūtâvâsa**, m. 'abode of beings,' N. of Vishṇu and Śiva, MBh.; Hariv.; Terminalia Bellerica (as the abode of evil b°), L.; the body (as the ab° of the elements), Mn.; MBh. &c. **Bhūtâvishṭa**, mfn. possessed by evil spirits, Lalit. **Bhūtâveśa**, m. demoniac possession, L. **Bhūtâsana**, n. 'seat of Bhūtas,' N. of a magic chariot, Kathās. **Bhūte-chád**, f. pl. N. of AV. xx, 135, 11–13, Vait. **Bhūtêjya**, mfn. worshipping the Bhūtas or demons, Bhag. (cf. *bhūta-yajña*). **Bhūtêndriya-jayin**, m. 'one who has subdued both the elements (of the body) and the senses,' a kind of ascetic or devotee, Cat. **Bhūtêśa**, m. 'lord of beings,' N. of Brahmā or Kṛishṇa, MBh.; of the Sun, Hcat.; 'lord of evil beings,' N. of Śiva, BhP. **Bhūtêśvara**, m. 'lord of (evil) beings,' N. of Śiva, Prab.; Rājat. **Bhūtêshṭakā**, f. a partic. kind of brick, TS. **Bhūtêshṭā**, f. 'liked by the Bhūtas,' N. of the 14th day of a half-month, L. **Bhūtôḍḍāmara**, m. or n. N. of a Tantra (cf. *bhūta-ḍāmara*). **Bhūt'-odana**, m. a dish of rice (eaten to counteract the influence of demons), R.; Suśr. **Bhūtônmāda**, m. insanity produced by the influence of evil spirits (20 kinds are enumerated), ŚārṅgS. **Bhūtôpadeśa**, m. referring to anything already occurring or existing, L. **Bhūtôpamā**, f. comparison with a living being or animal, Nir. iii, 16. **Bhūtôpasarga**, m. possession by an evil spirit, Subh. **Bhūtôpasṛishṭa**, mfn. possessed by an evil spirit, ĀśvŚr. **Bhūtôpahata**, mfn. id., R.; *-citta*, mfn. having the mind possessed by an evil spirit, ib.

Bhūtâyana, m. pl. N. of a school, L.

Bhūti or (RV.) **bhūtí**, f. existence, being, L.; well-being, thriving, prosperity, might, power, wealth, fortune, RV. &c. &c.; Welfare personified (= *lakshmī*), BhP.; superhuman power (as attainable by the practice of austerity and magical rites), W.; ornament, decoration, Megh. 19; ashes, Kāv.; Kathās.; fried meat, L. (?); = *bhūmi*, earth, ground, AitBr. (Sāy.); (with *marutām*) N. of a Sāman, ĀrshBr.; of various plants (Andropogon Schoenanthus or = *rohiṣha* &c.), L.; (also °*tī*), of the wife of Ruci or Kavi and the mother of Manu Bhautya, Hariv.; VP.; m. a class of deceased ancestors, MārkP.; N. of Vishṇu, MBh.; of Śiva, L.; of the father of Manu Bhautya, MārkP.; of a Brāhman, L. **-karman**, n. any auspicious rite or ceremony (performed at a birth, marriage &c.), GṛS.; MBh. **-kalaśa**, m. N. of a man, Rājat. **-kāma** (*bhūti-*), mfn. desirous of wealth or property, TS. &c. &c.; m. a king's councillor, L.; N. of Bṛihas-pati, W. **-kāla**, m. time of prosperity, a happy moment, MW. **-kīrtana**, n. 'praise of prosperity,' N. of ch. of ŚivaP. ii. **-kīla**, m. a hole, pit, L.; a cellar (for concealing wealth), W. **-kṛit**, m. 'causing welfare,' N. of Śiva, Śivag.; a class of deceased ancestors, MārkP. **-kṛitya**, n. = *-karman*, Mn. viii, 393. **-garbha**, m. N. of the dram. poet Bhava-bhūti, L. **-gaurī**, f. N. of Śiva's wife, VP. **-tīrthā**, f. N. of one of the Mātṛis attending on Skanda, MBh. **-da**, m. = *-kṛit* (in both meanings), Śivag.; MārkP. **-datta**, m. N. of a man, Col. **-nanda**, m. N. of a prince, VP. **-nidhāna**, n. 'receptacle of prosperity,' N. of the Nakshatra Dhanishṭhā, L. **-bali**, m. N. of a grammarian (cf. *bhūta-b*°). **-bhūshaṇa**, m. 'adorned with ashes,' N. of Śiva, Śivag. **-mat**, mfn. possessing welfare, fortunate, happy, MBh. **-malina**, mfn. soiled with ashes, MW. **-mitra**, m. N. of a king, VP. **-yuvaka**, m. pl. N. of a people, MārkP. **-rāja**, m. N. of a man, Cat. **-laya**, m. N. of a Tīrtha, MBh. **-vardhana**, mfn. increasing welfare, ĀpŚr. **-varman**, m. N. of a king of Prāg-jyotisha, Vās., Introd.; of a Rākshasa, Kathās. **-vāhana**, mfn. bringing welfare (said of Śiva), Śivag. (cf. *bhūta-v°*). **-śiva**, m. N. of a man, Kathās. **-śubhra** (Kathās.), **-sita** (Śiś.), mfn. white with ashes (said of Śiva). **-sṛij**, mfn. creating welfare, MārkP. **Bhūtîśvara-tīrtha**, n. N. of a sacred bathing-place, ŚivaP. **Bhūty-artham**, ind. for the sake of prosperity, Ml.

Bhūtika, m. or n. a species of plant, Suśr.; (L. m. n. Ptychotis Ajowan; n. Andropogon Schoenanthus, Gentiana Chirata &c.); n. camphor, L.

Bhūtīka, m. or n. a species of plant, Car. (L. Gentiana Chirata, Curcuma Zerumbet &c.)

Bhūmá, m. (in the formula *dhruvāya bhūmāya* [= *bhaumāya*] *namaḥ*), TĀr.; mostly ifc. for *bhūmi* or *bhūman* (cf. *udaka-*, *kṛishṇa-bh°* &c.); also ibc. in the next words. **-vidyā**, f. N. of ChUp. vii. **Bhūmânanda-sarasvatī**, m. N. of the teacher of Advaitânanda, Cat.

Bhūmaka-tṛitīyā, f. N. of the 3rd day in a partic. month, Cat.

Bhū́man, n. the earth, world, RV.; AV.; a territory, country, district, ĀśvGṛ.; a being, (pl.) the aggregate of all existing things, RV.; (*bhūmán*), m. abundance, plenty, wealth, opulence, multitude, majority, RV. &c. &c. (ifc. filled with, Mcar.; *bhūmnā*, ind. generally, usually, Kāv.; Rājat.; *bhūnā́*, ind. plentifully, abundantly, RV.); the plural number (*bhūmni*, in the plural), L.; N. of Kṛishṇa, BhP.; f. a collection, assembly, ŚāṅkhBr.

Bhūmanyu, m. N. of a king, MBh. (B. *sumanyu*; cf. *bhumanyu*).

2. **Bhūmaya**, Nom. P. *°yati* (for 1. see p. 761, col. 2), to augment, increase, make abundant, Bhaṭṭ.

Bhū́mi, f. (Ved. also nom. *bhū́mī*, gen. abl. *°myās*, loc. *°myām*) the earth, soil, ground, RV. &c. &c.; (pl. divisions of the world; cf. *bhūmi-traya*); a territory, country, district, ib.; a place, site, situation, ŚBr. &c. &c.; position, posture, attitude, MBh.; Kāv. &c.; the part or personification (played by an actor), Kathās.; the floor of a house, story, Megh.; Kathās.; the area, Śulbas.; the base of any geometrical figure, Col.; (metaph.) a step, degree, stage, Yogas. (with Buddhists there are 10 or 13 stages of existence or perfection, Dharmas. 45; 46); extent, limit, Kir.; (ifc.) a matter, subject, object, receptacle i. e. fit object or person for (cf. *viśvāsa-*, *sneha-bh°* &c., and *pātra*, *bhājana*); the tongue, L.; m. N. of a son or grandson of Yuyudhāna and father of Yugaṃdhara, Hariv.; VP. **-kadamba**, m. a kind of Kadamba, L. **-kandaka** or **-kandara**, n. a mushroom, L. **-kandalī**, f. a species of plant (= *kandalī*), L. **-kapāla** (*bhū́mi-*), mfn. having the earth for a vessel or receptacle, ŚBr. **-kampa**, m. an earthquake, Gaut.; MBh.; R.; Var.; N. of the 62nd AVPariś. **-kampana**, n. an earthquake, MBh.; R.; Hariv. **-kushmāṇḍa**, m. Convolvulus Paniculatus, L. **-kūsmaṇḍa**, m. liquorice, L. **-kshaya**, m. loss of land, Pañcat. **-khaṇḍa**, m. n. 'earth-section,' N. of the 2nd book of the PadmaP. **-kharjūrikā** (Bhpr.) or *°jūrī* (L.), f. a species of palm. **-gata**, mfn. fallen to the earth, MānŚr.; Mn. **-garta**, m. a pit or hole in the earth, Kathās. **-garbha**, m. N. of Bhava bhūti, Gal. **-guhā**, f. a hole in the earth, L. **-gṛiha**, n. an underground chamber, Kathās.; (*bhū́mi-*), mfn. whose house is the earth (said of a dead person), AV. **-gocara**, m. an inhabitant of the earth, a man, Uttamac. **-campaka**, m. Kaempferia Rotunda, Pañcar. **-cala**, m. (Kauś.; Gobh.; MBh.; R.) or **-calana**, n. (Kauś.; PārGṛ.; Mn.) an earthquake. **-cchattra**, n. a mushroom, L. **-ja**, mfn. produced from the earth, sprung from the ground, Suśr.; m. the planet Mars, MārkP.; a man, L.; a kind of snail, L.; a kind of Kadamba, L.; N. of the demon Naraka, L.; hell, MW.; (*ā*), f. metron. of Sītā, L.; n. a species of vegetable, L.; *-guggulu*, m. a species of bdellium, L. **-jambu** or *°bukā* or *°bū*, f. a species of plant, L.; Premna Herbacea, L. **-jāta**, mfn. produced or arisen on the earth, MBh. **-jīvin**, m. 'living by the soil,' a Vaiśya, L. **-joshaṇá**, n. the choice of soil, ŚBr.; PārGṛ. **-m-jaya**, m. 'earth-conquering,' N. of a son of Virāṭa, MBh. **-tanaya**, m. the planet Mars, Var. **-tala**, n. (ifc. f. *ā*) the surface of the earth, the ground (also pl.), R. **-tuṇḍika**, m. N. of a district, Kathās. **-traya**, n. = *bhuvana-tr°*, Hariv. **-tva**, n. the state of earth, earthiness (e.g. *-tvam eti*, 'he becomes earth'), TāṇḍyaBr.; MaitrUp. **-da**, mfn. giving landed property, Mn. **-dāna**, n. donation of landed property, Cat.; the 9th AVPariś. **-dundubhí**, m. 'earth-drum,' a pit or hole in the earth covered over with skins, TS.; Br. &c. **-dṛiṅhá**, mfn. firmly fixed on the ground, AV. **-deva**, m. 'earth-god,' a Brāhman, Mn.; MBh. &c.; (*ī*), f. N. of various women, Cat.; W. **-dhara**, m. 'earth-supporter,' a mountain, R.; Kum.; a symbolical expression for the number seven, Sūryas.; a king, prince, Mālav.; N. of a poet, Subh. **-nanda**, m. N. of a prince, VP. **-nātha**, m. 'earth-lord' (Vet.), and **-pa**, m. 'earth-protector' (Mn.; MBh. &c.), a king, prince. **-paksha**, m. a swift horse, L. **-pati**, m. 'e°-lord,' a king, prince, Kauś.; Gobh.; MBh. &c.; *-tva*, n. sovereignty, kingship, R. **-paridṛiṅhaṇa**, n. the making firm of the ground, ĀpŚr. **-parimāṇa**, n. square measure, Yājñ., Sch. **-pāla**, m. (ifc. f. *ā*) 'earth-guardian,' a king, prince, MBh.; R.; Suśr. &c. **-pāśá**, m. and **-pāśakā**, f. a species of plant, Br. **-piśāca**, m. Borassus Flabelliformis, L. **-putra**, m. 'earth-son,' the planet Mars, Sūryas.; N. of a king, VP. **-puraṃ-dara**, m. 'e°-Indra,' N. of Dilīpa, Ragh. **-pra**, mfn. filling the e° (as fame), AitĀr. **-pracala**, m. an earthquake, Āp. **-prâpta**, mfn. fallen on the ground, KātyŚr. **-budhna**, mfn. having the earth for a bottom, ChUp. **-bhāga**, m. (also n., R.) a portion or plot of land, place, spot, ĀśvGṛ.; Lāṭy.; MBh. &c. **-bhuj**, m. 'earth-possessor,' a king, prince, Kāv.; Rājat. **-bhūta**, mfn. being the bottom of anything, Rājat.; become earth; being on the ground, MW. **-bhṛit**, m. 'e°-supporter,' a king, prince, Rājat.; Kathās.; a mountain, W. **-bhedin**, mfn. differing from (what exists on) earth, Kathās. **-maṇḍa**, m. Vallaris Dichotomus, L.; (*ā*), f. Arabian jasmine, L. **-maṇḍapa-bhūshaṇā**, f. Gaertnera Racemosa, L. **-mat**, mfn. possessing land, g. *yavâdi*. **-maya**, mf(*ī*)n. made or consisting of earth; (*ī*), f. N. of Chāyā, L. **-mitra**, m. 'friend of the country,' N. of two kings, VP. **-rakshaka**, m. the guardian or protector of a country, MW.; a swift horse, L. **-rathika**, m. a young cartwright (who prepares himself for his future profession by drawing on sand), Nyāyam., Comm. **-ruha**, m. earth-growing, a tree, Svapnac. **-lābha**, m. 'gaining earth,' dying, death, L. **-lepana**, n. 'earth-ointment,' cow-dung, L. **-loká**, m. the terrestrial world, TS. **-vajramaṇi**, m. pl. land and diamonds and (other) gems, Mn. xi, 38. **-vardhana**, m. n. 'earth-increasing,' a dead body, corpse, L. **-valli**, f. N. of a plant, Bhpr. **-vāsin**, mfn. dwelling on the ground floor, Pat. **-śaya**, mfn. lying or living on the ground or in the earth; m. any animal living in the g° or e° (cf. *bhū-ś°*), Mn.; a wild pigeon, L.; N. of a king, MBh. **-śayana**, n. (MW.) or **-śayyā**, f. (L.) the act of sleeping on the (bare) ground. **-shṭha**, mfn. standing or remaining on the earth or on the ground, being or lying in the earth (*ambu bhūmi-shṭham*, 'stagnant water;' *bhūmi-shṭha-mātra-tah*, 'from the moment of being on the e°,' i. e. 'immediately after birth'), KātyŚr.; MBh.; Hariv. &c.; living or remaining in one's own country, Kām. (cf. *para-bh°*). **-sattra**, n. an offering consisting of a donation of land, MBh. **-saṃniveśa**, m. the general appearance or configuration of a country, Uttarar. **-sambhava**, mfn. produced on or from the earth, MW.; (*ā*), f. N. of Sītā, L. **-sava**, m. one of the 9 Vrātya-stomas, ŚāṅkhŚr. **-sāmrājya**, n. sovereignty over the earth, Kathās. **-suta**, m 'earth-son,' the planet Mars, Var.; Mṛicch. **-sena**, m. N. of one of the sons of the 10th Manu, MārkP.; of a scholar, Buddh. **-stoma**, m. N. of an Ekâha, ĀśvŚr.; Vait. **-snu**, m. an earthworm, L. **-spṛiś**, mfn. touching the ground, Lāṭy.; blind; cripple, lame, L.; m. a man, L.; a Vaiśya, L.; a thief who creeps along the ground, L. **-svāmin**, m. 'landlord,' a king, prince, Rājat. **Bhūmicchā**, f. desire for lying on the ground, Sāh. **Bhūmîndra**, m. 'earth-chief,' a king, prince, L. **Bhūmîśvara**, m. (in *eka-bh°*) 'sovereign over the earth,' Rājat.; *-māhātmya*, n. N. of a ch. in the BhavP.

Bhūmikā, f. earth, ground, soil, Kāś.; Kathās. &c.; (ifc.) a spot, place for (e. g. *āhāra-bh°*, an eating-place, Kathās.; *akshara-bh°*, a place i. e. a tablet for writing, Ragh.); a story, floor, Inscr.; Pañcat. (with *gṛihôpari*, the flat roof of a house, Śukas.); a step, degree, Yogas.; (in dram.) an actor's part or character, Vikr.; Mālatim. &c.; decoration (as of an image), L.; preface, introduction, ChUp., Sch.; Kāvyâd. **-gata**, m. a person who wears a theatrical dress, L. **-bhāga**, m. a floor, threshold, Mṛicch.

Bhūmī, in comp. for *bhūmi*. **-kadamba**, m. = *bhūmi-kadamba*, q. v. **-kurabaka**, m. a species of plant, Suśr. **-pati**, m. = *bhūmi-p°*, q. v., Uṇ., Sch. **-bhuj**, m. = *bhūmi-bh°*, q. v., Śṛiṅgār. **-bhṛit**, m. a mountain, Śatr. **-ruh**, m. (Gīt.) or **-ruha**, m. (Hcat.) 'earth growing,' a plant, tree. **-śayya**, mfn. sleeping on the ground, Bhartṛ. **-saha**, m. a species of tree, Bhpr.

Bhūmy, in comp. for *bhūmi*. **-anantara**, mfn. belonging to the next country, Kām.; Kathās.; m. the king of an adjacent country, Kām. **-anṛita**, n. false evidence concerning land, Mn. viii, 99. **-āmalakī** or **-āmalī**, f. Flacourtia Cataphracta, L.; Phyllanthus Niruri, L. **-āhulya**, n. a species of shrub, L. **-eka-deśa**, m. one portion of territory, MW.

Bhūmyá, mfn. belonging to the earth, terrestrial, RV.

Bhūya, n. (ifc.) becoming, being (see *amutra-*, *ātma-* &c.) **-tva**, n., see *brahma-bhūya-tva*. **-rūpa**, mfn., prob. w. r. for *ubhaya-rūpa*, Kap.

Bhūyaḥ, in comp. for *bhūyas*. **-palâyana**, n. fleeing once more, Kathās. **-saṃnivṛitti**, f. returning once more (see *a-bhūyaḥ-s°*), Ragh. **-stana** (*bhū́yaḥ-*), mfn. having more teats than (abl.), ŚBr.

Bhūyaś, in comp. for *bhūyas*. **-chandika**, mfn. having a great desire for anything.

Bhūyaśas, ind. mostly, generally, usually, MBh.; once more, again, Hariv.; BhP.

Bhū́yas, mfn. becoming (n. the act of becoming; see *brahma-bh°*); 'becoming in a greater degree' (in this meaning accord. to Pāṇ. vi, 4, 158 compar. of *bahu*) i.e. more, more numerous or abundant, greater, larger, mightier (also 'much or many, very numerous or abundant' &c.), RV. &c. &c.; abounding in, abundantly furnished with (instr. or comp.), Kathās.; Sāh.; (*as*), ind. (g. *svar-ādi*) more, most, very much, exceedingly, RV. &c. &c.; still more, moreover, besides, further on, GṛŚrS.; Up. &c. (also *bhūyasyā mātrayā*, Divyâv.; *pūrvam-bhūyaḥ*, first–next, R.; *ādau-paścāt-bhūyaḥ*, first–then–next, Prasaṅg.); once more, again, anew, Mn.; MBh. &c. (also *bhūyo 'pi*, *bhūyaś câpi*, *bhūyo bhūyaḥ* and *punar bhūyaḥ*); (*asā*), ind. exceedingly, in a high degree, Kālid.; mostly, generally, as a rule, R.; Kathās. (cf. *yad bhūyasā*). **-kara**, mfn. making or doing more, VS. **-kāma**, mfn. very desirous of anything (*-tā*, f.), L. **-kṛit**, mfn. augmenting, increasing, TS.; f. pl. N. of a partic. kind of brick, ĀpŚr. **-taram** or **-tarām**, ind. more, anew, again, R. **-tva**, n. the becoming or being more or much, increase, preponderance, abundance, multitude, GṛŚrS.; Gaut.; Suśr.; great extent, Sarvad.; (*ena*), ind. for the most part, mostly, L.

Bhūyasvin, mfn. preponderant, superior, TāṇḍBr.

Bhū́yishṭha, mf(*ā*)n. (accord. to Pāṇ. vi, 4, 158 superl. of *bahu*) most numerous or abundant or great or important, chief, principal, RV. &c. &c.; (ifc. = having anything as chief part or ingredient, chiefly filled with or characterised by, nearly all, almost; cf. *śūdra-bh°*, *nirvāṇa-bh°* &c.); (*am*), ind. for the most part, mostly, chiefly, RV. &c. &c.; abundantly, numerously, R.; in the highest degree, very much, Ragh.; (*ena*), ind. mostly &c., MBh. **-tara**, mfn. mostly consisting of (comp.), MBh. **-bhâj**, mfn. sharing principally, receiving most, TS.; ŚBr.; ĀpŚr. **-śas**, ind. in very large numbers, MBh.

Bhūyo, in comp. for *bhūyas*. **-'kshara** (*bhūyas* + *akshara*), mf(*ā*)n. having more syllables, TāṇḍBr.; *-tara*, mfn. id., AitBr. **-guṇa**, mfn. 'doubled' and 'having more virtues,' Naish. **-darśana**, n. (and *°na-vāda*, m.) N. of wks. **-'nāgamana** (*bhūyas* + *anāgamana*), n. non-return, Kathās. **-bhartṛi-samāgama**, m. meeting again with a husband, ib. **-bhāva**, m. increase, growth, progress, L. **-mātra**, n. the greatest part, most of (gen.), Kauś. **-ruci**, mfn. taking much delight in anything (*-tā*, f.), L. **-vidya**, mfn. knowing more, more learned, Nir.

Bhū́r, ind. (orig. = *bhūs*, nom. voc. of 2. *bhū*) one of the 3 Vyāhṛitis (q. v.), 'the earth' (the first of the 7 upper worlds; cf. *bhúvas*), VS. &c. &c.; hell, L.; = next, Hariv. **-bhuva**, m. N. of one of the mind-born sons of Brahmā, Hariv.; *-kara*, m. a dog, L.; *-tīrtha* and *°vêśvara-tīrtha*, n. N. of Tīrthas, Cat. **-bhūra** or **-bhūva**, m. N. of a Daitya, VP. **-loka**, m. the terrestrial world, earth, MBh.; Pur. &c.; the country south of the equator, Siddhântaś. (cf. *bhū-loka*).

Bhū́ri, mfn. much, many, abundant, frequent, numerous, great, important, strong, mighty, RV. &c. &c.; (*ī*), ind. much, abundantly, greatly, often, frequently, ib. (*bhū́ri kṛitvas*, many times, repeatedly, RV. iii, 18, 4); m. N. of Brahmā or Vishṇu or Śiva, L.; of a son of Soma-datta (king of the Bālhikas), MBh.; Hariv.; Pur.; m. n. gold, L.; f. (cf. Pāli *bhūrī*) reason, intellect, Lalit. **-karman** (*bhū́ri-*), mfn. doing much, very busy, RV.; TBr.; making many oblations, BhP. **-kālam**, ind. for a long time, Kathās. **-kṛitrima-māṇikya-maya**, mf(*ī*)n. consisting of many imitation rubies, Kathās. **-gadgadam**, ind. with much stammering, Pañcat. **-gandhā**, f. a partic. perfume, L. **-gama**, m. 'much-going,' an ass, L. **-gu**, mfn. (*gu=go*) rich in cattle, RV. **-guṇa**, mfn. multiplying greatly, bearing manifold fruit, Subh. **-cakshas** (*bhū́ri-*), mfn. 'much-seeing' or 'affording manifold appearances' (said of the sun), RV. **-ja**, mfn. born in great numbers, ŚāṅkhŚr. **-janman** (*bhū́ri-*), mfn. having many births, RV. **-jyeshṭha**, m. N. of a son of king Vicakshus, VP. **-tara**, mfn. more, more abundant or numerous, BhP. **-tā**, f. muchness, multitude, Kathās. **-tejas**, mfn. of great splendour, very glorious, Mn.; MBh.; m. N. of a prince, MBh. **-tejasa**, mfn. = prec. mfn. (said of fire), MBh. **-toka**, mfn. having many children, Nir. **-da**, mfn. 'much-giving,' liberal, munificent, BhP. **-dakshiṇa**, mfn. attended with rich presents or rewards, MBh.; bestowing rich presents (esp. on Brāhmans at a sacrifice), liberal, ib.; (*am*), ind. with rich offerings or pr°, ib. **-dā́**, mfn. = *-da*, RV.; TBr. **-dātra** (*bhū́ri-*), mfn. rich in gifts, RV. **-dā́vat**, mfn. 'much-giving,' munificent, RV.; *-tara*, mfn. id., ib. (cf. Pāṇ. viii, 2, 17, Vārtt. 2, Pat.) **-dā́van**, mf(*arī*)n. id., ib. **-dugdhā**, f. 'having much milk,' Tragia Involucrata, L. **-dyumna**, m. 'possessing great glory,' N. of a pious prince (son of Vīra-dyumna), MaitrUp.; MBh.; R.; of the sons of 2 Manus (v. l. *-dhāman*), Hariv.; MārkP. **-dhana** (*bhū́ri-*), mfn. having much wealth or property, AV. **-dhāman**, mfn. possessing great might or splendour, Kir.; m. N. of a son of the ninth Manu, Hariv. (cf. *-dyumna*). **-dhāyas** (*bhū́ri-*), mfn. nourishing or supporting many, RV.; AV. **-dhāra** (*bhū́ri-*), mf(*ā*)n. (fr. 1. *dhārā*) 'much-showering,' yielding abundant streams or rays of light, RV. **-nidhana**, mfn. perishing in many ways, Prab. **-pattra**, m. 'many-leaved,' a species of Andropogon, L. **-palita-dā**, f. a species of shrub, L. **-pāṇi** (*bhū́ri-*), mfn. many-handed, AV. **-pādāta**, mfn. possessing many foot-soldiers, MW. **-pāśa** (*bhū́ri-*), m. du. 'holders of many fetters,' N. of Mitra-Varuṇa, RV. **-putra** (*bhū́ri-*), mf(*ā*)n. having many sons or children, TĀr. **-pushpā**, f. Anethum Sowa, L. **-poshin**, mfn. 'much-nourishing,' cherishing multitudes, RV. **-prayoga**, mfn. much or variously used (*-tva*, n.), L.; m. N. of a dictionary; *-gaṇa-dhātu-ṭīkā*, f. N. of a Comm. on a Dhātu-pāṭha. **-preman**, m. 'full of affection,' Anas Casarca, L. **-phalī**, f. a species of shrub, L. **-phenā**, f. a species of plant (= *saptalā*), Bhpr. **-bala**, m. 'having much strength,' N. of a son of Dhṛita-rāshṭra, MBh.; (*ā*), f. Sida Cordifolia and Rhombifolia, L. **-bhaṭṭa**, m. N. of a scholar, Cat. **-bhāra** (*bhū́ri-*), mfn. heavily laden, RV. **-bhoja**, mfn. having many enjoyments, BhP. **-mallī**, f. a species of plant, L. **-māya**, m. 'possessed of much deceit,' a jackal (*ā*, f.), L. **-mūla** (*bhū́ri-*), mfn. rich in roots, AV. **-mūlikā**, f. 'id.,' a species of plant, L. **-rasa**, m. 'having much juice,' the sugar-cane, L. **-rāma**, m. a donkey, ass, L. **-retas** (*bhū́ri-*), mfn. abounding in seed, prolific, RV.; AV.; VS. **-lagnā**, f. Clitoria Ternatea, L. **-lābha**, mfn. having much profit, very profitable; m. great gain, W. **-loha**, n. a kind of brass or bell-metal, L. **-varcas**, mfn. very splendid, R. **-varpas** (*bhū́ri-*), mfn. 'many-shaped,' presenting many appearances, RV.; AV. **-vasu**, m. 'having much wealth,' N. of a minister or councillor, Mālatīm.; of a Brāhman, Kathās. **-vāra** (*bhū́ri-*), mf(*ā*)n. rich in gifts, RV. **-vikrama**, mfn. of great valour, R. **-viyoga**, mfn. having or causing many separations, MW. **-vṛishṭi**, f. excessive rain, ib. **-vetasa**, mfn. having many canes or reeds, L. **-śas**, ind. manifoldly, variously, MBh.; Kāv. &c. **-śṛiṅga** (*bhū́ri-*), mf(*ā*)n. many- or strong-horned, RV. **-śravas**, m. N. of a son of Soma-datta (king of the Bālhikas), MBh.; of Indra, L. **-śreshṭhaka** or °*ṭhika*, m. or n.(?) N. of a place near Benares, Prab. **-sháh** or **-shāh** (for *sāh*), mfn. bearing or carrying much, RV. **-sheṇa** (fr. *senā*), m. 'having many armies,' N. of a man, BhP.; of a son of the 10th Manu, Hariv.; of king Śaryāti, BhP. **-sakha**, mfn. 'having many friends' or 'dear to many,' Hiraṇy. **-sthātra** (*bhū́ri-*), mfn. having many stations, being at many places or spots, RV. **-han**, m. 'many-killer,' N. of an Asura, MBh.

Bhūrika, m. N. of a man, Divyâv.

Bhūry, in comp. for *bhūri*. **-akshá**, mfn. many-eyed, RV. **-āsuti** (*bhū́ry-*), mfn. much-excited or much exciting, ib. **-ojas** (*bhū́ry-*), mfn. having great power, very vigorous, ib.

Bhūvarī, f. N. of a goddess, ĀpŚr.

Bhūshṇu, mfn. (= *bhavishṇu*, *bhavitṛi*, L.) growing, thriving, AitBr.; wishing to thrive, desiring happiness or prosperity, Mn. iv, 135 (cf. *alam-bhūshṇu*).

भूःखार *bhūḥkhāra*, mfn. coming from Bokhāra (as horses &c.), Rājat. (cf. *bhuḥkhāra*).

भूक *bhūka*, m. n. (Uṇ. iii, 41, Sch.) a hole, L.; the head of a fountain, L.; time, L.; m. darkness, L.

भूकल *bhūkala*, m. a restive horse, L.

भूताली *bhūtalī*, f. N. of two plants (= *bhūpāṭali* and *mushalī*), L.

भूत्यकण्टक *bhūtyakaṇṭaka*, v. l. for *bhūrja-k°* (see *bhūrja*).

भूना *bhūnā*, f. N. of a place, Cat. (for *bhūnā* = *bhūmnā* see *bhūman*, p. 763, col. 1).

भूमि *bhūmi*, *bhūmī* &c. See p. 763.

भूमिआण *bhūmiāṇa* and *bhūmīyāṇa*(?), m. or n. N. of two places, Cat.

भूयस् *bhūyas*, *bhūyishṭha*. See p. 763.

भूरि *bhūri* &c. See col. 1.

भूरिज् *bhūrij*, f. the earth, L. (prob. w. r. for *bhurij*, q. v.)

भूर्ज *bhūrja*, m. a species of birch (the Bhoj tree, Betula Bhojpatra, the bark of which is used for writing on), Kaṭh.; Kāv.; Var. &c.; n. a leaf made of birch bark for writing on, Kāraṇḍ.; a written deed, document, Lokapr. [Cf. Slav. *brěza*; Lith. *bérżas*; Germ. *bircha*, *Birke*; Eng. *birch*.] **-kaṇṭaka**, m. a man of one of the mixed classes (the son of an out-caste Brāhman by a woman of the same tribe), Mn. x, 21 (v. l. *bhūtya-kaṇṭaka* and *bhrijja-k°*; cf. *bhṛijya-kaṇṭha*). **-druma** (ŚārṅgP.), **-pattra** (Pañcat.), m. the birch tree.

भूर्णि *bhū́rṇi*, mfn. (√*bhur*) restless, active, excited, angry, rash, wild, RV.; f. the earth, Uṇ. iv, 52; a desert, L.

भूष *bhūsh*, cl. 1. P. *bhū́shati* (pf. *bubhūsha*, Gr.; aor. *abhūshīt*, ib.; fut. *bhūshishyati*, *bhūshitā*, ib.; inf. *bhūshitum*, ib.), to strive after, use efforts for, be intent upon (dat.), RV. iii, 25, 2; 34, 2 &c.; to seek to procure (acc.) for (dat.), ib. ix, 94, 3; to adorn, Dhātup. xvii, 30: Caus. *bhūshayati* (Dhātup. xxxiii, 56, ep. also °*te*; aor. *abubhūshat*; inf. *bhūshayitum*), to adorn, embellish, attire (Ā. also 'one's self,' Pāṇ. iii, 1, 87, Vārtt. 18, Pat.), MBh.; Kāv. &c.

Bhūshaṇa, mf(*ī*)n. decorating, adorning (ifc.), MBh.; BhP.; Suśr.; m. N. of Vishṇu, MBh.; of a Daitya, Kathās.; n. (rarely m., e. g. MBh. iii, 8588; cf. g. *ardharcâdi*) embellishment, ornament, decoration (often ifc., with f. *ā*, 'having anything as ornament' i. e. adorned or decorated with), MBh.; Kāv. &c.; N. of various wks. **-kānti**, f., **-ṭīkā**, f. N. of wks. **-tā**, f. the being an ornament, ornature, Kathās. **-dāyaka**, mfn. bestowing ornaments, Kām. **-deva**, m. N. of a poet, Cat. **-peṭikā**, f. a jewel-casket, Daś. **-bhaṭṭa**, m. N. of an author, Cat. **-bhūshaṇa**, mfn. decorated with ornaments, BhP. **-vāsas**, n. pl. clothes and o°s, Mn. viii, 357. **-sāra**, m. N. of wk. (also *-darpaṇa*), Cat. **Bhūshaṇâcchādanâśana**, n. pl. (dainty) food, clothes and o°s, Mn. iii, 59. **Bhūshaṇêndra-prabha**, m. N. of a king of the Kiṃ-naras, L.

Bhūshaṇīya and **bhūshayitavya**, mfn. to be adorned or decorated, MBh.; Kāv. &c.

Bhūshā, f. ornament, decoration, Kāv.; Kathās. &c. **-peṭī**, f. a jewel-case, Kuval.

Bhūshāya, Nom. Ā. *-yate*, to serve as an ornament, Mcar.

Bhūshin, mfn. (ifc.) adorned with, MBh.; Hariv.

Bhūshya, mfn. to be adorned or decorated, Kum.

भूषिक *bhūshika*, m. pl. N. of a people, VP. (v. l. *mūshika*).

भूष्णु *bhūshṇu*. See col. 2.

भूस्तृण *bhū-s-triṇa*. See p. 763, col. 3.

भृ 1. *bhṛi*, cl. 1. P. Ā. (Dhātup. xxii, 1) *bhárati*, °*te*; cl. 3. P. Ā. (xxv, 5) *bíbharti* (*bibhárti* only RV. iv, 50, 7), *bibhṛite*; cl. 2. P. *bhárti*, RV. i, 173, 6 (pr. p. P. *bíbhrat*, q. v.; Ā. *bibhrāṇa* with act. meaning, Ragh., *bibhramāṇa* with pass. m°, RV.; pf. *jabhā́ra*, *jabhárat*; *jabhre*, *ajabhartana*, ib.; *babhā́ra*, *babhṛima*, Br. &c.; p. *babhrāṇá* with pass. meaning, RV.; *bibharām-babhūva*, Ragh., °*rām-āsa*, Bhaṭṭ.; aor. *abhār*, RV.; *bhartám*, *bhṛitám*, Br.; *abhṛita*, Gr.; *abhā́rsham*, Subj. *bharshat*, RV.; *abhārisham*, AV.; Prec. *bhriyā́sam*, °*yā́t*, Br.; fut. *bharishyati*, cond. *ábharishyat*, RV.; *bhartā́*, ŚBr.; inf. *bhártum*, *bhártave*, *bhártavai*, Ved.; *bhā́radhyai*, RV.; ind. p. *-bhṛítya*, ib. &c.), to bear, carry, convey, hold ('on' or 'in,' loc.), RV. &c. &c.; to wear i. e. let grow (hair, beard, nails), Mn.; MBh. &c.; to balance, hold in equipoise (as a pair of scales), Vishṇ.; to bear i. e. contain, possess, have, keep (also 'keep in mind'), RV. &c. &c.; to support, maintain, cherish, foster, ib.; to hire, pay, MBh.; to carry off or along (Ā. *bharate*, 'for one's self' i. e. gain, obtain, or = *ferri*, 'to be borne along'), RV.; AV.; to bring, offer, procure, grant, bestow, RV. &c. &c.; to endure, experience, suffer, undergo, ib.; to lift up, raise (the voice or a sound; Ā. *bharate*, also 'to rise, be heard'), RV.; to fill (the stomach), Pañcat.; (with *garbham*) to conceive, become pregnant (cf. under √*dhṛi*), RV.; (with *kshitim*) to take care of, rule, govern, Rājat.; (with *ājñām*) to submit to, obey, ib.; (with *ūrjām*) to exert, employ, Bhaṭṭ.: Pass. *bhriyáte* (ep. also °*ti*; aor. *abhāri*), to be borne &c., RV. &c. &c.: Caus. *bhārayati* (aor. *abībharat*), to cause to bear &c.; to engage for hire, MBh.: Desid. *búbhūrshati* (ŚBr.; MārkP.), *bibharishati* (Pāṇ. viii, 2, 49), to wish to bear or support or maintain: Intens. *báribharti* (3. pl. °*bhrati*, RV., where also 2. du. *jarbhṛitáḥ*), *barībharti* (Kāv.), to bear repeatedly or continually, carry hither and thither. [Cf. Zd. *bar*; Gk. *φέρω*; Lat. *fero*; Slav. *brati*; Goth. *bairan*; Germ. *beran*, *ge-bären*; Eng. *bear*.]

Bhṛit, mfn. bearing, carrying, bringing, procuring, possessing, wearing, having, nourishing, supporting, maintaining (only ifc.; cf. *ishu-*, *kshiti-*, *dharma-*, *vaṃśa-bhṛit* &c.) **-tva**, n., see *śastrâstra-bhṛit-tva*.

Bhṛita, mfn. borne, carried &c. (see prec.); gained, acquired, Kathās.; (ifc.) filled, full of, ib.; hired, paid (as a servant), Mn.; MBh. &c. (*bhakta-venayor bhṛitaḥ*, 'one who receives board and wages;' cf. *kshīra-bh°*); m. a hireling, hired servant or labourer, mercenary, Yājñ., Sch. **-bhūti**, mfn. possessing power or prosperity, W.; smeared with ashes, ib. **-randhra**, mfn. filled up (as a hole or depression), ib. **Bhṛitâdhyāpana**, v. l. for *bhṛityâdh°*, q. v.

Bhṛitaka, mfn. brought, fetched (see *drāg-bh°*); mfn. hired, receiving wages; m. a hired labourer, servant, Mn.; MBh. &c.; (*ikā*), f. hire, wages, Divyâv. **Bhṛitakâdhyayana**, n. learning from a hired teacher, Prâyaśc. **Bhṛitakâdhyāpaka**, m. a hired t°, Yājñ. **Bhṛitakâdhyāpana**, n. instruction given by a h° t°, ib. **Bhṛitakâdhyāpita**, mfn. taught by a hired teacher, Mn. iii, 156.

Bhṛiti (ŚBr. also *bhṛíti*), f. bearing, carrying, bringing, fetching (see *idhmá-bh°*); support, maintenance, nourishment, food, RV. &c. &c.; hire, wages or service for w°, Mn.; Yājñ.; MBh. **-karma-kara**, m. a hired labourer or servant, ĀpGṛ., Sch. **-bhuj**, mfn. enjoying or receiving wages; m. = prec., L. **-rūpa**, n. a reward given to a person in lieu of wages (for the performance of a duty for which payment is improper), MW. **Bhṛity-adhyāpana**, n. (prob.) w. r. for *bhṛityâdh°*, q. v. **Bhṛity-anna**, n. wages and board, Kathās. **Bhṛity-artham**, ind. on account of the maintenance of (gen.), Ragh. i, 18 (v. l. for *bhūty-artham*).

Bhṛitin. See *saṃvatsara-bhṛitin*.

Bhṛitya, mfn. to be nourished or maintained;

m. one who is to be m°, a dependent, servant (also the s° of a king, a minister), GṛS.; Mn.; MBh. &c.; (*ā*), f. support, maintenance, wages &c. (= *bhṛiti*), L.; nursing, care of (cf. *kumāra-bhṛityā*). **-kāma-kṛit**, mfn. acting kindly to servants, MW. **-jana**, m. a person (or persons) to be supported, a servant or servants, Kāv. **-tā**, f., **-tva**, n. servitude, dependence, Kāv.; Kathās.; Pañcat. **-paramâṇu**, m. a very humble (lit. 'an atom of a') servant, Hcar. (cf. *padāti-lava*). **-bharaṇa**, n. maintaining or cherishing s°s, MBh. **-bhartṛi**, m. one who maintains s°s, the master of a family, Yājñ. **-bhāva**, m. servitude, dependence, Ratnâv. **-bhāvin**, mfn. being or becoming a servant, Ragh. **-varga**, m. 's°-class,' the whole number of any one's s°s, household, MBh. **-vātsalya**, n. kindness to s°s, Hit. **-vṛitti**, f. subsistence of s°s or dependents, Mn. xi, 7. **-śālin**, mfn. having many s°s, W. **Bhṛityâdhyāpana**, n. teaching the Veda for hire, Mn. xi, 63 (v.l. *bhṛitâdh°*). 1. **Bhṛityā-bhāva**, m. a state of servitude or dependence, MW. 2. **Bhṛityâbhāva**, m. the absence of servants, ib.

Bhṛityāya, Nom. Ā. °*yate*, to behave like a servant, Kathās.

Bhṛityī-√bhū, P. *-bhavati*, to become a servant, enter upon service, Rājat.

Bhṛitra, m. (?), Siddh.

Bhṛithá, (prob.) m. offering, oblation (of Soma), RV.; a turtle, tortoise, L.

भृंश् *bhriṇś*, cl. 1. 10. P. *briṇśati*, °*śayati*, to speak or to shine, Dhātup. xxxiii, 114.

भृकुंश *bhṛi-kuṇśa*, *bhṛi-kuṭi* &c. See under *bhrū*.

भृक्ष् *bhṛiksh* or *bhraksh*, 1. P. Ā. *bhṛikshati* or *bhrakshati*, °*te*, to eat, Dhātup. xxi, 27 (v.l. for *bhaksh*).

भृग् *bhṛig*, an onomat. word used to express the crackling sound of fire, MBh.

भृगमात्रिक *bhṛigamātrika*, prob. w.r. for *mṛiga-m°*.

भृगल *bhṛigala* = *bṛigala*, KātyŚr., Sch.

भृगवाण *bhṛígavāṇa*. See col. 2.

भृगु *bhṛígu*, m. pl. (√*bhrāj*) N. of a mythical race of beings (closely connected with fire, which they find [RV. x, 46, 2] and bring to men [i, 58, 6; 195, 2] or enclose in wood [vi, 15, 2] or put in the navel of the world [i, 143, 4]; or which is brought to them and first kindled by Mātari-śvan [i, 60, 1; iii, 5, 10]; they are also said to fabricate chariots [iv, 16, 20] and are mentioned together with the Aṅgirasas, Atharvans, Ṛibhus, Maruts, Druhyus &c. [cf. Naigh. v, 5]; in Hcat. 12 Bhṛigus are enumerated among gods; cf. Gk. οἱ Φλεγύαι), RV.; AV.; ŚBr.; Kauś.; N. of one of the chief Brāhmanical families (to which the Aitaśāyanas are said to belong, RV. (esp. vii, 18, 6; viii, 3, 9 &c.); Br.; MBh.; Pur.; sg. N. of a Ṛishi regarded as the ancestor of the Bhṛigus, AV.; AitBr. (he has the patr. Vāruṇi and is the supposed author of RV. ix, 65; x, 19; he is enumerated among the 10 Maharshis created by the first Manu, Mn. i, 35; cf. IW. 46 &c.); of a son of Kavi, MBh.; of one of the Prajā-patis produced from Brahmā's skin, Hariv.; Pur.; of one of the 7 sages, Hariv.; of the father of Cyavana and 6 other sons, MBh.; of the f° of Dhātṛi and Vidhātṛi, Pur.; of the f° of Śrī (by Khyāti), ib.; of the author of a Dharma-śāstra (cf. *bhṛigu-smṛiti*), Mn. i, 59; of an astronomer, Cat. (cf. *bhṛigu-saṃhitā*); of a medical authority, ib.; of the Ṛishi Jamad-agni or his son, L.; of Śukra or the planet Venus (called either Bhṛigu or the son of Bh°; his day is Friday), Sūryas.; Var.; of Kṛishṇa or of Rudra, L.; of a son of Artha-pati and uncle of the poet Bāṇa, Vās., Introd.; of the top of the mountain Bhṛigu-tuṅga, Cat.; a declivity, slope, precipice, Hcat. (cf. *bhṛigu-patana*). **-kaccha**, m. n. or (*ā*), f. N. of a town and sacred place on the northern bank of the river Narma-dā (now called Broach), AVPariś.; BhP.; KāśīKh.; m. pl. its inhabitants, MārkP.; *-tīrtha*, n. N. of a Tīrtha, Cat. **-kulôdvaha**, m. patr. of Paraśu-rāma, Dhanaṃj. **-kshetra**, n. N. of a place, VP.; *-māhātmya*, n. N. of wk. **-gītā**, f. N. of wk. **-ja** (Sūryas.) or **-tanaya**, (Var.), m. 'son of Bh°,' the planet Venus. **-tīrtha-māhātmya**, n. N. of wk. **-tuṅga**, m. 'Bh°'s peak,' N. of a sacred mountain in the Himālaya (or in the Vindhya; also called *bhṛigos t°*, R.), MBh.; Hariv.; R. **-deva**, m. N. of an author, Cat. **-devata**, mfn. worshipping the Bhṛigus, BhP. **-nandana**, m. 'son of Bh°,' the planet Venus, L.; patr. of Śaunaka, MBh.; of Ruru, ib.; of Paraśu-rāma, MBh.; Uttarar. **-paṭala**, m. n. N. of wk. **-patana**, n. a fall from a precipice, Daś. **-pati**, m. 'chief of the Bh°s,' N. of Paraśu-rāma, Kāv. **-pāta**, m. committing suicide by precipitating one's self from a precipice, RTL. 350. **-putra**, m. 'son of Bh°,' the planet Venus, VarBṛS. **-prasravaṇa**, m. 'Bh°'s spring,' N. of a mountain (prob. = *-tuṅga*), R. **-bharata-saṃvāda**, m. N. of wk. **-bhavā**, f. Clerodendrum Siphonanthus, Bhpr. **-bhūmi**, m. N. of a son of Aṅgiras (belonging to the family of the Bhṛigus, cf. *bharga-bhūmi*, *bhārga-bhūmi*), Hariv. **-maṇḍala**, n. (in astron.) 'Bh°'s circle,' N. of a Karaṇa, q. v., Cat. **-rākshasa**, m. N. of a Ṛishi (said to have sacrificed men and cows), Buddh. **-rāja**, m. N. of a tutelary deity (v.l. for *bhṛiṅga-r°*), Hcat. **-vaṇśa**, m. 'race of Bh°,' N. of a family deriving their origin from Paraśu-rāma, MW. **-vallī**, f. N. of the 3rd Vallī in the TUp.; *-°lly-upanishad*, f. N. of the 9th Prapāṭh. in the TĀr. **-vāra**, m. the day of Venus, Friday, MW. **-vāruṇīyôpanishad-bhāshya**, n. N. of wk. **-vāsara**, m. = °*tā-vāra*, A. **-śārdūla**, **-śreshṭha**, m. 'best of Bhṛigus,' N. of Paraśu-rāma, MBh. **-saṃhitā**, f. (and *-sāra*, m.) N. of wks. **-sattama**, m. 'best of Bh°s,' N. of P°, MBh. **-siddhânta**, m. N. of wk. **-suta**, m. 'Bh°'s son,' the planet Venus, Var.; N. of Paraśu-rāma, L. **-sūtra**, n. N. of wk. **-sūnu**, m. 'Bh°'s son,' = *-suta*, MBh. **-smṛiti**, f. N. of wk. **-harītakī**, f. a partic. mixture, Bhpr. **Bhṛigûdvaha**, m. 'offspring of Bh°,' N. of Śaunaka, MBh.; of Paraśu-rāma, ib. **Bhṛigûpanishad**, f. N. of an Upanishad.

Bhṛígavāṇa, mfn. (prob.) shining, glittering (Sāy. 'acting like Bhṛigu'), RV.; (prob.) N. of a man, ib. i, 120, 5.

Bhṛigūṇā-pati, w. r. for *bhṛigūṇām p°*.

Bhṛigv, in comp. for *bhṛigu*. **-aṅgiras**, m. N. of a Ṛishi, AV.Anukr.; °*ro-vid*, mfn. knowing (the verses or hymns of) the Bhṛigus and Aṅgirasas, kn° the Atharva-veda, Kauś.; Vait. **-aṅgirasikā**, f. the matrimonial union between the descendants of Bhṛigu and those of Aṅgiras, Pat. **-īśvara-tīrtha**, n. 'Tīrtha of Bh°'s lord,' N. of a sacred bathing-place on the Narma-dā, Cat.

Bhṛigvandiya (!), m. N. of a man, Saṃskārak.

भृङ्ग *bhṛiṅga*, m. (√*bhram*) a species of large black bee, the humble bee, Kāv.; Pur.; a species of wasp, L.; the fork-tailed shrike or some similar bird, Vāgbh.; a libertine, L.; a golden vase or pitcher, L.; N. of a genius (= *bhṛiṅga-rāja*), Hcat.; (in music) a kind of measure, Saṃgīt.; m. or n. Eclipta Prostrata, L.; (*bhṛíṅgā*), f. a large black bee (see m.), AV.; a kind of pulse, L.; (*ī*), f. (cf. g. *gaurâdi*) id., Kāv.; Kathās.; Aconitum Ferox, L.; n. the bark or the leaf of Laurus Cassia, L.; talc, L.; N. of a man (brother of Maṅkha), Śrīkaṇṭh. **-ja**, m. Agallochum, L.; (*ā*), f. Clerodendrum Siphonanthus, L. **-parṇikā**, f. small cardamoms, L. **-priyā**, f. 'liked by bees,' Gaertnera Racemosa, L. **-mārī**, f. N. of a flower, L. **-mūlikā**, f. N. of a creeping plant, L. **-raja** (Bhpr.) or **-rajas** (Suśr.; Car. &c.), m. Eclipta Prostrata. **-rasa**, m. the juice of Eclipta P°, Suśr. **-rāja**, m. 'bee-king,' a species of large bee, the humble bee, L.; the fork-tailed shrike, MBh.; R.; Suśr. &c.; Eclipta Prostrata, Suśr.; ŚārṅgS.; Wedelia Calendulacea, L.; N. of a tutelary deity, Var.; Hcat.; a kind of oblation or sacrifice, L.; *-rasa*, m. the juice of Eclipta Prostrata, Suśr. **-rājaka**, m. a species of bird, MBh. **-vallabha**, m. 'favourite of bees,' Nauclea Cordifolia, L.; (*ā*), f. = *bhūmi-jambū*, L. **-vṛiksha**, m. 'bee-tree,' (accord. to a gloss) = *vāta-hara-vṛiksha*, Suśr. **-sârtha**, m. a swarm of bees, Ratnâv. **-sôdara**, m. Eclipta Prostrata, L. **-svāmin**, m. N. of a poet, Cat. **Bhṛiṅgâdhipa**, m. 'bee-chief,' the queen of the bees, BhP. **Bhṛiṅgânandā**, f. 'bee-joy,' Jasminum Auriculatum, L. **Bhṛiṅgâbhîshṭa**, m. 'liked by bees,' the Mango tree, L. **Bhṛiṅgâri**, m. 'bee-enemy,' a species of flower, L. **Bhṛiṅgâlī**, f. a swarm of bees, Ratnâv. **Bhṛiṅgâvalī**, f. a line or flight of bees, MW. **Bhṛiṅgâshṭaka**, n. N. of wk. **Bhṛiṅgâhva**, m. Eclipta Prostrata, L.; another plant (= *jīvaka*), L.; (*ā*), f. N. of a creeping pl°, L. **Bhṛiṅgī-phala**, m. Spondias Mangifera, L. **Bhṛiṅgêśa-saṃhitā**, f. N. of wk. **Bhṛiṅgêshṭā**, f. 'liked by bees,' N. of sev. plants (Aloe Indica; Clerodendrum Siphonanthus; = *kāka-jambū*; = *taruṇī*), L.

Bhṛiṅgaka, (ifc.) = *bhṛiṅga*, a bee, Kathās.; m. the fork-tailed shrike, L.; N. of a man, Inscr.

Bhṛiṅgariṭi or °**rīṭa** (Cat.) or °**rīṭi** (Hariv.), m. N. of one of Śiva's attendants (cf. *bhṛiṅgin*, *bhṛiṅgiriṭa* &c.)

Bhṛiṅgarola, m. (said to be fr. *bhṛiṅga* and √*ru*, to cry) a kind of wasp, Vās. (cf. *varola*); 'a bee' and 'a species of bird,' L.

Bhṛiṅgāṇa, m. a large black bee, L.

Bhṛiṅgāya, Nom. Ā. °*yate*, to behave like a bee, Kusum.

Bhṛiṅgāra, m. n. (said to be fr. √*bhṛi*) a golden pitcher or vase, MBh.; Hariv.; Kām. &c.; a vase used at the inauguration of a king (of 8 different substances and 8 different forms), L.; m. = *bhṛiṅga-rāja*, L.; (*ī*), f. a cricket, L.; n. cloves; gold, L.

Bhṛiṅgāraka, m. a pitcher or vase (= *bhṛiṅgāra*), Daś. °**rikā**, f. = *bhṛiṅgārī*, a cricket, L. °**rīṭa**, m. = *bhṛiṅgariṭa* (see *bhṛiṅgariṭi*), L. °**ru**, m. = *bhṛiṅgāra*, a pitcher or vase, Hariv.

Bhṛiṅgi, m. N. of one of Śiva's attendants (cf. next), VāmP.; RTL. 441.

Bhṛiṅgin, m. the Indian fig-tree, L.; N. of one of Śiva's attendants (cf. *bhṛiṅgariṭi*, °*giriṭa* &c.), Kathās.; pl. N. of a people, Var.; (*iṇī*), f. a species of tree, L. **Bhṛiṅgîśa**, m. 'lord of the Bhṛiṅgins,' N. of Śiva, Cat.

Bhṛiṅgiriṭa or °**ṭi** (Hariv.; Bālar.), °**giriṭi** (L.), °**giriṭi** (Hariv.), °**geriṭi** (L.), m. = *bhṛiṅgariṭi*, q. v.; °*giriṭau* (Hariv. 15421?) or °*riṭī* (ib. iii, 104, 15), du. N. of two of Śiva's attendants.

भृज् *bhṛij* (cf. √*bhrajj*), cl. 1. Ā. *bharjate* (pf. *babhṛije*: Caus. *bharjayati*; aor. *ababharjat* and *abībhṛijat*: Desid. *bibharjishate*: Intens. *barībhṛijyate*; *barībharkti* and *barbharkti*, Gr.), to fry, parch, Dhātup. vi, 17.

Bharjana, mfn. parching i. e. destroying, annihilating, frustrating (with gen.), BhP.; n. the act of roasting or frying, KātyŚr.; a frying-pan, ib., Sch.

Bharjita, mfn. (fr. Caus.) roasted, fried, Suśr.; destroyed, annihilated, BhP.

Bhṛikta, mfn. roasted, fried, L.

भृजायन *bhṛijāyana*, m. patr., Saṃskārak.

भृज्ज् *bhṛijj*, *bhṛijja*, *bhṛijjana*. See under √*bhrajj*.

भृड् *bhṛiḍ*, cl. 6. P. *bhṛiḍati*, to dive, plunge, Dhātup. xxviii, 100 (v.l. for *kruḍ*).

भृणीय *bhṛiṇīya*, Nom. Ā. °*yáte*, to be angry (= *krudhyate*), Naigh. ii, 12 (cf. √*bhrī* and *hṛiṇīya*).

भृण्टिका *bhṛiṇṭikā*, f. a species of plant, L. (prob. = *bhiriṇṭikā*, q. v.)

भृण्डि *bhṛiṇḍi*, a wave, L. (cf. *bhaṇḍi*).

भृत *bhṛita*, *bhṛitya* &c. See p. 764.

भृम *bhṛimá*, m. (√*bhram*) error, mistake, RV.

Bhṛimalá, mfn. stunned, torpid, AV.

Bhṛími, mfn. whirling round, restless, active, quick, RV. i, 31, 16 &c.; m. a whirlwind, hurricane, ib. ii, 34, 1 ('a moving cloud' or 'a kind of lute,' Sāy.); a whirlpool, eddy, L.; (*bhṛimí*), f. quickness, activity, ib. iii, 62, 1.

Bhṛimy-aśva, m. 'having quick horses,' N. of a man, Nir. ix, 24.

भृश् *bhṛiś*, cl. 4. P. *bhṛiśyati*, to fall, fall down, Dhātup. xxvi, 115 (cf. √*bhraṇś*, *bhraś*, of which √*bhṛiś* is only the weak form); cl. 6. P. *bhṛiśati*, to be strong or vehement, Vop. (rather Nom. fr. next).

Bhṛiśa, mfn. (perhaps the original meaning may be 'falling heavily,' cf. √*bhraś*) strong, vehement, mighty, powerful, frequent, abundant (often ibc., cf. below; rarely as an independent word; cf. *su-bhṛiśa*), Mn.; MBh. &c.; ibc. and (*am*), ind. strongly, violently, vehemently, excessively, greatly, very much, Mn.; MBh. &c.; harshly, severely, ChUp.; quickly, without hesitation, MBh.; often, frequently, R.; eminently, in a superior manner, L.; m. a partic. tutelary deity, VarBṛ. **-kopana**, mfn. extremely passionate, very wrathful, MBh. **-tā**, f. violence, intensity, Ragh. **-daṇḍa**, mfn. inflicting severe punishment on (loc.), Mn. vii, 32. **-dāruṇa**, mfn. very terrible or cruel, Nal. **-duḥkhita**, mfn. very much afflicted, very unfortunate or unhappy, Nal. **-nâstika**, mfn. very sceptical or impious, MBh. **-pattrikā**, f. 'strong-leaved,' a species of plant, L. **-pīḍita**, mfn. very much afflicted, MW. **-vismita**, mfn. excessively astonished or perplexed, R. **-vedanā**, f. violent pain, MW. **-śoka-vardhana**, mf(ī)n. greatly increasing grief or sorrow, MBh. **-saṃyuta**, mfn. very much engaged in (instr.), ib. **-saṃhṛishṭa**, mfn. very delighted or glad, ib. **-svid**, mfn. perspiring violently, Śiś.

Bhṛiśāya, Nom. Ā. °*yate*, to become powerful or strong or vehement, Bhaṭṭ.

Bhṛiśī-√bhū, P. *-bhavati*, id., Vop.

1. **Bhṛishṭa**, mfn. fallen &c., L.

Bhraśiman, m. potency, vehemence, strength, g. *dṛiḍhâdi*.

Bhraśishṭha, mfn. (superl.) most (very) powerful or strong or vehement, Pat. on Pāṇ. vi, 4, 161.

Bhraśīyas, mfn. (compar.) more (very) powerful &c., ib.

भृष्ट 2. *bhṛishṭa* &c. See under √*bhrajj*.

भृष्टि 1. *bhṛishṭí*, f. (cf. √*hṛish*; for 2. *bhṛishṭi* see under √*bhrajj*) a spike, point, top, corner, edge, RV.; AV.; GṛS. (cf. *sahásra-*, *kshura-bhṛ°* &c.); a deserted cottage or garden, L. **-mát**, mfn. pronged, toothed, RV.; m. N. of a Ṛishi.

भॄ *bhṝi*, cl. 9. P. *bhṛiṇāti*, to bear; to blame; to fry; to be crooked, Dhātup. xxxi, 21.

भेक *bheka*, m. (probably onomat.; but cf. Uṇ. iii, 43) a frog, Up.; Kāv. &c. (accord. to Kathās. xx, 77 the croaking of frogs was caused by the curse of Agni who was betrayed by them to the gods when he took refuge in the water); a cloud, L.; a timid man (= *bhīru*), L. (cf. *bhela*); N. of a Nishāda and a Brāhmaṇī, L.; (*ī*), f. a female frog, L.; Hydrocotyle Asiatica, L. **-parṇī**, f. 'frog-leaved,' a species of plant, L. **-bhuj**, m. 'frog-eater,' a snake, L. **-śabda**, m. the croaking of frogs, Cat. **Bhekīpati**, m. a male frog, Subh.

भेकुरि *bhekúri*, f. N. of a class of Apsaras, VS.; VP. (cf. *bākura* and *bhākuri*).

भेटक *bheṭaka*, m. buying, purchase, L.

भेड *bheḍa*, m. a ram, L. (cf. *eḍa*, *bheḍra* and *bheṇḍa*); a raft, float, L. (cf. *bhela*); N. of a lexicographer and a physician, Cat.; of a Ṛishi, L.; (*ī*), f. a ewe, L.; N. of one of the Mātṛis attending on Skanda, MBh. **-giri**, m. N. of a mountain, Rājat. **-saṃhitā**, f. N. of wk.

Bheḍara, m. N. of an Agra-hāra, Rājat.

Bheḍra, m. a ram, L.

Bheṇḍa, m. id. (cf. *bhaiṇḍaka*).

भेण्डा *bheṇḍā*, °*ḍī*, f. and °*ḍitaka*, m. Abelmoschus Esculentus, L. (*bheṇḍā* also 'lotus-seed,' ib.)

भेतव्य *bhetavya*. See p. 758, col. 3.

भेताल *bhetāla* = *vetāla*, Siṇhās.

भेत्तवै *bhéttavaí*, *bhettavya*, *bhettṛi*. See under √*bhid*, p. 757, col. 2.

भेद *bhedá*, m. (√*bhid*) breaking, splitting, cleaving, rending, tearing, piercing (also pass. the being broken &c.), KātyŚr.; Yājñ.; MBh.; Kāv. &c.; breaking open, disclosing, divulging, betrayal (of a secret, cf. *rahasya-bh°*); bursting asunder, opening, gaping, parting asunder, BhP.; Suśr.; bursting forth or out, expanding, blossoming, shooting out, sprouting, Kālid.; Bālar.; a cleft, fissure, chasm (cf. *śilā-bh°*; du. pudendum muliebre), RV.; rupture, breach, hurt, injury, seduction, Kām.; MBh.; Kathās.; shooting pain (in the limbs), paralysis (cf. *ardhabh°*), Suśr.; separation, division, partition, part, portion, Kāv.; Pur.; distinction, difference, kind, sort, species, variety, ŚrS.; Up.; MBh. &c.; disturbance, interruption, violation, dissolution, RPrāt.; KātyŚr.; Sāh.; disuniting, winning over to one's side by sowing dissension (cf. *upâya*), Mn.; Yājñ.; Kām.; disunion, schism, dissension between (instr.) or in (comp.), MBh.; Var.; Rājat.; change, alteration, modification, MBh.; Śak.; contraction (cf. *bhrū-bh°*); evacuation (of the bowels), ŚārṅgS.; (in astron.) a partic. crossing or conjunction of the planets; one of the ways in which an eclipse ends (cf. *kukshi-bh°*); (in math.) the hypothenuse of a right-angled triangle; (in dram.) = *saṃhati-bhedana* or = *prôtsāhana*, Sāh.; (in phil.) dualism, duality (cf. comp.); N. of a man, AV.; pl. N. of a people, RV. **-kara**, mf(*ī*)n. breaking through or down, Yājñ.; sowing dissension among or in (gen. or comp.), Kāv.; Kathās. **-kārin**, mfn. causing dissension or disunion, MārkP.; making or showing a difference, altered, Ratnâv. **-kṛit**, mfn. = *-kara*, Yājñ. **-khaṇḍana**, n. 'refutation of duality,' N. of a Vedânta wk. **-tas**, ind. separately, singly, individually, Kathās.; according to difference or diversities, MW. **-darpaṇa**, m. 'mirror of duality,' N. of wk. **-darśin**, mfn. = *-dṛishṭi*, A. **-dīpikā**, f. 'illustration of duality,' N. of wk. **-dṛishṭi**, mfn. viewing or holding the Universe and the deity to be different and distinct, MW. **-dhik-kāra**, m. 'refutation of duality,' N. of a Vedânta wk. by Nṛisiṇhâśrama; *-nyak-kāra-nirūpaṇa*, n., *-nyak-kāra-humkṛiti*, *-sat-kriyā*, f. N. of wks. **-dhik-kṛiti**, f. (in comp.) = *-dhik-kāra*; *-tattva-nivecana*, n. N. of wk. **-prakāra**, m., **-prakāśa**, m. N. of wks. **-pratyaya**, m. belief in dualism (cf. *-dṛishṭi*), W. **-buddhi**, f. perception or idea of a difference or distinction, MW. **-vādin**, m. one who maintains the duality of God and the Universe, Cat.; N. of Comm. on BhP.; °*di-vidāriṇī*, f. N. of wk. **-vidhi**, m. the faculty of discriminating or discerning (between two different objects), MW. **-vibhīshikā**, f. N. of wk. **-saha**, mfn. capable of being disunited or seduced, Kathās. **Bhedâbheda**, m. disunion and union, dualism and non-dualism; *-vādin*, m. a maintainer of the doctrine both of the difference and the identity of God and the Universe, Cat. **Bhedôkti-jīvana** and **Bhedôjjīvana**, n. N. of 2 wks. **Bhedônmukha**, mf(*ī*)n. just about to burst into blossom, Vikr.

Bhedaka, mfn. breaking into or through, piercing, perforating, R.; diverting (water-courses), Mn. iii, 163; destroying (boundary-marks), ib. ix, 291; seducing (ministers), ib. ix, 232, Kull.; making a difference, distinguishing, determining, defining, Daśar.; Kāvyâd.; Pañcar.; (*ikā*), f. the act of breaking down or asunder, destruction, annihilation, Siddh.; n. a determinative i.e. an adjective, Pāṇ. ii, 1, 57, Sch. (cf. *bhedya*).

Bhedana, mfn. breaking, cleaving, splitting, rending, piercing, dividing, separating, MBh.; R. &c.; (ifc.) causing to flow, giving free course (to a river), Pañcar.; causing pain in the joints or limbs, Suśr.; loosening (the fæces), cathartic, purgative, ŚārṅgS.; destroying, dissolving, relieving (cf. *hṛidaya-granthi-bh°*); m. a hog, L.; Rumex Vesicarius, L.; n. the act of breaking, cleaving &c.; MBh.; R. &c.; bursting, parting asunder, breach, fracture, KātyŚr.; Suśr.; Prâyaśc.; the passing (through an asterism), VarBṛS.; disclosure, betrayal (of a secret), Kathās.; embroilment, disunion, discord, MBh.; Kām.; Rājat.; discrimination, W.; a purgative, Suśr.; Asa Foetida, L.

Bhedanaka. See *ghaṭa-bh°*.

Bhedanīya, mfn. to be broken or split or cleft or divided, R. (*-tā*, f., HPariś.); causing the secretion of bad humours, Car.

Bhedita, mfn. (fr. Caus.) broken, split, cleft, MBh.; Kāv. &c.; (ifc.) divided into, Sāh.

Bhedin, mfn. breaking, splitting, piercing, perforating, MBh.; Kāv. &c.; beating or knocking out (see *dvi-netra-bh°*); shaking, penetrating, R.; causing to flow (as juice), MBh.; loosening (the bowels), cathartic, purgative, Suśr.; ŚārṅgS.; breaking, violating (an agreement &c.), Mn.; Kām.; interrupting (devotion), Ragh.; disturbing (a country), Kathās.; dividing, separating from (abl.), Sāh.; (fr. *bheda*) having a distinction or division, ib.; (in phil.) one who separates spirit and matter or holds the doctrine of dualism; m. Rumex Vesicarius, L.; (*inī*), f. (with Tāntrikas) N. of a partic. Śakti, Cat. **Bhedi-tva**, n. separation, division, parting asunder, Suśr.

Bhedira, n. = *bhidira*, a thunderbolt, W.

Bhedīya. See *dosha-bh°*.

Bhedya, mfn. to be broken or split or pierced or perforated, MBh.; Kāv.; to be cut or opened, Suśr.; to be set at variance or disunited, Kām.; Pañcat.; to be divided or penetrated or betrayed or refuted (see *a-*, *dur-*, *nir-bh°*); to be (or being) determined; n. a substantive, Pāṇ. ii, 1, 57, Sch. (cf. *bhedaka*). **-roga**, m. any disease treated by incision or cutting, Suśr. **-liṅga**, mfn. distinguished by gender, L.

Bhedyaka. See *utpala-bh°*.

भेन *bhêna*, *bhêsa*. See under 4. *bha*, p. 742.

भेम्पुर *bhem-pura*, n. N. of a Grāma, Kshitîś.

भेय *bheya*. See p. 758, col. 3.

भेयपाल *bheya-pāla* (?), m. N. of a prince, Buddh.

भेर *bhera*, m. (√*bhī*?) a kettle-drum, L.

Bherôtsa, see *pushpa-bh°*.

Bherī, f. (rarely °*ri*) a kettle-drum, MBh.; Kāv. &c. **-ghnat**, m. 'striking a k°-d°,' a kettle-drummer, Jaim., Sch. **-tāḍana**, n. 'drum-beating,' N. of wk. **-nāda**, m. the sound of a k°-d°, L. **-bhāṃ-kāra**, m. id., Daś.; N. of a poet (°*rīya*, n. his wk.), Cat. **-bhramaka**, m. supposed N. of a poet, Cat. **-svana-mahā-svanā**, f. 'loud-sounding like the sound of a kettle-drum,' N. of one of the Mātṛis attending on Skanda, MBh.

Bheruṇḍa, mf(*ā*)n. (often v.l. *bheraṇḍa*) terrible, formidable, awful, MBh.; m. a species of bird, MBh.; Hcar.; (also °*ḍaka*) a beast of prey (wolf, jackal, fox, or hyena), Lalit. (cf. *pheru*); a partic. form of Śiva (?), W.; (*ā*), f. N. of a goddess (= *kālī*), L.; of a Yakshiṇī, L.; n. (√*bhṛi*?) pregnancy, L.

Bhela, mfn. (only L.) timid; foolish, ignorant; tall; active, restless; (also °*laka*) = *laghishṭha*; m. a species of small tiger, L.; (also °*laka*, m. n.) a raft, boat, L.; N. of a physician, L. (cf. *bheḍa*).

Bhelana, n. swimming, L.

भेलु *bhelu*, m. or n. (?) a partic. high number, Buddh.

भेलुक *bheluka*, m. Śiva's servant, L.

भेलुपुरा *bhelūpurā*, f. N. of a suburb of Benares (?), Col.

भेष् *bhesh*, cl. 1. P. Ā. *bheshati*, °*te*, to fear, dread, Dhātup. xxi, 19 (others 'to move, go'). Cf. √*bhī*, *bhyas*.

भेषज *bheshajá*, mf(*ī*)n. (fr. 1. *bhishaj*) curing, healing, sanative, RV.; AV.; AitBr.; n. a remedy, medicine, medicament, drug, remedy against (gen. or comp.), RV. &c. &c.; a spell or charm for curative purposes (generally from Atharva-veda), ŚrS.; water, Naigh. i, 12; Nigella Indica, W. **-karaṇa**, n. preparation of drugs or medicine, Baudh. **-kalpa**, m., **-kalpa-sāra-saṃgraha**, m. N. of wks. **-kṛita**, mfn. healed, cured, ChUp. **-candra**, m. 'moon of medicine,' N. of a man, Kathās. **-tarka**, m. N. of wk. **-tā** (°*já-*), f. curativeness, healing power, PañcavBr. **-bhakshaṇa**, n. 'drug-eating,' the act of taking medicine, Cat. **-vīrya**, n. the healing power of m°, Suśr. **-sarvasva**, n. N. of wk. **Bheshajâgāra**, n. 'm°-room,' a druggist's or apothecary's shop, Suśr. **Bheshajâṅga**, n. anything taken with or after m° (as water gruel), L.

Bheshajya, mf(*ā*)n. curative, sanitary, TS.

भैक्ष *bhaiksha*, mf(*ī*)n. (fr. *bhikshā*) living on alms, subsisting by charity, MBh.; n. asking alms, begging, mendicancy (°*kshāya* with √*gam*, to beg for alms, °*ksham* [ifc.] with √*car*, to go about begging for; °*ksham* with *ā-√hṛi* or *sam-ā-√hṛi*, to collect alms or food; °*kshena* with Caus. of √*vṛit*, to subsist on alms), Mn.; MBh. &c.; anything obtained by begging, begged food, charity, alms, GṛS.; Mn.; MBh. &c.; a multitude of alms, L. **-kāla**, m. 'alms-time,' the time for bringing home anything obtained as alms, MW. **-caraṇa**, n. going about begging, collecting alms (°*ṇaṃ √car*, to practise mendicancy), Mn.; Gaut. **-carya**, n., **-caryā**, f. = prec., Mn.; Yājñ.; MBh. **-jīvikā**, f. subsisting by alms or charity, L. **-bhuj**, mfn. living on alms; m. a mendicant, MBh. **-vat**, ind. as or for alms, ib. **-vṛitti**, f. = *-jīvikā*, Ashṭāv.; mfn. living by charity, Kathās. **Bhaikshā-kula**, n. (°*kshâk°*?) a charitable house, Divyâv. **Bhaikshânna**, n. begged food, MārkP. **Bhaikshâśin**, mfn. eating b° f°, a mendicant, Mn. xi, 72. **Bhaikshâśya**, n. (fr. prec.) = °*ksha-jīvikā*, Kām. **Bhaikshâhāra**, mfn. = °*kshâśin*, Mn. xi, 256. **Bhaikshôpajīvin**, mfn. living on alms, MBh.

Bhaikshaka (ifc.) = *bhaiksha*, alms, R.

Bhaikshava, mfn. (fr. *bhikshu*) belonging to a religious mendicant, Hcar.

Bhaikshuka, n. (fr. *bhikshuka*) a multitude of beggars or mendicants, g. *khaṇḍikâdi;* m. (scil. *āśrama*) the fourth stage in the life of a Brāhman, the life of a religious mendicant, L.

Bhaikshya, w. r. for *bhaiksha*.

भैडक *bhaiḍaka* and *bhaiṇḍaka*, mfn. (fr. *bheḍa, bheṇḍa*) relating to or coming from a sheep, L.

भैदिक *bhaidika*, mfn. = *bhedam nityam arhati*, Pāṇ. v, 1, 64.

भैम *bhaima*, mf(ī)n. (fr. *bhīma*, of which it is also the Vṛiddhi form in comp.) relating or belonging to Bhīma; m. a descendant of Bh°, MBh.; (*ī*), f. Bhīma's daughter i. e. Damayantī, ib. (°*mī-pariṇaya*, n. 'D°'s wedding,' N. of a drama); N. of the 11th day in the light half of Māgha and a festival kept on it (= *bhīmâikādaśī*), W.; of a grammar. **-gava**, m. patr. fr. *bhīma-gava* or *bhīma-gu*, ĀśvŚr. **-pravīṇa**, m. the bravest or chief of the Bhīmas, MBh. **-ratha**, mf(*ī*)n. relating to Bhīma-ratha; (*ī*), f. (with *niśīthinī*) prob. = *bhīma-rathī* (q. v.), Hcar. **-sena** (*bhaima-*), m. patr. fr. *bhīma-s°*, MaitrS. **-seni**, m. (fr. *bhīma-sena*) patr. of Divo-dāsa, Kāṭh.; of Ghaṭôtkaca, MBh. **-senya**, m. patr. fr. *bhīma-sena*, Pāṇ. iv, 1, 114, Vārtt. 7, Pat.

Bhaimāyana, m. patr. fr. *bhaima*, Pāṇ. vi, 2, 34, Sch.

Bhaimi, m. (fr. *bhīma*) patr. of Ghaṭôtkaca, MBh.

भैयाभट्ट *bhaiyā-bhaṭṭa*, m. N. of an author, Cat.

भैरव *bhairava*, mf(*ā* and *ī*)n. (fr. *bhīru*) frightful, terrible, horrible, formidable (*am*, ind.), MBh.; R. &c.; relating to Bhairava, Cat.; m. N. of a form of Śiva (cf. RTL. 85), Prab.; Rājat.; Pur. (in the latter 8 Bh°'s are enumerated, viz. *mahā-, saṃhāra-, asitâṅga-, ruru-, kāla-, krodha-, tāmracūḍa-* or *kapāla-, candracūḍa-* or *rudra-bh°*; sometimes other names are given, e. g. *vidyā-rāja, kāma-r°, nāga-r°, svacchanda-r°, lambita-r°, deva-r°, ugra-r°, vighna-r°*); a man representing Bh°, W.; a jackal, L.; a mountain, L.; (in music) N. of a Rāga; N. of a chief of Śiva's host, KālP.; of a son of Śiva by Tārā-vatī (wife of Candra-śekhara, king of Karavīra-pura), ib.; of a Nāga, MBh.; of a Yaksha, Cat.; of a hunter, Hit.; of 2 kings and various teachers and authors (also with *tripāṭhin, daivajña, tilaka, dīkshita, ācārya, bhaṭṭa* and *miśra*), ib.; of a river, L.; pl. N. of a partic. sect, VP.; (*ā*), f. N. of Nirṛiti, VYogay.; pl. of a class of Apsaras, VP.; (*ī*), f., see below; n. terror or the property of exciting terror, W.; = *bhairava-tantra* below. **-kāraka**, mfn. causing terror, formidable, W. **-tantra**, n. N. of a Tantra. **-tarjaka**, m. 'threatening terrible things,' N. of Vishṇu (properly of Śiva), Pañcar. **-tva**, n. the state of being Bhairava or a form of Śiva, Cat. **-datta**, m. N. of various authors, ib. **-dīpa-dāna**, n., **-dīpana**, n., **-nava-rasa-ratna**, n., **-nātha-tantra**, n., **-nāmâvalī**, f., **-paddhati**, f., **-purāṇa**, n., **-prayoga**, m., **-prasāda**, m., **-prādurbhāva-nāṭaka**, n., **-mantra**, m. N. of wks. **-yātanā**, f. pain inflicted by Śiva (as a penance), MW. **-saṃhitā**, f., **-saparyā-vidhi**, m., **-sahasra-nāman**, n. N. of wks. **-siṇha**, m. N. of a son of Narasiṇha and patron of Ruci-pati, Cat. **-stava**, m., **-stotra**, n. N. of various hymns. **Bhairavâgratas**, ind. in the presence of Bhairava, MW. **Bhairavânanda**, m. N. of a Yogin, Bhpr.; of an author, Cat. **Bhairavârâdhana**, n., **Bhairavârcana-kalpa-latā**, f., **Bhairavârcā-pārijāta**, m. N. of wks. **Bhairavâshṭaka**, n. N. of a collection of 8 Tantras, Āryav. **Bhairavêndra**, m. N. of a king, Cat. **Bhairavêśa**, m. 'lord of terror,' N. of Vishṇu (properly of Śiva; cf. *bhairava-tarjaka*).

Bhairavī, f. of °*va;* N. of a partic. form of Durgā, RTL. 188; a girl of 12 years (representing Durgā at the D° festival), L.; (in music) N. of a Rāgiṇī. **-tantra**, n., **-paṭala**, m. or n., **-rahasya**, n., **-rahasya-vidhi**, m. N. of wks. **Bhairavyashṭôttara-śata-nāmâvalī**, f. N. of wk.

Bhairavīya, mfn. relating to Bhairava, Bālar. **-tantra**, n., **-pañca-saṃdhi**, m. N. of wks.

Bhairika, m. N. of a son of Kṛishṇa by Satyabhāmā, Hariv.

भैषज *bhaishaja*, m. (fr. *bheshaja*) Perdix Chinensis, L.; n. a drug, medicine, L.; mfn. relating to Bhaishajya, g. *kaṇvâdi*.

Bhaishajya, m. patr. fr. *bhishaj* or *bhishaja*, g. *gargâdi* (Kāś.); n. curativeness, healing efficacy, VS.; a partic. ceremony performed as a remedy for sickness, Kauś.; any remedy, drug or medicine ('against,' gen.), ŚBr.; Suśr.; the administering of medicines &c., MW. **-guru-vaiḍūrya-prabhā**, f. N. of a Buddh. wk. **-yajña**, m. a sacrifice performed as a remedy for sickness, GopBr. **-ratnâkara**, m., **-ratnâvalī**, f. N. of wks. **-rāja** and **-samudgata**, m. N. of 2 Bodhi-sattvas, Lalit. **-sāra**, m., **-sârâmṛita-saṃhitā**, f. N. of wks. **-sena**, m. N. of a Bodhi-sattva, Kāraṇḍ.

Bhaishṇaja, mfn., fr. *bhaishṇajya*, g. *kaṇvâdi* (v. l. *bhaishaja*).

Bhaishṇajya, m. patr. fr. *bhishṇaja*, g. *gargâdi* (v. l. *bhaishaja*).

भैष्मक *bhaishmaka*, mf(ī)n., fr. *bhīshmaka;* (*ī*), f. patr. of Rukmiṇī, Hariv.

भैस् *bhais*. See √1. *bhī*, p. 758.

भो *bho*. See *bhos*, p. 768, col. 2.

भोंसल *bhonsala*, m. N. of a royal family of Tanjore, Cat. **-vaṇśâvalī**, f. N. of a Campū, ib.

भोक्तव्य *bhoktavya*, °*tṛi*. See p. 760, col. 1.

भोक्ष्यक *bhokshyaka*, m. pl. N. of a people, VP.

भोग 1. *bhogá*, m. (√1. *bhuj*) any winding or curve, coil (of a serpent), RV. &c. &c.; the expanded hood of a snake, Hariv.; Kām.; Pañcat.; a partic. kind of military array, Kām.; a snake, Suparṇ.; the body, L. **-tva**, n. the state of being curved or winding, curvedness, Kām. **-1. -vát**, mfn. (for 2. see col. 3) furnished with windings or curves or rings, ringed, coiled (as a serpent), R.; furnished with a hood (cf. *mahā-bh°*); a serpent or s°-demon, Suparṇ.; (*atī*), f. a s°-nymph, MBh.; N. of one of the Mātṛis attending on Skanda, ib.; the city of the s°-demons in the subterranean regions, ib.; R.; Hariv.; RTL. 322 (also °*gā-vatī*, L.); the sacred river of the s°-demons (or a Tīrtha in that river sacred to the s°-king Vāsuki), MBh. **Bhogêśvara-tīrtha**, n. N. of a sacred bathing-place, Cat. (w. r. for *bhogîśv°*?).

Bhogi, in comp. for 1. *bhogin*. **-kānta**, m. 'dear to serpents,' air, wind, L. **-gandhikā**, f. a species of ichneumon plant, L. **-nandana**, m. patr. of Śāli-vāhana, Vcar. **-pura**, n. the city of serpent-demons, Dharmaś. **-bhuj**, m. 's°-eater,' an ichneumon, L. **-vallabha**, n. 'dear to s°s,' a kind of sandal, L. **Bhogîndra**, m. 's°-king,' N. of Ananta, L.; of Patañjali, Cat.; *-tanaya* and *-nandana*, m. patr. of Śāli-vāhana, Vcar. **Bhogîśa**, m. 's°-king,' N. of Ananta and Śesha, L.

1. **Bhogin**, mfn. (for 2. see col. 3) furnished with windings or curves or rings, curved, ringed (as a serpent), R.; BhP. &c.; m. a serpent or s°-demon, MBh.; Kāv. &c.; a kind of shrub, L.; (*inī*), f. a serpent nymph, R.

भोग 2. *bhoga*, m. (√3. *bhuj*) enjoyment, eating, feeding on, RV. &c. &c. (with Jainas 'enjoying once,' as opp. to *upa-bhoga*, q. v.); use, application, ŚBr.; GṛŚrS. &c.; fruition, usufruct, use of a deposit &c., Mn.; Yājñ.; sexual enjoyment, Mn.; MBh. &c.; enj° of the earth or of a country i. e. rule, sway, MārkP.; experiencing, feeling, perception (of pleasure or pain), Mn.; MBh. &c.; profit, utility, advantage, pleasure, delight, RV. &c. &c.; any object of enjoyment (as food, a festival &c.), MBh.; R.; possession, property, wealth, revenue, Mn.; MBh. &c.; hire, wages (esp. of prostitution), L.; (in astron.) the passing through a constellation, VarBṛS.; the part of the ecliptic occupied by each of the 27 lunar mansions, Sūryas.; (in arithm.) the numerator of a fraction (?), W.; N. of a teacher, Cat.; (*ā*), f. N. of a Surâṅganā, Siṇhâs.; n., w. r. for *bhogya* or *bhāgya*. **-kara**, mf(*ī*)n. producing or affording enjoyment, Bhartṛ. **-karman**, m. (with *kāśmīra*), N. of a poet, Cat. (= *bhogi-varman*). **-kārikā**, f. N. of wk. **-guccha**, n. hire of prostitution, W. **-gṛiha**, n. 'pleasure-chamber,' the women's apartments, harem, Sāy. on RV. x, 95, 4. **-grāma**, m. N. of a village, Buddh. **-ṃ-karā**, f. N. of a Dik-kanyā, Pārśvan. **-jāta**, mfn. produced by enjoyment or by suffering, MW. **-tṛishṇā**, f. desire of worldly enjoyments, Ragh.; selfish enj°, Mālatim. **-dattā**, f. N. of a woman, Kathās. **-dā**, f. 'granting enj°,' N. of the goddess of the Piṅgalas, Cat. **-deva**, m. N. of a man, Rājat. **-deha**, m. 'the body of feeling' (the intermediate body which a dead person acquires through the Śrāddha after cremation, and with which, according to his works, he either enjoys happiness or suffers misery, cf. *adhishṭhāna-d°, sambhoga-kāya*), RTL. 28, 292; MWB. 247. **-nātha**, m. a nourisher, supporter, Cat. **-nidhi**, f. N. of a Surâṅganā, Siṇhâs. **-pati**, m. 'revenue-lord,' the governor of a town or province, Hit. **-pāla**, m. a groom, L. (cf. *bhogika*). **-piśācikā**, f. hunger, L. **-prastha**, m. pl. N. of a people, Var.; MārkP. **-bhaṭṭa**, m. N. of a poet, Cat. **-bhuj**, mfn. enjoying pleasures, MārkP.; m. a wealthy man, AgP. **-bhūmi**, f. 'fruition-land,' the place where people enjoy the reward of their works (opp. to *karma-bh°*, land of works), VP. **-bhṛitaka**, m. a servant who works only for maintenance, W. **-maṇḍapa**, m. the part of the Jagan-nāth temple where the food for offerings is cooked, MW. **-mālinī**, f. N. of a Dik-kanyā, Pārśvan. **-lābha**, m. 'acquisition of profit,' welfare, Lāṭy.; the gain or profit made by the use of anything deposited or pledged, W. **-2. -vat**, mfn. (for 1. see col. 2) furnished with enjoyments, having or offering e°, delightful, happy, prosperous, MBh.; Hariv.; BhP.; m. dancing, mimics, L.; N. of Satya-bhāmā's residence, Hariv.; (*atī*), f. the night of the 2nd lunar day, Sūryapr.; N. of Ujjayinī in the Dvāpara age, Kathās.; of a town, Vet.; of a Dik-kanyā, Pārśvan.; of wk. **-vardhana**, m. pl. N. of a people, Var.; MārkP. **-varman**, m. N. of various men, Kathās. **-vastu**, n. an object of enjoyment, Pañcar. **-saṃkrānti-vidhi**, m. N. of a section of the Bhavishyôttara Purāṇa. **-sadman**, n. 'seat or abode of pleasure,' the women's apartments, L. **-sena**, m. N. of a man, Rājat. **-sthāna**, n. the body; the women's apartments, W. **-svāmin**, m. N. of a man, Inscr. **Bhogâdhi**, m. a pledge or deposit which may be used until redeemed, MW. **Bhogânta**, m. the end of enjoyment or of suffering, ib. **Bhogâyatana**, n. a place of enj°, Vedāntas. **Bhogârha**, mfn. fit for enj°, to be enjoyed or possessed, MW.; n. property, money, W. **Bhogârhya**, n. corn, grain, L. **Bhogâvalī**, f. the panegyric of professional encomiasts or bards, Bālar.; Pratāp.; w. r. for *bhogā-vatī*, L.; °*li-vṛitti*, f. N. of wk. **Bhogâvāsa**, m. 'abode of pleasure,' the women's apartments, L.; (ifc., f. *ā*) a sleeping-room, Vās.

Bhogika, m. a horse-keeper, groom (= *bhoga-pāla*), L.; a chief of a village, L.

2. **Bhogin**, mfn. (for 1. see col. 2) enjoying, eating, MārkP.; Prasaṅg.; having or offering enjoyments, devoted to enj°, wealthy, opulent, MBh.; Yājñ.; Var. &c.; suffering, experiencing, undergoing, Kap.; using, possessing, MW.; m. a voluptuary, MW.; a king, L.; the head man of a village, L.; a barber, L.; = *vaiyāvṛitti-kara* (?), L.; a person who accumulates money for a partic. expenditure, W.; N. of a prince, VP.; (*inī*), f. a kind of heroine, Bhar.; the concubine of a king or a wife not regularly consecrated with him, L.

Bhogīna, mfn. (ifc.), Pāṇ. v, 1, 9; Vārtt. 1 and 2, Pat. (cf. *pitṛi-bhogīṇa, mātṛi-bh°*).

Bhógya, mfn. to be enjoyed, to be used (in the sense 'to be eaten' *bhojya* is more common), what may be enjoyed or used, useful, profitable, AV. &c. &c.; to be endured or suffered, Megh.; Rājat.; (in astron.) to be passed, Sūryas.; (*ā*), f. a harlot, L.; n. an object of enjoyment, possession, money, L.; corn, grain, L.; a precious stone, L. **-tā**, f. (ŚāṅkhBr.; Kām.) or **-tva**, n. (Hariv.) the state of being used, usefulness, profitableness, enjoyableness. **Bhogyâdhi**, m. = *bhogâdhi* above. **Bhogyârha**, n. corn, grain, L. (cf. *bhogârhya*).

Bhoj, mfn. in *a-bhog-ghán*, q. v.

Bhojá, mfn. bestowing enjoyment, bountiful, liberal, RV.; enjoying, leading a life of enjoyment, BhP.; m. a king with uncommon qualities, AitBr.; (pl.) N. of a country (near the Vindhya mountain) or of a people (the descendants of Mahā-bhoja), MBh.; Hariv.; Pur. &c.; a king of the Bhojas, MBh.; N. of Bhoja-deva (q. v.), Daś.; Sāh.; Rājat.; of various kings and other men, Hariv.; Ragh. &c.; = *bhoja-kaṭa*, q. v., L.; (*ā*), f. a princess of the Bhojas, MBh.; Hariv. (v. l. *bhojyā*); N. of the wife of Vīra-vrata, BhP.; a cowherd, MW. **-kaṭa**, n. N. of a town, MBh.; Pur.; the country of Bhoja (the present Bhojpur, or the vicinity of Patnā and Bhāgalpur), W.; m. pl. the inhabitants of the town of Bhoja-kaṭa, VarYogay. — **kaṭīya**, m. pl. the inh° of Bh°-k°, Pāṇ. i, 1, 75, Sch. — **kanyā**, f. a girl of the race of the Bhojas, Ragh. — **kula-pradīpa**, m. 'lamp of the r° of Bh°,' N. of a king of Vidarbha, ib. — **campū**, f. and **-caritra**, n. N. of wks. — **duhitṛi**, f. a princess of the Bh°, Pāṇ. vi, 3, 70, Vārtt. 9, Pat. — **deva**, m. N. of a celebrated king of Dhārā (who was a great patron of learning at the beginning of the 11th century, and is the reputed author of sev. wks., esp. of a Comm. on the Yoga-sūtras, cf. IW. 92, n. 2; 532 &c.), Mn., Kull.; Gīt. &c.; of a king of Kaccha, Cat.; *-śabdânuśāsana*, n. N. of wk. — **nagara**, n. N. of a town, MBh. — **nanda**, m. N. of an author, Cat. (rather *bhajanânanda*). — **narêndra**, m. N. of Bhoja-deva, king of Dhārā, Rājat. — **nidhi**, f. N. of a Surâṅganā, Siṉhās. — **nṛipati**, m. = *-narêndra*, Cat. — **pati**, m. the king of the Bhojas, king Bhoja, Ragh.; N. of Kaṇsa, BhP.; = *-rāja*, Col. — **pitṛi**, m. the father of a king, AitBr. — **putrī**, f. a princess of the Bhojas, Pāṇ. vi, 3, 70, Vārtt. 9, Pat. — **pura**, n. (L.) and **-purī**, f. (Cat.) N. of towns. — **prabandha**, m. (and °*dhasāra*, m.) N. of wks. (celebrating the deeds of king Bhoja). — **rāja**, m. the king of the Bhojas, MBh.; N. of Kaṇsa, VP.; of Bhoja-deva (king of Dhārā, above), Pratāp.; Cat.; *-prabandha*, m., *-vārttika*, n., *-vijaya*, m., *-vṛitti*, f., *-sac-carita*, n. N. of wks. — **rājaka-vivarga**, m. N. of wk. — **rājīya**, mfn. relating to or coming from Bhoja-rāja, Cat. — **vyākaraṇa**, n. and **-smṛiti**, f. N. of wks. **Bhojâdhipa**, m. 'king of the Bhojas,' N. of Kaṇsa, L.; of Karṇa (the half brother of the Pāṇḍus), W. **Bhojâdhirāja**, m. a king of the Bh°, Rājat. **Bhojântā**, f. N. of a river, Hariv. **Bhojêndra**, m. a king of the Bhojas, MW.

Bhojaka, mfn. eating (see *bahu-bh°*); being about to eat, Pāṇ. iii, 3, 10, Sch.; (fr. Caus.) giving to eat, nourishing, Yājñ.; m. (perhaps) a waiter at table, Kām.; N. of a class of priests (or Sun-worshippers, supposed to be descended from the Magas by intermarriage with women of the Bhoja race), Cat.; an astrologer, Hcar.; N. of a king, VP.

Bhójana, mf(*ī*)n. feeding, giving to eat (said of Śiva), MBh.; voracious, R.; m. N. of a mountain, BhP.; n. the act of enjoying, using, RV.; the act of eating (exceptionally with acc. of object), RV. &c. &c.; a meal, food, ib. (ifc. f. *ā*, 'feeding on,' 'affording anything as food,' 'serving as food for;' *tri-dvy-eka-bh°*, mfn. 'taking food every 3rd day, every 2nd day and every day'); anything enjoyed or used, property, possession, RV.; AV.; Naigh.; enjoyment, any object of enj° or the pleasure caused by it, RV.; (fr. Caus.) the act of giving to eat, feeding, GṛŚrS.; R.; Mn. (v. l.); dressing food, cooking, Nal. — **kastūrī**, f. N. of wk. — **kāla**, m. meal-time, Pāṇ. i, 3, 26, Sch. — **kutūhala**, n. N. of a wk. on culinary art. — **gṛiha**, n. a dining-room, Sāy. — **tyāga**, m. abstinence from food, fasting, L. — **bhāṇḍa**, n. a dish of meat, Rājat. — **bhūmi**, f. a place for eating, Kathās. — **vidhi**, m. 'the ceremony of dining,' N. of various wks. (cf. RTL. 423). — **viśesha**, m. choice food, a dainty, delicacy, Hit. — **vṛitti**, f. pl. course or act of eating, a meal, ŚārṅgP. — **velā**, f. meal-time, Kathās. — **vyagra**, mfn. occupied or engaged in eating, Hit.; distressed or straitened for want of food, MW. — **vyaya**, m. expenditure for food, MBh. — **samaya**, m. meal-time, A. — **sūtra**, n. N. of wk. **Bhojanâcchādana**, n. food and raiment, A. **Bhojanâdhikāra**, m. superintendence over food or provisions, the office of a master of the kitchen, Hit. **Bhojanârthin**, mfn. desirous of food, hungry, Kathās. **Bhojanôttara**, mf(*ā*)n. to be taken after a meal (as pills), Car.

Bhojanaka, m. a species of plant, Suśr., Comm.

Bhojanakī-smṛiti, f. N. of wk.

Bhojanīya, mfn. to be eaten, eatable (see n.); (fr. Caus.) to be fed, to be made to eat, Mn.; MārkP.; one to whom enjoyment is to be afforded or service to be done, Nir.; n. food (esp. what is not masticated, as opp. to *khādanīya*), MBh.; Divyâv.; sea salt, L. — **mṛita**, mfn. one who has died from indigestion, KātyŚr., Comm.

Bhojayitavya, mfn. (fr. Caus.) to be made to eat, to be fed, MBh.; Mn.; Kull.

Bhojayitṛi, mfn. (fr. Caus.) causing to enjoy or eat, feeding, MW.; one who makes another enjoy or feel anything, Nīlak.; BrahmavP.; a promoter of enjoyment or amusement, MW.

Bhojayitvā, ind. having caused to eat, having fed, Lāṭy.

Bhojas. See *puru-bhójas*, *viśvá-bh°*, *su-bhójas* (cf. *bhójase* under 3. √*bhuj*, p. 759, col. 2).

Bhojika, m. N. of a Brāhman, Kathās.

Bhojin, mfn. (ifc.) enjoying, eating, Lāṭy.; Mn.; MBh. &c.; using, possessing, MW.; exploiting, MBh.; (cf. *a-śrāddha-bh°*, *gṛiha-bh°*, *bhujaṃga-bh°*, *saha-bh°*).

Bhojya, mfn. to be enjoyed or eaten, eatable, what is enjoyed or eaten, (esp.) what may be eaten without mastication, Bhpr.; MaitrUp.; MBh.; Yājñ. &c.; to be enjoyed or used, MBh.; Bālar. &c.; to be enjoyed sexually, Rājat.; to be enjoyed or felt, MBh.; Hariv.; to be suffered or experienced, MW.; to be fed, one to whom food must be given, MBh.; (fr. Caus.) to be made to eat, to be fed, MBh.; Mn., Kull.; m. pl. N. of a people, MārkP. (prob. w. r. for *bhoja*); (*ā*), f. a procuress, Gal.; a princess of the Bhojas, MBh.; Hariv.; Ragh.; BhP. (cf. *bhojā*); n. anything to be enjoyed or eaten, nourishment, food, MBh.; R. &c.; the act of eating, a meal, MBh.; Mn.; a festive dinner, L.; a dainty, MW.; a feast, a store of provisions, eatables, ib., enjoyment, advantage, profit, RV. — **kāla**, m. eating-time, meal-time, Pañcat. — **tā**, f. (Pañcat.) or **-tva**, n. (MaitrUp.) the condition of being eaten, the state of being food (*-tām*√*yā*, to become food). — **maya**, mfn., see *bhakshya-bhojya-maya*. — **sambhava**, m. 'having its origin in food,' chyle, chyme, the primary juice of the body (cf. *rasa*), L. **Bhojyânna**, mfn. one whose food may be eaten, Mn. iv, 253. **Bhojyôshṇa**, mfn. too hot to be eaten, Pāṇ. ii, 1, 68, Sch.

भोट *bhoṭa*, m. N. of a country, Bhoṭa, Tibet, Śatr. (cf. *mahā-bh°* and MWB. 261). — **go**, m. 'the Tibetan ox,' Bos Gavaeus, L. — **deśa**, m. the country of Bhoṭa, Cat. **Bhoṭâṅga**, m. N. of a country, Bhutān, L. **Bhoṭânta**, m. N. of a country, Cat. (cf. prec.)

Bhoṭiya, mfn. Tibetan, L. — **kośī**, f. N. of a river, ib.

Bhauṭa, m. a Tibetan, Rājat. (w. r. *bhauṭṭa*).

भोत *bhota*, w. r. for *bhoṭa*.

भोमीरा *bhomīrā*, f. coral, W.

भोल *bhola*, m. the son of a Vaiśya and of a Naṭī, L.

Bholā-nātha, m. N. of Śiva, ŚivaP.; of an author, Cat.

भोलि *bholi*, m. a camel, L.

भोस् *bhos* (fr. *bhavas*, voc. of *bhavat*, q. v.; before vowels and soft consonants *bho*; before hard consonants *bhos* and *bhoḥ*; the latter form also in pause, cf. Pāṇ. viii, 3, 17 &c.; but there is occasional confusion of these forms, esp. in later literature; often also *bho bhoḥ*), an interjection or voc. particle commonly used in addressing another person or several persons = O! Ho! Hallo!, in soliloquies = alas!, ŚBr. &c. &c. (according to L. a particle of sorrow and of interrogation). — **kāra**, m. rules of address, Divyâv.

Bho, in comp. for *bhos*. — **bhavat-pūrvakam**, ind. with *bhoḥ* and *bhavat* preceding, Mn. ii, 128. — **bhāva**, m. the nature of *bhoḥ*, ib. 124. — **vādin**, mfn. saying *bhoḥ*, Hariv.

Bhoḥ, in comp. for *bhos*. — **śabda**, m. the word *bhoḥ*, Mn. ii, 124.

भोहर *bhohara* (?), m. N. of a poet, Cat.

भौगक *bhaugaka*, m. patr. fr. *bhogaka*, g. *bidâdi*.

भौजकट *bhaujakaṭa*, mfn. relating to or coming from Bhoja-kaṭa, Siddh.

भौजंग *bhaujaṃga* (fr. *bhujam-ga*), mf(*ī*)n. relating to a snake, serpent-like, Kām.; n. (scil. *bha*) the serpent constellation, the Nakshatra Āślesha, VarBṛS.

भौजि *bhauji*, m. patr. fr. *bhoja*, g. *gahâdi*.

Bhaujīya, mfn. relating to Bhauji, ib.

Bhaujya, n. the rank of a king with the title of Bhoja, AitBr.

भौजिष्य *bhaújishya*, n. (fr. *bhujishya*) slavery, servitude, Suparṇ.

भौट *bhauṭa*, *bhauṭṭa*. See above.

भौणिक्या *bhauṇikyā*, f. patr. fr. *bhuṇika*, Kāś. on Pāṇ. iv, 1, 79.

भौण्ड *bhauṇḍa*, m. N. of a poet, Cat.

भौत *bhauta*, mf(*ī*)n. (fr. *bhūta*) relating to living beings, meant for them (as a sacrifice), Mn. iii, 70; (also °*ta-ka*) relating to or possessed by evil spirits or demons, crazy, mad, an idiot, Kathās.; formed of the elements, material, MārkP.; m. = *devalaka*, L.; (*ī*), f. 'time of ghosts,' night, L.; n. a multitude of Bhūtas, L. — **tulya** and **-prāya**, mfn. like an idiot, deranged, imbecile, Kathās.

Bhautika, mf(*ī*)n. = prec. mfn., Mn.; MBh. &c.; n. a pearl, L.; m. (fr. *bhūti*, ashes?) N. of Śiva, L.; a sort of monk, Cat.; n. anything elemental or material, MW.; a pearl, L.; pl. the qualities of the elements (5 with Buddhists), Dharmas. 40.

Bhautya, m. (fr. *bhūti*) N. of a Manu, Hariv.; mf(*ī*)n. relating to him, MārkP.

भौपाल *bhaupāla*, m. (fr. *bhū-pāla*) the son of a prince, a king, MārkP.

भौम *bhaumá*, mf(*ī*)n. relating or dedicated to the earth, produced or coming from the earth, earthly, terrestrial, VS. &c. &c. (with *naraka*, m. = hell on earth, MBh.; with *brahman*, n. = the Veda, ib.); consisting or made of earth, earthy, PañcavBr.; KātyŚr.; MBh. &c.; coming from the land (as revenue &c.), L.; (fr. *bhauma*, the planet Mars) relating to the pl° Mars or to his day, falling on Tuesday, Vet.; m. a red-flowering Punar-navā, L.; = *ambara*, L.; N. of the 27th Muhūrta, L.; metron. of a partic. earth-deity, GṛS.; of Atri, RAnukr.; of the Daitya Naraka, MBh.; of the planet Mars (whose day is Tuesday), ib.; Var.; Pur. &c.; m. or n. N. of AV. xii, 1; (*ī*), f. 'produced from the earth,' N. of Sītā, L.; n. dust of the earth (pl.), MBh.; corn, grain, Āpast.; (only ifc.) floor, story, MBh.; R. — **cāra**, m. 'the course of the planet Mars,' N. of a ch. of Bhaṭṭôtpala's Comm. on VarBṛS. — **darśana-cāra**, m. N. of a ch. of the Mīna-jātaka. — **deva-lipi**, f. N. of a kind of writing, Lalit. — **pūjā**, f., **-pūjā-vidhi**, m. N. of wks. — **ratna**, n. coral, L. — **vāra**, m. 'Mars-day,' Tuesday, KātyŚr., Sch.; *-vrata-vidhi*, m. N. of wk. — **vrata**, n. N. of a partic. observance or ceremony; *-kathā*, f., *-pūjā-vidhi*, m. N. of wks. — **śānti**, f., **-saṃhitā**, f., **-sûkta**, n., **-stotra**, n. N. of wks. **Bhaumâvatāra-varṇana**, n. N. of wk.

Bhaumaka, m. any animal living in the earth, AdbhBr.

Bhaumana, m. N. of Viśva-karman, MBh. (prob. w. r. for *bhauvana*).

Bhaumika, mf(*ī*)n. being on the earth, collected on the ground or any partic. piece of ground, Mn. v, 142.

Bhaumya, mfn. being on the earth, earthly, terrestrial, VP.

भौर *bhaura*, m. patr. fr. *bhūri*, g. *śivâdi*.

Bhaurika, m. (fr. *bhūri*, gold) a treasurer, L.; (pl.) N. of a country belonging to Prācya, L.; (*ī*), f. a mint, Gal.

भौरिकायणि *bhaurikāyaṇi*, m. patr. fr. next, g. *tikâdi*.

Bhauriki, m. patr. (f. *ī*), g. *gaurâdi*. — **vidha**, mfn. inhabited by Bhauriki, Pāṇ. iv, 2, 54.

Bhaurikika, mf(*ā* and *ī*)n., fr. *bhauriki*, Kāś. on Pāṇ. iv, 2, 116.

Bhaurikyā, f., g. *kraudy-ādi*.

भौलिकायनि *bhaulikāyani*, m. patr. fr. next, g. *tikâdi*.

Bhauliki, m. (f. *ī*), g. *gaurâdi*. — **vidha**, mfn. inhabited by Bhauliki, Pāṇ. iv, 2, 54.

Bhaulikyā, f., g. *kraudy-ādi*.

भौलिङ्गि *bhauliṅgi*, m. a king of Bhū-liṅga, g. *pailâdi*; (*ī*), f. a princess of Bh°, g. *gaurâdi*.

Bhauliṅgika, mf(*ā* and *ī*)n. relating to Bhauliṅgi, Kāś. on Pāṇ. iv, 2, 116.

भौली *bhaulī*, f. (in music) N. of a Rāga.

भौवन *bhauvaná*, mfn. (fr. *bhuvana*) belonging to the world, AV.; m. patr. of Viśva-karman (cf. *bhaumana*), of Sādhana &c., VS.; Br.; BhP.

Bhauvanāyana, m. patr. fr. *bhuvana* or *bhauvana*, VS.

भौवादिक *bhauvādika*, mfn. (fr. √*bhū* + *ādi*) belonging to that class of roots which begins with √*bhū*, belonging to the first class, Pāṇ. iii, 1, 75, Sch.

भौवायन *bhauvāyaná*, m. (fr. 2. *bhū́* or *bhuva*) patr. of Kapi-vana, MaitrS.; PañcavBr.

भ्यस् *bhyas*, cl. 1. Ā. (Dhātup. xvi, 27) *bhyásate* (only impf. *ábhyasetām*, RV.; Subj. *bhyásāt*, SV.; Gr. also pf. *babhyase*, fut. *bhyasishyati* &c.: Caus. *bhyāsayati*: Desid. *bibhyasishate*: Intens. *bābhyasyate, bābhyasti*), to fear, be afraid, tremble (cf. √*bhī*, of which this is a secondary form, prob. through *bhiyas*).

Bhyasa. See *sva-bhyasá*.

भ्रंश् *bhraṅś* or *bhraś* (sometimes written *bhraṅs*; cf. √*bhriś*), cl. 1. Ā. (Dhātup. xviii, 17) *bhraṅśate* (once in AV. P. °*ti*), cl. 4. P. (xxvi, 116; cf. √*bhriś*) *bhraśyati* (ep. also Ā. °*te*; pf. *babhraṅśa*, °*śe*, Gr.; aor. Subj. *bhraśat*, RV.; *abhraṅśishṭa*, Gr.; fut. *bhraṅśishyati*, °*te*; *bhraṅśitā*, ib.; ind. p. *bhraṅśitvā* and *bhrashṭvā*, ib.), to fall, drop, fall down or out or in pieces, AitBr. &c. &c.; to strike against (loc.), MBh.; to rebound from (abl.), ib.; to fall (fig.), decline, decay, fail, disappear, vanish, be ruined or lost, MBh.; Kāv. &c.; to be separated from or deprived of, lose (abl.), TS.; Mn.; MBh. &c.; to slip or escape from (gen.), Kād.; to swerve or deviate from, abandon (abl.), Ragh.: Caus. *bhraṅśayati* (or *bhrāśayati*; cf. *bhrāśya* and *ni-*√*bhraṅś*; aor. *ababhraṅśat*; Pass. *bhraṅśyate*), to cause to fall (lit. and fig.), throw down, overthrow, KātyŚr.; MBh. &c.; to cause to disappear or be lost, destroy, MBh.; R.; to cause to escape from (abl.), Ratnāv.; to cause to deviate from (abl.), BhP.; to deprive any one (acc.) of (abl.; e.g. *upavāsāt* or *vratāt*, 'of the reward for fasting or performing any observance'), MBh.; R. &c.: Desid. *bibhraṅśishati*, °*te*, Gr.: Intens. *bābhraśyate*, °*bhrashṭi*; *banībhraśyate* or °*bhraṅśyate*, ib.

Bhraṅśa, m. falling or slipping down or off, Kālid.; decline, decay, ruin, Kām.; Var. (*deśa-bh*°, ruin of a country); disappearance, loss, cessation, MBh.; Kāv. &c.; straying or deviating from, abandonment of (abl. or comp.), deprivation of (comp.), ib.; (in dram.) a slip of the tongue (due to excitement), Sāh.

Bhraṅśakalā-√kri, g. *ūry-ādi* (Kāś.)

Bhraṅśathu, m. = *pra-bh*°, q. v.

Bhraṅśana, mfn. (in most meanings from Caus.) causing to fall, throwing down, R.; n. the act of causing to fall or falling from i. e. deprivation or loss of (abl.), ib.

Bhraṅśita, mfn. (fr. Caus.) made to fall, thrown down, deprived of (abl.), MBh.; Hariv.; BhP.

Bhraṅśin, mfn. falling, dropping, falling down or from or off (comp.), Kāv.; Pur.; decaying, transitory (*a-bh*°), Kām.; causing to fall, ruining, annihilating (cf. *svārtha-bh*°).

Bhrashṭá, mfn. fallen, dropped, fallen down or from or off (abl. or comp.), AV. &c. &c.; (with or scil. *divaḥ*), fallen from the sky i. e. banished to the earth, Kathās.; Śukas.; broken down, decayed, ruined, disappeared, lost, gone, MBh.; Kāv. &c.; fled or escaped from, rid of (abl.), Kathās.; strayed or separated from, deprived of (abl. or comp.), MBh.; Kāv. &c.; depraved, vicious, a backslider, W.; (*ā*), f. a fallen or unchaste woman, MW. **-kriya**, mfn. one who has discontinued or omitted prescribed acts, Pañcat. **-guda**, mfn. suffering from prolapsus ani, Suśr. **-nidra**, mfn. deprived of sleep, Inscr. **-pariśrama**, mfn. free from weariness or exhaustion, R. **-mārga**, mfn. one who has lost his way, ib. **-yoga**, mfn. one who has fallen from devotion, a backslider, MW. **-rājya**, mfn. fallen from or deprived of a kingdom, MBh. **-vaishṇava-khaṇḍana**, n. N. of wk. **-śrī**, mfn. deprived of fortune, unfortunate, Pañcat. (v.l.) **Bhrashṭâdhikāra**, mfn. fallen from office, dismissed (*-tva*, n. dismission), Pañcat.

Bhrashṭaka, m. N. of a man; pl. his descendants, g. *upakâdi*. **-kapishṭhala**, m. pl., g. *tikakitavâdi*.

Bhrā́śya, mfn. (fr. Caus.) to be struck down or overthrown, RV.

भ्रंस् *bhraṅs*, v. l. for √*bhraṅś*.

भ्रकुंश *bhra-kuṅśa* or °*sa*, *bhra-kuñca*, *bhra-kuṭi* &c. See under *bhrū*, p. 771, col. 1.

भ्रक्ष् *bhraksh*. See √*bhriksh*, p. 765.

भ्रज् *bhraj*. See *giri-bhráj* and *mṛita-bhraj*.

भ्रज *bhrája*, n. fire (?), VS.; ŚBr.

भ्रजस् *bhrajas*. See *vāta-bhrajas*.

भ्रज्ज् *bhrajj*, cl. 6. P. Ā. (Dhātup. xxviii, 4; cf. √*bhṛij*) *bhṛijjáti*, °*te* (in Bhaṭṭ. only forms of the pr. P., and pf. *babhrajja*; Gr. also pf. *babhrajje* and *babharja*, °*je*; aor. *abhrākshīt*, *abhārkshīt*; *abhrashṭa*, *abharshṭa*; fut. *bhrakshyati*, °*te*, *bharkshyati*, °*te*; *bhrashṭā*, *bharshṭā*; inf. *bhrashṭum* and *bharshṭum*; ind. p. *bhṛishṭvā*), to fry, parch, roast (esp. grain), RV.; GṛŚrS. &c.: Pass. *bhṛijjyate* (ep. also °*ti*; p. *bhṛijjyamāna*, Nir.): Caus. *bharjayati* (cf. √*bhṛij*; Gr. also *bhrajjayati*; aor. *ababharjat* or *ababhrajjat*), to fry, roast, Suśr.; ĀpŚr., Sch.: Desid. *bibhrakshati*, *bibharkshati*; *bibhrajjishati*, *bibharjishati*, Gr.: Intens. *barībhṛijjyate*, *bābhrashṭi*, *bābharshṭi*, ib. [Cf. √*bhrāj*; Gk. φρύγω; Lat. *frīgere*.]

Bharshṭavya. See *bhrashṭavya*.

Bhṛijj (ifc., nom. *bhṛiṭ*) frying, roasting, baking, Pāṇ. viii, 2, 29, Sch. (cf. *bahu-bhṛijj*).

Bhṛijja, only in *uda-bhṛijja* (see *audabhṛijji*) and in comp. **-kaṇṭaka**, m. a partic. mixed tribe, Mn. x, 21 (v. l. *bhūrja-*, *bhūta-k*° &c.; cf. next). **-kaṇṭha**, m. a partic. mixed tribe, Gaut. (the son of a Brāhman Vrātya and a Brāhmaṇī, L.); a surgeon, L. **-kaṇṭhaka**, m. a person who uses medicinal roots for injurious purposes, L.

2. Bhṛishṭa, mfn. (for 1. see p. 766, col. 1) fried, broiled, grilled, roasted, baked, GṛŚrS.; MBh.; Suśr. &c.; n. roasted meat (see next). **-kāra**, m. a preparer of roasted or fried meat, R. **-taṇḍula**, m. roasted grain, Suśr. **-pishṭa**, n. roasted meal, Kauś. **-yava**, m. fried barley or rice, L. **Bhṛishṭânna**, n. rice boiled and then fried, W.

2. **Bhṛishṭi**, f. (for 1. see p. 766, col. 1) the act of frying or boiling or roasting, L.

2. **Bhrajj** (ifc.; nom. *bhraṭ*) roasting, frying, Pāṇ. viii, 2, 36.

Bhrajjana, n. the act of roasting or frying, L.

Bhrashṭavya or **bharshṭavya**, mfn. to be roasted or fried, Pāṇ. vi, 4, 47, Sch.

Bhrā́shṭra, n. a frying-pan, gridiron, MaitrS.

Bhrāshṭra, m. (n., L.) id., Nir.; Pañcat.; n. light, ether (cf. √*bhrāś*); mf(*ī*)n. fried or cooked in a frying-pan, Pāṇ. iv, 2, 16, Sch. **-krit**, see *bhrāshṭreya*. **-ja**, mfn. produced or cooked in a fr°-pan, L.; (*ā*), f. a pan-cake made of rice flour, L. **-m-indha**, mfn. heating the fr°-pan, one who fries or cooks, Pāṇ. vi, 3, 70, Vārtt. 6, Pat. **-vratin**, m. N. of a man, Pravar.

Bhrāshṭraka, m. or n.(?) a frying-pan, Pañcat. (v.l.); N. of a man (cf. next).

Bhrāshṭraki, m. patr. fr. prec., Pravar.

Bhrāshṭreya, m. pl. N. of a family, ib. (v. l. °*ṭra-krit*).

भ्रण् *bhraṇ*, cl. 1. P. *bhraṇati* (pf. *babhrāṇa* &c.), to sound, utter a sound, Dhātup. xiii, 9.

भ्रभङ्ग *bhra-bhaṅga*, m. = *bhrū-bhaṅga*, Uṇ. ii, 68, Sch.

भ्रम् *bhram*, cl. 1. P. (Dhātup. xx, 20) *bhramati* (ep. also °*te*) and cl. 4. P. (xxvi, 96), *bhrā́myati* (Pot. *bhramyāt*, PārGṛ.; pf. *babhrāma*, 3. pl. *babhramuḥ* or *bhremuḥ*, MBh.; Kāv. &c.; fut. *bhramitā*, Gr.; *bhramishyati*, MBh.; aor. *abhramīt*, ib.; inf. *bhramitum* or *bhrāntum*, MBh.; Kāv. &c.; ind. p. *bhramitvā*, *bhrāntvā*, *-bhrā́mya*, ib.), to wander or roam about, rove, ramble (with *deśam*, to wander through or over a country; with *bhikshām*, go about begging), MBh.; Kāv. &c.; to fly about (as bees), Kāv.; Var.; to roll about (as the eyes), Kāvyâd.; to wag (as the tongue), ŚārṅgP.; to quiver (as the fetus in the womb), BhP.; to move to and fro or unsteadily, flicker, flutter, reel, totter, ŚBr.; Kālid.; Pur.; to move round, circulate, revolve (as stars), MBh.; Hariv.; Sūryas.; to spread, be current (as news), Daś.; to waver, be perplexed, doubt, err, Bhag.; Pur.; Siddh.: Pass. aor. *abhrāmi* (impers., with *te*, 'you have wandered or roamed about'), R.: Caus. *bhrā́mayati* (m. c. also °*te*; aor. *abibhramat*: Pass. *bhrāmyate*), to cause to wander or roam, drive or move about, agitate, MBh.; Kāv. &c.; (with *paṭaham* or °*ha-ghoshaṇām*), to move a drum about, proclaim by beat of drum, Kathās.; to cause to move or turn round or revolve, swing, brandish, Up.; MBh.; Kāv. &c.; to drive through (acc.) in a chariot, Cat.; to disarrange, Kauś.; to cause to err, confuse, Hariv.; MārkP.; to move or roam about (aor. *abibhramat*; B. *ababhramat*), R.: Desid. *bibhramishati*, Gr.: Intens. *bambhramīti*, *bambhramyate* (also with pass. meaning) and *bambhrānti* (only Gr.), to roam about repeatedly or frequently, wander through, circumambulate, Hariv.; Var.; Śatr. [Cf. Gk. βρέμω; Lat. *fremere*; Germ. *brëmen*, *brimmen*, *brummen*; Eng. *brim*, *brim-stone*.]

Bhramá, m. (ifc. f. *ā*) wandering or roaming about, roving over or through (comp.), Kathās.; moving about, rolling (as of the eyes), Rājat.; turning round, revolving, rotation (acc. with √*dā* = to swing), MBh.; Sūryas.; Hcat.; a whirling flame, RV.; a whirlpool, eddy, Prab.; a spring, fountain, watercourse, L.; a potter's wheel, Sāṃkhyak.; (v. l. °*mi*), a grindstone (see comp.); a gimlet or auger, L.; a circle, Āryabh.; giddiness, dizziness, Suśr.; confusion, perplexity, error, mistake (ifc. mistaking anything for), Hariv.; Kāv.; Rājat. &c.; (*āt*), ind. by an error or mistake, Gīt. **-kuṭi**, f. a sort of umbrella, Gal. (cf. *bhramat-k*°). **-tva**, n. (in phil.) the being an error, erroneousness. **-bhūta**, mfn. being an error, erroneous, unreal, Ashṭāv. **Bhramâsakta**, m. 'occupied at the grindstone,' a sword-cleaner, armourer, L.

Bhramaṇa, n. wandering or roaming about, roving through, circumambulating (comp.), Kām.; Kāv.; Hit.; wavering, staggering, unsteadiness, Suśr.; turning round, revolution, the orbit (of a planet), MBh.; Var.; giddiness, dizziness, Vet.; Sāh.; a cupola, AgP.; erring, falling into error, MW.; (fr. Caus.) causing to go round (cf. *paṭaha-bhr*°); (*ī*), f. a sort of game (played by lovers), L.; a leech, L.; N. of one of the 5 Dhāraṇās or mental conceptions of the elements, Cat. **-vilasita**, n. N. of a metre, MW. (cf. *bhramara-v*°). **Bhramaṇârthe**, ind. for the sake of travelling, ib.

Bhramat, mfn. wandering about, roaming, MBh. **-kuṭi**, f. a sort of umbrella, L. (cf. *bhrama-kuṭi*).

Bhramara, m. (ifc. f. *ā*) a large black bee, a kind of humble bee, any bee, MBh.; Kāv. &c.; a gallant, libertine, L.; a young man, lad (= *baṭu*), L.; a potter's wheel, L.; a partic. position of the hand, Cat.; N. of a man, MBh.; (pl.) of a people, VP.; (*ā*), f. a kind of creeper, L.; (*ī*), f. a bee, Kālid.; a sort of game, L. (cf. *bhramaṇī*); a species of Oldenlandia, L.; a species of creeper, L.; N. of an Apsaras, Bālar. **-karaṇḍaka**, m. a small box containing bees (which are let out by thieves to extinguish lights in houses), Daś. **-kīṭa**, m. Vespa Solitaria, L. **-kuṇḍa**, n. N. of a sacred bathing-place on the mountain Nīla, Cat. **-gīta-ṭīkā**, f. N. of wk. **-cchallī**, f. a species of creeper, L. **-ja**, mfn. produced by bees (as honey), L. **-dūta-kāvya**, n. N. of a poem (= *-saṃdeśa-k*°). **-deva**, m. N. of a poet, Cat. **-nikara**, m. a multitude of bees, Pañcar. **-pada**, n. a kind of metre, Col. **-priya**, m. Nauclea Cordifolia, L. **-bādhā**, f. molestation by a bee, Śak. **-maṇḍala**, n. a circle or swarm of bees, Kāv. **-mārī**, f. 'bee-killing,' a species of flower (growing in Malwa), L. **-vilasita**, mfn. hovered round by bees, Chandom.; n. the hovering or sporting of bees, ib.; N. of a metre, ib. **-sadṛiśa-keśa-tā**, f. having hair dark like a bee (one of the 80 minor marks of a Buddha), Dharmas. 84. **-saṃdeśa-kāvya**, n. = *-dūta-k*°, q. v. **Bhramarâtithi**, m. 'bee-guest,' Michelia Champaka, L. **Bhramarânanda**, m. 'bee-joy,' Mimusops Elengi, L.; Gaertnera Racemosa, L.; the red-flowering globe-amaranth, L. **Bhramarâmbā-kshetra**, n. 'the bee-mother's i. e. Durgā's district,' N. of the Kanara coast (cf. *bhrāmarī*); *-māhātmya*, n. N. of wk. **Bhramarâmbâshṭaka**, n. N. of wk. **Bhramarâri**, m. 'bee-enemy' = *bhramara-mārī* (q. v.), L. **Bhramarâlaka**, n. 'bee-curl,' a curl on the forehead, L. **Bhramarâshṭaka**, n. N. of a poem (cf. *bhṛiṅgâshṭaka*). **Bhramarêshṭa**, m. 'loved by bees,' a sort of Bignonia, L.; (*ā*), f. Clerodendrum Siphonantus, L.; = *bhūmi-jambū*, L. **Bhramarôtsavā**, f. 'bee-delight,' Gaertnera Racemosa, L.

Bhramaraka, m. n. a curl on the forehead, L. (cf. *bhramarâlaka*); m. a bee, L.; a ball for playing with, L.; a whirlpool, L.; (*ikā*), f. wandering in all directions (*-drishṭi*, f. a w° glance, BhP.); n. a humming-top (*-bhrāmam* with Caus. of √*bhram*, to cause to spin like a humming-top, Bālar.); honey of the large black bee, L.

Bhramarāya, Nom. Ā. °*yate*, to resemble a bee, Subh. °**rita**, mfn. covered with bees, Naish.

Bhramāya (accord. to g. *bhriśâdi* fr. p. *bhra-*

mat), Nom. Ā. °*yate*, (prob.) to begin turning round or revolving, to roam about.

Bhrami, mfn. turning round, revolving (cf. *saṃvatsara-, svayam-bh*°); f. (L. also °*mī*) the act of turning round, Uttarar.; Naish.; a potter's wheel or a turner's lathe, Sāṃkhyak.; Pur. (v. l. °*ma*); a whirlpool, Kād.; a whirlwind, L.; a circular array of troops, Pur.; an error, mistake, L.; N. of a daughter of Śiśu-māra and wife of Dhruva, BhP.

Bhramita, mfn. (fr. Caus.; cf. *bhrāmita*) made to go round, whirled round &c., R.; (ifc.) falsely taken for, confounded with, Mṛicch.

Bhramin, mfn. turning round, whirling (as the wind), Bhaṭṭ.

Bhrānta, mfn. wandering or roaming about, MBh.; Kāv. &c.; having wandered about or through (with acc.), Kathās.; wandered about or through (n. impers. with instr., 'it has been w° ab° by'), ŚārṅgP.; Kathās.; moving about unsteadily, rolling, reeling, whirling, MBh.; Kāv.; perplexed, confused, being in doubt or error, ib.; m. an elephant in rut, L.; a species of thorn-apple, L.; n. roaming about, moving to and fro, Kāv.; Pañcat.; Suśr.; a partic. mode of fighting, Hariv.; error, mistake, Cāṇ. **-citta** or **-buddhi**, mfn. confused or perplexed in mind, puzzled, Kāv. **Bhrāntâkulita-cetana**, mfn. one whose mind is troubled by doubt or error, R.

Bhrānti, f. wandering or roaming about, moving to and fro, driving (of clouds), quivering (of lightning), staggering, reeling, Kāv.; Kām.; turning round, rolling (of wheels), Vikr.; (ifc.) moving round, circumambulating, Ratnâv.; perplexity, confusion, doubt, error, false opinion (ifc., false impression of, mistaking something for, supposing anything to be or to exist), Kāv.; Kathās.; Pur. &c. **-kara**, mf(*ī*)n. causing error or confusion, MW. **-darśana**, n. erroneous perception, Yogas. **-nāśana**, m. 'destroying error,' N. of Śiva, Śivag. **-mat**, mfn. roaming or wandering about, Bālar.; turning round, rolling (as a wheel), Mālav.; mistaking any one or anything for (comp.), Prâyaśc.; a partic. figure of rhetoric (describing an error), Kpr. **-vilāsa**, m. N. of a Campū. **-hara**, m. 'taking away delusion,' a counsellor, minister of a king, L.

Bhrāma, m. roaming about, unsteadiness, Gīt.

Bhrāmaka, mf(*ikā*)n. (fr. Caus.) causing error, deceitful, false, R., Sch.; m. n. 'causing (scil. iron) to turn round,' a magnet (also °*kâdri*, m.), L.; m. 'turning round (scil. towards the sun?),' a sunflower, heliotrope, L.; a deceiver, cheat, L.; (*akā*), f. a species of plant, L.

Bhrāmaṇa, n. (fr. Caus.) turning round, swinging, waving, MārkP.; Suśr.; giddiness, dizziness, Hcat.; (*ī*), f. N. of a female demon, MārkP.

Bhrāmara, mf(*ī*)n. (fr. *bhramara*) relating or belonging to a bee, MārkP.; m. n. a kind of magnet or loadstone, L. (cf. *bhrāmaka*); (*ī*), f. N. of Durgā, MārkP.; of a Yoginī or female attendant of D°, W.; n. (scil. *madhu*) honey, Suśr.; dancing round, L.; vertigo, giddiness, epilepsy, L.; a village, L.

Bhrāmarin, mfn. (fr. prec.) affected with vertigo or epilepsy, Mn. iii, 161; whirling round, revolving, W.; made of honey, ib.

Bhrāmita, mfn. (fr. Caus.; cf. *bhramita*) rolled (as eyes), Hariv.

Bhrāmin, mfn. confused, perplexed, Bhartṛ. (v.l. for *bhrānta*).

भ्रमन्त *bhramanta*, m. a small house, L.

भ्रमात्र *bhramātra*, m. or n. (?) a partic. high number, Buddh.

भ्रश् *bhraś.* See √*bhraṅś*, p. 769, col. 1.

भ्रशिमन् *bhraśiman, bhraśishṭha*, °*śiyas*. See p. 766, col. 1.

भ्रष *bhrasha*, m. the son of a Vaiśya and a Vindakī, L.

भ्रष्ट *bhrashṭa*, °*ṭaka*. See √*bhraṅś*, p. 769.

भ्रस्ता *bhrastā*, f. = *bhastrā*, a bag, ĀpŚr.

भ्राज् 1. *bhrāj*, cl. 1. Ā. (Dhātup. vi, 22) *bhrājate* (rarely P. °*ti*; pf. *babhrāja*, MBh.; *bhreje, babhrājire* and *bhrejire*, Gr.; aor. *ábhrāṭ, abhrāji*, RV.; *abhrājishṭa*, Gr.; Prec. *bhrājyāsam*, AV.; fut. *bhrājitā*, Gr.; *bhrājishyate*, MBh.; inf. *bhrājitum*, ib.), to shine, beam, sparkle, glitter, RV. &c. &c.; (with *na*), to be of no account, Cāṇ.: Caus. *bhrājayati* (aor. *ababhrājat* and *abibhrajat*), to cause to shine or glitter, illuminate, irradiate, MBh.; Kathās.; Bhaṭṭ.: Desid. *bibhrājishate*, Gr.; Intens. *bābhrājyate* or *bābhrāshṭi*, ib. [Cf. *bhṛigu*; Gk. φλέγω; Lat. *fulgere, flamma* for *flag-ma* &c.; Lith. *blizgù*; Germ. *bleichen*; Eng. *bleach*.]

2. **Bhrāj**, f. (nom. *bhrāṭ*) light, lustre, splendour, RV.; MaitrS.; ĀpŚr. [Cf. Gk. φλόξ.]

Bhrājá, mfn. shining, glittering, RV.; AV.; VS.; m. N. of one of the 7 suns, TĀr.; of a partic. kind of fire, Hariv.; of a Gandharva protecting the Soma, Sāy. on AitBr.; (pl.) N. of a wk. ascribed to Kātyāyana (also *-ślokāḥ*), Pat.; n. N. of 2 Sāmans, ĀrshBr. **-bhrishṭi**, (prob.) w. r. for *bhrājad-ṛishṭi*, GṛS.

Bhrājaka, mf(*ī*)n. (fr. Caus.) causing to shine, making bright (said of the digestive fire and bile as brightening the skin), Suśr.; n. the bile, bilious humour, gall, L.

Bhrājat, mfn. shining, gleaming, glittering, RV. **Bhrājaj-janman**, mfn. having a brilliant place of birth or origin (said of the Maruts), ib. **Bhrājad-ṛishṭi**, mfn. having bright spears (said of the same), ib.

Bhrājathu, m. brilliance, splendour, L. **-mat**, mfn. shining, beautiful (said of a woman), Bhaṭṭ.

Bhrājana, n. (fr. Caus.) the act of causing to shine, brightening, illuminating, Vāgbh.

Bhrājas, n. sparkling, flashing, glittering, lustre, brilliance, RV.; VS.; Br. **-vat** (*bhrā*°), mfn. sparkling, glittering, TS.; containing the word *bhrājas*, Kāṭh. **-vin**, mfn. sparkling, glittering, TS.; ŚāṅkhŚr.

Bhrāji, f. splendour, lustre, MaitrS.

Bhrājin, mfn. shining, glittering, Megh.

Bhrājira, m. pl. N. of a class of gods under Manu Bhautya, Pur.

Bhrājishṭha, mfn. (superl.) shining very brightly, VS.; m. N. of a son of Ghṛita-pṛishṭha, BhP.

Bhrājishṇu, mfn. shining, splendid, radiant, MBh.; Ragh.; BhP.; Suśr.; m. N. of Vishṇu, MBh.; of Śiva, Śivag. **-tā**, f. radiance, brightness, splendid appearance, Suśr.

Bhrājis = *bhrājas* above. **Bhrājish-mat**, mfn. splendid, shining, MBh.

Bhrājobhrādantya (?), m. pl. N. of a race, Saṃskārak.

भ्रातृ *bhrā́tṛi*, m. (connection with √*bhṛi* doubtful) a brother (often used to designate a near relative or an intimate friend, esp. as a term of friendly address), RV. &c. &c.; du. brother and sister, Pāṇ. i, 2, 68. [Cf. Zd. *brātar*; Gk. φράτηρ &c.; Lat. *frater*; Lith. *broter-ēlis*; Slav. *bratrŭ*; Goth. *brôthar*; Germ. *bruoder, Bruder*; Eng. *brother*.] **-gandhi** (R.), **-gandhika** (MBh.), m. a brother only in appearance, having merely the name of a b° (cf. Pāṇ. v, 4, 136). **-ja**, m. a b°'s son; (*ā*), f. a b°'s daughter, L. **-jāyā**, f. a b°'s wife, sister-in-law, Megh. (also °*tur-j*°, L.) **-tvá**, n. fraternity, brotherhood, RV. &c. &c. **-datta**, mfn. given by a brother; n. anything given by a b° to a sister on her marriage, Mn. ix, 92. **-dvitīyā**, f. a festival on the 2nd day in the light half of the month Kārttika (on which sisters give entertainments to b°s in commemoration of Yamunā's entertaining her b° Yama), Cat. **-patnī**, f. = *-jāyā*, L. **-padma-vana**, n. a group of lotus-like brethren, MW. **-putra**, m. a b°'s son, nephew, L. (also °*tush-p*°, g. *kaskâdi*). **-bhaginī**, du. a brother and sister; *-darśana-vidhi*, m. N. of wk. **-bhāṇḍa**, m. n. a twin-b°, HPariś. **-bhāryā**, f. = *-jāyā*; pl. the wives of b°s, Gaut. **-mat**, mfn. having a b° or b°s, Yājñ.; BhP. **-vadhū**, f. = *-jāyā*, L. **-vala**, mfn. possessing a b° or b°s, Pāṇ. v, 2, 112, Vārtt. 1, Pat. **-śvasura**, m. a husband's eldest b°, L. **-siṇha**, m. N. of a man, Rājat. **-sthāna**, m. 'taking the place of a b°,' a b°'s representative, ĀśvGṛ. **-hatyā**, f. fratricide, MW.

Bhrātṛika (ifc., with f. *ā*) = *bhrātṛi*, a brother, Kālid. (cf. *a-* and *sa-bh*°); mf(*ī*)n. coming from or belonging to a brother, brotherly, fraternal, Pāṇ. iv, 3, 78, Sch.

Bhrā́tṛivya, m. a father's brother's son, cousin, AV.; Rājat.; (mostly with *á-priya, dvishát* &c.) a hostile cousin, rival, adversary, enemy, AV.; VS.; Br.; R.; BhP.; n. (with *Indrasya*) N. of a Sāman, ĀrshBr. **-kshāyaṇa**, mfn. destroying rivals, AV. **-ghnī**, see *-hán*. **-cātana**, mfn. driving away rivals, AV. **-janman** (*bhrā́*°), mfn. having the nature or character of a r°, ŚBr. **-devatyá**, mf(*ā́*)n. having a r° for a deity, TS.; (°*tyà*), ŚBr. **-parāṇutti** (*bhrā́*°), f. the driving away a r°, TS. **-yajña**, m. a sacrifice performed against a rival, ĀpŚr. **-loká**, m. the world of a rival, ŚBr.; (*bhrā́*°*-loká*) TS. **-vat** (*bhrā́*°), mfn. having rivals, TS.; Br. **-sáhana**, n. overpowering a r°, Kapishṭh. **-hán**, mf(*ghnī*)n. killing r°s, AV. **Bhrātṛivyâpanutti**, f. = °*vya-parāṇutti*, TS. **Bhrātṛivyâbhibhūti**, f. = *vya-sahana*, ib.

Bhrātrá, m. a brother (see *mātur-bh*°); n. brotherhood, fraternity, RV.

Bhrātrīya, m. a (father's) brother's son, nephew, Pāṇ. iv, 1, 144; mfn. fraternal, belonging or relating to a brother, W.

Bhrātreya, m. = prec. m., BhP.

Bhrātrya, n. = *bhrātra*, n., MBh.

भ्रादिनी *bhrādinī*, f. (in music) a partic. Śruti, Saṃgīt.

भ्रान्त *bhrānta, bhrānti, bhrāma* &c. See under √*bhram*, col. 1.

भ्राश् *bhrāś* (v. l. *bhrās*; cf. √*bhlāś*), cl. 1. 4. Ā. *bhrāśate*, °*śyate*, Pāṇ. iii, 1, 70 (°*śyati*, Naigh.; pf. *babhrāśe* and *bhreśe*, Pāṇ. vi, 4, 125; fut. *bhrāśishyate*, °*śitā*, aor. *abhrāśishṭa*), to shine, glitter, Dhātup. xix, 76: Caus. *bhrāśayati* (aor. *ababhrāśat* or *abibhraśat*), Gr.: Desid. *bibhrāśishate*, ib.: Intens. *bābhrāśyate, bābhrāshṭi*, ib.

भ्राश्य *bhrāśya*. See p. 769, col. 1.

भ्राष्ट्र *bhrāshṭra*, °*ṭraka* &c. See p. 769, col. 2.

भ्रास् *bhrās*, v. l. for √*bhrāś*.

भ्रास्त्रेय *bhrāstreya*, v. l. for *bhrāshṭreya*, p. 769, col. 2.

भ्री *bhrī*, cl. 9. P. (Dhātup. xxxi, 34) *bhrīṇāti* or *bhriṇāti* (only pr. 3. pl. *bhrīṇánti*, RV. ii, 28, 7; Gr. also pf. *bibhrāya*; fut. *bhretā, bhreshyati*, aor. *abhraishīt*), to injure, hurt (Sāy. = √*hiṅs*; Naigh. 'to be angry,' cf. *bhriṇīya*; Gr. 'to fear' or 'to bear'): Caus. *bhrāyayati*, Gr.: Desid. *bibhrīshati*, ib.: Intens. *bebhrīyate, bebhrayīti, bebhreti*, ib.

भ्रुकुंश *bhru-kuṅsa, bhru-kuṭi*. See under *bhrū*.

भ्रुड् *bhruḍ*, cl. 6. P. *bhruḍati*, to cover or to collect, Dhātup. xxviii, 99; 102.

भ्रुभङ्ग *bhru-bhaṅga*. See 771, col. 1.

भ्रुव *bhruva*. See below.

भ्रू *bhrū*, f. (accord. to Uṇ. ii, 68 fr. √*bhram*) an eyebrow, the brow, RV. &c. &c. (ifc. m. *ŭ*, n. *u*; also *-bhrūka*). [Cf. Gk. ὀ-φρύς; Slav. *brŭvĭ*; Angl. Sax. *brû*; Eng. *brow*.] **-kuṅsa** or **-kuṇsa**, m. a male actor in female attire, Pat. **-kuṭi**, f. contraction of the brows, a frown (also *-kuṭi*, Pāṇ. vi, 3, 61, Vārtt. 3, Pat., and *-kuṭika*, mfn. ifc., L.), MBh.; R. &c.; acc. with √*kṛi* or *bandh*, to knit the eyebrows; *-kuṭila*, mfn. contracted, frowning (as a face), R.; °*lânana*, mfn. having a face wrinkled with frowns, MW.; *-bandha*, m. bending or knitting the eyebrows, A.; *-mukha*, n. (R.) and mf(*ī*)n. (Kathās.) = *bhru-kuṭī-m*°, q. v.; *-racanā*, f. = *-bandha*, A. **-kula**, n., Pāṇ. vi, 3, 61, Vārtt. 3, Pat. **-kshepa**, m. = *-kuṭi*, MBh.; R. (also °*paṇa*, n., Āpast.); *-jihma*, n. (with *vilocana*) a side look with contracted brows, Ṛitus.; °*pâlāpa*, m. the language of frowns, MW. **-cāpâkṛishṭa-mukta**, mfn. drawn and discharged from the bow of the eyebrows, ib. **-jāha**, n. the root of the eyebrows (perhaps the inner side), L. **-bhaṅga**, m. = *-kuṭi*, Kāv.; Pur. &c. **-bheda**, m. id., Ragh.; Śak.; °*din*, mfn. frowning, attended with frowns, Kum. **-maṇḍala**, n. the arch of the eyebrow, BhP. **-madhya**, n. the interval between the eyebrows, MBh. **-latā**, f. 'brow-creeper,' an arched eyebrow; *-kshepa*, m. = *bhrū-ksh*°, VarBṛS. **-vikāra**, m. (R.; Megh.), **-vikriyā**, f. (A.) change of the eyebrows, frowning. **-vikshepa**, m. = *-kshepa*, Bhartṛ.; °*pam*, ind. with a frown, Pāṇ. iii, 4, 54, Sch. **-viceshṭita**, n. playful movement of the eyebrows, R. **-vibheda** (Sāh.), **-vibhrama** (A.), **-vilāsa** (Megh.), m. id. **-saṃgataka**, n. the contact of the eyebrows, Hcar.

2. **Bhṛi** (1. see p. 764, col. 3), in comp. for *bhrū*. **-kuṅsa** or **-kuṇsa** or °**saka**, m. = *bhrū-kuṅsa*,

L. **-kuṭi** or **-kuṭī**, f. = *bhrū-kuṭi* (also °*ṭi-kuṭi-lânana*, °*ṭi-bandha*, °*ṭī-mukha*), MBh.; Kāv. &c.; °*ṭi-dhara*, mfn. contracting the brows, Mcar.; (*ī*), f. a species of frog, Suśr.; (with Jainas) N. of a goddess, L.; (*i*), m. (with Jainas) N. of the servant of the 20th Arhat of the present Avasarpiṇī, L.

Bhra, in comp. for *bhrū* (cf. Pāṇ. vi, 3, 61, Vārtt. 3, Pat.) **-kuṃsa** or **-kuṇsa**, m. = *bhrū-kuṃśa*, L. **-kuñca**, m. the son of a Kshatriya and a Jallī, L. **-kuṭi** (L.) or **-kuṭī** (MārkP.), f. = *bhrū-kuṭi*; °*ṭī-mukha*, mfn. with a frowning face, MBh.

Bhru, in comp. for *bhrū* (cf. Pāṇ. vi, 3, 61, Vārtt. 3, Pat.) **-kuṃsa** or **-kuṇsa**, m. = *bhrū-kuṃśa*, L. **-kuṭi** or **-kuṭī**, f. = *bhrū-kuṭi* (also °*ṭi-bandha*, °*ṭi-racanā* &c.), MBh.; Kāv. &c.; °*ṭī-kṛit*, mfn. contracting the brows, MBh.; °*ṭī-mukha*, n. and mfn. = *bhrū-kuṭī-m*°; m. (also) a kind of snake, Suśr. **-bhaṅga**, m. = *bhrū-bh*°, L.

Bhruva (ifc.) = *bhrū*, MBh.

Bhrauveya, m. metron. fr. *bhrū*, Pāṇ. iv, 1, 125.

भ्रूण् *bhrūṇ*, cl. 10. Ā. *bhrūṇayate*, to hope or wish or fear, Dhātup. xxxiii, 17.

भ्रूण *bhrūṇá*, n. (for *bhūrṇa*, fr. √*bhṛi*) an embryo, RV, x, 155, 2; m. a child, boy, L.; a very learned Brāhman, Hcat.; a pregnant woman (= *garbhiṇī*), L. **-ghna**, mfn. killing an embryo, one who produces abortion, Mn.; Pañcar. **-bhid**, mfn. id., Vām. v, 2, 38. **-vadha**, m. (Hcat.), **-hati**, f. (MBh.) the killing of an embryo. **-hatyā́**, f. id., Br.; Up.; MBh. &c.; the killing of a learned Brāhman, R., Sch. **-han**, mf(*ghnī*)n. = *-ghna*, Br. &c. &c.; one who kills a l° Br°, Āp. (Sch.); m. or n.(?) = *-hati*, Gaut. **-hanana**, n. = *-hati*, Baudh. **-hantṛi**, m. the killer of an embryo, any mean murderer, Car.

Bhrauṇaghna, mf(*ī*)n. (fr. *bhrūṇa-han*), Pāṇ. vi, 4, 135, Sch.

Bhrauṇahatya, n. (fr. id.) the killing of an embryo, Pāṇ. vi, 4, 174.

भ्रेज् *bhrej* (allied to √1. *bhrāj*), cl. 1. Ā. *bhrejate* (pf. *bibhreje* &c.), to shine, glitter, Dhātup. vi, 21: Caus. *bhrejayati* (aor. *abibhrejat*), Gr.

भ्रेष् *bhresh* (allied to √*bhraṃś* and *hresh*), cl. 1. P. Ā. (Dhātup. xxi, 20) *bhreshati*, °*te* (pf. *bibresha*, °*she* &c., Gr.), to totter, waver, slip, make a false step, RV.; AitBr.; to be angry, Naigh.; to fear, Vop.; to go, Bhaṭṭ. (*gatau*, Dhātup.)

Bhrésha, m. tottering, slipping, going astray or amiss, failure, TS.; Br.; ŚrS.; loss, deprivation, Yājñ.

Bhreshaṇa, n. the act of going, moving &c., W.

भ्रौणघ्न *bhrauṇaghna* &c. See under *bhrūṇa*.

भ्रौवेय *bhrauveya*. See above.

भ्लक्ष् *bhlaksh* (v. l. for √*bhaksh*), cl. 1. P. Ā. *bhlakshati*, °*te*, to eat, Dhātup. xxi, 27.

भ्लाश् *bhlāś* (connected with √*bhrāś*), cl. 1. 4. Ā. *bhlāśate*, °*śyate* (pf. *babhlāśe* or *bhleśe* &c.), to shine, beam, glitter, Dhātup. xix, 77.

भ्लास् *bhlās* (v. l. for √*bhlāś*), Vop. in Dhātup. xix, 77.

भ्लेष् *bhlesh* (v. l. for √*bhresh*), Dhātup. xxi, 20.

भ्व *bhva*. See *a-bhva*.

म MA.

म 1. *ma*, the labial nasal. **-1. -kāra**, m. the letter or sound *ma*, ŚāṅkhBr.; AVPariś. &c.; *-pañcaka*, n. = *pañca-makāra*, W.; °*râdi-sahasra-nāman*, n. N. of ch. of the Rudra-yāmala (containing 1000 names of Rāma beginning with *m*).

म 2. *ma*, m. (in prosody) a molossus. **-2. -kāra**, m. the foot called molossus; *-vipulā*, f. N. of a metre, Piṅg., Sch.

म 3. *ma*, base of the 1st pers. pron. in acc. sg. *mā́m* or *mā*; instr. *máyā*; dat. *máhyam* or *me*; abl. *mát* or *mád*; gen. *máma* or *me* (for the enclitic forms, cf. Pāṇ. viii, 1, 22 &c.) [Cf. 1. *mád*; Zd. *ma*; Gk. ἐ-μέ, μέ; Lat. *me*, *mihi* &c.]

Makat, familiar dimin. fr. prec. = *mát* in comp. **-pitṛika**, m. my father, Pāṇ. i, 1, 29, Pat.

म 4. *ma*, m. time, L.; poison, L.; a magic formula, L.; (in music) N. of the 4th note of the scale (abbreviated for *madhyama*); the moon, L.; N. of various gods (of Brahmā, Vishṇu, Śiva, and Yama), L.; (*ā*), f. a mother, L.; measure, L.; authority (*-tva*, n.), Nyāyam.; light, L.; knowledge, L.; binding, fettering, L.; death, L.; a woman's waist, L.; n. happiness, welfare, L.; water, L.

मंह् *maṇh* (cf. √*mah*), cl. 1. Ā. (Dhātup. xvi, 33) *máṇhate* (pf. *mamaṇhe* &c., Gr.), to give, grant, bestow (with *dānāya*, 'as a present'), RV.; ŚBr.; to increase, Dhātup.: Caus. *maṇhayati* (cl. 10 accord. to Dhātup. xxxiii, 124), to give &c., RV.; to speak or to shine, Dhātup.: Intens. *māmahe* &c.; see √*mah*.

Maṇhána, n. a gift, present, RV.; (*ā*), ind. (also with *dákshasya*) promptly, readily, willingly, ib.

Maṇhane-shṭhā, mfn. (prob.) liberal, RV. x, 61, 1 (*pradāne pravartamāna*, Sāy.)

Maṇhanīya, mfn. = *pūjanīya*, Nir. (cf. √*mah*).

Maṇhama, m. a partic. personification, Gaut.

Maṇhayád-rayi, mfn. (pr. p. of Caus. + *rayi*) granting wealth or treasures, RV.

Maṇhayú, mfn. (fr. Caus.) wishing to give, liberal, RV.

Máṇhishṭha, mfn. (superl.) granting most abundantly, very liberal or generous, RV.; exceedingly abundant, ib.; quite ready for (dat.), ib. **-rāti** (*máṇh*°), mfn. one whose gifts are most abundant, very rich or bountiful, ib.

Máṇhiyas, mfn. (compar.) giving more abundantly than (abl.), RV.

मक् *mak*, ind., g. *svar-ādi*.

मक *maka*, m. n., g. *ardharcâdi*; m. the son of a Vaiśya and a Māluki, L. **-datta**, m. N. of a man, Vās., Introd.

मकक *mákaka*, m. (prob.) a kind of animal, AV.

मकत् *makat*. See under 3. *ma*, col. 1.

मकन्दिका *makandikā*, f. N. of a woman, Pat.

मकमकाय *makamakāya* (onomat.), Ā. °*yate*, to croak (as a frog), Kāv.

मकर *mákara*, m. a kind of sea-monster (sometimes confounded with the crocodile, shark, dolphin &c.; regarded as the emblem of Kāma-deva [cf. *makara-ketana* &c. below] or as a symbol of the 9th Arhat of the present Avasarpiṇī; represented as an ornament on gates or on head-dresses), VS. &c. &c.; a partic. species of insect or other small animal, Suśr.; N. of the 10th sign of the zodiac (Capricornus), Sūryas.; Var. &c.; the 10th arc of 30 degrees in any circle, L.; an army of troops in the form of a M°, Mn. vii, 187; an ear-ring shaped like a M°, BhP. (cf. *makara-kuṇḍala*); the hands folded in the form of a M°, Cat.; one of the 9 treasures of Kubera, L.; one of the 8 magical treasures called Padminī, MārkP.; a partic. magical spell recited over weapons, R.; N. of a mountain, BhP.; (*ī*), f. the female of the sea-monster M°, Pañcat.; N. of a river, MBh. **-kaṭī**, f. 'dolphin-hipped,' N. of a woman, Kathās. **-kuṇḍala**, n. an ear-ring shaped like a M°, BhP. **-ketana**, **-ketu** and **-ketu-mat**, m. 'having the M° for an emblem' or 'having a fish on his banner,' N. of Kāma-deva, MBh.; Kāv. &c. **-daṇshṭrā**, f. 'Makara-toothed,' N. of a woman, Kathās. **-dhvaja**, m. = *-ketana*, MBh.; the sea, Harav.; a partic. array of troops, Kām.; a partic. medical preparation, L.; N. of a prince, Vcar. **-pāṭaka**, m. N. of a village, Inscr. **-māsa**, m. N. of a partic. month, TS., Sch. **-mukha**, m. = *makarâkāra-dhārin*, *jala-nirgamana-dvāra*, or *jānūrdhvâvayava*, L. **-rāśi**, m. the zodiacal sign Capricornus, MW. **-lāñchana**, m. = *-ketana*, Kād. **-vāhana**, m. 'having the M° for his vehicle,' N. of Varuṇa, L. **-vāhinī**, f. N. of a river, VP. **-vibhūshaṇa-ketana**, m. 'having the Makara for a characteristic ornament,' N. of Kāma-deva, Hariv. **-saṃkramaṇa**, n. the passage of the sun from Sagittarius into Capricornus, MW. **-saṃkrānti**, f., id.; N. of a festival (which marks the beginning of the sun's northern course), RTL. 428; *-tila-dāna*, n. and *-dāna-prayoga*, m. N. of wks. **-saptamī**, f. N. of the 7th day in the light half of the month Māgha, W. (cf. under *mākara*). **Makarâkara**, m. 'receptacle of M°s,' the sea, Kathās. **Makarâkāra**, m. 'formed like a M°,' a variety of Caesalpina Banducella, L. **Makarâksha**, m. 'M°-eyed,' N. of Rākshasa (son of Khara), R. **Makarâṅka**, m. 'having the M° for a symbol or mark,' N. of Kāma-deva, L.; the sea, L. **Makarânana**, m. 'Makara-faced,' N. of one of Śiva's attendants, L. **Makarâlaya**, m. 'M°-abode,' the sea, MBh.; R.; N. of the number 'four' (cf. under *samudra*). **Makarâvāsa**, m. 'M°-abode,' the sea, MBh. **Makarâśva**, m. 'having the M° for a horse,' N. of Varuṇa, L.

Makarāyaṇa, mfn. (fr. *makara*), g. *pakshâdi*.

Makarikā, f. a partic. head-dress, Kād.; a figure resembling the Makara, ib.

Makarin, m. 'full of Makaras,' the sea, L.

Makarī, f. of *makara*, in comp. **-pattra**, n. the mark of a Makarī (on the face of Lakshmī), Prab. (cf. *pattra-bhaṅga*). **-prastha**, m. N. of a town, g. *karky-ādi*. **-lekhā**, f. = *-pattra*, Prab. (v. l.)

मकरन्द *makaranda*, m. the juice of flowers, honey, Kāv.; Pur. &c.; a species of jasmine, L.; a fragrant species of mango, L.; a bee, L.; the Indian cuckoo, L.; (in music) a kind of measure, Saṃgīt.; N. of a man, Mālatīm.; of various authors and wks.; n. a filament (esp. of the lotus-flower), L.; N. of a pleasure-garden, Kathās. **-kaṇāya**, Nom. Ā. °*yate*, to be like drops or particles of flower-juice, Cat. **-kārikā**, f. pl., **-dīpikā**, f., **-pañcâṅga-vidhi**, m. N. of wks. **-pāla**, m. N. of a man (father of Tri-vikrama), Cat. **-prakāśa**, m. N. of wk. **-vat**, mfn. rich in flower-juice; (*atī*), f. the flower of Bignonia Suaveolens, L. **-vāsa**, m. a species of Kadamba, L. **-vivaraṇa**, n., **-vivṛiti**, f. N. of wks. **-śarman**, m. N. of a teacher, Cat. **Makarandôdyāna**, n. N. of a pleasure-garden near Ujjayinī, Ratnâv.

Makarandikā, f. a kind of metre, Col.; N. of the daughter of a Vidyā-dhara, Kathās.

मकष्टु *makashṭu*, m. N. of a man, g. *śubhrâdi*.

मकुआण *makuāṇa*, m. N. of a race of kings, Cat.

मकुट *makuṭa*, n. a crest (= *mukuṭa*), Divyâv. **-bandhana**, n. N. of a temple, Divyâv. **Makuṭâgama**, m. N. of wk.

मकुति *makuti*, m. or f. an edict addressed to the Śūdras (= *śūdra-śāsana*), L.

मकुर *makura*, m. a looking-glass, mirror, L.; the stick or handle of a potter's wheel, L.; Mimusops Elengi, L.; a bud, L.; Arabian jasmine, MW. (cf. *mukura*).

Makurāṇa, m. or n. N. of a place, Cat.

Makula, m. Mimusops Elengi, L.; a bud, L. (cf. *mukula*).

मकुष्ट *makushṭa* or °*ṭaka*, m. Phaseolus Aconitifolius, L.

Makushṭha, m. id., L. (also °*ṭhaka*); mfn. slow (= *manthara*), L. (cf. *mukushṭha*, *mapashṭha*).

मकूलक *makūlaka*, m. Croton Polyandrum, Car.

मकेरुक *makeruka*, m. a kind of parasitical worm, ib.

मक्क् *makk* (cf. √*mask*), cl. 1. Ā. *makkate*, to go, move, Dhātup. iv, 28, Vop.

मक्कल्ल *makkalla*, m. a dangerous abscess in the abdomen (peculiar to lying-in women), Suśr.; ŚārṅgS.

मक्कुल *makkula*, m. red chalk (= *śilā-jatu*), L.

Makkola, m. chalk, L. (= *sudhā*, VarBṛS., Sch.)

मक्वण *makvaṇa*, m. a small-limbed elephant or one who has not got his teeth at the proper time, L.

मक्ष् 1. *maksh* (cf. √*mraksh*), cl. 1. P. to collect, heap, Dhātup. xvii, 12 (v. l.); to be angry, Vop.

मक्ष् 2. *máksh*, m. or f. a fly, RV. iv, 45, 4; vii, 32, 2.

Mákshā, f. id., RV. x, 40, 6; AV. ix, 1, 17 [cf. Lat. *musca*].

Mákshikā, f. (m. c. also °*ka*, m.) a fly, bee, RV.

&c. &c. **-mala**, n. 'excretion of bees,' wax, L. **Makshikâśraya**, m. 'receptacle of bees,' id., L.

Makshīkā, f. = *makshikā*, L.

मक्ष *maksha*, m. the concealing of one's own defects, L. (prob. w. r. for *mraksha*).

मक्षवीर्य *maksha-vīrya*, m. Buchanania Latifolia (prob. w. r. for *bhaksha-* or *-bhakshya-bīja*).

मक्षु *makshu*, mfn. only instr. pl. *makshúbhiḥ* (or *makshū́bhiḥ*; cf. *makshū́*), quickly, promptly, RV. viii, 46, 6; m. N. of a man, AitĀr., Sch. (cf. *mākshavya*). **-ṃ-gamá**, mf(*ā́*)n. going quickly, RV. viii, 22, 16 (Sāy.)

Makshū́ (Padap. °*kshú*), ind. quickly, rapidly, soon, directly, RV. [cf. *maṅkshu* and Lat. *mox*]. **-javas** (°*kshū́-*), mfn. most rapid or prompt, RV. vi, 45, 14. **-tama** (°*kshū́*), mfn. id., ib. viii, 19, 12 (°*mebhir ahabhiḥ*, 'in the next days,' ix, 55, 3).

Makshūyú, mfn. quick, rapid, fleet (as horses), RV. vii, 74, 3.

मक्षुण *makshuṇa*, n. a partic. measure of weight (= 7 Māshas), L.

मख् *makh* (cf. √*maṅkh*), cl. 1. P. *makhati*, to go, move, Dhātup. v, 18.

मख 1. *makhá*, mfn. (prob. connected with √1. *mah* or √*maṇh*) jocund, cheerful, sprightly, vigorous, active, restless (said of the Maruts and other gods), RV.; Br.; m. a feast, festival, any occasion of joy or festivity, RV.; ŚāṅkhGṛ.; a sacrifice, sacrificial oblation, ŚBr. &c. &c. (Naigh. iii, 17); (prob.) N. of a mythical being (esp. in *Makhasya śiraḥ*, 'Makha's head'), RV.; VS.; ŚBr. (cf. also comp.) **-kriyā**, f. a sacrificial rite, L. **-traya-vidhāna**, n. N. of wk. **-trātṛi**, m. 'protector of Viśvā-mitra's sacrifice,' N. of Rāma (son of Daśa-ratha), L. **-dvish**, m. 'enemy of sacrifices,' a demon, Rākshasa, Ragh. **-dveshin**, m. 'enemy of (Daksha's, q. v.) sacrifice,' N. of Śiva, Śivag. **-mathana**, n. the disturbance of (Daksha's) s°, Ratnâv. **-maya**, mf(*ī*)n. containing or representing a s°, BhP. **-mukha**, mfn. beginning a s°, R. **-vat** (*makhá-*), mfn. companion of Makha (a word used to explain *maghávat*, q. v.), ŚBr.; a sacrificer, Hariv. **-vahni**, m. sacrificial fire, L. **-vedi**, f. a sacrificial altar, R. **-svāmin**, m. 'lord of sacrifice,' N. of an author, Cat. **-hán**, m. 'killer of Makha,' N. of Agni or Indra or Rudra, TS. **Makhâṇśa-bhāj**, m. 'partaker of a s°,' a god, Ragh. **Makhâgni**, m. = *makha-vahni*, L. **Makhânala**, m. id., L. **Makhânna**, n. 'sacrificial food,' the seed of Euryale Ferox, Bhpr. **Makhâpêta**, m. N. of a Rākshasa, BhP. **Makhâlaya**, m. a house or place for sacrifice, Cat. **Makhâsuhṛid**, m. = *makha-dveshin*, L. **Makhêśa**, m. 'lord of s°,' N. of Vishṇu, VP.

Makhas. See next and *sádma-makhas*.

Makhasya, Nom. P. Ā. °*syáti*, °*te*, to be cheerful or sprightly, RV. [cf. μαχέομαι].

Makhasyú, mfn. cheerful, sprightly, exuberant, ib.

Makhya, w. r. for 1. *makha*.

मख 2. *makha*, m. or n. (?) the city of Mecca, Kālac. **-vishaya**, m. the district of Mecca, ib.

मग *maga*, m. a magian, a priest of the sun, Var.; BhavP.; pl. N. of a country in Śāka-dvīpa inhabited chiefly by Brāhmans, Cat. **-vyakti**, f. N. of a wk. on the origin of the Śāka-dvīpin Brāhmans by Kṛishṇa-dāsa Miśra.

मगदिन् *magadin*, mfn., g. *pragady-ādi*.

मगध *magádha*, m. the country of the Magadhas, South Behār (pl. the people of that country), AV. &c. &c.; a minstrel who sings the praises of a chief's ancestry, L.; (*ā*), f. the town of the M°s, L.; long pepper, Suśr. **-deśa**, m. the country of M°, Hit. **-paribhāshā**, f. N. of wk. **-purī**, f. the city of M°, Lalit. **-pratishṭha**, mfn. dwelling in M°, Ragh. **-lipi**, f. the writing of M°, Lalit. **-vaṇśa-ja**, mf(*ā*)n. sprung from the race of M°, Ragh. **Magadhêśvara**, m. a king of the M°s, Ragh.; N. of a king of the M°s, Vet. **Magadhôdbhava**, mf(*ā*)n. born or grown in M°; (*ā*), f. long pepper, Suśr.

Magadhaka, Pat. on Pāṇ. i, 1, 4, Vārtt. 1; 6.

Magadhīya, mfn. relating to or coming from Magadha, g. *gahâdi*.

Magadhya, Nom. P. °*yati*, to surround (g. *kaṇḍv-ādi*), to serve, be a slave, Siddh.

मगन्द *maganda*, m. = *kusīdin*, a usurer, Nir. vi, 32.

मगल *magala*, m. N. of a man, Pravar.

मगव *magava*, m. or n. (?) a partic. high number, Buddh.

मगस *magasa*, m. pl. N. of the warrior caste in Śāka-dvīpa, BhavP.

मगु *magu*, m. = *maga*, a magian, Cat.

मगुन्दी *magundī*, f. N. of a mythical being (whose daughters are female demons), AV.

मग्न *magna*. See √*majj*.

मघ *maghá*, m. (√*maṇh*) a gift, reward, bounty, RV.; wealth, power, ib.; a kind of flower, L.; a partic. drug or medicine (also *ā*, f.), L.; N. of a Dvīpa (s. v.), L.; of a country of the Mlecchas, L.; (*ā́*), f. (also pl.) N. of the 10th or 15th Nakshatra (sometimes regarded as a wife of the Moon), AV. &c. &c.; N. of the wife of Śiva, L.; (*ī* or *ā*), f. a species of grain, L. **-gandha**, m. Mimusops Elengi, Kir., Sch. **-tti** (*maghá-*), f. (for *magha* + *datti*) the giving and receiving of presents, RV. **-déya**, n. the giving of presents, ib. **-rava**, m. N. of a Nishāda, Cat. **-vat**, mfn., see next. **-van** (*maghá-*), mfn. (middle stem *maghá-vat* [which may be used throughout], weak stem *maghón*; nom. m. *maghávā* or °*vān*, f. *maghónī* or *maghavatī* [Vop.]; n. *maghavat*; nom. pl. m. once *maghónas*; cf. Pāṇ. vi, 4, 128; 133), possessing or distributing gifts, bountiful, liberal, munificent (esp. said of Indra and other gods, but also of institutors of sacrifices who pay the priests and singers), RV.; AV.; TS.; ŚBr.; Up.; m. N. of Indra (also pl. °*vantaḥ*), MBh.; Kāv. &c.; of a Vyāsa or arranger of the Purāṇas, Cat.; of a Dānava, Hariv.; of the 3rd Cakra-vartin in Bhārata, L.; *-vat-tvá*, n. liberality, munificence, RV.; *-van-nagara*, n. 'Indra's city,' N. of a town, Rājat.; *-van-mukta-kuliśa*, m. or n. (?) the thunderbolt hurled by Indra, Bhartṛ. **-svāmin**, m., v. l. for *makha-sv°*, q. v.

Maghava, m. = *magha-van*, BhavP.

Maghā, f. of *magha*, in comp. **-trayodaśī**, f. the 13th day in the dark half of the month Bhādra, Col.; *-śrāddha*, n. a s° ceremony on that day, MW. **-bhava** or **-bhū**, m. 'offspring of Magha,' the planet Venus, L.

Maghī-prastha, m. N. of a town, g. *karky-ādi* (Kāś. for *maghnī-pr°*).

मघष्टु *maghashṭu*, m. N. of a man, g. *śubhrâdi*, Kāś. (cf. *makashṭu*).

मघ्नीप्रस्थ *maghnī-prastha*. See *maghī-pr°*.

मङ्क् *maṅk* (cf. √*maṅg*), cl. 1. Ā. *maṅkate*, to move or to adorn, Dhātup. iv, 15 (only pf. *mamaṅkire*, explained by *śuśubhire*, Bhaṭṭ. [v. l. *mamaṅgire*; cf. Pāṇ. iii, 1, 87]; Gr. also fut. *maṅkishyate*; aor. *amaṅkishṭa* &c.)

Maṅkú, mfn. shaking, vacillating, ŚBr. (cf. *durm°*); m. blotch, L.

मङ्कणक *maṅkaṇaka*, m. N. of a Ṛishi, MBh.; of a Yaksha, ib. (B. *macakruka*).

मङ्कि *maṅki*, m. N. of a man, MBh. **-gīta**, n. 'song of Maṅki,' N. of the 15th ch. of the Pārtha Itihāsa-samuccaya (containing episodes from the MBh.)

मङ्किल *maṅkila*, m. a forest-conflagration, L.

मङ्कुर *maṅkura*, m. = *makura*, a mirror, L.

मङ्कुश *maṅkuśa*, m. a person who knows dancing and singing (also called *māhishya*), L.

मङ्क्तव्य *maṅktavya*, °*tṛi*. See p. 773, col. 2.

मङ्क्षण *maṅkshaṇa*, n. armour for the legs or thighs, greaves, L. (cf. *maṅkhuṇa*, *matkuṇa*).

मङ्क्षु *maṅkshu*, ind. (cf. *makshu*) quickly, immediately, directly, instantly, Kāv.; Kathās.; very much, exceedingly, L.; truly, really, L.; m. N. of a man, g. *gargâdi*.

मङ्ख् *maṅkh* (cf. √*makh*), cl. 1. P. *maṅkhati*, to go, move, Dhātup. v, 19.

मङ्ख *maṅkha*, m. = *magadha*, a royal bard or panegyrist, L.; a mendicant of a partic. order, W.; N. of a man, Rājat.; of a lexicographer (*-kośa*, m. his work).

Maṅkhaka, m. N. of a man, Rājat.

Maṅkhanā, f. N. of a woman, ib.

Maṅkhāya, Nom. °*yate*, to act or be like a bard, Śrīkaṇṭh.

मङ्खुण *maṅkhuṇa*, n. = *maṅkhaṇa*, L.

मङ्ग् *maṅg* (cf. √*maṅk*), cl. 1. Ā. *maṅgate*, to go, move, Dhātup. v, 40.

मङ्ग *maṅga*, m. n. the head of a boat, L.; m. a mast or side of a ship, L. (cf. *maṇḍa*); pl. N. of a country in Śāka-dvīpa inhabited chiefly by Brāhmans, MBh. vi, 436 (B.; cf. *maga* and *mṛiga*).

Maṅginī, f. a boat, ship, HPariś.

मङ्गल *maṅgala*, n. (accord. to Uṇ. v, 70 fr. √*maṅg*) happiness, felicity, welfare, bliss (also pl.; ifc. f. *ā*), Mn.; MBh. &c.; anything auspicious or tending to a lucky issue (e. g. a good omen, a prayer, benediction, auspicious ornament or amulet, a festival or any solemn ceremony on important occasions &c.; cf. mfn. below), Kauś.; MBh.; Kāv. &c.; a good old custom, PārGṛ.; Mn.; a good work, MBh.; BhP.; (in music) a partic. composition, Saṃgīt.; N. of the capital of Udyāna, Buddh.; m. N. of Agni, Gṛihyas.; of the planet Mars, L.; of a king belonging to the race of Manu, Cat.; of a Buddha, Lalit.; of a poet, Cat.; of a chief of the Cālukyas, ib.; the smell of jasmine, L.; (*ā*), f. the white- and blue-flowering Dūrvā grass, L.; a sort of Karañja, L.; turmeric, L.; a faithful wife, L.; N. of Umā, Hcat.; of Dākshāyaṇī (as worshipped in Gayā), Cat.; of the mother of the 5th Arhat of the present Avasarpiṇī, L.; (*ī*), f., g. *gaurâdi*; mf(*ā*)n. auspicious, lucky, Hcat.; having the scent of jasmine, L. **-karaṇa**, n. 'luck-causing,' the act of reciting a prayer for success before the beginning of any enterprise, Madhus. **-karman**, n. id., Mālav. **-kalaśa**, m. = *-ghaṭa*, a vessel used at festivals, Gīt.; *-maya*, mfn. consisting of vessels of this kind, Hcar. **-kāraka**, mfn. (MBh.) or **-kārin**, mfn. (MW.) causing welfare. **-kārya**, n. a festive occasion, solemnity, MW. **-kāla**, m. an auspicious occasion, Śak. **-kuṭhāra-miśra**, m. N. of a door-keeper, Cat. **-kshauma**, n. du. a linen upper- and under-garment worn at festivals, Ragh. **-gāthikā**, f. a solemn song, Dhanaṃj. **-giri**, m. 'mountain of fortune,' N. of a m°; *-māhātmya*, n. N. of wk. **-gīta**, n. = *-gāthikā*, Pañcat. **-gṛiha**, n. an auspicious house or temple, Mālav.; Mālatim. (also °*haka*); the house of the planet Mars, Siṇhâs. **-graha**, m. an auspicious planet, a lucky star, MW. **-ghaṭa**, m. 'ausp° jar,' a vessel full of water offered to the gods on festivals, MW.; N. of an elephant, Kathās. **-caṇḍikā** or **-caṇḍī**, f. N. of Durgā, Cat.; W. **-cchāya**, m. Ficus Infectoria, L. **-tūrya**, n. a musical instrument used at festivals, Pañcat.; Ragh. **-daśaka**, m. or n. (?) N. of a prayer, Cat. **-devatā**, f. a tutelary deity (cf. *brahma-m°*). **-dvāra**, n. the principal gate of a palace (being opened on festive occasions), Lalit. **-dhvani**, m. an auspicious sound (e. g. marriage-music), L. **-nirṇaya**, m. N. of wk. **-pattra**, n. a leaf serving as an amulet, Śak. **-pāṭhaka**, m. 'blessing-reciter,' a professional well-wisher or panegyrist, Daś.; Pārśvan. **-pāṇi**, mfn. having auspicious hands, R. **-pātra**, n. an ausp° vessel, a vessel containing ausp° objects, Śak. **-pura**, n. 'city of prosperity,' N. of a town, Cat. (cf. *maṅgala*). **-pushpa-maya**, mf(*ī*)n. formed of ausp° flowers, Ragh. **-pūjā-prayoga**, m. and **-pūjā-vidhi**, m. N. of wks. **-pūjita**, mfn. honoured with a sacrificial fee or offering, MW. **-pratisara**, m. = *-sūtra*, Mālatim.; the cord of an amulet, Daś. **-prada**, mfn. bestowing welfare, ausp°, Cat.; (*ā*), f. turmeric, L. **-prastha**, m. 'ausp°-peak,' N. of a mountain, Pur. **-bherī**, f. a drum beaten on festive occasions, Siṇhâs. **-maya**, mf(*ī*)n. consisting of nothing but happiness &c., Kād.; Bhām. **-mayūkha-mālikā**, f. N. of wk. **-mātra-bhūshaṇa**, mfn. only adorned with turmeric or with the Maṅgala-sūtra (q. v.), Vikr. **-mālikā**, f. marriage-music, L. **-rāja**, m. N. of a king, Inscr. **-vacas**, n. a benedictory or congratulatory speech, congratulation, Caurap. **-vat**, mfn. auspicious, blessed; (*atī*), f. N. of a daughter of Tumburu, Kathās. **-vatsa**, m. N. of a poet, Subh. **-vāda**, m. 'benediction, congratulation;' *-ṭīkā*, f., °*dârtha*, m. N. of wks. **-vādin**, mfn. pronouncing a benediction, expressing congratulations, R. **-vāra** or **-vāsara**, m. 'Mars-day,' Tuesday, L. **-vidhi**, m. any ausp° ceremony or festive rite; preparations for a festival, Daś. **-vṛishabha**, m. an ox with ausp° signs, Pañcat. **-śaṇsana**, n. the act of wishing joy, uttering a congratulation, L. **-śabda**, m. auspicious word, felicitation, Var. **-śānti**, f. N. of wk. **-saṃstava**, mfn. felicitating, containing felicitations, R. **-samālambhana**, n. an ausp° unguent, Śak. **-sāman**, n. an ausp° Sāman, L. **-sūcaka**, mfn. auguring good luck, Daś. **-sūtra**, n. 'lucky thread,' the marriage-thread (tied by the bridegroom round the bride's neck, and worn as long as the husband lives), MW. **-stava**, m., **-stotra**, n. N. of wks. **-snāna**, n. any solemn ablution, L. **-svara**, m. a sea-shell, L. **Maṅgalâkshata**, m. pl. rice cast upon people by Brāhmans in bestowing a blessing at marriages &c., MW. **Maṅgalâguru**, n. a species of Agallochum, L. **Maṅgalâcaraṇa**, n. benediction, prayer for the success of anything, Kap.; Sāh.; Cat.; pronouncing a blessing, wishing joy, MW. **Maṅgalâcāra**, m. the repeating a prayer for success and observing other auspicious ceremonies, MBh.; a partic. composition, Saṃgīt.; *yukta*, mfn. accompanied with a pr° for success, attended with ausp° cer°, Mn. **Maṅgalâtodya**, n. = °*la-bherī*, Kathās. **Maṅgalâdeśa-vṛitta**, m. a fortune-teller, Mn. ix, 258. **Maṅgalâyana**, n. the way to happiness or prosperity, BhP.; mfn. walking on the path of prosp°, ib. **Maṅgalârambha**, mfn. causing an ausp° beginning (said of Gaṇêśa), Pañcar. **Maṅgalârcana-paddhati**, f. N. of wk. **Maṅgalârjuna**, m. N. of a poet, Cat. **Maṅgalârtham**, ind. for the sake of prosperity or happiness, MW. **Maṅgalârha**, mfn. worthy of prosp° or happ°, Pañcar. **Maṅgalâlaṃkṛita**, mfn. decorated with auspicious ornaments, Kālid. **Maṅgalâlabhanīya**, n., w. r. for °*lâlambhanīya* (q. v.), R. **Maṅgalâlambhana**, n. touching anything auspicious, MBh. **Maṅgalâlambhanīya**, n. an object whose touch is ausp°, R. **Maṅgalâlaya**, mfn. having an ausp° dwelling, MW.; m. a temple, A. **Maṅgalâlāpana**, n. felicitation, R. **Maṅgalâvaṭa** (or °*lā-vaṭa* [?]), n. N. of a place of pilgrimage, Cat. **Maṅgalâvaha**, mfn. auspicious, Hcat. **Maṅgalâvāsa**, m. 'ausp° dwelling,' a temple, Kathās. **Maṅgalâshṭaka**, m. (!) a term for 8 ausp° things, Hcat.; m. or n. (?) 8 lines of benediction pronounced for good luck by a Brāhman on a newly-wedded pair while a piece of cloth is held between them, MW.; n. N. of wks. **Maṅgalâhnika**, n. any daily religious rite for success, L.; a vase full of water carried in front of a procession, L. **Maṅgalêcchā**, f. benediction, felicitation; (*āyai*), ind. for the sake of an ausp° omen, MaitrS. iii, 8, 10. **Maṅgalêcchu**, mfn. wishing joy, w° prosperity, MW. **Maṅgalêśvara-tīrtha**, n. 'Tīrtha of the lord of prosperity,' N. of a sacred bathing-place, Cat. **Maṅgalôpêpsā**, f. the desire for prosperity or happiness, ŚBr.

Maṅgalā, f. of *maṅgala*, in comp. **-gaurī-pūjā**, f., °**rī-vrata-kathā**, f., °**rī-vratôdyāpana**, n., °**ry-ashṭaka**, n. N. of wks. **-vaṭa**, n., see *maṅgalâvaṭa* above. **-vrata**, n. the vow of Umā, Cat.; N. of ch. of the Kāśī-khaṇḍa of the Skanda Purāṇa; mfn. devoted to Umā (said of Śiva), Śivag. **-śāstra**, n. 'the book of Umā,' N. of wk.

Maṅgalikā, (prob. n.) pl. (perhaps) N. of the hymns of the 18th Kāṇḍa of the Atharva-veda, AV. xix, 23, 28.

Maṅgalīya, mfn. auspicious, MBh.

Maṅgalya, mf(*ā*)n. auspicious, lucky, conferring happiness, Kauś.; Mn.; MBh. &c.; beautiful, pleasing, agreeable, MW.; pious, pure, holy, Uttarar.; m. Cicer Lens, Suśr.; Aegle Marmelos, Sāh.; Ficus Religiosa, L.; Ficus Heterophylla, L. (correctly *maṅgalyârhā*); the cocoa-nut tree, L.; Feronia Elephantum, L.; a species of Karañja, L.; = *jīvaka*, L.; N. of a serpent demon, Buddh.; (*ā*), f. (only L.) a species of fragrant sandal; Anethum Sowa; Mimosa Suma; Terminalia Chebula; Andropogon Aciculatus; Curcuma Longa; a partic. bulb (*ṛiddhi*); Dūrvā grass; = *adhaḥ-pushpī*; = *jīvantī*; = *priyaṅgu*; = *māsha-parṇī*; Acorus Calamus; N. of a partic. yellow pigment (= *go-rocanā*), Bhpr.; a partic. resin, L.; N. of Durgā, DevīP.; n. an auspicious prayer, MārkP.; any ausp° thing, Gaut.; Suśr.; Var. (sg. collectively, Hcat.); bathing with the juice of all medicinal plants, L.; water brought from various sacred places for the consecration of a king &c., MW.; sour curds, L.; sandal wood, L.; a kind of Agallochum, L.; gold, L.; red lead, L. **-kusumā**, f. Andropogon Aciculatus, Bhpr. **-daṇḍa**, m. 'having an auspicious staff,' N. of a man, Rājat. **-nāman**, mfn., v. l. for *māṅg°*, q. v., MaitrS.; °*ma-dheyā*, f. Hoija Viridifolia, Bhpr. **-vastu**, n. any ausp° object, Pañcat. **Maṅgalyârhā**, f. Ficus Heterophylla, L.

Maṅgalyaka, m. Cicer Lens, Bhpr.

मङ्गीर *maṅgīra*, m. N. of a man, Vait. (*mandīra*, KātyŚr.)

मङ्गु *maṅgu*, m. N. of a prince, VP.

मङ्गुर *maṅgura*, m. a kind of fish, Bhpr.

मङ्गुल *maṅgula*, n. evil, sin (= *pāpa*), Kāv.

मङ्गुष *maṅgusha*, m. N. of a man, g. *kurv-ādi.*

मङ्घ् *maṅgh*, cl. 1. P. *maṅghati*, to adorn, decorate, Dhātup. v, 56; Ā. *maṅghate*, to go, start, begin; to blame; to cheat, iv, 37.

मच् *mac* (cf. √*mañc*), cl. 1. Ā. *macate* (pf. *mece* &c.), to cheat, be wicked or arrogant; to pound, grind, Dhātup. vi, 12.

मचकचातनी *macaka-cātanī*, prob. w. r. for *mecaka-c°*, q. v.

मचक्रुक *macakruka*, m. N. of a Yaksha and of a sacred spot guarded by him near the entrance to Kuru-kshetra, MBh. (cf. *maṅkaṇaka*).

मचर्चिका *macarcikā*, f. (ifc.) excellence, anything excellent or good of its kind (cf. *go-m°*), g. *matallikâdi* (Gaṇar.)

मच्चित्त *mac-citta* &c. See under 1. *mad*, p. 777, col. 2.

मच्छ *maccha*, m. (Prākr. for *matsya*) a fish, L. **Macchâkshâṅka**, mfn. marked with a fish-eye (said of a bad pearl), ib.

मज् *maj*. See *nir-maj* under *nir-√majj*, p. 556, col. 1.

मजमुदार *majamudāra*, m. = مجموع دار *majmū'-dār*, a record-keeper, document-holder, Kshitîś.

मजिरक *majiraka*, m. N. of a man, g. *śivâdi.*

मज्ज् *majj*, cl. 6. P. (Dhātup. xxviii, 122) *majjati* (Ved. *májjati*, ep. also °*te*; pf. *mamajja* [2. sg. *mamajjitha* or *mamaṅktha*], MBh.; aor. [*mā*] *majjīs*, ib.; *amāṅkshīt*, Bhaṭṭ.; Prec. *majjyāt*, ŚBr.; fut. *maṅkshyati*, °*te*, Br. &c.; *majjishyati*, MBh.; *maṅktā*, Gr.; inf. *majjitum*, MBh.; *maṅktum*, Gr.; ind. p. *maṅktvā* or *maktvā*, ib.; *-májjya*, AV.), to sink ('into,' acc. or loc.), go down, go to hell, perish, become ruined, RV. &c. &c.; to sink (in water), dive, plunge or throw one's self into (loc.), bathe, be submerged or drowned, ShaḍvBr.; KātyŚr.; MBh. &c.: Caus. *majjáyati* (aor. *amamajjat*, Gr.), to cause to sink, submerge, drown, overwhelm, destroy, ŚBr. &c. &c.; to inundate, MBh.; to strike or plant into (loc.), ib.: Desid. *mimaṅkshati* or *mimajjishati*, Gr. (cf. *mimaṅkshā*): Intens. *māmajjyate*, *māmaṅkti*, ib. [Cf. Lat. *mergere*, and under *majjan*.]

Magna, mfn. sunk, plunged, immersed in (loc. or comp.), KātyŚr.; Mn.; MBh. &c.; set (as the moon), R.; sunk into misfortune, ib.; (ifc.) slipped into, lurking in, Ragh.; sunken, flat (as breasts or a nose), Hariv.; R.; Suśr.; m. N. of a mountain, Buddh.

Maṅktavya, mfn. to be immersed or plunged, Pāṇ. vii, 1, 60, Sch.; n. (impers.) it is to be immersed or plunged by (any one), Kathās.

Maṅktṛi, mfn. one who dives or plunges &c., Pāṇ. vii, 1, 60, Sch.

1. **Majja**, mfn. sinking, diving (in *uda-majja*; see *audamajji*).

2. **Majja**, in comp. for *majjan*. **-kṛit**, n. 'producing marrow,' a bone, L. **-tas**, ind. = *majjām prati*, Lāṭy. **-rasa**, m. = *majjā-r°*, L. **-samudbhava**, m. 'produced from the marrow,' semen virile, L.

Majjaka. See *a-majjaka*.

Majján, m. (lit. 'sunk or seated within') the marrow of bones (also applied to the pith of plants), RV. &c. &c. (according to ŚBr. &c. one of the 5 elements or essential ingredients of the body; in the later medical system that element which is produced from the bones and itself produces semen, Suśr.); scurf, Kull. on Mn. v, 135. [Cf. Zd. *mazga*; Slav. *mozgŭ*; Germ. *marg*, *marag*, *Mark*; Angl. Sax. *mearg*; Eng. *marrow*.] **-vát**, mfn. marrowy (opp. to *a-majjaka*), TS.

Majjana, m. N. of a demon causing sickness or fever, Hariv.; of one of Śiva's attendants, L.; n. sinking (esp. under water), diving, immersion, bathing, ablution, GṛŚrS.; MBh. &c.; (with *niraye*), sinking into hell, MBh.; drowning, overwhelming, ib.; = *majjan*, marrow, L. **-gata**, mfn. plunged in a bath, MBh. **-maṇḍapa**, m. a bathing-house, bath, Siṇhās. **Majjanônmajjana**, m. du. 'Majjana and Unmajjana,' N. of two demons, Hariv.

Majjayitṛi, mfn. one who causes to sink or plunge, ŚBr.

Majjala, m. N. of one of Skanda's attendants, MBh. (v. l. *majjāna*; cf. *majjana*).

Majjas, n. = *majjan*, marrow, Suśr.

Majjā, f. id., ŚBr.; MaitrUp.; Hariv. (cf. *nir-majja*). **-kara**, n. 'producing marrow,' a bone, L. **-ja**, m. a species of bdellium, L. **-°ṭikā** (°*jjāṭ°*?), f. a partic. weight, Hcat. **-meha**, m. N. of a partic. disease of the urinary organs, ŚārṅgS. **-rajas**, n. a partic. hell, L.; bdellium, L. **-rasa**, m. 'marrow-secretion,' semen virile, L. **-sāra**, n. 'having marrow as its chief ingredient,' a nutmeg, L.

Majjāna. See *majjala*.

Majjikā, f. the female of the Indian crane, W.

Majjūka, mfn. repeatedly diving (used to explain *maṇḍūka*), Nir. ix, 5.

मज्जर *majjara*, m. a kind of grass, L. (v. l. *garjara*).

मज्जूषा *majjūshā*, f. = *mañjūshā*.

मज्मन *majmána*, n. greatness, majesty, RV.; AV.; (*ā*), ind. altogether, generally, at all (with *nákis*, 'no one at all'), RV.

मज्र *majra*. See *khara-majrá*.

मञ्च् *mañc* (= √*mac*; prob. artificial), cl. 1. Ā. *mañcate*, to cheat &c., Dhātup. vi, 12, v. l.; to hold; to grow high; to adore; to shine, vi, 13; to go, move, vii, 15, v. l.

Mañca, m. a stage or platform on a palace or on columns, raised seat, dais, throne, MBh.; Kāv. &c.; a bedstead, couch, Ragh., Sch.; Divyâv.; a pedestal, Baudh.; an elevated platform or shed raised on bamboos in a field (where a watchman is stationed to protect the crop from cattle, birds &c.), W.; (in music) a kind of measure, Saṃgīt. **-nṛitya**, n. a kind of dance, Saṃgīt. **-pīṭha**, n. a seat on a platform, Kāraṇḍ. **-maṇḍapa**, m. a sort of temporary open shed, a pl° erected for partic. ceremonies, W. **-yāpya**, m. N. of a man, Cat. (v. l. *-yayya*). **-yūpa**, m. a post supporting a pl°, R. **-vāṭa**, m. the enclosure of a pl°, Hariv. **-stha**, mfn. standing on a pl°, Pañcar. **Mañcâgāra**, n. (prob.) = *mañca-maṇḍapa*, Hariv. **Mañcârohaṇa**, n. ascending a platform, ib.

Mañcaka, m. n. a stage or platform &c. (see *mañca*), MBh.; a couch, bed, Kathās.; any frame or stand (esp. one for holding fire), TĀr., Sch.; m. (in music) a kind of measure, Saṃgīt.; (*ikā*), f. = *āsandī*, a chair, KātyŚr., Sch.; a kind of trough on legs, Suśr.; (in music) a kind of measure, Saṃgīt. **-gata**, mfn. gone to bed, Sāh. **Mañcakâśraya** or °**yin**, m. 'bed-infesting,' a bed-bug, house-bug, L. **Mañcakâsura**, m. N. of an Asura, Cat.; *-dundubhi-vadha*, m. N. of ch. of GaṇP.

Mañcana, m. (with *ācārya*) N. of a teacher (father of Siṅgāya), Cat.

Mañcayayya. See *mañca-yāpya* above.

Mañci-pattra, n. a species of plant, L.

Mañcukā. See *madana-m°*.

मञ्ज् *mañj* (prob. invented to account for the following words of more or less uncertain origin; cf. √*mārj*, *mṛij*), cl. 10. P. *mañjayati*, to cleanse or be bright; to sound, Dhātup. xxxii, 106, Vop.

Mañjana, m. the son of a Śūdra and a Vaṭī, L.

Mañjara, n. a cluster of blossoms, panicle (as of corn &c.), Bhpr.; a species of plant (= *tilaka*), L.; a pearl, L. (cf. *deva-*); (*ī*), f., see below.

Mañjaraya, Nom. P. °*yati*, to adorn with clusters of blossoms, Vās.

Mañjari, see *mañjarī*. **-dhārin**, mfn. having clusters of flowers, MBh.; R.

Mañjarikā, f. = *mañjarī* (see *kaṭu-m°* and *pushpa-m°*); N. of a princess, Rājat.

Mañjarita, mfn. 'having clusters of flowers' or 'mounted on a stalk,' Amar. (g. *tārakâdi*).

Mañjarī, f. a cluster of blossoms, MBh.; Kāv. &c. (also *°ri*; often at the end of titles of wks., cf. *pradīpa-m°* &c.); a flower, bud, Kāv. (also *°ri*); a shoot, shout, sprig, ib. (also *°ri*); foliage (as an ornament on buildings), Vāstuv.; a parallel line or row, Gīt.; Sāh.; a pearl, L.; N. of various plants (= *tilakā*, *latā*, or holy basil, L.); of 2 metres, Col.; of various wks. **—cāmara**, n. a fan-like sprout, Vikr. **—jāla**, n. a dense mass of buds or flowers, MBh.; *-dhārin*, mfn. thickly covered with b° or f°, ib. **—dīpikā**, f. N. of wk. **—namra**, m. 'bent down with clusters of flowers,' Calamus Rotang, L. **—piñjarita**, mfn. 'having pearls and gold' or 'yellowish coloured with clusters of flowers,' Daś. **—prakāśa** and **-sāra**, m. N. of wks.

Mañjarīka, m. a species of fragrant Tulasī, L.

Mañjarī-√kṛi, P. *-karoti*, to turn into flower-buds, Kāvyâd.

Mañjā, f. = *mañjarī*, a cluster of blossoms &c., L.; = *ajā*, a she-goat, L.

Mañji, f. a cluster of blossoms &c., L. (also *°jī*; cf. *aṅgāra-mañjī*). **—phalā**, f. Musa Sapientum, L.

Mañjikā, f. a harlot, courtezan, L.

Mañjiman, m. (fr. *mañju*) beauty, elegance, W.

Mañjishṭha, mf(*ā*)n. (superl. of *mañju*) very bright, bright red (as the Indian madder), MBh. (perhaps w. r. for *māñjishṭha*); (*ā*), f., see next.

Mañjishṭhā, f. Indian madder, Rubia Munjista, Kauś.; Suśr. **—°bha** (*°ṭhâbha*), mfn. having the colour of I° m°, VarBṛS. **—meha**, m. a disease in which the urine is of a light red colour, Suśr.; *°hin*, mfn. suffering from this disease, ib. **—rāga**, m. the colour or dye of the I° m°, Hariv.; an attachment pleasing and durable as the colour of the I° m°, Sāh.

Mañjī, f. a compound pedicle, L. (cf. *mañji*); a she-goat, L. (cf. *mañjā*).

Mañjīra, m. n. (ifc. f. *ā*) a foot-ornament, anklet, Kāv.; Pur.; m. N. of a poet, Cat.; (*ā*), f. N. of a river, L.; n. a post round which the string of the churning-stick passes, L.; a kind of metre, Col. **—kvaṇita**, n. the tinkling of anklets, Kāv. **—dhvani-komala**, n. N. of wk.

Mañjīraka, m. N. of a man, g. *śivâdi*.

Mañjīla, m. a village inhabited especially by washermen, W.

Mañju, mfn. beautiful, lovely, charming, pleasant, sweet, MBh.; Kāv. &c.; m. (with *bhaṭṭa*) N. of a Sch. on Amara-kośa. **—kula**, m. N. of a man, Buddh. **—keśin**, m. 'beautiful-haired,' N. of Kṛishṇa, L. **—gamana**, mfn. going beautifully or gracefully; (*ā*), f. a goose or a flamingo, L. **—garta**, m. or n. N. of Nepal, W. **—gir**, mfn. sweet-voiced, Kāvyâd. **—gīti**, f. N. of a metre, Col. **—guñja**, m. a charming murmur or humming, ŚārṅgP. **—guñjat-samīra**, mfn. exhaling a sweet-sounding breeze or breath, Śāntiś. **—ghosha**, mfn. uttering a sweet sound, BhP.; m. a dove, L.; = *-śrī*, SaddhP.; (*ā*), f. N. of an Apsaras, L.; of a Surâṅganā, Siṇhâs. **—tara**, mfn. more or most lovely or charming, Gīt. **—deva** and **-nātha**, m. = *-śrī*, Buddh. **—nāśī**, f. (w. r. for *-nārī*?) a beautiful woman, L.; N. of Indra's wife or Durgā, L. **—netra**, mfn. fair-eyed, Dhūrtas. **—paṭṭana** or **-pattana**, n. N. of a town built by Mañju-śrī, Buddh. **—pāṭhaka**, m. 'repeating beautifully,' a parrot, L. **—prâṇa**, m. N. of Brahmā, L. **—bhaṭṭa**, see under *mañju*. **—bhadra**, m. = *-śrī*, L. **—bhāshin**, mfn. sweetly speaking, Ragh.; Kathās.; (*inī*), f. N. of a metre, Col.; of various wks. **—mañjīra**, m. n. a beautiful foot-ornament, Rājat. **—maṇi**, m. 'beautiful gem,' a topaz, L. **—matī**, f. 'the b° one,' N. of a princess, Kathās. **—vaktra**, mfn. b°-faced, lovely, handsome, W. **—vacana** (Pañcar.), **-vāc** (Ragh.), mfn. = *-bhāshin*. **—vādin**, mfn. id.; (*ī*), f. N. of a woman, Daś.; of a metre, Col. **—śrī**, m. N. of one of the most celebrated Bodhisattvas among the northern Buddhists, MWB. 195 &c.; *-paripṛicchā*, f. N. of wk.; *-parvata*, m. N. of a mountain, SaddhP.; *-buddha-kshetra-guṇa-vyūha*, m., *-mūla tantra*, n., *-vikrīḍita*, n., *-vihāra*, m. N. of wks. **—saurabha**, n. a kind of metre, Col. **—svana**, mfn. sweet-sounding, Vikr. **—svara**, mfn. id., MBh.; m. = *-śrī*, Buddh.

Mañjula, mfn. beautiful, pleasing, lovely, charming, Kāv. (cf. g. *sidhmâdi*); m. a species of water-hen or gallinule, L.; (*ā*), f. N. of a river, MBh.; n. a bower, arbour, L. (also m.); a spring, well, L.; the fruit of Ficus Oppositifolia, L.; Blyxa Octandra, L.

Mañjulikā, f. N. of a woman, Kathās.

मञ्जूषा **mañjūshā**, f. (L., also *mañjushā*) a box, chest, case, basket, MBh.; Kāv. &c.; receptacle of or for (often ifc., rarely ibc. in titles of wks.; also N. of various wks. and sometimes abridged for the fuller names, e.g. for *dhātu-nyāya-m°* &c.); Rubia Munjista, Bhpr.; a stone, L. **—kuñcikā**, f. N. of wk.

Mañjūshaka, m. N. of a species of celestial flower, L. (*mañjushaka*, Kāraṇḍ.)

मट **maṭa**, m. (Prākr. for *mṛita*) the son of a Vaiśya and a Kuṭī, L.

Maṭaka, m. or n. a dead body, corpse, Kathās. (cf. *mṛitaka*).

मटची **maṭacī**, f. hail, ChUp. i, 10, 1 (*maṭacyo 'śanayaḥ*, Śaṃk.) **—hata**, mfn. struck by hail, ib.

मटती **maṭatī**, f. hail, W.

मटमटाय **maṭamaṭāya**, *°yati*, onomat., Pāṇ. viii, 1, 12, Vārtt. 8, Pat.

मटुतचण्डी **maṭutacaṇḍī**, f. N. of a Rākshasī, Buddh.

मटुस्फटि **maṭusphaṭi**, m. incipient arrogance or pride (= *darpârambha*), L.

मटूषिका **maṭūshikā**. See *maḍūshikā*.

मट्ट **maṭṭa**, m. a kind of drum, Saṃgīt. (cf. *maḍḍu*); a kind of dance, ib. (also *-nṛitya*, n.)

मट्टक **maṭṭaka**, m. the top of a roof, L.; Eleusine Coracana, L.

मट्मट **maṭmaṭá**, m. a class of demons or evil spirits, AV.

मठ् **maṭh** (prob. invented for the words below), cl. 1. P. *maṭhati*, to dwell or to be intoxicated, Dhātup. ix, 47 (Vop. 'to grind,' others 'to go'): Caus. *maṭhayati*, see *maṭhaya*.

Maṭha, m. n. (g. *ardharcâdi*; *ī*, f., g. *gaurâdi*) a hut, cottage, (esp.) the retired hut (or cell) of an ascetic (or student), MBh.; Kāv. &c.; a cloister, college (esp. for young Brāhmans), temple, ib.; m. a cart or carriage drawn by oxen, L. **—keśava-dhāriṇī**, f. N. of Nandā (the founder of the college of Keśava), Rājat. **—cintā**, f. the charge of a convent, Pañcat. **—pratishṭhā-tattva**, n. N. of wk. **—sthiti**, mfn. staying or residing in a college of priests, MW. **Maṭhâdhipati**, m. the superintendent of a monastery, principal of a college &c., Rājat. **Maṭhâdhyaksha**, m. id., MW. **Maṭhâyatana**, n. a monastery, college, Pañcat.

Maṭhaya, Nom. P. *°yati*, to build, erect, Hcat.

Maṭhara, mfn. (cf. g. *kaḍārâdi*) insisting on (loc.), Rājat.; hard, harsh (of sound), L.; intoxicated, Un. v, 39, Sch.; m. N. of a man (prob. of a saint), ib. (cf. g. *bidâdi* and *gargâdi*); hardness, harshness, L.

Maṭhikā, f. a hut, cell, Daś.; Kathās.; Rājat.

मठोशिलोठिका **maṭhośiloṭhikā**, f. N. of a woman, Rājat.

मडक **maḍaka**, m. Eleusine Corocana, L.; pl. N. of a people, MBh. (B. *māruta*).

मडमड् **maḍamaḍ**, onomat. (with *iti*), crack!, Bālar.

मडरकन्थ **maḍara-kantha**, n. N. of a town, g. *cihaṇâdi* (v.l. *mandar°*; Kāś. *maḍur°*).

मडरराज्य **maḍara-rājya**, n. N. of a district in Kaśmīra, Rājat. (v.l. *maḍava-r°*).

मडार **maḍāra**, g. *pragady-ādi*.

मडूषिका **maḍūshikā**, f. a dwarfish girl unfit for marriage, GṛS. (L. = *svalpa-dehā*; v.l. *maṭūshikā*, *maṇḍūshikā*, *madhūshikā* and *mandhūshikā*).

मड्डचन्द्र **maḍḍa-candra**, m. N. of a man, Rājat.

मड्डु **maḍḍu**, m. a kind of drum, L. (cf. *maṭṭa*). **—kairika**, m. the son of a Nishāda and a Māgadhī, L.

Maḍḍuka, m. = *maḍḍu*, Śiś. v, 29 (v.l. *maṇḍuka*).

मण् **maṇ**, cl. 1. P. *maṇati*, to sound, murmur, Dhātup. xiii, 5.

Maṇita, n. an inarticulate sound said to be uttered (by women, Śiś., Sch.) during cohabitation, murmur libidinosum, Kāv.

मण **maṇa**, m. or n.(?) (fr. Arabic من) a partic. measure of grain, Col.

मणऊ **maṇaū** (fr. Arabic منع), N. of the seventh Yoga (in astronomy).

मणि **maṇí**, m. (*i*, f. only L.; *ī*, f. Siṇhâs.; *maṇīva* = *maṇī* [du.] *iva*, Naish.) a jewel, gem, pearl (also fig.), any ornament or amulet, globule, crystal, RV. &c. &c.; a magnet, loadstone, Kap.; glans penis, Suśr.; N. of the jewel-lotus prayer, MWB. 372; clitoris, L.; the hump (of a camel), MBh.; the dependent fleshy excrescences on a goat's neck, VarBṛS.; thyroid cartilage, L. (cf. *kaṇṭha-m°*); the wrist (= *m°-bandha*), L.; a large water-jar, L.; N. of a Nāga, MBh.; of a companion of Skanda (associated with Su-maṇi), ib.; of a sage, ib.; of a son of Yuyudhāna, ib. (in Hariv. v.l. *tūṇi*); of a king of the Kim-naras, Kāraṇḍ.; of various wks. and a collection of magical formulas (also abridged for Tattva-cintāmaṇi and Siddhânta-śiromaṇi). [Cf. Gk. μάννος, μόννος; Lat. *monile*; Germ. *mane*, *Mähne*; Eng. *mane*.] **—kaṇṭha**, m. the blue jay, L.; N. of a Nāga, Buddh.; of an author, Cat. **—kaṇṭhaka**, m. a cock, L. **—karṇa**, mfn. 'jewel-eared,' having an ornament of any kind (as a mark) on the ear (of cattle &c.), Pāṇ. vi, 3, 115; m. N. of a Liṅga, KālP.; (*ī*), f. = *-karṇikā*, a sacred pool, RāmatUp.; *°ṇīśvara* (Kāśī Kh.) and *°ṇeśvara* (KālP.), m. N. of two Liṅgas. **—karṇikā**, f. an ear-ornament consisting of pearls or jewels; N. of a sacred pool in Benares (also written *-karṇikī*, RāmatUp.), Daś.; RTL. 308; 438; of a daughter of Caṇḍa-ghosha, ib.; *-mahiman*, m. N. of wk.; *-māhātmya*, n. N. of the 22nd ch. of the Uttara-khaṇḍa of the Śiva-Purāṇa; *-shṭaka* (*°kâsht°*), n., *-stotra*, n. N. of wks. **—kāca**, m. the feathered part of an arrow, L. **—kāñcana**, m. N. of a mountain, MBh.; *-prameya-saṃgraha*, m. N. of wk. **—kānana**, n. a wood or grove containing jewels, MW.; the neck (as covered with jewels), L. **—kārá**, m. a lapidary, jeweller, VS.; R. (*ī*, f., Kālac.); the adulterous offspring of Vaiśya parents whose mother's husband is still alive, L.; N. of various authors, Cat. **—kuṭṭikā**, f. N. of one of the Mātṛis attending on Skanda, MBh. **—kusuma**, m. N. of a Jina, W. **—kūṭa**, m. N. of two mountains, Pur. **—kṛit**, m. = *-kāra* (author of the Maṇi), Cat. **—ketu**, m. N. of a partic. comet or meteor, Var. **—khaṇḍa-dvaya-traya**, n. N. of wk. **—gaṇa**, m. pl. pearls, BrahmUp. **—garbha**, m. N. of a park, Divyâv. **—guṇa-nikara**, m. a multitude of strings of pearls, Piṅg.; N. of a metre, Chandom.; Col. **—grantha**, m. N. of wk. **—grāma**, m. N. of a place, Inscr. **—grīvá**, mfn. 'jewel-necked,' wearing a necklace, RV. i, 122, 14; m. N. of a son of Kubera, L. **—ghaṇṭā-kṛita-nyāya-ratna-prakaraṇa**, n. N. of wk. **—cīra**, n. (prob.) a garment adorned with jewels, MBh. **—cūḍa**, m. N. of a Vidyā-dhara, Śatr.; of a Nāga, Buddh.; of a king of Sāketa-nagara (= *ratna-cūḍa*), W.; (*ā*), f. N. of a Kiṃ-narī, Kāraṇḍ. **—cchidrā**, f. 'jewel-holed,' a root resembling ginger (= *medā*), L.; a partic. bulb growing on the Hima-vat (= *ṛishabha*), L. **—jalā**, f. 'having j°-like water,' N. of a river, MBh. **—tāraka**, m. 'jewel-eyed,' the Indian crane, L. (v.l. *-tārava*, *-bhārava*). **—tuṇḍaka**, m. a kind of bird living on the water, Car. **—tulā-koṭi**, f. a foot-ornament consisting of jewels, Kāv. **—daṇḍa**, mfn. having a handle adorned with jewels, R. **—datta**, m. N. of sev. men, Kathās.; Cat. **—dara**, m. N. of a chief of the Yakshas, Kathās. **—darpaṇa**, m. a mirror adorned with j°s or consisting of j°s, Rājat.; N. of sev. wks. **—dīkshitīya**, n. N. of wk. **—dīdhiti**, f. N. of wk.; *-gūḍhârtha-prakāśikā*, f. N. of Comm. on it. **—dīpa**, m. a lamp having j°s instead of a wick, Rājat. (also *°paka*, m.); N. of wk. **—dosha**, m. a flaw or defect in a j°, L. **—dvīpa**, m. 'j°-island,' the hood of the serpent Ananta, L.; N. of a mythical island in the ocean of nectar, Ānand. **—dhanu**, m. (AdbhBr.; Āpast.) or **-dhanus**, n. (Gaut.; PārGṛ.) 'j°-bow,' a rain-bow. **—dhara**, mfn. having a string of beads for counting, BhP.; m. a partic. Samādhi, Kāraṇḍ.; (*ā*), f. a partic. position of the fingers, ib. **—dhāna**, m. N. of a king, VP. (also read *-dhāna*, *-dhānya*, *-dhānyaka* or *-dhāra*).

-dhāriṇī, f. N. of a Kim-nara maid, Kāraṇḍ. **-dhāva,** m., v.l. for *-dhāna* or *-dhāra* (q.v.), VP. **-nanda,** m. N. of sev. authors, Cat. **-nāga,** m. N. of a snake-demon, MBh.; Hariv.; m. or n. (?) N. of a sacred bathing-place, MBh. **-niryātana,** n. the restitution of a jewel, R. **-pati-caritra,** n. N. of wk. **-padma,** m. N. of a Bodhi-sattva, W. **-parīkshā,** f. N. of wk. **-parvata,** m. 'jewel-mountain,' N. of a mythical mountain, Hariv. **-pālī,** f. a female keeper of jewels, g. *revaty-ādi.* **-puccha,** mf(*ī*)n. having lumps on the tail, Pāṇ. iv, 1, 55, Vārtt. 2, Pat. **-pura,** n. N. of town (= *-pūra,* n.), MBh.; *-purêśvara,* m. = *-pūr°,* q. v., Rājat. **-pushpaka,** m. N. of the conch-shell of Saha-deva, Bhag. **-pushpêśvara,** m. N. of one of Śiva's attendants, Kathās. **-pūra,** m. the navel, L.; a sort of bodice (worn by women and richly adorned with jewels), L.; n. a partic. mystical circle on the navel, Pañcar.; Ānand.; N. of a town in Kaliṅga situated on the sea-shore (also read *-pura,* n.), MBh.; Rājat.; *-pati,* m. N. of king Babhru-vāhana, Rājat.; BhP.; *-vibhedana,* n. N. of a jewel, MW.; *°rêśvara,* m. = *°rapati,* q. v., MBh. **-pūraka,** n. N. of a mystical circle on the navel, Cat. **-prakāśa,** m., **-prakāśaka-dīpti,** f., **-prakāśikā,** f., **-pratyaksha,** n. N. of wks. **-pradāna,** n. N. of the 34th ch. of the Sundara-kāṇḍa of the Rāmāyaṇa. **-pradīpa,** m. = *-dīpa* (q. v.), BhP.; ŚārṅgP.; N. of wk. **-prabhā,** f. 'jewel-splendour,' N. of a metre, Inscr.; of an Apsaras, Kāraṇḍ. (w. r. *-prastha*); of a lake, Cat.; of a wk. **-pravāla,** m. or n. (?) N. of wk. **-praveka,** m. a most excellent jewel, MBh. **-prastha,** (prob.) w. r. for *-prabhā* (q. v.), Kāraṇḍ. iii, 12. **-bandha,** m. the fastening or putting on of j°s, Ragh.; the wrist (as the place on which j°s are fastened), Suśr.; GāruḍaP.; a kind of metre, Col.; N. of a mixed race, ib. **-bandhana,** n. the fastening on of j°s, MW.; a string of pearls, an ornament of p°, MBh.; the part of a ring or bracelet where the j°s are set, MW.; the wrist, Śak.; Var.; Suśr.; &c. **-bīja,** m. the pomegranate tree, L. **-bhadra,** m. N. of a brother of Kubera and king of the Yakshas (the tutelary deity of travellers and merchants), MBh.; Kathās.; Daś. &c.; of a Śreshṭhin, Pañcat.; of a poet, Subh. **-bhadraka,** m. pl. N. of a race, MBh. (also read *pāri-bh°*); of a serpent-demon, Cat. **-bhava,** m. N. of one of the 5 Dhyāni-Buddhas, W. **-bhārava,** m., see *-tāraka.* **-bhitti,** f. 'jewel-walled,' N. of the palace of the serpent-demon Śesha, L. **-bhū,** f. a floor inlaid with j°s, L. **-bhūmi,** f. = prec., L.; a mine of j°s, L. **-bhūmikā-karman,** n. the inlaying or covering of a floor with j°s (one of the 64 arts; accord. to a Schol. = *kritrima-putrikā-nirmāṇa*), Cat. **-mañjarī,** f. rows of j°s or pearls, Gīt.; a species of metre, Col.; N. of sev. wks.; *-chedinī,* f. N. of wk. **-maṇḍapa,** m. a crystal hall or a h° on crystal pillars, Pañcar.; Rudray.; N. of the residence of Śesha, L.; of the residence of Nairṛita (the ruler of the south-west quarter), L.; *-māhātmya,* n. N. of wk. **-maṇḍita,** mfn. set or studded with j°s or pearls, MW. **-mat,** mfn. adorned with j°s, jewelled, BhP.; m. the sun, MW.; N. of a Yaksha, MBh.; of a servant of Śiva, BhP.; of a Rakshas, MBh.; of a Nāga, ib.; of a king (who was Vṛitra in a former birth), ib.; of a mountain, ib.; R.; Var.; of a Tīrtha, MBh.; (*atī*), f. N. of a town of the Daityas, MBh.; Hariv.; of a river, W. **-madhya,** n. N. of 2 metres, Śrutab.; Chandom.; Col. **-mantha,** m. N. of a mountain, MBh.; n. rock-salt, L. **-maya,** mf(*ī*)n. formed or consisting of jewels, crystalline, MBh.; Hariv.; Kāv. &c.; *°yī purī,* f. N. of a mythical town of the Nirvāta-kavacas, R.; *-bhū,* f. a jewelled floor, Megh. **-mahêśa,** m. N. of a Tīrtha, Cat. **-mālā,** f. a string or necklace of jewels or pearls, Chandom.; a circular impression left by a bite (esp. in amorous dalliance), L.; lustre, beauty, L.; a kind of metre, Chandom.; Col.; N. of Lakshmī, L.; of wk. **-māhātmya,** n. N. of wk. **-miśra,** m. N. of 2 authors, Cat. **-muktā,** f. N. of a river, Cat. **-mekhala,** mfn. girdled with gems, surrounded by j°s, Ṛitus. **-megha,** m. N. of a mountain, MārkP. **-yashṭi,** f. a string of pearls, Vikr.; a jewelled stick, MW. **-rata** (?), m. N. of a teacher, Buddh. **-ratna,** n. a jewel, gem, Hariv.; R. (with Buddhists 'one of a sovereign's 7 treasures,' Dharmaś. 85); *-maya,* mf(*ī*)n. formed or consisting of j°s, crystalline, MBh.; *-mālā,* f. 'garland of j°s,' N. of 2 wks.; *-vat,* mfn. containing jewels, MBh.; *-suvarṇin,* mfn. containing precious stones and gold, R.; *°nâkara,* m. N. of a wk. (also called *nāma-r°*). **-radana,** mfn. pearl-toothed, Bhām. **-rāga,** mfn. having the colour of a jewel, L.; m. the colour of a j°, Var.; a kind of metre, L.; n. vermilion, L.; a kind of ruby, L. **-rāja,** m. 'j°-king,' (prob.) a diamond (cf. *maṇîndra*), Pañcar.; N. of a king, Virac. **-rāma,** m. N. of sev. authors; *-kṛishṇa-dīkshitīya,* n. N. of wk. **-rūpya,** see *māṇirūpyaka.* **-rocanī,** f. N. of a Kim-nara maid, Kāraṇḍ. **-liṅgêśvara,** m. N. of one of the 8 Vīta-rāgas, W. **-vara,** m. N. of a man, Hariv.; n. a diamond, Bhpr. **-varman,** m. N. of a merchant, Kathās.; n. a talisman consisting of jewels, Divyâv. **-vâla,** mfn. (prob.) having beads (or lumps of excrement) on the tail (accord. to Mahī-dhara = *maṇi-śuddha-vāla* or *maṇi-varṇa-keśa*), VS. **-vāhana,** m. 'j°-bearer,' N. of Kuśâmba or Kuśa, MBh.; Hariv. **-viśesha,** m. a kind of j°, an excellent j°, MW. **-śaṅkha-śarkara,** mfn. having j°-like shells and gravel, ib. **-śabda,** m. N. of wk. **-śara,** see *-sara.* **-śilā,** f. a jewelled slab, MW. **-śṛiṅga,** m. the god of the sun, Hariv. **-śekhara,** m. N. of a Gandharva, Bālar. **-śaila,** m. 'j°-mountain,' N. of a m°, MārkP. **-śyāma,** mfn. dark-blue like a jewel (i. e. like a sapphire), MBh. **-sara,** m. a string or ornament of pearls, Gīt. (w. r. *-śara;* cf. *muktā-m°*). **-sānu,** m. 'jewel-ridged,' N. of mount Meru, L. **-sāra,** m. or n. (?), N. of a Nyāya wk.; *-khaṇḍana,* n., *-darpaṇa,* m., *-prāmāṇya-vāda,* m. N. of wks. **-sūtra,** n. a string of pearls, L. **-sopāna,** n. steps or stairs formed of j°s or crystal, Hariv.; a chain of golden beads, L. **-saupāna** (!), m. a staff or stick set with j°s, W. **-skandha,** m. N. of a snake-demon, MBh. (v. l. *maṇi* and *skandha* as 2 names). **-stambha,** m. a crystal post or column, BhP. **-sraj,** f. a garland of j°s, Pañcar. **-harmya,** n. 'jewelled palace, crystal p°,' N. of a p°, Vikr. **Maṇîndra,** m. 'jewel-chief,' a diamond, Pañcar. **Maṇîśvara-tīrtha,** n. N. of a Tīrtha, Cat. **Maṇy-āloka,** m. N. of wk.; *-kaṇṭakôddhāra,* m. N. of Comm. on it.

Maṇika, m. a jewel, gem, precious stone, MW.; (ifc. f. *ā*) a water-jar or pitcher, AdbhBr.; GṛS.; KātyŚr., Sch.; MBh.; pl. (accord. to Sāy.) globular formations of flesh on an animal's shoulder, AitBr.

Maṇilá, mfn. having fleshy excrescences (as on the dew-lap &c.), TS., Comm.

Maṇiva, mfn. in *a-m°,* q. v.; m. N. of a serpent-demon, Siddh.

Maṇica, n. a hand, L.; a flower, L.; a pearl, L.

Maṇīcaka, m. a king-fisher, halcyon, L.; n. a partic. jewel, = *candra-kānta,* L.; a flower, L. (cf. *maṇīvaka*).

Maṇīya, Nom. Ā. *°yate,* to resemble a jewel, Cat.

Maṇīvaka, m. N. of a son of Bhavya; n. N. of the Varsha ruled by that king, VP. (v. l. *shaṇīv°*); a flower, L.

Maṇivatī, f. N., g. *śarâdi.*

मणित्थ *maṇittha,* m. N. of an astronomer (= Manetho), VarBṛ. **-varsha-phala,** n. N. of wk.

मण्ट् *maṇṭ,* cl. 10. P. *maṇṭayati,* to act as an intermediator, TBr. (Sch.)

मण्टप *maṇṭapa,* m. n. = *maṇḍapa,* L.; (*ī*), f. a kind of purslain, L. (v. l. *maṇḍapī*).

मण्टि *maṇṭi,* m. N. of a man, Pravar. (prob. w. r. for *mānti*).

मण्ठ् *maṇṭh,* cl. 1. Ā. *maṇṭhate,* to long for, desire eagerly, Dhātup. viii, 10.

मण्ठ *maṇṭha,* m. a sort of baked sweet-meat, Bhpr.

Maṇṭhaka, m. id., ib.; a partic. musical air, Cat.

मण्ड् *maṇḍ,* cl. 1. P. *maṇḍati,* to deck, adorn, Dhātup. ix, 36; Ā. *maṇḍate,* to distribute or to clothe, viii, 19: Caus. *maṇḍayati* (ep. also *°te*), to adorn, decorate (Ā. 'one's self,' Pāṇ. iii, 1, 87, Vārtt. 18, Pat.), MBh.; Kāv. &c.; to glorify, extol, Prasannar.; to rejoice, exhilarate, L.

Maṇḍa, m. n. (ifc. f. *ā*) the scum of boiled rice (or any grain), Nir.; Uttarar.; Suśr.; the thick part of milk, cream, ŚvetUp.; MBh. &c. (cf. *dadhi-m°*); the spirituous part of wine &c., Hariv.; R. (W. also 'foam or froth; pith, essence; the head'); m. (only L.) Ricinus Communis; a species of potherb; a frog (cf. *maṇḍūka*); ornament, decoration; a measure of weight (= 5 Māshas); (*ā*), f. the emblic myrobalan tree, L.; spirituous or vinous liquor, brandy, L.; n., see *nau-maṇḍá.* **-karṇa,** m. N. of a man (see *māṇḍakarṇi*). **-kuṇḍa,** see *kuṇḍa-m°.* **-citra,** m. N. of a man; pl. his family, Saṃskārak. **-jāta,** n. the second change which takes place in sour milk when mixed with Takra, L. **-pa,** mfn. (Uṇ. iii, 145, Sch.) drinking the scum of boiled rice or of any liquor, Pañcar.; m. n. (g. *ardharcâdi;* L. also *ī,* f.; cf. *maṇṭapī*) an open hall or temporary shed (erected on festive occasions), pavilion, tent, temple; (ifc. with names of plants) arbour, bower, Hariv.; Kāv. &c.; m. N. of a man, Cat.; (*ā*), f. a sort of leguminous plant (= *nishpāvī*), L.; *-pa-kshetra,* n. N. of a sacred district, Kathās.; *-pa-druma,* m., *-pa-nirṇaya,* m., *-pa-pūjā-vidhi,* m. N. of wks.; *-pa-pratishṭhā,* f. the consecration of a temple, MW.; *-°pâroha,* m. a species of plant, L.; *°pikā,* f. a small pavilion, an open hall or shed, Kād.; Bālar. **-pīṭhikā,** f. two quarters of the compass, L. **-pūla,** m. or n. (?) a top-boot, L. **-maya,** mf(*ī*)n. made of cream or from the scum of any liquid, MBh. **-vāṭa,** m. a garden (?), Divyâv. (cf. *maṇḍala-v°*). **-hāraka,** m. a distiller of spirits &c. (the son of a Nishṭhya and a Śūdrā), L. **Maṇḍôdaka,** n. barm, yeast, Suśr.; the decorating of walls &c. on festive occasions, L.; 'mental excitement' or 'variegated colour' (*citta-* or *citra rāga*), L.

Maṇḍaka (ifc., with f. *ikā*), rice-gruel, Hariv.; m. a sort of pastry or baked flour, Pañcat.; Śukas.; Bhpr. (cf. *maṇṭhaka*); a partic. musical air, Saṃgīt. (cf. id.); pl. N. of a people, VP. (cf. *mandaka*).

Maṇḍana, mfn. adorning, being an ornament to (gen.), Kāv.; Pur.; m. N. of various authors and other men (also with *kavi, bhaṭṭa, miśra* &c.), Cat.; n. (ifc. f. *ā*) adorning, ornament, decoration, MBh.; Kāv. &c. **-kārikā,** f. N. of wk. **-kāla,** m. time for adorning, Ragh. **-priya,** mf(*ā*)n. fond of ornaments, Pañcat. (cf. *priya-m°*). **Maṇḍanârha,** mfn. worthy of ornaments, MW.

Maṇḍanaka. See *mukha-m°.*

Maṇḍayanta, m. (only L.) an ornament; an actor; an assembly of women; food; (*ī*), f. a woman, L.

Maṇḍika, m. pl. N. of a people, MBh. (B. *śuṇḍika;* cf. *maṇḍaka*).

Maṇḍita, mfn. adorned, decorated, MBh.; Kāv. &c.; m. (with Jainas) N. of one of the 11 Gaṇādhipas, L. **-putra,** m. = prec. m., L.

Maṇḍitṛi, mfn. adorning, one who adorns (= ornament), Bālar.

Maṇḍīlaka, m. a kind of cake, Divyâv.

मण्डप *maṇḍa-pa.* See under *maṇḍa* above.

मण्डर *maṇḍara,* m. or n., g. *aṅguly-ādi;* (*ī*), f. a sort of cricket, L. (cf. *māṇḍarika*).

मण्डल *máṇḍala,* mf(*ā*)n. circular, round, VarBṛS.; n. (rarely m., g. *ardharcâdi,* and f. *ī,* g. *gaurâdi*) a disk (esp. of the sun or moon); anything round (but in Hcat. also applied to anything triangular; cf. *maṇḍalaka*); a circle (instr. 'in a circle;' also 'the charmed c° of a conjuror'), globe, orb, ring, circumference, ball, wheel, ŚBr. &c. &c.; the path or orbit of a heavenly body, Sūryas.; a halo round the sun or moon, VarBṛS.; a ball for playing, MBh.; a circular bandage (in surgery), Suśr.; (also n. pl.) a sort of cutaneous eruption or leprosy with circular spots, ib.; a round mole or mark (caused by a finger-nail &c.) on the body, Lāṭy.; KātyŚr., Sch.; a circular array of troops, MBh.; Kām.; a partic. attitude in shooting, L.; a district, arrondissement, territory, province, country (often at the end of modern names, e. g. Coro-mandal), Inscr.; AVPariś.; MBh. &c.; a surrounding district or neighbouring state, the circle of a king's near and distant neighbours (with whom he must maintain political and diplomatic relations; 4 or 6 or 10 or even 12 such neighbouring princes are enumerated), Mn. (esp. vii, 154 &c.); Yājñ.; MBh. &c.; a multitude, group, band, collection, whole body, society, company, Yājñ.; MBh.; Kāv. &c.; a division or book of the Ṛig-veda (of which there are 10, according to the authorship of the hymns; these are divided into 85 Anuvākas or lessons, and these again into 1017, or with the 11 additional hymns into 1028 Sūktas or hymns; the other more mechanical division is into Ashṭakas, Adhyāyas and Vargas, q. v.), RPrāt.; Bṛih. &c.; m. a dog, L.; a kind of snake, L.; (*ī*), f. Panicum Dactylon, L.; Cocculus Cordifolius, Bhpr.; n. Unguis Odoratus, L.; a partic. oblation or sacrifice, L. **-kavi,** m. a poet for the crowd, bad poet, Dhanaṃj. **-kārmuka,** mfn. 'having a circular bow,' one whose bow is completely bent, MBh. **-cihna,** n. the sign or mark of a circle, Cat. **-tva**, n. roundness, Śiś. **-nābhi**, m. centre i.e. chief of the circle of neighbouring princes (*-tā*, f.), Ragh. **-nṛitya**, n. a circular dance (like that said to have been danced by the Gopīs round Kṛishṇa and Rādhā), L. (v. l. °*lī-n*°). **-nyāsa**, m. the putting down or drawing a circle (°*saṃ* √*kṛi*, to describe a circle), Kathās. **-pattrikā**, f. a red-flowering Punarnavā, L. (cf. *maṇḍali-p*°). **-pucchaka**, m. a species of insect, Suśr. **-bandha**, m. formation of a circle or roundness, Śiś. **-brāhmaṇa**, n. (and °*nôpanishad*), f. N. of wks. **-bhāga**, m. part of a circle, arc, Jyot. **-māḍa**, m. a pavilion, L. **-vaṭa**, m. an Indian fig-tree forming a circle, Pañcat. (cf. *maṇḍalin*). **-vartin**, m. the governor of a province, ruler of a small kingdom, BhP. (cf. *cakra-v*°). **-varsha**, n. (prob.) universal or lasting rain, VarBṛS. **-vāṭa**, m. a garden, Divyâv. (cf. *maṇḍa-v*°). **-śas**, ind. by circles, in rings, MBh. **Maṇḍalâgra**, mfn. round-pointed (as a sword), VarBṛS.; m. (n.) a bent or rounded sword, scimitar, Rājat.; n. (scil. *śastra*) a surgeon's circular knife, Suśr. **Maṇḍalâdhipa** (Kām.), °**lâdhīśa** (Pañcar.), m. the lord of a district, governor or king of a country. **Maṇḍalâbhisheka-pūjā**, f., °**lârcana**, n. N. of wks. **Maṇḍalâsana**, mfn. sitting in a circle, Śiś. **Maṇḍal'-īśa**, m. 'lord of rings' and = next, Śṛiṅgār. **Maṇḍalêśa**, m. the ruler of a country, sovereign (*-tva*, n.), Rājat. **Maṇḍalêśvara**, m. id., Vcar. **Maṇḍalêshṭakā**, f. a round or circular brick, TS.; ĀpŚr. **Maṇḍalôttama**, n. the best or principal kingdom, MW.

Maṇḍalaka, n. a disk, circle, orb &c. (= *maṇḍala*), Yājñ.; MBh. (also applied to a square, Hcat.); a sacred circle, Divyâv.; a cutaneous disease with round spots, L.; a circular array of troops, L.; a mirror, L.; a group, collection, mass, heap, MBh.; (*ikā*), f. a group, troop, band, crowd, Śiś.; m. a dog, L.; N. of a prince, VP. **-rājan**, m. the prince of a small district or province, L.

Maṇḍalaya, Nom. P. °*yati*, to whirl round, Kir.

Maṇḍalāya, Nom. Ā. °*yate*, to become or form one's self into a circle or ring, coil one's self, Ratnâv.

Maṇḍalika, w.r. for *māṇḍalika*, q.v.

Maṇḍalita, mfn. made round or circular (see next). **-hasta-kāṇḍa**, mfn. having a trunk formed in rings or circles (said of an elephant), Daś.

Maṇḍalin, mfn. forming a circle or ring, surrounding, enclosing (ifc.), Kathās.; (with *vāta*, m.) a whirlwind, R.; marked with round spots (as a snake), L.; possessing or ruling a country, Lalit.; m. the ruler of a province (with Śaivas, a partic. order or degree), Sarvad.; the sun, L.; a snake or a partic. species of snake (cf. above), MBh.; Var.; Suśr.; a chameleon, L.; a cat, L.; a polecat, L.; a dog, L.; the Indian fig-tree, L.; (*inī*), f. Cocculus Cordifolius, L.

Maṇḍali-pattrikā, f. = *maṇḍala-p*°, L.

Maṇḍalī, in comp. for *maṇḍala*. **-karaṇa**, n. rounding, gathering in a ball or circle, coiling, W. **-kāram**, ind. rounding, making round, Baudh. **-kṛita**, mfn. (√*kṛi*) made circular, curved, bent (as a bow), rounded, MBh.; R.; Hariv. **-nṛitya**, n., see *maṇḍala-n*°. **-bhāva**, m. circular form, roundness, Hcat. **-bhūta**, mfn. (√*bhū*) become round or circular, curved, bent (as a bow), MBh.; Var.

मण्डिक *maṇḍika*, *maṇḍita* &c. See p. 775, col. 3.

मण्डु *maṇḍu*, m. N. of a Ṛishi, ŚāṅkhGṛ. (cf. g. *gargâdi* and *māṇḍavya*).

Maṇḍuka, m. or n. = *saṃgraha*, Śiś. xviii, 21 (Sch.); v.l. for *madduka*, ib. v, 29 (see also *paṅka-maṇḍuka*); m. pl. N. of a people, VP.; (*ī*), f. the third part of an elephant's hind leg, L.

Maṇḍukeya, m., v.l. for *māṇḍukeya*, VP.

मण्डूक *maṇḍūka*, m. (ifc. f. *ā*) a frog, RV. &c. &c.; N. of a partic. breed of horses, MBh.; Calosanthes Indica, L.; a machine like a frog, L.; the sole of a horse's hoof, L.; N. of a Ṛishi, Pāṇ. iv, 1, 119; of a Nāga, L.; (*ī*), f. a female frog, RV.; N. of various plants (Hydrocotyle Asiatica, Clerodendrum Siphonantus, Ruta Graveolens &c.), L.; a wanton woman, L.; the sole of a horse's hoof, L.; n. a kind of coitus, L. **-kula**, n. a collection or assembly of frogs, Ritus. **-gati**, f. the gait of a frog (*-lālasa*, mfn. ardently desiring the gait of a frog), Pañcar.; mfn. (in gram.) leaping like a frog i.e. skipping several Sūtras, Pat. **-parṇa**, m. Calosanthes Indica, L.; = *kapītana*, L.; (*ī*), f. N. of various plants (Rubia Munjista, Clerodendrum Siphonantus &c.), Bhpr.; L. **-parṇikā**, f. a species of plant, L. **-pluta**, n. (prob.) = *-pluti*; *-sādhana*, n. N. of wk. **-pluti**, f. 'frog-leap,' (in gram.) the skipping of several Sūtras and supplying from a previous Sūtra, Pāṇ., Sch. **-brahmī-kalpa**, m. N. of wk. **-mātṛi**, f. 'frog-mother,' Clerodendrum Siphonantus, L. **-yoga**, m. 'frog-meditation' (in which an ascetic sits motionless like a f°); *-niyata*, mfn. intent upon the f°-med°, MBh.; *-śayana*, mfn. lying on the ground in the f°-med°, ib. **-śāyin**, mfn. lying like a f°, MBh. **-śikshā**, f. N. of wk. (cf. *māṇḍūkī-ś*). **-sarasa**, n. a f°-pond, Pāṇ. v, 4, 94, Sch. **Maṇḍūkânuvṛitti**, f. 'frog-course,' skipping over or omitting at intervals, MW. (cf. *maṇḍūka-pluti*).

Maṇḍūkikā, f. a female frog, Suparṇ.

मण्डूर *maṇḍūra*, n. rust of iron, L. **-dhāṇikī**, f. (prob.) having an impure pudendum, RV. x, 155, 4.

मत् *mát*. See 3. *ma* and 1. *mád*.

मत *mata*, *mataṃ-ga* &c. See under √*man*, p. 783, col. 1.

मतल्लिका *matallikā*, f. (ifc.) anything excellent of its kind (e.g. *go-m*°, 'an excellent cow'), g. *matallikâdi* (Gaṇar.); a kind of metre, Col.

Matallī, f. anything excellent &c. (= prec.), Sāh.

मतस्न *mátasna*, n. du. N. of partic. internal organs of the body, RV.; AV.; VS. (*hṛida-yôbhaya-pārśva-sthe asthinī*, two bones situated on either side of the heart, Mahīdh.)

मति *mati* &c. See p. 783, col. 2.

मतिनार *matināra*, m. N. of a king, MBh.; Hariv.; Pur.

मतिल *matila*, m. N. of a king, Inscr.

मतीकृ *matī-√kṛi*. See under *matya*.

मतुथ *matútha*, m. (√*man*) an intelligent person, RV. iv, 71, 5 (= *medhāvin*, Naigh. iii, 15).

मतुल *matula*, m. or n. (?) a partic. high number, Buddh.

मत्क 1. *matka*, m. (for 2. see p. 777, col. 2) a bug, L.

Matkuṇa, m. a bug, Kāv.; Pur.; Suśr. (*-tva*, n., Śiś.); a beardless man, L.; an elephant without tusks or of small stature, L.; a buffalo, L.; a cocoa-nut, L.; (*ā*), f. pudendum (of a young girl = *ajāta-loma-bhaga*), L.; N. of a river, VP.; n. armour for the thighs or legs, greaves, L. **-gandha**, mfn. having the smell of a bug, Suśr. **Matkuṇâri**, m. 'bug-enemy,' hemp, L.

Matkuṇikā, f. N. of one of the Mātṛis attending on Skanda, MBh. (B. °*kulikā*).

मत्कोटक *matkoṭaka*, m. a termite, HPariś.

मत्त *matta* &c. See p. 777, col. 3.

मत्य 1. *matyà*, n. (for 2. see p. 783, col. 2) a harrow, roller, TS.; Br.; a club (perhaps with iron points), AV.; harrowing, rolling, making even or level, L.

Matī-√kṛi, P. *-karoti*, to harrow, roll, make even by rolling, AitBr. (cf. *dur-matī-kṛita*).

मत्स *matsa*, m. (fr. √2. *mad*, 'the gay one') a fish (= *matsya*; cf. *maccha*), L. (*ī*, f. a female fish, Kāv.); the king of the Matsyas, MBh. iv, 145 (B. *matsya*). **-gaṇṭa** or **-gaṇṭha**, m. a kind of fish-sauce, L. (cf. *matsya-ghaṇṭa*). **Matsôdarī**, v.l. for *matsyôdarī*, q.v.

Matsará (prob. fr. √2. *mad*; cf. Uṇ. iii, 73), exhilarating, intoxicating, RV.; cheerful, joyous, gay, ib.; selfish, greedy, envious, jealous, hostile, wicked, Kāv.; m. the exhilarater, gladdener (Soma), RV.; selfishness, envy, jealousy, hostility, MBh.; Kāv. &c.; wrath, anger, ib.; passion for (loc. or comp.), MBh.; Hariv.; N. of a Sādhya, Hariv.; (also *ā*, f.) a fly, mosquito, L.; (*ī*), f. (in music) a partic. Mūrchanā, Saṃgīt. **-manas**, mfn. of envious disposition, ŚārṅgP. **-vat** (°*rá-*), mfn. exhilarating, intoxicating, RV. ix, 97, 32.

Matsarín, mfn. exhilarating, intoxicating, RV. (superl. °*rín-tama*); jealous, envious, wicked, bad, Mn.; MBh. &c.; addicted to, fond of (loc.), R. (cf. *a-m*°); m. an enemy, Harav.

Matsarī-kṛitā, f. (in music) a partic. Mūrchanā, Saṃgīt.

Matsin, mfn. containing fish, marked by water (as a boundary), Nār.

Mátsya, m. (cf. *matsa* and *maccha*) a fish, RV. &c. &c. (personified as a prince with the patr. *Sām-mada*, ŚBr.); a partic. species of f°, L.; (in astron.) the figure of a f° (= *timi*), Sūryas.; a partic. luminous appearance, VarBṛS.; (du.) the 12th sign of the zodiac (Pisces), Jyot.; a partic. figure (= *svastika-madhyâkṛiti*), Hcat.; (pl.) N. of a people and country (which accord. to Mn. ii, 19 forms part of Brahmarshi), RV. &c. &c.; a king of the Matsyas (cf. *matsa*); N. of Virāṭa (as having been found by fishermen, along with his sister Matsyā or Satya-vatī, in the body of the Apsaras Adrikā, metamorphosed into a fish), MBh.; N. of a pupil of Deva-mitra Śākalya, Cat.; (*ā*), f. a female fish, Uṇ. iv, 104, Sch.; N. of the sister of king Virāṭa (cf. above), MBh.; (*ī*), f., see *matsa* and g. *gaurâdi*. **-karaṇḍikā**, f. a fish-basket, any receptacle for fish, L. **-kūrmâdy-avatārin**, m. 'descending (and become incarnate) as a fish, tortoise &c.,' N. of Vishṇu, MW. **-gandha**, mf(*ā*)n. having the smell of f°, MBh.; m. (pl.) N. of a race, Saṃskārak.; (*ā*), f. N. of Satya-vatī (mother of Vyāsa, also called Mīna-gandha; see *matsya* above), MBh.; Commelina Salicifolia, L. **-gu**, m. N. of Cyavana, L. **-ghaṇṭa**, m. a kind of fish-sauce or a dish of fish, L. (cf. *matsa-gaṇṭa*). **-ghāta**, m. the killing or catching of f°, Mn. x, 45. **-ghātin**, mfn. killing f°; m. a fisherman, MBh. (also with *purusha*, Kathās.) **-jāla**, n. a fishing-net, L. **-jīvat** or **-jīvin** (v. l.), mfn. living by catching f°, a fisherman, Pañcat. **-tantra**, n. N. of wk. (prob. = *-sūkta*). **-deśa**, m. the country of the Matsyas (cf. above), Cat. **-dvādaśikā** or °**daśī**, f. N. of the 12th day in one of the halves of the month Mārgaśīrsha, ib. **-dvīpa**, m. 'fish-island,' N. of a Dvīpa, VP. **-dhānī**, f. 'fish-holder,' a fish-basket or a kind of snare for catching fish, L. **-dhvaja**, m. a f°-banner, Ragh.; N. of a mountain, KālP. **-nātha**, m. 'fish-lord,' N. of a man, Cat. (cf. *matsyêndra*). **-nārī**, f. 'f°-woman i.e. half f° half w°,' N. of Satya-vatī, Cat. **-nāśaka** and **-nāśana**, m. 'f°-destroyer,' a sea-eagle, osprey, L. **-pittā**, f. Helleborus Niger, L. **-purāṇa**, n. 'f°-Purāṇa,' N. of one of the 18 Purāṇas (so called as communicated by Vishṇu in the form of a fish to the 7th Manu; cf. *matsyâvatāra* and IW. 512). **-prādur-bhāva**, m. 'f°-manifestation,' Vishṇu's f° incarnation, N. of ch. of the NarasP. (cf. *matsyâ-vatāra*). **-bandha**, m. fish-catcher, a fisherman, MBh. **-bandhana**, n. a f°-hook, L.; (*ī*), f. a f°-basket, L. **-bandhin**, m. = *-bandha*, Pañcat.; (*inī*), f. a fish-basket (v. l. for *-bandhanī*), L. **-māṃsa**, n. f°-flesh, Mn. iii, 268. **-mādhava**, n. N. of a Tīrtha, Cat. **-raṅka** or **-raṅga**, °**gaka**, m. a halcyon, king-fisher, L. **-rāja**, m. pl. fish-kings, the best of fishes, Bhpr.; Cyprinus Rohita, L.; a king of the Matsyas, MBh. **-vid**, mfn. knowing fish, an ichthyologist, ŚāṅkhŚr. **-vinnā**, f. a species of plant, L. **-vedhana**, n. 'f°-piercing,' a f°-hook, angle, L.; (*ī*), f. id., L.; a cormorant, L. **-vratin**, mfn. one who lives in water, L. **-śakalā**, f. Helleborus Niger, Bhpr. **-sagandhin**, mfn. = *-gandha*, MBh. **-saṃghāta**, m. a shoal of young fry or small fish, L. **-saṃtānika**, m. a partic. dish of fish (eaten with condiments or oil), L. **-sūkta**, n. N. of wk. **-hán**, m. 'fish-killer,' a fisherman, ŚBr. **Matsyâkshaka**, m. 'f°-eyed (?),' a species of Soma plant, Car.; Suśr.; (*ā*), f. id., L.; (*ikā*), f. a kind of grass, L. **Matsyâkshī**, f. = prec. m., L.; Hincha Repens, L.; Solanum Indicum, L.; a kind of grass (= *gaṇḍa-dūrvā*), L. **Matsyâṅgī**, w.r. for *matsyâkshī*. **Matsyâṇḍa**, n. fish-roe, Bhpr. **Matsyâd**, mfn. 'fish-eating,' feeding on fish, L. **Matsyâda**, mfn. id., Mn.; Pañcat. **Matsyâdanī**, f. Commelina Salicifolia, L. **Matsyâvatāra**, m. 'fish-descent,' N. of the first of the 10 incarnations of Vishṇu (who became a fish to save the 7th Manu from the universal deluge; the conversation between them forms the Matsya-Purāṇa, q.v.; in MBh. i. the fish is represented as an incarnation of Brahmā; cf. IW. 327, 397 &c.); *-kathana*, n., *-prabandha*, m. N. of wk. **Matsyâśana**, m. 'feeding on fish,' a halcyon, king-fisher, L. **Matsyâśin**, mfn. eating fish, living on fish, Bhpr. **Matsyâsura**, m. 'fish-Asura,' N. of an As°, Cat.; *-śaila-vadha*, m. N. of ch. of GaṇP. ii. **Matsyêndra**, m. N. of a teacher of Yoga, Cat.; of an author (-*muhūrta*, m. or n. N. of his wk.), ib. **Matsyêśvara-tîrtha**, n. N. of a Tîrtha, Cat. **Matsyôtthā**, f. 'sprung from a fish,' N. of Satya-vatī, Gal. (see under *matsya* above). **Matsyô-darin**, m. N. of Matsya or Virāṭa (as the brother of Matsyôdarī), Cat. **Matsyôdarī**, f. 'sprung from a fish-belly,' N. of Satya-vatī, L. (see under *matsya* above); N. of a sacred bathing-place in Benares, Cat. **Matsyôdarīya**, mfn. relating to a fish-belly; m. N. of Vyāsa (son of Matsyôdarī, q.v.), MBh. **Matsyôpajīvin**, m. 'living by fish,' a fisherman, MBh.; R. (cf. *matsya-jīvat*, °*vin*).

Matsyaka, m. a little fish, MBh.

मत्सर *matsara*, °*rin*. See p. 776, col. 2.

मत्स्य *matsya* &c. See p. 776, col. 3.

मत्स्यण्डिका *matsyaṇḍikā*, f. inspissated juice of the sugar-cane, Mālav.; Car.; Suśr.

Matsyaṇḍī, f. id., Bhpr.

मथ् 1. *math* or *manth* (q.v.), cl. 1. 9. P. (Dhātup. xx, 18, iii, 5 and xxxi, 40) *má-thati*, *mánthati*, *mathnā́ti* (Ved. and ep. also Ā. *máthate*, *mánthate* and *mathnīte*; Impv. *math-nadhvam*, MBh.; pf. *mamātha*, AV.; 3. pl. *ma-mathuḥ*, Vop.; *methuḥ*, *methire*, Br.; *mamantha*, °*nthuḥ*, MBh.; aor. *mathīt*, RV.; *amanthishṭām*, ib.; *amathishata*, Br.; fut. *mathishyati*, °*te*; *man-thishyati*, Br. &c.; *mathitā*, MBh.; inf. *mathitum*, MBh. &c.; °*tos*, Br.; *mánthitavaí*, MaitrS.; ind. p. *mathitvā́*, -*máthya*, Br. &c.; *manthitvā*, Pāṇ. i, 2, 33; -*manthya* and -*mātham*, MBh. &c.), to stir or whirl round, RV. &c. &c.; (with *agnim*), to produce fire by rapidly whirling round or rotating a dry stick (*araṇi*) in another dry stick prepared to receive it, ib.; (with *araṇim*), to rotate the stick for producing fire, MBh.; Kāv.; Pur.; (with *ūrum*, *has-tam* &c.), to use friction upon any part of the body with the object of producing offspring from it, Hariv.; BhP.; to churn (milk into butter), produce by churn-ing, TS. &c. &c. (also with two acc., e.g. *sudhām kshīra-nidhim mathnāti*, 'he churns nectar out of the ocean of milk,' Siddh. on Pāṇ. i, 4, 51); to mix, mingle, Suśr.; to stir up, shake, agitate, trouble, dis-turb, afflict, distress, hurt, destroy, AV. &c. &c.: Pass. *mathyáte* (ep. also °*ti*), to be stirred up or churned &c., RV. &c. &c.: Caus. *manthayati* (Lāṭy.), *māthayati* (MBh.), to cause to be stirred up or churned &c.: Desid. *mimathishati*, *miman-thishati*, Gr.: Intens. *māmathyate*, *māmantti* &c., ib. [Cf. Gk. μίνθη; Lat. *mentha*, *menta*; Lit. *mentùrė*; Germ. *minza*, *Minze*; Angl. Sax. *minte*; Eng. *mint*.]

2. **Math**, (ifc.) destroying, a destroyer (cf. *madhu-math*); m., see *mathin*.

Matha, m. = *mātha*, g. *jvalâdi*.

Mathaka, m. N. of a man; pl. his descendants, g. *yaskâdi* (v.l. for *manthaka*).

Mathan (only instr. *mathnā*), a piece of wood for producing fire by attrition, BhP.

Mathana, mf(*ī*, once *ā*)n. rubbing, stirring, shaking, harassing, destroying (with gen. or ifc.), MBh.; R. &c.; m. Premna Spinosa (the wood of which is used to produce fire by attrition), L.; n. the act of rubbing, friction, BhP.; stirring or whirling round, churning or producing by churning, MBh.; R.; Pur.; hurting, annoying, injury, destruction, R.; Ratnâv. **Mathanâcala**, m. the mountain (Man-dara, q.v.) used as a churning-stick (by the gods and Dānavas in churning the ocean of milk), BhP. (cf. *mantha-śaila*).

Mathāya, Nom. P. °*yáti*, to produce fire by fric-tion, RV.; to tear off (a head), ib.; to shake, AV.

Mathi (ifc.; cf. Pāṇ. iii, 2, 27), see *urā-*, *vas-tra-* and *havir-māthi* (*mathīnām*, RV. viii, 53, 8 prob. w. r. for *matīnām*; cf. *mathin*).

Mathita, mfn. stirred round, churned or pro-duced by churning, RV.; shaken, agitated, afflicted, hurt, destroyed, MBh.; R.; Hariv.; dislocated, dis-jointed, Suśr.; m. N. of a descendant of Yama (and supposed author of RV. x, 19), RAnukr.; n. butter-milk churned without water, Kauś.; MBh. &c. **-pādapa**, mfn. (a wood) whose trees are damaged or destroyed, Hariv. **Mathitôrasa**, mfn. one whose breast is pierced or wounded (by arrows), ib. (v.l. *vyath*°).

Mathitṛi, mfn. (ifc.) crushing, destroying, Ānand.

Mathin, m. (strong stem *mánthan*, older *mán-thā*; middle *mathin* or *mathi* [q.v.]; sg. nom. *mánthās*, acc. *mánthām* [for *manthānam* see *manthāna* under √*manth*]; instr. *mathā́*, du. *ma-thibhyām*, pl. *mathibhyas* &c. [cf. *pathin* and Pāṇ. vii, 1, 83 &c.]; for *mathīnām* see *mathi* above) a churning-stick, any stick or staff for stirring or churn-ing, RV. &c. &c.; the penis, L.; a thunderbolt, L.; wind, L.

Mathīna, °*nati* (artificial Nom. fr. *mathin*), Siddh. on Pāṇ. vi, 4, 13.

Mathná (only *mathnā́*, RV. i, 181, 5), prob. w. r. for *mathrá*.

Mathya, mfn. to be rubbed out of (see *ulmuka-m*°); to be extracted or produced from (see *sindhu-m*°).

Mathrá, mfn. shaken, agitated, whirling, RV. (cf. *mathná*).

Mantha, **manthya** &c. See under √*manth*.

मथव्य *mathavyà*, prob. w.r. for *madh*°, AV.

मथा *mathā*, ind. a Nidhana formula, Lāṭy.

मथात *mathāta*. See *māthāta*.

मथु *mathu*, m. a proper N. (= *madhu*; cf. *māthava*).

मथुर *mathura*, m. (√*math*?) N. of a man (cf. *māthura*); (*ā*), f., see next.

Mathurā, f. N. of various towns (esp. of an an-cient town now called Muttra and held in great honour as the birthplace of Kṛishṇa; situated in the province of Agra on the right bank of the Yamunā or Jumnā; described in VP. xii, 1 as having been founded by Śatru-ghna; accord. to Kull. on Mn. ii, 19 it forms part of a district called Brahmarshi, be-longing to Śūra-sena), AVPariś.; Hariv.; Pur. &c. **-kāṇḍa**, n. **-guhya-varṇana**, n., **-campū**, f., **-tīrtha-māhātmya**, n. N. of wks. **-dāsa**, m. N. of the author of the drama Vṛishabhânujā. **-nā-ṭaka**, n. N. of a drama. **-nātha** (also °*ra-n*°), m. 'lord of Mathurā,' N. of Kṛishṇa, Pañcar.; N. of various men and authors (also with *śukla*, *cakra-vartin* and *tarka-vāg-īśa*); -*jāti-mālā*, f. N. of wk.; -*rāya*, m. N. of a man, Cat.; °*thīya*, n. N. of wk. **-mahiman**, m., **-māhātmya**, n., **-māhātmya-saṃgraha**, m., **-setu**, m. N. of wks. **Mathu-rêśa**, m. 'lord of Mathurā,' N. of Kṛishṇa, L.; of various authors (also with *vidyâlaṃkāra*), Cat.

Mathūrā, f. = *mathurā* above, L.

मद् 1. *mad*, base of the first pers. pron. in the sg. number (esp. in comp.) **-artha**, m. my pur-pose; (*am*), ind. for the sake of me, Bhag. **-deha**, m. my body, ib. **-bandhana-samudbhava**, mfn. caused by the binding of me i.e. by my bondage, ib. **-bhakta**, mfn. devoted to me, ib. **-bhāva**, m. my essence, ib. **-√bhū**, P. -*bhavati*, to become I, ib. **-vacana**, n. my word, my order; (*āt*), ind. in my name, from me, ib. **-1. -vat**, ind. (for 2. see p. 779, col. 2) like me, Kathās. **-vargīṇa** or **-vargīya** or **-vargya**, mfn. belonging to my class or party, connected with or related to me, Siddh. **-vidha**, mfn. like me, equal to me, of my sort or kind, MBh.; Kāv.; Pur. **-viyoga**, m. separation from me, Bhag. **-vihīna**, mfn. separated from me, ib.

Mac, in comp. for 1. *mad*. **-citta**, mfn. having the mind (fixed) on me, thinking of me, Bhag. **-charīra** (*mad* + *śar*°), n. my body, ib.

Mat, in comp. for 1. *mad*. **-kṛita** (*mát-*), mfn. done by me, RV.; MBh. **-tara**, mfn., compar., Pāṇ. vii, 2, 98, Sch. **-para**, **-parama** or **-parâ-yaṇa**, mfn. devoted to me, Bhag. **-putra**, m. the son of me, my son, MW. **-pūrva**, mfn. one who has lived before me, MārkP.; m. my elder brother, R. **-prasūta**, mfn. produced from me, MW. **-sakāśe**, ind. in my presence, ib. **-sakhi** (*mát-*), m. my companion, my friend, RV. **-saṃsthā**, f. union with me, Bhag. **-saṃdeśa**, m. news or tid-ings of me, ib. **-samaksham**, ind. in my sight or presence, ib. **-sama-tva** or **-sādṛiśya**, n. like-ness or resemblance of me, ib.

2. **Matka**, mfn. (for 1. see p. 776, col. 2) mine, my, Bālar.; Bhaṭṭ.

Madīya, mfn. my, my own, belonging to me, MBh.; Kāv. &c.

1. **Madya** (for 2. see p. 779, col. 1), Nom. P. °*yati*, Pāṇ. vii, 2, 98, Sch.

Madrik, ind. (fr. next) to me, towards me, RV.

Madryañc, mfn. directed towards me, RV.; (*âk*), ind. towards me, ib. (cf. *asmadryañc*).

Madryadrik, ind. = *madrik*.

Man, in comp. for 1. *mad*. **-manasa**, mf(*ā*)n. thinking of me, PārGṛ. **-maya**, mf(*ī*)n. consisting of or proceeding from me, full of me, like me, Bhag.; Hariv.

मद् 2. *mad* (cf. √*mand*), cl. 4. P. (Dhātup. xxvi, 99) *mádyati* (ep. also °*te*; Ved. also 1. P. Ā. *madati*, °*te*; 3. P. *mamátti*, °*ttu*, *mamá-dat*, *ámamaduḥ*; Ved. Impv. *mátsi*, °*sva*; pf. *ma-māda*; aor. *amādishuḥ*, *amatsuḥ*, *amatta*; Subj. *mátsati*, °*sat*; fut. *maditā*, *madishyati*, Gr.; Ved. inf. *maditos*), to rejoice, be glad, exult, delight or revel in (instr., gen., loc., rarely acc.), be drunk (also fig.) with (instr.), RV. &c. &c.; to enjoy heavenly bliss (said of gods and deceased ancestors), RV.; TBr.; to boil, bubble (as water), RV.; TS.; ŚBr.; Hariv.; to gladden, exhilarate, intoxicate, animate, inspire, RV.: Caus. *mādáyati*, °*te* (Dhātup. xxxiii, 31, xix, 54; aor. *ámīmadat* or *amamadat*; Ved. inf. *mā-dayádhyai*), to gladden, delight, satisfy, exhilarate, intoxicate, inflame, inspire, RV. &c. &c.; (Ā.) to be glad, rejoice, be pleased or happy or at ease, RV.; VS.; Kauś.; (Ā.) to enjoy heavenly bliss, RV.; TBr.; BhP.: Desid. *mimadishati*, Gr.: Intens. *māmad-yate*, *māmatti*, ib. [Perhaps orig. 'to be moist;' cf. Gk. μαδάω; Lat. *madere*.]

Matta, mfn. excited with joy, overjoyed, de-lighted, drunk, intoxicated (lit. and fig.), AV. &c. &c.; excited by sexual passion or desire, in rut, rut-tish (as an elephant), MBh.; R. &c.; furious, mad, insane, ib.; m. a buffalo, L.; the Indian cuckoo, L.; a drunkard, L.; a ruttish or furious elephant, L.; a madman, L.; a thorn-apple, L.; N. of a Rākshasa, R.; (*ā*), f. any intoxicating drink, spirituous or vinous liquor, L.; N. of a metre, Col. [cf. Lat. *mattus*, drunk]. **-kāla**, m. N. of a king of Lāṭa, Daś. **-kāśinī**, f. 'appearing intoxicated,' a be-witching or wanton woman (esp. used in address), MBh.; Kāv. &c. (also written -*kāsinī* or -*kāshiṇī*). **-kīśa**, m. an elephant, L. **-gāminī**, f. 'having the gait of an elephant in rut,' a woman with a rolling walk, a bewitching or wanton woman, L. **-dantin**, m. a furious or ruttish el°, W. **-nāga**, m. id., L.; N. of an author, Cat. **-mayūra**, m. a peacock in-toxicated with joy or passion, L.; m. N. of a man, L.; pl. = next, Nilak.; n. a kind of metre, Col. **-mayūraka**, m. pl. N. of a warrior-tribe, MBh. **-mātaṃga-līlâkara**, m. or n. (?) N. of a metre, Col. **-vāṅ-mauna-mūlikā**, f. N. of wk. **-vā-raṇa**, m. = -*dantin*, Vās. (-*vikrama*, mfn. having the might of a mad elephant, Ml.); m. or n. = *mat-tâlamba*, L.; n. a turret, pinnacle, pavilion, Vās.; a peg or bracket projecting from a wall, L.; a bed-stead, L. **-vāraṇīya**, mfn. attached to the turret (of a car), Bālar. **-vilāsinī**, f. N. of a metre, L. **-hastin**, m. = -*dantin*, Mālav. **Mattâkrīḍā**, f. N. of a metre, Col. **Mattâlamba**, m. a fence or hedge round the house of a rich man, L. **Mattê-bha**, m. = *matta-dantin*; -*kumbha-pariṇāhin*, mfn. round as the frontal globes of an elephant in rut, Pañcat.; -*gamanā*, f. = *matta-gāminī*, L.; -*vi-krīḍita*, n. N. of a metre, L.; °*bhâsya* (?), n. N. of wk.

Mattaka, mfn. somewhat drunk or intoxicated, MW.; somewhat proud or overbearing, Hariv.; m. N. of a Brāhman, Rājat. vi, 339 (perhaps *sumano-m*° in one word).

Máda, m. hilarity, rapture, excitement, inspira-tion, intoxication, RV. &c. &c.; (du. with *madasya*, N. of 2 Sāmans, ĀrshBr.); ardent passion for (comp.), MBh.; (ifc. f. *ā*) sexual desire or enjoyment, wanton-ness, lust, ruttishness, rut (esp. of an elephant), MBh.; Kāv. &c.; (ifc. f. *ā*), pride, arrogance, presumption, conceit of or about (gen. or comp.), ib.; any ex-hilarating or intoxicating drink, spirituous liquor, wine, Soma, RV. &c. &c.; honey, Ragh.; the fluid or juice that exudes from a rutting elephant's temples, MBh.; Kāv. &c.; semen virile, L.; musk, L.; any beautiful object, L.; a river, L.; N. of the 7th astrol. mansion, Var.; Intoxication or Insanity per-sonified (as a monster created by Cyavana), MBh.; N. of a son of Brahmā, VP.; of a Dānava, Hariv.; of a servant of Śiva, BhP.; (*ī*), f. any agricultural implement (as a plough &c.), L.; n. N. of 2 Sāmans, ĀrshBr. **-kara**, mf(*ī*)n. causing intoxication, in-toxicating, Suśr. **-karin**, m. an elephant in rut, Rājat. **-kala**, mfn. sounding or singing softly or indistinctly (as if intoxicated), MBh.; Kāv.; drunk, intoxicated (with liquor or passion), ruttish, furious, mad, Kālid.; m. an elephant, L.; -*kokila-kūjita*, n. the warbling of Kokilas during the breed-ing season, Vikr.; -*yuvati*, f. a young woman intoxicated with love, ib. **— kāraṇa,** n. a cause of pride or arrogance, MW. **— kārin** (ŚārṅgS.), **-kṛit** (Suśr.), mfn. = *-kara.* **— kohala,** m. a bull set at liberty (at a festival and allowed to range about at will), L. **— gandha,** m. Alstonia Scholaris, L.; (*ā*), f. an intoxicating beverage, L.; Linum Usitatissimum or Crotolaria Juncea, L. **— gamana,** prob. w. r. for *manda-g°.* **— guru-paksha,** mfn. having wings heavy with honey (as bees), Ragh. **— ghnī,** f. 'destroying intoxication,' a species of leguminous plant (= *pūtikā*), L. **— cyút,** mfn. reeling with excitement, wanton, intoxicated, exhilarated or inspired with Soma, RV.; gladdening, exhilarating, inspiriting, ib.; emitting temple-juice (as an elephant in rut), BhP. **— cyuta** (*máda-*), mfn. staggering or reeling with intoxication, RV. **— jala,** n. the temple-juice (of a ruttish el°), Prab. **— jvara,** m. the fever of passion or pride, Bhartṛ. **— durdina,** n. large exudation of t°-juice, Ragh. **— dvipa,** m. a ruttish or furious elephant, Kāv. **— dhāra,** m. N. of a king, MBh. **— paṭu,** mfn. ruttish, MBh.; ind. (to sing) loud or shrill, Ragh. **— pati,** m. 'lord of the Soma-juice,' N. of Indra and Vishṇu, RV. **— prada,** mfn. 'intoxicating' and 'causing arrogance,' Kāv. **— prayoga,** m. the issue of temple-juice (in a rutting elephant), L. **— praseka,** m. id.; R.; the aphrodisiacal fluid (of a woman), Mṛicch. iv, 14 (perhaps 'sprinkling with wine'). **— prasravaṇa,** n. = *-prayoga,* MBh. **— bhaṅga,** m. breach or humiliation of pride, Bhām. **— bhañjinī,** f. 'destroying intoxication,' Asparagus Racemosus, L. (cf. *-ghnī*). **— mattaka,** m. a kind of thorn-apple, L. **— mattā,** f. N. of a metre, Col. **— muc,** mfn. emitting temple-juice (as a rutting elephant), Uttarar. **— mohita,** mfn. stupefied by drunkenness, Mn. xi, 97; infatuated by pride, MW. **— rāga,** m. 'affected by passion or by intoxication,' the god of love, L.; a cock, L.; a drunken man, MW. **— rudra-datta,** m. N. of an author, Cat. **— lekhā,** f. a line formed by the rut-juice (on an elephant's temples), Chandom.; a kind of metre, Śrutab. **— vallabha,** m. N. of a Gandharva, Bālar. **— vāraṇa,** m. a furious elephant, Śrīkaṇṭh. **— vāri,** n. = *-jala,* Pañcat. **— vikshipta,** mfn. 'distracted by passion,' ruttish, furious (as an elephant), L. **— vihvala** or **°lita,** mfn. excited by passion, lustful, wanton, R. **— vīrya,** n. the power of passion or fury, Pañcat. **— vṛiddha** (*máda-*), mfn. invigorated or inspired by Soma-juice, RV. **— vyādhi,** n. = *madâtyaya,* L. **— śāka,** m. Portulaca Quadrifiga, L. **— śauṇḍaka,** n. a nutmeg, L. **— sāra,** m. Salmalia Malabarica, L. **— sthala** or **-sthāna,** n. 'place of intoxication,' a drinking-house, tavern, L. **— srāvin,** mfn. = *-muc,* MBh. **— hastinī,** f. a species of Karañja, L. **— hetu,** m. 'cause of intoxication,' Grislea Tomentosa, L. **Madâkula,** mfn. agitated by passion or lust, furious with rut, Ṛitus. **Madâgha,** m. N. of a man; pl. his descendants, g. *upakâdi.* **Madâḍhya,** mfn. rich in or filled with wine, intoxicated, drunk, W.; m. the wine-palm, L; Nauclea Cadamba, L.; a red-flowering Barleria, L. **Madâtaṅka,** m. = *madâtyaya,* L. **Madâtmânanda,** m. N. of an author, Cat. **Madâtyaya,** m. 'passing off of wine,' disorder resulting from intoxication (as head-ache &c.), Suśr. (cf. *pānâtyaya*); *°tyayita,* mfn. suffering from this disorder, Car. **Madândha,** mfn. blind through drunkenness or passion, infatuated, ruttish (as an elephant), MBh.; Kāv.; Pur.; (*ā*), f. N. of a metre, Col. **Madâpanaya,** m. removal of intoxication, Prab. **Madâmnāta,** m. a kettle-drum carried on an elephant, L. **Madâmbara,** m. the elephant of Indra or an el° in rut, L. **Madâmbu** and **°mbhas,** n. = *mada-jala,* Śiś. **Madâlasa,** mfn. lazy from drunkenness, languid, indolent, slothful, Kāv.; (*ā*), f. N. of the daughter of the Gandharva Viśvā-vasu (carried off by the Daitya Pātāla-ketu, and subsequently the wife of Kuvalayâśva), Pur.; of the daughter of the Rākshasa Bhramara-ketu, Uttamac.; of a poetess, Cat.; *°sa-campū,* f., *°sa-nāṭaka,* n., *°sâkhyāyikā* (or *°sâkh°*?), f., *°sā-pariṇaya,* m. N. of wks. **Madâlāpin,** m. 'uttering sounds of love or joy,' the Indian cuckoo or koil, L. **Madâ-vat,** mfn. intoxicated, drunk, AV. **Madâvasthā,** f. a state of passion, ruttishness, Kathās. **Madâhva,** m. musk, L. **Máderaghu,** mfn. (fr. loc. *made* + *r°*) eager with enthusiasm, RV. **Madôtkaṭa,** mfn. excited by drink, intoxicated, R.; excited by passion, furious, ib.; ruttish, MBh.; m. an elephant in rut, L.; a dove, L.; N. of a lion, Pañcat.; (*ā*), f. an intoxicating beverage, L.; Linum Usitatissimum, L.; N. of the goddess Dākshāyaṇī (as worshipped in Caitraratha), Cat.; n. an intoxicating drink made from honey or the blossoms of the Bassia Latifolia, L. **Madôdagra,** mf(*ā*)n. much excited, furious, Ragh.; arrogant, haughty, L. **Madôdarkā,** f. a collective N. of the 3 myrobolans (Terminalia Chebula, T. Bellerica and Phyllanthus Emblica), L. **Madôddhata,** mfn. intoxicated, L.; puffed up with pride, arrogant, Kām. **Madôdreka,** m. Melia Bukayun, L. **Madônmatta,** mfn. intoxicated with passion (rut) or pride, Pañcat. **Madôrjita,** mfn. swollen with pride, haughty with arrogance, Rājat. **Madôllāpin,** m. the Indian cuckoo, L. (cf. *madâlāpin*).

Mádana, m. (ifc. f. *ā*) passion, love or the god of love, MBh.; Kāv. &c.; a kind of embrace, L.; the season of spring, L.; a bee, L.; (?) bees-wax (see *-paṭṭikā*); Vanguiera Spinosa, Suśr.; a thorn-apple and various other plants (e.g. Phaseolus Radiatus, Acacia Catechu &c.), L.; a bird, L.; (in music) a kind of measure, Saṃgīt.; (in astrol.) N. of the 7th mansion, Var.; N. of various men and authors (also with *ācārya, bhaṭṭa, sarasvatī* &c.; cf. below), Rājat.; Inscr.; Cat.; (*ā*), f. any intoxicating drink, spirituous liquor, L.; (*ī*), f. id., L.; musk, L.; N. of a plant (= *atimukta*), L.; the civet-cat, L.; n. the act of intoxicating or exhilarating, MW.; (scil. *astra*), N. of a mythical weapon, R. (v. l. *mādana*); bees-wax, L.; mfn. = *mandrá,* Nir. **— kaṇṭaka,** m. erection of hair caused by a thrill of love, A.; Vanguiera Spinosa, L. **— kalaha,** m. a love-quarrel, Mālatīm. **— kāku-rava,** m. a pigeon, L. **— kīrti,** m. N. of a poet, Cat. **— klishṭa,** mfn. pained by love, Śak. **— gṛiha,** n. N. of a partic. Prākṛit metre, Col. **— gopāla,** m. 'herdsman of l°,' N. of Kṛishṇa, PadmaP.; N. of the preceptor of Vaikuṇṭha-purī, Cat.; *-vāda-prabandha,* m., *-vilāsa,* m. N. of wks. **— caturdaśī,** f. N. of a festival in honour of Kāma-deva on the 14th day in the light half of the month Caitra, L. **— tantra,** n. the science of sexual love, Daś. **— tṛishṇā,** f. 'love-thirst,' N. of a dancing girl, Kautukas. **— trayodaśī,** f. N. of a festival in honour of Kāma-deva on the 13th day in the light half of the month Caitra, L. **— daṇshṭrā,** f. N. of a princess, Kathās. **— damana,** m. 'Kāma-deva's subduer,' N. of Śiva, Daś. **— dahana,** m. 'K°'s burner or consumer,' N. of Śiva-Rudra (and so of the number eleven), Piṅg. **— dvādaśī,** f. the 12th day of the light half of the month Caitra (sacred to K°), MW. **— dvish,** m. 'enemy of K°,' N. of Śiva, Bālar. **— dhvajā,** f. the 15th day in the light half of the month Caitra, L. **— nālikā,** f. a faithless wife, L. **— nṛipa,** m. N. of an author (= *-pāla*), Cat. **— pakshin,** m. a kind of bird (= *sārikā*), L. **— paṭṭikā,** f. (prob.) a wax-tablet, Cat. **— parājaya,** m. N. of wk. **— pāṭhaka,** m. 'announcer of love or the spring,' the Indian cuckoo, L. **— pārijāta,** m. N. of a compendium of rules of morality and ritual composed by Viśvêśvara (see next). **— pāla,** m. N. of a king (patron of Viśvêśvara &c. and supposed author of various wks.); *-vinoda-nighaṇṭu,* m. = *madana-vinoda,* q. v. **— pīḍā,** f. = *-bādhā,* A. **— pura,** n. N. of a town, Kathās. **— prabha,** m. N. of a Vidyā-dhara, ib.; (*ā*), f. N. of a Surâṅganā, Siṅhās. **— phala,** n. the fruit of Vanguiera Spinosa, Suśr. **— bādhā,** f. the pain or disquietude of love, Vikr. **— bhavana,** n. 'abode of love or matrimony,' (in astrol.) a partic. station or state of the heavenly bodies, L. **— bhūshaṇa,** n. N. of a play. **— mañcukā,** f. N. of a daughter of Madana-vega and Kaliṅga-senā (the 6th Lambaka in the Kathās. is called after her), Kathās. **— mañjarī,** f. N. of a daughter of the Yaksha prince Dundubhi, ib.; of a Surâṅganā, Siṅhās.; of other women, Vcar.; of a Sārikā, Vet.; of a drama, Cat. **— manohara,** m. N. of an author (son of Madhu-sūdana Paṇḍita-rāja), Cat. **— maya,** mf(*ī*)n. entirely under the influence of the god of love, Kāv. **— maha,** m. a festival held in honour of Kāma-deva, Ratnâv.; *°hôtsava,* m. id., ib. **— mahârṇava,** m. N. of 2 wks. **— mālā** (Kathās.), **-mālinī** (Vās., Introd.), f. N. of two women. **— miśra,** m. N. of a man, W. **— mukha-capeṭā,** f. N. of wk. **— modaka,** m. a partic. medicinal powder, L. **— mohana,** m. 'the infatuater of the god of love,' N. of Kṛishṇa, PadmaP.; (*nī*), f. N. of a Surâṅganā, Siṅhās. **— yashṭi-ketu,** m. a kind of flag, Kād. **— ratna,** n. N. of wk.; *-nighaṇṭu,* m., *-pradīpa,* m. N. of wks. **— rāja,** m. N. of a man, Rājat. **— ripu,** m. = *-dvish,* Bhartṛ. **— rekhā,** f. N. of the supposed mother of Vikramâditya, Inscr.; of a divine female, Siṅhās. **— lalita,** mf(*ā*)n. amorously sporting or dallying, Chandom.; (*ā*), f. a kind of metre, ib. **— lekha,** m. a love-letter, Śak.; (*ā*), f. id., Sarvad.; N. of a daughter of Pratāpa-mukha (king of Vārāṇasi), Kath.; of another woman, ib. **— vatī,** f. N. of a town, Vcar. **— vaśa,** mfn. influenced by love, enamoured, A. **— vahni-śikhâvalī,** f. the flame of the fire of love, Śṛiṅgār. **— vinoda,** m. N. of a medical vocabulary (written in 1375 and attributed to Madana-pāla, q. v.) **— vega,** m. N. of a king of the Vidyā-dharas, Kathās. **— śalākā,** f. Turdus Salica (= *sārikā*), L.; the female of the Indian cuckoo, L.; an aphrodisiac, L. **— śikhipīḍā,** f. the pain of the fire of love, Kuval. **— saṃjīvana,** n. N. of a drama, Cat.; (*ī*), f. N. of a divine female, Siṅhâs.; of a treatise on erotics, Cat. **— saṃdeśa,** m. a message of love, Mālav. **— sārikā,** f. Turdus Salica, L. **— siṅha,** m. N. of various authors, Cat. **— sundarī** and **-senā,** f. N. of various women, Siṅhâs. **— harā,** f. (Prākṛit for *-gṛiha*) N. of a metre, Col. **Madanâgraka,** m. Paspalum Scrobiculatum, L. **Madanâṅkuśa,** m. the penis, L.; a finger-nail, L. **Madanâcārya,** m. N. of a teacher, Cat. **Madanâtapatra,** n. the vulva, Bhpr. **Madanâtura,** mfn. love-sick, Ragh. **Madanâditya,** m. N. of a man, Rājat. **Madanântaka,** m. 'Kāma-deva's destroyer,' N. of Śiva, Bhartṛ. **Madanândha-miśra,** m. N. of a man, Hāsy. **Madanâbhirāma,** m. N. of a prince, Caurap. **Madanâyudha,** n. pudendum muliebre, L. **Madanâyusha,** m. a species of shrub, L. **Madanâri,** m. = *°na-dvish,* Prasannar. **Madanârṇava,** m. 'sea of love,' N. of wk. **Madanâlaya,** m. 'love-dwelling,' pudendum muliebre, L.; a lotus, L.; a sovereign, prince, L.; = *°na-bhavana,* L. **Madanâvastha,** mfn. being in a state of love, enamoured, Śak.; (*ā*), f. the being in love, Ratnâv. **Madanâśaya,** m. sexual desire, VarBṛS. **Madanêcchā-phala,** n. a species of mango, L. **Madanôtsava,** m. Kāma-deva's festival (= *°na-maha*), the holy or vernal f°, L. (cf. RTL. 430); a partic. game, Cat.; (*ā*), f. a courtezan of Svarga, L. **Madanôtsuka,** mfn. pining or languid with love, Vikr. **Madanôdaya,** m. 'rising of l°,' N. of wk. **Madanôdyāna,** n. 'love's garden,' N. of a garden, Mālatīm.

Madanaka, m. Artemisia Indica, L. (prob. w. r. for *damanaka*); the thorn-apple, L.; n. bees-wax, Bhpr.; (*ikā*), f. N. of a woman, Mṛicch.

Madanāya, Nom. Ā. *°yate,* to resemble the god of love, Hariv.

Madanīya, mfn. intoxicating, Nir.; exciting passion or love, Ṛitus.

Madantikā, f. (in music) a partic. Śruti, Saṃgīt.

Mádantī, f. id., ib.; pl. (with or scil. *āpas*) bubbling or boiling water, RV.

Madayat, mfn. (fr. Caus.) intoxicating &c.; (*antī*), f. Arabian or wild jasmine, L.; N. of the wife of Kalmāsha-pāda or Mitra-saha, MBh.; Pur.

Madayantikā, f. Arabian jasmine, VarYogay.; N. of a woman, Mālatīm.

Madayitṛi, mfn. intoxicating, an intoxicater, maddener, delighter, Ragh.

Madayitnu, m. 'intoxicating &c.,' (only L.) the god of love; a distiller of spirituous liquor; a drunken man; a cloud; m. n. spirituous liquor.

Madāmada, mfn. being in perpetual excitement, KaṭhUp.

Madāra, m. (only L.; cf. Uṇ. iii, 134) a hog; an elephant (in rut); a thorn-apple; a lover, libertine; a kind of perfume; N. of a prince.

Madin, mfn. intoxicating, exhilarating, delighting, lovely (compar. *°din-tara,* superl. *°din-tama*), RV.; VS.; VPrāt.

Madira, mfn. = prec., RV. &c. &c.; m. a species of red-flowering Khadira, L.; (*ā*), f., see below. **— dṛiś,** mfn. 'having intoxicating or fascinating eyes,' lovely-eyed, Viddh.; f. a fascinating woman, ib. **— nayana,** mf(*ā*)n. id., Kautukas. **Madirâksha,** mf(*ī*)n. id., Vikr.; Kāvyâd.; m. N. of a younger brother of Śatânīka, MBh. **Madirâyata-nayanā,** f. a mistress with fascinating and lovely eyes, Śak. **Madirâśva,** m. N. of a Rājarshi and of a king (son of Daśâśva and grandson of Ikshvāku), MBh. **Madirêkshaṇa,** mf(*ā*)n. = *°ra-dṛiś,* Vikr.; *-vallabhā,* f. a mistress with fascinating eyes, Śak. (v. l.)

Madirā, f. spirituous liquor, any inebriating drink, wine, nectar, Mn.; MBh. &c.; a wagtail (esp. in the pairing season, = *matta-khañjana*), L.; a kind of metre, Col.; N. of Durgā, Hariv.; of the wife of Varuṇa, VP.; of one of the wives of Vasu-deva, ib.; Pur.; of the mother of Kādambarī, Kād. **— gṛiha,**

n. a drinking-house, tavern, L. **-madândha**, mfn. blind through drunkenness, dead drunk, BhP. **-maya**, mf(*ī*)n. consisting of intoxicating liquor, Hcar. **-°rṇava** (°*rârṇ*°), m. N. of wk. **-vatī**, f. N. of a girl (and of Kathās. xiii so called after her); of another girl, Hcar. **-vaśa-ga**, mfn. subdued by i.e. drunk with wine, Hariv. **-śālā**, f. = *-gṛiha*, MW. **-sakha**, m. 'friend of wine,' the mango tree, L. **-°sava** (°*râs*°), m. any intoxicating liquor, R. **Madirôtkaṭa**, mfn. excited or intoxicated with spirituous liquor, R. **Madirônmatta**, mfn. drunk with wine or spirituous liquor, MaitrUp.

Mádishṭha, mf(*ā*)n. (superl. of *madín*) very intoxicating or exhilarating &c., RV.; AV.; Pañcav-Br.; (*ā*), f. any intoxicating beverage, L.

Madishṇu, mfn. = *mandu*, Nir. iv, 12.

Madúgha, m. N. of a plant yielding honey or a species of liquorice, AV.; Kauś.

Madura, m. a bird, L.; N. of a prince, VP.

Maderú, mfn. 'very intoxicating' or 'worthy of praise,' RV. x, 106, 6 (Sāy.)

2. **Mádya**, mf(*ā*)n. (for 1. see p. 777, col. 2) intoxicating, exhilarating, gladdening, lovely, RV.; n. any intoxicating drink, vinous or spirituous liquor, wine, Mn.; MBh. &c. **-kīṭa**, m. a kind of insect or animalcule bred in vinegar &c., L. **-kumbha**, m. a vessel for intoxicating liquors, brandy-jar, Kāv. **-druma**, m. Caryota Urens, L. **-pa**, mf(*ā*)n. drinking intoxicating liquor, a drunkard, ChUp.; Mn. &c.; m. N. of a Dānava, Hariv.; -°*pâśana*, n. a drunkard's meal, L. **-paṅka**, m. vinous liquor for distilling, mash, L. **-pāna**, n. the drinking of intoxicating liquors, MBh.; Pañcat.; Suśr.; any int° drink, MārkP. **-pīta**, mfn. = *pīta-madya*, g. *āhitâgny-ādi*. **-pura**, n. du. (?), Divyâv. **-pushpā** or **-pushpī**, f. Grislea Tomentosa, L. **-bīja**, n. lees of wine, ferment, L. **-bhājana** (L.), **-bhāṇḍa** (Vas.). n. = *-kumbha*, q.v. **-maṇḍa**, m. yeast, barm, froth, L. **-maya**, mf(*ī*)n. consisting of intoxicating liquors, Jātakam. **-lālasa**, m. Mimusops Elengi, L. **-vāsinī**, f. = *-pushpā*, L. **-vikraya**, m. the sale of int° liquors, Yājñ., Sch. **-vīja**, see *-bīja*. **-saṃdhāna**, n. distillation of spirit, L. **Madyâkshepa**, m. addiction to drink, Car. **Madyâmoda**, m. Mimusops Elengi, L. **Madyâsattaka**, m. N. of a man, Rājat. (prob. w.r. for *madyâsaktaka*).

Madrá, m. a country to the north-west of Hindūstan proper, or a king (pl. the people) of this c°, ŚBr. &c. &c.; N. of a son of Śibi (the progenitor of the Madras), Pur.; (*ā*), f. N. of a daughter of Raudrāśva, Hariv.; (in music) a personification of the first Mūrchanā in the Gāndhāra-grāma; (*ī*), f. a princess of Madra, Pāṇ. iv, 1, 177, Sch.; n. joy, happiness (*madram tasya* or *tasmai*, 'joy to him!' cf. n. of *bhadra*), Pāṇ. ii, 3, 73. **-kāra**, mfn. causing joy or happiness, Pāṇ. iii, 2, 44; m., v.l. for *madra-gāra*, VBr. **-kūla**, g. *dhūmâdi*. **-gāra** or **-gāri**, m. N. of a man, VBr.; Pravar. **-m-kara**, mfn. = °*dra-kāra*, Pāṇ. iii, 2, 44. **-ja**, mfn. born in Madra, VP. **-nagara**, n. the city of the Madras, Pāṇ. vii, 3, 24, Sch. **-nābha**, m. a partic. mixed caste, MBh. **-pa**, m. a ruler of the Madras, ib. **-rāja**, m. a king of the Madras, Hariv. **-vāṇija**, m. a merchant who goes to Madra, Pāṇ. vi, 2, 13, Sch. **-sadeśa, -saniḍa, -samaryāda, -savidha, -saveśa**, n. neighbourhood of the M°, Pāṇ. vi, 2, 23, Sch. **-sutā**, f. 'daughter of the king of M°,' N. of Mādrī (the second wife of Pāṇḍu), L. **-strī**, f. a Madra woman, MBh. **-hrada**, m. N. of a lake, Pat. **Madrârma** and °**drâsmârma**, n., Pāṇ. vi, 2, 91. **Madrêśa** or °**śvara**, m. a sovereign of the Madras, Hariv.; Pur.

Madraka, mfn. = *mādro mādrau vā bhaktir asya*, Pāṇ. iv, 3, 100, Vārtt. 2, Pat.; belonging to or produced in Madra, W.; m. (pl.) N. of a degraded people (= *madra*), MBh.; Hariv.; Pur.; (sg.) a prince or an inhabitant of Madra, MBh.; N. of Śibi (see under *madra*), Hariv.; of a poet, Cat.; (*ikā*), f., see below; n. N. of a kind of song, Yājñ.; a kind of metre, Col. **-pati**, m. a ruler of the Madras, VarBṛS. **-gīti**, f. the song called Madraka, L. **Madrakâdhama**, mfn. the lowest or meanest of the Madras, MBh.

Madrā-√kṛi, P. *-karoti*, to shear, shave, Pāṇ. v, 4, 67 (cf. *bhadrā-√kṛi*).

Madrāya, Nom. Ā. °*yate*, to be glad, rejoice, g. *lohitâdi*.

Madrikā, f. a Madra woman, MBh. **-kalpa**, mfn. resembling a M° w°, Pāṇ. vi, 3, 37, Sch. **-bhārya**, m. 'having a M° w° for wife,' the husband of a M° w°, ib. **-mānin**, mfn. thinking (a person to be) a Madra woman, ib.

Madrikāya, Nom. Ā. °*yate*, to be like a Madra woman, Pāṇ. vi, 3, 37, Sch.

2. **Madvat**, mfn. (for 1. see p. 777, col. 2) intoxicating, gladdening, ŚāṅkhBr. (Sch.); containing a form or derivative of √2. *mad*, Br.

Mádvan, mfn. addicted to joy or intoxication, RV. viii, 81, 19; gladdening, intoxicating, ib. ix, 86, 35; m. N. of Śiva, Uṇ. iv, 112, Sch.

मददिन् *madadin*, g. *pragady-ādi*.

मदर्पतपुर *madarpata-pura* or °*pita-pura*, n. N. of a town, Rājat.

मदार्मद *madārmada*, m. a species of fish, L. (cf. *mahônmada*).

मदि *madi* or *madikā*, f. a kind of harrow or roller, Kṛishis. (cf. *matya*).

मदीणु *madīṇu*, N. of a place (Medina?), Romakas.

मदीय *madíya*. See p. 777, col. 2.

मद्ग *madga*. See *puru-madga*.

मद्गु *madgú*, m. (accord. to Uṇ. i, 7 fr. √*majj*) a diver-bird (a kind of aquatic bird or cormorant; cf. Lat. *mergus*), VS. &c. &c. (also °*guka*, R.); a species of wild animal frequenting the boughs of trees (= *parṇa-mṛiga*), Suśr.; a kind of snake, L.; a partic. fish, Nīlak.; a kind of galley or vessel of war, Daś.; a partic. mixed caste, Mn. x, 48 (the son of a Nishṭya and a Varuṭī, a Māhishya who knows medicine, or a Pāra-dhenuka who proclaims orders, L.); a person who kills wild beasts, L. (cf. Mn. x, 48); N. of a son of Śvaphalka, Hariv. **-bhūta**, w.r. for *maṅku-bh*°, Divyâv.

Madgura, m. (Uṇ. i, 42) a species of fish, Macropteronatus Magur, Lalit.; Bhpr. (*-priyā*, f. a female M°, L.); a diver, pearl-fisher (as a partic. mixed caste), MBh.; Hariv.

Madguraka, m. Macropteronatus Magur, L.

Madgurasī, f. a species of fish, L.

मद्धक *maddhaka*, m. (with *paṇḍita*) N. of a poet, Cat. (cf. *madraka*).

मद्भू *mad-√bhū*. See p. 777, col. 2.

मद्य 1. 2. *madya*. See pp. 777 and 779.

मद्र *madra* &c. See col. 1.

मद्रिक् *madrík*. See p. 777, col. 2.

मद्रुकस्थली *madruka-sthalī*, f., g. *dhūmâdi*.

मद्रुमरकन्थ *madrumara-kantha*, n., g. *cihaṇâdi*.

मद्र्यञ्च् *madryáñc*. See p. 777, col. 2.

मद्वचन *mad-vacana* &c. See p. 777, col. 2.

मधव्य *madhavyà*. See p. 781, col. 1.

मधु *mádhu*, mf(*ū* or *vī*)n. (gen. n. Ved. *mádhvas*, *mádhos* or *mádhunas*; instr. *mádhvā*; dat. *mádhune*; loc. *mádhau*) sweet, delicious, pleasant, charming, delightful, RV.; TS.; bitter or pungent, L.; m. N. of the first month of the year (= Caitra, March–April), ŚBr. &c. &c.; the season of spring, Var.; Kālid.; Bassia Latifolia, L.; Jonesia Asoka, L.; liquorice, L.; N. of Śiva, MBh.; of two Asuras (the one killed by Vishṇu, the other by Śatru-ghna), MBh.; Hariv.; Pur.; of one of the 7 sages under Manu Cākshusha, MārkP.; of a son of the third Manu, Hariv.; of various princes (of a son of Vṛisha, of Deva-kshatra, of Bindu-mat, of Arjuna Kārtavīrya), Hariv.; Pur.; of a son of Bhatta-nārāyaṇa, Kshitîś.; of a teacher (= *Madhva* or *Ānanda-tīrtha*), Col.; of a mountain, MārkP.; (pl.) the race of Madhu (= the Yādavas or Māthuras), MBh.; Hariv.; BhP.; (*u*), f. a partic. plant (= *jīvā* or *jīvantī*), L.; n. anything sweet (esp. if liquid), mead &c., RV.; AV.; TBr.; Soma (also *somyam madhu*), RV.; honey (said to possess intoxicating qualities and to be of 8 kinds; *madhuno leha*, m. licker of honey, a bee, W.), RV. &c. &c.; milk or anything produced from milk (as butter, ghee &c.), RV.; VS.; GṛŚrS.; the juice or nectar of flowers, any sweet intoxicating drink, wine or spirituous liquor, Kāv.; Var.; Sāh.; sugar, L.; water, L.; pyrites, Bhpr.; N. of a Brāhmaṇa, ŚBr.; a kind of metre, Col. [Cf. Gk. μέθυ, μέθη; Slav. *medŭ*; Lith. *midùs*, *medùs*; Germ. *Meth*; Eng. *mead*.] **-kaṇṭha**, m. the Indian cuckoo (= *kokila*), L.; N. of a poet, Cat. **-kara**, m. 'honey-maker,' a bee, Hariv.; Kāv. &c.; a lover, libertine, L.; Eclipta Prostrata or Asparagus Racemosus, L.; Achyranthes Aspera, W.; the round sweet lime, W.; (*ī*), f. a female bee, Kāv.; Pañcat. (v.l.) &c.; N. of a girl, Hcar.; *-gaṇa*, m. a swarm of bees, ŚārṅgP.; *-maya*, mfn. consisting of bees, Kād.; *-rājan*, m. the king of bees i.e. the queen b°, PraśnUp.; *-śreṇi*, f. a line of b°s, Megh.; *-sāha* (Cat.) and *-sāhi* (Inscr.), m. N. of two kings. **-karāya**, Nom. Ā. °*yate*, to represent a bee, Daś. **-karikā**, f. N. of woman, Mālav. **-karin**, m. a bee, Pañcat. (v.l.) **-karkaṭikā**, f. the sweet lime, L.; the date, L. **-karkaṭī**, f. the sw° l°, L.; the sw° cucumber, L. **-karṇa**, g. *kumudâdi*. **-kaśā**, f. 'whip of sweetness,' a kind of whip or lash belonging to the Aśvins with which they are said to sweeten the Soma juice (afterwards a symbol of plenty), RV.; AV.; TāṇḍyaBr.; KātyŚr. **-kāṇḍa**, n. N. of the first Kāṇḍa of the Bṛihad-āraṇyakôpanishad. **-kānana**, n. the forest of the Asura Madhu, Pañcar. **-kāra**, m. 'honey-maker,' a bee, BhP.; (*ī*), f. a female bee, R.; a partic. wind-instrument, Saṃgīt. **-kārin**, m. a bee, W. **-kiri**, f. N. of a Rāga, Saṃgīt. **-kukkuṭikā**, f. = *-kukkuṭī*, L.; another plant (= *madhurā*), L. **-kukkuṭī**, f. a kind of citron tree with ill-smelling blossoms, L. **-kumbhā**, f. N. of one of the Mātṛis attending on Skanda, MBh. **-kulyā**, f. a stream of honey, h° in str°s, ŚBr.; N. of a river in Kuśa-dvīpa, BhP. **-kūṭa**, m. N. of a poet. **-kūla** (*mádhu-*), mf(*ā*)n. whose banks consist of butter, AV. **-kṛít**, mfn. making honey or sweetness; m. a bee, AV.; TS.; Br.; ChUp. **-keśaṭa**, m. 'honey-insect,' a bee, L. **-kaiṭasa-sūdana**, m. N. of Vishṇu, Vishṇ. (w.r. for *-kaiṭabha-s*°). **-kośa**, m. 'h°-receptacle,' a bee-hive, L.; N. of sev. wks.; n. a honeycomb, ĀpŚr., Comm. **-krama**, m. a bee-hive, L.; a honeycomb, MW.; pl. a drinking bout, L. **-kroḍa**, m. or n. (?) a fritter with sweet stuffing, Car. **-kshīra** (L.) or °**raka** (A.), m. Phoenix Silvestris. **-kharjūrikā** or °**jūrī**, f. a kind of date, L. **-gandhika**, mfn. sweet-swelling, Suśr. **-gāyana**, m. the Indian cuckoo, L. **-guñjana**, m. Hyperanthera Moringa, L. **-grahá**, m. a libation of honey, ŚBr.; KātyŚr. **-gluntha**, m. a lump of honey (honeycomb?), ĀpŚr. **-ghosha**, m. 'sweetly-sounding,' the Indian cuckoo, L. **-cchattra**, m. or n. (?) = *vṛikshâdana*, L. **-cchada**, m. Flacourtia Sapida, L. (also *ā*, f.; Bhpr.) **-cchanda**, m. (mostly m. c.) = next, MBh.; Hariv.; R. **-cchandas**, m. N. of the 51st of Viśvā-mitra's 101 sons, AitBr.; ŚāṅkhŚr. &c.; pl. N. of all the sons of V°, BhP. **-cyut**, mfn. (MBh.; R. &c.) or **-cyuta**, mf(*ā*)n. (R.; BhP.) dropping sweets or honey. **-ja**, mf(*ā*)n. obtained from honey, L.; (*ā*), f. sugar made from h°, s°-candy, L.; the earth, L.; n. bees-wax, L. **-jambīra, -jambha** or **-jambhala**, m. a kind of sweet citron, L. **-jāta** (*mádhu-*), mf(*ā*)n. sprung or produced from h°, AV. **-jālaka**, n. a h°-comb, AVPariś. **-jit**, m. 'conqueror of the Daitya Madhu,' N. of Vishṇu, L. **-jihva** (*mádhu-*), mfn. h°-tongued, sweet-t°, sweetly-speaking, RV.; VS.; ŚBr. **-taru**, m. (Vās., Comm.) and **-tṛiṇa**, m. n. (Vās.) sugar-cane. **-traya**, n. the three sweet things (viz. *sitā*, *mākshika* and *sarpis*, q.v.), L. **-tva**, n. sweetness, MaitrUp. **-dalā**, f. Sanseviera Roxburghiana, L. **-dīpa**, m. 'lamp of spring,' the god of love, L. **-dúgha**, mf(*ā*)n. milking (i.e. yielding) sweetness, RV. **-dūta**, m. 'messenger of spring,' the mango tree, L.; (*ī*), f. Bignonia Suaveolens, Bhpr. **-doghá**, mfn. = *-dúgha*, RV. **-doham**, ind. milking out or obtaining honey, MBh. **-dra**, m. (√2. *drā*) 'hastening after honey or sweets,' a bee, L.; a libertine, L. **-drava**, m. a red-blossomed Hyperanthera Moringa, L. **-druma**, m. the mango tree, L.; Bassia Latifolia, L. **-dvish**, m. 'foe of the Daitya Madhu,' N. of Vishṇu-Krishṇa, Śiś.; BhP. **-dhā**, mfn. dispensing sweetness, RV. **-dhātu**, m. pyrites, L. **-dhāna** (*mádhu-*), mf(*ā*)n. pouring out sweetness, RV.; AV. **-dhārā**, f. a stream of honey, Kād.; BhP. &c.; a stream or plenty of sweet intoxicating drinks, Vcar.; N. of a mythical river, Hariv.; of wk. **-dhūli**, f. molasses, unrefined brown sugar, L. **-dhenu**, f. honey offered to Brāhmans in the form of a cow, Hcat. **-dhvaja** and **-nandi**, m. N. of

2 kings, VP. **-nāḍī**, f. a cell in a honeycomb, ChUp.; N. of RV. iii, 54, 55, ŚāṅkhŚr. **-nārikeraka, -nālikeraka** or °**rika**, m. a kind of cocoanut tree, L. **-nighātin**, m. N. of Vishṇu-Kṛishṇa, VP. **-nirgama**, m. the departure of spring, Ragh. **-nishūdana** (Hariv.), **-nihan** (MBh.), **-nihantṛi** (Hariv.), m. N. of Vishṇu-Kṛishṇa. **-netṛi**, m. a bee, L. **-pá**, mf(*ā*)n. drinking sweetness, honey-drinker, RV.; R.; m. (with or scil. *khaga*) a large black bee, Kāv.; Pañcat. &c.; a bee or a drunkard, Bhām.; *-dhvaja*, m. N. of a king, VP. **-paṭala**, m. a bee-hive, Nīlak. **-pati**, m. 'chief of the race of Madhu,' N. of Kṛishṇa, BhP. (cf. *-mati*). **-parká**, m. (n., L.) a mixture of honey, an offering of honey and milk, a respectful off° to a guest or to the bridegroom on his arrival at the door of the father of the bride (sometimes consisting of equal parts of curds, honey and clarified butter); the ceremony of receiving a guest with it, AV.; GṛŚrS. &c.; N. of a son of Garuḍa, MBh.; of wks.; *-dāna*, n. the offering of the Madhu-parka, MW.; *-nirṇaya*, m. N. of wk.; *-pāṇi*, mfn. having the M°-p° oblation in the hand, offering the M°-p°, MW.; *-prayoga*, m., *-mantra*, m. or n. N. of wks.; °*âcamana*, n. the tasting of the M°-p°. **-parkika**, mfn. presenting the offering of honey &c., MBh. (cf. *mādhup°*). **-parkya**, mfn. worthy of the h° offering, g. *daṇḍâdi*. **-parṇī** (Car., m. c.) or °**ṇī** (Suśr.; Bhpr.), f. N. of sev. plants (Gmelina Arborea, Indigofera Tinctoria, Cocculus Cordifolius &c., L.) **-parṇikā**, f. N. of various plants, Suśr.; Bhpr. (Gmelina Arborea, Indigofera Tinctoria &c., L.) **-pavana**, m. a vernal breeze, Gīt. **-pā**, mfn. = *-pá*, mfn.; *-tama*, mfn. drinking sweetness excessively, RV. **-pākā**, f. sweet melon, L. **-pāṇi** (*mádhu-*), mfn. having sweetness in the hand, RV. **-pātra**, n. a drinking vessel for intoxicating drinks, Vcar. **-pāna**, n. sipping the nectar of flowers (see comp.); a partic. sweet drink, MānGṛ.; *-kala*, mfn. sweet through the sipping of the n° of fl° (as the hum of bees), Kāvyâd. **-pāyin**, m. 'honey-drinker,' a bee, L. **-pārī**, f. = *-pātra*, Vcar. **-pāla**, m. a h°-keeper, R. **-pālikā**, f. Gmelina Arborea, L. **-piṅgâksha**, mfn. having eyes as yellow as h°, Var.; m. N. of a Muni, Cat. **-pīlu**, m. a species of tree, L. **-pura**, n. the city of the Asura Madhu, Hariv.; N. of a city in Northern India, Pañcat.; (*ī*), f. the city of the Madhus i. e. Mathurā, BhP.; Bhām.; *-ripu*, m. N. of Vishṇu, Hcat. **-pushpa** (only L.), m. Bassia Latifolia, Acacia Sirissa, Jonesia Asoka, Mimusops Elengi; (*ā*), f. Croton Polyandrum or C° Tiglium, Tiaridium Indicum. **-pū́**, mfn. purifying itself while becoming sweet, AV. **-pṛíc**, mfn. dispensing sweetness, RV.; AV. **-pṛishṭha** (*mádhu-*), mfn. whose back or surface consists of sw° or milk (said of Soma), RV. **-péya**, mfn. sweet to drink, RV.; n. the drinking of sweetness (as Soma &c.), ib. **-praṇaya**, m. addiction to wine, MW.; *-vat*, mfn. addicted to wine, ib. **-pratīka** (*mádhu-*), mf(*ā*)n. having a sweet mouth or sweetness in the m°, RV.; (*ā*), f. (with or scil. *siddhi*) N. of certain supernatural powers and properties of a Yogin, Cat. **-prapāta**, m. a precipice (met with) while seeking honey, MBh. **-prameha**, m. h°-like or saccharine urine, diabetes, MW. **-prasaṅga-madhu**, n. h° connected with spring, Ratnâv. **-prâśana**, n. putting a little honey into the mouth of a new-born male infant (one of the 12 Saṃskāras or purificatory rites of the Hindūs), RTL. 358. **-priya**, mfn. fond of h° or the juice of flowers, Hariv.; m. a kind of plant, = *bhūmi-jambu*, L.; N. of Akrūra, VP.; of Bala-bhadra, L. **-pluta**, mfn. swimming with honey, mixed w° h°, Vishṇ. **-psaras** (*mádhu-*), mfn. fond of sweetness, RV. **-phala**, m. a kind of cocoa-nut tree, L.; Flacourtia Sapida, L.; (*ā*), f. water-melon, L.; a kind of grape, L. **-phalikā**, f. a kind of date, L. **-bahulā**, f. Gaertnera Racemosa, L. **-bīja**, m. a pomegranate tree, L.; *-pūra*, m. a kind of citron, L. **-brāhmaṇa**, n. N. of a Brāhmaṇa. **-bhakshaṇa**, n. N. of ch. of the Bāla-kāṇḍa of the Rāmāyaṇa. **-bhadra**, m. N. of man, Rājat. **-bhāga** (*mádhu-*), mfn. whose lot or portion is sweetness, AV. **-bhāṇḍa**, n. = *-pātra*, Vcar. **-bhāva**, m. a partic. Prākrit metre, Col. **-bhid**, m. 'slayer of Madhu,' N. of Vishṇu, Kād. **-bhuj**, mfn. enjoying sweetness or gladness, BhP. **-bhūmika**, m. N. of a Yogin in the second order or degree, Sarvad. **-maksha**, m., **-makshā**, f. or **-makshikā**, f. 'honey-fly,' a bee, Kauś. **-majjan**, m. a walnut tree, L. **-mat** (*mádhu-*), mfn. possessing or containing sweetness, sweet; pleasant, agreeable (*-tama*, mfn.), RV.; AV.; VS. &c.; mixed with honey, Kum.; rich in h°, richly provided with the juice of flowers, Chandom.; containing the word *mádhu*, ŚBr.; ĀśvGṛ.; m. N. of a country, g. *kacchâdi* and *sindhv-ādi*; of a city (?), MW.; pl. N. of a people, MBh.; (*atī*), f. Gmelina Arborea, L.; Sanseviera Roxburghiana, L.; a partic. step or degree in the Yoga, Cat.; a partic. supernatural faculty belonging to a Yogin, Prab.; a kind of metre, Chandom.; N. of a daughter of the Asura Madhu (wife of Hary-aśva), Hariv.; of a female servant of Lakshmī (?), Pañcar.; of a river, Hariv.; Mālatīm.; of a city in Saurāshṭra, Śatr.; Daś.; of sev. wks.; °*tī-saṃgamêśvara-tīrtha*, n. N. of a Tīrtha, Rājat.; Cat. **-mati**, m. Mohammed, Kālac. (w.r. *-pati*); *-gaṇêśa*, m. N. of an author, Cat. **-matta**, mfn. drunk with wine, L.; intoxicated or excited by the spring, Hariv.; m. N. of a man, R.; pl. N. of a people, MBh. (v.l. *-mat*); (*ā*), f. a species of Karañja, L. **-math**, m. 'crusher or destroyer of Madhu,' N. of Vishṇu, Ragh. **-mathana**, m. = prec., Kāv.; BhP.; Chandom.; *-vijaya*, m. N. of wk. **-mada**, m. intoxication with wine, Kāv. **-madya**, n. intoxicating drink made from honey or from the blossoms of Bassia Latifolia, L. **-manta**, n. N. of a town, R. **-mantha**, m. a kind of drink mixed with honey, ĀśvGṛ.; Kauś.; Lāṭy. **-maya**, mf(*ī*)n. consisting of honey, Hcat.; sweet as honey, luscious, Hit.; Sāh. **-mallī** (also *-malli*, A.), f. Jasminum Grandiflorum, L. **-mastaka** (n., L.), N. of a partic. kind of sweetmeat, Suśr. **-māṇsa**, n. honey and meat, Mn. xi, 159. **-mādhava**, m. du. or n. sg. the two spring months (*kāle °ve*, 'in the spring'), MBh.; Suśr.; BhP. &c.; *-māsa*, m. sg. one of the 2 sp° m°, Pañcar.; *-sahāya*, m. N. of author, Cat. **-mādhavī**, f. any spring flower abounding in honey or a partic. species of fl°; (perhaps) Gaertnera Racemosa, BhP.; a kind of intoxicating drink, MBh.; a kind of metre, Col.; a partic. Rāgiṇī, Saṃgīt.; N. of Comm. **-mādhvīka**, n. any intoxicating drink, L.; a partic. int° d°, Hariv.; Bhaṭṭ. (v.l.) **-māraka**, m. 'destroyer of honey,' a bee, L. **-mālatī-nāṭaka**, n. N. of wk. (Mālatī-mādhava?). **-māla-pattrikā**, f. a species of small shrub, L. (uncertain reading). **-māsa**, m. a spring month; *-mahôtsava*, m. the spring festival, Kathās.; °*sâvatāra*, m. the setting in of the sp° m°, Prasannar. **-miśrá**, mfn. mixed with honey or sweet milk, TS.; Kauś.; Lāṭy.; N. of man, Cat. **-mura-naraka-vināśana**, m. 'destroyer of (the Daityas) Madhu, Mura and Naraka,' N. of Vishṇu-Kṛishṇa, Gīt. **-mūla**, n. the edible root of Amorphophallus Campanulatus, L. **-meha**, m. honey-like or saccharine urine, diabetes, Suśr.; *-tva*, n. the state of passing sacch° ur°, ib. **-mehin**, mfn. suffering from sacch° ur°, Car.; Suśr. **-maireya**, m. an intoxicating drink made of honey, BhP.; Pāṇ. vi, 2, 70, Sch. **-yashṭi**, f. sugar-cane, L.; liquorice, L.; = *tiktaparvan*, L. **-yashṭikā** or **-yashṭī**, f. liquorice, L. **-rasa**, m. the juice of honey, R.; sweetness, pleasingness, Bhartṛ. (v.l.); sugar-cane, L.; the wine palm, L.; (*ā*), f. Sanseviera Roxburghiana, Suśr.; Gmelina Arborea, Bhpr.; a vine, bunch of grapes, L.; a kind of Asclepias, L.; mfn. sweet, L.; *-maya*, mf(*ī*)n. full of the juice of honey, Hcar. **-ripu**, m. 'enemy of Madhu,' N. of Vishṇu-Kṛishṇa, Śiś. **-ruha**, m. N. of a son of Ghṛita-pṛishṭha, BhP. **-reṇu**, m. a species of plant, L. **-lagna**, m. a red-blossomed Moringa, L. **-latā**, f. a kind of liquorice, L. (cf. *madhura-l°*). **-lih**, mfn. (ifc.) one who has licked the honey of, BhP.; m. a bee, Kāv.; BhP.; Kuval. **-leha** (MW.), **-lehin** or **-lolupa** (L.), m. 'licking honey' or 'longing after honey,' a bee. **-vacas** (*mádhu-*), mfn. sweet-voiced, sweetly or friendly speaking, RV. **-vaṭī**, f. N. of a district, MBh. **-vat**, ind. as honey, BhP.; as through an intoxicating drink, ib. **-vana**, m. the Indian cuckoo, L.; n. N. of the forest of the ape Su-grīva (which abounded in honey), MBh.; R.; of the forest of the Asura Madhu on the Yamunā (where Śatru-ghna, after slaying Lavaṇa, son of Madhu, founded the city of Mathurā or Madhurā); *-vraja-vāsi-go-svāmi-guṇa-leśâshṭaka*, n. N. of wk. **-varṇa** (*mádhu-*), mfn. honey-coloured or having an agreeable aspect, RV.; m. N. of a being attending on Skanda, MBh. **-varṇana**, n. N. of wk. **-vallī**, f. liquorice, L.; a kind of grape, L.; sweet citron, L. **-vāc**, m. 'honey-voiced,' the Indian cuckoo, L. **-vātīya**, mf(*ā*)n. beginning with the words *mádhu-vātāḥ* (RV. i, 90, 6), ŚāṅkhGṛ. **-vāra**, m. tippling, carousing, Śiś.; Kir.; Dharmaśarm. **-váhana**, mfn. bearing or carrying sweet things (as honey, milk &c.; said of the chariot of the Aśvins), RV. **-vāhin**, mfn. bearing or carrying honey (a river), Hariv.; (*inī*), f. N. of a river, MBh. **-vidyā**, f. 'science of sweetness,' N. of a partic. mystical doctrine, BṛĀrUp.; Śaṃk.; SV., Sch. &c. **-vidvish**, m. 'enemy of Madhu,' N. of Vishṇu-Kṛishṇa, VP. **-vidhvaṇsa-bhāskara**, m. N. of wk. **-vṛiksha**, m. Bassia Latifolia, L. **-vṛídh**, 'abounding in sweetness,' (perhaps) a rain-cloud (others 'a partic. plant'), RV. x, 75, 8. **-vṛishá**, mfn. dropping or raining sw°, TBr. **-vrata** (*mádhu-*), mf(*ā*)n. occupied with sw°, RV.; m. a large black bee, Kāv.; BhP. &c.; (with *bodha-nidhi*), N. of author, Cat.; (*ī*), f. a bee regarded as female, Bālar.; Vcar.; *-pati*, m. 'king of bees' i.e. the queen bee, BhP.; *-varūtha*, m. n. a swarm of bees, ib. **-śarkarā**, f. honey-sugar, Suśr. **-śākha** (*mádhu-*), mfn. having sweet branches, VS.; m. Bassia Latifolia, L. **-śigru** (Suśr.) or °**ra** (Car.), m. Moringa Pterygosperma (Rubriflora). **-śishṭa**, n. wax, R. **-śīrshaka**, n., v.l. for *-mastaka*, q.v., Suśr., Comm. **-śukta**, n. a sour drink with honey, Suśr. **-śesha**, n. wax, Car.; Bhpr. **-ścút**, mfn. distilling sweetness, overflowing with sweets, RV.; AV.; VS. &c. **-ścyut**, mfn. id.; *-ścyun-nidhana*, n. N. of a Sāman (also called *Prajā-pater madhu-ścy°*, ĀrshBr.), TāṇḍyaBr.; Lāṭy. **-ścyuta**, mfn. = *-ścút*, MBh. **-śrava** and °**vā**, w.r. for *-srava* and °*vā*, q.v. **-śrī**, f. Beauty of Spring (personified), Vikr.; Kum. **-śreṇi**, m. the son of a Nishṭya and a Śūdrā (identical with a Śauṇḍika and Maṇḍa-hāraka), L.; f. Sanseviera Roxburghiana, L. **-śvāsā**, f. a species of plant (= *jīvantī*), L. **-shút**, mfn. (*shut* for *sut*) pressing out sweetness, RV.; emitting sw° (Soma), ib.; *-tama*, mfn., MW. **-shṭhāna**, n. = *-sthāna* (q.v.), Pāṇ. viii, 3, 106, Sch. **-shṭhālá**, n. a honey-pot, MaitrS.; Kāṭh.; ĀpŚr. **-shṭhīla**, m. Bassia Latifolia, L. **-shpanda** and **-shyanda**, m., see *-syanda*. **-sakha**, m. 'friend of spring,' the god of love, L. **-saṃkāśa** (*mádhu-*), mf(*ā*)n. looking sweet, appearing pleasant, AV. **-saṃdṛiśa** (*mádhu-*), mfn. sw°-looking, appearing lovely, AV. **-saṃdhāna**, n. any intoxicating drink, (esp.) brandy, L. **-sambhava**, m. pl. N. of partic. Jinas, Lalit.; n. wax, L. **-sammiśra**, mfn. mixed with h°, Mn. iii, 273. **-sarpis**, n. du. h° and ghee, ib. 274. **-sahāya**, m. 'having Spring for a companion,' the god of love, Cat. **-sāt**, ind. (with √*bhū*) to become honey, W. **-sārathi**, m. 'having Spring for a charioteer,' the god of love, L. **-sikthaka**, m. a kind of poison, L. **-suhṛid**, m. 'friend of spring,' the god of love, ib., Sch. **-sûkta**, n. N. of AV. ix, 1, Vait. **-sūdana**, m. 'destroyer of honey,' a bee, L.; 'destroyer of the demon Madhu,' N. of Vishṇu-Kṛishṇa, MBh.; R. &c.; N. of various scholars, Cat.; (*ī*), f. Beta Bengalensis, L.; N. of various authors (also with *guru, go-svāmin, ṭhakkura, dīkshita, dujanti, paṇḍita* and °*ta-rāja, vācas-pati-sarasvatī*), Cat.; *-śikshā*, f. N. of wk.; °*nâyatana*, n. a temple of Vishṇu, Prab. **-sena**, m. N. of a prince of Madhupura, Pañcat. **-skanda**, n. N. of a Tīrtha, Cat. **-stoká**, m. a drop of honey, ŚBr. **-sthāna**, n. 'bee-place,' a bee-hive, L. **-syanda**, m. N. of a son of Viśvā-mitra, R. (v.l. *-shpanda, -shyanda*). **-syandin**, m. a partic. stringed instrument, Saṃgīt. **-srava**, mfn. dropping sweetness, MBh.; BhP.; m. Bassia Latifolia, L.; Sanseviera Zeylanica, L.; (*ā*), f. Sanseviera Roxburghiana, L.; liquorice, L.; Hoya Viridiflora, Bhpr.; a kind of date, L.; = *jīvantī*, L.; = *haṇsa-padī*, L.; N. of the 3rd day in the light half of the month Śrāvaṇa, Cat.; N. of a river, Cat.; n. N. of a Tīrtha, MBh. **-sravas**, m. Bassia Latifolia, L. **-svara**, m. 'sweet-voiced,' the Indian cuckoo, L. **-han**, m. a collector of honey (accord. to Comm. 'destroyer of a bee-hive'), MBh.; Pur.; a partic. bird of prey, Vāgbh.; Car.; 'slayer of the Daitya Madhu,' N. of Vishṇu-Kṛishṇa, MBh.; BhP.; Pañcar.; a soothsayer, W. **-hantṛi**, m. 'slayer of the Daitya Madhu,' N. of Rāma as an incarnation of Vishṇu, R. **-hastya** (*mádhu-*), mfn. having honey or sweetness in the hand, RV. **Madhûcchishṭa**, n. bees-wax, MBh.; Yājñ.; Suśr. &c. (cf. *madhu-śishṭa, -śesha*); *-sthita*, mfn. covered on the outside with wax, MBh. **Madhûttha**, mfn. made or produced from honey, L.; n. bees-wax, Naish.; ib., Sch.; mead, Yājñ., Comm.

Madhûtthita, n. 'produced from honey,' wax, L. **Madhûtsava**, m. the spring festival (on the day of the full moon in the month Caitra), Śak. (v.l.) **Madhûdaka**, n. 'honey-water,' h° diluted in w°, Suśr.; *-prasravaṇa*, mfn. flowing with h° and w°, MW. **Madhûdaśvita**, n. buttermilk with h° or sweet milk with water, Kauś. **Madhûdyāna**, n. a spring garden, Kathās. **Madhûdyutá**, mfn. mixed with h°, MaitrS. **Madhûdvāpa**, m. pl. (?), Kauś. **Madhûpaghna**, n. (m., L.) N. of a city (= Mathurā or Madhurā), Ragh. **Madhûshita**, n. wax, L.

Madhavyà, mfn. fitted or authorized to drink Soma, TS.; TBr.; consisting of honey, Kāś. on Pāṇ. iv, 4, 139; m. = *mādhava*, the second month of spring, Pāṇ. iv, 4, 129.

Madhuka (ifc.) = *madhu*, g. *ura-ādi*; mfn. honey-coloured (only in *-locana*, 'having h°-c° eyes,' N. of Śiva), MBh.; sweet (in taste), W.; mellifluous, melodious, ib.; m. a species of tree, R.; Var. (Bassia Latifolia or Jonesia Asoka, L.); Parra Jacana or Goensis, L.; liquorice, L. (cf. n.); a kind of bard or panegyrist, L.; the son of a Maitreya and a married Āyogavī, L.; (*mádh°*) N. of a man, ŚBr.; (*ā*), f. Menispermum Glabrum, L.; Glycyrrhiza Glabra, L.; black Panic, L.; N. of a river, VP.; n. liquorice, Suśr. (cf. m.); old honey, L.; tin, L.

Madhunī, f. a species of shrub, L.

Madhún-tama, mf(*ā*)n. (a superl. of *madhu* formed analogously to *madin-tama*) very sweet, VS.; VPrāt., Sch.

Madhura, mf(*ā*)n. sweet, pleasant, charming, delightful, ĀśvGṛ.; R.; Suśr. &c.; sounding sweetly or uttering sweet cries, melodious, mellifluous, MBh.; Kāv. &c. (*am*, ind.); m. sweetness, L.; a kind of leguminous plant, Car.; the red sugar-cane, L.; a species of mango, L.; a Moringa with red flowers, L.; rice, L.; a partic. drug (= *jīvaka*), L.; molasses, L.; sour gruel (also f. *ā*), L.; N. of one of the attendants of Skanda, MBh.; of a Gandharva, SaddhP.; (with *ācārya*), of a teacher, Cat. (cf. *mādhura*); (*ā*), f. Anethum Sowa or Panmorium, L.; Beta Bengalensis, L.; Asparagus Racemosus and other plants, L.; liquorice, L.; a kind of root similar to ginger, L.; sour rice-water, L.; N. of a town (= *mathurā*), Pat. on Pāṇ. i, 2, 51, Vārtt. 5; of the tutelary deity of the race of Vandhula, Cat.; (*ī*), f. a kind of musical instrument, L.; n. kind or friendly manner (only *eṇa*, ind.), Hariv.; the quality of the throat which makes the voice sweet, L.; sweetness, syrup, treacle, L.; poison, L.; tin, L. **-kaṇṭaka**, m. 'having sweet bones,' a kind of fish, L. **-kaṇṭhin**, mfn. 'sweet-throated,' singing sweetly, R. **-kharjūrikā** or **-kharjūrī**, f. a species of plant, L. **-gātra**, mf(*ī*)n. 'sweet-limbed,' lovely, beautiful, Daś. **-cāru-mañju-svaratā**, f. the having a sweet and agreeable and pleasant voice (one of the 80 minor marks of a Buddha), Dharmas. 84. **-jambīra**, m. a species of citron or lime, L. **-tā**, f. sweetness, suavity, pleasantness, amiability, softness, Kāv.; Sāh. **-traya**, n. the three sweet things (sugar, honey and butter), L. **-tva**, n. sweetness (in taste), Suśr.; suavity, charm (of speech), Kāv. **-tvaca**, m. Grislea Tomentosa, L. **-nirghosha**, m. N. of an evil spirit or demon, Lalit. **-nisvana**, mf(*ā*)n. sweet-voiced, L. **-paṭolī**, f. a species of plant, L. **-pragīta**, mfn. singing sweetly (as a bird), Ṛitus. **-pralāpin**, mfn. singing sweetly, Vikr. **-priya-darśana**, m. 'of sweet and friendly aspect,' N. of Śiva, Śivag. **-phala**, m. a species of jujube, L.; (*ā*), f. the sweet melon, L. **-bīja-pūra**, m. a kind of citron, L. **-bhāshitṛi**, m. a sweet or kind speaker, Hariv. **-bhāshin**, mfn. speaking sweetly or kindly, MBh. **-maya**, mf(*ī*)n. consisting of or full of sweetness, Hcar. **-rāvin**, mfn. rumbling sweetly (as a cloud), VarBṛS. **-latā**, f. a kind of liquorice, L. **-vacana**, mfn. sweetly-speaking, MW. **-vallī**, f. a kind of citron, L. **-vāc**, mfn. = *-vacana*, L. **-vipāka**, mf(*ā*)n. sweet after digestion, Suśr. **-śīla**, m. N. of a poet, Cat. **-śukla-mūtra**, mfn. discharging sweet and light-coloured urine (*-tā*, f.), Suśr. **-sambhāsha**, mfn. discoursing agreeably, MW. **-sravā**, f. a kind of date tree, L. **-svana**, mfn. sweetly-sounding, L.; m. a conch, L. **-svara**, mfn. sweetly-sounding, sweet-voiced (*am*, ind.), MBh.; Kāv. &c.; m. N. of a Gandharva, SaddhP. **Madhurâkshara**, mf(*ā*)n. speaking or sounding sweetly, melodious, mellow (*am*, ind.), R.; n. pl. sweet or kind words, Pañcat. **Madhurâṅgaka**, mf(*ikā*)n. astringent, L.; m. astringent taste, ib. **Madhurâniruddha**, n. N. of a drama. **Madhurâmla**, mfn. sweet and sour, subacid, Suśr.; *-kaṭuka*, mfn. sw° and s° and pungent, ib.; *-kashāya*, mfn. sw° and s° and astringent, ib.; *-kāvya*, n. N. of a poem, Cat.; *-tikta*, mfn. sw° and s° and bitter, Suśr.; *-phala*, m. a species of fruit-tree, L.; *-lavaṇa*, mfn. sw° and s° and salty, Suśr. **Madhurâmlaka**, m. Spondias Mangifera, L. **Madhurâlāpa**, mfn. uttering sweet sounds, A.; m. sweet or melodious notes (*-nisarga-paṇḍita*, mfn. acquainted with the nature of sw° notes, i. e. skilled in sw° songs), Kum.; (*ā*), f. Turdus Salica, L. **Madhurâlābunī**, f. a kind of cucumber, L. **Madhurāvaṭṭa**, m. N. of a man, Rājat. **Madhurâshṭaka**, n. N. of a collection of 8 verses by Vallabhâcārya (in which various attributes of Kṛishṇa are described, each containing the word *madhura*), Cat. **Madhurâsvāda**, mfn. sweet in taste, ĀśvGṛ. **Madhurôdaka**, m. (scil. *samudra*) 'the sea of sweet or fresh water,' N. of the outermost of the seven great seas which encompass Jambu-dvīpa, L. **Madhurôpanyāsa**, m. kind address or speech, Mālatīm.

Madhuraka, mfn. sweet, pleasant, agreeable, L.; m. a partic. drug (= *jīvaka*), L.; (*ikā*), f. Anethum Panmorium (others 'a kind of fennel'), L.; Sinapis Racemosa, L.; (prob.) n. the seed of Anethum Panmorium, Suśr.

Madhuraya, Nom. P. °*yati* (°*rita*, mfn.), to sweeten, render sweet, Pañcar.

Madhuriman, m. sweetness, suavity, charm, Kāv.; Rājat.

Madhurila, g. *kāśâdi*.

Madhulá, mf(*ā*)n. = *madhura*, sweet, RV.; AV.; Kauś.; n. an intoxicating drink, spirituous liquor, L.

Madhulikā, f. black mustard, L.; N. of one of the Mātṛis attending on Skanda, MBh.

Madhuvilā, f. (*madhu* + *ila*?) N. of the river Samaṅgā, MBh.

Mádhus, n. = *madhu*, sweetness, TS.; TBr. (accord. to Uṇ. ii, 117 *madhús* = *pavitra-dravya*).

Madhusya, Nom. P. °*syati*, to wish for honey, Siddh. on Pāṇ. vii, 1, 51.

Madhūka, m. (fr. *madhu*) a bee, ŚāṅkhGṛ.; Bassia Latifolia (from the blossoms and seeds of which arrac is distilled and oil extracted), ib.; MBh.; Kāv. &c.; n. the blossoms or fruit of B° L°, L.; liquorice, L.; bees-wax, L. **-cchavi**, mfn. having the colour of the flower of B° L°, Gīt. **-pushpa**, n. the fl° of B° L°, MBh. **-mālā**, f. a garland of fl°s of B° L°, Ragh. **-rasa**, m. the juice of the seeds of B° L°, Suśr. **-vrata**, n. N. of a partic. observance, Cat. **-sāra**, m. the pith of the B° L°, Suśr.

Madhūya, Nom. P. °*yati* (fr. *madhu*), Pat.

Madhūyu, mfn. eager for sweetness, RV.

Madhūla, m. a kind of Bassia, L.; astringent, sweet and bitter taste, L.; (*ī*), f. a kind of grain, L.; a species of citron, L.; the mango tree, L.; a kind of drug, L.; liquorice, L.; pollen, L.; n. honey, L.; mfn. astringent, sweet and bitter, L.

Madhūlaka, mf(*ikā*)n. sweet, L.; m. sweetness, L. (cf. n.); a mountain species of the Bassia Latifolia, L.; (*ikā*), f. a kind of bee, Suśr.; a species of grain, ib.; a species of Bassia, L.; Sanseviera Zeylanica, L.; a kind of citron, L.; Aletris Hyacinthoides or Dracaena Nervosa, L.; liquorice, L.; arrac distilled from the blossoms of the Bassia tree or any intoxicating drink (also n.), L.; (*madhū́l°*), n. honey or sweetness, AV.

Madhūlika, mfn. astringent, sweet and pungent, L.; m. astr°, sw° and p° taste, ib.; (*ā*), f., see prec.

Madhv, in comp. for *madhu*. **-aksha**, mfn. having eyes of the colour of honey (said of Agni), MBh. (cf. *madhuka-locana*). **-añc**, mf(*dhūcī*)n. formed to explain *mádhūcī*, Mahīdh. on VS. xxxvii, 18. **-ád**, mfn. eating sweetness, RV. **-arṇas** (*mádhv-*), mfn. having sweet springs or waters (said of a river), ib. **-aśva**, see *mādhvaśvi*. **-ashṭaka**, n. N. of a Stotra (cf. *madhurâshṭaka*). **-ashṭhīlā**, f. a lump of honey, Kāṭh. (cf. *madhu-shṭhīlā*). **-ādhāra**, m. bees-wax, Bhpr. **-āpāta**, m. honey at first sight, Mn. xi, 9. **-āmra**, m. a kind of mango tree, L. **-ālu** or **-āluka**, n. a kind of sweet potato, Suśr. **-āvāsa**, m. the mango tree, L. **-āśin**, mfn. eating honey or sweets, KātySr. **-āsava**, m. a decoction of honey or of the blossoms of the Bassia Latifolia, sweet spirituous liquor; *-kshība*, mfn. drunk with sweet sp° l°, MBh.; R.; Suśr. **-āsavanika**, m. a preparer of sweet sp° l°, distiller, L. **-āsvāda**, mfn. having the taste of honey, MW. **-āhuti**, f. a sacrificial offering consisting of honey or other sweet things, MBh. **-ṛic**, f. pl. N. of partic. hymns, Vas.

Madhvaka, m. a bee, AdbhBr.

Madhvala, m. repeated tippling, carousing, L.

Madhvasya, P. °*syati*, to long for honey or anything sweet, L.

Madhvijā, f. any intoxicating drink, L. (prob. w.r.)

मध्य *mádhya*, mf(*ā*)n. middle (used like *medius*, e.g. *mádhye samudré*, 'in the midst of the sea'), RV.; VPrāt.; KaṭhUp.; middlemost, intermediate, central, Var.; Megh.; standing between two, impartial, neutral, Kām.; middle i. e. being of a middle kind or size or quality, middling, moderate (with *vṛitti*, f. 'a middle course'), Lāṭy.; Mn.; Suśr. &c.; (in astron.) mean i. e. theoretical (opp. to *spashṭa* or *sphuṭa*), Sūryas. (*-tva*, n.); lowest, worst, L.; m. n. (ifc. f. *ā*) the middle of the body, (esp.) a woman's waist, ŚBr. &c. &c.; (in alg.) the middle term or the mean of progression, Col.; (*ā*), f. a young woman, a girl arrived at puberty, Sāh.; the middle finger, L.; (in music) a partic. tone, Saṃgīt.; (also n.) a kind of metre, Col.; n. (m., g. *ardharcâdi*) the middle, midst, centre, inside, interior, RV. &c. &c. (*am*, ind. into the midst of, into, among, with gen. or ifc., MBh.; Kāv. &c.; *ena*, ind. in or through the midst of, on the inside, through, between, with gen., acc. or ifc., ŚBr.; MBh. &c.; *āt*, ind. from the midst of, out of, from among, R.; Hariv. &c.; *e*, ind., see s.v.); the middle of the sky (with or scil. *nabhasas*), Mn.; MBh.; space between (e.g. *bhruvos*, the eyebrows), MBh.; midday (with *ahnaḥ*), Mālav.; the meridian, Mālatīm.; intermediate condition between (gen.), R.; the belly, abdomen, Kum.; the flank of a horse, L.; (in music) mean time, Saṃgīt.; ten thousand billions, MBh.; cessation, pause, interval, L.; N. of a country between Sindh and Hindūstan proper, Cat. [Cf. Zd. *maidhya*; Gk. μέσσος, μέσος for μέθιος; Lat. *medius*; Goth. *midjis*; Eng. *mid* in *midland, midnight* &c.] **-karṇa**, m. a half diameter, radius, MW. **-kuru**, (prob.) m. pl. N. of a country, Cat. **-kaumudī**, f. = *madhya-siddhânta-kaumudī*, q.v. **-kshāmā**, f. 'slender-waisted' or 'slender in the centre,' N. of a kind of metre, Col. **-ga**, mf(*ā*)n. going or being in the middle or among (with gen. or ifc.), MBh.; Kāv. &c. **-gata**, mfn. id., ib.; n. the middle syllable, Śrutab. **-gandha**, m. 'having a middling scent (?),' the mango tree, L. **-grahaṇa**, n. the middle of an eclipse, MW. **-cārin**, mf(*iṇī*)n. going in the midst or among (gen.), Hit. **-cchāyā**, f. (in astron.) mean or middle shadow, MW. **-jihva**, n. the middle of the tongue (said to be the organ of the palatals), APrāt. **-jainêndra-vyākaraṇa**, n. N. of wk. **-jyā**, f. the sign of the meridian, Sūryas. **-tamas**, n. circular or annular darkness, central darkness, VarBṛS. **-tás**, ind. from or in the middle, centrally, centrically, RV. &c. &c.; out of, among (gen. or comp.), MBh.; R. &c.; of middle sort, Gaut.; *-taḥkārin*, m. N. of the 4 principal priests (viz. the Hotṛi, Adhvaryu, Brahman, and Udgātṛi), Lāṭy. **-tā**, f. the state of being in the middle, mediocrity, MBh. **-tāpinī**, f. N. of an Upanishad. **-tva**, n., see under *madhya*. **-danta**, m. a front tooth, L. **-dina**, for *madhyaṃ-dina*, q.v. **-dīpaka**, n. (in rhetoric) 'illuminating in the middle,' N. of a figure in which light is thrown on a description by the use of an emphatic verb in the middle of a stanza (e.g. Bhaṭṭ. x, 24), Vām. iv, 3, 18; 19. **-deśa**, m. middle region, middle space, the central or middle part of anything, ŚrS.; (= *madhyaṃ nabhasaḥ*), the meridian, MBh.; the middle of the body, waist, MBh.; Kāv. &c.; the trunk of the body, belly, abdomen, ib.; the midland country (lying between the Himâlayas on the north, the Vindhya mountains on the south, Vinaśana on the west, Prayāga on the east, and comprising the modern provinces of Allahabad, Agra, Delhi, Oude &c.), Mn.; MBh. (cf. IW. 226, n. 1); mfn. belonging to or living in the midland country, of m° origin, MBh.; m. pl. the inhabitants of the m° c°, Cat. **-deśīya** (MBh.) or **-deśya** (Pur.), mfn. = prec. mfn. **-deha**, m. the middle or trunk of the body, belly &c., Suśr. **-nagara**, n. the interior of a city, Pañcad. **-nihita**, mfn. placed in the middle, inserted, fixed into (anything), Pañcat. **-m-dina** (*madhyá-*), m. (n., L.) midday, noon, RV. &c. &c.; the midday offering (Savana or Pavamāna), Br.; ŚrS.; Bassia Latifolia, L.; N. of a disciple of Yājñavalkya, Cat.; n. Midday (personified as a son of Pushpârṇa by Prabhā), BhP.; mfn.

= *mādhyaṃdina* (q. v.); *-gata*, mfn. having reached the meridian (as the sun), MBh.; *-samaya*, m. midday-time, noon, Pañcat.; °*nârka-saṃtapta*, mfn. burnt by the midday-sun, Kāvyâd.; °*nīya*, mfn. meridional, meridian, belonging to noon or midday, Lāṭy. **-patita**, mfn. fallen in the middle, lying between or in the midst, Pāṇ. i, 1, 71, Sch. **-parimāṇa**, n. the middle measure or magnitude (or that between an atom and infinitude), MW. **-pāta**, m. falling or going in the midst, intercourse, commerce, Rājat.; (in astron.) the mean occurrence of the aspect. **-pravishṭa**, mfn. one who has stolen into another's confidence, Kathās. **-prasūtā**, f. (a cow) which has had a calf not very long ago, L. **-bha**, (in astron.) the meridian ecliptic point. **-bhakta**, mfn. eaten in the middle (a term applied to any medicine taken in the middle of a meal), Suśr. **-bhāga**, m. the middle part or portion, Kathās.; the middle of the body, waist, Bhartṛ. **-bhāva**, m. middle state or condition, mediocrity, MW.; a middling or moderate distance, ŚārṅgP. **-maṇi**, m. the central or principal gem of a necklace, MW. **-madhyā**, f. (in music) a partic. Mūrchanā, Saṃgīt. **-manoramā**, f. N. of a grammatical work (an abridgement of the Manoramā). **-mandira**, m. N. of the author of the Mahābhārata-tātparya-nirṇaya, Cat.; of Madhvâcārya, IW. 119; n. pudendum muliebre and anus, Subh. **-yava**, m. a weight of six white mustard seeds, W. **-yogin**, mf(*inī*)n. (in astron.) being in the middle of a conjunction, completely covered or obscured, VarBṛS. **-rātrá**, m. or **-rātri**, f. midnight (*au*, ind. at midnight), Br.; MBh. &c. **-rekhā**, f. the middle line, the central or first meridian (the line conceived by the Hindūs to be drawn through Laṅkā, Ujjayinī, Kurukshetra, and other places to mount Meru), Siddhântaś. **-lagna**, n. the point of the ecliptic situated on the meridian, ib. **-līlā**, f. N. of wk. **-loka**, m. the middle world, earth, abode of mortals; °*kêśa*, m. 'lord of the m° w° or e°,' a king, L. **-vayas**, mfn. middle-aged, Hariv. **-vartin**, mfn. being in the middle or between or among, middle, central, Kāv.; Kathās.; m. a mediator, W. **-vallī**, f. N. of a Vallī of the TUp. (probably from being in the middle of the book). **-vidaraṇa**, n. N. of one of the ten ways in which an eclipse ends, VarBṛS. **-vivartin**, mfn. = *-vartin*, L.; impartial, a mediator, L. **-vivekin**, mfn. of mediocre discernment, Sāṃkhyas., Sch. **-vṛitta**, n. the navel, L. **-śarīra**, mfn. having a middle-sized body or one of moderately full habit, Suśr. **-śāyin**, mfn. lying in the midst, lying within, Rājat. **-siddhânta-kaumudī**, f. 'the middle-sized Siddh.', N. of an abridgment of the Siddh. by Varada-rāja. **-sūtra**, n. the central meridian, Sūryas. (cf. *madhya-rekhā*). **-stha**, mf(*ā*)n. being in the middle, being between or among (gen. or comp.), Yājñ.; MBh. &c.; being in the middle space i.e. in the air, ŚāṅkhBr.; standing between two persons or parties, mediating, a mediator, Pāṇ. iii, 2, 179, Sch.; belonging to neither or both parties, (only) a witness, impartial, neutral, indifferent, Mn.; MBh. &c.; being of a middle condition or kind, middling, MBh.; Kāv.; m. 'arbitrator, umpire,' N. of Śiva, Śivag.; *-tā*, f. intermediate situation, indifference, impartiality, MBh.; R. &c. **-sthala**, n. (ifc. f. *ī*) a middle place or region, (esp.) the m° of the body, the waist or hip, L. **-sthāna**, n. the m° space i.e. the air (*-devatā*, f. a deity of the air, Nir.); a neutral soil, MW. **-sthita**, mfn. being in the middle, being among or between (gen.), Kathās.; (*ā*), f. indifference, MBh. (cf. *-stha-tā*). **-sthity-ardha**, m. or n. (in astron.) the mean half duration. **-svarita**, mfn. having the Svarita accent on the middle syllable, VPrāt., Sch. **Madhyâkshara-vistara-lipi**, f. N. of a partic. kind of written character, Lalit. **Madhyâṅguli** (or °*lī*), f. the middle finger, L. **Madhyâditya**, m. the midday sun (*-gate 'hani*, 'when the day has reached the mid-sun' i. e. at noon), R. **Madhyâdhidevaná**, n. the middle of a playing-ground, MaitrS. **Madhyânta**, (ibc.) middle and end; *-yamaka*, n. a Yamaka (s. v.) in the m° and end of a verse (e.g. Bhaṭṭ. x, 17); *-vibhaṅga-śāstra* or *-vibhāga-ś*°, n. N. of wk. **Madhyântika**, m. N. of an Arhat, Buddh. **Madhyâmla-kesara**, m. or n. the citron, L. **Madhyârjuna**, m. or n. N. of a district, Cat.; *-kshetra-māhātmya*, n. N. of wk., ib.; *-tīrtha*, n. N. of a Tīrtha on the southern bank of the Kaverī, ib. **Madhyā-varsha**, n. the middle of the rainy season, Br.; GṛŚrS. **Madhyâsthi**, n. Grewia Asiatica, L. **Madhyâhāriṇī-lipi**, f. N. of a partic. kind of written character, Lalit. (C. *adhyāh*°). **Madhyâhna**, m. midday, noon, Mn.; MBh. &c.; N. of a pupil of Saṃkarâcārya, Śaṃkar.; *-kāla*, m. midday time, noon, Kathās.; *-kṛitya*, n. midday duty or business or observance, Cat.; *-kriyā*, f. id., MW.; *-velā*, f. = *-kāla*, Pañcat.; *-saṃdhyā*, f. the m° Saṃdhyā, RTL. 407; *-samaya*, m. = *-kāla*, Pañcat.; *-savana*, n. m° sacrifice, Kathās.; *-snāna-vidhi*, m. m° ablution, Cat.; °*hnêndu-prabhā-karṇa*, m. or n. the hypotenuse of the moon's m° shadow, MW. **Madhyâhnika**, m. Pentapetes Phoenicea, Bhpr. **Madhyêbha-bandhana**, n. a band or rope round an elephant's body, L. **Madhyôdātta**, mfn. having the Udātta or acute accent on the middle syllable, VPrāt.

Madhyanya, mfn. occupying a middle place, having a m° rank or position (in any caste &c.), L.

Madhyamá, mf(*ā*)n. (superl. of *mádhya*) middle (used like Lat. *medius*, e.g. *madhyame gulme*, 'in the midst of the troop'), MBh.; R.; being or placed in the middle, middlemost, intermediate, central, RV. &c. &c.; middle-born (neither youngest nor oldest), Veṇīs.; of a middle kind or size or quality, middling, moderate, TS. &c. &c.; standing between two persons or parties, impartial, neutral, MBh.; Kāv. &c.; (in astron.) mean (cf. *madhya*), Sūryas.; relating to the meridian, ib.; m. the middlemost prince (whose territory lies between that of a king seeking conquest and that of his foe), Mn. vii, 155; the middle character in plays, IW. 473; the midland country (= *madhya-deśa*), L.; (in music) the 4th or 5th note, Saṃgīt.; the middlemost of the 3 scales, ib.; a partic. Rāga, ib.; (in gram.) the 2nd person (= *-purusha*), Pāṇ.; the governor of a province, L.; a kind of antelope, L.; N. of the 18th Kalpa (s. v.), Cat.; pl. a class of gods, ŚāṅkhŚr.; (with Buddhists) N. of a partic. Buddh. sect, Sarvad.; m. n. the middle of the body, waist, MBh.; R. &c.; (*ā*), f. the womb, TBr.; the middle finger, Kauś.; Suśr.; midnight, L.; a girl arrived at puberty, L.; the pericarp of a lotus, L.; a central blossom, W.; a kind of metre, L.; (in music) a partic. Mūrchanā, Saṃgīt.; n. the middle, APrāt.; mediocrity, defectiveness, Śriṅgār.; N. of the 12th (14th) Kāṇḍa of the ŚBr.; (in astron.) the meridian ecliptic point, Sūryas. **-kakshā**, f. the middle enclosure or courtyard, MBh. **-kāṇḍa**, n. N. of the 2nd Kāṇḍa of the MaitrS. **-khaṇḍa**, n. (in alg.) the middle term of an equation; N. of part ii of the ŚārṅgS. **-gati**, f. (in astron.) mean motion of a planet, Cat. **-grāma**, m. (in music) the middle scale, Saṃgīt. **-jāta**, mfn. middle-born, born between (two other children), middlemost. **-ṭīkā**, f. N. of a wk. by Kumārila, Cat. **-pada**, n. the middle number (which is sometimes omitted and requires to be supplied in a compound consisting of two words); *-lopa*, m. the omission of the middle member of a compound (as in *Śāka-pārthiva*, the king of the era, for *Śāka-priya-pārthiva*, the king dear to the era), Vām. v, 2, 16; *-lopin*, m. (scil. *samāsa*) a compound which omits the middle number, ib. **-parṇá**, n. (prob.) a middle-sized leaf, MaitrS. **-pāṇḍava**, m. 'the middlemost of the five Pāṇḍavas,' Arjuna, W. **-purusha**, m. a partic. personification, Gaut.; (in gram.) the second person in verbal conjugation, a termination of the second person (cf. *prathama-purusha, uttama-purusha*). **-pūrusha**, m. a mediocre person, MBh. **-bhṛitaka**, m. a husbandman, a farm-labourer who works both for his master and himself, W. **-yāna**, n. 'the middle passage,' the middle way to salvation, MWB. 159. **-rātra**, m. midnight, AitBr.; Kauś. **-rekhā**, f. (in astron.) the central meridian of the earth (a line conceived to be drawn through Laṅkā, Ujjayinī, Kuru-kshetra, and Meru; cf. *madhya-rekhā*). **-loka**, m. the middle world (between heaven and the nether world), the earth; *-pāla*, m. 'protector of the middle world,' a king, Kāv.; °*kêndu*, m. 'moon of the middle world,' a king, Rājat. **-vayas**, n. middle age, ŚBr. **-vayaska**, mfn. middle-aged, W. **-vāh**, mfn. driving at middling or slow speed (= *manda-gamanena vāhaka*), RV. ii, 29, 4, Sāy. (prob. 'driving in the middle,' scil. between gods and men). **-śī**, m. 'lying or being in the middle,' (prob.) an intercessor, RV. x, 97, 12. **-saṃgraha**, m. the middle method of intriguing with another's wife (presenting flowers &c.), W. **-sāhasa**, m. the middlemost penalty or amercement, punishment for crimes of a middle degree, Mn. viii, 138, 263; m. n. violence or outrage of the middle class (injuring buildings, throwing down walls &c.), W. **-stha**, mfn. standing or being in the middle, g. *brāhmaṇâdi*. **-sthā**, mfn. standing in the middle, forming the centre (of a community), VS. **-sthéya**, n. the state of standing in the middle or forming the centre, TS. **-svara**, m. the middle or dominant note, Mālav. i, 21; mfn. spoken in a m° tone (not too loud and not too low), R. **Madhyamâgama**, m. one of the 4 Āgamas, Buddh. **Madhyamâṅgiras**, m. the middle-sized Aṅgiras, Cat. **Madhyamâṅguli**, m. the m° finger, L. **Madhyamâtreya**, m. the m°-sized Ātreya, Cat. **Madhyamâdi**, m. or °**dī**, f. (in music) a partic. Rāgiṇī, Saṃgīt. **Madhyamâdhikāra**, m. N. of the 1st ch. of Sūryas. **Madhyamâharaṇa**, n. the elimination of the middle term of an equation, Col. **Madhyamêśvara**, m. N. of a Liṅga of Śiva in Benares, KūrmaP. **Madhyamêshā**, f. a partic. part of a chariot, MaitrS.; TS. **Madhyamôccais-tara**, mf(*ā*)n. half loud and very loud, Vait. **Madhyamôtkhāta**, m. a partic. division of time, L.

Madhyamaka, mf(*ikā*)n. middlemost, Mṛicch.; common (as property), KātyŚr., Sch.; (*ikā*), f. a marriageable woman, L.; N. of the 2nd or middle Grantha of the Kāṭhaka (cf. *mādhyamika*); n. the interior of anything (°*kam pra-√viś*, to enter), Mṛicch. **-vṛitti**, f. N. of wk. (also *madhyamika-v*°). **Madhyamakâlaṃkāra**, m., °**kâloka**, m. N. of 2 wks.

Madhyamakeya, m. pl. N. of a people, MBh.

Madhyamika, prob. w. r. for *mādhyamika*, q. v. **-vṛitti**, see under *madhyamaka*.

Madhyamīya, mfn. relating to the middle, middlemost, central, g. *gahâdi*.

Madhyame-shṭhá (MaitrS.), **-shṭhā́** (AV.), **-shṭhéya** (MaitrS.), mfn. = *madhyama-sthā*.

Madhyā́, ind. in the middle, between, among (gen.), RV. i, 89, 9 &c.; meanwhile, ib. x, 61, 6.

Madhyāyin, mfn. recited in the middle tone, SaṃhUp.

Madhyāyu (Padap. °*ya-yu*), mfn. intermediate, being a mediator or seeking a mediation, RV. i, 173, 10.

Madhye, ind. in the middle, in the midst, within, between, among, in the presence of (with gen. or ifc.; sometimes also ibc.; cf. Pāṇ. ii, 1, 18 and comp. below), Mn.; MBh. &c. (with √*kṛi* [ind. p. *-kṛitya* or *-kṛitvā*, Pāṇ. i, 4, 76], to place in the middle, make an intermediary of, Kull. on Mn. iv, 80; to count among, Kād.) **-kṛitya**, ind. with regard to, Mālav. v, 2. **-gaṅgam**, ind. in or into the Ganges, Pāṇ. ii, 1, 18, Sch. **-guru**, mfn. (prob.) having a long syllable in the middle, Pāṇ. vi, 3, 11. **-cchandas**, (prob. n.) said to mean 'the sun' or 'the middle of the year,' PārGṛ. iii, 3, 5, Sch. **-jaṭharam**, ind. in the m° of the body, Bhām. **-jalāt**, ind. from out of the m° of the water, Bhaṭṭ. **-jyotis**, f. a kind of Vedic metre, RPrāt. **-nagaram**, ind. in the m° of the city, Rājat. **-nadi**, ind. in or into the river, Kathās. **-narêśvara-sabham**, ind. in the m° of the assembly of princes, Bālar. **-nidhana**, mfn. having the passage called Nidhana (s. v.) in the m°, Lāṭy. **-padmam**, ind. in a lotus flower, Vām. **-pṛishṭham**, ind. having the sacrificial days called Pṛishṭhya (s. v.) in the m°, ŚāṅkhŚr.; n. a partic. Ajana, TāṇḍBr. **-madhyamâṅguli-karpūram**, ind. between middle finger and elbow, L. **-yajñam**, ind. in the middle of the sacrifice, ĀpŚr., Sch. **-raṇam**, ind. in the battle, Bhām. **-rathyam**, ind. in the m° of the street, ib. **-vāri**, ind. in or under the water, R. **-vārdhi**, ind. = *-samudram*, HPariś. **-vindhyâṭavi**, ind. in the forests of the Vindhya range, KāśīKh. **-vindhyântar**, ind. in the m° of the Vindhya, Kathās. **-vyoma**, ind. in the air, Bālar. **-śmaśānam**, ind. on the burial-place, Śvapnac. **-sabham**, ind. in the assembly, in public, Dhanaṃj. **-samudram**, ind. in the middle of the sea, Śiś.

मध्व *madhva*, m. N. of the founder of a sect of Vaishṇavas in the south of India (he was a Kanarese Brāhman otherwise called Ānanda-tīrtha, Bhagavat-pāda or Madhu, said to have been born about 1200; his doctrine is commonly called Dvaita, 'Duality,' in opposition to the A-dvaita, 'Non-duality,' of the great Vedântist Saṃkarâcārya, and his sect are called Mādhvas), RTL. 130 &c. **-guru**, m. the teacher Madhva, Cat. **-tantra-capeṭā-pradīpa**, m. and **-tantra-dūshaṇa**, n. N. of wks. **-mata**, n. the doctrine of M°; *-khaṇḍana*, n.,

-prakaraṇa, n., -pradarśana, n., -vidhvaṅsana, n., -saṃgraha-ṭīkā, f. N. of wks. **-māhātmya,** n., **-muktâvali,** f., **-mukha-bhaṅga,** m., **-mukha-mardana,** n., **-vaṅśâvalī,** f., **-vijaya,** m., **-vidhvaṅsana,** n., **-vedânta,** m., **-sahasra-nāma-bhāshya,** n., **-siddhânta,** m. (and °ta-bhañjana, n., °ta-sāra, m.), **-stuti,** f. N. of wks. **Madhvâcārya,** m. = madhva-guru, W. **Madhvârtha-dhvaṅsinī,** f., **Madhvâhnika,** n. N. of wks.

Madhvaka &c. See p. 781, col. 3.

Madhv-aksha &c. See p. 781, col. 2.

मन् man, cl. 8. 4. Ā. (Dhātup. xxx, 9; xxv, 67) manuté, mányate (ep. also °ti; 3. pl. manvaté, RV.; pf. mene, Br. &c.; mamnā́the, °nā́te, RV.; aor. ámata, ámanmahi, Subj. manāmahe, mananta, p. manānā́, q.v., RV.; maṅsi, amaṅsta, Subj. maṅsate, Prec. maṅsīshṭa, 1. pers. m. c. masīya, ib.; mā́ṅsta, AV., °stām, TĀr.; mandhvam, Br.; amanishṭa, Gr.; fut. maṅsyate, Br., °ti, MBh.; mantā, manitā, Gr.; manishyate, RV.; inf. mantum, MBh. &c., mántave, °tavai, RV., mántos, Br.; ind. p. matvā́, Up. &c.; manitvā, Gr.; -matya, Br. &c.; -manya, MBh. &c.), to think, believe, imagine, suppose, conjecture, RV. &c. &c. (manye, I think, methinks, is in later language often inserted in a sentence without affecting the construction; cf. g. câdi and Pāṇ. iv, 1, 106); to regard or consider any one or anything (acc.) as (acc. with or without iva, or adv., often in -vat; in later language also dat., to express contempt [cf. Pāṇ. ii, 3, 17], e.g. rājyaṃ triṇāya manye, 'I value empire at a straw,' i.e. I make light of it, = laghu √man and opp. to bahu or sādhu √man, to think much or well of, praise, approve), ib.; to think one's self or be thought to be, appear as, pass for (nom.; also with iva), ib.; to be of opinion, think fit or right, MBh.; Kāv. &c.; to agree or be of the same opinion with (acc.), MBh.; to set the heart or mind on, honour, esteem (with na, disdain), hope or wish for (acc. or gen.), RV. &c. &c.; to think of (in prayer &c., either 'to remember, meditate on,' or 'mention, declare,' or 'excogitate, invent'), RV.; AV.; to perceive, observe, learn, know, understand, comprehend (acc., Ved. also gen.), RV. &c. &c.; to offer, present, MBh.: Caus. (Dhātup. xxxiv, 36) mānayati (ep. also °te; aor. amīmanat; Pass. mānyate), to honour, esteem, value highly (also with uru, bahu and sādhu), AV. &c. &c.; (Ā.) stambhe, Dhātup. xxxiii, 35; garvake, ib., Vop.: Desid. (Dhātup. xxiii, 3) mīmāṅsate (rarely °ti; amīmāṅsishṭhās, ŚBr.; mīmāṅsyáte, AV.; mimaṅsate, mimanishate, Gr.), to reflect upon, consider, examine, investigate, AV.; Br. &c.; to call in question, doubt ('with regard to,' loc.), ib.: Desid. of Desid. mīmāṅsishate, Gr.: Intens. manmanyate, manmanti, ib. [Cf. Zd. man; Gk. μένω, μέμονα; Lat. meminisse, monere; Slav. and Lith. miněti; Goth. ga-munan; Germ. meinen; Eng. mean.]

Matá, mfn. thought, believed, imagined, supposed, understood, RV. &c. &c.; regarded or considered as, taken or passing for (nom. or adv.), Mn.; MBh. &c.; thought fit or right, approved, Yājñ.; Kāv.; Kām.; honoured, esteemed, respected, liked (with gen., Pāṇ. iii, 2, 188), Ragh.; Kām.; desired, intended, R.; m. N. of a son of Śambara, Hariv. (v.l. mana); n. a thought, idea, opinion, sentiment, view, belief, doctrine, MBh.; Kāv. &c.; intention, design, purpose, wish, MBh.; BhP.; commendation, approbation, sanction, L.; knowledge, W.; agallochum, L. **-khaṇḍana-stotra,** n. N. of wk. **-mga,** see s.v. **-catushṭaya-parīkshā,** f. N. of wk. **-jña,** mfn. knowing a person's intention, Śṛiṅgār. **-parīkshā,** f. N. of wk. **-bheda,** m. difference of opinion between (gen. and instr. with saha), VarBṛS., Sch. **-bhedana,** n. N. of wk. **-yogīśa,** m. N. of a man, L. **-vacas,** mfn. heeding words or prayers (said of the Aśvins), RV. (cf. mātavacasa). **-vat** (matá-), mfn. having an aim or purpose, ib. **Matâksha,** mfn. one well skilled in dice (as Śakuni), MBh. **Matânujñā,** f. admission of a fault in one's own reasoning while insisting on a similar one in that of the opponent, Nyāyas. **Matântara,** n. another opinion or creed or sect, MW. **Matâvalambana,** n. the embracing a particular doctrine, ib. **Matâvalambin,** mfn. holding the doctrines of a particular sect, ib.

Mataṃga, m. 'going wilfully' or 'roaming at will,' an elephant, MBh.; Śrutab.; a cloud, L.; N. of a Dānava, Hariv.; of a Muni and (pl.) his family, MBh.; Kāv. **-ja,** m. an elephant (-tva, n.), Kālid.; Kir.; (ā), f. (in music) a partic. Mūrchanā, Saṃgīt. **-tīrtha,** n. N. of a sacred bathing-place, Cat. **-deva,** m. N. of a fabulous being, Kathās. **-pāramêśvara,** m. N. of wk. **-pura,** n. N. of a city, Kathās. **-yajñâgni,** m. fire from the sacrifice of Mataṃga, Mcar. **-vāpī,** f. N. of a sacred tank or bathing-place, Vishṇ.; MBh. **-vṛitti,** f. N. of wk. **-sarasa,** m. N. of a lake, R. **-hataka,** m. N. of a man, Cat. **Mataṃgânúcara,** m. the keeper or driver of an elephant, Suparṇ.

Mataṃginī, f. N. of a daughter of Mandara, Kathās.

Matí (in ŚBr. also máti), f. devotion, prayer, worship, hymn, sacred utterance, RV.; VS.; thought, design, intention, resolution, determination, inclination, wish, desire (with loc., dat. or inf.), RV. &c. &c. (matyā, ind. wittingly, knowingly, purposely; matiṃ √kṛi or dhā or dhṛi or ā-√dhā or sam-ā-√dhā or ā-√sthā or sam-ā-√sthā, with loc., dat., acc. with prati, or artham ifc., to set the heart on, make up one's mind, resolve, determine; matim with Caus. of ni-√vṛit and abl. of a verbal noun, to give up the idea of; āhita-mati, ifc. = having resolved upon; vinivṛitta-mati with abl. = having desisted from); opinion, notion, idea, belief, conviction, view, creed, ŚrS.; Mn.; MBh. &c. (matyā, ind. at will; ifc., 'under the idea of,' e.g. vyāghra-m°, 'under the idea of its being a tiger'); the mind, perception, understanding, intelligence, sense, judgment, ŚBr. &c. &c. (in RV. also 'that which is sensible,' intelligent, mindful, applied to Aditi, Indra and Agni); esteem, respect, regard, Kir.; memory, remembrance, L.; Opinion personified (and identified with Subalâtmajā as one of the mothers of the five sons of Pāṇḍu, or regarded as a daughter of Daksha and wife of Soma, or as the wife of Viveka), MBh.; Hariv.; Prab.; a kind of vegetable or pot-herb, L.; m. N. of a king, Buddh. [Cf. Lat. mens; Angl.Sax. ge-mynd; Eng. mind.] **-karman,** n. a matter of the intellect, Kām. **-gati,** f. 'mental course,' mode of thought, Kāv. **-garbha,** mfn. 'filled with intelligence,' clever, intelligent, Śiś. **-citra,** m. N. of Aśva-ghosha, Buddh. **-datta,** m. N. of a man, Cat. **-darśana,** n. the act or faculty of seeing into the thoughts or intentions (of others), R. **-dā,** f. Cardiospermum Halicacabum or = śimṛiḍī, L. **-dvaidha,** n. difference of opinion, MBh. **-dhvaja,** m. N. of a nephew of Śaskya-paṇḍita, Buddh. **-nāra,** m. N. of a king, MBh.; Hariv.; Pur. **-nirṇaya,** m. N. of wk. **-niścaya,** m. a firm opinion, L. **-patha,** m. the path of reflection; °thaṃ √nī, to think over, Kāv. **-pura,** n. N. of a town, Buddh. **-pūrva** or °**vaka,** mfn. purposed, intended, Mn.; (°vam, °ve and °vakam) ind. purposingly, wittingly, ib.; Gaut. **-prakarsha,** m. superiority of mind, cleverness, talent, Hit. **-bhadra-gaṇi,** m. N. of a scholar, Cat. **-bheda,** m. change of opinion, MBh. **-bhrama,** m. (Śak.), **-bhrānti,** f. (L.) confusion of mind, perplexity, error, misapprehension. **-mat,** mfn. clever, intelligent, wise, MBh.; Kāv. &c.; m. N. of a son of Janam-ejaya, Hariv. **-mānusha** (?) and **-mukura,** m. N. of wks. **-ratna-muni,** m. N. of an author, Cat. **-rāja,** m. N. of a poet, ib. **-vat,** w.r. for -mat. **-vardhana,** m. N. of an author (also °na-gaṇi), Cat. **-vid,** mfn. knowing (one's) devotion or mind, VS.; TS.; AitBr. **-viparyaya,** m. an erroneous opinion, illusion, Vcar. **-vibhraṅśa,** m. failure or infatuation of mind, L. **-vibhrama,** m. = -bhrama, R. **-vibhrānti,** f. id., L. **-śālin,** mfn. 'possessing intelligence,' clever, wise, Pañcat. **-hīna,** mfn. deprived of sense, stupid, Hit. **Matīśvara,** m. 'lord of mind,' the wisest of the wise (Viśva-karman), Hariv.

2. **Matya,** n. (for 1. see p. 776, col. 2) the means of acquiring knowledge (= jñānasya kāraṇam), Kāś. on Pāṇ. iv, 4, 97.

1. **Mana,** m. Indian spikenard, Nardostachys Jatamansi, L.; N. of a son of Śambara, Hariv. (v.l. mata).

2. **Mana,** in comp. for manas. **-āpa,** mfn. gaining the heart, attracting, beautiful, L. (cf. Pāli manāpa). **-ṛiṅga** (mána-), mfn. (prob. fr. √2. ṛiñj) directing or guiding the mind, RV. x, 106, 8 (Sāy. manasā prasādhanaṃ yasya saḥ). **-nī,** see mananyà below. **-rañjana,** mf(ī)n. delighting the mind of (comp.), Subh. **-vasas** (?), m. N. of a prince, VP. **-haṅsa,** m. (w.r. for °no-h°?) a kind of metre, Col. **Manâpa,** mfn. = mana-āpa, Lalit.

Manaḥ, in comp. for manas. **-kānta,** mfn., see manas-k°. **-kshepa,** m. mental perplexity or confusion, Sāh. **-pati,** m. 'lord of the heart,' N. of Vishṇu, Pañcar. **-paryāya,** m. (with Jainas) 'the state of mental perception which precedes the attainment of perfect knowledge,' N. of the last stage but one in the perception of truth, Sarvad. **-pīḍā,** f. pain of mind, mental agony, MW. **-pūta,** mfn. pure in heart, mentally pure, Mn. vi, 46. **-praṇīta,** mfn. dear to the heart or mind, MBh. xiii, 3503. **-prasāda,** m. serenity or peace of mind, MBh.; Sāh.; Suśr. **-priya,** mf(ā)n. dear to the heart, Kir. **-prīti,** f. gladness of heart, delight, Kathās. **-śikshā,** f. N. of wk. (containing the Caitanya doctrine), Cat. **-śilā,** f. (L. also °la, m.; cf. comp.) realgar, red arsenic, MBh.; Kāv. &c.; -giri, v.l. for °lôccaya, R.; -guhā, f. a cave of red a°, MBh. (°la-guhā, Mṛicch. i, 12); -candana-dhāvana, n. a fluid prepared from r° a° and sandal, MW.; -vicchurita, mfn. inlaid with r° a°, Kum.; °lôccaya, m. a quantity of red arsenic, R. **-śīghra,** mfn. swift as thought, Kathās. **-śūka,** n. anguish of mind, Divyâv. **-shashṭha** (mánaḥ-), mfn. having the mind for a sixth organ (said of the 5 organs of sense), AV. **-saṃvara,** m. coercion of the mind, Lalit. **-saṃkalpa,** m. desire of the heart, R. **-saṅga,** m. attachment of the mind, fixing the thoughts (on a beloved one; second stage of love), Pratāp. **-saṃcetanâhāra,** m. one of the 4 kinds of food (in a material and spiritual sense), Buddh. **-sád,** mfn. seated or dwelling in the mind, VS. **-saṃtāpa,** m. mental anguish or grief, Śak. **-samunnati,** f. high-mindedness, R. **-samṛiddhi,** f. heart's content, BhP. **-sāra-maya,** mf(ī)n. forming the substance of the heart or mind, Hariv. **-siddhi,** f. N. of a goddess, Siṅhâs. **-silā,** w.r. for -śilā. **-sukha,** mfn. agreeable to the mind, of pleasant taste, Suśr.; n. joy of the heart, BhP. **-stha,** mf(ā)n. abiding or dwelling in the heart, R. **-sthirī-karaṇa,** n. the act of strengthening or confirming the mind, Cat. **-sthairya,** n. firmness of mind, Kāv. **-sparśa,** mfn. touching the heart, BhP. **-svāmin,** m. N. of a Brāhman, Kathās.

Manaka, m. N. of a man, HPariś.

Manána, mfn. thoughtful, careful, RV.; n. thinking, reflection, meditation, thought, intelligence, understanding (esp. intrinsic knowledge or science, as one of the faculties connected with the senses; Nir. viii, 6 = manman), Hariv.; Śaṃk.; Sarvad. (°nā́, ind. thoughtfully, deliberately, RV.); homage, reverence, Sāy. on RV. i, 165, 4. **-grantha,** m., **-prakaraṇa,** n. N. of wks. **-yukta** and **-vat,** mfn. attended with homage, Sāy. **Mananâdi-nighaṇṭu,** m. N. of wk.

Mananīya, mfn. (prob.) containing homage or praise (as a hymn), Nir. x, 5 (others 'estimable').

Mananyà, mfn. deserving praise, RV. x, 106, 8 (Sāy. = stútya, others 'fr. mana-nī, directing the mind').

Manayitṛi, mf(trī)n., Sāy. on RV. i, 124, 3.

Manaś, in comp. for manas. **-1. -cit,** mfn. (√1. ci) piled up or constructed with the mind (= manasā citaḥ), ŚBr. **-2. -cit,** mfn. (√2. cit) thinking or reflecting in the mind, RV. ix, 11, 8 (others 'knowing the heart').

Mánas, n. mind (in its widest sense as applied to all the mental powers), intellect, intelligence, understanding, perception, sense, conscience, will, RV. &c. &c. (in phil. the internal organ or antaḥ-karaṇa of perception and cognition, the faculty or instrument through which thoughts enter or by which objects of sense affect the soul, IW. 53; in this sense manas is always regarded as distinct from ātman and purusha, 'spirit or soul' and belonging only to the body, like which it is—except in the Nyāya—considered perishable; as to its position in the various systems see for Nyāya and Vaiśeshika, IW. 63; 67; 76, for Sāṃkhya and Vedânta, ib. 84; 109; 117; in RV. it is sometimes joined with hṛid or hṛidaya, the heart; Mn. vii, 6 with cakshus, the eye); the spirit or spiritual principle, the breath or living soul which escapes from the body at death (called asu in animals; cf. above), ib.; thought, imagination, excogitation, invention, reflection, opinion, intention, inclination, affection, desire, mood, temper, spirit, ib. (ifc. after a verbal noun or an inf. stem in °tu = having a mind or wishing to; cf. drashṭu-m° &c.; manaḥ √kṛi, to make up one's mind; with gen., to feel inclination for; *manaḥ* √*kṛi*, *pra*-√*kṛi*, √*dhā*, *vi*-√*dhā*, √*dhṛi*, √*bandh* and Caus. of *ni*-√*viś* with loc., dat., acc. with *prati*, or inf., to direct the mind or thoughts towards, think of or upon; *manaḥ* with *sam-ā*-√*dhā*, to recover the senses, collect one's self; with √*han*, see *mano-hatya*; *mánasā*, ind. in the mind; in thought or imagination; with all the heart, willingly; with gen., by the leave of; with *iva* = °*sêva*, as with a thought, in a moment; with √*man*, to think in one's mind, be willing or inclined; with *sam*-√*gam*, to become unanimous, agree; *manasi* with √*kṛi*, to bear or ponder in the mind, meditate on, remember; with *ni*-√*dhā*, to impress on the mind, consider; with √*vṛit*, to be passing in one's mind); N. of the 26th Kalpa (s.v.), Cat.; of the lake Mānasa, BhP.; *manaso dohaḥ*, N. of a Sāman, ĀrshBr. [Cf. Gk. μένος; Lat. *Miner-va.*] **-kānta**, mfn. dear to the heart, pleasant, agreeable, Suśr. **-kāra**, m. consciousness (esp. of pleasure or pain), L.; attention of the mind, Lalit.; devotion (see next); *-vidhi*, m. performance of devotion, Jātakam. **-ketá**, m. mental perception or conception, idea, notion, AV. **-tāpa**, m. 'burning of the mind,' mental pain, anguish, repentance, MBh.; R. &c. **-tāla**, m. N. of the lion on which Durgā is carried, L. **-tushṭi**, f. satisfaction of mind, heart's content, MW. **-tejas** (*mánas-*), mfn. endowed with vigour of mind, AV. **-tokā**, f. N. of Durgā, L. **-tva**, n. intellectual state, the state or condition of mind, Sarvad. **-pāpa**, n. mental sin, a sin committed only in mind, AV. **-máya**, mf(*ī*)n. spiritual (as opp. to 'material'), RV. **-vat** (*mánas-*), mfn. full of sense or spirit, RV.; TS.; Kāth.; KaushUp.; containing the word *manas*, TS.; Kāth.; (*atī*), f., w.r. for *ánas-vatī*, TāṇḍBr. **-vi**, in comp. for *-vin*; *-garhita*, mfn. censured by the wise, MW.; *-tara*, mfn. wiser, cleverer, Kāṭh.; *-tā*, f. intelligence, high-mindedness, magnanimity, Kir.; hope, expectation, dependance, W.; *-praśaṅsā*, f. praise of the wise, Cat. **-vín**, mfn. full of mind or sense, intelligent, clever, wise, TBr. &c. &c.; in high spirits, cheerful, glad (*a-man*°), R.; fixing the mind, attentive, W.; m. the fabulous animal called Śarabha, L.; N. of a Nāga, Lalit.; of a son of Devala, VP.; (*inī*), f. a virtuous wife, W.; Momordica Mixta, L.; N. of the mother of the moon, MBh. (cf. *manasi-ja*); of Durgā, L.; of the wife of Mṛikaṇḍu, Pur.

Manasá, m. N. of a Ṛishi, RV. v, 44, 10 (Sāy.); (*ā*), f., see 1. *manasā*; n. (ifc., with f. *ā*) = *manas*, mind, heart, PārGṛ.; MBh. &c.

Mánasas-páti, m. the lord or presiding genius of the mental powers and life of men, RV.; Br.; ŚrS.

1. **Manasā**, f. N. of a partic. goddess (described as consisting of a particle of Prakṛiti and as daughter of Kaśyapa, sister of the serpent-king Ananta, wife of the Muni Jarat-kāru, mother of the Muni Āstīka, and protectress of men from the venom of serpents; cf. *visha-harī*), Pañcar.; of a Kiṃ-narī, Kāraṇḍ. **-devī**, f. the goddess Manasā, L. **-pañcamī**, f. the 5th day in the dark half of the month Āshāḍha (when there is a festival in honour of the goddess Manasā), Col. **-rāma**, m. N. of a man, Cat.

2. **Manasā**, instr. of *manas*, in comp. **-guptā**, f. (prob.) N. of a woman, Pāṇ. vi, 3, 4, Sch. **-°jñāyin** (°*sājñ*°), mfn. perceiving with the soul or intellectually, ib. 5, Sch. **-dattā** and **-saṃgatā**, f. (prob.) N. of women, ib. 4.

Manasi, loc. of *manas*, in comp. **-kāra**, m. taking to heart, Lalit. **-ja**, m. 'heart-born,' love or the god of love, Kāv.; the moon, RāmatUp.; *-taru*, m.l°conceived as a tree, Mālav.; *-bṛisī*, f. the moon, Alaṃkārav. **-manda**, mfn. slow or inert in love, MW.; *-ruj*, f. pain of love, Vikr. **-śaya**, m. 'lying in the heart,' = *-ja*, Vikr.

Manasín, mfn. having a mind or soul, having intellect, TS.

Manaská, n. dimin. of *manas*, AV. vi, 18, 3; (ifc.) = *manas*; cf. *gata-m*°.

Manasya, Nom. P. Ā. °*syáti*, °*te* (g. *kaṇḍv-ādi*), to have in mind, intend, RV.; ChUp.; to think, reflect, TBr.; Nir.

Manasyú, mfn. (prob.) wishing, desiring, RV.; m. N. of a prince (son of Pravīra), MBh.; of a son of Mahānta, VP.

Maná, f. devotion, attachment, zeal, eagerness, RV.; envy, jealousy, ib. **-vasu**, mfn. rich in devotion, faithful, ib.

Manák, ind. (prob. fr. *manā* + *añc*, 'perceivably') a little, slightly, in a small degree (*dānam manāg api*, a gift however small; *kālam manāk*, a little time; *na m*°, not at all; *manāg asmi na pātitaḥ*, I was all but thrown down), Kāv.; Kathās. &c.; shortly, immediately, at once, Prasannar.; only, merely, Ratnâv. **-kara**, mfn. doing little, lazy, MW.; n. a kind of Agallochum, L. **-priya**, mfn. a little dear, MW.

Manāná, mfn. devout, pious, RV. vi, 67, 10.

Manānák, ind. (prob.) = *manāk*, a little, a short time, RV. x, 61, 6.

Manāya, Nom. P. °*yáti*, to be zealous or devoted, RV.; to think, consider, ib.

Manā́yī, f. (fr. *manu*) Manu's wife, MaitrS. (cf. *manāvī*).

Manāyú, mfn. (fr. *manā*) zealous, devoted, RV.; desirous, praying, ib.

Manāvī́, f. (fr. *manu*) Manu's wife, ŚBr. (cf. *manā́yī*).

Manita, mfn. known, understood, L.

Manī-√kṛi, P. *-karoti*, to take to heart, Vop.

Manīshá, f. thought, reflection, consideration, wisdom, intelligence, conception, idea (*páro manīsháyā*, beyond all conception), RV. &c. &c.; prayer, hymn, RV.; desire, wish, request, ib. **-pañcaka**, n. N. of two wks.

Manīshikā, f. wisdom, intelligence (*sva-manīshikayā*, 'according to one's own judgment'), BhP.; expectation, Bālar.

Manīshiṇā (?), f. a kind of metre, Śrutab.

Manīshita, mfn. desired, wished, MBh.; Kāv. &c.; n. wish, desire, ib. (cf. *yathā-m*°). **-varshin**, mfn. showering desired objects (like a rain), Rājat.

Manīshin, mfn. thoughtful, intelligent, wise, sage, prudent, RV. &c. &c.; devout, offering prayers or praises, RV.; m. a learned Brāhman, teacher, Paṇḍit, W.; N. of a king, VP. **Manīshi-tā**, f. wisdom, Veṇis.

Mánu, mfn. thinking, wise, intelligent, VS.; ŚBr.; m. 'the thinking creature (?)', man, mankind, RV.; VS.; AitBr.; TĀr. (also as opp. to evil spirits, RV. i, 130, 8; viii, 98, 6 &c.; the Ṛibhus are called *mánor nápātaḥ*, the sons of man, iii, 60, 3); the Man par excellence or the representative man and father of the human race (regarded in the RV. as the first to have instituted sacrifices and religious ceremonies, and associated with the Ṛishis Kaṇva and Atri; in the AitBr. described as dividing his possessions among some of his sons to the exclusion of one called Nābhā-nedishṭha, q.v.; called Sāṃvaraṇa as author of RV. ix, 101, 10–12; Āpsava as author of ib. 106, 7–9; in Naigh. v, 6 he is numbered among the 31 divine beings of the upper sphere, and VS. xi, 66 as father of men even identified with Prajā-pati; but the name Manu is esp. applied to 14 successive mythical progenitors and sovereigns of the earth, described Mn. i, 63 and in later wks. as creating and supporting this world through successive Antaras or long periods of time, see *manv-antara* below; the first is called Svāyambhuva as sprung from *Svayam-bhū*, the Self-existent, and described in Mn. i, 34 as a sort of secondary creator, who commenced his work by producing 10 Prajāpatis or Maharshis, of whom the first was *Marīci*, Light; to this Manu is ascribed the celebrated 'code of Manu,' see *manu-saṃhitā*, and two ancient Sūtra works on Kalpa and Gṛihya i.e. sacrificial and domestic rites; he is also called Hiraṇyagarbha as son of Hiraṇya-garbha, and Prācetasa, as son of Pra-cetas; the next 5 Manus are called Svārocisha, Auttami, Tāmasa, Raivata, Cākshusha, cf. IW. 208, n. 1; the 7th Manu, called *Vaivasvata*, Sun-born, or from his piety, *Satya-vrata*, is regarded as the progenitor of the present race of living beings, and said, like the Noah of the Old Testament, to have been preserved from a great flood by Vishṇu or Brahmā in the form of a fish: he is also variously described as one of the 12 Ādityas, as the author of RV. viii, 27–31, as the brother of Yama, who as a son of the Sun is also called Vaivasvata, as the founder and first king of Ayodhyā, and as father of Ilā who married Budha, son of the Moon, the two great solar and lunar races being thus nearly related to each other, see IW. 344; 373; the 8th Manu or first of the future Manus, accord. to VP. iii, 2, will be Sāvarṇi; the 9th Daksha-sāvarṇi; the 12th Rudra-s°; the 13th Raucya or Deva-s°; the 14th Bhautya or Indra-s°); thought (= *manas*), TS.; Br.; a sacred text, prayer, incantation, spell (= *mantra*), RāmatUp.; Pañcar.; Pratāp.; N. of an Agni, MBh.; of a Rudra, Pur.; of Kṛiśāśva, BhP.; of an astronomer, Cat.; (pl.) the mental powers, BhP.; N. of the number 'fourteen' (on account of the 14 Manus), Sūryas.; f. Manu's wife (= *manāvī*), L.; Trigonella Corniculata, L. [Cf. Goth. *manna*; Germ. *Mannus*, mentioned by Tacitus as the mythical ancestor of the West-Germans, *Mann, man*; Angl. Sax. *man*; Eng *man*.] **-kapāla**, n. Manu's bowl or dish, Kapishṭh. **-kulâditya**, m. N. of a king, Cat. **-ga**, m. N. of a son of Dyuti-mat, Pur.; n. N. of the Varsha ruled by him, ib. **-ja**, m. 'Manu-born,' a man, MBh.; Kāv. &c.; (*ā* or *ī*), f. a woman, ib.; *-nātha* (Daś.), *-pati* (R. &c.), m. 'lord of men,' a prince, king; *-loka*, m. 'world of men,' the earth, MBh.; *-vyāghra*, m. 'man-tiger,' any eminent or illustrious man, R.; *-°jâtmaja*, m. 'son of man,' a man, L.; (*ā*), f. a woman, MBh.; *-°jâdhipa* and °*pati*, m. 'sovereign of men,' a prince, king, MBh.; °*jī*-√*kṛi*, P. *-karoti*, to change into a man, Kathās.; *-°jêndra*, m. 'lord of men,' a prince, king, MBh. (°*dra-putra*, n., °*trī*, f. a prince, princess, Kathās.); *-°jêśvara*, m. = *-°jêndra*, VarBṛS.; *-°jôttama*, m. best of men, MBh. **-jāta** (*mánu-*), mfn. descended from men or from Manu, AV.; m. a man, MBh. **-jyeshṭha**, m. a sword, L. **-tantu**, m. N. of a man, ĀśvŚr. **-tīrtha**, n. N. of a Tīrtha, BhP. **-tva**, n. the rank or office of a Manu, ib. **-divi** (?), N. of wk. **-praṇīta**, mfn. taught or promulgated by Manu (*-tva*, n.), Kull. on Mn. i, 4. **-pravarha** or **-pravalha**, m. N. of RV. viii, 29, ŚāṅkhŚr. **-prīta** (*mánu-*), mfn. beloved by men, RV. **-bhū**, m. a man, L. **-muktāvali**, f. N. of wk. **-yuga**, n. the age or period of a Manu (= 311,040,000 years), Col. **-rāj**, m. 'king of men,' N. of Kubera, L. **-vát**, ind. like men or as becomes men, RV.; as with Manu, KātyŚr. **-vaśa**, m. N. of a king, VP. **-vṛita**, mfn. chosen by men, AitBr. **-śreshṭha**, m. 'best among men,' N. of Vishṇu, Pañcar. **-saṃhitā**, f. N. of the collection of laws commonly known as 'the laws or institutes of Manu;' of a Tantra wk.; Cat. **-savá**, m. = *manushya-sava*, TS. (others 'Manu's libation'). **-smṛiti**, f. Manu's law-book; *-māhātmya*, n. N. of wk.

Mánur-hita (°*nus* + *h*°), mfn. friendly to men, good for men, RV.

Mánusha (or °*shá*, MaitrS.), m. (fr. *manus*) a man, RV.; (*ī*), f. a woman, L. **Manushêndra**, w. r. for *manujêndra*, q. v.

Manushyà, mf(*ā*)n. human, manly, useful or friendly to man, RV.; AV.; ŚBr.; m. a man, human being, RV. &c. &c.; a man (as opp. to woman), Mn.; MārkP.; a husband, VarBṛS.; a class of deceased ancestors (those who receive the Piṇḍa offering), TBr. **-kāra**, m. the deed of a man, human exertion, MBh. **-kilbishá**, n. transgression against men, ŚBr. **-kṛita** (°*shyà-*), mfn. committed against men, VS. **-gandha**, m. human odour, AitBr. **-gandharva**, m. pl. the human Gandharvas (inferior to the Deva-g°), TUp. **-gavī**, f. pl. N. of partic. verses or formulas, ĀpŚr. **-granthi**, m. a knot formed by men, Kapishṭh. **-cará**, mfn. having dealings or intercourse with men, TS. **-cittá**, n. the thought or will of men, ŚBr. **-cchandasá**, n. the metre of men, TS. **-janman**, mfn. begotten by a man, Śiś. **-já**, mfn. born of men, RV. **-jāta**, n. the human race, mankind, Gaut. **-jātaka**, n. N. of wk. **-jāti**, f. = *-jāta*, Hit. **-tā**, f. manhood, humanity, the state or condition of man (acc. with *ā*-√*i*, to become a man), R.; MārkP. **-trá**, ind. among men, to men, ŚBr. **-tvá**, n. = *-tā*, f. (acc. with √*yā*, to become a man), TBr.; Mn. &c. **-durga**, mfn. inaccessible owing to men; n. a place inacc° &c., MBh. **-devá**, m. 'man-god,' a Brāhman, ŚBr.; a prince, king, Ragh. **-dharma**, m. the law or duty or state or character of man, MW.; (with *uttara*), highest condition, Divyâv. **-dharman**, m. 'having the nature or character of man,' N. of Kubera, Śiś.; = child of men, Jātakam. **-nāmá**, m. pl. N. of partic. verses or formulas, TĀr. **-nāmán**, n. a human name, ib. **-pātra**, n. cup or bowl of men, TāṇḍBr. **-pota**, m. a little boy, Mcar. **-prakṛiti**, mfn. of human origin, Āpast. **-mātra**, mfn. only a man, MBh. **-māraṇa**, n. manslaughter, (unintentionally) killing a man, Mn. viii, 296. **-yajñá**, m. 'man-offering,' the act of devotion due to men (i. e. *atithi-pūjana*, the honouring of guests or hospitality, one of the 5 *mahā-yajñas*, q.v.), ŚBr.; ĀśvGṛ. &c. **-yaśasá**, human glory or splendour, °*sin*, mfn. possessing h° gl°, TS. **-yāna**, n. a litter, palankin, MBh. **-yoni**, m. human womb, ŚBr. **-rathá**, m. chariot of men, TS.; AitBr. **-rājá**, m. a human king, VS. **-rājan**, m. id., Br. **-rūpá**, n. human form, ŚBr. **-loká**,

m. the world of men, VS.; ŚBr. &c. **-viś,** f. (AitBr.), **-viśá,** n. (TS.), **-viśā,** f. (Kāṭh.) mankind, the human race. **-śiras,** m. a partic. aquatic animal with a human head, Āpast. **-śṛiṅga,** n. 'man's-horn' (as an example of what cannot exist), impossibility, Sāṃkhyas., Sch. **-śoṇita,** n. human blood, R. **-sabhā,** f. an assembly or crowd or meeting-place of men, L. **-savá,** m. libation or sacrifice (performed) by men, TBr.; Kāṭh. **-sākshya,** n. the presence of men as witnesses; (*e*), ind. in the pr° of men, Nidānas. **-hāra,** m. man-stealing, Siṇhās. **-hārin,** m. a man-stealer, L. **Manushyâyusha,** n. the life-time of men, ŚBr. **Manushyâlaya,** (ibc.) human dwelling, house; *-candrikā,* f., *-lakshaṇa,* n. N. of wks. **Manushyêndra,** m. 'best of men' (in addressing a good man), Nal. xxii, 6. **Manushyêśvara,** m. 'lord of men,' a prince, king, Ragh. **Manushyêshu,** m. or f. (?) an arrow thrown by men, AV. **Manushyâinasá,** n. sin of men, ib.

Manushyát, ind. = next, AV. v, 12, 8 (printed *°shvát;* cf. APrāt. iv, 65).

Manush-vát, ind. (fr. *manus*) as (among or for or with) men, RV.; like or as (with) Manu, ŚBr.; KātyŚr.

Mánus, m. man or Manu (the father of men), RV.; VS. (cf. *mánur-hita, manush-vát,* and *mánusha*).

Mano, in comp. for *manas.* **-gata,** mfn. 'mind-gone,' existing or passing or concealed in the mind or heart, MBh.; Kāv. &c.; n. thought, opinion, notion, idea, wish, desire, ib. **-gati,** f. 'heart's course,' wish, desire, MBh.; mfn. going where one will, R. **-gamya,** mfn. accessible to (i.e. conceivable by) the mind, MW. **-gavī,** f. wish, desire, L. **-gupta,** mfn. cherished or concealed in the mind, thought or meditated on secretly, W.; (*ā*), f. red arsenic (= *manaḥ-śilā*), L.; a species of sugar-cane, L. **-gṛihītá,** mfn. seized by the mind, captivated by the m°, MaitrS.; Kāṭh. **-gráhaṇa,** n. the act of seizing or captivating the m°, MaitrS.; TS. **-grāhin,** mfn. captivating the m°, fascinating, MBh.; R. **-grāhya,** mfn. to be grasped by the m°, Bhāshāp.; = prec., MBh. **-glāni,** f. depression of m°, Daś. **-ghna,** mfn. intimidating the m°, Bhpr. **-ja,** m. 'm°-born,' love or the god of love, Kāv.; *-vṛiddhi,* f. a kind of shrub, L. **-janman,** m. = *-ja,* Kāv. **-jalpa,** m. 'mind-talk,' imagination, L. **-javá,** m. the speed or swiftness of thought, RV.; ŚBr.; (*máno-*), mfn. swift as thought, RV. &c. &c. (*am,* ind.; *-tā,* f.); quick in thought or apprehension, W.; resembling a father, fatherly, parental, L.; m. N. of a son of Anila or the Wind, MBh.; Hariv.; of a son of Rudra Īśāna, Pur.; of Indra in the 6th Manv-antara, ib.; of a son of Medhâtithi, BhP.; of a fabulous horse, Vās., Introd.; a person whose parents are a Brāhman and a Nishādī, L.; (*ā*), f. N. of one of the 7 tongues of Agni, MuṇḍUp.; Methonica Superba, L.; N. of one of the Mātṛis attending on Skanda, MBh.; of a river in Krauñca-dvīpa, VP.; m. or n. a kind of magic, Divyâv.; n. N. of a Tīrtha, MBh.; of the Varsha ruled by Medhâtithi, BhP. **-javas** (*máno-*), mfn. swift as thought, RV.; TS.; TBr.; N. of Yama, VS. (Mahīdh.) **-javasa,** mfn. resembling a father, fatherly, L. **-javin,** mfn. swift as thought (*°vi-tva,* n.), Cat. **-javishṭha** (*máno-*), mfn. very swift, as th°, RV. vi, 9, 6 (read so for *máno jáv°*). **-jātá,** mfn. 'mind-born,' sprung up in the mind or soul, VS.; ŚBr. **-jighra,** mfn. scenting out or guessing (a person's) thoughts, Sāh. **-jū́,** mfn. swift as thought, RV. **-jña,** mf(*ā*)n. agreeable to the mind, pleasing, lovely, beautiful, charming, MBh.; Kāv. &c.; m. a pleasant spot, Vishṇ.; Pinus Longifolia, L.; N. of a Gandharva, SaddhP.; (*ā*), f. (only L.) the senna plant; a kind of cumin; Jasminum Grandiflorum; = *vandhyā-karkoṭakī;* an intoxicating drink; red arsenic; a princess; n. the wood of Pinus Longifolia, L.; *-ghosha,* m. N. of a man, Buddh.; *-tā,* f. loveliness, beauty, Cāṇ.; *-śabdâbhigarjita,* m. N. of a Kalpa, Buddh.; *-svara;* m. N. of a Gandharva, Kāraṇḍ. **-jyotis** (*máno-*), mfn. one whose light is the intellect, ŚBr. **-jvalā,** f. Jasminum Auriculatum, L. **-daṇḍa,** m. complete control over the thoughts, Mn. xii, 10. **-datta,** mfn. 'given by the mind,' mentally given, wished, BhP.; N. of an author, Cat.; (*ā*), f. (prob.) N. of a woman, Pāṇ. vi, 3, 4, Sch. **-dāhin,** m. 'heart-inflamer,' the god of love, L. **-duḥkha,** n. heart-ache, mental affliction, MW. **-dushṭa,** mfn. defiled with evil thoughts, depraved in mind, Mn. v, 108. **-dūta-kāvya,** n., **-dūtikā,** f. N. of wks. **-dhara,** m. N. of an author, Cat. **-dhātu,** m. the sphere of the mind or intellect (with Buddh. one of the 18 elementary spheres), Dharmas. 25. **-'dhinātha,** m. 'heart-lord,' a lover, husband, MW. **-dhṛít,** mfn. 'having the mind restrained or controlled,' prudent, intelligent, RV. **-'navasthāna,** n. absence of m°, inattention, Sāṃkhyak. **-nāśa,** m. loss of m°, Cat. **-nīta,** mfn. 'taken by the m°,' chosen, approved, preferred, W. **-'nukūla,** mfn. pleasant to the m°, VarYogay. **-'nuga,** mfn. 'suiting the m°,' agreeable, pleasing, Hariv.; m. N. of a district, MBh. **-'pahārin,** mfn. ravishing or captivating the m°, gratifying, Kām. **-'pêta,** mfn. destitute of understanding, KaushUp. **-bhava,** mfn. 'm°-born,' arising or being in the m°, imaginary, BhP.; m. (ifc. f. *ā*) love (opp. to *krodha*), MBh.; sexual love or the god of l°, ib.; Kāv. &c.; *-druma,* m. love compared to a tree, Kāv.; *-śāsana,* m. 'chastiser of the god of love,' N. of Śiva, Bhām.; *°vâgāra,* n. 'abode of love,' pudendum muliebre, Bhpr. **-'bhidhā,** f. red arsenic, L. **-'bhiniveśa,** m. close application of mind, tenacity of purpose, MW. **-'bhiprâya,** m. heart's desire; *-ga,* mfn. agreeable, pleasant, MBh. **-'bhirāma,** mfn. pleasing the mind, delightful, Kāv.; m. N. of an author, Cat.; m. or n. (?) N. of the spot where Buddha Tamāla-pattra-candana-gandha (Mahā-maudgalyāyana) will appear, SaddhP. **-'bhilāsha,** m. the heart's desire or wish, MW. **-bhū,** m. 'mind-born,' love or the god of love, Kāv.; Kathās. **-bhṛít,** mfn. supporting the mind, ŚBr. **-mathana,** m. 'heart-agitator,' the god of love, Pañcar. **-máya,** mf(*ī*)n. consisting of spirit or mind, spiritual, mental, ŚBr.; Up. &c.; *-kośa,* m. the mental sheath (the 2nd of the subtle sheaths in which the soul is encased), Vedântas. **-múshi-gṛihīta,** mfn. seized by the stealer of the mind (a demon), ŚBr. **-múh,** mfn. perplexing or bewildering the m°, AV. **-mṛiga,** m. the heart conceived of as a deer, Subh. **-mohinī,** f. N. of a Surâṅganā, Siṇhās. **-yāyin,** mfn. going at will or wherever one likes (*°yi-tva,* n.), Pañcar. **-yúj,** mfn. yoked by a mere thought or wish (i.e. without effort), RV.; adapted to the understanding, wise, ib.; VS.; AV. **-yoni,** m. 'mind-born,' N. of the god of love, L. **-rañjana,** n., **-rañjinī,** f. N. of wks. **-ratha,** m. (ifc. f. *ā*) 'heart's joy' (see 2. *ratha*), a wish, desire (also = desired object), MBh.; Kāv. &c.; fancy, illusion, Śaṃk.; (in dram.) a wish expressed in an indirect manner, hint, Sāh.; the heart compared to a car (see 1. *ratha*), R.; N. of a teacher, Buddh.; of a poet, Cat.; of various men, Rājat.; (*ā*), f. N. of a woman (= *-prabhā*), Kathās.; *-kusuma,* n. wish or desire compared to a flower, MW.; *-kṛita,* mfn. chosen or taken at will (as a husband), Hariv.; *-tīrtha,* n. N. of a Tīrtha, Cat.; *-tṛitīyā,* f. the 3rd day in the light half of the month Caitra (*-vrata,* n. N. of wk.), Cat.; *-dāyaka,* m. 'fulfilling wishes,' N. of a Kalpa-vṛiksha, Kathās.; *-druma,* w. r. for *mano-bhava-dr°,* Mālav. iii, 11; *-dvādaśī,* f. the 12th day in a partic. half month, Cat.; *-prabhā,* f. N. of a woman, Kathās.; *-bandha,* m. the cherishing or entertaining of desires (*°âhubandhu,* m. the friend of [i.e. one who satisfies] wishes, Mālatīm. i, 34); *-maya,* mf(*ī*)n. consisting of wishes, having many w°, Bhām.; being the object of a w°, Naish.; *-siddha,* w. r. for *-siddhi,* Kathās.; *-siddhi,* f. the fulfilment of a w°, Kathās.; m. (also *°dhika*) N. of a man, ib.; *-sṛishṭi,* f. creation of the fancy, phantasm of the imagination, MW.; *°thântara,* m. 'innermost desire,' beloved object or person, Mṛicch. **-rama,** mf(*ā*)n. gratifying the mind, attractive, pleasant, charming, beautiful, MaitrUp.; MBh.; Kāv. &c.; m. N. of a Nāga, L.; of a mountain, ib.; (*ā*), f., see next; n. a kind of house, L.; N. of a pleasure-garden, HPariś. **-ramā,** f. a beautiful woman, L.; a kind of pigment (= *gorocanā*), L.; a kind of metre, Col.; N. of an Apsaras, MBh.; of a goddess, Buddh.; of a Gandharvī, Kāraṇḍ.; of a daughter of the Vidyā-dhara Indīvara (wife of Sva-rocis and mother of Vijaya), MārkP.; of various other women, Cat.; of a river, MBh.; of various wks., Cat.; *-kuca-mardinī,* f., *-khaṇḍa,* m. or n., *-pariṇayana-carita,* n., *-vyākhyā,* f. N. of wks. **-rāga,** m. affection, passion (of the heart), Mālatīm. **-rājya,** n. the realm of fancy, Sarvad. (*°jyāni √kṛi,* to build castles in the air, Rājat.) **-ruj,** f. pain or grief of the heart, Mālatīm. **-'rti** (fr. *ārti*), f. id., L. **-lakshaṇa,** n. N. of wk. **-laya,** m. loss of consciousness, Cat. **-laulya,** n. a freak of the mind, whim, caprice, Hit. **-vatī,** f. N. of a woman, Hariv.; of an Apsaras, ib.; of a daughter of the Vidyā-dhara Citrâṅgada, Kathās.; of a daughter of the Asura-pati Su-māya, ib.; of a mythical town on mount Meru, BhP., Sch. **-'valambikā,** f. N. of wk. **-vallabhā,** f. 'heart's beloved,' a beloved woman, Daś. **-vahā,** f. the heart-artery, MBh. **-vāk-karman,** n. pl. thoughts and words and deeds, Mn. xii, 242. **-vāg-deha-ja,** mfn. resulting from th° and w° and d° (lit. mind, speech and body), MW. **-vāñchā,** f., **-vāñchita,** n. heart's wish, the mind's desire, ib. **-vāta** (*máno-*), mfn. desired by the mind, agreeable, RV. **-vāda,** m. N. of wk. **-vikāra,** m. change or emotion of the mind, L. **-vid,** m. 'spirit-knower' (500 are reckoned as followers of the Jina Mahā-vīra), W. **-vinayana,** n. mental discipline, Inscr. **-vinoda** and *°da-kṛit,* m. N. of poets, Cat. **-viruddha,** m. pl. 'opposed to thought, incomprehensible,' N. of a group of divine beings, MBh. **-vṛitti,** f. activity or disposition of the mind, volition, fancy, Kāv.; Śaṃk. **-vega,** m. speed or velocity of thought, MW.; N. of a hero, Vcar. **-veda-śiras,** n. pl. N. of partic. verses or formulas, VarBṛS. **-vyathā,** f. mental pain or anguish, MW. **-hata,** mfn. frustrated in expectation, disappointed, L. **-hán,** mfn. mind-destroying, AV.; m. N. of a destructive Agni, ib.; PārGṛ. **-hara,** mf(*ā* or *ī*)n. 'heart-stealing,' taking the fancy, fascinating, attractive, charming, beautiful, Mn.; MBh. &c.; Jasminum Multiflorum or Pubescens, L.; the third day of the civil month (*karma-māsa*), Sūryapr.; N. of a poet, Cat.; of a wk., ib.; (*ā*), f. yellow jasmine or Jasminum Grandiflorum, L.; N. of an Apsaras, MBh.; of a Kim-narī, Kāraṇḍ.; of the wife of Varcasvin and mother of Śiśira, MBh.; of the wife of Dhara and mother of Śiśira, Hariv.; of a Comm. on the Rāmāyaṇa by Loka-nātha; (*ī*), f. Piper Longum, L.; n. gold, L.; *-kāvya,* n. N. of a poem; *-krishṇa,* m. N. of an author, Cat.; *-tara,* mfn. more or most fascinating or beautiful, MBh. (*°ratva,* n., Mālatīm.); *-dāsa,* m. N. of a king (patron of Sadā-śiva), Cat.; *-vīrêśvara,* m. N. of a teacher, ib.; *-śarman,* m. N. of an author, ib.; *-siṇha,* m. N. of a king, Inscr.; *°râkāra,* mfn. beautiful in form, Kāv. **-hartṛi,** m. a heart-stealer, BhP. **-hā,** m. = *-han,* m., MantraBr. **-hārikā,** f. N. of a woman, Kathās. **-hārin,** mfn. = *-hara,* MBh.; Kāv. &c. **-hārī,** f. an unfaithful or inconstant woman, L. **-hṛit,** mfn. 'stealing the life' and 'gladdening the heart,' Śiś. xix, 109. **-hlāda,** m. joy of the heart, R. **-hlādin,** mfn. gladdening the heart, Kām. **-'hvā** (fr. *āhvā*), f. red arsenic, L. (cf. *mano 'bhidhā*).

Manoka, m. N. of a poet, Cat.

Manota, prob. n. (ĀpŚr., Sch.) or **manótā,** f. (ŚāṅkhBr. &c.) the hymn RV. vi, 1 (containing the word *manótā,* nom. of *manotṛi,* and used in sacrificing; also *°tā-sûkta,* ŚāṅkhŚr.); the deity to whom the offering during the recitation of that hymn is dedicated (accord. to the Brāhmaṇas = Agni or = Vāc and Go), TS.; Br.; KātyŚr.

Manótṛi or **manotṛ́i,** m. (*√man, manute*) an inventor, discoverer, disposer, manager, RV. (in TS. nom. *°tā* also as f.)

Manonmanī, f. a form of Durgā, Hcat.

Manor-hata or **manor-hita,** m. N. of a patriarchal sage, Buddh. (cf. *mánur-hita*).

Mantavyà, mfn. to be thought, ŚBr. &c. &c.; to be regarded or considered as (nom.), Kāv.; Kathās.; Pañcat.; (with *dosheṇa*), to be accused of a fault, MBh. (v.l. *gantavya*); to be admitted or assumed or stated, MBh.; Kāv. &c.; to be approved or sanctioned, Hit. (v.l. *anu-m°*); n. (impers.) one should think or suppose, Yājñ., Sch.

Manti, f., g. *tanoty-ādi* (cf. *mati*).

Mántu, m. an adviser, manager, disposer, ruler, arbiter, RV. (also as f.); advice, counsel, ib.; a fault, offence, transgression, L.; a man, mankind, L.; lord of men (= *prajā-pati*), L.; a king, W.; f. thought, understanding, intellect, ib. **-mat,** mfn. (only voc. *mántu-mas*) wise, intelligent, RV.

Mantūya, Nom. P. Ā. *°yati, °te,* to become angry or to transgress against, L.; to be offended or be jealous, Bhaṭṭ.

Mantṛi, m. a thinker, adviser, counsellor, ŚBr.; KaushUp.; MBh.; one who consents or agrees, Āpast. [Cf. Gk. Μέντωρ.]

Mántra, m. (rarely n.; ifc. f. *ā*) 'instrument of thought,' speech, sacred text or speech, a prayer or song of praise, RV.; AV.; TS.; a Vedic hymn or sacrificial formula, that portion of the Veda which contains the texts called *ṛic* or *yajus* or *sāman* (q.v.) as opp. to the Brāhmaṇa and Upanishad portion (see IW. 5 &c.), Br.; GṛŚrS. &c.; a sacred formula addressed to any individual deity (e.g. *Om Śivāya namaḥ*), RTL. 61; a mystical verse or magical formula (sometimes personified), incantation, charm, spell (esp. in modern times employed by the Śāktas to acquire superhuman powers; the primary Mantras being held to be 70 millions in number and the secondary innumerable; RTL. 197–202), RV. (i, 147, 4); ĀśvŚr.; Mn.; Kathās.; Suśr.; consultation, resolution, counsel, advice, plan, design, secret, RV. &c. &c.; N. of Vishṇu, Vishṇ.; of Śiva, MBh.; (in astrol.) the fifth mansion, VarYogay. **-kamalâkara**, m. N. of wk. **-karaṇa**, n. the recital of a sacred text, Pāṇ. i, 3, 25; a Vedic text or verse, Cat. **-kalpa-druma**, m., **-kalpa-latā**, f. N. of wks. **-kāra**, m. a composer or reciter of s° t°, MānGṛ. **-kārya**, n. subject of consultation, MW. **-kāla**, m. the time of deliberation, Mn. vii, 149. **-kāśī-khaṇḍa**, m. or n. N. of wk. **-kuśala**, mfn. experienced in counsel, R.; Hariv. **-kṛit**, m. a composer of hymns, RV.; Br.; one who recites a s° t°, BhP.; a counsellor, adviser, Ragh.; an emissary, ambassador, BhP. **-kṛita**, mfn. consecrated by Mantras, MW. **-kovida**, mfn. knowing s° t°, ib. **-kośa**, m., **-kaumudī**, f., **-khaṇḍa**, m. or n., **-gaṇapati-tattva-ratna**, n. N. of wks. **-gaṇḍaka**, m. (prob.) a kind of amulet, Kād.; knowledge, L. **-gupta**, m. N. of a man, Daś. **-gupti**, f. secret counsel, Kām. **-gūḍha**, m. a secret agent, spy, L. **-gṛiha**, n. a council chamber, MBh. **-candrikā**, f., **-cintāmaṇi**, m., **-cūḍāmaṇi**, m. N. of wks. **-jala**, n. water consecrated by charms or s° t°, BhP. **-jāgara**, m. recital of Vedic texts (accord. to their different Pāṭhas) at night, L. **-jihva**, m. 'having s° t° for tongues,' fire or N. of Agni, Śiś.; L. **-jña**, mfn. knowing s° t°, Var.; BhP.; experienced in counsel, Mn.; R.; m. a spy, L.; a learned Brāhman, priest, W. **-jyeshṭha**, mfn. one whose superiority is dependent on his knowledge of s° t°, MBh. **-jyotis**, n. N. of wk. **-tattva**, n. the essence of counsel; *-netra*, n., *-prakāśa*, m. N. of wks. (v.l. *-tantra-n°* and *-pr°*); *-vid*, mfn. very experienced in counsel, MBh. **-tantra-meru-ratnâvalī**, f. N. of wk. **-tas**, ind. with respect to s° t°, from or by the Mantras, Mn.; R.; from advice, deliberately, W. **-toya**, n. water consecrated by Mantras or spells, Kathās. **-da**, mfn. teaching s° t°, Mn. ii, 153; giving advice, MārkP. **-darpaṇa**, m. N. of wk. **-darśin**, mfn. knowing s° t°, SaṃhitUp.; m. a Brāhman learned in the Vedas, Mn. iii, 212. **-dātṛi**, m. a teacher of s° t°, BrahmavP. **-dīdhiti**, m. 'having s° t° for rays,' fire, L. **-dīpaka**, n. and **-dīpikā**, f. N. of wks. **-dṛiś**, mfn. seeing i.e. knowing or composing s° t°, BhP.; skilled in counsel, a counsellor, ib. **-devatā**, f. the deity invoked in a s° t°; *-prakāśa*, m., *-prakāśikā* (also *-deva-pr°*), f. N. of wks. **-drashṭṛi**, m. a seer or composer of s° t°, Pāṇ. iv, 1, 114, Sch. **-druma**, m. N. of Indra in the 6th Manv-antara, BhP. **-dhara** (Hariv.), **-dhārin** (MBh.), m. a counsellor, adviser. **-nirṇaya**, m. decision or settlement of counsel, MW.; *-prabandha*, m. N. of wk. **-netra**, n. N. of wk. **-pati** (*mántra-*), m. lord or owner of a s° t°, TĀr. **-pattra**, n. a leaf inscribed with a s° t°, Vikr.; N. of wk. **-pada**, n. a sacred or magical word, Kir. **-paddhati**, f. N. of wk. **-pāṭha**, m. the recitation of a s° t°, KātyŚrS., Sch.; N. of wk. **-pāda**, m., **-pārâyaṇa**, n. (*°ṇa-krama*, m., and *°ṇe vidyârtha-dīpikā*, f.), **-puraścaraṇa-prakāra**, m. pl. N. of wks. **-pushpa**, n. flowers with recitation of s° t°, RTL. 415; *°pâñjali*, m. N. of wk. **-pustikā**, f. a book of spells, Kathās. **-pūta**, mfn. purified by s° t°, Ragh.; *°tâtman*, m. N. of Garuḍa, Gal. **-prakaraṇa**, n., **-prakāśa**, m., **-pradīpa**, m. N. of wks. **-prabhāva**, m. the power of a spell, Ratnāv. **-prayoga**, m. 'the employment of a s° t° or spell,' N. of wk. (also *-tantra*, n.); magical means or agency, Kathās. **-praśna**, m. (*°na-kāṇḍa*, n., *°na-bhāshya*, n.) and **-prastāra**, m. N. of wks. **-phala**, n. fruit of counsel or advice, W. **-bala**, n. the superiority or precedence of a s° t°, KātyŚr.; magical power, Kathās. **-bīja**, n. the seed (i.e. first syllable) of a spell, RāmatUp. (cf. RTL. 197–202); the germ or origin of counsel, Kām. **-brāhmaṇa**, n. the hymns and Brāhmaṇas (*-vid*, mfn. knowing them, Gaut.); N. of wk. **-bhāgavata**, n., **-bhāshya**, n., **-bhūshaṇa**, n. N. of wks. **-bheda**, m. breach of counsel, betrayal of a design, MBh.; Kāv. &c.; a partic. kind of spell or incantation, Cat. **-maya**, mf(*ī*)n. consisting of spells, MBh. **-mayūkha**, m., **-mahôdadhi**, m., **-mārtaṇḍa**, m. N. of wks. **-mālā**, f. N. of wks.; of a river in Kuśa-dvīpa, BhP. **-muktâvalī**, f. N. of various wks. **-mūrti**, m. 'whose body consists of sacred texts,' N. of Śiva, MBh. **-mūla**, mf(*ā*)n. rooted in counsel or in spells, Yājñ.; Kathās.; ŚārṅgP. **-yantra**, n. an amulet with a magical formula, Pañcar.; *-prakāśa*, m. N. of wk. **-yukti**, f. application of spells, magical means, Kathās. **-yoga**, m. employment of a sacred text, Var.; magic (?), Cat.; *-prakaraṇa*, n. N. of wk. **-ratna**, n. 'the jewel of magic;' *-kośa*, m., *-dīpikā*, f., *-prakāśa*, m., *-mañjūshā*, f., *°tnâkara*, m., *°tnâvalī*, f. (and *°lī-kośa*, m.) N. of wks. **-rahasya-prakāśikā**, f. N. of wk. **-rāja**, m. 'king of spells,' N. of a partic. magical formula, RāmatUp.; *-vidhi*, m., *°jâtmaka-stotra*, n., *°jânushṭhāna-krama*, m. N. of wks. **-rāmāyaṇa**, n. N. of a Tāntric text and Comm. by Nīla-kaṇṭha. **-vacana**, n. the recitation of a sacred text, KātyŚr. **-1. -vat**, ind. in conformity with or accompanied by the recitation of s° t°, Mn.; MBh.; R.; according to all rules of consultation, MBh. **-2. -vat**, mfn. attended with s° t° or hymns, ŚrS.; Mn.; Yājñ.; enchanted (as a weapon), Ragh.; entitled to use the Mantras, initiated, W.; having or hearing counsel, ib. **-varjam**, ind. without any s° t°, Mn. x, 127. **-varṇa**, m. the wording of a s° t°, GṛŚrS.; pl. the single letters of a s° t° or a magical formula, Pañcar.; Sarvad.; mf(*ī*)n. having the nature of i.e. resembling a s° t° or spell, BhP. **-varṇana**, n., **-vallarī**, f. N. of wks. **-vaśī-√1. kṛi**, P. *-karoti*, to subdue by a spell, HPariś. **-vaha**, m. N. of Vishṇu, Vishṇ. **-vāda**, m. the substance or contents of a s° t° (pl. with *ślokāḥ* = verses containing a s° t°), MBh.; magic art, Kāv. **-vādin**, m. a reciter of s° t° or spells, enchanter, Vet.; Pañcat. **-vid**, mfn. knowing s° t°, GṛŚrS. &c.; knowing magical formulas (superl. *-vit-tama*), Daś.; skilled in counsel, MBh.; m. a counsellor or a learned Brāhman or a spy, L. **-vidyā**, f. the science of Mantras, magic art, Kathās. **-vidhi**, m., **-vibhāga**, m., **-vishaya**, m. N. of wks. **-śakti**, f. magical power, charm, Kathās. **-śārīraka**, n. N. of wk. **-śāstra**, n. 'magic science,' N. of wk.; *-pratyaṅgirā*, f., *-sāra-saṃgraha*, m. N. of wks. **-śodhana**, n. N. of wk. **-śruti**, f. a consultation overheard, Kathās. **-śrútya**, n. following counsel, obedience, RV.; tradition respecting the correct use of sacred texts, MW. **-saṃvaraṇa**, n. concealment of a consultation or design, R. **-saṃskāra**, m. a (nuptial) rite performed with s° t°, Mn. v, 153; *-kṛit* (with *pati*), m. a consecrated husband, ib. **-saṃskriyā**, f. the preparation of magical formulas, Cat. **-saṃhitā**, f. the collection of the Vedic hymns, Cat.; 'coll° of mag° formulas,' N. of a Tāntric wk., ib. **-saṃkalanā**, f., **-saṃdhyā**, f., **-samuccaya**, m. N. of wks. **-sādhaka**, m. the performer of an incantation, magician, Kathās. **-sādhana**, n. (or *°nā*, f.) the performance of an incantation, ib.; Siṃhâs. **-sâdhya**, mfn. to be subdued or effected by incantations or spells (*-tva*, n.), Pañcat.; to be attained by consultation, Kathās. **-sāra**, m. (and *°ra-samuccaya*, m.) N. of wks. **-siddha**, mfn. accomplished by a spell, RāmatUp.; thoroughly versed in spells, MBh. **-siddhi**, f. the effect of a spell, Kathās.; the carrying out a resolution or advice, Hit. **-sūtra**, n. a charm fastened on a string, Kathās. **-snāna**, n. the recitation of partic. texts as a substitute for ablution, VP. **-spṛiś**, mfn. obtaining anything by means of spells (= *mantreṇa spṛiśati*), Pāṇ. iii, 2, 58, Sch. **-hīna**, mfn. destitute of hymns, contrary to sacred texts, MW. **-hemādri**, m. N. of wk. **Mantrâkshara**, n. a syllable in a spell, Sarvad.; *°ri-bhavānī-sahasra-nāma-stotra*, n. N. of wk. **Mantrâṅga-nāṭaka**, n. N. of a drama. **Mantrâdhirāja**, m. supreme over all spells (a Vetāla), Kathās. **Mantrânukramaṇikā**, f., **Mantrânushṭhāna**, n. (and *°nâṅga-tarpaṇa*, n.) N. of wks. **Mantrânta**, m. the end of a sacred text, MānŚr. **Mantrârādhana**, n. accomplishment by spells and incantations, conjuring, Bhartṛ. **Mantrârṇa**, m. = *mantrâkshara*, Sarvad. **Mantrârṇava**, m. N. of wk. **Mantrârtha**, m. 'the contents or object of a sacred text or a spell,' N. of wk.; *-kaumudī*, f., *-dīpa*, m., *-dīpikā*, f., *-paddhati*, f., *-bhāshya*, n., *-mañjarī*, f. N. of wks. **Mantrârshâdhyāya**, m. 'chapter on the Vedic Ṛishis,' a Ṛishy-anukramaṇī of the Kāṭhaka Yajur-veda, Cat. **Mantrâvalī**, f. a series of sacred texts, Git. **Mantrâśīrvāda-saṃhitā**, f. N. of wk. **Mantrêśa** or **°śvara**, m. 'supreme lord of spells,' (with Śaivas) N. of a partic. superhuman being, Sarvad. **Mantrôkta**, mfn. mentioned in a hymn, Vait. **Mantrôdaka**, n. water consecrated by holy texts, R. **Mantrôddhāra**, m. selection or extract from s° t° or magical formulas (?); *-kośa*, m., *-prakaraṇa*, n., *-vidhi*, m. N. of wks. **Mantrôpanishad**, f. N. of an Upanishad, Cat.; n. hymns and Upanishads, Up. **Mantrôpashṭambha**, m. encouragement by counsel, advice, direction, W.

Mantraṇa, n. consultation, deliberation, MBh.; R.; MārkP. (also *ā*, f., Pañcar.); advising, counselling in private, W. **Mantraṇârha**, g. *utkarâdi*. **Mantraṇârhīya**, mfn., ib.

Mantraṇaka, n. invitation, Divyāv.

1. **Mantri**, m. = *mantrin*, a king's counsellor, minister (only acc. pl. *°trīn*), R.

2. **Mantri**, in comp. for *mantrin*. **-tā**, f., **-tva**, n. the office or vocation of a minister, ministership, ministry, Kathās.; Rājat.; Pañcat. **-dhura**, mfn. able to bear the burden of the office of a counsellor, MW. **-pati**, m. a prime minister, R. **-putra**, m. the son of a m°, Kathās. **-prakâṇḍa**, m. an excellent counsellor or m°, Rājat. **-pradhāna**, **-mukhya**, m. = *-pati*, Kathās. **-vat**, ind. like a counsellor or m°, Rājat. **-vara** (Kathās.), **-śreshṭha** (R.), m. = *-pati*. **-śrotriya**, m. a m° who is also a Śrotriya (or conversant with the Vedas), MW. **-suta** or **-sūnu**, m. = *-putra*, Kathās.

Mantrika, (ifc.) = *mantrin* (see *sa-m°*).

Mantrikā, f. N. of an Upanishad (also *°kôpan°*; cf. *mantrôpanishad*).

Mantriṇī, f. of *°trin*. **-rahasya**, n. N. of wk.

Mantrita, mfn. discussed, deliberated, determined, MBh.; Kāv. &c.; advised, counselled (said of persons and things), ib.; consecrated with sacred texts, enchanted, charmed, MBh.; R.; n. counsel, deliberation, plan, ib.

Mantrin, mfn. wise or eloquent, VS.; m. 'knowing sacred texts or spells,' a conjurer, enchanter, Bhartṛ.; a king's counsellor, minister, Mn.; MBh. &c.; (in chess) the queen, Pañcad.; (in astrol.) the 12th mansion, VarYogay.

Manma, in comp. for *manman*. **-śás**, ind. each according to his heart's desire, RV. **-sâdhana**, mfn. accomplishing the heart's desires or wishes, ib.

Mánman, n. thought, understanding, intellect, wisdom, RV.; expression of thought i.e. hymn, prayer, petition, ib.

Manmoka, m. N. of a poet, Cat.

Manya, mfn. (only ifc.; cf. Pāṇ. iii, 2, 83; vi, 3, 68, Sch.) thinking one's self to be, passing for, appearing as (see *kālim-*, *dhanyam-*, *naram-m°* &c.)

Manyantī, f. N. of a daughter of Agni Manyu, MBh.

Manyú, m. (L. also f.) spirit, mind, mood, mettle (as of horses), RV.; TS.; Br.; high spirit or temper, ardour, zeal, passion, RV. &c. &c.; rage, fury, wrath, anger, indignation, ib. (also personified, esp. as Agni or Kāma or as a Rudra; *manyuṃ √kṛi*, with loc. or acc. with *prati*, 'to vent one's anger on, be angry with'); grief, sorrow, distress, affliction, MBh.; Kāv. &c.; sacrifice, Nalac.; N. of a king (son of Vitatha), BhP.; (with *Tāpasa*), N. of the author of RV. x, 83; 84; (with *Vāsishṭha*), N. of the author of RV. ix, 97, 10–12. **-tás**, ind. from anger, in a rage, AV. **-deva**, m. N. of a man, Cat. **-parīta**, mfn. filled with anger, MBh. **-parôpta** (*manyú-*), mfn. thrown away in a rage, MaitrS. **-pratikriyā**, f. venting of anger (*°yāṃ √kṛi*, with loc., 'to vent one's anger on'), Kathās. **-mát**, mfn. spirited, ardent, zealous, passionate, vehement, enraged (superl. *-mát-tama*), RV. &c. &c.; m. N. of Agni, MBh. **-maya**, mf(*ī*)n. formed or consisting of wrath, filled with resentment, MBh.; BhP. **-mí**, mfn. 'destroying hostile fury' or 'destroying in fury,' RV. **-śamana**, mfn. appeasing or pacifying anger, AV. **-shāvin** (for *sāv°*), mfn. preparing Soma in anger or with zeal, RV. **-sûkta**, n. the hymns of Manyu (prob. RV. x, 83; 84), Cat.; *-vidhāna*, n. N. of wk.

Manyūya, Nom. Ā. *°yate*. See *á-pratimanyū-yamāna*.

Manv, in comp. for *manu*. **-antara**, n. the period or age of a Manu (it comprises about 71 *mahā-yugas* [q.v.], which are held equal to 12,000 years of the gods or 4,320,000 human years or 1/14th of a day of Brahmā; each of these periods is presided over by its own special Manu [see *manu*, p. 784, col. 2]; six such Manv-antaras have already elapsed, and the 7th, presided over by Manu Vaivasvata, is now going on; 7 more are to come, making 14 Manv-antaras, which together make up one day of Brahmā), Mn. (esp. i, 79); Yājñ.; MBh. &c.; (*ā*), f. N. of various festivals (of the 10th day of the light half of the month Āshāḍha, of the 8th in the dark half of the same month, and of the 3rd in the light half of Bhādra), Col.; °*ra-varṇana*, n. N. of ch. of MatsyaP. **–artha-candrikā**, f., **-artha-muktâvalī**, f., **-artha-sāra**, m. N. of wks. **–iddha** (*mánv-*), mfn. kindled by men, Br. **–īśa**, prob. w. r. for *manīshā* (=°*shayā*), ŚvetUp. iii, 13.

मन 3. *maná*, m. du. (for 1. and 2. see p. 783, col. 2) a partic. ornament, RV. viii, 78, 2.

मनऊ *manaū*, m. (in astrol.) = منع, a partic. constellation.

मनाक् *manāk.* See p. 784, col. 1.

मनाका *manākā*, f. a female elephant, L.; a loving woman, L.

मनाग *manāga*, w. r. for *manâpa*, Lalit. (see under 2. *mana*, p. 783, col. 3).

मनाज्य *manājya* or *manādya*, n. du. (*Gotamasya* or *Gautamasya*) N. of 2 Sāmans, ĀrshBr.

मनायी *manāyī*, *manāvī.* See p. 784, col. 2.

मनिङ्गा *maniṅgā*, f. N. of a river, MBh. (*anaṅgā*, B.)

मनित्थ *manittha* and *manindha*, v. l. for *maṇittha*, q. v.

मनिष्ठका *manishṭhakā*, f. the little finger, L.

मनीक *manīka*, n. eye-salve, collyrium (powdered antimony or other substances used as an application and ornament to the eye), L.

मनीकृ *manī-√kṛi.* See p. 784, col. 2.

मनीमुषग्राम *manīmusha-grāma*, m. N. of a village, Rājat.

मनीवक *manīvaka*, m. N. of a son of Bhavya (son of Priya-vrata) and a Varsha named after him, MārkP.

मनीषा *manīshā* &c. See p. 784, col. 2.

मनु *mánu* &c. See p. 784, col. 2.

मनुष्य *manushyà* &c. See p. 784, col. 3.

मनोगत *mano-gata* &c. See p. 785, col. 1.

मन्तव्य *mantavyà*, *mántu*, *mantṛí.* See p. 785, col. 3.

मन्त्र् *mantr* (properly a Nom. fr. *mantra*, p. 785, col. 3), cl. 10. Ā. (Dhātup. xxxiii, 6) *mantrayate* (rarely P. °*ti*; Subj. *mantrayaithe*, °*te*, Pāṇ. iii, 4, 95, Sch.; Pot. *mantrayīta*, MBh.; inf. *mantrayitum*, Pañcat.), to speak, talk, say, RV. i, 164, 10; to deliberate, take counsel, consult with (instr. with or without *saha*) or about (dat.), ŚBr. &c. &c.; to resolve upon, determine to (inf.), MBh.; to deliberate on, discuss (acc.), Mn.; MBh. &c.; to counsel, advise, propose any measure, give any one advice (with acc. of pers., or with gen. of pers. and acc. of thing), MBh.; Kāv. &c.; to consecrate with sacred or magical texts, enchant with spells or charms, MBh.; R.

Mantra. See p. 785, col. 3.

Mantraṇa, mantrita, mantrin. See p. 786.

मन्थ् *manth*, strong form of √1. *math*, q. v.

Mantha, m. stirring round, churning, Kāv.; Kathās.; shaking about, agitating, Ragh.; Uttarar.; killing, slaying, Bālar.; a drink in which other ingredients are mixed by stirring, mixed beverage (usually parched barley-meal stirred round in milk; but also applied to a partic. medicinal preparation), RV. &c. &c.; a spoon for stirring, ĀśvGṛ.; Kauś.; a churning-stick, MBh.; Pāṇ. vii, 2, 18; a kind of antelope, ShaḍvBr.; the sun or a sun-ray, L.; a partic. disease of the eye, excretion of rheum, L.; (*ā*), f., see below; n. an instrument for kindling fire by friction, MBh. **–giri**, m. 'churning-mountain,' N. of the mountain Mandara (which served for a ch°-stick at the ch° of the ocean of milk), A. **–guṇa**, m. a ch°-cord (°*ṇī-kṛita*, mfn. made into a ch°-c°, said of the serpent Vāsuki), MW. **–ja**, n. 'produced by churning,' butter, L. **–daṇḍa** (Pañcar.), **-daṇḍaka** (L.), m. a ch°-stick; °*ḍī-kṛita*, mfn. made into a ch°-stick, MW. **–parvata**, m. = *-giri*, L. **–pātra**, n. a ch°-vessel, L. **–vishkambha**, m. a post round which the string of a ch°-stick is wound, L. **–śaila**, m. = *-giri*, L. **Manthâcala**, m. id., Kāv. **Manthâdri**, m. id., Kathās. **Manthôdaka**, m. 'ch°-water,' the ocean of milk, L. **Manthôdadhi**, m. 'churning-sea,' sea of milk, ib.

Manthaka, mfn. churning, Car.; m. N. of a man, pl. his descendants, g. *yaskâdi* (v. l. *mathaka*).

Manthan, form of the strongest cases of *mathin*; see p. 777, col. 1.

Manthana, mfn. kindling fire by friction, Nir. iii, 14; m. a churning-stick, Hariv.; (*ī*), f. a vessel for butter, L.; n. the act of kindling fire by rubbing pieces of wood together, ChUp.; ŚrS.; the act of shaking, shaking about, agitating, churning (milk into butter), MBh.; Kāv.; Suśr.; churning out (of Amṛita), MBh. (cf. *amṛita-m°*). **–ghaṭī**, f. a butter-vat, L. **–daṇḍa**, m. a churning-stick, Kāv.

Manthanīya. See *agni-m°*.

Mantharu, m. the wind raised by flapping away flies, L.

1. **Mánthā**, form from which comes nom. m. *mánthās*, acc. °*thām*; see *mathín*, p. 777, col. 1.

2. **Mánthā**, f. a churning-stick, B.; a mixed beverage, AV.; ŚāṅkhŚr.; Trigonella Foenum Graecum, L.

Manthāna, m. 'shaker (of the universe),' N. of Śiva, MBh.; a partic. instrument for stirring or rubbing (esp. for kindling fire), Car.; a churning-stick, MBh.; R.; Hariv.; Cassia Fistula, L.; a kind of metre, Col. **–bhairava**, m. N. of a teacher of Yoga and various authors, Cat.

Manthānaka, m. a species of grass, L.

Manthāvala, m. a partic. animal (prob. the flying fox), AitBr. (cf. *mānthālá*).

Manthi, in comp. for *manthin*. **–pá**, mfn. drinking stirred or mixed Soma, VS. **–pātrá**, n. the cup or bowl for the mixed S°, TS. **–vat**, mfn. connected with m° S°, KātyŚr. (also °*thī-vat*). **–śocis** (*manthí-*), mfn. sparkling like mixed Soma, VS. **Manthy-âgra**, mfn. beginning with mixed S°, TS.

Manthitavyà, mfn. to be produced by friction (as fire), MaitrS.

Mánthitṛi, m. a shaker, stirrer, agitator, AV.

Manthín, mfn. shaking, agitating, Bhaṭṭ.; paining, afflicting, W.; m. Soma-juice with meal mixed in it by stirring, RV.; TS.; Br.; ŚrS.; semen virile (cf. *ūrdhva-m°*); (*inī*), f. a butter-vat, L.; N. of one of the Mātṛis attending on Skanda, MBh.

Manthī-vat. See *manthi-vat*.

Manthu, m. N. of a man (son of Vīra-vrata and elder brother of Pramanthu), BhP.

Mánthya, mfn. to be rubbed or stirred or churned &c. (cf. *mathya*); to be kindled by friction (as fire), TS.

मन्थर *manthara*, mf(*ā*)n. (allied to √2. *mand* and *manda*, but in some meanings rather fr. √*math*) slow (lit. and fig.; often ifc. 'slow in'), lazy, tardy, indolent, dull, stupid, silly, Kāv.; Rājat.; Sāh. &c. (*am*, ind.); low, hollow, deep (as sound), W.; bent, curved, crooked, humpbacked (cf. *ā*, f. and *mantharaka*); broad, wide, large, bulky, L.; tale-bearing, L.; m. a treasure or hair or anger (= *kośa*, *keśa* or *kopa*), L.; fruit, L.; a spy, L.; an antelope, L.; of the month Vaiśākha, L.; a fortress, stronghold, L.; an obstacle, hindrance, L.; whirling, L.; a churning-stick, L.; the mountain Mandara, W. (cf. *mantha-parvata*); N. of a tortoise, Hit.; (*ā*), f. N. of a humpbacked female slave of Bharata's mother Kaikeyī (accord. to MBh. an incarnation of the Gandharvī Dundubhī; accord. to R. a daughter of Virocana); n. safflower. **–kaulika**, m. a stupid weaver (called Mantharaka, q. v.), Pañcat. **–gāmin**, mfn. slow-going, Rājat. **–tā**, f. slowness, tardiness, Kathās. **–viveka**, mfn. slow in judgment, void of discrimination, Mālatīm. **Mantharâksharam**, ind. (to pronounce) with slow or distinct syllables, Sāh. **Mantharêshaṇa**, m. N. of a man; pl. his descendants, Pāṇ. ii, 4, 66, Sch.

Mantharaka, m. N. of a man, Kathās.; of a tortoise, ib.; of a stupid weaver, Pañcat.; of a humpback, ib.

Mantharita, mfn. made slow or lazy, relaxed, Kathās.

मन्थरु *mantharu*, *manthya.* See above.

मन्द् 1. *mand* (cf. √2. *mad*), cl. 1. Ā. (Dhātup. ii, 12) *mándate* (Ved. also P. °*ti*; pf. *mamanda*, °*dat*, *amamanduḥ*, RV.; aor. *mandús*, °*dānā*; *amandīt*, *mandishta*, ib.; Subj. *mandishat*, Gr.; Prec. *mandishīmahi*, VS.; fut. *manditā*, °*dishyate*, Gr.; inf. *mandádhyai*, RV.), to rejoice, be glad or delighted, be drunk or intoxicated (lit. and fig.), RV.; AV.; VS.; (P.) to gladden, exhilarate, intoxicate, inflame, inspirit, RV.; to sleep (?), VS. (Mahīdh.); to shine, be splendid or beautiful, Naigh. i, 16; to praise or to go, Dhātup.: Caus. *mandáyati* (inf. *mandayádhyai*), to gladden, exhilarate, intoxicate, RV.; to be glad or drunk, ib.

Mandád-vīra, mfn. rejoicing men, RV.

Mandána, mf(*ā*)n. gay, cheerful, RV.; TS.; = *mandra*, Nir. vi, 23; m. N. of a pupil of Śaṃkarâcārya (also *-miśra*), W. (cf. *maṇḍana*); n. (with a sect of Pāśupatas) N. of a partic. limping gait, Sarvad.; praise, eulogium, L.

Mandayat, mf(*antī*)n. (fr. Caus.) delighting, rejoicing; (*antī*), f. N. of a Durgā, L. **Mandayát-sakha**, mfn. rejoicing friends, RV.

Mandayú, mfn. gay, cheerful, happy, RV.

Mandasāná, mfn. being delighted, joyous, glad, intoxicated, inspirited, RV.; m. (only L.) fire; life; sleep.

Mandasānu, m. sleep or life, L. (prob. w. r. for prec.)

Mandin, mfn. delighting, exhilarating, inspiriting (said of Soma), RV.; delighted, cheerful, inspirited, ib.

Mándishṭha, mfn. most exhilarating or delightful, RV.

1. **Mandú**, mfn. (for 2. see p. 788, col. 3) joyous, cheerful, pleased, ib.

Mandrá, mf(*ā*)n. pleasant, agreeable, charming, (esp.) sounding or speaking pleasantly &c., RV.; AV.; VS.; ŚāṅkhGṛ.; low, deep (of sound), hollow, rumbling (*am*, ind.), Br. &c. &c.; m. a low tone, the low or base tone (*sthāna*) of the voice (as opp. to the middle or *madhyama* and the high or *uttama*), RPrāt.; a kind of drum, L.; a species of elephant, L. **–kaṇṭha-garjita**, n. a deep or rumbling sound in the throat (of an elephant), Vikr. **–karshaṇa**, n. a partic. Svara, SaṃhUp. **–jihva** (*mandrá-*), mfn. 'pleasing-tongued,' pleasant-voiced, RV. **–tama** and **-tara** (*mandrá-*), mfn. most or more pleasant or charming, RV. **–dhvani**, m. a rumbling sound, roaring, Ragh. **–dhvāna**, m. id., Prab. **–bhadra**, m. a species of elephant (between a Mandra and Bhadra), L.; *-mṛiga*, m. an elephant between a M° and Bh° and Mṛiga, ib.; *-lakshaṇa*, n. the mark of a M° el° (whose special signs are coarseness, size and flaccidity), ib. **–snigdha**, mfn. deep and pleasant (rumblings), Megh. **–svana**, m. = *-dhvani*, VarBṛS. **–svara**, m. having the low or base tone, SaṃhUp. **Mandrâjanī**, f. 'uttering pleasant sounds,' the tongue or voice, RV. ix, 69, 2 (Naigh. i, 11).

Mandraya, Nom. Ā. °*dráyate*, to praise, honour (= *arcati*), Naigh. iii, 14.

Mandrayú, mfn. pleasant, RV. ix, 86, 17.

मन्द् 2. *mand* or *mad* (only *mamáttana*, *mamandhi*, *ámaman*), to tarry, stand still, pause, RV. (cf. *upa-ni-√mand* and *ni-√mad*): Caus., see *mandaya*.

Manda, mf(*ā*)n. slow, tardy, moving slowly or softly, loitering, idle, lazy, sluggish in (loc. or comp.), apathetic, phlegmatic, indifferent to (dat.), MBh.; Kāv. &c.; weak, slight, slack (as a bow), dull, faint (as light), low (as a voice), gentle (as rain or wind), feeble (as the digestive faculty), ib.; weak i. e. tolerant, indulgent to (loc.), MBh.; dull-witted, silly, stupid, foolish, KaṭhUp.; MBh. &c.; unhappy, miserable (L. = *kṛipaṇa*), MBh.; Hariv.; languid, ill, sick, Mālav.; bad, wicked, MārkP.; drunken, addicted to intoxication, L.; = *mandra*, L.; m. the planet Saturn, Var.; the (upper) apsis of a planet's course or (according to some) its anomalistic motion, Sūryas.; N. of Yama, L.; a stupid or slow elephant, L. (cf. *mandra*, *bhadra-manda*, *mṛiga-manda*); the end of the world (= *pralaya*), L.; (*ā*), f. a pot, vessel, inkstand, L.; N. of Dākshāyaṇī, Cat.; (scil. *saṃkrānti*) a partic. astron. conjunction, L.; (in music) N. of a Śruti, Saṃgīt.; n. the second change which takes place in warm milk when mixed with Takra, L.; (*am*), ind. slowly, tardily, gradually, slightly, faintly, softly (also *manda* ibc., and *mandam mandam*), MBh.; Kāv. &c. **–karṇa**, mfn. 'dull-eared,' slightly deaf (proverb *badhirān manda-karṇaḥ śreyān*, 'something is better than nothing'), A. **-karṇi**, m. N. of a Muni, R. (v. l. *māndak°* and *śātak°*). **-1. -karman**, n. the process for determining the apsis of a planet's course, Sūryas. **-2. -karman**, mfn. having little to do, inactive, Suśr. **-kānta**, m. slightly bright, of a dull lustre, W. **-kānti**, m. 'having a soft lustre,' the moon, ib. **-kārin**, mfn. acting slowly and foolishly, Kathās. **-kiraṇa**, mfn. weak-rayed (*°ṇa-tva*, n.), Suśr. **-ga**, mfn. moving or flowing slowly, Suśr.; m. the planet Saturn, L.; N. of a son of Dyuti-mat, VP.; (pl.) of the Śūdras in Śāka-dvīpa, MBh.; (*ā*), f. N. of a river, ib.; n. N. of the Varsha ruled by Manda-ga, VP. **-gati**, mfn. moving slowly (*-tva*, n.), Hit.; Dhūrtan. **-gamana**, mfn. moving slowly, W.; (*ā*), f. a buffalo-cow, L. **-gāmin**, mfn. = *-gati*, Sūryas. **-cārin**, mfn. moving slowly, Sūryas. **-cetas**, mfn. having little consciousness, hardly conscious, MBh.; dull-witted, silly, foolish, ib. **-cchāya**, mfn. of little brilliance, dim, faint, lustre-less, Megh. **-jananī**, f. the mother of Manda or Saturn (and wife of Sūrya), L. **-jaras**, mfn. slowly growing old, Vāgbh. **-jāta**, mfn. produced or arising slowly, Suśr. **-tara**, mfn. more or very slow &c. (*am*, ind.), MBh. **-tā**, f. slowness, indolence, Suśr.; weakness, feebleness, littleness, insignificance, Sūryas.; Sāh.; dulness, stupidity (*a-mand°*), Mālav. **-tva**, n. = prec., Kāv.; (with *agneḥ*) weakness of the digestive faculty, Suśr. **-dhāra**, mfn. flowing in a slow stream, Suśr. **-dhī**, mfn. slow-witted, simple, silly, MBh. **-nāga**, m. (prob. w. r. for *malla-nāga*) = *vātsyāyana*, L. **-paridhi**, m. (in astron.) the epicycle of the apsis, Sūryas. **-pāla**, m. N. of a Ṛishi, Mn.; MBh. **-pītha**, prob. w. r. for *bhadra-pīṭha*, Caur. **-puṇya**, mfn. unfortunate, ill-fated, Hcar. **-prajña**, mfn. = *-dhī*, MBh. **-prabodha**, m. N. of wk. **-prāṇa**, mfn. having slow or weak breath; *-viceshṭita*, mfn. breathless and motionless, MBh. **-preman**, mfn. having little affection, Kāvyād. **-1. -phala**, n. (in astron.) equation of the apsis or (according to some) the anomalous motion of a planet, Sūryas. **-2. -phala**, mfn. bearing little fruit or having unimportant results, Vet.; Var. **-bala**, mfn. having little strength, weak, MBh. **-buddhi**, mfn. = *-dhī*, Kathās. **-bhāgin**, mfn. unfortunate, ill-fated, unhappy, Kāv. **-bhāgya**, mfn. id., ib. &c.; n. (MBh.) = *-tā*, f. (Pañcat.) misfortune, ill-luck. **-bhāj**, mfn. = *-bhāgya*, MBh. **-bhāshiṇī**, f. a kind of metre (= *mañju-bh°*), L. **-mati**, mfn. = *-dhī*, Pañcat.; Hit.; m. N. of a wheelwright and a lion, ib. **-mandam**, ind. slowly, softly, in a low tone, Ṛitus. **-mandâtapa**, mfn. having very little heat, cool, Megh. **-medhas**, mfn. = *-dhī*, Mālav. **-raśmi**, mfn. = *-kiraṇa*, MBh. **-vāhinī**, f. 'gently-flowing,' N. of a river, ib. **-viceshṭita**, mf(*ā*)n. slowly-moving, Suśr. **-vibhraṇśa**, mfn. slightly purgative, Car. **-virikta**, mfn. not sufficiently purged, Suśr. **-viveka**, m. little judgment or discernment, Sāmkhyak., Sch.; *°kin*, mfn. having little j°, ib. **-visha**, mfn. having little venom, Suśr.; m. N. of a snake, Pañcat. **-visarpa**, m. N. of a snake, Hit. (cf. next; v. l. *manda-visha*). **-visarpin**, mfn. creeping slowly; (*iṇī*), f. N. of a louse, Pañcat. **-vīrya**, mfn. = *-bala*, R. **-vrishṭi**, f. slight rain, Var. **-vedana**, mfn. causing little pain (*-tā*, f.), Suśr. **-śiśira**, mfn. slightly cool, R. **-samīraṇa**, m. a gentle breeze, MW. **-subodhinī**, f. N. of wk. **-smita**, n. a gentle laugh, smile, W.; *-śataka*, n. N. of ch. of the Mūka-pañcaśatī (q. v.) **-hāsa**, mfn. gently laughing, smiling, Bhām. (*am*, ind., Daś.); m. = *-smita*, Pañcar. **-hāsya**, n. = prec. m., W. **Mandâkrānta**, mfn. slowly advancing; (*ā*), f. N. of a metre (like that of the Megha-dūta), Śrutab. &c. **Mandâksha**, mf(*ī*)n. weak-eyed, R.; n. bashfulness, excessive connivance, Hcar. **Mandâgni**, mfn. having weak digestion, dyspeptic, Kathās.; MārkP.; m. slowness of digestion, Suśr.; *-dhārâcala-māhātmya*, n., *-haramesha-dāna*, n. N. of wks. **Mandâcāra**, mfn. badly conducted, MārkP. **Mandâtman**, mfn. = *mandha-dhī*, MBh. **Mandâdara**, mfn. having little respect for, careless about (loc.), Hit. **Mandânala**, mfn. = *°dâgni*; *-tva*, n. dyspepsia, Kull. **Mandânila**, m. a gentle breeze, zephyr, Kāv. **Mandânusārin**, mfn. passing away slowly, Suśr. **Mandâbhinivesa**, mfn. having little inclination for (loc.), Daś. **Mandâyus**, mfn. short-lived, BhP. **1. Mandâri-tā**, f. (for 2. see below, col. 2) the having few enemies, Nalôd. **Mandâsu**, mfn. having slow or weak breath, one from whom the breath of life is departing, R. **Mandâsya**, prob. w. r. for *mandâksha*. **Mandôcca**, m. the upper apsis of the course of a planet, Sūryas. **Mandôtsāha**, mfn. unenergetic, indolent, Śak. **Mandôdaka**, mfn. deficient in water, Daś. **Mandôdarī**, f. N. of Rāvaṇa's favourite wife (daughter of Maya and mother of Indra-jit; she advised her husband to deliver Sītā to Rāma, but he did not heed her; she is regarded as one of the five very chaste women, the other four being Ahalyā, Draupadī, Sītā, and Tārā), MBh.; R. &c.; of one of the Mātṛis attending on Skanda, MBh.; of the mother of the lexicographer Jaṭā-dhara, Cat.; *°rīśa*, m. 'M°'s lord,' N. of Rāvaṇa, L.; *°rī-suta*, m. 'M°'s son,' N. of Indrajit, L. **Mandôpakāriṇī**, f. N. of wk. **Mandôshṇa**, mfn. tepid, lukewarm, L.; n. and *-tā*, f. gentle heat, warmth, L. **Mandôshman**, mfn. slightly warm, cool (*°ma-tā*, f.), Suśr. **Mandâutsukya**, mfn. having little inclination for (*prati*), Śak.

Mandaka, mfn. simple, silly, foolish, MBh.; scanty, little, Pat.; pl. N. of a people, MBh. (cf. *maṇḍaka*).

Mandaya, Nom. P. *°yati*, to weaken, lessen, allay (hunger), MBh.

Mandara, mfn. slow, tardy, sluggish (= *manda*), L.; large, thick, firm (= *bahala*), L.; m. a pearl chain consisting of 8 or 16 strings, L.; N. of a sacred mountain (the residence of various deities; it served the gods and Asuras for a churning-stick at the churning of the ocean for the recovery of the Amṛita and thirteen other precious things lost during the deluge), MBh.; Kāv. &c.; heaven (= *svarga*; cf. *meru*), L.; a mirror, L.; a kind of metre, Col.; N. of a Brāhman, Cat.; of a Vidyā-dhara, Kathās.; of a son of Hiraṇya-kaśipu (B. *mandāra*); of a tree of paradise or one of the 5 trees in Indra's heaven (= *mandāra*), L. **-kantha**, v. l. for *madara-k°*, Siddh. **-deva**, m. N. of a king of the Vidyā-dharas, Kathās.; (*ī*), f. a sister of M°-d°, ib.; *°vīya*, mfn. coming from or belonging to M°-d°, ib. **-droṇī**, f. a valley in the mountain M°, BrahmaP. **-maṇi**, m. N. of Śiva, L. (w. r. for *mandira-m°*?). **-vāsinī**, f. 'dwelling on M°,' N. of Durgā, MBh. **-hariṇa**, m. N. of one of the 8 Upadvīpas in Jambu-dvīpa, BhP. **Mandarâdri**, m. the mountain M°, L. **Mandarâvāsā**, f. = *°ra-vāsinī*, Hariv.

Mandarāya, Nom. P. *°yate*, to be like the mountain Mandara, Daś.

Mandāka, n. praising, praise, L.; a stream, current (accord. to Uṇ. iv, 13 fr. √*mand* + *aka*; but prob. an artificial word to explain the next).

Mandākinī, f. (fr. *manda* + 2. *añc*) 'going or streaming slowly,' N. of an arm of the Ganges (flowing down through the valley of Kedāra-nātha in the Himālayas) and of other rivers, MBh.; Pur.; (esp.) the heavenly Ganges, MBh.; Kāv. &c.; another river in heaven, BhP.; N. of a metre, Chandom.; (in astron.) N. of a partic. conjunction.

Mandāya, Nom. P. Ā. *°yati*, *°te* (g. *bhṛiśâdi* and *lohitâdi*), to go slowly, linger, loiter, Kālid.; to be weak or faint, ib.

Mandāra, m. (in some meanings also written *mandara*) the coral tree, Erythrina Indica (also regarded as one of the 5 trees of paradise or Svarga), MBh.; Kāv. &c.; a white variety of Calotropis Gigantea, L.; the thorn-apple, L.; heaven, L.; N. of a son of Hiraṇya-kaśipu, MBh. (C. *mandara*); of a Vidyā-dhara, MārkP.; of a hermitage and desert spot on the right bank of the Ganges where there are said to be 11 sacred pools, Cat.; of a mountain (v. l. *mandara*), R.; (*ī*), f. a kind of plant, Suśr.; n. = *-pushpa*, Kālid. **-deva**, m. N. of a prince, Kathās. **-pushpa**, n. a flower of the M° tree, MW. **-mañjarī**, f. N. of wk. **-mālā**, f. a garland of M° flowers, Kāv.; N. of a celestial woman (daughter of Vasu), Kathās. **-vatī**, f. N. of a woman, Vet.; *-vana-māhātmya*, n. N. of wk. **-shashṭhī** and **-saptamī**, f. N. of the 6th and 7th days in the light half of the month Māgha; *-vrata*, n. a partic. observance on these days, Cat.

Mandāraka, m. Erythrina Indica (cf. above), Pañcar. (*ikā*, f. N. of a woman, Mālatim.) **-dina**, n. N. of a partic. day, Cat.

Mandārava (Lalit.), *°ru* (L.), m. the coral tree.

2. **Mandāri-tā**, f. (fr. *mandārin*; for 1. see under *manda*, col. 1) the state of abounding in Mandāra trees, Nalôd.

Mandiman, m. slowness, Vās. (g. *pṛithv-ādi*).

Mandira, n. any waiting or abiding-place, habitation, dwelling, house, palace, temple, town, camp &c. (ifc. dwelling in), MBh.; Kāv. &c.; a stable for horses, L. (cf. *mandurā*); the body, L.; m. the sea, L.; the hollow or back of the knee, L.; N. of a Gandharva, L. **-paśu**, m. 'domestic animal,' a cat, L. **-maṇi**, m. 'temple-jewel,' N. of Śiva, L.

Mandī, in comp. for *manda*. **-√1. kṛi**, P. *-karoti*, to weaken, diminish, Kāv.; Rājat. **-kṛita**, mfn. slackened, Śak. **-bhāva**, m. slowness, tardiness, stupidity, MW. **-√bhū**, P. *-bhavati*, to move on more slowly, Vas.; to become weak or faint, MBh. **-bhūta**, mfn. become slow or dull, MBh.; lessened, diminished, Kād.

2. **Mandu** (for 1. see p. 787, col. 3) prob. = *mandurā* in comp. **-pāla**, m. 'groom,' the son of a Nishāda and a Ratha-kārī, L.

Mandura, in comp. = *mandurā*. **-ja**, mfn. (prob.) born in a stable, Pat.

Manduraka, n. a kind of mat, Divyâv.

Mandurā, f. a stable for horses, Kāv.; Rājat.; a mattress, sleeping-mat, bed, L. **-pati** (Siṇhâs.), **-pāla** (Kād.), m. an ostler, groom. **-bhūshaṇa**, n. a species of monkey, L.

Mandurika, m. = *māndurika*, an ostler, groom, Siṇhâs.

मन्दट *mandaṭa*, m. the coral tree, L.

मन्दन *mandana*, *mandayu* &c. See p. 787, col. 3.

मन्दर *mandara*. See col. 2.

मन्दसान *mandasānâ*. See p. 787, col. 3.

मन्दाक *mandāka*, *°kinī*, *mandâkrānta*, *mandāra* &c. See cols. 1 and 2.

मन्दिकुकुर *mandikukura*, m. a kind of fish, L. (v. l. *mallikukuḍa*).

मन्दिन् *mandin*, *mandira* &c. See above.

मन्दीर *mandīra*, m. (prob.) N. of a man, KātyŚr. (v. l. *maṅgīra*); n. w. r. for *mañjīra*.

मन्दु 1. 2. *mandu*, *mandura*, *°rā* &c. See above.

मन्देह *mandeha*, m. pl. (fr. *man* = *manas* + *deha*?) a kind of Rākshasa, R.; N. of the Śūdras in Kuśa-dvīpa, VP.

मन्दोक *mandoka*, m. N. of a poet, Cat.

मन्दोत्साह *mandôtsāha* &c. See col. 2.

मन्द्र *mandrá* &c. See p. 787, col. 3.

मन्ध *mandha*, m. a kind of antelope, ShaḍvBr. (Sch. *mantha*).

मन्धातृ *mandhātṛí*, m. (fr. *man* = *manas* + *dhātṛi*) a thoughtful or pious man, RV. (accord. to Naigh. = *medhā-vin*; accord. to Sāy. mostly a proper N.); N. of a man, ĀśvŚr. (also w. r. for *māndhātṛi*, q. v.)

मन्नुराम *mannurāma* (?), m. N. of an author, Cat.

मन्मथ *manmatha*, m. (either an intens. form fr. √*math*, or fr. *man* = *manas* + *matha*, 'agitating;' cf. *mandeha* and *mandhātṛi*) love or the god of love, amorous passion or desire (ifc. f. *ā*), MBh.; Kāv. &c.; Feronia Elephantum, L.; the 29th (3rd) year in a 60 years' cycle of Jupiter, VarBṛS.; N. of a physician and various other men, Cat.; (*ā*), f. N. of Dākshāyaṇī, ib. **-kara**, m. 'causing love,' N. of a being attending on Skanda, MBh. **-bandhu**, m. 'friend of love,' the moon, Vcar. **-math**, mfn. destroying the god of l°, Bālar. **-manmatha**, m. a god of l° agitating the god of l°, BhP. **-yuddha**, n. strife of l°, amorous strife or contest, R. **-lekha**, m. a l°-letter, Śak. **-vat**, mfn. being in love, enamoured, R. **-sakha**, m. friend of love, the spring, L. **-saṃjīvanī**, f. 'exciting l°,' N. of a Surāṅganā, Siṇhâs. **-samāna**, mfn. feeling similar love, Daś. **-suhṛid**, m. = *-sakha*, Bālar. **Manmathânanda**, m. 'love's joy,' a kind of mango, L. **Manmathânala**, m. the fire of l°, Śāntiś. **Manmathâyatana**, n. 'l°'s abode,' pudendum muliebre, MBh. **Manmathâlaya**, m. 'id.,' the mango tree, L.; = prec., A. **Manmathâvāsa**, m. 'id.,' a kind of mango, L. **Manmathâvishṭa**, mfn. penetrated or inflamed by l°, R. **Manmathêśvara-tīrtha**, n. N. of a sacred bathing-place, Cat. **Manmathôddīpana**, n. the act of kindling or inflaming love, Ṛitus.

Manmathin, mfn. enamoured, impassioned, in love, W.

मन्मन् *manman.* See p. 786, col. 3.

मन्मन *manmana,* m. confidential whisper (= *karṇa-mūle guptâlāpa*), Kāvyâd., Sch.; love or the god of love, ib. **-tva,** n. a partic. defect of the organs of speech, HYog.

मन्मनस *man-manasa* &c. See p. 777, col. 2.

मन्मोक *manmoka,* m. N. of a poet, Cat.

मन्या *mányā,* f. du. and pl. the back or the nape of the neck (musculus cucullaris or trapezius), AV.; VS.; Suśr.; m. (!) the middle of an elephant's goad, L. **-gata,** mfn. being on the nape of the neck, Suśr. **-graha,** m. spasm or contraction of the neck, Suśr.; SārṅgS. **-stambha,** m. stiffness or rigidity of the neck, ib.

Manyākā, f. the nape of the neck, L.

मन्यु *manyú* &c. See p. 786, col. 3.

मन्वन्तर *manv-antara* &c. See p. 786, col. 3.

मपष्ट *mapashṭa,* °*shṭaka, mapushṭaka* or °*shṭhaka,* m. a kind of bean, L.

मफिर *maphira* (?), N. of a place, Cat.

मभ्र् *mabhr,* cl. 1. P. *mabhrati,* to go, move, Dhātup. xv, 50.

मम *máma,* gen. sg. of 1st pers. pron. in comp. **-kāra,** m. interesting one's self about anything, Rājat. **-kṛitya,** n. id., Vajras. **-tā** (*mamá-*), f. the state of 'mine,' sense of ownership, self-interest, egotism, interest in (loc.), MBh.; Kāv.; Pur.; pride, arrogance, L.; N. of the wife of Utathya and mother of Dīrgha-tamas, RV. vi, 10, 2 (Sāy.); MBh.; BhP.; *-yukta,* mfn. filled with selfishness, a miser or egotist (= *kṛipaṇa*), L.; *-śūnya,* mfn. devoid of interest for us, Prab. **-tva,** n. = *-tā,* MBh.; Kāv. &c. (*-tvaṃ* √1. *kṛi,* P. *-karoti,* to be attached to, with loc., MBh.; to envy, with gen., MārkP.) **-satyá,** n. 'the being mine,' contest for ownership, RV. x, 42, 4.

Mámaka, mfn. my, mine, RV. i, 31, 11; 34, 6 (cf. Pāṇ. iv, 3, 3 and *māmaka*).

Mamāya, Nom. Ā. °*yate,* to envy (with acc.), MBh.

ममत् *mámat,* ind. (only repeated with *caná* or *cid*) at one time–at another time &c., RV. iv, 18, 8; 9.

ममत्तर *mamattara,* mfn. = *balavat-tara,* MBh. (Nīlak.)

ममाथ *mamātha,* n. N. of a Sāman (v.l. for *māthāla*).

ममापताल *mamāpatāla* (?), m. an object of sense (= *vishaya*), Uṇ. v, 50, Sch.

मम्ब् *mamb,* cl. 1. P. *mambati,* to go, move, Dhātup. xi, 35 (Vop.)

मम्म *mamma,* m. N. of a man, Rājat.; (with *bhaṭṭa*), N. of an author, Cat. **-svāmin,** m. N. of a temple built by Mamma, Rājat.

Mammaka, m. N. of a man, Rājat.

मम्मट *mammaṭa,* m. (for *mahima-bhaṭṭa*) N. of various writers (esp. of the author of the Kāvya-prakāśa), Cat.

मम्रि *mamri,* mfn. mortal (see *á-mamri*).

मय् *may,* cl. 1. Ā. to go, move, Dhātup. xv, 50.

मय 1. *maya,* m. (√3. *mā*) N. of an Asura (the artificer or architect of the Daityas, also versed in magic, astronomy and military science), MBh.; Kāv. &c.; N. of various teachers and authors (esp. of an astronomer and a poet), Cat.; (*ā*), f. medical treatment, L. **-kshetra,** n. N. of a place; *-māhātmya,* n. N. of wk. **-grāma,** m. N. of a village, Rājat. **-dānava** (?), m. N. of an author, Cat. **-dīpikā,** f. N. of a wk. (on sculpture), Hcat. **-nirmita,** mfn. made by Maya, MW. **-mata,** n., **-śilpa,** n., **-saṃgraha,** m. N. of wks. **-saras,** n. N. of a pool, Cat. **Mayârāma,** m. (with *miśra*) N. of an author, Cat. **Mayêśvara,** m. N. of the Asura Maya, Kathās.

मय 2. *máya,* m. (prob. fr. √2. *mā*) a horse, VS.; a camel, L.; a mule, L.; (*ī*), f. a mare, Lāṭy., Sch.

मय 3. *maya,* m. (√1. *mī*) hurting, injuring, W.

मयका *mayakā,* instr. sg. of 3. *ma* = *mayā,* by me, Bhadrab.

मयट *mayaṭa,* m. = *prasāda* (prob. *prās*°) or *tṛiṇa-harmya,* L.

मयन्त *máyanta* (MaitrS.) and *máyanda* (VS.), n. N. of a metre.

मयष्ट *mayashṭa* or °*ṭaka,* m. a kind of bean, L.

मयस् *máyas,* n. (prob. fr. √3. *mā*) refreshment, enjoyment, pleasure, delight, RV.; VS.; TBr. **-kará,** mfn. causing enjoyment, giving pleasure, VS.

Mayo, in comp. for *mayas.* **-bhavá,** mfn. causing pleasure, delighting, VS.; m. refreshment, delight, ĀpŚr.; N. of a man (pl. his descendants), Pravar. **-bhú** or **-bhú,** mf(*ú*)n. = *-bhava,* RV.; VS.; ŚBr.; ĀśvGṛ.; (*ū*), m. a partic. Agni, ŚāṅkhGṛ. **-bhuva,** mfn. = *-bhava,* ĀpŚr.

मयिवसु *mayi-vásu,* mfn. (fr. *mayi,* loc. sg. of 3. *ma* + *vasu*) good in me (used in partic. formulas), AitBr.; TS.

मयु *mayú,* m. (prob. fr. √2. *mā*) a Kim-purusha (s.v.) or a partic. man-like animal, VS.; TS.; ŚBr.; an antelope, deer, L. **-rāja,** m. 'king of the Kim-purushas,' N. of Kubera, L.

मयुष्टक *mayushṭaka,* m. a kind of bean, L. (cf. *makushṭaka* and *mayashṭaka*).

मयूक *mayūka,* m. = *mayūra,* L.

मयूख *mayúkha,* m. (prob. fr. √1. *mi*) a kind of peg (esp. for hanging woven cloth or skins upon), RV.; AV.; Br.; ŚrS.; the pin or gnomon of a sun-dial (= *kīla*), L.; a ray of light, flame, brightness, lustre, Up.; Kāv.; Var. &c. (also *ā,* f., L.; once n. in KaushUp.); a partic. Agni, GṛS.; N. of a wk. (by Śaṃkara-miśra). **-pṛikta,** mfn. touching (one another) with rays (as two planets), Var. **-mālā** or **-mālikā,** f. N. of wk. **-mālin,** m. 'wreathed with rays,' the sun, Kād. **-vat,** mfn. having rays, radiant, brilliant, Var. **Mayūkhâditya,** m. a form of the sun, Cat. **Mayūkhâvali,** f. N. of wk. **Mayūkhêśa,** m. 'lord of rays,' the sun, Hcat.

Mayūkhin, mfn. radiant, brilliant, MBh.

मयूर *mayūra,* m. (prob. fr. √2. *mā*) a peacock, VS.; Lāṭy.; MBh. &c.; a cock, L.; a species of plant, Suśr. (Celosia Cristata or Achyranthes Aspera, L.); a kind of instrument for measuring time, Sūryas.; a kind of gait, Saṃgīt.; N. of an Asura, MBh.; of a poet, Prasannar.; (also with *bhaṭṭa*), of various other writers, Cat.; (of the father of Śaṅkuka, ib.; of a mountain, MārkP.; (*ī*), f. a peahen, RV. &c. &c.; a species of pot-herb, L.; n. a partic. posture in sitting, Cat.; N. of a town, Buddh. **-karṇa,** m. 'peacock's ear,' N. of a man, g. *śivâdi;* pl. his descendants, g. *upakâdi.* **-ketu,** m. 'having a p° for emblem,' N. of Skanda, MBh. **-gati,** f. 'p°'s gait,' N. of a metre, Ked. **-grīva** or °**vaka,** n. 'p°'s neck,' a kind of blue vitriol, Bhpr. **-ghṛita,** n. 'p°'s fat,' a kind of medicine, ŚārṅgS. **-caṭaka,** m. the domestic cock, L. **-citraka,** n. N. of VarBṛS. xlvii and of another wk. **-cūḍa,** n. 'p°'s crest,' a kind of gall-nut, L.; (*ā*), f. Celosia Cristata, L. **-jaṅgha,** m. Bignonia Indica, L. **-tā,** f. (Kād.), **-tva,** n. (Kathās.) the state or condition of a peacock. **-tuttha,** n. a kind of blue vitriol, L. **-pattrin,** mfn. (an arrow) furnished with p°'s feathers, R. **-padaka,** n. a scratch or impression in the form of a p°'s foot made with the finger-nails, L. **-parvata,** m. N. of a mountain, MaitrS., Introd. **-piccha,** n. a p°'s tail-feather, Kād.; *-maya,* mf(*ī*)n. consisting of p°'s tail-f°s, ib. **-pura,** n. 'p°'s town,' N. of a hill; *-māhātmya,* n. N. of wk. **-poshaka,** m. 'breeder of p°s,' N. of the father of Candra-gupta, HPariś. **-maya,** mf(*ī*)n. consisting of p°s, Kād. **-ratha,** m. 'having a p° for a vehicle,' N. of Skanda, L. **-roman** (*mayūra-*), mfn. 'p°-haired' (said of Indra's horses), RV. **-varman,** m. N. of a king; °*ma-caritra,* n. N. of wk. **-vācaspati** and **-vāhana,** m. N. of authors, Cat. **-vidalā,** f. Hibiscus Cannabinus, Bhpr. **-vyaṃsaka,** m. = *dhūrta-mayūra,* Pāṇ. ii, 1, 71, Sch. **-śataka,** n. N. of a poem (= *sūrya-ś*°). **-śarman,** m. N. of a poet, Cat. **-śikhā,** f. 'p°'s crest,' Celosia Cristata, Bhpr. **-śepya** (*mayūra-*), mfn. 'p°-tailed' (said of Indra's horses), RV. **-sārin,** mfn. strutting like a peacock; (*iṇī*), f. N. of a metre, Col. **-stuti,** f., **-sthala-māhātmya,** n. N. of wks. **Mayūrâksha,** 'p°-eyed,' N. of a teacher, Cat. **Mayūrâṅkī,** f. a species of jewel, L. **Mayūrâri,** m. 'p°'s enemy,' a chameleon, lizard, L. **Mayūrâshṭaka,** n. N. of a poem. **Mayūrêśa,** m. 'peacock-lord,' N. of a man; *-vivāha-varṇana,* n. N. of ch. of the GaṇP. **Mayūrêśvara,** m. 'p°-lord,' m. N. of the father of Khaṇḍa-bhaṭṭa, Cat.; of a Liṅga, ib. **Mayūrôllāsaka,** m. 'peacock's joy,' the rainy season, L.

Mayūraka, m. a peacock, L.; a species of plant (= *mayūra*), Suśr.; N. of a poet, Cat.; m. or n. a kind of blue vitriol, L.; (*ikā*), f. a kind of venomous insect, Suśr.; Hibiscus Cannabinus, L.

Mayūrikā-bandham, ind., Pāṇ. ii, 4, 42, Sch.

Mayūrī-√bhū, P. *-bhavati,* to become a peacock, Kathās.

मर *mara,* m. (√*mṛi*) dying, death (see *pari-mara*); the world of death, i.e. the earth, AitUp.; mfn. killing (see *nṛi-mara*); m. pl. the inhabitants of hell, Āryabh.; w.r. for *narāḥ,* Hariv. 8464. **Marârāma,** m. N. of a Daitya, Kathās.

Maraka, m. an epidemic, plague, mortality, Var.; Suśr.; pl. N. of a people, MārkP.

Maraṭa, m. death, Uṇ. iii, 110, Sch.

Maraṇa, n. the act of dying, death (ifc. dying by; °*ṇaṃ* √1. *kṛi,* Ā. *kurute,* to die), ŚrS.; Mn.; MBh. &c.; passing away, cessation (as of lightning or rain), AitBr.; (in astrol.) the 8th mansion, VarBṛS., Sch.; a kind of poison, L. (prob. w.r. for *māraṇa*); a refuge, asylum, BhP. (prob. w.r. for *śaraṇa*). **-ja,** mfn. produced by death, MW. **-daśā,** f. the time or hour of d°, Mṛicch. **-dharma,** m. the law of d° (instr. with Caus. of √*yuj,* 'to put to d°'), R. **-dharman,** mfn. subject to the law of d°, mortal, Kathās. **-niścaya,** mfn. determined to die, Pañcat. **-bhaya,** n. the fear of d° (with Buddh. one of the 5 kinds of fear), Dharmas. 52. **-bhīruka,** mfn. afraid to die, Mṛicch. (in Prākṛit). **-vyādhi-śoka,** m. pl. death and sickness and sorrow, Hit. **-śīla,** mfn. liable to d°, mortal, MW. **-sāmāyika-nirṇaya,** m. N. of wk. **Maraṇâgresara,** mfn. preceding in d°, MW. **Maraṇâtmaka,** mf(*ikā*)n. causing d°, Vet. **Maraṇânta** and °**tika,** mfn. ending in d°, MBh. **Maraṇândha-tamasa,** n. the gloom or shadow of d°, Kād. **Maraṇâbhimukha,** mfn. on the point of d°, moribund, MW. **Maraṇâlasa,** n. N. of a partic. Yoga-posture (in which only one leg is stretched out; cf. *vahitra-karṇa*), L. **Maraṇônmukha,** mfn. = °*ṇâbhimukha,* MW.

Maraṇīya, mfn. 'to be died,' doomed to death, liable to die, MW.

Marāyin, m. (prob.) N. of a man, RV. x, 60, 4 (Sāy. 'destroying enemies' = *śatrūṇām mārakaḥ;* others 'brilliant, splendid').

Marāyu, mfn. mortal, perishable, RV. x, 106, 6; 7 (Sāy.; cf. *dur-marāyu*).

Mariman, m. death, dying, Uṇ. iv, 118, Sch.

Marishṇu, mfn. mortal (see *a-marishṇu*).

मरकत *marakata,* n. an emerald, R.; Var.; Pañcat. &c. [Cf. Gk. σμάραγδος; Lat. *smaragdus.*] **-pattrī,** f. a kind of climbing plant, L. **-maṇi,** m. the em° gem, VarBṛS. **-maya,** mf(*ī*)n. made of emerald, Śiś. **-vallī-pariṇaya,** m. N. of a drama. **-śilā,** f. an emerald slab, Megh. **-śyāma,** mfn. dark or green as an emerald, BhP.

Marakta, n. = *marakata,* L.

मरन्द *maranda,* m. (also pl.) the juice or nectar of flowers, Kāv. (also °*daka,* W.; cf. *makaranda*). **Marandâukas** or °**kasa,** n. 'nectar-abode,' a flower, L.

मराकाली *marākālī,* f. Tragia Involucrata, L.

मराय *marāya,* m. N. of an Ekâha, ŚrS.; n. N. of a Sāman, ĀrshBr.

मरायिन् *marāyin, marāyu.* See above.

मरार *marāra,* m. a corn-loft, granary, L.

मराराम *marârāma.* See above.

मराल *marāla,* mfn. (said to be fr. √*mṛi*) soft, mild, tender, L.; red with a little yellow, L.; = *vistṛita* and *śubha,* L.; m. a kind of duck or goose or flamingo, Kāv. (*ī,* f., L.; °*la-tā,* f., HPariś.); a partic. mode of joining the hands, Cat. (L. also a horse; an elephant; a grove of pomegranate trees;

white oleander; a villain; a cloud; lamp-black); m. or n. redness mixed with a little yellow, L. **-gamanā,** f. 'having the gait of a flamingo,' N. of a Surâṅganā, Siṇhās.

Marālaka, m. a kind of duck or goose or flamingo, L. (*ī*, f., Daś.); a partic. mode of joining the hands, Cat.

मरिच *marica,* m. the pepper shrub, R.; Var.; Suśr.; a kind of Ocimum, L.; Strychnos Potatorum, L. (v.l. *marīca*); N. of a man, Rājat.; n. black pepper, Suśr.; a partic. fragrant substance (= *kakkolaka*), L. **-kshupa,** m. the pepper shrub, Hariv. **-pattraka,** m. Pinus Longifolia, L.

Marīca, m. the pepper shrub (also *-kshupa*), Hariv.; Strychnos Potatorum, L. (v.l. *marica*); marjoram, L.; N. of the father of Kaśyapa, Cat.; of a son of Sunda, VP.; n. black pepper, L.

मरिष्टक *marishṭaka,* m. a kind of kidney bean, L. (cf. *mayashṭaka*).

मरी *marī.* See *kara-marī.*

मरीचि *márīci,* mf. (m. only in TĀr.; prob. connected with *marút,* q.v.) a particle of light, shining mote or speck in the air, RV.; AV.; a ray of light (of the sun or moon), RV. &c. &c.; (also °*cī;* f. with *Somasya* = moonlight, Hariv.); a mirage (= *marīcikā*), Kathās. (cf. *marīci-toya*); m. N. of a Prajā-pati or 'lord of created beings' (variously regarded as a son of Svayam-bhū, as a son of Brahmā, as a son of Manu Hairaṇyagarbha, as one of the 7 sages and father of Kaśyapa, or, accord. to Mn. i, 35 as the first of the ten Prajā-patis [q.v.] engendered by Manu Svāyambhuva), Mn.; MBh. &c.; of the star η in the great Bear, VarBṛS.; of Kṛishṇa (as a Marut), Bhag. x, 21; of a Daitya, Hariv.; of a Maharshi, Daś.; of the father of Paurṇamāsa, Pur.; of a king (son of Samrāj and father of Bindu-mat), ib.; of a son of Tīrtham-kara Ṛishabha, W.; of a son of Śaṃkarācārya and various other teachers and authors, Cat.; a miser, niggard (= *kripaṇa*), L.; f. N. of an Apsaras, MBh.; of a Comm. on Siddhântaś. **-garbha,** m. pl. 'containing particles of light within,' N. of a world, Hariv.; a class of gods under Manu Dākshasāvarṇi, VP. **-tantra,** n. N. of wk. **-toya,** n. a mirage, BhP. **-pá,** mfn. drinking in or absorbing particles of light, VS.; m. pl. rays of light, Naigh. i, 5; N. of a mythical race of Ṛishis, MBh.; R. **-paṭala,** n. N. of wk. **-pattana,** n. N. of a town, R. **-mat,** mfn. (ifc.) having rays, radiant or shining with, MBh.; m. the sun, Kathās. **-mālin,** mfn. garlanded with rays, radiant, Hit.; m. the sun, Kād. **-smṛiti,** f. N. of wk. **Marīcôpapurāṇa,** n. N. of an Upapurāṇa.

Marīcika, m. (with Buddhists) N. of a world; (*ā*), f. a mirage, illusory appearance of water in a desert, Prab.; Kathās.; N. of a Comm. on the Brahmasūtra.

Marīcin, mfn. having rays, radiant; m. the sun, MBh.

मरीमृज *marīmṛija,* mfn. (fr. Intens. of √*mṛij*) rubbing repeatedly or very much, Pāṇ. i, 1, 4, Sch.

मरीमृश *marīmṛiśa,* mfn. (fr. Intens. of √*mṛiś*) feeling about, groping, AV.

मरीयमि *marīyami,* f. Mary, Romakas. **-putra,** m. 'son of Mary,' N. of Christ, ib.

मरीस *marīsa,* n. milk (in *avi-m*°, q.v.)

मरु *marú,* m. (prob. fr. √*mṛi*) a wilderness, sandy waste, desert (often pl.), MBh.; Kāv. &c.; a mountain, rock, MBh.; MārkP.; 'the desert-like penance,' i.e. abstinence from drinking, MBh.; Hariv.; a species of plant, Bhpr.; a deer, antelope, L.; N. of a Daitya (usually associated with Naraka), MBh.; of a Vasu, Hariv.; of a prince (the son of Śīghra), ib.; R.; Pur.; of a king belonging to the Ikshvāku family, BhP.; of a son of Hary-aśva, R.; Pur.; pl. N. of a country (Marwar) and its inhabitants, TĀr.; R.; Var. &c. [Cf. Lat. *mare* (?); Angl. Sax. *mōr;* Germ. and Eng. *moor.*] **-kaccha,** m. N. of a country; *-nivāsin,* mfn. inhabiting it, MBh. **-kucca** (?), m. N. of a country, VarBṛS. **-gata,** mfn. being in a desert, ŚārṅgP. **-cchadā,** f. a kind of shrub, L. (cf. *madhu-cchadā*). **-ja,** m. Unguis Odoratus, L.; a tree akin to the Mimosa Catechu, L.; (*ā*), f. colocynth, L.; a kind of deer, L. **-jātā,** f. Carpopogon Pruriens or a similar plant, L. **-jush,** m. the inhabitant of a desert, Alaṃkāras. **-deśa,** m. N. of a country, KātyŚr., Sch. **-deśya,** m. bdellium, L. (cf. *marud-ishṭa*). **-druma,** m. Vachellia Farnesiana, L. **-dvipa,** m. 'desert-elephant,' a camel, L. **-dhanva,** m. a wilderness, sandy desert, BhP. **-dhanvan,** m. id., MBh.; Hariv.; N. of the father of the wife of the Vidyādhara Indīvara, MārkP. **-dhara,** m. N. of a country, MW. **-nandana,** m. N. of a prince, VP. **-patha,** m. a desert, wilderness, Rājat. **-pṛishṭha,** n. id., Ragh. **-prapatana,** n. the act of throwing one's self from a rock, MārkP. xl, 3 (printed *marut-pr*°). **-prapāta,** m. a rocky precipice, mountain-crag, MBh. **-priya,** m. 'the desert's friend,' a camel, L. **-bhava,** m. the inhabitant of a desert, VarBṛS. **-bhū,** f. a desert (cf. *bhū-ruha*); pl. N. of a country (prob. Marwar; accord. to some = *daśerakāḥ*), L.; *-ruha,* m. 'growing in deserts,' Capparis Aphylla, Bhpr. **-bhūti** or °**tika,** m. N. of a son of Yaugamdharāyaṇa, Kathās. **-bhūmi,** f. a desert, wilderness (*-tva,* n.), ib.; N. of a country (= Marwar), MBh. **-bhauma,** m. pl. N. of a people, VP. **-maṇḍala,** n. N. of a country, Uttamac. **-marīci** (pl.) and °**cikā** (sg.) f. a mirage, illusory appearance of water in a desert, Kathās. **-mahī,** f. = *-bhūmi,* Rājat. **-mārga,** m. a way through a desert, Kuval. **-sambhava,** n. 'produced in a d°,' a kind of horse-radish, L.; (*ā*), f. N. of two plants (a species of Alhagi and = *mahêndra-vāruṇī*), L. **-sthala,** n., °**lī,** f. a desert spot, wilderness, Kāv.; Kathās.; Hit. **-sthā,** f. a species of Alhagi, L. **-sthita,** mfn. living in a desert; m. the inhabitant of a d°, Rājat. **Marūdbhava,** m. 'produced in a d°,' a kind of ill-scented Mimosa, L.; (*ā*), f. Alhagi Maurorum, L.; a species of Khadira, L.

Marū-√bhū, P. *-bhavati,* to become a wilderness or sandy desert, Kathās.

मरुक *maruka,* m. (cf. *marūka*) a peacock, L.; a deer, antelope, L.

मरुचीपट्टन *marucī-paṭṭana,* n. N. of a town, VarBṛS. (cf. *marīci-pattana*).

मरुटा *maruṭā,* f. a woman with a high forehead, L. (cf. *maruṇḍā*).

मरुण्ड *maruṇḍa,* m. N. of a prince, Cat. (also *-rāja,* Siṇhâs.); pl. of a dynasty and a people, VP.; (*ā*), f. = *maruṭā,* L.

मरुत् *marút,* m. pl. (prob. the 'flashing or shining ones;' cf. *marīci* and Gk. μαρμαίρω) the storm-gods (Indra's companions and sometimes, e.g. Ragh. xii, 101 = *devāḥ,* the gods or deities in general; said in the Veda to be the sons of Rudra and Pṛiśni, q.v., or the children of heaven or of ocean; and described as armed with golden weapons i.e. lightnings and thunderbolts, as having iron teeth and roaring like lions, as residing in the north, as riding in golden cars drawn by ruddy horses sometimes called Pṛishatīḥ, q.v.; they are reckoned in Naigh. v, 5 among the gods of the middle sphere, and in RV. viii, 96, 8 are held to be three times sixty in number; in the later literature they are the children of Diti, either seven or seven times seven in number, and are sometimes said to be led by Mātariśvan), RV. &c. &c.; the god of the wind (father of Hanumat and regent of the north-west quarter of the sky), Kir.; Rājat. (cf. comp.); wind, air, breath (also applied to the five winds in the body), Kāv.; Pur. &c.; a species of plant, Bhpr.; = *ṛitvij,* Naigh. iii, 18; gold, ib. i, 2; beauty, ib. iii, 7; N. of a Sādhya, Hariv.; of the prince Bṛihad-ratha, MaitrUp.; f. Trigonella Corniculata, L.; n. a kind of fragrant substance (= *granthi-parṇa*), L. **-kara,** m. Dolichos Catjang, L. **-karman,** n. (Cat.) or **-kriyā,** f. (L.) breaking wind, flatulency. **-koṇa,** m. the north-west quarter of the sky, MW. **-tanaya,** m. 'son of the Wind,' N. of Hanumat, MW.; of Bhīma, A. **-tama** (*marút-*), mfn. very or altogether equal to the Maruts, as swift as the Maruts (said of the Aśvins), RV.; m., w.r. for *marutta,* Cat. **-taruṇī,** f. N. of a Vidyā-dharī, Bālar. **-paṭa,** m. 'wind-cloth,' a sail, Kathās. **-pati,** m. 'lord of the M°,' N. of Indra, MBh.; R.; BhP. **-patha,** m. the path or region of the air, Kād. **-pāla,** m. 'protector of the M°,' N. of Indra, L. **-putra,** m. 'son of the wind-god,' N. of Bhīma, L.; of Hanu-mat, MW. **-plava,** m. 'springing with the rapidity of w°,' a lion, L. **-phala,** n. 'fruit of the w°,' hail, W. **-mat,** mfn. = *-vat* (q.v.), g. *yavâdi.* **-vat** (*marút-*), mfn. attended by the Maruts, RV.; VS.; Br.; containing the word *marut,* Br.; m. N. of Indra, MBh.; Kāv.; of Hanu-mat, L.; of a son of Dharma by Marut-vatī, Hariv.; BhP.; a cloud, L.; pl. a class of gods regarded as children of Dharma or of Manu by Marut-vatī, MBh.; R.; Hariv.; (*atī*), f. N. of a daughter of Daksha, wife of Dharma (Manu), Hariv.; Pur. **-vatīya,** mfn. related or belonging to Indra Marut-vat (said esp. of 3 Grahas at the midday libation, the Śastra recited afterwards and the hymn forming the chief part of that Śastra), VS.; Br.; ŚrS. **-vatya,** mfn. = prec., Pāṇ. iv, 2, 32. **-sakha,** mfn. having the wind for a friend (clouds), Ragh.; m. N. of fire (cf. *vāyu-s*°), ib.; of Indra, L. **-sakhi** (*marút-;* only nom. m. f. *-sakhā*), having the Maruts for friends, RV.; ŚāṅkhŚr. **-sahāya,** mfn. having the w° for a companion (said of fire), VarBṛS. **-suta** (BhP.) and **-sūnu** (A.), m. 'son of the Wind,' N. of Hanumat; of Bhīma, A. **-stotra** (*marút-*), mfn. (a place) in which praise of the Maruts is common, RV. i, 101, 11. **-stomá,** m. a Stoma of the Maruts, TBr.; N. of an Ekâha, TāṇḍyaBr.; ŚrS.

Maruta, m. wind, Śak.; a god, L.; Bignonia Suaveolens, L.; N. of various men, MBh.; Hariv.; VP.; °*tôpanishad,* f. N. of an Upanishad.

Marútta (= *marud-datta* accord. to Pat. on Pāṇ. i, 4, 58. 59, Vārtt. 4), m. N. of various kings, Br.; ŚāṅkhŚr. &c.; wind, a gale (?), W.

Marud, in comp. for *marut.* **-āndola,** m. a kind of fan made of the skin of a deer or buffalo, L. **-ishṭa,** m. bdellium, L. (cf. *maru-deśya*). **-eva,** m. N. of a king, Pur.; of the father of the Arhat Ṛishabha, Śatr.; of a mountain, ib. (v.l. *mār*°); (*ā*), f. (L.) or (*ī*), f. (Śatr.) N. of the mother of Marudeva, grandmother of the Arhat Ṛish°. **-gaṇa,** m. (ifc. f. *ā*) the host or troop of the Maruts, the host of the gods, MBh.; R.; Hariv.; Bhartṛ.; (*marúd-*), mfn. being with or attended by the tr° of the M°, RV.; m. or n. (?) N. of a Tīrtha, MBh. **-datta,** mfn. given by the M°, Pāṇ. i, 4, 58; 59, Vārtt. 4, Pat. **-dvīpa-vatī,** f. N. of the Ganges, Dharmaśarm. **-dhvaja,** n. 'wind-sign, w°-banner,' the down of cotton floating in the air, flocculent seeds wafted by the w°, L. **-baddha,** m. (only L.) a kind of sacrificial vessel; a section of the Sāma-veda; N. of Vishṇu. **-bhavā,** f. (= *tāmra-mūlā*) a kind of plant, L.; (accord. to others) cotton. **-ratha,** m. a horse, L.; a car in which idols are dragged about, L. **-vartman,** n. the path or region of the air, L. **-vāha,** m. smoke, L.; fire, L. **-vidhā,** f., w.r. for *-vṛidhā* (below), Col. **-vṛitā,** f., w.r. for *-vṛidhā* (below), L. **-vṛiddhā,** f. N. of a river (= *-vṛidhā*), BhP. **-vṛidha** (*marúd-*), mfn. rejoicing in the wind or in the Maruts, RV.; ŚāṅkhŚr.; (*ā*), f. N. of a river in the Panjāb, RV.; Prâyaśc. **-vega,** m. 'having the velocity of wind,' N. of a Daitya, Kathās.

Marun, in comp. for *marut.* **-nāma,** mfn. containing names of the Maruts; pl. verses or formulas cont° n° of the M°, Kāṭh. **-maya,** mf(*ī*)n. consisting of wind, Hcar. **-mālā,** f. Trigonella Corniculata, Bhpr.; Medicago Esculenta, L.

Marunta, m., w.r. for *marutta,* Hariv.

Marul, in comp. for *marut.* **-loka,** m. the world of the gods, VP.

मरुत्तक *maruttaka,* m. a species of plant, Bhpr. (prob. w.r. for *maruvaka*).

मरुन्त *marunta,* w.r. for *marutta.*

मरुन्ध *marundha,* N. of a town, Cat. (cf. *marūndha* and *mārudha*).

मरुन्धव *marundhava,* m. the white Mimosa, L.

मरुल *marula,* m. a kind of duck, L. (cf. *marāla*); a beast of prey, L.; n. water, L.

मरुव *maruva,* m. marjoram, L.

Maruvaka, m. (also °*baka*) a kind of flower, Bālar. v, 35; (only L.) marjoram; a kind of Ocimum; Vanguieria Spinosa; Clerodendrum Phlomoides; a crane; a tiger; Rāhu or the ascending node personified; mfn. terrible.

मरूक *marūka,* m. (only L.) a kind of deer; a peacock; a frog; Curcuma Zerumbet.

मरून्ध *marūndha,* N. of a town, Śaṃkar. (v.l. *marundha,* q.v.)

मरोलि *maroli* or °*lika*, m. the sea monster Makara, L.

मर्क् *mark* (prob. invented to serve as the source of the words below), to go, move.

1. **Marka**, m. an ape, monkey, BhP.; N. of Vāyu, the wind, L.; the mind, L.

Markaka, m. Ardea Argala, L.; a spider, L.

Markáṭa, m. (Uṇ. iv, 81) a monkey, ape, VS. &c. &c.; a kind of bird, ShaḍvBr. (the adjutant or Indian crane, L.); a spider, L.; a sort of poison or venom, L.; a mode of coitus, L.; N. of a man, Pravar.; (*ī*), f., see 1. *markaṭī;* n. an iron monkey-shaped bolt, L. **-karṇa**, mfn. monkey-eared, L. **-joḍa**, mfn. m°-chinned, L. **-tinduka**, m. a kind of ebony, Bhpr. **-danta**, mf(*ā* or *ī*)n. m°-toothed, L. **-nāsa**, mfn. m°-nosed, L. **-nyāya**, m. the m°-rule (opp. to *mārjāra-n°*), RTL. 125. **-pati**, m. a young m°, A. **-pippalī**, f. Achyranthes Aspera, L. **-pota**, m. a young m°, MW. **-priya**, m. Mimosa Kauki, L. **-locana**, mfn. m°-eyed, Pañcat. **-vāsa**, m. a cobweb, L. **-śīrsha**, n. vermilion, L. **-hrada**, m. 'ape's pool,' N. of a pool in the neighbourhood of Vaiśālī, Buddh. **Markaṭâsya**, mfn. m°-faced; n. copper, L. **Markaṭêndu**, m. (prob. = °*ṭa-tindu*) Diospyros Tomentosa, L. **Markaṭôtplavana**, n. the act of springing like an ape, BhP.

Markaṭaka, m. a species of grain, ĀpŚr.; (only L.) an ape (*ikā*, f.); a spider; a kind of fish; a Daitya.

1. **Markaṭī**, f. a female ape, L.; N. of various plants, Suśr.; Bhpr. (= Galedupa Piscidia; Carpopogon Pruriens &c.); L.; an iron monkey-shaped bolt, L. **-vrata**, n. N. of a partic. observance, Cat.

2. **Markaṭī**, in comp. for *markaṭa*. **-bhūta**, mfn. one who has become an ape, Kathās.

Markaḍikā, f. a spider, Nalac., Sch. (cf. *markaṭaka*).

मर्क 2. *marká*, m. (√*mṛic*, cf. *marc* below) seizure i. e. eclipse (of sun), RV. x, 27, 20; (*márka*), N. of the Purohita of the Asuras (held to be a son of Śukra), VS.; TS.; Br.; a demon presiding over various sicknesses of childhood, PārGṛ.; N. of a Yaksha, Cat.

मर्क 3. *marka*, m. (accord. to Uṇ. iii, 43 fr. √*marc*) the vital breath which pervades the body, L. (others 'wind' and 'body').

मर्कर *markara*, m. Eclipta Prostrata, L. (cf. *mārkara*); (*ā*), f. (only L.) a hollow, hole made under ground; a vessel, pot; a barren woman.

मर्कस *markasa*, m. vapid spirituous liquor, L.

मर्कोटपिपीलिका *markoṭa-pipīlikā*, f. a kind of small black ant, L.

मर्ग *marga*, w. r. for *mārga*, ĀpGṛ.

मर्च् *marc* (cf. √*mṛic*), cl. 10. P. *marcayati*, to sound, Dhātup. xxxii, 106 (v. l. for *mārj*); to seize, take (cf. Uṇ. iii, 43).

मर्ज् *marj* (cf. √*mṛij*), cl. 1. 6. P. *marjati*, *mṛiñjati*, to sound, Dhātup. vi, 76; 77 (v. l. for *muj*, *muñj*).

मर्जू *marjū*, m. (√*mṛij*) a washerman, L.; = *pīṭha-marda*, a catamite, L.; f. washing, cleansing, purification, L.

Márjya, mfn. to be cleansed or prepared (said of Soma), RV.

मर्डितृ *marḍitṛi*, m. (√*mṛiḍ*) one who shows compassion or favour, pitier, comforter, RV.

मर्त *márta*, m. (√*mṛi*) a mortal, man, RV.; VS. (in later literature prob. w. r. for *martya*); the world of mortals, the earth, Uṇ. iii, 86, Sch. [Gk. μορτός, βροτός; Lat. *mortuus*, *mortalis*.] **-bhójana**, n. food of mortals, nourishment of men, RV. **-vat** (*márta-*), mfn. containing the word *márta;* (*atī*), f. a verse or formula c° the word *márta*, ŚBr. **Martôpanishad**, f. N. of an Upanishad.

Martavya, mfn. 'to be died,' liable to die; n. impers. 'it must be died' (°*vye sati*, death being inevitable; °*vye krita-niścaya*, mfn. determined to die), Mn.; MBh. &c.

Mártya, mfn. who or what must die, mortal, Br.; Kauś.; m. a mortal, man, person, RV. &c. &c.; the world of mortals, the earth, L.; (*ā*), f. dying, death (see *putra-martyā*); n. that which is mortal, the body, BhP. **-kṛita** (*mártya-*), mfn. done by mortals, RV. **-tā**, f. mortality, human condition (*-tām prâptaḥ*, one who has become man), MBh.; Kathās. **-trā**, ind. among mortal men, RV. **-tva**, n. = *-tā* (*-tvam āgataḥ* = *-tām prâptaḥ*), Kathās. **-tvaná**, n. the ways of man, RV. **-dharma**, m. pl. the laws or conditions of human life, Kathās. **-dharman** or °**min**, mfn. having the character or properties of a mortal, any human being, MBh. **-nivāsin**, m. a m° inhabitant (of the world), man, mankind, Hariv. **-bhāva**, m. human state or nature, Kathās.; Rājat. **-bhuvana**, n. the world of mortals, the earth, Śak. (v. l.) **-maṇḍala**, n. id., Bālar. **-mahita**, m. 'honoured by m°,' a god, L. **-mukha**, m. 'm°-faced,' a Kiṃ-nara or a Yaksha, L. **-loka**, m. = *-bhuvana*, KaṭhUp.; MBh. &c. **Martyâmṛita**, n. the immortality of mortals, Āpast. **Martyêndra-mātṛi**, f. Solanum Jacquini, L. **Mártyêshita**, mfn. instigated by mortals, RV.

Martyī-√bhū, P. *-bhavati*, to become a mortal, HPariś.

मर्द *marda*, mfn. (√*mṛid*) crushing, grinding, rubbing, bruising, destroying (ifc.; cf. *ari-*, *cakra-m°* &c.); m. grinding, pounding, violent pressure or friction, MBh.; VarBṛS. (cf. *graha-m°*); acute pain (cf. *aṅga-m°*); dispassion, L.

Mardaka, mfn. (ifc.) crushing, pounding &c.; causing violent pain in, Suśr.

Mardana, mf(*ī*)n. crushing, grinding, rubbing, bruising, paining, tormenting, ruining, destroying, MBh.; Kāv. &c. (cf. *candrârka-*, *samara-* and *samiti-m°*); N. of a king of the Vidyā-dharas; (*ī*), f. a cover for the feet, L.; n. the act of crushing or grinding or destroying, Kāv.; Kathās.; BhP.; rubbing, anointing, Kāv.; Pañcat. &c. (*-śālā*, f., Siṇhâs.), cleaning or combing (the hair; see *keśa-m°*); friction i. e. opposition (of planets; see *graha-m°*).

Mardanīya, mfn. to be crushed or trodden down, Kām.; to be rubbed or touched, W.

Mardala (and °*laka*, L.), m. a kind of drum, MBh.; Kāv. &c. **-dhvani**, m. the sound of a drum, L.

Marditavya, mfn. to be crushed or trodden down or laid waste, MBh.

Mardin, mfn. (ifc.) crushing, grinding, pounding, destroying, Mn.; MBh. &c. (cf. *ripu-* and *loshṭa-m°*); (*inī*), f. a kind of musical composition, Saṃgīt. (cf. *medinī*).

मर्ब् *marb* (cf. √*barb*), cl. 1. P. *marbati*, to go, move, Dhātup. xi, 25.

मर्मन् *márman*, n. (√*mṛi*) mortal spot, vulnerable point, any open or exposed or weak or sensitive part of the body (in Nir. reckoned to be 107), RV. &c. &c.; the joint of a limb, any joint or articulation, ib.; the core of anything, the quick, ib.; any vital member or organ (cf. *antar-m°*); anything which requires to be kept concealed, secret quality, hidden meaning, any secret or mystery, MBh.; Kāv. &c.

Marma, in comp. for *marman*. **-kīla**, m. a husband, L. **-ga**, mf(*ā*)n. going to the vitals, cutting to the quick, excessively poignant or painful, MBh. **-ghāta**, m. wounding the vitals, ŚārṅgS. **-ghātin**, mfn. = *-cchid*, L. **-ghnī**, see *-han*. **-cara**, n. the heart, L. **-cchid**, mfn. cutting through the joints or to the quick, wounding mortally, Kām. **-ccheda**, m. the act of cutting through the vitals or to the quick, causing intense suffering or pain, Prab. **-cchedin**, mfn. = *-cchid*, Nāg. **-ja**, n. blood, L. **-jña**, mfn. knowing weak or vulnerable points (lit. and fig.), MBh.; (ifc.) having a deep insight into, Rājat.; exceedingly acute or clever, Hit. **-jñāna**, n. knowledge of a secret, MW. **-tāḍana**, mf(*ā*)n. piercing or paining to the quick, BhP. **-tra**, n. 'vitals-protector,' a coat of mail, R. **-pāra-ga**, mfn. (ifc.) one who has penetrated into the interior of any matter, thoroughly conversant with, Naish. **-pīḍā**, f. pain in the inmost soul, MW. **-bheda**, m. = *-ccheda*, MārkP.; hitting the mark, L. **-bhedana**, m. 'piercer of the vitals,' an arrow, L. **-bhedin**, mfn. = *-cchid* (lit. and fig.), MBh.; R. &c.; m. an arrow, MBh. **-maya**, mf(*ī*)n. consisting of or relating to the v°, containing secrets, Pañcat. **-rāja**, m. N. of a man, Rājat. **-vid**, mfn. = *-jña*, Kathās. (cf. *para-marma-jña*). **-vidāraṇa**, mfn. tearing the v°, mortally wounding, R. **-vibhedin**, mfn. = *-bhedin*, ib. **-vegitā**, prob. w. r. for next. **-vedi-tā**, f. (fr. *-vedin* = *-vid*) knowing weak points or secrets, Kām. **-vedhin**, mfn. (°*dhi-tā*, f.), see *a-marma-vedhitā*. **-vyathā**, f. = *-pīḍā*, Gīt. **-saṃdhi**, m. pl. joints and articulations, Dhūrtas. **-sthala** or **-sthāna**, n. a vital part, vulnerable place, MW. **-spriś**, mfn. touching the v°, very cutting or stinging (lit. and fig.), Caṇḍ.; Kuval. **-han**, mf(*ghnī*)n. striking the v°, very cutting (as speech), Hariv. **Marmâtiga**, mfn. piercing deeply into the joints or v°, causing acute pain, MBh. **Marmânveshaṇa**, n. the act of seeking out vulnerable points; °*shin*, mfn. seeking out v° p°, MW. **Marmâbhighāta**, m. = *marma-ghāta*, Bhpr. **Marmâvaraṇa**, n. = *marma-tra;* *-bhedin*, mfn. penetrating a coat of mail, MBh.

Marmā-vidh, mfn. wounded in a vital spot, AV.; piercing through vulnerable places, very cutting, Mcar.; Bhaṭṭ.

Marmāvin, mfn., Pāṇ. v, 2, 122, Vārtt. 1, Pat.

Marmika, mfn. = *marma-vid*, L.; v. l. for *mārmika*, Bhām.

मर्मर *marmara*, mfn. (onomat.) rustling (as leaves or garments), murmuring, Kālid.; Rājat.; m. a rustling sound, murmur, Ragh.; a kind of garment, L.; (*ā*), f. coarse ground meal, L.; (*ī*), f. Pinus Deodora, L.; a partic. vein in the external ear, Vagbh. [Cf. Gk. μορμύρω; Lat. *murmurare;* Germ. *murmeln;* Eng. *murmur.*] **-pattra-moksha**, mfn. having leaves falling with a rustling sound, Kum.

Marmaraka, mf(*ikā*)n. (only f. *ikā* with *sirā*) a partic. vein in the tip of the ear, Suśr.

Marmarāya, Nom. Ā. °*yate*, to rustle, murmur, Ragh., Sch.

Marmarī-bhūta, mfn. rustling, murmuring, Ragh.

मर्मरीक *marmarīka*, m. (said to be fr. √*mṛi*) a low or wicked man, Uṇ. iv, 20, Sch.

मर्मृजेन्य *marmṛijénya*, mfn. (fr. Intens. of √*mṛij*) to be rubbed down or cleansed repeatedly (as a horse), RV. ii, 10, 1.

मर्मृत्यु *marmṛityu*, g. *vanas-paty-ādi*.

मर्य *márya*, m. (prob. fr. √*mṛi*) a mortal, man, (esp.) young man, lover, suitor, RV.; VS.; Br. (pl. people; voc. often used as a kind of particle; cf. VPrāt. ii, 16 and *bhos*); a stallion, RV. vii, 56, 16 &c.; a camel, L. (cf. *maya*). **-tas**, ind. from or among men or suitors, RV. x, 27, 1. **-śrī** (*márya-*), mfn. adorned as a lover or suitor, ib. ii. 10, 5.

Maryaká, m. a little man (a term applied to a bull among cows), RV. v, 2, 5.

मर्या *maryā*, f. (perhaps orig. something clear or shining; cf. *marīci* and *marut*) a mark, limit, boundary, L.

Maryā-da, m. 'one who sets marks or limits,' an arbiter, umpire (?), AV. v, 1, 8.

Maryādā, f. (doubtful whether fr. *maryā* + *dā* or *maryā* + *āda* [fr. *ā* + √*dā*]; fancifully said to be fr. *marya* + *ada*, 'devouring young men' who are killed in defending boundaries) 'giving or containing clear marks or signs,' a frontier, limit, boundary, border, bank, shore, mark, end, extreme point, goal (in space and time), RV. &c. &c. (*shaṇ-māsa-maryādayā*, within six months, VarBṛS.); the bounds or limits of morality and propriety, rule or custom, distinct law or definition, Mn.; MBh. &c.; a covenant, agreement, bond, contract, MBh.; Kāv. &c.; continuance in the right way, propriety of conduct, Kāv.; Pañcat.; N. of a kind of ring used as an amulet, AV. vi, 81, 2; N. of the wife of Avacīna (daughter of a king of Vidarbha), MBh.; of the wife of Devâtithi (daughter of a king of Videha), ib. **-giri** and **-°cala** (°*dâc°*), m. a mountain which serves as a frontier, BhP. **-dhāvana**, n. running towards a mark, TBr., Sch. **-parvata**, m. = *-giri*, Hcat.; *-vat*, mfn. having a range of mountains for a frontier, ib. **-bandha**, m. keeping within limits, Divyâv. **-bhedaka**, m. a destroyer of landmarks, Mn. ix, 291. **-maya**, mf(*ī*)n. consisting in (i. e. forming) limits or bounds, Kād. **-vacana**, n. statement of the limit, Pāṇ. iii, 3, 136. **-vyatikrama**, m. overstepping bounds or limits, Pañcat. **-sindhu**, m. N. of wk. **Maryādôkti**, f. = *maryādā-vacana*, Pāṇ. iii, 3, 136, Sch.

Maryādin, mfn. having or keeping within bounds, Vet.; a neighbour, borderer, Nir. iv, 2.

Maryādī-√kṛi, P. *-karoti*, to make anything

an end or limit, reach or attain anything as an end, Pāṇ. v, 2, 8, Sch.

मर्व् *marv* (cf. √*marb*), cl. 1. P. *marvati*, to fill, Dhātup. xv, 69; to go, move, Vop.: Caus. *marvayati*, to utter a partic. sound (v.l. for *mārj*), Dhātup. xxxii, 106.

मर्श *marśa*, m. (√1. *mṛiś*) any substance used to excite sneezing, a sternutatory, Bhpr. (cf. *prati-marśa*); counsel, advice, W.

Marśana, n. touching (esp. a woman), MBh.; inquiring into, examining (= *mīmāṉsā*), BhP.; advising, counselling, deliberating, W.; explaining, explication, MW.; rubbing off, removing, ib.

मर्ष *marsha*, m. (√*mṛish*) patience, endurance, L. (cf. *a-* and *dur-marsha*). °**shaṇa**, mfn. (ifc.) enduring, forgiving, BhP.; n. = prec., MBh.; R. °**shaṇīya**, mfn. to be forgiven or pardoned, ib.; deserving indulgence, MBh. °**shita**, mfn. borne, endured, forgiven, Bh. (*-vat*, mfn. one who has borne or forgiven, patient, enduring), W.; patient, content, W. (cf. *a-marshita*); n. patience, W. °**shin**, mfn. patient, forgiving, indulgent, MBh.; Kāv. &c.

मर्षिका *marshikā*, f. a kind of metre, RPrat.

मल् *mal* (cf. √*mall*), cl. 1. Ā. 10. P. *malate*, *malayati*, to hold, possess, Dhātup. xiv, 22; xxxv, 84, Vop.

Mali, f. holding, having, possession, W.

मल *mála*, n. (in later language also m.; prob. fr. √*mlai*) dirt, filth, dust, impurity (physical and moral), AV. &c. &c.; (in med.) any bodily excretion or secretion (esp. those of the Dhātus, q. v., described as phlegm from chyle, bile from the blood, nose-mucus and ear wax from the flesh, perspiration from the fat, nails and hair from the bones, rheum of the eye from the brain; cf. also the 12 impurities of the body enumerated in Mn. v, 135), Suśr.; Vāgbh. &c.; (with Śaivas), original sin, natural impurity, Sarvad.; camphor, L.; Os Sepiae, L.; m. the son of a Śūdra and a Mālukī, L.; (*ā*), f. Flacourtia Cataphracta, L.; n. tanned leather, a leathern or dirty garment (?), RV. x, 136, 2; a kind of brass or bell-metal, L.; the tip of a scorpion's tail, L. (v.l. *ala*); mfn. dirty, niggardly, L.; unbelieving, godless, L. [Cf. Gk. μέλας; Lat. *mălus*; Lith. *mėlis*, *mėlynas*.] **-karshaṇa**, mfn. removing dirt, Cat. **-kūṭa**, m. or n. (?) N. of a country, Buddh. (cf. *mālā-kuṭa*). **-koshṭhaka**, m. N. of a man, Rājat. (w.r. *-koshṭaka*; cf. *malla-koshṭaka*). **-gá**, m. (perhaps) a fuller, washerman, AV. **-grahi**, mfn., Vop. xxvi, 48. **-ghna**, mfn. removing dirt, cleansing, L.; m. the root of Salmalia Malabarica, L. (cf. *-hantṛi*); (*ī*), f. Artemisia Vulgaris or Alpinia Nutans, L. **-ja**, mfn. arising from filth or dirt, L.; m. pl. N. of a people, MBh. (VP.); R. (cf. *malaka*, *malada*, *malaya*); n. purulent matter, pus, L. **-jñu**, mfn. having dirty knees, MānGṛ. **-tva**, n. dirtiness, filthiness, Ragh. **-dāyaka**, mfn. casting a blemish upon any one, Kād. **-digdhâṅga**, mfn. having the limbs defiled with dirt, h° the body soiled with dust, MBh. **-dūshita**, mfn. soiled with dirt, filthy, L. **-drava**, m. the impure fluid which becomes separated from the chyle and produces urine, ŚārṅgS. **-drāvin**, mfn. dissolving impurity, L.; n. the seed of Croton Tiglium, L. **-dhātrī**, f. a nurse who attends to a child's bodily necessities, Buddh. **-dhārin**, m. a Jaina monk, L. **-paṅka**, m. or n. (?) dirt, MBh. **-paṅkin**, mfn. covered with dust and mire, MBh.; MārkP. **-pū**, f. Ficus Oppositifolia, Suśr.; Bhpr.; Car.; = *kshīra* and *vidārī*, L.; (prob. *u*), n. = *śriṅgī* and *nala*, L. **-pṛishṭha**, n. 'dust-page,' the outer or first page of a book (left unwritten because liable to be dirtied), MW. **-bhuj**, mfn. feeding on impurity, L.; m. a crow, L. **-bhedinī**, f. (prob.) Helleborus Niger, L. **-mallaka**, n. a piece of cloth passing between the legs and covering the privities (= *kaupīna*), Daś.; *-śesha*, mfn. having nothing left but a small piece of cl° to cover the pr°, MW. **-māsa**, m. an intercalary month, an intercalated 13th m° (in which no religious ceremonies should be performed), Cat. &c.; *-kathā*, f., *-tattva*, n., *-nirūpaṇa*, n., *-nirṇaya*, m. (and °*ya-tantra-sāra*, m.), *-pūjā*, f., *-māhātmya*, n., *-vicāra*, m. N. of wks.; *-vrata*, n. N. of a partic. ceremony, Cat.; of a ch. of the BhavP.; *-sāriṇī*, f.; °*sâgha-marshaṇī*, f. N. of wks. **-mūtra-parityāga**, m. evacuation of feces and urine, Subh. **-rodha**, m. or **-rodhana**, n. constipation of the bowels, L. **-vat**, mfn. dirty, filthy, Mn.; (*mála-vad*)-*vāsas*, mfn. wearing d° or impure clothes, MW.; f. a menstruous woman, TS.; GṛS. &c. (cf. *malôdvāsas*). **-vānara**, m. pl. N. of a people, VP. **-vārin**, m. a Jaina beggar, L. (w. r. for *-dhārin*?). **-vāhin**, mfn. carrying filth or soil, bearing or containing dirt, Hit. **-vināśinī**, f. 'dirt-destroyer,' Andropogon Aciculatus, L. **-viśodhana**, mfn. cleansing away filth, R. **-vishṭambha**, m. constipation (of the feces), L. **-visarga**, m. (MW.) or **-visarjana**, n. (W.) the act of removing dirt, cleansing (of a temple); evacuation of feces. **-vega**, m. diarrhoea, L. **-vaiśamya**, n. a kind of dysentery, Gal. (correctly *-vaiśadya*). **-śuddhi**, f. clearing away of feculent matter, evacuation of the bowels, MW. **-sruti**, f. evacuation of the feces, L. **-hantṛi**, m. the bulbous root of the Salmalia Malabarica, L. (cf. *-ghna*). **-hā**, f. N. of a daughter of Raudrāśva, Hariv. **-hāraka**, mfn. taking away impurity, removing sin, MW.; a person who knows how to please an elephant, L. **Malâkarshin**, m. 'dirt-remover,' a sweeper, scavenger, L. **Malâpakarshaṇa**, n. the act of removing dirt or impurity, removal of sin, L. **Malāpahā**, f. a partic. preparation, L.; N. of a river, L. **Malâbha**, mfn. dirty-looking, ŚārṅgS. **Malâyana**, n. the path of the excretions, i. e. the rectum, Car. **Malâri**, m. 'dirt-enemy,' a kind of natron, L. **Malâvarodha**, m. obstruction of the feces, MW. **Malâvaha**, mfn. bringing or causing defilement, Mn. xi, 70. **Malâśaya**, m. 'receptacle of feculent matter,' the bowels, ŚārṅgS. **Malôtsarga**, m. evacuation of the feces, Siṇhâs. **Malôdvāsās**, f. a woman who has put off her soiled clothes (after her impurity), ŚBr. **Malôpahata**, mfn. soiled, dirty, Śiś.

Malaka, m. pl. N. of a people, MārkP.

Malina, mfn. dirty, filthy, impure, soiled, tarnished (lit. and fig.), Yājñ.; MBh.; Kāv. &c.; of a dark colour, gray, dark gray, black, Śiś.; Rājat. &c.; m. a religious mendicant wearing dirty clothes (perhaps) a Pāśupata, Vishṇ.; N. of a son of Taṉsu, VP. (v.l. *anila*); (*ā* [Prâyaśc.] or *ī* [L.]), f. a woman during menstruation; n. a vile or bad action, Pañcat.; Bhartṛ.; Viddh.; buttermilk, L.; water, L.; borax, L. **-tā**, f. dirtiness, impurity, Sāh.; moral imp°, blackness, moral bl°, MW. **-tva**, n. blackness, Cāṇ.; moral bl°, wickedness, Vās. **-prabha**, mfn. whose light is obscured or clouded, W. **-manas**, mfn. having a foul mind, Prasaṅg. **-mukha** (only L.), mfn. 'dirty-faced, dark-f°,' vile, wicked; cruel, fierce; m. fire; a kind of ape; a departed spirit, ghost, apparition. **Malinâtman**, mfn. having a spotted nature (the moon), ŚārṅgP.; impure-minded, ŚārṅgP. **Malinâmbu**, n. 'black-fluid,' ink, L. **Malinâsya**, mfn. 'dirty-faced, dark-faced,' vulgar, low, wicked, L.; savage, cruel, W.

Malinaya, Nom. P. °*yati*, to soil, make dirty, defile, tarnish (lit. and fig.), Ragh.; Śak.; Kuval.

Malinita, mfn. dirtied, soiled, defiled, Bālar.; Rājat.; tainted, wicked, W.

Maliniman, m. dirtiness, impurity, MW.; blackness, Vās.; Śiś.; vileness, wickedness, Vās.

Malinī, in comp. for *malina*. **-karaṇa**, n. the act of soiling, staining; an action which defiles, Prâyaśc. **-karaṇīya**, mfn. fitted to cause defilement, Mn. xi, 125. **-√kṛi**, P. *-karoti*, to make dirty, soil, stain (properly and fig.), Hariv.; VP.; to darken, make obscure, Kathās. **-√bhū**, P. *-bhavati*, to become dirty, Śak.; to pass away, vanish, Naish., Comm.

Malishṭha, mfn. excessively dirty, filthy; (*ā*), f. a woman during menstruation, L.

Malīmasa, mf(*ā*)n. dirty, impure, soiled (lit. and fig.); of a dark or dirty gray colour, Kāv.; Hit.; Kathās. &c.; m. (!) iron, L.; m. (!) or n. yellowish vitriol of iron, L.

Maliyas, mfn. excessively dirty, filthy, W.; very sinful, wicked, ib.

मलद *malada*, m. Phaseolus Radiatus, L.; pl. N. of a people, MBh.; VP. (cf. *malaka*, *mala-ja*, *malaya*); (*ā*), f. N. of a daughter of Raudrāśva, Hariv. (v.l. *malandā*).

मलन *malana*, m. a tent, L.; (*ā*), f. the long cucumber, L.; n. crushing, grinding, L. (= *mardana*; cf. *pari-mala*).

मलप्रालदेश *malaprāla-deśa*, m. N. of a country (°*śīya*, mfn.), Cat.

मलबार *malabāra*, the country Malabar (also *-deśa*, m.), ib.

मलय *malaya*, m. (Uṇ. iv, 99) N. of a mountain range on the west of Malabar, the western Ghāts (abounding in sandal trees), MBh.; Kāv. &c.; of the country Malabar and (pl.) its inhabitants, ib.; of another country (= *śailâṅśa-deśaḥ* or *śailâṅgo d°*), L.; of an Upa-dvīpa, L.; of a son of Garuḍa, MBh. (B. *mālaya*); of a son of Ṛishabha, BhP.; of a poet, Cat.; a celestial grove (= *nandana-vana*), L.; a garden, L.; (in music) a kind of measure, Saṃgīt.; (*ā*), f. Ipomoea Turpethum, L.; N. of a woman, Vās., Introd. **-ketu**, m. N. of various princes, Vcar.; Mudr. **-gandhinī**, f. N. of a Vidyā-dharī, Cat.; of a companion of Umā, L. **-giri**, m. the Malaya mountains, Daś.; another mountain, Buddh.; N. of an author, Cat. **-ja**, mfn. growing on the M° m°; m. a sandal tree, MBh.; N. of a poet, Cat.; n. sandal, Kāv.; Suśr.; N. of Rāhu, L.; *-rajas*, n. the dust of s°, Bhartṛ.; *-rasa*, n. s° water, Vām.; *-jâlepa*, m. s° unguent, Śukas. **-deśa**, m. the country of M°, L. **-druma**, m. M° tree, a sandal tree, Ragh. **-dvīpa**, n. N. of one of the 6 islands of Anudvīpa, L. **-dhvaja**, m. N. of a king of the Pāṇḍyas, MBh.; BhP.; of a son of Meru-dhvaja, Kathās.; *-narapati*, m. a king of Malaya, Mudr. **-parvata**, m. the M° mountain, Kathās. **-pura**, n. N. of a town, ib. **-prabha**, m. N. of a king, ib. **-bhū-bhṛit**, m. = *-parvata*, ib. **-bhūmi**, f. N. of a district in the Himālaya, L. **-marut**, m. wind (blowing) from Malaya (an odoriferous wind prevalent in Southern and Central India during the hot season), Amar. **-mālin**, m. N. of a man, Kathās. **-rāja**, m. N. of a poet, Cat.; *-stotra*, n. N. of a hymn. **-ruha**, m. 'growing on the M° mountain,' a sandal tree, Śiś. **-vatī**, f. N. of a Surâṅganā, Siṇhâs.; of other women, Kathās.; Nāg. **-vāta**, m. = *-marut*, Vikr. **-vāsinī**, f. 'dwelling on the M° mountain,' N. of Durgā, Hariv. **-samīra**, m. = *-marut*, Gīt. **-siṇha**, m. N. of two princes, Kathās. **Malayâcala**, m. = °*ya-parvata*, ib.; *-khaṇḍa*, m. or n. N. of ch. of SkandaP. **Malayâdri**, m. = °*yâcala*; *-vāyu*, m. = next, Kāv. **Malayânila**, m. = °*ya-marut*, Ratnâv. **Malayāvatī**, f. N. of a woman, Cat. (cf. *malaya-vatī*). **Malayêndu**, m. (with *sūri*) N. of an author, Cat. **Malayôdbhava**, n. sandal wood, L. (cf. *malaya-ja*).

मलयू *malayū*, f. Ficus Oppositifolia, Bhpr. (cf. *mala-pū*).

मलर *malara*, m. or n. (?) a partic. high number, Buddh.

मलवदेश *malava-deśa*, m. N. of a country, Cat.

मलाका *malākā*, f. (only L.) a female messenger, confidante; an amorous woman; a female elephant.

मलिक *malika*, m. (= ملك) a king, Cat.

मलिन *malina* &c. See col. 2.

मलिम्लु *malímlu* or *malimlú*, m. (prob. a mutilated form) a robber, thief, AV.; VS.; MaitrS. **-sená**, f. a band of robbers, TS.

Malimluc, m. (fr. Intens. of √*mluc*) 'one who goes about in the dark,' a robber, thief, MānŚr.; a partic. demon, ĀpŚr. (cf. *deva-m°*).

Malimlucá, m. a thief, robber, Rājat. (Naigh. iii, 24); a demon, imp, AV.; PārGṛ.; a gnat, mosquito, L.; a Brāhman who omits the 5 chief devotional acts, L.; an intercalated 13th month (introduced every 5th year to approximate the lunar and solar modes of computation; cf. *mala-māsa*), ŚrS.; Sūryas.; fire, L.; wind, L.; frost or snow, L. **-tattva**, n. N. of wk. (= *mala-māsa-tattva*).

मलिह *malihá*, mfn. = *malhá*, MaitrS.

मलुक *maluka*, m. the belly, L.; a quadruped, L.

मलुद *maluda* and *maluma*, m. or n. (?) partic. high numbers, Buddh.

मलूक *malūka*, m. a kind of worm, L.; a bird, L. **-candrikā**, f. N. of wk.

मल्मलाभवत् *malmalā-bhávat*, mf(*antī*)n. flashing, glittering, TS.; MaitrS. (= *jvalat*, Naigh. i, 17).

मल्ल् *mall* (cf. √*mal*), cl. 1. Ā. *mallate*, to hold, have, Dhātup. xiv, 23.

Malli, m. the act of having, holding, possessing, W. (cf. *mali*); N. of the 19th Arhat of the present Avasarpiṇī, L.; f. (= *mallikā*) Jasminum Zambac (also *ī*), Prasannar.; earthenware, L.; a seat, L. **-gandhi**, mfn. smelling like Jasminum Zambac, L.; n. a kind of Agallochum, L. **-nātha**, m. N. of a poet and celebrated commentator (also called Kolâcala or Peḍḍa Bhaṭṭa, father of Kumāra-svāmin and Viśvêśvara; he lived probably in the 14th or 15th century and wrote commentaries on the Raghuvaṇśa, Kumāra-sambhava, Megha-dūta, Śiśupāla-vadha, Kirātārjunīya, Bhaṭṭi-kāvya, Naishadīya &c.); of two authors on medicine and grammar, L.; *-caritra*, n. N. of wk. **-pattra**, n. a mushroom or fungus, L. **-bhūshaṇa-deva** and **-sheṇa-sūri**, m. N. of two men, Cat.

मल्ल **malla**, m. a wrestler or boxer by profession (the offspring of an out-caste Kshatriya by a Ksh° female who was previously the wife of another out-caste, Mn. x, 22; xii, 45), an athlete, a very strong man, MBh.; Hariv.; Var. &c.; N. of a king called Nārāyaṇa, Cat.; of the 21st Arhat of the future Utsarpiṇī, L.; of an Asura (see *mallâsura*); of various men, Rājat.; a vessel, boiler, Divyâv. (also *ī*, f., L.); the remnant of an oblation, L.; a kind of fish (= *kapālin*), L.; the cheek and temples, L.; pl. N. of a people, MBh.; Hariv. &c.; (*ā*), f. a woman, L.; N. of two women, Rājat.; ornamenting the person with coloured unguents (= *pattra-vallī*), L.; Arabian jasmine (cf. *mallikā*), L.; mfn. strong, robust, L.; good, excellent, L. **-kūṭa**, m. or n. (?) N. of a village, Hcar. **-koshṭa** or °**ṭaka**, m. N. of a man, Rājat. (perhaps w. r. for *-koshṭha* and °*ṭhaka*). **-krīḍā**, f. a wrestling or boxing match, athletic sports, MW. **-ga**, m. N. of a son of Dyuti-mat; n. N. of a Varsha ruled by that prince, VP. **-ghaṭī**, f. a kind of pantomime, Vikr. **-ja**, n. black pepper, L. **-tāla**, m. (in music) a kind of measure, Saṃgīt. **-tūrya**, n. a kind of drum beaten during a wrestling match, L. **-deva**, m. N. of various men, Cat.; Inscr. **-dvādaśī**, f. N. of the 12th day in a partic. half month, Cat.; *-vrata*, n. N. of a partic. religious observance, MW. **-nāga**, m. N. of Vātsyāyana, author of the Kāma-sūtra, Vās.; Cat.; Indra's elephant, L.; a letter-carrier, L. **-nātha**, m. N. of a man L. **-pura**, n. N. of a city, Cat. **-prakāśa**, m. N. of wk. **-priya**, m. N. of Kṛishṇa, Hariv. **-bandhāntara**, (prob.) n. a partic. posture with wrestlers, MW. **-bhaṭī-tūrya**, n. = *-tūrya* (above), Bālar. **-bhaṭṭa**, m. N. of two authors, Naish., Comm.; Cat. **-bhāvana**, m. N. of Kṛishṇa, Hariv. **-bhū**, f. a wrestling ground, L.; the site of any conflict, a field of battle, W. **-bhūmi**, f. a wrestling ground, L.; N. of a country, R. **-malla**, m. N. of an author, Cat. **-yātrā**, f. a line or procession of wrestlers, L. **-yuddha**, n. 'a prize-fight,' pugilistic encounter, wrestling or boxing match, MBh. **-rāja**, m. a chief wrestler, VP.; N. of an author, Cat. **-rāshṭra**, n. N. of a kingdom, MBh. (VP.) **-vāstu**, n. N. of a place, Pāṇ. iv, 2, 120, Sch. (cf. *māllavāstava*). **-vidyā**, f. the art of wrestling, MW. **-vena**, m. N. of an author, Cat. **-veśa**, m. a wrestler's dress, MW. **-śālā**, f. a room for wrestling or boxing, ib. **-śilā-yuddha**, n. a fight with stones between wrestlers, Cat. **Mallâdarśa**, m. N. of wk. **Mallâdi**, m. N. of Kṛishṇa, Hariv. (v. l. °*lâri*). **Mallā-pura**, n. = *malla-pura* (above); *-māhātmya*, n. N. of wk. **Mallâri**, m. 'enemy of the Asura Malla,' N. of Kṛishṇa, Hariv. (v. l. °*lâdi*); of Śiva, RTL. 266, n. 1; of two authors, Cat.; *-kavaca*, n., *-paddhati-ṭīkā*, f., *-pratishṭhā*, f., *-bhujaṃga*, m., *-māhātmya*, n., *-sahasra-nāman*, n., *-hṛidaya*, n.; °*ry-ashṭaka*, n., °*ry-ashṭôttara-śataka*, n., °*ry-ashṭottara-śata-nāmâvalī*, f. N. of wks. **Mallârishṭā**, f. a kind of plant, L. **Mallârjuna**, m. N. of a king, Rājat. **Mallâsura**, m. N. of an Asura, RTL. 266. **Mallā-soma-yājin**, m. N. of an author, Cat.

Mallaka, m. a tooth, L.; a lamp-stand, L.; a lamp, L.; a vessel made out of a cocoa-nut shell, L.; any vessel, Divyâv.; a cup or leaf in which anything is wrapped, MW.; N. of a Brāhman, Rājat.; pl. N. of a people, MārkP.; (*ikā*), f. Jasminum Zambac (both the plant and the flower; ifc. f. *ikā*), MBh.; R.; Hariv. &c.; an earthenware vessel of a peculiar form, Mṛicch.; a lamp-stand, L.; a lamp, L.; any vessel made out of a cocoa-nut shell, L.; a species of fish, L.; N. of two metres, Col. **-sampuṭa**, m. or n. (prob.) a vessel consisting of two halves (a cup and a cover), Car.

Mallikā, f. of *mallaka*, in comp. **-kusuma-priyā**, f. a kind of citron, L. **-°ksha**, **-°khya**, see under *mallika* below. **-gandha**, n. a kind of Agallochum, L. **-chad** or **-chadana**, n. a lamp-shade, L. **-°pīḍa** (°*kâp*°), m. N. of a king, Prasannar. **-pushpa**, m. Citrus Decumana or Wrightia Antidysenterica, L. **-māruta**, n. N. of a drama. **-°moda** (°*kâm*°), m. (in music) a kind of measure, Saṃgīt. **-°rjuna**, see under *mallika*.

मल्लटसूत्रटीका *mallaṭa-sūtra-ṭīkā* (?), f. N. of wk.

मल्लयार्य *mallayārya*, m. N. of an author, Cat.

मल्लव *mallava*, m. pl. N. of a people, MBh. (B. *ballava*).

मल्लानकग्राम *mallānaka-grāma*, m. N. of a village, Cat.

मल्लार *mallāra*, m. (in music) N. of a Rāga, Saṃgīt.; (*ī*), f. (cf. *mallârī* under *malla*) N. of a Rāgiṇī, ib. (also °*rikā*).

मल्लिक *mallika*, m. a kind of goose with dark-coloured or brown legs and bill, L.; a shuttle, L.; the month Māgha, L.; (*ikā*), f., see under *mallaka*. **-pūrva**, mfn. preceded by the word *mallika* (e.g. *m°-p° arjuna* = *mallikârjuna*), Cat. **Mallikâksha**, m. N. of a partic. breed of horses (with white spots on the eyes), MBh.; Hariv.; a white spot on the eye of a horse (see *sa-m°*); a kind of goose, Suśr.; (*ī*), f. a female dog (with white spots on the eyes), VarBṛS. **Mallikâkhya**, m. a kind of goose, Mālatim.; Uttarar. **Mallikârjuna**, m. a form of Śiva (n. N. of a Liṅga consecrated to Śiva on the Śrī-śaila), Vās.; of an author, Cat.; of the Guru of Veṅkata, ib.; *-śriṅga*, n. N. of a place, Cat.; °*nīya*, n. N. of a Stotra by Mallikârjuna.

मल्लिनी *mallinī*, f. Gaertnera Racemosa, L.

मल्लिवार *mallivāra*, N. of a place, Cat.

मल्ली *mallī*. See under *malla* and *malli*.

मल्लीकर *mallīkara*, m. a thief, L.

मल्लु *mallu*, m. a bear, L. (cf. *bhalla*).

मल्लूर *mallūra*, prob. w. r. for *mandūra*, q. v.

मल्व *malvá*, mfn. unwise, foolish, silly, AV. (cf. *mālvya*).

मल्ह *malhá*, mf(*ā*)n. having a dew-lap, dew-lapped (as a cow or goat), TS.; ŚBr.; KātyŚr.

मल्हण *malhaṇa*, m. N. of a poet, Cat. **-stotra**, n. Malhaṇa's Stotra, Cat.

Malhaṇīya, n. = *malhaṇa-stotra*, Cat.

मव् *mav* (cf. √*mavy* and *mū*), cl. 1. P. (Dhātup. xv, 90) *mavati*, only pf. *mevuḥ* (v. l. *nehuḥ*), Bhaṭṭ.: Intens. *mammavyate*, *māmavyate*, Vop.

Mavita, mfn. bound, strung, tied, L.

मवर *mavara*, m. or n. (?) a partic. high number, Buddh.

मव्य् *mavy* (cf. √*mav*), cl. 1. P. (Dhātup. xv, 1) *mavyati* (fut. *mavyitā*, Pāṇ. vi, 4, 49, Sch.), to bind.

मश् *maś* (cf. √*miś*), cl. 1. P. *maśati*, to hum, buzz, make a noise, Dhātup. xvii, 75 (Vop. also 'to be angry').

Maśa, m. a hum, humming, L.; anger, L.; a gnat, mosquito, W. **-cchada**, m. Andropogon Serratus, L. **-hari**, f. = *maśaka-hari*, L.

Maśáka, m. a mosquito, gnat, any fly that bites or stings, AV. &c. &c.; a partic. skin disease (causing dark bean-like pustules or eruptions), VarBṛS.; Suśr.; a leather water-bag, KātyŚr.; N. of a preceptor with the patr. Gārgya (the composer of a Kalpa-sūtra), Lāṭy. (IW. 176); N. of the district in Śāka-dvīpa inhabited by Kshatriyas, MBh. **-kalpa**, m. N. of wk. **-kuṭi** or **-kuṭī**, f. a whisk for driving away mosquitoes, L. **-jámbhana**, mf(*ī*)n. driving away m°, AV. **-varaṇa**, m. or n. (?) = *-kuṭi*, L. **-hari**, f. a bed-curtain for protection against m°, L. **Maśakârtha**, mfn. used for m° (°*tho dhūmaḥ*, smoke for driving off m°), MW. **Maśakā-vatī**, f. N. of a district or a river, Pāṇ. iv, 2, 85, Sch. **Maśakôdumbara**, m. du. or n. sg. a m° and a fig-tree (often combined as connected with each other and yet very different), MBh. (cf. next).

Maśakin, m. 'swarming with mosquitoes,' Ficus Glomerata, L.

Maśana, n. a sound, L.

Maśāka, m. a bird, L.

मशर्शार *maśarśāra*, m. N. of a man, RV. i, 122, 15.

मशुन *maśuna*, m. a dog, L.

मशुलबर *maśulabara*, N. of a place, Cat.

मष् *mash* (prob. invented to serve as the source of the words below), cl. 1. P. *mashati*, to hurt, injure, Dhātup. xvii, 41.

Masham, ind. (with Caus. of √1. *kṛi*) to grind to powder, pulverize, ŚāṅkhGṛ. (v. l. °*shim*).

Mashi, m. or f. (or °*shī*, f.; cf. below) powder, (esp.) a black p° used to paint the eyes, soot, lampblack, ink, Kāv.; Var.; Suśr. &c. **-kūpī** or **-ghaṭī**, f. an ink-bottle, ink-stand, L. **-jala**, n. ink, L. **-dhāna**, n. an ink-stand, L. **-paṇya**, m. a writer, clerk, L. **-patha**, m. 'ink-path,' a pen, L. **-prasū**, f. an ink-bottle, L.; a pen, L. **-maṇi**, m. an ink-bottle, L. **-vardhana**, n. myrrh, L.

Mashī (= *mashi*), in comp. **-kūrcaka**, m. an ink-brush, Viddh. **-guḍikā**, f. a globule or blot of ink, Mṛicch. **-jala**, n. ink, L. **-dhanī**, f. an ink-stand, L. **-pātra** and **-bhāṇḍa**, n. id., Hcat. **-bhāvuka**, mfn. becoming as black as ink, Naish. **-maya**, mfn. consisting of lampblack, black as ink, ib. **-lipta**, mfn. smeared with ink, Kathās. **-varṇa**, mfn. ink-coloured, MW.

Mashmashā́-√kṛi, P. *-karoti*, to reduce to dust, grind to powder, AV. (cf. *masmasā* and *mṛismṛisā*).

Mashy, in comp. for *mashī*. **-abhāva**, m. absence of ink (°*vāt*, ind. from want of ink), Kathās. **-ādhāra**, m. an ink-stand, L.

मष्क् *mashk*, v. l. for √*mask*, q. v.

मष्णार *mashṇāra*, N. of a tract of country, AitBr.; BhP.

मस् 1. *mas* (prob. an artificial root), cl. 4. P. *masyati*, to measure, mete (*parimāṇe*, v. l. *pariṇāme*), Dhātup. xxvi, 112.

Masa, m. measure, weight, W.

Masana, n. (only L.) meting, measuring; hurting, injuring (cf. √*mash*); Vernonia Anthelmintica.

Masta, mfn. measured, MW.; n. (= *mastaka*) the head, Dhūrtas. **-dāru**, n. Pinus Deodora, Bhpr. **-mūlaka**, n. 'head-root,' the neck, L.

Mastaka, m. n. (Uṇ. iii, 148, Sch.) the head, skull, Mn.; MBh. &c.; the upper part of anything, top, summit (esp. of mountains or trees), ib. (°*kam*, ind. = on the top of, upon, e. g. *cullī-mastakam*, upon the hearth, Pañcat.); the tuft of leaves which grows at the top of various species of palm trees, Suśr.; N. of a partic. form of Śiva, Sarvad. **-jvara**, m. 'head-fever,' head-ache, BhP. **-piṇḍaka**, m. n. a round protuberance on the temples of an elephant in rut, MBh. **-mūlaka**, n. = *masta-m°*, W. **-luṅga**, m. or n. (?) the membrane of the brain, L. (cf. *mastu-luṅga*). **-śūla**, n. sharp or shooting pain in the head, head-ache, Vet. **-sneha**, m. 'h°-marrow,' the brain, L. **Mastakâkhya**, m. the top of a tree, L. **Mastakôdbhava**, m. 'produced in the head,' the brain, L.

Masti, f. meting, measuring, weighing, L.

Mastika, n. = *mastaka*, the head, L.

Mastishka, m. n. the brain, RV. &c. &c.; any medicine or substance acting upon the brain, Suśr. **-tvac**, f. the membrane surrounding the brain, MW.

Mástu, n. sour cream, TS. &c. &c.; the watery part of curds, whey, Suśr. **-luṅga** or **-luṅgaka**, m. n. the brain, Suśr.; ŚārṅgS. (cf. *mastaka-luṅga*). **Mastv-āmikshā**, f. du. whey and curds, MW.

मस् 2. *mas* = *mās* in *candrá-mas*.

मसक *masaka*, incorrectly for *maśaka*.

मसमसा *masamasā*, onomat., g. *ūry-ādi*.

मसरा *masarā*, f. a sort of lentil or pulse (= *masūra*), L.

मसार *masāra*, m. a sapphire or an emerald, MBh.; Hariv. (also °*raka*, L.); N. of a place, Cat.

– galvarka-maya, mf(*ī*)n. consisting of emerald (sapphire) and crystal, MBh.

मसि *masi* and *masī*, incorrectly for *mashi* and *mashī*, q. v. (*masī-√bhū*, to become black, Śiś. xx, 63; cf. *mashī-bhāvuka*); (*ī*), f. the stalk of the Nyctanthes Arbor Tristis, L.

Masika, m. a serpent's hole, L.; (*ā*), f. Nyctanthes Arbor Tristis, L. (cf. prec.; v. l. *malikā*).

Masina, mfn. well ground, finely pounded, L.; kinship through the right of presenting the Piṇḍa to a common progenitor (= *sa-piṇḍaka*), L.

मसीना *masīnā*, f. linseed, Linum Usitatissimum, L.

मसीर *masīra*, m. pl. N. of a people, MBh. (v. l. *samīra*).

मसुर *masura*, m. a sort of lentil or pulse, L.; (*ā*), f., see below. **– karṇa,** m. N. of a man, g. *śivâdi*.

Masurā, f. = *masura*, L.; a harlot, courtezan, L.

Masū́ra, m. = *masura*, VS. &c. &c.; a pillow, L.; (*ā* and *ī*), f., see below. **– karṇa,** m. N. of a man (pl. his descendants), g. *upakâdi*. **– vidala,** m. or n.(?) prob. 'a split lentil,' Rājat. vi, 187; (*ā*), f. Ipomoea Turpethum, L.; Ichnocarpus Frutescens, L. **– saṃghârāma,** m. N. of a monastery, Buddh. **Masūrâksha,** m. N. of a poet, Cat. **Masūrâbha,** mf(*ā*)n. resembling a lentil, L.

Masūraka, m. = *masura*, L.; a kind of pillow, Hcar.; (*ikā*), f. lentil, L.; eruption of lentil-shaped pustules, smallpox, Suśr.; a mosquito-curtain, L.; a procuress, L.; n. a kind of ornament on Indra's banner, L.

Masūrā, f. = *masurā*, L.

Masūri, f. hemorrhoids, Gal.

Masūrī, f. a kind of smallpox, L.; Ipomoea Turpethum, L.

मसुरक्षित *masu-rakshita* (?), m. N. of a king, Buddh.

मसूस्य *masū́sya*, n. a kind of grain growing in some northern country, TBr. (Sch.)

मसृण *masṛiṇa*, mfn. soft, smooth, tender, mild, bland, Kāv.; Kathās. &c.; (*ā* or *ī*), f. Linum Usitatissimum, L. **– tva,** n. softness, mildness, Vām. **– vāṇī,** f. 'soft-spoken,' having a soft or gentle voice, Gīt.

Masṛiṇaya, Nom. P. °*yati*, to make soft or smooth, Hcar.

Masṛiṇita, mfn. softened, smoothed, Uttarar. **– śila,** mfn. (mountains) whose rocks are polished (by water), Prab.

मस्क् *mask*, cl. 1. Ā. *maskate*, to go, move, Dhātup. iv, 28 (Vop. *mashk*).

मस्कर *maskara*, m. a bamboo; a hollow bamboo cane, L.

Maskarin, m. a religious mendicant, a Brāhman in the fourth order (who carries a bamboo cane), Kāv.; Kathās.; the moon, L.; N. of an author, Cat.; of another man, Buddh.

Maskarīya, n. N. of wk.

मस्त *masta* and °*taka*, *masti* &c. See p. 793.

मस्मसा *masmasā́*, v. l. for *mashmashā́*, q. v.

मस्मा *masmā*, f. N. of two princesses, Rājat.

मह् 1. *mah* (orig. *magh*; cf. also √*maṅh*), cl. 1. 10. P. (Dhātup. xvii, 81; xxxv, 15) *mahati*, *mahayati* (Ved. and ep. also Ā. *mahate*, °*hayate*; p. *mahát*, q. v.; pf. *mamāha*, Gr.; *māmahé*; Subj. *māmahanta*, *māmahas*, RV.; aor. *amahīt*, Gr.; fut. *mahitā*, *mahishyati*, ib.; ind. p. *mahitvā*, MBh.; inf. *mahe*, and *maháye*, q. v.) to elate, gladden, exalt, arouse, excite, RV.; Br.; Kauś.; ChUp.; MBh.; to magnify, esteem highly, honour, revere, MBh.; Kāv. &c.; (Ā.) to rejoice, delight in (instr. or acc.), RV. iii, 52, 6; vi, 15, 2; to give, bestow, ib. i, 94, 6; 117, 17; v, 27, 1 &c. [Cf. Gk. μέγ-ας; Lat. *magnus*, *mactus*; Old Germ. *michel*; Eng. *mickle*, *much*.]

2. **Máh,** mf(*ī* or = m.)n. great, strong, powerful, mighty, abundant, RV.; VS.; (with *pitṛi* or *mātṛi*) old, aged, RV. i, 71, 5; v, 41, 15 &c.; (*ī́*), f., see *mahī́*, p. 803, col. 2.

1. **Mahá,** mfn. great, mighty, strong, abundant, RV.; m. (cf. *makha*, *magha*) a feast, festival, MBh.; the festival of spring, Śiś.; Hariv.; Var.; a partic. Ekâha, ŚāṅkhŚr.; a sacrifice, L.; a buffalo, L.; light, lustre, brilliance, L.; (*ā*), f. a cow, L.; Ichnocarpus Frutescens, L.; n. pl. great deeds, RV. **– m-kāla** (?), m. = *mahā-kāla*, Siṇhâs. **– tā,** f. greatness, mightiness, ChUp. **– da,** mfn. giving greatness(?), Daś. (in *mahadâyudhāni*, 'weapons g° gr°'). **– dyuman,** m. or n. (?) N. of a Tīrtha (others 'of the sun'), MBh. i, 804. **– reṇu,** m. or n. (?) N. of a place, Cat. **– vīrya,** m. N. of a teacher, ib. **– sena,** m. N. of a prince, Priy.; *-narêśvara*, m. N. of the father of the 8th Arhat of the present Avasarpiṇī, L. **– soṇa** (?), m. N. of a man, Inscr.

2. **Maha,** in comp. for *mahā* before *ṛi* and before *r* for *ri*. **– ṛishí,** m. = *-rshi*, AV. **– rtvik-tva,** n. (fr. next) the state or office of the great priest, TBr. **– rtvij** (*mahá-*) or *-rtvij*, m. 'great priest,' N. of the 4 chief priests or Ṛitvij (viz. the Hotṛi, Udgātṛi, Adhvaryu and Brahman), Br.; ŚrS. **– rddhi,** f. great prosperity or power or perfection (in *-prâpta*, m. N. of a prince of the Garuḍas, Buddh.; *-mat*, mfn. possessing or conferring great pr° &c., Cat.; m. a great sage, L.); mfn. very prosperous or powerful, R.; Kathās. (also °*dhika*, L., and °*dhin*, MBh.); very sage, Rājat. **– rshabhá,** m. a great bull, AV. **– rshi,** m. a great Ṛishi, any great sage or saint (accord. to Mn. i, 34 ten Maharshis were created by Manu Svāyambhuva, viz. Marīci, Atri, Aṅgiras, Pulastya, Pulaha, Kratu, Pracetas, Vasishṭha, Bhṛigu, Nārada, also called the 10 Prajāpatis, q. v.; some restrict the number to 7, and some add Daksha, Dharma, Gautama, Kaṇva, Vālmīki, Vyāsa, Manu, Vibhāṇḍaka &c.), Mn.; MBh. &c. (IW. 206, n. 1); N. of Śiva, Śivag.; of Buddha, L.; of a poet, Cat.

Mahaka, m. (only L.) an eminent man; a tortoise; N. of Vishṇu; N. of a man (cf. *māhaki*).

Mahac, in comp. for *mahat*. **– chabda** (*śabda*), the word *mahat*, Kathās.

Mahát, mfn. (orig. pr. p. of √1. *mah*; strong form *mahā́nt*, f. *mahatī́*; in ep. often *mahat* for *mahāntam*; ibc. mostly *mahā*, q. v.) great (in space, time, quantity or degree), i. e. large, big, huge, ample, extensive, long, abundant, numerous, considerable, important, high, eminent, RV. &c. &c. (also ind. in *mahad-√bhū*, to become great or full [said of the moon], Śiś.); abounding or rich in (instr.), ChUp.; (ifc.) distinguished by, Śak.; early (morning), ib.; advanced (afternoon), MBh.; violent (pain or emotion), ib.; thick (as darkness), gross, ib.; loud (as noise), Lāṭy.; many (people, with *jana* sg.), MBh. (with *uktha*, n. a partic. Uktha of 720 verses; with *aukthya*, n. N. of a Sāman, MBh.; *mahānti bhūtāni*, the gross elements, Mn.; MBh.; cf. *mahā-bhūta*); m. a great or noble man (opp. to *nīca*, *alpa* or *dīna*), Kāv.; Kām.; Pañcat.; the leader of a sect or superior of a monastery, RTL. 87, n. 1; a camel, L.; N. of Rudra or of a partic. R°, BhP.; of a Dānava, Hariv.; (scil. *gaṇa*), a partic. class of deceased progenitors, MārkP.; of two princes, VP.; m. (rarely n., scil. *tattva*), 'the great principle,' N. of Buddhi, 'Intellect,' or the intellectual principle (according to the Sāṃkhya philosophy the second of the 23 principles produced from Prakṛiti and so called as the *great* source of Ahaṃkāra, 'self-consciousness,' and Manas, 'the mind;' cf. IW. 83, 91 &c.), MaitrUp.; Mn.; Sāṃkhyak.; MBh. &c.; (*atī*), f. the egg-plant, Bhpr.; the (7 or 100-stringed) lute of Nārada, Śiś.; (with *dvādaśī*), the 12th day in the light half of the month Bhādrapada, Pur.; Suśr.; n. anything great or important, ChUp.; greatness, power, might, ŚBr.; ĀśvGṛ.; dominion, L.; a great thing, important matter, the greater part, ĀśvGṛ.; advanced state or time (*mahatī rātriyai* or *rātryai*, in the middle of the night, TS.; Br.); sacred knowledge, MBh. **– katha,** mfn. talked about by the great, mentioned by them, BhP. **– kāṇḍá,** m. or n. (?) N. of a section of the Atharva-veda-saṃhitā, AV. **– kula,** n. a distinguished or noble family, Pañcad. **– kshetra,** mfn. occupying a wide district or territory, L. **– tattva,** n. 'the great principle,' Intellect (see above), BhP. **– tama,** mfn. greatest or very great; *-pada*, mfn. holding a great or high position (said of a saint), Divyâv. **– tara,** mfn. greater or very great or mighty or strong, MBh.; R.; Kathās.; m. the oldest, most respectable, chief, principal, R. (*ā*, f., Mṛicch.); the head or oldest man of a village, L.; a Śūdra (?), W.; a courtier, chamberlain, Kathās.; N. of a son of Kaśyapa (or of Kāśyapa), MBh.; (*ī*), f. N. of a form of the goddess Tārā, Buddh.; °*raka*, m. a courtier, chamberlain, Kathās.; (*ikā*), f. a lady of the bed-chamber, Kād. **– tā,** f. greatness, high rank or position, Kathās. **– tva,** n. id., Kāv.; Var.; great size or extent, magnitude, MBh.; Kāv. &c.; violence, intensity, Suśr.; moral greatness, Kathās.; *-rahita*, mfn. deprived of majesty or greatness, MW. **– pati,** m. 'great lord,' N. of Vishṇu, Vishṇ. **– sena,** m. N. of a prince, VP. **– sevā,** f. service of the great, homage (rendered) to great men, MW. **– sthāna,** n. a high place, lofty position (v. l. *mahā-sth°*), ib.

Mahad, in comp. for *mahat*. **– abhikhya,** mfn. having a high-sounding name, Daś. **– āyudha,** n. a great weapon, ib. **– āvāsa,** m. a great or roomy dwelling, R. **– āśā,** f. great expectation, high hope, Daś. **– āścaryam,** ind. very surprising, W. **– āśraya,** mfn. dependent upon or attached to the great; m. having recourse to the great, W. **– gata,** mfn. great, Divyâv. (cf. Pāli *mahaggato*). **– guṇa,** mfn. possessing the virtues of the great (*-tva*, n.), BhP. **– gaurava,** n. high respect or reverence, Pañcad. **– bila,** n. the atmosphere, ether (cf. *mahā-b°*), L. **– bhaya,** n. a great danger or emergency, MBh.; fear of great people, MW. **– bhū,** mfn. become great or full, Ml. (*mahad* used adverbially). **– bhūta,** mfn. id.; °*tâdhipati*, m. a partic. supernatural being, ShaḍvBr. **– vat,** mfn. connected with the word *mahat*, AitBr. **– vāruṇī,** f. a species of plant, L. **– vyatikrama,** m. a great transgression, BhP.

Mahā́n, n. greatness, might, power, abundance (only instr. sg. *mahnā́* and once pl. *mahā́bhiḥ*, which also = greatly, mightily, right heartily), RV.

Mahanīya, mfn. to be honoured, praiseworthy, illustrious, glorious, Kāv. **– kīrti,** mfn. of illustrious fame, Ragh. **– mūrti,** mfn. of a magnificent form or appearance, ŚārṅgP. **– śāsana,** mfn. ruling a glorious empire, Ragh.

Mahanta, m. the superior of a monastery, Inscr.

Mahayā́yya, n. (fr. Caus.) enjoyment, merriment, RV.

Maháye, Ved. inf. for joy, for enjoyment, RV.

Mahayya, mfn. to be gladdened or delighted, ChUp.

Mahar, ind. (fr. *mahas*) the fourth of the seven worlds which rise one above the other (supposed to be the abode of those saints who survive a destruction of the world, Pur.; Vedântas; cf. IW. 55, n. 2). **– jagat,** n. (NādapUp.), **-loka,** m. (BhP.) id.

Mahartvij, maharddhi &c. See col. 2.

Máhas, n. greatness, might, power, glory (instr. pl. greatly, mightily &c.), RV.; AV.; Br.; Up.; joy, gladness, pleasure, VS.; AV.; TBr. (°*ás*, ind. gladly, briskly, swiftly, RV.); a festival or a festive hymn, Pañcar.; a sacrifice, oblation, L.; light, splendour, majesty, Inscr.; Kāv.; Kathās.; BhP.; the fourth of the seven worlds (written *Mahar*; see above and cf. *vyāhṛiti*); = *udaka*, water, Naigh. i, 12; N. of a Sāman, ĀrshBr. **– tva,** n. greatness, mightiness, Up. **– vat** (*máhas-*), mfn. giving pleasure, gladdening, RV.; VS.; TBr.; great, mighty, glorious, splendid, ChUp.; BhP.; N. of a king, Pur. **– vin,** mfn. brilliant, splendid, glorious, Kathās.

Mahasa, n. knowledge, L.; kind, sort, manner, L.

Mahā́, in comp. for *mahat* (in RV. ii, 22, 1 and iii, 23; 49, 1 used for *mahat* as an independent word in acc. sg. *mahām* = *mahāntam*). **– kaṅkara,** m. or n. (?) a partic. high number, Buddh. **– kaccha,** m. a high Cedrena Toona, MBh.; 'having vast shores,' the sea, L.; Varuṇa, god of the sea, L.; a mountain, L. **– kaṭi-taṭa-śroṇī,** f. (a woman) having large hips and buttocks, MW. **– kaṇṭakinī,** f. 'having large thorns,' Cactus Indicus, L. **– °kathaha-cakra** (°*hâk°*), n. a partic. magical diagram, Cat. **– kadambaka,** m. a species of large Kadamba, L. **– kanda,** m. garlic, radish and other tuberous plants, L.; Hingtsha Repens; n. dry ginger, L. **– kanya,** m. N. of a man; pl. of his descendants, Pravar. **– kaparda,** m. a species of shell, MW. **– kapāla,** m. 'large-headed,' N. of a Rākshasa, R.; of one of the attendants of Śiva, L. **– kapi,** m. 'great ape,' N. of a king, Hariv.; of one of the attendants of Śiva, L.; of one of the 34 incarnations of Buddha, Jātakam. **– kapittha,** m. Aegle Marmelos, L.; red garlic, A. **– kapila-pañca-rātra,** n. N. of wk. **– kapota,** m. a species of serpent, Suśr. **– kapola,** m. 'great-cheeked,' N. of one of the attendants of Śiva, L. **– kambu,** mfn. stark naked (said of Śiva), MBh. **– kara,** m. a large hand, W.; a l° revenue or rent, MW.; 'having great rays,' N. of a Buddha, Lalit.; mfn. large-handed; having a large revenue, W.

-karañja, m. Galedupa Piscidia, Bhpr. **-karabha**, m. or n. (?) a partic. high number, Buddh. **-karambha**, m. a partic poisonous plant, Suśr. **-karuṇa**, mfn. very compassionate (*-tā*, f.), Buddh.; (*ā*), f. general compassionateness, Lalit.; *-puṇḍarīka*, n. N. of a Sūtra, Buddh.; °*ṇā-candri*, m. N. of a Bodhi-sattva, Lalit. **-karkāru**, m. a species of plant, Buddh. **-karṇa**, mfn. having large ears (said of Śiva), MBh.; m. N. of a Nāga, Hariv.; (*ī*), f. N. of one of the Mātṛis attending on Skanda, MBh. **-karṇi**, m. N. of a man, MBh.; *-kāra*, m. Cathartocarpus (Cassia) Fistula, L. **-karman**, n. a great work, AitBr.; mfn. accomplishing great works (said of Śiva), MBh. **-kalā**, f. the night of the new moon, Cat. **-kalopa**, m. pl. N. of a Śākhā or school, Caraṇ. (cf. *-kālopa*, *-kāpola*). **-kalpa**, m. a great cycle of time, MBh.; Pur.; Buddh.; N. of Śiva, MBh. (= *divya-bhūshaṇa*, Sch.) **-kalyāṇa**, n. a partic. drug, Suśr. (cf. *kalyāṇaka*). **-kalyāṇaka**, mfn. very excellent, Suśr.; Bhpr. **-kavi**, m. a great or classical poet, Piṅg., Comm. (cf. *-kāvya*); N. of Śukra, Cat. **-kātyāyana**, m. N. of a disciple of Buddha, Buddh. **-kānta**, m. 'very pleasing,' N. of Śiva, L.; (*ā*), f. the earth, L. **-kāpola**, m. pl. a partic. school of the Sāma-veda, Āryav. **-kāya**, mfn. large-bodied, of great stature, tall, bulky, MBh.; R.; Pañcat. &c. (*-tva*, n.); m. an elephant, L.; N. of Vishṇu, DhyānabUp.; of Śiva, MBh.; of a being attending on Śiva, MBh.; of a king of the Garuḍas, Buddh.; (*ā*), f. N. of one of the Mātṛis attending on Skanda, MBh.; *-śiro-dhara*, mfn. having a large body and strong neck, R. **-kāyika**, m. N. of Vishṇu, Vishṇ. **-°kāra** (°*hāk*°), mfn. 'large-formed,' great, extensive, Rājat.; m. pl. N. of a country belonging to Madhya-deśa, L. **-kāraṇa**, n. first cause; *-prakaraṇa*, n. N. of wk. **-kāruṇika**, mfn. exceedingly compassionate, Lalit. **-kārtayaśa**, n. N. of a Sāman, ĀrshBr. **-kārttikī**, f. the night of full moon in the month Kārttika (when the moon is in the constellation Rohiṇī), PadmaP.; Hcat. **-kāla**, m. a form of Śiva in his character of destroyer (being then represented black and of terrific aspect) or a place sacred to that form of Śiva, MBh.; Kāv. &c.; N. of one of Śiva's attendants, MBh.; Hariv.; Kathās. &c. (*-tva*, n., Hariv.); of Vishṇu, DhyānabUp.; = *vishṇu-rūpâkhaṇḍa-daṇḍāyamāna-samaya* (?), L.; N. of a teacher, Cat.; of a species of cucumber, Trichosanthes Palmata, Kāv.; the mango tree (?), W.; (with Jainas) one of the 9 treasures, L.; N. of a mythical mountain, Kāraṇḍ.; (*ī*), f. N. of Durgā in her terrific form, MBh.; Buddh.; of one of D°'s attendants, W.; (with Jainas) of one of the 16 Vidyā-devīs, Hemac.; of a goddess who executed the commands of the 5th Arhat of the present Avasarpiṇī, ib.; n. N. of a Liṅga in Ujjayinī, Kathās.; *-kavaca*, n., *-khaṇḍa*, m. n.(?), *-tantra*, n. N. of wks.; *-pura*, n. 'Mahā-kāla's city,' Ujjayinī, Inscr.; *-bhairava-tantre śarabha-kavaca*, n., *-mata*, n., *-yoga-śāstre khecarī-vidyā*, f., *-rudrôdita-stotra*, n., *-saṃhitā*, f. (and °*tā-kūṭa*, m. or n.), *-sahasra-nāman*, n., *-stotra*, n.; °*lī-tantra*, n., °*lī-mata*, n. N. of wks.; °*lī-yantra*, n. N. of a partic. magical diagram, MW.; °*lī-sūkta*, n. N. of wk.; °*lêśvara*, n. N. of a Liṅga at Ujjayinī, Cat. **-kālaveya** or **-kāleta**, m. pl. N. of a Śākhā or school, L. **-kāleya**, n. N. of a Sāman, ĀrshBr. **-kālopa**, m. pl. N. of a school (cf. *-kalopa*). **-kāvya**, n. a great or classical poem (applied as a distinguishing title to 6 chief artificial poems, viz. the Raghu-vaṃśa, Kumāra-sambhava and Megha-dūta by Kālidāsa, the Śiśupāla-vadha by Māgha, the Kirātârjunīya by Bhāravi and the Naishadha-carita by Śrī-harsha; accord. to some the Bhaṭṭi-kāvya is also a M°), Kāvyâd.; Pratāp. (IW. 452). **-kāśa**, m. N. of a Varsha, MBh. **-°kāśa-bhairava-kalpe śarabhêśvara-kavaca** (°*hâk*°), n. N. of wk. **-kāśī**, f. N. of the tutelary goddess of the Mataṃga-jas, Cat. **-kāśyapa**, m. N. of a disciple of Buddha, MWB. 193; 510. **-kīta-parvata**, m. N. of a mountain, Buddh. **-kīrtana**, n. a house, L. **-kīrti**, mfn. high-renowned, R. **-kuṇḍa**, m. N. of one of the attendants of Śiva, L.; of a man, Virac. **-kumāra**, m. an hereditary prince, L. **-kumudā**, f. Gmelina Arborea, L. **-kumbhī**, f. a species of plant, L. **-kula**, n. a great or noble family, MBh.; Hit. &c.; (*-kulá*), mfn. being of a gr° or n° f°, high-born, RV.; Kām. &c.; °*lôtpanna* (Sāy.; Kathās.) or °*lôdbhava* (MW.), mfn. sprung from a gr° or n° f°. **-kulīna**, mf(*ā*)n. = prec., Mn.; MBh.; Kāv.; *-tā*, f. noble birth, Pratāp. **-kuśa**, m. N. of a Cakra-vartin, Buddh. **-kushṭha**, n. 'severe cutaneous eruption,' N. of 7 forms of cut° er°, Suśr. **-kusumikā**, f. Gmelina Arborea, Bhpr. **-kuha**, m. a species of parasitical worm, Bhpr.; Car. (cf. *-guha*). **-kūpa**, m. a deep well, Cat. **-kūrma**, m. N. of a king, Hariv. **-kūla**, mf(*ā*)n. having high banks, Nir.; high-born (= *-kula*), L. **-kṛicchra**, n. great penance (used as N. of Vishṇu), MBh. **-kṛityā-parimala**, m. a kind of magical spell, Cat. **-kṛishṇa**, m. 'very black,' a species of serpent, Suśr. **-ketu**, mfn. having a great banner (said of Śiva), MBh. **-keśa**, mfn. having strong hair (said of Śiva), ib. **-kailāsa-daṇḍaka**, m. N. of wk. **-kośa**, m. a large sheath, R.; mfn. having a l° sh°, MW.; having a l° scrotum (said of Śiva), MBh.; (*ī*), f. N. of the tutelary goddess of the Mataṃga-jas, Cat. (v.l. *-kāśī*); of a river, Kum.; *-phalā*, f. a species of gourd, L. **-kośātakī**, f. a kind of gourd, Bhpr. **-kaushītaka**, n. N. of a Vedic wk., GṛS.; AVPariś. **-kaushītaki**, m. N. of a teacher; *-brāhmaṇa*, n. N. of a Brāhmaṇa, L. **-kaushṭhila** or °**ṭhilya**, m. N. of a disciple of Buddha, Buddh. **-kratu**, m. a great sacrifice, MBh.; R.; Ragh. (cf. *-yajña*). **-krama**, m. 'wide-striding,' N. of Vishṇu, L. **-krūrā**, f. N. of a Yoginī, Hcat. **-krodha**, mfn. very inclined to wrath, MBh.; N. of Śiva, RTL. 106, n. 1. **-°ksha** (°*hâksha*), mfn. having great eyes (N. of Śiva), MBh.; *-paṭalika*, m. a chief keeper of archives, Bālar. **-kshatrapa**, m. a great satrap, Inscr. **-kshapaṇaka**, m. N. of an author, Cat. **-kshāra**, m. a kind of natron, L. **-kshīra**, m. sugar-cane, L.; (*ā*), f. a female buffalo, L. **-°kshobhya** (°*hâk*°), m. or n.(?) a partic. high number, Buddh. **-°kshauhiṇī** (°*hâk*°; in alg.), f. id. (1 with twenty-four ciphers), L. **-khaṇḍana**, m. N. of two wks. **-kharva**, m. n. a high number, 10 billions (?), MW. **-khallava** or **-khalvala**, m. pl. N. of a school, L. **-khāta**, n. a deep ditch or moat, Hcar.; mfn. having a large d° or m°, Hit. **-khyāta**, mfn. greatly renowned, Pañcar. **-ga**, mfn. (?) great, prosperous, W. **-gaṅgā**, f. 'the great Gaṅgā,' N. of a river, MBh. **-gaja**, m. a gr° elephant, BhP.; one of the el°s that support the earth (cf. *dik-karin*), R.; *-lakshaṇa*, n. N. of wk. **-gaṇá**, m. a great multitude, gr° assembly or crowd, gr° corporate body, AV.; MBh.; Śāntik.; Var.; a partic. high number (1 with 14 ciphers), L.; *-pati*, m. 'gr° leader of (Śiva's) hosts,' N. of Gaṇêśa or a form of G°, Yājñ.; Hariv. (RTL. 217); °*ti-kalpe pañca-triṃśat-pīṭhikā*, f., °*ti-vidyā*, f., °*ti-sahasra-nāma-stotra*, n., °*ti-stava-rāja*, m., °*ti-stotra*, n. N. of wks. **-gaṇêśa**, m. N. of Gaṇêśa, Cat.; *-purāṇe gaṇêśa-gītā*, f. pl. N. of wk. **-gati**, (prob.) f. a partic. high number, Buddh. **-1. -gada** (°*hâg*°), m. 'gr° remedy,' a kind of drug, Suśr. **-2. -gada**, m. gr° sickness, Suśr.; Car.; fever, L.; a partic. sickness, Car. **-3. -gada**, mfn. having a gr° club, BhP. **-gandha**, mf(*ā*)n. having a strong odour, very fragrant, Hariv.; m. Calamus Rotang, L.; Wrightia Antidysenterica, L.; (*ā*), f. Uraria Lagopodioides, L.; N. of a flower, L.; of Cāmuṇḍā, L.; n. a kind of sandal-wood, L.; myrrh, L.; *-hastin*, m. N. of a very efficacious remedy, Car. **-gayá**, mfn. having a great household (said of Agni), RV. ix, 66, 20. **-garta**, m. N. of Śiva, Śivag. **-garbha**, mfn. 'having a large womb' (or m. 'a l° w°'), N. of Śiva, MBh.; m. N. of a Dānava, Hariv. **-gala**, mfn. long-necked or thick-n°, MBh. **-gava**, m. Bos Gavaeus, L. **-°gastya-saṃhitā** (°*hâg*°), f. N. of wk. **-giri**, m. a gr° mountain, Lāṭy.; TĀr.; R.; Pur.; N. of a Dānava, Hariv.; (with Jainas) of a Sthavira, L. **-gīta**, m. 'great singer,' N. of Śiva, MBh. **-guṇa**, m. a chief quality, cardinal virtue, Kām.; mfn. possessing gr° excellencies, distinguished, very meritorious, MBh.; Prab.; very efficacious, Suśr.; m. N. of a teacher, Buddh.; *-tva*, n. the possession of gr° properties or virtues, Suśr. **-guru**, m. a very venerable person, ĀśvGṛ.; KālP. &c. **-gulmā**, f. the Soma plant, L. **-guha**, m. a species of parasitical worm, ŚārṅgS. (cf. *-kuha*); (*ā*), f. Hemionitis Cordifolia, L. **-gṛishṭi**, f. a cow with a large hump, Pāṇ. **-gṛiha**, n. a large house, Mṛicch. **-godhūma**, m. coarse-grained wheat, Bhpr. **-gaurī**, f. one of the 9 forms of Durgā, Cat.; N. of a river, MBh.; MārkP. **-gaurīvita**, n. N. of a Sāman, ĀrshBr. **-°gni** (°*hâg*°), m., **-°gni-cayana**, n. (and °*na-kārikā*, f., °*na-prayoga*, m., °*na-vyākhyā*, f., °*na-sūtra*, n.), **-°gni-sarvasva**, n. N. of wks. **-granthika**, mfn. (in med.) forming great knots, Suśr. **-graha**, m. 'the great planet,' N. of Rāhu, Hariv.; of the planet Saturn, L. **-°grahāyaṇī** (°*hâgr*°), f. N. of the 15th day of the first half of the month Āgrahāyaṇa, L. **-grāmá**, m. a gr° multitude, RV.; a gr° village, Rājat.; N. of the ancient capital of Ceylon (said to be the Μαάγραμμον of Ptolemy and the modern Māgama), L.; pl. N. of a people, R. **-grāha**, m. a gr° shark, MBh. **-grīva**, mfn. long-necked (said of Śiva), MBh.; m. a camel, L.; N. of one of Śiva's attendants, Hariv.; pl. N. of a people, Var.; MārkP. **-grīvin**, m. 'long-necked,' a camel, L. **-ghaṭa**, m. a gr° pitcher, Cat. (accord. to others, a proper N.) **-ghaṇṭā-dhara**, mf(*ā*)n. having a large bell, R. **-ghasa**, m. 'great eater,' N. of one of Śiva's attendants, L. **-ghāsa**, mfn. abounding with grass or fodder, W.; m. = *mahato mahatyā vā ghāsaḥ*, Pāṇ. vi, 3, 46, Vārtt. 1. **-ghūrṇā**, f. spirituous liquor, L. **-ghṛita**, n. ghee kept a long time (used for medicinal purposes), Suśr. **-ghoṇṭā**, f. the big jujube, L. **-ghora**, mfn. very terrible or formidable, MBh.; R.; Kathās.; m. N. of a hell, L. **-ghosha**, mf(*ā*)n. loud-sounding, MBh.; m. a loud noise, L.; (*ā*), f. Boswellia Thurifera, L.; = *karkaṭa-śṛiṅgī* (or a kind of gall-nut), L.; = *śṛiṅgī*, L.; n. a market, L.; *-svara-rāja*, m. N. of a Bodhi-sattva, Buddh.; °*shânugā*, f. N. of a Tantra deity, ib.; °*shêśvara*, m. N. of a king of the Yakshas, ib. **-°ṅga** (°*hâṅga*), mfn. having a great body or limbs (said of Śiva), MBh.; m. (only L.) a camel; a kind of rat; Asteracantha Longifolia; Plumbago Zeylanica. **-cakra**, n. a great wheel, a gr° discus, RāmatUp.; MBh.; the mystic circle or assembly in the Śākta ceremonial, RTL. 196; m. 'having a gr° wh° or d°,' N. of a Dānava, Hariv. (v.l. *-vaktra*); *-praveśa-jñāna-mudrā*, f. N. of a Mudrā (q.v.), Buddh.; *-vartin*, m. a great emperor or universal monarch (°*ti-tā*, f. the rank of a gr° e°), Kathās.; *-vāḍa* or *-vāla*, m. N. of a mythical mountain, Buddh. **-cañcū**, f. a species of culinary plant, L. **-caṇḍa**, m. a very violent or passionate man, W.; N. of one of Yama's two servants, L.; of one of Śiva's attendants, L.; (*ā*), f. N. of Cāmuṇḍā, L.; (*ī*), f. N. of a female attendant of Durgā, L. **-caturaka**, m. N. of a jackal, Pañcat. **-candra**, m. N. of a man, Divyâv. **-capalā**, f. a kind of metre, Col.; Piṅg., Sch. **-camasa**, m. N. of a man; cf. *māhācamasya*. **-camū**, f. a large army, a gr° battalion, in *su-m*°, MBh. **-campā**, f. N. of a country or kingdom, Buddh. **-caryā**, f. 'great course of life,' the course of life of a Bodhi-sattva, Kathās. **-°cala** (°*hâc*°), m. a gr° mountain, R.; MārkP.; (with Buddhists) one of the 7 lower regions, Dharmas. 123. **-cārī**, f. the speaking of the Nāndī (q.v.), L. **-°cārya** (°*hâc*°), m. 'the gr° teacher,' N. of Śiva, Śivag.; (?) N. of an author, Cat. **-cit**, f. gr° intelligence (*-tva*, n.), Up.; **-citta**, g. *sutaṃgamâdi*; (*ā*), f. N. of an Apsaras, L. **-citra-pāṭala**, a species of plant, Buddh. **-cīna**, m. Great China; pl. the inhabitants of that country, Buddh.; Cat. **-cunda**, m. N. of a Buddhist mendicant, Buddh. **-cūḍā**, f. N. of one of the Mātṛis attending on Skanda, MBh. **-cūta**, m. a species of mango tree, L. **-caitanya**, mfn. being the gr° intellect, Up. **-chada**, m. Lipeocercis Serrata, L. **-chāya**, m. the Indian fig-tree, L. **-chidrā**, f. a species of medicinal plant, L. **-1. -°já** (°*hâja*), m. a large he-goat, ŚBr.; Yājñ. **-2. -ja**, mfn. high-born, noble, W. **-jaṅgha**, m. 'great-legged,' a camel, L. **-jajñu**, m. N. of a mythical teacher, Baudh. **-jaṭa**, mfn. wearing a gr° braid or coil of matted hair (N. of Śiva), MBh.; (*ā*), f. a species of plant, L. **-jatru**, mfn. having a gr° collar-bone (N. of Śiva), MBh. **-jana**, m. (sg.; rarely pl.) a gr° multitude of men, the populace (°*ne*, ind. in the presence of a gr° number of men, in public), MBh.; R.; Kāv. &c.; a gr° or eminent man, gr° persons, Pañcat.; the chief or head of a trade or caste, MW.; a merchant (?), Pañcat.; mfn. (a house) occupied by a gr° number of men, MBh. **-janīya**, mfn. = *mahāñ jano yasya*, Pāṇ., Vārtt. **-japá**, m. a partic. personification, MaitrS. **-jambu** or °**bū**, f. a species of plant, Bhpr. **-jambha**, m. N. of one of Śiva's attendants, L. **-jaya**, mfn. very victorious, MW.; m. N. of a Nāga, MBh.; (*ā*), f. N. of Durgā, L. **-java**, mf(*ā*)n. very impetuous, v° swift, v° fleet, very rapid, MBh.; R.; BhP.; m. an antelope, L.; (*ā*), f. N. of one of the Mātṛis attending on Skanda, MBh. (v.l. *mano-javā*). **-jātaka**, n. 'the great

Jātaka,' N. of one of the best and most often recited Jātakas of the Buddha, MWB. 113. — **jāti,** f. Gaertnera Racemosa, L. — **jātīya,** mfn. moderately large, Pāṇ. vi, 3, 46; of an excellent sort or species, W. — **jānu,** m. 'large-kneed,' N. of a Brāhman, MBh.; of one of Śiva's attendants, L. — **jābāla,** m. N. of a man, Pāṇ. vi, 2, 38. — **jālini** (m. c. for °*nī*), f. a species of plant, Car. — **jālī,** f. (only L.) a species of Ghoshā with yellowish flowers; a sp° of Kośātakī with red flowers; a sp° of creeper; a kind of factitious salt. — **jihva,** mfn. long-tongued (said of Śiva), MBh.; m. N. of a Daitya, Hariv. — **jñāna-gītā,** f. N. of a Tantra deity, Buddh. — **jñāna-yutā,** f. N. of the goddess Manasā, Cat. — **jñānin,** m. 'knowing much,' N. of Śiva, Śivag.; a great soothsayer, Kathās. — **jyaishṭhī,** f. N. of a night of full moon coinciding with certain phenomena in the heavens in the month Jyaishṭha, Tithyād. — **jyotis,** m. 'having great splendour,' N. of Śiva, Śivag.; °*tish-matī,* f. a species of plant, L. — **jvara,** m. great affliction, Kathās.; °*rāṅkuśa,* m. a mixture used as a remedy for fever, Bhpr.; Rasêndrac. — **jvāla,** mfn. blazing greatly (said of Śiva), MBh.; m. a sacrificial fire, L.; N. of a hell, VP.; (*ā*), f. a large flame, L. — **jhasha,** m. a big or strong fish, L. — °**ñjana** (°*hāñj*°), m. N. of a mountain, R. — °**ñji** (°*hāñji*), mfn. having broad spots, VS. — °**ṭavī** (°*hāṭ*°), m. pl. N. of a people, VarBṛS.; (*ī*), f. a gr° forest, Daś. — **ḍakara** (?), m. N. of a commentator, Cat. — **ḍīna,** n. a kind of flight, MBh. — °**ḍhya** (°*hāḍh*°), mfn. very rich, Kathās.; m. Nauclea Cadamba, L. — **ṇagnī** (!), f. see *-nagnā.* — **tattva,** n. 'the gr° principle,' Intellect (second of the Sāṃkhya Tattvas; see *mahat*); (*ā*), f. N. of one of Durgā's attendants, W. — **tantra,** n. N. of a Śaiva wk.; *-rāja,* m., see *brahma-jñāna-m*°. — **tapa** (m. c.), mfn. = *-tapas,* Hariv. — **tapana,** m. 'greatly burning,' N. of a hell, Buddh. — **tapas,** mfn. very afflicted, MBh.; practising severe penance or great religious austerities, Mn.; MBh.; R.; m. a great ascetic, MW.; N. of Vishṇu, L.; of Śiva, RTL. 83; of a Muni, Hit.; Kathās.; °*paḥ-saptamī,* f. 'the 7th (day in a partic. half month) of severe penance,' a partic. festival, Cat. — **tapasvin,** mfn. greatly afflicted, = *-tapas,* MBh. — **tamas,** n. 'gross (spiritual) darkness,' N. of one of the 5 degrees of A-vidyā, BhP.; °*maḥ-prabhā,* f. 'having thick darkness for light,' N. of the lowermost of the 21 hells, L. — **taru,** m. 'great tree,' Tithymalus Antiquorum, L.; Euphorbia of various kinds, W. — **tala,** n. N. of the 6th of the 7 lower worlds or regions under the earth inhabited by the Nāgas &c. (see *pātāla*), ĀruṇUp.; Pur. &c. (IW. 431, n. 1). — **tāpaścita,** n. N. of a Sattra, ŚrS. — **tārā,** f. N. of a Buddhist goddess, L. — **tālī,** f. a species of creeping plant (w. r. for *-jālī*), L. — **tālêśvara,** m. a partic. drug, L. — **tikta,** mfn. very bitter; with *sarpis,* n. a partic. drug, Car.; m. Melia Sempervirens, L.; (*ā*), f. Clypea Hernandifolia, L.; = *yava-tiktā,* L. — **tiktaka,** mfn. extremely bitter; (with *sarpis*), n. a partic. drug, Suśr. — **tiṭibha,** m. or n. (?) N. of a partic. high number, Buddh. — **tithi,** f. the great lunar day, the 6th day of a lunation, MBh. — **tīkshṇa,** mfn. exceedingly sharp (said of weapons, of perception &c.); very pungent (said of flavours), W.; (*ā*), f. the marking-nut plant, L. — **tushita,** m. N. of Vishṇu, Vishṇ.; MBh. — **tushṭi-jñāna-mudrā,** f. N. of a Mudrā (q. v.), Buddh. — **teja,** mfn. (m. c.) = next, mfn., BhP. — **tejas,** mfn. of great splendour, full of fire, of gr° majesty (said of gods and men), Mn.; MBh.; R.; m. a hero, demigod, W.; fire, L.; N. of Skanda, L.; of Su-brahmaṇya, L.; of a warrior, Cat.; of a king of the Garuḍas, Buddh.; n. quicksilver, L.; °*jo-garbha,* m. a kind of meditation, Buddh. — **taila,** n. any valuable or precious oil, (or perhaps) N. of a partic. kind of oil, Kathās. — °**todya** (°*hāt*°), n. a great drum, Kathās. — °**tman** (°*hāt*°), mfn. 'high-souled,' magnanimous, having a gr° or noble nature, high-minded, noble, Mn.; MBh.; R. &c.; highly gifted, exceedingly wise, Pañcat.; eminent, mighty, powerful, distinguished, MBh.; R.; Pañcat.; Suśr.; m. the Supreme Spirit, gr° soul of the universe, MaitrUp.; Mn.; the gr° principle i. e. Intellect, BhP.; (scil. *gaṇa*), N. of a class of deceased ancestors, MārkP.; of a son of Dhī-mat, VP.; °*ma-vat,* mfn. 'high-souled,' highly gifted, very wise, Kām.; °*tmya,* mfn. magnanimous, MW.; n., w. r. for *māhātmya* (q. v.), PadmaP.; Daś. — **tyaya** (°*hāt*°), m. any gr° evil or harm or pain, MBh.; mfn. causing gr° evil, very pernicious, ib.; (with *jvara,* m., used by Suśr.) = *mahā-kashṭa, gambhīra* or *cāturthika,* Bhpr.; *-tyayika,* mfn. connected with any gr° immediate evil or danger, Car. — **tyāga,** m. gr° liberality or generosity (in °*ga-maya* below); mfn. extremely liberal or generous (°*ga-citta,* mfn. of ext° liberal mind), Lalit.; m. N. of a man, Buddh.; *-maya,* mfn. consisting of great liberality, Kathās. — **tyāgin,** mfn. extremely liberal or generous (said of Śiva), Śivag. — **trikakud** or °**kubh,** m. N. of a Stoma, ŚrS. — **tripura-sundarī-kavaca,** n. N. of a kind of magical spell, Cat. — **tripura-sundarī-tāpanīyôpanishad** and °**dary-uttara-tāpanī,** f. N. of two Upanishads. — **tripura-sundarī-mantra-nāma-sahasra,** n. N. of a ch. of the Vāmakêśvara-tantra. — **triśūla,** n. a gr° trident, Rājat. — **daṇshṭra,** mfn. having gr° tusks or fangs, MBh.; R.; m. a species of big tiger, L.; N. of a Vidyā-dhara, Kathās.; of a man, ib. — **daṇḍa,** m. a long staff; (accord. to Sch.) a long arm, Prab.; severe punishment, MBh.; mfn. carrying a l° st°; N. of a servant or officer of Yama, L.; *-dhara,* mf(*ā*)n. (a ship) carrying a great mast, R. — **danta,** m. the tusk of an elephant, L.; (*mahā-*), mfn. having large teeth or tusks, MBh. (said of Śiva); Suparṇ.; m. an elephant with l° tusks, W. — **damatra,** m. N. of a teacher, ŚāṅkhGṛ.; AVPariś. — **dambha,** mfn. practising gr° deceit (said of Śiva), Śivag. — **daridra,** mfn. extremely poor, Pañcar. — **daśā,** f. the influence of a predominant planet, MW. — **dāna,** n. 'great gift,' N. of certain valuable gifts (16 are enumerated), Pañcar.; Cat.; mfn. accompanied by val° gifts (said of a sacrifice), Hariv.; *-nirṇaya,* m. N. of wk.; *-pati,* m. a very liberal man, Lalit.; *-paddhati,* f., *-prayoga-paddhati,* f., *-vākyâvalī,* f., °*nânukramaṇikā,* f. N. of wks. — **dāru,** n. Pinus Deodora, ŚārṅgS. — °**di-kaṭabhī** (°*hād*°), f. a species of Achyranthes, L. (v. l. *mahāli-k*°). — **divākīrtya,** n. N. of a Sāman, Br.; ŚrS. — **diś,** f. a chief quarter of the world (east, south, west, north), ĀpŚr., Comm. — **dīpa-dāna-vidhi,** m. N. of wk. — **duḥkha,** n. a gr° pain or evil, Subh. — **dundu,** m. a gr° military drum, L. — **durga,** mfn. very difficult to be crossed, MW.; n. a gr° calamity or danger, Pañcat. — **dūta,** m. or n. (?) N. of a Buddhist Sūtra wk. — **dūshaka,** m. a species of grain, Suśr. — **dṛiti,** m. a gr° leather bag or pouch, MBh. — **devá,** m. 'the gr° deity,' N. of Rudra or Śiva or one of his attendant deities, AV. &c. &c.; of one of the 8 forms of R° or Ś°, Pur.; of Vishṇu, MBh.; Hariv.; RāmatUp.; of various authors &c., Cat. (also *dīkshita-m*°, *dvi-vedi-m*°; cf. below); of a mountain, Vās., Introd.; (*ā*), f. N. of a daughter of Devaka, VP. (w. r. for *saha-devā*); (*ī*), f. N. of Śiva's wife Pārvatī, MBh.; Hariv. &c. (RTL. 186); of Lakshmī, MBh.; R.; of Dākshāyaṇī in the Śālagrāma, Cat.; the chief wife of a king, MBh.; Kathās. &c. (°*vī-tva,* n. the rank of chief wife, Kathās.); a kind of colocynth, L.; N. of various women, Vet.; Cat.; of sev. wks.; n. N. of a Tantra, Cat.; Āryav. (cf. *Śiva-tantra*); *-kavîśâcārya-sarasvatī,* m. N. of an author, Cat.; *-kṛityā,* f. a wrong act committed against Śiva, MBh.; *-giri,* m. N. of a mountain, Kathās.; *-gṛiha,* n. a temple of Śiva, Cat.; *-josī,* m. N. of an author, Cat.; *-tantra,* n. the Mahā-deva Tantra, Cat. (see above); *-tīrtha,* m. N. of a teacher, Cat.; *-tva,* n. the state or dignity of 'the gr° deity,' Up.; *-dīkshita,* m., *-daiva-jña,* m., *-dvi-vedin,* m., *-paṇḍita,* m., *-puṇya-stambha-kara* or *-puṇatāma-kara* (?), m. N. of authors, Cat.; *-pura,* n. N. of a city, Buddh.; *-bhaṭṭa* and *-bhaṭṭa-dina-kara,* m. N. of learned men, Cat.; *-maṇi,* m. a species of medicinal plant, L.; *-vājapeyin,* m., *-vādîndra,* m., *-vid,* m., *-vidyā-vāg-īśa,* m., *-vedânta-vāg-īśa,* m., *-vedântin,* m., *-śarman,* m., *-śāstrin,* m., *-sarasvatī,* m. (and °*tī-vedântin,* m.), *-sarva-jña-vādîndra,* m. N. of learned men, Cat.; *-sahasra-nāman,* n. N. of wk.; *-sahasra-nāma-stotra* and *-stotra,* n. N. of Stotras; *-hata,* mfn. slain by Rudra, ĀpŚr.; *-hārivaṇśa,* m., °*vânanda,* m., °*vâśrama,* m. N. of authors, Cat., °*vâshṭôttara-śata-nāman,* n. N. of wk.; °*vâhata,* mfn. hit by Mahā-deva, MaitrS.; °*vêndra-sarasvatī,* m. N. of an author, Cat. — **devīya,** mfn. composed by Mahā-deva, Cat.; n. N. of wk. — **deha,** mfn. having a great body, Bhpr. — **daitya,** m. 'the gr° Daitya,' N. of a D°, GāruḍaP.; of the grandfather of the second Candra-gupta, Inscr. — **dairghatamasa,** n. N. of a Sāman, L. — °**dbhuta** (°*hād*°), mfn. very wonderful, MBh.; n. a gr° marvel, AVPariś.; N. of the 72nd Pariśishṭa of the AV. — **dyuti,** mfn. of gr° splendour, very bright or glorious, Mn.; MBh.; R.; *-kará,* m. N. of the sun, TĀr. — **dyotā,** f. N. of a Tantra goddess, Buddh. — **drāvaka,** m. a kind of drug, L. — **druma,** m. a gr° tree, MBh.; Hariv. &c.; Ficus Religiosa, L.; N. of a son of Bhavya, Pur.; n. N. of the Varsha ruled by him, VP. — **droṇā** or °**ṇī,** f. a species of plant, L. — **dvandva,** m. = *-dundu* (q. v.), L. — **dvādaśī-vicāra,** m. N. of wk. — **dvāra,** m. n. a principal door or gate, Hariv.; (*ā*), f. (a woman) having a large vagina, Suśr. — **dhaná,** n. great spoil or booty (taken in battle), RV.; a gr° contest, gr° battle, ib.; Naigh.; great wealth or riches, Var.; Kathās.; agriculture, L.; mf(*ā*)n. costing much money, very costly or precious or valuable, MBh.; Hariv.; R.; Cāṇ.; having much money, rich, wealthy, R.; Pañcat.; Hit. &c.; m. N. of a merchant, Kathās.; Vet.; n. anything costly or precious, W.; gold, L.; incense, L.; costly raiment, L.; *-pati,* m. a very rich man, Kathās. — **dhanika,** mfn. excessively rich, VarBṛS., Sch. — **dhanus,** mfn. having a gr° bow (Śiva), Śivag.; °*nur-dhara,* m. (MaitrUp.) or °*nush-mat,* m. (MBh.) a gr° archer. — **dharma,** m. N. of a prince of the Kiṃ-naras, Buddh. — **dhavala-purāṇa,** n. N. of wk. — **dhātu,** m. 'great metal or element,' gold, L.; lymph, L.; N. of Śiva, MBh. (= *meru-parvata,* Nīlak.) — °**dhipati** (°*hâdh*°), f. N. of a Tantra deity, Buddh. — **dhī,** mfn. having a great understanding, Śiś.; Śrutab. — **dhur,** m. = *mahān dhūḥ sadṛiśaḥ pravāhaḥ,* MBh. (Nīlak.) — **dhura,** m., Pāṇ. v, 4, 74, Sch. — **dhurya,** m. a full-grown draught-ox, R. — **dhṛiti,** m. N. of a king, Pur. — **dhvaja,** m. a camel, L. — **dhvani,** m. 'making a loud noise,' N. of a Dānava, Hariv. — °**dhvanika** (°*hâdh*°), mfn. 'one who has gone a long journey,' dead, L. — °**dhvara** (°*hâdh*°), m. a great sacrifice, MW. — **dhvāna,** m. a loud sound, Hemac. — °**naka** (°*hān*°), m. a kind of large drum, MBh. — **nakha,** mfn. having great nails or claws (Śiva), MBh. — **nagara,** n. a gr° city or N. of a c°, Pāṇ. vi, 2, 89. — **nagná,** m. 'quite naked,' a paramour, AV.; ŚāṅkhŚr.; an athlete, Buddh.; Lalit.; (*ā,* f., ĀpŚr.; or *ī́,* AV. &c.), a kind of harlot (= *mahatī ca nagnī ca,* Sāy. on AitBr.; w. r. *mahā-nagnī* and *-naghnī*). — **naṭa,** m. 'gr° actor,' N. of Śiva, Cat. — **nada,** m. a gr° river or stream, MārkP.; N. of a river, VP.; (*ī*), f. a river, Lāṭy.; MaitrUp.; MBh. &c.; N. of the Ganges, MBh.; MārkP.; of a well-known river (which rises on the south-west of Bengal, and after an eastward course of 520 miles divides into sev. branches at the town of Cuttack, and falls by sev. mouths into the Bay of Bengal), MW.; of various streams, MBh.; Hariv. &c.; °*dī-sāgara-saṃgama,* m. 'confluence of the Mahā-nadī and the ocean,' N. of a place, Cat. — °**nana** (°*hān*°), mfn. having a gr° mouth or face, MBh. — °**nanda** (°*hān*° or °*hā-n*°), m. gr° bliss (*-tva,* n. state of great bliss), Up.; the gr° joy of deliverance from further transmigration, final emancipation, L.; a kind of flute, Saṃgīt.; N. of a disciple of Buddha, Buddh.; of a king, Pur.; of two authors, Cat.; of a river, L.; (*ā*), f. ardent spirits, L.; a species of plant (= *ārāma-śītalā*), L.; the 9th day in the light half of the month Māgha, Tithyād.; N. of a river, MBh.; *-dhīra,* m. N. of an author, Cat. — **nandi** or °**din,** m. N. of a king, Pur. — **naya-prakāśa,** m. N. of wk. — **naraka,** m. N. of a hell, Mn.; Yājñ. — **narêndra,** m. a gr° conjuror or magician, Kād. — **narman,** m. a Māhishya (q. v.) who knows medicine, L. — **naḍa,** m. Arundo Bengalensis, L. — **navamī,** f. the 9th day in the light half of the month Āśvina, KālP.; Tithyād.; the last of the 9 days or nights dedicated to the worship of Durgā, the l° d° of the D°-pūjā, MW.; *-pūjā,* f. N. of wk. — °**nasa** (°*hān*°), n. a heavy waggon or cart, ŚrS.; a kitchen (also m.), Gobh.; KātyŚr.; MBh. &c.; cooking utensils (?), KātyŚr.; m. N. of a mountain, BhP.; (*ī*), f. a cook, kitchen-maid, MBh.; °*sâdhyaksha,* m. a chief kitchen-superintendent, BhP. — **nāgá,** m. a great serpent, ŚBr.; Suparṇ.; a gr° elephant, Hariv.; one of the elephants that support the earth, R.; N. of Vātsyāyana, Gal.; *-hana* (?), m. N. of Śiva, MBh.; of a Śrāvaka, Buddh. — **nāṭaka,** n. a brilliant spectacle, Bālar.; N. of a kind of drama, Sāh.; of a drama in 14 acts fabled to have been composed by the monkey-chief Hanu-mat (= *hanuman-n*°, q. v.), IW. 367; 519. — **nāḍī,** f. a gr° tubular vessel, MW.; sinew, tendon, L. — **nāda,** m. a loud sound, l° cry, roaring, bellowing, MBh.; MārkP.; mf(*ā*)n. l°-sounding, roaring or bellowing loudly, making a loud noise, MBh.;

R.; m. a great drum, L.; a muscle, shell, L.; rain-cloud, L.; an elephant, L.; a lion, L.; a camel, L.; the ear, L.; = *śayānaka* (*bhayānaka*?), L.; N. of Śiva, MBh.; of a Rākshasa, R.; n. a musical instrument, W. — **nānā-tva**, n. N. of certain ceremonial rules, Lāṭy. — **nābha**, mfn. having a large navel-like cavity, R.; m. N. of a magical spell pronounced over weapons, R.; of two Dānavas, Hariv.; VP. — **nāman**, m. N. of a relation of Gautama Buddha, Buddh.; (*mahā́-nāmnī*), f. N. of a Pariśishṭa of the Sāma-veda, Cat.; pl. (scil. *ṛicas*), N. of 9 verses of the S°-v° beginning with the words *vidā maghavan*, AV.; VS.; Br. &c.; °*mnī-vrata*, n. a religious observance in which the Mahā-nāmnī verses are recited, Saṃskārak. — **nāmnika**, mfn. relating to the Mahā-nāmnī, MW.; rel° to the M° verses, Gobh.; Kull. on Mn. ii, 165. — **nāyaka**, m. a gr° head or chief, Inscr.; Vās.; a gr° gem in the centre of a string of pearls, Vās. — **nārāyaṇa**, m. 'the great Nārāyaṇa,' Vishṇu, Lalit.; °*ṇôpanishad*, f. N. of an Upanishad. — **nāsa**, mfn. having a gr° nose (Śiva), MBh. — **nidra**, mfn. sleeping soundly, sl° long, R.; (*ā*), f. 'the gr° sleep,' death, L. — **nidhi**, m., °**dhi-kumāra**, m. N. of two poets. — **ninàda**, m. N. of a Nāga, Buddh. — **nimitta**, n. N. of a partic. doctrine, W. — **nimna**, n. the intestines, abdomen, Car. — **nimba**, m. Melia Bukajun, Suśr.; *-rajas*, n. a partic. high number, Buddh. — **niyama**, m. 'great vow,' N. of Vishṇu, MBh. — **niyuta**, n. a partic. high number, Buddh. — **niraya**, m. N. of a hell, Yājñ. — **nirashṭa** (*mahā́-*), m. a gelded bull, TS.; Kāṭh.; ĀśvŚr. — **nirṇaya-tantra**, n. N. of wk. — **nirvāṇa**, n. 'the gr° Nirvāṇa,' total extinction of individual existence, Buddh.; *-tantra*, n. N. of a Tantra, IW. 525. — °**nila** (°*hān*°), m. N. of a serpent demon, VP. — **niś**, f. the dead of night, midnight, Mn. — **niśā**, f. = prec., BrahmavP.; Tithyād.; Hcat. &c.; N. of Durgā, L. — **niśitha**, m. pl. N. of a Jaina sect, W.; n. of a Jaina wk. — **nīca**, m. 'very low (in caste),' a washerman, fuller, L. — **nīla**, mfn. dark blue, deep black, MBh.; Bhartṛ.; m. a sapphire, Kāv.; Var. &c.; a kind of bdellium, Bhpr.; Verbesina Scandens, L.; N. of a Nāga, Hariv.; VP.; of a mountain, MārkP.; (*ā*), f. a species of plant, L.; (*ī*), f. a blue variety of Clitoria Ternatea, L.; = *bṛihan-nīlī*, L.; n. a lotion or ointment for the eyes, Car.; *-tantra*, n. N. of a Tantra; *-maya*, mfn. consisting or made of sapphire, Kathās.; °*lâbhra-jālīya*, Nom. P. °*yati*, to resemble a dense mass of black clouds, Vās., Introd.; °*lôpala*, m. 'dark-blue stone,' a sapphire, R. — °**nubhāva** (°*hān*°), mf(*ā*)n. of great might, mighty, MBh.; R.; Pañcat. &c.; high-minded, noble-m°, generous, Ratnāv.; Kād.; *-tā*, f. (Kād.; Mṛicch. [in Prākṛit]) or *-tva*, n. (Kathās.) magnanimity, generosity. — °**nurāga** (°*hān*°), m. gr° love, excessive affection, MW. — °**nuśaṇsaka** (°*hān*°), mfn. being of gr° comfort or advantage, Divyâv. — °**nūpa** (°*hān*°), mfn. having gr° swamps, R. — **nṛitya**, m. a great dancer (said of Śiva), MBh. — **netra**, mfn. large-eyed (Śiva), MBh. — **nemi**, m. a crow, L. — °**ntaka** (°*hān*°), m. 'the great finisher,' death (N. of Śiva), MBh. — °**ndha-kāra** (°*hān*°), m. thick darkness, gross spiritual darkness, MaitrUp. — °**ndhra** (°*hān*°), m. pl. N. of a people, Buddh. — °**ndhraka** (°*hān*°), m. N. of a king (v.l. *mahīdhraka*), R. — **nyāya**, m. a principal rule, ĀśvŚr. — **nyāsa**, m., °**sa-vidhi**, m. N. of wks. — °**nvaya** (°*hān*°), mf(*ā*)n. being of noble family, Kathās. — **paksha**, mfn. having a gr° party or numerous adherents, Mn.; Kām.; h° a gr° family, MW.; m. 'gr°-winged,' a kind of duck, L.; N. of Garuḍa, L.; (*ī*), f. an owl, L. — **pakshin**, m. the hooting owl, L. — °**pagā** (°*hâp*°), f. a gr° river or stream, MBh.; N. of a river (?), VP. — **paṅka**, m. or n. (?) deep mire, Hit. — **paṅkti**, f. a kind of metre, RPrāt. — **pañca-mūla**, n. a group of 5 various roots, Suśr. (cf. *pañca-m*°). — **pañca-visha**, n. the 5 strong poisons (viz. *śṛiṅgī, kāla-kūṭa, mustaka, vatsanābha, śaṅkha-karṇī*), L. — **paṭa**, m. the skin, Gal. — **paṇḍita**, mfn. extremely learned; m. a gr° scholar, Cat. — **pattra**, m. 'having large leaves,' a kind of pot-herb, W.; (*ā*), f. Uraria Lagopodioides, L. — **patha**, m. a principal road, high street (in a city), high road, highway (ifc. f. *ā*), AitBr.; Gaut.; Āpast. &c.; N. of Śiva, MBh.; the long journey, the passage into the next world (°*thaṃ*√*yā*, to die), Kathās.; the gr° pilgrimage (to the shrine of Śiva on mount Kedāra, or the same pilg° performed in spirit i.e. by deep absorption into Ś°), Cat.; the knowledge of the essence of Śiva acquired in this pilg°, Cat.; the mountain-precipices from which devotees throw themselves to obtain a speedier entrance into Śiva's heaven, ib.; N. of the book which treats of the above subjects; of a hell, Yājñ.; n. = *brahma-randhra* (q.v.), Cat.; mf(*ā*)n. having a great path or way, PārGṛ.; *-gama*, m. (L.) or *-gamana*, n. (MW.) 'the act of going the gr° journey,' dying; *-giri*, m. N. of a mountain, Kathās. — **pathika**, mfn. undertaking gr° journeys, MBh. — **pathi-kṛid-ishṭi**, f. a partic. sacrifice, ĀpŚr., Comm. — **padá**, n. (perhaps) gr° space, RV. x, 73, 2; *-paṅkti*, f. a kind of metre, RPrāt. — **padma**, m. (L.) or n. a partic. high number, MBh.; R.; Līl.; m. N. of one of the 9 treasures of Kubera, Cat.; L.; (with Jainas) N. of a partic. treasure inhabited by a Nāga, L.; of one of the 8 t°s connected with the Padminī magical art, MārkP.; of a hell, Divyâv. (one of the 8 cold hells, Dharmas. 122); a kind of serpent, Suśr.; N. of a Nāga dwelling in the Mahā-padma treasure mentioned above, Hariv.; VP. &c.; of the southernmost of the elephants that support the earth, MBh.; R. (IW. 432); of Nanda, Pur.; of a son of N°, Buddh.; of a Dānava, Hariv.; a Kiṃ-nara or attendant on Kubera, MW.; a species of esculent root, L.; n. a white lotus flower, L.; the figure of a wh° l° fl°, Kathās.; MārkP.; RāmatUp.; a partic. compound of oil, Car.; N. of a city on the right bank of the Ganges, MBh.; m. or n. (?) N. of a Kāvya; *-pati*, m. 'proprietor of millions,' N. of Nanda, BhP.; *-saras* or *-salila*, n. N. of a lake, Rājat. — **padya-shaṭka**, n. 'collection of 6 classical verses,' N. of a poem in praise of king Bhoja (ascribed to Kālidāsa). — **panthaka**, m. N. of a disciple of Buddha, Buddh. — **parāka**, m. a partic. penance, Hcat. — °**parādha** (°*hâp*°), m. a gr° offence, Hit. — °**parāhṇa** (°*hâp*°), m. a late hour in the afternoon, Pāṇ. vi, 2, 38 (cf. *-niśā, -rātra*). — **parinirvāṇa** or °**ṇa-sūtra**, n. N. of a Buddhist Sūtra. — **parvata**, m. a high mountain, R. — **pavitra**, mfn. greatly purifying (said of Vishṇu), MBh.; greatly protecting against unfavourable influences, VarBṛS.; °*trêshṭi*, f. N. of wk. — **paśu**, m. large cattle, Mn. — **pākajānī**, m. N. of an author, Cat. — **pāṭala**, m. or n. (?) a species of plant, Buddh. — **pāta**, m. a long flight, Pañcat.; mfn. far-flying (said of an arrow), Hariv. — **pātaka**, n. a great crime or sin (5 such are enumerated, viz. killing a Brāhman, drinking intoxicating liquors, theft, committing adultery with the wife of a religious teacher, and associating with any one guilty of these crimes), Mn. (esp. xi, 54); Yājñ. &c.; any gr° crime or heinous sin, W. — **pātakin**, mfn. guilty of a gr° crime, Mn.; Yājñ. &c. — **pātra**, n. a prime minister, Pañcar.; Sāh. — **pāda**, mfn. having large feet (Śiva), MBh. — **pāna**, n. an excellent drink, BhP. — **pāpa**, n. a great crime, MBh.; Yājñ. &c. — **pāpman**, mfn. doing much evil, Bhag. — **pāra**, m. a partic. personification, SāmavBr.; Gaut.; mfn. having distant shores, wide (the sea), MBh. — **pāraṇika**, m. N. of a disciple of Buddha, Lalit. — **pārishad**, m. one of the principal attendants (of a god), MBh. — **pārushaka**, m. or n. (?) a species of plant, Buddh. — **pārevata**, n. a species of fruit tree, L. — **pārśva**, mf(*ā*)n. having broad or thick sides, Suśr.; m. N. of a Dānava, MBh.; Hariv.; of a Rākshasa, R. — **pāla**, m. N. of a king, Buddh. — **pāśa**, m. N. of an officer of Yama, Pur.; of a Nāga, Buddh. — **pāśupata**, m. a zealous worshipper of Śiva Paśu-pati, Hcar.; n. (with *vrata*) the great religious vow connected with the worship of Śiva P°, Kathās. — **pāsaka**, m., w.r. for *mahôp*° (q.v.), L. — **piṇḍītaka**, m. a species of plant, L. — **piṇḍītaru**, m. a species of tree, L. — **pīṭha**, n. a high seat, Up. — **pīlu**, m. a species of tree, L.; *-pati*, m. (?), Uṇ. i, 38, Sch. — **puṇs**, m. (prob.) N. of a mountain, MBh. — **puṇsa**, m. a gr° man, Śatr. — **puṇya**, mf(*ā*)n. extremely favourable or auspicious (as a day), Hcat.; very good or beautiful; greatly purifying, very holy, MBh.; R. &c.; (*ā*), f. N. of a river, Cat. — **putra**, m., g. *sutaṅgamādi*. — **putrīya**, Nom. P. °*yati* (fr. *-putra*), Pat. — **purá**, n. a gr° fortress, TS.; Kāṭh.; AitBr.; N. of a Tīrtha, MBh.; (*ī*), f. a gr° fortress or city, R. — **puraś-caraṇa-prayoga**, m. N. of wk. — **purāṇa**, n. a gr° Purāṇa, MBh.; N. of the Bhāgavata and Vishṇu Purāṇas, IW. 515. — **purusha**, m. a gr° or eminent man (*-tā*, f. the state of being one), Hit.; Mcar.; Buddh. &c.; a gr° saint or sage or ascetic, MW.; the gr° Soul, the Supreme Spirit (identified with the year, AitĀr.; also as N. of Vishṇu), Gaut.; MBh.; R. &c.; N. of Gautama Buddha, MWB. 23; *-dantā* (Car.) or *-dantikā* (L.), f. Asparagus Racemosus; *-pāvana-kavaca*, n. a partic. magical formula, Cat.; *-lakshaṇa*, n. N. of wk.; *-vidyā*, f. a partic. mag° form°, BhP.; °*yāyām vishṇu-rahasye kshetra-kāṇḍe jagan-nātha-māhātmya*, n., *-stava*, m., *-stotra*, n. N. of wks. — **pushpa**, m. Bauhinia Variegata, L.; a kind of worm, Suśr.; (*ā*), f. Clitoria Ternatea, L. — **pūjā**, f. 'gr° honour,' a partic. religious ceremony, Hcat.; *-vidhi*, m. N. of wk. — **pūta**, mfn. exceedingly pure, Pañcar. — **pūrusha**, m. the Supreme Spirit (= *-purusha* above), BhP.; Pañcar. — **pūrṇa**, m. N. of a king of the Garuḍas, Buddh. — **pṛithivī**, f. the gr° earth (*-tva*, n.), Sāṃkhyapr. — **pṛishṭha**, mfn. having a gr° or broad back, MBh. (see comp.); m. a camel, L.; n. N. of 6 Anuvākas in the 4th Ashṭaka of the Ṛig-veda used at the Aśvamedha sacrifice (cf. *-pṛishṭhya*); *-gala-skandha*, mfn., w.r. for *mahā-vṛiksha-g*°, MBh. — **pṛishṭhya**, N. of partic. Anuvākas, TPrāt. — **paiṅgya**, n. N. of a Vedic text, GṛS. — **paiṭhīnasi**, m. N. of a preceptor, Cat. — **paiśācika**, n. (with *ghṛita*) a partic. ointment, Car. — **poṭagala**, m. a species of large rush or reed, L. — **paurava**, m. N. of a king, VP. — **paurṇamāsī**, f. a night in which Jupiter enters into conjunction with the full moon, Hcat. — **prakaraṇa**, n. the principal treatment of a subject, ĀpŚr., Comm. — **prakāśa**, m. N. of wk. — **prajāpati**, m. 'gr° lord of creatures,' N. of Vishṇu, MBh.; Vishṇ.; (*ī*), f. N. of Gautama Buddha's aunt and foster-mother (the first woman who embraced the Buddha's doctrines), Buddh. — **prajāvatī**, f. = *-prajā-patī*, Buddh. — **prajñā-pāramitā-sūtra**, n. N. of a Buddhist Sūtra wk. — **praṇāda**, m. N. of a Cakra-vartin, Buddh. — **pratāpa**, mfn. very dignified or majestic, very puissant, MW. — **pratibhāna**, m. N. of a Bodhisattva, Buddh. — **pratīhāra**, m. a chief door-keeper, Rājat. — **pradāna**, n. a gr° gift, R. — **pradīpa**, m. N. of a man, Lalit. — **prapañca**, m. the gr° universe or visible world, Vedāntas. — **prabandha**, m. a gr° literary wk., Pratāp. — **prabha**, mfn. shining brightly, exceedingly brilliant or splendid, MBh.; Hariv.; m. the light of a lamp, W.; (*ā*), f. gr° brightness, L.; N. of Comm.; °*bhā-maṇḍala-vyūha-jñāna-mudrā*, f. N. of a partic. Mudrā (q.v.), Buddh. — **prabhāva**, mf(*ā*)n. exceedingly mighty or powerful, MBh.; Prab. — **prabhāsa**, N. of a Tīrtha; °*sôtpatti-varṇana*, n. N. of wk. — **prabhu**, m. a gr° master, mighty lord, king, prince (*-tva*, n.), Up.; a very holy man or gr° saint, W.; a chief, W.; N. of Indra, L.; of Śiva, L.; of Vishṇu, L. — **pramāṇa**, mfn. of gr° extent, Pañcat. — **prayoga-sāra**, m. N. of wk. — **pralaya**, m. the total annihilation of the universe at the end of a Kalpa, VP.; Kād.; N. of a Hindī wk., RTL. 179. — **pravara-nirṇaya**, m. and °**ra-bhāshya**, n. N. of wks. — **pravṛiddha**, mfn. of lofty growth, Pāṇ. vi, 2, 38. — **praśna**, m. a knotty question, Kathās. — **prasāda**, m. a gr° favour or kindness, MW.; a gr° present (of food &c. distributed among the persons present at the worship of an idol), Matsyas.; mfn. of gr° kindness, exceedingly gracious, MBh. — **prasuta**, m. or n. (?) a partic. high number, Buddh. — **prasthāna**, n. setting out on the gr° journey, departing this life, dying, Hariv.; R.; Mn.; Kull. &c.; *-parvan*, n. N. of the 17th book of the Mahā-bhārata. — **prasthānika**, mfn. relating to the great journey or dying, MBh.; R.; *-parvan*, n. = *mahā-prasthāna-p*° above. — **prājña**, mfn. very wise, very clever or intelligent, MBh.; R. — **prāṇa**, m. the hard breathing or aspirate (heard in the utterance of certain letters), Pāṇ. i, 1, 9, Sch.; the aspirated letters themselves, A.; gr° spirit or power (see *su-mahā-p*°); mfn. pronounced with the hard breathing or aspirate, Pāṇ. viii, 4, 62, Sch.; of gr° bodily strength or endurance, Kād.; 'making a harsh breathing or cry,' a raven, L. (cf. *alpa-p*°, *mahāp*°). — **prāvrājya**, n. the hard life of a wandering religious mendicant, MārkP. — **prāsthānika**, mfn. = *-prasthānika*, MBh. (v.l. *-prasth*°). — **prīti-vega-sambhava-mudrā**, f. N. of a partic. Mudrā (q.v.), Buddh. — **prīti-harshā**, f. N. of a Tantra deity, ib. — **prêta**, m. a noble departed spirit, Rudray. — **plava**, m. a great flood, MārkP. — **phaṇaka**, m. N. of a Nāga, Buddh. — **phala**, n. a gr° fruit, Bhartṛ.; a testicle, Vishṇ.; gr° reward, Mn.; mf(*ā*)n. having gr° fruits, bearing much fruit, L.; bringing a rich reward, Mn.; m. Aegle Marmelos, L.; (*ā*), f. (only L.) a kind of colocynth; the big jujube; a species of Jambū; a citron tree; a kind of spear. — **phetkārīya**, n. N. of a Tantra, Cat. — **phenā**, f. Os Sepiae, L. — **bandha**, m. a peculiar position of the hands or feet (in Yoga), Cat. — **babhru**, m. a kind of animal living in holes, Suśr. — **bala**, mf(*ā*)n. exceedingly strong, very powerful or mighty, very efficacious, MBh.; R.; Hariv. &c.; m. wind, L.; borax, L.; a Buddha, L.; (scil. *gaṇa*), a partic. class of deceased ancestors, MārkP.; N. of one of Śiva's attendants (?), Hariv.; of Indra in the 4th Manv-antara, MārkP.; of a Nāga, Buddh.; of one of the 10 gods of anger, Dharmas. 11; of a king and various other persons, Hit.; VP. &c.; (*ā*), f. Sida Cordifolia and Rhombifolia, L.; N. of one of the Mātṛis attending on Skanda, MBh.; n. lead, L.; a partic. high number, Buddh.; N. of a Liṅga, Cat.; *-kavi*, m. N. of an author, L.; *-parākrama*, mfn. of great power and strength (Vishṇu), Vishṇ.; *-rāsa*, m. N. of wk.; *-śākya*, m. N. of a king, Buddh.; *-sūtra*, n. N. of a Buddhist Sūtra wk.; °*lāksha*, a partic. high number, Buddh.; °*lêśvara*, m. N. of Śiva, MW.; n. N. of a Liṅga temple; of a well-known Sanitarium called 'Mahābleshwar' in a range of hills near Poona in the Bombay Presidency, RTL. 348; Cat. — **bali**, m. N. of the giant Bali, MW. — **bādha**, mfn. causing gr° pain or damage, MBh. — **bārhata**, mfn. (fr. *-bṛihatī*) 'a kind of metre,' RPrāt.; RAnukr. — **bāhu**, mfn. long-armed, MBh.; R.; MārkP.; N. of Vishṇu, MBh.; of a Dānava, Hariv.; of a Rākshasa, R.; of one of the sons of Dhṛita-rāshṭra, MBh.; of a king, Kathās. — **bimbara**, m. or n. a partic. high number, Buddh. — **bila**, n. a deep cave or hole, MBh.; the atmosphere, ether, Cat.; a water-jar, W.; the heart or mind, W. (cf. *mahad-b*°). — **bīja**, mfn. having much seed (said of Śiva), MBh. (cf. *-retas*). — **bījya**, n. the Perinaeum, L. — **buddha**, m. the great Buddha, Buddh. — **buddhi**, f. the intellect, VP.; mfn. having gr° understanding, extremely clever, R.; Pañcat. (*-buddhe*, w. r. for *-yuddhe*, MBh.); m. N. of an Asura, Kathās.; of a man, ib. — **budhna** (*mahā́-*), mfn. having a wide bottom or base (said of a mountain), AV. — **busa**, m. a sort of rice (which takes a year to ripen), L.; barley, L. — **bṛihatī**, f. Solanum Melongena, L.; a kind of metre, RPrāt. — **bodhi**, m. or f. the gr° intelligence of a Buddha, Buddh.; m. a Buddha, L.; a partic. incarnation of B°, Jātakam.; *-saṃghārāma*, m. N. of a Buddhist monastery, Buddh.; °*dhy-aṅga-vatī*, f. N. of a Tantra deity, ib. — °**bja** (°*hāb*°), m. N. of a serpent demon, Kālac. — **brahma** or °**man**, m. the great Brahman, the Supreme Spirit, Buddh.; pl. (with Buddhists) one of the 18 classes of gods of the world of form, Dharmas. 128 (cf. MWB. 210 &c.) — **brāhmaṇá**, m. a gr° Brāhman, ŚBr.; Śak.; a gr° B° (in ironical sense), Mṛicch.; Ratnâv. (= *nindita-brahman*, L.); a priest who officiates at a Śrāddha or solemn ceremony in honour of deceased ancestors, W.; n. 'great Brāhmaṇa,' N. of the Tāṇḍya Br°; *-bhāgya*, w. r. for *brāhmaṇa-mahā-bh*°, MBh. — **bhaṭa**, m. a gr° warrior, Inscr.; BhP.; N. of a Dānava, Kathās.; of a warrior, ib. — **bhaṭṭārikā**, f. N. of Durgā; °*kârcā-ratna*, n. N. of wk. — **bhaṭṭi-vyākaraṇa**, n. N. of wk. — **bhadra**, m. N. of a mountain, MārkP.; (*ā*), f. Gmelina Arborea, L.; N. of the Gaṅgā, L.; Buddh.; n. N. of a lake, Pur. — **bhaya**, n. great danger or peril, AitBr.; MBh. &c.; m. Great Danger personified as a son of Adharma by Nirṛiti, MBh. (cf. *bhaya*); mf(*ā*)n. accompanied with gr° d° or peril, very dangerous or formidable, MBh. — **bharī**, f. Alpinia Galanga, Bhpr. — **bhāga**, mf(*ā*)n. one to whom a gr° portion or lot has fallen, highly fortunate, eminent in the highest degree, illustrious, highly distinguished (mostly of persons and frequently in address), Mn.; MBh.; Hariv. &c.; virtuous in a high degree, pure, holy, W.; m. gr° luck, prosperity, MW.; N. of a king, VP.; (*ā*), f. N. of Dākshāyaṇī in Mahâlaya, Cat.; *-tā*, f. (W.) or *-tva*, n. (MW.) high excellence, gr° good fortune, exalted station or merit; the possessing of the 8 cardinal virtues. — **bhāgavata**, m. a great worshipper of Bhagavat (Vishṇu), BhP.; n. (with or scil. *purāṇa*) the gr° Bhāgavata Purāṇa, Cat. — **bhāgin**, mfn. exceedingly fortunate, Kathās. — **bhāgya**, mfn. exceedingly fortunate (*-tā*, f.), Daś.; n. gr° luck or happiness, MW.; high excellence, exalted position, Mn.; MBh.; Pratāp. (cf. *māhābhāgya*). — **bhāṇḍa**, n. a gr° vessel, MBh.; °*ḍâgāra* (°*ḍâg*°), n. a chief treasury, Rājat.; Viddh. — **bhāra**, m. a gr° weight or burden, Pāṇ. — **bhārata**, m. or n. (with or scil. *āhava*, *yuddha* or any word signifying 'battle') the gr° war of the Bharatas, MBh.; Hariv.; n. (with or scil. *ākhyāna*), 'great narrative of the war of the Bh°,' N. of the gr° epic poem in about 215,000 lines describing the acts and contests of the sons of the two brothers Dhṛita-rāshṭra and Pāṇḍu, descendants of Bharata, who were of the lunar line of kings reigning in the neighbourhood of Hastinā-pura (the poem consists of 18 books with a supplement called Hari-vaṇśa, the whole being attributed to the sage Vyāsa), ĀśvGṛ.; MBh. &c. (IW. 370 &c.); *-kūṭôddāra*, m., *-tātparya*, n. (°*parya-nirṇaya*, m. and °*ya-pramāṇa-saṃgraha*, m., °*parya-prakāśa-saṃketa*, m., °*parya-raksha*, f., °*parya-saṃgraha*, m.), *-darpaṇa*, m., *-pañca-ratna*, n. pl., *-mañjarī*, f., *-mīmāṇsā*, f., *-vivaraṇa-stotra*, n., *-vyākhyāna*, n., *-śravaṇa-vidhi*, m., *-ślokôpanyāsa*, m., *-saṃgraha*, m., and °*ha-dīpikā*, f., *-saptati-śloka*, m. pl., *-samuccaya*, m., *-sāra*, m. n., *-sāra-saṃgraha* (?), m., *-sūci*, f., *-sphuṭa-śloka*, m. pl., °*ratâdi-śloka*, m. pl., °*ratâdhyāyânukramaṇī*, f., °*ratôddhṛita-sāra-śloka*, m. pl. N. of wks. — **bhāratika**, m. (prob.) one who knows the Mahā-bhārata, Cat. — **bhāshya**, n. 'Great Commentary,' N. of Patañjali's com° on the Sūtras of Pāṇini and the Vārttikas of Kātyāyana, Prab.; Rājat. &c. (IW. 167); *-kāra*, m. N. of Patañjali, ĀpŚr., Comm.; *-ṭīkā*, f., *-tri-padī*, f. (and °*dī-vyākhyāna*, n.), *-dīpikā*, f., *-prakāśikā*, f., *-pradīpa*, m., *-ratnâvalī*, f., *-vārttika*, n., *-vyākhyā*, f., *-sphūrti*, f. N. of commentaries on the Mahā-bhāshya. — **bhāsura**, mfn. extremely brilliant (said of Vishṇu), MBh. — **bhāskara-ṭīkā**, f. N. of wk. — **bhāsvara**, mfn. = *-bhāsura*, Vishṇ. — **bhikshu**, m. 'gr° monk,' N. of Gautama Buddha, Buddh. — °**bhijana** (°*hâbh*°), m. a high or noble descent; mfn. nobly born, A.; *-jāta*, mfn. of noble d°, Rājat. — °**bhijñā-jñânâbhibhū** (°*hâbh*°), m. N. of a Buddha, Buddh. — °**bhinishkramaṇa** (°*hâbh*°), n. 'the great going forth from home,' N. of Buddha's celebrated abandonment of his own family, MWB. 28; 308. — °**bhimāna** (°*hâbh*°), m. great self-conceit, gr° pride, arrogance, MW. — °**bhiyoga** (°*hâbh*°), m. a gr° accusation, Yājñ. — °**bhishava** (°*hâbh*°), m. the gr° distillation of Soma, ĀpŚr.; KātyŚr., Sch. — °**bhisheka** (°*hâbh*°), m. solemn sprinkling or unction, AitBr.; N. of Kathās. xv; *-prayoga*, m., *-vidhi*, m. N. of wks. — °**bhisyandin** (°*hâbh*°), mfn. generating hypertrophy, Suśr.; Car. (superl. °*di-tama*); °*di-tva* and °*di-tama-tva*, n. state of hyp°, Car. — **bhīta**, mfn. greatly terrified, Pañcar.; (*ā*), f. Mimosa Pudica, L. — **bhīti**, f. great danger or distress, L. — **bhīma**, m. N. of Śāṃtanu, L.; of one of Śiva's attendants, L. — **bhīru**, m. 'very timid,' a sort of dung-beetle, L. — °**bhīśu** (°*hâbh*°), mfn. very brilliant, Mcar. — **bhīshaṇaka**, mfn. causing great distress, exceedingly fearful, MBh.; Hariv.; R. — **bhīshma**, m. N. of Śāṃtanu, L. — **bhuja**, mfn. having long arms, MBh.; R.; Ragh. &c. — **bhūta**, mfn. being great, gr°, MBh.; m. a gr° creature or being, ib.; n. a great element, gross el° (of which 5 are reckoned, viz. ether, air, fire, water, earth, Up.; Nir.; Mn. &c. [cf. IW. 83, 221], as distinguished from the subtle el°s or Tanmātra, q. v.), IW. 221; *-ghaṭa*, m. a jar with a figurative representation of the 5 el°s, Hcat. (w. r. *-dhaṭa*); °*ta-dāna*, n. a kind of religious gift, Cat. — **bhūmi**, f. a gr° country, KaṭhUp.; the whole territory (of a king), Nyāyam. — **bhūmika**, mfn. (?), L. — **bhūshaṇa**, n. a costly ornament, BrahmavP. — **bhṛiṅga**, m. a species of Verbesina with blue flowers, L. — **bherī-hāraka**, m., °**ka-parivarta**, m. N. of certain Buddhist Sūtra wks. — **bhairava**, m. a form of Śiva or Bhairava, Prab.; Cat.; N. of a Liṅga, MW.; mf(*ī*)n. related to or connected with Mahā-bhairava, Prab.; Cat.; *-tantra*, n. N. of a Tantra, Cat. — 1. **-bhoga**, m. (fr. 1. *bhoga*) a great curve or coil, gr° hood (of a snake), gr° winding, MW.; mfn. (a snake) having gr° windings or coils, h° a gr° hood, MBh.; m. a gr° serpent, AshṭâvS.; *-vat*, mfn. having great windings &c., BhP. — 2. -°**bhoga** (°*hâbh*°), mfn. having a wide girth, h° a large compass, Kathās. — 3. **-bhoga**, m. (fr. 2. *bhoga*) gr° enjoyment, Kathās.; mf(*ā*)n. causing gr° enj°; (*ā*), f. N. of Durgā, Pur.; *-vat*, mfn. having gr° enj°s, MW. — **bhogin**, mfn. = 1. *-bhoga-vat*, BhP. — **bhoja**, m. a gr° monarch, BhP.; N. of a king, Pur. — **bhoṭa** or °**ṭa-deśa**, m. Great Tibet, Cat. — **bhauma**, m. N. of a king, MBh. — °**bhra** (°*hâbh*°), n. a great or dense cloud, ŚāṅkhGṛ. — **makha**, m. a great or principal sacrifice, Yājñ.; MBh. (cf. *-yajña*). — **magna**, w. r. for *-nagna* (q. v.), Kāraṇḍ. — **maṅgala**, n. N. of a Buddhist Sūtra. — **mañjushaka**, n. (!) or °**jūshaka**, m. N. of a partic. celestial flower, Buddh. — **maṇi**, m. a costly gem, precious jewel, MBh.; Śak.; BhP.; N. of Śiva, Śivag.; of a king, VP.; *-cūḍa*, m. N. of a serpent-demon, Buddh.; *-dhara*, m. N. of a Bodhi-sattva, Kāraṇḍ.; *-ratna*, m. N. of a fabulous mountain, ib. — **maṇḍapa**, n. N. of a vestibule in a celebrated Śaiva temple, RTL. 447. — **maṇḍala**, m. N. of a king, Buddh.; °*lêśvara*, m. a gr° chief of a province, L. — **maṇḍalika**, m. N. of a Nāga, Buddh. — **maṇḍūka**, m. a kind of large frog, L. — **mata**, mfn. highly esteemed or honoured, MW. — **mati**, mfn. great-minded, having a great understanding, clever, MBh.; R. &c.; m. the planet Jupiter, L.; N. of a king of the Yakshas, Buddh.; of a Bodhi-sattva, ib.; of a son of Su-mati, Kathās.; f. N. of a woman, Cat.; (*ī*), f. a partic. lunar day personified as a daughter of Aṅgiras, MBh. — **matta**, mfn. being in excessive rut (as an elephant), R. — **matsyá**, m. a large fish, ŚBr. — **mada**, m. gr° pride or intoxication, W.; excessive or violent rut (of an elephant), MārkP.; fever, Gal.; an elephant in strong rut, L. — **manas** (*mahā́-*), mfn. gr°-minded, high-m°, magnanimous, RV.; MBh.; R.; Śiś.; arrogant-minded, proud, haughty, ChUp.; MBh.; m. the fabulous animal Śarabha (q. v.), L.; N. of a king, Hariv.; Pur.; *-vin*, m. a partic. Samādhi, Kāraṇḍ. — **manaska**, mfn. = *-manas*, mfn., MW. — **manī**, m. N. of a king, VP. (w. r. for *-maṇi*, q. v.) — **manushya**, m. a man of high rank, Kathās.; N. of a poet, Cat. — **mantra**, m. any very sacred or efficacious text (of the Veda &c.), MW.; a great spell, very eff° charm (used esp. against a serpent's venom), Kād.; Gīt.; °*trâdi-sevā-prakāra*, m. N. of wk.; °*trânusāriṇī*, f. N. of a Buddhist goddess, Buddh.; W. — **mantrin**, m. a chief counsellor, prime minister, Hit.; Kathās.; a gr° statesman or politician, MW. — **mandārava**, m. N. of a partic. celestial plant, Buddh. — **mayūrī**, f. N. of a Buddhist goddess, Dharmas. 5 (= *-māyūrī*, q. v.) — **marakata**, m. a gr° emerald, BhP.; mfn. adorned with gr° em°s, BhP. (v. l. *-mārakata*, q. v.) — **marutvatīya**, m. (with *graha*) a partic. libation consisting of a cupful offered to Indra Marut-vat, ŚrS. — °**marsha** (°*hām*°), mfn. extremely wrathful, BhP. — **malaya-pura**, n. N. of the 7 pagodas hewn out of the rocks near Madras, L. — **mala-harī**, f. a partic. Rāgiṇī, Saṃgīt. — **malla**, m. N. of Kṛishṇa, Hariv. — 1. **-maha**, m. a great festive procession, Siṅhâs. — 2. **-mahá**, mfn. (prob. an old intens. form) very mighty, RV.; (*ā*), f. N. of a constellation, SkandaP.; a species of plant (w. r. for *-sahā*), Car.; (cf. the similar forms *ghanāghana*, *paṭāpaṭa*, *vadāvada*.) — **mahas**, n. a great light (seen in the sky), ŚārṅgP. — **mahiman**, m. excessive greatness, true greatness (°*hima-śālin*, mfn. possessing true gr°), Sāh.; mfn. extremely great, truly great (°*hima-tva*, n.), Pratāp. — **mahi-vrata** (*mahā́-*), mfn. exercising gr° power, RV. — **mahêśvara-kavi**, m. N. of an author, Cat. — **mahêśvarâyatana**, n. a partic. region of the gods, Buddh. — **mahôpâdhyāya**, m. a very great or venerable teacher (a title given to learned men), Hāsy. — **māṇsa**, n. 'costly meat,' N. of various kinds of meat and esp. of human flesh, Mālatim.; Kathās. &c.; (*ī*), f. a kind of little shrub, L.; *-vikraya*, m. selling human fl°, Pañcat. — **māghī**, f. (prob.) the day of full moon in the month Māgha when certain other celestial phenomena also occur, Hcat. — **mātṛi**, f. pl. 'the great mothers,' N. of a class of personifications of the Śakti or female energy of Śiva, RTL. 186; *-gaṇêśvara*, m. N. of Vishṇu, Pañcar. — °**mātya** (°*hām*°), m. the prime minister of a king, Kām.; Rājat. — **mātra**, mfn. great in measure, gr°, the greatest, best, most excellent of (comp.), MBh.; R.; m. a man of high rank, high official, prime minister, ib. &c.; an elephant-driver or keeper, Mn.; MBh.; Hariv. &c.; a superintendent of elephants, W.; (*ī*), f. a spiritual teacher's wife, L.; the wife of a prime minister or high official, great lady, W. — **mānasikā**, f. (with Jainas) N. of one of the 16 Vidyā-devīs, L. — **mānasī**, f. a goddess peculiar to the Jainas, L. — **mānin**, mfn. exceedingly proud, Inscr. — **māndāra**, m. or n. (?) a species of flower, Kāraṇḍ. — **mānya**, mfn. being in great honour with (gen.), Bhām. — **māya**, mf(*ā*)n. having great deceit or illusion, R.; practising gr° d° or ill°

very illusory, R.; Kathās.; m. N. of Vishṇu, Pañcar.; of Śiva, MBh. (RTL. 106); of an Asura, Kathās.; of a Vidyā-dhara, ib.; (*ā*), f. gr° deceit or illusion, the divine power of ill° (which makes the universe appear as if really existing and renders it cognizable by the senses), the illusory nature of worldly objects personified and identified with Durgā, Pur.; N. of a wife of Śuddhodana, Buddh.; (*ī*), f. N. of Durgā, L.; °*yā-dhara*, m. N. of Vishṇu, MBh.; °*yā-śambara* (or °*ra-tantra*), n. N. of a Tantra. — **māyūra**, n. a partic. drug, Car.; (only ifc.) a partic. prayer, Hcar.; (*ī*), f. (with Buddhists) N. of one of the 5 amulets and of one of the 5 tutelary goddesses (cf. *-mayūrī*); °*rī-stotra*, n. N. of a collection of Stotras. — **mārakata**, mf(*ā*)n. richly adorned with emeralds, BhP. (cf. *-marakata*). — **mārī**, f. 'gr° destroying goddess,' a form of Durgā and a spell called from her, Pur.; a pestilence causing great mortality, the cholera, MW. (cf. *mārī*). — **mārga**, m. a gr° road, high road, main street, Kām.; BhP. (cf. *-patha*); *-pati*, m. a superintendent of roads, Rājat. — **māla**, mfn. wearing a gr° garland (said of Śiva), MBh. — **mālikā**, f. a kind of metre, Col. — **māsha**, m. a species of large bean, Suśr. — **māheśvara**, m. a gr° worshipper of Maheśvara or Śiva, Rājat. — **mīna**, m. a large fish, Suśr. — **mukha**, n. a gr° mouth, Var.; the gr° embouchure of a river, Hariv.; mf(*ī*)n. large-mouthed (said of Śiva), MBh.; having a gr° embouchure, KātyŚr.; m. a crocodile, L.; N. of a Jina, Gal.; of a man, MBh. — **mucilinda**, a species of plant, Buddh.; m. N. of a mythical mountain, Kāraṇḍ.; *-parvata*, m. id., Buddh. — **muṇḍanikā** or **-muṇḍī**, f. a kind of Sphaeranthus, L. — **mudrā**, f. a partic. posture or position of the hands or feet (in the practice of Yoga, q. v.), Cat.; a partic. high number, Buddh. — **muni**, m. a gr° Muni or sage, (esp.) N. of a Buddha or Jina, MBh.; R.; BhP. &c.; Zanthoxylon Hastile, L.; N. of Vyāsa, W.; of Agastya, L.; of a Ṛishi in the 5th Manv-antara, VP.; n. the seed of Zanthoxylon H°, L.; Elaeocarpus Ganitrus, L.; any medicinal herb, L.; *-svādhyāya*, m. N. of wk. — **mūḍha**, mfn. very foolish or infatuated; m. a gr° simpleton, Pañcat.; Pañcar.; Kathās. — **mūrkha**, m. a gr° fool, Pañcar. — **mūrti**, mfn. large-formed, gr°-bodied (said of Vishṇu), MBh. — **mūrdhan**, mfn. gr°-headed, large-h° (N. of Śiva), MBh. — **mūla**, n. a large or full-grown radish, Buddh.; a species of onion, L. — **mūlya**, mfn. very costly, L.; m. n. a ruby, L.; (also *ā*, f.) very precious cloth, L. — **mūshaka** or °**shika**, m. a kind of rat, L. — **mṛiga**, m. a large animal, (esp.) any l° wild an°, Vāgbh.; an elephant, R.; the mythical animal Śarabha (q. v.), L. — **mṛityu**, m. the great death, KātyŚr., Sch.; N. of Śiva, L.; °*yuṃ-jaya* (with *lauha*), m. or n. (?) 'conquering gr° death,' a partic. drug, L.; m. N. of a sacred text addressed to Śiva (also °*ya-mantra*, m.), Cat.; °*yuṃ-jaya-kalpa*, m., °*yuṃ-jaya-vidhi*, m., °*yuṃ-jaya-homa*, m., °*yuhara-stotra*, n. N. of wks. — **mṛidha**, n. a gr° battle, MBh.; R.; Kathās. — **megha**, m. a gr° or dense cloud, AitĀr.; MBh.; R.; N. of Śiva, MBh.; of a man, MBh. (v. l. *megha-vega*); *-giri*, m. N. of a mountain, Hariv.; *-nibha-svana*, mfn. = *-svana* below, MW.; *-nivāsin*, m. 'dwelling in thick clouds,' N. of Śiva, MBh.; *-svana*, mfn. sounding like immense thunder-clouds, MBh.; °*ghâugha-nirghosha*, mfn. sounding like a multitude of large th°-cl°s, MW. — **meda**, m. Erythrina Indica, W.; m. (L.) or (*ā*), f. (Suśr.; Bhpr.) a species of medicinal plant. — **medha**, m. a gr° sacrifice, MBh. — **medhā**, f. 'great intelligence,' N. of Durgā, MārkP. — **meru** (*mahā-*), m. the gr° mountain Meru, TĀr.; VP.; N. of a Varsha, MBh.; *-dhara*, m. a partic. Samādhi, Kāraṇḍ. — **maitra**, m. N. of a Buddha, L.; (*ī*), f. great friendship, great attachment, great compassion, Buddh. (cf. Dharmas. 131); °*trī-samādhi*, m. N. of a partic. Samādhi, Buddh. — **moda**, m. a species of jasmine, L. — **moha**, m. great confusion or infatuation of mind, Pur.; Rājat. &c.; (*ā*), f. N. of Durgā, MārkP.; *-mantra*, m. a very efficacious charm (*-tva*, n.), Kathās.; *-svarôttara-tantra*, n. N. of wk. — **mohana**, mfn. very confusing or bewildering, MBh. — **mohin**, m. a thorn-apple, Bhpr. — **maudgalyāyana**, m. N. of a disciple of Buddha, Buddh. — °**mbuka** (°*hâm*°), m. N. of Śiva, L. (perhaps w. r. for *mahâmbu-da*; cf. *-megha*). — °**mbu-ja** (°*hâm*°), n. a partic. high number, a billion; L. — °**mla** (°*hâm*°), mfn. very acid or sour, W.; n. the fruit of the Indian tamarind, L.; acid seasoning, W. — **yaksha**, m. a gr° Yaksha, a chief of the Y°s, R. (cf. *yaksha-pati*); N. of the servant of the second Arhat of the present Avasarpiṇī, L.; pl. a class of Buddhist deities, MW.; (*ī*), f. a gr° female Yaksha, R.; *-senā-pati*, m. a general of the gr° Yaksha; N. of a Tantra deity, Buddh. — **yajña**, m. a great sacrifice or offering, a principal act of devotion (of these there are 5 accord. to Mn. iii, 69–71, viz. *brahma-*, *deva-*, *pitri-*, *manushya-*, and *bhūta-yajña*; cf. IW. 194 &c.; RTL. 411), ŚBr. &c. &c.; N. of Vishṇu, MBh.; pl. (with *pañca*) N. of wk.; *-kratu*, m. = *mahā-yajñá* above, Cat.; *-bhāga-hara*, m. 'receiving a share of the gr° sacr°,' N. of Vishṇu, MBh. — **yati**, m. a gr° ascetic, MārkP. — **yantra**, n. a gr° mechanical work, MBh.; *-pravartana*, n. the engaging in or erecting gr° mech° works, Mn. — **yamá**, m. the gr° Yama, AV. — **yamaka**, n. a verse in which all four Pādas contain words with exactly the same sounds, but different senses (e.g. Kir. xv, 52 or Bhaṭṭ. x, 20). — **yava**, m. a kind of large barley, L. — **yaśas**, mfn. very glorious or renowned or celebrated, MBh.; Hariv.; R. &c.; m. N. of the fourth Arhat of the past Utsarpiṇī, L.; of a learned man, Cat.; f. N. of one of the Mātṛis attending on Skanda, MBh. — **yaśaska**, mfn. = *-yaśas*, mfn., L. — °**yasa** (°*hây*°), mfn. having much iron (as an arrow which has a large point, Nīlak.), MBh. — **yāgika**, m. pl. N. of a school of the Sāma-veda, Divyâv. — **yātrā**, f. a great pilgrimage, the pil° to Benares, MW.; N. of wk. — **yātrika**, m. N. of a man, Hāsy. — **yāna**, n. 'great vehicle' (opp. to *hīna-y*°), N. of the later system of Buddhist teaching said to have been first promulgated by Nāgārjuna and treated of in the Mahā-yāna-sūtras, MWB. 66; 158–160 &c.; m. 'having a gr° chariot,' N. of a king of the Vidyādharas, Kathās.; *-deva*, m. an honorary N. of Hiouen-thsang, Buddh.; *-parigrahaka*, m. a follower of the Mahā-yāna doctrines, ib.; *-prabhāsa*, m. N. of a Bodhi-sattva, ib.; *-yoga-śāstra*, n., *-saṃgraha*, m., *-samparigraha-śāstra*, n. N. of wks.; *-sūtra*, n. N. of the Sūtras of the later Buddhist system, MW.; (°*tra-ratna-rāja*, m. N. of a highly esteemed Mahā-yāna-sūtra, Kāraṇḍ.); °*nâbhidharma-saṃgīti-śāstra*, n. N. of wk. — **yāma**, n. N. of a Sāman, ĀrshBr. — **yāmya**, m. N. of Vishṇu, MBh. — **yuga**, n. a gr° Yuga or Y° of the gods (= 4 Yugas of mortals or the aggregate of the Kṛita, Tretā, Dvāpara and Kali Yugas = 4,320,000 years; a day and a night of Brahmā comprise 2,000 Mahā-yugas), Sūryas. (IW. 178). — °**yuta** (°*hây*°), m. or n. (?) a partic. high number, Buddh. — **yuddha**, n. a gr° fight, MBh. — °**yudha** (°*hây*°), mfn. having great weapons (said of Śiva), MBh. — **yoga-pañcaratne āśvalāyanôpayogyâdhāna-prakaraṇa**, n. N. of wk. — **yogin**, m. a gr° Yogin (N. of Vishṇu or of Śiva, esp. when worshipped by Buddhists, MWB. 215), MBh.; a cock, L. — **yogêśvara**, m. a gr° master of the Yoga system, MBh. — **yoni**, f. excessive dilation of the female organ, ŚārṅgS.; Suśr. (*ati-m*°). — **yaudhājaya**, n. N. of a Sāman, ĀrshBr. — **rakshas**, n. a gr° Rākshasa, Śāntik. — **rakshā**, f. (with Buddhists) a gr° tutelary goddess (5 in number, viz. Mahā-pratisarā or Prat°, Mahā-māyūrī or M°-may°, M°-sahasra-pramardanī or °dinī, M°-śīta-vatī or M°-śeta-v° and M°-mantrânusāriṇī), Buddh.; W. — **rakshita**, m. N. of a man, Buddh. — **raṅga**, m. a large stage, Hariv. — **rajata**, n. gold, R.; MārkP.; m. a thorn-apple, L.; mfn., w. r. for next, mfn., Hariv. — **rajana**, n. the safflower, Daś.; gold, L. (cf. prec.); mfn. coloured with safflower, Hariv.; *-gandhi* or °*dhin*, n. a kind of ruby, L. — **rañjana**, n. the safflower, MBh. (w. r. for *-rajana*). — **raṇa**, m. a gr° battle, ĀpŚr., Sch.; MBh.; Pratāp.; v. l. for *mahī-raṇa*, (q. v.), VP. — °**raṇya** (°*hâr*°), n. a gr° forest, R.; Buddh. — **ratna**, n. a precious jewel, most pr° of all j°s, Kathās.; SaddhP.; Prasaṅg.; *-pratimaṇḍita*, m. N. of a Kalpa or cycle, Buddh.; *-maya*, mfn. consisting of pr° j°s, Kathās.; *-vat*, mfn. adorned with pr° j°s, MBh.; *-varshā*, f. N. of a Tantra deity, Buddh.; °*nâbhisheka-rāma-dhyāna*, n. N. of wk. — **rathá**, m. a gr° chariot, MBh.; R.; a gr° warrior (not a Bahu-vrīhi comp., as shown by the accent; cf. *ratha*, 'a warrior'), VS.; TS.; MBh. &c.; N. of a Rākshasa, R.; of a son of Viśvā-mitra, R.; of a king, MārkP.; Buddh.; of a minister, Rājat.; desire, longing, L. (cf. *mano-ratha*); mfn. possessing gr° chariots, Hariv.; *-tva*, n. the being a gr° warrior, MBh.; *-mañjarī*, f. N. of wk. — **rathyā**, f. (ifc. f. *ā*) a gr° street, high street (with *purī*, a city having large streets), MBh.; R. — °**rambha** (°*hâr*°), m. a gr° undertaking, Subh.; mfn. performing gr° und°s, enterprising, industrious, Kām.; n. a kind of salt, L. — **rava**, mf(*ā*)n. loud-sounding, uttering loud cries, MBh.; Hariv.; MārkP.; m. loud cries or roarings, Hit.; a frog, L.; N. of a Daitya, Hariv. (v. l. *-bala*); of a man, MBh. — **raśmi-jālâvabhāsa-garbha**, m. N. of a Bodhi-sattva, Buddh. — **rasa**, m. 'precious mineral' (N. of 8 metals or minerals used in med°), Cat.; L.; quicksilver, L.; flavour, R.; mfn. having much fl°, very savoury, MBh.; m. a sugar-cane, L.; Phoenix Sylvestris, L.; Scirpus Kysoor, L.; (*ā*), f. Indigofera Tinctoria, L.; Clitoria Ternatea, L.; Evolvulus Alsinoides, L.; n. sour rice-water, L.; *-vatī*, f. 'having much flavour,' a very savoury kind of food, Bharat.; °*sâyana-vidhi*, m. N. of wk. — **rājá**, m. a great king, reigning prince, supreme sovereign, Br. &c. &c.; N. of the moon, MaitrS.; of a partic. deity, MānGṛ. (*-rājan*!); Āpast.; of Kubera, TĀr.; of Vishṇu, BhP.; pl. (with Buddhists) a partic. class of divine beings (the guardians of the earth and heavens against the demons), MWB. 206; a Jina, Gal.; N. of Mañjuśrī, L.; of the successors of Vallabhâcārya (founder of a sect), RTL. 135 &c.; a finger-nail, L.; *-kulīna*, mfn. belonging to a race of gr° kings, R.; *-cūta*, m. a kind of mango, L.; *-druma*, m. Cathartocarpus Fistula, L.; *-nighaṇṭu*, m. N. of wk.; *-phala*, m. a kind of mango, L.; *-miśra*, m. N. of a man, Cat.; °*jâṅgaṇa* (or °*gana*), n. the courtyard in the palace of a reigning prince, R.; °*jâdhirāja*, m. a paramount sovereign, emperor, Kād. — **rājaka**, m. pl. = *-rājika-deva*, pl., L. — **rājika**, m. N. of Vishṇu, MBh.; *-deva*, pl. (with Buddhists) N. of a class of gods (the inhabitants of the lowest heaven), MWB. 206. — **rājñī**, f. a reigning queen, BhP.; N. of Durgā, Kathās.; *-stava*, m. N. of wk. — **rājya**, n. the rank or title of a reigning sovereign, MBh. — **rātra**, n. the time after midnight or near the close of night, (accord. to some also) midn°, ŚāṅkhBr.; ŚrS.; BhP. — **rātri** or °**trī**, f. = prec., L.; the gr° night of the complete destruction of the world, Devīm., Sch.; the 8th day in the light half of the month Āśvina, L.; N. of a festival (kept by the left-hand worshippers on the 14th day of the dark half of Māgha), RTL. 204; °*tri-caṇḍikā-vidhāna*, n. N. of wk.; (only °*trī*), f. N. of a Śakti of Śiva, VP. — **rāmāyaṇa**, n. the great Rāmāyaṇa, Cat. — **rāva**, m. loud cries, Hit. — **rāshṭra**, m. pl. the Marāṭha people, commonly called Mahrattas, Var.; MārkP. &c.; (*ī*), f. (scil. *bhāshā*) the Marāṭhī or Mahratta language, Sāh. &c.; a species of culinary plant, L.; Commelina Salicifolia, L.; n. a gr° kingdom, gr° country, (esp.) the land of the Marāṭhas in the west of India, W.; a kind of metre, Col.; *-varishṭha-bhāshā-maya*, mfn. composed in the excellent language of the Marāṭhas, Siṇhās.; °*traka*, mf(*ikā*)n. belonging to the Marāṭhas, Cat.; (m. pl. the Marāṭhas, Cat.); °*trīya*, mf(*ā*)n. id., Cat. — **rishṭa**, m. a species of tree allied to the Melia Bukayun, L. — **ruj** (ŚārṅgS.) or **-ruja** (Suśr.), mfn. causing gr° pain, very painful. — °**ruṇa** (°*hâr*°), m. N. of a mountain, R. — **rudra**, m. 'gr° Rudra,' a form of Śiva, Cat.; N. of an author (?), Cat.; (*ā*), f. a form of Durgā, Hcat.; (*ī*), f. id., W. (prob. w. r. for *-raudrī*, q. v.); *-karma-kalāpa-paddhati*, f., *-japa-vidhi*, m., *-nyāsa-paddhati*, f., *-paddhati*, f., *-pīṭha-devatā*, f. pl., *-prayoga*, m. (and °*ga-paddhati*, f.), *-vidhi*, m. N. of wks.; *-siṇha*, m. N. of an author, Cat. — **ruru**, m. a species of antelope, MBh. — **rūpa**, mfn. mighty in form (said of Śiva), MBh.; m. N. of a Kalpa or cycle, Buddh.; resin, W.; (*ā*), f. N. of one of Durgā's attendants, W. — **rūpaka**, n. a kind of drama, L. — **rūpin**, mfn. large-formed, great in shape, R. — **retas**, mfn. abounding in seed (N. of Śiva), MBh. — **roga**, m. a severe illness, ĀśvŚr. — **rogin**, mfn. suffering from a severe illness, Pañcar.; KūrmaP. — **roca**, m. or n. (?) a species of plant, Buddh. — **roman**, mfn. having large or thick hair on the body (said of Śiva), MBh.; m. N. of a king, R.; Pur.; of the superior of a Buddhist monastery, Buddh. (w. r. *-roma*; cf. *-loman*). — **romaśa**, mfn. having large or thick hair, Suśr. — **rohi**, m. a species of gr° gazelle, R. — **raudra**, mf(*ā*)n. very terrible, MBh.; MārkP. (*ati-m*°); (*ī*), f. a form of Durgā, Cat. (cf. *-rudrī*). — **raurava**, m. N. of a hell, AitUp.; Śaṃk.; Pur. &c. (one of the 8 hot hells, Dharmas. 121); n. N. of a Sāman, ĀrshBr. — **rauhiṇa**, m. N. of a demon, VarBṛS. — °**rgha** (°*hâr*°), mfn. high-priced, very precious or valuable, MBh.; Kathās. (also °*ghya*, Bharat.); costly, expensive, Bālar.; m. Perdix Chinensis, L.; *-tā*, f. gr° costliness, preciousness, high value, Var.; Śiś.; ŚārṅgP. (also °*ghya-tā*, Rājat.); *-rūpa*, mf(*ā*)n. of splendid form, Kathās. **— °rcis** (°*hâr*°), mfn. having gr° flames, flaming high, MBh. **— °rṇava** (°*hâr*°), m. 'mighty sea,' the ocean, MaitrUp.; R. &c.; N. of Śiva, L.; of sev. wks.; pl. 'dwelling by the ocean,' N. of a people, MārkP.; *-karma-vipāka*, m. N. of wk.; *-nipāna-vid*, m. N. of Śiva, MBh.; *-prakāśa*, m., *-vratârka*, m. N. of wks. **— °rtha** (°*hâr*°), m. a gr° thing, a gr° matter, DevīP.; weighty or important meaning, MW.; mf(*ā*)n. having large substance, rich, VarBṛS.; great, dignified, W.; having gr° meaning, significant, important, weighty, MBh.; R.; m. N. of a Dānava, Kathās.; n. = *mahā-bhāshya* (q.v.), Cat.; *-tā*, f. fullness of meaning or significancy, L.; *-prakāśa*, m., *-mañjarī*, f. N. of wks.; *-vat*, mfn. having gr° meaning, very significant, MBh.; of gr° consequence, very dignified, MW.; °*thaka*, mfn. valuable, L.; rich; having gr° meaning, very important &c., MW. **— °rdraka** (°*hâr*°), n. wild ginger, L. **— °rdha** (°*hâr*°), m. a species of plant, L. **— °rbuda** (°*hâr*°), n. 10 Arbudas = 1000 millions, Jyot. **— °rma** (°*hâr*°), Pāṇ. vi, 2, 90. **— °rya** (°*hâr*°), m. N. of a teacher, Cat.; *-siddhânta*, m. N. of wk. **— °rha** (°*hâr*°), mfn. very worthy or deserving, very valuable or precious, splendid, MBh.; R. &c.; n. white sandal-wood, L. **— lakshmī**, f. the gr° Lakshmī (properly the Śakti of Nārāyaṇa or Vishṇu, but sometimes identified with Durgā or with Sarasvatī; also N. of Dākshāyaṇī in Kara-vīra), Pañcar.; Kathās. (cf. RTL. 385); N. of a girl 13 years old and not arrived at puberty (who represents the goddess Durgā at the D° festival), L.; of a woman, Cat.; a kind of metre, Col.; *-kalpa*, m. N. of wk.; *-tīrtha*, n. N. of a Tīrtha, Cat.; *-nāma-vidhi*, m., *-paddhati*, f., *-ratna-kośa*, m. N. of wks.; *-vilāsa*, m. a partic. drug, L.; *-vrata*, n. a partic. religious observance, Cat.; (°*ta-pūjā*, f.), *-sûkta*, n., *-stotra*, n., *-hṛidaya*, n., (°*ya-stotra*, n.); °*my-ashṭaka*, n. N. of wks. **— °laya** (°*hâl*°), m. a great dwelling, MW.; a gr° temple, gr° monastery, ib.; a temple, W.; a monastery, L.; a place of refuge, sanctuary, asylum, W.; the Loka or world of Brahmā, W.; a tree &c. sacred to a deity, W.; a place of pilgrimage, L.; the gr° Universal Spirit, L.; a partic. half month, Tithyād.; N. of a place, Cat.; of a man, Cat.; (*ā*), f. N. of a partic. festival, the day of the moon's change in the month Bhādra and the last day of the Hindū lunar year, Col.; of a partic. deity, A.; (prob.) n. N. of a Liṅga, Cat.; *-prayoga*, m., *-śrāddha-paddhati*, f. N. of wks. **— lalāṭa**, mfn. having a gr° forehead, R. **— °lasā** (°*hâl*°), f. 'very lazy,' N. of a woman, Cat. **— °li-kaṭabhī**, f., v.l. for *-°di-k°*, q.v., L. **— liṅga**, n. a gr° Liṅga or phallus, Rājat.; N. of a place, Cat.; mfn. having a gr° male organ (N. of Śiva), MBh.; *-yogin*, m., *-śāstrin*, m. N. of authors, Cat. **— līlā-sarasvatī**, f. a form of the goddess Tārā, q.v., Tantras. **— lugi**, m. N. of an astronomer, Cat.; *-paddhati*, f. N. of wk. **— lodha** (W.) or **-lodhra** (L.), m. a species of Symplocos. **— loman**, m. N. of the superior of a Buddhist monastery, Buddh. (w.r. *-loma*; cf. *-roman*). **— lola**, mfn. excessively eager, L.; m. a crow, L. **— loha**, n. 'gr° iron,' magnetic iron, L. **— vaṇśa**, m. 'gr° lineage or race,' N. of a well-known wk. written in Pāli by a monk named Mahānāma in the 5th century, MWB. 65 &c.; mfn. sprung from a gr° race or family, MW.; *-samudbhava*, mfn. spr° or descended fr° a gr° r° or f°, MW.; °*śâvalī*, f. N. of wk.; °*śya*, mfn. springing from a high or noble race, Rājat. **— °vakāśa** (°*hâv*°), mfn. having great space, very spacious or roomy, Kauś. **— vaktra**, mfn. large-mouthed, MBh.; m. N. of a Dānava, Hariv. **— vakshas**, mfn. broad-breasted (said of Śiva), MBh. **— vajraka**, n. (with *taila*) a kind of oil mixed with other ingredients for medical purposes, Suśr. **— vaṭūrin** (*mahā́-*), mfn. very wide (accord. to Sāy.), RV. i, 133, 2. **— vaṇij**, m. a gr° merchant, Kathās. **— vada**, m. 'speaker of gr° words,' proclaimer or teacher of the highest Vedic knowledge, AitBr. (Sāy.) **— vadha** (*mahā́-*), m. a mighty or destructive weapon, dest° thunderbolt, MW.; mfn. carrying a mighty w° or dest° shaft, RV. **— vana**, n. a great forest, MBh.; R.; N. of a forest, L.; of a Buddhist monastery in a f° in Udyāna, Buddh.; mfn. having a gr° forest, Vop.; *-saṃghārāma*, m. N. of a Buddhist monastery, Buddh. **— vandhyā**, f. a wholly barren woman, Pañcar. **— vapa**, m. a species of plant, L. **— varā**, f. Dūrvā grass, L. **— varāha**, m. 'great boar,' N. of Vishṇu in his boar incarnation, Ragh.; of a king, Kathās.; of a wk. (cf. *-vārāha*). **— °varoha** (°*hâv*°), m. Ficus Infectoria, L. **— vartana**, n. high wages, large pay or allowance, W. **— varti**, f. a large wick, Vishṇ. **— valli**, f. a large climbing-plant, Kathās; Gaertnera Racemosa, L. **— vasa**, m. Delphinus Gangeticus, L. **— vasu** (*mahā́-*), mfn. possessing much substance, very wealthy, RV. **— vastu**, n. N. of a non-canonical work of northern Buddhism, MWB. 70. **— vākya**, n. any long continuous composition or literary wk. (*-tva*, n.), Sāh.; a principal sentence, gr° proposition, N. of 12 sacred utterances of the Upanishads (e.g. *tat tvam asi*, *aham brahmâsmi* &c., esp. of the mystic words *Tattvam* and *Om*), Vedântas.; Cat.; N. of an Upanishad; *-ṭippaṇa*, m. or n. (?), *-darpaṇa*, m., *-nirṇaya*, m., *-nyāsa*, m., *-pañcī-karaṇa*, n., *-mantrôpadeśa-paddhati*, f., *-muktâvalī*, f., *-ratnâvalī* or °*lī*, f., *-rahasya*, n., *-vicāra*, m., *-vivaraṇa*, n., *-viveka*, m., *-vivekârtha-sâkshi-vivaraṇa*, n., *-vyākhyā*, f., *-siddhânta*, m.; °*kyârtha*, m. (and m. pl. with *atharva-vedīyāḥ*, also °*tha-darpaṇa*, m., °*tha-prabandha*, m., °*tha-prabodha*, m., °*tha-vicāra*, m.), °*kyôpanishad*, f. N. of wks. **— vāta**, m. a gr° or stormy wind, Kām.; *-vyādhi*, m. a gr° or severe nervous disorder, Suśr.; *-samūha*, m. a tempest, MBh. **— vātsapra**, n. N. of a Sāman, ĀrshBr. **— vādin**, m. a gr° controversialist, Buddh. **— vāmadevya**, n. N. of a Sāman, ĀrshBr. **— vāyu**, m. a tempestuous wind, gale, Bhāshāp.; air (as one of the five elements), MW. **— vārāha**, m. N. of wk. (cf. *-varāha*). **— vāruṇī**, f. the festival on the 13th day of the moon's decrease in the month Caitra, SkandaP. **— vārttika**, n. 'great Vārttika or critical commentary,' N. of Kātyāyana's Vārttikas on the Sūtras of Pāṇini (cf. *mahâv*°). **— vārshikā**, f. a species of plant, Buddh. **— vāla-bhid**, m. N. of a Maharshi and of a transposition of Pādas in reciting the Vālakhilya (invented by him), AitBr.; Sāy.; ĀśvŚr. **— vāstu**, n. gr° space, Bhpr.; mfn. occupying gr° sp°, ib. **— vāhana**, m. or n. (?) a partic. high number, Buddh. **— vikrama**, mfn. very valorous or courageous, L.; m. N. of a lion, Hit.; of a Nāga, Buddh. **— vikramin**, m. N. of a Bodhi-sattva, Buddh. **— vighna**, m. or n. a gr° obstacle, MānGṛ.; R. **— vijña**, mfn. very wise or intelligent, Buddh. **— viḍa**, n. a kind of factitious salt, Cat. **— vidagdha**, mfn. very clever, L. **— videha**, n. N. of a mythical country, Campak.; Śatr.; (*ā*), f. (with *vṛitti*, in the Yoga system) N. of a certain condition of the Manas or mind, Cat. **— vidyā**, f. a gr° or exalted science, MW.; N. of Lakshmī, VP. (= *viśva-rūpôpāsanā*, Comm.); of Durgā, MārkP.; of a Mantra, Cat.; pl. of a class of personifications of the Śakti or female energy of Śiva (10 in number), RTL. 187; *-dīpa-kalpa*, m., *-prakaraṇa*, n., *-prayoga*, m., *-sāra-candrôdaya*, m., *-stava*, m., *-stotra*, n. N. of wks.; °*yêśvarī*, f. N. of a goddess (perhaps a form of Durgā), Cat. **— vidyut-prabha**, m. N. of a Nāga, Buddh. **— vipulā**, f. a kind of metre, Piṅg., Sch. **— vibhāshā**, f. a general alternative, a rule containing a gen° alt°, MW.; *-śāstra*, n. N. of wk. **— vibhūta**, m. or n. (?) a partic. high number, Buddh. **— vibhūti**, f. manifestation of gr° might, excessive might, BhP.; the gr° goddess of welfare, Lakshmī, BhP.; mfn. possessing gr° might, MBh. (said of Vishṇu); BhP. **— viraha**, m. a gr° separation, Pracaṇḍ. **— virāva**, mf(*ā*)n. loud-sounding, l°-crying, l°-roaring, Ragh. **— vivāha**, m. or n. (?) a partic. high number, Buddh. **— viśishṭa**, mfn. said to be for *mahad-v*°, 'distinguished among the great,' Pāṇ. vi, 3, 46, Vārtt. 1, Pat. **— visha**, n. 'gr° poison,' a kind of p°, Suśr.; mfn. very poisonous or venomous, R.; Suśr.; m. Coluber Naga, L. **— vishuva**, n. (VP., or °*va-saṃkrānti*, f., MW.) the vernal equinox, the moment of the sun's passing into Aries (differing by sev. days from European computation). **— vishṇu**, m. the great Vishṇu, RāmatUp.; Cat. (esp. N. of Vishṇu when worshipped by Buddhists, MWB. 215); N. of Kapila, L.; *-pūjā-paddhati*, f., *-stuti-ṭīkā*, f.; °*ṇor mahā-stuti*, f. N. of wks. **— vistara**, mfn. very extensive or copious, Bhartṛ. **— vihāra**, m. a gr° Buddhist monastery, Buddh.; N. of a Bud° mon° in Ceylon, ib.; *-vāsin*, m. pl. N. of a Bud° sect, ib. **— vīci**, m. N. of a hell, Mn. **— vīṇā**, f. a kind of lute, Lāṭy. **— °vīta** (°*hâv*°), m. N. of a son of Savana, Pur.; n. N. of the Varsha ruled by that king, VP.; (v.l. *-vīra*). **— vīrá**, m. a gr° hero, RV.; Kathās.; Tantras.; N. of Vishṇu, DhyānabUp.; an archer, bowman, L.; a lion, L.; N. of Garuḍa (the bird and vehicle of Vishṇu), L.; of Hanumat, A.; of Gautama Buddha, MWB. 23; sacrificial fire, BhP.; a sacrif° vessel, ŚBr.; thunderbolt, L.; a white horse, L.; the Indian cuckoo, L.; a kind of hawk, W.; Helminthostachys Laciniata, L.; = *jarāṭaka*, L.; N. of sev. kings, MBh.; R.; Pur.; of the last Arhat of the present Avasarpiṇī (the last and most celebrated Jaina teacher of the present age, supposed to have flourished in Behar in the 6th century B.C.), MWB. 529; (*ā*), f. a species of bulbous plant, L.; *-carita*, n. 'the exploits of the gr° hero (Rāma),' N. of a celebrated drama by Bhavabhūti, IW. 502; *-caritra*, n. = prec.; N. of another wk.; °*rânanda*, m. or n. (?) N. of a drama. **— vīrya** (*mahā́-*), mfn. of gr° strength or energy, very powerful, v° potent, v° efficacious, ŚBr.; MBh.; R. &c.; m. yam, L.; N. of Brahmā, W.; of Indra in the 4th Manv-antara, MārkP.; of a Buddha, L.; of a Jina, MW.; of sev. kings, R.; Pur.; of a Bhikshu, Buddh.; (*ā*), f. (only L.) the wild cotton-shrub; = *mahā-śatāvarī*, L.; N. of Saṃjñā (the wife of Sūrya); *-parākrama*, mfn. of gr° power and heroism, MBh. **— vṛikshá**, m. a gr° tree, AV.; TāṇḍyaBr. &c.; a species of Euphorbia, Suśr.; Car.; = *-pīlu* (q.v.), L.; *-kshīra*, m. n. the milky juice of the above tree, Suśr.; *-gala-skandha*, mfn. one whose neck and shoulders resemble corresponding parts of a gr° tree, MBh. **— vṛiddha**, mfn. very old or aged, R. **— vṛinda**, n. a partic. high number (= 100,000 Vṛindas), R. **— vṛishá**, m. a gr° bull, Rājat.; Phaseolus Radiatus, L.; pl. N. of a people, AV.; ChUp. **— vega**, mf(*ā*)n. greatly agitated (as the sea), R.; moving swiftly, flowing rapidly, flying sw°, very fleet or swift or rapid, MBh.; m. an ape, L.; the bird Garuḍa, L.; (*ā*), f. N. of one of the Mātṛis attending on Skanda, MBh.; *-labdha-sthāma*, m. N. of a king of the Garuḍas, Buddh.; *-vatī*, f. a species of plant, Suśr. **— vedânta-shaṭka**, n. N. of wk. **— vedi**, f. the gr° Vedi or altar i.e. the whole V°, ŚrS. **— vedha**, m. a partic. position of the hands or feet (in the practice of Yoga), Cat. **— vela**, mfn. having high tides or strong currents, billowy, surgy, MBh. **— vaipulya**, n. gr° magnitude, wide extent, Lalit.; *-sūtra*, n. N. of a Buddhist Sūtra wk. **— vaira**, n. gr° enmity, Kām. **— vairāja**, n. N. of a Sāman, Gaut.; (*ī*), f. a partic. religious observance (Ishṭi), ĀśvŚr. **— vaila-stha** (*mahā́-*), mfn. (perhaps) abiding in a very remote hiding-place, RV. i, 133, 3. **— vaiśvadeva** (*mahā́-*), m. N. of a Graha (q.v.), VS.; ŚBr.; KātyŚr. **— vaiśvānara-vrata**, n. N. of two Sāmans, ĀrshBr. **— vaiśvāmitra**, n. N. of two Sāmans, Br. **— vaishṭambha**, n. N. of a Sāman, ĀrshBr. **— vyasana-saptaka**, n. collection of seven vices (viz. *mṛigayā*, *aksha*, *strī*, *pāna*, *vāk-pārushya*, *artha-dūshaṇa*, and *daṇḍa-pārushya*), L. **— vyādhi**, m. a gr° or severe disease, Suśr.; the black leprosy, MW. **— vyāhṛiti**, f. the gr° Vyāhṛiti (q.v.), N. of the mystical formula *bhūr bhuvaḥ svàḥ*, ShaḍvBr.; GṛŚrS.; Nir. &c. **— vyutpatti**, f. N. of a Sanskṛit-Tibetan lexicon. **— vyūha**, m. N. of a Samādhi, Buddh.; of a Deva-putra, Lalit. **— vraṇa**, n. a serious wound, Vārāhīt. **— vratá**, n. a gr° duty, fundamental duty (5 in number, accord. to the Jaina system), HYog.; Yogas.; a gr° vow, Sāh.; a gr° religious observance, R.; Pur.; N. of a Sāman or Stotra appointed to be sung on the last day but one of the Gavām-ayana (applied also to the day itself or its ceremonies or, accord. to Comm., to the Śastra following the Stotra), AV.; Br.; TS. &c.; the relig° usages of the Pāśupatas, Prab., Sch.; W.; mf(*ā*)n. one who has undertaken solemn religious duties or vows, performing a gr° vow, MBh.; R. &c.; observing the rule of the Pāśupatas; also used to explain *máhi-vrata* (q.v.), Nir.; Sāy.; m. a Pāśupata, Kathās.; N. of a poet, Cat.; *-dhara*, mfn. one who has undertaken gr° religious duties or vows, BhP.; *-paddhati*, f., *-prayoga*, m. (and °*gânukrama*, m.), *-bhāshya*, n. N. of wks.; *-vat* (*-vratá-*), mfn. connected with the Mahā-vrata Sāman &c., TS.; KātyŚr., Sch.; *-vesha-bhṛit*, mfn. wearing the dress of a Pāśupata, Kathās.; *-hautra*, n. N. of wk. **— vratika**, mfn. related to the Mahā-vrata Sāman &c., ŚāṅkhŚr.; observing the rule of the Pāśupatas, a Pāśupata, Kathās.; (v.l., and perhaps more correctly *māhāv*°); *-vesha*, mfn. dressed as a Pāś°, Kathās. **— vratin**, mfn. practising the five fundamental duties of Jainas, observing the rule of the Pāś°s, Kathās.; Rājat.; Daś.; m. a Pāś°, ib.; N. of Śiva, L.; a devotee, ascetic (= *joṭiṅga*), L.; = *uraskaṭa* (?), L. **— vratīya**, mfn. relating to the Mahā-

vrata Sāman or to the Mahā-vrata day, Kāṭh.; Br. — **vrāta** (*mahā-*), mfn. accompanied by a gr° host (of Maruts; said of Indra), RV. — **vrīhi** (*mahā-*), m. large rice, TS.; AitBr. &c.; *-maya*, mfn. consisting of large rice, Hcat. — **°śa** (°*hāśa*), m. N. of a son of Kṛishṇa, BhP. — **śakuni**, m. N. of a Cakra-vartin, Buddh. — **śakti**, mfn. very powerful or mighty (said of Śiva), Śivag.; m. N. of Kārttikeya, L.; of a son of Kṛishṇa, BhP.; of a poet, Cat.; *-nyāsa*, m. N. of wk. — **śakya**, m., w.r. for *-śākya* (q.v.), Rājat. — **śaṅku**, m. the sine of the sun's elevation, Siddhāntaś. — **śaṅkha**, m. a great conch-shell, MBh.; the temporal bone, L.; a human bone, L.; a partic. high number (= 10 Nikharvas), L.; one of Kubera's treasures, L.; N. of a serpent-demon, BhP.; m. n. the frontal bone, L.; *-maya*, mf(*ī*)n. formed of temporal bones, L.; *-mālā-saṃskāra*, m. N. of wk. — **śaṭha**, m. a species of thorn-apple, L. — **śaṇa-pushpikā**, f. a species of plant, L. — **śata-koṭi**, f. N. of wk. — **śatā** or **-śatāvarī**, f. a species of plant, Bhpr. — **°śana** (°*hāś°*), mf(*ā*)n. eating much, voracious, a great eater, Nir.; MBh.; Suśr. &c.; m. N. of an Asura, BhP. — **°śani-dhvaja** (°*hāś°*), m. a banner with a gr° thunderbolt delineated on it, Ragh. — **śaphara**, m. a species of carp, Bhpr. — **śabda**, m. a gr° noise, loud sound, loud cry, MBh.; Kathās.; the word *mahā*, MBh.; Tithyād.; any official title beginning with the word *mahā* (5 such titles are enumerated), Inscr.; Rājat.; mf(*ā*)n. very noisy or loud, Kathās. — **śamī**, f. a large Acacia Suma, Pañcat. — **śambhu**, m. the gr° Śiva, Cat. — **°śaya** (°*hāś°*), m. 'great receptacle,' the ocean, L.; mfn. having a noble disposition, high-minded, magnanimous, noble, liberal, open, unsuspicious, AshṭāvS.; Hit.; Kathās. &c.; m. a respectable person, gentleman (sometimes a term of respectful address = Sir, Master), MW. — **śayana**, n. a gr° or lofty bed or couch, Buddh. — **śayyā**, f. a gr° or lofty or splendid couch, Bhartṛ. — **śara**, m. a species of reed, L. — **śarīra**, mfn. having a gr° body, Suśr. — **śarman**, m. N. of an author, Cat. — **śalka**, m. 'large-scaled,' a kind of prawn or sea crab, Mn.; Yājñ.; (*ā*), f. a kind of sweet citron, L. — **śalkalin**, mfn. large-scaled (a fish), Kull. on Mn. iii, 272. — **śastra**, n. a powerful weapon, MBh. — **śāka**, n. a kind of vegetable, Yājñ. — **śākya**, m. a gr° or noble Śākya, Lalit.; Rājat. — **śākha**, mfn. having gr° branches, L.; (*ā*), f. a gr° traditional recension of a Vedic text, L.; Uraria Lagopodioides, L. — **śānti**, f. an expiatory observance and recitation (for averting evil), GṛS.; VarBṛS. (also °*ti*, m. c.); N. of two wks.; *-nirūpaṇa*, n., *-paddhati*, f., *-viniyoga-mālā*, f. N. of wks. — **śāmbavaka**, m. N. of a man, ŚāṅkhGṛ. — **śārīrakôpanishad**, f. N. of an Upanishad. — **śāla**, m. a gr° Vatica Robusta, R. (*su-m°*); (*mahā-*), the possessor of a large house, a gr° householder, ŚBr.; Up. &c.; N. of a son of Janam-ejaya, Hariv. (cf. *-śīla*). — **śāli**, m. a kind of large rice, Suśr. — **śālīna**, mfn. very modest, BhP. — **śālvana**, n. 'gr° fomentation,' N. of a remedy, ŚārṅgS. — **śāsana**, n. gr° rule or dominion, Bhartṛ. (v.l.); gr° edict or order of government, MW.; mfn. exercising gr° dom°, having gr° power, Dhūrtas.; m. (perhaps) a minister who enforces the royal edicts, MW. — **śimbī**, f. a species of Dolichos, L. — **śiras**, mfn. large-headed, L.; m. a kind of serpent, Suśr.; a species of lizard, ib.; N. of a Dānava, MBh.; of a man, ib.; °*raḥ-samudbhava*, m. (with Jainas) N. of the 6th black Vāsudeva, L.; °*ro-dhara*, see *mahā-kāya-ś°*. — **śilā**, f. a kind of weapon (a Śata-ghnī with iron nails), L. — **śiva**, m. the gr° Śiva, Pañcar.; BrahmavP.; *-rātri*, f. N. of a festival (= *mahā-rātri*, q.v.); °*tri-nirṇaya*, m., °*tri-vrata*, n. (and °*ta-nirṇaya*, m.), °*try-udyāpana*, n. N. of wks. — **śīta-vatī**, f. (with Buddhists) N. of one of the 5 gr° tutelary goddesses (see *mahā-rakshā*), Buddh.; (*mahā-śetav° v.l.*) — **śītā**, f. Asparagus Racemosus, L. — **śīrsha**, m. N. of one of Siva's attendants, L. — **śīla**, m. N. of a son of Janam-ejaya, BhP. (cf. *-śāla*). — **śukti**, f. a pearl muscle, mother of p°, L. — **śuklā**, f. N. of Saras-vatī, L. — **śubhra**, n. silver, L. — **śūdra**, m. a Śūdra in a high position, an upper servant, Kauś.; a cowherd, Pāṇ. iv, 1, 4, Vārtt. 1, Pat.; (*ā*), f. = *mahatī śūdrā*, ib.; (*ī*), f. a female cow-keeper, (or) a cowherd's wife, ib.; L. — **śūnya**, n. 'great vacuity or vacancy,' N. of a partic. mental condition of a Yogin, Cat.; *-tā*, f. (with Buddhists) 'gr° void,' N. of one of the 18 vacuities or vacancies, Dharmas.
41 — **śriṅga**, m. a species of stag, L. — **śetavatī**, f. = *-śīta-vatī* above. — **śairīsha**, n. N. of two Sāmans, ĀrshBr. — **śaila**, m. a gr° rock or mountain, Bhartṛ.; N. of a m°, MārkP. — **śaiva-tantra**, n. N. of wk. — **śoṇa**, m. 'gr° Śoṇa,' N. of a river, MBh. — **śauṇḍī**, f. a species of Achyranthes, L. — **śaushira**, see *-saushira*. — **°śman** (°*hāś°*), m. a precious stone, Kir. — **śmaśāna**, n. a gr° cemetery or place for burning the dead, Kathās.; N. of the city of Benares (whither Hindūs are in the habit of going to die), Kāśīkh. — **śyāmā**, f. Ichnocarpus Frutescens, Suśr.; Dalbergia Sissoo, L. — **°śrama** (°*hāś°*), m. 'gr° hermitage,' N. of a sacred hermitage, MBh. — **śramaṇa**, m. 'gr° religious mendicant,' N. of Gautama Buddha, L.; a Jina, Gal. — **śrāvaka**, m. a gr° Śrāvaka or disciple (of Gautama Buddha or of a Jina), Lalit.; HYog. — **śrāvaṇikā**, f. a species of medicinal drug, L. — **śrāvaṇī**, f. a species of plant, (perhaps) Sphaeranthus Indicus, Suśr. — **śrī**, f. N. of Lakshmī, W.; of a Buddhist goddess, L. — **śruti**, m. N. of a Gandharva, Hariv. — **śrotriya**, m. a gr° theologian, ChUp.; BhP. — **ślakshṇā**, f. sand, L. (v.l.) — **°śva** (°*hāś°*), m. N. of a man, MBh.; *-śālā*, f. the principal royal stables or office of superintending them, Rājat. — **śvāsa**, m. 'great breathing or difficulty of br°,' a kind of asthma, Suśr.; ŚārṅgS.; *-sārin*, m. or n. (with *lauha*) a partic. preparation of iron, L. — **śveta**, mfn. very white, of a dazzling whiteness, L.; (*ā*), f. a species of plant, Suśr.; Batatas Paniculata, L.; Clitoria Ternatea, L.; a species of Achyranthes, L.; white or candied sugar, L.; N. of Durgā, DevīP.; of Sarasvatī, L.; of a goddess, Hcar. (accord. to some = *ravi-stha-devatā*); of a woman, Kād.; *-ghaṇṭī*, f. a species of plant, L. — **shaṭ-taila**, n. a partic. mixture, Bhpr. — **shashṭhī**, f. a form of Durgā, Tantras. — **shoḍhā-nyāsa**, m. (with Kaulikas) N. of a partic. position of the hands and feet, Cat.; of wk. — **°shṭamī** (°*hāsh°*), f. 'gr° 8th,' the 8th day in the light half of the month Āśvina (or festival in honour of Durgā, called D°-pūjā), KālP.; Cat.; *-nirṇaya*, m. N. of wk.; *-saṃdhi-pūjā*, f. the festival mentioned above, Col. — **saṃsṛishṭa**, m. N. of a mythical mountain, Kāraṇḍ. — **saṃhitā**, f. gr° connexion or combination, TUp. — **saṃkaṭa**, mfn. very intricate or difficult, full of great difficulties, very troublesome, MW.; n. a great danger or distress, Bhartṛ. — **saṃkalpa**, m. N. of wk. — **saṃkrānti**, f. 'gr° passing,' the sun's entrance into Capricorn, the winter solstice, MW. — **saṃghika**, w.r. for *-sāṃghika*, q.v. — **saṃjñā**, f. a partic. high number, Buddh. — **satī**, f. a highly virtuous or faithful woman, any w° who is a pattern of conjugal fidelity, Pañcat.; Hit.; Vet. — **sato-bṛihatī**, f. (RPrāt.; RAnukr.) and **-sato-mukhā**, f. (RPrāt.) two kinds of metre. — **sat-tā**, f. absolute being, abs° existence, RāmatUp. — **sattrá**, n. a gr° Soma sacrifice, a gr° festival on which S° is offered, ŚBr.; KātyŚr.; Āpast. — **sat-tva**, m. a gr° creature, large animal, MBh.; n. = *-sat-tā* above, Up.; mfn. steady, constant (see *-tā* below); having a gr° or noble essence, noble, good (of persons; with Buddhists, N. of a Bodhi-sattva), MBh.; R. &c.; extremely courageous, MBh.; Kathās.; containing large animals (see *-tā* below); m. a Buddha, L.; N. of Kubera, L.; of Gautama Buddha as heir to the throne, Buddh.; *-tā*, f. 'constancy of character' and 'the containing large animals,' Kāv.; *-vadha*, m. the killing of a gr° creature or large animal, R. — **satya**, m. N. of Yama, L. — **°sana** (°*hās°*), n. a splendid seat, MBh.; Kathās.; *-paricchada*, mfn. amply supplied with seats and furniture, MW. — **saṃdhi-vigraha**, m. the office of prime minister of peace and war, Rājat. (cf. *-sāṃdhivigrahika*). — **sanna**, m. N. of Kubera, L. (cf. *-sat-tva*). — **sanni**, m. (in music) a kind of measure, Saṃgīt. — **saptamī**, f. 'gr° 7th,' N. of a partic. 7th day, W. — **sabhā**, f. a large (dining) hall, Kathās. — **sama**, m. pl. N. of a school of the Sāma-veda, Divyâv. — **samaṅgā**, f. a species of plant, L. — **samaya**, m. or n. (?) N. of a Buddhist Sūtra. — **samāpta**, m. or n. (?) a partic. high number, Buddh. — **samudra**, m. 'great sea,' the ocean, Var. — **sambhava**, m. N. of a Buddhist world, Buddh. — **sammata**, m. 'highly honoured,' (with Buddhists) N. of the first king of the present age of the world; of a Turkish chief, Buddh. — **sammatīya**, m. pl. N. of a Buddhist school, Buddh. — **sammohana** or °**na-tantra**, n. 'greatly bewildering,' N. of a Tantra. — **sarasvatī**, f. the gr° Sarasvatī, Cat.; *-dvādaśa-nāma-stotra*, n., *-sūkta*, n., *-stava-rāja*, m., *-stotra*, n. N. of wks. — **saroja**, n. (with Buddhists) a partic. high number (= *mahāmbu-ja*), L. — **sarga**, m. a gr° or completely new creation (after a complete destruction of the world), Col. — **sarja**, m. Terminalia Tomentosa, L.; Artocarpus Integrifolia, L. — **sarpa**, m. 'gr° serpent,' N. of the Darvī-kara snake; n. N. of sev. Sāmans, ĀrshBr. — **saha**, mfn. much-enduring, bearing much, W.; m. Rosa Moschata, L.; (*ā*), f. N. of various plants, Car.; Suśr. (Gomphraena Globosa, Glycine Debilis, L.; Wrightia Antidysenterica &c., L.) — **sahasra-nāman**, n. a list of 1000 names of Rāma from the Rudray. — **sahasra-pramardana**, n. N. of a Sūtra, Buddh.; (*ī*), f. N. of one of the 5 gr° tutelary goddesses, Buddh. — **sahasra-pramardinī**, f. = prec. f., W. — **sāgara-prabhā-gambhīra-dhara**, m. N. of a king of the Garuḍas, Buddh. — **sāṃkhyāyana**, m. N. of a teacher, Cat. — **sāṃghika**, m. pl. N. of a Buddhist school, Buddh. (w. r. *-saṃghika*; cf. MWB. 157). — **sādhana-bhāga**, m. a great executive minister or officer of state, Rājat. — **sādhu**, mfn. very good, Buddh.; (*vī*), f. = *-satī* (q.v.), Kathās. — **sāṃtapana**, m. 'greatly tormenting,' a kind of severe penance (viz. subsisting for 6 successive days respectively on cow's urine, cow-dung, milk, curds, ghee and water in which Kuśa grass has been boiled, and fasting on the 7th; or instead of 1 day some authorities assign a period of 3 days to each penance, considering the first kind as the common Sāṃtapana [Mn. xi, 212]; others omit the 6th and 7th penance, making the whole last 15 days), Yājñ. — **sāṃdhivigrahika**, m. the prime minister of peace and war, Inscr. (cf. *-saṃdhi-vigraha*). — **sāman**, n. a great Sāman, L.; °*ma-rāja*, n. N. of a Sāman. — **sāmanta**, m. a great vassal, Inscr. — **sāmānya**, n. the widest universality, generality in the broadest sense, Sarvad. — **sāra**, mfn. 'having gr° sap or vigour,' firm, strong, R.; Mālav.; valuable, precious, R.; m. a tree akin to the Acacia Catechu, L.; n. N. of a city, Buddh. — **sārathi**, m. 'gr° charioteer (of the sun),' N. of Aruṇa or the Dawn, L. — **sārtha**, m. a gr° caravan, MBh. — **sāvetasa**, n. N. of two Sāmans, ĀrshBr. — **sāhasa**, n. excessive violence, gr° cruelty or outrage, brutal assault, W.; extreme audacity, MW. — **sāhasika**, mfn. extremely daring or foolhardy, one who goes to work very rashly, Sarvad.; m. a robber, Yājñ.; Pañcat.; an assaulter, violator, W.; *-tā*, f. great boldness or daring, MW.; gr° energy; (*ayā*), ind. in a very decided manner, Pañcat. — **sāhasin**, mfn. = *-sāhasika*, mfn. (q.v.), BhP. — **°si** (°*hāsi*), m. a large scimitar or sword, W. — **siṃha**, m. a gr° lion, R.; MārkP.; the fabulous animal Sarabha, L.; N. of two princes, Cat.; Inscr.; *-gati*, mfn. having the gait or bearing of a noble lion (said of Yudhi-shṭhira), MBh. (cf. IW. 381, n. 1); *-tejas*, m. N. of a Buddha, Lalit. — **sitā**, f. a species of Crotolaria, L. — **siddha**, m. 'very perfect,' a great saint, perfect Yogin, W.; °*dhānta*, m. N. of the younger Āryabhaṭa's wk. on astronomy. — **siddhi**, f. 'great perfection,' a partic. form of magical power, Prab.; Śāntiś. &c. — **sukha**, m. 'having gr° joy,' a Buddha, L.; n. 'gr° pleasure,' copulation, L. — **su-gandha**, mfn. very fragrant, L.; (*ā*), f. a species of plant, Suśr.; Piper Chaba, L.; = *sarpākshī*, L.; n. a fragrant unguent, Dhanv. — **su-gandhi**, m. a kind of antidote, Suśr. — **su-darśana**, m. N. of a Cakravartin, Buddh. — **sundarī-tantra**, n. N. of wk. — **suparṇá**, m. a gr° bird, ŚBr. — **su-bhiksha**, n. great abundance of food, good times, Rājat. (pl.) — **°sura** (°*hās°*), m. a gr° Asura, MBh.; R. &c.; N. of a Dānava, Hariv.; (*ī*), f. a gr° female demon, MBh.; N. of Durgā, MārkP. — **suhayá**, m. a high-spirited horse, ŚBr. — **sûkta**, n. a gr° hymn, AitBr.; pl. the gr° hymns of the 10th Maṇḍala of the Ṛig-veda (i. e. 1–128), ib.; m. the composer of the gr° h°s (of the 10th Maṇḍ°), GṛS.; *-vidhāna*, n. N. of wk. — **sūkshma**, mfn. very fine or minute or subtle, L.; (*ā*), f. sand, L. — **sūci**, m. (with *vyūha*) a partic. mode of arraying troops in battle, Kathās. — **sūta**, m. a military drum, W. — **setu**, m. 'gr° bridge,' N. of certain sacred syllables pronounced before a partic. mystical formula, Cat. — **sena** (*mahā-*), mfn. having a great army, RV. (Sāy.); MBh.; m. the commander of a large force, a general, W.; N. of Kārttikeya or Skanda, TĀr.; MānGṛ.; MBh. &c.; of Śiva, MBh.; the father of the 8th Jina of the present era, W.; N. of various sovereigns, Kathās.; (*ā*), f. a gr° army, Vas.; *-nareśvara*, m. N. of the father of the 8th Arhat of the present Avasarpiṇī, L. (cf. *mahasena-n°*); °*nā-vyūha-parākrama*, m. N. of a Yaksha, Buddh. — **soma**, m. a species of Soma plant, Suśr. — **saukhya**, mfn. feeling intense delight,

Sūryapr. **—saura**, n. N. of two wks. **—saushira**, m. a kind of scurvy in the mouth, Suśr. **—skandha**, m. 'large-shouldered, high-sh°,' a camel, W.; (*ā*), f. 'having a strong stem,' Eugenia Jambolana, L. **—skandhin**, m. the fabulous animal Śarabha, L. **—stūpa**, m. 'great Stūpa or pile,' a great Buddhist structure for containing relics, Buddh. **—stotra**, n. the great Stotra, Vait. **—stoma**, mfn. having a great Stoma, AitBr. **—°stra** (°*hâs*°), n. a gr° or powerful missile, p° bow, MuṇḍUp.; MBh.; Kathās. **—sthalī**, f. 'gr° ground,' the earth, L. **—sthavira**, m. 'gr° elder,' N. of a class of monks among Buddhists, MWB. 255. **—sthāna**, n. a high position or station, lofty rank, MBh.; *-prâpta*, m. (prob. w. r. for next) N. of a Bodhi-sattva, Buddh. **—sthāma-prâpta**, m. N. of a Bodhi-sattva, Buddh.; of Buddha, Lalit. **—sthāla**, m. or n.(?) a species of plant, Buddh. **—sthūla**, mfn. very coarse or gross, L. **—snāna**, n. a gr° washing, Hcat. **—snāyu**, m. a gr° artery, L. **—sneha**, m. combination of the 4 kinds of fat, Bhpr. **—°spada** (°*hâs*°), mfn. 'having a gr° position,' mighty, powerful, Hariv. **—smṛiti**, f. gr° tradition, MBh.; N. of Durgā, MārkP.; *-maya*, mf(*ā*, m.c.)n. containing gr° traditions, Hariv.; °*ty-upasthāna*, n. N. of a Buddhist Sūtra. **—°sya** (°*hâs*°), mfn. large-mouthed, AV. **—sragvin**, mfn. wearing a gr° garland (said of Śiva), MBh. (cf. *-māla*). **—srotas**, n. 'great stream,' the bowels, Car. **—svana**, m. a loud sound, R.; mf(*ā*)n. making a loud noise, loud-sounding, crying aloud, MBh.; R.; m. a kind of drum (= *malla-tūrya*), L.; N. of an Asura, Hariv.; (*am*), ind. noisily, loudly, MW. **—svapna**, m. the gr° dream, Sāṃkhyapr. **—svara**, mfn. loud-sounding, R. **—svāda** (°*hâs*°), mfn. very tasteful, savoury, Rājat. **—svāmin**, m. N. of a commentator, Cat. **—haṅsa**, m. 'great Haṅsa' (q.v.), N. of Vishṇu, MBh.; BhP.; Pañcar. **—hanu**, mfn. having large jaws, MBh.; Hariv.; m. N. of a Nāga, MBh.; of a Dānava, Hariv.; of a being attending on Śiva, ib. **—haya**, m. N. of a king, BhP. **—harmya**, n. a great building or palace, splendid mansion, Rājat. **—1. -°hava** (°*hâh*°), m. a gr° war or battle, MBh. **—2. -hava**, m. a gr° sacrifice, Śiś. **—havís**, n. the principal oblation at the Sākam-edha sacrifice, ŚBr.; ŚrS.; clarified butter, MārkP.; N. of Śiva, MBh. (cf. *havis*); (*mahā́*-), m. N. of a Hotṛi, MaitrS.; TĀr.; ŚāṅkhŚr. **—hasta**, mfn. having large hands (N. of Śiva), MBh. **—hastín**, mfn. having large hands, RV. **—hāsa**, m. loud laughter, L.; mfn. laughing loudly, R. **—°hi** (°*hâhi*), m. a gr° serpent, ŚBr.; Kathās.; *-gandhā*, f. Piper Chaba, L.; *-valaya*, mf(*ā*)n. wearing a gr° serpent as a bracelet (said of Durgā), MārkP.; *-śayana*, n. the sleeping (of Vishṇu) on the gr° serpent, Hit. **—hima-vat**, m. N. of a mountain, Śatr. **—hetu**, m. or n.(?) a partic. high number, Buddh. **—hema-vat**, mfn. richly adorned with gold, ŚāṅkhGṛ. **—hailihila**, Pāṇ. vi, 2, 38. **—°hna** (°*hâh*°), m. 'advanced time of day,' the afternoon, ŚāṅkhBr. (cf. *-niśā*, *-rātra*). **—hrada**, m. a gr° tank or pool, Mn.; R. &c.; N. of a Tīrtha, MBh.; of a mythical pool, Siddhântaś.; Gol.; of Śiva, Śivag. (cf. *tīrtha-m*°). **—hrasva**, mfn. very short, exceedingly low, L.; (*ā*), f. Mucuna Pruritus, L. **Mahêccha**, mfn. having high aims, magnanimous, ambitious, Ragh.; Pañcat.; *-tā*, f. ambition, Kathās. **Mahêndrá**, m. the great Indra, AV. &c. &c. (also applied to Vishṇu [R.] and Śiva [Śivag.]); a partic. star, VP.; a great chief or leader (*sarva-devānām*), Nal.; a partic. high number, Buddh.; N. of a younger brother (or son) of Aśoka (who carried the Buddhist doctrine into Ceylon), MWB. 59; of another prince (= Kumāra-gupta), Inscr.; of a poet, Cat.; of various other writers and teachers (also with *âcārya* and *sūri*), ib.; of a mountain or range of m°s (said to be one of the 7 principal chains in India, and sometimes identified with the northern parts of the Ghats), MBh.; Kāv. &c.; of a place, MW.; (*ā*), f. N. of a river, MBh.; (*ī*), f. a species of plant, L.; *-kadalī*, f. a species of banana, L.; *-ketu*, m. great Indra's banner, Var.; *-gupta*, m. N. of a prince, Inscr.; *-guru*, m. 'gr° I°'s teacher,' N. of the planet Jupiter (= Bṛihas-pati), Var.; *-cāpa*, m. 'gr° I°'s bow,' a rainbow, Hariv.; Kāv.; *-jit*, m. N. of Garuḍa, L.; *-tva*, n. the name or rank of gr° I°, AitBr.; MBh.; *-devī*, f. the wife of gr° I°, VarBṛS., Sch.; *-dhvaja*, m. = *-ketu*, VarBṛS.; *-nagarī*, f. 'gr° I°'s city,' i.e. Amarā-vatī, L.; *-nātha*, m. N. of an author, Cat.; *-pāla*, m. N. of a king (also called *nirbhaya-rāja*, the pupil and patron of Rāja-śekhara), Bālar., Introd.; *-mantrin*, m. 'gr° I°'s counsellor,' the planet Jupiter, Var. (cf. *-guru*); *-mandira*, n. gr° I°'s palace, Vikr.; *-mahôtsava*, m. a gr° festival in honour of gr° I°, Cat.; *-yāga-prayoga*, m. N. of wk.; *-yājin*, mfn. one who worships gr° I°, MānŚr.; *-varman*, m. N. of a prince, L.; *-vāruṇī*, f. a species of plant, L.; *-śakti*, m. N. of a man, Kathās.; *-siṅha*, m. N. of a king, Inscr.; °*drâcārya-śishya*, m. N. of an astronomer, Cat.; °*drâṇī*, f. 'the wife of gr° I°,' i.e. Śacī, MBh.; °*drâditya*, m. N. of a king, Kathās.; °*drâdri*, m. N. of a mountain, BhP.; °*driya*, mfn. sacred or belonging to gr° I°, Pāṇ. iv, 2, 29; °*drīya*, mfn. id., ib. (with *graha*, m., Kāṭh.); °*drôtsava*, m. festival of gr° I°, MW. **Mahêbhya**, m. a very rich man, Campak. **Mahêśa**, m. 'great lord or god,' N. of Śiva, Cāṇ.; of a Buddhist deity, W.; of various authors and other men (also with *kavi*, *ṭhakkura*, *bhaṭṭi* and *miśra*), Cat.; *-candra*, *-tīrtha*, *-nandin*, *-nārāyaṇa*, m. N. of authors, Cat.; *-netra*, n. 'Śiva's eyes,' N. of the number 'three,' Śrutab.; *-bandhu*, m. Aegle Marmelos, L.; *-liṅga*, n. N. of a Liṅga, Kshitīś.; *-saṃhitā*, f. N. of wk.; °*śâkhya*, mfn. having the name of 'great lord,' highly distinguished or eminent, Buddh. **Mahêśāna**, m. = *mahêśa*, N. of Śiva, Cat. (*-bandhu*, m. = °*śa-b*°, A.); (*ī*), f. 'great lady,' N. of Pārvatī, Pañcar. **Mahêśitṛi**, m. = *mahêśāna*, Cat. **Mahêśvara**, m. a great lord, sovereign, chief, ŚvetUp.; MBh. &c. (with *tridaśānām*, 'chief of the gods,' i.e. Indra); a god (opp. to *prakriti*), ŚvetUp.; N. of various gods (esp. of Śiva and of Kṛishṇa; pl. of the Loka-pālas or guardians of the world, viz. Indra, Agni, Yama and Varuṇa), MBh.; R. &c.; of a Deva-putra, Lalit.; of various authors and other men, Inscr.; Siddhântaś.; Cat.; bdellium, L.; (*ī*), f. N. of Durgā, Tantras. (IW. 522); of Dākshāyaṇī in Mahā-kāla, Cat.; a kind of brass or bell-metal, L.; Clitoria Ternatea, L.; *-kara-cyutā*, f. 'dropped from the hand of Śiva,' N. of the river Kara-toyā, L.; *-tīrtha*, m. N. of a Sch. on R. and of another author, Cat.; *-tva*, n. supreme lordship or dominion, Up.; *-datta*, m. N. of a merchant, HPariś.; *-dīkshita*, m. N. of an author (°*tīya*, n. his wk.), Cat.; *-dīpa*, m., *-dharmâdharma*, m. or n. N. of wks.; *nyāyâlaṃkāra*, m. N. of an author, Cat.; *-bhaṭṭa*, m. N. of an author (°*ṭīya*, n. his wk.), ib.; *-liṅga*, n. N. of a Liṅga, Kshitīś.; *-vaidya*, m. N. of a lexicographer, Col.; *-siṅha*, m. N. of a king of Mithilā (patron of Ratna-pāṇi), Cat.; *-siddhânta*, m. = *paśu-pati-śāstra*, q.v., Col.; °*rânanda*, m. N. of an author, Cat.; °*riya*, n. N. of wk. **Mahêshu**, m. a great arrow, MārkP.; mfn. armed with a great arrow, Pāṇ. vi, 2, 107, Sch. **Mahêshudhi**, f. a gr° quiver, MBh. **Mahêshvāsa**, m. a gr° archer, MBh. (also *-tama*); R.; N. of Śiva, Śivag. **Mahâikôddishṭa**, n. a kind of funeral ceremony, Cat. **Mahâitareya**, n. N. of the AitUp., GṛS. **Mahâiraṇḍa**, m. a species of Ricinus, L. **Mahâilā**, f. great cardamoms, L. **Mahâiśvarya**, n. gr° power, Pañcar. **Mahôkshá**, m. a large bull, ŚBr. &c. &c. (*-tā*, f., Ragh.) **Mahôgra-tantra**, n. N. of a Tantra. **Mahôcchraya**, mfn. of great height, very lofty, R. **Mahôcchrāya-vat**, mfn. id., Pañcat. **Mahôtkā**, f. (prob. w. r. for *mahôlkā*) lightning, L. **Mahôttama**, m. or n. (?) N. of a partic. fragrant perfume, Kathās. **Mahôtpala**, n. a large water-lily, Nelumbium Speciosum, MBh.; N. of Dākshāyaṇī in Kamalâksha, Cat. **Mahôtpāta** (in comp.) a gr° portent or prodigy; *-prâyaścitta*, n. N. of wk.; mfn. very portentous, having great prodigies, R. **Mahôtsaṅga**, m. or n. (?) a partic. high number, Buddh. **Mahôtsava**, m. (ifc. f. *ā*) a gr° festival, any gr° rejoicing, MBh.; Kāv. &c.; the god of love, L.; *-maya*, mf(*ī*)n. consisting of gr° festivals, Kathās.; *-vidhi*, m. N. of wk.; °*savin*, mfn. celebrating gr° f°s, Hcar. **Mahôtsāha**, mfn. having gr° power or strength or energy, Yājñ.; MBh. &c.; m. N. of Śiva, Śivag. **Mahôdadhi**, m. the gr° ocean, a gr° sea (4 in number), MBh.; Kāv. &c.; N. of a poet, Cat.; *-ja*, m. 'sea-born,' a muscle, shell, MBh. **Mahôdaya**, m. great fortune or prosperity, Kāv.; BhP.; pre-eminence, sovereignty, L.; final emancipation, L.; mfn. conferring gr° fortune or prosperity, very fortunate, Mn.; MBh. &c.; thinking one's self very lucky, BhP.; m. a lord, master, L.; sour milk with honey, L.; N. of a Vāsishṭha, R.; of a royal chamberlain (who built a temple), Rājat. (cf. below); of another man, MBh.; of a mountain, R.; (*ā*), f. N. of the city and district of Kānya-kubja, Bālar. (also m., L.); Uraria Lagopodioides, L.; an overgrown maiden, L.; N. of a mythical town on mount Meru, BhP., Sch.; of a hall or dwelling in the world of the moon, Kād.; *-svāmin*, m. N. of a temple built by Mahôdaya, Rājat. **Mahôdara**, n. 'large abdomen,' dropsy, L.; mf(*ī*)n. big-bellied, Ragh.; Car.; m. N. of a serpent-demon, MBh.; of a Dānava, ib.; of a Rākshasa, R.; of a son of Dhṛita-rāshṭra, MBh.; of a son of Viśvāmitra, R.; (*ī*), f. Asparagus Racemosus, Bhpr.; Cyperus Pertenuis, L.; N. of a daughter of Maya, VP.; °*ra-mukha*, m. N. of an attendant of Durgā, Kathās.; °*rêśvara*, n. N. of a Liṅga, Cat.; °*rya*, m. N. of a man, MBh. (v.l. °*daya*). **Mahôdāra**, mfn. mighty, powerful, W. **Mahôdyama**, m. great effort or exertion, W.; (with Jainas), a partic. Kalpa, Dharmaś.; mfn. very energetic or diligent or persevering, studiously occupied or busily engaged in (loc. or dat.), Śukas.; Rājat. **Mahôdyoga**, mfn. making gr° exertions, very laborious or industrious, MW. **Mahôdreka**, m. a partic. measure of capacity (= 4 Prasthas), L. **Mahôdhas**, mfn. 'large-uddered,' rich in clouds or water (said of Parjanya), Pat. **Mahônnata**, mfn. very high or lofty, ŚārṅgP.; m. the palm or palmyra tree, L. **Mahônnati**, f. great elevation, high rank or position, L. **Mahônmada**, m. excessive intoxication, great ecstasy, W.; a species of fish, L. **Mahônmāna**, mfn. very extensive or weighty, AV. **Mahôpakāra**, m. great aid or assistance, MW. **Mahôpanishad**, f. N. of an Upanishad; *-dīpikā*, f. N. of a Comm. on it. **Mahôpanishada**, n. a gr° science or mystical doctrine, Up. **Mahôpamā**, f. N. of a river, MBh. (v.l. *mahâpagā*). **Mahôpasthāna-prayoga**, m. N. of wk. **Mahôpâdhyāya**, m. 'gr° teacher,' N. of various scholars and authors (e.g. of Bhāravi, Vidyā-nātha, Raghu-nātha &c.), Cat. (cf. *mahā-mahôp*°). **Mahôpâsaka**, m. a lay-brother, Buddh. (w. r. *mahâp*°). **Mahôraga**, m. a gr° serpent (with Jainas and Buddhists a class of demons), MBh.; Kāv. &c. (cf. MWB. 220); n. the root of Tabernaemontana Coronaria, L.; *-dashṭa*, mfn. bitten by a gr° serpent, MaitrUp.; *-lipi*, f. a kind of writing, Lalit. **Mahôraska**, mfn. broad-chested, MBh.; R. **Mahôrmin**, mfn. having gr° waves, very billowy, MBh. **Mahôlkā**, f. a gr° firebrand, MBh.; a gr° meteor, Mn.; R.; lightning (?), see *mahôtkā*. **Mah'-oshṭha**, mfn. gr°-lipped (said of Śiva), MBh. **Mahâugha**, mf(*ā*)n. having a strong current, Kathās.; m. N. of a son of Tvashṭṛi, ib. **Mahâujas**, n. great might or power, W.; mfn. very vigorous or powerful or mighty, Mn.; MBh. &c.; m. a hero, champion, W.; N. of a king, MBh.; of Su-brahmaṇya, L.; pl. of a people, MBh.; °*jasa*, n. the discus of Vishṇu, L.; (*ī*), f. a species of plant, L.; °*jaska*, mfn. = *mahâujas*, L. **Mahâuṇḍanī**, f. Asparagus Racemosus, L. **Mahâuṇḍavāhi**, m. N. of a Vedic teacher, ĀśvGṛ. **Mahâushadha**, n. a very efficacious drug, a sovereign remedy, panacea, Kāv.; Kathās.; N. of certain very strong or pungent plants (such as dried ginger, garlic, long pepper &c.), Suśr.; Pañcar.; L. **Mahâushadhi**, f. a great or very efficacious medicinal plant, MBh.; Kāv. &c. (also °*dhī*); Dūrvā grass, L.; Mimosa Pudica, L.; N. of a serpent-maid, Kāraṇḍ.; (°*dhī*), f. N. of various medicinal plants (such as Hingtsha Repens, Aconitum Ferox &c.), Suśr.; Pañcar.; L.; °*dhi-sûkta*, n. N. of RV. x, 97, Cat.

1. **Mahânta**, mfn. great, Suparṇ.; m. N. of a prince, VP.

2. **Mahânta**, mfn. (for *mahar-anta*) ending with *mahar*, MBh.

1. **Máhi**, mfn. (only nom. acc. sg. n.) = *mahát*, great, RV.; AV.; VS.; ind. greatly, very, exceedingly, much, ib.; ŚāṅkhŚr.; m. n. greatness, BhP.; m. = *mahat*, intellect, ib.; f. = 1. *mahī́*, the earth, L. (in comp. not always separable from 1. *mahín*, q.v.) **—keru** (*máhi*-), mfn. praising highly, RV. i, 45, 4 (fr. √2. *kṛi*; Sāy. = *prâuḍha-karman*, fr. √1. *kṛi*). **—kshatra** (*máhi*-), mfn. possessing great power, RV. **—1. -tā**, f. (for 2. see p. 803, col. 1) greatness, BhP. **—tvá**, n. greatness, might, RV.; VS. &c. **—tvaná**, n. id. (*ā́*, ind. by greatness), RV. **—nadī**, f. (only in voc. *mahe-nadi*) a great river, ib. **—nasa**, m. a form of Śiva or Rudra, BhP. **—pa**, m. N. of a man, Cat. (cf. next). **—pati**, m. N. of an author, Cat. **—magha** (*máhi*-), mfn. rich in oblations or treasures, RV. i, 122, 8. **—mat**, mfn. much, abundant, MBh.; m. marriage-fire, L. **—mati**, mfn. (only in voc. *mahe-mate*) high-minded (said of Indra), RV. **—ratna**, mfn. possessing great treasures, RV. **—vṛidh**, mfn. greatly rejoicing, RV. vii, 31, 10 (Sāy. 'giving great wealth;' SV. *mahe-vṛidh*). **—vrata** (*máhi*-), mfn. having

great power, ruling mightily, RV.; AV. **-shváni** (for *-sv°*), mfn. very noisy, RV.

2. **Mahi,** in comp. for *mahī.* **-datta,** m. N. of a man, Vās., Introd. **-dāsa,** m. N. of a son of Itarā, AitĀr.; ChUp.; *-budha,* m. (prob. w. r. for *bhaṭṭa*) N. of an author, Cat. (cf. *mahī-dāsa-bhaṭṭa*).

3. **Mahi,** in comp. for 2. *mahin.* **-2. -tā,** f. (for 1. see p. 802, col. 3) festivity, Nalôd.

Mahita, mfn. honoured, celebrated &c., Inscr.; Kāv.; proper, right, W.; m. (scil. *gaṇa*) a class of deceased ancestors, MārkP.; N. of a Deva-putra, Lalit.; of Kailāsa, L.; of a man, g. *gargâdi; (ā),* f. N. of a river, MBh. (VP. *ahitā*); n. the trident of Śiva, L. **Mahitâmbhas,** mfn. whose waters are celebrated, Kir.

1. **Mahín,** mfn. = *mahát,* great, mighty, RV. (*-tama,* mfn., RV. x, 115, 6).

2. **Mahin,** mfn. keeping a feast, festive, Nalôd. (cf. 3. *mahi,* above).

Mahina, mf(*ā*)n. = 1. *mahín,* great, mighty, RV.; n. sovereignty, dominion, L.

Mahiná. See *mahimán.*

Mahima, in comp. for *mahiman.* **-taraṃga-ṭikā,** f. N. of wk. **-bhaṭṭa** and **-siṅha-gaṇi,** m. N. of two authors, Cat. **-sundara,** m. N. of a man, Cat. **-stava,** m. N. of a hymn (cf. under *mahimán*). **Mahimôdaya,** m. N. of wk.

Mahimán, m. greatness, might, power, majesty, glory, RV. &c. &c. (*°himnā* or *°hinā́,* ind. mightily, forcibly, RV.); the magical power of increasing size at will, Vet.; Pañcar. (cf. MWB. 245); magnitude (as one of Śiva's attributes; *°mnaḥ stava,* m., *stuti,* f., *stotra,* n. N. of hymns; cf. *mahima-stava*); N. of a man, Rājat.; a N. of Mammaṭa, q. v., Cat.; du. N. of two Grahas at the Aśva-medha sacrifice, ŚBr.; ŚrS.

Mahimā, f. = *mahimán,* greatness &c., R. **-taraṃga,** m. N. of wk. **-vat,** m. (scil. *gaṇa*) a class of deceased ancestors, MārkP.

Mahimna, m. N. of a poet, Cat.

Mahimnāra, m. N. of a prince, Hariv.

Mahishá, mf(*máhishī*)n. great, powerful, Naigh. iii, 3; m. (with *suparṇá*) the sun, AV.; (with or scil. *mṛigá,* once with *mṛigấṇām*) a buffalo, RV. &c. &c. (considered as the emblem of Yama and of a Jaina saint); a great priest, Mahīdh.; the son of a Kshatriya and a Tīvarī, L.; N. of an Asura (slain by Durgā or Skanda), MBh.; Pur.; of a Sādhya, Hariv.; of a sage (author of a Comm. on the Prāt. of the Yajur-veda), Cat.; of a mountain in Śālmala-dvīpa, VP.; pl. N. of a people, Hariv.; (*ī*), f., see below. **-kanda,** m. a species of bulbous plant, L. **-ga,** mfn. riding upon a buffalo (as Yama), VarBṛS. **-ghnī,** f. 'slayer of the demon Mahisha,' N. of Durgā, Hcat. **-cara,** mfn. = *-ga,* Caṇḍ. **-tva,** n. the state or condition of a b°, Kathās. **-dhvaja,** m. 'having a b° for an emblem,' N. of Yama, L. **-pāla** (Kathās.), *°laka* (Rājat.), m. a buffalo-herd, L. **-mardinī,** f. 'crusher of Mahisha,' N. of Durgā, Cat.; a prayer addressed to D°, ib.; *-tantra,* n. N. of a Tantra, ib. **-yamana,** m. 'buffalo-tamer,' N. of Yama, Dhūrtan. **-vallī,** f. a kind of creeper, L. **-vāhana,** m. 'having a buffalo for a vehicle,' N. of Yama, Kpr. **-śataka,** n. N. of a poem. **-sūdanī,** f. = *-ghātinī,* A. **Mahishâksha** or *°shaka,* m. a kind of bdellium, L. **Mahishânanā,** f. 'buffalo-faced,' N. of one of the Mātṛis attending on Skanda, MBh. **Mahishârdana,** m. 'tormenter of Mahisha,' N. of Skanda, MBh. **Mahishâsura,** m. the Asura or demon Mahisha (from whom the country of Mysore is said to take its name), RTL. 431; *-ghātinī,* f. 'slayer of the A° Mahisha,' N. of Durgā, Hariv.; *-majjôtthā,* f. 'produced from the marrow of the A° M°,' a kind of perfume, Gal.; *-mardinī,* f. = *-ghātinī* (*°dinī-stotra,* n. N. of a Stotra); *-sambhava,* m. 'produced from the A° M°' (cf. *-majjôtthā*) or 'pr° in Mysore,' a kind of bdellium, L.; f. *-sūdanī* (Kathās.); *°rāpahā* and *°rārdinī* (Hariv.) = *-ghātinī.* **Mahishôtsarga-vidhi,** m. N. of wk.

Mahishaka, m. pl. N. of a people, MBh. (B.); VarBṛS. (v. l. *māhisha*).

Mahishi, m. pl. N. of a people, VP.

Mahishita, mfn. changed into a buffalo, Kāv.

Máhishī, f. a female buffalo, b°-cow, Br.; Mn.; MBh. &c.; any woman of high rank, (esp.) the first or consecrated wife of a king (also pl.) or any queen, RV. &c. &c.; the female of a bird, BhP.; (with *samudrasya*), N. of the Gaṅgā, Hariv.; an unchaste woman or money gained by a wife's prostitution, L.; a species of plant, L.; N. of the 15th day of the light half of the month Taisha, L. **-kanda,** m. a species of bulbous plant (= *mahisha-k°*), L. **-goshṭha,** n. a stable for buffalo-cows, Pāṇ. v, 2, 29, Vārtt. 3, Pat. **-dāna,** n. N. of wk.; *-prayoga,* m., *-mantra,* m., *-vidhi,* m. N. of wks. **-pa,** m. N. of a man (orig. = next), Vcar. **-pāla,** m. a keeper of buffalo-cows, L. **-priyā,** f. a species of grass, L. **-bhāva,** m. the state or condition of a buffalo-cow, Kathās. **-śataka,** n. N. of a poem. **-stambha,** m. a pillar or column adorned with a buffalo's head, MW.

Mahishṭha, mfn. greatest, largest, BhP.

Mahishmat, mfn. (fr. *mahisha*) rich in buffaloes, Pāṇ. iv, 2, 87, Vārtt.; m. N. of a king, Hariv.; Pur.; (*atī*), f. N. of a partic. lunar day (personified as a daughter of Aṅgiras), MBh.

Máhishvanta, mfn. (fr. *mahis,* √1. *mah*?) refreshing, delighting, RV. vii, 68, 5 (others 'great;' Sāy. = *ribisa*).

1. **Mahī́,** f. (cf. 2. *máh*) 'the great world,' the earth (cf. *urvī, pṛithivī*), RV. &c. &c. (in later language also = ground, soil, land, country); earth (as a substance), Mn. vii, 70; the base of a triangle or other plane figure, Col.; space, RV. iii, 56, 2; v, 44, 6 &c.; a host, army, ib. iii, 1, 12; vii, 93, 5 &c.; a cow, RV.; VS. (Naigh. ii, 11); du. heaven and earth, RV. i, 80, 11; 159, 1 &c. (Naigh. iii, 30); pl. waters, streams, RV. ii, 11, 2; v, 45, 3 &c.; Hingtsha Repens, L.; a kind of metre, Col.; N. of a divine being (associated with Iḍā and Sarasvatī, RV. i, 13, 9, Sāy.; cf. Naigh. i, 11); of a river, MBh.; Hariv.; of the number 'one,' Gaṇit. **-kampa,** m. 'earth-tremor,' an earthquake, VarBṛS. **-kshit,** m. 'earth-ruler,' a king, prince, Mn.; MBh. &c. **-candra,** m. 'earth-moon,' N. of a king, Col. **-cara** or **-cārin,** mfn. moving on the earth, MBh. **-ja,** mfn. 'earth-born,' (prob.) born in the desert (said of horses), MBh.; m. a plant, tree, ib.; 'son of the Earth,' N. of the planet Mars, VarBṛS.; (*ā*), f. N. of Sītā, A.; n. green ginger, L. **-jīvā,** f. the horizon, Gol. **-taṭa,** n. N. of a place, VarBṛS. **-tala,** n. the surface of the earth, ground, soil, Mn.; MBh. &c.; *-visarpin,* m. 'earth-walker,' an inhabitant of the earth, Hariv. **-dāsa,** m. N. of various authors (also *-bhaṭṭa;* cf. *mahi-d°*), Cat. **-durga,** mfn. inaccessible through (the nature of) the soil; n. a fort inaccessible &c., Mn. vii, 70 (others 'a fort built of earth'). **-dhara,** mfn. 'e°-bearing,' supporting the earth, Hariv.; m. a mountain, MBh.; Kāv. &c.; N. of Vishṇu, VP.; of a Deva-putra, Lalit.; of various men and authors (esp. of a Sch. on VS.); *-datta,* m. N. of a man, Vās., Introd. **-dhra,** m. (for *-dhara*) a mountain, MBh.; Kāv. &c.; N. of the number 'seven,' Sūryas. (cf. *parvata*); N. of Vishṇu, BhP. **-dhraka,** m. (cf. prec.) N. of a king, R. (v. l. *mahândhraka*). **-°na** (*°hīna*), m. 'earth-ruler,' a king, prince, Ragh. **-nātha,** m. 'earth-lord,' = prec., Pañcat. **-°ndra** (*°hîndra*), m. id. (lit. 'earth-Indra'); *°drêndra,* m. an Indra among kings, MBh. **-pa,** m. 'earth-protector,' a king, MBh.; N. of a lexicographer, Cat. **-patana,** n. prostration on the ground, humble obeisance, R. **-pati,** m. 'e°-lord,' a king, sovereign (*-tva,* n.), Mn.; MBh. &c.; a kind of big lime, L. **-pāla,** m. 'e°-protector,' a king, MBh.; Kāv. &c.; N. of various princes (also *-deva*), Kathās.; Śatr.; *-putra,* m. a king's son, prince, MārkP. **-putra,** m. a son of the earth, Hariv.; the planet Mars, Yājñ.; (*ī*), f. N. of Sītā, A. **-pṛishṭha,** n. the surface of the e°, Bhartṛ. **-prakampa,** m. = *-kampa,* VarBṛS. **-pradāna,** n. a gift of land, Pañcat. **-praroha,** m. 'e°-growing,' a tree, MBh. **-praśāsana,** n. dominion over the e°, ib. **-prācīra,** m. n. 'earth-fence,' the sea, L. **-prāvara,** n. 'earth-enclosure,' the sea, L. **-bhaṭṭa,** m. N. of a grammarian, Col. **-bhartṛi,** m. 'e°-supporter,' a king, Kāv.; Rājat. **-bhāra,** m. a burden for the earth, Pañcar. **-bhuj,** m. 'earth-enjoyer,' a king, Kāv.; Kathās. **-bhṛit,** m. = *-bhartṛi,* MBh.; Kāv. &c.; a mountain, ib. **-maghavan,** m. 'earth-Indra,' a king, Naish.; Rājat. **-maṇḍala,** n. the circumference of the e°, the whole e°, Kād.; Sūryas. **-maya,** mf(*ī*)n. consisting of e°, earthen, Yājñ.; MBh. &c.; (*ī*), f. (with *nau*) the e° compared to a ship, BhP. **-mahikâṅśu,** m. 'e°-moon,' an illustrious king, Naish. **-mahêndra,** m. 'great Indra of the e°,' a king, Rājat. **-mṛiga,** m. the earthly antelope (opp. to *tārā-mṛiga*), R. iii, 49, 45. **-rajas,** n. 'e-dust,' a grain of sand, MārkP. **-raṇa,** m. N. of a son of Dharma (one of the Viśve Devāḥ), Hariv. **-rata,** m. N. of a king, Cat. (v. l. *bahīnara*). **-randhra,** n. a hole in the e°, MārkP. **-ruh,** m. (nom. *-ruṭ*) 'earth-grower,' a plant, tree, Kir. **-ruha,** m. id., MBh.; Kāv. &c.; Tectona Grandis, L. (prob. w. r. for *-saha*). **-latā,** f. an earth-worm, dew-worm, L. **-vallabha,** m. 'e°-lover,' a king, Daś. **-śāsaka,** m. pl. N. of a school, Buddh. **-°śvara** (*°hīśv°*), m. 'e°-lord,' a king, Cat. **-saṃgama,** m. N. of a place, ib. **-saha,** m. Tectona Grandis, L. (cf. *-ruha*). **-suta,** m. 'son of the earth,' the planet Mars, VarBṛS.; (*ā*), f. N. of Sītā, A. **-sura,** m. 'e°-god,' a Brāhman, Daś. **-sūnu,** m. = *-suta,* L. **-svāmin,** m. 'earth-lord,' a king, Pañcad. **Mahy-uttara,** m. pl. N. of a people, MBh. (v. l. *samantara* and *brahmôttara*).

2. **Mahī,** in comp. for *maha.* **-√kṛi,** P. *-karoti,* to make great, magnify, exalt, Śaṃk.

Mahīya, Nom. Ā. *°yáte,* to be joyous or happy, RV. &c. &c.; to prosper, TUp.; to be exalted, rise high, R.; to be highly esteemed or honoured, Kāv. (also pr. p. Pass. *mahīyyamāna,* Bhaṭṭ.)

Mahīyatva (?), g. *vimuktâdi* (cf. *māhīyatva*).

Mahīyas, mfn. greater, mightier, stronger (or 'very great, v° mighty &c.'), Up.; MBh.; Kāv. &c. (with *hāsa,* m. very loud laughter; with *kula,* n. a very noble family).

Mahīyā́, f. joyousness, happiness, exultation (dat. *°yai*), RV.; TS.; N. of a partic. verse, ĀpŚr., Sch.

Mahīyú, mfn. joyous, happy, RV.

Mahe-nadi, mahe-mati, mahe-vṛidh. See under 1. *mahi,* p. 802, col. 3.

Mahmán, m. greatness, AV.

Mahya, mfn. (prob.) highly honoured, MBh. (= *mahat,* Nīlak.); m. pl. N. of a people, VP.; (*ā*), f., see under *mahnya,* p. 804, col. 1.

महक्क *mahakka,* m. a wide-spreading fragrance, L.

महत् *mahát, mahán* &c. See p. 794, cols. 2, 3.

महमदएदल *mahamada-edala,* m. = محمد عادل N. of a prince, Cat.

महम्मद *mahammada,* m. = محمد N. of a king, ib.

महयाय्य *mahayā́yya, maháye* &c. See p. 794, col. 3.

महर् *mahar* &c. See p. 794, col. 3.

महल्ल *mahalla,* m. (fr. Arabic محل *mahall*) a eunuch in a king's palace or in a harem, L.

Mahallaka, mf(*ikā*)n. old, feeble, decrepit, Lalit.; Kāraṇḍ.; m. = prec., L.; a large house, mansion, L.; (*ikā*), f. a female attendant in the women's apartments, L.; N. of a daughter of Prahlāda, Kathās.

Mahallika, m. = *mahalla,* L.

महस् *mahas, mahasa* &c. See p. 794, col. 3.

महा *mahā, mahā-kaṅkara* &c. See p. 794, col. 3.

महाभिष *mahābhisha,* m. N. of a sovereign of the race of Ikshvāku, MBh.; Kād.; BhP.

महि *mahi, mahi-keru* &c. See p. 802, col. 3.

महिका *mahikā,* f. mist, frost (for *mihikā,* q. v.), L. **Mahikâṅśu,** m. the moon, Naish.

महित *mahita, mahin* &c. See col. 1.

महिन्धक *mahindhaka,* m. a rat, L.; an ichneumon, L.; the cord of a pole for carrying loads, L.

महिमन् *mahiman* &c. See col. 1.

महिर *mahira,* m. the sun (for *mihira*), L. **-kula,** m. N. of a prince, Buddh. (cf. *mihira-k°*).

महिला *mahilā,* f. (accord. to Uṇ. i, 55 fr. √1. *mah*) a woman, female, Hit.; Sāh. (cf. *mahelā*); a woman literally or figuratively intoxicated, L.; a partic. fragrant drug, L. (= *priyaṅgu,* Bhpr.); N. of a river, Siṃhâs. **-pāda,** mfn., g. *hasty-ādi,* Kāś. **Mahilâkhyā,** f. = *priyaṅgu* (cf. above), L. **Mahilâhvayā,** f. id., W.

Mahilā, f. a woman, L.

Mahīlukā, f. a cow, AV.

Mahelā, f. a woman, Nalac.; Nalôd. **-pāda,** mfn., g. *hasty-ādi* (Kāś. *mahilā-p°*).

Mahelikā, f. = *mahelā,* L.

महिलारोप्य *mahilāropya,* n. N. of a city in the south, Pañcat. (cf. *mihil°*).

महिष *mahisha* &c. See p. 803, col. 1.

मही *mahī, mahī-kampa* &c. See p. 803, col. 2.

महेच्छ *mahêccha* &c. See p. 802, col. 1.

महेत्थ *mahettha*, N. of a country, MBh.

महेन्द्र *mahêndra* &c. See p. 802, col. 1.

महेरणा *maheraṇā* or *maheruṇā*, f. Boswellia Thurifera, L.

महेश *mahêśa, °śvara* &c. See p. 802, col. 2.

महैकोद्दिष्ट *mahâikoddishṭa, mahâitareya* &c. See p. 802, col. 2.

महोक्ष *mahóksha, mahôcchraya* &c. See p. 802, col. 2.

महोटिका *mahoṭikā* or *mahoṭī*, f. the egg-plant, Bhpr.

महोविशीय *mahoviśīya*, n. du. (with *prajā-pateḥ*) N. of two Sāmans, ArshBr.

महौघ *mahâugha, mahâujas* &c. See p. 802, col. 3.

मह्न *mahna* in *puru-m°*. See *puru-madga*.

मह्न्या *mahnyā*, f. a partic. exclamation (v l. *mahyā*), Gobh.; pl. N. of the Mahā-nāmnī verses, TāṇḍBr. (v.l. *mahnyā*).

मह्मदखान *mahmada-khāna*, m. = محمد خان N of a man, Cat.

मह्मन् *mahmán, mahya*. See p. 803, col. 3.

मह्युत्तर *mahy-uttara*. See p. 803, col. 3.

मह्लण *mahlaṇa*, m. N. of a prince, Rājat. (cf. *malhaṇa*). **—svāmin**, m. N. of a temple founded by Mahlaṇa, ib.

Mahlāṇa-pura, n. N. of a town, Rājat. (prob. w. r. for *mahlaṇa-* or *malhaṇa-p°*).

मा 1. *mā́*, ind. (causing a following *ch* to be changed to *cch*, Pāṇ. vi, 1, 74) not, that not, lest, would that not, RV. &c. &c.; a particle of prohibition or negation = Gk. μή, most commonly joined with the Subjunctive i. e. the augmentless form of a past tense (esp. of the aor., e. g. *mā́ no vadhīr Indra*, do not slay us, O I°, RV.; *mā bhai-shīḥ* or *mā bhaiḥ*, do not be afraid, MBh.; *tapo-vana-vāsinām uparodho mā bhūt*, let there not be any disturbance of the inhabitants of the sacred grove, Śak.; often also with *sma*, e. g. *mā sma gamaḥ*, do not go, Bhag., cf. Pāṇ. iii, 3, 175; 176; in the sense of 'that not, lest' also *yathā mā*, e. g. *yathā mā vo mṛityuḥ pari-vyathā iti*, that death may not disturb you, PraśnUp.; or *mā yathā*, e. g. *mā bhūt kālâtyayo yathā*, lest there be any loss of time, R.; *mā na* with aor. Subj. = Ind. without a negative, e. g. *mā dvisho na vadhīr mama*, do slay my enemies, Bhaṭṭ., cf. Vām. v, 1, 9; rarely with the augmentless impf. with or without *sma*, e. g. *mâinam abhibhāshathāḥ*, do not speak to him, R.; *mā sma karot*, let him not do it, Pāṇ. vi, 4, 74, Sch.; exceptionally also with the Ind. of the aor., e. g. *mā kālas tvām aty-agāt*, may not the season pass by thee, MBh.; cf. Pāṇ. vi, 4, 75, Sch.); or with the Impv. (in RV. only viii, 103, 6, *mā no hṛiṇītām* [SV. *hṛiṇītās*] *agniḥ*, may Agni not be angry with us; but very often in later language, e. g. *mā kranda*, do not cry, MBh.; *gaccha vā mā vā*, you can go or not go, ib.; *ripur ayam mā jāyatām*, may not this foe arise, Śāntiś.; also with *sma*, e. g. *mā sva kiṃ cid vaco vada*, do not speak a word, MBh.); or with the Pot. (e. g. *mā Yamam paśyeyam*, may I not see Yama; esp. *mā bhujema* in RV.); or with the Prec. (only once in *mā bhūyāt*, may it not be, R. [B.] ii, 75, 45); or sometimes with the fut. (= that not, lest, e. g. *mā tvāṃ śapsye*, lest I curse thee, MBh., cf. Vop. xxv, 27); or with a participle (e. g. *mā jīvan yo duḥkha-dagdho jīvati*, he ought not to live who lives consumed by pain, Pañcat.; *gataḥ sa mā*, he cannot have gone, Kathās.; *mâivam prârthyam*, it must not be so requested, BhP.); sometimes for the simple negative *na* (e. g. *katham mā bhūt*, how may it not be, Kathās.; *mā gantum arhasi*, thou oughtest not to go, R ; *mā bhūd āgataḥ*, can he not i. e. surely he must have arrived, Amar.); occasionally without a verb (e. g. *mā śabdaḥ* or *śabdam*, do not make a noise, Hariv.; *mā nāma rakshiṇaḥ*, may it not be the watchmen, Mṛicch.; *mā bhavantam analaḥ pavano vā*, may not fire or wind harm thee, Vām. v, 1, 14; esp. = not so, e. g. *mā Prātṛida*, not so, O Pr°, ŚBr.; in this meaning also *mā mā, mā mâi-vam, mā tāvat*); in the Veda often with *u* (*mô*) = and not, nor (e. g. *mā́ maghónaḥ pári khyatam mô asmā́kam ṛishīṇām*, do not forget the rich lords nor us the poets, RV. v, 65, 6; and then usually followed by *shú = sú*, e. g. *mô shú ṇaḥ Nír-ṛitir vadhīt*, let not N° on any account destroy us, i, 38, 6); in ŚBr. *sma mā—mô sma* = neither—nor (in a prohibitive sense). **—kim**, ind., g. *câdi* (cf. *na-kim* &c.) **—kis** (*mā́-*), ind. (only in prohibitive sentences with Subj.) may not or let not (= Lat. *ne*), RV.; may no one (= *ne-quis*), ib. **—kīm** (*mā́-*), ind. may or let not (= *ne*), RV. **—ciram**, ind. 'not long,' shortly, quickly, MBh.; R.; Pur. (generally after an Impv. or augmentless aor., and almost always at the end of a verse; sometimes m. c. for *na-ciram*, q. v.) **—vilambam** (Pañcat.), **-vilam-bitam** (BhP.), ind. without delay, shortly, quickly (in commands).

मा 2. *mā*, cl. 3. P. *mímāti* (accord. to Dhātup. xxv, 6, Ā. *mimīte*; SV. *mimeti*; Pot. *mimīyāt*, Kāṭh.; pf. *mimāya*; aor. *ámīmet*, Subj. *mīmayat*; inf. *mā́tavai*), to sound, bellow, roar, bleat (esp. said of cows, calves, goats &c.), RV.; AV.; Br.: Intens., only pr. p. *mémyat*, bleating (as a goat), RV. i, 162, 2.

1. **Māyu**, m. (for 2. see p. 811, col. 2) bleating, bellowing, lowing, róaring, RV.; AV.; ŚrS.; 'the bleater or bellower,' N. of a partic. animal or of a Kim-purusha, ŚāṅkhŚr.

Māyūka, mfn. bellowing, roaring, L.

मा 3. *mā*, cl. 2. P. (Dhātup. xxiv, 54) *māti*; cl. 3. Ā. (xxv, 6) *mimīte*; cl. 4. Ā. (xxvi, 33) *māyate* (Ved. and ep. also *mimāti*, Pot. *mimīyāt*, Impv. *mimīhi*; Pot. *mimet*, Br.; pf. *mamau, mame, mamiré*, RV.; aor. *ámāsi*, Subj. *mā́sātai*, AV.; *amāsīt*, Gr.; Prec. *māsīshṭa, me-yāt*, ib.; fut. *mātā*; *māsyati, māsyate*, ib.; inf. *-mé, -mai*, RV.; *mātum*, Br.; ind. p. *mitvā́, -māya*, RV. &c. &c.), to measure, mete out, mark off, RV. &c. &c.; to measure across = traverse, RV.; to measure (by any standard, compare with (instr.), Kum.; (*māti*) to correspond in measure (either with gen., 'to be large or long enough for,' BhP.; or with loc., 'to find room or be contained in,' Inscr.; Kāv.; or with *na* and instr., 'to be beside one's self with,' Vcar.; Kathās.); to measure out, apportion, grant, RV.; to help any one (acc.) to anything (dat.), ib. i, 120, 9; to prepare, arrange, fashion, form, build, make, RV.; to show, display, exhibit (*amimīta*, 'he displayed or developed himself,' iii, 29, 11), ib.; (in phil.) to infer, conclude; to pray (*yācñā-kar-maṇi*), Naigh. iii, 19: Pass. *mīyáte* (aor. *amāyi*); to be measured &c., RV. &c. &c.: Caus. *māpayati*, *°te* (aor. *amīmapat*, Pāṇ. vii, 4, 93, Vārtt. 2, Pat.), to cause to be measured or built, measure, build, erect, Up.; GṛS.; MBh. &c.: Desid. *mitsati*, *°te*, Pāṇ. vii, 4, 54; 58 (cf. *nir-√mā*): Intens. *memī-yate*, Pāṇ. vi, 4, 66. [Cf. Zd. *mā*; Gk. μέτρον, μετρέω; Lat. *mētior, mensus, mensura*; Slav. *mĕra*; Lith. *mèrà*.]

4. **Mā**, f. See under 4. *ma*, p. 751, col. 2.

1. **Mātá**, mfn. (for 2. and 3. see pp. 806 and 807) formed, made, composed (?), RV. v, 45, 6 (others 'fr. √*man*,' others '*mātā*, mother;' cf. *deva-māta*).

Māti, f. measure, accurate knowledge, L.; a partic. part of the body, L.

Mātu, m. (in music) = *vāg-varṇa-samudāya*, Saṃgīt.

1. **Mātṛi**, m. (for 2. *mātṛi*, f., see p. 807, col. 1) a measurer, Nir. xi, 5; one who measures across or traverses, RV. viii, 41, 4 (cf. 10); a knower, one who has true knowledge, Cat.; N. of a partic. caste, ib. (w. r. for *māḍava*?); of an author, Bṛih.

Mātra, m. a Brāhman of the lowest order i. e. only by birth, Hcat.; (*ā*), f., see s. v.; n. an element, elementary matter, BhP.; (ifc.) measure, quantity, sum, size, duration, measure of any kind (whether of height, depth, breadth, length, distance, time or number, e. g. *aṅgula-mātram*, a finger's breadth, Pañcat.; *artha-mātram*, a certain sum of money, ib.; *krośa-mātre*, at the distance of a Kos, Hit.; *māsa-mātre*, in a month, Lāṭy.; *śata-mātram*, a hundred in number, Kathās.); the full or simple measure of anything, the whole or totality, the one thing and no more, often = nothing but, entirely, only (e. g. *rāja-mātram*, the whole class of kings, ŚāṅkhŚr.; *bhaya-m°*, all that may be called danger, any danger, VarBṛS.; *rati-m°*, nothing but sensuality, Mn.; *śabda-mātreṇa*, only by a sound, Śak.); mf(*ā* and *ī*)n. (ifc.) having the measure of, i. e. as large or high or long or broad or deep or far or much or many (cf. *aṅgushṭha-, tāla-, bāhu-, yava-, tāvan-, etāvan-m°*); possessing (only) as much as or no more than (cf. *prâṇa-yātrika-m°*); amounting (only) to (pleonastically after numerals; cf. *tri-m°*); being nothing but, simply or merely (cf. *padāti-, manushya-m°*; after a pp. = scarcely, as soon as, merely, just, e. g. *jāta-m°*, scarcely or just born, Mn.; *kṛishṭa-m°*, merely ploughed, KātyŚr.; *bhukta-mātre*, immediately after eating, Mn.) **—tas**, ind. (ifc.) from the first moment of (cf. *bhūmi-shṭha-m°*). **—tā**, f. (ifc.) the being as much as, no more nor less than anything, Śaṃkar. **—traya**, mfn. threefold, MārkP. **—tva**, n. = *-tā*, Vedântas. **—rāja**, m. (with *Anaṅga-harsha*) N. of a poet, Cat.

Mātraka (ifc.) = *mātra*, MBh.; Kāv. &c.; (*ikā*), f. = *mātrā*, a prosodial instant, RPrāt. (cf. *mātrika*).

Mā́trā, f. measure (of any kind), quantity, size, duration, number, degree &c., RV. &c. &c. (*bhū-yasyā mātrayā*, in a higher degree, Lalit.); unit of measure, foot, VarBṛS.; unit of time, moment, Suśr.; ŚārṅgS. (= *nimesha*, VP.; ifc. = lasting so many moments, Gaut.); metrical unit, a mora or prosodial instant, i.e. the length of time required to pronounce a short vowel (a long vowel contains 2 Mātrās, and a prolated vowel 3), Prāt.; musical unit of time (3 in number), Pañcat.; (only once ifc.) the full measure of anything (= *mātra*), Hariv. 7125; right or correct measure, order, RV.; ChUp.; a minute portion, particle, atom, trifle, ŚBr. &c. &c. (*ayā*, ind. in small portions, in slight measure, moderately, Daś.; Suśr.; *āyām*, ind. a little, Gaṇar.; *rājêti kiyatī mātrā*, of what account is a king? a king is a mere trifle, Pañcat.; *kā mātrā samudrasya*, what is the importance of the sea? the sea will easily be managed, ib.; an element (5 in number), BhP.; matter, the material world, MaitrUp.; MBh.; BhP.; materials, property, goods, household, furniture, money, wealth, substance, livelihood (also pl.), Vas.; Mn.; MBh. &c.; a mirror, Vishṇ.; an ear-ring, jewel, ornament, Kād.; the upper or horizontal limb of the Nāgarī characters, W. **—kṛita**, mfn. (a metre) regulated by moræ, L. **—kośa-bhāravikā**, f. N. of wk. **—guru**, mfn. (food) heavy on account of its quantity or ingredients, Suśr. **—cyutaka**, (prob.) n. 'dropping of moræ,' N. of a game (in which the dropped moræ are to be supplied), Kād. **—chandas**, n. a metre measured by the number of prosodial instants, Col. (cf. *ak-shara-* and *gaṇa-cch°*). **—°di-śrāddha-nirṇaya** (*°trâd°*), m. N. of wk. **—°dhika** (*°trâdh°*), mfn. a little more than (abl.), Dharmaś. **—prayoga**, m. N. of wk. **—bhastrā**, f. a money-bag, purse, Pañcat. **—°rdha** (*°trârdha*), n. half-measure, half of a prosodial instant, APrāt. **—lakshaṇa**, n. N. of a Sūtra wk. **—lābha**, m. pl. acquisition of wealth, MBh. **—vat**, mfn. containing a partic. measure, KātyŚr.; Suśr. **—vasti**, m. a kind of oily clyster, Car.; ŚārṅgS. **—vidhāna-sūtra**, n. N. of wk. (= *-lakshaṇa*). **—vṛitta**, n. = *-chandas*, Col. **—°śita** (*°trâś°*), n. eating moderately; *°tīya*, mfn. treating of it, Vāgbh. **—°śin** (*°trâś°*), mfn. eating moderately, ib. **—saṃsarga**, m. the mutual connection between the several parts (of a whole), ŚBr. **—saṅga**, m. attachment to household possessions or utensils, Mn. vi, 57. **—samaka**, n. N. of a class of metres, Col. **—°sura** (*°trâs°*), m. N. of an Asura, Vīrac. **—sparśa**, m. material contact, the concurrence of material elements, Bhag.

Mātrika (ifc.) all, every kind of (e. g. *mṛiga-mātrika*, pl. all kinds of deer), Suśr.; f. a prosodial instant, mora, RPrāt. (mfn. containing one pr° instant or mora, VPrāt., Sch.); a model, paragon, Bālar.

2. **Māna**. See p. 809, col. 3.

Māpaka. See p. 810, col. 3.

माउथ *mâutha*, m. or n. (?) N. of a place, Cat. (v. l. *mâuṇatha*).

मांश्चतु *māṅścatú*, mfn. (prob.) light yellow, dun-coloured, RV. vii, 44, 3 (Padap. and Prāt. *maṅścatú*); pl. (*°catvàs*) = *aśvāḥ*, Naigh. i, 14.

Māṇścatvá, mfn. (prob.) yellowish, RV. ix, 97, 52 (*māṇścalva*, ib. 54).

मांस् *māṇs*, n. flesh, meat &c. (= *māṇsa*, for which it is used in the weak cases accord. to Pāṇ. vi, 1, 63, Vārtt. 1, Pat.); it appears only in the following compounds. **-pácana**, mf(*ī*)n. used for cooking meat (as a cauldron), RV. i, 162, 13. **-pāka**, m. = *māṇsa-p°*, Kār. on Pāṇ. vi, 1, 144.

Māṇsá, n. sg. and pl. flesh, meat, RV. &c. &c. (also said of the fleshy part or pulp of fruit, Suśr.); m. N. of a mixed caste, MBh. (= *māṇsa-vikretṛi*, Nīlak.); a worm, L.; time, L.; (*ī*), f. Nardostachys Jatamansi, Var.; Suśr.; = *kakkolī*, f.; = *māṇsa-cchadā*, L. [Cf. Slav. *męso*; Pruss. *mensa*; Lith. *mėsà*.] **-kacchapa**, m. a fleshy abscess on the palate, Suśr. **-kandī**, f. a fleshy protuberance, ib. **-kara**, n. flesh-making, blood, L. **-kāma**, mfn. fond of fl°, Pāṇ. iii, 2, 1, Vārtt. 7, Pat. **-kārin**, n. = *-kara*, L. **-kīla**, m. a tumour, polypus (also °*laka*), L.; a wart, L. **-kshaya**, m. 'house of flesh,' the body, MBh. **-khaṇḍa**, n. a bit of flesh, Subh. **-gṛidhyin**, mfn. desirous of flesh, MBh. **-granthi**, m. flesh-swelling, a gland, MW. **-cakshus**, n. 'the fleshy eye,' Vajracch. (with Buddhists one of the 5 sorts of vision, Dharmas. 65). **-caru**, m. meat-broth, Gobh. **-cchadā**, f. a species of plant, L. **-ccheda**, m. 'fl°-cutter,' N. of a mixed caste (*ī*, f.), Cat. **-cchedin**, m. id., ib. **-ja**, mfn. 'flesh-born,' produced in the fl° (as an abscess), Suśr.; n. fat, ib. **-tas**, ind. on the fleshy side (of a hide; opp. to *loma-tas*), MānŚr. **-tāna**, m. a polypus in the throat, Suśr. **-tejas**, n. 'fl°-marrow,' fat, L. **-tva**, n. the being fl°, MBh.; the derivation of the word *māṇsa*, Mn. v, 55. **-dagdha**, n. cauterizing of the fl°, Suśr. **-dalana**, m. Amoora Rohitaka, L. **-drāvin**, m. Rumex Vesicarius, L. **-dhāvana**, n. water in which fl° has been washed, Suśr. **-dhauta**, mfn. cleaned with fl° i.e. with the hand, ĀpŚr. **-nirṇaya**, m. N. of wk. **-niryāsa**, m. the hair of the body, L. **-pa**, m. 'fl°-sucker,' N. of a Piśāca, Hariv.; of a Dānava, ib. **-pacana**, n. a vessel for cooking fl°, Vop. **-parivarjana**, n. abstaining from flesh or animal food, Mn. v, 34. **-parivikrayin**, m. a flesh-monger, MW. **-pāka**, m. a kind of disease (destroying the membrum virile), Suśr. **-piṭaka**, m. n. a basket-full or large quantity of flesh, Hariv. **-piṇḍa**, m. n. a lump of flesh, tumour, Suśr.; *-gṛihīta-vadana*, mfn. carrying a lump of fl° in the mouth, MW. **-pitta**, n. a bone, L. **-pīyūsha-latā**, f. N. of wk. **-pushpikā**, f. a species of plant, L. **-peśī**, f. a piece of fl°, Gobh.; N. of the fetus from the 8th till the 14th day, L.; a muscle, Bhpr. **-praroha**, m. a fleshy excrescence or protuberance, Suśr. **-phala**, m. Cucurbita Citrullus, L.; (*ā*), f. Solanum Melongena, L. **-budbuda-vat**, mfn. having fleshy protuberances, Suśr. **-bhaksha**, mfn. flesh-eating, carnivorous, Kāv.; Kathās. (also °*kshaka*); m. N. of a Dānava, Hariv. **-bhakshaṇa**, n. eating fl° or animal food; *-dīpikā*, f. N. of wk. **-bhikshá**, f. begging for fl° as alms, RV. **-bhūta**, mfn. being fl°, forming a bait, R.; °*t'-odana*, n. boiled rice mixed with meat, ib. **-bhettṛi**, mfn. piercing the fl°, Mn. viii, 284. **-maya**, mf(*ī*)n. consisting of fl°; °*yī peśī*, f. a piece of fl°, MBh. **-māshā**, f. Glycine Debilis, L. **-mīmāṇsā**, f. N. of wk. **-mukha**, mf(*ī*)n. having fl° in the mouth, MW. **-maithuna**, n. du. animal food and sexual intercourse, KātyŚr. **-yūtha**, n. a quantity of fl°, MW. **-yoni**, m. 'fl°-born,' a creature of fl° and blood, MBh. **-rasa**, m. fl°-broth, Suśr.; blood, Gal. **-ruci**, m. fond of fl°, Hit. **-ruhā, -rohā, -rohikā, -rohiṇī**, and **-rohī**, f. a species of fragrant plant, L. **-latā**, f. 'fl°-tendril,' a wrinkle, Bhartṛ. **-lubdha**, mfn. desirous of fl°, Hit. **-vat** (*māṇsa-*), mfn. having or possessing fl°, AV. **-varshin**, mfn. raining fl° (i.e. locusts?), MBh. **-vikraya**, m. the sale of fl°, Sukas. **-vikrayin** (Mn.), **-vikretṛi** (MBh.), m. a fl°-seller (the former also used as a term of reproach). **-viveka**, m. N. of wk. **-vṛiddhi**, f. increase or growth of fl°, Hit. **-śīla**, mfn. accustomed to eat animal food, Pāṇ. iii, 2, 1, Vārtt. 7, Pat. **-śukrala**, mfn. producing fl° and semen, Car. **-śoṇita**, m. fl° and blood, g. *gav-ādi*; *-paṅkin*, mfn. (a river) miry with flesh and blood, MBh. **-saṃghāta**, m. swelling of the flesh. **-sāra**, m. 'fl°-essence,' fat, L.; blood. Gal.; mfn. having the fl° predominant (among the 7 constituent parts of the body), VarBṛS. **-sneha**, m. 'fl°-marrow,' fat, L. **-hāsā**, f. skin, L. **Māṇsâd**, mfn. fl°-eating, carnivorous, L. **Māṇsâda**, mfn., id., Mn.; MBh. &c. **Māṇsâdin**, mfn. id., L. **Māṇsânaśana**, n. abstinence from animal food, ŚāṅkhŚr. **Māṇsârgala**, m. n. a piece of fl° hanging from the mouth (of a lion &c.), MBh. **Māṇsârbuda**, m. a partic. disease of the membrum virile, Suśr. **Māṇsâśana**, n. eating of meat or fl°, animal food, Mn. v, 73. **Māṇsâśā**, f. desire of fl°, ŚBr.; ĀpŚr. **Māṇsâśin**, mfn. eating fl°, living on animal food (°*śi-tva*, n.), R.; Pañcat. **Māṇsâshṭakā**, f. N. of the 8th day in the dark half of the month Māgha (on which meat or flesh is offered to deceased ancestors), Col. **Māṇsâhāra**, m. animal food, MW. **Māṇse-pad** (strong from *pād*), m. a species of animal, Kāṭh. **Māṇsêshṭā**, f. a species of flying animal (*valgalā*), L. **Māṇs'-odana**, m. = *māṇsâudana*, GṛS. **Māṇsônnati**, f. swelling of the flesh, Suśr. **Māṇsôpajīvin**, m. 'living by flesh,' a dealer in meat, R. **Māṇsâudana**, m. meat and boiled rice, ŚBr.; Kathās.; Suśr.; *-piṇḍa*, m. a ball of meat and boiled rice, MānGṛ.; °*danika*, mf(*ī*)n., g. *guḍâdi*.

Māṇsan-vát, mfn. (fr. *māṇsan* = *māṇsa*) fleshy (opp. to *a-māṇsaha*), TS.

Māṇsala, mfn. fleshy, VarBṛS.; Daś.; Suśr.; bulky, powerful, strong (also applied to sound), Uttarar.; Bālar.; pulpy (as fruit), MW.; m. Phaseolus Radiatus, L. **-phalā**, f. Solanum Melongena, L.

Māṇsi, m. sperm; mfn. having the smell of sperm, L.

Māṇsika, mfn. *māṇsāya prabhavati*, g. *saṃtāpâdi*; = *māṇsaṃ niyuktaṃ dīyate 'smai*, Kāś. on Pāṇ. iv, 4, 67; m. a butcher or a seller of meat, SaddhP.

Māṇsikā, māṇsinī or **māṇsī**, f. Nardostachys Jatamansi, L.

Māṇsīya, Nom. P. °*yáti*, to long for flesh, ŚBr.; ĀpŚr.

मांस्पृष्ट *māṃ-spṛishṭa*, mfn. (= *mām anuprâpta* or *mayā labdha*), ŚBr., Sch.

माकन्द *mākanda*, m. the mango tree, Kāv.; (*ī*), f. the Myrobolan tree, Myrobolan, L.; another species of plant, L.; yellow sanders, L.; N. of a city on the Ganges, MBh.

Mākandaka, mfn. belonging to the town Mākandī, Pāṇ. iv, 2, 123, Sch.; (*ikā*), f. N. of a city (= *mākandī*), Kathās.

Mākandika, m. (metron. fr. *makandikā*, Pat.) N. of a man, Buddh.

माकर *mākara*, mf(ī)n. relating or belonging to a Makara or sea-monster (with *ākara*, m. 'mine of M°s,' the sea, Nalôd.; with *āsana*, n. a partic. posture in sitting, Cat.; with *vyūha*, m. a partic. form of military array, Hariv.; with *saptamī*, f. = *makara-saptamī*, W.); m. pl. N. of a people, VarBṛS.

माकरन्द *mākaranda*, mf(ī)n. (fr. *makaranda*) coming from or consisting of the juice of flowers, Uttarar.; Mālatīm.

माकलि *mākali*, m. the moon, L.; N. of the charioteer of Indra, L. (cf. *mātali*).

माकष्टेय *mākashṭeya*, m. patr. fr. *makashṭu*, g. *śubhrâdi*.

माकारध्यान *mākāra-dhyāna*, n. (prob. fr. 1. *mā* + *k°* + *dh°*) a partic. method of abstract meditation, Cat.

माकिम् *mā-kim*, *mā́-kis*, *mā́kīm*. See under 1. *mā*, p. 804, col. 2.

माकी *mā́kī*, f. du. (prob.) heaven and earth, RV. viii, 2, 42 (Sāy. = *nirmātryau bhūtajātasya*; others 'the two great ones').

माकीन *mā́kīna*, mf(*ā*)n. (fr. 3. *ma*) my, mine, RV. viii, 27, 8.

माकुलि *mākuli*, m. a kind of snake, Suśr.

माकोट *mākoṭa*, N. of one of the places in which Dākshāyaṇī is worshipped, Cat.

माक्षव्य *mākshavya*, m. (patr. fr. *makshu*, g. *gargâdi*, Kāś.) N. of a teacher, AitĀr. (cf. *māṅkshavya*).

Mākshavyāyaṇī, f. of prec., g. *lohitâdi*, Kāś.

माक्षिक *mākshika*, mfn. (fr. *makshikā*) coming from or belonging to a bee, MārkP.; n. (scil. *madhu*) honey, Var.; Suśr.; a kind of h°-like mineral substance or pyrites, MBh. **-ja**, n. 'honey-born,' beeswax, L. **-dhātu**, m. pyrites, L. (also °*kaḥ dhātuḥ*). **-phala**, m. a species of cocoa-nut, L. **-svāmin**, m. N. of a place, Rājat. **Mākshikāśarkarā** (!), f. candied sugar, L. **Mākshikâśraya**, m. beeswax, L. (prob. w. r. for *makshik°*).

Mākshīka, m. a spider, BrahmUp. (also *ā*, f.); n. honey, L.; pyrites, L. (cf. *mākshika*). **-dhātu**, m. pyrites, VarBṛS. **-śarkarā**, f. candied sugar, L.

माख *mākha*, (prob.) n. (fr. *makha*) any relationship based upon an oblation offered in common, Hariv. (v.l. *maukha*).

माखनलाल *mākhana-lāla*, m. N. of a modern author, Cat.

मागद्य *māgadya*, mfn. (fr. *magadin*), g. *pragady-ādi*; n. N. of a city or of a place, Gaṇar.

मागध *māgadhá*, mf(ī)n. relating to or born in or living in or customary among the Magadhas or the Magadha country, AVPariś.; Lalit. &c.; m. a king of the M°, MBh.; Hariv.; N. of a mixed caste, AV. &c. &c. (accord to Mn. x, 11 the son of a Kshatriya mother and a Vaiśya father; he is the professional bard or panegyrist of a king, often associated with *sūta* and *bandin*, MBh.; Kāv. &c.; accord. to others one who informs a Rāja of what occurs in bazaars; also an unmarried woman's son who lives by running messages or who cleans wells or dirty clothes &c.; also opprobrious N. of a tribe still numerous in Gujarāt, and called the Bhāts, W.); white cumin, L.; N. of one of the seven sages in the 14th Manv-antara, Hariv.; of a son of Yadu, ib.; (pl.) N. of a people (= *magadhāḥ*), AVPariś.; MBh. &c.; of the warrior-caste in Śaka-dvīpa, VP.; of a dynasty, ib.; (*ā*), f. a princess of the Magadhas, PadmaP.; long pepper, L.; (*ī*), f. a princess of the M°, MBh.; R.; the daughter of a Kshatriya mother and a Vaiśya father, MBh.; a female bard, Kād.; (with or scil. *bhāshā*), the language of the M° (one of the Prākrit dialects), Sāh. &c. (cf. *ardha-m°*); Jasminum Auriculatum, L.; a kind of spice, Suśr. (long pepper; white cumin; anise; dill; a species of cardamoms grown in Gujarāt, L.); refined sugar, L.; a kind of metre, VarBṛS.; N. of a river (= *śoṇā*), R. **-deśīya**, mfn. belonging to or born in the land of the Magadhas, ŚrS. **-pura**, n. 'city of the Magadhas,' N. of a city, Cat. **-mādhava**, m. N. of a poet, ib.

Māgadhaka, mfn. belonging to Magadha, Kāraṇḍ.; m. pl. N. of a people (= *magadhāḥ*), Lalit.; (*ikā*), f. (sg. and pl.) long pepper, Suśr.; ŚārṅgS.

Māgadhika, m. a prince of the Magadhas, VarBṛS.

मागवी *māgavī*, f. yellow Panic, L.

माघ *māghá*, mf(ī)n. relating to the constellation Maghā, ŚārṅgS.; MBh.; m. (scil. *māsa*) the month Māgha (which has its full moon in the const° M°, and corresponds to our January-February), ŚBr. &c. &c.; N. of a poet (son of Dattaka and grandson of Suprabha-deva, author of the Śiśupāla-vadha, hence called Māgha-kāvya; cf. IW. 392, n. 2); of a merchant, Virac.; (*ī*), f., see below. **-kāvya**, n. M°'s poem; see above. **-caitanya**, m. N. of an author, Cat. **-pākshika**, mf(*ī*)n. belonging to one of the two halves of the month Māgha, MBh. **-purāṇa**, n. N. of wk. **-māsika**, mf(*ī*)n. relating to the month M°, MBh. **-māhātmya**, n. 'greatness of the m° M°,' N. of ch. of various Purāṇas; *-saṃgraha*, m. N. of wk. **-vallabhā**, f. and **-vyākhyā**, f. N. of Comms. on Śiś. **-śukla**, m. (scil. *paksha*) the light half of the month M°, Mn. iv, 96. **-snāna**, n. bathing or religious ablution in the m° M°; *-vidhi*, m. N. of wk. **Māghôtsava**, m. the chief festival kept by the Samājes (in commemoration of the founding of monotheistic worship by Rāmmohun Roy on the 11th of Māgha i.e. on the 23rd of January), RTL. 504. **Māghôdyāpana**, n. N. of wk.

Māghī, f. (scil. *tithi*) the day of full moon in the month Māgha, GṛŚrS.; MBh. &c.; Hingtsha Repens, L. **-paksha**, m. the dark half of the month M°, KātyŚr.; *-yajanīya*, n. the first day of the month Phālguna, ib.

Māghya, n. the flower of Jasminum Multiflorum or Pubescens, L.

माघमा *māghamā*, f. a female crab (= *karkaṭī*), L.

माघवत *māghavata*, mf(ī)n. (fr. *magha-vat*) relating or belonging to Indra, Pāṇ. vi, 4, 128, Sch.;

(*ī*), f. (scil. *diś*) the east, L. **—cāpa**, m. 'Indra's bow,' the rainbow, Uttarar.

Māghavana, mf(*ī*)n. belonging to or ruled by Indra, Pāṇ. vi, 4, 128, Sch.; (*ī*), f. (with *kakubh*) the east, Śiś.

Māghona, n. bountifulness, liberality, RV.; (*ī*), f. (scil. *diś*) the east, L.

माघष्टेय *māghashṭeya*, m. patr. fr. *maghashṭu*, g. *śubhrâdi*, Kāś.

माङ्कड *māṅkaḍa*, m. N. of a poet, L.

माङ्क्ष् *māṅksh*, cl. 1. P. *māṅkshati*, to wish, long for, desire, Dhātup. xvii, 18.

माङ्क्षव्य *māṅkshavya*, m. patr. fr. *maṅkshu*, g. *gargâdi*; °*vyāyaṇī*, f., g. *lohitâdi* (cf. *mākshavya*).

माङ्गल *māṅgala*, n. pl. (fr. *maṅgala*) N. of partic. verses addressed to Agni, ĀśvŚr. °**li**, m. patr. of a teacher, BhP. °**lika**, mf(*ī*)n. desirous of success, Pat.; auspicious, indicating good fortune, MBh.; Kāv. &c.; (prob.) n. any ausp° object (as an amulet &c.), Vet.; (*ā*), f. N. of a woman, Daś. °**likya**, mfn. auspicious, L.; (prob.) n. an ausp° object, Bālar.

Māṅgalya, mfn. conferring or indicating happiness, auspicious, MBh.; Kāv. &c.; m. Aegle Marmelos, L.; n. any ausp° object or ceremony, MBh.; Kāv.; VarBṛS.; welfare, propitiousness, Uṇ. v, 70, Sch.; du. N. of 2 partic. verses, MānGṛ. **—nāman** (°*lyá-*), mfn. having an ausp° name, MaitrS. (v.l. *maṅg*°). **—mṛidaṃga**, m. a drum beaten on ausp° occasions, Uttarar. **Māṅgalyârhā**, f. Ficus Heterophylla, L.

माङ्गुष्य *māṅgushya*, m. patr. fr. *maṅgusha*, g. *kurv-ādi*.

माच *māca*, m. a way, road, L. (cf. *māṭha*, *mātha*).

माचल *mācala*, m. (perhaps fr. 1. *mā* + *cala*) a thief, robber, L.; = *grāha* or *graha*, L.; sickness, L. (cf. *kari-* and *gaja-m*°).

माचाकीय *mācākīya*, m. N. of a grammarian, TPrāt.

माचाल *mācāla*. See *parṇa-m*°.

माचिका *mācikā*, f. a fly, L. (cf. *gṛiha-m*°); Hibiscus Cannabinus, Bhpr. (cf. *kāka-m*°).

Mācī, see *kāka-* and *dhvāṅksha-m*°. **—pattra**, n. a species of medicinal plant, L. (cf. *mañci-p*°).

माचिरम् *māciram*. See under 1. *mā*, p. 804, col. 2.

माजल *mājala*, m. the blue roller, L. **—pura**, n. N. of a city, Cat.

माजव *mājava*, m. pl. N. of a people, VP.

माजिक *mājika*, m. N. of a man, Rājat.

माजिरक *mājiraka*, m. patr. fr. *majiraka*, g. *śivâdi*.

माजीज *mājīja*, N. of a place, Cat. (v.l. *mājuja* and *mājūja*).

माञ्जिष्ठ *māñjishṭha*, mfn. (fr. *mañjishṭhā*) dyed with madder, red as m°, GṛS.; R. &c.; n. red, red colour, W.

Māñjishṭhaka (R.), °**ṭhika** (Uttarar.), mfn. = prec.

Māñjishṭhī-√kṛi, P. *-karoti*, to dye with madder, Bālar.

माञ्जीरक *māñjīraka*, m. patr. fr. *mañjīraka*, g. *śivâdi*.

माटङ्क *māṭaṅka*, m. a salt market, L.

माटाम्रक *māṭāmraka*, m. a species of tree, L.

माटि *māṭi*, f. armour, mail, L.

माटियारि *māṭiyāri* or *māṭīyāri*, N. of a city, Kshitîś.

माठ *māṭha* or *māṭhya*, m. a road, L. (cf. *māca*, *mātha*).

माठर *māṭhara*, m. (fr. *maṭha*) the superintendent of a monastic school or college, L.; a Brāhman, Gal.; (fr. *maṭhara*, g. *bidâdi*), N. of an ancient teacher, Kauś.; Vait.; of a disciple of Paraśu-rāma, Bāl.; of one of the Sun's attendants, MBh.; (with *ācārya*) of the author of the Sāṃkhya-kārikā-vṛitti, Cat.; of Vyāsa, L.; pl. N. of a people, MBh. (v.l. *rāmaṭha*); (*ī*), f. N. of a woman (cf. *kāśyapī-bālākyā-māṭharī-putra*).

Māṭharaka, mfn. (fr. *māṭhara*), g. *dhūmâdi*.

Māṭharāyaṇa, m. patr. fr. *māṭhara*, g. *haritâdi*.

Māṭharya, m. patr. fr. *maṭhara*, Uṇ. v, 39, Sch.

माठव्य *māṭhavya*, m. N. of a Brāhman, Śak.

माठी *māṭhī*, f. armour, mail, L. (cf. *māṭi*).

माठ्य *māṭhya*. See *māṭha*, col. 1.

माड् *māḍ*, cl. 1. P. Ā. *māḍati*, °*te*, to measure, weigh, Dhātup. xxi, 29 (v.l. for *māh*).

Māḍa, m. measure, weight, quantity, W.; Caryota Urens, L. (also *māḍā-druma*; cf. *madya-d*°).

माडव *māḍava*, m. a partic. mixed caste, L.

माडार्य *māḍārya*, mfn. (fr. *maḍāra*), g. *pragady-ādi*.

माडि *māḍi*, m. a palace, L.

माड्डुक *māḍḍuka* or *māḍḍukika*, m. (fr. *maḍḍuka*) a drummer, Pāṇ. iv, 4, 56.

माढि *māḍhi*, f. (only L.) the fibre or the germ of a leaf; honouring, reverencing (fr. √*mah*); dejection, sadness; a back or double tooth (also *māḍhī*); poverty, indigence; anger, passion; the hem or border of a garment; N. of a district.

माण *māṇa*, m. a species of plant (= *māṇaka*), L.

Māṇaka, m. Arum Indicum, L.; n. the bulb of Arum Indicum, L.

Māṇakī-vrata, n. N. of a partic. observance, Cat.

माणव *māṇava*, m. a youth, lad, youngster (esp. a young Brāhman; also contemptuously = little man, manikin), Kāty.; Kār. on Pāṇ. iv, 1, 161 &c. (cf. *daṇḍa-m*°); a pearl ornament of 16 strings, L.; (with Jainas) N. of one of the 9 treasures.

Māṇavaka, m. a youth, lad, fellow (= prec.), Gobh.; Kāv.; Pur. &c. (cf. *mādhavya-* and *māyā-m*°); a pupil, scholar, religious student, W.; a pearl ornament of 16 (accord. to L. also of 20 or 48) strings, VarBṛS.; Pañcad.; (*ikā*), f. a young girl, damsel, wench, Pāṇ. iii, 4, 72, Sch.; n. a kind of metre, Col. (also *-krīḍa* or °*ḍanaka*, n., °*ḍā*, f., °*ḍitaka*, n.)

Māṇavīna, mfn. proper for boys or lads, Pāṇ. v, 1, 11.

Māṇavya, n. a multitude or company of boys or lads, g. *brāhmaṇâdi*.

माणहल *māṇahala*, m. pl. N. of a people, VarBṛS.

माणि *māṇi*, Vṛiddhi form of *maṇi* in comp. **—cara**, m. a partic. deity, PārGṛ. **—cari**, m. N. of a Guhyaka (= Kubera?), L. **—cāra**, m. N. of a prince of the Yakshas (= *māṇibhadra*), R. **—pāra**, m. patr., Pravar. **—pāla**, mfn. = *maṇi-pālyā dharmyam*, g. *mahishy-ādi*. **—pālika**, m. metron. fr. *maṇi-pālī*, g. *revaty-ādi*. **—bandha**, n. = *māṇi-mantha*, L. **—bhadra**, m. N. of a prince of the Yakshas (= *maṇi-bh*°), SāmavBr.; MBh. **—mantha**, n. (fr. *maṇi-m*°) a kind of rock-salt, Bhpr. **—rūpya**, n. (fr. *maṇi-r*°) N. of a village, Pat.; °*pyaka*, mfn., ib. **—vara**, m. = *māṇibhadra*, MBh.

Māṇika, m. a jeweller, Campak.; (*ā*), f. a partic. weight (= 2 Kuḍavas, = 1 Śarāva, = 8 Palas), ŚārṅgS.

Māṇikâmbā, f. N. of a woman (mother of the Sch. Viṭṭhala), Cat.

Māṇikya, n. a ruby, Kāv.; Kathās. &c.; (*ā*), f. a kind of small house-lizard, L.; m. N. of a man, Rājat.; (with *sūri*) N. of an author, Cat. **—candra**, m. N. of a prince (patron of Keśava), Cat.; (with *sūri*) N. of an author, ib. **—candraka**, m. N. of a man, Vīrac. **—deva**, m. N. of a grammarian, Cat. **—puñja**, m. N. of a man, Vīrac. **—maya**, mf(*ī*)n. made or consisting of rubies, Kathās. **—malla**, m. N. of a prince (patron of Manohara-śarman), Cat. **—mālā**, f. N. of wks. (see *praśna-* and *vṛitta-m°-m*°). **—miśra**, m. N. of a man, Cat. **—mukuṭa**, **-mukha**, **-ratna**, m. N. of men, Vīrac. **—rāya** and **-sūri**, m. N. of men, Cat. **Māṇikyâditya**, m. N. of a man, Vīrac. **Māṇikyâdri**, m. N. of a mountain, Bālar. **Māṇikyântaka**, m. N. of a man, Vīrac.

माण्टि *māṇṭi*, m. N. of a teacher, ŚBr.; pl. his descendants, Cat.

माण्ड *māṇḍa*, m. N. of a man, Cat.

माण्डकर्णि *māṇḍakarṇi*, m. (fr. *maṇḍa-karṇa*) N. of a Muni, R.

माण्डप *māṇḍapa*, mf(*ī*)n. (fr. *maṇḍapa*) belonging to a temple, Cat.

माण्डरिक *māṇḍarika*, mfn. (fr. *maṇḍara*), g. *aṅguly-ādi*.

माण्डलिक *māṇḍalika*, mf(*ī*)n. (fr. *maṇḍala*) relating to a province, ib.; ruling a province (= *maṇḍalaṃ rakshati*), Uṇ. i, 106, Sch.; m. the governor of a province, Var.; Kām.

माण्डव *māṇḍava*, n. (fr. *maṇḍu*) N. of various Sāmans, ĀrshBr.

Māṇḍavī, f. fr. °*vya*, N. of Dākshāyaṇī in Māṇḍavya, Cat.; of a daughter of Kuśa-dhvaja and wife of Bharata, R. (cf. *vātsī-māṇḍavī-putra*).

Māṇḍavya, m. (patr. fr. *maṇḍu*, g. *gargâdi*) N. of a teacher (pl. his descendants), ŚBr. &c. &c.; of an astronomer, Var.; pl. N. of a people, Var.; of a school of the Bahv-ṛicas, Divyâv.; m. or n. (?) N. of a place, Cat. **—pura**, n. N. of a city on the Godā, Cat. **—śruti**, f., **-saṃhitā**, f. N. of wks. **Māṇḍavyêśvara**, n. N. of a Liṅga, Cat.; *-tīrtha*, n. N. of a place of pilgrimage, ib.

Māṇḍavyāyana, mf(*ī*)n. (fr. *māṇḍavya*), g. *lohitâdi*.

माण्डूक *māṇḍūka*, mf(*ī*)n. derived from the Maṇḍūkas (*śikshā*), L.; m. pl. N. of a Vedic school, ib.; (*māṇḍūkī*), f. N. of a woman; °*kī-putra*, m. N. of a teacher, ŚBr.

Māṇḍūkāyana, m. pl. N. of a school, L.; (*māṇḍūkāyanī*), f. N. of a woman; *-putra*, m. N. of a teacher, ŚBr.

Māṇḍūkāyani, m. N. of a teacher, ŚBr.

Māṇḍūki, m. patr. fr. *maṇḍūka*, Pāṇ. iv, 1, 119.

Māṇḍūkeya, m. patr. of a teacher (pl. his descendants), GṛS.; AitĀr.; n. the doctrine of M°, GṛS.

Māṇḍūkeyīya, mfn. relating to Māṇḍukeya, AitĀr.

Māṇḍūkya (prob. fr. *māṇḍūka*), in comp. **—śruti**, f. N. of wk. **Māṇḍūkyôpanishad**, f. N. of an Upanishad; *-āloka*, m., (°*shat*)*-kārikā*, f. pl., *-dīpikā*, f., *-bhāshya*, n., *-bhāshya-saṃgraha*, m. N. of wks.

मात 2. *māta*, m. (for 1. see p. 804, col. 2; for 3. under 2. *mātṛi*, p. 807, col. 2) metron. fr. *matī*; (*ī*), f. in *vāṅ mātī*, TS. (*mātyā*, VS.; MaitrS.; cf. Pāṇ. iv, 1, 85, Vārtt. 1, Pat.)

मातंग *mātaṃga*, m. (fr. *mataṃ-ga*) an elephant, MBh.; Kāv. &c. (ifc. = the chief or best of its kind, Hariv.); Ficus Religiosa, L.; (in astron.) N. of the 24th Yoga; a Caṇḍāla, man of the lowest rank, Daś.; Lalit.; a kind of Kirāta mountaineer, barbarian, Kathās.; N. of a serpent-demon, L.; of a Pratyeka-buddha, Lalit.; of the servant of the 7th and 24th Arhat of the present Avasarpiṇī, L.; of a writer on music, Ragh., Sch.; (*ī*), f., see below. **—kumārī**, f. a Caṇḍāla girl, Kād. **—ja**, mfn. coming from an elephant, elephantine, Suśr. **—tva**, n. the state or condition of a Caṇḍāla, Kād. **—divākara**, m. N. of a poet, Cat. **—nakra**, m. a crocodile as large as an elephant, Ragh. **—pati**, m. a Caṇḍāla chief, Kathās. **—makara**, m. a kind of marine monster, L. **—mātaṃga**, m. an excellent elephant, Bālar. **—rāja**, m. a Caṇḍāla king, Kathās. **—līlā**, f. N. of a medical wk.; *-prakāśikā*, f., *-vyākhyā*, f. N. of Comms. on it. **—sūtra**, n. N. of a Buddhist Sūtra. **Mātaṃgôtsaṅga**, m. the back of an elephant, MW.

Mātaṃgaka, m. N. of a Caṇḍāla chief, Kād.

Mātaṃgī, f. N. of the mythical mother of the elephant tribe, MBh.; R.; a Caṇḍāla or Kirāta woman, Kathās.; N. of a form of Durgā, Cat.; of one of the 10 Mahā-vidyās (q.v.), RTL. 188; of the mother of Vasishṭha, L. **—karṇāṭaka-kathā**, f., **-krama**, m., **-daṇḍaka**, m. or n., **-dīpa-dāna-vidhāna**, n., **-rahasya**, n., **-stotra**, n. N. of wks.

मातय *mātaya*. See p. 807, col. 2.

मातरपितरौ *mātara-pitarau*. See p. 807, col. 2.

मातरिपुरुष *mātari-purusha* &c. See p. 807, col. 2.

मातलि *mātali*, m. N. of Indra's charioteer,

MBh.; Kāv. &c. **– sārathi**, m. 'having Mātali for his charioteer,' N. of Indra, Ragh. **Mātalyupākhyāna**, n. N. of wk.

Mātalīya, mfn. relating to or concerning Mātali, MBh.

मातली *mātalī*, m. (only nom. sg. °*lī*, accord. to Sāy. from °*lin*) N. of a divine being associated with Yama and the Pitṛis, RV. (cf. *mātalī*, col. 3).

मातवचस *mātavacasa*, m. patr. fr. *matavacas*, ĀśvŚr.

मातवै *mātavai*. See under √2. *mā*.

माता 1. 2. *mātā*, *mātā-duhitṛi* &c. See col. 3.

मातालव *mātālavá*, m. (prob.) the flying fox, MaitrS. (Padap. *mānthālavá*; cf. *mānthālá*, *māndhāla*, *manthāvala*).

माति *māti*, *mātu*. See p. 804, col. 2.

मातुःष्वसृ *mātuḥ-shvasṛi*, *matur-bhrātrá*. See col. 3.

मातुर *mātura*. See col. 3.

मातुल *mātula* &c. See col. 3.

मातुलङ्ग *mātulaṅga*, m. a citron tree, Suśr.; n. a citron, ib. (also °*lāṅga*, Hcat.)

Mātuliṅga, m. (Hariv.), °**liṅgī**, f. (HPariś.) = prec. m.; n. = prec. n., Hariv.; Hcat.

Mātuluṅga, m. and n. = prec. m. and n., Suśr.; (*ā* or *ī*), f. another species of citron tree, sweet lime, ib. **– phala**, n. the fruit of the citron tree, a citron, Kathās. **– rasa**, m. the juice of the citron tree, Suśr. **Mātuluṅgâsava**, m. a liquor distilled from the citron tree, ib.

Mātuluṅgaka, m. = *mātuluṅga*, L.; (*ikā*), f. the wild citron tree, L.

मातृ 2. *mātṛí*, f. (derivation from √3. *mā* very doubtful; for 1. *mātṛi*, see p. 804, col. 2) a mother, any mother (applicable to animals), RV. &c. &c. (sometimes ifc., e.g. *Kuntī-m*°, having K° for a mother); du. father and mother, parents, RV. iii, 3, 33; vii, 2, 5 (also *mātárā-pitárā*, iv, 6, 7, and *pitárā-mātárā*, Pāṇ. vi, 3, 33; cf. *mātara-pitarau*, col. 2); the earth (du. heaven and earth), RV.; (with or scil. *lokasya*), a cow, MBh.; (du. and pl.) the two pieces of wood used in kindling fire, RV. (cf. *dvi-m*°); (pl.) the waters, RV. (cf. *sapta-m*° and Naigh. i, 13); (pl.) the divine mothers or personified energies of the principal deities (sometimes reckoned as 7 in number, viz. Brāhmī or Brahmāṇī, Māheśvarī, Kaumārī, Vaishṇavī, Vārāhī, Indrāṇī or Aindrī or Māhendrī, Cāmuṇḍā; sometimes 8, viz. Brāhmī, Māheśvarī, Kaumārī, Vaishṇavī, Vārāhī, Raudrī, Carma-muṇḍā, Kāla-saṃkarshiṇī; sometimes 9, viz. Brahmāṇī, Vaishṇavī, Raudrī, Vārāhī, Nārasiṇhikā, Kaumārī, Māhendrī, Cāmuṇḍā, Caṇḍikā; sometimes 16, viz. Gaurī, Padmā, Śacī, Medhā, Sāvitrī, Vijayā, Jayā, Deva-senā, Sva-dhā, Svāhā, Śānti, Pushṭi, Dhṛiti, Tushṭi, Ātma-devatā and Kula-devatā; they are closely connected with the worship of Śiva and are described as attending on his son Skanda or Kārttikeya, to whom at first only 7 Mātṛis were assigned, but later an innumerable number; also the 13 wives of Kaśyapa are called *lokānām mātaraḥ*), MBh.; R.; Pur.; Hcat. (RTL. 222 &c.); (pl.) the 8 classes of female ancestors (viz. mothers, grandmothers, great-grandmothers, paternal and maternal aunts &c., Saṃskārak.; but the word 'mother' is also applied to other female relatives and in familiar speech to elderly women generally); N. of Lakshmī, Bhartṛ.; of Durgā, L.; of Dakshāyaṇī in certain places, Cat.; accord. to L. also = a colocynth; Salvinia Cucullata, Nardostachys Jatamansi, Sphaerantus Indicus; air, space; the lower mill-stone; = *vibhūti*; = *revatī*. [Cf. Gk. μάτηρ, μήτηρ; Lat. *mater*; Lith. *motė*; Slav. *mati*; Germ. *muotar*, *Mutter*; Eng. *mother*.] **– ka-cchida**, m. 'the cutter off of his mother's head,' N. of Paraśu-rāma, L. **– kalpika**, mfn., Pat. **– kula**, m. N. of a man, L. **– kṛita** (*mātṛ́-*), mfn. done towards or by a mother, AV. **– kesaṭa**, m. a m°'s brother, L. **– gaṇa**, m. the assemblage of divine m°s (cf. above), MBh.; Var. &c. **– gandhinī**, f. 'having only the smell of a m°,' an unnatural m°, R. **– garbha**, m. a m°'s womb (*-stha*, mfn. being in it), L. **– gāmin**, mfn. 'going to a m°,' one who has committed incest with his m°, Pañcar. **– gupta**, m. N. of a king and poet, Rājat.; °*tâbhishechana*, n. an expedition against M°, MW. **– gṛiha**, n. a temple of the (divine) mothers, Kād. **– gotra**, n. a m°'s family (m. belonging to it); *-nirṇaya*, m. N. of wk. **– grāma**, m. 'the aggregate of m°s,' the female sex, Lalit.; any woman, L.; N. of a village, Rājat.; *-dosha*, m. pl. the faults of womankind, Lalit. **– ghāta** (L.); °**taka** (R.), °**tin** (Pañcar.), m. a matricide. **– ghātuka**, m., id.; N. of Indra, L. **– ghna**, m. = *-ghāta*, VarBṛS. **– cakra**, n. a kind of mystical circle, Rājat.; the circle or assemblage of (divine) mothers, Kathās.; *-pramathana*, m. 'afflicter of the circle of d° m°s,' N. of Vishṇu, Pañcar. **– ceṭa**, m. N. of a man, L. **– jña**, mfn. knowing i.e. honouring a m°, Lalit. **– tama** (*mātṛ́-*), mfn. very motherly or maternal (said of the waters), RV. **– tas**, ind. on the mother's side, in right of the m°, Mn. ix, 215. **– tā**, f. the state of a m°, BhP. **– datta**, m. 'm°-given,' N. of a man, Kathās.; of an author, Cat.; *ā*, f. N. of a woman, Kathās.; °*ttīya*, n. N. of wk. **– dāsa**, m. N. of a man, L. **– deva**, mfn. having one's m° for a deity, TUp. **– dosha**, m. the defect or inferiority of a m° (who is of a lower caste), Mn. x, 14. **– nandana**, m. 'm°'s joy,' N. of Kārttikeya, VarP. **– nandin**, m. a species of Karañja, L. **– nāman**, n. (scil. *sūkta*) N. of a class of sacred texts in the Atharva-veda, AVAnukr.; m. N. of the reputed author and deity of these texts, ib.; mf(*mnī*)n. named after a mother, MW. **– nivātam**, ind. at a m°'s side, Pāṇ. vi, 2, 8, Sch. **– paksha**, mfn. belonging to the m°'s side or maternal line, W. **– pālita**, m. N. of a Dānava, Kathās. **– pitṛi-kṛitâbhyāsa**, mfn. trained or exercised by father and m°, Hit., Introd. **– pūjana**, n., **-pūjā**, f. worship of the divine mothers, Saṃskārak. **– prayoga** (?), m. N. of wk. **– bandhu**, m. a relation on the m°'s side, Gaut.; (*ú*), n. blood relationship on the m°'s side, AV.; (*ū*), f. an unnatural m°, Mcar. (cf. *brahma-b*°). **– bāndhava**, m. = prec. m., L. **– bhakti**, f. devotion to a m°, Mn. ii, 233. **– bhāva**, m. the state of a m°, maternity, MW. **– bheda-tantra**, n. N. of a Tantra. **– bhogīṇa**, mfn., Pāṇ. v, 1, 9, Sch. **– maṇḍala**, n. the circle of (divine) m°s, Kād.; (*-vid*, m. the priest who acts for them), VarBṛS.; a partic. constellation, Kāśīkh. **– mát**, mfn. accompanied by a m°, possessing a m°, AV.; ŚBr. **– mātṛi**, f. 'm° of m°s,' N. of Pārvatī, L. **– mukha**, mfn. 'm°-faced,' foolish, scurrilous, L. **– mṛishṭa** (*mātṛ́-*), mfn. adorned by a m°, RV. **– modaka**, m. N. of Uvaṭa's Comm. on VPrāt. **– yajña** (Saṃskārak.), **-yāga** (ŚāṅkhGṛ.), m. a sacrifice to the m°s. **– vaṇsa**, m. the m°'s family, ŚāṅkhGṛ.; °*śya*, mfn. belonging to it, Kāv. **– vat**, ind. like (towards) a m°, Mn.; Cāṇ. **– vatsala**, mfn. m°-loving, Śak.; N. of Kārttikeya, MBh. **– vadha**, m. the murder of a mother, RāmatUp. (with Buddhists one of the 5 unpardonable sins, Dharmas. 60). **– vartin**, m. 'behaving well to a m°,' N. of a hunter, Hariv. **– vāhinī**, f. 'm°-carrying,' a bat, L. **– vidūshita**, mfn. tainted or impaired by a m°, R. **– vishṇu**, m. N. of a man, L. **– śāsita** or **-śishṭa**, m. 'taught by a m°,' foolish, simple, L. **– śrāddha**, n. an oblation offered to the m°s, Cat. **– shashṭha**, mfn. six with (i.e. inclusive of) a m°, MW. **– sheṇa**, m. N. of a poet, ib. **– shvasṛi**, f. (Pāṇ. viii, 3, 84) a m°'s sister, Mn.; MBh. &c. **– shvaseya**, m. (Pāṇ. iv, 1, 134) a m°'s sister's son, R.; (*ī*), f. a m°'s sister's daughter, MBh. **– shvasrīya**, m. = prec. m., Pāṇ. iv, 1, 134. **– siṇhī**, f. Justicia Gendarussa, L. **– svasṛi** and **-svaseyā**, w.r. for *-shvasṛi* and *-shvaseyī*. **– han**, m. = *-ghāta*, AVPaip.

3. **Māta** (for 1. and 2. see pp. 804 and 806), ifc. after a proper N. = *mātṛi*, Pāṇ. vi, 1, 14, Pat.

Mātaya, (artificial) Nom. P. °*yati* (*amamātat* = *mātaram ākhyat*), Pāṇ. vii, 4, 2, Sch.

Mātara-pitarau, m. (nom. du.) mother and father, parents, Pāṇ. vi, 3, 32.

Mātari, loc. of *mātṛi*, in comp. **– purusha**, m. a man (only when opposed) to his mother, a cowardly bully, g. *pātre-samitâdi* (cf. *pitari-śūra*). **– bhvarī** (*mātari-*), f. (fr. √*bhū*) = *mātari bhavantī*, RV. x, 120, 9 (Sāy.); AV. v, 29. **– śva**, m. (fr. *-śvan*) N. of a Ṛishi, ŚāṅkhŚr. **– śvaka**, mfn. containing the word *mātari-śvan*, g. *ghoshad-ādi*. **– śvan**, m. (*mātari-*; prob. 'growing in the m°,' i.e. in the fire-stick, fr. √*śvi*) N. of Agni or of a divine being closely connected with him (the messenger of Vivasvat, who brings down the hidden Fire to the Bhṛigus, and is identified by Sāy. on RV. i, 93, 6 with Vāyu, the Wind), RV.; AV.; (doubtful for RV.) air, wind, breeze, AV. &c. &c. (cf. Nir. vii, 26); N. of Śiva, Śivag.; of a son of Garuḍa, MBh.; of a Ṛishi, RV. **– śvarī**, prob. w.r. *-bhvarī*, AV. v, 2, 9.

1. **Mātā**, f. = *mātṛi* (see *kāka-* and *viśva-m*°). **– °lī** (°*tālī*), f. 'the m°'s friend,' N. of a being attending on Durgā, W. (2nd ed. *mātatī*).

2. **Mātā**, nom. of *mātṛi*, in comp. **– duhitṛi**, f. du. mother and daughter, Kathās. **– pitṛi**, m. du. (Pāṇ. vi, 3, 25, Sch.) mother and father, parents, ŚrS.; Mn.; MBh. &c. (pl. *mātā-pitáraḥ*, TS.); *-ghātaka*, m. one who kills m° and f°, Kāraṇḍ.; *-vihīna*, mfn. bereft of m° and f°, Mn. ix, 177; *-saṃjñin*, mfn. considering as m° and f°, Lalit.; *-sahasra*, n. pl. thousands of m°s and f°s, MBh. **– putra**, m. du. (Pāṇ. vi, 3, 25, Sch.) m° and son, R. **– maha**, m. (Pāṇ. iv, 2, 35, Vārtt. 2, Pat.) a maternal grandfather, MBh.; Kāv. &c.; (du.) mat° grandparents, PārGṛ.; (pl.) a mother's father, grandfather, and ancestors, Yājñ.; (*ī*), f. (Pāṇ. iv, 2, 36, Vārtt. 3, Pat.) a mat° grandmother, Mn. ix, 193; mf(*ī*)n. related or belonging to a mat° grandfather, R.; Hariv. (also °*hīya*, mfn., Hariv., Sch.)

Mātuḥ, in comp. for *mātur*. **– shvasṛi** or **-svasṛi**, f. the sister of a mother, Pāṇ. vi, 3, 24.

Mātur, gen. of *mātṛi*, in comp. **– bhrātrá**, m. a mother's brother, MaitrS.

Mātura, ifc. after a proper N. = *mātṛi*, Pāṇ. iv, 1, 115 (cf. *dvai-*, *bhādra-m*° &c.)

Mātula, m. a maternal uncle (often in respectful or familiar address, esp. in fables), GṛS.; Mn.; MBh. &c.; N. of the solar year, L.; the thorn-apple tree, L.; a species of grain, L.; a kind of snake, L.; (*ā*), f. the wife of a mat° uncle, mat° aunt, L.; (*ī*), f. id., L.; hemp, L.; mf(*ā* or *ī*)n. belonging to or existing in a mat° uncle, Śukas. (v.l.) **– putra** or °**traka**, m. the son of a mat° u°, L.; a thorn-apple (the fruit), L. **– sutā-pariṇaya**, m. N. of wk. **Mātulâtmaja**, m. the son of a maternal uncle, Gal. **Mātulâhi**, m. a kind of snake, L.

Mātulaka, m. a maternal uncle (a more endearing term than *mātula*), Pañcat.; the thorn-apple, L.; mfn. relating to or coming from a maternal uncle, Pat. on Pāṇ. iv, 2, 104.

Mātulānī, f. (Pāṇ. iv, 1, 49) the wife of a maternal uncle, Mn.; Yājñ.; BhP.; hemp or Crotolaria Juncea, L.; a kind of pulse (also °*nikā*), L.

Mātuleya, m. the son of a maternal uncle, BhP.; (*ī*), f. the daughter of a maternal uncle, ib.

Mātulya, n. (prob.) the house of a maternal uncle, R.

Mātṛika, mfn. coming from or belonging to a mother, maternal, Mn.; MBh. &c.; m. a maternal uncle, R.; (*ā*), f., see next; n. the nature of a mother, R.

Mātṛikā, f. a mother (also fig. = source, origin), Kāv.; Kathās.; Pur.; a divine mother (cf. under *mātṛi*), RTL. 188; a nurse, L.; a grandmother, Daś.; N. of 8 veins on both sides of the neck (prob. so called after the 8 divine m°s), Suśr.; N. of partic. diagrams (written in characters to which a magical power is ascribed; also the alphabet so employed; prob. only the 14 vowels with Anusvāra and Visarga were originally so called after the 16 div° m°s), RāmatUp.; Pañcar.; any alphabet, Hcat.; (pl.), Lalit.; a wooden peg driven into the ground for the support of the staff of Indra's banner, VarBṛS.; N. of the wks. included in the Abhidharma-piṭaka, Buddh.; of the wife of Aryaman, BhP.; = *karaṇa*, L. **– kośa**, m. N. of a wk. (on the employment of the alphabet in cabalistic diagrams). **– °kshara-nighaṇṭu** (°*kâksh*°), m., **-jagan-maṅgala-kavaca**, **-tantra**, n., **-nighaṇṭu**, m., **-nyāsa**, m., **-pushpa-mālikā**, f., **-pūjana**, n. (and °*na-vidhi*, m.), **-pravaṇa**, **-bīja-kośa**, m., **-bheda-tantra**, n. N. of wks. **– maya**, mf(*ī*)n. consisting of mystic characters, Hcat. **– maha**, see *pra-mātṛikā-maha* under 2. *pra-mātṛi*. **– yantra**, n. a kind of mystical diagram, Cat. **– °rṇava** (°*kârṇ*°), m., **-°rtha-cintana** (°*kârth*°), n., **-viveka**, m., **-sthāpana**, n., **-hṛidaya**, n. N. of wks. **Mātṛikôdaya**, m. N. of wk.

Mātṛi-√kṛi, P. *-karoti*, to adopt as a mother, Pāṇ. vii, 4, 27, Sch.

Mātṛiya, Nom. P. *-yati*, to consider or treat as a mother, VarYogay. (cf. Pāṇ. iii, 1, 10); Ā. *-yate*, to desire a mother, Pāṇ. vii, 4, 27, Sch.

मात्पुत्र *mātputra*, m.pl. (fr. *mat-putra*) the disciples of my son, Pat.

मात्या *mātyá.* See 2. *māta*, p. 806, col. 3.

मात्र *mātra*, °*traka* &c. See p. 804, cols. 2, 3.

मात्सर *mātsara*, mf(ī)n. (fr. *matsara*) envious, jealous, malicious, selfish, L. °**sarika**, mfn. envious, jealous, mal°, Kām. °**rya**, n. envy, jealousy, MaitrUp.; MBh. &c. (with Buddhists 5 kinds are named, Dharmas. 78; °*ryaṃ √kṛi*, to show jealousy, MBh.); displeasure, dissatisfaction, Kathās.

मात्सिक *mātsika*, m. (fr. *matsya*) a fisherman, Pāṇ. i, 1, 68, Vārtt. 8, Pat.

Mātsyá, mfn. relating to or coming from a fish, fish-like, fishy, ŚāṅkhGṛ.; Yājñ. &c.; m. a king of the Matsyas, ŚBr.; MBh.; Hariv.; N. of a Ṛishi, TBr.; MBh.; VP.; n. = *matsya-purāṇa*. **-gandha**, m. pl. (fr. *matsya-gandha*) N. of a race, L. **-purāṇa**, n. = *matsya-p°*.

Mātsyaka, mfn. = *mātsya*, MBh. °**syika**, m. a fisherman, Pāṇ. iv, 4, 35. °**syeya**, m. pl. the Matsya people, MBh.

माथ *mātha*, m. (√*math*) churning, stirring, W.; hurting, killing, destruction, Śatr.; illness, disease, L.; a way, road, L. (cf. *mātha*).

Māthaka, m. a destroyer, Bālar.

Māthitika, mfn. dealing in buttermilk (*mathita*), Pāṇ. v, 3, 83, Vārtt. 2, Pat.

माथव *māthavá*, m. patron. (= *mādhava*), ŚBr.

माथाथ *māthātha*, n. N. of two Sāmans, ĀrshBr.

माथिक *māthika*, m. Nimba Azadirachta, L.

माथुर *māthura*, mf(ī)n. coming from or born in or belonging to Mathurā, Hariv.; Kathās.; relating or belonging to Mathurā, Cat.; composed by Mathurā-nātha, ib.; m. an inhabitant of Mathurā, Hariv.; N. of a son of Citra-gupta, Cat.; of the keeper of a gambling house, Mṛicch.; (*ī*), f. N. of various wks. **-deśya**, mfn. coming from the Mathurā district, MBh.

Māthuraka, m. pl. the inhabitants of Mathurā, Cat.

माद *māda*, m. (√2. *mad*) drunkenness, exhilaration, delight, passion, stupor, L.; fighting, war, Sāy. (cf. *gandha-* and *sadha-m°*). **Mādānanda**, m. N. of a man, Cat.

Mādaka, mfn. intoxicating, exhilarating, gladdening, stupefying (*-tā*, f., *-tva*, n.), Kām.; Kap., Sch.; m. a gallinule (= *dātyūha*), L.

Mādana, mfn. exhilarating, delighting, RV.; maddening, intoxicating, Suśr.; m. the god of love, L.; Vanguiera Spinosa, L.; the thorn-apple, L.; (*ī*), f. N. of two plants (= *mākandī* and *vijayā*), L.; n. intoxication, exhilaration, L.; 'stupefier,' N. of a mythical weapon, R. (v. l. *madana*).

Mādanīya, mfn. intoxicating, inebriating, MBh.; n. an intoxicating drink, ib.

Mādayitṛi, m. an exhilarater, gladdener (f. °*trī*), Sāy.

Mādayitnú or °**yishṇú**, mfn. intoxicating, RV.; AV.

Mādāyana, m. patr. fr. *mada* (also pl.), Saṃskārak.

Mādin, mfn. intoxicating, stupefying (see *gandha-mādinī*); (*inī*), f. hemp, Bhpr.

माद्द्य *mādadya*, mfn. (fr. *madadin*), g. *pragady-ādi*.

मादानक *mādānaka*, n. a species of wood, Kauś. (w. r. for *mādanaka*?).

मादुक *māduka*, m. N. of a man, Pañcad.

मादुघ *mādugha*, mfn. relating to the plant called Madugha, L.

मादुर्णा *mādurṇā*, f. N. of a village, Kshitīś.

मादुष *mādusha*, n. (and *-tva*, n.) a word artificially formed for a partic. etymology, AitBr.

मादृश् *mā-dṛiś*, mf(ī)n. (fr. 3. *ma* + 2. *dṛiś*) like me, resembling me, MBh.; Kāv. &c. °**dṛiśa**, mf(*ī*)n. id., ib.

माद्य *mādya*, w. r. for *māndya*.

माद्र *mādra*, m. (fr. *madra*, of which it is also the Vṛiddhi form in comp.) a king of the Madras, Pat.; (*ī*), f., see below. **-kūlaka**, mfn. (fr. *madra-kūla*), g. *dhūmâdi*. **-nagara**, n. (fr. *madra-n°*), Pāṇ. vii, 3, 24, Sch. **-bāheya**, m. patr., Pat. **-vatī**, f. 'princess of the Madras,' N. of the wife of Parikshit, MBh.; of the second wife of Pāṇḍu, ib.; *-suta*, m. metron. of Saha-deva and Nakula, ib.

Mādraka, m. a prince of the Madras, Inscr.; (*ikā*), f. a Madra woman, MBh. (B. *madrikā*).

Mādri, m. c. for *mādrī* in comp. **-nandana**, m. metron. of Saha-deva and Nakula, MBh.

Mādrī, f. a species of plant (= *ativishā*), L.; 'princess of the Madras,' N. of the second wife of Pāṇḍu and mother of the twins Nakula and Saha-deva (who were really the sons of the Aśvins), MBh.; Hariv. &c.; of the wife of Saha-deva (also called Vijayā), MBh.; of the wife of Kroshṭu, Hariv.; of the wife of Kṛishṇa, ib.; VP. **-pati**, m. 'husband of Mādrī,' N. of Pāṇḍu, L. **-pṛithā-pati**, m. 'husband of Pṛithā and Mādrī,' N. of Pāṇḍu, W.

Mādreya, m. 'son of Mādrī,' metron. of Nakula and Saha-deva (du. of both together), MBh.; pl. N. of a people, AVPariś.; MBh.

माद्रुकस्थलक *mādrukasthalaka*, mfn. (fr. *madruka-sthalī*), g. *dhūmâdi*.

माधव *mādhava*, mf(ī)n. (fr. *madhu*; f. *ā* only in *mādhavā* [= *madhavyā*] *tanūḥ*, Pāṇ. iv, 4, 129, Sch.) relating to spring, vernal, Hariv.; Vikr.; Kathās.; belonging or peculiar to the descendants of Madhu i. e. the Yādavas, Hariv.; representing Kṛishṇa (as a picture), Hcat.; m. N. of the second month of spring (more usually called Vaiśākha, = April-May), TS. &c. &c.; spring, Kāv.; Pañcar.; Bassia Latifolia, L.; Phaseolus Mungo, L.; a son or descendant of Madhu, a man of the race of Yadu (sg. esp. N. of Kṛishṇa-Vishṇu or of Paraśu-rāma as an incarnation of this god; pl. the Yādavas or Vṛishṇis), MBh.; R.; Hariv.; BhP.; N. of Śiva, Śivag.; of Indra, Pañcat.; Vet. (w. r. for *vāsava*?); of a son of the third Manu, Hariv.; of one of the 7 sages under Manu Bhautya, MārkP.; of the hero of Bhava-bhūti's drama Mālatī-mādhava; of various other men, Kathās.; Hit. &c.; of various scholars and poets (also with *paṇḍita*, *bhaṭṭa*, *miśra*, *yogin*, *vaidya*, *sarasvatī* &c.; cf. *mādhavâcārya*); (*ī*), f., see below; n. sweetness, L.; (also m.) a partic. intoxicating drink, L. **-kara**, m. = *-candra-kara*. **-kāla-nirṇaya**, m., **-kośa**, m. N. of wks. **-gupta**, m. N. of a man, Hcar. **-candra-kara**, m. N. of a medical writer, Cat. **-campū**, f., **-carita**, n., **-cikitsā**, f. N. of wks. **-tīrtha**, m. N. of a chief of the Madhva sect (13th century), Cat. **-dāsa**, prob. w. r. for *mohana-d°*. **-deva**, m. N. of various authors, Cat. **-druma**, m. Spondias Mangifera, L. **-nandana**, m. N. of an author, Cat. **-nidāna**, n. N. of a medical wk. (also called *rug-* or *roga-viniścaya*). **-padâbhirāma**, m. N. of an author, Cat. **-pura**, n. N. of a city, L. **-purī**, m. N. of a poet, Cat. **-prācī**, f. N. of a locality, Cat. **-priya**, n. a species of sandal, Gal. **-bhaṭṭa-prayoga**, m. N. of wk. **-bhikshu**, m. N. of an author (= *mādhavâśrama*), Cat. **-māgadha**, m. N. of a poet, ib. **-māhātmya**, n. N. of wk. **-rāja**, m. N. of a king, L. **-rāmânanda-sarasvatī**, m. N. of a teacher, Cat. **-laghu-kārikā**, f. N. of wk. **-vallī**, f. Gaertnera Racemosa, Kathās. **-vijaya**, m. N. of a poem. **-śāstrin**, m. N. of Rāma-candra-tīrtha (who died in 1377), Cat. **-saṃgraha**, m. N. of wk. **-siṇha**, m. N. of a king and poet, Inscr. **-sena**, m. N. of a prince, Mālav.; of a poet, Cat. **-senā-rājan**, m. N. of a king, Daś. **-soma-yājin**, m. N. of a man (= *mādhavâcārya*), Cat. **-stava-rāja**, m., **-stuti**, f. N. of two hymns (from the VāyuP.) **Mādhavâcārya**, m. 'the learned M°,' N. of a celebrated scholar (author of the Sarva-darśana-saṃgraha, the Kāla-nirṇaya, the Nyāya-mālā-vistara &c.; he was the brother of Sāyaṇa with whom he is by some identified), IW. 118 &c.; of a pupil of Svarūpâcārya (belonging to the Nimbârka school), Cat. **Mādhavânanda-kāvya**, n. N. of a poem by Nanda-paṇḍita. **Mādhavânala**, m. N. of an author; n. N. of a love-story; *-kathā*, f. or *-kāma-kandala-kathā*, f. id.; *-nāṭaka*, n. N. of a play. **Mādhavâbhyudaya-kāvya**, n. N. of a poem. **Mādhavārya**, m. N. of an author (= *mādhavêndra-purī*), Cat. **Mādhavâśrama**, m., see *mādhava-bhikshu*. **Mādhavêndra-purī**, m., see *mādhavārya*. **Mādhavêshṭā**, f. a species of tuberous plant, L.; N. of Durgā, L. **Mādhavôcita**, n. a kind of perfume, L. **Mādhavôdbhava**, m. a species of tree, L. **Mādhavôllāsa**, m. N. of wk. **Mādhavôshita**, n. cubeb, L.

Mādhavaka, m. a spirituous liquor (prepared from honey or from the blossoms of the Bassia Latifolia), L.; (*ikā*), f. Gaertnera Racemosa, Gīt.; a kind of metre, Col.; N. of a woman, Mālav.

Mādhavi, m. patr. of Pradyumna, VP.

Mādhavī, f. the earth (also with *devī*), R.; 'spring-flower,' Gaertnera Racemosa, Kālid.; BhP.; honey-sugar, L.; an intoxicating drink, L.; a kind of grass, L.; sacred basil, L.; Anethum Sowa, L.; a procuress, L.; affluence in cattle or herds, L.; (in music) a partic. Rāgiṇī, Saṃgīt.; a woman of the race of Madhu or Yadu (e. g. An-antā, wife of Janam-ejaya; Sampriyā, w° of Vidūratha; Kuntī, w° of Pāṇḍu), MBh.; N. of Dākshāyaṇī in Śrī-śaila, Cat.; of Durgā, L.; of one of the Mātṛis attending on Skanda, MBh.; of a daughter of Yayāti, ib.; (with *śānti*) N. of wk. **-maṇḍapa**, m. or n. a bower formed of spring-flowers, Śak. **-latā**, f. a spring-creeper (esp. Gaertnera Racemosa, bearing white fragrant flowers), Ratnāv.; *-gṛiha*, n. = *mādhavī-maṇḍapa*, ib. **-vana**, n. N. of a forest; *-māhātmya*, n. N. of wk.

Mādhavīya, mfn. relating or belonging to or dedicated to or composed by Mādhava or Mādhavâcārya; see comp.; (*ā*), f. N. of a commentary; (with *avasthā*) the state or condition of Mādhava, Mālatīm.; m. pl. the disciples of Mādhavya, Pat.; n. a work of Mādhavâcārya. **-dhātu-vṛitti**, f. N. of a treatise on Sanskṛit roots by Sāyaṇa (dedicated to his brother Mādhava). **-nidāna**, n. N. of wk. (= *mādhava-n°*). **-vedārtha-prakāśa**, m. N. of Sāyaṇa's or Mādhava's Comms. on various Vedas.

Mādhavya, m. (patr. fr. *madhu*, Pāṇ. iv, 1, 106) N. of the Vidūshaka in Kālidāsa's drama Śakuntalā. **-māṇavaka**, m. the lad or fellow M°, ib.

Mādhu, Vṛiddhi form of *madhu* in comp. **-kara**, mf(*ī*)n. relating to or derived from a bee or honey, Prâyaśc.; resembling a bee, BhP.; (*ī*), f. collecting alms after the manner of a bee (i.e. by going from door to door), L.; alms obtained from five different places by the third class of religious mendicants, L. **-karṇika**, mf(*ī*)n. (fr. *madhu-karṇa*), g. *kumudâdi*. **-cchandasá**, mfn. relating to or coming from Madhu-cchandas, ŚBr.; ŚrS.; m. (patr. fr. *madhu-cchandas*) N. of Agha-marshaṇa and Jetṛi, RAnukr.; n. N. of a Sāman, ĀrshBr. **-tailika**, mfn. (fr. *madhu* + *taila*) prepared from honey and oil, Suśr. **-parkika**, mf(*ī*)n. relating to or presented at the Madhu-parka ceremony, ŚāṅkhGṛ.; Mn. **-matá**, mf(*ī*)n. derived from Madhu-mat, g. *kacchâdi* on Pāṇ. iv, 2, 133; m. pl. the inhabitants of Kaśmīra, L.; belonging to the river Madhu-matī, L. **-mataka**, mfn. (fr. *madhu-mat*), g. *kacchâdi* on Pāṇ. iv, 2, 134. **Mādhūkara**, mfn. (fr. *madhu-kara*) gathered or collected after the manner of bees, Cat. (cf. *mādhu-k°* above).

Mādhvaka, n. = *mādhavaka*, L.

Mādhvaśvi, m. (fr. *madhv-aśva*), Pat.

Mādhvika, m. a person who collects honey, MBh.

Mádhvī, f. (Pāṇ. vi, 4, 175) sweet, RV. (i, 90, 6; 8); ŚBr.; TS.; BhP.; a kind of intoxicating liquor, Mn. xi, 94; Gaertnera Racemosa, Vās.; a date, L.; a species of fish, L.; N. of a woman (an ardent worshipper of Vishṇu), W.; du. 'the two sweet ones,' N. of the Aśvins, RV.; VS.; AV.; TS.; pl. the waters, MaitrS.; TS. **-madhurā**, f. a species of date, L.

Mādhvīka, n. a kind of intoxicating drink, MBh.; Kāv. &c. (cf. *madhu-mādhvīka* and *mādhavaka*); (*ā*), f. Dolichos Sinensis, L. **-phala**, m. a species of cocoa-nut tree, L.

माधुक *mādhuká*, mfn. coming from or belonging to the Madhuka tree, TS.; m. pl. 'mead-makers,' N. of the Maireyakas or of a partic. mixed caste, MBh.

Mādhuki, m. patr. fr. *madhuka*, ŚBr.

माधुर *mādhura*, mf(ī)n. relating to or coming from Madhura or Madhurā, R.; (*ī*), f. sweetness, amiableness, loveliness, charm, Kāv.; mead, wine, ib.; N. of a Comm. on Gīt.; n. the blossom of Jasminum Zambac, L.

Mādhuri, f. = *mādhurī*, sweetness, loveliness, Bhojapr.

Mādhurya, n. sweetness, Kāv.; Suśr.; loveliness, exquisite beauty, charm, MBh.; Kāv. &c.; (with Vaishṇavas) a feeling of tender affection (for Kṛishṇa like that of a girl for her lover), RTL. 141; (in rhet.) grace of style (esp. consisting in the employment of separated words in a sentence, as opp. to *ślesha*, q.v.), Vām.; Kpr. &c.; mfn. sweetly speaking, Kull. on Mn. x, 33. **-kadambinī**, f. N. of wk.

माधूक *mādhūka*, mfn. (fr. *madhūka*) made from Bassia Latifolia, Kull. on Mn. xi, 95; (= *madhura-bhāshin*) sweet-voiced (said of the Maitreyakas), Mn. x, 33 (Kull.; cf. *mādhuka*); n. a kind of mead, Yājñ., Sch.

माधूची *mā́dhūcī*, f. du. (prob. formed after the analogy of *mādhvī*, q. v.) N. of the Aśvins, VS.

माधूल *mādhūla*, m. patr. fr. *madhūla* (also pl.), Saṃskārak.

माध्य *mādhya*, mfn. (fr. *madhya*, of which it is also the Vṛiddhi form in comp.) middle, central, mid, TS. **-ṃ-dina** (*mā́dh°*), mf(*ī*)n. (fr. *madhyaṃ-dina*) belonging to midday, meridional, RV. &c. &c.; m. = *mādhyaṃdinaḥ pavanaḥ*, ŚāṅkhŚr.; pl. N. of a branch of the Vājasaneyins, Inscr. &c. (cf. IW. 150; 245, 2); of an astron. school who fixed the starting-point of planetary movements at noon, Col.; of a family, Pravar.; (*ī*), f. (with *śikshā*) N. of wk.; n. = *mādhyaṃdinam savanam*, KātyŚr.; N. of a Tīrtha, Cat.; *-gṛihya*, n. N. of wk.; *-vat*, ind. as at the midday oblation, KātyŚr.; *-śākhā*, f. the school of the Mādhyaṃdinas (°*khīya*, mfn. belonging to it), Cat.; *-saṃhitā*, f., *-saṃdhyā-prayoga*, m.; °*nâraṇyaka-vyākhyā*, f. N. of wks. **-ṃ-dināyana**, m. (prob. fr. *madhyaṃ-dina*) N. of a teacher, BṛĀrUp. **-ṃ-dini**, m. (fr. id.) N. of a grammarian, Kār. on Pāṇ. vii, 1, 94. **-ṃ-dinīya**, mf(*ā*)n. (fr. *mādhyaṃdina*) usual at the midday oblation (also °*yaka*), ŚrS.; belonging to the school of the Mādhyaṃdinas, Cat. **-ṃ-dineya**, m. pl. the school of the M°, ib. **-stha**, mfn. (fr. *madhya-stha*) being in a middle state, indifferent, impartial, Kām.; n. indifference, impartiality, Mn. iv, 257. **-sthya**, n. (fr. *madhya-stha*) = prec. n., Dhūrtas.; intercession, mediation, W. **Mādhyāhnika**, mf(*ī*)n. (fr. *madhyâhna*) belonging to midday, taking place at noon, MārkP.; *-mantra*, m. or n., *-saṃdhyā-prayoga*, m. N. of wks.

Mādhyama, mfn. (fr. *madhyama*) relating to the middle, middlemost, central (also applied to the composers of the middle portion of the Ṛig-veda i.e. of books ii–vii), ŚāṅkhBr.; GṛS.; Pat.; middle-born, W.; m. pl. N. of a race, Pravar. **-sthya**, n. (fr. *madhyama-stha*) g. *brāhmaṇâdi*.

Mādhyamaka, mf(*ikā*)n. (fr. *madhyama*) relating to the middle region (i.e. the atmosphere), Nir.; (*ikā*), f. N. of the middle portion of the Kāṭhaka. °**keya**, m. pl. N. of a people, MBh. (v.l. *madhyamakeya*).

Mādhyamika, mfn. (fr. *madhyama*) = *mādhyamaka*, Nir. (also applied to a kind of cloth, Pat.); m. pl. N. of a Buddhist school, MWB. 157; 159; of a people in central India, VarBṛS. °**kīya**, mfn. = *madhyamikāyām bhavaḥ*, Pat.

Mādhyamineya, m. metron. fr. *madhyamā*, g. *kalyāṇy-ādi*.

माध्व *mādhva*, m. an adherent of Madhva (see p. 782, col. 3), W. **-siddhânta-sāra**, m. N. of wk.

माध्वक *mādhvaka*, °*vika*, *mā́dhvī*. See p. 808, col. 3.

मान् *mān*, cl. 1. 10. P. *mānati*, *mānayati*, to honour, respect, Dhātup. xxxiv, 36 (cf. √*man*, of which *mānayati* is the Caus.)

मान 1. *mā́na*, m. (√*man*) opinion, notion, conception, idea, Tattvas. (cf. *ātma-m°*); purpose, wish, design, AitBr.; self-conceit, arrogance, pride, KaushUp.; Mn. &c. (with Buddhists one of the 6 evil feelings, Dharmas. 67; or one of the 10 fetters to be got rid of, MWB. 127); (also n.) consideration, regard, respect, honour, Mn.; MBh. &c.; a wounded sense of honour, anger or indignation excited by jealousy (esp. in women), caprice, sulking, Kāv.; Daśar.; Sāh.; N. of the father of Agastya (perhaps also of A° himself; pl. the family of Māna), RV.; (in astron.) N. of the tenth house, VarBṛS. (W. also 'a blockhead; an agent; a barbarian'). **-kalaha**, m. quarrel arising from jealousy, rivalry, Kathās.; pl. N. of a people, MārkP. **-kali**, m. mutual disdain or ill-will, Amar. **-kṛit**, mfn. showing honour or respect (to others), MBh. **-kshati**, f. injury to h°, mortification, insult, Rājat. **-gṛiha**, n. N. of a place in Nepal. **-granthi**, m. violent or lasting anger, Caṇḍ. **-grahaṇa**, n. fit of sulkiness, Ratnâv. **-tantavya**, prob. w.r. for *mānut°*, Gobh. **-tas**, ind. from or through honour, for honour's sake, MBh. **-tā**, f. the being a proof, Nyāyam. **-tuṅga**, m. 'a man high in h°,' N. of various authors (also *-sūri* and °*gâcārya*), Cat. **-1. -tva**, n. haughtiness, arrogance, MW. **-1. -da**, mfn. (√*dā*) giving or showing honour (esp. voc. sg. 'honour-giver' in respectful address), MBh.; Kāv. &c.; m. a mystical N. of the letter *ā*, RāmatUp.; pl. N. of a people, MārkP.; (*ā*), f. the second Kalā or digit of the moon, Cat.; n. (scil. *astra*) N. of a partic. magical weapon, R. **-2. -da**, mfn. (√*do*) destroying arrogance or pride, MW. **-deva**, m. N. of a prince, L. **-dhana**, mfn. rich in honour, Ragh. **-dhmāta**, mfn. puffed up with pride, MW. **-para**, mf(*ā*)n. wholly addicted to pride, very proud or arrogant, Śiś.; (*ā*), f. N. of a woman, Kathās. **-parikhaṇḍana**, n. = *-bhaṅga*, Cāṇ. **-puraḥsaram**, ind. with (lit. 'preceded by') honour, Pañcat. **-prāṇa**, mfn. valuing h° like one's life, Kathās. **-bhaṅga**, m. breach or loss of honour, Cāṇ. **-bhaj**, mfn. receiving h° from (comp.), Mn. ii, 139. **-bhṛit**, mfn. possessing pride, Kir. **-mandara** or **-mandira**, m. N. of Rāvaṇa, L. **-maya**, m. a partic. article of enjoyment or luxury (?), Hariv. 8455 (Nīlak.) **-mahat**, mfn. great in pride, extremely proud, Bhartṛ. **-mātra**, n. mere honour, Pañcat. **-mānya**, mfn. (to be) held in h°, MBh. **-mauna**, n. silence caused by pride, MBh. **-yajña**, m. a sacrifice instituted through pride, ib. **-ratha**, m. N. of a king, VP. **-vat**, mfn. enjoying honour, rich in h°, TUp.; (*atī*), f. (a woman) angry from jealousy, Śiś.; Kathās. **-varjaka**, m. pl. N. of a people, MBh.; Pur. (v.l. *-vartika* and *valaka*). **-varjita**, mfn. destitute of h°, MBh.; dishonouring, BhP. **-vardhana**, mfn. increasing (a person's) h°, indicating respect, Mn. ix, 115. **-vikrayin**, mfn. selling one's h°, Kathās.; Rājat. **-1. -sāra**, m. or n. a high degree of pride, Daś.; m. N. of a king of Mālava, ib. **-siṅha**, m. N. of a king and various authors, Cat.; *-kīrti-muktâvalī*, f. N. of wk. **-sthiti**, f., see under 2. *māna*. **-svarūpa**, n. the nature of honour; °*pâbhijña-tva*, n. knowledge of the n° of h°, Rājat. **-han**, mf(*ghnī*)n. destroying pride, MārkP. **-hāni**, f. loss of honour, A. **Mānâgnihotra**, n. an Agnihotra instituted through pride, MBh. **Mānâṅka**, m. N. of an author, Cat. **Mānânanda**, m. N. of a teacher of Yoga, ib. **Mānândha**, mfn. blinded by pride, Veṇis. **Mānâpamāna**, n. du. honour and dishonour, Bhag.; w.r. for *mānâvabhaṅga*. **Mānârha**, mfn. worthy of h°, Mn. ii, 137. **Mānâvabhaṅga**, m. destruction of pride or anger, Vikr. iv, 25. **Mānâsa**, mfn. driving away pride or arrogance, Śiś. **Mānâsakta**, mfn. given to pride, haughty, VarBṛS. **Mānôtsāha**, m. energy arising from self-confidence, Pañcat. **Mānôtseka-parākrama-vyasanin**, mfn. possessing intense diligence, prowess, haughtiness and pride, Hit. **Mānônnata**, mfn. (a head) uplifted in pride, Ragh. **Mānônnati**, f. high honour, great respect, Bhartṛ. **Mānônmāda**, m. infatuation of pride, Pañcat. **Mānônmukta**, mfn. destitute of honour, VarBṛS.

Mānana, mfn. (fr. Caus.) honouring, serving as a token of respect, Nir.; n. and (*ā*), f. paying honour, showing respect, MBh.; Kāv. &c.

Mānanīya, mfn. to be honoured, deserving honour from (gen.), Kāv.; Pur.; Rājat.; m. an honourable man, Kād.

Mānayāna, mfn. (for *mānayamāna*, cf. Vām. v, 2, 83) showing honour or respect, MBh.; BhP.

Mānayitavya, mfn. to be honoured, deserving honour or respect, MBh.

Mānayitṛi, mfn. one who honours or respects, ib., Hariv. &c.

Māni, in comp. for 1. *mānin*. **-tā**, f. (ifc.) the fancying that one possesses, imaginary possession of (*jñāna-m°*), MBh.; honouring, esteeming, ib.; pride, Kir. **-tva**, n. (ifc.) the thinking one's self to be or have, MBh.; pride, arrogance (*a-m°*), Bhag.; the being honoured, receiving honour, MBh.

Mānika = 1. *mānin* in *paṇḍita-mānika*, q. v.

Mānita, mfn. (fr. Caus.) honoured, respected, MBh.; Kāv. &c.; n. showing honour or respect, Hariv. **-sena**, m. N. of a king, Buddh.

1. **Mānin**, mfn. (fr. √*man* or fr. 1. *māna*) thinking, being of opinion, KaṭhUp.; high-minded, haughty, proud towards (*prati*) or of (*-tas*), MBh.; Kāv. &c.; highly honoured or esteemed, ib.; (ifc.) thinking (esp. one's self) to be or have, appearing as or passing for (see *darśanīya-*, *paṇḍita-m°* &c.); highly esteeming or honouring (see f.); m. Marsilia Dentata, L.; (*inī*), f. a disdainful or sulky woman, Kāv.; (ifc.) the wife of (see *madhu-māninī*, lit. 'highly esteeming her husband'); Aglaia Odorata, L.; a kind of metre, W. (prob. w.r. for *mālinī*); N. of an Apsaras, VP.; of a daughter of Vidūrastha and wife of Rājya-vardhana, MārkP.

Mānya, mfn. to be respected or honoured, worthy of honour, respectable, venerable, Mn.; MBh. &c.; (*mānyá*), m. patr. fr. 1. *mā́na*, RV. i, 163, 14, &c., N. of Maitrāvaruṇi (author of RV. viii, 67), RAnukr. **-tva**, n. the being honoured by (gen.), respectability, worthiness, VarBṛS. **-sthāna**, n. a title to respect, Mn. ii, 136.

मान 2. *mā́na*, m. (√3. *mā*) a building, house, dwelling, RV.; an altar, Āpast.; (*mānā́*) a preparation, decoction (?), RV. x, 144, 5; (*ī*), f. measure (see *tiryaṅ-m°*); a partic. measure (= 2 Añjalis), L.; n. measuring, meting out, KātyŚr.; Hariv. &c.; measure, measuring-cord, standard, RV. &c. &c.; dimension, size, height, length (in space and time), weight, ib. (ifc. = fold, see *śatá-m°*); a partic. measure or weight (= *kṛishṇala* or *raktikā*; accord. to Sch. on TS. and KātyŚr. 100 Mānas = 5 Palas or Paṇas); form, appearance, RV.; likeness, resemblance, Śiś.; (in phil.) proof, demonstration, means of proof (= *pra-māṇa*, q. v.) **-kathana**, n. N. of wk. **-kanda**, m. Arum Indicum, Bhpr. **-2. -tva**, n. the being a measure or standard, L. **-3. -da**, mfn. (for 1. and 2. see under 1. *māna*) measuring, W. **-dīpikā**, f. N. of a Vedânta wk. **-dhānikā**, f. a species of gourd or cucumber, L. **-bhadraka**, m. a kind of pavilion, Vāstuv. **-mañjarī**, f. a dictionary of Sanskṛit and Bhāshā; *-guṇa-leśa-sūcaka-daśaka*, n. N. of wk. **-manohara**, m. or n. (?) N. of a wk. on the Mīmāṇsā by Vāg-īśvara. **-ṃ-paca**, mfn. (a vessel) cooking a partic. quantity of anything, Vop., Sch. **-yoga**, m. pl. the various methods or applications of measuring and weighing, Mn. ix, 330. **-randhrā** or **-randhrī**, f. a kind of water-clock or clepsydra, L. **-veda-campū**, f., **-samuccaya-ṭīkā**, f. N. of wks. **-2. -sāra**, m. N. of a wk. on architecture (or of a sage, its reputed author), IW. 185. **-sūtra**, n. a measuring-cord, Daś.; a cord or chain worn round the body, L. **-sthalaka**, mfn. (fr. *māna-sthalī*), g. *dhūmâdi*. **-sthiti**, f. 'right measure' or 'strong sentiment of honour' (the latter fr. 1. *māna*), Siṇhās. **Mānâṅgula-mahā-tantra**, n. N. of a Tantra. **Mānâdhika**, mfn. exceeding all measure, too large, VarBṛS. **Mānâdhyāya**, m. 'measurement-chapter,' N. of ch. of Sūryas. **Mānônmānikā**, f., g *śāka-pārthivâdi*, Siddh.

Mānaka, n. measure, weight, Hcat. (esp. ifc.); m. n. Arum Indicum (cf. *māṇaka* and *māna-kanda*); (*ikā*), f. a partic. weight or measure (= 2 Añjalis), Siddh. (cf. *mānī*); a partic. spirituous liquor, L.

2. **Mānin**, mfn. measuring, applying a measure, measurable, VP.

मानःशिल *mānaḥśila*, mf(*ī*)n. consisting of realgar or red arsenic, MBh.

मानन *mānana*, *mānanīya* &c. See col. 2.

मानव *mānavá*, mf(*ī*)n. (fr. *mánu*) descended from or belonging to man or Manu, human, RV. &c. &c.; favouring men, RV. ix, 98, 9; m. a human being, man, RV. &c. &c.; patr. fr. *mánu* (N. of Nābhā-nedishṭha, Śāryāta, Cakshus, Nahusha, Bhṛigu, Su-dyumna, Karūsha, and Deva-hūti), Br.; Pur. &c.; N. of a cosmic period, VP.; pl. the children of men, mankind, RV. &c. &c.; the races of men (of which 5 or 7 are reckoned), AV.; Br.; the subjects of a king, Mn.; R.; N. of a school of the black Yajur-veda, Hcat.; (*ī*), f. a daughter of man, a woman, RV. &c. &c.; Jasminum Auriculatum, L.; N. of a Vidyā-devī, L.; of a goddess (executing the commands of the 11th Arhat of the present Avasarpiṇī), L.; of a river, MBh. (v.l. *tāmasī*); pl. N. of partic. verses, Gaut.; n. a man's length (as a measure), VarBṛS.; a partic. penance, Prāyaśc.; N. of various

Sāmans, ĀrshBr.; of Manu's law-book, Vas.; of a Varsha, Cat. **-kalpa-sūtra**, n. incorrect N. of a Comm. on the first part of MānŚr. (IW. 205, 2). **-gṛihya-sūtra**, n. N. of one of the Sūtra wks. ascribed to Manu (q.v.) **-deva**, m. 'god among men,' a king, prince, Ragh. **-dharma-śāstra**, n. N. of the code of laws attributed to Manu (= *manu-saṃhitā*). **-pati**, m. 'man-lord,' a king, sovereign, VarBṛS. **-purāṇa**, n. N. of an Upapurāṇa. **-rākshasa**, m. a fiend in human shape, Bhartṛ. **-vāstu-lakshaṇa**, n. N. of wk. **-śrauta-sūtra**, n. N. of one of the Sūtra wks. attributed to Manu (q.v.) **-saṃhitā**, f. N. of ch. of the Āditya-purāṇa. **-sāra**, n. N. of wk. **-sūtra**, n. a Sūtra of M° (cf. *-gṛihya-* and *-śrauta-s°*). **Mānavâcala**, m. N. of a mountain, MārkP. **Mānavâdya**, n. N. of a Sāman, ĀrshBr. **Mānavêndīya-carita** (?), n. N. of a poem. **Mānavêndra**, m. = *mānava-deva*, R. **Mānavôttara**, n. N. of a Sāman, ĀrshBr. **Mānavâugha**, m. (with *guru*) N. of a class of composers of mystical prayers, Caṭ. (cf. *divyâugha-* and *siddhâugha*).

Mānavasya, Nom.P. (only p. °*syát*), to act like men, RV. i, 140, 4 (Sāy. 'to wish for men').

Mānavīya, mfn. descended or derived from Manu, Kull.; n. a kind of penance, ib. **-saṃhitā**, f. = *mānava-s°*, q.v.

Mānaveya, mfn. = *mānavīya*; m. patr., Hariv.

Mānavya, m. patr. fr. *manu*, g. *gargâdi*; n., w.r. for *māṇavya*.

Mānavyāyanī, f., g. *lohitâdi*.

मानवर्तिक *mānavartika*, *mānavalaka*. See *māna-varjaka* under 1. *māna*.

मानस *mānasá*, mf(*ī*, once *ā*)n. (fr. *mánas*) belonging to the mind or spirit, mental, spiritual (opp. to *śārīra*, corporeal), VS. &c. &c.; expressed only in the mind, performed in thought, i.e. silent, tacit (as a hymn or prayer), ŚrS.; Mn.; MBh.; conceived or present in the mind, conceivable, imaginable, R.; relating to or dwelling on the lake Mānasa (see n. below), BhP.; m. a form of Vishṇu, VP.; N. of a serpent-demon, MBh.; of a son of Vapush-mat, MārkP.; pl. a partic. class of deceased ancestors (regarded as sons of Vasishṭha), Cat.; a class of ascetics, RāmatUp.; N. of the Vaiśyas in Śāka-dvīpa, MBh.; of the worlds of the Soma-pa, Hariv.; (*ī*), f. (with *pūjā*) mental or spiritual devotion (opp. to *mūrti-p°*, adoration of images), RTL. 524; N. of a Kiṃ-narī, Kāraṇḍ.; of a Vidyā-devī, L.; n. (ifc. f. *ā*) the mental powers, mind, spirit, heart, soul (= *manas*, g. *prajñâdi*), KaṭhUp.; MBh.; Kāv. &c.; (in law) tacit or implied consent, W.; a kind of salt, KātyŚr., Sch.; the 25th mansion from that under which one is born, VarYogay.; (with or scil. *saras* or *tīrtha*) N. of a sacred lake and place of pilgrimage on mount Kailāsa (the native place of the wild geese, which migrate to it every year at the breeding season), MBh.; Kāv.; Pur.; N. of a work on Śilpa or art. **-karaṇa**, n., **-gaṇita-vidhi**, m. N. of wks. **-cārin**, m. 'frequenting lake Mānasa,' a wild goose, swan, Hariv. **-janman**, m. 'mind-born,' the god of love, Kathās. **-tva**, n. the state of spirit, spirituality, fulfilment of anything in mere thought, PañcavBr., Sch.; Sarvad. **-nayana**, n. N. of wk.; *-prasādinī*, f. N. of Comm. on it. **-pūjana**, n. N. of a Tāntric wk. **-pūjā**, f. N. of various wks.; *-prakāra*, m.; *-vidhi*, m. N. of wks. **-ruj**, f. mental disease, VarBṛS. **-vega**, mfn. swift as thought, Kād.; m. N. of a prince, Kathās. **-śuc**, f. mental sorrow or grief, VarBṛS. **-saṃtāpa**, m. id., Śak. **-haraṇa**, n. N. of wk. **Mānasâcala**, m. N. of a mountain, VP. **Mānasâlaya**, m. 'dwelling on lake Mānasa,' a wild goose or swan, L. **Mānasôtka**, m. eager to go to lake M°, Megh. **Mānasôttara**, n. N. of a mountain, Pur. (cf. *uttara-mānasa*). **Mānasôpacāra-pūjā-vidhi**, m. N. of wk. **Mānasôllāsa**, m. N. of various wks.; *-prabandha*, m., *-vṛittânta*, m., *-vṛittânta-vilāsa*, m., *-vyākhyā*, f. N. of Comms. **Mānasâukas**, mfn. dwelling on lake Mānasa, MBh.; m. a wild goose or swan, Rājat.

Mānasāyana, m. patr. fr. *manas*, g. *aśvâdi*.

Mānasika, mfn. (fr. *manas* or *mānasa*) committed (only) in thought (as a sin), Hcat.; conceived (only) in the mind, imaginary, Kāraṇḍ.; m. N. of Vishṇu, MBh.

Mānasoka (?), m. N. of an author or wk. on Vedânta, Cat.

Mānaskṛitā, m. (accord. to Mahīdh.) = *pūjāyā abhimānasya vā kartṛi*; (accord. to Sch. on TBr.) patr. fr. *manas-kṛit*, VS. xxx, 14.

Mānasya, m. patr. fr. *manas*, g. *gargâdi*.

मानस्तोकीय *mānastokīya*, n. the hymn beginning with *mā nas toke*, Baudh.

मानाप्य *mānāpya*, n. temporary degradation of a monk, Buddh.

मानायन *mānāyana*, m., g. *aśvâdi*.

मानाय्य *mānāyya*, m., *mānāyyāyanī*, f., g. *gargâdi* and *lohitâdi*.

मानिक *mānika*, *mānita*, 1. 2. *mānin*. See p. 809, cols. 2 and 3.

मानीन्ध *mānīndha*, m. N. of an astronomer (v.l. *mānindha*; cf. *maṇittha*).

मानुतन्तव्य *mā́nutantavya*, m. (fr. *manu-tantu*) patr. of Aikādaśâksha, AitBr.

मानुष *mā́nusha* or *mānushá*, mf(*ī*)n. (fr. *manus*) belonging to mankind, human, RV. &c. &c.; favourable or propitious to men, humane, RV.; AV.; m. (ifc. f. *ā*) a man, human being (pl. the races of men, 5 in number), RV. &c. &c.; N. of the signs of the Zodiac Gemini, Virgo, and Libra, VarBṛS.; (*ī*), f. a woman, MBh.; Kāv. &c.; (scil. *cikitsā*) 'human medicine,' a branch of med°, the administering of drugs (opp. to *āsurī* and *daivī cik°*), W.; n. the condition or manner or action of men, humanity, manhood, RV. &c. &c.; N. of a place, Cat. **-tā**, f., **-tva**, n. the state or condition or nature of man, manhood, manliness, humanity, MBh.; R.; Pur. **-daivika**, mfn. human and divine, Mn. i, 65. **-pradhana** (*mā́n°*), mfn. fighting for men, RV. **-māṃsâda**, mfn. eating man's flesh, MBh. **-rākshasa**, m. a fiend in human form, Bhartṛ.; (*ī*), f. a she-demon in human form, Kathās. **-laukika**, mfn. belonging to the world of men, human, MBh. **-sambhava**, mfn. coming from or produced by men, MW. **Mānushâda**, m. a man-eater; *-tva*, n. cannibalism, Kād. **Mānushôpêta**, mfn. joined with human effort, MBh.

Mānushaka. See *daiva-m°*.

Mānushi-buddha, m. a human Buddha (opp. to *dhyāni-b°*), Buddh.

Mānushī-√bhū, P. *-bhavati*, to become a man, Kathās.

Mānushya, n. (fr. *manushya*) human nature or condition, humanity, manhood, manliness, MBh.; Hariv. &c.; mf(*ā*)n. human, manly, Gobh.; MBh.; Hcat.

Mā́nushyaka, mfn. human, ŚBr. &c. &c.; n. human nature or condition, Daś. (loc. as far as lies in man's power, Kād.); a multitude of men, L.

मानोज्ञक *mānojñaka*, n. (fr. *mano-jña*) beauty, loveliness, Pāṇ. v, 1, 133.

मान्तव्य *māntavya*, m. patr. fr. *mantu*, g. *gargâdi*.

Māntavyāyanī, f. of prec., g. *lohitâdi*.

मान्त्र *māntra*, mf(*ī*)n. (fr. *mantra*) proper or peculiar to Vedic or magical texts, MW.

Māntravarṇika, mf(*ī*)n. (fr. *mantra-varṇa*) contained in the words of Vedic hymns, Bādar.; ŚrS., Sch. (°*kī-tva*, n., Nyāyam., Sch.)

Māntrika, m. a reciter of spells, enchanter, sorcerer, Rājat.; Vet.; Siṇhās.

Māntrita, mfn. (fr. next), g. *kaṇvâdi*.

Māntritya, m. patr. fr. *mantrita*, g. *gargâdi*.

मान्थ् *mānth*, cl. 1. P. *mānthati* = √*manth* or 1. *math*, to hurt, injure, Dhātup. iii, 9 (Vop.)

Mānthālá, m. (prob.) the flying fox, VS.; TBr. (cf. *manthāvala*, *mātālavá*, *māndhāla*, and next).

Mānthālavá (Padap. of MaitrS.) or **mānthīlava** (TS.), m. id.

Mānthya, mfn. (fr. *mantha*), g. *saṃkāśâdi*.

मान्थरेषणि *mānthareshaṇi*, m. patr. fr. *manthareshaṇa*, Pāṇ. ii, 4, 66, Sch.

Māntharya, n. (fr. *manthara*) weakness, Kāvyâd., Sch.

मान्द 1. *mánda*, mf(*ā*)n. (√1. *mand*) 'gladdening,' N. of water in partic. formularies, VS.; TS.; Kāṭh.

Māndra, mfn. (fr. *mandra*), g. *chattrâdi*.

मान्द 2. *mānda*, mfn. (fr. *manda*) relating to the higher apsis of a planet's course (°*daṃ karma*, the process of correction for the apsis; °*daṃ phalam*, the equation of the apsis), Sūryas.; n. = *māndya*, g. *prithv-ādi*.

Māndāra or °**rava**, m. a partic. mystical flower, Buddh. (cf. *mandāra*).

Māndāraka, mfn. belonging to the Mandāra tree, Divyâv.

Māndāryá, m. (fr. *mandāra*, g. *pragady-ādi*) N. of a man, RV. i, 165, 5.

Māndurika, m. (fr. *mandurā*) an ostler, groom, Siṇhâs.

Māndodareya, m. metron. fr. *mandôdarī*, Bālar.

Māndya, n. slowness, laziness, indolence, BhP.; Pañcat.; Sāh.; weakness, feeble state (as of understanding, digestion &c.), Daś.; Vedântas.; Hcat.; sickness, disease, Kathās. (°*dyaṃ* √*kṛi*, to make one's self ill); stateliness, Ml. **-vyāja**, m. simulation of illness, Kathās.

मान्धातकि *māndhātaki*, m. patr., g. *taulvaly-ādi* (Kāś.)

मान्धातृ *māndhātṛi*, m. (cf. *mandhātṛi*) N. of a king (son of Yuvanâśva, author of RV. x, 134), ĀśvŚr.; MBh. &c.; of another prince (son of Madana-pāla, patron of Viśvêśvara), Cat. **Māndhātā-pura**, n. N. of a city (also read *māndhāttā-tripura*), Cat.

Māndhātra, mfn. relating to Māndhātṛi (in °*trôpâkhyāna*, Cat.); m. patr. fr. *māndhātṛi*, ĀśvŚr.

मान्धाल *māndhāla*, m. (prob.) the flying fox, Gaut.; Vas. (cf. *mānthālá* &c.)

मान्धीर *māndhīra*, m. a bat, L. (cf. prec. and next).

Māndhīlava, m. a large bat, L.

मान्ध्योद *māndhyoda*, m. patr., Saṃskārak. (prob. w.r.)

मान्मथ *mānmatha*, mf(*ī*)n. (fr. *manmatha*) relating to or concerning love, produced by love, filled with love &c., Kāv.; belonging to the god of l°, Vcar.

मान्य *mānya*. See p. 809, col. 3.

मान्यमान *mānyamāná*, m. (fr. *manyamāna*, see √*man*) the proud one, RV. vii, 18, 20 (lit. 'the son of the proud;' Sāy. 'the son of Manyamāna').

मान्यव *mānyava*, mfn. relating to Manyu, Nir.

मान्यवती *mānyavatī*, f. N. of a princess, MārkP. (perhaps w.r. for *mālyavatī*).

मापक *māpaka*, mfn. (fr. Caus. of √3. *mā*) serving as a measure of (gen.), Nīlak.

Māpana, m. a pair of scales, balance, L.; (*ī*), f. measuring or meting out (esp. the place for a sacrifice), MBh.; n. the act of measuring or forming or shaping, ib.

Māpaya, °*yati*, see Caus. of √3. *mā*, 1. *mī* and *me*.

Māpya, mfn. measurable (in *a-m°*), Vajracch.

मापत्य *mā́patya*, n. (prob. fr. *mā* + *apatya*, 'by no means a child' or 'not a child,' scil. in the ordinary sense; accord. to others fr. Caus. of √*me*) N. of the god of love, L.

माबर *mābara*, N. of a place, Cat.

माभीद *mābhida*, m. a species of Rudrâksha with one berry, L.

माम् *mā́m*, acc. sg. of 3. *ma*, q. v. **-paśyá**, mfn. regarding or looking at me, AV.

माम *māma*, m. (fr. *mama*, lit. 'belonging to mine') dear friend, uncle (only in voc. sg. as a term of affection among animals in fables), Pañcat. (cf. *tāta*, *mātula* &c.) **-kesara**, m. a maternal uncle, Gal.

Māmaka, mfn. (Pāṇ. iv, 3, 3) my, mine, RV. &c. &c.; selfish, greedy, a miser, L.; a maternal uncle, L.; (*ī*), f. N. of one of the Buddhist Devīs, Dharmas. 4 (MWB. 216).

Māmakīna, mfn. (Pāṇ. iv, 3, 3) my, mine, Kāv.; Kathās.

Māmateyá, m. (fr. *mama-tā*) metron. of the mother of Dīrgha-tamas, RV.; AitBr.; BhP.

मामनसायति *māmanasāyati*, m. patr. (?), Pravar.

मामल्लदेवी *māmalla-devī*, f. N. of the mother of Śrī-harsha, Vās., Introd.

मामिडि *māmidi*, m. N. of a man, Cat.

मामुखी *māmukhī*, f. N. of a Buddhist Devī, W. (cf. *māmakī*).

मामुदगजनवी *māmuda-gajanavī*, m.=محمود غزنوی Mahmūd of Ghaznī, Kshitîś.

माय *māya*, mfn. (√3. *mā*) measuring (see *dhānya-m°*); creating illusions (said of Vishṇu), MBh.; (*ā*), f., see below. **–dāsa** (?), m. N. of an author, Cat. **–vat**, mfn. (comp. *māyá-vattara*) m. c. for *māyā́-vat*, Br.

Māyā́, f. art, wisdom, extraordinary or supernatural power (only in the earlier language); illusion, unreality, deception, fraud, trick, sorcery, witchcraft, magic, RV. &c. &c.; an unreal or illusory image, phantom, apparition, ib. (esp. ibc.=false, unreal, illusory; cf. comp.); duplicity (with Buddhists one of the 24 minor evil passions), Dharmas. 69; (in phil.) Illusion (identified in the Sāṃkhya with Prakṛiti or Pradhāna and in that system, as well as in the Vedânta, regarded as the source of the visible universe), IW. 83; 108; (with Śaivas) one of the 4 Pāśas or snares which entangle the soul, Sarvad.; MW.; (with Vaishṇavas) one of the 9 Śaktis or energies of Vishṇu, L.; Illusion personified (sometimes identified with Durgā, sometimes regarded as a daughter of Anṛita and Nirṛiti or Nikṛiti and mother of Mṛityu, or as a daughter of Adharma), Pur.; compassion, sympathy, L.; Convolvulus Turpethum, L.; N. of the mother of Gautama Buddha, MWB. 24; of Lakshmī, W.; of a city, Cat.; of 2 metres, Col.; du. (*Māye Indrasya*) N. of 2 Sāmans, ĀrshBr. **–kāpālika**, n. N. of a drama. **–kāra** or **-kṛit**, m. 'illusion-maker,' a conjurer, juggler, L. **–kshetra-māhātmya**, n. N. of wk. **–caṇa**, mfn. famous for juggling, Bhaṭṭ.; illusive, deceptive, W. **–°cāra** (*māyâc°*), mfn. practising illusion or deceit, Subh.; acting deceitfully, MBh. **–cid-yoga**, m. the union of Cit and Māyā, RTL. 37, n. 1. **–chadma-para**, mfn. only intent upon fraud and deceit, Subh. **–jīvin**, m. 'living by illusion,' a conjurer, juggler, L. **–tantra**, n. N. of a Tantra. **–°tmaka** (*māyâtm°*), mf(*ikā*)n. consisting of illusion, essentially illusory, W. **–da**, m. 'giving or causing illusion,' an alligator, crocodile, L. **–darśana**, n. N. of ch. of BhavP. **–devī**, f. N. of the mother of Gautama Buddha, Buddh.; of the wife of Pradyumna, VP.; *-suta*, m. 'son of Māyā-devī,' N. of Gautama Buddha, L. **–dhara**, mfn. possessing illusion, skilled in magic, R.; m. N. of a king of the Asuras, Kathās. **–°dhika** (*māyâdh°*), mfn. abounding in magic, R. **–°nvita** (*māyânv°*), mfn. possessing ill°, deceitful, MW. **–paṭu**, mfn. skilled in ill° or magical arts, Var. **–pati**, m. 'lord of ill°,' N. of Vishṇu, Pañcar. **–pur**, f. N. of a city, Kathās. (cf. *māyā*). **–purī**, f.=prec., ib.; *-māhātmya*, n. N. of sev. wks. **–prayoga**, m. the application or employment of magic, Pañcat.; deceitfulness, A. **–phala**, n. a gall-nut, L. **–baṭu**, m. N. of a king of the Śabaras, Kathās. **–bala-vat**, mfn. one who possesses or makes over to another the virtue of a partic. spell, R. **–bīja-kalpa**, m. N. of wk. **–°bhyudayana** (*māyâbh°*), m. N. of a Kāyastha, Rajat. **–mata**, m. or n. (?) N. of wk. **–maya**, mf(*ī*)n. consisting of illusion, formed of or creating ill°, illusive, unreal, magical, Up.; MBh.; R. &c.; m. N. of a Rākshasa, Bālar. **–māṇavaka**, mfn. appearing in an illusory way as a boy or dwarf, BhP. **–māhātmya**, n. N. of ch. of SkandaP. **–mṛiga**, m. an illusory antelope, phantom deer, R. **–moha**, m. 'illusion, bewilderment,' N. of a Jina or Buddha, VP. **–yantra**, n. 'instrument of illusion,' enchantment (ibc.=enchanted, magical, e.g. *°tra-vimāna*, m. n. an ench° chariot, magical car), Kathās. **–yoga**, m. the application or employment of illusion, empl° of magical arts, R.; BhP. **–yodhin**, mfn. fighting illusively or with deceitful artifices, MBh. **–rati**, f. N. of the wife of Pradyumna (=*-devī*), VP. **–rasika**, mfn. see *-vasika*. **–rāvaṇa**, m. Rāvaṇa in an illusory or disguised form, Cat. **–līlā-mata**, m. or n. (?) N. of wk. **–vacana**, n. a deceptive or hypocritical speech, Pañcat. **–vat** (*māyā́-*), mfn. having magical powers, employing deceit, sly, cunning, RV.; R.; Bālar. (*-tara*, AitBr.; more correctly *māyá-vat-tara*, ŚBr.); connected with many magical arts, BhP., Sch.; m. N. of Kaṇsa, L.; (*atī*), f. a partic. magical art personified, Kathās.; N. of the wife of Pradyumna, Hariv.; Pur. (cf. *-devī*); of the wife of a Vidyā-dhara, Kathās.; of a princess, ib.; of an authoress of certain magical incantations, Cat. **–°vani** (*māyâv°*), m. N. of a Vidyā-dhara, Bālar. **–vasika**, mfn.=*para-pratāraka*, L. (prob. w. r. for *-rasika*, 'fond of illusion or deceit'). **–vāda**, m. the doctrine affirming the world to be illusion (applied to the doctrine of the Vedânta and of Buddhism), Cat.; *-khaṇḍana*, n. (*°na-ṭippaṇī*, f., *°na-ṭīkā*, f.), *khaṇḍa-vivaraṇa*, n., *-saṃdūshaṇī*, f. N. of wks. **–vid**, mfn. experienced or skilled in magical arts, MBh. **–vidhi-jña**, mfn.=prec., Divyâv. **–vín**, mfn. possessing illusion or magical powers, employing deceit, deluding or deceiving others (*-vi-tā*, f.), RV.; MBh.; R. &c.; illusory, creating illusions, Nilak.; m. a magician, conjurer, juggler, MBh.; BhP.; a cat, L.; N. of a son of Maya, R.; n. a gall-nut, MW.; *°vi-mālikā*, f. N. of wk. **–śīla**, mfn. deceitful, Subh. **–°shṭaka** (*māyâsh°*), n. N. of wk. **–suta**, m. 'son of Māyā,' N. of Gautama Buddha, L. **–°sura** (*māyâs°*), m. N. of an Asura, Virac. **Māyôpajīvin**, mfn. living by fraud, Pañcat.

Māyāyin, mfn.=*māyā-vín* above, MW.

Māyi, in comp. for *māyin*. **–kāya**, m. N. of a grammarian, TPrāt. **–phala**, n. a gall-nut, L. **–bhairava-tantra**, n. N. of a Tantra (cf. *māyika-bhairava*). **–mata-khaṇḍana**, n. N. of wk.

Māyika, mfn. illusory, creating illusion, Pañcar.; practising deceit, deceiving others, L.; m. a conjurer, juggler, L.; n. or (*ā*), f. a gall-nut, L. **–bhairava**, n. N. of a Tantra.

Māyín, mfn. artful, skilled in art or enchantment, cunning, deceptive, illusory (*°yi-tā*, f.), RV.; AV.; ŚvetUp. &c.; subject to illusion, BhP.; m. a conjurer, juggler, magician, Kathās.; a cheat, deceiver, W.; N. of Brahmā, L.; of Śiva, L.; of Agni, L.; of Kāma, L.; n. magic, magical art, BhP. (cf. *dur-m°*); a gall-nut, L.

Māyīya, mfn. proceeding from Māyā, Harav.

Māyeya, mfn. (fr. *māyā*), g. *nady-ādi*.

मायण *māyaṇa*, m. N. of the father of Mādhava and Sāyaṇa, Cat.

मायव *māyavá*, m. a descendant of Mayu or Māyu, RV.

मायाति *māyāti* (?), m.=*nara-bali*, BrahmavP.

मायु 2. *māyu*, m. (√3. *mā*; for 1. *māyú* see p. 804, col. 2)=*āditya*, Nir.; sorcery, witchcraft, bad art (cf. *dur-m°*); (*ū́*), AV. xviii, 4, 4.

मायु 3. *māyu*, m. n. (accord. to Uṇ. i, 1 fr. √1. *mi*) gall, bile, the bilious humour, L.

मायुक *māyuka*, mfn.=*hrasva*, Naigh. (cf. *pra-māyu*, *°yuka*, under *pra-√mī*).

मायुराज *māyurāja*, m. N. of a son of Kubera, L. (cf. *mayu-r°*); of a poet (also read *mā-yū-r°*), Cat.

मायुस् *māyus*, m. N. of a son of Purū-ravas, VP.

मायूक *māyūka*. See under 1. *māyú*, p. 804, col. 2.

मायूर *māyūra*, mf(*ī*)n. (fr. *mayūra*) belonging to or coming from a peacock, MBh.; R. &c.; made of p°s' feathers, VarBṛS.; drawn by p°s, Hariv.; dear to p°s, Mālav.; (*ī*), f. a species of plant, L.; (in music) a partic. Rāgiṇī, Saṃgīt.; a partic. sternutatory, Car.; a flock of peacocks, Pāṇ. iv, 2, 44, Sch. **–karṇa**, m. patr. fr. *mayūra-k°*, g. *śivâdi*. **–kalpa**, m. N. of a partic. Kalpa or long period of time, Cat. **–vratin**, m. a member of a partic. sect, L.

Māyūraka, m. a peacock-catcher or one who makes various articles with p°s' feathers, R.; (*ikā*), f. (in music) a partic. Rāgiṇī, Saṃgīt.

Māyūri, m. patr. fr. *mayūra*, Pat.

Māyūrika, m. a peacock-catcher, R.

मायोभव *māyobhava* or *°vya*, n. (fr. *mayobhū*) well-being, gladness, enjoyment, GṛS.

माय्य *māyya*. See *puru-māyya*.

मार *māra*, mfn. (√*mṛi*) killing, destroying; m. death, pestilence, VarBṛS.; AVPariś.; slaying, killing, Rājat. (cf. *paśu-m°*); an obstacle, hindrance, Vās.; the passion of love, god of love, Hariv.; Kāv.; Kathās.; (with Buddhists) the Destroyer, Evil One (who tempts men to indulge their passions and is the great enemy of the Buddha and his religion; four Māras are enumerated in Dharmas. 80, viz. *skandha-*, *kleśa-*, *devaputra-*, and *mṛityu-m°*; but the later Buddhist theory of races of gods led to the figment of millions of Māras ruled over by a chief Māra), MWB. 208 &c.; the thorn-apple, L.; (*ī*), f. killing, slaughter, Prasannar.; pestilence (also personified as the goddess of death and identified with Durgā), AVPariś.; Kathās.; Pur. **–kāyika**, mfn. belonging to the retinue or attendants of Māra, Lalit. **–cittā**, f. N. of a Buddhist deity, Kālac. **–jit**, m. 'conqueror of Māra,' N. of Buddha, L. **–da**, n. 'death-giving,' flesh, Gal.; *-°dâkāra*, m. N. of a man, Cat. **–pa**, m. 'death-drinking (?),' N. of a man, Cat. **–pāpīyas**, m. the evil tempter, i.e. Māra, Lalit. **–putra**, m. a son of the Tempter, i.e. a tempter, ib. **–phī** (?), f. (in music) a partic. Rāgiṇī, Saṃgīt. **–bīja**, n. N. of a magical formula, Pañcat. **–mohita**, mfn. infatuated by the god of love, Kathās. **–ripu**, m. 'enemy of the god of love,' N. of Śiva, Prasannar. **–vat**, mfn. full of love, enamoured, Nalôd. **–siṇha**, m. N. of a prince, VP. **–hāṭī**, **-haṭṭā**, or **-hāṭhī** (?), f. (in music) a partic. Rāgiṇī, Saṃgīt. **Mārâṅka**, mfn. displaying tokens of passion, Gīt. **Mārâtmaka**, mfn. naturally murderous, Hit. **Mārâbhibhu**, m. 'overthrower of M°,' N. of a Buddha, L. **Mārâbhirāma**, mfn. fond of destroying, murderous, Dāś. **Mārâri**, m. =*māra-ripu*, Kathās.

Māraka, mfn. (ifc., f. *ā*), killing a killer, murderer (cf. *tri-* and *daśa-mārikā*); calcining (cf. *loha-māraka*); m. any deadly disease, plague, pestilence (personified as the god of death), Śaṃk.; a falcon, hawk, L.; (also n.) death of all creatures at the dissolution of the universe, L.; (*ikā*), f. a plague, pestilence, BhP.

Mā́raṇa, n. killing, slaying, slaughter, death, destruction, MaitrS.; Mn.; Hariv. &c. (*°ṇam pra-√āp*, to suffer death); a magical ceremony having for its object the destruction of an enemy (also *-karman* and *-kṛitya*, n.), RāmatUp.; Pañcar.; (scil. *astra*) 'slayer,' N. of a partic. mystical weapon, R.; calcination, Cat.; a kind of poison (cf. *maraṇa*); (*ī*), f. 'slayer,' N. of one of the 9 Samidhs, Gṛihyas.

Māri, f. death, pestilence, L. (also=*māraka*, m. n.); small-pox, L.; killing, slaying, L.; rain, L. **–vyasana-vāraka**, m. 'averting plague and distress,' N. of Kumāra-pāla, L.

Mārita, mfn. (fr. Caus.) killed, slain, destroyed, MārkP.; Pañcat.

Mārin, mfn. (only ifc.) dying (cf. *pūrva-* and *yuva-m°*); killing, destroying (cf. *jantu-m°*).

Mārī-mṛita, (prob. m.) a spectre, apparition, VarBṛS.

Mārīya, mfn. belonging to the god of love, Kathās.

Mā́ruka, mf(*ā*)n. dying, perishing, TS.; MānGṛ.; m. pl. N. of a people, VP.

मारकत *mārakata*, mf(*ī*)n. (fr. *marakata*) belonging to an emerald, having any of the properties or qualities of an e°, coloured like an e°, MBh.; Kāv.; Pur.; m. (with *dhātu*) an emerald, MBh. **–tva**, n. state or colour of an emerald, L.

मारजातक *mārajātaka*, m. a cat (?), W.

मारव *mārava*, mf(*ī*)n. (fr. *maru*) relating to a wilderness, forming a w°, being in a w°, Nalôd.; (*ī*), f. N. of a partic. musical scale, Col.

माराविक *mārāvika* or *mārāvida*, mfn. (applied to *śuka*), Pat. on Pāṇ. ii, 2, 11.

मारिच *mārica*, mfn. (fr. *marica*) made of pepper, peppery; n. (with *cūrṇa*) ground or pounded pepper, Hariv.

Māricika, mfn. prepared or seasoned with pepper, peppered, Pāṇ. iv, 4, 3, Sch. (cf. *vyakta-m°*).

मारित *mārita*, *mārin*. See above.

मारिष *mārisha*, m. (perhaps fr. Pāli *māri-sa*=*mādṛiśa*, 'colleague;' cf. *mārsha*) a worthy or respectable man (esp. in the voc. as a term of address = 'worthy friend' or 'dear sir;' in dram. applied to the manager or one of the principal actors), MBh.; Kāv.; BhP.; Amaranthus Oleraceus, Bhpr.; pl. N. of a people, MBh.; (*ā*), f. N. of the mother of Daksha, Hariv.; Pur.; of the wife of Śūra, Pur.; of a river, MBh.

मारी *mārī*. See under *māra*.

मारीच *mārīca*, mfn. belonging or relating to or composed by Marīci, Madhus; m. (patr. fr. *marīci*) N. of Kaśyapa, MBh.; R. &c.; a royal elephant, L.; a species of plant (= *kakkola*), L.; N. of a Rākshasa, MBh.; Hariv.; R.; (*ī*), f. N. of a Buddhist goddess, Dharmas. 4; of the mother of Gautama Buddha (= *māyā-devī*), L.; of an Apsaras, L.; of the wife of Parjanya, VP.; n. (fr. *marīca*) a grove of pepper plants, Ragh.; N. of Comm. on Siddhāntaś. **Mārīcôpapurāṇa**, n. N. of an Upapurāṇa.

Mārīci, m. patr. fr. *marīci*, Cat.; metron. fr. *marīcī*, g. *bāhv-ādi*; w.r. for *marīci*.

Mārīcya, m. pl. patr. fr. *marīci*, Mn. iii, 195.

मारुङ्ग *māruṅga*, m. softness, L.

मारुण्ड *māruṇḍa*, m. a serpent's egg, L.; cow-dung or a place spread with it, L.; a road, way, L.

मारुत *māruta* or *mārutá*, mf(*ī*)n. (fr. *marut*) relating or belonging to the Maruts, proceeding from or consisting of the M°, RV. &c. &c.; relating to or derived from the wind, windy, aerial, Mn.; Hariv. &c.; m. N. of Vishṇu, RV.; of Rudra, VarBṛS.; a son of the Maruts (applied to Vāyu, Ūrdhva-nabhas, Dyutāna or Nitāna), VS.; TS.; Br.; ŚrS.; (= *marut*) wind, air, the god of wind, Mn.; MBh. &c.; vital air, one of the 3 humours of the body, Suśr.; breath, Śiksh.; a chief of the Maruts, g. *parśv-ādi*; N. of a Marut, Yājñ.; Sch.; of Agni, Gṛihyas.; pl. the Maruts (regarded as children of Diti), MBh.; R.; N. of a people, MBh. (B.; C. *madaka*); (*ā*), f. N. of a woman, Vās., Introd.; (*ī*), f. (scil. *diś* or *vidiś*) the north-west quarter, VarBṛS.; n. (scil. *ṛiksha* or *nakshatra*) the constellation Svāti, L.; N. of a Sāman, ĀrshBr. **-kopana**, mfn. disturbing the wind (of the body), Suśr. (cf. *vāta-k°*). **-pūrṇa-randhra**, mfn. having cavities filled with wind (said of reeds), MW. **-maṇḍana**, n. N. of wk. **-maya**, mf(*ī*)n. consisting or having the essence of w°, Kuval. **-roga**, m. N. of a partic. disease (= *vāta-r°*), Suśr. **-vrata**, n. 'the having w°-like duties,' penetrating everywhere (as a king by means of spies), MW. (cf. Mn. ix, 306). **-suta** (A.), **-sūnu** (R.), m. 'son of the w°,' N. of Hanumat. **Mārutâtmaja**, m. 'son of the w°,' N. of fire, R.; of Hanumat, L. **Mārutândolita**, mfn. shaken by the w°, Ratnâv. **Mārutâpaha**, m. 'expelling the wind (of the body),' Capparis Trifoliata, L. **Mārutâpūrṇa**, mfn. filled with w°, MW. **Mārutâyana**, n. 'wind-passage,' a round window, Bhām. **Mārutâśana**, mfn. feeding on w° or air (alone), fasting, MBh.; m. a snake, L.; N. of one of Skanda's attendants, MBh.; of a Dānava, Hariv. **Mārutâśva**, m. having horses rapid as wind (?), RV. v, 33, 9 (patr. fr. *marutâśva*, Sāy.) **Mārutêśvara-tīrtha**, n. N. of a Tīrtha, Cat. **Mārutôtpatti**, f. N. of ch. of VāyuP. **Mārutôdvellita**, mfn. = *mārutândolita*, Ratnâv.

Māruti, m. (fr. *marut* or *māruta*) patr. of Dyutāna, RAnukr.; of Bhīma, MBh.; of Hanumat, Kāv. **-prashṭha**, mfn. led on or preceded by Hanumat, MW. **-mañjarī**, f. N. of a Stotra.

मारुतन्तव्य *mārutantavya*, w. r. for *mānvtantavya*, q. v.

मारुदेव *mārudeva*, N. of a mountain, Śatr. (v.l. for *marud-eva*, q.v.)

मारुध *mārudha*, N. of a place, MBh.

मारुला *mārulā*, f. N. of a poetess, Cat.

मारुवार *māruvāra*, N. of a country, ib.

मार्क *mārka*, m. = *mārkava*, L.

मार्कट *mārkaṭa*, mf(*ī*)n. (fr. *markaṭa*) peculiar to a monkey, m°-like, apish, Kathās. **-pipīlikā**, f. a small black ant, L.

Mārkaṭi, m. patr. fr. *markaṭa*.

मार्कण्ड *mārkaṇḍa*, m. = *mārkaṇḍeya*, Hariv.; mfn. composed by Mārkaṇḍa (as a Purāṇa), Cat.; (*ī*), f., see below. **Mārkaṇḍêśvara-tīrtha**, n. N. of a Tīrtha, Cat.

Mārkaṇḍikā or °*ḍī*, f. a species of plant, Bhpr.

Mārkaṇḍīya, n. a species of shrub, L.

Mārkaṇḍeya, m. (fr. *mṛikaṇḍu* or °*ḍa*; cf. g. *śubhrâdi*) patr. of an ancient sage (the reputed author or narrator of the Mārkaṇḍeya-purāṇa), MBh.; R. &c. (pl.) the descendants of M°, Saṃskārak.; (*ī*), f. N. of the wife of Rajas, VP.; n. N. of a Tīrtha, L.; mfn. composed by M°, Pur.; Madhus. **-kavindra**, m. N. of the author of the Prākṛita-sarvasva. **-carita**, n. N. of wk. **-tīrtha**, n. N. of a Tīrtha, Cat. **-darśana-stotra**, n. N. of ch. of Hariv. **-purāṇa**, n. N. of one of the 18 Purāṇas (so called from its supposed author M°; it expounds the nature of Kṛishṇa and explains some of the incidents of the Mahā-bhārata; it differs from the other Purāṇas in the form of its narrative rather than its sectarial character), IW. 387, n. 1; 514. **-saṃhitā**, f., **-stotra**, n., **-smṛiti**, f. N. of wks.

मार्कव *mārkava*, m. Eclipta Prostrata, L. (w.r. *mārkara*).

मार्ग *mārg* (properly Nom. fr. *mārga*; cf. √*mṛig*), cl. 1. 10. P. (Dhātup. xxxiv, 39) *mārgati*, *mārgayati* (ep. also Ā. *mārgate*; pf. *mamārga*, Gr.; aor. *amārgīt*, ib.; fut. *mārgitā*, ib.; *mārgishyati*, R.; inf. *mārgitum*, R.; ind. p. *mārgitvā*, ib.), to seek, look for, MBh.; Hariv.; R.; to search through, ib.; to seek after, strive to attain, MBh.; Var.; BhP.; to endeavour to buy, Kathās.; to request, ask, beg, solicit anything from any one (with abl. of pers. and acc. of thing, or with two acc.), MBh.; Kāv. &c.; to ask (a girl) in marriage, Śatr.; (cl. 10. P. *mārgayati*), to purify, adorn; to go (?), Dhātup. xxxii, 74.

Mārga, m. (in most meanings fr. *mṛiga*, of which it is also the Vṛiddhi form in comp.) seeking, search, tracing out, hunting, L.; (exceptionally also n.; ifc. f. *ā*) the track of a wild animal, any track, road, path, way to (loc. or comp.) or through (comp.), course (also of the wind and the stars), Mn.; MBh. &c. (*mārgam* √*dā* or *yam*, with gen. of pers., to give up the way to, allow to pass; *mārgeṇa*, ifc. = by way of i.e. through, across or along; with √*yā*, to go the way of i.e. suffer the same fate as; *mārgais*, ifc., through; *mārgāya*, with gen., in order to make way for any one; *mārge*, by the wayside or on the way; with *pra*-√*cal*, to set out on one's way; *nija-mārgam* √*gam*, to go one's way); a walk, journey, VarBṛS.; reach, range, Kir.; a scar, mark (left by a wound &c.), Ragh.; (in medic.) a way, passage, channel (in any part of the body, esp. the intestinal canal, anus); a way, expedient, means, Kām.; Kathās. (*mārgeṇa*, by means of, VarBṛS.); a way, manner, method, custom, usage, Up.; Yājñ.; MBh. &c.; the right way, proper course, MBh.; Hariv.; (cf. *a-mārga*); (with Buddhists) the way or path pointed out by Buddha for escape from the misery of existence (one of the 4 noble truths), MWB. 44 (cf. *āryâshṭâṅga-m°*); a title or head in law, ground for litigation, Mn. viii, 3, 9 &c.; a way of speaking or writing, diction, style, Kāvyâd.; Sāh.; a high (opp. to 'vulgar') style of acting or dancing or singing, Inscr.; Daśar.; (in dram.) pointing out the way, indicating how anything is to take place, Daśar.; Sāh.; (in astrol.) the 7th mansion, VarYogay.; (in geom.) a section, W.; musk, L. (cf. *mṛiga-mada*); the month Mārgaśīrsha (November–December), Rājat.; the constellation Mṛiga-śiras, L.; N. of Vishṇu (as 'the way,' scil. to final emancipation), MBh.; mf(*ī*)n. belonging to or coming from game or deer, R.; Var.; Suśr. **-kleśa**, m. the hardships of a journey, VarBṛS. **-tāla**, m. (in music) a partic. kind of measure, Saṃgīt. **-toraṇa**, n. a triumphal arch erected over a road, Ragh. **-dakshaka**, m. one skilled in making roads, R. (v.l. *-rakshaka*). **-darśaka**, m. 'way-shower,' a guide, Mṛicch. **-dāyinī**, f. 'giving up the way,' N. of Dākshāyaṇī at Kedāra, Cat. **-deśika**, m. = *-darśaka*, q. v., L. **-draṅga**, m. or °*gā*, f. a city on a road, Rājat. **-druma**, m. a tree growing by the wayside, Kathās. **-dhenu**, m. or °*nuka*, n. a Yojana, a measure of distance (perhaps originally 'a mile-stone in the form of a cow'), L. **-pa** or **-pati**, m. 'road-inspector,' N. of a partic. official, Rājat. **-patha**, m. a course, road, path, R. **-pariṇāyaka**, m. a guide, L. **-pālī**, f. 'road-protectress,' N. of a goddess, PadmaP. **-bandhana**, n. obstruction of a road or way, Kām. **-madhya-ga**, mfn. going in the middle of a road, being on the road, Rājat. **-marshi**, m. N. of a son of Viśvāmitra, MBh. (B. *mārdam°*). **-rakshaka**, m. a r°-keeper, guard, R. **-rodhin**, mfn. r°-obstructing, blocking up a r°, Kathās. **-vaṭī**, f. N. of a goddess who protects travellers, Cat. **-vartman**, n. pl. ways and paths; °*ma-su*, ind. everywhere, MBh. **-vaśâgata** (Kathās.), **-vaśânuga** (R.), **-vaśâyāta** (Kathās.), mfn. going or situated along the road. **-vāsas**, mfn. clad in an antelope's skin, MānGṛ. **-vighna**, m. an obstacle on the way, VarBṛS. **-vinodana**, n. entertainment on a journey, Kathās. **-śākhin**, m. a tree by the r°-side, Ragh. **-śira**, m. the month Mārgaśīrsha, Var.; BhP.; (*ī*), f. = *mārgaśīrshī* below, A.; *-lakshmī-vāra-vrata-kalpa*, m. N. of a Mantra. **-śiras**, m. the month Mārgaśīrsha, ŚāṅkhŚr., Sch. **-śīrsha**, mf(*ī*)n. born under the constellation Mṛiga-śiras, Pāṇ. iv, 3, 37, Sch.; m. (also with *māsa*) N. of the month in which the full moon enters the const° Mṛiga-ś°, the 10th or (in later times) the 1st month in the year = November-December, Kauś.; Mn.; MBh. &c.; (*ī* or *ā*), f. (with or without *paurṇamāsī*) the day on which the full moon enters the const° Mṛiga-ś°, the 15th d° of the first half of the month Mārgaśīrsha, GṛS; MBh.; *-māhātmya*, n.; °*shâdi-pūjā*, f. N. of wks. **-śīrshaka**, m. = *mārgaśīrsha*, m., Cat. **-śodhaka**, m. a r°-clearer, R. **-śobhā**, f. the clearing of a path in honour of some one, Divyâv. **-saṃdarśana**, m. a partic. Samādhi, Kāraṇḍ. **-stha**, mfn. being on the road, a traveller, MW.; staying on the right way (lit. and fig.), Kathās.; ŚārṅgP. **-sthiti**, f. wandering about, Gal. **-harmya**, n. a mansion or palace on a high road, Kathās. **Mārgâkhyāyin**, m. 'road-teller,' a guide, L. **Mārgâgata** (MBh.; Kathās.) or **mārgâyāta** (Kathās.), mfn. come from a journey; m. a traveller, wayfarer, L. **Mārgâlī**, f. a track, streak, Vcar. **Mārgâvalokin**, mfn. 'looking towards the road,' waiting for any one anxiously, Kathās. **Mārgêśa**, m. = *mārga-pa*, q. v., Rājat. **Mārgâishin**, mfn. searching for a road or path, MW. **Mārgôpadiś**, m. 'road-shower,' a guide, leader, Kām.

Mārgaka, m. the month Mārgaśīrsha, L. (cf. *prati-m°*).

Mārgaṇa, mfn. (ifc.) desiring, requiring, asking, MBh.; seeking, investigating, MW.; m. a beggar, suppliant, mendicant, Rājat.; an arrow, MBh.; R. &c.; a symbolical expression for the number 5 (derived from the 5 arrows of the god of love), Sūryas.; n. the act of seeking or searching for, investigation, research, inquiry, TBr., Comm.; MBh.; R. &c.; the act of begging, solicitation, affectionate sol° or inquiry (also *ā*, f.), L.; a bow (16384 Hastas long?), L. **-tā**, f. the being an arrow (°*tāṃ gataḥ*, become an arrow), Vikr. **-priyā**, f. N. of a daughter of Pradhā, MBh.

Mārgaṇaka, m. a beggar, solicitor, mendicant, L.

Mārgāyaṇī, f. N. of Mṛiga-śirsha (q. v.), L.

Mārgārá, m. patr. fr. Mṛigāri, VS. (Mahīdh.); metron. fr. Mṛigī, Pat.; 'one who catches fish with his hands,' TBr., Sch.

Mārgika, m. a hunter, Pāṇ. iv, 4, 35; a traveller, wayfarer, L.

Mārgita, mfn. sought, searched, searched through, pursued, hunted after, R.; Hariv.; SaddhP.; desired, required, Yājñ.; Kathās.

Mārgitavya, mfn. to be sought or s° after, R.; Hariv.; to be searched through, Hariv.; to be striven after, MBh.

Mārgin, m. one who clears or guards or shows the way, a pioneer or a guide, R.

1. **Mārgya**, mfn. (for 2. see under √*mārj* below) to be sought or searched for, W.

मार्गयथ *mārgayatha*, m. pl., patr., Saṃskārak.

मार्गव *mārgava*, m. a partic. mixed caste (born from a Nishāda and an Āyogavī), Mn. x, 34 (cf. *mārgāra*).

Mārgavīya, n. N. of a Sāman, ĀrshBr.

Mārgaveya, m. patr. or metron. of a Rāma, AitBr.

मार्गार *mārgārá*. See above.

मार्गीयव *mārgīyava*, n. N. of two Sāmans, ĀrshBr. (also *mārgīya-vādya*).

मार्ज *mārj* (rather Caus. of √*mṛij*, q.v.), cl. 10. P. (Dhātup. xxxii, 106, Vop.) *mārjayati*, to wipe, cleanse, purify; to sound (?), Dhātup. ib.

2. **Mārgya**, mfn. (for 1. see above) to be wiped away or removed, Bhaṭṭ.

Mārja, mfn. cleaning, a cleaner (see *astra-* and

śastra-m°); m. a washerman, L.; cleansing, purification, L.; smoothness, unctuousness, L.; N. of Vishṇu, L.; pl. N. of a people, VP.; (*ā*), f. a mixture of 3 oils, L.

Mārjaka, mfn. cleaning, a cleaner (see *keśa-m°*).

Mārjana, mf(*ī*)n. wiping away, cleaning, a cleaner (see *keśa-, gātra-, griha-m°*); m. Symplocos Racemosa, L.; (*ā*), f. wiping off, washing, purifying, Bālar.; the sound of a drum, Mālav.; Bālar.; (prob.) the parchment stretched at the ends of a drum, Bālar. ii, 1/2; performance with the fingers on a musical instrument (of which there are 3 kinds), L.; (*ī*), f. purification, ĀpŚr.; a broom, besom, brush, Kāv.; Kathās.; a washerwoman (as an abusive term), Lāṭy.; (in music) a partic. Śruti, Saṃgīt.; N. of one of Durgā's female attendants, L.; n. wiping away, rubbing, sweeping, cleansing, purifying, GṛŚrS.; Mn.; MBh. &c.; (also *ā*, f.), rubbing the ends of a drum with ashes or mud, Śiś.; 'purifying (one's self with water),' part of a religious ceremony at the morning Saṃdhyā, RTL. 403; (ifc.) removal, effacement of, amends for, Sāh.

Mārjanīya, mfn. to be cleaned or purified, W.

Mārjāra, m. a cat (prob. so called from its habit of constantly cleaning itself), Mn.; MBh. &c.; a wild cat, MBh.; R.; Suśr.; a civet-cat, L.; Plumbago Rosea, L.; Terminalia Katappa, L.; Agati Grandiflora, L.; N. of a poet, Cat.; (*ī*), f. a female cat, MārkP.; Rājat.; a civet-cat, L.; another animal (=*kodriṅga*), L.; musk, L. — **kaṇṭha**, m. 'having the throat or cry of a cat,' a peacock, L. — **karaṇa**, n. a partic. posture in sexual intercourse (also *°rī-kramaṇa*), MW. — **karṇikā** or **-karṇī**, f. 'cat-eared,' N. of Cāmuṇḍā, L. — **gandhā** or **°dhikā**, f. a species of Phaseolus, L. — **nyāya**, m. 'cat-hold theory,' a kind of doctrine held by a partic. sect of Vaishṇavas, RTL. 125 — **mūshaka**, n. sg. cat and mouse, Pāṇ. ii, 4, 9, Sch. — **liṅgin**, mfn. having the nature or character of a cat, Mn. iv, 197.

Mārjāraka, m. a cat, MBh.; a peacock (cf. *mārjāra*), L.; (*ikā*), f. a civet-cat, L.

Mārjāri, m. N. of a son of Saha-deva, BhP.

Mārjārī-kramaṇa. See *mārjāra-karaṇa*.

Mārjārīya, m. a cat, L.; a Śūdra, L.; one who continually cleanses his body, L.

Mārjāla, m. = *mārjāra*, a cat, L.

Mārjālīya, mfn. fond of ablution or purification (said of Śiva), MBh. (= *śuddha-deha* or *kirāta*, Nilak.); m. (scil. *dhishṇya*) a heap of earth to the right of the Vedi on which the sacrificial vessels are cleansed, VS.; Br.; ŚrS.; N. of the 17th Kalpa (q.v.), Cat.; = *mārjārīya* (in all meanings), L.

Mārjālya, mfn. fond of washing or ablution, delighting in purification, RV.

Mārjita, mfn. wiped, rubbed, swept, cleansed, purified (*°te*, ind. after purification), KātyŚr.; MBh. &c.; wiped away, removed, destroyed, Prab.; m. (or *ā*, f.) curds with sugar and spice, L.

Mārshṭavya, mfn. to be cleansed or swept or purified, Kull.

Mārshṭi, f. washing, ablution, purification, L.; anointing a person with oil or perfumes, L.; N. of the wife of Duḥ-saha, VP. (cf. *nir-mārshṭi*); m. N. of a son of Sāraṇa, VP. (v. l. *mārshi*). — **mat**, m. N. of a son of Sāraṇa, VP. (v. l. *mārshi-mat*).

मार्डाकव *mārḍākava*, m. patr. fr. *mṛiḍāku*, g. *biḍādi*.

Mārḍākavāyana, m. patr. fr. *mārḍākava*, g. *haritādi*.

मार्डीक *mārḍīká*, n. (fr. *mṛiḍīka*) mercy, pity, compassion, RV.

मार्ड्यर्थ *mārḍyartha*, m. N. of a man (pl. his descendants), Saṃskārak.

मार्णाल *mārṇāla*, mfn. (fr. *mṛiṇāla*) belonging to or being on a lotus-fibre, Dhūrtan.

मार्तण्ड *mārtaṇḍa*, m. (later form of *mārtāṇḍa*, q. v.) the sun or the god of the sun, MBh.; R. &c. (often ifc. in titles of books; cf. *chando-prameya-m°* &c.); a statue of the sun-god, Rājat.; N. of various authors (cf. comp.); pl. the Ādityas (and therefore a symbolical N. for the number 'twelve'), Śrutab.; a hog, boar, L. — **tilaka-svāmin**, m. N. of the teacher of the sage Vācaspati-miśra, Cat. — **dīpikā**, f. N. of wk. — **pratimā**, f. an image or statue of the sun-god, Rājat. — **maṇḍala**, n. the disc of the sun, Siṇhās. — **māhātmya**, n. N. of wk. — **vallabhā**, f. 'beloved of the sun,' Polanisia Icosandra, L.; N. of a Comm. — **vedôddhāra**, m. N. of wk. — **śataka**, n. N. of a Stotra.

Mārtaṇḍârcana, n. N. of wk.; *-candrikā*, f. of Comm. on it.

Mārtaṇḍīya, mfn. relating or belonging to the sun, solar, Bālar.

Mārtāṇḍá, m. (fr. *mṛitāṇḍa*) 'sprung from a (seemingly) lifeless egg,' a bird, RV.; Br.; 'bird in the sky,' the sun (= or v. l. for *mārtaṇḍa*), Rājat.

मार्तवत्स *mārtavatsa*, n. (fr. *mṛita-vatsā*) a still-born child, AV.

मार्त्तिक *mārttika*, mf(ī)n. (fr. *mṛittikā*) made of clay or loam, earthen, MānŚr.; Car.; m. n. an earthenware pot or dish, GṛŚrS. (m. also 'the lid of a pitcher,' W.); n. a clod or lump of earth, Bhām.

Mārttikāvata, (prob.) m. (fr. *mṛittikā-vatī*) N. of a country, MBh.; m. a prince of M°, Vās., Introd.; pl. N. of a people, MBh.; Var.; of a princely race, Hariv.; VP.; (prob.) n. N. of a town, MBh. **°vataka**, mfn. relating to the country M°, MBh. (v. l. *°vatika*).

मार्त्य *mārtya*, n. (fr. *martya*) the corporeal part (of man), mortality, BhP.

Mārtyavá, m. (fr. *mṛityu*) patr. of Antaka, AV. (*ī*, f., Kauś.)

Mārtyumjayī, f. (fr. *mṛityum-jaya*) patr., Kauś.

मार्त्स्न *mártsna*, mf(*ā*)n. (fr. *mṛitsnā*) ground fine or small, ŚBr.

मार्दंग *mārdaṃga*, m. (fr. *mṛidaṃ-ga*) a drummer, L.; N. of a town, L.

Mārdaṃgika, m. a drummer, R. — **pāṇavika**, n. sg. (fr. *mṛidaṃga + paṇava*) two players on different kinds of drums, Pāṇ. ii, 4, 2, Sch.

मार्दमर्षि *mārdamarshi*. See *mārga-marshi*, p. 812, col. 2.

मार्दलिक *mārdalika*, m. (fr. *mardala*) a drummer, Saṃgīt.

मार्दव *mārdava*, m. (fr. *mṛidu*) patr., g. *bidādi*; a partic. mixed caste, L. (prob. w. r. for *mārgava*, q. v.); n. (ifc. f. *ā*) softness (lit. and fig.), pliancy, weakness, gentleness, kindness, leniency towards (with gen., e.g. *m° sarva-bhūtānām*, leniency towards all beings), Āpast.; Yājñ.; R. &c. — **bhāva**, m. = prec. n., Hariv.

Mārdavāyana, m. patr. fr. *mārdava*, g. *haritâdi*.

Mārdavī-√kṛi, P. *-karoti* (p. p. *-kṛita*) to make soft or weak or indulgent, MBh.

मार्देय *mārdeya*, m. patr. or metron. fr. *mṛidi*, Siddh. — **pura**, n. N. of a town, Pāṇ. vi, 2, 101.

मार्द्वीक *mārdvīka*, mfn. (fr. *mṛidvīkā*) coming from or made of grapes, Suśr.; Bhaṭṭ.; n. wine, Śiś. viii, 30.

मार्मिक *mārmika*, mfn. (fr. *marman*) versed in, familiar or acquainted with anything (loc. or comp.), Bhām.

मार्ष *mārsha*, m. (cf. *mārisha*) an honourable man, respectable person, Buddh.; Amaranthus Oleraceus, Bhpr.

Mārshaka, m. (in dram.) a respectable person, L.

Mārshika, m. Amaranthus Oleraceus, L.

मार्षि *mārshi*, *mārshi-mat*. See under *mārshṭi*, *mārshṭi-mat*, col. 1.

मार्ष्टव्य *mārshṭavya*, *mārshṭi* &c. See col. 1.

माल *māla*, m. (derivation doubtful) N. of a district (lying west and south-west of Bengal), Megh.; of one of the 7 islands of Antara-dvīpa, L.; of Vishṇu, L.; of the son of a Śūdra and a Sūta, L.; pl. N. of a barbarous tribe or people, MBh.; (*ā*), f., see col. 3; n. a field, Inscr.; MBh.; a forest or wood near a village, L.; fraud, artifice, L.; (in some comp.) = *mālā*, a wreath, garland. — **kauśa** or **-kauśika**, m. (in music) a partic. Rāga, Saṃgīt. — **cakraka**, n. the hip-joint, L. — **jātaka**, m. a civet-cat, L. — **jit**, m. N. of Vedâṅga-rāya (author of the Pārasī-prakāśa), Cat. — **dhānya**, m. N. of a man, VP. — **bhañjikā**, f. 'breaking the garland,' N. of a game, Pāṇ. iii, 3, 109, Sch. — **bhārin**, m. bearing or wearing a garland, Mālatīm. (Pāṇ. vi, 3, 65, Sch.) — **maṅgala**, m. N. of an author; *-bhāṇa*, m. N. of a play composed by him. — **śrī**, f. (in music) a partic. Rāgiṇī, Saṃgīt.

Mālaka, m. (prob.) an arbour, bower, Siṇhās.; Melia Sempervirens, L.; a wood near a village, L.; pl. N. of a people, VP.; (*ā*), f. a garland, L.; (*akī*), f., g. *gaurâdi*; (*ikā*), f. a garland, Kāv.; Kathās.; a necklace, Hariv.; a row, series, collection of things arranged in a line, Kāv.; a white-washed upper-storied house, L.; N. of various plants (double jasmine, Linum Usitatissimum &c.), L.; a kind of bird, L.; an intoxicating drink, L.; a daughter, L.; N. of a river, L.; n. a garland, ring, Suśr.; Hibiscus Mutabilis, L.

1. Mālaya, Nom. (fr. *mālā*), P. *°yati* (for 2. see p. 814, col. 1), to crown or wreathe, Up. (cf. Pāṇ. vii, 4, 2, Sch.)

Mālā, f. a wreath, garland, crown, GṛŚrS.; MBh. &c.; a string of beads, necklace, rosary, Kāv.; Pañcat. (cf. *aksha-* and *ratna-m°*); a row, line, streak, MBh.; Kāv. &c.; a series, regular succession (with *nāmnām*, a collection of words arrayed in a series, a vocabulary, dictionary; cf. *nāma-m°*); a kind of Krama-pāṭha (cf. *krama-mālā*); N. of various metres, Col.; (in rhet.) a series of epithets or similes, W.; (in dram.) a series of offerings for obtaining any object of desire (Śak. iii, 17), Sāh.; (in astrol.) a partic. Dala-yoga (q. v.), VarBṛS., Sch.; Trigonella Corniculata, L.; N. of a river, MBh.; of a glossary. — **kaṇṭha**, m. Achyranthes Aspera, L. — **kanda**, m. a species of bulbous plant, L. — **kara**, m. = next, L. — **kāra**, m. a garland-maker, gardener, florist (also as a mixed caste), MBh.; Kāv. &c. (*ī*, f., VarBṛS.); N. of a son of Viśva-karman by a Śūdra woman or by Ghṛitācī, BrahmavP. — **kāriṇī**, f. a female g°-maker or florist, Pañcad. — **kuṭa**, N. of a kingdom, Buddh.; *-dantī*, f. N. of a Rākshasī, ib. — **guṇa**, m. the string of a g°, necklace; *-parikshiptā*, f. 'invested with the marriage-thread,' a marriageable woman, MW. — **guṇā**, f. (scil. *lūtā*) a species of venomous spider, Suśr. — **granthi**, m. = *-dūrvā*, L. — **°ṅka** (*mālâṅka*), m. N. of a king and author, Cat. — **tṛiṇa** and **-tṛiṇaka**, m. Andropogon Schoenanthus, L. — **dāman**, n. a garland of flowers, R. — **dīpaka**, n. (in rhet.) a partic. figure of speech, a closely linked or connected climax, Kāvyād.; Kpr. — **dūrvā**, f. a species of Dūrvā grass, L. — **dhara**, mfn. wearing a garland, crowned; m. N. of a class of divine beings, Buddh.; of a man, Kathās.; (*ī*), f. N. of a Rākshasī, Buddh.; n. a kind of metre, Col. — **dhāra**, m. N. of a class of divine beings, Divyâv. (cf. prec.) — **prastha**, m. N. of a city, Pāṇ. vi, 2, 88; *°sthaka*, mfn., ib. iv, 2, 122, Sch. — **phala**, n. the seed of Elaeocarpus Ganitrus (employed for rosaries), L. — **manu** or **-mantra**, m. a sacred text or spell written in the form of a wreath, RāmatUp. — **maya**, mf(*ī*)n. made or consisting of garlands, forming a line or series of (comp.), Rājat. — **°rishṭā** (*mālâr°*), f. a species of plant, L. (prob. w. r. for *mallār°*). — **rūpa**, mf(*ā*)n. forming a row or series (*-tā*, f., *-tva*, n.), Kpr.; Sāh. — **°likā** or **°lī** (*mālâl°*), f. Trigonella Corniculata, L. — **vat**, mfn. having a wreath or garland, garlanded, crowned, R., Sch.; m. (prob.) a gardener, Pāṇ. iv, 2, 72, Sch.; (*atī*), f. N. of the wife of Upa-barhaṇa, Cat.; of the w° of Kuśa-dhvaja, ib. — **vata**, n. the dwelling of the Mālāvats, Pāṇ. iv, 2, 72, Sch. — **vāda-khaṇḍa**, m. or n., **-śodhana**, n. N. of wks. — **saṃskāra**, m. 'consecration of rosaries with prayers,' N. of wk. (also *-varṇana*, n.)

Mālâsana-dīpikā, f. N. of wk. **Mālôpamā**, f 'string of comparisons,' a partic. figure of speech, Kāvyād. ii, 42.

Mālākā, f. = *mālikā* (see under *mālaka*), L.

Mālāyana, m. pl., patr., Saṃskārak.

Māli, mfn. (ifc.) = and v. l. for *mālin*, MBh. (cf. *yajña-*, *veda-* and *su-m°*); m. = *mālin*, N. of a son of the Rākshasa Su-keśa, R.

Mālika, m. a garland-maker, gardener, Kāv.; Pañcat.; a painter, dyer, L.; a kind of bird, L.; (*ā*), f., see under *mālaka*.

Mālita, mfn. (ifc.) garlanded, crowned, Vet.

Mālin, mfn. garlanded, crowned, encircled or surrounded by (instr. or comp.), Āpast.; MBh. &c.; (*ī*), m. a gardener, florist (cf. f.); N. of a son of the Rākshasa Su-keśa, R. (cf. *māli*); (*inī*), f., see next.

Mālinī, f. the wife of a garland-maker or gardener, female florist, Pañcat.; N. of two plants (= Alhagi Maurorum and *agni-śikhā*), L.; (in music) a partic. Śruti, Saṃgīt.; N. of various metres, Col.; of Durgā and one of her female attendants (also of a girl seven years old representing D° at her festival), L.; of a celestial maiden, MBh.; of one of the seven Mātṛis of Skanda, MBh.; of a Rākshasī (mother of Vibhīshaṇa), MBh.; N. assumed by Draupadī (while resident with king Virāṭa), MBh.; of the wife of Śveta-karṇa (daughter of Su-kāru), Hariv.; of the wife of Priya-vrata, Cat.; of the wife of Ruci and mother of Manu Raucya, MārkP.; of the wife of Prasena-jit, Buddh.; of various rivers, MBh.; of the celestial Ganges, L.; of a city (=*campā*), MBh.; Hariv.; =next, Āryav. **–tantra,** n. N. of a Tantra. **–vijaya,** m. N. of wk.

1. **Mālīya,** Nom. P. °*yati,* to wish one's self a garland, Pāṇ. vii, 4, 33, Sch.

2. **Mālīya,** mfn. fit or destined for a garland, Pāṇ. i, 1, 73, Sch.

Māleya, m. a garland-maker, florist, A.; (patr. fr. *māli*) N. of a Rākshasa, R.; (*ā*), f. great cardamoms, L.

Mālya, m. patr., PañcavBr. (also pl., Saṃskārak.); (*ā*), f. Trigonella Corniculata, L.; n. a wreath, garland, chaplet, GṛŚrS.; Up.; Mn. &c.; a flower, L.; mfn. relating to a garland, W. **–guṇāya,** Nom. Ā. °*yate* (fr. *mālya-guṇa*) to become the string of a g°, appear like a wreath, Bhartṛ. **–grathana,** n. the stringing together or winding of g°s, Cat. **–jīvaka** (Hariv.), °**vin** (L.), m. one who lives by making or selling garlands. **–dāman,** n. a g° of flowers, MBh. **–piṇḍaka,** m. N. of a serpent-demon, ib. **–pushpa,** m. Cannabis Sativa or Crotolaria Juncea, L. **–pushpikā,** f. a species of plant (=*śaṇa-pushpī*), L. **–vat,** mfn. crowned with garlands, garlanded, MBh.; m. N. of a Rākshasa (son of Su-keśa), R.; of one of Śiva's attendants, Kathās.; of a mountain or mountainous range (lying eastward of mount Meru), MBh.; (*atī*), f. N. of a river, R. **–vṛitti,** m. =*-jīvaka,* Hariv. **Mālyâpaṇa,** m. a garland or flower-market, MBh.; R.; Hariv.

मालति *mālati,* f.=*mālatī,* Gīt. (v.l.)

Mālatikā, f. N. of one of the Mātṛis attending on Skanda, MBh.; of a woman, Kathās.

Mālatī, f. Jasminum Grandiflorum (plant and blossom; it bears fragrant white flowers which open towards evening), Kāv.; Var.; Suśr.; Bignonia Suaveolens, W.; Echites Caryophyllata, L.; another species of plant (=*viśalyā*), L.; a bud, blossom, L.; =*kāca-mālī* (?), L.; a maid, virgin, L.; moonlight or night, L.; N. of various metres, Col.; of a river, VarBṛS.; of a woman (the heroine of the drama Mālatī-mādhava, q. v.); of Kalyāṇa-malla's comm. on Megha-dūta. **–kshāraka,** m. (prob.) borax, L. **–tīra** (ibc.) the banks of the Mālatī; *-ja* and *-sambhava,* m. or n. 'produced on the banks of the M°,' white borax, L. **–pattrikā,** f. the outer shell of a nutmeg, L. **–phala,** n. a nutmeg, Bhpr. **–mādhava,** n. 'Mālatī and Mādhava,' N. of a celebrated drama by Bhava-bhūti. **–mālā,** f. a garland of jasmine blossoms, Dhūrtas.; a kind of metre, Col.; N. of a lexicon.

मालद *mālada,* m.pl. N. of a people, MārkP. (v.l. for *māna-da*).

मालय 2. *mālaya,* mfn. (for 1. see p. 813, col. 3) coming from the Malaya mountains, Nalôd.; m. sandal-wood, L.; N. of a son of Garuḍa, MBh.; n. a caravansary, Sāh.; the unguent prepared from sandal, W.; =*malaya-dvīpa,* L.

मालव *mālava,* m. N. of a country (Malwa in central India; pl. its inhabitants), AVPariś.; MBh.; Kāv. &c.; m. (with or scil. *nṛipati*) a prince of the Mālavas, MBh.; Hariv.; Var.; a horse-keeper, L.; (in music) a partic. Rāga, Saṃgīt.; a white-flowering Lodhra, L.; N. of a man, Rājat.; (*ā*), f. N. of a river, MBh.; (*ī*), f. a princess of the M°, Pāṇ. v, 3, 114, Sch.; N. of the wife of Aśva-pati and progenitress of the M°, MBh.; (in music) a partic. Rāgiṇī, Saṃgīt. (printed *bhālavī*); a kind of Prākrit metre, Col.; Clypea Hernandifolia, L.; n. (with *pura*) N. of a city, Kathās.; mf(*ī*)n. relating or belonging to the M°, MBh.; Kāv. &c. **–gupta,** m. N. of an author (also °*tâcārya*), Cat. **–gauḍa,** m. in (music) a partic. Rāga, Gīt. **–deśa,** m. the country of Mālava or Malwa, Kathās. **–nṛipati,** m. a king of M°, MBh. **–bhadra,** m. N. of a poet, L. (w.r. for *rudra*?). **–maṇḍalâdhipati,** m. a ruler of the district of M°, Inscr. **–rudra,** m. N. of a poet, Cat. **–vishaya,** m. =*-deśa,* Hit. **–śrī,** f. (in music) a partic. Rāgiṇī, Saṃgīt. **–strī,** f. a M° woman, Kathās. **Mālavâdhīśa,** m. a king of M°, Daś.; Rājat. **Mālavêndra,** m. a ruler of M°, Cat. **Mālavôdbhava,** mf(*ā*)n. born or produced in Mālava, Kathās.

Mālavaka, mfn. worshipping Mālava, Pāṇ. iv, 2, 104, Vārtt. 18, Pat.; m. the country of M°, Inscr.; the adulterous offspring of Śūdra parents whose mother's husband is still alive, L.; (*ikā*), f. Ipomoea Turpethum, L.; N. of a woman (see next). **Mālavikâgnimitra,** n. 'Mālavikā and Agnimitra,' N. of a drama by Kālidāsa.

Mālavīya, mfn. native of or belonging to Mālava, Kathās.

Mālavya, mfn. relating or belonging to Mālava (*-deśa,* m. N. of a country, Cat.); m. a prince of the Mālavas, Pāṇ. v, 3, 114, Sch.; N. of 5 classes of extraordinary men (*mahā-purushāḥ*) born under partic. constellations, VarBṛS.

मालवर्ति *mālavarti,* m. pl. N. of a people, VP. (cf. *mānavartika*).

मालवानक *mālavānaka,* m. pl. N. of a people, MBh. (B. *mālavā narāḥ*).

मालसिका *mālasikā,* f. (in music) a partic. Rāgiṇī, Saṃgīt.

Mālasī, f. id., ib.; a species of plant, L.

मालहायन *mālahāyana,* m. patr., Pravar.

माला *mālā, mālin.* See p. 813, col. 3.

मालिन्द *mālindya,* m. N. of a mountain, VarBṛS.

मालिन्य *mālinya,* mfn. (fr. *malina*), g. *saṃkāśâdi;* n. foulness, dirtiness, impurity, Kāv.; Kathās.; Rājat.; darkness, obscurity, ŚārṅgP.; trouble, shame, affliction (cf. *vadana-m*).

मालु *mālu,* m. N. of a partic. mixed caste, BrahmavP. (v.l. *malla*); N. of one of Śiva's attendants, L.; f. a species of creeper (=*pattra-vallī* or *pattra-latā*), Uṇ. i, 5, Sch.; a woman, L. **–dhāna,** m. a species of animal, Hcar.; a kind of serpent, L.; (*ī*), f. a species of creeper (prob.=prec. and next), Bālar. **–latā,** f. the creeper called *mālu,* Lalit.

Māluka, m. pl. N. of a people (*ī,* f.), VP. (cf. *krishṇa-m°*). **Mālukâcchada,** m. a species of tree, L.

Mālūka, m. Ocimum Sanctum, L.

Mālorjara (?), m. id., L.

मालुद *māluda,* m. or n. a partic. high number, Buddh.

मालुवा *māluvā,* f. a kind of sweet potato, L.

मालूर *mālūra,* m. a species of plant, Hcar. (Aegle Marmelos or Feronia Elephantum, L.)

मालोक *māloka* and *māloji,* m. N. of two poets, Cat.

माल्य *mālya* &c. See col. 1.

माल्ल *malla,* m. (fr. *malla,* g. *sāṃkalâdi*) N. of a partic. mixed caste (cf. *mālu*). **–vāstava,** mfn. (fr. *malla-vāstu*), Pāṇ. iv, 2, 120, Sch.

Māllavī, f. a procession or expedition of wrestlers (=*malla-yātrā*), L.

माल्व्य *mālvya,* n. (fr. *malva*) foolishness, inconsiderateness, thoughtlessness (opp. to *dhairya*), MaitrS.; Kāṭh.

मावत् *mā-vat,* mfn. (for *ma-vat,* fr. 3. *ma*) like me, RV. (cf. Pāṇ. v, 2, 39, Vārtt. 1, Pat.)

माविलम्बम् *mā-vilambam,* °*bitam.* See under 1. *mā,* p. 804, col. 1.

मावेल्ल *māvella,* m. N. of a son of Vasu (prince of Cedi), MBh.

Māvellaka, m. pl. N. of a people, MBh. (v.l. *māvelaka* and *māvelvaka*).

माशब्दिक *mā-śabdika.* See under 3. *mā.*

माष *mâsha,* m. (n., g. *ardharcâdi*) a bean, RV. &c. &c. (sg. the plant; pl. the fruit; in later times =Phaseolus Radiatus, a valued kind of pulse having seeds marked with black and grey spots); a partic. weight of gold (=5 Kṛishṇalas=$\frac{1}{16}$ Suvarṇa; the weight in common use is said to be about 17 grains troy), Mn.; Yājñ.; a cutaneous eruption resembling beans, L.; a fool, blockhead, L.; N. of a man, g. *bāhv-ādi;* pl. (with or scil. *akṛishṭāḥ*) 'wild beans,' N. of a Ṛishi-gaṇa (the children of Su-rabhi, to whom RV. ix, 86, 1–10 is ascribed), RAnukr.; R.; Hariv.; (*ī*), f., see below. **–tilá,** m. du. sesamum and beans, TS. **–taila,** n. an oily preparation from beans, ŚārṅgS. **–pattrikā** and **-parṇī,** f. Glycine Debilis, Var.; Suśr. **–pishṭa,** n. ground beans, KātyŚr. **–pushpa,** n. the blossom of b°s, MBh. **–pesham,** ind. (with √*pish*) as if beans were ground, Mcar. **–prati,** ind., Pat. on Pāṇ. ii, 1, 19. **–mantha,** m. a beverage mixed with beans, Kauś. **–maya,** mf(*ī*)n. consisting of b°s, Hcat. **–mudga-maya,** mf(*ī*)n. consisting of Phaseolus Radiatus and Ph° Mungo, ib. **–rāśi,** m. a heap of blossoms, MBh. **–varṇa,** mfn. coloured like beans, Suśr. **–vardhaka,** m. a goldsmith, jeweller, L. **–śarāvi,** m. N. of a man, Lāṭy. (prob. patr. fr. *māsha-śarāvin;* cf. g. *bāhv-ādi*). **–śas,** ind. Māsha-wise, M° by M°, Siddh. **–sūpa,** m. b°-soup, Suśr. **–sthalaka,** mfn., **-sthalī,** f., g. *dhūmâdi* (Kāś.) **Māshâjya,** n. a dish of beans dressed or cooked with ghee, AV. **Māshâda,** m. 'b°-eater,' a tortoise, L. **Māshâśa** or °**śin,** m. 'id.,' a horse, L. **Māshôna** or **māshôna,** mfn. less by a Māsha, g. *giri-nady-ādi.*

Māshaka, m. a bean, Suśr.; m. n. a partic. weight of gold &c. (=7 or 8 Guñjās, acc. to some about 4½ grains), Mn.; VarBṛS.; Suśr. (cf. *pañca-m°*).

Māshi, m. patr. fr. *māsha,* g. *bāhv-ādi* (cf. *māsha-śarāvi*).

Māshika, mf(*ī*)n. See *pañca-m°.*

Māshī, f. N. of the wife of Śūra, VP.

Māshīṇa, mfn. sown with beans; n. a bean-field, Hcar. (Pāṇ. v, 2, 4).

Māshya, mfn. fit or suited for beans, Pāṇ. v, 1, 7; (ifc., after numerals) amounting to or worth a partic. number of Māshas, ib. v, 1, 34 (cf. *dvi-*, *adhyardha-m°*); n. a field of kidney-beans, W.

मास् 1. *mās,* n.=*māṇs,* flesh, meat, RV.

मास् 2. *mās,* m. (√3. *mā;* pl. instr. *mādbhís,* RV.; loc. *māssu,* PañcavBr., *māsú,* TS.) the moon, RV. (cf. *candra-* and *sūrya-mās*); a month, ib. &c. &c. [Cf. Gk. μήν, μήνη; Lat. *Mēna, mensis;* Slav. *měseci;* Lith. *menù, menesis;* Goth. *mêna;* Germ. *mâno, mâne, Mond;* Angl. Sax. *môna;* Eng. *moon.*]

Mâsa, m. (or n., Siddh.) the moon (see *pūrṇa-m°*); a month or the 12th part of the Hindū year (there are 4 kinds of months, viz. the solar, *saura;* the natural, *sāvana;* the stellar, *nākshatra,* and the lunar, *cāndra;* the latter, which is the most usual and consists of 30 Tithis, being itself of two kinds as reckoned from the new or full moon, cf. IW. 179; for the names of the months see ib. 173, n. 3), RV. &c. &c. (*māsam,* for a month; *māsam ekam,* for one month; *māsena,* in the course of a m°; *māse,* in a m°=after the lapse of a m°); a symbolical N. for the number 'twelve,' Sūryas. **–kālika,** mfn. lasting or available for a month, monthly, MBh. **–cārika,** mfn. practising anything for a m°, ib. **–jāta,** mfn. a m° old, Pāṇ. ii, 2, 5, Sch. **–jña,** m. 'knowing m°s,' a species of gallinule, L. **–tama,** mf(*ī*)n. forming or completing a m°, Pāṇ. v, 2, 57. **–tālā,** f. pl. (prob.) those parts of a calf skin from which the parchment stretched at the end of drums is made, MBh. **–tulya,** mfn. equal to a m° or to a number of m°s, MW. **–traya,** n. three m°s; °*yâvadhi,* ind. for the space of three m°s, Kathās. **–darpaṇa,** m. N. of wk. **–deya,** mfn. to be paid in a m° (as a debt), Pāṇ. ii, 1, 43, Sch. **–dvaya,** n. two m°s; °*yôdbhava,* m. a species of rice ripening within two m°s, L. **–dhā,** ind. by the m°, monthly, AitBr. **–nāman,** n. the name of a m°, MānŚr. **–nirṇaya,** m. N. of wk. **–pāka,** mfn. maturing or producing results in a m°, VarBṛS. **–pūrva,** mfn. earlier by a m°, Pāṇ. i, 1, 30, Sch. **–pramita,** mfn. measured by m°s, occurring once in a m° (as new moon), VarBṛS. (cf. Pāṇ. ii, 1, 28, Sch.) **–praveśa,** m. the beginning of a month; *-sāriṇī,* f., °*śânayana,* n. N. of wks. **–phala,** mf(*ā*)n. having results in a m°, VarBṛS. **–bhāj,** mfn. partaking of a m°, ŚBr. **–bhāvâdhyāya,** m. N. of wk. **–bhukti,** f. the (sun's) monthly course, BhP. **–māna,** m. a year, L. **–mīmāṇsā,** f. N. of wk. **–lokā** (*māsá-*), f. N. of partic. bricks, ŚBr. **–vartikā,** f. a species of wagtail (=*sarshapī*), L. **–śás,** ind. m° by m°, for m°s, Br.; KātyŚr.; MBh. **–śiva-rātri-vrata-kalpa,** m., **-śiva-rātry-udyāpana,** n. N. of wks. **–saṃcayika,** mfn. having provisions for a m°, Mn. vi, 18. **–stoma,** m. N. of an Ekâha, ŚāṅkhŚr. **Māsâgnihotra-vāda,** m. N. of wk. **Māsâdi** (ibc.) the beginning of a m°; *-nirṇaya,* m., *-bhāva-phala,* n. N. of wks.

Māsâdhipa, m. the regent or planet presiding over a month, Sūryas. **Māsâdhipati,** m. id. (°*tya,* n.),

VarBṛS. **Māsânumāsika**, mfn. performed or occurring every m°, monthly, Mn. iii, 122. **Māsânta**, m. the end of a month, day of new moon, Lāṭy. **Māsâpavarga**, mfn. lasting a m° at the most, ŚrS. (-*tā*, f., -*tva*, n., KātyŚr., Sch.) **Māsâvadhika**, mfn. happening in the period of a month at the latest, Daś. **Māsâhāra**, mfn. taking food only once a m°, R. **Māsêśvara-phala**, n. N. of wk. **Māsôpavāsa** or °**saka**, m. fasting for a m°, AgP. **Māsôpavāsin**, mfn. one who fasts for a m°, MBh.; (*inī*), f. a lascivious woman, procuress, L.

Māsaka, m. a month, Sūryas.; Śatr.

Māsala, m. a year, L.

Māsika, mf(*ī*)n. relating to or connected with a month (see *māgha-m*°); monthly (i.e. 'happening every month,' or 'lasting for a m°' or 'performed within a m°' &c.), Mn.; MBh. &c.; payable in a month (as a debt), Pāṇ. iv, 3, 47, Sch.; engaged for a m° (as a teacher), ib. v, 1, 80, Sch.; dedicated to a partic. month (as an oblation), ib. iv, 2, 34, Sch.; n. (with or scil. *śrāddha*) a partic. Śrāddha or oblation to deceased ancestors performed every new moon, Mn. v, 140 &c. **–śrāddha**, n. = prec. n.; -*nirṇaya*, m., -*paddhati*, f., -*prāyoga*, m. N. of wks. **Māsikânna**, n. food offered monthly to deceased progenitors, Mn. xi, 157. **Māsikârtha-vat**, mfn. happening or being done every month, Vishṇ.

Māsi-śrāddha, n. (fr. loc. of 2. *mās* + *ś*°) a Śrāddha or oblation to deceased ancestors performed every month, ĀpGṛ.

Māsī-√1. kṛi, P. -*karoti*, to turn into months, Sūryas.

Māsīna, mfn. monthly, Gobh.; one month old, Pāṇ. v, 1, 81.

Māsya, mfn. a month old, Pāṇ. v, 1, 81 (cf. *dvi-*, *pañca-m*° &c.)

मासन *māsana*, n. the seed of Vernonia Anthelminthica, L.

मासर *mā́sara*, n. a partic. beverage (a mixture of yeast, grapes, &c. with the water in which rice and millet have been boiled), KātyŚr.; Mahīdh. on VS. xix, 1 (accord. to Sāy. on TBr. 'm. the meal of slightly parched barley mixed with sour milk or buttermilk;' accord. to L. 'm. rice-gruel').

मासुरकर्ण *māsurakarṇa*, m. patr. fr. *masurakarṇa*, g. *śivâdi*.

मासुरी *māsurī*, f. a beard, L.

मासूर *māsūra*, mf(*ī*)n. (fr. *masūra*) lentil-shaped, Suśr.; made of lentils, Bhpr.

माह् *māh*, cl. 1. P. Ā. *māhati*, °*te*, to measure, mete, Dhātup. xxi, 29.

माहकस्थली *māhaka-sthalī*, f. N. of a place, g. *dhūmâdi*.

Māhakasthalaka, mfn. (fr. prec.), ib.

माहकि *māhaki*, m. (patr. fr. *mahaka*) N. of a teacher, Pravar.

माहकीप्रस्थ *māhakī-prastha*, mf(ī)n., Kāś. on Pāṇ. iv, 2, 110 (v.l. *māhikī-prastha*).

माहत *māhata*, mfn. (fr. *mahat*), g. *utsâdi*; n. greatness, g. *pṛithv-ādi*.

माहन *māhana*, m. a Brāhman, L.

माहनीय *māhanīya*, w.r. for *mahanīya*.

माहा 1. *māhā*, f. a cow, L. (cf. *mahā*, *mahī*, *māheyī*).

माहा 2. *māhā*, Vṛiddhi form of *mahā*, in comp. **–kula** and **-kulīna**, mfn. (fr. *mahā-kula*) nobly born, Pāṇ. iv, 1, 114. **–camasya**, m. patr. fr. *mahā-camasa*, TUp. **–citti**, mfn. (fr. *mahā-citta*), g. *sutaṃgamâdi*. **–janika** and **-janīna**, mfn. (fr. *mahā-jana*) fit for great persons or for merchants, Pāṇ. v, 1, 9, Vārtt. 6, Pat.; g. *pratijanâdi*. **–°tmika**, mfn. (fr. *mahâtman*) belonging to an exalted person, majestic, glorious, Mn. v, 94. **–°tmya**, n. (fr. *mahâtman*) magnanimity, high-mindedness, MBh.; Kāv. &c.; exalted state or position, majesty, dignity, ib.; the peculiar efficacy or virtue of any divinity or sacred shrine &c., W. (cf. RTL. 433); a work giving an account of the merits of any holy place or object, W. (cf. *devī-m*° &c.) **–nada**, mf(*ī*)n. (fr. *mahā-nada*) relating to a great river, g. *utsâdi*. **–°nasa**, mf(*ī*)n. (fr. *mahânasa*) relating to a large carriage or to a kitchen, ib. **–nāmana**, mf(*ī*)n. relating to the Mahā-nāmnī verses, AitBr. **–nāmika** or **-nāmnika**, mfn., id.; m. a Brāhman versed in the M° verses, Pāṇ. v, 1, 94, Vārtt. 1 and 2, Pat. **–putri**, mfn. (fr. *mahā-putra*), g. *sutaṃgamâdi*. **–prāṇa**, mfn. (fr. *mahā-pr*°), g. *utsâdi*. **–bhāgya**, n. = *mahā-bh*°, Nir. vii, 4 &c. **–rajaná**, mf(*ī*)n. (fr. *mahā-r*°) dyed with saffron, ŚBr. **–rājika**, mf(*ī*)n. (fr. *mahā-rāja*) attached or devoted to the reigning prince, Pāṇ. iv, 2, 35. **–rājya**, n. (fr. id.) the rank of a reigning prince or sovereign, AitBr. **–rāshṭra**, mf(*ī*)n. (fr. *mahā-r*°) belonging to the Marāṭhas; (*ī*), f. (with or scil. *bhāshā*) the M° language (Marāṭhī), Cāṇ.; Mṛicch., Introd. **–vārttika**, mf(*ī*)n. (fr. *mahā-v*°) familiar with (Kātyāyana's) Vārttikas, Pāṇ. iv, 2, 65, Vārtt. **–vratī**, f. (fr. *mahā-vrata*) the doctrine of the Pāśupatas, Prab.; °*tika*, mfn. adhering to it; m. a Pāśupata (v.l. for *mahā-vratika*); °*tīya*, w.r. for *mahā-vratīya*. **Māhendrá**, mf(*ī*)n. (fr. *mahêndra*) relating or belonging to great Indra, VS. &c. &c. (°*draṃ dhanus*, n. the rainbow; °*draṃ ambhas*, n. rain-water); eastern, running or flowing eastward, VarBṛS.; Rājat.; m. (with or scil. *graha*, q.v.) a partic. ladleful, ŚBr.; KātyŚr.; = *śubha-daṇḍa-viśesha*, L.; (in astron.) N. of the 7th Muhūrta; (with Jainas) N. of a Kalpa (q.v.), Dharmaś.; patr., Pravar.; pl. N. of a dynasty, VP.; (*ī*), f. (with or scil. *diś* or *āśā*) the east, MBh.; VarBṛS.; Rājat.; the Consort or Energy of Indra (one of the seven divine Mātṛis and one of the Mātṛis of Skanda), MBh.; a partic. Ishṭi, ĀśvŚr.; a large banana, L.; a cow, L. (cf. *māheyī*); pl. (scil. *ṛicas*) N. of partic. verses in praise of Indra, VarBṛS.; n. the asterism Jyeshṭha, VarYogay.; -*ja*, m. pl. (with Jainas) N. of a class of gods; -*vāṇī*, f. N. of a river, MBh.

Māheśa, m. (fr. *mahêśa*) one of the Mānavâughas (q.v.), Cat.; (*ī*), f. N. of Durgā, Pur. **Māheśvara**, mf(*ī*)n. (fr. *mahêśvara*) relating or belonging to the great lord Śiva, MBh.; Hariv.; Pur.; m. a worshipper of Śiva, Hariv.; Kathās.; Hcar.; (*ī*), f., see below; -*tantra*, n. N. of a Tantra; -*tā*, f. the worship of Śiva, Śivaism, Rājat.; -*pada*, n., -*pura*, n. N. of two Tīrthas, MBh.; °*rôpapurāṇa*, n. N. of an Upapurāṇa. **Māheśvarī**, f. the Consort or Energy of Śiva (one of the seven divine Mātṛis, also = Durgā), MBh. (cf. IW. 522); N. of a river, Śatr.; a species of climbing plant, L.; -*tantra*, n. N. of a Tantra.

माहिक *māhika*, m. pl. N. of a people, MBh.; VP. (v.l. *māhisha*).

Māhiki-prastha. See *māhakī-pr*°.

माहित्थि *māhitthi*, m. patr. of a teacher, ŚBr.

माहित्य *māhitya*, m. patr. fr. *mahita*, g. *gargâdi*.

Māhita, mfn. (fr. prec.), g. *kaṇvâdi*.

माहित्र *māhitra*, n. (scil. *sūkta*) N. of the hymn RV. x, 185 (beginning with the words *mahi trīṇām*), Mn. xi, 249.

माहिन *mā́hina*, mf(*ā*)n. (√1. *mah*) gladsome, blithe, causing or feeling joy (others 'great, powerful'), RV.; n. dominion, L.

Māhinā-vat, mfn. exhilarated, excited (others 'great, mighty'), RV.

माहिर *māhira*, m. N. of Indra, L. (v.l. *mihira*).

माहिष *māhisha*, mf(ī)n. (fr. *mahisha*, °*shī*) coming from or belonging to a buffalo or b°-cow, R.; MārkP.; m. N. of a district; pl. of a people, VarBṛS.; n. the female apartments, L.; -*sthalī*, f. N. of a place, g. *dhūmâdi* (°*laka*, mfn., ib.); °*shâḍḍaka* (?), m. son of a Māhishya and a Karaṇī, L. °**shaka**, m. a buffalo keeper, L.; pl. N. of a people, MBh.; Pur. °**shika**, m. = prec. sg., VP.; the paramour of an unchaste woman (others 'one who lives by the prostitution of his wife'), L.; (*ā* or *ī*), f. N. of a river, R. °**sheya**, m. a son of the first wife of a king, ĀpŚr.; N. of a grammarian and Sch. on TS., Cat. °**shya**, m. a partic. mixed caste (the son of a Kshatriya and a Vaiśyā mother whose business is attendance on cattle), Yājñ.; Gaut.

माहिष्म *māhishma*, m. pl. (cf. next) N. of a people, VP.

Māhishmatī, f. N. of a city (founded by Mahishmat or Mucukunda), MBh.; Kāv. &c.

Māhishmateyaka, mfn. (fr. prec.), g. *kattry-ādi*.

माहीन *mā́hīna*, m. (?) patr. (others mfn. = *māhina*), RV. x, 60, 1.

माहीयत्व *māhīyatva*, mfn. beginning with the word *mahīya-tva* (g. *vimuktâdi*; Kāś. *māhīyala*).

माहुण्डक *māhuṇḍaka*, m. (with *bhaṭṭa*) N. of a poet, Cat.

माहुरदत्त *māhura-datta*, N. of a place, ib.

माहुल *māhula*, m. patr., Pravar.

माहेन्द्र *māhendra*. See col. 2.

माहेय *māheya*, mf(ī)n. (fr. *mahī*) made of earth, earthen, MBh.; m. metron. of the planet Mars, VarBṛS.; coral, L.; pl. N. of a people, MBh.; (*ī*), f. a cow, L.

माहेल *māhela*, m. patr., Pravar.

माहेश *māheśa*, °*śvara*. See col. 2.

मि 1. *mi* (cf. √3. *mā* and *mī*), cl. 5. P. Ā. (Dhātup. xxvii, 4) *minóti*, *minute* (pf. P. *mimāya*, *mimyúḥ*, RV., *mamau*, Gr.; Ā. *mimye*, Gr.; aor. *amāsīt*, °*sta*, ib.; Prec. *mīyāt*, *māsīshṭa*, ib.; fut. *mātā*, *māsyati*, °*te*, ib.; p. *meshyat* [?], AitBr.; ind. p. -*mitya*, ib., -*māya*, Gr.), to fix or fasten in the earth, set up, found, build, construct, RV.; AV.; ŚBr.; ŚrS.; to mete out, measure, VarBṛS.; to judge, observe, perceive, know, MāṇḍUp.; MBh.; to cast, throw, scatter, Dhātup.: Pass. *mīyáte* (aor. *amāyi*, Gr.), to be fixed &c., AV.: Caus. *māpayati* (aor. *amīmapat*), Gr.: Desid. *mitsati*, °*te*, ib.: Intens. *memīyate*, *memayīte*, *memeti*, ib.

Mit, f. anything set up or erected, a post, pillar, RV. (cf. *garta-*, *upa-*, *prati-m*°).

1. **Mitá**, mfn. (for 2. see below) fixed, set up, founded, established, RV.; AV.; ŚāṅkhŚr.; firm, strong (see comp.); cast, thrown, scattered, W. **–jñu** (*mitá-*), mfn. having strong or firm knees, RV. **–dru** (*mitá*), mfn. strong-legged, running well, ib.; m. (perhaps fr. 2. *mita*, 'having a measured course') the sea, ocean, L. **–medha** (*mitá-*), mfn. having firmly established power, RV.

1. **Mití**, f. (for 2. see p. 816, col. 1) fixing, erecting, establishing, RV.

मि 2. *mi*. See √*mī*.

मिक्ष् 1. *miksh* or *mimiksh* (prob. Desid. from a lost √*miś*, contained in *miśra* and *miśla*; but referred by others to √*mih*, q.v.; only pr. *mimikshati*, pf. *mimikshátuḥ*, °*shé*, °*shire*, and Impv. *mimikshvá*; cf. *sam-√miksh*), to mix (Ā. intrans.), mingle with (instr.), prepare (an oblation of Soma &c.), RV.; VS.; Br.: Caus. *mekshayati*, to stir up, mix, mingle, ŚBr.

Mimiksha, **mimikshu**. See s.v.

मिक्ष् 2. *miksh*. See √*myaksh*.

मिघ् *migh* = √*mih* (only in *ni-méghamāna* and *meghá*, q.v.)

मिचिता *micitā*, f. N. of a river, VP. (v.l. for *niścitā*).

मिच्चक *miccaka* or *micchaka*, m. N. of the sixth patriarchal sage, Buddh.

मिछ् *mich*, cl. 6. P. *micchati*, to hurt, pain, annoy, Dhātup. xxviii, 16.

मिञ्ज् *miñj*, cl. 10. P. *miñjayati*, to speak or to shine, Dhātup. xxxiii, 83.

मिञ्जिकामिञ्जिक *miñjikā-miñjika*, n. sg. N. of two beings sprung from the seed of Rudra, MBh.

मिण्मिण *miṇmiṇa*, mfn. (onomat.) speaking indistinctly through the nose (-*tva*, n.), Suśr. (v.l. *minmina*).

मित् *mit*. See under √1. *mi*.

मित 2. *mita*, mfn. (√3. *mā*; for 1. *mita* see √1. *mi*) measured, meted out, measured or limited by, i.e. equal to (instr. or comp.), Sūryas.; VarBṛS.; BhP.; containing a partic. measure, i.e. measuring, consisting of (acc.), RPrāt.; Bhartṛ. (v.l.); measured, moderate, scanty, frugal, little, short, brief, Inscr.; Mn.; Kāv. &c.; measured i.e. investigated, known (see -*loka*); m. N. of a divine being (associated with Sammita), Yājñ.; of a Ṛishi in the third Manv-antara, VP. **–ṃ-gama**, mf(*ā*)n. taking measured steps, Pāṇ. iii, 2, 38, Vārtt. 1, Pat.; m. and (*ā*), f. an elephant, W. **-dakshiṇa**, mf(*ā*)n. that for which a partic. fee is fixed, TāṇḍBr. **-dhvaja**, m. N. of a prince, BhP. **-prakāśikā**, f. N. of wk. **-bhāshitṛi**, mfn. speaking measuredly or little, MBh. **-bhāshin**, mfn. id. (°*shi-tva*, n.), Ragh.; Siṇhās.; (*inī*), f. N. of various commentaries. **-bhukta** (MBh.), **-bhuj** (Mn.; Yājñ.), mfn. eating sparingly, moderate in diet. **-mati**, mfn. narrow-minded, Rājat. **-m-paca**, mf(*ā*)n. cooking a measured portion of food, Pāṇ. iii, 2, 34; small-sized (said of a cooking utensil), Daś.; sparing, stingy, a miser, Hit. **-rāvin**, mfn. roaring moderately (used to explain *marut*), Nir. xi, 13. **-rocin**, mfn. shining moderately (used to explain *marut*), ib. **-vāc**, mfn. = *-bhāshin*, W. **-vyayin**, mfn. spending little, frugal, economical, MW. **-śāyin**, mfn. sleeping little or sparingly, MārkP. **Mitâkshara**, mfn. having measured syllables, metrical, Nir.; RPrāt.; short and comprehensive (as a speech), Kum.; (*ā*), f. N. of various concise commentaries, (esp.) of a celebrated Comm. by Vijñānêśvara on Yājñavalkya's Dharmaśāstra (IW. 303 &c.); °*rā-kāra*, m. 'author of the M°,' N. of Vijñānêśvara; *-vyākhyāna*, n., *-sāra*, m., *-siddhânta-saṃgraha*, m. N. of wks. connected with the M°. **Mitâṅka**, m. or n.(?) N. of a wk. (containing rules for compiling almanacs); *-karaṇa*, n. N. of wk. **Mitârtha**, m. a well-weighed matter (*-bhāshin*, mfn. speaking deliberately), Sāh.; mfn. (also *-ka*) of measured meaning, speaking with caution (said of a partic. class of envoys), Kām.; Sāh. **Mitâśana**, mfn. = *mita-bhukta*, Yājñ. **Mitâhāra**, mfn. id., MBh.; m. moderate food, scanty diet, Daś. **Mitôkti**, f. moderate speech, Cat.

2. **Miti**, f. (for 1. see p. 815, col. 3) measuring, measure, weight, VarBṛS.; ŚārṅgS.; accurate knowledge, evidence, MāṇḍUp.

Mitya, n. what is to be measured or fixed, (prob.) price, Rājat.

मित्र 1. mitrá, m. (orig. *mit-tra*, fr. √*mith* or *mid*; cf. *medin*) a friend, companion, associate, RV.; AV. (in later language mostly n.); N. of an Āditya (generally invoked together with Varuṇa, cf. *mitrā-v°*, and often associated with Aryaman, q.v.; Mitra is extolled alone in RV. iii, 59, and there described as calling men to activity, sustaining earth and sky and beholding all creatures with unwinking eye; in later times he is considered as the deity of the constellation Anurādhā, and father of Utsarga), RV. &c. &c.; the sun, Kāv. &c. (cf. comp.); N. of a Marut, Hariv.; of a son of Vasishṭha and various other men, Pur.; of the third Muhūrta, L.; du. = *mitrā-varuṇa*, RV.; (*ā*), f. N. of an Apsaras, MBh. (B. *citrā*); of the mother of Maitreya and Maitreyī, Śaṃk. on ChUp.; BhP.; of the mother of Śatru-ghna (= *su-mitrā*), L. (W. *ī*); n. friendship, RV.; a friend, companion (cf. m. above), TS. &c. &c.; (with *aurasa*) a friend connected by blood-relationship, Hit.; an ally (a prince whose territory adjoins that of an immediate neighbour who is called *ari*, enemy, Mn. vii, 158 &c., in this meaning also applied to planets, VarBṛS.); a companion to = resemblance of (gen.; ifc. = resembling, like), Bālar.; Vcar.; N. of the god Mitra (enumerated among the 10 fires), MBh.; a partic. mode of fighting, Hariv. (v.l. for *bhinna*). **-karaṇa**, the making of friends, m° one's self fr°, Pāṇ. i, 3, 25, Vārtt. 1, Pat. **-karman**, n. a friendly office, friendship (°*ma* √*kṛi*, to join in friendship with [instr.]), Gaut.; Kām. **-kāma**, mfn. desirous of friends, MārkP. **-kārya**, n. the business of a fr°, a friendly office, MBh.; R. **-kṛit**, m. 'fr°-maker,' N. of a son of the 12th Manu, Hariv. **-kṛiti**, f. a kind or friendly office, AitBr. iii, 4 (Sāy.; but *mitra kṛityeva*, instead of being understood as °*tyeva*, could also be resolved into the words °*tya*, ind. 'making a friend,' and *iva*). **-kṛitya**, n. = *-kārya*, q.v., Ragh.; Pañcat. **-kaustubha**, m. N. of a man, Cat. **-krú** or **-krū**, m. or f. (prob.) N. of an evil being, RV. x, 89, 14. **-gupta** (*mitrá-*), mfn. protected by Mitra, ŚBr.; m. N. of a man, Daś. **-gupti**, f. protection of friends, MW. **-ghna**, mfn. 'fr°-killing,' treacherous, MW.; m. N. of a Rākshasa, R.; of a son of Divo-dāsa, VP.; (*ā*), f. N. of a river, Hariv. (v.l. *citra-ghnī*). **-jit**, m. N. of a son of Su-varṇa, VP. (v.l. *a-m°*). **-jña**, m. N. of a demon (said to steal oblations), MBh. **-tā**, f. friendship (°*tām samprâptaḥ*, one who has become a friend), MBh.; Pañcat. &c.; equalness, likeness with (comp.), Vcar. **-tūrya**, n. victory of friends, AV. **-tva**, n. friendship, TS.; Pañcat. &c. **-deva**, m. N. of one of the sons of the 12th Manu, Hariv.; of another man, MBh. **-drúh**, mfn. (nom. *-dhruk*) seeking to injure a friend, the betrayer of a fr°, a false or treacherous fr°, MaitrS.; TBr.; Mn. &c. [Cf. Zd. *mithra-druj*.] **-droha**, m. injury or betrayal of a fr°, MBh.; R. &c. (*-drohena*, w.r. for *-drohiṇā*, Kathās.) **-drohin**, mfn. = *-drúh*, MBh.; Pañcat. &c. **-dvish** (Pāṇ., Sch.) or **-dveshin** (MBh.), mfn. hating or injuring a friend; m. a treacherous fr°, W. **-dharman**, m. N. of a demon (said to steal oblations), MBh. **-dhā́**, ind. in a friendly manner, VS.; AV. **-dhita** (*mitrá-*), n. (RV.) or **-dhiti** (*mitrá-*), f. (ib.) or **-dhéya**, n. (VS.; ŚBr.) a covenant or contract of friendship. **-nandana**, mfn. gladdening one's friends, MBh. **-pati**, m. lord of friends or of friendship, RV. **-pathâdi-kuṇḍa-māhātmya**, n. N. of wk. **-pada**, n. 'Mitra's place,' N. of a locality, L. **-pratikshā**, f. regard for a friend, MBh. **-bandhu-hīna**, mfn. destitute of fr°s or relations, ib. **-bāhu**, m. N. of one of the sons of the 12th Manu, Hariv. (v.l. *-vāha*); of a son of Kṛishṇa, ib. **-bha**, n. a friendly constellation, Var.; Mitra's Nakshatra i.e. Anurādhā, Var.; Śatr. **-bhānu**, m. N. of a king, MBh. **-bhāva**, m. a state of friendship, friendly disposition, MBh.; Hariv. &c. **-bhū**, m. N. of a man, L. **-bhṛit**, mfn. entertaining or supporting a friend, TS. **-bheda**, m. separation of fr°s, breach of friendship, MBh.; Kām. &c.; N. of the first book of the Pañca-tantra. **-mahas** (*mitrá-*), mfn. (perhaps) having plenty of fr°s, rich in fr°s, RV. **-mitra**, n. 'a fr° of the fr°,' i.e. that king who is separated from another k° by an 'enemy' (the next neighbour) and the 'friend' (the neigh° of the prec°) and the 'friend of the enemy' (the neigh° of the prec°), Kām. **-miśra**, m. N. of an author, Cat. **-mukha**, mfn. speaking like a fr° (but not being really one), MBh. **-yajña**, m. N. of a man, Saṃskārak. **-yúj**, mfn. one who has made an alliance, leagued, RV.; m. N. of a man; pl. N. of his descendants, Saṃskārak. **-yuddha**, n. a contest of fr°s, L. **-labdhi**, f. = next, W. **-lābha**, m. acquisition of fr°s or of friendship, Var.; N. of the first book of the Hitôpadeśa. **-1. -vat**, mfn. having fr°s, MBh.; R.; Pañcat.; m. N. of a demon (said to steal oblations), MBh.; of a son of the 12th Manu, Hariv.; MārkP.; of a son of Kṛishṇa, Hariv.; (*atī*), f. N. of a daughter of Kṛ°, ib. **-2. -vat**, ind. like a fr° (acc.), Kāv. **-vatsala**, mfn. affectionate towards fr°s, devoted to fr°s, Mudr. **-vana**, n. 'Mitra's wood,' N. of a forest, L. **-varaṇa**, n. choice of fr°s, Var. **-varcas**, m. N. of a man, L. **-vardha**, g. *dhūmâdi* (v.l. *-vardhra*; cf. *maitravardhaka*). **-várdhana**, mfn. prospering fr°s, AV.; m. N. of a demon (said to steal oblations), MBh. **-vardhra**, see *-vardha*. **-varman**, m. N. of a man, MBh. **-vāha**, m. N. of a son of the 12th Manu, Hariv. (v.l. *-bāhu*). **-vid**, m. a spy, L. (w.r. for *mantra-vid*). **-vinda**, mfn. 'acquiring fr°s,' N. of an Agni, MBh.; m. N. of a son of the 12th Manu, MārkP.; of a son of Kṛishṇa, Hariv.; of a preceptor, Cat.; (*ā*), f. N. of an Ishṭi, ŚBr.; ŚrS.; MārkP.; of a wife of Kṛishṇa, Hariv.; Pur.; Pañcar.; of a river in Kuśa-dvīpa, BhP.; of wk.; °*dêshṭi*, f. (°*ṭi-prayoga*, m., °*ṭi-hautra*, n.), N. of wks. **-vishaya**, m. friendship, MW. **-vaira**, n. dissension among fr°s, Var. **-śarman**, m. N. of various persons, Pañcat.; Rājat. **-śis** (fr. √*śās*; cf. *āśis*), mfn., Kāś. on Pāṇ. vi, 4, 34. **-saptamī**, f. N. of the 7th day in the light half of the month Mārgaśīrsha, BhavP. **-samprâpti**, f. 'acquisition of friends,' N. of the 2nd book of the Pañca-tantra. **-saha**, m. 'indulgent towards friends,' N. of a king (also called Kalmāsha-pāda), MBh.; R. &c.; of a Brāhman, Hariv. **-sāha**, mfn. tolerant of fr°s, indulgent towards fr°s, MBh. **-sâhvayā**, f. N. of a divine being, ib. **-sûkta**, n. N. of wk. **-sena**, m. N. of a Gandharva, VP.; of a son of the 12th Manu, Hariv.; of a grandson of Kṛishṇa, ib.; of a king of the Draviḍa country, Cat.; of a Buddhist, Buddh. **-sneha**, m. affection towards fr°s, friendship, Mudr. **-hatyā**, f. the murder of a friend, MW. **-han** or **-hana**, mfn. one who kills or murders a fr°, MBh. (cf. *-ghna*). **-hū**, mfn. = *mitram hvayati*, Vop. **Mitrâkhya**, mfn. named after Mitra, Var. **Mitrâcāra**, m. treatment of fr°s, conduct to be observed towards a fr°, Kathās. **Mitrâtithi**, m. N. of a man, RV. **Mitrânugrahaṇa**, n. the act of favouring fr°s or causing them prosperity, MaitrUp. **Mitrâbhidroha**, m. = *mitra-droha*, R. **Mitrâmitra**, n. sg. friend and foe, Mn. xii, 79. **Mitrā́-váruṇa**, m. du. Mitra and Varuṇa, RV. &c. &c. (together they uphold and rule the earth and sky, together they guard the world, together they promote religious rites, avenge sin, and are the lords of truth and light, cf. under 1. *mitrá* above; °*ṇayor ayanam* and °*ṇayor ishṭiḥ*, N. of partic. sacrifices; °*ṇayoḥ saṃyojanam*, N. of a Sāman), RV.; VS.; Br. &c. (sg., w.r. for *maitrāvaruṇa*, Hariv.); *-vat*, mfn. accompanied by M° and V°, RV.; *-samīrita*, mfn. impelled by M° and V°, TBr. **Mitrāvaruṇīya**, w.r. for *maitr°* (q.v.), Pāṇ. v, 1, 135, Sch. **Mitrā-vasu**, m. N. of a son of Viśvā-vasu (king of the Siddhas), Kathās.; Nāg. **Mitrérū** (or *mitr'-eru?*), mfn. (accord. to Sāy.) troubling friends; (prob.) one who breaks an alliance, faithless, RV. **Mitrêśvara**, m. (with *Hara*) N. of a statue of Śiva erected by Mitra-śarman, Rājat. **Mitrôdaya**, m. sunrise, ŚārṅgP.; a friend's welfare, ib.; N. of wk. **Mitrôpasthāna**, n. worship of the sun (part of the morning Saṃdhyā service), RTL. 406.

2. **Mitra**, Nom. P. *mitrati*, to act in a friendly manner, Śatr.

Mitraka, m. N. of a man, Cat.

Mitraya, Nom. P. *mitrayati*, (prob.) to befriend (cf. next).

Mitrayu, mfn. (fr. prec.) friendly-minded, L.; winning or acquiring friends, attractive, W.; possessing worldly prudence, Uṇ. i, 38, Sch.; m. a friend, L.; N. of a teacher, Pur.; of a son of Divo-dāsa, Hariv.; pl. (said to be also pl. fr. *maitreya*) the descendants of Mitrayu, ĀśvŚr.; Pravar.

Mitrāya, Nom. Ā. *mitrāyate*, (prob.) to desire or wish for a friend (cf. next).

Mitrāyú, mfn. (fr. prec.) desiring a friend, seeking friendship, RV.; m. N. of a preceptor, BhP., Introd.; of a son of Divo-dāsa, Pur. (v.l. *mitreyu*).

Mitrín, mfn. befriended, united by friendship, RV.; AV.

Mitriya, mfn. friendly, coming from or relating to a friend, RV.; AV.

Mitrī, in comp. for *mitra*. **-√1. kṛi**, P. Ā. *-karoti, -kurute*, to make any one a friend, RAnukr.; Kām. &c. **-kṛita**, mfn. made a friend, won as a fr°, Kathās. **-√bhū**, P. *-bhavati* (ind. p. *-bhūya*), to become a friend, make friends with (instr.), ib.

Mitrīya, Nom. P. °*yati*, to seek to make any one a friend, RAnukr.; Bhaṭṭ.; to think any one a fr°, to treat any one as a fr° or companion, VarYogay.; to be inclined to friendship or to an alliance, Hcar.

Mitreyu. See *mitrāyú* above.

Mitreru. See under 1. *mitrá* above.

Mitryà, mfn. = *mitrīya*, RV.; ŚBr.; KātyŚr.; (ifc.) belonging to the friends of any one, g. *vargyâdi*.

मिथ् mith, cl. 1. P. Ā. (cf. Dhātup. xxi, 7) *méthati*, °*te* (pr. p. f. *mithatī́*, RV.; pf. *mimetha*, ib.; ind. p. *mithitvā*, BhP.), to unite, pair, couple, meet (as friend or antagonist), alternate, engage in altercation; (Ā.) to dash together, RV. i, 113, 3 (accord. to Dhātup. also 'to understand' or 'to kill').

Mitha, in comp. for *mithaḥ* = *mithas* **-spṛídhya**, ind. p. (√*spṛidh*) meeting together as rivals, mutually emulous, RV. i, 166, 9 (Padap. *mitha-spṛídhyā*).

Mithaḥ, in comp. for *mithas*. **-kṛitya**, n. mutual obligation, MBh. **-prasthāna**, n. mutual or common departure, Śak. **-samaya**, m. mutual agreement, ib. (v.l. *-samavāya*).

Mithatyā́, ind. alternately, emulously, RV. vii, 48, 3 (accord. to Sāy. and others instr. of *mithati* = *hiṇsā*).

Mitháḥ, ind. together, together with (instr.), mutually, reciprocally, alternately, to or from or with each other, RV. &c. &c.; privately, in secret, Mn.; Kālid.; Daś.; by contest or dispute, BhP. **-túr**, mfn. following one another, alternating (as day and night), RV.

Mithita, m. N. of a man, Saṃskārak.

Mithu, ind. (cf. *mithū*) alternately, pervertedly, falsely, wrongly, RV. (Padap. and Prāt.); TBr.; Kāṭh.

Mithuná, mf(*ā*)n. paired, forming a pair; m. a pair (male and female; but also 'any couple or pair,' RV. &c. &c., usually du., in later language mostly n.; ifc. f. *ā*); n. pairing, copulation, TS. &c. &c.; a pair or couple (= m.; but also 'twins'), MBh.; (also m.) the sign of the zodiac Gemini or the third arc of 30° in a circle, Sūryas.; Var.; Pur.; the other part, complement or companion of anything, MBh. (also applied to a kind of small statue at the entrance of a temple, VarBṛS.); honey and ghee, L.; (in gram.) a root compounded with a preposition, Siddh. **-tvá**, n.

the state of forming a pair, AV. &c. &c. **-bhāva**, m. id., Kap., Sch. **-yamaka**, n. a partic. kind of Yamaka (e.g. Bhaṭṭ. x, 12). **-yoni** (°*ná-*), mfn. produced by copulation, MaitrS. **-vratin**, mfn. devoted to cohabitation, practising copulation, MBh.

Mithunāya, Nom. Ā. °*yate*, to couple, pair, cohabit sexually, Pāṇ. viii, 1, 15, Sch.

Mithunin, m. 'going in pairs,' a wagtail, L.

Mithunī, in comp. for *mithuna*. **-√as** (only Pot. *-syām*), to become paired, cohabit sexually, ŚBr. **-√1. kṛi**, P. *-karoti*, to cause to pair, cause the union of the sexes, TS.; ŚBr. **-cārin**, mfn. coupling together, having sexual intercourse, BhP. **-bhāva**, m. copulation, sexual union, BhP. **-√bhū**, P. *-bhavati* (ind. p. *-bhūya*), = *-√as*, ŚBr.; ChUp.; to be joined or arranged in pairs, BhP.

Mithune-cara, m. 'going or living in pairs,' the Cakra-vāka, Hariv.

Mithuyā́, ind. 'conflictingly,' invertedly, falsely, incorrectly, RV.; AV. (with √1. *kṛi*, P. *-karoti*, to undo, Āpast.)

Míthus, ind. = *mithuyā́*, TS. (*mithus-√car*, P. *-carati*, to go astray, AV.; *mithur-√bhū*, P. *-bhavati*, to turn out badly, fail, TBr.)

Míthū, ind. = *mithu* in RV. (Saṃhitā-patha). **-kṛit**, mfn. fallen into trouble or danger, x, 102, 1. **-dṛiś**, mfn. seen or appearing alternately, i, 29, 3; ii, 31, 5.

Mitho, in comp. for *mithas* (cf. g. *svar-ādi*). **-avadya-pa** (*mithó-av°*), mfn. mutually averting calamities, RV. **-yodhá**, m. hand to hand fighting with one another, AV. **-viniyoga**, m. employing mutually in any occupation, Āpast.

Mithyā́, ind. (contracted from *mithūyā́*) invertedly, contrarily, incorrectly, wrongly, improperly, ŚBr. &c. &c. (with Caus. of √*kṛi*, to pronounce a word wrongly 'once' [P.] or 'repeatedly' [Ā.], Pāṇ. i, 3, 71; with *pra-√car*, to act wrongly, Mn. ix, 284; with *pra-√vṛit*, to behave improperly, MBh. iii, 2414); falsely, deceitfully, untruly, Mn.; MBh. &c. (often with √*brū*, *vac* or *vad*, to speak falsely, utter a lie; with √*kṛi*, to deny, MBh.; to break one's word, with *na* √*kṛi*, to keep it), R.; with √*bhū*, to turn out or prove false, MBh.; not in reality, only apparently, Madhus.; to no purpose, fruitlessly, in vain, MaitrUp.; MBh. &c. (ibc. often = false, untrue, sham; Mithyā is personified as the wife of A-dharma, KalkiP.) **-kárman**, n. a false act, failure, ŚBr. **-kāruṇika**, mfn. pretending to be false, Pañcat. **-kṛita** (*mithyā́-*), mfn. wrongly done, ib. **-kopa**, m. feigned anger, Vet. **-kraya**, m. a false price, Pañcat. **-krodha**, m. = *-kopa*, A. **-graha** (*mithyâg°?*), m. improper persistency, useless obstinacy, ib.; (also °*haṇa*, n.) misconception, misunderstanding, A. **-glaha**, m. a false game at dice, MBh. **-caryā**, f. false behaviour, hypocrisy, L. **-°cāra** (*mithyâc°*), m. improper conduct, wrong treatment (in medicine), Suśr.; mfn. acting falsely or hypocritically, Bhag.; m. a rogue, hypocrite; *-prahasana*, n. N. of a comedy. **-jalpita**, n. a false report or rumour, Pañcat. **-jīvātu**, m. N. of a man, Kautukas. **-jñāna**, n. a false conception, error, mistake, Yogas.; Pañcat. (cf. IW. 104); *-khaṇḍana*, n. N. of a drama. **-tva**, n. falsity, unreality, Kap., Sch.; (with Jainas) perversion (as one of the 18 faults) or illusion (as the lowest of the 14 steps which lead to final emancipation), Sarvad.; *-nirukti*, f. or *-nirvacana*, n., *-vāda-rahasya*, n.; *-°tvânumāna-khaṇḍana*, n. N. of wks.; *-°tvin*, mfn. being in a state of illusion, Śatr. **-darśana**, n. a false appearance, MaitrUp.; = next, L. **-dṛishṭi**, f. false doctrine, heresy, atheism, Lalit. (one of the 10 sins, Dharmas. 56). **-°dhīta** (*mithyâdh°*), n. recitation practised in a wrong manner, Āpast. **-°dhyavasiti** (*mithyâdh°*), f. a partic. figure of speech (in which the impossibility of a thing is expressed by making it depend upon some impossible contingency), Kuval. **-nirasana**, n. denial by oath, L. **-paṇḍita**, mf(*ā*)n. educated or learned only in appearance, Kathās. **-°pavāda** (*mithyâp°*), m. a false accusation. **-purusha**, m. a man only in app°, Cat. **-praṇidhāna**, n. (prob.) false exertion, Divyâv. **-pratijña**, mfn. false to one's promise, faithless, treacherous, Hariv.; R. **-pratyaya**, m. f° conception, error, illusion, Sāṃkhyas., Sch. **-prayukta**, mfn. employed in vain, Śiksh. **-pravādin**, mfn. speaking falsely, lying, Pañcar. **-pravṛitti**, f. wrong function (of the senses), Col. **-prasupta**, mfn. falsely asleep, feigning sleep, MW. **-phala**, n. an imaginary or vain advantage, Bhartṛ. **-°bhigṛidhna** (*mithyâbh°*), mfn. unjustly or eagerly covetous, MBh. **-°bhidhā** (*mithyâbh°*), f. a false name, BhP.; °*dhāna*, n. a false statement, MBh. **-°bhimāna** (*mithyâbh°*) = *-pratyaya*, Sāṃkhyas., Sch. **-bhiyoga** (*mithyâbh°*), m. a f° charge, L.; °*yogin*, mfn. making a f° charge, Yājñ. **-°bhiśaṃsana** (*mithyâbh°*), n. a false accusation, R. (v.l.); °*śaṃsin*, mfn. making a f° acc°, Yājñ.; BhP. **-°bhiśapta** (*mithyâbh°*), mfn. falsely accused, Prab. **-°bhiśasta** (*mithyâbh°*), mfn. id., Yājñ.; °*śasti*, mfn. a false charge, Hariv. **-°bhiśāpa** (*mithyâbh°*), m. id., ib.; a f° prediction, Tithyād. **-°bhishaṅga** (*mithyâbh°*), m. an unjust imprecation, MBh. **-mati**, f. a f° opinion, error, L. **-manorama**, mfn. beautiful only in appearance, MaitrUp. **-māna**, m. f° pride, L. **-yoga**, m. wrong use or employment, ŚārṅgS. **-°rambha** (*mithyâr°*), m. f° treatment (in medicine), Car. **-°rṇava** (*mithyârṇ°*), m. N. of a man, Hāsy. **-liṅga-dhara**, mfn. wearing false marks, being anything only in appearance, Cat. **-vacana**, n. telling an untruth, Gaut. **-vadhyânukīrtana**, n. the proclaiming that any one has been unjustly sentenced to death, MW. **-vākya**, n. a false statement, lie, R. **-vāc**, mfn. speaking falsely, lying, Sāh. **-vāda**, m. = *-vākya*, MBh.; mfn. = *-vāc*, Pañcat. (also *-vādin*, Mn.; R. &c.) **-vārttā**, f. false report, MW. **-vikalpa**, m. false suspicion, Jātakam. **-vyāpāra**, m. wrong occupation, meddling with another's affairs, Pañcat. **-vyāhārin**, mfn. = *-vāc*, MBh. **-sâkshin**, m. false witness; °*kshi-pradātṛi*, mfn. bringing forward false witnesses, Pañcar. **-stava**, m. pl., **-stotra**, n. pl. f° or unfounded praise, Kāv.; Rājat. **-°hāra** (*mithyâh°*), m. improper nourishment, wrong diet, Suśr.; *-vihārin*, mfn. taking improper n° and indulging in impr° enjoyments, ib. **Mithyôttara**, n. (in law) f° or prevaricating reply, L. **Mithyôpacāra**, m. a feigned or pretended service or kindness, Hit.; (in medicine) wrong treatment, Suśr. **Mithyôpayojita**, mfn. wrongly applied, Suśr.

मिथि *mithi*, m. N. of a son of Nimi and prince of Mithilā, R. (cf. IW. 511, n. 1).

Mithila, m. N. of a king (the founder of Mithilā) = *mithi*, BhP.; pl. N. of a people (prob. the inhabitants of Mithilā), MBh.; VarBṛS.; (*ā*), f. N. of a city said to have been founded by Mithi or Mithila (it was the capital of Videha or the modern Tirhut, and residence of King Janaka), MBh.; Kāv. &c.; of a school of law, IW. 302 &c. **Mithilâdhipati**, m. lord of Mithilā, i.e. Janaka, R. **Mithileśa**, m. (prob.) id.; *-carita*, n.; °*śâhnika*, n. N. of wks.

मिथुन *mithuna* &c. See p. 816, col. 3.

मिथ्या *mithyā́* &c. See col. 1.

मिद् 1. *mid* or *med*, cl. 1. P. Ā. = √*mith* ('to understand' or 'to kill'), Dhātup. xxi, 7.

मिद् 2. *mid* or *mind*, cl. 1. Ā. or 4. P. (Dhātup. xviii, 3 and xxvi, 133) *médate* or *médyati* (of the former only 3. sg. Impv. *medátām*, RV. x, 93, 11; pf. *mimeda*, *mimide*; aor. *amidat*, *amedishṭa*; fut. *meditā*, *medishyati*, °*te*; ind. p. *miditvā* or *meditvā*, Gr.; Pass. *midyate*, impers., Pāṇ. vii, 3, 82, Sch.), to grow fat, RV.; TS.; Br.; cl. 10. P. (Dhātup. xxxii, 8) *mindayati* or *medayati* (cf. MBh. viii, 1992 and *mitra*); the latter also as Caus. 'to make fat,' RV. vi, 28, 6.

Minna, mfn. become fat, fat, Pāṇ. vii, 2, 16 (impers. *minnam* or *meditam*, ib. 17).

मिद्ध *middha*, n. sloth, indolence, Lalit.; Divyâv. (one of the 24 minor evil passions, Dharmas. 69).

मिध् *midh* or *medh*, cl. 1. P. Ā. *medhati*, °*te*, = √*mith*, Dhātup. xxi, 7.

मिन्दा *mindā́*, f. a bodily defect, fault, blemish, TS.; N. of partic. verses, ĀpŚr. **-°huti** (°*dâh°*), f. a partic. sacrifice, Hiraṇy.

मिन्मिन *minmina*, mfn. = *miṇmiṇa*, L.

मिन्व् *minv* (cf. √*ninv*, *sinv*) = √*pinv*, Dhātup. xv, 80.

मिमङ्क्षा *mimaṅkshā*, f. (fr. Desid. of √*majj*) the wish to plunge into water, W. °**kshu**, mfn. being about to bathe or dive, Śiś.

मिमत *mimata*, m. N. of a man, Pāṇ. iv, 1, 150 (cf. *maimata*).

मिमन्थिषा *mimanthishā*, f. (fr. Desid. of √*math* or *manth*) the wish to stir up or shake or destroy, W. °**shu**, mfn. wishing to stir up &c., ib.

मिमर्दयिषु *mimardayishu* or °*dishu*, mfn. (fr. Desid. of √*mṛid*) wishing to crush or grind down, MBh.

मिमारयिषु *mimārayishu*, mfn. (fr. Desid. of Caus. of √*mṛi*) wishing to kill, HPariś.

मिमिक्ष *mimiksha*, mfn. (√1. *miksh*) mixed, RV. vi, 34, 4. °**kshú**, mfn. id. or 'mingling,' ib. iii, 50, 3.

मियेध *miyédha*, m. = *médha*, a sacrificial oblation, sacrifice, offering of food, RV.

Miyédhas, n. = *médhas*, ib. x, 70, 2.

Miyedhya, mfn. = *médhya*, partaking of the sacrificial food, RV.

मिरफ *mirapha*, m. or n. (?) a partic. high number, Buddh.

मिरा *mirā*, f. a limit, boundary, L. (cf. *mīra*). **-khāna**, m. (= خان) N. of a Paṭhān chief (the patron of Rudra-bhaṭṭa), Cat.

मिरिका *mirikā*, f. a species of plant, L.

मिर्मिर *mirmirá*, mfn. blinking, TBr. (Sch.); having fixed unwinking eyes, L.

मिल् *mil*, cl. 6. P. Ā. (Dhātup. xxviii, 71; 135; but cf. Vām. v, 2, 2) *milati*, °*te* (pf. *mimiluḥ*, Kāv.; fut. *milishyati*, Br.; aor. *amelīt*, *amelishṭa*, Gr.; ind. p. *militvā* and *-milya*, Kathās. &c.), to meet (as friends or foes), encounter, join, fall in with (instr. with or without *saha*; dat., gen., or loc.), come together, assemble, concur, Kāv.; Kathās.; Rājat. &c.: Caus. *melayati* (or *melāpayati*; cf. *melāpaka*), to cause any one to meet any one else (gen.), bring together, assemble, Kathās.

Milat, mfn. meeting, joining &c.; appearing, happening, occurring, Naish.; (ibc. or ifc.) joined or connected with, Kāv.; Pañcar. **Milad-vyādha**, mfn. joined or surrounded by huntsmen, Kathās.

Milana, n. coming together, meeting, contact, union, Amar.; Gīt.

Milā, **milikā**. See *dur-m°*.

Milita, mfn. met, encountered, united &c.; happened, occurred, Kāv.; (ifc.) connected or combined or mixed or furnished with, Pañcat.

मिलिन्द *milinda*, m. a bee, Bhām.; N. of a king (= Menander), Buddh. **-praśna**, m. N. of a Pāli wk. (containing a conversation on Nirvāṇa between king Milinda and the monk Nāga-sena), MWB. 141.

Milindaka, m. a kind of snake, Suśr.

मिलीमिलिन् *milīmilin*, m. N. of Śiva, MBh. (accord. to Sch. fr. a Mantra containing the word *mili* repeated twice).

मिल्ला *millā*, f. N. of a woman, Rājat.

मिश् *miś* (cf. √*maś* and 1. *miksh*), cl. 1. P. *meśati*, to sound or to be angry, Dhātup. xvii, 74.

मिशर *miśara*, m. or n. N. of a place, Cat. (cf. *misara*, p. 818, col. 2).

मिशि *miśi* or *miśī*, f. (only L.) Anethum Panmori and Anethum Sowa; Nardostachys Jatamansi (cf. *mishikā*); a species of sugar-cane.

Miśreyā, f. Anethum Panmori or dill, L.

मिशृष *miśṛisha*, m. or n. (?) N. of a place, Cat. (v.l. *miśrisha*).

मिश्र् *miśr* (also written *misr*, properly Nom. fr. *miśra* below), cl. 10. P. (Dhātup. xxxv, 67) *miśrayati* (or *miśrāpayati*, Vop.), to mix, mingle, blend, combine ('with,' instr.), KātyŚr.; MBh. &c.; to add, Sūryas. [Cf. Gk. μίσγω, μίγνυμι; Lat. *miscere*; Slav. *mĕsiti*; Lith. *misti*, *maisztas*; Germ. *misken*, *mischen*; Angl. Sax. *miscian*; Eng. *mix*.]

Miśrá, mf(*ā*)n. (prob. fr. a lost √*miś*; cf. under *miksh*) mixed, mingled, blended, combined, RV. &c.

&c. (*vacāṇsi miśrā* √1. *kṛi*, Ā. *-kṛiṇute*, to mingle words, talk together, RV. x, 93, 1); manifold, diverse, various, TS. &c. &c.; mixed or connected or furnished with, accompanied by (instr. with or without *samam*, gen. or comp.; rarely *miśra* ibc., cf. *miśra-vāta*), VS. &c. &c.; pl. (ifc. after honorific epithets = &c.; e. g. *ārya-miśrāḥ*, respectable or honourable people &c.; often also in sg. ifc. and rarely ibc. with proper names by way of respect, cf. *Kṛishṇa-, Madhu-m°*, and comp. below); mixing, adulterating (cf. *dhānya-m°*); m. a kind of elephant, L.; (in music) a kind of measure, Saṃgīt.; N. of various authors and other men (also abbreviation for some names ending in *miśra*, e. g. for Madana-, Mitra-, Vācaspati-m°), Cat.; n. principal and interest, Lalit. (cf. *-dhana*); a species of radish, L. **–keśava**, m. N. of an author, Cat. **–keśī**, f. N. of an Apsaras, MBh.; Kāv.; Pur. **–catur-bhuja**, m. N. of a man, L. **–cora** or **-caura**, m. an adulterator of grain, Vishṇ. **–ja**, m. 'mixed-born,' a mule, L. **–jāti**, mfn. being of mixed birth or breed, one whose parents belong to different castes, L. **–tā**, f. mixedness, mixture, MBh.; R. **–dāmodara**, m. N. of the supposed arranger of the Mahā-nāṭaka, IW. 367. **–dina-kara**, m. N. of a Sch. on Śiśupāla-vadha. **–dhana**, n. principal and interest, Lalit. **–dhānya**, n. mixed grain, Kauś.; (*miśrá-*), mfn. made by mixing various kinds of grain, AV. **–pushpā**, f. Trigonella Foenum Graecum, L. **–prakṛitika**, mfn. of a mixed nature, L. **–bhāva**, m. N. of the author of the Bhāva-prakāśa (also called Bhāva-miśra). **–laṭakana**, m. N. of the father of Miśra-bhāva, Cat. **–varṇa**, mfn. being of a mixed colour, L.; m. a species of sugar-cane, L.; (in music) a kind of measure, Saṃgīt.; n. a kind of black aloe-wood, L.; *-phalā*, f. Solanum Melongena, L. **–vṛitta**, n. a mixed story (partly popular and partly supernatural, as the source of a kind of drama), IW. 471. **–vyavahāra**, m. (in arithm.) investigation of mixed or combined quantities, ascertainment of anything combined (as of principal and interest, &c.), Col. **–śabda**, m. a mule, L. (cf. *miśra-ja*).

Miśraka, mfn. mixed (either 'not pure' or 'various, manifold'), Var.; Suśr. (with *guṇa-sthāna*, n. N. of the third degree on the way to final emancipation, Jain.); singing out of tune, Saṃgīt.; m. a mixer or adulterator (of grain &c.), Mn. xi, 50; salt produced from salt soil, L.; a pigment produced from clarified butter, L.; N. of a Tīrtha, MBh.; of a grove or garden of paradise, L. **–vyavahāra**, m. = *miśra-v°*, Līl. **Miśrakā-vana**, n. Indra's pleasure-grove, Pāṇ. viii, 4, 4 (cf. g. *koṭavādi*).

Miśraṇa, n. mixing, mixture, KātyŚr. (cf. *vāṇ-m°*); addition, Col.

Miśraṇīya, mfn. to be mixed or mingled, MW.

Miśrita, mfn. mixed, blended with (comp.), MBh.; Kāv. &c.; promiscuous, miscellaneous (as taste), VarBṛS.; added, W.; respectable, ib. **–māhātmya**, n. N. of wk.

Miśrin, m. N. of a serpent-demon, MBh.

Miśrī, in comp. for *miśra*. **–karaṇa**, n. the act of mixing, seasoning, an ingredient, Pāṇ. ii, 1, 35. **–√1. kṛi**, P. *-karoti*, to mix, mingle with (instr.), Mahīdh. **–bhāva**, m. mixing, mingling, mixture, Hit. (also *-karman*, n.); mingling carnally, sexual intercourse, Car. **–√bhū**, P. *-bhavati*, to become mixed, mix (also sexually), interwine, meet together, Hariv.; Kāv.; Rājat.

Miśla, mfn. = *miśra* (in *ā́-, ní-, sám-m°*).

मिष् 1. *mish*, cl. 6. P. (Dhātup. xxviii, 60) *misháti* (of the simple verb only pr. p. *mishát*; in Gr. also pf. *mimesha*; aor. *ameshīt*; fut. *meshitā, meshishyati* &c.; cf. *un-* and *ni-√mish*), to open the eyes, wink, blink, RV. &c. &c. (generally used in gen. = before the eyes of, in presence of, in spite of, e. g. *mishato bandhu-vargasya*, the whole number of friends looking on, i. e. before their very eyes, in spite of them); to rival, emulate (*spardhāyām*), Dhātup.

Misha, m. rivalry, emulation, L.; the son of a Kshatriya and a low woman, L.; n. false appearance, fraud, deceit (*mishena* or *mishāt* or *-tas* or ifc. under the pretext of), Kāv.; Kathās.; Rājat.

मिष् 2. *mish*, cl. 1. P. *meshati*, to sprinkle, moisten, wet, Dhātup. xvii, 48. **Mishṭa**, see col. 2.

मिषमिषाय *mishamishāya*, Nom. Ā. *°yate* (onomat.), to crackle, L.

मिषि *mishi*, f. = *misi* (q. v.), L.

Mishikā, f. Nardostachys Jatamansi, L.

मिष्ट *mishṭa*, mfn. (prob. fr. *mṛishṭa*) dainty, delicate, sweet (lit. and fig.), MBh.; Kāv. &c.; n. a sweetmeat, dainty or savoury dish, ib. **–kartṛi**, m. 'maker of dainties,' a skilful cook, MBh. **–tā**, f. sweetness, Naish. **–nimbū**, f. a sweet citron, Bhpr. **–pācaka**, mfn. cooking savoury food or delicacies, Cāṇ. **–bhuj**, mfn. eating dainties, MW. **–bhojana**, n. the eating of dainties, Kathās. **–vākya**, mfn. speaking pleasantly, VarBṛS. **Mishṭânna**, n. sweet or savoury food, MBh.; Kāv. &c.; a mixture of sugar and acids &c. eaten with rice or bread, W.; *-pāna*, n. du. sweet food and drink, Cāṇ. **Mishṭâśā**, f. desire for delicacies, MBh.

मिस् *mis*, cl. 4. P. *mísyati*, to go, Naigh. ii, 14.

मिसर *misara*, m. or n. (perhaps = مصر Misr, Egypt?) N. of a place, Cat.; (cf. *miśara*.)

Misaru, N. of a place, Cat.

Misaru-miśra, m. N. of an author (14th cent.), Cat.

मिसि *misi*, f. (only L.) Anethum Sowa and Panmori; Nardostachys Jatamansi; = *aja-modā*; = *uśīrī* (cf. *miśi*).

मिस्र् *misr*. See *miśr*, p. 817, col. 3.

मिह् 1. *mih*, cl. 1. P. (Dhātup. xxiii, 23) *méhati* (ep. also Ā. *°te*, p. *-meghamāna*, RV.; pf. *mimeha*, Gr.; aor. *amikshat*, ŚBr.; fut. *meḍhā*, Gr., *mekshyáti*, AV.; inf. *mihé*, RV.), to void or pass urine, make water upon (loc. or acc.) or towards (acc.), RV. &c. &c.; to emit seminal fluid, BhP.; (*mimiḍḍhi*) = *yācñā-karman*, Naigh. iii, 19: Caus. *mehayati* (aor. *amīmihat*, Gr.) to cause to make water, RV.: Desid. *mimikshati*, see √1. *miksh*: Intens. *mémihat*, see *ni-√mih*. [Cf. Gk. ὀμιχεῖν; Lat. *mingere, mejere*; Slav. *migla*; Lith. *mížti*; Angl. Sax. *mīgan*; Germ. *Mist*.]

2. **Mih**, f. mist, fog, downpour of water (also pl.; *mihó nápāt*, the demon of the mist), RV.

Mihikā, f. snow, BhP.; mist, fog, L.; camphor, L.

Mīḍha, mfn. urined, watered, L.; m. a ram, L.; (*ā*), f. N. of a woman, Subh.; (*mīḍhá* or *mīḷhá*) n. contest, strife, RV.; prize, reward, ib.; excrement, faeces, Lalit.

Mīḍhu, mīḷhú, m. = *dhana*, Naigh. ii, 10.

Mīḍhúsh or **mīḷhúsh**, in comp. for *mīḍhvás*. **–tama** (*°ḍhúsh-*), mfn. most bountiful or liberal (applied to various gods), RV. &c. &c.; m. the sun, W.; a thief, ib. **–mat** (*°ḍhúsh-*), mfn. bountiful, liberal, kind, RV.

Mīḍhusha, m. N. of a son of Indra by Paulomī, BhP.

Mīḍhvás, mf(*úshī*)n. (declined like a pf. p.; nom. *mīḍhvān*, voc. *mīḍhvas*, dat. *mīḍhúshe* or *mīḷhúshe* &c.), bestowing richly, bountiful, liberal, RV. &c. &c.; (*ushī*), f. N. of Devī (the wife of Īśāna), ĀpGṛ.

मिहिर *mihira*, m. (accord. to Uṇ. i, 52 fr. √1. *mih*, but prob. the Persian مهر) the sun, MBh.; Kāv. &c. (L. also 'a cloud; wind; the moon; a sage'); N. of an author (= *varāha-m°*), Cat.; of a family, VP. **–kula**, m. N. of a prince, Rājat. **–datta**, m. N. of a man, ib. **–pura**, n. N. of a city (built by Mihira-kula), ib. **–rati**, m. N. of a man, Cat. **Mihirâpad**, f. eclipse of the sun, Hcat. **Mihirêśvara**, m. N. of a temple (built by Mihira-kula), Rājat.

Mihirāṇa, m. N. of Śiva, L. (v. l. *miharāṇa*).

मिहिलारोप्य *mihilāropya*, n. N. of a city in the south of India, Pañcat. (cf. *mahilāropya*).

मी 1. *mī*, cl. 9. P. Ā. (Dhātup. xxxi, 4) *mīnā́ti, mīnīte* (Ved. also *mināti* and *minoti*; *mīyate* or *mīyáte* [Dhātup. xxvi, 28]; *mimītas, mimīyāt*[?]; pf. *mimāya*, RV.; *mīmaya*, AV.; *mamau, mimye*, Gr.; aor. *amāsīt, amāsta*, Gr.; *meshṭa*, AV.; aor. Pass. *ámāyi*, Br.; Prec. *mīyāt, māsīshṭa*, Gr.; fut. *mātā, māsyati, °te*, Gr.; *meshyate*, Br.; inf. *-mīyam, -miye*, RV.; *métos*, Br.; ind. p. *mītvā, -mīya, -māya*, Gr.), to lessen, diminish, destroy (Ā. and Pass. to perish, disappear, die), RV.; AV.; Br.; Up.; BhP.; to lose one's way, go astray, RV.; to transgress, violate, frustrate, change, alter, RV.; AV.: Caus. *māpayati*, aor. *amīmapat*, see *pra-√mī*: Desid. *mitsati, °te*, Gr.: Intens. *memīyate, memayīti, memeti*, ib. [Cf. Gk. μινύω; Lat. *minuere*; Slav. *mĭnij*; Germ. *minniro, minre, minder*; Angl. Sax. *min*.]

2. **Mī**. See *manyu-mī*.

Mīta. See under *pra-√mī*.

मी 3. *mī*, cl. 1. 10. P. *mayati* or *māyayati*, to go, move, Dhātup. xxxiv, 18; to understand, Vop.

मीडम् *mīḍam*, ind. in a low tone, softly, Kāṭh.

मीढ *mīḍha, mīḍhu, mīḍhúsh, mīḍhvás* &c. See col. 2.

मीन *mīna*, m. (derivation fr. √1. *mī* very doubtful in spite of Uṇ. iii, 3) a fish, Mn.; MBh. &c.; the sign of the zodiac Pisces, R.; VarBṛS.; Pur.; N. of a teacher of Yoga, Cat.; (*ā*), f. a stick, L.; N. of a daughter of Ushā and wife of Kaśyapa, Pur. **–ketana**, m. 'fish-bannered,' the God of love, L. **–ketu**, m. id., Vcar.; *°tūdaya*, m. N. of a poem. **–gandhā**, f. N. of Satyavatī, Cat. (cf. *matsya-g°*). **–godhikā**, f. a pond, pool of water, L. (v. l. *-gandhikā*). **–ghātin**, m. 'fish-killer,' a fisherman, L.; a crane, L. **–tā**, f. the state or condition of a fish, MW. **–dvaya**, n. a couple of fish, BhP. **–dhāvanatoya**, n. water in which fish have been washed, Suśr. **–dhvaja**, m. = *-ketana*, HYogaś. **–nayanâshṭaka**, n. N. of wk. **–nātha**, m. N. of a teacher of Yoga, Cat. **–netrā**, f. a species of grass, L. **–puccha**, m. or n. (?) a fish-tail; *-nibha*, mfn. resembling a fish-tail, VarBṛS. **–matsya**, m. du. the zodiacal sign Pisces, Var., Sch. **–raṅka** or **-raṅga**, m. a kingfisher, L. **–ratha**, m. N. of a king, VP. **–rāja**, m. the king of the f°, BhP.; (with *yavaneśvara*) N. of an astrologer, Cat.; *-jātaka*, n. his wk. **–lāñchana**, m. = *-ketana*, Vcar. **–vat**, mfn. abounding in fish, MBh. **Mīnâksha**, mfn. marked with a fish-eye, L.; m. N. of a Daitya, Hariv.; (*ā*), f. (prob.) w. r. for next. **Mīnâkshī**, f. a species of Soma-plant or of Dūrvā grass, L.; N. of a daughter of Kubera, Pur.; of a deity (the deified daughter of a Pāṇḍya king, esp. worshipped in Madurā and also called Mīnācī), RTL. 228; 442, n. 1; *-cūrṇikā*, f., *-pañca-ratna*, n., *-pariṇaya*, m. N. of wks.; *-sundareśvara*, m. N. of a temple sacred to Mīnâkshī and Śiva (considered as her husband), RTL. 441, n. 1; *-stava-rāja*, m., *-stotra*, n. N. of wks. **Mīnâghātin**, m. = *mīna-gh°*, L. **Mīnâṅka**, m. = *mīna-ketana*, L. **Mīnâṇḍa**, n. fish-spawn, roe, milt, W.; (*ī* or *ā*), f. moist or brown sugar, L. **Mīnâri**, m. 'enemy of fish,' a fisherman, Jātakam. **Mīnâlaya**, m. 'abode of fish,' the sea, ocean, L.

Mīnara, m. a kind of sea-monster (= *makara*), L.

Mīnāmṛiṇa, m. a kind of sauce or condiment, L.; a wagtail, L. (v. l. *mīnāstṛiṇa*).

मीम् *mīm*, cl. 1. P. *mīmati*, to move; to sound, Dhātup. xiii, 25.

मीमांसक *mīmāṇsaka*, m. (fr. Desid. of √*man*) as examiner, investigator, prover (cf. *kāvya-m°*); a follower of the Mīmāṇsā system (see below), TPrāt.; Śaṃk.; (*ikā*), f. the Mīmāṇsā system, Hcat.

Mīmāṇsā, f. profound thought or reflection or consideration, investigation, examination, discussion, ŚBr.; TĀr.; theory (cf. *kāvya-m°*); 'examination of the Vedic text,' N. of one of the 3 great divisions of orthodox Hindū philosophy (divided into 2 systems, viz. the Pūrva-mīmāṇsā or Karma-mīmāṇsā by Jaimini, concerning itself chiefly with the correct interpretation of Vedic ritual and text, and usually called the Mīmāṇsā; and the Uttara-mīmāṇsā or Brahma-m° or Śārīraka-m° by Bādarāyaṇa, commonly styled the Vedânta and dealing chiefly with the nature of Brahmā or the one universal Spirit), IW. 46; 98 &c. **–kutūhala**, n., **-kutūhala-vṛitti**, f., **-kusumâñjali**, m. N. of wks. **–kṛit**, m. 'author of the Mīmāṇsā system,' N. of Jaimini, Pañcat. **–kaumudī**, f., **-kaustubha**, m. n., **-jīva-rakshā**, f., **-tattva-candrikā**, f. N. of wks. **–tantra-vārttika**, n. N. of Kumārila's Comm. on Śabarasvāmin's Mīmāṇsā-bhāshya (see below). **–°dhikaraṇa** (*°sâdh°*), n. (ibc.); *-nyāya-vicārôpanyāsa*, m., *-mālā-ṭīkā*, f. N. of wks. **–naya-viveka**, m. N. of a Comm. on the Mīmāṇsā-sūtras (q. v.) by Bhava-nātha-miśra; *-gatârtha-mālikā*, f., *-śaṅkā-dīpikā*, f.; *°kālaṃkāra*, m. N. of wks. **–nyāya**, m. (ibc.); *-parimalôllāsa*, m., *-prakāśa*, m., *-ratnâkara*, m. N. of wks. **–padârtha-nirṇaya**, m., **-paribhāshā**, f., **-palvala**, n., **-pādukā**, f., **-prakriyā**, f., **-bāla-prakāśa** (also called *-sāra-saṃgraha*), m. N. of wks. **–bhaṭṭa**, m. N. of an author, Cat. **— bhāshya**, n. (also *-sūtra-bh°*) N. of the oldest existing Comm. on the M°-sūtra, by Śabara-svāmin. **— makaranda**, m., **-rasa-palvala**, n. N. of wks. **— °rtha** (*°sârtha*), m. (ibc.); *-dīpa*, m., *-saṃgraha*, m. N. of wks. **— vāda**, m. (or *°dârtha*, m.) N. of wk. **— vārttika**, n. = *°sā-tantra-vārttika*. **— vidhi-bhūshaṇa**, n., **-vivaraṇa-ratna-mālā**, f., **-vishaya**, m. N. of wks. **— śāstra**, n. (ibc.); *-dīpikā*, f., *-sarvasva*, n. N. of wks. **— śiromaṇi**, m. 'crest-gem of the M°,' N. of an author (also called Nīla-kaṇṭha), Cat. **— śloka-vārttika**, n. N. of a metrical paraphrase of Śabara's M°-bhāshya. **— saṃkalpa-kaūmudī**, f. N. of wk. **— saṃgraha**, m. = *°sârtha-saṃgraha*. **— sarvasva**, n. = *°sā-śāstra-sarvasva*. **— sāra**, m. and *°ra-saṃgraha*, m. N. of wks. (cf. *°sā-bāla-prakāśa*). **— siddhântâryā**, f. N. of wk. **— sūtra**, n. (= *jaimini-s°*) N. of the 12 books of aphorisms by Jaimini (see above); *-dīdhiti*, f., *-rahasya*, n. N. of wks. **— stabaka**, m. N. of an elementary treatise on the Mīmāṇsā by Rāghavânanda.

Mīmāṇsitavya, mfn. to be examined or investigated, Jātakam.

Mīmāṇsya, mfn. to be thought over or reflected upon, to be examined or considered, Gobh.; KenUp. (cf. *a-m°*).

मीर *mīra*, m. the sea, ocean, Uṇ. ii, 25, Sch. (L. also 'a partic. part of a mountain; a limit, boundary; a drink, beverage').

मीरमीरा *mīramīrā*, f. N. of a woman (*-suta*, m. N. of a lexicographer), Cat.

मील् *mīl*, cl. 1. P. (Dhātup. xv, 10) *mīlati* (rarely Ā. *°te*; pf. *mimīla*, Kāv.; aor. *amīlīt*, Gr.; fut. *mīlitā*, *mīlishyati*, ib.; ind. p. *-mīlya*, RV.), to close the eyes, Gīt.; to close (intrans., said of the eyes), wink, twinkle, Hariv.; Kāv.; Pur.; (= √*mil*) to assemble, be collected, Uttarar.: Caus. *mīlayati* (ep. also *°te*; aor. *amimīlat* or *amīmilat*, Pāṇ. vii, 4, 3), to cause to close, close (eyes, blossoms &c.), Kāv.; Pur.: Desid. *mimīlishati*, Gr.: Intens. *memīlyate*, *memīlti*, ib.

Mīlana, n. the act of closing the eyes, Kathās.; closing (intrans., said of eyes and flowers), Kir., Sch.; Sāh.; (in rhet.) a covert or concealed simile (cf. *mīlita*), Pratāp.

Mīlika, see *nīla-m°*; (*ā*), f. black brass, L. (v.l. *nīlikā*).

Mīlita, mfn. one who has closed his eyes, sleepy (only compar. *°tá-tara*), ŚBr.; closed, obstructed (opp. to *mukta*), PañcavBr.; closed, unblown, partly opened (as eyes, blossoms &c.), Kāv.; Pur.; disappeared, ceased to be, BhP.; met, assembled, gathered together, Rājat.; (in rhet.) an implied simile (in which the similarity between two objects is only implied, as in the example: 'women clothed in white are invisible in the moonlight, therefore they are as bright as moonlight'), Kpr.; Kuval.

मीव् 1. *mīv*, cl. 1. P. *mīvati*, to move (see *ā-*, *ni-*, *pra-*, *prati-*√*mīv*).

1. **Mūta**, mfn. (for 2. see √1. *mū*) moved (see *kāma-mūta*).

मीव् 2. *mīv* (cf. √*pīv*), cl. 1. P. *mīvati*, to grow fat or corpulent, Dhātup. xv, 56.

मीवग *mīvaga*, m. or n. (?) a partic. high number, Buddh.

मीवर *mīvara*, mf(ī)n. hurtful, injurious, Uṇ. iii, 1, Sch.; venerable, L.; m. a leader of an army, L.

मीवा *mīvā*, f. a tape-worm, Uṇ. i, 154, Sch. (others 'air, wind;' W. *mīvan*, m.)

मु *mu*, m. (only L.; cf. √*mū*) a bond; N. of Śiva; final emancipation; a funeral pile or pyre; a reddish-brown or tawny colour.

मुंसल *muṇsala*, m. or n. (?) N. of a place, Cat.

मुक *muka*, m. the smell of cowdung; mf(*ā*)n. having the smell of cowdung, L.

मुकन्दक *mukandaka*, prob. w.r. for *su-k°*, q.v.

मुकय *mukaya*, m. and *mukayī*, f. a partic. kind of living being, Pāṇ. iv, 1, 63, Vārtt. 1, Pat.

मुका *mukā*, f. N. of a town, VP.

मुकारिणा *mukāriṇā*, f. = مقارنة, (in astrol.) a partic. position or conjunction of the planets.

मुकाविला *mukāvilā*, f. = مقابلة, id.

मुकु *muku*, m. = *mukti* (a word formed to explain *mukun-da* as 'giver of liberation;' others assume an ind. *mukum*), L.

मुकुट *mukuṭa*, m. n. (ifc. f. *ā*) a tiara, diadem, crown (said to be crescent-shaped; the *kirīṭa* being pointed, and the *mauli* having three points), Inscr.; MBh.; Kāv. &c.; a crest, point, head (see *tri-m°*); N. of an author (= *rāya-m°*), Cat.; pl. N. of a people, MBh.; (*ā*), f. N. of one of the Mātṛis attending on Skanda, MBh.; (*ī*), f. snapping the fingers, L.; n. N. of a Tīrtha, Cat. **— tāḍitaka**, n. N. of a drama. **— ratna**, n. = *mukuṭôpala*, Ragh.

Mukuṭe-kārshāpaṇa, n. N. of a tax or tribute raised for a royal diadem (in the east of India), Pāṇ. vi, 2, 65, Sch. **Mukuṭêśvara**, m. N. of a king, Cat.; (*ī*), f. N. of Dākshāyaṇī in Mukuṭa, ib.; *-tīrtha*, n. N. of a Tīrtha, ib. **Mukuṭôpala**, m. a crest-gem, jewel on a diadem, MW.

Mukuṭin, mfn. crowned, wearing a diadem, MBh.; Hariv.; R.

मुकुट्ट *mukuṭṭa*, m. N. of a man, MBh.

मुकुण्टी *mukuṇṭī*, f. a kind of weapon, L. (prob. w.r. for *su-kuṇṭhī*).

मुकुण्ठ *mukuṇṭha*, m. pl. N. of a people, VP.

मुकुन्द *mukunda*, m. (cf. *muku*) N. of Vishṇu (sometimes transferred to Śiva), MBh.; BhP.; of a celebrated saint, RTL. 318; of a partic. treasure, MārkP.; a kind of precious stone, L.; a kind of grain, Car.; the resin of Boswellia Thurifera, Bhpr.; a kind of drum or kettle-drum, L.; (in music) a kind of measure, Saṃgīt.; N. of various scholars and authors (also with *miśra*, *paṇḍita*, *dīkshita*, *śarman*, *kavi*, *parivrājaka*; cf. comp.), Cat.; of a mountain, VP. **— govinda**, m. N. of the Guru of Rāmânanda, Cat. **— caturdaśa**, n. N. of a Stotra. **— dāsa**, m. N. of two authors; *-guṇa-leśâshṭaka*, n. N. of wk. **— deva**, m. N. of various princes of Orissa, Cat. **— priya**, m. N. of the son of Gadādhara and father of Rāmânanda, Cat. **— bhaṭṭa**, m. N. of various authors (also *gāḍagila* and *°ṭṭâcārya*); *°ṭṭīya*, n. N. of wk. **— mālā**, f. N. of a Stotra (in 22 verses, addressed to Vishṇu) by Kula-śekhara. **— muktā-ratnâvalī-stotra-ṭīkā**, f., **-muktâvalī**, f. N. of wks. **— muni** or **-rāja**, m., **-lāla**, m., **-vana**, m. N. of various men, Cat. **— vijaya**, m., **-vilāsa**, m. N. of wks. **— sena**, m. N. of a man, Cat. **Mukundânanda**, m. N. of a Bhāṇa (q.v.) by Kāśī-pati. **Mukundâshṭaka**, n. N. of a Stotra.

Mukundaka, m. a kind of grain (reckoned among the Ku-dhānyas), Suśr.; w.r. for *su-kandaka*.

Mukundu, m. the resin of Boswellia Thurifera, L.

मुकुम् *mukum*. See *muku* above.

मुकुर *mukura*, m. a mirror (= *makura*), Kāv. (cf. *karṇa-* and *mati-m°*); the stick or handle of a potter's wheel, L.; Mimusops Elengi, L.; Jasminum Zambac, L.; a bud, blossom, L. (g. *tārakâdi*).

Mukurāya, Nom. Ā. *°yate*, to become a mirror, Dharmaśarm.

Mukurita, mfn. (prob.) = *mukulita* (q.v.), g. *-tārakâdi*.

मुकुल *mukula*, n. (m., g. *ardharcâdi*; ifc. f. *ā*) a bud (also fig. 'a first tooth'), Kālid.; Pur.; Suśr. (in this sense also *makula*, L.); the body, L.; the soul, L.; (only n.) a kind of metre, Ked.; m. (with *hāsta*) a bud-like junction or bringing together of the fingers of the hand, Nalôd.; N. of a king and another man, Rājat.; (with *bhaṭṭa*) N. of an author, Cat.; mf(*ā*)n. closed (as eyes), Mālatīm., Sch.

Mukulâgra, n. a partic. surgical instrument with a bud-like point, Suśr.

Mukulaya, Nom. P. *°yati*, to cause to close or shut (the eyes), Mālatīm.

Mukulāya, Nom. Ā. *°yate*, to shut like a bud, resemble a closed bud, Hcar.; Kād.

Mukulâyita, mfn. budded, blossomed, Kāv.

Mukulikā, f. a low or humming sound made to lull a child to sleep, Vās., Introd.

Mukulita, mfn. budded, full of blossoms, R.; Gīt.; closed like a bud, shut, Kāv.; Var.; Sāh. **— nayana**, mf(*ā*)n. or **°tâksha**, mf(*ī*)n. having half-closed eyes, Kāv.

Mukulin, mfn. budding, full of buds, Mālatīm.

Mukulī, in comp. for *mukula*. **— √1. kṛi**, P. *-karoti*, to close in the form of a bud, Vcar. **— kṛita**, mfn. closed, shut (as a bud), Kum.; Amar. **— bhāva**, m. closing, the being closed (as a flower), Kum., Sch.

मुकुष्ठ *mukushṭha*, mfn. = *manthara*, L.; m. = next, L.

Mukushṭhaka, m. a species of bean, L.

मुकूलक *mukūlaka*, m. a species of plant (= *makūlaka*), L.

मुक्त *mukta*, *muktā*, *mukti*. See p. 816 &c.

मुक्षीजा *mukshījā*, f. a net, snare, RV. i, 125, 2.

मुख *mukha*, n. (m., g. *ardharcâdi*; ifc. *ā* or *ī*, cf. Pāṇ. iv, 1, 54, 58) the mouth, face, countenance, RV. &c. &c.; the beak of a bird, snout or muzzle of an animal, GṛS.; Mn.; MBh. &c.; a direction, quarter (esp. ifc., cf. *diṅ-m°*; mfn. turning or turned towards, facing, cf. *adho-m°*; also *am*, ind., cf. *prāṅ-mukham*); the mouth or spout of a vessel, KātyŚr.; opening, aperture, entrance into or egress out of (gen. or comp.), MBh.; Kāv. &c.; the mouth or embouchure (of a river), Ragh.; the fore part, front, van (of an army), TBr.; MBh.; the upper part, head, top, tip or point of anything, VS.; Br.; MBh. &c. (also mfn. in comp., cf. *payo-m°*); the edge (of an axe), Kāv.; the nipple (of a breast), Hariv.; the surface, upper side, Āryabh., Sch.; the chief, principal, best (ifc. = having any one or anything as chief &c.), ŚBr.; MBh. &c.; introduction, commencement, beginning (ifc. = beginning with; also *-mukhâdi*, cf. the use of *ādi*), Br.; MBh.; Kāv. &c.; source, cause, occasion of (gen. or comp.), MBh.; a means (*ena*, ind. by means of), Śaṃk.; (in dram.) the original cause or source of the action, Daśar.; Pratāp.; (in alg.) the first term or initial quantity of a progression, Col.; (in geom.) the side opposite to the base, the summit, ib.; the Veda, L.; rock salt, L.; copper, L.; m. Artocarpus Locucha, L. **— kamala**, n. 'face-lotus,' a lotus-like face, MW. **— khura**, m. 'mouth-razor,' a tooth, L. **— gata**, mfn. being in the mouth or in the face, Subh. **— gandhaka**, m. 'mouth-scenting,' an onion, L. **— grahaṇa**, n. kissing the mouth, Daś. **— ghaṇṭā**, f. 'mouth-bell,' a partic. sound made with the mouth, L.; *°ṭikā*, f. = *mukulikā*, col. 2. **— candra**, m. 'face-moon,' a moon-like face, Bhartṛ.; *-mas*, m. = prec., Kāvyâd. **— capala**, mf(*ā*)n. 'one whose mouth is ever moving,' loquacious, garrulous (*-tva*, n.), Var.; (*ā*), f. a kind of Āryā metre, Piṅg.; Col. **— capeṭikā**, f. a slap on the face, box on the ear (cf. *durjana-m°*). **— cāpalya**, n. loquacity, Dhūrtan. **— cāli**, f. an introductory dance, Saṃgīt. **— cīrī**, f. the tongue, L. **— cchada**, m. or n. (?) a face-cover, eye-bandage, Kir. **— cchavi**, f. 'face-colour,' complexion, Daś. **— ja**, mfn. produced from or in the mouth, L.; being on the face (with *abhinaya*, m. change of countenance, play of feature), Saṃgīt.; m. 'mouth-born,' a Brāhman (so called as produced from the mouth of Brahmā), Siṃhās.; a tooth, W. **— janman**, m. a Brāhman, Gal. (cf. prec.) **— jāha**, n. the root or point of issue of the mouth, the top of the pharynx, g. *karṇâdi*. **— 1. -tás**, ind. from or at the mouth, by means of the m°; at the head, in the front, from before, RV.; TS.; Br. &c.; *-taḥ-kāram*, ind., Pāṇ. iii, 4, 61, Sch. **— 2. -tas**, mfn. = *mukhe tasyati*, Pāṇ. ib. **— tuṇḍaka**, m. or n. (?) the mouth, Divyâv. **— daghná**, mfn. reaching to the mouth, ŚBr. **— dūshaṇa**, n. (L.) or *°ṇaka*, m. (Bhpr.) 'mouth-defiler,' an onion. **— dūshikā**, f. 'face-spoiler,' an eruption which disfigures the face, Bhpr.; ŚārṅgS. **— dhautā**, f. Clerodendrum Siphonanthus, L. **— nāsika**, n. sg. the mouth and nose, APrāt. **— nirīkshaka**, mfn. 'face-gazer,' idle, lazy, L.; m. an idler, W. **— nivāsinī**, f. 'dwelling in the mouth,' N. of Sarasvatī, L. **— paṅkaja**, m. 'face-lotus,' a lotus-like f°, Kāvyâd. **— paṭa**, m. 'face-cloth,' a veil, Megh. **— pāka**, m. inflammation of the mouth, Suśr.; ŚārṅgS. **— piṇḍa**, m. or n. (?) a lump or piece of food in the m°, Bhartṛ. **— pushpaka**, n. a kind of ornament, L. **— pūraṇa**, n. 'filling the mouth,' a mouthful of water, a mouth in general, L. **— poñchana** (for *-prôñchana*), n. a cloth or napkin for wiping the mouth, L. (w.r. *-pocchana*). **— pratimukha**, speech and reply (?), MW. **— prasāda**, m. the light of the countenance, graciousness of aspect. **— prasādhana**, n. decorating or painting the face, Mālav. **— priya**, mfn. pleasant in the mouth, Suśr.; m. an orange, Bhpr. **— prêksha** (MBh.) or **-prêkshin** (Rājat.), mfn. observing or watching the face (to detect any one's intentions). **-phullaka,** n. a kind of ornament, L. **-bandha,** m. 'head-composition,' preface, MW. **-bandhana,** n. 'top-fastening,' a lid, cover, L.; 'head-composition,' introduction, preface, Chandom.; the fifth change which takes place in warm milk when mixed with Takra, L. **-bâhûru-paj-ja,** mfn. sprung from the mouth, arms, thighs and feet, Mn. i, 87. **-bâhûru-pâdatas,** ind. from the m°, arms, thighs and feet, MW. **-bhagā,** f. (a woman) who suffers her mouth to be used as a vulva, Hariv. (cf. *mukhe-bhagā, bhagâsya*). **-bhaṅga,** m. a blow on the face (*upânan-m°*, a blow on the f° with a shoe), Cāṇ.; a face distorted by sickness, wry f°, grimace, Kād.; GāruḍaP. **-bhaṅgī,** f. the act of making wry faces, Naish., Comm. **-bhūshaṇa,** n. 'mouth-ornament,' betel, L.; tin(?), L. **-bheda,** m. distortion of the face, gaping, MBh. **-maṇḍana** or °**naka,** m. Clerodendrum Phlomoides, L. **-maṇḍala,** n. 'face-orb,' the face, countenance, Kāv. **-maṇḍikā** (MBh.; Suśr.) or °**ḍinikā** (ŚārṅgS.), f. a partic. disease or the deity presiding over it. **-maṇḍī,** f. N. of one of the Mātṛis attending on Skanda, Hariv. **-madhu,** mfn. honey-mouthed, sweet-lipped, Śak. **-mātra,** mf(*ī*)n. reaching to the mouth, VS., Comm.; (*e*), ind. as high as the m°, KātyŚr. **-mâdhurya,** n. a partic. disease of the phlegm, ŚārṅgS. **-māruta,** m. 'm°-wind,' breath, Kālid. **-mārjana,** n. washing or cleansing the m° (after meals &c.), MW. **-mudrā,** f. distortion of the face or (more prob.) silence, Naish. **-moda,** m. Hyperanthera Moringa, L. **-m-paca,** m. a beggar, L. **-yantraṇa,** n. 'mouth-curb,' the bit of a bridle, L. **-yoni,** m. = *āsekya*, Bhpr. **-rajju,** f. 'mouth-cord,' the bridle or bit of a horse, L. **-randhra,** n. the mouth of a flute, Saṃgīt. **-rāga,** m. colour of the face, Ragh.; Kathās. **-ruj,** f. any disease of the mouth, VarBṛS. **-rekhā,** f. feature, mien, air, Prasannar. **-roga,** m. = *-ruj* (q.v.), Suśr.; VarBṛS.; MārkP. **-rogika,** mfn. relating to mouth-disease, Suśr. **-rogin,** mfn. diseased in the m°, ib. **-lāṅgala,** m. 'using his snout for a plough,' a boar, hog, Harav. **-lepa,** m. anointing the m°, Bhartṛ.; an° the upper side of a drum, ib.; a partic. disease of the phlegmatic humour, ŚārṅgS. (cf. *âs-yôpalepa*). **-vat,** mfn. possessing a m°, MaitrUp. **-varṇa,** m. colour of the face, MBh.; R.; Pañcat. **-vallabha,** m. a pomegranate tree, L. **-vastrikā,** f. a piece of fine muslin or net held before the face while speaking, HPariś. **-vāṭikā,** f. a species of plant (= *amba-shṭhā*), L. **-vādya,** n. any musical instrument sounded with the mouth, L.; (in the worship of Śiva) a kind of musical sound made with the m° (by striking it with the hand), L. **-vāsa,** m. 'mouth-perfume,' a perf° used to scent the breath, Pañcat.; BhP.; Pañcar.; a partic. intoxicating drink, L.; fragrant grass, L. **-vāsana,** n. mouth-perfume (= *-vāsa*), L.; the smell of camphor, L.; mfn. having the smell of camphor, L. **-vipulā,** f. a kind of Āryā metre, Piṅg. **-viluṇṭhikā,** f. a she-goat, L. **-vishṭhā,** f. a species of cockroach, L. **-vairasya,** n. a bad taste in the mouth, Suśr. **-vyādāna,** n. the act of opening the m° wide, gaping, Hit. **-śapha,** mfn. foul-mouthed, scurrilous, L. **-śaśin,** m. = *-candra*, Ratnâv. **-śālā,** f. entrance-hall, waiting room, vestibule, L. **-śuddhi,** f. cleansing or purifying the mouth, Tithyād. **-śṛiṅga,** m. a rhinoceros, L. **-śesha,** mfn. having only the face left; m. N. of Rāhu, R. **-śodhana,** mfn. cleansing the mouth, L.; sharp, pungent, L.; m. pungency, sharp or pungent flavour, MW.; n. the cleansing of the m°, Cat.; cinnamon, L. **-śodhin,** mfn. cleansing the m°, L.; m. a lime or citron, citron tree, L. **-śobhā,** f. brilliancy of the face resulting from reading the Veda, L. **-śosha,** m. dryness of the m°, Suśr.; ŚārṅgS. **-śoshin,** mfn. suffering from dr° of the m°, Suśr. **-śrī,** f. beauty of countenance, a beautiful face, BhP.; Kāvyâd. **-shṭhila,** mfn. (prob. for *mukhâsh-ṭhila*) = *-sapha* (q.v.), L. **-saṃdaṃśa,** m. forceps, Suśr. **-saṃdhi,** m. (in dram.) N. of a kind of fugue, Sāh. **-sambhava,** m. 'mouth-born,' a Brāhman, L. (cf. *-ja*). **-sammita** (*múkha-*), mfn. reaching to the m°, ŚBr.; KātyŚr. **-sukha,** n. causing ease of pronunciation, Pāṇ. iii, 3, 57, Sch. **-sura,** n. lip-nectar, L. **-secaka,** m. N. of a serpent-demon, MBh. **-srāva,** m. flow of saliva, ŚārṅgS.; saliva, L. **Mukhâkāra,** m. 'form of the countenance,' mien, look, R. **Mukhâkshepa,** m. the act of throwing up soil with the ploughshare, (or) an invective (as uttered by the mouth), Kāv. **Mukhâgni,** m. a forest-conflagration, L.; a sort of goblin with a face of fire, W.; fire put into the mouth of a corpse at the time of lighting the funeral pile, W.; a sacrificial or consecrated fire, W. **Mukhâgra,** n. the extremity of a nose or snout; any extremity, L. **Mukhâṅga,** n. a part of the face, Kāvyâd. **Múkhâdāna,** mfn. seizing with the m°, MaitrS. **Mukhâdi-tva,** n., fr. *mukhâdi*, 'the face &c.,' Kāvyâd. **Mukhânila,** m. 'm°-wind,' breath, ĀpŚr., Comm. **Mukhâbja,** n. = *mukha-kamala* (q.v.), Bhaktâm. **Mukhâmaya,** m. disease of the m°, L. **Mukhâmṛita,** n. the nectar of the mouth or countenance, MW. **Mukhâmodā,** f. Boswellia Thurifera, L. **Mukhâmbuja,** n. = *mukha-kamala*, Kalyāṇam. **Mukhârcis,** n. 'm°-flame,' hot breath (?), Pañcar. **Mukhârjaka,** m. Ocimum Pilosum, L. **Mukhâlu,** n. a species of arum, L. **Mukhâvarī,** f. N. of a Rāgiṇī, Saṃgīt. **Mukhâvalepa,** m. clamminess of the mouth, Suśr. **Mukhâsava,** m. nectar of the lips, Ragh. **Mukhâstra,** m. 'mouth-armed,' a crab, L. **Mukhâsrāva,** m. 'flow of saliva,' Suśr. **Mukhâsvāda,** m. kissing the m°, Yājñ. **Mukhêndu,** m. a moon-like face, Śṛiṅgār.; Kāvyâd.; *-bimba*, n. id., Ratnâv. **Mukhe-balin,** m. a rhinoceros, L. **Mukhe-bhagā,** f. = *mukha-bhagā* (q.v.), MBh. **Mukhe-bhava,** mf(*ā*)n. formed in the mouth, RPrāt., Sch. **Mukhôcchvāsa,** m. breath, A. **Mukhôtkīrṇa,** m. N. of a man, Rājat. **Mukhôlkā,** f. a forest fire, L.

Mukhatīya, mfn. (fr. 1. *mukha-tás*) being in the mouth or in the front, g. *gahâdi*.

Mukhara, mf(*ā*)n. (fr. *mukha*; cf. Pāṇ. v, 2, 107, Vārtt. 1, Pat.) talkative, garrulous, loquacious (said also of birds and bees), Kāv.; Kathās.; noisy, tinkling (as an anklet &c.), Mṛicch.; Kālid.; sounding, resonant or eloquent with, expressive of (comp.), Kāv.; Kathās.; Rājat.; foul-mouthed, scurrilous, speaking harshly or abusively, L.; m. a crow, L.; a conch shell, L.; a leader, principal, chief, Hit.; N. of a Nāga, MBh.; of a rogue, Cat.; (*ā*), f. N. of a serpent-maid, Kāraṇḍ.; (*ī*), f. the bit of a bridle, KātyŚr., Sch. **-tā,** f. talkativeness, garrulity, noisiness, Kir.

Mukharaka, m. N. of a rogue, Kathās.; (*ikā*), f. the bit of a bridle, KātyŚr.; talking, conversation, BhP.

Mukharaya, Nom. P. °*yati*, to make talkative, cause to speak, Bālar.; to make noisy or resonant, Nāg.; Gīt.; to announce, notify, declare, MW. °**rita,** mfn. rendered noisy, made resonant, sounding, ringing, Kāv.; Kathās.; BhP.

Mukharī-√1. kṛi, P. *-karoti*, to make resonant, cause to resound, Kathās.

Mukhīna. See *brāhmaṇa-m°*.

Mukhī-√bhū (ind.p. *-bhūya*), Pāṇ. iii, 4, 61, Sch.

Mukhīya, mfn. (ifc.) being at the top or head, being foremost (see *śālā-, savana-m°* &c.)

Múkhya, mf(*ā*)n. being in or coming from or belonging to the mouth or face, AV. &c. &c.; being at the head or at the beginning, first, principal, chief, eminent (ifc. = the first or best or chief among, rarely = *mukha* or *ādi*, q.v.), TS. &c. &c.; m. a leader, guide, Kām.; N. of a tutelary deity (presiding over one of the 81 or 63 divisions or Padas of an astrological house), VarBṛS.; Hcat.; pl. a class of gods under Manu Sāvarṇi, Pur.; (*ā*), f. N. of the residence of Varuṇa, VP.; n. an essential rite, W.; reading or teaching the Vedas, ib.; the month reckoned from new moon to new moon, ib.; moustache, Gal. **-candra,** m. or n. (?) the principal lunar month (which ends with the conjunction, as opp. to the *gauṇa-c°* which ends with the opposition), Col. **-tas,** ind. principally, chiefly, particularly, Kap., Sch. **-tā,** f., **-tva,** n. pre-eminence, superiority, highest rank or position, MBh.; R. &c. **-nṛipa,** m. a paramount sovereign, reigning monarch, L. **-mantrin,** m. a prime minister (°*tri-tva*, n.), Hit. **-rāj** or **-rājan,** m. = *-nṛipa*, L. **-śas,** ind. principally, chiefly, before all, next, MBh. **-sadṛiśa,** mfn. similar to the principal matter, Bhpr. **Mukhyârtha,** m. the primary meaning of a word (as opp. to *gauṇârtha*, the secondary or metaphorical meaning), Saṃk.; Sāh.; mfn. employed in (or having) the original sense, Siddh. **Mukhyâśramin,** m. the pupil of a Brāhman, Gal. **Mukhyôpāya,** m. pl. the four chief stratagems (*sāman, dāna, bheda,* and *daṇḍa*), A.

मुखण्डी *mukhaṇḍī* or *mukhuṇḍhī*, f. a kind of weapon, L.

मुखुली *mukhulī*, prob. w.r. for *utkhalī*, q.v.

मुगदस *mugadasa, mugademu, mugala-sthāna*, N. of places, Cat.

मुगूह *mugūha*, m. a species of gallinule (= *dātyūha*), L.

मुग्ध *mugdha* &c. See p. 825, col. 1.

मुङ्ग *muṅga* and *muṅgaṭa*, m. N. of two men, Rājat.

मुच् 1. *muc*, cl. 1. Ā. *mocate*, to cheat, Dhātup. vi, 12 (= √*mac*, q.v.)

मुच् 2. *muc*, cl. 6. P. Ā. (Dhātup. xxviii, 136) *muñcáti*, °*te* (RV. also *mucánti, mucasva*; p. *muñcāna*, MBh.; pf. *mumóca, mumucé*, Ved. also *mumócat, mumocati, mumucas, mumoktu, amumuktam*; aor. *ámok*, AV.; Impv. *mogdhi*, TĀr.; *amauk*, Br.; *ámucat*, AV.; *amukshi, mukshata*, RV.; AV.; Prec. *mucīshṭa*, RV.; *mukshīya*, ib.; fut. *moktā*, Kālid.; *mokshyati*, °*te*, Br. &c.; inf. *moktum*, Br. &c.; ind. p. *muktvā*, ib., *-múcya*, RV., *mókam*, Br.), to loose, let loose, free, let go, slacken, release, liberate ('from,' abl. or *-tas*; Ā. and Pass. with abl. or instr., rarely with gen. 'to free one's self, get rid of, escape from'), RV. &c. &c. (with *kaṇṭham*, to relax the throat i.e. raise a cry; with *raśmīn*, to slacken the reins; with *prâṇān*, to deprive of life, kill); to spare, let live, R.; to set free, allow to depart, dismiss, despatch ('to,' loc. or dat.), MBh.; Kāv. &c.; to relinquish, abandon, leave, quit, give up, set aside, depose, ib. (with *kalevaram, deham, prâṇān* or *jīvitam*, to quit the body or give up the ghost, i.e. to die); to yield, grant, bestow, Rājat.; Campak.; to send forth, shed, emit, utter, discharge, throw, cast, hurl, shoot ('at' or 'upon,' loc., dat., or acc. with or without *prati*; with abl. and *ātmānam*, to throw one's self down from), Yājñ.; MBh.; R. &c.; (Ā.) to put on, Bhaṭṭ. (Sch.): Pass. *mucyáte* (or *múcyate*, ep. also °*ti* and fut. *mokshyati*; aor. *ámoci*), to be loosed, to be set free or released, RV. &c. &c.; to deliver one's self from, to get rid of, escape (esp. from sin or the bonds of existence), Mn.; MBh. &c.; to abstain from (abl.), Pañcat.; to be deprived or destitute of (instr.), MBh.: Caus. *mocayati* (m.c. also °*te*; aor. *amūmucat*), to cause to loose or let go or give up or discharge or shed (with two acc.), Megh.; Bhaṭṭ.; to unloose, unyoke, unharness (horses), MBh.; R.; to set free, liberate, absolve from (abl.), Mn.; MBh. &c.; to redeem (a pledge), Yājñ.; to open (a road), Prab.; to give away, spend, bestow, MārkP.; to gladden, delight, yield enjoyment, Dhātup. xxxiii, 66: Desid. of Caus. *mumocayishati*, to wish to deliver (from the bondage of existence), Saṃk. (cf. *mumocayishu*): Desid. *mumukshati*, °*te*, (P.) to wish or be about to set free, Pāṇ. vii, 4, 57, Sch.; to be about to give up or relinquish (life), Kathās.; to wish or intend to cast or hurl, Ragh.; (Ā.) to wish to free one's self, Pāṇ. vii, 4, 57, Sch.; to desire final liberation or beatitude, RV.; BhP. (cf. √*moksh*): Intens. *momucyate* or *momokti*, Gr. [Cf. Gk. μύσσω, μύκος, μυκτής; Lat. *mungo, mucus*.]

Mukta, mfn. loosened, let loose, set free, relaxed, slackened, opened, open, MBh.; Kāv. &c.; liberated, delivered, emancipated (esp. from sin or worldly existence), Mn.; MBh. &c. (with instr. or ifc. = released from, deprived or destitute of; cf. Pāṇ. ii, 1, 38); fallen or dropped down (as fruit), Hariv.; abandoned, relinquished, quitted, given up, laid aside, deposed, MBh.; Kāv. &c.; sent forth, emitted, discharged, poured out, hurled, thrown, ib.; left free (as a road), Megh.; uttered (as sound), MBh.; shed (as tears), Pañcat.; let fly, applied (as a kick), Ragh.; gone, vanished, disappeared (esp. ibc.; cf. below); m. N. of one of the 7 sages under Manu Bhautya, MBh.; of a cook, Rājat.; (*ā*), f. (with or scil. *diś*) the quarter or cardinal point just quitted by the sun, VarBṛS.; a pearl (as loosened from the pearl-oyster shell), Mn.; MBh. &c.; an unchaste woman, L.; a species of plant (= *rāsnā*), L.; N. of a river, VP.; n. the spirit released from corporeal existence, W.; (*e*), ind. beside (with instr.), Kāś. on Pāṇ. ii, 3, 72; iii, 2, 108 &c. **-kaccha,** m. 'one who lets the hem of the upper garment hang down or loose,' a Buddhist, Sarvad.; *-mata*, n. the doctrine of Buddhists, ib. **-kañcuka,** mfn. (a snake) that has cast its skin, L. **-kaṇṭha,** mfn. (BhP.) or °**ṭham,** ind. (Kāv.; Kathās.), with √*krand*, √*rud* &c., to cry aloud, cry or weep with all one's might. **-kara,**

mfn. open-handed, liberal, Kathās. **-keśa,** mf(*ā* or *ī*)n. 'loose-haired,' having the hair dishevelled or hanging down, Mn.; MBh.; R. &c. **-cakshus,** mfn. having the eyes opened, MW.; m. 'casting glances,' a lion, L. **-cintāmaṇi,** m. N. of wk. **-cetas,** mfn. one whose soul is liberated (from existence), emancipated, AshṭāvS. **-tā,** f. or **-tva,** n. emancipation, the being liberated from existence, MBh.; AshṭāvS. **-dhvani,** mfn. giving out thunder (as a cloud), Megh. **-nidra,** mfn. set free from sleep, awakened, Kathās. **-nirmoka,** mfn. = *-kañcuka* (q.v.), L. **-pushpa,** n. pl. flowers scattered, Divyâv. **-phūt-kāra,** mfn. uttering a scream, screaming, Kathās. **-phūt-kṛiti,** f. uttering a shriek, shrieking, hissing, ib. **-bandhana,** mfn. released from bonds, AshṭāvS.; (*ā*), f. Arabian jasmine, L. **-buddhi,** mfn. one whose soul is liberated, emancipated, ib. **-maṇḍūka-kaṇṭha,** mf(*ā*)n. having loudly croaking frogs, VarBṛS. **-mūrdhaja,** mf(*ā*)n. = *-keśa* (q.v.), MBh.; R.; BhP. **-rodho-nitamba,** mfn. quitting the hip-like bank, Megh. **-rosha,** mfn. one who has laid aside or relinquished anger, MW. **-lajja,** mfn. casting away shame, R.; Kum. **-vasana,** mfn. one who has put off his clothes, going about naked; m. a Jaina ascetic, Col. **-vyāpāra,** mfn. one who has resigned an office, L. **-śikha,** mfn. = *-keśa*, Gaut. **-śaiśava,** mf(*ā*)n. adult, grown up, Daś. **-saṃśaya,** mfn. free from doubt, certain, Pat. **-saṅga,** mfn. free from worldly or selfish attachment, disinterested, BhP. **-sūryā,** f. (with *diś*) the quarter just quitted by the sun, Var. **-svāmin,** m. 'lord of emancipation,' N. of a statue erected by a king, Rājat. **-hasta,** mf(*ā*)n. open-handed, liberal, Mn.; Hit.; loosed, let go, MW. **Muktâtman,** m. the emancipated soul, MW.; mfn. one whose soul is liberated, emancipated, AshṭāvS. **Muktânanda,** m. N. of an author, Cat. 1. **Muktâbharaṇa,** mfn. (for 2. *muktā-bh°* see under *muktā* below) having no ornament, Subh. **Muktâmukta,** mfn. hurled and not hurled (applied esp. to weapons which may be wielded and hurled, as clubs and javelins &c.), L. **Muktâmbara,** mfn. or m. = *mukta-vasana*, L. **Muktâsana,** mfn. one who has risen from a seat, Kāv.; n. the mode in which the emancipated are said to sit, a partic. posture of ascetics (= *siddhâsana*, q.v.), Cat. **Muktâharaṇa-vrata,** n. a partic. religious observance, Cat. 1. **Muktâhāra,** mfn. (for 2. *muktā-h°* see under *muktā* below) taking no food, Cat. **Muktêśvara,** n. N. of a Liṅga, Cat.

Muktaka, mfn. detached, separate, independent, Pur.; n. a missile, L.; a detached śloka (the meaning of which is complete in itself), Kāvyâd.; simple prose (without compound words), Sāh.

Muktā, f. of *mukta*, in comp. **-kaṇa,** m. N. of a man, Rājat. **-kalāpa,** m. an ornament made of strings of pearls, Kum.; Caurap.; *°pī*, ind., with √*kṛi*, to make anything an ornament of p°, Kum. **-°kāra** (*°tâk°*), mfn. having the look or appearance of a pearl (*-tā*, f.), Bhartṛ. **-kāvya,** n. N. of a Kāvya. **-keśava,** m. N. of a statue of Kṛishṇa, Rājat. **-°khya** (*°tâkh°*), m. a partic. mode of beating a drum, Saṃgīt. **-°gāra** (*°tâg°* or *°tâg°*), n. 'pearl-abode,' the p°-oyster, L. **-guṇa,** m. a string of p°s, Kāv.; the excellence of a p°, lustre or water of a p°, Ragh. **-caritra,** n. N. of wk. **-jāla,** n. an ornament of p°s, MBh.; R.; Kāv.; *-maya*, mf(*ī*)n. made or consisting of p°s, MBh. **-dāman,** n. a string of p°s, BhP. **-paṭala,** n. a mass of p°s, Ragh. **-°pīḍa** (*°tâp°*), m. 'pearl-crowned,' N. of a king, Rājat.; of a poet, Kshem. **-pura,** n. N. of a mythical city in the Himâlaya mountains, Kathās. **-pushpa,** m. Jasminum Multiflorum or Pubescens, L. **-pralamba,** m. = *-prālamba* (q.v.), L. **-prasū,** f. 'p°-bearing,' the p°-oyster, L. **-prālamba,** m. a string of pearls, p° ornament, L. **-phala,** n. a p°, Kāv. &c.; a species of flower, Buddh.; the fruit of the Lavalī plant, L.; camphor, L.; N. of wk.; m. N. of a king of the Śabaras, Kathās.; *-ketu*, m. N. of a king of the Vidyā-dharas, Kathās.; *-jāla*, n. = *muktā-j°* (q.v.), Kum.; *-tā*, f. the being a pearl, state of a p°, Mālav.; *-dhvaja*, m. N. of a king, Kathās.; *-parîkshā*, f. N. of ch. of wk.; *-maya*, mfn. formed of p°s, Hcat.; *-latā*, f. a string of p°s, MārkP. **-2. °bharaṇa** (*°tâbh°*), mfn. (for 1. see under *mukta* above) having a p° ornament, Subh. **-°bhā** (*°tâbhā*), m. Jasminum Zambac, L. **-maṇi,** m. 'p°-gem,' a p°, ShaḍvBr.; Suśr. &c.; *-sara*, m. a string of p°s, Uttarar. **-maya,** mf(*ī*)n. made or consisting of p°s, MBh.; Ragh. **-mātṛi,** f. mother of pearl, a p°-oyster, L. **-mālā,** f. N. of 2 wks. **-modaka,** m. a kind of pastry, Bhpr. **-ratna,** n. 'pearl-gem,' a p°, Kāv.; *-raśmi-maya*, mfn. consisting of p°-rays, Hcat. **-latā,** f. a string of p°s, L.; N. of a woman, Kathās. **-°vali** or **°lī** (*°tâv°*), f. a p° necklace, Kāv. &c. (*°li*, L.); N. of various wks.; (*°lī*) N. of the wife of Candra-ketu, Kathās.; *-kiraṇa*, m., *-ṭīkā*, f., *-dīpikā*, f., *-paddhati*, f., *-prakāśa*, m., *-prabhā*, f. N. of wks.; (*°lī*)*-maya*, mf(*ī*)n. formed of strings of p°s, Hcat.; *-vyākhyā*, f., *-vyāpti-vāda-dīpikā*, f. N. of wks. **-śukti,** f. a p°-oyster, Pañcar. **-sena,** m. N. of a king of the Vidyā-dharas, Kathās. **-sthūla,** mfn. big as a pearl, MW. **-sphoṭa,** m. or **°ṭā,** f. a p°-oyster, L. **-sraj,** f. a chaplet of pearls, L. **-2. -hāra,** m. (for 1. see under *mukta*, col. 1) a string of pearls, MBh.; R. &c.; *-latā*, f. id., Prab.

Mukti, f. setting or becoming free, release, liberation, deliverance from (comp.), ŚBr. &c. &c.; final liberation or emancipation, final beatitude (= *moksha*, q.v.), Kāv.; Kathās.; abandonment, putting off, giving up (comp.), ib.; throwing, casting, hurling, shooting, sending, Hariv.; discharge (of a debt; cf. *ṛiṇa-m°*); N. of a divine being (the wife of Satya), Cat. **-kalaśa,** m. N. of one of the ancestors of Bilhaṇa, Vcar.; (with *bhaṭṭa*) N. of a poet, Cat. **-kānta-vilāsa,** m. N. of a poem. **-kośaka** and **-koshṭaka,** m. N. of two poets, Cat. **-kshetra,** n. a place where final emancipation is attainable (esp. a partic. place south of the Kāverī); *-māhātmya*, n. N. of ch. of BrahmavP. **-khaṇḍa,** m. or n., **-grantha,** m., **-cintāmaṇi,** m. (and *°ṇi-māhātmya*, n.), **-tattva,** n., **-traya-bheda-nirūpaṇa,** n. N. of wks. **-pati,** m. lord of bliss or beatitude, BhP. **-pariṇaya,** m. N. of a drama. **-pura,** n. N. of a Dvīpa, Cat. **-pūr-dasyu,** m. a Dasyu in the city of emancipation, Subh. **-maṇḍapa,** m. N. of a temple, Cat. **-matī,** f. N. of a river, MBh.; Pur. (v.l. *bhukti-* and *śukti-m°*). **-mārga,** m. the path to liberation or final emancipation, Śāntiś. **-mukta,** m. frankincense, L. **-vat,** mfn. having freedom, freed from (abl.), Kathās. **-vāda,** m. (also *-ṭīkā*, f., *-rahasya*, n., *-vicāra*, m.), **-sapta-śatī,** f., **-sāra,** m. N. of wks. **-sena,** m. N. of a man, Buddh. **-sopāna,** n. N. of wk. **Muktîśvara,** m. (with *dīkshita*) N. of a poet, Cat.

Muktikā, f. a pearl, L. **Muktikôpanishad,** f. and **Muktikôpâkhyāna,** n. N. of wks.

Muktvā́, ind. having loosed or freed or let go or given up or discharged or sent forth or left or abandoned, ŚBr. &c. &c.; having liberated one's self, having attained final emancipation, Vedântas.; having put aside, excepting, except, save (with acc.), Kāv.; Pañcat.

3. **Muc,** mfn. freeing or delivering from (see *aṅho-m°*); letting go or letting fall, dropping, discharging, shooting, sending (see *jala-*, *parṇa-*, *sāyaka-m°* &c.); f. deliverance (see *a-múc*).

Muca, mf(*ī*)n. id. (see *á-mucī*, *nakha-muca*, *raśmi-muca*).

Mucira, mfn. liberal, munificent, Uṇ. i, 52, Sch.; m. charity, virtue, L.; wind, L.; a deity, L.

Mumukshā, f. (fr. Desid.) desire of liberation from (abl.) or of final emancipation, MBh.; Kāv.; Pur.

Mumukshú, mfn. desirous of freeing, wishing to deliver from (abl.), MBh.; eager to be free (from mundane existence), striving after emancipation, RV.; Up. &c.; wishing to let go or give up (acc.), Kathās.; wishing to discharge or shed or emit or shoot or hurl or send forth (acc. or comp.), MBh.; Ragh.; m. a sage who strives after emancipation, W. **-jana-kalpa,** m. N. of wk. **-tā,** f. (Cat.), **-tva,** n. (Vedântas.) desire of liberation or of final emancipation. **-māhātmya,** n., **-sarvasva,** n. (and *°sva-sāra-saṃgraha*, m.), **-sāra-saṃgraha,** m., **sāra-sarvasva,** n. N. of wks.

Mumucāna, m. a cloud, L.

Mumucu, m. N. of a Ṛishi (mentioned with Unmucu and Pramucu), MBh.; Hariv.

Mumokshayishu or **mumocayishu,** mfn. desirous of setting free or liberating, MBh.; R.

Moktavya, moktṛi. See p. 834, col. 3.

मुचक *mucaka,* m. gum-lac, L.

मुचलिन्द *mucalinda,* v.l. for *mucilinda,* q.v.

मुचि *muci,* m. N. of a Cakra-vartin, L.

मुचिलिन्द *mucilinda,* m. Pterospermum Suberifolium, L.; N. of a Nāga (who sheltered the Buddha from a violent storm by coiling himself round him), Lalit.; MWB. 39 &c.; of the sacred tree protected by this Nāga (under which B° seated himself), MWB. 232; of a Cakra-vartin, L.; of a mountain, Kāraṇḍ. (also *-parvata*, L.); (*ā*), f. N. of a serpent-maid, Kāraṇḍ.

मुचुकुन्द *mucukunda,* m. Pterospermum Suberifolium, L.; N. of a Daitya, L.; of an ancient king (or Muni), MBh.; BhP.; of a son of Māndhātṛi (who assisted the gods in their wars with the demons and was rewarded by the boon of a long and unbroken sleep), MBh.; Pur.; of a son of Yadu, Hariv.; of the father of Candra-bhāga, Cat.; of a poet of Kaśmīra, ib. **-kavi,** m. the poet Mucukunda, Bhojapr. **-prasādaka,** m. N. of Kṛishṇa, Pañcar. **-moksha,** m., **-stuti,** f. N. of wks.

मुचुटी *mucuṭī,* f. a pair of forceps, Vāgbh.; (also *°ṭi*) a closed hand, fist, L.; snapping the fingers, L.

मुचुलिन्द *muculinda,* m. a kind of big orange, L. (cf. *mucalinda* and *mucilinda*).

मुछ् *much,* cl. 1. P. *mucchati*, v.l. for √*yuch*, Dhātup. vii, 35.

मुज् *muj* or *muñj,* cl. 1. P. *mojati* or *muñjati*, to give out a partic. sound, Dhātup. vii, 76, 77; (accord. to Vop. also) cl. 10. P. *mojayati* or *muñjayati*, 'to sound' or 'to cleanse.'

मुञ्च् *muñc,* cl. 1. P. *muñcati*, to go, move, Dhātup. vii, 16 (Vop.); cl. 1. Ā. *muñcate*, to cheat, be wicked, Dhātup. vi, 12 (cf. √*mac* and √1. *muc*).

Muñcaka, m. a species of tree, L.

Muñcāta, m. N. of a family, VP.

मुञ्ज् *muñj.* See √*muj* above.

Múñja, m. 'sounding, rustling (?),' a species of rush or sedge-like grass, Saccharum Sara or Munja (which grows to the height of 10 feet, and is used in basket-work), ŚBr. &c. &c.; the Brāhmanical girdle formed of M° (cf. *mauñja*; Mn. ii, 27, 42 &c.) an arrow (?), W.; N. of a king of Dhārā, Daśar.; of a prince of Campā, Piṅg., Sch.; of a man with the patr. Sāmaśravasa, ShaḍvBr.; of a Brāhman, MBh.; of various authors &c., Cat.; (*ā*), f. N. of a river, VP.; = m. (see comp. below). **-kulāyá,** m. a kind of basket-work made of rush, ŚBr. **-ketu,** m. N. of a man, MBh. **-keśa,** m. 'M°-haired,' N. of Vishṇu (also *-vat*) or Śiva, MBh.; Pañcar.; of a king, MBh.; of a teacher, VP.; of a disciple of Vijitâsu, Kathās.; *°śin*, m. 'M°-haired,' N. of Vishṇu, L.; of a man, Pravar. **-grāma,** m. N. of a village, MBh. (B. *ramya-gr°*). **-dhārin,** mfn. holding M°-grass in the hand, Hariv. **-néjana,** mfn. purified from M°-grass, RV. i, 161, 8. **-m-dhaya,** mf(*ī*)n. sucking M°-grass, Vop. **-pṛishṭha,** m. N. of a place on the Himâlaya mountains, MBh. **-bandhana,** n. investiture with the Brāhmanical girdle, W. **-maya,** mf(*ī*)n. made of Muñja-grass, Kull. on Mn. ii, 42. **-mekhalin,** m. 'Muñja-girdled,' N. of Vishṇu or Śiva, Hariv. **-vaṭa,** N. of a place of pilgrimage, MBh. (cf. *muñjā-v°*). **-1. -vat,** ind. like M°-grass or rushes, MBh. **-2. -vat,** mfn. overgrown with rushes, Nir.; m. N. of a species of Soma plant (which are 20 in number), Suśr.; of a mountain of the Himâlaya range, MBh. **-valśá,** m. a shoot or sprout of M°-grass, ŚBr. **-vāsas,** m. 'rush-clothed,' N. of Śiva, MBh. **-vivayana,** mf(*ā*)n. matted or twisted out of M°-grass, ŚBr. **-sūnu,** m. 'son of Muñja,' N. of Dāsa-śarman (q.v.), Cat. **Muñjā-jyā-balbaja-maya,** mf(*ī*)n. made of M°-grass and a bow-string and Eleusine Indica, Vishṇ. **Muñjâṭavī,** f. a forest of M°-grass or rushes, BhP. **Muñjâditya,** m. N. of a poet, Cat. **Muñjâdri,** m. N. of a mountain, VarBṛS. **Muñjā-vaṭa** = *muñja-pṛishṭha*, MBh. (cf. *muñja-vaṭa*). **Muñjêshīka-tūla,** n. a panicle of Muñja-grass, Pāṇ. vi, 3, 63, Sch.

Muñjaka, m. a species of rush (= *muñja*), VarBṛS. (v.l. for *mauñjaka*). **Muñjana,** n. a sound, L. **°jara,** n. an edible lotus-root, L. **°jāta,** m. a species of plant, Suśr. **°jātaka,** m. a species of tree, MBh.; Suśr.; a kind of vegetable, Car.; Saccharum Munja, Bhpr. **°jāla,** m. N. of an astronomer, Cat.

Muñjī-√kṛi, P. *-karoti*, to reduce to Muñja-grass, i.e. to tear to shreds, MBh.

मुट् *muṭ,* cl. 1. 6. 10. P. *moṭati*, *muṭati*, *moṭayati*, to crush, grind, break, Dhātup. ix, 38; xxviii, 81; xxxii, 72 (cf. *prati-√muṭ*).

Muṭa, m. or n. (?) a basket or bundle, Kāraṇḍ. (v. l. *mūṭa*; cf. *nir-muṭa*, *moṭa*, and *mūṭa*).

Muṭṭa, m. (?), Subh.

मुड् *muḍ*, cl. 1. P. *moḍati*, to crush, grind, Dhātup. ix, 38 (v. l. for *muṭ*).

मुण् *muṇ*, cl. 6. P. *muṇati*, to promise, Dhātup. xxviii, 44.

मुण्ट् *muṇṭ*, cl. 1. P. *muṇṭati*, to crush, grind, Dhātup. ix, 38 (v. l. for *muṭ*).

मुण्ठ् *muṇṭh*, cl. 1. Ā. *muṇṭhate*, 'to run away' or 'to protect' (*palâyane*, v. l. *pālane*), Dhātup. viii, 12.

मुण्ड् *muṇḍ* (prob. artificial, to serve as the supposed source of the words below), cl. 1. P. to cut (*khaṇḍane* = *chidi*), Dhātup. ix, 40; to crush, grind, ix, 38 (v. l. for *muṭ*); cl. 1. Ā. 'to cleanse' or 'to sink' or 'to shave' (*mārjane*, v. l. *magne* and *muṇḍane*), viii, 22: Caus. *muṇḍayati* (or *muṇḍāpayati*, Divyâv.), see *muṇḍaya* below.

Muṇḍa, mf(*ā*)n. shaved, bald, having the head shaved or the hair shorn, Mn.; MBh. &c.; having no horns, hornless (as a cow or goat), Var.; stripped of top leaves or branches, lopped (as a tree), MBh.; pointless, blunt, Kathās.; without awns or a beard (a kind of corn), L.; low, mean, W.; m. a man with a shaven head, bald-headed man, Yājñ. i, 271 (also applied to Śiva), MBh.; the trunk of a lopped tree, W.; a barber, L.; N. of Rāhu, L.; of a Daitya, Hariv.; of a king, Buddh.; pl. N. of a people, MBh.; of a dynasty, VP.; (*ā*), f. a (close-shaved) female mendicant, L.; a widow, Gal.; a species of plant, L.; Bengal madder, W.; (*ī*), f. Sphaerantus Hirtus, Bhpr.; N. of one of the Mātṛis attending on Skanda, MBh.; n. (L. also n.) a shaven head, any head, Kāv.; Rājat.; iron, L.; myrrh, L. **–khaṇḍeyôpanishad** (?), f. N. of an Upanishad. **–caṇaka**, m. a kind of pulse, L. **–ja**, n. steel, L. **–dhānya**, n. a kind of grain without awns, Suśr. (v. l. *rūḍha-dh°*). **–dhārin**, mfn. wearing (a garland of) heads or skulls. **–pṛishṭha**, m. or n. (?) N. of a place, Cat. **–phala**, m. a cocoa-nut tree (the fruit being one step towards a human head made by Viśvāmitra, when attempting a creation in opposition to that of Brahmā), L. **–maṇḍalī**, f. a number of shaven heads, MW.; a collection of inferior troops, Hit. **–mathanā**, f. N. of Durgā, MārkP. **–mālā-tantra**, n. N. of a Tantra. **–mālinī**, f. a form of Durgā, W. **–loha**, n. iron, L. (cf. *muṇḍâyasa*). **–vedâṅga**, m. N. of a serpent-demon, MBh. **–śayanâsana-vārika**, m. a partic. official in a monastery, Buddh. **–śāli**, m. a species of rice, L. **–śṛiṅkhalika**, m. N. of a subdivision of the Pāśupatas, L. **Muṇḍâkhyā**, f. a species of plant, L. **Muṇḍâyasa**, n. iron, L. (cf. *muṇḍa-loha*). **Muṇḍâsana**, n. a partic. posture in sitting, Cat. **Muṇḍêśvara-tīrtha**, n. N. of a place of pilgrimage, ib.

Muṇḍaka, mfn. shaved, shorn, Divyâv.; m. the lopped trunk or stem of a tree, pollard, L.; a shaver, barber, L.; (*ikā*), f. a species of plant, L.; n. the head, L.; N. of the chapters into which the Muṇḍakôpanishad is divided. **Muṇḍakôpanishad**, f. N. of a well-known Upanishad of the Atharva-veda (called also Ātharvaṇôpanishad and said to take its former name from the word *muṇḍa*, because every one who comprehends its sacred doctrine is 'shorn,' i. e. liberated from all error, a similar idea being probably involved in the name of the Kshurikôpanishad or 'Razor Upanishad;' cf. IW. 35, 39 &c.); *°shat-khaṇḍârtha*, m.; *°shad-āloka*, m., *°shad-dīpikā*, f., and *°shad-bhāshya*, n. N. of Comms. on the MuṇḍUp.

Muṇḍana, n. shaving the head (with or scil. *śirasaḥ*), tonsure, MBh.; Kāv. &c.; protecting, defending (cf. √*muṇṭh*), L.; m. N. of one of Śiva's attendants, Kāśikh. **Muṇḍanêśa**, m. N. of Śiva, ib.

Muṇḍanaka, m. a species of rice, L. (cf. *muṇḍa-śāli*); (*ikā*), f., see *mahā-m°*.

Muṇḍaya, Nom. P. *°yati*, to shave, shear, Hariv.; Pañcat.

Muṇḍāra, n. N. of a place at which the sun is worshipped, Cat.

Muṇḍita, mfn. shaved, bald, shorn, lopped, Kāv.; Hit.; (*ā*), f. a window, Gal.; n. iron, L. **–prahasana**, n. N. of a drama. **–muṇḍa**, **-mūrdhan**, **-śiras**, mfn. shaven-headed, bald-pated, Kāv.; Kathās.

Muṇḍitikā, f. Sphaerantus Hirtus, L.

Muṇḍin, mfn. shaven, bald (also applied to Śiva), MBh.; Hariv.; Kām.; hornless, Bhpr.; m. a barber, L. **Muṇḍibhá**, m. N. of a man (the supposed author of VS. xxv, 9), ŚBr.; TBr.

Muṇḍī-kalpa, m. N. of wk.

Muṇḍīra, m. the sun, L.

Muṇḍīrikā and *°rī*, f. a species of plant, L.

Muṇḍīśvara-tīrtha, n. (fr. *muṇḍin* + *īśv°*) N. of a Tīrtha, Cat. (cf. *muṇḍêśv°*).

मुतव *mutava*, m. or n. (?) a species of grass, Gobh.

मुत्कल *mutkala*, m. N. of a man, Rājat.

मुत्खलिन् *mutkhalin*, m. N. of a Deva-putra, Lalit.

मुत्य *mutya*, n. a pearl, L.

मुथशिल *muthaśila* = مُتَّصِل, (in astrol.) N. of the third Yoga.

Muthaśilita and *°śilin*, mfn. from the prec.

Muthahā, an astrol. term.

मुद् 1. *mud*, cl. 10. P. *modayati*, to mix, mingle, blend, unite, Dhātup. xxxiii, 66.

मुद् 2. *mud*, cl. 1. Ā. (Dhātup. ii, 15) *módate* (ep. and m. c. also P. *°ti*; pf. *mumóda*, RV.; *mumude*, MBh. &c.; aor. *amodishṭa*, Gr.; Pot. *mudīmahi*, RV.; Prec. *modishīshṭhās*, AV.; fut. *moditā*, Gr.; *modishyate*, MBh.; ind. p. *-modam*, MBh.), to be merry or glad or happy, rejoice, delight in (instr. or loc.), RV. &c. &c.: Caus. *modayati*, *°te* (aor. *amūmudat*), to gladden, give pleasure, exhilarate, MBh.; Bhaṭṭ.: Desid. of Caus. *mumodayishati*, ŚBr.: Desid. *mumodishate* or *mumudishate*, Pāṇ. i, 2, 26: Intens. *momudyate*, *momudīti*, *momotti*, Gr.

3. **Múd**, f. joy, delight, gladness, happiness (also pl.), RV. &c. &c.; Joy personified (as a daughter of Tushṭi), BhP.; intoxication, frenzy, W.; a species of drug (= *vṛiddhi*), W.; a woman (?), L.; pl. N. of a class of Apsaras, VP. **–bhāj**, mfn. feeling joy or pleasure, VarBṛS.

Muda, mfn., see *hasā-mudá*; m. N. of a teacher, L.; (*ā*), f., see below.

Muda-kara (?), m. pl. N. of a people.

Mudā, f. pleasure, joy, gladness, MBh.; Kāv. &c. **–kara**, m. (with *sūri*) N. of an author, Cat. **–°nvita** (*°dânv°*), mfn. filled with joy, pleased, delighted, R. **–yukta** and **-yuta**, mfn. id., MBh. **–vat**, mfn. rejoicing, glad, delighted (see *nâti-mudâvat*), MBh.; (*atī*), f. N. of a daughter of king Vidūratha, MārkP. **–vasu**, m. N. of a son of Prajāti, ib.

Mudita, mfn. delighted, joyful, glad, rejoicing in (instr. or comp.), MBh.; Kāv. &c.; m. a partic. sort of servant, R.; (*ā*), f. joy, gladness, complacency, Lalit.; sympathy in joy, Divyâv.; n. a kind of sexual embrace, L.; a partic. Siddhi, Sāṃkhyas., Sch.; w. r. for *nudita* and *sūdita*. **–pushpā**, f. N. of a female Gandharva, Kāraṇḍ. **–bhadra**, m. N. of a man, Buddh. **–madâlasa**, m. or n. (?) N. of a drama.

Mudira, m. a cloud, Gīt.; Bhām.; a lover, L.; a frog, L. **–phala**, m. Asteracantha Longifolia, L.

Mudī, f. moonshine, L.

Mudgá, m. (accord. to Uṇ. i, 127 fr. √*mud*) Phaseolus Mungo (both the plant and its beans), VS. &c. &c.; a cover, covering, lid, L.; a kind of sea-bird, L. (prob. w. r. for *madgu*, q. v.) **–giri**, m. N. of a city, Buddh. **–parṇī**, f. Phaseolus Trilobus, Bhpr. **–bhuj** or **-bhojin**, m. 'bean-eater,' a horse, L. **–modaka**, m. a kind of sweetmeat, Bhpr. **–yūsha**, n. bean-soup, L. **–vat**, mfn. having beans &c., Nir. **Mudgâbha**, mfn. bean-coloured, VarBṛS. **Mudgârdraka-vaṭa**, m. a kind of sweetmeat, Bhpr. **Mudgâudana**, m. a soup made of beans and rice, ŚāṅkhGṛ.

Mudgapa, m. N. of a man, Col.

Mudgara, m. (prob. fr. *mudga*) a hammer, mallet, any hammer-like weapon or implement, MBh.; Kāv. &c.; a bud, L.; a kind of jasmine (n. its blossom), L.; a species of fish, L.; N. of a Nāga, MBh.; n. a partic. posture in sitting, Cat. **–gomin**, m. N. of a man, Buddh. **–parṇaka** and **-piṇḍaka**, m. N. of two Nāgas, MBh. **–phala**, m. Averrhoa Carambola, L. **Mudgarâkāra**, mfn. shaped like a hammer, MW.

Mudgaraka, ifc. (f. *ikā*) = *mudga*, a hammer, Kathās.; m. Averrhoa Carambola, L.

Múdgala, m. (prob. fr. *mudga*) N. of a Ṛishi with the patr. Bhārmyaśva (the supposed author of RV. x, 102), AV.; Nir.; MBh. &c.; of a disciple of Śākalya, VP.; of a son of Viśvāmitra, MBh.; of various authors and other men (also with *bhaṭṭa*, *sūri* &c.), Cat.; pl. the descendants of Mudgala, TBr.; N. of a people, MBh.; n. a species of grass, L.; = *mudgalôpanishad*. **–deva**, m. N. of an author (who translated the Prākṛit passages of the Ratnâvalī), Cat. **–purāṇa**, n., **-smṛiti**, f. N. of wks. **Mudgalâryā**, f. N. of wk. **Mudgalôpanishad**, f. N. of an Upanishad.

Mudgalânī, f. the wife of Mudgala, RV. x, 102, 2 (cf. Pāṇ. iv, 1, 49, Vārtt. 5, Pat.)

Mudgashṭa and *°ṭaka*, m. a species of bean, L.

Mudgashṭha and *°ṭhaka*, m. id., ib.

Mudrá, mfn. joyous, glad, AV.; (*ā*), f., see *mudrā* below.

मुदर *mudara*, v. l. for *mṛidura*.

मुदानादत *mudānādata*, m. N. of a divine being, HPariś.

मुद्ग *mudga* &c. See col. 2.

मुद्द *mudda*, an astrological term.

मुद्रा *mudrā*, f. (fr. *mudra*, see above) a seal or any instrument used for sealing or stamping, a seal-ring, signet-ring (cf. *aṅguli-m°*), any ring, MBh.; Kāv. &c.; type for printing or instrument for lithographing, L.; the stamp or impression made by a seal &c.; any stamp or print or mark or impression, MBh.; Kāv. &c.; a stamped coin, piece of money, rupee, cash, medal, L.; an image, sign, badge, token (esp. a token or mark of divine attributes impressed upon the body), Kāv.; Pur.; Rājat.; authorization, a pass, passport (as given by a seal), Mudr.; shutting, closing (as of the eyes or lips, gen. or comp.), Kāv.; a lock, stopper, bung, Amar.; Bhpr.; a mystery, Cat.; N. of partic. positions or intertwinings of the fingers (24 in number, commonly practised in religious worship, and supposed to possess an occult meaning and magical efficacy, Daś.; Sarvad.; Kāraṇḍ.; RTL. 204; 406); a partic. branch of education ('reckoning by the fingers'), Divyâv.; parched or fried grain (as used in the Śākta or Tāntrik ceremonial), RTL. 192; (in rhet.) the natural expression of things by words, calling things by their right names, Kuval.; (in music) a dance accordant with tradition, Saṃgīt. **–kara**, m. a maker of seals, engraver, coiner, MW. **–°kshara** (*°drâksh°*), n. type, print (often used in the title-pages of books). **–°kshepa** (*°drâksh°*), m. taking away or removing a seal, MW. **–°ṅka** (*°drâṅka*), mfn. stamped, sealed, marked, Rājat.; m. N. of a poet, Cat. **–°ṅkita** (*°drâṅk°*), mfn. = prec. mfn., Kāv.; Kathās. **–dhāraṇa**, n. 'wearing a seal-ring;' *-māhâtmya*, n., *-stotra*, n. N. of wks. **–prakāśa**, m. N. of two wks. **–bala**, n. a partic. high number, Buddh. **–mārga**, m. = *brahma-randhra*, Cat. **–yantra**, n. a printing-press; *°trâlaya*, m. n. a printing office (often in the title-pages of books). **–rakshaka**, m. a keeper of seals, MW. **–rākshasa**, n. 'Rākshasa (N. of a minister) and the seal-ring,' N. of a celebrated drama by Viśākha-datta; *-kathā-saṃgraha*, m.; *-kathā-sāra*, m., *-pūrva-pīṭhikā*, f., *-prakāśa*, m. N. of wks. **–°rṇava** (*°drârṇ°*), m. (and *°va-lakshana-ṭīkā*, f.), **-lakshaṇa**, n. N. of wks. **–lipi**, f. 'printed writing,' print, lithograph, L. **–vidhi**, m., **-vivaraṇa**, n. N. of wks. **–sthāna**, n. the place (on the finger) for a seal-ring, Śak.

Mudraṇa, n. the act of sealing up or closing or printing, Vcar.; Sāh.

Mudraṇī-pattra, n. a proof-sheet, Āryav., Introd.

Mudraya, Nom. P. *°yati*, to seal, stamp, print, mark, Hariv.; Kāv.

Mudrikā, f. a little seal, seal, seal-ring, MBh.; stamp, impression, stamped coin, L.; a sealed or signed paper, W.; a partic. surgical instrument, Suśr.; N. of partic. positions or intertwinings of the fingers (= *mudrā*, q. v.), Pañcar.

Mudrita, mfn. sealed, stamped, impressed, printed, marked, Kāv.; Kām.; contracted, closed, sealed up, Kāv.; Kathās. (*nidrā-m°*, sunk in sleep, Daś.); strung, bound, L.; unblown (as a flower), L.; intertwined in partic. forms (as the fingers; cf. *mudrā*), Pañcar.; n. impressing a seal on (loc.), Hit. **–pāṃsu**, mfn. making impressions on dust or sand (said of drops of water), Amar. **–mukha**, mfn. having the mouth closed or the lips sealed, Vikr. **Mudritâksha**, mf(*ī*)n. having the eyes closed, Subh.

मुधा *mudhā*, ind. (√*muh*) in vain, uselessly, to no purpose, MBh.; Kāv. &c.; falsely, wrongly, Bhartṛ. (v.l.)

मुनि *múni*, m. (accord. to Uṇ. iv, 122 fr. √*man*) impulse, eagerness (?), RV. vii, 56, 8; (prob.) any one who is moved by inward impulse, an inspired or ecstatic person, enthusiast, RV.; AV.; Br.; a saint, sage, seer, ascetic, monk, devotee, hermit (esp. one who has taken the vow of silence), ŚBr. &c. &c. (with *hṛidayeshu sthitaḥ*, the internal monitor or conscience, Mn. viii, 91); a Brāhman of the highest (eighth) order, Hcat.; N. of a son of Kuru, MBh.; of a son of Dyuti-mat, MārkP.; of Vyāsa, Kir.; of Bharata, Sāh.; of Agastya, L.; of a Buddha or Arhat, Lalit.; of Pāṇini &c. (cf. *-traya*); of other men, VP.; of various authors, Cat.; of various plants (Agati Grandiflora, Buchanania Latifolia, Butea Frondosa, Terminalia Catappa, the mango-tree and Artemisia Indica), L.; pl. 'the celestial Munis,' N. of the seven stars of Ursa Major (and therefore a symbolical N. for the number 'seven'), Var.; Sūryas.; Śrutab.; (*i*), f. a female Muni (also *ī*), Uṇ. iv, 122, Sch.; N. of a daughter of Daksha (and wife of Kaśyapa), mother of a class of Gandharvas and Apsaras (cf. *mauneya*), MBh.; Hariv.; Pur.; n. N. of a Varsha (called after a royal Muni), VP. **–kumāra**, m. a young sage, A. **–keśa** (*múni-*), mfn. wearing long hair like a Muni, AV. **–kharjūrikā**, f. a species of date, L. **–gāthā**, f. N. of a partic. sacred text, Divyâv. **–candra**, m. N. of a pupil of Vardhamāna, Gaṇar. **–cita**, g. *sutaṃgamâdi*. **–cchada**, m. 'seven-leaved,' Alstonia Scholaris, L. **–jñāna-jyanta**, m. N. of a scribe, MW. **–tanayā**, f. a Muni's daughter, Śak. **–taru**, m. Agati Grandiflora, L. **–tā**, f., **-tva**, n. the state or character of a Muni, Kāv. **–traya**, n. 'triad of Munis,' Pāṇini and Kātyāyana and Patañjali, Cat. **–dāraka**, m. = *-kumāra*, A. **–deva**, m. (also with *ācārya*) N. of an author. **–deśa**, m. N. of a place, MBh. **–druma**, m. Agati Grandiflora, L.; Calosanthes Indica, L. **–nirmita**, m. a species of plant (= *ḍiṇḍiśa*), Bhpr. **–pati-caritra**, n. N. of wk. **–patnī**, f. a Muni's wife, R. **–padī**, f., g. *kumbhapady-ādi*. **–paramparā**, f. a tradition handed down from Muni to Muni, uninterrupted tradition, VarBṛS. **–pittala**, n. copper, L. **–pishṭakin**, mf(*ī*)n. one who lives every day on 8 wild-rice cakes, L. **–puṃgava**, m. an eminent sage, VP. **–putra**, m. a Muni's son, VP.; Artemisia Indica, L. **–putraka**, m. a wagtail, L. **–pushpaka**, n. the blossom of Agati Grandiflora, L. **–pūga**, m. Areca Triandra, L. **–priya**, m. Panicum Miliaceum, L. **–bhāva-prakāśikā**, f. N. of wk. **–bheshaja**, n. 'sage's medicine,' fasting, L.; Agati Grandiflora, L.; Terminalia Chebula or Citrina, L. **–mata** (ibc.), the opinion or doctrine of sages; *-maṇi-mālā*, f., *-mīmāṅsā*, f. N. of wks. **–maraṇa**, n. N. of a district, PañcavBr. **–vana**, n. a forest inhabited by Munis, Ragh. **–vara**, m. the best of M°s or sages, MBh.; N. of Vasishṭha (as one of the stars of the Great Bear), VarBṛS. **–vākya**, n. a M°'s saying or doctrine, MW. **–vishṭara**, m. a species of plant, L. **–vīrya**, m. N. of one of the Viśve Devāḥ, MBh. **–vṛiksha**, m. N. of various kinds of trees (the Palāśa, Sarala, Śyonāka &c.), L. **–vesha**, m. a Muni's garment, R.; also = *-dhara*, mfn. wearing a Muni's garment, ib. **–vrata**, mfn. observing a M°'s vow, keeping perpetual silence, Śiś.; °*tin*, mfn. one who eats eight mouthfuls, L. **–sattra**, n. N. of a partic. Ishṭi, ŚāṅkhŚr. **–suta**, m. = *-putra*, R. **–suvrata**, m. (with Jainas) N. of the 12th Arhat of the past and the 20th of the present Avasarpiṇī, L. **–sevita**, m. a kind of wild grain or rice, L. **–sthala**, g. *kumudâdi*. **–sthāna**, n. an abode of Munis or ascetics, L. **–hata**, m. N. of king Pushya-mitra, Buddh. **Munîndra**, m. 'chief of Munis,' a great sage or ascetic (*-tā*, f.), Kathās.; N. of a Buddha or Jina, (esp.) of Gautama B°, L.; of Śiva, Vet.; of Bharata, Sāh.; of a Dānava, Hariv.; of an author, Cat.; (*ā*), f. N. of a Kim-narī, Kāraṇḍ. **Munī-vatī**, f., g. *śarâdi*. **Munī-vaha**, Pāṇ. vi, 3, 121, Sch. **Munîśa**, m. 'chief of Munis,' N. of Gautama Buddha or of a Jina, L.; of Vālmiki, R., Introd. **Munîśvara**, m. 'id.,' N. of Vishṇu or Buddha, Prasaṅg.; of a Sch. on the Siddhânta-śiromaṇi, Col.; of Viśva-rūpa (son of Raṅga-nātha), Cat.; °*rīya-pāṭī-sāra*, m. N. of wk.

Munika, m. N. of a man, VP.

Muniśa, mfn. full of ascetics, g. *lomâdi*.

Muny, in comp. for *muni*. **–anna**, n. the food of ascetics (consisting mostly of roots and fruits), Mn.; BhP. **–ayana**, n. N. of a partic. Ishṭi, ŚāṅkhŚr. **–ālaya-tīrtha**, n. N. of a Tīrtha, Cat.

मुन्थहा *munthahā* = منتهى, an astrol. term.

Munthā = prec. **–phala-vicāra**, m. N. of wk.

मुन्नभट्ट *munna-bhaṭṭa*, m. N. of a man, Cat.

मुमुक्षा *mumukshā*, °*kshu*, *mumucāna*, °*cu*. See p. 821, col. 2.

मुमुषिषु *mumushishu*. See p. 824, col. 2.

मुमूर्षा *mumūrshā*, °*shu*. See p. 827, col. 2.

मुमोक्षयिषु *mumokshayishu*, *mumocayishu*. See p. 821, col. 2.

मुम्मडिदेव *mummaḍi-deva*, m. N. of an author, Cat.

मुम्मुनि *mummuni*, m. N. of a man, Rājat.

मुर् 1. *mur* (fr. √*murch*), Pāṇ. vi, 4, 21, Sch.

मुर् 2. *mur* (fr. √*murv*), L.

मुर् 3. *mur*, cl. 6. P. *murati*, to encompass, entwine, bind together, Dhātup. xxviii, 53.

1. **Mura**, n. encompassing, surrounding, L.; (*ā*), f., see 2. *mura*.

मुर् 4. *múr*, m. (prob. fr. √*mṛī*; cf. *ā-mur*, *abhi-pra-mur*) a destroyer, slayer, enemy, RV. viii, 55, 2 (Sāy. 'a mortal,' others 'a wall').

2. **Mura**, m. N. of a Daitya slain by Kṛishṇa, MBh.; Hariv.; BhP. (cf. *muru*); (*ā*), f. a species of fragrant plant (named after the Daitya), Bhpr.; said to be the N. of the wife of Nanda and mother of Candra-gupta, VP.; n., see under 1. *mura*. **–gaṇḍa**, m. an eruption on the face, L. (v.l. *-maṇḍa*). **–jit**, m. 'conqueror of Mura,' N. of Kṛishṇa or Vishṇu, Kāv. **–da**, m. 'Mura-slaying,' the discus of Vishṇu, W. **–dvish**, m. 'foe of Mura,' N. of Kṛishṇa, Inscr. **–bhid**, **-mardana**, **-ripu**, **-vairin**, **-han**, m. 'slayer or foe of M°,' N. of Kṛishṇa or Vishṇu, Kāv. **Murâri**, m. 'enemy of Mura,' N. of Kṛishṇa or Vishṇu, Kāv.; Pur.; Kathās.; N. of the author of the Murâri-nāṭaka or Anargha-rāghava; of a Sch. on the Kātantra grammar and other authors &c. (also with *pāṭhaka*, *bhaṭṭa*, *miśra* &c.), Cat.; *-gupta*, m. N. of a disciple of Caitanya, Cat.; *-nāṭaka*, n. Murâri's drama i.e. Anargha-rāghava (*-vyākhyā*, f. and *-vyākhyā-pūrṇa-sarasvatī*, f. N. of Comms. on it); *-miśrīya*, n. N. of wk.; *-vijaya*, n. N. of a drama by Kṛishṇa-kavi (son of Nṛi-siṇha); *-śrī-pati*, m. (with *sārvabhauma*) N. of an author, Cat.

मुरङ्गी *muraṅgī*, f. Moringa Pterygosperma, Suśr. (cf. *muruṅgī*).

मुरची *muracī*, f. N. of a river, Ragh. (v.l.) **–pattana**, n. N. of a town in the Dekhan (also called *marīci-pattana*).

मुरज *muraja*, m. (fr. *mura* + *ja* ?) a kind of drum, tambourine (ifc. f. *ā*), MBh.; Kāv. &c.; a Śloka artificially arranged in the form of a drum, Sāh. (also *-bandha*, Kpr.); (*ā*), f. a great drum, L.; N. of Kubera's wife, L. **–dhvani**, m. the sound of a drum, L. **–phala**, m. Artocarpus Integrifolia, L. **–bandha**, see above.

Murajaka, m. N. of one of Śiva's attendants, Kathās.

मुरण्ड *muraṇḍa*, m. a country to the north-west of Hindūstān (also called Lampāka, and now Laghman in Cabul), L.; pl. N. of a people (cf. *muruṇḍa*).

मुरन्दला *murandalā*, f. N. of a river, L. (= *muralā*; thought by some to be Narma-dā).

मुरमण्ड *muramaṇḍa*. See *mura-gaṇḍa*.

मुरल *murala*, m. (prob. fr. √3. *mur*) a species of fresh-water fish, Suśr.; a king of the Muralas, Inscr.; pl. N. of a people, Kathās.; (*ā*), f. N. of a river in the country of the Keralas (= *murandalā*, L.), Ragh. (v.l. *muracī*); Uttarar.; (*ī*), f., see below.

Muralikā, f. N. of a woman, Vās., Introd.

Muralī, f. a flute, pipe, L. **–dhara**, m. 'flute-bearer,' N. of Kṛishṇa, L.; of a grandson of Kālidāsa Miśra, Cat. **–prakāśa**, m. 'instruction in flute-playing,' N. of wk.

मुरवार *muravāra*, m. N. of a king of the Turushkas, Kathās.

मुरसिदाबाद *murasidābāda* = مرشد آباد, Murshidabad, N. of a city, Kshitīś.

मुराद *murāda*, m. = مراد, N. of a man, ib.

मुरु *muru*, m. N. of a country, MBh.; of a Daitya (= *mura*), MBh. (C. *maru*); Hariv.; VP.; a species of plant (in explanation of *maurvī*), PārGṛ., Sch.; a kind of iron, L.; (*ū*), f. (in music) a kind of dance, Saṃgīt. **–deśa**, m. N. of a country, Cat. (cf. *maru-d°*).

मुरुङ्गी *muruṅgī*, f. Moringa Pterygosperma, Suśr. (cf. *muraṅgī*).

मुरुण्टक *muruṇṭaka*, m. pl. N. of a school, Buddh.

मुरुण्ड *muruṇḍa*, m. N. of a king, Vās., Introd.; pl. N. of a dynasty and a people (cf. Μαροῦνδαι in Ptolemy), VP. (v.l. *murūṇḍa*).

Muruṇḍaka, m. N. of a mountain in Udyāna, Buddh.

मुरुतानदेश *murutāna-deśa*, m. N. of a country, Cat.

मुरूण्ड *murūṇḍa*, v.l. for *muruṇḍa*.

मुर्छ् *murch* or *mūrch*, cl. 1. P. (Dhātup. vii, 32) *mūrchati* (pf. *mumūrcha*, MBh.; Kāv. &c.; aor. *amūrchīt*, Gr.; fut. *mūrchitā*, *mūrchishyati*, ib.; ind.p. *mūrtvā*, ib.), to become solid, thicken, congeal, assume shape or substance or consistency, expand, increase, grow, become or be vehement or intense or strong, AV. &c. &c.; to fill, pervade, penetrate, spread over, Kālid.; to have power or take effect upon (loc.), ib.; to grow stiff or rigid, faint, swoon, become senseless or stupid or unconscious, MBh.; Kāv. &c.; to deafen, Caurap.; to cause to sound aloud, MBh.: Caus. *mūrchayati* (m. c. also °*te*), to cause to thicken or coagulate (milk), Kauś.; to cause to settle into a fixed or solid form, shape, AitUp.; to strengthen, rouse, excite, MBh.; R.; to cause to sound loudly, play (a musical instrument), BhP.

Mūrkhá, mf(*ā́*)n. stupid, foolish, silly, dull, TS.; Mn. &c.; inexperienced in (loc.), Kathās.; = *gāyatrī-rahita* or *sârtha-gāyatrī-rahita*, L.; m. a fool, blockhead, Bhartṛ.; Phaseolus Radiatus, L.; N. of a poet, Cat. **–tā**, f., **-tva**, n. stupidity, foolishness, dulness, Kāv.; Pañcat. **–paṇḍita**, m. a learned fool, Pañcat. **–bhūya**, n. stupidity, L. **–bhrātṛika**, mfn. one who has a foolish brother, Pāṇ. v, 4, 157, Sch. **–maṇḍala**, n. a collection or assemblage of fools, Pañcat. **–vyasani-nāyaka**, mfn. having a foolish and vicious commander, MW. **–śata**, n. a hundred fools, Hit. **–śataka**, n. N. of a Kāvya. **–hā** (?), f. N. of a treatise on Prâyaścitta.

Mūrkhiman, m. dulness, stupidity, folly, g. *dṛiḍhâdi*.

Mūrkhī-√bhū, P. *-bhavati*, to become stupid or foolish, Kathās.

Mūrchana, mfn. stupefying, causing insensibility (applied to one of the 5 arrows of Kāma-deva), R.; (ifc.) strengthening, augmenting, confirming, Pañcar.; n. (m. c.) and (*ā*), f. fainting, swooning, syncope, Suśr.; Kir., Sch.; (in music) modulation, melody, a regulated rise or fall of sounds through the Grāma or musical scale (ifc. f. *ā*), Kāv.; Pur.; Saṃgīt.; n. vehemence, violence, prevalence, growth, increase (of diseases, fire &c.), MBh.; (also *ā*, f.) a partic. process in metallic preparations, calcining quicksilver with sulphur, Bhpr.; Rasar.

Mūrchā, f. fainting, a swoon, stupor, MBh.; Kāv. &c.; mental stupefaction, infatuation, delusion, hallucination, Kāv.; Sarvad.; congealment, solidification (of quicksilver), Kāv.; modulation, melody (= *mūrchanā*), Śiś., Sch. **–°kshepa** (°*châksh°*), m. (in rhet.) expression of vehement dissent or disapprobation by swooning, Kāvyâd. ii, 155. **–°pagama** (°*châp°*), m. the passing off of faintness, Ragh. **–paripluta**, mfn. overcome with faintness, insensible, MārkP. **–parita**, mfn. id., MBh. **–prada**, mfn. causing faintness, MārkP. **–maya**, mf(ī)n. swoon-like, Naish. **-vat**, mfn. suffering from faintness, swooning away, W.

Mūrchāya, m. faintness, a swoon, Car.

Mūrchāla, m. fainted, insensible, L.; liable to faint or swoon away, Bhpr.

Mūrchita, mfn. fainted, stupefied, insensible (n. impers.), MBh.; Kāv. &c.; calcined, solidified (said of quicksilver), Sarvad.; intensified, augmented, increased, grown, swollen (ifc. = filled or pervaded or mixed with), MBh.; Kāv.; Suśr.; tall, lofty, W.; reflected (as rays), Var.; agitated, excited, MBh.; n. a kind of song or air, BhP.

Mūrtá, mfn. coagulated, TS.; settled into any fixed shape, formed, substantial, material, embodied, incarnate, ŚBr. &c. &c.; real (said of the division of time in practical use, as opp. to *a-mūrta*), Sūryas. (IW. 177); stupefied, unconscious, insensible, Ragh. **-tva**, n. material form, incarnate existence, Bhāshāp.; MārkP.; *-jāti-nirākaraṇa*, n. N. of wk. **-mātra**, n. that which is merely material, MW.

Mūrtaya, m. N. of a son of Kuśa, BhP.

Mūrti, f. any solid body or material form (pl. material elements, solid particles; ifc. = consisting or formed of), Up.; Mn.; MBh. &c.; embodiment, manifestation, incarnation, personification, TBr.; Mn.; MBh. &c. (esp. of Śiva, Hcat.); anything which has definite shape or limits (in phil. as mind and the 4 elements earth, air, fire, water, but not *ākāśa*, ether, IW. 52, n. 1), a person, form, figure, appearance, MBh.; Kāv. &c.; an image, idol, statue, Kāv.; beauty, Pañcat.; N. of the first astrological house, VarBṛS.; of a daughter of Daksha and wife of Dharma, BhP.; m. N. of a Ṛishi under the 10th Manu, ib.; of a son of Vasishṭha, VP. **-tas**, ind. from the form, in bodily shape. **-tva**, n. the having a body, corporeal nature, materiality, Sūryas.; VarBṛS.; (in phil.) the having a finite or fixed measure or motion. **-dhara**, mfn. having a body, corporeal, incarnate, Kathās.; BhP. **-dhyāna**, n. N. of two wks. **-pa**, m. 'image-keeper,' a priest who guards an idol, Cat. **-pūjā**, f. adoration of images, RTL. 524. **-pratishṭhā**, f., **-pratishṭhāpana**, n. 'setting up of idols,' N. of wks. **-bhāva**, m. the state of assuming form, materiality, Dhātup. **-mat**, mfn. having a material form (ifc. = formed of), corporeal, incarnate, personified, Mn.; MBh. &c. **-maya**, mf(ī)n. possessing a partic. form (with gen. = poss° the form of), Hariv. **-mātrā**, f. a particle of matter, MW. **-lakshaṇa**, n. N. of wk. **-liṅga**, n. (prob.) = *prāg-jyotisha*, N. of the city of Naraka, Hariv. **-vighnêśa**, m. pl. the eight manifestations of Śiva and the various Gaṇeśas (with *mantrāḥ*, the verses or formulas addressed to them). Hcat. **-saṃcāra**, mfn. = *-dhara*, Mcar. **-sanātha**, mfn. (ifc.) possessing an idol of, Kathās. **-sevana**, n. (ifc.) worship of the idol of, Dhūrtas.

मुर्भिणी *murbhiṇī*, f. a chafing-dish, fire-pan, L.

मुर्मुर *múrmura*, m. (onomat.) an expiring ember, MaitrS.; burning chaff, Kāv. (v. l. *murmara*); the smell of the urine of a cow (mfn. smelling like the urine of a cow), L.; the god of love, L.; N. of one of the horses of the Sun, L.; (*ā*), f. N. of a river, MBh.

Murmurīya, Nom. P. °*yati* (fr. prec.), Pat.

मुर्व् *murv*, cl. 1. P. *mūrvati*, to bind, tie, Dhātup. xv, 66 (cf. *mūrvā*).

मुल् *mul*, v. l. for √*mūl* (q. v.), Dhātup. xxxii, 63.

मुलालिन् *mulālín*, m. or *mulālī́*, f. (prob.) a species of edible lotus, AV.

मुशटी *muśaṭī*, v. l. for *musaṭī*.

मुशल *muśala*, °*likā*, °*lin*. See *musala* &c.

मुशल्लह *muśallaha* = مصالحة 'reconciliation,' an astrol. term.

मुष् 1. *mush*, cl. 1. P. *moshati*, v. l. for √*mash*, q. v.

मुष् 2. *mush*, cl. 9. 1. P. (Dhātup. xxxi, 58 and xvii, 25 v. l.; cf. √1. *mūsh*) *mushṇā́ti*, *móshati* (ep. also cl. 6. P. *mushati*; 2. sg. Imp. *mushāṇa*, Śiś.; pf. *mumosha*; aor. *amoshīt*, 2. sg. *moshīs*, RV.; fut. *moshitā*, *moshishyati*, Gr.; ind. p. *mushitvā*, Daś.; Kathās.; *-mūshya*, RV.; inf. *mushé*, ib.; *moshitum*, Gr.), to steal, rob, plunder, carry off (also with two acc. = take away from, deprive of), RV. &c. &c.; to ravish, captivate, enrapture (the eyes or the heart), MBh.; Kāv. &c.; to blind, dazzle (the eyes), ib.; to cloud, obscure (light or the intellect), ib.; to break, destroy, Kāvyād. (cf. √*mus*): Pass. *mushyate* (ep. also °*ti*; aor. *amoshi*), to be stolen or robbed, MBh.; Kāv. &c.: Caus. *moshayati* (aor. *amūmushat*), Gr.: Desid. *mumushishati*, ib. (cf. *mumushishu*): Intens. *momushyate*, *momoshṭi*, ib. [For kindred words see under 2. *mūsh*, p. 827.]

Mumushishu, mfn. (fr. Desid.) wishing to steal, a thief (*-vat*, ind. like a thief), Bhaṭṭ.

3. **Mush** (ifc.; nom. *muṭ*), stealing, robbing, removing, destroying, MBh.; Kāv. &c.; surpassing, excelling, Megh.; Kād.; Bālar.; f. stealing, theft, MW.

Mushaka, m. = *mūshaka*, a mouse, L.

Mushā, f. = *mūshā*, a crucible, L.

Mushāya, Nom. P. °*yáti*, to steal, rob, carry off, RV.

Mushi, (ifc.) stealing, a stealer (see *mano-mushi-gṛihīta*).

Mushitá, mfn. stolen, robbed, carried off, RV. &c. &c.; plundered, stripped, naked, ŚBr.; GṛS.; bereft or deprived of, free from (acc.), RV.; removed, destroyed, annihilated, Ratnāv.; Kathās.; blinded, obscured, MBh.; seized, ravished, captivated, enraptured, MBh.; Kāv. &c.; surpassed, excelled, Kāvyād.; deceived, cheated, Ratnāv.; BhP.; made fun of, Rājat. **-cetas**, mfn. bereft of sense, deprived of consciousness, BhP. **-trapa**, mfn. one in whom the sense of shame has been destroyed (by love), Kathās. **-smṛiti**, mfn. bereft of memory, ib.; *-tā*, f. forgetfulness, L.

Mushitaka, mfn. stolen in a low or vile manner, MW.; n. stolen property, Daś.

Mushīván, m. a robber, thief, RV.

Mushká, m. (fr. *mush* = *mūsh* + *ka*?) 'little mouse,' a testicle, the scrotum, RV. &c. &c.; (du.) pudenda muliebria, AV.; VS.; TS.; an arm (?), L.; Schrebera Swietenioides, L.; a muscular or stout person, L.; a thief, L.; a crowd, heap, multitude, L. [Cf. Gk. μύσχον; Lat. *musculus*.] **-kacchū**, f. an eruption on the scrotum, Suśr. **-deśa**, m. the region of the scrotum, Hit. **-dvaya**, n. the two testicles, ib. **-bhāra** (*mushká-*), mfn. having large t°, RV. **-vat**, m. 'having t°,' N. of Indra (as author of RV. x, 38), RAnukr. **-śūnya**, m. 'destitute of t°,' a eunuch, L. **-śopha**, m. swelling of the t°, Suśr. **-srotas**, n. (in anat.) vas deferens or funiculus, ib. **Mushkâbarhá**, m. one who removes the testicles or gelds or castrates, AV.

Mushkaka, m. a species of tree (the ashes of which are used as a cautery), Suśr.

Mushkará, mfn. having testicles, TS.; Br.; m. (prob.) a species of small animal, AV.

Mushṭa, mfn. stolen, robbed &c. (a rarer form for *mushita*), Kāv.; Pañcat.; n. theft, robbery, W. **-dṛishṭi**, mfn. one whose eyes are caught by (instr.), BhP.

Mushṭā-mushṭi, ind. (see next) fist to fist, fighting hand to hand, Mcar. (cf. *kacā-kaci*, *keśā-keśi* &c.)

Mushṭi, m. f. stealing, filching, W.; the clenched hand, fist (perhaps orig. 'the hand closed to grasp anything stolen'), RV. &c. &c.; a handful, ŚBr. &c. &c.; a partic. measure (= 1 Pala), ŚārṅgS.; a hilt or handle (of a sword &c.), Kāv.; Kathās.; a compendium, abridgment, Sarvad.; the penis (?), Mahīdh. on VS. xxiii, 24. **-karaṇa** and **-karman**, n. clenching the fist, ŚrS. **-graha**, m. clasping with one hand, Harav. **-grāhya**, mfn. to be clasped with one hand (as a waist), Kathās. **-ghāta**, m. a blow with the fist, VP., Sch. (°*taṃ* √*han*, to strike with the fist), Śiś. **-tā**, f. firmness of grasp, MW. **-deśa**, m. the part of a bow which is grasped in the hand, the middle of a bow, Hariv. **-dyūta**, n. a kind of game, odd or even, L. **-ṃ-dhama**, mf(ī)n. blowing into the fist, Pāṇ. iii, 2, 30. **-dhaya**, mfn. sucking the fist, ib.; m. a boy, L. **-nyāsa**, m. N. of wk. **-pāta**, m. pummelling, boxing, W. **-praśna-cintana**, n. N. of wk. **-prahāra**, m. = *-ghāta*, Suśr. **-bandha**, m. = *-karaṇa*, L.; closing the hand (in taking hold of anything), L.; a handful, Pāṇ. iii, 3, 36, Sch. (°*dham*, ind., Kāś. on Pāṇ. iii, 4, 41). **-māndya**, n. slight loosening of the bow-string, L. (cf. *-deśa*). **-mukha**, mfn. having a fist-like face, Pāṇ. vi, 2, 168. **-meya**, mfn. to be measured or spanned with one hand (as a waist), Kathās. **-ṃ-paca**, see *nīvāra-* and *śyāmāka-m°*. **-yuddha**, n. a pugilistic encounter, MBh. **-yoga**, m. the offering of handfuls i. e. small quantities, Pracaṇḍ. **-vadha**, m. devastation of the crops, Daś. **-varcas**, n. the feces compacted into a ball, Suśr. **-visarga**, m. the opening of the fist or closed hand, KātyŚr. **-stha**, m. or n. (?) a kind of game, Siṃhās. **-hatyā́**, f. = *-yuddha*, RV. **-hán**, mfn. striking with the fist, fighting hand to hand, RV.; AV.

Mushṭika, m. a handful (see *catur-m°*); a partic. position of the hands, Cat.; a goldsmith, L.; N. of an Asura, Hariv.; (pl.) of a despised race (= *ḍombās*), R.; (*ā*), f., see *akshara-mushṭikā*; (prob.) n. a pugilistic encounter, MBh.; a partic. game, Siṃhās. **-ghna**, m. 'slayer of Mushṭika,' N. of Vishṇu, Pañcar. **-svastika**, m. a partic. position of the hands in dancing, Cat. **Mushṭikântaka**, m. 'annihilator of M°,' N. of Bala-deva (the brother of Kṛishṇa), L.

Mushṭikā, f. in comp. **-kathana**, n. talking with the fingers, Cat. **-cintāmaṇi**, m. N. of wk.

Mushṭī, in comp. for *mushṭi*. **-√1. kṛi**, P. *-karoti*, to close the hand, clench the fist, TS.; ŚBr. **-mushṭi**, ind. = *mushṭā-mushṭi*, Vop.

Mushṭy, in comp. for *mushṭi*. **-aṅgula**, m. n. a partic. measure of length, AmṛitUp. **-ashṭaka**, n. eight handfuls, L. **-āyojana**, n. seizing a bow with the hand, L.

Mustu, mfn. = *mushṭi*, the closed hand, fist, L.

मुषल *mushala*, °*lya*. See *musala* &c.

मुष्ठक *mushṭhaka*, m. black mustard, L.

मुस् *mus* (cf. √2. *mush*), cl. 4. P. *musyati*, to break or cut in pieces, destroy, Dhātup. xxvi, 111.

Músala, m. n. (often spelt *muśala* or *mushala*; cf. Uṇ. i, 108, Sch.) a pestle, (esp.) a wooden pestle used for cleaning rice, AV. &c. &c.; a mace, club, Mn.; MBh. &c. (cf. *cakra-m°*); the clapper of a bell, Kathās.; a partic. surgical instrument, Suśr.; a partic. constellation, VarBṛS.; the 22nd astron. Yoga or division of the moon's path, MW.; m. N. of a son of Viśvāmitra, MBh.; (*ī*), f. Curculigo Orchioides, L.; Salvinia Cucullata, L.; a house-lizard, L.; an alligator, L. **-pāṇi**, m. 'club-handed,' N. of Bala-deva, MW. **-yashṭika**, m. a long staff, L. **Musalâyudha**, m. 'club-armed,' N. of Bala-deva, MBh. **Musalôlūkhala**, n. sg. a pestle and mortar, Mn. iii, 88.

Musalaka, m. N. of a mountain, Buddh.; (*ikā*), f. a house-lizard, L.

Musalā-musali, ind. club against club, fighting hand to hand, Pāṇ. v, 4, 127, Sch. (cf. *mushṭā-mushṭi*).

Musalita, mfn. (fr. *musala*), g. *tārakâdi*.

Musalin, mfn. armed with a club, Gaut.; MBh.; m. N. of Bala-deva, Pañcar. (cf. IW. 332, n. 2).

Musalī-√bhū, P. *-bhavati*, to become a club, MBh.

Musalīya, mfn. deserving to be clubbed or pounded to death with a club, g. *apūpâdi*.

Musalya, mfn. id., Hcar. (g. *daṇḍâdi*).

Musra, n. = *musala*, a pestle, L.; (for *masru* = *aśru*?) a tear, Uṇ. ii, 13, Sch.

मुसटी *musaṭī*, f. a white variety of Panicum Italicum, L. (v. l. *muśaṭī* and *musuṭī*).

मुसल्लह *musallaha* = *muśallaha*, q. v.

मुसारगल्व *musāragalva*, m. or n. a kind of coral, Car.; Buddh.

मुसुण्ठी *musuṇṭhī*, f. = (or v. l. for) *bhuśuṇḍi*, L.

मुस्त् *must* (prob. artificial), cl. 10. P. *mustayati*, to gather, collect, Dhātup. xxxii, 87.

Musta, m. n. and (*ā*), f. a species of grass, Cyperus Rotundus, Kāv.; Var.; Suśr. (n. prob. the root of C° R°). **-giri**, m. N. of a mountain, Cat. **Mustâda**, m. 'grass-eater,' a hog, wild boar, L. **Mustâbha**, m. a species of Cyperus, L.

Mustaka, m. n. and (*ā*), f. = *musta*, Cyperus Rotundus, Var.; Suśr.; Bhpr.; m. a partic. vegetable poison, L.

मुस्तु *mustu*. See above.

मुस्र *musra*. See above.

मुह् 1. *muh*, cl. 4. P. (Dhātup. xxvi, 89) *múhyati* (rarely Ā. °*te*; pf. *mumoha*, Br.

&c.; *mumuhe*, MBh.; aor. *amuhat*, Br.; fut. *mohitā, mogdhā, moḍhā*, Gr.; *mohishyáti*, Br.; *mokshyati*, Gr.; inf. *muhé*, RV.; ind. p. *mohitvā, muhitvā; mugdhvā, mūḍhvā*, Gr.; *-móham*, Gr.), to become stupefied or unconscious, be bewildered or perplexed, err, be mistaken, go astray, RV. &c. &c.; to become confused, fail, miscarry (opp. to √*kḷip*), ŚBr. &c. &c.: Caus. *mohayati* (m. c. also °*te*; aor. *amūmuhat*; Pass. *mohyate*), to stupefy, bewilder, confound, perplex, cause to err or fail, RV. &c. &c.; (Ā., with *adhvānam*) to cause to go the wrong way, MBh.: Desid. *mumohishati, mumuhishati, mumukshati*, Gr.: Intens. *momuhyate* (MBh.), *momogdhi* and *momoḍhi* (Gr.), to be greatly bewildered or perplexed.

Mugdhá, mfn. gone astray, lost, RV.; VS.; perplexed, bewildered, AV.; Daś.; foolish, ignorant, silly, ŚBr. &c. &c.; inexperienced, simple, innocent, artless, attractive or charming (from youthfulness), lovely, beautiful, tender, young (esp. *ā*, f. a young and beautiful female, often in voc.; also in rhet. a variety of the Nāyikā), Kāv.; Kathās.; Rājat.; (ifc.) strikingly like, Vcar.; Bālar. **-kathā**, f. a tale about a fool, MW. **-kāntā-stana**, m. the bosom of a young mistress, Siś. **-gaṇḍa-phalaka**, mfn. (a face compared to a young lotus) whose pericarps are lovely cheeks, ib. **-tā**, f., **-tva**, n. ignorance, simplicity, artlessness, loveliness, Kāv. **-dūrvā**, f. young or tender Dūrvā grass, Śak. **-dṛiś**, mfn. fair-eyed, Sāh. **-dvīpa**, m. N. of an island, Uttamac. **-dhī**, mfn. foolish, silly, a simpleton, Kathās. **-prabodha**, m. instruction of the ignorant (only in °*dhe gṛiha-praveśa-vidhi*, m. N. of wk.). **-buddhi**, mfn. = *-dhī*, Kathās. **-bodha**, n. (scil. *vyākaraṇa*) 'instructing the ignorant,' N. of a celebrated grammar by Vopa-deva (supposed to have flourished in the 13th century, and regarded as a great authority in Bengal); of another wk. (on the consecration of new houses); *-kāra*, m. N. of Vopadeva, Cat.; *-pariśishṭa*, n., *-pradīpa*, m., *-subodhinī*, f. N. of wks. connected with Vop°'s grammar; °*dhâkhyā jvarâdi-roga-cikitsā*, f. N. of a medical wk. **-bodhinī**, f. (scil. *ṭīkā*) N. of 2 Comms. on the Amara-kośa and the Bhaṭṭi-kāvya by Bharatasena. **-bhāva**, m. stupidity, simplicity, BhP. **-mati**, mfn. = *-dhī*, A. **-mṛiga**, m. a young or harmless deer, Śāntiś. **-vat**, mfn. perplexed, embarrassed, ignorant of or inexperienced in (loc.), MBh. **-vadhū**, f. a young and lovely woman, Ragh. **-vilokita**, n. a beautiful glance; °*tôpadeśa*, m. instruction in b° glances, Śak. **-svabhāva**, m. artlessness, simplicity, Veṇis.; mfn. artless or charming by nature, Pañcat. **-hariṇī**, f. a young or tender antelope, Bhartṛ. **Mugdhâkshī**, f. a fair-eyed woman, Kāv.; Kathās. **Mugdhâgraṇī**, m. the chief of fools, Kathās. **Mugdhā-cakra**, n. a partic. mystical circle, Cat. **Mugdhâtman**, mfn. foolish, ignorant, Kāv. **Mugdhânana**, mfn. lovely-faced, W. **Mugdhâloka**, mfn. lovely to look at, Uttarar. **Mugdhêkshaṇā**, f. = *mugdhâkshī*, Priy. **Mugdhêndu**, m. the new moon, Kāv.

Mugdhiman, m. ignorance, simplicity, artlessness, Vām. v, 2, 56 (v. l.)

2. **Muh** (nom. *muk* or *muṭ*, Pāṇ. viii, 2, 33, Sch.) See *mano-múh*.

Muhira, m. a fool, blockhead, L. (cf. *muhera*); m. 'bewilderer,' N. of the god of love, L.

Múhu or **muhú**, ind. suddenly, in a moment, RV.; ŚBr.

Muhuḥ, in comp. = *muhur*. **-prôkta**, mfn. often told, L.

Muhuká, n. a moment, instant (*als*, ind. = prec.), RV.

Múhur, ind. (perhaps orig. 'in a bewildering manner') suddenly, at once, in a moment (often with a following *á*), RV.; AV.; for a moment, a while, RV. &c. &c.; at every moment, constantly, incessantly (*muhur-muhur*, now and again, at one moment and at another, again and again), MBh.; Kāv. &c.; on the other hand, on the contrary, Śak. **-gír**, mfn. swallowing suddenly, RV. **-bhāshā**, f. repetition of what has been said, tautology, L. **-bhuj** or **-bhojin**, m. 'constantly eating,' a horse, L. **-vacas**, n. = *-bhāshā*, L.

Muhuś, in comp. for *muhur*. **-cārin**, mfn. occurring repeatedly, recurring, Suśr.

Muhus, in comp. for *muhur*. **-kāma**, mf(*ā*)n. loving or desiring again and again, Pāṇ. viii, 3, 41, Vārtt. 1, Pat. **-tanais**, ind. at repeated intervals, repeatedly, constantly, MW.

Muhūrtá, m. n. a moment, instant, any short space of time, RV. &c. &c. (ibc., in a moment; *ena*, ind. after an instant, presently); a partic. division of time, the 30th part of a day, a period of 48 minutes (in pl. personified as the children of Muhūrtā), ŚBr. &c.; (*ā*), f. N. of a daughter of Daksha (wife of Dharma or Manu and mother of the Muhūrtas), Hariv.; Pur. **-kalpadruma**, m. (and °*mīya-saṃkrānti-saṃjñā-kusuma*, n.), **-kalpâkara**, m. N. of wks. **-kovida**, m. 'skilled in divisions of time,' an astrologer, Caurap. **-gaṇapati**, m., **-grantha**, m., **-cakrâvali**, f., **-candrakalā**, f., **-cintāmaṇi**, m. (and *-sāra*, m., *-sāriṇī*, f.), **-cūḍāmaṇi**, m. N. of wks. **-ja** (m. c. for °*tā-ja*), m. pl. the children of Muhūrtā, VP. **-ṭīkā**, f., **-tattva**, n., **-darpaṇa**, m., **-darśana**, n., **-dīpa** and **-dīpaka**, m., **-dīpikā**, f., **-nirṇaya**, m., **-padavī**, f., **-parīkshā**, f., **-bhāga**, m., **-bhuvanônmārtaṇḍa**, m., **-bhūshaṇa-ṭīkā**, f., **-bhairava**, m., **-mañjarī**, f., **-mañjūshā**, f., **-maṇi**, m., **-mādhavīya**, n., **-mārtaṇḍa**, m., **-mālā**, f., **-muktāmaṇi**, m., **-muktâvalī**, f., **-racana**, n., **-ratna**, n. (and °*na-mālā*, f., °*nâkara*, m.), **-rājīya**, n., **-lakshaṇa-paṭala**, m. n., **-vallabhā**, f., **-vidhāna-sāra**, m., **-vṛitta-śata**, n., **-śāstra**, n., **-saṃgraha**, m., **-sarvasva**, n., **-sāra**, m., **-sāriṇī**, f., **-siddhi**, f., **-sindhu**, m., **-skandha**, m. N. of wks. **-stoma**, m. pl. N. of a partic. Ekâha, ŚāṅkhŚr. **Muhūrtârka**, m., °**tâlaṃkāra**, m., °**tâvali**, f. N. of wks.

Muhūrtaka, m. or n. (?) a moment, instant, MBh.; an hour, Pañcar.

Muhé. See under √1. *muh*.

Muhera, m. = *muhira*, a fool, blockhead, L.

Mūḍhá, mfn. stupefied, bewildered, perplexed, confused, uncertain or at a loss about (loc. or comp.), AV. &c. &c.; stupid, foolish, dull, silly, simple, Mn.; MBh. &c.; swooned, indolent, L.; gone astray or adrift, ĀśvGṛ.; driven out of its course (as a ship), R.; wrong, out of the right place (as the fetus in delivery), Suśr.; not to be ascertained, not clear, indistinct, Āpast.; R.; perplexing, confounding, VP.; m. a fool, dolt, MBh.; Kāv. &c.; pl. (in Sāṃkhya) N. of the elements, Tattvas.; n. confusion of mind, Sarvad. **-garbha**, m. difficult delivery, a dead fetus, Suśr. **-grāha**, m. confused notion, misconception, infatuation, MW. **-cakshur-gada-cchetṛi**, m. the remover of the defect of vision of the foolish, ib. **-cetana** or **-cetas**, mfn. bewildered in mind, foolish, silly, MBh.; Kāv. **-tama**, mfn. very foolish or simple, MBh. **-tā**, f. bewilderment, perplexity, confusion, simplicity, folly, ignorance, Kāv.; Pur.; the gathering or drawing (of a tumour), Suśr.; degeneracy, morbid condition (of the wind in the body), ib. **-tva**, n. bewilderment, confusion, infatuation, folly, stupidity, MaitrUp.; Kathās.; Pañcat.; bewildering, confounding, Kap., Sch. **-dhī**, mfn. 'silly-minded,' simple, foolish, Kāv.; Kathās. **-prabhu**, m. the chief of fools, a great blockhead, Kathās. **-buddhi** (MBh.), **-mati** (Kathās.) and **-manas** (Siṃhâs.), mfn. = *-dhī*. **-ratha**, m. N. of a man, pl. his descendants, Saṃskārak. **-vat**, ind. like a fool, MBh. **-viḍambana**, n. N. of a Kāvya. **-śreshṭha**, m. = *-prabhu*, A. **-sattva**, mfn. foolish or silly by nature, MW. **Mūḍhâtman**, mfn. = *mūḍha-dhī*, Suśr. **Mūḍhêśvara**, m. 'lord of fools,' N. of a man, Cat.

मुहरपर्णक *muharaparṇaka*, w. r. for *mudgara-p°*, q. v.

मुहिष *muhisha*, m. N. of a mountain, VP.

मुहुर् *muhur*. See col. 1.

मुहूर्त *muhūrta*. See above.

मू 1. *mū* (cf. √*mav* and 1. *mīv*), cl. 1. Ā. *mavate*, to bind, tie, fix, Dhātup. xxii, 71: Caus. aor. *amīmavat*, Pāṇ. vii, 4, 80, Sch.: Desid. of Caus. *mimāvayishati*, ib.: Intens. *māmoti, māmavīti*, Siddh. on Pāṇ. vi, 4, 20.

2. **Mū**, mfn. binding, tying, fixing, Pāṇ. vi, 4, 20, Sch.; f. the act of binding or tying, L.

Mūka (ŚBr. *mūká*), mf(*ā*)n. 'tied or bound' (scil. tongue-tied), dumb, speechless, mute, silent, VS. &c. &c.; wretched, poor, L.; m. a fish, L.; the offspring of a mule and a mare, L.; N. of a Dānava, MBh.; of a serpent-demon, ib.; of a poet, Cat.; (*ā*), f. a crucible, L. (= or w. r. for *mūshā*). **-kavi**, m. the poet Mūka, Cat. **-tā**, f., **-tva**, n. dumbness, muteness, silence, MBh.; Pur.; Suśr. **-pañcaśatī**, f. N. of 5 poems in praise of Kāmâkshī, by Mūkakavi. **-praśna**, m. N. of wk. **-bhāva**, m. the state of being dumb, dumbness, MW. **-vat**, ind. like a mute, Pañcat. **Mūkâṇḍaja**, mfn. (a forest) whose birds are silent, Kum. **Mūkâmbikā**, f. (prob.) a form of Durgā (°*kāyāḥ sadana*, n. N. of a place), Cat.; *-stotra*, n. N. of a Stotra.

Mūkita, mfn. silenced, dumb, Nalac.

Mūkiman, m. dumbness, silence, g. *dṛiḍhâdi*.

Mūkī-√1. **kṛi**, P. *-karoti*, to make dumb, put to silence, Sāh.

2. **Mūta**, mfn. (for 1. see p. 819, col. 1) bound, tied, woven, Pāṇ. vi, 4, 20; m. n. a woven basket, TBr.; Kāṭh.; ŚrS.; pouring a little Takra into warm milk, L. **-kārya**, mfn. shaped like a basket, KātyŚr. **Mūtâkāra**, mfn. id., KātyŚr., Sch. **Mūtâvabaddha**, mfn. made of plaited work, Suśr.

Mūtaká, n. a little basket, ŚBr.; pouring a little Takra into warm milk, L.

मू 3. *mū*, weak form of √*mīv*, q. v.

मूकलराय *mūkalarāya*, m. N. of a king, Cat.

मूचीप *mūcīpa*, m. pl. N. of a people, ŚāṅkhŚr.

मूजवत् *mū́javat*, m. N. of a mountain, VS.; pl. N. of a people, AV.; ŚBr.

मूजालदेव *mūjāla-deva*, m. N. of a man, Cat.

मूट *mūṭa*, m. or n. a basket or bundle, Kāraṇḍ. (cf. *muṭa*).

Mūṭaka (Campak.), **mūḍaka** (Pañcad.), m. or n. id.

मूढ *mūḍha, mūḍha-garbha* &c. See col. 2.

मूत 1. 2. *mūta*. See under √1. *mīv* and above.

मूतिब *mūtiba*, m. pl. N. of a people, AitBr.

मूत्र *mūtra*, n. (prob. fr. √*mū* = *mīv*; but cf. Uṇ. iv, 162) the fluid secreted by the kidneys, urine (*mūtraṃ* √1. *kṛi*, to make water), AV. &c. &c. **-kara**, mfn. producing urine, Vāgbh. **-kṛicchra**, m. n. painful discharge of u°, strangury (°*rin*, mfn. suffering from it), Suśr.; a class of urinary affections (of which 8 kinds are enumerated), ŚārṅgS. **-kṛita**, mfn. steeped or soaked in urine, KātyŚr. **-kośa**, m. the scrotum, ŚārṅgS. **-kshaya**, m. insufficient secretion of urine, Suśr. **-granthi**, m. a knot or induration at the neck of the bladder, ib. **-ghāta**, prob. w. r. for *mūtrâghāta*. **-jaṭhara**, m. n. swelling of the abdomen in consequence of retention of urine, Suśr. **-dosha**, m. urinary disease, ib. **-nirodha**, m. obstruction of urine, GāruḍaP. **-patana**, m. the civet cat, L. **-patha**, m. = *-mārga*, MW. **-parīkshā**, f. uroscopy, N. of a ch. of the ŚārṅgS. **-puṭa**, m. 'u°-cavity,' the lower belly, L. **-purīsha**, n. sg. du. pl. urine and excrement, Mn. vi, 76; xi, 154 (cf. g. *gavâśvâdi*); °*shôccāra* and °*shôtsarga*, m. voiding urine and e°, Cat. **-pratighāta**, m. = *-nirodha*, Suśr. **-praseka**, m. the urethra, ib. **-phalā**, f. Cucumis Utilissimus or another species of cucumber, L. **-bhāvita**, mfn. = *-kṛita*, MW. **-mārga**, m. the urethra (*-nirodhana*, n. obstruction of it), Suśr. **-rodha**, m. = *-nirodha*, Bhpr. **-varti**, f. rupture of the scrotum, Suśr. **-vartma-rodha**, m. = *-mārga-nirodhana*, Gal. **-vardhaka**, mfn. increasing u°, diuretic, MW. **-vaha**, mfn. conveying urine, Suśr. **-vibandhaghna**, mfn. preventing suppression of urine, ib. **-visha**, mfn. poisonous with urine, ib. **-vṛiddhi**, f. copious secretion of urine, ib.; = *-varti*, ib. **-śakṛit**, n. urine and excrement, VarBṛS. (g. *gavâśvâdi*). **-śukra**, n. a partic. disease (in which urine and semen are ejected together), Suśr. **-śūla**, n. urinary colic, ib. **-saṃkshaya**, m. = *-kshaya*, ib. **-saṅga**, m. a painful and bloody discharge of u° (°*gin*, mfn. suffering from it), ib. **Mūtrâghāta**, m. urinary disease (of which 12 or 13 kinds), ib. **Mūtrâtīta**, m. a partic. kind of retention of u°, ib. **Mūtrâtīsāra**, m. diabetes, Rasar. **Mūtrârti**, f. pain in discharging u°, Suśr. **Mūtrâśaya**, m. u°-receptacle, ib.; the belly or bladder, L. **Mūtrâsāda**, m. = *mūtrâuka-sāda*, ŚārṅgS. **Mūtrôccāra**, m. voiding urine and excrement, Gaut. **Mūtrôtsaṅga**, m. = *mūtra-saṅga*, Car. **Mūtrôtsarga**, m. discharging urine, Pañcat. **Mūtrâukasāda**, m. a partic. disease (in which the urine assumes various colours and is voided with pain), Suśr.; Car.

Mūtraya, Nom. P. °*yati* (Dhātup. xxxv, 55; ep. also Ā. °*te*; ind. p. *mūtrya*), to discharge urine, make water against (acc.), MBh.; Var.; BhP.: Intens. *momūtryate*, Pat. on Pāṇ. iii, 1, 22.

Mūtrala, mfn. diuretic, Suśr.; (*ā*), f. Cucumis Utilissimus, L.; another species of cucumber (also n.), L.

Mūtrasāt, ind. into urine (°*sād-√bhū*, to become urine), HYogaś.

Mūtrita, mfn. one who has voided urine, Suśr.; discharged like urine, W.; soiled with urine, MW.; n. the voiding of urine, Cat.

Mūtrya, mfn. urinary, belonging or relating to urine, AitBr.

मूर 1. *mūrá*, mf(*ā*)n. (either = *mūḍha* or fr. √*mṛī*) dull, stupid, foolish, RV.; PañcavBr.

मूर 2. *mūrá*, mfn. (fr. √1. *mū* = *mīv*) rushing, impetuous (said of Indra's horses), RV. iii, 43, 6 (Sāy. = *māraka*).

3. **Mūra**, n. (prob. also fr. √1. *mū* and meaning 'something firm and fixed,' cf. Kāś. on Pāṇ. viii, 2, 18) = *mūla*, a root, AV. i, 28, 3. — **deva** (*mū́ra-*), m. pl. N. of a class of demons, RV. (accord. to Sāy. fr. 2. *mūra* = *māraṇa-krīḍā*).

मूरु *mūru*, N. of a country, Col.

मूर्ख *mūrkha* &c. See p. 823, col. 3.

मूर्खलिका *mūrkhalikā*, f. an arrow in the form of a bird's heart, L.

मूर्छन *mūrchana*. See p. 823, col. 3.

मूर्ण *mūrṇa*. See under √*mṛī*, p. 831, col. 2.

मूर्त *mūrta*, *mūrti*. See p. 824, col. 1.

मूर्त्सा *mūrtsā*, f. = *mūrchā*, fainting away, Gal.

मूर्धन् *mūrdhán*, m. (Uṇ. i, 158) the forehead, head in general, skull, (fig.) the highest or first part of anything, top, point, summit, front (of battle), commencement, beginning, first, chief (applied to persons), RV. &c. &c. (*mūrdhni* with √*vṛit* &c., to be above everything, prevail; with √*dhṛi* or *ā-√dā* = *mūrdhnā* √1. *kṛi*, to place on the head, hold in high honour); the base (in geom.; opp. to *agra*; perhaps w.r. for *budhna*), Col.; (in gram.) the roof or top of the palate (as one of the 8 Sthānas or places of utterance), Pāṇ. i, 1, 9, Sch.; (with Buddhists) 'the summit,' N. of a state of spiritual exaltation, Divyâv. — **vát**, mfn. containing the word *mūrdhan*, TS.; ŚBr.; m. N. of a Gandharva, TĀr.; of an Āṅgirasa or Vāmadevya (author of RV. x, 88), RVAnukr.

1. **Mūrdha**, in comp. for *mūrdhan*. — **karṇī**, f., -**karparī**, f., -**khola**, n. a broad-brimmed hat or an umbrella, L. — **ga**, mfn. sitting down on a person's head, Kāv. — **gata**, m. N. of a Cakra-vartin, Divyâv. — **ja**, m. pl. 'head-born,' the hair of the h°, MBh.; Kāv. &c.; the mane, Kathās.; N. of a Cakravartin, Buddh. — **jyotis**, n. = *brahma-randhra*, Cat. — **tás**, ind. out of the head, on the h°, MaitrS.; AV. — **tailika** (with *vasti*), m. N. of a kind of Errhine or remedy for promoting discharges from the nose, Suśr. — **dhara**, mf(*ā*)n. supporting the head; f. (with *sirā*) a vessel or vein which terminates in the head, Bhpr. — **pāta**, m. splitting of the skull, Jyot. — **piṇḍa**, m. the lump on the head (of an elephant in rut), L. — **pushpa**, m. Acacia Sirissa, L. — **bhinna** (*mūrdhá-*), mfn. one who has his head cleft, Suparṇ. — **rasa**, m. the scum of boiled rice, L. — **veshṭana**, n. 'h°-covering,' a turban, diadem, L. — **saṃhitá**, mf(*ā*)n. attached or fastened to the h°, ŚBr. **Mūrdhâgata**, n. a partic. state of ecstasy, Divyâv. **Mūrdhânta**, m. the crown of the head, Kathās. **Mūrdhâbhishikta**, mfn. having the h° sprinkled, anointed, consecrated, MBh.; universally, acknowledged (as a rule or example), Pat.; m. a consecrated king, Kāv.; Pur.; a man of the Kshatriya or warrior caste, L.; a royal counsellor, minister, L.; a partic. mixed caste (= *mūrdhâvasikta*), Yājñ. (v.l.) **Mūrdhâbhisheka**, m. 'h°-sprinkling,' consecration, inauguration, Rājat. **Mūrdhâvasikta**, m. N. of a partic. mixed caste (the son of a Brāhman and a Kshatriyā), Gaut.; Yājñ. (v.l. *mūrdhâbhishikta*); a consecrated king, L.; an officer in the army (or 'expert in the Dhanur-veda,' or 'one who carries arms, or knows the power of precious stones, Mantras, and medicinal herbs'), L.

2. **Mūrdha** (ifc.) = *mūrdhan*, the head (cf. *dvi-* and *tri-mūrdha*).

Mūrdhaka, m. a Kshatriya, L.

Mūrdhanya, mfn. being on or in the head, belonging to the head, capital, Kauś.; Kāv.; Pur.; 'formed on the roof or top of the palate,' N. of a class of letters (the so-called 'cerebrals' or 'linguals,' viz. *ṛi*, *ṝi*, *ṭ*, *ṭh*, *ḍ*, *ḍh*, *ṇ*, *r*, *sh*), Prāt.; Pāṇ.; highest, uppermost, pre-eminent, Inscr.; (*ā*), f. N. of the mother of Veda-śiras, VP.

Mūrdhvan, m. = *mūrdhan*, Uṇ. i, 158, Sch.

मूर्वा *mūrvā*, f. (cf. √*mūrv*) Sanseviera Roxburghiana (a sort of hemp from which bowstrings and the girdle of the Kshatriyas are made), Var.; Suśr. (cf. *maurva*). — **maya**, mf(*ī*)n. made of Mūrvā, Kull. on Mn. ii, 42. — **vaṇa** or -**vana**, Pāṇ. viii, 4, 6, Sch.

Mūrvikā, f. = *mūrvā*, L.

मूल् *mūl* (rather Nom. fr. *mūla* below), cl. 1. P. *mūlati* (accord. to Vop. also Ā. °*te*), to be rooted or firm, Dhātup. xv, 22: Caus. *mūlayati* (xxxii, 63; Vop. also *molayati*), to plant or to grow.

Mūla, n. (or m., g. *ardharcâdi*; ifc. f. *ā* or *ī*; prob. for 3. *mū́ra*, see above) 'firmly fixed,' a root (of any plant or tree; but also fig. the foot or lowest part or bottom of anything), RV. &c. &c. (*mūlaṃ √kṛi* or *bandh*, to take or strike root); a radish or the root of various other plants (esp. of Arum Campanulatum, of long pepper, and of Costus Speciosus or Arabicus), L.; the edge (of the horizon), Megh.; immediate neighbourhood (*mama mūlam* = to my side), R.; basis, foundation, cause, origin, commencement, beginning (*mūlād ārabhya* or *ā mūlāt*, from the beg°; *mūlāt*, from the bottom, thoroughly; *mūlaṃ kramataś ca*, right through from beginning, Divyâv.), Mn.; MBh. &c. (ibc. = chief, principal, cf. below; ifc. = rooted in, based upon, derived from); a chief or principal city, ib.; capital (as opp. to 'interest'), SāmavBr.; Prab.; an original text (as opp. to the commentary or gloss), R.; Kathās.; Suśr.; a king's original or proper territory, Mn. vii, 184; a temporary (as opp. to the rightful) owner, Mn. viii, 202; an old or hereditary servant, a native inhabitant, MW.; the square root, Sūryas.; a partic. position of the fingers (= *mūla-bandha*), Pañcar.; a copse, thicket, L.; also m. and (*ā*), f. N. of the 17th (or 19th) lunar mansion, AV. &c. &c.; m. herbs for horses, food, Divyâv.; N. of Sadā-śiva, Cat.; (*ā*), f. Asparagus Racemosus, L.; (*ī*), f. a species of small house-lizard, L.; mfn. original, first, Cat.; = *nija*, own, proper, peculiar, L. — **karman**, n. 'root-machination,' employment of roots for magical purposes, Mn. ix, 290 &c. (also °*ma-kriyā*, f., MBh.) — **kāra**, m. the author of an original wk., L. — **kāraṇa**, n. first or original cause, TPrāt., Comm.; Śaṃk. on BṛĀrUp.; Kathās. — **kārikā**, f. a fire-place, furnace, L. — **kṛicchra**, m. n. 'root-austerity,' a kind of penance, living solely on r°s, Vishṇ. — **kṛit**, mfn. preparing r°s (for magical uses), AV. — **kesara**, m. a citron, L. — **khānaka**, m. 'r°-digger,' one who digs for r°s, a collector of r°s, Mn. — **guṇa**, m. 'root-multiplier,' the co-efficient of a root (in alg.), MW.; -*jāti*, f. assimilation and reduction of the r°'s co-eff° with a fraction, ib. — **grantha**, m. 'original text,' N. of the very words uttered by Gautama Buddha, Buddh. — **granthi**, f. a species of Dūrvā grass, L. — **cchinna**, mf(*ā*)n. cut away with the r°, i.e. gone, lost (as hope), Daś. — **ccheda**, m. cutting away the r°s, c° up by the r°s, MBh.; VarBṛS. — **ja**, mfn. 'r°-born,' growing from a r°, L.; formed at the roots of trees, MBh.; m. a plant growing from a r° (as a lotus), W.; n. green ginger, L. — **jāta-śānti**, f. N. of a Pariśishṭa of the Mānava Gṛihya-sūtra. — **jāti**, f. chief or principal origin, L.; = -*guṇa-jāti* above, MW. — **tás**, ind. on the root, on the lower side, TBr.; Kauś. &c.; *ā m°*, from the r° upwards, Ṛitus.; from the beginning, Kathās. — **tā**, f. = -*tva*, Daś. — **trikoṇa**, n. the third astrological house, VarBṛS. — **tva**, n. the state of being a root or foundation or source, the having a f° (*tan-mūlatvāt prajānāṃ rājā skandhaḥ*, 'the king is the stem of his subjects through their being his root;' *veda-mūlatva*, 'the fact that the Veda is the original source of all knowledge;' *śāstra-m°*, 'the being founded upon the Śāstras'), Kām. (cf. *tan-m°*). — **deva**, m. = *mūra-d°* (q.v.); N. of Kaṇsa, L. (cf. -*bhadra*); of various men, Kathās. — **dravya**, n. original property, capital, stock, L. — **dvāra**, n. a principal door, VarBṛS.; -*vatī*, f. the original or ancient Dvāravatī, the older part of that city, Cat. (cf. *laghu-dv°*, *mūla-nagara*). — **dhana**, n. = -*dravya*, L. — **dhātu**, m. lymph, L. — **nakshatra-śānti**, f., °*ti-prayoga*, m. N. of wks. — **nagara**, n. the old part of a town (opp. to the suburbs), L. — **nāthīya**, n. N. of wk. — **nāśa** or -**nāśaka**, m. N. of a barber, Dhūrtas. — **nikṛintana**, mf(*ī*)n. 'cutting away the roots,' utterly destroying, Pañcar. — **parivāsa**, m. the original period for the continuance of the punishment called Par°, Mahāvy.; see *mūlâpakarsha-p°*. — **parṇī**, f. a species of plant (= *maṇḍūka-p°*), L. — **pāka**, m., g. *nyaṅkv-ādi*. — **purusha**, m. the male representative of a family, the last m° of a race, Śak. — **puliśa-siddhânta**, m. the original Siddhânta of Puliśa, VarBṛS., Comm. — **pushkara**, n. the root of Costus Speciosus or Arabicus, L. — **pushpikā**, f. Helianthus Indica, L. — **potī**, f. a species of plant, L. — **prakāśa**, m. N. of wk. — **prakṛiti**, f. (in phil.) the original root or germ out of which matter or all apparent forms are evolved, the primary cause or 'originant,' Sāṃkhyak.; Pañcar. &c. (IW. 82); pl. the 4 principal kings to be considered in time of war (viz. the Vijigīshu, Ari, Madhyama and Udāsīna; cf. *prakṛiti* and *śākhā-p°*), Mn. vii, 157, Kull.; Kām. — **praṇihita**, mfn. (perhaps) known of old by means of spies (thieves), Mn. ix, 269. — **phala**, n. sg. roots and fruits, ŚāṅkhGṛ.; VarBṛS.; the interest of capital, Āryabh.; -*da*, m. the Jaka or bread-fruit tree, L.; °*lâśana*, n. feeding on roots and fruits, MW. — **bandha**, mfn. deep-rooted (a sin), RāmatUp.; m. a partic. position of the fingers, Cat. — **bárhaṇa**, mf(*ī*)n. uprooting, AV.; n. and (*ī*), f. N. of the Nakshatra Mūla, TBr.; n. the act of uprooting, AV. — **bhaṭṭa-prayoga**, m. N. of wk. — **bhadra**, m. N. of Kaṇsa, L. (cf. -*deva*). — **bhava**, mf(*ā*)n. springing or growing from roots, Suśr. — **bhāga**, m. the lower part, Mṛicch., Comm. — **bhāra**, m. a load of roots, g. *vaṇsâdi*. — **bhāva-prakāśikā**, f. N. of wk. — **bhūta**, mfn. become the root or original, MW. — **bhṛitya**, m. an hereditary servant, one whose ancestors were servants before him (opp. to *āgantu*), Hit. — **mantra**, m. a principal or primary or fundamental text, BhP.; Hcat. &c.; a spell, Kād.; -*maya*, mf(*ī*)n. formed of spells i.e. producing the effect of a sp°, Hcar.; -*sāra*; °*trârtha-sāra*, m. n. N. of wks. — **māthurīya**, n. N. of wk. — **mādhava**, m. or n. (?) N. of a place, Cat.; -*tīrtha*, n. N. of a sacred bathing-place, MW. — **mitra**, m. N. of a man, L. — **rasa**, m. original taste (cf. under *rasa*); Sanseviera Zeylanica, L. — **rāja**, m. N. of a king, Cat. — **rāmāyaṇa**, n. the original Rāmāyaṇa i.e. Vālmīki's R°, Sarvad. — **rāśi**, m. a cardinal number, Piṅg., Comm. — **vacana**, n. primary words, a fundamental text, Cat. — **vaṇig-dhana**, n. a merchant's original property or capital, L. — **vat**, mfn. possessing (edible) roots, MBh.; standing upright, R.; m. a Rākshasa, R. (Sch.) — **vāpa**, m. one who plants (edible) roots, R. — **vārin**, m. N. of a man, Cat. — **vāsin**, mfn. (said of the Yavanās), Virac. — **vitta**, n. 'original property,' capital, L. — **vidyā**, f. 'principal science,' N. of a partic. Mantra (= *dvādaśâkshara*, q.v., Sch.), BhP. — **vināśana**, n. radical or entire destruction, R. — **vibhuja**, mfn. bending down roots, Pāṇ. iii, 2, 5, Vārtt.; m. a chariot, W. — **virecana**, n. a purgative prepared from r°s, Suśr. — **vyasana-vṛitti-mat**, mfn. one who gains his living by an hereditary debasing occupation, Mn. x, 38. — **vyādhi**, m. a principal disease, Bhpr. — **vratin**, mfn. living exclusively on roots, Hariv. — **śakuna**, m. (in augury) the first bird, VarBṛS. — **śākaṭa** or -**śākina**, n. a field planted with (edible) r°s, Pāṇ. v, 2, 29, Vārtt. 3, Pat. — **śānti**, f., °*ti-paddhati*, f., °*ti-vidhāna*, n., °*ti-vidhi*, m. N. of wks. — **śrī-pati-tīrtha**, n. N. of a sacred bathing-place, Cat. — **saṅgha**, m. N. of a society or sect (esp. of one of the groups of the Jaina-Siddhânta), W. — **sarvâsti-vāda** or °**din**, m. pl. N. of a Buddhist school, Buddh. — **sasya**, n. an esculent root, L. — **sādhana**, n. a chief instrument, principal expedient, Kum. — **sūtra**, n. an initial Sūtra, Cāṇ.; TPrāt., Comm.; a principal S°, MW.; (with Jainas) a partic. class of works. — **stambha-nirṇaya**, m. N. of wk. — **sthala**, n. N. of a place, Cat. — **sthāna**, n. foundation, base, Cat.; principal place, VarBṛS., Sch.; the air, atmosphere, L.; a god, L.;

Mooltan, Cat. &c.; (*ī*), f. N. of Gaurī, L.; *-tīrtha*, n. N. of a Tīrtha, Cat. **-sthāyin**, mfn. existing from the beginning (said of Śiva), MBh. **-srotas**, n. the fountain-head of a river, principal current, Rājat. **-svāmin**, m. du. the temporary and the rightful owner, Yājñ., Sch. **-hara**, mfn. taking away the roots of (gen.), i. e. utterly destroying, Mn.; R.; *-tva*, n. utter ruin, Daś. **Mūlâgra**, w.r., NṛisUp. (°*grau* for °*gnau*). **Mūlâcāra**, m., °**lâdi-śānti**, f. N. of wks. **Mūlâdhāra**, n. N. of a mystical circle situated above the generative organs, Pañcar.; Ānand.; the navel, RāmatUp. **Mūlâpakarsha-parivāsa**, m. the shortened period of the punishment called Parivāsa, see *mūla-p*°. **Mūlâbha**, n. a radish, L. **Mūlâbhidharma-śāstra**, n. the original Abhidharma-śāstra, Buddh. **Mūlâyatana**, n. an original residence, Ragh. **Mūlârtha-śekhara**, m. N. of wk. **Mūlâlavāla**, n. = *ālavāla*, Vikr. (*mūla* is prefixed in connection with the gen. *taroḥ*). **Mūlâvidyā-vināśaka**, mfn. destroying original ignorance, Pañcar. **Mūlâśin**, mfn. living upon roots, Kav. **Mūlâhva**, n. a radish, L. **Mūlôccheda**, m. 'cutting up the roots,' utter destruction, Pañcat. **Mūlôtkhāta**, mfn. dug up by the roots, utterly destroyed, Pañcat.; n. digging up r°s, MārkP. **Mūlôtpāṭana**, n. the digging up of roots, MW.; *-jīvin*, m. one who lives by digging for roots, ib. **Mūlôddharaṇa**, n. a means of plucking up anything (gen.) by the r° or of destroying, Vet. **Mūlaushadhi**, f. a species of plant, R.

Mūlaka, mf(*ikā*)n. (ifc.) rooted in, springing from (*-tva*, n.), MBh.; Jaim., Sch. &c.; born under the constellation Mūla, Pāṇ. iv, 3, 28; m.n. a radish, Mn.; Yājñ. &c.; a sort of yam, W.; m. a kind of vegetable poison, L.; N. of a prince (a son of Aśmaka), Pur.; (*ikā*), f. a root used in magic, Pañcat.; Siṃhâs.; n. a root, MBh.; Pañcar. **-paṇa**, m. a handful or bunch of radishes &c. (for sale), Pāṇ. iii, 3, 66, Sch. **-parṇī**, f. Moringa Pterygosperma, L. **-potikā** (Suśr.; Npr.; Bhpr.) or **-potī** (Npr.; Bhpr.), f. a radish. **-mūlā**, f. Lipeocercis Serrata, L. **-śākaṭa** or **-śākina**, m. n. and (*ā*), f. = *mūla-ś*°, L. **Mūlakâdi-suta**, m. n. and (*ā*), f. gruel made of the root of Mūlaka, L. **Mūlakôpadaṇśam**, ind. with a bite at a radish, Pāṇ. iii, 4, 47, Sch.

Mūlasa, mfn. fr. *mūla*, g. *tṛiṇâdi*.

Mūlika, mfn. original, Tattvas.; primary, principal, W.; living on roots, L.; m. an ascetic, L.; a seller of roots, Nār. (accord. to others = *mūlaṃ vipralambhas tat-kārī*); (*ā*), f. a multitude or collection of roots, MW. **Mūlikârtha**, m. a radical fact, MW. (cf. *yoga*).

Mūlin, mfn. having a root, ŚBr.; Suśr. (cf. *phala-m*°); = *mūla-kṛit*, q. v., AV.; m. a plant, tree, L.

Mūlī, in comp. for *mūla*. **-karaṇa**, n. the extraction of the square-root, Āryabh., Comm. **-karman**, n. = *mūla-karman*, q. v., L. **-√1. kṛi**, P. *-karoti*, to extract the square-root from (acc.), Āryabh., Comm. **-bhūta**, mfn. become a root, become a source or origin, MW.

Mūlera, m. a king, Uṇ. i, 62, Sch.; = *jaṭā*, Siddh.

Mūlya, mfn. being at the root, KātyŚr., Sch.; to be torn up by the r°s, Pāṇ. iv, 4, 88; = *mūlenânām-yam* and = *mūlena samaḥ*, ib. 91; to be bought for a sum of money, purchasable, W.; n. (ifc. f. *ā*) original value, value, price, worth, a sum of money given as payment (e.g. *dātum mūlyena*, to part with for a certain price, sell; *dattvā kiṃcin mūlyena*, having given something in payment; *mūlyena √grah*, to buy for a price, buy; *mūlyena √mārg*, to seek to buy), Mn.; MBh.; R. &c.; wages, salary, payment for service rendered, Rājat.; Kathās.; earnings, gain, Pañcat.; capital, stock, Kathās.; an article purchased, W. **-karaṇa**, n. making the worth or value of anything, turning into money, MārkP. **-tva**, n. the being of a certain value or price, ĀpŚr., Comm. **-dravya**, n. a purchase-sum, Siṃhâs. **-vivarjita**, mfn. devoid of price, priceless, invaluable, Pañcat. **Mūlyâdhyāya**, m., °**ya-vivaraṇa**, n. N. of wks.

Mūlyaka, n. price, worth, value, Āryabh., Comm.

मूलाट *mūlāṭa*, °*ṭī*, g. *gaurâdi*.

मूष् 1. *mūsh* (= √2. *mush*), cl. 1. P. *mūshati*, to steal, rob, plunder, Dhātup. xvii, 25.

2. **Mūsh**, m. f. 'stealer, thief,' a mouse, RV. i, 105, 8. [Cf. Gk. μῦς; Lat. *mus*; Slav. *myšĭ*; Germ. *mûs*, *Maus*; Eng. *mouse*.]

Mūsha, m. (*ā* and *ī*) f. a rat, mouse, Pañcat.; L.; a crucible, MārkP.; Kull.; L.; (*ā*), f., see below. **-vāhana**, mfn. 'rat-vehicled,' N. of Gaṇeśa, L.

Mūshaka, m. a thief, plunderer, BhP.; a rat, mouse, Yājñ.; R.; Var. &c.; a partic. part of the face (= *kara-viraka*), VarBṛS., Sch.; a kind of metre, L.; pl. N. of a people, MBh.; (*ikā*), f., see below. **-karṇikā** or **-karṇī**, f. Salvinia Cucullata or Anthericum Tuberosum, L. **Mūshakâda**, m. 'mouse-eater,' N. of a Nāga, MBh. (cf. *mūshikâda*). **Mūshakârāti**, m. 'mouse's foe,' a cat, L. (cf. *mūshikârāti*).

Mūshaṇa, n. stealing, pilfering, W.

Mūshā, f. Lipeocercis Serrata, Car.; a round window, air-hole, L. **-karṇī**, f. Salvinia Cucullata, L. **-tuttha**, n. a kind of vitriol, L.

Mūshika, m. a rat, mouse, Gaut.; MBh. &c.; Acacia Sirissa, L.; pl. N. of a people inhabiting the Malabar coast between Quilon and Cape Comorin, MBh. (B. *bhūshika*); (*ā*), f., see below. **-nirviśesha**, mfn. not differing from a mouse. **-parṇī**, f. Salvinia Cucullata, L. **-ratha**, m. 'rat-vehicled,' N. of Gaṇeśa, L. **-vishāṇa**, n. a mouse's horn (= an impossibility), Sarvad. **-sthala**, n. (prob.) a mole-hill, MārkP. **Mūshikâkṛiti**, mfn. formed like a rat's tail, Suśr. **Mūshikâṅka**, m. 'characterized by a rat,' N. of Gaṇeśa, L. **Mūshikâñcana**, m. 'riding on a rat,' id., L. **Mūshikâñcita**, m. = *mūshikâṅka*, L. **Mūshikâda**, m. = *mūshakâda*, MBh. **Mūshikântakṛit**, m. 'mouse-destroyer,' a cat, MBh. **Mūshikârāti**, m. = *mūshakârāti*, L. **Mūshikôtkara**, m. a mole-hill, Mṛicch.

Mūshikakā, f. (dimin. of next) little rat or mouse, Pāṇ. vii, 3, 46, Sch.

Mūshikā, f. a rat, mouse, VS. &c. &c.; a kind of leech, Suśr.; a spider, L.; Salvinia Cucullata or Anthericum Tuberosum, L.; a crucible, L. **-dat** or **-danta**, mfn. 'mouse-toothed,' having the teeth of a mouse, Pāṇ. v, 4, 145, Sch. **-hairaṇyika**, m. nickname of a man, Divyâv. **-°hvayā** (*mūshikâhv*°), f. Anthericum Tuberosum, Car.

Mūshikāra, m. a male mouse, Pāṇ. iv, 1, 120, Pat. (v.l.)

Mūshikikā, f. = *mūshikakā*, Pāṇ. vii, 3, 46, Sch.

Mūshita, mfn. = *mushita*, stolen, robbed, plundered, L.

Mūshi-parṇikā, f. Salvinia Cucullata, L.

Mūshī, f. a crucible (see also under *mūsha*). **-karaṇa**, n. melting in a crucible, Cat.

Mūshīka, m. and (*ā*) f. = *mūshika*, a rat, mouse, L. **-karṇī**, f. Salvinia Cucullata, L.

मूष्यायण *mūshyāyaṇa*, mfn. born of unknown parents (= *ajñāta-pitṛika*), L. (prob. w.r. for *āmushyāyaṇa*).

मूसरिफ *mūsarilpha* and *mūsarīpha* = مصرف, (in astrol.) N. of the fourth Yoga.

मृ *mṛi*, cl. 6. Ā. (Dhātup. xxviii, 110) *mriyáte* (ep. and m. c. also P. °*ti*; cl. 1. P. Ā. *marati*, *márate*, RV.; Impv. *mara*, Cāṇ.; pf. *mamā́ra*, *mamruḥ*, RV. &c. &c.; p. *mamṛivás*, RV.; Ā. *mamrire*, BhP.; aor. *amṛita*, Subj. *mṛithāḥ*, RV.; AV.; Pot. *murīya*, AV.; *mṛishīshṭa*, Pāṇ. i, 3, 61; fut. *martā*, Gr.; *marishyati*, AV. &c. &c.; °*te*, MBh.; inf. *martum*, MBh.; R. &c.; *martave*, AVPaipp.; ind. p. *mṛitvā*, Br.; *-māram*, MBh.), to die, decease, RV. &c. &c.: Pass. *mriyate* (cf. above; sometimes used impers. with instr.; pf. *mamre*; aor. *amāri*), Bhaṭṭ.: Caus. *mārayati* (m. c. also °*te*; aor. *amīmarat*): Pass. *māryate*, to cause to die, kill, slay, AV. &c. &c.: Desid. of Caus., see *mimārayishu*: Desid. *mumūrshati* (Pāṇ. vii, 1, 102), to wish or be about to die, face death, ŚrS. &c. &c.: Intens. *memrīyate*, *marmarti*, Gr. [Cf. Zd. *mar*, *mareta*; Gk. βροτός for μροτός; Lat. *mors*, *morior* &c.; Slav. *mrěti*; Lith. *mìrti*; Goth. *maurthr*; Germ. *Mord*, *morden*; Eng. *murder*.]

Mumūrshā, f. (fr. Desid.) desire of death, impatience of life, MBh.; R. &c.

Mumūrshu, mfn. wishing or being about to die, moribund, ib.

Mṛitá, mfn. dead, deceased, deathlike, torpid, rigid, RV. &c. &c.; departed, vanished (as consciousness), MBh.; vain, useless, Kāv.; calcined, reduced (said of metals), ib.; n. death, MBh.; R.; = *caitya*, a grave, L.; begging, food or alms obtained by begging, L. **-kambala**, m. a dead man's shroud, Caṇḍ. **-kalpa**, mfn. almost dead, apparently dead, Yājñ.; MBh.; Daś. **-garbhā**, f. (a woman) whose fetus dies, Hcat. **-gṛiha**, n. 'house of the dead,' a tomb, Buddh. **-cela**, n. the garments of the d°, Mn. x, 52. **-jāta**, mfn. born dead, Vishṇ.; Daś. **-jātaka**, n. N. of wk. **-jīva**, m. Clerodendrum Phlomoides, L. **-jīvana**, mf(*ī*)n. raising the dead to life, Kathās. **-dāra**, m. one whose wife is dead, a widower, MW. **-deha**, m. a dead body, corpse, Kathās. **-dhavā**, f. (a woman) whose husband is dead, Uṇ., Sch. **-dhāra** or °**raka**, mfn. bearing a corpse, MBh. **-nandana**, m. a kind of hall with 58 pillars, Vāstuv. **-nātha**, mfn. one whose lord is d°, MBh. **-niryātaka**, m. one who carries out d° bodies, ib. **-pa**, m. a person who guards a d° body, ib. (cf. Pāṇ. ii, 4, 10, Sch.) **-patnīkâdhāna**, n. N. of wk. **-pā**, m. a person who watches a d° body, a man of the lowest caste who collects d° men's clothes or conveys d° bodies to the river side to be burnt or executes criminals &c., W.; N. of an Asura, MBh. **-putra**, m. one whose son is d°, MW. **-purusha-śarīra**, n., **-pūrusha-deha**, m. a human corpse, Kathās. **-prajā**, f. (a woman) whose children are dead, Mn.; BhP. **-prâya**, mfn. well-nigh dead, MW. **-priyā**, f. whose beloved is d°, L. **-bhartṛikā**, f. (a woman) whose husband is d°, Kathās. **-bhāva**, m. a state of death, Vas. **-bhraj** (*mṛitá-*), mfn. one who has lost the power of erection, AV. **-matta** or °**taka**, m. a jackal, L. **-manas** (*mṛitá-*), mfn. unconscious, insensible, AV. **-mātṛika**, mfn. one whose mother is dead, Kathās. **-vat**, ind. like one d° (*ātmānam m° saṃdarśya*, feigning death), Hit. **-vatsakā**, w.r. for *-vatsikā*, q. v., Hcat. **-vatsā** (*mṛitá-*), f. whose offspring or new-born child dies, AV.; *-cikitsā*, f. N. of wk. **-vatsikā**, f. = *-vatsā*, L. **-vastra-bhṛit**, mfn. wearing a dead man's clothes, Mn. x, 35. **-vārshika**, m. or n. (?) the period of the short rains (which cease in 24 hours), Buddh. **-vāsara**, m. the day of any one's death, Hcat. **-śaṅkā**, f. the fear of a person's being dead, W. **-śabda**, m. report of any one's death, AitBr. **-saṃskāra**, m. funeral rites or ceremonies, L. **-saṃjīvana**, mfn. reviving the dead, Kathās.; (*ī*), f. revival of a d° person, Cat.; N. of sev. wks.; n. revival of a d° person or bringing the d° to life, MārkP. **-saṃjīvin**, mfn. reviving the d° (N. of various remedies), Bhpr.; Rasêndrac.; (*inī*), f. a species of shrub, L.; N. of Comm. **-sūtaka**, m. a partic. preparation of quicksilver, Sarvad.; n. bringing forth a still-born child, MaitrUp.; VarBṛS. **-strī**, mfn. one whose wife is d°, AitBr., Comm. **-snāta**, mfn. one who has bathed after a death or funeral, L.; dying immediately after ablution, W. **-snāna**, n. ablution after a death or funeral, L. **-sva-moktṛi**, m. 'letting alone (i.e. not taking) the property of deceased persons,' N. of Kumāra-pāla, L. **-hāra** or **-hārin**, m. a carrier of the dead, one who bears a corpse to the funeral pyre, MārkP. **Mṛitâṅga**, n. a dead body (°*ga-lagna*, prob. n. the clothing of a d° b°), Yājñ. **Mṛitâṅgāra**, m. N. of a man, Dhūrtas. **Mṛitâṇḍa**, n. a seemingly dead or lifeless egg (cf. *mārtāṇḍa*); (*ā*), f. (a woman) whose offspring dies, Hcat.; m. the sun, L. (cf. *mṛitaṇḍa*). **Mṛitâdhāna**, n. placing a dead body (on the pyre), MW. **Mṛitâśana**, mfn. 'having lost the power of eating (?),' being of the age of 90 to 100 years, L. (cf. *mṛita-bhraj*). **Mṛitâśauca**, n. impurity contracted through the death of any one, Cat. **Mṛitâha**, m. (Vishṇ.), °**han**, n. (MārkP.) or °**has**, n. (BhP.) the day of any one's death. **Mṛitôtthita**, mfn. died and risen again to life, BhP. **Mṛitôdbhava**, m. the sea, ocean, L. (for *am*°).

Mṛitaka, m. n. a dead man, a corpse, MBh.; BhP.; Vet.; n. death, decease, KātyŚr., Sch.; impurity contracted through the death of a relation, A. **Mṛitakântaka**, m. 'consumer of corpses,' a jackal, L.

Mṛiti, f. death, dying, Śrutab.; BhP. &c. **-tattva** and **-tattvânusmaraṇa**, n. N. of wks. **-rekhā**, f. a line (on the hand) denoting death, Daś. **-sādhana**, mfn. causing death, ib.

Mṛitiman, m. mortality, Kāṭh.

Mṛityú, m. (very rarely f.) death, dying, RV. &c. &c.; (deaths of different kinds are enumerated, 100 from disease or accident and one natural from old age; ifc. = 'd° caused by or through'); Death personified, the god of d° (sometimes identified with Yama or with Vishṇu; or said to be a son of Adharma by Nirṛiti or of Brahmā or of Kali or of Māyā; he has also the patronymics Prādhvaṇsana and Sāmparāyaṇa, and is sometimes reckoned among the 11 Rudras, and sometimes regarded as Vyāsa in the 6th Dvāpara or as a teacher &c.), ŚBr.; MBh.; Pur. &c.;

N. of the god of love, L.; of a partic. Ekâha, ŚāṅkhŚr.; of the 8th astrol. house, VarBṛS.; of the 17th astrol. Yoga, Col. (*mṛityor haraḥ* and *mṛityor vikarṇa-bhāse*, N. of Sāmans). **-kanyā**, f. the goddess of d°, BrahmavP. **-kara**, mfn. causing d°, VarBṛS. **-kāla**, m. hour of d°, MBh.; R.; *-cihna*, n. pl. N. of wk. **-jit**, m. 'conqueror of d°,' N. of an author (also called *-jid-amṛiteśa* and *-jid-bhaṭṭāraka*), Cat.; N. of wk. **-m-jaya**, mfn. overcoming d° (said of various remedies), Bhpr.; Rasêndrac.; m. (with or without *mantra*) N. of RV. vii, 59, 12, Pañcar.; N. of Śiva, Pañcar.; Prasaṅg.; Rājat.; of an author (also called °*ya-bhaṭṭāraka*), Cat.; N. of wk.; *-kokila*, m. N. of an author, Cat.; *-japa*, m. muttering the verse RV. vii, 59, 12, Kād.; N. of wk.; *-tā*, f. the state of overcoming d° or of being Śiva, Kāv.; *-tantra*, n. N. of wk.; *-tīrtha*, n. N. of a Tīrtha, Cat.; *-tva-prakaraṇa*, n., *-dhyāna*, n., *-paddhati*, f., *-mānasa*, n., *-yantra*, n., *-vidhāna*, n. (and °*na-paddhati*, f.), *-vidhi*, m., *-stotra*, n. (and °*tra-vidhāna*, n.); °*yâdi-homa-vidhi*, m. N. of wks. **-tīrtha**, n. N. of a Tīrtha, Cat. **-tūrya**, n. a kind of drum beaten at funeral ceremonies, Rājat. **-da**, mfn. death-giving, fatal, MW. **-dūta**, m. 'death-messenger,' one who brings the news of a death, AV. **-dvāra**, n. the door leading to death, R.; Hit. **-nāśaka**, m. 'd°-averter,' quicksilver, L. **-nāśana**, n. 'd°-destroying,' the nectar of immortality, Kathās. **-nivartaka**, mfn. destroying death (Vishṇu), Pañcar. **-patha**, m. a way leading to d°, R.; Rājat.; BhP. **-pā**, mfn. d°-quaffing (said of Śiva), MBh. **-pāśá**, m. d°'s noose (variously reckoned at 101 or even more than 1000 in number), AV.; TBr. &c. **-pushpa**, m. 'having fatal flowers,' the sugar-cane (so called because it dies after losing its flowers), L.; bamboo, L. **-pratibaddha**, mfn. subject or liable to d°, BṛĀrUp.; Śaṃk. **-phala**, m. a species of cucumber, L.; (*ā* or *ī*), f. Musa Sapientum, L.; n. a sort of fruit considered as poisonous, W. **-bándhu** (RV., or *mṛityú-bandhu*, TS.), m. companion of d°. **-bīja**, m. 'dying after production of seed,' the bamboo-cane, L. **-bhaṅguraka**, m. = *-tūrya*, q.v., L. **-bhaya**, n. fear of death, Kathās.; danger of death, VarBṛS. **-bhīta**, mfn. afraid of death, Kathās. **-bhṛitya**, m. 'servant of death,' sickness, disease, L. (cf. *-sevaka*). **-mat**, mfn. having death, subject to d°, PraśnUp.; dead, L. **-mahishī-dāna**, n., °**na-vidhi**, m. N. of wks. **-māra**, m. (with Buddhists) N. of one of the 4 Māras, L. **-mṛityu**, m. the death of d° i.e. a remover or preventer of d° (*-tva*, n.), Up. **-rāj**, m. the god of d°, MBh. **-rūpiṇī**, f. 'death-formed,' mystical N. of the letter *ś*, RāmatUp. **-laṅghanôpanishad**, f., **-lāṅgalôpanishad**, f. N. of an Upanishad. **-lāṅgula-stotra**, n. N. of a Stotra. **-lāṅgūla** = **-laṅghanôpanishad** above; *-mantra*, m. N. of wk. **-loka**, m. the world of d° (the 5th of the 7 w°s), ŚāṅkhBr.; w° of the dead, abode of Yama, MBh.; R. **-vañcana**, m. 'death-cheater,' N. of Śiva, L.; a raven, L.; Aegle Marmelos, L. **-vijaya**, m. N. of an elephant, Daś. **-samyamana**, m. or n. N. of two Yoga postures (= *cūlikā* or *vīrâsana*), L. **-saṃyuta** (*mṛityú-*), mfn. connected with death, subject to d°, TS. **-saṃjīvanī**, f. a spell which causes the dead to live, Cat.; *-vidhāna*, n. N. of wk. **-saṃdhita** or **-sammita** (v.l.), mfn. united with death, meeting with d°, MBh. **-sāt**, ind., with √*kṛi*, to deliver any one over to d°, MBh. **-suta**, m. 'death's son,' N. of a class of comets, VarBṛS.; (*ā*), f. patr. of Su-nīthā, Hariv. **-sūti**, f. 'dying in parturition,' a female crab, L. **-senā**, f. the army of the god of death, MBh. **-sevaka**, m. = *-bhṛitya*, q.v., Gal. **-hetu**, m. cause of death; (*ave*), ind. for the sake of death, in order to kill, BhP. **Mṛityv-ashṭaka**, n. N. of wk.

Mṛityuka, mfn. (ifc.) = *mṛityu*; cf. *sva-cchanda-m°*.

मृकण्ड *mṛikaṇḍa* (and °*ḍaka*, L.) or *mṛikaṇḍu*, m. N. of an ancient sage, the father of Mārkaṇḍeya, MārkP. (cf. Uṇ. i, 38, Sch.)

मृक्त *mṛikta* &c. See √*mṛic*.

मृक्ष् *mṛiksh*, weak form of √*mraksh*.

Mṛikshá, m. (prob.) a curry-comb, comb or any instrument for scraping, RV. viii, 66, 3.

Mṛikshaka-nāṭaka, n. N. of a drama.

Mṛikshiṇī, f. 'tearing up (scil. the ground),' a torrent, RV. x, 98, 6 (others 'a rain cloud').

मृग् *mṛig* (rather Nom. fr. *mṛiga*; cf. √*mārg*, *mṛij*), cl. 4. P., 10 Ā. (Dhātup. xxvi, 137; xxxv, 46) *mṛigyati*, *mṛigáyate* (m. c. also P. °*ti*; pr. p. *mṛigayāṇa*, MBh.), to chase, hunt, pursue, RV. &c. &c.; to seek, search for or through, investigate, examine, MBh.; Kāv. &c.; to visit, frequent, MBh.; to seek or strive after, aim at, endeavour to obtain (acc.), MBh.; Kāv. &c.; to desire or request or ask anything (acc.) from (abl., *-tas*, gen. with or without *sakāśāt*), Kathās.

Mṛigá, m. (prob. 'ranger,' 'rover') a forest animal or wild beast, game of any kind, (esp.) a deer, fawn, gazelle, antelope, stag, musk-deer, RV. &c. &c.; the deer or antelope in the moon (i. e. the spots on the disk supposed to resemble those of an antelope as well as a hare); the d° or ant° in the sky (either the Nakshatra Mṛiga-śiras or the sign of the zodiac Capricorn; also in general the 10th arc of 30° in a circle), Sūryas.; VarBṛS. &c.; an elephant with partic. marks (accord. to L. 'one the secondary marks of whose body are small'), R.; Var.; a large soaring bird, RV. i, 182, 7 &c.; N. of a demon or Vṛitra in the form of a deer slain by Indra, ib. i, 80, 7 &c.; of a celestial being (occupying a partic. place in an astrol. house divided into 81 compartments), VarBṛS.; Hcat.; of a partic. class of men whose conduct in coitus resembles that of the roebuck, L.; of the district in Śāka-dvīpa inhabited principally by Brāhmans, MBh. (B. *maṅga*); of the Brāhmans of Śāka-dvīpa themselves, VP. (v.l. *maga*); of a horse of the Moon, VP.; musk (= *mṛiga-nābhi* or *-mada*), VarBṛS.; a partic. Aja-pāla sacrifice, L.; search, seeking, asking, requesting, L.; (*ā*), f. = *mṛiga-vīthī*, L.; (*ī*), f. a female deer or antelope, doe, Hariv.; R. &c.; N. of the mythical progenitress of antelopes, MBh.; R.; Pur.; a partic. class of women, L.; a kind of metre, Col.; a partic. gait of a dancing girl, Saṃgīt.; demoniacal possession, epilepsy, L. **-kāka**, m. du. a deer and a crow, MW. **-kānana**, n. a forest abounding in game, park, Kathās. **-ketana**, m. the moon, Alaṃkārav. **-kshīra**, n. doe's milk, g. *kukkuṭy-ādi* (cf. *mṛigī-k°*). **-gartâśrayâpcara**, mfn. containing wild beasts and animals living in holes and aquatic animals, Mn. vii, 72. **-gāminī**, f. Embelia Ribes, L. **-grahaṇa**, n. the capture of a deer, Mn. v, 130. **-gharma-ja**, m. the substance called 'civet,' Gal. **-cakra**, n. the zodiac(?), Divyâv. **-carmīya**, m. N. of an author, Cat. **-caryā**, f. the acting like a deer (a kind of penance), MBh. **-cārin**, mfn. acting like a deer (as certain devotees; cf. *go-c°*), ib. **-cirbhiṭā**, f. coloquintida, L. **-caiṭaka** (!), m. a wild cat, pole-cat, W. **-jambuka**, m. du. a deer and a jackal, MW. **-jala**, n. 'deer-water,' mirage (see *-tṛish*), MW.; *-snāna*, n. bathing in the waters of a mir° (a term for any impossibility), ib. **-jāti**, f. pl. the deer species, whole race of d°, MBh. **-jālikā**, f. a net for snaring game, L. **-jīvana**, m. one who lives by hunting, a hunter, MBh. **-ṭaṅka**, m. 'a deer as a mark' or 'deer-marked,' the moon, Āryabh., Sch. **-tīrtha**, n. 'animal-track,' N. of the path by which the priests at the end of the Savana leave the sacred place to attend to their bodily wants, ŚrS. **-tṛish** (L.), **-tṛishā** (Kām.), **-tṛishṇā** (Hit.; Dhūrtas.), **-tṛishṇi** (BhP.), or **-tṛishṇikā** (R.; Śak. &c.), f. 'deer-thirst,' mirage, vapour floating over sands or deserts, fancied appearance of water in deserts. **-toya**, n. the water of a mirage, Nilak. **-tva**, n. the state or condition of a d°, R.; Pur. **-daṃśa** or °**śaka**, m. 'animal-biter,' a hunting-dog, dog, L. **-darpa**, m. musk, VarBṛS., Sch. **-dāva**, m. 'deer-park,' N. of the place where Gautama Buddha first preached, MWB. 402. **-dṛiś**, m. the zodiacal sign Capricorn, L.; f. a fawn-eyed woman, Pañcat.; Śiś.; Rājat. &c. **-dyut**, mfn. attacking or hunting a deer, Bhaṭṭ. **-dyū**, mfn. delighting or taking pleasure in d°, ib.; m. a hunter, W. **-dvija**, m. pl. beasts and birds, Mn. v, 20. **-dvish**, m. a lion, A. **-dhara**, m. 'having deer-like marks,' the moon, Śiś.; N. of a minister of Prasena-jit, Buddh. **-dharma** (TāṇḍyaBr., Sch.), **-dharman** (TāṇḍyaBr.), mfn. having the nature of game. **-dhūma**, m. or n. (?) N. of a Tīrtha, MBh. **-dhūrta** or °**taka**, m. 'animal-deceiver,' a jackal, L. **-nayanā**, f. a fawn-eyed woman, MW. **-nābhi**, m. 'deer's navel,' musk, Ṛitus.; Kum. &c.; a musk-deer, Ragh. (cf. *nābhi*); *-ja*, mf(*ā*)n. coming from the m°-d°, Subh.; (*ā*), f. musk, L.; *-maya*, mf(*ī*)n. made of musk, Hariv. **-nirmoka-vasana**, mfn. clothed in the cast-off skin of a deer, MBh. **-netra**, mf(*ā*)n. having the Nakshatra Mṛiga for a leader, BrahmaP.; Malamāsat.; (*ā*), f. a woman with eyes like a fawn's, L. **-pakshin**, m. pl. beasts and birds, Mn.; Suśr. **-pati**, m. 'lord of the beasts,' a lion, Hariv.; BhP. &c.; a tiger, MBh.; 'antelope's lord,' a roebuck, Hariv.; *-gamanā*, f. (with Buddhists) N. of a goddess, Kālac. **-pada**, n. = *mṛigyāḥ padam*, g. *kukkuṭy-ādi*. **-pālikā**, f. a jackal-like musk-deer, L. **-piplu**, m. 'deer-marked,' the moon, L. **-pota** (MW.) or °**taka** (R.), m. a young deer, fawn. **-prabhu**, m. 'lord of beasts,' the lion, Kathās. **-priya**, m. Jasminum Sambac, L.; a species of grass, L. **-prêkshin**, mfn. looking at (anything) like a deer, having the eyes of a d°, Ragh. (cf. *vṛika-p°*). **-bandhinī**, f. a net for snaring game, L. **-bālaka**, m. a young deer, BhP. **-bhakshā**, f. Nardostachys Jatamansi, L. **-bhojanī**, f. coloquintida, Suśr. **-mattaka**, m. a jackal, L. **-mada**, m. (also pl.) musk, Gīt.; Śrutab. &c.; *-vāsā*, f. a m°-bag, L. **-manda**, m. a class of elephants, R.; (*ā*), f. N. of the mythical progenitress of lions, Sṛimaras (and Camaras), MBh.; R. (cf. *-vatī*). **-mandra**, m. a class of elephants, R. **-maya**, mf(*ī*)n. produced or coming from wild animals, Nir. **-māṉsa**, n. deer's flesh, venison, MW. **-mātṛikā**, m., °**kā**, f. a species of wild animal, Car.; Suśr.; (*ā*), f. a kind of red-coloured hare-like deer, L. **-māsa**, m. the month Mārgaśīrsha, VarBṛS. **-mukha**, m. the zodiacal sign Capricorn, VarBṛ. (cf. *mṛigâsya*). **-yūtha**, n. a herd of deer, R.; *-pa*, m. lord of the herd of deer, MBh. **-rasā**, f. a species of plant, L. **-rāj**, m. 'king of beasts,' a lion, R.; BhP. &c.; the zodiacal sign Leo, L.; a tiger, Nal. **-rāja**, m. 'king of beasts,' a lion, MBh.; R.; Ragh. &c.; the zodiacal sign Leo, VarBṛS.; a tiger, MBh.; the moon (see °*ja-lakshman*); N. of a poet, Cat.; *-tā*, f. dominion over the beasts, Vcar.; *-dhārin*, m. N. of Śiva, Vikr.; *-lakshman*, mfn. having the mark or name of lion or the moon, Veṇis. **-rājinī**, f. N. of a Gandharva maid, Kāraṇḍ. **-rāṭikā**, f. a species of medicinal plant (eaten also as a pot-herb), L. **-ripu**, m. 'enemy of wild animals,' the lion, L.; the sign Leo, Gaṇit. **-rūpin**, mfn. deer-shaped, being in the form of an antelope, MW. **-rocanā**, f. a yellow pigment prepared from the bile of a deer, Vikr. (cf. *go-r°*). **-roma-ja**, mfn. 'produced from animal's hair,' woollen, L. **-rksha** (*m°* + *ṛiksha*), n. sg. an antelope or a bear, R. **-lakshman**, m. 'deer-marked,' the moon, Kathās. **-lāñchana**, m. id., Kād.; Vikr.; Dhūrtas.; *-ja*, m. 'son of the moon,' the planet Mercury, VarBṛS. **-lipsu**, mfn. wishing to catch or kill a deer, MBh. **-lekhā**, f. a deer-like streak on the moon, Ragh. **-locana**, m. 'deer-eyed,' the moon, MW.; (*ā* or *ī*), f. a fawn-eyed woman, L. **-lomika**, mfn. 'made of the hair of animals,' woollen, Vishṇ. **-vatī**, f. N. of the mythical progenitress of bears and Sṛimaras, R. **-vadhâjīva** or °**vin**, m. 'one who lives by killing wild animals,' a huntsman, L. **-vadhū**, f. a female deer, doe, Kāv. **-vana**, n. a forest abounding in wild animals, a park, Ragh.; *-tīrtha*, n. N. of a Tīrtha, Cat. **-varman**, m. N. of a man, L. **-vallabha**, m. 'liked by deer,' a species of grass, L. **-vāhana**, m. 'having a d° for a vehicle,' the god of wind (sometimes so represented), wind, L. **-vīthikā** or °**thī**, f. 'deer-track,' N. of that portion of the moon's course which includes the constellations Śravaṇā and Śata-bhishaj and Pūrva-bhadrapadā, VP. (cf. *mṛigâkhya*). **-vaiṇika**, n. a partic. posture in sitting, Cat. **-vyādha**, m. a huntsman, MBh.; Rājat.; the dog-star, Sirius, AitBr.; Sūryas.; N. of Śiva, MBh.; of one of the 11 Rudras, MBh.; Hariv.; VP.; *-kathānaka*, n. N. of ch. of the Nārada-purāṇa (called also *mṛigôpâkhyāna*); *-sarpa-sūkara*, m. pl. a deer, hunter, snake and boar, MW. **-vyādhīya**, n. N. of ch. of the Vāsishṭha-rāmāyaṇa. **-vyāla-nishevita**, mfn. infested by wild beasts and serpents, MBh. **-śaphá**, m. a stag's hoof, MaitrS. **-śāyikā**, f. the recumbent posture of an antelope (*śayīta °kām*, 'let him lie as still as an ant°'), MBh. **-śāva** (comp.) or (ifc.) **-śāvaka** (VarBṛS.), m. a young deer, fawn; °*vâkshī*, f. a fawn-eyed woman, MBh.; R. &c. **-śira**, n. (Jyot.) or °**rā**, f. (L.) the Nakshatra Mṛiga-śiras. **-śiras** (*mṛigá-*), n. N. of the 3rd (or 5th) Nakshatra (q.v.) containing 3 stars (one of which is λ Orionis; it is figured by an antelope's head), AV.; GṛŚrS.; VarBṛS.; mfn. born under that Naksh°, Pāṇ. iv, 3, 37, Sch.; m. a partic. position of the hands, Cat. **-śīrshá**, n. the Nakshatra Mṛiga-śiras, TS.; Br.; BhP.; mfn. born under that N°, VarBṛS. (v.l. mārgaś°, mārgaśira); m. the month Mārgaśīrsha, ib.; a partic. position of the hands (also °shaka), Cat.; N. of a serpent-king, Kāraṇḍ. **-śīrshan**, n. the Naksh° Mṛiga-śiras, L. **-śṛiṅga**, n. a stag's horn, Vait.; -vratin, m. pl. N. of a Buddhistic sect, Buddh. **-śreshṭha**, m. 'best of beasts,' 'chief of animals,' a tiger, MBh. **-saktha**, n. = mṛigasya sakthi, Pāṇ. v, 4, 98. **-sattama**, m. the best of antelopes, MW. **-sattra**, n. N. of a festival lasting 19 days, TāṇḍyaBr. **-siṅhaka**, m. a species of small lion, L. **-sūkara**, m. du. a deer and a boar, MW. **-han** or **-hantṛi**, m. 'deer-slayer,' a huntsman, MBh.; BhP. **Mṛigâkshī**, f. a fawn-eyed woman, Megh.; Rājat. &c.; coloquintida, L.; = tri-yāmā, L. **Mṛigâkhará**, m. the lair or den of a wild animal, TS.; TBr. &c. **Mṛigâkhya**, mf(ā)n. named after a deer (°yā vīthī, a portion of the moon's course which comprises 3 constellations beginning with Maitra), VarBṛS. **Mṛigâṅka**, m. 'deer-marked,' the moon, Mṛicch.; VarBṛ.; Rājat.; camphor, L.; the wind, L. (cf. mṛiga-vāhana); N. of a sword, Kathās.; of a man, Vās., Introd.; -gupta, m. N. of a man, Cat.; -tanaya, m. N. of the planet Mercury, VarBṛ., Comm.; -datta, m. N. of various men, Kathās.; Cat.; -dattīya, mfn. relating to Mṛigâṅka-datta, Kathās.; -bandhu, m. the god of love, Bālar.; -maṇi, m. the stone Candra-kānta, Kād.; -mālā, f. N. of a woman, Vāsant.; -mūrti, m. 'having a deer-spotted form,' the moon, Śiś.; -mauli, m. N. of Śiva, Prasannar.; -rasa, m. a partic. mixture, Cat.; -rksha (ṛik°), n. the Nakshatra Mṛiga-śiras, VarYogay.; -lekha, m., °kha-kathā, f. N. of wks.; -lekhā, f. N. of the daughter of a king of the Vidyā-dharas, Kathās.; of a woman, Hāsy.; -vatī, f. N. of various princesses (and of one of the Vidyā-dharas), Kathās.; Cat.; -śataka, n. N. of wk.; -sena, m. N. of a king of the Vidyā-dharas, Kathās. **Mṛigâṅkaka**, m. N. of a sword (= mṛigâṅka), Kathās. (w.r. mṛigâṅgaka). **Mṛigâṅganā**, f. a female deer, doe, Kum. **Mṛigâjina**, n. a deer-skin, W. **Mṛigâjīva**, m. 'subsisting by wild animals,' a huntsman, L.; a hyena, L. **Mṛigâṭavī**, f. = mṛiga-kānana, q.v., Kām. **Mṛigâṇḍakī** or °ḍa-jā, f. musk, L. **Mṛigâd**, m. 'animal-devourer,' a tiger, L. **Mṛigâda**, m. a hyena, L.; (ī), f. a thick cucumber, L. **Mṛigâdana**, m. 'animal-devourer,' a hyena, L.; a hunting leopard, L.; (ī), f. coloquintida, Suśr.; Sida Rhombifolia, L.; = saha-devī, L. **Mṛigâdhipa**, m. 'king of animals,' a lion, Hariv.; Pañcat. &c. **Mṛigâdhipatya**, n. 'dominion over wild animals,' Pañcat. **Mṛigâdhirāja**, m. = °dhipa, q.v., Ragh. **Mṛigântaka**, m. 'animal-destroyer,' a hunting leopard, L. **Mṛigârāti**, m. an enemy or pursuer of deer, a lion, Kathās.; a dog, L. **Mṛigâri**, m. 'enemy of wild animals,' a lion or tiger, Kathās.; a dog, L.; a species of Moringa with red blossoms, L. **Mṛigâvatī**, f. N. of Dākshāyaṇī on the Yamunā, Cat.; of sev. princesses, Kathās.; Rājat.; Inscr.; -caritra, n. N. of wk. **Mṛigâvidh** (or °gā-v°?), m. 'deer-killer,' a huntsman, L. **Mṛigâśana**, m. a lion, A. **Mṛigâshṭaka**, n. N. of wk. **Mṛigâsya**, mfn. having the face or head of a d°, VarBṛ.; m. the sign Capricorn, L. (cf. mṛiga-mukha). **Mṛigêkshaṇa**, n. a deer's eye, an eye like a deer's, Kāvyâd.; (ā), f. a fawn-eyed woman, VarBṛS.; coloquintida, L. **Mṛigêndra**, m. 'king of beasts,' a lion, Bhag.; Hariv.; R. &c.; the sign Leo, VarBṛS.; a tiger, MBh.; a partic. metre, Col.; a house lying to the south (?), L.; N. of a king, VP.; of an author, Sarvad.; (prob.) n. N. of Mṛigêndra's wk.; of a Tantra; -caṭaka, m. a falcon, L.; -tā, f. dominion over wild animals, Pañcat.; -mukha, n. a lion's mouth, MW.; a partic. metre, Col.; -vṛishabha, m. du. a lion and a bull, MW.; -svāti-karṇa, m. N. of a king, VP.; °râsana, n. 'lion's seat,' a throne, L. (cf. siṅhâs°); °râsya, mfn. lion-faced (N. of Śiva), Śivag.; °rôttara, n. N. of wk. **Mṛigêndrāṇī**, f. Gendarussa Vulgaris, L. **Mṛigêbha**, n. sg. an antelope and (or) an elephant, Mn. xii, 67. **Mṛig-'ervāru**, m. or n. (?) coloquintida, Suśr.; m. a species of animal, MW.; a white deer, W. **Mṛig-'ervāruka**, m. a species of animal dwelling in holes or caves, Suśr. **Mṛigêśa** or °śa-vara-varman, m. N. of a man, L. **Mṛigêśvara**, m. 'lord of beasts,' a lion, VarBṛS.; the sign Leo, VarBṛ. **Mṛigêshṭa**, m. a species of jasmine, L. **Mṛigâirvāru**, m. or n. coloquintida, Suśr. **Mṛigâirvāruka**, m. = mṛig-'erv°, q.v., Suśr. **Mṛigôttama**, m. best of antelopes, a very beautiful deer, R.; n. the Nakshatra Mṛiga-śiras, MBh.; °mâṅga, n. 'deer-head,' the Nakshatra Mṛiga-śiras, L. **Mṛigôdbhava**, m. musk, L. **Mṛigôpâkhyāna**, n. = mṛiga-vyādha-kathānaka.

Mṛigaṇā, f. seeking, research, L.

Mṛigaṇyú, mfn. hunting wild animals, RV. x, 40, 4.

Mṛigaya, m. N. of a demon conquered by Indra, RV.; (ā), f., see below.

Mṛigayás, m. a wild animal, RV. ii, 38, 7.

Mṛigayā, f. hunting, the chase (acc. with √aṭ, gam, car &c., dat. with √yā, nir-√yā and vi-√har, to go hunting), Mn.; MBh. &c.; Chase personified (as one of the attendants of Revanta), VarBṛS. **-krīḍana**, n., **-krīḍā**, f. the pleasure of hunting, Kām. **-dharma**, m. the law or rules of hunting, MBh. **-yāna**, n. the going out to hunt, hunting, Kām. **-°raṇya** (°yâr°), n. a hunting-forest, park, preserve, ib. (cf. mṛiga-kānana). **-rasa**, m. the pleasure of the chase, Vet. **-vana**, n. = -°raṇya, Kathās. **-vihāra**, m. = -krīḍā, Kāv.; mfn. = next, BhP. **-vihārin**, mfn. delighting in the chase, Śak. **-vesha**, m. a hunting-garment, ib. **-vyasana**, n. a hunting-accident, Kām. **-śīla**, mfn. devoted to the chase, addicted to hunting, Śak.

Mṛigayú, m. a huntsman, AV. &c. &c.; a jackal, L.; N. of Brahmā, L.

Mṛigava, m. or n. (?) a partic. high number, Buddh.

Mṛigavya, n. hunting, the chase, Rājat.; MārkP.; the butt or mark in archery, a target, W.

Mṛigāra, m. N. of the author of AV. iv, 23, 29, Anukr.; of a minister of Prasena-jit, Buddh.; n. (?) = next, Kauś. **-sûkta**, n. the hymns AV. iv, 23–29. **Mṛigārêshṭi**, f. N. of TS. iv, 7, 15 and (prob.) of AV. iv, 23–29; -paddhati, f., -prayoga, m., -hautra, n.; °ty-ādi-prayoga, m. N. of wks.

Mṛigita, mfn. chased, pursued, sought, searched for, L.

Mṛigī, f. (of mṛiga above) a female deer, doe. **-kuṇḍa**, n. N. of a Tīrtha, Cat. **-kshīra**, n. milk of a doe, Āpast. (cf. mṛiga-k°). **-tva**, n. the state or condition of a female deer or doe, MārkP. **-dṛiś**, f. a fawn-eyed woman, Bhartṛ.; Rājat. &c. **-pati**, m. 'husband of the woman called Mṛigī,' N. of Kṛishṇa, Pañcar. **-locanā**, f. = -dṛiś, q.v., Chandom.

Mṛigū, f. N. of the mother of Rāma Mārgaveya, AitBr. (Sāy.)

Mṛigya, mfn. to be hunted after or sought for or found out, Kāv.; Pur.; to be striven after or aimed at (a-m°), Kum.; to be investigated, questionable, uncertain, Vām.

मृच् 1. mṛic (cf. √marc), cl. 10. P. marcáyati (cl. 4. P. mṛicyati [?], JaimBr.; Prec. mṛikshīshṭa), to hurt, injure, annoy, RV.; AV.; GṛS.

Mṛiktá, mfn. hurt &c. (cf. á-mṛikta). **-vāhas** (mṛiktá-), m. (with Dvita Ātreya) N. of the author of RV. v, 18.

2. **Mṛic**, f. threatening or injury, RV. viii, 67, 9 (Sāy. 'a snare').

Mṛicaya, mfn. liable to destruction or decay, perishable, AitBr.

मृचय mṛic-caya &c. See under 1. mṛid, p. 830, col. 1.

मृछ् mṛich, cl. 6. Ā. mṛicchate, to pass away, perish, KaushUp.

मृज् 1. mṛij (cf. √marj, mārj and mṛiś), cl. 2. P. mārshṭi (Ved. also Ā. mṛishṭé and cl. 6. P. Ā. mṛijáti, °te, 3. pl. mṛiñjata, RV.; Pot. mṛiñjyāt, ŚBr.; cl. 1. P. Ā. mārjati, °te, MBh.; pf. mamārja, mamṛijé, AV. &c.; 3. pl. mamārjuḥ, MBh.; māmṛijuḥ, RV.; Ā. māmṛijé, °jīta, ib.; aor. amṛikshat, °shata, RV.; MBh.; amārkshīt and amārjīt, Br.; fut. mrashṭā, Br.; mārshṭā or mārjitā, Gr.; mrakshyate or mārkshyate, Br. &c.; mārjishyati, Gr.; inf. marshṭum, mārshṭum and mārjitum, MBh. &c.; ind. p. mṛishṭvā, AV.; -mṛijya, AV.; -mārjya, Kāv.), to wipe, rub, cleanse, polish, clean, purify, embellish, adorn (Ā. also 'one's self'), RV. &c. &c.; to make smooth, curry (e.g. a horse or other animal), RV.; to stroke, R.; to wipe off or out, remove, destroy, MBh.; Kāv. &c.; to wipe off or transfer (impurity, debt &c.) from one's self upon (loc.), AV.; to carry away, win, RV. i, 174, 4; (mārshṭi), to go, Naigh. ii, 14 (Nir. xiii, 3): Caus. or cl. 10. marjayati, °te (Ved., mārjayati, °te, Br. &c.; aor. amamārjat, Gr.; amīmṛijanta, Br.; Pass. mārjyate, Kāv.), to wipe, rub, cleanse, purify, adorn, RV. &c. &c.; to wipe off, remove, destroy, Yājñ.; Bhartṛ.; (marjayate), to move about, roam, RV. vii, 39, 3 (Sāy.): Desid. mimārjishati and mimṛikshati, Gr.: Intens. marmṛijiti (°jmá, °janta, p. °jānā), marmṛijyáte, RV.; AV.; marīmṛijyáte, Br.; marmārshṭi, Gr.; to rub or wipe off, clean, purify (Ā. also 'one's self'). [Cf. Gk. ὀ-μόργνυμι, ἀ-μέργω, ἀ-μέλγω; Lat. mulgere; Slav. mlěsti; Lith. mìlsti; Germ. melken, Milch; Eng. milk.]

2. **Mṛij** (ifc.), see dharma-mṛij.

Mṛija, mfn. (ifc.) wiping off, removing, destroying (in avadya-m°), BhP.; m. a kind of drum, L.; (ā), f., see next.

Mṛijā, f. wiping, cleansing, washing, purification, ablution, Hariv.; Naish.; purity, cleanliness, MBh.; Kāv.; a pure skin, clear complexion, Suśr.; complexion (= chāyā), VarBṛS. **-nagara**, n. N. of a town, Kshitîś. **-°nvaya** (mṛijânv°), mfn. possessing cleanliness, clean, Bhaṭṭ. **-vat**, mfn. possessed of cl°, MBh. **-varṇa-bala-prada**, mfn. causing a clear complexion, colour and strength, Suśr. **-vihīna**, mfn. destitute of cl°, uncleanly, unclean, R. **-hīna**, mfn. id., MBh. **Mṛijôpêta**, mfn. = mṛijā-vat, Pancar.

Mṛijita, mfn. wiped, wiped off, removed, BhP.

Mṛijya, mfn. to be wiped or wiped off or removed, Bhaṭṭ.

1. **Mṛishṭá**, mfn. (for 2. see p. 831, col. 1) washed, cleansed, polished, clean, pure (lit. and fig.), RV. &c. &c.; smeared, besmeared with (instr.), R.; Naish.; prepared, dressed, savoury, dainty, R.; Hariv.; Var. (cf. mishṭa); sweet, pleasant, agreeable, MBh.; Kāv. &c.; n. pepper, L. **-kuṇḍala**, mfn. wearing polished or bright earrings, BhP. **-gandha**, m. (prob.) an agreeable smell or savour, Suśr.; -pavana, m. a fragrant wind, VarBṛS. **-tama**, mfn. exceedingly delicate or savoury, Suśr. **-yaśas**, mfn. of pure glory or renown, BhP. **-luñcita**, mfn. torn up and washed (as a root), g. rāja-dantâdi. **-vat**, mfn. containing a form of √1. mṛij, ŚāṅkhŚr. **-vākya**, mfn. speaking sweetly, VarBṛS. (v.l. mishṭa-v°). **-śalāka**, prob. w.r. for ashṭa-śalāka, (an umbrella) having eight ribs, Hcat. **-salila**, mfn. having bright or pure water, MBh. **Mṛishṭânulepana**, mfn. smeared with ointment, R. **Mṛishṭâśana**, mfn. eating dainty food, Vishṇ., Sch. **Mṛishṭâśin**, mfn. id., Vishṇ.

1. **Mṛishṭi**, f. (for 2. see p. 831, col. 1) cleansing, preparation, dressing (of food), MaitrS.; Kāṭh.; a savoury repast, Mn. iii, 255.

Mṛishṭeruka, mfn. eating dainties or delicacies, luxurious, selfish, L.; liberal, L.

मृड् mṛiḍ (RV. mṛiḷ), cl. 6. P. (Dhātup. xxviii, 38) mṛiḍati (mṛiḷati; once Ā. mṛiḍase, Kāṭh.), cl. 9. P. mṛiḍnāti (xxxi, 44), cl. 10. mṛiḍayati (mṛiḷáyati), °te; mṛiṇḍayati (?), xxxii, 117 (pf. mamarḍa, Gr.; mamṛiḍyuḥ, RV.; aor. amarḍīt, Gr.; fut. marḍitā, °ḍishyati, ib.; inf. marḍitum, ib.; ind. p. mṛiḍitvā, Pāṇ. i, 2, 7), to be gracious or favourable, pardon, spare (with dat. of pers. and acc. of thing), RV. &c. &c.; to treat kindly, make happy, rejoice, delight (with acc.), BhP.: Caus. marḍayati (aor. amīmṛiḍat or amamarḍat), Gr.: Desid. mimarḍishati, ib.: Intens. marīmṛiḍyate, marīmartti, ib.

Mṛiḍa, mfn. showing compassion or mercy, gracious, Kāṭh.; ĀśvGṛ.; m. N. of Agni at the Pūrṇâhuti, Gṛihyas.; of Śiva, Śivag.; (ā or ī), f. N. of Pārvatī, L. °**ḍana**, n. showing comp°, pardoning, blessing, BhP. °**ḍaya**, see a-mṛiḍaya. °**ḍayat**, mfn. showing comp°, favouring (superl. °yát-tama), RV. °**ḍayāku**, mfn. merciful, kind, ib. °**ḍāku**, m. N. of a man, g. biḍâdi. °**ḍānī**, f. 'wife of Mṛiḍa or Śiva,' N. of Pārvatī, Kathās.; -kānta, m. 'P°'s loved one,' N. of Śiva, Bālar.; -tantra, n. N. of wk.; -pati and °nîśvara, m. 'P°'s lord,' N. of Śiva, Prab.; Gīt.; Hāsy. °**ḍitṛi**, mfn. one who shows compassion or favour, AV. (cf. marḍitṛi). °**ḍīká**, n. comp°, favour, RV.; N. of a Vāsishṭha (author of ix, 97, 25–27; x, 150), RAnukr.; N. of Śiva, L.; a deer, L.; a fish, L.

Mṛiḷaya, °ḷayāku, °ḷīka. See mṛiḍaya &c.

मृण् mṛiṇ (cf. √mṛī), cl. 6. P. (Dhātup. xxviii, 41) mṛiṇáti, to crush, smash, slay, kill, RV.; AV.; to thread, winnow, ŚBr.

Mṛiṇāla, n. (also m., g. ardharcâdi; and ī, f., MBh.; R.; cf. Uṇ. i, 117, Sch.) 'liable to be crushed,' the edible fibrous root of some kinds of lotus (f. according to some 'a smaller root'), a lotus-fibre, fibre attached to the stalk of a water-lily, MBh.; Kāv. &c.; n. the root of Andropogon Muricatus, L. **-kaṇṭha,** m. a partic. aquatic bird, Car. **-komala,** mfn. delicate like a lotus-fibre, Vikr. **-dhavala,** mfn. white like a l°-fibre, BhP. **-pattra,** n. sg. l°-fibre and leaves, Kāv. **-bhaṅga,** m. a bit of a l°-f°, Ragh. **-bhañjam,** ind. (with √*bhañj*) as if one were to break a l°-f°, Bālar. **-maya,** mf(*ī*)n. consisting of l°-f°s, Kād. **-latikā,** f. a l°-tendril or stalk, Kāv. **-vat,** mfn. possessing lotus-fibres, Śak. **-valaya,** m. or n. a l°-f° as a bracelet, ib. **-vallī,** f. = *-latikā*, Harav. **-sūtra,** n. (Kum.), **-hāra,** m. (Ratnāv.) a l°-f° as a necklace. **Mṛiṇālâṅgada,** n. = *mṛiṇāla-valaya*, Kathās. **Mṛiṇālâsava,** m. a decoction of lotus-fibres, Suśr.

Mṛiṇālaka, (ifc.) a lotus-root or fibre, Kathās.; (*ikā*), f., see next.

Mṛiṇālikā, f. id., Ratnāv.; N. of a woman, Vās., Introd. **-pelava,** mfn. as delicate as a lotus-fibre, Kum. **-maya,** mf(*ī*)n. consisting of lotus-fibres, Naish.; Kād.

Mṛiṇālin, m. a lotus, L.; (*inī*), f. a lotus plant or a group of lotuses, Ragh.; Kād.

मृण्मय *mṛiṇ-maya*, w.r. for *mṛin-m°*, col. 3.

मृत् *mṛit*, *mṛit-kaṇa* &c. See below.

मृत *mṛita* &c. See p. 827, col. 2.

मृतण्ड *mṛitaṇḍa*, m. N. of the father of the sun, L.; the sun, L. (cf. *mṛitâṇḍa*).

मृतामद *mṛitāmada*, m. blue vitriol, L.

मृतालक *mṛitālaka*, *mṛittāla* and °*laka*, n. a kind of loam or clay, L.

मृत्यव *mṛityava*, w.r. for *mṛit-paca*.

मृत्यु *mṛityu* &c. See p. 827, col. 3.

मृत्सा *mṛitsā*, *mṛitsna*. See col. 2.

मृद् 1. *mṛid* (cf. √*mrad* and *mṛid*), cl. 9. P. *mṛidnāti* (cl. 1. P. Ā. *márdati*, °*te*, MBh.; cf. Naigh. ii, 14; pf. P. *mamarda*, 3. pl. *mamṛiduḥ* or *mamarduḥ*, Ā. *mamṛide*, MBh.; aor. *amardīt*, Gr.; fut. *mardishyati*, °*te*, ib.; inf. *marditum*, MBh.; °*tos*, Br.; *-mradé*, ib.; ind. p. *mṛiditvā*, Pāṇ. i, 2, 7; *-mṛidya*, Br. &c.; *-mardam*, Kāv.), to press, squeeze, crush, pound, smash, trample down, tread upon, destroy, waste, ravage, kill, slay, MBh.; Kāv. &c.; to rub, stroke, wipe (e.g. the forehead), ib.; to rub into, mingle with (instr.), Suśr.; to rub against, touch, pass through (a constellation), VarBṛS.; to overcome, surpass, Bhaṭṭ.: Caus. *mardayati* (m.c. also °*te*; aor. *amīmṛidat* or *amamardat*), to press or squeeze hard, crush, break, trample down, oppress, torment, plague, destroy, kill, MBh.; Kāv. &c.; to rub, Kāv.; Kathās.; to cause to be trampled down, KātyŚr., Sch.: Desid. *mimardishati*, to desire to crush or pound, MBh.: Intens. *marmartti* (only Impv. °*ttu*, RV. ii, 23, 6), to crush, grind down, destroy; *marīmartti* and *marīmṛidyate*, Gr. [Cf. Gk. ἀ-μαλδ-ύνω and under *mṛidu*.]

3. **Mṛic,** in comp. for 2. *mṛid*. **-caya,** m. a heap of earth, KātyŚr., Sch. **-chakaṭikā** (for *śak*°), f. 'clay-cart,' N. of a celebrated Sanskṛit drama (supposed to be one of the oldest) by king Śūdraka; *-setu*, m. N. of a Comm. on it by Lallā-dīkshita. **-chilā-maya** (for *śil*°), mf(*ī*)n. made of clay and stone, Pañcar.

Mṛit, in comp. for 2. *mṛid*. **-kaṇa,** m. a small lump or clod of earth or clay (*-tā*, f.), Kāv. **-kara,** m. a worker in clay, potter, L. **-karman,** n. work in clay; °*ma-sampanna*, mfn. coated with clay, Car. **-kāṇsya,** n. an earthen vessel, L. **-kirā,** f. 'earth-scattering,' an earth-worm or kind of cricket, L. **-kshāra,** n. a radish, L. **-khana,** m. a clay-pit, ĀpŚr. **-khalinī,** f. a species of plant (= *carmakaśā*), L. **-toya,** n. pl. earth and water. **-paca,** m. 'clay-moulder,' a potter, MaitrUp. **-pātrá,** n. an earthen vessel, MaitrS. **-piṇḍá,** m. a clod of earth, lump of clay, ŚBr. &c.; *-tas*, ind. from a lump of clay, MBh.; *-buddhi*, m. 'clod-pated,' a fool, blockhead, Śak. **-prakshepa,** m. scattering earth over anything (for purification), Mn. v, 125. **-phalī,** f. Costus Speciosus or Arabicus, L. **-stoma,** m. a heap of earth, VarYogay., Sch.

Mṛittikā, f. earth, clay, loam, VS. &c. &c. (ibc. also *a*); a kind of fragrant earth, L.; aluminous slate, L. **-cūrṇa,** n. mould, powdered earth, L. **-vata,** n. (VP.), **-vatī,** f. (Kād.) N. of a town.

Mṛitsā, f. good earth or soil, Pāṇ. v, 4, 40; a kind of fragrant earth, L.; aluminous slate, L.

Mṛitsna, m. n. dust, powder, Suśr.; (*ā*), f., see next.

Mṛitsnā, f. clay, loam, BhP.; good earth or clay, excellent soil, Pāṇ. v, 4, 40; a kind of fragrant e°, L.; aluminous slate, Bhpr. **-bhāṇḍaka,** n. a partic. earthenware vessel, L.

2. **Mṛid,** f. earth, soil, clay, loam, VS. &c. &c.; a piece of e°, lump of clay, Mn. v, 136; a kind of fragrant e°, L.; aluminous slate, L. **-āhvayā,** f. a k° of frag° e°, L. **-ga,** m. being in the e°, growing in clay, Kāv. **-ghaṭa,** m. an earthen pot or pitcher, Pañcat. **-dāru-śaila,** mfn. made of clay or wood or stone, Hcat. **-bhāṇḍa,** n. a vessel of clay, earthenware; °*dâvaśesham*, ind. (to steal) so that only an earthen vessel is left, Daś.

Mṛidaṃga, m. (prob. fr. *mṛidam* + *ga*, 'going about while being beaten;' cf. *mardala* and Uṇ. i, 120, Sch.) a kind of drum, tabour, MBh.; Kāv. &c.; noise, din, L.; a bamboo cane, L.; (*ī*), f. a species of plant (= *ghoshātakī*), L. **-phala,** m. the bread fruit-tree, L.; n. Luffa Acutangula, Car. **-phalinī,** f. = *mṛidaṃgī*, L.

Mṛidaṃgaka, n. a species of metre, Piṅg., Sch.

Mṛidava, n. (in dram.) contrasting excellence or merit of any kind with demerit, Daśar.; Pratāp.

Mṛidā, f. clay, loam, earth, ŚvetUp. **-kara,** m. a thunderbolt, W.

Mṛidi, m. N. of a man (cf. *mārdeya*).

Mṛiditá, mfn. pressed, squeezed, crushed, broken, trampled down, laid waste, AV. &c. &c.; rubbed, Kāv.; Suśr.; rubbed off, wiped away, removed, destroyed, ChUp.; BhP. **-kukshika,** mfn. (with *dāva*) N. of a forest, Divyâv.

Mṛidinī, f. good earth or soil, L.

Mṛidishṭha, w.r. for *mradishṭha*.

Mṛidú, mf(*ú* or *vī́*)n. soft, delicate, tender, pliant, mild, gentle, VS. &c. &c.; weak, feeble, AV.; slight, moderate, Suśr.; slow (gait), MBh.; Kāv. &c.; (in astron.) situated in the upper apsis, Gaṇit.; m. the planet Saturn, VarBṛS.; N. of a king and various other men, VP. (cf. g. *bidâdi*); (*u*), f. Aloe Perfoliata, L.; (*vī*), f. a vine with red grapes, L. (cf. *mṛidvīkā*); n. softness, mildness, gentleness, MBh.; Kāv. &c. (also m., Pāṇ. ii, 2, 8, Vārtt. 3, Pat.) [Cf. Gk. βραδύς; Lat. *mollis*.] **-kaṇṭaka,** m. a kind of sheat-fish, L. **-karman,** n. = *mandak*°, n. (q.v.), Gol. **-kārshṇāyasa** (A.) or **-kṛishṇāyasa** (L.), n. 'soft-iron,' lead, L. **-kopa,** mfn. mild in wrath, of a gentle nature, VarBṛS. **-koshṭha,** mfn. having relaxed bowels, relaxed, Car. **-kriyā,** f. the act of softening, mollifying, Suśr. **-gaṇa,** m. = *-varga* below, L. **-gandhika,** m. a species of plant, Buddh. **-gamanā,** f. 'having a slow gait,' a goose, female swan, L. **-gātra-tā,** f. having soft limbs (one of the 80 minor marks of a Buddha), Dharmas. 84. **-gāmin,** mfn. going softly, having a soft or gentle gait, MBh.; MārkP.; (*inī*), f. = *-gamanā* above, L. **-gir,** mfn. soft-voiced, Mṛicch. **-granthi,** m. a species of grass, L. **-carmin,** m. Betula Bhojpatra, L. **-cāpa,** m. N. of a Dānava, Hariv. **-cāru-bhāshin,** mfn. emitting soft and sweet sounds, VarBṛS. **-cchada,** m. (only L.) Betula Bhojpatra; a species of Pilu tree; Blumea Lacera; a tree similar to the vine-palm; Amphidonax Karka; a species of grass, = *śilpikā*. **-jātīya,** mfn. somewhat soft, slightly weak, Pāṇ. vi, 1, 217, Sch.; APrāt., Sch. **-jihva-tā,** f. having a soft tongue (one of the 80 minor marks of a Buddha), Dharmas. 84. **-taruṇa-hasta-pāda-tala-tā,** f. having the palms and soles of the feet soft and tender (one of the 32 signs of perfection), Dharmas. 83. **-tā,** f. softness, tenderness, mildness, weakness (*-tām* √*gam* or √*vraj*, to become mild or weak), MBh.; Ragh. &c. **-tāla,** m. a species of tree related to the vine-palm, L. **-tīkshṇa,** mfn. mild and violent, gentle and harsh (*-tara*, mfn.), Mālav.; n. sg. the Nakshatras Kṛittikā and Viśākhā, VarBṛS. **-tva,** n. softness, tenderness, mildness, MBh.; R. &c. **-tvac,** m. Betula Bhojpatra, L.; Saccharum Munja, L. **-pattra,** m. 'soft-leafed,' a rush, reed, L.; (*ī*), f. a species of pot-herb of the nature of spinage, L. **-parusha-guṇa,** m. du. 'mild and harsh qualities,' mildness and harshness, Kāv. **-parvaka** or **-parvan,** m. 'soft-jointed,' a reed, cane, L. **-pāṇi,** mfn. having a delicate hand, W. **-pīṭhaka,** m. a kind of sheat-fish, Silurus Pelorius, L. **-pushpa** or °**paka,** m. Acacia Sirissa, L. **-pūrva,** mf(*ā*)n. 'beginning softly,' gentle, tender (as a speech), MBh.; (*am*), ind. softly, tenderly, ib.; R. **-prayatna,** mfn. (to be pronounced) with a slight effort, APrāt., Sch. **-priya,** m. N. of a Dānava, Hariv. **-prauḍha,** mfn. full of gentleness, MBh.; mild and haughty, MW. **-phala,** m. Flacourtia Sapida, L.; Asteracantha Longifolia, L.; a species of cocoa-nut tree, L. **-bhāva,** m. softness, mildness, HYog. **-bhāshin,** mfn. speaking sweetly (°*shi-tā*, f.), Vikr.; VarBṛS.; Daś. **-madhyā,** f. N. of a Mūrchanā, Saṃgīt.; of a Kshānti, Divyâv. **-madhyâdhimātra,** mfn. moderate, middling and (or?) excessive (*-tva*, n.), Yogas. **-mṛitsna,** mfn. consisting of soft or fine particles or atoms, Suśr. **-yuddha,** mfn. fighting lazily (*-tā*, f.), MBh. **-romaka** or °**man** (A.) or °**ma-vat** (L.), m. 'having soft hair,' a hare. **-latā,** f. a species of grass (= *śūlī*), L. **-lomaka,** m. = *-romaka*, q.v., L. **-varga,** m. the group of Nakshatras called *mṛidu* (viz. Anurādhā, Citrā, Revatī and Mṛiga-śiras), VarBṛS. **-vāc,** mfn. mild in speech, Mn.; VarBṛS. &c. **-vāta,** m. a gentle breeze, W. **-vid,** m. N. of a son of Śvaphalka, BhP. **-sārā,** f. Thespesia Populnea, L. **-sūrya,** mfn. (a day) on which the sun shines mildly, R. **-sparśa,** mf(*ā*)n. soft to the touch, MBh.; Kāv. **-hṛidaya** (*mṛidú-*), mfn. tender-hearted (superl. *-tama*), ŚBr. **Mṛidûcca,** n. the upper apsis of a planet's course, Gaṇit. **Mṛidûtpala,** n. Nymphaea Cyanea, L.

Mṛiduka, mfn. soft, tender, SaddhP.; (*a*), f. N. of an Apsaras, Kāraṇḍ.; (*am*), ind. softly, gently, tenderly, Lāṭy.

Mṛidura, m. a species of aquatic animal, Āpast. (= *makara*, Comm.); N. of a son of Śvaphalka, Hariv. (v.l. *mudara*); Pur. **-svana,** m. N. of an Asura, Hariv. (v.l.)

Mṛiduri, m., v.l. for *mṛidu-vid*, q.v., VP.

Mṛidula, mfn. soft, tender, mild, Kāv.; BhP.; Kuval.; m. Amyris Agallocha, L.; n. water, W.; a variety of aloe-wood, A.

Mṛidū, in comp. for *mṛidu*. **-√as,** P. *-asti*, to become or be soft, Pāṇ. vii, 4, 26, Sch. **-bhāva,** m. the becoming soft, Nir.; subsiding (of a fever), Car. **-√bhū,** P. *-bhavati*, to become soft, ŚārṅgP.

Mṛidv, in comp. for *mṛidu*, q.v. **-aṅga,** mf(*ī*)n. 'tender-limbed,' delicately formed, Mn.; Kathās.; (*ī*), f. a delicate woman, W.; n. tin, L. **-avagraha,** m. a partic. slight separation of the members of a compound, RPrāt.

Mṛidvīkā, f. a vine, a bunch of grapes (esp. a reddish one), Suśr.; VarBṛS. &c.

Mṛin, in comp. for *mṛid*. **-máya,** mf(*ī*)n. made of earth or clay, earthen, RV. &c. &c. (with *gṛihá*, n. the grave; with or scil. *pātra*, an earthenware vessel). **-mayaka,** mfn. id., Hcat. **-maru,** m. a stone, rock (?), L. **-māna,** used to explain *kūpa*, L. **-mūshā,** f. an earthenware crucible, Bhpr.

Mṛil, in comp. for *mṛid*. **-loshṭa,** n. a lump of clay, clod of earth, Mn. iv, 70.

मृदङ्कुर *mṛidaṅkura* or °*kuru*, m. Columba Hariola, L.

मृदङ्ग *mṛidaṅga* &c. See *mṛidaṃga*, col. 2.

मृदर *mṛidara*, m. 'a hole' or 'a disease,' Uṇ. v, 41; mfn. sportive, sporting, W.; passing quickly away, transient, ib.

मृदानी *mṛidānī*, w.r. for *mṛiḍānī*.

मृदु *mṛidu* &c. See col. 2.

मृदुन्नक *mṛidunnaka* (?), n. gold, L.

मृदुर *mṛidura*, °*dula*. See above.

मृध् 1. *mṛidh*, cl. 1. P. Ā. (Dhātup. xxi, 10) *márdhati*, °*te* (Ved. also cl. 6. P. Ā. *mṛidhati*, °*te*; aor. *mardhīs*, *mardhishát*, RV.; Pot. *mṛidhyās*, ib.), to neglect, forsake, abandon, RV.; GṛŚrS.; to be moist or moisten (*undane*), Dhātup.

Mṛiddhá, mfn. forsaken, helpless, MaitrS.

2. **Mṛidh,** f. fight, battle, RV. i, 174, 4 (Sāy.); a contemner, adversary, foe, RV.; VS.; Br.

Mṛidha, m. n. fight, battle, war, MBh.; Kāv. &c. **-bhū,** f. field of battle, Mcar.

Mṛidhas, n. disdain, contempt (only °*dhas*-√*kṛi*, to disdain, contemn, injure), RV.; fight, battle, L.

Mṛidhrá, n. contempt or one who contemns or injures, adversary, foe, RV. — **vāc** (*mṛidhrá-*), mfn. speaking injuriously or contumeliously, insulting, ib.

मृधा *mṛidhā*, ind. = *mṛishā*, L.

मृन्मय *mṛin-maya, mṛil-loshṭa.* See p. 830, col. 3.

मृळ् *mṛiḷ.* See √*mṛiḍ.*

मृश 1. *mṛiś* (often confounded with √1. *mṛish*), cl. 6. P. (Dhātup. xxviii, 131) *mṛiśáti* (rarely Ā. °*te*; pf. P. *mamarśa, mamṛiśuḥ*, MBh.; *māmṛiśuḥ*, RV.; Ā. *mamṛiśe*, Br.; aor. *ámṛikshat*, RV. &c.; *amārkshīt* or *amrākshīt*, Gr.; fut. *marshṭā, mrashṭā*, ib.; *markshyati, mrakshyati*, ib.; inf. *marshṭum*, MBh. &c.; *-mṛiśe*, RV.; ind. p. *-mṛiśya*, ib.; *-marśam*, Br.), to touch, stroke, handle, AV.; to touch mentally, consider, reflect, deliberate, BhP.: Intens. *marmṛiśat* (see *abhi-*√*mṛiś*), RV.; *marīmṛiśyate*(?), to seize, grasp, ŚBr. [Cf. Lat. *mulceo.*]

2. **Mṛiś** (ifc.) one who strokes or touches, MW.

Mṛiśita, mfn. See under *vi-*√*mṛiś.*

2. **Mṛishṭa,** mfn. (for 1. and 3. see under √*mṛij* and 3. *mṛish*) touched, W.

2. **Mṛishṭi,** f. (for 1. and 3. see ib.) touching, contact, W.

मृशय *mṛiśaya*, v. l. for *mṛicaya.*

मृशाखान *mṛiśākhāna*, v. l. for *mūśā-kh*°.

मृष 1. *mṛish* (often confounded with √1. *mṛiś*), cl. 4. P. Ā. (Dhātup. xxvi, 55) *mṛishyati*, °*te* (in RV. only Ā.; accord. to Dhātup. xvii, 57 also cl. 1. P. Ā. *marshati*, °*te*, cf. √3. *mṛish*; pr. p. *mṛishat*, BhP.; pf. *mamársha*, RV., *mamṛishe*, MBh. &c.; aor. *mṛishṭhās, mṛishantta*, RV.; *marshishṭhās*, ib.; *amṛishat*, MBh.; *amarshīt*, Gr.; fut. *marshitā*; *marshishyati*, °*te*, ib.; inf. *-mṛishe*, RV.; ind. p. *marshitvā, mṛishitvā* or *mṛishṭvā*, Gr.; *-mṛishya*, MBh.), to forget, neglect, RV.; MaitrS.; to disregard, not heed or mind, bear patiently, put up with (acc.), ŚBr. &c. &c.; to pardon, forgive, excuse, bear with (gen.), MBh.; to suffer, permit to (inf.), Daś.; to like (with *na*, dislike), MBh.: Caus. (or cl. 10, Dhātup. xxxiv, 40) *marshayati*, °*te* (aor. *amīmṛishat* or *amamarshat*), to cause to forget, MaitrS.; to bear, suffer, overlook, pardon, excuse, RV. &c. &c. (mostly with acc.; sometimes with Pot. or fut. or with Pot. after *yad, yac ca, yadi, yadā, jātu*, e. g. *na marshayāmi yat*—, I cannot endure that—; or with fut. after *kiṃ kila*, Pāṇ. iii, 3, 145 &c.); to put up with anything from (gen.), R.; (with *na*), not to let alone, molest, MBh.: Intens. *māmṛishat*, to bear, suffer, Kauś.

2. **Mṛish** (ifc.) one who bears or endures, bearing, MW.

Mṛíshā, ind. in vain, uselessly, to no purpose, RV. &c. &c.; wrongly, falsely, feignedly, lyingly, AV. &c. &c. (with √*kṛi*, to feign; with √*jñā* or *man*, to consider false or untrue; *mṛishâiva tat*, that is wrong; *varjanīyam mṛishā budhaiḥ*, untruthfulness is to be avoided by the wise); 'Untruth' personified as the wife of A-dharma, BhP. — **jñāna,** n. false knowledge, ignorance, folly, Kathās. — **tva,** n. incorrectness, falsity, Śaṃk. — **dāna,** n. 'false gift,' feigned or insincere promise of a gift, MBh. — **dṛishṭi,** mfn. having a false view or opinion, BhP. — **dhyānin** or **-dhyāyin,** m. 'feignedly meditative,' Ardea Nivea (a species of crane compared to a religious hypocrite), L. — °**nuśāsin** (*mṛishân*°), mfn. punishing unjustly, MBh. — **bhāshin,** mfn. speaking falsely, a liar, Rājat. — °**rtha** (*mṛishâr*°), mfn. having a false sense or meaning, untrue, absurd, Pracaṇḍ.; *-ka*, mfn. id., L.; n. an impossibility, absurdity (e.g. horn on a rabbit &c.), W. — **vacana,** n., **-vāc,** f. untrue speech, sarcasm, irony, Kāv. — **vāda,** m. id., MBh.; lying (with Buddhists one of the 10 sins), Dharmas. 56; mfn. = next, R. — **vādin,** mfn. speaking falsely, a liar, R.; m. a false accuser, W. — **sākshin,** mfn. false witness, L. **Mṛishôdya,** mfn. speaking untruthfully, a liar, L.; to be spoken falsely, uttered untruthfully, Śiś.; n. untrue speech, lying, a lie, Āpast.

Mṛishāya, Nom. Ā. °*yate*, to err, be mistaken, hold a wrong notion or opinion, BhP.

Mṛishita. See *apa-mṛishita.*

मृष 3. *mṛish* (cf. √1. *mṛish*), cl. 1. P. Ā. *marshati*, °*te*, to sprinkle, pour out, Dhātup. xvii, 57.

3. **Mṛishṭa,** mfn. (for 1. and 2. see under √*mṛij* and *mṛiś*) sprinkled, W.

3. **Mṛishṭi,** f. (for 1. and 2. see ib.) sprinkling, W.

मृषालक *mṛishālaka*, m. the mango tree, L.

मृष्ट *mṛishṭa, mṛishṭi.* See under √*mṛij*, *mṛiś* and 3. *mṛish.*

मॄ *mṝi* (cf. √*mṛi* and *mṛiṇ*), cl. 9. P. (Dhātup. xxxi, 22; 26) *mṛiṇāti* (Impv. *mṛiṇīhi*, AV.; Subj. *mumurat*, RV.; pf. *mamāra*, Gr.; aor. *amārīt*, ib.; Caus. aor. *ámīmṛiṇan*, AV.: Pass. *mūryáte*, ŚBr.), to crush, smash, break, kill, destroy, RV.; AV.; Br.

Mūrṇá, mfn. crushed, broken, AV.; Br.; = *mūta*, bound, tied, L.

मे 1. *me*, cl. 1. Ā. (Dhātup. xxii, 65) *mayate* (ep. also P. *mayati*; pf. *mame*, Gr.; aor. *amāsta*, ib.; fut. *mātā, māsyate*, ib.; ind. p. *-mitya* or *-māya*, ib.), to exchange, barter (cf. *apa-* and *ni-*√*me*): Caus. *māpayati*, ib.: Desid. *mitsate*, ib.: Intens. *memīyate, māmeti, māmāti*, ib.

मे 2. *me*, (onomat.) imitative of the sound of a bleating goat (*me-me-*√*kṛi*, to bleat), Kāv. — **nāda,** m. 'making the sound *me*,' a goat, L.; a cat, L.; a peacock, L.

1. **Meka,** m. a goat, L.

मेक 2. *meka.* See *su-méka*

मेकल *mekala*, m. N. of a mountain in the Vindhya, VP.; Harav.; (?) of a Ṛishi (father of the river Narma-dā), ib.; pl. of a people, MBh.; of a dynasty, VP.; (*ā*), f. N. of the river Narma-dā (Nerbudda), ib.; of a town, ib. — **kanyakā,** f. 'daughter of Mekala,' N. of the river Nar° (also *-kanyā*, L.); *-taṭa*, m. or n. N. of a district, Cat. — **prabhava,** mfn. arising or having its source in the M° mountain, Hariv. — **śaila,** m. the M° mountain, *-kanyā*, f. = *mekala-kanyakā*, Bālar. **Mekalâdri,** m. the M° mountain, *-jā*, f. N. of the river Narma-dā, L.

Mekalaka, m. pl. = *mekala*, N. of a dynasty, VP.

मेक्षण *mekshaṇa*, n. (√*miksh*) a wooden stick or spoon for stirring up the Caru (q.v.) or taking small portions from it, Br.; GṛŚrS.

मेखल *mekhala*, m. or n. a girdle, belt, R.; m. pl. N. of a people, VarBṛS. (prob. w. r. for *mekala*); (*ā*), f., see below. — **kanyakā,** f., w. r. for *mekala-k*°, L.

Mékhalā, f. a girdle, belt, zone (as worn by men or women, but esp. that worn by the men of the first three classes; accord. to Mn. ii, 42 that of a Brāhman ought to be of *muñja* [accord. to ii, 169 = *yajñôpavīta*, q.v.]; that of a Kshatriya, of *mūrvā*; that of a Vaiśya, of *śaṇa* or hemp, I. W. p. 240), AV. &c. &c.; the girth of a horse, Kathās.; a band or fillet, L.; (ifc., f. *ā*) anything girding or surrounding (cf. *sāgara-m*°); investiture with the girdle and the ceremony connected with it, VarBṛS.; a sword-belt, baldric, L.; a sword-knot or string fastened to the hilt, L.; the cords or lines drawn round an altar (on the four sides of the hole or receptacle in which the sacrificial fire is deposited), BhP.; the hips (as the place of the girdle), L.; the slope of a mountain (cf. *nitamba*), Kālid.; a partic. part of the fire-receptacle, Hcat.; Hemionitis Cordifolia, L.; N. of the river Narma-dā (prob. w. r. for *mekalā*), L.; of a place(?), Vās., Introd.; of various women, Viddh.; Kathās. — **dāman,** n. 'girdle-band,' a girdle, R. — **pada,** n. 'g°-place,' the hips, Kathās. — **paddhati,** f. N. of wk. — **bandha,** m. investiture with the g° and the rites connected with it, VarBṛS. — **maṇi,** m. the jewel on a g°, Kām. — **vat,** mfn. having a g°, wearing a fillet, KātyŚr. — **vin,** mfn. wearing a g°, APrāc., Sch. **Mekhalôttha,** mfn. (tinkling) produced by a girdle, Bhartṛ.

Mekhalāla, mfn. 'adorned with a girdle,' N. of Śiva-Rudra, Hariv. (Nīlak.)

Mekhalika, mfn. wearing a girdle, g. *vrīhy-ādi.*

Mekhalin, mfn. id. (ifc. = wearing a girdle of), MBh.; Hariv.; m. a Brāhmanical student or Brahmacārin, MBh. (gen. pl. °*līnām*, B.); N. of Śiva, Śivag.

Mekhalī-√1. **kṛi,** P. *-karoti*, to put on a girdle or sacred cord, MBh.; Kām.

मेघ *megha*, m. (fr. √*migh* = *mih*, cf. *meghamāna*) 'sprinkler,' a cloud, RV. &c. &c. (also = cloudy weather); a mass, multitude (see *gṛiha-m*°); Cyperus Rotundus, L.; (in music) a partic. Rāga, Col.; a Rākshasa (?), L.; N. of a king (pl. of a dynasty), VP.; of an author (= *-bhagīratha*), Cat.; of a poet, ib. (v. l. *meca*); of the father of the 5th Arhat of the present Avasarpiṇī, L.; of a mountain (cf. *-giri* and *-parvata*); n. talc, L. — **kapha,** m. 'cloud-lump,' hail, L. — **karṇā,** f. N. of one of the Mātṛis attending on Skanda, MBh. — **kāla,** m. 'cl°-time,' the rainy season, VarBṛS. — **kumāra-carita,** n. N. of a Jaina wk. — **kumāra-deva,** m. N. of a divine being, Siṇhās. — **kūṭâbhigarjitêśvara,** m. N. of a Bodhi-sattva, Lalit. — **gambhīra,** mfn. deep as (the rumbling of) a cloud, MBh. — **garjana,** n. or °**nā,** f. 'cloud-rumbling,' thundering, thunder, L.; °*na-vidhi*, m. N. of wk. — **garjita-ghosha-tā,** f. having a voice like the rolling of a cloud (one of the 80 minor marks of a Buddha), Dharmas. 84. — **giri,** see *mahā-m*°*-g*°. — **ṃ-kara,** mfn. producing cl°s, Bhaṭṭ. — **candra-śishya,** m. N. of an author, Cat. — **cintaka,** m. 'anxious for cl°s,' the Cātaka bird (supposed to drink only rain-water), L. — **jā,** mfn. 'cl°-born,' coming from cl°s (*-jam ambu*, rain), R.; m. a large pearl, W.; n. water, L. — **jāla,** n. 'cloud-collection,' a mass of clouds, thick clouds, L.; talc, L. — **jīvaka** or °**vana,** m. 'living on cl°s,' the Cātaka bird, L. — **jyotis,** n. 'cl°-light,' lightning, a flash of l°, L. — **ḍambara,** m. thunder, Kāv. (cf. *meghâḍ*°). — **taru,** m. 'cl°-tree,' a partic. form of cl°, VarBṛS. — **timira,** n. 'cl°-darkness,' darkness resulting from a clouded sky, cloudy or rainy weather, L. — **tva,** n. the being a cloud (*-tvam upa-*√*gam*, to become a cl°), MārkP. — **dīpa,** m. 'cloud-light,' lightning, L. — **dundubhi,** m. N. of an Asura, BhP.; *-nirghosha* (MBh.) or *-rāvin* (R.), mfn. roaring as a cl° or a kettle-drum; *-svara-rāja*, m. N. of a Buddha, Buddh. — **dūta,** m. 'cl°-messenger,' N. of a celebrated poem by Kāli-dāsa; *-pāda-samasyā*, f. N. of wk.; °*tâbhidha*, mfn. entitled 'cloud-messenger,' MW.; °*târtha-muktâvalī*, f., °*tâvacūri*, f. N. of wks. — **dvāra,** n. 'cl°-gate,' heaven, the sky, Cat. — **nāda,** m. 'cl°-noise,' thunder, MBh.; R.; mfn. sounding or rumbling like th°, R.; Inscr.; m. N. of Varuṇa, L.; Amaranthus Polygonoides, L.; Butea Frondosa, L.; N. of one of Skanda's attendants, MBh.; of a Dānava or Daitya, Hariv.; Virac.; of a son of Rāvaṇa (afterwards called Indra-jit), R.; Ragh.; Inscr.; of a man, Kād.; of a frog, Pañcat.; (*ā*), f. N. of a Yoginī, Hcat.; *-jit*, m. 'conqueror of Meghanāda or Indra-jit,' N. of Lakshmaṇa, L.; *-tīrtha*, n. N. of a Tīrtha, Cat.; *-maṇḍapa*, m. a kind of pavilion, Pañcad.; °*dânulāsaka* or °*sin*, m. 'rejoicing in the rumbling of clouds,' a peacock, L.; °*dâri*, m. N. of an author, Cat. — **nādin,** mfn. sounding like thunder, R.; crying (with joy) at the appearance of clouds, Hariv.; m. a car which rumbles, MBh.; N. of a Dānava, Hariv. — **nāman,** m. 'cl°-named,' Cyperus Rotundus, L. — **nirghosha,** m. the rumbling of cl°s, thunder, L.; mfn. sounding like thunder, MBh. — **nīla,** m. N. of a Gaṇa of Śiva, Harav. — **paṅkti,** f. a line or succession of cl°s, MW. — **patha,** m. 'path of cl°s,' atmosphere, A. — **parvata,** m. N. of a mountain, MārkP. — **pāli-tṛitīyā-vrata,** n. a partic. ceremony, Cat. — **pushpa,** n. 'cl°-blossom,' water, L.; a partic. medicinal plant, L.; river-water, L.; m. N. of one of the 4 horses of Vishṇu or Kṛishṇa, MBh.; Hariv.; BhP. — **pṛishṭha,** m. N. of a son of Ghṛita-pṛishṭha; n. N. of the Varsha ruled by him, BhP. — **pradīpa,** m. N. of wk. — **pravāha,** m. N. of one of Skanda's attendants, MBh. — **prasara** or **-prasava,** m. water, L. — **baddha,** m. a partic. mixture, Cat. — **bala,** m. N. of a man, Kathās. — **bhagīratha-ṭhakkura** and **-bhaṭṭa,** m. N. of authors, Cat. — **bhūti,** m. 'cl°-born,' a thunderbolt, L. — **mañjarī,** f. N. of a princess, Rājat. — **maṭha,** m. N. of a monastery or college, ib. — **maṇḍala,** n. 'cl°-sphere,' cl°-region, atmosphere, MW. — **maya,** mf(*ī*)n. formed or consisting of cl°s, Hariv.; Hcar. — **mallārikā,** f. N. of a Rāga, Saṃgīt. — **mārga,** m. = *-patha*, q.v., A. — **māla,** m. 'cl°-capped, crowned with cl°s,' N. of a mountain, BhP.; of a Rākshasa, R.; of a son of Kalki, KalkiP.; (*ā*), f. a line or succession or gathering of cl°s, MBh.; Kām.; N. of a Mātṛi attending on Skanda, MBh.; of sev. wks. — **mālin,** m. 'cloud-wreathed,' N. of one of Skanda's attendants, MBh.; of an Asura, Śatr.; of a king, Kathās. — **medura,** mfn. (darkness) dense with cl°s, Uttarar. — **modinī,** f. Eugenia Jambolana, L. — **yāti,** m. N. of a king, VP. — **yoni,** m. 'cl°-source,' smoke, fog, L. — **raṅgikā** or °**gī,** f. N. of a Rāga, Saṃgīt. — **ratha,** m. N. of a Vidyā-dhara, HPariś. — **rava,** m. 'cl°-noise,' thunder, MBh.; Hariv.; (*ā*), f. 'thundering like a cl°,' N. of a Mātṛi attending on Skanda, MBh. — **rāga**, m. (in music) N. of a Rāga, Saṃgīt. — **rāja**, m. N. of a Buddha, Lalit. — **rājī** (MW.) or °**jī** (Mālav.), f. a line of cl°s. — **rāva**, m. 'having a note like that of a cl°,' a kind of water-bird, Suśr.; Car. — **rekhā**, f. a line of cl°s, VarBṛS. — **latā**, f. N. of wk. — **lekhā**, f. = *-rekhā*, q. v., MBh. — 1. **-vat**, mfn. enveloped in cl°s, overcast with cl°s, Lalit.; m. N. of a mountain, VarBṛS. — 2. **-vat**, ind. like a cl°, MBh. — **vana**, m. or n.(?) N. of an Agra-hāra, Rājat. — **vapus**, n. 'cl°-body,' a mass of cl°s of any shape, MBh. — **varṇa**, mfn. having the hue of a cl°, MBh.; m. N. of a man, Cat.; of a crow, Pañcat.; Hit.; Kathās.; (*ā*), f. the indigo plant, L. — **vartman**, n. 'cl°-path,' the atmosphere, L. — **varsha**, m. N. of an author, Cat. — **vahni**, m. 'cloud-fire,' lightning, L. — **vāta**, m. wind with cl° or rain, Ratnāv. — **vāsas**, m. 'clad in cl°s,' N. of a Daitya, MBh.; Hariv. — **vāhana**, m. 'having cl°s for a vehicle,' N. of Indra, Śiś.; of Śiva, W.; of various kings, MBh.; Rājat.; of the 22nd Kalpa, Cat. — **vāhin**, m. 'producing clouds,' smoke, L.; (*inī*), f. 'riding upon a cloud,' N. of a Mātṛi attending on Skanda, MBh. (v. l. *mesha-v*°). — **vijaya**, m. N. of an author, Cat. — **vitāna**, m. n. 'cl°-canopy,' an expanded mass of cl°s, a sky overcast with cl°s, VarBṛS.; n. a partic. metre, Ked. — **visphūrjita**, n. the rumbling of cl°s, thundering, Chandom.; (*ā*), f. a partic. metre, Ked. — **vṛinda**, n. a mass of cl°s, MBh. — **vega**, m. N. of a man, MBh. — **veśman**, n. 'cl°-abode,' the sky, atmosphere, L. — **śyāma**, mfn. dark as a cl°, R.; Pañcar. — **sakha**, m. 'cl°-friend,' N. of a mountain, Hariv.; (*meghá-*), mf(*ā*)n. having a cl° for a friend, Suparṇ. — **saṃghāta**, m. an assemblage or multitude of cl°s, MBh. — **saṃdeśa**, m. = *-dūta*, q. v. — **saṃdhi**, m. N. of a king, MBh. — **sambhava**, m. 'cl°-produced,' N. of a Nāga, Buddh. — **sāra**, n. 'cloud-essence,' a kind of camphor, L. — **suhṛid**, m. 'cloud-friend,' a peacock (delighting in rainy weather), L. — **skandin**, m. the fabulous animal Śarabha, L. — **stanita**, n. 'cloud-rumbling,' thunder, MBh.; °*tôdbhava*, m. Asteracantha Longifolia, L. — **svanā**, f. 'sounding like a thunder-cl°,' N. of a Mātṛi attending on Skanda, MBh. — **svara**, °**ra-rāja**, m. N. of two Buddhas, Buddh. — **svāti**, m. N. of a king, Pur. — **hīna**, mfn. cloudless, without rain, Subh. — **hrit**, w. r. for *mesha-h*°, q. v., MBh. — **hrāda**, mfn. shouting or roaring like a thunder-cl°, MBh. **Meghâksha**, m. N. of a Persian king, Mudr. **Meghâkhya**, m., v. l. for prec. (in Prākrit *mehākkho*); n. Cyperus Rotundus, L.; talc, L. **Meghâgama**, m. 'approach of cl°s,' the rainy season, Rājat.; *-priya*, m. Nauclea Cordifolia, L. **Meghâcchanna** (MW.) or °**cchādita** (Pañcat.), mfn. overspread or covered with clouds. **Meghâṭopa**, m. 'cloud-mass,' a dense cloud, Kathās. **Meghâḍambara**, m. 'cl°-drum,' thunder, Cat. (cf. *megha-ḍamb*°). **Meghâdhvan**, m. 'cloud-path,' atmosphere, A. **Meghânandā**, f. 'rejoicing in cl°s,' a kind of crane, L. **Meghânandin**, m. 'rejoicing in clouds,' a peacock, L. (cf. *megha-suhṛid*). **Meghânayana**, n. N. of certain wks. **Meghânta**, m. 'coming at the end of the rainy season,' autumn, L. **Meghâbha**, m. 'resembling a cl°,' N. of a partic. kind of small Jambu, L. **Meghâbhyudaya**, m. N. of wk. **Meghârāva**, m., v. l. for *megha-rāva*, q. v., Car. **Meghâri**, m. 'cl°-enemy,' the wind, L. **Meghâloka**, m. the appearance or sight of cl°s, Megh. **Meghâvatata**, mfn. overspread with cl°s, overcast, Suśr. **Meghâvalī**, f. N. of a princess, Rājat. **Meghâsthi**, n. 'cl°-lump,' hail, L. **Meghâspada**, n. 'cl°-region,' the atmosphere, sky, L. **Meghêśvara-tīrtha**, n. N. of a Tīrtha, Cat. **Meghêśvara-nāṭaka**, n. N. of wk. **Meghôdaka**, n. 'cl°-water,' rain, Mṛicch. **Meghôdaya**, m. rising of cl°s, Nal.; Vikr. **Meghôdara**, w. r., L. **Meghôpala**, m. 'cl°-stone,' hail, L. **Meghônmukhya**, n. the looking up eagerly or longing for clouds (said of peacocks), Rājat.

Meghamāna. See √*mih*.

Meghaya, Nom. P. *meghdyati*, to make cloudy, cause cloudy weather (only pr. p.; see next).

Megháyat, mfn. making cloudy, TS.; (*antī*), f. N. of one of the 7 Kṛittikās, TS., Comm.; TBr.

Meghāya, Nom. Ā. °*yate* (= *megham karoti*, Pāṇ. iii, 1, 17), to form clouds, become cloudy (only p. dat. °*yaté*, °*yishyaté*, °*ghitāya*), TS.; to resemble clouds, rise like cl° (°*yita*, n. impers.), Hcat.; Dhanaṃj.

Meghya, mfn. being in a cloud, VS.; TS.; (ifc.) = *megham arhati*, g. *daṇḍâdi*; = *megha iva*, g. *śākhâdi*.

Maígha, mf(*ī*)n. descended from clouds, VS.; belonging to clouds, cloudy, MW.

मेङ्गनाथ *meṅga-nātha*, m. N. of various authors (also with *bhaṭṭa* and *sarva-jña*), Cat.

मेच *meca*, v. l. for *megha* (N. of a poet).

मेचक *mecaka*, mf(*ā*)n. dark-blue, black, MBh.; Kāv. &c. (in alg. applied to the 15th unknown quantity, Col.); m. dark-blue colour, blackness, L.; the eye of a peacock's tail, Mālatim.; a kind of gem, L.; smoke, L.; a cloud, L.; Moringa Pterygosperma, L.; (also n.) a teat, nipple, L.; n. darkness, L.; sulphuret of antimony, L. — **gala**, m. 'blue-necked,' a peacock and N. of Śiva, Harav. — **cātanī**, w. r. for *macaka-c*°. **Mecakâpagā**, f. 'dark-blue river,' N. of the Yamunā, L. **Mecakâbhidhā**, f. a species of creeper, L.

Mecakita, mfn. furnished with decorations which resemble the eyes of a peacock's tail, Hcat.; having a dark blue-colour, Kād.; Hcar.

मेचटिक *mecaṭika*, m. the smell of bad oil, L.; mfn. having the smell of bad oil, L.

मेचुरुदि *mecurudi* (?), N. of a place, Buddh.

मेट् *meṭ*, cl. 1. P. *meṭati*, to be mad, Dhātup. ix, 3 (v. l. *mreṭ* and *mleṭ*).

मेट *meṭa*, m. a whitewashed storied house, L.

मेटि *meṭi* and *meṭī*, v. l. for *methi* and *meḍhī*.

मेटुला *meṭulā*, f. the myrobolan tree, L.

मेठ *meṭha*, m. (cf. *meṇḍa*) an elephant-keeper, Hcar.; a ram, L.

मेठि *meṭhi* and *meṭhī*, v. l. for *meḍhī*, *methi*, and *methī*.

मेड् *meḍ*, cl. 1. P. *meḍati*, to be mad, Dhātup. ix, 4 (v. l. *mreḍ* and *mleḍ*).

मेडि *meḍí* or *melí*, m. crackling, roaring, sounding (said of wind, fire &c.), RV.; TS.; AV. (in Kāṭh. v. l. *meḍu*).

मेढ *meḍha*, m. an elephant-keeper, Gal. (cf. *meṭha*).

मेढी *meḍhī*, f. = *methi*, *methī*, q. v. — **bhūta**, mfn. being the central point round which everything turns, BhP.

मेढ्र *méḍhra*, n. or (L.) m. (fr. √1. *mih* + *tra*) membrum virile, penis, AV. &c. &c.; m. a ram, L. — **carman**, n. the fore-skin, prepuce, Suśr. — **ja**, m. N. of Śiva, MBh. — **tvac**, f. = *-carman*, Suśr. — **nigraha**, m. N. of wk. — **roga**, m. venereal disease, ib. — **śṛiṅgī**, f. Odina Pinnata (whose fruit is like a ram's horn), L.

Meḍhraka, m. the penis, L.; a ram, L.

Meṇḍha, m. a ram, L. **Meṇḍhaka**, m. id., L.; N. of a man, Buddh. **Meṇḍhra**, m. the penis, BhP.; a ram, L.

मेण्ठ *meṇṭha*, m. an elephant-keeper, HPariś.; N. of a poet (= *bhartṛi-m*°), Rājat.

मेण्ड *meṇḍa*, m. = *meṭha*, L.

मेतार्य *metārya*, m. (with Jainas) N. of one of the eleven Gaṇâdhipas, L.

मेतृ *métṛi*, m. (√1. *mi*) one who erects a column, builder, architect, RV. iv, 6, 2 (Sāy. *metā*, f. = *sthūṇā*, a column, pillar).

मेत्थित *metthitá*, mfn. (for *methita* fr. √*mith*?) associated, TBr.

मेथ् *meth*, strong form of √*mith*, q. v.

Methana, n. abusive speech, Vait.

मेथि *methí*, m. (perhaps fr. √1. *mi*) a pillar, post (esp. a pillar in the middle of a threshing-floor to which oxen are bound, but also any central point or centre), AV. &c. &c. (also *methī*, f.; v. l. *meḍhī*, *meḍhī*, *meṭhī*; *meḍhī-bhūta*, mfn. forming a solid pillar or centre, MBh.); a cattle-shed, AV. (*methī*, f., TāṇḍBr.); a prop for supporting carriage-shafts, AV. &c. &c. (also *methī*, f.) — **shṭha**, mfn. standing at the post to which cattle are bound, TS.

Methika, m. the 17th or lowest cubit (*aratni*) from the top of the sacrificial post, L.; (*ā*), f., see next.

Methikā or **methinī**, f. Trigonella Foenum Graecum, L.

Methī, f. id., Pañcad.

मेद् *med*, strong form of √*mid*.

1. **Meda**, m. fat (= *medas*), R.; Kām.; a species of plant (= *alambushā*), L.; a partic. mixed caste (the son of a Vaideha and a Kāravara or a Nishāda female, accord. to some 'any person who lives by degrading occupations'), Mn.; MBh. &c.; N. of a serpent-demon, MBh.; (*ā*), f. a root resembling ginger (said to be one of the 8 principal medicines), Suśr.; (*ī*), f., g. *gaurâdi*. — **kṛit**, n. 'fat-producer,' the flesh, Gal. — **ja**, m. 'fat-produced,' a kind of bdellium, L. — **pāṭa**, N. of a country, Uttamac. — **pāṭha**, m. N. of a branch of the Vatsa family, ib. — **bhilla** (?), m. N. of a degraded tribe, Col. — **śiras**, m. N. of a king, BhP. **Medôdbhavā**, f. a plant resembling ginger, L.

2. **Meda**, in comp. for *medas*. — **āhuti**, f. an oblation of fat, ŚBr.

Medaḥ, in comp. for *medas*. — **puccha** or **-pucchaka**, m. the fat-tailed sheep, Suśr. — **sāra**, mfn. one among whose Dhātus (q. v.) fat predominates, Var.; (*ā*), f. a species of medicinal plant, L.

Medaka, m. spirituous liquor used for distillation, Bhpr.; Car.

Médana, n. the act of fattening, RV. x, 69, 2.

Medaś, in comp. for *medas*. — **cheda**, m. the removal of fat (from the body), Śak.

Médas, n. fat, marrow, lymph (as one of the 7 Dhātus, q. v.; its proper seat is said to be the abdomen), RV. &c. &c.; excessive fatness, corpulence, ŚārṅgS.; a mystical term for the letter *v*, Up. — **kṛit**, n. 'fat-producer,' the body, flesh, L. — **tás**, ind. from the fat, VS. — **tejas**, n. 'strength of the Medas,' bone, L. — **piṇḍa**, m. a lump of fat, g. *kaskâdi*. — **vat** (*médas-*), mfn. possessed of fat, fat, AV.; TS. — **vin**, mfn. 'having Medas,' fat, corpulent, robust, strong, Śiś.; Suśr.

Medin, mfn. having Medas, possessing vigour or energy (= *medasā yukta* = *bala-vat*), Sāy.; m. 'one who is unctuous or sticks close(?),' a friend, companion, partner, ally, RV.; AV.; Br.; (*ī*), f., see next.

Medinī, f. 'having fatness or fertility,' the earth, land, soil, ground, TĀr.; MBh. &c.; a place, spot, Hariv.; a kind of musical composition, Saṃgīt.; Gmelina Arborea, L.; = *medā*, L.; N. of a lexicon (also *-kośa* or *medini-k*°). — **kara**, m. N. of the author of the Medinī-kośa, Cat. — **kośa**, m., see above. — **ja**, m. 'earth-born,' the planet Mars, VarBṛS. — **dāna**, n. N. of wk. — **dina**, n. a natural day, Gaṇit. — **drava**, m. dust, L. — **dhara**, m. 'earth-supporter,' a mountain, Bhām. — **nandana**, m. = *-ja*, Hāsy. — **pati**, m. 'earth-lord,' a king, prince, Rājat. — **śa** (°*nīśa*), m. id., ŚārṅgP.; *-tantra*, n. N. of a Tantra.

Medurá, mfn. fat, ŚBr.; Suśr.; smooth, soft, bland, unctuous, L.; thick, dense, thick like (comp.), Uttarar.; thick with, full of (instr. or comp.), Kāv.; (*ā*), f. a partic. medicinal plant, L.

Medurita, mfn. thickened, made dense by or with (comp.), Uttarar.; unctuous, MW.

Medo, in comp. for *medas*. — **gaṇḍa**, m. a kind of fatty excrescence, ŚārṅgS. — **gala**, m. a species of plant resembling the Mimosa Pudica, Bhpr. — **granthi**, m. a fatty tumour, Suśr. — **ghna**, mfn. destroying or removing fat, Suśr. — **ja**, n. 'produced by Medas,' bone, L. — **dosha**, m. excessive fatness, corpulency, ŚārṅgS. — **dharā**, f. a membrane in the abdomen containing the fat, the omentum, ib. — **bhava**, n. = *-ja*, Bhpr.; (*ā*), f. = *-vatī*, L. — **rūpa** (*médo-*), mfn. appearing as fat, TS. — **roga**, m. = *-dosha*, Suśr. — **'rbuda**, n. a fatty tumour unattended with pain, W. — **vatī**, f. a species of plant resembling ginger, Bhpr. — **vaha**, n. a vessel conveying fat, a lymphatic, W. — **vṛiddhi**, f. corpulence, ib.; enlargement of the scrotum, ib.

Medya, mfn. fat, thick, consistent, Suśr.

मेध् *medh*, strong form of √*midh*.

Médha, m. the juice of meat, broth, nourishing or strengthening drink, RV.; ŚBr.; KātyŚr.; marrow (esp. of the sacrificial victim), sap, pith, essence, AV.; TS.; Br.; a sacrificial animal, victim, VS.; Br.; ŚrS.; an animal-sacrifice, offering, oblation, any sacrifice (esp. ifc.), ib.; MBh. &c.; N. of the reputed author of VS. xxxiii, 92, Anukr.; of a son of

Priya-vrata (v.l. *medhas*), VP.; (*ā*), f., see below; mfn., g. *pacâdi*. **-ja**, m. 'sacrifice-born,' N. of Vishṇu, MBh. **-jit**, see *medhā-jit*. **-pati** (*médha-*, TBr.; *medhá-*, RV.), m. lord of sacrifice. **-sāti** (*medhá-*), f. the receiving or offering of the oblation, sacrificial ceremony, RV. (Sāy.; others 'the offering of devotion, service or worship of the gods;' others 'the gaining or deserving of a reward or praise'). **Medhâtithi**, m. N. of a Kāṇva (author of RV. i, 12-23, viii, 1 &c.), RV. viii, 8, 20; of the father of Kaṇva, MBh.; R.; of a son of Manu Svāyambhuva, Hariv.; of one of the 7 sages under Manu Sāvarṇa, ib.; of a son of Priya-vrata, Pur.; (also with *bhaṭṭa*) of a lawyer and commentator on the Mānava-dharma-śāstra, Kull. on Mn. ix, 125 (IW. 303); of a river, MBh.; a parrot, L.

Medhayú, mfn. eager for war, RV. iv, 38, 3 (others 'desirous of reward or praise').

Médhas, n. = *medha*, a sacrifice, ŚBr.; ŚāṅkhŚr.; m. N. of a son of Manu Svāyambhuva, Hariv.; of a son of Priya-vrata (v.l. *medha*), VP.; (ifc.) = *medhā*, intelligence, knowledge, understanding.

Medhasa, m. N. of a man, Cat.

Medhā́, f. mental vigour or power, intelligence, prudence, wisdom (pl. products of intelligence, thoughts, opinions), RV. &c. &c.; Intelligence personified (esp. as the wife of Dharma and daughter of Daksha), MBh.; R.; Hariv.; Pur.; a form of Dākshāyaṇī in Kaśmīra, Cat.; a form of Sarasvatī, W.; a symbolical N. of the letter *dh*, Up.; = *dhana*, Naigh. ii, 10. **-kāma**, mfn. wishing intelligence to or for (gen.), MānGṛ. **-kārá**, mfn. causing or generating intel°, RV. **-kṛit**, mfn. id.; m. a species of culinary plant, L. **-cakra**, m. N. of a king, Rājat. **-janana**, mfn. generating intel° or wisdom, MBh.; n. N. of a rite (and of its appropriate sacred text) for producing mental and bodily strength in a new-born child or in a youth, GṛŚrS. **-jit**, m. N. of Kātyāyana, L. (v.l. *medha-jit*). **-°tithi**, see under *medha*. **-dhṛiti** or **-mṛiti**, m. N. of a Ṛishi in the 9th Manv-antara. **-rudra**, m. N. of Kālidāsa, L. **-vat**, mfn. possessing wisdom, intelligent, wise, Pāṇ. v, 2, 121, Sch.; (*atī*), f. a species of plant, L.; N. of a woman, Kathās. **-vara**, m. N. of a man, ib. **-vin**, mfn. = *-vat*, AV. &c. &c.; m. a learned man, teacher, Pandit, L.; a parrot, L.; an intoxicating beverage, L.; N. of Vyāḍi, L.; of a Brāhman, MBh.; of a king, son of Su-naya (Su-tapas) and father of Nṛipaṃ-jaya (Puraṃ-jaya), VP.; of a son of Bhavya and (n.) of a Varsha named after him, MārkP.; (*inī*), f. N. of the wife of Brahmā, L.; Turdus Salica, L.; a species of Jyotish-matī, L.; *-vi-ka*, n. N. of a Tīrtha, MBh.; *-vi-tā*, f. cleverness, judiciousness, Var.; *-vi-rudra*, m. N. of an author, Cat. **-sûkta**, n. N. of a partic. Vedic hymn.

Medhin. See *griha-medhin*.

Médhira, mfn. (fr. *medhā*) intelligent, wise (said of Varuṇa, Indra, Agni &c.), RV.

Medhishṭha and **medhīyas**, mfn. (superl. and compar. of *medhā vin*) wisest, wiser, Vop.

Médhya, mf(*ā*)n. (fr. *medha*) full of sap, vigorous, fresh, mighty, strong, AV.; fit for a sacrifice or oblation, free from blemish (as a victim), clean, pure, not defiling (by contact or by being eaten), Br.; Mn.; MBh. &c.; (fr. *medhā*), wise, intelligent, RV.; AV.; VS.; = *medhām arhati*, g. *daṇḍâdi*; m. a goat, L.; Acacia Catechu, L.; Saccharum Munja, L.; barley, L.; N. of the author of RV. viii, 53; 57; 58, Anukr.; (*ā*), f. N. of various plants (thought to be sacrificially pure), L.; the gall-stone of a cow (= *rocanā*), L.; a partic. vein, Pañcar.; N. of a river, MBh. **-tama**, mfn. most pure, purest, Mn. i, 92. **-tara**, mfn. more pure, purer, ib. **-tā**, f. (MārkP.), **-tvá**, n. (TS.; TBr.) ritual purity. **-mandira**, m. N. of a man, Cat. **-maya**, mf(*ī*)n. consisting of pure matter, BhP. **Medhyâtithi**, m. N. of a Ṛishi (a Kāṇva and author of RV. viii, 1, 3-29; 3, 33; ix, 41-43), Anukr. (cf. *medhâtithi* and *maidhyātitha*).

मेधि *medhi*. See *methi*.

Medhī, f. (cf. *methi*) a partic. part of a Stūpa, Divyâv.

मेन *mena*, m. N. of Vṛishaṇ-aśva (father of Menakā or Menā), ShaḍvBr.; (*ā*), f., see below.

Menakā, f. N. of the daughter of Vṛishaṇ-aśva, ShaḍvBr.; of an Apsaras (wife of Hima-vat), MBh.; Kāv. &c. **-°tmajā** (°*kâtm*°), f. 'daughter of M°,' N. of Pārvatī, L. **-prâṇêśa**, m. 'husband of M°,' N. of Hima-vat, L. **-hita**, n. N. of a Rāsaka (kind of drama), Sāh.

Ménā, f. a woman (also the female of any animal), RV.; speech (= *vāc*), Naigh. i, 11; N. of the daughter of Vṛishaṇ-aśva, RV. i, 51, 13 (Sāy.); of an Apsaras (= *menakā*, wife of Hima-vat and mother of Pārvatī), Hariv.; R.; Pur.; of a river, MBh. **-jā**, f. 'daughter of M°,' N. of Pārvatī, L. **-dhava**, m. 'husband of M°,' N. of Hima-vat, L.

Menilā, f. N. of a princess, Rājat.

Menula, m. N. of a man, Pravar.

मेनाद *me-nāda*. See 2. *me*.

मेनि *mení*, f. (√*mī*) a missile weapon, thunderbolt, RV.; AV.; Br. (others 'wrath,' 'vengeance,' 'punishment'); speech (= *vāc*), Naigh. i, 11 (v.l. for *menā*).

मेन्धिका *mendhikā* or *mendhī*, f. Lawsonia Alba (a plant used for dyeing), L.

मेप् *mep*, cl. 1. P. *mepati*, to go, Dhātup. x, 9.

मेब् *meb*, v.l. for √*mev*.

मेम *mema*, m. or n. (?) a partic. high number, Buddh.

मेमिष *memisha*, mfn. (fr. Intens. of √1. *mish*) opening the eyes wide, staring (in *âti-m*°), TBr.

मेम्यत् *memyat*. See √2. *mā*.

मेय *méya*, mfn. (√3. *mā*) to be measured, measurable, discernible, AV.; Mn.; MBh. &c.

मेरक *meraka*, m. or n. a seat covered with bark, Divyâv.; N. of an enemy of Vishṇu, L.

मेरण्डु *meraṇḍu* (?) = *melândhu*, an inkstand, Karaṇḍ.

मेरु *meru*, m. (Uṇ. iv, 101) N. of a fabulous mountain (regarded as the Olympus of Hindū mythology and said to form the central point of Jambu-dvīpa; all the planets revolve round it and it is compared to the cup or seed-vessel of a lotus, the leaves of which are formed by the different Dvīpas, q.v.; the river Ganges falls from heaven on its summit, and flows thence to the surrounding worlds in four streams; the regents of the four quarters of the compass occupy the corresponding faces of the mountain, the whole of which consists of gold and gems; its summit is the residence of Brahmā, and a place of meeting for the gods, Ṛishis, Gandharvas &c.; when not regarded as a fabulous mountain, it appears to mean the highland of Tartary north of the Himâlaya), MBh.; Kāv. &c.; a partic. kind of temple, VarBṛS.; the central or most prominent bead in a rosary, L.; the most prominent finger-joint in partic. positions of the fingers, L.; N. of the palace of Gāndhārī (one of the wives of Kṛishṇa), Hariv.; of a Cakra vartin, L.; (with *śāstrin*) of a modern teacher, Cat.; of another man, Rājat.; f. N. of the wife of Nābhi and mother of Ṛishabha, VP. (cf. *-devī*). **-kalpa**, m. N. of a Buddha, Buddh. **-kūṭa**, m. n. the summit of Meru, MBh.; m. N. of a Buddha, Buddh. **-gaṇḍa**, m. pl. N. of a mountain range near M°, L. **-candra-tantra**, n. and **-tantra**, n. N. of a Tantra. **-tuṅga**, m. N. of a Jaina, Cat. **-duhitṛi**, f. a daughter of the mountain M°, Pāṇ. vi, 3, 70, Vārtt. 9, Pat.; a d° of M° (wife of Nābhi), BhP. **-dṛiśvan**, mfn. one who has seen or visited M°, Pāṇ. iii, 2, 94, Sch. **-devī**, f. N. of a daughter of M° (wife of Nābhi and mother of Ṛishabha, who was an incarnation of Vishṇu), BhP. **-dhāman**, mfn. having M° for a habitation (said of Śiva), MBh. **-dhvaja**, m. N. of a king, Kathās. **-nanda**, m. N. of a son of Sva-rocis, MārkP. **-parvata**, m. the mountain M°, MW. **-putrī**, f. a daughter of the mountain M°, Pāṇ. vi, 3, 70, Vārtt. 9, Pat. **-pṛishṭha**, n. the summit of M°, Hariv.; heaven, the sky, L. **-prabha**, n. 'shining like M°,' N. of a forest, Hariv. **-prastāra**, m. a partic. representation of all the possible combinations of a metre in such a form as to present a fancied resemblance to mount M°, AgP. **-bala-pramardin**, m. N. of a king of the Yakshas, Buddh. **-bhūta**, m. pl. N. of a people, MBh. **-mandara**, m. N. of a mountain, Pur. **-mahī-bhṛit**, m. mount M°, MW. **-yantra**, n. (in math.) a figure shaped like a spindle, Col. **-vardhana**, m. N. of a man, Rājat. **-varsha**, n. N. of a Varsha, MārkP. **-viraha-tantre bhuvanêśvarī-sahasra-nāma-stotra**, n. N. of a Stotra. **-vraja**, n. N. of a city, MBh. **-śikhara-dhara-kumāra-bhūta**, m. N. of a Bodhi-sattva, Buddh. **-śṛiṅga**, n. the summit of M°, heaven, Gal. **-śrī**, f. N. of a serpent-maiden, Kāraṇḍ.; *-garbha*, m. N. of a Bodhi-sattva, Buddh. **-sarshapa**, m. du. mount Meru and a mustard-seed, MBh. **-sāvarṇa**, m. a general N. for the last 4 of the 14 Manus (*-tā*, f.), Hariv. **-sāvarṇi**, m. id. (*-tā*, f.), ib.; VP.; N. of the 11th Manu, VP. **-susambhava**, m. N. of a king of the Kumbhâṇḍas, Buddh. **Merv-adri-karṇikā**, f. 'having mount Meru for a seed-vessel,' the earth, L.

Meruka, m. fragrant resin, incense, L.; m. or n. (?) N. of a people or country, VarBṛS.

मेरुटू *meruṭū*, (prob. f.) a partic. high number, Buddh. (also *merudu*).

मेरुण्डा *meruṇḍā*, prob. w.r. for *bheruṇḍā*.

मेल *mela*, m. (√*mil*) meeting, union, intercourse, Kāv.; Kathās.; (*ā*), f., see below.

Melaka, m. id., Kāv.; Pañcat. (°*kaṃ* √*kṛi*, to assemble together); conjunction (of planets, in *graha-m*°), Sūryas. **-lavaṇa**, n. a kind of salt, L.

Melana, n. meeting, union, junction, association, Kathās.

Melā, f. an association, assembly, company, society, Pañcat.; a musical scale, Cat. (perhaps *mela*, m.); a partic. high number, Buddh.; any black substance used for writing, ink, L.; antimony, eye-salve, L.; the indigo plant, L. **-nanda**, m. (and *ā*, f.) an ink-bottle, L. (cf. *-mandā*); °*dāya*, Nom. Ā. °*yate*, to become an ink-bottle, Vās. **-°ndhu** or **-°ndhuka** (*melândh*°), an ink-bottle, L. **-maṇi**, m. f. ink, L. **-mandā**, f. an ink-bottle, L. **-°mbu** (*melâmbu*), n. ink, L.

Melāpaka, m. (fr. Caus.) uniting, bringing together, KātyŚr., Sch.; conjunction (of planets), Cat.

Melāyana, n. conjunction, Cat. (perhaps w.r. for prec.)

मेलु *melu* or *meluda*, N. of two high numbers, Buddh.

मेव् *mev*, cl. 1. Ā. *mevate*, to worship, serve, Dhātup. xiv, 34.

मेवार्य *mevārya*, w.r. for *metārya*, q.v.

मेशिका *meśikā*. See *kāla-m*°.

मेशी *méśī*, f. (v.l. *meshī*) N. of water in a partic. formula, TS.

मेष *meshá*, m. (√2. *mish*) a ram, sheep (in the older language applied also to a fleece or anything woollen), RV. &c. &c.; the sign of the zodiac Aries or the first arc of 30° in a circle, Sūryas.; Var.; BhP.; a species of plant, Suśr.; N. of a partic. demon, L. (cf. *nejam*°); (*ā*), f. small cardamoms, L.; (*ī*), f. (cf. *méśī*) a ewe, RV.; VS.; Kauś.; Nardostachys Jatamansi, L.; Dalbergia Ougeinensis, L. **-kambala**, m. a sheep's fleece serving for an outer garment, a woollen rug or blanket, L. **-kusuma**, m. Cassia Thora, L. **-carman**, n. a sheep-skin, Rājat. **-pāla** or **-pālaka**, m. a shepherd, MW. **-pushpā**, f. a species of plant, L. **-māṇsa**, n. the flesh of sheep, mutton, MW. **-yūtha**, n. a flock of sheep, Pañcat. **-locana**, m. Cassia Thora, Bhpr. **-vallī**, f. Odina Pinnata, L. **-vāhinī**, f. 'riding on a ram,' N. of a Mātṛi attending on Skanda, MBh. (v.l. *megha-v*°). **-vishaṇikā**, f. Odina Pinnata, L. **-vṛishaṇa**, m. du. a ram's testicles, R.; mfn. having a ram's t°, ib. **-śṛiṅga**, m. a species of tree, MBh.; Suśr.; a species of poisonous plant, L.; (*ī*), f. Odina Pinnata or Gymnema Sylvestre, L. **-saṃdhi**, w.r. for *megha-s*°. **-hṛit**, m. N. of a son of Garuḍa, MBh. **Meshâkshi-kusuma**, m. Cassia Thora, L. **Meshâṇḍa**, m. 'having ram's testicles,' N. of Indra, L. **Meshânana**, mfn. ram-faced, Suśr.; N. of a demon noxious to children, Cat. **Meshântrī**, f. Argyreia Speciosa or Argentea, L. **Meshâlu**, m. a species of plant, L. **Meshâsya**, mfn. ram-faced, Suśr. **Meshâhvayā**, f. Cassia Thora, L.

Meshaka, m. a species of vegetable, L. (cf. *jīva-m*°); (*ikā*), f. a ewe, L.

Meshāya, Nom. Ā. °*yate*, to act like a ram (°*yita*, mfn. acting like a ram), BhP.

मेषूरण **meshūraṇa**, n. (Gk. μεσουράνημα) N. of the 10th astrological house, VarBṛS.

मेष्क **meshka**, m. a partic. beast of prey, ĀpŚr.

मेह **meha**, m. (√*mih*) urine (*meham* √*kṛi*, to make water), Br. (cf. *á-meha*); MārkP.; urinary disease, excessive flow of urine, diabetes, Suśr.; a ram (= *mesha*), L. — **ghnī**, f. 'curing diabetes,' Indian saffron, L. — **pāṭa**, m. or n. N. of a place, Cat. (cf. *meda-p*°). — **mudgara-rasa**, m. a partic. mixture serving as remedy against urinary disease, L. — **vat**, mfn. suffering from ur° d°, Hcat.

Mehatnū, f. N. of a river, RV.

Méhana, n. membrum virile, RV. &c. &c.; the urinary duct, AV.; urine, Suśr.; the act of passing ur°, W.; copulation, L.; m. Schrebera Swietenioides, L.; (*ā*), f. = *mahilā*, L.

Mehánā, ind. in streams, abundantly, RV. — **vat** (*mehánā-*), mfn. bestowing abundantly, ib.

Mehala, m. the smell of urine, L.; mfn. having the smell of urine, L.

Mehin, mfn. (only ifc.) voiding urine, making water; suffering from a partic. urinary disease (cf. *ikshu-*, *udaka-*, *geha-*, *nīla-m*° &c.); m. a species of small tiger or panther, L.

मैघ **maigha**. See p. 832, col. 2.

मैण्मिण्य **maiṇmiṇya**, n. = *miṇmiṇa-tva*, Car.

मैत्र **maitrá**, mf(*ī*)n. (fr. *mitra*, of which it is also the Vṛiddhi form in comp.) coming from or given by or belonging to a friend, friendly, amicable, benevolent, affectionate, kind, Mn.; MBh. &c.; belonging or relating to Mitra, VS. &c. &c.; m. 'friend of all creatures,' a Brāhman who has arrived at the highest state of human perfection, L.; a partic. mixed caste or degraded tribe (the offspring of an out-caste Vaiśya; cf. *maitreyaka*), Mn. x, 23; (scil. *saṃdhi*) an alliance based on good-will, Kām.; a friend (= *mitra*), Pāṇ. v, 4, 36, Vārtt. 4, Pat.; N. of the 12th astrol. Yoga, Col.; the anus, Kull. on Mn. xii, 72; a man's N. much used as the N. of an imaginary person in giving examples in gram. and philos. (cf. *Caitra* and Lat. *Caius*); N. of an Āditya (= *mitra*), VP.; of a preceptor, Cat.; (*ī*), f., see below; n. (ifc. *ā*) friendship, ŚBr. &c. &c.; a multitude of friends, MBh. (Nīlak.); = *-nakshatra*, Sūryas.; an early morning prayer addressed to Mitra, BhP.; evacuation of excrement (presided over by Mitra; *maitram* √1. *kṛi*, to void excr°), Mn. iv, 152; = *-sūtra*. — **kanyaka**, m. N. of a man, Buddh. — **citta**, n. benevolence, Kāraṇḍ.; mfn. benevolent, kind, Lalit. — **tā**, f. friendship, benevolence, L. — **nakshatra**, n. the Nakshatra Anurādhā (presided over by Mitra), MBh. — **bala**, m. N. of a man, Jātakam. — **bha**, n. = *-nakshatra*, L. — **vardhaka**, mfn. (fr. *mitra-v*°), g. *dhūmâdi*. — **vardhraka**, mfn. (fr. *mitra-v*°), ib. (v. l.) — **śākhā**, f. N. of a school, Cat. — **sūtra**, n. N. of a Sūtra. **Maitrâksha-jyotika**, m. N. of a partic. class of evil beings, Mn. xii, 72. **Maitrābārhaspatyá**, mfn. belonging to Mitra and Bṛihas-pati, ŚBr. 1. **Maitrâyaṇa**, n. (for 2. see below) 'kind or friendly way,' benevolence, MBh. **Maitrāvaruṇá**, mf(*ī*)n. descended from Mitra and Varuṇa, belonging to them, AV.; TS.; VS.; Br.; relating to the priest called Maitrāvaruṇa, PañcavBr.; m. a patr., RV. vii, 33, 11 (of Agastya or of Vālmīki, L.; *ī*, f., ŚBr.); N. of one of the officiating priests (first assistant of the Hotṛi), Br.; ŚrS.; *-camasīya*, mfn. being in the cup of this priest, ĀpŚr.; *-prayoga*, m., *-śastra*, n., *-śruti*, f., *-soma-prayoga*, m., *-hautra*, n. N. of wks.; °*ṇi*, m. a patr. of Mānya or Agastya, RAnukr.; MBh.; of Vasishṭha, ib.; of Vālmīki, Uttarar.; °*ṇīya*, mfn. relating to the priest called Maitrāvaruṇa, ŚāṅkhBr.; n. his office, Siddh.

Maitraka, m. a person who worships in a Buddhist temple, L.; n. friendship, Uttarar.

Maitrāya, P. *-yati*, to be kind or friendly, Divyâv.

2. **Maitrāyaṇa**, m. (for 1. see under *maitra*) patr. fr. *mitra*, g. *naḍâdi*; pl. N. of a school (called after Maitri), MaitrUp., Introd.; (*ī*), f., see below. — **gṛihya-paddhati**, f. N. of wk. **Maitrāyaṇôpanishad**, f. = *maitry-up*°.

Maitrāyaṇaka, mfn. (fr. 2. *maitrāyaṇa*), g. *arīhaṇâdi*.

Maitrāyaṇi, m. N. of Agni, MānGṛ.; N. of an Upanishad (prob. w. r. for °*ṇī*).

Maitrāyaṇī, f. of 2. *maitrāyaṇa*, q. v.; N. of the mother of Pūrṇa, Buddh.; of a female teacher, Col. — **pariśishṭa**, n. N. of wk. — **putra**, m. metron. of Pūrṇa, Buddh. — **brāhmaṇa-bhāshya-dīpikā**, f., **-brāhmaṇôpanishad**, f. N. of wks. — **śākhā**, f. N. of a branch of the Black Yajur-veda. — **saṃhitā**, f. N. of the Saṃhitā of the Maitrāyaṇīyas (q. v.) **Maitrāyaṇy-upanishad**, f. = *maitry-up*°.

Maitrāyaṇīya, m. pl. N. of a school of the Yajur-veda (closely connected with the Kaṭhas and Kalāpas), Caraṇ. — **śākhā**, f. and **-saṃhitā**, f. = °*ṇī-ś*° and *-s*°. **Maitrāyaṇīyôpanishad**, f. = *maitry-up*°. **Maitrāyaṇīyâūrdhvadehika-paddhati**, f. N. of wk.

Maitri, m. a metron. of a teacher, MaitrUp. **Maitry-upanishad**, f. N. of an Upanishad, IW. 44.

Maitrika, (ifc.) a friendly office, Pañcar.

Maitrin, mfn. friendly, benevolent, Pañcar.

Maitrī, f. friendship, friendliness, benevolence, good will (one of the 4 perfect states with Buddhists, Dharmas. 16; cf. MWB. 128), MBh.; Kāv. &c.; Benevolence personified (as the daughter of Daksha and wife of Dharma), BhP.; close contact or union, Megh.; Vcar.; (ifc.) equality, similarity, Prasannar.; N. of the Nakshatra Anurādhā, L.; N. of an Upanishad (cf. under *maitri*). — **karuṇā-mudita**, m. a partic. Samādhi, Kāraṇḍ. — **dāna**, n. friendliness (with Buddhists, one of the three forms of charity), Dharmas. 105. — **nātha**, m. N. of an author, Buddh. — **paksha-pāta**, m. a partiality for any one's friendship, Pañcat. — **pūrva**, mfn. preceded by friendship, MW. — **bala**, m. 'whose strength is benevolence,' a Buddha, L.; N. of a king (regarded as an incarnation of Gautama Buddha), Buddh.; v. l. for *maitra-b*°, Divyâv. — **maya**, mf(*ī*)n. benevolent, friendly, kind, Hcar.

Maitreya, mfn. (fr. *maitrī*) friendly, benevolent, MBh.; m. (fr. *mitrayu*, Pāṇ. vi, 4, 174) patr. of Kausharava, AitBr.; of Glāva, ChUp. (accord. to Sch. metron. fr. *mitrā*); of various other men, MBh.; Pur.; N. of a Bodhi-sattva and future Buddha (the 5th of the present age), Lalit. (MWB. 181 &c.); of the Vidūshaka in the Mṛic-chakaṭikā; of a grammarian (= *-rakshita*), Cat.; of a partic. mixed caste (= *maitreyaka*), Kull. on Mn. x, 33; (*ī*), f., see below. — **rakshita**, m. N. of a grammarian, Cat. — **vana**, n. N. of a forest, ib. — **sūtra**, n. N. of a Sūtra wk. **Maitreyôpanishad**, f. = *maitry-up*°.

Maitreyaka, m. N. of a partic. mixed caste or degraded tribe (the offspring of a Vaideha and an Ayogavī, whose business is to praise great men and announce the dawn by ringing a bell), Mn. x, 33; (*ikā*), f. descent from Mitrayu, Pāṇ. vii, 3, 2, Sch.; a contest between friends or allies, L.

Maitreyī, f. N. of the wife of Yājñavalkya, ŚBr.; of Ahalyā, ShaḍvBr.; of Sulabhā, ĀśvGṛS. — **brāhmaṇa**, n. N. of ŚBr. xiv, 5 &c. — **śākhôpanishad**, f. = next. **Maitreyy-upanishad**, f. = *maitry-up*°.

Maitrya, n. friendship, Kāv.; Kathās.; Pañcat. **Maitryâbhimukha**, m. a partic. Samādhi, Kāraṇḍ.

Maitry-upanishad. See *maitri* above.

मैथिल **maithila**, mf(*ī*)n. relating or belonging to Mithilā, MBh.; Kāv. &c.; m. a king of M° (pl. the people of M°), ib.; (*ī*), f., see below. — **kāyastha**, m. N. of a poet, Cat. — **paddhati**, f. N. of wk. — **vācaspati** and **-śrī-datta**, m. N. of two men, Cat. — **saṃgraha**, m. N. of wk.

Maithilika, m. pl. the inhabitants of Mithilā, MW.

Maithilī, f. N. of Sītā (daughter of Janaka, king of M°), R.; Kālid. — **nāṭaka**, n., **-pariṇaya**, m., **-śaraṇa**, n. N. of wks.

Maithileya, m. metron. fr. *maithilī*, Ragh.

मैथुन **maithuná**, mf(*ī*)n. (fr. *mithuna*) paired, coupled, forming a pair or one of each sex, BhP.; connected by marriage, PārGṛ.; relating or belonging to copulation, KaṭhUp.; Mn.; MBh. (with *bhoga*, m. carnal enjoyment; with *dharma*, m. 'sexual law,' copulation; with *vāsas*, n. a garment worn during cop°); n. (ifc. f. *ā*) copulation, sexual intercourse or union, marriage, ŚBr. &c. &c. (acc. with √*ās*, *i*, *gam*, *car*; dat. with *upa-√gam* or *upa-√kram*, to have sexual intercourse); union, connection, L. — **gata**, mfn. engaged in copulation, MBh. — **gamana**, n. sexual intercourse, Suśr. — **jvara**, m. sexual passion, MBh. — **dharmin**, mfn. cohabiting, copulating, BhP. — **vairāgya**, n. abstinence from sexual intercourse, MW. **Maithunâbhāshaṇa**, n. a conversation in which allusions are made to sexual int°, Mahāvy. **Maithunâbhighāta**, m. prohibition of sex° int°, Suśr. **Maithunôpagamana**, n. = °*na-gamana*, ib.

Maithunika, (ifc.) having sexual intercourse, MBh.; (*ikā*), f. union by marriage, Pāṇ. iv, 3, 125.

Maithunin, mfn. = prec. mfn., Mn.; MārkP.; m. Ardea Sibirica, L.

Maithunī-bhāva, m. copulation, sexual union, R.

Maithunya, mfn. proceeding from or caused by or relating to copulation, Mn.; BhP.

मैधातिथ **maidhātitha**, mf(*ī*)n. relating to Medhâtithi, ŚāṅkhŚr.; n. N. of a Sāman, ĀrshBr. (also *maidhyātitha*).

Maidhāva, m. (fr. *medhā-vin*) the son of a wise man, Pāṇ. vi, 4, 164, Sch. °**vaka**, n. intelligence, wisdom, g. *manojñâdi*.

मैनवी **mainavī**, f. (prob. fr. *mīna*) a kind of gait or movement, Saṃgīt.

मैनाक **maināká**, m. (fr. *menā*) N. of a mountain (son of Hima-vat by Menā or Menakā, and said to have alone retained his wings when Indra clipped those of the other mountains; accord. to some this mountain was situated between the southern point of the Indian peninsula and Laṅkā), TĀr. (v. l. *mai-nāgi*); AVPariś.; MBh. &c.; N. of a Daitya, Hariv. — **prabhava**, m. N. of the river Śoṇa, VP. — **bhaginī** and **-svasṛi**, f. 'sister of Maināka,' N. of Pārvatī, L.

मैनाल **maināla**, m. (fr. *mīna*) a fisherman, VS. (Sch.)

Mainika, m. id., Pāṇ. iv, 4, 35, Sch.

मैनेय **maineya**, m. pl. N. of a people, Lalit.

मैन्द **mainda**, m. N. of a monkey-demon killed by Kṛishṇa, MBh.; R. — **mardana** and **-han**, m. 'slayer of Mainda,' N. of Kṛishṇa, L.

मैमत **maimata**, m. patr. fr. *mimata*, Pāṇ. iv, 1, 150.

Maimatāyana (g. *naḍâdi*) and °**ni** (Car.; cf. Pāṇ. iv, 1, 150), m. patr. fr. *mimata*.

मैरव **mairava**, mf(*ī*)n. (fr. *meru*) relating to mount Meru, Prab.

मैराल **mairāla**, m. N. of a mythical being, L.

मैरावण **mairāvaṇa**, m. N. of an Asura (*-caritra*, n. N. of wk.), Cat.

मैरेय **maireya**, m. n. a kind of intoxicating drink (accord. to Suśr., Sch. a combination of *surā* and *āsava*), MBh.; R. &c.

Maireyaka, m. n. id., MBh.; m. pl. N. of a mixed caste, MBh. (cf. *maitreyaka*).

मैलिन्द **mailinda**, m. (fr. *milinda*) a bee, L.

मैश्रधान्य **maiśradhānya**, n. (fr. *miśra-dhānya*) a dish prepared by mixing various grains, Kauś.

मैहिक **maihika**, mf(*ī*)n. (fr. *meha*) relating to urinary disease, Suśr.

मो **mŏ** = *má* + *u* (see under 3. *má*).

मोक **moka**, n. (√2. *muc*) the stripped-off skin of an animal, MBh. (cf. *nir-m*°); a quadruped, L.; a pupil, L.; (*mókī*), f. 'releaser,' night, RV. ii, 38, 3 (Naigh. i, 7).

Moktavya, mfn. to be set free or liberated, MBh.; Kāv.; to be let go or given up or delivered, Mn.; Yājñ.; to be renounced or resigned, Campak.; to be flung or hurled or thrown upon or against (loc. or acc. with *prati*), MBh.; MārkP.

Moktu-kāma, mfn. wishing to let go, desiring to shoot or cast, MW.

Moktṛi, mfn. one who releases or liberates &c.; one who pays or discharges, Suśr.

Mokya. See *a-mokyá*.

मोकलिन् **mokalin**, m. N. of a man, Cat.

मोक्ष् **moksh**, cl. 1. Ā. *mokshate* (rather Desid. fr. √2. *muc*; fut. *mokshishyate*, MBh.), to wish to free one's self, seek deliverance, Kāṭh. (cf. Pāṇ. vii, 4, 57); to free one's self from (acc.), shake off, MBh.; cl. 10. P. (Dhātup. xxxiii, 57; rather Nom. fr. *moksha*, below), *mokshayati* (m. c. also Ā. °*te*; Impv. *mokshayadhvam*, MBh.; fut. *mokshayishyati*, °*te*, ib.; inf. *mokshitum*, Hariv., v. l.), to free or deliver from (abl.), Gaut.; Yājñ.; MBh. &c.; to liberate, emancipate (from transmigration), Hariv.; to loosen, untie, undo, Suśr.; to detach, extract, draw out of (abl.), AitBr.; to wrest or take away anything from (abl.), Hariv.; to shed, cause to flow (blood), Suśr.; to cast, hurl, fling, Dhātup.

Mumokshayishu, mfn. See under √2. *muc*, p. 821, col. 2.

Moksha, m. (ifc. f. *ā*) emancipation, liberation, release from (abl., rarely gen. or comp.), MBh.; Kāv. &c.; release from worldly existence or transmigration, final or eternal emancipation, Up.; Mn.; MBh. &c. (IW. 39); death, L.; N. of partic. sacred hymns conducive to final eman°, Yājñ.; (in astron.) the liberation of an eclipsed or occulted planet, the last contact or separation of the eclipsed and eclipsing bodies, end of an eclipse, Sūryas.; VarBṛS.; falling off or down, Kum.; VarBṛS. (cf. *garbha-*); effusion, VarBṛS.; setting free, deliverance (of a prisoner), Gaut.; loosing, untying (hair), Megh.; settling (a question), Kathās.; acquittance of an obligation, discharge of a debt (cf. *ṛiṇa-*); shedding or causing to flow (tears, blood &c.), MārkP.; Suśr.; casting, shooting, hurling, MBh.; Kāv.; Pur.; strewing, scattering, Kum.; Kathās.; utterance (of a curse), R.; relinquishment, abandonment, Kathās.; N. of the Divine mountain Meru, L.; Schrebera Swietenioides, L. **-kāṅkshin,** mfn. desirous of liberation or of final emancipation, MW. **-kāṇḍa,** N. of ch. of the Kṛitya-kalpataru by Lakshmī-dhara. **-kāraṇatā-vādârtha,** m., **-kārikā,** f. pl. N. of wks. **-kriyā-samācāra,** mfn. accomplishing the act of liberation, Pañcat. **-khaṇḍa,** m. or n. N. of wk. **-jñāna,** n. knowledge of final beatitude or emancipation, MW. **-tīrtha,** n. N. of a Tīrtha, Cat. **-dā,** f. N. of a female ascetic, Kathās. **-deva,** m. N. of Hiouen-thsang, Buddh. **-dvāra,** n. 'gate of eman°,' N. of the sun, MBh. **-dharma,** m. law or rule of eman°, MBh.; N. of a section of the 12th book of the Mahābhārata (from Adhyāya 174 to the end; also *-parvan*, n.), IW. 374; *-ṭīkā*, f., *-dīpikā*, f., *-vyākhyā*, f., *-vyākhyāna*, n., *-sārôddhāra*, m.; °*mârtha-dīpikā*, f. N. of wks. **-nirṇaya,** m. N. of wk. **-pati,** m. (in music) a kind of measure, Saṃgīt. **-parāyaṇa,** mfn. having eman° as chief object, Bhag. **-purī,** f. 'city of eman°,' N. of the city of Kāñcī, Cat. **-praveśa-vyavasthāna,** m. a partic. Samādhi, Kāraṇḍ. **-bhāgīya,** mfn. having to do with eman°, Divyâv. **-bhāj,** mfn. attaining final eman°, Cat. **-bhāva,** m. liberation, final eman°, MBh. **-mahāparishad,** f. 'great eman°-assembly,' the Buddhist general council, Buddh. **-mārga,** m. N. of a Jaina wk. **-lakshmī-vilāsa,** m. N. of a temple, Cat.; N. of wk. **-lakshmī-sāmrājya-tantra,** n., °**ya-siddhi,** f. N. of wks. **-vat,** mfn. connected with final eman°, MārkP. **-vāda,** m., °**da-mīmāṅsā,** f. N. of wks. **-vārttika,** mfn. reflecting upon final eman°, MBh. **-viṇśaka** or °**ka-stotra,** n. '20 verses on eman°,' N. of the verses Hariv. 14348 &c. **-śāstra,** n. the doctrine of final eman°, Up. **-sādhana,** n. means of eman°, ib.; °*nôpadeśa*, m. N. of wk. **-sāmrājya-siddhi,** f., **-siddhi,** f., **-hetutā-vāda,** m., **-mokshâgama,** m. N. of wks. **Mokshântaraṅga,** mfn. nearest or next to final eman°, MW. **Mokshâvalambin,** m. resting (hopes) on eman°, a heretic, L. **Mokshêcchā,** f. desire of eman°, MBh. **Mokshêśvara,** m. N. of a man; of an author, Cat. **Mokshôpāya,** m. means of eman°, Hariv.; a sage, saint, devotee (?), W.; *-niścaya*, m., *-sāra*, m. or n. (?) N. of wks.

Mokshaka, mfn. one who looses or unties or sets free, Mn.; (ifc.) final emancipation, L.; m. a species of tree, VarBṛS.; Suśr.; Bhpr.; Schrebera Swietenioides, Bhpr.

Mokshaṇa, mfn. liberating, emancipating, Cat.; n. liberation, releasing, rescuing, MBh.; Mṛicch.; setting at liberty (a criminal), Mn. ix, 249; loosing, untying, Pañcat.; shedding, causing to flow, Mālav.; Suśr. (cf. *rakta-m*°); giving up, abandoning, deserting, Pañcat.; Hit. (v. l.); squandering, W.; (*ī*), f. the magic art of releasing any one, HPariś.

Mokshaṇīya, mfn. to be given up or resigned, to be disregarded or neglected (*a-m*°, inevitable), MBh.; R.

Mokshayitavya, mfn. to be emancipated, Bādar., Sch.

Mokshayitṛi, mfn. one who frees or liberates from (abl.), R.

Mokshāya, Nom. Ā. °*yate*, to become a means of emancipation, Cat.

Mokshita, mfn. set free, liberated, MBh.; Hariv.; wrested away, Hariv.

Mokshin, mfn. striving after emancipation, MBh.; MārkP.; emancipated, RāmatUp.

Mokshya, mfn. to be liberated, to be saved, Hariv.

मोग *moga*, m. the chicken-pox or some similar disease, L.

मोघ *mógha* (or *moghá*, MaitrS.), mf(*ā*)n. (√1. *muh*) vain, fruitless, useless, unsuccessful, unprofitable (ibc. and *am*, ind. in vain, uselessly, without cause), RV. &c. &c.; left, abandoned, MBh.; idle, ib.; m. a fence, hedge, L.; (*ā*), f. Bignonia Suaveolens, L.; Embelia Ribes, L. **-karman,** mfn. one whose actions are fruitless, observing useless ceremonies, Bhag. **-jñāna,** mfn. one whose knowledge is useless, cultivating any but religious wisdom, ib. **-tā,** f. vainness, uselessness, Kathās. **-pushpā,** f. a barren woman, L. **-hāsin,** mfn. laughing causelessly, Kāth. **Moghâśa,** mfn. one whose hopes are vain, Bhag.

Moghāya, Nom. Ā. °*yate*, to become vain or useless or insignificant, Alaṃkārav.

Moghī, in comp. for *mogha*. **-√1. kṛi,** P. *-karoti*, to make vain, frustrate, disappoint, Kālid. **-bhūta,** mfn. become useless, rendered vain, MBh.

Mogholi, m. an enclosure, hedge, fence, L.

मोच *moca*, m. (√2. *muc*) the juice of a tree; L.; Moringa Pterygosperma, MBh.; (prob.) Musa Sapientum, Suśr.; (*ā*), f. Musa Sapientum, Naish.; the cotton shrub, L.; the indigo plant, L.; (*ī*), f. Hingtsha Repens, L.; n. a plantain, banana (the fruit), Vāgbh. **-niryāsa,** m., **-rasa,** m., **-sāra,** m., **-srāva,** m., **-srut,** m. the resin of Gossampinus Rumphii, L. **Mocâhva,** m. id., Bhpr.

Mocaka, mfn. liberating, emancipating, Pañcar.; one who has abandoned all worldly passions and desires, an ascetic, devotee, L.; m. (only L.) Moringa Pterygosperma, L.; Musa Sapientum, L.; Schrebera Swietenioides, L.; (*ikā*), f. a species of plant, L.; a species of fish, Bhpr.; n. a kind of shoe, L.

Mocana, mf(*ī*)n. (ifc.) releasing from, BhP.; casting, darting, Gīt.; (*ī*), f. a species of plant (= *kaṇṭa-kārī*), L.; n. release, liberation, freeing or delivering from (abl. or comp.), Daś.; Śukas. (cf. *ṛiṇa-m*°); unyoking (a car), MBh.; (ifc.) discharging, emitting, Gobh. **-paṭṭaka,** m. or n. 'a clearing cloth,' filter, L.

Mocanaka, mf(*ikā*)n. releasing, setting free (see *bandha-m*°); (*ikā*), f. N. of a woman, Kathās.

Mocanīya, mfn. to be released or set free, Pañcat.

Mocayitavya, mfn. id., Mālav. (v. l. *mocit*°).

Mocayitṛi, mfn. freeing, releasing, Kull. on Mn. viii, 342.

Mocāṭa, m. (only L.) the pith or core of the banana; the fruit of the banana tree; Nigella Indica; sandal wood.

Moci. See *hila-m*°.

Mocika, m. a tanner or shoemaker (cf. Hind. *mochī*), L.

Mocita, mfn. caused to be released, set free, Hit.

Mocin, mfn. setting free, liberating (see *bandha-mocinī*).

Mocya, mfn. = *mocanīya*, Yājñ.; to be given up or restored, ib.; to be deprived of (acc.), Gaut.

मोजकेशिन् *mojakeśin*, w. r. for *muñja-k*°.

मोट *moṭa*, m. or n. a bundle (= Hindī *moṭh*), Divyâv. (also written *mūḍha*, *muṭa*, *mūṭa*).

मोटक *moṭaka*, m. n. (√*muṭ*) a globule or pill to be used as a remedy against (gen.), Cat. (cf. *modaka*); m. N. of an author, Cat.; (*ī*), f. (in music) a partic. Rāgiṇī, L.; n. a broken or crushed leaf, L.

Moṭana, mfn. crushing, grinding, destroying (see *gaja-m*°); m. wind, air, L.; n. the act of crushing, breaking, snapping, wringing, strangling, Mṛicch.; Śukas. (cf. *aṅguli-m*°).

Moṭanaka, n. crushing, entire destruction, Chandom.; a kind of metre, ib.

Moṭamāna, n. a partic. Siddhi, Sāṃkhyas., Sch.

मोटपल्ली *moṭa-pallī*, f. N. of a country, Uttamac.

मोटा *moṭā*, f. Sida Cordifolia, L.; Sesbania Aegyptiaca, L.

मोटि *moṭi* or *moṭī*. See *karṇa-m*°.

मोट्टायित *moṭṭāyita*, n. showing affection in the absence of a loved object, the silent expression of returned affection, Daśar.; Sāh.

मोढ *moḍha*, m. N. of a family, Cat. **-śataka,** n. N. of a poem.

Moḍhaka, m. N. of a man, Cat.

मोण *moṇa*, m. dried fruit, L.; a kind of fly, L.; a basket in which snakes are carried, L.

Moṇaka, a word used to explain *ḍimbikā*, L.

मोतीराम *motīrāma*, m. (with *kavi*) N. of a poet (author of the Kṛishṇa-vinoda-kāvya), Cat.

मोद *móda*, m. (√2. *mud*) joy, delight, gladness, pleasure, RV. &c. &c.; fragrance, perfume, BhP. (cf. *āmoda*); N. of a partic. formula, ĀpŚr.; of a Muni, Cat.; (*ā*), f. a species of plant (= *aja-modā*), L.; a kind of Andropogon, L. **-kara,** m. N. of a Muni, R. **-nātha,** m. N. of an author, Cat. **-mañjarī-guṇa-leśa-mātra-sūcakâshṭaka,** n. and **-mañjarī-guṇa-leśa-sūcaka-daśaka,** n. N. of Stotras. **-modinī,** f. Eugenia Jambolana, L. (prob. w. r. for *megha-m*°). **Modâkhya,** m. the mango tree, L. **Modā-giri,** m. N. of a country, MBh. **Modâdhyā,** f. a species of plant (= *aja-modā*), L. **Modā-pura,** n. N. of a town, MBh.

Modaka, mfn. (ifc.) gladdening, exhilarating, MBh.; m. n. a small round sweetmeat, any sweetmeat, MBh.; R. &c.; (in medicine) a kind of pill, Suśr.; Bhpr.; m. a partic. mixed caste (the son of a Kshatriya by a Śūdra mother), L.; (*ī*), f. N. of a partic. mythical club, R.; n. a kind of metre, Col. **-kāra,** m. a sweetmeat-maker, confectioner, R. **-maya,** mf(*ī*)n. composed of sweetmeats, Pāṇ. v, 4, 22, Sch. **-vallabha,** m. 'fond of sweetmeats,' N. of Gaṇeśa, Gal.

Modakikā, f. a sweetmeat (only ifc. after numerals, e. g. *dvi-modakikām dadāti*, he gives always two sweetmeats), Pāṇ. v, 4, 1, Vārtt. 1, Pat.

Modana, mfn. (fr. Caus.) gladdening, delighting, gratifying (mostly ifc.), MBh.; R.; Hariv.; (*ī*), f. musk, L.; n. the act of gladdening &c., Dhātup.; wax (= *ucchishṭa-m*°), L.

Modanīya, mfn. to be rejoiced at, delightful, KaṭhUp.

Modamāna, mfn. rejoicing, being glad, ChUp.; m. (prob.) a proper N. (cf. *maudamānika*).

Modayat, mfn. (fr. Caus.) rejoicing, delighting; (*antī*), f. Ptychotis Ajowan, L. (also °*tikā*).

Modāki and °**kin,** v. l. for *maudākin*.

Modāyani, m. patr. fr. *moda*, Prav. (prob. w. r. for *maudāyani*).

Modita, mfn. (fr. Caus.) pleased, delighted, W.; n. pleasure, delight, ib.

Modin, mfn. rejoicing, glad, cheerful, MaitrUp.; (ifc.) gladdening, delighting, MBh.; (*inī*), f. Jasminum Zambac or Auriculatum, L.; = *aja-modā*, L.; musk, L. (cf. *modana*); an intoxicating drink, L. **Modinīśa,** n. N. of a Tantra, Āryav. (cf. *medinīśa*).

मोदोष *modosha*, m. N. of a preceptor, BhP.

मोमहण *momahaṇa*, m. N. of an author (15th century), Cat. **-vilāsa,** m. N. of M°'s wk.

मोमुघ *momughá*, mfn. (fr. Intens. of √1. *muh*) mad, insane, ŚBr.

मोर *mora*, m. a peacock (= *mayūra*), L.; (*ī*), f. N. of a family, Cat. **Morêśvara,** m. (with *bhaṭṭa*) N. of an author, ib.

मोरक *moraka*, n. a kind of steel, L.; the milk of a cow seven days after calving, L. (cf. next).

मोरट *moraṭa*, m. a species of plant with sweet juice, L.; (also n.) the milk of a cow seven days after calving, Suśr. (also 'sour buttermilk' = *moraṇa*, Bhpr.); (*ā*), f. Sanseviera Roxburghiana, L.; n. the root of the sugar-cane, L.; the flower and root of Alangium Hexapetalum, L.

Moraṭaka, n. the root of the sugar-cane, L.

मोरण *moraṇa*, m. sour buttermilk, Suśr., Sch. (cf. *moraṭa*).

मोराक *morāka*, m. N. of king Pravarasena's minister, Rājat. — **bhavana**, n. N. of a temple built by M°, ib.

मोरिका *morikā*, f. a side-door, postern-gate, Gal.; N. of a poetess, Cat.

मोर्वणीकर *morvaṇī-kara*, m. N. of Nara-hari-dikshita, Cat.

मोष *mosha*, m. (√2. *mush*) a robber, thief, plunderer, BhP.; Gīt.; robbery, theft, stealing, plundering, Mn.; Var. &c. (also *ā*, f., L.); anything robbed or stolen, stolen property, Mn. ix, 278. — **kṛit**, mfn. proclaiming or predicting a theft, VarBṛS. **Moshâbhidarśana**, n. seeing or witnessing a robbery, Mn. ix, 274.

Moshaka, m. a thief, robber, L.

Moshaṇa, mfn. (ifc.) robbing, plundering, carrying off, BhP.; n. the act of robbing &c., Nir.; defrauding, embezzling, Kull. on Mn. viii, 400.

Moshayitṛi, m. (fr. Caus.) a Brāhman, L.; the Indian cuckoo, L.

Moshṭṛi, m. a robber, thief, L.

Moshya, mfn. liable to be stolen, Vas.

मोह *móha*, m. (√1. *muh*; ifc. f. *ā*) loss of consciousness, bewilderment, perplexity, distraction, infatuation, delusion, error, folly, AV. &c. &c. (*moham* √*brū*, to say anything that leads to error; *moham* √*yā*, to fall into error; *mohāt*, ind. through folly or ignorance); fainting, stupefaction, a swoon, MBh.; Kāv. &c.; (in phil.) darkness or delusion of mind (preventing the discernment of truth and leading men to believe in the reality of worldly objects); (with Buddhists) ignorance (one of the three roots of vice, Dharmas. 139); a magical art employed to bewilder an enemy (= *mohana*), Cat.; wonder, amazement, L.; Infatuation personified (as the off-spring of Brahmā), VP. — **kalila**, n. thicket or snare of illusion, Bhag.; spirituous liquor, L. — **kārin**, m. Caryota Urens, L. — **cūḍôttara** or °**ra-śāstra**, n. N. of wk. — **jāla**, n. net of illusion, mundane fascination, Yājñ.; MBh. — **nidrā**, f. 'sleep of infatuation,' thoughtless confidence, ŚārṅgP. — **parâyaṇa**, mf(*ā*)n. thoroughly stupefied, Kum. — **parimuktā**, f. N. of a Gandharva maid, Kāraṇḍ. — **pāśa**, m. the snare of (worldly) illusion, MW. — **mantra**, m. a spell or charm causing infatuation or delusion, Kathās. — **maya**, mf(*ī*)n. consisting of infatuation or delusion, Kāv. — **mudgara**, m. 'hammer of ignorance or infatuation,' N. of two wks. — **rāja-parājaya**, m. N. of a drama. — **rātri**, f. 'night of bewilderment,' the n° when the world is to be destroyed, BrahmavP. — **vat**, mfn. filled with infatuation, MBh.; Sāṃkhyak., Sch. — **śāstra**, n. false doctrine, KūrmaP. — **śūlôttara**, n. N. of wk. **Mohâtmaka**, mfn. causing delusion, Up. **Mohântá**, m. deep bewilderment of mind, ŚBr. **Mohândha-sūrya**, m. a partic. medicament, Rasêndrac. **Mohôpanishad**, f. N. of wk. **Mohôpamā**, f. 'delusion-comparison,' (in rhet.) a comp° which leads to confusing the subject and object of comparison (e.g. 'regarding thy face, O dear one, as the moon, I run after the moon as if it were thy face'), Kāvyâd.

Mohaka, mfn. bewildering, infatuating, causing ignorance or folly, MW.

Mohana, mf(*ī*)n. depriving of consciousness, bewildering, confusing, perplexing, leading astray, infatuating, MBh.; R. &c.; m. the thorn-apple, L.; N. of Śiva, R.; N. of one of the 5 arrows of the god of love, Vet.; of various other authors and men, Kathās.; Śukas.; Cat.; (*ā*), f. the flower of a sort of jasmine, L.; Trigonella Corniculata, L.; (*ī*), f. Portulaca Quadrifida, L.; a partic. illusion or delusion, Sarvad.; a partic. incantation, Kathās.; N. of an Apsaras, Pañcar.; of a female demon (daughter of Garbha-hantṛi), MārkP.; of one of the nine Śaktis of Vishṇu, L.; n. the being deluded or infatuated, delusion, infatuation, embarrassment, mistake, Nir.; Bhag.; Gīt.; stupor, being stupefied, Suśr.; sexual intercourse, Kāv.; Sāh.; the act of perplexing, puzzling, bewildering, R.; Gīt.; MārkP.; any means employed for bewildering others, Daś.; temptation, seduction, W.; a magical charm used to bewilder an enemy; the formula used in that process (esp. the hymns AV. iii, 1, 2), Kauś.; N. of a town, MBh. — **canda**, m. N. of a man, MW. — **dāsa**, m. N. of two authors, Cat. — **prakṛiti**, m. N. of a pupil of Śaṃkarācārya, Śaṃkar. — **bhoga**, m. a partic. kind of sweetmeat, L. — **latā**, f. a plant which has the power of fascinating, MW. — **lāla**, m. N. of an author, Cat. — **vallikā** (Suśr.) or — **vallī** (Npr.), f. a species of plant. — **sapta-śatī**, f. N. of a poem. **Mohanâstra**, n. N. of one of the 5 arrows of the god of love, Kathās.; a weapon which stupefies or fascinates the person against whom it is directed, MW.

Mohanaka, m. the month Caitra, L.; (*ikā*), f. a species of plant, Suśr.

Mohanīya, mfn. 'to be deluded,' resulting from illusion or error or infatuation, MBh.; producing delusion, bewildering, puzzling, ib.; Sarvad.

Mohama, m. a partic. personification, SāmavBr.

Mohayitṛi, mfn. one who bewilders or perplexes, MBh.

Mohita, mfn. stupefied, bewildered, infatuated, deluded (often in comp., e.g. *kāma-m°*, infatuated by love), MBh.; R. &c.

Mohin, mfn. deluding, confusing, perplexing, illusive, MBh.; R. &c.; (*inī*), f. a fascinating woman, MW. (cf. RTL. 65, n. 1); the flower of a species of jasmine, L.; N. of an Apsaras, Pañcar.; of a daughter of Rukmâṅgada, VP.; °*nī-mantra*, m., *-rāja-sahasra-nāmâvalī*, f. N. of wks.

Móhuka, mfn. falling into confusion, TS.

मौक *mauka*, m. patr. fr. *mūka*, ĀśvŚr.

मौकलि *maukali*, m. a raven, L. (cf. *maukuli*; *maudgali*).

Maukalya, m. a Vaidehaka who sews and dyes clothes (also called a Rāmaka), L.

मौकुन्द *maukunda*, mfn. relating to Mukunda i.e. Vishṇu, Pañcar.

मौकुलि *maukuli*, m. a crow, Uttarar. (cf. *maukali*).

मौक्तिक *mauktika*, mfn. (fr. *mukti*) striving after final emancipation, Pañcat.; m. (only in MBh.) n. (fr. *muktā*; comp. f. *ā*) a pearl (properly 'a collection of p°s'), MBh.; Kāv. &c. — **gumphikā**, f. a female stringer of p°s, Kāśikh. — **taṇḍula**, m. a kind of white Yavanāla, L. — **dāman**, n. a string of p°s, L.; a kind of metre, Col. — **prasavā**, f. a pearl muscle, L. (cf. *muktā-prasū*). — **maya**, mf(*ī*)n. consisting of pearls, Śriṅgār. — **māraṇa**, n. N. of a subject treated of in the Dhātu-ratna-mālā, Cat. — **mālā**, f. a pearl necklace, L.; a species of metre, Col. — **ratna**, n. a pearl gem, pearl (*-tā*, f.), Rājat. — **śukti**, f. a pearl oyster, L. — **sara**, m. a string of p°s, Nalac.; Uttarar. **Mauktikâbha**, mfn. like p°s, MW. **Mauktikâvali** (Kir.) or °**lī** (Kathās.), f. a pearl necklace. **Mauktikā-hāra**, m. id., Mālatīm.

मौक्य *maukya*, n. (fr. *mūka*) dumbness, speechlessness, Mn. xi, 51.

मौक्ष *mauksha*, n. (fr. *moksha*) N. of a Sāman, Lāṭy.

Maukshika, mfn. relating to the release of a planet (from eclipse) or to the end of an ecl°, Sūryas.

मौख *maukha*, mfn. (fr. *mukha*) relating to the mouth, oral (n.[?] a fault or defect connected with the mouth), Hariv.; based on oral instruction, Pat.

Maukhika, mfn. (fr. *mukha*), L.

Maukhya, n. precedence, pre-eminence, Hit. (w.r.)

मौखर *maukhara*, m. (fr. *mukhara*) N. of a family or race, Hcar.

Maukhari, m. a patr., Vās., Introd.

Maukharī, f. = next, MW.

Maukharya, n. talkativeness, garrulity, Pañcar.; scurrility, defamation, abusiveness, calumny, MW.; (*ā*), f. of *maukhari* above, Pāṇ. iv, 1, 79, Sch.

मौग्ध *maugdha* (w.r., Sāh.; Uttarar.) or *maugdhya* (ib.; Kathās. &c.), n. (fr. *mugdha*), simplicity, innocence, inexperience, a feminine grace (asking a lover to tell what is already known); charm, beauty, MW.

मौघ्य *maughya*, n. (fr. *mogha*) vanity, unprofitableness, uselessness, BhP.

मौच *mauca*, n. (fr. *moca*) the fruit of the banana or plantain tree, Suśr.

मौजवत *maujavatá*, mfn. coming from or produced on the mountain Mūja-vat, RV.; Nir.; m. (said to be) a patr. of Aksha (author of RV. x, 34).

मौञ्ज *mauñjá*, mf(*ī*)n. (fr. *muñja*) made of Muñja-grass or its fibres, TS. &c. &c.; resembling Muñja-grass or living on it, RV. i, 191, 3; m. a blade of Muñja-grass, MW.; N. of a village of the Bāhīkas, L.; (*ī*), f., see below. — **vivāna**, mfn. twisted or fabricated out of Muñja-grass, ĀpŚr.

Mauñjaka, m. blades of Muñja-grass, VarBṛS. (v.l. *muñjaka*).

Mauñjakāyana, m. a patr., Pravar.

Mauñjavata, mf(*ī*)n. coming from the mountain Muñja-vat, Siddh. on Pāṇ. iv, 4, 110.

Mauñjāyana, m. patr. fr. *muñja*, g. *naḍâdi*; N. of a man, MBh.; pl. N. of a warlike family, g. *dāmany-ādi*; (*ī*), f. a princess of the Mauñjāyanas, g. *śārṅgaravâdi*. °**nīya**, m. a prince of the Mauñjāyanas, g. *dāmany-ādi*.

Mauñjin, mfn. girt with or wearing a girdle of Muñja-grass, Hariv. (cf. *nāga-m°*).

Mauñjī-bandhana, n. = *mauñjī-bandhana*, Mn. ii, 169, 171; Yājñ. i, 39.

Mauñjī, f. (scil. *mekhalā*, m. c. also *mauñji*) a Brāhman's girdle or cord made of a triple string of Muñja-grass; any girdle, MBh.; Kāv. &c. — **tṛiṇâkhya**, m. Muñja-grass, L. — **dhara**, mfn. wearing or carrying Muñja-grass, MBh. — **nibandhana**, n. the binding on of the girdle of Muñja-grass or of the sacred cord, Mn. ii, 27. — **pattrā**, f. Eleusine Indica, L. — **bandhana**, n. = *-nibandhana*; °*na-cihnita*, mfn. distinguished by the binding of the Muñja girdle, Mn. ii, 170.

Mauñjīya, mfn. made of Muñja-grass, BhavP.

Mauñjya, m. a partic. personification, Gaut.

मौडी *mauḍī*, f. coarse ground meal, L.

मौढ्य *mauḍhya*, m. (fr. *mūḍha*) patr., g. *kurv-ādi*; n. stupidity, ignorance, folly, MBh.; Kāv. &c.; swoon, stupor, L.

मौण्डिनिकाय *mauṇḍi-nikāya*, m. (*mauṇḍi* fr. *muṇḍa*) a proper N., Pāṇ. vi, 2, 94, Sch.

Mauṇḍika, n. shaving, L.

Mauṇḍya, n. shaving the head, tonsure, baldness, Mn.; MBh. &c.

मौत्र *mautra*, n. (fr. *mūtra*) a quantity of urine, GṛŚrS. (cf. *a-mautra-dhauta*).

Mautra-kṛicchrika, mf(*ī*)n. (fr. *mūtra kṛicchra*) resembling strangury, Car.

मौद *mauda*, m. pl. (fr. *muda*) N. of a school, Pāṇ. iv, 2, 66, Sch.; sg. a pupil of this school (see *maudaka*). — **paippalāda**, m. pl., g. *kārta-kaujapâdi*. — **hāyana**, m. a patr. (also pl.), Saṃskārak.

1. **Maudaka**, n. a partic. version of a sacred text adopted by Mauda, Pat.

मौदक 2. *maudaka*, mf(*ī*)n. (fr. *modaka*) relating to sweetmeats, dealing with them, Cat. °**kika**, mf(*ī*)n. consisting or composed of sw°, Pāṇ. v, 4, 22, Sch.; m. a confectioner, Pāṇ. v, 4, 21, Sch.

Maudanika, mf(*ā* or *ī*)n. (fr. *modana*), g. *kāśy-ādi*. °**neyaka**, mfn., g. *kattry-ādi*.

मौदमानिक *maudamānika*, mf(*ā* or *ī*)n. (fr. *modamāna*), g. *kāśy-ādi*.

मौदाकिन् *maudākin*, m. (prob.) N. of a mountain, MBh. (v.l. *modakin*); of a son of Bhavya and (n.) a Varsha ruled by him, VP. (v.l. *maudaki*).

मौद्ग *maudga*, mf(*ā*)n. (fr. *mudga*) relating to a bean, consisting of beans, KātyŚr.; Suśr.; m. N. of a preceptor, VP. **Maudgika**, mf(*ī*)n. purchased with beans, Pāṇ. v, 1, 37, Vārtt. 3, Pat. °**gīna**, mf(*ī*)n. sown with beans, Pāṇ. v, 2, 1, Sch.

मौद्गल *maudgali*, m. (fr. *mudgala*) a crow, L. — **kera**, m. a patr., L.

Maudgalīya, mfn. (fr. *maudgalya*), g. *kṛiśâśvâdi*.

Maúdgalya, mfn. descended or sprung from Mudgala, BhP.; m. patr. of Nāka, ŚBr.; of Śatabalâksha, Nir.; of Lāṅgalāyana, AitBr.; N. of a chamberlain, Mālav.; m. a partic. mixed caste, MBh.

Maudgalyāyana, m. (patr. fr. prec.) N. of a pupil of Gautama Buddha, Lalit.

मौद्रिक *maudrika*, m. (fr. *mudrā*) a maker of seal rings (?), L.

मौन *mauná*, m. (fr. *muni*) a patr., ĀśvŚr.; pl. N. of a dynasty, VP.; (*ī*), f. N. of the 15th day in the dark half of the month Phālguna (when a partic. form of ablution is performed in silence), Col.;

n. the office or position of a Muni or holy sage, ŚBr.; MBh.; silence, taciturnity, ChUp.; Mn.; MBh. &c. (*maunaṃ* with √*kṛi* or *vi-√dhā* or *sam-ā-√car*, to observe silence, hold one's tongue). **—gopāla**, N. of wk. **—tyāga**, m. breaking silence, Cat. **—dhārin**, mfn. observing silence, Kathās. **—bhaṭṭa**, m. N. of various men, Cat. **—mantrâvabodha**, m. N. of wk. **—mudrā**, f. the Mudrā or attitude of silence, MW. **—vṛitti**, mfn. observing a vow of silence, Subh. **—vrata**, mfn. id., Pañcat.; n. a vow of silence, MBh.; *-dhara* (MBh.), *-dhārin* (R.); °*tin* (MārkP.), mfn. = *-vṛitti*. **—sammati**, f. tacit assent, MW. **—sūtra**, n. N. of wk.

Mauni, Vṛiddhi form of *muni*, in comp. **—citi** (fr. *muni-cita*), g. *sutaṃ-gamâdi*. **—sthalika**, mfn. (fr. *muni-sthala*), g. *kumudâdi*. **Maunīndra**, mfn. (fr. *munīndra*), Divyâv.

Maunika, mfn. like a Muni, g. *aṅguly-ādi*.

Maunin, mfn. observing silence, silent, taciturn, MBh.; Kāv. &c.; m. = *muni* (sometimes ifc. in proper names, e. g. *gopīnātha-m*°). **Mauni-tva**, n. silence, Kāv.

Mauneya, m. metron. of a class of Gandharvas and Apsaras, MBh.; Hariv.; Pur.; pl. N. of a school, L.; (*maún*°), n. the position or office of a Muni, RV. x, 136, 3.

Maunya, a patr., w. r. for *mauna*.

मौन्द *maunda*, m. N. of a teacher, Cat. (v. r. *moda*, *maudga*).

मौरजिक *maurajika*, m. (fr. *muraja*) a drum-beater, drummer, L.

मौरव *maurava*, mf(ī)n. (fr. *muru*) relating to the demon Muru, MBh.

1. **Maurva**, mf(ī)n. made from the iron called *muru*, BhP.

मौर्ख्य *maurkhya*, n. (fr. *mūrkha*) stupidity, folly, fatuity, Kāv.; Kathās.; Suśr.

मौर्य *maurya*, m. patr. fr. *mura* and metron. fr. *murā*, VP.; HPariś. (cf. g. *kaṇvâdi*); pl. N. of a dynasty beginning with Candra-gupta, Pur. **—datta**, m. N. of a man, Daś. **—putra**, m. (with Jainas) N. of one of the eleven Gaṇâdhipas, W.

मौर्व 2. *maurva*, mf(ī)n. (fr. *mūrvā*) made of the Sanseviera Roxburghiana, coming from or relating to Mūrvā or bow-string hemp, GṛŚrS.; Mn.; MBh.; (*ī*), f., see below.

Maurvikā, f. (in geom.) the sine of an arc, Sūryas.; a bow-string, L.

Maurvī, f. a string or girdle made of Mūrvā (see comp.); a bow-string, MBh.; (in geom.) the sine of an arc, Sūryas. **—mekhalin**, mfn. wearing a girdle made of Mūrvā, MBh.

मौल *maula*, mf(ā)n. (fr. *mūla*) derived from roots (as poison), Hcar.; handed down from antiquity, ancient (as a custom), MBh.; holding office from previous generations, hereditary (as a minister or warrior), Mn.; MBh. &c.; aboriginal, indigenous, Mn. viii, 62; 259; m. an hereditary minister (holding his office from father and grandfather), Ragh.; Daś.; pl. aboriginal inhabitants who have emigrated, L.; (with *pārthivāḥ*) = *mūlaprakṛitayaḥ*, Kām.

Maulabhārika, mfn. (fr. *mūla-bhāra*) carrying a load of roots, g. *vaṅśâdi*.

Mauli, m. the head, the top of anything, Hariv.; Kāv.; Hit. &c. (*maulau ni-√dhā*, to place on the head, receive respectfully); chief, foremost, best, Bhām.; Jonesia Asoka, L.; patr., Pravar.; pl. N. of a people, MārkP.; m. f. a diadem, crown, crest, MBh.; Kāv. &c.; a tuft or lock of hair left on the crown of the head after tonsure, a top-knot (= *cūḍā*), Kum. (v. l.); hair ornamented and braided round the head (= *dhammilla*), Veṇīs.; (also *ī*), f. the earth, L. **—kapha**, m. the phlegm secreted in the head, ŚārṅgS. **—pṛishṭha**, n. the crown of the h°, L. **—bandha**, m. a diadem for the h°, Var. **—maṇi**, m. a crest gem, jewel worn in a diadem, Kālid. **—maṇḍana**, n. head ornament, Pañcar.; *-mālikā*, f. a garland worn as a h° orn°, Kathās. **—mālā** and **-mālikā**, f. a wreath worn on the h°, Kāv.; Kathās.; °*lin*, mfn. (ifc.) having anything for a crest, MārkP. **—mukuṭa**, n. a diadem, tiara, Dhūrtas. **—ratna**, n. = *-maṇi*, MW. **Maulindu**, m. the moon on (Śiva's) h°, Hcat. **Mauly-ābharaṇa**, n. a h° ornament, BhP.

Maulika, mfn. (fr. *mūla*) producing roots &c., g. *vaṅśâdi*; derived from a root, original, Sāṃkhyapr., Introd.; inferior, of low origin (opp. to *kulīna*), Col.; m. a digger or vendor of roots, VarBṛS.; pl. N. of a people, MārkP.; n. = *garbhâdhāna*, L.

Maulikya, n. (fr. *mūlika*), g. *purohitâdi*.

Maulin, mfn. (fr. *mauli*) having anything uppermost or turned upwards (see *cakra-m*°); being at the head, chief, Kāv.; having a diadem or crown, diademed, crested (also applied to Śiva), MBh.; Hcat.

Mauleya, m. pl. N. of a people, MBh.

Maulya, mfn. being at the root, KātyŚr.; n. = *mūlya*, price, Vet.; Pañcad. **Maulyâdhyāya**, m. N. of wk.

मौलुगि *maulugi*, m. N. of an author, Cat.

मौशल *mauśala*, *maushala*, w. r. for *mausala* below.

मौषिक *maushika*, mfn. (fr. *mūshikā*) relating or belonging to a mouse, Pañcat.

Maushikāra, m. a male mouse, Pat. on Pāṇ. iv, 1, 120.

Maushiki, m. metron. fr. *mūshikā*, g. *bāhv-ādi*.

Maúshikī-putra, m. N. of a teacher, ŚBr.

मौष्टा *maushṭā*, f. (fr. *mushṭi*) a combat with fists, boxing match, L.

Maushṭika, m. a cheat, rogue, sharper, Buddh.; a goldsmith, L.

मौसल *mausala*, mf(ī)n. (fr. *musala*) club-shaped, club-formed, ĀśvŚr.; R.; fought with clubs (as a battle), MBh.; Hariv.; relating to the battle with clubs (cf. *-parvan*); N. of a Madhu-parka (composed of ghee and spirituous liquor), Kauś.; relating to Mausalya, g. *kaṇvâdi*; m. pl. N. of a family, Saṃskārak. **—parvan**, n. 'Musala-section,' N. of the 16th book of the Mahā-bhārata (so called after the self-slaughter in a club-fight of Kṛishṇa's family, the Yādavas, through the curse of some Brāhmans, IW. 374).

Mausalya, m. patr. fr. *musala*, g. *gargâdi*.

मौसुल *mausula*, m. = مسلم a Moslim, Musalmān, Cat.

मौहनिक *mauhanika*, m. (fr. *mohana*) N. of Caitra, L.

मौहूर्त *mauhūrta*, m. (fr. *muhūrta*) an astrologer, MBh.

Mauhūrtika, mfn. lasting for a moment, momentary, BhP.; relating to a particular time or hour, ib.; skilled in astrology, Kāv.; m. an astrologer, Kāv.; Kathās.; Hit.; pl. N. of a class of celestial beings (children of Muhūrtā), BhP.

म्ना *mnā* (cf. √*man*, with which *mnā* was originally identical), cl. 1. P. Dhātup. xxii, 31; *manati* (Gr. also pf. *mamnau*; aor. *amnāsīt*; Prec. *mnayat* or *mneyāt*; fut. *mnātā* and *mnāsyati*; inf. *mnātum*: Caus. *mnāpayati*, aor. *amimnapat*: Desid. *mimnāsati*: Intens. *māmnāyate*, *māmnāti*, *māmneti*), only in *anu-*, *ā-*, *praty-ā-*, *sam-ā-*, *pari-√mnā*.

Mnāta. See *ā-*, *sam-ā-mnāta*.

म्यक्ष *myaksh*, cl. 1. P. *myákshati* (pf. *mimyaksha*, *mimikshúḥ*, °*kshire*; aor. *amyak*, Pass. *amyakshi*), to be fixed or situated in (loc.), rest firmly, RV.; to be present, exist, ib. (cf. *apa-*, *ā-*, *ni-*, *sam-√myaksh*).

म्रक्ष *mraksh* or *mṛiksh*, cl. 1. P. (Dhātup. xvii, 12) *mrakshati* or *mṛiksháti* (pf. *mimṛikshúḥ*), to rub, stroke, curry, RV. viii, 74, 13; to smear, Lalit.; to accumulate, collect, Dhātup.: Caus. (or cl. 10, Dhātup. xxxii, 119) *mrakshayati* or *mṛikshayati*, to rub, smear, anoint, KātyŚr.; Buddh.; to accumulate, Dhātup.; to speak indistinctly or incorrectly, ib.; to cut, ib.

Mraksha, mfn. rubbing, grinding down, destroying (cf. *tuvi-mr*°); m. concealment of one's vices, hypocrisy (with Buddhists, one of the 24 minor evil qualities), Dharmas. 69. **—kṛitvan**, mfn. rubbing to pieces, destroying, RV.

Mrakshaṇa, n. rubbing in, anointing, Dhātup.; ointment, oil, Suśr.

Mrakshita, mfn. rubbed in, smeared, Hariv.

Mrakshya, n. ill-feeling (?), Divyâv.

म्रद् *mrad* (cf. √1. *mṛid*), cl. 1. Ā. *mradate* (Gr. also pf. *mamrade*, fut. *mraditā* &c.), only in *pra-* and *vi-√mrad*: Caus. *mradayati* (aor. *amamradat*, Pāṇ. vii, 4, 95), to smooth: Desid. *mimradishate*, Gr.: Intens. *māmradyate*, *māmratti*, ib.

Mrada, **mradas**. See *ūrṇa-mrada* and *ūrṇā-mradas*.

Mradiman, m. softness, Naish.; tenderness, mildness, Śiś.; Rājat. **Mradimânvita**, mfn. endowed with softness, mild, kind, W.

Mradishṭha, mfn. (superl. of *mṛidu*) very soft or mild, Pāṇ. vi, 4, 161, Sch.

Mradīyas, mfn. (compar. of *mṛidu*) softer, milder, APrāt., Sch.; Pāṇ. vi, 4, 161, Sch.

म्रातन *mrātana*, n. Cyperus Rotundus, L.

म्रित् *mrit*, cl. 4. P. *mrityáti*, to decay, be dissolved, ŚBr.

म्रुच् *mruc* (cf. √*mluc*), cl. 1. P. *mrocati* (aor. *amrucat* and *amrocīt*, Pāṇ. iii, 1, 58), to go, move, Dhātup. vii, 13: Desid. *mumrucishati* and *mumrocishati*, Pāṇ. i, 2, 26 (cf. *ni-* and *abhi-ni-√mruc*).

Mrukta. See *abhi-ni-mrukta*.

Mroká, m. N. of a destructive Agni, AV. (*mrokânumroka*, ii, 24, 3).

म्रुञ्च् *mruñc* (= √*mruc*, Dhātup. vii, 11), cl. 1. P. *mruñcati*.

म्रेट् *mreṭ* (cf. √*mleṭ*), v. l. for next.

म्रेड् *mreḍ*, cl. 1. P. *mreḍati*, to be mad, Dhātup. ix, 4 (cf. *ā-* and *upa-ri-√mreḍ*).

म्लक्त *mlakta* (?), mfn. stolen, L.

म्लक्ष् *mlaksh*, cl. 10. P. *mlakshayati*, to cut, divide, Dhātup. xxxii, 119 (v.l.)

म्लात *mlāta*, *mlāna*, *mlāyin*, *mlāsnu*. See p. 838, col. 1.

म्लिछ् *mlich*, *mlishṭa*. See √*mlech*.

म्लुच् *mluc* (cf. √*mruc*), cl. 1. P. (Dhātup. vii, 14) *mlócati* (aor. *amlucat* and *amlocīt*, Pāṇ. iii, 1, 58), to go, move; to go down, set, ŚBr.: Desid. *mumlucishati* and *mumlocishati*, Pāṇ. i, 2, 26: Intens. *malimlucāmahe*, to bring to rest, allay, MānGṛ. (cf. *anu-*, *upa-*, *ni-*, *abhi-ni-√mluc*).

Mlukta. See *ápa-mlukta*.

म्लुञ्च् *mluñc* (= √*mluc*, Dhātup. vii, 12), cl. 1. P. *mluñcati*.

म्लुप् *mlup*, another form of √*mluc*, only in *abhi-ni-* and *upa-mlupta*, q. v.

म्लेछ् *mlech* (= √*mlich*), cl. 1. P. (Dhātup. vii, 25) *mlecchati* (Gr. also pf. *mimleccha*, fut. *mlecchitā* &c.; Ved. inf. *mlecchitavai*, Pat.), to speak indistinctly (like a foreigner or barbarian who does not speak Sanskṛit), ŚBr.; MBh.: Caus. or cl. 10. P. *mlecchayati*, id., Dhātup. xxxii, 120.

Mlishṭa, mfn. spoken indistinctly or barbarously, Pāṇ. vii, 2, 18; withered, faded, faint (= *mlāna*), L.; n. indistinct speech, a foreign language, L. **Mlishṭôkti**, f. indistinct or barbarous speech, Vop.

Mlecchá, m. a foreigner, barbarian, non-Aryan, man of an outcast race, any person who does not speak Sanskṛit and does not conform to the usual Hindū institutions, ŚBr. &c. &c. (*ī*, f.); a person who lives by agriculture or by making weapons, L.; a wicked or bad man, sinner, L.; ignorance of Sanskṛit, barbarism, Nyāyam., Sch.; n. copper, L.; vermilion, L. **—kanda**, m. Allium Ascalonicum, L. **—jāti**, m. a man belonging to the Mlecchas, a barbarian, savage, mountaineer (as a Kirāta, Śabara or Pulinda), MBh. **—taskara-sevita**, mfn. infested by b°s and robbers, Ml. **—tā**, f. the condition of b°s, VP. **—deśa**, m. a foreign or barbarous country, Hariv. **—dvishṭa**, m. bdellium, Gal. **—nivaha**, m. a host or swarm of b°s, Gīt. **—bhāshā**, f. a foreign or barbarous language, MBh. **—bhojana**, n. 'food of b°s,' wheat, L. (also °*jya*); n. = *yāvaka*, half-ripe barley, L. **—maṇḍala**, n. the country of the Mlecchas or b°s, W. **—mukha**, n. = *mlecchâsya*, L. **—vāc**, mfn. speaking a barbarous language (i.e. not

Sanskṛit; opp. to *ārya-vāc*), Mn. x, 43. **Mlecchâkhya,** n. 'called Mleccha,' copper, L. **Mlecchâśa,** m. = *mleccha-bhojana,* L. **Mlecchâsya,** n. 'foreigner-face,' copper (so named because the complexion of the Greek and Muhammedan invaders of India was supposed to be copper-coloured), L.

Mlecchana, n. the act of speaking confusedly or barbarously, Dhātup.

Mlecchita, mfn. = *mlishṭa,* Pāṇ. vii, 2, 18, Sch.; n. a foreign tongue, L.

Mlecchitaka, n. the speaking in a foreign jargon (unintelligible to others), Cat.

म्लेट् *mleṭ* (cf. √*mreṭ*), cl. 1. P. *mleṭati,* to be mad, Dhātup. ix, 3 (accord. to Vop. also *mleḍ, mleḍati*).

म्लेव् *mlev* (cf. √*mev*), cl. 1. Ā. *mlevate,* to serve, worship, Dhātup. xiv, 33.

म्लै *mlai,* cl. 1. P. (Dhātup. xxii, 8) *mlāyati* (ep. also °*te* and *mlāti*; pf. *mamlau,* MBh.; *mamle,* Pāṇ. vi, 1, 45, Sch.; aor. *amlāsīt,* 2. sg. *mlāsīḥ,* MBh.; Prec. *mlāyāt* or *mleyāt,* Pāṇ. vi, 4, 68, Sch.; fut. *mlātā, mlāsyati,* Gr.; Cond. *amlāsyatām,* Br., °*syetām,* Up.; inf. *mlātum,* Gr.), to fade, wither, decay, vanish, ŚBr. &c. &c.; to be languid or exhausted or dejected, have a worn appearance, ib.: Caus. *mlāpáyati,* to cause to wither or fade, enfeeble, make languid, AV.; *mlapayati,* to crush, Kāv.

Mlātá, mfn. (leather &c.) made soft by tanning, RV.; faded, withered, Kāv. &c.

Mlāna, mfn. faded, withered, exhausted, languid, weak, feeble, MBh.; Kāv. &c.; relaxed, shrunk, shrivelled, Car.; dejected, sad, melancholy, Daś.; vanished, gone, Naish.; black, dark-coloured, Prab.; foul, dirty, L.; m. a house frog, L.; n. withered or faded condition, absence of brightness or lustre, VarBṛS. **-kshīṇa,** mfn. withering and languishing, Rājat. **-tā,** f. = next, Dhūrtas. **-tva,** n. withered or faded condition, dejectedness, languor, R. **-manas,** mfn. depressed in mind, dispirited, MBh. **-vaktra,** mfn. having a blackened countenance, Prab. **-vrīḍa,** mfn. one whose shame is gone, shameless, Bhartṛ. (v.l. for *vīta-vr*°). **-sraj,** mfn. having a withered or faded garland, MBh. **Mlānâṅga,** mf(*ī*)n. having enfeebled limbs, weak-bodied; (*ī*), f. a woman during the menses, L. **Mlānêndriya,** mfn. having enfeebled senses, Bhartṛ.

Mlāni, f. withering, fading, decay, languishing, perishing, Kāv.; Kathās.; depression, melancholy, sadness, Kathās.; disappearance, Kād.; foulness, filth, Kāv.; blackness, ib.; vileness, meanness, ib.

Mlāniman, m. withered or faded condition, Vās.

Mlāpin, mfn. (fr. Caus.) causing to fade or wither, Naish.

Mlāyat, mfn. fading, withering, languishing &c. **Mlāyad-vaktra,** mfn. having a haggard or sorrowful face, Rājat.

Mlāyin, mfn. fading, withering away, languishing, Bhartṛ.; Suśr.

Mlāsnu, mfn. id., L.

य YA.

य 1. *ya,* the 1st semivowel (corresponding to the vowels *i* and *ī,* and having the sound of the English *y,* in Bengal usually pronounced *j*). **-kāra,** m. the letter or sound *ya,* TPrāt.; °*râdi-pada,* n. a word beginning with *ya* (euphemistically applied to any form of √*yabh*), Kāvyâd. **-tva,** n. the being the sound *ya,* TPrāt., Sch.

य 2. *ya,* m. (in prosody) a bacchic (⏑ – –), Piṅg.

य 3. *ya,* the actual base of the relative pronoun in declension [cf. *yád* and Gk. ὅς, ἥ, ὅ]. **-tamá,** mfn. (superl.; n. °*mat,* m. pl. °*me*; cf. Pāṇ. v, 3, 93) who or which (of many), RV.; AV.; Br.; °*má-thā,* ind. in which of many ways, ŚBr. (*yatamathā kathamathā,* in the same way as always, ShaḍvBr.) **-tará,** mfn. (compar.; cf. Pāṇ. v, 3, 92) who or which (of two), RV.; AV.; Br.; Up.; °*rá-tra,* ind. in which of the two places, MaitrS.; °*rá-thā,* ind. in which of two ways, ŚBr.

Yaká, mf(*ā́*)n. (cf. Pāṇ. vii, 3, 45) = 3. *ya,* who, which, RV.; VS.

य 4. *ya,* m. (in some senses fr. √1. *yā,* only L.) a goer or mover; wind; joining; restraining; fame; a carriage (?); barley; light; abandoning; (*ā*), f. going; a car; restraining; religious meditation; attaining; pudendum muliebre; N. of Lakshmī.

यकन् *yakán.* See next.

यकृत् *yákṛit,* n. (the weak cases are optionally formed fr. a base *yakan,* cf. Pāṇ. vi, 1, 63; nom. acc. *yákṛit,* AV.; abl. *yaknás,* RV.; *yakṛitas,* Suśr.; instr. *yaknā́,* VS.; loc. *yakṛiti,* Suśr.; ibc. only *yakṛit*) the liver, RV. &c. &c. [Cf. Gk. ἧπαρ; Lat. *jecur.*] **-kośa,** m. n. the cyst or membrane enveloping the liver, MW. **-tas,** ind. from the liver, Nir. iv, 3.

Yakṛid, in comp. for *yakṛit.* **-ari-lauha,** n. a partic. drug, L. **-ātmikā,** f. a kind of cockroach, L. **-udara,** n. an enlargement of the liver, Suśr. **-dālya,** n. or **-dāly-udara,** n. id., ib. **-varṇa,** mfn. liver-coloured, ib. **-vairin,** m. Andersonia Rohitaka, L.

Yakṛin, in comp. for *yakṛit.* **-medas,** n. liver and fat, g. *gavâśvâdi.*

Yakṛil, in comp. for *yakṛit.* **-loma** or **-loman,** m. pl. N. of a people, MBh.

यक्ष् *yaksh* (perhaps Desid. of a √*yah,* from which *yahu* and *yahva*), cl. 1. P. Ā. *yákshati,* °*te,* (prob.) to be quick, speed on (only in *pra-*√*yaksh,* q. v.; and once in *yakshāmas,* to explain *yaksha,* R. vii, 4, 12), cl. 10. Ā. *yakshayate,* to worship, honour, Dhātup. xxxiii, 19.

Yakshá, n. a living supernatural being, spiritual apparition, ghost, spirit, RV.; AV.; VS.; Br.; GṛŚrS. (accord. to some native Comms. = *yajña, pūjā, pūjita* &c.); m. N. of a class of semi-divine beings (attendants of Kubera, exceptionally also of Vishṇu; described as sons of Pulastya, of Pulaha, of Kaśyapa, of Khasā or Krodhā; also as produced from the feet of Brahmā; though generally regarded as beings of a benevolent and inoffensive disposition, like the Yaksha in Kālidāsa's Megha-dūta, they are occasionally classed with Piśācas and other malignant spirits, and sometimes said to cause demoniacal possession; as to their position in the Buddhist system see MWB. 206, 218), Up.; GṛS.; Mn.; MBh. &c.; (with Jainas) a subdivision of the Vyantaras; N. of Kubera, VarYogay.; of a Muni, R.; of a son of Śvaphalka, VP.; of Indra's palace, L.; a dog, L.; (*ā*), f. N. of a woman, HPariś.; (*ī*), f. a female Yaksha, MBh.; R. &c. (*yakshīṇām prathamā yakshī* = *Durgā,* Hariv.); N. of Kubera's wife, L. **-kardama,** m. an ointment or perfumed paste (consisting of camphor, agallochum, musk, sandalwood and Kakkola), KātyŚr., Sch.; Dhanv.; Hcat. **-kūpa,** m. 'Yaksha-tank,' N. of a place, Cat. **-graha,** m. 'the being possessed by Y°s,' a partic. kind of insanity, MBh.; *-paripīḍita,* mfn. afflicted with it, Suśr. **-taru,** m. the Indian fig-tree, L. **-tā,** f. (Kathās.) or **-tva,** n. (R.) the state or condition of a Y°. **-dattā,** f. N. of a woman, HPariś. **-dara,** N. of a district, Rājat. **-dāsī,** f. N. of a wife of Śūdraka, Daś. **-dig-vijaya,** m. N. of wk. **-dṛiś,** mfn. having the appearance of a Y° (accord. to Sāy. = *utsavasya drashṭā*), RV. **-deva-gṛiha,** n. a temple dedicated to the Y°s, Kathās. **-dhūpa,** m. a partic. incense, Hcat.; the resin of Shorea Robusta, L.; resin in general, W. (also °*paka,* Gal.) **-nāyaka,** m. N. of the servant of the 4th Arhat of the present Avasarpiṇī, L. **-pati,** m. a king of the Y°s, Kathās.; N. of Kubera, Hariv.; BhP. **-pāla,** m. N. of a king, Buddh. **-praśna,** m. N. of wk. **-bali,** m. an oblation to the Y°s (a partic. nuptial ceremony), ĀpGṛ., Comm. **-bhavana,** n. a temple dedicated to Y°s, Kathās. **-bhṛit,** mfn. supporting or nourishing living beings (?), RV. i, 190, 4. **-malla,** m. (with Buddhists) N. of one of the 5 Lokêśvaras, W. **-rasa,** m. a kind of intoxicating drink, L. **-rāj,** m. 'king of the Y°s,' N. of Kubera, R.; BhP.; of Maṇi-bhadra, MBh.; a palaestra or place prepared for wrestling and boxing, L.; (*-rāṭ*)*-purī,* f. N. of Alakā, the capital of Kubera, L. **-rāja,** m. 'Y°-king,' N. of Kubera, MBh. **-rātri,** f. 'night of the Y°s,' N. of a festival (= *dīpâlī,* q. v.), L. **-varman,** m. N. of a commentator, Śākaṭ., Sch. **-vitta,** mfn. one whose property is like that of the Y°s, one who has merely the guardianship of property and does not make use of it himself, BhP. **-sena,** m. N. of a king, Buddh. **-sthala,** m. (!) N. of a place, Cat. **Yakshâṅganā,** f. a Y° woman, Megh. **Yakshâṅgī,** f. N. of a river, Śatr. **Yakshâdhipa** (MBh.) or °**pati** (ShaḍvBr.), m. 'lord of the Y°s,' N. of Kubera. **Yakshâmalaka,** n. the fruit of a species of date, L. **Yakshâyatana,** n. a temple dedicated to the Y°s, Kathās. **Yakshâvāsa,** m. 'abode of the Y°s,' the Indian fig-tree, L. **Yakshêndra,** m. a king of the Y°s, R.; MārkP.; N. of Kubera, MBh.; R. **Yakshêś,** m. N. of the servants of the 11th and 18th Arhat of the present Avasarpiṇī, L. **Yakshêśa,** m. = next, W. **Yakshêśvara,** m. a king of the Y°s, Megh.; N. of Kubera, Hit.; *-medhīya,* n. N. of wk. **Yakshôdumbaraka,** n. the fruit of the Ficus Religiosa, L. (w. r. *yakshôd*°).

Yakshaka, m. = *yaksha,* N. of certain mythical beings attending on Kubera, R.

Yakshaṇa, n. = *jakshaṇa* (q. v.), MārkP.

Yakshan, prob. w. r. for *yakshman* (q. v.), MārkP.

Yakshiṇī, f. of *yakshin*; a female Yaksha, MBh.; R. &c.; Kubera's wife, L.; a sort of female demon or fiend (attached to the service of Durgā and frequently, like a sylph or fairy, maintaining intercourse with mortals), W. **-kavaca,** m. or n. (?), **-tantra,** n. N. of wks. **-tva,** n. the state or condition of a female Y°, Kathās. **-paṭala,** m. or n. (?), **-mantra,** m., **-vetāla-sādhana,** n., **-sādhana,** n. N. of wks.

Yakshín, mfn. having life, living, really existing (accord. to Sāy. = *pūjanīya*), RV.; (*iṇī*), f., see above.

Yakshī, f. of *yaksha* above. **-tva,** n. the state or condition of a female Yaksha, Kathās.

Yákshu, m. sg. or pl. N. of a race or tribe, RV.

1. **Yákshma,** m. sickness, disease in general or N. of a large class of diseases (prob. of a consumptive nature), RV.; AV.; VS.; pulmonary disease, consumption, TS.; Kāṭh. &c. **-nā́śana,** mf(*ī*)n. destroying or removing sickness, AV.; m. the reputed author of the hymn RV. x, 161.

2. **Yakshma,** in comp. for °*man.* **-gṛihīta,** mfn. seized or afflicted with consumption, ĀśvGṛ. **-grasta,** mfn. attacked by cons°, BhP. **-graha,** m. an attack of cons°, cons°, ib. **-ghnī,** f. 'destroying consumption,' grapes, raisins, L.

Yakshman, m. pulmonary consumption, consumption, KātyŚr., Sch.; MBh. &c.

Yakshmin, mfn. consumptive, phthisical, MW.; one who suffers from pulmonary consumption, Mn.; MBh.

Yakshmodhā́, f. (prob.) the seat of a disease, AV. (*yakshmaḥ-dhā,* Pada-pāṭha).

Yákshya, mfn. (prob.) active, restless, RV. viii, 60, 3 (Sāy. = *yashṭavya*).

यङ् *yaṅ,* (in gram.) a term for the Intensive suffix *ya,* Pāṇ. iii, 1, 22 &c. **-anta,** m. the Ātmanepada Intens. formed by reduplication and the suffix *ya,* ib. vi, 1, 9, Sch. **-luk,** the dropping of the Intensive suffix *ya* (or a blank substituted for it), ib. ii, 4, 74; (*-lug*)*-anta,* m. the Parasmaipada Intens. formed without *ya*; °*ta-śiromaṇi,* m. N. of wk.

यच्छन्दस् *yac-chandas* &c. See p. 844, col. 3.

यज् 1. *yaj,* cl. 1. P. Ā. (Dhātup. xxiii, 33) *yájati,* °*te* (1. sg. *yajase,* RV. viii, 25, 1; Ved. Impv. *yákshi* or °*shva*; pf. *iyāja,* MBh.; *ījé,* RV.; *yejé* [?], AV., cf. Kāś. on Pāṇ. vi, 4, 120; Ved. aor. *ayākshīt* or *ayāṭ*; *ayashṭa*; Subj. *yakshat, yakshati,* °*te*; 3. sg. *ayakshata,* ĀśvGṛ.; Prec. *ijyāt,* Pāṇ. iii, 4, 104; *yakshīya,* MaitrS.; fut. *yashṭā,* Br.; *yakshyati,* °*yáte,* RV. &c. &c.; inf. *yáshṭum, ījitum,* MBh.; Ved. °*ṭave*; *yájadhyai* or *yajádhyai*; p.p. *ishṭa,* ind. p. *ishṭvā́,* AV.; *ishṭvīnam,* Pāṇ. vii, 1, 48; *-ijya,* Gr.; *yájam,* AV.), to worship, adore, honour (esp. with sacrifice or oblations); to consecrate, hallow, offer (with acc., rarely dat., loc. or *prati,* of the deity or person to whom; dat. of the person for whom, or the thing for which; and instr. of the means by which the sacrifice is performed; in older language generally P. of Agni or any other mediator, and Ā. of one who makes an offering on his own account, cf. *yája-māna*; later properly P. when used with reference to the officiating priest, and Ā. when referring to the institutor of the sacrifice), RV. &c. &c.; to offer, i. e. to present, grant, yield, bestow, MBh.; BhP.; (Ā.) to sacrifice with a view to (acc.), RV.; to invite to sacrifice by the Yājyā verses, ŚBr.; ŚāṅkhŚr.: Pass. *ijyate* (p. Ved. *ijyamāna* or *yajyamāna* Pat. on Pāṇ. vi, 1, 108; ep. also pr. p. *ijyat*), to be sacrificed or worshipped, MBh.; Kāv. &c.: Caus. *yājáyati* (ep. also °*te*; aor. *ayīyajat*), to assist any one (acc.) as a priest at a sacrifice (instr.), TS.; Br.; to cause any one (acc.) to sacrifice anything (acc.) or by means of any one (instr.), MBh.; R.: Desid. *yíyakshati*, °*te* (cf. *íyakshati*), to desire to sacrifice or worship, MBh.; R.: Intens. *yāyajyate*, *yāyajīti*, *yāyashṭi*, Pāṇ. vii, 4, 83, Sch. [Cf. Zd. *yaz*; Gk. ἁγνός, ἅγος, ἅζομαι.]

2. **Yaj**, (ifc.; cf. Pāṇ. viii, 2, 36) sacrificing, worshipping, a sacrificer (see *divi-* and *deva-yáj*).

Yaja, m. a word formed to explain *yajus*, ŚBr.; (*ā*), f. N. of a female tutelary being (mentioned with Sitā, Samā and Bhūti), PārGṛ.

Yajatá, mf(*ā́*)n. worthy of worship, adorable, holy, sublime, RV. [cf. Zd. *yazata*]; m. a priest (= *ṛitv-ij*), L.; the moon, L.; N. of Śiva, L.; (with Ātreya) of a Ṛishi (author of RV. v, 67, 68), Anukr.

Yajati, m. N. of those sacrificial ceremonies to which the verb *yajati* is applied (as opp. to *juhoti*), KātyŚr. (cf. Kull. on Mn. ii, 84). — **deśa**, m., -**sthāna**, n. the place or position of the Vedi or sacrificial altar, KātyŚr., Sch.

Yájatra, mf(*ā*)n. worthy of worship or sacrifice, deserving adoration, RV.; VS.; AV.; m. = *agni-hotrin*, L.; = *yāga*, L.; n. = *agni-hotra*, L.

Yajátha, (only in dat. = °*thāya*, construed like an inf.) worship, sacrifice, RV.

Yajadhyai. See under √1. *yaj*.

Yajana, n. the act of sacrificing or worshipping, Mn; MBh. &c. (*tava yajanāya*, to worship thee, BhP.); a place of sacrifice, R.; BhP.; N. of a Tīrtha, MBh. **Yajanâdhyayana**, n. du. sacrificing and studying the Veda (the duties incumbent on all twice-born), Vishṇ.

1. **Yajanīya**, mfn. (fr. prec.) relating to sacrifice or worship; n. (with or scil. *ahan*) a day of sacrifice or consecration, GṛŚrS.

2. **Yajanīya**, mfn. (√*yaj*) to be sacrificed or worshipped, Ml.

Yajanta, m. a sacrificer, worshipper(?), W.

Yaja-praísha, mfn. having a Praisha (or form of invitation to a priest) containing the Impv. *yaja*, KātyŚr.

Yájamāna, mfn. sacrificing, worshipping &c.; m. the person paying the cost of a sacrifice, the institutor of a s° (who to perform it employs a priest or priests, who are often hereditary functionaries in a family), ŚBr. &c. &c. (*ī*, f. the wife of a Y°, BhP.); any patron, host, rich man, head of a family or tribe, Pañcat. — **camasa**, n. the cup of a Y°, AitBr. — **tva**, n. the rank or position of a Y°, Śaṃk. — **devatyà**, mfn. having the Y° for a deity, TBr. — **prayoga**, m. N. of wk. — **brāhmaṇá**, n. the Brāhmaṇa of the Y°, AV. — **bhāgá**, m. the share of a Y°, ŚBr. — **mantrânukramaṇī**, f. N. of wk. — **loká**, m. the world of the Y°, TS.; AitBr. (*yáj°-l°*, MaitrS.) — **vākya**(?), n., -**vaijayantī**, f. N. of wks. — **sishya**, m. the pupil of a Brāhman who defrays the expenses of a sacrifice, Śak. (v.l.) — **havis**, n. the oblation of a Y°, BhP. — **hautrânukramaṇī**, f. N. of wk. **Yajamānâyatana**, n. the place of a Y°, MaitrS.

Yajamānaka, m. = *yajamāna*, a sacrificer or institutor of a sacrifice, Cāṇ.

Yájas, n. worship, sacrifice, RV. viii, 40, 4 (= *yāga*, Sāy.)

Yajāka, mfn. making offerings, munificent, liberal, L.

Yaji, mfn. sacrificing, worshipping (see *deva-y°*); m. worship, sacrifice, Pat. on Pāṇ. i, 3, 72; the root *yaj*, KātyŚr., Sch. — **mat**, mfn. being denoted by the verb *yajati*, Jaim., Sch.

Yajin, m. a worshipper, sacrificer, MBh.

Yájishṭha, mfn. (superl.) worshipping very much or in the highest degree, RV.

Yajishṇu, mfn. worshipping the gods, sacrificing, MBh.

Yájīyas, mfn. (compar.) worshipping more or most, sacrificing excellently, RV.

Yaju, m. N. of one of the ten horses of the Moon, L.

Yajuḥ, in comp. for *yajus*. — **śākhin**, mfn. familiar with a Śākhā of the Yajur-veda, Cat. — **śrāddha**, n. a Śrāddha performed by a Brāhman versed in the Y°-v°, ib. — **saṃdhyā**, f. N. of wk. — **svāmin**, m. N. of a Purohita, Kathās.

Yajur, in comp. for *yajus*. — **āraṇyaka**, n. = *taittirīyâraṇyaka*, Cat. — **uttama** (*yájur-*), mfn. ending with verses of the Yajur-veda, MaitrS. — **gati**, m. N. of Kṛishṇa, Pañcar. — **brāhmaṇa-bhāshya**, n., -**mañjarī**, f. N. of wks. — **máya**, mf(*ī*)n. consisting of verses of the Y°-v°, Br.; Up.; MBh. — **yukta** (*yájur-*), mfn. harnessed during the recitation of a verse of the Y°-v°, AitĀr. — **vallabhā**, f., -**vāṇī-mantra**, m. pl. N. of wks. — **víd**, mfn. knowing the Yajus or sacrificial formulas, AV. — **vidhāna**, n. rules about the application of sacr° formulas, AgP.; N. of wk. — **vivāha-paddhati**, f. N. of wk. — **vedá**, m. 'the sacrificial Veda,' the collective body of sacred Mantras or texts which constitute the Yajur-veda (these Mantras, though often consisting of the prose Yajus, are frequently identical with the Mantras of the Ṛig-veda, the Yajur-veda being only a sort of sacrificial prayer-book for the Adhvaryu priests formed out of the Ṛig-veda, which had to be dissected and rearranged with additional texts for sacrificial purposes; the most characteristic feature of the Yajur-veda is its division into two distinct collections of texts, the Taittirīya-saṃhitā and the Vājasaneyi-saṃhitā, q.v.; the former of which is also called Kṛishṇa, i.e. 'Black,' because in it the Saṃhitā and Brāhmaṇa portions are confused; and the latter Śukla, i.e. 'White,' because in this, which is thought the more recent of the two recensions, the Saṃhitā is cleared from confusion with its Brāhmaṇa and is as it were white or orderly; the order of sacrifices, however, of both recensions is similar, two of the principal being the Darśa-pūrṇa-māsa or sacrifice to be performed at new and full moon, and the Aśva-medha or horse-sacrifice; cf. IW. 6; 245, n. 2), Br.; GṛŚrS.; Mn. &c.; -*kriyā-svara-lakshaṇa*, n., -*jaṭâvali*, f., -*tri-kāṇḍa-bhāshya*, n., -*pada*, n., -*brāhmaṇa*, n., -*bhāshya*, n., -*mañjarī*, f., -*mantra-saṃhitā-sukha-bodhana*, n., -*lakshaṇa*, n., -*śākhā*, f., -*śrāddha*, n., -*śrauta*, n., -*saṃhitā*, f. (and °*tânukramaṇikā*, f., °*tā-brāhmaṇa*, n.), -*smārta*, n.; °*dâraṇyaka*, n., °*dârṇava*, m., °*dâśīr-vāda*, m., °*dôpanishad*(?), f. N. of wks. — **vedin**, mfn. familiar with the Yajur-veda, Kull. on Mn. iii, 145; °*di-vṛishôtsarga-tattva*, n., °*di-śrāddha-tattva*, n., N. of wks. — **vedíya**, mfn. relating to the Yajur-veda; -*dakshiṇa-dvāra*, n. N. of wk.

Yajush, in comp. for *yajus*. — **kalpa**, mfn., Pāṇ. viii, 3, 39, Sch. — **kāmya**, Nom. P. °*yati*, to be fond of sacrificial formulas, ib. — **kṛita** (*yájush-*), mfn. performed or consecrated with s° f°, TS. — **kṛiti** (*yájush-*), f. consecration with a s° f°, ib.; Br. — **kriyā**, f. a ceremony connected with a Yajus, KātyŚr. — **ṭama** and -**ṭara**, mfn., Pāṇ. viii, 3, 101, Sch. — **ṭás**, ind. from or in relation to a Y°, on the authority of the Yajur-veda, ŚBr.; ĀśvŚr.; ChUp. — **ṭā**, f. (Kāś.), -**ṭva**, n. (Vop.) the state of a Yajus. — **pati**, m. 'lord of the Y°,' N. of Vishṇu, BhP. — **pātra**, n., g. *kaskâdi*. — **priya**, mfn. fond of the Y° (said of Kṛishṇa), Pañcar. — **mat** (*yájush-*), mfn. having or accompanied with a Y°, Nir. (°*tya ishṭakāḥ*, N. of partic. bricks used in the building of the sacrificial altar, ŚBr.)

Yajusha. See *ṛig-yajusha*.

Yajushka, mfn., Pāṇ. viii, 3, 39 (occurs only in *a-yajushka*).

Yajushyà, mfn. relating to ceremonial, AV.

Yájus, n. religious reverence, veneration, worship, sacrifice, RV.; a sacrificial prayer or formula (technical term for partic. Mantras muttered in a peculiar manner at a sacrifice; they were properly in prose and distinguished from the *ṛic* and *sāman*, q.v.), RV. &c. &c.; N. of the Yajur-veda, q.v. (also pl.); of a partic. sacrificial text, NṛisUp.; m. N. of a man, Kathās. — **sāt**, ind. to the state of a Yajus, APrāt.

Yajûdara, mfn. (*yajus* + *udara*) having the Yajus for a belly (said of Brahman), KaushUp.

Yajñá, m. worship, devotion, prayer, praise; act of worship or devotion, offering, oblation, sacrifice (the former meanings prevailing in Veda, the latter in post-Vedic literature; cf. *mahā-y°*), RV. &c. &c.; a worshipper, sacrificer, RV. iii, 30, 15; 32, 12); fire, L.; = *ātman*, L.; Sacrifice personified, MBh.; Hariv.; (with *Prājāpatya*) N. of the reputed author of RV. x, 130, Anukr.; N. of a form of Vishṇu, Pur.; of Indra under Manu Svāyambhuva, ib.; of a son of Ruci and Ākūti, ib. — **karman**, mfn. engaged in a sacrifice, R.; n. sacrificial rite or ceremony, KātyŚr.; Mn. &c.; °*mârha*, mfn. worthy of a sacrifice, L. — **kalpa**, mfn. resembling a s°, BhP. — **kāma** (*yajñá-*), mfn. desirous of s° or worship, RV. &c. &c. — **kāra**, mfn. occupied in a s°, MBh. — **kāla**, m. time for s°, Lāṭy.; the last lunar day in each half of a month, L. — **kīlaka**, m. 's°-post,' the post to which a victim is fastened, L. — **kuṇapī**, f. a partic. bird, MaitrS. — **kuṇḍa**, n. a hole in the ground for receiving the s°al fire, L.; -*cakra*, n. pl. N. of wk. — **kṛit**, mfn. worshipping, performing a s°, TS.; BhP.; causing or occasioning s°s (said of Vishṇu), MBh.; m. N. of a king, BhP. (also -*kṛita*). — **kṛintatrá**, n. pl. the dangers connected with a s°, ŚBr. — **ketu** (*yajñá-*), mfn. giving a sign by a s°, RV.; m. N. of a Rākshasa, R. — **kopa**, m. N. of a Rākshasa, R. — **kratú**, m. s°al rite or ceremony, a complete rite or chief ceremony, TS.; Br.; ŚrS.; a personification of Vishṇu, BhP.; pl. the Yajña and Kratu s°s, RāmatUp. — **kriyā**, f. s°al act or rite, Kathās. — **gamya**, mfn. accessible by s° (Vishṇu-Kṛishṇa), Vishṇ. — **gāthā**, f. a memorial verse connected with a s°, AitBr.; GṛŚrS. — **giri**, m. N. of a mountain, Hariv. — **guhya**, m. N. of Kṛishṇa, Pañcar. — **ghosha**, m. N. of a poet, Cat. — **ghna**, m. 's° destroying,' N. of a malicious demon, R.; BhP. — **cchāga**, m. a goat for a s°, Mn. — **jāgara**, m. a kind of small s°al grass, L. — **jña**, mfn. skilled in worship or s°, Nir. — **tati**, f. performance of a s°, APrāt. — **tanū**, f. a form of worship or s°, Kauś.; N. of partic. Vyāhṛitis, ŚBr.; of partic. s°al bricks, TS. — **tantra**, n. extension of a s°, Āpast.; -*sudhā-nidhi*, m., -*sūtra*, n. N. of wks. — **tā** (*yajñá-*), f. state or condition of a s°, MaitrS. — **turaṃga**, m. a horse for a s°, Mālav. — **tyāgin**, mfn. one who has abandoned a s°, L. — **trātṛi**, m. s°-protector, N. of Vishṇu, Pañcar. — **dakshiṇā**, f. a s°al gift or donation, a fee given to priests for performing a s°, R. — **datta**, m. 's°-given,' N. of a man (commonly used in examples = Latin *Caius*), R.; Kathās.; Kaṇ.; (*ā*), f. N. of a woman (cf. *yajña-dattaka*); -*vadha*, m. 'Yajña-datta's death,' N. of an episode of the Rāmāyaṇa; -*śarman*, m. N. of a man (often used in examples), KātyŚr., Sch. — **dattaka**, m. (and *ikā*, f.) endearing forms of -*datta*, -*dattā*, Pat. — **dattīya**, mfn. (fr. *yajña-datta*) Pāṇ. i, 1, 73, Vārtt. 5, Pat. — **dāsī**, f. N. of a woman, Daś. — **dīkshā**, f. initiation into s°s, due performance of a s°, Mn.; R. — **dīkshita**, m. N. of an author, Cat. — **dugdha** (*yajñá-*), mfn. milked or drawn out by a s°, TS. — **dṛiś**, mfn. looking on at a s°, MBh. — **deva**, m. N. of a man, Kathās. — **dravya**, n. anything used for a s°, R. — **druh**, m. 'enemy of s°s,' a Rākshasa, W. — **dhara**, m. 's°-bearer,' N. of Vishṇu, L. — **dhīra** (*yajñá-*), mfn. conversant with worship or s°, R. — **nārāyaṇa**, m. (also with *dīkshita*) N. of various authors, Cat. — **nidhana**, m. N. of Vishṇu, Vishṇ. — **nishkṛit**, mfn. arranging the s°, RV. — **ní**, mfn. conducting worship or s°, ib. — **nemi**, m. 'surrounded by s°s,' N. of Kṛishṇa, Pañcar. — **pati** (*yajñá-*), m. lord of s° (applied to any one who institutes and bears the expense of a s°), RV.; Br.; ŚrS.; N. of Soma and Vishṇu (as gods in whose honour a s° is performed), VS.; BhP.; of an author (also with *upâdhyāya*), Cat. — **patnī**, f. the wife of the institutor of a s° (as taking part in the ceremony), MBh. (-*tva*, n.); BhP. — **pathá**, m. the path of worship or s°, ŚBr. — **padī**, f. (prob.) taking a step or steps with the feet during a s°, AV. — **paribhāshā**, f. N. of a Sūtra work by Āpastamba (also -*sūtra*, n.) — **parús**, n. a section or part of a s°, TS. — **paśu**, m. an animal for s°, victim, BhP.; a horse, L.; -*mīmāṃsā*, f. N. of wk. — **pātrá**, n. a s°al vessel, ŚBr.; GṛŚrS. &c.; -*kārikā*, f., -*lakshaṇa*, n. N. of wks.; °*trīya*, mfn. fit for a s°al v°, ŚBr. — **pārśva**, n. N. of wk. — **puṃs**, m. 'soul of s°,' N. of Vishṇu, BhP. — **pucchá**, n. the tail (i.e. the last part) of a s°, ŚBr. — **puraścaraṇa**, n. N. of wk. — **purusha**, m. = -*puṃs* (also -*pūr°*), BhP.; -*vājapeya-yāji-kārikā*, f. N. of wk.; °*shâsammita*(?), mfn., MaitrS. — **prayāṇa**, n. N. of the 85th ch. of the Uttara-kāṇḍa of the Rāmāyaṇa. — **prâpya**, mfn. to be attained by s°s (said of Kṛishṇa), Pañcar. — **prâyaścitta-vivaraṇa**, n., -**prâyaścitta-sūtra**, n. N. of wks. — **priya**, mfn. fond of s° (Kṛishṇa), Pañcar. — **prī**, mfn. delighting in s°, RV. — **phala-da**, mfn. granting the fruit or reward of s° (Vishṇu), Pañcar. — **bandhu** (*yajñá-*), m. associate in s°, RV. — **bāhu**, m. 'arm of s°,' fire or Agni, BhP.; N. of a son of Priya-vrata, ib. — 1. -**bhāga**, m. a share in a s°, Hariv.; Kāv.; Pur.; -*bhuj*, m. enjoyer of a share in a s°, a god, Kum.; Pur. — 2. -**bhāga**, mfn. having a share in a s°, MārkP.; m. a god, in °*geśvara,* m. 'lord of the gods,' N. of Indra, Śak — **bhājana** (L.), -**bhāṇḍa** (R.), n. = -*pātra.* — **bhāvana,** mfn. promoting s° (Vishṇu), BhP.; Pañcar. — **bhāvita,** mfn. honoured with s° (as the gods), MW. — **bhuj,** m. 's°-enjoyer,' a god (esp. Vishṇu), MBh.; Pur. — **bhūmi,** f. a place for s°, R.; Kathās. — **bhūshaṇa,** n. 's°-ornament,' white Darbha grass, Bhpr. — **bhṛit,** m. 's°-bearer,' the institutor of a s°, VarBṛS.; N. of Vishṇu, MBh. — **bhairava,** m. N. of an author, Cat. — **bhoktṛi,** m. = -*bhuj,* Pañcar. — **mañjūshā,** f. N. of wk. — **maṇḍala,** n. circle or place for a s°, R. — **manas,** mfn. intent on s°, ĀśvŚr. — **manman** (*yajñá-*), mfn. ready for s°, RV. — **maya,** mf(*ī*)n. containing the s°, Hariv. — **mahôtsava,** m. a great s°al feast or ceremony, BhP. — **māli,** m. N. of a man, Cat. — **mukhá,** n. mouth i. e. commencement of or introduction to a s°, TS.; Br. — **músh,** m. 's°-stealer,' N. of a malicious demon, TS.; MBh. — **muh,** mfn. disturbing a s°, ŚāṅkhBr. — **mūrti,** m. N. of Vishṇu, Vishṇ.; of a man (ancestor of Kāśī-nātha), Cat. — **mení,** f. s° compared to an angry or malicious demon, ŚBr. — **yaśasa,** n. s°al splendour, TS. — **yoga,** m. N. of Vishṇu, Vishṇ. — **yogya,** m. Ficus Glomerata, L. — **rasa,** m. 'juice of s°,' the Soma, Hariv. — **rāj,** m. 'king of s°,' the moon, L. (cf. under *yajvan*). — **ruci,** m. N. of a Dānava, Kathās. — **rūpá,** n. the form or attribute of a s°, ŚBr.; KātyŚr. (-*dhṛik,* m. N. of Kṛishṇa, Pañcar.); mfn. having the form of a s°, MuṇḍUp. — **retas,** n. 'seed of s°,' the Soma, BhP. — **rta** (for -*ṛita; yajñá-*), mfn. suitable or proper for s° (?), AV. — **liṅga,** m. 'having s° for an attribute,' N. of Vishṇu, BhP. — **lih,** m. 's°-taster,' a priest, L. — **vacas** (*yajñá-*), m. N. of a teacher (with the patr. Rāmastambāyana; pl. his family), ŚBr.; (-*vacás*), AV. xi, 3, 19, w.r. for *yajña-vatas* (Paipp.; cf. next). — **vat** (*yajñá-*), mfn. worshipping, sacrificing, RV.; AV. — **vanas** (*yajñá-*), mfn. loving s°, RV. — **varāha,** m. Vishṇu in the boar-incarnation, W. — **vardhana,** mfn. increasing or promoting s°, AV. — **varman,** m. N. of a king, Inscr. — **valka,** m. N. of a man, Saṃk. — **vallī,** f. Cocculus Cordifolius, L. — **vaha,** m. du. 'conducting the s° to the gods,' N. of the two Aśvins, L. — **vāṭa,** m. a place enclosed and prepared for a s°, MBh.; Kāv.; Pur. — **vāma,** m. N. of a man, VāyuP. — **vāstú,** n. = -*bhūmi,* TS.; Br.; a partic. ceremony, Gaut.; Gobh. — **vāha,** mfn. conducting the s° to the gods, MBh.; m. N. of one of Skanda's attendants, ib. — **vāhana,** mfn. performing a s° (as a Brāhman), MBh.; m. 'having s° for a vehicle,' N. of Vishṇu, ib.; of Śiva, Śivag. — **vāhas** (*yajñá-*), mfn. offering or receiving worship or s°, RV.; AV.; TS. — **vāhin,** mfn. = -*vāha,* MBh. (only *a-y°-v°*). — **víd,** mfn. skilled in s°, ŚBr. — **vidyā,** f. skill in s°, Prab. — **vibhráṅśa,** m. failure of a s°, ĀpŚr. — **vibhrashṭa** (*yajñá-*), mfn. failing or unsuccessful in s°, TS.; -*tva,* n., ĀpŚr., Sch. — **vīrya,** m. 'whose might is s°,' N. of Vishṇu, BhP. — **vṛiksha,** m. 's°-tree,' Ficus Indica, L. — **vṛiddha** (*yajñá-*), mfn. exalted or delighted with s°, RV. — **vṛidh,** mfn. pleased with or abounding in s°, AV. — **vedi** or -**vedī,** f. an altar for s°, MW. — **veśasá,** n. disturbance or profanation of worship or s°, TS.; Br. — **vaibhava-khaṇḍa,** m. or n. N. of wk. — **voḍhave** (for *yajñam* + *v°,* Ved. inf. fr. √*vah*), to convey the s° to the gods, Nidānas. — **vrata** (*yajñá-*), mfn. observing the ritual of s°, TS. — **śatru,** m. 'enemy of s°,' N. of a Rākshasa, R. — **śamalá,** n. a fault in a s°, TS. — **śaraṇa,** n. 's°-shed,' a building or temporary structure under which s°s are performed, Mālav. — **śālā,** f. a s°al hall, BhP.; = *agni-śaraṇa,* Sch. — **śāstra,** n. the science of s° (-*vid,* mfn. familiar with it), Mn. iv, 22. — **śishṭa,** n. the remnants of a s° (°*ṭâśana,* n. the eating of them), Mn. iii, 118. — **śīla,** mfn. frequently or zealously performing s°, Mn. xi, 20; m. N. of a Brāhman, Cat. — **śesha,** m. what is left (to be performed) of a s°, Lāṭy.; = -*śishṭa,* Mn. iii, 285. — **śrí,** mfn. promoting s°, RV. i, 4, 7; m. N. of a prince, Pur. — **śreshṭha,** m. the best of s°s, Kauś.; (*ā*), f. Cocculus Cordifolius, L. — **saṃśita** (*yajñá-*), mfn. excited or impelled by s°, AV. — **saṃsiddhi,** f. success of a s°, Gobh. — **saṃsthā,** f. the basis or fundamental form of a s°, ŚāṅkhGṛ. — **sac,** see *á-yajña-sac.* — **sadana,** n. = -*śālā,* MBh.; BhP. — **sadas,** n. an assembly of people at a s°, BhP. — **sammita** (*yajñá-*), mfn. corresponding to the s°, ŚBr. — **sā́dh,** mfn. performing s°, RV. — **sā́dhana,** mfn. id., RV.; occasioning or causing s° (said of Vishṇu), MBh. — **sāra,** m. 'essence of s°,' N. of Vishṇu, Pañcar.; Ficus Glomerata, L. — **sārathi,** n. N. of a Sāman, ĀrshBr. — **siddhânta-vigraha,** m., -**siddhânta-saṃgraha,** m., -**siddhi,** f. N. of wks. — **sūkara,** m. = -*varāha,* BhP. — **sūtra,** n. the s°al thread or cord (see *yajñôpavīta*), R.; -*vidhāna,* n. N. of wk. — **sena** (*yajñá-*), m. N. of a man, TS.; Kāṭh.; of Drupada, MBh.; of a king of Vidarbha, Mālav.; of a Dānava, Kathās.; of Vishṇu, MBh. — **soma,** m. N. of various Brāhmans, Kathās. — **stha,** mfn. engaged in a s°, Yājñ. — **sthala,** n. = -*bhūmi,* Cat.; N. of an Agra-hāra, Kathās.; of a Grāma, ib.; of a town, Cat. — **sthāṇú,** m. a s°al post or stake (over which the priest stumbles), TBr. — **sthāna,** n. = -*bhūmi,* L. — **svāmin,** m. 'lord of s°,' N. of a Brāhman, Kathās. — **hán,** mfn. destroying or disturbing s° or worship, TS.; Br.; m. N. of Śiva, MBh. — **hana,** mfn. = prec.; m. N. of a Rākshasa, R. — **hartṛi,** m. 'spoiler of s°,' N. of Kṛishṇa, Pañcar. — **hut,** m. a s°al priest, Vishṇ. — **hṛidaya,** mfn. 'whose heart is in s°,' loving s°, BhP. — **hotṛi,** m. the offerer at a s°, RV.; N. of a son of Manu Uttama, BhP. **Yajñâṅśabhuj,** m. 'enjoying a share in the s°,' a god, deity, Kum. **Yajñâgāra,** n. = *yajña-śaraṇa,* ŚāṅkhŚr. **Yajñâgni,** m. s°al fire, L. **Yajñâṅga,** n. 's°-limb,' a part or means or instrument or requisite of a s°, ŚrS.; Kum.; m. the black-spotted antelope, L.; N. of Vishṇu-Kṛishṇa, MBh.; Ficus Glomerata, L.; Acacia Catechu, L.; Clerodendrum Siphonantus, L.; (*ā*), f. Cocculus Cordifolius, L. **Yajñâḍhya,** m. 'rich in s°,' N. of Parāśara, L. **Yajñâtita,** m. 'surpassing s° (?),' N. of Kṛishṇa, Pañcar. **Yajñâtman,** m. 'soul of s°,' N. of Vishṇu, BhP.; (with *miśra*), N. of the father of Pārtha-sārathi, Cat. **Yajñânukāśín,** mfn. looking at or inspecting s°, TBr. **Yajñânta,** m. the end or conclusion of a s° (-*kṛit,* m. 'one who causes the end of a s°, i. e. one who spoils a s°,' N. of Kṛishṇa, Pañcar.); a supplementary s°, W.; mfn. ending with the word *yajña,* PārGṛ. **Yajñâpêta,** m. 'destitute of s°,' N. of a Rākshasa, VP. **Yajñâyatana,** n. a place for s°, MBh.; R. **Yajñâyudhá,** n. any vessel or utensil employed at a s° (10 are usually enumerated), AV.; TS.; Br.; N. of a partic. litany, TS. **Yajñâyudhin,** mfn. furnished with s°al utensils, ŚBr. **Yajñâyus,** n. the life (i. e. duration) of a s°, TBr. **Yajñâraṇyá,** n. s° compared to a wilderness (pl. the dangers connected with s°), Br. **Yajñârâdhya,** mfn. to be propitiated by s° (said of Vishṇu), VP. **Yajñâri,** m. 'foe of s°,' N. of Śiva, L. **Yajñârha,** mfn. deserving or fit for a s°; m. du. N. of the Aśvins, L. **Yajñâvakīrṇa,** mfn. one who has violated (or falsely performed) a s°, TāṇḍBr. **Yajñâvacará,** mfn. having its sphere in the s°, MaitrS. **Yajñâvayava,** mfn. whose limbs are s°s (said of Vishṇu), BhP. **Yajñâvasāna,** n. N. of the 93rd ch. of the Uttara-kāṇḍa of the Rāmāyaṇa. **Yajñâvṛitti,** f. repetition of a s°, Kauś. **Yajñâśana,** m. 's°-eater,' a god, L. **Yajñā-sáh** (strong form -*sā́h*), mfn. mighty in s°, RV. **Yajñêśa,** m. lord of s°, Mahīdh.; N. of Vishṇu, BhP.; Pañcar.; of the sun, MārkP. **Yajñêśvara,** m. 'lord of s°,' N. of Vishṇu, VāyuP.; of the wind-god, Hcat.; of the moon, ib.; (also with *ārya, bhaṭṭa* and *dīkshita*) of various authors and other men, Cat.; (*ī*), f. N. of a goddess; °*rī-vidyā-māhātmya,* n. N. of wk. **Yajñêshu,** m. N. of a man, TBr. **Yajñêshṭa,** n. a kind of fragrant grass, L. **Yajñôtsava,** m. a s°al festival, Cāṇ.; -*vat,* mfn. abounding in s°s and festivals, MBh. **Yajñôdumbara,** m. Ficus Glomerata (also written °*dumbara*). **Yajñôpakaraṇa,** n. an implement useful or necessary for s°, MBh. **Yajñôpavītá,** n. the investiture of youths of the three twice-born castes with the sacred thread or (in later times) the thread itself (worn over the left shoulder and hanging down under the right; originally put on only during the performance of sacred ceremonies but its position occasionally changed [cf. *prācīnāvītin, nivītin*]; in modern times assumed by other castes, as by the Vaidyas or medical caste in Bengal; cf. *upanayana* and IW. 192), TBr. &c. &c. (-*dāna,* n., -*dhāraṇa-mantra,* m., -*nāśa-prāyaścitta-prayoga,* m., -*nirmāṇa-paddhati,* f., -*paddhati,* f., -*pratishṭhā,* f., -*pratishṭhā-sañcikā,* f., -*mantra,* m., -*vidhi,* m. N. of wks.); °*ta-ka,* n. the sacred thread, L. (cf. *bāla-yajñôpav°*); °*ta-vat,* mfn. invested with the s° th°, MBh.; Hariv.; °*tín,* mfn. id., ŚBr.; GṛS.; MBh. **Yajñôpâsaka,** m. an honourer of s°s, one who performs a s°, Kap. **Yajñôpêta,** w.r. for *yajñâpêta.*

Yajñaka, m. endearing form of *yajña-datta,* Pat.; (*ā*), f. id. of *yajña-dattā,* ib.

Yajñāya, Nom. P. °*yáti,* to be diligent in worship or in sacrifices, RV.

Yajñāyajñíya, n. (fr. *yajñā-yajñā,* the beginning of RV. i, 168, 1) N. of various Sāmans (also called *Agnishṭoma-s°,* from coming at the end of an Agni-shṭoma), AV.; VS.; Br. &c.

Yajñāraṅgêśa-purī, f. N. of a town, Nir., Introd. (perhaps for *yajña-r°*).

Yajñika, m. Butea Frondosa, L.; = *yajña-dattaka,* Pāṇ. v, 3, 78, Sch.

Yajñin, mfn. abounding in sacrifices (said of Vishṇu), MBh.

Yajñíya, mf(*ā*)n. worthy of devout worship or sacrifice, sacred, godly, divine (applied to gods and to anything belonging to them), RV.; AV.; MBh.; BhP.; active or eager in worship and sacrifice, pious, devoted, holy, RV.; AV.; TS.; Hariv.; belonging to worship or sacrifice, sacrificial, sacred, RV. &c. &c.; m. a god, Nir.; N. of the Dvāpara or third Yuga, L.; Ficus Glomerata, L. — **deśa,** m. 'sacrificial country,' the country of the Hindūs (or that region in which sacrificial ceremonies can be duly performed, the country in which the black antelope is indigenous; cf. Mn. ii, 23), W. — **śālā,** f. a sacrificial hall, L.

Yajñiyát, mfn. = *adhvaryát,* ŚBr.

Yajñīya, mfn. suitable or fit for sacrifice, sacrificial, MBh. (with *bhāga,* m. share of a sacrifice, v.l. *yajñiya,* Hariv.); m. Ficus Glomerata, L.; Flacourtia Sapida, L.

Yajya, mfn. to be worshipped &c.; n. and (*ā*), f., see *deva-y°.*

Yájyu, mfn. worshipping, devout, pious, RV.; worthy of worship, adorable, ib.; m. an Adhvaryu priest, L.; the institutor of a sacrifice (= *yajamāna*), L.

Yájvan, mf(*arī*; accord. to Pāṇ. iv, 1, 7, Vārtt. 1, Pat.)n. worshipping, a worshipper, sacrificer, RV. &c. &c. (*yajvanām patiḥ,* the moon, L.); sacrificial, sacred, RV. i, 3, 1; m. an offerer, bestower, Hcat.

Yajvin, mfn. = *yajvan,* worshipping, a worshipper, MBh.; Pur.

Yañjá, m. a word invented to explain *yajñá,* ŚBr.

Yáshṭave. See under √*yaj.*

Yashṭavya, m. to be worshipped or adored (n. impers.), MaitrUp.; MBh. &c.

1. **Yashṭi,** f. (for 2. see p. 848, col. 3) sacrificing, Pāṇ. iii, 3, 110, Sch. (prob. w.r. for *ishṭi*).

Yashṭu-kāma, mfn. desiring to sacrifice, R.

Yashṭrí or **yáshṭṛi,** mf(*trī,* ĀpŚr., Sch.)n. worshipping, a worshipper, RV. &c. &c. — **tara,** mfn. one who worships more or most, Nir. — **tā,** f., -**tva,** n. the state of a worshipper, Nyāyam., Sch.

Yiyakshat (R.), °**kshamāṇa** and °**kshu** (MBh.), mfn. (fr. Desid.) wishing to worship or sacrifice.

यण् *yaṇ,* (in gram.) a term for the semivowels *y, r, l, v,* Pāṇ. — **ādeśa-sūtra,** n. N. of wk.

यण्व *yaṇva,* n. N. of a Sāman (*yaṇvâpatye,* n. du.), ĀrshBr.

यत् 1. *yát,* mfn. (pr. p. of √5. *i*) going, moving, RV. &c. &c. (*abde yati,* in this year, L.)

यत् 2. *yat,* cl. 1. Ā. (prob. connected with √*yam* and orig. meaning 'to stretch;' Dhātup. ii, 29) *yátate* (Ved. and ep. also P. °*ti*; p. *yátamāna, yátāna* and *yatāná,* RV.; pf. *yete,* 3. pl. *yetire,* ib. &c.; aor. *ayatishṭa,* Br.; fut. *yatishyate,* Br., °*ti,* MBh.; inf. *yatitum,* MBh.; ind.p. -*yátya,* MBh.), (P.) to place in order, marshal, join, connect, RV.; (P. or Ā.) to keep pace, be in line, rival or vie with (instr.), ib.; (Ā.) to join (instr.), associate with (instr.), march or fly together or in line, ib.; to conform or comply with (instr.), ib.; to meet, encounter (in battle), ib.; Br.; to seek to join one's self with, make for, tend towards (loc.), ib.; to endeavour to reach, strive after, be eager or anxious for (with loc., dat., acc. with or without *prati,* once with gen.; also with *arthe, arthāya, artham* and *hetos* ifc.; or with inf.), Mn.; MBh.; Kāv. &c.; to exert one's self, take pains, endeavour, make effort, persevere, be cautious or watchful, ib.; to be prepared for (acc.), R.: Caus. (or cl. 10, Dhātup. xxxiii, 62) *yātáyati* (or °*te*; aor. *ayīyatat*; Pass. *yātyate*), to join, unite (Ā. intrans.), RV.; to join or attach to (loc.), PañcavBr.; to cause to fight, AitBr.; to strive to obtain anything (acc.) from (abl.), Mālav.;

(rarely Ā.) to requite, return, reward or punish, reprove (as a fault), RV. &c. &c.; (Ā.) to surrender or yield up anything (acc.) to (acc. or gen.), MBh.; (P. Ā.) to distress, torture, vex, annoy, BhP.; accord. to Dhātup. also *nikāre* (others *nirākāre* or *khede*) and *upaskāre:* Desid. *yiyatishate*, Gr.: Intens. *yāyatyate* and *yāyatti*, ib.

Yatana, n. making effort or exertion, W.

Yataniya, mfn. to be exerted or persevered or striven after (n. impers. with loc.), Sarvad.

Yatavyà, mf(*ā*)n. (fr. *yatu;* applied to *tanú*) = *prayatna-vat*, TS. (Sch.; Kāṭh. *yātavya* fr. *yātu*).

1. **Yáti**, m. (for 2. and 3. see col. 2 and p. 845) a disposer, RV. vii, 13, 1 (Sāy. 'a giver'); 'a striver,' an ascetic, devotee, one who has restrained his passions and abandoned the world, Up.; Mn.; MBh. &c. (cf. IW. 131); N. of a mythical race of ascetics (connected with the Bhṛigus and said to have taken part in the creation of the world), RV. &c. &c.; N. of a son of Brahmā, BhP.; of a son of Nahusha, MBh.; Hariv.; Pur.; of a son of Viśvāmitra, MBh.; N. of Śiva, MBh.; = *nikāra* or *kāra*, L. **–kartavya-gaṅgā-stuti**, f. N. of wk. **–cāndrâyaṇa**, n. N. of a partic. kind of penance, Mn. xi, 218. **–tva**, n. the state of a Yati or ascetic, Cat. **–dharma**, m. the duty of a Y°; *-prakāśa*, m., *-saṃgraha*, m., *-samuccaya*, m. N. of wks. **–dharman** or **-dharmin**, m. N. of a son of Śvaphalka. **–pañcaka**, n. N. of 5 stanzas on the subject of ascetics (attributed to Śaṃkarâcārya). **–pātra**, n. an ascetic's bowl, a wooden vessel for collecting alms (sometimes a hollow bamboo or an earthen bowl or a gourd is used for that purpose), W. **–prativandana-khaṇḍana**, n., **-prayoga**, m., **-pravana-kalpa**, m., **-bhāgavata**, n., **-bhūshaṇī**, f. N. of wks. **–maithuna**, n. the unchaste life of ascetics, L. **–rāja**, m. 'king of ascetics,' N. of Rāmânuja (RTL. 119 &c.); *-daṇḍaka*, m. or n., *-viṃśati*, f., *-vijaya*, m. (also called *vedânta-vilāsa*), *-śatakaṭīkā*, f., *-saptati*, f.; °*jīya*, n. N. of wks. **–liṅga-samarthana**, n., **-vandana-nishedha**, m., **-vandana-śata-dūshaṇī**, f., **-vandana-samarthana**, n. N. of wks. **–varya**, m. N. of an author, Cat. **–vilāsa**, m. N. of a man, Cat. **–saṃskāra**, m. N. of ch. of wk.; *-prayoga*, m., *-vidhi*, m., *-vidhinirṇaya*, m. N. of wks. **–samārādhana-vidhi**, m. N. of wk. **–sāṃtapana**, n. N. of a partic. kind of penance (a *pañca-gavya* lasting for three days), Prâyaśc. **–svadharma-bhikshā-vidhi**, m. N. of a wk. (containing rules for the regulation of life on the part of religious mendicants, attributed to Śaṃkarâcārya). **Yatindra**, m. = *yati-rāja; -mata-dīpikā*, f., *-mata-dūshaṇī*, f., *-mata-bhāskara*, m. N. of wks. **Yatiśa**, m. N. of various authors (also with *paṇḍita*), Cat. **Yatiśvara**, m. = *yati-rāja; -prârthanā*, f. N. of a Stotra; *-svāmin*, m. N. of an author, Cat.

Yatita, mfn. striven, endeavoured, attempted, tried (with inf., e.g. °*to hantum*, attempted to be killed), MBh.; n. also imp. (e.g. °*tam mayā gantum*, it was tried by me to go), ib.

Yatitavya, mfn. to be endeavoured, to be striven for or after (n. impers. with loc.), R.; Pañcat.

Yatin, m. an ascetic, devotee, Pañcar.; (*inī*), f. a widow, L.

Yatu. See *yatavyà*.

Yatúna, mfn. (prob.) moving, active, restless, RV. v, 44, 8.

1. **Yatta**, mfn. (for 2. see under √*yam*) endeavoured, striven, MBh.; Kāv. &c.; engaged in, intent upon, prepared for, ready to (loc., dat., acc. or inf. with *prati*), MBh.; R.; Hariv.; on one's guard, watchful, cautious, ib.; attended to, guided (as a chariot), MBh.

Yatna, m. activity of will, volition, aspiring after, Kaṇ.; Bhāshāp.; performance, work, Bhar.; (also pl.) effort, exertion, energy, zeal, trouble, pains, care, endeavour after (loc. or comp.), Mn.; MBh. &c. (*yatnaṃ* with √*kṛi*, *ā-*√*sthā*, *samā-*√*sthā*, *ā-*√*dhā* and loc. or inf., 'to make an effort or attempt,' 'take trouble or pains for;' *yatnena* or °*tnais*, 'with effort,' 'carefully,' 'eagerly,' 'strenuously' [also *yatna*, ibc.]; *yatnenâpi*, 'in spite of every effort;' *yatnair vinā*, 'without eff°;' *yatnāt*, with or notwithstanding eff°; *mahato yatnāt*, 'with great eff°,' 'very carefully'); a special or express remark or statement, ĀpŚr., Sch. **–tas**, ind. through or with effort, diligently, zealously, carefully, Mn.; R. &c. **–pratipādya**, mfn. to be explained with difficulty, not easy, MW. **–vat**, mfn possessing energy (*-tva*) n., making effort, taking pains about (loc.), strenuous, diligent, Mn.; MBh. &c. **Yatnâkshepa**, m. an objection raised notwithstanding an eff° to stop it, Kāvyâd. **Yatnântara**, n. another eff° or exertion, Kāś. on Pāṇ. vi, 1, 26.

Yaty, in comp. for 1. *yati.* **–anushṭhāna**, n. (and °*na-paddhati*, f.), **-anta-karma-paddhati**, f., **-ācāra-saṃgrahīya-yati-saṃskāra-prayoga**, m., **-ācāra-saptarshi-pūjā**, f. N. of wks.

Yatya, mfn. to be striven or exerted, Pat. on Pāṇ. iii, 1, 97.

यत *yata.* See under √*yam*, p. 845.

यतम *ya-tama, ya-tara.* See under 3. *ya.*

Yátas, ind. (fr. 3. *ya*, correlative of *tátas*, and often used as abl. or instr. of the relative pron.) from which or what, whence, whereof, wherefrom, RV. &c. &c. (*yáto yataḥ*, 'from whichever,' 'from whatever,' 'whencesoever;' *yatas tataḥ*, 'from any one soever,' 'from any quarter whatever;' *yata eva kutaś ca*, 'from this or that place,' 'whencesoever'); where, in what place, AV. &c. &c.; whither, Kāv.; Var.; Kathās. (*yato yataḥ*, 'whithersoever;' *yatas tataḥ*, 'any whither,' 'to any place whatever'); wherefore, for which reason, in consequence whereof, R.; BhP.; as, because, for, since, AV. &c. &c. (often connecting with a previous statement); from which time forward, since when (also with *prabhṛiti; yato jātā*, 'ever since birth'), MBh.; Kāv. &c.; as soon as, RV. iii, 10, 6; that (= ὅτι, also to introduce an oratio recta), Kāv.; Pur.; in order that (with Pot.), BhP.

2. **Yáti** (fr. 3. *ya*, correlative of *táti;* declined only in pl., nom. acc. *yáti*), as many as (= Lat. *quot*), as often, how many or often, RV. (for 1. and 3. *yati* see col. 1 and p. 845).

Yatithá, mf(*ī*)n. 'the as manieth,' ŚBr.

Yatidhā, ind. in as many parts or ways, AV.

Yato, in comp. for *yatas.* **–já**, mfn. produced from which, VS. **–dbhava** (irreg. for *yata-udbh°*), mfn. id., Hariv. **–mūla**, mfn. originating in or from which, R.

Yátra, ind. (in Veda also *yátrā;* fr. 3. *ya*, correlative of *tátra*, and often used for the loc. of the relative pron.) in or to which place, where, wherein, wherever, whither, RV. &c. &c. (*yatra yatra*, 'wherever,' 'whithersoever;' *yatra tatra* or *yatra tatrâpi*, 'anywhere whatever' or = *yasmiṃs tasmin*, 'in whatever;' *yatra tatra dine*, 'on any day whatever;' *yatra kutra*, with or without *cit* or *api*, 'everywhere' or = *yasmin kasmin*, 'in whatever;' *yátra kvà ca* or *yatra kva cana*, 'wherever,' 'in any place whatever,' 'whithersoever;' *yatra kva ca*, 'anywhere whatever;' *yatra kvâpi*, 'to any place,' 'hither and thither;' *yatra vā*, 'or elsewhere'); on which occasion, in which case, if, when, as, RV. &c. &c. (*yatra tatra*, 'on every occasion,' *yatra kva ca*, 'whenever'); in order that, RV. iii, 32, 14; ix, 29, 5; that (with Pot. after 'to doubt, wonder &c.'), Pāṇ. iii, 3, 148; (with Pres.), Hit. i, 176 (v.l.) **–kāmam**, ind. wherever one pleases, accord. to pleasure or wish, ŚBr. **–kāmâvasāya**, m. the supernatural power of transporting one's self anywhere one likes (said to belong to Yogins), Cat.; °*sāyin*, mfn. (in °*sāyi-tā*, f. and *-tva*, n.) possessing that power, Pur. **–tatra-śaya**, mfn. lying down or sleeping anywhere, MBh. **–sāyaṃ-gṛiha** and **-sāyam-pratiśraya**, mfn. taking up an abode wherever evening overtakes one, ib. **–stha**, mfn. where staying, in which place abiding, ib. **Yatrâkūṭá**, n. the aim or object in view, TS. **Yatrâstamita-śāyin**, mfn. lying down to sleep wherever sunset finds one, MBh. **Yatrêcchaka**, mfn. wherever one likes, ib. **Yatrôdbhūta**, mfn. wherever arisen, Kāvyâd.

Yatratya, mfn. where being or dwelling, relating to which place, Mālatim.; BhP.

Yatha for *yathā* before *ṛi* and *r* = *ṛi.* **–ṛishi**, ind. according to the Ṛishi, AitBr.; ĀśvŚr. **–rcam**, ind. acc° to the Ṛic, Lāṭy. **–rtu**, ind. acc° to the season or any fixed time, AitBr.; GṛŚrS.; *-pushpita*, mfn. bearing flowers or blossoms at the right season, R. **–rtuka**, mfn. corresponding to the season of the year, MBh. **–rshi**, ind. = *-ṛishi*, KātyŚr.; acc° to the number of Ṛishis, ĀpGṛ.; °*shy-ādhāna*, n. N. of partic. verses or formulas, ĀpŚr.

Yáthā, ind. (in Veda also unaccented; fr. 3. *ya*, correlative of *táthā*) in which manner or way, according as, as, like (also with *cid, ha, ha vai, iva, ivâṅga, iva ha, eva*, and followed by correl. *tathā, tathā tathā, tadvat, evam*, Ved. also *evā*), RV. &c. &c. (*yathâtat* or *yathâvâtat*, 'as for that;' *yathā-tathā* or *yathā—tena satyena*, 'as surely as' —'so truly'); as, for instance, namely (also *tad yathā*, 'as here follows'), Up.; GṛŚrS.; Nir.; as it is or was (elliptically), BhP.; that, so that, in order that (with Pot. or Subj., later also with fut., pres., imperf. and aor.; in earlier language *yathā* is often placed after the first word of a sentence; sometimes with ellipsis of *syāt* and *bhavet*), RV. &c. &c.; that (esp. after verbs of 'knowing,' 'believing,' 'hearing,' 'doubting' &c.; either with or without *iti* at the end of the sentence), Up.; MBh.; Kāv. &c.; as soon as, Megh.; as, because, since (*yathā-tathā*, 'as'—'therefore'), MBh.; Kāv. &c.; as if (with Pot.), Daś.; Śak.; how (= *quam*, expressing 'admiration'), Pāṇ. viii, 1, 37, Sch.; according to what is right, properly, correctly (= *yathâvat*), BhP. (*yáthā yathā–táthā tathā* or *evâiva*, 'in whatever manner,'—'in that manner,' 'according as' or 'in proportion as,'—'so,' 'by how much the more'—'by so much,' 'the more'—'the more;' *yathā tathā*, 'in whatever manner,' 'in every way,' 'anyhow;' with *na*, 'in no way,' 'really not;' *yathā kathaṃcit*, 'in any way,' 'somehow or other;' *yathâiva*, 'just as;' *tad yathâpi nāma*, 'just as if'). **–°ṃśa-tas** (°*thâṅ°*), ind. (W.) or **-°ṃśam** (°*thâṅ°*), ind. (A.) according to shares or portions, in due proportion, proportionably. **–kathita**, mfn. as (already) mentioned, Vikr. **–kanishṭham**, ind. acc° to the age from the youngest to the oldest, PārGṛ. **–kartavya**, mfn. proper to be done (under any partic. circumstances), Hit. **–karmá**, ind. acc° to actions, ŚBr.; ŚrS. &c.; acc° to circumstances, MW.; *-guṇam*, ind. acc° to actions and qualities, BhP. **–kalpam**, ind. in conformity with ritual or ceremonial, R. **–kāṇḍam**, ind. acc° to chapters, L. **–kāma** (*yáthā-*), mfn. conformable to desire, ŚBr.; acting acc° to wish, Hcat.; (*-kāmam*, RV.; *-kāmám*, ŚBr.) ind. acc° to wish, as one likes, at pleasure, easily, comfortably, RV. &c. &c.; *-cāra*, n. action acc° to pleasure or without control, ChUp.; *-jyeya*, mfn. to be oppressed at pl°, AitBr.; *-prayāpya*, mfn. to be sent away at pl°, ib.; *-vadhya*, mfn. to be chastised or punished at pl°, ib.; *-vicārin*, mfn. roaming at pl°, MBh.; R.; °*mârcitârthin*, mfn. honouring suppliants by conforming to their desires, Ragh. **–kāmin**, mfn. acting acc° to will or pleasure (°*mi-tva*, n.), GṛŚrS.; Śaṃk. on AitUp.; Yājñ. **–kāmya**, n., w. r. for *yathâk°*, q. v., Pāṇ. viii, 1, 66, Vārtt. 1. **–kāyam**, ind. 'according to body or form,' acc° to the dimensions (of the Yūpa), KātyŚr. **–kāram**, ind. in such a way, in whatever way, Pāṇ. iii. 4, 28. **–kārin**, mfn. acting in such or in whatever way, ŚBr. **–kārya**, mfn. = *-kartavya*, Hit.; Vet. **–kāla**, m. the proper time (for anything), suitable moment (*dvitīyo y°*, 'the second meal-time'), MBh.; ibc. or (*am*), ind. acc° to time, in due t°, at the right or usual t°, KātyŚr. &c. &c.; *-prabodhin*, mfn. watchful in proper seasons, waking at the right t°, Ragh. **–kulam**, ind. acc° to families, ĀpGṛ., Comm.; °*la-dharmam*, ind. acc° to family usage, GṛS. **–kṛita**, mfn made or done acc° to rule, in *a-y°*, MBh.; VarBṛS.; agreed, Yājñ.; (*ám*), ind. acc° to usual practice, RV.; as happened, Kathās.; in the way agreed upon, Mn. viii, 183; acc° as anything has been done, KātyŚr. **–kṛishṭam**, ind. acc° to furrows, f° after f°, KātyŚr. **–klṛipti**, ind. in a suitable or fitting way, R. (v. l. *-jñapti*). **–kratu** (*yáthā-*), mfn. forming such a plan, ŚBr. **–krama** (ibc.; Kathās.), °**mam** (Mn.; Kāv. &c.), or °**meṇa** (MaitrUp.; VarBṛS.), ind. acc° to order, in due succession, successively, respectively. **–kriyamāṇa**, mf(*ā*)n. 'as being done,' usual, customary, Hcar. **–krośam**, ind. acc° to the number of Krośas, KātyŚr. **–kshamam**, ind. acc° to power or ability, as much as possible, Kathās. **–°ksharam** (°*thâk°*), ind. acc° to syllables, syl° after syl°, SaṃhUp. **–kshipram**, ind. as quickly as possible, R. **–kshemeṇa**, ind. safely, comfortably, peaceably, R. **–khātam**, ind. as dug or excavated, ŚBr.; KātyŚr. **–khelam**, ind. playfully, Vikr. **–°khyam** (°*thâkh°*), ind. acc° to names, as named, KātyŚr. **–°khyāta** (°*thâkh°*), mfn. as previously told or described or mentioned, R.; Daś.; MārkP. **–°khyānam** (°*thâkh°*), ind. acc° to any narrative or statement, as narrated or stated, Kathās. **–1. -gata**, mfn. as gone, as previously gone, MW. **–2. -°gata** (°*thâg°*), mfn. as come, by the way one came, R.; Hariv. &c.; as one came (into the world), without sense, stupid, L. (cf. *-jāta, yathôdgata*); *am* (MBh.; R. &c.) or *ena* (MBh.), ind. by the way one came. **–°gama**

(°*thâg°*), mfn. orthodox, ŚāṅkhGṛ.; (*am*), ind. acc° to tradition, Āpast.; MBh. &c. — °**gamanam** (°*thâg°*), ind. acc° to the way in which anything has come or has been found, Śak. — **gātram**, ind. acc° to every limb, limb after l°, Kauś. — **guṇam**, ind. acc° to qualities or endowments, ChUp.; Saṃk.; Rājat. — **gṛiham**, ind. acc° to houses (*yānti yathā-g°*, they go to their respective homes), MBh. — **gṛihītám**, ind. just as taken or laid hold of, as come to hand, ŚBr.; ŚrS.; in the order mentioned, RPrāt. — **gotra-kula-kalpam**, ind. acc° to the usages of a family or race, Gobh. — °**gni** (°*thâg°*), ind. acc° to (the size of) the fire, KātyŚr.; acc° to the digestive power, Car. — **grahaṇam**, ind. acc° to any statement, acc° to what was mentioned, ĀśvŚr. — °**ṅgám** (°*thâṅ°*), ind. = -*gātram* (q. v.), AV.; ŚBr.; GṛŚrS. — **camasám**, ind. Camasa after C°, ŚBr.; ŚāṅkhŚr.; Vait. — °**cāram** (°*thâc°*), ind. acc° to custom, as usual, R.; Prayogar.; Saṃskārak. — **cārín**, mfn. as proceeding, as acting, ŚBr. — **citi**, ind. layer after l°, KātyŚr. — **cittam**, ind. acc° to a person's thought or will, Mālatim. — **cintita**, mfn. as previously considered, Pañcat.; VarBṛS.; Kathās.; °*tânubhâvin*, mfn. judging by one's own state of mind, Śak. — **coditam**, ind. acc° to precept or injunction, ŚrS. — **chandasam**, ind. acc° to metre, one metre after another, AitBr.; ŚāṅkhŚr. — **janapadam**, ind. acc° to countries, ĀpGṛ., Sch. — **jāta**, mfn. just as born (ibc.); stupid, foolish, Kād.; barbarous, outcast, W.; (*ám*), ind. acc° to race or family, f° by f°, ŚBr.; -*rūpa-dhara*, mfn. stark naked, JābālUp. — **jāti**, ind. acc° to kind or class, sort by sort, Lāṭy. — **jātīyaka**, mfn. of such a kind, of whatever kind, Pat.; Nyāyad., Sch. — **josham**, ind. acc° to will or pleasure, acc° to one's satisfaction, MBh. — °**jñapta** (°*thâj°*), mfn. as before enjoined, before directed, R. — °**jñapti** (°*thâj°*), ind. acc° to injunction, R. — **jñānam**, ind. acc° to knowledge, to the best of one's kn° or judgment, Gobh.; Pañcar. — **jñeyam**, ind. id., Hcat. — °**jya-gāna** (°*thâj°*), n. a song corresponding to the Ājya, Lāṭy. — **jyeshṭham**, ind. acc° to the oldest, by seniority, from the oldest to the youngest, Lāṭy.; Gobh.; Pañcat. — **tattva**, ibc. (MBh.) or -**tattvam**, ind. (ib.; R.; Kathās.) in accordance with truth, acc° to actual fact, exactly, accurately. — **tatha**, mfn. conformable to truth or the exact state of the case, right, true, accurate, W.; (*am*), ind. in conformity with truth or reality, precisely, exactly; as is becoming or proper, fitly, duly, MBh.; Pur.; Kathās.; n. a detailed account of events, W. — **tathyam** (MBh.; R.) or °**yena** (R.; Hariv.), ind. in accordance with the truth, really, truly. — **tṛipti**, ind. to the heart's content, MW. — °**tmaka** (°*thât°*), mfn. conformable to or having whatever nature, Pañcar. — **datta**, mfn. as given, R. — **dadhi-bhaksham**, ind. acc° to the Dadhi-bhaksha, ŚāṅkhŚr. — **darśana**, ibc., or -**darśanam**, ind. acc° to every occurrence, in every single case, Sāh. — **darśitam**, ind. as has been shown, Mālav. — **dāyam**, ind. acc° to shares or portions, BhP. — **dik** (ĀśvGṛ.; VarBṛS.) or -**diśam** (MBh.; Var.; BhP.), ind. acc° to the quarters of the compass; in all directions, MW. — °**dishṭa** (°*thâd°*), mfn. corresponding to what has been enjoined or directed, R.; Kathās.; (*ám*), ind. acc° to a direction or injunction, ŚBr.; Kauś.; RPrāt. — **dīksham**, ind. acc° to the prescribed observances, MBh. — **drishṭam** (Mn.; Kathās.) or °**ṭi** (Cat.), ind. as seen or observed. — **devatám**, ind. deity after d°, TS.; Br. — 1. -**deśam**, ind. acc° to places, ŚrS.; Mn.; BhP.; -°*śa-kāla-dehâvasthāna-viśesham*, ind. acc° to differences of place, time, and bodily constitution, BhP. — 2. -°**deśam** (°*thâd°*), ind. acc° to direction or injunction, GṛŚrS.; BhP. — **dosham**, ind. acc° to damage, ĀpŚr., Comm. — **dravya**, mfn. acc° to property, acc° to the kinds of wealth, KātyŚr. — **dharmám**, ind. acc° to duty or right, in proper form or order, ŚBr.; R. &c.; acc° to nature or character, Śulbas. — °**dhikāra** (°*thâdh°*), ibc. according to office or rank or position, Jātak.; acc° to authority, BhP.; (*am*), ind. acc° to auth°, Gaut. — **dhishṇyám**, ind. acc° to the position or arrangement of the Dhishṇya, ŚBr.; Vait. — °**dhīta** (°*thâdh°*), mfn. as read, conformable to the text; (*am*), ind. acc° to the text, Lāṭy.; BhP. — °**dhyāpakam** (°*thâdh°*), ind. acc° to a teacher, agreeably to a t°'s instructions, Pāṇ. ii, 1, 7, Sch. — **nāma**, mf(*ā*)n. having whatever name, ĀpŚr.; (°*má*), ind. n° by n°, AV. — **nārada-bhāshita**, mf(*ā*)n. being just as Nārada announced, BhP. — **niḥsṛiptam**, ind. as gone forth or out, ŚāṅkhŚr. — **nikāyam**, ind. acc° to the body, ŚvetUp. — **niruptam**, ind. as scattered or offered, GṛS. — **nirdishṭa**, mfn. as mentioned or described or directed, Kāv. — **nilayam**, ind. each in its own resting-place or lair, R. — **nivāsin**, mfn. wherever dwelling or abiding, R. — **niveśam**, ind. each in his own dwelling-place, R. — **niśāntam**, ind. in the received or usual manner, ĀśvŚr. — °**nīkam** (°*thân°*), ind. acc° to the extent of the army, as far as the host extended, MW. — °**nupūrvam** (°*thân°*, BhP.) ind., or -°**nupūrvya** (°*thân°*, KātyŚr.) ibc., or °**vyā** (VarBṛS.), ind. acc° to a regular series, successively, respectively. — °**nubhūtam** (°*thân°*), ind. acc° to experience, R.; BhP. — °**nurūpam** (°*thân°*), ind. acc° to form or rule, in exact conformity, VarBṛS.; Kathās. — °**ntaram** (°*thân°*), ind. acc° to the intermediate space, Kauś. — **nyastam**, ind. as deposited, Mn. — **nyāyam**, ind. acc° to rule or justice, rightly, fitly, GṛŚrS.; Mn.; MBh. &c. — **nyāsam**, ind. acc° to the text of a Sūtra, as written down, Pat. — **nyupta**, mfn. as placed on the ground or offered, Mn. iii, 218; (*ám*), ind. throw by throw, TBr.; KātyŚr. — **paṇyam**, ind. acc° to the (value or kind of the) commodities, Mn. viii, 398. — **padam**, ind. acc° to word, w° by w°, RPrāt. — **param**, ind. (prob.) as otherwise, MBh. — °**parādham** (°*thâp°*), ind. acc° to the offence, BhP.; °*dha-daṇḍa*, mfn. inflicting punishment in proportion to the crime, Ragh. — **paridhi**, ind. Paridhi after P°, MānSr. — **parilikhitam**, ind. acc° to the outline or sketch, KātyŚr. — **parīttam**, ind. as delivered up, ŚāṅkhGṛ. — **parú**, ind. joint after j°, limb by l°, AV.; Kauś. — **paryukshitam**, ind. as sprinkled, KātyŚr. — **parva**, ind. acc° to each Parvan, ŚāṅkhŚr. — **pāṭha**, mfn. conformable to the enumeration or recitation, VarBṛS., Sch.; (*am*), ind. acc° to the recit°, MBh. — **puṃsam**, ind. man by man, ĀpGṛ., Sch. — **puram**, ind. as before, GopBr.; GṛŚrS. &c. — **purusham**, ind. man by man, L. — **pūrva**, mfn. being as before (-*tva*, n.), Kāṭh.; Ragh.; (*ám*), ind. in succession, one after another, RV.; TS.; Br. &c.; as before, as previously, R.; Pañcat.; BhP. — **pūrvaka**, mfn., °**kam**, ind. = -*pūrva*, °*vam*, A. — **pṛishṭhya**, mfn. conformable to the Pṛishṭhya, ŚāṅkhŚr. — **paurāṇa**, mfn. being as before, in the former state, Jātak. — **prakṛiti**, ind. acc° to a scheme or rule, ŚrS. — **prajñam**, ind. acc° to knowledge, Cat. — **pratiguṇam** (MW.) or °**ṇais** (Hariv.), ind. acc° to qualities, to the best of one's abilities. — **pratijñam**, ind. acc° to promise or agreement, MBh.; (*ābhis*), ind. acc° to ag°, as arranged, MBh. — **pratirūpám**, ind. as is suitable or fitting, ŚBr. — **pratyaksha-darśanam**, ind. as if in one's view, as if one saw it with one's eyes, MBh. — **pratyarham**, ind. acc° to merit, Buddh. — **pradānam**, ind. in the same order as the offering (was made), Jaim. — **pradishṭam**, ind. acc° to precept, as suitable or proper, R. — **pradeśam**, ind. acc° to place, in a suitable or proper pl°, Kālid.; Pañcad.; on all sides, R.; = -*pradishṭam* above, MBh.; Hariv. — **pradhānam**, ind. acc° to precedence or superiority or rank, ŚāṅkhGṛ.; MBh. &c.; acc° to size, Kād.; °*na-tas*, ind. acc° to precedence &c., Hariv. — **prapannam**, ind. as each one entered, ŚāṅkhŚr. — **prabhāvam**, ind. acc° to strength or power, ŚBr. — **prayogam**, ind. acc° to usage or practice, TPrāt.; ĀpŚr., Comm. — **pravṛitam**, ind. as chosen, KātyŚr. — **praveśam**, ind. accord. as each one entered, Daś. — **praśnam**, ind. acc° to the questions, BhP.; Suśr. — **prasṛiptam**, ind. as each one crept in, ĀśvŚr. — **prastaram**, ind. as in the Prastara, Lāṭy. — **prastāvam**, ind. on the first suitable occasion, Jātak. — **prastutam**, ind. as already begun or commenced, at last, at length, Mālatim.; conformably to the circumstances, MW. — **prāṇam** (MBh.) or °**ṇena** (R.), ind. with the whole soul, with all one's might. — **prâpta**, mf(*ā*)n. as met with, the first that is met or occurs, Kād.; in conformity with a partic. state, suitable or conformable to circumstances, R.; Hit.; following from a previous grammatical rule, Kāś. on Pāṇ. iii, 2, 135; (*am*), ind. in conformity with a previous rule, regularly, Kāś. on Pāṇ. iii, 2, 108; °*ta-svara*, m. a regular accent, Anup. — **prâpti**, mfn. w. r. for -*prâpta*, R. — **prârthitam**, ind. as desired, acc° to wish, Ragh. — **prâsu**, ind. as quickly as possible, ĀpŚr. — **prīti**, mfn. in accordance with love or affection, MBh. — **prêshitam**, ind. accord. as called upon or invited to take part (in liturgical ceremonies), ŚrS. — **praisham**, ind. id., Vait. — **phalam**, ind. acc° to fruit, Pañcat. — **balám**, ind. acc° to power, with all one's might, AV.; MBh. &c.; in relation to p°, R.; acc° to the (condition of the) army, acc° to the (number of) forces, Mn.; Kām. — **bījam**, ind. acc° to the seed or germ, Mn.; BhP. — **buddhi**, ind. acc° to knowledge, to the best of one's judgment, R. — **bhaktyā** (instr. of *bhakti*), ind. with entire devotion, BhP. — **bhakshitam**, ind. as eaten, KātyŚr. — **bhavanam**, ind. acc° to houses, house by house, VarBṛS. — **bhāgám**, ind. acc° to shares or portions, each acc° to his share, AV.; VS. &c.; each in his respective place or in the proper pl°, MBh.; Ragh.; °*gaśas*, ind. = °*gam*, A. — **bhājanam**, ind. each in his proper place or position, AitBr. — **bhāva**, m. proper condition or relation, Mn.; Kull. on Mn. viii, 95; conformity to any destined state, destiny, R.; mfn. having whatever nature, BhP. — °**bhikāmam** (°*thâbh°*), ind. acc° to wish or desire, BhP. — °**bhijñāya** (°*thâbh°*), mfn. as desired, Car.; (°*jñāyam*), ind. as perceived or ascertained, TBr. — °**bhinivishṭa** (°*thâbh°*), mfn. as acknowledged by each, Jātak. — °**bhiprêta** (°*thâbh°*), mfn. as wished or intended or desired, see *a-y°*; (*am*), ind. acc° to one's (gen.) desire or wish, Lāṭy.; Pañcat. &c. — °**bhimata** (°*thâbh°*), mfn. as desired, as pleasing or agreeable to each, Hit.; Yogas.; Kathās.; (*am*), ind. acc° to wish or will, at pleasure, wherever desire leads, Pañcat.; Hit.; Kathās. — °**bhirāmam** (°*thâbh°*), ind. acc° to loveliness, acc° to the degree of l° (belonging to each), MW. — °**bhirucita** (°*thâbh°*), mfn. agreeable to taste or liking, agreeable, pleasant, Kathās. — °**bhirūpam** (°*thâbh°*), ind. = *abhirūpasya yogyam*, Pāṇ. ii, 1, 7, Sch. — °**bhilashita** (°*thâbh°*), mfn. as desired, R.; BhP. &c. — °**bhilikhita** (°*thâbh°*), mfn. painted or written in the manner stated, VarBṛS. — °**bhivṛishṭam** (°*thâbh°*), ind. as far as it has rained, ib. — °**bhihitam** (°*thâbh°*), ind. as spoken, MW. — °**bhishṭa** (°*thâbh°*), mfn. as liked or desired (°*ṭa-diśaṃ jagmuḥ*, they went to the quarter that each wished), Pañcat.; Kathās. — **bhūtam**, ind. in accordance with fact, acc° to what has happened, acc° to the truth, MBh.; Lalit.; °*ta-darśin*, mfn. looking at things as they are, L. — **bhūmi**, ind. in or into the respective country (of each), Kād. (w. r. °*mim*). — **bhūyas**, ind. acc° to seniority, Vishṇ.; °*yaso-vāda*, m. a general rule, Lāṭy. — °**bhyarthita** (°*thâbh°*), mfn. as previously asked for, Śak. — **maṅgalam**, ind. acc° to custom, PārGṛ. — **mati**, ind. acc° to opinion, as seems fit to (gen.), R.; to the best of one's judgment, TPrāt.; BhP.; Vedāntas. — **manasam**, ind. to the heart's content, Āpast. — **manīshitam**, ind. acc° to wish, Hariv. — **mantra-varṇam**, ind. acc° to the words of a formula or hymn, KātyŚr. — **mātram**, ind., see *a-y°*. — **mānam**, ind. acc° to a partic. measure or dimension, MBh. — **mukham**, ind. from face to f°, Pāṇ. v, 2, 6. — **mukhīna**, mfn. looking straight at (gen.), Bhaṭṭ. (Pāṇ. ib.) — **mukhyam**, ind. acc° to the chief persons, with respect to the chief per°, MBh.; (*ena*), ind. acc. to precedence above or before all, chiefly, ib. — **mūlya**, mfn. worth the price, accordant with the price or value, Hcat. — °**mnātam** (°*thâm°*, KātyŚr.; BhP.) or -**mnāyam** (Lāṭy.; BhP.), ind. as handed down or in accordance with sacred tradition, acc° to the tenour of the sacred text. — **yajús**, ind. acc° to the Yajus, TS.; TBr. — °**yatanám** (°*thây°*), ind. each in his own place or abode, TS.; ŚBr.; Up.; (*ât*), ind. each from his own pl°, TS.; TBr. — **yathám**, ind. (fr. *yathā + yathā*) in a proper manner, as is fit or pr°, rightly, suitably, fitly; one after another, by degrees, gradually, AV.; TS. &c. — **yācita**, mfn. acc° as asked for, Siṃhās. — **yukta**, mfn. as joined, TPrāt.; directed to (loc.), concerning, MBh.; (*am*), ind. = next, Kathās. — **yukti** or -**yukti-tas**, ind. acc° to circumstances, VarBṛS. — **yūtham**, ind. acc° to the herds, Hariv. — **yūpam**, ind. acc° to the Yūpas, KātyŚr. — **yogam** (KātyŚr.; Mn.; MBh. &c.) or °**gena** (Kām.), ind. as is fit, acc° to circumstances, acc° to requirements; in due order, MW.; (*am*), ind. acc° to usage, as hitherto, usual, MBh. — **yogya**, mfn. consonant with propriety, MW.; (*am*), ind. suitably, properly, fitly, Hit. — **yoni**, ind. acc° to the womb, BhP.; in the original manner, Lāṭy. — °**rabdha** (°*thâr°*), mfn. as previously begun, VāyuP. — °**rambham** (°*thâr°*), ind. acc° to the beginning, in the same order or succession, KātyŚr. — **rasam**, ind. acc° to the sentiments, Mālav. — **rucam**, ind. acc° to taste or liking, BhP. — **ruci**, ind. acc° to pleasure or liking, acc° to taste, BhP.; Sāh.;

Kathās. **-rūpa,** mf(*ā*)n. as constituted, Lāṭy.; of whatever form, of a corresponding form or appearance, extremely beautiful, MBh.; R.; exceedingly great, R.; (*ám*), ind. in a suitable way, properly, duly, ŚBr.; ŚāṅkhGṛ.; BhP.; acc° to the form or appearance, of the same f° or app°, BhP. **-°rtha** (°*thâr*°), mf(*ā*)n. accordant with reality, conformable to truth or the true meaning, true, genuine, right (with *svapna*, m. a dream which is fulfilled; with *janman*, n. a life in the true meaning of the word), Kāv.; Pañcat. &c.; ibc. or (*ám*), ind. acc° to the aim or object, suitably, fitly, ŚBr.; GṛŚrS.; Nir.; acc° to pleasure or liking, GṛŚrS.; RPrāt.; Drāhy.; acc° to truth or fact, truly, really, MBh.; R. &c.; *-krita-nāman*, mfn. appropriately named, R.; *-tattvam*, ind. in accordance with truth or reality, MBh.; *-tas*, ind. id., Hariv.; R.; AshṭāvS.; *-tā*, f. suitableness, rectitude, accordance of a name with its meaning, Kir.; Kathās.; *-nāmaka*, mfn. having an appropriate name (*-tva*, n.), Kir., Sch.; *-nāman*, mfn. id., Kāv. &c.; *-bhāshin*, mfn. speaking fitly or truly, Ragh.; *-mañjarī*, f. N. of wk.; *-varṇa*, m. 'having a true colour or appearance,' a spy, secret emissary, MW. (cf. *-°rha-v°*); °*rthâkshara*, mfn. having letters expressive of the true sense, Vikr.; °*rthâkhya*, mfn. having an appropriate name, Kathās. **-°rthaka** (°*thâr*°), mfn. right, true, real (with *svapna*, m. a dream which is fulfilled), Kathās. **-°rthita** (°*thâr*°), mfn. as asked, as previously asked for, ib. **-°rthi-tvam** (°*thâr*°), ind. acc° to design or purpose, Sāh. **-°rpita** (°*thâr*°), mfn. as delivered, Yājñ. **-°rsham** (°*thâr*°), ind. acc° to divine descent (?), MānŚr. (prob. w. r. for *yathârtham*, q. v.) **-°rha** (°*thâr*°), mfn. as deserving, having suitable dignity, MBh.; accordant with merit or deserts, as is fit or right, appropriate, R.; Kathās.; ibc. or (*am*), ind. acc° to merit or dignity or worth, suitably, fitly (*-krita-pūja*, mfn. honoured acc° to m°), Kauś.; PārGṛ.; Mn. &c.; *-tas*, ind. acc° to worth or merit, as is proper or suitable, justly, Mn.; MBh. &c.; *-varṇa*, m. 'having a suitable appearance,' a spy, secret agent, L. **-°rhaṇam** (°*thâr*°), ind. acc° to merit or worth, BhP. **-labdha,** mfn. as obtained or met with, as actually in hand, R.; Kathās. **-lābha** (ibc.), acc° to what is met with, just as it happens to occur, Yājñ.; (*am*), ind. id., ib.; VarBṛS. &c.; acc° to gain or profit, MW. **-°likhitânubhāvin** (°*thâl*°), mfn. perceiving that anything is (only) painted, Śak. **-liṅgam,** ind. acc° to the characteristic marks or tokens, acc° to the cha° words, GṛŚrS. **-lokám,** ind. acc° to room or place, each in its respective pl° (also *-loka*, ibc.), AV.; MaitrS. &c. **-°vakāśám** (°*thâv*°), ind. acc° to room or space, TBr.; GṛS.; RPrāt.; in the proper place, Ragh.; acc° to opportunity, on the first op°, Hit. **-vacanam,** ind. acc° to the statement or word expressed, Nir.; °*na-kārin*, mfn. performing any one's orders, obedient, R. **-vat,** ind. duly, properly, rightly, suitably, exactly, RPrāt.; Mn.; MBh. &c.; as, like (= *yathā*), MārkP.; *-vad-grahaṇa*, n. right comprehension, Sarvad. **-°vattam** (°*thâv*°), ind. (*avatta*, p. p. of *ava-√do*) as cut off, KātyŚr. **-°vadānam** (°*thâv*°), ind. part by part, portion by p°, MānŚr. **-°vaniktam** (°*thâv*°), ind. as cleansed, KātyŚr. **-°vabhṛitham** (°*thâv*°), ind. acc° to the Avabhṛitha, ib. **-vayas,** ind. acc° to age, MBh.; Hariv.; R.; BhP.; of the same age, BhP. **-vayasam,** ind. acc° to age, Lāṭy.; Gobh. **-varṇam,** ind. acc° to caste, BhP.; Vait.; °*ṇa-vidhānam*, ind. acc° to the rules or laws of caste, BhP. **-vaśám,** ind. acc° to pleasure or inclination, RV.; AV. **-vashaṭ-kāram,** ind. acc° to the Vashaṭ-kāra, ŚāṅkhŚr. **-°vasaram** (°*thâv*°), ind. acc° to opportunity, on every occasion, Hit. **-vastu,** ind. acc° to the state of the matter, precisely, accurately, Prab.; Kathās. **-°vastham** (°*thâv*°), ind. acc° to state or condition, whenever the same circumstances occur, Sāh.; Kathās. **-°vasthitârtha-kathana** (°*thâv*°), n. the representation of a matter as it is in reality, Yājñ., Sch. **-vāsa,** m. N. of a man, MBh. **-°vāsam** (°*thâv*°), ind. each to his own abode, R. **-vāstu,** ind. in accordance with the site or ground, BhP. **-vitānam,** ind. acc° to the Vitānas, Kauś. **-vittam,** ind. acc° to what is found, AitBr.; acc° to possession, in proportion to substance, BhP.; °*tânusāram* or °*reṇa*, ind. acc° to one's circumstances or means, Hcat. **-vidyam,** ind. acc° to knowledge, KaushUp. **-vidha,** mfn. of whatever kind or sort (= Lat. *qualis*), MBh.; Ragh.; of such a kind or sort, such as, MW. **-vidhānam** (Pañcar.) or °**nena** (Yājñ.), ind. acc° to prescription or rule. **-vidhi,** ind. id., Kauś.; Mn. &c. (°*dhim*, m. c., Hariv.); fitly, suitably, acc. to the merit of (gen.), R. **-viniyogam,** ind. in the succession or order stated, Nyāyas., Sch. **-vibhava,** ibc. (Pañcat.) or **-vibhavam,** ind. (MārkP.; Hcat.) acc° to property or resources; *vibhava-tas*, *-mānena*, *-vistaram*, *-vistarais*, *-vistāram* or *-sambhavāt*, ind. id., Hcat. **-vibhāgam,** ind. acc. to share or portion, ŚāṅkhGṛ. **-vishayam,** ind. acc° to the subject or point under discussion, Kāś. **-vīrya,** mfn. of whatever strength, MBh.; (*am*), ind. acc° to strength or vigour, in respect of manliness or courage, R.; BhP. **-vṛitta,** mfn. as happened or occurred, as ensued, R.; as behaving or conducting one's self, Mn.; MBh.; n. a previous occurrence or event, MBh.; R.; Kathās.; the circumstances or details of an event, MBh.; R. &c.; ibc. or (*am*), ind. acc° to the circumstances of an ev°, as anything happened, circumstantially, ib.; acc° to the metre, Piṅg.; °*ttânta*, m. n. an event or adventure, Hcar.; Kathās. **-vṛitti,** ind. in respect to way or mode of living or subsistence, MBh. **-vṛiddha,** ibc. or **-vṛiddham,** ind. acc° to age or seniority, R.; Kum. **-vṛiddhi,** ind. acc° to the increase (of the moon), R. **-vedam,** ind. acc° to the Veda, KātyŚr.; Vait. **-vedi,** ind. acc° to the Vedi of each, KātyŚr. **-vyavasitam,** ind. as has been determined, Mṛicch. **-vyavahāram,** ind. acc° to usage, Hit. **-vyādhi,** ind. acc° to the (nature of a) disease, Malamāsat. **-vyutpatti,** ind. acc° to the degree of education or culture, Sāh.; acc° to the derivation or etymology, MW. **-śakti** (GṛŚrS. &c.) or **-tyā** (MBh.; Hariv. &c.), ind. acc° to power or ability, to the utmost of one's power. **-°śayam** (°*thâś*°), ind. acc° to intention or wish, BhP.; Rājat.; acc° to stipulation or presumption, BhP. **-śarīrám,** ind. body by body, TBr. **-śāstra,** ibc. (Mn.; ChUp.; Śaṃk.) or **-śāstram,** ind. (APrāt.; Mn. &c.) acc° to precept or rule, acc° to the codes of law; °*rânusārin*, mfn. observing the Śāstras, following the precepts of the sacred book, MW. **-°śisham** (°*thâś*°), ind. acc° to the prayer, Lāṭy. **-śīlam,** ind. in conformity with character, BhP. **-śobham,** ind. so that it has a good appearance, Hcat. **-śraddhám,** ind. acc° to inclination, Br.; KātyŚr. &c.; acc° to faith, in all faith or fidelity, confidently, MW. **-°śramam** (°*thâś*°), ind. acc° to the period of life (see *āśrama*), BhP. **-°śrayam** (°*thâś*°), ind. in respect of or in regard to the connection, MBh.; Kathās. **-śrāddham,** ind. acc° to the Śrāddha (q. v.), Kauś. **-śruta,** mfn. corresponding to (what has been) heard, agreeing with a report, Kathās.; n. a relative tradition, ChUp.; Śaṃk.; (*am*), ind. as heard, acc° to report, Mn.; Pur.; Kathās.; acc° to knowledge, KaṭhUp.; BhP.; acc° to Vedic precept, Śak. (w. r. for next). **-śruti,** ind. acc° to the precepts of the sacred books, Śak.; Cat. **-śreshṭhám,** ind. in order of merit, so that the best is placed first, in order of precedence, ŚBr.; Hariv. **-ślakshṇa,** mfn. pl. behaving in such a way as that the weaker is placed first, Āryabh. **-saṃvṛittam,** ind. as has happened, Mṛicch. **-saṃvedam,** ind. acc° to agreement or stipulation, KātyŚr. **-saṃstham,** ind. acc° to circumstances, BhP. **-saṃhitam,** ind. acc° to the Saṃhitā, RPrāt. **-sakhyam,** ind. acc° to friendship, BhP. **-saṃkalpam,** ind. acc° to wish, MBh. **-saṃkalpita,** mfn. as wished for, fulfilling wishes, PraśnUp.; Mn. **-saṃkhya,** n. 'relative enumeration,' (in rhet.) N. of a figure (which separating each verb from its subject so arranges verbs with verbs and subjects with subjects that each may answer to each), Kpr.; *am* (APrāt.; VPrāt.; KātyŚr. &c.) or *ena* (BhP.; Pāṇ., Sch.), ind. acc° to number, n° for n° (so that in two series composed of similar n°s, the several n°s of one correspond to those of the other, e. g. the first to the first &c.) **-saṅgam,** ind. acc° to need or exigency, suitably, opportunely, MBh. **-satyam,** ind. in accordance with truth, MBh.; R. **-°sanam** (°*thâs*°), ind. each in proper place or seat, accord. to pr° position, ŚrS.; Vas. **-saṃdishṭa,** mfn. as agreed or directed, MW.; (*am*), ind. acc° to direction or order, R.; Kathās. **-saṃdhi,** ind. acc° to Saṃdhi, RPrāt. **-°sannam** (°*thâs*°), ind. acc° as any one approaches, MBh. **-sabhaksham,** ind. in the order of each messmate, ĀśvŚr. **-samayam,** ind. acc° to agreement, acc° to established custom, MW.; acc° to time, at the proper t°, MBh.; Prab. **-samarthitam,** ind. as has been thought good, Mālav. **-samāmnātam,** ind. acc° to what has been mentioned or specified, VPrāt. **-samīhita,** mfn. as desired, corresponding to wish, Pañcat.; (*am*), ind. acc° to wish, Ratnâv. (in Prākrit). **-samuditám,** ind. as agreed or stipulated, ŚBr. **-sampad,** ind. acc° to the event, as may happen, Kauś. **-samprakīrṇam,** ind. as mingled or mixed, ŚāṅkhŚr. **-sampratyayam,** ind. acc° to agreement, MBh. **-sampradāyam,** ind. acc° to tradition, Siddh. **-samprêshitam,** ind. as called upon or invited, ŚāṅkhŚr. **-sambandham,** ind. acc° to relationship, BhP. **-sambhava,** mfn. accordant with possibility, as far as possible, compatible, Sāh.; (*am*), ind. compatibly, acc° to the connexion, respectively, VPrāt., Sch.; BṛĀrUp.; Śaṃk. &c. **-sambhavin** (Kathās.) or °**bhāvita** (MārkP.), mfn. as far as possible, compatible or corresponding. **-sarvam,** ind. as everything is, in all particulars, MBh. **-savanam,** ind. acc° to the order of the Savana, Vait.; according to the time or season, BhP. **-savam,** ind. acc° to the Sava, Kauś. **-sāma,** ind. acc° to the order of the Sāman, AitBr. **-sāmarthyam,** ind. acc° to ability or power, MW. **-sāram,** ind. acc° to quality or goodness, Hariv. **-siddha,** mfn. as effected or accomplished, MW.; as happening to be prepared, R. **-sukha,** m. the moon, L.; (ibc., AVPrāy.) or *am* (ŚāṅkhGṛ.; Mn.; MBh. &c.), ind. acc° to ease or pleasure, at ease, at will or pl°, comfortably, agreeably; °*kha-mukha*, mfn. having the face turned in any direction one pleases, Mn. iv, 51. **-sûktam,** ind. hymn by hymn, ŚāṅkhGṛ. **-sūkshma,** mfn. pl. behaving in such a way as that the smaller precedes, Āryabh.; (*am*), ind., Kād. **-sūtram,** ind. acc° to the Sūtra, Baudh. **-°stam** (°*thâs*°), ind. each to his respective home, MānGṛ. **-stut,** ind. Stut by Stut, KātyŚr. **-stutam,** ind. = *-stomam*, q. v., ŚrS.; Vait. **-stotriyam,** ind. acc° to the order of the Stotriya (or °*yā*), ŚāṅkhŚr. **-stomam,** ind. acc° to the order of the Stoma, AitBr.; ŚrS. **-stri,** ind. woman by woman, ĀpGṛ., Sch. **-sthāna,** n. (only loc. sg. and pl.) the respective place, the right or proper pl°, R.; Pañcar.; mfn. each in proper pl°, ŚāṅkhŚr.; (*ám*), ind. acc° to pl°, each acc° to the right pl°, TS.; Br. &c.; instantly, MW.; (*e*), ind. as at first, Divyâv. **-sthāmá,** ind. in the proper place (= *-sthānam*), AV. **-sthita,** mfn. accordant with circumstances, standing properly; right, proper, fit, true, MW.; (*am*), ind. accord. to the place, KātyŚr.; in statu quo, MW.; certainly, assuredly, BhP.; Kathās. **-sthiti,** ind. acc° to usage, as on previous occasions, Kathās. **-sthūla,** ibc. (Car.) or *am*, ind. (MBh.; Suśr.; Car.) in the rough, without detail. **-smṛiti,** ind. acc° to recollection, as called to mind, MBh.; acc° to the precepts of the law-books, Śak.; *-maya*, mf(*ī*)n. as fixed in the memory, Hariv. **-sva,** mf(*ā*)n. each acc° to (his, her, their) own, every one possessing his own, MBh.; Suśr.; ibc. or (*am*), ind. each on (his, her, their) own account, e° for himself or in his own way, individually, properly, ŚrS.; Gaut.; MBh. &c. **-svaram,** ind. accord. to the sound, Vait. **-svaira,** ibc. or *am*, ind. acc° to one's inclination or wish, at pleasure, freely, MBh. **-°hāra** (°*thâh*°), mfn. eating anything that comes in the way, R. **-°hṛitam** (°*thâh*°), ind. as fetched, Lāṭy.

Yathêkshitam, ind. as beheld with one's own eyes, Kathās. **Yathêccha,** mfn. agreeable to wish or desire, Pañcar.; ibc. (ib.) or *am* (MBh.; Pañcat. &c.) or *ayā* (Pañcat.; Kathās.) or °*chakam* (MBh.), ind. acc° to wish, at will or pleasure, agreeably. **Yath'êtám** (°*thā* + 1. *ēta*), ind. as come, ŚBr.; ŚrS.; Bādar. **Yathêpsayā,** ind. acc° to wish, at pleasure, MBh. **Yathêpsita,** mfn. agreeable to wish, wished for, MBh.; R. &c.; (*am*), ind. acc° to wish or desire, agreeably, ad libitum, ib. **Yathêshṭa,** mfn. agreeable to wish, desired, agreeable (*-tva*, n.), Mn.; VarBṛS. &c.; ibc. (Pañcat.; Kathās.) or *am* (GṛŚrS.; MBh. &c.), ind. acc° to wish or inclination, at pleasure, agreeably; (*am*), ind. acc° to the order of sacrifices, KātyŚr. (in this sense fr. 2. *ishṭa*); *-gati*, mfn. going as one wishes, Ragh.; *-cārin*, m. a bird, L.; *-tas*, ind. acc° to wish, at pleasure, MBh.; R.; *-saṃcārin*, mfn. = *-gati* above, ŚārṅgP.; °*ṭâcāra*, mfn. doing as one likes, unrestrained, MW.; °*ṭâsana*, mfn. sitting down as one likes, Mn. **Yathêshṭi,** ind. acc° to the sacrifice called *ishṭi*, ŚBr. **Yathâika-divasam,** ind. as if it were or had been only one day, MBh. **Yathâitam,** ind. = *yath'-ētam* above, ŚāṅkhŚr. **Yathôkta,** mf(*ā*)n. as said or told, previously t° or prescribed, above mentioned, Kauś.; Mn. &c.; ibc. (Mn.; MBh.; R.) or *am*

(KātySr.; Āp.; R. &c.) or *ena* (Mn.), ind. acc° to what has been stated, as mentioned before, in the above-mentioned way; *-vādin*, mfn. speaking as told, reporting accurately what has been said, MBh. **Yathôcita,** mfn. accordant with propriety or equity, fit, suitable, becoming, R.; Hit. &c.; ibc. (Kathās.) or *am*, ind. (R.; BhP. &c.) suitably, fitly. **Yathôcchritam,** ind. as raised or erected, KātySr. **Yathôjjitam,** ind. accord. to the victory gained, AitBr. **Yathôḍham,** ind. as led or brought along, in regular order or succession, ĀpGṛ. **Yathôttara,** mfn. following in regular order, succeeding one another, VarBṛS.; (*am*), ind. in reg° order or succession, one after another, ib.; Mn. &c. **Yathôtpatti,** ind. acc° to accomplishment, Kauś. **Yathôtsāha,** mfn. corresponding to power or strength of effort, Lāṭy.; (*am*), ind. acc° to p°, with all one's might, ŚrS.; Mn. &c. **Yathôdaya,** mfn. (that) on which anything may follow, RPrāt.; (*am*), ind. in proportion to one's income, acc° to means or circumstances, BhP.; Yājñ. **Yathôdita,** mfn. as said or told, previously stated, before mentioned, RPrāt.; Mn. &c.; (*am*), ind. as ment° bef°, acc° to a previous statement, Mn.; Pur.; Kathās. **Yathôdgata,** mfn. as arisen, MW.; as one came (into the world), without sense, stupid, L. (cf. *yatkâgata*). **Yathôdgamana,** ibc. in ascending proportion, the higher the more, Kād. **Yathôddishṭa,** mfn. as mentioned or described, as directed by (instr.), Mn.; R.; Śak.; (*am*), ind. in the manner stated, R. **Yathôddeśam,** ind. acc° to direction, MBh.; R.; Hariv. **Yathôdbhavam,** ind. acc° to origin, BhP. **Yathôpakīrṇam,** ind. as strewed or scattered down, ŚBr. **Yathôpacāram,** ind. as politeness or courtesy requires, Jātak. **Yathôpajosham,** ind. acc° to inclination or pleasure, MBh.; R.; BhP. **Yathôpadishṭa,** mfn. as indicated, as before stated, R.; (*am*), ind. in the manner before mentioned or prescribed, R.; Pāṇ. i, 4, 12. **Yathôpadeśam,** ind. acc° to advice or suggestion, acc° to precept or instructions, KātySr.; Āp. &c. **Yathôpapatti,** ind. acc° to the event or occasion, as may happen, ĀśvSr. **Yathôpapanna,** mfn. just as may happen to be at hand, just as happened, just as occurring, unconstrained, natural, MBh.; BhP. **Yathôpapātam,** ind. w.r. for next, ĀpŚr. **Yathôpapādam,** ind. just as or where anything may occur or happen, ŚāṅkhBr.; GṛŚrS. (°*pāde* [!], Kauś.) **Yathôpapādin,** mfn. the first that appears to be the best, Kauś. **Yathôpamā,** f. (in rhet.) a comparison expressed by *yathā*, MW. **Yathôpamuktam,** ind. as put on, KātySr. **Yathôpayoga,** ibc. (Kathās.) or *am*, ind. (MārkP.; Rājat.) acc° to use or need, acc° to circumstances. **Yathôpalambham,** ind. just as one happens to lay hold of or set about anything, GṛŚrS. **Yathôpasthitam,** ind. as come to or approached, Lāṭy. **Yathôpasmāram,** ind. acc° to recollection, as one may happen to remember, ŚBr. **Yathôpâdhi,** ind. acc° to the condition or supposition, BhP., Comm. **Yathôpta,** mfn. as sown, in proportion to the seed sown, Mn. **Yathâukasam,** ind. each acc° to (his) abode, AV. **Yathâucityam** (Pañcat.; Kathās.) or °**tyāt** (Sāh.), ind. in a suitable manner, acc° to propriety, fitly, suitably, duly.

Yadā, ind. (fr. 3. *ya*) when, at what time, whenever (generally followed by the correlatives *tadā*, *tatas*, *tarhi*, in Veda also by *ād*, *ād it*, *ātha*, *ádha* and *tád*), RV. &c. &c. (*yadā yadā*, followed by *tadā* or *tadā tadā*, 'as often as—so often,' 'whenever;' *yadā—tadā*, id., with repeated verbs, e.g. Hit. i, 197; *yadâiva—tadâiva*, 'when indeed—then indeed,' Śak.; *yadā prabhṛiti—tadā prabhṛiti*, 'from whatever time—from that time forward,' R.; *yadâiva khalu—tadā prabhṛity eva*, 'as soon as—thenceforward,' Śak.; *yadā kadā ca*, 'as often as,' 'whenever,' RV.; *yadā kadā cit*, 'at any time,' Kauś.; *yadā tadā*, 'always,' Naish.; the copula after *yadā* is often dropped, esp. after a participle, e.g. *yadā kshayaṃ gatam sarvam*, 'when all had gone to ruin,' R. *Yadā* is sometimes joined with other relatives used indefinitely, e.g. *yo 'tti yasya yadā māṅsam*, 'when any one eats the flesh of any one,' Hit.) — **nikāmam,** ind. when it pleases, ŚBr. — **vāja-dāvarī,** f. pl. N. of a Sāman, PañcavBr.

यतीयस *yatīyasa* (?), n. silver, L.

यतुका *yatukā* or *yatūkā*, f. a species of plant, L.

यतुन *yatuna*. See p. 841, col. 1.

यत्कर *yat-kara*, *yat-kāma*, *yat-kāraṇam* &c. See col. 3.

यत्न *yatna*, *yatya*. See p. 841, cols. 1 and 2.

यथऋषि *yatha-ṛishi*, *yatharcam* &c. See p. 841, col. 2.

यथा *yathā*, *yathâṅsa-tas* &c. See p. 841, cols. 2 and 3 &c.

यद् *yád* (nom. and acc. sg. n. and base in comp. of 3. *ya*), who, which, what, whichever, whatever, that, RV. &c. &c. (with correlatives *tad*, *tyad*, *etad*, *idam*, *adas*, *tad etad*, *etad tyad*, *idaṃ tad*, *tad idam*, *tādṛiśa*, *īdṛiśa*, *īdṛiś*, *etāvad*, by which it is oftener followed than preceded; or the correl. is dropped, e.g. *yas tu nârabhate karma kshipram bhavati nirdravyaḥ*, '[he] indeed who does not begin work soon becomes poor,' R.; or the rel. is dropped, e.g. *andhakam bhartāraṃ na tyajet sā mahā-satī*, 'she who does not desert a blind husband is a very faithful wife,' Vet. *Yad* is often repeated to express 'whoever,' 'whatever,' 'whichever,' e.g. *yo yaḥ*, 'whatever man;' *yā yā*, 'whatever woman;' *yo yaj jayati tasya tat*, 'whatever he wins [in war] belongs to him,' Mn. vii, 96; *yad yad vadati tad tad bhavati*, 'whatever he says is true,' or the two relatives may be separated by *hi*, and are followed by the doubled or single correl. *tad*, e.g. *upyate yad dhi yad bījam tat tad eva prarohati*, 'whatever seed is sown, that even comes forth,' Mn. ix, 40; similar indefinite meanings are expressed by the relative joined with *tad*, e.g. *yasmai tasmai*, 'to any one whatever,' esp. in *yadvā tadvā*, 'anything whatever;' or by *yaḥ* with *kaśca*, *kaścana*, *kaścit*, or [in later language, not in Manu] *ko 'pi*, e.g. *yaḥ kaścit*, 'whosoever;' *yāni kāni ca mitrāṇi*, 'any friends whatsoever;' *yena kenâpy upâyena*, 'by any means whatsoever.' *Yad* is joined with *tvad* to express generalization, e.g. *śūdrāṅs tvad yāṅs tvad*, 'either the Śūdras or anybody else,' ŚBr.; or immediately followed by a pers. pron. on which it lays emphasis, e.g. *yo 'ham*, 'I that very person who;' *yas tvaṃ kathaṃ vettha*, 'how do you know?' ŚBr.; it is also used in the sense of 'si quis,' e.g. *striyaṃ spṛiśed yaḥ*, 'should any one touch a woman.' *Yad* is also used without the copula, e.g. *andho jaḍaḥ pīṭha-sarpī saptatyā sthaviraś-ca yaḥ*, 'a blind man, an idiot, a cripple, and a man seventy years old,' Mn. viii, 394; sometimes there is a change of construction in such cases, e.g. *ye ca mānushāḥ* for *mānushāṅś-ca*, Mn. x, 86; the nom. sg. n. *yad* is then often used without regard to gender or number and may be translated by 'as regards,' 'as for,' e.g. *kshatraṃ vā etad vanaspatīnāṃ yan nyag-rodhaḥ*, 'as for the Nyag-rodha, it is certainly the prince among trees,' AitBr.; or by 'that is to say,' 'to wit,' e.g. *tato devā etaṃ vajraṃ dadṛiśur yad apaḥ*, 'the gods then saw this thunderbolt, to wit, the water,' ŚBr. *Yad* as an adv. conjunction generally = 'that,' esp. after verbs of saying, thinking &c., often introducing an oratio directa with or without *iti*; *iti yad*, at the end of a sentence = 'thinking that,' 'under the impression that,' e.g. Ratnâv. ii, $\frac{1}{8}$. *Yad* also = 'so that,' 'in order that,' 'wherefore,' 'whence,' 'as,' 'in as much as,' 'since,' 'because' [the correlative being *tad*, 'therefore'], 'when,' 'if,' RV. &c. &c.; *ádha yád*, 'even if,' 'although,' RV.; *yad api*, id., Megh.; *yad u—evam*, 'as—so,' ŚvetUp.; *yad uta*, 'that,' Bālar.; 'that is to say,' 'scilicet,' Kāraṇḍ.; Divyâv.; *yat kila*, 'that,' Prasannar.; *yac ca*, 'if,' 'that is to say,' Car.; *yac ca—yac ca*, 'both—and,' Divyâv.; 'that' [accord. to Pāṇ. iii, 3, 148 after expressions of 'impossibility,' 'disbelief,' 'hope,' 'disregard,' 'reproach' and 'wonder']; *yad vā*, 'or else,' 'whether,' Kāv.; Rājat.; [*yad vā*, 'or else,' is very often in commentators]; 'however,' Bālar.; *yad vā—yadi vā*, 'if—or if,' Bhag.; *yad bhūyasā*, 'for the most part,' Divyâv.; *yat satyam*, 'certainly,' 'indeed,' 'of course,' Mṛicch.; Ratnâv.; *yan nu*, with 1st pers., 'what if I,' 'let me,' Divyâv.); m. = *purusha*, Tattvas. — **anna,** mfn. eating which food, R. — **abhâve,** ind. in the absence or in default of which, MW. — **artha,** mfn. having which object or intention, BhP.; (*am* or *e*), ind. on which account, for which purpose, wherefore, why, MBh.; Kāv. &c.; as, since, because, whereas, ib. — **avadhi,** ind. since which time, Bhām. — **avasāna,** mfn. terminating in which, Lāṭy. — **aśana,** mfn. = *-anna*, R. — **aśanīya,** n. anything that may be eaten, ĀpGṛ. — **ātmaka,** mfn. having which essence or existence, BhP. — **ārsheya,** mfn. of which divine descent, L. — **ṛiccha,** mf(*ā*)n. spontaneous, accidental, ĀpGṛ.; (*ā*), f. self-will, spontaneity, accident, chance (ibc. or *ayā*, ind. spontaneously, by accident, unexpectedly), ŚvetUp.; Mn.; MBh. &c.; (in gram.), see *-śabda*, below; *-tas*, ind. by chance, accidentally, BhP.; *-°bhijña* (°*cchâbh*°), m. a voluntary or self-offered witness, Nār.; *-mātra-tas*, ind. only quite by accident, Kathās.; *-lābha-saṃtushṭa*, mfn. satisfied with obtaining what comes spontaneously, easily satisfied, Bhag.; *-śabda*, m. 'chance-word,' a word neither derived from authority nor possessing meaning, Śiś.; *-saṃvāda*, m. accidental or spontaneous conversation, Uttarar.; °*cchika*, m. (scil. *putra*) a son who offers himself for adoption, MW. — **gotra,** mfn. belonging to which family, ChUp. — **devata** (ŚrS.) or **-devatyà** (ŚBr.), mfn. having which godhead or divinity. — **dvaṃdva,** n. N. of a Sāman, Lāṭy. — **dhetos** (for *-hetos*), ind. from which reason, on which account, BhP. — **bala,** mfn. of which strength or power, MBh. — **bhavishya,** mfn. one who says 'what will be will be,' Fatalist (N. of a fish), Hit. — **bhūyas,** (ibc.) the greatest part (°*sā*, ind., see col. 2); *kārin*, mfn. doing anything for the most part, L. — **rūpa-vicāra,** m. N. of wk. — **vat,** ind. in which way, as (correlative of *tad-vat* and *evam*), MBh.; Kāv. &c. — **vada,** mfn. talking anything, saying no matter what, L. — **vāhishṭhīya,** n. (fr. *yad vāhishṭham*, the first two words of RV. v, 25, 7) N. of a Sāman, ĀrshBr. (also *agner-yadv*°). — **vidha,** mfn. of which kind, R. — **vīrya,** mfn. of which valour, MBh. — **vṛitta,** n. anything that has occurred, event, adventure, Hariv.; Kathās.; any form of *yad*, Pāṇ. viii, 1, 66.

Yac, in comp. for *yad* — **chandas,** mfn. having which metre, ŚāṅkhGṛ. — **chīla** (for *-śīla*), mfn. having which disposition, MBh. — **chraddha** (for *-śraddha*), mfn. having which faith or belief, Bhag.

Yat, in comp. for *yad*. — **kara,** mf(*ā*)n. doing or undertaking which, Pāṇ. iii, 2, 21, Vārtt. — **kāma** (*yát-*), mfn. desiring or wishing which, RV.; (°*myā*), ind. with which view or design, ŚBr. — **kāraṇam,** ind. for which cause or reason, wherefore, why, MārkP.; as, because, since (also °*ṇāt*), Pañcat. — **kārin,** mfn. doing or undertaking which, TBr. — **kāryam,** ind. with which intention, MārkP. — **kiṃ-cana,** see col. 2 under *yád*; *-kāraka*, mfn. doing anything whatever, acting at random, MBh.; *-kārin*, mfn. acting at random or precipitately (*ri-tā*, f.), Kād.; Divyâv.; *-pralāpin*, mfn. talking at random, R.; *-vāda*, m. a r° assertion, Nyāyas., Sch. — **kiṃ-cid,** see under *yad* above; *-cic-cāraka*, m. a servant of all work, L.; *-cid-api-saṃkalpa*, m. desire for anything whatever, Yogavās.; *-cid-duḥkha*, n. pl. pains of whatever kind, Mcar. — **kiṃ-cêdam,** n. the first words of the verse RV. vii, 89, 5 (w. r. *kiṃcidam*). — **kula,** mfn. of which family, Hariv. — **kṛite,** ind. for which reason, wherefore, why, MBh.; Kathās. — **kratu,** mfn. having which resolution, forming which plan, BṛĀrUp. — **parākrama,** mfn. of which valour, being so courageous, MBh. — **pṛishṭha,** mfn. connected with which Pṛishṭha (kind of Stotra), ŚāṅkhŚr. — **prathama,** mfn. doing which for the first time, Pāṇ. vi, 2, 162, Sch. — **saṃkhyāka,** mfn. having which number, so numerous, Yājñ., Sch. — **sena,** mfn. having which (or so strong an) army, MBh. — **svabhāva,** mfn. being of which nature or character, ib.

Yan, in comp. for *yad*. — **nāman,** mfn. having which name, Hariv. — **nimitta,** mfn. caused or occasioned by which, MBh.; (*am*), ind. for which reason, in consequence of which, wherefore, why, R.; MārkP. — **maṅhishṭhīya,** n. N. of a Sāman, ĀrshBr. (also *agner-yanm*°). — **madhye,** ind. in the centre of which, MW. — **maya,** mf(*ī*)n. formed or consisting of which, Kāvyâd.; Pur. — **mātra,** mfn. having which measure or circumference &c., MBh.; VarBṛS. — **mūrdhan,** mfn. the head of whom, MW. — **mūla,** mfn. rooted in which, dependent on whom or which, MBh.

Yada = *yad* (only in the form *yadam* at the end of an adverbial comp.), g. *śarad-ādi*.

Yádi, ind. (in Veda also *yadī*, sometimes *yadi cit*, *yadi ha vai*, *yádī*, *yády u*, *yady u vai*) if, in case that, RV. &c. &c. In the earlier language *yadi* may be joined with Indic., Subj. or Leṭ, Pot., or Fut., the consequent clause of the conditional sentence being generally without any particle. In the later language *yadi* may be joined with Pres. (followed in cons° cl° by another Pres., e.g. *yadi jīvati bhadrāṇi paśyati,* 'if he lives he beholds prosperity,' or by fut. or by Impv. or by Pot. or by no verb); or it may be joined with Pot. (e.g. *yadi rājā daṇḍam na praṇayet,* 'if the king were not to inflict punishment,' followed by another Pot. or by Cond. or by Pres. or by Impv. or by fut. or by no verb); or it may be joined with fut. (e.g. *yadi na karishyanti tat,* 'if they will not do that,' followed by another fut. or by Pres. or by Impv. or by no verb); or it may be joined with Cond. (e.g. *yady anujñām adāsyat,* 'if he should give permission,' followed by another Cond. or by Pot. or by aor.); or it may be joined with aor. (e.g. *yadi Prajā-patir na vapur arsrākshīt,* 'if the Creator had not created the body,' followed by Cond. or by Pot. or by pf.); or it may be joined with Impv. or even with pf. (e.g. *yady āha,* 'if he had said'). There may be other constructions, and in the consequent clauses some one of the following may be used: *atha, atra, tad, tena, tatas, tataḥ param, tadā, tarhi, tadānīm.* Observe that *yadi* may sometimes = 'as sure as' (esp. in asseverations, followed by Impv. with or without *tathā* or *tena* or followed by Pot. with *tad*), MBh.; Kāv. &c.; or it may = 'whether' (followed by Pres. or Pot. or no verb, e.g. *yadi-na vā,* 'whether-or not,' and sometimes *kim* is added), ib.; or it may = 'that' (after verbs of 'not believing' or 'doubting,' with Pres. or Pot., e.g. *nâśanse yadi jīvanti,* 'I do not expect that they are alive,' cf. Pāṇ. iii, 3, 147, Sch.); or if placed after *dushkaram* or *katham cid* it may = 'hardly,' 'scarcely,' MBh.; R.; or it may = 'if perchance,' 'perhaps' (with Pot. with or without *iti,* or with fut. or Pres.), MBh.; Kāv. &c. The following are other combinations:—*yadi tāvat,* 'how would it be if' (with Pres. or Impv.); *yadi nāma,* 'if ever;' *yadi cêt* (*cêt* being added redundantly) = 'if' (e.g. *yadi cêt syāt,* 'if it should be'); *purā yadi* = 'before' (e.g. *purā yadi paśyāmi,* 'before that I see'); *yády ápi* (rarely *api yadi*), 'even if,' 'although' (followed by *tathâpi* or *tad api* or sometimes by no particle in the correlative clause); *yadi—yadi ca—yady api,* 'if—and if—if also; *yádi—yádi-vā,* or *yádi vā—yádi vā,* or *yádi vā—yádi,* or *yadi vā—vā,* or *vā—yadi vā,* or *yad vā—yadi vā,* 'if—or if,' 'whether—or;' *yádi vā—ná vā,* 'whether—or not;' *vā—yadi vā—yadi vā—tathâpi,* 'whether—or—or—yet;' *vā yadi* = 'or if,' 'or rather;' *yadi vā,* id. or = 'yet,' 'however.'

Yadīya, mfn. relating to whom, belonging to which or what, whose, Inscr.; Rājat.; BhP.

Yadriyañc (TS.) or **yadryañc** (MaitrS.), mfn. moving or turning in which direction, reaching whither.

Yadvan, m. pl. N. of a class of Ṛishis, Pat.

यदा *yadā́.* See p. 844, col. 1.

यदु *yádu,* m. N. of an ancient hero (in the Veda often mentioned together with Turvaśa [or Turvasu], q.v., and described as preserved by Indra during an inundation; in epic poetry he is a son of Yayāti and brother of Puru and Turvasu, Kṛishṇa being descended from Yadu, and Bharata and Kuru from Puru; Yadu is also called a son of Vasu, king of Cedi, or a son of Hary-aśva), RV.; MBh.; Hariv.; Pur.; N. of a country on the west of the Jumnā river (about Mathurā and Vṛindā-vana, over which Yadu ruled; according to others the Deccan or Southern peninsula of India), W.; pl. the people of Yadu or the descendants of king Yadu (cf. *yādava*), ib. **–kulôdvaha,** m. 'supporter of the Yadu family,' N. of Kṛishṇa, Pañcar. **–girîśâshṭôttara-śata,** n. N. of a Stotra. **–dhra,** m. N. of a Ṛishi, Hariv. **–nandana,** m. N. of Akrūra, VP. **–nātha,** m. 'lord of the Yadus,' N. of Kṛishṇa, L.; (also with *miśra*) N. of an author, Cat. **–pati,** m. 'lord of the Yadus,' N. of Kṛishṇa, Cāṇ.; of various authors, Cat. **–puṃgava,** m. a chief of the Yadus, MBh. **–bharata,** m. N. of an author, Cat. **–maṇi,** m. N. of a man (father of Parama), ib. **–vaṇśa,** m. the family of Yadu, Cat.; *-kāvya,* n. N. of a poem. **–vīra-mukhya,** m. 'leader of the Yadu heroes,' N. of Kṛishṇa, MBh. **–śreshṭha,** m. 'best of Yadus,' N. of Kṛishṇa, Pañcar. **Yadûdvaha,** m. 'supporter of the Yadus,' N. of Kṛishṇa, ib.

यदृच्छा *yad-ṛicchā, yad-gotra* &c. See p. 844, col. 3.

यद्रियञ्च् *yadriyañc, yadryañc, yadvan.* See col. 1.

यद्वा *yadvā,* f. = *buddhi,* perception, mind, intelligence (?), L.

यन्तवे *yántave* (see under √*yam* below), *yantavyà, yanti* &c. (see col. 3).

यन्त्र् *yantr* (rather Nom. fr. *yantra,* see col. 3), cl. 10. P. (Dhātup. xxxii, 3) *yantrayati* (or 1. P. *yantrati*), to restrain, curb, bind (*saṃkocane*), Dhātup.; to bind up, bandage, Suśr.

Yantra. See col. 3.

Yantraṇa, yantrita, yantrin. See p. 846, col. 1.

यन्नामन् *yan-nāman, yan-nimitta* &c. See p. 844, col. 3.

यभ् *yabh,* cl. 1. P. (Dhātup. xxiii, 11) *yábhati* (or Ā. °*te,* Vet.; pf. *yayābha,* Gr.; aor. *ayāpsīt,* ib.; fut. *-yapsyáti,* TBr.; inf. *yabhitum,* BhP., *-yabdhum,* TBr., Sch.), to have sexual intercourse, futuere, AV. &c. &c.: Desid. *yiyapsati,* °*te,* to desire sexual intercourse, ŚrS.

Yabhana, n. copulation, sexual intercourse, Vop.

Yabhya, f. to be carnally known (see *á-* and *su-yabhyā*).

Yiyapsu, mfn. (fr. Desid.) desiring sexual intercourse, Sāy. on RV. x, 86, 17.

Yiyapsyamānā, f. desiring to be carnally known, ŚāṅkhŚr.

यम् *yam,* cl. 1. P. (Dhātup. xxiii, 15) *yácchati* (Ved. also °*te,* and Ved. ep. *yámati,* °*te;* pf. *yayāma, yeme;* 2. sg. *yayantha,* 3. pl. *yemúḥ, yemiré,* RV. &c. &c.; 3. du. irreg. *-yamatuḥ,* RV. v, 67, 1; aor. *áyān, áyamuh;* Impv. *yaṇsi, yandhi;* Pot. *yamyās, yamīmahi,* RV.; *ayaṇsam, ayaṇsi, ayaṇsta,* Subj. *yaṇsat,* °*satas,* °*sate,* ib.; Br.; 3. sg. *-yámishṭa,* RV. v, 32, 7; *ayaṇsisham,* Gr.; fut. *yantā,* ib.; *yaṇsyati, yamishyati,* Br. &c., inf. *yántum, yamitum,* ib.; *yántave, yámitavaí,* RV.; ind. p. *yatvā, yamitvā,* MBh.; Kāv. &c.; *-yátya,* AV.; Br.; *-yamya,* GṛŚrS.; *-yámam,* RV.; Br.), to sustain, hold, hold up, support (Ā. 'one's self'; with loc. 'to be founded on'), RV.; Br.; ChUp.; to raise, wield (a weapon &c.; Ā. with *āyudhaiḥ,* 'to brandish weapons'), RV.; to raise, extend or hold (as a screen &c.) over (dat.), RV.; (Ā.) to extend one's self before (dat.), AitBr.; to raise (the other scale), weigh more, ŚBr.; to stretch out, expand, spread, display, show, RV.; to hold or keep in, hold back, restrain, check, curb, govern, subdue, control, ib. &c. &c.; to offer; confer, grant, bestow on (dat. or loc.), present with (instr.), RV. &c. &c.; (with *mārgam*), to make way for (gen.), MBh.; (with *prati* and abl.), to give anything in exchange for anything, Kāś. on Pāṇ. ii, 3, 11; (Ā.) to give one's self up to, be faithful to, obey (dat.), RV.; to raise, utter (a sound &c.), ib.; to fix, establish, ib.; (Ā.) to be firm, not budge, RV.; to catch fire, TBr. (Sch.): Pass. *yamyáte* (aor. *áyāmi*), to be raised or lifted up or held back or restrained, RV. &c. &c.: Caus. *yāmayati* (AV.); *yamayati* (Br. &c.; °*te,* MBh.; aor. *ayīyamat*), to restrain, hold in, control, keep or put in order: Desid. *yiyaṇsati,* to wish to restrain &c., Br.: Intens. *yaṃyamīti* (see *ud-√yam*) or *yaṃyamyate* (Pāṇ. vii, 4, 85, Vārtt. 2, Pat.) [Cf. Gk. ζημία, 'restraint, punishment.']

Yatá, mfn. restrained, held in, held forth, kept down or limited, subdued, governed, controlled &c., RV. &c. &c. (cf. comp. below); n. restraint (?), see *yataṃ-kará;* the spurring or guiding of an elephant by means of the rider's feet, L. **–krit,** m. N. of a man, Cat. (prob. w.r.) **–gir,** mfn. one who restrains speech, silent, Ragh. **–ṃ-kará,** m. (prob.) a restrainer, subduer, conqueror, RV. v, 34, 4. **–cittâtman,** mfn. one who controls his soul and spirit, Bhag. **–cittêndriyânala,** mfn. one who conquers the fire of his thoughts and senses, BhP. **–cetas,** mfn. restrained or subdued in mind, Bhag. **–manyu,** mfn. restraining or controlling anger, BhP. **–mānasa,** mfn. = *-cetas,* MārkP. **–maithuna,** mfn. abstaining from sexual intercourse, R. **–raśmi** (*yatá-*), mfn. having well held or guided reins, RV. **–vāk-tva,** n. (fr. next) reticence, silence, KātyŚr., Sch. **–vāc,** mfn. = *-gir,* MaitrUp.; BhP. **–vrata,** mfn. observing vows, firm of purpose, MBh.; MārkP. **–sruc** (*yatá-*), mfn. raising or stretching out the sacrificial ladle, RV. **Yatâkshâsu-mano-buddhi,** mfn. one who controls his eyes and breath and soul and mind, BhP. **Yatâtman,** mfn. self-restrained, Mn.; MBh.; R. (also °*tmavat*). **Yatâhāra,** m. temperate in food, abstemious, R. (v.l. *yathâh*°). **Yatêndriya,** mfn. having the organs of sense restrained, of subdued passions, chaste, pure, MBh.

3. **Yáti,** f. (for 1. and 2. see p. 841, cols. 1 and 2) restraint, control, guidance, TS.; Br.; stopping, ceasing, a pause (in music), Saṃgīt.; a cæsura (in prosody), Piṅg.; (also *ī*), f. a widow, L. **–tāla,** m. (in music) a kind of measure, Gīt. **–nṛitya,** n. a kind of dance, Saṃgīt. **–bhrashṭa,** mfn. wanting the cæsura (in prosody), Kāvyâd.; Vām. **–rekhā,** f. a partic. attitude in dancing, Saṃgīt. **–lagna,** m. (in music) a kind of measure, ib. **–śekhara,** m. a kind of measure, ib.

Yantavyà, mfn. to be restrained or checked or controlled, MaitrS.; MBh.

Yanti, f., Pāṇ. vi, 4, 39, Sch.

Yantu. See *su-yántu.*

Yantúr, m. (only acc. °*túram*) a ruler, regulator, guide, RV.

Yantṛí, mfn. restraining, limiting, withholding from (loc.), Āpast.; fixing, establishing, RV.; AV.; VS. (f. *yántrī*); granting, bestowing, RV.; m. (ifc. also °*tṛika*) a driver (of horses or elephants), charioteer, ib. &c. &c.; a ruler, governor, manager, guide, RV.; Hariv.; *yantāraḥ* among the *yácñā-karmāṇaḥ,* Naigh. iii, 19.

Yantra, n. any instrument for holding or restraining or fastening, a prop, support, barrier, RV. &c. &c.; a fetter, band, tie, thong, rein, trace, Mn.; MBh.; a surgical instrument (esp. a blunt one, such as tweezers, a vice &c., opp. to *śastra*), Suśr.; Vāgbh.; any instrument or apparatus, mechanical contrivance, engine, machine, implement, appliance (as a bolt or lock on a door, oars or sails in a boat, &c.), MBh.; Kāv. &c. (cf. *kūpa-, jala-, taila-y*°; ibc. or ifc. often = mechanical, magical); restraint, force (*eṇa,* ind. forcibly, violently), MW.; an amulet, mystical diagram supposed to possess occult powers, Kathās.; Pañcat. (cf. RTL. 203). **–karaṇḍikā,** f. a kind of magical basket, Kathās. **–karman,** n. the employment or application of instruments, Vāgbh.; °*ma-krit,* m. a maker or employer of instruments, a machinist, artisan, R. **–garuḍa,** m. an image of Garuḍa (mechanically contrived to move by itself), Pañcat. **–gṛiha,** n. an oil-mill or any manufactory, L.; a torture chamber, Divyâv. **–gola,** m. a kind of pea, L. **–cintāmaṇi,** m. N. of various wks. **–ceshṭita,** n. anything effected by magical diagrams, enchantment, Kathās. **–cchedya,** n. N. of a partic. art, Kād. (prob. w.r. for *pattra-cch*°). **–ṇī,** see *yantraṇa.* **–takshan,** m. a constructor of machines or of magical diagrams, Kathās. **–toraṇa,** n. a mechanical arch (fitted with contrivances to move it), A. **–dṛiḍha,** mfn. secured by a lock or bolt (as a door), Mṛicch. **–dhārā-gṛiha,** n. a room fitted up with a kind of shower-bath, a bath-room (*-tva,* n.), Megh. **–nāla,** n. a mechanical pipe or tube, tubular instrument, MārkP. **–pattra,** n. N. of wk. **–pīḍā,** f. the pressing (of grain &c.) by any mechanical contrivance, HYog. **–putraka,** m. (Rājat.), °**trikā,** f. (Kathās.) a mechanical doll or puppet (fitted with strings or any mechanism for moving the limbs). **–pūjana-prakāra,** m. N. of wk. **–pūta,** mfn. (water) cleared by any mechanical contrivance, Gṛihyas. **–peshaṇī,** f. a hand-mill, L. **–prakāśa,** m., **-pratishṭhā,** f. N. of wks. **–pravāha,** m. an artificial stream of water, machine for watering, Ragh. **–maya,** mf(*ī*)n. consisting of machinery or mechanism, artificially constructed, BhP.; Kathās. **–mayūraka,** m. an artificial peacock, Kād. **–mātṛikā,** f. N. of one of the 64 Kalās (q.v.), Cat. **–mārga,** m. an aqueduct, canal, Prab. **–mālikā-ṭīkā,** f. N. of wk. **–mukta,** mfn. thrown by any kind of machine, MBh.; R.; n. a kind of weapon, L. **–moha,** m. N. of wk. **–yukta,** mfn. furnished with (all necessary) implements or apparatus, MBh. **–ratnâvalī,** f., **-rahasya,** n., **-rāja,** m. (also °*ja-ghaṭanā,* f., *-paddhati,* f., *-racanā,* f., *-racanā-prakāra,* m., *-vyākhyāna,* n., and °*jâgama,* m.) N. of wks. **–vat,** mfn. possessing or furnished with instruments or machines, Kām. **–vidhi,** m. the science of surgical instruments, Suśr. **–vimāna,** m. or n. a chariot moving by itself, Kathās. **–vedha-vicāra,** m. N. of wk. **–śara,** m. a missile shot off by machinery,

Kathās. — **saṃgraha,** m., -**sāra,** m. or n. N. of wks. — **sadman,** n. an oil-mill, Gal. — **sūtra,** n. the cord attached to the mechanism of a doll or puppet, Rājat.; N. of a Sūtra-work on war-engines. — **haṅsa,** m. an automatic goose or flamingo, Kathās. — **hastin,** m. an automatic elephant, ib. **Yantrâkāra,** m. N. of wk. **Yantrâdhyāya-vivṛiti,** f. N. of wk. **Yantrâpīḍa,** mfn. suffering from feverish convulsions, Bhpr. **Yantrârūḍha,** mfn. fixed or mounted on the revolving engine (of the universe), Bhag. **Yantrâlaya,** m. a printing-office, press (often in titles of books). **Yantrâvalī,** f. N. of wk. **Yantrôtkshiptôpala,** m. a stone shot off by a machine, R. **Yantrôddhāra,** m. (and *-vidhi,* m.) N. of wks. **Yantrôpala,** m. n. a mill-stone, (pl.) a mill, L.

Yantraka (ifc.) any instrument or mechanical contrivance, Hcat.; m. (and *ikā,* f.) a restrainer, tamer, subduer, PañcavBr.; a machinist, artisan, R.; n. a bandage (in medicine), Suśr.; a turner's wheel, lathe, L.; a hand-mill, Hcat.

Yantraṇa, n. (or *ā,* f.) restriction, limitation, restraint, constraint, force, compulsion (often ifc.), Kāv.; Kathās.; Suśr.; the application of a bandage, Suśr.; pain, anguish, affliction, W.; (*ī*), f. = *yantriṇī,* L.; n. guarding, protecting, L.

Yantraya, Nom. P. °*yati.* See √*yantr.*

Yantrita, mfn. restrained, curbed, bound, fettered, confined (lit. and fig.), MBh.; Kāv. &c. (cf. *a-* and *su-y*°); subject to, compelled by, depending on (instr., abl., or comp.), ib.; bandaged, placed in splints, Suśr.; one who takes pains or strenuously exerts himself for (*krite,* ifc.), R.; Pañcat. — **katha,** mfn. restrained in speech, constrained to be silent, R. — **sāyaka,** mfn. one who has fixed an arrow (in a kind of self-acting bow or machine which discharges itself when touched), Kathās.

Yantrin, mfn. furnished with harness or trappings (as a horse), KātyŚr.; furnished with an amulet, Cat.; m. a tormentor, harasser, painer, R.; (*iṇī*), f. a wife's younger sister, L. (cf. *yantraṇī*).

Yáma, m. a rein, curb, bridle, RV. v, 61, 2; a driver, charioteer, ib. viii, 103, 10; the act of checking or curbing, suppression, restraint (with *vācam,* restraint of words, silence), BhP.; self-control, forbearance, any great moral rule or duty (as opp. to *niyama,* a minor observance; in Yājñ. iii, 313 ten Yamas are mentioned, sometimes only five), Mn.; MBh. &c.; (in Yoga) self-restraint (as the first of the eight Aṅgas or means of attaining mental concentration), IW. 93; any rule or observance, PārGṛ.; (*yamá*), mf(*ā́* or *ī*)n. twin-born, twin, forming a pair, RV. &c. &c.; m. a twin, one of a pair or couple, a fellow (du. 'the twins,' N. of the Aśvins and of their twin children by Mādrī, called Nakula and Saha-deva; *yamau mithunau,* twins of different sex), ib.; a symbolical N. for the number 'two,' Hcat.; N. of the god who presides over the Pitṛis (q. v.) and rules the spirits of the dead, RV. &c. &c.; IW. 18; 197, 198 &c.; RTL. 10; 16; 289 &c. (he is regarded as the first of men and born from Vivasvat, 'the Sun,' and his wife Saraṇyū; while his brother, the seventh Manu, another form of the first man, is the son of Vivasvat and Saṃjñā, the image of Saraṇyū; his twin-sister is Yamī, with whom he resists sexual alliance, but by whom he is mourned after his death, so that the gods, to make her forget her sorrow, create night; in the Veda he is called a king or *saṃgamano janānām,* 'the gatherer of men,' and rules over the departed fathers in heaven, the road to which is guarded by two broad-nosed, four-eyed, spotted dogs, the children of Saramā, q. v.; in Post-vedic mythology he is the appointed Judge and 'Restrainer' or 'Punisher' of the dead, in which capacity he is also called *dharma-rāja* or *dharma* and corresponds to the Greek Pluto and to Minos; his abode is in some region of the lower world called Yama-pura; thither a soul when it leaves the body, is said to repair, and there, after the recorder, Citra-gupta, has read an account of its actions kept in a book called Agra-saṃdhānā, it receives a just sentence; in MBh. Yama is described as dressed in blood-red garments, with a glittering form, a crown on his head, glowing eyes, and, like Varuṇa, holding a noose, with which he binds the spirit after drawing it from the body, in size about the measure of a man's thumb; he is otherwise represented as grim in aspect, green in colour, clothed in red, riding on a buffalo, and holding a club in one hand and noose in the other; in the later mythology he is always represented as a terrible deity inflicting tortures, called *yātanā,* on departed spirits; he is also one of the 8 guardians of the world as regent of the South quarter; he is the regent of the Nakshatra Apa-bharaṇī or Bharaṇī, the supposed author of RV. x, 10; 14, of a hymn to Vishṇu and of a law-book; *Yamasyârkah,* N. of a Sāman, ĀrshBr.); N. of the planet Saturn (regarded as the son of Vivasvat and Chāyā), Hariv.; BhP.; of one of Skanda's attendants (mentioned together with Ati-yama), MBh.; a crow, L. (cf. *-dūtaka*); a bad horse (whose limbs are either too small or too large), L.; (*ī́*), f. N. of Yama's twin-sister (who is identified in Post-vedic mythology with the river-goddess Yamunā), RV. &c. &c.; n. a pair, brace, couple, L.; (in gram.) a twin-letter (the consonant interposed and generally understood, but not written in practice, between a nasal immediately preceded by one of the four other consonants in each class), Prāt.; Pat. on Pāṇ. i, 1, 8; pitch of the voice, tone of utterance, key, Prāt. — **kālindī,** f. N. of Saṃjñā (mother of Yama), L. — **kiṃkara,** m. Y°'s servant, MārkP.; Pañcat. — **kīṭa,** m. a wood- or earth-worm, L. — **kīla,** m. N. of Vishṇu, L. — **ketu,** m. 'Y°'s ensign,' a sign of death, BhP. — **koṭi** or °**ṭī,** f. N. of a mythical town (fabled as situated 90° east of the meridian of Laṅkā; also °*ṭi-pattana,* n., °*ṭi-purī,* f.), VP.; Sūryas. &c. (cf. *yava-koṭi*). — **kshaya,** m. Y°'s abode, MBh.; R.; BhP. — **gāthā́,** f. a verse or hymn treating of Y°, TS.; Kāṭh.; PārGṛ.; N. of RV. x, 10. — **gītā,** f. 'hymn of Y°,' N. of ch. of the Vishṇu-Purāṇa. — **gṛiha,** n. Y°'s abode, Pañcad. — **ghaṇṭa,** m. N. of an astronomical Yoga, Cat. — **ghna,** mfn. destroying Yama or death (N. of Vishṇu), Śaṃk. — **ja** (MBh.; Hariv. &c.) or -**jāta,** °**taka** (R.), mfn. twin-born; m. du. twins. — **jit,** m. 'conqueror of Y°,' N. of Śiva, L. — **jihvā,** f. N. of a Yoginī, Hcat.; 'Yama's tongue,' N. of a procuress, Kathās. — **tarpaṇa,** n. presenting libations to Y° on the 14th day of the dark half of the month Āśvina, MW. — **tā,** f. the being god of death (*-tām* √*yā,* to become god of death; with gen., to cause any one's d°), Hcar. — **tīrtha,** n. N. of a Tīrtha, Cat. — **tvá,** n. the being Y°, TS.; MBh.; Pañcar. — **daṇshṭra,** m. N. of an Asura, Kathās.; of a Rākshasa, ib.; of a warrior on the side of the gods, ib.; (*ā*), f. Y°'s tooth (°*ṭrântaram gatah,* one who has fallen into the jaws of Y° or Death), MBh.; (prob.) a stab from a dagger, Pañcad.; a kind of poison, Rasêndrac.; f. pl. the last 8 days of the month Āśvina and the whole of Kārttika considered as a period of general sickness, MW. — **daṇḍa,** m. Y°'s rod, R.; Kathās. — **diś,** f. Y°'s quarter, the south, Hcat. — **dūtá,** m. Y°'s messenger or minister (employed to bring departed spirits to Y°'s judgment-seat, and thence to their final destination), AV.; PārGṛ. &c.; a crow (as boding evil or death), MW.; pl. N. of a race or family, Hariv.; (*ī*), f. N. of one of the 9 Samidhs, Gṛihyas. — **dūtaka,** m. Y°'s messenger or minister, L.; a crow, L.; (*ikā*), f. Indian tamarind, L. — **devata** (*yamá-*), mfn. having Y° for deity, ŚBr.; Gobh.; n. or (*ā*), f. N. of the lunar asterism Bharaṇī (as presided over by Y°), L. — **devatyà,** mfn. having Y° for deity, MaitrS. — **daivata,** mfn. having Y° for lord or ruler, VarBṛS. — **druma,** m. 'Y°'s tree,' Bombax Heptaphyllum, L. — **dvitīyā,** f. N. of the 2nd day in the light half of the month Kārttika, Cat.; *-vrata,* n. a partic. ceremony, ib. — **dvīpa,** m. N. of an island, VP. (cf. *yava-d*°). — **dharma-nirbhaya-stotra,** n. N. of a Stotra. — **dhānī,** f. Y°'s dwelling or abode, Bhartṛ. — **dhāra,** m. a kind of double-edged weapon, L. — **nakshatrá,** n. Y°'s asterism or lunar mansion (see above under *yamá*), TBr. — **nagarâtithi,** m. 'guest in Y°'s city,' i. e. dead, Daś. — **netra** (*yamá-*), mfn. having Y° as guide or leader, VS.; TS. — **paṭa,** m. a piece of cloth or canvas on which Y° with his attendants and the punishments of hell are represented, Mudr. — **paṭika,** m. one who carries about the above Y°-paṭa, Hcar. — **pada,** n. a repeated word, Bhāshik. — **pālaka,** m. Y°'s servant, Kāraṇḍ. — **pāla-purusha,** m. id., ib. — **pāśa,** m. the snare or noose of Y°, MW. — **pura,** n. the city or abode of Y° (see under *yamá*), MW. — **purāṇa,** n. N. of a Purāṇa. — **purusha,** m. Y°'s servant, ĀśvGṛ.; BhP. — **prastha-pura,** n. N. of a town (where Y° was especially worshipped), Cat. — **priya,** m. 'beloved by Y°,' Ficus Indica, L. — **bhaginī,** f. 'Y°'s sister,' the river Yamunā or Jumnā, L. — **bhaṭa,** m. Y°'s servant, AgP. — **mandira,** n. Y°'s dwelling, Hariv. — **mārga,** m. Y°'s road; *-gamana,* n. the entering on Y°'s road, receiving the recompense for one's actions, Cat. — **yajña,** m. a partic. sacrifice, TĀr., Sch. — **yāga,** m. N. of a Yājyā, Sāy. — **yātanā,** f. the torment inflicted by Y°, L. — **ratha,** m. 'Y°'s vehicle' i. e. a buffalo, MW. — **rāj,** m. king Y°, L. — **rāja,** m. id., L.; N. of a physician, Cat. — **rājan,** m. king Y°, BhP.; (*yamá-*), mfn. having Y° as king, subject to Y°, RV.; AV. &c. — **rā́jya,** n. Y°'s dominion, AV.; VS. &c. — **rāshṭra,** n. Y°'s kingdom, Suśr.; Rājat. — **ṛksha** (for *-ṛiksha*), n. the lunar mansion Bharaṇī supposed to be under Y°, VarBṛS. — **loká,** m. Y°'s world, MaitrS.; TāṇḍyaBr. &c. — **vat,** mfn. one who governs himself and his passions, self-restrained, Ragh. — **vatsā,** f. a cow bearing twin calves, Kauś. — **vāhana,** m. = *-ratha,* q. v., L. — **vishaya,** m. Y°'s realm, MaitrUp.; R. — **vrata,** n. a religious observance or vow made to Y°, Kauś.; a partic. ceremony of the Brahma-cārin, Kauś., Sch.; Y°'s method (i. e. punishing without respect of persons and without partiality, as one of the duties of kings), Mn.; R.; MārkP.; N. of a Sāman, ĀrshBr. — **śānti,** f. N. of wk. — **śikha,** m. N. of a Vetāla, Kathās. — **śrāya,** m. the residence of Y°, the Southern quarter, Bhaṭṭ. — **śreshṭha** (*yamá-*), mfn. among whom Y° is the chief (said of the Pitṛis), AV. — **śvá,** m. Y°'s dog (see under *yamá*), Kāṭh.; MaitrS. (du.) — **saṃhitā,** f. N. of a Saṃhitā. — **sattva-vat,** mfn. having Y°'s nature, Suśr. — **sadana,** n. Y°'s seat or abode, Pañcat.; Bhartṛ.; BhP. — **sabha,** n. (Pāṇ.) or -**sabhā,** f. (Kathās.) Y°'s tribunal. — **sabhīya,** mfn. relating to Y°'s court of justice, Pāṇ. — **sāt,** ind. with √*kri,* to deliver over to the god of death, Bhaṭṭ.; *yamasāt-krita,* made over to or sent to Y°, MW. — **sādaná,** n. = *-sadana,* q. v., AV.; TĀr. &c. — **sū́,** f. bringing forth twins, RV.; VS. &c.; m. Y°'s father, the Sun, L. — **sûkta,** n. a hymn in honour of Y°, PārGṛ.; Yājñ.; N. of RV. x, 14. — **sūrya,** n. a building with two halls (one with a western, the other with a northern aspect), VarBṛS. — **stotra,** n. N. of a Stotra. — **stoma,** m. N. of an Ekâha, ŚāṅkhŚr. — **smṛiti,** f. N. of a code of law. — **svasṛi,** f. 'Y°'s sister,' N. of the river Yamunā or Jumnā, Hariv.; Hcar.; of Durgā, L. — **hārdikā,** f. N. of one of Devī's female attendants, W. — **hāsêśvara-tīrtha,** n. N. of a Tīrtha, Cat. **Yamâṅgikā,** f. N. of a Yoginī, Hcat. (v. l. *yamântikā*). **Yamâtirātra,** m. N. of a Sattra of 49 days' duration, TāṇḍyaBr.; ĀśvŚr.; Maś. **Yamâdarśana-trayodaśī,** f. a partic. 13th lunar day; *-vrata,* n. a religious observance on the above day (those who perform it are said to be exempted from appearing before Y°), Cat. **Yamâditya,** m. a partic. form of the sun, Cat. **Yamânuga,** mfn. following Y°, being in attendance on Y°, MārkP. **Yamânucara,** m. a servant of Y°, BhP. **Yamântaka,** m. Y° (regarded as the destroyer or god of death, MBh.; R.; Buddh. (cf. *kālântaka*); 'Y°'s destroyer,' N. of Śiva, L.; du. Y° and the god of d°, MārkP.; (*ikā*), f., see *yamâṅgikā* above. **Yamâri,** m. 'Y°'s enemy,' N. of Vishṇu, Pañcar. **Yamâlaya,** m. Y°'s abode, BhP. **Yamêśa,** n. 'having Y° as ruler,' the Nakshatra Bharaṇī, VarBṛS. **Yamêśvara,** n. N. of a Liṅga, Cat. **Yamêshṭa,** n. an oblation made to Y°, TS.

Yamaka, mfn. twin, doubled, twofold, MBh.; m. a religious obligation or observance (= *vrata*), L.; (scil. *sneha*) two similar greasy substances, oil and ghee, Suśr.; m. or n. restraint, check (= *yama*), L.; (*ikā*), f. (scil. *hikkā*) a kind of hiccough, Bhpr.; n. (in med.) a double band or bandage, Suśr.; (in rhet.) the repetition in the same stanza of words or syllables similar in sound but different in meaning, paronomasia (of which various kinds are enumerated), Kāvyâd.; Vām. &c. (cf. IW. 457); a kind of metre, Col. — **kāvya,** n. N. of an artificial poem (ascribed to Ghaṭa-karpara). — **tva,** n. (in rhet.) the being a Yamaka, Sāh. — **bhārata,** n. a summary of the Mahā-Bhārata in alliterative verse (by Ānanda-tīrtha). — **ratnâkara,** m., -**śikhāmaṇi,** m. N. of wks. — **śāla-vana,** n. N. of a place, Divyâv. **Yamakârṇava,** m. N. of a poem. **Yamakâvalī,** f. an uninterrupted series of Yamakas (e. g. Bhaṭṭ. x, 9). **Yamakâshṭaka,** n. N. of wk.

Yámana, mf(*ī*)n. restraining, governing, managing, VS.; m. the god Yama, L.; n. the act of restraining &c., Hariv.; Rājat.; binding, tying, L.; cessation, end, L.

Yamala, mf(*ā*)n. twin, paired, doubled, Suśr.; m. a singer in a duet, Saṃgīt.; N. of the number 'two,' Sūryas.; du. twins, a pair, couple, brace, MBh.; Kāv. &c.; (*ā*), f. a kind of hiccough, Suśr.; N. of a Tantra deity, Cat.; of a river, Śatr.; a sort of dress (consisting of body and petticoat), W. (also *ī*, f., Divyâv.); n. a pair, L. **-cchada,** m. Bauhinia Variegata, L. **-janana-śānti,** f. N. of wk. on the purificatory ceremonies after the birth of twins. **-pattraka,** m. Bauhinia Tomentosa, L. **-śānti,** f. N. of a Pariśishṭa of the MānGṛS. (cf. *-janana-ś°*). **-sū,** f. bringing forth twins, Hcat. **Yamalârjuna** or **°naka,** m. du. two Arjuna trees (which obstructed the path of Kṛishṇa, when a child, and were uprooted by him; afterwards personified as the enemies of Kṛishṇa, and in the later mythology regarded as metamorphoses of Nala-kūbara and Maṇi-grīva, two sons of Kubera), R.; Hariv.; Pur.; *-bhañjana* (Pañcar.), *-han* (W.), m. 'breaker or destroyer of the two Arjuna trees,' N. of Kṛishṇa or Vishṇu. **Yamalôdbhava,** m. the birth of twins, VarBṛS.

Yamalaka, m. a singer in a duet, Saṃgit.; a twin, L.

Yamasāná, mfn. champing the bit (as a horse), RV. vi, 3, 4.

Yamānikā or **yamānī,** f. Ptychotis Ajowan, Suśr. (cf. *kshetra-y°* and *yavānikā*).

Yamāya, Nom. Ā. *°yate,* to represent or be like Yama (the god of death), Gīt.

Yamika, n. du. (with *Agastyasya*) N. of two Sāmans, ĀrshBr.

Yamita, mfn. (fr. Caus.) restrained, checked &c. (cf. *a-yamita*).

Yamitrī, f. (prob.) holding together, ĀpŚr.

Yamin, mfn. restraining, curbing &c.; one who restrains himself or has subdued his senses, Kāv.; (*inī*), f. bringing forth twins, AV.

Yámishṭha, mfn. (superl.) guiding or managing best, most skilful in restraining or guiding (horses), RV.

Yamúnā, f. N. of a river commonly called the Jumnā (in Hariv. and MārkP. identified with Yamī, q. v.; it rises in the Himālaya mountains among the Jumnotri peaks at an elevation of 10,849 feet, and flows for 860 miles before it joins the Ganges at Allahabad, its water being there clear as crystal, while that of the Ganges is yellowish; the confluence of the two with the river Sarasvatī, supposed to join them underground, is called *tri-veṇī,* q. v.), RV. &c. &c.; of a daughter of the Muni Mataṃga, Kathās.; of a cow, KātyŚr., Sch. **-°cārya,** see *yāmunâcārya.* **-janaka,** m. 'father of Yamunā,' N. of the god of the sun, L. **-tīrtha,** n. N. of a Tīrtha; *-māhātmya,* n. N. of wk. **-datta,** m. N. of a frog, Pañcat. **-dvīpa,** n. N. of a district, Buddh. **-pati,** m. 'lord of Y°,' N. of Vishṇu, Pañcar. **-pūjā,** f. N. of wk. **-prabhava,** m. the source of the river Y° (celebrated as a place of pilgrimage), MBh. **-bhāj,** mfn. living on the Y°, MW. **-bhid,** m. N. of Bala-deva (so called from having divided the river into two parts with his ploughshare), L. **-bhrātṛi,** m. 'brother of Y°,' N. of Yama, L. **-māhātmya,** n. N. of ch. of PadmaP. **-varṇana,** n. N. of a poem (by Jagan-nātha Paṇḍita-rāja). **-°shṭaka** (*°nâsht°*), n. N. of two poems; *-ṭīkā,* f. N. of a Comm. on prec. **-°shṭapadī** (*°nâsht°*), f. N. of a short poem. **-stotra,** n. N. of a Stotra.

1. **Yamya,** mfn. restrainable, to be curbed or controlled, Pāṇ. iii, 1, 100.

2. **Yamyà** (?), mfn. (fr. *yama*) being a twin, belonging to twins, RV.; (*ā*), f. night, Naigh. i, 7.

यमदग्नि *yamadagni,* w. r. for *jamad-agni.*

यमन्वा *yamanvā,* f. (in gram.) a term for a form increased by Vṛiddhi.

यमया *yamayā,* said to = جمعة, N. of the 6th astronomical Yoga.

यमयिष्णु *yamayishṇu,* w. r. for *namayishṇu.*

यमल *yamala.* See p. 846, col. 3.

यमुन्द *yamunda,* m. N. of a man, Pāṇ. iv, 1, 149, Sch.

यमुषदेव *yamushadeva,* N. of a kind of woven cloth, Rājat.

यमेरुका *yamerukā,* f. a kind of drum or gong on which the hours are struck, L.

ययाति *yayā́ti,* m. (prob. fr. √*yat*) N. of a celebrated monarch of the lunar race (son of king Nahusha whom he succeeded; from his two wives came the two lines of the lunar race, Yadu being the son of Devayānī, daughter of Uśanas or Śukra, and Puru of Śarmishṭhā, daughter of Vṛisha-parvan; Yayāti Nāhusha is also represented as the author of RV. ix, 101, 4–6), RV.; MaitrUp.; MBh.; Kāv. &c. **-carita,** n. 'the story of Yayāti,' N. of a Nāṭaka (by Rudra-deva). **-jā,** f. patr. of Mādhavī, MBh. **-patana,** n. 'fall of Y°,' N. of a place of pilgrimage, ib. **-vát,** ind. like Y°, RV. **-vijaya,** m. 'Y°'s victory,' N. of wk.

Yayātika, m. (m. c.) = *Yayāti,* AgP.

ययावर *yayāvará,* v. l. for *yāyāvará.*

ययि *yayí,* mfn. (√*yā*) going, hastening, quick, RV.; m. a cloud, ib.

Yayin, mfn. = prec. (see *ni-yayín*); m. N. of Śiva, L.

Yayī́, mfn. = *yayi,* RV.; m. a horse, L.; N. of Śiva, L.

Yáyu, mfn. (*yayú* in a corrupted passage, AV. iv, 24, 2) going, moving, swift (applied to a horse), VS.; m. a horse (esp. 'one fit for sacrifice'), L.; N. of one of the horses of the Moon, VP.; the way of final beatitude, L.; f. obtaining, L.; mfn. having a long stick, L.

यरादेवीरहस्य *yarādevī-rahasya,* n. N. of wk.

यर्हि *yárhi,* ind. (fr. 3. *ya;* correlative of *tárhi, etárhi,* but also followed by *tadā, tatra, atha* &c.) when, at which time, whenever, while, whereas (with pres. or Pot., impv., aor. or pf.; sometimes also with no verb), TS.; AitBr.; BhP.; since, as, because, BhP.

यल्ल *yalla,* m. N. of various authors (also with *bhaṭṭa* and *ārya*), Cat. **-bhaṭṭa-suta,** m. N. of the author of Comm. on ĀśvŚr. **-bhaṭṭīya,** n. N. of wk.

Yallaya and **°yârya,** m. N. of two authors, Cat.

Yallāji, m. N. of an author; *°jīya,* n. his wk.

यव 1. *yáva,* m. the first half of a month (generally in pl.; accord. to Comm. = *pūrva-pakshāḥ;* also written *yāva*), VS.; ŚBr.; Kāṭh.

Yávan, m. id., ŚBr.

1. **Yavyá,** m. (for 2. see p. 848, col. 1) a month (as containing a Yava), ŚBr.

यव 2. *yáva,* mfn. (√1. *yu*) warding off, averting, AV.; Yājñ.

Yavayā́van, m. one who keeps off or averts, AV.

यव 3. *yáva,* m. barley (in the earliest times, prob. any grain or corn yielding flour or meal; pl. barley-corns), RV. &c. &c.; a barley-corn (either as a measure of length = ⅙ or ⅛ of an Aṅgula, VarBṛS.; or as a weight = 6 or 12 mustard seeds = ½ Guñjā, Mn.; Yājñ.); any grain of seed or seed corn, Bhpr.; (in palmistry) a figure or mark on the hand resembling a barley-corn (supposed to indicate good fortune), VarBṛS.; N. of a partic. astron. Yoga (when the favourable planets are situated in the 4th and 10th mansions and the unfavourable ones in the 1st and 7th), ib.; speed, velocity, W. (prob. w. r. for *java*); a double convex lens, ib. [Cf. Zd. *yava;* Gk. ζειά; Lith. *javaī.*] **-koṭi** or **-koṭī,** f. = *yama-k°,* Āryabh. **-krin,** m. = *-krīta,* MBh. **-krī,** m. a buyer or purchaser of barley, MW.; = next, MBh. **-krīta,** m. 'purchased with barley,' N. of a son of Bharad-vāja, MBh.; R. &c. **-kshāra,** m. an alkali prepared from the ashes of burnt green barley-corns, Suśr.; ŚārṅgS. **-kshetra,** n. a field of barley, Kathās. **-kshoda,** m. b°-meal, L. **-khada,** g. *vrīhy-ādi.* **-khadika,** mfn. (fr. *-khada*), ib. **-khala,** m. a barn-floor, ŚāṅkhŚr. **-godhūma-ja,** mfn. produced from barley and wheat, MW. **-godhūma-vat,** mfn. sown with b° and wh°, R. **-grīva,** mfn. having a neck like a b°-corn, VarBṛS. **-caturthī,** f. a sort of game played on the 4th day in the light half of the month Vaiśākha (when people throw b°-meal over one another), Cat. **-cūrṇa,** n. barley-meal, ŚāṅkhŚr. **-ja,** m. = *-kshāra,* L.; Ptychotis Ajowan, L. **-tiktā,** f. a species of plant, Suśr.; Car. **-dvīpa,** m. the island Yava, R. (v. l. *jala-d°*); Buddh. **-nāla,** m. Andropogon Bicolor or Sorghum, Suśr.; barley-straw (?), W.; *-ja,* m. an alkali made from the ashes of the above plant, L. (cf. *yava-kshāra*). **-pāla,** m. one who guards a b°-field, Pāṇ. vi, 2, 78. **-pishṭa,** n. barley-meal, Gobh.; MānŚr. (pl.); Suśr.; *°ṭaka,* m. b°-cake, L. **-prakhyā,** f. a partic. eruption or small tumour like a b°-corn, Bhpr. **-praroha,** m. a shoot or ear of b°, Kum. **-phala,** m. (only L.) the bamboo cane; Nardostachys Jatamansi; Wrightia Antidysenterica; Ficus Infectoria; an onion (?). **-busa,** n. the husk of barley, Pāṇ. iv, 3, 48. **-busaka,** mfn. (to be paid) at the time of producing chaff from b° (as a debt), ib. **-maṇi,** m. a partic. amulet, Kauś. **-mat** (*yáva-*), mfn. containing b°, mixed with b°, TS.; Kāṭh. &c.; m. one who cultivates grain, RV.; N. of a Gandharva, ŚBr.; of the author of VS. ii, 19, Anukr.; (*atī*), f. a kind of metre, Piṅg.; Col.; n. abundance of grain, RV. **-matya,** Nom. P. *°yati,* = *yava-mān ivâcarati,* Pat. **-madhya** (*yáva-*), mf(*ā*)n. being like a barley-corn in the middle, i. e. broad in the centre and thin or tapering at the ends, ŚBr.; RPrāt. &c.; m. a partic. Pañca-rātra, ŚBr.; a kind of drum, L.; (*ā*), f. a kind of metre, W.; n. a partic. measure of length, MārkP.; a kind of Cāndrâyaṇa, Prâyaśc.; Kull. on Mn. xi, 217. **-madhyama,** m. a partic. measure of length, AgP.; n. a kind of Cāndrâyaṇa or lunar penance, Mn. xi, 217. **-máya,** mf(*ī*)n. consisting of barley, made of b°, TS.; ŚBr. **-mardana,** n. a barn-floor, ŚāṅkhŚr., Comm. **-mātra,** mfn. of the size of a barley-corn, KātyŚr. **-mushṭi,** m. f. a handful of b°, Gobh. **-lāsa,** m. nitre, saltpetre, W. **-vaktra,** mf(*ā*)n. having a head or point like a grain of b°, Suśr. **-velā,** f. the time of the barley-harvest, Lāṭy. **-śasya** (for *-sasya*), n. a species of corn, Divyâv. **-śiras,** mfn. having a head shaped like a grain of b°, VarBṛS., Comm. **-śūka** or **-śūka-ja,** m. = *-kshāra,* q. v., L. **-saktú,** m. pl. b°-groats, ŚBr. **-sâhva,** see under *yavasa.* **-surā,** f. an intoxicating drink prepared from b°-meal, Madanav. **Yavâkāra,** mfn. b°-shaped, shaped like a b°-corn, MW. **Yavâgraja,** m. = *yava-kshāra,* Car.; Bhpr.; Ptychotis Ajowan, L. **Yavâgrayaṇa,** n. the first-fruits of b°, KātyŚr., Sch. **Yavâṅkura,** m. a shoot or blade of b°, Ragh. **Yavâcitá,** mfn. laden with b° (or corn), TS.; Br.; ŚrS. **Yavâd,** mfn. eating b°, RV. **Yavântara,** n. a partic. measure of time, Lāṭy., Comm. **Yavânna,** n. b°-food, boiled barley, Suśr. **Yavânvita,** mfn. having b°, L. **Yavâpatya,** n. = *yava-kshāra,* L. **Yavâmlaja,** n. sour b°-gruel, L. **Yávâśir,** mfn. mixed with corn, RV. **Yavâhāra,** mfn. having b° for food, living on b°, Mn. xi, 199. **Yavâhva,** m. = *yava-kshāra,* Suśr. **Yavôttha,** n. = *yavâmlaja* above, L. **Yavôdara,** n. the body or thick part of a grain of b° (used as a measure of length), MārkP. **Yavôrvarā,** f. a field sown with barley, ŚrS.

Yavaka, mfn. being of the nature of barley, g. *sthūlâdi;* m. barley, VarBṛS.; Vāgbh.

Yavakya, mfn. sown with barley, Pāṇ. v, 2, 3.

Yavakshā, f. N. of a river, MBh.

Yavayú, mfn. desiring corn, RV.

Yavalaka (?), m. a species of bird, Suśr.

Yávasa, m. n. grass, fodder, pasturage, RV. &c. &c. **-prathama** (*yávasa-*), mfn. beginning with or depending on good past°, well-nurtured (accord. to Mahīdh., 'first or best of all kinds of food'), VS. xxi, 43. **-mushṭi,** m. f. a handful of grass, ŚāṅkhŚr. **Yavasâd,** mfn. eating gr°, grazing, pasturing, RV. **Yavasânnôdakêndhana,** n. grass, corn, water and fuel, MW. **Yavasâhva,** m. Ptychotis Ajowan, L. **Yavasôdaka,** n. du. grass and water, KātyŚr.

Yavasin, yavasyu. See *sū-yavasin, sū-yavasyú.*

Yavāgū, f. (in Uṇ. iii, 81 said to come fr. √2. *yu*) rice-gruel; any weak decoction of other kinds of grain &c. (accord. to some, a dec° in which 4 measures of an ingredient are steeped in 64 meas° of water and the whole boiled down to half the original quantity; frequently in comp. with the ingredient from which the gruel is made), TS.; Br. &c. **-cāraka,** m. the lay-brother who prepares the rice-gruel, L. **-maya,** mf(*ī*)n. consisting of Yavāgū, Pāṇ. v, 4, 21, Sch.

Yavānikā, f. Ptychotis Ajowan, Car.

Yavānī, f. Ptychotis Ajowan, Suśr.; ŚārṅgS. &c.; a kind of bad barley, Pāṇ. iv, 1, 49, Sch.

Yavāsa, m. (said to be fr. √2. *yu*) Alhagi Maurorum, L.; a species of Khadira, L.; (*ā*), f. a kind of grass, L. (prob. w. r. for *jala-vāsā*). **-śarkarā,** f. a kind of sugar made from Yavāsa, Suśr.; Madanav.

Yavāsaka, m. Alhagi Maurorum, Suśr.; Car. &c.

Yavāsinī, f. a district abounding in Yavāsa, g. *pushkarâdi.*

Yavika, yavin, or **yavila,** mfn., fr. 3. *yava,* g. *tundâdi.*

2. **Yávya**, mfn. (for 1. *yavyá* see p. 847, col. 2) suitable for barley, Pāṇ. v, 1, 7; sown with b°, L.; m. (accord. to Mahīdh.) a stock of barley or of fruit, MaitrS.; VS.; pl. N. of a family of Ṛishis, MBh. (v.l.); n. of a field of b°, MW.; (*yavyá*), n. N. of certain Homa-mantras, TBr.; (*á*), f. a stock of b° or of fruit, TS.; (accord. to Naigh.) a river, RV.; (*á* or *ábhis*), ind. in streams, in abundance, ib.

Yavyá-vatī, f. N. of a river or a district, RV.; TāṇḍyaBr.

यवगण्ड *yavagaṇḍa*, m. = *yuva-gaṇḍa* (q.v.), L.

यवन 1. *yavana*, mfn. (√1. *yu*) keeping away, averting (see *dvesho-yávana*).

यवन 2. *yavana*, n. (√2. *yu*) mixing, mingling (esp. with water), Nyāyam.

यवन 3. *yavana*, mfn. quick, swift; m. a swift horse, L. (prob. w.r. for *javana*).

Yavāna, mfn. quick, swift, L. (prob. w.r. for *javāna*).

यवन 4. *yavana*, w.r. for *paijavana*, Mn. vii, 41.

यवन 5. *yavana*, m. an Ionian, Greek (or a king of the Greeks, g. *kambojâdi*; in later times also a Muhammadan or European, any foreigner or barbarian), Mn.; MBh. &c.; N. of a caste, Gaut. (accord. to L. 'the legitimate son of a Kshatriya and a Vaiśyā' or 'an Ugra who is an elephant catcher'); of a country (= *yavana-deśa*, sometimes applied to Ionia, Greece, Bactria, and more recently to Arabia), W.; wheat, L.; a carrot, L.; olibanum, L.; pl. the Ionians, Greeks (esp. the Greek astrologers), MBh.; VarBṛS. &c.; N. of a dynasty, Pur.; (*ī*), f. the wife of a Yavana, a Greek or Muhammadan woman, Kālid.; Śiś. (Yavana girls were formerly employed as attendants on kings, esp. to take charge of their bows and quivers); = *javanī*, a curtain, L.; n. salt from saline soil, L. — **jātaka**, n. N. of wk. — **deśa**, m. the country of the Yavanas; *-ja*, mfn. growing or produced in the country of the Y°s, Bhpr.; styrax or benzoin, ib.; °*ôdbhava*, mfn. born in the c° of the Y°s, Prâyaśc. — **dvishṭa**, n. 'disliked by Y°s,' bdellium, L. — **pura**, n. 'city of Y°s,' (prob.) Alexandria, VarBṛS., Introd. — **priya**, n. 'dear to Y°s,' pepper, L. — **mata-golâdhyāya**, m. N. of wk. — **muṇḍa**, m. a bald Y°, one with a shaven head, g. *mayūra-vyaṅsakâdi*. — **śāstre 'mala-praśna**, m., -**sāra**, m. N. of wks. — **sena**, m. N. of a man, Kathās. — **horā**, f. N. of wk. **Yavanâcārya**, m. N. of an astronomer (also called Yavanêśvara, author of various wks.; perhaps any Greek astronomer), Var., Sch. **Yavanâri**, m. 'enemy of the Y°s,' N. of Kṛishṇa, L.; of a king of Vārāṇasī, Cat. **Yavanêśvara**, m. N. of a prince of the Y°s, Hcar.; of an astronomer (see *yavanâcārya*). **Yavanêshṭa**, m. 'liked by Y°s,' a kind of onion or garlic, Bhpr.; Azadirachta Indica, L.; (*ā*), f. the wild date tree, L.; n. lead, L.; an onion, L.; pepper, L.

Yavanaka, m. a partic. kind of grain, L.; (*ikā*), f. a Yavana woman, Śak. (v.l.); a screen of cloth or a veil, Kāv.; BhP. (cf. *javanikā*).

Yavanānī, f. the writing of the Yavanas, Pāṇ. iv, 1, 49, Vārtt. 3, Pat.

Yavanīya-ramala-śāstra, n. N. of wk.

यवनाल *yava-nāla* &c. See p. 847, col. 2.

यवय *yavaya*, Nom. fr. *yuvan*, P. *yavayati*, L.

यवयस *yavayasa*, m. N. of a son of Idhmajihva and (n.) of the Varsha in Plaksha-dvīpa ruled by him, BhP.

यवस *yavasa* &c. See p. 847, col. 3.

यवागू *yavāgū* &c. See p. 847, col. 3.

यवान *yavāna*. See above.

यवानिका *yavānikā*. See p. 847, col. 3.

यवाष *yavāsha*, m. (cf. *yévāsha*) a partic. noxious insect, Kāṭh.; g. *kumudâdi* (on Pāṇ. iv, 2, 80).

Yavāshika and **yavāshin**, mfn., g. *kumudâdi* and *prêkshâdi*.

यवास *yavāsa* &c. See p. 847, col. 3.

यविष्ठ *yávishṭha*, mfn. (superl. of *yuvan*) youngest, very young, last-born (esp. applied to Agni when just produced from wood or placed on the altar after everything else; Agni Yavishṭha is also the supposed author of RV. viii, 91), RV.; BhP.; Pañcar.; m. a younger brother, L.; N. of a Brāhman (pl. his descendants), Cat. — 1. -**vat** (*yáv*°), mfn. containing the word *yávishṭha*, ŚBr. — 2. -**vat**, ind. like a youth, ŚBr.

Yávishṭhya, mfn. youngest (only at the end of a Pada = *yávishṭha*), RV.

Yavīyas, mfn. (compar. of *yuvan*) younger, Mn.; MBh. &c. (with *mātṛi*, *jananī* or *ambā*, a younger stepmother; with *bhūta* opp. to *mahā-bh*°; also applied to a Śūdra as opp. to one of the three higher castes; m. c. acc. sg. m. also *yavīyasam*; nom. pl. m. also *yavīyasas*); lesser, worse, MBh.; m. a younger brother, L.; (*asī*), f. a younger sister, L.

Yavīyasa, m. N. of a preceptor, Cat.

यवीनर *yavīnara*, m. N. of a son of Ajamīḍha (Hariv.) or of Dvi-mīḍha (BhP.) or of Bharmyâśva (ib.) or of Vāhyâśva (ib.)

यवीयुध् *yavīyúdh*, mfn. (fr. Intens. of √1. *yudh*) eager to fight, fond of war, RV. (also written *yavyudh*, ŚatarUp.)

यव्य 1. 2. *yavya*. See p. 847 and col. 1.

यश *yaśa*, *yaśaḥ* &c. See below.

यशद *yaśada*, n. zinc, Bhpr.

यशस् *yáśas*, n. beautiful appearance, beauty, splendour, worth, RV.; AV.; VS.; ŚBr.; GṛŚrS.; honour, glory, fame, renown, AV. &c. &c. (also personified as a son of Kāma and Rati, Hariv.; or of Dharma and Kīrti, Pur.); an object of honour, a person of respectability, ŚBr.; favour, graciousness, partiality, RV.; N. of various Sāmans, ĀrshBr.; = *udaka*, water, or *anna*, food, or *dhana*, wealth, Naigh.; (*yaśás*), mfn. beautiful, splendid, worthy, excellent, RV.; AV.; honoured, respected, venerated, ib.; pleasant, agreeable, estimable, ib. — **kara**, mf(*ī*)n. causing renown; (ifc.) conferring glory on, glorious for, Mn.; MBh. &c.; m. N. of an author, Cat.; of various men, Kathās.; Rājat.; *-svāmin*, m. N. of a temple founded by Yaśas-kara, Rājat. — **kāma** (*yáśas*-), mfn. desirous of fame or glory, ambitious, TS.; Br.; ŚrS.; m. N. of a Bodhi-sattva, SaddhP. — **kāmya**, Nom. P. °*yati*, to desire honour or fame, Bhaṭṭ. — **kṛit**, mfn. conferring dignity or renown, TS. — **tama** and -**tara** (*yaśás*-), mfn. most (more) renowned or resplendent, RV. — **vat** (*yáśas*-), mfn. glorious, famous, honourable, RV.; splendid, magnificent, excellent, ib.; TS.; pleasant, dear, AV.; (*atī*), f. N. of a woman, Kathās. — **vin**, mfn. beautiful, splendid, illustrious, famous, celebrated, AV. &c. &c. (superl. *-vi-tama*); m. (with *kavi*) N. of a poet, Cat.; *-(inī)*, f. N. of an artery, Cat.; of various plants (wild cotton, = *yava-tikta*, = *mahā-jyotishmatī* &c.), L.; of one of the Mātṛis attending on Skanda, MBh.

Yaśa, mfn. (ifc.) = *yaśas* (see *ati-yaśa*).

Yaśaḥ, in comp. for *yaśas*. — **karṇa** (Inscr.), -**ketu** (Kathās.), m. N. of two princes. — **kāya**, m. a body of fame or glory, fulness of glory or reputation, Bhartṛ. — **khaṇḍin**, mfn. destroying fame, Pracaṇḍ. — **paṭaha**, m. a drum, double drum, L. — **pāla**, m. N. of a prince, Col.; of the author of the Moha-rāja-parājaya, Cat. — **prakhyāpana**, n. spreading abroad or proclaiming the glory (of any one), Daś. — **śarīra**, n. = *-kāya*, Ragh. — **śesha**, mfn. having nothing left but glory or fame, i.e. dead (*-tām* with *pra-√yā*, to die, Kathās.; with √*nī*, to die; °*shī-bhūta*, mfn. dead, Kāv.); m. death, dying, W.

Yaśaś, in comp. for *yaśas*. — **candra**, m. N. of a king, Inscr.

Yaśasa, n. (ifc.) = *yaśas* (see *deva-*, *manushya-* and *śrī-yaśasá*).

Yaśasin, mfn. See *deva-* and *manushya-yaśasin*.

Yaśasya, mfn. conferring fame or renown, famous, creditable, glorious, TS. &c. &c.; honoured, celebrated, R.; stately, decent, Car.; (*ā*), f. N. of various plants (= *ṛiddhi*, *jīvantī* &c.), L.

Yaśasyú, mfn. seeking favour, AV.

Yaśo, in comp. for *yaśas*. — **gopi**, m. N. of a Sch. on KātyŚr. — **ghna**, mfn. destroying fame or reputation, Mn.; BhP. — **da**, mfn. conferring fame or renown, L.; m. quicksilver, L. (cf. *yaśo-dhā*); (*ā*), f., see 1. *yaśo-dā*. — **datta**, m. N. of a man, Lalit. — **darpaṇikā**, f. N. of wk. — 1. -**dā**, f. (of *yaśo-da*) N. of the daughter of a class of deceased ancestors, Hariv.; of the wife of the cowherd Nanda (Kṛishṇa's foster-mother who nursed him immediately after his birth, cf. IW. 332), Hariv.; Pur. &c.; of the wife of Mahā-vīra (and daughter of Samara-vīra), W.; *-garbha-sambhūtā*, f. N. of Durgā, MBh.; *-nanda* (Hariv.), *-nandana* (Pañcar.), *-suta* (Cāṇ.), m. 'Yaśo-dā's son,' metron. of Kṛishṇa. — 2. -**dā́**, mfn. bestowing fame or honour, TS.; f. N. of partic. bricks, ib.; ĀpŚr. — **deva**, m. N. of a Buddhist mendicant, Lalit.; of a son of Rāma-candra, Cat.; (*ī*), f. N. of a daughter of Vainateya and wife of Bṛihan-manas, Hariv. — **dhana**, n. a fund or stock of fame, MW.; mfn. whose wealth is fame, renowned, famous, Inscr.; MBh.; Kāv. &c.; m. N. of a king, Kathās.; of the author of the Dhanamjaya-vijaya. — **dhara**, mfn. maintaining or preserving glory, BhP.; m. N. of the fifth day of the civil month, L.; of a son of Kṛishṇa by Rukmiṇī, MBh. (v.l. *yaśo-vara*); (with Jainas) of the 18th Arhat of the preceding and of the 19th of the future Utsarpiṇī, L.; of various other men, Kathās.; Rājat.; (also with *bhaṭṭa* and *miśra*) of various authors, Cat.; (*ā*), f. N. of the fourth night of the civil month, L.; of the mother of Rāhula, Buddh.; of several other women, MBh.; Kathās.; Pur. — **dhareya**, w.r. for *yāśodh*°. — **dhā́**, mfn. conferring splendour or fame, TBr.; BhP.; m. quicksilver (?), L. — **dhāman**, n. site or abode of glory, PhP. — **nandi**, m. N. of a prince, ib. — **nidhi**, mfn. = *-dhana*, Pracaṇḍ. — **bhagín**, mfn. rich in glory, famous, renowned, VS. — **bhagīna** or -**bhagya**, mfn., Pāṇ. iv, 4, 131 &c. — **bhadra**, m. (with Jainas) N. of one of the six Śruta-kevalins, HPariś. — **bhṛit**, mfn. possessing or conferring renown, MBh. — **maṅgala-stotra**, n. N. of wk. — **matī**, f. N. of the third lunar night, L. — **matya**, m. pl. N. of a people, MārkP. — **mādhava**, m. a form of Vishṇu, Cat. — **mitra**, m. N. of an author, Buddh.; of various other men, HPariś. — **medhā-samanvita**, mfn. possessing fame and intelligence, Mn. iii, 263. — **yuta**, mfn. possessing fame, renowned, VarBṛS. — **rāja**, m. N. of a man, Rājat. — **rāta**, m. N. of a man, Inscr. — **rāśi**, m. a heap or mass of glory, a glorious deed, Vikr. — **lekhā**, f. N. of a princess, Kathās. — **vat**, mfn. possessing fame or glory; (*atī*), f. N. of various women, Rājat.; Vās., Introd.; (m. c. also *ati*) of a district (originally a stream), VarBṛS.; of a mythical town on mount Meru, BhP., Sch. — **vara**, m. N. of a son of Kṛishṇa by Rukmiṇī, MBh. (B. *-dhara*). — **vartman**, n. the path of glory, MW. — **vardhana**, m. N. of a man, Inscr. — **varmaka** (ifc.) = next, Kathās. — **varman**, m. N. of a king of Kanyā-kubja (who reigned about A.D. 720), IW. 499; of a poet (also °*ma-deva*), Cat.; of various other men, Kathās.; Rājat. — **han**, mf(*ghnī*)n. destroying beauty, PārGṛ.; destroying fame or glory, BhP. — **hara**, mfn. depriving of reputation, MBh.; R.; m. or n. (?) N. of a place, Kshitîś.; *-jit*, m. N. of Kacu-rāya, ib. — **hīna**, mfn. shorn of glory, MW.

यष्टव्य *yashṭavya*, *yashṭṛi*. See p. 840, col. 3.

यष्टि 2. *yashṭí*, m. (only L.) or f. (also *yashṭī*, cf. g. *bahv-ādi*; prob. fr. √*yach* = *yam*; for 1. *yashṭi*, see p. 840, col. 3) 'any support,' a staff, stick, wand, rod, mace, club, cudgel; pole, pillar, perch, ŚBr. &c. &c.; a flag-staff (see *dhvaja-y*°); a stalk, stem, branch, twig, Hariv.; Kāv.; (ifc.) anything thin or slender (see *aṅga-*, *bhuja-y*°), MBh.; Kāv. &c.; the blade of a sword (see *asi-y*°); a thread, string (esp. of pearls; cf. *maṇi-*, *hāra-y*°), Kālid.; a partic. kind of pearl necklace, VarBṛS.; liquorice, Suśr.; sugar-cane, L.; Clerodendrum Siphonantus, L.; any creeping plant, W. — **gṛiha**, n. N. of a district, Vās., Introd. (cf. *-grāma*). — **graha**, mfn. carrying a stick or staff, Pāṇ. iii, 2, 9, Vārtt. 1. — **grāma**, m. N. of a district, Hcar. (v.l. *-grihaka*). — **grāham**, ind. seizing sticks, Pāṇ. iii, 4, 53, Sch. — **nivāsa**, m. a pole serving as a perch, a pigeon-house standing on upright poles, Ragh. (cf. *vāsa-yashṭi*). — **prāṇa**, mfn. one whose strength lies (only) in his staff, powerless, feeble, out of breath, MBh. (cf. *yashty-utthāna*). — **mat**, mfn. having a stick or staff, furnished with a flag-staff (as a chariot), MBh. — **madhu** and -**madhuka**, n., -**madhukā**, f. liquorice, L. — **maudgalya**, m. Maudgalya with the staff (= *yashṭi-pradhāna-m*°), Pat. — **yantra**, n. a partic. astronomical instrument, Sūryas. — **latā**, f. a kind of plant (= *bhramarâri*), L.

Yashṭika (ifc.) = *yashṭi*, a string of pearls (see *śata-yashṭika*): a species of water-fowl, L.; a bird, the lapwing, W.; (*ā*), f. a staff, stick, club, R.; Suśr.; a partic. pearl ornament or necklace, L.; an oblong pond or tank, L.; liquorice, Suśr.

Yashṭī, f. = *yashṭi*. Also in comp. for *yashṭi*. **-pushpa**, m. Putranjiva Roxburghii, L. **-madhu** or °**dhuka**, n. liquorice, Suśr.

Yashṭīka, n. liquorice, L.

Yashṭy, in comp. for *yashṭi* or *yashṭī*. **-āghāta**, m. a blow with a stick, cudgeling, beating, MW. **-āhva** and **-āhvaya**, m., **-āhvā**, f. liquorice, Suśr.; Car.; Bhpr. **-utthāna**, n. rising with the help of a staff, Bhartṛ.

यष्ट्रस्क *yashṭraska*, m. pl. N. of a people, L.

यस् *yas*, cl. 4. P. (Dhātup. xxvi, 101) *yásyati* (rarely *yasati*, cf. Pāṇ. iii, 1, 71; Impv. *-yayastu*, RV.; Gr. also pf. *yayāsa*; aor. *ayasat*; fut. *yasitā*, *yasishyati*; inf. *yasitum*; ind. p. *yasitvā* or *yastvā*) to froth up, foam, RV. (cf. √*yesh*); to heat or exert one's self, Car.; to strive after (dat.), Kāvyâd. ii, 83 (v. l.): Caus. *yāsayati* (aor. *ayīyasat*), Gr.: Desid. *yiyasishati*, ib.: Intens. *yāyasyate*, *yāyasti*, ib. [Cf. Gk. ζέω &c.]

Yaska, m. N. of a man (pl. his descendants and a partic. school; cf. *yāska*), Kāṭh.; ĀśvŚr. (cf. Pāṇ. ii, 4, 63).

Yasta, mfn. entrusted, deposited, L. (cf. *ā-*, *pra-y°* &c.)

Yasya, mfn. to be endeavoured &c.; to be killed (*-tva*, n.), Bhaṭṭ.

यस्मात् *yasmāt*, ind. (abl. of 3. *ya*, correlative of *tasmāt*, *tatas*, *tad* &c.) from which, from which cause, since, as, because, Mn.; MBh. &c.; that, in order that, R.

यहस् *yáhas*, n. (prob. fr. a lost √*yah*, to speed, be quick), water, Naigh. i, 12; strength, power, ib. ii, 9.

Yáhu, mfn. (prob.) 'restless, swift,' or 'mighty, strong,' RV. (= *mahat*, Sāy.); m. offspring, a child (= *apatya*), Naigh. ii, 2 (*sáhaso yahúḥ*, RV. viii, 60, 13 = *sahaso putraḥ*, Sāy.)

Yahvá, mf(*ī*)n. restless, swift, active (applied to Agni, Indra and Soma), RV.; continually moving or flowing (applied to the waters), ib. (= *mahat*, Sāy.); m. = *yajamāna*, a sacrificer, Uṇ. i, 134, Sch.; (*ī*), f. du. heaven and earth, RV.; pl. the flowing waters (with *sapta*, 'the seven great rivers'), ib. (cf. Naigh. i, 15).

Yahvát, mf(*átī*)n. ever-flowing (waters), RV.

या 1. *yā* (collateral form of √5. *i*), cl. 2. P. (Dhātup. xxiv, 41) *yā́ti* (1. pl. *yāmahe*, MBh.; impf. 3. pl. *ayuḥ*, Br.; *ayān*, Pāṇ. iii, 4, 111, Sch.; pf. *yayaú*, *yayā́tha*, *yayá*, *yayúḥ*, RV. &c. &c.; *yaye*, Kāv.; aor. *ayāsam* or *ayāsisham*; Subj. *yā́sat*, *yeshám*, *yāsishat*, RV.; Br.; Prec. *yāsishīshṭhās*, Br.; fut. *yātā*, MBh. &c.; *yāsyati*, AV.; °*te*, MBh.; inf. *yātum*, MBh. &c.; Ved. inf. *-yai*, *yā́tave* or °*vai*; ind. p. *yātvā́*, Br. &c.; *-yā́ya*, *-yā́yam*, ib.), to go, proceed, move, walk, set out, march, advance, travel, journey (often with instr. or acc. of the way, esp. with *gatim*, *mārgam*, *adhvānam*, *panthānam*, *padavīm*, *yātrām*), RV. &c. &c.; to go away, withdraw, retire, MBh.; Kāv. &c.; (also with *palāyya*) to flee, escape, R.; Kathās. (with *kshemeṇa* or *svasti*, to escape unscathed, Pañcat.; BhP.); to go towards or against, go or come to, enter, approach, arrive at, reach, RV. &c. &c. (with acc. often followed by *prati*, e.g. with *gṛiham*, to enter a house; with *ripum prati*, to march against the enemy; with *mṛigayām*, to go out hunting; with *śirasā mahīm*, to bow down to the ground with the head; with *prakṛitim*, to return to one's natural state; with *karṇau*, to come to the ears, be heard; with *utsavād utsavam*, to go from one festival to another; with *hastam* ifc., to fall into the hands of; with *patham* or *gocaram* ifc., to come within range of; esp. with the acc. of an abstract noun = to go to any state or condition, become, be, e. g. *vināśam yāti*, he goes to destruction, i. e. he is destroyed; *kāṭhinyam yāti*, it becomes hard; *dveshyatām yāti*, he becomes hated; similarly *nidhanam* √*yā*, to die; *nidrām* √*yā*, to fall asleep; *udayam* √*yā*, to rise, said of stars &c.; sometimes also with loc., e. g. *yāhi rājñaḥ sakāśe*, go into the presence of the king, R.; or even with dat., e. g. *yayatuḥ sva-niveśāya*, both went home, Kathās.; *na câtmane kṛipaṇasya dhanam yāti*, nor does the wealth of the miser go to [i. e. benefit] himself, Hit.; *phalebhyo yāti*, he goes to [fetch] fruits, Pāṇ. ii, 3, 14, Sch.); to go to for any request, implore, solicit (with two acc.), RV.; (with *striyam*) to go to a woman for sexual intercourse, MBh.; to go to for any purpose (inf.), Bhaṭṭ.; Vop.; often with adverbs, e.g. with *bahir*, to go out, Kathās.; with *adho*, to go down, sink, BhP.; with *khaṇḍaśo* or *dalaśo*, to fall to pieces, Kathās.; with *śata-dhā*, to fall into a hundred pieces, ib.; to extend to (acc.), VarBṛS.; to last for (acc.), Hit.; to pass away, elapse (said of time), MBh.; Kāv. &c.; to vanish, disappear (as wealth), Mṛicch.; to come to pass, prosper, succeed, BhP.; to proceed, behave, act, MBh.; to find out, discover, MBh.; to receive or learn (a science) from (abl.), BhP.; to undertake, undergo (acc.), RV.; Impv. *yātu*, be it as it may, Hit.: Pass. *yāyate*, to be gone or moved, MBh.: Caus. *yāpáyati* (aor. *ayīyapat*), to cause to depart, cause to go or march, dismiss, Kāv.; BhP.; to cause to go towards (acc.), Pāṇ. i, 4, 32, Sch. (cf. *yāpita*); to direct (the gaze) towards (loc.), Bhartṛ. (v. l. *pātayati*); to drive away, remove, cure (a disease), Suśr.; to cause to pass or elapse, pass or spend (time), MBh.; Kāv. &c.; to live (Pāli *yāpeti*), Divyâv.; to cause to subsist, support, maintain, Divyâv.; to induce, MW.: Desid. *yiyāsati*, to intend or be about to go, desire to proceed, MBh.; Kāv. &c.: Intens. *īyāyate* (?), to move, PraśnUp.; *yāyāyate*, *yāyeti*, *yāyāti*, Gr.

2. **Yā** (ifc.) going, moving (see *riṇa-*, *eva-*, *tura-*, *deva-yā́*).

1. **Yāt**, mfn. (nom. *yān*, *yātī* or *yāntī*, *yāt*; for 2. *yāt* see p. 851, col. 1) going, moving &c. (in RV. i, 32, 15, 'travelling,' as opp. to *áva-sita*, 'resting'). **-sattra**, n. 'continuous sacrifice,' N. of partic. solemn ceremonies (which go on for a long period, also called Sārasvata), ŚrS.

Yātá, mfn. gone, proceeded, marched (n. also impers.), RV. &c. &c.; gone away, fled, escaped, MBh.; Kāv. &c.; passed by, elapsed, Hariv.; Var.; entered upon, pursued (as a path), R.; gone to, come or fallen into (acc., loc. or comp.), Mn.; MBh. &c.; situated (as a heavenly body), VarBṛS.; become, turned out (*kva tad yātam*, what has become of this?), Hariv.; known, understood, Pat.; n. motion, progress, gait, course, drive, RV. &c. &c.; the place where a person has gone, Pāṇ. ii, 3, 68, Sch.; the past time (opp. to *an-āgatam*, the future), VarBṛS.; the guiding or driving of an elephant with a goad, L. **-yāma** or **-yāman** (*yātá-*), mfn. 'having completed its course,' used, spoiled, useless, rejected, Br.; GṛS.; MBh. &c.; raw, half-ripe, W.; exhausted, old, aged, BhP.; °*ma-tva*, n. uselessness, old age, Gobh. **Yātânuyāta**, n. (prob.) the going and following, g. *śāka-pārthivâdi*. **Yātâyāta**, n. going and coming, BhP.; ebb and flow, Sadukt. **Yātôpayāta**, n. going and coming; °*tika*, mfn. g. *aksha-dyūtâdi*.

1. **Yātavya**, mfn. to be gone or marched (n. impers.), MBh.; Hariv. (°*vyāya*, ind. for departure, Kām.; *-tā*, f. the necessity for setting out on a journey, ib.); to be marched against, to be attacked or assailed, Mālav.

2. **Yātavyà**, mf(*ā*)n. (fr. *yātú*) serviceable against witchcraft or against Rākshasas, MaitrS.; Kāṭh. (cf. Pāṇ. iv, 4, 121).

Yāti. See *aham-yāti*.

Yātika, m. a traveller, L. (prob. w. r. for *yātrika*).

Yātú, m. one who goes, a traveller, L.; 'going against, attack (?),' sorcery, witchcraft, RV.; AV.; Kāṭh.; ŚBr.; a kind of evil spirit, fiend, demon, RV.; AV.; Kauś.; wind, L.; time, L.; n. = *rakshas*, L. **-ghna**, n. 'destroying Yātus,' bdellium, L. **-câtana**, mfn. driving away Y°s, AV. **-jambhana**, mfn. devouring Y°s, ib. **-jū́**, mfn. incited or possessed by Y°s, RV. **-dhā́na**, m. = *yātu*, a kind of evil spirit or demon (*ī*, f.), RV. &c. &c.; *-kshayaṇa*, mfn. destroying Y°s, AV.; *-prêshita* (°*dhā́na-*), mfn. hurled by Y°s, ŚBr. **-mát** or **-mā́vat**, mfn. practising witchcraft or sorcery, injurious, malignant, RV. **-víd**, mfn. skilful in sorcery, ŚBr. **-hán**, mfn. destroying witchcraft, AV.

1. **Yātṛi**, mfn. going, travelling, marching, being on a journey, RV.; going for, seeking, ib.; (ifc.) going to or in, riding on, MBh.; Hariv. &c.; m. a charioteer (?), RV. i, 70, 11; (*yā́tṛi*), an avenger (?), RV. i, 32, 14 (= *hantṛi*, Sāy.)

Yātṛika, w. r. for *yātrika*.

Yātrā, f. going, setting off, journey, march, expedition, MBh.; Kāv. &c. (with *prāṇāntikī* or *aurdhvadehikī* = death; *yātrām* √*yā* or *dā*, to undertake an expedition, take the field; *yātrām* √*prich*, to wish luck, Divyâv.); going on a pilgrimage (cf. *gaṅgā-* and *tīrtha-y°*); a festive train, procession, Kathās.; Rājat.; Hit. (cf. *deva-y°*); a feast, festival (= *utsava*), Bālar.; support of life, livelihood, maintenance, Mn.; MBh. &c.; intercourse (with *laukikī*, worldly intercourse = *jagad-y°*), Mn. xi, 184; way, means, expedient, L.; passing away time, W.; practice, usage, custom, W.; N. of a partic. kind of astronomical wk. (cf. *yoga-y°*); of a sort of dramatic entertainment (popular in Bengal), W. **-kara**, mfn. supporting life, subsisting, Car. **-karaṇa**, n. the setting forth on a journey or march, W. **-kāra**, m. the author of an astrological Yātrā, VarBṛS. **-gamana**, n. the going on a journey or expedition, R. **-prakaraṇa**, n. (and *-ṭīkā*, f.), **-prabandha**, m. N. of wks. **-prasaṅga**, m. engaging in or performing a pilgrimage, W. **-phala**, n. the fruit of an expedition, success of a campaign, MW. **-maṅgala**, n. N. of wk. **-mahôtsava**, m. a great festive procession, Rājat.; Pañcat. **-°rtham** (°*trâr°*), ind. for the sake of marching, MW. **-śiromaṇi**, m. N. of wk. **-śrāddha**, n. a Śrāddha performed before setting out on a journey, VP. **Yātrôtsava**, m. a festive procession, Kathās.; Hit.

Yātrika, mfn. relating to a march or campaign &c., Mn. vii, 184; relating to the support of life, requisite for subsistence, ib. vi, 27; customary, usual, W.; m. a traveller, pilgrim, ib.; n. a march, expedition, campaign, MBh.; provisions for a march, supplies &c., MW.; N. of a partic. class of astrological wks. (cf. *yātrā*).

Yātrin, mfn. being on a march or in a procession, Kām.

Yātha. See *dīrgha-yāthá*.

Yā́na, mfn. leading, conducting (said of a road; 'to,' gen. or adv. in °*trā́*), RV.; (*yā́nī*), f. a path, course, TS.; MaitrS.; Kāṭh. (cf. g. *gaurâdi*); n. (ifc. f. *ā*) a journey, travel; going, moving, riding, marching &c. to (loc. or comp.) or upon (instr. or comp.) or against (acc. with *prati*), Mn.; MBh. &c.; a vehicle of any kind, carriage, waggon, vessel, ship, litter, palanquin, RV. &c. &c.; (with Buddhists) the vehicle or method of arriving at knowledge, the means of release from repeated births (there are either 3 systems, the *Śrāvaka-yāna*, the *Pratyeka-buddha-y°* or *Pratyeka-y°*, and the *Mahā-y°*; or more generally only 2, the *Mahā-yāna* or 'Great method' and the *Hīna-y°* or 'Lesser method;' sometimes there is only 'One Vehicle,' the *Eka-yāna*, or 'one way to beatitude'), SaddhP.; Dharmas. 2 (cf. MWB. 159 &c.) **-kara**, m. 'carriage maker,' a wheelwright, carpenter, VarBṛS. **-ga**, mfn. riding in a carriage, Mn. iv, 120. **-pātra**, n. 'vessel for going,' a ship, boat, Hariv.; Kathās.; Pañc. **-pātraka**, n. (MW.), **-pātrikā**, f. (Kathās.) a small vessel, boat. **-bhaṅga**, m. 'fracture of a vessel,' shipwreck, Ratnâv. **-mukha**, n. the fore part of a waggon or chariot, L. **-yātrā**, f. 'going in a vessel,' a sea-voyage, Divyâv. (printed *-pātra*). **-yāna**, n. riding on horseback or going in a carriage, Car. **-vat**, mfn. having a carriage or travelling in a carriage, MBh.; Kāv. &c. **-śayyâsanâśana**, n. sg. carriage and bed and seat and food, Mn. vii, 220. **-śālā**, f. a coach house, cart shed, R. **-svāmin**, m. the owner of a vehicle, Mn. viii, 290. **Yānâsana**, n. du. marching and sitting quiet, ib. vii, 162. **Yānâstaraṇa**, n. a carriage-cushion, Mṛicch.

Yānaka, n. a vehicle, carriage, BhP.

Yānī-√kṛi, P. *-karoti*, to make one's self familiar with, L.

Yāpa (fr. Caus.), see *kāla-yāpa*. °**paka**, mfn. causing to go or come, bringing, bestowing, BhP. °**pana**, mfn. causing to go or pass away, bringing to an end, BhP.; mitigating, alleviating, curing (as an injection), Car.; prolonging or supporting life, MBh.; m. (with *saṃgha*) N. of a partic. Jaina sect, Bhadrab.; n. and (*ā*), f. causing to go, driving away, L.; causing time to pass away, delay, procrastination, Kām.; Kāv.; cure, alleviation (of a malady), Car.; maintenance, support, MBh.; exercise, practice, MBh.

Yāpanīya, mfn. = *yāpya*, L.; m. a partic Jaina sect (cf. °*pana*), L.; *-tara*, n. better state, Divyâv. °**paniyaka**, mfn. = *yāpya*, L. °**payitavya**, mfn. trifling, unimportant, Pat. °**pita**, mfn. caused to go or to attain (acc.), VarBṛS.; removed, cured (as a disease), Suśr. **Yāpya**, mfn. to be caused to go, to be expelled or discharged (as a witness), Gaut.; to be removed or cured (as a disease), Suśr. (*-tva*, n.); trifling, unimportant, VarBṛS.; mean, base (as an action), Gaut.; m. the father's elder brother, Gal.; *-yāna*, m. a palanquin, litter, L.

1. **Yāma**, m. (for 2. see below, for 3. see p. 851, col. 3) motion, course, going, progress, RV.; AV.; Br.; a road, way, path, ib.; a carriage, chariot, RV.; (ifc. f. *ā*) a night-watch, period or watch of 3 hours, the 8th part of a day, Mn.; MBh. &c.; pl. N. of a partic. class of gods, MBh.; Hariv.; Pur. (*yāma-syârkaḥ*, w. r. for *yam°*, q. v.); (*ī*), f. N. of a daughter of Daksha (wife of Dharma or Manu; sometimes written *yāmi*), Hariv.; Pur.; of an Apsaras, Hariv. **-kareṇukā**, f. a female elephant standing ready at a certain place and at appointed hours, Kād. **-kuñjara**, m. a male elephant standing ready &c. (see prec.), ib. **-kośá**, m. a carriage-box, RV. iii, 30, 15 (Sāy. 'mfn. obstructing the way'). **-ghosha**, m. 'proclaiming the watches,' a cock, L.; (also *ā*, f.) a metal plate on which the night-watches or hours are struck, a drum or gong used for a similar purpose, L. **-ceṭī**, f. a female servant on guard or watch, Car. **-tūrya**, n. (Ragh.), **-dundubhi**, m. (R.) a kind of drum or clock on which the night-watches are struck. **-nādin**, m. 'proclaiming the watches,' a cock, Bhpr. (v. l.) **-nālī**, f. = *-tūrya*, L. **-nemi**, m. N. of Indra, L. **-bhadra**, m. a kind of pavilion, Vāstuv. **-mātra**, n. a mere watch, only three hours, MW. **-yama**, m. a regular or stated occupation for every hour, BhP. **-vatī**, f. 'possessing watches,' night, Kād. (cf. *yāminī*). **-vṛitti**, f. the being on watch, standing on guard, Kām. **-stamberama**, m. = *-kuñjara*, Kād. **Yāmâvasthita**, mfn. standing ready at a certain place and at stated hours, Kād.; Hcar.

2. **Yāma**, in comp. for 2. *yāman*. **-śruta** (*yā́ma-*), mfn. renowned for going or speed, RV. (others 'heard while going along'). **-hū**, mfn. one who allows himself to be invoked by devout approach or prayers, RV. (others 'invoked during the sacrifice'). **-hūti** (*yā́ma-*), f. invocation for assistance, cry for help, ib. (others 'invocation during the sacrifice').

1. **Yāmaka** (for 2. see p. 851, col. 3), in comp. = 1. *yāma*. **-kareṇukā**, f., **-kuñjara**, m. = *yāma-ka°* and *yāma-ku°*, Kād.

1. **Yā́man**, n. (for 2. see p. 851, col. 3) going, coming, motion, course, flight, RV.; march, expedition, ib.; approaching the gods, invocation, prayer, sacrifice &c., ib.; AV.; TS. (loc. *yāman* sometimes = this time or turn).

1. **Yāmi** (for 2. see p. 851, col. 3) = *yāmī*; see under 1. *yāma*.

Yāmika, mfn. being on watch or guard; m. (also with *purusha*) a night-watcher, watchman, Kād.; Naish.; Kathās.; (*ā*), f. = *yāminī*, night, L. **-tā**, f. the state or office of a watchman, Vcar. **-bhaṭa**, m. a night-watcher, watchman, L. **-sthita**, mfn. = *yāmâvasthita*, Kād.

Yāminaya, Nom. (fr. next), P. *°yati*, to appear like night, Kpr.

Yāminī, f. (fr. 1. *yāma*) 'consisting of watches,' night, MBh.; Kāv. &c.; N. of a daughter of Prahlāda, Kathās.; of the wife of Tārksha (mother of Śalabha), BhP. **-dayita** (Vcar.), **-nātha** (Viddh.), **-pati** (BhP.), m. 'the beloved or the husband of night,' the moon. **-pūrṇa-tilakā**, f. assumed N. of a princess, Caurap. **-priyatama** or **-ramaṇa**, m. 'lover of night,' the moon, Vcar. **-virahin**, mfn. separated by night; m. (with *vihaga*) the bird Cakravāka, Kir. **-°śa** (*°nīśa*), m. = *-pati*, Dharmaś.

Yāmīra, m. the moon, L.; (*ā*), f. night, L.

1. **Yāmeya**, m. (for 2. see p. 851, col. 3) metron. fr. 1. *yāmi*, BhP.

Yāmyā, f. night, L. (cf. under *yāmya*, p. 851, col. 3).

Yāyāvará, mfn. (fr. Intens.) going about, having no fixed or permanent abode, TS. &c. &c.; m. a vagrant mendicant, saint, Bhaṭṭ.; a Brāhman who has preserved his household-fire (?), W.; 'wandering at large,' a horse selected for a horse-sacrifice, L.; pl. (also with *gaṇāḥ*) N. of a family of Brāhmans (to which Jarat-kāru belongs), MBh. (sg. = *jarat-kāru*, L.); n. the life of a vagrant mendicant, BhP.

Yāyin, mfn. (mostly ifc.) going, moving, riding, driving, flying, travelling, marching, taking the field, going to war (also applied to planets opposed to each other in the *graha-yuddha*, q.v.), MBh.; Kāv. &c.

1. **Yāvan**, m. (for 2. see p. 852, col. 3) a rider horseman, invader, aggressor, foe, R.; (ifc.) going, driving, riding (cf. *akshṇa-*, *agra-*, *eka-y°* &c.)

Yiyāsā, f. (fr. Desid.) desire of going, HPariś. **°su**, mfn. wishing to go or move or ride or drive or fly &c.; intending to set off or depart, desirous of marching or taking the field (with dat. or acc. with or without *prati*), MBh.; Kāv. &c.

या 3. *yā*, f. of 3. *ya*, q.v.

याकृत्क *yākṛitka*, mfn. (fr. *yakṛit*), Pāṇ. vii, 3, 51, Sch.

Yākṛilloma, mfn. (fr. *yakṛil-loma*), g. *paladyādi*.

याक्ष *yāksha*, mf(ī)n. (fr. *yaksha*) belonging or peculiar to the Yakshas, Sāṃkhyak., Sch.

याग *yāga*, m. (√1. *yaj*) an offering, oblation, sacrifice; any ceremony in which offerings or oblations are presented, Yājñ.; Ragh.; Rājat. &c.; presentation, grant, bestowal, Hcat. **-kaṇṭaka**, m. 'sacrifice-thorn,' a bad sacrificer (who does not know the god, metre, glossarial explanation, Brāhman, Ṛishi, Kṛit and Taddhita affixes of the Vedic verses), L. **-karman**, n. a sacrificial rite or ceremony, MārkP. **-kāla**, m. time of sacrifice, Jyot. **-maṇḍapa**, m. n. 'hall for sacrifices,' a temple, Cat. **-maya**, mf(*ī*)n. consisting of sacrifices, L. **-saṃtāna**, m. N. of Jayanta (son of Indra), L. **-sampradāna**, n. the recipient of a sacrifice, Kāś. on Pāṇ. iv, 2, 24. **-sūtra**, n. the sacrificial cord, sacred thread, Up. (cf. *yajña-sūtra*).

याच् *yāc*, cl. 1. P. Ā. (Dhātup. xxi, 3) *yācati*, *°te* (usually Ā. in sense of 'asking for one's self;' pf. *yayāca*, Gr., *yayāce*, Br. &c.; aor. *ayācīt*, *°cishṭa*, Subj. *yācishat*, *°shāmahe*, RV.; Prec. *yācyāt*, Gr.; fut. *yācitā*, ib.; *yācishyati*, *°te*, Br. &c.; inf. *yācitum*, AV. &c.; ind. p. *yācitvā*, *-yācya*, Br. &c.), to ask, beg, solicit, entreat, require, implore (with double acc.; or with abl., rarely gen. of pers.; the thing asked may also be in acc. with *prati*, or in dat., or ibc. with *arthe* or *artham*), RV. &c. &c.; (with *pún*ar) to ask anything back, TBr.; (with *kanyām*) to be a suitor for a girl, to ask a girl in marriage from (abl., rarely acc.) or for (*kṛite* or *arthe*; also with *vivāhârtham*), MBh.; Kāv. &c.; to offer or tender anything (acc.) to (dat.), AV.; to promise (?), ib.: Pass. *yācyate*, to be asked ('for,' acc.; rarely of things), MBh.; Kāv. &c.; Caus. *yācayati* (*°te*, AV.; aor. *ayayācat*, Pāṇ. vii, 4, 2), to cause to ask or woo, MBh.; to request anything (acc.) for (*arthe*), Pañcat.: Desid. *yiyācishate*, Pāṇ. vi, 1, 8, Vārtt. 3, Pat.: Intens. *yāyācyate*, *yāyākti*, Gr.

Yācaka, m. a petitioner, asker, beggar, Yājñ.; MBh. &c.; (*ī*), f. a female beggar, MBh. **-vṛitti**, f. the occupation or profession of a beggar, MW.

Yācana, n. begging, soliciting, asking (also in marriage), ŚārṅgP.; Sāh.; Vet.; (*ā*), f. asking, soliciting, request, petition, entreaty for or solicitation of (comp.), R.; Kālid. &c. (*°nām* √*kṛi*, to fulfil a request). **°naka**, m. an asker, petitioner, beggar, Mn.; MBh.; Hariv. **°nīya**, mfn. to be asked, to be desired or requested (n. also impers.), MBh.; Pañcat.

Yāci or **yācikā**, f. a petition, request, Kāś. on Pāṇ. iii, 3, 110.

Yācita, mfn. asked, begged (borrowed), Mn.; MBh. &c.; solicited or asked for (anything, acc.), entreated, importuned, ib.; asked in marriage, Vet.; required, requisite, necessary, MW.; n. alms obtained by begging, L. **°taka**, mfn. borrowed, Naish.; n. anything borrowed, Yājñ., Sch. **°tavya**, mfn. to be asked, MBh.; to be asked for (a girl, acc.) by (instr.), Kum.

Yācitṛi, m. an asker, petitioner, Gobh.; R.; a suitor, wooer, Kum.

Yācin, mfn. (ifc.) asking, requesting, Nir.

Yācishṇu, mfn. habitually asking or begging, importuning, an importunate person, MBh.; BhP.; *-tā*, f. the habit of soliciting favours, Mn. xii, 33.

Yācñā́, f. begging, asking for (comp.), asking alms, mendicancy, any petition or request, prayer, entreaty, TS. &c. &c. (*yācñām* √*kṛi*, to fulfil a request); the being a suitor, making an offer of marriage, Kathās. **-jīvana**, n. subsisting by begging or mendicancy, Hit. **-prāpta**, mfn. obtained by begging or asking, L. **-bhaṅga**, m. failure of a request, useless request, Bhartṛ. **-vacas**, n. pl. words used in begging or entreating, Śāntiś.

Yācñyá, m. (AV.), **yācñyā́**, f. (ŚBr.) = *yācñā*, asking, begging, request.

Yācya, mfn. to be asked (esp. for alms), Mn. viii, 181 &c.; to be wooed (*-tā*, f.), MBh.; to be required, ib., Hariv.; n. asking, making a request, MBh.

याच्छ्रेष्ठ *yāc-chreshṭha*. See under 2. *yāt*.

याज् *yāj*, m. (√1. *yaj*; nom. *yāṭ*) a sacrificer, BhP. (cf. *hayamedha-yāj*).

Yāja, m. a sacrificer (in *ati-yājá*), RV.; m. a sacrifice (cf. *upâṅśu-*, *ṛitu-y°* &c.); boiled rice or any food, L.; N. of a Brahmarshi, MBh.

Yājaka, m. (fr. Caus.) a sacrificer, (ifc.) one who offers sacrifices or oblations for or to (cf. *grāma-*, *nakshatra-y°*), Mn.; MBh. &c. (*-tva*, n.); a royal elephant (also *-gaja*), L.; an elephant in rut, L.

Yājana, n. (fr. Caus.) sacrificing for others, the act of performing a sacrifice for (gen. or comp.), Mn.; MBh. &c. **-pratigraha**, m. du. the performance of sacrifices for others and the acceptance of gifts (as the two privileges of Brāhmans), Vishṇ.

Yājanīya, mfn. (fr. Caus.) to be made or allowed to sacrifice, to be assisted at a sacrifice, Kull. on Mn. ix, 238.

Yājamāna, n. (fr. *yajamāna*) the part of a sacrificial ceremony performed by its institutor, ŚrS.

Yājamānika, mfn. belonging or relating to the institutor of a sacrifice, Śaṃk. on BṛĀrUp.

Yājayitṛi, m. (fr. Caus.) the officiating priest at a sacrifice, Cat.

Yāji, f. a sacrifice, Pāṇ. iii, 3, 110, Sch.; m. = *yashṭṛi*, a sacrificer, Uṇ. iv, 124.

Yājikā, f. a sacrifice, oblation, Pāṇ. iii, 3, 110, Sch.

Yājin, mfn. (mostly ifc.) worshipping, sacrificing, a sacrificer, TS. &c. &c.

Yājuka. See *ishṭi-yā́juka*.

Yājña, mfn. (fr. *yajña*, of which it is also the Vṛiddhi form in comp.) relating or belonging to sacrifice, Nir. **-turá**, m. (fr. *yajña-tura*) patr. of Ṛishabha, ŚBr.; N. of a Sāman, ĀrshBr. **-datta**, mfn. (fr. *yajña-datta*), Pāṇ. i, 1, 73, Vārtt. 5, Pat.; *°ttaka*, mfn., g. *arīhaṇâdi*; *°tti*, m. patr., Pāṇ. iv, 1, 157, Sch. (f. *°ttyā*, Pat.) **-deva**, m. (prob.) w. r. for *yājñika-deva*. **-pata**, mfn. (fr. *yajña-pati*), g. *aśvapaty-ādi*. **-valka**, mfn. composed by or derived from Yājñavalkya, Pāṇ. iv, 2, 111. **-valkīya**, mfn. id.; n. (scil. *dharma-śāstra*) the code of Y°; *-kāṇḍa*, m. or n. N. of chs. 3 and 4 of the BṛĀrUp. in the Kāṇva-śākhā; *-dharma-śāstra-nibandha*, m. N. of wk. **-valkya**, m. (*yā́°*, fr. *yajñavalka*) N. of an ancient sage (frequently quoted as an authority in the ŚBr.; the first reputed teacher of the Vājasaneyi-saṃhitā or White Yajur-veda, revealed to him by the Sun; he is also the supposed author of a celebrated code of laws, which is only second in importance to that of Manu, and with its well-known commentary, the Mitâksharā, is the leading authority of the Mithilā school; cf. IW. 291), ŚBr. &c. &c.; pl. the family of Y°, Hariv.; mfn. relating to or derived by Y°; n. N. of an Upanishad; *-gītā*, f., *-ṭīkā*, f., *-dharma-śāstra*, n., *-mahima-varṇana*, n., *-yoga*, m., *-śikshā*, f., *-smṛiti*, f.; *°kyôpanishad*, f. N. of wks. **-sena**, m. (fr. *yajña-sena*) patr. of Śikhaṇḍin, KaushBr. (also *°ni*, MBh.); (*ī*), f. patr. of Draupadī, MBh.

Yājñāyani, m. a patr. fr. *yajña*, g. *tikâdi*.

Yājñiká, mf(*ī*)n. relating or belonging to sacrifice, sacrificial, ŚrS.; R.; BhP.; m. a sacrificer, one versed in s°al ritual, ŚBr. &c. &c. (cf. g. *ukthâdi*; = *yājaka* or *yajña-kartṛi*, L.); N. of various plants used at a s° (a species of Kuśa-grass, barley, Ficus Religiosa, Butea Frondosa &c.), L. **-kitava**, m. (prob.) one who wishes to perform a s° for persons not worthy of it (*ayājya-yājana-tṛishṇā-paraḥ*), Kāś. on Pāṇ. ii, 1, 53. **-deva**, m. N. of the author of a Comm. on KātyŚr. &c. (he is also named *deva-yājñika* or *śrī-deva* or *deva*), Cat. **-nātha**, m. N. of an author, Cat. **-paddhati**, f., **-vallabhā**, f., **-sarvasva**, n. N. of wks. **Yājñikânanta**, m. N. of an author (also called *ananta-yājñika*), Cat. **Yājñikâśraya**, m. 'refuge of sacrificers,' N. of Vishṇu, Pañcar. **Yājñikâśva**, m. the horse given to the sacrificer, Kāś. on Pāṇ. vi, 2, 65. **Yājñikyupanishad**, f. N. of ch. x of TĀr. (also called *nārāyaṇīyôp°*).

Yājñikya, n. sacrificial or ritualistic rules, Kāś. on Pāṇ. ii, 3, 36 (*°kyaka*, n. a bad Yājñikya, Pat.)

Yājñiya, mfn. belonging to or suitable for a sacrifice, MBh.; BhP.; m. one skilled in the performance of sacrifice or ritual, Hariv. (v.l. for *yājñika*).

Yājñīya, mfn. = prec. mfn., Śaṃk. **-mantra**, m. N. of a partic. sacred text; *-ṭīkā*, f. N. of Comm. on it.

Yājya, mfn. to be made or allowed to sacrifice, one on whose behalf a sacrifice is performed, AitBr. &c. &c.; to be sacrificed, sacrificial (see *a-yājya*); m. a sacrificer, the master or institutor of a sacrifice (*-tā*, f., *-tva*, n.), Mn.; MBh. &c.; (*ā̀*), f. (scil. *ṛic*) sacrificial text or verse, the words of consecration used at a sacrifice, VS.; ŚrS.

Yājyà-vat, mfn. having the Yājyā or consecrating text, ŚBr.

Yājyā-vat, ind. like the Yājyā or consecrating text, ŚāṅkhŚr.

Yājvana, m. (fr. *yajvan*) the son of a sacrificer, Vop.

याजुर्वेदिक *yājurvedika* or °*vaidika*, mfn. belonging or relating to the Yajur-veda, KātyŚr., Sch.

Yājusha, mf(*ī*)n. relating to the Yajus or Yajur-veda, TBr.; m. an observer of religious ceremonies as prescribed in the Yajur-veda, MW.; a partridge (cf. *taittirīya-saṃhitā*), L.

Yājushmata, mf(*ī*)n. (fr. *yajush-mat*); only (*ī*), f. (with *ishṭakā*) N. of a kind of brick used for the sacrificial altar, Śaṃk. on BṛĀrUp.

याज्ञ *yājña*, *yājñika*, *yājya*. See above.

यात् 2. *yā́t*, ind. (obs. abl. of 3. *ya*, cf. *tā́t*; for 1. *yāt* see p. 849, col. 2) inasmuch as, so far as, as long as, since, RV.; AV. [Cf. Gk. ὡς.]

Yāc-chreshṭhá, mf(*ā*)n. (*yāt + śr*°) the best possible, RV. iii, 53, 21 (cf. *yāvac-chr*°).

Yād-rādhyàm, ind. (prob.) as far or as well or as quickly as possible, RV. ii, 38, 8.

यात् 3. *yāt* (√2. *yat*). See *riṇa-yā́t*.

यात *yāta* &c. See p. 849, col. 2.

यातऊतीय *yā-ta-ūtīya*, n. the hymn RV. vi, 25 (beginning with *yā ta ūtir*), ŚāṅkhŚr.

यातन *yātana*, n. (√2. *yat*) requital, retaliation, return (with *vairasya*, revenge, vengeance), MBh.; (*ā*), f., see next.

Yātanā, f. id. (°*nāṃ* √*dā*, to make requital, revenge; *vaira-y*°, vengeance; cf. above), MBh.; Hariv.; Pañcat.; acute pain, torment, agony, (esp.) punishment inflicted by Yama, the pains of hell (in BhP. personified as the daughter of *Bhaya* and *Mṛityu*, Fear and Death), Mn.; MBh. &c. **-gṛiha**, m. torture-chamber, Pañcar. **-°rthīya** (°*nār*°), mfn. destined to suffer or susceptible of the torments of hell, Mn. xii, 16.

Yātayáj-jana, mfn. (fr. *yātayat*, pr. p. of Caus. of √2. *yat*, and *jana*) 'bringing or arraying men together' or 'impelling men to exertion' (esp. said of Mitra, Varuṇa, and Aryaman), RV.

Yātya, m. (fr. Caus. of √2. *yat*) 'to be tormented,' an inhabitant of hell, L.

यातयाम *yāta-yāma*, °*man*. See p. 849, col. 2.

यातलराय *yātalarāya*, m. N. of a king, Cat.

यातव्य 1. 2. *yātavya*. See p. 849, col. 2.

यातसुच *yātasruca*, n. (fr. *yata-sruc*) N. of a Sāman, ĀrshBr.

यातानप्रस्थ *yātānaprastha*, °*thaka*, w.r. for *pāt*°, Pat. on Pāṇ. iv, 2, 104, Vārtt. 26.

यातु *yātu* &c. See p. 849, col. 2.

यातृ 2. *yātṛi*, f. (acc. *yātaram*, nom. acc. du. °*rau*, nom. pl. °*ras*, Vop.; for 1. *yātṛi* see p. 849, col. 2) a husband's brother's wife, Sāh. [Cf. Gk. εἰνάτηρ; Lat. *janitrices*; Lit. *jentė*; Slav. *jętry*.] **Yātā-nanāndṛi**, m. du. a husband's brother's wife and a husband's sister, Pāṇ. vi, 3, 25, Sch.

यात्निक *yātnika*, m. pl. (fr. *yatna*) 'making effort,' N. of a Buddhist school, Buddh.

यात्रा *yātrā*, *yātrika* &c. See p. 849, col. 3.

यात्सत्त्र *yāt-sattra*. See p. 849, col. 2.

याथ *yātha*. See *dīrgha-yāthá*.

याथा *yāthā*, Vṛiddhi form of *yathā*, in comp. **-kathāca**, n. (fr. *yathā kathā ca*) the happening under any circumstances, Pāṇ. v, 1, 98. **-kāmī**, f. (ŚrS.), **-kāmya**, n. (ib.; Śaṃk.; fr. *yathā-kāma*) the acting according to will or desire, arbitrariness. **-tathya**, n. (fr. *yathā-tatham*) a real state or condition, propriety, truth, MBh.; R. &c. (*am* or *ena*, ind. according to truth, in reality); *-tás*, ind. from the truth, truly, really, VS. **-°tmya**, n. (fr. *yathâtman*) real nature or essence, Hariv.; Ragh.; BhP. **-°rthika**, mfn. (fr. and) = *yathârtha*, W. **-°rthya**, n. (fr. id.) conformity with truth, the true or real meaning, Kum.; Sāh.; application, use, accomplishment, attainment of an object, W. **-saṃstarika**, mfn. (fr. *yathā-saṃstara*) letting a covering lie according (to its original position), Buddh.

याद् *yād* (only pr. p. Ā. *yā́damāna*), to be closely united or connected with (instr.), meet in (loc.), RV. (The meaning of this root, as well as its connection with the following words, is very doubtful.)

Yāda, in comp. for *yādas*. **-īśa**, m. 'lord of marine animals,' the sea, L.

Yādaḥ, in comp. for *yādas*. **-pati**, m. = *yādaīśa*, L.; N. of Varuṇa, L.

Yā́das, n. 'close union (?),' voluptuousness, VS.; TBr.; any large aquatic animal, sea monster, MBh.; Kāv. &c. (°*sāṃ nāthaḥ*, 'lord of aq° an°,' N. of Varuṇa, L.; °*sāṃ prabhuḥ*, id., Rājat.; °*sāṃ patiḥ*, id. or 'the sea,' L.); water, Naigh. i, 12; semen, Nir., Sch.; a river, Siddh. **-pati**, m. = *yādasāṃ pati*, L.

Yādú, m. water, Naigh. i, 12.

Yā́dura, mf(*ī*)n. embracing voluptuously (with copious effusion), RV. i, 126, 6 (Sāy. *yādurī* = *bahu-reto-yuktā*).

Yādo, in comp. for *yādas*. **-nātha**, m. 'lord of sea animals,' N. of Varuṇa, Ragh.; the sea, L. **-nivāsa**, m. 'abode of sea animals,' the sea, L.

यादव *yādava*, mf(*ī*)n. (fr. *yadu*) relating to or descended from Yadu, MBh.; Kāv. &c.; m. a descendant of Y° (also pl.), ib.; N. of Kṛishṇa, L.; N. of various authors (cf. comp.), Cat.; (*ī*), f. a female descendant of Y°, MBh.; Hariv.; N. of Durgā, L.; n. a stock of cattle, L. **-kośa**, m. N. of a dictionary (= *vaijayantī*; cf. *yādava-prakāśa*). **-giri**, m. N. of a place; *-māhātmya*, n. N. of wk. **-campū**, f. N. of an artificial poem. **-paṇḍita**, m. N. of an author (also called *yādava-vyāsa*). **-putra**, m. 'son of Y°,' N. of Kṛishṇa, MBh. **-prakāśa**, m. N. of an ascetic and author (also called *govinda-dāsa*), Cat.; of the author of the Vaijayantī (see *yādava-kośa*), ib.; *-svāmin*, m. N. of a poet, ib. **-rāghava-pāṇḍavīya**, n., **-rāghavīya**, n. N. of two poems. **-rāya**, m. N. of a king, Inscr. **-vyāsa**, m. N. of an author, Cat. **-śārdūla**, m. 'tiger or chief of the Y°s,' N. of Kṛishṇa, MBh. **Yādavâcārya**, m. N. of a teacher, Cat. **Yādavâbhyudaya**, m. 'rise of the Y°s,' N. of a history of Kṛishṇa. **Yādavêndra**, m. 'lord of the Y°s,' N. of Kṛishṇa, Pañcar.; of various authors (also with *bhaṭṭa* and *purī*), Cat. **Yādavôdaya**, m. 'rise of the Yādavas,' N. of a drama.

Yādavaka, m. pl. the descendants of Yadu, Hariv.

Yādavī-putra, m. metron. of Yudhi-shṭhira, MBh.

Yā́dva, mfn. belonging to the family of Yadu, RV.; m. a descendant of Yadu, ib.

यादायनि *yādāyani*, m. a patr. fr. *yad*, Pat.

यादृक्ष *yādṛiksha*, mf(*ī*)n. (for *yad-dṛ*°) looking or appearing like which, which like, as like (used correlatively to *tādṛiksha*, q. v.), Pāṇ. vi, 3, 90, Sch.

Yādṛig, in comp. for *yādṛiś*. **-guṇa**, mfn. of whatever qualities, Mn. ix, 21.

Yādṛ́iś, mfn. (for *yad-dṛiś*; nom. in Veda *yādṛín*, Pāṇ. vii, 1, 83; *yādṛik*, RV. v, 44, 6; loc. *yādṛiśmin*, ib. 8), which like, as like, of whatever kind or nature, RV. &c. &c.; *yādṛik kīdṛik ca*, quale tale, TBr.

Yādṛiśa, mf(*ī*)n. = prec., ŚBr. &c. &c.; *yādṛiśa tādṛiśa* (Pañcat.) or *yādṛiśa-t*° (MBh.; Kathās.), 'any one whatever,' 'anybody whatsoever.'

यादृच्छिक *yādṛicchika*, mf(*ī*)n. (fr. *yadṛicchā*) spontaneous, accidental, unexpected, MBh.; Daś. &c.; having no particular object, acting at random, BhP.; m. an officiating priest who does as he pleases, W.

याद्राध्यम् *yād-rādhyam*. See under 2. *yā́t*.

याद्व *yādva*. See above.

यान *yāna* &c. See p. 849, col. 3.

यान्त्रिक *yāntrika*, mfn. (fr. *yantra*) relating to instruments or to (blunt) surgical instruments, Suśr.; mechanically refined (said of sugar), ib.

याप *yāpa*, *yāpaka*, *yāpana*. See p. 849, col. 3.

याप्ता *yāptā*, f. twisted or plaited hair (= *jaṭā*), L.

याप्य *yāpya* &c. See p. 850, col. 1.

याभ *yābha*, m. (√*yabh*) sexual intercourse, BhP. **-vat**, mfn. having sexual intercourse, Kāvyâd.

याभिस् *yā́bhis*, ind. (instr. pl. f. of 3. *ya*) whereby, that, in order that, RV. viii, 1, 8.

याम 3. *yā́ma*, m. (√*yam*; for 1. 2. *yāma* see p. 850, col. 1) cessation, end, TS.; restraint, forbearance (= *yama*, *saṃyama*), L.; (*yāmá*), mf(*ī*)n. (fr. *yama*, of which it is also the Vṛiddhi form in comp.) relating to or derived from or destined for Yama, Br.; Kauś.; Mn.; n. N. of various Sāmans, ĀrshBr. **-dūta**, m. pl. (fr. *yama-dūta*) N. of a family, Hariv. **-nemi**, m. N. of Indra, L. **-ratha**, n. (fr. *yama-ratha*) N. of a partic. observance, Hariv. **Yāmôttara**, n. N. of a Sāman, ĀrshBr.

2. **Yāmaka**, m. du. (for 1. see p. 850, col. 1) N. of the Nakshatra Punarvasu, L.

2. **Yāman**, n. (for 1. see p. 850, col. 1) = *niyamana*, TāṇḍBr., Sch.

Yāmāyana, m. (fr. *yama*) patr. of various authors of Vedic hymns (viz. of Ūrdhva-kṛiśana, of Kumāra, of Damana, of Deva-śravas, of Mathita, of Śaṅkha, and of Saṃkasuka), RAnukr.

Yāmin. See *antar-yāmin* (for *yāminī* see p. 850, col. 1).

Yā́mya, mf(*ā*)n. relating or belonging to Yama, GṛŚrS., Mn.; MBh. &c.; southern, southerly (also applied to a kind of fever; *e* or *ena*, ind. in the south or to the south), TS. &c. &c.; m. the right hand (cf. *dakshiṇa*), Hcat.; (scil. *nara* or *purusha* or *dūta*) a servant or messenger of Yama, ShaḍvBr.; ŚāṅkhGṛ.; MārkP.; N. of Śiva or Vishṇu, MBh.; of Agastya, L.; the sandal-tree, L.; (*ā*), f. (cf. *yāmyā* on p. 850, col. 1) the southern quarter, south, Hariv.; R.; Var. &c. (also with *diś* or *āśā*); = n., VP.; n. (also with *ṛiksha*) the Nakshatra Bharaṇī (presided over by Yama), Var.; MārkP.; Suśr. **-tas**, ind. from the south, VarBṛS. **-tīrtha**, n. N. of a Tīrtha, Cat. **-pāśa**, m. the noose or fetter of Yama, BhP. **-sattva-vat**, mfn. having the nature or character of Yama, Suśr. (v. l. *yama-s*°). **Yāmyâyana**, n. the sun's progress south of the equator, the winter solstice (= *dakshiṇâyana*), L. **Yāmyôttara**, mfn. southern and northern, Sūryas.; going from south to north, VarBṛS.; *-vṛitta*, n. s° and n° circle, the solstitial colure, MW.; °*râyata*, mfn. extended from s° to n°, VarBṛS. **Yāmyôdbhūta**, n. 'growing in the south,' a species of tree, L.

यामकिनी *yāmakinī*, f. = 2. *yāmi* below.

यामल *yāmala*, n. = *yamala*, a pair, L.; N. of a class of Tantra works (of which 3 or 7 or 8 are mentioned; cf. *rudra-yāmala*), Cat. **-sāra**, m. N. of wk. **Yāmalânusāri-praśna**, m., °**lâshṭaka-tantra**, n. N. of wks.

Yāmalāyana, mfn. (fr. *yamala*), g. *pakshâdi*.

Yāmalīya, n. N. of a work or of a class of works, Cat.

यामातृ *yāmātṛi*, m. = *jāmātṛi*, a daughter's husband, son-in-law, L.

Yāmātṛika, m. id., Vet.

यामि 2. *yāmi* (or °*mī*), f. (for 1. see p. 850, col. 1) = *jāmi* (Uṇ. iv, 43, Sch.), a sister, female relation, Mn. iv, 180, 183 (v. l. *jāmi*); MārkP.; = *kula-strī*, a woman of rank or respectability, L.

2. **Yāmeya**, m. (for 1. see p. 850, col. 1) a sister's son, nephew, L.

यामिक *yāmika*. See p. 850, col. 1.

यामित्र *yāmitra*, n. = *jāmitra*, a diameter, VarBṛS.

यामिनी *yāminī*, *yāmira*. See p. 850, col. 1.

यामी *yāmī*. See under 1. *yāma*, p. 850, col. 1, and 2. *yāmi* above.

यामुन *yāmuná*, mfn. (fr. *yamunā*) belonging or relating to the river Yamunā (commonly called Jumna), coming from it, growing in it &c., MBh.; Hariv.; R.; m. a metron., Pāṇ. iv, 1, 113, Sch.; N. of a mountain, MBh.; R.; of an author (also called *yāmunâcārya* and °*rya-svāmin*), Cat.; pl. N. of a people, MBh.; Var.; Pur.; n. (scil. *añjana*) antimony, collyrium, AV.; N. of a Tīrtha, MBh. **-stuti-ṭīkā**, f. N. of wk. **Yāmunâcārya**, m., see above; *-stotra*, n. N. of wk. **Yāmunêsh-ṭaka**, n. lead, L. (cf. *yavanêshṭa*).

यामुन्दायनि *yāmundāyani*, m. patr. fr. *ya-munda*, g. *tikâdi*.

Yāmundāyanika or °**dāyanīya**, m. patr. fr. *yāmundāyani* (used contemptuously), Pāṇ. iv, 1, 149.

याम्य *yāmya* &c. See p. 851, col. 3.

यायजूक *yāyajū́ka*, mf(*ā*)n. (fr. Intens. of √1. *yaj*) constantly sacrificing, devout, ŚBr.; m. a performer of frequent sacrifices, L.

Yāyashṭi, f. the frequent performance of sacrifices, Pāṇ. i, 1, 58, Vārtt. 7, Pat.

यायात *yāyāta*, mf(*ī*)n. (fr. *yayāti*) relating or belonging to Yayāti, MBh.; Hariv.; n. the history of Yayāti (N. of ch. of BhP.)

Yāyātika, m. one conversant with the history of Yayāti, Pat. on Pāṇ. iv, 2, 60.

यायावर *yāyāvara, yāyin*. See p. 850, col. 1.

यार्कायण *yārkāyaṇa*, m. (also pl.), a patr., Saṃskārak.

याव 1. *yā́va*, m. = 1. *yava*, TS.

याव 2. *yāva*, mf(*ī*)n. (fr. 3. *yava*, of which it is also the Vṛiddhi form in comp.) relating to or consisting of or prepared from barley, KātyŚr.; m. a kind of food prepared from b°, L.; (*ī*), f. Andrographis Paniculata, L. **-krītika**, m. one conversant with the history of Yava-krīta, Pat. on Pāṇ. iv, 2, 60. **-nāla**, m. = *yava-n*° (*ī*, f. sugar extracted from Yāvanāla); *-nibha* or *-śara*, m. a kind of cane or reed resembling the Yāvanāla. **-śūka**, m. (fr. *yava-śūka*) a kind of alkaline salt prepared from the ashes of burnt barley-straw, L.

1. **Yāvaka**, m. n. a partic. food prepared from barley, Gaut.; n. grains of b°, MBh. (Nīlak.) **-kṛic-chra**, m. a kind of penance, Prâyaśc. **-vratin**, mfn. living only on the grains of barley found in cow-dung, Nīlak.

Yāveya, n. a field of barley, Gal.

याव 3. *yāva*, m. lac or the red dye prepared from the cochineal insect, Naish.

2. **Yāvaka**, m. id., Kāv.; Kathās.; Rājat.

यावत् *yā́vat*, mf(*atī*)n. (fr. 3. *ya*; correlative of *tāvat*, q. v.) as great, as large, as much, as many, as often, as frequent, as far, as long, as old &c. (or how great &c. = quantus, quot or qualis), RV. &c. &c. (*yā́vantaḥ kiyantaḥ*, 'as many as,' TBr.; *yā́vad vā yāvad vā*, 'as much as possible,' ŚBr.; *yāvat tāvat*, 'so much as,' in alg. applied to the first unknown quantity [= x] or so much of the unknown as its co-efficient number; in this sense also expressed by the first syllable *yā*, cf. IW. 182; *iti yāvat* in Comms. 'just so much,' 'only so,' 'that is to say,' 'such is the explanation'); ind. as greatly as, as far as, as much or as many as; as often as, whenever; as long as, whilst; as soon as, the moment that, until that, till, until, RV. &c. &c. (in these senses used with either pres., Pot., fut., impf., or aor., or with the simple copula). *Yā́vat* with the 1st sg. of pres., rarely of Pot., may denote an intended action and may be translated by 'meanwhile,' 'just;' *yā́vad yāvad-tā-vat tāvat*, 'as gradually as-so,' ŚBr.; *yā́van na*, 'while not,' 'before,' 'till;' 'if not,' 'whether not;' *na yāvat-tāvat*, 'scarcely-when,' 'no sooner-than;' *na param* or *na kevalam-yāvat*, 'not only-but even.' Sometimes *yāvat* is also used as a preposition with a prec. or following acc., or with a following abl., rarely dat., e. g. *māsam ekaṃ yāvat*, 'during one month;' *sūryôdayaṃ yāvat*, 'until sunrise;' *sarpa-vivaraṃ yāvat*, 'up to the serpent's hole;' *yāvad* or *yāvad-ā samāpanāt*, 'until the completion;' *yāvad garbhasya paripākāya*, 'until the maturity of the fetus.' Sometimes also with a nom. followed by *iti*, e. g. *anta iti yāvat*, 'as far as the end;' *pañca yāvad iti*, 'up to five;' or with another ind. word, e. g. *adya yāvat*, 'up to this day.' *Yāvatā*, ind. as far as, as long as, Āpast.; R.; BhP.; till, until (with Pot.), Lāṭy. (with *na*, as long as not, before, BhP.); as soon as, the moment that, Cat.; inasmuch as, Pat.; *yā́vati*, ind. as long as, as far as &c., ŚBr.; TBr.; *yāvati-tāvati*, Daś. **-kapālam**, ind. according to the circumference of the cup or bowl, KātyŚr. **-kartṛi**, ind. according to the number of the persons acting or sharing in a sacrifice, KātyŚr., Comm. **-kāmam**, ind. as long as one likes, AitBr. **-kā-lam**, ind. as long as anything may last, ŚāṅkhGṛ.; for a while, Kathās. **-kṛitvas** (*yā́vat-*), ind. as often as, ŚBr.; Kauś. **-kratu** (*yā́vat-*), mfn. having as many purposes, ŚBr. **-tarasám**, ind. according to power or ability, MaitrS.; TĀr. (*yā́vat-tarásam*). **-tāvat-kalpana**, n. the putting down of the algebraic formula = x, Bījag. **-tmūtám**, ind. as far as soaked in grease, TS. **-pramāṇa**, mfn. as great, as large, BhP. **-priya** (*yā́vat-*), mfn. as dear, MaitrS. **-saṃsāram**, ind. as long as the world lasts, MW. **-sattvam**, ind. as far as one's ability goes, to the best of one's understanding, BhP. **-sá-bandhu**, ind. as far as relationship extends, inclusive of all relations, AV. **-samasta**, mfn. as many as form the whole, as far as complete, as large as anything is, MW. **-sampātam**, ind. as long as possible, ChUp. **-sāmidheni**, mfn. consisting of as many Sāmidhenī verses, KātyŚr. **-smṛiti**, ind. as many as one remembers, ib. **-svam**, ind. as much as one possesses, ib.

Yāvac, in comp. for *yāvat*. **-chakti** (for *-śak*°; A.) or °**ti-tas** (Kād.), ind. according to power. **-chakya** (for *-śak*°), mfn. as far &c. as possible, ĀpŚr., Comm.; (*am*), ind. according to ability, Hit. **-charāva** (for *-śar*°), mfn. consisting of the requisite number of measures of corn called Śarāva, ĀśvŚr. **-charkaram** (for *-śar*°), ind. proportionately to the quantity of gravel, ĀpŚr. **-chás** (for *-śas*), ind. as many times as, in as many ways or manners as, TS.; ŚBr. **-chastram** (for *-śas*°), ind. as far as the Śastra extends, ŚāṅkhŚr. **-chesham** (for *-śesh*°), ind. as much as is left, KātyŚr. **-chresh-ṭhá** (for *-śr*°), mfn. the best possible, AV. **-chlo-kam** (for *-śl*°), ind. proportionately to the number of the Ślokas, Vop.

Yāvaj, in comp. for *yāvat*. **-janma**, ind. as long as life, all one's life long, MārkP. **-jīva**, ibc. (Hcat.; Cat.), or °**vám** (ŚBr.; ŚrS. &c.), °**vena** (MBh.), ind. during the whole of life, for life. **-jīvika**, mfn. life-long, lasting for life, ĀśvŚr.; ĀpŚr., Comm.; Jaim.; *-tā*, f. the lasting for life, KātyŚr., Sch.

Yāvatitha, mfn. (a kind of ordinal of *yāvat*; cf. Pāṇ. v, 2, 53) 'the how-manieth,' 'as manieth,' to whatever place or point, in how many soever (degrees advanced), Mn. i, 20.

Yāvad, in comp. for *yāvat*. **-aṅgīna**, mfn. having as large a member or limb, AV. **-adhya-yanam**, ind. during the recitation, Mn. ii, 241. **-antam** (BhP.) or °**tāya** (Gṛihyas.), ind. as far as the end, to the last. **-antya**, mfn. life-long, lasting for life, MBh. **-abhīkshṇam**, ind. for a moment's duration, Nir. **-amatram**, ind. corresponding to the number of the vessels, Pāṇ. ii, 1, 8, Sch. **-artha**, mfn. as many as necessary, corresponding to requirement, Mn.; Śiś.; BhP.; devoted to anything (loc.), as much as is nec°, BhP.; ibc. (BhP.) or (*am*), ind. (Bhartṛ.), as much as may be useful, according to need. **-ahá**, n. the corresp° day ('the how-manieth day'), ŚBr.; ŚrS. **-ādishṭa**, mfn. as much as related, ŚāṅkhŚr. **-ābhūta-samplavam**, ind. up to the dissolution of created things, to the end of the world, Siṃhās. **-āyusham**, ind. as long as life lasts, for the whole of life, ChUp. **-āyus**, ind. id., Vikr.; Rājat.; °*yuḥ-pramāṇa*, mfn. measured by the duration of life, lasting for life, Kām.; Hit. **-āhūta-samplavam**, ind. w. r. for *-ābhūta-s*° above, Yājñ.; BṛNārP. **-iccham**, ind. according to desire, Car. **-ittham**, ind. as much as necessary, Bhartṛ. (v. l.) **-ishṭakam**, ind. according to the number of bricks, KātyŚr. **-ishṭam**, ind. = next, A. **-īpsitam**, ind. as far as agreeable, as much as desired, R. **-ukta**, mfn. as much as stated, KātyŚr.; (*am*), ind., ib. **-uttamam**, ind. up to the furthest limit or boundary, MBh. **-upani-shad** (?), f. N. of wk. **-aupamya**, n. a mere comparison, Vajracch. **-gamam**, ind. as fast as one can go, BhP. **-gṛihītin**, mfn. as often as one has taken or ladled out, Lāṭy. **-grahaṇam**, ind. until taking, PārGṛ. **-deya**, ibc. (in law) until paying a debt. **-devatyà**, mfn. directed to as many divinities, ŚBr. **-deha-bhāvin**, mfn. lasting as long as the body, Sāṃkhyas., Sch. **-dhavis** (for *-havis*), ind. according to the number of oblations, KātyŚr. **-dhā**, ind. as often, as many times, ŚrS. **-balam**, ind. as far as strength goes, with all one's might, TĀr., Comm. **-bhāshita**, mfn. as much as has been said, Sāh. **-yajus**, mfn. as far as the whole Yajus extends, Lāṭy. **-rājyam**, ind. for the whole reign, Rājat. **-vacanam**, ind. as far as the statement goes, Lāṭy. **-viṉśati**, mfn. up to 20, to the 20th, R. **-vīrya-vat** (*yā́vad-*), mfn. as far as possessed of power, as effective, ŚBr. **-vedam**, ind. as much as gained or obtained, Pāṇ. **-vyāpti**, ind. to the utmost reach or extent, Nir.

Yāvan, in comp. for *yāvat*. **-mātrá**, mf(*ā*)n. having which measure, of w° size, as large, extending as far, ŚāṅkhBr.; Kum.; Hcat.; moderate, insignificant, diminutive, little, ŚBr.; MBh.; Rājat.; (*am*), ind. as long, RV.; in some measure or degree, a little, Br.

यावन् 2. *yāvan* (for 1. see p. 850, col. 1), in *á-yāvan*, q. v.

यावन् 3. *yāvan*, in *ṛiṇa-yā́van*, q. v.

यावन 1. *yāvana*, mf(*ī*)n. (fr. *yavana*; for 2. and 3. see p. 853, col. 1) born or produced in the land of the Yavanas, Prâyaśc.; m. olibanum, L.

यावनाल *yāvanāla, yāvaśūka*. See under 2. *yāva*.

यावन्तिका *yāvantikā*, f. See *riti*.

यावयत् *yāvayat* &c. See under √1. *yu*.

यावयितृ *yāvayitṛi*. See under √2. *yu*.

यावस *yāvasa*, m. (fr. *yavasa*) a quantity or heap of grass, fodder, provisions, L.

Yāvasika, m. a mower of grass, Lalit.

यावास *yāvāsa*, mfn. (fr. *yavāsa*), g. *palā-śâdi*.

याविहोत्र *yāvi-hotrá*, n. a partic. sacrifice, ŚBr.

याव्य *yāvya*. See p. 853, col. 1.

याशु *yā́śu*, n. embracing, embrace, sexual union (or effusion), RV. i, 126, 6 (Sāy.)

याशोधरेय *yāśodhareya*, m. (fr. *yaśo-dhara*) metron. of Rāhula, L.

याशोभद्र *yāśobhadra*, m. (fr. *yaśo-bhadra*) N. of the fourth day of the civil month, L.

याष्टि *yāshṭi*, f. (fr. Caus. of √1. *yaj*) assistance at a sacrifice, Pāṇ. i, 1, 58, Vārtt. 7, Pat.

याष्टीक *yāshṭīka*, mf(*ī*)n. (fr. *yashṭi*) armed with a stick or club, Rājat. (cf. Pāṇ. iv, 4, 59; iv, 1, 15, Pat.)

यास् 1. *yās* = *yas* (only in *avayāsisishṭhām*), Kāṭh.

2. **Yās**, mfn. See *a-yā́s*.

यास *yāsa*, m. = *yavāsa*, Alhagi Maurorum, L. (*-śarkarā*, f. = *yavāsa-ś*°, Car.); (*ā*), f. Turdus Salica, L.

Yāsaka, m. Alhagi Maurorum, L.

यास्क *yāská*, m. (fr. *yasku*) patr. of the author of the Nirukta (or commentary on the difficult Vedic words contained in the lists called Nighaṇṭus; he is supposed to have lived before Pāṇini; cf. IW. 156 &c.), ŚBr.; RPrāt.; MBh.; pl. the pupils of Yāska, Pāṇ. ii, 4, 63, Sch.; (*ī*), f. (and pl. *yāskyaḥ*), ib. **-nirukta**, n. Yāska's Nirukta, Cat.

Yāskāyani, m. patr. fr. Yāska, Pāṇ. iv, 1, 91, Sch.

Yāskāyanīya or °**kīya**, m. pl. the pupils of Yāskāyani, ib.

यित्थ *yittha*, m. N. of a man, Rājat.

यियक्षत् *yiyakshat*. See p. 840, col. 3.

यियप्सु *yiyapsu*. See p. 845, col. 2.

यियविषु *yiyavishu*. See p. 853, col. 1.

यियासा *yiyāsā*, °*su*. See p. 850, col. 2.

यु 1. *yu* (cf. √*yuch*) cl. 3. P. *yuyóti* (Impv. 2. sg. *yuyodhi*, RV.; *yuyudhi*, Pāṇ. iii, 4, 88, Sch.; 2. du. *yuyotam* or *yuyutám*, RV.; 2. pl. *yu-yóta* or °*tana*, ib.; Ā. Subj. 2. sg. *yuyothās*, ib.; Ā. impf. 3. pl. *ayuvanta*, AV.; aor. P. *yaus*, *a-yaushīt*; Subj. *yoshati, yoshat*, RV.; *yūshat*, AV.; *yūyāt, yūyātām*, Br.; *yūyot*, RV.; *yāvīs*, ib.; Ā. *yoshṭhās*, Br.; *yavanta*, RV.; Pass. *ayāvi*, ib.; inf. *yótave*, °*taval*, °*tos*, ib.; *-yāvam*, AV.), to separate, keep or drive away, ward off (acc.), exclude or protect from (abl.), RV.; AV.; VS.; Br.; to keep aloof, to be or remain separated from (abl.), RV.; AV.;

ŚāṅkhŚr.: Caus. *yavā́yati* or *yāvā́yati*, to cause to separate or remove or keep off &c., RV.; AV.; VS.; ŚBr.: Intens. *yoyavīti* (impf. *áyoyavīt*; p. *yóyuvat*), to retreat back, recede, RV.; to be rent, gape asunder, ib.; to keep off from (abl.), MaitrS.

2. **Yāvana**, n. (fr. Caus.; for 1. see p. 852, col. 3; for 3. below) keeping off, removing, Nir.; Sāy.

Yāvayat, mfn. (fr. Caus.) warding off, protecting (see comp.) – **sakhá**, m. a protecting friend or companion, RV.

Yāvayád-dveshas, mfn. (cf. prec.) driving away enemies, ib.

1. **Yut**, mfn. (for √2. *yut* see s. v.) keeping off, in *dvesho-yút*, q. v.

1. **Yuta**, mfn. (for 2. see below) kept off, removed (see comp.); separate (= *prithak*), L. – **dveshas** (*yutá-*), mfn. delivered from enemies, RV.

1. **Yutaka**, n. = *yautaka* (q. v.), L.

Yúyuvi or **yū́yuvi**, mfn. setting aside, removing, RV.

यु 2. *yu* (cf. √*yuj*), cl. 2. P. (Dhātup. xxiv, 23) *yauti* (Ved. also Ā. *yuté* and cl. 6. *yuváti*, °*te*; accord. to Dhātup. xxxi, 9 also cl. 9. *yunāti*, *yunīte*; pf. *yuyāva*, 2. sg. *yuyavitha*, Pāṇ. vi, 4, 126, Sch.; *yuyuvé*, RV.; aor. *-yāvishṭam* (?), ib.; *ayavishṭa*, Gr.; Prec. *yūyāt*, ib.; fut. *yuvitā*, ŚBr.; *yavitā*, *yavishyati*, °*te*, Gr.; ind. p. *yutvā*, Pāṇ. vii, 2, 11, Sch.; *-yūya*, RV.; *-yutya*, GṛŚrS.), to unite, attach, harness, yoke, bind, fasten, RV.; to draw towards one's self, take hold or gain possession of, hold fast, AV.; TS.; ŚBr.; to push on towards (acc.), AV.; to confer or bestow upon (dat.), procure, RV.; (*yauti*), to worship, honour, Naigh. iii, 14: Pass. *yūyate* (aor. *ayāvi*), Gr.: Caus. *yāvayati* (aor. *ayīyavat*), ib.: Desid. of Caus. *yiyāvayishati*, ib.: Desid. *yúyūshati* (RV.), *yiyavishati* (Gr.), to wish to unite or hold fast: Intens. *yoyūyate*, *yoyoti*, *yoyavīti* &c. (see *ā-*, *ni-√yu*).

3. **Yāvana**, n. (fr. Caus.) uniting, joining, mixing (see *a-y*°).

Yāvayitṛi, mf(*trī*)n. procuring, bestowing, Sāy.

Yāvya, mfn. to be joined or mixed &c., Pāṇ. iii, 1, 126; = *yāpya*, unimportant, insignificant, L.

Yiyavishā, f. (fr. Desid.) the wish to mix or blend, W. °**shu**, mfn. wishing to mix or fill or cover with (instr.), Bhaṭṭ.

2. **Yuta**, mfn. (for 1. see above) attached, fastened (ifc.), Bhartṛ.; added, Sūryas.; united, combined, joined or connected or provided or filled or covered with, accompanied by, possessed of (instr. or comp.), Mn.; MBh. &c.; (ifc.) standing in conjunction with, VarBṛS.; made or consisting of, R.; (with instr.) occupied in, performing (sacrifices), L.; (ifc.) connected with, concerning, R.; BhP.; n. a partic. measure of length (= 4 Hastas), L.

2. **Yutaka**, mfn. (for 1. see above) joined, connected, L.; n. (only L.) a pair; a sort of cloth or dress; the edge of a cloth or dress; the edge of a winnowing basket; doubt or an asylum (*saṃśaya* or *saṃśraya*); friendship or forming friendship.

Yuti, f. uniting, junction, union or meeting with (in astron. 'conjunction'), Sūryas.; VarBṛS.; the being furnished with or obtaining possession of (instr. or comp.), VarBṛS.; the sum, total number, Sūryas.; the number to be added, Bījag.

यु 3. *yú*, mfn. (√*yā*) going, moving, RV. i, 74, 7; x, 176, 3 (viii, 18, 13?).

यु 4. *yu*, the actual base of the du. and pl. numbers of the 2nd pers. pron. (see *yushmad*).

युक् *yuk* or *yut* (?), ind. badly, ill, W.

युक्त *yukta*, *yukti* &c. See cols. 2, 3.

युग *yuga*, *yugma*, *yugya* &c. See p. 854.

युगत् *yugat*, v. l. for *dyu-gat* (q. v.), Naigh.

युग्वन् *yugvan*. See *abhi-*, *sa-*, *sva-y*°.

युङ्ग् *yuṅg*, cl. 1. P. *yuṅgati*, to desert, relinquish, abandon, Dhātup. v, 50.

युङ्ग *yuṅga*. See *á-yuṅga*.

युङ्गिन् *yuṅgin*, m. N. of a partic. mixed caste, BrahmavP.

युछ् *yuch* (cf. √1. *yu*), cl. 1. P. (Dhātup. vii, 35) *yucchati*, to go away, depart, keep aloof, vanish, RV. (Dhātup. 'to err, be negligent;' cf. *pra-√yuch*).

युज् 1. *yuj* (cf. √2. *yu*), cl. 7. P. Ā. (Dhātup. xxix, 7) *yunákti*, *yuṅkté* (ep. also *yuñjati*, °*te*; Ved. *yojati*, °*te*; *yuje*, *yujmahe*, 3. pl. *yujata*, Impv. *yukshvá*; Pot. *yuñjīyāt*, R.; pf. *yuyója*, *yuyujé*, RV. &c. &c., 3. sg. *yuyojate*, RV. viii, 70, 7; aor. Class. P. *ayokshīt*, *ayaukshīt* or *ayujat*; Ved. also Ā. *áyuji*; Ved. and Class. *ayukshi*, *ayukta*; fut. *yoktā*, Br.; *yokshyati*, ib.; °*te*, AV. &c. &c.; inf. *yoktum*, Br.; *yujé*, RV.; ind. p. *yuktvā́*, ib. &c. &c.; *yuktvā́ya*, RV.; Br.; *-yujya*, MBh. &c.), to yoke or join or fasten or harness (horses or a chariot), RV. &c. &c.; to make ready, prepare, arrange, fit out, set to work, use, employ, apply, ib.; to equip (an army), R.; to offer, perform (prayers, a sacrifice), BhP.; to put on (arrows on a bow-string), MBh.; to fix in, insert, inject (semen), ŚBr.; to appoint to, charge or intrust with (loc. or dat.), MBh.; VP.; to command, enjoin, BhP.; to turn or direct or fix or concentrate (the mind, thoughts &c.) upon (loc.), TS. &c. &c.; (P. Ā.) to concentrate the mind in order to obtain union with the Universal Spirit, be absorbed in meditation (also with *yogam*), MaitrUp.; Bhag. &c.; to recollect, recall, MBh.; to join, unite, connect, add, bring together, RV. &c. &c. (Ā. to be attached, cleave to, Hariv.); to confer, or bestow anything (acc.) upon (gen. or loc.), BhP.; MārkP. (Ā. with acc., to become possessed of, MBh.; with *ātmani*, to use for one's self, enjoy, Mn. vi, 12); to bring into possession of, furnish or endow with (instr.), Mn.; MBh.; R. &c.; to join one's self to (acc.), RV.; (in astron.) to come into union or conjunction with (acc.), VarBṛS.: Pass. *yujyáte* (ep. also °*ti*; aor. *áyoji*), to be yoked or harnessed or joined &c., RV. &c. &c.; to attach one's self to (loc.), Hit.; to be made ready or prepared for (dat.), Bhag.; to be united in marriage, Gaut.; MBh.; to be endowed with or possessed of (instr. with or without *saha*), Mn.; MBh. &c.; (in astron.) to come into conjunction with (instr.), VarBṛS.; to accrue to, fall to the lot of (gen.), Pañcat.; to be fit or proper or suitable or right, suit anything (instr.), be fitted for (loc.), belong to or suit any one (loc. or gen.), deserve to be (nom.), Mn.; MBh. &c.; (with *na*) not to be fit or proper &c. for (instr.) or to (inf., also with pass. sense = 'ought not to be'), Kāv.; Kathās.; Pañcat.: Caus. *yojayati* (m. c. also °*te*; aor. *ayūyujat*; Pass. *yojyate*), to harness, yoke with (instr.), put to (loc.), Kauś.; MBh. &c.; to equip (an army), draw up (troops), MBh.; R. &c.; to use, employ, set to work, apply, undertake, carry on, perform, accomplish, Mn.; Yājñ.; MBh. &c.; to urge or impel to, Bhartṛ.; Prab.; to lead towards, help to (loc.), Sarvad.; to set (snares, nets &c.), MBh.; Hit.; to put or fix on (esp. arrows), ĀśvGṛ.; MBh. &c.; to aim (arrows) at (loc.), R.; to fasten on or in, attack, adjust, add, insert, Kauś.; Kāv.; Pur.; (with *manas*, *ātmānam* &c.) to direct the thoughts to, concentrate or fix the mind upon (loc.), MBh.; Hariv.; Pur.; to join, unite, connect, combine, bring or put together (also = write, compose), R.; Var.; Rājat. &c.; to encompass, embrace, MBh.; to put in order, arrange, repair, restore, Rājat.; to endow or furnish or provide with (instr.), MBh.; Kāv. &c.; to mix (food) with (instr.), Mn. vii, 218; to confer anything upon (loc.), BhP.; (in astron.) to ascertain or know (*jānāti*) the conjunction of the moon with an asterism (instr.), Pāṇ. iii, 1, 26, Vārtt. 11, Pat.; (Ā.) to think little of, esteem lightly, despise, Vop. in Dhātup. xxxiii, 36: Desid. *yuyukshati*, to wish to harness or yoke or join &c.; to wish to appoint or institute, MBh.; to wish to fix or aim (arrows), BhP.; (Ā.) to wish to be absorbed in meditation, devout, Bhaṭṭ.: Intens. *yoyujyate*, *yoyujīti* or *yoyokti*, Gr. [Cf. Gk. ζεύγνυμι, ζυγόν; Lat. *jungere*, *jugum*; Lith. *jùngus*; Slav. *igo*; Goth. *juk*; Germ. *joh*, *Joch*; Angl. Sax. *geoc*; Eng. *yoke*.]

Yuktá, mfn. yoked or joined or fastened or attached or harnessed to (loc. or instr.), RV. &c. &c.; set to work, made use of, employed, occupied with, engaged in, intent upon (instr., loc. or comp.), ib.; ready to, prepared for (dat.), MBh.; absorbed in abstract meditation, concentrated, attentive, RV. &c. &c.; skilful, clever, experienced in, familiar with (loc.), MBh.; R.; joined, united, connected, combined, following in regular succession, RV.; ŚāṅkhŚr.; Var.; BhP. (*ám*, ind. in troops, ŚBr.); furnished or endowed or filled or supplied or provided with, accompanied by, possessed of (instr. or comp.), Mn.; MBh. &c.; come in contact with (instr.), R.; (in astron.) being in conjunction with (instr.), ĀśvGṛ.; (ifc.) added to, increased by (e. g. *catur-yuktā viṃśatiḥ*, twenty increased by four, i. e. 24), VarBṛS.; (ifc.) connected with, concerning, KātyŚr.; (ifc.) subject to, dependent on, MBh.; fitted, adapted, conforming or adapting one's self to, making use of (instr., e. g. *yuktaḥ kālena yaḥ*, one who makes use of the right opportunity), Kām.; fit, suitable, appropriate, proper, right, established, proved, just, due, becoming to or suitable for (gen., loc. or comp., e. g. *āyati-yukta*, suitable for the future; or ibc., see below; *yuktam* with *yad* or an inf. = it is fit or suitable that or to; *na yuktam bhavatā*, it is not seemly for you), Mn.; MBh. &c.; auspicious, favourable (as fate, time &c.), Mn.; R.; prosperous, thriving, R.; (with *tathā*) faring or acting thus, MBh.; (in gram.) primitive (as opp. to 'derivative'), Pāṇ. i, 2, 51; m. N. of a son of Manu Raivata, Hariv.; of a Ṛishi under Manu Bhautya, ib.; (*ā*), f. N. of a plant, L. (cf. *yukta-rasā*); n. a team, yoke, ŚBr.; junction, connection, Pāṇ. ii, 3, 4; 8 &c.; fitness, suitableness, propriety (*am*, ind. fitly, suitably, justly, properly, rightly; *ena*, properly, suitably, RV. v, 27, 3; *buddhi-yuktena*, conformably to reason, Rājat.) – **karman**, mfn. invested with any office or function, MW.; serving the purpose, suitable, appropriate (°*ma-tā*, f.), Bhpr. – **kārin** (Kām.), -**kṛit** (BhP.), mfn. acting properly or suitably. – **grāvan** (*yuktá-*), mfn. having set the stones (for bruising the Soma) in motion, RV. – **ceshṭa**, mfn. behaving properly, Bhag. – **tama**, mfn. most fit or intent upon, devoted to, BhP. – **tara**, mfn. more fit &c. (also °*raka*, L.); very much on one's guard against any one (loc.), Mn. vii, 186. – **tva**, n. application, employment, KātyŚr.; fitness, propriety (*a-y*°), Vedāntas. – **daṇḍa**, mfn. applying punishment, punishing justly, R.; Kām.; *-tā*, f., R. – **mada**, mfn. intoxicated, Mālav. – **manas** (*yuktá-*), mfn. fixing the mind, ready-minded, attentive, ŚBr. – **māṇsala**, mfn. properly stout or fleshy, VarBṛS. – **yoga**, m. (in astrol.) being in conjunction, Laghuk. – **ratha**, m. N. of a partic. kind of purging enema, Suśr.; n. a sort of elixir, ib. – **rasā** and -**rāsnā**, f. a kind of plant, L. – **rūpa**, mfn. suitably formed, fit, proper (with loc. or gen.), MBh.; Hariv.; Kāv.; (*am*), ind. suitably, MBh. – **rūpaka**, n. an appropriate metaphor, Kāvyād. – **vat** (*yuktá-*), mfn. containing a form of √1. *yuj*, ŚBr. – **vādin**, mfn. speaking properly or suitably, Veṇīs. – **śītôshṇa**, mfn. of moderate cold and heat, R. – **sena**, mfn. one whose army is ready (for marching), Suśr.; °*nīya*, mfn. relating to him, ib. – **svapnâvabodha**, mfn. moderate in sleeping and waking, Bhag.

Yuktâtman, mfn. concentrated in mind, Bhag.; (ifc.) wholly intent upon, Pañcat. **Yuktâyas**, n. 'bound with iron,' a sort of spade or shovel, W. **Yuktâyukta**, n. the proper and improper, right and wrong, MW. **Yuktârohin**, mfn., Pāṇ. vi, 2, 81. **Yuktârtha**, mfn. having a meaning, sensible, significant, rational, R. **Yuktâśva**, mfn. having (or 'brought by') yoked horses (as wealth), RV. v, 41, 5. **Yuktâhāra-vihāra**, mfn. moderate in diet and pleasure, Bhag.

Yuktaka, n. a pair, Pat.

Yukti, f. union, junction, connection, combination, AitBr.; TāṇḍBr.; preparation, going to, making ready for (loc. or comp.), R.; application, practice, usage, Kathās.; Suśr.; trick, contrivance, means, expedient, artifice, cunning device, magic, Kāv.; Kathās.; Pañcar. (*yuktim √kṛi*, to find out or employ an expedient; *yukti*, ibc.; °*tyā*, °*tibhis*, and °*ti-tas*, ind. by device or stratagem, artfully, skilfully, under pretext or pretence; *yuktyā* &c. ifc. = by means of); reasoning, argument, proof, influence, induction, deduction from circumstances, Kap.; Kāv.; Var. &c. (*-tas*, by means of an argument); reason, ground, motive, BhP.; MārkP.; suitableness, adaptedness, fitness, propriety, correctness, MBh.; Kāv. &c. (*yuktyā* and °*ti-tas*, properly, suitably, fitly, justly, duly); meditation on the supreme being, contemplation, union with the universal spirit, Sāṃk. (cf. IW. 111, 3); (in law) enumeration of circumstances, specification of place and time &c., Yājñ. ii, 92; 212; (in rhet.) emblematic or mystical expression of purpose, W.; (in dram.) connection of the events in a plot, concatenation of incidents, intelligent weighing of the circumstances, Daśar.; Sāh.; Pratāp.; (in astron.) conjunction, Jyot.; (in gram.) connection of words, a sentence, Nir.; connection of letters,

Vishṇ.; supplying an ellipsis, W.; mixture or alloying of metals, VarBṛS.; sum, total, Sūryas. **— kathana,** n. statement of argument, giving reasons, Hit. **— kara,** mfn. suitable, proper, fit; (or) established, proved, R. **— kalpa-taru,** m. N. of wk. **— kṛita,** mfn. acquired, gained (opp. to *saha-ja*), Car. **— jña,** mfn. skilled in mixing (perfumes), VarBṛS.; knowing the proper means, Kām. **— tas,** see under *yukti*, p. 853. **— dīpikā,** f., **-prakāśa,** m. N. of wks. **— bāhya,** mfn. ignorant of the proper application (of remedies), Car. **— bhāshā,** f. N. of wk. **— mat,** mfn. joined or united or tied to (comp.), R.; possessing fitness, ingenious, clever, inventive (with inf.), Kathās.; furnished with arguments, based on arg°, proved (*-tva*, n.), BhP.; suitable, fit, Naish. **— mallikā** (?), f., **-mālikā,** f., **-muktâvalī,** f. N. of wks. **— yukta,** mfn. experienced, skilful (see *a-y°*); suitable, proper, fit; established, proved, very probable, ŚārṅgP.; Bālar.; argumentative, A. **— ratna-mālā,** f. N. of wk. **— śāstra,** n. the science of what is suitable or proper, MBh. **— sneha-prapūraṇī,** f. N. of wk.

Yugá, n. a yoke, team (exceptionally m.), RV. &c. &c.; (ifc. f. *ā*), a pair, couple, brace, GṛŚrS.; MBh. &c.; (also with *mānusha* or *manushya*) a race of men, generation (exceptionally m.), RV. &c. &c.; a period or astronomical cycle of 5 (rarely 6) years, a lustrum (esp. in the cycle of Jupiter), MBh.; Var.; Suśr.; an age of the world, long mundane period of years (of which there are four, viz. 1. Kṛita or Satya, 2. Tretā, 3. Dvāpara, 4. Kali, of which the first three have already elapsed, while the Kali, which began at midnight between the 17th and 18th of Feb. 3102 B.C. [O.S.], is that in which we live; the duration of each is said to be respectively 1,728,000, 1,296,000, 864,000, and 432,000 years of men, the descending numbers representing a similar physical and moral deterioration of men in each age; the four Yugas comprise an aggregate of 4,320,000 years and constitute a 'great Yuga' or Mahā-yuga; cf. IW. 178), AV. &c. &c.; a measure of length = 86 Aṅgulas, Śulbas. (= 4 Hastas or cubits, L.); a symbolical N. for the number 'four,' Sūryas.; for the number 'twelve,' Jyot.; N. of a partic. position or configuration of the moon, VarBṛS.; of a partic. Nābhasa constellation (of the class called Sāṃkhya-yoga, when all the planets are situated in two houses), ib.; of a double Śloka or two Ślokas so connected that the sense is only completed by the two together, Rājat. **— kīlaka,** m. the pin of a yoke, L. **— kshaya,** m. the end of a Yuga, destruction of the world, R.; BhP. **— carman,** n. a leather pad attached to a yoke, MBh. **— dīrgha,** mfn. as long as a chariot yoke, Ragh. **— dhāra,** m. (prob.) the pin by which a yoke is fastened to the pole, MānGṛ. **— dhur,** f. the pin of a yoke, ĀpŚr. **— m-dhara,** mf(*ā*)n. holding or bearing the yoke (?), MBh.; m. n. the pole of a carriage or wood to which the yoke is fixed, MBh.; m. a partic. magical formula spoken over weapons, R.; N. of a king, Hariv.; Pur.; of a mountain, MBh. (with Buddhists one of the 8 mountains, Dharmas. 125); of a forest, Pañcar.; pl. N. of a people, MBh.; VarBṛS.; VP. **— pa,** m. N. of a Gandharva, MBh.; Hariv. **— pattra,** m. Bauhinia Variegata, L. **— pattraka,** m. id., Bhpr.; (*ikā*), f. Dalbergia Sissoo, L. **— pad,** ind. 'being in the same yoke or by the side of each other,' together, at the same time, simultaneously ('with,' instr., Pāṇ. ii, 1, 6, Sch.; cf. *yuga-śāram*), GṛŚrS. &c. &c.; (*-pat*)*-karman*, n. a simultaneous action, Lāṭy.; (*-pat*)*-kāla*, mfn. taking place at the same time, ĀpŚr.; (*-pat*)*-prâpti*, f. reaching simultaneously, ĀśvGṛ.; (*-pad*)*-bhāva*, m. simultaneousness, KātyŚr. **— pārśvaka** or **°va-ga,** mfn. going at the side of the yoke (said of a young ox in training), L. **— purāṇa,** n. N. of a section of the Garga-saṃhitā. **— pradhāna-svarūpa,** n. or **°na-paṭṭâvalī-sūtra,** n., **-pramāṇa,** n. N. of wks. **— bāhu,** mfn. having arms like a yoke, long-armed, Kum. **— bhaṅga,** m. the breaking of a yoke, Kathās. **— mātra,** n. the length of a yoke, 1° of 4 hands, MBh.; VP.; (*-mātrá*), mf(*ī*)n. as large as a y°, 4 hands long, ŚBr.; KātyŚr.; *-darśin* (Lalit.), *-dṛiś* (Car.) or *-prêkshin* (Lalit.), mfn. looking as far as a y° or towards the ground. **— varatra,** n. (or **°trā,** f.) the strap of a y°, g. *khaṇḍikâdi*. **— vyāyata-bāhu,** mfn. having arms long as a y°, long-armed, Ragh. **— vyā-vat,** w. r. for *-vyāyatā*, ib., Comm. **— śamyá,** n. a yoke together with the pin, ŚBr. **— śāram,** ind. together with (instr.), MaitrS.; Kāṭh. (cf. *-pad*). **— saṃvatsara,** m. the lunar year serving for the completion of the Yuga of 5 years, Sūryapr. **— sahasrāya,** Nom. Ā. *°yate*, to become a thousand mundane periods, i. e. appear infinitely long, Kād. **Yugâṅśaka,** m. 'part of a Yuga or lustrum,' a year, L. **Yugâdi,** m. the commencement of a Yuga, the beginning of the world, Cat.; *-kṛit*, m. N. of Śiva, Śivag.; *-jina* (Śatr.), *-deva* and *-purusha* (Siṇhâs.), or *°dīśa* (Śatr.), m. N. of the Jina Ṛishabha. **Yugâdyā,** f. (scil. *tithi*) the first day of a Yuga or age of the world, VP.; the anniversary of it, MW. **Yugâdhyaksha,** m. 'superintendent of a Y°,' N. of Prajā-pati, Jyot.; of Śiva, Śivag. **Yugânta,** m. the end of the yoke, R.; the meridian (*°tam adhirūḍhaḥ savitā* = it is noon-time), Śak.; the end of a generation, MBh.; the end of an age or Yuga, destruction of the world, R.; Hariv. &c.; *-bandhu*, m. a real and constant friend, MW.; *°tâgni*, m. the fire at the end of the world, MBh.; R.; Bhartṛ. **Yugântaka,** m. the end of an age or of the w°, Cat. **Yugântara,** n. a special yoke, peculiar y°, L.; the second half of the arc described by the sun and cut by the meridian (*°ram ārūḍhaḥ savitā* = midday is past), Śak.; another generation, a succeeding gen°, Bhartṛ. **Yugâvadhi,** m. end or destruction of the world, Śiś. **Yugêśa,** m. the lord of a lustrum, VarBṛS. **Yugôrasya,** m. N. of a partic. array of troops, Kām.

Yugala, n. (rarely m.; ifc. f. *ā*) a pair, couple, brace, Kāv.; Pur.; Pañcat. &c. (*°lo √bhū*, to be yoked or united with); 'double prayer,' N. of a prayer to Lakshmī and Nārāyaṇa, L. **— kiśora-sahasra-nāma-stotra,** n., **-kiśora-stotra,** n., **-sahasra-nāman,** n. N. of Stotras containing 1000 names of Kṛishṇa. **— ja,** m. du. twins, HPariś. **— bhakta,** m. pl. N. of a subdivision of the Caitanya Vaishṇavas, W. **Yugalâksha** or **°lâkhya,** m. a species of plant, L.

Yugalaka, n. a pair, couple, brace, Kathās.; a double Śloka (= *yuga*, q. v.), Rājat.

Yugalāya, Nom. Ā. *°yate*, to be like or represent a pair (of anything), Kāv.

Yugalāyita, mfn. (ifc.) representing or like a pair, ib.

Yugalin, mfn. (prob.) egoistical, Siṇhâs.

Yugāya, Nom. Ā. *°yate*, to appear like a Yuga i. e. like an immense period of time, BhP.

Yugin. See *vastra-yugin*.

Yugma, mf(*ā*)n. even (as opp. to 'odd'), GṛŚrS.; Mn. &c.; n. a pair, couple, brace, ŚāṅkhGṛ.; Yājñ.; R. &c.; twins, Suśr.; (in astron.) the sign of the zodiac Gemini; a double Śloka (cf. *yuga*), Rājat.; junction, confluence (of two streams), R.; often w. r. for *yugya*. **— kṛishṇala,** m. or n. a double Kṛishṇala, Kauś. **— cārin,** mf(*iṇī*)n. going about in pairs, Uttarar. **— ja,** m. du. twins, L. **— janana-śānti,** f. N. of wk. **— janman,** m. du. twins, HPariś. **— dharman,** mfn. (?), Śatr. **— pattra,** m. Bauhinia Variegata, L. **— pattrikā,** f. Dalbergia Sissoo, L. **— parṇa,** m. Bauhinia Variegata, L.; Alstonia Scholaris, L. **— phalā,** f. coloquintida, L.; Tragia Involucrata, L.; = *gandhikā* (?), L.; *°lôttama*, m. Asclepias Rosea, L. **— lāṅgalin,** mfn. possessing two ploughs, Hcat. **— vipulā,** f. a kind of metre, Ked. **— śukra,** n. two white spots in the dark portion of the eye, Suśr. **Yugmâpatyā,** f. one who is the mother of twins, Kathās.

Yugmaka, mfn. even (= *yugma*), Ked.; n. (ifc. f. *ā*), a pair, couple, brace, Vet.; a double Śloka (= *yuga*), Rājat.

Yugmát, mfn. even, TS.; Br. &c. **Yúgmad-ayujá,** mfn. even and odd, MaitrS.

Yugmán, mfn. even, ŚBr.

Yugmin, mfn. (fr. *yugma*), Śatr.

Yugya, mfn. yoked or fit to be yoked, L.; (ifc.) drawn by (e. g. *aśva-y°*), L.; n. a vehicle, chariot, car, Mn.; MBh. &c.; (also m.) any yoked or draught animal, Yājñ.; MBh. &c. (cf. Pāṇ. iv, 4, 76); (with *Jamad-agneḥ*) N. of a Sāman, ĀrshBr. **— vāha,** m. a coachman, driver, Rājat. **— stha,** mfn. being in a carriage, Mn. viii, 284. **Yugyâsana-praseva,** m. the nose-bag containing a horse's food, L.

2. **Yúj,** mfn. (mostly ifc.; when uncompounded, the strong cases have a nasal, e. g. nom. *yuṅ*, *yuñjau*, *yuñjas*, but *aśva-yuk* &c., Pāṇ. vii, 1, 71) joined, yoked, harnessed, drawn by, RV. &c. &c. (cf. *aśva-*, *hari-*, *hayôttama-yuj*); furnished or provided or filled with, affected by, possessed of (instr., mostly comp.), MBh.; Kāv. &c.; bestowing, granting (e. g. *kāma-yuj*, 'g° wishes'), Hariv.; exciting, an exciter (e. g. *yuṅ bhiyaḥ*, an exc° of fear), Bhaṭṭ.; being in couples or pairs, even (not odd or separate), Lāṭy.; Mn.; MBh. &c.; m. a yoke-fellow, companion, comrade, associate, RV.; AV.; Br.; a sage who devotes his time to abstract contemplation, W.; a pair, couple, the number 'two,' Pañcar.; du. the two Aśvins, L.; (in astron.) the zodiacal sign Gemini.

Yuja. See *a-yujá* and *yúgmad-ayujá*.

Yújya, mfn. connected, related, allied, RV.; AV.; homogeneous, similar, equal in rank or power, RV.; suitable, proper, capable, RV.; VS.; n. union, alliance, relationship, RV.; (with *Jamad-agneḥ*) N. of a Sāman, ĀrshBr. (v. l. *yugya*).

Yuñjaka, mfn. applying, performing, practising (e. g. *dhyāna-y°*, practising devotion), Cat.

Yuñjāna, mfn. uniting, joining, arranging, performing, Kathās.; BhP.; appointing to, charging or entrusting with (loc.), MBh.; suitable, proper, MW.; successful, prosperous, ib.; m. a driver, coachman, L.; a Yogin, L.

Yuñjānaka, mfn. containing the word *yuñjāna*, g. *goshad-ādi*.

Yuyujāná-sapti, mfn. one who has yoked his horses (in du. applied to the Aśvins), RV. vi, 62, 4.

Yoktavyà, mfn. to be joined or yoked or united &c.; to be concentrated (as the mind), MBh.; to be prepared or employed or practised or applied, TS.; Bhag. (n. impers.); to be inflicted (as punishment), MBh.; to be entrusted or charged with (loc.), ib.; to be furnished or provided with (instr.), ib.; Hariv.

Yoktṛi, mfn. one who yokes or harnesses, a charioteer, MBh.; one who excites or rouses, VS.; one who applies effort to (loc.), Āpast.

Yóktra, n. any instrument for tying or fastening, a rope, thong, halter, RV. &c. &c. (also *yoktra-pāśa*, m.); the thongs by which an animal is attached to the pole of a carriage, MBh.; the band round a broom, ĀśvŚr.; the tie of the yoke of a plough, L.

Yoktraka, n. = *yoktra*, VarBṛS.

Yoktraya, Nom. P. *°yati*, to tie, bind, fasten, wind round, MBh.

Yoga, yogya &c. See pp. 856, 858.

Yojana, yojayitṛi, yojitṛi, yojya &c. See pp. 858, cols. 1, 2.

युञ्जन्द *yuñjanda*, m. or n. (?) N. of a place, Cat.

युञ्जवत् *yuñjavat*, w. r. for *muñja-vat*.

युत् 2. *yut* (fr. √*dyut*; cf. √*jut* and *jyut*; for 1. *yut* see p. 853, col. 1), cl. 1. Ā. *yotate*, to shine, Dhātup. ii, 30.

युत *yuta*, *yutaka*, *yuti*. See under √1. 2. *yu*.

युत्कार *yut-kāra*, *yud-bhū* &c. See under 1. *yudh* below.

युध 1. *yudh*, cl. 4. Ā. (Dhātup. xxvi, 64) *yúdhyate* (rarely P. *°ti*; cl. 1. P. *yodhati*, AV.; Br.; Impv. *yôtsi*, RV.; pf. *yuyódha*, *yuyudhé*, RV. &c. &c.; aor. Ved. *yodhi*, *yodhat*, *yodhānā*; *ayodhīt*, *yodhishat*; *yutsmahi*; ep. *yotsīs*; Class. *ayuddha*; fut. *yoddhā*, MBh.; *yotsyati*, *°te*, Br. &c.; inf. *yudhé* or *yudháye*, RV.; *yudham*, Br.; *yoddhum*, MBh.; ind. p. *-yuddhvī*, RV.; *-yudhya*, MBh.), to fight, wage war, oppose or (rarely) overcome in battle; to fight with (instr., also with *saha*, *samam*) or for (loc.) or against (acc.), RV. &c. &c.; (*yúdhyati*), to go, Naigh. ii, 14; to move, fluctuate (as waves), MaitrS. (cf. Pat. on Pāṇ. iii, 1, 85): Pass. *yudhyate*, to be fought (also impers.), Hit. (v. l.): Caus. *yodháyati* (Pāṇ. i, 3, 86; m. c. also *°te*; aor. *ayūyudhat*, MBh.; Pass. *yodhyate*, ib.), to cause to fight, lead to war, engage in battle, RV. &c. &c.; to oppose or overcome in war, be a match for (acc.), MBh.; Kāv. &c.; to defend, MBh. iii, 639: Desid. *yúyutsati*, *°te* (P. in Class. only m. c.), to be desirous or anxious to fight, wish to fight with (instr.), RV. &c. &c.: Caus. of Desid. *yuyutsayati*, to make desirous of fighting, Bhaṭṭ.: Intens. *yoyudhyate*, *yoyoddhi* (cf. *yavīyúdh*), Gr. [Cf. Zd. *yud*; Gk. ὑσ-μίνη.]

3. **Yut** (for 1. see p. 853, col. 1; for 2. see above), in comp. for 2. *yudh*. **— kārá,** mfn. making war, fighting, RV. x, 103, 2.

Yud, in comp. for 2. *yudh*. **— bhū** or **-bhūmi,** f. battle-ground, a field of battle, L.

Yuddha, mfn. fought, encountered, conquered, subdued, MBh.; m. N. of a son of Ugra-sena, VP.; (*yuddhá*), n. (ifc. f. *ā*) battle, fight, war, RV. &c. &c.; (in astron.) opposition, conflict of the planets,

Sūryas.; VarBṛS. **-kāṇḍa**, n. 'battle-section,' N. of the 6th book of Vālmiki's Rāmāyaṇa; of the 6th book of the Adhyātma-rāmāyaṇa; of a ch. of the Skanda-purāṇa. **-kārin**, mfn. making war, fighting (°*ri-tva*, n.), Hit. **-kāla**, m. time of war, Pañcat. **-kīrti**, m. N. of a pupil of Saṃkarācārya, Cat. **-kutūhala**, n., **-kauśala**, n. N. of wks. **-kshmā**, f. a place of combat, Kāv. **-gāndharva**, n. battle-music, MBh.; a b° like the dance of the Gandharvas, MW. **-cintāmaṇi**, m., **-jaya-prakāśa**, m., **-jayârṇava**, m., **-jayôtsava**, m., **-jayôpâya**, m. N. of wks. **-jit**, mfn. victorious in battle, MBh. **-tantra**, n. military science, Viddh. **-dyūta**, n. 'game of war,' chance of w°, luck of battle, MBh. **-dharma**, m. the law of b°, law of w°, Mcar. (pl.) **-dhvāna**, m. battle-cry, L. **-parāṅmukha**, mfn. averse from fighting, Hariv. **-paripāṭī**, f. N. of wk. **-purī**, f. N. of a town; *-māhātmya*, n. N. of ch. of the Skanda-purāṇa. **-pravīṇa**, mfn. skilled in war, Pracaṇḍ. **-bhū** (Kathās.) or **-bhūmi** (MBh.; Hariv. &c.), f. battle-ground, a field of b°. **-maya**, mf(*ī*)n. resulting from battle, relating to war, MBh. **-mārga**, m. (sg. and pl.) a mode of fighting, MBh.; Hariv.; Kām. **-mushṭi**, m. N. of a son of Ugra-sena, VP. **-medinī**, f. = *-bhū*, q. v., Hariv.; R. **-yogya**, mfn. fit for war (*-tā*, f.), R. **-yojaka**, mfn. preparing for war, eager for battle, MBh. **-raṅga**, m. 'b°-arena,' field of b°, MBh.; Hariv.; 'whose ar° is b°,' N. of Kārttikeya, L. **-ratnasvara**, m., °**nâvalī**, f. N. of wks. **-vat**, mfn. fr. *yuddhá*, g. *balâdi*. **-varṇa**, m. a sort of battle, Ml. **-vastu**, n. an implement of war, Kām. **-vidyā**, f. the science of war, military art, MW. **-vinoda**, m. N. of wk. **-viśārada**, mfn. skilful in war, Bhag. **-vīra**, m. 'battle-hero,' a valiant man, warrior, hero, Sāh.; heroism (as one of the Rasas, q. v.), ib. **-vyatikrama**, m. violation of the rules of combat, Hariv. **-śakti**, f. warlike vigour or prowess, Cat. **-śālin**, mfn. warlike, valiant, R. **-sāra**, m. 'battle-goer,' a horse, L.; mfn. instinct with combativeness, warlike, provoking (as speech), MBh. **-sûkta**, n. N. of the hymn RV. vi, 75. **Yuddhâcārya**, m. 'war-preceptor,' one who teaches the use of arms, Mn. iii, 162. **Yuddhâji**, m. (N. of a descendant of Aṅgiras), w. r. for *yudhāji* below. **Yuddhâdhvan**, mfn. going or resorting to battle, Kathās. **Yuddhânivartin**, mfn. not turning the back (in battle), heroic, valiant, L. **Yuddhârthin**, mfn. desirous of war, seeking war, MW. **Yuddhâvasāna**, n. cessation of war, truce, ib. **Yuddhâvahārika**, n. booty, MBh. **Yuddhôdyama** or °**yoga**, m. preparing for battle, vigorous and active preparation for war, ib. **Yuddhônmatta**, mfn. 'battle-mad,' fierce or frantic in battle; m. N. of a Rākshasa, R.; Bhaṭṭ. **Yuddhôpakaraṇa**, n. any war implement, accoutrements, Nir. ix, 11.

Yuddhaka, n. = *yuddha*, war, battle, Kathās.

2. **Yudh**, m. a fighter, warrior, hero, MBh.; Hariv.; (*yúdh*), f. war, fight, combat, struggle, contest, RV. &c. &c.

Yudhā, instr. of 2. *yudh*, in comp. **-ji**, m. (prob. for *-jit*; but cf. *yaudhājaya*) N. of a man (v. l. *yuddhâji*). **-jit**, mfn. conquering or vanquishing by means of war, PañcavBr.; MBh.; N. of a son of Kroshṭu by a woman called Mādrī, Hariv.; of a son of Kekaya (uncle of Bharata), R.; of a son of Vṛishṇi, VP.; of a king of Ujjayinī, Cat. **-jīva**, m. (w. r. for *yuddhâj*°?) N. of a man. **-manyu**, m. N. of a warrior on the side of the Pāṇḍavas, MBh.; BhP. **-sura**, m. (w. r. for *yuddhâs*°?) N. of a king.

Yudhām-śraushṭi, m. N. of a man, AitBr.

Yudhāna, m. a man of the second or military order, a warrior, W.; an enemy, Uṇ. ii, 90, Sch.

1. **Yudhi**, fighting, battle (only in dat. *yudháye*; see under √1. *yudh*). **-m-gama**, mfn. going to battle, AV.

2. **Yudhi**, loc. of 2. *yudh*, in comp. **-shṭhira**, m. (for *-sthira*) 'firm or steady in battle,' N. of the eldest of the 5 reputed sons of Pāṇḍu (really the child of Pṛithā or Kuntī, Pāṇḍu's wife, by the god Dharma or Yama, whence he is often called Dharma-putra or Dharma-rāja; he ultimately succeeded Pāṇḍu as king, first reigning over Indra-prastha, and afterwards, when the Kuru princes were defeated, at Hastinā-pura; cf. IW. 379 &c.), MBh.; Hariv.; Pur.; of a son of Kṛishṇa, Hariv.; of two kings of Kaśmīra, Rājat.; of a potter, Pañcat.; (with *mahôpâdhyāya*) of a preceptor, Cat.; pl. the descendants of Yudhi-shṭhira (son of Pāṇḍu), Pāṇ. ii, 4, 66, Sch.; *-vijaya* (or *-dig-v*°), m. N. of a poem by Vāsudeva Parama-śiva-yogin of Kerala.

Yudhika, mfn. fighting, contending, L.

Yudhénya, mfn. to be fought with, to be overcome in battle, RV.

Yudhmá, m. a warrior, hero, RV.; (only L.) a battle; an arrow; a bow; = *śesha-saṃgrāma*; = *śarabha*.

Yudhyāmadhí, m. N. of a man, RV. vii, 18, 24.

Yúdhvan, mfn. warlike, martial, a warrior, RV.

Yuyutsā, f. (fr. Desid.) the wishing to fight, desire for war, pugnacity, combativeness, MBh.; Hariv.; R.; *-rahita*, mfn. without wish or intention to fight, cowardly, W. °**tsu**, mfn. wishing to fight ('with,' instr., also with *saha*, *sârdham* &c.), eager for battle, pugnacious, MBh.; Kāv. &c.; m. a combatant, W.; N. of one of the sons of Dhṛita-rāshṭra, MBh.; BhP.

Yuyudhan, m. N. of a king of Mithilā, BhP.

Yuyudhāna, m. N. of a son of Satyaka (one of the allies of the Pāṇḍavas), MBh.; Hariv.; Pur.; a Kshatriya, warrior, L.; N. of Indra, L.

Yúyudhi (or *yū́y*°), mfn. warlike, martial, pugnacious, RV.

Yoddhavya, mfn. to be fought or contended with or overcome in battle (n. impers.), MBh.; R. &c.

Yoddhu-kāma, mfn. wishing to fight, anxious for battle, Bhag.

Yoddhṛi, m. a fighter, warrior, soldier, MBh.; R. &c.

Yodha, yodhin, yodhya. See p. 858, col. 2.

युन्थ् *yunth*, v. l. for √*punth*.

युप् *yup*, cl. 4. P. (Dhātup. xxvi, 124; cf. *yūpa*) *yupyati* (only in pf. *yuyópa*; Gr. also aor. *ayupat*; fut. *yopitā*, *yopishyati*), to debar, obstruct, disturb, trouble, confuse, efface, remove, destroy, RV.; AV.; to be effaced or concealed, RV. i, 104, 4: Caus. *yopáyati* (aor. *ayūyupat*), to efface, obliterate, conceal, remove, destroy, RV.; TS.; Br.: Intens. *yoyupyáte*, to make level, smooth, TS.; ŚBr.

Yupitá, mfn. effaced, removed, AV.; confused, troubled (cf. *á-yupita*).

Yopana, n. effacing, removing, confusing, destroying &c. (only ifc.; cf. *jana-*, *jīvita-*, *pada-*, *śapatha-y*°).

Yoyupana, n. (fr. Intens.) smoothing, levelling, TS., Sch.

युयु *yuyu*, m. a horse, L. (prob. w. r. for *yayu*).

युयुक्खुर *yuyukkhura*, m. = *kshudra-vyāghra*, L. (a hyena, W.)

युयुत्सा *yuyutsā*, °*tsu*; *yuyudhāna*, °*dhi*. See above.

युयुवि *yuyuvi*. See under √1. *yu*.

युव 1. *yuvá*, actual base of the 2nd pers. pron. in the dual number (from which the forms *yuvā́m*, *yuvā́bhyām*, *yuváyos*; Ved. also *yuvā́m*, *yuvā́bhyām*, *yuvát*, *yuvós*, are derived). **-drik**, ind. directed towards both of you, RV. **-dhita** (*yuvá-*), mfn. placed or arranged by you both, ib.

Yuvad-devatyà, mfn. having (both of) you for a divinity, ŚBr.

Yuvayú or **yuvā́yú**, mfn. longing for you both, RV.

1. **Yuvā** (for 2. see col. 3), in comp. for 1. *yuva*. **-datta** (*yuvā́-*), mfn. given to both of you, RV. **-nīta** (*yuvā́-*), mfn. brought by both of you, ib. **-yúj**, mfn. yoked or harnessed by (or for) both of you, ib. **-vat** (*yuvā́-*), mfn. belonging to both of you, ib.

Yuvā́ku, mfn. (sometimes ind., with gen. or dat.) belonging or devoted to both of you, RV.

युवक *yuvaka*. See col. 3.

युवन् *yúvan*, mf(*yūnī* or *yuvatí*, q. v.)n. (prob. fr. √2. *yu*) young, youthful, adult (applied to men and animals), strong, good, healthy, RV. &c. &c.; m. a youth, young man, young animal (in Veda often applied to gods, esp. to Indra, Agni, and the Maruts), ib.; (in gram.) the younger descendant of any one (an elder being still alive), Pāṇ. i, 2, 65, &c.; N. of the ninth year in Jupiter's cycle of 60 years, Jyot.; an elephant 60 years old, Gal. [Cf. Lat. *juvenis*, *juventa*; Slav. *junŭ*; Lith. *jáunas*; Goth. *juggs*; Germ. *junc*, *jung*; Angl. Sax. *geong*; Eng. *young*.]

2. **Yuva**, in comp. for *yuvan*. **-khalati**, mfn. bald in youth; (*ī*), f. bald in girlhood, Pāṇ. ii, 1, 67, Sch. **-gaṇḍa**, m. an eruption on the face of young people L. **-jarat**, mf(*atī*)n. appearing old in youth, Pāṇ. ii, 1, 67, Sch. **-jāni** (*yúva-*), mfn. having a young wife, RV. viii, 2, 19. **-tā**, f. (Subh.), **-tva**, n. (Sāy.) youthfulness, youth. **-palita**, mf(*ā*)n. grey-haired in youth, Pāṇ. ii, 1, 67, Sch. **-pratyaya**, m. a suffix forming the so-called Yuvan patronymics, Pāṇ. ii, 4, 59 &c., Sch. **-mārin**, mf(*iṇī*)n. dying in youth, Āpast. (cf. *a-yuvam*°). **-rāja**, m. 'young king,' an heir-apparent associated with the reigning sovereign in the government, crown prince, R.; VarBṛS. &c.; N. of Maitreya (the future Buddha), L.; of various authors, Cat.; *-tva*, n. the rank or position of an heir-apparent to a throne, R.; Kathās.; Rājat.; *-divākara*, m. N. of a poet, Cat. **-rājan**, m. = *-rāja*, Hariv. **-rājya**, n. = *-rāja-tva*, Kathās.; Pañcat. **-valina**, mf(*ā*)n. having wrinkles in youth, Pāṇ. ii, 1, 67, Sch. **-sena**, m. N. of a poet, Cat. **-han**, mf(*ghnī*)n. child-murdering, infanticide, Car.

Yuvaka, m. a youth, young man, Śaktān.

Yúvat, mfn. young, RV.; Suparṇ.

Yuvati, f. a girl, young woman, any young female animal, RV. &c. &c. (in RV. applied to Ushas, Night and Morning, Heaven and Earth &c.; with *śaryā*, prob. 'an arrow just shot off;' but cf. *yuvá*; ifc. as f. for *yuvan*, a youth, e. g. *sa-bāla-vṛiddha-yuvatiḥ purī*, a town with boys, old and young men, Hariv.); turmeric, L. **-jana**, m. a young woman, Bhartṛ. **-dā**, f. bestowing young women, ĀpŚr. **Yuvatishṭā**, f. yellow jasmine, L.

Yuvatī, f. = *yuvati*, a girl, young woman, MBh.; R. &c.; (in astron.) the zodiacal sign Virgo. **-jana**, m. = *yuvati-j*°, MBh. **-sambhoga-kāra**, m. N. of a poet, Cat. **-sârtha**, m. a multitude of young women, Ratnâv. (in Prākṛit °*thaka*).

Yuvanyú, mfn. youthful, juvenile, RV.

Yuvaśá, mfn. young, youthful, juvenile; m. a youth, RV.

Yuvānaka, mfn. young, Hcat.

Yuvī-bhūta, mfn. become young, Kathās.

युवन *yuvana* (?), m. the moon, L.

युवनाश्व *yuvanāśva*, m. N. of the father of Māndhātṛi and of various other men, MBh.; R.; Hariv.; Pur. **-ja**, m. 'son of Y°,' patr. of Māndhātṛi (an early sovereign of the solar dynasty), L.

युवन्यु *yuvanyu*, *yuva-palita* &c. See above.

युवा 2. *yuvā*, f. (for 1. see col. 2) N. of one of Agni's arrows, TS.

युवाकु *yuvāku*, *yuvā-datta* &c. See col. 2.

युवाम *yuvāma*, N. of a town, Vās., Introd.

युष्टग्राम *yushṭa-grāma*, m. N. of a village, Rājat.

युष्म *yushma* (fr. *yu* + *sma*), the actual base of the 2nd pers. pron. in the plural number (from which all cases except the nom. *yūyám* are derived, viz. *yushmā́n*, *yushmā́bhis*, *yushmā́bhyam*, *yushmát*, *yushmā́kam*, in Ved. also acc. f. *yushmā́s*; loc. *yushmé*, and gen. *yushmāka*; cf. Gk. ὔμμες, fr. ὔσμες).

Yushmat, in comp. for *yushmad*. **-tas**, ind. (afraid) of you, R.

Yushmad, the base of the 2nd pers. pron. as used in comp.; also considered by native grammarians to be the base of the cases *yushmā́n* &c. (see above). **-artham**, ind. for you, on your account, MW. **-āyatta**, mfn. dependent upon you, at your disposal, ib. **-vācya**, n. (in gram.) the second person. **-vidha**, mfn. of your kind or sort, like you, BhP.

Yushmadīya, mfn. (Pāṇ. iv, 31) belonging to you, your, yours, Kathās.; m. a countryman of yours, Ratnâv.

Yushmaya, Nom. (fr. *yushma*) P. °*yati* (only in pr. p. *yushmayát*, seeking you, addressed to you), RV.

Yushmā, in comp. for *yushma* or *yushmad*. **-datta** (*yushmā́-*), mfn. given by you, RV. **-dṛiś** or **-dṛiśa**, mf(*ī*)n. like you, similar to you, one such as you, Kathās. **-nīta** (*yushmā́-*), mfn. accompanied by you, RV. **-vat** (*yushmā́-*), mfn. belonging to you, RV. **Yushmêshita**, mfn. excited or instigated by you, ib. **Yushmōta,** mfn. protected or loved by you, ib.

Yushmāka, mf(*ā*)n. your, yours, RV. (cf. *yushmākam* under *yushma*).

यू *yū*, m. (or f.) soup, pease-soup, broth (=*yūsha*), L.

यूक *yūka*, m. or (more commonly) *yūkā*, f. a louse, Mn.; Kathās.; Suśr. &c.

Yūka-devī, f. N. of a princess, Rājat.

Yūkā-liksha, n. sg. a louse and its egg or the egg of a louse (as a measure of length), VarBṛS.; MārkP.

यूकर *yūkara*, g. *kṛiśāśvâdi*.

यूति *yūti*. See *go-* and *bahir-yūti*.

यूथ *yūthá*, m. n. (in the older language only n.; fr. √2. *yu*) a herd, flock, troop, band, host, multitude, number, large quantity (ifc. f. *ā*), RV. &c. &c.; (*ī*), f. a kind of jasmine (=*yūthikā*), L. **–ga,** m. pl. N. of a class of gods under Manu Cākshusha, MārkP. **–cārin,** mf(*iṇī*)n. going about in troops (as monkeys), Kathās. **–tvā,** f. the forming or going in troops, Kauś. (dat. *āyai*); AVPariś. **–nātha,** m. the lord or leader of a herd or band or troop (esp. the chief elephant of a herd), R.; BhP.; Hit. **–pa,** m. (ifc. f. *ā*), id., MBh.; Kāv. &c. **–pati,** m. id., R.; BhP.; *-sakāśam*, ind. into the presence of the chief of the h°, Hit. **–paribhrashṭa,** mfn. fallen out or strayed from a h°, R. **–paśu,** m. N. of a partic. tax or tithe (*kāra*), Pāṇ. vi, 3, 10, Sch. **–pāla,** m. = *-pa*, R. **–bandha,** m. a flock or herd or troop, R. **–bhrashṭa,** mfn. = *-paribhrashṭa*, MBh.; BhP. **–mukhya,** m. the chief or captain of a troop, Hariv. **–vibhrashṭa,** mfn. = *-paribhrashṭa*, Kathās. **–śas,** ind. in troops or bands or flocks or herds, gregariously, MBh.; BhP. **–hata,** mfn. = *-paribhrashṭa*, R. **Yūthâgra-ṇī,** m. the leader of a herd or band, BhP.

Yūthaka (ifc.) = *yūtha*, BhP.

Yūthara, mfn. (fr. *yūtha*), g. *aśmâdi*.

Yūthikā, f. a kind of jasmine, Jasminum Auriculatum, Kālid.; BhP.; globe-amaranth, L.; Clypea Hernandifolia, L.

Yūthī-√1. kṛi, P. *-karoti*, to make or form into a herd, unite in a flock, BhP.

Yūthyà, mfn. belonging to a herd or flock, RV.; (ifc.) belonging to the troop or herd of, g. *vargyâdi*; (*ā*), f. a herd, pack, MBh.

Yūna, n. a band, cord, string, KātyŚr.

Yūni, f. connection, union, L.

यूनर्वन् *yūnarvan*, m. (a word of which the sense is doubtful), PañcavBr.; Lāṭy.

यूप *yūpa*, m. (prob. fr. √*yup*; but according to Uṇ. iii, 27, fr. √2. *yu*) a post, beam, pillar, (esp.) a smooth post or stake to which the sacrificial victim is fastened, any sacrificial post or stake (usually made of bamboos or Khadira wood; in R. i, 13, 24; 25, where the horse sacrifice is described, 21 of these posts are set up, 6 made of Bilva, 6 of Khadira, 6 of Palāśa, one of Uḍumbara, one of Śleshmātaka, and one of Deva-dāru), RV. &c. &c.; a column erected in honour of victory, a trophy (=*jaya-stambha*), L.; N. of a partic. conjunction of the class Ākṛiti-yoga (i. e. when all the planets are situated in the 1st, 2nd, 3rd and 4th houses), VarBṛS. **–kaṭaka,** m. a wooden ring at the top of a sacrificial post (or an iron ring at its base), L. **–karṇa,** m. the part of a s° post which is sprinkled with ghee, L. **–ketu,** m. N. of Bhūri-śravas, MBh. **–keśin,** m. N. of a demon, MānGṛ. **–cchedana,** n. the cutting of a s° p°, KātyŚr. **–dāru,** n. the wood for a s° p°, Pāṇ. i, 2, 43, Sch. **–dru** and **-druma,** m. Acacia Catechu, L. **–dhvaja,** m. 'having the s° p° as an emblem,' N. of the Sacrifice (personified), Hariv. **–madhya,** n. the middle part of the s° p°, L. **–mūrdha,** m. the head or top of a s° p°, MānŚr. **–lakshaṇa,** n. N. of the 1st Pariś. of Kātyāyana. **–lakshya,** m. a bird, L. **–vat,** mfn. having a s° p°, Ragh. **–vāsas,** n. a garment hanging on a s° p°, Vaitān. **–vāhá,** mfn. carrying or bearing a s° p°, RV. **–veshṭana,** n. the winding of a covering round a s° p°, KātyŚr.; the pieces of cloth used for covering a s° p°, ib. **–vraská,** mfn. cutting the s° p°, RV. **–śakalá,** m. a splinter from a s° p°, ŚBr. **–saṃskāra,** m. the consecration of a s° p°, L. **Yūpâksha** or **Yūpâkhya,** m. N. of a Rākshasa, R. **Yūpâgra,** n. the top of a s° post, L. **Yūpâṅga,** n. anything belonging to a s° p°, Jaim. **Yūpâvaṭa,** m. the pit in which a s° p° is fixed, ŚrS.; °*tya*, m. (scil. *śaṅku*), KātyŚr. **Yūpâhuti,** f. an oblation at the erection of a s° p°, ŚrS. **Yūpâikādaśinī,** f. a collection of eleven s° p°s, ŚBr. **Yūpôcchraya,** m. the ceremony of erecting a s° p°, MBh. **Yūpôlūkhalika,** mfn. having sacrificial posts and mortars (for pounding), MBh.

Yūpaka, m. = *yūpa* (m. c., esp. ifc.), Nyāyam.; n. a species of wood, L. **–vat,** mfn. having a sacrificial post, ĀśvŚr., Sch.

Yūpī-√1. kṛi, P. *-karoti*, to make into a sacrificial post, Nyāyam., Sch.

Yūpīya (Nyāyam., Sch.) or *yūpya* (ŚāṅkhBr.), mfn. fit or suitable for a sacrificial post.

यूयम् *yūyám*. See under *yushma*, p. 855, col. 3.

यूयुधि *yūyudhi*, *yūyuvi*. See *yuy*°.

यूष् *yūsh* (cf. √*jūsh*), cl. 1. P. *yūshati*, to hurt, kill, Dhātup. xvii, 29.

यूष *yūsha*, m. n. (fr. √2. *yu*) soup, broth, pease-soup, the water in which pulse of various kinds has been boiled, GṛŚrS.; Kathās.; Suśr.; m. the Indian mulberry tree, L. [Cf. Lat. *jūs*; Slav. *jucha*.]

Yūshán (only in the weak cases *yūshṇā*, °*ṇás*; cf. Pāṇ. vi, 1, 63), id., RV.; VS.; TS.

Yūs (only nom. sg. *yūs*), id., TS. (cf. *yū*).

येन *yena*, ind. (instr. of 3. *ya*) by whom or by which, by means of which, by which way, RV. &c. &c.; in which direction, whither, where, MBh.; Kāv. &c.; in which manner, PārGṛ.; Mn.; on which account, in consequence of which, wherefore, MBh.; R.; Kathās.; because, since, as, RV. &c. &c.; that, so that, in order that (with pres. or fut. or Pot.)

येमन *yemana*, n. = *jemana*, eating, L.

येयजामह *yeyajāmahá*, m. N. of the expression *ye yajāmahe* (which immediately precedes the Yājyā or formula of consecration), VS.; ŚrS. &c.

येयज्ञेनेतिसूक्त *yeyajñenétisūkta*, N. of the hymn RV. x, 62 (beginning with *ye yajñena*), Cat.

येयायेय *yeyāyeya*, n. (√1. *yā*) that which is to be gone after and not to be gone after, MW.

येवाष *yévāsha*, m. N. of a noxious insect, AV. (cf. *yavāsha*).

येष् *yesh*, cl. 1. P. *yéshati*, to boil up, bubble, RV.; AV.; (Ā.) *yeshate*, to exert one's self, endeavour, Dhātup. xvi, 14 (v.l. for √*pesh*).

येष्टिह *yeshṭiha* (?), N. of partic. Muhūrtas, KaushUp.

येष्ठ *yeshṭha*, mfn. (superl. fr. √1. *yā*) going best, very swift or rapid, RV.

योक् *yok*, ind. = *jyok*, for a long time, g. *svar-ādi*.

योक्तव्य *yoktavya*, *yoktṛi*, *yoktra*. See p. 854, col. 3.

योग *yóga*, m. (√1. *yuj*; ifc. f. *ā*) the act of yoking, joining, attaching, harnessing, putting to (of horses), RV.; MBh.; a yoke, team, vehicle, conveyance, ŚBr.; Kauś.; MBh.; employment, use, application, performance, RV. &c. &c.; equipping or arraying (of an army), MBh.; fixing (of an arrow on the bow-string), ib.; putting on (of armour), L.; a remedy, cure, Suśr.; a means, expedient, device, way, manner, method, MBh.; Kāv. &c.; a supernatural means, charm, incantation, magical art, ib.; a trick, stratagem, fraud, deceit, Mn.; Kathās. (cf. *yoga-nanda*); undertaking, business, work, RV.; AV.; TS.; acquisition, gain, profit, wealth, property, ib.; Kauś.; MBh.; occasion, opportunity, Kām.; MārkP.; any junction, union, combination, contact with (instr. with or without *saha*, or comp.), MBh.; Kāv. &c. (*yogam* √*i*, to agree, consent, acquiesce in anything, R.); mixing of various materials, mixture, MBh.; R.; VarBṛS.; partaking of, possessing (instr. or comp.), Mn.; R.; Hariv.; connection, relation (*yogāt*, *yogena* and *yoga-tas*, ifc. in consequence of, on account of, by reason of, according to, through), KātyŚr.; ŚvetUp.; Mn. &c.; putting together, arrangement, disposition, regular succession, Kāṭh.; ŚrS.; fitting together, fitness, propriety, suitability (*yogena* and *yoga-tas*, ind. suitably, fitly, duly, in the right manner), MBh.; Kāv. &c.; exertion, endeavour, zeal, diligence, industry, care, attention (*yoga-tas*, ind. strenuously, assiduously; *pūrṇena yogena*, with all one's powers, with overflowing zeal), Mn.; MBh. &c.; application or concentration of the thoughts, abstract contemplation, meditation, (esp.) self-concentration, abstract meditation and mental abstraction practised as a system (as taught by Patañjali and called the Yoga philosophy; it is the second of the two Sāṃkhya systems, its chief aim being to teach the means by which the human spirit may attain complete union with Īśvara or the Supreme Spirit; in the practice of self-concentration it is closely connected with Buddhism), Up.; MBh.; Kāv. &c. (IW. 92); any simple act or rite conducive to Yoga or abstract meditation, Sarvad.; Yoga personified (as the son of Dharma and Kriyā), BhP.; a follower of the Yoga system, MBh.; Śaṃk.; (in Sāṃkhya) the union of soul with matter (one of the 10 Mūlikârthās or radical facts), Tattvas.; (with Pāśupatas) the union of the individual soul with the universal soul, Kulârṇ.; (with Pāñcarātras) devotion, pious seeking after God, Sarvad.; (with Jainas) contact or mixing with the outer world, ib.; (in astron.) conjunction, lucky conjuncture, Lāṭy.; VarBṛS.; MBh. &c.; a constellation, asterism (these, with the moon, are called *cāndra-yogāḥ* and are 13 in number; without the moon they are called *kha-yogāḥ* or *nābhasa-yogāḥ*), VarBṛS.; the leading or principal star of a lunar asterism, W.; N. of a variable division of time (during which the joint motion in longitude of the sun and moon amounts to 13° 20′; there are 27 such Yogas beginning with Vishkambha and ending with Vaidhṛiti), ib.; (in arith.) addition, sum, total, Sūryas.; MBh.; (in gram.) the connection of words together, syntactical dependence of a word, construction, Nir.; Suśr. (ifc. = dependent on, ruled by, Pāṇ. ii, 2, 8, Vārtt. 1); a combined or concentrated grammatical rule or aphorism, Pāṇ., Sch.; Siddh. (cf. *yoga-vibhāga*); the connection of a word with its root, original or etymological meaning (as opp. to *rūḍhi*, q. v.), Nir.; Pratāp.; KātyŚr., Sch.; a violator of confidence, spy, L.; N. of a Sch. on the Paramârthasāra; (*ā*), f. N. of a Śakti, Pañcar.; of Pīvarī (daughter of the Pitṛis called Barhishads), Hariv. **–kakshā,** f. = *-paṭṭa*, q. v., BhP. **–kanyā,** f. N. of the infant daughter of Yaśo-dā (substituted as the child of Devakī for the infant Kṛishṇa and therefore killed by Kaṃsa, but immediately raised to heaven as a beautiful girl), Hariv. **–kara,** m. a partic. Samādhi, Kāraṇḍ. **–karaṇḍaka,** m. N. of a minister of Brahma-datta, Kathās.; (*ikā*), f. N. of a female religious mendicant, ib. **–kalpa-druma,** m., **-kalpa-latā,** f. N. of wks. **–kuṇḍalinī** or **-kuṇḍalyupanishad,** f. N. of an Upanishad. **–kshemá,** m. sg. and pl. (in later language also m. du. and n. sg.) the security or secure possession of what has been acquired, the keeping safe of property, welfare, prosperity, substance, livelihood, RV. &c. &c. (generally explained as a Dvaṃdva meaning 'acquisition and preservation of property,' cf. *kshema-yoga*; °*maṃ* √*vah* with dat. = to procure any one a livelihood, support, maintain, Śak.); the charge for securing property (from accidents), insurance, Mn. vii, 127; property destined for pious uses and sacrifices, Gaut. xxviii, 46; Mn. ix, 219 (others 'the means of securing protection, i. e. councillors, family priests and the like'); *-kara*, mfn. causing gain and security, causing protection of what is acquired, one who takes charge of property, MBh.; R.; *-vat*, mfn. possessing property which is designed for pious purposes, L.; *-vaha* (R.), *-samarpitṛi* (MBh.), mfn. offering or procuring sustenance or a livelihood. **–gati,** f. state of union, the being united together, BhP. **–gāmin,** mfn. going (through the air) by means of magical power, VP. **–grantha,** m. N. of two wks. **–cakshus,** mfn. 'contemplation-eyed,' one whose eye is meditation (N. of Brahmā), MārkP. **–candra-ṭīkā,** f., **-candrikā,** f. (and °*kā-vilāsa*, m.) N. of wks. **–cara,** m. N. of Hanumat, L. **–caryā,** f., **-cikitsā,** f., **-cintāmaṇi,** m., **-cūḍāmaṇi,** m., °**nyupanishad** or **-cūḍôpanishad,** f. N. of wks. **–cūrṇa,** n. magical powder, Daś.; Mudr. **–ja,** mfn. produced by or arising from Yoga or meditation, Bhāshāp.; n. agallochum, Bhpr. **–jñāna,** n. N. of wk. **–tattva,** n. the principle of Yoga, YogatUp.; N. of an Upanishad (also °*tvôpanishad*, f.); *-prakāśa* or

°*śaka,* m. N. of wk. **-tantra,** n. a wk. treating of the Yoga philosophy, Hariv.; BhP.; (with Buddhists) N. of a class of writings. **-taraṃga,** m., **-taraṃgiṇī,** f. N. of wks. **-talpa,** n. 'Yoga-couch,' = *-nidrā,* q.v., BhP. **-tas,** ind. conjointly, W.; suitably, properly, Mn.; conformably to, in accordance with, by means of, in consequence of (comp.), Ragh.; Kathās.; with application of effort, with all one's powers, Mn. ii, 100; seasonably, in due season, W.; through devotion, by the power of magic &c., ib. **-tārakā** (Sūryas.; VarBṛS.) or **-tārā** (Sūryas.; Col.), f. the chief star in a Nakshatra; °*râvalī,* f. N. of sev. wks. **-tva,** n. the state of Yoga, Sarvad. **-daṇḍa,** m. a magic wand, Siṇhâs. **-darpaṇa,** m. N. of wk. **-dāna,** n. gift of the Y°, communicating the Y° doctrine, W.; a fraudulent gift; *-pratigraha,* n. a fraudulent gift or acceptance, Mn. viii, 165. **-dīpikā,** f., **-dṛishṭi-samuccaya-vyākhyā,** f. N. of wks. **-deva,** m. N. of a Jaina author, Sarvad. **-dharmin,** mfn. doing homage to the Y°, MBh.; Hariv. &c. **-dhāraṇā,** f. continuance or perseverance in meditation, Bhag.; BhP. **-nanda,** m. the false Nanda, Kathās. **-nātha,** m. 'Yoga-lord,' N. of Śiva, Cat.; of Datta, BhP. **-nāvika,** m. a kind of fish, L. **-nidrā,** f. 'meditation-sleep,' a state of half med° half sleep (which admits of the full exercise of the mental powers; it is peculiar to devotees), light sleep, (esp.) the sleep of Vishṇu at the end of a Yuga, V°'s Sleep personified as a goddess and said to be a form of Durgā, MBh.; Ragh. &c.; (accord. to others) the great sleep of Brahmā during the period between the annihilation and reproduction of the universe, MW. **-nidrālu,** m. N. of Vishṇu, L. **-nilaya,** m. N. of Śiva, Śivag. **-m-dhara,** m. N. of a partic. magical formula recited over weapons, R. (v. l. *yaugaṃdh*°); N. of various men, Kathās.; Buddh. **-nyāsa,** m. N. of wk. **-paṭṭa** (Hcat.; PadmaP.) or **-paṭṭaka** (Hcar.; PadmaP.), m. the cloth thrown over the back and knees of a devotee during meditation. **-pati,** m. 'Yoga-lord,' N. of Vishṇu, Pañcar. **-patnī,** f. 'wife of Y°,' N. of Pivarī (also called *yogā* and *yoga-mātṛi*), Hariv. **-patha,** m. the road leading to Y°, BhP. **-pada,** n. a state of self-concentration or meditation, DhyānabUp. **-padaka,** n., w. r. for *-paṭṭaka,* q.v., L. **-paddhati,** f. N. of wk. **-pātañjala,** m. a follower of Patañjali as teacher of the Yoga doctrine, Madhus. **-pādukā,** f. a magical shoe (supposed to carry the wearer wherever he wishes), Siṇhâs. **-pāraṃ-ga,** m. 'conversant with Y°,' N. of Śiva, Śivag. **-pīṭha,** n. a partic. posture during religious meditation, Pañcar.; KālP. **-prakāra,** m., **-prakāśa-ṭīkā,** f., **-pradīpa,** m., °**pikā,** f., **-praveśa-vidhi,** m. N. of wks. **-prâpta,** mfn. obtained through abstract meditation, MW. **-bala,** n. the force of devotion, the power of magic, supernatural p°, R.; BrahmaP.; Kathās. **-bindu-ṭippaṇa,** m. or n. (?), **-bīja,** n., **-bhadrā,** f. N. of wks. **-bhāraka,** m. a shoulder-yoke for carrying burdens, Hcar. **-bhāvanā,** f. (in alg.) composition of numbers by the sum of the products, Col. **-bhāshya,** n., **-bhāskara,** m. N. of wks. **-bhrashṭa,** mfn. one who has fallen from the practice of Yoga or self-concentration, ĀpŚr., Comm. **-mañjarī,** **-maṇi-pradīpikā,** **-maṇi-prabhā,** f. N. of wks. **-maya,** mf(*ī*)n. resulting from self-c° or Yoga, MBh.; Pañcar.; BhP.; m. N. of Vishṇu, Pañcar.; *-jñāna,* n. knowledge derived from self-c° or meditation, Hariv. **-mahiman,** m. N. of sev. wks. **-mātṛi,** f. the mother of Yoga, MārkP.; N. of Pivarī, Hariv. **-māyā,** f. magic, Kathās.; the Māyā or magical power of abstract meditation, BhP.; the power of God in the creation of the world personified as a deity; N. of Durgā, A. **-mārga,** m. = *-patha,* q.v., Śiś.; Bādar., Sch. **-mārtaṇḍa,** m., **-mālā,** f., **-muktâvalī,** f. N. of wks. **-mūrti-dhara,** m. pl. 'bearing the form of the Yoga,' N. of a class of deceased ancestors, MārkP. **-yājñavalkya,** n., °**kya-gītā,** f., °**kya-smṛiti,** f. N. of wks. **-yātrā,** f. the road or way to union with the Supreme Spirit, the way of profound meditation, Bhartṛ.; N. of an astrological wk. by Varāha-mihira; of another wk. **-yukta,** mfn. immersed in deep meditation, absorbed in Yoga, MBh.; Pañcat. &c. **-yukti,** f. the being absorbed in Yoga, Kāśīkh. **-yuj,** mfn. one who has given himself to Yoga, VP. **-yogin,** mfn. = *-yukta* above, MBh. **-raṅga,** m. the orange tree, L. **-ratna,** n. a magical jewel, Cat.; N. of a wk. on med.; *-mālā,* f., *-samuccaya,* m.; °*nâkara,* m., °*nâvalī,* f. N. of wks. **-ratha,** m. the Yoga as a vehicle, BhP. **-rasâyana,** n., **-rahasya,** n. N. of wks. **-rāja,** m. 'king of medicines,' N. of a partic. med° preparation, Car.; Bhpr. &c.; a king or master in the Y°, Cat.; N. of various learned men and authors, Śrīkaṇṭh. &c.; *-guggulu,* m. a partic. med° preparation, Bhpr.; °*jôpanishad,* f. N. of an Upanishad. **-rūḍha,** mfn. having a special as well as etymological and general meaning (said of certain words, e.g. *paṅka-ja* means 'growing in mud' and 'a lotus-flower'), Bhāshāp., Sch.; *-tā,* f., KapS., Sch. **-rūḍhi-vāda,** m., **-rūḍhi-vicāra,** m. N. of wks. **-rocanā,** f. N. of a kind of magical ointment (making invisible or invulnerable), Mṛicch. **-rddhi-rūpa-vat** (*yoga* + *ṛiddhi-r*°), mfn. having the embodied form of the perfect Yoga, MBh. **-vat,** mfn. connected, united, joined, MārkP.; one who applies himself to contemplation or Yoga, Hariv. **-varṇana,** n. N. of wk. **-vartikā,** f. a magical wick, Daś. **-vaha,** mfn. (ifc.) bringing about, promoting, furthering, MBh. **-vācaspatya,** n., **-vārttika,** n. N. of wks. **-vāsishṭha,** n. N. of a wk. (also called Vāsishṭha-rāmāyaṇa, in the form of a dialogue between Vasishṭha and his pupil Rāma, treating of the way of obtaining happiness, cf. IW. 368); *-tātparya-prakāśa,* m., *-śāstra,* n., *-saṃkshepa,* m., *-sāra,* m., *-sāra-candrikā,* f., *-sāra-vivṛiti,* f., *-sāra-saṃgraha,* m. N. of wks. **-vāsishṭhīya,** mfn. relating to the Yoga-vāsishṭha, Cat. **-vāha,** m., w. r. for *a-y*°, q.v., VPrāt.; (*ī*), f. alkali, L.; honey, L.; quicksilver, L. **-vāhaka,** mfn. resolving (chemically), L. **-vāhin,** mfn. receiving into or assimilating to one's self, Bhpr.; (perhaps) contriving artifices, plotting (°*hi-tva,* n.), Rājat.; n. a menstruum or medium for mixing medicines, Suśr. **-vikraya,** m. a fraudulent sale, W. **-vicāra,** m. N. of a ch. of the Kāśi-khaṇḍa. **-vid,** mfn. knowing the right means or proper method, knowing what is fit or suitable, Hariv.; R. &c.; conversant with the Yoga, MBh.; BhP. &c.; m. N. of Śiva, Śivag.; a follower of the Y° doctrines; a practiser of abstract meditation; a magician; a compounder of medicines, W. **-vidyā,** f. knowledge of the Y°, the science of Y°, Prasannar. **-vibhāga,** m. the disuniting or separation of that which is usually combined, the sep° of one grammatical rule into two, making two rules of what might be stated as one, Pāṇ., Sch. **-viveka,** m. (and °*ka-ṭippaṇa*), **-vishaya,** m., **-vṛitti-saṃgraha,** m., **-śata,** n., **-śataka,** n., °**ka-vyākhyāna,** n., °**kâkhyāna,** n. N. of wks. **-śabda,** m. the word Yoga, Sarvad.; a word the meaning of which is plain from the etymology, Kāś. **-śarīrin,** mfn. (one) whose body is Y°, MBh. **-śâyin,** mfn. half asleep and h° absorbed in meditation, Rājat. **-śāstra,** n. any wk. on the Y° doctrine (esp. that of Patañjali), MBh.; Yājñ. &c.; N. of sev. wks.; *-pattra,* n. pl., *-sūtra-pāṭha,* m. N. of wks. **-śikshā,** f. N. of wk.; °*kshôpanishad,* f. = next. **-śikhā** or **-śikhôpanishad,** f. N. of an Upanishad. **-saṃsiddhi,** f. perfection in Y°, Bhag. **-saṃgraha,** m. N. of sev. wks. **-samādhi,** m. absorption of the mind in profound meditation peculiar to the Yoga system, Ragh. **-sāgara,** m., **-sādhana,** n. N. of wks. **-sāra,** m. or n. (?) a universal remedy, GāruḍaP.; Bhpr.; N. of sev. wks.; *-tantra,* n., *-saṃgraha,* m., *-samuccaya,* m.; °*râvali,* f., °*râvalī,* f. N. of wks. **-siddha,** mfn. perfected by means of Y°, BhP.; Col.; m. N. of an author, Cat.; (*ā*), f. N. of a sister of Bṛihas-pati, VP.; °*dhānta-candrikā,* f., °*ta-paddhati,* f. N. of wks. **-siddhi,** f. simultaneous accomplishment, Jaim.; *-prakriyā,* f. N. of wk.; *-mat,* mfn. experienced in the art of magic, Kathās. **-sudhâkara,** m., **-sudhānidhi,** m. N. of wks. **-sūtra,** n. the aphorisms of the Y° system of philosophy ascribed to Patañjali; *-gūḍhârtha-dyotikā,* f., *-candrikā,* f., *-bhāshya,* n., *-vṛitti,* f., *-vyākhyāna,* n.; °*rârtha-candrikā,* f. N. of wks. relating to the Yoga-sūtra. **-sevā,** f. the practice or cultivation of religious abstraction, Bhag.; YogatUp. **-stha,** mfn. absorbed in Y°, Bhag. **-svarôdaya,** m. N. of wk. **-svāmin,** m. a master in the Y°, Hcat. **-hṛidaya,** n. N. of wk. **Yogâkshara-nighaṇṭu,** m., **yogâkhyāna,** n. N. of wks. **Yogâgni-maya,** mfn. filled with the fire of the Y°, attained through the ardour of devotion, ŚvetUp. **Yogâṅga,** n. a constituent or part of the Y°, means of attaining it (generally said to be 8 in number, viz. *yama, niyama, āsana, prâṇâyāma, pratyāhāra, dhāraṇā, dhyāna,* and *samādhi,* or according to another authority 6, viz. *āsana, prâṇa-saṃrodha,* with the last four as enumerated above), Yogas.; Sarvad. **Yogâcāra,** m. the observance of the Y°, Cat.; a partic. Samādhi, Kāraṇḍ.; N. of wk.; = *yogin,* q.v., L.; a follower of a partic. Buddhist sect or school; pl. the disciples of that school, Buddh. &c.; *-bhūmi-śāstra,* n. (for *yogâcārya-bh*°) N. of wk. **Yogâcārya,** m. a teacher of the Y° system of philosophy, MBh.; Hariv.; BhP.; a teacher of the art of magic (also said to be a t° of the art of thieving), Mṛicch.; w. r. for *yogâcāra* above. **Yogâñjana,** n. a healing ointment, Suśr.; the Y° as a h° ointment, Prab.; N. of wk. **Yogâtman,** mfn. (one) whose soul or essence is Y° or who fixes his mind on Y°, MBh. **Yogâdhamana-vikrīta,** n. a fraudulent pledge or sale, Mn. viii, 165. **Yogâdhikāra,** m. N. of wk. **Yogânanda,** m. 'delight of the Y°,' N. of two authors, Cat.; w. r. for *yoga-nanda,* Vās., Introd.; *-prahasana,* n. N. of wk. **Yogânugatā,** f. N. of a Kiṃ-nara maid, Kāraṇḍ. **Yogânuśāsana,** n. 'Y°-instruction,' the doctrine of the Y° by Patañjali, Madhus.; N. of two wks.; *-sūtra,* n., °*tra-vṛitti,* f. N. of wks. **Yogânta** (in comp.) or °**gântikā,** f. (scil. *gati*) N. of the 7 divisions into which (accord. to Parāśara) the orbit of Mercury is divided, VarBṛS. **Yogâpatti,** f. modification of usage or application, ĀśvŚr. **Yogâbhyāsa-krama,** m., °**sa-prakaraṇa,** n., °**sa-lakshaṇa,** n., **yogâmṛita,** n., °**ta-taraṃgiṇī,** f. N. of wks. **Yogâmbara,** m. N. of a Buddhist deity, W. **Yogâyoga,** m. pl. a proper quantity, Suśr. (v. l.); du. suitableness and unsuitableness, Kāvyâd. **Yogâraṅga,** m. = *yoga-raṅga,* q.v., L. **Yogârūḍha,** mfn. absorbed in profound or abstract meditation, NṛisUp. **Yogârṇava,** m., °**gâvali,** f., °**valī,** f., °**lī-jātaka,** n., °**lī-tantre kula-dīpinī,** f. N. of wks. **Yogâvāpa,** m. the first attitude of an archer, L. **Yogâsana,** n. a mode of sitting suited to profound meditation or similar to that of the Yoga, Amṛit-Up.; Bhaṭṭ. &c.; *-lakshaṇa,* n. pl. N. of wk. **Yogêndra,** m. a master or adept in the Yoga, W. **Yogêśa,** m. id., BhP.; N. of Yājñavalkya, L.; of Śiva, W.; of the city of Brahmā, L.; °*śârṇava,* m., °*śī-sahasra-nāma-stotra,* n. N. of wks. **Yogêśvara,** m. a master in magical art (said of a Vetāla), Kathās.; a master or adept in the Yoga, MBh.; Hariv.; Pañcat. &c.; a deity, the object of devout contemplation, W.; N. of Kṛishṇa, MW.; of Yājñavalkya, Cat.; of a son of Deva-hotra, BhP.; of a Brahma-rākshasa, Kathās.; of various authors and learned men, Cat. &c.; of wk.; (*ī*), f. a fairy, Rājat.; Kathās.; a mistress or adept in the Yoga, Kathās.; a form of Durgā, Hcat.; a species of plant, Bhpr.; N. of a goddess, Cat.; of a Vidyā-dharī, Kathās.; *-tīrtha,* n. N. of a Tīrtha, Cat.; *-tva,* n. mastery of the Y°, MBh.; BhP.; *-paddhati,* f., *-mantra,* m. N. of wks. **Yogêshṭa,** n. tin, L.; lead, L. **Yogâiśvarya,** n. mastery of the Y°, BhP. **Yogôdvahana,** n. support (with food and clothes), Divyâv. **Yogôpadeśa,** m., °**panishad,** f. N. of wks.

Yogas, n. meditation, religious abstraction, Uṇ. iv, 215, Sch.; the half of a lunar month, ib.

Yogāya, Nom. Ā. °*yate,* to become Yoga, to be changed into religious contemplation or devotion, Cat.

1. **Yogi** (m.c.) = *yogin* (only in gen. pl. *yoginām*).

2. **Yogi,** in comp. for *yogin.* **-tā,** f. the being connected with (ifc.), connection, relation, Bhāshāp.; the state or condition of a Yogī (cf. *yogin*), MW. **-tva,** n. = prec., Sāh.; MārkP. **-daṇḍa,** m. a kind of reed or cane (= *vetra*), L. **-nidrā,** f. 'a Yogī's sleep,' light sleep, wakefulness, W. **-patnī** and **-mātṛi,** v. l. for *yoga-p*° and *-m*° (q.v.), Hariv. **-bhaṭṭa,** m. N. of an author, Cat. **-mārga,** m. 'a Y°'s path,' the air, atmosphere, Gal. **-yājñavalkya** = *yoga-yā*°, q.v. **-rāj,** m. a king among Y°s, Cat. **Yogîndra,** m. id., Kathās.; N. of Yājñavalkya, Yājñ.; of Vālmīki, Bālar. **Yogîśa,** m. a king among Y°s, MārkP.; N. of Yājñavalkya, L. **Yogîśvara,** m. = prec., Kāv.; Yājñ.; a master in sorcery, Kathās.; (*ī*), f. N. of a goddess, Cat. **Yogîshṭa,** n. lead, L.

Yogita, mfn. bewitched, enchanted, mad, crazy, wild, L.

Yogin, mfn. joined or connected with, relating to, accompanied by, possessed of (comp.), KātyŚr.; MBh.; Hariv.; being in conjunction with (e.g. *candra-y*°), MārkP.; possessed of superhuman powers, W.; m. a follower of the Yoga system, a Yogin (usually called Yogī) or contemplative saint, devotee, ascetic, MaitrUp.; Bhag. &c. (cf. RTL. 87);

a magician, conjurer, W.; a partic. mixed caste, Cat. (v.l. *yuṅgin*); an orange tree, L.; natron, alkali, L.; N. of Yājñavalkya, Cat.; of Arjuna, L.; of Vishṇu, MBh.; of Śiva, L.; of a Buddha, L.; (*inī*), f., see next.

Yoginī, f. a female demon or any being endowed with magical power, a fairy, witch, sorceress (represented as eight in number and as created by Durgā and attendant on her or on Śiva; sometimes 60, 64 or 65 are enumerated), Hariv.; Kathās. &c. (cf. RTL. 188, 189); N. of Durgā, L.; (with Tāntrikas) a partic. Śakti; (with Buddhists) a woman representing any goddess who is the object of adoration. **— cakra-pūjana**, n., **-jātaka**, n., **-jāla-śambara**, n., **-jñānârṇava**, m., **-tantra**, n. N. of wks. **— daśā**, f. state or condition of a Yoginī; *-krama*, m., *-cintāmaṇi*, m., *-jñāna*, n., *-°dhyāya* (*°śādh°*), m., *-prakaraṇa*, n., *-vicāra*, m. N. of wks. **— pura**, n. N. of a city, Siṉhās. **— bhairava-tantra**, n., **-sādhana**, n., **-stava-rāja**, m., **-hṛidaya**, n. and **°ya-setu-bandha**, m. N. of wks.

Yoginy, in comp. for *yoginī*. **— ashṭa-daśā-krama**, m., **-ādi-pūjana-vidhi**, m. N. of wks.

Yogīya, Nom. Ā. *°yate*, to regard or treat as Yoga, Cat.

Yógya, mfn. (fr. *yoga* and √1. *yuj*) fit for the yoke, Pāṇ. v, 1, 102; belonging to a partic. remedy, ŚārṅgS.; useful, serviceable, proper, fit or qualified for, able or equal to, capable of (gen., loc., dat., inf. with act. or pass. sense, or comp.), KātyŚr.; MBh.; Kāv. &c.; perceptible, Kap.; fit for Yoga, proper for religious meditation, L.; m. a draught animal, AV.; ŚBr.; a calculator of expedients, W.; the constellation Pushya, L.; (*ā*), f. preparation, contrivance, RV.; exercise, practice, (esp.) bodily exercise, gymnastics, drill, MBh.; Kāv.; Suśr.; (pl.) the straps with which horses are attached to the yoke of a carriage, traces (?), RV. iii, 3, 6; the earth, L.; N. of Bharaṇī, L.; of the wife of Sūrya, L.; n. (only L.) a vehicle or any machine; a cake; sandal; a kind of drug. **— tā**, f. suitableness, fitness, propriety, ability, R.; Kathās. &c.; *-grantha rahasya*, n., *-pūrva-paksha-rahasya*, n., *-rahasya*, n., *-vāda*, m., *-vicāra*, m. N. of wks. **— tva**, n. = *-tā*, Kap.; Vedântas. **— viśesha-guṇa-vicāra**, m. N. of wk. **Yogyânupalabdhi-rahasya**, n. or **°dhi-vāda**, m. N. of wks. **Yogyā-ratha**, m. a carriage employed in military exercises, L.

Yojaka, m. a yoker, harnesser, MBh.; BhP.; a user, employer, Kāv.; an arranger, preparer, contriver, effecter (cf. *yuddha-y°*); N. of Agni (as the nuptial fire), Gṛihyas.

Yójana, n. joining, yoking, harnessing, PārGṛ.; Hariv.; that which is yoked or harnessed, a team, vehicle (also applied to the hymns and prayers addressed to the gods), RV.; course, path, ib.; (sometimes m.; ifc. f. *ā*) a stage or Yojana (i.e. a distance traversed in one harnessing or without unyoking; esp. a partic. measure of distance, sometimes regarded as equal to 4 or 5 English miles, but more correctly = 4 Krośas or about 9 miles; according to other calculations = 2½ English miles, and according to some = 8 Krośas), RV. &c. &c.; instigation, stimulation, Sāh.; mental concentration, abstraction, directing the thoughts to one point (= *yoga*), Up.; the Supreme Spirit of the Universe (= *paramâtman*), L.; a finger, L.; n. and (*ā*), f. use, application, arrangement, preparation, RV.; KātyŚr.; MBh.; Sāh.; erecting, constructing, building, Rājat.; Kathās.; junction, union, combination, Sāh.; Vedântas.; (*ā*), f. application of the sense of a passage, grammatical construction, Śaṃk. **— gandhā**, f. 'diffusing scent or fragrance to the distance of a Yojana,' musk, L.; N. of Satya-vatī (mother of Vyāsa), MBh.; Kād. (also *°dhikā*, L.); of Sītā, L. **— parṇī**, f. Rubia Munjista, L. **— bāhu**, m. 'having arms a Y° long,' N. of Rāvaṇa, Mcar.; Kād. **— bhāj**, mfn. effective at the distance of a Y°, AV.Pariś. **— vallikā** or **-vallī**, f. Rubia Munjista, L. **— śata**, n. a hundred Yojanas, MW.

Yojanaka, mfn. (ifc., f. *ikā*) = next (cf. *pada-yojanikā*).

Yojanika, mfn. (ifc. after a numeral) so many Yojanas long, measuring so many Yojanas, R.

Yojanīya, mfn. to be joined or united with (instr.; with *karmaṇā*, to be set at work, Kām.; with *mṛishā-doshaiḥ*, to accuse falsely, Bālar.); to be used or employed, Kāv.; to be grammatically corrected or arranged, MaitrUp., Sch.; n. it is to be connected with or thought of in connection with (instr.), Sāy.

Yojanya. See *shashṭi-yojanya*.

Yojayitavya, mfn. (fr. Caus. of √1. *yuj*) to be joined or connected or furnished with (instr.), Sāṃkhyak., Sch.; to be made use of or chosen or selected, VarBṛS.

Yojayitṛi, mfn. one who joins or connects &c.; m. a setter (of precious stones), Pañcat.

Yojita, mfn. yoked, harnessed, BhP.; used, employed, applied, performed, MBh.; undertaken, begun, Yājñ.; appointed to, charged with (loc.), BhP.; tied or fastened to, put or placed in (loc.), ib.; joined, connected, put together, arranged, composed, MBh.; R.; supplied or furnished with (instr. or comp.), VarBṛS.; Rājat.

Yojitṛi, mfn. (√1. *yuj*) one who joins or unites or connects, VarBṛS.

Yojya, mfn. (√1. *yuj*) to be joined or united &c.; to be fixed on or directed to (loc.), Pañcat.; (ifc.) to be appointed to or entrusted with, Pañcat.; (ifc.) to be led towards or urged to, R.; to be used or employed or set to work, Yājñ.; Var. &c.; to be pronounced or uttered, Śak. (v.l.); to be added to (loc.), Sūryas.; Kām.; to be supplied or furnished with (instr.), MBh.; R.; to be shared in, MW.; to be connected or construed, Ml.; one on whom the mind is to be fixed or concentrated, MBh. (Nīlak.)

योटक *yoṭaka*, m. a combination of stars &c., constellation, L.

योतवे *yótave*, *°tavaí*, *°tos*. See √1. *yu*.

योतिमत्सक *yotimatsaka*, m. pl. N. of a people, MBh.

योतु *yotu*, m. (√2. *yu* ?) = *parimāṇa*, L.; (1. *yu*?) cleaning, purifying, W.

योत्र *yotra*, n. (√2. *yu*) = *yoktra*, a fastening, tie, rope, R.; the cord that fastens the yoke of a plough to the neck of an ox, L.

योत्रप्रमाद *yotra-pramāda*, m. (= *yo 'tra pr°*?) a proper N., Cat.

योद्धव्य *yoddhavya*, *yoddhṛi*. See p. 855, col. 2.

योध *yodhá*, m. (accord. to Gaṇar. ii, 26 also n.) a fighter, warrior, soldier, RV. &c. &c. (with *vṛishaḥ*, a bull trained or fit for war, VarBṛS.); battle, war (see *dur-* and *mitho-y°*); a kind of metre, Col.; pl. the third astrological mansion, VarYogay. **— dharma**, m. the law of soldiers, duty of the Kshatriya caste, Mn. vii, 98. **— mukhya**, m. a chief warrior, leader, Bhag. **— vīra**, m. a hero, warrior, ib. **— samrāva**, m. challenging to battle, mutual defiance of combatants, L. **— hara**, mfn. carrying soldiers, W. **Yodhâgāra**, m. a soldier's dwelling, barrack, MBh.

Yodhaka, m. = *yodha*, a fighter, warrior, MBh.; R.

Yodhana, n. the act of fighting, battle, war, MBh.; Pur.; battle-cry, L. **— pura-tīrtha**, n. N. of a Tīrtha, Cat.

Yodhanī-pura, n. N. of a town, Cat.

Yodhanīya, mfn. to be fought or overcome, Bālar.

Yodhika, n. a partic. mode of fighting, Hariv. (v.l. *yaudhika*).

Yodhin, mfn. (ifc.) fighting, combating, MBh.; R.; m. a warrior, conqueror, ib.

Yodhi-vana, n. N. of a place, R.

Yódhīyas, mfn. more warlike or martial, RV.

Yodheya, m. a warrior, combatant, L.; N. of a race, Hariv. (v.l. *yaudheya*).

Yódhya, mfn. to be fought or overcome or subdued, RV.; MBh. (cf. *a-y°*); m. pl. N. of a people, MBh.

योनल *yonala*, m. = *yava-nāla*, L.

योनि *yóni*, m. f. (in RV. only m.; f. sometimes also *yonī*; fr. √2. *yu*) the womb, uterus, vulva, vagina, female organs of generation, RV. &c. &c. (together with the *liṅga*, a typical symbol of the divine procreative energy, RTL. 224); place of birth, source, origin, spring, fountain (ifc. = sprung or produced from), ib.; place of rest, repository, receptacle, seat, abode, home, lair, nest, stable, RV.; AV.; ŚBr.; family, race, stock, caste, the form of existence or station fixed by birth (e.g. that of a man, Brāhman, animal &c.; ifc. = belonging to the caste of), Mn.; MBh. &c.; seed, grain (cf. *yoni-poshaṇa*); a partic. part of a fire-pit, Hcat.; a mine, L.; copper, L.; water, Naigh.; the regent of the Nakshatra Pūrva-phalgunī, VarBṛS.; N. of the sound *e*, Up.; of a partic. verse or formula, KātyŚr.; (*ī*), f. N. of a river in Śālmala-dvīpa, VP. **— kuṇḍa**, n. N. of a partic. mystical diagram, Cat. **— gāna**, n. N. of the first part of the Sāma-saṃhitā, Nyāyam., Sch. **— guṇa**, m. the property of a womb, quality of a place of origin, MW. **— grantha**, m. = *-gāna*, Nyāyam., Sch. **— cikitsā**, f. N. of wk. **— ja**, mfn. produced from the womb, viviparous, MBh.; R. &c. **— tantra**, n. N. of wk. **— tás**, ind. out of a place of rest or stable, MaitrS. **— tva**, n. the being an origin or source, NṛisUp.; Kum.; (ifc.) the arising from or being based on, Suśr.; Sarvad. **— dushṭā**, f. pl. sexually defiled (said of women), Hariv. **— devatā**, f. N. of the Nakshatra Pūrva-phalgunī, L. **— deśa**, m. the region of the womb or the generative organs, MW. **— dosha**, m. sexual defilement, Hariv.; a defect of the female organ; *-cikitsā*, f. N. of wk. **— dvāra**, n. the orifice of the womb, Suśr.; N. of a sacred bathing-place, MBh. **— nāsā**, f. the upper part of the female organ, W. **— niraya**, m. the womb compared to a hell, Hcat. **— poshaṇa**, n. the growing of seed or grain, Vishṇ. **— bhraṇśa**, m. fall of the w°, prolapsus uteri, Suśr. **— mat** (*yóni-*), mfn. connected with the womb, TBr.; Kāṭh.; sprung from a womb, MaitrS.; descended from a good race, Hcat. **— mantra**, m. the text VS. viii, 29, Hcat. **— mukta**, mfn. released from birth or from being born again, ŚvetUp. **— mukha**, n. the orifice of the womb, Suśr. **— mudrā**, f. N. of a partic. position of the fingers, L. **— rañjana**, n. the menstrual excretion, W. **— roga**, m. disease of the female organs of generation, Suśr. **— liṅga**, n. the clitoris, L. **— vyāpad**, f. N. of wk. **— śas**, ind. fundamentally, thoroughly, Lalit.; wisely, Divyâv. **— śāstra**, n. N. of a class of wks., VP. **— saṃvaraṇa**, n. (Bhpr.), **-saṃvṛiti**, f. (W.) contraction of the vagina. **— saṃkaṭa**, n. 'passage through the womb,' re-birth, MBh. **— saṃkara**, m. 'confusion of births,' mixture of caste by unlawful marriage, misalliance, Mn.; R. **— sambandha**, m. a blood-relation, Āpast. **— sambhava**, mfn. = *-ja*, Cat. **— ha**, mfn. injuring the womb, MantraBr. **Yony-arśas**, n. a fleshy excrescence in the female organ (= *kanda*), L.

Yonika. See *a-yonika*.

Yonin (ifc.) = *yoni*, MBh.; Hariv. (cf. *nīca-y°*); n. (*Gṛitsamadasya yoninī dve*) N. of Sāmans.

Yonyá, mfn. forming a womb or receptacle, RV.

योपन *yopana*, *yoyupana*. See p. 855, col. 2.

योषणा *yóshaṇā* (once *yoshánā*), f. (prob. fr. √2. *yu*; cf. *yuvan*) a girl, maiden, young woman, wife, RV. (accord. to Sāy. also = *stuti*, a hymn, praise).

Yóshan, f. id., ib. (also applied to the fingers).

Yóshā, f. = *yoshaṇā*, RV. &c. &c. (esp. applied to Ushas; accord. to Sāy. also 'a mare'); (with *dāru-mayī*) a wooden doll, MBh.

Yoshij-jana, m. (fr. *yoshit* + *j°*) womenfolk, women, Ratnâv.

Yoshít, f. = *yoshaṇā* (also applied to the females of animals and to inanimate things, e.g. *yoshito mantrāḥ*, 'female magical texts'), RV. &c. &c. **— kṛita**, mfn. done by a woman, contracted by a female, W. **— pratiyātanā**, f. the image or statue of a woman, Ragh. **— priyā**, f. turmeric, Bhpr. **— sarpā**, f. a serpent-like woman, MW.

Yoshitā, f. a woman, wife, MuṇḍUp., Sch.

Yoshitvā, ind. (a kind of ind. p. fr. *yoshā* or *yoshit*) having made into a woman, BhP.

Yoshid, in comp. for *yoshit*. **— grāha**, m. one who takes the wife of a deceased man, Yājñ. **— ratna**, n. a jewel of a woman, a most excellent woman, MBh.

Yoshin-maya, mf(*ī*)n. formed like a woman, representing a woman, BhP.

योस् *yós*, ind. (only in *śám yóḥ* and *śáṃ ca yóś ca*) welfare, health, happiness, RV.

योहिभाष्य *yohi-bhāshya*, n. and *yohi-śikshā*, f. N. of wks.

योहुल *yohula* (?), m. N. of a man, Pravar.

यौकरीय *yaukarīya*, mfn. (fr. *yūkara*), g. *kriśâśvâdi*.

यौक्तस्रुच *yauktasruca*, n. (fr. *yukta* + *sruc*) N. of a Sāman, ĀrshBr.

Yauktāśva, n. N. of a Sāman, ĀrshBr.

यौक्तिक *yauktika*, mfn. (fr. *yukti*) suitable, proper, fit, logical, reasonable (*a-y°*), Kap.; connective, binding, W.; usual, customary, ib.; m. a king's companion or associate (= *narma-saciva*), L.

यौग 1. *yauga*, m. (fr. *yoga*) a follower of the Yoga system of philosophy, L.

2. **Yauga**, Vṛiddhi form of *yuga* in comp. **-m-dhara**, mfn. relating to Yugaṃ-dhara (also °*raka*), Pāṇ. iv, 2, 130. **-m-dharāyaṇa**, m. (fr. *yugaṃ-dhara* and *yogaṃ-dhara*) patr., Pravar. (cf. g. *naḍādi*); N. of a minister of king Udayana, Mṛicch.; Ratnâv.; Kathās.; °*ṇīya*, mfn. relating to Yaugaṃ-dharāyaṇa, Kathās. **-m-dhari**, m. a prince of the Yugaṃ-dharas, Pāṇ. iv, 1, 173, Sch. **-pada**, n. = next, BhP. **-padya**, n. (fr. *yuga-pad*) simultaneousness, ŚāṅkhŚr.; Sāh.; Pratāp. &c.; (*ena*), ind. simultaneously, together, MBh. **-varatra**, n. = *yuga-varatrāṇām samūhaḥ*, g. *khaṇḍikâdi*.

Yaugaka, mfn. (fr. *yoga*), Siddh.

Yaugika, mf(*ī*)n. (fr. *yoga*; cf. Pāṇ. v, 1, 102) useful, applicable (*a-y°*), Kām.; belonging to a remedy, remedial, Suśr.; connected with or suiting the derivation, having an etymological meaning (*yaugikī saṃjñā*, f. a word retaining that signification which belongs to it according to its etymology), Pratāp.; Sarvad.; relating to or derived from the Yoga, Pañcar. **-rūḍha**, mfn. (a word) which has both an etymological and a conventional meaning, Bhāshāp. (cf. *yoga-r°*). **-tva**, n. accordance (of the meaning of a word) with its derivation or etymology, L.

यौजनशतिक *yaujanaśatika*, mf(*ī*)n. (fr. *yojana* + *śata*) one who goes a hundred Yojanas, Pāṇ. v, 1, 74, Vārtt. 1, Pat.; one who deserves to be approached from a distance of a hundred Yojanas, ib., Vārtt. 2, Pat.

Yaujanika, mfn. going or extending a Yojana, Pāṇ. v, 1, 74.

यौट् *yauṭ* (v.l. *yauḍ*), cl. 1. P. *yauṭati*, to join or fasten together, Dhātup. ix, 2 (cf. *yoṭaka*).

यौतक *yautaka*, mf(*ī*)n. (fr. 1. *yutaka*) rightfully or exclusively belonging to any one, being the property of any one, MBh.; n. a present, Bhojapr.; private property, (esp.) property given at marriage, a woman's dowry, presents made to a bride at her marriage by her father and friends (accord. to some also 'a gift to the bridegroom'), Yājñ.; MBh.; Rājat.

Yautaki, m. patr. (f. °*kyā*), g. *krauḍy-ādi*.

Yautuka, n. = *yautaka*, Mn. ix, 131.

यौतव *yautava*, n. measure in general (= or v. l. for *pautava*, q. v.), L.

यौत्र *yautra*, n. = *yotra*, a tie, rope, Pat.

यौथिक *yauthika*, m. (fr. *yūtha*) 'belonging to a troop or herd,' a companion, comrade, BhP.

Yauthya, mfn., g. *saṃkāśâdi*.

यौध *yaudha*, mf(*ī*)n. (fr. *yodha*) warlike, martial, Lāṭy.

Yaudhājaya, n. N. of various Sāmans, Br.

Yaudhika. See *yodhika*, p. 858, col. 2.

Yaudhishṭhira, mf(*ī*)n. relating or belonging to Yudhi-shṭhira, MBh.; Sāh.; Rājat.; m. a descendant of Yudhi-shṭhira (also pl. and f. *ī*), MBh.; Hariv.

Yaudhishṭhiri, m., patr. fr. *yudhi-shṭhira*, MBh. (g. *bāhv-ādi*).

Yaudheya, m. (prob. fr. *yodha*) a warrior, soldier, L.; (pl.) N. of a warlike race, MBh.; Hariv. &c.; a king of the Yaudheyas (f. *ī*), Pāṇ. iv, 1, 178; N. of a son of Yudhi-shṭhira, MBh.

Yaudheyaka, m. pl. = *yaudheya*, VarBṛS.

यौन 1. *yauna*, mf(*ī*)n. (fr. *yoni*) relating to the womb or place of birth, uterine, W.; relating to or resulting from or connected by marriage, Mn.; MBh. &c.; n. matrimonial connection, conjugal alliance, relationship by marriage, ib.; the ceremony on conception (= *garbhâdhāna*), L.; matrimonial duties, Gobh., Sch.; (ifc.) produced from (e.g. *agni-y°*), MBh. **-sambandha**, m. relationship by marriage, affinity, MW.

Yaunika, m. moderate wind (neither too mild nor too strong), L.

यौन 2. *yauna*, m. pl. N. of a people (prob. = *yavana*), MBh.

यौप *yaupa*, mf(*ī*)n. relating to a sacrificial post, Bṛih.

Yaupya, mfn., g. *saṃkāśâdi*.

यौयुधानि *yauyudhāni*, m. patr. fr. *yuyudhāna*, MBh.

यौवत 1. *yauvata*, n. (fr. *yuvati*) a number of girls or young women, Gīt. (Pāṇ. iv, 2, 38).

Yauvateya, m. the son of a young woman, Vop.

यौवत 2. *yauvata* = *yautava*, L.

यौवन *yauvana*, n. (fr. *yuvan*) youth, youthfulness, adolescence, puberty, manhood (also pl. = juvenile deeds or indiscretions; ifc. f. *ā*), AV. &c. &c.; a number of young people (esp. of young women), Pāṇ. iv, 2, 38; N. of the third stage in the Śākta mysteries, Cat. **-kaṇṭaka**, m. n. an eruption or pimples on the face (esp. of young people), L. **-darpa**, m. juvenile pride or indiscretion, Hit. **-daśā**, f. the period of youth, ib. **-padavī**, f. the path of youth (°*vīm ārūḍhaḥ*, having entered on adolescence), Pañcat. **-piḍakā**, f. = *-kaṇṭaka*, Suśr. **-prânta**, m. the extreme verge or end of youth, ib. **-bhinna-śaiśava**, mfn. whose childhood is separated off by youth, passing from childhood to manhood, MW. **-mattā**, f. 'intoxicated with (the pride of) youth,' N. of a metre, Col. **-lakshaṇa**, n. 'sign of youth,' the female breast, L.; loveliness, grace, L. **-vat**, mfn. possessing youth, young, youthful, Vet.; Hit.; Kathās. **-śrī**, f. the beauty of youthfulness, Bhartṛ. **-sukha**, n. the joys of youth or of love, Mṛicch. **-stha**, mfn. being in the (bloom of) youth, arrived at puberty, marriageable, MBh. **Yauvanânta**, mfn. ending in youth, having youthfulness at the end, Kum. **Yauvanârambha**, m. the prime of youth, first bloom of youth, juvenility, Mālatīm. **Yauvanârūḍha**, mfn. one who has arrived at adolescence or puberty, Kathās. **Yauvanâvasthā**, f. the state of youth, youthfulness, puberty, MW. **Yauvanôdbheda**, m. the ardour of youthful passion, L.; the god of love, L.

Yauvanaka, n. = *yauvana*, g. *manojñâdi*.

Yauvanāśva, m. (fr. *yuvanāśva*) patr. of Māndhātṛi, Pravar.; MBh. &c.; of a grandson of Māndhātṛi, BhP. (accord. to Pāṇ. vi, 2, 107, Sch., fr. *yauvana* + *aśva*).

Yauvanāśvaka, m. patr. of Māndhātṛi, L.

Yauvanāśvi, m. id., MBh.; R.

Yauvanika, m. (?) and (*ā*), f. = *yauvana*, youth, L.

Yauvanin, mfn. youthful, Hariv.; MārkP.

Yauvanīya, mfn. youthful, juvenile (with *dvār*, f. the gates of youth or adolescence), Naish.

यौवराजिक *yauvarājika*, mf(*ā* or *ī*)n. (fr. *yuva-rāja*), g. *kāśy-ādi*.

Yauvarājya, n. (fr. *yuva-rāja*; ifc. f. *ā*) the rank or office or rights of an heir-apparent, the right of succession to a kingdom, MBh.; R. &c.

यौषिण्य *yaushiṇya*, n. (cf. *yoshan*) womanhood, BhP.

यौष्माक *yaushmāka*, mf(*ī*)n. (fr. *yushma*) your, yours, Kathās. (Pāṇ. iv, 3, 1; 2).

Yaushmākīna, mf(*ā*)n. id., HPariś. (Pāṇ. ib.)

य्वागुली *yvāgulī* or *yvāgulyā*, f. sour scum of boiled rice, L. (cf. *yavāgū*).

र RA.

र 1. *ra*, the 2nd semivowel (corresponding to the vowels *ṛi* and *ṝī*, and having the sound of *r* in *ring*). **-kāra**, m. the letter or sound *ra*, R.; °*râdi-rāma-sahasra-nāman*, n. N. of a collection of the thousand names of Rāma (from the Brahmayāmala). **-pratyāhāra**, m. N. of a partic. Pratyāhāra (q. v.); *-khaṇḍana*, n., *-maṇḍana*, n., *-varṇana*, n. N. of wks. **Rôdara**, m. 'containing an *r*,' N. of the Cakra-vāka (q. v.), Vām. v, 1, 15 (v. l.)

र 2. *ra*, (in prosody) a cretic (– ◡ –), Piṅg. **-vipulā**, f. 'abounding in cretics,' N. of a metre, Col.

र 3. *ra*, mfn. (√*rā*) acquiring, possessing, Naish.; giving, effecting, Śiś.; m. (only L.) fire, heat; love, desire; speed; (*ā*), f. (only L.) amorous play (= *vibhrama*); giving; gold; (*ī*), f. going, motion, L.; n. brightness, splendour (used in explaining an etymology), L.

रंसु *ránsu*, mfn. (fr. √*ran* or *ram*) cheerful, delightful (only *u*, ind. delightfully), RV. ii, 4, 5. **-jihva** (*ránsu-*), mfn. having a pleasing tongue or voice, RV.

रंह् *raṅh* (for *raṅgh*; cf. √*laṅgh* and *raghu*, *laghu*), cl. 1. P. (Dhātup. xvii, 83) *ráṅhati* (RV. also Ā. *ráṅhate*, *ráṅhamāṇa*; pf. *raraṅhá*, Bhaṭṭ.; fut. *raṅhitā*, °*hishyati*; aor. *araṅhīt*, Gr.), to hasten, speed (trans. and intrans.); to cause to go or flow; to go or flow, RV.; Śaṃk.; Bhaṭṭ.: Caus. *raṅháyati*, °*te* (aor. *araraṅhat*, Gr.), to hasten, speed, run or cause to run, RV.; (cl. 10. P.) *raṅhayati*, to speak or to shine, Dhātup. xxxiii, 123 (v. l. *vaṅh°*): Intens., see *rārahāṇá*.

Raṅha = *raṅhas* (see *vāta-raṅha*).

Raṅhaṇa, n. going swiftly, hastening, MW.

Raṅhati, f. speed, velocity (of a chariot), W.

Raṅhas, n. speed, quickness, velocity, MBh.; Kāv. &c.; eagerness, impetuosity, BhP.; m. N. of Śiva (Vehemence personified), MBh.; of Vishṇu, Hariv.

Raṅhasa (ifc.) = *raṅhas* (e.g. *mano-māruta-r°*, having the swiftness of thought or of the wind, Hariv.)

Ráṅhi, f. running, flowing, hastening, speed, velocity, eagerness, impetuosity, RV.; AV.; VS.; ŚBr.; a flowing stream, RV.; a running horse, courser, ib.

Raṅhita, mfn. hastening, quick, rapid, Kauś.

1. **Rahas**, n. (for 2. see p. 871, col. 1) swiftness, speed, velocity, BhP.

Rārahāṇá, mfn. (fr. Intens.) id., R.

रक् *rak*, cl. 10. P. *rākayati*, to taste, relish; to obtain, get, Dhātup. xxxiii, 63 (v. l. *rag*, *ragh*).

Raka, m. the sun gem; crystal; a hard shower, W.

रकसा *rakasā*, f. a form of leprosy, Suśr.

रक्क *rakka*, m. N. of a man, Rājat. **-jayā**, f. N. of an image of Śrī erected by Rakka, ib.

रक्ष् 1. *raksh*, cl. 1. P. (Dhātup. xvii, 6) *rákshati* (Ved. and m.c. also °*te*; pf. *rarákṣha*, RV. &c. &c.; aor. *arakshīt*, AV. &c.; *arākshīt*, Br.; Prec. *rakshyāt*, Gr.; fut. *rakshitā*, MBh.; *rakshishyati*, Cond. *arakshishyat*, ib.; *rakshye*, R.; inf. *rakshitum*, MBh.), to guard, watch, take care of, protect, save, preserve ('from,' abl.), RV. &c. &c.; to tend (cattle), Mn.; MBh.; R.; to rule (the earth or a country), MBh.; Rājat.; to keep (a secret), Kathās.; to spare, have regard to (another's feelings), Mālav.; to observe (a law, duty &c.), RV.; MBh.; to guard against, ward off, keep away, prevent, frustrate, injure, AV. v, 1; to beware of, Kathās.; (Ā.) to heed, attend to (loc.), RV. i, 72, 5; (Ā.) to conceal, hide (?), RV. ix, 68, 4; to conceal one's self, be afraid (?), ib. x, 68, 1: Caus. *rakshayati*, °*te* (aor. *ararakshat*, Pāṇ. vii, 4, 93, Sch.), to guard, watch, save or protect from (abl.), Kāv.; Pañcat.: Desid. *rirakshati*, to wish to guard, intend to protect from (abl.), MBh.: Intens., see *rārak shāṇá*. [Prob. a kind of Desid. of some root like *raj* or *rajj*; cf. Gk. ἀ-λέξω, ἀρκέω; Lat. *arx*, *arceo*.]

2. **Raksh**, (ifc.) guarding, watching &c. (see *go-raksh*).

1. **Rakshá**, mf(*ī*)n. (*ā*, f., see p. 860) guarding, watching, protecting, serving; a watcher, keeper, Suparṇ.; MBh. &c. (mostly ifc.; cf. *kshetra-*, *go-*, *cakra-r°* &c.) **-pāla**, m. a protector, guard, Pañcat. **-pālaka**, m. id. (f. *ikā*), Pañcad. **-purusha**, w. r. for *rakshā-p°*, Pañcat. **-bhagavatī**, f. = *prajñā-pāramitā*, Buddh.

2. **Raksha**, in comp. for *rakshas*. **-īśa**, m. 'lord of the Rākshasas,' N. of Rāvaṇa, L.

Rakshaḥ, in comp. for *rakshas*. **-pati**, m. 'lord of the Rākshasas,' N. of Rāvaṇa, Subh. **-pāla**, mfn. protecting from R°, MatsyaP. **-sabha**, n. an assemblage or multitude of Rākshasas, L.

Rakshaka, mf(*ikā*)n. = 1. *raksha*, Kathās.; Pañcat.; Hit. (cf. *aṅga-*, *go-*, *dhana-r°* &c.); (*ikā*), f. an amulet, charm, anything worn as a preservative, L. **Rakshakâmbā**, f. N. of a woman, Cat.

Rakshaṇa, m. 'protector,' N. of Vishṇu, MBh.; (*ā*), f. guarding, protection, Śak. (v. l.); Pañcar.; (*ī*), f. a rein, bridle, L.; Ficus Heterophylla, L.; (*rá°*), n. the act of guarding, watching, protecting, tending (of cattle), preservation ('of,' gen., loc. or comp.), Mn.; MBh. &c.; a ceremony performed for protection or preservation, MārkP. **Rakshaṇârtham,** ind. for the sake of guarding or protecting, MW. **Rakshaṇôpâya,** ib. a means of safety, ib.

Rakshaṇāraka, m. morbid retention of urine, L. (v. l. *rakshaṇīraka*).

Rakshaṇīya, mfn. to be guarded or preserved or protected from (abl.), MBh.; Kāv. &c.; to be ruled by (gen. or instr.), R.; Kathās.; to be guarded against or prevented or avoided, Kathās.

Rakshaṇīraka. See *rakshaṇāraka.*

Rákshas, mfn. guarding, watching (see *pathi-r°*); n. 'anything to be guarded against or warded off,' harm, injury, damage, RV.; (in RV. and AV. also *rakshás,* m.) an evil being or demon, a Rākshasa (q. v.; in VP. identified with Nirṛiti or Nairṛita), RV. &c. &c.; pl. N. of a warlike race, g. *parśv-ādi.* — **tvá,** n. the nature of a Rākshasa, fiendishness, malice, RV. — **pāśa,** m. a contemptible R° or demon, W. (cf. under *pāśa*). — **vín,** mfn. demoniacal, evil-disposed, malignant, RV.; AV.

Rakshasyà, mf(*ā*)n. useful for (keeping off) Rākshasas, anti-demoniacal, TS. (cf. Pāṇ. iv, 4, 121).

Rakshā, f. the act of protecting or guarding, protection, care, preservation, security, Mn.; MBh. &c.; a guard, watch, sentinel, Mṛicch.; Kām.; any preservative, (esp.) a sort of bracelet or amulet, any mysterious token used as a charm, BhP.; Suśr.; a tutelary divinity (cf. *mahā-r°*); ashes (used as a preservative), L.; (*ā* or *ī*), f. a piece of thread or silk bound round the wrist on partic. occasions (esp. on the full moon of Śrāvaṇa, either as an amulet and preservative against misfortune, or as a symbol of mutual dependence, or as a mark of respect), MW. — **karaṇḍaka,** n. an amulet in the shape of a small box, Śak. — **gaṇḍaka,** m. a kind of amulet or talisman, ib. — **gṛiha,** n. 'watch-room,' a lying-in chamber, Ragh. — °**dhikṛita** (°*kshâdh°*), mfn. entrusted with the protection or superintendence (of a country &c.), Mn. vii, 123; m. = next, ib. ix, 272. — °**dhipati** (°*kshâdh°*), m. a superintendent of police, Śāntik. — **paṭṭolikā,** f. a cluster or collection of amulets, BhavP. — **pati,** m. = *rakshâdhipati,* VarBṛS. — **pattra,** m. Betula Bhojpatra, L. — **parigha,** m. a protective bar or bolt, Ragh. — **purusha,** m. a watchman, guard, protector, Pañcat. (w. r. *raksha-p°*). — °**pêkshaka** (°*kshâp°*), m. a doorkeeper or porter, W.; a guard of the women's apartments, ib.; a catamite, ib.; an actor, mime, ib. — **pratisara,** m. (or °*rā,* f.) an amulet, MBh. — **pradīpa,** m. a light kept burning for protection (against evil spirits &c.), Kathās. — **bandhana-vidhi,** m. N. of wk. — **bhūshaṇa,** n. an ornament worn for protection (against evil spirits &c.), Suśr. — °**bhyadhikṛita** (°*kshâbh°*), mfn. and m. = *rakshâdhikṛita,* MBh. — **maṅgala,** n. a ceremony performed for protection (against evil spirits &c.), Śak.; Suśr. — **maṇi,** m. a jewel worn as a preservative (against evil spirits &c.), Kathās.; N. of various wks. — **mantra,** m. N. of a collection of Vedic hymns (chanted at weddings in order to protect the bridal pair from evil influences). — **malla,** m. N. of a king, Col. — **mahâushadhi,** f. a sovereign remedy serving as a preservative (against evil spirits &c.), Kathās. — **ratna,** n. = *-maṇi,* Kathās.; Rājat.; *-pradīpa,* m. a lamp shining or brilliant with gems used as a preservative (against evil spirits &c.), Kathās. — °**rtham** (°*kshârth°*), ind. for the sake of protection, MW. — **vat,** mfn. enjoying protection, guarded, Ragh.; Prab. — **sarshapa,** m. mustard as a preservative (against evil spirits &c.), Rājat. — **sūtra,** n. a carrying-girth, Harav.

1. **Rakshi** (ifc.) guarding, protecting (see *pathi-, paśu-, soma-r°*).

2. **Rakshi,** in comp. for *rakshin.* — **jana,** m. an assemblage or force of policemen, Jātak. — **varga,** m. an assemblage of guards or sentinels, body-guard, L.

Rakshika, m. (fr. *rakshā*) a guard, protector, policeman, Daś. — **purusha,** m. id., ib.

Rakshitá, mfn. guarded, protected, saved, preserved, maintained, kept, RV. &c. &c.; m. N. of a teacher of medicine, Suśr.; of a grammarian, Siddh.; of various other men, HPariś.; (*ā*), f. N. of an Apsaras, MBh. — **vat,** mfn. containing the idea of *raksh* or 'protecting &c.,' ĀśvŚr.

Rakshitaka, mfn., only in *dāra-s°,* q. v.; (*ikā*), f. N. of a woman, Kathās.

Rakshitavya, mfn. to be guarded or protected or taken care of or kept, Mn.; MBh. &c.; to be guarded against or kept off, Nir. iv, 18.

Rakshitṛi, mfn. one who guards or protects, a guard, protector, watch, sentinel, RV. &c. &c.

Rakshin, mfn. id. (often ifc.; °*shi-tva,* n.), ŚrS.; MBh. &c.; (ifc.) guarding against, avoiding, keeping off, preventing, R.

Raksho, in comp. for *rakshas.* — **gaṇa,** m. a class or company of Rākshasas; *-bhojana,* n. N. of a hell (in which human beings are devoured by R°), BhP. — **ghna,** mfn. driving back or destroying R°, Kauś.; R.; Suśr. &c.; m. (scil. *mantra*) a spell or incantation destructive of R°, Kathās.; (*-mantra,* m., *-sûkta,* n. N. of wks.); Semecarpus Anocardium, L.; white mustard, L.; n. sour rice-gruel, L.; Asa Foetida, L. (for *raksho-ghnī* see under *-han*). — **jana,** m. the Rākshasa race, Gobh. — **jananī,** f. 'producing R°,' night, L. — **devatā,** f. pl. the R° compared to deities, the divine R°, Vas. — **devatyà** (MaitrS.; Kauś.) or **-daivata** (Vas.), mfn. having the R° for deities, sacred to them. — °**dhidevatā,** f. the chief goddess of the R°, Kathās. — **nātha,** m. 'lord of the R°,' N. of Rāvaṇa, A. — **bhāsh,** mfn. yelling or making a noise like Rākshasas, AitBr. — **mukha,** m. N. of a man; pl. his descendants, g. *yaskâdi.* — **yúj,** mfn. associated with Rākshasas, RV. — **vāha,** m. pl. N. of a race, MBh. — **vikshobhiṇī,** f. 'R°-agitating,' N. of a goddess, Cat. — **vidyā,** f. the science of dealing with Rākshasas, ŚāṅkhŚr. — **haṇa,** mfn. = *-han,* g. *goshad-ādi;* °*ṇaka,* mfn. containing the word *raksho-haṇa,* ib. — **hátya,** n. the killing of R°, RV. — **hán,** mf(*ghnī*)n. killing or destroying R°, RV.; VS.; ŚBr.; m. a partic. spell, Kauś. (cf. *raksho-ghna*); bdellium, L.; (with *Brâhma*) N. of the author of RV. x, 162, Anukr.; (*ghnī*), f. Acorus Calamus, L.

Rakshṇa, m. (Pāṇ. iii, 3, 90) protection, guard (°*ṇam* √*kṛi,* with abl. 'to protect from'), Bhaṭṭ.

Rakshya, mfn. to be guarded or protected or taken care of, Āpast.; MBh. &c.; to be prevented from (abl.), Kathās.; to be guarded against or avoided, ib.; Rājat. — **tama,** mfn. to be most carefully guarded, most worthy of protection, Mn.; MBh.; R.

Rārakshāṇá, mfn. (fr. Intens. of √*raksh*) protecting most carefully, RV.

रख् *rakh* (cf. √*raṅkh*), cl. 1. P. *rakhati,* to go, move, Dhātup. v, 22.

रग् *rag,* cl. 1. P. *ragati* (pf. *rarāga,* aor. *aragīt* &c., Gr.), to doubt, suspect, Dhātup. xix, 23; cl. 10. P. *rāgayati* (v. l. for √*rak, rākayati*), Dhātup. xxxiii, 63.

रघ् *ragh,* v. l. for √*rak,* q. v.

रघु *raghú,* mf(*vī*)n. (√*raṅh;* cf. *laghu*) hastening, going speedily, fleet, rapid, RV.; light, fickle, ib.; m. a racer, fleet courser, ib.; N. of an ancient king and ancestor of Rāma (described in Raghu-vaṅśa as son of Dilīpa and Su-dakshiṇā; he was father of Aja who was father of Daśa-ratha; hence he was great-grandfather of Rāma; in the Rāmāyaṇa Raghu is said to be son of Kakutstha; in the Hari-vaṅśa two Raghus are mentioned among the ancestors of Rāma), R.; Hariv.; Ragh.; Pur. (IW. 344); of a son of Gautama Buddha, Buddh.; of various authors (also with *daiva-jña* and *sūri*), Cat.; = the poem *raghu-vaṅśa* (cf. next); pl. the descendants of Raghu, Ragh.; Rājat. — **kāra,** m. 'author of the Raghu-vaṅśa,' N. of Kālidāsa, L. — **kulôttaṅsa,** m. 'crest-jewel of the race of Raghu,' N. of Rāma, Prasannar. — **já,** mfn. produced from a fleet courser or racer, RV. — **ṭippaṇī,** f. N. of a Comm. on Ragh. — **tanaya,** m. 'son of Raghu,' N. of Rāma, MW. — **tilaka,** m. 'ornament of the Raghus,' id., Prasannar. — **deva,** m. N. of various authors (also with *bhaṭṭâcārya* and *nyāyâlaṃkāra-bh°*), Cat.; (*ī*), f. N. of a Comm. by Raghu-deva. — **drú,** mfn. running like a race-horse, RV. — **nandana,** m. 'son or descendant of Raghu,' N. of Rāmacandra, R.; N. of various authors (also with *dīkshita, miśra, bhaṭṭâcārya* &c.), Cat.; *-kośa,* m. N. of wk. — **nātha,** m. 'lord of the Raghus,' N. of Rāma, Ragh.; N. of various authors and others (also with *dīkshita, bhaṭṭa, ārya, ācārya, upâdhyāya, kavi, yati, yatīndra, paṇḍita, sūri, cakravartin, bhūpāla* &c.), Inscr.; Cat.; *-carita,* n., *-pañca-ratna,* n., *-bhaṭṭa-gosvāmi-guṇa-leśâshṭaka,* n., *-bhūpālīya,* n., *-vilāsa,* n., *-vrata-kathā,* f., *-nāthâbhyudaya,* m., *-nāthīya,* n. N. of works. — **nāyaka,** m. 'chief of Raghus,' N. of Rāma, Cat. — **pati,** m. id., Kāv.; Kathās.; N. of various authors and teachers (also with *upâdhyāya* and *mahôpâdhyāya*), Cat.; *-rahasya-dīpikā,* f. N. of wk. — **pátma-jaṅhas,** mfn. light-winged, having a light-falling foot, RV. — **pátvan,** mfn. flying or moving quickly, RV. — **pratinidhi,** m. an image or counterpart of Raghu, Ragh. — **pravara,** m. 'best of Raghus,' N. of Rāma, R. — **maṇi,** m. 'gem of R°,' N. of an author, L. — **manyu,** mfn. quick-tempered, eager, zealous, RV. — **māhātmya,** n. N. of wk. — **mukha,** m. N. of a man, Vīrac. — **yā́man,** mfn. going quickly, moving lightly, RV. — **rāja-siṅha,** m. N. of an author, Cat. — **rāma,** m. N. of a man, Kshitīś.; (with *bhaṭṭa*) of an author, Cat. — **lāla-dāsa,** m. N. of an author, Cat. — **vaṅśa,** m. Raghu's race, R.; N. of Kālidāsa's celebrated poem (cf. *mahā-kāvya*); *-tilaka,* m. 'ornament of the race of Raghu,' N. of Rāma, MW.; *-saṃkshepa,* m. N. of an abridgment of the Raghu-vaṅśa, Cat.; *-saṃjīvanī,* f., *-subodhinī,* f. N. of two Comms. on Raghu-vaṅśa. — **vara,** m. = *-pravara,* R.; N. of an author, Cat.; *-śaraṇa,* n., *-saṃhitā,* f. N. of wks. — **vartani** (*rághu-*), mfn. lightly rolling or turning (said of a chariot and of a horse), RV. — **varya** and **-varya-tīrtha,** m. N. of two authors, Cat. — **vilāpa-nāṭaka,** n. N. of a drama. — **vīra,** m. 'Raghu-hero,' N. of Rāma, RāmatUp.; of two authors (also with *dīkshita*), Cat.; *-gadya,* n., *-carita,* n., *-viṅśati,* f. N. of wks. — **shyád,** mfn. (*r°* + *syad*) moving quickly, speedy, rapid, RV.; AV. — **suta,** m. 'Raghu's son,' patr. of Rāma, Bhaṭṭ. — **syada,** m. the act of moving or gliding quickly, Pat. on Pāṇ. viii, 2, 18 (cf. *-shyad*). — **svāmin,** m. = *-pati,* N. of Rāma, Vcar. **Raghûttama,** m. 'best of the Raghus,' N. of Rāma, R.; (with *yati* and °*ma-tīrtha*) N. of two authors, Cat. **Raghûdvaha,** m. 'offspring of Raghu,' N. of Rāma, Ragh.; Bālar.

Raghīyas, mfn. (compar. of *raghu*) more rapid or fleet, very swift, TS.

Raghuyát, mfn. (pr. p. fr. an unused Nom. *raghuya*) moving fleetly or rapidly, RV. (dat. *raghūyaté,* TBr.)

Raghuyā́, ind. (fr. *raghu*) quickly, swiftly, lightly, RV.

Raghūyat. See *raghuyat.*

रङ्क *raṅka,* mfn. niggardly, avaricious, Uṇ. iii, 40; slow, dull, ib.; poor, miserable, hungry (e. g. *kaṅka-raṅka,* a hungry or half-starved crane), Prab.; m. a beggar, starveling (*prêta-r°*), Mālatīm.

Raṅkaka, m. = prec. m., Bharat.

रङ्कु *raṅku,* m. a species of deer or antelope, Vās.; Nalac.; N. of a place, g. *kacchâdi.* — **mālin,** m. N. of a Vidyā-dhara, Kathās.

Raṅkuka, m. = *raṅku,* Śrīkaṇṭh.

Raṅkuṭi, f. a kind of vetch, L.

रङ्क्तृ *raṅktṛi.* See *raktṛi,* p. 862, col. 2.

रङ्क्षु *raṅkshu,* N. of a river, MārkP. (prob. w. r. for *vaṅkshu*).

रङ्ख् *raṅkh* (cf. √*rakh*), cl. 1. P. *raṅkhati,* to go, move, Dhātup. v, 23.

रङ्ग् *raṅg,* cl. 1. P. (Dhātup. v, 36) *raṅgati,* to move to and fro, rock, Nalac.

रङ्ग *raṅga, raṅgita, raṅgin.* See p. 862.

रङ्घ् *raṅgh* (cf. √*raṅh*), cl. 1. Ā. (Dhātup. iv, 33) *raṅghate,* to hasten, run, Bhaṭṭ. (cf. Ragh. iii, 21): Caus. or cl. 10 (Dhātup. xxxiii, 120) to speak; to shine.

Raṅghas, n. = *raṅhas,* haste, speed, velocity, Kāv.

Raṅghyā, f. a kind of disease, Kāśikh.

रच् *rac,* cl. 10. P. (Dhātup. xxxv, 12) *racayati* (pf. *racayām-āsa,* Kathās.; irr. fut. *racishyati,* Hariv. [with v. l. *karishyati*]; and ind. p. *racayitvā,* Vet.), to produce, fashion, form, make, construct, complete, cause, effect, R.; Var. &c. (with *cintām* or *cintāḥ,* to be anxious, Prab.); to make into (with double acc.), Bālar.; to compose, write (a book or any literary work), Śak.; Var.; Pañcat.; to place in or on (loc.), Kāv.; Kathās.; to adorn, decorate, Megh.; to cause to make or do (with double acc.), Uttarar.; to cause to move, put in motion (a horse), MBh.

Racana, n. the act of making, forming, arranging, preparing, composing, Kāv.; mostly (*ā*), f.

arrangement, disposition, management, accomplishment, performance, preparation, production, fabrication, MBh.; Kāv. &c.; a literary production, work, composition, VarBṛS.; Sāh.; style, Sāh.; putting on, wearing (of a garment), Mṛicch.; arrangement (of troops), array, Pañcat.; contrivance, invention, Kathās.; BhP.; a creation of the mind, artificial image, Jaim.; fixing the feathers on an arrow, L.; dressing the hair (cf. *keśa-r°*), L.; stringing flowers or garlands, W. (often ifc. with concrete meaning, e.g. *nivāsa-racanā*, a building, Mṛicch.; *gīti-racanā*, a song, Rājat.; *kūṭa-racanā*, an artifice, trick, Kathās.; accord. to L. also = *pari-spanda* or *pari-syanda, prati-yatna, granthana, gumpha, vyūha, niveśa, sthiti*; also = *pāśa, bhāra* &c., abundance, quantity, ifc. after a word meaning 'hair;' cf. Pāṇ. ii, 3, 44, Sch.); (*ā*), f. N. of the wife of Tvashṭṛi, BhP.

Racayitṛi, m. an author, composer, Cat.

Racita, mfn. produced, fashioned, constructed, performed, arranged, prepared, made of (instr. or comp.), Kāv.; Var.; BhP.; made or chosen for (nom.), Bhaṭṭ.; placed, inserted, inlaid, fixed on or in (loc.), Kāv.; Kathās.; BhP.; set out, displayed in (loc. or comp.), Kālid.; directed towards (loc.), BhP.; furnished, provided, set or studded with (instr. or comp.), Hariv.; Kālid.; Suśr.; (ifc.) occupied with, engaged in, Bālar.; (with *mṛishā*) invented, Kathās.; m. N. of a man, g. *biḍâdi*. **-tva**, n. the being composed or written, Sarvad. **-dhī**, mfn. one whose mind is directed to (loc.), intent upon, BhP. **-paṅkti**, mfn. forming a line, MW. **-pūrva**, mfn. what has been prepared or performed before, Śak. (v. l.) **-maṅgala**, mfn. one who has performed an auspicious ceremony, Kathās. **-śikhara**, mfn. having the summit adorned, Megh. **-svāgata**, mfn. one who has offered a welcome, Kathās. **Racitâtithya**, mfn. one who has shown hospitality, ib. **Racitânati**, mfn. one who has made his obeisance, ib.

Racitârtha, mfn. one who has obtained his object, ib. **Racitôtsava**, mfn. one who has celebrated a festival, ib.

रज् *raj.* See √*rañj.*

Raja, rajani &c. See p. 863, col. 1.

रजि 1. *rají*, m. N. of a demon or king subdued by Indra, RV. vi, 26, 6 (Sāy. 'a maiden or a kingdom called Raji'); of an Āṅgirasa, ĀrshBr.; of a son of Āyu, MBh.; *ubhé raji* (RV. x, 105, 2), 'heaven and earth' or 'the sun and moon,' Sāy.

रजि 2. *rájī*, f. (cf. *ṛiju*) direction, RV. x, 110, 12.

Rájishṭha, mfn. (superl. of *ṛiju*; cf. *ṛijishṭha* and Pāṇ. vi, 4, 162) straightest, RV.; most honest or upright, ib.

Rajīyas, mfn. (compar. of *ṛiju*) = *ṛijīyas*, Pāṇ. vi, 4, 162.

रजीकृ *rajī-kṛi, rajo-gātra* &c. See p. 863, col. 2.

रज्जु *rájju*, f. (ifc. sometimes m.; in earlier language also *rajjū*, f.; Ved. acc. *rajjvam*; gen. *rajjvās*, Mn. xi, 168; probably fr. an unused √*rasj* or *rajj*; cf. *rasanā* = *raśanā*) a rope, cord, string, line, RV. &c. &c. (*rajjum ā-√sthā*, to have recourse to the rope, to hang one's self, MBh.); N. of partic. sinews or tendons proceeding from the vertebral column, Suśr.; a lock of braided hair, braid (= *veṇī*), L.; N. of a partic. constellation, VarBṛS.; Caryota Urens, L.; a measure of 8 Hastas or 192 inches, L. [Cf. Lith. *rezgù*, 'I plait.'] **-kaṇṭha**, m. N. of a preceptor, g. *śaunakâdi*. **-kriyā**, f. rope-work, rope-maker's work, ĀpGṛ., Sch. **-dāla** (*rájju-*), m. Cordia Myxa Latifolia, ŚBr.; = next, Vishṇ.; Mn. **-dālaka**, m. a kind of wild-fowl, Yājñ. **-dhāna**, n. the part of the neck of a domestic animal around which a rope is fastened, Kauś. **-pīṭhikā**, f. a stool or bench suspended by ropes, Kathās. **-peḍā**, f. a rope-basket, ib. **-bandha**, m. binding with ropes, tying with cords (*°dhena* √*bandh*, to bind with ropes), ib. **-bhāra**, m. N. of a teacher, g. *śaunakâdi*. **-maya**, mf(*ī*)n. consisting of ropes, ĀpŚr. **-mātra-tva**, n. the condition of being merely a rope, MW. **-yantra**, n. a contrivance with cords, any mechanism worked with strings (as a doll), Kathās. **-lamba**, m. a hanging r°, ib. **-vartana**, n. the twisting of r°s, Jātakam. **-vāla**, v. l. for *-dāla*, Mn. v, 12. **-śārada**, mfn. newly drawn up by a r° (as water), Pāṇ. vi, 2, 9, Sch. **-s[illegible]dāná**, n. rope and foot-fetter, ŚBr. **-sarjá**, m. a rope-maker, VS. **Rajjûta**, mf(*ā*)n. twisted or plaited out of r°s, KātyŚr. **Rajjûddhṛita**, mfn. drawn up by means of a rope, Uṇ. i, 16, Sch. **Rajjv-avalambin**, mfn. hanging by a string, MW.

Rajjavyà, n. material for a rope, ŚBr.

Rajjuka (ifc.) = *rajjū*, Kathās.

Rajjū-√kṛi, P. *-karoti*, to use as a rope, A.

रञ्छ् *rañch.* See *ni-rañchana.*

रञ्ज् *rañj* or *raj*, cl. 1. 4. P. Ā. (Dhātup. xxiii, 30; xxvi, 58) *rajati, °te* (only Gr.; *-rañjati*, R. vii, 99, 11) or *rajyati, °te* (Gr. also pf. P. *rarañja*, 3rd du. *rarajatuḥ* or *rarañjatuḥ*; Ā. *rarañje*; aor. *arāṅkshīt, araṅkta*; Prec. *rajyāt, raṅkshīshṭa*; fut. *raṅktā*; *raṅkshyati, °te*; inf. *raṅktum*; ind. p. *raktvā* or *raṅktvā*), to be dyed or coloured, to redden, grow red, glow, AV.; Kāv.; to be affected or moved, be excited or glad, be charmed or delighted by (instr.), be attracted by or enamoured of, fall in love with (loc.), MBh.; Kāv. &c.; (*rajati, °te*), to go, Naigh. ii, 14: Caus. *rajayati* (only AV.) and *rañjayati, °te* (aor. *arīrajat* or *ararañjat*; Pass. *rajyate*; aor. *arañji* or *arāñji*), to dye, colour, paint, redden, illuminate, AV. &c. &c.; to rejoice, charm, gratify, conciliate, MaitrUp.; Mn.; MBh. &c.; to worship, Naigh. iii, 14 (*rajayati mṛigān* = *ramayati mṛigān*, Pāṇ. vi, 4, 24, Vārtt. 3, Pat.): Desid. *rirāṅkshati, °te*, Gr.: Intens. *rārajīti* (Gr. also *rārajyate* and *rāraṅkti*), to be greatly excited, exult, RV. ix, 5, 2 (others 'to shine bright'). [Cf. Gk. ῥέζω, 'to dye,' ῥεγεύς, 'dyer.']

Rakta, mf(*ā*)n. coloured, dyed, painted, Br.; GṛŚrS.; Mn. &c. (cf. Pāṇ. iv, 2, 1); reddened, red, crimson, ŚāṅkhGṛ.; MBh.; Kāv. &c. (said of 5 or 7 parts of the body which ought to be red, MBh. iv, 253; VarBṛS. lxviii, 84); 'coloured or modified by nasalization,' nasalized (said of a vowel), RPrāt. (cf. *raṅga*); excited, affected with passion or love, impassioned, enamoured, charmed with (instr.), attached or devoted to, fond of (loc., gen. or comp.), Mn.; MBh. &c.; beloved, dear, lovely, pleasant, sweet, Kāv.; fond of play, engaging in pastime, sporting, L.; m. red colour, L.; safflower, L.; Barringtonia Acutangula, L.; N. of Śiva, MBh.; of the planet Mars, VarBṛS., Sch.; (*ā*), f. lac (= *lākshā*), Suśr.; Abrus Precatorius (or its seeds as a measure or weight, = *raktikā*), Car.; Rubia Munjista, L.; Echinops Echinatus, L.; N. of one of the 7 tongues of fire, L.; (in music) N. of a Śruti, Saṃgīt.; n. blood, Mn.; Hariv. &c.; a partic. disease of the eyes, Hcat.; the menstrual fluid, L.; copper, L.; vermilion, L.; cinnabar, L.; saffron, L.; the fruit of Flacourtia Cataphracta, L.; = *padmaka*, L. **-kaṅgu**, m. Panicum Italicum, L. **-kaṇṭa**, m. a species of Celastrus, L. **-kaṇṭha**, mf(*ī*)n. sweet-voiced (said of a bird), BhP.; m. = *kokila*, the Indian cuckoo, ib., Sch. **-kaṇṭhin**, mfn. = *-kaṇṭha*, MBh.; R. **-kadamba**, m. a red-flowering Kadamba, Vikr. **-kadalī**, f. a species of Musa or plantain, L. **-kanda**, m. coral, L.; Dioscorea Purpurea, L.; a kind of bulbous plant (= *rāja-palāṇḍu*), L. **-kandala**, m. coral, L. **-kamala**, n. a red lotus flower, L.; *°linī*, f. a group of red lotus f°s, Vās. **-kambala**, n. = *-kamala*, L. **-karavīra** or *°raka*, m. Nericum Odorum Rubro-simplex, L. **-kallola**, m. N. of a man, Hasy. **-kāñcana**, m. Baubinia Variegata, L. **-kāṇḍā**, f. a red-flowering Punarnavā, L. **-kāla**, n. a species of earth, L. **-kāshṭha**, n. Caesalpina Sappan, L. **-kuṇḍala** or **-kumuda**, n. the flower of Nymphaea Rubra, red lotus, L. **-kṛimijā**, f. red lac, L. **-kṛishṇa**, mfn. dark red, ŚāṅkhGṛ. **-kesara**, m. Rottleria Tinctoria, L.; the coral-tree, L. **-kairava** or **-kokanada**, n. = *-kumuda*, L. **-kośātakī**, f. a species of plant (= *mahā-jālī*), L. **-khadira**, m. a red-flowering Khadira, L. **-khādava**, m. a species of foreign date, L. **-gandhaka**, n. myrrh, L. **-garbha**, f. Lawsonia Alba, L. **-gulma**, m. a particular form of the disease called *gulma*, GāruḍaP.; *°minī*, f. a female suffering from it, Suśr. **-gairika**, n. a kind of ochre, L. **-gaura**, mfn. reddish yellow or white, DhyānabUp. **-granthi**, m. a kind of Mimosa, L.; a partic. form of urinary disease, Car. **-graha**, m. a kind of demon, L. **-grīva**, m. 'red-necked,' a kind of pigeon, L.; a Rākshasa, L. **-ghna**, m. 'blood-corrupting,' Andersonia Rohitaka, L.; (*ī*), f. a kind of Dūrvā grass, L. **-candana**, n. red sandal, Bhpr.; Caesalpina Sappan, ib.; saffron, L. **-citraka**, m. Plumbago Rosea, L. **-cillikā**, f. a kind of Chenopodium, L. **-cūrṇa**, n. vermilion, L. **-cūrṇaka**, m. the red powder on the capsules of Rottleria Tinctoria, L. **-cchada**, mfn. red-leaved (*-tva*, n.), Subh. **-cchardi**, f. vomiting or spitting blood, ŚārṅgS. **-ja**, mfn. produced from bl°, Suśr. **-jantuka**, m. a kind of worm, an earth-worm, L. **-jihva**, mfn. red-tongued; m. a lion, L. **-tara**, mfn. more red or attached &c. (see *rakta*); n. = *rakta-gairika*, L. **-tā**, f. redness, MBh.; the nature of blood, ŚārṅgS.; the being affected by passion, MW. **-tuṇḍa**, m. 'red-beaked,' a parrot, L. **-tuṇḍaka**, m. a kind of worm, L. **-tṛiṇā**, f. a species of grass, L. **-tejas**, n. flesh, L. **-trivṛit**, f. a red-flowering Ipomoea, L. **-tva**, n. redness, Bhartṛ.; = *-tā*, f., W. **-dat** or **-dant**, mfn. having red or discoloured teeth, Āpast. **-dantikā** (MarkP.) or **-dantī** (L.), f. 'red-toothed,' N. of Durgā. **-dalā**, f. a species of small shrub, L.; = *nalikā*, L. **-dūshaṇa**, mfn. corrupting or vitiating the blood, Suśr. **-dṛiś** or **-dṛishṭi**, m. 'red-eyed,' a pigeon, L. **-druma**, m. a red-flowering Terminalia, L. **-dhātu**, m. red chalk or opiment, earth, ruddle, L.; copper, L. **-nayana**, mfn. red-eyed; m. Perdix Rufa, L. **-nāḍī**, f. a fistulous ulcer on the gum caused by a bad state of blood, ŚārṅgS. **-nāla**, m. or n. a kind of lotus, L.; = *jīvantī*, L. **-nāsika**, m. 'red-beaked,' an owl, L. **-niryāsaka**, m. = *-druma*, L. **-nīla**, mfn. blue-red, L. **-netra**, mfn. red-eyed, Pañcat.; Suśr.; *-tā*, f. (Suśr.), *-tva*, n. (ŚārṅgS.) the state of having red or blood-shot eyes. **-pa**, mfn. blood-drinking, blood-sucking, L.; m. a Rākshasa, L.; f. a leech, L.; a Ḍākinī or female fiend, L. **-paksha**, m. 'red-winged,' N. of Garuḍa, L. **-paṭa**, m. 'wearing red garments,' a kind of mendicant (= *sāṃkhya-bhikshu*), Var.; *-maya*, mf(*ī*)n. made of red cloth, Vās. (v. l.); *-vrata-vāhinī*, f. a Buddhist nun, Kād.; *°ṭī-kṛita*, mfn. changed into a Rakta-paṭa mendicant, Bhartṛ. (v. l.) **-patana**, n. a flow of blood, VarBṛS. **-pattra**, m. a kind of bulbous plant, L.; (*ā*), f. Boerhavia Erecta Rosea, L.; *°ttrâṅga*, n. a kind of red sandal, L.; *°ttrikā*, f. = *-parṇa*, L.; = *nākulī*, L. **-paḍī**, f. a species of plant, L. **-padma**, n. a red lotus flower, VarBṛS. **-parṇa**, m. or n. (?) a red-flowering Punarnavā, L. **-pallava**, m. Jonesia Asoka, L. **-pākī**, f. the egg-plant, L. **-pāta**, m. bloodshed, spilling of blood, L.; (*ā*), f. a leech, L. **-pāda**, mfn. red-footed; m. a bird with red feet, Yājñ.; MBh. &c.; a parrot, L.; an elephant, L.; a war-chariot, L.; (*ī*), f. Mimosa Pudica, L. **-pāyin**, mfn. blood-drinking; m. a bug, L.; (*inī*), f. a blood-sucker, leech, L. **-pārada**, m. n. cinnabar, L. **-piṭikā**, f. a red boil or ulcer, ŚārṅgS. **-piṇḍa**, m. Hibiscus Rosa Sinensis, L.; n. its flower, L. (W. also 'discharge of blood from the nose and mouth; a red pimple; the plant Ventilago Madraspatana'). **-piṇḍaka** or **-piṇḍâlu**, m. = *raktâlu*. **-pitta**, n. 'bile-blood,' a partic. disturbance of the blood caused by bile, plethora, spontaneous hemorrhage from the mouth or nose, Suśr. &c.; *-kara*, mfn. causing the above disease, ib.; *-kāsa*, m. the cough connected with it, Car.; *-hā*, f. 'removing it,' a kind of Dūrvā grass, ib.; *°ttika* or *°ttin*, mfn. subject to or suffering from it, Car. **-pītâsita-śyeta**, mf(*nī*)n. red-yellow-blackish white; m. r°-y°-bl° whiten[illegible], L. **-pucchaka**, mf(*ikā*) n. red-tailed; (*ikā*), f. a kind of lizard, L. **-punarnavā**, f. a red-flowering Punarnavā, L. **-pushpa**, n. a red flower, Vet.; mfn. red-flowered, bearing red flowers, VarBṛS.; m. (only L.) Bauhinia Variegata Purpurescens; Nerium Odorum; the pomegranate tree; Rottleria Tinctoria; Pentapetes Phoenicea; Andersonia Rohitaka; = *baka*; (*ā*), f. Bombax Heptaphyllus, L.; (*ī*), f. (only L.) Grislea Tomentosa; Bignonia Suaveolens; Hibiscus Rosa Sinensis; the senna plant; Artemisia Vulgaris or Alpinia Nutans; Echinops Echinatus; = *karuṇī*. **-pushpaka**, m. (only L.) Butea Frondosa; Salmalia Malabarica; Andersonia Rohitaka; Oldenlandia Herbacea; (*ikā*), f. (only L.) Mimosa Pudica; a red-flowering Punarnavā; Bignonia Suaveolens; = *bhū-pāṭalī*. **-pūya**, n. N. of a hell, Cat. **-pūraka**, n. the dried peel or integument of the Mangosteen, L. **-pūrṇa**, mfn. field of blood (*-tva*, n.), MW. **-paitta** or **-paittika**, mfn. relating to *rakta-pitta* (q. v.), Suśr. **-pradara**, m. a flow of blood from the womb, ŚārṅgS. **-prameha**, m. a disease of the bladder, the passing of blood in the urine, MW. **-pravāha**, m. a stream of blood, Ragh. **-prasava**, m. Nerium Odorum

Rubro-simplex, L.; red globe-amaranth, L.; Pterospermum Suberifolium, L. — **phala**, mfn. having or bearing red fruit, VarBṛS.; m. the Indian fig-tree, L.; (*ā*), f. Momordica Monadelpha, L.; = *svarṇa-vallī*, L. — **phena-ja**, m. (prob.) the lungs, L. — **bindu**, m. a red spot forming a flaw in a gem, W.; a drop of blood, MārkP. — **bīja**, m. the pomegranate tree, L.; N. of a physician, MārkP. — **bījakā**, f. a kind of thorny plant, L. — **bhava**, n. 'blood-produced,' flesh, L. — **bhāva**, mfn. being in love, amorous, enamoured, Hariv. — **mañjara**, m. Barringtonia Acutangula, L. — **maṇḍala**, mfn. having a red disk (said of the moon), Kāvyâd.; having devoted subjects, ib.; m. a species of red-spotted or red-ringed snake, Suśr.; (*ā*), f. a partic. venomous animal, ib.; n. a red lotus-flower, W.; *-tā*, f. the appearance of red spots on the body caused by a bad state of the blood, ŚārṅgS. — **matta**, mfn. drunk or satiated with blood (said of a leech), Vāgbh. — **matsya**, m. a species of red fish, L. — **maya**, mf(*ī*)n. consisting of blood, full of blood, bloody, W. — **mastaka**, m. 'red-headed,' Ardea Sibirica, L. — **mādrī**, f. a kind of woman's disease, L. — **mukha**, mf(*ā* or *ī*)n. red-faced, having a red mouth; m. a kind of fish, Bhpr.; N. of an ape, Pañcat. — **mūtra-tā**, f. the voiding of blood with urine, ŚārṅgS. — **mūlaka**, m. a kind of tree, L. — **mūlā**, f. Mimosa Pudica, L. — **meha**, m. the voiding of blood with urine, ŚārṅgS.; °*hin*, mfn. suffering from this disease, Car. — **moksha**, m. or **-mokshaṇa**, n. bloodletting, bleeding, venesection &c., Suśr. — **yashṭi** or **-yashṭikā**, f. Rubia Munjista, L. — **yāvanāla**, m. = *tubara-yāvanāla*, L. — **rāji**, m. a partic. venomous insect, Suśr.; a partic. disease of the eye, ib. — **rājī**, f. a partic. venomous insect, ib.; cress, Lepidium Sativum, L. — **reṇu**, m. vermilion, L.; a bud of Butea Frondosa (also °*ṇukā*), L.; Rottleria Tinctoria, L.; a sort of cloth, W.; an angry man, ib. — **raivataka**, m. a species of fruit tree, L. — **lasuna**, m. a kind of garlic, L. — **locana**, m. 'red-eyed,' a pigeon, L. — **vaṭī** or **-varaṭī**, f. small-pox, L. (the former also 'hemorrhoids,' Gal.) — **varga**, m. (only L.) lac; the pomegranate tree; Butea Frondosa; Pentapetes Phoenicea; Rubia Munjista; two kinds of saffron; safflower. — **varṇa**, m. red colour or the c° of blood, Cat.; mfn. red-coloured, Suśr.; the cochineal insect, L.; n. gold, L.; °*ṇaka*, mfn. red-coloured; m. (scil. *varga*) = *rakta-varga*, L. — **vartmaka**, m. a kind of bird, Vāgbh. — **vardhana**, m. 'blood-increasing,' Solanum Melongena, L. — **varshābhū**, f. = *rakta-punarnavā*, L. — **vasana**, m. 'clad in reddish garments,' a religious mendicant, L. — **vastrin**, m. = *yogin*, Gal. — **vāta**, m. a partic. disease, GāruḍaP. — **vārija**, n. a red lotus flower, L. — **vāluka**, n. or (*ā*), f. vermilion, L. — **vāsas**, mfn. wearing red garments, Mn. viii, 256. — **vāsin**, mfn. id., R. — **vikāra**, m. alteration or deterioration of blood, MW. — **vidradhi**, m. a boil filled with blood, Suśr. — **vindu**, **-vīja**, **-vījakā**, see *-bindu*, *-bīja*, *-bījakā*. — **virakta**, mfn. passionate and dispassionate (said of Śiva), MBh. — **vṛiksha**, m. a kind of tree, Suśr. — **vṛintā**, f. Nyctanthes Arbor Tristis, L. — **śāli**, m. red rice, Oryza Sativa, L. — **śāsana**, n. vermilion, L. — **śigru**, m. red-flowering Śigru, L. — **śīrshaka**, m. a kind of heron, Car.; Pinus longifolia or its resin, L. — **śukra-tā**, f. bloody condition of the semen, Suśr. — **śūla**, m. or n. (?) N. of a partic. disease (of women), Hcat. — **śṛiṅgaka**, n. (or °*gī*, f.) poison, venom, L. — **śmaśru**, mfn. having a red beard, MBh.; *-śiroruha*, mfn. having a red beard and hair, ib. — **śyāma**, mfn. dark-red, Var. — **shṭhīvana-tā** or **-shṭhīvī**, f. the spitting of blood, ŚārṅgS. — **saṃkoca**, m. safflower, L. — **saṃkocaka**, n. a red lotus flower, L. — **saṃjña**, n. saffron, L. — **saṃdaṇśikā**, f. a blood-sucker, leech, L. — **saṃdhyaka**, n. the flower of Nymphaea Rubra, L. — **saroruha**, n. id., L. — **sarshapa**, m. Sinapis Ramosa; pl. its seed, Suśr. — **sahā**, f. the red globe-amaranth, L. — **sāra**, mfn. whose essence is blood, having a sanguinary nature, VarBṛS.; m. a species of plant, Suśr. (= *amla-vetasa* or *rakta-kadhira*, L.); n. red sandal or Caesalpina Sappan, Bhpr. — **sūrya-maṇi**, m. a beautiful red-flowering shrub (Hibiscus Phoeniceus), MW. — **sūryāya**, Nom. Ā. *-sūryāyate*, to represent or be like a red sun, Hariv. — **saugandhika**, n. a red lotus flower, L. — **srag-anulepin**, m. (prob.) 'wearing a red garland and being anointed,' N. of Śiva, MBh. — **srāva**, m. a flow of blood, hemorrhage, VarBṛS.; a kind of acid sorrel or dock, L. — **haṇsa**, m. (in music) N. of a Rāga, Saṃgīt; (*ā*), f. N. of a Rāgiṇī, ib. — **hīna**, mfn. bloodless, cold-blooded, W. **Raktâṇśuka**, m. a red ray of light, Vās.; n. a red garment, ib. **Raktâkāra**, m. 'having a red appearance,' coral, L. **Raktâkta**, mfn. dyed red, W.; sprinkled or besmeared with blood, ib.; n. red sandal or Caesalpina Sappan, L. **Raktâksha**, mf(*ī*)n. red-eyed, having red or blood-shot eyes, R.; BhP. (*-tā*, f., Dharmaś.); fearful, dreadful, L.; m. a buffalo, L.; Perdix Rufa, L.; a pigeon, L.; the Indian crane, L.; N. of a sorcerer, Buddh.; N. of the minister of an owl-king, Kathās.; Pañcat.; n. N. of the fifty-eighth year in a Jupiter's cycle of sixty years, VarBṛS. (also °*kshi* or °*kshin*, m., Cat.); (*ī*), f. N. of a Yoginī, Hcat. **Raktâṅka**, m. coral, L. **Raktâṅga**, m. 'red-bodied,' a species of bird, R.; a bug, L.; the red pollen on the capsules of the Rottleria Tinctoria, L.; the planet Mars, L.; the disk of the sun and moon, L.; N. of a serpent demon, MBh.; (*ā*), f. a species of plant (= *jīvantī*), L.; (*ī*), f. Rubia Munjista, L.; coral, L.; n. coral, L.; saffron, L.; the red pollen on the capsules of the Rottleria Tinctoria, L. **Raktâtisāra** or **raktâtīsāra**, m. flow of blood, dysentery, bloody flux, ŚārṅgS. **Raktâdharā**, f. a Kiṃ-narī, Daś. **Raktâdhāra**, m. 'blood-receptacle,' the skin, L. **Raktâdhimantha**, m. inflammation of the eyes, ophthalmia with discharge of blood, L. **Raktânta**, mfn. having red extremities, having the corners (of the eyes) inflamed, MW. **Raktâpaha**, n. myrrh, L. **Raktâpāmārga**, m. a red-flowering Achyranthes, L. **Raktâbha**, mfn. red-looking, having a red appearance, R. **Raktâbhishyanda**, m. ophthalmia brought on by the state of the blood, redness of the vessels of the eye with a watery discharge, Suśr. **Raktâmishâda**, mfn. eating blood and flesh, R. **Raktâmbara**, n. a red garment (*-dhara*, mfn. wearing a red g°), MBh.; mfn. clad in red g°s; m. any vagrant religious mendicant wearing red g°s (*-tva*, n.), Sarvad. **Raktâmbupūra**, m. a stream or flow of blood, MBh. **Raktâmburuha**, n. a red lotus flower, R. **Raktâmbhoja**, n. id., L. **Raktâmra**, m. a species of plant, L. **Raktâruṇa**, mfn. blood-red, red as blood, Kathās. **Raktârti**, f. a partic. disease of the blood, L. **Raktârbuda**, n. a bloody tumour, L. **Raktârman**, n. a partic. disease of the eyes, L. **Raktârśas**, n. a form of hemorrhoids, Bhpr. **Raktâlu** or **raktâluka**, m. a species of red yam, Dioscorea Purpurea, L. **Raktâśaya**, m. 'blood-receptacle,' any organ containing or secreting blood (as the heart, liver, spleen), W.; = *uras*, the breast, Bhpr. **Raktâśoka**, m. red-flowering Aśoka, Megh.; Kathās. **Raktêkshu**, m. red sugar-cane, L. **Raktairaṇḍa**, m. the red Ricinus or castor-oil plant, L. **Raktairvāru**, m. a kind of cucumber, L. **Raktôtklishṭa**, m. a partic. disease of the eyes, ŚārṅgS. **Raktôtpala**, m. Bombax Heptaphyllum, L.; n. a red lotus, VarBṛS.; °*lâbha*, mfn. resembling the red lotus, L. **Raktôdara**, mfn. red-bellied, Bhpr. **Raktôpala**, n. red chalk, red ochre or orpiment, L.

Raktaka, mfn. red, VarBṛS.; passionately attached to, fond of, enamoured, L.; pleasing, amusing, L.; bloody, L.; m. a red garment, L.; an amorous or impassioned or sporting man, L.; a player, L.; Pentapetes Phoenicea, L.; globe-amaranth, L.; a red-flowering Moringa, L.; red Ricinus, L.; Caesalpina Sappan, L.; (*ikā*), f. Abrus Precatorius (its seed or grain is used as a weight = $\frac{1}{8}$, $\frac{1}{6}$, or $\frac{2}{15}$ Māshaka), ŚārṅgS.; KātyŚr., Sch.; (in music) a partic. Śruti, Saṃgīt.

Raktalā, f. Sanseviera Roxburghiana, L.; = *kākâdanī*, L.

Rakti, f. (only L.) pleasingness, loveliness; affection, attachment, devotion; Abrus Precatorius (cf. *raktikā*). — **mat**, mfn. charming, lovely, Kathās.

Raktiman, m. redness, red colour, Kuval; Sarvad.

Raktri, m. a dyer, painter, L. (prob. w. r. for *raṅktṛi*).

Raṅga, m. colour, paint, dye, hue, MBh.; Suśr.; Lalit.; the nasal modification of a vowel, Śiksh.; a place for public amusement or for dramatic exhibition, theatre, play-house, stage, arena, any place of assembly, MBh.; Kāv. &c.; the members of an assembly, audience, Śak.; Sāṃkhyak.; Daśar.; a dancing-place, L.; a field of battle, L.; diversion, mirth, L.; love, L.; (in music) a kind of measure, Saṃgīt.; borax, L.; an extract obtained from Acacia Catechu, L.; N. of a man, Rājat.; of various authors (also with *bhaṭṭa* and *jyotir-vid*), Cat.; (*ā*), f. N. of a river, Divyâv.; n. (m.) tin (= *vaṅga*), L. — **kāra** (BhP.), **-kāraka** (Hariv.), m. 'colour-maker,' a painter, colourist. — **kāshṭha**, n. Caesalpina Sappan, L. — **kshāra**, m. borax, L. — **kshetra**, n. N. of a place, Cat. — **cara**, m. 'stage-goer,' a player, actor, gladiator &c., VarBṛS. — **ja**, n. vermilion, L. — **jīvaka**, m. 'living by colours,' a dyer, painter, L.; 'living by the stage,' an actor, L. — **taraṃga**, m. N. of an actor, Vṛishabhân.; °*giṇī*, f. N. of a poem. — **tāla**, m. (in music) a kind of measure, Saṃgīt. — **da**, m. borax, L.; an extract from Acacia Catechu, L.; (*ā*), f. alum, L. — **datta**, (prob.) n. N. of a drama. — **dāyaka**, m. a partic. kind of earth, L. — **dṛiḍhā**, f. alum, L. — **devatā**, f. a goddess supposed to preside over sports and diversions, the genius of pleasure, MW. — **dvār**, f. a stage-door, the entrance of a theatre, Hariv.; BhP. — **dvāra**, n. 'id.,' the prologue of a play, Sāh. — **dhātu**, m. red ochre, L. — **nātha**, m. (also with *bhaṭṭa*, *dīkshita*, *ācārya*, *yajvan*, *sūri*) N. of various authors and other men, (esp.) of a Sch. on the Vikramôrvaśī (A. D. 1656) and a Sch. on the Sūrya-siddhânta; of a place, Cat.; *-deśikâhnika*, n., *-nāṭaka*, n., *-nāma-ratna*, n., *-pādukā-sahasra*, n., *-maṅgala-stotra*, n., *-māhātmya*, n., *-stotra*, n.; °*thânuśāsana*, n., °*thâshṭaka*, n., °*thâshṭôttara-śata*, n., °*thīya*, n. N. of wks. — **nāmaka** or **-nāyaka**, n. a partic. kind of earth, L. — **patākā**, f. N. of a woman, Daś. — **pattrī** or **-pushpī**, f. the indigo plant, L. — **pīṭha**, n. a place for dancing, Daś. — **pradīpaka**, m. (in music.) a kind of measure, Saṃgīt. — **praveśa**, m. entering on the stage, engaging in theatrical performances, Mṛicch. — **prasādana**, n. propitiation of the audience (of a theatre), Pratāp. — **pluta-lakshaṇa**, n. N. of wk. — **bhūti**, f. the night of full moon in the month Āśvina, L. — **bhūmi**, f. a place for acting, stage, theatre, arena, battle-field, MBh.; Pañcat. — **bhṛiṅga-vallī**, f. N. of wk. — **maṅgala**, m. N. of an actor, Vṛishabhân.; n. a festive ceremony on the stage, Sāh. — **maṇḍapa**, m. n. a play-house, theatre, Kathās. — **madhya**, n. the middle of an arena, MW. — **malla**, m. N. of a man, Cat.; (*ī*), f. the Indian lute, L. — **māṇikya**, n. a ruby, L. — **mātṛi**, f. lac (= *lākshā*), L. (also °*tṛikā*); a bawd, L.; = *truṭi*, L. — **māhātmya**, n. N. of wk. — **rāja**, m. N. of the patron of Sāyaṇa, Cat.; of various authors (also with *dīkshita*, *-adhvarin*, *-adhvari-vara* and *-adhvarîndra*), ib.; *-stava*, m. N. of a Stotra. — **rāṭ-chandas**, n. N. of a wk. on metres. — **rāmânuja**, m. N. of an author (also °*jâcārya*); °*jīya*, n. his wk. — **latā**, f. the senna plant, L. — **lāsinī**, f. Nyctanthes Arbor Tristis, L. — **līla**, m. (in music) a kind of measure, Saṃgīt. — **vatī**, f. N. of a woman (who killed her husband Ranti-deva), Vās., Introd. — **vallikā** or **-vallī**, f. a kind of plant used at sacrifices, Saṃskārak. — **vastu**, n. any colouring substance, paint, dye, Pañcar. — **vāṭa**, m. a place or arena enclosed (for contests, plays, dancing &c.), MBh.; Hariv. — **vārâṅganā**, f. a kind of dancing-girl, Śṛiṅgār. — **vidyā-dhara**, m. a master in the art of acting, Cat. — **śālā**, f. a play-house, theatre, dancing-hall, L. — **saṃgara**, m. contest on the stage, Prasannar. — **stotra**, n. N. of a Stotra. **Raṅgâṅgana**, n. an arena or place of public contest, MBh. **Raṅgâṅgā**, f. alum, L. **Raṅgâcārya**, m. N. of a teacher (who died in 1344), Cat.; of various authors, ib. **Raṅgâjīva**, m. 'living by colours or by the stage,' a painter or an actor, L. **Raṅgâbharaṇa**, m. (in music) a kind of measure, Saṃgīt. **Raṅgâri**, m. a fragrant oleander, L. **Raṅgârohaṇa**, n. N. of a poem. **Raṅgâvataraṇa**, n. 'entering on the stage,' the profession of an actor, MBh. **Raṅgâvatāraka** or °**rin**, m. (cf. prec.) a stage-player, actor, Mn. iv, 215; Yājñ. i, 161 (the latter also 'an actor who dresses like Rudra,' L.) **Raṅgâvali**, f. a row of stages or arenas, Dharmaś. **Raṅgêśa**, m. N. of a king (patron of Parāśara Bhaṭṭa), Cat.; *-pura*, n. N. of a city (Seringapatam), VBr. **Raṅgêśvarī**, f. (prob.) N. of the wife of Raṅgêśa, Cat. **Raṅgêshṭālu** or °**luka**, n. a kind of bulbous root or onion, L. **Raṅgôddyota**, m. (in music) a kind of measure, Saṃgīt. **Raṅgôpajīvin** (R.), °**vya** (VarBṛS.), m. 'living by the stage,' a stage-player, actor. **Raṅgôpamardin**, m. 'injuring the stage,' an actor who dresses like Rāvaṇa, L.

Raṅgaṇa, n. (prob.) dancing, merry-making &c., MW.

Raṅgita, mfn. well-coloured, handsome, pretty, Hcat.; Nalac.

Raṅgin, mfn. colouring, dyeing, painting, W.; passionate, impassioned, ib.; (ifc.) attached to, delighting in, fond of, Śatr.; entering the stage, BhP.; (*inī*), f. Asparagus Racemosus, L.

1. **Raja,** m. (g. *pacâdi*) = *rajas,* dust (cf. *nī-, vi-r°*); the pollen of flowers, Prasaṅgâbh.; the menstrual excretion (also n.), L.; emotion, affection, L.; the quality of passion, Uṇ. iv, 216, Sch.; N. of one of Skanda's attendants, MBh.; of a king (son of Viraja), VP.

2. **Raja,** in comp. for *rajas.* — **udvāsā,** f. a woman who has put off her soiled clothes (after her impurity), Kauś. (cf. *malôdvāsas*). **Rajā-śaya,** mfn. (for *rajaḥ-ś°,* q. v.), ĀpŚr. **Rájêshita,** mfn. (for *raja-ish°*) driven by camels or asses, RV. viii, 46, 28 (Sāy.) **Rajôtsava-māhātmya,** n. (for *raja-uts°*) N. of ch. of BhavP. **Rajônmiśra,** mfn. (for *raja-unm°*) mixed with the pollen of flowers, R. **Rajôpama,** mfn. (irreg. for *raja-up°*) resembling dust, Hit.

Rajaḥ, in comp. for *rajas.* — **kaṇa,** m. a grain of dust; pl. dust, Ragh. — **paṭala,** n. a coating of dust, MW. — **putra,** m. 'son of passion,' a vulgar person of low origin, Cat. — **pluta,** mfn. filled with (the quality of) passion, BhP. — **śayá,** mf(*ā*)n. silver, made of silver, MaitrS.; VS. (= *rajasi śete,* Mahidh.); m. a dog, W. — **śuddhi,** f. a pure or right condition of the menses, Suśr. — **suvāsinī,** f. a girl that has menstruated but still lives in her father's house, MānGṛ. — **spṛiś,** mfn. touching the dust or the earth, Kathās.

Rajaka, m. a washerman (so called from his cleaning or whitening clothes; regarded as a degraded caste; accord. to L. either 'the son of a Pāra-dhenuka and a Brāhmaṇī' or 'the son of a Nishṭhya and an Ugrī'), MBh.; Kāv. &c.; a parrot or a garment (*śuka* or *aṅśuka*), L.; N. of a king, VP. (prob. w. r. for *rājaka*); (*ikā*), f. a washerwoman, Pāṇ. iii, 1, 145, Pat.; (*akī*), f. id. or the wife of a washerman, ib.; N. of a woman on the third day of her impurity, Bhpr. — **sarasvatī,** f. N. of a poetess, Cat.

Rajatá, mfn. (cf. 2. *ṛijra*) whitish, silver-coloured, silvery (*°tám hiraṇyam,* 'whitish gold,' i. e. silver), RV.; TS.; VS.; silver, made of silver, Br.; ĀśvŚr.; ChUp.; n. (m., g. *ardharcâdi*) silver, AV. &c. &c.; (only L.) gold; a pearl ornament; ivory; blood; an asterism; N. of a mountain and of a lake. — **kumbha,** m. a silver jar, MW. — **kūṭa,** m. or n. N. of a peak on the Malaya mountains, Kathās. — **daṅshṭra,** m. N. of a son of Vajra-daṅshṭra (king of the Vidyā-dharas), Kathās. — **dāna-prayoga,** m. N. of wk. — **dyuti,** m. N. of Hanumat, L. — **nābha,** m. N. of a partic. fabulous being, Hariv. — **nābhi** (*rajatá-*), mfn. having a white navel, VS.; m. N. of a descendant of Kubera, AV. — **padma-dāna,** n. N. of wk. — **parvata,** m. a silver mountain, R.; N. of a partic. mountain, Hariv. — **pātrá,** n. a silver cup or vessel of any kind, AV.; Rājat. — **prastha,** m. N. of Kailāsa, L. — **bhājana,** n. = *-pātra,* Suśr. — **maya,** mf(*ī*)n. made of silver, silver, VarBṛS.; Kathās. — **vāha,** m. N. of a man; pl. his descendants, Saṃskārak. **Rajatâkara,** (prob.) m. 'silver-mine,' N. of a place, Cat. **Rajatâcala** or **°tâdri,** m. 'silver-mountain,' N. of Kailāsa, Kāv. **Rajatânvita,** mfn. adorned with silver, Mn. iii, 202.

Rájana, mf(*ī*)n. colouring, dyeing, AV.; m. a ray, ŚāṅkhBr.; N. of a man with the patr. Kauṇeya, TS.; PañcavBr. (also *°naka*); n. safflower, L.; (*ī*), f., see s. v.

Rajani, f. (m. c. and ibc.) = *rajanī,* night. — **kara and -kṛit,** m. 'night-maker,' the moon, Kāv. — **cara,** m. 'night-rover,' a Rākshasa, MBh.; R.; a night-watcher, Viddh. — **puraṃdhrī,** f. a form of the Upamā, Vām. iv, 3, 32, Sch. — **m-manya,** mfn. thinking itself to be night (said of day), Bhaṭṭ. — **rākshasī,** f. night regarded as a Rākshasī, Kathās.

Rajanī, f. 'the coloured or dark one,' night, AV. &c. &c.; Curcuma Longa (du. = *-dvaya*), Suśr.; the indigo plant, L.; a grape or lac (*drākshā* or *lākshā*), L.; N. of Durgā, Hariv.; of a partic. personification, MānGṛ.; (in music) of a partic. Mūrchanā, Saṃgīt.; of an Apsaras, Bālar.; of a river, BhP. — **kara,** m. = *rajani-k°,* Gīt.; BhP.; *-nātha,* w. r. for *rajanī-cara-n°.* — **gandha,** m. (and *ā,* f.) Polianthes Tuberosa, L. — **cara,** mfn. wandering in the night (as the moon), Hariv.; m. a n°-rover (*-nātha,* m. 'lord of the n°-r°s,' the moon; w. r. *rajanī-cara-n°*), Hit.; a Rākshasa, R.; a n°-watcher, W.; a thief, ib. — **jala,** n. 'n°-dew,' rime, hoar-frost, L. — **dvaṃdva,** n. a period of two nights with the intermediate day, MW. — **dvaya,** n. Curcuma Longa and Aromatica, Suśr. — **pati,** m. 'lord of night,' the moon, Kathās. — **bhujaṃga,** m. 'lover of n°,' id., Śrīkaṇṭh. — **mukha,** n. 'night-beginning,' the evening, Rājat. — **ramaṇa,** m. 'husband of night,' the moon, Kathās. — **°śa** (*°nīśa*), m. = *-pati,* Vcar. — **hāsā,** f. Nyctanthes Arbor Tristis, L.

Rajanīya, w. r. for *mahanīya,* MBh.

Rajayitrī, f. (fr. Caus.) a female painter or colourist, VS.

Rájas, n. 'coloured or dim space,' the sphere of vapour or mist, region of clouds, atmosphere, air, firmament (in Veda one of the divisions of the world and distinguished from *div* or *svar,* 'the sphere of light,' and *rocanā divaḥ,* 'the ethereal spaces,' which are beyond the *rajas,* as ether is beyond the air; often *rajas* = 'the whole expanse of heaven or sky,' divided into a lower and upper stratum, the *rajas uparam* or *pārthivam* and the *rajas uttamam* or *paramam* or *divyam;* hence du. *rajasī,* 'the lower and higher atmospheres;' sometimes also three and RV. i, 164, 6 even six such spheres are enumerated, hence pl. *rajāṅsi,* 'the skies'), RV.; AV.; TS.; VS.; Br.; vapour, mist, clouds, gloom, d[arkn]ess, darkness, RV.; AV.; impurity, dirt, dust, any small particle of matter, RV. &c. &c. (cf. *go-r°*); the dust or pollen of flowers, Kālid.; BhP.; cultivated or ploughed land (as 'dusty' or 'dirty'), arable land, fields, RV.; the impurity, i. e. the menstrual discharge of a woman, GṛS.; Mn.; MBh.; Suśr. &c.; the 'darkening' quality, passion, emotion, affection, MBh.; Kāv. &c.; (in phil.) the second of the three Guṇas or qualities (the other two being *sattva,* goodness, and *tamas,* darkness, cf. IW. 85; *rajas* is sometimes identified with *tejas,* q. v.; it is said to predominate in air, and to be active, urgent, and variable), Sāṃkhyak.; VarBṛS.; Suśr. &c.; 'light' or 'day' or 'world' or 'water,' Nir. iv, 19; a kind of plant (= *parpaṭa*), Bhpr.; tin, L.; autumn, L.; sperm, L.; safflower, L.; m. N. of a Ṛishi (son of Vasishṭha), VP. [Cf. Gk. ἔρεβος; Goth. *riqis.*] — **tamaska,** mfn. (any one or any thing) under the influence of the two qualities *rajas* and *tamas* (see above), BhP. — **tamo-maya,** mf(*ī*)n. made up or consisting of *r°* and *t°* (cf. prec.), MārkP. — **tas,** ind. from the dust, Pracaṇḍ. — **túr,** mfn. penetrating the sky, hastening through the air, RV. — **toka,** m. n. 'offspring of passion,' avarice, greediness, BhP. — **vala,** mf(*ā*)n. covered with dust, dusty, MBh.; BhP.; full of the quality *rajas,* full of passion, Mn. vi, 77; having water (= *udaka-vat*), Nir., Sch.; m. a buffalo, L.; = *ushṭra* or *gardabha,* Sāy. (cf. *rajêshita* under 2. *raja,* col. 1); (*ā*), f. a menstruating or marriageable woman, GṛS.; Mn.; MBh. &c. — **vin,** mfn. dusty, full of dust or pollen, Cat.; full of the quality *rajas,* ib.

Rajasá, mfn. unclean, dusty, dark, AV.; living in the dark, ib.; ifc. (f. *ī*) the menstrual excretion (= *rajas*), Gṛihyas.

Rajasaya, Nom. P. *°yati* = *rajasvinam âcashṭe,* Pat.

Rajasānu, m. a cloud, L.; soul, heart (= *citta*), L.

Rajaska, ifc. (f. *ā*) = *rajas,* in *nī-* and *vi-r°.*

1. **Rajasya,** Nom. P. *°syati,* to become dust, be scattered as dust, Gaṇar. [Cf. Goth. *riqizja.*]

2. **Rajasyà,** mfn. dusty, VS.; having the quality *rajas,* MW.

Rajā-śaya. See under 2. *raja,* col. 1.

Rajita, mfn. (fr. Caus.) affected, moved, captivated, allured, Śiś.

Rajī-kṛi, P. *-karoti,* to change or turn into dust, Vop.

Rajo, in comp. for *rajas.* — **gātra,** m. N. of a son of Vasishṭha, MārkP. — **guṇa-maya,** mf(*ī*)n. having the quality *rajas* (q. v.), ib. — **grahi,** mfn., Vop. xxvi, 48. — **jush,** mfn. connected with the quality *rajas* (q. v.), Kād. — **darśana,** n. (first) appearance of the menstrual excretion, Saṃskārak.; *-śānti,* f. N. of wk. — **'dhika,** mfn. one in whom the quality *rajas* predominates, VarBṛS. — **nimīlita,** mfn. blinded by passion or desire, MW. — **bandha,** m. suppression of menstruation, MW. — **bala** (or *-vala*), n. darkness, L. — **megha,** m. a cloud of dust, MBh.; R. — **rasa,** m. darkness, L. — **vala,** see *-bala.* — **virikta-manas,** mfn. one whose mind is free from passion, Ragh. — **hara,** m. 'remover of impurity,' a washerman, L.; (with Jainas) 'the broom,' HPariś. — **haraṇa,** n. = prec. (with Jainas), L.; *-dhārin,* m. = *-vratin,* L.

Rañja, m., see *jala-r°;* (*ā*), f. a kind of drum, Saṃgīt.

Rañjaka, mf(*ikā*)n. colouring, dyeing, ŚārṅgS.; exciting passion or love, charming, pleasing, Cat.; m. a colourist, dyer, painter, Mn. iv, 216; an inciter of affection &c., stimulus, W.; the red powder on the capsules of the Rottleria Tinctoria, L.; biliary humour on which vision depends, W.; (*akī*), f. a female colourer or dyer, Cat.; n. cinnabar, L.; vermilion, L.

Rañjana, mf(*ī*)n. colouring, dyeing (*-tva,* n.), Sarvad.; (ifc.) pleasing, charming, rejoicing, delighting, Gīt. (cf. *jana-rañjanī*); conciliating, befriending, MW.; m. Saccharum Munja, L.; (*ī*), f. (prob.) friendly salutation, Buddh.; the indigo plant, L.; Nyctanthes Arbor Tristis, L.; turmeric, L.; saffron, L.; a kind of fragrant perfume, L.; red arsenic, L.; (in music) a partic. Śruti, Saṃgīt.; n. the act of colouring or dyeing, Vāgbh.; colour, dye, paint, R.; (in gram.) nasalization, VPrāt., Sch.; the act of pleasing, delighting, conciliating, giving pleasure, MBh.; Kāv. &c.; a partic. game, L.; red sandal-wood, L.; cinnabar, L. — **dravya,** n. any colouring substance, Kum., Sch. — **dru,** m. a kind of tree, L. — **druma,** m. Shorea Robusta, L. — **vallī,** f. Momordica Charantia, L.

Rañjanaka, m. a kind of tree, L.

Rañjanīya, mfn. to be coloured or dyed, MW.; to be rejoiced or pleased or made happy, Kathās.; to be rejoiced at, pleasant, delightful, Sarvad.

Rañjita, mfn. coloured, dyed, painted, tinted, MBh.; Kāv. &c.; illumined, BhP.; affected, moved, charmed, delighted, MBh.; Kāv. &c.

Rañjinī, f. N. of various plants (the indigo plant, Rubia Munjista &c.), L. (cf. *rañjanī*).

रट् *raṭ,* cl. 1. P. (Dhātup. ix, 10) *raṭati* (pf. *rarāṭa;* fut. *raṭitā* &c., Gr.), to howl, shout, roar, yell, cry, Kāv.; Var.; Kathās.; to crash (as an axe), Prab.; to ring (as a bell), Mālatīm.; to lament, wail, HPariś.; to proclaim aloud, Kṛishṇaj.: Caus. *raṭayati* (aor. *arīraṭat*), to howl, shout &c., Daś.: Intens. *rāraṭīti,* to scream aloud, roar, yell, caw &c.; R.; Kāśikh.; Bhojapr.

Raṭana, n. shouting, shout, applause, Rājat.

Raṭantī, f. N. of the 14th day in the dark half of the month Māgha, W.

Raṭaraṭāya, Ā. *°yate* (onomat.), to croak, Subh. (v. l.)

Raṭita, mfn. screamed, shouted &c.; received with shouts, applauded, Inscr.; n. shouting, roaring, yelling, screaming, creaking, crying, Kād.; Hcar.; Rājat.

रट्टा *raṭṭā,* f. N. of a princess, Rājat.

रठ् *raṭh* (cf. √*raṭ*), cl. 1. P. *raṭhati,* to speak, Dhātup. ix, 50.

रडि *raḍi,* f. (with *rati*) play, sport (= *krīḍā*), Kāṭh., Sch. (omitted in other texts).

रड्ड *raḍḍa,* m. N. of a man, Rājat.; (*ā*), f. N. of a princess, ib.

रण 1. *raṇ* or *ran* (cf. √*ram*), cl. 1. 4. P. *ráṇati, ráṇyati* (2. du. *raṇyáthaḥ,* RV. i, 112, 18; pf. *rāraṇa,* RV.; aor. *arāṇishuḥ, raṇishṭana,* ib.), to rejoice, be pleased, take pleasure in (loc., rarely acc.), RV.; to gladden, delight, gratify, ib.: Caus. *randyati, °te,* to cheer, gladden, exhilarate with (instr. or loc.), RV.; to be at ease, be pleased or satisfied with, delight in (loc.), ib.; TS.; AV.: Intens. (Subj. *rāraṇat, rāraṇ;* Impv. *rārandhi, rārantu*) = Caus. (as well in the trans. as in the intrans. meanings), RV.

1. **Ráṇa,** m. delight, pleasure, gladness, joy, RV.; VS.; AV.; (also n.) battle (as an object of delight), war, combat, fight, conflict, RV. &c. &c. — **karman,** n. 'war-business,' battle, fighting, R.; MārkP. — **kāmin,** mfn. desirous of war, wishing to fight, W. — **kāmya,** Nom. P. *°yati,* to wish for battle, be desirous of battle, Śiś.; Bhaṭṭ. — **kārin,** mfn. causing b° or strife, VarBṛS. — **kṛit,** mfn. causing joy, delighting, RV.; fighting, a fighter, MBh. — **kshiti,** f., **-kshetra,** n., **-kshoṇi** or **-kshauṇi,** f., **-kshmā,** f., **-khala,** m. or n. (?) place of battle, battle-field, MBh.; Kāv. &c. — **gocara,** mfn. engaged in war, fighting, MārkP. — **jambuka,** m. N. of a man, Hāsy. — **jaya,** m. victory in battle, MW. — **m-jaya,** m. (*raṇam,* acc.) N. of a king, Pur. — **tūrya,** n. a war-drum, L. — **dara,** m. N. of a man, Cat. — **dundubhi,** m. a military drum, Hariv.; Siṃhās. — **durgā,** f. N. of Durgā, Hariv.; *°gādhāraṇa-yantra,* n. N. of a partic. amulet, Cat. — **dhur,** f. (R.) or **-dhurā,** f. (Veṇīs.) the heavy burden of fighting, the brunt of battle. — **dhṛishṭa,** m. N. of various men, VP.

-pakshin, m. a species of falcon, L. **-paṇḍita**, m. 'skilled in battle,' a warrior, W. **-pura-svāmin**, m. N. of a partic. image of Sūrya, Rājat. **-priya**, mf(*ā*)n. fond of war or battle, warlike, Hariv.; Kām.; m. a falcon, L.; n. the fragrant root of Andropogon Muricatus, L. **-bahādura-sāha-virudrâvalī**, f. N. of wk. **-bhaṭa**, m. N. of a man, Kathās. **-bhū** (BhP.) or **-bhūmi** (MBh.; Ragh.), f. a battle-ground, field of battle. **-matta**, mfn. furious in b°, L.; m. an elephant, L. **-mārga-kovida**, mfn. experienced in the art or ways of war, BhP. **-mukha**, n. the jaws of battle, MBh.; the van of b° or of an army, ib.; BhP. &c. **-mushṭikā**, f. a species of plant, L. **-mūrdhan**, m. the front or van of a battle, MBh.; R.; Kathās. **-yajña**, m. a b° regarded as a sacrifice, Veṇīs. **-raṅka**, m. the space between the tusks of an elephant, L. **-raṅga**, m. 'battle-stage,' a place or field of b°, BhP.; Rājat.; *-malla*, m. = *bhoja-rāja*, q. v., Col. **- 1. -raṇa**, n. (for 2. see col. 2), a longing, desire, wish, regret (for a lost object), L. **-raṇaka**, m. (Mālatīm.; Uttarar. &c.) or n. (L.) or (*ā*), f. (Daś.) longing, anxiety, anxious regret for some beloved object; m. n. desire, love, W.; m. the god of love, Dhūrtan. **-rasika**, mfn. fond of fighting, desirous of f° with (comp.), Bālar. **-lakshmī**, f. the fortune of war, goddess of battle, Kathās. **-vaṅga-malla**, m. (prob.) w. r. for *-raṅga-m°*, q. v., Col. **-vanya**, m. N. of a king, MārkP. **-vādya**, n. a military musical instrument, martial music, MW. **-vikrama**, m. N. of a man, Inscr. **-vigraha**, m. id., ib. **-viśārada**, mfn. skilled in war, MBh. **-vṛitti**, mfn. having war or battle for a profession, Hariv. **-śikshā**, f. the art or science of war, MBh. **-śiras**, n. the front or van of a battle, Kāv. **-śīrsha**, n. id., R. **-śūra**, m. a hero in war, warrior, R. **-śauṇḍa**, mfn. skilled in war, MBh. **-saṃrambha**, m. the fury of battle, Rājat. **-saṃkula**, n. the confusion or noise of battle, a mixed or tumultuous combat, L. **-sajjā**, f. military accoutrement, MW. **-sattra**, n. war or battle regarded as a sacrifice, MBh. **-sahāya**, m. 'war-helper,' an ally, MW. **-stamba-bhramara**, N. of a country, VP. **-stambha**, m. 'battle-pillar,' a monument of war or battle, L.; N. of a country, VP.; Cat. (prob. w. r.; cf. prec.) **-stha**, mfn. engaged in w° or b°, fighting, MBh. **-sthāna**, n. place or field of b°, ib. **-svāmin**, m. an image of Śiva as lord of b°, Rājat. **-hastin**, m. N. of an author, Cat. **Raṇâgni**, m. b° regarded as fire, MBh. **Raṇâgra**, n. the front or van of a battle, Kathās. **Raṇâṅga**, n. 'war-implement,' weapon of war or b°, a sword, Bhaṭṭ. **Raṇâṅgana**, n. a battle-arena, field of b° (also °*gaṇa*), MBh.; Rājat. **Raṇâji**, m. N. of a Sādhya, Hariv. **Raṇâjira**, n. area or arena for fighting, b°-field, MBh.; R. &c. **Raṇâtodya**, n. a b°-drum, Kathās. **Raṇâditya**, m. N. of various men, Rājat.; Subh. **Raṇânta-kṛit**, mfn. making an end of b° (N. of Vishṇu), R. **Raṇâpêta**, mfn. flying away from b°, Kir. **Raṇâbhiyoga**, m. engaging in battle, warlike encounter, W. **Raṇâyudha**, m. a cock, Bhpr. **Raṇârambhā**, f. N. of the wife of Raṇâditya, Rājat.; *-svāmi-deva*, m. N. of a statue erected by Raṇārambhā, ib. **Raṇâlaṃkaraṇa**, m. a heron, L. **Raṇâvani**, f. battle-ground, a field of b°, Hariv. **Raṇâśva**, m. N. of a king, VP. **Raṇe-cara**, mfn. going or moving about in the field of b° (said of Vishṇu), Pañcar. **Raṇêśa** or °**śvara**, m. = *raṇa-svāmin*, q. v., Rājat. **Raṇe-svaccha** (!), m. a cock, L. **Raṇâîshin**, mfn. eager for b°, Cat. **Raṇôtkaṭa**, mfn. furious or mad in b°, R.; m. N. of one of Skanda's attendants, MBh.; of a Daitya, Hariv. **Raṇôtsāha**, m. prowess in b°, R. **Raṇôddāma**, mfn. eager for b°, MW. **Raṇôddīpa-siṅha**, m. N. of a man, Cat. **Raṇôddeśa**, m. a field of b°, R.; a partic. spot or quarter of a battle-field, MW.

Raṇaka, m. N. of a king, BhP.

Rāṇitri, mfn. delighting in (loc.), RV.

Rāṇya, mfn. delectable, pleasant, RV.; AV.; fit for fighting, warlike, RV.; n. joy, pleasure, ib.; war, battle, ib. **-jit**, mfn. victorious in battle, ib. **-vāc**, mfn. speaking agreeably, ib.

1. **Raṇvá**, mf(*ā́*)n. pleasant, delightful, agreeable, lovely, RV.; joyous, gay, ib. **-samdṛiś** (*raṇvá-*), mfn. appearing beautiful, ib.

2. **Raṇva**, Nom. P. °*vati*, to rejoice, delight, TS.

Rā́ṇvan, mfn. agreeable, pleasant, RV. v, 4, 10 (= *ramaṇīya*, Sāy.)

Raṇvitá, mfn. joyous, gay, RV. ii 3, 6 (only f. du. *raṇvite*; Sāy. = *śabdite, stute*, or *paras-param gacchantyau*; cf. √*raṇv*).

रण् 2. *raṇ*, cl. 1. P. (Dhātup. xiii, 2) *raṇati* (Gr. also pf. *rarāṇa*, fut. *raṇitā* &c.), to sound, ring, rattle, jingle, Kāv.; Pur.: Caus. *raṇayati* (aor. *arīraṇat* or *ararāṇat*, Pat. on Pāṇ. vii, 4, 3), to make resound, BhP.: Desid. *rirāṇishati*, Gr.: Intens. *raṃraṇyate, raṃraṇti*, ib.

2. **Raṇa**, m. (for 1. see p. 863, col. 3) sound, noise, L.; the quill or bow of a lute (= *koṇa*), L. **- 2. -raṇa**, m. (for 1. see col. 1) a gnat, L. **-raṇâyita**, mfn. rattling or sounding aloud, Kād.

Raṇat, mfn. sounding, ringing, rattling &c., Kāv.; Pur. **-kāra**, m. a rattling or clanking sound, Mālatīm.; Prab.; humming (of bees), Rājat.

Raṇita, mfn. sounded, sounding, ringing &c., Kāv.; n. any ringing or rattling sound, ib.; Rājat.; BhP.; humming (of bees), Gīt.

रण् 3. *raṇ*, cl. 10. P. *raṇayati*, to go, Dhātup. xix, 33; 56.

3. **Raṇa**, m. going, motion, L.

रण्ड *raṇḍa*, mfn. (cf. *baṇḍa*) maimed, crippled, L.; faithless (see *śākhā-r°*); m. a man who dies without male issue, MW.; a barren tree, ib.; (*ā*), f. a term of abuse in addressing women, a slut (others 'a widow;' *bāla-r°*, 'a young widow'), Kāv.; Pañcat.; Salvinia Cucullata, L.; Anthericum Tuberosum, L.; a kind of metre, Col. **Raṇḍânanda** (°*ḍān°*?), m. N. of a poet, Cat. **Raṇḍâśramin**, m. one who loses his wife after the 48th year, BhavP.

Raṇḍaka, m. a barren tree, L.

रण्य *raṇya*. See col. 1.

रण्व् *raṇv* (cf. *ramb, riṇv, rimb*), cl. 1. P. *raṇvati*, to go, Dhātup. xv, 87.

रण्व 1. 2. *raṇva, raṇvita*. See col. 1.

रत *rata, rati* &c. See under √*ram*, p. 867, cols. 2, 3.

रताम्बुक *ratāmbuka* (?), n. du. the two cavities immediately above the hips, L.

रतू *ratū*, f. (cf. √*ṛit*) the river of heaven, the celestial Ganges, Uṇ. i, 94, Sch.; true speech, L.

रत्न *rátna*, n. (√1. *rā*) a gift, present, goods, wealth, riches, RV.; AV.; ŚBr.; a jewel, gem, treasure, precious stone (the nine j°s are pearl, ruby, topaz, diamond, emerald, lapis lazuli, coral, sapphire, Gomeda; hence *ratna* is a N. for the number 9; but accord. to some 14), Mn.; MBh. &c.; anything valuable or best of its kind (e. g. *putra-r°*, an excellent son); a magnet, loadstone, Kap., Sch. (cf. *maṇi*); water, L.; = *ratna-havis*, ŚBr.; m. (with *bhaṭṭa*) N. of a man, Cat. **-kaṇṭha**, m. N. of various authors, Cat. **-kandala**, m. coral, L. **-kara**, m. N. of Kubera, L. **-karaṇḍaka**, m. N. of wk. **-karṇikā**, f. an ear-ring with jewels, Divyâv. **-kalaśa**, m. N. of a man, Rājat. **-kalā**, f. N. of a woman, Cat.; *-caritra*, n. N. of wk. **-kirīṭin**, m. N. of a king of the Kiṃ-naras, Kāraṇḍ. **-kīrti**, m. N. of a Buddha, Lalit. **-kumbha**, m. a jar set with jewels, Mṛicch. **-kūṭa**, m. N. of a mountain, L.; of a Bodhi-sattva, Buddh.; n. N. of an island, Kathās.; *-sūtra*, n. N. of a Buddhist Sūtra wk. **-ketu**, m. N. of a Buddha, Buddh.; of a Bodhi-sattva, ib.; a N. common to 2000 future Buddhas (also °*tu-rāja*), ib.; °*tûdaya*, m. N. of a drama. **-koṭi**, m. N. of a Samādhi, Buddh. **-kośa**, m. N. of a lexicon and various wks.; *-kāra-mata-vāda*, m. (and *-kāra-vādârtha*, m.), *-kārikā-vicāra*, m., *-parishkāra*, m., *-mata-rahasya*, n., *-vāda* or *-vicāra*, m., *-vāda-rahasya*, n., and *-vādârtha*, m. N. of wks. **-kshetra-kūṭa-saṃdarśana**, m. N. of a Bodhi-sattva, Lalit. (v. l. *-cchattra-kū°*). **-khacita**, mfn. set or studded with gems, MW. **-khani**, f. a mine for precious stones, Śatr. **-kheṭa**, m. (with *dīkshita*) N. of an author, Cat. **-garbha**, mfn. filled with precious stones, containing jewels, set with j°, MBh.; R.; m. the sea, L.; N. of Kubera, L.; of a Bodhi-sattva, Lalit.; W.; of a commentator, Cat.; W.; (with *sārvabhauma*) of another author, Cat.; (*ā*), f. the earth, Prasannar.; Siṅhâs. **-giri**, m. N. of a mountain, Buddh.; *-rasa*, m. a partic. medicament, Rasêndrac. **-grīva-tīrtha**, n. N. of a Tīrtha, Cat. **-candra**, m. N. of a god (said to be guardian of a jewel-mine), Śatr.; of a Bodhi-sattva, Buddh.; of a son of Bimbi-sāra, ib.; °*rāmati*, m. N. of a Bhikshu, Kathās. **-cūḍa**, m. N. of a Bodhi-sattva, Buddh.; of a mythical king, W.; *-muni*, m. N. of a man, W.; °*ḍâ-paripṛicchā*, f., °*ḍôpâkhyāna*, n. N. of wks. **-cūra-muni**, °**rôpâkhyāna**, n. prob. w. r. for *-cūḍa-m°*, °*ḍôpâkhy°* above. **-cchattra**, n. an umbrella (adorned) with jewels, Pañcar.; *-kūṭa-saṃdarśana*, m., v. l. for *ratna-kshetra kūṭa-s°*, q. v., Lalit.; °*râbhyudgatâvabhāsa*, m. N. of a Buddha, ib. **-cchāyā**, f. glitter or splendour of jewels, Megh. **-jātaka**, n. N. of wk. **-talpa**, m. a couch adorned with j°, Daś. **-tūlikā**, f. N. of wk. **-tejo-'bhyudgata-rāja**, m. N. of a Buddha, Buddh. **-traya**, n. 'j°-triad,' the three j° or excellent things (with Buddhists, viz. *buddha, dharma* and *saṃgha*; or with Jainas, viz. *samyag-darśana, s°-jñāna* and *samyak-cāritra*; *-jaya-mālā* (prob. w. r. for *-japa-m°*), f. N. of a Jaina wk.; *-parīkshā*, f. N. of a Vedânta wk.; *-vidhāna-kathā*, f.; °*yôdyāpana*, n. N. of Jaina wks.; °*yôddyota*, m. N. of a Śaiva wk. **-daṇḍâtapatrin**, mfn. having a staff and an umbrella adorned with jewels, Hcat. **-datta**, m. N. of various men, Buddh.; Kathās.; Cat. **-darpaṇa**, m. 'j°-mirror,' a looking-glass consisting of jewels, Pañcar.; N. of a Comm. **-dīpa**, m. 'j°-lamp,' a lamp in which j°s give out light, a gem serving as a light (such gems are fabled to be in Pātāla), Kathās.; BhP. &c.; *-viśva-prakāśa*, m. N. of wk. **-dīpaka**, m., **-dīpikā**, f., **-dyota**, m. N. of wks. **-druma**, m. (prob.) coral; *-maya*, mf(*ī*)n. (prob.) made or composed of coral, MBh. **-dvīpa**, m. 'j°-island,' N. of an island, Hariv.; Rājat.; Tantras. **-dhá**, mfn. = *-dhā́*, q. v. **-dhara**, m. N. of various men, Cat. **-dhā́**, mfn. procuring wealth, distributing riches or precious things (*-tama*, mfn. dist° great riches), RV.; AV.; ŚBr.; possessing wealth, RV. **-dhenu**, f. a cow symbolically represented by j°s, Cat. **-dhéya**, n. distribution of wealth, RV. **-dhvaja**, m. N. of a Bodhi-sattva, Buddh. **-nadī**, f. 'j°-river,' N. of a river, Kathās. **-nātha**, m. N. of an author, Cat. **-nābha**, mfn. one whose navel is a jewel (said of Vishṇu), MBh. **-nāyaka**, m. a ruby, L. **-nicaya**, m. a heap or collection of j°s &c., MW. **-nidhi**, m. 'receptacle of pearls,' the sea, MBh.; N. of Meru, ib.; of Vishṇu, Pañcar.; a wagtail (w. r. for *rata-n°*), L. **-pañcaka**, n. the 5 jewels (viz. gold, silver, pearls, a kind of diamond [*rājâvarta*] and coral), Hcat.; N. of wk. **-pati**, m. N. of a man, Cat. **-pariṇāma**, m., **-parīkshā**, f. N. of wks. **-parvata**, m. a mountain containing j°s, R.; N. of Meru, Hariv. **-pāṇi**, m. N. of a Bodhi-sattva, MWB. 203; of various authors, Cat. **-pāla**, m. N. of a king, Madanav. **-pīṭhā**, f. N. of a Gandharva maiden, Kāraṇḍ. **-pura**, n. N. of a town, Kathās.; Virac. **-purī-bhaṭṭāraka**, m. N. of an author, Cat. **-prakāśa**, m. N. of a lexicon and sev. wks. **-pradīpa**, m. = *-dīpa*, q. v. (ifc. °*paka*), Megh.; BhP. &c.; N. of wks.; *-nighaṇṭu*, m. N. of wk. **-prabha**, m. N. of a class of deities, Buddh.; of a king, Kathās.; (*ā*), f. the earth, Sūryapr.; (with Jainas) N. of a hell, L.; of various women, Hit.; Rājat.; Kathās.; of a Nāgī, Kathās.; of an Apsaras, Bālar.; of the 7th Lambaka of the Kathā-sarit-sāgara. **-prāsāda**, m. a palace adorned with jewels, Kathās. **-bandhaka**, m. a jeweller, Hcar., Sch. **-bāhu**, m. 'jewel-armed,' N. of Vishṇu, L. **-bhā́j**, mfn. distributing gifts or wealth, RV.; possessing jewels, R. **-bhūta**, mfn. being a gem or jewel, Nal. **-bhūti**, m. N. of a poet, Subh. **-mañjarī**, f. N. of a Vidyādharī, Hit.; of a woman, ib.; of wk.; *-guṇa-leśa-mātra-sūcakâshṭaka* and °*śa-sūcaka-daśaka*, n. N. of Stotras. **-mati**, m. N. of a grammarian, Gaṇar.; of another man, Buddh. **-maya**, mf(*ī*)n. made or consisting of j°s, studded with precious stones, R.; Bhartṛ. &c. **-mālā**, f. a jewel necklace, pearl n° &c. (ifc. f. *ā*), Ratnâv.; Pañcat.; Pañcar.; N. of a Gandharva maid, Kāraṇḍ.; N. of various wks.; *-vatī*, f. 'having a necklace of jewels,' N. of one of Rādhā's female attendants, Pañcar. **-mālikā**, f. in *kula-r°*, q. v. **-mālin**, mfn. adorned with a necklace of jewels, RāmatUp. **-mālīya-puṇḍroka** (Sadukt.) and **-mitra** (Subh.), m. N. of poets. **-mukuṭa**, m. N. of a Bodhi-sattva, Buddh. **-mukhya**, n. 'chief of jewels,' a diamond, L. **-mudrā**, f. N. of a Samādhi, Buddh.; *-hasta*, m. N. of a Bodhi-sattva, ib. **-megha-sūtra**, n. N. of a Buddhist Sūtra wk. **-yashṭi**, m. N. of a Buddha, Lalit. **-yugma-tīrtha**, n. N. of a Tīrtha, Cat. **-rakshita**, m. N. of a scholar, Buddh. **-ratna**, n. the pearl of pearls, Daś. **-rāj**, m. 'jewel-king,' a ruby, L. **-rāji**, f. a string of pearls, Rājat. **-rāśi**, m. a heap of precious stones, collection of pearls, MBh.; Śak. &c.; the sea, L. **-rekhā**, f. N. of a princess, Kathās. **-lakshaṇa**, n., **-liṅga-sthāpana-vidhi**, m. N. of wks. **-liṅgêśvara**, m. (with Buddhists) N. of Svayam-bhū in his visible form, W. **-vat** (*rátna-*), mfn. accompanied with gifts, RV.; abounding in or decorated with precious stones or pearls, MBh.; R. &c.; m. N. of a mountain, MārkP.; (*atī*), f. the earth, Harav.; N. of various women, Daś.; Kathās. **-vara**, n. 'best of precious stones,' gold, L. **-vardhana**, m. N. of a man, Rājat.; °*nêśa*, m. an image of Śiva erected by Ratna-vardhana, ib. **-varman**, m. N. of a merchant, Kathās. **-varsha**, m. N. of a king of the Yakshas, ib. **-varshuka**, n. the mythical car Pushpaka (supposed to rain or pour out jewels; see *pushpaka*), L. **-viśuddha**, m. (with Buddhists) N. of a world, Buddh. **-vṛiksha**, m. = *vidruma* (in another sense than 'coral'), L. **-śalākā**, f. a sprout or sprig of j°, Kum. **-śāṇa**, m., **-śāstra**, n. N. of wks. **-śikhaṇḍa**, m. N. of a mythical bird (companion of Jaṭāyu), Bālar. **-śikhara**, m. N. of a Bodhi-sattva, Buddh. **-śikhin**, m. N. of a Buddha, ib. **-śilā**, f. mosaic (?), Divyâv. **-śekhara**, m. N. of a Jaina author (15th century), Cat. **-śeṇā**, f. N. of wk. **-shashṭhī**, f. the 6th day of a partic. fortnight, MW.; a partic. religious ceremony, Mṛicch., Sch. **-saṃgraha**, m. N. of various wks. **-saṃghāta**, m. a number or collection of jewels; *-maya*, mf(*ī*)n. made or consisting of a number of j°, MBh. **-samuccaya**, m. N. of wk. **-samudgala** (*-samudgaka?*), m. N. of a Samādhi, Buddh. **-sambhava**, m. N. of a Buddha, (esp.) of a Dhyāni-buddha, MWB. 203; of a Bodhi-sattva, Lalit.; of a place, Buddh. **-sāgara**, m. N. of wk. **-sānu**, m. N. of the mountain Meru, Kāv.; Siṃhās. **-sāra**, m. or n.(?) N. of wk.; *-cintāmaṇi*, m., *-jātake jyotisha-sāra-saṃgraha*, m. N. of wks.; *-parvata*, m. N. of Meru, Siṃhās.; *-śataka*, n., *-samuccaya*, m. N. of wks. **-siṇha**, m. N. of various men, Buddh. **-sū**, mfn. producing jewels, Ragh.; Rājat.; f. the earth, L. **-sūti**, f. the earth, Rājat. **-sūtra-bhāshya**, n. N. of wk. **-sena**, m. N. of a king, Inscr. **-sthala-nagara**, n. N. of a town, ib. **-svāmin**, m. N. of an image erected by Ratna, Rājat. **-havis**, n. a partic. oblation in the Rāja-sūya (having reference to persons who may be reckoned among a king's most valuable treasures), KātyŚr. (cf. *ratnin*). **-hasta**, m. N. of Kubera, L. (cf. *-garbha*). **Ratnâkara**, m. (ifc. f. *ā*) a jewel-mine (*-tva*, n.), Pañcar.; BhP. &c.; the sea, ocean, Kāv. &c.; N. of a Buddha, Buddh.; of a Bodhi-sattva, ib.; of various other persons, Rājat.; Cat. &c.; of a mythical horse, Kathās.; of various wks.; of a town (in this sense perhaps n.), Kathās.; pl. N. of a people, MBh.; *-nighaṇṭa*, m., *-paddhati*, f. N. of wks.; *-mekhalā*, f. 'sea-girded,' the earth, Daś.; *-sa-pāda-śataka*, n. N. of wk.; °*rāyita*, mfn. resembling a jewel-mine, (or) res° the sea, Hcat. **Ratnâṅka**, m. N. of Vishṇu's car, L. **Ratnâṅkura**, m. 'sprout of a pearl,' a small pearl, Mṛicch. **Ratnâṅga**, m. coral, L. **Ratnâṅgurīyaka** (Pañcar.) or °**gulīyaka** (Kathās.), n. a finger-ring (set) with gems. **Ratnâḍhya**, mfn. abounding in jewels or precious stones, R. **Ratnâdi-nandin**, m. N. of a Muni, Bhadrab. **Ratnâdi-parīkshā**, f. N. of wk. **Ratnā-devī**, f. N. of a princess, Rājat. **Ratnâdri**, m. N. of a mythical mountain, RāmatUp. **Ratnâdhipati**, m. 'superintendent of treasures,' N. of Agastya, Bālar.; of a king, Kathās. **Ratnânuviddha**, mfn. set or studded with jewels, A. **Ratnâpaṇa**, m. N. of wk. **Ratnā-pura**, n. N. of a town, Rājat. **Ratnâbharaṇa**, n. an ornament made of j°s, MW. **Ratnâbhisheka-mantra**, m. N. of wk. **Ratnârcis**, m. N. of a Buddha, Lalit. **Ratnârṇava**, m., °**tnârpaṇa**, n. N. of wks. **Ratnâloka**, m. the lustre or brilliance of a gem, MW. **Ratnā-vatī**, f. N. of a woman, Hcar.; of a town, Cat. **Ratnâvabhāsa**, m. (with Buddhists) N. of a Kalpa, Buddh. **Ratnâvalī**, f. a string of pearls, Mṛicch.; Hit.; Kathās.; a partic. rhetorical figure, Kuval.; N. of various women, Kathās.; Rājat. &c.; of a drama by king Harsha-deva (or rather by the poet Bāṇa; cf. IW. 505, n. 1); of other wks. (also °*vali*); *-nibandha*, m., *-paddhati*, f. N. of wks. **Ratnâshṭaka**, n. N. of wk. **Ratnâsana**, n. a throne ornamented with jewels, RāmatUp. **Ratnêndra**, m. 'jewel-chief,' a precious j°, Pañcar. **Ratnêśaka**, m. N. of an author, Cat. **Ratnêśvara**, m. N. of various men, Cat.; n. of a Liṅga, ib. **Ratnôjjvala**, mfn. shining with pearls, Rājat. **Ratnôttama**, m. N. of a Buddha, Kāraṇḍ.; (*ā*), f. N. of a Tantra deity, Buddh. **Ratnôdbhava**, m. N. of a Buddhist saint, W.; of the son of a Padmôdbhava, Daś. **Ratnôlkā**, f. N. of a Tantra deity, Buddh.

Ratnaka, m. N. of a man, Buddh.

Ratnin, mfn. possessing or receiving gifts, RV.; m. pl. N. of certain persons in whose dwelling the Ratna-havis (q. v.) is offered by a king (viz. the Brāhmaṇa, Rājanya, Mahishī, Parivṛiktī, Senā-nī, Sūta, Grāma-ṇī, Kshattṛi, Saṃgrahītṛi, Bhāga-dugha, and Akshâvāpa), TBr.; ŚBr. (°*ni-tva*, n., TBr.)

रत्नि *ratni*, m. f. (a corrupt form of *aratni*; cf. Uṇ. iv, 2) the elbow, ĀśvŚr.; a measure of length (= the distance from the elbow to the end of the closed fist, a cubit), ShaḍvBr.; m. the closed fist, W. **-pṛishṭhaka**, n. the elbow, L.

रत्यङ्ग *raty-aṅga*. See under *rati*, p. 867.

रथ 1. *rátha*, m. (√4. *ṛi*) 'goer,' a chariot, car, esp. a two-wheeled war-chariot (lighter and swifter than the *anas*, q. v.), any vehicle or equipage or carriage (applied also to the vehicles of the gods), waggon, cart, RV. &c. &c. (ifc. f. *ā*); a warrior, hero, champion, MBh.; Kathās.; BhP.; the body, L.; a limb, member, part, L.; Calamus Rotang, L.; Dalbergia Ougeinensis, L.; = *paurusha*, L.; (*ī*), f. a small carriage or waggon, cart, Śiś. **-kaṭyā** (Pārśvan.) or **-kaḍyā** (Vop.; L.), f. a quantity of chariots. **-kara**, m. = *-kārá* below, L. **-kalpaka**, m. the arranger or superintendent of a king's or a great man's equipages, MBh. **-kāmya**, Nom. P. °*yati*, to long for a ch°, wish to be yoked (said of a horse), Kāṭh. **-kāya**, m. the whole body or collection of ch°s (constituting one division of an army), Buddh. **-kārá**, m. a ch°-maker, carriage-builder, wheelwright, carpenter (regarded as the son of a Māhishya by a Karaṇī), AV.; VS.; Br. &c. (cf. IW. 149, n. 2); *-kulá*, n. the caste of carriage-builders, ŚBr.; *-tva*, n. the trade or business of a carriage-b°, Pañcat. **-kāraka**, m. = *-kārá* above, L. (accord. to some, 'the son of a Vaidehaka by a Kshatriyā'). **-kuṭumba** (BhP.) or °**bika** (L.) or °**bin** (R.), m. a carriage-driver, charioteer, coachman. **-kūbara**, m. n. a ch°-shaft, pole of a carriage, MBh. **-kṛicchra**, m. N. of a Yaksha, VP. **-kṛit**, m. = *-kārá* above, KātyŚr.; N. of a Yaksha, VP. **-kṛitsná**, m. a partic. character or personification, MaitrS. (*-gritsá*, VS.) **-ketu**, m. the flag or banner of a ch°, R. **-krānta**, mf(*ā*)n. travelled over by ch°s, TĀr.; m. (in music) a kind of measure, Saṃgīt. **-krītá**, mfn. purchased for the price of a ch°, AV. **-kshaya** (*rátha-*), mfn. sitting in a ch°, RV. **-kshobha**, m. the shaking about of a ch°, Ragh. **-gaṇaka**, m. 'ch°-numberer,' (prob.) an officer who numbers or counts a great man's ch°s, g. *udgātr-ādi*. **-garbhaka**, m. 'embryo-carriage,' a litter, sedan-chair, L. **-gupti**, f. 'car-preservative,' a fence of wood or iron protecting a war-ch° from collisions &c., L. **-gṛitsá**, m. a skilful charioteer, royal coachman (as a partic. character), VS.; AitBr. (*-kṛitsná*, MaitrS.) **-gopana**, n. = *-gupti* above, L. **-granthi**, m. the knot of a ch°, Hariv. **-ghosha**, m. the rattling or rumbling of a ch°, MBh. **-cakrá**, n. (m., w. r., MBh.) a ch°-wheel, Br.; Kauś.; MBh. &c.; N. of wk.; *-cit*, mfn. arranged in the form of a ch°-wh°, TS.; ŚBr. &c.; °*râkṛiti*, mfn. having the f° of a ch°-wh°, KātyŚr., Paddh. **-caraṇa**, m. a ch°-wheel, BhP.; Anas Casarca, L. **-caryā**, f. 'ch°-course,' travelling or going by carriage (frequently in pl.), MBh.; R. &c. (*-carya*, w. r. for *-varya*, MBh.) **-cárshaṇa**, m. or n. a partic. part of a ch°, RV. **-carshaṇi**, mfn. = *-gamana*, Nir. v, 12, Sch. **-citra**, m. N. of a Yaksha, VP.; (*ā*), f. of a river, MBh.; VP. **-jaṅghā**, f. a partic. part of a chariot, the hinder part, Lāṭy. **-1. -jit**, mfn. (for 2. see under 2. *ratha*) conquering ch°s, obtaining ch°s by conquest, RV.; m. N. of a Yaksha, VP. **-jūti** (*rátha-*), mfn. rushing along in a chariot; (or) m. a proper N., AV. **-jñāna**, n. knowledge of carriages and c°-driving, Kathās.; °*nin*, mfn. skilled in it, ib. **-jvara**, m. a crow, MW. **-túr**, mfn. urging or drawing (others, 'overtaking') a ch°, RV. **-dāna-vidhi**, m. N. of wk. **-dāru**, n. wood suitable for carriage-building, Pāṇ. vi, 2, 43, Sch. **-durga**, n. throng or crowd of ch°s, MBh. **-dru** or **-druma**, m. Dalbergia Ougeinensis, L. **-dhur**, f. the pole of a ch°, MBh.; *-dhūr-gata*, mfn. standing upon the fore-part of a ch°, ib. **-dhurya**, m. an excellent fighter, MBh.; *-tā*, f. the state of an e° f°, Jātak. **-nābhí**, f. the nave of a ch°-wheel, VS.; ŚBr.; MuṇḍUp. **-nirghosha** (Nal.) or **-nirhrāda** (BhP.) or **-nisvana** (Nal.), m. the sound or rattling of a ch°. **-nīḍa**, m. n. the seat or the inner part of a ch°, KātyŚr.; MBh.; BhP. **-nemi**, f. the rim or circumference of a ch°-wheel, ŚBr.; MBh. **-ṃ-tará**, n. (*ratham*, acc.) N. of various Sāmans, RV. &c. &c.; m. a form of Agni (regarded as a son of Tapas), MBh.; a partic. cosmic period, Hcat.; N. of a Sādhya, VP.; (*ī*), f. N. of a daughter of Taṃsu, MBh.; *-caraṇa-bhāshya*, n., *-pāda*, m. N. of wks.; *-pṛishṭha*, mfn. having the Sāman Rathaṃtara for a Stotra called Pṛishṭha, ŚrS.; *-varṇa*, mf(*ā*)n. being of the kind of the Sāman Rath°, Lāṭy.; *-sāman*, mfn. having a Rath° for a Sāman, ŚrS. **-patha**, m. a carriage road, Lāṭy.; AmṛitUp. **-pada**, n. 'carriage-foot,' a wheel, L. **-paddhati**, f. N. of wk. **-paryāya**, m. Calamus Rotang, L. **-pāda**, m. = *-pada*, L.; a discus, VarYogay. **-puṃgava**, m. chief of warriors, MBh. **-pratishṭhā-vidhi**, m. N. of ch. of the Pañca-rātra. **-prashṭha**, m. any one who goes before or leads a ch°, Ragh. **-prá**, mfn. (accord. to Sāy.) filling a ch° (with riches; said of Vāyu), RV.; f. N. of a river, Cat. **-prôta** (*rátha-*), m. 'fixed in a car,' a partic. personification, VS.; MaitrS. **-proshṭha** (*rátha-*), m. N. of a man; pl. of his family, RV. **-psā**, f. N. of a river, L. **-bandha**, m. 'ch°-fastening,' anything that holds a ch° together, MBh.; a league of warriors, ib. **-bhaṅga**, m. the breaking or fracture of a chariot, ib. **-bhṛit**, m. N. of a Yaksha, VP. **-maṇḍala**, m. n. a number of ch°s, MBh. **-madhya**, mf(*ā*)n. occupying the centre of a car, RV. v, 87 = MānGṛ. ii. 13; *-stha*, mfn. standing in the centre of a car, MW. **-mahôtsava**, m. a great car-festival, the solemn procession of an idol on a car, Cat. **-mārga**, m. a carriage-road, MBh. **-mitra**, m. N. of a Yaksha, VP. **-mukhá**, n. the front or fore-part of a c°, AV.; TS. **-yātaka**, n. (*ena* instr.) by carriage, in a c°, Cat. **-yātrā**, f. 'car-procession,' the festive proc° of an idol on a car (esp. the proc° of the c° of Jagan-nātha; also °*trā-mahôtsava*, m.), W.; Cat.; *-prayoga*, m. N. of wk. **-yâna**, n. the going by c°, AV.; R. **-yâvan**, mfn. going by c°, RV. **-yuga**, m. (!) a ch° yoke, BhP. **-yúj**, mfn. yoking or yoked to a ch°, RV.; m. a charioteer, Ragh. **-yuddha**, n. a fight (between combatants mounted) on ch°s, MBh. **-yūtha**, m. n. a quantity or number of ch°s, Hariv.; *-pa*, m. a chief warrior, MBh.; Hariv. &c. **-yoga** (*rátha-*), m. a team (of horses &c.) on a ch°, ŚBr.; MBh.; use of a ch°, art of driving it, MBh. **-yojaka**, m. the yoker or harnesser of a ch°, MBh. **-yodha**, m. one who fights from a ch°, MBh. **-raśmi**, m. the trace or traces of a carriage or ch°, ch°-rein, Ragh. **-rāja**, m. N. of an ancestor of Gautama Buddha, Buddh. **-reṇu**, m. the dust whirled up by a ch° (as a partic. cubic measure = 8 Trasa-reṇus), AgP. **-reshá**, m. injury done to a chariot, MaitrS. **-lakshaṇa**, n. N. of wk. **-vaṇśa**, m. a number of chariots, MBh. **-vat** (*rátha-*), mfn. having ch°s, accompanied with ch°s, RV.; containing the word *ratha*, AitBr.; n. abundance of ch°s, RV.; ind. like a ch°-wheel, TBr. (w. r. *-vṛit*). **-vara**, m. the best warrior, MBh.; an excellent ch°, MW.; N. of a king, VP. **-vartman**, n. a ch°-road, highway, R.; Ragh. **-vāraka**, m. the son of a Śūdra and a Sairandhrī, L. (v. l. *-kāraka*, q. v.) **-vāhá**, mf(*ī*)n. drawing a ch°, ŚBr.; KātyŚr.; m. a ch°-horse, a h° yoked in a ch°, MBh.; = next, Kathās. **-vāhaka**, m. a coachman, charioteer, MBh. **-vāhana**, see next. **-vâhana**, m. N. of a man, MBh.; n. a movable platform on which ch°s may be placed (also *-vāhana*; cf. Pāṇ. viii, 4, 8), RV.; VS. &c.; *-vāhá*, m. an ox for drawing such a platform, TS. **-vijñāna**, n. (Kathās.) or **-vidyā**, f. (ib.; KātyŚr., Comm.) the art of driving chariots. **-vimocana**, n. the unyoking of a ch°; °*nīya*, mfn. relating to the unyoking of a ch°, Br.; KātyŚr. **-vīti** (*rátha-*), m. N. of a man, RV. **-vīthī**, f. a carriage way, high road, BhP. **-vṛit**, see *-vat*, ind. **-vega**, m. the speed of a ch°, MW. **-vraja** or **-vrāta**, m. = *-vaṇśa*, q. v., MBh. **-śakti**, f. (prob.) the staff which supports the banner of a war-ch°, MBh.; Hariv.; R. **-śālā**, f. a coach-house, carriage-shed, MBh. **-śikshā**, f. the art of driving a ch°, R. **-śiras** (ŚrS.; Mcar.) or **-śīrshá** (ŚBr.), n. = *-mukha*, q. v. **-śreṇi**, f. a row of ch°s, ŚBr. **-saṅgá**, m. the meeting or encounter of war-ch°s, RV. **-sattama**, m. a most excellent ch°, MW.; the best of warriors, MBh. **-saptamī**, f. N. of the 7th day in the light half of the month Āśvina (so called as the beginning of a Manv-antara when a new Sun ascended his car), W.; *-kāla-nirṇaya*, m., *-pūjā*, f., *-vrata*, n., *-snāna-vidhi*, m. N. of wks. **—sārathi**, m. a charioteer, MBh. **—sūtra**, n. rules or directions about carriage-building, KātyŚr., Sch.; MBh. **—stha**, mfn. being on a ch°, mounted on a car, R.; Prasaṅg.; (*ā*), f. N. of a river, MBh. **—s-páti** (*ráthas-*), m. (*ráthas* prob. a form of the gen.; cf. *vánas-páti*) the 'lord of chariots,' a deity presiding over ch°s or over pleasure and enjoyment, RV. **—spashṭa** (*rátha-*), mfn. knowable or conspicuous by cartways, TS. **—spṛiś**, mfn. touching the ch°, RV. **—svana**, m. (ifc. f. *ā*) the sound or rattling of ch°s, Kathās.; (°*ná*) 'having the sound of a ch°(?), h° a sounding ch°,' a partic. personification, VS.; N. of a Yaksha, BhP. **Rathâkshá**, m. a ch°-axle, TS.; Kāṭh. &c.; a measure of length, = 104 Aṅgulas (*-mātra*, mfn. having that length), KātyŚr.; ib., Sch. &c.; N. of one of Skanda's attendants, MBh. **Rathâgra**, m., w. r. for °*thâgrya* below; n. the fore-part of a ch°, MBh.; *-tas*, ind. in the fore-part of a ch°, ib. **Rathâgrya**, m. the chief or best warrior, ib. **Rathâṅkā**, f. N. of a river, VarBṛS. (v. l. °*thâhvā*). **Rathâṅgá**, n. any part of a ch°, GṛS.; MBh.; a ch°-wheel, MaitrS.; Kāv.; Sāh.; a discus (esp. that of Kṛishṇa or Vishṇu), MBh.; Hariv.; BhP.; a potter's wheel, MBh.; m. the Anas Casarca or ruddy goose (= *cakra-vāka*, q. v.), Vikr.; Rājat.; N. of a poet, Sadukt.; (*ā*), f., see *rathâhvā*; (*ī*), f. a species of medicinal plant, L.; *-tulyâhvayana*, m. 'having the same name as a ch°-wheel,' the above bird, Hariv.; *-dhvani*, m. the rattling of ch°-wheels, Ragh.; *-nāmaka* (L.) or *-nāman* (Kāv.; Kathās.), m. = °*ga-tulyâhvayana* above; *-nemi*, f. the circumference or felly of a ch°-wheel, Śak.; *-pāṇi*, m. 'having a discus in his hand,' N. of Vishṇu, Hariv.; BhP. &c.; *-bhartṛi*, m. 'discus-bearer,' ib., MW.; *-śroṇi-bimbā*, f. having circular or rounded buttocks, MW.; *-samjña* (R.) or *-sâhva* (MBh.), or °*gâhva* (R.) or °*gâhvaya* (L.), m. = °*ga-tulyâhvayana* above; °*gâhvayana*, mfn. having the name 'wheel'; (with *dvija*), m. the ruddy goose, R.; °*gin*, m. 'one who possesses a discus,' N. of Vishṇu, Pracaṇḍ. **Rathânīka**, n. an array or army of war-ch°s, MBh. **Rathântara**, m., w. r. for *rathītara*, q. v. (VP.), or for *ratham-tara*, 'a partic. cosmic period' (AgP.); n. another ch°, TS., Comm. **Rathâbhirūḍhā**, f. N. of a serpent-maiden, Kāraṇḍ. **Rathâbhra**, m. Calamus Rotang (also *-pushpa*), L. **Rathâyudhaka**, m. a kind of bow, L. **Rathā-rathi**, ind. (fr. *ratha* + *r*°) ch° against ch°, MBh. (cf. *nakhā-nakhi* &c.) **Rathârūḍha**, mfn. mounted on a ch°, Kathās. **Rathâroha**, m. 'mounted on a ch°,' one who fights from a ch°, MBh.; the mounting or ascending a ch°, Śak. **Rathârohin**, mfn. one who fights from a ch°, L. **Rathârbhaka**, m. a small carriage, W. **Rathâvaṭṭa**, m. N. of a man, Rājat. **Rathâvayava**, m. any part of a ch°, a wheel; °*yavâyudha*, m. 'wheel- or discus-armed,' N. of Vishṇu (Kṛishṇa), Śiś. **Rathâvarta**, m. N. of a place of pilgrimage, MBh.; of a mountain, HPariś. **Rathâśman**, m. the son of a Brāhman by a Ratha-kārī, L. **Rathâśva**, m. a ch°-horse, Kathās.; n. a ch° and horse, Mn. vii, 96. **Rathā-sáh**, mfn. (the same stem in the strong cases) able or fit to draw a ch°, RV. **Rathâhas**, n. or °**hna**, (prob.) m. (ŚrS.) or °**hnyá**, n. (ŚBr.; ĀpŚr.) a day's journey by carriage. **Rathâhvā**, f. N. of a river, VarBṛS. (v. l. *rathâṅkā*, °*thâṅgā*). **Ráthe-citra**, m. 'glittering on a ch°,' a partic. personification, VS. **Rathêśa**, m. 'ch°-lord,' the owner of a ch°, a warrior fighting from a ch°, Ragh. **Rathe-śúbh**, mfn. flying along in a ch°, RV. **Rathêshā**, f. a ch°-pole, MBh.; Hariv. **Rathêshu**, m. a kind of arrow, Hariv. **Rathe-shṭhá** (RV.) or **-shṭhā** (RV.; VS.), mfn. standing on a ch°, a warrior fighting from a ch°; [cf. Zd. *rathaestā*.] **Rathôḍupa**, m. or n. the body of a carriage, the 'boot' or interior receptacle of a c°, MBh. **Rathôḍha** or **°thôḷha**, mfn. carried on a ch°, RV. **Rathôttama**, m. an excellent chariot, Bhag. **Rathôtsava**, m. a car-festival, a solemn procession of an idol mounted on a car, Cat. **Rathôddhata**, mfn. behaving arrogantly in (his) ch°, VarBṛS.; (*ā*), f. N. of a kind of metre, Śrutab.; Piṅg., Sch.; N. of wk. **Rathôdvaha**, m. a ch°-horse, L.; the Indian cuckoo, L. (w. r. for *ratôd*°); = next, MW. **Rathôpasthá**, m. the seat of a ch°, driving-box (as lower than the main body of the car), the hinder part of a car, AV.; Br. &c. **Rathôraga**, m. pl. N. of a people, MBh. **Rathôshmā**, f. N. of a river, Hariv. **Rathâugha**, m. a number of carriages, VarBṛS. **Ráthâujas**, m. 'having the strength of a ch°,' a partic. personification, VS.; MaitrS.; N. of a Yaksha, VP.

Rathaka, m. a small chariot or cart, Jātak.; pl. partic. parts of a house, AgP.

Ratha-garuta (?) m. (prob. w. r. for *ratni-g*°) the ninth cubit (*aratni*) from the bottom or the eleventh from the top of a sacrificial post, L.

Rathayá, f. desire for carriages or chariots, RV. °**yú**, mfn. desiring or wishing for carriages, ib.

Ratharya, Nom. P. °*yáti*, to go or travel by carriage or chariot, RV.

Ráthas-páti. See col. 1.

Rathika, mf(*ī*)n. going by carriage or chariot, the driver or owner of a car or chariot, VarBṛS.; HPariś.; m. a cartwright (see *bhūmi-r*°); Dalbergia Ougeinensis, L.

Rathita, mfn. furnished with a chariot, MaitrUp.

Rathin, mfn. possessing or going in a chariot or carriage, fighting in a war-ch° (superl. °*thi-tama*), RV. &c. &c.; consisting of ch°s, MBh.; carried in ch°s (as goods), RV.; accustomed to ch°s (as horses), ib.; m. an owner of a carriage or ch°, charioteer, warrior who fights from a ch°, RV. &c. &c.; a Kshatriya, MBh.; a driver, HPariś.; (*inī*), f. a number of carriages or ch°s, g. *khalâdi* on Pāṇ. iv, 2, 51, Vārtt.

Rathina, mfn. possessing or riding in a chariot, Vop.

Rathirá, mfn. id., RV.; speedy, quick, ib.

Rathirāya, Nom. P. (only p. °*yát*) to hasten, speed, RV.

Rathī́, mfn. (nom. sg. m. and f. *rathīs*; acc. sg. *rathyàm*, pl. *rathyàs*) going or fighting in a chariot (as subst. = a carriage-driver, charioteer, car-fighter, champion, hero, leader, lord), RV.; AitBr.; carried on a waggon, forming a cart-load, RV.; belonging to a chariot, ib. **—tama** (*rathī́-*), mfn. driving or fighting best in a chariot, chief of charioteers, RV. **—tara** (*rathī́-*), mfn. a better or superior charioteer, ib.; m. N. of a teacher; pl. his descendants, Pravar.

Rathīkara, m. N. of a man, Cat.

Rathīnara, w. r. for *rathī-tara*, VP.

Rathīya, Nom. P. (only p. °*yát*) to wish to go or travel in a chariot, RV.

Ráthya (or *rathyà*), mfn. belonging or relating to a carriage or chariot, accustomed to it &c. (with *ājī*, 'a chariot-race'), RV.; ŚBr.; (?) delighting in roads (see f. and *rathya-virathya*); m. a carriage or chariot-horse, RV.; Śak.; (*ā*), f., see below; n. carriage equipments (trappings, a wheel &c.), RV.; Lāṭy.; a chariot-race or match, RV.; a carriage, vehicle (?), ib. **—caya**, m. a team of horses, Daś. **—carya**, w. r. for *ratha-c*°, R. **—virathya**, m. 'delighting in roads and by-roads,' N. of Śiva, MBh.

Rathyā, f. a carriage-road, highway, street, Yājñ.; MBh.; Kāv. &c.; a number of carriages or chariots, Śiś. xviii, 3. **—°ntar** (°*thyântar*), ind. in the street, Śāntiś. **—paṅkti**, f. a row of streets, Bhartṛ. **—mukha**, n. entrance to a road or street, Ratnâv. **—mṛiga**, m. 'street-animal,' a dog, L. **—°li** (°*thyâli*), f. = *-paṅkti*, Amar. **—°vasarpaṇa** (°*thyâv*°), n. going down to the street, MW. **Rathyôpasarpaṇa**, n. walking in a street, Yājñ.

रथ 2. *ratha*, m. (√*ram*) pleasure, joy, delight (cf. *mano-ratha*); affection, love (cf. next). **—2. -jit**, mfn. (for 1. see under 1. *ratha*) winning affection, charming, lovely, AV.

रद् *rad*, cl. 1. P. (Dhātup. iii, 16) *rádati* (rarely Ā. °*te*; Ved. Impv. *ratsi*; pf. *rarâda*, RV.; aor. *arādīt*, Gr.; fut. *raditā*, °*dishyati*, ib.), to scratch, scrape, gnaw, bite, rend, dig, break, split, divide, RV.; AV.; Suśr.; to cut, open (a road or path), RV.; to lead (a river) into a channel, ib.; to convey to, bestow on, give, dispense, RV.; AV.; Br. [Cf. Lat. *rad-o*, *rod-o*; Eng. *rat*.]

Rada, mfn. (ifc.) scratching, splitting, gnawing at, Ghaṭ.; m. the act of splitting or gnawing, L.; a tooth (and therefore N. of the number 32), Kāv.; Var.; the tusk of an elephant, Var.; Nalôd. **—khaṇḍana**, n. a tooth-bite, Gīt. **—cchada**, m. 'tooth-covering,' a lip, Viddh. **Radâṅkura**, m. the point of a tooth, L. **Radâyudha**, m. 'armed with tusks,' a wild boar, L. **Radâvali** (ibc.) a row of teeth; *-dvandva*, Nom. P. °*vati*, to appear like two rows of teeth, Naish. **Radā-vasu**, mfn. (Padap. *rada-v*°) dispensing wealth, RV.

Radana, m. a tooth, Suśr. (cf. comp.); an elephant's tusk, Hariv.; Ragh.; n. the act of splitting, tearing &c., W. **—cchada**, m. 'tooth-covering,' a lip, MBh.; Kāv. &c.

Radanikā, f. N. of a woman, Mṛicch.

Radanin or **radin**, m. 'tusked,' an elephant, L.

रद्द *radda*, m. (in astrol.) N. of the eleventh Yoga.

रद्ध *raddha*, *raddhṛi*. See below.

रध् *radh* or *randh*, cl. 4. P. (Dhātup. xxvi, 84) *rádhyati* (pf. *rarandha*, 1. pl. *rarandhima* or *redhma*, Gr.; 3. pl. *rāradhúḥ*, RV.; aor. *aradhat*, ib.; Subj. *randhīs*, Impv. *randhi* for *randdhi*, ib.; fut. *radhitā*, *raddhā*, Gr.; *radhishyati*, *ratsyati*, ib.; inf. *radhitum*, Bhaṭṭ.), to become subject to (dat.), be subdued or overthrown, succumb, RV.; AV.; to be completed or matured, MW. (cf. √*rādh*); to bring into subjection, subdue, RV.; to deliver into the hand of (dat.), ib.; to hurt, torment, Bhaṭṭ.: Caus. *randháyati* (Ved. also °*te*; aor. *rīradhat*, RV.; *ararandhat*, Gr.), to make subject, deliver over to (dat.), RV.; AV.; to torment, afflict, R.; to destroy, annihilate, BhP.; to cook, prepare (food), MānGṛ.: Desid. *riradhishati*, *riratsati*, Gr.: Intens. *rāradhyate*, *rāraddhi*, Gr. (in RV. vi, 25, 9 *rārandhi* for *rāranddhi*, and v, 54, 13 *rāranta* for *rārantta*) to hand over to, deliver.

Raddhá, mfn. subdued, overcome, RV.; hurt, injured, W.

Raddhṛi, m. a subduer, tormentor, Bhaṭṭ.

Radhita, mfn. injured, hurt, MW.

Radhitṛi, mfn. injurious, hurtful, ib.

Radhrá, mfn. willing, pliant, obedient, RV. (others 'weary' or 'wealthy' or 'a miser' or 'officious' or 'active' &c.) **—codá** or **-codaná**, mfn. furthering or encouraging the obedient, RV. **—túr**, mfn. (prob.) id., ib.

Randha, m. (prob.) subjection, destruction, Kāś. on Pāṇ. vii, 1, 61.

Randhaka, mfn. subduing, destroying, id.; m. n. and (*ikā*), f. the sheath of a knife, L.

Randhana, mfn. destroying (in *abhadra-r*°), BhP.; n. destruction, ib.; cooking, TS., Sch.

Randhanāya, Nom. P. °*yati*, to make subject, deliver into the power of (dat.), RV.

Randhas or °**dhasa**, m. N. of a man belonging to the family of Andhaka (cf. *rāndhasa*).

Rándhi, f. (for *ránddhi*) subjection, subjugation, RV.; the being prepared or cooked, BhP.

Randhita, mfn. subdued, destroyed, MW.; cooked, dressed (as food), L.

Randhin. See *sādhu-r*°.

Randhisha, m. = *hantṛi*, a destroyer, VS.

रन् 1. *ran*. See √1. *raṇ*.

रन् 2. *rán* (meaning doubtful), RV. i, 120, 7 (accord. to Sāy. = *rātārau* or *dātārau*, 'givers,' fr. √*rā*, the sg. being substituted for the du.)

रन्तव्य *rantavya*, 2. *ranti*, *rantu*, *rantṛi*. See under √*ram*, p. 868, col. 1.

रन्ति 1. *ránti*, m. (√1. *raṇ*) a fighter, warrior (?), RV. vii, 18, 10; ix, 102, 5.

Rántya, mfn. (√*ram*?) pleasant, comfortable, RV.; AV.

रन्दला *randalā*, f. N. of Samjñā (wife of the Sun), Cat.

रन्ध् *randh*. See √*radh*.

रन्ध्र *rándhra*, n. rarely m. (prob. fr. √*rad*) a slit, split, opening, aperture, hole, chasm, fissure, cavity, RV. &c. &c. (nine openings are reckoned in the human body, cf. under *kha*; and sometimes a tenth in the skull, as in the fontanel of an infant); the vulva, BhP.; a partic. part of a horse's head, VarBṛS.; Śiś. (cf. *upa-r*°); a defect, fault, flaw, imperfection, weak part, Yājñ.; MBh. &c. (cf. *chidra*); N. of the 8th astrological mansion, VarBṛS.; of the number 'nine' (cf. above), MW.; m. N. of a son of Manu Bhautya, VP. (v. l. *bradhna*); the offspring of a Brāhman and a Maitrī, L. **—kaṇṭa**, m. a species of acacia, L. **—gupti**, f. concealing one's weak points, Kām. **—prahārin**, mfn. attacking the weak places (of an enemy), Ragh. **—babhru**, m. a rat, L. **—vaṃśa**, m. hollow bamboo, L. **Randhrâgata**, n. a disease which attacks the throat of horses, MBh. **Randhrânusârin**, mf(*iṇī*)n. seeking for weak or assailable points, Mṛicch. **Randhrânveshaṇa**, n. the act of seeking for weak places, MW. **Randhrânveshin**, mfn. = *randhrânusârin*, ib. **Randhrâpêkshin**, mfn. watching for weak places, spying out holes, ib. **Randhrôpanipâtin**, mfn. rushing in through holes or weak places (said of misfortunes), Śak.

Randhraka, mf(*ikā*)n. = *randhra*, in *bahu-randhrikā*, q. v.

रप् *rap* (cf. √*lap*), cl. 1. P. (Dhātup. xi, 7) *rápati* (pf. *rarāpa* &c., Gr.), to talk, chatter, whisper, RV.: Intens. *rārapīti*, id., ib.

Rāpya, mfn. to be talked or whispered, Pāṇ. iii, 1, 126.

रपस् *rápas*, n. (cf. *repas* fr. √*rip*) bodily defect, injury, infirmity, disease, RV.; VS. (accord. to Sāy. also = *rakshas*).

रप्श् *rapś* (only occurring in the pr. p. below and in *pra-* and *vi-*√*rapś*, q. v.), to be full, RV.

Rapśád-ūdhan, mfn. having a full or distended udder, RV. ii, 34, 5.

रप्सु *rapsu* = *rūpa*, Mahīdh. on VS. xxxiii, 19.

Rapsúdā, f. du. (of unknown meaning), RV. viii, 72, 12.

रफ् *raph* (cf. √*ṛiph* and *ramph*), cl. 1. P. *raphati*, to go, Dhātup. xi, 19 (accord. to Vop. also 'to injure, kill').

Raphitá, mfn. hurt, injured, wretched, miserable, RV.

रब्ध *rabdha*, *rabdhṛi*. See below.

रभ् *rabh* or *rambh* (mostly comp. with a prep.; cf. √*grabh* and see √*labh* with which *rabh* is connected), cl. 1. Ā. (Dhātup. xxiii, 5) *rábhate* (m. c. also °*ti*, and ep. *rambhati*, °*te*; pf. *rebhé*, RV.; also *rārabhe* and 1. pl. *rarabhmá*; aor. *árabdha*, RV.; fut. *rabdhā*, Gr.; *rapsyati*, MBh.; °*te*, ib. &c.; inf. *rabdhum*, MBh.; Ved. *rábham*, *rábhe*; ind. p. *rábhya*, RV. &c.), to take hold of, grasp, clasp, embrace, BhP. (*arabhat*, Hariv. 8106, w. r. for *ārabhat*); to desire vehemently, MW.; to act rashly, ib. (cf. *rabhas*, *rabhasa*): Pass. *rabhyate*, aor. *arambhi*, Pāṇ. vii, 1, 63: Caus. *rambhayati*, °*te*, aor. *ararambhat*, ib.: Desid. *ripsate*, Pāṇ. vii, 4, 54: Intens. *rārabhyate*, *rārabhīti*, *rārabdhi* (as far as these forms really occur, they are only found after prepositions; cf. *anv-ā-*, *ā-*, *prâ-*, *vy-ā-*, *pari-*, *sam-*√*rabh* &c.)

Rabdha, mfn., see *ā-*, *prâ-*, *pari-r°* &c.; (*ā*), f. food, HPariś.

Rabdhṛi, mf(*rī*)n. one who seizes or takes hold of, Mahīdh.

Rabha, m. N. of a monkey, R.

Rábhas, n. violence, impetuosity, zeal, ardour, force, energy, RV.; (°*sā*), ind. violently, impetuously, forcibly, roughly, MBh.; Pur. **-vat** (*rábhas-*), mfn. violent, impetuous, zealous, RV.

Rabhasá, mf(*ā*)n. (fr. prec.) impetuous, violent, rapid, fierce, wild, RV. &c. &c.; (ifc.) eager for, desirous of, Kālid.; strong, powerful (said of the Soma), RV.; shining, glaring, ib.; m. impetuosity, vehemence, hurry, haste, speed, zeal, passion, eager desire for (comp.), MBh.; Kāv. &c. (also *ā*, f., L.; *rabhasa*, ibc.; *āt* and *ena*, ind. violently, impetuously, eagerly, quickly); joy, pleasure, Gīt.; regret, sorrow, W.; poison, L.; N. of a magical incantation recited over weapons, R.; of a Dānava (v. l. *raśmisa*); of a king (son of Rambha), BhP.; of a Rākshasa, L.; of a lexicographer (also called *rabhasa-pāla*), Cat.; of a monkey, R. **-kośa**, m. Rabhasa's dictionary, Cat. **-nandin**, m. N. of a Buddhist author, ib. **-pāla**, m. N. of a lexicographer (cf. above), ib.

Rabhasāná, mfn. shining, glaring, RV.

Rábhi, f. a partic. part of a chariot, RV. (accord. to Sāy. 'mfn. supporting').

Rábhishṭha, mf(*ā*)n. most violent or impetuous or strong, RV.; VS.

Rábhīyas (VS.) or **rábhyas** (RV.), mfn. more violent, very strong.

Rabhū, m. (nom. *ūs*) a messenger, L.

Rabho-dá, mfn. (fr. *rabhas* + *dā*) bestowing strength or force, RV.

1. **Rambhá**, m. (for 2. see p. 868, col. 2) a prop, staff, support, RV. viii, 45, 20; a bamboo, L.; N. of the fifth Kalpa (q. v.), Cat.; of the father of the Asura Mahisha and brother of Karambha, ib.; of a Nāga, VP.; of a son of Āyu, Hariv.; Pur.; of a son of Viviṇśati, BhP.; of a king of Vajra-rātra, Kathās.; of a monkey, R.; (*ā*), f., see next.

Rambhā, f. the plantain (Musa Sapientum), Kāv.; Kathās. &c.; a sort of rice, L.; a cotton string round the loins, L.; a courtezan, Kāv. (v. l. for *veśyā*); a kind of metre, Col.; N. of Gaurī or of Dākshāyaṇī in the Malaya mountains, Cat.; of a celebrated Apsaras (wife of Nala-kūbara and carried off by Rāvaṇa; sometimes regarded as a form of Lakshmī and as the most beautiful woman of Indra's paradise), MBh.; Kāv. &c. **-tṛitīyā**, f. N. of the third day of the first half of the month Jyaishṭha (so called because Hindū women on this day imitate Rambhā, who bathed on the same day with partic. ceremonies), Cat. **-°bhisāra** (°*bhâbh*°), m. and **-mañjarī**, f. N. of two dramas. **-vrata**, n. N. of a partic. ceremony (cf. *-tṛitīyā*), Cat. **-stambha**, m. the trunk of a plantain tree, Naish. **-stambhana**, n. the turning of R° into a pillar, Mcar. (cf. R. i, 64).

Rambhôru, mf(*ū*)n. having thighs (smooth and tapering) like (the stem of) a plantain tree, full, round, lovely (said of women, esp. in the voc. *rambhôru*, cf. Vām. ii, 49), MBh.; Kāv. &c.

Rambhin, mfn. carrying a staff or stick (m. an old man, a doorkeeper, Sāy.), RV.; (*iṇī*), f. (prob.) the shaft of a spear, RV.

Ripsu, mfn. (fr. Desid.) wishing to seize or grasp, Vop.

रम् *ram*, cl. 1. Ā. (Dhātup. xx, 23) *ramate* (Ved. also P. *rámati* or *ramṇāti*, pf. *rarāma*, MBh.; *reme*, Br. &c.; aor. 3. pl. *ranta*, RV.; *araṇsīt*, Kāv.; *araṇsta*, RV.; *raṇsisham*, SV.; fut. *rantā*, Gr.; *raṇsyati*, Br.; °*te*, ib. &c.; inf. *ramitum*, MBh.; *rantum*, ib. &c.; *rantos*, Br.; ind. p. *ratvā́*, ib.; *rantvā*, Kāv.; *-ramya* or *-ratya*, Pāṇ. vi, 4, 38), to stop, stay, make fast, calm, set at rest (P.; esp. pres. *ramṇāti*), RV.; VS.; (P. Ā.) to delight, make happy, enjoy carnally, MBh.; Hariv.; Śukas.; (Ā.) to stand still, rest, abide, like to stay with (loc. or dat.), RV. &c. &c.; (Ā.; P. only m. c.) to be glad or pleased, rejoice at, delight in, be fond of (loc., instr. or inf.), RV. &c. &c.; to play or sport, dally, have sexual intercourse with (instr. with or without *samam*, *saha*, *sākam* or *sârdham*), ChUp.; MBh. &c.; to couple (said of deer), Pāṇ. iii, 1, 26, Vārtt. 8, Pat. (cf. Caus.); to play with i. e. put to stake (instr.), Bhaṭṭ.: Caus. *ramáyati* or *rāmáyati* (aor. *árīramat*), to cause to stay, stop, set at rest, RV.; TS.; PañcavBr.; KātyŚr.; (*ramayati*, m. c. also °*te*) to gladden, delight, please, caress, enjoy carnally, MBh.; Kāv. &c. (3. sg. *ramayati-tarām*, Ratnâv. iii, 9); to enjoy one's self, be pleased or delighted, MBh.; Hariv.; *mṛigān ramayati*, he tells that the deer are coupling, Pāṇ. iii, 1, 26, Vārtt. 8, Pat.: Desid. in *riraṇsā*, °*su*, q. v.: Desid. of Caus. in *riramayishu*, q. v.: Intens. *raṇramyate* or *raṇramīti*, Pāṇ. vii, 4, 85. [Cf. Zd. *ram*; Gk. ἠρέμα, ἔραμαι, ἐρατός; Lith. *rìmti*; Goth. *rimis*.]

Ratá, mfn. pleased, amused, gratified, BhP.; delighting in, intent upon, fond or enamoured of, devoted or attached or addicted or disposed to (loc., instr. or comp.), ŚBr. &c. &c.; (ifc.) having sexual intercourse with, BhP.; loved, beloved, MW.; (*ā*), f. N. of the mother of Day, MBh.; n. pleasure, enjoyment, (esp.) enjoyment of love, sexual union, copulation, Kāv.; Var. &c.; the private parts, L. **-kila**, m. a dog, Vās. **-kūjita**, n. lascivious murmur, L. **-guru**, m. a husband, L. **-gṛiha**, n. pudendum muliebre, Gal. **-jvara**, m. a crow, L. **-tālin**, m. a libertine, voluptuary, L. **-tālī**, f. a procuress, bawd, L. **-nārāca** or **-nārīca**, m. (only L.) a voluptuary; a dog; the god of love; lascivious murmur. **-nidhi**, m. the wagtail, L. **-bandha**, m. sexual union, L. **-mānasa**, mfn. having a delighted mind or heart, Cat. **-rddhika** (for *-ṛid*°), n. (only L.) a day; bathing for pleasure; the aggregate of eight auspicious objects. **-vat**, mfn. pleased, gratified, happy, R.; containing a form of √*ram*, AitBr. **-viśesha**, m. pl. the various kinds of sexual union, Cat. **-vraṇa** and **-śāyin**, m. a dog, L. **-hiṇḍaka**, m. a seducer of women, libertine, L. **Ratânta**, m. the end of sexual enjoyment, Kathās. **Ratânduka**, m. a dog, L. **Ratândhrī** (?), f. mist, fog, L. **Ratâmarda**, m. a dog, L. **Ratâmbuka** (?), n. du. the two deep places immediately over the hips, L. **Ratâyanī**, f. a prostitute, harlot, L. **Ratârambhâvasānika**, mfn. relating to the beginning and end of sexual enjoyment, Cat. **Ratârthin**, mfn. wishing for s° enj°, amorous, lascivious; (*inī*), f. a wanton woman, W. **Rate-madā**, f. an Apsaras, L. **Ratôtsava**, m. the feast of sexual enj°, Śak. **Ratôdvaha**, m. the Indian cuckoo, L. **Ratôparata-saṃsupta**, mfn. sleeping after the cessation of sexual enjoyment, R.

Ráti, f. rest, repose, VS.; ŚāṅkhGṛ.; pleasure, enjoyment, delight in, fondness for (loc. or comp.; *ratim* with √*āp*, *labh*, *upa-labh*, *adhi-gam*, *vid*, *kṛi* or *bandh* and loc., 'to find pleasure in'), Up.; Mn.; MBh. &c.; the pleasure of love, sexual passion or union, amorous enjoyment (often personified as one of the two wives of Kāma-deva, together with Prīti, q. v.), Mn.; MBh. &c.; the pudenda, L.; = *rati-gṛiha*, pleasure-house, VarBṛS.; N. of the sixth Kalā of the Moon, Cat.; of an Apsaras, MBh.; of the wife of Vibhu (mother of Prithu-sheṇa), BhP.; of a magical incantation recited over weapons, R.; of the letter *n*, Up.; of a metre, Col. **-kara**, mf(*ī*)n. causing pleasure or joy, R.; BhP.; being in love, enamoured (= *kāmin*), VarBṛS.; m. a partic. Samādhi, L.; (*ā*), f. N. of an Apsaras, Kāraṇḍ. **-karman**, n. sexual intercourse, MW. **-kānta-tarka-vāg-īśa**, m. N. of a Sch. on the Mugdha-bodha, Col. **-kāma-pūjā**, f. N. of wk. **-kuhara**, n. pudendum muliebre, L. **-kriyā**, f. = *-karman*, Kām. **-kheda**, m. the languor of sexual enjoyment; *-khinna*, m. fatigued by s° enj°, Pañcat.; *-supta*, mfn. sleeping after the fatigue of s° enj°, Vikr. **-guṇa**, m. N. of a Deva-gandharva, MBh. **-gṛiha**, n. a pleasure-house, VarBṛS.; pudendum muliebre, L. **-caraṇa-samanta-svara**, m. N. of a Gandharva, L. **-janaka**, m. N. of a prince, Cat. **-jaha**, m. N. of a Samādhi, L. **-jña**, mfn. skilled in the art of love, Hit. **-taskara**, m. 'stealer of s° enj°,' a ravisher, seducer, Hariv. **-tāla**, m. (in music) a kind of measure, Saṃgīt. **-da**, mf(*ā*)n. causing pleasure or comfort, VarYogay. **-deva**, w. r. for *ranti-d*°. **-nāga**, m. a kind of coitus, L. **-pati**, m. 'Rati's husband,' Kāma-deva, the god of love, Kāv.; Pur. **-paricaya**, m. frequent repetition of s° enj°, Śiś. **-pāśa**, m. a kind of coitus, L. **-prapūrṇa**, m. N. of a partic. Kalpa or age, Buddh. **-priya**, mfn. pleasant during coition, Vās.; 'beloved by Rati,' N. of Kāma-deva, L.; (*ā*), f. N. of Dākshāyaṇī, Cat. (v. l. *ravi-p*°); of a Surâṅganā, Siṇhâs. **-prīti**, f. du. Rati and Prīti (the wives of Kāma-deva), Kathās. **-phala**, mfn. productive of sexual pleasure, aphrodisiacal, Ml. **-bandhu**, m. a husband, lover, ib. **-bhavana**, n. = *-gṛiha*, VarBṛS.; a brothel, L.; pudendum muliebre, VarBṛS. **-bhoga**, m. sexual enjoyment, ib. **-mañjarī**, f. N. of an erotic wk.; *-guṇa-leśa-sūcakâshṭaka*, n. N. of a Stotra. **-mat**, mfn. having enjoyment or pleasure, cheerful, glad, delighting in (loc.), Kathās.; enamoured, Ratnâv.; accompanied by Rati, ib. **-madā**, f. an Apsaras, L. (cf. *rate-m*°). **-mandira**, n. a pleasure-house, Pañcar.; pudendum muliebre, L. **-manmatha**, (prob. n.) N. of a Nāṭaka; *-pūjā*, f. N. of wk. **-mitra**, m. a kind of coitus, L.; N. of a poet, Subh. **-raṇa-dhīra**, mfn. bold or energetic in Love's contests, MW. **-ratna-pradīpikā**, f. N. of wk. **-ramaṇa**, m. 'lover of Rati,' N. of Kāma-deva, Mālatīm. **-rasa**, m. the taste or pleasure of love, Amar.; mfn. as sweet as love, Megh.; *-glāni*, f. lassitude after sexual enjoyment, MW. **-rahasya**, n. 'mysteries of love,' N. of an erotic wk. by Kokkoka; *-dīpikā*, f. N. of another wk. (prob. a Comm. on the former). **-laksha**, m. sexual intercourse, L. **-lampaṭa**, mfn. desirous of s° int°, lascivious, lustful, Cat. **-līla**, m. (in music) a kind of measure, Saṃgīt.; (*ā*), f. N. of a Surâṅganā, Siṇhâs. **-lola**, m. N. of a demon, Buddh. **-vara**, m. 'Rati's husband,' N. of Kāma-deva, L.; a gift or offering vowed to R°, Cat. **-vardhana**, mfn. increasing love, BhP. **-vallī**, f. love compared to a creeper, Kathās. **-śakti**, f. the faculty of sexual enjoyment, virile power, Cāṇ. **-śūra**, m. 'love-hero,' a man of great generative power, Pañcar. **-saṃyoga**, m. sexual union, R. **-saṃhita**, mfn. accompanied with love, abounding in affection, MW. **-saṃgraha-vyākhyā**, f. N. of wk. **-satvarā**, f. Trigonella Corniculata, L. **-sarvasva**, n. the whole essence of love, Śak.; N. of wk. **-sahacara**, m. 'R°'s consort,' N. of Kāma-deva, Daś. **-sāra**,

m. or n. N. of wk. **-sundara,** m. a kind of coitus, L. **-sena,** m. N. of a king of the Colas, Rājat.; of a poet, Cat. **Ratîśa,** m. = *rati-pati,* Naish.

Raty-aṅga, n. pudendum muliebre, L.

Ratikā, f. (in music) a kind of Śruti, Saṃgīt.

Ratī, f., m. c. for *rati,* the goddess of love, MBh.; Hariv.

Rantavya, mfn. to be rejoiced at or enjoyed, to be toyed with or carnally known, Mṛicch.; n. pleasure, enjoyment, play, MW.

2. **Ránti,** f. (for 1. see p. 866, col. 3) loving to stay, abiding gladly with (loc.), AV.; VS.; pleasure, delight (used as a term of endearment for a cow), TS.; VS.; PañcavBr.; m. N. of a lexicographer (= *ranti-deva*), Śiś., Sch. **-deva,** m. N. of Vishṇu, L.; of a king of the lunar race (son of Saṃkṛiti; he spent his riches in performing grand sacrifices, and the blood which issued from the bodies of the slaughtered victims was changed into a river called *carmaṇ-vatī;* Sch. on Megh. 46), MBh.; Kāv.; Pur.; of another king, Hcar.; of a teacher of Yoga and various authors, esp. of a lexicographer (= *ranti*), Cat.; a dog, W. **-nāra** or **-bhāra,** m. N. of a king, BhP.

Rantu, f. a way, road, L.; a river, L.

Rantu-manas, mfn. inclined to take pleasure, wishing to enjoy sexual intercourse, MW.

Rántri, mfn. gladly abiding with, delighting in (loc.), RV.

Rantos. See √*ram* and *a-rantos.*

Rama, mfn. pleasing, delighting, rejoicing (only ifc.; cf. *mano-r°*); dear, beloved, W.; m. (only L.) joy; a lover, husband, spouse; Kāma-deva, the god of love; the red-flowering Aśoka; (*ā*), f., see s. v.

Ramaka, mfn. sporting, dallying, toying amorously; m. a lover, suitor, MW. **-tva,** n. love, affection, ib.

Ramaṇa, mf(*ī*)n. pleasing, charming, delightful, BhP.; m. a lover, husband (cf. *kshapā-r°*), MBh.; Kāv. &c.; Kāma-deva, the god of love, L.; an ass, L.; a testicle, L.; a tree similar to the Melia Bukayun, L.; = *tinduka,* L.; N. of Aruṇa or the charioteer of the Sun, L.; of a mythical son of Manoharā, MBh.; Hariv.; of a man, Pravar.; pl. N. of a people (cf. *ramaṭha*), MBh.; (*ā*), f. a charming woman, wife, mistress, L.; a kind of metre, Col.; N. of Dākshāyaṇī in Rāma-tīrtha, Cat.; (*ī*), f., see s. v.; n. pleasure, joy, Subh.; dalliance, amorous sport, sexual union, copulation, Nir.; Śukas.; decoying (of deer), Śiś. vi, 9 (cf. Pat. on Pāṇ. vi, 4, 24, Vārtt. 3); (ifc.) gladdening, delighting, BhP.; the hinder parts, pudenda (= *jaghana*), L.; the root of Trichosanthes Dioeca, L.; N. of a forest, Hariv.; of a town, Divyâv. **-pati,** m. N. of a poet, Cat. **-vasati,** f. the dwelling-place of a lover, Megh.

Ramaṇâsakta, mfn. addicted to pleasure, Subh.

Ramaṇaka, m. N. of a son of Yajña-bāhu, BhP.; of a son of Vīti-hotra, ib.; of a Dvīpa, ib.; n. N. of a Varsha (ruled by Ramaṇaka), MBh.; BhP.; of a town, Divyâv.

Ramaṇī, f. a beautiful young woman, mistress, wife, Kāv.; Kathās.; BhP.; Aloe Indica, L.; a kind of metre, Col.; N. of a serpent-maid, Rājat. **-sakta,** mfn. devoted to a mistress or wife, Subh.

1. **Ramaṇīya,** mf(*ā*)n. to be enjoyed, pleasant, agreeable, delightful, charming, Up.; MBh. &c.; (*ā*), f. N. of a singer, Mālav.; of a town, HPariś. **-caraṇa,** mfn. of pleasant conduct or behaviour, ChUp. **-janman,** mfn. of auspicious birth, born under an auspicious star, Mālatīm. **-ḍāmara,** mfn. charming and amazing (*-tva,* n.), ib. **-tama,** mfn. most charming, MW. **-tara,** mfn. more charming or lovely (*-tva,* n.), Jātakam. **-tā,** f. loveliness, beauty, charm, Kāv.; Sāh. **-tāraka,** (prob.) m. N. of a Mantra. **-tva,** n. = *-tā,* R.; Śak. **-rāghava,** (prob.) n. N. of a poem.

2. **Ramaṇīya,** Nom. (fr. *ramaṇī*) Ā. °*yate,* to represent a wife, be the mistress of (gen.), Sāh.

Ramaṇîyaka, m. or n. (?) N. of an island, Suparṇ.; w. r. for *rāmaṇīyaka,* q. v.

Ramaṇya, mfn. = 1. *ramaṇīya* (in *su-ramaṇya,* q. v.)

Ramáti, f. a place of pleasant resort, AV.; TBr.; (*rám°*), mfn. liking to remain in one place, not straying (said of a cow), AV.; TS.; m. (only L.) a lover; paradise, heaven; a crow; time; Kāma-deva, the god of love.

Ramayantikā, f. N. of a dancing girl, Daś.

Ramā, f. of *rama,* q. v.; a wife, mistress, W.; N. of Lakshmī, the goddess of fortune, Bhartṛ.; BhP.; good luck, fortune, splendour, opulence, Cāṇ.; splendour, pomp, Bhām.; N. of the 11th day in the dark half of the month Kārttika, Cat.; of the syllable *śrīm* (also *rama*), Sarvad.; of a daughter of Śaśi-dhvaja and wife of Kalki, KalkiP. **-kānta** (Pañcat.) or **-dhava** (L.), m. 'lover or husband of Ramā,' N. of Vishṇu. **-dhipa** (°*mâdh°*), m. 'lord of R°,' id., Cat. **-nātha,** m. id., MBh.; N. of various authors (also with *vaidya* and *rāyi*), Cat. **-pati,** m. = *ramâdhipa,* Kathās.; BhP.; N. of various authors (also with *miśra*), Cat. **-priya,** n. 'dear to R°,' a lotus, L. **-veshṭa,** m. turpentine, L. **-śaṃkara,** m. N. of an author, Cat. **-śraya** (°*mâś°*), m. 'refuge of R°,' N. of Vishṇu, BhP. **Ramêśa** (Kāv.) or **Ramêśvara** (Pur.), m. = *ramâdhipa.*

Ramita, mfn. (fr. Caus.) gladdened, delighted, rendered happy, Gīt.; n. (prob.) pleasure, delight (see next). **-m-gama,** m. a proper N., Pāṇ. iii, 2, 47, Sch.

Ramyà, mf(*ā*)n. to be enjoyed, enjoyable, pleasing, delightful, beautiful, ŚBr. &c. &c.; = *bala-kara,* L.; m. Michelia Champaka, L.; another kind of plant (= *baka*), L.; N. of a son of Āgnīdhra, VP.; m. or n. (?) a pleasant abode, Vishṇ.; (*ā*), f. night, Hariv.; Hibiscus Mutabilis, L.; = *mahêndra-vāruṇī,* L.; (in music) a kind of Śruti, Saṃgīt.; N. of a daughter of Meru (wife of Ramya), BhP.; of a river, W.; n. the root of Trichosanthes Dioeca, L.; semen virile, L. **-grāma,** m. N. of a village, MBh. **-tā,** f. (Pratāp.), **-tva,** n. (R.) pleasantness, loveliness, beauty. **-dāruṇa,** mfn. beautiful and terrible, MBh. **-deva,** m. N. of a man the father of Loshṭa-deva, Śrīkaṇṭh. **-patha,** mfn. furnished with pleasant roads, Laghuk. **-pushpa,** m. Bombyx Heptaphyllum, L. **-phala,** m. Strychnos Nux Vomica, L. **-rūpa,** mfn. having a lovely form, beautiful, Bhām. **-śrī,** m. N. of Vishṇu, Pañcar. **-sānu,** mfn. having pleasant peaks or summits (said of a mountain), MW. **Ramyâkshi,** m. N. of a man, Pravar. **Ramyântara,** mfn. pleasant at intervals, pleasantly diversified (said of a journey), Śak.

Ramyaka, m. Melia Sempervirens, Bhpr.; N. of a son of Āgnīdhra, BhP.; n. (in Sāṃkhya) one of the 8 perfections or Siddhis, Tattvas.; Sāṃkhyak., Sch. (also *ā,* f., scil. *siddhi*); the root of Trichosanthes Dioeca, Suśr.; n. N. of a Varsha called after Ramyaka, Pur.

Ramra, m. N. of Aruṇa (the charioteer of the Sun), L. (cf. *ramaṇa*); beauty, splendour (= *śobhā*), L.

रमठ *ramaṭha,* m. pl. N. of a people in the west of India (also read *ramaṭa, rāmaṭha*), MBh.; VarBṛS.; n. = *rāmaṭha,* Asa Foetida, L. **-dhvani,** m. Asa Foetida, L.

रमल *ramala,* m. or n. (cf. Arabic رمال, *rammāl*) a mode of fortune-telling by means of dice (a branch of divination borrowed from the Arabs), Cat.; N. of various wks. **-grantha,** m., **-cintāmaṇi,** m., **-tattva-sāra,** m., **-tantra,** n., **-nava-ratna,** n., **-paddhati,** f., **-praśna,** m., **-praśna-tantra,** n., **-bhūshaṇa,** n., **-yantrikā,** f., **-rahasya,** n., **-rahasya-sāra-saṃgraha,** m., **-śāstra,** n., **-sāra,** m., **-siktā** (?), f. N. of wks. **Ramalâbhidheya,** °**lâmṛita,** °**lêndu-prakāśa,** m., °**lôtkarsha,** m. N. of wks.

रम्फ् *ramph* (cf. √*riph* and *raph*), cl. 1. P. *ramphati,* to go, Dhātup. xi, 20 (accord. to Vop. also 'to kill').

रम्ब् 1. *ramb* (cf. √*lamb*), cl. 1. Ā. *rámbate,* to hang down, RV. [Cf. Lith. *rambùs, rambókas.*]

रम्ब् 2. *ramb* (cf. √2. *rambh*), cl. 1. Ā. *rambate,* to sound, Dhātup. x, 14; cl. 1. P. *rambati,* to go, xv, 87 (cf. √*raṇv*).

रम्भ् 1. *rambh.* See √*rabh.*

1. **Rambha, rambhin,** &c. See p. 867, col. 2.

रम्भ् 2. *rambh* (cf. √2. *ramb*), cl. 1. Ā. *rambhate,* to sound, roar, Dhātup. x, 24 (only p. *rambhamāṇa,* BhP.)

2. **Rambha,** mfn. sounding, roaring, lowing &c. (see *go-r°*); (*ā*), f. a sounding, roaring, lowing &c., L.

Rambhaṇa or °**bhita,** n. a lowing, L.

रम्य *ramya, ramra.* See above.

रय् *ray* (cf. √*lay*), cl. 1. Ā. *rayate,* to go, Dhātup. xiv, 10.

रय *raya,* m. (√*rī*) the stream of a river, current, MBh.; Kāv. &c.; quick motion, speed, swiftness (*eṇa* and *āt,* ind. quickly, immediately, straightway), Kāv.; Pur.; course (cf. *saṃvatsara-r°*); impetuosity, vehemence, ardour, zeal, Śiś.; BhP.; N. of a son of Purū-ravas, BhP.; of another king, Cat. **-praśna-sūtra-siddhânta,** m. N. of wk. **-maṇi,** m. N. of two Sāmans, ĀrshBr. **-vat,** mfn. of rapid course, swift, MW.

Rayaṇa-sāra, m. N. of wk.

Rayishṭha, mfn. very swift or fleet or vehement, W.; m. N. of Agni or Kubera or Brahman, ib.; n. N. of various Sāmans, ĀrshBr.

रयक *rayaka,* v. l. for *ravaka,* q. v.

रयस् *rayas.* See *amūrta-rayas.*

रयि *rayí,* m. or (rarely) f. (fr. √*rā;* the following forms occur in the Veda, *rayis,* °*yim,* °*yibhis,* °*yīṇām; rayyā́,* °*yyai,* °*yyām;* cf. 2. *rai*), property, goods, possessions, treasure, wealth (often personified), RV.; AV.; VS.; Br.; ŚrS.; ChUp.; stuff, materials, PraśnUp.; v. l. for *raji,* q. v.; (?) mfn. rich, RV. viii, 31, 11; ix, 101, 7. **-dá** or **-dā́,** mfn. bestowing wealth, RV. **-dhāraṇa-piṇḍa,** m. a lump of earth, Kauś. **-páti,** m. lord of w°, ib. **-mát,** mfn. = *-vat* (q. v.), ib.; VS.; ŚBr.; ChUp.; containing the word *rayi,* ŚBr. **-vát,** mfn. possessing wealth, rich, RV. (cf. *revat*). **-vid,** mfn. obtaining or possessing w°, RV. **-vṛidh,** mfn. enjoying w°, ib. **-shác** (*-shā́c*), mfn. possessing w°, ib. **-sháh** (*-shā́h*), mfn. ruling over w°, ib. **-shṭhā́** or **-shṭhā́na** (AV.), **-sthā́na** (RV.), possessed of wealth, wealthy; m. a rich man.

Rayikva, v. l. for *raikva,* q. v.

Rayín-tama, mfn. (superl. of an unused form *rayin;* cf. Pāṇ. viii, 2, 17) possessing much property, very wealthy, RV.

Rayīyát, mfn. (p. from a Nom. *rayīyati*) wishing for wealth or riches, RV.

Rayīshin, mfn. desiring treasures, SV. (prob. w. r.)

रय्यावट्ट *rayyāvaṭṭa,* m. N. of a man, Rājat. (cf. *rathāvaṭṭa* under 1. *ratha*).

रराट *rarā́ṭa,* n. = *lalāṭa,* the forehead, brow, VS.; TBr.; Kāṭh.; PārGṛ.; (*ī*), f. id., BhP.; twisted grass used for the Havir-dhāna, Br.; ŚrS.

Rarāṭya, mf(*ā*)n. belonging or relating to the forehead, PārGṛ.; (*ā*), f. twisted grass &c. (= *rarāṭī,* q. v.), ŚāṅkhBr.; ŚrS.; the horizon, ŚāṅkhBr.

रराण *rárāṇa,* mfn. (√*rā*) distributing, bestowing, bountiful, liberal, RV.

Rárāvan, mfn., id., ib. (others 'w. r. for *drāvan*').

रर्फ् *rarph* (cf. √*raph*), cl. 1. P. *rarphati,* to go, Dhātup. xi, 18 (v. l.)

रलमानाथ *ralamā-nātha,* m. N. of a poet, Cat.

रलरोल *ralarola,* (prob.) m. howling, wailing, lamenting, HPariś.

रला *ralā,* f. a species of bird, VarBṛS.

रल्लक *rallaka,* m. a species of stag or deer with a shaggy or hairy body, Kād.; a woollen cloth, coverlet, blanket, ŚārṅgS.; the eyelashes, L.

रव *ráva,* m. (√1. *ru*) a roar, yell, cry, howl (of animals, wild beasts &c.), RV. &c. &c.; song, singing (of birds), MBh.; R. &c.; hum, humming (of bees), Ragh.; Kathās.; clamour, outcry, Kathās.; thunder, RV.; MBh.; talk, MW.; any noise or sound (e.g. the whizz of a bow, the ringing of a bell &c.), MBh.; Kāv. &c.; (*ā*), f., see s.v.

Ravaṇa, mfn. roaring, yelling, crying, howling, singing &c., Bhaṭṭ.; sonorous (= *śabdana*), L.; sharp, hot (= *tīkshṇa*), L.; unsteady, fickle (= *cañcala*), L.; m. a sound, L.; a camel, L.; the Koïl or Indian cuckoo, L.; a wagtail (= *bhaṇḍaka*), L.; a bee, L.; a big cucumber, L.; N. of a man, g. *śivâdi;* of a serpent-king, L.; n. brass, bell-metal, L.

Ravat, ravamāṇa, ravāṇa. See under √1. *ru.*

Ravata, m. = *rava,* roaring, yelling &c., ĀpŚr.

Ravátha, m. id., RV.; ŚBr.; Lāṭy.; the Indian cuckoo, L.

Ravas. See *purū-* and *bṛihad-r°.*

Ravasa. See *purū-r°.*

Ravitṛi, mfn. one who cries or calls out, crier, screamer, AitBr.

रवक *ravaka,* m. N. of a Dharaṇa or partic.

weight of pearls (30 making the Dh°; v.l. *rayaka, rivaka*), VarBṛS.; Hcat.

रवणक *ravaṇaka*, m. or n. (?) a filter made of cane or bamboo, Buddh.

रवा *ravā*, f. Gossypium Herbaceum, L.

रवि *ravi*, m. (accord. to Uṇ. iv, 138, Sch. fr. √1. *ru*) a partic. form of the sun (sometimes regarded as one of the 12 Ādityas; hence *ravi* is also a N. of the number 'twelve'), Var.; Hariv. &c.; the sun (in general) or the sun-god, Mn.; MBh. &c.; = *ravi-dina*, Sunday, Inscr.; Calotropis Gigantea, L.; a mountain, L.; N. of a Sauvīraka, MBh.; of a son of Dhṛita-rāshṭra, ib.; of the author of a Comm. on the Kāvya-prakāśa, Cat.; of the author of the Horā-prakāśa, ib.; the right canal for the passage of the vital air (?), W. **-kara**, m. N. of an author, Cat. **-kānta**, m. sun-stone, a sort of crystal (= *sūrya-kānta*), L.; *-maya*, mf(ī)n. consisting of sun-stones, Naish. **-kiraṇa**, m. a sunbeam, Śak.; *-kūrcikā*, f. N. of wk. **-kīrti**, m. N. of a poet (of the 7th century), Cat. **-kula dīpa prakāśa**, m N of wk. **-gupta**, m. (with *bhadanta*) N. of a poet, Cat. **-graha**, m., **-grahaṇa**, n. an eclipse of the sun, Cat. **-grāvan**, m. = *-kānta*, L. **-cakra**, n. a partic. astronomical diagram (the sun represented as a man carrying the stars on the various parts of his body), GāruḍaP.; *-kshepaka-dhruvāṅkāḥ*, pl. N. of astronomical tables. **-candra**, m. N. of the author of a Comm. on the Amaru-śataka. **-ja**, m. 'sun-born,' N. of the planet Saturn, VarBṛS.; of Yama, Subh.; pl. N. of partic. meteors or comets, ib. **-tanaya**, m. 'son of the sun,' N. of the planet Saturn, ib.; of Yama, VP. **-tīrtha**, n. N. of a Tīrtha, Cat. **-tejas**, n. the radiance of the sun, MW. **-datta**, m. N. of a priest and of a poet, Cat. **-dāsa**, m. N. of a poet, ib. **-dina**, n. day of the sun, Sunday, Inscr. **-dīpta**, mfn. lighted or illuminated by the sun, VarBṛS. **-dugdha**, n. the milk of Calotropis Gigantea, Bhpr. **-deva**, m. N. of a poet, Cat. **-dharman**, m. N. of the author of a Comm. on the Kavi-rahasya, ib. **-dhvaja**, m. 'having the sun for a banner,' day, L. **-nandana**, m. 'son of the sun,' N. of Manu Vaivasvata, BhP.; of the ape Su-grīva, L. **-nāga**, m. N. of a poet, Cat. **-netra**, m. 'sun-eyed,' N. of Vishṇu, A. **-pati-guru-mūrti**, f. N. of wk. **-pattra**, m. Calotropis Gigantea, L. **-putra**, m. 'son of the sun,' N. of the planet Saturn, VarBṛS. **-prabhu**, m. N. of a Brāhman, Vīrac. **-praśna**, m. N. of wk. **-priya**, m. (only L.) Calotropis Gigantea; Nerium Odorum Rubro-simplex; Artocarpus Locucha; (*ā*), f. N. of Dākshāyaṇī in Gaṅgā-dvāra, Cat. (v. l. *rati-priyā*); n. a red lotus-flower, L.; copper, L. **-bimba**, n. the sun's disk, VarBṛS. **-maṇi**, m. = *-kānta*, ŚārṅgP. **-maṇḍala**, n. = *-bimba*, BhP. **-māsaka**, m. a solar month, Sūryas. **-muhūrta**, m. or n. N. of wk. **-ratna**, n. = *-kānta*, Rājat. **-ratnaka**, n. 'sun-jewel,' a ruby, L. **-ratha**, m. the Sun's chariot, Siṃhâs. **-locana**, m. 'sun-eyed,' N. of Śiva, Śivag.; of Vishṇu, L. **-loha**, n. 'sun-metal,' copper, L. **-vaṃśa**, m. the solar race (of kings), Naish. **-varman**, m. N. of a man, Inscr. **-vāra**, m. = *-dina*, W.; *-vrata-vidhi*, m. N. of wk. **-vāsara**, m. n. = *-dina*, Cat. **-saṃkrānti**, f. the sun's entrance into a sign of the zodiac, MārkP.; *-nirṇaya*, m. N. of wk. **-saṃjñaka**, n. 'called after the sun,' copper, L. (cf. *-loha*). **-sama-prabha**, mfn. radiant as the sun, MW. **-sārathi**, m. 'the Sun's charioteer,' N. of Aruṇa or the Dawn, L. **-suta**, m. 'son of the sun,' N. of the planet Saturn, VarBṛS.; of the ape Su-grīva, Ragh. **-sundara-rasa**, m. N. of a partic. elixir, Cat. **-sūnu**, m. 'son of the sun,' the planet Saturn, L. **-sena**, m. N. of a poet, Cat. **Ravindra**, m. N. of an author, Cat.; w.r. for *su-rêndra*, Hariv. **Ravishṭa**, m. 'loved by the sun,' an orange, L.; (*ā*), f. Polanisia Icosandra, L.

रवित *ravita*, n. precipitation, hurry, L.

रवितृ *ravitṛi*. See p. 868, col. 3.

रविन्द *ravinda*, n. = *aravinda*, a lotus flower, L.

रविपुला *ra-vipulā*. See under 2. *ra*.

रवीषु *ravīshu*, m. the god of love, Kāma-deva, L. (v. l. *varīshu*).

रशना *raśanā́*, f. (prob. connected with *raśmi* and *rāśi* and derived from a lost √*raś*) a rope, cord, strap; rein, bridle; girth, girdle, zone (esp. of woman), RV. &c. &c. (also fig. applied to the fingers; cf. Naigh. ii, 5); a ray of light, beam, ŚāṅkhBr.; the tongue (w. r. for *rasanā*), L.; (ifc.) girt by, dependent on, Hariv.; BhP. **-kalāpa** or °**paka**, m. a woman's girdle formed out of several strings or threads, Kāv. (cf. *raśmi-kalāpa*). **-°kṛita** (°*nā́k*°), mfn. guided or led by a cord or bridle, Kauś. **-guṇa**, m. the cord of a girdle; °*nâspada*, n. 'place for the c° of a g°,' the waist, Kum. **-pada**, n. 'place for the girdle,' the hip, L. **Raśanôpamā**, f. 'string of comparisons,' a form of simile (when the object to which anything is compared is made the subject of another comparison, which again leads to a third and so on), Sāh.

Raśana, in comp. for *raśanā*. **-sammita** (°*nā́-*), mfn. as long as the rope (on the sacrificial post), TS.; ĀpŚr.

Raśanāya, Nom. Ā. °*yate* (only p. *raśanāyá-māna*), to be guided by a rein, AV.

रश्मि *raśmí*, m. (exceptionally f.; cf. *ra-śanā* and Uṇ. iv, 46) a string, rope, cord, trace, rein, bridle, leash, goad, whip (also fig. applied to the fingers), RV. &c. &c.; a measuring cord, RV. viii, 25, 18; a ray of light, beam, splendour, RV. &c. &c.; = *anna*, food, VS. xv, 16; = *paksha* or *pakshman*, L. **-kalāpa**, m. a pearl-necklace consisting of 54 or 56 threads, VarBṛS. **-ketu**, m. 'beam-bannered,' a partic. comet, ib.; N. of a Rākshasa, R. **-krīḍa**, m. N. of a Rākshasa, R. **-jāla**, n. a net or garland of rays, VarBṛS. **-pa**, m. pl. N. of a partic. class of deceased ancestors, VP. **-páti**, mfn. drunk by the rays of the sun (= *āditya-raś-maya eva pātāro yāsām*, scil. *apām*, Sch.; lit. 'ray-lord'), TĀr.; m. Calotropis Gigantea, L. **-pavitra** (°*mí-*), mfn. purified by rays or beams, TBr. **-puñja**, m. a heap or mass of rays, VP. **-prabhāsa**, m. N. of a Buddha, Buddh. **-maṇḍala**, n. a circle or garland of rays, AVPariś. **-mat**, mfn. having rays or beams, radiant, R.; m. the sun, MBh.; m. N. of a man, Kathās. **-maya**, mf(ī)n. formed or consisting of rays, BhP. **-mālin**, mfn. encircled or garlanded with rays, R.; the sun, L. **-muca**, m. 'ray-emitting,' the sun, MBh. **-rasa-prayoga**, m. N. of wk. **-rāja**, m. 'ray-lord,' N. of a man, Buddh. (cf. *raśmi-páti*). **-vát**, mfn. = *-mat*, TBr.; MBh. &c.; m. the sun, MBh.; (*atī*), f. a verse containing the word *raśmi*, Kāṭh. **-śata-sahasra-paripūrṇa-dhvaja**, m. N. of a Buddha, Buddh.

Raśman, m. = *raśmi*; only in instr. *raśmā́* (RV. vi, 67, 1) and ifc. (cf. *a-raśmán* and *sthā́-raśman*).

Raśmin, (ifc.) = *raśmi*, a rein, bridle, BhP.

Raśmisa, m. N. of a Dānava, Hariv. (v. l. *ra-bhasa* and *nabhasa*).

Raśmī-vát, mfn. = *raśmi-vát*, VS.

रस 1. *ras* (cf. √1. *rās*), cl. 1. P. (Dhātup. xvii, 63) *rasati* (rarely Ā. °*te*; pf. *rarāsa, resuḥ*, MBh. &c.; aor. *arāsīt*, Gr.; fut. *rasitā, rasishyati*, ib.; inf. *rasitum*, ib.), to roar, yell, cry, sound, reverberate, ŚBr. &c. &c.; to praise, Naigh. iii, 14: Caus. *rāsayati* (aor. *arīrasat*), Gr.: Desid. *rirasishati*, ib.: Intens. *rārasyate* (or *rārasti*, Gr.), to cry out loudly, scream aloud, Bhaṭṭ.

1. **Rasana**, n. (for 2. see p. 870, col. 3) the act of roaring or screaming or rumbling or thundering, any sound or noise, VarBṛS.; Bālar.; croaking (of frogs), VarBṛS.

1. **Rasita**, mfn. (for 2. see p. 871, col. 1) sounded, resounding, uttering inarticulate sounds, Kād.; Gīt.; n. a roar, scream, cry, noise, sound, thunder, Kāv.; Rājat. **Rasitâśin**, mfn. consuming or destroying by mere noise, MW.

1. **Rasitṛi**, mfn. (for 2. see p. 871, col. 1) one who roars or bellows, Sāh.

रस 2. *ras* (rather Nom. fr. *rasa* below), cl. 10. P. (Dhātup. xxxv. 77) *rasáyati* (rarely Ā. °*te*, ep. also *rasati* and *rasyati*), to taste, relish, ŚBr.; Up.; MBh. &c.; to feel, perceive, be sensible of, Sāh.; to love, Dhātup.: Desid. *rirasa-yishati*, to desire to taste, Śiś.

Rása, m. (ifc. f. *ā*) the sap or juice of plants, juice of fruit, any liquid or fluid, the best or finest or prime part of anything, essence, marrow, RV. &c. &c.; water, liquor, drink, MBh.; Kāv. &c.; juice of the sugar-cane, syrup, Suśr.; any mixture, draught, elixir, potion, R.; BhP.; melted butter, L.; (with or scil. *gavām*) milk, MBh.; (with or scil. *vishasya*) poison, Daś.; Rājat.; nectar, L.; soup, broth, L.; a constituent fluid or essential juice of the body, serum, (esp.) the primary juice called chyle (formed from the food and changed by the bile into blood), ib.; mercury, quicksilver (sometimes regarded as a kind of quintessence of the human body, elsewhere as the seminal fluid of Śiva), Sarvad.; semen virile, RV. i, 105, 2; myrrh, L.; any mineral or metallic salt, Cat.; a metal or mineral in a state of fusion (cf. *upa-*, *mahā-r*°); gold, L.; Vanguieria Spinosa, L.; a species of amaranth, L.; green onion, L.; resin, L.; = *amṛita*, L.; taste, flavour (as the principal quality of fluids, of which there are 6 original kinds, viz. *madhura*, sweet; *amla*, sour; *lavaṇa*, salt; *kaṭuka*, pungent; *tikta*, bitter; and *kashāya*, astringent; sometimes 63 varieties are distinguished, viz. beside the 6 original ones, 15 mixtures of 2, 20 of 3, 15 of 4, 6 of 5, and 1 of 6 flavours), ŚBr. &c. &c.; N. of the number 'six,' VarBṛS.; Śrutab.; any object of taste, condiment, sauce, spice, seasoning, MBh.; Kāv. &c.; the tongue (as the organ of taste), BhP.; taste or inclination or fondness for (loc. with or scil. *upari*, or comp.), love, affection, desire, MBh.; Kāv. &c.; charm, pleasure, delight, ib.; (in rhet.) the taste or character of a work, the feeling or sentiment prevailing in it (from 8 to 10 Rasas are generally enumerated, viz. *śṛiṅgāra*, love; *vīra*, heroism; *bībhatsa*, disgust; *raudra*, anger or fury; *hāsya*, mirth; *bhayānaka*, terror; *karuṇa*, pity; *adbhuta*, wonder; *śānta*, tranquillity or contentment; *vātsalya*, paternal fondness; the last or last two are sometimes omitted; cf. under *bhāva*), Bhar.; Daśar.; Kāvyâd. &c.; the prevailing sentiment in human character, Uttarar.; Rājat.; (with Vaishṇavas) disposition of the heart or mind, religious sentiment (there are 5 Rasas or Ratis forming the 5 degrees of *bhakti*, q. v., viz. *śānti*, *dāsya*, *sākhya*, *vātsalya*, and *mādhurya*), W.; a kind of metre, Piṅg.; N. of the sacred syllable 'Om,' ŚāṅkhGṛ.; the son of a Nishāda and a Śanakī, L.; (*ā*), f., see s. v. **-kaṅkāli**, m. N. of a medical wk. by Kaṅkāli. **-kadamba-kallolinī**, f. N. of a Comm. on Gīta-govinda. **-karpūra**, n. sublimate of mercury, Bhpr. **-karman**, n. a sacrificial rite connected with (the sipping of) liquids, Kauś.; = *-kalpanā*, Sarvad. **-kalikā**, f. N. of a wk. on rhetoric. **-kalpanā**, f. preparation of quicksilver, Cat. **-kalpa-latā**, f., **-kalpa-sāra-stava**, m. N. of wks. **-kalyāṇī-vrata**, n. N. of a partic. ceremony and of various wks. **-kashāya**, m. or n. N. of a medical wk. **-kulyā**, f. N. of a river in Kuśa-dvīpa, BhP. **-ketu**, m. N. of a prince, L. **-kesara**, n. camphor, L. **-komala**, n. a partic. mineral, Cat. **-kautuka**, n. N. of a medical wk. **-kaumudī**, f. N. of various wks. **-kriyā**, f. the inspissation and application of fluid remedies or fomentations, Suśr. **-gaṅgā-dhara**, m. N. of an author; °*rīya*, n. his wk. **-gandha**, m. or n. myrrh, L. (v. l. *-bhaṅga*); N. of wk. **-gandhaka**, m. myrrh, L.; brimstone, sulphur, L. **-garbha**, n. a collyrium made from the juice of Curcuma Xanthorrhiza, Bhpr.; an ointment made from the calx of brass, L.; cinnabar, L. **-gāndhāra**, m. or n. N. of wk. **-guṇa**, mfn. possessing the quality of taste, Mn. i, 78. **-govinda**, m. N. of wk. **-graha**, mfn. apprehending flavours, having a taste for enjoyments, BhP.; m. the organ of taste, ib. **-grāhaka**, mfn. apprehending or perceiving flavours, Tarkas. **-ghaná**, mfn. full of juice, consisting entirely of juice, ŚBr. **-ghna**, m. borax, L. **-candra**, m., **-candrikā**, f., **-cintāmaṇi**, m. N. of wks. **-cūḍāmaṇi**, m. a partic. preparation, L. **-ja**, mfn. bred in fluids, Mn. xi, 143; proceeding from chyle, L.; m. sugar, molasses, L.; any insect engendered by the fermentation of liquids, W.; n. blood, L. **-jāta**, n. an ointment prepared from the calx of brass, L. **-jña**, mfn. knowing tastes or the taste of, appreciative (gen. or comp.), Kāv.; Pur.; Kathās.; familiar with (loc. or comp.), Ragh.; Uttarar.; m. a poet or any writer who understands the Rasas, W.; an alchemist who understands the magical properties of mercury, ib.; a physician or any preparer of mercurial and chemical compounds, ib.; n. and *ā*), f. the tongue, Kāv.; BhP.; *-tā*, f. or *-tva*, n. knowledge of flavours, poetical skill or taste, discrimination, judgment, experience, familiarity with (gen. or comp.), Kāv.; Kām.; Kathās.; alchemy, W. **-jñāna**, n. knowledge of tastes (a branch of medical science), Suśr. **-jyeshṭha**, m. the first or best taste, sweet taste, sweetness, L.; the sentiment of love, W. **-jvara**,

m. (prob.) a gastric fever, HPariś. **-tattva-sāra,** m. N. of wk. **-tanmātra,** n. the subtle element or rudiment of taste, Tattvas. **-tama** (*rása-*), m. the juice of all juices, essence of essences, ŚBr.; ChUp. **-taraṃgiṇī,** f. N. of various wks. **-tas,** ind. according to taste or flavour, MBh. **-tā,** f. juiciness, fluidity, MBh.; Kād. &c. (*-tām upêtam,* become fluid). **-tejas,** n. 'strength of the chyle,' blood, L. **-tva,** n. the being chyle, state of chyle, MBh.; *-jāti-pramāṇa,* n. N. of wk. **-da,** mfn. emitting juice or sap, exuding resin, Nalôd.; m. 'giver of fluids or mixtures,' a physician, MBh. **-daṇḍa,** m. (prob.) a magic wand, Pañcad. **-darpaṇa,** m. N. of wk. **-dālikā,** f. a kind of sugar-cane, L. **-dīpikā,** f., **-dīrghikā,** f. N. of wks. **-drāvin,** m. a kind of citron, L. **-dhātu,** m. 'fluid metal,' quicksilver, L. **-dhenu,** f. a cow consisting of fruit-juice, Hcat. **-nātha,** m. 'chief of fluids,' quicksilver, L. **-nābha,** n. = *-jāta,* L. **-nāyaka,** m. 'lord of the feelings,' N. of Kāma-deva, Vcar.; of Śiva, L. **-nibandha,** m., **-nirū-paṇa,** n. N. of wks. **-nivṛitti,** f. cessation or loss of taste, W. **-netrikā** or **-netrī,** f. realgar, red arsenic, L. **-n-tamá,** m. = *rása-tama,* ŚBr. **-pati,** m. = *-nātha,* L. **-paddhati,** f., **-padma-candri-kā,** f., **-padmâkara,** m. (and °*ra-campū,* f.), **-pari-mala,** m. N. of wks. **-parpaṭī,** f. a partic. preparation of mercury, Bhpr. **-pāka-ja,** m. 'produced by the maturing of juices,' sugar, L. **-pācaka,** m. 'cooker of sauces or flavours,' a cook, MBh. **-pārijāta,** m. N. of wk. **-pushpa,** n. a partic. preparation of mercury, a kind of muriate (formed by subliming a mixture of sulphur, mercury, and common salt in closed vessels), W. **-prakāśa,** m. (and °*śa-sudhâkara,* m.), **-pradīpa,** m. N. of various wks. **-prabandha,** m. 'connection of Rasas,' any poetical composition, (esp.) a drama, Vikr. **-prâśanī,** f. N. of the verse AV. v, 2, 3, Kauś. **-phala,** m. a cocoa-nut tree (the fruit of which contains a fluid), L. **-bandhana,** n. (prob.) a partic. part of the intestines, R. **-bodha,** m. knowledge of taste (esp. in poetical composition), MW. **-bhaṅga,** m. interruption or cessation of passion or sentiment, W.; v.l. for *-gandha,* q.v. **-bhava,** n. = *-ja,* n. **-bhasman,** n. calx or oxide of mercury, W.; °*ma-vidhi,* m. N. of wk. **-bhāva-vid,** mfn. knowing the sentiments and passions, Śiś. **-bheda,** m. a variety of different mixtures (°*dīya,* mfn. relating to them), Līl.; a partic. preparation of quicksilver, MBh. **-bhedin,** mfn. of different taste or flavour, MBh.; discharging juice (said of fruits which burst with ripeness), MW. **-bheshaja-kalpa,** m., **-bhoga-muktâvalī,** f. N. of wks. **-bhojana,** mfn. feeding on liquids or fluids, VarBṛS.; n. an entertainment given to Brāhmans in which they are feasted with the juice of mangoes, MW. **-mañjarī,** f. N. of various wks.; *-guṇa-leśa-sūcakâshṭaka,* n., *-parimala,* m., *-prakāśa,* m., *-sthūla-tātparyârtha,* m. N. of wks. **-maṇi,** m. N. of a medical wk. **-maya,** mf(*ī*)n. formed of juice, consisting of fluid, liquid, Kathās.; BhP.; consisting of quicksilver, Sarvad.; whose essence is taste, savoury (as water), BhP.; delightful, charming, MārkP. **-mala,** m. or n. the refuse of juices (of the body), impure excretions, Kap. **-ma-hârṇava,** m. N. of wk. **-mātṛi** or **-mātṛikā,** f. 'mother of taste,' the tongue, L. **-mātra,** n. = *-tanmātra,* BhP. **-miśra,** mfn. mixed with fluids, Kauś. **-mīmāṉsā,** f., **-muktâvali,** f. N. of wks. **-mūlā,** f. N. of a Prākṛit metre, Col. **-yāmala,** n. N. of a medical wk. **-yoga,** m. pl. scientifically mixed juices, prepared mixtures, MBh.; *-muktâvalī,* f. N. of wk. **-yoni,** m. borax, L. **-ratna,** n. 'jewel of Rasas,' N. of a medical wk.; (ibc.) juice and pearls (cf. *-maya*); *-kośa,* m., *-dīpikā,* f., *-pradīpa,* m., *-pradīpikā,* f. N. of various wks.; *-maya,* mf(*ī*)n. consisting of juices and pearls, Hcat.; *-mālā,* f., *-samuccaya,* m., *-hāra,* m.; °*tnâkara,* m., °*tnâvalī,* f. N. of various wks. **-rasârṇava,** m., **-rahasya,** n. N. of medical wks. **-rāja,** m. = *-nātha,* L.; = *rasâñjana,* L.; N. of a wk. on medicine; *-lakshmī,* f., *-śaṃkara,* m., *-śiromaṇi,* m., *-haṉsa,* m. N. of medical wks. **-leha** (prob. w.r.) or **-loha,** m. quicksilver, L. **-vat** (*rása-*), mfn. full of juice or sap, juicy, succulent, strong, RV. &c. &c.; moist, well watered (as a field), MBh.; filled with juice (as a cup), Kauś.; overflowing with (instr.), Pañcar.; tasty, charming, elegant, graceful, lovely, MBh.; Kāv. &c.; possessing love and the other Rasas, impassioned, full of feeling, affected by emotions of love or jealousy &c., MW.; spirited, witty, ib.; (*ī*), f., see below; n. a tasteful style, Bhaṭṭ., Sch.; *-tara,* mfn. more savoury, more delightful, Vikr.; *-tā,* f. juiciness, savouriness, sapidity; tastefulness, elegance, beauty, Vās.; Sāh. **-vatī,** f. a kitchen, Kāv.; a meal, HPariś.; N. of various wks.; *-śataka,* n. N. of a poem. **-vara,** m. = *-nāyaka,* L. **-varja,** m. avoidance of tastes or flavours; (*am*), ind. except taste, Bhag. **-vaha,** mfn. bringing or producing juice, Suśr. **-vāda,** m. alchemy, Subh. **-vikraya,** m. the sale of stimulating juices or liquors, W. **-vikrayin** (Mn.), **-vikretṛi** (Kull.), m. a syrup seller, liquor seller, a dealer in essences or spices. **-vid,** mfn. knowing tastes or flavours, having good taste, discriminating, BhP. **-viddha,** n. artificial gold, L. **-vilāsa,** m., **-viveka,** m. N. of wks. **-viśesha,** m. a more excellent juice or flavour, MW. **-vaiśeshika,** (prob.) n., **-śabda-sāraṇi-nighaṇṭu,** m. N. of wks. **-śārdūla,** m. a partic. preparation of quicksilver, Rasêndrac. **-śāstra,** n. 'science of Rasas,' alchemy, Sarvad. **-śukta,** n. a sour beverage prepared from the juice of fruit, Suśr. **-śodhana,** m. borax, L.; n. purification of quicksilver, Cat.; N. of wk. **-saṃskāra,** m., **-saṃketa,** m. (and °*ta-kalikā,* f.), **-saṃgraha,** m. (and °*ha-siddhânta,* m.) N. of various wks. **-saṃgrāhī,** f. N. of a Yoginī, Hcat. **-sadana,** n., **-samuccaya,** m., **-sarvasva,** n., **-sāgara,** m., **-sāra,** m. (°*ra-saṃgraha,* m., °*ra-samuccaya,* m.; °*râmṛita,* n.) N. of wks. **-siddha,** mfn. brought to perfection by means of quicksilver, skilled in alchemy, Rājat.; Sarvad.; conversant with the poetical Rasas, accomplished in poetry, Bhartṛ. **-siddhânta-saṃgraha,** m., **-siddhânta-sāgara,** m. N. of wks. **-siddhi,** f. perfection attained by means of quicksilver, skill in alchemy, Rājat.; *-prakāśa,* m. N. of a medical wk. **-sindūra,** n. a sort of factitious cinnabar (used as an escharotic), W. **-sindhu,** m., **-sudhâkara,** m., **-sudhā-nidhi,** m., **-sudhâmbhodhi,** m., **-sūtra-sthāna,** n., **-setu,** m. N. of wks. **-sthāna,** n. cinnabar or vermilion, L. **-haraṇa,** n. the sucking up or imbibing of juice, Nir.; mf(*ī*)n. = *-vaha,* Car. **-hārin,** mfn. id., ib. **-hṛidaya,** n., **-heman,** n. N. of wks.

Rasâkara, m. N. of a work on the poetical Rasas. **Rasâgraja,** n. an ointment prepared from the calx of brass, L. **Rasâṅgaka,** m. the resin of Pinus Longifolia, L. **Rasâñjana,** n. vitriol of copper or a sort of collyrium prepared from it with the addition of Curcuma or (accord. to some) from the calx of brass with Amomum Anthorrhiza or (accord. to others) from lead ore, Suśr. **Rasâḍhya,** m. 'abounding in juice or sap,' Spondias Mangifera, L.; (*ā*), f. a species of plant, L. **Rasâtmaka,** mf(*ikā*)n. having juice for its essence, consisting of nectar (as the moon), Kum.; characterized by sapidity or savour (as water), Cat.; tasteful, elegant, charming, beautiful, Sāh. **Rasâdāna,** n. the taking up of moisture, absorption of fluid, suction, L. **Rasâdi-śuddhi,** f. N. of a medical wk. **Rasâdvaita,** n. N. of a wk. on the Vedânta. **Rasâdhāra,** m. 'receptacle of fluids or moisture,' the sun, L. **Ra-sâdhāraṇa,** n. retention of moisture (by the sun's rays), MW. **Rasâdhika,** mfn. full of taste, abounding in enjoyments, Śak.; m. borax, L.; (*ā*), f. a species of grape without seeds or stones, L. **Ra-sâdhikāra,** m. N. of a medical wk. **Rasâdhy-aksha,** m. a superintendent of liquors or fluids, R., Sch. **Rasâdhyāya,** m. N. of a medical wk. **Rasânupradāna,** n. the bestowing of moisture (one of the functions of Indra), Nir. **Rasântara,** n. difference of taste (*-vid,* mfn. knowing different tastes or flavours), Kpr.; another pleasure or enjoyment, Kathās.; different passion or emotion, Kum.; difference of the poetical Rasa or sentiment, Vām. **Rasâbdhi,** m. N. of a poem. **Rasâbhāsa,** m. the mere semblance or false attribution or improper manifestation of a sentiment, Sāh. **Rasâbhiniveśa,** m. accession of sentiment, intentness of feeling or passion, W. **Rasâbhivyañjanā** and °**vyañjikā,** f. N. of wks. **Rasâbhyantara,** mfn. filled with water or love, Ml. **Rasâmṛita,** n. (and °*ta-sindhu,* m.), **Rasâmbhodhi,** m., **Rasâmbhonidhi,** m. N. of wks. **Rasâmla,** m. Rumex Vesicarius, L.; (*ā*), f. a species of creeper, L.; vinegar made from fruit, Bhpr.; sour sauce, (esp.) tamarind sauce, MW. **Rasâyana,** m. a partic. drug used as a vermifuge (Embelia Ribes), L.; an alchemist, L.; N. of Garuḍa, L.; (*ī*), f. a canal or channel for the fluids (of the body), Car.; Suśr.; N. of various plants (Solanum Indicum; Cocculus Cordifolius; a species of Karañja; = *goraksha-dugdhā*; = *māṉsa-cchadā* &c.), L.; n. (sometimes following the gender of the word to which it refers) a medicine supposed to prevent old age and prolong life, an elixir, elixir vitae (also applied to the first fructifying rains), MBh.; Kāv. &c.; buttermilk, L.; poison, L.; long pepper (?), L.; the employment of mercury as a remedy or for magical purposes, W.; *-kara,* mfn. forming an elixir, L.; *-tantra,* n., *-taraṃgiṇī,* f., *-nidhāna,* n. N. of wks.; *-phalā,* f. Terminalia Chebula or Citrina, L.; *-vidhi,* m. N. of wk.; *-śreshṭha,* m. 'best of elixirs,' mercury, L.; °*nâmṛita-lauha,* m. a partic. medicinal preparation, L.; °*nin,* mfn. employing elixirs, L. **Rasârṇava,** m. 'ocean of Rasas,' N. of a medical wk.; *-kalā,* f., *-sudhâkara,* m. N. of wks. **Rasâlaṃkāra,** m. aesthetics, Caurap.; N. of a wk. on medicine. **Rasâlaya,** m. the seat of the Rasas or of enjoyments, Cat.; pl. N. of a people, MārkP. **Rasâ-vatāra,** m. N. of a medical wk. **Rasâveshṭa,** m. the resin of Pinus Longifolia, L. **Rasâśā,** °**śin,** see *a-ras*°. **Rásâśir,** mfn. mixed with juice or milk, RV. **Rasâsvāsā,** f. a kind of creeper (= or w.r. for *rasâmlā*), L. **Rasâsvāda,** m. 'sipping of juice' or 'perception of pleasure,' Vedântas.; °*din,* m. 'juice-sipper,' a bee, L. **Rasâhva,** m. the resin of Pinus Longifolia, L.; (*ā*), f. Asparagus Racemosus, L. **Rasêkshu,** m. sugar-cane, L. **Rasêndra,** m. 'chief of fluids,' quicksilver, Caṇḍ.; the philosopher's stone (the touch of which turns iron to gold), W.; *-kalpadruma,* m., *-cintāmaṇi,* m., *-cūḍāmaṇi,* m., *-maṅgala,* n., *-saṃhitā,* f., *-sāra-saṃgraha,* m. N. of wks. **Rasêśvara,** m. 'lord of fluids,' quicksilver; *-darśana,* n. the science of the application of mercury, the doctrine of alchemy; N. of wk., Sarvad. (RTL. 206, n. 1); *-siddhânta,* m. N. of a wk. (establishing the efficacy of mercury in alchemy), ib. **Rasôttama,** m. quicksilver, L.; Phaseolus Mungo, L.; milk, L. **Rasôtpatti,** f. production of taste or flavour, W.; development of passion or sentiment, ib.; generation of the vital fluids, ib. **Rasôdadhi,** m. 'ocean of Rasas,' N. of various wks. **Rasôdbhava,** n. a pearl, L.; cinnabar, L.; blood, L. **Rasôna,** see *rasona,* p. 871. **Rasôparasa,** m. or n. (?) N. of a medical wk. (also *-śodhana,* n.) **Rasôpala,** m. or n. (?) 'water-stone,' a pearl, L. **Rasôllāsa,** m. the springing up of desire for (comp.), Gīt., Sch. (°*sin,* mfn. feeling the awakening of desire, Cat.); (*ā*), f. (scil. *siddhi*) 'spontaneous evolution of the fluids (or juices of the body, without nutriment from without),' N. of one of the 8 Siddhis or states of perfection, VP.; *-bhāṇa,* m. N. of a drama. **Rasâudana,** n. rice boiled in meat-broth, Bhpr.

Rasaka, m. or n. soup made from meat, Kathās.

2. **Rasana,** m. (for 1. see p. 869, col. 2) phlegm or saliva (regarded as the cause of taste to the tongue), ŚārṅgS.; (*ā*), f., see below; n. tasting, taste, flavour, savour, Yājñ.; MBh. &c.; the tongue as organ of taste, Tarkas.; the being sensible of (anything), perception, apprehension, sense, Sāh. **Rasanêndriya,** n. 'organ of taste,' the tongue, Suśr.

Rasanā, f. the tongue as organ of taste, MaitrUp.; MBh. &c.; N. of two plants (= *gandha-bhadrā* and *rāsnā*), Bhpr. **-nigraha,** m. N. of wk. **-ma-la,** n. any impurity on the tongue, L. **-mūla,** n. the root of the tongue, Subh. **-rada,** m. 'having-the tongue for teeth,' a bird, L. **-lih,** m. 'licking with the tongue,' a dog, L.

Rasanīya, mfn. to be tasted, tasty, palatable, MBh.

Rasayati, m. or f. taste, flavour, BṛĀrUp.

Rasayitavya, mfn. = *rasanīya,* PraśnUp.

Rasayitṛi, mfn. one who tastes, a taster, ŚBr.

Rasā́, f. moisture, humidity, RV.; N. of a river, ib.; a mythical stream supposed to flow round the earth and the atmosphere, ib. (Nir. xi, 23); the lower world, hell, MBh.; Pur. (cf. *-tala*); the earth, ground, soil, Kāv.; the tongue, L.; N. of various plants (Clypea Hernandifolia; Boswellia Thurifera; Panicum Italicum; a vine or grape; = *kākolī*), L. **-khana,** m. 'digging or scratching in the soil,' a cock, L. **-tala,** n. N. of one of the seven hells or regions under the earth, MBh.; Pur. &c. (RTL. 102, n. 1); the lower world or hell in general (not to be confounded with Naraka or the place of punishment), MBh.; Kāv. &c.; the 4th astrological mansion, VarBṛS.; the earth, ground, soil, Subh.; m. N. of a poet, ib. **-°dhipatya** (*rasâdh*°), n. dominion over the lower world, BhP. **-pāyin,** m. 'drinking with the tongue,' a dog, L. — **push**, m. 'acquiring moisture i.e. honey (?),' a bee, Śrīkaṇṭh.

Rasāyaka, m. a kind of grass, L.

Rasāyya, mfn. juicy, tasteful, savoury, RV.

Rasārasā, f. = *rasālasā*, Lalit.

Rasāla, m. the mango tree, Prasannar.; the sugar-cane, L.; the bread-fruit tree, L.; a kind of grass, L.; wheat, L.; a kind of mouse, Cat.; (*ā*), f. curds mixed with sugar and spices, MBh.; Hariv.; R.; the tongue, L.; Dūrvā grass, L.; Desmodium Gangeticum, L.; a vine or grape, L.; N. of wk.; (*ī*), f. sugar, L.; n. myrrh or frankincense, L.

Rasālasā, f. any tubular vessel of the body (esp. one conveying the fluids), vein, artery &c., L.

Rasālihā, f. Hemionitis Cordifolia, L.

Rasika, mf(*ā*)n. tasteful, elegant, Bhartṛ.; having a discriminating taste, æsthetic, Kāv.; Kathās.; having a taste for or a sense of, fond of, devoted to, delighting in (loc. or comp.), ib.; Rājat.; Sāh.; sentimental, W.; fanciful, MW.; lustful, ib.; m. a man full of taste or feeling (cf. *a-r°*); a libertine, W.; Ardea Sibirica, L.; a horse, L.; an elephant, L.; unboiled juice of sugar-cane, L.; (*ā*), f., see below. — **candrikā**, f., **-jīvana**, n., **-jīvanī**, f. N. of wks. — **tā**, f., **-tva**, n. sense of, taste or fondness for, devotion or addiction to (loc.), Kāv. — **prakāśa**, m., **-priyā**, f., **-bhūshaṇa**, n., **-rañjana**, n., **-rañjinī**, f., **-ramaṇa**, n., **-saṃjīvinī**, f., **-sarvasva**, n. N. of wks.

Rasikā, f. an emotional wife (cf. comp.); the juice of sugar-cane, molasses, L.; curds with sugar and spice, L.; chyle, L.; the tongue, L.; a woman's girdle, L. (cf. *raśanā*). — **bhārya**, m. one who has a wife liable to strong emotions or feelings, Vop.

Rasikêśvara, m. 'lord or husband of a passionate wife,' N. of Kṛishṇa, BrahmavP.

2. **Rasita**, mfn. (for 1. see p. 869, col. 2) tasted, Kāv.; covered or overlaid with gold, gilded, plated, L.; having taste or flavour or sentiment, W. — **vat**, mfn. one who has tasted &c., Śis.

2. **Rasitṛi**, mfn. (for 1. see p. 869, col. 2) = *rasayitṛi*, a taster, MBh.

Rasin, mfn. juicy, liquid (as Soma), RV.; VS.; impassioned, W.; having good taste, æsthetic, Nalôd.

Rasya, mfn. juicy, tasty, savoury, palatable, MBh.; (*ā*), f. N. of two plants (= *rāsnā* and *pāṭhā*), L.; n. blood (supposed to be produced from chyle), L.

Rasyamāna, mfn. being tasted or perceived (*-tā*, f.), Sāh.

रसुन *rasuna*, m. Allium Ascalonicum, L. (cf. *laśuna*).

Rasona or **°naka**, m. id., Suśr., L.

रस्न *rasna*, n. (said to be fr. √1. *ras*) a thing, object, Uṇ. iii, 12, Sch.; (*ā*), f. = *rasanā*, the tongue, L.

रह् *rah*, cf. 1. P. (Dhātup. xvii, 82) *rahati* (pf. *rarāha* &c., Gr.; inf. *-rahitum*, see *vi-√rah*), to part, separate, MBh. i, 5199 (v.l.); to leave, quit, abandon, Dhātup.; Caus. or cl. 10. P. (xxxv. 6) to leave, abandon, Kāv.; to cause to give up or abandon, Bālar. [Cf. λαθ in λανθάνω.]

Raha, m. = 2. *rahas*, L. — **rūḍha-bhāva**, mfn. withdrawn into privacy, being private or in secret, BhP. — **sū**, f. (a woman) bringing forth a child in secret, RV. — **stha**, mfn. = (and v.l. for) *rahaḥ-stha*, q.v. **Rahâṭa**, m. 'gone to a secret place (?),' a counsellor, minister, W.; a ghost, spirit, ib.; a spring (?), ib.

Rahaḥ, in comp. for 2. *rahas*. — **śīla**, mfn. of a reserved or silent disposition, not talkative, Āpast. — **śuci**, mfn. one who has executed a secret commission, Kathās. — **sakhī**, f. a secret female friend, Ragh. — **stha**, mf(*ā*)n. standing or being in a lonely place or in private, being apart or alone, Kathās.; Pañcat.; being in the enjoyment of love, VarBṛS.

Rahaṇa, n. desertion, abandonment, separation, Nalôd.

2. **Rahas**, n. (for 1. see p. 859, col. 3) a lonely or deserted place, loneliness, solitude, privacy, secrecy, retirement (*rahas*, *°si* and *°ssu*, ind. privately, in secret), Mn.; MBh. &c.; a secret, mystery, mystical truth, Kāv.; Pur.; sexual intercourse, copulation, L. — **kara**, mfn. executing a secret commission, BhP. — **kāma**, m. fond of solitude (*-tā*, f.), Car. — **tas**, ind. out of retirement, Harav.

Rahasa. See *anu-*, *ava-*, and *tapta-r°*.

Rahasa-nandin or **rahasā-nandin**, m. N. of a grammarian, Col.

Rahasya, mfn. secret, private, clandestine, concealed, mysterious, Vas.; MBh. &c. (*°syāni romāṇi*, hair on the private parts, Mn. iv, 144); (*ā*), f. = *rāsnā* or *pāṭhā*, L.; N. of a river, MBh.; n. a secret, any secret doctrine or mystery, any subtle or recondite point, mystical or esoteric teaching, Mn.; MBh. &c.; an Upanishad (see *sa-r°*); full or abridged N. of various wks.; (*am*), ind. in secret, secretly, privately, MBh. — **gāna**, n. = *ūhya-g°*, q.v. — **chalâkshara**, n. N. of wk. — **traya**, n. the three categories of Rāmânuja and his school (defining the universe as consisting of Īśvara, Cit and A-cit, cf. RTL. 119); N. of wk.; *-kārikā-vyākhyā*, f., *-culuka*, m., *-cūdāmaṇi*, m., *-mīmāṃsā*, f., *-vidhi*, m., *-vyākhyârtha*, m., *-saṃgraha*, m., *-sāra*, m., *-sāra-saṃgraha*, m.; *°yârtha*, m. N. of wks. — **dhārin**, mfn. one who is in possession of a secret or mystery, initiated into a secret rite or mystery, Kathās.; (*iṇī*), f. a confidante, Ml. — **navanīta**, n. N. of wk. — **nikshepa**, m. one who is entrusted with (lit. 'the deposit of') a secret, Vikr. — **padavī**, f., **-puraścaraṇa-vidhi**, m., **-brāhmaṇa**, n. N. of wks. — **bheda**, m., **-bhedana**, n. the disclosure of a secret or mystery, Kāv.; Kathās. — **mañjarī**, f., **-mātṛikā**, f., **-rakshā**, f. N. of wks. — **vibheda**, m. = *-bheda*, MW. — **vrata**, n. 'mystical vow,' the mystic science of obtaining command over magical weapons, ib. — **shoḍaśī-ṭīkā**, f. N. of wk. — **saṃrakshaṇa**, n. the keeping of a secret, Kathās. — **saṃdeśa-vivaraṇa**, n., **-sāra**, m. N. of wks. **Rahasyâkhyāyin**, mfn. whispering (as it were) a secret, Śak.; making secret reports, Mn. vii, 223. **Rahasyâtirahasya-puraścaraṇa**, n. N. of wk. **Rahasyâlocana**, n. the pondering over secret things, L.; (*ā*), f. id., R.; (*°nā-para*, mfn. addicted to p° over s° things, ib. **Rahasyêshṭi**, f. (and *°ṭi-paddhati*, f.), **°syôcchishṭa-sumukhī-kalpa**, m., **°syôpanishad**, f. N. of wks.

Rahasyu, m. N. of a man, PañcavBr.

Rahāya (fr. 2. *rahas*), Nom. Ā. *°yate*, to be lonely or private, g. *bhṛiśâdi*.

Rahita, mfn. left, quitted, forsaken, deserted, lonely, solitary, MBh.; R. &c. (*e* or *eshu*, ind. in secret, secretly, privately); deserted by, separated or free from, deprived or void or destitute of (instr. or comp.), Yājñ.; MBh. &c.; (ibc.) wanting, absent (cf. below). — **tva**, n. (ifc.) want or lack of, Campak. — **ratna**, mfn. destitute of gems, MW. (also *ratna-rahita*). — **ratna-caya**, mfn. destitute of heaps of gems, Kir. **Rahitâsura**, mfn. destitute of divinity, BhP.

Rahī, in comp. for *raha* or 2. *rahas*. — **√kṛi**, P. *-karoti*, to withdraw to a solitary place, Vop. — **√bhū**, P. *-bhavati*, id., ib. — **bhūta**, mfn. withdrawn to a lonely place, retired, Bhaṭṭ.

Raho, in comp. for 2. *rahas*. — **gata**, mfn. being in a lonely place, alone, secret, concealed, private, Mn.; MBh. &c. — **mānin**, mfn. thinking one's self hidden, Jātak.

रहूराज *rahu-rāja*, m. N. of a man, Inscr.

रहूगण *rahū-gaṇa*, m. (pl.) N. of a family belonging to the race of the Āṅgirasas, RV.; ĀśvŚr.; (sg.) N. of the author of the hymns RV. ix, 37; 38, Anukr.

रा 1. *rā* or *rās*, cl. 2. P. (Dhātup. xxiv, 49) *rāti* (Ved. also Ā. *rāté*; Impv. *rirīhi*, *rarāsva*, *rarīdhvam*; p. *rarāṇa*; 3. sg. *rárate* and *rāsate*; pf. *rarimá*, *raré*; aor. *árāsma*, Subj. *rāsat* &c., Pot. *rāsīya*; Class. forms are only pr. *rāti*; fut. *rātā*, BhP.; *rāsyati*, Vop., and inf. *rấtave*, BhP.), to grant, give, bestow, impart, yield, surrender, RV. &c. &c.

Rarāṇa and **rarāvan**. See p. 868, col. 3.

2. **Rā**, (ifc.) granting, bestowing, BhP.

3. **Rá**, f., see 3. *rai*.

Rākā, f. (Uṇ. iii, 40) the goddess presiding over the actual day of full moon (or regarded as the Full Moon's consort; Anumati is supposed to preside over the previous day), Jyot. (cf. IW. 158); the day of full moon, full moon, RV. &c. &c.; N. of a daughter of Aṅgiras and Smṛiti, Pur.; of a daughter of Aṅgiras and Śraddhā, ib.; of the wife of Dhātṛi and mother of Prātṛi, ib.; of a Rākshasī (the mother of Khara and Śūrpa-ṇakhā), MBh.; of a daughter of Su-mālin, R.; of a river, BhP.; itch, scab, L.; a girl in whom menstruation has begun, L. — **°gama** (*°kāg°*), m. N. of wk. — **candra**, m. full moon, Kathās. — **niśā**, f. the night of f° m°, ib. — **pati**, m. 'husband of R°,' full moon, BhP. — **yajña**, m. f° m° sacrifice, PañcavBr. — **ramaṇa**, m. = *-pati*, Kathās. — **vibhāvarī**, f. = *-niśā*; *-jāni*, m. f° m°, Sāh. — **śaśāṅka** (Kathās.), **-śaśin** (Kāv.), m. = *-candra*. — **sudhākara**, m. id., Mcar.; N. of a poem. **Rākêndīvara-bandhu**, m. full moon, Cat. **Rākêndra**, m. = *rākā-pati*, Bhām. **Rākêśa**, m. id., BhP.; N. of Śiva, Śivag.

Rātá, mfn. given, presented, bestowed, RV. &c. &c. (often ifc.; cf. *asmad-*, *deva-*, *brahma-r°* &c.); m. N. of a teacher, Piṅg., Sch. — **manas** (*rātá-*), mfn. ready-minded, willing to (dat.), ŚBr. — **havis** (*rātá-*), mfn. one who willingly presents offerings, a liberal offerer or worshipper (of the gods), RV. — **havya** (*rātá-*), mfn. id., ib.; one to whom the offering is presented, one who receives the oblation, ib.; ŚāṅkhŚr.; m. (with *Ātreya*) N. of the author of RV. v, 65; 66, Anukr.

Rāti, mfn. ready or willing to give, generous, favourable, gracious, RV.; AV.; VS.; Br.; f. a favour, grace, gift, oblation, RV. &c. &c. (in RV. also 'the Giver' conceived of as a deity and associated with Bhaga; *Indrasya rātī*, v.l. *°tiḥ*, N. of a Sāman, ĀrshBr.) — **shāc** (for *-sāc*), mfn. granting favours, dispensing gifts, liberal, generous, RV.; AV.; ŚāṅkhŚr.

Rātin, mfn. containing gifts or oblations (as a sacrificial ladle), RV.

1. **Rāvan**, mfn. (for 2. see p. 879, col. 1) granting, bestowing, VS. (cf. *a-r°*).

रा 4. *rā*. See under 3. *ra*.

राउल *rāüla*, m. N. of a man, Cat.

राकिणी *rākiṇī*, f. N. of a Tantra goddess, Cat. (cf. *ḍākinī* and *lākinī*).

राक्य *rākya*, mfn. coming or descended from Raka, g. *śaṇḍikâdi*.

राक्षस *rākshasa*, mf(*ī*)n. (fr. *rakshas*) belonging to or like a Rakshas, demoniacal, infested by demons, AitBr. &c. &c. (with *vivāha* or *dharma* or *vidhi*, m. 'one of the 8 forms of marriage,' the violent seizure or rape of a girl after the defeat or destruction of her relatives, see Mn. iii, 33); m. a Rakshas or demon in general, an evil or malignant demon (the Rākshasas are sometimes regarded as produced from Brahmā's foot, sometimes with Rāvaṇa as descendants of Pulastya, elsewhere they are styled children of Khasā or Su-rasā; according to some they are distinguishable into 3 classes, one being of a semi-divine benevolent nature and ranking with Yakshas &c.; another corresponding to Titans or relentless enemies of the gods; and a third answering more to nocturnal demons, imps, fiends, goblins, going about at night, haunting cemeteries, disturbing sacrifices and even devouring human beings; this last class is the one most commonly mentioned; their chief place of abode was Laṅkā in Ceylon; in R. v, 10, 17 &c. they are fully described; cf. also IW. 310; RTL. 237), Kauś.; Up. &c.; a king of the Rakshas, g. *parśv-ādi*; (with Jainas) one of the 8 classes of Vyantaras, L.; N. of the 30th Muhūrta, L.; of one of the astronomical Yogas, Col.; of a minister of Nanda, Mudr.; of a poet, Cat. (cf. below); m. n. the 49th year in the Jupiter cycle of 60 years, VarBṛS.; (*ī*), f. a Rākshasī or female demon, MBh.; Kāv.; Kathās.; the island of the Rākshasas, i.e. Laṅkā or Ceylon, Buddh.; N. of a malignant spirit supposed to haunt the four corners of a house, VarBṛS.; of a Yoginī, Hcat.; night, L.; a kind of plant (= *caṇḍā*), L.; a large tooth, tusk, L. — **kāvya**, n. N. of a poem in 20 stanzas (also called *kāvya-rākshasa*, and attributed to 3 authors, to Kālidāsa, to Ravideva and to Vararuci). — **graha**, m. 'Rākshasa-demon,' N. of a partic. kind of insanity or seizure, MBh. — **ghna**, m. 'R°-slayer,' N. of Rāma, L. — **tā**, f., **-tva**, n. the state or condition of a R°, fiendishness, R.; Kathās. **Rākshasâlaya**, m. 'R°-abode,' N. of Laṅkā or Ceylon, Sūryas. **Rākshasêndra** (MBh.), **°sêśa** (L.), **°sêśvara** (MBh.), m. 'R°-king,' N. of Rāvaṇa. **Rākshasôtpatti**, f. N. of a poem.

Rākshasī, in comp. for *rākshasa*. — **karaṇa**, n. the act of changing into a Rākshasa, Cat. — **bhūta**, mfn. become or changed into a R°, Kathās.

राक्षा *rākshā*, f. = *lākshā*, lac, Uṇ. iii, 62, Sch.

राक्षोघ्न rākshoghná, mf(ī)n. (fr. raksho-ghna) relating to the slayer of a Rakshas, TS.; AitBr. &c.; n. N. of various Sāmans, ĀrshBr.

Rākshosura, mf(ī)n. (fr. raksho'sura) relating to or treating of the Rakshas and Asuras, g. *devâsurâdi*; containing the words *raksho'sura*, g. *vimuktâdi*.

राख् rākh (cf. √lākh), cl. 1. P. rākhati, 'to be dry' or 'to suffice' (*śoshaṇâlam-arthayoḥ*), Dhātup. v, 8.

राखडी rākhaḍī (?), f. a partic. kind of ornament, Pañcad.

राग rāga, m. (fr. √rañj; ifc. ā or ī) the act of colouring or dyeing (cf. *mūrdhaja-r°*); colour, hue, tint, dye, (esp.) red colour, redness, MBh.; Kāv. &c.; inflammation, Car.; any feeling or passion, (esp.) love, affection or sympathy for, vehement desire of, interest or joy or delight in (loc. or comp.), Up.; Mn.; MBh. &c.; loveliness, beauty (esp. of voice or song), Śak.; Pañcat.; a musical note, harmony, melody (in the later system a partic. musical mode or order of sound or formula; Bharata enumerates 6, viz. *Bhairava, Kauśika, Hindola, Dīpaka, Śrī-rāga*, and *Megha*, each mode exciting some affection; other writers give other names; sometimes 7 or 26 Rāgas are mentioned; they are personified, and each of the 6 chief Rāgas is wedded to 5 or 6 consorts called Rāgiṇis; their union gives rise to many other musical modes), Bhar.; Saṃgīt.; Rājat.; Pañcat. &c.; nasalization, RPrāt.; a partic. process in the preparation of quicksilver, Sarvad.; seasoning, condiment, Car.; a prince, king, L.; the sun, L.; the moon, L.; (*ā*), f. Eleusine Coracana (a sort of grain, commonly called Rāggy, and much cultivated in the south of India), L.; N. of the second daughter of Aṅgiras, MBh.; (*ī*), f. Eleusine Coracana, L. **–kāshṭha,** n. the wood of Caesalpina Sappan, L. **–khāḍava,** w.r. for next or *-shāḍava*, q.v. **–khāṇḍava,** m. or n. a kind of sweetmeat, MBh.; R.; °*vika*, m. a maker of it, MBh. **–graha-vat,** mfn. containing passions compared to crocodiles, Bhartṛ. **–candrôdaya,** m. N. of wk. **–cūrṇa,** m. Acacia Catechu (a tree yielding an astringent resin, the wood of which is used in dyeing), L.; a red powder (which Hindūs throw over each other at the Holī festival), L.; lac, L.; Kāma-deva, god of love, L. **–cchanna,** m. 'love-covered,' N. of the god of l°, L.; of Rāma, L. **–tattva-vibodha,** m. N. of wk. **–da,** mfn. colour-giving, colouring, passion-inspiring, W.; m. a kind of shrub, L.; (*ā*), f. crystal, L. **–dāli,** m. a kind of lentil, L. **–dṛiś,** m. a ruby, L. **–dravya,** n. 'colour-substance,' paint, dye, Pāṇ. iv, 2, 1, Sch. **–dvesha,** m. du. love and hatred, Mn. xii, 26; *-prakaraṇa*, n. N. of wk.; *-moha-parimokshaṇa*, m. a partic. Samādhi, Kāraṇḍ. **–dhyānâdi-kathanâdhyāya,** m. N. of wk. **–paṭṭa,** prob. w.r. for *rāja-p°*, q.v. **–pushpa,** m. Pentapetes Phoenicea, L.; the red globe-amaranth, L.; (*ī*), f. the Chinese rose, L. **–prasava,** m. Pentapetes Phoenicea, L.; the red globe-amaranth, L. **–prastāra,** m. N. of wk. **–prāpta,** mfn. conformable to desire, gratifying the senses, ĀpŚr., Sch. **–bandha,** m. connection of the Rāgas, expression or manifestation of affection, passion, Kālid. **–bandhin,** mfn. exciting or inflaming the passions, Ragh. **–bhañjana,** m. N. of a Vidyā-dhara, Kathās. **–mañjarikā,** f. a diminutive from *rāga-mañjarī* below ('wicked Rāga-mañjarī'), Daś. **–mañjarī,** f. N. of a woman, ib.; N. of wk. **–maya,** mf(*ī*)n. 'consisting of colour or of a red colour,' red-coloured, red, Kāvyâd.; dear, beloved, ib. **–mālā,** f. 'string or series of musical Rāgas,' N. of various wks. **–yuj,** m. a ruby, L. **–rajju,** m. Kāma-deva, the god of love, Vās. **–ratnâkara,** m., **-rāgiṇī-svarūpa-velā-varṇana,** n., **-lakshaṇa,** n. N. of wks. **–latā,** f. 'Passion-creeper,' N. of Rati (wife of Kāma-deva), L. **–lekhā,** f. a streak or line of paint, stroke, the mark of dye, Mālav.; N. of a woman, Vās. **–vat,** mfn. having colour, coloured, red, Gīt.; impassioned, enamoured, Śiś.; m. Areca Catechu, L. **–vardhana,** m. (in music) a kind of measure, Saṃgīt. **–vibodha,** m., **-vibodha-viveka,** m., and **-viveka,** m. N. of musical wks. **–vihiṅsana-vrata-nirṇaya,** m. N. of wk. **–vṛinta,** m. 'Passion-stem,' N. of Kāma-deva, the god of love, L. **–shāḍava** (or *-shāḍhava*), m. a kind of sweetmeat or syrup compounded of grapes and pomegranates and the juice of Phaseolus Mungo (or of half ripe mango fruit with ginger, cardamoms, oil, butter &c.), R.; Suśr. (also written *rāga-khāḍava*, cf. *rāga-khāṇḍava*). **–sūtra,** n. (only L.) any coloured thread or string; a silk thread; the string of a balance (also °*traka*). **Rāgâṅgī** or **rāgâḍhyā,** f. Rubia Munjista (= *mañjishṭhā*), L. **Rāgâtmaka,** mf(*ikā*)n. composed of or characterized by passion, impassioned, Bhag. **Rāgânugā,** f. (with *vivṛiti*) N. of a Comm. on a musical wk. **Rāgândha,** mfn. blind with passion or desire, MaitrUp. **Rāgânvita,** mfn. having colour or dye, coloured, W.; affected by passion or desire, ib. **Rāgâyāta,** n. the uprising of passion, excess of p°, MW. **Rāgârṇava,** m. N. of a wk. on the musical Rāgas. **Rāgârha,** mfn. worthy of affection, any suitable object of affection, W. **Rāgâśani,** m. a Buddha or Jina, L. **Rāgôtpatti,** f. N. of wk. **Rāgôdreka,** m. excess of passion, MW.

Rāgāru, mfn. one who raises hopes of a gift which he afterwards disappoints, L.

Rāgi, in comp. for *rāgin*. **–taru,** m. 'the red or passionate tree,' Jonesia Asoka, L. **–tā,** f. the state of being coloured or impassioned, fondness or desire for, longing after (loc. or comp.), Kām.; Kathās.

Rāgin, mf(*iṇī*)n. (fr. √*rañj* and *rāga*) coloured, having a partic. colour (applied to a kind of Amaurosis or blindness when it affects the second membrane of the eye, as opp. to *a-rāgin*, which affects the first), Suśr.; colouring, dyeing, L.; red, of a red colour, Pañcat.; Kathās.; impassioned, affectionate, enamoured, passionately fond of or attached to or hankering after (loc. or comp.), MBh.; Kāv. &c.; gladdening, delighting, Mālatīm.; m. a painter, L.; a lover, libertine, ib.; a sort of grain, L.; (*iṇī*), f. a modification of the musical mode called Rāga (q.v.; 35 or 36 Rāgiṇis are enumerated), Saṃgīt.; Pañcar.; Śukas.; a wanton and intriguing woman, W.; N. of the eldest daughter of Menakā, Pur.; of a form of Lakshmī, ib.

राघ् 1. rāgh (cf. √lāgh), cl. 1. Ā. rāghate (pf. rarāghe &c.; Caus. rāghayati, aor. ararāghat, Gr.), to be able or competent, Dhātup. iv, 38.

2. **Rāgh,** m. (nom. *rāk*) an able or efficient person, MW.

राघव rāghava, m. (fr. raghu) a descendant of Raghu, patr. of Aja, of Daśa-ratha, and (esp.) of Rāma-candra (du. *rāghavau* = Rāma and Lakshmaṇa), R.; Ragh. &c.; N. of various authors and others (also with *ācārya, bhaṭṭa, pañcânana-bhaṭṭâcārya, cakravartin, rāya* &c.), Cat.; of a serpent-demon, L.; the sea, ocean, L.; a species of large fish, L. **–caritra,** n. N. of a modern abridgment of the Rāmāyaṇa. **–caitanya,** m. N. of a poet, Cat. **–deva,** m. N. of various authors, ib. **–nandana,** m. N. of an astronomer, ib. **–paṇḍita,** m. N. of a poet; °*tīya*, n. his wk. **–pāṇḍava** (ibc.) the Rāghavas and the Pāṇḍavas; *-prakāśa*, m.; *-yādavīya*, n. N. of poems. **–pāṇḍavīya,** n. N. of an artificial poem by Kavi-rāja (giving a narrative of the acts of both Rāghavas and Pāṇḍavas in such a way that it may be interpreted either as the history of one or the other); of another poem by Veṅkaṭâcārya. **–prabandha,** m. N. of a musical wk. **–yādava-pāṇḍavīya,** n., **-yādavīya,** n., **-yādavīya-carita,** n. N. of poems. **–rahasya,** n., **-vilāsa,** m. N. of wks. **–siṅha,** m. 'R°-lion,' N. of Rāma-candra, R. **Rāghavânanda,** m. N. of various authors and others (also with *muni, yati, śarman*, and *sarasvatī*), Cat.; of a drama by Veṅkaṭêśvara. **Rāghavânuja,** mfn. referring to the younger brother of Rāma, MW. **Rāghavâbhyudaya,** m. 'rise of Rāma,' N. of a drama. **Rāghavâshṭaka,** n. N. of a wk. by Śaṃkarâcārya. **Rāghavêndra,** m. 'R°-chief,' N. of various authors and others (also with *ācārya, muni, yati, śatâvadhāna*, and *sarasvatī*), Cat.; *-stotra-vyākhyā*, f.; °*drīya*, n. N. of wks. **Rāghavêśvara,** 'R°-lord,' N. of one of Śiva's Liṅgas, Kshitîś. **Rāghavôllāsa,** m. N. of a poem.

Rāghavāyaṇa, n. Rāma's history, i.e. the Rāmāyaṇa, AgP.

Rāghavīya, n. (with or scil. *kāvya*) the poem composed by Rāghava, Cat.

राङ्कल rāṅkala, m. a thorn, L.

राङ्कव rāṅkava, mf(ī)n. belonging to the Raṅku deer, MBh.; made from the hair of the R° deer, woollen, ib., R.; coming from Raṅku (said of animals), Pāṇ. iv, 2, 100; m. a woollen cover or blanket, MBh.; R. **–kūṭa-śāyin,** mfn. lying on a heap of woollen rugs, MBh. **Rāṅkavâjina,** n. a woollen skin; *-śāyin*, mfn. lying upon a w° skin, ib.; *-saṃsparśa*, m. the touch of a woollen skin, MBh. **Rāṅkavâstaraṇa,** n. a w° coverlet, R. **Rāṅkavâstṛita,** mfn. covered with a woollen rug, ib.

Rāṅkavaka, mf(*ī*)n. coming from Raṅku (said of men), Pāṇ. iv, 2, 134.

Rāṅkavāyaṇa, mf(*ī*)n. coming from Raṅku (said of animals), Pāṇ. iv, 2, 100.

राङ्ग rāṅga, m. (fr. raṅga) an actor (?), Dhūrtas.

राङ्गण rāṅgaṇa, n. a kind of flower (commonly called Rangan), L.

राचित rācita, m. patr. fr. racita, g. bidâdi.

Rācitāyana, m. patr. fr. *rācita*, g. *haritâdi* (v.l.)

राज् 1. rāj (prob. originally two roots; cf. √raj, rañj, ṛiñj), cl. 1. P. Ā. (Dhātup. xix, 74) *rājati*, °*te* (Ved. also *rāshṭi, rāṭ*; pf. *rarāja*; *rarāje* or *reje*, 2. sg. P. *rarājitha* or *rejitha*, MBh. &c.; aor. *arājishuḥ*, RV.; *arājishṭa*, Gr.; fut. *rājitā, rājishyati*, ib.; inf. *rājáse*, RV.), to reign, be king or chief, rule over (gen.), direct, govern (acc.), RV. &c. &c.; to be illustrious or resplendent, shine, glitter, ib.; to appear as or like (*iva*), Kum. vi, 49: Caus. *rājayati*, °*te* (aor. *ararājat*), to reign, rule, AV.; MBh.; to illuminate, make radiant (cf. *rājita*): Desid. *rirājishati*, °*te*, Gr.: Intens. *rārājyate, rārāshṭi*, ib. [For cognate words see under *rājan*.]

2. **Rāj** (ifc.) shining, radiant &c.; (*rā́j*), m. (nom. *rā́ṭ*) a king, sovereign, chief (in later language only ifc.), RV. &c. &c.; anything the best or chief of its kind (cf. *śaṅkha-r°*); N. of an Ekâha, ŚrS.; a kind of metre, RPrāt.; f. N. of a goddess (explained by *rājamānā*), TBr.

1. **Rāja,** m. (ifc.) = 1. *rājan*, a king, sovereign, chief or best of its kind, MBh.; Kāv. &c.

2. **Rāja,** in comp. for 1. *rājan*. **–ṛishi** = *-rshi*, BhP. **–kathā,** f. history of kings, royal h°, Rājat. **–kadamba,** m. Nauclea Cadamba or a similar tree, L. **–kandarpa,** m. N. of a writer on music, Cat. **–kanyakā,** f. a king's daughter, Kathās.; Rājat. **–kanyā,** f. id., ib.; a kind of flower, L. **–kara,** m. king's tax, tribute paid to a king, Siṉhās. **–karaṇa,** n. a law-court, Mṛicch. **–karkaṭī,** f. a kind of cucumber, L. **–karṇa,** m. an elephant's tusk, Col. **–kartṛi,** m. 'king-maker,' pl. those who place a king on the throne, AitBr.; R. **–karman,** n. the business or duty of a k°, Pat.; royal service, Mn. vii, 125; the Soma ceremony, Kauś.; pl. royal or state affairs, Pañcat. **–karmin,** mfn. working for a prince, Pāṇ. i, 4, 49, Vārtt. 2, Pat. **–kalaśa,** m. N. of the father of Bilhaṇa, Rājat.; of another man, Vcar. **–kalā,** f. the 16th part of the moon's disk, Sāh. **–kali,** m. a bad king who does not protect his subjects, MBh. xii, 363. **–kaseru,** m. or f. Cyperus Rotundus, L. (also °*rukā*, Car.); n. the root of Cyperus Pertenuis, L. **–kārya,** n. a king's duty or business, state affairs, MBh.; R. &c.; royal command, Yājñ., Sch. **–kilbishin,** mfn. one who being a king has committed a transgression, MBh. **–kīra,** m. a species of parrot, L. **–kuñjara,** m. 'king-elephant,' a great or powerful monarch. **–kuṇḍa,** m. N. of a Sch. on the Kirātārjunīya. **–kumāra,** m. a king's son, prince, Vet.; Sāh.; °*rikā*, f. a princess, Kathās. **–kula,** n. a king's race, royal family (pl. = kings, princes), Kāv.; BhP.; a royal palace or court (where also law is administered), ShaḍvBr.; MBh. &c.; a main road or street, R. (B.); *-prajāta*, mfn. born from a race of kings, R.; *-bhaṭṭa*, m. N. of a poet, Cat.; *-vivāda*, m. a contest among kings, ShaḍvBr.; °*lânumantavya*, mfn. to be approved by k°s, Inscr.; °*lya*, mfn. of royal race or descent, MW. **–kushmāṇḍa,** m. Solanum Melongena, L. **–kṛit,** m. = *-kartṛi*, AV.; ŚBr. **–kṛita** (*rāja-*), mfn. made or performed by a k°, AV.; *-pratijña*, mfn. one who has fulfilled the k°'s conditions, MW. **–kṛitya,** n. a k°'s duty or business, state affairs, Kathās.; Pañcat. **–kṛitvan,** mfn. (with acc.) = *-kartṛi*, Bhaṭṭ. (Pāṇ. iii, 2, 95). **–kṛishṇa,** m. Oldenlandia Herbacea, L. **–kola,** m. a kind of jujube, L. **–kolāhala,** m. (in music) a kind of measure, Saṃgīt. **–kośa-nighaṇṭu,** m. N. of a dictionary by Raghu-nātha Paṇḍita (also called *rāja-vyavahāra-kośa*). **–kośātaka,** n. a gourd or cucumber, L.; (*ī*), f. Luffa Foetida or some

other species, Car. **—kaustubha**, n. = *-dharma-kaustubha*, q.v. **—kraya**, m. purchase of Soma, ŚrS. **—krayaṇī**, f. a cow which serves as the price of the Soma-plant (= *soma-kr°*), Lāṭy. **—kriyā**, f. the business of a king, royal or state affairs, Pañcat. **—kshavaka**, m. a kind of mustard, Suśr. **—kharjūrī**, f. a kind of date tree, L. **—gaṇa**, m. a host of kings, MW. **—gavī**, f. Bos Grunniens, TĀr., Sch. **—gāmin**, mfn. coming to or brought before the king (as slander), Mn. xi, 56; devolving or escheating to the king (as property &c. to which there are no heirs), W. **—giri**, m. 'king's hill,' N. of a place, Daś.; a species of vegetable, L. **—girī-ya**, m. N. of a school, Buddh. **—guru**, m. a king's minister or counsellor, R. **—guhya**, n. a royal mystery, Bhag. **—gṛiha**, n. a king's house, palace, Kathās.; (once *ī*, f.) N. of the chief city in Magadha, MBh.; Kāv. &c.; mfn. belonging to the city Rāja-gṛiha, VāyuP.; *-nirmāṇa*, n. *-māhātmya*, n. N. of wks.; *°haka*, mfn. belonging or relating to a k°'s palace, g. *dhūmâdi*. **—geha**, n. a k°'s palace, Suśr. **—grīva**, m. a species of fish, L. **—gha**, m. a slayer of hostile k°s, Naish. (others 'best of k°s' or = *tīkshṇa*). **—ghātaka**, m. a king-killer, regicide, Gaut. **—cakra**, n. the wheel of a k°'s chariot (*°kram pra-√vrit*, Caus. to cause it to roll over the earth, obtain sovereignty), MBh. **—candra**, m. N. of a lexicographer, Cat. **—campaka**, m. a kind of Campaka, L. **—cihna**, n. pl. the insignia of royalty, Siṃhâs.; *°naka*, n. the organs of generation, L. **—cūḍāmaṇi**, m. (in music) a kind of measure, Saṃgīt.; (with *dīkshita*) N. of an author, Cat. **—jakshman**, w.r. for *-yakshman*. **—jambū**, f. a species of Jambū or date tree, Vikr. **—jhaṃkāra**, m. (in music) a kind of measure, Saṃgīt. **—tanaya**, m. 'a k°'s son,' prince, Kathās.; (*ā*), f. a princess, ib. **—taraṃgiṇī**, f. 'stream (i.e. continuous history) of k°s,' N. of a celebrated history of the k°s of Kaśmīra or Cashmere by Kalhaṇa (written A.D. 1148) and of some other chronicles of that country; N. of a woman, Vās.; *-saṃgraha*, m. N. of wk. **—taraṇī**, f. globe amaranth, L. **—taru**, m. a kind of tree, Suśr. (accord. to L. Cathartocarpus Fistula or Pterospermum Acrifolium). **—tas**, ind. from the k°, Mn. iv, 33. **—tā**, f. kingship, royalty, sovereignty, government, Kāv.; Kathās. &c. **—tāla**, m. the Areca-nut tree, L. (also *ī*, f., Ragh.); (in music) a kind of measure, Saṃgīt. **—timisha**, m. Cucumis Sativus, L. **—tīrtha**, n. N. of a Tīrtha, W. **—tuṅga**, m. N. of a man, Rājat. **—temisha**, m. = *-timisha*, L. **—tva**, n. = *-tā*, f., MBh.; Kāv. &c. **—daṇḍa**, m. a k°'s sceptre or authority, punishment inflicted by a k°; *-bhayâkula*, mfn. afraid of it, Rājat. **—dattā**, f. N. of a woman, Kathās. **—danta**, m. (for *danta-rājaḥ = dantānāṃ rājā*, Pāṇ. ii, 2, 31) a principal tooth, front tooth, Naish.; N. of a man (cf. next). **—danti**, m. patr. fr. *-danta*, Pāṇ. iv, 1, 160, Sch. **—darśana**, n. the sight of a king, royal audience (*māṃ °naṃ kāraya*, 'let me see the k°'), Hit.; N. of an artificial poem. **—dāra**, m. pl. a k°'s wife or wives, R.; *°rikā*, f. a k°'s daughter, princess, Mālav. **—duhitṛi**, f. a k°'s daughter, princess, Kathās.; Pañcat. (*-maya*, mf(*ī*)n. consisting or full of princesses, Pañcat.); the musk rat, Yājñ., Sch. **—dūrvā**, f. a kind of high-growing Dūrvā grass, Prayogar. **—dṛishad**, f. (prob.) the larger or lower mill-stone, Pāṇ. vi, 1, 223, Sch. **—deva**, m. N. of a lexicographer, Cat. **—daivika**, mfn. (misfortune) proceeding from the k° or fate, Yājñ. **—druma**, m. = *-vṛiksha*, Suśr. **—droha**, m. oppression, tyranny, W.; rebellion, ib.; *°hin*, m. a rebel, traitor, ib. **—dvār**, f. (Hit.), *-dvāra*, n. (Hariv. &c.) the k°'s gate, gate of a royal palace; *°rika*, m. a royal porter or gate-keeper, Pañcat. **—dhattūra** or *°raka*, m. a kind of thorn-apple, L. **—dharma**, m. a k°'s duty; pl. rules or laws relating to kings, Mn.; MBh. &c.; = *°mânuśāsana*, Cat.; *-kāṇḍa*, m. or n., *-kaustubha*, m., *-prakaraṇa*, n. N. of wks.; *-bhṛit*, mfn. maintaining or fulfilling a k°'s duties, MBh.; *-lakshaṇa*, n. N. of wk.; *-vid*, mfn. knowing a k°'s duties, MBh.; *-sāra-saṃgraha*, m. N. of wk.; *°mânuśāsana*, n. 'instruction in a k°'s duties,' N. of MBh. xii, 1. **—dharman**, m. N. of the k° of the cranes or herons (son of Kaśyapa), MBh. **—dhāna** or *°naka*, n., *°nikā*, f. a king's residence, metropolis, capital, palace, L. **—dhānī**, f. id., MBh.; Kāv. &c.; *-tas*, ind. from the k°'s residence, Kathās. **—dhānya**, n. 'royal grain,' Panicum Frumentaceum or a kind of rice, VarBṛS. **—dhāman**, n. a k°'s residence, royal palace, Rājat. **—dhīra**, m. N. of a man, Kshitîś. **—dhura**, m. 'k°'s yoke,' the burden of government, Pāṇ. v, 4, 74, Sch. (*ā*, f., Vop. vi, 73). **—dhustūraka** or **-dhūrta**, m. a species of large Datura or thorn-apple, L. (cf. *-dhattūra*). **—nagarī**, f. a royal city, MW. **—nandana**, m. a k°'s son, prince, Yājñ. **—naya**, m. royal conduct or policy, politics, R. **—nātha**, m. N. of an author, Cat. **—nāpita**, m. a royal barber, a first-rate barber, Pāṇ. vi, 2, 63, Sch. **—nāman**, m. Trichosanthes Dioeca, L. **—nārāyaṇa**, m. (in music) a kind of measure, Saṃgīt.; (with *mukhôpâdhyāya*) N. of an author, Cat. **—nighaṇṭu** (also called *nighaṇṭu-rāja* or *abhidhāna-cintāmaṇi*), m. N. of a dictionary of materia medica (including many herbs and plants) by Harahari-paṇḍita. **—nindaka**, m. a scorner or reviler of a k°, Rājat. **—nirdhūta-daṇḍa**, mfn. one who has undergone punishment inflicted by a k°, Mn. viii, 318. **—niveśana**, n. a k°'s abode, palace, R. **—nīti**, f. royal conduct or policy, statesmanship, politics, MBh.; Kathās. &c.; *-prakāśa*, m., *-mayūkha*, m., *-śāstra*, n. N. of wks. **—nīla**, m. an emerald, L. **—nīlikā**, f. a kind of plant, L. **—paṭola**, m. Trichosanthes Dioeca, L. (also *°laka*); (*ī*), f. a kind of plant (= *madhura-paṭolī*), L. **—paṭṭa**, m. a kind of precious stone or diamond of inferior quality (said to be brought from Virāṭa-deśa in the north-west of India), Uttarar.; Mālatīm.; a royal fillet or tiara, W. **—paṭṭikā**, f. (prob.) intercourse with k°s, Vet. (= *-pāṭikā*); the bird Cātaka, L. **—pati** (*rā́ja-*), m. a lord of kings, ŚBr. **—patnī**, f. a king's wife, royal consort, queen, R.; VarBṛS. **—patha**, m. (ifc. f. *ā*) the k°'s highway, a main road, public road or street, Hariv.; R. &c. **—pathāya**, Nom. Ā. *°yate*, to represent or be like a main road, Cat. **—pada**, n. the rank of a k°, royalty, MW. **—paddhati**, f. a main road, principal street, Sarvad. **—parivarta**, m. change of k° or government, Mṛicch. **—parṇī**, f. Paederia Foetida, L. **—palāṇḍu**, m. a kind of onion, L. **—pāṭikā**, f. = *-paṭṭikā*, Pañcad. **—pāla**, m. N. of a k°, Col.; of a royal family, Cat. **—piṇḍā**, f. a species of date, L. **—pitṛi**, m. a king's father, AitBr. **—pīlu**, m. a species of tree (= *mahā-pīlu*), L. **—puṃs**, m. a royal servant or minister, Var. **—putra**, m. a k°'s son, prince, RV. &c. &c. (*-tā*, f., MBh.); a Rājput (who claims descent from the ancient Kshatriyas), IW. 210, n. 1; the son of a Vaiśya by an Ambashṭhā, or the son of a Kshatriya by a Karaṇī, Kathās.; Rājat. &c.; the planet Mercury (regarded as son of the Moon), MatsyaP.; a kind of mango, L.; N. of a writer on Kāma-śāstra, Cat.; (*ī*), f. a k°'s daughter, princess, MBh.; Kāv. &c.; a Rājput female, Cat.; N. of various plants (a kind of wild cucumber; Jasminum Grandiflorum; = *jātī*), L.; a kind of perfume (= *reṇukā*), Bhpr.; a kind of metal (= *rīti*), L.; a musk-rat, L.; the belly or the amputated limb of an animal, L.; (*ā*), f. (*rā́ja-*) 'having kings for sons,' a mother of k°s, RV.; *°tra-tā*, f. the condition of a Rājput, MBh.; *°tra-parpaṭi*, m. N. of a poet, Cat.; *°tra-loka*, m. a number of princes, Hcar.; *°trârgaṭa*, m. N. of a poet, Cat. **—putraka**, m. a k°'s son, prince, Kathās.; (*ikā*), f. a k°'s daughter, princess, Hariv.; a species of bird, L.; n. = *°tra-loka*, Pāṇ. iv, 2, 39. **—putrīya**, n. N. of a wk. **—pura**, n. 'king's-town,' N. of a city, MBh.; (*ī*), f. N. of a city, Rājat. **—purusha**, m. = *-puṃs*, MBh.; Kāv. &c.; *-vāda*, m. N. of wk. **—pushpa**, m. Mesua Roxburghii, L.; (*ī*), f. a species of plant (= *karuṇī*), L. **—pūga**, m. a kind of Areca-nut palm, BhP. **—pūrusha**, m. = *-purusha*, Kathās.; HPariś. **—paurushika**, mf(*ī*)n. being in a k°'s service, MBh. **—paurushya**, n. the state of a royal servant, the being a k°'s minister, g. *anuśatikâdi*. **—prakṛiti**, f. a k°'s minister, R. **—pratyenas**, m. (prob.) the nearest heir to the throne, Pāṇ. vi, 2, 60. **—prathamâbhisheka**, m. N. of the 2nd Pariś. of AV. **—prasāda**, m. royal favour; *-paṭṭaka*, n. any grant or document granted by royal favour, royal letters patent, Lokapr. **—priya**, m. a kind of onion, L.; (*ā*), f. a k°'s mistress or favourite wife, Kāv.; the moon's f° w°, ib.; a species of plant (= *karuṇī*), L. **—preshya**, m. a king's servant, MBh.; n. (for *praishya*) royal service, ib. **—phaṇijjhaka**, m. an orange tree, L. **—phala**, n. 'royal fruit,' the fruit of Trichosanthes Dioeca, L.; m. 'bearing royal fruit,' Mangifera Indica, L.; a species of tree (= *rājâdanī*), L.; (*ā*), f. Eugenia Jambolana, L. **—badara**, m. a species of Jujube tree, L.; n. = *rakta-melaka*, L.; salt, L. **—bandin**, m. N. of a man, Kathās. (printed *-vandin*). **—bandha**, m. imprisonment by the k°, Hariv. **—balā**, f. Paederia Foetida, L. **—balêndra-ketu**, m. N. of a man, Buddh. **—bāndhava**, m. (and *ī*, f.) a male or female relation of a king, GṛS.; Rājat. **—bījin**, mfn. of royal descent, ib. **—brāhmaṇa**, m., Pāṇ. vi, 2, 59. **—bhaksha**, m. a kind of plant, L. **—bhaṭa**, m. a k°'s soldier, soldier of the royal army, Kāv.; Kathās. &c.; a messenger, envoy (= *dūta*), VP., Sch. **—bhaṭṭikā**, f. a species of water-fowl, L. **—bhadraka**, m. Costus Speciosus or Arabicus, L.; Azadirachta Indica, L. **—bhaya**, n. 'k°'s risk,' danger from or fear of a k°, VarBṛS.; Pañcat. **—bhavana**, n. a k°'s abode, royal palace, R.; Kathās. &c. **—bhāj**, mfn. belonging to or claimed by the king, W. **—bhāryā**, f. a king's wife, queen, MW. **—bhūya**, n. = *rāja-tā*, royalty &c., L. **—bhūshaṇī**, f. N. of a wk. on royal polity. **—bhṛiṅga**, m. a large shrike (bird), L. **—bhṛit**, g. *saṃkalâdi*. **—bhṛita**, mfn. (fr. prec.) ib.; m. = *-bhaṭa*, a k°'s soldier, MBh.; R. **—bhṛitya**, m. a k°'s servant, royal servant or minister, R.; Rājat. **—bhoga**, m. a k°'s meal, royal repast, W. **—bhogīna**, mfn. fit for a k°'s enjoyment, suitable for a k°'s use, Pāṇ. v, 1, 9, Vārtt. 3, Pat. **—bhogya**, m. Buchanalia Latifolia, L.; n. nutmeg, L. **—bhojana**, mfn. eaten by k°s, Pāṇ. vi, 2, 150, Sch. **—bhauta**, m. a k°'s fool or jester, MW. (others 'an idiotic k°'). **—bhrātṛi**, m. a k°'s brother, ŚBr. **—maṇi**, m. a royal gem or precious stone, VarBṛS. **—maṇḍūka**, m. a species of large frog, L. **—mantra-dhara**, m. a k°'s counsellor, royal minister, Hariv. **—mantrin**, m. a minister of state, MW. **—mandira**, n. a k°'s palace, royal mansion, Kām.; Kathās.; Rājat.; N. of the chief town of Kaliṅga, Inscr. **—malla**, m. a royal wrestler, L.; N. of a k°, Cat. **—mahila**, N. of a town, L. **—mahishī**, f. the chief wife of a k°, Hcar. **—mahêndra-tīrtha**, n. N. of a Tīrtha, Cat. **—mātaṃgī-paddhati**, f., *-mātaṃgī-stotra*, n. N. of wks. **—mātṛi**, f. a k°'s mother, Pañcat. **—mātra**, mfn. any one who claims the title of king or enjoys royal authority, ŚāṅkhBr.; Car.; Divyâv. **—mānasôllāsa**, m. N. of wk. **—mānusha**, m. a royal officer or minister, Yājñ. **—mārga**, m. the k°'s highway, a royal or main road, principal street (passable for horses and elephants), Mn.; MBh. &c.; (met.) the great path, Sarvad.; the way or method of k°s, procedure of k°s (as warfare &c.; *-viśārada*, mfn. skilled in it), Hariv.; *°gī-√kri*, P. *-karoti*, to make into a main road, Jātak. **—mārtaṇḍa**, m. (in music) a kind of measure, Saṃgīt.; N. of various wks. (esp. of a Comm. by Bhoja-deva on Patañjali's Yoga-sūtras). **—māsha**, m. a kind of bean, Dolichos Catjang, MBh.; *°shya*, mfn. suited to the cultivation of it, consisting of or sown with this plant (a field &c.), Pāṇ. v, 1, 20, Vārtt. 1, Pat. **—māsa**, w.r. for *māsha*, MBh. **—mukuṭa**, m. N. of an author, Cat. **—mukhá**, n. a k°'s face, TBr. **—mudga** or *°gaka*, m. a kind of bean, Hcat. **—mudrā**, f. a royal signet or seal, MW. **—muni**, m. = *rājarshi*, Śak. **—mṛigâṅka**, m. (in music) a kind of measure, Saṃgīt.; N. of a partic. medicinal compound, Bhpr.; of an astronomical and of a medical work, Cat. **—m-bhavya**, mfn. destined for the succession to the throne, heir-apparent, ĀpŚr. **—yakshmá** or **-yakshman**, m. a partic. kind of dangerous disease (later 'pulmonary consumption, atrophy'), RV. &c. &c. (*-yakshman* also 'N. of a divine being,' Hcat.); *-nāman*, m. N. of a partic. mythical being (said to be connected with the foundation of a house), VarBṛS.; *°min*, mf(*iṇī*)n. suffering from consumption, consumptive, Suśr. **—yajña**, m. a k°'s sacrifice, royal offering, KātyŚr.; Mālav. **—yājaka**, mfn. one who has a warrior for sacrificer, MBh. **—yāna**, n. a royal vehicle, palanquin, BhP. **—yudhvan**, m. an enemy, rebel, one who makes war against a k°, Pāṇ. iii, 2, 95; a k°'s soldier, royal warrior, MW. **—yoga**, m. a constellation under which princes are born or a configuration of planets &c. at birth denoting a person destined for kingship, VarBṛS.; a partic. stage in abstract meditation, or an easy mode of meditation, Cat. (cf. *yoga*); N. of various wks. (also with *yavana-praṇīta*); *-vidhi*, m.; *°gâdhyāya*, m. N. of wks. **—yogya**, mfn. befitting a king, suitable for royalty, princely, W. **—yoshit**, f. a k°'s wife, queen, R. **—raṅga**, n. 'royal tin,' silver, L. **—ratha**, m. a royal carriage, MBh. **—rākshasa**, m. a 'Rākshasa-like king,' a bad king, Rājat. **—rāj**, m. a king of kings, supreme sovereign, R.; BhP.; N. of the moon, Hariv. **—rāja**, m. 'k° of k°s,' a supreme sovereign, emperor, MBh.; Kāv. &c.; N. of Kubera, ib.; of the moon, L.; of a man, Rājat.; *-giri*, m. N. of Himavat, Daś.; *-tā*, f. (Kathās.), *-tva*, n. (MBh.)

the rank of a supreme sovereign or emperor, dominion over all other princes, universal sovereignty; °*jêśvara*, m. (prob.) N. of Śiva (*-yoga-kathā*, f. N. of wk.); °*jêśvarī*, f. (prob.) N. of Durgā (*-kavaca*, n., *-tantra*, n., *-daṇḍaka*, m. or n., *-mantra*, m., *-stotra*, n. N. of wks.); °*jya*, n. = *-rāja-tā*, Hariv. **-rāṇaka**, m. a k°'s vassal, L. **-rāma**, m. N. of various authors (also with *dikshita*; cf. *rājârāma*), Cat.; *-nagara*, n. N. of a city, Cat. **-rīti**, f. a kind of brass or bell-metal, L. **-rshabha** (for *-ṛish°*), the chief of k°s, Nal. **-rshi** (for *-ṛishi*), m. a royal Ṛishi or saint, Ṛishi of royal descent, that holy and superhuman personage which a k° or man of the military class may become by the performance of great austerities (e.g. Purū-ravas, Viśvā-mitra &c.; cf. *deva-rshi* and *brahma-rshi*), ŚrS.; Mn.; Mbh. &c.; N. of a son of Kalyāṇa and of various authors, Cat.; *-bhaṭṭa*, m. N. of an author, ib.; *-loka*, m. the world of the Rājarshis, R. **-rshin**, m. (only gen. pl. °*shiṇām*) = *rājarshi*, Hariv. **-lakshaṇa**, n. a royal sign or token, any mark on the body &c. indicating a future k°, Daś.; royal insignia, regalia, W. **-lakshman**, n. a royal token, sign of royalty (in *a-r°*), Pañcat.; m. 'having the marks of royalty,' N. of Yudhi-shṭhira, Dhanaṃj. **-lakshmī**, f. the Fortune or Prosperity of a king (personified as a goddess), royal majesty or sovereignty, Kālid.; Rājat. &c.; N. of a princess, Rājat. **-liṅga**, n. a kingly mark, royal token, L. **-līlā-nāman**, n. pl. N. of Vallabhâcārya's collection of epithets borne by Kṛishṇa (having reference to 118 of his diversions when he had attained to royal rank), Cat. **-lekha**, m. 'k°'s writing,' a royal letter or edict, W. **-loka**, m. an assemblage of k°s, Hcar.; Pañcad. **-vaṇsa**, m. a family of k°s, dynasty, R.; Kathās.; *-kāvya*, n. N. of a poem; °*śâvalī*, f. 'royal pedigree,' N. of wk.; °*śīya*, mfn. of royal race or descent, MW.; °*śya*, mfn. id.; m. a Kshatriya, Mcar. **-1. -vat**, ind. like a king, Kāv.; Suśr.; as towards a king, R. **-2. -vat**, mfn. having a k°, possessing k°s, MBh. (*vati*, ind. in the presence of k°s, Āpast.); having a bad k°, L.; m. N. of a son of Dyutimat, VP.; (*vatī*), f. N. of the wife of the Gandharva Devaprabha, Kathās. **-vadana**, m. N. of a man, Rājat. **-vadhá**, m. a k°'s weapon, AV. **-vandin**, see *-bandin*. **-varcasa**, n. kingly rank or dignity, Pāṇ. v, 4, 78, Vārtt.; °*sin*, mfn. being in royal service, HPariś. **-varṇaka**, n. N. of wk. **-varta**, m. cloth of various colours, L. **-vartman**, n. a k°'s high road, L.; a partic. gem, Hcat. **-vardhana**, w.r. for *rājya-v°*. **-vallabha**, m. a k°'s favourite, MārkP.; a kind of Jujube tree, L.; a kind of Āmra, L.; = *rājâdanī*, L.; a kind of incense, L.; N. of various wks. and authors, Cat.; *-tā*, f. the state of being a k°'s favourite (*-tām eti*, 'he becomes a k°'s f°,' Pancar.); *-turaṃgama*, m. the f° horse of a k°, Kād.; *-maṇḍana*, n. N. of wk. **-vallī**, f. Momordica Charantia, L. **-vaśī-bhūta**, mfn. subject to a k°, loyal, MW.; *-tā*, f. loyalty, allegiance, ib. **-vasati**, f. dwelling in a k°'s court, MBh.; a royal residence, palace, ib. **-vahana**, mfn. carrying k°s, ridden by k°s, MBh.; n. the vehicle on which the Soma is carried, Vait. **-vahikā**, v.l. for *-vāhikā*, q.v. **-vādhavya** (?), m. a patr., Pravar. **-vārttika**, n. N. of wk. **-vāha**, m. a horse, L. **-vāhana**, m. N. of a son of king Rāja-haṇsa, Daś. **-vāhikā**, f. (prob.) the diary of a k°, Siṇhâs. **-vāhya**, m. a royal elephant, L. **-vi**, m. 'royal bird,' the blue jay, L. **-vijaya**, m. (in music) a partic. Rāga, Saṃgīt.; N. of wk. **-vidyā**, f. royal science, state policy, statesmanship, Kām.; *-dhara*, m. (in music) a kind of measure, Saṃgīt. **-vinoda**, m. N. of wk.; *-tāla*, m. (in music) a kind of measure, Saṃgīt. **-vihaṃgama**, m. = *-vi*, L. **-vihāra**, m. a royal pleasure-seat, Virac.; a royal convent, Rājat. **-vījin**, see *-bījin*. **-vīthī**, f. = *-vartman*, Ragh. **-vīrya**, n. the power of a k°, MW. **-vṛiksha**, m. 'royal tree,' N. of a kind of tree, Car.; Bhpr. (accord. to L., Cathartocarpus Fistula; Buchanania Latifolia; or Euphorbia Tirucalli). **-vṛitta**, n. the conduct or occupation of a k°, R. **-vetrin**, m. a king's staff-bearer, Pañcad. **-veśman**, n. a king's palace, MBh.; R.; Kathās. **-vesha**, m. a royal garment, Ragh. **-vyavahāra-kośa**, m. = *kośa-nighaṇṭu*, q.v. **-śaṇa**, m. Corchorus Olitorius (from the fibres of which a coarse cordage and canvas are prepared), L. **-śaphara**, m. Clupea Alosa (a kind of fish), L. **-śayana**, n. (Pāṇ. vi, 2, 151, Sch.) and *-śayyā*, f. (L.) a k°'s couch, royal seat or throne. **-śāka**, n. Chenopodium (a kind of pot-herb), L. **-śākaṇikā** or **-śākinī**, f. a kind of vegetable, L. **-śārdūla**, m. k°-tiger, a great k°, MBh. **-śāsana**, n. a royal edict or order, Mn. x, 55. **-śāstra**, n. = *-vidyā*, MBh. **-śīrshaka**, m. (in music) a kind of measure, Saṃgīt. **-śuka**, m. a kind of parrot (with red stripes on the neck and wings), L. **-śṛiṅga**, m. Macropteronatus Magur (a kind of fish), L.; n. a royal Chattar or golden-handled umbrella, L. **-śekhara**, m. (also with *kavi*, *sūri* &c.) N. of various authors and teachers; (esp.) of a poet (son of Durdaka and Śīla-vatī, tutor of Mahêndra-pāla, king of Kanyakubjā; he lived in the 10th century and wrote 4 plays, viz. Pracaṇḍa-pāṇḍava or Bāla-bhārata, Bāla-rāmāyaṇa, Viddhaśāla-bhañjikā, and Karpūra-mañjarī). **-śaila**, m. N. of a mountain, MārkP. **-śyāmalôpâsaka**, m. N. of a sect, Cat. **-śyāmāka**, m. a kind of grain, MārkP. **-śravas**, m. N. of a Vyāsa, VP. (v.l. *-sravas*). **-śrī**, f. = *-lakshmī*, Hariv.; R.; Rājat.; N. of a Gandharva maiden, Kāraṇḍ. **-saṃśraya**, mfn. having k°s for a refuge or protection, Pañcat. **-saṃsad**, f. a k°'s assembly, court of justice, Kathās. **-sattra**, n. a k°'s sacrifice, ib. **-sadana** (L.), **-sadman** (Kathās.), n. a k°'s palace. **-saṃnidhāna**, n. the royal presence, MW. **-sabhā**, f. = *-saṃsad*, Kāv.; Kathās.; *-stha*, mfn. being at a k°'s court, a courtier, MW. **-sarpa**, m. a species of large serpent, L. **-sarshapa**, m. (or *ā*, f., L.) black mustard, Sinapis Ramosa (the seed used as a weight = 3 Likshās = ⅓ of a Gaura-sarshapa), Mn.; Yājñ. **-sākshika**, mfn. testified by the k° (as a document), Vishṇ. **-sāt**, ind. to the state or power of a k°, MW.; *-√kṛi*, to make dependent on a k°, ib.; *-√bhū* (HPariś.) or *-sam-√pad* (Vop.), to fall to a k°'s share. **-sāman**, n. pl. N. of partic. Sāmans, TāṇḍBr. **-sāyujya**, n. 'close union with royalty,' sovereignty, L. **-sārasa**, m. 'royal crane,' a peacock, L. **-siṇha**, m. 'king-lion,' an illustrious king, MBh.; R.; N. of various kings, Inscr.; Cat.; *-sudhā-saṃgraha*, m. N. of a medical wk. (written by Mahādeva, at the request of king Rāja-siṇha, and also called *-sudhā-sindhu*). **-sukha**, n. a k°'s happiness or welfare, Caurap. **-suta**, m. a k°'s son, prince, Kāv.; Kathās.; (*ā*), f. a princess, ib. **-sundara-gaṇi**, m. N. of a preceptor, Cat. **-sū**, f. creating or making a king, VS. **-sūnu**, m. a k°'s son, prince, R.; Kathās. **-sūya**, m. a great sacrifice performed at the coronation of a k° (by himself and his tributary princes, e.g. the sacrifice at the inauguration of Yudhi-shṭhira, described in MBh. ii), AV. &c. &c.; N. of various wks. (esp. of ŚBr. vii, in the Kāṇva-śākhā); n. (only L.) a lotus-flower; a kind of rice; a mountain; mfn. relating &c. to the R°-s° ceremony (e.g. °*yo mantraḥ*, a Mantra recited at the R°-s° c°), Pāṇ. iv, 3, 66, Vārtt. 5, Pat.; *-yājin*, mfn. a priest who officiates at a R°-s° sacrifice, ŚBr.; *-sūtra*, n. N. of a Sūtra wk.; °*yârambha-parvan*, n. N. of MBh. ii, 12–18; °*yêshṭi*, f. the R°-s° sacrifice, MBh. **-sūyika**, mf(*ī*)n. relating to the R°-s° sacrifice, ŚrS.; MārkP. **-sena**, m. N. of a man, Mudr. **-sevaka**, m. a k°'s servant, Kathās.; BhP.; a Rājput, Pañcat. **-sevā**, f. royal service, Kuval.; °*vôpajīvin*, m. = next, Kathās. **-sevin**, m. a k°'s servant, Hariv.; Pañcat. **-saudha**, m. or n. a k°'s palace, Pañcad. **-skandha**, m. a horse, L. **-stamba**, m. N. of a man (cf. next). **-stambâyaná** (or °*bâyana*, ŚBr.) and **-stambi** (Pravar.), m. patr. fr. prec. **-strī**, f. a k°'s wife, queen, R. **-sthalaka**, mfn. (fr. next), g. *dhūmâdi*. **-sthalī**, f. N. of a place, ib. **-sthānâdhikāra**, m. viceroyalty, Rājat. **-sthānīya**, m. a viceroy, governor, Inscr. **-sravas**, see *-śravas*. **-sva**, n. the property of a k°, Mn. viii, 149. **-svarṇa**, m. a kind of thorn-apple, L. **-svāmin**, m. 'lord of k°s,' N. of Vishṇu, Rājat. **-haṇsa**, m. (ifc. f. *ā*) 'k°-goose,' a kind of swan or goose (with red legs and bill, sometimes compared to a flamingo), Hariv.; R. &c. (*ī*, f., Kālid.; Kathās.); an excellent k°, L.; N. of a k° of Magadha, Daś.; of an author, Cat.; of a servant, Kathās.; *-sudhā-bhāshya*, n. N. of wk.; °*sāya*, Nom. Ā. °*yate*, or °*sīya*, Nom. P. °*yati*, to behave like a Rāja-haṇsa bird, Alaṃkārat. **-hatyā**, f. assassination of a k°, regicide, MW. **-harmya**, n. a k°'s palace, Kām. **-harshaṇa**, n. Tabernaemontana Coronaria, L. **-hastin**, m. a royal elephant, excellent el°, Pāṇ. vi, 2, 63, Sch. **-hāra**, m. a bearer or bringer of Soma, Kāṭh. **-hāsaka**, m. Cyprinus Catla (a species of fish), L. **Rājâṅgana**, n. the court-yard of a palace, Kathās. **Rājâjñā**, f. a k°'s edict, royal decree, MW. **Rājâtmaka-stava**, m. N. of a panegyric of Rāma. **Rājâtyāvartaka**, w.r. for *rājanyâv°*. **Rājâdana**, m. (and *ī*, f., L.) N. of a kind of tree, Hcar.; Suśr. &c. (accord. to L., Buchanania Latifolia [n. its nut]; Mimusops Kauki [n. its fruit]; Butea Frondosa). **Rājâditya**, m. N. of an author, Cat. **Rājâdri**, m. a species of vegetable, L. **Rājâdhara**, m. N. of a man, Cat. **Rājâdhikārin** or °**kṛita**, m. 'royal official,' a judge, Kathās. **Rājâdhideva**, m. N. of a Śūra, Hariv.; (*ī*), f. of a daughter of Ś°, ib.; Pur. **Rājâdhirājá**, m. a king of kings, paramount sovereign, TĀr. **Rājâdhishṭhāna**, n. (with *nagara*) a royal residence, Pañcat. **Rājâdhīna**, m. the servant of a k°, Āpast. **Rājâdhvan**, m. a royal road, principal street, Rājat. **Rājânaka**, m. an inferior k°, petty prince, ib.; N. of Mammaṭa, Cat.; *-mahimâcārya*, m. N. of an author, ib. **Rājânujīvin**, m. the dependent of a king, a king's servant, MatsyaP. **Rājântakaraṇa**, mfn. causing the destruction of k°s, Mn. ix, 221 (v.l.) **Rājânna**, n. food obtained from a k° or Kshatriya, Mn. iv, 218; a kind of rice of a superior quality (grown in Andhra), L. **Rājânya-tva**, n. a change of k°s, VarBṛS. **Rājâpatyā**, f. (with *śānti*) N. of wk. **Rājâpasada**, m. a degraded or outcast king, Nal. **Rājâbharaṇa**, n. a k°'s ornament, regalia, MW. **Rājâbhisheka**, m. 'consecration of a k°,' N. of wk.; *-paddhati*, f., *-prayoga*, m. N. of wks. **Rājâmra**, m. a superior kind of mango, L. **Rājâmla**, m. Rumex Vesicarius, L. **Rājârāma**, m. (also with *bhaṭṭa*) N. of various authors, Cat. **Rājârka**, m. Calotropis Gigantea, L. **Rājârha**, mfn. fit for or worthy of or due to a k°, royal, noble, R.; (*ā*), f. Eugenia Jambolana, L.; n. aloe wood, Agallochum, L.; a kind of rice (= *rājânna*), L. **Rājârhaṇa**, n. a royal gift or offering of honour, L. **Rājâlābū**, f. a species of cucumber, L. **Rājâluka**, m. a species of tuberous plant or yam, L. **Rājâvarta**, m. (once n.) Lapis Lazuli, Bālar.; a kind of diamond or other gem (of an inferior quality, said to come from the country Virāṭa, and regarded as a lucky possession though not esteemed as an ornament); = *rāja-maṇi*, VarBṛS., Sch.; also °*tôpala*, m., Kathās.); n. cloth of various colours, L. (cf. *rāja-v°*). **Rājâvali**, f. = °*valī*; *-patākā*, f. N. of a continuation of the Rāja-taraṃgiṇī by Prâjya-bhaṭṭa. **Rājâvalī**, f. 'line of kings,' N. of various chronicles; *-phala-grantha*, m. N. of wk. **Rājâvavāda**, m. a sermon for a k°, Jātak.; °*daka*, n. N. of a Buddhist wk. **Rājâśvá**, m. a large or powerful stallion, AV. **Rājâsana**, n. a royal seat, throne, MBh.; R. **Rājâsandī**, f. a stool or stand on which the Soma is placed, ŚBr. **Rājâhi**, m. a kind of large snake, L. **Rājêndra**, m. a lord of k°s, supreme sovereign, emperor, MBh.; R. &c.; a partic. Samādhi, Kāraṇḍ.; N. of a poet and other men, Cat.; *-karṇa-pūra*, m. or n. N. of a poem in praise of Harsha-deva of Kaśmīra; *-gir*, m. N. of a man, W.; *-daśâvadhāna*, m. (with *bhaṭṭâcārya*) N. of an author, Cat. **Rājêśvara**, m. 'lord of kings,' N. of a man, Rājat.; *-mahôdaya*, m. N. of wk. **Rājêshṭa**, m. 'liked by k°s,' a kind of onion, L.; (*ā*), f. Musa Sapientum, L.; a species of date, L.; n. a kind of rice, L. **Rājôdvejana-saṃjñaka**, m. a species of tree, L. **Rājôpakaraṇa**, n. pl. the paraphernalia of a k°, ensigns of royalty, VarBṛS.; Kathās. **Rājôpacāra**, m. attention paid to a k°, Vikr.; Kathās. **Rājôpajīvin**, m. pl. the subjects of a k°, MW. **Rājôpasevā**, f. royal service, Mn. iii, 64. **Rājôpasevin**, m. a king's servant, VarBṛS.

Rājaka, mfn. illuminating, irradiating, splendid, W.; (°*ká*), m. a little king, petty prince, RV.; Hariv.; a king, prince (= *rājan*, esp. ifc.), MBh.; Kāv. &c.; N. of various men, Rājat.; Lalit.; n. a number of kings, Kāv.; Pur. (cf. Pāṇ. iv, 2, 39).

Rājakīya, mfn. (fr. prec.) of or belonging to a king, princely, royal, Rājat.; Sāh. &c.; m. (scil. *purusha*) a king's servant, Vet.; *-nāman*, n. the royal name, Vet. **-saras**, n. a pond or lake belonging to a king, Kathās.

1. **Rājan**, m. (ifc. mostly *-rāja*, esp. in Tat-purushas; f. *-rājan*, °*jā* or °*jñī*; cf. Pāṇ. iv, 1, 28, Sch.) a king, sovereign, prince, chief (often applied to gods, e.g. to Varuṇa and the other Ādityas, to Indra, Yama &c., but esp. to Soma [also the plant and juice] and the Moon), RV. &c. &c.; a man of the royal tribe or the military caste, a Kshatriya, ĀśvŚr.; ChUp.; Mn. &c. (cf. *rājanya*); a Yaksha, L.; N. of one of the 18 attendants on Sūrya (identified with a form of Guha), L.; of Yudhi-shṭhira, MBh. (*rājñām indra-mahôtsavaḥ* and *rājñām*

pratibodhaḥ, N. of wks.); (*rā́jñī*), f., see s. v. [Cf. Lat. *rex;* Kelt. *rīg*, fr. which Old Germ. *rīk;* Goth. *reiks;* Angl.-Sax. *rīce;* Eng. *rich.*] **-vat,** mfn. (anomalous for *rāja-vat;* cf. Pāṇ. viii, 2, 14) having a good king, governed by a just monarch, Ragh.; Kāvyâd.; Hcar.; Siṇhâs.

2. **Rājáṇ,** (only in loc. *rājáni*) government, guidance, RV. x, 49, 4.

Rājana, mfn. belonging to a royal family (but not to the warrior caste), Siddh. on Pāṇ. iv, 1, 137; (*ī*), f. N. of a river, MBh.; = *gautamī*, L.; (°*ná*), n. N. of various Sāmans, ĀrshBr.

Rājanyà, mf(*ā*)n. kingly, princely, royal, RV. &c. &c.; m. a royal personage, man of the regal or military tribe (ancient N. of the second or Kshatriya caste), ib. (cf. IW. 228); N. of Agni or Fire, Uṇ. iii, 100, Sch.; a kind of date tree (= *kshīrikā*), L.; pl. N. of a partic. family of warriors, VarBṛS.; (*ā*), f. a lady of royal rank, MBh.; Hariv. **-kumāra,** m. a prince, R. **-tva,** n. the being a warrior or belonging to the military caste, Sāy. **-bandhu** (°*nyà-*), m. the friend or connection of a prince (generally used in contempt), ŚBr.; Lāṭy.; a Kshatriya, Mn. ii, 65. **-rshi** (for *-ṛishi*), m. a Ṛishi of royal descent, TāṇḍBr. **-vat** (°*nyà-*), mfn. connected with one of royal rank, TS. **Rājanyâvartaka,** m. Lapis Lazuli, L.

Rājanyaka, mfn. inhabited by warriors, Pāṇ. iv, 2, 53; n. a number or assemblage of warriors, Ragh.; Daś. (cf. Pāṇ. iv, 2, 39).

Rājamāna, mfn. shining, radiant (*-tva*, n.), Vedântas.

Rājáse. See under √*rāj*.

Rājāna (fr. 1. *rājan*), Nom. P. °*nati*, Siddh. on Pāṇ. vi, 4, 15.

Rājāya (fr. id.), Nom. Ā. °*yate*, to act or behave like a king, consider one's self a king, MBh.

Rājika, mfn., see *shoḍasa-r*°; m. = *narêndra*, L.; N. of a Muni, Cat.; (*ā*), f., see *rājikā* under *rāji*, col. 2.

Rājita, mfn. illuminated, resplendent, brilliant, adorned or embellished with (instr. or comp.), MBh.; Kāv. &c.

Rājīya (fr. 1. *rājan*), Nom. P. °*yati*, Pāṇ. i, 4, 13, Sch.

1. **Rājīva,** mfn. (for 2. see col. 3) living at a king's expense (= *rājôpajīvin*), L.

Rājoka, m. N. of a poet, L.

Rā́jñī, f. (see 1. *rājan*) a queen, princess, the wife of a king, VS. &c. &c.; N. of the western quarter or that which contains the Soul of the Universe, ChUp. iii, 15, 2; of the wife of the Sun, Pur.; deep-coloured or yellowish-red brass (consisting of three parts of copper to one of zinc or tin), L. **-devī-pañcâṅga,** n., *-devī-māhātmya*, n. N. of wks. **-pada,** n. the rank or dignity of a queen, VarBṛS. **-stava,** m. N. of wk.

Rājyá, mfn. kingly, princely, royal, TBr.; n. (also *rā́jya* or *rājyà*) royalty, kingship, sovereignty, empire ('over,' loc. or comp.; 'of,' gen. or comp.; acc. with √*kṛi* or Caus. of √*kṛi* or with *upa-*√*ās* or *vi-* √*dhā*, to exercise government, rule, govern), AV. &c. &c.; kingdom, country, realm (= *rāshṭra*), ib. **-1. -kara,** mfn. exercising government, ruling, MBh. **-2. -kara,** m. the tribute paid by tributary princes, Kshitîś. **-kartṛi,** w. r. for *rāja-k*°, q. v. **-kṛit,** mfn. = 1. *-kara*, Pañcat. **-khaṇḍa,** n. a kingdom, country, R. **-cyuta,** mfn. fallen from sovereignty; m. a dethroned or deposed monarch, W. **-cyuti,** f. loss of sov°, dethronement, Daś. **-tantra,** n. (sg. and pl.) the science or theory of government, R.; Rājat. **-tyāga,** m. abandonment of rule or gov°, Cat. **-devī,** f. N. of the mother of Bāṇa, Vās., Introd. (v. l. *rāshṭra-d*°). **-dravya,** n. a requisite of sov°, any object necessary for a king's consecration; *-maya*, mf(*ī*)n. consisting of or belonging to the requisites of royalty, R. **-dhara,** m. 'kingdom supporter,' N. of a man, Kathās. **-dhurā,** f. burden of government, administration, W. **-pada,** n. royal rank, majesty, L. **-parikriyā,** f. exercise of government, administration, Pañcat. **-paribhrashṭa,** mfn. = *-cyuta*, MBh. **-pāla,** m. N. of a king (v. l. for *rāja-p*°, q. v.) **-prada,** mfn. giving or conferring a kingdom, Rājyat. **-bhaṅga,** m. subversion of sovereignty, Hit. **-bhāj,** m. 'kingdom-possessor,' a king, MBh. **-bhāra,** m. the weight of (the duties of) government, MW. **-bheda-mara,** mfn. causing division or discord in a government, Hit. **-bhoga,** m. possession of sovereignty, MBh. **-bhraṇśa,** m. = *-cyuti*, R. **-bhrashṭa,** mfn. = *-cyuta*, MW. **-raksha,** f. protection or defence of a kingdom, Vcar. **-lakshmī,** f. the good fortune of a kingdom, glory of sov°, R. **-lābha,** m. obtainment of sov°, succession to the throne; *-stotra*, n. N. of a Stotra. **-līlā,** f. 'king-play,' pretending to be a king; Nom. Ā. °*yate* (only °*yita*, n. the playing at kings), Kathās. **-loka,** w. r. for *rājya-l*°, Kathās. **-lobha,** m. desire for royalty, ambition, R. **-laulya,** n. id., L. **-vatī,** f. N. of a princess, L. **-vardhana,** m. N. of a king (son of Dama), Pur.; of another k° (son of Pratāpa-śila or Prabhākara-vardhana), Vās., Introd. **-vibhava,** m. (Kathās.), **-vibhūti,** f. (BhP.) the might or power of royalty. **-vyavahāra,** m. government business, MW. **-śrī,** f. = *-lakshmī*, HPariś. (personified, Hcar.); N. of a daughter of Pratāpa-śila, Hcar. **-sukha,** n. the pleasure of royalty, enjoyment of a kingdom, VarBṛS. **-sena,** m. N. of a king of Nandi-pura, Cat. **-stha** (R. &c.) or **-sthāyin** (Pañcat.), mfn. being in a kingly office, ruling. **-sthiti,** f. the being in a kingly office, government, Rājat. **-hara,** mfn. spoiling a kingdom, the spoiler of an empire, R. **Rājyâṅga,** n. 'limb of royalty,' a requisite of regal administration (variously enumerated as 7, 8, or 9, viz. the monarch, the prime minister, a friend or ally, treasure, territory, a stronghold, an army, the companies of citizens, and the Puro-hita or spiritual adviser), L. **Rājyâdhikāra,** m. authority over a kingdom, right or title to a sovereignty, MW. **Rājyâdhideva,** m. N. of a king, VP. **Rājyâdhidevatā,** f. the tutelary deity of a kingdom, Kād. **Rājyâpaharaṇa,** n. the taking away or deprivation of a king, usurpation, Nal. **Rājyâpahāraka,** m. a usurper, MW. **Rājyâbhishikta,** mfn. inaugurated to a kingdom, crowned, RāmatUp. **Rājyâbhisheka,** m. inauguration to a k°, coronation, Pañcat.; *-dīdhiti*, f., *-paddhati*, f., *-prakaraṇa-ṭīkā*, f., *-mantra*, m., *-vidhi*, m. N. of wks. **Rājyâśrama-muni,** m. 'monk of a royal hermitage,' a pious king, Ragh. **Rājyâika-sesheṇa,** ind. with the single exception of the kingdom, MW. **Rājyôpakaraṇa,** n. pl. the instruments or paraphernalia of government, insignia of royalty, MBh. (cf. *rājôp*°).

Rāshṭra. See s. v.

राजकिनेय *rājakineya*, m. metron. fr. *rajakī*, Vop.

राजत *rājata*, mf(*ī*)n. (fr. *rajata*) silvery, made of silver, silver, ŚrS.; MBh. &c.; n. silver, Mn.; R. &c. **Rājatâdri,** m. 'silver-m°,' N. of the Kailāsa mountain, Śiś. (cf. *rajatâdri*). **Rājatânvita,** mfn. covered or overlaid with silver, Mn. iii, 202.

राजनि *rājani*, m. patr. fr. *rajana*, TĀr.

राजस *rājasa*, mf(*ī*)n. belonging or relating to the quality *rajas* (q. v.), endowed with or influenced by the quality of passion, passionate (*-tva*, n.), MaitrUp.; Mn.; MBh. &c.; m. pl. N. of a class of gods in the 5th Manv-antara, VP.; (*ī*), f. N. of Durgā, L.

Rājasika, mfn. = *rājasa*, Pañcat.

राजसाइ *rājasāi*, N. of a country, Kshitîś.

राजासलखण *rājasalakhaṇa*, m. N. of a man, Inscr. (prob. corrupted fr. *rājasa-lakshaṇa*).

राजि *rā́ji*, f. (prob. fr. √*raj, rañj*) a streak, line, row, range, ŚBr. &c. &c.; a line parting the hair, MW.; the uvula or soft palate, L.; a striped snake, L.; a field, L.; Vernonia Anthelminthica, L. (cf. *rājī*); m. N. of a son of Āyu, MBh. (B. *raji*). **-citra,** m. a kind of striped snake, Suśr. **-tas,** ind. in long rows or lines, VarBṛS. **-phalā** or **-phalī,** f. 'having striped fruit,' a kind of cucumber, L. **-mat,** mfn. possessing stripes, striped, Hariv.; Kathās.; m. a species of snake, Suśr.

Rājikā, f. (for *rājika* see col. 1) a stripe, streak, line, L.; a field, L.; Sinapis Ramosa (a grain of it = ⅓ Sarshapa), Suśr.; ŚārṅgS.; a partic. eruption (enumerated among the Kshudra-rogas), ŚārṅgS. **-phala,** m. Sinapis Glauca, L.

Rājin, m. N. of a horse of the Moon, VP.

Rājila, m. 'striped,' a species of snake, Ragh.; Kathās.; Suśr.; m. an elephant, Gal.

Rājī, f. = *rāji*, a streak, line, row, MBh., Kāv. &c.; Vernonia Anthelminthica, L.; black mustard, L. **-kṛita,** mfn. formed into lines, striped, Kāv.; Kathās. **-phala,** m. Trichosanthes Dioeca, L. **-mat,** mfn. striped, Suśr.; a kind of snake, Cat.; *-matī-parityāga*, m. N. of wk.

2. **Rājīva,** mf(*ā*)n. (for 1. see col. 1) streaked, striped, ŚrS.; m. a species of fish, Mn. v, 16; Yājñ.; Suśr.; a kind of striped deer, Bhpr.; the Indian crane, L.; an elephant, L.; N. of the pupil of Viśva-nātha, MW.; n. a blue lotus-flower, Yājñ.; MBh. &c. **-netra,** mfn. lotus-eyed, blue-eyed, MBh. **-pṛiśni,** mfn. having l°-coloured spots or streaks, KātyŚr. **-phala,** m. a species of cucumber, L. **-mukha,** mfn. lotus-faced, Vcar.; (*ī*), f. a l°-f° or beautiful woman, ib. **-locana,** mfn. = *-netra*, MBh.; Hariv. &c.; (*ā*), f. N. of a daughter of Jarā-saṃdha, MBh. **-vilocana,** mfn. = *-netra*, Vcar. **-śubha-locana,** mfn. having eyes resembling the lotus-flower, blue-eyed, R.

Rājīvaka, m. a kind of fish, L.

Rājīvinī, f. the lotus plant or a group of lotuses (Nelumbium Speciosum), g. *pushkarâdi*. **-jīvita-vallabha,** m. 'beloved of the lotus plant,' the moon, Vcar.

Rājeya, mfn. derived from Raji or Rāji, Hariv.

राजीक *rājika*, m. pl. N. of a people, R. (v. l.)

राजेयु *rājeyu*, m. N. of a man, VP. (v. l. for *riteyu*).

राज्जु *rājju*, Vṛiddhi form of *rajju*, in comp. **-kaṇṭhin,** m. pl. the school of Rajju-kaṇṭha, g. *śaunakâdi*. **-dāla,** mf(*ī*)n. (*rā́jju-*) coming from the Rajju-dāla tree, made of its wood, ŚBr.; TBr.; KātyŚr. **-bhārin,** m. pl. the school of Rajju-bhāra, g. *śaunakâdi*.

राज्ञी *rājñī, rājya* &c. See col. 1.

राटि *rāṭi*, f. (√*raṭ*) war, battle, L.

Rāṭikā, f. See *mṛiga-rāṭikā*.

Rāṭu, m. N. of a preceptor, Cat.

राठ *rāṭha*, m. Vangueria Spinosa, Car. (cf. *rāḍha*).

राढा *rāḍhā*, f. beauty, splendour, L.; (sometimes written *rārā*) N. of a district in the west of Bengal (= *suhma*) and its capital, Kathās.; Prab. **-pura,** n. N. of a town, Cat.

Rāḍha, mf(*ī*)n. belonging to the district of Rāḍhā; m. N. of a tribe of Brāhmans belonging to that district, IW. 210, n. 1; Vangueria Spinosa, L. (cf. *rāṭha*).

Rāḍhīya, mfn. (also written *rārīya*) belonging to Rāḍhā, Prab., Sch.

राण *rāṇa*, m. n. (√2. *raṇ*) murmuring, L.; n. a leaf, L.; a peacock's tail, L. (cf. *rāja-rāṇaka*); (*ā*), f. (prob.) N. of a goddess. **Rāṇā-devī-māhātmya,** n. N. of wk.

Rāṇaka, m. N. of a poet, Cat.; of a Comm. on the Tantra-vārttika (also called *nyāya-sudhā* or *vārttika-yojanā* or *sarvânavadya-kāriṇī*); (*ikā*), f. a bridle, L. (cf. *rāja-rāṇaka*). **Rāṇakôjjivinī,** f. N. of wk.

Rāṇāyana, m. patr. fr. *rāṇa*, g. *naḍâdi;* (*ī*), f., see next.

Rāṇāyanī-putra, m. N. of a preceptor, Lāṭy.

Rāṇāyanīya, m. N. of a preceptor, Cat.; pl. the school of Rāṇāyana, Śaṃk. **-sūtra,** n. = *gobhila-gṛihya-sūtra*, Hcat.

Rāṇāyanīyi, m. N. of a preceptor, Cat.

Rāṇi, m. patr. fr. *raṇa*, g. *pailâdi*.

राणड्य *rāṇaḍya*, m. N. of Dāmôdara, Cat.

राणा *rāṇā*, m. (corruption of *rājan*, q. v.) a king.

Rāṇī, f. (corruption of *rājñī*, q. v.) a queen.

राणाक *rāṇāka*, m. N. of a man, MW.

राणिग *rāṇiga*, m. N. of a man (father of Keśava, Jayâditya and Kṛishṇa), Cat.

राण्ड्य *rāṇḍya* or *rāṇḍrya*, mfn. = *ramaṇīya*, agreeable, gratifying, Sāy. on RV. vi, 23, 6.

रात *rāta, rāti* &c. See p. 871, col. 3.

रातन्ती *rātanti* (?), a festival on the fourteenth day of the second half of the month Pausha (when people bathe at the first appearance of dawn), MW.

रातुल *rātula*, m. N. of a son of Śuddhodana, VP. (cf. *rāhula*).

रात्न *rātna*, mf(ī)n. consisting of pearls, HPariś.

रात्र *rātra, rātraka*. See below.

रात्रि *rā́tri* or (older) *rā́trī*, f. (prob. 'bestower,' fr. √*rā*; or 'season of rest,' fr. √*ram*) night, the darkness or stillness of night (often personified), RV. &c. &c. (*rātrau* or °*tryām*, ind. at n°, by n°; *rātrau śayanam*, a festival on the 11th day of the first half of the month Āshāḍha, regarded as the night of the gods, beginning with the summer solstice, when Vishṇu reposes for four months on the serpent Śesha); = *ati-rātra*, ŚBr.; = *rātri-paryāya*, ib.; = *rātri-sāman*, Lāṭy.; (only *rātri*) one of the 4 bodies of Brahmā, VP.; = *haridrā*, turmeric, MBh.; Suśr.; (with the patr. *Bhāradvājī*) N. of the authoress of RV. x, 127, Anukr. **— kara**, m. night-maker, the moon, Inscr. **— kāla**, m. n°-time, MW. **— cara**, m. 'n°-wandering,' a thief, robber, L.; a n°-watcher, watchman, W.; a Rākshasa, L. (*ī*, f., Bhaṭṭ.) **— caryā**, f. = *-cāra*, MBh.; a n° ceremony, Kathās. **— cāra**, m. n°-roving, Śṛiṅgār. **— cchandas**, n. a metre employed at the Atirātra, ŚāṅkhBr. **— ja**, n. 'night-born,' a star, L. **— jala**, n. 'n°-water,' dew, mist, L. **— jāgara**, m. n°-watching, Ragh.; 'night-watcher,' a dog, L.; *-da*, m. 'causing n°-watching,' a mosquito, L. **— jāgaraṇa**, n. n°-watching, MW. **— m-cara**, m. = *rātri-c°*, a Rākshasa, L. **— tarā**, f. (compar. of *rātri*) the depth or dead of n°, Pāṇ. vi, 3, 17, Sch. **— tithi**, f. a lunar night, Sūryapr. **— divam**, w.r. for *rātriṃ-d°*, Kathās. **— devata**, mf(*ā*)n. having the n° as a deity, ĀśvGṛ. **— dvish**, m. 'n°-hater,' the sun, L. **— nātha**, m. 'n°-lord,' the moon, Vāstuv. **— nāśana**, m. 'n°-destroyer,' the sun, L. **— m-diva**, n. n° and day, Kālid.; (*am* or *ā*), ind. by n° and day, Kāv.; Kām. **— m-divasa**, n. n° and day, Divyâv. **— pada-vicāra**, m. N. of wk. **— pariśishṭa**, n. = *-sūkta*, q.v. **— paryāya**, m. the three recurring ritual acts in the Atirātra ceremony, ŚāṅkhBr. **— paryushita**, mfn. anything which has stood over-night, stale, not fresh, Suśr. **— pushpa**, n. 'n°-flower,' a lotus-flower which opens at n°, L. **— pūjā**, f. the nocturnal worship of a deity, W. **— bala**, m. 'powerful by n°,' a Rākshasa, L. **— bhujaṃga**, m. 'night-lover,' the moon, Vcar. **— bhṛit**, mfn. one who maintains the Dīkshā only for a few n°s, Śulbas. **— bhojana**, n. eating at n°, MW.; *-nishedha*, m. N. of wk. **— m-aṭa**, m. = *rātry-aṭa*, Vop. **— maṇi**, m. 'n°-jewel,' the moon, L. **— maya**, mf(*ī*)n. nightly, nocturnal, Hcat. **— māraṇa**, n. murder (committed) at n°, L. **— m-manya**, mfn. being regarded as or appearing like n°, L. **— yoga**, m. night-fall, the coming on of n°, MW. **— rakshaka**, m. a n°-watcher, watchman, Kathās. **— rāga**, m. n°-colour, darkness, L. **— lagna-nirūpaṇa**, n. N. of a treatise ascribed to Kālidāsa. **— loka** (*rā́tri-*), mf(*ā*)n. representing n°, ŚBr. **— vāsas**, n. n°-dress, Tantras.; the garment of n°, i.e. darkness, obscurity, L. **— vigama**, m. 'n°-departure,' dawn, daylight, L. **— viślesha-gāmin**, m. 'separating at n°,' the ruddy goose (= *cakravāka*, q.v.), L. **— vihārin**, mfn. roaming at n°, Mālatīm. **— veda** or **-vedin**, m. 'n°-knower,' a cock, L. **— śṛita**, mfn. cooked by n°, KātyŚr. **— śesha**, m. the remainder or last part of night, ĀśvGṛ. **— shāman**, n. = *-sāman*, PañcavBr. **— sattra**, n. a sacrifice or ceremony at n°, ŚrS. **— sahasrá**, n. a thousand n°s, ŚBr. **— sācayá**, mfn. coming together or united at n°, ib. **— sāmán**, n. a Sāman belonging to the Atirātra, ib. **— sūkta**, n. N. of the hymn interpolated after RV. x, 127, ŚāṅkhGṛ.; *-vidhāna*, n. N. of wk. **— hāsa**, m. 'laughing,' i.e. opening at n°,' the white lotus, L. **— hiṇḍaka**, m. 'moving about at n°,' a guard of the women's apartments, L. **— huta**, n. a n° sacrifice, KātyŚr.

Rātra, m. n. (ifc.) = *rātri*, Pāṇ. iv, 2, 29 (cf. *ati-, tri-, divā-r°* &c.; also used alone in *trīṇi rātrāṇi*, MBh. xiii, 6230).

Rātraka, mf(*ikā*)n. nocturnal, nightly, lasting a night, Rājat.; Pañcat. (cf. *pañca-r°*); m. a man who dwells for a whole year in a harlot's house, L.; n. = *pañca-rātra*, N. of the sacred books of various Vaishṇava sects, L. (others 'a period of 5 nights' collectively).

Rātrika, mfn. nocturnal, nightly, Pañcad.; (ifc. after a numeral) lasting or sufficient for or completed in a certain number of nights or days (cf. *eka-, dvai-, pañca-r°*); (*ā*), f. night, MW.

Rātrī (= *rātri*), in comp. **— karaṇa**, mfn. turning into night, HPariś. **— daivodāsa**, n. N. of a Sāman, ĀrshBr. (v.l. *rātrīhava-daiv°*). **— sūkta** = *rātri-s°*, Cat.

Rātrīṇa. See *eka-* and *dvi-r°*.

Rātrau-bhava, mfn. (fr. *rātrau*, loc. of *rātri* + *bhava*) happening or occurring at night, ĀpŚr. Sch.

Rātry, in comp. for *rātrī*. **— aṭa**, m. 'night-rover,' a Rākshasa or a thief, L. **— andha**, mfn. n°-blind, unable to see at n°, Pañcat.; Suśr.; *-tā*, f. = *-āndhya*, q.v. **— ahanī**, n. du. n° and day, Mn.; R. &c. **— ākhyā**, f. Turmeric Curcuma, L. **— āgama**, m. the coming on or approach of n°, Bhag. **— āndhya**, n. n°-blindness, SārṅgS. **— upâya**, m. = *-āgama*, Lāṭy.

राथ 1. *rātha*, Vṛiddhi form of 1. *ratha*, in comp. **— kārika**, mf(*ī*)n. (fr. *ratha-kāra*), g. *kumudâdi*. **— kārya**, m. patr. (fr. id.), g. *kurv-ādi*. **— gaṇaka**, n. the occupation or office of a Ratha-gaṇaka, g. *udgātr-ādi*. **— m-tara** (*rā́th°*), mf(*ī*)n. relating to the Ratham-tara Sāman, TS.; ŚBr. &c.; m. patr., g. *bidâdi*; (*ī*), f. N. of a female teacher, Bṛih.; °*tarāyaṇa*, m. patr. fr. *rāthaṃtara*, g. *haritâdi*; °*tari*, m. N. of Airāvata, L. **— proshṭha**, m. patr. of A-samāti, L.

Rāthītara, m. (fr. *rathī-tara*, g. *bidâdi*) patr. of Satya-vacas, TUp.; °*rāyaṇa*, m. patr. fr. *rāthītara*, g. *haritâdi*.

Rā́thītarī-pútra, m. N. of a preceptor, ŚBr.

Rā́thya, n. possession of chariots (Padap. *ráthya*), RV. i, 157, 6; (*rāthyá*), mfn. fit for a carriage, VS.

राथ 2. *rātha*, Vṛiddhi form of 2. *ratha*, in comp. **— jiteyī**, f. pl. (fr. 2. *ratha-jit*) N. of a class of Apsarases, AV.

राध *rādh* (cf. √*ṛidh* and *radh*), cl. 5. 4. P. (Dhātup. xvii, 16; xxvi, 71) *rādhnóti, rā́dhyati* (Ved. also pr. *rā́dhati* and *rā́dhyate*; pf. *rarā́dha*, RV. &c. &c. [2. sg. *rarā́dhitha* or *redhita*, cf. Pāṇ. vi, 4, 123]; aor. *arātsīt, rādhishi*, AV.; Br.; Prec. *rādhyāsam*, ib.; fut. *rāddhā*, Gr.; *rātsyati*, AV.; Br.; ind. p. *rāddhvā, -rā́dhya*, Br.), to succeed (said of things), be accomplished or finished, VS.; TS.; AV.; to succeed (said of persons), be successful with (instr.), thrive, prosper, RV.; TS.; Br.; GṛŚrS.; to be ready for, submit to (dat.), AV.; to be fit for, partake of, attain to (dat. or loc.), Āpast.; TUp.; (*rādhyati*) to prophesy to (dat.), Pāṇ. i, 4, 39, Kāś.; to accomplish, perform, achieve, make ready, prepare, carry out, RV.; VS.; Br.; to hit, get at (acc.), TS.; to propitiate, conciliate, gratify, RV.; AitBr.; to hurt, injure, destroy, exterminate, Bhaṭṭ. (cf. Pāṇ. vi, 4, 123): Pass. *rādhyate* (aor. *árādhi*), to be conciliated or satisfied, RV. (cf. *rādhyate* above): Caus. *rādháyati* (aor. *arīradhat*, Br.; Pass. *rādhyate*, MBh.), to accomplish, perform, prepare, make ready, AV. &c. &c.; to make favourable, propitiate, satisfy, TS.; TBr.: Desid. of Caus. *rirādhayishati*, Br.: Desid. *-rirātsati* or *-ritsati*, Pāṇ. vii, 4, 54, Vārtt. 1, Pat.: Intens. *rārādhyate, rārāddhi*, Gr. [Cf. √*iradh*; Goth. *garēdan, rathjō*; Slav. *raditi*.]

Rāddhá, mfn. accomplished, brought about, perfected, achieved, prepared, ready (n. impers. 'it has been achieved by,' with instr.), KātyŚr.; BhP.; successful, fortunate, happy, Br.; Kauś.; fallen to the share or lot of any one, BhP.; propitiated, conciliated, MW.; perfect in mysterious or magical power, adept, initiated, ib. **Rāddhânta**, m. = *siddhânta*, an established end or result, demonstrated conclusion or truth, doctrine, dogma, Sarvad.; BhP.; *-muktā-hāra*, m. N. of wk.; °*tita*, mfn. logically demonstrated, proved, established, PañcavBr., Sch. **Rāddhânna**, n. dressed food, HPariś.

Rā́ddhi, f. accomplishment, perfection, completion, success, good fortune, AV.; Br.; ŚrS.

Rādha, m. or n. = *rā́dhas*, a gift, favour (only in *rā́dhānām patiḥ*, N. of Indra), RV.; m. (fr. *rādhā*) N. of the month Vaiśākha (= April–May), Rājat.; of a man, Buddh.; (with *Gautama*) N. of two teachers, Cat.; (*ā*), f., see below. **— gupta**, m. (for *rādhā-g°*; cf. Pāṇ. vi, 3, 63) N. of a minister of Aśoka, Buddh. **— raṅka**, m. = *sīra, sīraka*, and *ghanôpala*, L. **— raṅku**, m. = *sāra, sīkara*, and *jaladôpala*.

Rādhaka, mfn. liberal, bountiful, MW.

Rādhana, n. (only L.), propitiating, conciliating; pleasure, satisfaction; obtaining, acquisition; the means or instrument of accomplishing anything (*-dravya*, n. = *pācala*); (*ā*), f. speech, L.; (*ī*), f. worship, A.

Rā́dhas, n. favour, kindness, bounty, a gift of affection, any gift, RV.; AV.; munificence, liberality, ib.; accomplishment of one's wishes, success, BhP.; striving to accomplish or gain, ib.; wealth, power, ib. **— pati**, m. a lord of gifts or wealth, RV.

Rādhā, f. prosperity, success, L.; (also du.) N. of the 21st Nakshatra Viśākhā (containing 4 stars in the form of a curve supposed to be α, ι, ν Librae, and γ Scorpionis, cf. *nakshatra*), L.; lightning, L.; a partic. attitude in shooting (standing with the feet a span apart; cf. *-bhedhin, -vedhin*), Pracaṇḍ.; Emblic Myrobolan, L.; Clytoria Ternatea, L.; N. of the foster-mother of Karṇa (q.v.; she was the wife of Adhiratha, who was Sūta or charioteer of king Śūra), MBh. (cf. IW. 377); of a celebrated cowherdess or Gopī (beloved by Kṛishṇa, and a principal personage in Jaya-deva's poem Gīta-govinda; at a later period worshipped as a goddess, and occasionally regarded as an Avatāra of Lakshmī, as Kṛishṇa is of Vishṇu; also identified with Dākshāyaṇī), Gīt.; Pañcat. &c. (cf. IW. 332); of a female slave, Lalit. **— kavaca**, m. n. N. of wk. **— kānta**, m. 'lover of Rādhā,' N. of Kṛishṇa, BrahmavP.; (with *śarman* and *tarka-vāg-īśa*) N. of two authors; *-deva*, m. N. of a lexicographer (author of the Śabda-kalpadruma). **— kṛishṇa**, m. N. of various authors and teachers (also with *vedânta-vāg-īśa, go-svāmin* and *śarman*), Cat.; du. R° and Kṛishṇa, RTL. 184; *-kośa*, m., *-pada-cihna*, n., *-rūpa-cintāmaṇi*, m., *-līlā*, f.; °*nârcana-dīpikā*, f. N. of wks. **— caraṇa**, m. (with *kavîndra cakra-vartin*) N. of a man, Cat. **— janmâshṭamī**, f. N. of the 8th day of a partic. fortnight (commemorating the birthday of R°), Cat. (cf. *kṛishṇa-j°*). **— tanaya**, m. 'R°'s son,' N. of Karṇa, L. **— tantra**, n. N. of a Tantra. **— dāmôdara**, m. N. of various authors, Cat. **— nagarī**, f. N. of a town in the neighbourhood of Ujjayinī, L. **— nātha**, m. (with *śarman*) N. of an author, Cat. **— °nurādhīya** (*rādhân°*), mfn. relating to the Nakshatras R° and Anurādha, Pāṇ. iv, 2, 6, Sch. **— paddhati**, f. N. of wk. **— bhartṛi**, m. 'R°'s husband,' N. of Adhiratha, MBh. **— bhedin**, m. N. of Arjuna, L. (cf. *-vedhin*). **— mantra**, m. N. of wk., L. **— mādhava**, m. N. of an author, Cat.; *-rūpa-cintāmaṇi*, m. N. of wk. (= *rādhā-kṛishṇa-rūpa-c°*); *-vilāsa*, m. N. of a Campū by Jaya-rāma Kavîśvara. **— māna-taraṃgiṇī**, f. N. of a poem (written in 1696). **— mohana**, m. (with *śarman* and *go-svāmin bhaṭṭâcārya*) N. of two authors, Cat. **— ramaṇa**, m. 'lover of R°,' N. of Kṛishṇa, Cat.; *-dāsa*, m. (with *go-svāmin*) N. of an author, ib. **— rasa-mañjarī**, f., **-rasa-sudhā-nidhi**, m., **-rahasya-kāvya**, n. N. of poems. **— vat**, mfn. wealthy, rich, Nalôd. **— vallabha**, m. N. of a man, Cat.; (with *tarka-pañcânana bhaṭṭâcārya*) of an author, ib.; °*bhôpanishad*, f. N. of wk. **— vinoda-kāvya**, n., **-vilāsa**, m. N. of two poems. **— vedhin**, mfn. shooting in a partic. attitude (cf. *rādhā*), Siṇhâs.; m. N. of Arjuna, L. (cf. *-bhedin*). **— °shṭaka** (°*dhâshṭ°*), n. N. of a Stotra. **— sahasra-nāman**, n. N. of wk. **— suta**, m. = *-tanaya*, MBh. **— sudhā-nidhi**, m. N. of a poem (= *rasa-sudhā-nidhi*). **— saundarya-mañjarī**, f. N. of a poem. **Rādhêśa** and **Rādhêśvara**, m. 'lord of R°,' N. of Kṛishṇa, Pañcar. **Rādhôttara-tāpanīyôpanishad**, f., **Rādhôdbhava-saṃvāda**, m. N. of wks. **Rādhôpâsaka**, m. a worshipper of Rādhā, Cat.

Rādhi and **rādhī**, f., g. *bahv-ādi* (cf. *kṛishṭá-rādhi*).

Rādhika, m. N. of a king (son of Jaya-sena), BhP.; (*ā*), f., see next.

Rādhikā, f. endearing form of Rādhā (the Gopī), Gīt.; Pañcar. **— vinoda**, m. N. of a poem (= *rādhā-vinoda-kāvya*).

Rādheya, m. metr. of Karṇa (cf. under *rādhā*), MBh.; R.; Rājat.; of Bhīshma, L.

Rādho, in comp. for *rādhas*. **— gūrta** (*rā́dho-*), mfn. agreeable through kindness or gifts, VS. **— déya**, n. bestowal of gifts or favour, RV.

Rā́dhya, mfn. to be accomplished or performed, RV.; to be obtained or won, ib.; to be appeased or propitiated, ib.; to be worshipped, AitBr.

राध्रेवकि *rādhrevaki* (?), m. patr., Saṃskārak.

रान्द्र्य rāndrya. See rāṇḍya.

रान्धस rāndhasa, m. patr., Pāṇ. iv, 1, 144, Sch.

राप्य rāpya. See p. 867, col. 1.

राभसिक rābhasika, mfn. (fr. *rabhas*) impetuous, vehement (= *āyaḥśūlika*, q.v.), L. **-tā**, f. vehemency, impetuosity, Kād.

Rābhasya, n. (fr. *rabhasa*) velocity, impetuosity, Dhātup.; delight, joy, pleasure, MW.

राम rāma, mf(*ā*)n. (prob. 'causing rest,' and in most meanings fr. √*ram*) dark, dark-coloured, black (cf. *rātri*), AV.; TĀr. (*rāmaḥ śakuniḥ*, a black bird, crow, KāṭhGṛ.; Vishṇ.); white (?), L.; pleasing, pleasant, charming, lovely, beautiful, MBh.; Kāv. &c.; m. a kind of deer, Car.; a horse, L.; a lover, VarBṛS.; pleasure, joy, delight, BhP.; N. of Varuṇa, L.; N. of various mythical personages (in Veda two Rāmas are mentioned with the patr. Mārgaveya and Aupatasvini; another R° with the patr. Jāmadagnya [cf. below] is the supposed author of RV. x, 110; in later times three R°s are celebrated, viz. 1. Paraśu-rāma [q.v.], who forms the 6th Avatāra of Vishṇu and is sometimes called Jāmadagnya, as son of the sage Jamad-agni by Reṇukā, and sometimes Bhārgava, as descended from Bhṛigu; 2. Rāma-candra [see below]; 3. Bala-rāma [q.v.], 'the strong Rāma,' also called Halâyudha and regarded as elder brother of Kṛishṇa [RTL. 112]; accord. to Jainas a Rāma is enumerated among the 9 white Balas; and in VP. a R° is mentioned among the 7 Ṛishis of the 8th Manv-antara), RV. &c. &c.; N. of a king of Malla-pura, Cat.; of a king of Śṛiṅga-vera and patron of Nāgêśa, ib.; of various authors and teachers (also with *ācārya, upâdhyāya, kavi, cakra-vartin, jyotir-vid, jyautishaka, tarka-vāg-īśa, dīkshita, daiva-jña, paṇḍita, bhaṭṭa, bhaṭṭâcārya, vājapeyin, śarman, śāstrin, saṃyamin, sūri* &c.), Cat.; N. of the number 'three' (on account of the 3 Rāmas), Hcat. (*rāmasya ishuḥ*, a kind of cane = *rāma-kaṇḍa*, L.); pl. N. of a people, VP.; (*ā*), f. a beautiful woman, any young and charming woman, mistress, wife, any woman, KaṭhUp.; MBh. &c. (for comp. see p. 878); a dark woman i. e. a woman of low origin, TS.; TĀr.; N. of various plants (Jonesia Asoka; Aloe Perfoliata; Asa Foetida &c.), L.; vermilion, L.; red earth, L.; a kind of pigment (= *gorocanā*), L.; a river, L.; a kind of metre, L.; (in music) a kind of measure, Saṃgīt.; N. of an Apsaras, L., Sch.; of a daughter of Kumbhâṇḍa, Hariv.; of the mother of the ninth Arhat of the present Ava-sarpiṇī, L.; (*ī*), f. darkness, night, RV.; n. id., ib.; the leaf of Laurus Cassia, L.; Chenopodium Album, L.; = *kushṭha*, L. **-ṛishi**, see *rāma-rshi*. **-kaṇṭha**, m. N. of an author, Cat. **-kathā**, f. N. of wk. (also °*thâmṛita*, n. and °*thā-saṃgraha*, m.) **-karī**, f. (in music) N. of a Rāgiṇī, W. (prob. w.r. for *-kirī*, q.v.) **-karṇâmṛita**, n. N. of a poem. **-karpūra** or °**raka**, m. a species of fragrant grass, L. **-kalpa**, m. N. of a ch. of the Agastya-saṃhitā; *-druma*, m. N. of wk. **-kavaca**, n. 'R°'s breastplate or charm,' N. of a ch. of the Brahma-yāmala-tantra. **-kāṇḍa**, m. a species of cane, L. **-kānta**, m. = (or w. r. for) prec., L.; N. of various authors (also with *vācas-pati* and *vidyā-vāg-īśa*), Cat.; *-tanaya*, m. N. of an author, ib. **-kāvya**, n. N. of a poem. **-kiṃkara**, m. N. of various authors (also with *sarasvatī*), Cat. **-kirī**, f. (in music) N. of a Rāgiṇī, Saṃgīt. (also written *-kīrī* or *-karī*). **-kilbisha**, n. an offence against Rāma, MW. **-kiśora**, m. (with *śarman nyāyâlaṃkāra*) N. of an author, Cat. **-kīrī**, see *-kirī*. **-kīrti-mukundamālā**, f. N. of wk. **-kutūhala**, n. N. of a poem. **-kumāra**, m. (with *miśra*) N. of a man, Cat. **-kṛit**, m. (in music) N. of a Rāga, Saṃgīt. **-kṛishṇa**, m. N. of various authors and other men (also with *ācārya, dīkshita, daiva-jña, paṇḍita, bhaṭṭa, bhaṭṭâcārya, bhāva, miśra, vaidya-rāja, śesha* &c.), Cat.; *-kāvya*, n. = *-viloma-kāvya*; *-dīkshitīya*, n. N. of wk.; *-deva*, m. N. of a Sch. on Bhāskara's Līlāvatī; *-paddhati*, f. N. of wk.; *-viloma-kāvya*, n. N. of an artificial poem (by the astronomer Sūrya Paṇḍita) celebrating the praises of Rāma and Kṛishṇa (read either backwards or forwards; cf. *vilomâkshara-kāvya*); *-saṃvāda*, m., *-stotra*, n. N. of wks.; °*ṇânanda*, m. N. of a Sch. on the Mahā-bhāshya; °*ṇânanda-tīrtha*, m. N. of a teacher, Cat.; °*ṇīya*, n. N. of various wks. **-keli**, f. (in music) N. of a Rāgiṇī, Saṃgīt. **-keśava-tīrtha**, n. N. of a Tīrtha, Cat. **-kautuka**, n., **-kautūhala**, n. N. of wks. **-krī**, f. (in music) N. of a Rāga, Saṃgīt. **-kshetra**, n. N. of a district, Prâyaśc. **-gaṅgā**, f. N. of a river, Inscr. **-gāyatrī**, f. N. of a partic. hymn on Rāma Dāśarathi, RāmatUp. **-giri**, m. 'R°'s mountain,' N. of sev. mountains (esp., accord. to some, of Citra-kūṭa in Bundelkhand and of another hill near Nagpore, now called Ramtek). Megh.; VP. **-gīta-govinda**, m. N. of a poem (an imitation of the Gīta-govinda, attributed to a Jaya-deva). **-gītā**, f. N. of a ch. of the Adhyātma-rāmāyaṇa (in which spiritual knowledge is shown to be better than ritualistic observances; also pl.); of a ch. of the SkandaP. **-guṇâkara**, m. N. of a poem. **-gopāla**, m. N. of authors (also with *śarman*), Cat. **-govinda**, m. N. of authors (also with *śarman*), ib.; *-kīrtana*, n. N. of a Stotra; *-tīrtha*, m. N. of a teacher, Cat. **-grāma**, m. N. of a kingdom, Buddh. **-cakra**, n. N. of a partic. mystical circle, Cat. (also read *rāmâc*°). **-candra**, m. 'R°-moon,' N. of the principal Rāma called Dāśarathi, as son of Daśa-ratha, and Rāghava, as descended from Raghu (although the affix *candra* seems to connect him with the moon, he is not, like Kṛishṇa and Bala-rāma, of the lunar but of the solar race of kings; he forms the 7th Avatāra of Vishṇu and is the hero of the Rāmāyaṇa, who, to recover his faithful wife Sītā, advanced southwards, killed the demon Rāvaṇa and subjugated his followers the Rākshasas, the poetical representatives of the barbarous aborigines of the south), RāmatUp. (IW. 330; RTL. 110); N. of various kings and authors &c. (also with *ācārya, kavi, kshiti-pati, cakra-vartin, daṇḍin, dīkshita, naimisha-stha* or *vājapeyin, nyāya-vāg-īśa, parama-haṃsa, pāṭhaka, bhaṭṭa, bhaṭṭâcārya, bhārgava, bhishaj, miśra, yajvan, yatîśvara, vācas-pati, śāstrin, sārasvatī, siddha* &c.), Cat.; *-karuṇā-sāgara-candrikā*, f., *-kavaca*, n., *-kāvya*, n. N. of wks.; *-gaṇeśa*, m. N. of an author, Cat.; *-catuḥ-sūtrī*, f., *-candrikā*, f., *-campū*, f., *-carita*, n., *-caritra-sāra*, m., *-jyotsnā*, f. N. of wks.; *-tīrtha*, m. (formerly *mādhava śāstrin*) N. of the successor of Vāg-īśa-tīrtha (of the Madhva school; he died in 1377), Cat. (cf. RTL. 130); of two other scholars, Cat.; *-dāsa*, m. N. of a poet, ib.; *-nāṭaka*, n. N. of a drama (= *rāma-nāṭaka*); *-nāmâshṭôttara-śata*, n., *-pañcadaśī*, f., *-pūjā-vidhi*, m., *-mahôdaya*, m., *-yaśaḥ-prabandha*, m., *-stava-rāja*, m., *-stotra*, n.; °*drârya-maṅgalâśāsana*, n. N. of wks.; °*drâśrama*, m. N. of an author, Cat.; n. of a Tīrtha, ib.; °*drâśrita-pārijāta*, m., °*drâshṭaka*, n., °*drâhnika*, n., °*drikā*, f. N. of wks.; °*drêndra*, m. (with *sarasvatī*) N. of a teacher, Cat.; °*drôdaya*, m. 'rise of Rāma-candra,' N. of various wks. **-cara**, m. N. of Bala-rāma, L. **-caraṇa**, m. N. of various authors (also with *tarka-vāg-īśa*), Cat. **-carita**, n. 'R°'s exploits,' N. of various wks. **-cchardanaka**, m. a species of plant (v. l. *rāmâcch*°). **-ja**, m. N. of a man, Rājat. **-jananī**, f. R°'s mother, MW. **-janman**, n. the birth or birthday of R°, ib. **-jayanti-pūjā**, f., **-jātaka**, n., and °**ka-mahā-yantra**, n. N. of wks. **-jit**, m. N. of an author, Cat. **-jīvana**, m. N. of a king (son of Rudra-rāya), Kshitîś.; (with *tarka-vāg-īśa*) N. of an author, Cat. **-tattva-prakāśa**, m., **-tattva-bhāskara**, m., **-tantra**, n., **-tapana**, n. N. of wks. **-taraṇi** or **-taruṇī**, f. a species of plant, L. **-tāpanī**, f., °**panīya**, n., °**panôpanishad**, f., and °**pini**, f. N. of a well-known Upanishad (belonging to the Atharva-veda). **-tāraka-brahmôpanishad**, f. N. of an Upanishad. **-tāraka-mantra-ṭīkā**, f. N. of a Comm. **-tīrtha**, n. N. of a Tīrtha, MBh.; R. &c.; m. N. of various authors and other men (also with *yati*), Cat.; *-māhātmya*, n. N. of wk. **-toshaṇa**, m. (with *śarman*) N. of a modern author, Cat. **-trayodaśâksharī**, f., **-triṇśan-nāma-stotra**, n., **-trailokya-mohana-kavaca**, n. N. of wks. **-tva**, n. the being Rāma, Hariv.; R. **-daṇḍaka**, m. or n. N. of a Stotra. **-datta**, m. N. of a minister of Nṛi-siṇha (king of Mithilā), Cat.; (also with *mantrin*) of various authors, ib. **-dayā**, f. N. of a wk. on Bhakti. **-dayālu**, m. N. of various authors, Cat. **-darśanâdi-tas**, ind. after having seen Rāma, R. **-dāsa**, m. N. of a minister of Akbar, Cat.; of the father of Dharma-gupta, ib.; of the son of Ratnâkara (father of Mahī-dhara; he is also called Rāma-bhakta), ib.; of another man, ib.; (also with *miśra* and *dīkshita*) of various authors, ib. **-durga**, n. N. of a Stotra (attributed to Viśvāmitra). **-dūta**, m. 'R°'s messenger,' N. of Hanumat, L.; a monkey, L.; (*ī*), f. a kind of basil, L. **-deva**, m. N. of R° Dāśarathi, RāmatUp.; (also with *miśra* and *ciram-jīva*) N. of various authors and other men, Cat. **-dvādaśa-nāma-stotra**, n. N. of a Stotra. **-dvādaśī**, f. N. of the 12th day in one of the halves of the month Jyaishṭha, Cat. **-dhara**, m. N. of a man, Vās., Introd. **-dhyāna**, n. N. of wk.; *-stotra*, n. N. of a Stotra. **-nagara**, n. N. of a town, Cat. **-navamī**, f. N. of the 9th day in the light half of the month Caitra (being the birthday of Rāma-candra), RāmatUp.; RTL. 430; *-nirṇaya*, m., *-pūjā*, f., *-vrata-kathā*, f., *-vrata-māhātmya*, n. N. of wks. **-nava-ratna-sāra**, m. N. of wk. **-nāṭaka**, n. = *rāma-candra-nāṭaka*, q. v. **-nātha**, m. 'R's lord,' N. of R° Dāśarathi, W.; (with *hosalâdhîśvara*) of a king of Deva-giri (also called Rāma-candra), Cat.; of a teacher (also called Rāma-candra), ib.; of another man, ib.; (also with *cakra-vartin, vidyā-vācas-pati*, and *siddhânta*) of various authors, ib.; *-stotra*, n. N. of a ch. of the SkandaP. **-nāma**, 'R°'s name' (in comp. for *-nāman*); *-paddhati*, f., *-māhātmya*, n., *lekhana-vidhi*, m., *-lekhanôdyāpana-vidhi*, m. N. of wks.; *-vrata*, n. a partic. religious observance, Cat.; °*mâshṭôttara-śata*, n., °*môdyāpana*, n. N. of wks. **-nārāyaṇa**, m. N. of a man (son of Ghana-śyāma), Cat.; (also with *śarman* and *bhaṭṭâcārya cakra-vartin*) of various authors, ib.; *-jīva*, m. N. of a king, ib. **-nidhi**, m. (with *śarman*) N. of an author, ib. **-nibandha**, m. N. of wk. **-nṛi-pati**, m. N. of a king, Cat. **-nyāyâlaṃkāra**, m. N. of an author, ib. **-pañcadaśī-kalpa-latikā**, f., **-pañcâṅga**, n., **-paṭala**, n., **-paṭṭâbhisheka**, m. N. of wks. **-pati**, m. N. of the father of Vishṇu-pati, Cat.; of an author, ib. **-paddhati**, f., **-para**, m. or n., **-pāda-stava**, m. N. of wks. **-pāla**, m. N. of a man, Rājat. **-putra**, m. patr. of Rudraka, Lalit. **-pura**, n. N. of a village, L. **-pūga**, m. Areca Triandra, L. **-pūjā**, f. worship of R°; *-paddhati*, f., *-vidhāna-paddhati*, f., *-vidhi*, m., *-saraṇi*, f. (= *rāma-paddhati*), *-stotra*, n. N. of wks. **-pūrva-tāpanīya**, n. the first part of the Rāma-tāpanīya, q.v. **-prakāśa**, m. N. of wk. **-prasāda**, m. N. of various authors (also with *tarkâlaṃkāra* and *vidyâlaṃkāra bhaṭṭâcārya*), Cat. **-bāṇa**, m. a species of cane, L.; a partic. medicinal preparation, Bhpr. **-bāla-caritra**, n., **-bāhu-śataka**, n. N. of wks. **-brahmânanda-svāmin**, m. N. of an author, Cat. **-bhakta**, m. a worshipper of R°, RāmatUp.; N. of a man (= *rāma-dāsa*, q.v.), Cat. **-bhaginī**, f. 'R°'s sister,' N. of Pārvatī, L. **-bhadra**, m. N. of R° Dāśarathi, Uttarar.; Kathās.; of two kings, Cat.; of various authors and teachers (also with *dīkshita, bhaṭṭa, bhaṭṭâcārya, miśra, yajvan, yati, sarasvatī, sārvabhauma* &c.), ib.; °*drâmbā*, f. N. of a poetess, ib.; °*drâśrama*, m. N. of two authors, ib. **-bhujaṃga** and **-maṅgala**, n. N. of two Stotras. **-maṇi-dāsa**, m. N. of an author, Cat. **-mantra**, m. n. a verse addressed to R° Dāśarathi, RāmatUp.; *-paṭala*, n., *-paṭhana-vidhi*, m., *-paddhati*, f.; °*trârtha*, m., °*trârtha-nirṇaya*, m. N. of wks. **-maya**, m. (with *śarman*) N. of a Sch. on Mṛicch. and Vikr. **-mahiman**, m. the greatness or glory of R° (°*mnaḥ stotra*, n. N. of a Stotra). **-mānasika-pūjā**, f. N. of wk. **-mohana**, m. N. of an author, Cat. **-yantra**, n. a partic. diagram, RāmatUp.; *-pūjā-paddhati*, f. N. of wk. **-yaśas**, m. N. of a man, Cat. **-rakshā**, f. N. of a Stotra (also called *vajra-pañjara*); *-kavaca*, n., *-stotra*, n. and *-stotra-mālā*, f. N. of wks. **-ratnâkara**, m., **-rasâmṛita**, n. N. of two poems. **-rahasya**, n. or **-rahasyôpanishad**, f. N. of an Upanishad. **-rāja**, m. N. of an author, Bhpr. **-rāma**, m. N. of a preceptor, Cat.; of another man, ib.; (with *nyāyâlaṃkāra*) of a Scholiast. **-rāsa**, m. N. of wk. **-rudra**, m. (with *bhaṭṭa* and with *nyāya-vāg-īśa bhaṭṭâcārya*) N. of two authors, Cat. **-rshi**, m. N. of a Scholiast (also called *-ṛishi*), ib. **-lavaṇa**, n. a kind of salt, L. **-liṅga**, m. N. of two authors, Cat.; *-varṇana*, n. and °*gâmṛita*, n. N. of two poems. **-līlā**, f. N. of the dramatic representation of Sītā's abduction by Rāvaṇa and her recovery by R°-candra (performed at the annual festival which takes place in Northern India in the beginning of October and corresponds to the Durgā-pūjā of Bengal), IW. 365, n. 1; °*mṛita* (°*lām*°), n., *-sūci*, f. and °*lôdaya*, m. N. of wks. **-lekhā**, f. N. of a princess, Rājat. **-vacana**, n., **-vajra-pañjara-kavaca**, n., **-varṇana-**

stotra, n. N. of wks. **-vardhana**, m. N. of a man, Rājat. **-varman**, m. N. of the author of the Tilaka (a Comm. on the Rāmāyaṇa). **-vallabha**, n. cinnamon, L.; m. (with *śarman*) N. of an author, Cat. **-vāṇa**, see *-bāṇa*. **-vijñāpana-stotra**, n. N. of a Stotra. **-vinoda**, m. N. of wk.; *-karaṇa*, n. (also called *pañcâṅga-sādhanôdāharaṇa*), N. of a wk. composed by Rāma-candra in 1614. **-vilāsa-kāvya**, n., **-viśva-rūpa-stotra**, n. N. of wks. **-vīṇā**, f. 'R°'s lute,' a kind of lute (said to be also applicable ironically to the horn blown by Bala-rāma), L. **-vyākaraṇa**, n. N. of a grammar by Vopadeva. **-vratin**, m. pl. N. of a partic. school, Buddh. **-śaṃkara**, m. (also with *rāya*) N. of various authors, Cat. **-śataka**, n. N. of a poem. **-śara**, m. a kind of sugar-cane, L. **-śarman**, m. N. of the author of the Uṇādi-kośa (a metrical wk. on words formed with Uṇādi suffixes), Cat. **-śāstrin**, m. secular N. of Nara-hara-tīrtha (who died in 1214), ib. **-śilā-māhātmya**, n. N. of a ch. of the SkandaP. **-śishya**, m. N. of an author, Cat. **-śītalā**, f. = *ārāma-śītalā*, L. **-śesha**, m. N. of an author, Cat. **-śrī-krama-candrikā**, f. N. of a wk. on Bhakti. **-śrī-pāda**, m. N. of an author, Cat. **-shaḍ-akshara-mantra-rāja**, m., **-shaḍ-akshara-vidhāna**, n., **-shoḍaśa-nāman**, n. N. of wks. **-sakha**, m. 'R°'s friend,' N. of Sugrīva, L. **-saparyā-sopāna**, n., **-sapta-ratna**, n. N. of wks. **-samuddhāra**, m. N. of a man, Kshitīś. **-saras**, n. N. of a sacred lake, Cat. (cf. *-hrada*). **-sahasra-nāman**, n. 'R°'s thousand names,' N. of chs. of the BrahmaP. and LiṅgaP.; °*ma-vivaraṇa*, n., °*ma-stotra*, n. N. of similar wks. **-sāhi**, m. N. of a king, Inscr. **-siṇha**, m. N. of a king (son of Jaya-siṇha), Cat.; *-deva*, m. N. of a king of Mithilā and of the patron of Ratnêśvara, ib.; *-varman*, m. N. of a king of Jaya-pura (who passes as the author of the Dhātu-ratna-mañjarī), ib. **-siddhânta-saṃgraha**, m. N. of a wk. on Bhakti. **-subrahmaṇya**, m. (with *śāstrin*) N. of an author, Cat. **-sūkta**, n. N. of a hymn. **-setu**, m. 'R°'s bridge,' the ridge of coral rocks by which Rāma crossed to Ceylon (now called Adam's bridge, cf. Rāmêśvara below), Cat.; N. of a poem (= *setu-bandha*); *-pradīpa*, m. N. of wk. **-sena**, m. N. of the author of the Rasa-sārâmṛita, Cat. **-senaka**, m. Gentiana Cherayta, L.; Myrica Sapida, L. **-sevaka**, m. N. of a son of Devī-datta, ib.; of an author, ib. **-stava-rāja**, m., **-stuti**, f., **-stotra**, n. N. of wks. **-svasṛi**, f. = *-bhaginī*, L. **-svāmin**, m. N. of a statue of Rāma, Rājat.; of various authors, L. **-hari**, m. N. of an author, Cat. **-hṛidaya**, n. 'R°'s heart,' N. of a wk. on Bhakti (°*yâspada*, n. N. of a Comm. on it); of a ch. of the Adhyātma-rāmāyaṇa (revealing the supposed mythical essence of Rāma). **-hrada**, m. 'R°'s lake,' N. of a sacred bathing-place, MBh.; Hariv.; BhP. **Rāmâkheṭaka**, m. or n. N. of a poem by Padma-nābha. **Rāmâgnicit**, see *rāmâṇḍāra*. **Rāmâgni-ja** (?), m. N. of an author, Cat. **Rāmâṅka-nāṭikā**, f. N. of a drama. **Rāmâtmâikya-prakāśikā**, f. N. of wk. **Rāmâdvaya** and **Rāmâdhāra**, m. N. of two authors, L. **Rāmâdhikaraṇa**, mfn. relating to Rāma, R. **Rāmânanda**, m. N. of a disciple of Rāmânuja (see below) and founder of a subdivision of his sect, W.; (also with *ācārya*, *yati*, *vācas-pati*, *sarasvatī* &c.) of various authors and other men, Cat.; *-tīrtha*, m. N. of a preceptor (also called *tīrtha-svāmin*), ib.; *-rāya* and *-svāmin*, m. N. of two authors, ib.; °*dīya*, n. N. of a Vedânta wk. by Rāmânanda. **Rāmânuja**, m. 'younger brother of Rāma' (this title would be applicable to Kṛishṇa as born after Bala-rāma of the same father); N. of a celebrated Vaishṇava reformer (founder of a particular Vedantic school which taught the doctrine of *Viśishṭâdvaita* or qualified non-duality i. e. that the human spirit is separate and different from the one Supreme Spirit though dependent on it and ultimately to be united with it; he lived at Kāñcī-puram and Śrī-raṅgam in the South of India, in the 12th century, and is believed by his followers to have been an incarnation of Śesha; he is also called Rāmânujâcārya and Yati-rāja; n. or °*jam matam*, Rāmânuja's doctrine), RTL. 119, 448 &c.; (with *dīkshita*) N. of another author, Cat.; *-guru-paramparā*, f., *-grantha*, m., *-campū*, f., *-carita*, n., *-caritra*, n., *-daṇḍaka*, m. or n., *-darśana*, n. N. of wks.; m. N. of an author, Cat.; *-divya-caritra*, n., *-bhāshya-gāmbhīrya*, n., *-mata-khaṇḍana*, n., *-mata-dhvaṇsana*, n., *-mauktika*, n., *-vaṇśâvali*, f., *-vijaya*, m., *-śataka-ṭīkā*, f., *-siddhânta-padavī*, f., *-siddhânta-vijaya*, m., *-siddhânta-saṃgraha*, m., *-su-prabhāta*, n., *-stotra*, n. N. of wks.; *-svāmin*, m. N. of an author, Cat.; °*jârādhana-vidhi*, m., °*jâshṭôttara*, n., °*jīya*, n., °*jīya-siddhânta*, m. N. of wks. **Rāmânushṭubh**, f. N. of a partic. prayer addressed to Rāma, RāmatUp. **Rāmânusmṛiti**, f. N. of a ch. of the BrahmâṇḍaP. **Rāmâbhinanda**, m. N. of a Nāṭaka, Sāh. **Rāmâbhisheka**, m. 'R°'s consecration,' N. of a poem by Keśava Paṇḍita. **Rāmâbhyudaya**, m. N. of a Nāṭaka by Yaśo-varman, Sāh.; of a poem by Veṅkaṭêśa; *-tilaka*, n., *-vyākhyāna*, n. N. of wks. **Rāmâmātya**, m. N. of an author, Cat. **Rāmâyaṇa**, see *rāmāyaṇa*, col. 3. **Rāmârcana**, n. worship of Rāma; *-candrikā*, f., *-dīpikā*, f., *-paddhati*, f., *-ratnâkara*, m., *-vidhi*, m., *-sopāna*, n. N. of wks. **Rāmârcā**, f. N. of a ch. of the Agastya-saṃhitā; *-paddhati*, f. N. of a wk. by Rāmânuja. **Rāmârya**, m. N. of the Guru of Śaṃkara, Cat.; (*ā*), f. N. of a poem by Rāma-candra; *-vijñapti*, f., *-śataka*, n. N. of wks. **Rāmâśrama**, m. N. of various authors (also with *ācārya*), Cat.; °*môddhāra-kośa*, m. N. of a dictionary. **Rāmâśvamedha**, m. 'R°'s horse-sacrifice,' N. of the PadmaP.; °*dhika*, mfn. relating to R°'s h°-s°, Cat. **Rāmâshṭaka**, n. 'eight verses of R°,' N. of various Stotras; *-vyākhyā*, f. N. of wk. **Rāmâshṭaviṇśati-nāma-stotra**, n., **Rāmâshṭôttara-śata-nāman**, n. N. of wks. **Rāmêndra**, m. (with *yati*, *yogin* and *sarasvatī*) N. of 3 teachers, Cat.; *-vana*, m. N. of the Guru of Rāmânanda, ib. **Rāmêśa**, m. (with *bhāratī*) N. of an author, ib.; (with *bhaṭṭa*) of another man, ib.; n. N. of a Liṅga, ib. **Rāmêśvara**, m. (also with *bhaṭṭa*, *bhāratī*, *maithila*, *yogîndra*, *śarman*, *śāstrin*, *śukla* &c.) N. of various authors and other men; n. N. of a Liṅga, RāmatUp.; of a Tīrtha, ib.; of an island (which with its coral reef or bridge of rocks nearly connects the South of India with Ceylon) and of the celebrated Śaiva temple and town on it (this is the place where Rāma is supposed to have crossed to Ceylon and one of the most sacred places of pilgrimage in India), RTL. 443; *-datta*, m. N. of an author, Cat.; *-pūjā*, f., *-stava*, m. N. of wks. **Rāmêshu**, m. 'R°'s arrow,' N. of a species of sugar-cane, L.; of a man, Daś. **Rāmôttara-tāpanīya**, n. the second part of Rāma-tāpanīya, q. v. **Rāmôda**, m. N. of a man, g. *aśvâdi*. **Rāmôdanta**, m. N. of a poem. **Rāmôdaya**, m. N. of a drama. **Rāmodāyana**, m. patr. fr. *rāmôda*, g. *aśvâdi*. **Rāmôpanishad**, f. N. of an Upanishad (°*shat-pañcaka*, n., Cat.) **Rāmôpākhyāna**, n. 'episode of R°,' N. of an abridged story of Rāma in MBh. iii, 15872–16601 (cf. IW. 366). **Rāmôpâdhyāya**, m. N. of a preceptor, Caurap., Introd. **Rāmôpâsaka**, m. a worshipper of Rāma Dāśarathi, Cat. **Rāmôpâsana-krama**, m. N. of wk.

Rāmaka, mfn. (fr. Caus. of √*ram*) delighting, gratifying, Pāṇ. vii, 3, 34; = *ramaka*, enjoying one's self, playing, sporting, Vop.; m. a partic. form of a temple, Hcat.; a partic. mixed caste, Vas. (either 'a Vaidehaka who sews and dyes clothes,' or 'a Māgadha who lives as a messenger,' L.); N. of Rāma Rāghava, AgP.; of a mountain, MBh.

Rāmakāyanā́, m. (wrongly printed °*nā́*), patr., MaitrS.

Rāmaṭha, m. n. Asa Foetida, L.; m. Alangium Hexapetalum, L.; pl. N. of a people, MBh.; (*ī*), f. the resin of Gardenia Gummifera, L.

Rāmaṇa, m. Diospyros Embryopteris, L. (v. l. *ramaṇa*); a tree resembling the Melia Bukayun, L.; (*ā*), f. N. of an Apsaras, R. (v. l. *vāmanā*).

Rāmaṇi, m. patr., Pravar.

Rāmaṇīyaka, n. (fr. *ramaṇīya*) loveliness, charm, beauty, Kāv.; m. or n. N. of a Dvīpa, MBh.; mfn. = *ramaṇīya*, lovely, beautiful, pleasing, L.

Rāmaṇyaka, n. loveliness, beauty, R. (B.)

Rāmala, m. N. of a man, Rājat.

Rāmā, f. (of *rāma*) a lovely or charming woman. **-cakra**, prob. w. r. for *rāma-cakra*, Cat. **-devī**, f. N. of the mother of Jaya-deva, Gīt. **-°liṅgana-kāma** (*rāmāl°*), m. 'longing for the embrace of a beautiful person,' N. of the red-flowering globe-amaranth, L. **-vakshojôpama**, m. 'resembling the breasts of a beautiful woman' (which are not separated from each other), N. of the ruddy goose or Cakra-vāka (q. v.), L.

Rāmâṇḍāra, m. N. of a Sch. on ĀpŚr. (also called Rāmâgnicit).

Rāmāyaṇa, mf(*ī*)n. relating to Rāma (Dāśarathi), ŚārṅgP.; (*ī*), f. the female descendant of the Black One (*rāma*), AV. vi, 83, 3; n. (*Rāmāyaṇa*) N. of Vālmīki's celebrated poem, describing the 'goings' [*ayana*] of Rāma and Sītā (it contains about 24000 verses in 7 books called Kāṇḍas, viz. 1. Bāla-kāṇḍa or Ādi-k°; 2. Ayodhyā-k°; 3. Araṇya-k°; 4. Kishkindhyā-k°; 5. Sundara-k°; 6. Yuddha-k°; 7. Uttara-k°; part of the 1st book and the 7th are thought to be comparatively modern additions; the latter gives the history of Rāma and Sītā after their re-union and installation as king and queen of Ayodhyā, afterwards dramatized by Bhava-bhūti in the Uttara-rāma-caritra; Rāma's character, as described in the Rāmâyaṇa, is that of a perfect man, who bears suffering and self-denial with superhuman patience; the author, Vālmīki, was probably a Brāhman connected with the royal family of Ayodhyā; and although there are three recensions of the poem, all of them go back to a lost original recension, the groundwork of which, contained in books 2–6, in spite of many amplifications and interpolations, may be traced back to one man, and does not, like the Mahābhārata, represent the production of different epochs and minds), MBh.; Hariv. &c. (cf. IW. 335). **-kathā**, f. 'the story of the Rāmāyaṇa,' N. of an abridgment of the Rāmāyaṇa; *-praśna*, m. N. of wk.; *-sāra*, m. or *-sāra-mañjarī*, f. N. of a poem based on the R°, by Kshemêndra (11th century). **-kāla-nirṇaya-candrikā**, f. N. of wk. **-kūṭa-ṭīkā**, f. N. of a Comm. by Rāmânanda-tīrtha. **-campū**, f. N. of a poetical paraphrase of the R° in 7 books (attributed to Bhoja and Kālidāsa, and also called *campū-rāmāyaṇa* or *bhoja-campū*). **-tattva-darpaṇa**, m., **-tātparya-dīpikā**, f., **-tātparya-nirṇaya**, m., **-tātparya-saṃgraha**, m., **-nāṭaka**, n., **-nirvacana**, n., **-paṭhana-phala**, n., **-prabandha**, m., **-bhārata-sāra-saṃgraha**, m., **-mahimâdarśa**, m., **-māhātmya**, n., **-rañjanī**, f., **-rahasya**, n., **-vidhi**, m., **-viveka**, m., **-saṃkshepa**, m., **-saṃgraha**, m., **-sāra**, m., **-sāra-saṃgraha**, m., **-sūtra-dīpikā**, f., **-stotra**, n. N. of wks. **Rāmâyaṇâyodhyā-kāṇḍa**, m. N. of a poem based upon the 2nd book of the R°. **Rāmâyaṇôpanyāsa-śloka**, m. pl. N. of wk.

Rāmâyaṇika, mfn. one who recites the Rāmāyaṇa, Gaṇar.

Rāmâyaṇīya, mfn. relating or belonging to the Rāmāyaṇa, Cat.

Rāmi, m. patr. fr. *rāma*, g. *bāhv-ādi*.

Rāmin. See *kshaṇa-rāmin*.

Rāmila, m. a lover, husband, L.; the god of love, L.; (also °*laka*), N. of a poet, Cat.

Rāmī. See under *rāma*.

Rā́myā (RV.) or **rāmyā́** (AV.), f. night.

रामुष *rāmusha*, m. or n. N. of a place, Rājat.

राम्भ *rāmbha*, m. (fr. 1. *rambha*) the bamboo staff of a religious student, L.

राय 1. *rāya*. See *á-rāya*.

राय 2. *rāya*, m. (at the beginning or end of a proper N. used as a title of honour = *rājan*, of which it is a corruption) a king, prince; N. of a son of Purū-ravas, W. (prob. w. r. for *raya*). **-nara-siṇha-paṇḍita**, m., **-madana-pāla**, m., **-mukuṭa**, m., **-m-bhaṭṭa**, m. N. of authors, Cat. **-raṅgāla**, n. (in music) a kind of dance, Saṃgīt. **-rāghava**, m. N. of a king (patron of Raghu-nātha), Cat. **-vaṅkola**, m. (in music) a kind of measure, Saṃgīt. **-vaṅgāla**, see *raṅgāla*. **-siṇhôtsava**, m. N. of a medical wk. by Rāyasiṇha (also called *vaidyaka-sāra-saṃgraha*).

रायण *rāyaṇa*, n. = *pīḍā*, L.

Rāyaṇêndra-sarasvatī, f. N. of a Scholiast, Cat.

रायभाटी *rāyabhāṭī*, f. the stream of a river, L. (cf. *raya*).

रायस्काम *rāyas-kāma* &c. See p. 888, col. 1.

रायाणनीय *rāyāṇanīya*, m. N. of a preceptor, Cat. (v. l. *rāṇāyanīya*).

रायान *rāyāna* (?), m. N. of a cow-herd, Cat. (v. l. *rāyana*).

रायोवाज *rāyo-vāja* &c. See p. 888, col. 1.

रारा *rārā*, *rārīya*. See *rāḍhā*, °*ḍhīya*.

राल rāla, rālaka or rāli, m. the resin of Shorea Robusta, L.

Rālakārya (?), m. Shorea Robusta, L.

राव rāva, m. (√1. ru) a cry, shriek, roar, yell, any sound or noise, MBh.; Kāv. &c.

Rāvaṇa, mfn. (fr. Caus.) causing to cry (with gen. or ifc.; only in this sense to explain the name of the famous Rākshasa), MBh.; R. &c.; m. N. of the ruler of Laṅkā or Ceylon and the famous chief of the Rākshasas or demons whose destruction by Rāma-candra forms the subject of the Rāmāyaṇa (as son of Viśravas he was younger brother of Kubera, but by a different mother, Ilavilā being the mother of Kubera, and Keśinī of the three other brothers, Rāvaṇa, Vibhīshaṇa, and Kumbha-karṇa; he is one of the worst of the many impersonations of evil common in Hindū mythology; he has ten heads and twenty arms, symbolizing strength; this power was, as usual, acquired by self-inflicted austerities, which had obtained from Brahmā a boon, in virtue of which R° was invulnerable by gods and divine beings of all kinds, though not by men or a god in human form; as Vishṇu became incarnate in Rāma-candra to destroy R°, so the other gods produced innumerable monkeys, bears, and various semi-divine animals to do battle with the legions of demons, his subjects, under Khara, Dūshaṇa, and his other generals), MBh.; R.; Hariv. &c. (IW. 353); patr. fr. *ravaṇa*, g. *śivâdi*; N. of a prince of Kaśmīra, Rājat.; of various authors, Cat.; (*ī*), f. (with *cikitsā*) N. of a medical wk.; n. the act of screaming &c., MW.; N. of a Muhūrta, Cat. **-gaṅgā**, f. 'R°'s Ganges,' N. of a river in Laṅkā, GāruḍaP. **-caritra**, n., **-bhaiṭ** (or *chalâkshara*), N. of wks. **-vadha**, m. 'killing of R°,' original N. of the Bhaṭṭi-kāvya. **-vaha**, m. (Prākṛit = prec.) another N. of the Setu-bandha (q.v.) **-sūdana**, m. 'destroyer of R°,' N. of Rāma, L. **-hasra**, m. or n. a partic. stringed instrument, L., Sch. **-hrada**, m. N. of a lake (from which the Śata-dru or Sutlej takes its rise), Buddh. **Rāvaṇâri**, m. 'R°'s enemy,' N. of Rāma, L. **Rāvaṇārjunīya**, n. N. of a grammatical poem, by Bhaumaka Bhaṭṭa (quoted in Kāś.)

Rāvaṇi, m. (patr. fr. *rāvaṇa*, g. *taulvaly-ādi*), N. of Indra-jit, MBh.; R.; of Siṇha-nāda, Bālar.; of any son of Rāvaṇa (pl. the sons of R°), Bhaṭṭ.

2. **Rāvan**, mfn. (for 1. see p. 871, col. 3) crying, sounding (in *bṛihad-r°*, q.v.)

Rāvita, mfn. (fr. Caus.) sounded, made to resound, filled with sound or noise, MBh.; R.; VarBṛS.; n. sound, noise, R.

Rāvin, mf(*iṇī*)n. screaming, crying, roaring, bellowing, MBh.; R.; VarBṛS.

रावट् rávaṭ, ind. (a word occurring in a partic. formula), MaitrS.

रावौट rāvauṭa, m. N. of a royal race, Cat.

राश् rāś, v.l. for √*rās*, q.v.

राशभ rāśabha, w.r. for *rāsabha*.

राशि rāśí, m. (L. also f.; once m.c. in R. *ī*, f.; derivation doubtful, but cf. Uṇ. iv, 32) a heap, mass, pile, group, multitude, quantity, number, RV. &c. &c.; (in arithm.) a sum or the figure or figures put down for an operation (such as multiplying, dividing &c.), Col.; a measure of quantity (= *droṇa*), ŚārṅgS.; a sign of the zodiac (as being a certain sum or quantity of degrees), one-twelfth part of the ecliptic, an astrological house, MBh.; VarBṛS. &c. (cf. IW. 178); a heap of corn, L.; N. of an Ekâha, ŚrS. **-gata**, mfn. placed in a heap, heaped, piled up, MW.; summed up, computed, algebraic or arithmetical, Col. **-cakra**, n. the zodiacal circle, zodiac, Col.; N. of a partic. mystical circle, Cat. **-traya**, n. 'triad of numbers,' (in arithm.) the rule of three. **-dāśā-phala**, n. N. of wk. **-nāman**, n. a name given to a child taken from the Rāśi under which he is born, MW. **-pa**, m. the regent of an astrological house, VarBṛS. **-pravibhāga**, m. a division or distribution of the 12 signs of the zodiac under the 28 Nakshatrás (N. of VarBṛS. cii). **-prâyaś-citta**, n. N. of wk. **-bhāga**, m. a fraction, Col.; *°gânubandha*, m. the addition of a fr°, ib.; *°gâpavāha*, m. the subtraction of a fr°, ib. **-bheda**, m. a portion or division of a zodiacal sign or astrological house, VarBṛS. **-bhoga**, m. the passage of the sun or moon or any planet through the sign of a planet, W. **-marāya**, n. N. of two Sāmans, ĀrshBr. **-vyavahāra**, m. (in arithm.) the method for finding the quantity contained in a heap, Līl. **-śas**, ind. in heaps, Śiś. **-stha**, mfn. standing in a heap, heaped up, accumulated, Kathās.

Rāśika, mfn. (ifc. after a numeral) consisting of a partic. sum or number of quantities, Col. (cf. *rāśi*).

Rāśī, in comp. for *rāśi*. **-karaṇa**, n. the making into a heap, piling together, Pāṇ. iii, 3, 41, Sch.; *-bhāshya*, n. N. of a wk. of the Pāśupatas (also called *-kara-bhāshya*), Sarvad.; Cat. **-√kṛi**, P. Ā. *-karoti*, *-kurute*, to form into a heap, pile up, accumulate, Kathās. **-kṛita**, mfn. made into a heap, heaped up, accumulated, R. **-√bhū**, P. *-bhavati*, to become a heap or mass, be piled up or accumulated, Megh. **-bhūta**, mfn. become a heap, piled up, accumulated, ib.; *-dhana*, mfn. one who has piled up treasures, Rājat.

Rāśy, in comp. for *rāśi*. **-aṇsa**, m. = *navâṇsa*, q.v. **-adhipa**, m. the regent of an astrological house, VarBṛS. **-abhidhāna**, n. N. of wk.

राष्ट्र rāshṭrá, m. n. (fr. √*rāj*; g. *ardharcâdi*; m. only MBh. xiii, 3050) a kingdom (Mn. vii, 157 one of the 5 Prakṛitis of the state), realm, empire, dominion, district, country, RV. &c. &c.; a people, nation, subjects, Mn.; MBh. &c.; any public calamity (as famine, plague &c.), affliction, L.; m. N. of a king (son of Kāśi), BhP. **-karshaṇa**, n. distressing or oppressing a kingdom, Mn. vii, 112. **-kāma** (*rāshṭrá-*), mfn. desiring a k°, TS. **-kūṭa**, m. N. of a man, HPariś.; of a people, Inscr. **-gupti**, f. protection of a k°, MBh. **-gopa**, m. a guardian or protector of a k°, AitBr. **-tantra**, n. system of government, administration, R. **-dá**, mfn. conferring dominion, MaitrS. **-dipsú**, mfn. intending to injure a k°, menacing a country, AV. **-devī**, f. N. of the wife of Citra-bhānu, Vās., Introd. **-pata**, mfn. (fr. next), g. *aśvapaty-ādi*. **-pati** (*rāshṭrá-*), m. 'lord of a k°,' a sovereign, ŚBr.; MBh. **-pāla**, m. 'protector of a k°,' a sovereign, BhP.; N. of a son of Ugra-sena, Hariv.; Pur.; of another man, Buddh.; (*ī*), f. N. of a daughter of Ugra-sena, Hariv.; Pur.; *°la-paripṛicchā*, f. N. of wk. **-pālikā**, f. = *-pālī*, BhP. **-bhaṅga**, m. breaking up or dissolution of a k°, Dhūrtas. **-bhaya**, n. fear for a k°, danger threatening a country, VarBṛS. **-bhṛit**, m. 'bearing sway,' (prob.) a tributary prince, AV.; AitBr.; Kāṭh.; N. of dice, AV.; of a son of Bharata, BhP.; f. N. of an Apsaras, AV.; of partic. prayers and oblations (*-tvá*, n.), TS.; ŚBr.; GṛŚrS. **-bhṛiti**, f. (TS.), **-bhṛitya**, n. (AV.) maintenance of government or authority. **-bheda**, m. division of a k°, Kathās. **-bhedin**, m. 'subverter of a k°,' a rebel, ib. **-mukhya**, m. the chief of a k° or country, Daś. **-vardhana**, mfn. increasing a k°, exalting dominion, R.; m. N. of a minister of Daśa-ratha and Rāma, ib. **-vāsin**, m. an inhabitant of a k°, subject, L. **-viplava**, m. calamity or ruin of a k°, Cāṇ. (v.l.) **-vivṛiddhi**, f. increase or prosperity of a k°, VarBṛS. **-saṃvarga**, m. N. of a Pariś. of the AV. **Rāshṭrânta-pāla**, m. the protector of the borders of a k°, Kām. **Rāshṭrâbhivṛiddhi**, f. increase or exaltation of a kingdom, VarBṛS.

Rāshṭraka (ifc.) = *rāshṭra*, a kingdom, country &c., MBh.; mfn. dwelling in a k° or c°, BhP.; (*ikā*), f. a kind of solanum (= *bṛihatī*), L.

Rāshṭri, f. = *rāshṭrī*, a female ruler, proprietress, Gobh.

Rāshṭrika, mfn. belonging to or inhabiting a kingdom, MW.; m. an inhabitant of a k°, subject, Mn. x, 61; the ruler of a k°, governor, Hariv.

Rāshṭrín, mfn. possessing or occupying a kingdom, ŚBr.

Rāshṭriya, mfn. relating to or dealing with a kingdom, Pāṇ. iv, 3, 87, Sch.; m. an heir-apparent or pretender, MaitrS. (v.l.); a king's brother-in-law (also *-syāla*), Mṛicch.; Śak.

Rāshṭrī, f. a female ruler or sovereign or proprietress, RV.; AitBr.

Rāshṭriya, mfn. (cf. *rāshṭriya*) belonging to a country or kingdom, ŚBr.; m. an heir-apparent or pretender, MaitrS.; a king's brother-in-law, MBh.

रास 1. rās (cf. √1. *ras*), cl. 1. Ā. (Dhātup. xvi, 25) *rāsate* (pf. *rarāse*, Kāv.; fut. *rāsitā*, *rāsishyate*, Gr.; aor. *arāsishṭa*, ib.), to howl, cry, MBh.; R. &c.: Intens. *rārāsyate*, to cry aloud, utter loud lamentations (only p. *rārāsyamāna*; B. *vāvāśyamāna*), MBh.

Rāsa, m. uproar, noise, din, L.; N. of a partic. rustic dance practised by cowherds, (esp.) the dance practised by Kṛishṇa and the Gopīs, Hariv.; Pur.; Gīt. &c. (cf. *rāsaka*); any sport or play, L.; a legend (?), in *narmadā-sundarī-r°* (q.v.); = *bhāshā-śṛiṅkhalaka*, L. **-krīḍā**, f. = *-goshṭhī*, BhP.; Pañcar.; N. of a ch. of the BhP.; *-māhātmya*, n. N. of wk. **-gītikā**, f. N. of a ch. of the Rāsôllāsa-tantra. **-goshṭhī**, f. the sportive dance of Kṛishṇa and the cowherdesses, BhP. **-pañcâdhyāyī**, f. N. of a ch. of the BhP. **-praṇetṛi**, m. leader of the dance called Rāsa, Hariv. **-mañjarī**, f. N. of wk. **-maṇḍala**, n. Kṛishṇa's circular dancing ground, BhP.; Pañcar. **-mahôtsava**, m. = *-goshṭhī*, Pañcar. **-yātrā**, f. a festival in honour of Kṛishṇa and his dances with the Gopīs (kept on the full moon of the month Kārttika), W.; *-paddhati*, f., *-viveka*, m. N. of wks. **-vilāsa**, m., **-sundara-mahākāvya**, n. N. of wks. **Rāse-rasa**, m. = *utsava* or = *parihāsa*, L. **Rāsôllāsa-tantra**, n. N. of a Tantra.

Rāsaka, m. a kind of dance, Hcar.; a kind of song, ib.; (in music) a kind of measure, Saṃgīt.; m. n. a kind of dramatic entertainment, Sāh.

1. **Rāsana**. See *ghora-r°*.

Rā́sabha, m. (√1. *rās*) 'the brayer,' an ass, jackass, donkey, RV. &c. &c.; (*ī*), f. a she-ass, MBh.; Pañcat. **-dhūsara**, mfn. grey as an ass, light brown, MW. **-yukta**, mfn. yoked with asses, R. **-vandinī**, f. Arabian jasmine, W. **-sena**, m. N. of a king, Inscr. **Rāsabhârāva**, m. the braying of asses, MBh. **Rāsabhâruṇa**, mfn. brown as an ass, ib.

Rāsin. See *ghora-rāsin*.

Rāsya. See *go-rāsya*.

रास् 2. rās. See √1. *rā*.

रासन 2. rāsana, mfn. (fr. *rasanā*) relating to or perceptible by the tongue, savoury, palatable, Pāṇ. iv, 2, 92, Sch.

रासभ rāsabha. See above.

रासायन rāsāyana, mfn. (fr. *rasâyana*) relating to an elixir &c., Suśr.

रास्ना rā́snā, f. a girdle (cf. *raśanā*, *raśmi*), VS.; ŚBr.; the ichneumon plant, Suśr.; ŚārṅgS. (v.l. *rāshṇā*); N. of various other plants (Mimosa Octandra; Acampe Papillosa &c.), L.; bdellium, Bhpr.

Rāsnākā, f. a small girdle or band, Kāṭh.

Rāsnāvá, mfn. having a girdle, girdled, girt, ŚBr.

रास्प rāspa. See *rāspira* below.

रास्पिन rāspiná, mfn. (prob. connected with √1. *ras*, 1. *rās*, *rap*, and said to mean 'sounding, noisy, loud,' RV. i, 122, 4; cf. Nir. vi, 21).

Rāspirá, mfn. (prob.) id., RV. v, 43, 14 (Sāy. 'the Hotṛi who holds the sacrificial ladle,' fr. a word *rāspa* = 2. *jukū*).

राहक्षति rāhakshati, m. patr., g. *pailâdi* (Kāś. *rohakshiti*).

राहडी rāhaḍi, f. (in music) a kind of composition, Saṃgīt.

राहवि rāhavi, °viya. See p. 880, col. 1.

राहित्य rāhitya, n. (fr. *rahita*, ifc.) destituteness, non-possession, the being destitute of or free from or without, Sāh.; Sarvad.

राहिल rāhila, m. N. of a man, Rājat.

राहु rāhú, m. (fr. √*rabh*; cf. *graha* and √*grah*) 'the Seizer,' N. of a Daitya or demon who is supposed to seize the sun and moon and thus cause eclipses (he is fabled as a son of Vipra-citti and Siṇhikā and as having a dragon's tail; when the gods had churned the ocean for the Amṛita or nectar of immortality, he disguised himself like one of them and drank a portion; but the Sun and Moon revealed the fraud to Vishṇu, who cut off Rāhu's head, which thereupon became fixed in the stellar sphere, and having become immortal through drinking the Amṛita, has ever since wreaked its vengeance on the Sun and Moon by occasionally swallowing them; while at the same time the tail of the demon became Ketu [q.v.] and gave birth to a numerous progeny of comets and fiery meteors; in astron. Rāhu is variously regarded as a dragon's head, as the ascending node of the moon [or point where the moon intersects the ecliptic in passing northwards], as one of the planets [cf. *graha*], and as the regent of the south-west quarter [Laghuj.]; among Buddhists many demons are called Rāhu), AV. &c. &c.; an eclipse or (rather) the moment of the beginning of an occultation or obscuration, VarBṛS. **-kanya**, w.r. for *rāhūgaṇya*, q.v. **-kālāvalī**, f. N. of wk. **-ketu**, m. du. R° and Ketu, MBh. (cf. IW. 180, n. 1; RTL. 344). **-gata**, mfn. 'gone to Rāhu,' darkened, eclipsed, VarBṛS. **-gamya**, mfn. liable to be obscured or eclipsed, L. **-grasana**, n. 'the being swallowed by R°,' an eclipse, Kāv. **-grasta**, mfn. 'swallowed by R°,' eclipsed; *-niśā-kara*, mfn. (a night) whose moon has been sw° by R°, MBh. **-graha**, m. the demon (lit. 'seizer') R°, Kāv. **-grahaṇa**, n. 'seizure by R°,' an eclipse, R. **-grāsa** or **-grāha**, m. = *-grasana* or *-grahaṇa*, L. **-cāra**, m. N. of two wks. **-cchattra**, n. green ginger, L. **-darśana**, n. 'appearance of R°,' an eclipse, Āpast. **-parvan**, n. the day or period of an eclipse, MW. **-pīḍā**, f. 'seizure by R°,' an eclipse, ib. **-pūjā**, f. 'worship of R°,' N. of wk. **-bhedin**, m. 'severing (the body of) R°,' N. of Vishṇu, L. **-mukha**, n. R°'s mouth, Mṛicch. **-mūrdha-bhid** or **-mūrdha-hara**, m. 'R°'s decapitator,' N. of Vishṇu, L. **-ratna**, n. 'R°'s jewel,' the hyacinth, L. **-śatru**, m. 'R°'s enemy,' N. of Vishṇu (according to others 'the moon'), R. ii, 114, 3. **-samsparśa**, m. 'contact with R°,' an eclipse, L. **-suta**, m. pl. 'R°'s sons,' N. of partic. Ketus or comets &c., VarBṛS. **-sûkta**, n. N. of wk. **-sūtaka**, n. 'birth or appearance of R°,' an eclipse, Yājñ. **Rāhûcchishṭa** or **Rāhûtsṛishṭa**, n. Allium Ascalonicum, L.

Rāhavi, m. patr. fr. *rāhu*, g. *pailâdi*.

Rāhavīya, mfn. relating or belonging to Rāhu, Bālar.

Rāhula, m. N. of a man, Pravar.; of a son of Gautama Buddha, MWB. 25; 193; of a son of Śuddhodana, VP. (v. l. for *rātula*); of a minister, Buddh. **-bhadra**, m. = *rāhula*, N. of a son of Gautama B°, Buddh. **-sū**, f. 'father of R°,' N. of Gautama B°, L.

Rāhulaka, m. N. of a poet, Cat.

Rāhulata (?), m. N. of a Buddhist patriarch.

राहूगण *rāhūgaṇa*, mfn. (fr. *rāhūgaṇya*), g. *kaṇvâdi*; m. patr. fr. *rahū-gaṇa*, ŚBr.; ĀśvŚr.

Rāhūgaṇya, m. patr. fr. *rahū-gaṇa*, g. *gargâdi*.

रि 1. *ri*. See √1. *ri*.

रि 2. *ri* (ifc.) = 3. *rai* (cf. *ati-ri*, *bṛihad-ri*).

रि 3. *ri* (for *ṛishabha*), the second note of the Hindū gamut.

रिःफ *riḥpha*, n. (for ῥιφή) N. of the 12th astrological house, VarBṛS.

रिक्णस् *rikṇas*, n., w. r. for *rekṇas*, Uṇ. iv, 198, Sch.

रिक्त *riktá*, *rikthá* &c. See col. 2.

रिक्वन् *ríkvan*, m. = *stena*, a thief, Naigh. iii, 24.

रिक्षा *rikshā*, f. a nit (= *likshā*), L.; a mote in a sunbeam, W.

रिख *rikh*, cl. 1. P. *rekhati*, to go, move, Dhātup. v, 33, Vop. (cf. √*riṅkh*); cl. 6. P. *rikhati*, to scratch, scrape (cf. *ā*-√*rikh* and √*likh*).

रिङ्ख *riṅkh* (cf. prec.), cl. 1. P. (Dhātup. v, 33, Vop.) *riṅkhati*, to go, move, crawl (said of young children), BhP.; to go or advance slowly, Cat.

Riṅkha, m. (only L.) disappointing, deceiving; a horse's hoof; one of a horse's paces; dancing; sliding; slipping; a hammock, swing; (*ā*), f. (only L.) one of a horse's paces; dancing; Carpopogon Pruriens.

Riṅkhaṇa, n. the crawling of children, L.

Riṅkhola or °**lana**, n. a hammock, swing, L.

रिङ्ग *riṅg* (cf. √*riṅkh*), cl. 1. P. (Dhātup. v, 47) *riṅgati* (pr. p. *riṅgat* or *riṅgamāṇa*), to move, creep, crawl, advance with difficulty or slowly, Inscr.; BhP.; Pañcar.: Caus. *riṅgayati*, to cause to creep, BhP.

Riṅgaṇa, n. = *riṅkhaṇa*, L.; (*ī*), f. a species of plant (= *kaivartikā*), L.; Phaseolus Trilobus, L.

Riṅgi, f. going, motion, BhP.

Riṅgita, n. motion, surging (of waves), Chandom.

Riṅgin, mf(*iṇī*)n. creeping, crawling (said of young children), Hariv.

रिच *ric*, cl. 7. P. Ā. (Dhātup. xxix, 4) *riṇákti*, *riṅkte*, cl. 1. P. (Dhātup. xxxiv, 10) *recati*; cl. 4. Ā. (cf. Pass.) *ricyate* (ep. also °*ti*; pf. *riréca*, *riricé*, RV. &c. &c.: *riricyām*, *arirecīt*, RV.; p. *ririkvás*, *riricāná*, ib.; aor. *áraik*, RV.; *arikshi*, ib.; Br.; *aricat*, Kāv.; fut. *rektā*, Gr., *rekshyati*, °*te*, Br. &c.; inf. *rektum*, Gr.), to empty, evacuate, leave, give up, resign, RV.; to release, set free, ib.; to part with i.e. sell ('for,' instr.), ib. iv, 24, 9; to leave behind, take the place of (acc.), supplant, AV.; TS.; Br.; to separate or remove from (abl.), Bhaṭṭ.: Pass. *ricyáte* (aor. *areci*), to be emptied &c., RV.; ŚBr. &c.; to be deprived of or freed from (abl.), Vikr.; BhP.; to be destroyed, perish, R.: Caus. (or cl. 10, Dhātup. xxxiv, 10; aor. *arīricat*), to make empty, Daś.; to discharge, emit (as breath, with or scil. *mārutam*), AmṛitUp.; Pañcar.; to abandon, give up, Kāv.: Desid. *ririkshati*, °*te*, Gr.: Intens. *rericyate*, *rerekti*, ib. [Cf. Zd. *ric*; Gk. λείπω, λοιπός; Lat. *linquo*, *licet*; Lith. *likti*; Goth. *leihwan*; Angl. Sax. *león*; Eng. *loan*, *lend*; Germ. *lîhan*, *leihen*.]

Riktá, mfn. (accord. to Pāṇ. vi, 1, 208, also *rikta*) emptied, empty, void, AV. &c. &c.; bared (as an arm), Megh.; hollow, hollowed (as the hands), Cat.; poor, indigent, MBh.; BhP.; idle, worthless, Pāṇ. viii, 1, 8, Sch.; (ifc.) devoid or destitute of, free from, without, MBh.; Kāv. &c.; m. (in augury) N. of one of the four wagtails which serve for omens, VarBṛS.; of a man, Pat.; (*ā*), f. (scil. *tithi*) N. of the 4th, 9th, or 14th day of the lunar fortnight, VarBṛS. (cf. *riktârka*); n. an empty place, desert, wilderness, wood, L. **-kumbhá**, n. pl. '(the sound of) an empty vessel,' (prob.) empty or senseless language, AV. **-kṛit**, mfn. making empty, causing a vacuum, VarBṛS. **-guru**, see Pāṇ. vi, 2, 42. **-tā**, f. emptiness, vacuity, Śiś.; Kathās. **-pāṇi**, mfn. empty-handed, having nothing in the hand, Āpast.; bringing no present, ib.; MBh. &c. **-bhāṇḍa**, n. an empty vessel, Mn.; VarBṛS.; having no vessels or effects, W. **-mati**, mfn. empty-minded, thinking of nothing, BhP. **-hasta**, mfn. empty-handed, bringing no present, Pañcad.; Kathās.; carrying away no pr°, Cāṇ. **-hāra**, w. r. for *riktha-h°*, q.v., BhP. **Riktârka**, m. a Sunday falling on one of the Rikta days, Cat.

Riktaka, mfn. empty, void, L.; unladen, unburdened, Mn. viii, 404.

Rikti, in comp. for *rikta*. **-√kṛi**, P. *-karoti*, to make empty or void, Kāv.; to leave, quit, Hcar.; Kād.; to remove, take away, Bhaṭṭ., Sch.; to steal, MW.; to get back, recover, ib. **-kṛita-hṛidaya**, mfn. emptied or deprived of heart, Pañcat.

Rikthá, n. (sometimes written *ṛik°*) property left at death, inheritance, RV.; AitBr. &c.; any prop°, possessions, wealth, Mn.; BhP.; gold, MW. **-grāha**, mfn. receiving an inheritance, inheriting property; m. an inheritor, heir, Yājñ. **-jāta**, n. the aggregate of a prop°, collected estate (of a deceased person), MW. **-bhāgin** (Mn.) or **-bhāj** (ib.; Gaut.; ŚāṅkhGṛ., Sch.), mfn. inheriting or sharing property, an heir. **-vibhāga**, m. the division or sharing of (a deceased person's) prop°; a share in an inheritance, Cat. **-hara** (Mn.) or **-hāra** (BhP.), mfn. or m. = *-grāha* above. **-hārin**, mfn. or m. id., Yājñ., Sch.; m. a maternal uncle, W.; the seed of the Indian fig-tree, ib. **Rikthâda**, mfn. receiving an inheritance; m. a son and heir, BhP.

Rikthin, mfn. or m. inheriting property, an heir, Yājñ.; Dāyabh.; mfn. possessing property, wealthy, W.; m. a testator, Yājñ.

Rikthīya, mfn. in *a-r°*, q. v.

Ririkyás, **riricāná**. See above under √*ric*.

Reka, **reca**, **recita** &c. See p. 887, col. 1.

रिज् *rij* (cf. √1. *riñj*), cl. 1. Ā. *rejate*, to fry, parch, Dhātup. vi, 19, Vop.

रिटि *riṭi*, f. (only L.) the crackling or roaring of flames; a musical instrument; black salt (cf. *bhṛiṅgi-* and *bhṛiṅgī-r°*).

रिणिनगर *riṇi-nagara*, n. N. of a town, Cat.

रिण्व् *riṇv*, cl. 1. P. *riṇvati*, to go, Dhātup. xv, 86 (v. l. *rimb*).

रित् *rít*, mfn. (√*ri*, *rī*) running, flowing, RV. vi, 37, 4 (Sāy. = *gantṛi*).

रितक्वन् *ritakvan*, m. a thief, Naigh. iii, 24 (v.l. for *takvan*).

रिद्ध *riddha*, mfn. (prob. for *ṛiddha*) ripe (as grain), L.

रिधम *ridhama*, m. spring, L.; love, L.

रिप् 1. *rip* (cf. √*lip*; only pf. *riripúḥ*), to smear, adhere to (loc.), RV. (cf. *riptá*); to deceive, cheat, ib.

2. **Rip**, f. injury, fraud, deceit, RV.; an injurer, deceiver, enemy, ib.; the earth (?), RV. iii, 5, 5; x, 79, 3 (Sāy.; cf. Naigh. i, 1).

Ripú, mfn. deceitful, treacherous, false, RV.; m. a deceiver, cheat, rogue, ib.; an enemy, adversary, foe, Mn.; MBh. &c.; (in astrol.) a hostile planet, VarBṛS.; N. of the 6th astrological house, ib.; a gall-nut, L.; N. of a son of Ślishṭi, Hariv.; of a son of Yadu and Babhru, Pur. **-kāla**, m. the god of death (as invoked against enemies), Jātakam. **-ghātin**, mfn. slaying an en°, L.; (*inī*), f. Abrus Precatorius, W. **-ghna**, mfn. killing an en°, VarBṛS. **-m-jaya**, mfn. conquering a foe, Cāṇ.; BhP.; m. N. of several kings, Hariv.; Pur.; of an author, Cat. **-tā**, f. enmity, hostility, Hit. **-nipātin**, mfn. causing an enemy to fall, destroying a foe, MBh. **-paksha**, mfn. being on the side of an en°; m. an en°, Mcar. vii, ½ (perhaps w.r. for *-pakshe*, 'on the side of the en°'). **-bala**, n. an en°'s army, VarBṛS. **-bhaya**, n. fear or danger from an en°, ib. **-bhavana**, n. (ib.) or **-bhāva**, m. (Cat.) N. of the 6th astrological house. **-mardin**, mfn. harassing or destroying enemies, Hariv. **-malla**, m. N. of a king, Śatr. **-rakta**, n. an en°'s blood, Pañcat. **-rakshin**, mfn. preserving from an en°, MW. **-rākshasa**, m. N. of an elephant, Kathās. **-rāśi**, m. the 6th astrological house, VarYogay. **-varjita**, mfn. freed from an en°, MW. **-vaśa**, mfn. subject to an en°; *-tva*, n. subjection to an en°, VarBṛS. **-sūdana**, mfn. destroying en°s, R. **-sthāna**, n. the 6th astrological house, Cat.

Riptá, mfn. smeared, adhering to (loc.), RV. i, 162, 9. **-lepa**, m. what sticks or adheres (to the hand), ĀpŚr.

Riprá, n. dirt, impurity (lit. and fig.), RV.; AV.; m. N. of a son of Ślishṭi, Hariv. (v.l. *vipra*); mfn. vile, bad, W. **-vāhá**, mfn. removing impurity or sin, RV.

Repa, mfn. low, vile, wicked, cruel, savage, L.

Répas, n. a spot, stain, fault, RV.; mfn. = prec. L.; miserly, niggardly, L.

रिफ् *riph*, cl. 6. P. (Dhātup. xxviii, 23) *riphati* (p. *-rephat*, ŚāṅkhBr.; pf. *rirepha* &c., Gr.; ind. p. *rephitvā*, Pāṇ. i, 2, 23, Sch.), to snarl, AV.; (only L.) to speak or boast (*kathane* or *katthane*); to blame; to fight; to give; to hurt, kill (cf. √*rimph*): Pass. *riphyate*, to be murmured or spoken in a guttural or burring manner (like the letter *r*); to have or take the pronunciation of the letter *r*, ĀśvŚr. (cf. *repha*).

Riphitá, mfn. pronounced with a guttural roll (as the letter *r*), burred, rolled in the throat like *r*, VS.; ŚāṅkhŚr.

Repha, m. a burring guttural sound, the letter *r* (as so pronounced), Prāt.; ŚrS.; a word, BhP.; (in prosody) a cretic (– ◡ –), Piṅg.; passion, affection of the mind, L.; mfn. low, vile, contemptible, L. (cf. *repa*). **-vat**, mfn. giving a burring sound, having the sound of *r* (said of the vowel *ṛi*), RPrāt. **-vipulā**, f. a kind of metre (= *ra-v°*), Piṅg., Sch. **-samdhi**, m. the euphonic junction of *r*, Prāt.

Rephas, mfn. (only L.) low, vile; wicked; cruel; niggardly (cf. *repas*).

Rephin, mfn. having or containing the letter *r*, having the nature of *r*, ĀśvŚr.

रिभ् *ribh* or *rebh*, cl. 1. P. *rébhati* (accord. to Dhātup. x, 22, Ā. °*te*; pf. *rirébha*, RV.; aor. *arebhīt*, Gr.; fut. *rebhitā*, *rebhishyati*, ib.), to crackle (as fire), RV.; to creak (as a car), TS.; to murmur (as fluids), RV.; to chatter, talk aloud, AitBr.; to shout, sing, praise, RV.

Ribhvan, m. = *stena*, a thief, Naigh. iii, 24 (cf. *rihvan*).

Rebhá, mfn. creaking, crackling, murmuring, resounding, RV.; m. a praiser, panegyrist, celebrator, ib.; AV.; a prattler, chatterer, VS.; N. of a Ṛishi (who was cast into a well by the Asuras and lay there for ten nights and nine days until rescued by the Aśvins; he is the supposed author of ṚV. viii, 97, having the patr. *Kāśyapa*), RV.; (*ā*), f. = *śobhā*, Āpast., Sch. (cf. *rebhāya*). **-sūnu**, m. du. two sons of Rebha, authors of RV. ix, 99; 100.

Rebhaṇa, n. the lowing of kine, L.

Rebhāya, Nom. P. °*yati*, to shine, beam, Āpast.

Rebhin, mfn. (ifc.) causing to resound, Śiś.

Rebhila or °**laka**, m. N. of a man, Mṛicch.

रिमेद *rimeda*, m. = *ari-meda*, L.

रिम्फ् *rimph* (cf. √*riph*), cl. 6. P. *rimphati*, to hurl, kill, Dhātup. xxviii, 30.

Rimpha, n. the zodiac, W.

रिम्ब् *rimb*. See √*riṇv*.

रिय *riya*, Nom. P. °*yati* (fr. *rai*), Pat. (cf. √1. *rī*).

रिरंसा *riraṅsā*, f. (fr. Desid. of √*ram*) desire of pleasure or of sexual enjoyment, lasciviousness, lustfulness, MBh.; Kathās.; Pur.

Riraṅsu, mfn. wishing for sport or sexual pleasure, wanton, lustful, Hariv.; Kāv.; Suśr.; wishing to enjoy (any one, acc.) carnally, HPariś.

Riramayishu, mfn. (fr. Desid. of Caus.) wishing to cause or give (sexual) pleasure, Uṇ. i, 99, Sch.

रिरक्षिषा *rirakshishā* (fr. Desid. of √*raksh*) the desire to watch or guard or protect or maintain, Hariv.; (ungrammatical form *rirakshā*, BhP.) °**kshishu**, mfn. desiring to watch &c., MBh. (°*kshu* incorrect, BhP.)

रिरिक्षु *ririkshu*. See below.

रिरी *rirī*, f. yellow or pale brass, prince's metal, L. (cf. *rīrī*, *rīti*).

रिल्हण *rilhaṇa*, w. r. for *bilhaṇa*.

रिवक *rivaka*, w. r. for *ravaka*.

रिश् *riś* (cf. √*rish*, from which it is not in all forms distinguishable), cl. 6. P. (Dhātup. xxviii, 126) *riśáti* (Ved. also °*te*; pf. *rireśa* &c., Gr.), to hurt, tear, pluck off, crop, RV.: Caus. *reśayati* (aor. *aririśat*), Gr.: Desid. *ririkshati*, ib. (cf. √*rish*): Intens. *reriśyate*, *rereshṭi*, ib.

Riśá, mfn. tearing; m. an injurer, enemy (cf. *riśā́das*); (*ā*), f. N. of a partic. small animal, AV.

Riśā́das, mfn. (prob. fr. *riśa* + *adas*, √*ad*) devouring or destroying enemies, RV.

1. **Rishṭá**, mfn. (for 2. see below) torn off, broken, injured, RV.; AV.

रिश्य *riśya*, m. = *ṛiśya*, a deer, antelope, L. **-pad** (*rísya-*), mf(*padī*)n. deer-footed, AV. i, 18, 4.

रिष् 1. *rish* (cf. √*riś*), cl. 1. 4. P. (Dhātup. xvii, 43 and xxvi, 120, v. l.) *reshati* or *rishyati* (ep. also *rishyate*; aor. *riḍhvam*, TĀr.; *arishat*, Subj. *rishātha*, p. *rishat*, RV.; *areshīt*, Gr.; fut. *reshitā*, *reshṭā*, ib., *reshishyati*, ib.; inf. *reshitum* or *reshṭum*, ib.; Ved. inf. *rishé*, *rishás*), to be hurt or injured, receive harm, suffer wrong, perish, be lost, fail, RV. &c. &c.; to injure, hurt, harm, destroy, ruin, RV.; AV.; Bhaṭṭ.; Caus. *reshá yati* (aor. *arīrishat*; Ved. forms *rīrishīshṭa*, *ririsheḥ*, *rishayádhyai*), to hurt, injure, harm, cause to miscarry or fail, RV.; AV.; TBr.; MBh.; (Ā. *rīrishīshṭa*), to fail, meet with misfortune or disaster, BhP.: Desid. *ririkshati* (RV.; *ririshishati* or *rireshishati*, Gr.), to wish to injure or harm (cf. √*riś*): Intens. *rerishyate*, *rereshṭi*, Gr.

2. **Rish**, f. injury or an injurer, RV. (for *rishé*, *rishás* see under √1. *rish*).

Risha. See *naghā-rishá*.

1. **Rishaṇya**. See *á-rishaṇya*.

2. **Rishaṇya**, Nom. P. °*yáti*, to fail, miscarry, RV.

Rishaṇyú, mfn. injurious, deceitful, false, RV.

Rishīka, mfn. (prob.) destructive, injurious, Hariv.

Rishīkara, mfn. = *hiṅsra*, Nīlak.

2. **Rishṭá**, mfn. hurt, injured, wounded (cf. *á-rishṭa* and 1. *rishṭa*); failed, miscarried, ŚBr.; m. a sword, L. (cf. *rishṭi*); Sapindus Detergens, L. (cf. *a-rishṭa*); N. of a Daitya, Hariv.; of a king, MBh.; of a son of Manu, MārkP.; (*ā*), f. N. of the mother of the Apsarases, ib. (prob. w. r. for *a-rishṭā*); n. misfortune, calamity, VarBṛS., Sch.; a bad omen, Suśr.; good luck, fortune, L. **-tāti**, f. causing prosperity, auspicious, L. (cf. *śiva-tāti*). **-deha**, mfn. wounded in body, MW. **-navanīta**, n., **-samuccaya-śāstra**, n. N. of wks.

Rishṭaka, m. Sapindus Detergens, L.

Rishṭi, f. injury, damage, TBr.; failure, miscarriage, bad luck, AitBr.; ŚBr.; KātyŚr.; m. = *ṛishṭi*, a sword, L.

Rishṭīya, Nom. P. °*yati*, = 2. *rishaṇya*, Pāṇ. vii, 4, 36, Sch.

Rishva, mfn. = *hiṅsra*, Uṇ. i, 153, Sch.

रिषि *rishi*, m. = *ṛishi*, L.

रिष्फ *rishpha*, n. = *riḥpha*, L.

रिष्य *rishya*, m. = *ṛishya*, *ṛiśya*, L. **-mūka**, m. = *rishya-mūka*, VarBṛS.

रिस्सु *rissu*, m. N. of a poet, Cat.

रिह् *rih* (Vedic form of √*lih*), cl. 6. 2. P. *riháti*, *réḍhi* (or *rélhi*; 3. pl. Ā. *rihaté*; pr. p. *rihāṇá* or *rílhāṇa*), to lick, kiss, caress, RV.; AV.; VS.; (*rihati*) to praise, worship, Naigh. iii, 14; (Imp. *ririḍḍhi*, *rirīhi*) to ask, implore, ib. iii, 19; also v. l. for √*riph*, Dhātup. xxviii, 23: Intens. *rerihyáte* (*rérihat*, °*hāṇa*, see s. v.), to lick or kiss again and again, caress repeatedly, RV.; AV.; ŚBr.

Rihāyas, m. a thief, robber, Naigh. iii, 24 (v. l. *rihvan*; cf. *ribhvan*).

Riḍha, mfn. licked (see *á-rīḍha*), RV.; (*ā*), f. disregard, contempt, irreverence, Harav. (cf. *avalīḍhā*).

Reriha &c. See s. v.

रिहम् *riham*, ind. little, Naigh. iii, 2 (v. l. for *rihat*).

री 1. *rī* or *ri* (cf. √*lī*), cl. 9. P. (Dhātup. xxxi, 30) *riṇā́ti*, cl. 4. P. (Dhātup. xxvi, 29) *rīyate* (*riṇīte*, RV.; Br.; GṛŚrS.; *riyati*, Dhātup. xxviii, 111; impf. *ariṇvan*, MaitrS.; Gr. pf. *rirāya*, *ririye*; aor. *araishīt*, *areshṭa*; fut. *retā*; *reshyati*, °*te*; inf. *retum*), to release, set free, let go, RV.; to sever, detach from (abl.), ib.; to yield, bestow, AV.; (Ā.) to be shattered or dissolved, melt, become fluid, drop, flow, RV.: Caus. *repayati* (aor. *arīripat*), Gr.: Desid. *rirīshati*, °*te*, ib.: Intens. *rerīyate*, *rerayīti*, ib.

Rīṇa, mfn. melted, dissolved, vanished, Śiś.

Rīti, f. going, motion, course, RV.; a stream, current, ib.; a streak, line, row, PārGṛ.; Hariv.; Naish.; limit, boundary (= *sīman*), L.; general course or way, usage, custom, practice, method, manner, Kāv.; Kathās.; Sarvad.; natural property or disposition, L.; style of speaking or writing, diction (three are usually enumerated, viz. *vaidarbhī*, *gauḍī*, *pāñcālī*, to which a fourth is sometimes added, viz. *lāṭikā*, and even a fifth and sixth, viz. *āvantikā* or *yāvantikā* and *māgadhī*), Vām.; Kāvyād.; Sāh. &c.; yellow or pale brass, bell-metal, Rājat.; Kathās.; rust of iron, L.; scoria or oxide formed on metals by exposure to heat and air, L. **-kusuma**, n., and **-ja**, n. calx of brass, L. **-jña**, mfn. acquainted with established usages or customs, MW. **-pushpa**, n. calx of brass, L. **-prastha**, m. n. a Prastha weight of brass, MW. **-baddha**, mfn. brass-bound, studded or inlaid with brass, ib. **-vṛitti-lakshaṇa**, n. N. of a wk. on rhet.

Rītika, n. calx of brass, L.; (*ā*), f. brass, bell-metal.

Rīti-bhūta, mfn. being in a row, standing in a line, PārGṛ.

Rīty-àp, mfn. streaming with water, RV.

री 2. *rī* = *rai* in *ṛidhád-rī*, q. v.

री 3. *rī*, f. See under 3. *ra*, p. 859, col. 3.

रीज्या *rījyā*, f. (cf. *rīḍhā* above) contempt, disgust, L.; shame, L.

रीटि *rīṭi*. See *bhṛiṅgirīṭi*.

रीठा *rīṭhā*, f. a species of Karañja (al o -*karañja*, m.), L.

रीढ *rīḍha*. See under √*rih* above.

रीढक *rīḍhaka*, m. (√*rih*?) the back-bone, L.

रीर *rīra*, m. N. of Śiva, Cat.

रीरी *rīrī*, f. = *rirī*, yellow brass, L.

रीव् *rīv*, cl. 1. P. Ā. *rīvati*, °*te*, to take, Dhātup. xxi, 15; to cover, ib. (v. l. for √*cīv*, q. v.)

रु 1. *ru*, cl. 2. P. (Dhātup. xxiv, 24; cf. Pāṇ. vii, 3, 95) *rauti* or *ravīti* (Ved. also *ruvátiand ravati*, °*te*; p. *rúvat*, *ravat*, *ravamāṇa*, *ravāṇa*; pf. *rurāva*, MBh.; *ruruvire*, Br.; aor. *árāvīt*, RV.; Prec. *rūyāt*, Gr.; fut. *ravitā* or *rotā*, ib.; *ravishyati*, ib.; inf. *ravitum*, ib., *rotum*, Kāv.), to roar, bellow, howl, yelp, cry aloud, RV. &c. &c.; to make any noise or sound, sing (as birds), hum (as bees), MBh.; Kāv. &c.; (*rauti*) to praise, Naigh. iii, 14: Caus. *rāvayati* (aor. *arūruvat* with the sense of the Intens., BhP.; or *arīravat*, Pāṇ. vii, 4, 80, Sch.), to cause to bellow or roar, cause an uproar, ĀśvŚr.; MBh. &c.: Desid. of Caus. *rirāvayishati*, Gr.: Desid. *rurūshati*, ib.: Intens. (Ved.) *róravīti* (p. *róruvat* and *róruvāṇa*) or (ep.) *rorūyate*, °*ti* or (Gr.) *roroti*, to bellow or roar &c. loudly, scream aloud, vociferate. [Cf. Gk. ὠρύομαι; Lat. *raucus*; Angl. Sax. *rȳn*.]

2. **Ru**, m. (only L.) sound, noise; fear, alarm; war, battle.

1. **Rutá**, mfn. sounded, made to resound, filled with cries (of animals), AV. &c. &c.; n. (often pl.) any cry or noise, roar, yell, neigh (of horses), song, note (of birds), hum (of bees), KātyŚr.; MBh.; Kāv. &c. **-jña**, mfn. understanding the cries (of beasts or birds), MBh.; m. an augur, VarBṛS. **-vettṛi**, m. = prec. m., Cat. **-vyāja**, m. simulated cry or sound, W.; mimicry, ib. **Rutâbhijña**, mfn. = *ruta-jña*, Kathās.

Rutāyata, mfn. (w. r. for °*yita*?) rendered vocal (by the sound of birds &c.), W.

Ruvaṇya (fr. an unused *ruvaṇa*), Nom. P. °*yati*, to cry, utter harsh or loud cries, RV.

Ruvaṇyú, mfn. sounding, clamouring, RV.

Ruvatha, m. the bellowing of a bull, Kāṭh.; a dog, Uṇ. iii, 116, Sch.

Roravaṇa &c. See s. v.

रु 3. *ru*, cl. 1. Ā. (Dhātup. xxii, 63) *ravate* (only *rāvisham*, RV. x, 86, 5; *ruruvishe*, *aravishṭa*, *aroshṭa*, Vop.), to break or dash to pieces, RV. (Dhātup. also 'to go; to kill; to be angry; to speak'): Intens. (only p. *róruvat*) to break, shatter, RV. i, 54, 1; 5.

4. **Ru**, m. cutting, dividing, L.

2. **Rutá**, mfn. broken to pieces, shattered, divided, RV.; AV.; VS.

रुंश् *ruṅś*, cl. 1. 10. P. *ruṅśati*, *ruṅśayati*, to speak, Dhātup. xxxiii, 115.

रुंष् *ruṅsh*, only *ruṅshita*, mfn. covered with dust, Kir. (cf. *adhi-* and *prati-r*°).

रुक *ruka*, mfn. liberal, bountiful, L.

रुक्काम *ruk-kāma* &c. See under 1. *ruk*.

रुक्केश *ruk-keśa* &c. See under 2. *ruk*, p. 882, col. 3.

रुक्म *rukma*, *rukmin*. See next page.

रुक्ष 1. *rukshá*, m. (prob.) a tree (cf. *vṛiksha*), RV. vi, 3, 7.

रुक्ष 2. *ruksha*, w. r. for *rūksha*, q. v.

रुग्ण *rugṇa*, *rugna*. See p. 882, col. 3.

रुङ्मत् *ruṅ-mat*. See p. 882, col. 1.

रुच् 1. *ruc*, cl. 1. Ā. (Dhātup. xviii, 5) *rocate* (Ved. and ep. also °*ti*; pf. *ruroca*, *rurucé*, RV. &c. &c.; Subj. *rurucanta*, Pot. *rurucyā́s*, RV.; p. *rurukvás*, *rurucānā́*, ib.; aor. *arucat*, Rājat.; *arocishṭa*, Br. &c.; *arukta*, TĀr.; p. *rucānā́*, RV.; aor. Pass. *aroci*, RV.; Prec. *rucīya*, TĀr.; *rocishīya*, Br.; *rucishīya*, AV.; fut. *rocitā*, Gr.; *rocishyate*, MBh.; inf. *rocitum*, ib.; *rucé*, RV.; ind. p. *rucitvā* or *rocitvā*, Pāṇ. i, 2, 26), to shine, be bright or radiant or resplendent, RV. &c. &c.; (only in pf. P.) to make bright or resplendent, RV.; to be splendid or beautiful or good, AV.; Mn.; MBh. &c.; to be agreeable to, please (dat. or gen.), Mn.; MBh. &c.; to be pleased with, like (acc.), MBh.; R.; to be desirous of, long for (dat.), Hariv.: Caus. *rocáyati*, °*te* (aor. *árūrucat*, °*cata*; Pass. *rocyate*), to cause to shine, RV.; to enlighten, illuminate, make bright, ib.; ŚBr.; BhP.;

to make pleasant or beautiful, AV.; AitBr.; Kum.; to cause any one (acc.) to long for anything (dat.), Gīt.; to find pleasure in, like, approve, deem anything right (acc. or inf.), Mn.; MBh. &c.; to choose as (double acc.), R.; to purpose, intend, Hariv.; (Pass.) to be pleasant or agreeable to (dat.), R.: Desid. *ru-rucishate* or *rurocishate*, Gr.: Intens. (only p. *ró-rucāna*), to shine bright, RV. [Cf. Gk. λευκός, ἀμφιλύκη; Lat. *lux, luceo, luna, lumen;* Goth. *liuhath, lauhmuni;* Germ. *lioht, lieht, licht;* Angl. Sax. *leóht;* Eng. *light.*]

1. **Ruk** (for 2. see under √1. *ruj*, col. 3), in comp. for 2. *ruc*. — **kāma** (*rúk-*), mfn. desiring splendour, eager for lustre, TS.; Kāṭh. — **mat** (*rúk-*), mfn. possessed of brightness, shining (said of Agni), TS.

Rukmá, m. 'what is bright or radiant,' an ornament of gold, golden chain or disc, RV.; AV. (here n.); VS.; Br.; ŚrS.; Mesua Roxburghii, L.; the thorn-apple, L.; N. of a son of Rucaka, BhP.; n. gold, L.; iron, L.; a kind of collyrium, L. — **kavaca**, m. N. of a grandson of Uśanas, Hariv.; VP. — **kāraka**, m. a worker in gold, goldsmith, L. — **keśa**, m. N. of a son of Bhīshmaka, BhP. — **dhara**, m. N. of a king, VP. — **pāśá**, m. a string on which golden ornaments are worn, ŚBr.; KātyŚr. — **puṅkha**, mfn. gold-shafted (as an arrow), R. — **pura**, n. 'city of gold,' N. of the city inhabited by Garuḍa, Pañcat. — **purushá**, m. du. N. of partic. bricks, ŚBr. — **pṛishṭha**, mfn. having a gold surface, coated with g°, g°-plated, gilded, MBh.; R. — **prastaraṇa** (*rukmá-*), mfn. having a g°-ornamented outer garment, AV. — **bāhu**, m. N. of a son of Bhīshmaka, BhP. — **maya**, mf(*ī*)n. made of gold, golden, MBh.; Hariv. — **mālin**, m. N. of a son of Bhīshmaka, BhP. — **ratha**, m. a golden chariot; the chariot of Rukma-ratha i. e. of Droṇa, MBh.; mfn. having a g° ch°; m. N. of Droṇa, ib.; of various men (also pl.), ib.; Hariv.; BhP. — **lalāṭa**, mfn. having a golden ornament on the forehead (said of a horse), KātyŚr. — **loha** or -**lauha**, n. a partic. drug, Bhpr. — **vakshas** (*rukmá-*), mfn. golden-breasted, having g° ornaments on the breast (said of the Maruts), RV.; AV. — **vat**, mfn. possessing gold, ornamented with g°, L.; m. N. of the eldest son of Bhīshmaka (= *rukmin*), Hariv.; (*atī*), f. a partic. metre, Piṅg.; N. of a granddaughter of Rukmin and wife of Aniruddha, Hariv. — **vāhana**, mfn. having a golden chariot, L.; m. N. of Droṇa, MBh. — **steya**, n. stealing gold, Mn. xi, 58. **Rukmâṅgada**, mfn. wearing a golden bracelet on the upper arm, L.; m. N. of various men, MBh.; Hit.; Cat.; -*carita* or °*tra*, n.; °*dīya*, n. N. of wks. **Rukmâbha**, mfn. shining like gold, bright as the purest g°, Mn. xii, 122. **Rukmêshu**, m. 'golden-arrowed,' N. of a king, Hariv.; Pur.

1. **Rukmi**, m. (only acc. *rukmim*) = *rukmin* (son of Bhīshmaka), Hariv.

2. **Rukmi**, in comp. for *rukmin*. — **darpa**, m. N. of Bala-deva (so called as proud of having overcome Rukmin), W. — **dāraṇa**, -**dārin** or -**bhid**, m. 'destroyer of R°,' N. of Bala-deva, L. — **śāsana**, m. 'chastiser of R°,' N. of Vishṇu-Kṛishṇa, Pañcar.

Rukmiṇi-nandana, m. (for *rukmiṇī-n°*) N. of Pradyumna, MBh. (cf. next).

Rukmiṇī, f. (of *rukmin*) a species of plant (= *svarṇa-kshīrī*), L.; N. of a daughter of Bhīshmaka and sister of Rukmin (betrothed by her father to Śiśu-pāla but a secret lover of Kṛishṇa, who, assisted by Bala-rāma, carried her off after defeating her brother in battle; she is represented as mother of Pradyumna, and in later mythology is identified with Lakshmī), MBh.; Kāv.; Pur.; N. of Dākshāyaṇī in Dvāravatī, Cat.; of various other women, HPariś. — **kalyāṇa**, n., -**kṛishṇa-vallī**, f., -**campū**, f. N. of wks. — **tīrtha**, n. N. of a Tīrtha, Cat. — **nāṭaka**, n., -**pariṇaya**, m. N. of two dramas. — **vrata**, n. a partic. observance and N. of a ch. of the KalkiP., Cat. — °**śa** (°*ṇīśa*), m. 'lord of R°,' N. of Vishṇu-Kṛishṇa, Pañcar.; -*vijaya*, m. N. of a poem. — **svayam-vara**, m., -**haraṇa**, n. N. of wks. — **hrada**, n. N. of a Tīrtha, Cat.

Rukmin, mf(*iṇī*)n. wearing golden ornaments, adorned with gold, RV.; Br.; m. N. of the eldest son of Bhīshmaka and adversary of Kṛishṇa (he was slain by Bala-rāma; see *rukmiṇī* above), MBh.; Hariv.; Pur.; N. of a mountain, L.; (*iṇī*), f., see above.

Rúṅ-mat, mfn. (*ruṅ* for 2. *ruc* + *mat*) containing the word *ruc;* (*atī*), f. a verse containing that word, ŚBr.

2. **Rúc**, f. light, lustre, brightness, RV. &c. &c.; splendour, beauty, loveliness, VS.; ŚBr. &c.; colour, hue, VarBṛS.; Kālid.; BhP.; (ifc.) appearance, resemblance, BhP.; Kāvyâd.; pleasure, delight, liking, wish, desire, VS.; MBh.; pl. N. of a partic. class of Apsarases, VP.

Rucá, mfn. bright, radiant, brilliant, VS.; (*ā*), f. liking, desire, MBh.; light, lustre, beauty, L.; the note of the parrot or Maina, L.

Rucaka, mfn. very large, L. (W. also 'agreeable, pleasing; sharp, acid; tonic, stomachic'); m. n. a tooth, Suśr.; a kind of golden ornament or necklace, Daś.; a ring, L.; any object or substance supposed to bring good luck, Suśr.; a citron, L.; m. a dove, pigeon, L.; Ricinus Communis, L.; N. of one of the five remarkable personages born under partic. constellations, VarBṛS.; a kind of four-sided column, ib.; N. of a son of Uśanas, BhP.; of a king, VP. (v. l. *ruruka*); of an author, Pratāp., Sch.; of a mountain, Pur.; Śatr.; n. a horse-ornament, L.; a garland, L.; Embelia Ribes, L.; sochal salt, L.; natron, L.; sweet juice, L.; a bright yellow pigment = *go-rocanā*, q. v., L.; a kind of tonic (see above); a sort of building or temple having terraces on three sides and closed only on the north side, VarBṛS.

Rúci, f. (*rucī*, MaitrS.) light, lustre, splendour, beauty, AV. &c. &c.; colour, Kāv.; liking, taste, relish, pleasure, appetite, zest, AV. &c. &c. (ifc. taking pleasure in, desirous of, longing for; with loc., *prati*, inf. or comp.; *rucim* √*dā* or *rucaye* √*bhū*, to please; *rucim ā-*√*vah*, with dat., to excite a desire for; *rucyā* or *sva-rucyā*, at pleasure, at will); a kind of coitus, L.; a kind of pigment (= *rocanā*), L.; N. of an Apsaras, MBh.; of the wife of Deva-śarman, ib.; m. N. of a Prajā-pati (the husband of Ākūti and father of Yajña or Su-yajña and of Manu Raucya), Pur.; of a son of Viśvāmitra, MBh.; of a king, VP.; mfn. pleasant, agreeable (= *rucira*), R. — **kara**, mfn. causing pleasure, exciting desire, Kir.; causing an appetite or relish, Suśr.; m. N. of a king, Cat. — **kṛit**, mfn. causing a relish, relishing, MW. — **tā**, f. (Mn.; MBh. &c.) or -**tva**, n. (R.) the having a taste or liking or desire for, taking pleasure in (ifc.; e. g. *ārambha-ruci-tā*, 'fondness or taste for new enterprises;' cf. *samāna-r°*, *hiṅsā-ruci-tva;* *adharma-ruci-tā*, MBh. xiii, 5628 [w. r. *adharme r°*]). — **datta**, m. N. of various authors, Cat.; -*bhāshya*, n.; °*ttīya*, n. N. of wks. — **deva**, m. N. of a man, Kathās. — **dhāman**, mfn. having light for an abode, MW.; n. 'abode of light,' the sun, Śiś. — **nātha**, m. N. of an author, Cat. — **pati**, m. N. of various men, Cat. — **parvan**, m. N. of a man, MBh. — **prada**, mfn. giving an appetite, appetizing, Suśr. — **prabha**, m. N. of a Daitya, MBh. — **phala**, n. a pear, L.; the fruit of Momordica Monadelpha, L. — **bhartṛi**, m. 'lord or bearer of light,' the sun, Śiś.; 'lord of pleasure,' a husband, ib. — **rañjana**, m. Moringa Pterygosperma, L. — **ruci**, m. N. of a man, ĀrshBr. — **vadhū-gala-ratna-mālā**, f. N. of wk. — **vaha**, mfn. bringing light, Pāṇ. vi, 3, 121, Vārtt. — **sampraklṛipta**, mfn. prepared with good taste, Bhaṭṭ. — **stava**, m. N. of a ch. of the Mārkaṇḍeya Purāṇa. — **stha**, mfn. w. r. for *rucishya*, 'causing an appetite,' Suśr.

Rucika, m. a kind of ornament, Ṛiktantr. (prob. w. r. for *rucaka*).

Ruciṭa, m. the son of a Kshatriya and a Caṇḍālī, L.

Rucitá, mfn. shone upon (by the sun &c.), bright, brilliant, glittering, ŚBr.; ŚrS.; pleasant, agreeable, ŚāṅkhGṛ.; MBh.; sweet, delicate, dainty, Uṇ. iv, 185, Sch.; sharpened (as appetite), W.; digested, ib.; (*ā*), f. a kind of metre, W. (prob. w. r. for *rucirā*); n. an exclamation used at a Śrāddha, Mn. iii, 254. — **vat**, mfn. containing the meaning or any form of √1. *ruc*, AitBr.

Rucira, mf(*ā*)n. bright, brilliant, radiant, splendid, beautiful, MBh.; Kāv. &c.; pleasant, charming, agreeable to, liked by (gen. or comp.), ib.; sweet, dainty, nice, L.; stomachic, cordial, ŚārṅgS.; m. N. of a son of Sena-jit, Hariv.; (*ā*), f. a kind of pigment (= *go-rocanā*), L.; N. of a woman (see col. 3); of two metres, Col.; of a river, R.; n. (only L.) saffron (prob. w. r. for *rudhira*), a radish; cloves (prob. w. r. for *sushira*). — **ketu**, m. N. of a Bodhi-sattva, Buddh. — **deva**, m. N. of a prince, Kathās. — **dhī**, m. N. of a king, VP. — **prabhāva-sambhava**, m. N. of a serpent-demon, Buddh. — **bhāshaṇa**, mfn. of pleasant speech, eloquent, Daś. — **mud**, mfn. exquisite, affording great pleasure, W. — **mūrti**, mfn. of pleasant form or appearance, Daś. — **vadana**, mfn. sweet-faced, MW. — **śrī-garbha**, m. N. of a Bodhi-sattva, Buddh. **Rucirânana**, mfn. = °*ra-vadana*, W. **Rucirâpâṅgī**, f. a fair-eyed woman, ib. **Rucirâśva**, m. N. of a son of Sena-jit, Pur.

Rucirā, f. (of °*ra*) N. of a woman. — **tanaya**, m. a metron. of Kakshīvat, Gal. — **suta**, m. a metron. of Pālakāpya, L.

Rucishya, mfn. pleasant, agreeable, liked, Hariv.; giving an appetite, tonic, stomachic, Suśr.; dainty, nice, L.; n. white salt, L.

Rucī, f. pl. (m. c.) = *ruci*, light, splendour, Naish.

Rucu, m. a deer with black horns (either white like a sheep or yellow like a boar), L.

Rucé. See p. 881 under √1. *ruc*.

Rucya, mf(*ā*)n. bright, radiant, beautiful, pleasing, Naish.; giving an appetite, tonic, Suśr.; Bhpr.; m. (only L.) a lover, husband; Strychnos Potatorum; Aegle Marmelos; rice; (*ā*), f. (only L.) black cumin; a species of cucumber; n. a kind of tonic, W.; sochal salt, L. — **kanda**, m. Arum Campanulatum, L. — **vāhana**, m. N. of one of the 7 Ṛishis under Manu Rohita, Hariv. (v. l. *havya-v°*).

रुज् 1. *ruj*, cl. 6. P. (Dhātup. xxviii, 123) *rujáti* (ep. also °*te;* pf. *rurója*, RV. &c. &c.; aor. 2. sg. *rok*, VS.; *ruk*, MaitrS.; *araukshīt*, Gr.; fut. *roktā*, *rokshyati*, ib.; inf. -*rúje*, RV.; ind. p. *ruktvā*, -*rújya*, Br.), to break, break open, dash to pieces, shatter, destroy, RV. &c. &c.; to cause pain, afflict, injure (with acc. or gen.; cf. Pāṇ. ii, 3, 54), VS. &c. &c.: Caus. *rojayati* (aor. *arūrujat*), to cause to break &c.; to strike upon (loc.), BhP.; (cl. 10, Dhātup. xxxiii, 129) to hurt, injure, kill: Desid. *rurukshati*, Gr. (see *rurukshâṇi*): Intens. *rorujyate*, *rorokti*, Gr. [Cf. Gk. λυγρός; Lat. *lugeo*.]

2. **Ruk** (for 1. see col. 1), in comp. for 2. *ruj*. — **keśa**, m. a partic. medical compound, L. — **pratikriyā**, f. counteraction or treatment of disease, curing, remedying. — **sadman**, n. 'seat of disease,' excrement, feces, L.

Rug, in comp. for 2. *ruj*. — **anvita**, mfn. attended with pain, painful. — **ārta**, mfn. afflicted with pain, ill, Veṇīs. — **dāha**, m. a kind of fever, Bhpr. — **bhaya**, n. fear of disease, MW. — **bheshaja**, n. 'disease-drug,' any medicine or drug, VarBṛS. — **viniścaya**, m. (also called *roga-v°* or *mādhava-nidāna* or simply *nidāna*) 'determination of disease,' N. of a wk. by Mādhava (treating of the causes and diagnosis of 80 kinds of disease).

Rugṇá, mfn. (sometimes incorrectly written *rugnâ*) broken, bent, shattered, injured, checked, MBh.; Kāv. &c.; diseased, sick, infirm, W.; n. a cleft, fissure, RV. iii, 31, 6. — **tā**, f. and -**tva**, n. brokenness, crookedness, MW.; infirmity, sickness, disease, ib. — **raya**, mfn. checked in an onset, foiled in an attack, ib.

Ruṅ, in comp. for 2. *ruj*. — **nivartana**, n. cessation of disease, recovery of health, L.

2. **Ruj** (ifc.), breaking, crushing, shattering, MBh.; pain, illness, disease, Mn.; MBh. &c.; fracture, MW.; toil, trouble, ib.; Costus Speciosus, Bhpr.

Rujá, mf(*ā*)n. breaking, crushing, destroying, RV.; VS. (cf. *valam-r°*); m. of doubtful meaning, AV. xvi, 3, 2; (*ā*), f., see below.

Rujas-kara, mfn. (acc. pl. of 2. *ruj* + 1. *kara*) causing or producing pain, MBh.

Rujā, f. breaking, fracture, Megh.; pain, sickness, disease, MBh.; Kāv. &c.; Costus Speciosus or Arabicus, L.; an ewe, L. — **kara**, mfn. causing pain, sickening, Kāvyâd.; m. sickness, disease, L.; sickness induced by passion or love (said to be one of the Bhāvas, q. v.), MW.; the fruit of Averrhoa Carambola, L. — °**paha** (*rujâp°*), mfn. keeping off pain, removing sickness, Suśr. — **vat** (Suśr.), -**vin** (Pāṇ. v, 2, 122, Vārtt. 1), mfn. painful. — **saha**, m. Grewia Elastica, L.

Rujānā, f. a river, RV. i, 36, 6 (cf. Naigh. i, 13; Nir. vi, 4).

Rujāya, Nom. Ā. °*yate*, to be sick or ill, MW.

Rurukshâṇi, mfn. (fr. Desid.) wishing or able to destroy, RV.

रुट् *ruṭ* (cf. √*ruṭh* and *luṭ*), cl. 1. Ā. *roṭate*, to strike against, Dhātup. xviii, 7; to shine, ib.; cl. 10. P. *roṭayati*, to be angry, xxxii, 131 (v. l.); to speak or to shine (*bhāshârthe* or *bhāsârthe*), xxxiii, 110.

रुठ् *ruṭh* (cf. √*ruṭ* and *luṭh*), cl. 1. P. *roṭhati*, to strike down, fell, Dhātup. ix, 51;

cl. 1. Ā. (xxviii, 9, v.l.), to torment, pain (only p. *roṭhamāna*, R.)

रुणस्करा *ruṇaskarā*, f. a cow easily milked, a gentle cow, L.

रुणा *ruṇā*, f. N. of a river flowing into the Sarasvatī, MBh.

रुण्ट् *ruṇṭ* (v.l. *ruṇḍ*), cl. 1. P. *ruṇṭati*, to steal, rob, Dhātup. ix, 41 (v.l. *ruṇḍ*).

रुण्ठ् *ruṇṭh* (cf. √*luṇṭh*), cl. 1. P. *ruṇṭhati*, to go, Dhātup. ix, 61; to be lame; to be idle, 58, v.l.; to strike against; to steal, 41, v.l.

रुण्ड् *ruṇḍ*. See √*ruṇṭ*.

Ruṇḍa, mfn. maimed, mutilated; m. a headless body, Uttarar.; Kathās. (L. also n.); the offspring of a mule and a mare, L.

Ruṇḍaka, m. = *ruṇḍa*, a headless body (only ifc.), Kathās.; the son of a Śūdra and a Varuṭī, L.; (*ikā*), f. (only L.) a field of battle; a female messenger or go-between; the threshold of a door; superhuman power (= *vibhūti*).

रुत 1. 2. *ruta* &c. See p. 881, col. 3.

रुथ *rutha*, m. N. of a man, MārkP.

रुद् 1. *rud* (cf. √1. *ru*), cl. 2. P. (Dhātup. xxiv, 59; cf. Pāṇ. vii, 2, 76) *roditi* (Ved. and ep. also *rudati*, °*te* and *rodati*, °*te*; pf. *ruroda*, *rurude*, MBh.; aor. *árudat*, AV. &c.; *arodīt*, °*dishuḥ*, Gr.; *araudishīt*, BhP.; fut. *roditā*, Gr.; *rodishyati*, Kāv.; inf. *roditum*, ib.; ind. p. *ruditvā* or *roditvā*, MBh.; *-rudya*, Kathās.), to weep, cry, howl, roar, lament, wail, RV. &c. &c.; to bewail, deplore, ib.: Pass. *rudyate* (aor. *arodi*; *rudyamāne*, 'while weeping is heard,' Mn. iv, 108): Caus. *rodáyati* (aor. *arūrudat*), to cause to weep or lament, RV. &c. &c.: Desid. *rurudishati*, Gr. (cf. *rurudishā*, °*shu*): Intens. *rorudyate*, *rorotti* (p. *rorudyamāna*, *rorudat*), MBh. [Cf. Lat. *rudere*; Lith. *rù̃dis*, *raudà*, *raudóti*; Angl. Sax. *reótan*.]

2. **Rud** (ifc.), weeping, crying &c. (see *agharúd* and *bhava-rud*); f. cry, wail; sound; grief, pain; disease, W.

Rudatha, m. (only L.) a child, pupil, scholar; a dog; a cock.

Rudana, n. the act of crying, weeping, lamentation, Hariv.

Rudantikā and **rudantī**, f. 'weeper,' N. of a species of small succulent plant (= *amṛita-sravā*), L.

Rudita, mfn. wept, lamented, MBh.; Kāv. &c.; weeping, crying, lamenting, ib.; wet with tears, MBh.; n. weeping, crying, lamentation, Kāv.; VarBṛS.; Kathās. &c.

Rudrá, mfn. (prob.) crying, howling, roaring, dreadful, terrific, terrible, horrible (applied to the Aśvins, Agni, Indra, Mitra, Varuṇa, and the *spáśaḥ*), RV.; AV. (accord. to others 'red, shining, glittering,' fr. a √*rud* or *rudh* connected with *rudhira*; others 'strong, having or bestowing strength or power,' fr. a √*rud* = *vṛid*, *vṛidh*; native authorities give also the following meanings, 'driving away evil;' 'running about and roaring,' fr. *ru* + *dra* = 2. *dru*; 'praiseworthy, to be praised;' 'a praiser, worshipper,' = *stotṛi*, Naigh. iii, 16); m. 'Roarer or Howler,' N. of the god of tempests and father and ruler of the Rudras and Maruts (in the Veda he is closely connected with Indra and still more with Agni, the god of fire, which, as a destroying agent, rages and crackles like the roaring storm, and also with Kāla or Time, the all-consumer, with whom he is afterwards identified; though generally represented as a destroying deity, whose terrible shafts bring death or disease on men and cattle, he has also the epithet *śiva*, 'benevolent' or 'auspicious,' and is even supposed to possess healing powers from his chasing away vapours and purifying the atmosphere; in the later mythology the word *śiva*, which does not occur as a *name* in the Veda, was employed, first as an euphemistic epithet and then as a real name for Rudra, who lost his special connection with storms and developed into a form of the disintegrating and reintegrating principle; while a new class of beings, described as eleven [or thirty-three] in number, though still called Rudras, took the place of the original Rudras or Maruts: in VP. i, 7, Rudra is said to have sprung from Brahmā's forehead, and to have afterwards separated himself into a figure half male and half female, the former portion separating again into the 11 Rudras, hence these later Rudras are sometimes regarded as inferior manifestations of Śiva, and most of their names, which are variously given in the different Purāṇas, are also names of Śiva; those of the VāyuP. are Ajâikapad, Ahir-budhnya, Hara, Nirṛita, Īśvara, Bhuvana, Aṅgāraka, Ardha-ketu, Mṛityu, Sarpa, Kapālin; accord. to others the Rudras are represented as children of Kaśyapa and Surabhi or of Brahmā and Surabhi or of Bhūta and Su-rūpā; accord. to VP. i, 8, Rudra is one of the 8 forms of Śiva; elsewhere he is reckoned among the Dik-pālas as regent of the north-east quarter), RV. &c. &c. (cf. RTL. 75 &c.); N. of the number 'eleven' (from the 11 Rudras), VarBṛS.; the eleventh, Cat.; (in astrol.) N. of the first Muhūrta; (in music) of a kind of stringed instrument (cf. *rudrī* and *rudra-vīṇā*); of the letter *e*, Up.; of various men, Kathās.; Rājat.; of various teachers and authors (also with *ācārya*, *kavi*, *bhaṭṭa*, *śarman*, *sūri* &c.), Cat.; of a king, Buddh.; du. (incorrect acc. to Vām. v, 2, 1) Rudra and Rudrāṇī (cf. also *bhavā-r°* and *somā-rudra*); pl. the Rudras or sons of Rudra (sometimes identified with or distinguished from the Maruts who are 11 or 33 in number), RV. &c. &c.; an abbreviated N. for the texts or hymns addressed to Rudra, GṛŚrS.; Gaut.; Vas. (cf. *rudra-japa*); of a people (v.l. *puṇḍra*), VP.; (*ā*), f. a species of creeping plant, L.; N. of a wife of Vasu-deva, VāyuP.; of a daughter of Raudrāśva (v.l. *bhadrā*), VP.; pl. a hundred heat-making suns' rays, L.; (*ī*), f. a kind of lute or guitar, L. (cf. m. and *rudra-vīṇā*). **–ṛiṇ-mantra-dhyāna**, n. N. of wk. **–kalaśa**, m. 'Rudra's jar,' a partic. receptacle for water used in making oblations to the planets, Cat.; *-snāna-vidhi*, m. N. of wk. **–kalpa**, m. (and *-taru*, m., *-druma*, m.), and **-kavaca**, n., and °**ca-stotra**, n. N. of wks. **–kavindra**, m. N. of an author, Cat. **–kāṭi**, f., w.r. for *-koṭi*. **–kālī**, f. a form of Durgā, VP. **–kumāra**, m. N. of a man, Cat. **–koṭi**, f. N. of a place of pilgrimage, MBh.; *-māhātmya*, n. N. of ch. of the Bhavishyôttara Purāṇa. **–kośa**, m. N. of a lexicon by Rudra. **–gaṇa**, m. the class of (beings called) Rudras (see under *rudra*), VarBṛS. **–garbha**, m. 'Rudra's offspring,' N. of Agni, MBh. **–gāyatri** (m.c.) or °**trī**, f. N. of the text *tatpurushāya—tan no rudraḥ pracodayāt* (TĀr. i, 10, 5) and of a modification of it, Hcat. **–gīta**, n. (BhP.) or (*ā*), f. sg. or pl. (RāmatUp.; Cat.) the song of Rudra (in which Agastya repeats a dialogue between himself and R°). **–caṇḍikā**, n. of a partic. text or formula, Cat. **–caṇḍī**, f. a form of Durgā, Cat.; N. of a section in the Rudra-yāmala and of a Stotra. **–candra**, m. N. of a king, Cat.; *-deva*, m. N. of an author, ib. **–cchattra**, m. N. of a man, ib. **–ja**, m. 'produced from R°,' quicksilver (supposed to be the semen of Śiva), L. **–jaṭā**, f. 'R°'s hair,' a species of creeper, Bhpr. **–japa**, m. N. of a prayer or hymn addressed to R°, VarBṛS.; NṛisUp.; *-kalpa*, MānŚr.; *-pañcâdhyāya*, m. pl., *-vidhi*, m. N. of wks. **–japana**, n. the recitation of the R°-japa in a low tone, Cat. **–jāpaka** (NṛisUp.) or °**pin** (ib.; Yājñ.), mfn. one who recites the R°-japa in a low tone. **–jāpa-viniyoga**, m. N. of wk. **–jāpya**, n. = *-japa* above, Cat. **–jābālôpanishad**, f. N. of an Upanishad. **–ḍamarûdbhava-sūtra-vivaraṇa**, n. N. of wk. **–tanaya**, m. 'R°'s son,' N. of Punishment, MBh.; of a sword, L.; (with Jainas) of the third black Vāsudeva, L. **–tri-pāṭhin**, m. N. of an author, Daśar., Introd. **–tri-śatī**, f. N. of a Stotra. **–tva**, n. the being Rudra, Kāṭh.; MaitrUp. &c. **–datta**, m. N. of an author, Cat.; of a wk. on medicine; *-vṛitti*, f.; °*ttīya*, n. N. of wks. **–darśana**, mfn. of dreadful appearance, terrific, R. **–dāna-vidhi**, m. N. of a section of the Vāyu Purāṇa. **–dāman**, m. N. of a king, Inscr. **–dīpikā**, f. N. of various wks. **–deva**, m. N. of various persons, Inscr.; Cat. **–dhara**, m. N. of various authors, Cat. **–dhyāna-varṇana**, n. N. of wk. **–nandin**, m. (Sadukt.), **-nātha**, m. (Cat.) N. of authors. **–nārāyaṇa**, m. N. of a man, Cat. **–nirmālya**, n. a species of plant, Bhpr. **–nyāya-vācas-pati-bhaṭṭâcārya**, m. N. of an author, Cat. **–nyāsa**, m., **-pañcâṅga-nyāsa**, m. N. of wks. **–paṇḍita**, m. N. of an author, Cat. **–patnī**, f. Rudra's wife, the goddess Durgā, L.; Linum Usitatissimum, L. **–paddhati**, f., **-pāṭha**, m., **-pāda-mahiman** (prob. w.r. for *-pāṭha-m°*), m. N. of wks. **–pāla**, m. N. of a man, Rājat. **–putra**, m. R°'s son, a patr. of the 12th Manu, MārkP. (cf. *-sāvarṇi*). **–pura**, n. N. of a province, W. **–purāṇa**, n. N. of wk. **–pushpa**, n. the China rose, Rosa Sinensis, L. **–pūjana**, n., **-pūjā**, f. N. of wks. **–pratāpa**, m. N. of a king, Cat. **–pratishṭhā**, f., **-pradīpa**, m. N. of wks. **–prayāga**, m. N. of the sacred place where the river Mandākinī joins the Ganges, Cat. **–praśna**, m. N. of wk. **–priyā**, f. 'dear to R°,' Terminalia Chebula, L.; the goddess Pārvatī, W. **–bali**, m. an oblation of flesh &c. presented to the R°s, W. **–bhaṭṭa**, m. (also with *ācārya*), N. of various scholars and authors, Cat. **–bhāshya**, n. N. of various wks. **–bhū**, f. 'R°'s ground,' a cemetery, L. **–bhūti**, m. N. of a preceptor, L.; of a chief, Inscr. **–bhūmi**, f. = *-bhū* above, MW. **–bhairavī**, f. a form of Durgā, Cat. **–maṇi**, m. (also with *tri-pāṭhin*), N. of authors, Cat. **–mantra** and °**tra-vibhāga**, m. N. of wks. **–maya**, mf(*ī*)n. having the essence of R°, Hariv. **–mahā-devī**, f. N. of a princess, Cat. **–mahā-nyāsa**, m. N. of wk. **–yajña**, m. an oblation or sacrifice offered to R°, Kathās. **–yāmala**, n. N. of a Tantra wk. in the form of a dialogue between Bhairava and Bhairavī; *-tantra*, n. id. (cf. IW. 525); °*lâdi-saṃgraha*, m., °*līya-cikitsā*, f. N. of wks. **–yāmila**, n. = *-yāmala* above. **–rāya**, m. N. of a king, Kshitîś. **–rāśi**, m. N. of a man, Inscr. **–rodana**, n. 'R°'s tears,' gold, BhP. **–roman**, f. N. of one of the Mātṛis attending upon Skanda, MBh. **–latā**, f. a species of creeper, L. **–loka**, m. R°'s world, Hariv.; VP. **–vaṭa**, N. of a Tīrtha, MBh. **–vat** (*rudrá-*), mfn. having R° or the R°s, VS.; TS. &c.; *-vadgaṇa* (*rudrá-*), mfn. surrounded by the R° troop (said of Soma), TS. **–vartani** (*rudrá-*), m. du. 'moving in terrific paths,' N. of the Aśvins, RV. (others 'moving on red or shining paths,' scil. after the rising of the dawn). **–viṃśati**, f. N. of the last 20 years in the Jupiter cycle of 60 y°, L. **–vidhāna**, n. (and *-paddhati*, f.), **-vidhi**, m. N. of wks. **–vīṇā**, f. a kind of lute, Saṃgīt. **–vrata**, n. a partic. religious observance, Cat.; °*tin*, m. a Kshatriya who stands on one foot, L. **–śarman**, m. N. of a Brāhman, Kathās. **–saṃhitā**, f. N. of wk. **–sakha**, m. 'Rudra's friend,' N. of Kubera, L. **–sampradāyin**, m. pl. N. of a sect, W. **–sammita**, mfn. equal to eleven, L. **–saras**, n. N. of a lake, Cat. **–sarga**, m. R°'s creation, VarP.; the cr° of the 11 R°s, Cat. **–sahasra-nāman**, n. N. of a Stotra. **–sāman**, n. N. of a partic. Sāman, Saṃskārak. **–sāvarṇi**, m. N. of the 12th Manu, BhP. (cf. *-putra*, col. 2). **–sāvarṇika**, mfn. belonging or relating to Rudra-sāvarṇi, being under R°-s°, MārkP. **–sāvitrī**, f. a partic. imitation of the Sāvitrī, AVPariś. **–siṇha**, m. N. of various men, Cat. **–sīha**, m. (Prākṛit for *-siṇha*) N. of a king, Inscr. **–suta**, m. a patr. of Skanda, Kād. **–sundarī**, f. N. of a goddess, Cat. **–sū**, f. a mother of 11 children, L. **–sûkta**, n. N. of a partic. hymn, Saṃskārak.; *-japa*, m. N. of wk. **–sūtra**, n. N. of wk. **–sūri**, m. N. of an author, Cat. **–sṛishṭi**, f. R°'s creation, (or) the cr° of the 11 R°s, Cat. (cf. *-sarga*). **–sena**, m. N. of a warrior, MBh.; (*ā*), f. R°'s army, ŚāṅkhŚr. (pl.) **–soma**, m. N. of a Brāhman, Kathās.; (*ā*), f. N. of the wife of a Soma-deva, HPariś. **–skanda** or **-skanda-svāmin**, m. N. of a commentator, Cat. **–snāna-vidhi**, m. N. of wk. **–svarga**, m. R°'s heaven, Cat. **–svāmin**, m. N. of a man, Inscr. **–havana**, m. or n. (?) N. of wk. **–hāsa**, m. N. of a partic. divine being, Bālar. **–himâlaya**, m. N. of a peak of the Himâlaya mountains, L. **–hūti** (*rudrá-*), mfn. invoked by the R°s (or accord. to Mahīdh. 'by praisers'), VS. (cf. *rudrá-hotṛi*). **–hṛidaya**, n., °*yôpanishad*, f. N. of wks. **–hotṛi** (*rudrá-*), mfn. having the R°s for invokers, being invoked by the R°s, TĀr. (cf. *rudrá-hūti*). **Rudrâkrīḍa**, m. 'Rudra's pleasure-ground,' a cemetery or burning-ground for corpses (R° being supposed to dance in such places at evening twilight), Bhaṭṭ. **Rudrâksha**, m. 'R°-eyed,' Elaeocarpus Ganitrus or its berry (used for rosaries), W. (cf. RTL. 67, 82); a rosary (gender doubtful), Rājat.; N. of an Upanishad (gender d°); *-kalpa*, m., *-dhāraṇa*, n., *-parīkshā*, f. N. of wks.; *-mālā* (Hcar.) or *-mālikā* (Kād.), f. a rosary; *-māhātmya*, n., °*ya-varṇana*, n. N. of wks.; *-valaya*, m. or n. (?) a rosary, Kād.; °*shôpanishad*, f. N. of an Upanishad. **Rudrâgni**, see *raudrâgna*. **Rudrâṅkuśa**, m. R°'s trident, Bālar. **Rudrâcārya**, m. N. of a man, Cat. **Rudrâtharvaṇa-śirshôpanishad**, f. N. of an Upanishad. **Rudrâdhyāya**, m. N. of partic. prayers addressed to R°, Hcat.; *-ṭīkā*, f. N. of wk.; °*yāyin*, mfn. reciting the above prayers, Up. **Rudrânuja**, m. N. of an author, Cat. **Rudrânu-**

shṭhâna-paddhati, f., **Rudrâbhisheka**, m., **°kavidhi**, m. N. of wks. **Rudrâyatana**, n. a temple dedicated to R°, VarBṛS. **Rudrâri**, m. R°'s enemy, L.; N. of Kāma-deva, L.; mfn. having R° for an enemy, L. **Rudrârcana-candrikā**, f. N. of wk. **Rudrâvarta**, N. of a place of pilgrimage, MBh. **Rudrâvasṛishṭa**, mfn. hurled by R°, TS. **Rudrâvāsa**, m. R°'s abode i.e. Kāśī or Benares, Kāśīkh.; the mountain Kailāsa, A.; a cemetery, A. **Rudrâśva**, see *raudrāśva*. **Rudrâhva**, mfn. having 11 names, L. **Rudrâikādaśaka-mantra**, m. pl. (Hcat.) or **°daśinī**, f. (Yājñ.) the 11 Rudra hymns (Anuvāka in the Taittirīya Saṃhitā). **Rudrâikādaśa-vastradāna-vidhi**, m. N. of wk. **Rudrôpanishad**, f. N. of 2 Upanishads. **Rudrôpastha**, m. 'R°'s generative organ,' N. of a mountain, Hariv.

Rudraka, m. N. of a man, Buddh. (v. l. *udraka*).

Rudraṭa, m. (with *śatânanda*) N. of a writer on rhetoric (son of Vāmuka), Cat.

Rudrāṇī, f. Rudra's wife, the goddess Durgā, ŚāṅkhŚr.; MBh. &c.; N. of a girl eleven years of age (in whom menstruation has not yet commenced, representing the goddess D° at the D° festival), L.; a species of plant (= *rudra-jaṭā*), L.

Rudrāyaṇa, m. N. of a king of Roruka, Buddh.

Rudríya, mf(*ā*)n. relating to Rudra or the Rudras, coming from them &c., RV.; ŚBr.; ŚāṅkhŚr. (cf. *śata-r°*); terrific, fearful, impetuous, RV. (Sāy. 'uttering praise' or 'giving pleasure;' cf. *rudrá*); m. (sg. and pl.) the Maruts, RV.; ŚBr.; n. Rudra's majesty or power, ib. (Sāy. 'pleasure, delight,' = *sukha*).

Rudrīya, mfn. = *rudríya*, Kapishṭh.

Rurudishā, f. wish or inclination to weep, Śiś. **°shu**, mfn. wishing to weep, inclined to cry, Bhaṭṭ.

Róda, m. weeping, wailing, lamentation, AV.; ChUp.

Rodana, n. id., Āpast.; R.; Suśr. &c. (in ŚārṅgS. reckoned among the diseases of children); a tear, tears, L.; (*ī*), f. Alhagi Maurorum, L.

Rodanikā, f. Alhagi Maurorum, L.

Rodas, **rodasī**. See p. 889, cols. 1, 2.

Roditavya, mfn. to be bewailed or lamented (n. impers. it is to be wept or cried), MBh.; Kāv. &c.

Rorudat, **°dyamāna**. See Intens. of √1. *rud*.

Rorudā, f. (fr. Intens.) violent weeping (-*vat*, mfn. weeping violently or intensely), Bhaṭṭ.

रुद्ध *ruddha* &c. See col. 2.

रुद्र *rudra* &c. See p. 883, col. 1.

रुध् 1. *rudh* (cf. √1. *ruh*, of which this seems to be only another form), cl. 1. P. *ródhati*, to sprout, shoot, grow (only *ródhati*, RV. viii, 43, 6; and *viródhat*, i, 67, 9; accord. to some also p. *rudhat*, i, 179, 4, in *nadásya rudhatáḥ kā́maḥ*, 'the desire of the growing reed' i.e. of the membrum virile; others, 'of the husband who keeps me away,' fr. √2. *rudh*; cf. also *nada*).

1. **Rodha** (ifc.) sprouting, growing &c. (cf. 2. *ava-rodha* and *nyag-r°*); m. growing, ascending, moving upwards (cf. next). **Rodhâvarodha**, m. (prob.) moving up and down, Kauś.

1. **Rodhana**. See 2. *ava-*, *ud-*, *-pra-r°*.

रुध् 2. *rudh*, cl. 7. P. Ā. (Dhātup. xxix, 1) *ruṇáddhi*, *runddhé* (1. pl. *-rudhmas*, AV.; *rundhati*, °*te*, Br. &c.; *rodhati*, MBh.; pf. *rurodha*, *rurudhe*, RV. &c. &c.; *rurundhatuḥ*, MBh.; aor. *araut*, AV.; *arautsīt*, Br. &c.; *rotsīs*, Up.; *arutsi*, *aruddha*, Br.; Up.; *arautsi*, AitBr.; *arodham*, RV.; *arudhma*, MaitrS.; p. *rudhát*, cf. √1. *rudh*; *arudhat*, RV. &c. &c.; Prec. *rudhyā́t*, Kāv.; fut. *roddhā*, Gr.; *rotsyati*, °*te*, Br. &c.; inf. *roddhum* or *rodhitum*, MBh.; *roddhos*, Br.; ind. p. *ruddhvā*, MBh. &c.; *-rúdhya*, RV. &c. &c.; *-rundhya*, MBh.; *-rúdham*, AV.; Br.; *-rúndham*, Br.; *-ródham*, ib.), to obstruct, check, arrest, stop, restrain, prevent, keep back, withhold, RV. (always with *na*), &c. &c.; to avert, keep off, repel, Bhaṭṭ. (cf. *rudhat* under √1. *rudh*); to shut, lock up, confine in (loc.), Mn.; MBh. &c. (accord. to Vop. also with double acc.); to besiege, blockade, invest, Pat.; MBh. &c.; to close, block up (a path), R.; to cover, conceal, veil, obscure, MBh.; Kāv. &c.; to stop up, fill, ib.; to lay (dust), Ragh.; to touch, move (the heart), Bālar.; to torment, harass, R.; to lose, be deprived of (acc.), TS.; ŚBr.; to tear, rend asunder (?), AV. xix, 29, 3: Caus. *rodhayati* (ep. also °*te* and *rundhayati*; aor. *arūrudhat*; Pass. *rodhyate*), to stop, arrest, MBh.; to cause to be confined by (acc.), Pañcar.; to cause to be besieged by (instr.), Ragh.; to close (with a cover or lid), Bhpr.; to fetter, enchain, influence, BhP.; to oppress, torment, harass, MBh.; R.: Desid. *rorutsate* (Br.), °*ti* (MBh.), to wish to obstruct &c.: Intens. *rorudhyate*, *roroddhi*, to obstruct intensely or repeatedly &c., Gr. (only *rorudhaḥ*, MBh.)

Ruddhá, mfn. obstructed, checked, stopped, suppressed, kept back, withheld, RV. &c. &c.; shut, closed, covered, MBh.; Kāv. &c.; invested, besieged, blockaded, R.; Pañcat.; secured, held, taken possession of, Kāv.; BhP.; obstructed in its effect, ineffectual (as a spell), Sarvad.; (*ā*), f. a siege, W.; (prob.) n. N. of a town, Cat. **-gir**, mfn. having the utterance choked or impeded, BhP. **-taṭâbhimukhya**, mfn. obstructed (in its motion) towards the shore (said of the sea), Rājat. **-dṛiś**, mfn. having the sight impeded by (tears &c.), VarBṛS. **-pravāha**, mfn. obstructed in (its) flow, Rājat. **-mukha**, mfn. having the mouth filled or stuffed, Kathās. **-mūtra**, mfn. having suppressed urine, suffering from retention of urine, Suśr. **-vaktra**, mfn. having the face covered or hidden, Mṛicch. **-vadana**, mfn. having the mouth filled full (with food), VarBṛS. **-vasudha**, mfn. filling the earth, Rājat.; covering i.e. touching the e°, Amar. **-vīrya**, mfn. one whose strength is impeded, Ragh. **Ruddhâpâṅga-prasara**, mfn. having the space in the outer corner (of the eye) obstructed, Megh. **Ruddhâloka**, mfn. obstructing the sight, dark, ib.

Ruddhaka, n. a citron, Nīlak. (w. r. for *rucaka*).

3. **Rudh** (ifc.) impeding, holding (see *kara-r°*).

Rudha (ifc.) id. (see *á-go-r°*).

Rudhi-krā́, m. N. of an Asura conquered by Indra, RV. (cf. *dadhi-krā*).

Rurutsā, f. (fr. Desid.) the wish to obstruct or check or prevent, Harav. **°tsu**, mfn. wishing to obstruct or oppose or keep back, Naish.; wishing to bind or tie up (as the hair), W.

Roddhavya, mfn. to be closed or shut, Kathās.

Roddhṛi, mfn. one who stops or obstructs or shuts in, a besieger, Ragh.

Roddhos. See √2. *rudh*, col. 1.

2. **Rodha**, m. (for 1. see above, col. 1) the act of stopping, checking, obstructing, impeding; suppressing, preventing, confining, surrounding, investing, besieging, blockading, MBh.; Kāv. &c.; obstruction of the bowels, costiveness, Car.; attacking, making war upon (gen.), R.; a dam, bank, shore, Rājat.; Suśr. (cf. *rodhas*); an arrow, L.; a partic. hell, VP.; N. of a man, g. *śivâdi*. **-kṛit**, m. N. of the 45th year in the Jupiter cycle of 60 years, VarBṛS. **-cakra** (*ródha-*), mf(*ā*)n. (prob.) forming eddies on the bank, RV.; AV. **-vakrā**, v. l. for *rodho-v°*. **-vedī**, f. a river, L. **-stha**, mfn. standing on the bank of a river, Rājat.

Rodhaḥ, in comp. for *rodhas*. **-patana-kalusha**, mfn. (rendered) muddy by the falling in of a bank, MW. **-stha**, v. l. for *rodha-stha*, Rājat.

Rodhaka, mfn. stopping, holding back, restraining, shutting up, besieging, blockading, Kāv.

2. **Rodhana**, mf(*ī*)n. (for 1. see above, col. 1) obstructing, impeding, being an obstacle or hindrance, W.; m. the planet Mercury, L.; (*ā*), f. a dam, bank, wall (= *rodhas*), RV. ii, 13, 10; (*ró°*), n. shutting up, confinement, RV.; BhP.; stopping, restraining, checking, preventing, impeding, Kāv.; Pur.

Ródhas, n. a bank, embankment, dam, mound, wall, shore, RV. &c. &c.; a mountain slope, R.; Hariv.; the steep wall or bank (of a cloud), Kathās.; the brink (of a well), BhP.; the flank, side, a woman's hips, BhP. (cf. *taṭa*). **-vat** (*ródhas-*), mfn. having high banks, RV.; (*atī*), f. N. of a river, BhP.

Rodhin, mfn. (ifc.) = *rodhaka*, Kāv.; Kathās. &c.; obstructing, overpowering or drowning (one sound by another), Rājat.; filling, covering, Kathās.

Rodho, in comp. for *rodhas*. **-bhū**, mfn. growing on the bank of a river, Kir. **-vakrā**, f. 'winding along its banks,' a river, L. **-vatī**, f. 'having banks,' id., L. **-vapra**, m. a rapid river, L.

Rodhya, mfn. to be stopped or checked or restrained (see *a-r°*).

रुध् 4. *rudh*, prob. a root of this form once existed with a meaning 'to be red.'

Rudhirá, mfn. (prob. fr. the above lost root *rudh*, 'to be red;' cf. *rohita* and also under *rudra*) red, blood-red, bloody, AV. v, 29, 10; m. the blood-red planet or Mars, VarBṛS.; Pañcat.; a kind of precious stone (cf. *rudhirâkhya*); (*rú°*), n. (ifc. f. *ā*) blood, ŚBr. &c. &c.; saffron, Car.; N. of a city, Hariv. (cf. *śonita-pura*). [Cf. Gk. ἐρυθρός, ἔρευθος; Lat. *ruber*, *rubeo*, *rufus*; Lith. *rùdas*, *raùdas*, *raudónas*; Slav. *rŭdrŭ*, *rŭdĕti*; Goth. *rauths*; Angl. Sax. *reád*; Eng. *red*; Germ. *rôt*, *rot*.] **-carcita-sarvâṅga**, mf(*ī*)n. having the whole body smeared with blood, Vet. **-tāmrâksha**, mf(*ī*)n. having b°-red eyes, R. **-pāta**, m. a 'flow of b°,' Kautukar. **-pāyin**, m. 'b°-drinking,' a Rākshasa or demon, W. **-pradigdha**, mfn. besmeared with blood, Bhag. **-plāvita**, mfn. swimming with blood, soaked in b°, Pañcat. **-bindu**, m. a drop of b°, ib. **-maya**, mf(*ī*)n. bloody, Anargh. **-rūshita**, mfn. covered with b°, R. **-lālasa**, mfn. b°-thirsty, sanguinary, MBh. **-lepa**, m. a spot of blood, MBh. **-varsha**, n. b°-shower, ShaḍvBr. **-sāra**, mfn. one who essence is b°, sanguine, Laghuj. **Rudhirâksha** or **°râkhya**, n. 'blood-named, red in b°,' a partic. precious stone, Var. **Rudhirâdāna**, n. 'removal of b°,' bleeding, Kāv. **Rudhirâdhyāya**, m. N. of a ch. of the Kālikā Purāṇa. **Rudhirânana**, n. N. of one of the 5 retrograding motions of Mars, VarBṛS. **Rudhirândha**, m. 'b°-blind,' N. of a hell, VP. **Rudhirâmaya**, m. 'b°-disease,' hemorrhage, Suśr.; hemorrhoids, A. **Rudhirâvila**, mfn. stained or soiled with b°, MW. **Rudhirâśana**, mfn. feeding on b° (said of demons and arrows), R. **Rudhirôdgārin**, mf(*iṇī*)n. 'emitting b°,' N. of the 57th year in Jupiter's cycle of 60 years, Cat.

रुन्द्र *rundra*, mfn. (ifc.) rich in, L.

रुन्ध् *rundh*. See √2. *rudh*, col. 1.

रुप् 1. *rup* (cf. √*lup*), cl. 4. P. (Dhātup. xxvi, 125) *rúpyati* (pf. *ruropa*, aor. *arupat* &c., Gr.), to suffer violent or racking pain (in the abdomen), TBr.; Kāṭh.; to violate, confound, disturb, Dhātup.: Caus. *ropayati* (aor. *arūrupat*), to cause acute or violent pain, AV.; to break off, TBr. [Cf. Lat. *rumpere*; Angl. Sax. *reófan*; Germ. *roubôn*, *rauben*; Eng. *reave*.]

Rupita. See *á-rupita*.

Ropa, 1. **ropaṇa** &c. See p. 889, col. 2.

रुप् 2. *rúp*, f. the earth, RV. (Sāy.)

रुप *rupá*, m. v. l. for *rūpa*, AV. xviii, 3, 40.

रुप्यक *rupyaka* and *rairupyaka*, m. N. of a poet, L.

रुभेटि *rubheṭi*, f. fog, vapour, L.

रुम *rúma*, m. N. of a man, RV.; (*ā*), f., s. v.

Rumaṇa, m. N. of an ape, R.

Ruman-vat, m. N. of various men, MBh.; Kāv.; Kathās.; 'possessing salt,' N. of a mountain, Pāṇ. viii, 2, 12, Sch.

Rumā, f. N. of a river, Suśr., Sch.; of a place, Kāśīkh.; of a salt-mine or salt-lake (in the district of Sambhar in Ajmere), L.; of a wife of Su-grīva (the ape), R. **-bhava**, n. salt (obtained from the salt-lake of Rumā), L.

रुम्र *rumra*, mfn. tawny (or 'the dawn,' = *aruṇa*), Uṇ. ii, 14, Sch.; beautiful (= *śobhana*), ib.

रुय्यक *ruyyaka*, m. N. of a teacher (v. l. for *rucaka*), Cat.

रुरु *rúru*, m. (cf. √1. *ru*; Uṇ. iv, 103) a species of antelope (picta), VS. &c. &c.; a kind of savage animal, BhP. (cf. *raurava*); a dog, L.; a species of fruit tree, g. *plakshâdi*; a form of Bhairava, Cat.; N. of a son of the Ṛishi Pramati by the Apsaras Ghṛitācī, MBh.; Kathās.; of a son of Ahina-gu, VP.; of one of the Viśve Devāḥ, Hariv.; of one of the 7 Ṛishis under Manu Sāvarṇi (with the patr. Kāśyapa), ib.; of a Dānava or Daitya (said to have been slain by Durgā), Kathās. **-nakha-dhārin**, m. N. of Kṛishṇa, Pañcar. **-pṛishata**, n. sg. or m. pl. Rurus and Pṛishatas (two kinds of deer), Pāṇ. ii, 4, 12, Vārtt. 1, Pat. **-bhairava**, m. a form of Bhairava (cf. above), Cat. **-muṇḍa**, m. N. of a mountain, Buddh. (v. l. *uru-m°*). **-vidāriṇī**, f. N. of Durgā, Kathās. **-śīrshan** (*rúru-*), mfn. 'deer-headed,' having a deer's horn or a destructive point (said of an arrow), RV.

Ruruka, m. N. of a king, Hariv.; VP.

रुरुक्वस् *rurukvas*. See √1. *ruc*, p. 881.

रुरुक्षणि *rurukshaṇi.* See under √*1. ruj.*

रुरुत्सा *rurutsā*, °*tsu.* See p. 884, col. 2.

रुरुदिषा *rurudishā*, °*shu.* See p. 884, col. 1.

रुवण्य *ruvaṇya*, °*ṇyu; ruvatha.* See p. 881, col. 3.

रुवु *ruvu*, m. (cf. *uruvu*) the castor-oil tree, Ricinus Communis, ŚārṅgS.

Ruvuka or **ruvūka**, m. id., L. (cf. *rūvuka, uruvuka, uruvūka*).

रुश् *ruś* (cf. √*rush* and *riś*), cl. 6. P. (Dhātup. xxviii, 126) *ruśáti* (pf. *rurośa*; fut. *roshṭā, rokshyati*; aor. *arukshat*, Gr.; only pr. p. *ruśát*, q.v.), to hurt, injure, annoy (*hinsāyām*, Dhātup.): Caus. *rośayati* (aor. *arūruśat*), Gr.: Desid. *rurukshati*, ib.: Intens. *roruśyate, roroshṭi*, ib.

1. **Ruśát**, mf(*ántī* or *atī*)n. cropping, browsing on, AV. iv, 21, 7 (RV. *riśántī*); hurting, injuring, mortifying, detestable, disagreeable, AV.; Kauś.; MBh. (v.l. *rushat*); BhP.

रुशङ्गु *ruśaṅgu*, m. (cf. *rushaṅgu* and *ruśad-gu*) N. of a Ṛishi, Cat. (v.l. *nṛishaṅgu*).

रुशत् 2. *rúśat*, mf(*atī*)n. (cf. √*1. ruc*) brilliant, shining, bright, white, RV. — **paśu** (*rúśat-*), mfn. having glistening waves...

Rúśad, in comp. for 2. *ruśat.* — **ūrmi** (*rúśad-*), mfn. having glistening waves, RV. — **gu** (*rúśad-*), mfn. having white or bright cattle, ib.; m. N. of a man (cf. *ruśaṅgu, rushaṅgu*). — **ratha**, m. 'having a white chariot,' N. of a prince, BhP. — **vatsa** (*rúśad-*), mfn. having white calves, RV.

रुशना *ruśanā*, f. N. of one of the wives of Rudra, BhP.

रुशम *rúśama* (or *ruśáma*), m. N. of a man, RV.; (*ruśámās*), pl. his descendants, ib.; (*ā*), f. N. of a woman (said to have contended with Indra as to which of the two would run fastest round the earth, and to have won by the artifice of only going round Kuru-kshetra), PañcavBr.

रुशेकु *ruśeku*, m. N. of a king, BhP. (v.l. *rushadru, ushadgu, ṛishadgu* &c.)

रुष् 1. *rush* (cf. √*ruś*), cl. 1. 4. P. (Dhātup. xvii, 42; xxvi, 120) *roshati* or *rushyati* (rarely °*te*, and *rushati*, cf. *rushat*; Gr. also pf. *rurosha*; aor. *arushat* or *aroshīt*; fut. *roshitā, roshṭā*; *roshishyati*; inf. *roshitum* or *roshṭum*; ind. p. *rushya*, MBh.), to hurt, injure, kill (*hinsāyām*), Dhātup.; (cl. 1.) to be hurt or offended by, take offence (acc.), RV. viii, 99, 4; to displease, be disagreeable to (gen.), ib. viii, 4, 8; AitBr. iv, 10 (cf. *rushat* and 1. *ruśat*); (cl. 4.) to be vexed or cross, be angry with (gen.), MBh.; R. &c.: Caus. (or cl. 10., Dhātup. xxxii, 131) *roshayati*, °*te* (aor. *arūrushat*; Pass. *roshyate*), to vex, annoy, displease, irritate, exasperate, MBh.; Kāv. &c.; to be furious or angry, Divyāv.: Desid. *rurushishati, ruroshishati*, Gr.: Intens. *rorushyate, roroshṭi*, ib. [Cf. Gk. λύσσα &c.]

2. **Rush**, f. (nom. *ruṭ*, Siddh.) anger, wrath, rage, fury, passion, MBh.; Kāv. &c.

Rushaṅgu, m. N. of a Brāhman, MBh. (prob. w.r. for *ruśad-gu*).

Rushat, mf(*atī*)n. (cf. 1. *ruśat*) hurting, injuring, displeasing, MBh.; Hariv.

Rushad, in comp. for *rushat.* — **gu**, m. N. of a king, VP. (prob. w.r. for *ruśad-gu*). — **ratha**, m. N. of a king, ib. (v.l. *ushad-ratha*; cf. *ruśad-r*°).

Rushā, f. = 2. *rush* (mostly ifc.) — °**nvita** (*rushânv*°), mfn. filled with anger, full of wrath, MW.

Rushita, mfn. injured, offended, irritated, furious, angry, MBh.; Kāv. &c.

Rushṭa, mfn. id., ib.; m. N. of a Muni, Cat.

Rushṭi, f. = 2. *rush*, W. — **mat**, mfn., g. *madhv-ādi.*

Rushya, °**shya-mat**, g. *madhv-ādi.*

Rosh, mfn. (nom. *roṭ*) one who hurts or injures or irritates or enrages, L.

Rosha, m. anger, rage, wrath, passion, fury, Āpast.; MBh. &c. (*rosham* √*kṛi* with *prati*, 'to be angry with'). — **tāmrâksha**, mf(*ī*)n. having eyes red with anger, MBh. — **dṛishṭi**, f. an angry look, BhP. — **parīta**, mfn. filled with wrath, R. — **bhāj**, mfn. angry, Śiś. — **bhāshaṇa**, n. angry speech, Daśar. — **maya**, mf(*ī*)n. consisting of anger, proceeding from fury, Hariv.; BhP. — **rūksha**, mfn. rough or harsh through wrath, Daś. — **vāhana**, mfn. 'being a vehicle of anger,' bearing or feeling wrath, W. **Roshâkulita**, mfn. troubled or perplexed by passion, Hariv. **Roshâkshepa**, m. (in rhet.) angry expression of dissent, angry reproach, ironical taunt, Kāvyâd. **Roshâgni**, m. the fire of passion or fury, Mṛicch. **Roshâvaroha**, m. N. of a warrior on the side of the gods in the war against the Asuras, Kathās. **Roshôkti**, f. angry speech, L.

Roshaka, mfn. furious, angry, Divyâv.

Roshaṇa, mfn. angry, wrathful, passionate, enraged at or against (gen. or comp.), MBh.; Hariv.; MārkP. (-*tā*, f., Śak.); m. (only L.) a touchstone; quicksilver; an arid or desert soil containing salt; Grewia Asiatica.

Roshāṇa, mfn. (cf. prec.) angry, furious, L.; m. a touchstone for gold, L.; quicksilver, L.

Roshita, mfn. (fr. Caus.) enraged, exasperated, irritated, MBh.; Kāv. &c.

Roshin, mf(*iṇī*)n. angry, wrathful, furious, passionate, Hariv.

Roshṭṛi, mfn. id., Bhaṭṭ.; m. an injurer, MW.

रुह् 1. *ruh* (cf. √1. *rudh*), cl. 1. P. (Dhātup. xx, 29) *róhati* (m. c. also °*te* and *ruhati*, °*te*; Ved. and ep. impf. or aor. *aruhat*; Pot. *ruheyam, -ruhethās, -ruhemahi*; Impv. *ruha*, p. *rúhāṇa*; pf. *ruroha, ruruhúḥ*, RV. &c. &c.; *ruruhe*, BhP.; aor. *árukshat*, RV.; AV. &c.; fut. *roḍhā*, Gr.; *rokshyáti*, °*te*, Br. &c.; *rohishye*, MBh.; inf. *roḍhum*, Br. &c.; *rohitum*, MBh.; *róhishyai*, TS.; ind. p. *rūḍhvā́*, AV., -*rúhya*, ib. &c.; -*rūhya*, AitBr.; -*rúham*, RV.; -*róham*, Br.), to ascend, mount, climb, RV.; AV.; Br.; ŚrS.; to reach to, attain (a desire), ŚBr.; to rise, spring up, grow, develop, increase, prosper, thrive, RV. &c. &c. (with *na*, 'to be useless or in vain,' MBh.); to grow together or over, cicatrize, heal (as a wound), AV.; Kathās.; Suśr. &c.: Caus. *roháyati* or (later) *ropayati*, °*te* (aor. *arūruhat* or *arūrupat*, Gr.; Pass. *ropyate*, MBh., aor. *aropi*, Kāv.), to cause to ascend, raise up, elevate, RV.; AV.; Rājat.; to place in or on, fix in, fasten to, direct towards (with acc. or loc.), MBh.; Kāv.; Kathās.; to transfer to, commit, entrust, Ragh. (cf. *ropita*); to put in the ground, plant, sow, MBh.; R.; VarBṛS.; to lay out (a garden), MBh.; to cause to grow, increase, Rājat.; to cause to grow over or heal, AV.; Kathās.; Suśr.: Desid. *rúrukshati*, see *ā*-√*ruh*: Intens. *roruhyate, roroḍhi*, Gr.

2. **Rúh**, f. rising, growth, sprout, shoot, RV.; AV.; ŚāṅkhŚr.; (ifc.) shooting, sprouting, growing, produced in or on (cf. *ambho-, avani-, kshiti-r*° &c.)

Ruha, mf(*ā*)n. (ifc.) = prec. (cf. *aṅga-, ambu-, kara-, jala-r*° &c.); mounted, ascended, W.; (*ā*), f. Panicum Dactylon, L.; = *rohiṇī*, Bhpr.

Ruhaka, n. a hole, vacuity, chasm, L. (cf. 1. *ropa*).

Ruharuhikā (Hcar., Sch.) or **ruhiruhikā** (L.), f. longing, desire.

Ruhvan, m. a plant, tree, Uṇ. iv, 113, Sch.

Rūḍhá, mfn. mounted, risen, ascended, AV. &c. &c.; lifted up, imposed on, laden (see -*paricchada*); grown together, healed, R.; Suśr.; sprung up, grown, increased, developed, produced from (comp.), MBh.; Kāv. &c.; budded, blown, W.; large, great, MW.; high, noble (see -*vaṇśa*); diffused, spread about, widely known, current, notorious, famous, Kāv.; Sāh.; traditional, conventional, popular (opp. to *yaugika* and said of words which have a meaning not directly connected with their etymology; esp. in pl. applied to names of warrior tribes which also denote the country inhabited by them), Śiś.; Pāṇ., Sch. &c.; acquainted or conversant with (loc.), Gaṇit.; certain, ascertained, W.; obscure, MW.; m. a scar (also n. and *ā*, f.); barley, L. — **granthi**, mfn. forming a knot, Uttarar. — **tṛiṇâṅkura**, mfn. (a palace) on the roof of which young grass has sprouted, Ragh. — **paricchada**, mfn. laden with chattels, BhP. — **paryāya**, mfn. (a ceremony) in which the regularly returning formulas are constantly increasing, Lāṭy. — **praṇaya**, mfn. one whose love or affection has grown strong, MW. — **manyu**, mfn. one whose passion has grown strong, BhP. — **mūlatva**, n. having taken firm root, firmness (*a-r*°), Mālav. — **yoga**, mfn. one whose Yoga or devotion has increased, ib. — **yauvana**, mfn. one who has attained to youth or adolescence, ib.; Kathās. &c. — **rāga-pravāla**, mfn. (the tree of love) in which the sprouts of affection have grown strong, Mālav. — **vaṇśa**, mfn. of a high family, Daśar. — **vacana**, n. = *rūḍhi-śabda*, MW. — **vraṇa**, mfn. one whose wounds are healed, R. — **śādvala**, mfn. (a wood) whose grass has grown high, Hariv. — **śmaśru**, mfn. one whose beard has grown, R. — **sauhṛida**, mfn. one whose friendship is grown or increased, firm in friendship, Vikr. — **skandha**, mfn. (a tree) whose stem or trunk has grown, high, lofty, R.

Rūḍhi, f. rise, ascent (lit. and fig.), increase, growth, development, Kāv.; Rājat.; birth, production, W.; decision, Rājat.; fame, celebrity, notoriety, Śiś.; tradition, custom, general prevalence, current usage (esp. of speech), Nyāyam.; Rājat.; (in rhet.) the more amplified or popular or conventional meaning of words, the employment of a word in such a meaning (as opp. to *yoga*, q.v.), Kāś. on Pāṇ. i, 2, 55; Sāh.; Kpr. &c. — **śabda**, m. a word used in its conventional sense (as opp. to *yoga-ś*°; thus *śatru* as a Rūḍhi-śabda means 'enemy,' but as a Yoga-ś° 'destroyer'), APrāt.; Bhar. &c.; -*tā*, f. the state of being used in a conventional sense, Rājat.

Roḍhṛi, 2. **ropa** &c. See p. 889, cols. 1, 2.

रूक्ष् *rūksh* (rather Nom. fr. *rūksha*), cl. 10. P. *rūkshayati* (Vop. also *rūkshāpayati*; aor. *arurūkshat*), to be rough or harsh, Dhātup. xxxv, 56; to make dry or emaciated, ŚBr.; to soil, smear, VarBṛS.; to injure, offend, exasperate, Jātak.

1. **Rūkshá**, mf(*ā*)n. (prob. fr. √*rūsh*; cf. 2. *rukshá*) rough, dry, arid, dreary, ŚBr. &c. &c.; emaciated, thin, Suśr.; rough to the taste, astringent, MBh.; Suśr.; not greasy or oily (as food or medicine), Kathās.; Suśr.; hard, harsh, unkind, cruel (as a person or speech), MBh.; Kāv. &c.; unpleasant, disagreeable, not soft (to the sight, smell &c.), ib.; dismal (as a house), Pañcat.; soiled, smeared, dirtied, R.; Mudr.; having the smell of an elephant in rut, L.; m. hardness, harshness, L.; the smell of the rut of an elephant, L.; a kind of grass (= *varaka*), L.; (*ā*), f. Croton Polyandrum or Tiglium, L.; n. a good kind of iron, L.; the thick part of curds, L. — **gandha** or -**gandhaka**, m. bdellium, L. — **tā**, f. (Kāv. &c.), -**tva**, n. (Śaṃk.) roughness, dryness, aridity, harshness, unkindness. — **darbha**, m. a kind of Kuśa-grass, L. — **durbala**, mfn. emaciated and feeble, Suśr. — **nishṭhura-vāda**, m. harsh and rough language, ib. — **pattra**, m. Trophis Aspera, L. — **pesham**, ind. (√*pish*, to pound) having pounded (anything) into dry powder (without adding butter or any liquid), Pāṇ. iii, 4, 35. — **priya**, m. a species of bulbous plant (growing on the Himavat), L. — **bhāva**, m. harsh or unfriendly behaviour, Ratnâv. — **mlānâṅga**, mfn. having emaciated and withered limbs, Suśr. — **varṇa**, mfn. dark-coloured (as clouds), MBh. — **vāc**, f. rough speech, MBh. — **vādin**, mfn. speaking roughly, R. — **vāluka**, n. honey of a small bee, L. — **vāsin**, mfn. screaming or crying harshly, Kām. — **svara**, mfn. harsh-sounding (*am*, ind.), Mṛicch.; m. an ass, L. — **svādu-phala**, m. Grewia Elastica, L. **Rūkshâbhibhāshin**, mf(*iṇī*)n. speaking harshly or unkindly, Hariv.

Rūkshaṇa, mfn. making thin, attenuating, ŚārṅgS.; n. the act of making thin, (esp.) medical treatment for reducing fat or corpulence, Suśr.

Rūkshaṇīya, m. rum, spirit distilled from molasses, L.; (*ā*), f. Coix Barbata, L.

Rūkshita, mfn. made rough, rough (see *a-r*°); soiled, smeared, VarBṛS.; injured, offended (-*tva*, n.), Jātak.

Rūkshī-kṛita, mfn. made rough, soiled, besmeared, covered with (comp.), Mṛicch.

रूक्ष 2. *rūksha*, m. (prob. for Prākṛit *rukkha* = *vṛiksha*) a tree, L.

रूखर *rūkhara*, m. pl. N. of a Śaiva sect, W.

रूचक *rūcaka*, w.r. for *rucaka*, q.v.

रूढ *rūḍha, rūḍhi.* See col. 2 and above.

रूप् *rūp* (prob. Nom. fr. *rūpa*), cl. 10. P. (Dhātup. xxxv, 79) *rūpayati*, to form, figure, represent (esp. on the stage), exhibit by gesture, act, feign, Hariv.; Kāv.; BhP. &c.; to view, inspect, contemplate, Kir. viii, 26; Pāṇ. iii, 1, 25, Sch.; (Ā. °*yate*) to show one's self, appear, Vop.

Rūpá, n. (perhaps connected with *varpa, varpas*; ifc. f. *ā*, rarely *ī*) any outward appearance or phenomenon or colour (often pl.), form, shape, figure,

RV. &c. &c. (*rūpeṇa*, ifc. in the form of; *rūpam* √*kṛi* or √*bhū*, to assume a form; often ifc. = 'having the form or appearance or colour of,' 'formed or composed of,' 'consisting of,' 'like to;' sometimes used after an adj. or p. p. to emphasize its meaning or almost redundantly, cf. *ghora-r°*; or connected with a verb, e.g. *pacati-rūpam*, he cooks very well, cf. Pāṇ. viii, 1, 57); dreamy or phantom shapes (pl.), VS.; ŚBr.; handsome form, loveliness, grace, beauty, splendour, RV. &c. &c.; nature, character, peculiarity, feature, mark, sign, symptom, VS. &c. &c.; likeness, image, reflection, Mn.; Kathās.; circumstances (opp. to 'time' and 'place'), Mn. viii, 45; sort, kind, R.; Suśr.; mode, manner, way, Kap.; (ifc.) trace of, R.; a single specimen or exemplar (and therefore a term for the number 'one'), VarBṛS.; Gaṇit.; a partic. coin (prob. a rupee), VarBṛS.; a show, play, drama, Daśar.; (in alg.) the arithmetical unit; (pl.) integer number; known or absolute number, a known quantity as having specific form (and expressed by *rū* i. e. first syllable of *rūpa*), IW. 182; (in gram.) any form of a noun or verb (as inflected by declension or conjugation), Pāṇ. i, 1, 68 &c.; (in phil.) the quality of colour (one of the 17 or 24 Guṇas of the Vaiśeshikas), IW. 68; (with Buddhists) material form i. e. the organized body (as one of the 5 constituent elements or Skandhas), Dharmas. 22; MWB. 109; (in dram.) a reflection or remark made under partic. circumstances when the action is at its height (*garbhe*), Bhar.; Daśar. &c.; (only L.) cattle; a beast; a sound, word; re-reading a book (= *granthâvṛitti*); m. a word of unknown meaning, AV. xviii, 3, 40; (pl.) N. of a people, MBh.; m. or n. N. of a place (v. l. *rūma*), Cat.; (*ā*), f. N. of a river, VP. — **kartṛi**, m. 'maker of forms or figures,' N. of Viśva-kṛit, R. — **kavi-rāja-go-svāmi-guṇa-leśa-sūcakâshṭaka**, n. N. of wk. — **kāntā**, f. N. of a Surâṅganā, Siṉhâs. — **kāra**, m. a maker of images, sculptor, Kathās. — **kṛit**, mfn making forms or figures (N. of Tvashṭṛi), TS.; ŚBr.; KātyŚr.; m. a sculptor, Kathās. — **guṇa**, mfn. possessing the quality of colour, Mn. i, 77; (ibc.) beauty of form; *°ṇôpêta*, mfn. endowed with it, MBh. — **go-svāmin**, m. N. of an author, Cat.; *°mi-guṇa-leśa-sūcaka-nāma-daśaka*, n. N. of wk. — **graha**, mfn. apprehending forms, perceiving colours, L.; m. the eye, L. — **candra**, m. N. of an author, Cat. — **cintāmaṇi**, m. N. of wk. — **jīva**, mfn., w. r. for *rūpâj°* below, R. — **jīvanā**, f. 'subsisting by beauty of form,' a prostitute, L. — **jña**, mfn., see *á-r°*. — **tattva**, n. 'reality of form,' inherent property, nature, essence, L. — **tama** (*rūpá-*), n. the best form or colour, ŚBr. — **taraṃgiṇī**, f. N. of sev. wks. — **tarka**, m. (prob.) an assaye-master or inspector of a mint, Pat. — **tas**, ind. according to form, by shape, in form, Nal. — **tā**, f. (ifc.) the state of being formed or composed of (e.g. *duḥkha-r°*, 'the consisting of pain'), Nilak. — **tva**, n. id. or the state of having form or figure, Sarvad.; = *-tā*, Kap.; *-jāti-pramāṇa*, n. N. of wk. — **dīpaka-piṅgala**, m. N. of wk. — **deva**, m. N. of two poets, Sadukt.; Cat. — **dhara**, mfn. having the form or shape of, being of the colour of (ifc.; e.g. *go-r°*, cow-shaped; cf. *kāma-r°*), Ragh.; VP. &c.; m. N. of a king, Kathās. — **dhātu**, m. the element of form, original seat or region of f° (with Buddhists; the other two el°s being *kāma-dh°*, q. v., and *arūpa-dh°*, 'the el° of formlessness'), Buddh. — **dhārin**, mfn. bearing a form, assuming a shape (*catur-guṇa-r°*, 'having a 4 times greater sh°'), Pañcad.; endowed with beauty, VāmP.; *°ri-tva*, n. the power of assuming any f° or sh°, Kām. — **dhṛik**, mfn. (see *dhṛik*, p. 519) = next, MW. — **dhṛit**, mfn. having the form or shape of (ifc.; e.g. *kapi r°*, 'monkey-shaped;' cf. *vividha-r°*), Kathās. — **dhéya**, n. form and colour, external appearance, AV.; beauty, Naish.; (cf. *nāma-dh°*.) — **nayana**, m. N. of a commentator, Cat. — **nārāyaṇa**, m. N. of two authors, Cat.; (?) of wk.; *-cakra-vartin*, *-sena*, m. N. of men, Cat. — **nāśana**, m. 'form-destroying,' an owl, L. — **nāśin**, mfn. destroying form or beauty, disfiguring, MBh. — **pa**, m. pl. N. of a people, MārkP. — **pati** (*rūpá-*), m. lord of forms (N. of Tvashṭṛi), ŚBr.; KātyŚr. — **pari-kalpanā**, f. the assuming of a shape, R. — **pura**, n. N. of a town, Cat. — **praśna**, m. N. of wk. — **bhāgânubandha**, m. addition of the fraction of an unit, Col. — **bhāgâpavāha**, m. subtraction of the fraction of an unit, ib. — **bhāj**, mfn. endowed with beauty, Vishṇ. — **bhṛit**, mfn. having form or beauty, MW.; (ifc.) having the appearance of, VarYogay. — **bheda**, m. diversity or variety of forms or manifestations, Kṛishṇaj.; (in gram.) div° of phonetic form or sound; n. N. of a Tantra wk.; *-prakāśa*, m. N. of a glossary. — **mañjarī**, f. N. of sev. wks.; of a woman, Cat.; *-guṇa-leśa-sūcakâshṭaka*, n., *-pādâmbuja-sevā-prârthanā*, f. N. of Stotras. — **maṇḍana**, n. N. of wk. — **matī** (?), f. N. of a princess, Inscr. — **mātra**, n. only beauty, MW. — **mālā**, f. N. of a grammatical wk. (also *-vyākaraṇa*); (*ī*), f. N. of a metre, Col. — **yauvana-vat**, mfn. possessing beauty and youth, Hit.; Kathās. — **yauvanôtsāhin**, mfn. poss° b° y° and energy, Sāh. — **ratnâkara**, m. N. of wk. — **rasa-gandha-sparśa-vat**, mfn. having colour and taste and smell and palpability, Kaṇ. — **rasa-sparśavat**, mfn. having col° and t° and pal°, ib. — **rāga**, m. (with Buddh.) craving for life in a material form (either on earth or in heaven; one of the 10 fetters or Saṃyojanas), MWB. 127. — **latā**, f. N. of a princess, Kathās. — **lāvaṇya**, n. beauty of form, elegance, loveliness, W. — **vajrā**, f. N. of a Buddhist goddess, Kālac. — **vat**, mfn. having form or colour, formed, embodied, corporeal, R.; BhP.; Kathās.; having a beautiful form or col°, handsomely formed, handsome, beautiful (superl. *-tama*), PārGṛ.; MBh.; Nir. &c.; having the form or appearance of (ifc.), MBh.; MārkP.; (*atī*), f. a handsome woman (N. of various women), Buddh.; Kathās.; of a river, BhP. — **vāsika** (VP.) or **-vāhika** (MBh.), m. pl. N. of a people. — **vicāra**, m. N. of wk. — **viparyaya**, m. a morbid change of bodily form, Mn.; R. — **vibhāga**, m. the dividing of an integer number into fractions, Col. — **śas**, ind. in various forms, according to peculiarity, RV.; Kauś. — **śālin**, mfn. possessed of beauty, handsome, beautiful, MārkP.; Hcat.; Kathās. — **śikhā**, f. N. of a daughter of the Rākshasa Agni-śikha, Kathās. — **sanātana**, m. N. of an author, L. — **samṛiddha** (*rūpá-*), mfn. perfect in form, AitBr.; perfectly beautiful, TS.; ŚBr. — **samṛiddhi**, f. perfection of form, suitable form, AitBr.; Sāy. — **sampatti** (MW.) or **-sampad** (MBh.), f. perfection or excellence of form, beauty. — **sampanna**, mfn. endowed with beauty, MBh.; R.; modified, Nir. — **siddhi**, m. N. of a man, Kathās.; of a grammatical wk. — **sena**, m. N. of a Vidyā-dhara, Kathās.; of a king, Vet. — **saubhāgya-vat**, mfn. having beauty of form, Vishṇ.; Hcat.; Campak. — **skandha**, m. (with Buddhists) a physical element (of which there are 11), Dharmas. 26. — **stha**, mfn. possessed of form or shape, RāmatUp. — **sparśa-vat**, mfn. possessing colour and palpability, Kaṇ. — **hāni**, f. loss of form (in the Nyāya one of the 7 preventives of classification), MW. **Rūpâjīva**, mf(*ā*)n. making a living by beauty of form, living by prostitution, Kām.; Daś.; (*ā*), f. a harlot, R. **Rūpâdhibodha**, m. the perception of form or of any visible object (by the senses), W. **Rūpâbhigrāhita**, mfn. caught in the act, c° red-handed, A. **Rūpâyatana**, n. (with Buddhists) form as one of the 12 Āyatanas (or organs and objects of sense), Dharmas. 24. **Rūpâyudha-bhṛit**, mfn. (men) possessing beauty and bearing weapons, VarBṛS. **Rūpâvacara**, m. pl. (with Buddhists) N. of one of the 18 classes of gods of the world of form, Dharmas. 128 (cf. *kāmâv°*). **Rūpâvatāra**, m. N. of wk. **Rūpâvalī**, f. a list or series of (grammatical) forms or of the variations of (grammatical) forms (caused by declension, conjugation &c.), MW.; N. of various wks. **Rūpâśraya**, m. a repository or receptacle of beauty; (or) mfn. exceedingly handsome, BhP. **Rūpâstra**, m. 'having beauty for a weapon,' the god of love, L. **Rūpêndriya**, n. the organ which perceives form and colour, the eye, Suśr. **Rūpêśvara**, m. N. of a god, Cat.; (*ī*), f. N. of a goddess, DevibhP. **Rūpôccaya**, m. a collection of lovely forms, Śak. **Rūpôpajīvana**, n. the gaining a livelihood by a beautiful form, MBh. **Rūpôpajīvin**, mfn. gaining a livelihood by a b° f°, VarBṛS.

Rūpaka, mfn. having form, figurative, metaphorical, illustrating by figurative language, Sāh.; m. a partic. coin (prob. a rupee), Var.; Pañcat. &c.; (in music) a kind of measure, Saṃgīt. (cf. *-tāla*); (*rūpakā*), f. a female fox or jackal, AV. xi, 9, 15 [cf. Zd. *urupi*]; (*ikā*), f. swallow-wort, Asclepias Lactifera; n. form, figure, shape, appearance (mostly ifc., with f. *ā*, = having the form of, composed or consisting of, similar to), MBh.; Kāv. &c.; image, likeness, AitBr.; Kathās.; feature, sign, symptom, W.; kind, species, MaitrUp.; (in rhet.) a figure of speech, metaphor, comparison, simile (esp. one in which *iva*, *vat* &c. are omitted, e.g. *bāhu-latā*, 'a creeper-like arm,' *pāṇi-padma*, 'a lotus-like hand;' there are 3 or 4 varieties of Rūpaka, e.g. the *ardha-r°*, 'partial metaphor,' *khaṇḍa-r°*, 'imperfect m°,' and *lalāma-r°*, 'flowery m°'), Kāvyâd.; Sāh. &c. (cf. IW. 458); a drama, play, theatrical performance (esp. of the principal class, as opp. to the *upa-rūpakas* or inferior dramas; of the former there are 10 species including the Nāṭaka or higher order of play and the Prahasana or farce), Daśar.; Sāh. &c. (IW. 471); a partic. weight (= 3 Guñjās), L.; = *mūrta* or *dhūrta*, L. — **tāla**, n. (in music) a kind of measure, Gīt. (w. r. *-tala*). — **nṛitya**, n. (in music) a kind of dance, Saṃgīt. — **paribhāshā**, f. N. of wk. — **rūpaka**, n. a partic. kind of Rūpaka (metaphor), Kāvyâd. — **vākya**, n., **-śabda**, m. a figurative expression, MW. **Rūpakâkhya-shaḍ-aṅga**, n. N. of a collection of Mantras.

Rūpaṇa, n. figurative illustration, metaphorical description, Kāvyâd.; Sāh.; examination, investigation, proof, Sāh.

Rūpasvin, mfn. (fr. an unused *rūpas* = *rūpa* + *vin*) handsome, beautiful (superl. *°vi-tama*), PārGṛ.; Vet.; (*inī*), f. N. of a woman, Siṉhâs.

Rūpâvata, m. N. of a prince, Divyâv.; (*ī*), f. N. of a woman, ib.

Rūpâvaty-alaṃkaraṇa, n. (fr. prec. f. + *al°*) N. of a poem, Cat.

Rūpika, m. or n. (?) coined gold or silver, money, L.

Rūpiṇa, m. N. of a son of Aja-mīḍha, MBh.

Rūpiṇikā, f. (dimin. fr. *rūpiṇī*) N. of a courtezan, Kathās.

Rūpita, mfn. formed, represented, exhibited, imagined, Kāv.; Sarvad.

Rūpi-dāraka, m. (fr. *rūpin* + *d°*) a fine boy, Mṛicch.

Rūpin, mf(*iṇī*)n. having or assuming a partic. form or figure, embodied, corporeal, MBh.; Kāv. &c.; having a beautiful form or figure, well-shaped, handsome, beautiful, ŚBr. &c. &c.; (ifc.) having the form or nature or character of, characterised by, appearing as, MBh.; Kāv. &c.

Rūpī-√kṛi, P. *-karoti*, to make rough, soil, besmear, A.

Rūpya, mfn. well-shaped, beautiful, Pāṇ. v, 2, 120; stamped, impressed, ib.; to be denoted (or capable of being denoted) figuratively or metaphorically, Sāh.; (ifc.) formerly in the possession of or possessed by, Pāṇ. v, 3, 54; proceeding from or originating with (= *tasmād āgataḥ*), ib. iv, 3, 82; m. N. of a man, g. *tikâdi*; of a mountain, Śatr.; (*ā*), f. a partic. fragrant substance, Gal.; n. silver, Mn.; MBh. &c.; wrought silver or gold, stamped coin, rupee, L.; collyrium, L. — **da**, mfn. one who gives silver, Mn. iv, 230. — **dhauta**, n. silver, L. — **maya**, mf(*ī*)n. made or consisting of silver, containing s°, Pañcat. — **mākshika**, n. s° Mākshika, Hepatic pyrites of iron, MW. — **māsha**, m. a s° Māsha (= 2 Kṛishṇalas), Yājñ. i, 363. — **rajju**, f. a cord or rope made of s°, Mṛicch. — **ratna-parîkshā**, f. 'test of silver and jewels,' N. of one of the 64 Kalās, Cat. — **rukma-maya**, mf(*ī*)n. made or consisting of s° or gold, MBh. — **śata-māna**, n. a partic. weight (= $3\frac{1}{2}$ Palas), L. — **svarṇa-maṇi-maya**, mf(*ī*)n. consisting of silver and gold and (or) jewels, HPariś. **Rūpyâcala**, m. 's°-mountain,' N. of the m° Kailāsa, Śaṃkar. **Rūpyâdhyaksha**, m. a superintendent of silver or silver coinage, master of the mint, L.

Rūpyaka. See *suvarṇa-r°*.

रूम *rūma*, m. or n. N. of a place, Cat. (v. l. *rūpa*).

रूर *rūrá*, mfn. hot, burning (as fire, fever &c.), AV.; TāṇḍBr.

रूवुक *rūvuka*, m. the castor-oil tree, Ricinus Communis, L. (cf. *ruvuka*).

रूष् *rūsh*, cl. 1. P. *rūshati*, to adorn, decorate, Dhātup. xvii, 27; to cover, strew, smear (see *rūshita*): Caus. (or cl. 10. P.) *rūshayati*, 'to tremble' or 'to burst' (*visphuraṇe*), Dhātup. xxxv, 84, Vop.

Rūsha, m. bitter and sour taste, L.; mf(*ā*)n. bitter and sour, L. (cf. *rūksha*).

Rūshaka, m. Gendarussa Vulgaris, L.

Rūshaṇa, n. covering, strewing, Chandom.; soiling, L.; adorning, decoration, MW.

Rūshita, mfn. (sometimes confounded with *rushita*) strewed, covered, soiled, smeared with (comp.), MBh.; Kāv. &c.; adhering to (comp.), BhP.; perfumed with (comp.), MBh.; pounded, reduced to powder, L.; adorned, decorated, L.; = *nashṭa*, Prab., Sch.; made rough or rugged (cf. *rūksha*), W.

रे *re*, ind. a vocative particle (generally used contemptuously or to express disrespect; often doubled), Kāv.; Kathās. &c.

रेउइ *reüi*, N. of a village, Kshitīś.

रेक् *rek*, cl. 1. Ā. *rekate*, to suspect, doubt, Dhātup. iv, 6.

1. **Reka**, m. (only L.) suspicion, doubt, fear; a man of low caste; a frog (cf. *bheka*); a kind of fish.

रेक 2. *reka*, m. (√*ric*) emptying, loosening, purging, Bhpr.

Réku, mfn. empty, void, deserted, RV.

Rékṇas, n. property left by bequest, inherited possession, any property or valuable object, wealth, gold, RV. **-vat** (*ré°*), mfn. possessed of valuable property, wealthy, rich, ib.

Reca, m. the emptying of the lungs by exhalation (see next), emission of breath, AmṛitUp.

Recaka, mf(*ikā*)n. emptying, purging, aperient, cathartic, L.; emptying the lungs, emitting the breath, L.; m. the act of breathing out, exhalation, VarBṛS.; (esp.) expelling the breath out of one of the nostrils (one of the three Prāṇāyāmas [q. v.] or breath-exercises performed during Saṃdhyā), AmṛitUp.; BhP. &c.; RTL. 402; a syringe, BhP.; a partic. movement of the feet, VP.; saltpetre, L.; Croton Jamalgota, L.; Clerodendrum Phlomoides, L.; N. of a forester, Vikr. (v.l. *redhaka*); pl. N. of a people, MBh. (B. *ārocaka*); n. a kind of soil or earth, L.; the fruit of the yellow myrobolan, L.; a purge, cathartic, W.; m. or n. (?) = *bhramaṇa*, Harav. (cf. next).

Recakita, mfn. = *bhramita*, Vām. iv, 1, 2.

Recana, mf(*ī*)n. purging, cathartic, aperient, Suśr.; clearing (the head), Car.; (*ī*), f. N. of various plants (Ipomoea Turpethum; Croton Polyandrum; = *kālāñjanī, gundrā, kāmpilla* &c.), L.; n. the act of emptying, lessening, exhausting, Kām.; emission of breath, exhalation, Yogas., Sch. (cf. *reca* and *recaka*); purging, evacuation, Suśr.; Sarvad.; clearing (the head), Car.; a kind of earth, L.; mucus, Gal.

Recanaka, m. a kind of red powder, L. (cf. *recin*).

Recita, mfn. (fr. Caus.) emptied, purged, cleared, W.; left, abandoned, Ragh.; Śiś.; m. (scil. *hasta*) N. of a partic. position of the hands in dancing, Cat.; (*ā*), f. contraction of one eye-brow, L.; n. N. of one of a horse's paces, cantering, Kād.

Recin, m. Alangium Hexapetalum, L.; a kind of red powder, L. (cf. *recanaka*).

Recya, m. = *reca*, L.

रेख *rekha*, m. (m. c. for *rekhā*, fr. √*rikh* = *likh*) a scratch, line, Caurap.; N. of a man, g. *śivādi*; (*ā*), f., see below.

Rekhaka. See *bindu-r°*.

Rekhā, f. a scratch, streak, stripe, line, Gṛihyas.; Yājñ.; MBh. &c.; a continuous line, row, range, series, MBh.; Kāv. &c.; the first or prime meridian (considered to be a line drawn from Laṅkā to Meru, i. e. from Ceylon [supposed to lie on the equator] to the north pole), Sūryas.; a right or straight position of all the limbs in dancing, Saṃgīt.; delineation, outline, drawing, sketch, Kāv.; Kathās.; appearance (*rekhayā*, ifc. under the app° of, Bālar.; *rekhām na* √*labh*, not to attain even to the app° of, not to be at all equal to, Vcar.); deceit, fraud (= *chadman*), L.; fulness, satisfaction (= *ābhoga*), L.; a small quantity, little portion, L. (cf. *-mātram*). **-°ṅśa** (*rekhāṅśa*), m. a degree of longitude, L. **-°kāra** (*rekhāk°*), mfn. formed in lines, striped, MW. **-gaṇita**, n. 'line-reckoning, geometry,' N. of a wk. by Bhāskarācārya; *-kshetra-vyavahāra*, m. 'geometry and mensuration,' N. of a wk. by Jagan-nātha (18th century). **-jātaka-sudhākara**, m. N. of a wk. (on prognostications from lines on various parts of the body). **-°ntara** (*rekhānt°*), n. geographical longitude, distance east or west from the first meridian, L. **-nyāsa**, m. the marking down of lines or lineaments, outline, sketch, Kāv. **-pratiti**, f., **-pradīpa**, m. N. of astron. wks. **-mātram**, ind. even by a line or by a hair's breadth, Ragh.

Rekhāya, Nom. Ā. °*yate*, g. *kaṇḍv-ādi*.

Rekhāyani, m. patr. (also pl.), Saṃskārak.

Rekhin, mfn. having lines on the hand, lined (*bahu-r°*), VarBṛS.

रेच *reca, recaka* &c. See col. 1.

रेज् 1. *rej*, cl. 1. P. Ā. *réjati*, °*te*, (P.) to go, Naigh. ii, 14; to cause to tremble or shake, RV.; (Ā.) to shine (cf. √*rāj*), Dhātup. vi, 23; to shake, tremble, quiver, RV.: Caus. *rejáyati*, to cause to tremble or quake, to shake, RV.

2. **Réj**, mfn. (nom. *reṭ*; cf. 2. *resh*) trembling, quaking, VS.; MaitrS.; m. fire, L.

Reja, mfn. = *tejishṭha*, Śiś. xix, 102 (Sch.)

रेट् *reṭ*, cl. 1. P. Ā. *reṭati*, °*te* (pf. *rireṭa*, *rireṭe* &c., Gr.), to speak; to ask, request, Dhātup. xxi, 4: Caus. *reṭayati* (aor *arireṭat*), Gr.: Desid. *rireṭishati*, °*te*, ib.: Intens. *rereṭyate, rereṭṭi*, ib.

Reṭi, f. the sound of fire, L.; harsh or unrestrained speech, L.

रेट्टमत *reṭṭa-mata*, n. N. of an astron. wk.

रेड् *reḍ* or *reḷ*, cl. 1. Ā. *réḷate*, to be angry (= *krudhyati*), Naigh. ii, 12 (only in *á-reḍat* = *anādaram akurvat*, TS., Sch.)

रेणा *reṇā*, f. N. of a woman, HPariś.

रेणु *reṇú*, m. (or f., Siddh.; or n., g. *ardharcādi*; fr. √*ri, rī*) dust, a grain or atom of dust, sand &c., RV. &c. &c.; the pollen of flowers, MBh.; Kāv. &c.; powder of anything, Śiś.; a partic. measure, Lalit. (= 8 *trasa-reṇus*, L.); m. N. of a partic. drug, Piper Aurantiacum, VarBṛS.; Suśr. (cf. *reṇukā*); Oldenlandia Herbacea, L.; N. of the author of RV. ix, 70 and x, 81 (with the patr. *Vaiśvāmitra*), AitBr.; ŚrS.; of a descendant of Ikshvāku, Hariv.; of a son of Vikukshi, R.; f. N. of a wife of Viśvāmitra, Hariv. **-kakāṭa** (*reṇú-*), mfn. whirling up dust (?), RV.; VS. (others 'having the head covered with dust;' cf. *kakāṭikā*). **-kadambaka**, m. a species of Kadamba, L. **-kārikā**, f. N. of a Kārikā. **-garbha**, m. 'sand-vessel,' (prob.) a kind of hour-glass (used for astron. purposes), MW. **-guṇṭhita**, mfn. covered with dust, MBh. **-jāla**, n. a dense mass or cloud of dust, Hariv. **-tva**, n. the state of being dust (*reṇu-tvam* √*i*, to become dust), Ragh. **-dīkshita**, m. N. of an author, Cat. **-pa**, m. pl. N. of a people, MBh. (B. *veṇu-pa*). **-padavī**, f. a path of dust, MW. **-pālaka**, m. N. of a man, Pravar. **-mat**, m. N. of a son of Viśvāmitra by Reṇu, Hariv. **-rūshita**, m. 'covered with d°, dusty,' an ass, L. **-lakshman**, m. 'marked by d°,' the wind, Harav. **-vāsa**, m. 'covered with d° or with the pollen of flowers,' a bee, L. **-śas**, ind. to d°, into d° (*-śaḥ* √*kṛi*, to make into d°, turn to d°), Rājat. **-sāra** or **-sāraka**, m. 'essence of dust,' camphor, L. **-sahasra**, n. N. of a Stotra. **Reṇûtpāta**, m. rising or sudden appearance of dust, VarBṛS.

Reṇuka, m. a partic. formula recited over weapons, R.; N. of a Yaksha, MBh. (Nīlak.); of a son of Reṇu, VP.; of a mythical elephant, MBh.; (*ā*), f., see below; n. a species of gem, L. **Reṇukâcārya**, m. N. of an author (who lived in the 13th century).

Reṇukā, f. a partic. drug or medicinal substance (said to be fragrant, but bitter and slightly pungent in taste, and of greyish colour; cf. *reṇu*), L.; N. of a Kārikā (composed by Hari-hara; cf. *reṇu-kārikā*), Cat.; of the wife of Jamad-agni and mother of Paraśu-rāma (she was the daughter of Reṇu and of king Prasena-jit), MBh.; Hariv.; Pur.; of a river, VP. **-kavaca**, n. N. of a partic. Kavaca. **-tanaya**, m. 'son of Reṇukā,' patr. of Paraśu-rāma (*-tā*, f.), Śiś. **-tīrtha**, n. N. of a Tīrtha, MBh. **-mālāmantra**, m., **-māhātmya**, n., **-°shṭaka** (°*kâshṭ°*), n., **-sahasra-nāman**, n. N. of wks. **-suta**, m. = *-tanaya*, MBh. **-stotra**, n. N. of a Stotra.

Reta = *retas*, semen virile, L. **-ja**, mfn. born from (one's own) seed, one's own or beloved (son), MBh.

Retaḥ, in comp. for *retas*. **-kulyā**, f. a stream or river of semen virile (in a partic. hell), BhP. **-pāta**, m. effusion of s° v°, Kull. on Mn. v, 63. **-pātin**, mfn. discharging s°, having sexual intercourse with (loc.), ib. **-pīta**, mfn. one who has swallowed s°, TĀr. **-sic**, mfn. discharging s°; f. N. of partic. Ishṭakās, ŚBr.; TS. **-sicya**, n. discharge of s°, ŚāṅkhBr. **-seka**, m. id., sexual intercourse with (loc.), Mn. xi, 58. **-sektṛi**, m. 'impregnator,' one who has offspring, Nīlak. **-skandana** (Gaut.), **-skhalana** (Kull.), n. effusion of semen.

Retana, n. semen virile, L.

Rétas, n. (√*ri, rī*) a flow, stream, current, flow of rain or water, libation, RV.; AV.; flow of semen, seminal fluid, sperm, seed, RV. &c. &c. (*retaḥ* √*sic* or *ni*-√*sic* or *ā*-√*dhā* with loc., 'to discharge semen into,' impregnate; *reto* √*dhā*, Ā., to conceive; *retaso 'nte*, after the discharge of s°); offspring, progeny, descendants, TS.; ŚBr.; quicksilver (regarded as Śiva's semen), L.; water, L.; sin (?), Sāy. on RV. iv, 3, 7. **-vat** (*rétas-*), mfn. possessed of seed, prolific, impregnating, MaitrS.; m. N. of Agni, ŚāṅkhŚr. **-vín**, mfn. abounding in seed, prolific, productive, TS.

Retasa (ifc.) = *retas* (cf. *agni-* and *kapota-r°*).

Retasya, mf(*ā*)n. conveying seed, AitBr.; (*ā*), f. (with or without *ṛic*) N. of the first verse of the Bahish-pavamāna Stotra, ShaḍvBr.; Lāṭy.

Retín, mfn. abounding in seed, prolific, impregnating, RV.

Reto, in comp. for *retas*. **-dhas**, mfn. impregnating, fertilizing, begetting offspring; m. (with or without *pitṛi*) 'a begetter,' natural father, Āpast.; MBh.; Kāv. &c. **-dhā́**, mfn. = prec. mfn., RV.; AV.; TS. &c.; f. = next, Kauś. **-dheya**, n. discharge of semen, impregnation, Br. **-mārga**, m. the seminal duct or canal, Suśr. **-'vasikta**, mfn. 'sprinkled with seed' (said of ascetics who live on the flesh of animals killed by other animals), Baudh. **-vaha**, m. conveying or producing semen, Bhpr.

Retoka, m. N. of a poet, Cat.

Retya, n. = *rīti*, bell-metal, L.

Retra, n. (only L.) semen virile; quicksilver; nectar, ambrosia; perfumed or aromatic powder (cf. *vetra*).

रेधक *redhaka*, m. N. of a man, Vikr. (v.l. *recaka*).

रेप् *rep*, cl. 1. Ā. *repate*, to go; to sound, Dhātup. x, 10.

रेप *repa, repas*. See p. 880, col. 3.

रेफ *repha*, °*phas*, °*phin*. See ib.

रेफाय *rephāya*, v.l. for *rebhāya*, Āpast.

रेब् *reb*. See √*rev*.

रेभ् *rebh, rebha* &c. See √*ribh*, p. 880, col. 3.

रेभटि *rebhaṭi*, f. deceit, L.

रेमि *remi* (√*ram*), Pat. on Pāṇ. iii, 2, 171, Vārtt. 2.

रेरिवन् *rerivan*, mfn. = *prêrayitṛi*, TUp. (Śaṃk.)

रेरिह *rerihá*, mfn. (fr. Intens. of √*rih*) continually or repeatedly licking, AV.

Rérihat, mfn. excessively licking, licking up, consuming, RV.; AV.

Rérihāṇa, mfn. repeatedly licking or caressing, RV.; m. N. of Śiva, L. (cf. *lelihāna*); a thief, L.; = *ambara, vara* or *asura*, L.

रेव् *rev* or *reb* (prob. artificial and of doubtful connection with the following words; Dhātup. xiv, 39; x, 14), to go, move; to leap, jump.

Reva, m. N. of a son of Ānarta and father of Raivata, Hariv.; (*ā*), f., see below; n. N. of various Sāmans, ĀrshBr.

Revaṭa, m. (only L.) a boar; a bamboo or dust (*veṇu* or *reṇu*); a whirlwind; a doctor skilled in antidotes; oil of the Morunga tree; the fruit of the plantain; n. a muscle or a conch-shell which coils from right to left, L.

Revaṇa, m. N. of a writer on Mīmāṅsā, Cat.

Revā, f. the indigo plant, L.; N. of Rati (the wife of Kāma-deva), L.; (in music) a partic. Rāga, Saṃgīt.; N. of the Narma-dā or Nerbudda river (which rises in one of the Vindhya mountains called Āmra-kūṭa or more commonly Amara-kaṇṭak in Gondwana, and after a westerly course of about 800 miles falls into the sea below Broach), Kāv.; Var. &c. **-khaṇḍa**, m. n., **-māhātmya**, n. N. of wks.

Revôttaras, m. N. of a man, ŚBr.

रेवत *revata*, m. a species of plant (the citron tree or Cathartocarpus Fistula, L.), Suśr.; N. of various persons, Buddh. (cf. *revataka*); of a son of Andhaka, Hariv. (v.l. *raivata*); of a son of Ānarta, BhP. (cf. *reva*); of the father of Revatī and father-in-law of Bala-rāma, MBh.; of a Varsha(?), ib.; (*i* and *ī*), f., see under *revát* below. **Revatôttara**, prob. n. N. of wk. (v.l. *revantôttara*).

Revataka, m. N. of a man, Buddh.; n. a species of date, L. (prob. w.r. for *raivataka*).

रेशय *reśaya*, mfn. (√*riś*) injuring, hurting (= *hiṇsat*), Nir. vi, 14, Sch. — **dārin**, mf(*iṇī*)n. destroying those who injure, ib. (used to explain *riśâdas*; v.l. *-dāśin*).

रेशी *réśī*, f. N. of water, MaitrS.; TS.

रेष् 1. *resh*, cl. 1. Ā. *reshate* (pf. *rireshe* &c., Gr.), to howl, roar, yell (as wolves), Dhātup. xvi, 19 (others 'to neigh' or 'to utter any inarticulate sound').

2. **Resh**, mfn. (nom. *reṭ*; cf. 2. *rej*) any animal that howls or yells or neighs, howling, neighing, W.

1. **Reshaṇa**, n. the howl of a wolf, howling, yelling, roaring, L.

Reshā, f. id., L.

Reshita, mfn. yelled, sounded; n. neighing, roaring, W.

रेष *resha*, m. (√1. *rish*) injury, hurt, Śaṃk. on ChUp. (cf. *ratha-r°*).

2. **Reshaṇá**, mfn. injuring, hurting, RV.; n. injury, damage, failure, Nir.; Dhātup.

Reshin, mf(*iṇī*)n. = prec. (see *purusha-r°*).

Reshṭṛi, mfn. one who injures or hurts, an injurer, Bhaṭṭ.

Reshma, in comp. for *reshman*. — **chinna** (*reshmá-*), mfn. rent or torn up by a storm, AV. — **mathita**, mfn. id., Kauś.

Reshmaṇyà, mfn. = *reshmya*, MaitrS.

Reshmán, m. a storm, whirlwind, storm-cloud, AV.; VS. (Mahīdh. 'the dissolution or destruction of the world').

Réshmya, mfn. being in a storm or in a storm-cloud, VS.

रेहत् *rehat*, g. *bhṛiśâdi* (Kāś. *rehas*).

Rehāya, Nom. P. °*yate* (fr. prec.), ib.

रै 1. *rai*, cl. 1. P. (Dhātup. xxii, 23) *rāyati*, to bark, bark at (acc.), RV. [Cf. Lat. *latrare*; Lith. *rěti*, *lóti*; Slav. *lajati*; Goth. *laian*.]

2. **Rai**, m. (nom. *rās*?) barking, sound, noise, MW.

रै 3. *raí*, m., rarely f. (fr. √*rā*; nom. *rā́s*, acc. *rā́yam* or *rā́m*, instr. *rāyā́*, dat. *rāyé*; abl. gen. *rāyás*, loc. *rāyí*; du. *rā́yau*, *rābhyā́m*, *rāyós*; pl. nom. *rā́yas*; acc. *rāyás* or *rā́s*; instr. *rābhís*; dat. abl. *rābhyás*, gen. *rāyā́m*, loc. *rāsú*; cf. the cognate stems 3. *rā* and *rayí*, and Lat. *rēs*, *rēm*), property, possessions, goods, wealth, riches, RV.; AV.; Br.; ŚrS.; BhP.; (*rai*), ind., g. *cādi*. — √**kṛi**, P. *-karoti*, to convert into property, Uṇ. ii, 66, Sch.

Rāyas, gen. of *rai*, in comp. — **kāma** (*rāyás-*), mfn. desirous of property, anxious to become rich, RV. — **posha**, m. increase of property or wealth or prosperity, Prāt. (cf. *bahu-r°*); mfn. increasing riches (said of Kṛishṇa), MBh.; *-dā́* (VS.), *-dā́van* (TS.), mfn. granting increase of wealth or prosperity; *-váni*, mfn. procuring increase of riches, VS. — **poshaka**, mfn. (fr. *-posha*), g. *arīhaṇâdi*.

Rāyo, in comp. for *rāyas*. — **vāja**, m. N. of a man, PañcavBr. — **vājīya**, n. (fr. prec.) N. of a Sāman, ĀrshBr.

Revát, mfn. (prob. contracted fr. *rayi-vat*) wealthy, opulent, rich, prosperous, RV.; AV.; abundant, plentiful, ib.; brilliant, splendid, beautiful (*át*, ind.), ib.; MBh. xiii, 1853 (here applied to the Gaṅgā); (*átī*), f., see below; n. wealth, prosperity, RV.; N. of a Sāman, ĀrshBr.

Revati, f. = *revatī*, the wife of Bala-rāma, Hariv.; N. of Rati (wife of Kāma-deva), L. — **putra**, m. a son of Revati, L.

Revátī, f. of *revát* above; (also pl.) N. of the fifth Nakshatra, RV. &c. &c.; a woman born under the N° Revatī, Pāṇ. iv, 3, 34, Vārtt. 1, Pat.; (in music) a partic. Rāgiṇī, Saṃgit.; N. of a female demon presiding over a partic. disease or of a Yoginī (sometimes identified with Durgā or with Aditi), MBh.; Kathās.; Suśr. &c.; of the wife of Mitra, BhP.; of a daughter of the personified light (*kānti*) of the Nakshatra Revatī and mother of Manu Raivata, MārkP.; of the wife of Bala-rāma (daughter of Kakudmin), Hariv.; Megh.; Pur.; of a wife of Amṛitodana, Buddh.; of various other women, HPariś.; Tiaridium Indicum, L.; Jasminum Grandiflorum, L.; pl. 'the wealthy ones' or 'the shining ones' (applied to cows and the waters), RV.; VS.; GṛŚrS.; N. of the verse RV. i, 30, 13 (beginning with *revatī*), VS.; TS.; Br. &c.; of the Sāman formed from this verse, ĀrshBr.; ChUp. ii, 18, 1; 2; of the divine mothers, L. — **kānta**, m. 'beloved of Revatī,' N. of Bala-rāma, L. — **graha**, m. N. of a demon presiding over diseases, Buddh. — **tantra**, n. N. of a Tantra. — **dvīpa**, m. N. of an island, L. — **pṛishṭha**, mfn. whose Pṛishṭha (q.v.) consists of the R° verses, Lāṭy. — **bhava**, m. 'son of R°,' N. of the planet Saturn, L. — **ramaṇa**, m. 'husband of R°,' N. of Bala-rāma, L.; of Vishṇu, Pañcar. — °**śa** (°*tīśa*), m. 'lord of R°,' N. of Bala-rāma, L. — **suta**, m. 'son of R°,' N. of Skanda, MBh. — **hālânta**, m. N. of a drama.

Revatyà, n., Pāṇ. iv, 4, 122.

Revanta, m. N. of a son of Sūrya and chief of the Guhyakas, VarBṛS.; Pur.; the 5th Manu of the present Kalpa (cf. next and *raivata*). — **manu-sū**, f. 'mother of Manu Revanta,' N. of Saṃjñā (wife of Sūrya), L. **Revantôttara**, prob. n. N. of wk. (v.l. *revatôttara*).

Raikva, m. N. of a man, ChUp. (cf. *rayikva*). — **parṇa**, m. pl. N. of a place, ib.

Raiya, Nom. P. °*yati*, to desire riches, Pāṇ. vi, 1, 79, Sch.

Raiva, m. N. of a king, BhP.

Raivatá, mf(*ī*)n. (fr. *revát*) descended from a wealthy family, rich, RV.; relating to Manu Raivata, Pur.; connected with the Sāman R°, TS.; VS.; m. a cloud, Naigh. i, 10; a kind of Soma, Suśr.; a species of tuberous vegetable (= *suvarṇâlu*), L.; N. of Śiva, L.; (as patr. of *revata* and metron. of *revatī*) N. of a demon presiding over a partic. disease of children, MBh.; of one of the 11 Rudras, Hariv.; Pur.; of a Daitya, L.; of the 5th Manu, Mn. i, 62; Hariv.; Pur.; of a Ṛishi, MBh.; of a Brahmarshi, Lalit.; of a king, MBh.; of Kakudmin (the ruler of Ānarta), Pur.; of a son of Amṛitodana by Revatī, Buddh.; of a mountain near Kuśa-sthalī (the capital of the country Ānarta), MBh.; Hariv.; Pur.; (with *ṛishabha*) N. of a Sāman, PañcavBr.; Lāṭy.; (*ī*), f. (with *ishṭi*) N. of a partic. Ishṭi (= *pavitrêshṭi*, Nīlak.); n. N. of various Sāmans, ĀrshBr.; Vas. — **garbha**, n. N. of a Sāman, ŚāṅkhŚr. — **giri**, m. N. of a mountain (cf. above), Cat. — **pṛishṭha**, mfn. = *revatī-pṛ°*, ib. — **madanikā**, f. N. of a drama. — **stotra**, n. N. of a Stotra. **Raivatâcala** and °**tâdri**, m. = °*ta-giri*, Śatr.

Raivataka, m. N. of a mountain (= *raivata*), MBh.; Hariv.; Pur. (pl. the inhabitants of it, VarBṛS.); of a Parama-haṇsa (q.v.), JabālUp. (v.l. *raivatika*); of a doorkeeper, Śak.; of a prince, VP.; n. a species of date, L.

Raivatika, m. metron. fr. *revatī*, Pāṇ. iv, 1, 46; 3, 131; v.l. for prec. (q.v.) — °**tikīya**, mfn. (fr. prec.), Pāṇ. iv, 3, 131. — °**tyà**, mfn. (fr. *revat*); m. (with *ṛishabha*) N. of a Sāman (v.l. for *raivata*, q.v.); n. riches, wealth, RV.

रैख *raikha*, m. patr. fr. *rekha*, g. *śivâdi*.

रैचीक्य *raicīkya*, m. N. of a man, Hcat.

रैणव *raiṇava*, m. patr. fr. *reṇu*, ĀśvŚr.; n. N. of a Sāman, ĀrshBr. (v.l. *vaiṇava*).

Raiṇukeya, m. (fr. *reṇukā*) metron. of Paraśu-rāma, L.

रैतस *raitasá*, mf(*ī*)n. (fr. *retas*) belonging to seed or semen, seminal, ŚBr.

रैतिक *raitika*, mf(*ī*)n. (fr. *rīti*) of or belonging to brass, brazen, Suśr.

Raitya, mfn. made of brass, brazen, Mn. v, 114.

रैभ *raibha*, m. patr. fr. *rebha*, Cat.; (*raíbhī*), f. N. of partic. ritualistic verses (esp. of AV. xx, 127, 4–6; containing several repetitions of the word *rebha*).

Raíbhya (or *raibhyá*), m. (fr. *rebha*) N. of various men, ĀśvŚr.; MBh. &c.; of a son of Sumati and father of Dushyanta, BhP.; of an astronomer, Cat.; of a class of gods, Hariv. (Nīlak.)

रैवत *raivata* &c. See above.

रैष्णायन *raishṇāyana*, m. patr., Saṃskārak.

रोक 1. *roká*, m. (√1. *ruc*) light, lustre, brightness, RV. iii, 6, 7; = *kraya-bhid*, L. (buying with ready money, W.); n. (only L.) a hole, vacuity; a boat, ship; = *cara* or *cala*; = *kṛipaṇa-bheda*.

2. **Róka**, m. or **rókas**, n. light, splendour, RV. vi, 66, 6.

Rokya, n. blood, L.

रोग *róga*, m. (√1. *ruj*) 'breaking up of strength,' disease, infirmity, sickness (also personified as an evil demon), AV. &c. &c.; a diseased spot, Suśr.; Costus Speciosus or Arabicus, L. — **grasta**, mfn. seized with any disease or sickness, W. — **ghna**, mfn. removing disease, Śiś.; Suśr.; n. medicine, L.; ([*ī*], f., see *-han*). — **jña**, m. a physician, Gal. — **jñāna**, n. knowledge of d°, Cat. — **da**, mfn. giving or causing d°, VarBṛS. — **nāśana**, mfn. destroying or removing d°, AV. — **nigrahaṇa**, n. suppression of d°, Suśr. — **nirṇaya**, m. N. of wk. — **pālaka**, m. one who has the care of the sick, Subh. — **pushṭa**, m. fever, Gal. — **prada**, mfn. causing d°, VarBṛS. — **pradīpa**, m. N. of various wks. — **preshṭha**, m. fever, L. (v.l. *-śreshṭha*). — **bhaya**, n. fear of d°, VarBṛS. — **bhāj**, mfn. possessing d°, ill, sick, ib.; Pañcat. — **bhū**, f. the place or seat of d°, the body, L. — **mukta**, mfn. freed or recovered from a d°, Cat. — **murāri**, m., *-mūrti-dāna-prakaraṇa*, n. N. of wks. — **rāj**, m. 'king or chief of d°s,' fever, Car.; Suśr. — **rāja**, m. 'king or chief of d°s,' consumption, L. — **lakshaṇa**, n. the sign or symptoms of a d°, pathology, Cat.; N. of wk. — **viniścaya**, m. N. of wk. — **vairūpya**, n. disfigurement caused by d°, Kathās. — **śama**, m. recovery from sickness, Car. — **śāntaka**, m. 'disease-alleviator,' a physician, L. — **śānti**, f. alleviation or cure of d°, W. — **śilā**, f. realgar, red arsenic, L. — **śilpin**, m. a species of plant, L. — **śreshṭha**, m. 'chief of d°s,' fever, L. (v.l. *-preshṭha*). — **saṃghāta**, m. an attack of fever, Suśr. — **sambaddha**, mfn. 'affected by d°,' sick, Āpast. — **sambandha**, mfn., w.r. for prec. — **ha**, n. 'destroying disease,' a drug, medicament, W. — **han**, mf(*ghnī*)n. removing disease, Suśr.; m. a physician, W. — **hara**, mfn. taking away d°, curative, Suśr.; VarBṛS.; n. medicine, L. — **hārin**, mf(*iṇī*)n. = prec. mfn., L.; m. a physician, L. — **hṛit**, mfn. curing d°, L.; m. a physician, Rājat. **Rogâkhya**, n. Costus Speciosus or Arabicus, L. (cf. *roga*). **Rogâdhīśa**, m. = *roga-rāja* above. **Rogânīka**, n. a class of d°s, a species of d°, Car.; *-rāj*, m. 'chief of all d°s,' fever, Suśr. **Rogântaka**, mfn. 'd°-destroying,' curative; m. a physician, W.; *-sāra*, N. of wk. **Rogânvita**, mfn. affected by d°, sick, W. **Rogâbhyāgama**, m. the symptom of a d°, VarYogay. **Rogâyatana**, n. abode or seat of d°, the body, Mn. **Rogârambha**, m. N. of wk. **Rogârta**, mfn. suffering from d°, sick, Mn.; MBh. **Rogârdita**, mfn. id., MBh. **Rogâvishṭa**, mfn. attacked or affected by d°, sick, Āpast. **Rogâhvaya**, n. Costus Speciosus or Arabicus, Bhpr. (cf. *roga*). **Rogônmādita**, mfn. maddened by disease (said of a dog), L. **Rogôpaśama**, m. alleviation or cure of disease, Cat. **Rogôlbaṇatā**, f. the spreading or raging of diseases, VarBṛS.

Rogi, in comp. for *rogin*. — **taru**, m. 'tree of the sick,' the Aśoka tree, L. (prob. w.r. for *rāgi-t°*). — **tā**, f. sickness, disease, W. — **vallabha**, n. 'friend of the sick,' medicine, a drug, L.

Rogita, mfn. (fr. *roga*; g. *tārakâdi*) diseased, suffering from sickness, VarBṛS.; mad (said of a dog), L.

Rogin, mfn. sick, diseased, ill, Mn.; MBh. &c.

Rogishṭha, mfn. (superl. fr. prec.) always sick or ill, MW.

Rogya, mfn. (adj.; or fut. p. fr. √1. *ruj*, Vop.) related to or connected with disease, producing sickness, unwholesome, L.

रोच् *róc*, ind. (√1. *ruc*) used in a partic. formula, MaitrS.

Rocá, mfn. shining, radiant, AV.; one who lightens or makes bright, MW.; m. N. of a king, Buddh.; (*ī*), f. Hingtsha Repens, L.

Rocaka, mfn. brightening, enlightening, W.; giving an appetite, Suśr.; pleasing, agreeable, W.; m. a worker in glass or artificial ornaments, R.; (only L.) hunger, appetite; a stomachic or stimulant; a sack; Musa Sapientum; a kind of onion; = *granthi-parṇa-bheda*.

Rocakin, mfn. having desire or appetite, taking delight in (loc.), Bālar. (cf. *a-roc°*).

Rocaná, mf(*ī* or *ā*)n. bright, shining, radiant, AV.; Br.; GṛS.; MBh.; Hariv.; giving pleasure or satisfaction, pleasant, charming, lovely, Bhaṭṭ.; BhP.; sharpening or stimulating the appetite, stomachic,

Suśr.; m. N. of various plants (Andersonia Rohitaka; Alangium Hexapetalum; the pomegranate tree &c.), L.; a partic. yellow pigment (v.l. for *rocanā*), MBh. (C.); a stomachic, W.; N. of a demon presiding over a partic. disease, Hariv.; of one of the 5 arrows of the god of love ('exciter'), Cat.; of a son of Vishṇu by Dakshiṇā, BhP.; of Indra under Manu Svārocisha, ib.; of one of the Viśve Devāḥ, VP.; of a mountain, MārkP.; (*ā́*) and (*ī*), f., see below; n. light, brightness, (esp.) the bright sky, firmament, luminous sphere (of which there are said to be three; cf. under *rajas*), RV.; AV.; Br. (in this sense sometimes *ā*, f.); pl. lights, stars, AV.; (ifc.) the causing a desire for, BhP.; (*Ruci-ruce r°*) N. of a Sāman, ĀrshBr. **-phala**, m. the citron tree, L.; (*ā*), f. a species of cucumber, L. **-sthá**, mfn. abiding in light or in the firmament, RV.

Rocanaka, m. the citron tree, L.; (*ikā*), f. N. of various plants, L.; = *vaṇśa-rocanā*, bamboo manna or Tabāshīr, L.

1. **Rocanā́**, f. the bright sky or luminous sphere (= *rocana*, m.), AV.; TBr.; a partic. yellow pigment (commonly called *go-rocanā*), Mn.; Yājñ.; MBh.; Suśr.; a handsome woman, L.; a red lotus-flower, L.; bamboo manna or Tabāshīr, L.; dark Śālmali, L.; N. of a wife of Vasu-deva, BhP.; of a Surâṅganā, Siṇhâs. **-mukha**, m. N. of a Daitya, MBh. **-vat** (*rocanā́-*, Padap. °*ná-*), mfn. shining, bright, AV.

2. **Rocanā**, ind. (in *rocanā-√kṛi*, ind. p. *-kṛitvā* or *-kṛitya*), g. *sākshād-ādi*.

Rocanī, f. a partic. yellow pigment (= 1. *rocanā*), Pañcat. (v.l.); red arsenic, realgar, L.; N. of various plants (Convolvulus Turpethum; the myrobolan tree; Croton Polyandrum; = *kāmpilla*), L.; (with Buddhists) N. of one of the four Devīs, Dharmas.

Rócamāna, mfn. shining, bright, splendid, RV. &c. &c.; pleasing, agreeable, MBh.; Kāv. &c.; m. a tuft or curl of hair on a horse's neck, Śiś.; Kathās.; N. of a king, MBh.; (*ā*), f. N. of one of the Mātṛis attending on Skanda, ib.

Rócas, n. light, lustre, MaitrS. (cf. *svá-r°*).

Roci, f. light, a beam, ray, Hariv.; MārkP.

Rocin. See *mita-r°*.

Rocisha, m. (fr. *rocis*) N. of a son of Vibhāvasu by Ushas, BhP.

Rocishṇú, mfn. shining, bright, brilliant, splendid, gay, VS. &c. &c.; giving an appetite, stomachic, Suśr. **-mukha**, mfn. having a bright countenance, MW.

Rocish-mat, mfn. (fr. *rocis* + *mat*) possessing or giving light, Hariv.; m. N. of a son of Manu Svārocisha, BhP.

Rocis, n. light, lustre, brightness, RV. &c. &c.; grace, loveliness, BhP.

Rocī. See under *rocá*.

Rócuka, mfn. causing pleasure or delight, MaitrS. (cf. *arocuká*).

Rocyà, mfn. used in a partic. formula, MaitrS. (cf. *rócá*).

रोट *roṭa*. See *pūga-roṭa*.

Roṭaka-vrata, n. a partic. religious observance, Cat.

Roṭikā, f. bread or a kind of bread, wheaten cakes toasted on an earthen or iron dish, Bhpr. (cf. next).

Roṭī, f. bread (see *phiraṅga-r°*; cf. the similar Hindī word).

रोड् *roḍ*, cl. 1. P. *roḍati*, to be mad, Dhātup. ix, 73 (cf. *√loḍ*); to despise, disrespect, ib. ix, 72, v.l. (cf. *√rauḍ, rauṭ*).

रोड *roḍa*, mfn. satisfied, contented (= *tṛipta*), L.; m. crushing, pounding (= *ksheda*), L.

रोढृ *roḍhṛi*, mfn. (√1. *ruh*) one who grows or ascends &c., L.

रोणी *roṇī*, f., Pāṇ. iv, 2, 78.

Roṇika, °**kīya**, prob. w.r. for *eṇika*, °*kīya*, Pat. on Pāṇ. iv, 2, 141.

रोद *roda*, *rodana* &c. See p. 884, col. 1.

रोदर *ródara*. See under 1. *ra*, p. 859, col. 2.

रोदस् *ródas*, n. du. (prob. connected with *rudra*; cf. *rodasī*) heaven and earth (only ibc. and in gen. *ródasoḥ*, RV. ix, 22, 5); the earth (see *svarga-rodaḥ-kuhara*). **-tvá**, n. a word used to explain *rodasī*, TBr.

Rodaḥ, in comp. for *rodas*. **-kandara-kuhara**, n. the void or hollow space between heaven and earth, Bālar. **-kuhara**, n. id., Nalôd.

Rodasi-prā́, mfn. (for °*sī-prá*) filling heaven and earth, RV.

Ródasī, f. (du., once sg.) heaven and earth, RV. &c. &c.; (sg.) N. of lightning as wife of Rudra and companion of the Maruts (also *rodasí*), RV.; the earth, R.; Hcat.

Rodo, in comp. for *rodas*. **-gṛiha** (Bālar.) o. **-randhra** (Śiś.), n. the void or hollow space between heaven and earth.

रोदाका *rodākā*, f. (a word of unknown meaning), Vait.

रोद्धव्य *roddhavya*, *roddhṛi*. See p. 884.

रोध 1. *rodha*, *rodhana*. See p. 884, col. 1.

रोध 2. *rodha*, *rodhaka* &c. See p. 884, col. 2.

रोध्र *rodhra*, m. (prob. connected with *rudhira*) the tree Symplocos Racemosa (it has yellow flowers, and the red powder scattered during the Holī festival is prepared from its bark), Kāv.; Var.; Suśr.; n. sin (also m.), L.; offence, L. **-pushpa**, m. Bassia Latifolia, L.; a species of ringed snake, Suśr. **-pushpaka**, m. a kind of grain (said to be a sort of Śāli), Suśr.; a species of snake (= *-pushpa*), ib. **-pushpiṇī**, f. Grislea Tomentosa, L. **-śūka**, m. a kind of rice (having ears coloured like Rodhra flowers), L.

रोप 1. *ropa*, m. (√1. *rup*) confusing, disturbing, W.

1. **Ropaṇá**, mfn. causing bodily pain, AV.; n. = *vimohana* or *upadrava*, TBr., Sch.

Ropayishṇu, mfn. rending, tearing, lacerating, Vait.

Rópi, f. acute or racking pain, AV.

1. **Ropita**, mfn. bewildered, perplexed, W.

Rópushī, f. (prob.) female destroyer, RV. i, 191, 13 (Sāy.)

रोप 2. *ropa*, m. (fr. Caus. of √1. *ruh*) the act of raising, setting up, planting, fixing in &c., MBh.; an arrow, Śiś.; Naish.; n. a fissure, hole.

Ropaka, m. a planter (see *vṛiksha-r°*); a weight of metal or a coin ($\frac{1}{70}$ of a Suvarṇa), W. (cf. *rūpaka*).

2. **Ropaṇa**, mf(*ī*)n. causing to grow, causing to grow over or cicatrize, healing, Suśr.; putting on, Kathās.; m. an arrow, L.; n. the act of setting up or erecting, raising, Kṛishis.; the act of planting, setting, sowing, transplanting, Pañcat.; Kṛishis.; healing or a healing application (used for sores), Suśr.

Ropaṇīya, mfn. to be set up or erected or raised, Kṛishis.; to be planted or sown, VarBṛS.; useful for healing or cicatrizing, Suśr.

Ropayitṛi, mfn. one who sets up or erects, an erecter (with acc. or gen.), R.; a planter, Kull. on Mn. iii, 163.

Ropita, mfn. caused to grow, raised, elevated &c.; fixed, directed, aimed (as an arrow), Ragh.; Sāh.; set (as a jewel), Hit.; committed, entrusted, Ragh.; set, planted, Kull. on Mn. i, 46.

Ropin, mf(*iṇī*)n. (ifc.) raising, erecting, setting planting, MBh.; Kull.

Ropya, mfn. to be planted or sown or transplanted, MBh.; Suśr.

रोपणाका *ropaṇākā*, f. a kind of bird, RV.; AV. (Sāy. 'a thrush,' = *śārikā*).

रोम 1. *roma*, m. (of uncertain derivation, but cf. 1. *ropa*) a hole, cavity, L.; n. water, L.

रोम 2. *roma*, m. the city Rome, Cat. (cf. *bṛihad-roma* and next); pl. N. of a people, VP.

1. **Romaka**, m. Rome, Siddhântaś.; 'the Roman,' N. of a partic. astronomer, Var.; N. of a village in the north of India, g. *palady-ādi*; of a partic. mixed caste (v.l. for *rāmaka*), Vas.; = *romaka-siddhânta* below; pl. N. of a people, MBh. ii, 1837 (cf. 2. *roman*); the people of the Roman empire, the Romans, VarBṛS. **-pattana** or **-pura**, n. the city of Rome, Siddhântaś.; Gol. &c. **-vishaya**, m. the country or empire of the Romans, Āryabh. **-siddhânta**, m. N. of Romakâcārya's Siddhânta (one of the 5 chief astronomical Siddhântas current in the age of Varāha-mihira); of a modern fiction, Cat.

Romakâcārya, m. N. of a teacher of astronomy (author of the above Siddhânta).

Romakāyana, m. N. of an author, Bṛih.

रोम 3. 4. *roma*. See under 1. *roman*.

रोमक 2. *romaka*, n. (fr. *rumā*) a kind of saline earth and the salt extracted from it (accord. to some 'the salt from the lake Sambar in Ajmere'), Suśr. &c. (cf. *raumaka*); a kind of magnet, L.

रोमक 3. *romaka*. See under 1. *roman*.

रोमन् 1. *róman*, n. (prob. connected with √1. *ruh*; cf. *loman*) the hair on the body of men and animals, (esp.) short hair, bristles, wool, down, nap &c. (less properly applicable to the long hair on the head and beard of men, and to that of the mane and tail of animals), RV. &c. &c.; the feathers of a bird, R. (cf. *mayūra-r°*); the scales of a fish (see *pṛithu-r°*).

3. **Roma**, in comp. for *roman*. **-kanda**, m. Dioscorea Globosa, L. **-karṇaka**, m. 'hair-eared,' a hare, L. **-kūpa**, m. n. 'hair-hole,' a pore of the skin (*bhavatāṃ roma-kūpāni prahṛishṭāny upalakshaye*, 'I observe that the hairs on your bodies bristle'), MBh.; R. &c. (cf. *-randhra*). **-kesara**, n. (said to be) = *-gutsa*, q.v., L. **-garta**, m. = *-kūpa* above, GopBr.; BhP. **-guccha**, m. or **-gutsa**, n. the tail of the Yak used as a Chowrie (cf. *cāmara*), L. **-ja**, n. 'produced from h° or wool,' a kind of cloth, L. **-tyaj**, mfn. losing hair (said of a horse), VarBṛS. **-pāda**, m. N. of two kings, Pur. **-pulaka**, m. = *-harsha*, q.v., BhP.; Caurap. **-phalā**, f. a species of plant, Npr. **-baddha**, mfn. 'h°-bound,' woven with h°, Yājñ. **-bandha**, m. h°-texture, ib. (v.l.) **-bhū** or **-bhūmi**, f. 'hair-place,' the skin, L. **-mūrdhan**, mfn. covered with h° or down on the head (said of insects), Suśr. **-ratâdhāra**, m. the belly, L. (v.l. *ratâsāra* and *rasâsāra*). **-randhra**, n. 'h°-hole,' a pore of the skin, MW. **-rasâsāra**, see *-ratâdhāra*. **-rāji** or **-rājī**, f. a row or line or streak of hair (esp. on the abdomen of women just above the navel, said to denote puberty), R.; Suśr. &c.; °*ji-patha*, m. the waist, Śiś. **-latā** (L.) or **-latikā** (Sāh.), f. a winding line of hair above the navel (in women). **-vat**, mfn. possessed of hair, covered with h°, Suśr. **-vallī**, f. Mucuna Pruritus, L. **-vāhin**, mfn. cutting off h°, sharp enough to cut a h°, Vāgbh. **-vikāra**, m. (L.) or **-vikriyā**, f. (Kum.; Sāh.; Pratāp.) 'changed condition of the h°,' bristling or erection of the h° of the body. **-vidhvaṇsa**, m. 'h°-destroying,' a louse, W. **-vibheda**, m. = *-harsha*, Kir. **-vivara**, n. = *-kūpa* above, BhP.; m. n. N. of partic. mythical regions, Kāraṇḍ. **-vedha**, m. N. of an author, Cat. **-śātana**, n. a depilatory for removing the hair, Cat. **-śuka**, n. a species of fragrant plant, Bhpr. **-saṃvejana**, n. the bristling of the hair of the body, Suśr. **-sūcī**, f. the quill of the porcupine, a hair-pin, ĀpGṛ., Sch. **-harsha**, m. the bristling of the h° of the body, thrill (caused by joy, fear, cold &c.), MBh.; R. &c. **-harshaṇa**, mfn. causing the h° to bristle or stand erect (through excessive joy or terror), MBh.; R. &c.; m. Terminalia Bellerica (the nuts of which are used as dice), L.; N. of Sūta (the pupil of Vyāsa and supposed narrator of the Purāṇas), Pur.; of the father of Sūta, BhP.; n. = *-harsha* above, L.; °*naka*, mf(*ikā*)n. w.r. for *raumah°*, q.v., VP.; °*shaṇi* or °*shiṇi*, m., w.r. for *raumaharshaṇi*, q.v., Cat. **-harshita**, mfn. having the h° of the body bristling or erect (through excessive joy or terror), PadmaP. **-harshin**, mfn. id., Śiś. **-hṛit**, n. 'hair-destroying,' sulphuret of arsenic, L. **Româṅka**, m. a mark of hair, Ragh. **Româṅkura**, m. a bristling hair of the body, Kād. 1. **Româñca**, m. (ifc. f. *ā*) thrill of the hair, Kāv.; Hariv. &c.; *-kañcuka*, m. a coat of mail consisting (as it were) of the down of the body erect through delight, Kathās.; °*mâñcôdgata-rāji-mat*, mfn. surrounded with erect rows of bristling hair, Hariv. 2. **Româñca** (fr. the prec.), Nom. P. °*cati*, to feel a thrill of joy or horror, Gīt. **Româñcakin**, m. N. of a serpent-demon, L. **Româñcikā**, f. a species of small shrub, L. **Româñcita**, mfn. having the hair of the body erect or thrilling with joy or terror (*ūrdhva-r°*, id.), Hariv.; Kāv. &c. **Româñcin**, mfn. id., Kād. **Românta**, m. the hairy side i.e. the upper side of the hand, ĀśvGṛ. **Româla-viṭapin**, m. a species of tree, L. **Romālī**, f. a line of hair (above the navel in women; cf. *roma-rāji*), Kāv.; puberty, L. **Româlu**, m. Dioscorea Globosa, L.; Mucuna Pruritus, L.; *-viṭapin*, m. a species of plant, L. **Româvalī**, f. a

line of hair (above the navel; cf. *româlī*), Kāv.; *-śataka*, n. N. of various wks. **Româśraya-phalā**, f. a species of shrub, L. (w. r.) **Romôtpāta**, m. (Hcat.) or **romôdgati**, f. (Veṇīs.) = *roma-harsha* above. **Romôdgama**, m. (ifc. f. *ā*) id. (*vyakta-romôdgama-tva*, n.), Kum.; Pañcar. &c. **Romôdbheda**, m. id., Prab.

4. **Roma** (ifc.) = *roman* (cf. *a-*, *dīrgha-*, *sa-r°*).

3. **Romaka**, n. hair (= *roman*), Hcat. (esp. ifc., f. *ikā*).

Romaṇ-vat, mfn. (for 1. *roman* + *vat*) covered with hair, hairy (= *roma-vat*), RV.

Romaśá, mf(*ā́*)n. (cf. *lomaśa*) having thick hair or wool or bristles, hairy, shaggy, RV. &c. &c.; applied to a faulty pronunciation of vowels, Pat.; m. a sheep, ram, L.; a hog, boar, L.; N. of two plants (= *kambhī* and *piṇḍâlu*), L.; = *dullala* (?), L.; N. of a Ṛishi, BhP.; of an astronomer (cf. *-siddhânta*); (*ā*), f. Cucumis Utilissimus, L.; another plant (= *dagdhā*), L.; N. of the reputed authoress of RV. i, 126, 7, RAnukr.; (*ī*), f. a squirrel, L.; n. the pudenda, RV. x, 86, 16. **-pucchaka**, m. a species of rodent animal (= *kaśa*), L. **-phala**, m. a species of plant (= *tiṇḍiśa*), Bhpr. **-siddhânta**, m. N. of an astron. work.

रोमन् 2. *roman*, m. pl. N. of a people, MBh.; VP.

रोमन्थ *romantha*, m. (perhaps for *ruj-m°*; cf. cognate words below) ruminating, chewing the cud, Kālid.; VarBṛS. &c.; chewing (of betel), Rājat.; frequent repetition, ib. (cf. *gagaṇa-r°*). [Cf. Gk. ἐρεύγειν, ἐρυγή; Lat. *e-rugere*, *ructare*, *ruminare*, fr. *rugminare*; Slav. *rygati*; Lith. *atrûgas*; Germ. *itarucchen*, *itrücken*; Angl. Sax. *roccettan*, *edroccian*.]

Romanthana, n. ruminating, L.

Romanthāya, Nom. P. *°yate*, to ruminate, chew the cud, Pāṇ. iii, 1, 15.

रोमाञ्च *româñca*. See p. 889, col. 3.

रोम्बिल्लवेङ्कटबुध *rombilla-veṅkaṭa-budha*, m. N. of an author, Cat.

रोर 1. *róra*, m. a partic. part of the body, MaitrS. (du.); VS. (= *aṇsa-granthi*, Mahīdh.)

रोर 2. *rora* or *raura*, m. a worker, labourer (?), HPariś.

रोरवण *roravaṇa*, n. (fr. Intens. of √1. *ru*) a loud roaring or bellowing, Nir.

Rorūya, mfn. crying much, Vop.

रोरुक *roruka*, m. or n. (?) N. of a country or a town, Buddh.

रोरुदा *rorudā*. See p. 884, col. 1.

रोल *rola*, m. Flacourtia Cataphracta, L.; green ginger, L.; (*ā*), f. a kind of metre (= *lolā*), Col. **-deva**, m. N. of a painter, Kathās.

रोलम्ब *rolamba*, mfn. distrustful, unbelieving (?), W.; m. a bee, Kāv.; Sāh.; dry or arid soil (?), W. **-kadamba**, n. a swarm of bees, Sāh. **-rāja**, m. N. of an author; *°jīya*, n. his wk.

रोलिचन्द्रू *rolicandrū* (?), m. N. of a man, Cat.

रोशंसा *rośaṇsā* or *rosaṇsā* (?), f. wish, desire, W.

रोष् *rosh*, *rosha* &c. See p. 885, col. 1.

रोह *róha*, mfn. (√1. *ruh*) rising, mounting, ascending &c.; Kāv.; Rājat.; ifc. riding on (cf. *aśva-r°*); m. rising, height, AV.; mounting, ascending (gen.), AitBr.; growth, increase, ŚrS.; the increasing of a number from a smaller to a higher denomination, MW.; sprouting, germinating, MBh.; a shoot, sprout, bud, blossom, L. **-kshiti**, w. r. for *rauhakshiti*, q. v. **-ga**, m. N. of a mountain (= *rohaṇa*), W. **-pūrva**, mfn. having the tones or accents ascending, SaṃhUp. **-śikhin**, m. fire which mounts upwards, ascending flame, Rājat. **-sena**, m. N. of a boy, Mṛicch.

Rohaka, mfn. one who mounts or rises (= *roḍhṛi*), L.; (ifc.) riding on, a rider (see *kaṭi-r°*); growing on (see *grāva-r°*); m. a kind of spirit or goblin, L.

Róhaṇa, m. N. of a mountain (Adam's Peak in Ceylon), Rājat.; (*ī*), f. a medicine for healing or cicatrizing, AV.; n. a means of ascending, RV.; the act of mounting or ascending or riding or sitting or standing on (comp.), Yājñ.; the putting or fastening on (of a bowstring), Cat.; the growing over, healing (of a wound; cf. *kshata-r°*), MBh.; the proceeding from, consisting of, Vās.; Sāh.; semen virile, L. **-druma**, m. the sandal tree, L. **-parvata**, m. Adam's Peak in Ceylon, Śatr. **Rohaṇâcala**, m. id., Sarvad.

Róhat, mfn. rising, mounting, ascending, growing, RV. &c. &c. **-parvā**, f. a species of Dūrvā grass, L. (v. l. *rohit-p°*).

Rohanta, m. a partic. tree (others 'any tree'), L.; (*ī*), f. a partic. creeper (others 'any creeper'), L.

Róhas, n. height, elevation, RV.; ŚāṅkhŚr.

Rohāya (fr. *rohat*), Nom. Ā. *°yate*, g. *bhṛiśâdi*.

Rohin, mf(*iṇī*)n. rising, Nir.; (ifc.) mounting, ascending towards, Śiś.; grown, shot up, long, tall, MBh.; (ifc.) grown on or in, R.; Ragh.; growing, increasing (in number), Nidānas.; m. Andersonia Rohitaka, L.; Ficus Indica and Religiosa, L.; (*iṇī*), f., see s. v.

Róhishyai. See √1. *ruh*.

रोहि *rohi*, m. (prob. fr. a √*ruh* for 4. *rudh*, 'to be red') a kind of deer, R.; (only L.) a seed; a tree; a pious or religious man (= *vratin*). **-māṇsa**, n. the flesh of the deer called Rohi, R.

Rohiṇa, mfn. born under the asterism Rohiṇī, Pāṇ. iv, 3, 37, Sch.; m. N. of Vishṇu, Hariv.; of a man, g. *aśvâdi* (pl. his descendants, ĀśvŚr.); of various plants, Mālatīm. (Andersonia Rohitaka; Ficus Indica; Andropogon Schoenanthus, L.); n. N. of the ninth Muhūrta (a part of the forenoon extending to midday, in which Śrāddhas are especially to be performed), W.; (*ī*), f., see below.

Rohiṇi, f. (m. c. and ibc.) = *rohiṇī*. **-tva**, n. = *rohiṇī-tva*, TBr. (cf. Pāṇ. vi, 3, 64, Sch.) **-nandana**, m. 'son of Rohiṇī,' metron. of Bala-rāma, MBh. **-putra**, m. son of Rohiṇī (as a proper N.), Pāṇ. vi, 3, 63. **-sheṇa** or **-sena**, m. N. of a man, Pāṇ. viii, 3, 100, Sch.

Rohiṇikā, f. inflammation of the throat, ŚārṅgS.; a woman with a red face (either from anger or from being coloured with pigments), L.

Róhiṇī, f. (f. of *rohita*, 'red,' below; also f. of *rohin* above) a red cow or [later] any cow (represented as a daughter of Surabhi and mother of cattle, esp. of Kāma-dhenu, 'cow of plenty;' in the Veda, Rohiṇī may perhaps also mean 'a red mare'), RV. &c. &c.; N. of the ninth Nakshatra or lunar asterism and of the lunar day belonging to it (in this sense it may optionally have the accent on the last syllable; it is personified as a daughter of Daksha, and as the favourite wife of the Moon, called 'the Red one' from the colour of the star Aldebaran or principal star in the constellation which contains 5 stars, prob. α, β, γ, δ, ε, Tauri, and is figured by a wheeled vehicle or sometimes by a temple or fish; it is exceptionally pl., and in TS. and TBr. there are 2 Nakshatras of this name; it may also be used as an adj. and mean 'born under the Nakshatra Rohiṇī,' Pāṇ. iv, 3, 34, Vārtt. 1); lightning, L.; a young girl (in whom menstruation has just commenced; others 'a girl nine years of age'), Gṛihyas.; Pañcat.; N. of various plants, Suśr.; Bhpr. (= Helleborus Niger; Acacia Arabica; Gmelina Arborea &c., L.); inflammation of the throat (of various kinds), Suśr.; (in music) a partic. Śruti, Saṃgīt.; a partic. Mūrchanā, ib.; a kind of steel, L.; N. of two wives of Vasudeva and the mother of Bala-rāma, MBh.; Pur.; of a wife of Kṛishṇa, Hariv.; of the wife of Mahā-deva, Pur.; of a daughter of Hiraṇya-kaśipu, MBh.; of one of the 16 Vidyā-devīs, L.; of a river, VP. **-kānta**, m. 'lover of Rohiṇī,' the Moon, Kṛishṇaj. **-candra-vrata** and *°dra-śayana*, n. N. of two religious observances, Cat. **-tanaya**, m. the son of Roh°, i. e. Bala-rāma, RāmatUp.; Śiś. **-tapas**, n. N. of wk. **-taru**, m. a species of tree, Kathās. **-tīrtha**, n. N. of a Tīrtha, Cat. **-tvá**, n. the state or condition of the Nakshatra R°, ŚBr. **-pati**, m. 'husband of R°,' the Moon, Vcar. **-priya**, m. 'lover of R°,' the Moon, L. **-bhava**, m. 'son of R°,' the planet Mercury, L. **-yoga**, m. the conjunction of the moon with the Nakshatra R° (more completely *candra-r°*), Vikr.; VarBṛS. **-ramaṇa**, m. 'cow-lover,' a bull, L.; 'lover or husband of R°,' the Moon, Gīt.; Hcar.; Vāsant. **-vallabha**, m. 'lover of R°,' the Moon, L. **-vrata**, n. N. of a partic. religious observance, Cat.; *°tôdyāpana*, n. N. of wk. **-°śa** (*°nīśa*), m. 'lord or husband of R°,' the Moon, Śiś. **-śakaṭa**, m. n. an asterism (prob. α, β, γ, δ, ε, Tauri), Pañcat.; VarBṛS.; Siṇhâs. **-śānti**, f. N. of wk. **-sheṇa**, m. N. of a man, g. *sushāmâdi* (cf. *rohiṇi-sh°*). **-suta**, m. 'son of R°,' the planet Mercury, L. **Rohiṇy-ashṭamī**, f. the 8th day in the dark half of the month Bhādra when the moon is in conjunction with the Nakshatra R°, Cat.

Rohít, mfn. red (in *rohid-aśva*, q. v.); m. the sun, L.; Cyprinus Rohita, L.; f. a red deer or a red mare, VS.; TS.; AV.; a woman in her courses, Sāy.; a kind of creeper, L.; pl. the rivers, Naigh. i, 13; the fingers, ib. ii 5. **-parvā**, v. l. for *rohat-p°*, q. v.

Róhita, mf(*ā* or *iṇī*, q. v.)n. (cf. *lohita*) red, reddish, RV. &c. &c.; m. a red or chestnut horse, RV.; TS.; Br. (applied to the Sun, AV. xiii, 1 &c., and therefore in pl. N. of these hymns); a kind of deer, VarBṛS.; Uttarar.; Suśr.; a kind of fish, Cyprinus Rohitaka, Mn.; MBh. &c.; a kind of tree, Andersonia Rohitaka, Suśr.; a sort of ornament made of precious stones, L.; a partic. form of rainbow (cf. n.), VarBṛS.; N. of a son of Hari-ścandra, AitBr.; BhP.; of a Manu, Hariv.; of a son of Kṛishṇa, ib. (v. l. *rauhita*); of a son of Vapush-mat (king of Śālmala), MārkP.; of a river, Buddh.; pl. N. of a class of Gandharvas, R.; of a class of gods under the 12th Manu, MārkP.; n. a kind of metre, AitBr.; a kind of rainbow appearing in a straight form, Indra's bow unbent and invisible to mortals, VarBṛS.; L. (cf. *rohitêndra-dhanus*); blood, L.; saffron, L.; N. of the Varsha ruled by Rohita (son of Vapush-mat), VP. **-kūla**, N. of a place, PañcavBr. **-kūlīya**, n. N. of a Sāman, ĀrshBr. (also *°yâdya* and *°yôttara*, n.) **-giri**, m. N. of a mountain; *rīya*, m. pl. its inhabitants, Pāṇ. iv, 3, 91, Sch. **-pura**, n. N. of a town (founded by Rohitaka, the son of Hari-ścandra), Hariv. **-matsya**, m. Cyprinus Rohitaka, VarBṛS. **-rūpá**, n. the red colour, MaitrS. **-vat**, mfn. having a red horse, Lāṭy. **-vastu**, N. of a place, Lalit. (also read *-vastra*). **-vṛiksha**, m. Andersonia Rohitaka, VarBṛS. **Rohitâksha**, mf(*ī*)n. red-eyed, R.; m. N. of a man, Mudr. **Róhitâñji**, mfn. marked with red, VS. **Rohitâśva**, m. 'having red horses,' Agni, the god of fire, L.; N. of a son of Hari-ścandra, VP. **Rohitâsya**, prob. w. r. for prec., MārkP. **Rohitêndra-dhanus**, n. pl. imperfect and perfect rainbows, Mn. i, 38. **Rohitâita**, m. (fr. *r°* + 2. *eta*) marked with red and other colours, TS.

Rohítaka, m. N. of a tree, Andersonia Rohitaka, MaitrS. (v. l. *rohītaka*); of a river, Buddh.; of a Stūpa, ib.; pl. N. of a people, MBh. **Rohitakâraṇya**, n. N. of a place, MBh.

Rohitāyana, m. patr., Saṃskārak. (prob. w. r. for *rauhitāyana* or *rauhiṇāyana*).

Rohiteya, m. Andersonia Rohitaka, L.

Rohíd-aśva, mfn. (*rohít* + *a°*) having red horses (said of Agni), RV. (cf. *rauhidaśva*).

Rohish, m. a kind of deer, L.; f. a doe, L.

Rohisha, m. a kind of fragrant grass, Suśr.; a kind of fish, L.; a kind of deer, L.

Rohī, f. a doe, MBh. (v. l. *rauhī*); N. of a river, ib.

Rohītaka, m. Andersonia Rohitaka, MaitrS. (v. l. *rohitaka*), VarBṛS.; Bhpr.; N. of a place or a mountain, MBh. (accord. to some a stronghold on the borders of Multan is so called).

रोहिन् *rohin*, mf(*iṇī*)n. See under *roha*, col. 2.

रौक्म *raukma*, mf(*ī*)n. (fr. *rukma*) golden, adorned with gold, Mn.; MBh. &c.

Raukmiṇeya, m. 'descendant of Rukmiṇī,' N. of Pradyumna, MBh.

रौक्षचित्त *rauksha-citta*, mfn. (fr. *rūksha-c°*) harsh-tempered, Divyâv.

Raukshya, n. (fr. *rūksha*) roughness, hardness, dryness, aridity, Yājñ.; Suśr.; harshness, cruelty, uncouthness, MBh.; Ragh.

रौक्षक *raukshaka*, m. (also pl.) patr., Pravar.

Raukshāyaṇa, m. (also pl.) id., ib.

रौचनिक *raucanika*, mf(*ī*)n. (fr. *rocanā*) coloured with or like (the pigment) Rocanā, yellowish, Kir.; n. the tartar of the teeth, W.

Raucya, m. (fr. *rucya* = *bilva*) a staff of Bilva wood, L.; an ascetic with a staff of B° w°, W.; (fr. *ruci*) N. of the 13th (9th) Manu, Hariv.; Pur.; mfn. belonging to Manu Raucya, MārkP.

रौट् *raut* or *rauḍ* (cf. √*roḍ*), cl. 1. P. *rauṭati, rauḍati*, to despise, treat with disrespect, Dhātup. ix, 72.

रौडि *rauḍi*, m. patr., Pat.

रौढीय *rauḍhīya*, m. pl. (prob. fr. *rūḍhi*) N. of a grammatical school, Siddh.

रौद्र *raúdra* or *raudrá*, mf(*ā* or *ī*)n. (fr. *rudra*) relating or belonging to or coming from Rudra or the Rudras, Rudra-like, violent, impetuous, fierce, wild (*am*, ind.), RV. &c. &c.; bringing or betokening misfortune, inauspicious, R.; Var.; m. a descendant of Rudra, MBh.; a worshipper of Rudra, W.; (pl., or sg. with *gaṇa*) a class of evil spirits, Hariv.; (scil. *rasa*) the sentiment of wrath or fury, Sāh.; Pratāp.; N. of Yama, L.; the cold season of the year, winter, L.; a partic. Ketu, VarBṛS.; N. of the 54th year of the Jupiter cycle of 60 years, ib.; (pl.) N. of a people, MBh.; (also n.) heat, warmth, sunshine, L.; (also n. and *ī*, f.) N. of the Nakshatra Ārdrā when under Rudra, VarBṛS.; (*ī*), f. N. of Gaurī, L.; one of the 9 Samidhs, Gṛihyas.; a partic. Śakti, Hcat.; (in music) a partic. Śruti, Saṃgīt.; a partic. Mūrchanā, ib.; a species of creeper, L.; N. of the Comms. on the Tattva-cintāmaṇi-didhiti and the Nyāya-siddhânta-muktâvalī by Rudra Bhaṭṭâcārya; (with *megha-mālā* and *śānti*) of two older wks.; n. savageness, fierceness, formidableness Kathās.; Suśr.; N. of a Liṅga, Cat.; of various Sāmans, ĀrshBr. **—karman**, n. a terrible magic rite or one performed for some dreadful purpose, Cat.; mfn. doing t° acts, MBh.; m. (also °*min*) N. of a son of Dhṛita-rāshṭra, ib. **—tā**, f. wild or savage state, dreadfulness, R.; Mālatīm. **—daṇshṭra**, mfn. having terrible tusks or fangs, BhP. **—darśana**, mfn. of dreadful appearance, terrific, W. (cf. *rudra-d*°). **—netrā**, f. N. of a Buddhistic goddess, Kālac. **—pāda**, (prob.) N. of the Nakshatra Ārdrā, Kṛishis. **—manas** (*raúdra-*), mfn. savage-minded, fierce, ŚBr. **Raudra-rksha**, n. N. of the Nakshatra Ārdrā, VarBṛS.

Raudraka, n. Rudra's work (= *rudreṇa kṛitam*), g. *kulālâdi*.

Raudrāksha, mf(*ī*)n. (fr. *rudrâksha*) made from Elæocarpus Ganitrus, Anarghar.

Raudrāgna, mf(*ī*)n. (fr. *rudrâgni*) relating to Rudra and Agni, ĀśvŚr.

Raudrāṇī, (prob.) w.r. for *rudrāṇī*.

Raudrāyaṇa, m. (also pl.) patr. fr. *rudra*, Pravar.

Raudrāśva, m. (prob. fr. *rudrâśva*) N. of a son or a more distant descendant of Puru, MBh.; Hariv.; Pur.; of a Ṛishi, Cat.

Raudri, m. patr. fr. *rudra*, Hariv.

Raudrī, in comp. for *rudra*. **—karaṇa**, n. the doing dreadful acts, performing horrors, MānŚr. **—bhāva**, m. 'terribleness,' the character of Rudra or Śiva, MBh.

रौध *raudha*, m. patr. fr. *rodha*, g. *śivâdi*.

रौधादिक *raudhādika*, mf(*ī*)n. (fr. *rudh-ādi*) belonging to the class of roots beginning with *rudh* (i.e. the 7th class), Pāṇ. viii, 2, 56, Sch.

रौधिर *raudhira*, mf(*ī*)n. (fr. *rudhira*) bloody, consisting of or caused by blood, MBh.; Suśr.

रौप्य *raupya*, mfn. (fr. *rūpya*) made of silver or resembling silver, silvery, silver, Yājñ.; MBh. &c.; (*ā*), f. N. of a place, MBh.; n. silver, GāruḍaP. **—nābha**, m. N. of a Rākshasa, VP. **—maya**, mf(*ī*)n. consisting or made of silver, Hariv.; Rājat. **—māshaka**, m. a Māshaka weight of silver, Mn. viii, 135. **—rukma-maya**, mf(*ī*)n. consisting or made of silver and gold, MBh. **Raupyâyasa-hiraṇ-maya**, mf(*ī*)n. consisting or made of silver and iron and gold, BhP.

Raupyaka, mfn. silvery, silver, Hcat.

Raupyāyaṇa, m. (also pl.) patr., Saṃskārak.

Raupyāyaṇi, m. patr. fr. *rūpya*, g. *tikâdi*.

रौम *rauma*, m. (fr. *ruma*) N. of a man, Rājat.; (pl.) = *raumya*, VP.; n. (fr. *rumā*) a kind of salt procured from the Rumā district, L. **—lavaṇa**, n. = prec. n., L.

1. **Raumaka**, n. (cf. 2. *romaka*) = prec. n., Suśr. **—lavaṇa**, n. id., L.

Raumya, n. N. of partic. evil demons in the service of Śiva, MBh. (cf. *rauma*).

रौमक 2. *raumaka*, mfn. (fr. 2. *romaka*), g. *palady-ādi*; Roman, spoken by the inhabitants of the Roman empire, Col.; derived or coming from the astronomer Romaka, Cat.

Raumakīya, mfn., g. *kṛiśāśvâdi*.

रौमण्य *raumaṇya*, mfn. (fr. 1. *roman*), g. *saṃkāśâdi*.

Raumaśīya, mfn. (fr. *romaśa*), g. *kṛiśâśvâdi*.

Raumaharshaṇaka, mf(*ikā*)n. made or composed by Roma-harshaṇa, BhP., Introd. (cf. *lauma-h*°).

Raumaharshaṇi, m. patr. of Sūta, BhP. (cf. *lauma-h*°).

Raumāyaṇa, mfn. (fr. 1. *roman*), g. *pakshâdi*.

रौम्य *raumya*. See col. 1.

रौर *raura*. See 2. *rora*, p. 890, col. 1.

रौरव *raurava*, mf(*ī*)n. (fr. *ruru*) coming from or made of the skin of the deer called Ruru, GṛŚrS.; MBh. &c.; fearful, L.; unsteady, dishonest, L.; m. N. of one of the hells, Mn.; MBh. &c. (personified as husband of Vedanā and father of Duḥkha, MārkP.; with Buddhists, one of the 8 hot hells, Dharmas. 121); N. of the fifth Kalpa (q.v.); a savage, monster, W.; n. the fruit of the Ruru tree, g. *plakshâdi*; N. of various Sāmans, ĀrshBr. **—tantra**, n. N. of a Tantra.

Rauravaka, n. = *ruruṇā kṛitam*, g. *kulālâdi*.

Raurukin, m. pl. (fr. *ruruka*) the school of Ruruka, Gobh.; Lāṭy.; n. pl. the Yajus handed down by this school, Lāṭy.

Raurukīya, mfn. (fr. prec.), Lāṭy., Sch.

रौशदश्व *rauśadaśva*, m. (fr. *ruśad-aśva*) patr. of Vasu-manas (the supposed author of RV. x, 179, 3), Ml. (cf. *rauhidaśva*).

रौशर्मन् *rauśarman*, m. N. of a man, Cat.

रौहक्षिति *rauhakshiti*, m., g. *pailâdi* (Kāś.)

रौहिक *rauhika*, mfn. = *ruha iva*, g. *aṅguly-ādi*.

रौहिण *rauhiṇá*, mf(*ī*)n. (fr. *rohiṇī*) connected with the Nakshatra Rohiṇī, born under it, Pāṇ. iv, 3, 37, Sch.; m. the sandal tree (accord. to others 'the Indian fig-tree'), Suparṇ.; MBh.; Hariv.; N. of partic. Puroḍāsas used in the Pravargya ceremony, ŚBr.; N. of Agni, ŚBr.; of a demon slain by Indra, RV.; AV.; of a man (with the patr. *Vāsishṭha*), ĀśvŚr.; TĀr.; pl. N. of a grammatical school, Pāṇ. vi, 2, 36, Sch.; n. sandal-wood, MW.; the 9th Muhūrta of the day, L.; N. of various Sāmans, ĀrshBr. **—kapālá**, n. the dish for the Rauhiṇa cakes, ŚBr. **—hávanī**, f. the ladle for the R° c°, ib.

Rauhiṇêśvara-tīrtha, n. N. of a Tīrtha, Cat.

Rauhiṇaka, n. N. of a Sāman, Lāṭy.

Rauhiṇāyana, m. (also pl.) patr. fr. *rohiṇa*, ŚBr.; Pravar.

Rauhiṇi, m. id. (°*ṇer ekarshe rājanam*, N. of a Sāman), L.

Rauhiṇika, n. a jewel, L.

Rauhiṇeya, m. (fr. *rohiṇī*) a calf, L.; metron. of Bala-rāma, MBh.; Hariv.; of the planet Mercury, VarBṛS., Sch.; n. an emerald, L.

Rauhiṇya, m. (also pl.), patr., Saṃskārak.

Rauhita, mf(*ī*)n. (fr. *rohita*) coming from the animal or fish called Rohita, Suśr.; relating to Manu Rohita, Hariv.; m. N. of a son of Kṛishṇa, Hariv. (v. l. *rohita*).

Rauhitaka, mfn. (fr. *rohitaka*) made of the wood of the Andersonia Rohitaka, KātyŚr.; Car.

Rauhityāyani, m. patr., Saṃskārak.

Rauhidaśva, m. (fr. *rohid-aśva*) patr. of Vasumanas, RAnukr. (cf. *rauśadaśva*).

Rauhish, m. (cf. *rohish*) a kind of deer, L.

Rauhisha, m. (cf. Uṇ. i, 48) id., L.; Cyprinus Rohita, L.; a kind of medicinal plant, L.; (*ī*), f. (only L.) a doe of the Rauhisha species; a creeper; Dūrvā or some other kind of grass.

Rauhī, f. the female of a partic. kind of deer, MBh.

Rauhītaka, mfn. = *rauhitaka*, ŚrS.; coming from the district Rohītaka, Rājat.; m. Andersonia Rohitaka, MBh.

Rauheya, mfn. (fr. *roha*), g. *sakhy-ādi*.

ल LA.

ल 1. *la*, the 3rd semivowel (corresponding to the vowels *lṛi, lṛī*, and having the sound of the English *l*); a technical term for all the tenses and moods of a finite verb or for the terminations of those tenses and moods (also applied to some forms with *kṛit* affixes construed like a finite verb, Pāṇ. ii, 3, 69; cf. iii, 2, 124, and when accompanied by certain indicatory letters denoting each tense separately, see *laṭ; laṅ; liṅ; loṭ; liṭ; luṭ; lṛiṭ; luṅ; lṛiṅ; leṭ*), Pāṇ. iii, 4, 69; 77, Sch. **—kāra**, m. the letter or sound *la*, APrāt. (applied in naming the 10 tenses and moods as above, Pāṇ. iii, 4, 77, Sch.); *-vāda*, m., *-viśeshârtha-nirūpaṇa*, n.; °*rârtha-prakriyā*, f., °*rârtha-vāda*, m. N. of wks.

ल 2. *la*, m. N. of Indra, L.; cutting (?cf. *lava*), W.; (*lā*), f., see s.v.

ल 3. *la* (in prosody) = *laghu*, a short syllable.

लक् *lak* (cf. √*rak*), cl. 10. P. *lākayati*, to taste; to obtain, Dhātup. xxxiii, 63, v.l. (Prob. artificial and of very questionable connection with the following words.)

Laka, n. the forehead, W.; the ear or spike of wild rice, W.

Lakaca (L.) or **lakuca** (MBh.; Suśr. &c.), m. a kind of bread-fruit tree, Artocarpus Lacucha (a tree containing a large quantity of sticky milky juice); n. the fruit of this tree.

लकुट *lakuṭa*, m. = *laguḍa*, a club, ĀpŚr.; Car.

Lakuṭin, mfn. carrying a club, armed with a club, L.; MārkP.

लकुल *lakula*, °*lya*, g. *balâdi*.

Lakulin, m. N. of a Muni, Cat.

लक्कक *lakkaka*, m. N. of a man, Rājat.

लक्त *lakta*, m. = *rakta*, red, MW. (cf. *gūtha-l*°). **—karman**, m. a red variety of the Lodh tree (used in dyeing), W.

Laktaka, n. = *naktaka*, a dirty and tattered cloth, a rag, Suśr.; (?) = *alaktaka*, lac, the red dye, W.

लक्नचन्द्र *lakvana-candra*, m. N. of a man, Rājat.

लक्ष् *laksh*, cl. 1. Ā. *lakshate*, to perceive, observe, BhP.; Kathās.; (P. °*ti*), to recognise, MBh.; cl. 10. P. Ā. (Dhātup. xxxii, 5; xxxiii, 23; rather Nom. fr. *laksha* below) *lakshayati*, °*te* (aor. *alalakshat*, °*ta*; inf. *lakshayitum*; ind. p. *lakshayitvā*, *-lakshya*), to mark, sign, MBh.; to characterize, define (in Comms.); to indicate, designate indirectly, Śaṃk.; Kpr.; Sāh.; Sarvad.; to aim at (as to aim an arrow at any object), direct towards, have in view, mean, Kāś. on Pāṇ. ii, 3, 37 &c.; to consider or regard any one (acc.) as (acc. with or without *iva*), MBh.; Hariv.; Pur.; to suppose of any one (acc.) that he will &c. (oratio recta with *iti*), MBh. iii, 10375; to know, understand, recognise by (instr.) or as (acc.) or that &c. (oratio recta with *iti*), MBh.; Kāv.; Pur.; to notice, perceive, observe, see, view, MaitrUp.; Mn.; MBh. &c.: **Pass.** *lakshyate*, to be marked &c.; to be meant or intended, Kāś. on Pāṇ. ii, 3, 14 &c.; to be named or called (with double nom.), BhP.; to be perceived or seen, appear, seem, look like (nom. with or without *iva*), MBh.; Kāv. &c.: Desid., see *lilakshayishita*.

Lakshá, m. or n. (prob. fr. √*lag* as 'that which is attached or fixed') a mark, sign, token, (esp.) a mark to aim at, target, butt, aim, object, prey, prize, RV. ii, 12, 4 &c. &c. (cf. *labdha-l*°; *ākāśe laksham* √*bandh*, to fix the gaze vaguely on space, look into space as if at some object barely visible in the distance, Śak.; cf. also *ākāśa-baddha-laksha*); appearance, show, pretence (cf. *-supta*); a kind of citron, L.; a pearl, L.; (also n., or *ā*, f.) a lac, one hundred thousand, Yājñ.; Hariv. &c. **—tā**, f. the state of being a mark or aim, MW. **—tulasī-vratôdyāpana**, n., **-tulasy-udyāpana-vidhi**, m. N. of wks. **—datta**, m. N. of a king, Kathās. **—dīpa-kalpa**, m., **-dīpa-vratôdyāpana**, n., **-namaskāra-vidhi**, m., **-namaskāra-vrata**, n., **-padma-vratôdyāpana**, n., **-pārthiva-liṅga-vratôdyāpana**, n. N. of wks. **—pura**, n. N. of a town, Kathās. **—pushpa-pūjôdyāpana**, n., **-pushpa-vrata**, n., **-pushpavratôdyāpana-vidhi**, m., **-pushpôdhyāpana**, n., **-pūjā-māhātmya**, n., **-pūjôdyāpana**, n., **-pradakshiṇa-vidhi**, m., **-pradakshiṇa-vrata-vidhi**, m. N. of wks.

-bhūta, mfn. that which has become the aim or object (of all), sought by all, Cat.; (ifc.) liable or subject to, Jātakam. **-rāma-nāma-lekhana-vrata**, n., **-varti-kathā**, f., **-vartikôdyāpana-vidhi**, m., **-varti-dīpa-vrata-kalpa**, m., **-varti-vrata**, n., **-varty-udyāpana**, n., **-varty-udyāpana-vidhāna**, n. N. of wks. **-vedhin**, mfn. piercing or hitting the mark, Vikr. (cf. *lakshya-v°*). **-śas**, ind. by hundreds of thousands, by lacs, MW. **-śloka**, mfn. containing 100,000 verses, Pañcar. **-supta**, mfn. pretending to be asleep, feigning sleep, Mṛicch. (v.l. *laksha-s°*). **-svastika-vrata-kalpa**, m., **-svastika-vratôdyāpana**, n. N. of wks. **-homa**, m. a partic. sacrifice offered to the planets, AgP.; *-paddhati*, f., *-vidhi*, m. N. of wks. **Lakshâdhîśa**, m. a person possessed of a lac (or of 100,000 rupees), MW. **Lakshânta-purī**, f. N. of a town, Cat. **Lakshântara**, n. a distance of 100,000 (Yojanas), Vcar. **Lakshâvatāra**, m. N. of wk. **Laksheśa**, m. = *lakshâdhîśa*, Kāv.

Lakshaka, mfn. indicating, hinting at, expressing indirectly or elliptically or by metonymy, Sāh.; N. of two men, Rājat.; n. a lac, one hundred thousand, Pañcar.

Lakshaṇa, mfn. indicating, expressing indirectly, Vedântas.; m. Ardea Sibirica, L.; N. of a man, Rājat. (often confounded with *lakshmaṇa*); (*ā*), f., see s.v.; n. (ifc. f. *ā*) a mark, sign, symbol, token, characteristic, attribute, quality (ifc. = 'marked or characterized by,' 'possessed of'), Mn.; MBh. &c.; a stroke, line (esp. those drawn on the sacrificial ground), ŚBr.; GṛŚrS.; a lucky mark, favourable sign, GṛŚrS.; Mn.; MBh. &c.; a symptom or indication of disease, Cat.; a sexual organ, MBh. xiii, 2303; a spoon (?), Divyâv.; accurate description, definition, illustration, Mn.; Sarvad.; Suśr.; settled rate, fixed tariff, Mn. viii, 406; a designation, appellation, name (ifc. = 'named,' 'called'), Mn.; MBh.; Kāv.; a form, species, kind, sort (ifc. = 'taking the form of,' 'appearing as'), Mn.; Saṃk.; BhP.; the act of aiming at, aim, goal, scope, object (ifc. = 'concerning,' 'relating to,' 'coming within the scope of'), APrāt.; Yājñ.; MBh.; BhP.; reference, quotation, Pāṇ. i, 4, 84; effect, operation, influence, ib. i, 1, 62 &c.; cause, occasion, opportunity, R.; Daś.; observation, sight, seeing, W. **-karman**, n. statement of marks or qualities, accurate description, definition, Āpast. **-kāṇḍa**, m. or n., **-grantha**, m. N. of wks. **-jña**, mfn. sign-knowing, understanding marks (esp. those on the body), able to interpret or explain them, R.; VarBṛS.; (ifc.) understanding a person's lucky marks or signs, BhP. **-tva**, n. the being a mark or definition, Sāh. **-dīpikā**, f., **-prakāśa**, m. N. of wk. **-praśasta**, mfn. celebrated on account of good or lucky marks, Gobh. **-bhrashṭa**, mfn. deprived of good marks, fallen into misfortune, ill-fated, unhappy, Yājñ. iii, 217 (v.l. *alakshaṇā bhrashṭāḥ* for *lakshana-bhr°*). **-ratna**, n., **-ratna-mālikā**, f., **-rāji**, f. N. of wks. **-lakshaṇā**, f. N. of a partic. figure of speech (in which the proper meaning of a word gives place to the figurative one, cf. *lakshaṇā* below, and *jahal-l°*), Kpr.; Sāh. **-vat**, mfn. possessing marks or signs, marked or characterized by (instr.), MBh.; endowed with auspicious marks, MānGṛ.; R.; giving correct definitions, Car.; (ifc. after a numeral) having a partic. number of marks or characteristics, BhP. **-vāda**, w.r. for *lakshaṇā-v°*. **-vṛitti**, f., **-śataka**, n., **-saṃgraha**, m. N. of wks. **-saṃnipāta** (R.), **-saṃniveśa** (Mahān.), m. the impressing or fixing of a mark, branding, stigmatizing. **-samuccaya**, m. N. of a wk. on the characteristic marks of deities (attributed to Hemâdri). **-sampad**, f. a multitude of marks or characteristics, Vajracch. **-sāra-samuccaya**, m. N. of a wk. (containing rules for the construction of Liṅgas of Śiva). **Lakshaṇânvita**, mfn. endowed with good marks, lucky, Mn. iii, 4. **Lakshaṇâmṛita** (or °*ṇâm°*?), n. N. of wk. **Lakshaṇâlakshaṇa-tas**, ind. with regard to characteristics and non-ch°s, Vajracch. **Lakshaṇâvalī**, see under *lakshaṇā*. **Lakshaṇôttamā**, f. N. of a Kiṃ-narī, Kāraṇḍ. **Lakshaṇôru**, mf(*ū*)n., Pāṇ. iv, 1, 70 (cf. *lakshmaṇôru*).

Lakshaṇaka (ifc., f. *ikā*) = *lakshaṇa*, a mark, sign, Piṅg., Sch.

Lakshaṇā, f. aiming at, aim, object, view, Hariv.; indication, elliptical expression, use of a word for another word with a cognate meaning (as of 'head' for 'intellect'), indirect or figurative sense of a word (one of its three Arthas; the other two being *abhidhā* or proper sense, and *vyañjanā* or suggestive s°; with *sâropā*, the placing of a word in its figurative sense in apposition to another in its proper s°), Sāh.; Kpr.; Bhāshāp. &c.; the female of the Ardea Sibirica (= *lakshmaṇā*), Suśr.; a goose, Uṇ. iii, 7, Sch.; N. of an Apsaras, MBh.; Hariv. **-°valī** (°*ṇāv°* or °*ṇâv°*?), f. N. of various wks. **-vāda**, m. N. of two wks. (by Gadā-dhara and Raghu-deva); *-rahasya*, n. N. of a wk. (by Mathurā-nātha). **-vṛitti-prakaraṇa**, n. N. of wk.

Lakshaṇin, mfn. possessing marks &c.; = *lakshana-jña*, R. ii, 29, 9.

Lakshaṇīya, mfn. to be perceived, visible, Ragh.; to be expressed figuratively or elliptically, anything so expressed, L.

Lakshaṇya, mfn. serving as a mark or token, PārGṛ.; having auspicious marks or signs, Yājñ.; MBh. &c.; m. a diviner, Divyâv.

Lakshita, mfn. marked, indicated, distinguished or characterized by (instr. or comp.), Mn.; MBh. &c.; vaguely indicated or expressed, equivocal, ambiguous (as a word which is indecent only in its figurative sense, e.g. *janma-bhūmi*, 'place of birth' and 'the female organ'), Vām. ii, 1, 18; (ifc.) aimed at (as a target or object aimed at by an arrow), R.; called, named, Śrutab.; considered or regarded as, taken for (nom.), BhP.; enquired into, examined, Mn.; Sāh.; recognised, MBh.; perceived, observed, beheld, seen, evident, MBh.; Kāv. &c.; known, understood, Ratnâv.; proved, Jātak.; excellent, ib. **-tva**, n. the state of being marked or expressed indirectly, Vedântas.; excellence, Jātak. **-lakshaṇa**, mfn. having the marks (of anything) perceived or evident, MW.

Lakshitavya, mfn. to be marked or indicated or defined, Sāh.

Lakshin, mf(*iṇī*)n. (fr. *laksha*) having good marks or signs, R.

Lakshī, in comp. for *laksha*. **-√kṛi**, P. Ā. *-karoti*, *-kurute*, to make a mark or object, aim or point or look at, Kālid.; Dhūrtas.; to set out towards, Naish.; to calculate (cf. next). **-kṛita**, mfn. made a mark, aimed at, directed towards (*-nāsa*, mfn. fixing the gaze on the tip of the nose), MW.; amounting to (instr.), Naish. **-√bhū**, P. *-bhavati*, to become a mark or aim or object, Kull. (v.l. *lakshyī-bhū*).

Lakshma. See *deva-lakshmá*.

Lakshmaka, m. N. of a man, Rājat.

Lakshma-kaṇikā, f. a little spot, Kāv.

Lakshmaṇá, mf(*ā́*)n. having marks or signs or characteristics, TS.; endowed with auspicious signs or marks, lucky, fortunate, L.; m. Ardea Sibirica, Āpast.; N. of a Vāsishṭha, g. *śubhrâdi*; of a son of Daśa-ratha by his wife Su-mitrā (he was younger brother and companion of Rāma during his travels and adventures; L° and Śatru-ghna were both sons of Su-mitrā, but L° alone is usually called Saumitri; he so attached himself to Rāma as to be called R°'s second self; whereas Śatru-ghna attached himself to Bharata), R.; Pur. &c.; N. of various authors and other persons (also with *ācārya*, *kavi*, *deśika*, *dvivedin*, *paṇḍita*, *bhaṭṭa*, *śāstrin*, *sūri* &c.), Cat.; (*ā*), f. the female of the Ardea Sibirica, MBh.; a goose, Uṇ. iii, 7, Sch.; a kind of potherb, Car.; N. of various other plants (Hemionitis Cordifolia; Uraria Lagopodioides; = *putra-kandā* and a white-flowering Kaṇṭakâri), L.; N. of a wife of Kṛishṇa, Hariv.; Pur.; of a daughter of Dur-yodhana (carried off by Sāmbha, a son of Kṛishṇa), BhP.; of an Apsaras, Hariv.; of a Buddhist Devī, Kālac.; of the mother of the 8th Arhat of the present Avasarpiṇī, L.; n. a mark, sign, token, MBh.; R. &c. (often v.l. *lakshaṇa*), a name, L. **-kavaca**, n. N. of a hymn in praise of Lakshmaṇa. **-kuṇḍaka**, n. N. of a place, Cat. **-khaṇḍa-praśasti**, f. N. of wk. **-candra**, m. N. of a king, Cat. **-campū**, f. N. of a poem (= *campū-rāmāyaṇa*, q.v.) **-cūrṇikā**, f. N. of wk. **-dāsa**, m., **-deva**, m., **-pati**, m. N. of three men, Cat. **-prasū**, f. 'mother of L°,' N. of Su-mitrā (cf. above), L. **-bhaṭṭīya**, n. N. of a wk. on the Vedânta. **-rāja-deva**, m. N. of a king, Inscr. **-siṅha**, m. N. of an author, Cat. **-sena**, m. N. of various men (esp. of a son of Ballāla-sena, who gave his name to an Era which commenced in 1119–20). **-svāmin**, m. N. of a man, Inscr.; of an image of L°, Rājat. **Lakshmaṇâditya**, m. (with *rāja-putra*) N. of a poet and pupil of Kshemêndra, Cat. **Lakshmaṇâbharaṇīya**, n. N. of a Campū. **Lakshmaṇôtsava**, m. N. of a medical wk. by Lakshmaṇa. **Lakshmaṇôru**, mf(*ū*)n., Vop. iv, 30 (cf. *lakshaṇôru*).

Lakshmaṇyà, mfn. serving as a mark, visible far and wide, ĀpGṛ.; m. N. of a man, RV. v, 33, 10 (Sāy. 'son of Lakshmaṇa').

Lákshman, n. a mark, sign, token, characteristic, AV. &c. &c.; a good or lucky mark, excellence, MBh.; a bad mark, stain, blemish, Bālar.; definition (as 'the marks or characteristics collectively'), Sarvad.; = *pradhāna*, the chief, principal, L.; a pearl, L.

Lakshmi, (m.c.) in comp. for *lakshmī*. **-vardhana**, mfn. increasing good fortune, R. **-sampanna**, mfn. possessed of good fortune, ib.

Lakshmī́, f. (nom. *īs*, rarely *ī*; also ifc. as m. f., but n. *i*; cf. *lakshmika*) a mark, sign, token, RV. x, 71, 2; Nir. iv, 10; (with or without *pāpī*) a bad sign, impending misfortune, AV.; ĀpŚr.; (but in the older language more usually with *púṇyā*) a good sign, good fortune, prosperity, success, happiness (also pl.), AV. &c. &c.; wealth, riches, Kāv.; Rājat.; beauty, loveliness, grace, charm, splendour, lustre, MBh.; Kāv. &c.; N. of the goddess of fortune and beauty (frequently in the later mythology identified with Śrī and regarded as the wife of Vishṇu or Nārāyaṇa; accord. to R. i, 45, 40–43 she sprang with other precious things from the foam of the ocean when churned by the gods and demons for the recovery of the Amṛita, q.v.; she appeared with a lotus in her hand, whence she is also called Padmā; accord. to another legend she appeared at the creation floating over the water on the expanded petals of a lotus-flower, she is also variously regarded as a wife of Sūrya, as a w° of Prajā-pati, as a w° of Dharma and mother of Kāma, as sister or mother of Dhātṛi and Vidhātṛi, as w° of Dattâtreya, as one of the 9 Śaktis of Vishṇu, as a manifestation of Prakṛiti &c., as identified with Dākshāyaṇī in Bharatâśrama, and with Sītā, wife of Rāma, and with other women), ib. (cf. RTL. 103; 108 &c.); the Good Genius or Fortune of a king personified (and often regarded as a rival of his queen), royal power, dominion, majesty, Kāv.; Kathās.; Rājat.; a partic. verse or formula, NṛisUp.; N. of various plants (Hibiscus Mutabilis; Mimosa Suma; turmeric; a white Tulasī; = *ṛiddhi*, *vriddhi*, *priyaṅgu*, and *phalinī*), L.; of the eleventh Kalā of the moon, Cat.; of two kinds of metre, Col.; the wife of a hero, L.; = *dravya*, L.; a pearl, L.; N. of the wife of king Candra-siṅha of Mithilā and patroness of various authors (also called *lakhamā*, *lashamā*, *lakhimā* or *lachimā*), Cat.; of a poetess, ib.; of another woman, Śukas. **-kalpa**, m. a partic. period of time, Hcat. **-kavaca**, n. N. of various Kavacas, Cat. **-kānta**, m. 'beloved of Lakshmī,' N. of Vishṇu, ib. (cf. *kallāleśo lakshmī-k°*); a king, A.; N. of an author, Cat.; (with *nyāya-bhūshaṇa bhaṭṭâcārya*) of another author, ib.; *-śikshā*, f. N. of wk. **-kumāra-tātâcārya**, m. N. of an author, Cat. **-kula-tantra**, n., **-kulârṇava**, m., **-khaṇḍa**, N. of wks. **-gṛiha**, n. 'abode of Lakshmī,' a mint, Gal.; a red lotus-flower, L. **-candra-miśra**, m. N. of an author, Cat. **-caritra**, n. N. of wk. **-janârdana**, n. sg. L° and Janârdana, BrahmavP. **-tantra**, n. N. of wk. **-tāla**, m. a tree resembling the vine-palm, L.; (in music) a kind of measure, Saṃgīt. **-tva**, n. the being L° (of Sītā), R., Sch. **-datta**, m. (also with *ācārya*) N. of various authors, Cat. **-dāsa**, m. N. of various men, ib.; Col. **-deva**, m. N. of a man, Śrīkaṇṭh.; (*ī*), f. N. of a learned woman, Cat. **-dvādaśa-nāma-mahiman**, m., and °**ma-stotra**, n. N. of wks. **-dhara**, m. (also with *ācārya*, *kavi*, *dīkshita*, *deśika*, *bhaṭṭa*, *sūri*) N. of various authors and other persons, Kathās.; Cat. &c.; (prob.) n. a partic. metre, Col.; m. or n. (?) N. of a commentary; *-kāvya*, n. N. of wk.; *-sena*, m. N. of a man, Cat. **-nara-siṅha**, m. N. of a king, Inscr.; of various authors, Cat. **-nātha**, m. 'lord of Lakshmī,' N. of Vishṇu, BhP.; (also with *bhaṭṭa*, *miśra*, *śarman*) of various authors, Cat. **-nāmâmṛita**, n. N. of a Stotra. **-nārāyaṇa**, m. du. or n. sg. L° and Nārāyaṇa, Hcat. (cf. RTL. 151; 184); m. N. of a prince, Inscr.; (also with *nyāyâlaṃkāra*, *paṇḍita*, *yati*) of various authors and other men, Cat.; mfn. belonging to L° and Nārāyaṇa, Hcat.; *-pañcâṅga*, n., *-pūjā-vidhāna*, n. N. of wks.; *-vrata*, n. a partic. religious observance, Cat.; °*ta-kalpa*, m., *-saṃvāda*, m., *-sahasra-nāman*, n., *-stava*, m., *-stotra*, n., *-hṛidaya*, n.; °*ṇârcā-kaumudī*, f., °*ṇīya*, N. of wks. **-niketana**, n. the bathing with fragrant myrobolan powder, L. **-nivāsa**, m. the abode of the goddess of fortune, Cat.; N. of a commentator, ib.; °*sâbhidhāna*, n. N. of wk. **-nṛi-siṅha**, n. sg. L° and Vishṇu as the man-lion, BrahmavP.; m. N. of a king, Cat.; (also with *kavi* or *bhaṭṭa*) of various authors and other men, ib.; *-kavaca*, n., *-pañca-ratna-mālikā*, f., *-mahāshṭôttara*, n. (and °*ra-bhāshya*, n.), *-sahasra-nāman*, n., *-stava-rāja*, m., *-stotra*, n. N. of wks. **— m-dadā**, f. N. of a Kiṃnarī, Kāraṇḍ. **— pañcāśat**, f. N. of wk. **— pati**, m. 'husband or lord of L°,' a king or prince, Kir.; N. of Vishṇu-Kṛishṇa, Vishṇ.; the betel-nut tree, L.; the clove tree, L.; (also with *śarman*) N. of various authors and other persons, Cat. **— putra**, m. 'son of L°,' N. of Kāma, L.; of Kuśa and Lava (the sons of Rāma), L.; a horse, Śiś., Sch.; a wealthy man, L. **— pura**, n. N. of various towns, Campak.; Cat.; *-māhātmya*, n. N. of ch. in the Brahmâṇḍa-purāṇa. **— purusha-kāra**, m. N. of wk. **— pushpa**, n. 'L°'s flower,' a clove, Gal.; a ruby, L. **— pūjana**, n. the ceremony of worshipping L° performed by a bridegroom along with his bride (at the conclusion of the marriage after the bride has been brought to her husband's house), MW. **— pūjā**, f. 'worship of L°,' N. of a festival on the 15th day in the dark half of the month Āśvina (celebrated in modern times by bankers and traders to propitiate Fortune), Col.; N. of wk.; *-viveka*, m. N. of wk. **— praṇayin**, mfn. dear to L°, a favourite of fortune, Rājat. **— phala**, m. Aegle Marmelos, L. **— bahish-kṛita**, mfn. excluded from fortune, destitute of wealth, Rājat. **— mantra**, m. N. of wk. **— mandira**, n. a fictitious N. of a town, Caurap. **— yajus**, n. N. of a partic. sacred text (more correctly *lakshmī* and *yajus* as N. of two sacred texts), NṛisUp. **— ramaṇa**, m. the husband of L°, i. e. Vishṇu, Kāv. **— lahari**, f. N. of wk. **— vat**, mfn. possessed of fortune or good luck, lucky, prosperous, wealthy, MBh.; R. &c.; handsome, beautiful, Hariv.; R. &c.; m. Artocarpus Integrifolia, L.; Andersonia Rohitaka, L.; (*atī*), f. N. of a woman, HParis. **— varma-deva**, m. N. of a king, Col.; Inscr. **— vallabha**, m. 'favourite of L°,' N. of an author, Cat. **— vasati**, f. 'abode of L°,' N. of the lotus-flower (Nelumbium Speciosum), ŚārṅgP. **— vākya**, n. N. of wk. **— vāra**, m. 'L°'s day,' Thursday, MW. **— vinaya**, m. du. good fortune and modest conduct, Kathās. **— vilāsa**, m. a partic. compound, Rasêndrac.; N. of various wks.; pl. royal behaviour (personified), Uttarar. **— vivarta**, m. change of fortune, Dhūrtas. **— veshṭa**, m. the resin of Pinus Longifolia, L. **— vrata-pūjā**, f. N. of wk. **— °śa** (°*mīśa*), m. 'lord of L°,' N. of Vishṇu, Vop.; a prosperous man, W.; the mango tree, L.; (in music) a kind of measure, Saṃgīt.; (with *sūri*) N. of a man, Cat. **— śreshṭhā**, f. Hibiscus Mutabilis, L. **— °svara-siṃha** (°*mīs*°), m. N. of a king, Cat. **— saṃhitā**, f. N. of wk.; of ch. in the Nārada-pañca-rātra; of ch. in the Vāyu-purāṇa. **— sakha**, m. a friend or favourite of the goddess of fortune, Rājat. **— sanātha**, mfn. endowed with beauty or fortune, MW. **— saparyā-sāra**, N. of wk. **— samāhvayā**, f. 'having the name of Lakshmī,' N. of Sitā, L. **— sarasvatī**, f. du. L° and Sarasvatī, Kathās.; *-saṃvāda*, m. N. of wk. **— saha-ja**, m. 'produced together with L°,' the moon (supposed to have arisen together with L° from the ocean when churned by the gods and Asuras, see *lakshmī* above), L. **— sahasra-nāman**, n., °*ma-stotra*, n. N. of wks. **— sahôdara**, m. = *-saha-ja* (q. v.), A. **— sûkta**, n. a partic. hymn addressed to L°, Cat. **— sena**, m. N. of a man, Kathās. **— stava**, m., **-stuti**, f. N. of wks. **— stotra**, n. praise of L°, W.; N. of various Stotras. **— svayaṃvara-nāṭaka**, n., **-hṛidaya**, n.; °**ya-stotra**, n. N. of wks.

Lakshmīka (ifc.) = *lakshmī*, g. *uraḥ-prabhṛiti* (cf. *gata-*, *pūrṇa-l°* &c.)

Lakshmy, in comp. for *lakshmī*. **— ashṭôttara-śata-nāman**, n., **-ashṭôttara-śata-stotra**, n. N. of wks. **— ārāma**, m. 'garden of Lakshmī,' N. of a forest, L.

Lakshya, mfn. to be marked or characterized or defined, Kap., Sch.; to be indicated, indirectly denoted or expressed, Sāh.; Vedāntas.; (to be) kept in view or observed, VarBṛS.; Kathās.; to be regarded as or taken for (nom.), Śiś.; Hit.; to be recognised or known, recognisable by (instr. or comp.), Hariv.; Kālid.; Dhūrtas.; observable, perceptible, visible, MBh.; Kāv. &c.; m. N. of a magical formula or spell recited over weapons, R.; n. an object aimed at, prize, MBh.; R.; Kām.; (exceptionally also n., with m. as v. l.) an aim, butt, mark, goal, Up.; Gaut.; MBh. &c. (*lakshyaṃ* √*labh*, to attain an object, have success; *lakshyam* √*bandh* with loc., 'to fix or direct the aim at,' with *ākāśe* = *ākāśe lakshaṃ* √*bandh*, see under *laksha*); the thing defined (opp. to *lakshaṇa*), A.; an indirect or secondary meaning (that derived from *lakshaṇā*, q. v.), Kpr.; a pretence, sham, disguise, Ragh.; Kām. (cf. *-supta*); a lac or one hundred thousand, Rājat.; an example, illustration (?), Sāh.; often v. l. or w. r. for *laksha* and *lakshman*. **— krama**, mfn. having an indirectly perceptible method, MW. **— graha**, m. taking aim, L. **— jña-tva**, n. knowledge of a mark or of examples, Cat. **— tā**, f. the being visible, visibility (acc. with √*nī*, to make visible, show), Rājat.; the being an aim or object (acc. with √*yā*, to become an aim), Kathās. **— tva**, n. the being indirectly expressed, Sarvad.; (ifc.) the being an aim or object of, Kathārṇ. **— nirṇaya**, m. N. of wk. **— bhūta**, mfn. that which has become a mark or aim, BhP. **— bheda**, m. the cleaving or hitting of a mark, Kir. **— lakshaṇa-bhāva**, m. the connection of the indicated and indicator, Ml. **— vīthī**, f. the visible or universally recognisable road, Hariv. (= *brahma-loka-mārga* or *deva-yāna*, Nīlak.) **— vedha**, m. = *-bheda*; °*dhin*, mfn. piercing or hitting a mark, MW. (cf. *laksha-vedhin*). **— siddhi**, f. the attainment of an object, Kām. **— supta**, mfn. pretending to be asleep, Daś.; Mṛicch. (cf. *laksha-supta*). **— han**, m. 'hitting the mark,' an arrow, L. **Lakshyâbhiharaṇa**, n. the carrying off of a prize, MBh. **Lakshyârtha**, m. indirectly expressed meaning, Kāv. **Lakshyâlakshya**, mfn. visible and not visible, scarcely visible, MBh.

Lakshyī, in comp. for *lakshya*. **— √kṛi**, P. *-karoti*, to make an aim or object, Kālid. (cf. *lakshī-√kṛi*). **— √bhū**, P. *-bhavati*, to become an aim or object (v. l. for *lakshī-√bhū*, q. v.)

लख् *lakh* (cf. √*laṅkh* and *liṅkh*), cl. 1. P. *lakhati*, to go, move, Dhātup. v, 24.

लखमादेवी *lakhamā-devī* or *lakhimā-devī*, f. N. of a princess, Cat. (cf. under *lakshmī*).

लग् *lag* (cf. √*laksh*, *laksha* &c.), cl. 1. P. (Dhātup. xix, 24) *lagati* (accord. to Nir. iv, 10 also *lagyati*; pf. *lalāga*, Gr.; aor. *alagīt*, ib.; fut. *lagitā*, ib.; *lagishyati*, Pañcat.; ind. p. *lagitvā*, *-lagya*, Kāv.), to adhere, stick, cling or attach one's self to (loc.), MBh.; Kāv. &c. (with *hṛidi* and gen., 'to penetrate to a person's heart,' Kathās.); to take effect upon (loc.), Śiś.; to meet, come in contact, cut (as lines), Gol., Sch.; to follow closely, ensue or happen immediately, Kathās.; to pass away (as time), Pañcat.: Caus. or cl. 10. (Dhātup. xxxiii, 63) *lāgayati*, 'to taste' or 'to obtain' (*āsvādane* or *āsādane*). [In Hindī this root often means 'to begin.']

Laganīya, mfn. to be attached or clung to, Cat.

Lagita, mfn. attached to, adhered, W.; obtained, got, ib.; entered, Hit. (v. l. *calita*).

1. **Lagna**, mfn. (for 2. see p. 895, col. 2) adhered, adhering or clinging to, attached to, sticking or remaining in, fixed on, intent on, clasping, touching, following closely (with gen. or ifc.), MBh.; Kāv. &c. (with *pṛishṭhe*, *pṛishṭha-tas*; or *pṛishṭha* ibc., following on a person's heels; with *mārge*, sticking to i. e. following the road; with *hṛidaye*, one who has penetrated the heart); one who has entered on a course of action, one who has begun to (inf.), Pañcat.; meeting, intersecting, cutting (said of lines), Gol.; immediately ensuing, Pañcat.; passed (as days), Vet.; consumed by, spent in (instr.), Kull. on Mn. vii, 127; auspicious (see comp.); furious through being in rut (an elephant), L.; m. a bard or minstrel (who awakes the king in the morning), L.; m. n. (ifc. f. *ā*) the point of contact or intersection (of two lines), the point where the horizon intersects the ecliptic or path of the planets, Sūryas.; VarBṛS.; the point or arc of the equator which corresponds to a given point or arc of the ecliptic, ib.; the division of the equator which rises in succession with each sign in an oblique sphere, ib.; the point of the ecliptic which at a given time is upon the meridian or at the horizon (*kshitije lagnam*, horizon Lagna; *madhya-lagnam*, meridian Lagna), ib.; the moment of the sun's entrance into a zodiacal sign, ib.; the rising of the sun or of the planets, ib.; (in astrol.) a scheme or figure of the 12 houses or zodiacal signs (used as a horoscope); the whole of the first astrological house; (also with *śubha*, *śobhana*, *anukūla* &c.) an auspicious moment or time fixed upon as lucky for beginning to perform anything, Rājat.; Kathās.; Hit.; the decisive moment or time for action, decisive measure, Kathās. **— kāla**, m. the time or moment pointed out by astrologers as auspicious, Kathās. **— graha**, mfn. insisting firmly on anything, persistent, obtrusive, ib. **— grahaṇa**, n. the computation of the moment favourable for any undertaking, Camp. **— candrikā**, f. N. of wk. **— cintā**, f. thinking of the auspicious moment, Kāv. **— darpaṇa**, m. N. of wk. **— dina**, n., **-divasa**, m. an auspicious day (fixed upon as favourable for beginning any undertaking), Kathās. **— devī**, f. N. of a fabulous cow of stone, Śatr. **— dvādaśa-bhāva**, m. pl. N. of wk. **— nakshatra**, n. any auspicious constellation in the moon's path, MW. **— pañcâṅga-bhāshya**, n. N. of wk. **— pattrikā**, f. a paper on which the auspicious moment for a marriage &c. is noted down, MW. **— bhuja**, m. (in astron.) ascensional difference i. e. the d° between the time of rising of a heavenly body at Laṅkā and at any other place, W. **— maṇḍala**, n. 'circle of signs,' the zodiac, MW. **— māsa**, m. an auspicious month, ib. **— muhūrta**, n. the auspicious moment for a marriage &c., ib. **— yāna**, n., **-vāda**, m. N. of wks. **— vāsara**, m. = *-dina*, A. **— velā**, f. = *-kāla*, Kathās.; Hit. **— śuddhi**, f. auspiciousness of the signs &c. for the commencement of any contemplated work, MW. **— samaya**, m. = *-kāla*, Pañcat. **— sāriṇī**, f., **-horā-prakāśa**, m. N. of wks. **Lagnâṅka**, m. N. of wk. **Lagnâsu**, m. pl. (in astron.) ascensional equivalents in respirations, MW. **Lagnâha**, m. = *lagna-dina*, Kathās. **Lagnôddyota**, m. N. of wk.

Lagnaka, m. a (fixed) surety, bondsman, bail, L.; (*ikā*), f., w. r. for *nagnikā*, q. v.

लग *laga*, (in prosody) an iambus. **Lagâlikā**, f. 'series of iambi,' a kind of metre (four times ⏑ – ⏑ –, cf. *nagānikā* &c.), MW.

लगड *lagaḍa*, mfn. beautiful, handsome, L. (cf. *laḍaha*). **Lagaḍâcārya**, m. N. of an astronomer, Āryabh.

लगण *lagaṇa*, m. a partic. disease of the eyelid, Suśr.; (*ā*), f. the heart pea, Cardiospermum Halicacabum, L.

लगत *lagata*, prob. w. r. for next.

लगध *lagadha*, m. N. of the author of the Vedâṅga called Jyotisha.

लगुड *laguḍa*, m. (cf. *lakuṭa*) a stick, staff, club, MBh.; Kāv. &c.; n. Nerium Odorum, L. **— vaṃśikā**, f. a kind of small bamboo, L. **— hasta**, m. 'staff-in-hand,' a man armed with a stick or mace, a staff-bearer, MW.

Laguḍin, mfn. armed with or holding a club or staff, Kād.

Lagura, m. = *laguḍa* above, W. **— hasta**, m. = *laguḍa-h°*, ib.

लग्न 1. and 2. *lagna*. See col. 2 and p. 895, col. 2.

लघट् *laghaṭ* or *laghaṭi*, m. (fr. √*laṅgh*?) the wind, Uṇ. i, 134, Sch.

Laghantī, f. N. of a river, MBh. (B. *laṅghatī*).

लघय *laghaya*, *laghiman*. See p. 894, col. 3.

लघु *laghú*, mf(*vī* or *u*)n. (a later form of *raghu*, q. v.) light, quick, swift, active, prompt, nimble, Mn.; MBh. &c. (also said of a partic. mode of flying peculiar to birds, Pañcat.; applied to the Nakshatras Hasta, Aśvinī, and Pushya, VarBṛS.); light, easy, not heavy or difficult, AV. &c. &c.; light in the stomach, easily digested, Suśr.; easy in mind, light-hearted, Hariv.; Kālid.; causing easiness or relief, Sāṃkhyak.; well, in good health, L.; unimpeded, without attendance or a retinue, MBh. iii, 8449; short (in time, as a suppression of the breath), MārkP.; (in prosody) short or light (as a vowel or syllable, opp. to *guru*); (in gram.) easily pronounced or articulated (said of the pronunciation of *va*, as opp. to *madhyama* and *guru*); small, minute, slight, little, insignificant, ŚBr. &c. &c.; weak, feeble, wretched, humble, mean, low (said of persons), Mn.; MBh. &c.; young, younger (see *-bhrātṛi*); clean, pure (see *-vāsas*); soft, gentle (as sound), Kathās.; BhP.; pleasing, agreeable, handsome, beautiful, MBh.; Kālid.; m. bdellium, L.; (*u*), f. Trigonella Corniculata, L.; (*vī*), f. id., L.; a light carriage, L.; a slender or delicate woman, W.; n. a partic. measure of time (= 15 Kāshṭhās = $\frac{1}{15}$ Nāḍikā), L.; a partic.

species of agallochum, L.; the root of Andropogon Muricatus, L.; (*u*), ind. lightly, quickly, easily &c., Śak. (*laghu* √*man*, to think lightly of, Śak.) [Cf. Gk. ἐ-λαχύς; Lat. *lĕvis* for *lēvis*, *lenhuis;* Lith. *lengvùs, lèngvas;* Angl. Sax. *lungre*, 'quickly;' Eng. *lungs*, 'lights.'] — **kaṅkola**, m. Pimenta Acris, Npr. — **kaṇṭakā**, f. Mimosa Pudica, ib. — **karkandhu**, m. f. a small kind of Zizyphus, ib. — **karṇikā**, f. Sanseviera Roxburghiana, L. — **karṇī**, f. a species of plant, L. — **kāya**, mfn. light-bodied; m. a goat, L. — **kārikā**, f., **-kāla-nirṇaya**, m. N. of wks. — **kāśmarya**, m. a kind of tree (= *kaṭphala*), L. — **kāshṭha**, m. a light stick for defence against another stick, L. — **koshṭha**, mfn. having a light stomach, having little in the st°, Kām. — **kaumudī**, f. 'the short or easy Kaumudī,' N. of an easy epitome of the Siddhânta-k° by Varada-rāja. — **krama**, mfn. having a quick or rapid step, going quickly, Hariv.; MārkP.; (*am*), ind. with quick step, quickly, hastily, Kathās. — **kriyā**, f. a small matter, trifle, MW. — **khaṭvikā**, f. a small couch, easy chair, L. — **khartara**, m. N. of a family, W. — **ga**, m. 'moving quickly,' N. of Vāyu, the god of the wind, L. — **gaṅgā-dhara**, m. a partic. powder (used in diarrhœa), ŚārṅgS. — **gati**, mfn. having a quick step, Megh. — **garga**, m. a species of fish, L. — **gītā**, f. N. of wk. — **godhūma**, m. a small kind of wheat, L. — **graha-mañjarī**, f. N. of wk. — **caccarī**, f. (in music) a kind of measure, Saṃgīt. — **candrikā**, f., °**kā-paddhati**, f., **-cāṇakya-rāja-nīti**, f. N. of wks. — **citta**, mf(*ā*)n. light-minded, little-minded, fickle, MBh.; *-tā*, f. light-mindedness, fickleness, R. — **citra-hasta**, mfn. light and ready-handed, possessing unusual manual skill, MBh. — **citrâlaṃkara**, m., **-cintana**, n. N. of wks. — **cintāmaṇi**, m. N. of wk.; *-rasa*, m. a partic. fluid compound, Cat. — **cirbhiṭā**, f. colocynth, L. — **cetas**, mfn. little-minded, low-m°, Bhartṛ.; Pañcat. &c. — **cchadā**, f. a kind of asparagus, L. — **cchedya**, mfn. easy to be cut or extirpated, easily destroyed, Pañcat. (prob. w.r. for *laghûcchedya*). — **jaṅgala**, m. Perdix Chinensis, L. — **jātaka**, n., **-jāti-viveka**, m., **-jānakīya**, n., **-jñāna-vāsishṭha**, n. N. of wks. — **tara**, mfn. more quick, lighter, easier &c. (= *laghīyas*), Pañcat. — **tā**, f. quickness, promptness, agility, dexterity, MBh.; MārkP.; lightness, ease, facility, Suśr.; Ṛitus.; feeling of ease, f° of bodily freshness, Kāraṇḍ.; prosodial shortness, VarBṛS.; smallness, littleness, meanness, insignificance, MBh.; Rājat.; Śiś.; light-mindedness, thoughtlessness, levity, wantonness, R.; want of rank or dignity, humbleness, disregard, disrespect, Kāv.; Pañcat. &c. — **tāla**, m. (in music) a kind of measure, Saṃgīt. — **tva**, n. quickness, agility, dexterity, MBh.; lightness, ease, facility, ŚvetUp.; Suśr.; feeling of ease, Mṛicch.; prosodial shortness, Piṅg., Sch.; levity, thoughtlessness, wantonness, MBh.; want of dignity, humbleness, disregard, disrespect, Kāv.; Pañcat. &c. — **dantī**, f. a kind of Croton, Bhpr. — **dīpikā**, f. N. of sev. wks. — **dundubhi**, m. a small drum, L. — **drākshā**, f. a small stoneless grape, L. — **drāvin**, mfn. fusing or liquefying easily, flowing rapidly (said of quicksilver), Sarvad. — **dvāra-vatī**, f. the young or recent Dvāra-vatī, (or) the more modern part of the town D°, Cat. — **nābha-maṇḍala**, n. a partic. mystic circle, Cat. — **nāman**, n. Agallochum, L. — **nāradīya**, n., **-nārāyaṇôpanishad**, f. N. of wks. — **nālika**, n. a musket, L. — **nidāna**, n., **-nyāya-sudhā**, f., **-nyāsa**, m. N. of wks. — **pañca-mūla**, n. a compound of five different roots, L. — **paṇḍita**, m. N. of an author, Cat.; °*tīya*, n. N. of wk. — **patanaka**, m. 'quickly flying,' N. of a crow, Pañcat.; Hit. — **pattraka**, m. a kind of plant (= *rocanī*), L. — **pattra-phalā**, f. Ficus Oppositifolia, L. — **pattrī**, f. the small Pippala tree, L. — **paddhati**, f. N. of various wks. — **parākrama**, mfn. of quick resolution, R. — **parāmarśa**, m. N. of wk. — **parāśara**, m. the shorter Parāśara, Cat. — **parikrama**, mfn. moving quickly (= *tvarita-gati*, Comm.), Kām. — **paribhāshā-vṛitti**, f. N. of Comm. — **parṇikā**, f. Asparagus Racemosus, L. — **parṇī**, f. a species of plant, L. — **pāka**, m. easy digestion, digestibility, ŚārṅgS.; mfn. growing old rapidly, Bhpr.; easy of digestion, easily digested, Suśr.; ŚārṅgS. — **pākin**, mfn. easily digested, Suśr. — **pātin**, m. 'quickly flying,' N. of a crow, Kathās. — **pārāśarya**, n. N. of wk. — **picchila**, m. Cordia Myxa, L. — **pulastya**, m. the shorter Pulastya, Cat. — **pushpa**, m. a kind of Kadamba, L. — **pūjā-prakāra**, m. N. of wk. — **pramāṇa**, mf(*ā*)n. of little magnitude, short, VarBṛS. — **prayatna**, mfn. using little effort, indolent, impotent, W.; pronounced with slight articulation (*-tara*, mfn.), Pāṇ. viii, 3, 18. — **prâyaścitta**, n. N. of wk. — **badara**, m. or (*ī*), f. a kind of jujube tree, L. — **bindu-śekhara**, m., **-buddha-purāṇa**, n., **-bodha**, m., **-bodhinī**, f., **-brahma-vaivarta**, n. N. of wks. — **brāhmī**, f. a kind of Rue, L. — **bhava**, m. (in *a-laghu-bh*°) m. low or humble station, Bhartṛ. (v. l.) — **bhāgavata**, n. N. of wk. — **bhāva**, m. light state, lightness, ease, facility, Cat.; *-prakāśikā*, f. N. of wk. — **bhāskarīya**, n. N. of various wks. — **bhuj**, mfn. eating little, VarBṛS. — **bhūta-druma**, m. Cordia Myxa, L. — **bhūshaṇa-kānti**, f. N. of Comm. — **bhojana**, n. a light repast, slight refreshment, Pañcat. — **bhrātṛi**, m. a younger brother, Pañcat. — **mañjūshā**, f. N. of Comm. — **manas**, mfn. = *-citta* above, A. — **mantha**, m. Premna Spinosa, L. — **māṇsa**, m. 'having light (i.e. easily digested) flesh,' a kind of partridge, L.; (*ī*), f. a kind of Valerian, L. — **mātra**, n. an unimportant matter, trifle, ĀśvŚr.; mfn. having small property, MBh. — **mānasa**, n. N. of various wks. — **mitra**, n. a slight or weak friend, an ally of little power or value, W. — **mīmāṇsā-vārttika-ṭīkā**, f. N. of wk. — **mūla**, n. (in alg.) the least root with reference to the additive quantities, W.; (or) the lesser root of an equation, L.; mfn. having a small root or beginning, small in the beg°, MBh.; R. — **mūlaka**, n. a radish, Bhpr. — **meru**, m. (in music) a kind of measure, Saṃgīt. — **yama**, m. N. of a short version of Y°'s law-book, Cat. — **yoga-ratnâvalī**, f., **-ratnâkara**, m. N. of wks. — **rāśi**, m. (with *paksha;* in arithm.) a set of fewer terms, Col. — **laksha-homa**, m. a partic. sacrifice, Cat.; N. of the 30th Pariśishṭa of the Atharva-veda. — **laya**, n. the root of Andropogon Muricatus, L. — **lalita-vistara**, m., **-vasishṭha-siddhânta**, m., **-vākya-vṛitti**, f., °**tti-prakāśikā**, f., **-vādârtha**, m., **-vāyu-stuti**, f., **-vārttika**, n. N. of wks. — **vāsas**, mfn. wearing a light or clean dress, Mn. ii, 70. — **vāsishṭha**, n., °**ṭha-siddhânta**, m. N. of wks. — **vikrama**, m. a quick step, R.; mfn. having a qu° st°, quick-footed, Hariv.; R. — **vimarśinī**, f. N. of wk. — **vivaratva**, n. narrowness of an aperture or opening, Pañcat. — **vishṇu**, m. N. of a short version of Vishṇu's law-book, Cat. — **vṛitti**, f. 'short commentary,' N. of Comm.; mfn. having a light nature, light in conduct or behaviour, RPrāt.; light-minded, W.; ill-conducted or conditioned, ib.; ill-done, mismanaged, ib.; *-kārikā*, f. N. of wk.; *-tā*, f. insignificance, meanness, W.; light-mindedness, Kir.; bad conduct, mismanagement, W.; °*tty-avacūrikā*, f. N. of wk. — **vedhin**, mfn. easily piercing, cleverly hitting, MBh. — **vaiyākaraṇa-bhūshaṇa**, n., °**shaṇa-siddhânta-mañjūshā**, f., **-vyākaraṇa-bhūshaṇa-sāra**, N. of wks. — **vyāsa**, m. N. of an author, Cat. — **śaṅkha**, m. a kind of small shell, Madanav. — **śabda-ratna**, n., °**dêndu-śekhara**, m. N. of wks. — **śamī**, f. a kind of Acacia, MW. — **śānti-purāṇa**, n., °**ti-vidhāna**, n. N. of wks. — **śikhara-tāla**, m. N. of a partic. time in music, Cat. — **śiva-purāṇa**, n. N. of wk. — **śīta**, m. Cordia Myxa, L. — **śekhara**, m. (in music) a kind of measure, Saṃgīt. — **śaunaka**, m. or n., °**nakī**, f., **-saṃgraha**, m., °**haṇī-sūtra**, n. N. of wks. — **sattva**, mfn. 'weak-natured,' having a w° or fickle character, VarBṛS.; *-tā*, f. weakness of char°, fickleness, MBh.; R. — **sadā-phalā**, f. Ficus Oppositifolia, L. — **saṃtāpa**, mfn. having the pain (of sickness) alleviated, Śak. — **saṃdeśa-pada**, mf(*ā*)n. (speech) expressing a request in few words, Ragh. viii, 76. — **sapta-śatikā-stava**, m., **-sapta-śatikā-stotra**, n., **-sapta-śatī**, f., °**tī-stotra**, n. N. of wks. — **samutthāna**, mfn. rising quickly to work, active, alert, Kām.; Daś. — **samudīraṇa**, mfn. moving easily; *-tva*, n. mobility (of the body), Buddh. — **saralā**, f., **-sahasra-nāma-stotra**, n., **-sāṃkhya-vṛitti** or °**khya-sūtra-v**°, f. N. of wks. — **sāra**, mfn. of little importance, insignificant, worthless, Inscr.; °*râvalī*, f. N. of wk. — **siddhânta-kaumudī**, f., °**ta-candrikā**, f. N. of easy versions of the Siddhânta-k°, see *laghu-k*°. — **su-darsana**, n. a partic. medicinal powder, Cat. — **sūtra-vṛitti**, f., **-stava**, m., °**va-ṭippaṇaka**, **-stotra**, n. N. of wks. — **sthāna-tā**, f. w.r. for *laghûtthāna-tā*, q.v., Kāraṇḍ. — **syada**, m. the act of moving or gliding quickly, MBh. (= *raghu-sy*°, Kāś.) — **hasta**, mfn. light-handed, ready-h°, possessing skill in the hands (as an archer, writer &c.), MBh.; Suśr. &c.; m. a good archer, W.; *-tā*, f. (MBh.; Ragh.) or *-tva*, n. (Kathās.) ready-handedness, skilful-h°; *-vat*, mfn. = *laghu-hasta*, Hariv.; BhP. — **hārīta**, m. 'short Hārīta,' N. of a partic. recension of H°'s law-book; *-smṛiti*, f. N. of wk. — **hṛidaya**, mfn. light-hearted, fickle, Kād. — **hema-dugdhā**, f. Ficus Oppositifolia, L. — **homa-paddhati**, f., **-horā**, f. N. of wks. **Laghū-karaṇa**, n., see *laghū-kṛi*. **Laghûkti**, f. a brief mode of expression, Kull. on Mn. v, 64. **Laghûtthāna**, mfn. easily set about or begun, Kām.; making active efforts, doing work rapidly, MW.; *-tā*, f. bodily vigorousness or activity, good health, Divyâv. **Laghûtthita**, mfn. promptly ready or at hand, Kām. **Laghûdumbarikā**, f. Ficus Oppositifolia, L.

Laghaya, Nom. P. °*yati*, to make light, lessen, diminish, mitigate, soften, alleviate, Kālid.; Kir.; to cause to appear light, Subh.; to make light of, slight, despise, Kir.; to excel, surpass, Hcar.

Laghiman, m. lightness, levity, absence of weight, MBh.; Kāv.; Pur.; a kind of *siddhi* or supernatural faculty of assuming excessive lightness at will, Vet.; MārkP.; Pañcar. (cf. RTL. 427); lowness, meanness (of spirit), Kād.; thoughtlessness, frivolity, Bhaṭṭ.; slight, disrespect, ŚārṅgP.

Laghishṭha, mfn. (superl. of *laghu*, q. v.) most light or quick, very light or quick &c. [Cf. Gk. ἐ-λάχιστος.]

Lághīyas, mfn. (compar. of *laghu*, q. v.) more or very quick or light, AV. &c. &c. — **tva**, n. extreme insignificance, want of authority, HYog.

Laghuka, mfn. = *laghu*, light, unimportant, insignificant, Harav.

Laghū, in comp. for *laghu*. — **karaṇa**, n. the act of making light, lessening, diminishing, diminution, Sarvad.; thinking little of, contemning, W. — √**kṛi**, P. *-karoti*, to make light, reduce in weight, diminish, alleviate, Mālatīm.; Veṇīs.; Śiś.; to lessen, shorten (days), Naish.; to reduce in importance, slight, humiliate, ib.; to think lightly of, despise, Mṛicch., Sch. — **kṛita**, mfn. made light, reduced in weight &c. (cf. prec.); 'shortened' and 'reduced in importance or authority,' ŚārṅgP.

Laghūya, Nom. P. °*yáti*, to think lightly of, despise, ŚBr.

Laghv, in comp. for *laghu*. — **akshara**, mfn. short-syllabled, RPrāt. — **aksharaka**, m. a space of two Truṭis (a partic. measure of time), L. — **añjira**, n. a species of fig, L. — **atri**, m. N. of a short version of Atri's law-book. — **amara**, m. N. of an abbreviation of Amara's dictionary. — **ashṭavarga**, m. N. of wk. — **ācārya**, m. N. of an author, Cat. — **ādy-udumbarâhvā**, f. = *laghûdumbarikā*, L. — **āryabhaṭa-siddhânta**, m. N. of an astron. wk. (= *mahā-siddhânta*). — **āśin** and **-āhāra**, mfn. eating little, moderate in diet, abstemious, MBh. — **āhnika**, n. N. of wk.

लङ् *laṅ*, (in gram.) a technical term for the terminations of the Imperfect or for that tense itself (cf. 1. *la*).

लङ्क *laṅka*, m. N. of a man, g. *naḍâdi;* (*ā*), f., see below. — **taṅkaṭā**, f. N. of a daughter of Saṃdhyā (wife of Vidyut-keśa and mother of Sukeśa), R. — **śāntamukha**, m. pl. the descendants of Laṅka and Śānta-mukha, g. *tika-kitavâdi*.

Laṅkaka, m. abridged N. of Alaṃ-kāra (brother of Maṅkha, minister of Jaya-siṇha of Kaśmīra, 1129–1150), Śrīkaṇṭh.

Laṅkā, f. N. of the chief town in Ceylon or of the whole island (renowned as the capital of the great Rākshasa Rāvaṇa, q. v.; accord. to some accounts L° was much larger than the island of Ceylon is at present, or was even distinct from it, the first meridian of longitude which passed through Ujjayinī being supposed to pass through L° also), MBh.; R. &c.; N. of a lake (= *rāvaṇa-hrada*), R.; of a Yoginī, Hcat.; of a Śākinī or evil spirit, L.; an unchaste woman, L.; a branch, L.; a kind of grain, L. — **kāṇḍa**, m. or n. N. of wk. — **dāhin**, m. 'burner of Laṅkā,' N. of Hanumat (as having set fire to the city with his burning tail), L. — **deśa**, m. the place or district of L°, Gol. — °**dhipati** (*laṅkâdh*°), m. 'lord of L°,' N. of Rāvaṇa, R. — °**dhirāja** (*laṅkâdh*°), m. 'id.,' N. of Vibhīshaṇa (brother of Rāvaṇa), Rājat. iii, 73. — **nagarī**, f. the city of L°, Gaṇit. — **nātha**, m. N. of Rāvaṇa and of Vibhīshaṇa, Ragh. xv, 103; N. of an author (also called Rāvaṇa), Cat. — °**nila** (*laṅkân*°), m. the wind blowing from L°, south-wind, Vcar. — **pati**, m. 'lord of L°,' N. of Rāvaṇa and of Vibhīshaṇa, L. — **purī**,

f. the city of L°, AV.Pariś. **-°ri** (*laṅkâri*); m. 'enemy of L°,' N. of Rāma-candra, Kālid. **-°vatāra** (*laṅkâv°*), m. N. of a Sūtra wk. of the Northern Buddhists (one of their 9 canonical scriptures, also called *sad-dharma-l°*, see *Dharma*, MWB. 69). **-sthāyin**, mfn. residing or being in L°, W.; m. Euphorbia Tirucalli, ib. **Laṅkêndra**, m. N. of Rāvaṇa, Rājat. **Laṅkêśa**, m. N. of Rāvaṇa, Hariv.; Ragh.; *-vanâri-ketu*, m. 'having the enemy of the grove of L° (i.e. the monkey Hanumat) for an ensign,' N. of Arjuna, MBh. iv, 1294 (Nīlak.) **Laṅkêśvara**, m. N. of Rāvaṇa, R.; Ragh. &c.; N. of an author (cf. *laṅkā-nātha*), Cat.; (*ī*), f. N. of a Yoginī, L. **Laṅkôdaya**, m. 'ascension at L°,' the equivalents of the signs in right ascension, Sūryas.

Laṅkāpikā or **°kāyikā** or **°kārikā** or **°koṭikā** or **°kopikā** or **°koyikā**, f. Trigonella Corniculata, L.

लङ्ख् *laṅkh* (cf. √*lakh* and *liṅkh*), to go, Dhātup. v, 25.

लङ्खनी *laṅkhanī*, f. the bit of a bridle, W.

लङ्ग् *laṅg*, cl. 1. P. *laṅgati*, to go, Dhātup. v, 37; Nir. vi, 26; to limp, Vop. (cf. 2. *vi-lagita*).

1. **Laṅga**, mfn. lame, limping, KātyŚr., Sch.; m. limping, lameness, W.

Laṅgana, n. leaping across, L. (cf. *laṅghana*).

Laṅgin, mfn. lame, limping, L.

लङ्ग 2. *laṅga*, m. (prob. fr. √*lag*) union, association, L.; a lover, paramour (also °*gaka*), L.; =*jāra*, L. **-datta**, m. N. of a poet, Cat.

Laṅganī, f. a stick or rope on which to hang clothes, L.

Laṅgiman, m. union (°*ma-maya*, joined), Dhūrtas.

लङ्गल *laṅgala*, n.=*lāṅgala* (q.v.), a plough, Kāṭh.; N. of a country, Buddh. (v.l. *lāṅgala*).

लङ्गुरा *laṅgurā*, f. millet, Gal.

लङ्गूला *laṅgūlā*, f.=*lāṅgūla* (q.v.), L.

लङ्घ् *laṅgh* (cf. √*raṅh* and *laghu*) cl. 1. P. Ā. (Dhātup. iv, 34; v. 55) *laṅghati*, °*te* (Gr. also *lalaṅgha*, °*ghe*; aor. *alaṅghīt*, °*ghishṭa*; fut. *laṅghitā*; °*ghishyati*, °*te*; inf. *laṅghitum*), to leap over, go beyond (Ā.), Pañcad.; to ascend, mount upon (P.), Bhaṭṭ.; to pass over meals, abstain from food, fast (P.), Dhātup.; to dry, dry up, waste, consume, L.: Caus. or cl. 10. P. (Dhātup. xxxiii, 87; 121) *laṅghayati* (m.c. also A. °*te*; Pass. *laṅghyate*), to leap over, cross, traverse, Mn.; MBh. &c.; to mount, ascend, tread upon, enter, Kāv.; Kathās.; to overstep, transgress, violate, neglect, Yājñ.; Kāv.; Rājat.; to get over, avoid, shun, escape from, Kāv.; Kathās.; to frustrate, prevent, avert, R.; Mṛicch.; to disregard, slight, offend, insult, injure, Mn.; MBh. &c.; to excel, surpass, outshine, obscure, eclipse, R.; Ragh.; Rājat.; to remove, transport, Kāraṇḍ.; to cause to pass over meals i.e. fast, Suśr.: Desid. of Caus. *lilaṅghayishati*, to intend to step over, Kāvyâd., Sch.

Laṅghaka, mfn. one who leaps over or transgresses, a transgressor or offender, VarBṛS.

Laṅghatī, f. N. of a river, MBh. (v.l. *laghantī*).

Laṅghana, n. the act of leaping or jumping, leaping over, stepping across, crossing, traversing (gen. or comp.), PārGṛ.; R. &c.; one of a horse's paces, curvetting, bounding, L.; (ifc.) rising to or towards, ascending, mounting, attaining, Kālid.; sexual union, impregnating, Daś.; attack, conquest, capture, Kāv.; Pur.; transgression, violation, disdain, neglect, R.; Rājat.; (also *ā*, f.) insult, offence, injury, wrong, MBh.; Kāv. &c.; fasting, hunger, starving system, Suśr. **-pathya-nirṇaya**, m. N. of a medical wk.

Laṅghanaka, (prob.) n. means of crossing (?), Divyâv.

Laṅghanīya, mfn. to be lept or passed over, to be crossed or traversed, Kathās.; to be reached or caught or overtaken (*a-l°*), Śak.; to be transgressed or violated, Cat.; to be insulted or injured, Pañcat. **-tā**, f. (Śiś.), **-tva**, n. (Rājat.) capability of being stepped over or transgressed or violated or injured.

Laṅghita, mfn. lept over, overstepped, traversed, transgressed, violated, disregarded, insulted, MBh.; Kāv. &c.; made to fast, Car.

Laṅghitavya, mfn.=*laṅghanīya*, MW.

Laṅghiman, v.l. for *laṅgiman*, q.v.

Laṅghya, mfn. to be lept or passed over or crossed or traversed, Kāv.; Kathās.; attainable, Rājat.; to be transgressed or violated or neglected, ib.; BhP.; Pañcar.; to be injured or offended or wronged, MBh.; Kāv. &c.; to be made to fast, Suśr.; to be cured by fasting, Car.

लछ् *lach* (cf. √*laksh* and *lāñch*), cl. 1. P. *lacchati*, to mark, Dhātup. vii, 26.

लछिमा *lachimā*, f. N. of a woman (=*lakshmī*, q.v.), Cat.

लज् 1. *laj* (cf. √*lajj*), cl. 6. Ā. *lajate* (only 3. pl. pf. *lejire*, Bhaṭṭ.), to be ashamed, Dhātup. xxviii, 10.

Laja-kārikā, f. (*laja* for *lajjā*) the sensitive plant, Mimosa Pudica, W.

लज् 2. *laj* (cf. √1. *lañj*), cl. 1. P. *lajati*, 'to fry' or 'to blame' (*bharjane*, v.l. *bhartsane*), Dhātup. vii, 64.

लज् 3. *laj* (cf. √2. *lañj*), cl. 10. P. *lajayati*, to appear (*prakāśane*), Dhātup. xxxv, 66.

लज्ज् *lajj*, cl. 6. Ā. (Dhātup. xxviii, 10) *lajjate* (ep. also °*ti*; pf. *lalajje*, 3. pl. °*jjire*, Kathās.; fut. *lajjitā*, *lajjishyate*, Gr.; aor. *alajjishṭa*, Bhaṭṭ.; inf. *lajjitum*, MBh. &c.), to be ashamed, blush, MBh.; Kāv. &c.: Caus. *lajjayati* (or *lajjāpayati*?), to cause any one (acc.) to be ashamed, inspire with shame, Kāv.; Rājat.: Desid. *lilajjishate*, Gr.: Intens. *lālajjyate*, ib.

2. **Lagna**, mfn. (also referable to 1. *laj*; for 1. *lagna* see p. 893, col. 2) ashamed, Pāṇ. vii, 2, 14, Sch.

Lajja, m. N. of a man; pl. his descendants, Vop.; (*ā*), f., see below.

Lajjakā, f. the wild cotton tree, Gossypium, L.

Lajjarī, f. a white sensitive plant, L.

Lajjā, f. shame, modesty, bashfulness, embarrassment (also Shame personified as the wife of Dharma and mother of Vinaya), MBh.; Kāv. &c.; the sensitive plant, Mimosa Pudica, L. **-kara**, mf(*ī*)n. causing shame, shameful, disgraceful, Kāvyâd. **-kārin**, mf(*iṇī*)n. id., W. **-°kṛiti** (*lajjâk°*), mfn. feigning modesty, Śṛiṅgār. **-°dhāra** (*lajjâdh°*), m. N. of a mountain, VP. (prob. w.r. for *jalâdh°*). **-°nvita** (*lajjânv°*), mfn. possessed of shame, modest, bashful, W. **-rahita**, mfn. void of shame, shameless, immodest, ib. **-vat**, mfn. ashamed, embarrassed, bashful, perplexed, MBh.; Kāv. &c.; *-tva*, n. bashfulness, modesty, Sāh. **-vaha**, mf(*ā*)n. causing shame, disgraceful, Rājat. **-vinamrânana**, mf(*ā*)n. bending down the face with shame, VarBṛS. **-śīla**, mfn. of a modest disposition, bashful, humble (*-tva*, n.), TBr., Sch. **-śūnya**, mfn. destitute of shame, shameless, impudent, MW. **-hīna**, mfn. id., W. **Lajjôjjhita**, mfn. id., Rājat. **Lajjôdvahana**, n. possession or sentiment of shame; °*nâkshama*, mfn. incapable of feeling shame, ib.

Lajjāpayitṛi, mfn. (Prākṛit °*trika*, see √*lajj*) causing shame, Śak.

Lajjāya, Nom. (prob. Ā.) *lajjāyate*, to be ashamed (see next).

Lajjāyita, mfn. ashamed, abashed, embarrassed, BhP.; n. pl. shame, embarrassment, perplexity, Kād.

Lajjālu, mfn. shameful, bashful, timid (in Prākṛit °*luka*), Ratnâv.; f. Mimosa Pudica, Bhpr.

Lajjinī and **lajjirī**, f. Mimosa Pudica, L. (cf. *lajjarī*).

Lajyā, f.=*lajjā*, shame, modesty, L.

लञ्चा *lañcā*, f. a present, bribe, Nīlak.

लञ्छन *lañchana*, m. Eleusine Corocana, L.

लञ्ज् 1. *lañj* (cf. √2. *laj*), cl. 1. P. *lañjati*, 'to fry' or 'to blame' (*bhartsane*, v.l. *bharjane*), Dhātup. vii, 65.

लञ्ज् 2. *lañj* (cf. √*luñj*), cl. 10. P. *lañjayati*, to be strong; to strike; to dwell; to give, Dhātup. xxxii, 30 (v.l.); to speak; to shine, xxxiii, 111; to manifest (also *lañjāpayati*), xxxv, 66 (v.l.)

लञ्ज *lañja*, m. (only L.) a foot, a tail; =*kaccha*; =*paṅgu*; (*ā*), f. (only L.) an adulteress; sleep; a current; N. of Lakshmī.

Lañjikā, f. a harlot, prostitute, L.

लट् 1. *laṭ* (cf. √*raṭ*), cl. 1. P. *laṭati*, 'to be a child' or 'to cry,' Dhātup. ix, 11.

Laṭa, m. (only L.) a thief; one who speaks like a child or like a fool (=*pramāda-vacana*); a fault, defect. **-parṇa**, n.=*tvaca*, large cinnamon.

Laṭaka, m. a bad man, contemptible person. **-melana-prahasana**, n. N. of a drama.

Laṭṭa, m. (cf. *laḍḍa*)=*laṭaka*, a bad man, L.

Laṭya, Nom. P. °*yati*, to speak foolishly, g. *kaṇḍv-ādi*.

लट् 2. *laṭ*, (in gram.) a technical term for the terminations of the Present or for that tense itself (cf. 1. *la*).

Laḍ-artha-vāda, m. N. of a treatise on the meaning of the Present tense.

लटकन *laṭakana*, m. (with *miśra*) N. of the father of Bhāva-miśra (author of the Bhāva-prakāśa), Cat.

लटभ *laṭabha*, mfn. (cf. next and *laḍaha*) handsome, pretty, lovely, Vcar.; (*ā*), f. a handsome girl, beautiful woman, ib.

Laṭaha, mfn. handsome, pretty, VarBṛS., Sch.

लटूषक *laṭūshaka*. See *laḍūshaka*.

लट्टुन *laṭṭunu*, m. (with *bhaṭṭa*) N. of a poet, Cat.

लट्व *laṭva*, m. (accord. to Uṇ. i, 151 fr. √*laṭ*; only L.) a horse; a partic. caste (said to be a tribe of mountaineers); a dancing boy; a big boiler; (in music) a partic. Rāga; (*ā*), f. a kind of bird, Suśr.; (only L.) safflower; a kind of Karañja; any fruit; a game, gambling; a curl on the forehead (=*bhramaraka*); =*śilī*; =*vādya* or *avadya*; =*tūlikā* or *tulikā*.

Laṭvākā, f.=*laṭvā*, a kind of bird, MBh. (C. *laḍvākā*).

लड् *laḍ* (cf. √*lal*), cl. 1. P. (Dhātup. ix, 76) *laḍati*, to play, sport, dally, Rājat. vii, 928; cl. 10. P. *laḍayati*, to loll the tongue, put out the tongue, lick, Dhātup. xix, 53; (*lāḍayati*), to throw, toss, ib. xxxv, 81; to cherish, foster, ib. xxxii, 7; (*lāḍayate*), to wish, desire, ib. xxxii, 15, Vop.

Laḍita, mfn. moving hither and thither, Jātak.

लडक *laḍaka*, m. pl. N. of a people, MBh. (B. *dhenuka*).

लडह *laḍaha*, mfn. (cf. *laṭabha* and *laṭaha*) handsome, pleasing, beautiful, Kād.; Bālar.; pl. N. of a people, VarBṛS. (v.l. *lahara*). **-candra**, m. N. of a poet, Cat.

लडितमहेश्वर *laḍita-mahêśvara*, m. N. of a temple of Śiva, Inscr.

लडुक *laḍuka*, m. N. of a poet, Cat.

लड्ड *laḍḍa*, m. a wretch, villain, L. (cf. *laṭṭa*).

लड्डु *laḍḍu* or *laḍḍuka*, m. a kind of sweetmeat (made of coarsely ground gram or other pulse, or of corn-flour, mixed with sugar and spices, and fried in ghee or oil), AgP.; Hcat.

लड्वा *laḍvā*, f. N. of a woman, Rājat.

लड्वाका *laḍvākā*. See *laṭvākā*.

लण्ड् *laṇḍ* (cf. *olaṇḍ*), cl. 10. P. *laṇḍayati*, to throw or toss up, Dhātup. xxxii, 9; to speak, ib. xxxiii, 125.

लण्ड *laṇḍa*, n. (cf. *leṇḍa*) excrement, BhP. x, 37, 8 ('hard excrement, as of horses,' L.)

लण्ड्र *laṇḍra* (prob. fr. the French *Londres*), London, L. **-ja**, mfn. born or produced in London, ib.

लता *latā*, f. a creeper, any creeping or winding plant or twining tendril, Mn.; MBh. &c. (the brows, arms, curls, a slender body, a sword-blade, lightning &c. are often compared to the form of a creeper, to express their graceful curves and slimness of outline; cf. *bhrū-l°*, *bāhu-l°*, *taḍil-l°* &c.); the Mādhavī-creeper, Gaertnera Racemosa, Bhpr.; Trigonella Corniculata, ib.; Panicum Italicum, L.; Cardiospermum Halicacabum, L.; Panicum Dactylon, L.; =*kaivartikā*, L.; =the plant *sārivā*, L.; musk-creeper, L.; a slender woman, any woman, Naish.; Tantras.; the thong or lash of a whip, whip, Pañcat.; Suśr.; a string of pearls, VarBṛS.; a streak, line (*vārām latāḥ*, thin jets of water), Bālar.; a kind of metre, Col.; N. of an Apsaras, MBh.; of a daughter of Meru and wife of Ilāvṛita, BhP. **-kara**, m. a partic. position of the hands in dancing, Saṃgīt. (du.) **—karañja**, m. Guilandina Bonduc, L. **—kastūrikā** or °**rī**, f. musk-creeper, a kind of aromatic medicinal plant; (accord. to some 'Hibiscus Moschatus'), Suśr.; Bhpr. &c. **—kuśa**, m. the sacrificial grass creeper, L. **—koli**, f. the Jujube creeper, L. **—gahana-vat**, mfn. thickly overspread with creepers, R. **—gṛiha**, n. (ifc. f. *ā*) a creeper-bower, arbour of cr°s, MBh.; Kāv.; Kathās. **—°ṅkura** (°*tâṅ*°), m. the marshy date palm, L. **—°ṅgī** (°*tâṅ*°), f. a kind of gall-nut, L. **—°ṅguli** (°*tâṅ*°), f. 'cr°-finger,' a branch serving as a f°, MW. **—jihva**, m. 'cr°-tongued,' a snake, L. **—taru**, m. N. of various trees (Shorea Robusta; Borassus Flabelliformis; the orange tree), L. **—druma**, m. Shorea Robusta, L. **—°nana** (°*tân*°), m. a partic. position of the hands in dancing, Cat. **—°nta** (°*tân*°), n. 'end of a creeper,' a flower, L.; *-bāṇa*, m. the god of love, Daś. **—panasa**, m. the water-melon, L. **—parṇa**, m. N. of Vishṇu, L.; (*ī*), f. Curculigo Orchioides, Dhanv.; Trigonella Foenum Graecum, ib. **—pāśa**, m. a snare or festoon formed of cr°s, Ratnâv. **—puṭakī**, f. Cardiospermum Halicacabum, Car., Sch. **—pūga**, n. the Areca creeper, L. **—pṛikkā**, f. Trigonella Corniculata, L. **—pratāna**, m. the tendril of a cr°, Ragh. **—phala**, n. the fruit of Trichosanthes Dioeca, BrahmavP. **—bāṇa**, m. c. creeper-arrowed. N. of Kāma-deva. **—bṛihatī**, f. the creeper egg-plant, L. **—bhadrā**, f. Paederia Foetida, L. **—bhavana**, n. = *-gṛiha* above, in *apa-l°*, q. v. **—maṇi**, m. 'cr°-jewel,' coral, L. **—maṇḍapa**, m. a cr°-bower, Kāv. **—marut**, f. Trigonella Corniculata, L. **—mādhavī**, f. Gaertnera Racemosa, Śak. **—mārisha**, m. the Amaranth creeper, L. **—mṛiga**, m. an ape, monkey, W. **—°mbuja** (°*tâm*°), n. a kind of cucumber, L. **—yashṭi**, f. Rubia Munjista, L. **—yāvaka**, n. a shoot, sprout, young or tender pasturage, L. **—rada**, m. an elephant, Gal. **—rasana**, m. 'cr°-tongued,' a snake, L. **—°rka** (°*târ*°), m. a green onion, L. **—°laka** (°*tâl*°), m. an elephant, L. **—°laya** (°*tâl*°), m. 'cr°-abode,' arbour of cr°s, Kathās. **—liṅga** (?), Cat. **—valaya**, m. or n. (?) = *-gṛiha* above, Śak.; *-vat*, mfn. possessed of bowers made of cr°s, ib. **—vitāna**, m. or n. a canopy made of cr°s, ib. **—vṛiksha**, m. the cocoa-nut tree, Npr.; Shorea Robusta, ib. **—veshṭa**, m. N. of a mountain, Hariv.; a kind of coitus, L. **—veshṭana**, n. 'cr°-embrace,' an embrace, L. **—veshṭita**, m. N. of a mountain (= *-veshṭa*), Hariv. **—veshṭitaka**, n. the winding (embrace) of a creeper, Naish. **—śaṅku-taru**, m. Shorea Robusta, Npr. (correctly *latā-taru* and *śaṅku-t°*). **—śaṅkha**, m. id., L. (w. r.) **Latôdgama**, m. (as an explanation of *avaroha*) a shoot or root sent down from a branch, L.; the upward climbing of a creeper, MW.

Latāya, Nom. Ā. °*yate*, to resemble a creeping plant, Kāv.

Latikā, f. a delicate or slender creeper or small winding tendril (to which the graceful curve of a slim figure is compared), Kāv.; Kām.; a string of pearls, Sāh.

लतु *latu*, m. N. of a man, Uṇ. i, 78, Sch. (cf. *lātavya*).

लट्टादिनिर्णय *laṭṭādi-nirṇaya*, m. N. of a wk. by Govinda.

लट्टिका *laṭṭikā*, f. a kind of lizard, Uṇ. iii, 147, Sch.

लदनी *ladanī*, f. N. of a female poet, Cat.

लदूषक *ladūshaka* (or *laṭūshaka*?), m. a kind of bird, Car.; Suśr.

लड्डी *laddī*, f. = *laḍḍu* (?), Divyâv.

लड्डनदेव *laddhana-deva*, m. N. of a man, Cat.

लद्धा *laddhā*, w. r. for *laṭvā*.

लप् 1. *lap* (cf. √*rap*), cl. 1. P. (Dhātup. x, 8) *lapati* (ep. also °*te* and *lapyati*; pf. *lalāpa*, *lepus*, MBh. &c.; aor. *alāpīt*, Gr.; fut. *lapitā*, ib.; *lapishyati*, Br. &c.; inf. *laptum*, MBh.; *lapitum*, Kāv.; ind. p. *-lapya*, MBh.), to prate, chatter, talk (also of birds), MBh.; Hariv.; to whisper, Gīt.; Pañcar.; to wail, lament, weep, Nalôd.: Caus. *lāpayati*, °*te* (aor. *alīlapat* or *alalāpat*, Gr.), to cause to talk, ChUp.: Desid. *lilapishati*, Gr.: Intens. *lā́lapīti*, to prate senselessly, AV.; Kāṭh.; *lālapyate* (m.c. also °*ti*), to wail, lament, MBh.; R.; MārkP.; to address repeatedly, MBh.; *lā́lapti*, Gr. [Cf. Gk. ὀ-λοφ-ύρομαι; perhaps Lat. *lāmentum* for *lap-mentum*.]

2. **Lap**, (ifc.) speaking, uttering (see *abhilāpa-lap*).

Lapana, n. the mouth, Śiś.; speaking, talking, W.

Lapita, mfn. chattered, spoken, said, L.; (*ā*), f. N. of a Śārṅgikā (a kind of bird) with which Mandapāla is said to have allied himself, MBh.; (°*tá*), n. chatter, hum, AV.

Lāpa, m. speaking, talking, W.

Lāpikā. See *antar-* and *bahir-l°*.

Lāpin, mfn. (ifc.) speaking, uttering, Hariv.; wailing, lamenting, MārkP.

Lāpinikā, f. (prob.) talk, conversation, Siṃhâs.

Lāpya, mfn. to be spoken &c., Pāṇ. iii, 1, 126.

लपेटिका *lapeṭikā*, f. N. of a place of pilgrimage, MBh.

लपेत *lapeta*, m. N. of a demon presiding over a partic. disease of children, PārGṛ.

लप्सिका *lapsikā*, f. N. of a kind of prepared food, Bhpr.

लप्सुद *lapsuda*, n. = *kūrca*, the beard (of a goat &c.), KātyŚr., Sch.

Lapsudin, mfn. having a beard, bearded (said of a goat), TS.; ŚBr.; KātyŚr.

लब *labá*, m. a quail, VS.; (with *Aindra*) N. of the supposed author of RV. x, 119, Anukr. **—sûkta**, n. N. of the hymn RV. x, 119, Nir.

लभ् *labh* (cf. √*rabh*), cl. 1. Ā. (Dhātup. xxiii, 6) *labhate* (ep. also °*ti* and *lambhate*; pf. *lebhé*, ep. also *lalābha*; aor. *alabdha*, *alapsata*, Br.; Prec. *lapsīya*, Pāṇ. viii, 2, 104, Sch.; fut. *labdhā*, Gr.; *lapsyate*, °*ti*, Br. &c.; *labhishyati*, Kāv.; inf. *labdhum*, MBh.; ind. p. *labdhvā́*, AV. &c.; *-labhya*, *-lambham*, Br. &c.; *lābham*, Pāṇ. vii, 1, 69), to take, seize, catch; catch sight of, meet with, find, Br. &c. &c. (with *antaram*, to find an opportunity, make an impression, be effective; with *avakāśam*, to find scope, be appropriate; with *kālam*, to find the right time or moment); to gain possession of, obtain, receive, conceive, get, receive ('from,' abl.; 'as,' acc.), recover, ib. (with *garbham*, 'to conceive an embryo,' 'become pregnant;' with *padam*, to obtain a footing); to gain the power of (doing anything), succeed in, be permitted or allowed to (inf. or dat., e.g. *labhate drashṭum* or *darśanāya*, 'he is able or allowed to see'), ChUp.; MBh. &c.; to possess, have, Sāh.; MārkP.; to perceive, know, understand, learn, find out, Kathās.; Kull.: Pass. *labhyáte* (ep. also °*ti*; aor. *alābhi* or *alambhi*, with prep. only *alambhi*; cf. Pāṇ. vii, 1, 69, Kāś.), to be taken or caught or met with or found or got or obtained, Br. &c. &c.; to be allowed or permitted (inf. sometimes with pass. sense, e.g. *nâdharmo labhyate kartum*, 'injustice ought not to be done,' cf. above), Kathās.; to follow, result, Sāh.; Sarvad.; to be comprehended by (abl.), Bhāshāp.: Caus. *lambhayati*, °*te* (aor. *alalambhat*), to cause to take or receive or obtain, give, bestow (generally with two acc.; rarely with acc. and instr. = to present with; in Kir. ii, 55 with two acc. and instr.; cf. Vām. v, 2, 10), MBh.; Kāv. &c.; to get, procure (cf. *lambhita*); to find out, discover, Mn. viii, 109; to cause to suffer, MW.; Desid. *lípsate* (m. c. also °*ti*; TBr. *līpsate*), to wish to seize or take or catch or obtain or receive (with acc. or gen.; 'from,' abl.), TBr. &c. &c.: Intens. *lālabhyate*, *lālambhīti* or *lālabdhi*, Gr. [Gk. λάφ-υρον, λαμβ-άνω; Lat. *labor*; Lith. *lábas*, *lóbis*.]

Labdha, mfn. taken, seized, caught, met with, found &c.; got at, arrived (as a moment), Kathās.; obtained (as a quotient in division), Col. (cf. *labdhi*); (*ā*), f. N. of a partic. heroine, L.; a woman whose husband or lover is faithless, W. **—kāma**, mfn. one who has gained his wishes, MW. **—kīrti**, mfn. one who has won fame or glory, ib. **—cetas**, mfn. one who has recovered his right mind, restored to sense, recovered, W. **—janman**, mfn. one who has obtained birth, born, ib. **—tīrtha**, mfn. one who has gained an opportunity, BhP. **—datta**, m. 'restoring what has been received,' N. of a man, Kathās. **—dhana**, mfn. one who has acquired wealth, wealthy, W. **—nāman**, mfn. one who has gained a name, well spoken of, famous, celebrated, Kām.; Ratnâv. ('for,' loc.; in Prākṛit). **—nāśa**, m. the loss of what has been acquired, MBh. **—nidrā-sukha**, mfn. enjoying the pleasure of sleep, Ml. **—para-bhāga**, mfn. one who has gained pre-eminence over (abl.), ib. **—praṇāśa**, m. id., N. of the 4th book of the Pañca-tantra. **—pratishṭha**, mfn. one who has acquired fame or renown, Kum. **—pratyaya**, mfn. one who has won confidence, one who has firm belief in (*-tā*, f.), Ratnâv. (in Prākṛit). **—praśamana**, n. the securing of what has been acquired, keeping acquisitions in safety, Mn.; MBh.; Hariv.; (accord. to Kull. 'bestowing acquisitions on a proper recipient'); *-svastha*, mfn. at ease by (reason of) the securing or secure possession of acquisitions, Ragh. **—prasara**, mf(*ā*)n. that which has obtained free scope, moving at liberty, unimpeded, Mudr.; Ratnâv. (in Prākṛit). **—laksha**, mfn. one who has hit the mark, one who has obtained the prize, proved, tried, tested in (loc.), Mn.; MBh.; Hariv.; Kathās.; skilled in the use of missiles, MW.; m. N. of a man, MBh. **—lakshaṇa**, mfn. one who has gained an opportunity for (doing anything), Daś. **—lakshya**, mfn. = *-laksha* above, R.; Kām. **—lābha**, mf(*ā*)n. one who has gained a profit or advantage, one who has attained his aim, satisfied, Kāraṇḍ.; one who has gained possession of (comp.), ib.; happily obtained or reached, ib. **—vat**, mfn. one who has obtained or gained or received, MBh. **—vara**, mfn. one who has obtained a boon or favour, MBh.; m. N. of a dancing master, Kathās. **—varṇa**, mfn. one who has gained a knowledge of letters, lettered, learned in (comp.), Ragh.; Pārśvan.; famous, renowned, Mṛicch.; *-bhāj*, mfn. honouring the learned, Ragh. **—vidya**, mfn. one who has acquired knowledge or wisdom, learned, educated, W. **—śabda**, mfn. = *-nāman* (q. v.), R. **—saṃhāra**, mfn. brought together, b° about, Divyâv. **—saṃjña**, mfn. one who has recovered his senses, restored to consciousness, MBh.; R. **—sambhāra**, mfn. = *-saṃhāra* above, Divyâv. **—siddhi**, mfn. one who has attained perfection, W. **Labdhâtiśaya**, mfn. one who has obtained the possession of supernatural power, Sāṃkhyas. **Labdhânujña**, mfn. one who has obtained leave of absence, L. **Labdhântara**, mfn. one who has found an opportunity (*-tva*, n.), Śak.; one who has got access or admission, Ragh. **Labdhâvakāśa** (Śak.; Kathās.) or °**vasara** (Kaush-Up.; HPariś.), one who has found an opportunity or gained scope, one who has obtained leisure. **Labdhâspada**, mfn. one who has gained a footing or secured a position, Mālav. **Labdhôdaya**, mfn. one who has received birth or origin, Kum.; one who has attained prosperity, Rājat.

Labdhaka, mf(*ikā*)n. = *labdha*, obtained, got (see *duḥkha-labdhikā*).

Labdhavya, mfn. to be obtained or received, obtainable &c., MBh.; Śaṃk.

Labdhi, f. obtaining, gaining, acquisition, Yājñ.; Kathās.; Pur.; gain, profit, VarBṛS.; in (arithm.) the quotient, Col.

Labdhṛi, mfn. one who obtains or receives, a receiver, gainer, recipient, KaṭhUp.; MārkP.

Labha. See *īshal-*, *dur-*, *su-l°*.

Labhana, n. the act of obtaining or getting or gaining possession of (in *ātma-l°*), BhP.; the act of conceiving, conception, Jaim., Sch.

Labhasa, n. (only L.) a horse's foot-rope (= *vājibandhana*); wealth, riches; one who asks or solicits, a solicitor.

Labhya, mfn. to be found or met with, KaṭhUp.; Pat.; Kum.; capable of being reached or attained, obtainable, acquirable, procurable, MBh.; Kāv. &c.; to be understood or known, intelligible, Up.; MBh. &c.; suitable, proper, fit, Kālid.; Kathās.; Rājat.; to be allowed to (inf. with pass. sense), MBh. ii, 921; to be furnished or provided with (instr.), MBh. xiii, 5081.

Lambha, m. (for *lambham* see √*labh*) the obtaining or attaining, meeting with, finding, recovery, ChUp.; MBh. &c.; capture (of a fortress), VarBṛS.; (*ā*), f. a sort of fence or enclosure, L. °**bhaka**, mfn. one who finds, a finder, Pāṇ. vii, 1, 64, Sch. (cf. *varsha-lambhaka*).

Lambhana, n. the act of obtaining or receiving, attainment, recovery, MBh.; R.; causing to get, procuring, Daś.; HPariś. °**bhanīya**, mfn. to be attained, attainable, KaṭhUp. °**bhayitavya**, mfn. to be applied or set to work, Mālav.

Lambhita, mfn. (fr. Caus.) caused to obtain or receive, given, procured, gained, MBh.; Kāv. &c. (W. also 'heightened, improved; cherished; applied, adapted; addressed, spoken to; abused'). **—kānti**, mfn. one who has acquired lustre or beauty, MW. **-lobha**, mfn. one who has a desire of (comp.), Gīt.

Lambhuka, mfn. one who is accustomed to receive (acc.), ChUp.

Lābha, m. meeting with, finding, Mn.; Kathās.; obtaining, getting, attaining, acquisition, gain, profit, Mn.; MBh. &c.; capture, conquest, Hariv.; VarBṛS.; apprehension, perception, knowledge, Śaṃk.; Sāh.; BhP.; enjoying, MW.; N. of the 11th astrological house or lunar mansion VarBṛS. (also *-sthāna*, Cat.) **-kara** (MW.) or **-kṛit** (W.), mfn. causing gain, making profit, gainful, profitable. **-kāraṇāt**, ind. for the sake of gain or profit, MBh. **-tas**, ind. = *yathā-lābham*, Car. **-lipsā**, f. greediness of gain, avarice, covetousness, ŚārṅgP. **-vat**, mfn. one who has gain or advantage, Ragh.; (ifc.) one who has got possession of, Kathās. **Lābhâlābha**, m. du. profit and loss, gain and detriment, Mn. ix, 331.

Lābhaka, m. gain, profit, advantage, VarBṛS.

Lābham. See under √*labh*.

Lābhin, mfn. (ifc.) obtaining, meeting with, finding, Rājat.; Pracaṇḍ.; Kāraṇḍ.

Lābhya, n. = *lābha*, L.

Lipsā, f. (fr. Desid.) the desire to gain, wish to acquire or obtain, longing for (loc. or comp.), MBh.; Kāv. &c.

Lipsita, mfn. wished to be obtained, desired, R. **Lipsitavya**, mfn. desirable to be obtained, wished for, MBh. **Lipsu**, mfn. wishing to gain or obtain, desirous of, longing for (acc. or comp.), MBh.; Kāv. &c. (*lipsu-tā*, f. 'desire of gaining').

Lipsya, mfn. to be wished to be obtained, desirable to be acquired, Vop.

Līpsitavya, mfn. worthy to be acquired, desirable, AitBr.

लम् *lam* (= √*ram*; not in Dhātup.; only pf. *lalāma*), to delight in, sport, enjoy sexually, Hariv.

Lamaka, m. a lover, gallant, W.; = *tīrtha-śodhaka*, Uṇ. ii, 33, Sch.; N. of a man; pl. his descendants, g. *upakâdi*.

लम्न *lamna*, m. pl. N. of a partic. tribe, Rājat.

लम्पक *lampaka*, m. pl. N. of a Jaina sect, W.

लम्पट *lampaṭa*, mf(*ā*)n. covetous, greedy, lustful, desirous of or addicted to (loc. or comp.), Inscr.; Kāv.; Pur.; m. a libertine, lecher, dissolute person, W.; (*ā*), f. a partic. personification, L. **-tā**, f., **-tva**, n. greediness, dissoluteness, lewdness.

Lampāka, mfn. = *lampaṭa*, Nalac.; pl. N. of a people and country (= *muraṇḍa*; accord. to some the district of Lamghan in Cabul), MBh.; MārkP.; (*ī*), f. a woman from the country of the Lampākas, Bālar.; (prob. n.) N. of a wk. on accents (*svara-śāstra*) by Padma-nābha.

लम्पा *lampā*, f. the black banana, L.; N. of a town and of a kingdom, Kathās.; Buddh. **-paṭaha**, m. a kind of drum, L. (cf. *lambā-p°*).

लम्फ *lampha*, m. a leap, spring, jump, L. (cf. *jhampa*).

Lamphana. See *ul-* and *pra-l°*.

लम्ब 1. *lamb* (cf. √1. *ramb*), cl. 1. Ā. (Dhātup. x, 15) *lámbate* (m.c. also °*ti*; pf. *lalambe*, MBh. &c.; aor. *alambishṭa*, Gr.; fut. *lambitā*, ib.; *lambishyati*, MBh.; inf. *lambitum*, ib.; ind. p. *-lambya*, ib.), to hang down, depend, dangle, hang from or on (loc.), Suparṇ.; MBh. &c.; to sink, go down, decline, fall, set (as the sun), MBh.; Kāv. &c.; to be fastened or attached to, cling to, hold or rest on (loc.), ib.; to fall or stay behind, be retarded, Sūryas.; to lag, loiter, delay, tarry, MBh.: Caus. *lambayati* (aor. *alalambat*), to cause to hang down or depend, let down, Kathās.; to hang up, suspend, ib.; to cause to be attached or joined, MW.; to stretch out, extend (the hand) for (dat.), Ragh.; (prob.) to depress, discourage, MBh. i, 1445 (C. *laṅghayitvā* for *lambayitvā*): Desid. *lilambishate*, to be about to sink or decline, Hcar., v.l. [Cf. Gk. λοβός; Lat. *labi, labare, labes*; Germ. *lappa, Lappen*; Eng. *lap, limp*.]

Lamba, mf(*ā*)n. hanging down, pendent, dangling, hanging by or down to (comp.), MBh.; Kāv. &c.; long, large, spacious (see comp.); m. (in geom.) a perpendicular, Col.; (in astron.) complement of latitude, co-latitude, the arc between the pole of any place and the zenith, Sūryas.; N. of a partic. throw or move (at a kind of chess or backgammon or draughts), L.; a present, bribe, L. (prob. w.r. for *lañcā*); = *nartaka, aṅga*, or *kānta*, L.; N. of a Muni, Cat.; of a Daitya, Hariv.; (*ā*), f., see s. v.; (*ī*), f. a kind of food prepared from grain, Madanav.; a flowering branch, Harav. **-karṇa**, mf(*ā* or *ī*)n. having pendulous ears, long-eared, MBh.; R.; m. a he-goat, goat, L.; an elephant, L.; a hawk, falcon, L.; a Rākshasa, L.; Alangium Hexapetalum, L.; N. of one of Śiva's attendants, L.; of an ass, Pañcat.; of a hare, ib. **-keśa**, mfn. having hanging or flowing hair, Gṛihyas. **-keśaka**, m. 'long-haired,' N. of a Muni, Cat. **-guṇa**, m. (in astron.) the sine of the co-latitude, Gol. **-jaṭhara**, mfn. big-bellied, MBh. **-jihva**, mfn. letting the tongue hang out; m. N. of a Rākshasa, Kathās. **-jyakā** or **-jyā**, f. (in astron.) the sine of the co-latitude, Sūryas. **-dantā**, f. a kind of pepper, L. **-payo-dharā**, f. a woman with large or pendent breasts, MBh.; N. of one of the Mātṛis attending upon Skanda, ib. **-bījā**, f. a kind of pepper, L. **-māla**, mfn., (prob.) w.r. for *lambamāna*, Hariv. **-rekhā**, f. (in astron.) the complement of latitude, co-lat°, Gol. **-stanī**, f. a woman with flaccid breasts, Suśr. **-sphic**, mfn. having large or protuberant buttocks, MBh. **Lambâksha**, m. 'long-eyed,' N. of a Muni, Cat. **Lambâlaka**, mfn. having pendulous curls, Daś.; *-tva*, n. pendulosity of curls, MW. **Lambôdara**, mf(*ī*)n. having a large or protuberant belly, pot-bellied (*-tā*, f.), MBh.; Kād.; Kathās.; voracious, L.; m. N. of Gaṇeśa, Pañcar.; Kathās.; of a king, Pur.; of a Muni, Cat.; (*ī*), f. N. of a female demon, Suśr.; of a river, Cat.; °*ra-prahasana*, n., °*rī-nadī-māhātmya*, n. N. of wks. **Lamb'oshṭha** (Śiksh.) or °**bâushṭha** (L.), mfn. having a large or prominent under-lip; m. a camel, L.

Lambaka, m. (in geom.) a perpendicular, Āryabh.; (in astron.) the complement of latitude, co-latitude, Gol.; a partic. implement or vessel, L.; N. of the 15th astrological Yoga, L.; N. of the larger sections or books in the Kathā-sarit-sāgara (there are 18 Lambakas containing 124 Taraṃgas or chapters); w.r. for *lambhaka*, Kathās. lxi, 24; (*ikā*), f. the uvula or soft palate (cf. *lambikā-kokilā*).

Lambana, mfn. hanging down or causing to hang down (said of Śiva), MBh.; m. a camp-follower, soldier's boy, Hcar.; phlegm, the phlegmatic humour, L.; N. of a son of Jyotish-mat, VP.; n. hanging down, depending, falling, W.; a partic. mode of fighting, Hariv.; the moon's parallax in longitude, the interval of the lines between the earth's centre and surface, Sūryas.; Gol.; a fringe, L.; a long necklace (depending from the neck to the navel), L.; N. of a Varsha in Kuśa-dvīpa, MārkP. **-vidhi**, m. (in astron.) the rule for calculating the moon's parallax in longitude.

Lambara, m. a kind of drum, BṛĀrUp.

Lambā, f. of *lamba*, q. v.; a kind of bitter gourd or cucumber, Suśr.; a present, bribe, L. (perhaps w.r. for *lañcā*); N. of Durgā and Gaurī, Hariv.; of Lakshmī, L.; of one of the Mātṛis attending upon Skanda, MBh.; of a daughter of Daksha and wife of Dharma (or Manu), Hariv.; Pur.; of a Rākshasī, Buddh. **-paṭaha**, m. a kind of drum, Hcar. **-viśvavayasau**, m. du., w.r. for *bambā-v°*, g. *vanaspaty-ādi*.

Lambika, m. the Indian cuckoo, Kāraṇḍ.

Lambikā-kokilā, f. N. of a goddess, Cat.

Lambita, mfn. hanging down, pendent, MBh.; hanging by (instr.), ib.; sunk, gone down, glided down, fallen off, MBh.; Kāv. &c.; (ifc.) clinging or adhering to, supported or resting on, R.; Ragh.; = *vi-lambita*, slow (of time in music), L.

Lambin, mfn. hanging down, pendent, hanging by or down to (comp.), Kālid.; (*inī*), f. N. of one of the Mātṛis attending on Skanda, MBh.

Lambuka, m. N. of the 15th astrological Yoga, Col. (cf. *lambaka*); N. of a serpent-demon, Buddh.

Lambushā, f. a necklace of seven strings, L.

लम्ब 2. *lamb* (cf. √2. *ramb*), cl. 1. Ā. *lambate*, to sound, Dhātup. x, 15.

लम्भ *lambh* (cf. √2. *rambh*), cl. 1. Ā. *lambhate*, to sound, Dhātup. x, 24 (Vop.)

लम्भ *lambha*, °*bhaka*, °*bhana* &c. See p. 896, col. 3.

लय् *lay* (cf. √*ray*), cl. 1. Ā. *layate*, to go, Dhātup. xiv, 10 (Vop.)

लय *laya*, *layana* &c. See p. 903, col. 2.

लर्द् *lard*, cl. 10. P. *lardayati*, to load, Divyâv. (cf. Hindī *lād*).

लर्ब् *larb*, cl. 1. P. *larbati*, to go, Dhātup. xi, 37.

लल् *lal* (cf. √*laḍ*), cl. 1. P. (Dhātup. ix, 77) *lalati* (m.c. also °*te*), to play, sport, dally, frolic, behave loosely or freely, MBh.; Kāv. &c.; to loll or wag the tongue (see below): Caus. *lālayati*, °*te* (Pass. *lālyate*), to cause to sport or dally, caress, fondle, foster, cherish, ib.; to wave, flourish, Hariv.; to favour, Sāh.; (Ā.) to desire, Dhātup. (cf. under √*laḍ*).

Lala, mfn. sporting, playful, W.; lolling, wagging, ib.; wishing, desirous, ib.; m. a partic. fragrant substance, Gal.; n. a shoot, sprout, L.; a garden, L.

Lalaj-jihva, mf(*ā*)n. (fr. pr. p. *lalat* + *j°*) lolling the tongue, moving the tongue to and fro, Kathās.; Hcat.; fierce, savage, L.; m. a camel, L.; a dog, L.

Lalad-ambu, m. (fr. pr. p. *lalat* + *a°*) the citron tree, L.

Lalana, mfn. sporting, playing, coruscating (as light or colour), BhP.; m. Vatica Robusta, L.; Buchanania Latifolia, L.; (*ā*), f., see below; n. play, sport, dalliance, L.; the lolling or moving the tongue to and fro, MārkP. **Lalanâksha**, m. 'having quivering eyes,' a kind of animal, L.

Lalanā, f. a wanton woman, any woman, wife, MBh.; Kāv. &c.; the tongue, L.; N. of various metres, Col.; of a mythical being, R. (v.l. *analā*). **-priya**, mfn. dear to women, L.; m. Nauclea Cadamba, L.; a kind of Andropogon, L. **-varūthin**, mfn. surrounded by a troop of women, BhP.

Lalanikā, f. (dimin. fr. *lalanā*) a little woman, miserable woman, Kāvyâd.

Lalantikā, f. (fr. *lalantī*, f. of pr. p. *lalat*) a long pendulous necklace, L.; a lizard, chameleon, W.

Lalalla, (onomat.) indistinct or lisping utterance, Kathās.

Lalita, mfn. sported, played, playing, wanton, amorous, voluptuous, Kāv.; Kathās.; Rājat.; artless, innocent, soft, gentle, charming, lovely (*am*, ind.), ib. &c.; wished for, desired, MBh.; Mṛicch.; BhP.; quivering, tremulous, Bālar.; m. a partic. position of the hands in dancing, Cat.; (in music) a partic. Rāga, Sāh.; (*ā*), f. a wanton woman, any woman, W.; musk, L.; N. of various metres, Col.; (in music) a partic. Mūrchanā, Saṃgīt.; a partic. Rāga, ib.; N. of a gram. wk.; N. of a Durgā or a partic. form of her, Hcat.; Cat.; of a Gopī (identified with Durgā and Rādhikā), PadmaP.; of the wife of a Śatāyudha, HPariś.; of a river, KālP.; n. sport, dalliance, artlessness, grace, charm, R.; Kpr.; languid gestures in a woman (expressive of amorous feelings, 'lolling, languishing' &c.), Daśar.; Sāh.; N. of 2 metres, Piṅg., Sch.; of a town, Rājat. (cf. *-pura*); a kind of necklace (?), L. **-caitya**, m. N. of a Caitya, W. **-tāla**, m. a partic. time (in music), Cat. **-tri-bhaṅga**, m. N. of wk. **-pada**, mf(*ā*)n. consisting of amorous or graceful words, elegantly composed, VarBṛS.; n. a kind of metre, VarBṛS.; *-bandhana*, n. an amorous composition in verse, a metrical composition treating of love, MW. **-pura**, n. N. of a town, W. **-purāṇa**, n. = *-vistara-purāṇa*. **-prahāra**, m. a soft or gentle blow, MW. **-priya**, m. (in music) a kind of measure, Saṃgīt. **-mādhava**, n., **-ratna-mālā**, f. N. of dramas. **-lalita**, mfn. excessively beautiful, Uttarar.; Pañcar. **-locana**, mf(*ā*)n. beautiful-eyed, MBh.; Rājat.; (*ā*), f. N. of a daughter of the Vidyā-dhara Vāma-datta, Kathās. **-vanitā**, f. a lovely woman, MW. **-vistara**, m. or °**ra-purāṇa**, n. N. of a Sūtra wk. giving a detailed account of the artless and natural acts in the life of the Buddha. **-vyūha**, m. (with Buddh.) a partic. kind of Samādhi or meditation, Lalit.; N. of a Deva-putra, ib.; of a Bodhisattva, ib. **-sva-cchanda**, m. N. of wk. **Lalitâṅga**, m. N. of a man, HPariś.; (*ī*), f. a beautiful woman, Vcar.; *-nareśvara-carita*, n. N. of wk.

Lalitâditya, m. N. of a king of Kaśmīra, Rājat.; *-pura*, n. N. of a town founded by him, ib. **Lalitânurāga**, m. N. of a poet, Subh. **Lalitâpīḍa**, m. N. of a king, Rājat. **Lalitâbhinaya**, m. erotic performance, representation of love scenes, Bhar. **Lalitârtha**, mfn. having an amorous meaning; *-bandha*, mfn. composed in words of love or in words having an amorous meaning, Vikr.

Lalitaka, n. N. of a Tīrtha, MBh. (v.l. *lalitika*).

Lalitā, f. (see *lalita*) in comp. **-krama-dīpi-**

kā, f., **-khaṇḍa**, n., **-gadya-nirūpaṇa**, n., **-tantra**, n. N. of wks. **— tṛitīyā**, f. N. of a partic. third day; *-vrata*, n. a partic. religious ceremony, Cat. **— tri-śatī**, f. N. of wk. **— °dikīrti** (°*tâd*°), m. N. of a man, Bhadrab. **— °di-pūjā-vidhi** (°*tâd*°), m. N. of wk. **— pañcamī**, f. the 5th day of the moon's increase in the month Āśvina (when the goddess Lalitā or Pārvatī is worshipped), MW. **— pañca-śatī**, f., **-pañcâṅga**, n., **-paddhati**, f., **-pūjā-khaṇḍa**, n., °**jā-vidhāna**, n., **-bhaṭṭa-bhāskara**, m., **-bhāshya**, n., **-mādhava**, n. (= *lalita-m*°); **-māhātmya**, n., **-rahasya**, n.; **-°rcana-candrikā** (°*târ*°), f., °**na-dīpikā**, f., °**na-vidhi**, m.; **-°ryā-dvi-śatī** (°*târ*°), f. N. of wks. **— vrata**, n. a partic. religious observance, Cat. **— shashṭhī**, f. a partic. sixth day; *-vrata*, n. a partic. rel° obs°, Cat. **— °shṭôttara-śata-nāman** (°*tâsh*°), n. pl., **-saparyā-paddhati**, f. N. of wks. **— saptamī**, f. N. of the 7th day in the light half of the month Bhādra, L. **— sahasra**, n., °**sra-nāman**, n. pl., °**ma-bhāshya**, n., **-siddhânta**, m., **-stavaratna**, n., **-hṛidaya**, n. N. of wks. **Lalitôpâkhyāna**, n. N. of wk. and of chs. of Purāṇas.

Lalitoka, m. N. of a poet, Cat.

Lalittha, m. pl. N. of a people (sg. a prince of this people), MBh.

Lalītikā, f. N. of a place of pilgrimage, MBh.

Lāla, m. the son of a Maitreya and a Brāhmaṇī, L.; N. of an astronomer in Kānyakubja, Cat.; (with *paṇḍita* and *vihārin*) of two other authors, ib.; (*ā*), f., see below; n. (only L.) persuasion; a secret matter; the wife of another. **— candra**, m. N. of an author, Cat. **— bhārata-kāvya**, n. N. of a poem. **— maṇi**, m. N. of various authors (also with *tri-pāṭhin* and *bhaṭṭâcārya*), Cat. **— matī**, f. N. of a princess, Inscr. **— miśra**, m. N. of a man, Cat. **— vat**, mfn. (for *lālā-vat*) causing saliva to flow, Suśr. **— siṇha**, m. N. of an astronomer, Col. (cf. *lalla*).

Lālaka, mf(*ikā*)n. (fr. Caus.) fondling, caressing, Nalôd.; m. a king's jester, VarBṛS., Sch.; also (n. and *ikā*), f. an infant's attempts at speaking, L.; (*ikā*), f. a rope round the nostrils of a horse, L.; a jesting or evasive reply, equivoque, W.

Lālana, mfn. caressing, fondling, coaxing, L.; m. a partic. venomous animal resembling a mouse, Suśr.; resin, L.; n. the act of caressing, fondling, coaxing, indulging, Kāv.; BhP.; Rājat.

Lālanīya, mfn. to be caressed or fondled or indulged, Hariv.; R.; Kathās.

Lālayitavya, mfn. id., MBh.; Hariv.

Lālā, f. saliva, spittle, slobber, Kāv.; Var.; Suśr. &c.; a species of myrobolan, L. **— klinna**, mfn. wet with saliva, Bhartṛ. **— pāna**, n. drinking saliva, sucking the thumb, Subh. **— pūrṇârṇava**, m. a sea full of s°, BhP. **— bhaksha**, m. 'having s° for food,' N. of a partic. hell (assigned to those who eat their meals without offering portions of food to the gods, deceased ancestors, and guests), Pur. **— meha**, m. passing mucous urine, ŚārṅgS. **— visha**, mfn. having poisonous saliva (said of venomous insects), L. **— srava**, m. 'distilling saliva,' a spider, L. **— srāva**, m. id., L.; flow of saliva, Suśr.; °*vin*, mfn. causing a flow of saliva, ib.

Lālāya, Nom. Ā. °*yate*, to let saliva fall from the mouth, slobber, drivel, Bhartṛ.

Lālāyita, mfn. emitting saliva, slobbering, drivelling, L.

Lālālu, id., Car.

Lālika, m. a buffalo (cf. *lāvikā*), L.; (*ā*), f., see under *lālaka*.

Lālita, mfn. (fr. Caus.) caressed, fondled, coaxed, indulged, cherished, MBh.; Kāv. &c.; n. pleasure, joy, love, MW.

Lālitaka, m. a favourite, pet, Rājat. (perhaps in some places a proper N.)

Lālitya, n. (fr. *lalita*) grace, beauty, charm, amorous or languid gestures, Inscr.; Sāh.; Hcat.

Lālin, mfn. caressing, fondling, coaxing, Śiś.; m. a seducer, W.; (*inī*), f. a wanton woman, ib.

Lālilá, m. N. of Agni, TĀr.

Lālya, mfn. = *lālanīya*, Hit.

ललाट *lalāṭa*, n. (later form of *rarāṭa*, q.v.) the forehead, brow, AV. &c. &c. (*e*, ind. on the forehead, in front; the destiny of every individual is believed by the Hindūs to be written by Brahmā on his forehead on the 6th day after birth, see RTL. 370). **— taṭa**, m. the slope or surface of the forehead, Rājat. **— deśa**, m. the region of the f°, Pañcat. **— ṃ-tapa**, mfn. scorching the f° (as the sun), Kālid.; Hcar. **— paṭṭa** or **-paṭṭaka**, m. (Kād.), **-paṭṭikā**, f. (Pārśvan.) the flat surface of the f°; a tiara, fillet, W. **— pura**, n. N. of a town, Pāṇ. v, 4, 74, Sch. **— phalaka**, n. the flat surface of the f°, MārkP. **— rekhā**, f. (only W.) a line on the f° supposed to indicate long life; a wrinkled or corrugated brow; a coloured sectarial mark on the f°. **— likhita**, mfn. written (by Brahmā) on the f° (see above), Bhartṛ. **— lekhā**, f. the lines written on the f°, Mahān.; a line-like or very narrow forehead, Śiś. **Lalāṭâksha**, mf(*ī*)n. having an eye in the forehead, MBh.; m. N. of Śiva, ib.

Lalāṭaka, n. the forehead, brow, AgP.; a beautiful f°, L.; (*ikā*), f. an ornament worn on the f°, L. (cf. Pāṇ. iv, 3, 65, Sch.); a mark made with sandal or ashes on the forehead, Kād.

Lalāṭika, mfn. being in front, ĀpŚr.; (*ā*), f., see prec.

Lalāṭikāya, Nom. Ā. °*yate*, to represent or be like a mark on the forehead, Cat.

Lalāṭūla, mfn. having a high or handsome forehead, g. *sidhmâdi*.

Lalāṭya, mfn. (cf. *rarāṭya*) belonging to the forehead, frontal, Pāṇ. iv, 3, 55, Sch.; suitable for the forehead, ib. v, 1, 6, Sch.

ललाम *lalā́ma*, mf(*ī*)n. having a mark or spot on the forehead, marked with paint &c. (as cattle), AV.; TS.; having any mark or sign, MBh.; beautiful, charming, L.; eminent, best of its kind (f. *ā*), L.; m. n. ornament, decoration, embellishment, MBh.; Kāv. &c.; (*ī*), f. N. of a female demon, AV.; a kind of ornament for the ears, L.; n. (only L.) a coloured mark on the forehead of a horse or bull; a sectarial mark; any mark or sign or token; a line, row; a flag, banner; a tail; a horse; = *prabhāva*. **— gu** (*lalā́ma-*), m. a facetious term for the penis, VS. **— vat**, mfn. having a mark or spot or ornament, L.

Lalāmaka, n. a chaplet or wreath of flowers worn on the forehead, L. **— rūpaka**, n. (in rhet.) a flowery metaphor.

Lalāman, n. an ornament, decoration, Vcar.; (only L.) a sectarial mark; any mark or sign; a banner, flag; a tail; a horn; a horse; chief or principal; a species of stanza (having 10 syllables in the first two Pādas, 11 in the third, and 13 in the fourth); = *ramya* or *sukha*.

ललित *lalita* &c. See p. 897, col. 3.

लल्यान *lalyāna*, m. or n. (?) N. of a place, Rājat.

लल्ल *lalla*, m. N. of an astronomer, Gol.; of a writer on law, Cat.; of a minister, Rājat.; (*ā*), f. N. of a courtezan, ib. **— vārāha-suta**, m. N. of an astronomer, Cat.

Lallā-dīkshita, m. N. of a modern commentator on the Mṛicchakaṭikā.

लल्लर *lallara*, mf(*ā*)n. (onomat.) stammering, L.

लल्लिय *lalliya*, m. N. of a man, Rājat.

लल्लुजीलाल *lalluji-lāla*, m. N. of an author, Cat.

लव *láva*, m. (√1. *lū*) the act of cutting, reaping (of corn), mowing, plucking or gathering (of flowers &c.), Daś.; Nalôd.; that which is cut or shorn off, a shorn fleece, wool, hair, Mn.; Ragh.; anything cut off, a section, fragment, piece, particle, bit, little piece (*am*, ind. a little; *lavam api*, even a little), MBh.; Kāv. &c. (cf. *padāti-l*°); a minute division of time, the 60th of a twinkling, half a second, a moment (accord. to others $\frac{1}{4000}$ or $\frac{1}{5400}$ or $\frac{1}{20250}$ of a Muhūrta), ib.; (in astron.) a degree, Gol.; (in alg.) the numerator of a fraction, Col.; the space of 2 Kāshṭhās, L.; loss, destruction, L.; sport, L. (cf. *lala*); Perdix Chinensis, W.; N. of a son of Rāmacandra and Sītā (he and his twin-brother Kuśa were brought up by the sage Vālmīki and taught by him to repeat his Rāmāyaṇa at assemblies; cf. *kuśī-lava*), R.; Ragh.; Uttarar.; Pur.; of a king of Kaśmīra (father of Kuśa), Rājat.; n. (only L.) nutmeg; cloves; the root of Andropogon Muricatus; a little (cf. m.). **— rāja**, m. N. of a Brāhman, Rājat. **— vat**, mfn. lasting only for a moment, Śāntiś. **— śas**, ind. in small pieces, bit by bit, Mn.; MBh.; in minute divisions or instants, after some moments, MBh. **Lavâpavāha**, m. (in alg.) subtraction of fractions, Līl. **Lavêpsu**, mfn. wishing to cut or reap.

Lavaka, mfn. reaping, a reaper, Pāṇ. iii, 1, 14; N. of a partic. substance (see *sa-l*°).

Lavaṃga, m. (Uṇ. i, 119) the clove tree; n. cloves, Kāv.; Var.; Kathās.; (*ī*), f. N. of an Apsaras, Bālar.; of another woman, Nalac. **— kalikā**, f. cloves, L. **— pushpa**, n. the flower of the clove tree, Ragh. **— latā**, f. Limonia Scandens, L.

Lavaṃgaka, n. cloves, L.; (*ikā*), f. N. of a woman, Vās., Introd.

Lavana, mfn. one who cuts &c., a cutter, reaper, g. *nandy-ādi*; (*ī*), f. Anona Reticulata, L.; n. the act of cutting, reaping, mowing &c., KātyŚr.; an implement for cutting, sickle, knife &c., Kauś. (see *darbha-l*°). **— kartṛi**, m. a mower, reaper, Kull. on Mn. vii, 110. **— kalāyī**, **-sādhikā**, see *lavaṇa-k*°, *lavaṇa-s*°.

Lavanīya, mfn. to be cut or reaped or mown, Bhaṭṭ., Sch.

Lavanya, m. N. of a partic. tribe of men, Rājat.

Lavaya, Nom. P. °*yati* = *lavam ācashṭe*, Pāṇ. i, 1, 58, Vārtt. 2, Pat.

Lavāka, m. (prob. w. r. for next) an implement for cutting, sickle, reaping-hook, L.; the act of cutting, L.

Lavānaka, m. an implement for cutting, sickle reaping-hook &c., Uṇ. iii, 83, Sch.

Lavi, mfn. cutting, sharp, edged (as a tool or instrument), W.; m. an iron instrument for cutting or clearing, Uṇ. iv, 138.

Lavitavya, mfn. to be cut (*-tva*, n.), Nyāyam., Sch.

Lavitra, n. = *lavānaka* above, Pāṇ. iii, 2, 184.

Lavya, mfn. to be cut or mown or hewn down, Bhaṭṭ. (cf. *eka-* and *duḥkha-l*°).

लवट *lavaṭa*, m. N. of a man, Rājat.

लवण *lavaṇá*, mf(*ā*)n. (derivation doubtful) saline, salt, briny, brinish, ŚBr. &c. &c. (°*ṇaṃ kṛitvā* or *kṛitya*, g. *sākshâdi*); tasteful, graceful, handsome, beautiful, W.; m. saltness, saline taste, W.; the sea of salt water (in MBh. vi, 236 &c. one of the seven oceans which surround the Dvīpas in concentric belts), IW. 420; N. of a hell, VP. (v. l. *savana*); of a Rākshasa or Daitya, MBh.; Hariv.; Pur.; of a king belonging to the family of Hariścandra, Cat.; of a son of Rāma (= *lava*, q.v.), Śatr.; of a river, L.; = *bala* and *asthi-deva*, L.; (*ā*), f. lustre, grace, beauty, L. (cf. *lāvaṇya*); Cardiospermum Halicacabum, L.; N. of a river, Mālatīm.; (*ī*), f. (g. *gaurâdi*) N. of various rivers, L.; n. (according to some also m. and *ā*, f.) salt (esp. sea-salt, rock or fossil salt; but also factitious salt or salt obtained from saline earth), AV. &c. &c.; over-salted food, L.; lustre, beauty, charm, grace (ifc., see *nir-l*° and *lava-ṇâkara*); a partic. mode of fighting (prob. w. r. for *lambana*), Hariv. **— kaṭuka**, mfn. saline and acrid, Suśr. **— kalāyī** (prob. w. r. for *lavaṇa-kalāpī*), f. (perhaps) a trough, Hcar. (v. l. *-sādhikā*). **— kashāya**, mfn. saline and astringent, Suśr. **— kiṃśukā**, f. Cardiospermum Halicacabum, L. **— krītaka**, m. a Cākrika (q. v.) who sells salt, L. **— kshāra**, m. a kind of salt, L.; a partic. preparation made of sugar-cane juice, L. **— khāni**, f. a salt-mine, L.; the district of Sambher in Ajmere celebrated for its fossil salt, W. **— jala**, mfn. having salt water, MBh.; m. the sea, ocean, ib.; *-dhi* (BhP.) or *-nidhi* (R.), m. 'receptacle of s° w°,' sea, ocean; °*lôdbhava*, m. 'sea-born,' a muscle, shell, MBh. **— tā**, f. saltness, brinishness, Suśr. **— tikta**, mfn. saline and bitter, ib. **— tṛiṇa**, n. a kind of grass, L. **— toya**, mfn. having salt water; m. the sea, ocean, R. **— tva**, saltness, MBh. **— dāna-ratna**, n. N. of sev. wks. **— dhenu**, f. an offering of salt, a cow symbolically represented with salt, Cat. **— parvata**, m. a mountain symb° repr° with salt, Cat. **— pāṭalikā**, f. a salt-bag, Buddh. **— pura**, n. N. of a town, Cat. **— pragāḍha**, mfn. strongly impregnated with salt, Suśr. **— mada**, m. a kind of salt, L. **— mantra**, m. a prayer accompanied with an offering of salt, Cat. **— meha**, m. a kind of urinary disease (discharging saline urine), L.; °*hin*, mfn. suffering from it, Suśr. **— lāyikā**, f. an instrument by which salt is given to a horse, L. **— vāri**, mfn. having salt water; m. sea, ocean, ŚārṅgP. **— śrāddha**, n. N. of wk. **— samudra**, m. the salt-sea, sea, ocean, Sūryapr. **— sādhikā**, f. (prob. for *lavaṇa-s*°), see *-kalāyī*. **— sindhu**, m. the salt-sea, sea, ocean, Śiś., Comm. **— sthāna**, n. N. of a place, Cat. **Lavaṇâkara**, m. a salt-mine, L.; (met.) treasure of grace or beauty, Daśar. **Lavaṇâcala**, m. = *lavaṇa-parvata*, q.v., Cat. **Lavaṇân-**

taka, m. 'slayer of the Rākshasa Lavaṇa,' N. of Śatru-ghna, Ragh.; Pañcar. **Lavaṇâpaṇa**, m. a salt market, L. **Lavaṇâbdhi**, m. 'receptacle of salt water,' the sea, ocean, MārkP.; *-ja*, n. 'sea-born,' sea-salt, L. **Lavaṇâmbu-rāśi**, m. 'mass of salt water,' the sea, ocean, Kāv. **Lavaṇâmbhas**, n. salt water, MW.; m. 'having salt w°,' the sea, ocean, MBh.; Hariv.; Kāv. **Lavaṇârṇava** (R.; Rājat.; BhP.) or **lavaṇâlaya** (R.), m. 'sea of salt w°,' the ocean. **Lavaṇâśva**, m. N. of a Brāhman, MBh. **Lavaṇâsura**, m. N. of an Asura, Virac.; *-ja*, n. a kind of salt, L. **Lavaṇôtkaṭa**, m.n. and (*ā*), f. oversalted food, L. **Lavaṇôttama**, n. 'best salt,' river or rock s°, Suśr.; Bhpr.; nitre, W. **Lavaṇôttha**, n. a kind of salt, L. **Lavaṇôtsa**, n. N. of a town, Rājat. **Lavaṇôda**, n. salt water, brine (comp.); m. 'containing salt w°,' the sea of salt w°, ocean, Sūryapr.; Cat.; °*dhi*, m. 'receptacle of salt w°,' the sea, ocean, R.; Pur. **Lavaṇôdaka**, n. salt w°, brine, L.; mfn. having or containing salt water, MBh.; m. the sea, ocean, Buddh.

Lavaṇaya, Nom. P. °*yati*, to salt, season with salt, Pāṇ. iii, 1, 21.

Lavaṇasya, Nom. P. °*yati*, to desire salt, long for salt, Pāṇ. vii, 1, 51.

Lavaṇita, mfn. salted, seasoned with salt, Car.

Lavaṇiman, m. saltness, g. *dṛiḍhâdi*; grace, beauty, Prasannar.

Lavaṇīya, Nom. P. °*yati*, Pāṇ. vii, 1, 51, Sch.

लवन *lavana* &c. See p. 898, col. 3.

लवलि *lavali*, f. Averrhoa Acida, Viddh.

Lavalī, f. id., Śiś.; Vās.; Bhpr.; a kind of metre, Col.; (prob.) N. of a woman (see next). **-pariṇaya**, m. N. of a drama. **-phala-pāṇḍura**, mfn. pale as the fruit of the Lavalī tree, Vikr.

लवेटिका *laveṭikā*, f. corn, L.

लवेरणि *laveraṇi*, m. N. of a man; pl. his descendants, Saṃskārak. (prob. w.r. for *lāveraṇi*).

लव्य *lavya*. See p. 898, col. 3.

लश् *laś*, cl. 10. P. *lāśayati*, to exercise an art, Dhātup. xxxvi, 55 (v.l. for *las*).

लश *laśa*, m. gum, resin, L.

लशुन *laśuna*, n. or (rarely) m. (Uṇ. iii, 57; sometimes written *lasuna*, cf. *rasuna*) garlic, Gaut.; Mn.; MBh. &c.; one of the 10 kinds of onion, L.

Laśunīya, mfn. garlicky, W.

लष *lash* (cf. √*las*), cl. 1. 4. P. Ā. (Dhātup. xxi, 23; cf. Pāṇ. iii, 1, 70) *lashati*, °*te*, *lashyati*, °*te* (pf. *lalāsha*, *leshe*; aor. *alāshīt*, *alashishṭa*; fut. *lashitā*; °*shishyati*, °*te*; inf. *lashitum*), to wish, desire, long for (acc.), MBh.; Kāv. &c. (mostly with prepos. *abhi*); to strive after, approach (acc.), VarBṛS., Sch.: Caus. or cl. 10. P. *lāshayati* (aor. *alīlashat*), to exercise an art, Dhātup. xxxiii, 55 (v.l. for *las*): Desid. *lilashishati*, Gr.: Intens. *lālashyate*, *lālashṭi*, ib.

Lashaṇa, mfn. one who desires or longs for, Pāṇ. iii, 2, 150.

Lashaṇā-vatī, f. N. of a place, Cat.

Lashita, mfn. wished, desired &c., MBh.

Lashva, m. a dancer, actor, Uṇ. i, 153, Sch.

लषमण *lashamaṇa*, m. (= *lakshmaṇa*) N. of a man, Inscr.

Lashamā-devī, f. = *lakshmī-devī*, N. of a princess, Inscr.

लस 1. *las*, cl. 1. P. (Dhātup. xvii, 64) *lasati* (only p. *lasat*, *lasamāna*, and pf. *lalāsa*; Gr. also aor. *alasīt*; fut. *lasitā*, *lasishyati*), to shine, flash, glitter, MBh.; Kāv. &c.; to appear, come to light, arise, Kathās.; to sound, resound, ib. (cf. √*ras*); to play, sport, frolic, Chandom.; to embrace, Dhātup.: Caus. or cl. 10 (Dhātup. xxxiii, 55), *lāsayati* (aor. *alīlasat*; Pass. *lāsyate*), to dance, R.; to cause to teach to dance, Vikr.; to exercise an art (cf. √*laś*), Dhātup. [Cf. Lat. *lascivus*, *lascivire*.]

2. **Las**, mfn. shining, glittering (see *a-las*).

Lasa, mfn. shining, playing, moving hither and thither (cf. *a-lasá*); having the smell of bell-metal, L.; m. fever in a camel, L.; smell of bell-metal, L.; (*ā*), f. saffron, turmeric, L.; n. red sandal-wood, L.

Lasaka, mfn. = *lāsaka*, L.; m. a kind of tree, L.; (*ikā*), f. spittle, saliva, L.; a tendon, muscle, L. (cf. *lasīkā*); n. a partic. drug, L.

Lasad-aṇśu, mfn. (p. *lasat* + *a*°) having flashing or glancing rays (as the sun), MW.

Lasita, mfn. played, sported &c., MBh.

Lasīkā, f. watery humour in the body, lymph, serum &c., Car.; Bhpr.; the juice of the sugar-cane, L.; a tendon, muscle, L.

Lasta, mfn. embraced, grasped, W.; skilled, skilful, ib.

Lastaka, m. the middle of a bow (the part grasped), L. **-graha**, m. seizing the m° of a bow, L.

Lastakin, m. a bow, L.

Lāsa, m. the act of jumping, sporting, dancing, Ṛit. (cf. *rāsa*); dancing as practised by women, L.; soup, broth (= *yūsha*), L.; saliva (?), in *alāsa*, q.v. **-vatī**, f. N. of a woman, Kathās.

Lāsaka, mfn. moving hither and thither, playing, gamboling, L.; m. a dancer, actor (with *nartaka*, among the names of Śiva), R.; a peacock, L.; N. of a dancer, Kathās.; embracing, surrounding (= *veshṭa*), L.; m. or n. a kind of weapon, Kād.; (*ikā*), f. a female dancer, Kathās.; Vcar.; a harlot, wanton, L.; a kind of dramatic performance (= *vilāsikā*), Sāh.; (*akī*), f. a dancing girl, L.; n. a turret, tower, room on the top of a building (= *aṭṭa*), L.

Lāsana, n. moving hither and thither, MBh.

Lāsika, mfn. dancing, Śiś.

Lāsin, mfn. moving to and fro, dancing, MW. (cf. *raṅga-lāsinī*).

Lāsya, n. dancing, a dance (esp. accompanied with instrumental music and singing), a dance representing the emotions of love dramatically (this was at one time a principal part of the drama, and as such accord. to Bharata and the Daśa-rūpa consisted of 10 divisions or Aṅgas, viz. *geya-pada*, *sthita-pāṭhya*, *āsīna*, *pushpa-gaṇḍikā*, *pracchedaka*, *tri-gūḍha* or *tri-mūḍhaka*, *saindhava*, *dvigūḍhaka* or *vi-mūḍhaka*, *uttamôttamaka*, and *ukta-pratyukta*; including also a style of dramatic composition in which there is abrupt transition from Sanskṛit to Prākṛit and from Prākṛit to Sanskṛit; the term *lāsya* is also applied to the Nāch [Nautch] dance of the Indian dancing girls, consisting chiefly of gesticulation with a shuffling movement of the feet forwards and backwards, as invented by Pārvatī and opposed to the boisterous masculine dance called Tāṇḍava practised by Śiva and his followers; cf. IW. 467), MBh.; Kāv. &c.; m. a dancer, MārkP.; N. of a king, VP.; (*ā*), f. a dancing girl, L. **Lāsyâṅga**, n. a division of the Lāsya (cf. above).

Lāsyaka, n. = *lāsya*, a dance, L.

लसोफरञ्ज *lasopharañja*, m. or n. (?) N. of a place, Cat.

लस्त *lasta*, *lastaka* &c. See above.

लस्पूजनी *laspūjanī́*, f. a large needle, ŚBr.; KātyŚr. (here ibc. °*ni*).

लहका *lahakā*, f., g. *kshipakâdi* on Pāṇ. vii, 3, 45, Vārtt. 5 (6).

लहड *lahaḍa*, m. pl. N. of a people, VarBṛS. (v.l. *laḍaha* and *lahara*).

Lahara, m. pl. N. of a people (see prec.); of a province in Kaśmīra (perhaps the present Lahore), Rājat.

लहरि *lahari* or °*rī*, f. a large wave, billow, Kāv.; Kathās. &c.

लहलहाय *lahalahāya*, °*yate*, onomat., to breathe, snort, Pañcad.

लहिक *lahika*, m. dimin. fr. next, Pāṇ. v, 3, 83, Vārtt. 3, Pat. (cf. *kahika*).

Lahoḍa, m. N. of a man, ib. (cf. *kahoḍa*).

लह्य *lahya*, m. N. of a man, g. *śivâdi*; pl. his descendants, g. *kaskâdi*.

लह्वा *lahvā*, f. a kind of bird, Suśr. (prob. w.r. for *laṭvā*).

ला 1. *lā*, cl. 2. P. (Dhātup. xxiv, 50) *lāti* (pf. *lalau*, Bhaṭṭ.; aor. *alāsīt*, ib.; fut. *lātā*, *lāsyati*, Gr.; ind. p. *lātvā*, Śatr.), to take, receive, obtain, Kāv.; Sāh.; HPariś.; to undertake, begin, Campak.; to give, Dhātup. [Cf. Hind. *lenā*.]

2. **Lā**, f. the act of taking or giving, L.

Lāta, mfn. taken, received, obtained, MW.

Lāti, f. taking, receiving (cf. *deva-l*°).

Lātvā, ind. having taken, taking (often = 'with,' accompanied by), Kāv.

लाकिनी *lākinī*, f. N. of a Tantra goddess, Cat. (cf. *ḍākinī*).

लाकुच *lākuca*, mf(*ī*)n. (fr. *lakuca*) belonging or relating to the tree Arthocarpus Locucha, Vāgbh.

Lākuci, m. patr. fr. *lakuca* (also pl.), Saṃskārak.

लाकुटिक *lākuṭika*, m. (fr. *lakuṭa*) 'staff-bearer,' a servant, attendant, Pañcat. (B.; v.l. *lāguḍika*).

लाक्षकी *lākshakī*, f. N. of a Sītā, L.

लाक्षण *lākshaṇa*, mf(*ī*)n. (fr. *lakshaṇa*) relating to or acquainted with characteristic signs or marks, APrāt., Sch.

Lākshaṇi, m. patr. fr. *lakshaṇa*, Pāṇ. iv, 1, 153.

Lākshaṇika, mf(*ī*)n. knowing marks, acquainted with signs, an interpreter of marks or signs, R.; indicatory, expressing indirectly or figuratively, metaphorical, secondary, technical (*-tva*, n.), Śaṃk.; Kpr.; Sarvad.

Lākshaṇya, mfn. = *lākshaṇa*, R.; m. patr., Pāṇ. iv, 1, 152.

लाक्षा *lākshā*, f. (cf. *rākshā* and Uṇ. iii, 62, Sch.) a species of plant, AV.; a kind of red dye, lac (obtained from the cochineal or a similar insect as well as from the resin of a partic. tree), Mn.; MBh. &c.; the insect or animal which produces the red dye, MW. **-gṛiha**, n. = *jatu-g*° (q.v.), Veṇis. **-cūrṇa**, n. lac-powder, Suśr. **-taru**, m. the tree Butea Frondosa (in which the above insect is especially found), L. **-taila**, n. a particular medicinal oil, L. **-pura**, n. N. of a town, Virac. **-prasāda**, m., **-prasādana**, n. the red Lodh tree (an astringent infusion prepared from its bark is used to fix colour in dyeing), L. **-bhavana**, n. = *-gṛiha*, BhP. **-rakta**, mfn. coloured or dyed with lac, Kauś. **-rasa**, m. (prob.) = *-taila*, Suśr. **-vāṇijya**, n. dealing in lac or similar articles, HYog. **-vṛiksha**, m. Butea Frondosa, L.; Mangifera Sylvatica, L.

Lākshika, mf(*ī*)n. relating to or dyed with lac, Bhaṭṭ.; (fr. *laksha*) relating to a large number or to a lac, MW.

लाक्षेय *lāksheya*, m. patr., Saṃskārak.

लाक्ष्म *lākshma*, mf(*ī*)n. (fr. *lakshmī*) addressed to Lakshmī, L.

लाक्ष्मण *lākshmaṇa*, mf(*ī*)n. (fr. *lakshmaṇa*) relating to the plant Lakshmaṇā, Vāgbh.; a patr. fr. *lakshmaṇa*, Saṃskārak.

Lākshmaṇi, m. patr. fr. *lakshmaṇa*, Pravar.

Lākshmaṇeya, m. patr. fr. id., g. *śubhrâdi*.

लाक्ष्यिक *lākshyika*, mf(*ī*)n. = *lakshyam adhīte veda vā*, Pāṇ. iv, 2, 60, Vārtt.

लाख् *lākh*, cl. 1. P. *lākhati* = √*rākh* (q.v.), Dhātup. v, 9.

लागनृत्त *lāga-nṛitta*, n. (in music) a kind of dance, Saṃgīt.

लागुडिक *lāguḍika*. See *lākuṭika*.

लाघ् *lāgh*, cl. 1. Ā. *lāghate* = √*rāgh* (q.v.), Dhātup. iv, 39.

लाघरकोलस *lāgharakolasa*, m. a partic. form of jaundice, Suśr.

लाघव *lāghava*, n. (fr. *laghu*) swiftness, rapidity, speed, MBh.; R.; alacrity, versatility, dexterity, skill, MBh.; Kāv. &c.; lightness (also of heart), ease, relief, Mn.; Yājñ.; Suśr.; levity, thoughtlessness, inconsiderateness, rashness, R.; Kathās.; insignificance, unimportance, smallness, R.; Mālav.; MārkP.; (in prosody) shortness of a vowel or syllable (opp. to *gaurava*), Piṅg.; shortness of expression, brevity, conciseness, Sarvad.; Kāty., Sch.; lack of weight or consequence, derogation of dignity, slight, disrespect, MBh.; Kāv. &c. **-kārin**, mfn. degrading, disgraceful, Pañcat. **-gaurava-vicāra**, m. N. of wk. **Lāghavânvita**, mfn. possessed of brevity, MW.

Lāghavāyana, m. N. of an author, Cat.

Lāghavika, mfn. being short or brief, KātyŚr.

Lāghavin, n. a juggler, Siṇhâs.

लाङ्काकायनि *lāṅkākāyani*, m. metron. fr. *laṅkā*, g. *vākinâdi*.

Lāṅkāyana, m. patr. fr. *laṅka*, g. *naḍâdi*.

लाङ्गल *lā́ṅgala*, n. (cf. √*lag* and *laṅg*) a plough, RV. &c. &c.; a kind of pole used in gathering fruit from a tree, R.; Sch.; a plough-shaped beam or timber (used in the construction of a house), L.; a partic. appearance presented by the moon, VarBṛS.; the palm tree, L.; a kind of flower, L.; membrum virile, L. (cf. *lāṅgūla*); (*ī*), f. N. of various plants, Pañcar.; Suśr. (accord. to L. Jussiæa Repens; Hemionitis Cordifolia; Rubia Munjista; Hedysarum Lagopodioides; the cocoa-nut tree; = *rāsnā*); of a river, MBh.; m. a kind of rice, Car.; N. of a son of Śuddhoda and grandson of Śākya, BhP.; pl. N. of a school, SaṃhUp.; of a people, VP. (v.l. for *jāṅgala*). **-graha**, m. 'plough-holder,' a ploughman, peasant, L. **-grahaṇa**, n. the act of holding or guiding the plough, ploughing, W. **-cakra**, n. a partic. pl°-shaped diagram, L. **-daṇḍa** or **-daṇḍaka**, m. the pole or beam of a pl°, L. **-dhvaja**, m. 'plough-bannered,' N. of Bala-rāma (q.v.), MBh. **-paddhati**, f. 'pl°-path,' a furrow, L. **-phāla**, m. n. a ploughshare, MW. **Lāṅgalâkhya**, m. 'pl°-named,' Jussiæa Repens, Suśr. (cf. under *lāṅgala*). **Lāṅgalâpakarshin**, mf(*iṇī*)n. drawing the plough (said of an ox), Pañcat. **Lāṅgalâhvā**, f. = °*lâkhya*, Suśr. **Lāṅgal'īshā**, f. (for °*lêshā*) the pole of a pl°, g. *śakandhv-ādi* on Pāṇ. vi, 1, 94, Vārtt. 4.

Lāṅgalaka, mfn. plough-shaped (as an incision in surgery), Suśr.; (*ikā* or *akī*), f. Methonia Superba or Jussiæa Repens, L.; n. a plough (cf. *pañca-l°*). **-mārga**, m. 'plough-path,' a furrow, Hcat. (cf. *lāṅgala-paddhati*).

Lāṅgalāyana, m. patr. fr. *lāṅgala* (pl. N. of a school), AitBr.

Lāṅgali, m. patr. of a certain preceptor, VP.

Lāṅgalika, mfn. relating or belonging to a plough, W.; m. a partic. vegetable poison, L.; pl. N. of a school of the Sāma-veda, Āryav.; (*ī*), f. Methonia Superba, L. (*ikā*, f., see under *lāṅgalaka*).

Lāṅgalin, mfn. furnished with or possessing a plough (cf. *phāla-kuddāla-l°* and *yugma-l°*); m. N. of Bala-deva (q.v.), MBh.; Hariv.; of a preceptor, Pāṇ. vi, 4, 144, Vārtt. 1, Pat.; the cocoa-nut tree, L.; (*inī*), f. Methonica Superba, L.

Lāṅgale-gṛihya, ind. (loc. of *lāṅgala* + *gṛ°*) seizing by the plough, g. *mayūra-vyaṃsakâdi*, Kāś.

लाङ्गुल *lāṅgula*, n. = *lāṅgūla*, Pañcat.; BhP.; membrum virile, L.

Lāṅgulikā, f. Uraria Lagopodioides, L.

Lāṅgulinī, f. N. of a river, VP. (cf. *lāṅgūlinī*).

Lāṅgule-gṛihya, ind. seizing by the tail, g. *mayūra-vyaṃsakâdi* (cf. *lāṅgale-gṛihya*).

Lāṅgūla, n. (Uṇ. iv, 90, Sch.) a tail, hairy tail, ŚāṅkhŚr.; MBh. &c.; membrum virile, L.; (*ī*), f. Uraria Lagopodioides, L. **-gṛihya**, ind. seizing by the tail, g. *mayūra-vyaṃsakâdi*. **-cālana**, n. wagging or waving the tail, MBh. **-vikshepa**, m. id., Kum.

Lāṅgūlikā (L.), °**kī** (Car.), f. Hemionitis Cordifolia, L.

Lāṅgūlin, mfn. tailed, having a tail, W.; m. a monkey, L.; a kind of bulbous plant which grows on the Hima-vat, L.; (*inī*), f. N. of a river, MārkP. (cf. *lāṅgulinī*).

लाज् *lāj* (cf. √2. *laj* and *lāñj*), cl. 1. P. *lājati*, 'to fry' or 'to blame' (*bharjane* or *bhartsane*), Dhātup. vii, 66.

Lājá, m. (or *ā*, f.) pl. fried or parched grain (esp. rice grain), VS. &c. &c.; n. the root of Andropogon Muricatus, L. **-peyā**, f. water with parched grain, rice-gruel, Car. **-maṇḍa**, m. the scum of parched grain, Suśr. **-sphoṭam**, ind. (with √*sphuṭ*) to crack asunder like parched grain, Bālar.

Lājāya, Nom. Ā. °*yate*, to resemble parched grain, Bālar.

Lāji, m. a quantity of parched grain, VS. xxiii, 8, Mahīdh. (accord. to TBr., Sch. *lāji* is voc. fr. *lājin* = *lājôpalakshita*).

Lājī, f. N. of a place, Cat.

लाञ्चि *lāñci*, a species of plant, Dharmaś.

लाञ्छ् *lāñch* (cf. √*lach*), cl. 1. P. *lāñchati* (pf. *lalāñcha* &c.), to mark, distinguish, characterize, Dhātup. vii, 27: Caus. *lāñchayati*, id., Hcat.

Lāñchana, n. a mark, sign, token (ifc. = marked or characterized by, furnished or provided with), Kālid.; BhP.; a mark of ignominy, stain, spot, Vcar.; a name, appellation, L. **-tā**, f. the condition of being marked or stained, Subh.

Lāñchanāya, Nom. Ā. °*yate*, to become a mark or sign, Nalac.

Lāñchita, mfn. marked, decorated, characterized by, endowed or furnished with (comp.), Kāv.; Pur.; Kathās.; Rājat.

लाञ्ज् *lāñj*, cl. 1. P. *lāñjati* = √*lāj*, Dhātup. vii, 67.

लाट *lāṭa*, m. pl. (fr. *rāshṭra*) N. of a people and of a district inhabited by them (= Λαρικη of Ptolemy), MBh.; Var. &c.; (sg.) a king of the Lāṭas, Kathās.; the country of the Lāṭas, Uttamac.; m. or n. (only L.) clothes, dress; worn-out clothes, shabby ornaments; idle or childish language; (in rhet.) repetition of words in the same sense but in a different application; mf(*ī*)n. relating to the Lāṭas or belonging to Lāṭa, Rājat.; Sāh.; old, worn, shabby (as clothes), W.; childish, ib. **-jana**, m. an inhabitant of Lāṭa or the people of L°, Sāh. **-diṇḍīra**, m. N. of a poet, Cat. **-deśa**, m. the country of the L°s, Kathās. **-nārī**, f. a Lāṭa woman, ib. **-bhāshā**, f. the language of the Lāṭas, Cat. **-vishaya**, m. = *-deśa*, Kathās. **Lāṭâcarya**, m. 'teacher of the L°s,' N. of an astronomer, VarBṛS., Introd. **Lāṭânuprâsa**, m. 'Lāṭa repetition,' the repetition of a word in the same sense but with a different application, Kāvyâd.; Sāh. **Lāṭânvaya**, m. the offspring or family of the Lāṭas, Inscr. **Lāṭêśvara**, m. a king of the Lāṭas, Daś.

Lāṭaka, mf(*ikā*)n. of or belonging to the Lāṭas, customary among them; (*ikā*), f. (with or scil. *rīti*) = *lāṭī*, Sāh.

Lāṭāyana, w. r. for *lāṭyāyana*, Col.

Lāṭī, f. (with or scil. *rīti*) a partic. style of speech or composition, Sāh.

Lāṭīya, mfn. = *lāṭaka*, Cat.

लाट्याय *lāṭyāya*, Nom. P. *lāṭyāyati*, to live, g. *kaṇḍv-ādi*.

लाट्यायन *lāṭyāyana*, m. N. of the author of a Sūtra wk., IW. 146. **-śrauta-sūtra**, n. the Śrauta-sūtra of Lāṭyāyana.

लाड् *lāḍ* (cf. √*laḍ*), cl. 10. P. *lāḍayati*, to throw, Dhātup. xxxv, 81 (v. l.)

लाड *lāḍa*, m. N. of a man, Rājat.; of a royal race, Cat. **-khāna**, m. N. of a king, ib.

Lāḍana, m. N. of a man (also *-malla*), Cat.; n. = (and v. l. for) *lālana*, fondling, caressing, cherishing, Cāṇ.

लाडम *lāḍama*, m. N. of a man, Cat.

लाडि *lāḍi*, m. patr., g. *krauḍy-adi* (*lāḍyā*, f., ib.)

लाडिक *lāḍika* or *lāḍīka*, m. a boy, servant, slave, L.

लाढाचार्य *lāḍhâcārya*, w. r. for *lāṭâcarya*, Col.

लात *lāta*, *lāti*. See under √1. *lā*.

लातक *lātaka*, m. a kind of globe amaranth, L.

लातव्य *lātavya*, m. patr. of various men, Br.; Vikr.

लान्त *lānta*, m. a mystical N. for the letter *va*, RāmatUp.

लान्तकज *lāntaka-ja*, m. pl. (with Jainas) N. of a class of deities, L.

लान्तव *lāntava*, m. (with Jainas) a partic. Kalpa (q. v.), Dharmaś.

लान्द्र *lāndra*, g. *yavâdi*.

Lāndraka, mfn., ib.

लाप *lāpa*, *lāpin*. See p. 896, col. 2.

लापु *lā́pu*, m. or n. a partic. instrument, MaitrS.

लाप्य *lāpya*. See p. 896, col. 2.

लाब *lāba* (often written *lāva*), m. Perdix Chinensis, R.; Suśr. (also *ā*, f.); a partic. gait, Saṃgīt. **Lābâksha** or °**shaka**, m. 'quail-eyed,' a kind of rice, Suśr.

Lābaka, m. Perdix Chinensis, Suśr.

लाबु *lābu* or *lābū*, f. = *alābu*, L.

Lābukī, f. a kind of lute, L. (cf. *alābu-vīṇā*).

लाबुकायन *lābukāyana*, m. N. of a philosophical writer (mentioned in the Mīmāṃsā-sūtras).

लाभ् *lābh*, cl. 10. P. *lābhayati*, to throw, direct, Dhātup. xxxv, 81.

लाभ *lābha* &c. See p. 897, col. 1.

लामकायन *lāmakāyana*, m. patr. fr. *lamaka*, g. *naḍâdi*; N. of a teacher, Nidānas.; pl. the descendants of Lamaka, g. *upakâdi*.

Lāmakāyani, m. a patr., Pravar.

Lāmakāyanin, m. pl. the school of Lāmakāyana, Cat.

Lāmagāyana, m. = *lāmakāyana*, GopBr.

Lāmagāyani, m. = *lāmakāyani*, Cat.

लामज्जक *lāmajjaka*, n. the root of Andropogon Muricatus, Hcar.; Suśr.

लाम्पट्य *lāmpaṭya*, n. (fr. *lampaṭa*) lasciviousness, lustfulness, dissoluteness, Nalac.

लाय *lāya*, m. (perhaps fr. √*lī* = *ri*, to set in motion, throw) a missile, weapon, RV. x, 42, 1 (accord. to Sāy. = *saṃśleshaṇa*, *hṛidaya-vedhin*).

लाल *lāla*, *lālaka*, *lālana* &c. See p. 898, col. 1.

लालस *lālasa*, mf(*ā*)n. (fr. Intens. of √*las*) eagerly longing for, ardently desirous of, delighting or absorbed in, devoted or totally given up to (loc. or comp.), MBh.; Kāv. &c. (*-tā*, f.); m. and (*ā*), f. longing or ardent desire, fond attachment or devotion to (loc.), Bhartṛ.; Bālar. (L. also 'regret, sorrow; asking, soliciting; the longing of a pregnant woman; dalliance'); (*ā*), f. a kind of metre, Piṅg., Sch.

Lālasaka, mf(*ikā*)n. = *lālasa*, Vikr. (in Prākṛit).

Lālasīka, n. sauce, gravy, W.

ललाट *lālāṭa*, mf(*ī*)n. (fr. *lalāṭa*) being in or on the forehead, relating to it &c., Prab.; (*ī*), f., see below.

Lālāṭi, m. a patr. (also pl.), Saṃskārak.

Lālāṭika, mf(*ī*)n. = *lālāṭa*, q. v., KātyŚr., Sch.; relating to fate or destiny (supposed to be written on the forehead), W.; useless, low, vile, ib.; m. an attentive servant (as 'one who watches his master's face or countenance'), L.; an idler (prob. as 'one who is always gazing at the countenance of others'), L.; a mode of embracing, L.

Lālāṭī, f. the forehead, Suśr.

लालाध *lālādha*, m. epilepsy, the falling sickness, L.

लालामिक *lālāmika*, mf(*ī*)n. = *lalāmaṃ gṛihṇāti*, Pāṇ. iv, 4, 40.

लालिक *lālika*, *lālita* &c. See p. 898, col. 1.

लालि *lāli*, f. the being possessed by a demon, Gal.

लालीला *lālīlá*. See p. 898, col. 1.

लालुका *lālukā*, f. a sort of necklace, W.

लाव 1. *lāva*, *lāvaka* &c. See p. 905, col. 2.

लाव 2. *lāva*, *lāvaka*, w. r. for *lāba*, *lābaka*.

लावण *lāvaṇa*, mf(*ī*)n. (fr. *lavaṇa*) saline, salt, salted, cooked or dressed with salt, Hariv.; Suśr.; m. N. of the salt sea which surrounds Jambudvīpa, L. **-saindhava**, mf(*ī*)n. situated on the sea-coast, Śiś.

Lāvaṇika, mf(*ī*)n. = *lāvaṇa* (cf. *uda-* and *daka-l°*); dealing in salt, Śiś.; charming, lovely, ib.; n. a vessel holding salt, salt-cellar, L.

Lāvaṇya, n. (ifc. f. *ā*) saltness, the taste or property of salt, Amar.; beauty, loveliness, charm, Inscr.; Kāv.; Kathās. &c. **-kalita**, mfn. endowed with beauty, MW. **-mañjarī**, f. N. of a woman, Kathās. **-maya**, mf(*ī*)n. consisting entirely of beauty, Kād.; lovely, charming, Kum. **-lakshmī**, f. 'wealth of b°,' great beauty, Kathās. **-laharī**, f. N. of a Surâṅganā, Siṇhâs. **-vat**, mfn. = *-maya*; (*vatī*), f. N. of a Surāṅganā, Siṇhâs.; of another woman, Kathās.; of a poem by Kshemêndra. **-śarman**, m. N. of an author, Cat. **-śesha**, mfn. having only beauty left (*-tā*, f.), Kathās. **-śrī**, f. = *-lakshmī*, MW. **Lāvaṇyârjita**, mfn. obtained through beauty;

n. (in law) the private property of a married woman (consisting of that which has been presented to her at her marriage as a token of respect or kindness by her father or mother-in-law).

लावणक *lāvaṇaka*, m. or n. N. of a place, Ratnâv.

Lāvāṇaka, m. N. of a district adjacent to Magadha, Kathās. (sometimes written *lāvān°*); N. of the 3rd Lambaka of the Kathā-sarit-sāgara.

लावली *lāvalī*, f. a species of myrobolan, L.

लाविक *lāvika*, m.=*lālika*, a buffalo, W.

लावु *lāvu*, *lāvū* &c. See *lābu*, p. 900, col. 3.

लावेरणि *lāveraṇi*, m. a patr., g. *gahâdi*.

Lāveraṇīya, mfn., ib.

Lāveriṇi (?), m. patr., Pravar.

लाव्य *lāvya*. See p. 905, col. 2.

लाषुक *lāshuka*, mfn. (√*lash*) covetous, greedy, Pāṇ. iii, 2, 154.

लास *lāsa*, *lāsin*, *lāsya*. See p. 899, col. 2.

लास्फोटनी *lāsphoṭanī*, f.= *āsphoṭanī*, a gimlet, auger, L.

लाहरिमल्ल *lāhari-malla*, m. N. of a general, Kshitîś.

लाहल *lāhala*, m.= *śabara-viśesha*, L.

लाह्य *lāhya*, m. patr. fr. *lahya*, Śaṃk. (cf. g. *śivâdi*).

Lāhyāyani, m. (fr. *lāhya*) patr. of Bhujyu, ŚBr.

लि *li*, m. (only L.; perhaps connected with √*lī*) weariness, fatigue; loss, destruction; end, term; equality, sameness; a bracelet; (in gram.) abbreviated form of *liṅga* (see *li-dhu*).

लिकुच *likuca*, m.=*lakuca*, Artocarpus Lacucha, Daś.; Car.; n. vinegar, L.

Likuci, m. N. of a man, Cat.

लिक्षा *likshā*, f. (also written *likkā*) a nit, young louse, the egg of a louse (as a measure of weight = 8 Trasa-reṇus), Mn.; Yājñ. (m. c. also *liksha*, VarBṛS.)

Likshikā, f.= *likshā*, a nit, L.

Likhya, m. and (*ā*), f. id. (also a measure of weight), ŚārṅgS.; Bhpr.; AgP.

लिख् *likh* (cf. the earlier form √*rikh*), cl. 6. P. (Dhātup. xxviii, 72) *likháti* (rarely Ā. °*te*; pf. *lilékha*, Br. &c.; aor. *alekhīt*, ib.; fut. *lekhitā*, *lekhishyati*, Gr.; *likhishyati*, Hariv.; inf. *lekhitum* or *likhitum*, Gr.; ind. p. *lekhitvā*, ib.; *likhitvā*, Hariv.; *-líkhya*, Br. &c.), to scratch, scrape, furrow, tear up (the ground), AV. &c. &c.; to pick, peck (said of birds), VarBṛS.; Hit.; to scarify, lance, Suśr.; to produce by scratching &c., draw a line (with or scil. *lekhām*), engrave, inscribe, write, copy, trace, sketch, delineate, paint, Br. &c. &c.; to make smooth, polish, MārkP.; to graze, touch, MW.; to unite sexually with a female (?), MBh. xiii, 2456 (Nīlak.): Pass. *likhyate* (aor. *alekhi*), to be written, Kathās.; Pañcat.: Caus. *lekhayati* (or *likhāpayati*; aor. *alīlikhat*), to cause to scratch or write or copy or paint, ŚāṅkhŚr.; Mn. &c.; to scratch, lance, Suśr.; to write, paint, Yājñ.: Desid. *lilikhishati* or *lilekhishati*, Pāṇ. i, 2, 26. [Cf. Gk. ἐρείκω; Lith. *rě́kti*, 'to cut.']

Likha, mfn. scratching, writing; a writer &c., Pāṇ. iii, 1, 135.

Likhana, n. the act of scratching, furrowing &c., Kāv.; Sāh.; writing, inscribing, MārkP.; Pañcar.; scarifying, W.; a written document, ib.

Likhitá, mfn. scratched, scraped, scarified, AV. &c. &c.; written, Pañcat.; Kathās. (=mentioned, Inscr.); drawn, delineated, sketched, painted, Kāv.; VarBṛS.; m. N. of a Ṛishi and author of a work on law (frequently mentioned together with Śaṅkha, q.v.), MBh. (IW. 302); N. of Śaṅkha's brother (whose hands were cut off by king Su-dyumna as a punishment for having eaten some fruit in Śaṅkha's hermitage without leave, described in MBh. xii, 668 &c.); n. a writing, written document, scripture, Yājñ., Sch. (IW. 297). **-tva**, n. the condition of being written down, Yājñ., Sch. **-pāṭha**, m. the reading of written words, learning from books, Sarvad. **-pāṭhaka**, m. one who reads from manuscript, Śiksh. **-rudra**, m. N. of a grammarian, Cat. **-smṛiti**, f. N. of a law-book (cf. above).

Likhitavya, mfn. to be painted, Śak.

Likhitṛi, m. a painter, Viddh.

Lekha, m. (cf. *rekha*) a line, stroke, MānGṛ.; (also pl.) a writing, letter, manuscript, written document of any kind, Hariv.; Kāv.; VarBṛS. &c. (cf. *kūṭa-l°*); a god, deity, Śiś.; =*ābhoga*, L.; N. of a man, g. *śivâdi*; of a poet, Cat.; pl. N. of a class of gods under Manu Cākshusha, Pur.; (*ā*), f., see below. **-pañcāśikā**, f. N. of wk. (containing 50 forms of letters, deeds, bonds &c., composed A.D. 1232). **-pattra**, n. (Mālatīm.), and **-pattrikā**, f. (Kathās.) a written document, letter, writ, deed. **-pratilekha-lipi**, f. a partic. kind of writing, Lalit. **-rshabha** (for *-ṛish°*), m. 'best of gods,' N. of Indra, L. **-śālā**, f. a writing-school, Camp. **-śālika**, m. a pupil in a writing-school, ib. **-saṃdeśa-hārin**, mf(*iṇī*)n. taking or conveying a written message or instructions, Kathās. **-sādhana**, v. l. for *lekhana-s°*, q. v. **-hāra** or **-hāraka**, m. a letter-carrier, the bearer of a letter, Kathās. **-hārin**, mf(*iṇī*)n. taking or conveying a letter (*-tva*, n.), Kull. on Mn. vii, 153. **Lekhâkshara**, n. writing (opp. to *ālekhya*, painting), MW. **Lekhâdhikārin**, m. 'presiding over written documents,' a king's secretary, Rājat. **Lekhâbhra**, m. N. of a man (g. *śubhrâdi*); pl. his descendants, g. *upakâdi*. **Lekhâbhru**, see *lekhā-bhrū* under *lekhā*. **Lekhârambha**, m. N. of a tale (=*vikrama-carita*, q. v.) **Lekhârha** or °**hya**, m. 'fit for writing,' a kind of palm-tree (the leaves of which are used for writing on), L. **Lekhêśa**, m.= *lekha-rshabha*, Dhūrtan.

Lekhaka, m. a writer, scribe, clerk, secretary, Yājñ.; MBh. &c.; one who delineates or paints, MW.; (*ikā*), f. a little stroke, Kād.; n. a writing, written message, Subh.; a calculation (°*kaṃ* √*kṛi*, to make a calculation, reckon), Mṛicch. **-pramāda**, m. error in writing, mistake of a copyist, MW. **-muktā-maṇi**, m. 'pearl-gem for scribes,' N. of a treatise by Hari-dāsa on letter-writing and on secretarial art.

Lekhana, mf(*ī*)n. scratching, scraping, scarifying, lancing, Suśr.; exciting, stimulating, attenuating, ib.; ŚārṅgS.; Bhpr.; m. Saccharum Spontaneum (a sort of reed of which pens are made), W.; (*ī*), f. id., L.; an instrument for writing or painting, reed-pen, painting-brush, pen, pencil, MBh.; VarBṛS.; Hcat. (m. c. also °*ni*); a spoon, ladle (cf. *ghṛita-l°*); n. the act of scratching or scraping, lancing, scarifying, Car.; Suśr.; touching, coming in contact (said of heavenly bodies), AV. Pariś.; writing down, transcribing, Kathās.; Pañcat.; an instrument for scraping or furrowing, Kauś.; Betula Bhojpatra (the bark of which is used for writing), L.; the leaf of the palm tree (used for the same purpose), W.; making thin, attenuating, reducing corpulency (see next). **-vasti**, f. a kind of enema for reducing corpulency, Suśr.; ŚārṅgS. **-sādhana**, n. writing materials, Śak. (v. l. *lekha-s°*).

Lekhani. See under *lekhana* above.

Lekhanika, m. one who makes a deputy sign a document, signing by proxy or making a mark (from inability to write), L.; a letter-carrier, bearer of a letter, L. (cf. *lekhīlaka*).

Lekhanikā. See *citra-l°*.

Lekhanīya, mfn. to be written or drawn or painted, Yājñ., Sch.; useful as a remedy for reducing corpulency or for scarifying, Suśr.; Car.; n. (in law) an accusation or defence (required to be made in writing), W.

Lékhā, f. (cf. *rekhā*) a scratch, streak, line, stroke, stripe, furrow, ŚBr. &c. &c.; the pale or faintly discernible streak of the young moon's crescent, Kir. (cf. *candra-* and *śaśâṅka-l°*); the act of delineation, drawing, painting, Śak. (v. l.); writing, handwriting, L.; a drawing, likeness, figure, impression (cf. *mṛiga-* and *savya-pāda-l°*); the drawing of lines with fragrant substances (on the face, arms, breast &c.), L.; a hem, border, rim, edge, horizon, Kām.; VarBṛS.; the crest (=*śikhā* or *cūḍâgra*), L. **-bhrū**, f. N. of a woman, g. *śubhrâdi* (v. l. for *lekhâbhra*); *-bhrum-manya*, mfn. passing for Lekhā-bhrū, Pāṇ. vi, 3, 68, Sch. **-valaya**, m. n. an encircling line, MW. **-vidhi**, m. the act of drawing or painting, Mālatīm. **-saṃdhi**, m. the point where the eyebrows meet, MantraBr.; Gobh. **-stha-vṛitta**, mfn. conforming to prescription, Car.

Lekhāya, Nom. P. °*yati* (fr. *lekha* or *lekhā*, g. *kaṇḍv-ādi*), 'to be wanton' or 'to waver.'

Lekhita, mfn. (fr. Caus.) caused to be written, Mn. viii, 168; written, Yājñ. ii, 86.

Lekhin, mfn. scratching, grazing, touching (*ambara-l°*, 'touching the sky'), Ragh.; (*inī*), f. a spoon, ladle (see *ghṛita-l°* and cf. *lekhana*).

Lekhīlaka, m. a letter-carrier, L.

1. **Lekhya**, Nom. P. °*yati*=*lekhāya*, g. *kaṇḍv-ādi*.

2. **Lekhya**, mfn. to be scratched or scraped or scarified, Suśr.; to be written or transcribed, Yājñ.; MārkP.; to be drawn or painted, Yājñ.; to be portrayed, painted, BhP.; to be written down or numbered among (loc.), Kāvyâd.; favourable to the gods (said of Vishṇu), Vishṇ. (Sch.); n. the act or the art of writing, MBh.; R.; copying, transcribing, VarBṛS.; delineation, drawing, painting, ib.; a writing, letter, manuscript, Kām.; Kathās.; Sāh.; (in law) any written document (esp. a written accusation or defence), Vishṇ.; Yājñ. (cf. IW. 293); an inscription, MBh. xiii, 6330; (*gaṇanā-*) a catalogue, list of, Ragh.; a painted figure, BhP. **-kṛita**, mfn. done in writing, signed, executed, W. **-gata**, mfn. represented in painting, painted, MBh.; Hariv. **-cūrṇikā**, f. a pencil for writing or drawing, paint-brush, L. **-dala**, m.= *lekhârha*, L. **-pattra**, m. the palmyra or palm tree, L.; n. a written document, writing, scripture, letter, Mudr.; a leaf or sheet of anything for writing, L. **-pattraka**, m. and n.=prec., L. **-padma**, n. a painted lotus-flower, Kāv. **-prasaṅga**, m. a written contract, record, document, MW. **-maya**, mf(*ī*)n. delineated, painted, BhP., Sch. **-rūpa**, mfn. id., Kāv. **-sthāna**, n. a writing-place, office, L. **Lekhyârūḍha**, mfn. committed to writing, recorded, W.

Lekhyaka, mfn. written, epistolary, W.

लिखिखिल्ल *likhikhilla* (?), m. a peacock, L.

लिख्य *likhya*. See col. 1.

लिगी *ligī*. See *á-* and *ví-ligī*.

लिगु *ligu*, n. (√*lag* ?) the mind, heart, Uṇ. i, 37, Sch.; m. a fool, blockhead, L.; a deer, L.; = *bhū-pradeśa*, L.; N. of a man, g. *nadâdi* and *gargâdi*.

लिङ् *liṅ*, (in gram.) N. of the terminations of the Potential and Precative Moods or N. of those Moods themselves (the Precative being usually distinguished by the fuller term *liṅ āśishi* or *āśir-liṅ*; cf. under 1. *la*). **-artha-vāda** and **-artha-vicāra**, m. 'explanation of the sense of Liṅ,' N. of grammatical treatises.

लिङ्कवाराहतीर्थ *liṅka-vārāha-tīrtha*, n. N. of a Tīrtha, Cat.

लिङ्ख् *liṅkh* (cf. √*lakh*, *laṅkh*), cl. 1. P. *liṅkhati*, to go, move, Dhātup. v, 34.

लिङ्ग् *liṅg* (cf. *ā-*√*liṅg*), cl. 1. P. *liṅgati*, to go, Dhātup. v, 48; cl. 10. P. *liṅgayati*, to paint, variegate (*citrī-karaṇe*), ib. xxxiii, 65; to change or inflect a noun according to its gender, Vop., Sch.

Liṅga, n. (once m. in NṛisUp.; ifc. f. *ā*, *ī* only in *vishṇu-liṅgī*; prob. fr. √*lag*; cf. *laksha*, *lakshaṇa*) a mark, spot, sign, token, badge, emblem, characteristic (ifc.=*tal-liṅga*, 'having anything for a mark or sign'), Up.; MBh. &c.; any assumed or false badge or mark, guise, disguise, MBh.; Kāv. &c.; a proof, evidence, Kaṇ.; KātyŚr.; Sarvad.; a sign of guilt, corpus delicti, Yājñ., Sch.; the sign of gender or sex, organ of generation, Mn.; Hariv.; Pur. &c.; the male organ or Phallus (esp. that of Śiva worshipped in the form of a stone or marble column which generally rises out of a *yoni*, q. v., and is set up in temples dedicated to Śiva; formerly 12 principal Śiva-liṅgas existed, of which the best known are Soma-nātha in Gujarāt, Mahā-kāla at Ujjayinī, Viśvêśvara at Benares &c.; but the number of Liṅgas in India is estimated at 30 millions, IW. 322, n. 1; RTL. 78, 1; 90), MBh.; R. &c.; gender (in gram.; cf. *pum-l°*), Prāt.; Pāṇ.; the image of a god, an idol, VarBṛS.; (in logic) = *vyāpya*, the invariable mark which proves the existence of anything in an object (as in the proposition 'there is fire because there is smoke,' smoke is the *liṅga*; cf. IW. 62); inference, conclusion, reason (cf. *kāvya-l°*); = *liṅga-śarīra* (in Vedânta) anything which has an origin and therefore liable to be destroyed again, Kap.; = *ākāśa*, Karaṇḍ.; (in Sāṃkhya) = *prakṛiti* or *pradhāna*, 'the eternal procreative germ,' L.; = *vyakta*, L.; cf. RTL. 30; = *prātipadika*, the crude base or uninflected stem of a noun (shortened into *li*), Vop., Sch.; (in rhet.) an indication (word that serves to fix the meaning of another word; e. g. in the passage *kupito makara-dhvajaḥ* the word *kupita* restricts the meaning of *makara-dhvaja* to 'Kāma'), Kpr.; = *liṅga-purāṇa*, BhP.; the order of the religious student, W.; a symptom, mark of disease, W. – **kāraṇa-vāda**, m., °**ṇa-tā-pūrva-paksha-rahasya**, n., -°**tā-vāda**, m., °**tā-siddhânta-rahasya**, n.; -**kārikā**, f. pl., °**rikā-vṛitti**, f. N. of wks. – **klṛipta**, mfn. having the right mark, ŚāṅkhŚr. – **guṇtama-rāma**, m. N. of an author, Cat. – **caraṇa-bhāshya**, n. N. of wk. – **ja**, m. (mucus) secreted on the penis, Gal.; (*ā*), f. a kind of plant, L. – **jyeshṭha**, m. (in Sāṃkhya) the great principle or intellect, L. – **tas**, ind. from a mark or sign, according to marks &c. (see comp.); (*-to*)-*bhadra*, n. a partic. magical circle, Cat.; N. of wk.; °*ra-kārikā*, f. pl., °*ra-prayoga*, m., °*ra-lakshaṇa*, n. N. of wks. – **tva**, n. the state of being a mark, BhP. – **durbheda**, N. of a drama. – **deha**, m. n. the subtle body (see *liṅga* above and *l°-śarīra* below), Bālar. – **dvādaśa-vrata**, n. a partic. religious ceremony, Cat. – **dhara**, mfn. (ifc.) wearing or having marks or mere marks, having the mere appearance of, simulating anything (*mithyā-l°*, wearing false marks, a hypocrite; cf. *suhṛil-l°*), R.; BhP. – **dhāraṇa**, mfn. wearing a badge, MW.; n. the act of w° a b° or any characteristic mark, MBh.; *-candrikā*, f., *-dīpikā*, f. N. of wks. – **dhārin**, mfn. wearing a badge, w° the Liṅga of Śiva, MW.; m. = *-vat*, m., ib.; (*inī*), f. N. of Dākshāyaṇī in Naimisha, Cat. – **nāśa**, m. loss of what is characteristic or of the real essence, ŚvetUp. (Śaṃk.); a partic. disease of the eyes (loss of vision from cataract &c., considered to be a discolouration of the pupil), Suśr.; ŚārṅgS.; loss of the penis, W. – **nirṇaya**, m., °**ya-bhūshaṇa**, n. N. of wks. – **parāmarśa**, m. (in log.) the groping after or seeking for a sign or token, the inference drawn from an invariable sign or characteristic (e. g. as of the existence of fire from smoke), MW. – **pīṭha**, n. the pedestal of a Śiva-Phallus, Rājat. – **purāṇa**, n. N. of one of the 18 Purāṇas (in which Śiva, supposed to be present in the Agni-liṅga or great fiery Liṅga, gives an account of the creation &c. as well as of his own incarnations in opposition to those of Vishṇu). – **pūjā-paddhati**, f., °**jā-phala**, n., °**jôdyāpana**, n.; **-prakāśa**, m. N. of wks. – **pratishṭhā**, f. the setting up or consecration of a Phallus of Śiva (see comp.); N. of sev. wks.; *-paddhati*, f. N. of wk.; *-vidhi*, m. rules for setting up a Phallus of Śiva, Cat. – **bhaṭṭa**, m. N. of an author, Cat. – **bhaṭṭīya**, n. (written also *liṅgā-bh°*), **-bhāshā-purāṇa**, n. N. of wks. – **mātra**, n. the intellect, Yogas. – **māhātmya**, n. N. of a section of sev. Purāṇas; *-dīpikā*, f. N. of wk. – **mūrti**, mfn. (represented) in the form of a Phallus (said of Śiva), Cat. – **līlā-vilāsa-caritra**, n. N. of wk. – **lepa**, m. a partic. disease, Cat. – **vat**, mfn. having marks, containing a characteristic, Vait.; BhP.; having various sexes or genders, MaitrUp.; having or wearing a small model of the Phallus of Śiva in a casket suspended round the neck; m. N. of a partic. Śaiva sect who so wear the Ph° (commonly called Liṅgaits and sometimes Jaṅgamas), RTL. 88. – **varti**, f. a partic. disease of the genital organs, Bhpr. – **vardhana**, mfn. causing erections of the male organ, L.; m. Feronia Elephantum, L. (also *-vardha*). – **vardhin**, mfn. causing erections, L.; (*inī*), f. Achyranthes Aspera, L. – **vāda**, m., **-vidhi**, m. N. of wks. – **viparyaya**, m. change of gender, RāmatUp. – **viśeshaṇa**, n. N. of wk. – **viśesha-vidhi**, m. rules for the different genders, N. of a grammatical treatise. – **vṛitti**, mfn. making a livelihood by false appearance or assumed outward marks, hypocritical, L.; m. a religious hypocrite, one who assumes the dress &c. of an ascetic to gain a livelihood, W.; f. N. of various wks. – **vedī**, f. the pedestal of a Śiva-Phallus, MW. – **śarīra**, n. the subtle body which accompanies the individual spirit or soul in all its transmigrations and is not destroyed by death (it is also called *sūkshma-ś°*, q. v., and since it is the sign and accompaniment of individuality it can never perish till the individualized soul is finally merged in the Universal), Kap.; Vedântas. (IW. 53, n. 2). – **śāstra**, n. a grammatical treatise on gender; N. of various wks. – **śopha**, m. swelling on the penis, L. – **sambhūtā**, f. N. of a plant, L. – **stha**, m. a religious student, Mn. viii, 65 (Kull.) – **hanī**, f. Sanseviera Roxburghiana, L. **Liṅgâgama-tantra**, n. N. of wk. **Liṅgâgra**, n. the end or glans of the penis, L. **Liṅgâdi-pratishṭhā-vidhi**, m. N. of wk. **Liṅgânuśāsana**, n. the doctrine or laws of grammatical gender, Pañcad.; N. of various wks.; *-vṛitti*, f. N. of wk. **Liṅgā-bhaṭṭīya**, n. N. of wk. (cf. *liṅga-bh°*). **Liṅgârcana**, n. worship of the Phallus of Śiva, W.; *-candrikā*, f., *-tantra*, n. N. of wks. **Liṅgârcā-pratishṭhā-vidhi**, m. N. of wk. **Liṅgârśas**, n. a partic. disease of the genital organs, Bhpr. **Liṅgâshṭaka**, n. N. of a Stotra. **Liṅgôtpatti**, f. N. of wk. **Liṅgôddhāra**, m. the excision or removal of the male organ, Gaut. **Liṅgôpadaṇśa**, m. = *liṅgârśas*, Bhpr. **Liṅgôpadhāna-vādârtha**, °**panishad**, f., °**pahita-laiṅgika-bhāna-nirāsa-rahasya**, n., °**ka-bhāna-vicāra**, m., °**ka-vādârtha**, N. of wks.

Liṅgaka (ifc.) = *liṅga*, Sarvad.; Hcat.; m. Feronia Elephantum, L.; (*ikā*), f. a species of plant, Bhpr.

Liṅgana, n. = *ā-liṅgana*, embracing, an embrace, W.

Liṅgaya-sūri, m. N. of an author, Cat.

Liṅgin, mfn. having a mark or sign, wearing a distinguishing mark; (ifc.) having the marks or appearance of, characterized by, Mn.; MBh. &c.; bearing false marks or signs, a hypocrite, (ifc.) only having the appearance or acting the part of, ib. (cf. *dvija-l°*); having a right to wear signs or badges, one whose external appearance corresponds with his inner character, ib.; having a subtle body, BhP.; m. a Brāhman of a partic. order, religious student, ascetic, MBh.; Kāv. &c.; pl. 'possessing or furnished with a Liṅga,' N. of a Śaiva sect (see *liṅga-vat*), Col.; 'sustaining the Liṅga or Pradhāna,' N. of Parameśvara, LiṅgaP.; (in logic) = *vyāpaka*, that which possesses an invariable characteristic mark (as in the proposition 'there is fire because there is smoke,' fire is the *liṅgin*; cf. IW. 62); original source or germ, Kap., Sch.; an elephant, L.; (*inī*), f. a female ascetic, Daśar.; a species of plant, L.

Liṅgi-vesha, m. (fr. *liṅgin* + *v°*) the dress or the insignia of a religious student, Mn. iv, 200.

Liṅgya, ind. = 2. *ā-liṅgya*, having embraced, MBh. xii, 6089.

लिङ्गालिका *liṅgālikā*, f. a kind of mouse, L.

लिङ्गिक *liṅgika* and *liṅgita*, n. lameness, L. (prob. w. r. for *laṅgika*, °*gita*).

लिच्छवि *licchavi* or *licchivi*, m. N. of a regal race (accord. to L. 'the son of a Kshatriya Vrātya and a Kshatriyā'), MWB. 409; 410.

लिट् *liṭ*, (in gram.) N. of the terminations of the Reduplicated Perfect Tense or N. of that Tense itself.

लिट्य *liṭya*, Nom. P. *liṭyati*, 'to be little' or 'to think little of,' g. *kaṇḍv-ādi*.

लिधु *li-dhu*, (in gram.) a term for nominal verbs (abbreviated from *liṅga*, 'the crude base or stem of a noun,' and *dhātu*, 'a root'), Vop.; IW. 169, n. 1.

लिन्दु *lindu*, mfn. = *picchala*, slimy, slippery, ChUp. viii, 14, Śaṃk.

लिप् *lip* (cf. √*rip*), cl. 6. 1. P. Ā. (Dhātup. xxviii, 139) *limpáti*, °*te* (pf. *lilepa*, Br. &c.; aor. *alipat*, Kathās.; *alipata*, *alipta*, Gr.; *-alipsata*, RV.; fut. *leptā*, *lepsyati*, °*te*, Gr.; inf *leptum*, ib.; ind. p. *-lipya*, Br. &c.), to smear, besmear, anoint with (instr.), stain, soil, taint, pollute, defile, TBr. &c. &c.; to inflame, kindle, burn, Bhaṭṭ.: Pass. *lipyaṭe* (ep. also °*ti*; aor. *alepi*), to be smeared &c.; to be attached to (loc.), stick, adhere, ĪśUp.: Caus. *lepayati* (aor. *alīlipat*), to cause to smear &c.; to smear or anoint anything (acc.) with (instr.) or on (loc.), Hcat.; Suśr.; to cover, R.; to cast blame on any one, Sāy.; (*limpayati*), to smear anything (acc.) with (instr.): Des. *lilipsati*, °*te*, Gr.: Intens. *lelipyate*, *lelepti*, ib. [Cf. Gk. ἀ-λείφω, λιπαρός; Lat. *lippus*; Lith. *lìpti*; Goth. *bileiban*; Germ. *bilîban*, *blîben*, *bleiben*, *leben*, *Leib*; Angl. Sax. *libban*; Eng. *to live*, *life*.]

Lipa, m. smearing, anointing, plastering, W.

Lipi, f. (accord. to L. also *lipī*) smearing, anointing &c. (see *-kara*); painting, drawing, L.; writing, letters, alphabet, art or manner of writing, Kāv.; Kathās.; anything written, manuscript, inscription, letter, document, Naish.; Lalit.; outward appearance (*lipim* √*āp*, with gen., 'to assume the appearance of;' *citrāṃ lipiṃ* √*nī*, 'to decorate beautifully'), Vcar. – **kara**, m. an anointer, whitewasher, plasterer, R.; a writer, scribe, MBh.; Vās.; an engraver, MW. – **karman**, n. drawing, painting; °*ma-nirmita*, mfn. painted, Śiś. – **kāra**, m. a writer, scribe, copyist, L. – **jña**, mfn. one who can write, Kām. – **jñāna**, n. the science or art of writing, Daś. – **tva**, n. the condition of being anything written, Hcat. – **nyāsa**, m. 'the act of putting down written characters,' writing, transcribing, Kathās. – **phalaka**, n. a writing-tablet, leaf for writing on, Lalit. – **viveka**, m. N. of a wk. on the art of wr°. – **śālā**, f. a wr°-school, Lalit. – **śāstra**, n. the art of wr°, ib. – **saṃkhyā**, f. a number of written characters, L. – **sajjā**, f. implements or materials for writing, W. – **saṃnāha**, m. 'writing belt,' a belt worn on the fore-arm, L.

Lipika, m. a scribe, clerk, Divyâv.; (*ā*), f. = *lipi*, a writing, written paper &c., L.

Liptá, mfn. smeared, anointed, soiled, defiled, AV. &c. &c.; sticking or adhering to (loc.), ŚBr.; joined, connected, Uṇ. v, 55, Sch.; envenomed, L.; eaten, L.; (*ā*), f., see *liptā* below. – **vat**, mfn. one who has smeared or anointed &c., W. – **vāsita**, mfn. anointed and perfumed, Bhaṭṭ. (cf. g. *rāja-dantâdi*). – **hasta**, mfn. having the hands smeared or stained, W. **Liptâṅga**, mfn. having the body anointed with unguents &c., MW.

Liptaka, mfn. smeared, covered with poison; m. a poisoned arrow, L.; (*ikā*), f., see *liptikā* below.

Lipti, f. ointment, Naish.

Libi. See *livi*.

Limpa, m. smearing, anointing, plastering, Pāṇ. iii, 1, 138; m. N. of one of Śiva's attendants, L.

Limpaṭa, mfn. libidinous, lustful, lecherous; m. a libertine, L. (cf. *lampaṭa*).

Limpāka, m. an ass, L.; a citron or lime tree (n. its fruit), L.

Limpi, f. = *lipi*, a writing &c., Pañcar.

Livi, f. = prec., Uṇ. iv, 119, Sch. (accord. to L. also °*vī*). – **kara**, m. a writer, scribe, Pāṇ. iii, 2, 21. – **m-kara**, m. id., L.

Lepa, m. the act of smearing, daubing, anointing, plastering, Yājñ.; Kāv.; Pur.; anything smeared on, ointment, unguent, plaster, MBh.; Hariv.; Suśr. &c.; a coating of paint &c.; spot, stain, impurity (lit. and fig.), any grease or dirt sticking to vessels, (esp.) particles or remnants wiped from the hand after offering oblations to three ancestors (these remnants being considered as an oblation to paternal ancestors in the 4th, 5th and 6th degrees), ŚrS.; Gaut. &c.; food, victuals, Bhadrab.; a kind of disease, Car. – **kara**, m. a plaster-maker, bricklayer, whitewasher, R. – **kāminī**, f. a moulded figure of a woman, L. – **bhāgin**, m. 'sharing the Lepa,' a paternal ancestor (in the 4th, 5th, and 6th degrees; cf. above), Mn. iii, 216. – **bhuj**, m. id., MatsyaP.

Lepaka (ifc.) = *lepa* (see *a-lepaka*); m. a plasterer, bricklayer, one who moulds or models, L.

Lepana, n. the act of smearing, anointing, plastering, spreading on, ĀśvGṛ.; MBh. &c.; ointment, plaster, mortar (ifc. = smeared or plastered with), Mn.; MBh. &c.; flesh, meat, L.; m. olibanum, incense, L.

Lepanīya, mfn. to be smeared or anointed, fit to be plastered, MW.

Lepin, mfn. besmearing or covering, L.; (ifc.) smeared or covered with, Kālid.; m. = *lepaka*, L.

Lepya, mfn. to be smeared or anointed or stained or defiled, MaitrUp.; moulded, modelled, BhP.; n. plastering, moulding, modelling, L. – **kāra** (Hcar.), **-kṛit** (L.), m. one who makes moulds or models, a bricklayer, plasterer. – **nārī**, f. a moulded figure of a woman, L. – **maya**, mf(*ī*)n. made of mortar or clay, moulded, HPariś.; (*ī*), f. a doll, puppet, L. – **yoshit**, f. = *-nārī*, L. – **strī**, f. a perfumed woman, L.

लिप्ता *liptā*, f. = λεπτή, a minute, the 60th part of a degree, Jyot. (cf. IW. 173, n. 2).

Liptikā, f. id., ib.

Liptī-√kṛi, P. *-karoti*, to reduce to minutes, VarBṛS.

लिप्सा *lipsā*, *lipsu*, *lipsya* &c. See p. 897, col. 1.

लिबि *libi, libī.* See *livi*, p. 902, col. 3.

लिबुजा *libujā*, f. a creeping plant, creeper, RV.; AV.; PañcavBr.

लिम्प *limpa*, °*pi.* See p. 902, col. 3.

लिम्बभट्ट *limba-bhaṭṭa*, m. N. of a man, Cat.

लिलक्षयिषित *lilakshayishita*, mfn. (fr. Desid. of √*laksh, lakshayati*) wished or intended to be indicated, had in view, meant, Śaṃk.

लिश् 1. *liś* (later form of √*riś*, in *ā*-√*liś*, *vi*-√*liś*); cl. 4. Ā. *liśyate* (pf. *liliśe* &c.), to be or become small, lessen, Dhātup. xxvi, 70; cl. 6. P. *liśati* (pf. *leleśa* &c.), to go, move, ib. xxviii, 127: Caus. *leśayati* (aor. *alīliśat*), Gr.: Desid. *lilikshate*, ib.: Intens. *leliśyate, leleshṭi.*

2. **Liś**, mfn. (nom. *liṭ*), Pāṇ. viii, 2, 36, Sch.

Liśa. See *ku-liśa.*

Lishṭa, mfn. lessened, wasted, decayed, L. (cf. *vi-lishṭa*).

Leśa, m. a small part or portion, particle, atom, little bit or slight trace of (gen. or comp.; *-tas* and *ena*, ind. = very slightly or briefly; *leśa-śas*, in small pieces, R.), Prāt.; ChUp.; MBh. &c.; smallness, littleness, W.; a partic. division or short space of time (= 2 or 12 Kalās), L.; a kind of song, L.; (in rhet.) a figure of speech in which a statement is made indirectly (e.g. Veṇīs. ii, 4), Sāh.; a figure of speech in which what is usually considered as an advantage is represented as a disadvantage and vice versâ), Kuval.; N. of a prince (a son of Su-hotra), VP.

Leśôkta, mfn. briefly said, only hinted or insinuated, Suśr.

Leśika, m. a grass-cutter, Hcar.

Leśin, mfn. (ifc.) containing small portions or particles of, ib.

Leśya, m. or n., °**śyā**, f. light, Sūryapr.

Leshṭavya, mfn. (prob.) to be torn off or injured, Pāṇ. viii, 2, 36, Sch.

Leshṭu, m. a clod, lump of earth, MBh.; Hariv.; Hcat. (cf. *loshṭa, loshṭu*). **-ghna** or **-bhedana**, m. a clod-breaker, a harrow or other agricultural implement used for breaking clods, L.

Leshṭukā, f. (in Prākṛit) = *leshṭu*, Mṛicch.

लिश्व *lishva*, m. = *lashva*, a dancer, actor, L.

लिह् 1. *lih* (later form of √*rih*), cl. 2. P. Ā. (Dhātup. xxiv, 6) *leḍhi, līḍhe* (ep. also *lihati*; pf. *leleha, lilihe*, Gr.; fut. *leḍhā, lekshyati*, °*te*, ib.; aor. *alikshat, alikshata* and *alīḍha*, ib.; inf. *leḍhum*, ib.; ind. p. *līḍhvā*, ib.), to lick, lap, lick at (loc.), taste, sip, take any food by licking or lapping, Br. &c. &c.; to lick up = destroy (said of an arrow), Daś.: Caus. *leháyati* (aor. *alīlihat*), to cause to lick, Br.; Suśr.; to apply as an electuary, Car.: Desid. *lilikshati*, °*te*, Gr.: Intens. *lelihyati, leleḍhi* (p. *lelihat*, °*hyat*, °*hyamāna* or °*hāna*, q.v.), to lick frequently or constantly, play with the tongue, MBh.; R. &c. [Cf. Gk. λείχω; Lat. *lingo*; Slav. *lizati*; Lith. *lëžti*; Germ. *lëcchôn, lecken*; Angl. Sax. *liccian*; Eng. *lick.*]

2. **Lih** (ifc.) licking (cf. *madhu-l*°); perceiving (*nayanayoḥ*, 'in the eyes'), Sāh.; m. mild wind, L.

Liha (ifc.) 'licking' or 'being licked' (see *abhram-l*° and *go-l*°).

Līḍha, mfn. licked, tasted, eaten, devoured, consumed, destroyed, MBh.; Kāv. &c. **-mukta**, mfn. rejected after being tasted, W.

Leḍhṛi, m. 'licker,' a mild wind, L.

Leliha, mfn. (fr. Intens.) 'constantly licking,' a kind of parasitical worm, Car.; ŚārṅgS.; a serpent, snake, MBh.; BhP.; (*ā*), f. a partic. Mudrā or position of the fingers, L.

Lelihāna, mfn. frequently licking or darting out the tongue, MBh.; m. N. of Śiva, ib.; (*ā*), f. a partic. Mudrā or position of the fingers, L.

Leha, m. one who licks, a licker, sipper (*madhuno lehaḥ*, 'sipper of honey,' a bee), Bhaṭṭ.; anything to be taken by licking or sipping or sucking, an electuary, syrup, Suśr.; food, L.; N. of one of the 10 ways in which an eclipse can take place, VarBṛS.; (*ī*), f. a partic. disease of the tips of the ears, ŚārṅgS.; (*am*), ind., see *kshīra-leham.* **-cintāmaṇi**, m. N. of a medical wk.

Lehaka, m. one who licks or tastes, MW.

Lehana, n. the act of licking, tasting or lapping with the tongue, Sarvad.

Lehanīya, mfn. = *lehya*, MW.

Lehin, mfn. licking, a licker (see *madhu-l*°).

Lehina, m. borax, L.

Lehya, mfn. to be licked, lickable, to be lapped or licked up or eaten by licking, MBh.; R. &c.; n. nectar, sipped food, any food, L.; a syrup, electuary, W.

ली 1. *lī* (cf. √*rī*), cl. 9. P. (Dhātup. xxxi, 31) *lināti*, to adhere, obtain (not usually found); cl. 1. P. *layati* (xxxiv, 6), to melt, liquefy, dissolve (not usually found); cl. 4. Ā. (xxvi, 30) *līyate* (Ved. also *láyate*; pf. *lilye, lilyuḥ*, Br. &c.; *lilāya, lalau*, Gr.; aor. *aleshṭa*, ŚBr.; *alaishīt, alāsīt, alāsta*, Gr.; fut. *letā, lātā*; *leshyati* or *lāsyati*, °*te*, ib.; inf. *letum* or *lātum*, ib.; ind. p. *-lāyam*, AV.; Br.; *-līya*, MBh.; Kāv. &c.), to cling or press closely, stick or adhere to (loc.), MBh.; R. &c.; to remain sticking, Suśr.; to lie, recline, alight or settle on, hide or cower down in (loc.), disappear, vanish, MBh.; Kāv. &c.: Caus. P. *lāpayati* or *lāyayati*, to cause to cling &c., Br. &c.; Ā. *lāpayate*, to deceive; to obtain honour; to humble, Pāṇ. i, 3, 70; Desid. *lilīshati*, °*te*, Gr.: Intens. *lelīyate, lelayīti, leleti*, ib. (cf. *lelāya*).

Laya, m. the act of sticking or clinging to (loc.), Śiś. (*layam* √*gā* with loc., 'to become attached to any one,' Kuval.); lying down, cowering, MBh.; melting, dissolution, disappearance or absorption in (loc. or comp.), Up.; Kap. &c. (*layam* √*gam* or *yā*, 'to disappear, be dissolved or absorbed;' *layam sam*-√*gam*, 'to hide or conceal one's self'); extinction, destruction, death, MBh.; Kāv. &c. (*layam* √*yā*, 'to be destroyed, perish'); rest, repose, Śiś.; BhP. (cf. *a-laya*); place of rest, residence, house, dwelling, W.; mental inactivity, spiritual indifference, Kap.; Vedântas.; sport, diversion, merriness, Vās.; delight in anything, Harav.; an embrace, L.; (in music) time (regarded as of 3 kinds, viz. *druta*, 'quick,' *madhya*, 'mean or moderate,' and *vilambita*, 'slow'), Kālid.; Daśar.; Pañcat. &c.; a kind of measure, Saṃgīt.; the union of song, dance and instrumental music, L.; a pause, MW.; a partic. agricultural implement (perhaps a sort of harrow or hoe), VS.; a swoon, L.; the quick (downward) movement of an arrow, L.; (*ā*), f. N. of a Yoginī, Hcat. (v.l. *jayā*); n. the root of Andropogon Muricatus, Bhpr.; mfn. making the mind inactive or indifferent, BhP. **-kāla**, m. time of dissolution or destruction, MW. **-gata**, mfn. gone to dissolution, dissolved, melted, ib. **-nālika**, m. a Buddhist or Jaina temple, L. **-putrī**, f. 'daughter of (musical) time,' a female dancer, actress, L. **-madhya**, mfn. to be performed in mean or moderate time (as a piece of music), Mālav. **-yoga**, m. N. of wk. **-śuddha**, mfn. to be performed in clear or right time (cf. *laya* above), Śak. **-sthāna**, n. place of dissolution, Vedântas. **Layârambha** or **layâlamba**, m. 'moving according to time,' a dancer, actor, L. **Layârka**, m. the sun at the dissolution of the world, BhP. **Layâlaya**, m. du. destruction and non-destruction, R.

Layana, n. the act of clinging, adhering, lying &c., rest, repose, Śiś., Sch.; a place of rest, house, cell &c., Śiś.; Prab.; Kāraṇḍ.

Lāyaka, mfn. clinging, sticking, adhering &c., APrāt., Sch.

2. **Lī**, f. clinging to, adhering &c., L.; = *capala*, L.

Līna, mfn. clung or pressed closely together, attached or devoted to, merged in (loc. or comp.), R.; Sarvad.; sticking, Mahīdh.; lying or resting on, staying in, lurking, hiding, MBh.; Kāv. &c.; dissolved, absorbed in (loc. or comp.), disappeared, vanished, ŚvetUp.; MBh. &c.; n. the clinging to, being dissolved or absorbed in, disappearance, Pañcar. **-tā**, f. = prec. n.; (ifc.) concealment in, Śak.; complete retirement or seclusion, HYog. **-tva**, n. (ifc.) sticking or concealment in, Suś. **Linâli**, mfn. having bees adhering (to anything), embraced or clung to by bees, MW.

Līnaya, Nom. P. °*yati*, to dissolve, melt (trans.), Pāṇ. vii, 3, 39, Sch.

Lelya, n. (fr. Intens.) clinging or adhering very closely, Vop.

लीका *likā*, f. pl. N. of partic. evil spirits, MārkP.

लीक्षा *līkkā* or *līkshā*, f. = *likshā*, L.

लीला *līlā*, f. (derivation doubtful) play, sport, diversion, amusement, pastime, MBh.; Kāv. &c.; mere sport or play, child's play, ease or facility in doing anything, ib.; mere appearance, semblance, pretence, disguise, sham, Kāv.; Kathās.; Pur. (ibc. sportively, easily, in sport, as a mere joke; also = *līlayā*, ind. for mere diversion, feignedly); grace, charm, beauty, elegance, loveliness, Kālid.; Kathās.; Rājat.; (in rhet.) a maiden's playful imitation of her lover, Daśar.; Sāh.; Pratāp.; a kind of metre (4 times ⏑⏑–⏑⏑–⏑⏑–⏑⏑–), Col.; N. of a Yoginī, HPariś. **-kamala**, n. a woman's toy-lotus, a lotus-flower held in the hands as a plaything, Kāv. **-kara**, m. a partic. metre, VarBṛS., Sch. **-kalaha**, m. a quarrel or dispute in play, sham-fight, Śṛiṅgār. **-khela**, mfn. moving or sporting playfully, Ragh.; n. a kind of metre, Col. **-°gāra** (°*lâg*°; Ragh.) or **-gṛiha** (Kathās.; Naish.) or **-geha** (Kathās.), n. a pleasure-house, place of amusement or sport. **-°ṅga** (°*lâṅga*), mfn. (accord. to Nīlak.) = *vilasitâṅga*, having playful limbs (said of a bull; but prob.) w.r. for *nīlâṅga*, q.v., MBh. **-catura**, mfn. sportively charming, Kum. **-candra**, m. N. of a poet, Subh. **-°cala** (°*lâc*°), m. N. of a district, Cat. **-tanu**, f. a form assumed for mere sport or pleasure, BhP. **-tāṇḍava-paṇḍita**, mfn. skilled in sportive dances (said of Śiva), MW. **-tāmarasa**, n. = *-kamala* above, Kāv. **-tāla**, m. (in music) a kind of measure, Saṃgīt. **-dagdha**, mfn. burnt or consumed without effort, Bhartṛ. **-devī**, f. N. of a princess, Inscr. **-°dri** (°*lâdri*), m. = *līlâcala* above, Cat. **-dhara-bhaṭṭa**, m. N. of an author, Cat. **-naṭana**, n. a sportive dance, MW.; a sham or pretended dance, Pañcat. **-nṛitya**, n. id., Kāvyâd. **-padma**, n. = *-kamala* above, Sāh.; Kāvyâd. **-parvata**, m. N. of a mountain, Kathās. **-pura**, n. N. of a town, Inscr. **-°bja** (°*lâbja*), n. = *-kamala* above, Kuval. **-°bharaṇa** (°*lâbh*°), n. an ornament worn for mere pleasure (of no intrinsic value, as a bracelet of lotuses), Śak. **-madhu-kara**, m. N. of a drama (IW. 471). **-manushya**, m. a sham man, one not really a man, BhP. **-mandira**, n. a pleasure-house, Daś. **-maya**, mfn. consisting of or relating to play or amusement (comp.), Cat. **-mātreṇa**, ind. out of mere sport, in mere play, without the least effort, Pañcar. **-mānusha-vigraha**, mfn. having or taking a human form merely for amusement or in mere semblance (said of Kṛishṇa), ib. **-°mbuja** (°*lâm*°), n. = *-kamala* above, Kathās. **-°yudha** (°*lây*°), m. pl. N. of a people, MBh. (v.l. *nīlây*°). **-rati**, f. sportive amusement, am° with (loc.), Kāv. **-°ravinda** (°*lâr*°), n. = *-kamala* above, Ragh.; Kathās. **-rasa-krama-stotra**, n. N. of wk. **-vajra**, n. an implement or instrument shaped like a thunderbolt, Kathās. **-vat**, mfn. possessed of grace or beauty, graceful, charming, Hcat. (only f.); Col.; (*atī*), f. a beautiful and charming woman, Bhartṛ.; Hit. &c.; N. of Durgā, Cat.; of the wife of the Asura Maya, Kathās.; of a Surâṅganā, Siṇhās.; of a wife of Avīkshita, MārkP.; of a merchant's daughter, Hit.; a kind of metre, Col.; N. of various wks. (esp. of a well-known treatise on arithmetic, algebra, and geometry by Bhāskarâcārya, Col.; IW. 176, 183; also abbreviated for *nyāya-l*°); °*tī-prakāśa*, m., °*tī-rahasya*, n., °*tī-vyākhyā*, f., °*tī-sāra*, N. of wks. **-°vatāra** (°*lâv*°), m. the descent (of Vishṇu on the earth) for his own amusement, BhP. **-°vadhūta** (°*lâv*°), mfn. gracefully waved about, Megh. **-vāpī**, f. a pleasure-tank or lake, Kathās. **-veśman**, n. a pleasure-house, Rājat. **-śuka**, m. 'pleasure-parrot,' a parrot kept for pl°, A.; N. of the poet Bilva-maṅgala, Cat. **-sampādana-krama**, m. N. of wk. **-sādhya**, mfn. to be effected with ease, Kathās. **-svâtma-priya**, m. N. of an author held in esteem by the Tāntrikas, Cat. **Līlêśvara-deva**, m. N. of a sanctuary, Inscr. **Līlôdyāna**, n. a pleasure-garden, Kathās.; the garden of gods, Indra's paradise, A.

Līlāya, Nom. P. Ā. °*yati*, °*te*, to play, sport, dally, amuse one's self, R.; Hariv. &c.

Līlāyita, mfn. sporting, dallying, rejoicing, Bālar.; (ifc.) pretending to be, representing, resembling, Bhojapr.; n. sport, amusement, Siṇhās.; an exploit easily accomplished, Bālar.

Lilopavatī (?), f. a kind of metre, Col.

लीसुष *lisusha*, m. a partic. taste (bitter, sweet, sour and pungent); mfn. so tasting, L.

लुक् 1. *luk* (only *lukishyasi* and *lukita*), prob. invented to explain the following word.

Lukêśvara, n. N. of a Tīrtha, Cat.

लुक् 2. *luk* (prob. fr. √*luñc*), a gram. term to express 'the dropping out' or 'disappearance' of

Pratyayas or affixes (the symbols *luk*, *lup*, and *ślu* are distinguished from *lopa*, q.v., and are called *lu-mat*, as containing the syllable *lu*).

लुगि *lugi*. See *mahā-lugi*.

लुङ् *luṅ*, (in gram.) N. of the terminations of the Aorist or Third Preterite and N. of that Tense itself.

लुङ्ग *luṅga* = *mātuluṅga*, a citron, L.

लुञ्च् *luñc*, cl. 1. P. (Dhātup. vii, 5) *luñcati* (pf. *luluñca*, °*ce*, MBh.; Kāv. &c.; aor. *aluñcīt*, Gr.; fut. *luñcitā*, *luñcishyati*, ib.; ind. p. *luñcitvā* or *lucitvā*, Pāṇ. i, 2, 24; *-lucya*, MBh.), to pluck, pull out, tear off, MBh.; Kāv. &c.; to peel, husk, Pañcat.

Luc, f. plucking out or off, MW.

Luñca, mfn. one who plucks or pulls (in *a-* and *ku-l*°, q.v.)

Luñcaka, mfn. id. (see *keśa-l*°); m. (prob.) a kind of grain, Suśr.

Luñcana, mfn. = prec. (see *keśa-l*°); n. plucking or tearing out, Bhpr.; (*ā*), f. concise speech, L.

Luñcita, mfn. plucked, pulled; husked, peeled, MBh.; Suśr.; Pañcat. **-keśa** or **-mūrdhaja**, m. 'having the hair torn out,' N. of a Jaina ascetic (so called as pulling out the hair of the head and body by way of self-mortification), Sarvad.

लुञ्ज् *luñj*, v.l. for √*lañj*, q.v.

लुट् 1. *luṭ* (cf. √*ruṭ* and 1. *luṭh*), cl. 1. Ā. *loṭate*, to resist; to suffer pain; to shine, Dhātup. xviii, 8; cl. 10. P. *loṭayati*, to speak; to shine, xxxiii, 81.

लुट् 2. *luṭ* (connected with √2. *luṭh*), cl. 1. 4. P. *loṭati*, *luṭyati* (only p. *luṭyat*, rolling, in Bhaṭṭ.; Gr. also pf. *luloṭa* &c.), to roll, roll about, wallow, Dhātup. ix, 27; xxvi, 113; cl. 1. Ā. *loṭate*, to go, Naigh. ii, 14: Caus. or cl. 10. P. *loṭayati*, see under √1. *luṭ*.

Loṭana, n. tumbling, rolling, W. (cf. *loḍana*); (*ā*), f. persuasive speech, complaisance, L.

लुट् 3. *luṭ*, (in gram.) N. of the terminations of the First Future or N. of that Tense itself.

लुट्टक *luṭṭaka*, m. N. of a poet, Cat.

लुठ् 1. *luṭh*, cl. 1. P. *loṭhati* (pf. *luloṭha* &c.), to strike, knock down, Dhātup. ix, 52; to roll, wallow, Dharmaś. (see √2. *luṭh*); cl. 1. Ā. *loṭhate* (pf. *luluṭhe*; aor. *aluṭhat*, *aloṭhishṭa*, Pāṇ. i, 3, 91), to resist; to suffer pain, Dhātup. xviii, 9; to go, Naigh. ii, 14: Caus. or cl. 10. P. *loṭhayati*, to rob, pillage, sack, Dhātup. xxxii, 27, Vop.

लुठ् 2. *luṭh*, cl. 6. P. (Dhātup. xxviii, 87) *luṭhati* (pf. *luloṭha*, Hit.; aor. *aloṭhīt*, °*thishṭa*, Gr.; fut. *luṭhitā*, *loṭhishyati*, ib.), to roll, move about or to and fro, wallow, welter, flutter, dangle, Kāv.; Pur.; Rājat. &c.; to roll down from (abl.), HPariś.; to touch, BhP.; to agitate, move, stir, ib.: Caus. *loṭhayati* (aor. *alūluṭhat* or *aluloṭhat*), to set in motion, stir, agitate, BhP., Sch.; to sound, make resound, Viddh.; to deal blows round about, Bhaṭṭ.: Desid. *lulutḥishate*, to wish to roll, be on the point of rolling, Pat.: Intens. *loluṭhīti*, to roll about (said of a drunken man), Bālar.

Luṭhat, mfn. rolling, falling down, W.; flowing, trickling (?), ib.

Luṭhana, n. the act of rolling, rolling or wallowing on the earth, Mudr. **Luṭhaneśvara-tīrtha**, n. N. of a Tīrtha, Cat.

Luṭhita, mfn. rolled, rolled down, rolling on the ground (as a horse), fallen, Kathās.; Pañcat.; n. the rolling on the ground (of a horse), L.

Luṭheśvara, n. = *luṭhaneśvara*, Cat.

Loṭha, m. rolling, rolling on the ground, Vop. **-bhū**, f. a place where a horse is rolling in dust, L.

Loṭhaka, m. N. of a poet, Cat.

Loṭhana, n. wagging of the head, Car.; Bhpr.; m. N. of a man, Rājat.

Loṭhitaka, m. N. of a poet, Cat. (cf. *loṇitaka*).

लुड् *luḍ* (connected with √*lul* and √2. *luṭh*), cl. 1. P. *loḍati*, to agitate, move, stir, Dhātup. ix, 27; cl. 6. P. *luḍati*, to adhere; to cover, xxviii, 87; to cover, Vop.: Caus. *loḍayati* (ind. p. *-loḍya*; Pass. *loḍyate*), to set in motion, agitate, disturb, MBh.; R. &c.

Loḍana, n. the act of agitating or disturbing, Dhātup. ii, 4 (v.l. *loṭana*).

Loḍita, mfn. (fr. Caus.) agitated, troubled, MBh.

लुणिग *luṇiga*, m. N. of a man (the father of Mahā-deva; he wrote notes on his son's book), Cat.

लुण्ट् *luṇṭ* (cf. √*ruṇṭ* and *luṇḍ*), cl. 1. P. (Dhātup. ix, 42) *luṇṭati*, to rob, plunder, HPariś.; cl. 10. P. *luṇṭayati*, id., Dhātup. xxxii, 27 (Vop. 'to despise').

Luṇṭaka, m. a kind of vegetable, L.; N. of a man, Cat.

Luṇṭā, f. rolling, MW.; = *luṭhana*, L.

Luṇṭāka, m. a robber, thief, Vcar.; HPariś.; a crow, L.

Luṇṭita, mfn. robbed, plundered, MW.; v.l. (or w.r.) for *luñcita*, q.v.

लुण्ठ् *luṇṭh* (cf. √*ruṇṭh*), to stir, agitate, MBh.; to go, Dhātup. ix, 61; to be idle; to be lame; to resist, ix, 58; to rob, plunder, ix, 41 (cf. *nir-* and *vi-*√*luṇṭh*): Caus. *luṇṭhayati* (Pass. *luṇṭhyate*), to cause to rob or plunder, Siṃhās.; to rob, steal, plunder, sack, Rājat.; Kathās.

Luṇṭha, m. a kind of grass, Gobh. **-nadī**, f. N. of a river, Hariv. (v.l. *kuṇḍa-n*°).

Luṇṭhaka, m. a robber, plunderer, Hcar.

Luṇṭhana, n. the act of plundering, pillaging (see *grāma-l*°); w.r. for *luñcana*, Śak., Sch.; v.l. for *luṭhana*, L.

Luṇṭhā, f. = *luṭhana*, L.

Luṇṭhāka, m. a robber, plunderer (*-tā*, f.), Bālar.; a crow, L.

Luṇṭhi, f. plundering, pillaging, sacking, Rājat.

Luṇṭhita, mfn. plundered, pillaged, robbed, stolen, Hariv.; Kathās. (also w.r. for *luñcita*).

Luṇṭhī, f. = *luṭhana*, L.

लुण्ड् *luṇḍ*, v.l. for √*luṇṭ*, q.v.

लुण्डिका *luṇḍikā*, f. a ball, round mass (of anything); = *leṇḍa*, q.v.; = next, L.

Luṇḍī, f. proper behaviour, acting and judging rightly, L.; = *nigama*, L.

Luṇḍī-kṛita, mfn. made into a ball, rolled up together, L.

लुन्थ् *lunth* (cf. √1. *luṭh*), cl. 1. P. *lunthati*, to strike, hurt, cause or suffer pain, Dhātup. iii, 8.

लुप् 1. *lup* (cf. √*rup*), cl. 6. P. Ā. (Dhātup. xxviii, 137) *lumpáti*, °*te* (pf. *lulopa*, *lulupe*, Br. &c.; aor. *alupat*, *alupta*, Gr.; Prec. *lopsīya*, ChUp.; fut. *loptā*, *lopsyati*, °*te*, Gr.; inf. *loptum*, Hit.; ind. p. *luptvā*, MBh. &c.; *-lúpya*, AV.; *-lúmpam*, MaitrS.; *lopam*, Kauś.), to break, violate, hurt, injure, spoil, Hariv.; VarBṛS.; to seize, fall or pounce upon (acc.), MBh.; Hit.; to rob, plunder, steal, Kathās.; BhP.; to cheat (said of a merchant), Campak.; to take away, suppress, waste, cause to disappear, ŚārṅgS.; Śatr.; BhP.; to elide, erase, omit (a letter, word &c.), Prāt.; Pāṇ., Kār.; cl. 4. P. *lupyati* (pf. *lulopa*; fut. *lopitā*, *lopishyati*, &c.), to disturb, bewilder, perplex, confound, Dhātup. xxvi, 126: Pass. *lupyáte* (TS. *lúpyate*; aor. *alopi*), to be broken &c., AV. &c. &c.; to be wasted or destroyed, Hcar.; (in gram.) to be suppressed or lost or elided, disappear; to be confounded or bewildered, MaitrUp.: Caus. *lopayati*, °*te* (aor. *alūlupat*, MBh.; *alulopat*, Gr.; Pass. *lopyate*), to cause to break or violate, cause to swerve from (abl.), Ragh.; to break, violate, infringe, neglect, Mn.; MBh. &c.; (Ā.) to cause to disappear, efface, MānGṛ.: Desid. *luluptsati* or *lulopishati*, °*te*, Gr.: Intens. *lolopti* (p. *lolupat*), to confound, bewilder, perplex, KaṭhUp.; *lolupyate* = *garhitam lumpati*, Pāṇ. iii, 1, 24; to be greedy, in *a-lolupyamāna*, q.v. [For cognate words, see under √*rup*.]

2. **Lup**, (in gram.) falling out, suppression, elision (cf. 2. *luk*); mfn. = *lupta*, fallen out, dropped, elided, VPrāt.

Lupta, mfn. broken, violated, hurt, injured, VarBṛS.; robbed, plundered, (ifc.) deprived of, Kauś.; MBh. &c.; suppressed, lost, destroyed, annihilated, disappeared, ĀśvŚr.; MBh. &c.; (in gram.) dropped, elided, Prāt.; Pāṇ. &c.; (in rhet.) elliptical (as opp. to *pūrṇa*, 'complete'), Vām.; Kpr.; n. stolen property, plunder, booty, L.; (prob.) disappearance (cf. *śaśa-l*°). **-tā**, f. the state of being cut off or divided, disappearance, non-existence, W. **-daṇḍaka**, m. (prob.) an arch-rogue, Mṛicch. **-dharma-kriya**, mfn. excluded from or deprived of religious ordinances, Mn. viii, 226. **-pada**, mfn. wanting (whole) words, W. **-piṇḍôdaka-kriya**, mfn. deprived of funeral rites, Bhag. **-pratibha**, mfn. deprived of reason, Rājat. **-visarga**, mfn. dropping the Visarga, Sāh.; n. = next, Pratāp.; *-ka*, n. (ib.); *-tā*, f. (Sāh.) absence of Visarga. **Luptâhata-visarga**, mfn. having Visarga dropped or coalesced (with a preceding *a*) into *o* (*-tā*, f.), Sāh. **Luptôpama**, mfn. wanting or omitting the particle of comparison, Nir.; (*ā*), f. (in rhet.) a mutilated or imperfect simile (the conjunction expressing comparison or the common attribute being omitted), Vām.; Kpr. &c. (IW. 458). **Luptôpamāna**, mfn. = prec. mfn., Mahīdh.

Lopa, m. breaking, hurting, injury, destruction, interruption, MBh.; Kāv. &c.; neglect, violation, transgression (of a vow or duty), Mn.; Yājñ. &c.; robbing, plundering, MBh.; want, deficiency, absence, disappearance, ŚrS.; Ragh.; (in gram.) dropping, elision (generally as distinguished from the terms *lup*, *ślu*, *luk*, which are only applicable to affixes; when *lopa* of an affix takes place, a blank is substituted, which exerts the same influence on the base as the affix itself, but when either *luk* or *lup* or *ślu* of an affix is enjoined, then the affix is not only dropped but it is also inoperative on the base; thus in the 1st pl. of *kati*, where *jas* is said to be elided by *luk*, the change of the final of the base to Guṇa does not take place, i.e. both the affix and its effect on the base are abolished; moreover, *lopa* refers only to the last letter of an affix, whereas by *luk* &c. the dropping of the whole affix is implied), Nir.; Prāt.; Pāṇ. &c.; (*lópā*), f. a partic. bird, TS.; a kind of bird, L.; = *lopā-mudrā* below. **Lopâpatti**, f. the being cut off or dropped or elided, MW.

Lopaka, mfn. (ifc.) interrupting, violating, destroying (see *vidhi-l*°); m. violation, MW.; (*ikā*), f. a kind of sweetmeat, AgP.; Hcat.

Lopana, n. the act of omitting or violating, violation (see *vrata-l*°); the mouth, Gal. (prob. w.r. for *lapana*).

Lopāka, m. a kind of jackal, Suśr.

Lopāpaka, m. id. (*ikā*, f.), L.

Lopā-mudrā, f. N. of the reputed wife of the sage Agastya (she is said to have been formed by the sage himself and then secretly introduced into the palace of the king of Vidarbha, where she grew up as his daughter; she asked her husband to acquire immense riches; so he went to the rich demon Ilvala, and having conquered him, satisfied his wife with his wealth; she is considered as the authoress of RV. i, 179, 4), RV.; MBh.; Hariv. &c.; *-kavi*, m. N. of a poet, Cat.; *-pati* or *-sahacara*, m. husband of Lopā-mudrā, N. of Agastya, L.

Lopāyikā, f. a kind of bird, L.

Lopāśá, m. a jackal, fox, or a similar animal, RV.; VS. [Cf. Gk. ἀλώπηξ.] °**śaka**, m. N. of a man, Buddh.; (*ikā*), f. a female jackal or fox, L.

Lopin, mfn. (ifc.) injuring, diminishing, impairing, MBh.; Ragh.; liable or subject to elision, Pat. (cf. *madhyama-pada-l*°).

Loptṛi, mfn. one who interrupts or violates (with gen.), MBh.; (*trī*), f. a lump of dough or paste, Bhpr.

Loptra, n. stolen property, plunder, booty, Yājñ.; MBh.

Lopya, mfn. to be broken &c.; to be omitted or elided, Vop.; being among thickets or inaccessible places, VS. (Mahīdh.)

लुभ् *lubh*, cl. 6. P. *lubhati* (only Dhātup. xxviii, 22) or cl. 4. P. (xxvi, 124) *lúbhyati* (pf. *lulubhe*, R.; aor. *alubhat* or *alobhīt*, Gr.; fut. *lobdhā* or *lobhitā*, *lobhishyati*, ib.; inf. *lobdhum*, MBh.; ind. p. *lobhitvā*, *lubhitvā*, *lubdhvā*, Gr.), to be perplexed or disturbed, become disordered, go astray, AitBr.; to desire greatly or eagerly, long for, be interested in (dat. or loc.), Mn.; MBh. &c.; to entice, allure, R.: Caus. *lobháyati*, °*te* (aor. *alūlubhat*, Br.; Pass. *lobhyate*, MBh.), to confound, bewilder, perplex, derange, ŚBr.; to cause to desire or long for, excite lust, allure, entice, attract, MBh.; Kāv. &c.; to efface, ĀpŚr. (cf. Caus. of √*lup*): Desid. of Caus. *-lulobhayishati*, see *ā-*√*lubh*: Desid. *lulubhishati* or *lulobhishati*, Gr.: Intens. *lolubhyate* (Gr. also *lolobdhi*), to have a vehement desire for (loc.), Kām. [Cf. Lat. *lubet*, *libet*, *libido*; Goth. *liufs*; Germ. *liob*, *lieb*, *lieben*; Angl. Sax. *leóf*; Eng. *lief*, *love*.]

Lubdha, mfn. bewildered, confused, AitBr. (*am*, ind.); greedy, covetous, avaricious, desirous of or longing for (loc. or comp.), Gaut.; MBh. &c.; n. a hunter, MBh.; R.; a lustful man, libertine, W. **-jana**, mfn. having covetous followers, MW. **-jātake varsha-vardhāpana-vidhāna**, n. N. of wk. **-tā**, f., **-tva**, n. greediness, covetousness, ardent desire for (loc.), Rājat.; Kathās.

Lubdhaka, m. a hunter, MBh.; Kāv. &c.; a covetous or greedy man, L.; the star Sirius (so called because Śiva in the form of a hunter shot an arrow [represented by the three stars in the belt of Orion] at Brahmā transformed into a deer and pursuing his own daughter metamorphosed into a doe; cf. *mṛiga-vyādha*), Gaṇit.; Kathās.; N. of the hinder parts, BhP.

Lubhita, mfn. perplexed, disturbed, fascinated, Pāṇ. vii, 2, 54.

Lobha, m. perplexity, confusion (see *a-l°*); impatience, eager desire for or longing after (gen., loc. or comp.), Mn.; MBh. &c.; covetousness, cupidity, avarice (personified as a son of Pushṭi or of Dambha and Māyā), ib. **-tas**, ind. from greediness or desire, Kathās. **-mañjarī**, f. 'flower of avarice,' nickname of a courtezan, Daś. **-mohita**, mfn. beguiled by covetousness or avarice, Hit. **-viraha**, m. absence of avarice, ib.; mfn. = next. **-śūnya**, mfn. free from avarice (*-tva*, n.), Vishṇ. **Lobhâkṛishṭa**, mfn. attracted by greediness or covetousness, Hit. **Lobhâtman**, mfn. greedy-minded, avaricious, A. **Lobhânvita**, mfn. possessed of covetousness, avaricious, greedy, MW. **Lobhâbhipātin**, mfn. hastening through eager desire, rushing greedily, MBh. **Lobhôtkarsha**, m. excess of avarice or greed, MW.

Lobhana, mfn. alluring, enticing, attracting, L.; (*ī*), f. a kind of Sphaerantus, L.; n. allurement, enticement, temptation, R.; Kām.; gold, L.

Lobhanīya, mfn. to be desired or longed for, alluring, seductive, MBh. **-tama**, mfn. most attractive; *°mâkṛiti*, mfn. having a most attr° figure, ib.

Lobhayāna, mfn. alluring, enticing, seducing, Hariv.

Lobhāyana, m. a patr., Pravar.

Lobhita, mfn. allured, enticed, seduced, Kām. **-vat**, mfn. one who has allured &c., MBh.

Lobhin, mfn. covetous, avaricious, desirous of, eager after, longing for (often ifc.), Rājat.; BhP.; Campak. (*°bhi-tā*, f.); alluring, enticing, charming, R.

Lobhya, mfn. = *lobhanīya*, L.; m. Phaseolus Mungo, L.

लुमत् **lu-mat.** See under 2. *luk*.

लुम्ब् **lumb**, cl. 1. P. *lumbati*, to torment, harass, Dhātup. xi, 37; cl. 10. P. *lumbayati*, id., xxxii, 113; to be invisible, ib. (*adarśane*, v.l. for *ardane*).

लुम्बिका **lumbikā**, f. a kind of drum, L.

लुम्बिनि **lumbini** (m.c.) or *°nī*, f. N. of a princess and a grove named after her, Buddh. (cf. MWB. 389). *°nīya*, mfn. relating to the above, Lalit.

लुल् **lul** (connected with √*lud*, and √1. *lu*), cl. 1. P. (Dhātup. ix, 27, v.l.) *lolati* (only pr. and pr. p. P. Ā. *lolat* and *lolamāna*), to move to and fro, roll about, stir, Śiś.; Pañcar.; to disappear, Śiś. x, 36: Caus. *lolayati*, to set in motion, agitate, confound, disturb, R.; Śiś.

Lulita, mfn. moved or tossed about, agitated, swinging to and fro, dangling, fluttering, heaving, waving, tremulous, MBh.; Kāv. &c.; (ifc.) touched by, come in contact with, Śak. (v.l.); BhP.; disarranged, dishevelled (as hair), Ṛitus.; hurt, injured, crushed, destroyed, MBh.; R. &c.; fatigued, unnerved, Mālatim.; agreeable, pleasing, beautiful, W. (w.r. for *lalita*?); n. movement, motion, Uttarar. **-kuṇḍala**, mfn. having dangling earrings, Kathās. **-pallava**, mfn. (a wood) with waving twigs, Bhaṭṭ. **-makaranda**, mfn. (flowers) whose sap is disturbed (by bees), Veṇis. **-maṇḍana**, mfn. having ornaments tossed about in confusion, MW. **-srag-âkula**, mfn. (a bed) strewn with scattered garlands, Ragh. **Lulitâkula-keśânta**, mfn. one whose hair is disordered and dishevelled, R. **Lulitâlaka-keśânta**, mfn. one whose curls and locks are dishevelled, Kathās.

Lola, mf(*ā*)n. moving hither and thither, shaking, rolling, tossing, dangling, swinging, agitated, unsteady, restless, MBh.; Kāv. &c.; changeable, transient, inconstant, fickle, Kāv.; Kathās.; desirous, greedy, lustful, (ifc.) eagerly desirous of or longing for (loc., inf. or comp.), Kāv.; Var. &c.; m. the penis, Gal.; N. of a man, MārkP.; (*ā*), f. the tongue, L.; lightning, Prab. (v.l.); 'the fickle or changeable one,' N. of the goddess of fortune or Lakshmī, Pañcar.; of Dākshāyaṇī in Utpalâvartaka, Cat.; of the mother of the Daitya Madhu, R.; of a Yoginī, Hcat.; of two metres, Chandom.; Col.; (*ī*), f. (in music) a kind of composition, Saṃgīt. **-karṇa**, mf(*ī*)n. listening to everybody, Rājat. **-kuṇḍala**, mfn. having dangling or pendent earrings, MW. **-ghaṭa** (?), the wind, ib. **-cakshus**, mfn. having a rolling eye, W.; looking wantonly upon (loc.), Śiś. **-jihva**, mfn. having a rolling or restless tongue, insatiable, greedy, W. **-tā**, f., **-tva**, n. movableness, fickleness, restlessness, wantonness, cupidity, eager desire, Kāv.; Sāh.; Suśr. **-nayana**, **-netra**, and **-locana**, mfn. having rolling eyes, W. **-lāṅgūla**, n. 'wagging tail,' N. of a hymn in praise of Hanumat. **-lola**, mfn. being in constant motion, ever restless, Śāntiś. **Lolâkshikā** or **lolâkshī**, f. (a woman) with a rolling eye, Kāv. **Lolâpâṅga**, mfn. having tremulous or quivering outer corners (said of eyes), MW. **Lolârka**, m. a form of the sun, VāmP. **Lolêkshaṇa**, mf(*ā*)n. = *lola-nayana*, Hāsy. **Lol'-oshṭha**, mfn. having moving or restless lips, Śiś.

Lolat, mf(*antī*)n. moving to and fro, rolling &c. (cf. √*lul*). **-karâṅguli**, mfn. having restless or tremulous fingers, Pañcar.

Lolad, in comp. for *lolat*. **-bhuja**, mfn. having swinging arms, Śiś.

Lolana, m. pl. N. of a people, MārkP.

Lolita, mfn. (fr. Caus.) moved hither and thither, shaken, agitated, tremulous, Śiś.

लुलाप **lulāpa**, m. a buffalo, Hcat.; Dhūrtan. **-kanda**, m. a kind of plant with a tuberous root, L. **-kāntā**, f. a buffalo cow, L.

Lulāya, m. a buffalo, Bālar. **-ketu**, m. 'having a buffalo for an emblem,' N. of a Gaṇa of Śiva, Harav. **-lakshman**, m. id., N. of Yama, Bālar.

लुश **luśa**, m. N. of a Ṛishi with the patr. Dhānāka (author of RV. x, 35; 36), PañcavBr.

Luśâkapi, m. N. of a man, ib.

लुष् **lush** (cf. √*lūsh*), cl. 1. P. *loshati*, to rob, steal, Dhātup. ix, 42.

लुष **lusha**, m. the son of a Nishāda and a Chāṇakī, L.

लुषभ **lushabha**, m. an elephant in rut, Uṇ. iii, 124, Sch.

लुस्त **lusta**, n. the end of a bow, L.

लुह् **luh** (cf. √*lubh*), cl. 1. P. *lohati*, to covet, Dhātup. xxvi, 128 (Vop.)

लू 1. **lū**, cl. 9. P. Ā. (Dhātup. xxxi, 13) *lunāti*, *lunīte* (Ved. also *lunoti*; pf. *lulāva*, Kathās.; 2. sg. *lulavitha*, Pāṇ. vi, 1, 196, Sch.; 2. pl. *luluvidhve* or *°viḍhve*, ib. viii, 3, 79, Sch.; aor. *alāvīt*, *alavishṭa*, Gr.; fut. *lavitā*, *lavishyati*, *°te*, ib.; inf. *lavitum*, ib.; ind. p. *lūtvā*, ib.; *-lāvam*, Kāv.), to cut, sever, divide, pluck, reap, gather, TBr. &c. &c.; to cut off, destroy, annihilate, Kāv.; Rājat.: Pass. *lūyate* (aor. *alāvi*), to be cut, Gr.: Caus. *lāvayati* (aor. *alīlavat*, *°vata*), to cause to cut, Gr.: Desid. of Caus. *lilāvayishati*, ib.: Desid. *lulūshati*, *°te*, ib.: Intens. *lolūyate*, *loloti*, ib.: Desid. of Intens. *lolūyishate* (ind. p. *°yam*), ib. [Cf. Gk. λύω; Lat. *so-luo*, *solvo*; Goth. *fra-liusan*; Germ. *vir-liosan*, *ver-lieren*; Angl.Sax. *for-leósan*; Eng. *lose*.]

Lava, **lavana** &c. See p. 898, cols. 2, 3.

Lāva, mf(*ī*)n. (ifc.) cutting, cutting off, plucking, reaping, gathering, Ragh.; Sāh.; cutting to pieces, destroying, killing, Bhaṭṭ.

Lāvaka, m. a cutter, reaper, Śaṃk.; MārkP.

Lāvin. See *pushpa-l°*.

Lāvya, mfn. to be cut or reaped &c., Pāṇ. iii, 1, 125, Sch.

2. **Lū**, mfn. cutting, dividing &c., Pāṇ. vi, 4, 83, Sch. (cf. *eka-lū*).

Lūta, mfn. = *pūrva-vicchinna*, TS. (Sch.)

Lūna, mfn. cut, cut off, severed, lopped, clipped, reaped, plucked, MBh.; Kāv. &c.; nibbled off, Hit.; knocked out, Kathās.; stung, Rājat.; pierced, wounded, Ragh.; destroyed, annihilated, Rājat.; n. a tail, L. (cf. *lūma*). **-dushkṛita**, mfn. one who has destroyed or annihilated his sins, Rājat. **-dos**, m. N. of Vṛishaṇa (one of Śiva's attendants), L. **-paksha**, mfn. one whose wings have been clipped, R. **-bāhu**, mfn. one whose arms have been cut off, Kathās. **-māṃsa**, mfn. one whose flesh is stung by (instr.), Rājat. **-yavam**, ind. after the barley has been cut, after barley-harvest, g. *tishṭhad-gu*. **-visha**, mfn. having poison in the tail, L.

Lūnaka, m. cut, divided &c. (= *bhinna* or *bhedita*), L.; m. an animal, L.; a cut, wound, anything cut or broken, W.; sort, species, difference, W.

Lūni, f. the act of cutting or reaping &c., Pāṇ. viii, 2, 44, Vārtt. 1, Pat.; rice (= *vrīhi*), Uṇ. iv, 105, Sch.

Lūnī, mfn. (fr. next), Pāṇ. vi, 1, 112, Sch.

Lūnīya, Nom. (fr. *lūna*), ib.

Lūyamāna, mfn. being cut or plucked or gathered. **-yavam**, ind. when the barley is cut, g. *tishṭhad-gu*.

Loluva, mfn. (fr. Intens.) cutting much or often, Pāṇ. i, 1, 4, Sch.

Lolūya, mfn. (fr. id.) = prec., Vop. xxvi. 29; (*ā*), f., see next.

Lolūyā, f. determination to cut, W. **-vat**, mfn. resolved to cut or cut off, ib.

लूक्ष **lūkshá**, mfn. = *rūksha*, rough, harsh, TS.; ĀpŚr.

लूता **lūtā**, f. a spider, Mn.; Var.; Suśr. &c.; an ant, L.; a kind of cutaneous disease (said to be produced by the moisture from a spider), Rājat. **-tantu**, m. a spider's web, cobweb, MW. **-paṭṭa**, m. a spider's egg, L. **-°maya** (*lūtâm°*), m. the skin disease called *lūtā*, Rājat. **-markaṭaka**, m. (only L.) an ape; Arabian jasmine; = *putrī*. **-°ri** (*lūtâri*), m. 'spider-enemy,' a kind of shrub, L.

Lūtāta, m. an ant, L.

Lūtikā, f. a spider, L.

लूम **lūma**, n. a tail, a hairy tail (as a horse's or monkey's), L. (cf. *lūna*). **-visha**, m. 'having poison in the tail,' an animal that stings with the tail (as a scorpion), L.

Lūman, n. = *lūma*, L.

लूलुक **lūluka**, m. a frog, L.

लूष् **lūsh** (cf. √*lush* and *rūsh*), cl. 1. P. *lūshati*, to adorn, decorate, Dhātup. xvii, 26; cl. 10. P. *lūshayati* (aor. *alūlushat*), to hurt, injure, kill, Dhātup. xxxii, 70; to steal, xxxii, 27 (Vop.)

Lūsha. See *arka-l°*.

लूह **lūha**, mfn. bad (?), L.; N. of a man, Buddh.

Lūha-sudatta, m. N. of a man (= *lūha*), Buddh.

लृ **lṛi**, (in gram.) N. of the terminations of the Conditional Mood or N. of that Mood itself.

लृट् **lṛiṭ**, (in gram.) N. of the terminations of the Second Future or N. of that Tense itself.

लेक **léka**, m. (said to be) N. of an Āditya, TS.

लेकुञ्चिक **lekuñcika**, m. N. of a man, Buddh.

लेख **lekha, lekhana, lekhin** &c. See p. 901, cols. 2, 3.

लेट् **leṭ**, (in gram.) N. of the terminations of the Vedic Subjunctive Mood or N. of that Mood itself.

लेट **leṭa**, m. N. of a partic. mixed caste, BrahmavP.

लेट्य **leṭya** or **loṭya**, Nom. P. *°yati*, to deceive; to be first; to sleep; to shine, g. *kaṇḍv-ādi*.

लेढृ **leḍhṛi**. See p. 903, col. 1.

लेण्ड **leṇḍa**, n. (cf. *laṇḍa*) excrement, BhP.

लेत **leta**, m. n. (cf. *lota*) tears, L.

लेदरी **ledarī**, f. N. of a river, Rājat.

लेप् **lep**, cl. 1. Ā. *lepate*, to go; to serve, Dhātup. x, 11.

लेप **lepa, lepana, lepin** &c. See p. 902, col. 3.

लेय *leya*, m. (fr. Gk. λέων) the sign of the zodiac Leo, VarBṛS.

लेलाय *lelāya* (either a kind of Intens. fr. √*lī*, or Nom. fr. *lelā*, cf. next), P. Ā. *leláyati*, °*te* (pr. p. *leláyantī*, gen. *leláyatas*; impf. *álelā-yat*, *lelāyat*; pf. *leláya*), to move to and fro, quiver, tremble, shake, MaitrS.; TS.; Br.; Up.; ĀpŚr. [Cf. Goth. *reiraith.*]

Lelā, f. (only instr. *leláyā*, cf. above) quivering, flickering, shaking about, ŚBr.

Lelāyamānā, f. N. of one of the seven tongues of fire, MuṇḍUp.

लेलितक *lelitaka* or *lelītaka*, m. or n.(?) sulphur, Car.

लेलिह *leliha*, °*hāna* &c. See p. 903, col. 1.

लेल्य *lelya*. See p. 903, col. 2.

लेवार *levāra*, m. N. of an Agra-hāra, Rājat.

लेश *leśa*, *leśya*, *leshṭavya* &c. See p. 903, col. 1.

लेसक *lesaka* or *lesika*, m. a rider on an elephant, L.

लेह *leha*, *lehana* &c. See p. 903, col. 1.

लैख *laikha*, m. patr. fr. *lekha*, g. *śivâdi*.

Laikhābhreya, m. patr. fr. *lekhâbhra* or metron. fr. *lekhā-bhrū*, g. *śubhrâdi*.

लैगवायन *laigavāyana*, m. a patr. fr. *ligu*, g. *naḍâdi*.

Laigavya, m. id., g. *gargâdi*.

Laigavyāyanī, f. a patr. fr. *laigavya*, g. *lohitâdi*.

लैङ्ग *laiṅga*, mf(*ī*)n. (fr. *liṅga*) relating to grammatical gender, Pat.; (*ī*), f. a species of plant, L.; n. N. of a Purāṇa and an Upapurāṇa. — **dhūma**, m. an ignorant priest (who does not know the god, metre &c. of Vedic hymns), L. **Laiṅgôdbhava**, n. (the tale of) the origin of the Liṅga, Bālar.

Laiṅgika, mfn. based upon a characteristic mark or evidence or proof, Sāy.; m. a sculptor, Kap., Sch. — **bhāva-vāda**, m. N. of wk.

Laiṅgika, w. r. for *laiṅgika*.

लैण *laiṇ*, cl. 1. P. *laiṇati*, to go; to send; to embrace, Dhātup. xiii, 15 (w. r. for *paiṇ*).

लैशिक *laiśika*, n. the offence of a monk who taking advantage of an apparent transgression committed by a fellow monk wrongfully accuses him of it, Buddh.

लो *lo*, mfn. (fr. *lavaya*; nom. *laus*), Pāṇ. i, 1, 58; Vārtt. 2, Pat.; m. N. of a man, Rājat.

लोक् *lok* (connected with √1. *ruc*), cl. 1. Ā. (Dhātup. iv, 2) *lokate* (pf. *luloke*, Bhaṭṭ.; inf. *-lokitum*, Kathās.), to see, behold, perceive: Caus. or cl. 10. (Dhātup. xxxiii, 103) *lokayati* (aor. *alulokat*), id., ŚBr.; Sāh.; to know, recognize, R.; LiṅgaP. [Cf. Eng. *look.*]

Loká, m. (connected with *roka*; in the oldest texts *loka* is generally preceded by *u*, which accord. to the Padap. = the particle 3. *u*; but *u* may be a prefixed vowel and *ulokά* a collateral dialectic form of *loka*; accord. to others *u-loka* is abridged from *uru-* or *ava-loka*), free or open space, room, place, scope, free motion, RV.; AV.; Br.; ĀśvŚr. (acc. with √*kṛi* or √*dā* or *anu-*√*nī*, 'to make room, grant freedom;' *loke* with gen., 'instead of'); intermediate space, Kauś.; a tract, region, district, country, province, ŚBr.; the wide space or world (either 'the universe' or 'any division of it,' esp. 'the sky or heaven;' 3 Lokas are commonly enumerated, viz. heaven, earth, and the atmosphere or lower regions; sometimes only the first two; but a fuller classification gives 7 worlds, viz. Bhūr-l°, the earth; Bhuvar-l°, the space between the earth and sun inhabited by Munis, Siddhas &c.; Svar-l°, Indra's heaven above the sun or between it and the polar star; Mahar-l°, a region above the polar star and inhabited by Bhṛigu and other saints who survive the destruction of the 3 lower worlds; Janar-l°, inhabited by Brahmā's son Sanat-kumāra &c.; Tapar-l°, inh° by deified Vairāgins; Satya-l° or Brahma-l°, abode of Brahmā, translation to which exempts from re-birth; elsewhere these 7 worlds are described as earth, sky, heaven, middle region, place of re-births, mansion of the blest, and abode of truth;' sometimes 14 worlds are mentioned, viz. the 7 above, and 7 lower regions called in the order of their descent below the earth—A-tala, Vi-t°, Su-t°, Rasā-t°, Talā-t°, Mahā-t°, and Pātāla; cf. RTL. 102, n. 1; IW. 420, 1; 431, 1), AV. &c. &c.; N. of the number 'seven' (cf. above), VarBṛS., Sch.; the earth or world of human beings &c., Mn.; MBh. &c. (*ayám lokáḥ*, 'this world;' *asaú* or *páro lokáḥ*, 'that or the other world;' *loke* or *iha loke*, 'here on earth,' opp. to *para-tra*, *para-loke* &c.; *kṛitsne loke*, 'on the whole earth'); (also pl.) the inhabitants of the world, mankind, folk, people (sometimes opp. to 'king'), Mn.; MBh. &c.; (pl.) men (as opp. to 'women'), Vet.; Hit.; a company, community (often ifc. to form collectives), Kāv.; Vas.; Kathās. &c.; ordinary life, worldly affairs, common practice or usage, GṛS.; Nir.; Mn. &c. (*loke* either 'in ordinary life,' 'in worldly matters;' or 'in common language, in popular speech,' as opp. to *vede*, *chandasi*); the faculty of seeing, sight (only in *cákshur-l°*, q. v.); *lokānāṃ sāmanī*, du. and *lokānāṃ vratāni*, pl. N. of Sāmans, ĀrshBr. [Cf. Lat. *lūcus*, originally 'a clearing of a forest;' Lith. *laúkas*, a field.] — **kaṇṭaka**, m. 'man-thorn,' a wicked man (who is a 'curse' to his fellow-men), Mn.; MBh.; R.; N. of Rāvaṇa, MW. — **kathā**, f. a popular legend or fable, ib. — **kartṛi**, m. 'world-creator' (N. applied to Vishṇu and Śiva as well as to Brahmā), MBh.; R. — **kalpa**, mfn. resembling or appearing like the world, becoming manifested in the form of the w°, BhP.; regarded by the world, considered by men as (nom.), ib.; m. a period or age of the world, ib. — **kānta**, mfn. w°-loved, liked by every one, pleasing to all, MBh.; R.; (*ā*), f. a kind of medicinal herb, L. — **kāma**, mfn. longing for a partic. world, MBh. — **kāmyā**, f. love towards men, ib. — **kāra**, m. creator of the w° (N. of Śiva), Śivag. — **kāraṇa-karaṇa**, n. cause of the causes of the w° (N. of Śiva), MW. — **kṛít** (also *uloka-k°*), mfn. making or creating free space, setting free, RV.; AV.; TS. &c.; m. the creator of the w°, MBh.; R.; MārkP. — **kṛitnú**, mfn. creating space, RV. (prob. *uloka-k°*). — **kshit**, mfn. inhabiting heaven, ChUp. — **gati**, f. 'way of the world,' actions of men, Hariv.; R. — **gāthā**, f. a verse or song (handed down orally) among men, Sarvad. — **guru**, m. a teacher of the world, instructor of the people, R.; BhP. — **cakshus**, n. 'eye of the world,' the sun, L. (accord. to some m.); pl. the eyes of men, Sāh. — **cara**, mfn. wandering through the w°s, MBh. — **cāritra**, n. the way or proceedings of the world, R. — **cārin**, mfn. = *-cara*, q. v., MBh. — **jananī**, f. 'mother of the world,' N. of Lakshmī, Cat. — **jit**, mfn. winning or conquering any region, ŚBr.; winning Heaven (*loka-jitám svargám* = *svarga-loka-jitam*), AV.; Mn.; m. conqueror of the world, W.; a sage, ib.; N. of a Buddha, L. — **jña**, mfn. knowing the w°, understanding men; *-tā*, f. knowledge of the w°, kn° of mankind, Prasaṅg. — **jyeshṭha**, m. 'the most distinguished or excellent among men,' N. of Buddha, Buddh.; a monk of a partic. order, ib. — **tattva**, n. 'w°-truth,' knowledge of the w°, kn° of mankind, R. — **tantra**, n. the system or course of the w°, MBh.; Hariv.; Śak.; Pur. — **tas**, ind. by men, from people, from people's talk, R.; Kathās.; (ifc.) on the part of the people of (*jñāti-l°*, on the part of the collective body of relations), VarBṛS.; as usual or customary in the world, ŚāṅkhGṛ. — **tā**, f. (in *tal-loka-tā*) the being possessed of one's world, BhP. (MBh. vii, 6519, read *gantā sa-lokatām*). — **tushāra**, m. 'earth's dew,' camphor, L. — **traya**, n. (MBh.; Ragh.) or (*ī*), f. (Kuval.) 'world-triad,' the three w°s (heaven, earth and atmosphere, or h°, earth and lower regions). — **dambhaka**, mfn. deceiving the w°, cheating mankind, Mn. iv, 195. — **dūshaṇa**, mfn. damaging mankind, R. — **dvaya**, n. both w°s (heaven and earth), Kām.; Rājat. — **dvāra**, n. the door or gate of heaven, ChUp.; °*rīya*, n. N. of a Sāman, KātyŚr., Sch. — **dharma**, m. a worldly matter, Lalit.; worldly condition (eight with Buddhists), Dharmas. 61. — **dhātu**, m. f. a region or part of the world, Buddh.; N. of a partic. division of the w°, ib.; °*tv-īśvarī*, f. N. of Mārīcī, wife of Vairocana, Tantr. — **dhātṛi**, m. creator of the w° (N. of Śiva), MBh.; (*trī*), f. N. of the earth (?), Caṇḍ. (perhaps for *-dhartrī*; cf. next). — **dhāriṇī**, f. N. of the earth, TĀr. — **nātha**, m. 'lord of worlds,' N. of Brahmā, Cat.; of Vishṇu-Kṛishṇa, MBh.; BhP.; of Śiva, Kum.; of the gods in general, BhP.; of the sun, Cat.; a protector or guardian of the people, king, sovereign, R.; BhP. &c.; a Buddha, L.; N. of a Buddha, Rājat.; of Avalokitêśvara, ib.; Inscr.; of various authors, Cat.; a partic. mixture, Rasêndrac.; mfn. being under the guardianship of mankind, Kāv.; *-cakra-vartin*, m. N. of a Scholiast, Cat.; *-bhaṭṭa*, m. N. of an author, Cat.; *-rasa*, m. a partic. medicinal preparation, Cat.; *-śarman*, m. N. of an author, Cat. — **nāyaka**, m. leader of the worlds (the sun), Hcat. — **nindita**, mfn. blamed by the w°, generally censured, Sarvad. — **netṛi**, m. guide of the w° (N. of Śiva), Śivag. — **nyāyâmṛita**, n. N. of wk. — **pa**, m. a w°-guardian, world-protector (8 in number; see *l°-pāla*), MBh.; BhP. — **pakti**, f. the mental evolution of the w°, ŚBr.; worldly reward or esteem, Jātakam. — **paṅkti**, f. w. r. for prec., Sāṃkhyak., Sch. — **pati**, m. 'lord of the world,' N. of Brahmā, VarBṛS.; of Vishṇu, BhP.; a lord or ruler of people, king, sovereign, R.; BhP. — **patha**, m. way of the world, general or usual way or manner, MBh. — **paddhati**, f. general or universal way, Sarvad. — **paro'ksha**, mfn. hidden from the world, MBh. — **pārya**, m. N. of a man, Inscr. — **pālá**, m. a world-protector, guardian of the w°, regent of a quarter of the w° (the Loka-pālas are sometimes regarded as the guardian deities of different orders of beings, but more commonly of the four cardinal and four intermediate points of the w°, viz. accord. to Mn. v, 96, 1. Indra, of the East; 2. Agni, of South-east; 3. Yama, of South; 4. Sūrya, of South-west; 5. Varuṇa, of West; 6. Pavana or Vāyu, of North-west; 7. Kubera, of North; 8. Soma or Candra, of North-east; others substitute Nir-ṛiti for 4 and Īśānī or Pṛithivī for 8; according to Dharmas. the Buddhists enumerate 4 or 8 or 10 or 14 Loka-pālas), ŚBr. &c. &c.; a protector or ruler of the people, king, prince, Ragh.; Rājat.; N. of various kings, Bhadrab.; Col.; of Avalokitêśvara, MWB. 198; protection of the people (?), R.; *-tā*, f. (MārkP.) or *-tva*, n. (Hariv.; R.) the being a guardian of the world; °*lâshṭaka-dāna*, n. N. of wk. — **pālaka**, m. a world-protector, BhP.; a king, sovereign, ib. — **pālinī**, f. 'world-protectress,' N. of Durgā, Kautukar. — **pitāmaha**, m. 'progenitor of the w°, great forefather of mankind,' N. of Brahmā, R.; BhP. — **puṇya**, N. of a place, Rājat. — **purusha**, m. 'w°-man,' the World personified, L. — **pūjita**, mfn. honoured by the world, universally worshipped, L.; m. N. of a man, Lalit. — **prakāśa**, m. and °*śaka*, n. N. of wks. — **prakāśana**, m. 'world-illuminator,' the sun, L. — **pratyaya**, m. world-currency, universal prevalence (of a custom &c.), KātyŚr. — **pradīpa**, m. 'light of the world,' N. of a Buddha, Buddh.; °*pânvaya-candrikā-nidāna*, n. N. of wk. — **pravāda**, m. popular talk, common saying, commonly used expression, R.; Hit. — **pravāhin**, mfn. flowing through the world, MBh. — **prasiddha**, mfn. celebrated in the world, generally established, universally known, Kām. — **prasiddhi**, f. universal establishment or reception (of any custom &c.), general prevalence (°*dhyā*, ind. according to prevalent usage), VarBṛS. — **bandhu**, m. 'universal friend, friend of all,' N. of Śiva, Śivag.; of the sun, L. — **bāndhava**, m. 'friend of all,' N. of the sun, Cat. — **bāhya**, mfn. excluded from the w°, excluded from society, excommunicated, L.; differing from the w°, singular, eccentric, MW.; m. an outcast, ib. — **bindusāra**, n. N. of the last of the 14 Pūrvas or most ancient Jaina writings, L. — **bhartṛi**, m. supporter of the people, R. — **bhāj**, mfn. occupying space, ŚBr. — **bhāvana** (MBh.; Hariv.; BhP.) or °**vin** (R.), mfn. promoting the welfare of the world or of men; w°-creating, MW. — **bhās-kara**, m., **-manoramā**, f. N. of wks. — **máya**, mf(*ī*)n. containing space or room, spacious, ŚBr.; containing the worlds or the universe, Hariv.; BhP. — **maryādā**, f. 'bounds of the w°,' popular observance, established usage or custom, Śaṃkar. — **mahā-devī**, f. N. of a princess, Inscr. — **maheśvara**, m. N. of Kṛishṇa, Bhag. — **mātṛi**, f. the mother of the w°, Sāh.; BhP.; N. of Lakshmī, BhP.; of Gaurī, Kāv. — **mātṛikā**, f. (pl.) the mother of the w°, Hcat. — **mārga**, m. general or universal way, prevalent custom, Pañcat. — **m-pṛiṇa**, mfn. filling the world, penetrating everywhere, Bhām.; (*ā́*), f. (scil. *ishṭakā*), N. of the bricks used for building the sacrificial altar (set up with the formula *lokám pṛiṇa* &c., those which have a peculiar formula being called *yajush-matī*, q.v.), ŚBr.; TS.; ĀpŚr.; Jaim.; (scil. *ṛic*), N. of the formula *lokám pṛiṇa* &c., ŚBr.; TS.; KātyŚr. **-yātrā**, f. the business and traffic of men, worldly affairs, conduct of men, ordinary actions, Mn.; MBh.; Kāv. &c.; worldly existence, career in life, Mālav.; support of life, Hit. **-yātrika**, mfn. relating to the business or traffic of the world, MW. (said to be also employed to explain the word *de-vayu*, L.) **-raksha**, m. 'protector of the people,' a king, sovereign (°*kshâdhirāja*, m. a king supreme over all rulers), R. **-rañjana**, n. pleasing the world, satisfying men, gaining public confidence, Yājñ., Comm. **-rava**, m. the talk of the world, popular report, MBh. **-lekha**, m. an ordinary letter, Cat. **-locana**, n. (accord. to some m.) 'eye of the world,' the sun, Vās.; BhP.; pl. the eyes of men, Kathās.; °*nâpāta*, m. the glancing of men's eyes, i. e. the prying eyes of men, ib. **-vacana**, n. people's talk, public rumour, Pañcat. **-** 1. **-vat**, mfn. containing the worlds, MaitrUp. **-** 2. **-vat**, ind. as in the ordinary life, Jaim.; TPrāt., Comm. **-vartana**, n. the means by which the world subsists, Kathās. **-vāda**, m. the talk of the world, public rumour, MBh.; Kāv. &c. **-vādhin**, mfn. occupying space, Śulbas. **-vārttā**, f. the world's news, popular report or rumour, Cat. **-vikrushṭa**, mfn. abused by the w°, universally blamed or contemned, Mn. **-vijñāta**, mfn. universally known, Pat. **-víd**, mfn. possessing or affording space or freedom, MaitrS.; knowing the w°s, MBh.; kn° or understanding the w° (N. of a Buddha), Buddh. **-vidvishṭa**, mfn. hated by men, universally hated, Mn.; Yājñ.; R. **-vidhi**, m. the creator of the world, disposer of the universe, MBh.; order or mode of proceeding prevalent in the world, BhP. **-vināyaka**, m. pl. a partic. class of deities presiding over diseases, VahniP. **-vindu**, mfn. possessing or creating or affording space or freedom, TāṇḍyaBr. **-viruddha**, mfn. opposed to public opinion, notoriously at variance, Vām. **-virodha**, mfn. opposed to the people's opinion, R. **-viśruta**, mfn. universally celebrated, famous, Mn.; R. **-viśruti**, f. world-wide fame, notoriety, W.; unfounded rumour or report, ib. **-visarga**, m. the end of the world, MBh.; the creation of the w°, BhP. **-visargika**, mf(*ī*)n. bringing about or leading to the creation of the w°, MBh. **-visargin**, mfn. creating the w°, ib. **-vistāra**, m. universal spreading, general extension or diffusion, Kull. on Mn. vii, 33 (v. l. *loke v°*). **-vīra**, m. pl. the w°'s heroes, BhP. **-vṛitta**, n. a universal custom, Mn.; Śak.; the conduct of the common people or of the public, MBh.; worldly intercourse, idle conversation, W. **-vṛittânta**, m. the events or occurrences of the world, course or proceedings of the w°, R.; Śak. **-vyavahāra**, m. id., Kull. on Mn. ix, 27; usual or commonly current designation, Pāṇ. i, 2, 53, Sch. **-vrata**, n. general practice or way of proceeding, gen° mode of life, BhP.; N. of several Sāmans, ĀrshBr. **-śabda**, m. the noise of the world, bustle of the day, Dhūrtan. **-śruti**, f. world-wide fame, universal notoriety, R.; a popular report, A. **-śreshṭha**, mfn. best in the world, Mālatīm. **-saṃvṛitti**, f. right conduct (in the world), Divyâv. **-saṃvyavahāra**, m. commerce or intercourse with the w°, worldly business, Mn.; MārkP.; *-nāmakâṅka*, m. N. of wk. **-saṃsṛiti**, f. passage through worlds, course through the world, events of the w° or life, BhP. **-saṃ-skṛita** (?), N. of wk. **-saṃkara**, m. confusion of mankind or among men, R. **-saṃkshaya**, m. the destruction of the w°, MBh. **-saṃgraha**, m. experience gained from intercourse with men, Cat.; the propitiation or conciliation of men, Bhag.; R. (v. l.); BhP.; the whole of the universe, aggregate of worlds, VP.; the welfare of the world, MW.; N. of wk. **-saṃgrāhin**, mfn. propitiating men, Kām. **-sáni**, mfn. causing room or space, effecting a free course, VS.; Vait. **-sampanna**, mfn. experienced in the world, possessed of worldly wisdom, MBh. **-sākshika**, mfn. having the world as a witness, attested by the world or by others, MBh.; (*am*), ind. before or in the presence of witnesses, ib.; R. **-sākshin**, m. witness of the world, universal witness (said of Brahman, of Fire &c.), R.; Cat.; mfn. = *-sākshika* above, Hariv. **-sāgara**, m. N. of wk. **-sāt**, ind. for the general good, for the sake of the public; *-kṛita*, mfn. made or done for the gen° good, made common property, Kathās. **-sādhaka**, mfn. creating worlds, Cat. **-sādhāraṇa**, mfn. common (as a topic), Daś. **-sāman**, n. N. of a Sāman, Lāṭy. **-sāraṅga**, m. N. of Vishṇu, MBh. **-siddha**, mfn. world-established, current among the people, usual, common, Sarvad.; universally admitted, generally received, MW. **-sīmâtivartin**, mfn. passing beyond ordinary limits, extraordinary, supernatural, Sāh. **-sundara**, mf(*ī*)n. thought beautiful by all, generally admired, R.; m. N. of a Buddha, Lalit. **-sthala**, n. an incident of ordinary life, common or ordinary occurrence, L. **-sthiti**, f. duration or existence of the world, Kāv.; a universal law, generally established rule, Śaṃk. on BṛĀrUp. **-spṛít**, mfn. = *-sáni* above, TS. **-smṛit**, mfn., v. l. for prec. (accord. to Comm. = *pṛithivī-lokasya smartā*), MaitrUp. **-hāsya**, mfn. world-derided, universally ridiculous, any object of general ridicule; *-tā*, f. state of being so, Kathās. **-hita**, mfn. beneficial to the world or to mankind, A.; n. the welfare of the world, Śak.; BhP. **Lokâkâśa**, m. space, sky, Sarvad.; (accord. to the Jainas) a worldly region, the abode of unliberated beings, MW. **Lokâkshi** (VP.) or °**kshin** (Cat.), m. 'eye of the world,' N. of a preceptor. **Lokâcāra**, m. usage or practice of the world, common practice, general or popular custom, Pañcat. **Lokâcārya**, m. N. of an author, Cat.; *siddhânta*, m. N. of wk. **Lokâtiga** (Sāh.) or °**tiśaya** (ib.) or °**tita** (Kād.), mfn. = *loka-sīmâtivartin* above. **Lokâtman**, m. the soul of the universe, R. **Lokâdi**, m. the beginning of the w°, i. e. the creator of the w°, MBh. **Lokâdhāra**, mf(*ā*)n. depending on the people or on the support of the p°, Pañcat.; Kām. **Lokâdhika**, mfn. extraordinary, uncommon, Kir.; Bhām. **Lokâdhipa**, m. a ruler of the w°, a god, Buddh.; a king, A. **Lokâdhipati**, m. the ruler or lord of the w°, Up.; °*teya*, n. conduct suited to public opinion, Jātakam. **Lokânanda**, m. N. of an author, Cat. **Lokânukampaka**, mfn. pitying the w°, Lalit. **Lokânugraha**, m. the welfare of the world, prosperity of mankind, Kāv.; *-pravṛitta*, m. N. of Gautama Buddha, Divyâv. **Lokânurāga**, m. the love of mankind, universal love or benevolence, Sāh. **Lokânuvṛitta**, n. obedience of the people, Kāv. **Lokânuvṛitti**, f. accommodating one's self to others, dependence on others, Śiś. **Lokântara**, n. another world, the next w°, a future life (°*raṃ √gam* or *√yā*, to go into the next w°, die), Kāv.; BhP. &c.; *-gata* (Rājat.), *-prâpta* (W.), or *-stha* (Mṛicch.), mfn. gone to another w°, deceased, dead. **Lokântarika**, mf(*ā*)n. dwelling or situated between the worlds, Buddh. **Lokântarita**, mfn. deceased, dead, Kād. **Lokântâdri**, m. the range of mountains forming a border round the world (= *lokâloka* below, cf. *cakra-vāla*), L. **Lokâpavāda**, m. the reproach or censure of the world, general evil report, public scandal, MBh.; Kāv. &c. **Lokâbhidhāna**, n. N. of wk. **Lokâbhibhāvin**, mfn. overcoming the w°, MW.; overspreading or pervading the w° (said of light), ib. **Lokâbhilashita**, mfn. w°-desired, universally coveted, generally liked; m. N. of Buddha, Lalit. (w. r. °*lāshita*). **Lokâbhilāshita** (w. r. for prec.) or °**shin**, m. N. of a Buddha, Buddh. **Lokâbhyudaya**, m. the prosperity of the world, general welfare, Ragh. **Lokâyata**, mfn. 'world-extended (?),' materialistic; m. a materialist, Buddh.; Nīlak.; Āryav. (°*tī-√kṛi*, P. *-karoti*, to consider as materialistic); n. (scil. *śāstra* or *mata* or *tantra*), materialism, the system of atheistical philosophy (taught by Cārvāka), Prab.; Sarvad. &c. **Lokâyatana** (!), m. a materialist, Col. **Lokâyatika**, m. id., Śaṃk. on BṛĀrUp. and PraśnUp. &c.; (perhaps) a man experienced in the ways of the world, MBh.; Hariv.; *-paksha-nirāsa*, m. N. of wk. **Lokâyana**, m. 'refuge of the w°,' N. of Nārāyaṇa, Hariv. **Lokârya-pañcâśat**, f. N. of a Stotra. **Lokâloka**, n. sg. or m. du. (also m. sg.?) the world and that which is not the w°, i. e. world and non-w°, MBh.; Pur.; m. N. of a mythical belt or circle of mountains surrounding the outermost of the seven seas and dividing the visible world from the region of darkness (as the sun is within this wall of mountains they are light on one side and dark on the other; see IW. 420; cf. *cakra-vāla*), Sūryas.; Ragh.; Pur. &c. **Lokâlokin**, mfn. looking through the worlds, Śiś. **Lokâvekshaṇa**, n. consideration for the world, anxiety or care for the welfare of the public, Rājat. **Lokêśa**, m. lord of the world, KaushUp.; Mn.; R. &c.; N. of Brahmā, L.; of a Buddha, Buddh.; W.; quicksilver, L.; *-kara*, m. N. of a commentator, Cat.; *-prabhavâpyaya*, mfn. having both origin and end subject to the lords of the world, MW. **Lokêśvará**, m. the lord of the world, ŚBr.; MBh.; R.; N. of a Buddha (also °*ra-rāja*), W.; Buddh.; of Avalokitêśvara, Inscr.; *-śataka*, n. N. of a poem; °*rât-majā*, f. 'Lokêśvara's daughter,' N. of a Buddhist goddess, L. **Lokêshṭakā**, f. N. of partic. bricks, ĀpŚr. (cf. *logêshṭakā*). **Lokêshṭi**, f. N. of a partic. Ishṭi, ĀśvŚr. **Lokâika-bandhu**, m. 'the only friend of the world,' N. of Gotama and of Śākya-muni, W. **Lokâishaṇā**, f. desire or longing after heaven, ŚBr.; NṛisUp. &c. **Lokôkta-muktâvalī**, f. N. of wk. **Lokôkti**, f. people's talk, Pañcad.; a general or common saying, any s° commonly current among men, proverb, Pañcat. **Lokôttara**, mf(*ā*)n. excelling or surpassing the w°, beyond what is common or general, unusual, extraordinary, Kathās.; Rājat. &c.; (ibc.), ind., HPariś.; m. an uncommon person, Uttarar.; m. or n. (?) N. of wk.; *-parivarta*, m. N. of wk.; *-vādin*, m. pl. N. of a Buddhist school (prob. so called from their pretending to be superior to or above the rest of the world), Buddh. **Lokôddhāra**, n. N. of a Tīrtha, MBh. **Lokôpakāra**, m. a public advantage, Pañcad.; °*rin*, mfn. useful to the p°, ib.

Lokana, n. the act of looking, seeing, viewing, MW.

Lokanīya, mfn. to be seen or perceived, visible, worthy of being looked at, W.

Lokita, mfn. seen, beheld, viewed, ib.

Lokín, mfn. possessing a world, possessing the best world, ŚBr.; ChUp.; m. pl. the inhabitants of the universe, MuṇḍUp.

Lokyà, mf(*ā*)n. granting a free sphere of action, bestowing freedom, ĀśvGṛ.; diffused over the world, world-wide, MBh. (C. *laukya*); conducive to the attainment of a better world, heavenly, BhP.; customary, ordinary, correct, right, real, actual, ŚBr.; MBh.; usual, every-day, MBh.; n. free space or sphere, ŚBr. **-tā** (*lokyà-*), f. the attainment of a better world, ŚBr.

लोग *logá*, m. (perhaps connected with √1. *ruj*) a clod of earth, lump of clay, clod, RV.; ŚBr. (= *loshṭa*, Sāy.) **Logâksha**, m. 'clod-eyed,' N. of a man (cf. *laugâkshi*). **Logêshṭakā**, f. a brick made from a lump of clay, ŚBr.

लोच् *loc* (connected with √*ruc* and √*lok*), cl. 1. Ā. (Dhātup. vi, 3) *locate* (pf. *luloce*; fut. *locitā* &c., Gr.), to see, behold, perceive (see *ā-* and *nir-√loc*): Caus. or cl. 10. P. *locayati* (aor. *alulocat*), to speak; to shine (*bhā-shârthe* or *bhāsârthe*), Dhātup. xxxiii, 104: Desid. *lulocishate*, Gr.: Intens. *lolocyate*, ib.

Loca, m. sight (?), MW.; n. tears, L. (cf. *lota*). **-markaṭa** or **-mastaka**, m. cock's comb, Celosia Cristata, L. **-mālaka**, m. a dream before midnight, L.

Locaka, mfn. 'gazing, staring,' stupid, senseless, L.; one whose food is milk, L.; m. the pupil of the eye, Śiś.; (only L.) lamp-black; a dark or black dress; a lump of flesh; a partic. ornament worn by women on the forehead; a partic. ear-ornament; a bow-string; a wrinkled skin or contracted eyebrow; the cast-off skin of a snake; the plantain tree, Musa Sapientum; (*ikā*), f. a kind of pastry, L.

Locana, mfn. illuminating, brightening, BhP.; m. N. of an author, Cat.; (*ā* or *ī*), f. N. of a Buddhist goddess, Dharmas. 4; (*ī*), f. a species of plant, L.; n. (ifc. f. *ā*) 'organ of sight,' the eye, MBh.; Kāv. &c.; N. of wk. **-kāra**, m. N. of an author, Cat. **-gocara**, m. the range or horizon of the eye; mf(*ā*)n. being within the range of vision, visible, Bhartṛ. **-traya-patha**, m. the range of the three eyes (of Śiva), Ratnâv. **-patha**, m. = *-gocara*, Amar. **-parusha**, mfn. looking fiercely, Daś. **-pāta**, v. l. for *locanâpāta*, q. v. **-maya**, mf(*ī*)n. consisting of eyes, Kād. **-mārga**, m. = *-gocara*, MW. **-hita**, mfn. useful for the eyes; (*ā*), f. a kind of medicinal preparation, L.; Dolichos Uniflorus, L. **Locanâñcala**, m. (ifc. f. *ā*) a corner of the eye, Bhartṛ. **Locanânanda**, m. delight of the eye, Kathās. **Locanâpāta**, m. 'eye-fall,' a glance, Kathās. **Locanâmaya**, m. eye-disease, L. **Locanôddāraka**, m. or n. (?) N. of a village, Rājat. **Locanôtsa**, m. or n. (?) N. of a place, ib.

लोट् 1. *loṭ* (or *loḍ*), cl. 1. P. *loṭati* or *loḍati*, to be mad or foolish, Dhātup. ix, 74.

लोट् 2. *loṭ*, (in gram.) N. of the terminations of the Imperative and N. of that Mood itself.

लोट *loṭa*, see *upa-* and *śaka-l°*; (*ā*), f. sorrel, L.

Loṭikā, f. sorrel, L.; N. of a princess, Rājat.

लोटुल *loṭula*, m. = *abhi-loṭaka* (?), L.

लोट्य loṭya. See leṭya, p. 905, col. 3.

लोठ loṭha, loṭhaka &c. See p. 904, col. 1.

लोड् loḍ. See √1. loṭ.

लोडन loḍana, loḍita. See p. 904, col. 2.

लोड्य loḍya. See aṅka-l°, aṅga-l° &c.

लोण loṇa, in comp. for lavaṇa. — **triṇa**, n. a species of grass, L. **Loṇâmlā**, f. Oxalis Pusilla, L.
Loṇā, f. = loṇâmlā, L.
Loṇāra, m. a kind of salt, L.
Loṇikā, f. Portulacca Oleracea, L.; = loṇâmlā, L.
Loṇī. See amla-l°.
Loṇīkā, f. = loṇikā, Car.

लोणितक loṇitaka, m. N. of a poet (cf. loṭhitaka, p. 904, col. 1).

लोत lota, m. tears, Uṇ. iii, 86, Sch. (cf. leta); a mark, sign, ib.; n. = loptra, plunder, booty, L.
Lotra, n. tears, L.; plunder, booty, Uṇ. iv, 172, Sch.

लोदी lodī, N. of a family or race, Cat.

लोध lodha, m. (prob.) a species of red animal, RV. iii, 53, 23 (cf. rudhira; Nir. and Sāy. = lubdha); m. = next, L.
Lodhra, m. = rodhra, Symplocos Racemosa, MBh.; Kāv. &c. — **tilaka**, n. (in rhet.) a species of Upamā (subdivision of the Saṃsṛishṭi), Vām. iv, 3, 23. — **pushpa**, m. Bassia Latifolia, L. — **prasava-rajas**, n. pollen of Lodhra blossoms, Ml.
Lodhraka, m. Symplocos Racemosa, Bhpr.

लोप lopa, lopaka &c. See p. 904, col. 3.

लोभ lobha, lobhana &c. See p. 905, col. 1.

लोमन् loman, n. (later form of roman, q.v.) the hair on the body of men and animals (esp. short hair, wool &c.; not so properly applicable to the long hair of the head or beard, nor to the mane and tail of animals), RV. &c. &c.; a tail, L.; du. (with Bharad-vājasya), N. of Sāmans, ĀrshBr.

1. **Loma**, in comp. for loman. — **karaṇī**, f. a species of plant, L. — **karṇa**, m. 'hair-eared,' a hare, L. — **kīṭa**, m. 'hair-insect,' a louse, Kālac. — **kūpa** (Pañcar.) or **-gartá** (ŚBr.), m. 'hair-hole,' a pore of the skin. — **ghna**, n. 'hair-destruction,' loss of hair through disease, L. — **tás**, ind. on the hairy side (of a skin; opp. to mā̃sa-tas), MānŚr. — **dvīpa**, m. a species of parasitic worm, Car. — **pāda**, m. N. of a king of the Aṅgas, MBh.; R.; -pur or -purī, f. N. of Campā, the capital of Loma-pāda, L. — **pravāhin**, mfn. = loma-vāhin, MBh. — **phala**, n. the fruit of Dillenia Indica, L. — **maṇi**, m. an amulet made of hair, Kauś. — **yūka**, m. a hair-louse, Kālac. — **randhra**, n. = -kūpa above, A. — **rāji**, f. = lomâvali below, A. — **ruha**, mf(ā)n. (any surface) having short hair growing (on it), Car. — **latâdhāra**, m. the belly, Gal. — **vat** (lóma-), mfn. having hair, hairy, TS.; AV.; ŚBr. — **vāhana**, mfn. (cf. next) sharp enough to cut a hair, MBh. (v. l.) — **vāhin**, mfn. either 'bearing or having feathers, feathered,' or 'sharp enough to cut a hair' (said of an arrow), MBh. — **vivara**, n. 'hair-hole,' a pore of the skin, Pañcar.; N. of partic. mythical regions (= roma-v°), Kāraṇḍ. — **visha**, mfn. having poisonous hair, L. — **vetāla**, m. N. of a demon, Hariv. — **śātana**, n. 'hair-remover,' a depilatory, Cat. — **saṃharshaṇa**, mfn. causing the hair of the body to bristle or stand erect, MBh. — **sātana**, w.r. for -śātana above, L. — **sāra**, m. an emerald, L. — **harsha**, m. the bristling or erection of the hair of the body, thrill or shudder (caused by excessive joy, fear &c.), MBh. (cf. roma-h°); N. of a Rākshasa, R. — **harshaṇa**, mf(ā)n. causing the hair to bristle, exciting a thrill of joy or terror, thrilling, MBh.; Hariv.; R.; Uttarar.; m. N. of Sūta (the pupil of Vyāsa), MBh.; VP.; of the father of S°, Cat.; n. the bristling of the hair, horripilation, thrill or shudder, L.; °ṇaka, mf(ikā)n., w.r. for laumah°, q.v., Cat. — **harshin**, mfn. = -harshaṇa, mfn., above, R. — **hārin**, mfn. = -vāhin, MBh. — **hṛit**, mfn. hair-removing, depilatory; n. yellow orpiment, L. **Lomâñca**, m. = româñca, curling or erection of the hair, a thrill of rapture or terror, shudder &c., W. **Lomâda**, m. a species of parasitic worm, Car. **Lomâli** or **lī°**, f. = lomâvali, A. **Lomâlikā**, f. a fox, L. **Lomâvali** or **°lī**, f. the line of hair from the breast to the navel, MW.

2. **Loma** (ifc.) = loman (see aja-lomá); n. a hairy tail, tail, L.
Lomaka (ifc.) = loman (see a-, prati-, mṛidu-l°).
Lomakā-khaṇḍa, m., Pāṇ. vi, 3, 63, Sch.
Lomakā-gṛiha, n. ib.
Lomakin, m. a bird, L.
Lomaṭaka, m. a fox, Śīl.
Lomadhi, m. N. of a prince, BhP.
Lomana, m. n., g. ardharcâdi (v. l.)
Lomaśá, mf(ā)n. hairy, woolly, shaggy, bristly, covered or mixed with hair, made of hair, containing hair, TBr. &c. &c.; consisting in sheep or other woolly animals (as property), TUp.; overgrown with grass, Kāṭh.; GṛŚrS.; m. a ram, sheep, L.; N. of a Ṛishi, MBh.; of a cat, ib.; m. or n. N. of a partic. plant or its root, Car.; (ā), f. (only L.) a fox; a female jackal; an ape; N. of various plants (Nardostachys Jatamansi; Leea Hirta; Carpopogon Pruriens &c.); green vitriol, L.; N. of a Śākinī or female attendant of Durgā, L.; (ī), f. spikenard, L.; (with or scil. śikshā) = lomaśa-śikshā; n. a kind of metre, Nid. — **karṇa**, m. a species of animal living in holes, Suśr. — **kāṇḍā**, f. Cucumis Utilissimus, L. — **pattrikā**, f. a species of gourd, L. — **parṇinī** or **-parṇī**, f. Glycine Debilis, L. — **pushpaka**, m. Acacia Sirissa, L. — **mārjāra**, m. the civet cat, L. — **vakshaṇa**, mf(ā)n. covered with hair on the body, shaggy, AV. — **śikshā**, f. N. of a Śikshā attributed to Garga. — **saṃhitā**, f. N. of wk. — **saktha** (lomaśá-) or **-sakthi**, mfn. having hair or bristles on the thighs or hind feet, VS.; ŚBr. (Mahīdh., 'having a hairy tail').
Lomaśya, n. hairiness, woolliness, MW.; n. 'roughness,' N. of a partic. pronunciation of the sibilants, RPrāt.
Lomāyayaṇi (?), patr., Pravar.
Lomâśa, m. a jackal or fox, VarBṛS. (cf. lomaśā, lopāśa).
Lomâśikā, f. the female of the jackal or fox, ib.

लोराय lorāya, Nom. P. °yati (said to be vilocane), g. kaṇḍv-ādi (Gaṇar.)

लोल lola, lolita &c. See p. 905, cols. 1, 2.

लोलम्ब lolamba, m. a large black bee, L. (cf. rolamba).

लोलिका lolikā, f. a sort of sorrel, Oxalis Pusilla, L. (cf. loṭikā and loṇikā).

लोलिम्बराज lolimba-rāja, m. N. of an author, Cat.

लोलुप lolupa, mf(ā)n. (fr. Intens. of √1. lup) very destructive, destroying, MW.; (prob. corrupted fr. lolubha) very desirous or eager or covetous, ardently longing for (loc. or comp.), MBh.; Kāv. &c.; (ā), f. eager desire, appetite, longing for (loc.), MBh.; N. of a Yoginī, Hcat. — **tā**, f., **-tva**, n. eager desire or longing for (comp.), greediness, cupidity, lust, Kāv; Pur.; Suśr.

लोलुभ lolubha, mf(ā)n. (fr. Intens. of √lubh) very desirous, eagerly longing for or greedy after (comp.), Kathās. (cf. lolupa).

लोलुव loluva, lolūya &c. See p. 905, col. 3.

लोलोर lolora, n. N. of a town, Rājat.

लोल्लट lollaṭa, m. (also with bhaṭṭa) N. of an author, Cat.

लोशशरायणि lośaśarāyaṇi (?), m. N. of an author, Cat.

लोष्ट् losht (prob. artificial), cl. 1. Ā. loshṭate, to heap up, gather into a heap or lump, Dhātup. viii, 5.
Loshṭá, m. n. (prob. connected with √1. ruj; said to be fr. √1. lū, Uṇ. iii, 92) a lump of earth or clay, clod, TS. &c. &c.; a partic. object serving as a mark, VarBṛS., Sch.; n. rust of iron, L.; m. N. of a man, Rājat. — **kapāla**, mfn. having a lump of earth serving as a cup, KātyŚr. — **guṭikā**, f. a pellet of clay, Mṛicch. — **ghāta**, m. a blow with a clod, Hāsy.; (°taṃ √han, to kill with clods, i.e. stone to death, Mudr.) — **ghna**, m. an agricultural instrument for breaking clods, harrow, L. — **cayana**, n., **-citi-prayoga**, m. N. of wks. — **deva**, m. N. of an author, Cat. — **dhara**, m. N. of a man, Rājat. — **bhañjana**, m., **-bhedana**, m. n. = -ghna, L. — **maya**, mf(ī)n. made of clay, earthen, Mn. viii, 289. — **mardin**, mfn. crushing or breaking clods, ib. iv, 71. — 1. **-vat**, ind. like a clod, BhP. — 2. **-vat**, mfn. containing or mixed with lumps or particles of earth, Suśr. — **sarva-jña**, m. N. of a poet, Cat.
Loshṭâksha, m. N. of a man, Saṃskārak.
Loshṭaka, m. = loshṭa, a clod, MBh.; Mṛicch. (°kaḥ kṛitaḥ = 'hewn down,' 'cut up,' Rājat.); m. or n. (?) a partic. object serving as a mark, VarBṛS., Sch.; m. N. of various men, Rājat.
Loshṭan, m. or n. (only in instr. pl. loshṭabhis) = loshṭa, a clod, MBh. iii, 2559.
Loshṭaśa, m. N. of a man, Rājat.
Loshṭāya, Nom. Ā. °yate, to resemble a clod of earth (i. e. to be quite valueless), Alaṃkāras.
Loshṭu, m. a clod, L.
Loshtra, **loshṭha**, **loshṭhaka**, incorrect for loshṭa, °ṭaka.

लोस्तानी lostānī or lostonī, f. a proper N., Rājat.

लोह lohá, mfn. (prob. fr. a √ruh for a lost √rudh, 'to be red;' cf. rohi, rohiṇa &c.) red, reddish, copper-coloured, ŚrS.; MBh.; made of copper, ŚBr. (Sch.); made of iron, Kauś.; m. n. red metal, copper, VS. &c. &c.; (in later language) iron (either crude or wrought) or steel or gold or any metal; a weapon, L.; a fish-hook, L.; blood, L.; m. the red goat (cf. lohâja), Gaut.; Mn.; Yājñ.; (prob.) a kind of bird, MārkP.; N. of a man, g. naḍâdi; (pl.) N. of a people, MBh.; (ī), f. a pot, Divyâv.; n. any object or vessel made of iron, Kāv.; aloe wood, Agallochum, L. — **kaṭaka**, m. or n. (?) an iron chain, KātyŚr., Comm. — **kaṇṭaka**, m. Vanguiera Spinosa, L. — **kānta**, m. or °**taka**, n. magnetic iron, L. — **kāra**, m. a worker in iron, smith, blacksm°, R.; Hit.; (ī), f. N. of the Tantra goddess Atibalā, Kālac.; °ra-bhastrā, f. a blacksmith's bellows, Pañcat. — **kāraka**, m. = -kāra, m. (q.v.), L. — **kārshāpaṇa**, m. a partic. coin or weight (= 20 Māshas), L. — **kiṭṭa**, n. rust of iron, Suśr. — **kīla**, m. an iron bolt, KātyŚr., Comm. — **giri**, m. N. of a mountain, Cat. — **gola-khaṇḍana**, n. N. of wk. — **ghātaka**, m. 'iron-striker,' a blacksmith, Uṇ. i, 62, Sch. — **carma-vat**, mfn. covered with plates of iron or metal, MBh. — **cāraka**, m. N. of a hell, Mn. iv, 90 (v. l. -dāraka). — **cāriṇī**, f. N. of a river, VP. (v. l. -tāraṇī, °riṇī, and lohitâraṇī). — **cūrṇa**, n. rust of iron, VarBṛS. — **ja**, mf(ā)n. iron, made of i°, Śiś.; n. steel (from Damascus), L.; brass, bell-metal, L.; rust of i°, L. — **jaṅgha**, m. N. of a Brāhman, Kathās.; pl. N. of a people, MBh. — **jāla**, n. an iron net, a coat of mail, Hariv.; Kām. — **jit**, m. 'conquering iron (in hardness),' a diamond, L. — **tāraṇī** (MBh.; VP.) or °**riṇī** (MBh.), f. N. of a river (cf. -cāriṇī). — **daṇḍa**, m. an iron staff, Gaut.; a battle-axe, L. — **dāraka**, m., see -cāraka). — **drāvin**, mfn. melting copper or iron, fusing metal, L.; m. borax, L. — **nagara**, n. N. of a town, Kathās. — **nāla**, m. an iron arrow, L. — **paṭṭikā**, f. an iron plate, KātyŚr., Paddh. — **pāśa**, m. an i° chain, Hariv. — **pura**, n. N. of a place, Cat. — **pṛishṭha**, m. 'iron-backed,' a species of bird reckoned among the Pratudas, Car.; a heron, L. — **pratimā**, f. an i° image, L.; an anvil, W. — **baddha**, mfn. studded with iron (as a war-club), MBh. — **bhāraka**, v. l. for -cāraka, q.v. — **máya**, mf(ī)n. made of iron or copper, ŚBr.; ChUp.; Suśr. &c. — **mala**, n. rust of i°, L. — **mātra**, m. a spear, L. — **māraka**, mfn. calcining metal, L.; m. Achyranthes Triandra, L. — **mālaka**, m. N. of a partic. tribe (the son of a Maitreya and a Śūdrā or Nishādī), L. — **muktikā**, f. a red pearl, Buddh. — **mukha**, m. pl. N. of a people, R. — **mekhala**, mfn. wearing a metal girdle; (ā), f. N. of one of the Mātṛis attending on Skanda, MBh. — **yashṭi**, f. N. of a place, Cat. — **rajas**, n. iron-dust, rust of i° or i° filings, Suśr. — **ratnâkara**, m. N. of wk. — **rājaka**, n. silver, W. — **liṅga**, n. a boil or abscess filled with blood, Buddh. — **lekhya**, mfn. liable to be scratched with iron, Sāṃkhyas., Sch. — **vat**, mfn. a little reddish, ĀśvGṛ. — **vara**, n. the most precious metal, gold, L. — **varman**, n. iron armour, mail, W. — **vila**, m. a kind of rice, Car.; Vāgbh. — **śaṅku**, m. an iron stake or spike, MW.; 'iron-spiked,' N. of a hell, Mn.; Yājñ. — **śayana**, n. an iron bed, Gaut. — **śāstra**, n. N. of wk. — **śuddhi-kara**, m. borax, L. — **śṛiṅkhala**, m. an iron chain for elephants, L. — **śleshaṇa**, mfn. uniting metals; m. = next, L. — **saṃśleshaka**, m. borax, L. — **saṃkara**, m. composition or union of various metals, L.; n. steel (from Damascus), L. — **siṅhānikā** (?), f. rust of iron, Bhpr. – **stha**, mfn. being in iron, Kāv. **Lohâkara**, N. of a town, Cat. **Lohâkhya**, n. black pepper, L.; Agallochum, L. **Lohâṅgāraka**, N. of a hell ('pit of red-hot charcoal'), MW. **Lohâcala**, m. N. of a mountain, Cat.; *-māhātmya*, n. N. of wk. **Lohâcārya**, m. N. of an Ādyâṅgadhārin, Jain. **Lohâja**, m. the red goat; *-vaktra*, m. N. of one of Skanda's attendants, MBh. **Lohâṇḍa** (or °*hâṇ*°), mf(*ī*)n., g. *gaurâdi.* **Lohâbhisāra**, m. N. of a military ceremony performed on the 10th day after the Nīrājana, L.; = next, L. (cf. *lauhâbhisārikā-prayoga*). **Lohâbhihāra**, m. = *nīrājana*, q. v., L. **Lohâmisha**, n. the flesh of the red-haired goat, Mn. **Lohâyasá**, mfn. made of a reddish metal, made of copper, MānŚr.; n. any metal mixed with cop°, (or) cop°, Br.; KātyŚr. **Lohârgala**, n. N. of a Tīrtha, Cat. **Lohârṇava**, m. N. of wk. **Lohâsava**, m. a partic. preparation of iron, Bhpr. (cf. *lauhāsava*). **Lohâsura-māhātmya**, n. N. of wk. **Lohôttama**, m. 'best metal,' gold, L.

Lohaka. See *indu-*, *tri-*, *pañca-l*°.

Lohara, m. or n. (?) N. of a district, Rājat.

Lohala, mfn. iron, made of iron, W.; lisping, speaking inarticulately, L.; m. the principal ring of a chain, W. (= *srinkhalâdhārya* or °*lâcārya*, L.)

Lohi, n. a kind of borax, L.

Lohikā, f. an iron pot or vessel (being a sort of large shallow bowl, usually of wood and bound with iron, used for washing rice &c.), L.

1. **Lóhita**, mf(*ā* or *lóhinī*)n. (cf. *rohita*) red, red-coloured, reddish, AV. &c. &c.; made of copper, copper, metal, AV.; Kauś.; m. red (the colour), redness, L.; a partic. disease of the eyelids, ŚārṅgS.; a kind of precious stone, Pañcat.; a species of rice, Bhpr.; a sort of bean or lentil, L.; Dioscorea Purpurea, L.; Cyprinus Rohita, L.; a sort of deer, L.; a snake, serpent, L.; the planet Mars, VarBṛS.; N. of a serpent-demon, MBh.; of a man (pl. his descendants), Pravar.; Hariv. (cf. Pāṇ. iv, 1, 18); of a country, MBh.; of a river (the Brahma-putra), ib.; of a sea, ib.; R.; of a lake, Hariv.; (pl.) of a class of gods under the 12th Manu, VP.; (*ā*), f. N. of one of the 7 tongues of Agni, Gṛihyas.; Mimosa Pudica, L.; a Punar-navā with red flowers, L.; (*lohinī*), f. a woman with a red-coloured skin or red with anger, L.; n. any red substance, ŚBr.; ChUp.; (also m., g. *ardharcâdi;* ifc. f. *ā*), blood, VS. &c. &c. (°*taṃ* √*kṛi*, to shed blood); ruby, L.; red sanders, L.; a kind of sandal-wood, L.; a kind of Agallochum, L.; an imperfect form of rainbow, L.; a battle, fight, L. – **kalmāsha**, mfn. variegated with red, red-spotted, Pāṇ. vi, 2, 3, Sch. – **kūṭa**, N. of a place, Hariv. – **kṛitsna**, n. N. of one of the 10 mystic exercises called Kṛitsna, Buddh. – **kṛishṇa**, mfn. of a reddish black colour; *-varṇa*, mf(*ā*)n. id., ŚvetUp. – **kshaya**, m. loss of blood, Suśr. – **kshayaka**, mfn. suffering from loss of bl°, ŚārṅgS. – **kshīra** (*lóhita-*), mf(*ā*)n. yielding red or bloody milk, AV. – **gaṅga**, N. of a place, Hariv.; (*am*), ind. where the Ganges appears red, Pāṇ. ii, 1, 21, Sch. – **gaṅgaka**, N. of a place, KālP. – **gātra**, m. 'red-limbed,' N. of Skanda, AV. Pariś. – **grīva**, mfn. red-necked; m. N. of Agni, MBh.; MārkP. – **candana**, n. saffron, Hariv.; Bhpr. – **jahnu**, m. N. of a man (pl. his descendants), ĀśvŚr. – **tā**, f. redness, MW. – **tūla**, mfn. having red tufts, Kāṭh. – **tva**, n. redness, red colour, L. – **darśana**, n. the appearing or flowing of blood, Gaut. – **dalā**, f. a kind of Chenopodium, L. – **drapsa**, m. a drop of blood, Kauś. – **dhvaja**, mfn. having a red flag; m. pl. N. of a partic. association of persons, Pāṇ. v, 3, 112, Sch. – **nayana**, mfn. red-eyed, having eyes reddened with anger or passion, MW. – **pacanīya**, mfn. becoming red when boiled, ĀpŚr. – **pāṇsu**, mfn. having red earth, Gobh. – **pātra**, mfn. having a red vessel in one's hand, Gaut. – **pādaka**, mf(*ikā*)n. one having the soles of the feet still red (as in early childhood), Pat. – **pāda-deśa**, m. N. of a place, Cat. – **piṇḍá**, m. a red lump, ŚBr. – **pittin**, mfn. subject to hemorrhage, suffering from h°, Suśr. (cf. *rakta-p*°). – **pura**, n. N. of a place, Cat. – **pushpa** (*lóhita-*), mfn. r°-flowering, bearing r° flowers, ŚBr.; (*ī*), f. Echinops Echinatus, L. – **pushpaka**, mfn. r°-flowering, L.; m. the granate tree, Bhpr. – **pravāṇa**, mfn. having a r° border, Lāṭy. – **maya**, mf(*ī*)n. blood-red, Hcar. – **miśrá**, mfn. mixed with blood, ŚBr. – **mukti**, f. a kind of precious stone, Buddh. – **mṛittikā**, f. red earth, r° chalk, ruddle, L. – **rasa** (*lóhita-*), mfn. having red juice, ŚBr. – **rāga**, m. a red colour, red hue, MW. – **lavaṇa**, n. red salt, Kauś. – **vat** (*lóhita-*), mfn. containing blood, TS. – **varsha**, m. or n. (?) a shower of blood, bloody rain, Kauś. – **vāsas** (*lóhita-*), mfn. having red or blood-stained garments, AV.; ŚrS. – **śata-pattra**, n. a red lotus-flower, BhP. – **śabala**, mfn. variegated or dappled with r°, Pāṇ. ii, 1, 69, Sch. – **śukla-kṛishṇa**, mf(*ā*)n. red, white and black, ŚvetUp. – **sāraṅga** (*lóhita-*), mfn. = *-śabala*, q. v., ŚBr.; ŚrS. – **smṛiti**, f. N. of a law-book. 1. **Lohitâksha**, m. a red die (used in gaming), MBh. 2. **Lohitâkshá**, mf(*ī*)n. r°-eyed, ŚBr.; ŚvetUp. &c.; m. a kind of snake, Suśr.; the Indian cuckoo, L.; N. of Vishṇu, L.; of another deity, MānGṛ.; of one of Skanda's attendants, MBh.; of a man (pl., his descendants), ĀśvŚr.; (*ī*), f. N. of one of the Mātṛis attending on Skanda, MBh.; n. a part of the arm and of the thigh, the place where these are joined to the body, joint of the arm, thigh-j°, Suśr.; Bhpr.; °*ksha-saṃjñā*, f. (scil. *sirā*) an artery or vein situated either at the thigh-joint or at the arm-j°, Suśr. **Lohitâkshaka**, m. a kind of snake, L. **Lohitā-giri**, m. (*lohitā* for *lohita*) N. of a mountain, g. *kiṃśulukâdi.* **Lohitâṅga**, m. 'red-limbed,' the planet Mars, MBh.; Hariv. &c.; a partic. red powder, L. **Lohitâja**, m. a reddish he-goat, Kauś.; (*ā*), f. a red she-goat, ib. **Lohitâda**, mfn. consuming blood, MantraBr. **Lohitâdhipa**, m. the planet Mars, VP. **Lohitânana**, mfn. red-faced, r°-mouthed; m. an ichneumon, L. **Lohitā-mukhī**, f. N. of a club, R. **Lohitâyas**, n. 'red metal,' copper, L. **Lohitâyasá**, mfn. made of r° metal; m. or n. (?) a razor m° of r° met°, MaitrS.; TBr.; n. copper, MaitrS. **Lohitâraṇī**, f. N. of a river, MBh. (v. l. *loha-tāraṇī*, q. v.) **Lohitârcis**, m. 'red-rayed,' the planet Mars, VP. **Lohitârṇa**, m. N. of a son of Ghṛita-pṛishṭha, BhP.; n. N. of the Varsha ruled by that prince, ib. **Lohitârdra**, mfn. wet or dripping with blood, soaked in bl°, MBh. **Lohitârman**, n. a red swelling or blood-shot appearance in the whites of the eyes, Suśr. **Lohitâlaṃkṛita**, mfn. adorned with red, Kauś. **Lohitâlu**, m. a red-coloured sweet potato, L. **Lohitâvabhāsa**, mfn. having a red appearance, reddish, Suśr. **Lohitâśoka**, m. a red-flowering Aśoka, Kathās. **Lohitâśva**, mfn. having or driving r° horses, MBh.; m. fire, Kir.; N. of Śiva, Śivag. **Lohitâśvattha**, m. a species of tree, Kauś. **Lohitâsya**, mfn. having a red or blood-stained mouth, AV. **Lohitâhí**, m. a red snake, VS. **Lohitêkshaṇa**, mfn. r°-eyed, MBh. **Lohitêkshu**, m. r° sugar-cane, L. **Lohitaíta**, mfn. variegated with r° (= *roh*°), Pāṇ. vi, 2, 3, Sch. **Lohitôtpala**, n. the flower of Nymphaea Rubra, BhP. **Lohitôda**, mf(*ā*)n. having red water, having blood instead of w°, MBh.; R.; m. N. of a hell, Yājñ. **Lohitôrṇá**, mf(*ī*)n. having r° wool, VS. **Lohitôshṇīsha**, mfn. wearing a red turban, ŚrS.; *-tā*, f., Jaim., Comm.

2. **Lohita**, Nom. P. °*tati*, to be or become red, Vop.

Lohitaka, mf(°*tikā* or *lohinikā*)n. red, of a red colour, reddish, Āpast.; MBh. &c. (in arithm. said of the 5th unknown quantity, Col.); m. n. a ruby, Śiś. xiii, 52; m. a sort of rice, Suśr.; the planet Mars, L.; N. of a Stūpa, Buddh.; (°*tikā*), f. a partic. vein or artery, Suśr.; a species of plant, ib.; n. bell-metal or calx of brass, L.

Lohitāya, Nom. P. Ā. °*yati*, °*te*, to be or become red, redden, MBh.; Hariv.; Kād.

Lohitāyana, m. patr., Hariv.; pl., Saṃskārak.

Lohitāyani (m. c. for °*nī*), f. patr., MBh.

Lohitiman, m. redness, red colour, ŚāṅkhBr.; Gobh.

Lohitīka, n. a partic. weight or coin (3 Māshas), L.

Lohitī-√bhū, P. *-bhavati*, to be or become red, Vop.

Lohitya, m. a kind of rice, L.; N. of a man, Hariv. (v. l. *lauh*°); of the Brahma-putra river, VarBṛS. (v. l. for *lauh*°); of a village, R.; of the blood sea near Kuśa-dvīpa, L.; (*ā*), f. N. of a celestial female, Hariv. (with *jana-mātā;* v. l. *lohityāyana-m*°); of a river, MBh.

Lohinikā. See under *lohitaka* above.

Lóhinī. See under 1. *lóhita*, col. 1.

Lohinīkā, f. red glow or lustre, TBr.

Lohinya (?), m. patr., Pravar.

Lohya, n. brass, L.

लौकाक्ष **laukâksha**, m. pl. N. of a school, Divyâv. (g. *kārta-kaujapâdi*).

लौकायतिक **laukāyatika**, m. (fr. *lokâyata*) a follower of Cārvāka, a materialist, atheist, R.

लौकिक **laukika**, mf(ī)n. (fr. *loka*) worldly, terrestrial, belonging to or occurring in ordinary life, common, usual, customary, temporal, not sacred (as opp. to *vaidika*, *ārsha*, *śāstrīya*; *laukikeshu*, ind. = *loke* 'in ordinary or popular speech,' opp. to *vaidikeshu*, Nir.), ŚrS.; Mn.; MBh. &c.; (ifc.) belonging to the world of (cf. *brahma-l*°); m. common or ordinary men (as opp. to 'the learned, initiated' &c.), Śaṃk.; Sarvad.; men familiar with the ways of the world, men of the world, Uttarar.; men in general, people, mankind, MBh.; n. anything occurring in the world, general custom, usage, Śak.; MārkP.; a person's ordinary occupation, BhP. – **jña**, mfn. knowing the ways of the world, Śak. – **tva**, n. worldliness, commonness, usual custom, general prevalence, Sāh. – **nyāya**, m. a general rule or maxim; *-muktāvalī*, f., *-ratnâkara*, m., *-saṃgraha*, m. N. of wks. – **bhāna-vāda-rahasya**, n., **-vishayatā-vāda**, m., **-vishayatā-vicāra**, m. N. of wks.

Laukyà, mfn. belonging to the world, mundane, AV.; extended through the world, generally diffused, MBh.; general, usual, common, commonplace, ib.; m. N. of a man, ŚāṅkhŚr.

लौगाक्षि **laugākshi**, m. patr. fr. *logâksha*, N. of a teacher and author of a law-book, KātyŚr. – **bhāskara**, m. N. of a modern author, Cat. – **mīmāṇsā**, f., **-smṛiti**, f. N. of wks.

लौठरथ **lauṭharatha**, m. N. of a man, Rājat.

लौड् **lauḍ** (cf. √*loṭ*, *loḍ*), cl. 1. P. *lauḍati*, to be foolish or mad, Dhātup. ix, 74 (v. l.)

लौप्स **laupsa**, v. l. for *lauśa*, q. v.

लौम **lauma**, mfn. (fr. *loman*), g. *saṃkalâdi* and *śarkarâdi*.

Laumakāyana, mfn. (fr. *lomaka*), g. *pakshâdi*.

Laumakāyani, m. patr. fr. *lomaka*, g. *tikâdi*.

Laumakīya, mfn. (fr. *lomaka*), g. *kṛiśâśvâdi*.

Laumana (cf. Pāṇ. vi, 4, 167) and °**nya**, mfn. (fr. *loman*), g. *saṃkāśâdi*.

Laumaśīya, mfn. (fr. *lomaśa*), g. *kṛiśâśvâdi*.

Laumaharshaṇaka, mf(*ikā*)n. composed by Loma-harshaṇa, BhP., Introd.

Laumaharshaṇi, m. patr. fr. *loma-harshaṇa*. MBh.

Laumāyana, mfn. (fr. *loman*), g. *pakshâdi;* pl., see next.

Laumāyanya, m. patr. fr. *loman*, g. *kuñjâdi* (pl. *laumāyanāḥ*, ib.)

Laumi, m. patr. fr. *loman*, g. *bāhv-ādi*.

लौयमानि **lauyamāni**, m. patr. fr. *lūyamāna*, Pat.

लौलक **laulaka** or **laulika**, m. N. of a poet, Cat.

लौलाह **laulāha**, m. or n. (?) N. of a place, Cat.

लौल्य **laulya**, n. (fr. *lola*) restlessness, Suśr.; unsteadiness, inconstancy, fickleness, Hariv.; lustfulness, eagerness, greediness, passion, ardent longing for (loc. or comp.), MBh.; Kāv. &c. – **tā**, f. lustfulness, eager desire, BhP. – **vat**, mfn. eagerly desirous, avaricious, lustful, Kathās.

लौश **lauśa**, n. (fr. *luśa*) N. of various Sāmans, ĀrshBr. (cf. *laupsa*).

लौह **lauha**, mf(ī)n. (fr. *loha*) made of copper or iron or any metal, coppery, iron, metallic, GṛŚrS.; MBh. &c.; red, MBh.; belonging to or coming from the red-coloured goat, MārkP.; (*ā*), f. a metal or iron cooking-pot, kettle, pan, L.; n. iron, metal, Bhaṭṭ. – **kāra**, m. = *loha-k*°, a blacksmith, Hit. – **cāraka**, m. N. of a hell, L. (cf. *loha-dāraka*). – **ja**, n. = *loha-ja*, the rust of iron, L. – **pradīpa**, m. N. of a wk. on the application of metals or minerals (in medicine). – **bandha**, n. an iron chain, iron fetters, W. – **bhāṇḍa**, n. an iron vessel, metal mortar, L. – **bhū**, f. a metal pan, boiler, caldron, L. – **mala**, n. rust of iron, L. – **śaṅku**, m. = *loha-ś*°, L. – **śāstra**, n. a Śāstra treating of metals, Cat. – **sāra**, m. or n. (?) salts of iron, L. **Lauhâcārya**, m. a teacher of metallurgy or the art of working metals, ib. **Lauhâtman**, m. = *lauha-bhū*, L. **Lauhâbhisārikā-prayoga**, m. N. of wk. **Lauhâsava**, m. a partic. preparation of iron, L. **Lauhêsha**, mfn. having a metal pole (said of a carriage), Pāṇ. vi, 3, 39, Sch.

Lauhāyana, m. patr. fr. *loha*, g. *naḍâdi*.
Lauhāyasa, mfn. (fr. *lohâyasa*) made of metal or copper, GṛS.
Lauheyī, f. N. of an Apsaras, VP.

लौहि *lauhi*, m. N. of a son of Ashṭaka, Hariv.

लौहित *lauhita*, m. (fr. 1. *lohita*) the trident of Śiva, L.
Lauhitadhvaja, m. a follower of the Lohita-dhvajas, Pāṇ. v, 3, 112, Sch.
Lauhitāśva, w.r. for *lohitâśva*.
Lauhitīka, mfn. (fr. 1. *lohita*) reddish, having a reddish lustre, Pāṇ. v, 3, 110, Sch.; m. rock-crystal, Harav.
Lauhitya, m. (fr. id.) a kind of rice, Car. (cf. *lohitya*); patron. (also pl.), Hariv. (cf. g. *gargâdi*); N. of a river, the Brahma-putra, MBh.; Hariv.; of a sea, ib.; of a mountain, MBh.; (prob. n.) of a Tīrtha, ib.; n. red colour, redness, Sāh. — **bhaṭṭa-gopāla**, m. N. of an author, Cat.
Lauhityāyanī, f. (feminine form of the patr. *lauhitya*), Pāṇ. iv, 1, 18.

ल्पी *lpī* or *lyī*, cl. 9. P. *lpināti*, *lyināti*, to join, unite, mix with, Dhātup. xxxi, 31 (v.l. for √1. *lī*).

ल्यप् *lyap*, (in gram.) N. of the affix *ya* (of the ind. p.)

ल्युट् *lyuṭ*, (in gram.) N. of the Kṛit affix *ana*.

ल्वी *lvī*, cl. 9. P. *lvināti*, *lvīnāti*, to go, move, approach, Dhātup. xxxi, 32 (v.l. for √*vlī* or *plī*).
Lvīna, mfn. gone, MW.

व VA.

व 1. *va*, the 3rd semivowel (corresponding to the vowels *u* and *ū*, and having the sound of the English *v*, except when forming the last member of a conjunct consonant, in which case it is pronounced like *w*; it is often confounded and interchanged with the labial consonant *b*). — **kāra**, m. the letter or sound *va*, TPrāt.; *-bheda*, m. N. of a treatise on the proper spelling of words beginning with *v* or *b*.

व 2. *va*, (only L.) m. air, wind; the arm; N. of Varuṇa; the ocean, water; addressing; reverence; conciliation; auspiciousness; a dwelling; a tiger; cloth; the esculent root of the water-lily; (*ā*), f. going; hurting; an arrow; weaving; a weaver (?); n. a sort of incantation or Mantra (of which the object is the deity Varuṇa); = *pra-cetas*; mfn. strong, powerful.

व 3. *va*, ind. = *iva*, like, as, MBh.; Kāv. &c. (in some more or less doubtful cases).

वंश *vaṇśá*, m. (derivation doubtful) the bamboo cane or any cane (accord. to L. also 'sugar-cane' and 'Shorea Robusta'), RV. &c. &c.; the upper timbers or beams of a house, the rafters or laths fastened to the beams (of a roof; cf. *prācīna-v°*), AV. &c. &c.; a cross-beam, joist, joint, VarBṛS.; a reed-pipe, flute, fife, Kāv.; Rājat.; the back-bone, spine, VarBṛS.; BhP.; a hollow or tubular bone, BhP. (B.), Sch.; the upper nasal bone, L.; the central projecting part of a scimitar or sabre, VarBṛS.; the line of a pedigree or genealogy (from its resemblance to the succession of joints in a bamboo), lineage, race, family, stock, ŚBr. &c. &c. (esp. a noble race, a dynasty of kings, a list of teachers &c.; cf. Pāṇ. ii, 1, 19, Sch.); offspring, a son, BhP.; (ifc.) a succession or collection of similar things, assemblage, multitude, host (as of chariots, stars &c.), MBh.; Kāv. &c.; a partic. measure of length (= 10 Hastas), Līl.; a partic. musical note, Śiś.; pride, arrogance, Vās.; bamboo-manna, L.; N. of Vishṇu, L.; (*ā*), f. N. of an Apsaras (daughter of Prādhā), MBh.; (*ī*), f., see s.v. — **ṛishi**, m. a Ṛishi mentioned in a Vaṇśa-Brāhmaṇa (or list of ancient teachers), Śaṃk. — **kaṭhina**, m. a clump or thicket of bamboos, Pāṇ. iv, 4, 72, Sch. (cf. *vāṇśakaṭhinika*). — **kapha**, n. 'bamboo-phlegm,' cottony or flocculent seeds floating in the air, L. — **kara**, m. making or founding a family, propagating or perpetuating a race, MBh.; R.; m. an ancestor, ib.; a son, Vikr.; N. of a man, Cat.; (*ā*), f. N. of a river rising in the Mahêndra mountains, MārkP. — **karpūra-rocanā**, f. = *vaṇśa-rocanā*, L. — **karman**, n. bamboo-work, manufacture of baskets &c.; °*ma-kṛit*, mfn. doing bamboo- or basket-work, R. — **kīrti**, mfn. having family renown, celebrated, W. — **kṛit**, mfn. = *vaṇśa-karma-kṛit*, R.; m. the founder of a family, BhP. — **kṛitya**, n. flute-playing, Ragh. — **kramâgata**, mfn. descended or inherited lineally, coming from a family in regular succession, obtained by family inheritance, Kām.; Hit. — **kramâhita-gaurava**, mfn. highly esteemed by the successive generations of a family, Hcar. — **kshaya**, m. family decay, W. — **kshīrī**, f. b°-manna, L. — **ga**, f. id., L. — **gulma**, N. of a sacred bathing-place, MBh. — **goptṛi**, m. the supporter or preserver of a family, MBh. — **ghaṭikā**, f. a kind of children's game, Divyâv. — **carita**, n. family history, the history of a race or dynasty, genealogy, W. — **carma-kṛit**, m. a worker in b° and leather, R. — **cintaka**, m. an investigator of pedigrees, genealogist, Hariv. — **cchettṛi**, m. one who cuts off the line of descent, the last of a family or race, VarBṛS. — **ja**, mfn. made of or produced from b°, W.; born in the family of, belonging to the family of (loc. or comp.), Kāv.; Var.; Rājat.; belonging to the same family (plur. with *prāktanāḥ* = forefathers, ancestors), Kāv.; sprung from a good family, W.; m. the seed of the bamboo, L.; n. and (*ā*), f. b°-manna, L. — **taṇḍula**, m. the seed of the b°, L. — **dalā**, f. a kind of plant or grass (= *vaṇśa-pattrī*, *jīrikā*), L. — **dhara**, mfn. carrying or holding a b°-cane &c., W.; maintaining or supporting a family, MBh.; R. &c.; m. the continuer of a family, VP.; a descendant, BhP.; (with *miśra*) N. of an author, Cat. — **dhānya**, m. n. the seed of the b°, L. — **dhārā**, f. N. of a river rising in the Mahêndra mountains, VP. — **dhārin**, mfn. = *vaṇśa-dhara*, Pañcar. — **nartín**, m. 'family-dancer,' a buffoon, VS. — **nāḍikā** or **-nāḍī**, f. a pipe or tube made of bamboo, Kathās. — **nātha**, m. the head of a family, chief of a race, R. — **nālikā**, f. a pipe made of b°, a reed, flute, L. (cf. *nāḍikā*). — **niśreṇī**, f. a ladder made of b°, Pañcat. — **netra**, n. a kind of sugar-cane, the root of s°-c° (= *ikshu-mūla*), L. — **pattra**, n. a b°-leaf, VarBṛS.; sulphuret of arsenic, L.; a kind of metre (= *vaṇśa-pattra-patita*), Col.; m. a reed, L.; (*ī*), f. a partic. kind of grass, L.; the resin of Gardenia Gummifera, Bhpr.; *-patita*, mfn. fallen on a b°-leaf; n. a species of metre, VarBṛS.; *-haritāla*, n. bamboo-leaved orpiment, L. — **pattraka**, m. (only L.) a reed; white sugar-cane; a sort of fish, Cynoglossus Lingua; n. yellow orpiment, L. — **paramparā**, f. family succession, lineage, descent, W. — **pātra**, n. a bamboo vessel (also *ī*, f.), KātyŚr., Sch.; *-kāriṇī*, f. a woman who makes b° vessels or baskets, MW. — **pīta**, m. a kind of bdellium, L. — **pushpā**, f. a species of creeper, L. — **pūraka**, n. the root of the sugar-cane (= *ikshu-mūla*), L. — **pota**, m. 'b°-shoot' and 'child of a good family,' Vās. — **pratishṭhāna-kāra**, m. one who establishes his family on a firm foundation, R. — **bāhya**, mf(*ā*)n. repudiated by a family, Hcar. — **brāhmaṇa**, n. N. of a Brāhmaṇa (belonging to the Sāma-veda and containing a chronological list of ancient teachers); of a part of the Śata-patha Brāhmaṇa (xiv, 5, 5, 20–22). — **bhava**, mfn. 'made of b°' and 'descended from a noble race,' Bhām. — **bhāra**, m. a load of b°s, Pāṇ. v, 1, 50. — **bhṛit**, m. the supporter or perpetuator of a family, head of a race, MBh.; Kathās. — **bhojya**, mfn. to be possessed by a family, hereditary; n. (with *rājya*) an hereditary estate, MBh. — **maya**, mf(*ī*)n. made of b°, KātyŚr., Sch. — **mūla**, n. the root of the sugar-cane, L. — **mūlaka**, n. N. of a sacred bathing-place, MBh. — **mṛin-maya**, mf(*ī*)n. made of b° and clay, L. — **yava**, m. the grain of b°, L. — **rāja**, m. a high or lofty b°, Hariv.; N. of a king (*-kula*, n. his race), Lalit. — **rājya-dhara**, mfn. perpetuating race and dominion, Kathās. — **rocanā** or **-locanā**, f. an earthy concretion of a milk-white colour formed in the hollow of a b° and called b°-manna, L. (also *-locana*, Car.) — **lakshmī**, f. the family fortune, MW. — **lūna**, mfn. cut off from one's family, alone in the world, Ml. — **varṇa**, m. the chick pea, Cicer Arietinum, L. — **vartin**, m. a partic. class of gods in the third Manv-antara, VP. — **vardhana**, mf(*ī*)n. increasing or prospering a family, Vikr.; n. the act of causing prosperity to a family, R.; m. a son, Daś. — **vardhin**, mfn. = prec., MBh. — **vitati**, f. a clump or thicket of bamboos, Kir.; family descent, W. — **vidāriṇī**, f. a woman whose employment is to split b°, MW. — **viśuddha**, mfn. (made) of a good b°, W.; of a pure or good family, ib. — **vistara**, m. a complete genealogy, VP. — **vṛiddhi**, f. prosperity of a family, W. — **śarkarā**, f. = *-rocanā*, L. — **śalākā**, f. a b° peg or screw at the lower end of a Vīṇā or lute, (accord. to some) the b° pipe that forms the body of the lute, L.; any small b° pin or stake (as the bar of a cage &c.), W. — **samâcāra**, m. family usage, W. — **stanita**, v.l. for *-sthavila*, Chandom. — **stūpa**, n. the uppermost beam of a house (that supports the roof), ĀpGṛ., Sch. — **stha**, n. (or *ā*, f.?) a partic. metre (= *vaṇśa-sthavila*), Piṅg. — **sthavila**, n. the hollow or cavity of a b° cane; N. of a species of Jagatī metre (used in the beginning of the Ṛitu-saṃhāra), Chandom. — **sthiti**, f. the state or condition of a family, Kālid. — **hīna**, mfn. destitute of family or descendants, having no kindred, Hit. **Vaṇśâgata**, mfn. coming from one's family, inherited, obtained by inheritance, Kām. **Vaṇśâgra**, n. the point or end of a b° cane, the shoot of a bamboo, Sāy. **Vaṇśâṅkura**, m. a b° shoot or sprout, L. **Vaṇśânukīrtana**, n. the recounting or proclaiming a family or a genealogy, Cat. **Vaṇśânukrama**, m. family succession, genealogy, lineal inheritance, Ragh. **Vaṇśânuga**, mfn. being on or along the central projecting part of a sword, VarBṛS.; passing from family to family, Rājat. **Vaṇśânucarita**, n. the history of a family or dynasty, a genealogical list (one of the five distinguishing marks of a Purāṇa), BhP.; IW. 511. **Vaṇśânuvaṇśa-carita**, n. the history of both old and recent families (see prec.), L. **Vaṇśântara**, m. Amphidonax Karka, L. **Vaṇśā-vatī**, f. a proper N., g. *śarâdi* on Pāṇ. vi, 3, 120. **Vaṇśâvalī**, f. the line of a family, pedigree, genealogy, L. **Vaṇśâhva**, m. bamboo-manna, L. **Vaṇśôdbheda**, N. of a Tīrtha, MatsyaP.

Vaṇśaka, m. a kind of large sugar-cane, Suśr.; a tubular bone, R. (B.), Sch.; a small fish, Cynoglossus Lingua, L.; N. of a prince, VP.; (*ikā*), f. a kind of pipe or flute, L.; aloe wood, Agallochum, L.; n. Agallochum, L.

Vaṇśika, mfn. belonging or relating to a bamboo, pertaining to a family &c., lineal, genealogical, W.; m. a measure of 4 Stomas, L.; the son of a Śūdra and a Veṇī, L.; n. aloe wood, L.

Vaṇśin, mfn. belonging to a family (cf. *sva-v°*).

Vaṇśi-vādya, prob. w.r. for *vaṇśī-v°* (q.v.)

Vaṇśī, f. a flute, pipe, Pañcar.; an artery, vein, L.; a partic. measure (cf. *vaṇśika*), L.; a partic. weight (= 4 Karshas), L.; bamboo manna, L. — **gīta**, n. playing on a flute, Vṛishabhān. — **dāsa**, m. N. of an author, Cat. — **dhara**, mfn. holding a flute (said of Kṛishṇa), Pañcar.; m. (also with *daiva-jña* and *śarman*) N. of various authors and other men, Cat. — **rava**, m. the sound of a flute, Gīt. — **vadana**, m. (with *śarman*) N. of an author, Cat. — **vādya** (?), n. a flute, Tithyâd. (cf. *vaṇśi-v°*).

Vaṇśīya, mfn. belonging to a family, of a good family, of the same family, BhP.

Vaṇśya, mfn. = prec., peculiar to a family, genealogical, lineal, Mn.; MBh. &c.; belonging or attached to a main beam, BhP.; connected with the back-bone or spine (as subst. 'a bone in the arm or leg'), BhP.; preceding any one (gen.) in a science (loc.), being a person's teacher in anything, Āpast.; m. any member of a family, a son, lineal descendant; an ancestor, forefather; a kinsman from seven generations above and seven below, Mn.; MBh. &c.; a pupil, scholar, W. (cf. Pāṇ. ii, 1, 19); pl. the members of a family, ancestors or descendants, Mn.; MBh. &c.; a cross-beam, joist, BhP.; (*ā*), f. coriander, L. **Vaṇśyânucarita**, v.l. for *vaṇśân°*, BhP.

वंसग *váṇsaga*, m. a bull, RV.; AV.

वंह् *vaṇh*. See √*baṇh*, p. 719.
Vaṇhishṭha, **vaṇhīyas**. See *baṇh°*, ib.

वक् 1. *vak* = √*vac*, in the Vedic form *vivakmi*.

वक् 2. *vak* or *vaṅk* (connected with √*vañc*, q.v.), cl. 1. Ā. *vaṅkate*, to be crooked, go crookedly, Dhātup. iv, 14; to go, roll, ib. 21 (only 3. pl. pf. *vāvakre*, 'they rolled,' RV. vii, 21, 3).

Vaka &c. See *baka*, p. 719.

Vakrá, mf(*ā*)n. crooked, curved, bent, tortuous, twisted, wry, oblique, AV. &c. &c.; curled, curly (as hair), AV. &c. &c.; having an apparently backward motion, retrograde (said of planets), Sūryas.;

Var. &c.; (in prosody) long (the form of the long mark being curved); crooked in disposition, cunning, fraudulent, dishonest, evasive, ambiguous, KaṭhUp.; MBh. &c.; hostile, cruel, malignant, inauspicious, Kāv.; Kathās.; Sāh.; m. a nose, L.; the planet Mars, VarBṛS.; the planet Saturn, L.; a partic. drug (=*parpaṭa*), L.; N. of Rudra, L.; of the Asura Bāṇa, L.; of a prince of the Karūshas, MBh. (v.l. *vaktra*); of a Rākshasa, R.; pl. N. of a people, VP. (v.l. *cakra*); (*ā*), f. a partic. musical instrument, Lāṭy.; (scil. *gati*) a partic. variation in the course of Mercury, VarBṛS.; n. the winding course of a river, the arm or bend of a stream, ŚvetUp.; the apparent retrograde motion of a planet, MBh.; Hariv.; VarBṛS.; a form of fracture (when a bone is bent or only partially broken), Suśr.; w.r. for *vaktra*. **–kaṇṭa**, m. 'having crooked thorns,' the jujube tree, L.; = next, L. **–kaṇṭaka**, m. Acacia Catechu, L. **–kīla**, m. a curved iron for striking an elephant, L. **–khaḍga** or **-khaḍgaka**, m. a curved sword, scimetar, sabre, L. **–ga** or **-gata**, mfn. having a retrograde motion (as a planet), Sūryas.; VarBṛS. **–gati**, mfn. = prec., BhP.; = *-gāmin*, Hariv.; f. crooked or winding course, apparent retrograde motion or retrogression (said of the course of a planet), Sūryas. **–gandha-nibandha-kṛit**, m. N. of the poet Bāṇa, Cat. **–gamana**, n. = *-gati*, f., MBh. **–gāmin**, m. going crookedly, fraudulent, dishonest, Hariv. **–grīva**, m. 'having a curved neck,' a camel, L. **–cañcu**, m. 'having a curved beak,' a parrot, L. **–tā**, f. crookedness, curvedness, tortuousness, Śiś.; MārkP.; (in astron.) retrograde motion, Sūryas.; the going crookedly or wrong, failure, mishap, L.; ambiguity, perverseness, falseness, Prasannar. **–tāla**, n. or **-tālī**, f. a partic. wind-instrument, L. (cf. *-nāla*). **–tuṇḍa**, mfn. having a curved beak, BhP.; m. a parrot, L.; N. of Gaṇeśa (as having an elephant's curved trunk), TĀr.; *-gaṇa-nāyaka-prakaraṇa*, n., *-pūjā-vidhi*, m., *-stavana*, n., *-stotra*, n.; °*dâshṭaka*, n. N. of wks. **–todin**, mfn. stinging or pricking treacherously, MantraBr. **–tva**, n. = *-tā*, Kāv.; Kathās. **–daṇshṭra**, m. 'having curved tusks,' a boar, L. (w.r. *vaktra-d*°). **–danta**, m. N. of a prince of the Karūshas, MBh. (v.l. *danta-vakra* and *danta-vaktra*). **–dantī-bīja**, m. Croton Jamalgota, L. **–dala**, w.r. for *vaktra-d*°. **–dṛiś**, mfn. looking obliquely, squinting, Gal. **–dṛishṭi**, mfn. id.; jealous, envious, MW.; f. oblique vision, an oblique look, malignant regard, hostile view, ib. **–dhī**, mfn. deceitful, dishonest, BhP.; f. deceitfulness, dishonesty, ib. **–nakra**, m. 'having a curved beak,' a parrot, L.; a low or depraved man, L. **–nāla**, n. a sort of wind-instrument, L. (cf. *-tāla*). **–nāsa**, mfn. having a curved nose or beak, R.; Pañcat.; m. N. of the councillor of an owl-king, Kathās.; Pañcat. **–nāsika**, m. 'having a curved beak,' an owl, L. **–paksha**, mfn. having bent or curved wings, Śulbas. **–pada**, n. a cloth marked with various patterns, L. **–pāda**, mfn. crooked-legged, Kathās.; m. N. of Gaṇeśa, Gal. **–puccha** or **-pucchika**, m. 'curly-tailed,' a dog, L. **–pura**, n. N. of a town, Kathās. **–pushpa**, m. Butea Frondosa, L.; Agati Grandiflora, L.; another plant (=*baka*), L. **–pluta**, mfn. leaping in curves, Kathās. **–buddhi**, mfn. 'crooked-minded,' deceitful, false, Hcat. **–bhaṇita**, n. indirect speech, equivocation, evasion, Ratnāv. (in Prākṛit). **–bhāva**, m. curvature, crookedness, Piṅg., Sch.; cunning, craft, deceit, Prab. **–bhuja**, m. 'crooked-armed,' N. of Gaṇeśa, Gal. **–mati**, mfn. = *-buddhi*, MBh. **–yodhin**, m. 'fighting deceitfully,' N. of a Dānava, VP. **–rekhā**, f. a curved line, MW. **–lāṅgūla**, m. = *-puccha*, L. **–vaktra**, m. 'having a curved snout,' a boar, L. **–vākya**, n. ambiguous speech, Śiś. (w.r. *vaktra-v*°). **–vāladhi**, m. = *-puccha*, L. **–śalyā**, f. Capparis Sepiaria, L.; Abrus Precatorius, L. **–śriṅga**, mf(*ī*)n. having crooked or curved horns, Col. **–saṃstha**, mfn. placed transversely, MW. **Vakrâkhya**, n. tin, L. **Vakrâgra**, n. N. of a plant, L. **Vakrâṅga**, n. (ifc. f. *ī*) a crooked limb, Hariv.; w.r. for *vakrâṅghri* (q.v.), Rājat.; m. 'having a curved body,' a goose; the ruddy goose, L.; a snake, L. **Vakrâṅghri**, m. a crooked foot; *-saṃgrāma*, m. (prob.) a treacherous fight, Rājat. **Vakrêtara**, mfn. 'other than crooked,' straight, not curled (as hair), Ragh. **Vakrôkti**, f. indirect mode of expression, Kull. on Mn. iii, 133; a figure of speech consisting in the use of evasive speech or reply (either by means of a pun, or by an affected change of tone, e.g. Mudr. i, 1), Kpr.; *-jīvita*, n., *-pañcāśikā*, f. N. of wks. **Vakr'-oshṭhi**, f. (L.), °**shṭhika**, n. (L.) or °**shṭhikā**, f. (HPariś.) a slight smile, one in which the lips are drawn on one side without the teeth being shown.

Vakratu, m. N. of a deity, MārkP.

Vakri, mfn. equivocating, prevaricating, lying, L.

Vakrita, mfn. curved, crooked, bent, Amar.; Naish.; entering on an apparently retrograde course (as a planet), VarBṛS.

Vakrin, mfn. crooked, W.; bending the neck (as a singer), Saṃgīt.; retrograding, moving apparently backwards (said of Mars and other planets), Sūryas.; dishonest, fraudulent, W.; m. a weakling of a partic. kind, Car.; a Jaina or Buddha, L.

Vakrima, mfn. bent, curved, Amar. (v.l. for *vakrita*).

Vakriman, m. crookedness, curvature, Kāv.; ambiguity, duplicity, Sāh.

Vakrī, in comp. for *vakra*. **–karaṇa**, n. curving, bending, distorting, W. **–√kṛi**, P. *-karoti*, to make crooked or curved, bend (a bow), Bālar. **–kṛita**, mfn. made crooked or curved, bent, Gol., Sch. **–bhāva**, m. curvature, curve, W.; fraudulent or dishonest disposition, ib. **–√bhū**, P. *-bhavati*, to become crooked or bent, Suśr.; to retrograde (said of planets), MBh., Sch. **–bhūta**, mfn. bent, crooked, W.; dishonest, ib.; inauspicious, hostile, adverse, Cāṇ.

Vákva, mfn. winding about, rolling, bubbling (as Soma), RV.

Vákvan, mf(*arī*)n. id., ib.

Vaṅka, m. 'roaming about,' a vagabond, Bhadrab.; crookedness, W.; the bend or elbow of a river, L.; = *nadī-pātra*, L.; = f., L.; (*ā*), f. the pummel of a saddle, L. **–sena**, m. a kind of tree (cf. *vaṅga-s*°).

Vaṅkaṭaka, m. N. of a mountain, Kathās.

Vaṅkara, m. = *vaṅka*, the bend of a river, L.

Vaṅkâlakâcārya, m. (Prākṛ. for *vakrâl*°?) N. of an astronomer (who wrote in Prākṛit), Cat.

Vaṅkālā, f. N. of a place, Rājat.

Vaṅkinī, f. a species of plant, L.

Vaṅkima-dāsa, m. (Prākṛ. for *vakrima-d*°?), with *kavi-rāja*, N. of an author, Cat.

Vaṅkila, m. a thorn, L.

Vaṅkú, mfn. going crookedly or hurriedly, hastening, rash, RV.

Vaṅkya, mfn. crooked, curved, flexible, pliant, Pāṇ. vii, 3, 63, Sch.

Vaṅkri, f. a rib, the rib of any animal (as of a horse, said to have 34 ribs, or of an ox, said to have 26, &c.), RV.; Br.; ŚrS.; BhP. (also *ī*, f.); the ribs or timber of a roof, L.; a partic. musical instrument, L.

वकल *vákala*, m. inner rind or bark, bast, TBr.; ŚāṅkhBr.

वकसुहाण *vakasuhāṇa*, m. or n. (?) N. of a place, L.

वकुल *vakula* &c. See *bakula*.

वकुश *vakuśa*, m. a partic. animal living in the foliage of trees, Suśr.

वकेरुका *vakerukā*, *vakoṭa*. See *bak*°.

वक्क् *vakk*, cl. 1. Ā. *vakkate*, to go, Dhātup. iv, 27 (v.l.)

वक्कलिन् *vakkalin*, m. (Prākṛ. for *valkalin*) N. of a Ṛishi, Buddh.

वक्कस *vakkasa*, prob. w.r. for *vakvasa*.

वक्कुल *vakkula*, m. N. of a man, Buddh. (v.l. *vatkula* and *vakula*).

वक्तव्य *vaktavya*, *vaktṛi*, *vaktra* &c. See p. 912, cols. 1, 2.

वक्र *vakra* &c. See p. 910, col. 3.

वक्रम *va-krama*, m. (for *ava-krama*) flight, retreat, L.

वक्रय *va-kraya*, m. (for *ava-kraya*), price, L.

वक्रातप *vakrātapa*, m. pl. N. of a people, MBh. (B. *cakrāti*).

वक्रोलक *vakrolaka*, m. N. of a village, Kathās.; of a town, ib.

वक्व *vákva*, *vákvan*. See above.

वक्वस *vakvasa*, m. a partic. intoxicating drink, Suśr. &c.

वक्ष् *vaksh* (cf. √1. *uksh*), cl. 1. P. (Dhātup. xvii, 11) *vakshati* (pf. *vavaksha*, fut. *vakshitā* &c., Gr.; really there occur only the pf. forms *vavákṣha*, *vavákshitha*, *vavakshatuḥ*, *vavakshúḥ*, *vavakshé*, *vavakshire*), to grow, increase, be strong or powerful, RV.; to be angry, Dhātup.: Caus. *vakshayati*, to make grow, cause to be strong, RV. [Cf. Gk. ἀέξω, αὐξάνω; Lith. *áugti*; Goth. *wahsjan*; Germ. *wahsan*, *wachsen*; Angl. Sax. *weaxan*; Eng. *wax*; see also under √1. *uksh*.]

Vakshaḥ, in comp. for *vakshas*. **–sammardinī**, f. a wife (as 'pressing or reclining on her husband's breast'), MW. **–stha**, mfn. being on or in the breast, Kathās. **–sthala**, n. the place of the breast, bosom, heart, MW.

1. **Vákshaṇa**, mf(*ī*)n. strengthening, refreshing, invigorating, RV. x, 64, 9 (cf. *vi-* and *vīra-v*°); n. refreshment, invigoration, ib. vi, 23, 6; the breast, L. (cf. *vakshas*); (*ṇá*), f. 'nourisher,' the stomach, abdomen, interior, cavity; the sides, flank, RV.; AV.; Kauś. (others also 'udder,' = *yoni*, lit. and fig., &c.); the bed of a river, RV. iii, 33, 12; a river, Naigh. i, 13; refreshment, oblation, RV. v, 52, 15.

Vakshaṇi, mfn. strengthening, making strong, RV.

Vakshátha, m. invigoration, increase, growth, ib.

Vakshas, in comp. for *vakshas*. **–chada**, m. 'breast-cover,' armour, L.

Vákshas, n. sg. and pl. (cf. *vakshaṇa* and *pakshas*) the breast, bosom, chest, RV. &c. &c.; m. an ox, bullock, L. **–kāra**, m. a bag, sack or bag-like receptacle (prob. for keeping valuable things, and so called from being borne upon the breast, applied to sections of Jaina wks.; cf. *karaṇḍaka* and *piṭaka*). **–kārikā**, f. (prob.) id., Uttamac. **–taṭâghāta**, m. a blow on the region of the chest, MW.

Vakshasi-ja, m. = *vaksho-ja*, L.

Vaksho, in comp. for *vakshas*. **–grīva**, m. N. of a son of Viśvāmitra, MBh. **–ja**, m. du. 'rising out of the chest,' the female breast, Kāv.; Sāh. (*-tā*, f., Bhām.) **–maṇi**, m. a jewel worn on the breast, Śiś. **–maṇḍalin**, m. (scil. *hasta*) a partic. position of the hands in dancing, Cat. **–ruh** (Dhūrtas.) or **-ruha** (L.), m. = *-ja*.

वक्षण 2. *vakshaṇa*, m. (√*vah*), prob. 'rushing along,' N. of Agni (see next). **Vakshaṇeshṭhá**, mfn. being in Agni or fire, RV. v, 19, 5 (Sāy.)

Vakshī, f. a flame, RV. v, 19, 5 (cf. prec.)

वक्षु *vakshu*, (prob.) m. the Oxus, VarBṛS. (cf. *vaṅkshu*).

वक्ष्यमाण *vakshyamāṇa*. See p. 912, col. 2.

वख् *vakh* (cf. √*vaṅkh*), cl. 1. P. *vakhati*, to go, move, Dhātup. v, 16.

वगला *vagalā*, f. a goddess worshipped by the Tāntrikas, Cat. **–kalpa**, m., **-paṭala**, m. or n., **-mantra-sādhana**, n., **-vidhāna**, n., **-sahasra-nāman**, n. N. of wks. **–mukhī**, f. = *vagalā*, Cat.; *-kavaca*, n., *-dīpa-dāna*, n., *-pañcâṅga*, n., *-paddhati*, f., *-prakaraṇa*, n., *-stotra*, n. N. of wks.

वगाह *va-gāha*, m. (for *ava-gāha*) bathing, ablution, Vop.

Va-gāhya, ind. having bathed or dipped into or entered, MW.

वग्नु *vagnu*, *vagvana*, *vagvanu*. See p. 912, col. 2.

वघा *vághā*, f. a kind of noxious animal, AV. **–pati**, m. the male of the Vaghā, ib.

वङ्क् *vaṅk*. See √2. *vak*.

Vaṅka, **vaṅkaṭaka** &c. See under √2. *vak*, col. 2.

वङ्क्षण *vaṅkshaṇa*, n. (cf. 1. *vakshaṇa*) the groin, the pubic and iliac regions (also *ā*, f.), VarBṛS.; Suśr.; the thigh-joint, MW.

वङ्क्षु *vaṅkshu*, f. an arm or branch of the Ganges, W. (cf. *vaṅka*, *vaṅku*); the Oxus, MBh.; Pur. (cf. *vakshu*).

वङ्ख् *vaṅkh* (cf. √*vakh*), cl. 1. P. *vaṅkhati*, to go, move, Dhātup. v, 17.

वङ्खर *vaṅkhara*, mfn. = *cāru* (applied to a body), Pañcar.; m. N. of a man (see next). **–bhaṇ-**

dîratha, m. the descendants of Vaṅkhara and Bhaṇḍīratha, g. *tika-kitavâdi.*

वङ्ग् *vaṅg*, cl. 1. P. *vaṅgati*, to go, Dhātup. v, 39; to go lamely, limp, Vop.

वङ्ग *vaṅga*, m. Bengal proper or the eastern parts of the modern province (pl. its inhabitants), AV.Pariś.; MBh. &c.; N. of a king of the lunar race (son of Dīrgha-tamas or Dīrgha-tapas and Su-deshṇā, regarded as the common ancestor of the people of Bengal), MBh.; Hariv.; Pur.; a tree, AitĀr.; a species of tree, Hcar. (v.l. *vaṅgaka*); N. of a mountain, Jātak.; m. n. cotton, L.; Solanum Melongena, L.; n. tin or lead, L. **-ja**, n. brass, red-lead, L. **-jīvana**, n. silver, L. **-datta-vaidyaka** (?), N. of a wk. by Vaṅga-sena. **-dāsa**, m. N. of an author, Cat. **-deśa**, m. the country of Bengal, MW. **-lipi**, f. Bengal writing, Lalit. **-śulbaja** (?), n. brass, bell-metal, L. **-sena**, m. a kind of tree, L. (cf. *vaṅka-s°*); N. of a medical writer (author of the Cikitsā-sāra-saṃgraha), Bhpr.; of a grammarian, Cat. **-senaka**, m. Agati Grandiflora, L. **Vaṅgâri**, m. yellow orpiment, L. **Vaṅgêśvara-rasa**, m. a partic. medical preparation, L.

Vaṅgaka, m. a species of tree, Hcar. (v.l. *vaṅga*).

Vaṅgana, m. the egg-plant, Solanum Melongena, W. (cf. *vaṅga*).

Vaṅgīya, mfn. relating or belonging to Vaṅga, Bengal, g. *gahâdi.*

वङ्गर *vaṅgara*, m. N. of a prince, VP.

वङ्गला *vaṅgalā*, f. (in music) a partic. Rāgiṇī, L.

Vaṅgāla, m. N. of a son of the Rāga Bhairava, L.; (*ī*), f. N. of the wife of the Rāga Bhairava (also *ikā*, f.), ib.

Vaṅgulā, f. = *vaṅgalā*, W.

वङ्गिरि *vaṅgiri*, m. N. of a king, BhP.

वङ्गृद *váṅgṛida*, m. N. of a demon, RV.

वङ्गेरिका *vaṅgerikā*, f. a small basket, Daś.

वङ्घ् *vaṅgh*, cl. 1. Ā. *vaṅghate*, to go; to set out; to begin; to move swiftly; to blame or censure, Dhātup. iv, 36.

वङ्घ *vaṅgha*, m. a kind of tree, Kauś. (cf. *vaṅga*).

वच् *vac*, cl. 2. P. (Dhātup. xxiv, 55) *vakti* (occurs only in sg. *vacmi, vakshi, vakti*, and Impv. *vaktu*; Ved. also cl. 3. P. *vívakti*; pf. *uvắca, ūcé*, RV. &c. &c.; *uváktha*, AV.; *va-vāca, vavakshé*, RV.; aor. *avocat*, °*cata*, RV. &c. &c.; in Veda also Subj. *vocati*, °*te, vocāti*; Pot. *vocét*, °*ceta*; Impv. *vocatu*; Prec. *ucyāsam*, Br.; fut. *vaktā*, ib. &c.; *vakshyáti*, RV. &c. &c.; °*te*, MBh.; Cond. *avakshyat*, Br.; Up.; inf. *váktum*, Br. &c.; °*tave*, RV.; °*tos*, Br.; ind. p. *uktvā*, Br. &c.; *-úcya*, ib.), to speak, say, tell, utter, announce, declare, mention, proclaim, recite, describe (with acc. with or without *prati*, dat. or gen. of pers., and acc. of thing; often with double acc., e. g. *tam idaṃ vākyam uvāca*, 'he spoke this speech to him;' with double acc. also 'to name, call,' Ā. with nom. 'one's self;' with *punar*, 'to speak again, repeat;' or 'to answer, reply'), RV. &c. &c.; to reproach, revile (acc.), Hariv.; R.: Pass. *ucyáte* (aor. *avāci*, or in later language *avoci*), to be spoken or said or told or uttered &c., RV. &c. &c. (*yad ucyate*, 'what the saying is'); to resound, RV.; to be called or accounted, be regarded as, pass for (nom., L. also loc.), Mn.; MBh. &c.: Caus. *vācayati*, °*te* (Pot. *vācayīta*, ĀśvGṛ.; aor. *avīvacat*; Pass. *vācyate*), to cause to say or speak or recite or pronounce (with double acc.; often the object is to be supplied), Br.; GṛS.; MBh. &c.; to cause anything written or printed to speak, i. e. to read out loud, Hariv.; Kāv.; Kathās. &c.; (Dhātup. xxxiv, 35) to say, tell, declare, Bhaṭṭ.; to promise, MBh.: Desid. *vivakshati*, °*te* (Pass. *vivakshyate*), to desire to say or speak or recite or proclaim or declare, MBh.; Kāv. &c.; (Pass.) to be meant, Saṃk.; Sarvad.: Intens. (only *ávāvacīt*) to call or cry aloud, RV. x, 102, 6. [Cf. Gk. ἐπ for Ϝεπ in ἔπος, εἶπον, ὄψ, ὄσσα &c.; Lat. *vocare, vox*; Germ. *gi-waht, gi-wahinnen, er-wähnen.*]

Váktave, Ved. inf. of √*vac* (cf. above), RV. vii, 31, 5 (Sāy. '*váktu*, mfn. speaking harshly, reviling').

Vaktavyà, mf(*ā*)n. to be (or being) spoken or said or uttered or declared, fit to be said or spoken &c., ŚBr. &c. &c. (n. impers. 'it should be said' &c.); to be named or called, VarBṛS.; to be spoken to or addressed, to be told (with acc. of thing), MBh.; Kāv. &c.; to be spoken about or against, objectionable, reprehensible, vile, low, bad, Mn.; MBh. &c.; liable to be called to account, accountable or answerable or responsible or subject to, dependent on (gen. or comp.), MBh.; R.; n. speaking, speech, Pañcat.; blame, censure, Mṛicch.; a rule, dictum, aphorism, W. **-tā**, f., **-tva**, n. the state of being fit or proper to be said or spoken or spoken to or about or against, reproachableness, blamableness, the having a bad name, accountableness or subjection to, dependence, Mn.; MBh. &c. **-hṛidaya**, mfn. (ifc.) one whose heart is accountable to or dependent on, R.

Vakti, f. speech (cf. *ukti*), BṛĀrUp. (ŚBr. *vacas*).

Vaktu, in comp. for inf. *vaktum*. **-kāma**, mfn. desirous of speaking, intending to speak, ŚārṅgP. **-manas**, mfn. having a mind to speak, being about to speak, MW.

Vaktṛí, mfn. one who speaks, a speaker, proclaimer of (Ved. gen.; Class. gen., acc., or comp.) RV. &c. &c.; croaking (said of frogs), Subh.; speaking sensibly, eloquent, L.; learned, wise, W.; honest, sincere, ib.; loquacious, talkative, ib.; m. a speaker, orator, MBh.; Kāv. &c.; an expounder, teacher, Sarvad. **-tā**, f. ability to speak, talkativeness, eloquence, Śatr. **-tva**, n. id., Kshem.; *-śakti*, f. power of speech, MW.

Vaktṛika (ifc.) = *vaktṛi*, speaking, a speaker, Kap., Sch.

Váktos. See under √*vac.*

Vaktra, n. 'organ of speech,' the mouth, face, muzzle, snout, proboscis, jaws, beak &c., Mn.; MBh. &c. (*vaktraṃ* √*kṛi*, to open the mouth, gape); the point (of an arrow), MBh.; the spout (of a jug or vessel, see *a-vaktra*); beginning, commencement, Gaṇit.; (in alg.) the initial quantity or first term of a progression, Col.; a metre containing 4 × 8 syllables, Kāvyâd.; a sort of garment, L.; the root of Tabernaemontana Coronaria, L.; m. N. of a king of the Karūshas, MW. (v.l. *vakra*). **-khura**, m. (prob. for *-kshura*, 'mouth-razor') a tooth, L. **-cchada**, m. a cloth covering the face (of an elephant), Śiś. **-ja**, m. 'mouth-born,' a tooth, L.; 'sprung from the m° (of Brahmā),' a Brāhman, L. **-tāla**, n. a wind-instrument (said also to mean 'making a noise by striking the m° with the hand at the moment of uttering sound'), L. (cf. *vakra-t°*). **-tuṇḍa**, m. 'having a proboscis on the face,' N. of Gaṇêśa, L. (cf. *vakra-t°*). **-daṇshṭra**, w.r. for *vakra-d°*. **-dala**, n. 'part of the mouth,' the palate, L. **-dvāra**, n. the aperture of the mouth, Pañcat. **-paṭa**, (ifc. f. *ā*) a veil, Rājat. **-paṭṭa**, m. 'nose-bag,' a bag containing corn tied round a horse's head, L. **-parispanda**, m. 'm°-motion,' speech, discourse, MBh. i, 2233. **-bhedin**, mfn. 'mouth-cutting,' pungent, bitter, L. **-yodhin**, m. 'fighting with the mouth,' N. of an Asura, Hariv. **-ruha**, m. or n. (?) 'face-growing,' hair growing on the face or on the proboscis of an elephant, VarBṛS. **-roga**, m. 'm°-disease;' °*gin*, mfn. suffering from it, ib. **-vākya**, Śiś. x, 12, prob. w.r. for *vakra-v°*, q. v. **-vāsa**, m. 'mouth-scenting,' an orange, L. **-śodhana**, n. 'm°-cleansing,' the fruit of Dillenia Speciosa or of Averrhoa Carambola, L. **-śodhin**, m. 'id.,' the citron tree, L.; n. a citron, L. **Vaktrâmbuja**, n. a lotus-like face, Kāvyâd. **Vaktrâsava**, m. 'mouth-liquor,' saliva, L. **Vaktrêndu**, m. a moon-like face, Ratnâv.

Vaktraka (ifc.) = *vaktra*, Hariv.

Váktva, mfn. to be uttered or spoken, RV.

Vákman, n. utterance, speech, hymn of praise (?), RV. i, 132, 2.

Vakma-rája-satya, mfn. faithful to those who are the rulers or ordainers of hymns (of praise), RV. vi, 51, 10.

Vákmya, mfn. to be praised, worthy of celebration, RV.

Vakshyamāṇa, mfn. about to be said or described, to be mentioned hereafter or subsequently. **-tva**, n. the being about to be mentioned, subsequent mention, Pāṇ. i, 2, 48, Sch.

Vagnú, m. a cry, call, roar, sound (esp. of animals; but also applied to the noise produced by dice), RV.; TBr.; a speaker, W.; mfn. loquacious, talkative, L.

Vagvaná, mfn. talkative, chattering, RV.

Vagvanú, m. a sound, noise, ib.

Vaca, mfn. speaking, talking (see *ku-v°*); m. a parrot, L.; = *sūrya*, the sun, L.; = *kāraṇa*, L.; (*ā*), f. a kind of talking bird, Turdus Salica (= *sārikā*), L.; a kind of aromatic root (accord. to some = Acorus Colamus), Hcar.; n. the act of speaking, speech (see *dur-v°*). **Vacâcārya**, m. N. of a preceptor, Cat. (cf. *vacchâc°*). **Vacā-cchada**, m. a kind of white basil, L. **Vacârca**, m. a sun-worshipper, Parsee, ib.

Vacaḥ, in comp. for *vácas*. **-krama**, m. course of speech, discourse (m.pl. series of discourses), Kathās.

Vacaka. See *dur-v°*.

Vacaknu, mfn. talkative, loquacious, eloquent, Uṇ. iii, 81; m. a Brāhman, L.; N. of a man, Śaṃk.

Vacakru, w.r. for prec.

Vacaṇḍā or °**ḍī**, f. (only L.) a kind of talking bird, Turdus Salica; the wick of a lamp (= *varti*); a dagger, knife.

Vacaná, mfn. speaking, a speaker, eloquent, RV.; (ifc.) mentioning, indicating, expressing, meaning, Pāṇ.; KātyŚr.; Sarvad. (*-tā*, f., *-tva*, n.); being pronounced, RPrāt. (*-tva*, n.); n. (ifc. f. *ā*) the act of speaking, utterance, Sāṃkhyak.; pronunciation, Pāṇ.; Prāt.; statement, declaration, express mention, AitBr.; ŚrS.; Pāṇ. &c.; speech, sentence, word, Mn.; MBh. &c.; (in gram.) the injunction of a teacher, rule, Kāś.; advice, instruction, direction, order, command, MBh.; Kāv. &c. (°*naṃ* √*kṛi* or °*ne* √*sthā* with gen. = to do the bidding of any one, follow a person's advice, obey; °*nena* or °*nāt*, with gen. = in the name of); sound, voice, APrāt.; Megh.; Hit.; (in gram.) number, Pāṇ.; Vop. (cf. *eka-, dvi-, bahu-v°*); rumour, L.; dry ginger, L. **-kara**, mf(*ī*)n. making a speech, speaking, W.; doing what one is told, obedient, Pañcat.; m. the author or enunciator of a precept, W. **-kāra** and **-kārin**, mfn. doing what one is commanded, obeying orders, obedient, MBh. **-krama**, m. order of words, discourse, W. **-gocara**, mfn. forming a subject of conversation, BhP. **-gaurava**, n. respect for an order, deference to a command, R. **-grāhin**, mfn. accepting or obeying orders, obedient, submissive, humble, L. **-paṭu**, mfn. skilful in speech, eloquent, VarBṛS.; Pañcat. **-bhūshaṇa**, n., **-mālikā**, f. N. of wks. **-mātra**, n. mere words, assertion unsupported by facts, MW. **-racanā**, f. skilful arrangement of speech, eloquence, Pañcat. **-viruddha**, mfn. opposed to a declaration or precept, contrary to a text, W. **-virodha**, m. inconsistency of precepts or texts, incongruity, contradiction, ib. **-vyakti**, f. distinctness or perspicuity of a text, ib. **-śata**, n. a hundred speeches, repeated speech or declaration, Pañcat. **-saṃgraha**, m., **-samuccaya**, m., **-sampuṭa**, m. N. of wks. **-sahāya**, m. a companion to converse with, any sociable companion, Pañcat. **-sāra-saṃgraha**, m. N. of wk. **Vacanânuga**, mfn. following advice or orders, obedient, submissive, MārkP. **Vacanâbādha**, m. an obstacle to speech, Pāṇ. vi, 2, 21, Sch. **Vacanârtha**, m. N. of wk. **Vacanâvakshepa**, m. scornful or abusive speech, Śak. (in Prākṛit). **Vacaná-vat**, mfn. (for °*ná-vat*) possessed of speech, eloquent, RV. **Vacanôpakrama**, m. commencement of a speech, exordium, MW. **Vacanôpanyāsa**, m. suggestive speech, insinuation, Śak. (in Prākṛit).

Vacanī-kṛita, mfn. made an object of (reproachful) speech, exposed to censure or abuse, R.

Vacanīya, mfn. to be spoken or uttered, mentionable, Mn.; R.; to be called or named, Nir.; to be spoken about or against, censurable, liable to reproach, Hariv.; n. reproach, censure, blame, Kālid.; Uttarar. **-tā**, f., **-tva**, n. liability to be spoken about or against, rumour, report, (esp.) evil report, blame, reprehension, Kāv. **-dosha**, m. the fault of being censurable or reprehensible, Mṛicch.

Vacane-sthita, mfn. (loc. of *vacana* + *sth°*) abiding in a command, obeying orders, complaint, obedient, L.

Vacara, m. a cock, L.; a low person, L.

Vacalu, m. = *śatru*, an enemy, L.; offence, fault (?), L.

1. **Vácas**, n. (for 2. see p. 914, col. 2) speech, voice, word, RV. &c. &c. (°*casāṃ patiḥ*, N. of Bṛihaspati, Laghuj.); singing, song (of birds), Ṛitus.; advice, direction, command, order, MBh.; Kāv. &c. (*vacaḥ* √*kṛi*, with gen., 'to follow the advice of;' *vacasā mama*, 'on my advice'); an oracular utterance (declarative of some future fate or destiny), VarBṛS.; a sentence, L.; (in gram.) number (see *dvi-v°*). **-kara**, mfn. = *vacana-k°*, L. **-vin**, mfn. possessed of speech, eloquent, Śiś.

1. **Vacasa**, mfn. (for 2. see p. 914, col. 2) talka-

tive, eloquent, wise, MW.; (ifc.) = 1. *vacas* (see *ā-cārya-v°*).

1. **Vacasya** (fr. 1. *vacas*), Nom. Ā. *°syate*, to be audible, to murmur (said of the sound of the trickling Soma), RV.

2. **Vacasyà**, mfn. worthy of mention, praiseworthy, celebrated, AV.

Vacasyā́, f. (fr. 1. *vacasya*) desire of speaking, readiness of speech, eloquence, RV.

1. **Vacasyú**, mfn. (for 2. see p. 914, col. 2) eloquent, RV.

Vaci (ibc.) = *vacana*, statement, mention, declaration (only in *-bhedāt*), KātyŚr.

Vaco, in comp. for 1. *vacas*. — **graha**, m. 'receiving words,' the ear, L. — **mārgâtita**, mfn. 'gone beyond the path of words,' greater than words can tell, Siṇhâs. — **yúj**, mfn. yoked by a (mere) word (said of Indra's steeds), RV. — **víd**, mfn. skilful in speech, eloquent, ib. — **viparilopá** (*váco-*), m. loss of speech or of words, ŚBr. — **hara**, m. 'receiver of words,' a messenger, envoy, Śiś.

वच्छ *vaccha*, m. and (*ā*), f. = *vatsa*, child (esp. in familiar address), Pañcad.

Vacchâcārya, m. N. of the maternal grandfather of Nīla-kaṇṭha, Cat. (cf. *vacâcārya*).

Vacchikā. See *dīrgha-v°*.

वच्छिय *vacchiya*, m. N. of an author, Cat.

वज् *vaj* (prob. corrupted fr. √*vraj*), cl. 1. P. *vajati* (pf. *vavāja*, fut. *vajitā* &c., Gr.), to go, Dhātup. vii, 78: Caus. or cl. 10. P. *vājayati*, to prepare the way; to trim or feather an arrow (*mārga-* or *mārgaṇa-saṃskāre*), Dhātup. xxxii, 74.

Another √*vaj* or *uj*, 'to be hard or strong,' may be inferred from *ugra*, *ojas*, *vajra*, *vāja* (qq. vv.), the last of which gave rise to the Nom. *vājaya*, q. v. [For cognate words see under *ugra* and *ojas*.]

Vajja-deva, m. (prob. for *vajra-d°*) N. of a king, Inscr.

Vájra, m. n. 'the hard or mighty one,' a thunderbolt (esp. that of Indra, said to have been formed out of the bones of the Ṛishi Dadhīca or Dadhīci [q.v.], and shaped like a circular discus, or in later times regarded as having the form of two transverse bolts crossing each other thus ×; sometimes also applied to similar weapons used by various gods or superhuman beings, or to any mythical weapon destructive of spells or charms, also to *Manyu*, 'wrath,' RV., or [with *apām*] to a jet of water, AV. &c. &c.; also applied to a thunderbolt in general or to the lightning evolved from the centrifugal energy of the circular th° of Indra when launched at a foe; in Northern Buddhist countries it is shaped like a dumb-bell and called Dorje; see MWB. 201; 322 &c.), RV. &c. &c.; a diamond (thought to be as hard as the th° or of the same substance with it), ShaḍvBr.; Mn.; MBh. &c.; a kind of talc, L.; a kind of penance (feeding for a month on only barley prepared with cow's urine), L.; sour gruel, W.; m. a form of military array, Mn.; MBh. &c. (cf. *-vyūha*); a kind of column or pillar, VarBṛS.; a partic. form of the moon, ib.; a partic. Ekâha, Vait.; a kind of hard mortar or cement (*kalka*), VarBṛS. (cf. *-lepa*); N. of the 15th of the 27 Yogas or astronomical divisions of time, ib.; a partic. Soma ceremony, ShaḍvBr.; Euphorbia Antiquorum and another species, L.; Asteracantha Longifolia, L.; white-flowering Kuśa grass, L.; N. of a mountain, R.; of an Asura, Vīrac.; of a son of Aniruddha, MBh.; Hariv.; Pur.; of a son of Viśvāmitra, MBh.; of a son of Manu Sāvarṇa, Hariv.; (with Jainas) of one of the 10 Daśa-pūrvins, L.; of a Ṛishi, VarBṛS. (v. l. for *vātsya*); of a minister of Narêndrâditya, Rājat.; of a son of Bhūti, ib.; of a heretical king, Buddh.; (*ā*), f. Cocculus Cordifolius, L.; Euphorbia Antiquorum or Tirucalli, L.; N. of Durgā, DevīP.; of a daughter of Vaiśvānara, VP.; (*ī*), f. a kind of Euphorbia, L.; n. denunciation in strong language (compared to thunder), R.; Sāh.; Pratāp. (cf. *vākya-* and *vāg-v°*); a kind of hard iron or steel, L.; a partic. posture in sitting, Cat. (cf. *vajrâsana*); N. of a partic. configuration of the planets and stars (in which favourable planets are situated in the 1st and 7th houses and unfavourable in the 4th and 10th), VarBṛS.; myrobolan, L.; the blossom of the sesamum or of any plant called Vajra, L.; Andropogon Muricatus, L.; = *bālaka*, a child, pupil, L.; mfn. adamantine, hard, impenetrable, W.; shaped like a kind of cross (cf. above), forked, zigzag, ib. [Cf. Zd. *vazra*, 'a club.'] — **kaṅkaṭa**, m. 'having adamantine armour,' N. of Hanumat, L. — **kanṭa**, m. Euphorbia Neriifolia or Antiquorum, L. — **kanṭaka**, m. id., L.; Asteracantha Longifolia, L.; *-śālmalī*, f. 'having hard-thorned Ś°-trees,' N. of a hell, BhP. — **kanda**, m. a species of bulbous plant, L. — **kandaka**, m. = *-kanṭa*, Hcar., Sch. — **kapāṭa-mat**, mfn. having adamantine doors, BhP. — **kapāṭa-rasa**, m. a kind of medicament, L. — **karṇa**, m. = *-kanda*, L. — **karshaṇa**, m. N. of Indra, Mcar. — **kavaca**, m. or n. adamantine mail, Kāraṇḍ.; m. a partic. Samādhi, ib. — **kāmā**, f. N. of a daughter of Maya, VP. — **kālikā**, f. N. of the mother of Gautama Buddha, L. — **kālī**, f. N. of a Jina-śakti, L. — **kīṭa**, m. a kind of insect (which bores holes in wood and stones), Śiś., Sch. (cf. *-daṇshṭra*). — **kīla**, m. a thunderbolt, Mcar. — **kīlāya**, Nom. Ā. *°yate*, to act or be like a th° (*°yita*, n. impers.), Uttarar. — **kukshi**, N. of a cave, Kāraṇḍ.; a partic. Samādhi, ib. — **kuca**, m. a partic. Samādhi, ib. — **kūṭa**, m. 'diamond-peak,' a mountain consisting of diamonds, BhP.; N. of a mountain, ib.; of a mythical town on the Himâlaya, Kathās. — **kṛita**, mfn. caused by a thunderbolt, Rājat. — **ketu**, m. 'having a Vajra for ensign,' N. of the demon Naraka, Pur. — **kshāra**, n. an alkaline earth, impure carbonate of soda, L. — **garbha**, m. N. of a Bodhisattva, Buddh. — **gopa**, m. = *indra-gopa*, L. — **ghāta**, m. a thunder-stroke, MBh. — **ghosha**, mfn. sounding like a thunderbolt, Ragh. — **cañcu**, m. 'hard-beaked,' a vulture, L. (cf. *-tuṇḍa*). — **carman**, m. 'hard-skinned,' a rhinoceros, L. — **cihna**, n. a Vajra-like mark, VarBṛS. — **cchedaka-prajñā-pāramitā**, f. N. of a Buddhist Sūtra wk. (also *-cchedikā*). — **jit**, w. r. for *vajri-jit*. — **jvalana**, n. thunder-flash, lightning, Kām. — **jvālā**, f. id., L.; N. of a granddaughter of Vairocana, R. — **ṭaṅka**, m. N. of an author (also with *śāstrin*); *°kīya*, n. N. of his wk. — **ṭīka**, m. N. of a Buddha, L. — **ṇakhā**, f. a proper N., Pāṇ. iv, 1, 58, Sch. (cf. *-nakha*). — **tara**, m. N. of a kind of very hard cement (= *kalka*), VarBṛS. — **tā**, f., or **-tva**, n. great hardness or impenetrableness, severity, MW. — **tīrtha-māhātmya**, n. N. of a wk. — **tuṇḍa**, mfn. 'hard-beaked,' BhP.; m. (only L.) a vulture; a mosquito, gnat; N. of Garuḍa; of Gaṇeśa; Cactus Opuntia. — **tulya**, m. 'resembling a diamond,' lapis lazuli, beryl, L. — **daṇshṭra**, mfn. having teeth as hard as adamant, BhP.; m. N. of a Rākshasa, R.; of an Asura, BhP.; of a king of the Vidyā-dharas, Kathās.; of a lion, Pañcat.; = *-kīṭa*, Cat. — **dakshiṇa** (*vájra-*), mfn. holding a thunderbolt in the right hand, RV.; m. N. of Indra, L. — **daṇḍa**, mfn. having a handle or staff studded with diamonds, BhP. — **daṇḍaka**, m. Cactus Opuntia. — **datta**, m. N. of a son of Bhaga-datta, MBh.; of a prince, Hcar.; of a king of Puṇḍarīkiṇī, HPariś.; (*śrī-*), N. of an author, Buddh. — **danta**, mfn. 'hard-tusked,' a hog, boar, L.; a rat, L. — **daśana**, m. 'id.,' a rat. — **dṛiḍha-netra**, m. N. of a king of the Yakshas, Buddh. — **deśa**, m. N. of a district, Cat. — **deha**, mfn. having an adamantine frame or a very hardy body, MW.; (*ā*), f. N. of a goddess, Kālac. — **dehin**, mfn. = prec., MW. — **dru** or **-druma**, m. N. of various kinds of the Euphorbia plant, L. — **druma-kesara-dhvaja**, m. N. of a king of the Gandharvas, Buddh. — **dhara**, mfn. holding a thunderbolt; m. N. of Indra, MBh.; Kāv. &c.; of a Bodhi-sattva (= *vajra-pāṇi*), MWB. 195; 201; of a king, Rājat.; *-prabhāva*, m. having the power of Indra, Ragh. — **dhātrī** or **-dhātvī**, f. N. of a Buddhist Śakti, Dharmas. 4; MWB. 216. — **dhātvīśvarī**, f. N. of Vairocana's wife and of a Tantra deity, L. — **dhāra**, mfn. whose edge or point is as hard as a diamond. — **dhāraṇa**, n. artificial gold, L. — **dhṛik**, mfn. wielding a th°, MBh. — **nakhá**, mf(*ī*)n. having hard claws, TĀr. (cf. *-ṇakhā*). — **nagara**, n. N. of the city of the Dānava Vajra-nābha, Hariv. — **nābha**, mfn. having a hard nave (said of a wheel &c.), MBh.; R.; m. Kṛishṇa's discus, MW.; N. of one of Skanda's attendants, MBh.; of a Dānava, Hariv.; of several princes (a son of Uktha; of Unnābha; of Sthala), Kāv.; Pur.; *°bhīya*, mfn. relating to the Dānava Vajra-nābha, treating of him, Hariv. — **nirghosha**, m. a clap of thunder, L. — **nishkambha**, w. r. for *-vishkambha*. — **nishpesha**, m. the clashing or concussion of thunder-clouds, a thunder-clap. — **pañjara**, m. 'adamantine cage,' a secure refuge for, protector of (gen. or comp.), Hcar.; Rājat.; (prob. n.) N. of partic. prayers addressed to Durgā, Cat. (cf. *nṛisiṇha-pañjara* and *nṛisiṇha-vajra-p°*); m. N. of a Dānava, Kathās. — **patana**, n. the fall or stroke of a thunderbolt, Mālatīm. — **pattrikā**, f. Asparagus Racemosus, L. — **parīkshā**, f. the testing a diamond, VarBṛS. — **pāṇi**, mfn. 'thunderbolt-handed,' wielding a th°; whose th° is the hand (said of Brāhmans), MBh.; m. N. of Indra, ShaḍvBr.; MBh. &c.; of a Bodhi-sattva (also called *vajra-dhara*, and corresponding in some respects to Indra), MWB. 195; 201 &c.; *-tva*, n. the state of a wielder of a thunderbolt, VarBṛS. — **pāṇin**, mfn. 'th°-handed,' wielding a th°, Hariv. — **pāta**, mfn. falling like a th°, R.; m. the fall of a th°, stroke of lightning, Kāv.; Prab.; *-dāruṇa*, mfn. terrible as a clap of thunder, Pañcat.; *-duḥ-saha-tara*, mfn. more dangerous than a th°-clap, ib.; *-sadṛiśa*, mfn. like a th°-clap, ib.; *°tāya*, Nom. Ā. (only *°yita*) to fall like a thunderbolt, Pārśvan. — **pātana**, n. the hurling of a thunderbolt, MBh. — **pāshāṇa**, m. diamond stone, a kind of spar or precious stone, L. — **pura**, n. N. of the city of the Dānava Vajra-nābha, Hariv. (cf. *-nagara*). — **pushpa**, n. 'diamond-flower,' a valuable flower, W.; the blossom of sesamum, L.; (*ā*), f. a kind of fennel, Anethum Sowa, L. — **prabha**, m. N. of a Vidhyā-dhara, Kathās. — **prabhāva**, m. N. of a king of the Karūshas, Vās., Introd. — **prastāriṇī** or **-prastāvinī**, f. N. of a Tantra goddess; *-mantra*, m. pl. N. of partic. magical formulas, Cat. — **prākāra**, m. a partic. Samādhi, Kāraṇḍ. — **prâya**, mfn. like adamant, adamantine, exceedingly hard, MW. — **badha**, see *-vadha*. — **bāhu** (*vájra-*), mfn. 'th°-armed,' wielder of a th° (said of Indra, Agni and Rudra), RV.; m. N. of a king of Orissa and of another person, Cat. — **bījaka**, m. Guilandina Bonduc, L. — **bhaṭṭīya**, n. N. of wk. — **bhūmi**, f. N. of a place; *-rajas*, n. a partic. precious stone, L. — **bhṛikuṭi**, f. (with Buddhists) one of the 6 goddesses of magic, Dharmas. 13. — **bhṛit**, mfn. carrying or wielding a th°; m. N. of Indra, RV.; MBh. &c. — **maṇi**, m. 'th°-gem,' a diamond, Bhartṛ. — **maṇḍa**, f. N. of a Dhāraṇī, Buddh. — **mati**, m. N. of a Bodhi-sattva, Kāraṇḍ. — **maya**, mf(*ī*)n. made of diamond, hard as diamond, adamantine, Kāv.; Kathās.; hard-hearted, W. — **māra**, m. the calcining of a diamond, Bhpr. — **mālā**, f. a partic. Samādhi, Kāraṇḍ.; N. of a Gandharva maiden, ib. — **mitra**, m. N. of a king, Pur. — **mukuṭa**, m. N. of a son of Pratāpa-mukuṭa, Kathās.; Vet.; *°ṭi-vilāsa*, m. N. of a drama. — **mukha**, m. a partic. Samādhi, Kāraṇḍ. — **mushṭi**, m. 'grasping a th°,' or 'one whose clenched fist is like adamant,' N. of Indra, R.; of a Rākshasa, ib.; of a Kshatriya or warrior, Kathās.; m. or f. an adamantine clenched fist or a kind of weapon, Hariv.; N. of a Gaṇa of Śiva, ib.; f. a partic. position of the hand in shooting an arrow, ŚārṅgP. — **mūlī**, f. Glycine Debilis, L. — **yoginī**, f. N. of a goddess, Buddh. — **ratha**, mfn. one whose th° is a war-chariot (said of a Kshatriya), MBh. — **rada**, m. 'having adamantine tusks,' a hog, boar, L. — **rātra**, n. N. of a town, Kathās. — **rūpa**, mfn. shaped like a Vajra or cross (see *v°*), VarBṛS. — **lipi**, f. a partic. style of writing, Lalit. — **lepa**, m. a kind of hard mortar or cement, Vcar.; Ratnâv.; Vās.; *-ghaṭita*, mfn. joined with adamantine cement, Vikr.; Mālatīm. — **lepāya**, Nom. Ā. *°yate*, to be like Vajra-lepa, i.e. as hard as cement (*°yamāna-tva*, n.), Sarvad. — **lohaka**, m. or n. a magnet, loadstone, L. — **vadha**, m. death by a th° or by lightning, W.; oblique or cross multiplication, Col. — **vara-candra**, m. N. of a king of Orissa, Cat. — **varman**, m. N. of a poet, ib. — **vallī**, f. a species of sun-flower, Heliotropium Indicum, L. — **váh** (or *-vā́h*), m. wielding a th°, RV. — **vāraka**, m. a title of respect applied to certain sages, L. — **vārāhī**, f. N. of a Tantra goddess, MWB. 491; 526 (cf. *-kālikā*). — **vidrāviṇī**, f. N. of a Buddhist goddess, W. — **vishkambha**, m. N. of a son of Garuḍa, MBh. — **vihata** (*vájra-*), mfn. struck by a th° or lightning, ŚBr. — **vījaka**, see *-bījaka*. — **vīra**, m. N. of Mahā-kāla, W. — **vṛiksha**, m. Cactus Opuntia, Suśr.; Euphorbia Antiquorum, L. — **vega**, m. 'having the swiftness of a thunderbolt or of lightning,' N. of a Rākshasa, MBh.; of a Vidyā-dhara, Kathās. — **vyūha**, m. a kind of military array, Kathās. — **śarīra**, mfn. = *-deha*, MW. — **śalya**, m. 'having hard quills or bristles,' a porcupine, L.; (*ā*), f. a species of plant, L. — **śākhā**, f. N. of a branch or sect of the Jainas (founded by Vajra-svāmin), W. — **śīrsha**, m. N. of a son of Bhṛigu, MBh. — **śuci**, w. r. for *-sūci*. — **śṛiṅkhalā**, f. (with Jainas) N. of one of the 16 Vidyā-devīs, L.; *°likā*, f. Asteracantha

Longifolia, L. **-śrī**, f. N. of a Gandharvī, Kāraṇḍ. **-saṃhata**, m. N. of a Buddha, Lalit. **-saṃghāta**, mfn. having the hardness or compactness of adamant (said of Bhīma), MBh. i, 4775; m. N. of a kind of hard cement, VarBṛS. **-sattva**, m. 'having a soul or heart of adamant,' N. of a Dhyāni-buddha, Dharmas. 3; °*ttvâtmikā*, f. N. of Vajra-sattva's wife, W. **-samādhi**, m. a partic. Samādhi, Buddh. **-samāna-sāra**, mfn. having a diamond-like essence or nature, hard as adamant, MBh. **-samutkīrṇa**, mfn. perforated by a diamond or any hard instrument, Ragh. **-sāra**, mfn. having the essence or nature of a diamond, R.; Pañcat.; adamantine, MBh.; m. or n. a diamond, ib.; Mālatīm.; m. N. of various men, Kathās.; Rājat.; *-maya*, mf(*ī*)n. hard as a diamond, adamantine (*-tva*, n.), MBh.; Kāv.; Kathās.; °*rī-√kṛi*, P. *-karoti*, to make as hard as adamant, Śak. **-siṇha**, m. N. of a king, Pañcat. **-sūci** or **-sūcī**, f. a diamond-pointed needle, MBh.; Hcar.; N. of an Upanishad ascribed to Śaṃkarācārya (also °*cikā* or °*cy-upanishad*); of a wk. by Aśva-ghosha. **-sūrya**, m. N. of a Buddha, L. **-sena**, m. N. of a Bodhi-sattva, Kāraṇḍ.; of a king of Śrāvastī, Śatr.; of a preceptor, Cat. **-sthāna**, n. N. of a place, R. **-svāmin**, m. (with Jainas) N. of one of the seven Daśapūrvins, Śatr. **-hasta** (*vájra-*), mfn. 'thunderbolt-handed,' wielding a th° (said of Indra, Agni, the Maruts), RV.; m. N. of Śiva, Śivag.; (*ā*), f. N. of one of the nine Samidhs, Gṛihyas.; of a Buddhist goddess, W. **-hūna**, m. N. of a place, Cat. **-hṛidaya**, n. an adamantine heart, A.; N. of a Buddhist wk. **Vajrâṇśu**, m. N. of a son of Kṛishṇa, Hariv. (v.l. *vajrâsu*). **Vajrâṇśuka**, n. cloth marked with various patterns, L. **Vajrâkara**, m. a diamond mine, Ragh.; N. of a place, Cat. **Vajrâkāra** (VarBṛS.) or **vajrâkṛiti** (Vop.), mfn. shaped like a thunderbolt or Vajra, having transverse lines (see *v*°); a cross-shaped symbol (formerly used in grammars to denote Jihvāmūlīyas). **Vajrâkshī**, f. Asteracantha Longifolia, L. **Vajrâkhya**, mfn. named or called Vajra, MBh.; VarBṛS.; m. a kind of mineral spar, L. (cf. *vajra-pāshāṇa*). **Vajrâghāta**, m. the stroke of a thunderbolt or of lightning, W.; any sudden shock or calamity, ib. **Vajrâṅkita**, mfn. marked with a Vajra-like symbol (see *v*°), VarBṛS. **Vajrâṅkuśa**, m. N. of a mountain, Kāraṇḍ.; (*ī*), f. N. of a goddess, Buddh. **Vajrâṅga**, m. (prob. for *vakrâṅga*) a snake, L.; (*ī*), f. Coix Barbata, L.; Heliotropium Indicum, L. **Vajrâcārya**, m. N. of a preceptor, Buddh. **Vajrâṇḍī** (?), f. a species of plant, Bhpr. **Vajrâditya**, m. N. of a king of Kaśmīra, Rājat. **Vajrâbha**, m. 'diamond-like,' a kind of spar or precious stone, (perhaps) opal, L. (cf. *vajrâkhya*). **Vajrâbhishavaṇa**, n. a partic. penance lasting for 3 days (eating only food prepared with barley), L. **Vajrâbhyāsa**, m. cross or zigzag multiplication, Bījag. **Vajrâbhra**, n. a species of dark-coloured talc, L. **Vajrâmbujā**, f. N. of a goddess, Buddh. **Vajrâyudha**, m. 'thunderbolt-armed,' N. of Indra, Hariv.; BhP.; of a poet, Cat.; of another man, Kathās. **Vajrâvalī**, f. N. of a Tantra wk. **Vajrâśani**, mfn. Indra's th°, L.; *-nipāta*, m. the fall of Indra's th°, R.; *-vibhūshita*, mfn. adorned with Indra's th°, ib.; *-sama-svana*, mfn. sounding like Indra's th°, ib. **Vajrâsana**, n. a diamond seat, Buddh.; a partic. posture in sitting (the hands being placed in the hollow between the body and the crossed feet), HYog.; m. N. of Buddha, Inscr. **Vajrâsu**, see *vajrâṇśu*. **Vajrâsura**, m. N. of an Asura, Vcar. **Vajrâsthi**, f. Asteracantha Longifolia, L. **Vajrâhata**, mfn. struck by a th°, Kathās. **Vajrâhikā**, f. Carpopogon Pruriens, L. **Vajrêndra**, m. N. of various men, Rājat. **Vajrêśvarī**, f. N. of a Buddhist goddess, W.; *-kāvya*, n. N. of a poem. **Vajrôdarī**, f. N. of a Rākshasī, R. **Vajrôdgata**, m. a partic. Samādhi, Kāraṇḍ.

Vajraka, mfn. (with *taila*) a kind of oil (prepared with various substances and used for curing skin diseases), Suśr.; m. N. of a mountain, Divyâv.; (*ikā*), f. (in music) a partic. Śruti, Saṃgīt.; n. a diamond, L.; = *vajra-kshāra*, L.; a partic. phenomenon in the sky, L.

Vajrāya, Nom. Ā. °*yate*, to become a thunderbolt, MBh.; Vcar.

Vajri, in comp. for *vajrin*. **-jit**, m. 'conqueror of Indra,' N. of Garuḍa, L. **-vat**, for *vajra-vat* (only in voc. *vajri-vas*; cf. *adri-vas*, *hari-vas*), having or wielding a thunderbolt, RV.

Vajrin, mf(*iṇī*)n. holding or wielding a thunderbolt (said of various gods), RV.; MBh.; containing the word *vajra*, PañcavBr.; m. 'thunderer,' N. of Indra, ib.; MBh. &c.; a Buddha or Jaina deified saint, L.; one of the Viśve Devāḥ, MBh.; (*iṇī*), f. N. of partic. Ishṭakās, TS.

Vajrī, in comp. for *vajra*. **-karaṇa**, n. the making into a Vajra or into the form of a thunderbolt, Cat. **-bhūta**, mfn. become or turned into a thunderbolt, Sāy. on RV. viii, 14, 13.

वजञाण *vajaāṇa* and *vajahuṇa*, N. of places, Cat. (cf. *vajra-hūṇa*).

वज्रट *vajraṭa*, m. N. of the father of Uvaṭa, Cat.

वज्रोली *vajrolī*, f. a partic. position of the fingers, Cat.

वञ्च् *vañc* (cf. √2. *vak*), cl. 1. P. (Dhātup. vii, 7) *váñcati* (Gr. also pf. *vavañca*; fut. *vañcitā*, °*cishyati*; aor. *avañcīt*; Prec. *vacyāt*; inf. *vañcitum*; ind. p. *vañcitvā*, *vacitvā*, or *vaktvā*), to move to and fro, go crookedly, totter, stagger, waver, AV.; VS.; ŚBr.; ŚāṅkhŚr.; to go, go to, arrive at (acc.), Bhaṭṭ.; to go slyly or secretly, sneak along, VS.; to pass over, wander over, go astray, MW.: Pass. *vacyáte*, to move or rock to and fro, hurry along, speed, RV.; AV.; to be moved (in the heart), be poured forth, issue forth (as hymns or prayers), RV.: Caus. *vañcayati*, °*te* (aor. *avavañcat*), to move or go away from, avoid, shun, escape (mostly P. and with acc.), MBh.; Kāv. &c.; to cause to go astray, deceive, cheat, defraud of (instr. or abl.; in these senses more properly Ā., but sometimes also P.; Pass. *vañcyate*), ib.: Desid. *vivañcishate*, Gr.: Intens. *vanīvacyate*, *vanīvañcīti*, ib.

2. **Vacas**, mfn. (for 1. see p. 912, col. 3) in *adhó-vacas*, q.v.

2. **Vacasá**, mfn. (for 1. see p. 912, col. 3) moving about, rolling (said of a carriage), RV.

2. **Vacasyú**, mfn. (for 1. see p. 913, col. 1) tottering, staggering, wavering, RV.

Vañcaka, mf(*ā*)n. (fr. Caus.) deceiving, a deceiver, fraudulent, crafty, Mn.; MBh. &c.; m. a jackal, Vās.; Hit.; a tame or house-ichneumon, L.; a low or vile man, W.

Vañcatha, m. (only L.) deceit; a deceiver; the Indian cuckoo; time.

Vañcana, n. (or °*nā*, f.; fr. Caus.) cheating, deception, fraud, MBh.; Kāv. &c. (°*naṃ* or °*nāṃ* √*kṛi*, to practise fraud, cheat, take in; °*nāṃ* √*labh* or *pra-√āp*, to be deceived); illusion, delusion, hallucination, MW.; (*ā*), f. lost labour or time, Kālid. (cf. *śīla-v*°). **-cañcutā**, f. skill in fraud or deception, Pañcat. **-tā**, f. trickery, deception, roguishness (in *a-v*°), Cāṇ. **-pravaṇa**, mfn. inclined to fraud or deception, Kathās. **-yoga**, m. practice of fraud or deception, MBh. **-vat**, mfn. deceitful, crafty, fraudulent, Nir.

Vañcanā, f. (see prec.) in comp. **-paṇḍita**, mfn. clever at cheating; *-tva*, n. cleverness at cheating, roguishness, Mṛicch. **-mati**, m. N. of a man, Campak.

Vañcanīya, mfn. to be avoided or shunned, R.; to be deceived, capable of being cheated, ib.; Pañcat.

Vañcayitavya, mfn. to be deceived, MBh.; Hit. (n. impers.)

Vañcayitṛi, mfn. one who deceives, a deceiver, cheater, Hariv.

Vañcita, mfn. deceived, tricked, imposed upon, MBh.; Kāv. &c.; (*ā*), f. a kind of riddle or enigma, Cat.

Vañcitaka. See *paksha-v*°.

Vañcin. See *āgata-v*°.

Vañcuka or **vañcūka**, mfn. deceptive, fraudulent, dishonest, L.

Vañcya, mfn. to be cheated or deceived &c.; to be gone, Pāṇ. vii, 3, 63.

वञ्चति *vañcati* (?), m. fire, L. (cf. *añcati*).

वञ्जरा *vañjarā*, f. N. of a river, Prāyaśc.

वञ्जुल *vañjula*, m. N. of various trees and other plants (accord. to L. Dalbergia Ougeinensis, Jonesia Asoka, Calamus Rotang or Hibiscus Mutabilis), MBh.; Kāv. &c.; a sort of bird, R.; VarBṛS.; N. of a river (written *bañjula*), VP.; (*ā*), f. a cow that yields abundance of milk, L.; N. of a river, MārkP. **-druma**, m. the Aśoka tree, L. **-priya**, m. the ratan, Calamus Rotang, L.

Vañjulaka, m. a kind of plant, BhP. (also *-druma*, Hariv.); a sort of bird, R.; (*ikā*), f. Oldenlandia Herbacea, L.

वट् 1. *vaṭ* (prob. invented to serve as a root for the words below; cf. √1. *vṛit*), cl. 1. P. *vaṭati* (pf. *vavāṭa* &c.), to surround, encompass, Dhātup. ix, 13; cl. 10. P. *vaṭayati*, to tie, string, connect, xxxv, 5; to divide, partition, xxxv, 65; to speak, xix, 17: Pass. *vaṭyate* (only *vaṭyante*, Vishṇ. xliii, 34), to be crushed or pounded or ground down.

Vaṭa, m. (perhaps Prākṛit for *vṛita*, 'surrounded, covered;' cf. *nyag-rodha*) the Banyan or Indian fig-tree (Ficus Indica), MBh.; Kāv. &c.; RTL. 337 (also said to be n.); a sort of bird, BhP.; a small shell, the Cypræa Moneta or cowry, L.; a pawn (in chess), L.; sulphur, L.; = *sāmya*, L.; N. of a Tīrtha, Vishṇ.; of one of Skanda's attendants, MBh.; the son of a Vaiśya and a Venukī, L. (also n. and *ī*, f.); a string, rope, tie, L. (only *vaṭa* ibc., and *pañca-v*°, q.v.); a small lump, globule &c. = *vaṭaka*, ŚārṅgS.; (*ī*), f. a kind of tree, Rājan.; (with *gāḍhā*) a partic. position in the game of Catur-aṅga or chess, L.; a little round ball, L. **-kaṇikā** or **-kaṇikā**, f., **-kaṇiya**, (prob.) n. a very minute portion of the Indian fig-tree, MBh. **-kalikā**, f. N. of wk. **-ja**, m., Pāṇ. vi, 2, 22. **-tīrtha-nātha**, N. of a Liṅga; *-māhātmya*, n. N. of a ch. of the SkandaP. **-nagara**, n. N. of a town, L. **-pattra**, n. a kind of white basil, L.; (*ā*), f. a kind of jasmine, L.; (*ī*), f. a partic. plant (= *irā-vatī*), Madanav. **-yakshiṇī-tīrtha**, n. N. of a Tīrtha, Cat. **-vatī**, f., g. *madhv-ādi*. **-vāsin**, m. 'dwelling in the Banyan tree,' a Yaksha, L. **-sāvitrī-pūjā**, f., **-sāvitrī-vrata**, n., and **-sāvitrī-vrata-kāla-nirṇaya**, m. N. of wks. **Vaṭâkara**, m. a cord, string, L. (cf. *vaṭāraka*). **Vaṭâraṇya-māhātmya**, n. N. of ch. of the AgniP. **Vaṭâśraya**, m. 'dwelling in the Indian fig-tree,' N. of Kubera, L. (cf. *vaṭa-vāsin*). **Vaṭâśvattha-vivāha**, m. the marriage (generally by engrafting) of the Ficus Indica with the Ficus Religiosa (a religious ceremony), Cat.; cf. RTL. 335-337. **Vaṭêśa**, m. N. of a man (the father of Śisu), Cat. **Vaṭêśvara**, m. N. of a Liṅga, Rājat.; of a poet and of various other men, Cat.; *-datta*, m. N. of a man (the father of Pṛithu and grandfather of Viśākha-datta who wrote the Mudrā-rākshasa), Cat.; *-māhātmya*, n., *-siddhânta*, m. N. of wks. **Vaṭôdakā**, f. N. of a river, BhP.

Vaṭaka, m. n. a small lump or round mass, ball, globule, pill, round cake made of pulse fried in oil or butter, Vas.; Suśr.; m. a particular weight (= 8 Māshas or 2 Śāṇas), ŚārṅgS.; (*akā*), f. = m. n., Dhūrtan.; (*ikā*), f. id., Pañcat. (B.); Lalit.; a pawn (at chess), L.

Vaṭakinī, f. (fr. prec.) N. of a partic. night of full moon (when it is customary to eat Vaṭaka cakes), Pāṇ. v, 2, 82, Vārtt. 1, Pat.

Vaṭāraka, m. a cord, string (cf. *vaṭâkara* and *varāṭaka*), MBh. (also *ā*, f.); N. of a man; (pl.) his descendants, g. *upakâdi*. **-maya**, mf(*ī*)n. made of a rope or of string, MBh.

Vaṭi, f. a sort of ant (= *divī* and *upajihvā*), L.; a kind of louse or other insect, L.

Vaṭika, m. a pawn (at chess), L.; (*ā*), f., see under *vaṭaka*.

Vaṭin, mfn. stringed, having a string, L.; circular, globular, L.; m. = *vaṭika*, BhavP.

Vaṭibha, mfn. having or containing the insect Vaṭi, Pāṇ. v, 2, 139.

Vaṭī. See under *vaṭa* above.

Vaṭūrin, mfn. broad, wide, RV. i, 133, 2 (Sāy.)

Vaṭya, mfn. belonging to the Banyan or Indian fig-tree, g. *balâdi*; m. or n. a kind of mineral, Cat.

वट् 2. *váṭ*, ind. an interjection or exclamation used in sacrificial ceremonies, TS.

वटर *vaṭara*, mfn. wicked, villainous, unsteady, L.; m. (only L.) a thief; a cock; a turban; a mat; a fragrant grass, Cyperus; a churning-stick; (?) a kind of bee (cf. *vāṭara*).

वटाकु *vaṭāku*, m. N. of a man (cf. *vāṭākavi*).

वटावीक *vaṭāvīka*, m. 'one who assumes a false name' or 'a notorious thief' (= *nāma-caura*), L.

वटु *vaṭu* &c. See *baṭu*.

वट्कु vaṭku, prob. w. r. for barku, Nyāyam., Sch.

वट्ट् vaṭṭ, cl. 1. P. vaṭṭati, Pat. on Pāṇ. i, 3, 1, Vārtt. 12.

वट्ट vaṭṭa or baṭṭa, m. N. of a man (also -deva), Rājat.

वट्टक vaṭṭaka, m. a pill, bolus, Bhadrab. (cf. vaṭaka).

वठ् vaṭh (also written baṭh), cl. 1. P. vaṭhati, to be big or fat, Dhātup. ix, 46; to be powerful or able, ib.

वठर vaṭhara, mfn. stupid, dull, a fool, blockhead, Hcar.; (only L.) wicked, vile (cf. vaṭara); m. a physician; a water-pot; =vakra; =ambashṭha; =śabda-kāra.

वडब vaḍabá, m. (also written vaḍavá, baḍavá, baḍabá) a male horse resembling a mare (and therefore attracting the stallion), Vait.; (ā), f., see next. **-dhenu**, f. a mare, KātyŚr.

Váḍabā, f. (also written váḍavā, báḍavā, báḍabā) a female horse, mare, TS. &c. &c.; the nymph Aśvinī (who, in the form of a mare as wife of Vivasvat or the Sun, became the mother of the two Aśvins; cf. aśvinī), Pur.; Daś.; a partic. constellation represented by a horse's head, W.; a female slave, L.; a harlot, prostitute, L.; = dvija-strī, L.; N. of a woman (having the patr. Prātitheyī), GṛS.; of a wife of Vasu-deva (called Paricārikā), Hariv.; of a river, MBh.; of a place of pilgrimage, Vishṇ. **-°gni** (°bāgni or °vāgni), m. 'mare's fire,' submarine fire or the fire of the lower regions (fabled to emerge from a cavity called the 'mare's mouth' under the sea at the South pole; cf. aurva), MBh.; Kathās.; -mala, n. a partic. foamy substance on the sea, L. **-°nala** (°bān°), m. = vaḍabāgni, Gol.; Kāv. (also personified, Virac.); a partic. powder (prepared from pepper and other pungent substances to promote digestion), Bhpr. **-bhartṛi**, m. 'mare's husband,' N. of the mythical horse Uccaiḥ-śravas (q. v.), Śiś. **-bhṛita**, v.l. for -hṛita (q.v.) **-mukha**, n. 'mare's mouth,' N. of the entrance to the lower regions at the South pole, Āryabh.; MBh.; Hariv.; m. (with or scil. agni) = vaḍabāgni (also identified with Śiva or the Maharshi Nārāyaṇa), ib.; R.; Kathās.; pl. N. of a mythical people, VarBṛS.; MārkP.; (ī), f. N. of a Yoginī, Hcat. **-ratha**, m. a chariot drawn by mares, L. **-vaktra**, n. = -mukha, n., MBh.; -huta-bhuj, m. = vaḍabāgni, Uttarar. **-suta**, m. du. 'the two sons of Vaḍabā,' N. of the Aśvins, L. **-hṛita**, mfn. said of a kind of slave, Yājñ., Sch.

Vaḍabin, mfn. (fr. vaḍabā), g. vrīhy-ādi.

वडभा vaḍabhā, f. a kind of bird (belonging to the class Pratuda, q.v.), Car.

वडभि vaḍabhi or °bhī, f. = valabhi, °bhī (q.v.), Hariv.; R.; Megh.

Vaḍabhī-kāra, m. N. of a man, g. kurv-ādi (cf. bāḍabhī-kara).

वडव vaḍavá, váḍabā. See vaḍabá, váḍabā.

वडहंसिका vaḍahaṅsikā or °sī, f. (in music) a partic. Rāgiṇī, Saṃgīt.

वडा vaḍā, f. (cf. = vaṭa) a small lump, globule, round mass or cake, L.

वडिश vaḍiśa. See baḍiśa.

वडेरु vaḍeru, m. N. of a man, Cat.

वडौसक vaḍausaka, m. or n.(?) N. of a place, Rājat.

वड्ढ् vaḍḍh, cl. 1. P. vaḍḍhati, Pat. on Pāṇ. i, 3, 1, Vārtt. 12.

वड्र vaḍra, mfn. large, great, L.

वण् vaṇ (also written baṇ), cl. 1. P. vaṇati (pf. vavāṇa &c.; Caus. aor. avīvaṇat or avavāṇat), to sound, Dhātup. xiii, 3.

Vaṇa, m. sound, noise, MW. (cf. dhig-v°).

Vaṇita, mfn., v.l. for veshṭita, KātyŚr., Sch.; = vyūta, ib.

वणथलग्राम vaṇathala-grāma, m. (prob. for vana-sthala-gr°) N. of a village, Cat.

वणिज् vaṇíj, m. (also written baṇij) a merchant, trader, RV. &c. &c.; the zodiacal sign Libra, VarBṛS.; N. of a partic. Karaṇa (q.v.), ib.; trade, traffic, commerce, Gaut.; Mn.

Vaṇik, in comp. for vaṇij. **-kaṭaka**, m. a company of merchants, caravan, Daś. **-karman**, n. (Pañcat.), **-kriyā**, f. (VarBṛS.) the business or occupation of a m°, trade. **-tva**, n. the position of a m°, Mudr. **-patha**, m. 'm°'s path,' trade, traffic, Mn.; MBh. &c.; a m°'s shop, Śiś.; Rājat.; a m°, BhP.; the zodiacal sign Libra, ib. **-putra**, m. a m°'s son, m°, Kathās.; Kāraṇḍ. **-purusha**, m. a m°, Kāraṇḍ. **-sārtha**, m. = -kaṭaka, BhP. **-suta**, m. a m°'s son, Kathās.; (ā), f. a m°'s daughter, ib. **-sūnu**, m. = -suta, ib.

Vaṇig, in comp. for vaṇij. **-gṛiha**, n. a merchant's house, L. **-grāma**, m. an association or guild of merchants, Daś. **-jana**, m. a commercial man, merchant, the m°-class, VarYogay. **-bandhu**, m. 'm°'s friend,' the indigo plant, L. **-bhāva**, m. 'condition of a m°,' trade, L. **-vaha**, m. 'm°'s vehicle,' a camel, L. **-vīthī**, f. a market-street, bazaar, Caṇḍ. **-vṛitti**, f. 'm°'s business,' trade, traffic, business, Bhartṛ.

Vaṇiṅ, in comp. for vaṇik fr. vaṇij. **-mārga**, m. a market-street, bazaar, L.

Vaṇija, m. = vaṇij, a merchant, trader, L.; N. of Śiva, MBh.; the zodiacal sign Libra, Laghuj.; N. of a Karaṇa (q.v.), VarBṛS.; (ā), f. traffic, commerce, L.

Vaṇijaka, m. a merchant, trader, L.

Vaṇijya, n. trade, traffic, L.; (ā), f. id., ŚBr. &c. &c.

वण्ट् vaṇṭ (also written baṇṭ), cl. 1. 10. P. vaṇṭati or vaṇṭayati (accord. to some also vaṇṭāpayati), to partition, apportion, share, divide, Dhātup. ix, 43; xxxii, 48 (only vaṇṭyate, Cāṇ., and vaṇṭyamāna, Hcar., v.l.)

Vaṇṭa, mfn. tailless, having no tail, Gaut. (cf. baṇḍa); unmarried, L.; m. an unmarried man, L.; a portion, share, L.; the handle of a sickle, L.

Vaṇṭaka, m. a portion, share, L.; dividing, MW.; an apportioner, distributer, ib.

Vaṇṭana, n. apportioning, distributing, partition, dividing into shares, L.

Vaṇṭanīya, mfn. to be apportioned or divided, W.

Vaṇṭita, mfn. divided into shares, partitioned, MW.

वण्टाल vaṇṭāla or vaṇṭhāla or vaṇḍāla, m. (only L.) a spade, shovel, hoe; a boat; a kind of contest or partic. mode of fighting.

वण्ठ् vaṇṭh, cl. 1. Ā. vaṇṭhate (pf. vavaṇṭhe &c.), to go or move alone, go unaccompanied, Dhātup. viii, 9.

Vaṇṭha, mfn. crippled, maimed, L.; unmarried, L.; m. an unmarried man, L.; a servant, L.; a dwarf, L.; a javelin, L.

Vaṇṭhara, m. (only L.) the new shoot of the Tāl or palm tree; the sheath that envelopes the young bamboo; a rope for tying a goat &c.; the female breast; a dog's tail; a dog; a cloud.

वण्ड् vaṇḍ (connected with √vaṇṭ), cl. 1. Ā. vaṇḍate, to partition, share, divide, Dhātup. viii, 18; to surround, cover, ib. (v.l. veshṭane for vibhājane); cl. 10. P. vaṇḍayati, to partition, share, divide, xxxii, 48 (v.l.)

वण्डर vaṇḍara, m. (cf. baṇḍa) a niggard, miser, W.; a eunuch or attendant on the women's apartments, ib.

वत् 1. vat, an affix (technically termed vati; see Pāṇ. v, 1, 115 &c.) added to words to imply likeness or resemblance, and generally translatable by 'as,' 'like' (e.g. brāhmaṇa-vat, like a Brāhman; pitṛi-vat = pitêva, pitaram iva, pitur iva and pitarîva). **-kāra**, m. the affix vat, Saṃk.

वत् 2. vat. See api-√vat.

वत vata. See 1. bata.

वतंस va-taṅsa, m. (ifc. f. ā) = ava-taṅsa, a garland, ring-shaped ornament, crest (also °saka), Kāv.; Chandom.

Va-taṅsita, mfn. = ava-taṅsita, Harav.

वतण्ड vataṇḍa, m. N. of a man, g. lohitâdi on Pāṇ. iv, 1, 18; pl. his descendants, Pravar. (cf. taṇḍa-vataṇḍa); (ī), f. a female descendant of Vataṇḍa, Pāṇ. iv, 1, 109.

वतरणी vataraṇī, w.r. for vaitaraṇī.

वतायन vatāyana, w.r. for vātāyana.

वति vati. See under √1. van, p. 917.

वतु vatu or vatū, ind. an interjection = hush! silence! Hcar.

वतू vatū, f. a river of heaven, L.; m. (only L.) one who speaks the truth; a road; a disease of the eyes.

वतोका va-tokā, f. = ava-tokā, a cow miscarrying from accident, L.

वत्स vatsá, m. (prob. originally 'yearling,' fr. a lost word vatas) a calf, the young of any animal, offspring, child (voc. vatsa often used as a term of endearment = my dear child, my darling), RV. &c. &c.; a son, boy (see bāla-v°); a year (see tri-v°); N. of a descendant of Kaṇva, RV.; PañcavBr.; ŚāṅkhŚr.; of an Āgneya (author of RV. x, 187), Anukr.; of a Kāśyapa, Kathās.; of the step-brother of Maitreya (who passed through fire to prove the falseness of Maitreya's allegation that he was the child of a Śūdrā), Mn. viii, 116 (Sch.); of a son of Pratardana, MBh.; Hariv.; of a son of Sena-jit, Hariv.; of a son of Aksha-mālā, Cat.; of a son of Uru-kshepa, VP.; of a son of Soma-śarman, Kathās.; of the author of a law-book, Cat.; (with carakâdhvaryu-sūtra-kṛit) of another author, ib.; of a serpent-demon, VP.; N. of a country (whose chief town is Kauśāmbī), Kathās.; Nerium Antidysentericum, L.; the Kuṭaja tree, L.; pl. the descendants of Vatsa, ĀśvŚr. (cf. Pāṇ. ii, 4, 64, Sch.); the inhabitants of the country called Vatsa, MBh.; Kathās.; (ā), f. a female calf, little daughter (voc. vatse = my dear child), Kālid.; Uttarar.; Prab.; m. n. the breast, chest, L. [Cf. vatsara and ἔτος for ϝέτος; Lat. vetus, vetus-tus, vitulus; Germ. widar, Widder; Eng. wether.] **-kāmā**, f. 'affectionate towards offspring,' a cow longing for her calf or a mother for her child, L. **-guru**, m. a teacher of children, preceptor, W. **-cchavi**, f. a calf's skin, ŚāṅkhBr.; ŚrS. **-jānu** or **-jñu**, mfn. formed like a calf's knee, ŚrS. **-tantī** (Āpast.; Gaut.) or **-tantrī** (Vas.; Vishṇ.; Mn.), a long rope to which calves are tied (by means of shorter ropes). **-tará**, m. (and ī, f.) more than a calf, a weaned calf, a young bull or heifer (also applied to goats and exceptionally to sucking calves and even to full grown animals which have not yet copulated), TS.; VS.; AitBr. &c.; °tarârṇa (°ra-ṛiṇa), n. the debt or loan of a bullock (?), Pāṇ. vi, 1, 89, Vārtt. 7, Pat. **-tva**, n. the state or condition of a calf, BhP. **-danta**, m. 'calf-toothed,' a kind of arrow (having a point like a calf's tooth), MBh.; R. (also °taka); N. of a mythical person, Virac.; n. an arrow point like a calf's tooth, ŚārṅgP. **-devī**, f. N. of a princess of Nepāl, Inscr. **-napāt** (vatsá-), m. N. of a descendant of Babhru, ŚBr. **-nābha**, m. a partic. tree, MBh.; Hariv. (also °bhaka); N. of a mythical being, Hariv. (v.l. rajata-n°); m. n. (also °bhaka) a partic. strong poison prepared from the root of a kind of aconite (said to resemble the nipple of a cow; it is also called Mīṭhā zahr), Suśr.; Bhpr.; n. a cavity of a partic. shape in the frame of a bedstead, VarBṛS. **-nābhi**, m. a calf's navel, Bhpr. **-nikānta** (vatsá-), mfn. affectionate towards offspring, MaitrS. **-pa** (vatsá-), m. a keeper of calves, BhP.; N. of a demon, AV. **-pati**, m. a king or lord of the Vatsas, (or) N. of a king, Vās., Introd.; N. of Udayana, Hcar. **-pattana**, n. 'Vatsa town,' N. of a city in the north of India (also called Kauśāmbī), L. **-pāla** or **°laka**, m. a keeper of calves (also applied to Krishṇa and Bala-deva), Hariv.; BhP.; HPariś. **-pālana**, n. the keeping or tending of calves, Pañcar. **-pītā**, f. (a cow) at which a calf has sucked, MBh. **-pracetas**, mfn. mindful of Vatsa or the Vatsas, RV. **-prī** (Sāy.), **-prí** (TS.) or **-prīti** (BhP.), m. N. of the author of RV. ix, 68; x, 45; 46 (his patr. is Bhālandana). **-prīya**, n. N. of the hymn RV. ix, 68, Sāy. (cf. prec. and vātsapriya). **-bandhā**, w.r. for baddha-vatsā (q.v.), MBh. **-bālaka**, m. N. of a brother of Vasu-deva, VP. **-bhūmi**, f. the country of the Vatsas, MBh.; m. N. of a son of Vatsa, Hariv. **-mitra**, m. N. of a certain Gobhila, VBr.; (ā), f. N. of a celestial virgin (Dik-kumārī), Harav. **-mukha**, mfn. calf-faced, Pāṇ. vi, 2, 168. **-rāja**, m. a king of the Vatsas,

MBh.; Ratnâv.; Kathās.; N. of various authors and other men (also *-deva*), Cat. **–rājya**, n. sovereignty or authority over the Vatsas, Kathās. **–rūpa**, m. a small calf, Hcar. **–lāñchana** and **-varadâcārya**, m. N. of two authors, Cat. **–vat**, mfn. having a calf, Hariv.; m. N. of a son of Śūra, ib. **–vinda**, m. N. of a man; pl. his descendants, Pravar. **–vṛiddha**, m. N. of a son of Uru-kriya, BhP. **–vyūha**, m. N. of a son of Vatsa, VP. **–śāla**, mfn. (fr. next) born in a calf-shed, Pāṇ. iv, 3, 36. **–śālā**, f. a calf-shed, ib. **–smṛiti**, f. N. of wk. **–hanu**, m. N. of a son of Sena-jit, VP. **Vatsâkshī**, f. Cucumis Maderaspatanus, L. **Vatsâjīva**, m. 'gaining a livelihood by keeping calves,' N. of a Piṅgala, Buddh. **Vatsâdana**, m. 'eating calves,' a wolf, L.; (*ī*), f. Cocculus Cordifolius, Car. **Vatsânusāriṇī**, f. (scil. *vivṛitti*) a hiatus between a long and short syllable, MāṇḍŚ. **Vatsânusṛij** (perhaps w.r. for °*sṛit*), a common N. for prec. and next, TPrāt., Sch. **Vatsânusṛitā** (MāṇḍŚ.), °**ti** (TPrāt., Sch.), f. a hiatus between a short and long syllable. **Vatsâsura**, m. N. of an Asura, Pañcar. **Vatsâhvaya**, m. Wrightia Antidysenterica, Suśr. **Vatsêśa**, m. a king of Vatsa, Kathās. **Vatsêśvara**, m. id., ib.; Ratnâv.; N. of two authors, Cat. **Vatsôddharaṇa**, (prob.) n. N. of a place, g. *takshaśilâdi*.

Vatsaka, m. (ifc. f. *ā*) a little calf, any calf or young animal, Mn.; BhP.; Hcat. (in voc. as a term of endearment; cf. *vatsa*); Wrightia Antidysenterica, L.; N. of an Asura, BhP.; of a son of Śūra, ib.; (*ikā*), f. a female calf, heifer, young cow, Yājñ.; n. green or black sulphate of iron, L.; the seed of Wrightia Antidysenterica (also *-bīja*), L.; = *vatsanābha*, n., Vāstuv.

Vatsará, m. the fifth year in a cycle of 5 or 6 years, (or) the sixth year in a cycle of 6 years, VS.; TS.; PārGṛ.; a year, Mn.; Yājñ.; VarBṛS. &c. (also n., MaitrUp. and *ī*, f., HPariś.); the Year personified, Mn. xii, 49 (as a son of Dhruva and Bhrami, BhP.; also applied to Vishṇu, MBh.); N. of a Sādhya, Hariv. (v.l. *matsara*); of a son of Kaśyapa, Cat. (v.l. *vatsāra*). **–phala**, n. N. of wk. **Vatsarâdi**, m. the first month of the Hindū year, Mārgaśīrsha, L. **Vatsarântaka**, m. the last month of the Hindū year, Phālguna, L. **Vatsarârṇa** (°*ra-ṛiṇa*), n. a debt or a loan for a year(?), Vop. ii, 9.

Vatsala, mf(*ā*)n. child-loving, affectionate towards offspring (*ā*, f. with or scil. *go* or *dhenu*, a cow longing for her calf), MBh.; R.; BhP.; kind, loving, tender, fond of or devoted to (loc., gen., acc. with *prati*, or comp.), MBh.; Kāv. &c.; m. (with *rasa*) the tender sentiment in a poem, Sāh.; a fire fed with grass (i.e. quickly burning away), L.; N. of one of Skanda's attendants, MBh.; n. = next, W. **–tā**, f., **-tva**, n. affectionateness, tenderness towards or delight in (loc. or comp.), MBh.; Kāv. &c.

Vatsalaya, Nom. P. °*yati*, to make tender or affectionate (esp. towards offspring or children), Śak.

Vatsāya, Nom. P. °*yati*, to represent or be like a calf, BhP.

Vatsāra, m. N. of a son of Kaśyapa, Cat. (cf. *vatsara* and *avatsāra*).

Vatsikā, f., see under *vatsaka* above.

Vatsin, mfn. having a calf, RV.; m. 'having many children(?),' N. of Vishṇu, MBh.

Vatsiman, m. childhood, early youth, Naish. (g. *pṛithv-ādi*).

Vatsi-putra, °**trīya**, w.r. for *vātsī-p*°.

Vatsīya, mfn. proper or fit for a calf, tending calves, Pāṇ. v, 1, 5, Sch. **–bālaka**, m. a boy who understands tending calves, cowherd, Hcar.

Vatsya, m. pl. = *vatsa-deśāḥ*, R. (B.); w.r. for *vatsa*, MBh.

वत्सणुरकतीर्थ *vatsaṇuraka-tīrtha*, n. N. of a Tīrtha, Cat.

वथ्सर *vathsara*, m. = *vatsara* (accord. to the grammarian Paushkarasādi).

वद् *vad*, cl. 1. P. Ā. (Dhātup. xxiii, 40) *vádati*, °*te* (ep. m. c. also *vādati*; Pot. *udeyam*, AV.; pf. *uvāda*, pl. *ūdimá*, RV.; *ūde* &c., Br.; Up.; *veditha*, °*dathuḥ*, °*duḥ*, Vop.; aor. *avādīt*, °*dishuḥ*, RV. &c. &c.; Subj. *vādishaḥ*, AV.; *avādiran*, ib.; *vadishma*, °*shṭhāḥ*, Br.; Prec. *udyāt*, ib.; fut. *vadishyáti*, °*te*, AV. &c.; inf. *váditos*, Br.; *vaditum*, ib. &c.; ind. p. *uditvā*, GṛŚrS.; *-udya*, Br.), to speak, say, utter, tell, report, speak to, talk with, address (P. or Ā.; with acc. of the thing said, and acc. [with or without *abhi*] or gen., or loc. of the person addressed; also followed by *yad*, 'that,' or by *yadi*, 'whether'), RV. &c. &c.; (P.) to praise, recommend, MBh.; to adjudge, adjudicate, TS.; BhP.; to indicate, designate, VarBṛS.; to proclaim, announce, foretell, bespeak, ĀśvGr.; MBh.; Kāv. &c.; to allege, affirm, ib.; to declare (any one or anything) to be, call (two acc. or acc. and nom. with *iti*), AV. &c. &c.; (with or scil. *vācam*) to raise the voice, sing, utter a cry (said of birds &c.), RV. &c. &c.; (Ā.) to say, tell, speak to (acc.), ŚBr. &c. &c.; to mention, state, communicate, name, TS.; R.; Hariv.; to confer or dispute about, RV.; TS.; to contend, quarrel, ŚBr.; to lay claim to (loc.), AitBr.; to be an authority, be eminent in (loc.), Pāṇ. i, 3, 47; to triumph, exult, Bhaṭṭ.: Pass. *udyáte* (aor. *avādi*), to be said or spoken &c., AV. &c. &c.: Caus. *vādáyati*, m. c. also °*te* (cf. Pāṇ. i, 3, 89; aor. *avīvadat*; Pass. *vādyate*, ep. also °*ti*), to cause to speak or say, MBh.; to cause to sound, strike, play (with instr., rarely loc. of the instrument), ŚBr.; MBh. &c.; to play music, MBh.; R.; Hariv.; (with *bahu*) to make much ado about one's self, Subh.; to cause a musical instrument (acc.) to be played by (instr.), Pāṇ. i, 1, 58, Vārtt. 2, Pat.; to speak, recite, rehearse, Hariv.: Desid. *vivadishati*, °*te*, to desire to speak, Br.; Gobh.: Intens. *vâvadīti* (RV.; AV.), *vāvadyáte* (ŚBr.), *vāvatti* (Gr.), to speak or sound aloud. [Cf. Lit. *vadìnti*.]

Udita. See 2. *udita*, p. 186.

Vada, mfn. speaking, a speaker (only ifc.; see *ku-v*°, *priyaṃ-v*°); speaking well or sensibly, L.; m. N. of the first Veda (with the Magians), Cat.

Vadaka. See *dur-v*°.

Vádana, n. (ifc. f. *ā*) the act of speaking, talking, sounding, ŚBr.; ŚrS.; the mouth, face, countenance, MBh.; Kāv. &c. (°*naṃ* √*kṛi*, to make a face or grimace, °*nī-*√*bhū*, to become a face); the front, point, R.; Suśr.; (in alg.) the first term, initial quantity or term of a progression, Col.; (in geom.) the side opposite to the base, the summit or apex of a triangle, Āryabh. **–kaṃja**, n. a lotus-face, MW. **–cchada**, w.r. for *radana-cch*°, R. **–dantura**, m. pl. N. of a people, MārkP. **–paṅka-ja**, n. = *-kaṃja*, Kāvyâd. **–pavana**, m. 'mouth-wind,' breath, Śiś. **–madirā**, f. the wine or nectar of the mouth, Megh. **–māruta**, m. = *-pavana*, Śak. **–mālinya**, n. a troubled face, shame-faced appearance, Bālar. **–roga**, m. mouth-disease, VarBṛS. **–śyāmikā**, f. 'blackness of the face,' a kind of disease, Cat. **–saroja**, n. = *-kaṃja*, W. **Vadanâmaya**, m. mouth-disease, face-sickness, L. **Vadanâsava**, m. 'mouth-liquor,' saliva, spittle, L. **Vadanêndu**, m. 'face-moon,' the face, W. **Vadanôdara**, n. 'mouth-hole,' the jaws, Bhartṛ.

Vadanta, °**ti**, or °**tī**. See *kiṃ-v*°.

Vadantika, m. pl. N. of a people, MārkP.

Vadanya, mfn. = *vadānya*, L.

Vadamāna, mfn. speaking, saying &c.; glorifying, boasting, W.

Vadānya, mf(*ā*)n. bountiful, liberal, munificent, a m° giver, MBh.; Kāv. &c.; eloquent, speaking kindly or agreeably, affable, L.; m. N. of a Ṛishi, MBh. **–śreshṭha**, m. 'best of givers,' N. of Dadhyac (q.v.), Gal.

Vadāvada, mfn. (prob. an old Intens.; cf. *carācara*, *calācala* &c.) speaking much or well, a speaker, Pāṇ. vi, 1, 12, Vārtt. 6, Pat. (cf. *a-vadāvada*).

Vadāvadin, mfn. id., Lāṭy.

Vaditavya, mfn. to be said or spoken (n. impers.), AitBr.; Sarvad.

Vaditṛi, mfn. speaking, saying, telling (with acc.), Śiś.; m. a speaker (with gen.), AitBr.; MBh.

Váditos. See √*vad* above.

Vadishṭha, mfn. speaking best or very well, PañcavBr.

Vadmán, mfn. speaking, a speaker (said of Agni), RV.

Vadya, mfn. to be spoken &c. (see *a-v*° and *an-av*°); N. of the days of the dark lunar fortnight; n. speech, speaking about, conversing (see *brahma-v*°, *satya-v*°). **–paksha**, m. the dark fortnight of the lunar month (in which the moon is waning), MW.

वदर *vadara*, °*rika* &c. See *badara*.

वदाम *vadāma*, m. (fr. Persian بادام) an almond, L. (cf. *bādāma*).

वदाल *vadāla*, m. a kind of Silurus or sheat-fish, L.; an eddy or whirlpool, L.

Vadālaka, m. = *vadāla*, a kind of sheat-fish, L.

वदि *vadi*, ind. (g. *svar-ādi*; accord. to some for *badi*, contracted fr. *bahula-dina*, but cf. *vadya*) in the dark half of any month (affixed to the names of months in giving dates; see *vaiśākha-v*°).

वट्टक *vaddaka*, v.l. for *vaṭṭaka* (q.v.)

वड्डिवास *vaddivāsa*, m. or n.(?) N. of a place, Rājat.

वद्ध्री *vaddhrī*, v.l. for *vadhrī* (q.v. under *vadhra*).

वध् *vadh* (also written *badh*; cf. √*bādh*; properly only used in the aor. and Prec. tenses *avadhīt* and °*dhishṭa*; *vadhyāt* and *vadhishīshṭa*, Pāṇ. ii, 4, 42 &c.; vi, 4, 62; the other tenses being supplied by √*han*; cf. Dhātup. xxiv, 2; but in Ved. and ep. poetry also pres. *vadhati*; Pot. *vadhet*; fut. *vadhishyati*, °*te*; other Ved. forms are aor. *avadhīm*, *vádhīm*, Subj. *vadhishaḥ*; *badhīḥ*, TĀr.; Prec. *badhyāsam*, °*suḥ*, AV.), to strike, slay, kill, murder, defeat, destroy, RV. &c. &c.: Pass. *vadhyate*, °*ti* (aor. *avadhi*), to be slain or killed, MBh.; Kāv. &c.: Caus. *vadhayati*, to kill, slay, MBh. [Cf. Gk. ὠθέω.]

Vadhá, m. one who kills, a slayer, vanquisher, destroyer, RV.; VS.; TS.; ŚBr.; a deadly weapon (esp. Indra's thunderbolt), RV.; AitBr.; ŚāṅkhGr.; the act of striking or killing, slaughter, murder, death, destruction, RV. &c. &c.; (in law) capital or (more commonly) corporal punishment, Mn.; Yājñ. &c. = *vadha-bhūmi*, place of execution, Caurap., Introd.; stroke, hurt, injury, Nir.; paralysis, Suśr.; annihilation, disappearance (of inanimate things), MBh.; Kāv. &c.; frustration, prevention, Gaut.; a defect, imperfection (28 are enumerated), VP.; multiplication, Gaṇit.; a product, Bījag.; N. of a Rākshasa, VP.; (*ā*), f. a kind of pot-herb, Convolvulus Repens, L. **–karmâdhikārin**, m. 'one who superintends the act of putting to death,' an executioner, hangman, Rājat. **–kāṅkshin**, mf(*iṇī*)n. wishing for death, W. **–kāma**, mfn. desirous of killing, Gobh. **–kāmyā**, f. desire to kill, intention to hurt, Mn. iv, 165. **–kshama**, mfn. deserving death, MBh. **–jīvin**, m. 'living by killing (animals),' a butcher, hunter &c., Yājñ. **–1. -trá**, mfn. (for 2. *vádhatra* see below) protecting from death or destruction, PārGṛ. **–daṇḍa**, m. capital or corporal punishment Mn. viii, 129. **–nigraha**, m. capital punishment, Kathās. **–nirṇeka**, m. expiation for killing, atonement for murder or manslaughter, Mn. xi, 139. **–bandha**, m. du. death and bonds, Mn. v, 49. **–bhūmi**, f. a place of execution, Caurap., Sch. (cf. *vadhya-bh*°). **–rata**, mfn. fond of killing, L. **–sthalī**, f., **-sthāna**, n. a place of execution, L.; a slaughter-house, L. **Vadhâṅgaka**, n. a prison, L. **Vadhârha**, mfn. deserving death, W. **Vadhâśaṅka**, m. or n. (BṛĀrUp.); (*ā*), f. (ŚBr.) fear of death or destruction. **Vadhâishin**, mf(*iṇī*)n. desirous of killing, MBh. **Vadhôdarka**, mfn. resulting in death, MW. **Vadhôdyata**, mfn. prepared or ready to kill, murderous; m. an assassin, murderer, L. **Vadhôpâya**, m. an instrument or means of putting to death, Mn. ix, 248.

Vádhaka, mfn. killing, destructive, Uṇ. ii, 36; intending to strike or kill, Jātak.; m. a murderer, assassin, MBh.; VarBṛS.; Rājat.; an executioner, hangman, Kathās.; a partic. sort of reed or rush, AV.; ŚBr.

2. **Vádhatra**, n. (for 1. *vadha-trá* see under *vadhá* above) 'instrument of death,' deadly weapon, dart, RV.

Vadhánā, f. a deadly weapon, RV.

Vádhar, n. (only this form) a destructive weapon (esp. the thunderbolt of Indra), RV.

Vadharya, Nom. P. °*yáti*, to hurl a thunderbolt (only f. of pr. p. *vadharyántī*, 'casting a bolt,' prob. = lightning), RV.

Vadhasná, m. or n. (only in instr. pl.) = *vádhar*, RV.

Vadhasnu, mfn. wielding a deadly weapon, RV.

Vadhika, m. or n. musk, L.

Vadhitra, n. sexual love or the god of love, Uṇ. iv, 172, Sch.

Vadhin, mfn. incurring death, killed by (ifc.), L.

Vádhya, mfn. (frequently written *bádhya*) to be slain or killed, to be capitally punished, to be corporally chastised (cf. under *vadha*), sentenced, a criminal, AV. &c. &c.; to be destroyed or annihilated, MBh.; Kāv. &c.; m. an enemy, MW.; (*ā*), f., see below. **-ghātaka** (L.), **-ghna** (MBh.), mfn. killing one sentenced to death, executing criminals. **-cihna**, n. the mark or attribute of one sentenced to be killed, Nāg. **-ḍiṇḍima**, m. or n.(?) a drum beaten at the time of the execution of a criminal, Mṛicch. **-tā**, f., **-tva**, n. the state of being sentenced to death, fitness to be killed, MBh. **-paṭa**, m. the red garment of a criminal during his execution, Śrīkaṇṭh. **-paṭaha**, m. = *-ḍiṇḍima*, Mṛicch. **-paryāya**, m. (a hangman's) turn to execute a criminal, Mṛicch. **-pāla**, m. 'guardian of criminals,' a jailer, VP. **-bhū** or **-bhūmi**, f. a place of public execution, Kathās. **-mālā**, f. a garland placed on the head of one sentenced to death, Mṛicch. **-vāsas**, n. the clothes of a criminal who has been executed (given to a Caṇḍāla), Mn. x, 56. **-śilā**, f. a stone or rock on which malefactors are executed, scaffold, slaughter-house, shambles, Nāg.; Kathās.; Pañcat.; N. of wk. **-sthāna**, n. = *-bhū*, Pañcat. **-sraj**, f. = *-mālā*, Mudr.

Vadhyat, mfn. = *vadhyamāna*, being struck or killed, MBh. iii, 805.

Vadhyā, f. killing, murder (see *ātma-* and *brahma-v°*).

Vádhri, mfn. 'one whose testicles are cut out,' castrated, emasculated, unmanly (opp. to *vṛishan*), RV.; AV.; ŚBr. **-matī**, f. a woman who has an impotent husband, RV. **-vāc** (*vádhri-*), mfn. speaking unmanly or useless words, idly talking, ib. **Vadhry-aśvá**, m. 'having castrated horses,' N. of a man, RV.; Br. &c. (in PañcavBr. he has the patr. *Ānūpa*); pl. the family of Vadhry-aśva, ŚrS. (cf. *vādhryaśva* and *bradhnaśva*).

Vadhrikā, m. a castrated person, eunuch, Kāś. on Pāṇ. vi, 1, 204.

वधा *vadhā*, ind., g. *câdi*.

वधिर *vadhira*. See *badhira*.

वधू *vadhū*, f. (fr. √*vadh* = *vah*; cf. *ūḍhā*) a bride or newly-married woman, young wife, spouse, any wife or woman, RV. &c. &c.; a daughter-in-law, HPariś.; any younger female relation, MBh.; R. &c.; the female of any animal, (esp.) a cow or mare, RV. v, 47, 6; viii, 19, 36 (cf. *vadhū-mat*); N. of various plants (Trigonella Corniculata; Echites Frutescens; Curcuma Zerumbet), L. **-kāla**, m. the time during which a woman is held to be a bride, R. **-gṛiha-praveśa**, m. the ceremony of the entrance of a bride into the house of her husband, Cat. **-jana**, m. a woman or wife (also collectively 'women'), Ratnâv. **-tva**, n. condition of a bride, Vcar. **-darśá**, mfn. looking at a bride, AV. **-dhana**, n. a wife's private property, ĀpGṛ., Sch. **-pathá**, m. the path or way of a bride, ib. **-praveśa**, m. = *-gṛiha-pr°*, Cat. **-mat** (*vadhū́-*), mfn. (prob.) drawn by mares, RV. **-vára**, n. sg. or m. pl. bride and bridegroom, a newly-married couple, HPariś.; m. pl. brides and bridegroom, ib. **-vastra**, n. bridal apparel, MW. **-vāsas**, n. a bride's undergarment, ĀpGṛ. **-samyāna**, n. a woman's vehicle, Mṛicch. **-sarā**, f. N. of a river (fabled to have sprung from the weeping eyes of Pulomā, wife of Bhṛigu), MBh.; *-kṛitāhvayā*, f. id., ib.

Vadhu, f. a young wife or woman. Śiś.; a daughter-in-law, L.

Vadhukā, f. a young woman or wife, L.

Vadhuṭī, f. a young woman living in her father's house, L.; a daughter-in-law, L.

Vadhūka (ifc.) = *vadhū*, a wife, HPariś. (cf. *sa-v°*).

Vadhūṭikā, f. a young wife or woman, Prasannar.

Vadhūṭī, f. id., Bālar.; a daughter-in-law, L. **-śayana**, n. 'resting-place of women,' a lattice, window, Gal.

Vadhūyú, mfn. one who loves his wife or longs for a wife, uxorious, lustful, a wooer, suitor, bridegroom, RV.; AV.

Vadhvaṭī, f. = *vadhūṭī*, L.

वध्न *vadhna*, m. pl. N. of a people, MBh. (B. *vadhra*).

वध्य *vadhya* &c. See p. 916, col. 3.

वध्योष *vadhyosha*, m. N. of a man, Kāś. in g. *bidâdi* on Pāṇ. iv, 1, 104 (cf. *badhyoga*).

वध्र *vadhra*, m. n. (also written *badhra*; cf. √*bandh*) a leathern strap or thong, Suparṇ.; MBh.; (*ī*), f. (also written *vaddhrī*) id., L.; (prob.) a slice of bacon (see *varāha-v°*); n. lead, L.

Vadhraka, n. lead, L.

Vadhraśva, v.l. for *vadhry-aśva*.

Vadhrya, m. (also written *badhrya*) a shoe, slipper, L.

वध्रि *vadhri* &c. See col. 1.

वध्वा *vadhvā*, ind., g. *câdi*.

वन् 1. *van*, cl. 1. P. (Dhātup. xiii, 19; 20; xix, 42) *vánati* (Ved. also °*te*, and *vanáti*); cl. 8. P. Ā. (xxx, 8) *vanóti*, *vanuté* (pf. *vāvā́na*, *vāvántha*, *vavanmá*, *vavné*; p. *vavanvás*, RV.; aor. *vanta*, *váṇsva*, ib.; *vaṇsat*, °*sate*, ib.; *vanishat*, AV.; °*shanta*, TS.; *vanushanta*, RV.; Pot. *vaṇsīmahi*, *vasīmahi*, ib.; Prec. *vanishīshṭa*, RV.; *vaṇsishīya*, AV.; fut. *vanitā*, Gr.; *vanishyate*, ŚāṅkhŚr.; inf. *vanitum*, Gr.; *-vantave*, RV.), to like, love, wish, desire, RV.; AV.; ŚBr.; Kāṭh.; ŚāṅkhŚr.; to gain, acquire, procure (for one's self or others), RV.; AV.; ŚBr.; to conquer, win, become master of, possess, RV.; AV.; to prepare, make ready for, aim at, attack, RV.; to hurt, injure, MW. (Dhātup. also 'to sound;' 'to serve, honour, worship, help, aid'): Caus. *vanayati* or *vānayati*, Dhātup. xix, 68; xxxix, 33, v.l. (cf. *sam-√van*): Desid. *vivāsati*, °*te*, to attract, seek to win over, RV.: Intens. (only *vāvánaḥ* and *vāvandhi*; but cf. *vanīvan*) to love, like, RV. [Cf. Lat. *venia*, *Venus*; Got. *gawinnan*; Germ. *gewinnen*; Eng. *to win*.]

Vata, mfn. uttered, sounded, spoken, W.; asked, begged, ib.; killed, hurt, MW.; (ind.), see *bata*.

Vati, f. (prob.) asking, begging, Pāṇ. vi, 4, 37, Sch.

2. **Ván** = *vána* (only in gen. and loc. pl. *vanā́m*, *váṇsu*), 'wood' or 'a wooden vessel,' RV.; love, worship, L.

1. **Vána**, n. (once m., R. v, 50, 21; for 2. see p. 919, col. 1) a forest, wood, grove, thicket, quantity of lotuses or other plants growing in a thick cluster (but in older language also applied to a single tree), RV. &c. &c.; plenty, abundance, R.; Kathās.; a foreign or distant land, RV. vii, 1, 19 (cf. *araṇya*); wood, timber, RV.; a wooden vessel or barrel (for the Soma juice), RV. (?); a cloud (as the vessel in the sky), ib.; (prob.) the body of a carriage, RV. viii, 34, 18; water, Naigh. i, 12; a fountain, spring, L.; abode, Nalôd.; Cyperus Rotundus, VarBṛS.; = *raśmi*, a ray of light, Naigh. i, 4; (prob.) longing, earnest desire, KenUp.; m. N. of a son of Uśīnara, BhP.; of one of the 10 orders of mendicants founded by Śaṃkarâcārya (the members of which affix *vana* to their names, cf. *rāmêndra-v°*), W.; (*ā*), f. the piece of wood used for kindling fire by attrition (= *araṇi*, q.v.; sometimes personified), RV. iii, 1, 13; (*ī*), f. a wood, forest, Sāh. **-ṛikshá**, w.r. for *-krakshá*. **-kacu**, m. Arum Colocasia, L. **-kaṇā**, f. wild pepper, L. **-kaṇḍūla**, m. a kind of bulbous plant, L. **-kadalī**, f. wild banana or plantain, L. **-kanda**, m. N. of two kinds of tuberous plant (= *dharaṇī-kanda* or *vana-śuraṇa*), L. **-kapi**, m. a wild monkey, Kāś. on Pāṇ. ii, 3, 68. **-kapīvat**, m. N. of a son of Pulaha, VP. (v.l. *ghana-* and *dhana-k°*). **-karin**, m. a wild elephant, Kād. **-kāma**, mfn. fond of (or living in) a forest, MBh. **-kārpasī** (Suśr.), °**sī** (L.), f. the wild cotton tree. **-kāshṭhikā**, f. 'forest-twig,' a piece of dry wood in a forest, Pañcat. **-kukkuṭa**, m. a wild fowl, jungle fowl, L. **-kuñjara**, m. = *-karin*, BhP. **-kusuma**, n. a forest-flower, Subh. **-kokilaka**, n. a kind of metre, Chandom. **-kodrava**, m. a kind of inferior grain, L. **-koli**, f. the wild jujube, L. **-kauśāmbī**, f. N. of a town, g. *nady-ādi*. **-krakshá**, mfn. (prob.) crackling or bubbling in a wooden vessel (said of Soma), RV. **-khaṇḍa**, n. 'group of trees,' copse, wood, MBh. (also written *-shaṇḍa*). **-ga**, m. inhabitant of a forest, MBh. **-gaja**, m. a wild elephant, MBh.; Kāv. &c.; *-mada*, m. the fluid exuding from the temples of a wild el° in rut, Megh. **-gamana**, n. retiring to a forest, leading the life of an anchorite, Vikr. **-gava**, m. Bos Gavæus, L. **-gahana**, n. the depth or thick part of a forest, Pañcat. **-gupta**, m. 'forest-protected,' a spy, emissary, L. **-gulma**, m. a forest-shrub or bush, MBh. **-go**, m. = *-gava*, L. **-gocara**, mf(*ā*)n. dwelling in a f°, denizen or inhabitant of forests (said of men and animals), Mn.; MBh. &c; living in water, BhP.; m. a hunter, forester, W.; n. a forest, ib. **-grahaṇa**, n. the act of occupying a forest (cf. *-grāhin*), Śak.; *-kolāhala*, m. or n. the din of oc° a forest, hunting cries, Śak. **-grāmaka**, m. a forest village, a poor small v°, Hcar. **-grāhin**, m. 'occupying or searching a forest,' a hunter, Śak. (cf. *-grahaṇa*). **-gholi**, f. = *araṇya-gh°*, MW. **-ṃ-kāraṇa**, n. a partic. part of the body (with *mehana*), RV. x, 163, 5. **-candana**, n. aloe wood or Agallochum, L.; Pinus Deodora, L. **-candrikā**, f. Jasminum Sambac, L. **-campaka**, m. the wild Campaka tree, L. **-cara**, mf(*ī*)n. roaming in woods, living in a forest, MBh.; Kāv. &c.; m. a woodman, forester, ib.; a wild animal, ib.; the fabulous eight-legged animal Śarabha, MW. **-carya**, n. (SaṃjUp.), **-caryā**, f. (R.) the roaming about or dwelling in a forest. **-cārin**, mfn. = *-cara*, Mn.; MBh. &c. **-cohāga**, m. a wild goat, L.; a boar, hog, L. **-cchid**, mfn. cutting wood, felling timber; m. a woodcutter, Hariv.; Bhaṭṭ. **-ccheda**, m. cutting timber, W. **-ja**, mfn. f°-born, sylvan, wild, Śiś.; m. a woodman, forester, R.; (only L.) an elephant; Cyperus Rotundus; the wild citron tree; a partic. bulbous plant (= *vana-śūraṇa*); coriander; (*ā*), f. (only L.) Phaseolus Trilobus; the wild cotton tree; wild ginger; Physalis Flexuosa; a kind of Curcuma; Anethum Panmori; a species of creeper; n. 'water-born,' a blue lotus-flower, Hariv.; *-pattrâksha*, mf(*ī*)n. (MBh.) and *-°jâksha*, mf(*ī*)n. (Prasannar.) lotus- (leaf-) eyed; *-°jâyata*, mfn. long and resembling a blue lotus-flower, Subh. **-jāta** = *-ja*, mfn., Hit. **-jīra**, m. wild cumin, L. **-jīvikā**, f. forest-life (i.e. living by gathering leaves and fruit &c.), HPariś. **-jīvin**, m. 'living in a forest,' a woodman, forester, W. **-jyotsnī**, f. 'Light of the Grove,' N. of a plant, Śak. (in Prākrit). **-taraṃgiṇī**, f. N. of wk. **-tikta**, m. Terminalia Chebula, L.; (*ā*), f. a kind of plant (accord. to L. Symplocos Racemosa or = *śveta-buhnā*), Vāgbh. **-tiktikā**, f. Clypea Hernandifolia, L. **-da**, m. 'rain-giving,' a cloud, L. **-damana**, m. a wild Artemisia, L. **-dāraka**, m. pl. N. of a people, MārkP. **-dāha**, m. a forest-conflagration; °*hâgni*, m. fire from a f°-c°, R. **-dīpa**, m. = *-campaka*, L. **-dīya-bhaṭṭa**, m. N. of a Commentator, Col. **-durga**, mfn. made inaccessible by (reason of) a forest; n. a place made so inac°, MBh.; R. **-durgā**, f. (prob.) a form of the goddess Durgā; *-kalpa*, m., *-tattva*, n., *-prayoga*, m., *-mantra*, m.; °*gôpanishad*, f. N. of wks. **-devatā**, f. a f°-goddess, Dryad, Kāv.; Kathās. **-druma**, m. a f°-tree, Bharṭṛ. (v.l.) **-dvipa**, m. = *-karin*, Ragh.; Kathās. **-dhānya**, n. pl. grains of wild corn, HPariś. **-dhārā**, f. an avenue of trees, Vikr. **-dhiti** (*vaná-*), f. (prob.) a layer of wood to be laid on an altar, RV. **-dhenu**, f. the cow or female of the Bos Gavæus, L. **-nitya**, m. N. of a son of Raudrâśva, Hariv. **-pá**, m. a forest-protector, woodman, VS.; MBh. **-pannaga**, m. a forest-snake, MBh. **-parvan**, n. 'F°-section,' N. of MBh. iii (describing the abode of the Pāṇḍava princes in the Kāmyaka f°). **-pallava**, m. Hyperanthera Moringa, L. **-pāṇsula**, m. a hunter, deer-killer, L. **-pādapa**, m. a f°-tree, L. **-pārśva**, m. f° side or region, R. **-pāla**, m. = *-pa* (°*lâdhipa*, m. high-forester), R.; N. of a son of Deva-pāla, Satr.; of a son of Dharma-pāla, Buddh. **-pālaka**, m. = *-pa*, Dhūrtan. **-pippalī**, f. wild pepper, L. **-pushpa**, n. a f°-flower, wild flower (*-maya*, mf[*ī*]n. made or consisting of wild fl°s), Kathās.; (*ā*), f. Anethum Sowa, L. **-pūraka**, m. the wild citron tree, L. **-pūrva**, m. N. of a village, Rājat. **-prakshá**, v.l. for *-krakshá*, SV. **-praveśa**, m. entering a forest, (esp.) a solemn procession into a forest (for cutting wood for an idol), VarBṛS.; commencing to live as a hermit, W. **-prastha**, m. or n. (?) a forest situated on elevated or table land, MBh.; N. of a place, Rājat.; mfn. retiring into a forest, living the life of an anchorite, MW. **-priya**, m. 'fond of woods,' the Indian cuckoo, Pārvat.; n. the cinnamon tree, L. **-phala**, n. wild fruit, R. **-barbara**, m. Ocimum Sanctum, L. **-barbarikā**, f. Ocimum Pilosum, L. **-barhiṇa**, m. a wild peacock (*-tva*, n.), Ragh. **-bāhyaka**, m. pl. N. of a people, MārkP. **-biḍāla**, m. a kind of wild cat, Felis Caracal, Kautukas. **-bīja**, m. the wild citron tree (also °*jaka*), L.; *-pūraka*, m. id., L. **-bhadrikā**, f. Sida Cordifolia, L. **-bhuj**, m. a partic. bulbous plant (growing on the Himavat), L. **-bhū** or **-bhūmi**, f. 'forest-region,' the neighbourhood of a wood, Kāv. **-bhūshaṇī**, f. 'wood-adorning,' the female of the Indian cuckoo, L. **-bhojana-puṇyâha-vācana-prayoga**, m., **-bhojana-prayoga**, m., **-bhojana-vidhi**, m. N. of wks. **-makshikā**, f. a gad-fly, L. **-mallikā**, f. Jasminum Sambac, L. **-mallī**, f. wild jasmine,

L. **-mātaṃga,** m. = *-karin,* Daś. **-mānusha,** m. 'wild-man,' the orang-utang, MW.; °*shikā* (Kād.), °*shī* (Hcar.), f. a (little) f°woman. **-māya,** m. aloe wood, Agallochum, L. **-māla,** mfn. wearing a garland of f°-flowers (said of Vishṇu-Kṛishṇa), Hariv. **-mālā,** f. a garland of f°-flowers, (esp.) the chaplet worn by Kṛishṇa, Kāv.; VarBṛS. &c.; a kind of metre, Col.; N. of a wk. on Dharma; of various women, HPariś.; *-dhara,* (prob.) n. a kind of metre; *-miśra,* m. N. of an author, Cat. (°*rīya,* n. his wk.); *-vijaya,* m., *-stotra,* n. N. of wks. **-mālikā,** f. a garland of wild flowers, BhP.; yam, L.; a kind of metre, Piṅg., Sch.; N. of one of Rādhā's female attendants, Pañcar.; of a river, Hariv. **-mālin,** mfn. = *-māla* (said of Vishṇu-Kṛishṇa), MBh.; Kāv. &c.; m. (in music) a kind of measure, Saṃgīt.; N. of various authors (also with *bhaṭṭa*), Cat.; (*inī*), f. Dioscorea or = *varāhī* (prob. a kind of plant, accord. to others 'the female energy of Kṛishṇa'), L.; N. of the town Dvārakā, L.; °*li-kīrti-chando-mālā,* f. N. of a poem; °*li-dāsa* and °*li-miśra,* m. N. of two authors, Cat.; °*līśā,* f. 'having Kṛishṇa as husband,' N. of Rādhā, Pañcar. **-muc,** mfn. pouring forth rain, Ragh.; m. a cloud, L. **-mudga,** m. Phaseolus Trilobus (also *ā,* f.) or Aconitifolius, L. **-mūta,** m. a cloud, L. **-mūrdhajā,** f. gall-nut, L. **-mūla,** m. Tetranthera Lanceifolia, MW.; *-phala,* n. roots and fruits of the forest, VarBṛS. **-mṛiga,** m. a forest deer, R. **-methikā,** f. Melilotus Parviflora, L. **-mocā,** f. wild plantain, L. **-yamānī,** f. Cnidium Diffusum, L. **-rakshaka,** m. a forest-keeper, MW.; (*ā*), f. N. of a woman, Vṛishabhân. **-rāja,** m. 'forest-king,' a lion, L.; Verbesina Scandens, L. **-rāji,** mf(*ī*)n. embellishing or beautifying a f°, W.; (°*jī*), f. a row of trees, a long track of f° or a path in a f°, MBh.; Kāv. &c.; (only °*jī*), a female slave belonging to Vasu-deva, VP. **-rājya,** n. N. of a kingdom, VarBṛS. **-rāshṭra** or °**raka,** m. pl. N. of a people, VarBṛS.; MārkP. **-ṛddhi** (for *-ṛiddhi*), f. an ornament of the forest, BhP. **-lakshmī,** f. 'f°-ornament,' Musa Sapientum, L. **-latā,** f. a f°-creeper, Śak. **-lekhā,** f. = *-rāji,* Śiś. **-varāha,** m. a wild hog, MW. **-vartikā,** f. a kind of quail, Mālatīm. **-vartin,** mfn. residing in the forest, W. **-varbara, -varbarikā, -varhiṇa,** see *-barbara* &c. **-vallarī,** f. a kind of grass, L. **-vahni,** m. a forest-conflagration, Kathās. **-vāta,** m. a f°-wind, Śak. **-vāsa,** m. dwelling or residence in a forest, wandering habits, R.; Kām.; MārkP.; N. of a country, Cat.; mfn. residing in a f°, wood-dweller, Śak.; °*saka,* m. pl. N. of a people, MBh. (B. °*sika*). **-vāsana,** m. 'f°-dweller,' a civet-cat, L. **-vāsin,** mfn. living in a f°; m. a forest-dweller, hermit, anchorite, Mn.; MBh. &c.; N. of various plants or roots (= *ṛishabha, mushkaka, varāhī-kanda* &c.), L.; a crow, L.; N. of a country in the Dekhan (also °*simaṇḍala*), Inscr.; °*sī,* f. N. of the chief town of that country, ib. **-vāsya,** (prob.) n. N. of a country, Hariv. (cf. *-vāsin*). **-vāhyaka, -viḍāla,** see *-bāh°, -biḍ°.* **-virodhin,** m. 'forest-enemy,' N. of one of the Hindū months (that succeeding the Nidāgha, q. v.), L. **-vilāsinī,** f. Andropogon Auriculatus, L. **-vīja** &c., see *-bīja.* **-vṛitti,** f. = *-jīvikā,* HPariś. **-vṛintākī,** f. the egg-plant, L. **-vrīhi,** m. wild rice, L. **-śikhaṇḍin,** m. = *-barhiṇa,* L. **-śūkarī,** f. Mucuna Pruritus, L. **-śūraṇa,** n. a kind of bulbous plant, L. **-śṛiṅgâṭa** and °**ṭaka,** m. Tribulus Lanuginosus, L. **-śobhana,** n. 'water-beautifying,' a lotus-flower, L. **-śvan,** m. 'f°-dog,' a jackal, Śiś.; a tiger, L.; a civet-cat, L. **-shaṇḍa,** see *-khaṇḍa.* **-shad,** v.l. for *-sad,* PārGṛ. **-saṃkaṭa,** m. lentil, L. **-sád,** mfn. abiding in wood or in a f°, VS.; PārGṛ.; m. a forest-dweller, forester, Kir. **-saṃnivāsin,** mfn. dwelling in a forest; m. a forester, Kir. **-samûha,** m. a thick forest or wood, L. **-sampraveśa,** m. = *vana-praveśa,* VarBṛS. **-sarojinī,** f. the wild cotton plant, L. **-sâhvayā,** f. a kind of creeping plant, L. **-sindhura,** m. = *-karin,* HPariś. **-stamba,** m. N. of a son of Gada, Hariv. **-stha,** mfn. forest-abiding; m. a f°-dweller, hermit, ascetic, Mn.; R. &c.; a deer, gazelle, L.; (with *gaja*) a wild elephant, Hariv.; (*ā*), f. the holy fig-tree, L.; the small Pippala tree, L.; a kind of creeper, L. **-sthalī,** f. f°-region, a wood, Hariv.; Kālid. **-sthāna** (?), n. N. of a country, Buddh. **-sthāyin,** mfn. being or abiding in a forest, W.; m. a hermit, anchorite, ib. **-sthita,** mfn. situate or being in a f°, ib. **-s-páti** (*vánas-*), m. (*vanas* prob. a form of the gen.; cf. 2. *van* and *ráthas-páti*) 'king of the wood,' a forest-tree (esp. a large tree bearing fruit apparently without blossoms, as several species of the fig, the jack tree &c., but also applied to any tree), RV. &c. &c.; a stem, trunk, beam, timber, post (esp. the sacrificial post), RV.; VS.; Br.; 'lord of plants,' the Soma plant, ib.; GṛS.; BhP.; the Indian fig-tree, L.; Bignonia Suaveolens, L.; an offering made to the sacrificial post, ŚBr.; ŚrS.; anything made of wood (esp. partic. parts of a car or carriage, a wooden drum, a wooden amulet, a block on which criminals are executed, a coffin &c.), RV.; AV.; VS.; an ascetic, W.; N. of Vishṇu, Vishṇ.; of a son of Ghṛita-pṛishṭha, BhP.; du. pestle and mortar, RV. i, 28, 6; f. N. of a Gandharvī, Kāraṇḍ.; n. N. of the Varsha ruled by Vanas-pati, BhP.; *-kāya,* m. the whole body or world of plants, L.; *-yāga,* m. and *-sava,* m. N. of partic. sacrificial rites, Vait. **-sraj,** f. a garland of forest-flowers, BhP. **-hari,** m. (prob.) a lion, Rājat. **-haridrā,** f. wild turmeric, L. **-hava,** m. a partic. Ekâha, ŚrS. **-hāsa,** m. Saccharum Spontaneum (also °*saka*), L.; a kind of jasmine, L. **-hutâśana,** m. = *vana-dāha,* Cat. **-homa,** m. a partic. oblation, ĀpŚr. **Vanâkampa,** m. the shaking of f°-trees by the wind, W. **Vanâkhu,** m. 'forest rat,' a hare, L.; °*khuka,* m. Phaseolus Mungo, L. **Vanâgni,** m. = *vana-dāha,* R. **Vanâcārya,** m. N. of an author, Cat. **Vanâja,** m. the wild goat, L. **Vanâṭana,** n. roaming about in a f° (also pl.), Rājat. **Vanâṭu,** m. 'forest-roamer (?),' a kind of blue fly, L. **Vanâdhi-vāsin,** mfn. dwelling in a forest, Kir. **Vanânta,** m. 'forest-region,' a wood, MBh.; Kāv. &c.; mfn. bounded by a f°, Hariv.; *-bhū,* f. neighbourhood of a f°, Kir.; *-vāsin,* mfn. dwelling in a f°, Rājat.; *-stha,* mfn. standing or situate in a forest (as a town), Kathās.; *-sthalī,* f. a forest-region, Bhartṛ. **Vanântara,** n. interior of a forest, Kāv.; VarBṛS.; Kathās. (°*re,* in the f°; °*rāt,* out of the f°; °*ram,* into the f°, with *pra-√viś* or *√āp,* to enter or reach a f°); *āṇi,* pl. forests, Vcar.; *-cara* and *-cārin,* mfn. roaming about in a f°, Kāv.; VarBṛS. **Vanâpaga** (ibc. for °*gā*), a forest stream, river, R. **Vanâbjinī,** f. lotus growing in a f°, Kathās. **Vanâbhilāva,** mfn. f°-destroying, W. **Vanâmala,** m. Carissa Carandas, L. **Vanâmbikā,** f. N. of a tutelary deity in the family of Daksha, Cat. **Vanâmra,** m. Mangifera Sylvatica, L. **Vanârishṭā,** f. wild turmeric, L. **Vanârcaka,** m. 'f°-worshipper,' a florist, maker of garlands, L. **Vanârdraka,** n. the root of wild ginger, L.; (*ā*), f. wild ginger, L. **Vanâlakta** or °**ktaka,** n. 'wild lac,' red earth, ruddle, L. **Vanâlaya,** m. forest-habitation; *-jīvin,* mfn. living in f°s, Hariv. **Vanâlikā,** f. Heliotropium Indicum, L. **Vanâlī,** f. = *vana-rāji,* Prab. **Vanâlu,** m. Marsilia Dentata, L. **Vanâśa,** mfn. living on water, MBh. (Nīlak.); m. a kind of small barley, L. **Vanâśrama,** m. abode in the f° (the third Āśrama [q. v.] in a Brāhman's life), Hariv.; *-nivāsin* (ib.) or °*śramin* (BhP.), m. a Vānaprastha or Brāhman dwelling in a forest, an anchorite. **Vanâśraya,** mfn. living in a f°; m. a f°-dweller, MārkP.; a sort of crow or raven, L. **Vanêjya,** m. a highly valued species of mango, L. **Vanâika-deśa,** m. a part or spot of a f°, Hit. **Vanôtsarga,** m. N. of a wk. (on the dedication of temples, tanks, groves &c.) by Vishṇu-śarman. **Vanôtsāha,** m. a rhinoceros, L. **Vanôddeśa,** m. a partic. spot in a f°, MBh. **Vanôdbhava,** mfn. produced or existing in a f°, growing wild, MBh.; m. (with *mārga*) a path in a f°, ib.; (*ā*), f. the wild cotton plant, L.; Phaseolus Trilobus, L.; the wild citron, L. **Vanôpaplava,** m. = *vana-dāha,* Megh. **Vanôpala,** m. 'forest-stone,' shaped and dried cow-dung, Bhpr. **Vanôpêta,** mfn. one who has retired to the forest, VarBṛS. **Vanôrvī,** f. = *vana-bhū,* Rājat. **Vanâuka,** m. = next, MBh.; BhP. **Vanâukas,** mfn. living in a forest; m. a f°-dweller, anchorite, MBh.; Kāv. &c.; a f°-animal, (esp.) a wild boar, BhP.; an ape, L. **Vanâugha,** m. a mass of water, Śiś.; 'thick f°,' N. of a district or mountain in the west of India, VarBṛS. **Vanâushadhi,** f. a medicinal herb growing wild, Cat.

Vanád (only pl. *vanádaḥ*), longing, earnest desire, RV. ii, 4, 5 (Sāy. = *vanantaḥ* = *sambhaktāraḥ;* others translate *me van-ádaḥ,* 'of me, the wood-devourer').

Vanana, n. longing, desire, Nir. v, 5; (*ánā*), f. (prob.) wish, desire, RV. ix, 86, 40.

Vananīya, mfn. to be desired, desirable, Nir.; Śaṃk.

Vánanva, Nom. P. °*vati,* to be in possession, be at hand, RV. viii, 102, 19; x, 92, 15; pr. p. °*nvat,* possessing, ib. vii, 81, 3; viii, 6, 34; being in possession, ib. viii, 1, 31.

Vanayitṛi, mfn. (superl. °*tṛi-tama*) one who causes to ask &c., Nir.

Vanar, in comp. for *vanas* (= *vana*). **-gú,** mfn. moving about in woods, wandering in a forest or wilderness, a savage, RV.; AV.; a thief or robber, Naigh. **-ja,** m. a kind of plant (= *śṛiṅgī*), L. **-shád,** mfn. sitting on trees or in the forest (as birds), RV.; MaitrS.

Vánas, n. loveliness, RV. x, 172, 1; longing, desire (cf. *yajña-vanas* and *gir-vaṇas*); = *vana,* a wood (cf. *vanar*).

Vanasa, mfn., g. *tṛiṇâdi.*

Vánas-páti. See col. 1.

Vanasyā. See *sajāta-v°.*

Vanasyú. See *gir-vaṇasyú.*

Vanāyu, m. N. of a country (see comp.); of a son of Purū-ravas, MBh.; Hariv. (also °*yus,* VP.); of a Dānava, MBh. **-ja** (Hcar.) or **-deśya** (Ragh.), mfn. produced or bred in Vanāyu (as horses).

Vaní, f. wish, desire, AV.; m. fire, L.; (*váni,* ifc.) procuring, bestowing (cf. *rāyas-posha-v°* and Pāṇ. iii, 2, 27).

Vanikā, f. a little wood, grove, MBh.; R. &c. (only in *aśoka-v°;* once in R. *-vanika,* n.)

Vanikâvāsa (or °*kâv°*?), m. N. of a village, Rājat.

Vanita, mfn. solicited, asked, wished for, desired, loved, L.; served, W.; (*ā*), f. a loved wife, mistress, any woman (also applied to the female of an animal or bird), MBh.; Kāv. &c.; a kind of metre, Col.

Vanitā, f. (see prec.) in comp. **-dvish,** m. hating women, a misogynist, MBh. **-bhoginī,** f. a woman like a serpent, MW. **-mukha,** m. pl. 'woman-faced,' N. of a people, MārkP. **-rājya,** n. the kingdom of women, L. (cf. *strī-r°*). **-vilāsa,** m. the wantonness of women, MW.

Vanitāya, Nom. Ā. °*yate,* to be or act like a woman, Śṛiṅgār.

Vanitāsa, m. N. of a family, Cat.

Vanitṛi, mfn. one who owns or possesses (with acc.), RV. (cf. *vantṛi*).

1. **Vanin,** mfn. (fr. *√van*) asking, desiring, RV.; granting, bestowing, ib.

2. **Vánin,** m. (fr. 1. *vana*) a tree, RV.; the Soma plant, ib. iii, 40, 7; (perhaps) a cloud, ib. i, 73, 8; 130, 4; 'living in a wood,' a Brāhman in the third stage of his life, a Vānaprastha, Kull. on Mn. vi, 38.

Vanina, n. a tree or a wood, RV. x, 66, 9.

Vanila, mfn. (fr. 1. *vana*), g. *kāśâdi.*

Vánishṭha, mfn. (superl.) obtaining or imparting most, very munificent or liberal, RV.

Vanī. See under 1. *vana.*

Vanīka (L.) or **vanīpaka** (L. and Siṃhâs., v. l.), m. a beggar, mendicant.

Vanīya, Nom. P. °*yati,* to beg, ask alms, Uṇ. iv, 139, Sch.

Vanīyaka, m. a mendicant, beggar, R. (B.); Dhūrtan.; Siṃhâs. (v. l. *vanīpaka*). **-jana,** m., id., Śiś.

Vánīyas, mfn. (compar.) obtaining most, imparting more, RV.; very munificent or liberal, BhP.

Vánīvan, mfn. (an intens. form) asking for, demanding, RV. x, 47, 7.

Vanú, m. 'zealous, eager,' (either) an assailant, injurer, enemy, RV. iv, 30, 5; (or) an adherent, friend, ib. x, 74, 1.

Vanusha (fr. *vanús*), Nom. Ā. °*shate* (only *vanushanta*), to obtain, acquire, RV. x, 128, 3.

Vanushya (fr. *vanús*), Nom. P. Ā. °*shyáti,* °*te,* to plot against, attack, assail, RV. i, 132, 1 &c.; (Ā.) to wish for, desire, ib. ix, 7, 6.

Vanús, mfn. zealous, eager; (either) anxious for, attached or devoted to, a friend; (or) eager to attack, a foe, enemy, RV.

Vane, loc. of 1. *vana,* in comp. **-kiṃśuka,** m. pl. 'Butea Frondosa in a wood,' anything found unexpectedly, Pāṇ. ii, 1, 44, Sch. (cf. *-bilvaka*). **-kshudrā,** f. Pongamia Glabra, L. **-cara,** mf(*ī*)n. wandering or dwelling in a wood, inhabitant of a forest (applied to men, animals and demons), MBh.; Kāv. &c.; °*râgrya,* m. 'chief of forest-dwellers,' an ascetic, anchorite, sage, W. **-já,** mfn. born or existing in woods, RV. **-bilvaka,** m. pl. 'Aegle Marmelos in a forest,' anything found unexpectedly, Pāṇ. ii, 1, 44, Sch. (cf. *-kiṃśuka*). **-ráj,** mfn. shining or blazing in a wood, RV. vi, 12, 3. **-vāsin,** m. 'forest-dweller,' a Brāhman in the third stage of his life, a Vānaprastha, L. **-śaya,** mfn. living in woods, W. **-shāh** (*-sháh*), mfn. prevailing in woods, RV. x, 61, 20. **-sad,** m. a forest-dweller, Kir. (cf. *vana-sad*). **-sarja,** m. Terminalia Tomentosa, L.

Vaneyu, m. N. of a son of Raudrāśva, MBh.

Vanti, f., Pāṇ. vi, 4, 39, Sch.

Vantṛi, m. an enjoyer, owner, possessor (with gen.), RV. (cf. *vánitṛi*).

Ványa, mf(*ā*)n. growing or produced or existing in a forest, wild, savage, VS. &c. &c.; greenish (?), AV. vi, 20; being or existing in woods (said of Agni), TS.; made of wood, wooden, RV.; m. a wild animal, R.; VarBṛS.; a wild plant, R.; N. of partic. wild plants (= Arundo Bengalensis; *varāhī-kanda; vana-śūraṇa*), L.; a Buddhist novice, Gal.; (*ā*), f. a multitude of groves, large forest, L.; abundance of water, a flood, deluge, Kṛishis.; N. of various plants (Physalis Flexuosa; Abrus Precatorius; a kind of Curcuma; a kind of gourd or cucumber; a kind of Cyperus; dill), L.; n. anything grown in a wood, the fruit or roots of wild plants, MBh.; R. &c.; = *tvaca*, L. (cf. also *cakshur-v°* and *a-jīta-punar-vaṇya*). **-damana,** m. a species of Artemisia, L. **-dvipa,** m. a wild elephant, MW. **-pakshin,** m. a wild bird, forest-bird, ib. **-vṛitti,** f. forest-food, f°-produce, ib.; mfn. living on forest-food, Ragh. **Vanyânna-bhojana,** m. 'eating forest-food,' a Brāhman in the third stage of his life, Gal. **Vanyâśana,** mfn. = *vanya-vṛitti*, mfn., VarBṛS. **Vanyâśrama,** w.r. for *vanâśrama*, Hariv. **Vanyêtara,** mfn. different from wild, tame, civilized, Ragh. **Vanyêbha,** m. a wild elephant, Śiś. **Vanyôpôdakī,** f. a species of creeper, L.

वन 2. *vana*, ind., g. *câdi*.

वनर *vanara*, m. = *vānara*, an ape, L.

वनर्गु *vanar-gu* &c. See p. 918, col. 3.

वनहबन्दि *vanahabandi*, N. of a place, Cat.

वनाहिर *vanāhira*, m. a hog, wild boar, L.

वनिष्ठु *vanishṭhu*, m. a part of the entrails of an animal offered in sacrifice (accord. to Sch. either 'the rectum' or 'a partic. part of the intestines near the omentum'), RV.; AV.; Br.; ŚrS. **-sava,** m. a partic. Ekâha, ŚāṅkhŚr.

Vanishṇu, m. (prob. w.r. for *vanishṭu*) = *apâna*, the anus, Uṇ. iv, 2, Sch.

वनीवाहन *vanīvâhana*, n. (anom. intens. form fr. √1. *vah*) the act of carrying or moving hither and thither, ŚBr.; ŚrS.

Vanīvāhitá, mfn. carried hither and thither, ŚBr.

वनोद्देश *vanôddeśa, vanôpaplava, vanâukas*. See p. 918, col. 2.

वन्तव *vantava* (?), m. N. of a man, Pravar.

वन्द् *vand* (cf. √*vad*), cl. 1. Ā. (Dhātup. ii, 10) *vándate* (ep. also *°ti*; pf. *vavanda, °dé*, RV. &c. &c.; Prec. *vandishīmahi*, RV.; fut. *vanditā, vandishyate*, Gr.; inf. *vanditum*, MBh. &c.; *vandádhyai*, RV. i, 27, 1; 61, 5; ind. p. *vanditvā, -vandya*, MBh. &c.), to praise, celebrate, laud, extol, RV.; AV.; ŚāṅkhŚr.; to show honour, do homage, salute respectfully or deferentially, venerate, worship, adore, RV. &c. &c.; to offer anything (acc.) respectfully to (dat.), MārkP.: Pass. *vandyate* (aor. *avandi, vandi*), to be praised or venerated, RV. &c. &c.: Caus. *vandayati* (aor. *avavandat, °data*), to show honour to any one, greet respectfully, MārkP.: Desid., see *vivandishu*.

Vanda, mfn. praising, extolling (see *deva-vandá*); (*ā*), f., see below.

Vandaka, m. a parasitical plant, L. (also *ā*, f.); a Buddhist mendicant, Gal.

Vandatha, m. 'a praiser' or 'one deserving praise,' L.

Vandád-vāra, w.r. for *vánde dārúm*, SV.

Vandád-vīra, w.r. for *mandád-vīra*, ib.

Vandádhyai. See under √*vand*.

Vándana, m. N. of a Ṛishi (who was cast into a well, along with Rebha, by the Asuras, and rescued by the Aśvins), RV.; (*ā*), f. praise, worship, adoration, L.; (with Buddhists) one of the 7 kinds of Anuttara-pūjā or highest worship (the other 6 being *pūjanā, pāpa-deśanā, anumodanā, adhyeshaṇā, bodhi-cittôtpāda* and *pariṇamanā*), Dharmas. 14; a mark or symbol impressed on the body (with ashes &c.), Vas.; (*ī*), f. (only L.) reverence; a drug for resuscitating the dead (= *jīvātu*); begging or thieving (*yācana-* or *mācala-karman*); the hip or a species of tree (*kaṭī* or *vaṭī*); = *go-rocana*; n. the act of praising, praise, RV.; reverence (esp. obeisance to a Brāhman or superior by touching the feet &c.), worship, adoration, Mn.; MBh. &c.; a parasitical plant, AV.; Bhpr.; a disease attacking the limbs or joints, cutaneous eruption, scrofula (also personified as a demon), RV.; = *vadana*, L. **-mālā** (L.), **-mālikā** (Kāv.; Pañcat.), f. a festoon of leaves suspended across gateways (in honour of the arrival of any distinguished personage, or on the occasion of a marriage or other festival). **-śrut,** mfn. listening to praise, a hearer of praises, RV. **Vandane-shṭhā,** mfn. mindful of praises, ib.

Vandanaka, n. respectful salutation, Śil.

Vandanīya, mfn. to be respectfully greeted, Vajracch.; m. a Verbesina with yellow flowers, L.; (*ā*), f. a yellow pigment (= *go-rocanā*).

Vandā, f. (only L.) a parasitical plant (esp. Epidendrum Tesselatum); a female mendicant; = *bandī*, a prisoner.

Vandāka, m., **°kā** or **°kī,** f. Vanda Roxburghii, L.

Vandāra, m. a parasitical plant, L.

Vandā́ru, mfn. praising, celebrating, RV.; VS.; respectful, reverential, civil or polite to (comp.), Mcar.; Prab.; Dhūrtan.; m. N. of a man, Cat.; n. praise, RV.

Vandi, °dī. See 1. 2. *bandin*.

Vanditá, mfn. praised, extolled, celebrated, AV. &c. &c.

Vanditavya, mfn. to be praised, Nir.; to be respectfully greeted, R.

Vanditṛi or **vánditṛi,** mfn. one who praises or celebrates, a praiser, RV.; ŚBr.

Vandin, mfn. to praise or honour (ifc.), Kum. (cf. 1. *bandin*).

Vandinikā or **°nīyā,** f. N. of Dākshāyaṇī, Cat.

Vándya, mfn. to be praised, praiseworthy, RV. &c. &c.; to be saluted reverentially, adorable, very venerable, Kāv.; Kathās.; to be regarded or respected, L.; m. N. of a man, Cat.; (*ā*), f. a parasitical plant, L.; = *go-rocanā*, L.; N. of a Yakshī, Kathās. **-ghaṭīyā,** f. N. of a Comm. on the Amarakośa. **-tā,** f. laudability, praiseworthiness, venerableness, Rājat. **-bhaṭṭīya,** n. N. of wk.

Vandra, mfn. praising, doing homage, worshipping, Uṇ. ii, 13, Sch.; m. a worshipper, votary, follower, W.; n. prosperity, plenty, abundance, L.

वन्दीक *vandīka*, m. (also written *bandh°*) N. of Indra, L.

वन्धा *vandhā*, ind., g. *ūry-ādi*.

वन्धुर *vandhúra*, n. (also written *bandhura*; rather fr. 2. *van* + *dhura* than fr. √*bandh*) the seat of a charioteer, the fore part of a chariot or place at the end of the shafts, a carriage-seat or driver's box, RV.; AV.; MBh.; Hariv.; BhP. (cf. *tri-v°*). **Vandhure-shṭhá,** mfn. standing or sitting on the chariot-seat, RV.

Vandhúr, m. = *vandhúra*, RV. i, 34, 9.

Vandhurāyú, mfn. having a standing-place in front or seat for driving (said of the car of the Aśvins), RV.

वन्धुल *vandhula*, m. N. of a Ṛishi (see *bandhula*).

वन्ध्य *vandhya*, mf(*ā*)n. (also written *bandhya*, q.v., and perhaps to be connected with √*bandh*) barren, unfruitful, unproductive (said of women, female animals and plants), Mn.; MBh. &c.; fruitless, useless, defective, deprived or destitute of (instr. or comp.), MBh.; Kāv. &c.; (*ā*), f., see below. **-tā,** f., **-tva,** n. barrenness, sterility, uselessness, deficiency, lack of (loc. or comp.), Hariv.; Kāv.; Rājat. **-parvata,** m. N. of a district, Cat. **-phala,** mfn. fruitless, useless, idle, vain (*-tā*, f.), Bhartṛ.

Vandhyā, f. a barren or childless woman, Mn.; Yājñ. &c.; a barren cow, L.; a partic. fragrant substance, L. **-karkaṭakī,** f. a species of medicinal plant (given to barren women), L. **-garbha-dhāraṇa-vidhi,** m. N. of wk. **-tanaya,** m. = *-putra*, L. **-tva,** n. the barrenness of a woman, Suśr.; Hcat.; *-kārakôpadrava-hara-vidhi*, m. N. of wk. **-duhitṛi,** f. the daughter of a barren woman, a mere chimera or anything merely imaginary, L. **-putra,** m. the son of a b° w°, i.e. anything merely imaginary, an impossibility, Śaṃk. **-prakāśa,** see *pañcadhā-bandhyā-pr°*. **-prāyaścitti-vidhi,** m. N. of wk. **-roga,** m., **-°valī** (*°dhyâv°*), f. N. of wks. **-suta,** or **-sūnu,** m. = *-tanaya*, L.

Vandhyāya, Nom. Ā. *°yate*, to become barren or useless, Cat.

वन्ना *vannā*, f. N. of a woman, Cat.

वन्र *vanra*, m. (prob. fr. √1. *van*) a co-partner, co-heir (= *vibhāgin*), Uṇ. ii, 28, Sch.

वप् 1. *vap*, cl. 1. P. Ā. *vápati, °te* (only pres. stem and ind. p. *uptvā, -upya*), to shear, shave (Ā. 'one's self'), cut off, AV.; TS.; Br.; GṛŚrS.; to crop (herbage), mow, cut (grass), graze, RV. vi, 6, 4: Caus. *vāpayati, °te* (Pot. *vāpayīta*, ĀśvŚr.), to cause (Ā. 'one's self') to be shorn, GṛŚrS.

1. **Upta,** mfn. shorn, shaved, GṛŚrS. **-keśa,** mfn. one who has his hair shorn, MānGṛ.; *-śmaśru*, mfn. one who has his hair and beard shorn, Kauś.

1. **Vapa,** m. shaving, shearing, W.

1. **Vapana,** n. the act of shearing or shaving or cutting off, ŚBr. &c. &c.; a razor, L.; (*ī*), f. a barber's shop, L. **-nirṇaya,** m. N. of wk. **-prayoga,** m. N. of a treatise on the ceremony of shaving the Brahma-cārin for the first time. **-vidhi,** m. N. of ch. of TS.

1. **Vapanīya.** See *keśa-v°*.

1. **Vaptṛi** or **váptṛi,** m. one who shears, a shearer, cutter, shaver, RV.; AV.; TBr.; GṛS.

वप् 2. *vap*, cl. 1. P. Ā. (Dhātup. xxiii, 34) *vápati, °te* (Pot. *upet*, GṛS.; pf. *uvāpa, ūpúḥ*; *ūpe*, RV. &c.; *vavāpa*, MBh.; *-vepe*, Kāś. on Pāṇ. vi, 4, 120; aor. *avāpsīt*, Br. &c.; *avapta*, Gr.; Pot. *upyāt*, ib.; fut. *vaptā*, ib.; *vapsyáti*, Br.; *vapishyati*, MBh. &c.; inf. *vaptum*, Gr.; ind. p. *uptvā*, MBh.; *-úpya*, RV. &c.), to strew, scatter (esp. seed), sow, bestrew, RV. &c. &c.; to throw, cast (dice), ib.; to procreate, beget (see *vapus* and 2. *vaptṛi*); to throw or heap up, dam up, AV.: Pass. *upyáte* (aor. *vāpi*, Br.), to be strewn or sown, RV. &c. &c.: Caus. *vāpayati* (aor. *avīvapat*, Gr.), to sow, plant, put in the ground, MBh.: Desid. *vivapsati, °te*, Gr.: Intens. *vāvapyate, vāvapti*, ib.

Upita, mfn. scattered, sown, MBh.

2. **Uptá,** mfn. scattered, sown, planted, put in the ground, RV. &c. &c.; bestrewed or covered with (instr. or comp.), BhP.; thrown down, lying, AV.; presented, offered, BhP.; n. a sown field, Gal. **-kṛishṭa,** mfn. ploughed after sowing, Gal. **-gāḍha,** mfn., g. *rāja-dantâdi*.

Upti, f. sowing seeds, L. **-vid,** mfn. an agriculturist, Mn. ix, 330.

Uptrima, mfn. sown, cultivated, Pāṇ. iii, 3, 88, Sch.

Upya, mfn. (cf. under √2. *vap*) to be scattered or sown, KātyŚr.

2. **Vapá,** m. one who sows, a sower, VS. (cf. g. *pacâdi*); (*ā*), f., see below.

2. **Vapana,** n. the act of sowing seed, L.; semen virile, W.; placing, arranging, L.

2. **Vapanīya,** mfn. to be scattered or sown (n. impers.), Kull. on Mn. ix, 41.

Vapā́, f. a mound or heap thrown up by ants (see *valmīka-v°*); a cavity, hollow, hole, L.; the skin or membrane investing the intestines or parts of the viscera, the caul or omentum, VS. &c. &c. (the horse has no omentum accord. to ŚBr.); the mucous or glutinous secretion of the bones or flesh, marrow, fat (= *medas*), L.; a fleshy prominent navel, L. **-kṛit,** m. marrow, L. **-°dhiśrayaṇī** (*vapâdh°*), f. du. = *vapā-śrapaṇī*, L. **-°nta** (*vapânta*), m. the end of the offering of the omentum, ŚrS. **-mārjana,** n. the wiping or separating off of the omentum, Vait.; mf(*ā*)n. that on which the om° is wiped or separated off, ib. **-vat** (*vapā́-*), mfn. furnished with or enveloped in the om°, RV.; VS.; ŚBr. **-śrapaṇī,** f. du. a two-pronged fork on which the om° is fried, ŚBr. **-śravaṇī,** w.r. for prec., MaitrS. **-°huti** (*vapâh°*), f. (AitBr.), **-homa** (KātyŚr.), m. the offering of om°. **Vapôdara,** mfn. fat-bellied, corpulent (said of Indra), RV. **Vapôddharaṇa,** n. the aperture through which the om° is taken out, GṛŚrS.

Vapāka. See *a-vapāka*.

Vapila, m. a procreator, father, L.

Vapu, m. = *vapus*, a body, MW.; f. N. of an Apsaras, MBh.; MārkP. **-nandana,** m. N. of a poet, Cat.

Vapuḥ, in comp. for *vapus*. **-prakarsha,** m.

excellence of form, personal beauty, Ragh. **-srava,** m. humour of the body, chyle, L.

Vapuna, m. a god, L.; n. knowledge, L. (w.r. for *vayuna*).

Vapur, in comp. for *vapus*. **-dhara,** m. having form, embodied, BhP.; having beautiful form, handsome, MBh. **-mala-samâcita,** mfn. having the body covered with dirt, ib. &c.

Vapush, in comp. for *vapus*. **-ṭama,** mfn. most beautiful or handsome or wonderful, AV.; (*ā*), f. Hibiscus Mutabilis, L.; N. of the wife of Janamejaya, MBh.; Hariv. **-ṭara** (*vápush-* or *vapúsh-*), mfn. more or most beautiful or wonderful (*vápusho vapushṭara*, most wonderful of all), RV. **-mat,** mfn. having a body, embodied, corporeal, Kir.; having a beautiful form, handsome, Mn.; MBh. &c.; containing the word *vapus*, AitBr.; m. N. of a deity enumerated among the Viśve Devāḥ, Hariv.; of a son of Priya-vrata, Pur.; of a Ṛishi in the 11th Manv-antara, VP.; of a king of Kuṇḍina, ib.; (*atī*), f. N. of one of the Mātṛis attending upon Skanda, MBh.; *-tā*, f. beauty, Divyâv. **-mata,** m. (only acc. *-matam* m. c. for *-mantam*) N. of a king of Kuṇḍina, MārkP.

Vápusha, mfn. wonderfully beautiful, RV.; (*ā*), f. = *havushā*, Bhpr.; n. marvellous beauty (dat. with *darśatá*, wonderful to look at), RV.; (°*shī*), f., see under *vapus*.

1. **Vapushya,** Nom. P. °*yáti*, to wonder, be astonished, RV.

2. **Vapushyà,** mfn. wonderfully beautiful, wonderful, RV.

Vapushyā́, f. (the same form as instr.) wonder, astonishment, RV.

Vápus, mfn. having form or a beautiful form, embodied, handsome, wonderful, RV.; n. form, figure, (esp.) a beautiful form or figure, wonderful appearance, beauty (*vápushe*, ind. for beauty; *vápur dṛiśáye*, a wonder to see), RV. &c. &c.; nature, essence, Mn. v, 96; x, 9 &c.; (ifc. f. *ushī*) the body, Mn.; MBh. &c.; f. Beauty personified as a daughter of Daksha and Dharma, VP.; MārkP.; N. of an Apsaras, VP. **-sât,** ind. into the state of a body, APrāt, Sch.

Vaptavya, mfn. = *vapanīya*, Mn. ix, 41; 42.

2. **Vaptṛi,** m. a sower, Mn.; MBh. &c.; a procreator, progenitor, father, Dharmaś.; a poet, L.

Vaptṛika. See *prakhyāta-v°*.

Vapya-nīla, N. of a country, Rājat.

Vapra, m. n. a rampart, earthwork, mound, hillock, mud wall, earth or bank raised as a wall or buttress or as the foundation of a building, MBh.; Kāv. &c.; a high river-bank (also *nadī-v°*), any shore or bank, MBh.; R.; Kir.; the slope or declivity of a hill, table-land on a mountain, Kir.; Śiś.; a ditch, VarBṛS.; the gate of a fortified city, W.; the circumference of a sphere or globe, Gol.; a sown field, any field, Dharmaś.; dust, L.; = *nishkuṭa*, *vanaja*, n., *vājikā*(?) and *pāṭīra*, L.; the butting of an elephant or of a bull (see *-kriyā* and *-krīḍā*); m. a father, L. (cf. 2. *vaptṛi*); = *prajā-pati*, L.; N. of a Vyāsa, VP.; of a son of the 14th Manu, Hariv.; (*ā*), f. a flat bank of earth, garden-bed (*vaprā-vat*, ind. as in a level bank, i.e. as in levelling or arranging a place for the fire, Mahīdh.); Rubia Munjista, L.; N. of the mother of the Arhat Nimi, L.; (*ī*), f. a hillock, ant-hill (cf. *vamrī*), MW.; n. lead, L. (cf. *vardhra*). **-kriyā** (Ragh.), **-krīḍā** (Megh.), f. the playful butting of an elephant or of a bull against a bank or mound of any kind. **-kshetra-phala,** n. the circumference of a sphere or globe, Gol. **-phala,** n. id., ib. **Vaprânata,** mfn. bound or stooping to butt at a bank or wall, W. **Vaprântar,** ind. in or between banks or mounds, ib. **Vaprâbhighâta,** m. butting at a bank or mound, Kir., Sch. (cf. *taṭâghāta*). **Vaprâmbhas,** n. the water flowing along a bank, W.; °*bhaḥ-sruti*, f. the stream of water flowing along or issuing from a bank, a rivulet, MW. **Vaprâvanī,** f. cultivated land, Dharmaś.

Vapraka, m. the circumference of a sphere, Gol.

Vapri (only L.) = *kshetra*, *durgati*, or *samudra*.

Vaprīvan, m. N. of a Vyāsa, VP.

Vapsas, n. a beautiful form or appearance, RV. i, 181, 8 (Sāy.)

Vāpita, mfn. (fr. Caus.) scattered, sown, VarBṛS.

वपाटिका *vapāṭikā*, f. = *ava-pāṭikā*, laceration of the prepuce, Suśr.

वप्प *vappa*, *vappaka*. See *bappa*.

वप्पटदेवी *vappaṭa-devī* or *vapyaṭa-devī*, f. N. of a princess, Rājat.

Vappiya or °**yaka,** m. N. of a king, ib.

वप्पीह *vappīha*, m. Cuculus Melanoleucus, L.

वभ्र् *vabhr* (or *babhr*), cl. 1. P. *vabhrati* (aor. *avabhrīt*, Pāṇ. vii, 2, 2, Sch.), to go, go astray, Dhātup. xv, 49.

वभ्रुक *vábhruka*, v. l. for *bábhruka*, MaitrS.

वम् *vam*, cl. 1. P. (Dhātup. xx, 19) *vamati* (Ved. also *vāmiti*; impf. *avamat* or *avamīt*; pf. *vavāma*, *vemuḥ*, MBh. &c.; *vavamuḥ*, Pāṇ. vi, 4, 126; 2. sg. *vemitha* or *vavamitha*, ib.; Siddh.; 3. sg. *uvāma*, ŚBr.; aor. *avān*, ŚāṅkhBr.; fut. *vamitā*, *vamishyati*, Gr.; inf. *vamitum*, ib.; ind. p. *vamitvā*, Mn. iv, 121; *vāntvā*, Vop.), to vomit, spit out, eject (lit. and fig.), emit, send forth, give out, RV. &c. &c.; to reject, i.e. repent (a word), RV. x, 108, 8: Pass. *vamyate* (aor. *avāmi*, Gr.), to be vomited &c.: Caus. *vāmayati*, *vamayati* (cf. Dhātup. xix, 68; aor. *avīvamat*, Gr.), to cause to vomit, Suśr.: Desid. *vivamishati*, Gr.: Intens. *vaṃvamyate*, *vaṃvanti*, ib. [Cf. Gk. ἐμέω for ϝεμέω; Lat. *vomere*; Lith. *vémti*.]

Vama, mf(*ī*)n. vomiting, ejecting, giving out, W.; m. = *vāma*, g. *jvalâdi*.

Vamati, m. the act of vomiting, L.

Vamathu, m. id., Suśr.; qualmishness, nausea, Car.; water ejected from an elephant's trunk, Hcar.; a cough (?), L.

Vamana, m. hemp, L.; pl. N. of a people, MārkP.; (*ī*), f. a leech, L.; the cotton shrub, L.; N. of a Yoginī, Hcat.; n. the act of vomiting or ejecting from the mouth, Suśr.; emitting, emission, Kālid.; 'causing vomiting,' an emetic, Kathās.; Suśr. &c.; offering oblations to fire, L.; pain, paining, L. **-kalpa,** m. N. of a ch. of the Ashṭâṅga-hṛidaya-saṃhitā. **-dravya,** n. an emetic, Suśr. **Vamanârthīya,** mfn. serving as an emetic, Car.

Vamanīya, mfn. to be vomited &c.; (*ā*), f. a fly, L.

Vami, f. vomiting, nausea, qualmishness (also *ī*), Suśr.; an emetic, W.; m. (only L.) fire; a thorn-apple; a rogue, cheat. **Vamy-âśânti** (?), f. N. of wk.

Vamita, mfn. vomited, made to vomit, sickened, W. (cf. Vop. xxvi, 103).

Vamitavya, mfn. to be vomited or ejected from the mouth, Kull. on Mn. xi, 160.

Vamin, mfn. vomiting, being sick, Pāṇ. iii, 2, 157.

Vamya, mfn. to be made to vomit (in *a-v°*), Car.

Vānta, *vānti* &c. See s. v.

वम्भ *vambha*, m. = *vaṃśa*, a bamboo &c., L.

वम्भारव *vambhā-rava*. See *bambh°*.

वम्मागदेश *vammāga-deśa*, m. N. of a place, Cat.

वम्र *vamrá*, m. (and *ī*, f., accord. to some also *ā*; derivation fr. √*vam* very doubtful, cf. *valmī*) an ant, RV.; Br.; m. N. of a man, RV. (with *Vaikhānasa*, the supposed author of x, 99).

Vamraká, m. a small ant, RV.; mfn. small, little (= *hrasva*), Naigh. iii, 2.

Vamrī-kūṭa, n. an ant-hill, L.

वय् *vay*, cl. 1. Ā. *vayate*, to go, Dhātup. xiv, 2 (for cl. 1. P. *vayati*, see √*ve*).

वय *vaya*, m. (fr. √*ve*) one who weaves, a weaver, L.; (*ī*), f. a female weaver, RV.

Váyat, mf(*antī*)n. weaving, interweaving, RV. &c. &c.; m. N. of a man, Sāy. on RV. vii, 33, 3.

Vayana, n. the act of weaving &c., Vop.

1. **Váyas,** n. a web (?), RV. ii, 31, 5.

Vayitrī, f. a female weaver, TāṇḍBr.

Vayíyu, vayúna. See col. 3.

वयम् *vayám*, nom. pl. of 1. pers. pron., we (cf. *asma*).

वयस् 2. *váyas*, n. (cf. 2. *ví*) a bird, any winged animal, the winged tribe (esp. applied to smaller birds), RV. &c. &c.

1. **Vayasá,** m. = 2. *váyas*, a bird, TS.

Váyo-vidha, mfn. (*vayo* for 2. *váyas*) of the kind or nature of birds, ŚBr.

वयस् 3 *váyas*, n. (√*vī*) enjoyment, food, meal, oblation, RV.; AV. (cf. *vīti*); energy (both bodily and mental), strength, health, vigour, power, might, RV.; AV.; VS. (often with *bṛihát*, with √*dhā* and dat. or loc. of pers. 'to bestow vigour or might on'); vigorous age, youth, prime of life, any period of life, age, RV. &c. &c. (*sarvāṇi vayāṇsi*, animals of any age; *vayasâtīta* or *vayasâtīta*, aged, old); degree, kind (in *vayāṇsi pra-brūhi*), ŚBr. **-kara,** mf(*ā* or *ī*)n. causing life or health; of mature age (?), MW. **-kṛit,** mfn. causing strength, preserving health or youth, RV.; VS. **-vat** (*váyas-*), mfn. possessed of power or vigour, mighty, vigorous, ib.

Vayaḥ, in comp. for 3. *vayas*. **-pariṇati,** f. ripeness of age, MW. **-pramāṇa,** n. measure or duration of life, age, MBh. **-śata,** n. an age of a hundred years, BhP. **-saṃdhi,** m. 'life-juncture,' puberty, Cat.; *-matī*, f. a girl arrived at puberty, Gal. **-sama,** mfn. equal in age, R. **-stha,** mf(*ā*)n. being in the bloom of age, grown up, full-grown, strong, vigorous, MBh.; R.; aged, old, MBh.; nourishing (as flesh), Vāgbh.; m. a contemporary, associate, friend, W.; (*ā*), f. a female friend or companion, L.; N. of various plants, Suśr.; Car. (accord. to L. Emblica Officinalis; Terminalia Chebula or Citrina; Cocculus Cordifolius; Bombax Heptaphyllum; = *atyamla-parṇī*, *kākolī*, *kshīra-kākolī*, and *brāhmī*); small cardamoms, L. **-sthāna,** n. the firmness or freshness of youth, Kām. **-sthāpana,** mfn. maintaining or preserving the freshness of youth, Suśr.

Vayasá (ifc.) = 3. *vayas* (see *uttara-*, *pūrva-*, *madhyama-v°*).

Vayasín. See *pūrva-* and *prathama-v°*.

Vayaska. See *abhinava-* and *madhyama-v°*.

Vayasya, mfn. being of an age or of the same age, contemporary, MBh.; Kāv. &c.; m. a contemporary, associate, companion, friend (often used in familiar address), ib.; (*ā*), f. a female friend, a woman's confidante, Mṛicch.; Kathās.; (scil. *ishṭakā*) N. of 19 bricks used for building the sacrificial altar (so called from the word *vayas* in the formula of consecration), TS.; Kāṭh.; ŚBr. **-tva,** n. (MBh.), **-bhāva,** m. (R.) the condition of being a contemporary, companionship, friendship.

Vayasyaka, m. a contemporary, friend, Kathās.; (*ikā*), f. female friend, faithful female servant, Mālav. **-tva,** n. companionship, friendship, Ratnâv.

Vayā́, f. a branch, twig, RV. (also fig. = offspring, posterity); vigour, strength, power (?), ib. i, 165, 5. **-vat** (*vayā́-*), mfn. rich in offspring (others 'mighty, powerful'), ib. vi, 2, 5.

Vayāka, m. a little branch, tendril, creeper (= *latā*), Sāy. (cf. next).

Vayākín, mfn. having little branches or tendrils, ramifying (said of the Soma plant), RV. v, 44, 5.

Vayíyu, mfn. (prob.) = *váyas-vat*, mighty, powerful, RV. viii, 19 ('anything woven, clothes,' fr. √*ve*, Nir. iv, 15, Sch.)

Vayúna, mfn. (rather fr. √*vī* than fr. √*ve*) moving, active, alive, ŚBr.; waving, agitated, restless (applied to the sea), TS.; MaitrS.; clear (as an eye), BhP. (cf. *a-vayuna*); a path, way (= *mārga* also fig. either = 'means, expedient,' or 'rule, order, custom'), RV.; AV.; VS. (instr. 'according to rule,' RV. i, 162, 18); distinctness, clearness, brightness, RV. ii, 19, 3; iii, 29, 3 &c. (loc. pl. 'clearly, distinctly,' ii, 34, 4); a mark, aim (?), RV. i, 182, 1; ii, 19, 8 &c.; knowledge, wisdom, BhP.; a temple, Uṇ. iii, 61, Sch.; (*ā*), f. a mark, aim, goal (?), RV. iv, 5, 13; x, 49, 5; knowledge, wisdom, BhP.; N. of a daughter of Svadhā, BhP.; m. N. of a son of Kṛiśâśva and Dhishaṇā, BhP. **-vat** (*vayúna-*), mfn. clear, distinct, bright, RV. **-śás,** ind. according to rule or order, in due order, ib. **Vayunā-dhá** or **-dhā́** (for *vayuna-dhā́*), mfn. establishing rule or order, MaitrS. **Vayunā-víd** (Padap. *vayuna-víd*), mfn. learned in rules, well versed in ordinances, RV.

Vayo, in comp. for 3. *vayas*. **-gata,** mfn. advanced in years, aged, old, AitUp.; n. advanced age (*e*, ind. 'when youth is passed'), Kāv. **-jū,** mfn. exciting or increasing strength, RV. **-'tiga** or **-'tita,** mf(*ā*)n. advanced in age, exceedingly old or decrepit, Mn.; MBh. &c.; passing beyond or liberated from all periods or stages of existence, MBh. **-dhás,** mfn. = *-dhā́*, AV.; VS.; ŚBr.; ŚrS.; young, fresh, Uṇ. iv, 228, Sch. **-dhā́,** mfn. bestowing or possessing health or strength, strong, vigorous, RV.; AV.; TS.; m. a young or middle-aged man, W.; f. strengthening, invigorating (*dhai* as inf.), RV. **-'dhika,** mfn. superior in years, older in age, VarBṛS.; advanced in years; m. an old man, Mn.; R. **-dhéya**, n. bestowing strength or vigour, RV. **-nādhá**, mfn. (√*nah*) establishing or preserving health, VS. **-bāla**, mfn. young in years, R. **-rūpa-samanvita**, mfn. endowed with youth and beauty, Mn. viii, 182. **-'vasthā**, f. a stage or state of life (generally considered to be three, viz. *bāla-tva*, childhood, *taruṇa-tva*, youth, and *vṛiddha-tva*, old age), Kāv.; Pur.; Suśr. **-vidyā**, f., see *vāyovidyiká*. **-viśesha**, m. difference of age, Āpast. **-vṛiddha**, mfn. advanced in years, old, ib.; Ragh. **-vṛídh**, mfn. increasing strength or energy, invigorating, RV. **-hāni**, f. loss of youth or vigour, the growing old, Dhātup.; Sāy.

वयोवङ्ग *vayovaṅga*(?), n. lead, MW.

वय्य *vayyà*, m. a companion, friend, RV. ix, 68; N. of an Asura, ib. i, 112, 6; patr. of Turvīti, ib. i, 54, 6 (Sāy.)

वर 1. *vára*, m. (fr. √1. *vṛi*) 'environing,' 'enclosing,' circumference, space, room, RV.; AV.; TS. (*vára á pṛithivyáḥ*, on the wide earth); stopping, checking, RV. i, 143, 5. **-ga**, m. or n. (?) N. of a place, Cat. **-ja** = *vare-ja*, Pāṇ. vi, 3, 16. **-sád**, mfn. sitting in a circle or in the wide space, RV. iv, 40, 5. **Vare-ja** = *vara-ja*, Pāṇ. vi, 3, 16.

1. **Varaka**, m. a cloak, L.; n. cloth, L.; the cover or awning of a boat, L.

1. **Varaṇa**, m. a rampart, mound, L.; a causeway, bridge, L.; the tree Cratæva Roxburghii (also called *varuṇa* and *setu*; it is used in medicine and supposed to possess magical virtues), MaitrS. &c. &c.; any tree, W.; a camel, L.; a kind of ornament or decoration on a bow, MBh.; a partic. magical formula recited over weapons, R. (*varuṇa*, B.); N. of Indra, L.; N. of a country, Buddh.; (pl.) of a town, Pāṇ. iv, 2, 82 (cf. Kāś. on Pāṇ. i, 2, 53); (*ā*), f. N. of a small river (running past the north of Benares into the Ganges and now called Barnā), Up.; Pur.; n. surrounding, enclosing, L.; keeping off, prohibiting, L.

Varaṇaka, mfn. covering, covering over, concealing, Sāṃkhyak.

Varaṇasī (L.) and **Varaṇāśī** (Gal.), f. Benares (more usually *varāṇasī* and *vārāṇasī*, qq. vv.)

Varaṇā-vatī, f. (prob.) N. of a river, AV.

Varaṇḍa, m. (Uṇ. i, 128) the string of a fish-hook (cf. *-lambuka*), Mṛicch.; (only L.) a multitude; an eruption on the face; a rampart separating two combatant elephants; a heap of grass; a packet, package; (*ā*), f. (only L.) Turdus Salica; a dagger, knife; the wick of a lamp. **-lambuka**, m. the string of a fish-hook (?), Mṛicch. **Varaṇḍâlu**, m. a kind of bulbous plant (= *phala-puccha*), L.; the castor-oil tree, Ricinus Communis, L.

Varaṇḍaka, mfn. (only L.) round; large, extensive; miserable, wretched; fearful, terrified; m. a small mound of earth, KātyŚr., Sch.; a rampart separating two combatant elephants, Śiś.; Vās.; the seat or canopy on an elephant, a howdah, L.; a wall, L.; an eruption on the face, L.; a multitude, L.

Varaṇya, Nom. P. °*yati*, g. *kaṇḍv-ādi*.

Varatrā, f. a strap, thong, strip of leather, RV. &c. &c. (once in BhP. °*tra*, prob. n.); an elephant's or horse's girth, L. **-kāṇḍa**, m. or n. (?) a piece of a strap or thong, KātyŚr.

Váras, n. width, breadth, expanse, room, space, RV. [Cf. Gk. εὖρος.]

Varāka, mf(*ī*)n. wretched, low, miserable, pitiable (mostly said of persons), Kāv.; Kathās. &c.; vile, impure (as money), Kathās.; m. (only L.) N. of Śiva; battle, war; a kind of plant.

Varākaka, mf(*ikā*)n. wretched, low, vile, Pañcad.

Varāṭa, m. a cowry (used as a coin), Pañcat.; a rope, L.; (*ī*), f. (in music) a partic. Rāga, Col. (cf. *varāḍī* below).

Varāṭaka, m. a cowry, Cypræa Moneta (= $\frac{1}{20}$ of a Kākiṇī or $\frac{1}{80}$ of a Paṇa), Kāv.; Kathās.; Sāh. &c. (also *ikā*, f.); the seed vessel of a lotus-flower, Naish.; a rope, cord, string (only ifc., with f. *ā*), MBh. xii, 2488, v.l. *varārakā*; (*ikā*), f. Mirabilis Jalapa, L.; n. a partic. vegetable poison, Suśr. **-rajas**, m. Mesua Roxburghii, L.

Varāḍī or **varāḍī**, m. (in music) a partic. Rāga (cf. *varāṭī* above).

Varāṇa, m. Cratæva Roxburghii, L.; N. of Indra, L.

Varāṇasa, mfn. (fr. prec.), g. *tṛiṇâdi*; (*ī*), f. N. of a river, MBh.; the city of Benares (more usually written *vārāṇasī*, cf. *varaṇasī*; two small rivers, the Varaṇā and Asī are said to join or give rise to the name, see RTL. 434).

Varāla, m. or n. cloves, L.; m. a black-yellow-whitish whiteness, L.; mfn. black-yellowish-whitish white, L.; (*ā*), f. a female goose, L.

Varālaka, m. or n. cloves, L.; Carissa Carandas, L.

1. **Varitṛi**, mfn. one who covers or screens, Pāṇ. vii, 2, 34, Sch. (cf. 1. *varītṛi*).

Varimát (RV.) or **várimat** (AV.) = next.

1. **Varimán** or **váriman**, m. (abstract noun of *urú*, q.v.) expanse, circumference, width, breadth, space, room, RV.; VS.; AV.; ŚāṅkhŚr.

Várivas, n. room, width, space, free scope, ease, comfort, bliss, RV.; VS.; TS. (acc. with √*kṛi*, *dhā* or *vid* and dat., 'make room for, clear the path to'); wealth, treasure (= *dhana*), Naigh. **-kṛít**, mfn. procuring space, affording relief, delivering, RV.; TS.

Varivasita, mfn. = *varivasyita*, L.

Varivasya, Nom. P. °*syáti*, to grant room or space, give relief, concede, permit, RV.; to show favour, wait upon, cherish, tend, Bhaṭṭ.; Sāy. (p. °*syamāna* = *varivasyita*, Daś.)

Varivasyā́, f. service, honour, devotion, attendance, RV.; Kāv.; obedience to a spiritual teacher, L. **-rahasya**, n. N. of various wks.

Varivasyita, mfn. served, cherished, adored, L.

Varivo, in comp. for *varivas*. **-dá** (VS.), **-dhā́** and **-víd** (RV.), mfn. granting space or freedom or relief or repose or comfort.

1. **Várishṭha**, mfn. (superl. of *urú*, q.v.) widest, broadest, largest, most extensive, RV.; VS.; TBr.; R.

1. **Varītṛi**, mfn. one who covers or screens, Pāṇ. vii, 2, 34, Sch. (cf. 1. *varitṛi*).

1. **Várīman**, n. = 1. *variman*, expanse, width, breadth, room, RV.

1. **Várīyas**, mfn. (compar. of *urú*, q.v.) wider, broader ('than,' abl.); freer, easier, ib.; ŚBr.; (*as*), ind. farther, farther off or away, RV.; n. wider space ('than,' abl.), ib.; free space, freedom, comfort, ease, rest, ib.

Váruṇa, m. (once in the TĀr. *varuṇá*) 'All-enveloping Sky,' N. of an Āditya (in the Veda commonly associated with Mitra [q.v.] and presiding over the night as Mitra over the day, but often celebrated separately, whereas Mitra is rarely invoked alone; Varuṇa is one of the oldest of the Vedic gods, and is commonly thought to correspond to the Οὐρανός of the Greeks, although of a more spiritual conception; he is often regarded as the supreme deity, being then styled 'king of the gods' or 'king of both gods and men' or 'king of the universe;' no other deity has such grand attributes and functions assigned to him; he is described as fashioning and upholding heaven and earth, as possessing extraordinary power and wisdom called *māyā*, as sending his spies or messengers throughout both worlds, as numbering the very winkings of men's eyes, as hating falsehood, as seizing transgressors with his *pāśa* or noose, as inflicting diseases, especially dropsy, as pardoning sin, as the guardian of immortality; he is also invoked in the Veda together with Indra, and in later Vedic literature together with Agni, with Yama, and with Vishṇu; in RV. iv, 1, 2, he is even called the brother of Agni; though not generally regarded in the Veda as a god of the ocean, yet he is often connected with the waters, especially the waters of the atmosphere or firmament, and in one place [RV. vii, 64, 2] is called with Mitra *Sindhu-pati*, 'lord of the sea or of rivers;' hence in the later mythology he became a kind of Neptune, and is there best known in his character of god of the ocean; in the MBh. Varuṇa is said to be a son of Kardama and father of Pushkara, and is also variously represented as one of the Deva-gandharvas, as a Nāga, as a king of the Nāgas, and as an Asura; he is the regent of the western quarter [cf. *loka-pāla*] and of the Nakshatra Śata-bhishaj [VarBṛS.]; the Jainas consider Varuṇa as a servant of the twentieth Arhat of the present Ava-sarpiṇī), RV. &c. &c. (cf. IW. 10; 12 &c.); the ocean, VarBṛS.; water, Kathās.; the sun, L.; a warder off or dispeller, Sāy. on RV. v, 48, 5; N. of a partic. magical formula recited over weapons, R. (v.l. *varaṇa*); the tree Cratæva Roxburghii, L. (cf. *varaṇa*); pl. (prob.) the gods generally, AV. iii, 4, 6; (*ā*), f. N. of a river, MBh. **-kāshṭhikā**, f. wood of the Ficus Religiosa (used for kindling fire by rubbing), L. **-kṛicchraka**, n. a partic. penance (in which for a month only ground rice with water is eaten), L. **-gṛiha-pati** (*vá*°), mfn. having Varuṇa for a house-lord (i.e giving V° precedence at a great sacrifice), MaitrS. **-gṛihīta** (*vá*°), mfn. seized by V°, afflicted with disease (esp. dropsy; see under *varuṇa*), ŚBr.; TS. **-graha**, m. 'seizure by V°,' paralysis, L. **-grāha**, m. seizure by V° (in *á-v*°), TS.; TBr. **-japa**, m. N. of wk. **-jyeshṭha** (*vá*°), m. pl. having V° for chief, TBr. **-tīrtha**, n. N. of a Tīrtha, Cat. **-tejas** (*vá*°), mfn. one whose vital power is V° i.e. water, AV. **-tva**, n. the state or nature of V°, R. **-datta**, m. N. of a man, Pāṇ. v, 3, 84, Sch. **-deva**, n. 'having V° as deity,' the Nakshatra Śata-bhishaj, VarBṛS. **-devatyà**, mfn. having V° as deity, MaitrS. **-daiva** or **-daivata**, n. = *-deva*, VarBṛS. **-dhrút**, mfn. deceiving V°, RV. vii, 60, 9. **-pāśá**, m. V°'s snare or noose, TS.; Br.; a shark, L. **-purāṇa**, n. N. of wk. **-purusha**, m. a servant of V°, ĀśvGṛ. **-praghāsá**, m. pl. the second of periodical oblations offered at the full moon of Āshāḍha for obtaining exemption from V°'s snares (so called from eating barley in honour of the god V°), TS.; Br.; ŚrS.; (sg.) a partic. Ahīna, ŚāṅkhŚr.; °*sika*, mfn. relating to the above oblation, Lāṭy., Sch. **-praśishṭa** (*vá*°), mfn. ruled over or guided by V°, RV. **-priyā**, f. V°'s wife, L. **-bhaṭṭa**, m. N. of an astronomer, Col. **-mati**, m. N. of a Bodhi-sattva, L. **-mitra**, m. N. of a Gobhila, VBr. **-mení**, f. V°'s wrath or vengeance, punishment or injury inflicted by V°, TS.; Kāṭh. **-rājan** (*vá*°), mfn. having V° as king, TS.; ŚrS. **-loka**, m. V°'s world or sphere, KaushUp.; his province, i.e. water, Tarkas. **-vidhi**, m. N. of wk. **-vegā**, f. N. of a Kiṃ-narī, Kāraṇḍ. **-śarman**, m. N. of a warrior on the side of the gods in their war against the Daityas, Kathās. **-śeshas** (*vá*°), mfn. having descendants capable of protecting, RV. v, 65, 5 (Sāy.; others 'being V°'s posterity, i.e. sinless'). **-śrāddha**, n. N. of a partic. Śrāddha offering, Cat.; *-vidhi*, m. N. of wk. **-savá**, m. 'V°'s aid or approval,' a partic. sacrificial rite, TBr.; ŚBr. **-sāman**, n. N. of various Sāmans, ĀrshBr. **-srotasa**, m. N. of a mountain, MBh. (C. *śrotasa*). **Varuṇâṅgaruha**, m. 'V°'s offspring or scion,' patr. of Agastya, VarBṛS. **Varuṇâtmajā**, f. 'V°'s daughter,' spirituous or vinous liquor (so called as produced from the ocean when it was churned), L. **Varuṇâdri**, m. N. of a mountain, Pañcat. **Varuṇârishṭaka-maya**, mf(*ī*)n. made from Cratæva Roxburghii and the soap-berry tree, Suśr. **Varuṇâlaya**, m. 'V°'s habitation,' the sea, ocean, R. **Varuṇâvāsa**, m. 'V°'s abode,' the sea, ocean, R. **Varuṇêśa**, mfn. having V° as lord or governor; n. the Nakshatra Śata-bhishaj, VarBṛS.; *-deśa*, m. the district or sphere governed by V°, Gaṇit. **Varuṇêśvara-tīrtha**, n. N. of a Tīrtha, Cat. **Varuṇôda**, n. 'V°'s water,' N. of a sea, MārkP. **Varuṇôpanishad**, f. N. of an Upanishad. **Varuṇôpapurāṇa**, n. N. of an Upapurāṇa.

Varuṇaka, m. = *varuṇa*, Cratæva Roxburghii, MBh.; Suśr.

Varuṇānī, f. Varuṇa's wife, RV.; AV. (also pl., Kāṭh.); °*nyāḥ sāman*, n. N. of a Sāman, ĀrshBr.

Varuṇāvi or °**vis**, f. N. of Lakshmī, Cat.

Varuṇika, °**niya** and °**nila**, m. endearing forms of *varuṇa-datta*, Pāṇ. v, 3, 84, Sch.

Varuṇyà, mf(*ā*)n. coming from Varuṇa, belonging to him &c., RV.; ŚBr. (f. pl. with *āpaḥ*, 'stagnant water').

Varutṛi, mfn. = *varūtṛi*, Pāṇ. vii, 2, 34.

Varutra, n. an upper and outer garment, cloak, mantle, Uṇ. iv, 172, Sch. [Cf. Gk. ἔλυτρον for Ϝέλυτρον.]

Varūtṛi, mfn. one who wards off or protects, protector, defender, guardian deity (with gen.), RV.; N. of an Asura priest (mentioned together with Trishṭha), Kāṭh.; (*várūtrī*), f. a female protector, guardian goddess (applied to a partic. class of divine beings), RV.; TS.; VS.; ŚBr. [Cf. Gk. ῥύτωρ for Ϝερύτωρ.]

Várūtha, n. protection, defence, shelter, secure abode, RV.; AV.; VS.; TBr.; a house or dwelling, Naigh.; armour, a coat of mail, L.; a shield, L.; (also m.) a sort of wooden ledge or guard fastened round a chariot as a defence against collision, ŚāṅkhŚr.; MBh. &c.; any multitude, host, swarm, quantity, assemblage (also of sons &c.), BhP.; m. the Indian cuckoo, L.; time, L.; = *nija-rāshṭraka* (?), L.; N. of a Grāma, R.; of a man, MārkP. **-pa**, m. the leader of a multitude or host, chief, general, BhP. **-vati**, f. a host, army, Harav. **-śas**, ind. in multitudes or heaps, BhP. **Varūthâdhipa**, m. the leader of an army, ib.

Varūthaka. See *sāpta-dhātu-v*°.

Varūthín, mfn. wearing defensive arms or armour, VS.; furnished with a protecting ledge, having a guard, MBh.; R.; Hariv.; affording protection or shelter, GṛS.; MBh.; Hariv.; seated in a chariot, Ragh.; (ifc.) surrounded by a quantity or heap of, BhP. (cf. *lalanā-v°*); m. a guard, defender, W.; a car, Śiś.; (*inī*), f., see next.

Varūthinī, f. a multitude, troop, army, MBh.; Kāv. &c. **-pati**, m. the leader of an army, BhP.

Varūthyà, mfn. affording shelter or protection, safe, secure, RV. **-deśe**, ind. in a secure abode, ŚāṅkhGṛ.

Vártave, Ved. inf. fr. √1. *vṛi*, q.v.

1. **Vartu**. See *dur-v°*.

Vartṛi, mfn. one who keeps back or wards off, expeller (with gen.), RV.

Vártra, mf(*ī*)n. keeping or warding off, protecting, defending, ĀśvGṛ.; n. a dike, dam, AV.; TS.

वर 2. **vará**, mf(*ā*)n. (fr. √2. *vṛi*) choosing (see *patiṃ-varā, svayam-varā*); m. 'chooser,' one who solicits a girl in marriage, suitor, lover, bridegroom, husband (rarely 'son-in-law'), RV. &c. &c.; a bridegroom's friend, MW.; a dissolute man (= *viṭa* or *shiḍga*), L.; (*vára*), mf(*ā*)n. 'select,' choicest, valuable, precious, best, most excellent or eminent among (gen., loc., abl., or comp.) or for (gen.), ŚrS.; MBh. &c.; (ifc.) royal, princely, Jātakam.; better, preferable, better than (abl., rarely gen.) or among (abl.), Mn.; MBh. &c.; eldest, W.; (*am*), ind. (g. *svar-ādi*) preferably, rather, better (also = preferable, sometimes with abl. which in Veda is often followed by *ā*, e.g. *agníbhyo váram*, 'better than fires,' RV.; *sákhibhya ā́ váram*, 'better than companions,' ib.; exceptionally with acc., e.g. *śishyaiḥ śata-hutān homān ekaḥ putra-huto varam*, 'better one sacrifice offered by a son than a hundred offered by disciples,' ShaḍvBr.), RV. &c. &c.; it is better that, it would be best if (with pres., e.g. *varam gacchāmi*, 'it is better that I go;' or with Impv., e.g. *varaṃ naye sthāpyatām*, 'it would be better if he were initiated into our plan,' Kathās.; or without any verb, e.g. *varaṃ siṇhāt*, 'better [death caused] by a lion,' Pañcat.; sometimes with Pot., e.g. *varaṃ tat kuryāt*, 'better that he should do that,' Kām.), Kāv.; Kathās. &c.; it is better than, rather than (in these senses *varam* is followed by *na, na ca, na tu, na punaḥ, tad api na* or *tathâpi na*, with nom., e.g. *varaṃ mṛityur na câkīrtiḥ*, 'better death than [lit. 'and not'] infamy;' exceptionally with instr., e.g. *varam eko guṇī putro na ca mūrkha-śatair api*, 'better one virtuous son than hundreds of fools,' Hit.; *na hi—varam*, 'by no means—but rather'), Mn.; MBh. &c.; m. (rarely n.; ifc. f. *ā*) 'act or object of choosing,' choice, election, wish, request; boon, gift, reward, benefit, blessing, favour (*várāya, váram ā́, práti váram* or *váraṃ varam*, 'according to wish, to one's heart's content;' *mad-varāt*, 'in consequence of the boon granted by me;' *váraṃ* √*vṛi*, 'to choose a boon;' *varaṃ* √*yāc* or *ā-*√*kāṅksh* or √*brū* or Caus. of *pra-*√*arth*, 'to prefer a request;' *váraṃ* √*dā*, 'to grant a boon or blessing;' *varam pra-*√*dā* or *pra-*√*yam*, id.; *varaṃ* √*labh*, 'to receive a boon or reward'), RV. &c. &c.; a benefit, advantage, privilege, Daś.; charity, alms, VarBṛS.; a dowry, Pañcat.; m. a kind of grain (= *varaṭa*), KātyŚr., Sch.; bdellium, L.; a sparrow, L.; N. of a son of Śvaphalka, VP.; (*ā*), f. N. of various plants and vegetable products (accord. to L. 'the three kinds of myrobolan;' Clypea Hernandifolia; Asparagus Racemosus; Cocculus Cordifolius; turmeric; Embelia Ribes; a root similar to ginger; = *brāhmī* and *reṇukā*), Suśr.; N. of Pārvatī, L.; N. of a river, BhP.; (*ī*), f. Asparagus Racemosus, L.; N. of Chāyā (the wife of Sūrya), L.; n. saffron, BhP. (In comp. not always separable from 1. *vara*.) **-kalyāṇa**, m. N. of a king, Buddh. **-kāshṭhakā**, f. the plant Clerodendrum Siphonanthus, Npr.; a grain similar to Varāṭikā, ib. **-kīrti**, m. N. of a man, Pañcat. **-kratu**, m. N. of Indra, L. **-ga**, N. of a place, Cat. **-gātra**, mf(*ī*)n. fair-limbed, beautiful, Mṛicch. **-ghaṇṭa**, m. N. of Skanda, AV.Pariś. **-ghaṇṭikā** or °**ṭī**, f. Asparagus Racemosus, L. **-candana**, n. a sort of dark sandal-wood, L.; Pinus Deodora, L. **-candrikā**, f. N. of a Commentary. **-ja**, see under 1. *vara*, p. 921. **-jānuka**, m. N. of a Ṛishi, MBh. **-tanu**, mf(*ū*)n. having a beautiful body, Kālac.; (*ū*), f. a beautiful woman, Kāv.; a kind of metre, Piṅg. **-tantu**, m. N. of an ancient preceptor, Ragh.; Hcat.; pl. his descendants, Cat. **-tama**, mfn. most preferable or excellent, L. **-tara**, mfn. more or most excellent, Siṇhâs. **-tā**, f. the being a blessing, Kād. **-tikta**, m. Wrightia Antidysenterica, L.; Azadirachta Indica, L.; = *parpaṭa*, Bhpr. **-tiktaka**, m. Azadirachta Indica, Dhanv.; a species of medicinal plant, = *parpaṭa*, ib.; (*ikā*), f. Clypea Hernandifolia, L. **-toyā**, f. 'having excellent water,' N. of a river, Śatr. **-tvac** or **-tvaca**, m. Azadirachta Indica, L. **-dá**, mf(*ā́*)n. granting wishes, conferring a boon, ready to fulfil requests or answer prayers (said of gods and men), AV.; ŚvetUp.; TĀr. &c.; m. a benefactor, W.; N. of Agni in Śāntika, Gṛihyas.; fire for burnt offerings of a propitiatory character, W.; N. of one of Skanda's attendants, MBh.; of a partic. class of deceased ancestors, MārkP.; of a partic. Samādhi, Kāraṇḍ.; of one of the 7 Ṛishis in the 4th Manv-antara, VP.; of a Dhyāni-buddha, W.; (mostly with *ācārya, kavi, deśika, bhaṭṭāraka* or *deś° āc°*) N. of various authors and other men, Cat.; pl. N. of a people, R.; (*ā*), f. a young woman, girl, maiden, L.; N. of a guardian goddess in the family of Vara-tantu, Cat.; of a Yoginī, Hcat. (cf. *vara-pradā*); of various plants, Physalis Flexuosa, Bhpr.; Npr.; Polanisia Icosandra, L.; Helianthus, Npr.; Linum Usitatissimum, Bhpr.; the root of yam, ib.; = *tri-parṇī*, Npr.; N. of a river, MBh.; Kāv.; *-gaṇapati-stotra, -gaṇeśa-stotra*, n. N. of Stotras; *-caturthī*, f. N. of the 4th day in the light half of the month Māgha, Cat. (prob. w.r. for *varadā-caturthī*); *-nātha*, °*thâcārya-sūnu*, *-nāyaka-sūri* (Cat.), *-bhaṭṭa* (V.P.), *-mūrti* (Cat.), m. N. of authors; *-rāja*, m. (also with *ācārya, cola-paṇḍita, bhaṭṭa, bhaṭṭāraka*) N. of various authors and other persons, Cat. (°*ja-campū*, f., *-daṇḍaka*, *-pañcāśat*, f., *-maṅgala*, *-mahishī-stotra*, n., *-mūla*, n., *-śataka*, n., *-su-prabhāta*, *-stava*, m., *-stotra*, n.; °*jâshṭaka*, n., °*jâshṭôttara-śata*, n. N. of wks.; °*jīya*, mfn. coming from or relating to or composed by Varada-rāja; n. N. of wk.); *-vishṇu-sūri*, m. N. of a Commentator, Cat.; *-hasta*, m. the beneficent hand (of a deity or benefactor of any kind), MW.; °*dā-caturthī*, see *varada-c°* above, L.; °*dā-tantra*, n. N. of wk.; °*dâdhīśa-yajvan*, m. N. of an author, Cat.; °*dârka*, m., °*dôpanishad-dīpikā*, f. N. of wks. **-dakshiṇā**, f. a present made to the bridegroom by the bride's father in giving her away, MW.; a term for expense or costs incurred in fruitless endeavours to recover a loss, ib.; mfn. (with *kratu*, a sacrifice) at which excellent fees are given, Yājñ. i, 358 (cf. Mn. viii, 306). **-datta**, mfn. given as a boon, granted in consequence of a request, R.; presented with the choice of a boon, ib.; m. N. of a man, Cat. **-darśinī**, f. prob. incorr. for *-varṇinī* (q.v.), R. **-dātu**, m. Tectona Grandis, Bhpr. **-dātṛi**, mfn. = *-da* (q.v.), Pañcar. **-dāna**, n. the granting a boon or request, MBh.; R.; the giving compensation or reward, ĀśvŚr.; N. of a place of pilgrimage, MBh.; *-maya*, mf(*ī*)n. caused by the granting of a request, arising from the bestowal of a favour or boon, R.; °*nika*, mfn. id., ib. **-dāyaka**, m. a partic. Samādhi, Kāraṇḍ. **-dāru**, Tectona Grandis, Npr.; Bhpr. **-dāruka**, a kind of plant with poisonous leaves, Suśr. **-dāsvas**, mfn. = *-da* (q.v.), BhP. **-druma**, m. Agallochum, L. **-dharma**, m. a noble act of justice, excellent work &c.; °*mī* √*kṛi*, P. *-karoti*, to do a noble act towards any one (acc.), R. **-dharmin**, m. N. of a king, VP. **-nārī**, f. the best woman, a most excellent woman, MW. **-nimantraṇa**, n. a journey undertaken by the parents of the bride to recall the bridegroom (who pretends to go to Kāśī), L. **-niścaya**, m. the determining or choosing of a person to be a husband, choice of a bridegroom, MW. **-paksha**, m. the party or side of a bridegroom at a wedding, Ragh.; °*shiya*, mfn. belonging to the p° of the br°, a relation of the br°, Pañcad. **-pakshiṇī**, f. N. of a Tantra goddess, Cat. **-paṇḍita**, m. (with *śrī* prefixed) N. of an author, Cat. **-parṇâkhya**, m. Lipeocercis Serrata, L. **-pāṇḍya**, m. N. of a man, W. **-pītaka**, talc, L. **-purusha**, m. the best of men, Mṛicch. **-pota**, m. a kind of antelope, Car.; (prob.) n. a kind of vegetable, Npr. **-prada**, mfn. granting wishes, Kathās.; (*ā*), f. N. of Lopāmudrā, L.; of a Yoginī, Hcat.; *-stava*, m. N. of a hymn. **-pradāna**, n. the bestowal of a boon, MBh.; Hit. &c. **-prabha**, mf(*ā*)n. having excellent brightness; m. N. of a Bodhi-sattva, Buddh. **-prasthāna**, n. the setting out of a bridegroom in the procession towards the bride's house, MW. **-prârthanā**, f. the desiring a husband, Śak. **-phala**, mfn. possessing or yielding the best fruits, L.; m. the cocoa-nut tree, L. **-bālhika**, n. saffron, L. (written *vāhlīka*). **-mukhī**, f. a kind of drug, L. **-yātrā**, f. the procession of a suitor or bridegroom (to the bride's house), L. **-yuvati** or °**tī**, f. a beautiful young woman or girl, L.; a kind of metre, Piṅg. **-yogya**, mf(*ā*)n. worthy of a boon or reward, MārkP.; fit for marriage, Priy. **-yonika** = *kesara*, Npr. **-yoshit**, f. a beautiful woman, Hcat. **-ruci**, mfn. taking pleasure in boons (N. of Śiva), Śivag.; m. N. of a grammarian (also a poet, lexicographer, and writer on medicine, sometimes identified with Kātyāyana, the reputed author of the Vārttikas or supplementary rules of Pāṇini; he is placed by some among the nine gems of the court of Vikramâditya, and by others among the ornaments of the court of Bhoja; he was the author of the Prākṛit grammar called Prākṛita-prakāśa, and is said to be the first grammarian who reduced the various dialects of Prākṛit to a system), Pañcat.; Kathās. &c.; *-kārikā*, f., *-kośa*, m., *-prākṛita-sūtra*, n., *-liṅga-kārikā*, f., *-vākya*, n. N. of wks. **-rūpa**, mfn. having an excellent form, L.; m. N. of a Buddha, Lalit. **-lakshmī-kathā**, f., °**mī-pūjā**, f., °**mī-māhātmya**, n., °**mī-vrata**, n., °**ta-kathā**, f., °**ta-kalpa**, m. N. of wks. **-labdha**, mfn. one who has obtained a boon (= *labdha-vara*), R.; received as a boon, L.; m. Michelia Champaka, L.; Bauhinia Variegata, Npr. **-vatsalā**, f. a mother-in-law, L. **-varaṇa**, n. the act of choosing or requesting, ŚrS.; the choosing a bridegroom, Viddh. **-vara-muni**, m. N. of an author, Cat.; *-śataka*, n. N. of wk. **-varṇa**, m. or n. 'best-coloured,' gold, Hariv. (cf. *su-v°*). **-varṇin**, mf(*iṇī*)n. having a beautiful complexion or colour, MBh.; (*iṇī*), f. a woman with a beautiful compl°, an excellent or handsome woman, any woman, MBh.; R. &c.; N. of Durgā, MBh.; of Lakshmī, L.; of Sarasvatī, L.; turmeric, Bhpr.; lac, L.; = *go-rocanā*, L.; a kind of plant (= *priyaṅgu, phalinī*), L. **-vastra**, n. a beautiful garment, Mṛicch. **-vāraṇa**, m. a fine elephant, MBh. **-vāsi**(?), m. pl. N. of a people, VP. **-vāhlīka**, see *-bālhīka*. **-vṛita**, mfn. received as a boon, AitBr. **-vṛiddha**, m. N. of Śiva, L. **-śāpa**, m. du. blessing and curse, BhP. **-śikha** (*vará-*), m. N. of an Asura whose family was destroyed by Indra, RV. vi, 27, 4; 5. **-śīta**, cinnamon, Npr. **-śreṇī**, f. a kind of plant, ib. **-sāvitrī-caritra**, n. N. of a Kāvya. **-sundarī**, f. a very beautiful woman, Caurap.; a kind of metre, Piṅg. **-surata**, mf(*a*)n. well acquainted with the secrets of sexual enjoyment, Hit. **-strī**, f. an excellent or noble woman, MBh.; VarBṛS.; Kathās. **-sraj**, f. a bridegroom's garland, the g° placed by a maiden round the neck of a chosen suitor, Rājat. **Varâkāṅkshin**, mfn. soliciting a boon, preferring a request, ib. **Varâṅga**, n. 'best member of the body,' the head, R.; VarBṛ.; the female pudenda, Kathās.; the principal piece or part, VarBṛS.; an elegant form or body, MW.; mfn. having an excellent form, excellent or beautiful in all parts, L.; m. an elephant, Divyâv.; (in astron.) a Nakshatra year consisting of 324 days; N. of Vishṇu, L.; of a king, VP.; (*ī*), f. turmeric, L.; N. of a daughter of Dṛishadvat, MBh.; n. Cassia bark, green cinnamon, Bhpr.; sorrel, L.; *-rūpin*, m. a great hero, L.; *-rūpôpeta*, mfn. handsome and well shaped; (accord. to others, 'shaped like an elephant'), L. **Varâṅgaka**, n. = *varâṅga*, Cassia bark, L. **Varâṅganā**, f. a beautiful woman, MBh.; R. &c. **Varâṅgin**, m. sorrel, L. **Varâjīvin**, m. an astrologer, Col. **Varâjya**, n. the choicest ghee or clarified butter, MW. **Varâtisarga**, m. the granting a boon or request, MBh. **Varâdana**, n. the nut of Buchanania Latifolia, L. **Varânanā**, f. a lovely-faced woman, R.; N. of an Apsaras, VP. **Varânanda-bhairava-tantra**, n. N. of wk. **Varâbhidha**, m. one who has a good name, MW.; (*ā*), f. sorrel, L. **Varâmra**, m. Carissa Carandas, L. **Varâraṇi**, m. a mother, R. vii, 23, 22. **Varâroha**, m. an excellent rider, L.; a rider on an elephant, L.; a rider in general, L.; mounting, riding, MW.; mf(*ā*)n. having fine hips, MBh.; R.; BhP.; m. N. of Vishṇu, L.; (*ā*), f. a handsome or elegant woman, MW.; the hip or flank, L.; N. of Dākshāyaṇī in Someśvara, Cat. **Varârthā**, f. (a woman) who wishes for a husband, BhP. **Varârthin**, mfn. asking for a boon, Kathās. **Varârdhya**, w.r. for *avar°*, ĀpGṛ. xxi, 9. **Varârha**, mf(*ā*)n. worthy of a boon, MW.; exceedingly worthy, being in high esteem,

R.; very costly, R.; Hariv. **Varâli**, m. the moon, W.; a partic. Rāga, W. (cf. *varāḍī*). **Varâlikā**, f. N. of Durgā, L. (cf. *vār°*). **Varâsana**, n. an excellent or chief seat, a throne, MBh.; BhP.; N. of a town, KālP.; Hibiscus Rosa Sinensis, L.; a cistern, reservoir, W. (for *vār-âs°*, q.v.); mfn. having an excellent seat, L.; m. a door-keeper, L.; a lover, paramour, L. **Vare-ja**, see under 1. *vara*, p. 921. **Varêndra**, m. a chief, sovereign, MW.; Indra, ib.; m. n. N. of a part of Bengal, Buddh.; (*ī*), f. ancient Gauḍa or Gaur, the capital and district so named (accord. to some), MW.; *-gati*, m. N. of an author, Cat. **Varêśa**, mfn. presiding over boons, able to grant wishes, BhP. **Varêśvara**, mfn. id. (*sarva-kāma-var°*, 'able to grant all wishes'), ib.; m. N. of Śiva, L. **Varêshudhi**, mfn. wearing an excellent quiver, R. **Varôru**, m. a beautiful thigh, VarBṛS.; mf(*u* or *ū*)n. (a woman) having b^c th^os, Kāv.; BhP.

2. Varaka, m. one who asks a female in marriage, ŚāṅkhGṛ.; a wish, request, boon, MBh.; N. of a prince, VP. (v.l. *dhanaka* and *kanaka*), Phaseolus Trilobus, L.; a kind of rice, L.; =*parpaṭa* or *śara-parṇikā*, L.

Varaṭa, m. a kind of grain, (prob.) the seed of safflower, Carthamus Tinctorius, = 2. *vara*), Gṛihyas.; KātyŚr., Sch.; a kind of wasp, L.; a gander, L.; an artisan of a partic. class (reckoned among Mlecchas or Barbarians), L. (cf. *varuṭa*, *varuḍa*); pl. N. of a barbarous tribe, L.; (*ā*), f. the seed of Carthamus Tinctorius, L.; a kind of wasp, L.; a goose, Pat.; Hcar.; (*ī*), f. a kind of wasp, Suśr.; n. a jasmine flower, L.

Varaṭaka, m. (KātyŚr., Sch.) and **varaṭṭikā**, f. (Bhpr.) = *varaṭa*, the seed of safflower.

2. Varaṇa, n. the act of choosing, wishing, wooing, choice of a bride, KātyŚr.; MBh. &c.; honouring &c. (*pūjanâdi*), L.; m. pl. the sacred texts recited at the choice of a priest, ĀpŚr. **-mālā**, f. (Kathās.), **-sraj**, f. (Naish.) the garland placed by a maiden round the neck of a selected suitor.

Varaṇīya, mfn. to be chosen or selected, KaṭhUp.; Kathās.; Sarvad.; to be solicited (for a boon) &c., W.

Varayitavya, mfn. to be chosen or selected, Nir.; MBh. (*-tva*, n., ĀpŚr., Sch.)

Varayitṛi, m. a suitor, lover, husband, L.

Varayu, m. N. of a man, MBh.

Varala, m. a sort of gad-fly or wasp, L.; (*ā*), f. id., L.; a goose, L.; (*ī*), f. = *varaṭā*, L.

Varasyā, f. wish, desire, request, RV.

Varāya, Nom. (only °*yita*, n. impers.) to be or represent a boon, Kathās.

2. Varitṛi, mfn. choosing, a chooser, MW.

Varin, m. 'rich in gifts(?),' N. of a divine being enumerated among the Viśve Devāḥ, MBh.

2. Variman, m. the most excellent, best, BhP. (lit. 'excellence, superiority, worth').

2. Várishṭha, mf(*ā*)n. (superl. of 2. *vara*) the most excellent or best, most preferable among (gen. or comp.), RV. &c. &c.; better than (abl.), Mn. vii, 84; chief (in a bad sense) = worst, most wicked, MBh. xiv, 879; iii, 12590. **Varishṭhâśrama**, m. N. of a place, Cat.

Varishṭhaka, mfn. = prec., most excellent or best, Pañcar.

2. Varītṛi, m. a wooer, suitor (°*tā*, as fut. 'he will woo'), Bālar.

2. Varīman, m. = 2. *variman*, BhP.

2. Varīyas, mfn. (compar. of 2. *vara*) better, more or most excellent, chief or best or dearest of (gen.), MBh.; BhP.; m. (in astrol.) N. of a Yoga; of Śiva, Śivag.; of a son of Manu Sāvarṇa, Hariv.; of a son of Pulaha by Gati, BhP.; (*asī*), f. Asparagus Racemosus, L.

Vareṇ (fr. *vareṇyaya*), Uṇ. iii, 98, Sch.

Váreṇya, mfn. to be wished for, desirable, excellent, best among (gen.), RV. &c. &c.; m. a partic. class of deceased ancestors, MārkP.; N. of a son of Bhṛigu, MBh.; (*ā*), f. N. of Śiva's wife, L.; n. supreme bliss, VP.; saffron, L. **-kratu** (*vá°*), mfn. having excellent understanding, intelligent, wise, RV.; AV.

Vareṇyaya, Nom. °*yayati* (fr. *vareṇya*), Uṇ. iii, 98, Sch.

Vareya, Nom. P. °*yáti* (fr. 2. *vara*), to be a suitor, ask in marriage (inf. °*yám*), RV.

Vareyú, m. a wooer, suitor, RV.

वरण्ट *varaṇṭa*. See *jala-v°*.

वरत्करी *varatkarī*, f. a sort of perfume (= *reṇukā*), L.

वरम्बरा *varambarā*, f. the Nux Vomica plant, L.

वरसान *varasāna*, m. = *dārika*, Uṇ. ii, 86, Sch.

वरहक *varahaka*, m. or n.(?) N. of a place, Cat.

वराडिराग *varāḍi-rāga*. See *varāḍi*, p. 921.

वराणस *varāṇasa*. See p. 921, col. 1.

वरारक *varāraka*, n. a diamond, L.

वराशि *varāśi*, *varāsi*. See *barāsī*.

वराह *varāha*, m. (derivation doubtful) a boar, hog, pig, wild boar, RV. &c. &c. (ifc. it denotes 'superiority, pre-eminence;' see g. *vyāghrâdi*); a cloud, Naigh. i, 10; a bull, Col.; a ram, L.; Delphinus Gangeticus, L.; N. of Vishṇu in his third or boar-incarnation (cf. *varāhâvatāra*), TĀr.; MBh. &c.; an array of troops in the form of a boar, Mn. vii, 187; a partic. measure, L.; Cyperus Rotundus, L.; yam, manioc-root, L.; = *varāha-purāṇa* and °*hôpanishad* (q.v.); N. of a Daitya, MBh.; of a Muni, ib.; of various authors (also with *paṇḍita* and *śarman*), Cat.; abridged fr. *varāha-mihira*, ib.; Uṇ., Sch.; of the son of a guardian of a temple, Rājat.; of a mountain, MBh.; R.; of one of the 18 Dvīpas, L.; (*ī*), f. a species of Cyperus, L.; Batatas Edulis, L. **-kanda**, m. an esculent root, a sort of yam, L. **-karṇa**, m. 'boar-eared,' N. of a kind of arrow, MBh.; R.; N. of a Yaksha, MBh.; (*ī*), f. Physalis Flexuosa, L. **-karṇikā**, f. a kind of missile weapon, L. **-kalpa**, m. the period during which Vishṇu assumed his boar-form, MBh. **-kavaca**, n. N. of a Kavaca (q.v.), Cat. **-kāntā**, f. a kind of yam, L. **-kālin**, m. a kind of sunflower, Helianthus Annuus, L. **-krāntā**, f. a sort of sensitive plant, Mimosa Pudica, L. (accord. to some 'Lycopodium Imbricatum'). **-danshṭra**, m. and (*ā*), f. 'boar-toothed,' N. of a disease (reckoned among the Kshudra-rogas), ŚārṅgS. **-dat** or **-danta**, mfn. having b^o's teeth, L. **-datta**, m. N. of a merchant, Kathās. **-dāna-vidhi**, m. N. of wk. **-deva**, m. N. of a man, Rājat.; *-svāmin*, m. N. of an author. **-dvādaśī**, f. N. of a festival in honour of the boar-incarnation of Vishṇu (observed on the twelfth day in the light half of Māgha), W. **-dvīpa**, N. of a Dvīpa, VāyuP. **-nāman**, m. Mimosa Pudica, L.; an esculent root, yam, L.; °*mâshṭôttara-śata*, n. N. of a Stotra. **-pattrī**, f. Physalis Flexuosa, L. **-parvata**, m. N. of a mountain, Vishṇ. **-purāṇa**, n. N. of the fifteenth Purāṇa (celebrating Vishṇu in his boar-incarnation; cf. *purāṇa* and IW. 514). **-māhātmya**, n. N. of wk. **-mihira**, m. N. of an astronomer (son of Āditya-dāsa and author of the Bṛihaj-jātaka, Bṛihat-saṃhitā, Laghu-jātaka, Yoga-yātrā, Pañca-siddhāntikā; in the last of these wks. he takes 506 A.D. as the epoch of his calculations), IW. 176 &c. **-mūla**, n. N. of a place having an image of Vishṇu in his boar-form, Rājat. **-yūtha**, m. a herd of wild boars, Ṛitus. **-vat**, ind. like a boar, MW. **-vadhrī**, f. (prob.) a flitch, R. **-vapusha**, n. the body of a boar, ib. **-vasā**, f. hog's grease, Suśr. **-śṛiṅga**, m. 'boar-horned,' N. of Śiva, Śivag. **-śaila**, m. N. of a mountain, Cat. **-saṃhitā**, f. N. of wk. (the Bṛihat-saṃhitā of Varāha-mihira). **-stuti**, f. N. of ch. of the BrahmâṇḍaP. **-sphuṭa**, m. or n. N. of wk. **-svāmin**, m. N. of a mythical king, Kathās. **Varāhâdri**, m. N. of a mountain, MārkP. **Varāhâvatāra**, m. the boar-incarnation (in which Vishṇu, in boar-form, raised up on one of his tusks the earth which lay buried beneath the waters when the whole world had become one ocean), IW. 327; RTL. 109. **Varāhâśva**, m. N. of a Daitya, MBh. **Varāhôpanishad**, f. N. of an Upanishad. **Varāhôpānah**, f. du. shoes made of pig's leather, Kāty.

Varāhaka, m. N. of a serpent-demon, MBh.; (*ikā*), f. Physalis Flexuosa, L.; n. N. of an Upanishad.

Varāhayú, mfn. eager after boars, useful or fit for boar-hunting, RV.

Varāhú, m. a boar, hog, RV.; pl. N. of partic. winds, TĀr.; N. of a class of gods belonging to the middle sphere, Sāy.

वरितृ 1. *varitṛi*, *varimán*, *várishṭha*. See p. 921, col. 2.

वरितृ 2. *varitṛi*, °*riman* &c. See p. 923, col. 1.

वरिवस् *várivas*, *varivo-dá* &c. See p. 921, col. 2.

वरिशी *variśī*. See *bariśī*.

वरिष *varisha*, m. = *varsha*, rain &c., Uṇ. iii, 62, Sch.; (*ā*), f. pl. the rains, rainy season, L. **Varishā-priya**, m. 'friend of the rainy season,' the Cātaka bird (being supposed to drink only rain-water), L.

वरी *varī*, f. pl. (see also under 2. *vara*) streams, rivers, Naigh. i, 13 (cf. *vār*, *vāri*). **-tāksha**, m. N. of a Daitya, MBh. **-dāsa**, m. N. of the father of the Gandharva Nārada, Hariv. **-dharā**, f. a kind of metre, L.

वरीमन् 1. *várīman*, *várīyas*. See p. 921, col. 2.

वरीमन् 2. *varīman*, °*rīyas*. See p. 923, col. 1.

वरीवर्द *varīvarda* = *balivárda* (see under *balivarda*).

वरीवृजत् *várīvṛijat*. See under √*vṛij*.

वरीवृत *varīvṛitá*, mfn. (fr. Intens. of √1. *vṛit*) turning frequently, rolling, AV.

वरीषु *varīshu*, m. N. of Kāma-deva, the god of love, L. (cf. *ravīshu*).

वरु *varu*, (accord. to Sāy.) N. of a man, RV. viii, 23, 28; 24, 28; 25, 2 (only in *varo*, which is always followed by *sushāmṇe*, and should be a voc., but, accord. to others, ought to form the one word *Varosushāman* a proper N.)

वरुक *varuka*, m. a species of inferior grain, Suśr.

वरुट *varuṭa*, m. N. of a class of Mlecchas, L. (accord. to some 'the son of an out-caste Kshatriya,' = *karaṇa*, q. v.)

Varuḍa, m. N. of a low mixed caste (one of the 7 low castes called Antya-ja, whose occupation is splitting canes), Kull. on Mn. iv, 215; (*ī*). f. a woman of the above caste, Yājñ., Sch.

वरुण *váruṇa* &c. See p. 921, col. 2.

वरुतृ *varutṛi*, *varutra*. See p. 921, col. 3.

वरुल *varula* = *sambhakta*, L.

वरूक *varūka*, m. = *varuka*, Car.

वरूतृ *varūtṛí*, *várūtha* &c. See p. 921, col. 3.

वरेण् *vareṇ*, *váreṇya*, *vareya* &c. See col. 1.

वरेण *vareṇa*, m. a wasp, L. (cf. *varola*); (*ā*), f. (prob.) w. r. for *vareṇya*.

वरेणुक *vareṇuka*, m. corn, L.

वरेन्द्र *varêndra*, *varêśa* &c. See col. 1.

वरोट *varoṭa*, m. N. of a plant (= *maruvaka*), L.; n. its flower.

वरोरु *varôru*. See col. 1.

वरोल *varola*, m. a kind of wasp, L.; (*ī*), f. a smaller kind of wasp, L.

वर्कर *varkara*. See *barkara*.

वर्कराट *varkarāṭa*, m. (only L.) a side glance; the rays of the ascending sun; the marks of a lover's finger-nails on the bosom of a woman.

वर्करीकुण्ड *varkarī-kuṇḍa*, m. or n.(?) N. of a place, Cat.

वर्कुट *varkuṭa*, m. a pin, bolt, L.

वर्ग *várga* (accented only in Nigh.), m. (fr. √*vṛij*) one who excludes or removes or averts, KaushUp.; (ifc. f. *ā*) a separate division, class, set, multitude of similar things (animate or inanimate), group, company, family, party, side (mostly ifc., e.g. *catur-*, *tri-v°*, q. v.; often pl. for sg.), KātyŚr.; Prāt. &c.; (esp.) any series or group of words classified together (as *manushya-v°* *vanas-pati-v°* &c.), or a class or series of consonants in the alphabet (seven such classes being given, viz. *ka-varga*, 'the class of Guttural letters;' *ca-kāra-v°* or *ca-v°*, 'the Palatals;' *ṭa-v°*, 'the Cerebrals;' *ta-v°*, 'the Dentals;' *pa-v°*, 'the Labials;' *ya-v°*, 'the Semivowels;' *śa-v°*, 'the Sibilants,' and the aspirate *h*, cf. *varga-dvitīya* and *-prathama*), Prāt.; VarBṛS.; Vop.; everything comprehended under any department or head, everything included under a category, province or sphere of, VarBṛS.; = *tri-varga* (q. v.), BhP.; a section, chapter, division of a book, (esp.) a subdivision of an Adhyāya in the Ṛig-veda (which, accord. to the mere mechanical division, contains 8 Ashṭakas or 64 Adhyāyas or 2006 Vargas; cf. *maṇḍala*) and a similar subdivision in the Bṛihad-devatā; (in alg.) the square of a number, Col. (e. g. *pañca-v°*, square of five, cf. *bhinna-v°*); = *bala*, strength, Naigh. ii, 9; N. of a country, Buddh.; (*ā*), f. N. of an Apsaras, MBh. **-karman**, n. N. of an indefinite problem or of an operation relating to square numbers, Līl. **-ghana**, n. the square of a cube, W.; *-ghāta*, m. (in arithm.) the fifth power. **-dvitīya**, m. (in gram.) the second letter of a Varga (see above). **-pada**, n. a square root, Col. **-prakṛiti**, f. (in arithm.) an affected square, Col. **-prathama**, m. (in gram.) the first letter of a Varga (see above). **-praśaṅsin**, mfn. praising one's own class or set (relatives, dependants &c.), Nilak. **-mūla**, n. (in arithm.) square root, Col. **-varga**, m. (in arithm.) the square of a square, a biquadratic number; *-varga*, m. the square of a squared square. **-śas**, ind. accord. to divisions, in groups, BhP. **-stha**, mfn. standing by or devoted to a party, partial, MBh. **Vargầntya**, m. (in gram.) the last letter of a Varga, a nasal, APrāt., Sch. **Vargâshṭaka**, n. the eight groups of consonants i. e. the consonants collectively, RāmatUp., Sch. **Vargôttama**, m. = *vargântya*, APrāt., Sch.; (in astrol.) 'chief of a class,' N. of the Ram and the Bull and the Twins (being the first in a partic. grouping of the zodiacal signs), Var.

Vargaṇā, f. division, class, Sil.; multiplication, VarBṛS.

Vargaya, Nom. P. *°yati*, to raise to a square, Līl. (*°gita*, mfn. squared, ib.)

Vár̥gas, n., among the *bala-nāmāni*, Naigh. ii, 9.

Vargin, mf(*iṇī*)n. belonging to a class, devoted to a side or party, MBh.

Vargī-kṛita, mfn. made into classes, classified, arranged, MW.; (in alg.) raised to a square, squared.

Vargīṇa, mfn. (ifc.) belonging to the class or category or family or party of, Pāṇ. iv, 3, 64.

Vargīya, mfn. (ifc.) id., ib. (e. g. *ka-vargīya*, a guttural, *pa-vargīya*, a palatal, Sch.; cf. *artha-*, *mad-v°* &c.)

Vargya, mfn. (ifc.) id., Pāṇ. iv, 3, 54 (cf. *mad-v°*); m. a member of a society, colleague, Mālatīm.

Varja, mf(*ā*)n. (ifc.) free from, devoid of, excluding, with the exception of, MBh.; BhP.; m. leaving, leaving out, excepting, W.; (*am*), see below. **°jaka**, mfn. (ifc.) shunning, avoiding, MBh.; Hcat.; excluding, exclusive of, MW. **°jana**, n. excluding, avoiding, leaving, abandoning, Mn.; MBh. &c.; neglect, Pañcar.; omission, ĀśvŚr.; exception, Pāṇ. i, 4, 88 &c.; hurting, injury, L. **°janīya**, mfn. to be excluded or shunned or avoided, improper, censurable, Mn.; MBh. &c. **°jam**, ind. (mostly ifc., exceptionally with acc.) excluding, excepting, except, without, with the exception of, GṛŚrS.; Mn. &c. **°jayitavya**, mfn. to be shunned or avoided, VarBṛS. **°jayitṛi**, mfn. one who excludes or avoids or shuns, MBh.; one who pours out, discharger (of rain), Sāy.

Varjita, mfn. excluded, abandoned, avoided, MBh.; Kāv. &c.; (with instr. or ifc.) deprived of, wanting, without, with the exception of, Mn.; MBh. &c. **°jin**, mfn. avoiding, shunning, MBh. **°jya**, mfn. to be excluded or shunned or avoided or given up, Mn.; MBh. &c.; (ifc.) with the exception of, exclusive of, without, MBh.; MārkP.; n. a stage in each lunar mansion during which no business should be begun, W.

वर्च् **varc** (prob. artificial, to serve as the source of the words below), cl. 1. Ā. *varcate*, to shine, be bright, Dhātup. vi, 1.

Varca, m. N. of an ancient sage, MBh. (= *su-varcaka*, Nilak.)

Varcaḥ-sthāna, n. (for *varcas + sth°*) a place for voiding excrement, Car.

Varcala. See *su-varcala*.

Várcas, n. (√*ruc*) vital power, vigour, energy, activity, (esp.) the illuminating power of fire or the sun, i. e. brilliance, lustre, light, RV. &c. &c.; colour, R.; BhP.; splendour, glory, Kāv.; Pur.; form, figure, shape, L.; excrement, ordure, feces, Rājat.; Suśr.; m. N. of a son of Soma, MBh.; of a son of Su-tejas or Su-ketas, ib.; of Rākshava, BhP. (Sch.) **-vat** (*várcas-*), mfn. vigorous, fresh, AV.; VS.; shining, bright, VS.; containing the word *varcas*, Pāṇ. iv, 4, 125, Sch. **-vin**, mfn. vigorous, active, energetic, AV.; VS. &c.; m. an energetic man, ŚBr.; N. of a son of Varcas and grandson of Soma, MBh.; Hariv.

Varcasá, n. (ifc.) = *varcas*, light, lustre, colour, AV.; MBh.; R. &c. (cf. *brahma-v°*).

Varcasín. See *brahma-* and *su-v°*.

Varcaska, m. n. (g. *ardharcâdi*) power, vigour, brightness &c., MBh.; Hariv.; ordure, excrement, Pāṇ. vi, 1, 148. **-sthāna**, n. = *°caḥ-sthāna*, Car.

Varcasyà, mfn. bestowing vital power or vigour, VS.; AV.; ŚāṅkhGṛ.; relating to *varcas*, Kauś.; acting on the excrement, Suśr.; (*ā*), f. (scil. *ishṭakā*) N. of partic. sacrificial bricks (at the laying of which certain Mantras containing the word *varcas* are used), Pāṇ. iv, 4, 125, Sch.

Varcāya, Nom. Ā. *°yate*, to shine, g. *bhṛiśâdi*.

Varcā-vasu, m. a partic. sunbeam, VP., Sch. (in a quotation); N. of a Gandharva, VP.

Varcita, w.r. for *carcita*, Pañcat.

Varcín, m. N. of a demon (slain by Indra or by Indra and Vishṇu jointly), RV.

Varco, in comp. for *varcas*. **-graha**, m. obstruction of the feces, constipation, Suśr. **-dā́** (AV.), **-dhā́s** (AV.), **-dhā́** (AV.; VS.), mfn. granting power, bestowing vigour or energy. **-bheda**, m. diarrhœa, Car.; *°din*, mfn. suffering from it, ib. **-mārga**, m. the anus, L. **-vinigraha**, m. = *-graha*, Car.

वर्चटी **varcaṭī** (?), f. a kind of rice, W.; a harlot, ib.

वर्ज् **varja** &c. See col. 1.

वर्ण् **varṇ** (rather Nom. fr. *varṇa*), cl. 10. P. (Dhātup. xxxv, 83) *varṇayati* (m. c. also *°te*; aor. *avavarṇat*; inf. *varṇayitum* or *varṇitum*), to paint, colour, dye, Yājñ.; Daś.; to depict, picture, write, describe, relate, tell, explain, MBh.; Kāv. &c.; to regard, consider, Kathās.; to spread, extend, MBh.; to praise, extol, proclaim qualities, W.: Pass. *varṇyate* (aor. *avarṇi*), to be coloured or described &c., MBh.; Kāv. &c.

Várṇa, m. (or n., g. *ardharcâdi*, prob. fr. √1. *vṛi*; ifc. f. *ā*) a covering, cloak, mantle, L.; a cover, lid, Yājñ. iii, 99; outward appearance, exterior, form, figure, shape, colour, RV. &c. &c.; colour of the face, (esp.) good colour or complexion, lustre, beauty, Mn.; MBh. &c.; colour, tint, dye, pigment (for painting or writing), MBh.; Kāv. &c.; colour = race, species, kind, sort, character, nature, quality, property (applied to persons and things), RV. &c. &c.; class of men, tribe, order, caste (prob. from contrast of colour between the dark aboriginal tribes and their fair conquerors; in RV. esp. applied to the Āryas and the Dāsas; but more properly applicable to the four principal classes described in Manu's code, viz. Brāhmans, Kshatriyas, Vaiśyas, and Śūdras; the more modern word for 'caste' being *jāti*; cf. IW. 210, n. 1), ib.; a letter, sound, vowel, syllable, word, Br.; Prāt. &c.; a musical sound or note (also applied to the voice of animals), MBh.; R.; Pañcat.; the order or arrangement of a song or poem, W.; praise, commendation, renown, glory, Mṛicch.; Kum; Rājat.; (in alg.) an unknown magnitude or quantity; (in arithm.) the figure 'one;' (accord. to some) a co-efficient; a kind of measure, L. (cf. *-tāla*); gold, L.; a religious observance, L.; one who wards off, expeller, Sāy. on RV. i, 104, 2; (*ā*), f. Cajanus Indicus, L.; n. saffron, L. [Cf., accord. to some, Slav. *vranŭ*, 'black,' 'a crow;' Lith. *várnas*, 'a crow.'] **-kavi**, m. N. of a son of Kubera, L. **-kūpikā**, f. any vessel containing colour or paint, an ink-bottle, ink-stand, L. **-kṛit**, mfn. causing or giving colour, Suśr. **-krama**, m. order or succession of colours, KātyŚr., Sch.; order of castes (*eṇa*, ind. according to the order of castes), Prab.; order or series of letters, alphabetical arrangement, alphabet, W.; a partic. Krama or method of reciting Vedic texts (see under *krama*), TPrāt.; *-darpaṇa*, m., *-lakshaṇa* and *-vivaraṇa*, n. N. of wks. **-gata**, mfn. 'gone to colour,' coloured, described, W.; algebraical, Col. **-guru**, m. 'father or chief of the castes,' a king, prince, Rājat. **-grathanā**, f. a partic. artificial method of writing verses, Vās. **-ghanasāriṇī**, f. N. of wk. **-cāraka**, m. a painter, L. **-citrita**, mfn. painted with colours, Śak. **-caura**, m. a stealer of colour, L. **-ja**, mfn. produced from castes, VarBṛS. **-jyāyas**, mfn. higher in caste, Āpast. **-jyeshṭha**, mf(*ā*)n. highest in caste, Hit. iv, 21 (v.l.); m. a Brāhman, L. **-tanu**, f. N. of a partic. Mantra addressed to Sarasvatī, Cat. **-tantra-mālā**, f. a grammar or N. of a partic. grammar, Cat. **-tarṇaka**, n. or *°ṇikā*, f. woollen cloth used as a mat, L. **-tas**, ind. by or with or according to colour &c., RPrāt.; AgP. **-tā**, f. (MBh.), **-tva**, n. (Suśr.; Kull. &c.) the state of colour, colour (*anya-varṇa-tva*, the being of another colour); the state or condition of caste, division into classes; the state or condition of a letter or sound. **-tāla**, m. N. of a king, Vār., Introd.; (in music) a kind of measure, Saṃgīt. **-tūli**, **-tūlikā**, or **-tūlī**, f. 'letter-brush,' a pen, pencil, paint-brush, L. **-da**, mfn. giving colour, colouring, dyeing, W.; giving tribe &c., ib.; n. a kind of fragrant yellow wood, L. **-dātrī**, f. 'giving colour,' turmeric, L. **-dīpikā**, f. 'letter-explainer,' N. of a wk. on the mystical meaning of letters. **-dūta**, m. 'letter-messenger,' a letter, epistle, L. **-dūshaka**, mf(*ikā*)n. violating or disturbing the distinctions of caste, Mn. x, 61. **-devatā**, f. the deity presiding over any partic. letter, VPrāt. **-deśanā**, f. 'instruction in letters,' N. of a treatise (by Deva-kīrti on the proper spelling of words with certain cognate consonants, such as *ś*, *sh*, *s*; *j* and *y*; *gh* and *h*), and of some similar wks. **-dvaya-maya**, mf(*ī*)n. consisting of two syllables, Cat. **-dharma**, m. the partic. duty or occupation of any caste or tribe, Gaut.; Mn. &c. **-nātha**, m. the planetary regent of a caste, Vāstuv. **-paṭala**, m. or n. (?) N. of a Pariśishṭa of the AV. **-pattra**, n. 'colour-leaf,' a pallet, L. **-paricaya**, m. skill in song or music, Śak. **-paridhvaṅsa**, m. (Sch.) or *°sā*, f. (Āpast.) loss of caste. **-pāṭha**, m. 'letter-register,' the alphabet, Pat. **-pāta**, m. the dropping or omission of a letter in pronunciation, MW. **-pātra**, n. 'colour-vessel or receptacle,' a paint-box, L. **-pushpa**, n. the blossom of globe-amaranth, L.; (*ī*), f. Echinops Echinatus, L. **-pushpaka**, m. globe-amaranth, L. **-prakarsha**, m. excellence or beauty of colour, MW. **-prakāśa**, m., **-prabodha**, m. N. of wks. **-prasādana**, n. aloe wood, Agallochum, L. **-buddhi**, f. the idea or notion connected with partic. letters or sounds, Sarvad. **-bhinna** and **-bhīru**, m. (in music) two kinds of measure, Saṃgīt. **-bheda-vidhi**, m. method of letter-division, N. of wk. **-bhedinī**, f. millet, L. **-bhairava**, m. or n. (?) N. of a wk. on the terrible importance of the mystical meaning of letters. **-mañcikā**, f. (in music) a kind of measure, Saṃgīt. **-maya**, mf(*ī*)n. consisting of colours, MW.; consisting of symbolical letters or sounds, Cat. **-mātṛi**, f. 'letter-mother,' a pen, pencil &c., L. **-mātṛikā**, f. N. of Sarasvatī, L. **-mātra**, n. only the colour, nothing but colour, Hit.; (*ā*), f. a kind of metre, Sāh. **-mālā**, f. order or series of letters (esp. rows of letters written on a board or in a diagram), the alphabet, L.; *-praśna-grantha*, m. N. of wk. **-yati**, f. (in music) a kind of measure, Saṃgīt. **-ratna-dīpikā**, f. N. of wk. **-rāśi**, m. 'multitude or series of letters,' the alphabet, RPrāt., Introd.; Sarvad. **-rekhā**, f. chalk or a white substance often confounded with chalk, L. **-līla**, m. (in music) a kind of measure, Saṃgīt. **-lekhā** or **-lekhikā**, f. = *-rekhā*, L. **-vat**, mfn. having colour &c., MW.; (*-vatī*), f. turmeric, L. **-varti** or **-vartikā**, f. a writing-pen, pencil &c., L. **-vādin**, m. a speaker of praise, panegyrist, L. **-vikriyā**, f. enmity against the castes, Ragh. **-viparyaya**, m. the change or substitution of one letter for another, MW. **-vilāsa**, m. N. of wk. **-vilāsinī**, f. turmeric, L. **-viloḍaka**, m. a plagiarist, L.; a house-breaker, L. **-viveka**, m. distinction of sounds, N. of a treatise on the different spelling of nouns. **-vṛitta**, n. N. of a class of metres regulated by the number of syllables in the half-line (such as the Anushṭubh, Indra-vajrā &c.; cf. *mātrā-vṛitta*), Col. **-vaikṛita**, n. degeneracy of caste, Cat. **-vyatikrāntā**, f. a woman that has transgressed by intercourse with a man of lower caste, Āpast. **-vyavasthā** (Siṃhās.), **-vyavasthiti** (Gol.), f. caste-system, institution of caste. **-śāsana**, n. N. of wk. **-śreshṭha**, mfn. belonging to the best of tribes, W.; m. a Brāhman or member of the highest caste, R. **-saṃyoga**, m. 'union of tribe or caste,' matrimonial connection or marriage between persons of the same caste, MārkP. **-saṃsarga**, m. mixture or confusion of castes, matrimonial connection or marriage with members of other castes, Mn. viii, 172. **-saṃhāra**, m. an assemblage or mixture of different castes, an assembly in which all the four tribes are represented, Bhar.; Daśar.; Sāh. **-saṃhitā**, f. a kind of Saṃhitā (q. v.), TPrāt. **-saṃkara**, m. mixture or blending of colours, MBh.; mixture or confusion of castes through intermarriage, Mn.; MBh.; (*-tā*), f. a tribe of different origin, a man descended from a father and mother of different castes, W.; *-jāti-mālā*, f. N. of a wk. on mixed c°s; °*rika*, mfn. one who causes confusion of castes by intermarriage, MBh. **-saṃghāṭa** or **-saṃghāta** (Pat.), **-samāmnāya** (VPrāt. &c.), m. 'assemblage or aggregate of letters,' the alphabet. **-sāra-bhūta-varṇa-krama**, m., **-sāra-maṇi**, m., and **-sūtra**, n. N. of wks. **-sthāna**, n. the place or organ of utterance of any sound or letter (eight in number, as 'the throat' &c.; see under *sthāna*), Ragh. **-hīna**, mfn. deprived of caste, out-caste, W. **Varṇâgama**, m. the addition of a letter to a word, MW. **Varṇâṅkā**, f. 'letter-maker,' a pen, L. **Varṇâtman**, m. 'consisting of sounds or letters,' a word, L.; °*tmaka*, mfn. having articulate sound, Tarkas. **Varṇâdhipa**, m. 'caste-lord,' a planet presiding over a class or caste, L. **Varṇânuprāsa**, m. alliteration, paronomasia, Vām. **Varṇântara**, n. another caste, Āpast. (*-gamana*, n. the passing into another caste, Gaut.); another letter, change of sound, Jaim. **Varṇânyatva**, n. change of complexion or colour, Sāh. **Varṇâpasada**, m. one who is excluded from caste, an out-caste, W. **Varṇâpêta**, mfn. = *varṇa-hīna*, Mn. x, 57. **Varṇâbhidhāna**, n. N. of a glossary of monosyllables by Nandana Bhaṭṭa. **Varṇârha**, m. a sort of bean, Phaseolus Mungo, L. **Varṇâvara**, mfn. inferior in caste, Mālav. **Varṇâśrama**, n. caste and order, class and stage of life (see *āśrama*), Śak.; *-guru*, m. 'chief of caste and order,' N. of Śiva, L.; *-dharma*, m. the duties of caste and order, W.; N. of wk. (also °*madipa*, m.); °*śrama-vat* or °*śramin*, mfn. possessed of caste and order, BhP. **Varṇêśvarī**, f. N. of a goddess, Cat. **Varṇôdaka**, n. coloured water, Ragh. **Varṇôdaya**, m., °*ṇôddhṛiti*, f. N. of wks. **Varṇôpanishad**, f. N. of an Upanishad. **Varṇôpêta**, mfn. having tribe or caste, W.

Varṇaka, mf(*ikā*)n. painting, picturing, representing, Rājat.; m. a strolling player or singer, L.; a species of plant, Suśr.; fragrant ointment, L.; N. of a man (pl. his descendants), g. *upakâdi*; m. or n. a model or specimen, Kathās.; m. n. and (*ikā*), f. colour for painting, paint, pigment, unguent, anything for smearing on the body, AitĀr.; ŚāṅkhGṛ. &c. (ifc. f. *akā*); sandal, L.; (*akā*), f. woven cloth, L.; (*ikā*), f. a mask, dress of an actor &c. (*-parigraha*, m. the assumption of a mask or part), Mālatim.; a pencil or brush for painting or writing, L.; kind, description, HPariś.; a woman's fragrant ointment, L.; (*akā* or *ikā*), f. fine gold, purity of gold, L.; n. a chapter, section of a book, Nyāyam., Sch.; a circle, orb, HPariś.; orpiment, L.; the red colouring or paint with which bride and bridegroom are marked at weddings, the painting of the bride by the bridegroom and of the bridegroom by the bride, L.; (ifc.) a letter or syllable, Śrutab. **-citrita**, mfn. painted with colours or with a brush, Śak. (cf. *varṇac*°). **-daṇḍaka**, m. or n. 'a stick used in painting' and 'a kind of metre,' VarBṛS. **-dāru**, n. sandal-wood, Harav. **-maya**, mf *ī*)n. composed or consisting of colours, painted, Śāntik.

Varṇakita, mfn. (fr. *varṇaka*), g. *tārakâdi*.

Varṇaṭa, m. N. of a man, Rājat.

Varṇana, n. and °*ṇā*, f. the act of painting, colouring &c.; delineation, description, explanation, Kāv.; Pur.; Kathās. &c.; writing, MW.; embellishment, decoration, ib.; (*ā*), f. praise, commendation, L.

Varṇanīya, mfn. to be painted or coloured or delineated or described, BhP.; Sāh.; Sarvad. (cf. *śoṇita-v*°).

Varṇayitavya, mfn. = prec., Śaṃk.

Varṇasa, mfn. (fr. *varṇa*), g. *triṇâdi*.

Varṇāṭa, m. (only L.) a painter; a singer; one who makes his living by his wife; a lover.

1. **Varṇi** (gender doubtful), gold, Uṇ. iv, 123, Sch.; m. fragrant ointment, L.

2. **Varṇi**, in comp. for *varṇin*. **-liṅgin**, m. one wearing the marks of a religious student, W. **-vadha**, m. killing or occasioning the death of a man belonging to one of the four castes, MW.

Varṇika, mfn., in *aika-v*°, q. v.; m. (v. l. for *vārṇika*) a writer, scribe, secretary, L.; (*ikā*), f., see under *varṇaka*.

Varṇita, mfn. painted, delineated, described, explained, MBh.; Kāv. &c.; praised, eulogized, extolled, W.; spread, MBh. **-vat**, mfn. one who has painted or described &c., W.

Varṇin, mf(*inī*)n. having a partic. colour, coloured, AgP.; (ifc.) having the colour or appearance of, R.; belonging to the caste or tribe of (see *jyeshṭha-v*°); m. a painter, L.; a writer, scribe, L.; a person belonging to one of the four castes, Yājñ.; Kām.; a religious student or Brahma-cārin (q. v.), Kum.; Kathās. (cf. Pāṇ. v, 2, 134); a partic. plant (?), MBh. xii, 2652; pl. N. of a partic. sect, Vās., Introd.; (*inī*), f. a woman belonging to one of the higher castes, Vāgbh.; any woman or wife, L.; turmeric, L.

Varṇila, mfn. (fr. *varṇa*), g. *picchâdi*.

Varṇī-√bhū, P. *-bhavati*, to become or be changed into an articulate sound, RPrāt.

1. **Varṇya**, mfn. to be (or being) delineated or described or pictured, describable, Sāh. **-sama**, m. (scil. *pratishedha*) a kind of sophism, Nyāyam.; Sarvad.; Car. (cf. *a-varṇya-sama*).

2. **Varṇya**, mfn. relating to or useful for or giving colour, Suśr.; n. saffron, L.

वर्णसि *varṇasi*, m. or f.(?) water, Uṇ. iv, 107, Sch.

Varṇāśā, f. N. of two rivers, VP.

Varṇu, m. N. of a river and the adjacent district, Uṇ. iii, 38, Sch. (cf. *vārṇava*); the sun, L.

वर्त *varta*, m. (fr. √*vṛit*) subsistence, livelihood, L. (mostly ifc.; see *andhaka-*, *kalya-*, *bahu-*, *brahma-v*°); the urethra, Kauś., Sch. (v. l. for 1. *varti*). **-janman**, m. a cloud, L. **-tīkshṇa** or **-loha**, n. a sort of brass or steel, L.

Vartaka, mfn. who or what abides or exists, abiding, existing, living, W.; (ifc.) given up or devoted or attached to (cf. *guru-v*°), R.; m. a quail, Car.; a horse's hoof, L.; (*ā*), f. a quail, L.; (*vártikā*), f. (see also s. v.) id., RV.; MBh.; Suśr. (here of a different kind fr. the m.); (*ī*), f. id., L.; n. a sort of brass or steel, L. [Cf. Gk. ὄρτυξ, ὀρτυγία.]

Vartana, mfn. (also fr. Caus.) abiding, staying &c. (= *vartishṇu*), L.; setting in motion, quickening, causing to live or be (also applied to Vishṇu), Hariv.; BhP.; m. a dwarf, L.; (*ā*), f., see under n.; (*ī*), f. staying, abiding, living, life, L.; a way, road, path (= *vartani*), HPariś.; 'grinding' or 'despatching' (= *peshaṇa* or *prêshaṇa*), L.; a spindle or distaff, Lalit.; n. the act of turning or rolling or rolling on or moving forward or about (trans. and intrans.), Nir.; KātyŚr.; BhP.; Car. &c. (also *ā*, f., Harav.); twisting (a rope), L.; staying, abiding in (loc.), Uttarar.; living on (instr.), livelihood, subsistence, occupation, earnings, wages, Kāv.; Rājat.; Kathās.; Hit.; commerce, intercourse with (*saha*), Kām.; proceeding, conduct, behaviour, Sāh.; (ifc.) application of, Kir.; a distaff or spindle, L.; a globe or ball, L.; an often told word, L.; a place where a horse rolls, L.; decoction, L. **-dāna**, n. the gift of means of subsistence or wages, W. **-viniyoga**, m. appointment of means of s°, salary, wages, ib. **Vartanâbhāva**, m. want of means of s°, destitution, ib. **Vartanârthin**, mfn. seeking an occupation, Hit.

Vartanī, f. the circumference or felloe of a wheel, RV.; Br.; the track of a wheel, rut, path, way, course, ib.; AV.; ChUp.; the course of rivers, RV.; TS.; the eyelashes, ŚBr. (cf. *vartman*); the eastern country, L.; = *stotra*, g. *uñchâdi*.

Vartanin. See *eka-*, *ubhaya-* and *sahasra-v*°.

Vartanīya, mfn. to be stayed or dwelt in; n. (impers.) it should be applied or attended to (loc.), Vcar.

Vartamāna, mfn. turning, moving, existing, living, abiding &c.; present, KātyŚr.; (*ā*), f. the terminations of the present tense, Kāt.; n. presence, the present time, Kāv.; BhP.; (in gram.) the present tense. **-kavi**, m. a living poet, Mālav. **-kāla**, m. the present time (*-tā*, f.), Kāś.; VP. **-tā**, f., **-tva**, n. the being present, the condition of present time, Śaṃk.; Sarvad.; the dwelling or abiding in (with loc.), TPrāt. **-vat**, ind. like the present time, Pāṇ. iii, 3, 131. **Vartamānâkshepa**, m. denying or not agreeing with any present event or circumstances, Kāvyâd.

Vartayádhyai. See under √*vṛit*.

1. **Varti** (or °*tī*), f. anything rolled or wrapped round, a pad, a kind of bandage bound round a wound, Suśr.; any cosmetic prepared from various substances (used as a remedy in the form of a paste or pill), ib.; ointment, unguent, collyrium, Uttarar.; Kathās.; a suppository, ib.; the wick of a lamp, MBh.; VarBṛS.; Kathās.; a magical wick, Pañcat.; a lamp, L.; the projecting threads or unwoven ends of woven cloth, a kind of fringe, L.; a projecting rim or protuberance round a vessel, KātyŚr.; a swelling or polypus in the throat, Suśr.; a swelling or protuberance formed by internal rupture, ib. (cf. *mūtra-v*°); a surgical instrument, bougie, L.; a streak, line (see *dhūma-v*°).

2. **Varti**, in comp. for *vartin*. **-tā**, f. (ifc.) conduct or behaviour towards, R. **-tva**, n. (ifc.) treatment as of, Kām.

Vartika, m. = *vartaka*, a quail, L.

Vartikā, f. (fr. 1. *varti*; cf. under *vartaka*) a stalk, MBh.; the wick of a lamp, KālP. (cf. *yoga-v*°); a paint-brush, Śak. (cf. *citra-v*°); colour, paint, ib. (prob. w. r. for *varṇikā*); Odina Pinnata, L.

Vartita, mfn. (fr. Caus.) turned, rounded (see *su-v*°); turned about, rolled (as a wheel), BhP.; caused to be or exist, brought about, accomplished, prepared, MBh.; Pañcat.; spent, passed (as time or life), MBh.; BhP. **-janman**, mfn. one in whom existence has been brought about, begotten, procreated, BhP. **-vat**, mfn. one who has passed or spent (time), MBh.

Vartitavya, mfn. to be dwelt or stayed in, BhP.; to be carried out or practised or observed, R.; to be treated or dealt with, MBh.; n. (impers.) it should be abided or remained in (loc.; with *asmad-vaśe*, 'in obedience to us' = 'we ought to be obeyed'), BhP.; Kathās.; Pañcat.; it should be applied (by any one) to (loc.), MBh.; R.; it should be lived or existed, Pañcat.; (with an adv. or instr.) it should be proceeded or behaved towards or dealt in any way with any one (loc., gen., or instr. with *saha*), MBh.; Kāv. &c. (*mātṛi-vat* = *mātarīva*, 'as with a mother').

Vartin, mfn. abiding, staying, resting, living or situated in (mostly comp.) Kāv.; Kathās. &c.; (ifc.) being in any position or condition, engaged in, practising, performing, MBh.; R. &c.; obeying, executing (an order; cf. *nideśa-v*°); conducting one's self, behaving, acting, Mn.; MBh. &c.; (ifc.) behaving properly towards, ib. (cf. *guru-v*°; *guru-vat* = *gurāv iva*); turning, moving, going, MW.; m. the meaning of an affix (= *pratyayârtha*), Pat.

Vartira, m. = *vartīra*, L.

Vartishṇu, mfn. = *vartana* or °*tin*, L.

Vartishyamāṇa, mfn. about to be or take place, future, Sarvad.

Vartis, n. circuit, orbit, RV.; lodging, abode, ib. (= *mārga*, Mahīdh.; = *gṛiha*, Sāy.)

Vartī = 1. *varti*, q. v. **-√kṛi**, P. *-karoti*, to make into a paste or pill, &c., ŚārṅgS.

Vartīra, m. a sort of quail or partridge, Suśr.

2. **Vartu**. See *tri-vártu* (for 1. *vartu* see p. 922, col. 1).

Vartula, mf(*ā*)n. round, circular, globular, BhP.; Vet.; Hcat.; m. a kind of pea, Madanav.; a ball, L.; N. of one of Śiva's attendants, L.; (*ā*), f. a ball at the end of a spindle to assist its rotation, L.; (*ī*), f. Scindapsus Officinalis, L.; n. a circle, Cat.; the bulb of a kind of onion, L. **Vartulâkāra** or °*lâkṛiti*, mfn. of circular shape, round, Pañcar. **Vartulâksha**, m. 'having circular eyes,' the brown hawk, L.

Vartulā-tantra, n. N. of a Tantra.

Vartuli (gender doubtful), a kind of bean, Buddh.

Varttavya, n. (impers.) it should be acted or behaved, R.

Vartma, in comp. for *vartman*. **-karman**, n. the business or science of road-making, R. **-da**, m. pl. N. of a school of the Atharva-veda. **-pāta**, m. coming into the way, Gīt. **-pātana**, n. waylaying, HPariś. **-bandha**, m. a disease which obstructs the movement of the eyelids, L. **-roga**, m. a disease of the eyelids, Suśr. **-vibandhaka**, m. = *-bandha*, ib. **-śarkarā**, f. hard excrescences on the eyelids, ib. **Vartmâbhihoma**, m. a libation poured on the track of a wheel, Vait. **Vartmâyāsa**, m. 'road-fatigue,' weariness after a journey, Cat. **Vartmâvabandhaka** and °*varoha*, m. = *vartma-bandha*, Suśr.

Vártman, n. the track or rut of a wheel, path, road, way, course (lit. and fig.), RV. &c. &c. (instr. or loc., ifc. = by way of, along, through, by); an edge, border, rim, Suśr.; an eyelid (as encircling the eye), AV.; ChUp.; Suśr.; basis, foundation, RPrāt. (cf. *dyūta-v*°).

Vartmani, f. = *vartani*, L.

1. **Vartsyat**, mfn. about to be or take place, Bhaṭṭ.

वर्तरूक vartarūka, m. (only L.) standing water, a pool; a crow's nest; a doorkeeper; N. of a river.

वर्तृ vartri, vartra. See under √1. vri.

वर्त्स vartsa, (prob.) w.r. for bārsva (adj. vartsya).

वर्त्स्यत् 2. vartsyat, mfn. (fut. p. of √vridh) intending or going to augment, about to increase or grow, Pañcat.

वर्ध् vardh, cl. 10. P. vardhayati (also vardhāpayati; cf. below), to cut, divide, shear, cut off, Dhātup. xxxii, 111; to fill, ib. (in this sense rather Caus. of √vridh).

1. **Vardha**, m. (for 2. see below) cutting, dividing, W.; n. lead, L. (cf. vardhra).

Vardhaka, mfn. cutting, dividing, cutting off, shearing (see māsha- and śmaśru-v°); m. a carpenter, R.

Vardhaki, m. a carpenter, MBh.; R.; Hariv.; VarBṛS. (also °kin). **-hasta**, m. a carpenter's measure of 42 inches, L.

1. **Vardhana**, n. the act of cutting or cutting off (see nābhi-v°); ifc. after a proper N. prob. = 'town' (cf. puṇḍra-v°, and Old Persian vardana).

1. **Vardhāpaka**, m. (prob.) one who performs the ceremony of cutting the umbilical cord, L.; (prob.) the presents distributed at this ceremony, L.

1. **Vardhāpana**, n. (for 2. see col. 2) the act of cutting the umbilical cord, (or) the ceremony in commemoration of that act, Vet.; Pur.; (prob.) = vardhāpaka, presents distributed at the ceremony of cutting the umbilical cord, L. **-prayoga**, m. N. of wk.

1. **Vardhāpanaka**, n. the cutting of the umbilical cord, (or) a ceremony commemorating it, Pañcat.

1. **Vardhita**, mfn. cut off, L.; carved or fashioned (as timber for a building); fabricated, built, Vāstuv.; filled, full, L.

Várdhra, m. 'what is cut out or off (?),' a strap, thong, leather band of any kind, AV.; ŚBr.; (ī), f. a sinew, leather thong, L.; n. id., Śiś.; leather, L.; lead, L. **-kaṭhina**, n. a strap or band by means of which anything is carried, Kāś. on Pāṇ. iv, 4, 72. **-vyuta** (vá°), mfn. intertwisted with bands or thongs, ŚBr.

Vardhrikā, f. 'strap, thong,' a person as supple or flexible as leather, Pāṇ. vi, 1, 204, Sch. (Kāś. vadhrikā).

वर्ध 2. várdha, mfn. (fr. √vridh; for 1. vardha see above) increasing, augmenting, gladdening (see nandi- and mitra-v°); m. the act of increasing, giving increase or prosperity, RV.; increase, augmentation, W.; Clerodendrum Siphonantus, L. **-phala**, m. Pongamia Glabra, L. **-māla**, m. N. of a Brāhman, Buddh.

2. **Várdhana**, mf(ī)n. increasing, growing, thriving, MBh.; (often ifc.) causing to increase, strengthening, granting prosperity, RV. &c. &c.; (mostly ifc.) animating, gladdening, exhilarating, MBh.; R.; BhP.; m. a granter of increase, bestower of prosperity, ib.; a tooth growing over another tooth, Suśr.; (in music) a kind of measure, Saṃgīt.; N. of Śiva, MBh.; of one of Skanda's attendants, ib.; of a son of Kṛishṇa and Mitra-vindā, BhP.; (ī), f. a broom, brush, L.; a water-jar of a partic. shape, Pur.; Hcat. (cf. vārdhanī); the act of increasing, increase, growth, prosperity, success, MBh.; R.; enlarging, magnifying, strengthening, promoting, KātyŚr.; Hit.; a means of strengthening, restorative, comfort, RV.; educating, rearing, Kathās. **-śīla**, mfn. having a tendency to increase or grow, increasing, growing, MW. **-sūri**, m. N. of a Jaina preceptor, W. **-svāmin**, m. N. of a partic. temple or image, Rājat.

Vardhanaka, mf(ikā)n. exhilarating, gladdening (see cakshur-vardhanikā); (ikā), f. a small vessel in which sacred water is kept, Buddh.

Vardhanīya, mfn. to be increased or strengthened, to be made prosperous or happy, Inscr.; MBh.; Hariv. **-tā**, f., **-tva**, n. augmentability, MW.

Várdhamāna, mfn. increasing, growing, thriving, prosperous, RV. &c. &c.; m. Ricinus Communis (so called from its vigorous growth), Suśr.; sweet citron, L. (also ā, f.); a partic. way of joining the hands, Cat.; a partic. attitude in dancing, Saṃgīt.; a kind of riddle or charade, L.; N. of Vishṇu, L.; of a mountain and district (also of its town, now called Bardwān or Burdwān), VarBṛS.; Pur.; of a Grāma, Rājat.; of various authors and other men, Cat.; of the last of the 24 Arhats or Jinas, Jain.; of the elephant who supports the eastern quarter, L.; (pl.) of a people, MārkP.; m. or n. a kind of mystical figure or diagram, VarBṛS.; Lalit.; a dish or platter of a partic. shape (sometimes used as a lid or cover for water-jars &c.), MBh.; Suśr.; a house having no entrance on the south side, VarBṛS.; MatsyaP.; (ā), f. a species of Gāyatrī metre, RPrāt.; N. of the town of Bardwān, Vet.; (ī), f. N. of a Comm. written by Vardhamāna; n. = vardhamāna-pura, Kathās.; Pañcat.; a kind of metre, Col. **-dvāra**, n. 'gate leading to Vardhamāna,' N. of a gate in Hastināpura, MBh. **-pura**, n. the town of Bardwān, ib.; Kathās.; Pañcat.; -dvāra, n. the gate leading to the town of B°, MBh. **-purīya**, mfn. coming from or born in V°-pura, Kathās. **-pūraṇa**, n., **-prakriyā**, f., and **-prayoga**, m. N. of wks. **-mati**, m. N. of a Bodhi-sattva, Buddh. **-miśra**, m. N. of a grammarian, L. **-svāmin**, m. N. of a Jina, L. **Vardhamānêndu**, m. N. of a Comm. on the Vardhamānī. **Vardhamānêśa**, m. N. of a partic. temple or an image, Rājat.

Vardhamānaka, m. a dish or saucer of a partic. shape, lid or cover, MBh.; a partic. way of joining the hands, Cat.; N. of a class of persons following a partic. trade, MBh. (Nīlak.); of a district or of a people, AV.Pariś.; of a serpent-demon, Buddh.; of various men, Mṛicch.; Pañcat.

Vardhayitṛi, mfn. one who causes to grow or increase &c.; m. (ifc.) an educator, rearer of (ī, f.), Kathās.

2. **Vardhāpaka** = kañcuka, pāṃsu-cāmara, and pūrṇa-pātra, L.; (ikā), f. a nurse, HPariś. (cf. prec.)

2. **Vardhāpana**, n. (for 1. see col. 1; possibly 1. and 2. ought not to be separated) a birthday ceremony, festival on a birthday or any festive occasion, L. °**naka**, n. id.; congratulation, congratulatory gift, Campak. °**nika**, mfn. congratulatory, auspicious, ib.

Vardhāya, ind. having congratulated, Hariv. (v. l. and prob. more correct vardhāpya).

2. **Vardhita**, mfn. increased, grown, expanded, augmented, strengthened, promoted, gladdened, MBh.; Kāv. &c.; n. a kind of dish (?), Mn. iii, 224.

Vardhitavya, mfn. to be increased &c.; n. (impers.) it should be grown or increased, Pat.

Vardhin, mfn. augmenting, increasing (ifc., always f. inī), MBh.; R. &c.

Vardhishṇu, mfn. increasing, growing, Śiś.; enlarging, expanding, W.

Vardhma (or °man), m. internal rupture, hernia, Car.; Bhpr. (cf. antra-vardhman). **-roga**, m. the above disease, ŚārṅgS. **-vṛiddhy-adhikāra**, m. N. of ch. of wk.

वर्धिपथक vardhi-pathaka, m. or n. (?) N. of a district, Inscr.

वर्पस् várpas, n. (prob. connected with rūpa) a pretended or assumed form, phantom, RV.; any form or shape, figure, image, aspect, ib.; artifice, device, design, ib.

Várpa-nīti, mfn. (fr. varpa = varpas + nīti) taking a pretended form, acting artfully, RV.

Varphas, n. = varpas, Uṇ. iv, 200.

वर्पेयु varpeyu, m. N. of a son of Raudrāśva, VP.

वर्फ् varph, cl. 1. P. varphati, 'to go' or 'to kill,' L.

वर्मती varmatī, f. N. of a place, Pāṇ. iv, 3, 94.

वर्मन् varman, n. (or m., Siddh.; fr. √1. vri) 'envelope,' defensive armour, a coat of mail, RV. &c. &c.; a bulwark, shelter, defence, protection, ib. (often at the end of the names of Kshatriyas); bark, rind, VarBṛS.; N. of partic. preservative formulas and prayers (esp. of the mystic syllable hum), BhP.

1. **Varma**, in comp. for varman. **-kaṇṭaka**, m. Gardenia Latifolia or Fumaria Parviflora, L. (v. l. karma-k°). **-kaśā** or **-kashā**, f. a species of plant, L. **-mantra**, m. a partic. formula or prayer (cf. under varman), Cat. **-vat**, mfn. having armour or a coat of mail, mailed, MBh.; n. an unfortified (?) town, MārkP. **-śarman**, m. N. of various men, Inscr. **-hara**, mfn. wearing armour or mail, being young or of a military age, Ragh.: Kathās. (cf. kavaca-h°); one who bears arms or despoils another of them, W.

2. **Varma** (ifc., f. ā) = varman, MBh.

Varmaka, m. pl. N. of a people, MBh.

Varmaṇa, m. the orange tree, L.

Várman-vat, mfn. = varma-vat, RV.

Varmaya, Nom. P. °yati, to provide with a coat of mail, Śiś.

Varmāya, Nom. Ā. °yate, Pāṇ. iv, 1, 15, Sch.

Varmika, mfn. clad in armour, mailed, accoutred, g. vrīhy-ādi.

Varmita, mfn. id., g. tārakâdi. **Varmitâṅga**, mfn. having the body clad in armour, R.

Varmin, mf(iṇī)n. clad in armour, mailed, AV. &c. &c.; m. N. of a man, Pat. on Pāṇ. iv, 1, 158, Vārtt. 2.

वर्मि varmi, m. a kind of fish (commonly called vāmi), Suśr. **-matsya**, m. the fish Varmi, ib.

Varmusha, m. a kind of fish (commonly vāmi-rūsha), L.

वर्य várya, mf(ā)n. (fr. √2. vri) to be chosen, eligible, to be asked or obtained in marriage, Pāṇ. iii, 1, 101, Sch.; excellent, eminent, chief, principal, best of (gen. or comp.), MBh.; Kāv. &c.; m. the god of love, L.; (ā), f. a girl who chooses her husband, L.

वर्व varva, m. or n. (prob.) a partic. coin, Kām.

वर्वट varvaṭa. See barbaṭa.

वर्वणा varvaṇā, f. (also written barb°) a kind of fly, L. (v. l. carmaṇā).

वर्वर varvara &c. See barbara.

Varvaraka, m. (more correct barb°) N. of a man, Mudr.

Varvari, m. N. of a man, Cat.

वर्वि varvi, mfn. voracious, gluttonous (= ghasmara), Uṇ. iv, 53, Sch.

वर्वूर varvūra, m. Acacia Arabica, L.

Varvurika, varvūraka. See jāla-v°.

वर्श्मन् varśman, m. = Zd. bareśman, Cat.

वर्ष varshá, mf(ā)n. (fr. √vrish) raining (ifc., e. g. kāma-v°, raining according to one's wish), BhP.; m. and (older) n. (ifc. f. ā) rain, raining, a shower (either 'of rain,' or fig. 'of flowers, arrows, dust &c.;' also applied to seminal effusion), RV. &c. &c.; (pl.) the rains, AV. (cf. varshā, f.); a cloud, L.; a year (commonly applied to age), Br. &c. &c. (ā varshāt, for a whole year; varshāt, after a year; varshena, within a year; varshe, every year); a day (?), R. vii, 73, 5 (Sch.); a division of the earth as separated off by certain mountain ranges (9 such divisions are enumerated, viz. Kuru, Hiraṇmaya, Ramyaka, Ilāvṛita, Hari; Ketu-māla, Bhadrâśva, Kiṃnara, and Bhārata; sometimes the number given is 7), MBh.; Pur. (cf. IW. 420); India (= Bhārata-varsha and Jambu-dvīpa), L.; m. N. of a grammarian, Kathās.; (ā́), f., see p. 927, col. 2. **-kara**, mfn. making or producing rain, L.; m. a cloud, MW.; (ī), f. a cricket (this animal chirping in wet weather), L. **-karman**, n. the act of raining, Nir. **-kāma**, mfn. desirous of rain; °**mêshṭi**, f. an offering made by one desirous of rain, GṛŚrS.; Nir. **-kārī**, f. (accord. to L. = sravat-pāṇipādā) 'a girl with moist hands and feet, unfit for marriage' (but of doubtful meaning), GṛS. **-kṛitya**, mfn. to be done or completed in a year, Cat.; n. N. of various wks.; -kaumudī, f., -taraṃ-ga, m. N. of wks. **-ketu**, m. a red-flowering Punar-navā, L.; N. of a son of Ketu-mat, Hariv. **-kośa**, m. (also written -kosha) a month, L.; an astrologer, L. **-gaṇa**, m. a long series of years (pl.), Mn. xii, 54; N. of a grammarian, Cat. **-gaṇita-paddhati**, f. N. of wk. **-giri**, m. a mountain bounding a V° (see -parvata), BhP. **-ghna**, mfn. keeping off rain, protecting from rain, R. **-caryā-varṇana**, n. N. of wk. **-ja**, mfn. born or produced in the rainy season, MW.; coming from rain, Sāh.; arisen a year ago, one year old, RāmatUp. **-tantra**, n. N. of various wks. **-tra**, n. 'rain-protector,' an umbrella, R. **-trāṇa**, n. id., L. **-daśā-prakaraṇa**, n., **-daśā-phala**, n., **-dīdhiti**, f. N. of wks.

—dhara, m. 'rain-holder,' a cloud, L.; a mountain bounding a Varsha, Śatr.; the ruler of a Varsha, BhP.; 'withholding generative fluid,' a eunuch, attendant on the women's apartments, Kāv.; Pañcat. &c. **—dharsha**, m. a eunuch, W. **—dhāra**, m. N. of a serpent demon, Buddh. **—dhārā-dhara**, mfn. containing torrents of rain, Cāṇ. **—nakshatra-sūcaka**, m. a weather-prophet and astrologer, Nār. **—nirṇij** (*varshá-*), mfn. clothed with rain (said of the Maruts), RV.; ŚāṅkhŚr. **—m-dhara**, m. N. of a Ṛishi, ĀrshBr., Sch. **—pa** or **-pati**, m. the ruler of a Varsha, BhP. **—pada**, n. a calendar, L. **—paddhati**, f. N. of various wks. **—parvata**, m. one of the mountainous ranges supposed to separate the Varshas or divisions of the earth from each other (6 in number, viz. Himavat, Hema-kūṭa, Nishadha, Nīla, Śveta and Śṛiṅgin or Śṛiṅga-vat; Meru constitutes a 7th, and others are given), L. **—pasu-prayoga**, m. N. of wk. **—pākin**, m. Spondias Mangifera, L. **—pāta**, m. (pl.) fall of rain, Mṛicch. **—purusha**, m. an inhabitant of a Varsha, BhP. **—pushpa**, m. N. of a man, Saṃskārak.; (*ā*), f. a kind of creeping plant, L. **—pūga**, m. n. (sg. or pl.) quantity of rain, BhP.; a series or succession of years, MBh.; BhP. **—pratibandha**, m. stoppage of rain, drought, Pāṇ. iii, 3, 51. **—pradīpa**, m. N. of wk. **—praveśa**, m. the entrance into a new year, MW. **—prāvan** (*varshá-*), mfn. giving plenty of rain, TBr. (Sch.) **—priya**, m. 'fond of rain,' the Cātaka, Cuculus Melanoleucus, L. **—phala**, n., °**la-paddhati**, f., °**la-rahasya**, n., **-bhās-kara**, m. N. of wks. **—bhuj**, m. the ruler of a Varsha, BhP. **—mañjarī**, f. N. of wk. **—maryādā-giri**, m. = *-giri*, (q.v.), BhP. **—mahôdaya**, m. N. of wk. **—mātra**, n. one year only, MW. **—medas** (*varshá-*), mfn. thick or plentiful through rain, AV. xii, 1, 42 (*-medhas*, AV.Paipp.) **—rātra** or °**tri**, w.r. for *varshā-r°* below, R. **—ṛtu** (for *-ṛitu*), m. the rainy season, MW.; *-māsa-pakshâho-velā-deśa-pradeśavat*, mfn. containing a statement of the place and country and time and day and fortnight and month and season and year, Yājñ., Sch.; *-varṇana*, n. N. of wk. (prob. the Ṛitu-saṃhāra). **—lambhaka**, m. (prob.) = *-parvata* (q.v.), MBh. **—vat**, ind. as in rain, ŚāṅkhGṛ. iv, 7. **—vara**, m. a eunuch, one employed in the women's apartments, Kād. **—vardhana**, mfn. causing increase of years, Uttarar.; n. increase of years, MW. **—vardhāpana-vidhāna**, n. N. of a section of the Lubdha-jātaka. **—vasana**, n. (more correctly *varshā-v°*) the dwelling in houses (of the Buddhist monks) during the rainy season, Buddh. **—vicāra**, m. N. of wk. **—vṛiddha** (*varshá-*), mfn. grown up in or through rain, AV.; VS.; ŚBr.; Kauś. **—vṛiddhi**, f. 'year-increase,' birthday, L.; N. of wk.; *-prayoga*, m. N. of wk. **—śata**, n. a century, ChUp.; Mn. &c.; °*tâdhika*, mfn. more than a century, Vet.; °*tin*, mfn. 100 years old, Hariv. **—sahasrá**, n. 1000 years, ŚBr.; R.; °*raka*, n. id., Hariv.; mfn. living or lasting 1000 y°, MBh.; Pañcar.; °*rāya*, Nom. Ā. °*yate*, to appear like 1000 years, Kād.; °*rika*, mf(*ā*)n. lasting 1000 y°, MBh.; °*rin*, mfn. 1000 years old, becoming 1000 years old, MBh.; °*rīya*, mfn. id., MBh. **—sthāla**, n. a rain-vessel (?), Divyâv. **Varshâṇsa** or °**śaka**, m. 'year-portion,' a month, L. **Varshâṅga**, n. 'y°-member,' a month, L.; (*ī*), f. Bœrhavia Procumbens, L. **Varshâjya**, mfn. 'having ghee for rain' or 'having rain for ghee,' AV. **Varshâdhipa**, m. the regent of a year, Gaṇit. **Varshâmbu**, n. rain-water; *-pravaha*, m. a receptacle or reservoir of rain-water, Yājñ. **Varshâmbhaḥ-pāraṇa-vrata**, m. 'breaking fast on rain-water,' the Cātaka bird, L. **Varshâyuta**, n. 10,000 years, MBh. **Varshârdha**, m. a half year (*āt*, after a h° y°), VarBṛS. **Varshârha**, mfn. sufficient for a year, Hcat. **Varshâhika**, m. a kind of venomous snake, Suśr. **Varshe-ja**, mfn. = *varsha-ja*, Pāṇ. vi, 3, 16. **Varshêśa**, m. the regent of a year, L. **Varshâika**, mfn. yearly, annual, W. **Varshôpala**, m. 'rain-stone,' hail, VarBṛS. **Varshâugha**, m. a torrent, sudden shower of rain, Kāv.

Varshaka, mfn. raining, falling like rain, Pāṇ.; Siddh.; m. or n.(?) a summer-house, Buddh.; (ifc.) = *varsha*, a year (e.g. *pañca-v°*, 5 years old), MBh.

Varshaṇa, mf(*ī*)n. (mostly ifc.) raining (with *astram*, a missile causing rain), Hariv.; R.; BhP.; Inscr.; n. raining, causing to rain, pouring out, shedding out gifts upon (comp.), Hariv.; VarBṛS.; Pañcat. &c.; sprinkling, MW.

Varshaṇi, f. (only L.) raining; abiding; action; sacrifice.

Várshat, mfn. raining (*varshati*, loc. 'while it rains'), AV. &c. &c.; m. rain, ŚBr.; m. or n.(?) a summer-house, MW.

Varsháyantī, f. (fr. Caus. of √*vṛish*) causing to rain; N. of one of the 7 Kṛittikās, TS.

Varshā́, f. rain, ŚāṅkhGṛ.; VarBṛS.; pl. (exceptionally sg.) the rains, rainy season, monsoon (lasting two months accord. to the Hindū division of the year into six seasons [see *ṛitu*], the rains falling in some places during Śrāvaṇa and Bhādra, and in others during Bhādra and Āśvina; and in others for a longer period), TS. &c. &c.; Medicago Esculenta, L. [Cf. Gk. ἐέρσαι, 'rain-drops.'] **—kāra**, m. N. of a Brāhman, Divyâv. **—kāla**, m. the rainy season, R.; Vās.; Hit.; °*lika*, mfn. relative to the rainy season, R., Sch.; °*līna*, mfn. belonging to or produced in the r° s°, MW. **—°gama** (*varshâg°*), m. beginning of the rainy s°, VarBṛS. **—°ghosha** (*varshâgh°*), m. 'uttering cries in the r° s°,' a large frog, L. **—cara**, mfn. (of obscure meaning), MBh. **—dhṛita**, mfn. worn in the rainy season (as a garment), KātyŚr. **—nadī**, f. a river which becomes swollen in the rainy season, Bhām. **—prabhañjana**, m. 'rain-scattering,' a high wind, gale, W. **—bīja**, n. hail, L. **—bhava**, m. a red-flowering Bœrhavia, L. **—bhū**, m. 'produced in the rains,' a frog, L.; an earth-worm, L.; a lady-bird, L.; (*ū*), f. a female frog, L.; Bœrhavia Procumbens, Suśr.; (*vī*), f. id., L.; (*ū* or *vī*), f. an earth-worm, MW. **—mada**, m. 'rejoicing in the rains,' a peacock, L. **—rātra**, m. or °**tri**, f. the rainy season, R. **—°rcis** (*varshâr°*), m. the planet Mars (as visible in the r° s°), L. **—laṅkāyikā** (?), f. Trigonella Corniculata, L. **—°vasāna** (*varshâv°*), m. (?) or °**sāya**, m. the close of the rainy season, autumn, L. **—vastu**, n. N. of a section in the Vinaya, Buddh. **—°vāsa** (*varshâv°*), m. the residence during the rains, Divyâv. **—śarád**, f. du. the rainy season and autumn, ŚBr. (once *-śaradáu*). **—śāṭī**, f. a garment worn in the rainy s° (also °*ṭī-cīvara*; °*ṭī-gopaka*, m. a keeper of such garments), Buddh. **—samaya**, m. the rainy season, HPariś.; Vās.; Kathās. **Varshâsu-ja**, mfn. arising or appearing in the rainy s°, Pāṇ. vi, 3, 1, Vārtt. 6, Pat. **Varshā-hū**, f. Bœrhavia Procumbens, TS.; a frog, VS. **Varshôpanāyikā**, f. the first residence in houses during the rainy season (when Buddhist monks suspend their peregrinations), Divyâv. **Varshôshita**, mfn. one who has spent the rainy season, Divyâv.

Varshālī, ind. with √*kṛi*, *bhū*, *as*, g. *ūry-ādi*.

Varshika, mfn. raining, rainy, relating or belonging to the rains, W.; shedding, showering, pouring down, ib.; (ifc.) = *varsha*, a year (e.g. *dvādaśa-v°*, 12 years old), ĀśvŚr.; n. Agallochum, MW.

Varshita, mfn. fallen like rain, VarBṛS.; n. rain, Hariv. (v.l. *varshaṇa*; for °*tā* see under *varshin*).

Varshitṛi, mfn. raining, one who makes rain, Nir.

Varshin, mfn. raining, discharging like rain, pouring out, showering down, distributing (anything good or evil; mostly ifc.), ŚāṅkhGṛ. &c. &c. (°*shitā*, f.); shedding profuse tears, Kāv.; (ifc.) attended with a rain of (see *sâśma-v°*); (ifc.) having (so many) years (e.g. *shashṭi-v°*, 60 years old), MBh.

Varshikā, f. a kind of metre, Nidānas.

Varshiṇa, mfn. (ifc.) so many years old, Pāṇ. v, 1, 86 &c.

Varshīya, mfn. (ifc.) id. (e.g. *tri-v°*, 3 years old), MBh.; Pañcar.

Varshu, mfn. 'lasting' or 'produced by rain,' VS. (Sch.)

Várshuka, mf(*ā*)n. rainy, abounding in rain, TS.; Br.; Bhaṭṭ.; raining, causing to rain, pouring out, Śiś. (cf. *ratna-v°*); m. N. of a man; pl. his descendants, g. *yaskâdi*. **Varshukâbda**, m. a rainy cloud, MW. **Varshukâmbuda**, m. a rain-cloud, ib.

Várshṭri, mfn. one who rains, TS.

Varshyà, or **várshya**, mf(*ā*)n. of rain or belonging to rain, rainy, RV.; VS.; TS. &c.; to be rained or showered, MW.; to be sprinkled, ib.; (*vârshyā*), f. pl. rain-water, Kauś.

वर्षिमन् *varshiman*, m. (prob. in some of the following senses connected with √*vṛi*, 'to cover') height, length, width, breadth, VS. [Cf. Slav. *vrĭchŭ*; Lith. *virshùs*.]

Várshishṭha, mfn. (accord. to Pāṇ. vi, 4, 157 superl. of *vṛiddha*) highest, uppermost, longest, greatest, very great, RV.; Br.; BhP.; oldest, very old, L. **—kshatra** (*vá°*), mfn. having the greatest power or might, RV.

Várshīyas, mfn. (compar. of *vṛiddha*; cf. prec.) higher, upper, longer, greater than (abl.), RV.; AV.; VS.; Br.; better than (abl.), Āpast.; very great, considerable, important, BhP.; thriving, prosperous, ib.; aged, old, Bhadrab.

1. **Varshma**, m., PārGṛ. i, 3, 8 (*varshmo 'smi* prob. w.r. for *varshmâsmi*); n. body, form, = *várshman*, MW.

2. **Varshma**, in comp. for *varshman*. **—vat**, mfn. having a body, MBh. **—vīrya**, n. vigour of body, MW. **—seka**, m. pouring water upon the body (to cool it), HPariś. **Varshmâbha**, mfn. resembling the body or form (of anything), MW.

Varshmán, m. height, top, RV.; AV.; the vertex, RV.; n. (*várshman*) height, top, surface, uttermost part, RV.; VS.; TS. &c.; height, greatness, extent, MBh.; Hariv. &c.; measure, W.; body, MBh.; Hariv.; Yājñ. &c.; a handsome form or auspicious appearance, L.; mfn. holding rain, W.

Varshmala, mfn. fr. *varshman*, g. *sidhmâdi*.

वर्ह् *varh*. See √*barh*.

वर्ह *varha*, *varhishṭha*, *varhis*. See *barha* &c.

वल् *val* (cf. √*bal*, *vall*, and *vṛi*), cl. 1. Ā. (Dhātup. xiv, 20) *valate* (oftener P. *valati*; cf. Vām. v, 2, 3; pf. *vavale*; ind. p. *valitvā*, Kāv.; aor. *avalishṭa*; fut. *valitā* &c., Gr.), to turn, turn round, turn to (with *abhimukham* and acc., or loc.), Kāv.; Kathās. &c.; to be drawn or attached towards, be attached to (loc.), Nalôd., Gīt.; to move to and fro, Hcat.; to go, approach, hasten, Mcar.; Śiś.; to return i. e. come back or home, Uttamac.; to return i. e. depart or go away again, ib.; HPariś.; to break forth, appear, Gīt.; to increase, Sāh.; to cover or enclose or to be covered (cf. √1. *vṛi*), L.: Caus. *valayati* or *vālayati* (Dhātup. xix, 58; aor. *avīvalat*), to cause to move or turn or roll, Śiś.; HPariś.; Naish., Sch.; to cherish &c., W. (rather *bâlayati*; see √2. *bal*): Desid. of Caus. in *vivālayishu*, q.v.

1. **Valá**, m. 'enclosure,' a cave, cavern, RV.; AV.; Br.; a cloud, Naigh. i, 10; a beam or pole, KātyŚr., Sch.; N. of a demon (brother of Vṛitra, and conquered by Indra; in later language called *Bala*, q.v.) **—m-rujá**, mfn. shattering caverns, RV. **—krama**, m. N. of a mountain, VP. **—gá**, n. a partic. charm or spell hidden in a pit or cavern, any secret charm or spell, AV.; VS.; (*-ga-*)*hán*, mfn. destroying secret charms, VS. **—gin**, mfn. versed in secret charms, AV. **—nāśana**, **-bhid**, **-sūdana** &c., see under *bala*. **—rasā**, f. sulphur, L. **—vat**, mfn. containing the word *vala*, AitBr.

2. **Vala** = *vali* (see *śata-vala*).

Valaka (cf. *balaka*), m. or n.(?) a beam, pole, KātyŚr., Sch.; n. a procession, Kathās.; m. N. of one of the seven sages under Manu Tāmasa, MārkP.

Valakêśvara-tīrtha, n. N. of a Tīrtha, Cat.

Valana, n. (ifc. f. *ā*) turning, moving round in a circle, waving, undulation, agitation, Kāv.; Sāh.; Rājat.; (also *ā*, f.) deflection (in astron.), Sūryas.; VarBṛS. **Valanâṇśa**, m. degree of deflection, MW.

Valantikā, f. a partic. mode of gesticulation, Vikr. (v.l. *valabhikā*).

Valabhi or (more usual) °**bhī**, f. (perhaps abbreviated fr. *vala-bhid*, 'cloud-splitting') the ridge of a roof, top or pinnacle of a house, MBh.; Kāv. &c.; a turret or temporary building on the roof of a house, upper room, L.; N. of a town in Saurāshṭra, Daś. (also °*bhi-pura*). **Valabhī-niveśa**, m. an upper room, Dharmaś.

Valaya, m. n. (ifc. f. *ā*) a bracelet, armlet, ring (worn by men and women on the wrist), MBh.; Kāv. &c. (also applied to waves as compared to bracelets); a zone, girdle (of a married woman), MW.; a line (of bees), Śiś.; a circle, circumference, round enclosure (ifc. often = 'encircled by'), Gol.; Kāv.; Kathās.; m. a sore throat, inflammation of the larynx, Suśr.; a kind of circular military array, Kām.; a branch, MW.; pl. N. of a people, AV.Pariś.; n. N. of certain round bones, Bhpr.; multitude, swarm, Kād. **—vat**, mfn., see *latā-valaya-vat*.

Valayita, mfn. encircled, surrounded, encompassed, enclosed by (instr. or comp.), Kāv.; Chandom.; put round (the arm, as a bracelet), Śiś.; forming a circle, curling, whirling round, Kād.; Mālatim.

Valayitṛi, mfn. encircling, surrounding, Dharmaś.

Valayin, mfn. provided with a bracelet, BhP.; (ifc.) encircled by, studded with (see *jyotir-lekhā-v°*).

Valayī, in comp. for *valaya.* — **√kṛi,** P. -*karoti,* to make into or use as a bracelet, Śiś. — **kṛita,** mfn. made into or used as a br°; -*vāsuki,* m. 'one who has made the serpent Vāsuki his br°,' N. of Śiva, MW.; °*tāhi,* mfn. girdled with a serpent as with a br° (as Śiva's hand), Kum. — **√bhū,** P. -*bhavati,* to become a circle or circular enclosure, Kir.

Valāka &c. See *balāka.*

Vali (cf. *bali* and *valī*), f. (once m.) a fold of the skin, wrinkle, MBh.; Kāv. &c. (cf. *tri-v°*); a line or stroke made with fragrant unguents on the person, L.; the edge of a roof, VP.; sulphur, L.; a partic. musical instrument, L. — **mat,** mfn. wrinkled, shrivelled, BhP. — **mukha,** m. 'having a wrinkled face,' a monkey, L.

Valika, m. n. the edge of a thatched roof, W.

Valita, mfn. bent round, turned (n. impers.), Kāv.; turned back again, Uttamac.; broken forth, appeared, Gīt.; (ifc.) surrounded or accompanied by, connected with; Ṛitus.; Pañcar.; wrinkled, MW.; m. a partic. position of the hands in dancing, Cat.; n. black pepper, L. — **kaṃdhara,** mfn. having the neck bent, Mālatim. — **grīva,** mfn. id., Kathās. — **dṛiś,** mfn. having the eyes turned towards, Kathās. **Valitânana,** mfn. having the face turned, ib. **Valitâpâṅga,** mf(*ī*)n. having the (corners of the) eyes turned or directed towards anything, ib.

Valitaka, m. a kind of ornament, Buddh.

Valina, mfn. shrivelled, wrinkled, flaccid, ŚāṅkhŚr.

Valibha, mfn. id., Śiś. (cf. Pāṇ. v, 2, 139).

Valira, mfn. squint-eyed, squinting, L.

Valī, f. = *vali,* a fold, wrinkle, MBh.; Kāv. &c.; a wave, L. — **palita,** n. wrinkles and grey hair, Mn. vi, 2. — **bhṛit,** mfn. curled, having curls (as hair), R. (B.) — **mat,** mfn. curled, Ragh. — **mukha,** m. = *vali-m°,* R.; N. of a monkey, Kathās.; n. the sixth change which takes place in warm milk when mixed with Takra, L.; -*mukha,* m. pl. N. of a people, Pracaṇḍ. — **vadana,** m. a monkey, Mālatīm.

Valīka, ifc. = *valī* (cf. *tri-valīka*); n. a projecting thatch, Kauś.; Gaut.; reed, sedge (used for a torch), Kauś.

Valinaka, m. Pandanus Odoratissimus, L.

Valūka, mfn. (Uṇ. iv, 40) red or black, PañcavBr.; ŚrS. (Sch.); m. a bird, L.; m. n. the root of a lotus, L.

Valūla. See *balūla,* p. 723, col. 2.

वलक्ष *valaksha* &c. See *balaksha.*

वलग्न *va-lagna,* m. n. = *ava-lagna,* the waist, middle, L.

वलम्ब *va-lamba,* m. = *ava-lamba,* a perpendicular, W.

वलम्भ *valambha,* m. or n. (?) N. of a country, Cat.

वलाक *valāka* &c. See *balāka.*

वलाट *valāṭa,* m. Phaseolus Mungo, L.

वलासक *valāsaka,* m. (prob. for *ava-l°*) the koïl or Indian cuckoo, W.; a frog, L.

वलाहक *valāhaka.* See *balāhaka.*

वलिवण्ड *valivaṇḍa,* m. N. of a king, Cat.

वलिश *valiśa,* °*śi,* °*śī.* See *baliśa.*

वलिशान *valiśāná,* m. a cloud, Naigh. i, 10.

वल्क् *valk,* cl. 10. P. *valkayati,* to speak, Dhātup. xxxii, 35.

1. **Valka,** m. (for 2. see below) = *vaktṛi,* a speaker, Śaṃk. on BṛĀrUp. (in explaining *Yajña-valka*).

वल्क 2. *valka,* m. n. (prob. connected with √*val,* 'to cover;' for 1. see above) 'covering,' the bark of a tree, TS. &c. &c.; n. the scales of a fish, L. — **ja,** m. pl. N. of a people, VP. — **taru,** m. the Areca palm, Areca Catechu, L. — **druma,** m. Betula Bhojpatra, L. — **pattra,** m. Phoenix Paludosa, L. — **phala,** m. the pomegranate tree, L. — **rodhra** or -**lodhra,** m. a kind of Lodhra tree, L. — **vat,** mfn. having bark or scales, W.; m. a fish, L. — **vāsas,** n. clothing made of bark, Ragh.; Kir.

Valkala, m. n. (ifc. f. *ā*) the bark of a tree, a garment made of bark (worn by ascetics &c.), Yājñ.; MBh. &c.; m. = *valka-rodhra,* L.; N. of a Daitya, BhP. (prob. w. r. for *balvala*); pl. N. of a school of the Bahv-ṛicas (cf. *bāshkala*), Divyâv.; (*ā*), f. = *śilā-valka,* a medicinal substance said to be of cooling and lithonthryptic properties, Suśr.; n. the bark of Cassia, L. — **kshetra,** n. N. of a sacred district; -*māhātmya,* n. N. of wk. — **cīrin,** m. N. of a man, HPariś. — **vat,** mfn. clad in bark, Ragh. — **saṃvīta,** mfn. clothed in a bark dress, MW. **Valkalâjina-dhāraṇa,** n. the wearing of clothes of bark and deer-skin, R. **Valkalâjina-vāsas,** mfn. clad in bark and deer-skin, R. **Valkalâjina-saṃvṛita,** mfn. id., MW.

Valkalin, mfn. yielding bark (as a branch), Bhartṛ.; clothed in a bark-dress, MBh.; Ragh.

Valkita, m. a thorn, L.

Valkuta, n. bark, rind, L.

वल्कल *valkala* &c. See col. 1.

वल्ग् *valg,* cl. 1. P. (Dhātup. v, 35) *vál-gati* (m.c. also °*te*; pf. *vavalga,* MBh.; aor. *avalgīt,* Gr.; fut. *valgitā,* °*gishyati,* ib.), to spring, bound, leap, dance (also of inanimate objects), VS. &c. &c.; to sound, Pañcat. i, 71 (v.l.); (Ā.) to take food, eat, Śiś. xiv, 29 (*vavalgire,* v.l. *vavalbhire*).

Valgaka, m. a jumper, dancer, Mālav.

Valgana, n. bounding, jumping, galloping, Ragh.

Valgā, f. a bridle, rein, Mṛicch.; Rājat.; N. of a woman, Rājat. — °**ṅka** (*valgâṅka*), mfn. holding a bridle, MW. — **maṭha,** m. the college founded by Valgā, Rājat.

Valgita, mfn. leaped, jumped, gone by bounds or leaps (n. impers.), Hariv.; VarBṛS.; fluttering, moving to and fro, Kāvyâd.; BhP.; sounding well, Hariv.; n. a bound, jump, spring, gallop of a horse, MBh.; R.; motion, gesture, Bhar.; leaping for joy, MBh.; Śiś.; shaking, fluttering, BhP. — **kaṇṭha,** mfn. uttering a pleasant sound (in the throat), BhP. — **bhrū,** mfn. moving the eyebrows playfully, Kāvyâd.

Valgú, mfn. (Uṇ. i, 20) handsome, beautiful, lovely, attractive (*ú,* ind. beautifully), RV. &c. &c.; m. a goat, L.; N. of one of the four tutelary deities of the Bodhi tree, Lalit.; (prob.) N. of a place, g. *varaṇâdi*; n. an eyelash, L. — **ja,** m. or -**jā,** f. = *avalguja,* L. — **jaṅgha,** m. 'handsome-legged,' N. of a son of Viśvāmitra, MBh. — **danti-suta,** m. metron. of Indra, Sch. on Kām. — **nāda,** mfn. singing sweetly (said of a bird), R. — **pattra,** m. Phaseolus Trilobus, L. — **podakī,** f. Amaranthus Polygamus or Oleraceus, L.

Valguka, mfn. = *valgu,* handsome, beautiful, L.; m. a kind of tree, Pañcar.; n. (only L.) sandal; a wood; price (= *paṇa*).

Valgula, m. the flying fox, W.; (*ā*) f. a species of night-bird, L.; (*ī*), f. id. or a kind of bat, VarBṛS.; Suśr.

Valgulikā, f. a box, chest, Kathās.; = *valgulī,* Nalac.

Valgūya, Nom. P. °*yáti,* to treat kindly, RV. iv, 50, 7; to exult, Bhaṭṭ.

वल्भ् *valbh,* cl. 1. Ā. to take food, eat, Dhātup. x, 31 (cf. √*valg*).

Valbhana, n. the act of eating, L.; food, W.

Valbhita, mfn. eaten, W.

वल्मी *valmī,* f. (cf. *vamra* and *vamrī* for *varmī*; often w. r. for *vallī*) an ant. — **kalpa,** m. N. of the 11th day in the dark half of Brahmā's month, L. (cf. under *kalpa*). — **kūṭa,** n. an ant-hill (cf. *vamrī-kūṭa*), L.

Valmika or °**kī,** m. n. an ant-hill, L.

Valmīka, m. and n. (g. *ardharcâdi*) an ant-hill, mole-hill, a hillock or ground thrown up by white ants or by moles (cf. *vamrī-kūṭa*) &c., VS. &c. &c.; swelling of the neck or of the chest and other parts of the body, elephantiasis, Suśr.; m. = *sâtapo meghaḥ* or = *sūryaḥ,* Megh., Sch.; N. of the father of Vālmīki, BhP.; the poet Vālmīki, L.; n. N. of a place, Kathās. — **janman** and -**bhava,** m. patr. of Vālmīki, Kāv. — **bhauma,** n. an ant-hill, ShaḍvBr. — **mātra,** mfn. having the size of an ant-hill, MW. — **rāśi,** m. (Kauś.), -**vapā,** f. (TS.) an ant-hill. — **śīrsha,** n. antimony, L. — **śṛiṅga,** n. (the top of) an ant-hill; -*vat,* ind. like an ant-hill, Kāśīkh. — **sambhavā,** f. a kind of cucumber, L. **Valmīkâgra,** n. N. of a peak of Rāma-giri, Megh.

वल्युल *valyula* or °*yūla,* Nom. P. °*layati* = *palyula,* Dhātup. xxxv, 29, Vop.

वल्ल् *vall* (prob. artificial; cf. √*val* and *vell*), cl. 1. P. *vallate,* 'to be covered' or 'to go,' Dhātup. xiv, 21.

Valla, m. a kind of wheat, VarBṛS.; Śaṃk.; a partic. weight (3 or 2 or 1½ Guñjas), ŚārṅgS.; Līl.; covering, W.; winnowing corn, ib.; prohibiting, ib. — **karañja,** m. Pongamia Glabra, L. — **brahmasūtra-bhāshya** (?), n., -**māhātmya,** n. N. of wks.

Vallaka, m. a sea-monster, Divyâv. (cf. *valla-bhaka*).

Vallakī, f. a kind of lute (often mentioned with the Vīṇā), MBh.; Kāv. &c. (also °*ki*); N. of a partic. configuration of the stars caused by the position of the planets in seven houses, VarBṛS.; Boswellia Thurifera, L.

Vallana, m. N. of a poet, Cat.

Vallabha, mf(*ā*)n. (Uṇ. iii, 125) beloved above all, desired, dear to (gen., loc., or comp.), MBh.; Kāv. &c.; dearer than (abl.), Pañcat. iv, $\frac{3}{4}\frac{3}{4}$; supreme, superintending, L.; a favourite, friend, lover, husband, Kāv.; Kathās. &c.; a cowherd, L. (prob. w. r. for *ballava*); a horse (esp. one with good marks or a favourite horse), L.; a kind of Agallochum, Gal.; N. of a son of Balākâśva, MBh.; of the founder of a Vaishṇava sect = *Vallabhâcārya,* q.v.); of a grammarian and various other writers and teachers (also with *gaṇaka* and *nyāyâcārya*), Cat.; (*ā*), f. a beloved female, wife, mistress, R.; Kālid.; N. of two plants (= *ativisha* and *priyaṅgu*), L.; (*ī*), f. N. of a city in Gujarāt (the capital of a line of kings). — **gaṇi,** m. N. of a lexicographer, Cat. — **jana,** m. a beloved person, mistress, Ragh. — **jī,** m. N. of various authors (also = *Vallabhâcārya*), Cat. — **tama,** mfn. most beloved, dearest, Bhartṛ. — **tara,** mfn. more or most beloved, Caurap. (-*tā,* f., Kād.) — **tā,** f. (MBh. &c.), -**tva,** n. (Mālav.) the being beloved or a favourite, love, favouriteship, popularity with (gen., loc., or comp.) — **dāsa,** m. N. of an author, Cat. — **dīkshita,** m. N. of a teacher (= *Vallabhâcārya*), Cat. — **deva,** m. N. of a poet and others (esp. of the compiler of the Subhāshitâvali, 16th cent.) — **nṛisiṇha,** m. N. of a man, Cat. — **pāla** (Śiś.) or -**pālaka** (L.), m. a horse-keeper, groom. — **pura,** n. N. of a town and of a village, Kshitīś. — **rāja-deva** (Inscr.), -**śakti** (Kathās.), m. N. of kings. — **siddhânta-ṭīkā,** f. N. of a wk. on Bhakti. — **svāmin,** m. N. of a teacher, Cat. **Vallabhâkhyāna,** n. N. of a wk. in Prākrit (by Gopāla-dāsa). **Vallabhâcārya,** m. N. of a celebrated Vaishṇava teacher (successor of a less celebrated teacher Vishṇu-svāmin; he was born, it is said, in the forest of Campâraṇya in 1479; at an early age he began travelling to propagate his doctrines, and at the court of Kṛishṇa-deva, king of Vijaya-nagara, succeeded so well in his controversies with the Śaivas that the Vaishṇavas chose him as their chief; he then went to other parts of India, and finally settled down at Benares, where he composed seventeen works, the most important of which were a commentary on the Vedânta and Mīmāṇsā Sūtras and another on the Bhāgavata-Purāṇa, on which last the sect rest their doctrines; he left behind eighty-four disciples, of each of whom some story is told, and these stories are often repeated on festive occasions. He taught a non-ascetical view of religion and deprecated all self-mortification as dishonouring the body which contained a portion of the supreme Spirit. His followers in Bombay and Gujarāt, and their leaders, are called Mahā-rājas; they are called the epicureans of India), RTL. 134–137; -*vaṇśâvalī,* f. N. of wk. **Vallabhânanda,** m. N. of a grammarian, Cat. **Vallabhâshṭaka,** n. N. of a Stotra (by Viṭṭhala-dīkshita); -*vivṛiti,* f. N. of Comm. on it. **Vallabhêndra,** m. N. of two authors, Cat. **Vallabhêśvara,** m. N. of a king, Piṅg., Sch.

Vallabhaka, m. a sea-monster, Divyâv. (cf. *val-laka*).

Vallabhāyita, n. a kind of coitus, MW. (cf. *purushāyita*).

Vallara, n. = *vallura,* L.

Vallari or °**rī,** f. a creeper, any climbing or creeping plant (also fig. applied to curled hair), Kāv.; VarBṛS. &c.; a branching foot-stalk, compound pedicle, L.; Trigonella Foenum Graecum, Bhpr.; a kind of metre, Col.; (only °*rī*) a partic. musical instrument, Divyâv.

Vallarīka (ifc.) = *vallarī,* a creeping plant, Bālar.; (*ā*), f. thin hair, L.

Vallava. See *ballava.*

Vallā-pura, n. N. of a town, Rājat.

Vallāra, m. the son of a Nishṭya and Kirāṭikā, L.; (*ī*), f. (in music) a partic. Rāgiṇī, Saṃgīt.

Valli, f. the earth, L. (mostly m. c. and in comp.

for *vallī*). — **kaṇṭa-kārikā**, f. Jasminum Jacquini, L. — **ja**, m. a species of plant with poisonous blossoms, Suśr. ('pepper' or 'tabāshīr,' L.; cf. *vallī-ja*). — **dūrvā**, f. a kind of Dūrvā grass, L. — **mat**, mfn. (ifc.) having anything (as locks, eyebrows &c.) resembling a creeper, Gīt. — **rāshṭra**, m. pl. N. of a people, VP. (v. l. for *malla-r°*). — **śākaṭa-potikā**, f. a kind of plant, L. — **śāstrin**, m. N. of a poet, Cat. — **sūraṇa**, m. a species of creeper, L.

Vallikā, f., dimin. fr. *vallī* (mostly ifc.; cf. *aṅghri-vallikā* &c.) **Vallikâgra**, n. coral, L.

Vallikī, f. a partic. musical instrument, Divyâv.

Vallinī, f. = *valli-dūrvā*, L.

Vallī (or *valli*, q.v.), f. a creeper, creeping plant (often fig. applied to arms, eyebrows, lightning &c.), Mn.; MBh. &c.; a class of medicinal plants (= *vidārī*, *sārivā*, *rajanī*, and *guḍūcī*), Suśr.; N. of various other plants (esp. = *aja-modā*, *kaivartikā*, and *cavya*), L.; (only *ī*) N. of the sections of partic. Upanishads (e.g. of the Kaṭha); = *phala-vallī* (q.v.), Āryabh., Sch. — **karṇa**, m. a partic. deformity of the ear, Suśr. — **gada**, m. a kind of fish (commonly called *bhola* or *bālikuḍā*), MW. — **ja**, m. N. of a class of plants (accord. to L. 'pepper'), VarBṛS. — **pada**, n. a kind of cloth with various markings or patterns, L. — **badarī**, f. a species of jujube, L. — **mudga**, m. Phaseolus Aconitifolius, L. — **vṛiksha**, m. Shorea Robusta, L.

Vallura, n. (only L.) an arbour, bower; a field; a thicket or wilderness; a place destitute of water; a cluster of blossoms; a compound pedicle.

Vallūra, n. (L. also m. and *ā*, f.) dried flesh, Mn.; Yājñ.; Suśr.; hog's flesh, L.; m. (only L.) an uncultivated field; a desert; a thicket; = *nakshatra*, white water.

Vallūraka, m. a partic. deformity of the ear, Suśr.

Vallyā, f. Emblic Myrobalan, L.

वल्व *valva*. See *balva*.

वल्वज *valvuja* &c. See *balbaja*.

वल्श *válśa*, m. (also written *bálśa*) a shoot, branch, twig, RV.; AV.; BhP.

वल्ह् *valh* (also written *balh*; cf. √*barh*), cl. 1. Ā. *valhate*, to be excellent, Dhātup. xvi, 38; to speak; to kill; to hurt; 'to give' or 'to cover' (*dāna*, v.l. *chādana*), ib. 40; cl. 10. P. *valhayati*, 'to speak' or 'to shine' (*bhāshârthe* or *bhāsârthe*), Dhātup. xxxiii, 97.

वल्हि *valhi*, *valhika*. See *balhi*.

वव *vava*. See *bava*.

ववाङ्ग *vavāṅga*, w.r. for **varâṅga**, L.

ववूल *vavūla*, m. Acacia Arabica, Madanav. (cf. *vavvola*).

वव्र *vavrá*, mfn. (fr. √1. *vṛi*) hiding or concealing one's self, RV.; m. 'hiding-place,' a cavern, hole, cave, ib.

Vavrāya, Nom. Ā. °*yate*, to retire or shrink from, keep aloof, RV. viii, 40, 2.

Vavrí, m. a lurking-place, RV.; a cover, vesture, ib.; the body, ib.; N. of the supposed author of RV. v, 19, Anukr. — **vāsas** (*vavrí-*), mfn. (prob.) dwelling in the body, AV.

वव्वोल *vavvola*, m. Acacia Arabica, L. (cf. *vavūla*).

वश् *vaś*, cl. 2. P. (Dhātup. xxiv, 71) *váshṭi* (1. pl. *uśmási* or *śmasi*, RV.; 3. pl. *uśánti*, ib.; p. *uśát*, *uśāná* and *uśámāna*, ib.; cl. 1. *vásati* and cl. 3. *vivashṭi* [also *vavásḥṭi*], 2. sg. *vavákshi*, ib.; pf. *vāvaśúḥ*, °*śe*; p. °*śāná*, ib.; *uvāśa*, *ūśuḥ*, Gr.; aor. *avāśīt*, ib.; 2. sg. *vaśīḥ*, MBh.; Prec. *uśyāt*, Gr.; fut. *vaśitā*, °*śishyati*, ib.), to will, command (p. *uśámāna*, 'having at command'), RV.; AV.; to desire, wish, long for, be fond of, like (also with inf.), RV. &c. &c. (p. *uśát* and *uśāná*, 'willing, glad, eager, zealous, obedient;' the former with superl. *uśat-tama*, also = charming, lovely, BhP. [accord. to Sch. also = *śuddha*, *dedīpyamāna*, and *sv-arcita*]); to aver, maintain, affirm, declare for (two acc.), MaitrUp.; VarBṛS.; BhP.: Caus. *vāśayati* (aor. *avīvaśat*), to cause to desire &c.; to get in one's power, subject, Cat.: Desid. *vivaśishati*, Gr.: Intens. *vāvaśyate*, *vāvaśīti*, or *vāvashṭi*, ib.; p. *vāvaśānā*, 'willing, eager,' RV. [Cf. Gk. ἑκών for Ϝεκων, 'willing.']

1. **Vàśa**, m. will, wish, desire, RV. &c. &c. (also pl. *vàśān ánu* or *ánu vàśa*, 'according to wish or will, at pleasure'); authority, power, control, dominion (in AV. personified), ib. (acc. with verbs of going, e.g. with √*i*, *anu-*√*i*, √*gam*, *ā-*√*gam*, √*yā*, *ā-*√*pad*, *ā-*√*sthā* &c., 'to fall into a person's [gen.] power, become subject or give way to;' acc. with √*nī*, *ā-*√*nī* and *pra-*√*yuj*, or loc. with √*kṛi*, √*labh* or Caus. of √*sthā* or *sam-*√*sthā*, 'to reduce to subjection, subdue;' loc. with √*bhū*, √*vṛit*, √*sthā* and *sam-*√*sthā*, 'to be in a person's [gen.] power;' *vaśena*, °*śāt*, and °*śa-taḥ*, with gen. or ifc., 'by command of, by force of, on account of, by means of, according to'); birth, origin, L.; a brothel, L. (cf. *veśa*); Carissa Carandas, L.; the son of a Vaiśya and a Karaṇī, L.; N. of a Ṛishi preserved by the Aśvins, RV.; (with *Aśvya*) of the supposed author of RV. viii, 46 (in ŚBr. &c. also of this hymn itself); = *Vālmīki*, Gal.; pl. N. of a people, AitBr.; MBh.; (*ā*), f., see below; mf(*ā*)n. willing, submissive, obedient, subject to or dependent on (gen.), Kathās.; BhP.; Pañcat.; docile, L.; free, licentious, L. — **ṃ-vada**, mfn. (mostly ifc.) submissive to the will of another, obedient, compliant, devoted or addicted to, actuated or transported or overcome with (*svêcchā-v°*, dependent on one's own will), Kāv.; Sāh. &c.; *-tva*, n. submission to the will of another, complaisance, Ragh.; °*dita*, mfn. made compliant, fascinated, Bhām. — **kara**, mf(*ī*)n. subjugating, winning, MBh.; Hit. — **kāraka**, mfn. leading to subjection, Pañcat. — **kriyā**, f. the act of subduing or bewitching (esp. by charms, incantations, drugs, gems), L.; the charms &c. so used, MW. — **ga**, mf(*ā*)n. being in the power of, subject, obedient, dependent on (gen. or comp.), MBh. &c. &c.; (ifc.) subjugating, Pañcar.; (*ā*), f. an obedient wife, MW.; *-tva*, n. (ifc.) dependence on, BhP. — **gata**, mfn. subject to the will (of another), being in the power of, obedient (ifc.), Pañcat.; VarBṛS.; BhP. — **gamana**, n. the coming into the power (of another), Nir. — **gāmin**, mfn. coming into the power (of another), becoming subject or obedient, MārkP. — **ṃ-kara**, mfn. (ifc.) subjugating, Pañcar. — **ṃ-kṛita**, mfn. brought into subjection, R. — **ṃ-gata**, mfn. = *vaśa-gata* above, MW. — **ṃ-gama**, mfn. subjected, influenced (said of partic. Saṃdhis), RPrāt.; m. du. N. of a partic. text, Gobh. — **tas**, ind. (ifc.) in consequence of, on account of, through the influence of, Bhartṛ.; Gol. — **tā**, f. subjection, the being under control of, dependence on (gen. or comp.), MBh.; Cat.; the having power over (loc.), Kāv. (v. l.) — **tva**, n. (ifc.) the being under the control of, VarBṛS. — **nī**, mfn. performing the will (of another), subject, vassal of (with gen.), RV. x, 16, 2. — **vartin**, mfn. being under the control of, acting obediently to the will of, obsequious, subject (with gen. or comp.), MBh.; R. &c.; (ifc.) having power over, ruling, Lalit.; having power over all, too powerful, ib.; m. N. of Vishṇu, Vishṇ.; of a Brāhman or Mahā-Br°, Lalit.; sg. (scil. *gaṇa*) or pl. a partic. class of gods in the third Manv-antara, VP. — **stha**, mfn. being under the control (of another), MBh. **Vaśâgata**, mfn. gone or lying along (a road; see *mārga-v°*). **Vaśâdhyaka**, w.r. for *vasâdh°*, q.v. **Vaśânuga**, mf(*ā*)n. following one's own will, CūlUp.; obedient or subject to the will of, submissive to (with gen. or ifc.), Mn.; MBh.; R.; Pur.; = *-vaśâgata* above (in *mārga-vaśânuga*); m. (*ā*), f. a male or female servant, MW. **Vaśâpāyin**, w.r. for *vasā-p°* (q.v.) **Vaśâyāta**, mfn. (ifc.) come in consequence of, Kathās.; lying along (cf. *mārga-v°*). **Vaśâroha**, w.r. for *vasâr°* (q.v.) **Vaśêndriya**, mfn. one who has the command of his senses (*-tva*, n.), R.

Vaśakā, f. an obedient wife, L.

Vaśana, n. wishing, desiring, willing &c., Pāṇ. iii, 3, 58, Vārtt. 3, Sch.

Vaśanīya, mfn. to be wished or willed, MW.

Vaśayita, mfn. (?), L.

1. **Vaśi**, mfn. = *kānta*, VS. (Mahīdh.); m. subjugation, fascination, bewitching, holding others in magical submission to the will, MW.; n. = *vaśi-tva*, L.; the state of being subject, subjection, MW.

2. **Vaśi**, in comp. for *vaśin*. — **tā**, f. subjugation, dominion, W.; the supernatural power of subduing all to one's own will, unbounded power of (comp.; a Bodhi-sattva is said to have 10 Vaśitās, viz. *āyur-*, *citta-*, *parishkāra-*, *dharma-*, *ṛiddhi-*, *janma-*, *adhimukti-*, *praṇidhāna-*, *karma-*, and *jñāna-v°*, Dharmas. 74), BhP.; Buddh.; subduing by the use of magical means, fascinating, bewitching, W. — **tva**, n. freedom of will, the being one's own master, MBh.; Hariv.; power or dominion over (loc.), Sarvad.; the supernatural power of subduing to one's own will, MārkP.; Pañcar. &c.; mastery of one's self, self-command, Kum.; MārkP.; subduing by magical means, fascinating, bewitching, MW. — **prāpta**, mfn. having power over (also ifc.), Divyâv. — **man**, m. the supernatural power of subduing to one's own will, MārkP.

Vaśika, mfn. void, empty, Hcar. (written also *vasika*; cf. *vaśin*); (*ā*), f. aloe wood, MW.

Vaśitṛi, mfn. having one's will free, independent, BhP.

Vaśin, mfn. having will or power, having authority, a ruler, lord ('over,' gen.), RV.; AV.; Br. &c.; compliant, obedient, VS.; TS.; Vet.; master of one's self, having the mastery of one's passions, MBh.; Kāv. &c.; void, empty (properly 'at disposal'), KātyŚr.; m. a ruler, see above; a sage with subdued passions, W.; N. of a son of Kṛiti, BhP.; (*inī*), f. a mistress, RV.; a parasite plant, L.; Prosopis Spicigera or Mimosa Suma, L.

1. **Vaśī**, f., in *urvásī*, q.v.

2. **Vaśī**, in comp. for 1. *vaśa*. — **kara**, mfn. bringing into subjection, subjugating, (ifc.) making any one subject to one's will, MBh.; Pañcar.; *-prakaraṇa*, n., *-vārāhī*, f. N. of wks. — **karaṇa**, n. the act of making subject, subjugating, bewitching (by means of spells &c.), overcoming by charms and incantations &c. (with gen. or ifc.), PārGṛ.; R.; Pañcat. &c. — **kāra**, m. id., Yogas.; Kathās. &c. — √**kṛi**, P. Ā. *-karoti*, *-kurute*, to reduce to subjection, subdue, TBr. &c. &c. — **kṛita**, mfn. brought into subjection, subdued, MBh.; Hariv.; Pur. &c.; bewitched, enchanted, fascinated, W. — **kṛiti** (MBh.) or **-kriyā** (Cat.), f. = *-karaṇa* above. — √**bhū**, P. *-bhavati*, to become subject to another's will, Kām.; Vcar.; Inscr. — **bhūta**, mfn. become subject, subject, obedient, Cāṇ.; Pañcar.; become powerful, Buddh.

Vaśīra, m. Achyranthes Aspera, L.; Scindapsus Officinalis, L. (cf. *vasira*).

Vaścika, m. N. of an Agra-hāra, Rājat.

Vaśmasā, ind., g. *ūry-ādi*.

Vaśya, mfn. to be subjected &c.; subdued, tamed, humbled; being under control, obedient to another's will, dutiful, docile, tame, humble, at the disposal of (gen. or comp.), MBh.; Kāv. &c.; m. a dependent, slave, MW.; N. of a son of Āgnīdhra, MārkP.; (*ā*), f. a docile and obedient wife, W.; (*ā*), f. (Cat.) or n. (ib.; Prab.) the supernatural power of subjecting to one's own will, any act (such as the repetition of spells) performed with that object, VarBṛS.; Gṛihyas.; cloves, W. — **kara**, mfn. giving power over others, Cat. — **karman**, n. the act of subjecting to one's will (by spells &c.), Cat. — **kārin**, mfn. = *-kara*, L. — **tā**, f. (MBh.; Hariv.; R. &c.) or **-tva**, n. (MBh.; R.) the being under the control of (gen. or comp.), fitness for subjection, obedience, humility. **Vaśyâtman**, mfn. of subdued mind, Bhag.

Vaśyaka, mf(*ā*)n. obedient, dutiful, L.; = *vaśya* above, MW.; (*ā*), f. an obedient wife, ib.; n. = *vaśya-karman* above, Cat.

Vashṭi, mfn. (fr. √*vaś*) eager, desirous, RV. v, 79, 5.

वश 2. *vaśa*, n. (cf. *vasā*) liquid fat, grease, AV.; AitBr.; Kāṭh.

वशा *vaśā́*, f. (rather fr. √*vāś*, as 'the lowing animal,' than fr. √*vaś*) a cow (esp. barren), RV.; AV.; Br.; GṛŚrS.; (with *ávī*) a ewe, TS.; TBr.; a female elephant, Vikr.; Kathās.; a barren woman, Mn. viii, 28; any woman or wife, L.; a daughter, L.; Premna Spinosa and Longifolia, L. [Cf., accord. to some, Lat. *vacca*.] — **jātá**, n. a kind of cow, AV. — **tvá**, n. the being a cow, MaitrS. — °**nna** (*vaśânna*), mfn. eating cows, RV. — **bhogá**, m. use of a cow, AV. — **makha**, m. the son of a Śūdra and a Kuvādushkī (?), L. — **mat**, mfn., g. *yavâdi*.

Vaśā-tamā, f. (for *vaśā-t°*) the best cow, AV. xii, 4, 42.

वशाकु *vaśāku*, w.r. for *vāśāku*.

वशातल *vaśātala*, m. pl. N. of a people, MBh.

वशाति *vaśāti* &c., w.r. for *vasāti*.

वशिर *vaśira*, w.r. for *vasira*.

वशिष्ठ *vaśishṭha*, w.r. for *vasishṭha*.

वशीर *vaśīra*, m. Achyranthes Aspera, L.; Scindapsus Officinalis, L. (cf. *vasira*).

वश्चिक *vaścika*, m. N. of an Agra-hāra, Rājat.

वश्मसा *vaśmasā*, ind., g. *ūry-ādi*.

वष् *vash* (also written *bash*), cl. 1. P. *vashati*, to hurt, strike, kill, Dhātup. xvii, 40.

वषट् *vávashaṭ*, ind. (accord. to some fr. √1. *vah*; cf. 2. *vaṭ* and *vaushaṭ*) an exclamation uttered by the Hotṛi priest at the end of the sacrificial verse (on hearing which the Adhvaryu priest casts the oblation offered to the deity into the fire; it is joined with a dat., e.g. *Pūshṇe vashaṭ*; with √*kṛi*, 'to utter the exclamation *vashaṭ*'), RV.; VS.; Br.; ŚrS.; Mn.; MBh.; Pur. **-karaṇa**, n. the utterance of Vashaṭ, Jaim., Sch. **-kartṛí**, m. the priest who makes the oblation with V°, ŚBr.; ŚrS. **-kārá**, m. the exclamation V° (also personified as a deity), VS.; AV.; Br. &c.; *-kriyā*, f. an oblation accompanied with the utterance of V°, ĀśvŚr.; *-nidhana*, n. N. of various Sāmans, ĀrshBr.; °*rin*, m. = *-kartṛi*, Lāṭy. **-kṛita** (*váshaṭ-*), mfn. offered in fire with V°, RV. **-kṛiti** (*váshaṭ-*), f. = *-kāra*, ib. (ind., i, 14, 8). **-kṛitya**, n. (ind.) V° should be uttered, AitBr. **-kriyā**, f. = *-kāra-kriyā*, MārkP.

वष्क् *vashk*, cl. 1. Ā. *vashkate*, to go, Dhātup. iv, 27 (v.l. for *vask*).

वष्कय *vashkaya*, °*kayaṇī*, °*kiha*. See *bashkáya* &c.

वस् 1. *vas* (encl.) acc. dat. gen. pl. of 2nd pers. pron. (cf. Pāṇ. viii, 1, 21, 24 &c.), RV. &c. &c.

वस् 2. *vas* (a Vedic root connected with √1. *ush*, q.v.; not in Dhātup.), cl. 6. P. *uccháti* (pf. *uvā́sa*, *ūshúḥ*, RV. &c.; aor. *avāt* [?], AV.; *avasran*, RV.; Cond. *avatsyat*, ŚBr.; Ved. inf. *vástave*, *-úshi*), to shine, grow bright (esp. applied to the dawn), RV.; to bestow by shining upon (dat.), ib. i, 113, 7; (with *dūré*) to drive away by shining, ib. vii, 77, 4: Caus. *vāsáyati*, to cause to shine, RV. [Cf. *vasar* in *vasar-han*; Gk. ἔαρ for ϝέσαρ; Lat. *vēr* &c.]

Ush, usha, ushás, 1. ushita. See under √1. *ush*.

Vasantá, m. (n., g. *ardharcâdi*) 'brilliant (season),' spring (comprising, accord. to some, the months Caitra and Vaiśākha or from the middle of March to that of May, see *ṛitu*; often personified and considered as a friend or attendant of Kāma-deva, the god of love), RV. &c. &c.; a partic. metre (4 times ⏑–⏑⏑–⏑) Col.; a partic. time (in music), L.; diarrhœa, L.; N. of a man, Rājat. **-kāla**, m. sp°-time, vernal season, R. **-kusuma**, m. 'having blossoms in spring,' Cordia Latifolia or Myxa, L.; °*mâkara*, m. a partic. mixture, L. **-gandhi** or °**dhin**, m. N. of a Buddha, Lalit. **-ghosha** or **-ghoshin**, m. 'singing in spring,' the Koïl or Indian cuckoo, L. **-ja**, mfn. born or produced in sp°, W.; (*ā*), f. a kind of jasmine, L.; a festival in honour of the god of love, W. (cf. *vasantôtsava*). **-tilaka**, n. the ornament of spring, Chandom.; the blossom of the Tilaka, VarBṛS.; a partic. mixture, L.; (also *ā*, f.) a kind of metre (four times ––⏑–⏑⏑⏑–⏑⏑–⏑––), Piṅg.; m. N. of a man, Kathās.; *-tantra*, n. N. of a Buddhist wk.; *-bhāṇa*, m. N. of a drama. **-dūta**, m. (only L.) 'sp°-messenger,' the Indian cuckoo (see *kokila*); the mango tree; the month Caitra (March-April); the 5th Rāga or the musical mode Hindola; (*ī*), f. the female of the Indian cuckoo; Gærtnera Racemosa; Bignonia Suaveolens; a plant like the Premna Spinosa. **-deva**, m. N. of a king and poet, Cat. **-dru** or **-druma**, m. 'spring-tree,' the mango (blossoming in March or April), L. **-pañcamī**, f. a festival held on the 5th of the light half of the month Māgha, RTL. 429; *-pūjā*, f., *-prayoga*, m. N. of wks. **-pura**, n. N. of a town, HPariś. **-pushpa**, n. a spring-flower, Kum.; a kind of Kadamba, L. **-bandhu**, m. 'friend of Spring,' N. of Kāma-deva (god of love), Daś. **-bhānu**, m. N. of a king, ib. **-bhūshaṇa**, n. N. of a Stotra. **-madana**, n. a plant resembling the Premna Spinosa, L. **-mahôtsava**, m. the great sp°-festival (in honour of the love-god), Ratnâv. (cf. *vasantôtsava*). **-mādanī**, f. = *-madanā*, L. **-mālati-rasa**, m. a partic. mixture, L. **-mālikā**, f. a kind of metre, Piṅg. **-māsa**, m. N. of the 9th month, L. **-yātrā**, f. a spring-procession, W. **-yodha**, m. 'spring-combatant,' the god of love, Ṛitus. **-rāja**, m. spring compared to a king, Siṅhâs.; N. of a king of Kumāra-giri (author of the *-rājīya-nāṭya-śāstra*), Cat.; (also with *bhaṭṭa*) of various authors; *-cikitsā*, f. N. of a medical wk. **-rtu** (for *ṛitu*), m. spring-season, Cat. **-latā** or **-latikā** (Dhūrtan.), **-lekhā** (Sāh.), f. N. of women. **-varṇana**, n. 'description of spring,' N. of a poem. **-vitala**, m. N. of a form of Vishṇu, W. **-vilāsa**, m. N. of a poem. **-vraṇa**, n. 'sp°-pustule,' small-pox, L. **-vrata**, n. sp°-observance, Cat. **-śākhin**, m. = *-dru*, Dharmaś. **-śekhara**, m. N. of a Kiṃ-nara, Cat. **-śrī**, f. the pomp or beauty of spring, Kāvyâd. **-sakha**, m. = *-bandhu*, L.; N. of the wind blowing from the Malaya mountains, Vikr. **-samaya**, m. = *-kāla*, Ratnâv.; °*yôtsava*, m. the festive time of spring, Kathās. **-sahāya**, m. = *-bandhu*, Daś. **-sena**, m. N. of a king, Kathās.; (*ā*), f. N. of various women, Mṛicch.; Vās., Introd. **Vasantâcārya**, m. N. of a teacher, Cat. **Vasantâdhyayana**, n. studying in spring, Pat. on Pāṇ. iv, 2, 63. **Vasantôtsava**, m. spring-rejoicings, spring festival (formerly held on the full moon of Caitra, but now of Phālguna, and = Dola-yātrā or Holī, IW. 430), Śak.; Kathās.; *-carita*, n. N. of wk.

Vasantaka, m. (ifc. fem. *ā*) spring, Ratnâv.; a partic. tree, a species of Śyonāka, L.; N. of a man, Ratnâv.; (*ikā*), f., w.r. for *vāsantikā*.

Vasántā (or °*tā́*), ind. in spring, TS.; ŚBr. &c. (cf. Pāṇ. vii, 1, 39, Sch.)

Vasar = *ushar*, q.v. **-hán**, striking in the dawn, destroying (nocturnal demons) at dawn, RV. i, 122, 3.

Vásavāna, m. (fr. 1. *vasu*) a possessor or preserver of wealth (also with *vásvas*), RV.

Vasavyà, mfn. (prob.) wealthy, affluent (applied to Agni, Soma and Sūrya), TS.; n. riches, wealth, RV.

Vásā or **vasā́** (sometimes written *vaśā*), f. 'shining,' 'white,' the serum or marrow of the flesh (considered by some as distinct from that of the bones, by others as the same), marrow, fat, grease, lard, suet, melted fat, any fatty or oily substance, VS. &c. &c.; brain, Kathās.; a partic. root similar to ginger, L.; N. of a river, MBh. **-ketu**, m. a partic. comet, VarBṛS. **-graha**, m. a ladleful of melted fat, KātyŚr. **-chaṭā**, f. the mass of the brain, MW. **-°ḍhya** or **-°ḍhyaka** (*vasâḍh°*), m. Delphinus Gangeticus, L. **-°danī** (*vasâd°*), f. 'fat-eating (?),' Dalbergia Sissoo, L.; Gendarussa Vulgaris, L. **-pāyin**, m. 'drinker of melted fat,' a dog, L. **-pāvan**, mfn. drinking melted fat, VS. **-maya**, mf(*ī*)n. consisting of fat, Prab. **-mūra**, m. or n. (?) N. of a place, Cat. **-meha**, m. a kind of diabetes (°*hin*, mfn. suffering from it), Suśr. **-roha** (or *vasār°*?), m. a mushroom, L. **-°vaśesha-malina** (*vasâv°*), mfn. soiled with the remains of fat, Hit. **-homá**, m. an offering of fat, TS.; ŚBr. &c.; *-śesha*, m. n. the remains of an offering of fat, MānGṛ.; *-hávanī*, f. the ladle used at an offering of fat, ŚBr.; ĀpŚr.

Vasāti, (prob.) f. (cf. *ushā*) dawn, Nir. xii, 2 (in a quotation; Sch. = *jana-pada*); m. N. of a son of Janam-ejaya, MBh.; of a son of Ikshvāku, Hariv. (v.l. *vaśāti*); pl. N. of a people (also °*tika*), MBh.

Vasātīya, mfn. relating to the Vasātis, MBh.; m. a king of the Vasātis, ib.

Vasávi or °**vī**, f. (fr. 1. *vasu*) a treasury, RV. x, 73, 4.

Vasin, m. (fr. *vasā*) an otter, L.

Vásishṭha, mfn. (superl. fr. 1. *vásu*; cf. *vásīyas* and under √3. *vas*) most excellent, best, richest, RV.; AV.; Br.; ChUp.; MBh.; m. (wrongly written *vaśishṭha*), 'the most wealthy,' N. of a celebrated Vedic Ṛishi or sage (owner of the 'cow of plenty,' called Nandinī, offspring of Surabhi, which by granting all desires made him, as his name implies, master of every *vasu* or desirable object; he was the typical representative of Brāhmanical rank, and the legends of his conflict with Viśvā-mitra, who raised himself from the kingly or Kshatriya to the Brāhmanical class, were probably founded on the actual struggles which took place between the Brāhmans and Kshatriyas; a great many hymns of the RV. are ascribed to these two great rivals; those of the seventh Maṇḍala, besides some others, being attributed to Vasishṭha, while those of the third Maṇḍala are assigned to Viśvā-mitra; in one of Vasishṭha's hymns he is represented as king Su-dās' family priest, an office to which Viśvā-mitra also aspired; in another hymn Vasishṭha claims to have been inspired by Varuṇa, and in another [RV. vii, 33, 11] he is called the son of the Apsaras Urvaśī by Mitra and Varuṇa, whence his patronymic Maitrāvaruṇi; in Manu i, 35, he is enumerated among the ten Prajā-patis or Patriarchs produced by Manu Svāyambhuva for the peopling of the universe; in the MBh. he is mentioned as the family priest of the solar race or family of Ikshvāku and Rāma-candra, and in the Purāṇas as one of the arrangers of the Vedas in the Dvāpara age; he is, moreover, called the father of Aurva [Hariv.], of the Sukālins [Mn.], of seven sons [Hariv.; Pur.], and the husband of Aksha-mālā or Arundhatī [MBh.] and of Ūrjā [Pur.]; other legends make him one of the 7 patriarchal sages regarded as forming the Great Bear in which he represents the star ζ, see *ṛishi*), RV. &c. &c. (cf. IW. 361; 402, n. 1 &c.); N. of the author of a law-book and other wks. (prob. intended to be ascribed to the Vedic Ṛishi above); pl. the family of Vasishṭha, RV.; ŚBr.; ŚrS. (*Vasishṭhasyâṅkuśaḥ* &c., N. of Sāmans, ĀrshBr.); N. of an Anuvāka, Pat. on Pāṇ. iv, 3, 131, Vārtt. 2; n. flesh, Gal. **-kalpa**, m. N. of wk. **-kaśyapikā**, f. a matrimonial alliance between the descendants of Vasishṭha and those of Kaśyapa, Pat. **-tantra**, n. N. of a Tantra. **-tva**, n. the state or condition of being V°, MBh. **-nihava**, m. N. of a Sāman, Lāṭy. **-putra**, m. pl. 'the sons or descendants of V°,' N. of the authors of RV. vii, 33, 10–14. **-pramukha**, mfn. preceded or led by V°, MW. **-prācī**, f. N. of a place, Cat. **-bhṛigv-atri-sama**, mfn. equal to (the three great saints) V° and Bhṛigu and Atri, MW. **-yajña** (*vá°*), m. N. of a partic. sacrifice, ŚBr. **-liṅga-purāṇa**, n. N. of a Purāṇa. **-vát**, ind. like V°, RV.; MBh. **-śapha**, m. du. N. of a Sāman, Lāṭy. **-śikshā**, f. N. of a Śikshā. **-śilā**, f. N. of a place, GopBr. **-śrāddha-kalpa**, m. N. of wk. **-saṃsarpa**, m. a partic. Catur-aha, ŚrS. **-saṃhitā**, f., **-siddhânta**, m., **-smṛiti**, f., **-homa-prakāra**, m. N. of wks. **Vasishṭhôkta-vidhi**, m. N. of wk. **Vasishṭhôpapurāṇa**, n. N. of an Upapurāṇa.

Vasishṭhaka, m. the sage Vasishṭha (see above).

Vásīyas, mfn. (compar. of 1. *vásu*; cf. *vasishṭha* and *vasyas*) more wealthy or opulent, more excellent, better than (abl.), TS.; Br.; Gobh.

Vasīyo-bhūya, n. better condition, superiority, MaitrS.

1. **Vásu**, mf(*u* or *vī*)n. (for 2. see p. 932, col. 3) excellent, good, beneficent, RV.; GṛŚrS.; sweet, L.; dry, L.; N. of the gods (as the 'good or bright ones,' esp. of the Ādityas, Maruts, Aśvins, Indra, Ushas, Rudra, Vāyu, Vishṇu, Śiva, and Kubera), RV.; AV.; MBh.; R.; of a partic. class of gods (whose number is usually eight, and whose chief is Indra, later Agni and Vishṇu; they form one of the nine Gaṇas or classes enumerated under Gaṇa-devatā, q.v.; the eight Vasus were originally personifications, like other Vedic deities, of natural phenomena, and are usually mentioned with the other Gaṇas common in the Veda, viz. the eleven Rudras and the twelve Ādityas, constituting with them and with Dyaus, 'Heaven,' and Pṛithivī, 'Earth' [or, according to some, with Indra and Prajā-pati, or, according to others, with the two Aśvins], the thirty-three gods to which reference is frequently made; the names of the Vasus, according to the Vishṇu-Purāṇa, are, 1. Āpa [connected with *ap*, 'water']; 2. Dhruva, 'the Pole-star;' 3. Soma, 'the Moon;' 4. Dhava or Dhara; 5. Anila, 'Wind;' 6. Anala or Pāvaka, 'Fire;' 7. Pratyūsha, 'the Dawn;' 8. Prabhāsa, 'Light;' but their names are variously given; Ahan, 'Day,' being sometimes substituted for 1; in their relationship to Fire and Light they appear to belong to Vedic rather than Purānic mythology), RV. &c. &c.; a symbolical N. of the number 'eight,' VarBṛS.; a ray of light, Naigh. i, 15; a partic. ray of light, VP.; = *jina*, Śil. (only L. the sun; the moon; fire; a rope, thong; a tree; N. of two kinds of plant = *baka* and *pīta-madgu*; a lake, pond; a kind of fish; the tie of the yoke of a plough; the distance from the elbow to the closed fist); N. of a Ṛishi (with the patr. Bharad-vāja, author of RV. ix, 80–82, reckoned among the seven sages), Hariv.; of a son of Manu, ib.; of a son of Uttāna-pāda, ib.; of a prince of the Cedis also called Upari-cara, MBh.; of a son of Īlina, ib.; of a son of Kuśa and the country called after him, RV.; of a son of Vasu-deva, BhP.; of a son of Kṛishṇa, ib.; of a son of Vatsara, ib.; of a son of Hiraṇya-retas and the Varsha ruled by him, ib.; of a son of Bhūta-jyotis, ib.; of a son of Naraka, ib.; of a king of Kaś-

mira, Cat.; (*u*), f. light, radiance, L.; a partic. drug, L.; N. of a daughter of Daksha and mother of the Vasus (as a class of gods), Hariv.; VP.: (*vī*), f. night, Naigh. i, 7; n. (in Veda gen. *vásos*, *vásvas* and *vásunas*; also pl., exceptionally m.) wealth, goods, riches, property, RV. &c. &c. (*vasosh-pati*, m., prob. 'the god of wealth or property,' AV. i, 1, 2 [Paipp. *asosh-p°*, 'the god of life']; *vásor-dhārā*, f. 'stream of wealth,' N. of a partic. libation of Ghṛita at the Agni-cayana, AV.; TS.; Br. &c.; of the wife of Agni, BhP.; of the heavenly Gaṅgā, MBh.; of a sacred bathing-place, ib.; of a kind of vessel, ib.; *°rā-prayoga*, m. N. of wk.); gold (see *-varma-dhara*); a jewel, gem, pearl (see *-mekhala*); any valuable or precious object, L.; (also f.) a partic. drug, L.; a kind of salt (= *romaka*), L.; water, L.; a horse (?), L.; = *śyāma*, L. **-karṇa**, m. N. of a Ṛishi with the patr. Vāsukra (author of RV. x, 65; 66). **-kalpa** and **°pa-datta**, m. N. of poets, Sadukt. **-kīṭa**, m. 'money-worm,' a suppliant, beggar, L. **-kṛit**, m. N. of a Ṛishi with the patr. Vāsukra (author of RV. x, 20–26). **-kṛimi**, m. = *-kīṭa* above, MW. **-kra**, m. N. of a Ṛishi with the patr. Aindra (author of RV. x, 27, 29 and part of 28); of another Ṛishi with the patr. Vāsishṭha (author of RV. ix, 97, 28–30); (with prefix *śrī*) of a grammarian, Gaṇar.; *-patnī*, f. N. of the authoress of RV. x, 28, 1. **-gupta** or **°tâcārya**, m. N. of an author, Sarvad. **-candra**, m. N. of a warrior, MBh. **-carita**, n. N. of a Campū. **-cchidrā**, f. N. of a medicinal plant, Bhpr. **-jit**, mfn. gaining wealth, AV. **-jyeshṭha**, m. N. of a king, VP. **-tā** or **-tāti** (*vasú-*), f. wealth, riches (or) liberality, RV. **-tti** (*vásu-*), f. (for *-datti*; cf. *bhaga-tti*, *magha-tti*) the granting of wealth, enrichment, RV. **-tvá** or **-tvaná**, n. wealth, riches, RV. **-da**, mf(*ā*)n. granting w° or treasures, VarBṛS.; m. N. of Kubera, Hariv.; (*ā*), f. the earth, MBh.; N. of a goddess, Cat.; of one of the Mātṛis attending on Skanda, MBh.; of a Gandharvī, R. **-datta**, m. N. of various men, Pat.; Kathās.; (*ā*), f. N. of various women (esp. of the mother of Vara-ruci), Kathās.; *-pura*, n. N. of a town, ib. **-dattaka**, m. an endearing form of *-datta*, L. **-dā́**, mfn. granting wealth, generous, RV.; AV. (said of the earth). **-dā́na**, mfn. id., AV.; ŚBr.; m. N. of various men, MBh.; VP.; (prob.) n. N. of a Varsha called after a Vasu-dāna, BhP. **-dāma**, m. N. of a partic. divine being, Pañcar.; (*ā*), f. N. of one of the Mātṛis attending on Skanda, MBh. **-dāman**, m. N. of a son of Bṛihad-ratha, Cat. **-dā́van**, mfn. (also with gen. *vásoḥ*) = *-dā́*, RV.; TS. **-déya**, n. the granting of wealth, liberality, RV.; AV. **-deva**, m. N. of the father of Kṛishṇa (he was the son of Śūra, a descendant of Yadu of the lunar line, and was also called Ānaka-dundubhi, q. v., because at his birth the gods, foreseeing that Vishṇu would take a human form in his family, sounded the drums of heaven for joy; he was a brother of Kuntī or Pṛithā, the mother of the Pāṇḍu princes, who were thus cousins of Kṛishṇa; see 1. *Kṛishṇa*), MBh.; Hariv.; BhP. &c.; of a king of the Kaṇva dynasty, Pur.; Vās., Introd.; of Kṛishṇa, Pañcar.; of the grandfather of the poet Māgha, Cat.; (also with *brahma-prasāda*) of two authors, Cat.; (*ā*), f. N. of a daughter of Śva-phalka, VP.; n. the lunar mansion Dhanishṭhā, VarBṛS.; *-janman*, m. N. of Kṛishṇa, Śiś.; *-tā*, f. a goddess granting w°, Hariv. (cf. *vasu-devatā* below); *-putra*, m. N. of Kṛishṇa, Kāv.; *-brahma-prasāda*, m. N. of an author, Cat.; *-bhū*, m. 'son of Vasu-deva,' N. of Kṛishṇa, L.; *°vâtma-ja*, m. id., Pañcar. **-devatā**, n. (VarBṛS.) or (*ā*), f. (L.) the lunar mansion Dhanishṭhā (presided over by the Vasus). **-devyā**, f. id., L.; the 9th day of a fortnight, L. **-daiva** or **°vata**, n. = *-devata* above, VarBṛS. **-dhara**, m. N. of a poet, Subh.; (*ā*), f. (with Buddhists) N. of a goddess, Buddh. **-dharman**, m. N. of a man, MBh. **-dharmikā**, f. crystal, L. **-dhā́**, mfn. producing wealth, liberal (*-tama*, *-tara*, mfn. more or most l°), AV.; VS.; TS.; (*ā*), f. the earth; a country, kingdom, Mn.; MBh.; Kāv. &c.; the ground, soil, VarBṛS.; earth (as a material), R.; N. of Lakshmī, Vishṇ.; an anapæst, Piṅg.; *-kharjūrikā*, f. a kind of date, L.; *-°gama* (*-dhāg°*), m. the products of the soil, VarBṛS.; *-tala*, n. the surface of the earth, the e°, Kāv.; Kathās.; the ground, soil, VP.; *-dhara*, mfn. bearing or supporting the e° (said of Vishṇu), MBh.; m. a mountain, ib.; Kāv.; a prince, king, Siṇhâs.; *-dhava*, m. a king, prince, ib.; *-dhātri*, m. id., Hariv.; *-°dhipa* (*-dhâdhipa*, MBh.; Kāv. &c.) or *°pati* (R.; Rājat.; Inscr.), m. lord of the earth, a king; *-°dhipatya* (*-dhâdhip°*), n. kingdom, royalty, Śāntiś.; Inscr.; *-nagara*, n. the capital of Varuṇa in the western ocean, MW.; *-nāyaka*, m. 'earth-leader,' a king, Kautukas.; *-pati*, m. id., Hariv.; Kālid.; *-paripālaka*, m. earth-guardian (N. of Kṛishṇa), Pañcar.; *-reṇu*, m. earth-dust, MBh.; Megh.; *-vilāsin*, m. a king, prince, Śrikaṇṭh.; *-suta*, m. the planet Mars, VarBṛS. **-dhātu-kārikā**, f. N. of wk. **-dhā́na**, mf(*ī*)n. containing or keeping wealth, AV.; ChUp.; Nir.; n. granting w°, Nir.; VS.; Mahīdh. **-dhāra**, mfn. holding w° or treasure, Hit.; m. N. of a mountain, MārkP.; (*ā*), f. (with Buddhists) N. of a goddess, Buddh.; a female Śakti peculiar to the Jainas, MW.; N. of a river, Hariv.; of the capital of Kubera, L.; a stream of wealth, st° of gifts, MBh.; Hcar.; HPariś.; *°rā-maya*, mfn. consisting of a st° of w°, Hcar. **-dhāriṇī**, f. 'treasure-holding,' the earth, MBh. **-dhita**, (prob.) n. possession of w°, Pāṇ. vii, 4, 45, Sch. (Ved.) **-dhiti** (*vásu-*), mfn. possessing w°, bestowing w°, RV.; VS.; ŚāṅkhŚr.; Nir.; f. the bestowal of w° or a treasury, RV. iv, 8, 2. **-dhéya**, n. (in a formula) the bestowal of w°, (or) possession of w°, VS.; Br.; ŚāṅkhŚr; Nir. **-nanda**, m. N. of a king, Rājat. **-nandaka** = *kheṭaka*, L. **-nāga**, m. N. of a poet, Subh. **-nīti** (*vásu-*), mfn. bringing wealth, AV. xii, 2, 6. **-nītha**, mfn. id., VS. xii, 44. **-netra**, m. N. of a Brāhman, Buddh. **-nemi**, m. N. of a serpent-demon, Kathās. **-m-dhara**, mfn. containing w°, Hariv.; m. N. of a poet, ŚārṅgP.; Sadukt. &c.; of another man, Kathās.; pl. N. of the Vaiśyas in Śālmala-dvīpa, BhP.; of a people, MW; (*ā*), f., see below; *°reśā*, f. 'having the keeper of wealth (Kṛishṇa) for lord,' N. of Rādhā, Pañcar. **-m-dharā**, f. the earth; a country, kingdom, NṛisUp.; MBh.; Kāv. &c.; the soil, the ground (also *°rā-pṛishṭha*, n.), MBh.; R. &c.; N. of a minute portion of Prakṛiti, Cat.; (with Buddhists) N. of a goddess, W.; of a daughter of Śva-phalka, Hariv.; of a princess, Daś.; of another woman, Ratnâv.; du. N. of the two Kumāris (set up with Indra's banner, see *kumārī*), VarBṛS.; *-dhara*, m. a mountain, MBh.; Bālar.; *-dhava*, m. a king, prince, Rājat.; *-bhṛit*, m. a mountain, Vcar.; *-śunāsīra*, a prince, king, Prasannar. (w. r. *-sunā-s°*). **-pati** (*vásu-*), m. lord of wealth or of good things (also with *vásūnām*; N. of Agni, Indra, Savitṛi and Kubera), RV.; Pañcar.; 'lord of the Vasus,' N. of Kṛishṇa, Pañcar. **-pátnī**, f. (said of the cow) mistress of wealth (also with *vásūnām*), RV. i, 164, 27. **-pātṛi**, mfn. 'protector of the Vasus,' N. of Kṛishṇa, Pañcar. **-pāla**, m. 'protector of wealth,' a king, BhP. **-pālita**, m. N. of various men, Daś.; HPariś. **-pūjya-rāj**, m. N. of the father of the 12th Arhat of the present Avasarpiṇī, Jain. **-prada**, mfn. bestowing w°, Vishṇ.; MBh.; m. N. of one of Skanda's attendants, MBh. **-prabhā**, f. one of the 7 tongues of fire, L.; N. of Kubera's capital, L. **-prāṇa**, m. 'breath of the Vasus,' fire, L. **-bandhu**, m. N. of a celebrated Buddhist scholar, Hcar.; Buddh. (w. r. *-bandha*). **-bha**, n. the constellation Dhanishṭhā (presided over by the Vasus), VarBṛS.; N. of a town, Virac. **-bhaṭṭa**, m. Aeschynomene or Sesbana Grandiflora, L. **-bharita**, mfn. full of treasures, Pañcar. **-bhāga**, m. N. of a poet, Sadukt. **-bhūta**, m. N. of a Gandharva, Cat. **-bhūti**, m. N. of various men, Mn., Kull.; Ratnâv.; Kathās.; W. **-bhṛid-yāna**, m. N. of a son of Vasishṭha, BhP. **-mat** (*vásu-*), mfn. having or possessing or containing treasures, wealthy, rich (*-tara*, compar.), RV.; ŚāṅkhGṛ.; MBh. &c.; attended by the Vasus, TS.; Kāṭh.; AitBr. &c.; m. N. of a son of Manu Vaivasvata, Pur.; of Kṛishṇa, BhP.; of a king, MBh.; of various other persons, Śak.; BhP.; of a mountain in the North, VarBṛS.; MārkP.; (*atī*), f., see below; *-tā*, f. the state of being wealthy, wealth, MBh.; *-(mad)-gaṇa* (*vá°*), mfn. having or attracting the troop consisting of the Vasus (said of Soma), TS.; N. of TS. iii, 2, 5, 2 (as beginning with this word), ĀpŚr. **-mati**, m. N. of a Brāhman, Kathās. **-matī**, f. (of *-mat*) the earth; a country, kingdom, region, MBh.; Kāv. &c.; the ground, Kāv.; N. of two kinds of metre, Ked.; Col.; N. of various women, Śak.; Kathās.; *-citra-senā-vilāsa*, m., *-citra-senīya*, n., *-citrâsana*, n. N. of wks.; *-pati*, m. a prince, king, Rājat.; *-pariṇaya*, m. N. of wk.; *-pṛishṭha*, n. the surface of the (spherical) earth, Gol.; *-sūnu*, m. metron. of Naraka, Bālar. **-manas**, m. N. of a king of Kosala, MBh.; (with *Rauhidaśva*) N. of the author of RV. x, 179, 3. **-máya**, mf(*ī*)n. consisting of wealth or of good things, ŚBr. **-mitra**, m. N. of various men, MBh.; Mālav.; Pur. &c. **-mekhala**, mfn. wearing a jewelled girdle, Pañcar.; **-rakshita**, m. N. of a man, Daś. **-raṇva**, mfn. delighted with wealth, NṛiUp. **-ratha**, m. N. of a poet, Sadukt. **-rāja**, m. the king Vasu, HYog. **-rāta**, m. N. of a man, MārkP. **-rúc**, mfn. (perhaps) bright like the Vasus or the gods, RV. ix, 110, 6; a proper N., MW. **-ruci** (*vásu-*), m. N. of a Gandharva, AV. **-rūpa**, mfn. having the nature of the Vasus (said of Śiva), MBh. (also applied to an ancestor on offering the Piṇḍa, Saṃskārak.) **-retas**, m. fire or the god of fire, MBh.; R.; N. of Śiva (also *°taḥ-su-vapuḥ*), MBh. **-rocis** (*vásu-*), m. N. of a man; (pl.) of his family, RV.; SāmavBr.; n. = *yajña*, Uṇ. ii, 112, Sch.; a religious ceremony in which the Vasus are esp. worshipped, MW. **-lakshmī**, f. N. of a sister-in-law of Agni-mitra, Mālav. (in Prākṛit); *-kalyāṇa*, n. N. of a Kāvya. **-vat** (*vásu-*), mfn. united with the Vasus (said of Agni), AV. **-ván**, mfn. = *-váni* (with *vasu-dhéyasya*), VS.; Br. &c. **-vana**, n. N. of a mythical country, VarBṛS. **-váni**, mfn. asking wealth (or) bestowing wealth, RV.; AV.; f. a request or prayer for w°, MW. **-varma-dhara**, mfn. wearing a golden armour, MBh. **-vallikā**, f. Serratula Anthelmintica, L. **-vāha**, m. N. of a Ṛishi, Cat. **-vā́hana**, mfn. carrying w°, bringing treasures, RV. **-víd**, mfn. bestowing w°, RV.; AV. &c.; (*-vit*)*-tama*, mfn. one who bestows great w°, MW. **-vinda**, mfn. gaining w°, Gaut. **-vīrya**, n. (prob.) the power of the Vasus, MānGṛ. **-vṛishṭi**, f. a shower of w° or of treasures, Cat. **-vrata**, n. a kind of penance (eating only ground rice for twelve days), L. **-śakti**, m. N. of a man, Pañcat. **-śravas** (*vásu-*), mfn. (perhaps) famous for wealth (or 'flowing with w°'), RV. v, 24, 2; N. of Śiva, Śivag. **-śrī**, f. N. of one of the Mātṛis attending on Skanda, MBh. **-śruta**, m. (prob.) a person renowned for w°, MW.; (with *Ātreya*) N. of the author of RV. v, 3–6. **-śreshṭha**, mfn. the best of the Vasus (said of Kṛishṇa), Pañcar.; m. N. of a king, VP.; n. 'best of treasure,' silver, L.; wrought gold, MW. **-sheṇa**, m. N. of Vishṇu, Vishṇ.; of Karṇa (half brother of the Pāṇḍu princes by the same mother, Pṛithā; the name is supposed by some to have reference to his wealth which he distributed liberally; cf. *karṇa*), MBh.; of a merchant, HPariś. **-sampatti**, f. accession or acquisition of wealth, Vait. **-sampūrṇa**, mfn. filled with wealth, MBh. **-sāra**, m. N. of a man, Buddh.; (*ā*), f. Kubera's capital, L. **-sena**, m. N. of a poet, Sadukt. **-sthalī**, f. the capital of Kubera, L. **-haṭṭa** (Car., Sch.) or **-haṭṭaka** (L.), m. a kind of tree = *baka*; = *baka-pushpa* or Sesbana Grandiflora, MW. **-homa**, m. N. of a king of the Aṅgas, MBh. **Vasū-jū́**, mfn. raising wealth, RV. viii, 88, 8. **Vasûttama**, m. 'best of the Vasus,' N. of Bhīshma, BhP. **Vasûdreka**, m. N. of a man, Cat. **Vasûpamāna**, mfn. resembling or equal to Kubera, MW. **Vasū-matī** (m.c. *vasu-m°*), f. a rich or wealthy woman, Hariv.

Vasuna, m. a sacrifice, L.

Vasura, mfn. (fr. 1. *vasu*) valuable, rich, L.

Vasula, m. (fr. id.) a god, L.; an endearing form for *vasu-datta*, Pāṇ. v, 3, 83, Pat.

Vasūya, Nom. P. *°yáti*, to desire wealth, RV. **°yā́**, ind. through desire of wealth, ib. **°yú**, mfn. desiring wealth, ib.

Vásor-dhā́rā and **vasosh-pati.** See col. 1 under 1. *vásu*.

1. **Vástu**, f. (for 2. see p. 932, col. 3) becoming light, dawning, morning, RV.; VS. (gen. *vástoḥ*, in the m°; *vástor vastoḥ*, every m°; *vástor asyā́ḥ*, this m°; *prā́ti vástoḥ*, towards m°; dat. *vástave*, see under √2. *vas*).

1. **Vastṛi**, mfn. (for 2. see p. 932, col. 1) shining, illumining (see *doshā-* and *prātar-v°*).

1. **Vasná**, n. (L. also m.; for 2. see p. 932, col. 2) wealth, riches, L.; price, value, RV.; AV.; VS.; hire, wages, L. [Cf. Gk. ὦνος for Fοσ-νος; ὠνή, ὠνέομαι; Lat. *venum*, *veneo*, *vendo*.]

Vasnaya, Nom. P. *°yáti* (only pr. p. *°yát*), to higgle, haggle, RV. vi, 47, 21.

Vasnika, mfn. earning wages, mercenary, Pāṇ. iv, 4, 13; purchasable (?), ib. i, 51; (*ā*), f. a valuable deposit, TāṇḍBr.

Vásnya, mfn. precious, valuable, RV. x, 34, 1.

Vásya-ishṭi, f. (fr. *vasyas* + *ishṭi*) seeking or desire for the better i. e. for welfare, RV.

Vásyashṭi, f. (for prec.) attaining to welfare, TS.; MaitrS.; Br. (in a formula).

Vásyas, mfn. = *vásīyas*, better, more excellent or glorious, wealthier or richer than (abl.), RV.; VS.; TBr.; TUp.; n. increasing wealth or prosperity, welfare, RV.; AV.

Vasyasa. See *pāpa-* and *śvo-v°*.

Vasyo-bhūya, n. (fr. *vasyas* + *bhūya*) increasing wealth, welfare, AV.

1. **Vasra**, m. (for 2. see p. 933, col. 1) a day, L.

Vasv, in comp. for 1. *vasu*. — **ananta**, m. N. of a son of Upagupta, BhP. — **anta**, mfn. ending with the word *vasu*, Gobh. — **okasārā** or **-aukasārā**, f. N. of a river, MBh.; R.; of the residence of Kubera, MBh.; Kāv.; of the city of Indra, VP.

Vasvī. See under 1. *vasu*, p. 931, col. 1.

वस् 3. *vas*, cl. 10. P. *vāsayati* (aor. *avīvasat*), to love; to cut off; to accept, take; to offer; to kill (*ni-vāsita*, killed), Dhātup. xxxiii, 70 (only with prep.; see *pari-√vas*; but accord. to some the Impv. *vasishva* [RV. viii, 70, 10] and *usha*, 'a lover' [x, 95, 5], and *vásishtha* [ib. 17] belong also to this root, which has developed an obscene meaning = Gk. κεντέω, futuere).

वस् 4. *vas*, cl. 2. Ā. (Dhātup. xxiv, 13) *váste* (Impv. *vasishva*, RV.; *vaddhvam*, Kauś.; p. *vásāna*, once *usāná* and *usámāna*, RV.; pf. *vavase*, Śiś.; *vāvase*, p. *°sāná*, RV.; aor. *avasishṭa*, ib.; fut. *vasitā*, Gr.; *vasishyate*, ib.; *vatsyati*, Hariv. 11206; inf. *vasitum*, MBh.; R.; ind. p. *vasitvā*, Mn.; BhP.; *-vasya*, MBh.), to put on, invest, wear, (clothes &c.), assume (a form &c.), enter into, RV. &c. &c.: Caus. *vāsáyati*, *°te* (Pass. *vāsyate*), to cause or allow to put on or wear (clothes), clothe (Ā. 'one's self') with (instr.), RV.; GṛŚrS.; Mn.: Desid. *vivasishate*, Gr.: Intens. *vāvasyate*, *vāvasti*, ib. [Cf. Gk. ἕννυμι for ϝεσ-νυμι, εἷμα; Lat. *vestis*; Goth. *wasjan*; Angl. Sax. *werian*; Eng. *wear*.]

Vas (ifc.), clothed in, wearing (e. g. *prêta-cīvara-vas*, 'wearing the garments of dead men'), Ragh.

1. **Vásana**, n. (for 2. see col. 3) cloth, clothes, dress, garment, apparel, attire (du. an upper and lower garment), RV. &c. &c. (ifc., f. *ā* = clothed in, surrounded by, engrossed by i. e. wholly devoted or attached to, e. g. to a doctrine, Kāv.; Pur.); investment, siege, L.; a leaf of the cinnamon tree, L.; (also *ā*, f.) an ornament worn by women round the loins, L. — **paryāya**, m. change of clothes, Mṛicch. — **maya**, mf(*ī*)n. consisting or made of cloth, Lāṭy. — **vat**, mfn. clothed, Gobh. — **sadman**, n. 'cloth-house,' a tent, Śiś. **Vasanârṇa**, n. (*°na* + *ṛiṇa*) the debt of a cloth, Pāṇ. vi, 1, 89, Vārtt. 7, Pat. **Vasanârṇava**, mf(*ā*)n. sea-girt (the earth), R.

1. **Vasi**, m. or f. (for 2. see col. 3) = *vastra*, clothes &c., L.

1. **Vasita**, mfn. (for 2. see col. 3) worn, put on, MBh.; n. cloth, L.

Vasitavya, mfn. to be worn or put on, R.

Vasitṛi, mfn. one who wears or puts on (*-tama*, mfn. = *ācchādayitṛi-tama*, used to explain *vasishṭha*), Śaṃk. on ChUp. v, 1, 2.

Vasuká, m. (in a formula) is said to = *vāsayitṛi* (prob. 'one who clothes'), MaitrS.; TāṇḍBr.; N. of various plants (accord. to L. = Calotropis Gigantea; Agati Grandiflora; Adhatoda Vasika and Chenopodium), Suśr.; a kind of measure (in music); n. a kind of salt, L.

Vasūka, m. a species of tree (= *baka*), L.; n. its flower, L.; a kind of salt, L.

1. **Vasti**, m. or f. (for 2. see col. 2) the ends or skirt of a cloth (also pl.), L.

2. **Vastṛí**, mfn. (for 1. see p. 931; for 3. p. 933) clothing, covering, RV. iii, 49, 4 (Sāy.); putting on (clothes), Kauś.

Vastra, n. (or m., g. *ardharcâdi*; ifc. f. *ā*) cloth, clothes, garment, raiment, dress, cover, RV. &c. &c.; (*ā*), f. N. of a river, VP.; n. a leaf of the cinnamon tree, L. — **kuṭṭima**, n. 'cloth-covering,' an umbrella, L.; a tent, L. — **kośa**, n. a clothes-bag, L. — **knopam**, ind. so that the clothes are thoroughly wetted, Śiś. — **gṛiha**, n. 'cloth-house,' a tent, L. — **gopana**, n. pl. N. of one of the 64 arts, Cat. — **granthi**, m. a piece of cloth wrapped round the waist, L.; the knot which fastens the lower garments above the hips, W. — **gharghari**, f. a sieve or cloth for straining, L. — **cchanna**, mfn. clad in clothes, Vop. — **da**, mfn. giving clothes, MBh. — **daśā**, f. the border of a garment, Gobh. — **dá**, mfn. = *-da*, RV. — **dāna**, n. N. of wk.; *-kathā*, f. N. of a tale. — **dhāraka**, w.r. for *vastrâdh°*, q.v. — **dhāraṇī**, f. a stick or rope to hang clothes upon, L. — **dhāvin**, mfn. washing clothes, Kathās. — **nirṇejaka**, m. a washer of cl°, washerman, W. — **pa**, m. pl. N. of a people, MBh. — **pañjala**, m. N. of a bulbous plant, L. — **paridhāna**, n. the putting on of cl°, dressing, Cat. — **putrikā**, f. a doll or puppet made of cloth, L. — **pūta**, mfn. purified with a cl°, strained through a cl°, Mn. vi, 46. — **peṭā**, f. a cl°s-basket, Kathās. — **peśī**, f. a fringe, L. — **bandha**, m. a cl° used for binding round, L. — **bhūshaṇa**, m. a kind of plant, L.; (*ā*), f. a kind of pl°, MW. — **bhedaka** or **°din**, m. a cl°-cutter, tailor, W. — **máthi**, mfn. tearing off or carrying off clothes, RV. iv, 38, 5. — **mukhya**, mfn. having clothes as the chief thing, Ml. — **yugala**, n. two garments, Pañcat. — **yugin**, mfn. clad in an upper-g° and under-g°, Pāṇ. viii, 4, 13, Sch. — **yugma**, n. a pair of garm° or clothes of any kind, Kathās. — **yoni**, f. the basis or material of cloth (as cotton &c.), L. — **raṅgā**, f. a species of plant, L. — **rajaka**, n. 'cl°-colourer,' safflower, Bhpr. — **rajanī**, f. Rubia Munjista, ib. — **rañjana**, n. = *-rajaka* above, L. — **vat**, mfn. having fine clothes, well-dressed, MBh. — **vidyā**, w.r. for *vāstu-v°*, q. v. — **vilāsa**, m. foppery in dress, MW. — **veśa**, m. or **-veśman**, n. a tent, L. — **veshṭita**, mfn. covered with clothes, well clad, Hit. **Vastrâgāra**, m. n. a clothier's shop, MW.; a tent, ib. **Vastrâñcala**, m. the end or hem of a garment, Kathās.; Hit. **Vastrâdhāraka**, a layer or stratum of cloth (placed underneath), Suśr. **Vastrânta**, m. the end or hem of a garm°, ŚāṅkhGṛ.; MBh.; R. &c. **Vastrântara**, n. (ifc. f. *ā*) an upper-garm°, Kathās. **Vastrâpatha-kshetra**, n. N. of a place, Cat. **Vastrâpahāraka** (Mn.) or **°hārin** (MW.), m. a stealer of clothes. **Vastrârdha**, n. the half of a garm°; *-prâvṛita* (MBh.) or *-saṃvīta* or *-saṃvṛita* (MW.), mfn. covered or clothed with half a garm°. **Vastrâvakarta**, m. a fragment of a garm°, MBh. **Vastrôtkarshaṇa**, n. the act of taking off clothes, MBh.

Vastraka, n. cloth (in *sūkshma-v°*), MBh.

Vastraya, Nom. P. *°yati*, Pāṇ. iii, 1, 21.

Vastrāya, Nom. Ā. *°yate*, to represent a garment, Vām. iv, 1, 9 (in a quotation).

2. **Vasna**, n. (for 1. see p. 931, col. 3) a garment, cloth, L.; the skin, L.

Vasnana, n. an ornament for a woman's loins, a zone, girdle (= *kaṭī-bhūshaṇa*), L.

1. **Vásman**, n. (for 2. see p. 933, col. 1) a cover, garment, RV. iv, 13, 4.

Vasya, mfn. to be put on (see *snāta-v°*).

वस् 5. *vas*, cl. 1. P. (Dhātup. xxiii, 36) *vásati* (m. c. also *°te*; pf. *uvāsa*, *ūshuḥ*, RV. &c. &c.; p. *vāvasāna*, RV. i, 46, 13; *-vāsāṃ cakre*, Up.; aor. *avātsīt*, AV.; *avākṣam*, AitBr. [where it is artificially connected with *vāc*]; *avāstam*, Up.; fut. *vastā*, Gr.; *vatsyati*, *°te*, Br. &c.; *vasishyati*, MBh.; inf. *vastum*, *vasitum*, MBh. &c.; ind. p. *ushitvā*, Br.; *ushṭvā*, MBh.; *-úshya*, Br. &c.), to dwell, live, stop (at a place), stay (esp. 'overnight,' with or without *rātrim* or *rātrīs*), RV. &c. &c.; to remain, abide with or in (with loc. of pers.; loc. or acc. of place, esp. with *vāsam* or *vasatim*), ŚBr. &c. &c.; to remain or keep on or continue in any condition (with a pp., e. g. with *channa*, 'to continue to be covered,' KātyŚr.; or with an acc., with *brahmacaryam*, 'to practise chastity,' AitBr.; or with an adv., e. g. with *sukham*, 'to live pleasantly or at ease;' with or without *dūratas*, 'to keep aloof'), TS. &c. &c.; to have sexual intercourse with (loc.), Hariv.; to rest upon (loc.), Subh.; to charge or entrust with (instr.), Hariv.; cl. 10. P. *vasayati*, to dwell, Dhātup. xxxv, 84, e: Pass. *ushyate* (aor. *avāsi*), to be dwelt &c., MBh.; Kāv. &c.: Caus. *vāsáyati*, *°te* (cf. Pāṇ. i, 3, 89; aor. *avīvasat*, MaitrS.: Pass. *vāsyáte*, Br., *°ti*, MBh.), to cause to halt or stay (overnight), lodge, receive hospitably or as a guest, ŚBr.; MBh. &c.; to cause to have sexual intercourse with (loc.), MatsyaP.; to let anything stand overnight (with *tisro*, scil. *ratrīs*, 'three nights'), Kauś.; to cause to wait, keep in suspense, RV.; to delay, retard, Kām.; to cause to exist, preserve, ŚBr.; to cause to be inhabited, populate (a country), Hit.; to put in, place upon (loc.), MBh.; Hariv.; Kāv. (*anadhyāyam mukhe*, to put restraint on the mouth, refrain from speaking); to produce, Sarvad.: Desid. *vivatsati*, to wish to dwell, ŚBr.: Intens. *vāvasyate*, *vāvasti*, to remain, be in, be engaged in, MW. [Cf. Goth. *wisan*; Germ. *wēsan*, *ge-wesen*, *war* &c.; Angl. Sax. *wēsan*; Eng. *was*, *were*.]

2. **Ushita** (ep. also *ushṭa*), mfn. (for 1. see p. 220) past, spent (as time; n. impers. 'time has been spent'), MBh.; Kāv. &c.; retired or resorted to (as a place), Kāv.; one who has halted or stayed (esp. 'overnight') or has been absent or lived or remained or waited in any place (loc. or comp.) or for any time (acc. or comp.), MBh.; Kāv. &c.; one who has had sexual intercourse with (*saha*), BrahmaP.; what has stood or lain (esp. 'overnight' said of things), VarBṛS.; Suśr.; one who has fasted, VarBṛS. — **m-gavīna**, mfn. (a place) where cows have been for a time, L. (cf. *āśitaṃ-g°*).

6. **Vás** (only in gen. *vásām*), prob. either 'an abode' or 'a dweller,' RV. v, 2, 6.

Vasa, m. or n. dwelling, residence (see *dur-vasa*); (*ā́*), f. (accord. to some) id. (?), RV. v, 2, 6.

Vasatí, f. staying (esp. 'overnight'), dwelling, abiding, sojourn, ŚBr. &c. &c. (*tisro vasatīr ushitvā*, 'having passed three nights;' *vasatiṃ √kṛi* or *√grah*, 'to pass the night, take up one's abode in,' with loc.); a nest, RV.; a dwelling-place, house, residence, abode or seat of (gen. or comp.), ib. &c. &c.; a Jaina monastery, L.; night, MBh.; mfn. (accord. to some) dwelling, abiding (with *vasām*), fixing one's residence (?), RV. v, 2, 6. — **druma**, m. a tree under which a night is passed, Ragh.

Vasatī, f. = *vasati*, staying, dwelling, a dwelling-place, &c., L. — **vári**, f. pl. (scil. *āpas*) water left standing overnight (drawn from a stream on the eve of the Soma sacrifice), TS.; Br.; ŚrS. (ibc. *°ri*, KātyŚr.)

Vasatha, m. a house, Gal.

2. **Vasana**, n. (for 1. see col. 1) dwelling, abiding, sojourn, residence in (comp.), MBh. — **sadman**, see under 1. *vasana*.

2. **Vasi**, m. (for 1. see col. 1) dwelling or a dwelling-place, W.

2. **Vasita**, mfn. (for 1. see col. 1) = 2. *ushita*, inhabiting &c.; stored (as grain), W.; n. abiding, abode, residence, ib.

2. **Vasu**, m. or n. (for 1. see p. 930, col. 3) dwelling or dweller (see *sám-vasu*).

Vasta, n. a house, L. (cf. also *upa-vasta*).

Vastavya, mfn. to be stayed or dwelt or lived in or with (loc.; n. impers. 'one should stay' &c.), MBh.; R. &c.; to be spent or passed (as time), ib. — **tā**, f. abode, residence, R.

2. **Vasti**, f. (for 1. see col. 1, for 3. see p. 933, col. 1) abiding, dwelling, staying, W.

2. **Vastu**, n. (for 1. see p. 931, col. 3) the seat or place of (see *kapila-*, *vraṇa-v°*); any really existing or abiding substance or essence, thing, object, article, Kāv.; VarBṛS.; Kathās. &c. (also applied to living beings, e. g. Śak. ii, 7); (in phil.) the real (opp. to *a-v°*, 'that which does not really exist, the unreal;' *a-dvitīya-v°*, 'the one real substance or essence which has no second'), IW. 53, n. 1; 103 &c.; the right thing, a valuable or worthy object, object of or for (comp.), Kāv.; goods, wealth, property (cf. *-vinimaya* and *-hāni*); the thing in question, matter, affair, circumstance, MBh.; Kāv. &c.; subject, subject-matter, contents, theme (of a speech &c.), plot (of a drama or poem), Kāv.; Daśar.; Sāh. &c.; (in music) a kind of composition, Saṃgīt.; natural disposition, essential property, W.; the pith or substance of anything, W. — **kṛita**, mfn. practised, cherished, Buddh. — **kośa**, m. N. of a dictionary. — **kshaṇāt**, ind. at the right moment, MW. — **jāta**, n. the aggregate of things, Sarvad. — **tattva**, n. and **-tattva-prakāśikā**, f. N. of wks. — **tantra**, mfn. dependent on things, objective (*-tva*, n.), Śaṃk. — **tas**, ind. owing to the nature of things, BhP.; in fact, in reality, actually, verily, essentially, ib.; Rājat.; Sarvad. — **tā**, f. (ifc.) the state of being the object of, Pañcat.; = next, BhP. — **tva**, n. reality, Kap. — **dharma**, m. sg. and pl. the true nature of things (*-tva*, n.), Kap.; Kathās.; Sāh.; *°min*, mfn. dependent on the nature of a thing, objective, Kpr. — **nirdeśa**, m. table of contents, register, Kāvyād.; Sāh. — **patita**, mfn. become real or corporeal, Vajracch. — **pāṇi**, mfn. holding the (necessary) things in one's hand, BhP. — **pāla**, m. N. of a minister of king Vīra-dhavala (died A.D. 1241), Cat.; of a poet, ib. — **bala**, n. the power of things, Sarvad. — **bhāva**, m. reality, truth (instr. pl. 'really'), Rājat. — **bhūta**, mfn. substantial, VP. — **bheda**, m. an actual or essential difference, ib. — **mātra**, n. the mere outline of any subject, skeleton of a discourse, W. — **racanā**, f. arrangement of matter, elaboration of a plot, Ratnâv.; Sāh.

-vat, mfn. supplied with commodities, MW. **-vicāra**, m. essential discrimination (personified), Prab. **-vijñāna-ratna-kośa**, m. N. of a dictionary (=*ratna-kośa*). **-vinimaya**, m. exchange of goods, barter, MW. **-vivarta**, mfn. the developing of the one real Essence (so as to create the illusory external world), Vedântas. **-vṛitta**, n. the actual fact, real matter, Mālatīm.; Rājat.; n. a beautiful creature, Mālav., Sch. **-śakti**, f. sg. and pl. the power of things, force of circumstances (*-tas*, ind. through the force of c°), Kāv. **-śāsana**, n. a genuine or original edict, Rājat. **-śūnya**, mfn. devoid of reality, unreal, Yogas. **-sthiti**, f. reality (instr. 'in reality'), Sāṃkhyas., Sch. **-hāni**, f. loss of substance or property, W. **Vastûtthāpana**, n. or °**nā**, f. invention of things or of incidents through supernatural causes (in a drama), Bhar.; Daśar.; Sāh. **Vastûpamā**, f. comparison of things (a kind of comparison where the common quality is omitted, e.g. thy face is like the lotus, where the word 'beautiful' is omitted), Kāvyâd. **Vastûpahita**, mfn. placed on a good or worthy object (as trouble or care), Ragh.

Vastuka (ifc.) = 2. *vastu*, substance, essence (in *an-ūna-v°*, 'of perfect substance or nature,' Mālav. i, ⅑); n. Chenopodium Album, W.

Vastūkī, f. a kind of potherb, L.

3. **Vástṛi** (for 2. see p. 931, col. 3), mfn. (only in superl. *vástṛi-tama*, 'dwelling most,' used in giving an etymology), ŚBr.

Vastya, n. a house, abode, L. (cf. *pastya*).

Vastv, in comp. for 2. *vastu*. **-antara**, n. another thing, another object or subject, W. **-abhāva**, m. absence of reality, unsubstantial essence, ib.; loss or destruction of property, ib.

2. **Vásman**, n. (for 1. see p. 932, col. 2) a nest, RV. ii, 31, 1.

2. **Vasra**, n. (for 1. see p. 932, col. 1) a house, abode, L.; a cross-road, L.

वस् 7. *vas* (only *vasishva*, [*anu*]-*vāvase*, *vāvasānā*, and *vástos*), to rush or aim at, attack, RV. viii, 70, 10 (cf. under √3. *vas*); viii, 4, 8; i, 51, 3; vi, 11, 6 (?); i, 174, 3.

वस् 8. *vas* (also written *bas*), cl. 4. P. *vasyati*, to be or make firm, Dhātup. xxxiii, 70.

वसति *vasati* &c. See p. 932, col. 3.

वसन 1. 2. *vasana*. See p. 932, cols. 1 and 3.

वसन्त *vasanta* &c. See p. 930, col. 1.

वसा *vasā*, *vasāti* &c. See p. 930, col. 2.

वसार *vasāra*(?), n. wish, purpose, W.

वसिक *vasika*, mfn. empty, L. (cf. *vaśika*, *vaśin*); one who sits in the Padmâsana posture, L.

वसिर *vasira*, m. Scindapsus Officinalis (n. its fruit), Suśr.; Bhpr. (v.l. *vasīra* and *vaśira*); Achyranthes Aspera, L.; n. sea salt (v.l. *vaśira* and *vaśīra*), L.

वसिष्ठ *vasishṭha*, *vasīyas*. See p. 930.

वसु 1. 2. *vasu*. See pp. 930 and 932.

वसुर *vasura*, *vasula*, *vasūya* &c. See p. 931.

वसूरा *vasūrā*, f. a harlot, prostitute, W.

वस्क् *vask* (cf. √*vashk*), cl. 1. Ā. *vaskate*, to go, Dhātup. iv, 27.

Vaska, m. going, motion, W.; application, perseverance, ib. (= *adhyavasāya*, L.)

वस्कय *vaskaya*, °*yaṇī*. See *bashkáya*.

वस्कराटिका *vaskarāṭikā*, f. a scorpion, L.

वस्त् *vast*, cl. 10. Ā. *vastayate*, to waste, hurt, Dhātup. xxxiii, 10; to go, W.; to ask, ib.

वस्त *vasta*, *vastavya*. See p. 932, col. 3.

वस्ति 3. *vastí*, m. f. (also written *basti*; perh. connected with 2. *vasti*, see p. 932, col. 3) the bladder, AV. &c. &c.; the lower belly, abdomen, VarBṛS.; Kāśikh.; the pelvis, MW.; an injection-syringe made of bladder or the injection itself, Kathās.; Suśr. &c. [Cf. Lat. *venter*, *vesica*; Germ. *wanast*, *Wanst*.] **-karman**, n. the application of an enema or injection, Cat. **-karmâḍhya**, m. the soap berry, Sapindus Detergens, L. **-kuṇḍala**, n. (Car.), **-kuṇḍalikā**, f. (ŚārṅgS.) a partic. disease of the bladder. **-kośa**, m. a bladder, bag, Suśr. **-pīḍā**, f. spasm in the bladder, ib. **-bilá**, n. aperture of the bl°, AV. **-mala**, n. 'bladder-excretion,' urine, L. **-mūla**, n. 'bl°-root,' aperture of the bl°, MBh. **-ruj** (Suśr.) or **-vyāpad** (Cat.), f. disease of the bl°. **-śiras**, n. the tube of an enema, W.; = next, ib. **-śīrsha**, n. sg. (Yājñ.) or m. du. (Vishṇ.) the neck of the bl°. **-śodhana**, m. 'bl°-cleanser,' Vangueria Spinosa, L.

Vasty, in comp. for 3. *vasti*. **-artham**, ind. for an enema, Kathās. **-aushadha**, n. 'remedy for the lower belly,' injection, enema, Cat.

वस्तु 1. 2. *vastu*. See pp. 931 and 932.

वस्तृ 1. 2. 3. *vastṛi*. See pp. 931, 932, & col. 1.

वस्न 1. 2. *vasna*. See pp. 931 and 932.

वस्नसा *vasnasā*, f. (cf. *snāyu*) a tendon, nerve, fibre (described as a hollow, string-like tube, attached to the bones and supposed to serve as a passage for the vital air), L.

वस्निक *vasnika*, *vasnya*. See p. 931, col. 3.

वस्मन् 1. 2. *vasman*. See pp. 932 and 933.

वस्यस् *vasyas* &c. See p. 932, col. 1.

वस्र 1. 2. *vasra*. See p. 932, and col. 1.

वह् 1. *vah*, cl. 1. P. Ā. (Dhātup. xxiii, 35) *váhati*, °*te* (in later language Ā. only m. c.; Vedic forms which may partly belong to the aor. are *vákshi*, *voḍham*, °*ḍhām* or *voḷham*, °*ḷhām*, *uhīta*, *vákshva*, *voḍhvam*, *ūḍhvam*, *úhāna*; pf. *uvāha*, *ūhúḥ*; *ūhé*, RV. &c. &c.; *vavāha*, °*hatuḥ*, MBh; aor. Ved. *ávākshīt* or *ávāṭ*, Subj. *vākshat*, °*ati*, Prec. *uhyāt*; *avakshi*, *avoḍha*, Gr.; fut. *voḍhā*, Br.; *vakshyáti*, °*te*, AV. &c.; *vahishyati*, MBh. &c.; inf. *voḍhum*, RV. &c. &c. [Ved. also °*ḍhave* and °*ḍhavai*]; *vāhe*, RV.; *váhadhyai*, ib.; ind. p. *ūḍhvā*, Br.; *-úhya*, AV. &c. &c.; cf. √1. *ūh*), to carry, transport, convey (with instr. of vehicle), RV. &c. &c.; to lead, conduct (esp. offerings to the gods, said of Agni), ib.; to bear along (water, said of rivers), ib.; to draw (a car), guide (horses &c.), ib.; to lead towards, to bring, procure, bestow, Kāv.; Kathās.; to cause, effect, BhP.; to offer (a sacrifice), ib.; to spread, diffuse (scent), Kathās.; to shed (tears), BhP.; to carry away, carry off, rob, MBh.; Kāv. &c.; to lead home, take to wife, marry, RV. &c. &c.; to bear or carry on or with (loc. or instr.), MBh.; Kāv. &c.; to take or carry with or about one's self, have, possess, Kāv.; Pur.; Rājat.; to wear (clothes), Mṛicch.; (with *śiras*) to bear one's head (*uccais-tarām*, 'high'), Hariv.; (with *vasumdharām* or *kshmā-maṇḍalam*) to support i.e. rule the earth, Rājat.; (with *garbham*) to be with child, Pañcat.; to bear, suffer, endure, Kāv.; Pur.; to forbear, forgive, pardon, BhP.; to undergo (with *agnim*, *visham*, *tulām*, 'the ordeal of fire, poison, and the balance'), Yājñ.; to experience, feel, MBh.; Kāv. &c.; to exhibit, show, betray, ib.; to pay (a fine), Yājñ.; to pass, spend (time), Rājat.; (intrans.) to drive, ride, go by or in (with instr. of the vehicle), be borne or carried along, run, swim &c., RV. &c. &c.; to draw (scil. a carriage, said of a horse), Mn. viii, 146; to blow (as wind), Kāv.; Sāh.; to pass away, elapse, Hcar.: Pass. *uhyáte* (ep. also °*ti*; aor. *avāhi*), to be carried (*uhyamāna*, 'being c°') &c.; to be drawn or borne by (instr.) or along or off, RV. &c. &c.: Caus. *vāhayati* (m. c. also °*te*; aor. *avīvahat*; Pass. *vāhyate*), to cause to bear or carry or convey or draw (with two acc., Pāṇ. i, 4, 52, Vārtt. 6, Pat.), drive (a chariot), guide or ride (a horse), propel (a boat), go or travel by any vehicle, MBh.; Kāv. &c.; to cause to guide (two acc.), Vop.; to cause any one (acc.) to carry anything (acc.) on (loc.), MBh.; to cause to take in marriage, ib.; to cause to be conveyed by (instr.), Ragh.; Rājat.; to traverse (a road), Ragh.; to accomplish (a journey), Megh.; to employ, keep going or in work, Mn. iii, 68; iv, 86; to give, administer (see *vāhita*); to take in, deceive (see id.): Desid. *vivakshati*, °*te*, Gr.: Intens. *vanīvāhyáte*, to carry hither and thither (cf. *vanīvāhana* and *vanīvāhitá*); *vāvahīti*, to bear (a burden), Subh.; *vāvahyate*, *vāvoḍhi*, Gr. [Cf. Gk. ὄχος for Ϝόχος, ὀχέομαι; Lat. *vehere*, *vehiculum*; Slav. *vesti*; Lith. *vèžti*; Goth. *gawigan*; Germ. *wëgan*, *bewegen*; Eng. *weigh*.]

Ūḍhá, mfn. (cf. √1. 2. *ūh*, p. 223) carried, conveyed, borne off or along, RV. &c. &c.; stolen, robbed, Mn. ix, 270; washed away (by water), ib. viii, 189; borne or carried on (instr.), MBh.; Kāv. &c.; led home, taken in marriage, married, ib.; advanced (see comp.); exhibited, betrayed, BhP.; (*ā*), f. a married woman, wife, L. **-pūrva**, mf(*ā*)n. married before, Śak. **-bhārya**, mfn. one who has taken a wife, married, g. *āhitâgny-ādi*. **-ratha**, mfn. drawing a carriage, Laghuk. **-vayas**, mfn. advanced in years, full grown, BhP.

Ūḍhaya, Nom. P. °*yati* (fr. *ūḍha* and *ūḍhi*), Kāś. on Pāṇ. viii, 2, 1.

Ūḍhi, f. bearing, carrying, bringing, Rājat.

2. **Vah** (ifc.; strong form *vāh*, weak form *ūh*, which with a preceding *a* coalesces into *au*; cf. Pāṇ. iii, 2, 64; iv, 1, 61) carrying, drawing, bearing, holding (cf. *anaḍ-uh*, *apsu-vah*, *indra-vah* &c.).

Váha, mf(*ā*)n. (ifc.) carrying, bearing, conveying, bringing, causing, producing, effecting (cf. *gandha-*, *dāru-*, *puṇya-v°* &c.); flowing through or into or towards (cf. *para-loka-v°*, *sarva-loka-v°* &c.); bearing along (said of rivers), Hcat.; bearing (a name), Kull. on Mn. iv, 203 (in a quotation); exposing one's self to (heat &c.), MBh.; m. the act of bearing or conveying (cf. *dur-*, *sukha-v°*); the shoulder of an ox or any draught animal, AV.; VS.; Br.; MBh.; the shoulder-piece of a yoke, AV.; ŚBr.; a horse, L.; a male river, L.; a road, way, L.; wind, L.; the breathing of a cow, L.; a weight or measure of four Droṇas, L.; (*ā*), f. a river, stream in general, L. **-m-liha**, mf(*ā*)n. licking the shoulder, Hcar. (cf. Pāṇ. iii, 2, 32). **-rāvin**, mfn. groaning under a yoke, AitBr. (Sāy.)

Vahát, f. (prob.) a vessel, ship, RV. iii, 7, 4 (Sāy. 'a stream').

Vahata, m. an ox, L.; a traveller, L.

Vahati, m. (only L.) wind; a friend; an ox; (*ī*), f. a river.

Vahatú, m. the bridal procession (to the husband's house), nuptial ceremony, RV.; AV.; AitBr. (pl. the objects constituting a bride's dowry, TBr.); means of furthering, RV. vii, 1, 17 (= *stotra* and *śastra*, Sāy.); an ox, L.; a traveller, L.

Vahad-gu, ind. (pr. p. of √*vah* + *go*) at the time when the oxen are yoked, g. *tishṭhad-gv-ādi*.

Váhadhyai. See √1. *vah*, col. 2.

Vahana, mfn. bearing, carrying, conveying (see *rāja-v°*); n. the act of bearing, carrying, conveying, bringing, MBh.; Kāv.; VarBṛS.; the flowing (of water), Nir. vi, 2; a ship, vessel, boat, Kathās.; the undermost part of a column, VārBṛS.; a square chariot with a pole, L. **-bhaṅga**, m. shipwreck, Ratnâv.; Kathās.

Vahanī-√kṛi, P. *-karoti*, to turn into a vehicle, Kathās.

Vahanīya, mfn. to be carried or borne or drawn or conducted, Vop.

Vahanta, m. air, wind, L.; an infant, L.

Vahantī, f. (of pr. p. of √1. *vah*) flowing water, TS.; Kāṭh.; ŚrS.

Vahalá, mf(*ā*)n. accustomed to the yoke, broken in, ŚBr.; n. a ship, L. (prob. w.r. for *vahana*).

Váhas, n. the shoulder of a draught animal, ŚBr. (v.l. for *vahá*).

Vahi, m. (artificial) N. of a Piśāca, MBh.

Vahikā. See *rāja-v°*.

Vahitra, n. 'instrument of conveying,' a boat, vessel, Git. (also °*traka*, L.); a square chariot with a pole, L. **-karṇa**, m. N. of a partic. Yoga posture (in which the two legs are stretched out together in front on the ground), L. (cf. *maraṇḍalasa*). **-bhaṅga**, m. shipwreck, Sāh.

Vahin, mfn. bearing the yoke, drawing well, TBr.; ŚrS.; m. an ox, L.

Váhishṭha, mfn. (superl.) drawing or driving or carrying best, swiftest, RV.; PañcavBr.

Váhīyas, mfn. (compar.) drawing or driving or carrying better, swifter, RV.; ShaḍvBr.

Váhni, m. any animal that draws or bears along, a draught animal, horse, team, RV.; AV.; VS.; TBr.; any one who conveys or is borne along (applied to a charioteer or rider, or to various gods, esp. to Agni, Indra, Savitṛi, the Maruts &c.), RV.; AV.; N. of Soma (as 'the flowing or streaming one'), RV. ix, 9, 6 &c.; the conveyer or bearer of oblations to the gods (esp. said of Agni, 'fire,' or of the three sacrificial fires, see *Agni*), RV.; a partic. fire, Gṛihyas.; fire (in general or 'the god of fire'), Mn.; MBh. &c. (*vahninā saṃ-√skṛi*, to hallow by fire, burn solemnly); the fire of digestion, VarBṛS.; N. of the number 'three' (fr. the three sacred fires), L.; N. of various plants (accord. to L. Plumbago Ceylanica; Semecarpus Anacardium; Poa Cynosuroides; and the citron tree), Suśr.; a mystical N. of the letter *r*, Up.; N. of the 8th Kalpa (q.v.), Cat.; of a Daitya, MBh.; of a son of Kṛishṇa, BhP.; of a son of Turvasu, ib.; of a son of Kukura, ib. **—kanyā,** f. a daughter of the god of fire, Hariv. (pl.) **—kara,** mfn. making fire, igniting, lighting, W.; promoting digestion, stomachic, L.; (*ī*), f. Grislea Tomentosa, L. **—kārya,** mfn. to be performed or achieved through fire, VarYogay. **—kāshṭha,** n. a kind of Agallochum used as incense, L. **—kuṇḍa,** n. a pit in the ground for receiving the sacred fire, Kathās. **—kumāra,** m. pl. (with Jainas) a partic. class of gods, L. **—kṛit,** mfn. causing a fire, VarBṛS. **—koṇa,** m. the south-east quarter, Pañcar. **—kopa,** m. the raging of fire, a conflagration, VarBṛS. **—gandha,** m. the resin of Shorea Robusta, L.; incense, W. **—garbha,** m. a bamboo, L.; a partic. Gaṇa of Siva, Harav.; (*ā*), f. Mimosa Suma, L. **—gṛiha,** n. a fire-chamber, VarBṛS. **—cakrā,** f. Methonica Superba, Bhpr. **—caya,** m. a fire-place, hearth, Kāty. **—cūḍa,** n. = *sthūpaka* (?), L. **—jāyā,** f. the wife of Vahni (called Svāhā), Sarvad. **—jvāla,** m. N. of a hell, VP.; (*ā*), f. Grislea Tomentosa, Bhpr. **—tama** (*váhni-*), mfn. carrying or leading best, VS.; bearing an oblation (to the gods) in the best manner, PraśnUp.; most luminous, brightest, MW. **—taskara-pārthiva,** m. pl. fire and thieves and the king, MW. **—da,** mfn. giving heat (to the body), Suśr. **—dagdha,** mfn. burned, ŚārṅgS. **—damanī,** f. Solanum Jacquini, L. **—dāha-samudbhava,** mfn. produced by burning, MW. **—dīpaka,** m. safflower, L.; (*ikā*), f. = *aja-modā*, L. **—daivata,** mfn. having Agni for a deity, MBh. **—dhauta,** mfn. pure like fire, Siṅhās. (cf. *-śuddha*). **—nāman,** m. 'called after fire,' the marking-nut plant, W.; lead-wort, ib. **—nāśana,** mfn. extinguishing the heat (of the body), Suśr. **—nī,** f. Nardostachys Jatamansi, L. **—netra,** m. 'having 3 eyes,' N. of Śiva, L. **—patana,** n. 'entering the fire,' self-immolation, Mālatīm. **—purāṇa,** n. N. of a Purāṇa (= *agni-p°*). **—pushpī,** f. Grislea Tomentosa, L. **—priyā,** f. the wife of Fire (called Svāhā), Hariv. **—bīja,** n. 'fire-seed,' gold, L.; a citron-tree, L.; a N. of the mystical syllable *ram* (repeated as the peculiar Mantra of fire in the Tantra system), RāmatUp.; RTL. 197. **—bhaya,** n. danger of fire, conflagration, VarBṛS.; *-da*, mfn. bringing danger of fire, ib. **—bhogya,** n. 'that which is to be consumed by fire,' ghee or clarified butter, L. **—mat,** mfn. containing fire, Tarkas; *-tva*, n., ib. **—mantha,** m. the tree Premna Spinosa (the wood of which when rubbed produces fire). L. **—maya,** mf(*ī*)n. consisting of fire, Hcar.; Kuval. **—māraka,** mfn. destroying fire; n. water, L. **—mitra,** m. 'f°-friend,' air, wind, L. **—rasa,** m. a partic. mixture, Cat. **—retas,** m. 'fire-semen,' N. of Śiva, L. **—rohiṇī,** f. a kind of disease, Suśr.; ŚārṅgS. **—lakshaṇa,** n. N. of wk. **—loka,** m. the world of Agni, Cat. **—loha** or **-lohaka,** n. 'fire-like iron,' copper, W.; (°*haka*), white brass, L. **—vaktrā,** f. Methonica Superba, Bhpr. **—vat,** mfn. containing the word *vahni*, AitBr. **—vadhū,** f. the wife of Agni (Svāhā), L. **—varṇa,** mfn. fire-coloured; n. a flower of the red water-lily, L. **—vallabha,** m. 'fire-favourite,' resin, L.; (*ā*), f. the wife of Agni, Pañcar. **—veśa,** m. N. of a physician, = *agni-v°*, Car. **—śālā,** f. a fire-chamber, MārkP. **—śikha,** n. safflower, L.; saffron, L.; Echites Dichotoma, MW.; (*ā*), f. a flame, L.; Methonica Superba, L.; Grislea Tomentosa, L.; Commelina Salicifolia and other species, L. (v.l. for *bahu-ś°*). **—śikhara,** m. Celosia Cristata, L. **—śuddha,** mfn. pure as fire, Pañcar. **—śekhara,** n. saffron, L. **—saṃskāra,** m. the religious rite of cremation (of a corpse), Kathās. **—sakha,** m. 'fire-friend,' the wind, L.; cumin, L. **—saṃjñaka,** m. = *citraka*, q.v., MW. **—sākshikam,** ind. so that fire is or was witness, Kathās. **—suta,** m. chyle, L. **—sthāna,** n. a fire-place, hearth, Kāty. **—sphuliṅga,** m. a spark of fire, Vām. **Vahnīśvarī,** f. N. of Lakshmī, Pañcar. **Vahny-utpāta,** m. an igneous meteor, L.

Vahnika, m. heat, L.; mfn. hot, L.

Vahni-sāt-√kṛi, P. *-karoti*, to consume with fire, burn, Veṇis.

Vahnīya, Nom. Ā. °*yate*, to become fire, Nalac.

Vahyá, mfn. fit to bear or to be borne or to draw or to be drawn &c., ĀśvŚr.; (*ā*), f. the wife of a Muni, L.; n. a portable bed, litter, palanquin, AV. **—śīvan,** mf(*arī*)n. reclining on a couch or palanquin, AV.

Vahyaka, mfn. = *vahya*; m. a draught animal, KātyŚr.; (*ā*), f. N. of a woman, g. *tikâdi*.

Vahyaska, m. N. of a man, g. *bidâdi*.

Vahye-śayá, mf(*ā*)n. = *vahya-śīvan*, RV.

वहिस् *vahís.* See *bahís.*

वहीनर *vahīnara.* See *bahīnara.*

वहेडक *vahedaka*, m. Terminalia Belerica, KātyŚr., Sch. (cf. *baheṭaka*).

वह्नि *vahni* &c. See p. 933, col. 3.

वह्लि *vahli, vahlika* &c. See *balhi.*

वा 1. *vā*, ind. or (excluded, like the Lat. *ve*, from the first place in a sentence, and generally immediately following, rarely and only m.c. preceding, the word to which it refers), RV. &c. &c. (often used in disjunctive sentences; *vā—vā*, 'either'—'or,' 'on the one side'—'on the other;' *na vā—vā* or *na—vā*, 'neither'—'nor;' *vā na—vā*, 'either not'—'or;' *yadi vā—vā*, 'whether'—'or;' in a sentence containing more than two members *vā* is nearly always repeated, although if a negative is in the first clause it need not be so repeated; *vā* is sometimes interchangeable with *ca* and *api*, and is frequently combined with other particles, esp. with *atha, athô, uta, kim, yad, yadi*, q.v. [e.g. *atha vā*, 'or else']; it is also sometimes used as an expletive); either—or not, optionally, KātyŚr.; Mn. &c. (in gram. *vā* is used in a rule to denote its being optional, e.g. Pāṇ. i, 2, 13; 35 &c.); as, like (= *iva*), PārGṛ.; MBh. &c.; just, even, indeed, very (= *eva*, laying stress on the preceding word), KātyŚr.; Kāv.; but even if, even supposing (followed by a future), Pañc. v, $\frac{38}{39}$; however, nevertheless, Bādar.; Bālar.; (after a rel. or interr.) possibly, perhaps, I dare say, MBh.; Kāv. &c. (e.g. *kim vā Śakuntalêty asya mātur ākhyā*, 'is his mother's name perhaps Śakuntalā?,' Śak. vii, $\frac{20}{21}$; *ko vā* or *ke vā* followed by a negative may in such cases be translated by 'every one, all,' e.g. *ke vā na syuḥ paribhava-padaṃ nishphalârambha-yatnāḥ*, 'everybody whose efforts are fruitless is an object of contempt,' Megh. 55).

वा 2. *vā*, cl. 2. P. (Dhātup. xxiv, 42) *vā́ti* (pf. *vavau*, Br.; MBh. &c.; aor. *avāsīt*, Br.; fut. *vāsyati*, Megh.; inf. *vātum*, Hariv.), to blow (as the wind), RV. &c. &c.; to procure or bestow anything (acc.) by blowing, RV. i, 89, 4; to blow towards or upon (acc.), MBh. xii, 2798; to emit an odour, be diffused (as perfume), ŚBr.; to smell (trans.), Vikr. iv, 41 (v.l.); to hurt, injure, Vop.: Caus. *vāpayati*, see *nir-√vā* and cf. *vājaya*: Desid. *vivāsati*, see √1. *van*. [Cf. Gk. ἄημι for ϝαημι; Lat. *ventus*; Slav. *vejati*; Goth. *waian, winds*; Germ. *wâjan, wæjen, wehen, Wind*; Angl.Sax. *wâwan*; Eng. *wind*.]

1. **Vāta,** mfn. (for 2. see p. 939, col. 3) blown &c.; (*vā́ta*), m. wind or the wind-god (pl. also 'the Maruts,' cf. *vāyu*), RV. &c. &c.; wind, air, Hit.; wind emitted from the body, MBh. iv, 117; wind or air as one of the humours of the body (also called *vāyu, māruta, pavana, anila, samīraṇa*), Kathās.; Suśr. &c.; morbid affection of the windy humour, flatulence, gout, rheumatism &c., VarBṛS.; Śṛiṅgār.; N. of a people (see *vāta-pati* and *vātâdhipa*); of a Rākshasa, VP.; of a son of Śūra, ib. **—kaṇṭaka,** m. a partic. pain in the ankle, Suśr.; ŚārṅgP. **—kara,** mfn. producing wind (in the body), causing flatulence, Bhpr. **—karman,** n. breaking wind, VarP. **—kalākalā,** f. the particles of w° or air distributed in the body (°*līya*, mfn. relating to them), Car. **—kuṇḍalikā** (Car.) or °**lī,** f. (Suśr.) scanty and painful flow of urine. **—kumbha,** m. the part of an elephant's forehead below the frontal sinuses, L. **—kṛit,** mfn. = *-kara*, Bhpr. **—ketu,** m. 'w°-sign,' dust, L. **—keli,** m. amorous sport or murmur, L.; = *shiḍgānām danta-lekhanam*, L.; the marks of finger-nails on a lover's person, W. **—kopana,** mfn. exciting w° (in the body), Suśr. **—kshobha,** m. disturbance or movement of w° (in the body), Kathās. **—khuḍakā,** f. a partic. rheumatic disease, Car. **—khuḍā,** f. = *vātyā, picchila-sphoṭa, vāmā*, and *vāta-śoṇita*, L. **—gajâṅkuśa,** m. a partic. drug, L. **—gaṇḍa,** mfn. relating to the company called *vāta-gaṇḍā*, Rājat.; (*ā*), f. N. of a partic. company or association, ib. **—gāmin,** m. 'wind-goer,' a bird, L. **—gulma,** m. 'w°-cluster,' a gale, high wind; acute gout or rheumatism, MārkP.; Suśr.; *-vat* (Vishṇ., Sch.), °*min* (Vishṇ.; Suśr.), suffering from the above disease. **—gopa** (*vā́ta-*), mfn. having the w° for a guardian, AV. **—grasta,** mfn. 'w°-seized,' epileptic or rheumatic, W. **—graha,** m. 'w°-seizure,' a partic. disease, Pañcar. **—ghna,** mf(*ī*)n. removing disorders of the w°, Suśr.; m. the shrub Hedysarum Gangeticum and other plants, L.; N. of a son of Viśvāmitra, MBh.; *-tvâdi-nirṇaya*, m. N. of wk. **—cakra,** n. 'w°-circle,' the circular markings of a compass, VarBṛS. **—codita** (*vā́ta-*), mfn. driven by the w°, RV. **—ja,** mfn. produced by w°, Suśr.; n. a kind of colic, Gal. **—java,** mfn. fleet as w°, MBh.; N. of a demon, Lalit. **—jā́,** mfn. arisen from w°, AV. **—jāma** (?), m. pl. N. of a people, MBh. **—jit,** mfn. = *-ghna*, Suśr. **—jūta** (*vā́ta-*), mfn. w°-driven, swift as w°, RV.; AV. **—jūti,** m. (with *vāta-raśana*, q.v.) N. of the author of RV. x, 136, 2, Anukr. **—jvara,** m. 'w°-fever,' fever arising from vitiated w°, Cat.; *-pratīkāra*, m. the remedying or counteraction of the above disease, MW. **—tūla,** n. cottony or flocculent seeds floating in the air, L. **—tejas** (*vā́ta-*), mfn. strong as w°, AV. **—trāṇa,** n. shelter from w°, Pāṇ. vi, 2, 8. **—tvish** (*vā́ta-*), mfn. impetuous as wind (said of the Maruts), RV. **—thuḍā,** w.r. for *-huḍā*. **—dhrāji-gati,** mfn. sweeping along like w°, TĀr. **—dhvaja,** m. 'wind-sign,' a cloud, L. **—nāmán,** n. pl. N. of partic. invocations of the wind (connected with partic. libations), TS.; ŚBr.; Kāṭh. **—nāśana,** mfn. = *-ghna*, Suśr. **—ṃ-dhama,** mfn. w°-blowing, Vop. **—paṭa,** m. 'wind-cloth,' a sail, Kathās. **—paṇḍa,** m. an impotent man or eunuch of a partic. kind, Dasar., Sch. (cf. *vātaka-piṇḍaka*). **—pati,** m. 'lord of the Vātas,' N. of a son of Sattra-jit, Hariv. **—patnī** (*vā́ta-*), f. the Wind's wife, AV. **—paryāya,** m. a partic. inflammation of the eyes, Suśr. **—pāta,** m. a gust of wind, L. **—pā́na,** n. 'shelter from wind (?),' a partic. part of a garment, TS. **—pālita,** m. N. of Go-pālita, Uṇ. iv, 1, Sch. **—pitta,** n. 'wind-bile,' a form of rheumatism, W.; *-ja*, mfn. arising from the w° and from the b°, GāruḍaP.; (*-ja-śūla*, n. a form of the disease called *śūla*, ib.); *-jvara*, m. a fever arising from the w° and from the b°, Cat. **—pittaka,** mfn. arising from the w° and from the b°, ŚārṅgS. **—putra,** m. 'son of the Wind,' N. of Bhīma, L.; of Hanumat, L.; a cheat, swindler, L. **—pū́,** mfn. (prob.) purified by the wind, AV. **—potha** or **-pothaka,** m. the tree Butea Frondosa, L. **—prakopa,** m. (in medicine) excess of wind, MW. **—prabala,** mfn. (in medicine) having an excess of wind, ib. **—pramī** (*vā́ta-*), mfn. outstripping the wind, RV. iv, 58, 7; m. a kind of antelope, L.; a horse, L.; an ichneumon, L. **—prameha,** m. a kind of urinary disease (cf. *vāta-meha*); *-cikitsā*, f. N. of a medical wk. **—phullântra,** n. 'air-inflated organ,' the lungs, L. (colic, flatulence, W.) **—balāsa,** m. a kind of disease, Cat. **—bahula,** mfn. causing flatulence, VarBṛS. **—bhaksha,** mfn. feeding on wind, R. **—bhrajas** (*vā́ta-*), mfn. (prob.) w.r. for *vāta-dhrajas*, following the course of the w°, AV. i, 12, 1. **—m-aja,** mfn. wind-driving, swift as w°, Bhaṭṭ.; m. an antelope, L. **—maṇḍalī,** f. 'w°-circle,' a whirlwind, L. **—maya,** mf(*ī*)n. consisting of w°, MaitrUp., Sch. **—mṛiga,** m. a kind of antelope, L. **—meha,** m. a kind of rheumatic urinary disease, Car. **—yantra,** n. 'wind-machine,' an apparatus for ventilating, ib.; *-vimānaka*, n. a mechanical car or other vehicle driven by the w°, Kathās. **—raṃha,** mfn. = next, MBh. **—raṃhas** (*vā́ta-*), mfn. fleet as w°, RV.; MBh. &c. **—rakta,** m. w° (in the body) and blood, Suśr.; acute gout or rheumatism (ascribed to a vitiated state of w° and blood), ib. (cf. *-śoṇita*); *-ghna*, m. 'gout-destroyer,' Blumea Lacera, L.; °*târi*, m. 'enemy of gout,' Cocculus Cordifolius, L. **—raṅga,** m. the holy fig-tree (= *aśvattha*), MW. **—rajju,** f. pl. the bands or fetters of the winds, MaitrUp., Sch. **—ratha,** mfn. w°-borne (as odour), BhP.; m. a cloud, L. **—raśana** (*vā́ta-*), mfn. wind-girt, having (only) air for a girdle (said of Munis and Ṛishis), RV.; TĀr.; m. a naked monk (= *dig-ambara, dig-vāsas*), BhP.; patr. of seven Ṛishis (viz. of Ṛishya-śṛiṅga, Etaśa, Karikrata, Jūti, Vāta-jūti, Vipra-jūta, and Vṛishāṇaka), RAnukr. **—rūpā,** f. N. of a female demon (the daughter of Likā), MārkP. **—rūsha,** m. (only L.) a gale, storm; a rainbow; = *utkoca* or *utkaṭa*. **—recaka,** m. a gust of wind, Hariv.; an empty boaster, braggart, MBh. **—reṇu-suvarṇa,** mfn. (said of a cow), Hcat. **—roga,** m. 'wind-disease,' any disease supposed to arise from a diseased state of the wind in the body (e.g. gout, rheumatism, paralysis &c.), Suśr.; ŚārṅgS.; *-hara-prâyaścitta*, n. N. of wk.; °*gin*, mfn. suffering from gout or rheumatism &c., VarBṛS. **—rddhi** (for *-ṛiddhi*), m. (also written *vātardi*) a sort of cup made

of wood and iron, (or) a wooden vessel with an iron stand, L.; a mace or iron-bound club, W. **-vat**, mfn. windy, gusty, Pāṇ. v, 2, 129, Sch. (cf. *vātā-vat*); m. N. of a man (cf. *vātavata*; *dṛiti-vātavator ayanam*, N. of a Sattra, PañcavBr.) **-varsha**, m. (sg. and pl.) rain and wind, Pañcat.; Rājat. **-vasti**, f. suppression of urine, Suśr.; ŚārṅgS. **-vaha**, m. N. of a village (°*haka*, mfn.), Pat. **-vikāra**, m., °**rin**, mfn. = *-roga*, °*gin*, Suśr. **-vṛiddhi**, f. swelled testicle, W. **-vṛishṭi**, f. = *-varsha*, VarBṛS. **-vega**, mfn. 'fleet as wind,' N. of a son of Dhṛita-rāshṭra, MBh.; of Garuḍa, ib. **-veṭaka**, v.l. for *-recaka*, MBh. **-vairin**, m. 'enemy of wind-disease,' the castor-oil tree &c., L. (cf. *vātāri*). **-vyādhi**, m. = *-roga*, Suśr.; *-karma-prakāśa*, m. N. of wk.; *-cikitsā*, f., *-nidāna*, n. the cure of any morbid affection of the w°, MW. **-śīrsha**, n. 'wind-source,' the lower belly, L. **-śukra-tva**, n. a morbid state of the semen (also in women), MārkP. **-śūla**, n. 'w°-pain,' colic with flatulence, Suśr. **-śoṇita**, n. diseased state of w° and blood, Suśr.; °*taka*, mf(*ī*)n. applied in that disease, Car.; °*tin*, mfn. suffering from it, Cat. **-śleshma-jvara**, m. a fever ascribed to the w° and phlegm, ib. **-sakha**, mfn. (fire) having w° as friend or companion, BhP. **-saṃcāra**, m. hiccough, L. **-saha**, mf(*ā*)n. bearing or enduring the wind (as a ship), MBh.; suffering from gout or rheumatism, L. **-sārathi**, m. 'having the Wind as charioteer,' Agni or Fire, L. **-suta**, m. a dissolute companion of a king or of a courtezan who knows one art (*kalā*), L. (cf. *-putra*). **-skandha**, m. 'wind-region,' the quarter from which the w° blows (seven are enumerated), R.; N. of a Ṛishi, MBh. **-svana** (*vāta-*), mfn. sounding like w°, RV. (also °*nas*); m. N. of a mountain, MārkP. **-hata**, mfn. smitten by the w° (with *vartman*, n. a partic. disease of the eyelid), Suśr.; mad, Buddh. **-han**, mfn. = *-ghna*, Suśr.; (*-ghnī*), f. Physalis Flexuosa, L.; Desmodium Gangeticum, L.; Sida Cordifolia, L.; a species of shrub (= *śimṛiḍī*), L. **-hara**, mfn. = *-ghna*, Suśr. **-hudā**, f. = *-khudā* (with v.l. *rāja-śoṇita* for *vāta-ś°*), L. **-homá**, m. air-oblation (offered with the hollowed hand), ŚBr.; Kāṭh. **Vātâkhya**, n. a house with two halls (one looking south and the other east), VarBṛS. **Vātâgara** (*āgara* prob. for *āgāra*), g. *utkarâdi* (°*rīya*, mfn., ib.) **Vātâgrá**, n. the point of the w°, TS. **Vātâṭa**, m. 'wind-goer,' a horse of the sun, L.; an antelope, L. **Vātâṇḍa**, m. swelling of the testicles (mfn. suffering from it), L. **Vātâtapika**, mfn. occurring in w° and sunshine, Car. **Vātâtisāra**, m. dysentery produced by vitiated w°, MW. **Vātâtmaka**, mfn. having a rheumatic nature, Car. **Vātâtmaja**, m. 'son of the Wind,' patr. of Hanu-mat, R.; of Bhīma-sena, MBh. **Vātâtman**, mfn. having the nature of wind or air, airy, Mahidh. **Vātâda**, m. 'air-eater,' a kind of animal, Car.; the almond tree, L. (cf. *bādāma*). **Vātâdhipa**, m. = *vāta-pati*, MBh. **Vātâdhvan**, m. 'wind-way,' air-hole, a round window, BhP. (cf. 1. *vātāyana*). **Vātânulomana** or °**min**, mfn. forcing the w° in the right direction or downwards (as in inflating the lungs), Suśr. **Vātā-parjanyá**, m. du. w° and rain (or the gods Vāta and Parjanya), RV. x, 66, 10. **Vātâpaha**, mfn. = *vāta-ghna*, Suśr. **Vātâpi**, mfn. (*âpi* fr. *ā-√pyai*) w°-swelled, fermenting, RV. i, 187, 8; m. (fr. *āpi*, 'friend, ally') 'having the w° as an ally,' N. of an Asura (son of Hrāda; he is said to have been devoured by the Muni Agastya), MBh.; R. &c. (also °*pin*); (*ī*), f. N. of a town (also called °*pi-purī*), Inscr.; *-dvish*, *-sūdana* or *-han*, m. N. of Agastya, L. **Vātâpya**, mfn. = *vātâpa*, RV.; n. swelling, fermentation, ib. **Vātâbhra**, n. a w°-driven cloud, Inscr. **Vātâmodā**, f. musk, L. 1. **Vātâyana**, mfn. (for 2. see col. 2) moving in the w° or air, MBh.; m. 'moving or fleet as w°,' a horse, L.; n. 'w°-passage,' a window, air-hole, loop-hole, Kāv.; Kathās. &c.; a balcony, portico, terrace on the roof of a house, Vcar.; Kathās. &c. (*-valabhī*, VarBṛS., Sch.); *-gata*, mfn. gone to or being at a window, R.; *-cchidra-rajas* or *-rajas*, n. a partic. measure of magnitude (= 7 Truṭis), Lalit.; *-stha*, mfn. standing or being at the window, MW. **Vātâri**, m. 'enemy of w°-disease,' N. of various plants (esp. Ricinus Communis; Asparagus Racemosus; Ptychotis Ajowan; Embelia Ribes &c.), L.; *-taṇḍulā*, f. Embelia Ribes, L. **Vātâlī**, f. a whirlwind, gale, Kathās. **Vātá-vat**, mfn. windy, airy, TS.; Br.; m. N. of a man (cf. *vātāvata*, col. 2). **Vātâvalī**, f. = *vātâlī*, Ratnâv. **Vātâśa** or °**śin**, m. 'w°-eater,' a serpent, Kāv.; Rājat. **Vātâśva**, m. a horse swift as the wind, Kathās. **Vātâshṭhīlā**, f. 'w°-globe,' a hard globular swelling in the lower belly, Car. **Vātā-saha**, mfn. = *vāta-s°*, rheumatic, gouty, L. **Vātâsṛij** or **vātâsra**, n. a partic. class of diseases (= *vāta-rakta*, q.v.), Bhpr. **Vātâhata**, mfn. stirred or shaken by the w° (*-nau*, f. a ship tossed by the w°), MW.; struck by w°-disease, affected by rheumatism, W. **Vātâhati**, f. 'w°-stroke,' a violent gust of w°, Kathās.; an attack of rheumatism or gout, W. **Vātâhāra**, mfn. one who feeds only on air, L. **Vātâika-bhaksha**, mfn. feeding only on air, fasting, Ml. **Vātêśvara-tīrtha**, n. N. of a Tīrtha, Cat. **Vātôttha**, mfn. = *vāta-ja*, Suśr. **Vātôdarin**, mfn. 'wind-bellied,' having the belly swollen from flatulence, ib. **Vātôna**, mfn. deficient in w° or windy humour, MW.; (*ā*), f. a species of plant, L. (v.l. *pratānā*). **Vātôpajūta**, mfn. = *vāta-jūta*, MW. **Vātôpadhūta**, mfn. shaken or impelled by the w°, RV. x, 91, 7. **Vātôpasṛishṭa**, mfn. affected with w°-disease, rheumatic, gouty &c., Suśr. **Vātôrmi**, f. a wave moved by the wind, Chandom.; a kind of metre, ib.

Vātaka, m. Marsilea Quadrifolia, L. **-piṇḍaka**, m. an impotent man (born without testicles), Car. (cf. *vāta-paṇḍa*).

Vātaki, m. N. of a man, g. *kurv-ādi*.

Vātakin, mfn. suffering from wind-disease, rheumatic, gouty, Pāṇ. v, 2, 129.

Vātakya, m. patr. fr. *vātaki*, g. *kurv-ādi*.

Vātaya, Nom. P. °*yati* (cf. √2. *vāt* and Dhātup. xxxv, 30), to fan, ventilate, Kāś.

Vātara, mfn. windy, stormy, W.; swift as the wind, ib.

Vātarāyaṇa, m. pl. N. of a partic. school (cf. next); (only L.) an arrow; arrow's flight, bow-shot; a saw; a mountain peak; a madman; an idler; the Sarala tree.

Vātarāyaṇīya, m. pl. N. of a partic. school, AV.Paipp.

Vātala, mf(*ā*)n. windy, stormy (= *vātula*), L.; flatulent, Suśr.; m. a sort of pulse, Cicer Arietinum, L.; (*ā*), f. (with or scil. *yoni*) a morbid state of the uterus, Suśr.; ŚārṅgS. **-maṇḍalī**, f. a whirlwind, L.

Vātavata, m. patr. fr. *vāta-vat*, PañcavBr.

2. **Vātāyana**, m. (for 1. see above, col. 1) patr. of Anila and Ulu, RAnukr. (also pl., Pravar.); a partic. school of the Sāma-veda, Āryav.; N. of a chamberlain, Śak.; pl. N. of a people, MBh.

Vātāyu, m. an antelope, L.

Vātāvata, m. patr. fr. *vātā-vat*, AitBr.

Vāti, m. (only L.) air, wind; the sun; the moon.

Vātika, mf(*ī*)n. windy, stormy, L.; affected by wind-disease, rheumatic, L.; exciting or allaying wind (in the body), Pat.; produced by or proceeding from disorder of the wind, Suśr.; mad, MW.; m. a man of mere words, noisy talker, flatterer, MBh.; a juggler or conjurer, MBh.; Hcar.; a person who cures poison, dealer in antidotes, L.; the bird Cātaka, Sāh. (cf. *vātīka*); N. of an attendant of Skanda, MBh. **-khaṇḍa**, m. N. of a pass leading to lake Mānasa, MBh. **-piṇḍaka**, m. = *vātaka-p°*, Car. **-shaṇḍa**, m. = *-khaṇḍa*, MBh. (B.)

Vātiga, mfn. acquainted with or working in minerals, L.; m. a mineralogist, metallurgist, or = next, L. **-gama**, m. Solanum Melongena, L. **-mgaṇa**, m. id., L.

Vātī, in comp. for 1. *vāta*. **-kārá**, m. a partic. disease of the eyes, AV. **-kṛita** (*vātī-*), n. id., ib.; *-nāśana*, mfn. curing the above disease, ib.

Vātīka, m. a kind of bird, Car. (cf. *vātika*).

Vātīya, mfn. windy, relating or belonging to wind &c., W.; sour rice-gruel, L.

Vātula, mfn. windy, L.; affected by wind-disease, gouty, rheumatic, W.; mad, crazy, Bhartṛ.; m. N. of certain leguminous plants causing flatulence, (Cicer Arietinum, Panicum Italicum &c.), L.; a whirlwind, gale, L.; n. N. of a Tantra, Hcat. (also written *vātūla* and *vāthula*). **-bhedâdika-tantra**, n., **-śuddhâgama**, m. N. of Tantric wks.

Vātulānaka, m. or n.(?) N. of a place, Rājat.

Vātuli, f. a large bat ('the flying fox'), L.

Vātūla, mf(*ā*)n. inflated with wind or affected with wind-disease, gouty, rheumatic &c., L.; mad, insane, Rājat.; (ifc.) entirely devoted to or bent upon, HPariś.; m. a whirlwind, gale, hurricane, L.; N. of a Mantra(?), Pat.; n. N. of a Tantra (cf. *vātula*). **-sūtra**, n. N. of wk.

Vātūli-bhrama, m. a whirlwind, Nalac.

Vātṛi, m. 'blower,' air, wind, L.

Vātoka, m. N. of a poet, L.

1. **Vātya**, mfn. (for 2. see *sa-vātya*) being in the wind &c., VS.

Vātyā, f. a strong wind, gale, storm, hurricane, Kāv.; Kathās. &c. **-cakra**, n. a whirlwind, Veṇīs. **Vātyâupamya**, mfn. resembling a storm, BhP.

Vātyāya, Nom. Ā. °*yate*, to resemble a storm, Kathās.

1. **Vāna**, mfn. (for 2. see p. 940) blown &c. (cf. *nir-vāṇa*); n. blowing, L.; a perfume, fragrance, L.; living, ib.; going, moving, rolling, W.; the rolling of water or of the tide (esp. the high wave in Indian rivers, commonly called 'the Bore'), ib.

वांश *vāṅśa*, mf(*ī*)n. (fr. *vaṅśa*) relating or belonging to sugar-cane, Car.; made of bamboo, W.; (*ī*), f. bamboo-manna, Car.; Bhpr. **-kaṭhinika**, mfn. (fr. *vaṅśa-kaṭhina*) dealing in bamboo-poles, Pāṇ. iv, 4, 72, Sch. **-bhārika**, mfn. (fr. *vaṅśa-bhāra*) carrying a load of bamboos, Pāṇ. v, 1, 50.

Vāṅśika, mfn. = *vāṅśa-bhārika*, Pāṇ.ib.; m. a flute-player, piper, L.; a bamboo-cutter, W.

वाःकिटि *vāḥ-kiṭi*, *vāḥ-pushpa* &c. See under *vār*, p. 943, col. 1.

वाक *vāka*. See *bāka* and p. 936, col. 2.

वाकलराशि *vākala-rāśi*, m. N. of a Śaiva ascetic, Inscr.

वाकारकृत् *vākāra-kṛit*, m. N. of a man, Saṃskārak.

वाकिन *vākina*, m. N. of a man, Pāṇ. iv, 1, 158; (*ī*), f. N. of a Tantra deity, Cat. (cf. *ḍākinī*, *rākinī*, *lākinī*).

Vākinakāyani or **vākini**, m. patr. fr. *vākina*, Pāṇ. iv, 1, 158.

वाकुची *vākucī*, f. Vernonia Anthelmintica, L.

वाकुल *vākula*. See *bākula*.

वाकोपवाक *vākôpavāka* &c. See p. 936, col. 2.

वाक्कलह *vāk-kalaha* &c. See p. 936, col. 1.

वाक्य *vākya* &c. See p. 936, col. 2.

वागतीत *vāg-atīta* &c. See p. 936, col. 3.

वागर *vāgara*, m. (only L.) ascertainment; a scholar, Paṇḍit; a hero, brave man; one desirous of final emancipation; submarine fire; an obstacle; a wolf; = *vāṭa-veshṭaka*; = *śāṇa*.

वागा *vāgā*, f. a bridle, L. (prob. w.r. for *valgā*).

वागायन *vāgāyana*, m. patr., Saṃskārak. (cf. *vāgmāyana*).

वागु *vāgu*, (prob.) f. N. of a river, Cat.

वागुजि *vāguji* or *vāgujī*, f. = *vākucī*, L.

वागुञ्जार *vāguñjāra*, m. a species of fish, L.

वागुण *vāguṇa*, n. Averrhoa Carambola, L.

वागुरा *vāgurā*, f. a net (for catching deer or wild animals), trap, toils, snare, noose, MBh.; Kāv. &c. **-vṛitti**, mfn. one who lives by snaring animals, Mn. x, 32; f. livelihood obtained by snaring or catching animals, W.

Vāgura, m. the son of a Vaiśya and a Venī, L.; N. of a poet, Cat.

Vāguri, m. N. of a writer on medicine, Cat.

Vāgurika, m. a deer-catcher, hunter, Ragh.

वागुलि *vāguli* = *pati*, L.

वागुस *vāgusa*, m. a species of large fish, L.

वागोयान *vāgoyāna*, m. or n.(?) N. of a place, Kshitîś.

वाग्गुण *vāg-guṇa*, *vāg-guda* &c. See p. 936, col. 3.

वाघत् *vāghát*, m. (prob. fr. a √*vāgh* = *vāh* = *vah*; cf. Ved. inf. *vā́he*) the institutor of a sacrifice, RV. (accord. to Nigh. = *ṛitvij* or *medhāvin*).

वाघेल्ल *vāghella*, N. of a family, Cat.

वाङ्क *vāṅka*, m. (cf. √2. *vak*, and *vaṅka*) the ocean, sea, L.

वाङ्क्ष् *vāṅksh* (connected with √*vāñch*, cf. *kāṅksh*), cl. 1. P. *vāṅkshati*, to wish, desire, long for, Dhātup. xvii, 17.

वाङ्ग *vāṅga*, m. a king of the Vaṅgas, VarBṛS. (cf. Pāṇ. iv, 1, 170, Sch.); N. of a poet, Cat.

Vāṅgaka, m. a reverer of the Vaṅgas or of their king, Pāṇ. iv, 3, 100, Sch.

Vāṅgāri, m. patr., Pravar.

Vāṅgāla, m. (in music) a partic. Rāga, Saṃgīt.; (*ī*), f. a partic. Rāgiṇī, ib.

वाङ्निधन *vāṅ-nidhana, vāṅ-matī* &c. See p. 937, cols. 1 and 2.

वाच् *vāc*, f. (fr. √*vac*) speech, voice, talk, language (also of animals), sound (also of inanimate objects as of the stones used for pressing, of a drum &c.), RV. &c. &c. (*vācam* √*ṛi, īr*, or *ish*, to raise the voice, utter a sound, cry, call); a word, saying, phrase, sentence, statement, asseveration, Mn.; MBh. &c. (*vācaṃ* √*vad*, to speak words; *vācaṃ vyā-*√*hṛi*, to utter words; *vācam* √*dā* with dat., to address words to; *vācā satyaṃ* √*kṛi*, to promise verbally in marriage, plight troth); Speech personified (in various manners or forms, e.g. as Vāc Ambhṛiṇī in RV. x, 125; as the voice of the middle sphere in Naigh. and Nir.; in the Veda she is also represented as created by Prajā-pati and married to him; in other places she is called the mother of the Vedas and wife of Indra; in VP. she is the daughter of Daksha and wife of Kaśyapa; but most frequently she is identified with Bhāratī or Sarasvatī, the goddess of speech; *vācaḥ sāma* and *vāco vratam*, N. of Sāmans, ĀrshBr.; *vācaḥ stomaḥ*, a partic. Ekâha, ŚrS.) **-chalya**, w.r. for *vāk-ch*°, MBh. xii, 530.

Vāk, in comp. for *vāc*. **-kalaha**, m. 'speech-strife,' quarrel, dispute, Prab. **-kīra**, m. 'parrot or repeater of what has been said,' i.e. 'always officious or obliging (?),' a wife's brother, L. **-kūṭa**, m. N. of a poet, Sadukt. **-keli** or °**lī**, f. a word-jesting, witty conversation, Daśar.; Sāh.; Pratāp. **-koka**, m. N. of a poet, Sadukt. **-kshata**, n. injurious speech, MBh.; Pañcat. **-cakshus**, n. sg. speech and sight, Yājñ. **-capala**, mfn. talking flippantly or idly, a careless talker, Mn.; MBh. **-cāpalya**, n. flippancy of speech, idle talk, Yājñ. **-cít**, mfn. arranged in layers with certain formularies of speech, ŚBr. **-chala**, n. the mere semblance of a voice, Kād.; (sg. or pl.) untruthful talk, Hariv. (v.l.); Kathās.; prevarication or perversion of the words of an opponent in disputation, Nyāyas.; °*lônvita*, mfn. equivocating, evasive, W. **-chalya**, n. = *-śalya*, q.v., Hariv. **-tvaca**, n. sg. (said to be a Dvandva comp.), Pāṇ. v, 106, Sch. **-tvisha**, n. sg. (said to be a Dvandva comp.), ib. **-paṭu**, mfn. skilled in speech, eloquent, Hit.; ŚārṅgP.; Cāṇ.; *-tā*, f. or *-tva*, n. skill in sp°, eloquence, Kāv.; Hit. &c. **-páti**, m. a lord of sp°, VS.; Kāṭh. &c.; N. of Bṛihas-pati or the planet Jupiter, R.; Var. &c.; a master of sp°, eloquent man, L.; a Śaiva saint of a partic. degree of perfection, Bādar., Sch.; N. of a poet, Sadukt.; mf(*i* or *tnī*)n. eloquent, L.; *-rāja*, m. N. of a poet, Rājat.; ŚārṅgP. &c.; °*ja-deva*, m. N. of a king of Mālava, Inscr.; N. of a poet, Daśar., Sch. **-patí-ya** (TBr.) or **-patya** (Kāṭh.), n. mastery of speech. **-patha**, mfn. suitable or seasonable for discourse, W; m. an opportunity or moment fit for speech, MBh.; the compass or range of sp° (*vāk-patha-pāram avâpita*, passed beyond the range of speech, indescribable; *atīta-v*°, id.), Śiś.; Naish. **-pavitra** (*vā́k-*), mfn. having speech as a means of purifying, TS. **-pā́**, mfn. protecting sp°, TS.; AitBr. **-pāṭava**, n. skilfulness in sp°, eloquence, Cat.; *-nir-ukti*, f. N. of a Kāvya. **-pārushya**, n. harshness of sp°, ŚārṅgP.; abusive words, insulting or scurrilous language, Mn.; Pañcat. **-pushṭā**, f. N. of a princess, Rājat.; °*ṭāṭavī*, f. N. of a forest called after her, ib. **-pushpa**, n. pl. 'sp°-flowers,' high-soaring words, Hariv.; Kathās. **-pūta** (*vā́k-*), mfn. purified by sp°, MaitrS. **-pracodana**, n. a command expressed in words; (*āt*), ind. in consequence of a command, in obedience to an order, R. **-pratoda**, m. goading words, cutting or taunting language, R. **-pradā**, f. N. of the river Sarasvatī, L. **-pralāpa**, m. readiness of speech, eloquence, MBh. **-pravadishu**, mfn. coming forward as a speaker, ĀśvŚr. **-praśasta**, mfn. consecrated or declared pure by certain formularies of speech, Gaut. **-prasārin**, mfn. spreading out or exuberant in speech, eloquent; °*ri-kāma* (prob. w.r. for *-prasārikā-kāma* or *-prasāra-k*°), mfn. wishing that (a child) may advance in speaking, PārGṛ. **-śalākā**, f. 'pointed speech,' injurious speech, MBh. **-śalya**, n. 'sp°-dart,' injurious speech, MBh.; R.; Kathās. (cf. *-chalya*). **-śava-hū**, mfn. (said of a Saṃhitā), SaṃhUp. **-śasta**, mfn. = *-praśasta* above, Yājñ. **-saṃyama**, m. restraint or control of sp°, MBh. **-saṃvara**, m. restraint of sp°, caution in speaking, Lalit. (w.r. *vākya-vara*). **-saṅga**, m. sticking fast or impediment in speech, impeded or slow speech (of aged persons), MBh.; paralysis of speech, Suśr. **-sāyaka**, m. an arrow-like word, MBh.; Śiś. **-sāra**, m. vigour of sp°, eloquence, VarBṛS. **-siddha**, n. supernatural perfection in sp°, Pañcar. **-stambha**, m. paralysis of speech, Vāgbh.

Vāká, mfn. sounding, speaking (ifc.; cf. *cakra-v*°, *cīrī-v*°); m. (RV. &c.) or (*ā́*), f. (VS.; MaitrS.) a text, recitation or formula (in certain ceremonies), rite; m. pl. chattering, murmuring, humming, AV.; n. N. of various Sāmans, ĀrshBr. **Vākôpavāka**, n. speech and reply, dialogue, Sāh. **Vākovākyà**, n. id. (also N. of partic. Vedic texts), ŚBr.; ChUp. &c. (cf. IW. 295, n. 1).

Vākāṭaka, m. pl. N. of a family of princes, Inscr.

Vāku. See *kṛika-vā́ku* and *ni-vāku*.

Vākya, n. (ifc. f. *ā*) speech, saying, assertion, statement, command, words (*mama vākyāt*, in my words, in my name), MBh. &c. &c.; a declaration (in law), legal evidence, Mn.; an express decl° or statement (opp. to *liṅga*, 'a hint' or indication), Sarvad.; betrothment, Nār.; a sentence, period, RāmatUp.; Pāṇ., Vārtt. &c.; a mode of expression, Cat.; a periphrastic mode of expression, Pāṇ., Sch.; Siddh.; a rule, precept, aphorism, MW.; a disputation, MBh.; (in logic) an argument, syllogism or member of a syllogism; the singing of birds, Hariv.; (in astron.) the solar process in computations, MW. **-kaṇṭha**, mfn. one whose speech is in the throat, being on the point of speaking anything, MBh. **-kara**, mfn. (ifc.) executing the words or commands (of another), R. **-karaṇa-siddhânta**, m. N. of wk. **-kāra**, m. the author of (a Vedânta wk. called) Vākya, Sarvad. **-khaṇḍana**, n. refutation of an argument, W. **-garbhita**, n. insertion of a parenthesis, Pratāp. **-graha**, m. paralysis of speech, Suśr. **-candrikā**, f., **-tattva**, n. N. of wks. **-tas**, ind. conformably to the saying, MW. **-tā**, f. in *gadgada-v*°, a stammering utterance, Suśr. **-tva**, n. the being a word or speech, Sāy.; the consisting of words, Sarvad.; the being a sentence or period, Sāh.; (ifc.) pronunciation, Suśr. **-dīpikā**, f. N. of wk. **-dhṛik**, mfn. having a commission from any one (gen.), R. **-pañcâdhyāyī**, f. N. of wk. **-pada**, n. a word in a sentence, MW.; (*ī*), f. N. of wk. **-padīya**, n. N. of a celebrated wk. on the science of grammar by Bhartṛi-hari (divided into Brahma-kāṇḍa or Āgama-samuccaya, Vākya-kāṇḍa, Pada-kāṇḍa or Prakīrṇaka). **-paddhati**, f. the manner or rule of constructing sentences, MW. **-pūraṇa**, mfn. the filling up of a sentence, Nir. **-prakaraṇa**, n., **-prakāśa**, m. N. of wks. **-pradīpa**, w.r. for *-padīya*, q.v., Cat. **-prabandha**, m. connected flow of words, connected composition or narrative, Dhātup. **-prayoga**, m. employment or application of speech or language, W. **-bheda**, m. difference of assertion, Jaim.; division of a sentence (*vākya-bhedād a-nighātaḥ*, because there is a division of the sentence there is no grave [but an acute] accent), Ml.; pl. contradictory statements, Mudr.; *-vāda*, m. N. of wk. **-mañjarī**, f. N. of sev. wks. **-mālā**, f. connection or sequence of several sentences, Kāvyâd.; N. of a Comm. **-racanā**, f. formation of speech, speaking, talking, R., Sch.; the arrangement or construction of sentences, syntax, MW. **-ratna**, n. N. of wk. **-vajra**, n. (sg. or pl.) words which fall like a thunderbolt, crushing words, strong language, R.; *-vishama*, mfn. rough or harsh (through the use of such words), BhP. **-vara**, w.r. for *vāk-saṃvara*, q.v., Lalit. **-vāda**, m. N. of sev. wks. **-vinyāsa**, m. the arrangement or order of a sentence, syntax, W. **-vivaraṇa**, n. N. of wk. **-viśārada**, mfn. skilled in speech, eloquent, W. **-viśesha**, m. a particular or special statement, W. **-vṛitti**, f., °**ti-prakāśikā**, f., °**ti-vyākhyā**, f. N. of wks. **-śalākā**, f. = *vāk-ś*°, q.v., MBh. **-śesha**, m. 'speech-remainder (in an ellipsis),' the part of a sentence which is wanting and has to be supplied, the words needed to complete an elliptical sentence (also *-tva*, n.), Jaim.; ĀpŚr., Sch.; Vikr. **-śruti**, f. (with *aparokshânubhūti*) N. of wk. **-saṃyoga**, m. grammatical construction, Nir. **-saṃkīrṇa**, n. confusion of two sentences, Pratāp. **-saṃgraha**, m., **-sāra**, m. or n. N. of wks. **-sārathi**, m. a chief speaker, spokesman, R. **-siddhânta-stotra**, n., **-sudhā**, f. N. of wks. **-stha**, mfn. (ifc.) attentive to words, obsequious, Suśr.; = next, W. **-sthita**, mfn. being or contained in a sentence, ib.; attentive to what is said, MW. **-sphoṭa**, see *sphoṭa*. **-svara**, m. the accent in a word or sentence, Cat. **-hāriṇī**, f. a female messenger, f° m° of love, L. **Vākyâḍambara**, m. bombastic language, turgidity, Pratāp. **Vākyâdhyāhāra**, m. supplying what is wanting in a sentence, Pāṇ. **Vākyâmṛita**, n. N. of various wks. **Vākyârtha**, m. the meaning or contents of a sent°, VS.; Prāt., Sch.; Tarkas.; Kāvyâd.; *-candrikā*, f., *-darpaṇa*, *-dīpikā*, f., *-bodha*, m., *-viveka*, m. N. of wks.; °*thôpamā*, f. a simile in which the resemblance of two things is specified in detail, Kāvyâd. **Vākyâlaṃkāra**, m. ornament of speech, L. **Vākyâlāpa**, m. talking together, conversation, MW. **Vākyôpacāra**, m. practice or employment of words, speaking, R.

Vāksha-sád, mfn. (in a formula; accord. to Sch. *vāksha* = *vāc*), TS.

Vāg, in comp. for *vāc*. **-atīta**, m. a partic. mixed caste, Cat. **-adhipa**, m. 'lord of speech,' N. of Bṛihas-pati, Kir. **-anta**, m. the end or pitch of voice, the highest voice, KātySr.; mfn. ending with *vāc*, ib. **-apahāraka**, mfn. 'word-stealer,' one who appropriates to himself what has been spoken or written by others, a reader of prohibited works or passages, Mn.; Yājñ. **-apêta**, mfn. destitute of speech, dumb, KaushUp. **-artha**, m. du. a word and its sense (between which, accord. to the Mīmāṃsā, there is an eternal connection), Ragh. **-asi**, m. 'speech-sword,' sharp or cutting sp°, W. **-āḍambara**, m. boastful or bombastic language, Śiś., Sch. **-ātman**, mfn. consisting of words, Uttarar. **-ādipitrya**, n. (with *ṛitūnām*) N. of a Sāman, ĀrshBr. **-ālambana**, n. depending on mere words or on some merely verbal difference, MW. **-āśīrdatta**, m. N. of a man, Pāṇ. v, 3, 84, Vārtt. 3, Pat. **-indra**, m. N. of a son of Prakāśa, MBh. **-īśa**, mfn. one who is a master of language, eloquent, an orator, author, poet &c. (frequently at the end of names of scholars), MBh.; Kāv.; N. of Bṛihas-pati or the planet Jupiter, VarBṛS.; of Brahmā, Kum.; BhP.; (also with *bhaṭṭâcārya*) N. of various authors, Cat.; (*ā*), f. N. of Sarasvatī, Sāy.; *-tīrtha*, m. N. of a scholar, Cat.; *-tva*, n. mastery of language, eloquence, Pañcar. **-īśvara**, m. a master of language, an orator, GāruḍaP.; Pañcar.; (with Buddhists) a deified sage (= Mañju-ghosha), MW.; N. of Brahmā, L.; of a Jina, Buddh.; (also with *bhaṭṭa*) of various authors, Sarvad.; Cat.; (*ī*), f. N. of Sarasvatī, Cat.; *-kīrti*, m. N. of a teacher, Buddh.; *-stotra*, n. N. of a Stotra; °*rī-datta*, m. N. of an author, Cat.; °*rī-stotra*, n. N. of a Stotra. **-uttara**, n. the last word, end of a speech, MBh.; speech and reply, MW. **-ṛishabha**, m. any one eminent in speech, an eloquent man; *-tva*, n. eminence in speaking, eloquence, R. **-guṇa**, m. excellence of speech, L. **-guda**, m. a kind of bat or bird, Mn. xii, 64. **-gumpha**, m. pl. 'word-weaving,' artificial language, Cat. **-guli** or °**lika**, m. the betel-bearer (of a king or prince &c.), L. **-ghastavat** (*vāc* + *hasta*), mfn. possessed of speech and hands, Pañcat.; Hit. **-jāla**, n. a confused mass or multitude of words, Śiś. **-jyotis** (*vā́g-*), mfn. receiving light or enlightenment by sp°, ŚBr. **-ḍambara**, m. n. loud-sounding or boastful language, grandiloquence, Kāv.; graceful or eloquent language, MW. **-daṇḍa**, m. verbal rebuke or reprimand, reproof, admonition, Mn.; Yājñ.; du. insult and assault (°*ḍayoḥ pārushyam* or °*ḍa-pārushye*, violence both by words and blows, violence both of language and bodily assault), Mn.; Gaut.; Hit.; speech-control, restraint of sp°, Mn. xii, 10; *-ja*, mfn. arising from insulting lang° and bodily assault (with *pārushyam* see above), Mn. vii, 48. **-daṇḍaka**, (prob. m.) pl. long-extended speeches, Car. **-datta**, mf(*ā*)n. 'given by word of mouth,' promised, W.; (*ā*), f. a betrothed virgin, Kull. on Mn. v, 72. **-daridra**, mfn. poor in speech, of few words, L. **-dala**, n. 'speech-leaf,' a lip, L. **-dā**, mfn. bestowing voice (in a formula), ĀpŚr. **-dāna**, n. 'gift by word of mouth,' the promise or betrothment of a maiden in marriage, Siṇhâs.; Kull.; *-prayoga*, m. N. of wk. **-dur-ukta**, n. hard or injurious words, MBh. **-dushṭa**, mfn. speaking badly or ill; m. a rude or insulting speaker, Mn.; MBh.; Hariv.; = *vrātya*, an out-caste or a Brāhman who has passed the proper time of life without investiture with the sacred thread &c., L.; N. of a Brāhman, Hariv. **-devatā**, f. the divinity of speech, Sarasvatī, Vcar.; Sāh.; Tantras.; *-guru*, m. 'master of words,' N. of Kāli-dāsa, Piṅg., Sch. (in a quot.); *-stava*, m. N. of wk. **-devatāka**, mfn. sacred to Sarasvatī, Kull. on Mn. viii, 105. **-devatya**, mfn. consecrated to speech, ŚāṅkhŚr. **-devī**, f. the goddess of sp°, Sarasvatī, Kāv.; Rājat. &c.; *-kula*, n. science, learning, eloquence, MW. **-daivatya**, mfn. sacred to Sar°, Mn. viii, 105. **-dosha**, m. 'speech-fault,' speaking badly or ill, abusive or ungrammatical speech, W.; uttering a disagreeable sound, Hit. **-dvāra**, n. entrance to sp° (*kṛita-v°*, mfn. anything to the description of which a way has been facilitated), Ragh.; N. of a place, W. **-baddha**, mfn. suppressing sp°, saying nothing, silent, Kathās. **-bandhana**, n. the obstruction or suppression of sp°, silencing, silence (°*nam pra-√kṛi*, to silence), Amar. **-bali**, m. N. of a man, Cat. **-brāhmaṇa**, n. a Brāhmaṇa which treats of Vāc, AitĀr. **-bhaṅga**, m., v. l. for *vāk-saṅga* (q. v.) **-bhaṭa**, m. N. of a writer on rhetoric (author of the Vāg-bhaṭâlaṃkāra), Cat.; of a writer on medicine, ib.; of other authors and learned men, ib.; *-kośa* (?), m., *-śārīra-sthāna*, n., *-sūtra-sthāna*, n.; °*ṭâlaṃkāra*, m. N. of wks. **-bhaṭṭa**, w. r. for *-bhaṭa*, Cat.; *-maṇḍana*, n. N. of wk. **-bhūshaṇa-kāvya**, n. N. of wk. **-bhṛit**, mfn. bearing or supporting speech, ŚBr. **-manasa**, see *vāṅ-m°*. **-min**, mfn., see below. **-mūla**, see *vāṅ-m°*. **-yajña**, m. an offering made in words, Siṇhās. **-yata**, mfn. restrained in speech, reserved, silent, ŚāṅkhBr.; GṛŚrS. &c. **-yama**, m. one who has controlled his sp°, a sage, A. **-yamana**, n. restraint of speech, silence, ŚrS. **-yāma**, mfn. = *-yata*, Pāṇ. iii, 2, 40, Sch.; m. a dumb man, one silent from necessity, W. **-yuddha**, n. war of words, controversy, vehement debate or discussion, MW. **-yoga**, m. correct use of words, Pat. **-rodha**, m. = *-bandhana*, MW. **-vajra**, n. words which fall like a thunderbolt, violent or strong language, Śiksh.; R.; BhP.; mfn. one whose words are like thunderbolts, BhP. **-vaṭa**, m. N. of an author, Cat. **-vat**, mfn. having speech, connected with sp°, AitBr.; *-vatī-tīrtha-yātrā-prakāśa*, m. N. of wk. **-vada**, m. (prob.) a kind of bat, Gaut., Sch. (v. l. *valgu-da*). **-vāda**, m. N. of a man, Pāṇ. vi, 3, 109, Vārtt. 2, Pat. **-vādinī**, f. N. of a goddess, Cat.; *-stotra*, n. N. of a Stotra. **-vid**, mfn. skilled in speech, eloquent, Kāvyâd.; Śiś. **-vidagdha**, mfn. id. (*-tā*, f.), Vet.; (*ā*), f. a kindly-speaking or agreeable woman, MW. **-vidheya**, mfn. to be effected by (mere) words, to be recited from memory, R. **-vin**, mfn. eloquent, AV. **-viniḥsṛita**, mfn. emitted or put forth by speech, Mn. iv, 256. **-viprusha**, n. sg. (said to be a copulative comp.), Pāṇ. v, 4, 106, Sch. **-vibhava**, m. stock of words, power of description, command of language, Kāv. **-virodha**, m. verbal dispute, controversy, Hcat. **-vilāsa**, m. play of words, ŚārṅgP.; graceful or elegant speech, W. **-vilāsin**, m. a pigeon, dove, L. **-visarga**, m. the emitting of the voice, breaking of silence, speaking, Gobh.; BhP. **-visarjana**, n. id., KātyŚr. **-vistara**, m. prolixity, diffuseness, Hāsy. **-vīṇa**, m. N. of a poet, Sadukt. **-vīra**, m. a master of speech, MBh. **-vīrya** (*vā́g-*), mfn. vigorous in voice, TS. **-vyaya**, m. expenditure of words or sp°, waste of breath, MW. **-vyavahāra**, m. employment of many words, a long discussion or altercation, Mālav. **-vyāpāra**, m. the practice of speaking, talking, talk, Sāh.; Hit.; manner of speaking, style or habit of speech, W.; customary phraseology, ib.

Vāgāyana, m. a patr., Saṃskārak. (pl.)

Vāgāru, mfn. breaking promise or faith, disappointing, a deceiver, L.

Vāgāśani (?), m. a Buddha, L.

Vāgmāyana, m. patr. fr. *vāgmin*, g. *aśvâdi*.

Vāgmi-tā, f. (Kām.; Sāh.) or °**mi-tva**, n. (MBh.; Kām.; Rājat.) eloquence (see next).

Vāgmin, mfn. speaking well, eloquent, ŚBr.; Lāṭy.; MBh. &c.; speaking much, loquacious, talkative, wordy, L.; m. a parrot, L.; N. of Bṛihas-pati or the planet Jupiter, L.; of a son of Manasyu, MBh.

Vāgya (?), mfn. (perhaps fr. *vāc + ya* fr. *√yam*; cf. *vāg-yata*) speaking little, speaking cautiously or humbly, L.; sp° truly, L.; m. modesty, humility, self-disparagement, L.; doubt, alternative, L. **-tas**, ind. silently, W.

Vāgvin, mfn. See under *vāg* above.

Vāṅ, in comp. for *vāc*. **-nidhana**, mfn. having *vāc* as the burden or refrain (in a recitation), Nid.; Lāṭy.; (with *krauñca*, n. or *sauhavisha*, n. N. of Sāmans.) **-niścaya**, m. settlement by word, affiance by word of mouth, marriage contract, MW. **-nishṭhā**, f. abiding by one's words, punctuality in fulfilling a promise, faithfulness, ib. **-matī**, f. N. of a sacred river, W. **-matsara**, m. envious or jealous speech, ŚāṅkhŚr. **-madhu**, n. pl. sweet words, Śak. **-madhura**, mfn. sweet in speech, speaking sweet words, Hit. **-manas**, n. du. (KaṭhUp.; Mn.; Vās.) or **-manasa**, n. (sg. [Pāṇ.; Vop.] or in comp. [Gaut.; Vedântas.] or du. [MW.]) speech and mind. **-máya**, mf(*ī*)n. consisting of speech, depending on sp°, whose essence is sp°, relating to sp° (also *-tva*, n.), ŚBr.; VS. Prāt.; ChUp. &c.; eloquent, rhetorical, W.; (*ī*), f. the goddess of speech, Sarasvatī, L.; n. sp°, language, Kum.; eloquence, rhetoric, manner of sp°, RPrāt.; Sāh. &c.; *-devatā*, f. the goddess of sp°, Siṇhās.; *-viveka*, m. N. of wk.; °*yâdhikṛita-tā*, f. the state of presiding over sp° or eloquence (said of the goddess of sp°), MW. **-mātra**, n. mere words, only sp°, Hariv. **-mādhurya**, n. sweetness of speech or voice, ŚārṅgP. **-mālā**, f. N. of wk. **-miśraṇa**, n. exchanging words, conversation with (instr.), Prab. **-mukha**, n. the opening of a speech, an exordium, L. **-mūrti**, mfn. having sp° for a body; (with *devatā*), f. Sarasvatī, Pracaṇḍ. **-mūla**, mfn. having root or origin in sp°, Mn. iv, 256.

Vācam, in comp. for *vācam*. **-yama**, mf(*ā*)n. restraining speech or voice, silent, Br.; Up. &c.; m. a sage who practises silence, L.; N. of a man, Cat.; *-tva*, n. silence, Ragh.; Kuval.

Vācaka, mf(*ikā*[*akā*, w. r.])n. speaking, saying, telling anything (gen.), Hit.; BhP.; speaking of, treating of, declaring (with gen. or ifc.), RāmatUp.; MBh. &c.; expressive of, expressing, signifying, RPrāt.; RāmatUp.; MBh. &c.; verbal, expressed by words, MW.; m. a speaker, reciter, MBh.; R. &c.; a significant sound, word, W.; a messenger, ib. **-tā**, f. (BhP.; Sarvad.) or **-tva**, n. (RāmatUp.; Pat.; Sāh. &c.) the speaking or treating of, expressing, significance. **-pada**, mfn. containing expressive (not senseless) words, Yājñ., Sch.; n. an expr° or significant word, explicit term, W. **-mukhya**, N. of wk. **-lakshaka-vyañjaka-tva**, n. direct or indirect or implicit designation of a thing, Pratāp.

Vācakâcārya, m. N. of a teacher (also *umā-svāti-v°*), Sarvad.

Vācakūṭī, f. (prob.) w. r. for next, Col.

Vācaknavī, f. (fr. *vacaknu*) N. of a preceptress with the patr. Gārgī, ŚBr.; GṛS.; AV. Pariś.

Vācana, n. the causing to recite, ŚrS.; the act of reciting, recitation, Yājñ.; Varāhit.; the act of reading, Bālar.; the act of declaring or designating, Sāh.; (*ā*), f. a lesson, chapter, HPariś.

Vācanaka, n. recitation (esp. of *svasti*), Hcat.; an enigma, riddle, MW.; a kind of sweetmeat, L.

Vācanika, mf(*ī*)n. founded on an express statement, mentioned expressly, Saṃk.; ĀpŚr., Sch.; VarBṛS., Sch.

Vācam, acc. of *vāc*, in comp. **-īnva**, mfn. 'word-moving,' singing, reciting, MaitrS. **-īṅkhayá**, mfn. id. (said of Soma), RV.

Vācayitṛi, mfn. one who causes to recite, the director of a recitation, Saṃskārak.

Vāca-śravas, m. N. of a man, Cat. (perhaps w. r. for *vāja-ś°*).

1. **Vācas**. See *vi-vācas* and *sá-vācas*.

2. **Vācas**, gen. of *vāc*, in comp. **-pata**, m. patr. fr. next, ŚāṅkhBr. **-páti** (*vācás-*), m. 'lord of voice or speech,' N. of a divine being (presiding over human life which lasts as long as there is voice in the body; applied to Soma, Viśva-karman, Prajā-pati, Brahmā &c., but esp. to Bṛihas-pati, who is lord of eloquence, preceptor of the gods, and regent of the planet Jupiter), RV.; AV. &c.; a master of speech, orator, BhP.; N. of a Ṛishi, a lexicographer, a philosopher &c., Sarvad.; Uṇ., Sch. &c.; *-kalpa-taru*, m. N. of wk.; *-govinda* (Cat.), *-bhaṭṭâcārya*, m. N. of authors; *-miśra*, m. N. of various authors (esp. of a philosopher and celebrated lawyer), IW. 92, n. 2; 305; *-vallabha*, m. a topaz, L. **-patya**, mfn. relating to Vācas-pati (N. of Śiva), MBh.; composed by V°, Cat.; declared by V°, MW.; n. eloquence, Śiś.; Hit.; fine language, eloquent speech, harangue, MW.

Vācasām-pati, m. N. of Bṛihas-pati or the planet Jupiter, L. (w. r. for *vacasām-p°*).

1. **Vācā**, f. speech, a word, Pañcat.; KātyŚr., Sch. &c.; the goddess of sp°, Uṇ. ii, 57, Sch.; a holy word, sacred text, MW.; an oath, ib.; w. r. for *vacā*, MBh. xiii, 6149. **-°rambhaṇa** (*vācâr°*), n. (said to be) = *vāg-ālambana*, ChUp.; Vedântas.; N. of wk. **-viruddha**, mfn. unsuitable to words, not describable with words; m. pl. a partic. class of divine beings, MBh. **-vṛitta** or **-vṛiddha**, m. pl. N. of a class of gods in the 14th Manv-antara, VP. **-sahāya**, m. a conversable or sociable companion, R.

2. **Vācā**, instr. of *vāc*, in comp. **-karman**, n. an act performed only by the voice, ĀpŚr., Sch. **-karmīṇa**, mfn. performed only by the voice, ib. **-stena** (*vācā́-*), mfn. (prob.) one who makes mischief by his words, RV. x, 87, 15.

Vācāṭa, mf(*ā*)n. talkative (said also of birds), Kāv.; Kathās. &c.; boastful, grandiloquent (*-tā*, f.), Bālar.; Prasannar.; (ifc.) filled with the song of, resounding with, Vās.

Vācāyana, m. N. of an author, HYog.

Vācāla, mf(*ā*)n. talkative, chattering (said also of birds), Kāv.; Kathās.; boasting, VarBṛ., Sch.; Rājat.; full of noise and bustle, (ifc.) filled with the song or noise of, R.; Vās. &c. **-tā**, f. (Kāv.; Bhpr.) or **-tva**, n. (Viddh.) talkativeness, loquacity.

Vācālanā, f. the act of making talkative, Kād.

Vācālaya, Nom. P. °*yati*, to make talkative, cause to speak, Bālar.; Kād.; Kathās.; to make full of noise, Kād.; Rājat.

Vācika, mfn. verbal, effected or caused by words, consisting in words, communicated by speech (with *abhinaya*, m. a declamatory speech; with *vināśa*, m. threatened destruction; *pārushye daṇḍa-vācike*, the two violences i.e. blows and words, or assault and slander), Mn.; MBh. &c.; m. a short expression for *vāg-āśīr-datta*, Pāṇ. v, 3, 84, Vārtt. 3, Pat.; n. a verbal commission or message, Naish.; Śiś.; Rājat.; news, tidings, intelligence, W. **-pattra**, n. a written agreement or contract, L.; a letter, dispatch, W.; a newspaper, gazette, ib. **-praśna**, m. N. of wk. **-hāraka**, m. a letter, epistle, L.; a messenger, courier, MW.

Vācin, mfn. (ifc.) asserting, supposing, Sarvad.; Kāś.; expressing, signifying (°*ci-tva*, n.), APrāt.; TPrāt., Sch. &c.

Vācī, f. See *ambu-v°*.

Vāco, in comp. for 2. *vācas*. **-yukti**, f. fit or appropriate speech, Mālatim.; Pat.; mfn. (?) possessing fitness of speech, eloquent, L.; *-paṭu*, mfn. skilled in speech, eloquent, Śiś., Sch.

1. **Vācya**, Nom. P. °*yati*, fr. *vāc*, Pāṇ. i, 4, 15, Sch.

2. **Vācya**, mfn. to be spoken or said or told or announced or communicated or stated or named or predicated or enumerated or spoken of, Up.; Mn.; MBh. &c. (n. impers. it is to be spoken or said &c.); to be addressed or spoken to about anything (acc. or nom. with *iti*), Mn.; Hariv.; Kāv. &c.; to be directed that (with *yathā*), MBh.; to be told about (= still untold), KātyŚr.; to be expressed or designated or meant expressly by (gen. or comp.), ChUp.; Saṃk.; Sāh. &c.; to be spoken against, blamable, censurable by (gen. or instr.), Mn.; MBh.; Kāv. &c.; used as a substantive, Vop.; (*vācyá*), belonging to the voice &c., VS.; (*vācyá*), m. metron. of the Ṛishi Prajā-pati, RV.; n. what may be said against any one or anything, blame, censure, reproach, fault (*vācyam √gam*, to undergo blame), MBh.; Kāv.; that of which anything is predicated, a substantive, Vop.; a predicate, W.; the voice of a verb (e.g. *kartari-v°*, the active voice; *karmaṇi-v°*, the passive voice), ib.; = *pratipādana*, L. **-citra**, mfn. fanciful in sense (as a poetical expression), MW.; n. a play upon words, Sāh. **-tā**, f. the being to be said or spoken, the being predicated of or the quality of being predicable, BhP.; blamableness, ill repute, infamy, MBh.; VarBṛS. &c.; conjugation, W. **-tva**, n. = prec.; (esp.) the being to be said or expressly stated, KātyŚr.; the being expressed or expressly meant by or by means of, Saṃk. on ChUp.; Sarvad. &c. **-liṅga** or °**gaka**, mfn. following or having the gender of the substantive, adjectival (°*ga-tva*, n., Pāṇ. ii, 4, 18, Sch.), L. **-vajra**, n. 'thunder-like words,' violent or strong language, MW. **-vat**, ind. like the substantive (see above), according to the gender of the substantive, adjectively, Vop. **-varjita**, n. an elliptical expression, Pratāp. **-vācaka-tā**, f. (BhP.) and **-vācaka-tva**, n. (RāmatUp.) and **-vācaka-bhāva**, m. (KapS.) the state of the signified and the signifier. **Vācyârtha**, m. the directly expressed meaning (*-tva*, n. direct expression of meaning), Vedântas.

Vācyāya, Nom. Ā. *vācyāyate*, to appear as if really expressed, Sāh.

Vācyāyaná, m. patr. of Vācya, TS.

वाच *vāca*, m. (only L.) a species of fish; a species of plant; = *madana*.

वाछोक *vāchoka*, m. N. of a poet, Cat.

वाज *vā́ja*, m. (fr. √*vaj*; cf. *ugra*, *uj*, *ojas* &c.) strength, vigour, energy, spirit, speed (esp. of a horse; also pl.), RV.; AV.; VS.; ŚāṅkhŚr. (*vā́jebhis*, ind. mightily, greatly; cf. *sahasā*); a contest, race, conflict, battle, war, RV.; VS.; GṛŚrS.; the prize of a race or of battle, booty, gain, reward, any precious or valuable possession, wealth, treasure, RV.; VS.; AV.; PañcavBr.; food, sacrificial food (= *anna* in Naigh. ii, 7 and in most of the Commentators), RV.; VS.; Br.; = *vāja-peya*, ŚāṅkhŚr.; (?) a swift or spirited horse, war-horse, steed, RV.; AV.; the feathers on a arrow, RV.; a wing, L.; sound, L.; N. of one of the 3 Ṛibhus (pl. = the 3 Ṛibhus), RV.; of the month Caitra, VS.; of a son of Laukya, ŚāṅkhŚr.; of a son of Manu Sāvarṇa, Hariv.; of a Muni, L.; n. (only L.) ghee or clarified butter; an oblation of rice offered at a Śrāddha; rice or food in general; water; an acetous mixture of ground meal and water left to ferment; a Mantra or prayer concluding a sacrifice. — **karman** (*vā́ja-*), mfn. (prob.) active in war, SV. (v. l. for *-bharman*). — **karmīya**, n. (with *Bharadvājasya*) N. of a Sāman, ĀrshBr. — **kṛitya**, n. a warlike deed, battle, fight, RV. — **gandhya** (*vā́ja-*), mfn. (prob.) forming or possessing a cart-load of goods or booty, RV. ix, 98, 12 (cf. *gadhā* and *gádhya*; others 'whose gifts are to be seized or held fast'). — **candra**, m. N. of an author, Cat. — **jaṭhara** (*vā́ja-*), mfn. containing food (in the interior), RV. v, 19, 4 (= *havir-j°*, Sāy.) — **jit**, mfn. conquering in a contest, winning in a race, winning booty, VS.; TBr.; n. N. of various Sāmans, ĀrshBr. — **jiti** (Kāṭh.), -**jityā́** (TBr.), f. a victorious course or contest. — **dā́**, mfn. bestowing vigour or speed, RV. — **dā́van**, mfn. bestowing the prize, granting wealth, ib.; (°*varī*), f. N. of a Sāman, PañcavBr. — **draviṇas** (*vā́ja-*), mfn. finding rich reward, RV. — **pati** (*vā́ja-*), m. the lord of booty or reward (said of Agni), RV.; VS.; GṛŚrS. — **patnī** (*vā́ja-*), f. the queen of booty or treasure, RV.; Kauś. — **pastya** (*vā́ja-*), mfn. possessing or bestowing a house full of wealth or treasure, RV. — **pīta**, mfn. one who has acquired strength by drinking, Lāṭy. — **péya**, m. n. 'the drink of strength or of battle,' N. of one of the seven forms of the Soma-sacrifice (offered by kings or Brāhmans aspiring to the highest position, and preceding the Rāja-sūya and the Bṛihaspati-sava), AV.; Br.; ŚrS.; MBh.; R.; Pur.; N. of the 6th book of the Śatapatha-Brāhmaṇa in the Kāṇva-śākhā; m. = *vājapeye bhavo mantraḥ* or *vājapeyasya vyākhyānaṃ kalpaḥ*, Pat. on Pāṇ. iv, 3, 66, Vārtt. 5 &c.; -*klṛipti*, f., -*krator udgātṛi-prayoga*, m. N. of wks.; -*grahá*, m. a ladleful taken at the Vājapeya, ŚBr.; -*paddhati*, f., -*prayoga*, m. N. of wks.; -*yājin*, m. one who offers (or has offered) a V°, TBr.; -*yūpá*, m. the sacrificial post at the V°, ŚBr.; -*rahasya*, n., -*rāja-sūya*, m. or n., -*sarva-pṛishṭhâptoryāmôdgātra-prayoga*, m. N. of wks.; -*sāman*, n. N. of a Sāman, Lāṭy.; -*stoma-prayoga*, m., -*hotṛi-saptaka*, n., -*hautra*, n.; °*yâdi-saṃśaya-nirṇaya*, m., °*yârcika*, n., °*yârcika-prayoga*, m., °*yôdgātra-prayoga*, m. N. of wks. — **peyaka**, mfn. belonging or relating to the Vāja-peya sacrifice, R. — **peyika**, mf(*ī*)n. id., KātyŚr., Sch. (cf. Pāṇ. iv, 3, 68, Sch.) — **peyin**, mfn. one who has performed a Vāja-peya sacrifice, Cat. — **peśas** (*vā́ja-*), mfn. adorned with precious gifts, RV. — **pramahas**, mfn. (prob.) superior in courage or strength, ib. — **prasavī́ya** (TS.) or °**vyà** (MaitrS.), mfn. beginning with the words *vāja* and *prasava*; n. (scil. *karman*) a rite so beginning, TS.; ŚBr.; (°*vīya*)-*homa*, m. a sacrifice so beginning, Vait. — **prasuta** (*vā́ja-*), mfn. started for a race or impelled by courage, RV. — **bandhu**, m. an ally in battle (or N. of a man), ib. — **bastya** (*vā́ja-*), v. l. for -*pastya*, TBr. (*vājenânnena janyam bastyam balam tad-yogyaḥ*, Sch.) — **bharman** (*vā́ja-*), mfn. winning a prize or reward, RV. — **bharmīya** or -**bhṛit** (also with *Bharad-vājasya*), n. N. of a Sāman, Lāṭy. — **bhojin**, m. = -*peya*, L. — **m-bhará**, mfn. carrying off the prize or booty, RV.; m. (with *Sapti*) N. of the author of RV. x, 79. — **ratna** (*vā́ja-*), mf(*ā*)n. rich in goods or treasure (as the Ṛibhus), RV.; m. N. of a man (cf. next). — **ratnāyana**, m. patr. of Soma-śushman, AitBr. — **vat** (*vā́ja-*), mfn. consisting of a prize or of treasures, connected with them &c., RV.; vigorous, strong, ib.; consisting of steeds or race-horses, ib.; accompanied by Vāja or by the Vājas (i. e. Ṛibhus), ib.; VS.; AitBr.; KātyŚr.; furnished with food, ŚāṅkhŚr.; containing the word *vāja*, TS.; PañcavBr. — **vāla**, m. an emerald, L. — **śrava**, m. N. of a man, VP. — **śravas** (*vā́ja-*), mfn. famous for wealth or steeds, RV.; (-*śrávas*), m. N. of a teacher, ŚBr. — **śruta** (*vā́ja-*), mfn. famous for swiftness, RV. — **sana**, see s. v. — **sáni**, mfn. winning a prize or booty or wealth, granting strength or vigour, victorious, RV.; bestowing food, Mahīdh.; m. N. of Vishṇu, MBh. — **saneya** &c., see s. v. — **saṃnyasta**, mfn., BhP. xii, 6, 74 (prob. corrupted). — **sā́**, mfn. (superl. -*tama*) = -*sáni*, RV.; VS. — **sāta**, n. or -**sāti**, f. (*vā́ja-*) the winning of a prize or of booty, battle, victory, RV.; VS.; AV. — **sāman**, n. N. of a Sāman, Vait. — **sṛít**, mfn. racing, a racer, race-horse, RV.; TS. — **srajâksha** (Cat.), -**srava** or -**sravas** (VP.), m. N. of Vena. **Vājâpya**, n. 'connection with food or strength (?),' a word formed to explain *vāja-peya*, TBr. **Vājédhyā**, f. (*vāja* + *idhyā́*) = *dīpti*, Mahīdh. on VS. i, 29 (perhaps w. r. for *vājétyā*, race, course).

Vājapya, m. N. of a man, g. *naḍâdi*.

Vājapyāyana, m. patr. of a teacher, Sarvad.

Vājaya (cf. √*vaj*), Nom. P. Ā. °*yáti*, °*te* (inf. *vājayádhyai*), to race, speed, hasten, run, contend, vie, RV.; to urge on, incite, impel, ib.; AV.; PañcavBr.; P. (*vājáyati*), to worship, Naigh. iii, 14; to fan, kindle (considered as Caus. of √*vā*), Pāṇ. vii, 3, 88.

Vājayú, mfn. eager for a race or contest, swift, active, energetic, vigorous, RV.; winning or bestowing wealth or booty, ib.

Vājavata, m. (fr. *vāja-vat*) N. of a man, g. *tikâdi* (Kāś. *dhvājavata*).

Vājavatāyani, m. patr. fr. prec., ib. (Kāś. *dhvājavatāyani*).

Vājasana, mf(*ī*)n. relating or belonging to Vājasaneya (said of Śiva and Vishṇu), MBh.; R.; BhP.

Vājasaneyá, m. patr. of Yājñavalkya (m. pl. the school of V°), ŚBr. — **gṛihya-sūtra**, n., -**pariśishṭa-nigama**, m. N. of wks. — **brāhmaṇa**, n. the Brāhmaṇa of the V°, i. e. the Śatapatha-brāhmaṇa, Kull. — **śākhā**, f. the branch or school of the V°s, Inscr. — **saṃhitā**, f. = *vājasaneyi-s°*, Cat.

Vājasaneyaka, mfn. belonging or relating to Vājasaneya, devoted to him, composed by him &c., ŚrS.; BṛĀrUp.; n. N. of the ŚBr., KātyŚr.

Vājasaneyi, in comp. for °*yin*. — **prātiśākhya**, n. the Prātiśākhya of the Vājasaneyins. — **brāhmaṇa**, n. = *śata-patha-br°* (cf. above); °*ṇôpanishad*, f. N. of an Upanishad. — **śākhā**, f. the branch or school of the V°s, Cat. — **saṃhitā**, f. 'the Saṃhitā or continuous text of the Vājasaneyins' (i. e. of the hymns of the White Yajur-veda ascribed to the Ṛishi Yājñavalkya and called *śukla*, 'white,' to distinguish it from the Black or Dark Yajur-veda, which was the name given to the Taittirīya-saṃhitā [q.v.] of the Yajur-veda, because in this last, the separation between the Mantra and Brāhmaṇa portion is obscured, and the two are blended together; whereas the White Saṃhitā is clearly distinguished from the Brāhmaṇa; it is divided into 40 Adhyāyas with 303 Anuvākas, comprising 1975 sections or Kaṇḍikās: the legend relates that the original Yajus was taught by the Ṛishi Vaiśampāyana to his pupil Yājñavalkya, but the latter having incurred his teacher's anger was made to disgorge all the texts he had learnt, which were then picked up by Vaiśampāyana's other disciples in the form of partridges [see *taittirīya-saṃhitā*]; Yājñavalkya then hymned the Sun, who gratified by his homage, appeared in the form of a *vājin* or horse, and consented to give him fresh Yajus texts, which were not known to his former master; cf. *vājin*); °*tôpanishad*, f. N. of an Upanishad (forming the 40th Adhyāya of the VS. and also called Īśā or Īśā-vāsyopanishad, q. v.)

Vājasaneyin, m. pl. the school of Vājasaneya, Hariv. (g. *śaunakâdi*); mfn. belonging to that school, Sāy.

1. **Vāji** (for 2. see col. 3), in comp. for *vājin*. — **keśa**, m. pl. N. of a mythical people, MārkP. — **gandhā**, f. the plant Physalis Flexuosa, L. — **grīva**, m. N. of a prince, MBh. — **tā**, f. the state of having strength or food or wings, Śiś.; the state or nature of a horse, ib. — **tva**, n. = prec., MW. — **danta** and -**dantaka**, m. Adhatoda Vasika, L. — **daitya**, m. N. of an Asura (also called Keśin), Hariv. — **nīrājana-vidhi**, m. N. of wk. — **pakshin**, m. a partic. bird, L. — **pīta**, mfn. drunk by the Vājins, ĀpŚr. (in a quotation; cf. *vāja-p°*). — **pṛishṭha**, m. the globe-amaranth, L. — **bha**, n. N. of the Nakshatra Aśvinī, VarBṛS. — **bhakshya**, m. the chick-pea, Cicer Arietinum, L. — **bhū** (Kām.) or -**bhūmi** (Kir.), f. a place where horses are bred or a spot abounding in or suitable for horses. — **bhojana**, m. Phaseolus Mungo, L. — **mat**, mfn. joined or connected with the Vājins, Vait.; m. Trichosanthes Dioeca, L. — **medha**, m. a horse-sacrifice, MBh.; R.; Pur. — **mesha**, m. pl. 'horse-rams,' a partic. class of Ṛishis, R. (accord. to Sch. they can at will assume the shape of a horse or a ram). — **yojaka**, m. 'h°-yoker,' a driver or groom, MBh. — **rāja**, m. N. of Vishṇu, Pañcar. — **vāraṇa-śālā**, f. pl. stables for h°s and elephants, R. — **vāhana**, n. h° and chariot, MBh.; a kind of metre, Col. — **vishṭhā**, f. 'horse's station,' the Indian fig-tree, Suśr. (cf. *aśva-ttha*). — **vega** (*vā́ji-*), mfn. having the swiftness of a h°, Suparṇ. — **śatru**, m. a species of plant, L. — **śālā**, f. a horse-stable, Rājat. — **śiras**, m. 'horse-head,' N. of a Dānava, Hariv.

Vājita, mfn. having feathers, feathered (as an arrow), MBh. (cf. *gṛidhra-v°*).

Vājín, mfn. swift, spirited, impetuous, heroic, warlike, RV. &c. &c. (with *ratha*, m. a war-chariot; superl. *vājín-tama*); strong, manly, procreative, potent, RV.; TS.; Br.; winged, (ifc.) having anything for wings, BhP.; feathered (as an arrow), Hariv.; m. a warrior, hero, man, RV. (often applied to gods, esp. to Agni, Indra, the Maruts &c.); the steed of a war-chariot, ib.; a horse, stallion, Mn.; MBh. &c.; N. of the number 'seven,' Gol. (cf. *aśva*); a bridle, L.; a bird, L.; an arrow, L.; Adhatoda Vasika, L.; pl. 'the Coursers,' a class of divine beings (prob. the steeds of the gods, but accord. to TBr. Agni, Vāyu and Sūrya), RV.; Br.; ŚrS. (*vājināṃ sāma*, N. of a Sāman, ĀrshBr.); the school of Vājasaneya (so called because the Sun in the shape of a horse revealed to Yājñavalkya partic. Yajus verses called *a-yātayāmāni*, q. v.), VP.; (*inī*), f., see below.

Vājina, mfn. belonging to the Vājins, VS.; m. N. of a Ṛishi, Br.; n. race, contest, emulation, RV.; VS.; AV.; curds or the scum of curdled milk, Lāṭy., Sch. (curds of two-milk whey or whey from which the curds have been separated, W.); the ceremony performed with curds for the Vājins, ĀśvŚr. — **brāhmaṇa**, m. the priest who performs the Vājina ceremony, ĀpŚr., Sch.

Vājinī, f. (of *vājin*) a mare, L. (cf. comp.); Physalis Flexuosa, L. — **vat** (*vājínī-*), mfn. possessing or driving swift mares, rich in horses (applied to various gods, and to the rivers Sindhu and Sarasvatī), RV.; AV.; TBr. (accord. to others 'strong,' 'spirited,' 'rich in sacrifices' &c.); m. the sun, AV.; pl. the steeds of the gods, ib. — **vasu** (*vājínī-*), mfn. = prec., RV.; bestowing strength or power, TĀr.

Vājineyá, m. the son of a hero or warrior, RV. vi, 26, 2.

Vājī, in comp. for *vāja*. — **kara**, mfn. strengthening, stimulating, producing virility, Suśr.; n. an aphrodisiac, ib. — **karaṇa**, mf(*ī*)n. = prec. (also n.), ib.; Kām. &c.; N. of wk.; -*tantra*, n.; °*ṇâdhikāra*, m. N. of wks. — **kārya**, n. = -*kriyā*, Cat. — √**kṛi**, P. -*karoti*, to strengthen, excite, produce virility, Suśr. — **kriyā**, f. the use or application of aphrodisiacs, Suśr. — **vidhāna**, n. id., Cat.

Vājya, m. patr. fr. *vāja*, g. *gargâdi*.

वाजि 2. *vāji* (?), m. (for 1. see col. 2) a partic. manner of cutting the hair, Saṃskārak.

वाज्रेय *vājreya*, mfn. (fr. *vajra*), g. *sakhyâdi*.

वाञ्चेश्वर *vāñceśvara*, m. (prob.) w. r. for *vāñcheśvara*.

वाञ्छ् *vāñch* (cf. √*van*), cl. 1. P. (Dhātup. vii, 28) *vāñchati* (occurring only in forms from the present stem, and in pr. p. Pass. *vāñchyamāna* [Kathās.]; but accord. to Gr. also pf. *vavāñcha*; aor. *avāñchīt*; fut. *vāñchitā*, *vāñchishyati* &c.), to desire, wish, ask for, strive after, pursue, RV. &c. &c.; to state, assert, assume, VarBṛS.: Caus. -*vāñchayati* (see *abhi-*√*vāñch*), MBh. [Cf. Germ. *wunsc*, *Wunsch*, *wünschen*; Angl. Sax. *wýscan*; Eng. *wish*.]

Vāñchaka, mfn. wishing, desiring; a wisher &c., MW.

Vāñchana, n. the act of desiring or wishing, W.

Vāñchanīya, mfn. to be wished for, desirable, ib.

Vāñchā, f. (ifc. f. *ā*) wish, desire, longing for (acc. with *prati*, loc. or gen.; *vāñchām* √*kri* with loc., 'to desire or long for'), Kāv.; Kathās.; Rājat. &c.; statement, assumption, Sarvad. — **kalpa**, m., -**kalpa-latā**, f. N. of wks. — **nātha**, m. N. of two authors, Cat.; °*thīya-sūtra*, n. N. of wk. **Vāñchêśa**, m. N. of a man (the father of Saṃkarânanda), Cat. **Vāñchêśvara**, m. (with *kavi*) N. of a poet (also called Vāñchā-nātha), ib.; (with *Hośa-nikarṇā-ṭaka*) of an author whose date is about 1800 A.D.; -*māhātmya*, n. N. of ch. of the SkandaP. **Vāñ-chôddhāra**, m. N. of a Tantric wk.

Vāñchāka, m. N. of a poet, Cat.

Vāñchita, mfn. wished, desired, beloved, longed for, MBh.; Kāv. &c.; n. wish, desire, ib.; m. (in music) a kind of measure.

Vāñchitavya, mfn. to be wished or desired, desirable, MW.

Vāñchin, mfn. wishing, desirous, lustful, W.; (*inī*), f. a libidinous woman, ib.

Vāñchya, mfn. = *vāñchitavya*, MW.

वाट् **vāṭ**, ind. (g. *cādi*) an exclamation on performing a sacrifice (prob. = 'bring' or 'take,' fr. √*vāh* = *vah*), VS.; Br.; ŚrS. — **kāra**, m. the exclamation *vāṭ*, KātyŚr.

वाट **vāṭa**, mf(ī)n. (fr. *vaṭa*) made or consisting of the Banyan or Indian fig-tree or its wood &c., Mn. ii, 45; m. an enclosure, (either) a fence, wall, (or) a piece of enclosed ground, garden, park, plantation, MBh.; Kāv. &c.; a district, Daś.; a road, Vās.; the site of a house, L.; Panicum Spicatum, W.; the groin, W.; the son of a Vaiśya and a Maitrī, L.; (also n. and [*ī*], f.) an enclosure of a (low-caste) village consisting of boundary trees, L.; (*ī*). f. a piece of enclosed ground, garden, Hariv.; Sāh.; BhP.; the site of a house, L.; a hut, L.; a species of bird, Car.; n. = *varaṇḍa*, *aṅga*, and *anna-bheda*. — **dhāna**, m. the descendant of an out-caste Brāhman by a Brāhman mother, Mn. x, 21; an officer who knows the disposition of his army, L.; pl. N. of a people, MBh.; VarBṛS.; BhP. (sg. a prince of the V°s; n. the country of the V°s, MBh.) — **mūla**, mfn. being at the root of the Ficus Indica, Hariv. — **śriṅkhalā**, f. a chain fixed round an enclosure, a sort of fence(?), L.

Vāṭaka, m. an enclosure, garden, plantation, Kathās.; Hcat.; (*ikā*), f. id., Kāv.; Kathās.; Pañcad.; the site of a house, L.; a hut, L.

Vāṭi, (prob.) f. a piece of enclosed ground, Kāty.

Vāṭi-dīrgha or **vāṭī-dīrgha**, m. a sort of grass or reed, L.

Vāṭīya. See *brahma-* and *sṛigāla-v°*.

Vāṭya, mfn. (fr. *vaṭa*) made of the Indian fig-tree, Suśr.; m. fried barley, Car. (cf. *vaṭṭaka*); (*ā*), f. = *vāṭyālaka*, Bhpr. — **pushpikā** (L.) or -**push-pī** (Car.), f. Sida Rhomboidea or Cordifolia. — **maṇ-ḍa**, m. scum of fried barley, L.

Vāṭyāyanī, f. a species of Sida with white flowers, Car.

Vāṭyāla or °**laka**, m., °**lī**, f. Sida Rhomboidea or Cordifolia, L.

वाटर **vāṭara**, n. (prob.) a sort of honey, Pāṇ. iv, 3, 119 (cf. *vaṭara*).

वाटाकवि **vāṭākavi**, m. patr. fr. *vaṭāku*, g. *bāhv-ādi*.

वाटु **vāṭu**, m. N. of a man, Kshitīś.

वाट्टक **vāṭṭaka**, n. fried barley, L. (cf. *vāṭya*).

वाट्टदेव **vāṭṭa-deva**, m. N. of a man, Rājat.

वाड् **vāḍ**. See √*bāḍ*.

वाडब **vāḍaba** (or *vāḍava*), mfn. (fr. *vaḍaba*) coming from a mare (as milk), Suśr.; m. a stallion, stud-horse, Pāṇ. vi, 2, 65, Sch.; submarine fire (cf. under *vaḍaba* and *aurva*), Kāv.; Pur.; a Brāhman, MBh.; Kāv. &c. (cf. *vāḍabya*); N. of a grammarian, Pat. on Pāṇ. viii, 2, 106; m. or n. the lower world, hell, L.; n. a stud, g. *khaṇḍikâdi*; a partic. Muhūrta, Cat.; a kind of coitus, L. — **karsha**, m. N. of a village (°*shīya*, mfn.), Pāṇ. iv, 2, 104, Vārtt. 2, Pat. — **haraṇa**, n. the fodder given to a stud-horse, Pāṇ. vi, 2, 65, Sch. — **hāraka**, m. a shark or other sea-monster, L. — **hārya**, n., Siddh. on Pāṇ. vi, 2, 65.

Vāḍabâgni, m. submarine fire (supposed to be at the south-pole), Kāv. **Vāḍabânala**, m. id., Pañcar.

Vāḍabīya, mfn. (with *jyotis*) submarine fire, Bālar.

Vāḍabeya, m. a stallion, stud-horse, g. *nady-ādi*; a Brāhman, L.; a bull, W.; du. the two Aśvins as the sons of Vaḍabā (or Aśvinī, q.v.), L.

Vāḍabya, n. a number of Brāhmans, Pāṇ. iv, 2, 42; the state of a Brāhman, g. *brāhmaṇâdi*.

वाडभीकार **vāḍabhīkāra**. See *bāḍ°*.

Vāḍabhīkārya, m. patr. fr. *vaḍabhīkāra*.

वाडव **vāḍava**. See *vāḍaba*.

वाडेयीपुत्र **vāḍeyī-pútra**. See *bāḍ°*.

वाड्डौत्स **vāḍḍautsa**, m. N. of a man, Rājat.

वाड्वलि **vāḍvali**, m. (said to be) patr. fr. *vāg-vāda*, Pāṇ. vi, 3, 109, Vārtt. 2, Pat.

वाढ **vāḍhá**. See *bāḍhá*.

वाण 1. **vāṇá**, m. (fr. √*vaṇ*; often written *bāṇa*, q.v.) sounding, a sound, Kir. xv, 10; an arrow (see *bāṇa*, p. 727 for comp.), RV. ix, 50, 1; music (esp. of flutes, harps &c.), RV. i, 85, 10 &c.; AV. x, 2, 17 (here written *bāṇá*); a harp with 100 strings, TS.; Br.; ŚrS.; (*ī*), f., see below; n. the sound of a partic. little hand-drum, L. — **vat**, mfn. containing the word *vāṇa* (a harp), TāṇḍBr. — **śabda**, m. the sound of a lute (or 'the whizz of an arrow'), Mn. iv, 113. — **śāla**, m. (or *ā*, f.) N. of a fortress, Rājat.

Vāṇitā, f. N. of a metre, Ked.

Vāṇin, mfn. (cf. *bāṇin*) speaking, W.; (*inī*), f. an actress, dancer, L.; a clever or intriguing woman, Hcar.; an intoxicated woman, R.; N. of two metres, Ked.; Col.

1. **Vā́ṇī**, f. sound, voice, music (pl. a choir of musicians or singers), RV. (the *sapta vāṇīs* are referred by the Comms. to the seven metres or to the seven notes of the gamut &c.); speech, language, words, diction, (esp.) eloquent speech or fine diction, MBh.; Kāv. &c.; a literary production or composition, Uttarar.; Bhām.; praise, laudation, MW.; the goddess of speech, Sarasvatī, R.; BrahmavP.; N. of a metre consisting only of long syllables, Kāvyâd., Sch.; of a river (accord. to some the Sarasvatī), VP. — **kavi**, -**kūṭa-lakshmī-dhara**, -**nātha**, m. N. of certain authors, Cat. — **pūrva-paksha**, m. N. of a Vedânta wk. — **bhūshaṇa**, n. N. of a wk. on metrics (by Dāmôdara). — **vat**, mfn. rich in words, Pañcar. — **vāda**, m. a kind of bird, MBh. — **vilāsa**, m. N. of two authors, Cat.

Vā́ṇīcī, f. (prob.) a partic. musical instrument, RV. v, 75, 4 ('speech,' Naigh.)

वाण 2. **vāṇa**, w.r. for *vāna* in *vānadaṇḍa* and *vānaprastha* (see 3. and 6. *vāna*).

वाणकि **vāṇaki**, m. N. of a man, Saṃskārak.

वाणारसी **vāṇārasī**, f. = *vārāṇasī* (q.v.), the city of Benares, Vcar.; Śatr. (w.r. *vāṇar°*).

वाणार्णी **vaṇārṇī**, w.r. for *bāṇa parṇī*, Kauś.

वाणि **vāṇi**, f. (only L.; cf. 1. 2. *vāṇī*) weaving; a weaver's loom; voice, speech; a species of metre; a cloud; price, value. — **bhūshaṇa**, n., w.r. for *vāṇī-bh°*.

वाणिकाज्य **vāṇikājya**, w.r. for *vāl°*.

वाणिज **vāṇijá**, m. (also written *bāṇijá*; fr. *vaṇij*) a merchant, trader, TBr.; MBh. (cf. Pāṇ. vi, 2, 13); the submarine fire (supposed to be at the south-pole), L.

Vāṇijaka, m. a merchant, MBh.; Hariv.; the submarine fire, L. — **vidha**, mfn. inhabited by merchants, g. *bhauriky-ādi*.

Vāṇijika, m. a merchant, trader, Mn. iii, 181 (v.l. *vāṇijaka*).

Vāṇijya, n. (Āpast.; Gaut. &c.), **vāṇijyā**, f. (Kathās.) traffic, trade, commerce, merchandise.

Vāṇijyaka, m. a merchant, trader, Hcat. (cf. *dharma-v°*).

वाणी 2. **vāṇī**, f. (cf. *vāṇi*) weaving, L.

वाणी 3. **vāṇī**, f. reed, RV. v, 86, 1; du. the two bars of a car or carriage, ib. i, 119, 5.

वाण्यविद **vāṇyavida** or **vāṇyovida**, m. N. of a Ṛishi, Car. (cf. *vāyovida*).

वात् 1. **vāt**, ind., g. *cādi*.

वात् 2. **vāt**, cl. 10. P. *vātayati*, to fan (cf. *vātaya*, p. 935, col. 2); to fan; to serve, make happy; to go, Dhātup. xxxv, 30.

वात 1. **vāta** &c. See p. 934, col. 2 &c.

वात 2. **vāta**, mfn. (fr. √*van*) = *vanita*, solicited, wished for, desired (cf. *vivasvad-v°*); attacked, assailed, injured, hurt (cf. 3. *a-v°* and *ni-vāta*).

वातण्ड **vātaṇḍa**, m. patr. fr. *vataṇḍa*, g. *śivâdi*; (*ī*), f., Pāṇ. iv, 1, 109, Sch.

Vātaṇḍya, m. patr. fr. *vataṇḍa*, g. *gargâdi*.

Vātaṇḍyāyanī, f. of prec., g. *lohitâdi*.

वातरशन **vāta-raśana**. See p. 934, col. 3.

वातर्दि **vātardi**. See *vātarddhi*, ib.

वातव्य **vātavya**. See under √*ve*.

वातश्चिक **vātaścika**, prob. w.r. for *vātâś-vika*, mfn. one whose horses are swift as the wind, Kām. xvi, 12.

वाताम **vātāma**, m. the almond-tree, Car.; Bhpr. (cf. *bādāma*).

वाति **vāti**, *vātula*, *vatūla*, *vātya* &c. See p. 935, col. 2 &c.

वात्स 1. **vātsa**, m. patr. fr. *vatsa*, VarBṛS. (v.l.); (*ī*), f., see below; n. N. of a Sāman, PañcavBr.; Lāṭy.

2. **Vātsa**, Vṛiddhi form of *vatsa*, in comp. — **prá**, m. (fr. *vatsa-prī*) patr. of a grammarian, TPrāt.; n. N. of RV. x, 45 (= VS. xii, 18 &c.) and the ceremony connected with it, TBr.; ŚBr.; KātyŚr.; N. of a Sāman, ĀrshBr. — **priya**, mfn. (fr. prec.) containing the hymn of Vatsa-prī and the ceremony connected with it, ŚBr. — **preya**, m. patr. fr. *vatsa-prī*, Pat. — **bandhá**, n. pl. (fr. *vatsa-b°*) a partic. text, TS.; -*vid*, mfn. knowing the text called Vātsa-bandha, ib. (*vātsambandha-vid*, MaitrS.) — **śāla**, mfn. (fr. *vatsa-śālā*) born in a cow-shed, Pāṇ. iv, 3, 36. **Vātsoddharaṇa**, mfn. born in Vatsôddharaṇa, g. *takshaśilâdi*.

1. **Vātsaka**, n. (fr. *vatsa*) a herd of calves, Pāṇ. iv, 2, 39.

2. **Vātsaka**, mfn. (fr. *vatsaka*) coming or made from the Wrightia Antidysenterica, Suśr.

3. **Vātsaka**, mfn. (fr. *vātsya*), Pat. on Pāṇ. iv, 2, 104, Vārtt. 18; 22.

Vātsalya, n. (fr. *vatsala*) affection or tenderness (esp. towards offspring), fondness or love for (gen., loc. or comp.), R.; Kālid. &c. — **tā**, f. (ifc.) id., BhP. — **bandhin**, mfn. showing tenderness, displaying affection, Vikr.

Vātsāyana, w.r. for *vātsyāyana*.

Vātsi, m. (fr. *vatsa*) patr. of Sarpi, AitBr.

Vātsī, f. of *vātsya* (q.v.), Pāṇ. iv, 1, 16, Sch.; (prob.) N. of a woman (see comp.; W. 'the daughter of a Śūdra woman by a Brāhman'). — **pútra** (*vātsī-*), f. N. of an ancient teacher, ŚBr.; Buddh.; of a serpent-demon, Kāraṇḍ.; a barber, L. — **putrīya**, m. pl. the sect or school of Vātsī-putra, Buddh. — **māṇ-davī-pútra** (*vā́tsī-*), m. N. of a preceptor, ŚBr.

Vātsīya, m. pl. N. of a school, Pāṇ. iv, 1, 89, Sch.

Vā́tsya, mfn. treating of Vatsa, ŚāṅkhŚr.; m. patr. fr. *vatsa*, g. *gargâdi*; N. of an ancient teacher, KātyŚr.; of an astronomer, Hcat.; pl. N. of a people, MBh.; (*ī*), f., see above; n., g. *prithv-ādi*. — **khaṇḍa**, m. N. of a man, Pat. on Pāṇ. ii, 2, 38. — **gulmaka**, m. pl. N. of a people, Cat.

Vātsyāyana, m. patr. of *vātsya*, g. *śārṅgarava-âdi* (*ī*, f., ib.); N. of various authors (esp. of the Kāma-sūtras and of the Nyāya-bhāshya, Pañcat.; Vās., Introd.; Cat.; mf(*ī*)n. relating to or composed by Vātsyāyana, Cat. — **bhāshya**, n. N. of V°'s Comm. on the Nyāya-sūtras. — **sūtra**, n. = *kāma-s°* (q.v.); -*sāra*, m. N. of a wk. by Kshemêndra. **Vātsyā-yani**, m. N. of a law-giver, Cat.

Vātsyāyanīya, n. a wk. composed by Vātsyāyana (esp. the Kāma-sūtras), Cat.

वाद **vāda**, mfn. (fr. √*vad*) speaking of or about (see *brahma-v°*); causing to sound, playing (see *vīṇā-v°*); m. speech, discourse, talk, utterance, statement, Mn.; MBh. &c.; (ifc.) speaking about, mentioning, MBh.; Hariv.; BhP.; advice, counsel, MBh.; a thesis, proposition, argument, doctrine, Sarvad.; Suśr.; discussion, controversy, dispute, contest, quarrel, Mn.; MBh. &c.; agreement, Daś.; cry, song, note (of a bird), AitBr.; sound, sounding (of a musical instrument), Pañcat.; demonstrated conclusion, result, W.; a plaint, accusation, ib.; a reply, ib.; explanation, exposition (of holy texts &c.), MW.; report, rumour, ib. **-kathā**, f. N. of a wk. on the Vedânta. **-kara**, mfn. making a discussion, causing a dispute, W. **-kartṛi**, m. a player on a musical instrument, Saṃgīt. **-kalpaka**, m. or n., **-kutūhala**, n. N. of wks. **-kṛit**, mfn. = *-kara*, MW. **-kautūhala**, n., **-grantha**, m. N. of wks. **-cañcu**, mfn. clever in repartee, a good jester, Bhartṛ. **-ḍiṇḍima**, m., **-taramgiṇī**, f. N. of wks. **-da**, mfn. emulating, vying with (comp.), Śiś. **-nakshatra-mālā-sūryôdaya**, m., **-nakshatra-mālikā**, f. (also called *nakshatra-vāda-mālikā* or *nakshatra-vādâvalī*), a defence of the Vedânta against the Mīmāṇsā doctrine. **-paricchedа**, m. N. of wks. **-prativāda**, m. (sg. and du.) a set disputation, assertion and counter assertion, statement and contradiction, controversy, disputation, MW. **-phakkikā**, f., **-mañjarī**, f., **-mahârṇava**, m. N. of wks. **-yuddha**, n. war of words, controversy, dispute, Mn. xii, 46; *-pradhāna*, mfn. skilled in controversial discussion, ib. **-raṅga**, m. Ficus Religiosa, L. **-rata**, mfn. adhering to or following any partic. proposition or doctrine, W.; addicted to controversy, disputatious, ib. **-ratnâvalī**, f. N. of wk. **-vatī**, f. N. of a river, L. **-vāda**, mfn. causing a controversy, BhP.; an assertion about a proposition, ib. **-vādin**, see *syād-vāda-vādin*. **-vivāda**, m. sg. or du. discussion about a statement, argument and disputation, MW. **-saṃgraha**, m. N. of wk. **-sādhana**, n. proof of an assertion, maintaining of an argument, controversy, W. **-sudhâkara**, m., **-sudhā-ṭīkā-ratnâvalī**, f. N. of wks. **Vādâdri-kuliśa**, m. or n. N. of wk. **Vādânuvāda**, m. du. assertion and reply, plea and counterplea, accusation and defence, controversy, dispute, disputation, W. **Vādârtha**, m. N. of various wks.; *-khaṇḍana*, n., *-cūḍāmaṇi*, m., *-dīpikā*, f. N. of wks. **Vādâvalī**, f. N. of wk.

Vādaka, mfn. (fr. Caus. of √*vad*) making a speech, speaking, a speaker, MW.; m. a musician, Saṃgīt.; a partic. mode of beating a drum, ib.

Vādana, m. a player on any musical instrument, musician, R.; n. = *-daṇḍa*, ŚrS.; (ifc. f. *ā*) sound, sounding, playing a mus° instr°, music, Mn.; MBh. &c. **-daṇḍa**, m. a stick for striking a mus° instr°, L. **-paricchеda**, m. N. of wk.

Vādanaka, n. playing a musical instrument, MBh.

Vādanīya, m. 'to be made to resound,' a reed, L.

Vādānya, mfn. = *vadānya*, L.

Vādâyana, m. patr. fr. *vada*, g. *aśvâdi*.

1. **Vādi**, mfn. speaking, Uṇ. iv, 124, Sch.; learned, wise, ib.

2. **Vādi** (not always separable from prec.), in comp. for *vādin*. **-karaṇa-khaṇḍana**, n., **-khaṇḍana**, n., **-ghaṭa-mudgara**, m. N. of wks. **-candra**, m. (with *sūri*) N. of a Jaina, Cat. **-tarjana**, n. N. of wk. **-tva**, n., see *satya-vāditva*. **-bhīkarâcārya**, m. N. of an author. **-bhūshaṇa**, n. N. of wk. **-rāj**, m. 'king among disputants,' an excellent disputant, Pañcat.; a Bauddha sage (also N. of Mañju-ghosha or Mañju-śrī), L. **-rāja**, m. N. of various authors (also *-tīrtha*, *-pati*, *-śishya*, *-svāmin*). **-vāg-īśvara**, m. N. of an author, L. **-vinoda**, m. N. of a wk. by Śaṃkara-miśra. **-śrī-vallabha**, m. N. of an author, Cat. **-siṇha**, m. 'lion of disputants,' N. of Buddha, L. **Vādîndra**, m. N. of a philosopher and a poet, ib. **Vādîbha-siṇha**, m. N. of a Jaina, ib. **Vādîśvara**, m. = *vādi-rāj*, an excellent disputant, Dhanaṃj. **Vādy-adhyāya**, m. N. of a ch. of the Saṃgīta-ratnâkara.

Vādika, mfn. talking, speaking, asserting, maintaining (a theory &c.), MBh.; m. a conjurer, magician, Hcat. (v. l. *vātika*).

Vādita, mfn. (fr. Caus. of √*vad*) made to speak or to be uttered &c.; made to sound, sounded, played, BhP.; n. instrumental music, ŚâṅkhBr.; Gobh.

Vāditavya, mfn. to be said or spoken &c.; n. instrumental music, MBh.

Vāditra, n. a musical instrument, Āpast.; music, musical performance, ib.; Gobh.; Gaut. &c.; a musical choir, Uttamac. **-gaṇa**, m. a band of music, MW. **-laguḍa**, m. a drum-stick, L. **-vat**, mfn. accompanied by music, KātyŚr.

Vādin, mfn. saying, discoursing, speaking, talking, speaking or talking about (often ifc. or sometimes with acc. of object), declaring, proclaiming, denoting, designating (or sometimes = designated as, addressed by a title &c.), Mn.; MBh. &c.; producing sounds, ŚâṅkhŚr.; m. a speaker, asserter, (ifc.) the teacher or propounder or adherent of any doctrine or theory, MaitrUp.; Saṃk.; Sarvad.; a disputant, MBh.; Hariv. &c.; a plaintiff, accuser, prosecutor (du. plaintiff and defendant), Yājñ.; Nār.; an alchemist, Kālac.; a player on any musical instrument, musician (see f.), the leading or key-note, W.; N. of Buddha (as 'the disputant'), L.; (*inī*), f. a female musician, R.; (prob.) N. of a Comm. on the Amara-kośa.

Vādiśa, mfn. (prob. for *vâdiśa*) = *sādhu-vādin*, L.; m. a learned and virtuous man, sage, seer, W.

Vā́dya, mfn. to be said or spoken or pronounced or uttered, AitBr.; to be sounded or played (as a musical instrument), Cat.; n. a speech, ŚBr.; instrumental music, Mālav.; Kathās. &c.; m. or n. a musical instrument, R.; Kathās.; Pañcat. **-kara** (MW.), **-dhara** (BhP.), m. 'performer on a mus° inst°,' a musician. **-nirghosha**, m. the sound of mus° inst°s, W. **-bhaṇḍa**, n. a mus° inst°, SaddhP.; a multitude of mus° inst°s, band, L.; *-mukha*, n. the mouth or top part or point of a mus° inst°, L. **-maṇḍa**, w. r. for *vātya-m°*. **-vādaka-sāmagrī**, f. the whole collection of mus° inst°s and those who play upon them, L.

Vādyaka, n. instrumental music, BhP.

Vādyamāna, mfn. (fr. Caus. of √*vad*) being made to speak or sound &c.; n. instrumental music, Hariv.

Vādyoka, m. N. of a poet, Cat.

वादर *vādara*, °*rāyaṇa*. See *bādara*.

वादल *vādala*, m. liquorice, L.; a dark day, L. (cf. *bādara*).

वादाम *vādāma*. See *bādāma*.

वादाल *vādāla*, m. the sheat-fish (= *vadāla*), L.

वादिर *vādira*, m. N. of a partic. tree (resembling the Badarī), L.

वादुलि *vāduli*, m. N. of a son of Viśvāmitra, MBh. (v. l. *vāhuli*).

वाद्गल *vādgala* (?), n. the lip, Gal.

वाध् *vādh*, *vādha* &c. See √*bādh*.

वाधव *vādhava*, n. (fr. *vadhū*), g. *udgātrādi*.

Vādhavaka, n. (fr. id.), g. *kulâlâdi*.

Vādhukya, n. (fr. id.) the taking a wife, marriage, L.

Vā́dhūya, mfn. (fr. id.) relating to a bride, bridal; n. a bridal dress, wedding garment, RV.; AV.; Kauś.

वाधावत *vādhāvata*, v. l. for *vātāvata*, q. v.

वाधिन् *vādhin*. See *loka-vādhin*.

वाधुल *vādhula*, m. N. of a man, Saṃskārak.

Vādhūla (cf. *bādhūla*), m. N. of a man, Cat.

Vādhūleya, m. a patr., g. *kārta-kaujapa* (Kāś. *vārcaleya*).

Vādhaula, m. patr., ĀśvŚr.

वाधू *vādhū*, f. (fr. √*vadh* = *vah*) a vessel, boat, raft, W.

वाधून *vādhūna*, m. N. of a teacher (prob. w. r. for *vādhūla* above).

वाध्योषायण *vādhyoshāyaṇa*, m. patr. fr. *vadhyosha*, g. *bidâdi*.

वाध्रिय *vādhriya* (?), m. patr., Pravar.

Vā́dhryaśva, m. patr. fr. *vadhry-aśva*, RV.; ĀśvŚr.

Vādhryaśvi, m. patr., ĀrshBr.

वाध्रीणस *vādhrīṇasa* or °*saka*, m. a rhinoceros, MBh.; R.; MārkP. (accord. to a Sch. also 'a kind of goat, bull, or bird;' cf. *vardhrāṇasa* and *vārdhrīṇ°*).

वान 2. *vāna*, mfn. (fr. √*vai*; for 1. see p. 935, col. 3) dried &c.; n. dry or dried fruit, L.; a kind of bamboo manna, L.

वान 3. *vāna*, n. (fr. √*ve*) the act of weaving or sewing, Nyāyam.; Sāy. (reckoned among the 64 Kalās); a mat of straw, L. **-daṇḍa**, m. a weaver's loom, L. (w. r. *vāṇa-d°*).

Vānīya, mfn. to be woven &c., Pat.

वान 4. *vāna*, m. or n. (?) a hole in the wall of a house, L.

वान 5. *vāna*, m. an intelligent man, L.; N. of Yama, L.

वान 6. *vāna*, mf(*ī*)n. (fr. 1. *vana*, p. 917) relating to a wood or to a dwelling in a wood &c., W.; n. a dense wood, Nalôd.; a multitude of woods or groves or thickets, W.

Vānaka, n. the state of a Brahma-cārin, L.

Vānakauśāmbeya, mfn. (fr. *vana-kauśāmbī*), g. *nady-ādi*.

Vānaprastha, m. (fr. *vana-prastha*) a Brāhman in the third stage of life (who has passed through the stages of student and householder and has abandoned his house and family for an ascetic life in the woods; see *āśrama*), hermit, anchorite (mentioned by Megasthenes under the name ὑλόβιοι), Āpast.; Mn.; MBh. &c.; RTL. 362; a class of supernatural beings, MW.; Bassia Latifolia or Butea Frondosa, L.; mfn. relating to a Vānaprastha; m. (scil. *āśrama*) the third stage of a Brāhman's life, forest-life, MBh.; R.; Hariv. **-dharma**, mfn. the law or duty of a V°, MW. **Vānaprasthâśrama**, m. the order of a V°, ib.

Vānaprasthya, n. the condition of a Vānaprastha, Āpast.

Vānara, m. (prob. fr. *vanar*, p. 918) 'forest-animal,' a monkey, ape (ifc. f. *ā*), Mn.; MBh. &c.; a kind of incense, Olibanum, L.; (with *ācārya*) N. of a writer on medicine, Cat.; (*ī*), f. a female ape, MBh.; R.; Kathās.; Carpopogon Pruriens, L.; mf(*ī*)n. belonging to an ape or monkey, m°-like &c., MBh.; R. **-ketana**, m. 'm°-bannered,' N. of Arjuna, MBh. **-ketu**, m. the m°-banner, ib.; = prec., ib. **-dhvaja**, m. = *-ketana*, ib. **-priya**, m. 'dear to m°s,' the tree Mimusops Kauki, L. **-rāja**, m. 'm°-king,' a strong or excellent m°, MBh. **-vīra-māhātmya**, n. N. of a ch. of the SkandaP. **Vānarâksha**, m. 'm°-eyed,' a wild goat, L. (v. l. *bālavāhya*). **Vānarâkhya**, n. Olibanum, VarBṛS., Sch. **Vānarâghāta**, m. 'm°-stroke,' i. e. 'struck or injured by m°s,' the tree Symplocos Racemosa (commonly called Lodhra or Lodh), L. **Vānarâpasada**, m. a contemptible m°, MW. **Vānarâshṭaka**, n. N. of eight verses (supposed to be spoken by a m°). **Vānarâsya**, m. pl. 'm°-faced,' N. of a people, VP. **Vānarêndra**, m. 'm°-chief,' N. of Sugrīva or of Hanumat, L. **Vānarêśvara-tīrtha**, n. N. of a Tīrtha.

Vānary-ashṭaka, n. N. of a poem (cf. *vānarâshṭaka*).

Vānala, m. the black species of Tulasī or holy basil (Ocymum Sanctum), L.

Vānavāsaka, mf(*ikā*)n. belonging to the (people of the) Vana-vāsakas, Cat.; m. the son of a Vaiśya and a Vaidehī, L.; (*ikā*), f. a kind of metre, Col.

Vānavāsī, f. N. of a city, Daś. **-māhātmya**, n. N. of ch. of the SkandaP., Cat.

Vānavāsya, m. a king of Vānavāsī, ib.

Vānaspatyá, mf(*ā*)n. (fr. *vanas-pati*) coming from a tree, wooden, AV.; VS.; Br.; GṛŚrS.; prepared from trees (as Soma), AitBr.; performed under trees (as a sacrifice), BhP.; living under trees or in woods (said of Śiva), R.; belonging to a sacrificial post; m. a tree or shrub or any plant, AV. (accord. to L. any flowering fruit-tree, such as the Mango, Eugenia &c.); n. the fruit of a tree, Br.; Mn. viii, 2, 39; a multitude or group of trees, Pāṇ. iv, 1, 85, Vārtt. 10, Pat.

Vānā, f. a quail, L.

Vānâvāsya, w. r. for *vānavāsya*.

Vānika, mfn. (prob.) living in the wood, Bhav.

Vānīra, m. (ifc. f. *ā*) a sort of cane or reed, Calamus Rotang, MBh.; Kāv. &c.; = *citraka*, L. **-gṛiha**, n. an arbour of reeds, Ragh. **-ja**, m. Saccharum Munjia, L.; Costus Speciosus or Arabicus, L.

Vānīraka, m. Saccharum Munjia, L.

Vāneya, mf(*ī*)n. living or growing in a wood, sylvan, MBh.; R.; relating or belonging to water &c., W.; n. Cyperus Rotundus, L. **-pushpa**, n. a forest flower, MBh.

Vānya, mf(*ā*)n. relating to a wood, sylvan, Baudh.; (*ā*), f., see next.

1. **Vānyā**, f. (for 2. see p. 941, col. 1) a dense wood or a collection of woods, L.

वानमन्तर *vānamantara*, m. pl. (with Jainas) a class of gods, L.

वानव *vānava*, m. pl. N. of a people, MBh.

वानायु *vānāyu*, m. = *vanāyu*, N. of a country (pl. a people) to the west of India, VP.; an antelope, L. (v. l. *vātāyu*). **-ja**, mfn. 'Vānāyu-born,' a V°

horse (regarded as of a particularly good breed), MBh.; R.

वानीर *vānīra.* See p. 940, col. 3.

वान्त *vānta*, mfn. (fr. √*vam*) vomited, ejected from the mouth, effused, Br.; MBh.; Pur. (*e*, ind. when one has v°); dropped, Ragh. vii, 6; one who has v°, Mn. v, 144; m. N. of a family of priests, Cat. **-vṛishṭi**, mfn. (a cloud) that has shed its rain, Megh. **Vāntâda**, m. 'eating what is vomited,' a dog, L.; (prob.) a kind of bird, Car. **Vāntânna**, n. vomited food, L. **Vāntâśin**, mfn. eating v° food, a foul feeder, Mn.; BhP.; HPariś.; a person who tells his Gotra &c. for the sake of getting food, L.; a foul-feeding demon, MW.

Vānti, f. the act of vomiting, ejecting from the mouth, L. **-kṛit**, mfn. causing vomiting, emetic, L.; m. Vanguieria Spinosa, L. **-da**, mfn. = prec., L.; (*ā*), f. N. of various plants (Helleborus Niger, Wrightia Antidysenterica or Calotropis Gigantea &c.), L. **-śodhanī**, f. Nigella Indica, L. **-hṛit**, w.r. for *-kṛit*.

Vāntī, in comp. for *vānta*. **-√kṛi**, P. *-karoti*, to reject, give up, resign, Buddh. **-bhāva**, m. the being given up, ib.

1. **Vāma**, m. (for 2. and 3. see col. 2) the act of vomiting, g. *jvalâdi*; (*ī*), f. id., Gal.

1. **Vāmaka**, mfn. (for 2. see col. 3) one who vomits, MW.

Vāmanīya, mfn. causing vomiting, emetic, Suśr.; to be cured with emetics, ŚārṅgS.

1. **Vāmin**, mfn. (for 2. see col. 3) vomiting, ejecting from the mouth, TS.; ŚBr.; (*inī*), f. (with *yoni*) a vulva ejecting the semen virile, Suśr.

1. **Vāmya**, mfn. (for 2. and 3. see cols. 2, 3) to be cured with emetics, ŚārṅgS.

वान्दन *vāndana*, m. patr. fr. *vandana*, ĀśvŚr.

वान्या 2. *vānyā*, f. (for 1. see p. 940, col. 3) a cow whose calf is dead, TBr. (cf. *api-*, *abhi-*, *ni-v°*).

वाप 1. *vāpa*, m. = 1. *vāya*, 'weaving' or 'a weaver' (see *tantu-*, *tantra-*, *sūtra-v°*). **-daṇḍa**, m. a weaver's loom, L. (cf. *vāna-* and *vāya-d°*).

Vāpaka. See *paṭṭikā-v°*.

वाप 2. *vāpa*, m. (fr. √1. *vap*) the act of shearing or shaving (see *kṛita-v°*).

1. **Vāpana**, n. the act of causing to shave or of shaving, GṛŚrS.

1. **Vāpita**, mfn. (fr. Caus.) shaven, shorn, L.

वाप 3. *vāpa*, m. (fr. √2. *vap*) a sower (see *bīja-v°*); the act of sowing seed, W.; the act of pouring in or mixing with, Nyāyam.; seed, MBh.; (ifc.) sown with, L. (cf. Pāṇ. viii, 4, 11, Sch.)

2. **Vāpana**, n. the act of scattering or sowing, SaṃhUp.

Vāpi, f. = *vāpī*, a pond, BhP. (cf. Uṇ. iv, 124).

Vāpikā, f. id., Kāv.

2. **Vāpita**, mfn. (fr. Caus.) caused to be sown, sown (as seed), VarBṛS.

Vāpin, mfn. (ifc.) sowing, Pāṇ. viii, 4, 11, Sch.

Vāpima, n. an unannealed vessel, L. (cf. next).

Vāpī, f. any pond (made by scattering or damming up earth), a large oblong pond, an oblong reservoir of water, tank, pool, lake, Mn.; MBh. &c. (cf. *krīḍā-v°*); a partic. constellation, VarBṛS. **-kūpa-taṭâka-śānti**, f., **-kūpa-taḍāgâdi-paddhati**, f. N. of wks. **-jala**, n. lake-water, Ml. **-vistīrṇa**, (prob.) n. a hole (made by a thief in a wall) resembling a pond, Mṛicch. **-ha**, m. 'abandoning lakes,' the Cātaka bird, Cuculus Melanoleucus, L. **Vāpy-utsarga**, m. N. of wk.

Vāpīka, (ifc.) = *vāpī*, Kathās.; m. N. of a poet, Cat.

Vāpya, mfn. to be scattered or sown or cast or thrown, Kauś.; coming from ponds or tanks (as water), Suśr.; m. a father(?), L.; n. Costus Speciosus or Arabicus, L. (v.l. *vyāpya*).

Vāpyāya, Nom. P. °*yate* (only pr. p. *vāpyāyamāna*), to become or resemble a pond, Divyâv.

वापुष *vāpusha*, mfn. (fr. *vapus*) wonderful, admirable, RV.

वाभट *vābhaṭa*, m. N. of a lexicographer, L. (prob. w.r. for *vāg-bhaṭa*).

वाभि *vābhi.* See *ūrṇa-vābhi.*

वाम् *vām*, (encl.) acc. dat. gen. du. of 2nd pers. pron. (cf. Pāṇ. viii, 1, 20; 24 &c.), RV. &c. &c. (the accented *vā́m* in RV. vi, 55, 1 is thought to be = *āvām*, nom. du. of 1st pers. pron.)

वाम 2. *vāmá*, mf(*ī* or *ā*)n. (fr. √1. *van*; for 1. see col. 1) lovely, dear, pleasant, agreeable, fair, beautiful, splendid, noble, RV. &c. &c.; (ifc.) striving after, eager for, intent upon, fond of, Kāv.; Kathās.; Rājat.; m. the female breast, L.; the god of love, L.; N. of Śiva, BhP.; of a Rudra, ib.; of Varuṇa, L.; (with Śaivas) = *vāma-deva-guhya*, Sarvad.; of a son of Ṛicīka, MBh. (B. *rāma*); of a son of Kṛishṇa and Bhadrā, BhP.; of a prince (son of Dharma), Cat.; of a son of Bhaṭṭa-nārāyaṇa, Kshitîś. (cf. *-deva*); of one of the Moon's horses, VP.; m. or n. a kind of pot-herb, Chenopodium Album, L.; (*ā*), f. a beautiful woman, any woman or wife, Pañcar.; Sāh.; a partic. form of Durgā, Pur.; a partic. Śakti, Hcat.; N. of Lakshmī, W.; of Sarasvatī, ib.; of one of the Mātṛis attending on Skanda, MBh.; of the mother of Pārśva (the 23rd Arhat of the present Avasarpiṇī), L.; (*áyā*), ind. in a pleasant or lovely manner, RV. viii, 9, 7; (*ī*), f. a mare, L. (*vāmī-ratha*, mfn., Pat. on Pāṇ. iv, 2, 104, Vārtt. 20); a she-ass, L.; a female camel (cf. *ushṭra-v°*); a young female elephant, L.; the female of the jackal, L.; n. a lovely thing, any dear or desirable good (as gold, horses &c.), wealth, fortune, RV.; AV.; Br.; ChUp.; mfn. relating to a mare, Pat. (cf. under *ī*, f. above). **-jāta** (*vāmá-*), mfn. lovely or dear by nature, RV. x, 140, 3. **-1. tā**, f., **-tva**, n. (for 2. see col. 3) loveliness, W. **-datta**, m. 'given by Śiva,' N. of a man, Kathās.; (*ā*), f. N. of a woman, ib. **-dṛiś** (nom. *k*) or **-dṛishṭi**, f. a fair-eyed woman, Kāv. **-deva** (*vāmá-*), m. N. of an ancient Ṛishi (having the patr. *Gautama*, author of the hymns RV. iv, 1-41; 45-48, comprising nearly the whole fourth Maṇḍala; pl. his family), RV. &c. &c.; of a minister of Daśa-ratha, MBh.; R.; of a king, MBh.; Hariv.; of a son of Nārāyaṇa (father of Viśva-nātha), Cat.; of a lawyer, a poet &c. (also with *upâdhyāya* and *bhaṭṭâ-cārya*), ib.; of a form of Śiva, Hariv.; BhP.; of a demon presiding over a partic. disease, Hariv.; of a mountain in Śālmala-dvīpa, BhP.; of the third day or Kalpa in the month of Brahmā (see under *kalpa*); (*ī*), f. a form of Durgā, Hcat.; mf(*ī*)n. relating to the Ṛishi Vāma-deva, MBh.; *-guhya*, m. (with Śaivas) one of the five forms of Śiva, Sarvad.; *-rathá*, m. V°-d°'s chariot, MaitrS.; *-saṃhitā*, f. N. of wk. **-devyá**, mfn. coming or descended from the Ṛishi Vāma-deva, ŚBr.; m. patr. of Aṅho-muc (author of RV. x, 127), Anukr.; of Bṛihad-uktha and Mūrdhanvat, ib.; n. N. of various Sāmans, ĀrshBr.; *-vidyā*, f. N. of wk. **-dhvaja**, m. N. of an author, Cat. **-nayanā**, f. a fair-eyed woman, Kāv. **-1. -nī**, mfn. (for 2. see p. 942, col. 1) bringing wealth, ChUp.; *-tva*, n. the attribute of bestowing w°, Śaṃk. **-nīti** (*vāmá-*), mfn. conducting to wealth or to the good, RV. **-netra**, n. a mystical N. of the vowel *ī*, L.; (*ā*), f. = *-nayanā*, L. **-bhā́j**, mfn. partaking of goods or of the good, RV. **-bhṛit**, f. a kind of brick (*-tvá*, n.), TS.; MaitrS. **-1. -bhrū́**, f. (for 2. see col. 3) a woman (with fine eyebrows or eyes), Kāv. **-moshá**, mfn. stealing precious things, TS. **-ratha**, m. N. of a man (pl. his family), g. *kurv-ādi*. **-rathya**, m. patr. fr. prec., ib.; a branch of the Ātreyas, KātyŚr. **-locana**, mfn. fair-eyed, Śak.; (*ā*), f. = *-dṛiś*, Hit.; N. of a woman (the daughter of Vīra-ketu), Daś. **-śiva**, m. N. of a man, Kathās. **-svabhāva**, mf(*ā*)n. of noble character or disposition, BhP. **Vāmâkshi**, n. = *vāma-netra*, L.; (*ī*), f. = *vāma-dṛiś*, Kāv.; Kathās. **Vāmâpīḍana** (or °*mā-p°*?), m. Careya Arborea or Salvadora Persica, L. **Vāmêkshaṇā**, f. = *vāma-nayanā*, Hāsy. **Vāmôru** or **vāmôrū**, f. (Nom. °*rūs*, Śiś. viii, 24; voc. °*rū*; cf. Vām. v, 2, 49; compar. °*rū-tarā*, Vop.) a handsome-thighed woman, MBh.; Kāv.; BhP.

Vāmila, vāmīya-bhāshya. See col. 3.

2. **Vāmya**, mfn. (for 1. see col. 1, for 3. col. 3) belonging to Vāma-deva, MBh.

वाम 3. *vā́ma*, mf(*ā*)n. (perhaps originally identical with 2. above) left, not right, being or situated on the left side, ŚBr. &c. &c. (the quivering of the left eye or arm is supposed to be a good omen in women and of the left arm a bad omen in men); reverse, adverse, contrary, opposite, unfavourable, Kāv.; Kathās.; crooked, oblique (*am*, ind. sideways), BhP.; refractory, coy (in love), Sāh.; acting in the opposite way or differently, Śak. iv, 18; hard, cruel, Kāv.; Pur.; vile, wicked, base, low, bad, Kir.; m. or n. the left side (*vāmād dakshiṇam*, from the left to the right; *vāmena*, on the left side), Kāv.; Kathās.; m. the left hand, RāmatUp.; a snake, L.; an animal, sentient being, L.; n. adversity, misfortune, Kathās.; the left-hand practices of the followers of the Tantras (= *vāmâcāra*, q.v.), Cat. **-kaṭistha**, mfn. lying or situated on the left side, Siṇhâs. **-kirīṭin**, mfn. one whose crest or diadem is turned towards the left, VarBṛS. **-kukshi**, m. the left side of the abdomen, Siṇhâs. (v.l. *-pārśva*). **-cūḍa** or **-cūla**, m. pl. 'left-crested,' N. of a people, Hariv. **-jushṭa**, n. = *vāmakêśvara-tantra*, Āryav. **-tantra**, n. N. of a Tantra. **-tas**, ind. from or on the left, MBh.; Kāv. &c. **-2. -tā**, f. (also pl., Kāv.; Rājat.), **-tva**, n. (for 1. see col. 2) contrariety, disfavour, refractoriness, coyness. **-nata**, mfn. bent or turned to the left, VarBṛS. **-pārśva**, m. the l° side, Siṇhâs. (see *-kukshi*). **-bhāshin**, mf(*iṇī*)n. speaking ill or adversely, R. **-2. -bhrū**, f. (for 1. see col. 2) the left eyebrow, PratijñāS. **-mārga**, m. the left-hand doctrine (see *vāmâcāra*), Cat.; °*gin*, m. = *vāmâcārin*, RTL. 185. **-śīla**, mfn. of bad character or disposition, Kir.; refractory or timid (in love), coy, Mālatīm. **-stha**, mfn. standing on the left, Kathās. **-hasta**, m. the dew-lap of a goat, Aryav. **Vāmâgama**, m. = next, W. **Vāmâcāra**, m. the left-hand practices or doctrines of the Tantras (i.e. the worship of the Śakti or Female Energy personified as the wife of Śiva, as opposed to *dakshiṇâcāra*, q.v.), Cat.; mfn. behaving badly or in the wrong way, Suśr.; Pañcar.; °*rin*, m. an adherent of the left-hand practices of the followers of the Tantras, IW. 523, n. 1. **Vāmârambha**, mfn. refractory, stubborn, Mālatīm. **Vāmârcana-candrikā**, f. N. of a Tantric wk. **Vāmârcis**, mfn. (a fire) flaming towards the left (and so foreboding evil), MBh. **Vāmâvacara**, mfn. keeping on the left side, Lalit. **Vāmâvarta**, mfn. winding or wound towards the left, Bhpr.; turned towards the left or west, Hcat. **Vāmêtara**, mfn. 'different from left,' right, Ragh. **Vāmâika-vṛitti**, mfn. always acting perversely (*-tva*, n.), Kathās.

2. **Vāmaka**, mf(*ikā*)n. (for 1. see col. 1) left, not right, VarBṛS.; Mālatīm.; adverse, cruel, rough, hard, KālP.; m. a partic. mixed tribe, MBh.; N. of a king of Kāśi, Car.; of a son of Bhajamāna, VP.; of a Cakra-vartin, Buddh.; (prob.) n. a kind of gesture, Vikr.; (*ikā*), f. N. of Durgā, MW. **Vāmakêśvara-tantra**, n. and **Vāmakêśvara-saṃhitā**, f. N. of wks.

Vā́makakshāyaṇa (once °*yaṇá*), m. patr., ŚBr.

2. **Vāmin**, mfn. (for 1. see this page, col. 1) = *vāmâcarin*, W.

Vāmila, mfn. = *vāma* or *dāmbhika*, L.

Vāmī-√kṛi, P. *-karoti*, to turn or direct towards the left side, VarBṛS.

Vāmīya-bhāshya, n. N. of wk.

3. **Vāmya**, n. (for 1. and 2. see cols. 1, 2) perverseness, refractoriness, Naish.; Sāh.

वामन् *vāman* (g. *pāmâdi*), prob. invented to explain *vāmana*.

वामन *vāmaná*, mf(*ā*)n. (of doubtful derivation) dwarfish, small or short in stature, a dwarf, VS. &c. &c.; small, minute, short (also of days), MBh.; Kāv. &c.; bent, inclined, HPariś.; relating to a dwarf or to Vishṇu (cf. below), treating of him, Pur.; descended from the elephant Vāmana (see below), R.; m. 'the Dwarf,' N. of Vishṇu in his fifth Avatāra or descent (undertaken to humble the pride of the Daitya Bali [q.v.]; the germ of the story of this incarnation seems to be contained in the 1st book of the ŚBr.; the later legend is given in R. i, 32, 2); N. of a partic. month, VarBṛS.; of Śiva, MBh. xiv, 193; a dwarfish bull, MaitrS.; TS.; a goat with partic. marks, VarBṛS.; a person born under a partic. constellation, ib.; = *kāṇḍa*, L.; Alangium Hexapetalum, L.; N. of a serpent-demon, MBh.; of a son of Garuḍa, ib.; of a son of Hiraṇya-garbha, Hariv.; of one of the 18 attendants of the Sun, L.; of a Dānava, Hariv.; of a Muni, Cat.; of a poet (minister under Jayâpīḍa), Rājat.; (also with *bhaṭṭa*, *ācārya* &c.) of various other scholars and authors &c. (esp. of one of the authors of the Kāśikā-vṛitti, the other being Jayâditya, and of the author of the Kāvyâlaṃkāra-vṛitti); of the elephant that supports the south (or west) quarter, MBh.; of a mountain, MBh.; (pl.) N. of a people, ib. (B. *ambashṭha*); (*ā*), f. N. of an Apsaras (v.l. *rāmaṇā*), R.; (*ī*), f. a female dwarf,

W.; N. of a Yoginī, Hcat.; a partic. disease of the vagina, W. (prob. w. r. for *vāminī*, q. v. under 1. *vāmin*); a sort of woman, W.; a mare, MW.; n. = *vāmana-purāṇa* and °*nôpapurāṇa* (q.v.); N. of a place of pilgrimage (called after the dwarf form of Vishṇu), MBh. — **kārikā**, f., **-citra-caritra**, n., **-jayantī-vrata**, n., **-jātaka**, n., **-tattva**, n. N. of wks. — **tanu**, mfn. dwarf-bodied, MW. — **tā**, f. (GāruḍaP.), **-tva**, n. (ŚārṅgS.) shortness, dwarfishness (*-tvaṃ* √*gam*, to assume the form of a dwarf, R.) — **datta** and **-deva**, m. N. of two authors, Cat. — **dvādaśī**, f. N. of the 12th day in the light half of the month Caitra (on which a festival is held in honour of Vishṇu), L.; *-kathā*, f., *-vrata*, n. N. of wks. — **nighaṇṭu**, m. N. of a dictionary. — **purāṇa**, n. N. of one of the 18 Purāṇas (said to have been related by Pulastya to Nārada, and containing an account of the dwarf-incarnation of Vishṇu), IW. 514. — **prādur-bhāva**, m. 'the Dwarf manifestation or incarnation (cf. above),' N. of a ch. of the Hari-vaṇśa. — **rūpin**, mfn. dwarf-formed, being in the form of a dwarf, MW. — **vṛitti**, f. = *kāśikā-vṛ°* or = *kāvyâlaṃkāra-vṛ°*; *-ṭīkā*, f. N. of Maheśvara's Comm. on the latter wk. — **vrata**, n. N. of a partic. Vrata to be observed on the 12th day of Śrāvaṇa in celebration of Vishṇu's dwarf-incarnation, L. (cf. *vāmana-dvādaśī-vrata*). — **sûkta**, n. N. of a partic. Vedic hymn, Cat. — **sūtra-vṛitti**, f. = *kāvyâlaṃkāra-vṛitti*. — **stava**, m. N. of a ch. of the Hari-vaṇśa. — **svāmin**, m. N. of a poet, Cat. **Vāmanâkṛiti**, mfn. dwarf-shaped, dwarfish, MW. **Vāmanânanda**, m. N. of an author, Cat. **Vāmanânvaya**, m. 'descended from the elephant Vāmana,' an el° with partic. marks, Gal. **Vāmanâvatāra**, m. the dwarf-incarnation; *-kathana*, n. N. of a ch. of the PadmaP. **Vāmanâśrama**, m. N. of a partic. hermitage, Ragh. **Vāmanêndra-svāmin**, m. N. of a preceptor, Cat. **Vāmanêbhī**, f. the female of the elephant Vāmana, L. **Vāmanôpapurāṇa**, n. N. of an Upapurāṇa.

Vāmanaka, mf(*ikā*)n. dwarfish, small, Hariv.; BhP.; m. a dwarf, VarBṛS.; Kād.; a person born under a partic. constellation, VarBṛS.; N. of a mountain, MBh.; (*ikā*), f. N. of one of the Mātṛis attending on Skanda, ib.; a female dwarf, Nalac.; a sort of woman, ib.; n. dwarfishness (°*kaṃ* √*kṛi*, to assume the form of a dwarf), BhP.; N. of a place of pilgrimage, MBh.

2. **Vāmanī** (for 1. see p. 941, col. 2), in comp. for *vāmana*. — **kṛita**, mfn. turned into a dwarf (said of Vishṇu), ŚārṅgP.; pressed down, flattened, Amar. — **bhūta**, mfn. become a dwarf, lowered, bent or broken down, Śiś.

वामरिन् *vāmarin*, w.r. for *cāmarin*, L.

वामलूर *vāmalūra*, m. an ant-hill, Kāśīkh.

वामिल *vāmila*. See p. 941, col. 3.

वाम्नी *vāmnī*, f. N. of a woman (cf. next).

Vāmneya, m. metr. fr. prec., PañcavBr.

वाम्र *vāmra*, m. (fr. *vamra*) N. of a Ṛishi, Br.; n. N. of a Sāman, Lāṭy.

वाय 1. *vāya*, m. (fr. √*ve*; cf. 1. *vāpa*) 'weaving' or 'a weaver' (see *tantu-*, *tantra-*, *tunna-*, *vāso-v°*); a thread, strap (see *tiraścīna-v°*). — **daṇḍa**, m. a weaver's loom, L.

1. **Vāyaka**, m. a weaver, sower, Kāv.; Kathās.; BhP.

Vāyana-kriyā, f. weaver's work, weaving, ĀpGṛ., Sch.

Vāya-rajju, f., g. *deva-pathâdi* (Kāś. *cāmar°*).

Vāyin, mfn. weaving, sowing, MW.

वाय 2. *vāya*, m. (said to be) patr. fr. *vi*, a bird, Nir. vi, 28.

वाय 3. *vāya*, m. (fr. √*vī*) a leader, guide (see *pada-vāyá*).

वायक 2. *vāyaka*, m. (said to be fr. √*vay*) a heap, multitude, number, L.

वायत *vāyata*, m. (fr. *vayat*), patr. of Pāśadyumna, RV. vii, 33, 2.

वायन *vāyana* or °*naka*, n. sweetmeats or cakes which may be eaten during a religious feast, presents of sweetmeats &c. (forming part of an offering to a deity or prepared on festive occasions, such as marriages &c.), L.; a kind of perfume.

Vāyanin (?), m. patr. (also pl.), Saṃskārak.

वायव *vāyava* &c. See p. 943, col. 1.

वायस *vāyasá*, m. (fr. *vayas*) a bird, (esp.) a large bird, RV. i, 164, 52 (cf. Nir. iv, 17); a crow, Br.; MBh. &c.; a prince of the Vayas, g. *pārśvâdi*; Agallochum or fragrant aloe, L.; turpentine, L.; a house facing the north-east, L.; (*ī*), f. a female crow, Mṛicch.; Pañcat.; Hit.; N. of various plants (accord. to L. Ficus Oppositifolia, Agati Grandiflora, = *kāka-tuṇḍī* and = *mahā-jyotishmatī*), Suśr.; mf(*ī*)n. relating or peculiar to crows, MBh.; Kāv. &c.; consisting of birds, Nalôd.; containing the word *vayas*, g. *vimuktâdi*; n. a multitude of crows, Pāṇ. iv, 2, 37, Sch. — **jaṅghā**, f. a species of plant (= *kāka-j°*), L. — **tīra**, n. (prob.) N. of a place (°*rīya*, mfn.), Pāṇ. iv, 2, 104, Vārtt. 2, Pat. — **tuṇḍa**, mfn. resembling the beak of a crow; m. (with *saṃdhi*) the joint of the jaw, Processus Coronoideus, Suśr. — **pīlu**, m. a partic. tree (= *kāka-p°*), Car. — **vidyā**, f. 'the science of (augury from observing) crows,' N. of a ch. of VarBṛS.; °*dyika*, mfn. versed in the above science, Pat. on Pāṇ. iv, 2, 60. — **śānti**, f. N. of wk. **Vāyasâdanī**, f. (only L.) N. of various plants or trees (Agati Grandiflora; Cardiospermum Halicacabum; Capparis Sepiaria; = *kāka-tuṇḍī*). **Vāyasântaka**, m. 'crow-destroyer,' an owl, MBh. **Vāyasâri** or °*sârāti*, m. 'crow's enemy,' id., L. **Vāyasâhvā**, f. (only L.) Agati Grandiflora; Solanum Indicum; Capparis Sepiaria. **Vāyasêkshuka**, m. Saccharum Spontaneum, L.

Vāyasi, in comp. for *vāyasa*. — **kṛita**, mfn. turned into a crow, Subh. — **bhūta**, mfn. become or being a crow, Kathās.

Vāyasolikā or °*lī*, f. a medicinal root (= *kākolī*), Bhpr.

वायस्क *vāyaska*, Uṇ. iv, 188, Sch.

वायु 1. *vāyú*, m. (fr. √2. *vā*) wind, air (as one of the 5 elements; in MBh. 7 winds are reckoned), RV. &c. &c.; the god of the wind (often associated with Indra in the Ṛig-veda, as Vāta [q.v.] with Parjanya, but although of equal rank with Indra, not occupying so prominent a position; in the Purusha-sûkta he is said to have sprung form the breath of Purusha, and elsewhere is described as the son-in-law of Tvashṭṛi; he is said to move in a shining car drawn by a pair of red or purple horses or by several teams consisting of ninety-nine or a hundred or even a thousand horses [cf. *ni-yút*]; he is often made to occupy the same chariot with Indra, and in conjunction with him honoured with the first draught of the Soma libation; he is rarely connected with the Maruts, although in i, 134, 4, he is said to have begotten them from the rivers of heaven; he is regent of the Nakshatra Svāti and north-west quarter, see *loka-pāla*), ib.; breathing, breath, VPrāt.; ĪśUp.; the wind of the body, a vital air (of which 5 are reckoned, viz. *prâṇa*, *apâna*, *samāna*, *udāna*, and *vyāna*; or *nāga*, *kūrma*, *kṛikara*, *devadatta*, and *dhanaṃ-jaya*), Hariv.; Sāṃkhyak.; Vedântas.; (in medicine) the windy humour or any morbid affection of it, Suśr.; the wind as a kind of demon producing madness, Kād.; Vcar. (cf. *-grasta*); (in astron.) N. of the fourth Muhūrta; a mystical N. of the letter *ya*, Up.; N. of a Vasu, Hariv.; of a Daitya, ib.; of a king of the Gandharvas, VP.; of a Marut, R.; pl. the Maruts, Kathās.; MārkP. — **kṛitsna**, n. one of the ten mystical exercises called Kṛitsna, L. — **ketu**, m. 'wind-sign,' dust, L. — **keśa** (*vāyú-*), mfn. (prob.) having waving hair (said of the Gandharvas), RV. iii, 38, 6. — **koṇa**, m. 'wind-corner,' the north-west quarter, W. — **gaṇḍa**, m. 'w°-swelling,' flatulence, indigestion, L. — **gati**, mfn. going like the w°, swift as w°, fleet, W. — **gadya**, N. of a Stotra. — **gīta**, mfn. sung by the w° (i.e. universally known), Mn. ix, 42. — **gulma**, m. 'wind-cluster,' a whirlwind, hurricane, W.; a whirlpool, eddy, L. — **gocara**, m. the track or range of the w°, MW.; the north-west, Hcat. — **gopa** (*vāyú-*), mfn. having the wind as protector, RV. x, 151, 4. — **gopā**, mfn. id., MW. — **granthi**, m. a lump or swelling caused by disturbance of the air in the body, MārkP. — **grasta**, mfn. 'wind-seized,' affected by w°, mad, VarBṛS.; Daś.; flatulent; gouty, A. — **ghna**, mfn. 'wind-destroying,' curing windy disorders, W. — **cakra**, m. N. of one of the 7 Ṛishis (said to be fathers of the Maruts), MBh.; n. the range of the w°, Vīrac. — **citi**, f. Vāyu's pile or layer, ŚBr. — **ja**, (prob.) m. 'air-born,' N. of a tree (?), Pañcat. i, $\frac{3\,2\,3}{3\,2\,4}$. — **jāta**, m. 'wind-born,' N. of Hanu-mat, W. — **jvāla**, m. N. of one of the 7 Ṛishis (see *-cakra*), MBh. — **tanaya**, m. = *-putra*, MW. — **tejas** (*vāyú-*), mfn. having the sharpness of w°, AV. x, 5, 26. — **tva**, n. the notion or idea of air, Sarvad. — **datta**, m. N. of a man, g. *śubhrâdi*; *-maya*, mf(*ī*)n. and *-rūpya*, mfn., Pāṇ. iv, 2, 104, Vārtt. 23, Sch. — **dattaka**, m. endearing form of *-datta*, Pat. — **datteya**, mfn. (fr. *-datta*), g. *sakhy-ādi*; m. patr. (fr. id.), g. *śubhrâdi*. — **dāra**, m. a cloud, L. — **dāru**, m. 'air-tearer, air-scatterer,' id., W. — **diś**, f. the north-west, VarBṛS. — **dīpta**, mfn. (said of animals in the practice of augury), VarBṛS. — **deva**, n. the lunar mansion Svāti (presided over by Vāyu), ib. — **daivata** or **-daivatya**, mfn. having Vāyu as a deity, VarBṛS. — **dvāra**, n. the door of breath, AmṛitUp. — **dhātu**, m. the element air or wind, Sarvad. — **dhāraṇa**, mfn. (with *divasa*, m.) N. of partic. days in the light half of the month Jyaishṭha, VarBṛS. — **nandana**, m. = *-putra*, MW. — **nānā-tva**, n. diversity of air (said to be caused by the concurrence [*sammūrchana*] of two winds), MW. — **nighna**, mfn. 'subject to wind,' mad, Daś. — **nivṛitti**, f. 'cessation of w°,' a calm, lull, W.; cure of windy disorders, ib. — **pañcaka**, n. the set of five vital airs, MW. — **patha**, m. 'wind-path,' N. of a partic. region in the atmosphere, Hariv.; R.; N. of a king, Kathās. — **paramâṇu**, m. a primary aerial atom, MW. — **putra**, m. 'son of the w°,' N. of Hanumat, RāmatUp.; R.; of Bhīma, L. — **putrāya** (only °*yita*, n. impers.), to represent or act the part of Hanumat, Rājat. — **pura**, n. N. of a town, W. — **purāṇa**, n. N. of one of the 18 Purāṇas (prob. one of the oldest, and supposed to have been revealed by the god Vāyu; it treats of the creation of the world, the origin of the four classes, the worship of Śiva &c.), IW. 514. — **pūta**, mfn. purified by the wind, NṛisUp. — **pracyuta** (*vāyú-*), mf(*ā*)n. driven by the wind, TS. — **praṇetra** (*vāyú-*), mfn. having the wind as leader, ŚBr. — **pratyaksha-vāda**, °*sha-vicāra*, m. N. of wks. — **phala**, n. 'wind-fruit,' hail, L.; the rainbow, L. — **bala**, m. N. of one of the 7 Ṛishis (see *-cakra*), MBh.; of a warrior who fought on the side of the gods against the Asuras, Kathās. — **bīja**, n. seed or germ of the air, Sarvad. (accord. to some N. of the syllable *jam*). — **bhaksha**, mf(*ā*)n. eating (only) air, living on air, MBh.; R.; BhP.; m. a snake, L.; an ascetic, W.; N. of a Muni, MBh. — **bhakshaka**, mfn. = *-bhaksha*, Hit. — **bhakshaṇa**, n. the act of eating or living on air, fasting, W.; m. = *-bhuj*, A. — **bhakshya**, mfn. = *-bhaksha*, R.; m. a snake, L. — **bhāratī-stotra**, n. N. of a Stotra. — **bhuj**, m. one who feeds only on air (as an ascetic, a snake &c.), A. — **bhūta**, mfn. become air, become like the wind, W.; going everywhere at will, ib. — **bhūti**, m. (with Jainas) N. of one of the eleven Gaṇâdhipas, L.; W. — **bhojana**, mfn. = *-bhaksha*, q. v., BhP. — **maṇḍala**, m. N. of one of the 7 Ṛishis (see *-cakra*), MBh.; n. a whirlwind, ib. — **mát**, mfn. attended with wind, AV.; ŚrS.; containing the word *vāyu* &c., TS. — **maya** (*vāyú-*), mf(*ī*)n. having the nature of the wind or of air, ŚBr.; MBh. — **marullipi** (fr. *-marut* + *l°*), f. a partic. mode of writing, Lalit. — **mārga**, m. the path or track of the wind, MW.; the atmosphere, Gal. — **rugṇa**, mfn. broken off by the w°, R. — **rujā**, f. 'w°-disease,' inflammation (of the eyes), MBh. — **retas**, m. N. of one of the 7 Ṛishis (see *-cakra*), MBh. — **roshā** (?), f. 'raging with wind,' night, L. (prob. for *vāsurôshā*, i. e. *vāsurā* + *ushā*). — **lakshaṇa**, n. the character or property of air (viz. touch), MW.; N. of wk. — **loka**, m. the world of Vāyu, ŚāṅkhBr.; KaushUp. — **vat**, ind. like w°, MBh. — **vartman**, m. (?) or n. 'wind-path,' the atmosphere, L. — **valana-pañca-taraṃgiṇī-māhātmya**, n., **-vāda**, m. N. of wks. — **vāha**, m. 'having the wind for a vehicle,' smoke, vapour, L. — **vāhana**, m. 'id.,' N. of Vishṇu, L.; of Śiva, Śivag. — **vāhinī**, f. the air-conveying (vessel of the body), L. — **vega**, m. the velocity of the wind, a gust of w° (see below); mfn. having the vel° of w°, fleet as the w°, L.; m. N. of one of the 7 Ṛishis (see *-cakra*), MBh.; of a son of Dhṛita-rāshṭra, MBh.; (*ā*), f. N. of a Yoginī, Kālac.; of a Kiṃ-nara maiden, Kāraṇḍ.; *-yaśas*, f. N. of a sister of Vāyu-patha, Kathās.; *-sama*, mfn. equal to the velocity of wind, swift as the wind, R. — **vegaka**, mf(*ikā*)n. swift as the w°, Hcat. — **vegin**, mfn. id., NādabUp. — **śānti**, f., **-saṃhitā**, f. N. of wks. — **sakha** or °*khi*, m. 'having the w° for a friend,' fire, L. — **sama**, mfn. resembling the wind, PārGṛ.; swift as wind, W.; like air or wind, unsubstantial, ib.

-sambhava, m. 'wind-born,' N. of Hanumat, W.; (*ā*), f. a red cow, L. **-savitrí** or °*trá*, m. du. Vāyu and Savitṛi, MaitrS. (cf. *vāyosāvitrá*). **-suta,** m. = *-putra*, MW. **-sūnu,** m. patr. of Hanumat, RāmatUp.; R. **-skandha,** m. the region of the wind, Hariv.; VarBṛS. &c. **-stuti,** f. N. of two hymns. **-han,** m. N. of one of the 7 Ṛishis of the Maruts, MBh. **-hīna,** mfn. destitute of wind, MW.

Vāyava, mf(*ī*)n. relating or belonging to the wind or air, given by or sacred to the god of wind &c., PārGṛ.; MBh.; north-western; (*ī*), f. (with or scil. *diś*) the north-west (cf. under *vāyu*), ĀśvGṛ.

Vāyavīya, mfn. relating to the air or the wind or the god of the wind, windy, aerial, Yājñ.; Suśr. &c. **-tantra,** n., **-saṃhitā,** f. N. of wks.

Vāyavī-saṃhitā, f. N. of wk. (= *vāyavīya-s*°).

Vāyavyà, mf(*ā*)n. = *vāyava* (in both meanings), MaitrS.; VarBṛS.; Mārk.; n. (with or scil. *pātra*) N. of partic. Soma vessels shaped like mortars, TS.; Br.; GṛŚrS.; the Nakshatra Svāti (of which Vāyu is the regent), VarBṛS.; (also m. and [*ā*], f.) the north-west (as presided over by V°), VarBṛS.; MārkP. **-purāṇa,** n. N. of a Purāṇa.

Vāyuka, m. endearing form for *vāyu-datta*, Pat.

Vāyúra, mfn. windy, ŚBr. (Sch.)

Vāyv, in comp. for 1. *vāyu*. **-agni,** m. du. Vāyu and Agni, MW. **-adhika,** mfn. 'having an excess of wind,' gouty, Divyâv. (w. r. *vāyv-ādh*°). **-abhibhūta,** mfn. = *vāyu-grasta*, Sarvad. **-aśva,** mf(*ā*)n. having the winds for horses, TĀr. (w. r. *vāyav-aśva*). **-āspada,** n. 'wind-place,' the atmosphere, sky, L.

वायु 2. *vāyú*, mfn. (fr. √*vai*) tired, languid, RV. vii, 91, 1.

वायु 3. *vāyú*, mfn. (fr. √*vī*) desirous, covetous, greedy (for food, applied to calves), TS.; desirable, desired by the appetite, RV.

वायुन *vāyuna*, m. a god, deity, L.

वायुष *vāyusha*, m. a kind of fish, L.

वायोधस *vāyodhasa*, mfn. relating or belonging to Vayo-dhas (i. e. Indra), KātyŚr.

वायोयानी *vāyoyānī*, f. N. of a kind of brick, MaitrS.

वायोर्विद *vāyorvida*, prob. w.r. for *vāyovida*.

वायोविद *vāyovida*, m. (fr. *vayo-vid*) N. of a Ṛishi, Car.

Vāyovidyiká, m. (fr. *vayo-vidyā*) a bird-catcher, fowler, ŚBr.

वायोसावित्र *vāyosāvitrá* (in °*tráḥ*, said to be = *vāyu-savitṛibhyām*), TS.

वाय्य *vāyyá*, m. (fr. *vayya*) patr. of Satyaśravas (represented as a poet and an Ātreya), RV.

वाय्वग्नि *vāyv-agni* &c. See above.

वार् *vār*, n. (said to be fr. √1. *vṛi*) water, RV. &c. &c. (n. pl. once in BhP. *vāras*, as if m. or f.; *vārāṃ nidhiḥ*, 'receptacle of waters,' the ocean, Prab.); stagnant water, a pond, RV. iv, 19, 4; viii, 98, 8; ix, 112, 4; m.(?) a protector, defender, i, 132, 3; x, 93, 3. [Cf., accord. to some, Gk. οὖρον, οὐρέω; Lat. *urina*, *urinari*.] **-āsana,** n. a water-reservoir, L. **-kāryà,** mfn. (prob.) producing w° or rain, RV. i, 88, 4 (Sāy. 'to be performed with w°'). **-gara,** m. 'w°-swallower (?),' a wife's brother, Gal. (cf. *vādgala*). **-ghaṭi-yantra-cakra,** n. a wheel for drawing water, Dharmas. **-da,** m. 'w°-giving,' a rain-cloud, Śatr. **-dara, -dala** &c., see s. v. **-dhānī,** f. a water-jar, HPariś. **-dhārā,** f. a jet of water, Divyâv. **-dhi,** m. w°-holder, the sea, ocean, Kāv.; BhP.; *-phena*, n. Os Sepiæ, L.; *-bhava*, n. = next, L. **-dheya,** n. a kind of salt, L. **-bhaṭa,** m. 'w°-fighter,' an alligator, L. **-muc,** m. 'w°-discharger,' a cloud, BhP. **-rāśi,** m. 'water-heap,' the ocean, L. **-vaṭa,** m. 'water-exclosure (?),' a boat, vessel, L. (also written *vārbaṭa*). **-vatī,** f. containing w°, a river, Naigh. i, 13 (v. l. for *pārvatī*). **-vāha,** m. 'water-bearer,' a rain-cloud, Mcar.

Vāḥ, in comp. for *vār*. **-kiṭi,** m. 'water-pig,' the Gangetic porpoise, W. **-pushpa,** n. cloves, ib. **-sadana,** n. water-receptacle, L. **-stha,** mfn. standing in water, MW.

1. **Vāri,** n. = *vār*, water, rain, fluid, fluidity, Mn.; MBh. &c.; a species of Andropogon, Bhpr.; a kind of metre, RPrāt. **-kaṇṭaka,** m. Trapa Bispinosa, L. **-karṇikā,** f. Pistia Stratiotes, L. **-karpūra,** m. a kind of fish, Clupea Alosa, L. **-kubja** (W.) or °*jaka* (L.), m. Trapa Bispinosa. **-kūṭa,** m. a turret or mound protecting the access to the gate of a town, L. **-kośa,** m. the consecrated water employed at ordeals, Kathās. **-krimi,** m. 'water-worm,' a leech, W.; a water-fly, L. **-kheḍa-grāma,** m. N. of a village, Inscr. **-garbha,** m. 'filled with water,' a cloud, Harav.; °*bhôdara*, mfn. pregnant inside with rain (as a cloud), Śak. **-catvara,** m. a piece of water, W.; Pistia Stratiotes, L. **-cara,** mfn. or m. living in or near water, aquatic, an aquatic animal, MBh.; R.; Kathās.; m. a fish, MBh.; BhP.; pl. N. of a people, VarBṛS.; MārkP. **-cāmara,** m. Vallisneria (Blyxa) Octandra, L. **-cārin,** mfn. living or moving on w°, Car. **-ja,** mfn. born or produced in or by w°, L.; m. a conch-shell, MBh.; R.; any bivalve shell, W.; (perhaps) a lotus, MBh. i, 3373 (Nīlak. 'a fish'); n. a lotus, Kāv.; Kathās.; BhP.; a kind of pot-herb, L.; cloves, L.; a kind of salt, L.; °*jâksha*, mfn. lotus-eyed, Cat.; °*sha-caritra*, n. N. of a ch. of the Brahmâṇḍa-purāṇa. **-jāta,** m. a conch-shell, MBh. **-jīvan,** Vop. xxvi, 69. **-jīvaka,** mfn. gaining a livelihood by water, VarBṛS. **-taraṃga,** m. a wave, Bhartṛ. **-tas,** ind. 'from water' (and 'restrained;' cf. *vārita*, p. 944, col. 1), ŚārṅgP. **-taskara,** m. 'water-thief,' N. of the sun (as absorbing water), MārkP.; a cloud, L. **-trā,** f. 'protecting from rain,' an umbrella, L. **-da,** mfn. giving w° or rain, Mn.; VarBṛS.; m. a rain-cloud, Kāv. &c.; Cyperus Rotundus, VarBṛS.; Suśr. &c. (in Bhpr. also n. or *ā*, f.); n. a sort of perfume (= *vālā* or *bāla*), L.; °*dâgama*, m. the rainy season, Vcar.; °*dânta*, m. 'end of the rainy season,' autumn, Bālar. **-durga,** mf(*ā*)n. inaccessible or difficult of access by reason of water, Hariv. **-dra,** m. the Cātaka bird, W. **-dhara,** mf(*ā*)n. holding water, MBh.; m. a rain-cloud, ib.; Kāv. &c. **-dhānī,** f. a w°-receptacle or reservoir, Kathās. **-dhāpayanta,** m. a patr. (also pl.), ĀśvŚr. **-dhāra,** m. N. of a mountain, Pur.; (*ā*), f. (sg. or pl.; ifc. f. *ā*) a torrent of w° (*galad-aśru-v*°, a t° of flowing tears), Kāv. &c.; a shower of rain, MW. **-dhi,** m. 'w°-holder,' the sea, ocean (sometimes four, sometimes seven oceans are enumerated), Kāv.; Kathās. &c.; N. of the number four, the fourth, Ked. **-nātha,** m. 'lord of waters,' the god Varuṇa, W.; the ocean, L.; a cloud, L.; the habitation of the Nāga or serpent race, L. **-nidhi,** m. 'w°-receptacle,' the ocean, Bālar.; Caṇḍ. **-1.-pa,** mfn. drinking water, one who has drunk w°, MBh.; Naish. **-2.-pa,** mfn. protecting w°, Naish. **-patha,** m. a water-way, communication by water, Kām.; Pat. (see *-pathika*); a voyage, MBh.; °*thôpajīvin*, mfn. living by sea-traffic, Śak. **-pathika,** mfn. going by water, conveyed or imported by w°, Pāṇ. v, 1, 77, Vārtt. 1, Pat. **-parṇī** or **-pālikā,** f. Pistia Stratiotes, L. **-piṇḍa,** m. a frog in the middle of a stone (*aśma-madhya-ja*), L. **-pūra,** m. pl. a w°-stream, Nāg. **-pūrṇī,** f. Pistia Stratiotes, Col. **-pūrvam,** ind. after having first poured out water, Śiś. xiv, 34. **-pṛiśnī,** f. = *-pūrṇī*, L. (w. r. *-praśnī*). **-pravāha,** m. a waterfall, cascade, L. **-praśnī,** w. r. for *-prīśnī*, q. v., L. **-badara,** n. the fruit of Flacourtia Cataphracta, L.; (*ā*), f. the plant Fl° C°, W. **-bandhana,** n. the damming or banking up of w°, Vāstuv. **-bālaka,** n. a perfume (= *bāla*), W. **-bindu,** m. a w°-drop, HPariś. **-bīja,** n. the seed or germ of water, Sarvad.; N. of the mystical syllable *bam*. **-bhava,** n. antimony, L.; (prob.) a kind of plant, MW. **-mat,** mfn. abounding in w°, MBh. **-maya,** mf(*ī*)n. consisting of water, MBh.; Hariv.; VarBṛS.; inherent in or peculiar to w°, MBh. **-masi** (more correctly *-mashi*), f. 'w°-ink,' a rainy cloud, L. **-muc,** mfn. discharging w° or rain (*prabhūta-v*°), VarBṛS.; m. a rain-cloud, ib.; Kāv. **-mūlī,** f. Pistia Stratiotes, L. **-yantra,** n. a water-engine, machine for drawing up water, Mālav. **-ra,** mfn. giving or shedding water, W.; m. a cloud, Śiś.; °*râva*, mfn. sounding like clouds or like thunder, MW. **-ratha,** m. 'water-carriage,' a boat, ship, L. **-rāja,** m. N. of Varuṇa, Hariv. **-rāśi,** m. a great mass of w°, Ragh.; the sea, ocean, Kāv.; Kathās.; Hit. &c.; a lake, MW. **-ruha,** n. 'w°-growing,' a lotus-flower, Kāv.; Hariv.; Kathās. **-leśa,** m. a drop of w° (see *śrama-v*°). **-loman,** m. 'having watery hair,' N. of Varuṇa, L. **-vadana,** n. = (or w. r. for) *-badara*, L. **-vara,** m. Carissa Carandas (n. its fruit), L. **-varṇaka,** (perhaps) sand, Kṛishṇaj. **-vallabhā,** f. Batatas Paniculata, L. **-vaha,** mf(*ā*)n. carrying water, running with water, R. (in *ramya-vāri-vaha*, *śiva v*°*-v*°). **-vāraṇa,** m. 'w°-elephant,' a kind of aquatic monster, Vcar. **-vālaka,** n. a kind of Andropogon, L. **-vāsa,** m. a distiller of spirit or spirituous liquors, L. **-vāna,** mf(*ā*)n. carrying water, running with w° (in *kūlâtikrānta-vāri-vāha*), VarBṛS.; m. a rain-cloud, Kāv.; the god of rain, Siṃhâs.; *-jāla*, n. a mass of clouds, MW. **-vāhaka,** mfn. carrying or bringing w°, Pañcat. **-vāhana,** m. a rain-cloud, L. **-vāhin,** mfn. carrying water, running with w°, Hariv. **-vindī** (?), f. a blue lotus, L. **-vihāra,** m. sporting and splashing one another in the w°, Ragh. **-śa,** m. (said to be fr. *vāri* + *śa* fr. √*śī*, to sleep) N. of Vishṇu, L.; n. N. of a Sāman, SV. **-śaya,** mfn. living in w°, Car. **-śukti,** f. a bivalve shell (found in fresh water), L. **-sheṇa,** m. (fr. *vāri* + *senā*) N. of a king, MBh. (v. l. *-sena*); °*ṇâcārya*, m. N. of a Jina, Inscr. **-sheṇya,** m. patr. fr. *-sheṇa*, Pat. **-saṃjña,** m. a kind of Andropogon, VarBṛS., Sch. **-sambhava,** mf(*ā*)n. produced in or from w°, R.; Suśr.; a kind of cane, L.; n. (only L.) cloves; the root of the plant Andropogon Muricatus; sulphuret of antimony. **-sāgara,** m. a partic. mixture, Rasêndrac. **-sāmya,** milk, L. **-sāra,** m. N. of a son of Candra-gupta, BhP. **-sena,** m. N. of a king, MBh.; Inscr.; (v. l. *-sheṇa*); of a Jina, W. **-stha,** mfn. standing in water, reflected in the w°, Mn. iv, 37. **Vārīśa,** m. 'lord of waters,' the ocean, L.

Vāríti, mfn. growing near the water (said of water-plants), VS.; TBr.

1. **Vārin** (ifc.) = 1. *vāri*, water, R. (for 2. *vārin* see p. 944, col. 1).

Varīya, Nom. Ā. °*yate*, to resemble water, Sāh.

Vāry, in comp. for 1. *vāri*. **-ayana,** n. a reservoir of water, pond &c., BhP. **-āmalaka,** m. a kind of Myrobolan growing near water, R. **-udbhava,** n. 'w°-born,' a lotus-flower, L. **-upajīvin,** mfn. or m. gaining one's living by w°. a w°-carrier, fisherman &c., VarBṛS. **-oka,** m. (W.) or **-okas,** (prob.) f. (Mn.; Suśr.) 'dwelling in water,' a leech.

1. **Vārya,** mfn. (for 2. and 3. see p. 944, col. 1) watery, aquatic, L.

वार 1. *vā́ra*, m. (earlier form of *vāla*, q. v.) the hair of any animal's tail (esp. of a horse's tail, = οὐρά), RV.; m. n. sg. and pl. a hair-sieve, ib. **-vat** (*vā́ra-*), mfn. long-tailed (as a horse), RV. **-vantīya,** n. (fr. prec.) N. of a Sāman, MaitrS.; Br.; ŚrS. (also *indrasya vāravantīyam*, *vāravantīyâdyam*, and *vāravantīyôttaram*).

वार 2. *vāra* (fr. √1. *vṛi*), m. keeping back, restraining (also mfn. ifc. = difficult to be restrained, TBr.; cf. *dur-v*°); anything which covers or surrounds or restrains, a cover, MW.; anything which causes an obstruction, a gate, door-way, W.; anything enclosed or circumscribed in space or time, esp. an appointed place (e. g. *sva-vāraṃ samā-√sthā*, to occupy one's proper place), R.; the time fixed or appointed for anything (accord. to some fr. √2. *vṛi*, to choose), a person's turn, MBh.; Kāv. &c. (often, esp. with numerals, = times, e. g. *vārāṃs trīn* or *vara-trayam*, three times; *bhūribhir vāraiḥ* or *bhūri-vārān* or *bahu-vāram* or *vāraṃ vāram* or *vāraṃ vāreṇa*, many times, often, repeatedly); the turn of a day (under the regency of a planet), a day of the week (they are Āditya-, Soma-, Maṅgala-, Budha-, Guru-, Śukra-, and Śani-v°; cf. IW. 178, n. 1), Gaṇit.; Yājñ., Sch.; Kāv. &c. (cf. *dina* and *divasa-v*°); a moment, occasion, opportunity, W.; a multitude, quantity (see *bāṇa-v*°); an arrow, L.; Achyranthes Aspera, L.; N. of Śiva, L.; (*ā*), f. a harlot, courtezan, MBh. vi, 5766 (cf. *-kanyakā* &c.); n. a vessel for holding spirituous liquor, L.; a partic. artificial poison, L. **-kanyakā,** f. 'girl (taken) in turn,' a harlot, courtezan, Daś. **-nārī,** f. id. (ifc. °*rīka*), Kathās. **-pāśi** or **-pāśya,** m. pl. N. of a people, MBh.; VP. (cf. *-vāsi*). **-bāṇa,** m. or n. (?) an armour, mail, Ragh.; Śiś. &c. (cf. *bāṇa-v*°). **-bushā** or **-bṛishā,** f. Musa Sapientum, L. (cf. *vāraṇa busā*). **-matha,** m. N. of a prince, VP. **-mukhya,** m. (prob.) a singer, dancer, MārkP.; (*ā*), f. the chief of a number of harlots, a royal courtezan, MBh.; R. &c. **-yuvati,** f. = *-kanyakā*, Daś. **-yoga,** m. ground flour or meal, powder, Gal. **-yoshit,** f. = *-kanyakā*, Kāv.; Pur.; °*shin-mukhyā* = *vāra-mukhyā*, Daś. **-rāmā** (Kuṭṭanim.), **-vadhū** (Śiś.; Kathās.), **-vanitā** (Ratnâv.; Dhūrtan.), f. a harlot, prostitute. **-vāṇa,** see *-bāṇa*.

-vāṇi, m. (only L.) a player on the flute; a principal singer, musician; a judge; a year; (also *ī*), f. a harlot. **-vāraṇa**, w.r. for *-bāṇa*. **-vāla**, m. N. of an Agra-hāra, Rājat. **-vāsi** or **-vāsya**, m. pl. N. of a people, MBh.; VP. (cf. *-pāśi*. **-vilāsinī** (Kāv.), **-sundarī** (L.), f. = *-kanyakā*. **-sevā**, f. practice of harlotry or a set of harlots, W. **-strī**, f. = *-kanyakā*, L. **Vārâṅganā**, f. id., Kāv. **Vārâvaskandin**, mfn. (said of Agni), Lāṭy.

Vāraka, m. a restrainer, resister, opposer, an obstacle, MBh.; a kind of vessel, Hcat.; a person's turn or time (°*keṇa*, ind. in turn), HPariś. (cf. *śata-vārakam*); one of a horse's paces, L.; a sort of horse or any h°, L.; n. a sort of perfumed or fragrant grass, L.; the seat of pain (= *kashṭha-sthāna*), L.

Vārakin, m. (only L.) an opposer, obstructor, enemy; a piebald horse or one with good marks: a hermit who lives on leaves; the sea, ocean.

1. **Vāraṇá**, mf(*ī*)n. warding off, restraining, resisting, opposing, MBh.; Kāv. &c.; all-resisting, invincible (said of the Soma and of Indra's elephant), RV. ix, 1, 9; Hariv. 1700; relating to prevention, Suśr.; shy, wild, RV.; AV. (with *mṛiga*, accord. to some = elephant, RV. viii, 33, 8; x, 40, 4); dangerous, RV.; ShaḍvBr.; forbidden, AitBr.; m. (ifc. f. *ā*) an elephant (from its power of resistance), MBh.; Kāv. &c.; an el°-hook, Daś.; armour, mail, L.; a kind of ornament on an arch, MBh. iv, 1326; (*ī*), f. a female elephant, L.; w.r. for *vāruṇī*, HYog.; n. the act of restraining or keeping back or warding off from (abl.); resistance, opposition, obstacle; impediment, KātyŚr.; MBh. &c.; a means of restraining. Bhartṛ.; = *hari-tāla*, L.; N. of a place, MBh. **-kara**, m. an elephant's 'hand' i.e. trunk, Bhām. **-kṛicchra**, m. 'el°'s penance,' a penance consisting in drinking only rice-water, Prâyaśc. **-kesara**, m. Mesua Roxburghii, Suśr. **-pushpa**, m. a species of plant, MBh. **-busā** or **-vallabhā**, f. Musa Sapientum, L. **-veśa**, m. (with *śāstrin*) N. of an author, Cat. **-śālā**, f. an elephant-stable, R. **-sâhvaya**, n. (with or without *pura*) 'the town called after el°s,' N. of Hastināpura, MBh.; Hariv. **-sthala**, n. N. of a place, R. **-hasta**, m. a partic. stringed instrument, Saṃgīt. **Vāraṇânana**, m. 'el°-faced,' N. of Gaṇêśa, Kathās. **Vāraṇâhvaya**, n. = *vāraṇa-sâhvaya*, MBh. **Vāraṇêndra**, m. 'elephant-chief,' a large and excellent elephant, MW.

Vāraṇāvata, n. N. of a town (situated on the Ganges at a distance of 8 days' journey from Hastināpura), MBh. °**taka**, mfn. inhabiting the town Vāraṇāvata, MBh.

Vāraṇīya, mfn. to be checked or restrained (see *a-v°*); belonging to an elephant (m. with *kara*, an elephant's-trunk), Kathās.

Vārayitavya, mfn. to be kept off from (acc.), MBh.

1. **Vārayitṛi**, m. a protector, MW.

2. **Vāri**, f. (for 1. see p. 943, col. 1) a place for tying or catching an elephant, Vās.; Śiś. (also *ī*); a rope for tying an elephant, Dharmaś. (also *ī*); a captive, prisoner, W.; a water-pot, pitcher, jar, L. (also *ī*); N. of Sarasvatī (the goddess of speech), L.

Vārika. See *nāga-v°*.

Vārita, mfn. (fr. Caus.) warded off, prevented, hindered, impeded, restrained, MBh.; Kāv. &c.; forbidden (see next). **-vāma**, mfn. eager for forbidden things, Kathās.; Rājat.

Vāritra, n. observance of that which is forbidden, Buddh.

Vārīṭa, m. an elephant, L.

Vāru, m. a royal elephant, war-elephant (carrying a standard, = *vijaya-kuñjara*), L.; a horse, L.

2. **Vārya**, mfn. (for 1. see p. 943, col. 3) to be warded off or prevented or checked or impeded, MBh.; Kāv. &c.; m. a wall, R.

वार 3. *vā́ra*, m. (fr. √2. *vṛi*) choice (see *vā́re-vṛita*); anything chosen or choice or exquisite, goods, treasure, RV. (often ifc.; cf. *aśasta-*, *ṛidhad-*, *dāti-v°* &c.); N. of a poet, Cat.

2. **Vārayitṛi**, m. 'chooser,' a husband, MW.

2. **Vārin.** See *kāṇḍa-vāriṇī* and *mūla-vārin*; (for 1. *vārin* see p. 943, col. 3.)

Vā́ruka, mfn. choosing (with acc.), MaitrS.

Vā́re-vṛita, mfn. chosen, TS.

3. **Vā́rya**, mfn. to be chosen, Pāṇ. iii, 1, 101, Sch.; precious, valuable, RV.; n. treasure, wealth, goods, ib. **-vṛita** (*vā́rya-*), mfn. received as a boon, MaitrS.; Kāṭh. (cf. *vara-vṛita* and *vā́re-vṛita*).

वारकीर *vārakira*, m. (only L.) a wife's brother; the submarine fire; a louse; a small comb; a war-horse, charger; = *vāra-grāhin* or *dvāra-grāhin*.

वारङ्क *vāraṅka*, m. a bird. L.

वारङ्ग *vāraṅga*, m. the handle of a sword or knife &c.; Suśr. (cf. Uṇ. 1, 121, Sch.)

वारट *vāraṭa*, n. a field, L.; a number of fields, L.; (*ā*), f. a species of bird belonging to the Vikiras, Vāgbh.; a goose, L. (cf. *vāralā*).

वारण 2. *vāraṇá*, mfn. (fr. *varaṇa*; for 1. see col. 1) consisting of or made from the wood of the Crataeva Roxburghii, ŚBr.; Kauś.

वारणसी *vāraṇasī*, f. = *vārāṇasī* below.

वारतन्तव *vāratantava*, m. patr. fr. *vara-tantu*, Pravar.

Vāratantavīya, m. pl. the school of Vara-tantu (belonging to the Black Yajur-veda), Āryav. (cf. Pāṇ. iv, 3, 102).

वारत्र *vāratra*, n. = *varatrā*, a leather thong, L.; (*ā*), f. a species of bird (= or w.r. for *vāraṭā*), Car.

Vāratraka, mfn. (fr. *varatrā*), g. *rājanyâdi*.

वारधान *vāradhāna*, (prob.) w.r. for *vāṭa-dh°*, MBh.

वाररुच *vāraruca*, mfn. composed by Vararuci, Pat.

वारलक *vāralaka*. See *nandi-v°*.

वारला *vāralā*, f. (cf. *vāraṭā*) a kind of gadfly, L.; a goose, L.

वारलीक *vāralīka*, m. Eleusine Indica, L.

वाराटकि *vārāṭaki*, m. a patr., g. *gahâdi*.

Vārāṭakīya, mfn. (fr. prec.), ib.

वाराणसी *vārāṇasī*, f. the city Benares (more properly written Banāras; accord. to JābālUp. so called after the names of two rivers, *varaṇā* and *asi* or *asī*; also written *vāṇārasī*, q.v., *varāṇasī* or *vāraṇasī*), MBh.; Kāv. &c.; cf. RTL. 434. **-darpaṇa**, m., **-māhātmya**, n. N. of wks. **-°śvara** (°*sīśv°*), m. N. of an author.

Vārāṇaseya, mfn. produced or born in Benares &c., g. *nady-ādi*.

वारालिका *vārālikā*, f. N. of Durgā, L.

वाराह *vā́rāha*, mf(ī)n. (fr. *varāha*) coming from or belonging to a boar (with *upānahau*, du. shoes made of pig's leather; with *māṅsa*, n. pig's flesh), Br.; Yājñ. &c.; relating to the Boar form of Vishṇu, MBh.; Kāv. &c.; taught or composed by Varāha i.e. Varāha-mihira (see comp.); m. 'the Boar' (i.e. Vishṇu in his third incarnation, as a *Varāha*, q.v.), MBh.; Pañcar. (v.l. *varāha*); a banner with the representation of a boar, MBh.; a kind of bulbous plant, Dioscorea (cf. *-kanda*); N. of a mountain, MBh.; Hariv. (v.l. *varāha*); pl. N. of a school of the Black Yajur-veda, Hcar.; Āryav.; (*ī*), f., see below; n. N. of a Sāman (*vārāham uttaram*), ĀrshBr.; of a Tīrtha, MBh.; = *varāha-dvīpa*, L. **-kanda**, n. the esculent root of Dioscorea, Suśr. **-karṇī**, f. Physalis Flexuosa. **-kalpa**, m. 'Boar-Kalpa,' N. of the now existing Kalpa or day of Brahmā (being the first of the second Parârdha of Brahmā's existence), MW. **-tīrtha**, n. N. of a Tīrtha, Cat.; *-māhātmya*, n. N. of wk. **-dvādaśī**, f. = *varāha-dv°*, ib. **-pattrī**, f. Physalis Flexuosa, L. **-purāṇa**, n. N. of one of the 18 Purāṇas (said to have been revealed to the Earth by Vishṇu in his form of *Varāha*, q.v.; it contains an account of the creation, the various forms or incarnations of Vishṇu, and a number of legends and directions relating to the Vaishṇava sect), IW. 514 &c. **-prayoga-vidhi**, m., **-mantra**, m., **-māhātmya**, n. N. of wks. **-saṃhitā**, f. N. of Varāha-mihira's Bṛihat-saṃhitā. **Vārāhâṅgī**, f. Croton Polyandrium or Tiglium, L.

Vārāhaka, mfn. (fr. *varāha*), Pāṇ. iv, 2, 80.

Vārāhī, f. a sow, W.; the Śakti or female Energy of the Boar form of Vishṇu, Yājñ., Sch.; N. of one of the Mātṛis attending on Skanda, MBh.; a kind of bulbous plant, Dioscorea, VarBṛS.; the earth, W.; a measure, ib.; N. of a river, Cat. **-kanda**, m. = *-mūla*, MW. **-tantra**, n., **-nigrahâshṭaka**, n. N. of wks. **-putra**, m. = *vārāhyā-p°*, Pat. **-praśna**, m., **-sahasra-nāma-stotra**, n., **-stotra**, n. N. of wks. **Vārāhy-anugrahâshṭaka**, n. N. of wk.

Vārāhīya, N. of wk.

Vārāhyā, f. patr. fr. *varāha*, Pāṇ. iv, 1, 78, Sch.

वारुठ *vāruṭha*, m. (fr. √1. *vṛi*?) a bier, the bed on which a corpse is carried, L.

वारुड *vāruḍa*, m. = *varuḍa*, Pāṇ. v, 4, 36, Vārtt. 1, Pat.

Vāruḍaka, n. (fr. *varuḍa*), g. *kulâlâdi*.

Vāruḍaki, m. patr. (fr. *varuḍa*), Pāṇ. iv, 1, 97, Vārtt. 1, Pat.

वारुण *vāruṇá*, mf(*ī*)n. (fr. *varuṇa*) relating or belonging or sacred to or given by Varuṇa, AV. &c. &c. (in MBh. and R. also said of partic. weapons); relating to the sea or to water, marine, oceanic, aquatic, MBh.; Kāv. &c. (with *bhūta*, n. an aquatic animal); western (cf. under *varuṇa*), AdbhBr.; R.; VarBṛS.; relating to Vāruṇi i.e. Bhṛigu, MBh.; m. an aquatic animal, fish. MBh. xiii, 4142 (perhaps also RV. ii, 38, 8, where *varuṇa* seems to be w.r.); patr. of Bhṛigu (cf. *vāruṇi*), MBh.; (pl.) Varuṇa's children or people or warriors, Hariv.; N. of a Dvīpa (see n.), VP.; (in astron.) N. of the 15th Muhūrta; (*ī*), f., see below; n. water, L.; the Nakshatra Śata-bhishaj (presided over by Varuṇa), MBh.; VarBṛS. &c.; n. or m. the west (°*ṇe*, in the west), Pañcar.; (with *khaṇḍa*) N. of one of the 9 divisions of Bhārata-varsha, Gol. **-karman**, n. 'Varuṇa's work,' any work connected with the supply of water (e.g. the digging of tanks or wells &c.), VahniP. **-tīrtha**, n. N. of a Tīrtha, Cat. **-paddhati**, f. N. of wk. **-pāśaka**, m. a sea-monster, L. **-praghāsika**, mf(*ī*)n. (fr. *varuṇa-praghāsa*), ŚrS. **Vāruṇêndra**, m. N. of a man, Cat. **Vāruṇêśvara-tīrtha**, n. N. of a Tīrtha, ib. **Vāruṇôpapurāṇa**, n. N. of an Upa-purāṇa.

Vāruṇānī, w.r. for *varuṇānī*.

1. **Vāruṇi**, m. 'son of Varuṇa,' patr. of various persons (esp. of Bhṛigu, Satya-dhṛiti, Vasishṭha, Agastya &c.), Br.; RAnukr.; MBh.

2. **Vāruṇi**, f. (m. c.) = *vāruṇī*, spirituous liquor, Hariv.

Vāruṇī, f. the western quarter or region (presided over by Varuṇa), the west (with or without *diś*), VarBṛS.; N. of partic. serpents, GṛS.; (pl.) of partic. sacred texts, Gaut.; Varuṇa's female Energy (personified either as his wife or as his daughter, produced at the churning of the ocean and regarded as the goddess of spirituous liquor), TĀr.; MBh.; R.; Pur.; a partic. kind of spirit (prepared from hogweed mixed with the juice of the date or palm and distilled), any spirituous liquor, MBh.; Kāv. &c.; N. of Śiva's wife, L.; a partic. fast-day on the thirteenth of the dark half of Caitra, Col.; Dūrvā grass or a similar species, L.; colocynth, L.; the Nakshatra Śata-bhishaj (ruled by Varuṇa), L.; N. of a river, R. **-vallabha**, m. N. of Varuṇa, L. **-°śa** (°*ṇīśa*), m. N. of Vishṇu, Pañcar. **Vāruṇy-upanishad**, f. N. of TĀr. viii and ix.

Vāruṇya, mfn. relating to Varuṇa; n. illusion, MW.

वारुण्ड *vāruṇḍa*, m. n. the excretion of the eyes and the ears, L.; a vessel for baling water out of a boat, L.; m. = *gaṇistha-rāja* or *phaṇināṃ rājakaḥ*, L.; (*ī*), f. a door-step, L.

वारूढ *vārūḍhā*, f. (only L.) fire; a viaticum (*śambala*); a cage; the edge of a garment; the leaf of a door.

वारेण्यायनि *vāreṇyāyani*, m. patr. fr. *varenya*, g. *tikâdi*.

वारेन्द्र *vārêndra*, m. n., and °*drī*, f. = *varêndra*, °*drī*, L.

वार्क *vārka*, Vṛiddhi form of *vṛika*, in comp. **-khaṇḍi**, m. patr. fr. *vṛika-khaṇḍa*, Gobh. **-grāhika**, m. patr. fr. *vṛika-grāha*, g. *revaty-ādi*. **-jambha**, m. patr. fr. *vṛika-jambha*, Cat.; n. N. of various Sāmans, ĀrshBr. **-bandhavika**, m. patr. fr. *vṛika-bandhu*, g. *revaty-ādi*. **-rūpya**, mfn. (fr. *vṛika-rūpya*), Kāś. on Pāṇ. iv, 2, 106. **-vañcaka**, m. patr. fr. *vṛika-vañcin*, g. *revaty-ādi*.

Vārkeṇī, f. of next, Pāṇ. v, 3, 115, Sch.

Vārkeṇya, m. a king of the Vṛikas, Pāṇ. ib.

वार्कलि *vā́rkali*, m. metron. fr. *vṛikalā*, ŚBr. (cf. g. *bāhv-ādi*).

Vārkaleya, m. metron. fr. *vṛikalā* or patr. fr. *vārkali*, Saṃskārak. (cf. g. *taulvaly-ādi*).

वार्कारुणीपुत्र *vā́rkāruṇī-pútra,* m. N. of a preceptor, ŚBr.

वार्कार्य *vār-kārya* &c. See under *vār,* p. 943, col. 1.

वार्क्ष *vā́rksha,* mf(ī)n. (fr. *vṛiksha*) relating or belonging to trees, consisting or made of trees, coming from or growing on trees, arboreous, Mn.; MBh. &c.; made of wood, wooden, KātyŚr.; Gobh.; MBh.; made of bark, MW.; (*ī*), f. 'daughter of the trees,' N. of the wife of Pracetas, MBh.; n. a forest, L.

Vārkshāyaṇa, m. N. of an author, Cat.

Vārkshya, mfn. = (or w. r. for) *vārksha,* wooden, Suśr.; m. patr., g. *gargâdi;* n. a forest, L. (prob. w. r. for *vārksha*).

Vārkshyāyaṇī, f. of the patr. *vārkshya,* g. *lohitâdi.*

वार्च *vārca,* m. (said to be fr. *vār* + *cara* fr. √*car*) a goose, Vop.

वार्चलीय *vārcalīya,* mfn. (fr. *varcala*), g. *kṛiśâśvâdi.*

वार्जिनीवत *vārjinīvata,* m. patr. fr. *vṛijinī-vat,* Hariv.

Vārjyaka, mfn. (fr. *varjya*), g. *dhūmâdi.*

वार्ढ्य *vārḍhya.* See *bārḍhya.*

वार्ण *vārṇa,* mfn. (fr. *varṇa*) relating to a sound or letter (in gram.)

Vārṇaka, mfn. (fr. next), g. *kaṇvâdi* (v. l.)

Vārṇakya, m. patr. fr. *varṇaka,* g. *gargâdi.*

Vārṇava or °**vaka,** mfn. (fr. *varṇa*), g. *suvāstv-ādi* and g. *kṛicchrâdi.*

Vārṇika, m. a scribe, writer, L.

वार्तक *vártaka,* m. (fr. √1. *vṛit*) a quail (cf. *vartaka*), L.; (*tikā*), f. id., ib.

Vārtana, mfn. = *vartanīshu bhavaḥ,* Pāṇ. iv, 2, 125, Sch.

Vārtanâksha, m. patr. fr. *vartanâksha,* g. *śivâdi.*

Vārtamānika, mfn. (fr. *vartamāna*) relating to the present, now existing, Śaṃk.

Vārtāka, m. = *vārtaka,* a quail, L.; (also °*kī* or °*ku,* f.) the egg-plant, Uṇ. iii, 79; iv, 15 (prob. w. r. for *vārttāka* &c.)

Vārtika, m. a kind of bird, Vāgbh. (= *vartika,* L.)

Vārtīka, m. a kind of quail, Bhpr.

Vārtīra, m. id., Vāgbh.

Vārtta, mfn. (fr. *vṛitti* and *vṛitta*) having means of subsistence, practising any business or profession, L.; healthy, well, Sarvad.; ordinary, middling, ĀśvGṛ.; worthless, vain, Sarvad.; right, correct (see *-taraka*), Pat.; m. N. of a man, MBh.; (*ā*), f., see below; n. health, welfare, Kāv.; chaff, W. **–taraka,** mfn. all correct, quite in order, Pat.

Vārttaya, Nom. P. °*yati,* to talk to, converse with (acc.), HPariś.

Vārttā, f. livelihood, business, profession (esp. that of a Vaiśya, i. e. agriculture, breeding of cattle, and trade; ifc. living on or by), Mn.; MBh. &c.; (sometimes pl.) an account of anything that has happened, tidings, report, rumour, news, intelligence, story of or about (gen. or comp.), Kāv.; Kathās. &c. (*vārttām* √*kīrt* with gen., 'to give an account of, talk about;' *kā vārttā,* 'what is the news?'); talking or talk about (gen., loc., acc. with *uddiśya,* or comp.), ib. &c. (*kā vārttā* with loc., 'what talk or question can there be about that?' *vārttayā* √*kṛi* with acc., 'to talk about;' *anayā vārttayâpi kiṃ kāryam,* 'what is to be done with her even in mere words?') the mere mention of facts without poetical embellishment (in rhet.), MW.; staying, abiding, W.; occurrence, event, L.; the egg-plant, L. (cf. *vārttāka*); a female monster, Car. (v. l. *vātā*); N. of Durgā, DevīP. **–karman,** n. the practice of agriculture and keeping cattle and trade (cf. above), Mn. x, 80. **–**°**nukarshaka** (°*ttân*°), m. 'news-bringer,' a spy, emissary, MBh. **–**°**nujīvin** (°*ttân*°), mfn. living by trade or business, Kām. **–**°**nuyoga** (°*ttân*°), m. inquiring after news or health, MW. **–pati,** m. 'lord or granter of a livelihood,' an employer, BhP. **–mātra,** n. mere report; °*trâvabodhana,* n. knowledge based only on hearsay, Daś. **–mālā,** f. N. of a wk. on Bhakti. **–mūla,** mfn. based on business or profession, R. **–**°**yana** (°*ttây*°), m 'going for news,' an emissary, spy, L. **–**°**rambha** (°*ttâr*°), m. commercial enterprise, business, Mn. vii, 43. **–**°**vaśesha** (°*ttâv*°), mfn. 'having nothing left but to be talked about,' dead, gone, Pārvat. **–vaha,** m. 'news-bearer,' a pedlar, L. **–vṛitti,** m. 'living by business or profession,' a householder, (esp.) a Vaiśya (cf. *-karman*), BhP. **–vyatikara,** m. bad news, Pañcat.; general report, common rumour, MW. **–**°**śin** (°*ttâśin*), m. 'news-eater,' a talker, prattler, L. **–hara** (Mālatīm.), **-hartṛi** (BhP.), **-hāra** (Mcar.), m. a carrier of tidings, messenger, courier. **–hārin,** mfn. (ifc.) bringing a message from, Mṛicch.; (*iṇī*), f. a female messenger, Mcar.

Vārttāka, m. (rarely *ī,* f.; prob. fr. *vṛitta,* round) the egg-plant, Solanum Melongena and another species (n. its fruit), Hariv.; Suśr.; MārkP. **–śākaṭa** or **-śākina,** m. n. or (*ā*), f. a field producing the egg-plant, L.

Vārttākin, m. and (*inī*), f. = *vārttāka,* L.

Vārttāku, m. id., Suśr.

Vārttika, mfn. (fr. *vārttā* and *vṛitti*) skilled in a profession or business (= *vṛittau sādhuḥ* or *vṛittim adhīte veda vā*), g. *kathâdi* and g. *ukthâdi;* relating to news, bringing or conveying intelligence, W.; explanatory, glossarial, containing or relating to a critical gloss or annotation (see n.); m. a business-man, trader, Kathās.; an emissary, envoy, MBh.; one who knows antidotes, conjurer, physician, L.; the egg-plant, L.; (*ā*), f. business, trade (ifc. = occupied with, practising), MBh.; BhP.; a sort of quail (prob. w. r. for *vārtikā,* q. v.); n. an explanatory or supplementary rule, critical gloss or annotation (added to a grammatical or philosophical Sūtra and defined to be 'the exposition of the meaning, of that which is said, of that which is left unsaid, and of that which is ill or imperfectly said;' the term Vārttika is, however, especially applied to Kātyāyana's critical annotations on the aphorisms of Pāṇini's grammar, the object of which is to consider whether Pāṇini's rules are correct or not, and to improve on them where this may be found to be necessary; and also to similar works on various matters by Kumārila, Surêśvara &c.; cf. *tantra-v*°, *śloka-v*°); a marriage feast, L. **–kāra,** m. 'composer of Vārttikas,' N. of Kātyāyana, Kumārila &c., Cat.; of a poet, ib. **–kāśikā** (?), f. N. of wk. **–kṛit,** m. = *-kāra,* ib. **–ṭippana,** n., **-tātparya-ṭīkā,** f., **-tātparya-śuddhi,** f., **-pāṭha,** m., **-yojanā,** f., **-sāra,** m., **-sāra-vyākhyā,** f., **-sāra-saṃgraha,** m. N. of wks. **–sūtrika,** mfn. one who studies the Vārttikas and Sūtras, Pat. **Vārttikâbharaṇa,** n. N. of a Comm. on the Ṭupṭīkā (q. v., also called *ṭupṭīkā-vyākhyāna*). **Vārttikêndra,** m. an alchemist, VarYogay.

Vārttikâhya, n. (for °*kâkhya*?) N. of a Sāman, L.

वार्तन्तवीय *vārtantavīya* and *vārtātaveya,* m. pl. N. of two Vedic schools (cf. *vāratantavīya*).

वार्त्र *vārtra,* Vṛiddhi form of *vṛitra* in comp. **–ghna** (*vā́rtra-*), mf(*ī*)n. (fr. *-vṛitra-han*) relating or belonging to the slayer of Vṛitra i. e. Indra (n. with *havis,* an oblation for victory), VS.; TS.; Br.; BhP.; containing the word *vṛitra-han,* g. *vimuktâdi;* m. patr. of Arjuna (as son of Indra), Kir.; n. (with *indrasya*) N. of Sāmans, ĀrshBr. **–tura,** n. (fr. *vṛitra-tur*) N. of a Sāman, ĀrshBr. **–hatya** (*vā́rtra-*), mfn. (fr. *vṛitra-hatya*) fit for slaying Vṛitra, RV.; n. the slaying of Vṛitra, ib.

वार्दर *vārdara,* n. (only L.; cf. *bādara;* prob. in some meanings from *vār* + *dara*) the berry of the Abrus Precatorius or the plant itself; the seed of the Mangifera Indica; silk; water; a conch shell (= *dakshiṇâvarta*); a sort of curl on the right side of a horse's neck (regarded as an auspicious mark); = *vīra* (prob. w. r. for *vāri;* cf. above).

वार्दल *vārdala,* m. n. (only L.; cf. prec.; prob. in the first meaning fr. *vār* + *dala,* accord. to some fr. *vārda* + *la*) a rainy day, bad weather; an inkstand; m. ink.

Vārdālikā, f. rainy weather, Divyâv. (printed *vardālikā*).

1. **Vārdālī,** f. N. of a plant, Gaṇar. **–vat,** mfn., ib.

2. **Vārdālī,** ind. (*prākāśye hiṇsāyām ca*), ib.

वार्द्ध *vārddha,* m. (fr. *vṛiddha*) patr., g. *bidâdi.*

Vārddhaka, m. an old man, Naish.; n. old age, senility, MBh.; Kāv. &c. (°*kaṃ* √*dhā,* to grow old); the infirmity or imbecility of old age, L.; a multitude of old men, Pat. on Pāṇ. iv, 2, 39. **–bhāva,** m. advanced age, old age, senility, Pañcat. (B.)

Vārddhakya, n. old age, senility, MBh.; Hāsy.

Vārddhakshatri, m. (fr. *vṛiddha-kshatra*), patr. of Jayad-ratha, MBh.

Vārddhakshemi, m. patr. (fr. *vṛiddha-kshema*), MBh.

Vārddhāyana, m. patr. fr. *vārddha,* g. *haritâdi.*

Vārddhya, n. old age, senility, Subh.

वार्द्धुष *vārddhusha,* m. (prob. fr. *vṛiddhi,* interest) one who exacts high interest, a usurer, MBh. °**ddhushi,** m. id., Vās.; Mn.; Yājñ.; a debt with accumulated interest, SāmavBr. °**ddhushika** (Āpast.; Vās.), °**ddhushin** (MBh.), m. a usurer. °**ddhushī,** f. (MBh.), °**ddhushya,** n. (Mn.; Yājñ.) usurious loan, usury.

वार्धनी *vār-dhanī, vār-dhi* &c. See under *vār,* p. 943, col. 1.

वार्ध्र *vārdhra,* mf(ī)n. (fr. *vardhra*) fit for straps (as a hide), Pāṇ. v, 1, 15, Sch.; consisting of leather, leathern, Pāṇ. iv, 3, 151; n. and (*ī*), f. a leather thong, PañcavBr. **–kaṭhinika,** mfn. dealing in leather straps, Kāś. on Pāṇ. iv, 4, 72.

Vārdhrāṇasá, m. a rhinoceros (cf. next), TS.; Āpast. (accord. to Sch. also 'an old white he-goat' or 'a kind of crane').

Vārdhrīṇasa (also written °*nasa*), m. (fr. *vārdhrī* + *nasa* for *nāsā*) a rhinoceros (prob. so called as having a leather-like snout), Mn.; Yājñ. (accord. to some also 'a bird with a black neck, red head, and white wings'); mfn. (fr. prec.), Gaut.

Vārdhrīnasá, mfn. (prob.) having streaks on the nose or snout, VS. (Mahīdh. 'having pendulous excrescences on the neck'); m., see *vārdhrīṇasa.*

वार्बट *vārbaṭa,* m. (also written *vārvaṭa;* cf. *vāvuṭa*) a ship, boat, L.

वार्मण *vārmaṇa,* n. (fr. *varman*) a collection of coats of mail, L.

Vārmika, m. the son of an Āyogava and a Kshatriyā, L.

Vārmikāyaṇi, m. patr. fr. *varmin,* Pāṇ. iv, 1, 158, Vārtt. 2, Pat.

Vārmikya, n. (fr. *varmika*), g. *purohitâdi.*

Vārmiṇa, n. (fr. *varmin*) a multitude of men in armour, L.

वार्मतेय *vā́rmateya,* mfn. born in Varmatī, Pāṇ. iv, 3, 94.

Vārmateyaka, mfn. (fr. prec.), g. *kattry-ādi.*

वार्य 4. *vārya,* m. (for 1. 2. 3. see pp. 943, col. 3, and 944, col. 1) patr. (?), ĀrshBr.

वार्ययन *vāry-ayana* &c. See p. 943, col. 3.

वार्वट *vārvaṭa.* See *vārbaṭa.*

वार्वणा *vārvaṇā,* f. = *varvaṇā,* a kind of blue fly, L.

वार्वती *vār-vatī, vār-vāha.* See p. 943, col. 1

वार्वर *vārvara,* °*raka.* See *bārbara.*

वार्श *vārśa,* n. (fr. *vṛiśa*) N. of a Sāman, PañcavBr.

वार्ष 1. *vārshá,* mf(*í*)n. (fr. *varsha* or *varshā*) belonging to the rainy season, VS.; belonging to a year, yearly, annual, W.; (*ī*), f. = *varshā,* the rainy season, L.

2. **Vārsha,** Vṛiddhi form of *varsha* in comp. **–śatika,** mfn. (fr. *varsha-śata*) 100 years old, Pāṇ. v, 1, 58, Vārtt. 5, Pat.; bestowing a life of 100 years, Kauś. **–sahasrika,** mfn. (fr. *varsha-sahasra*) 1,000 years old, Pāṇ., ib.

Vārshaka, n. (fr. *varsha,* division of the world) N. of one of the 10 parts into which Su-dyumna divided the world, VahniP.

Vārshakī-praśna, m. N. of wk.

Vā́rshika, mf(*ī*)n. belonging to the rainy season, rainy, AV. &c. &c. (with *āpas,* f. pl. rain-water, with *dhanus,* n. a rainbow); growing in the rainy season or fit for or suited to it, W.; others 'a river, the water of which lasts the whole year i. e. does not dry up in the hot season'); having water only during the rains (as a river), MBh. (cf. *vārshikôdaka*); versed in calculating the rainy season, g. *vasantâdi;* sufficient or lasting for a year, Yājñ.; MBh. &c.; yearly, annual, Gaut.; Pur.; (ifc. after a numeral) lasting a certain number of years, being so many years old (cf. *tri-*, *pañća-v°* &c.); n. or m. N. of various wks., Cat.; (*ī*), f. Jasminum Sambac, L. — **praśna**, m. N. of wk. **Vārshikôdaka**, mf(*ā*)n. having water only during the rainy season, MBh.

Vārshikya, mfn. yearly, annual, BhP.; n. the rainy season, R.

Vārshilā, f. hail, L.

Vārshuka, mfn. = (or w. r. for) *varshuka*, raining, L.

वार्ष 3. *vārsha*, n. (fr. *vṛisha* of which it is also the Vṛiddhi form in comp.), g. *pṛithv-ādi*; N. of a Sāman, L. — **gaṇa**, m. (*vārsha-*, fr. *vṛisha-gaṇa*) patr. of Asita, ŚBr.; pl. the descendants of Vārshagaṇa, g. *kaṇvâdi*. — **gaṇī-pútra** (*vā́rsha-*), m. N. of a preceptor, ŚBr. — **gaṇya**, m. patr. (fr. *vṛisha-gaṇa*), Lāṭy.; MBh. (g. *gargâdi*); N. of a philosopher, Cat. — **da**, mfn. (fr. *vṛisha-da*), g. *utsâdi* (v. l.) — **daṇśa**, mfn. (fr. *vṛisha-daṇśa*) made of cat's hair, MBh. ii, 1823 (Nīlak.); m. a patr. Uṇ. v, 21, Sch. (accord. to some two distinct patr., *vārshada* and *āṇsa*). — **m-dhara**, n. N. of two Sāmans, ĀrshBr. — **parvaṇa**, mfn. coming from Vṛisha-parvan, Śiś.; (*ī*), f. patr. of Śarmishṭhā, MBh.; Hariv.; BhP. — **bhāṇavī**, f. (fr. *vṛisha-bhāṇu*) patr. of Rādhā, L. (more correctly *-bhānavī*).

Vārshākapa, mfn. (fr. *vṛishā-kapi*), AitBr.

Vārshāgirá, m. pl. (fr. *vṛishā-gir*) patr. of Ambarīsha, Ṛijrâśva, Bhajamāna, Saha-deva, and Surādhas (authors of RV. i, 100), Anukr. (cf. i, 100, 17).

Vārshāyaṇi, m. patr. of an author, VP. (cf. g. *tikâdi*).

Vārshāyaṇī-putra, m. N. of a preceptor, ĀrshBr.

Vārshāhara, n. N. of various Sāmans (also *°rā-dya* and *°rôttara*, n.), ĀrshBr.

Vārshyāyaṇi, m. patr. of a grammarian and of a lawyer, Āpast.

Vārshyāyaṇīya, mfn. (fr. prec.), Apast.

वार्षभ *vārshabha*, mfn. (fr. *vṛishabha*) relating or belonging to a bull, Cat.

वार्षल *vārshala*, mfn. (fr. *vṛishala*) relating or peculiar to a Śūdra, Nār.; n. the condition or occupation of a Śūdra, g. *yuvâdi*.

Vārshali, m. (fr. *vṛishalī*) the son of a Śūdra woman, g. *bāhv-ādi*.

वार्ष्टिहव्य *vārshṭihavya*, m. (fr. *vṛishṭi-havya*) patr. of Upastuta (author of RV. x, 115), Anukr.

Vārshṭya, mfn. (fr. *vṛishṭi*), g. *saṃkāśâdi*.

वार्ष्ण *vā́rshṇa* or *vārshṇá*, m. (fr. *vṛishṇi*, *vṛishan*, or *vṛishṇa*) patr. of Go-bala and Barku, TBr.; ŚBr.

Vārshṇi, m. patr., Nyāyam. — **vṛiddha**, mfn. = *vṛishṇi-vṛiddheshu jātaḥ*, KaushBr., Sch.

Vārshṇika, m. patr. fr. *vṛishṇika*, g. *śivâdi*.

Vārshṇeya, m. (fr. *vṛishṇi*) patr. of Śūsha, TBr.; of Cekitāna, MBh.; of Kṛishṇa, Bhag.; of Nala's charioteer (who afterwards became a servant of Ṛitu-parṇa), Nal.; pl. the race descended from Vārshṇeya, MBh.; (*ī*), f. patr., ib.; mfn. relating or belonging to Kṛishṇa, ib. — **sahita**, mfn. accompanied by Vārshṇeya, Nal. — **sārathi**, mfn. having Vārshṇeya for a charioteer, ib.

Vārshṇyá, m. patr., ŚBr. (v. l. *vārshmá*).

वार्ष्मण *vārshmaṇa*, mfn. (fr. *varshman*) being uppermost, Kauś. (accord. to others 'a tree struck at the top by lightning').

वार्हत् *vārhat*, *vārhata*, *vārhadagna* &c. See *bārhat* &c.

वार्हस्पत *vārhaspata*, *°patya* &c. See *bārhas-p°*.

वाल 1. *vā́la*, m. (later form of 1. *vāra*; also written *bāla*, q. v.) the hair of any animal's tail (esp. of a horse's tail), any tail or hair, TS. &c. &c.; bristle, Kathās.; a hair-sieve, VS.; ŚBr.; m. n. a kind of Andropogon, VarBṛS.; Suśr.; (*ā*), f. the cocoa-nut, L.; a kind of jasmine, L.; Pavonia Odorata, L.; = *śiphā*, L.; N. of a Yoginī, Hcat.; (*ī*), f. a post, pillar, Anup. (= *medhi*, L.); a kind of ornament, L.; a pit, cavern, L. — **kūrcāla**, m. young growing hair, L. — **keśī**, f. a kind of sacrificial grass, L. — **ja**, mfn. consisting of hair, hairy, MBh. — **tushá**, m. (of unknown meaning), MaitrS. — **dā́man**, n. a hair-thread, ŚBr. — **dhāna**, n. a tail, TS.; ŚrS. — **dhi**, m. id., ShaḍvBr.; Mn.; MBh. &c.; N. of a Muni, MBh. (B. and C. *bāla-dhi*); *-priya*, m. 'fond of its tail,' a buffalo, the Yak or Bos Grunniens, L. (cf. *vāla-priya*). — **nāṭaka**, n. a kind of inferior grain, L. — **pāśaka**, m. a partic. part of an elephant's tail, L. — **pāśyā**, f. a string of pearls or other ornament for the hair, L. — **putra**, m. a moustache, L. — **priya**, mfn. (an animal) fond of its tail (*-tva*, n.), Kum.; m. the Yak or Bos Grunniens, L. — **bandha**, m. 'tail-band,' a crupper, MBh.; N. of a partic. performance, Cat. — **bandhana**, n. a crupper (cf. prec.), MBh. — **bhid**, see *mahā-vāla-bhid*. — **maya**, mf(*ī*)n. consisting of hair, KātyŚr. — **mātrá**, n. the thickness of a hair, ŚBr. — **mūlaka**, see *bāla-m°*. — **mṛiga**, m. 'tail-animal,' the Yak or Bos Grunniens, L. — **varti**, f. a hair-compress, Suśr. — **vāya**, m. a hair-weaver, Pāṇ. vi, 2, 76, Sch.; N. of a mountain, ib. 67, Sch.; *-ja*, n. 'produced on the Vāla-v° mountain,' the cat's eye, lapis lazuli, Śiś. xiii, 58. — **vāsas**, n. a garment of hair, Mn.; Yājñ. — **vījya**, m. a wild goat, L. — **vyajana**, n. a chowrie (= *cāmara*, q. v.) made from the tail of the Yak or Bos Grunniens, SaddhP.; *°nī-√bhū*, P. *-bhavati*, to become a chowrie, Ragh. — **hasta**, m. a tail, L. **Vālâkshī**, f. a species of plant, L. **Vālâgra**, n. the point of a hair (as a measure = 8 Rāgas = 64 Paramâṇus), VarBṛS.; MārkP.; mfn. having a hair-like point, ShaḍvBr.; n. a kind of dove-cot, L. (cf. *bālâgra*); *-potikā*, f. a kind of pleasure-house floating on a lake, L.

Vālaka, m. the tail of a horse or of an elephant, L.; m. n. a kind of Andropogon, Kāv.; VarBṛS.; Suśr.; a bracelet, L.; n. a finger-ring, L.; (*ikā*), f. a seal-ring, Hcar., Sch. (L. also m.); sand, L.; a kind of ornament for the ears, L.; the rustling of leaves, L.

1. **Vāli**, m. (also written *bāli*) = *vālin*, N. of a monkey, R.; of a Muni, Cat.

2. **Vāli**, in comp. for *vālin*. — **śikha**, m. N. of a serpent-demon, MBh. — **sambhava**, m. 'sprung from Vālin,' N. of a monkey, MW. — **hantṛi**, m. 'killer of Vālin,' N. of Rāma-candra, ib.

Vālika, m. pl. (also written *bālika*) N. of a people, MārkP.; (*ā*), f., see under *vālaka*.

Vālin, m. (also written *bālin*) 'haired or tailed,' N. of a Daitya, MBh.; of a monkey (son of Indra and elder brother of the monkey-king Su-grīva, during whose absence from Kishkindha Vālin usurped the throne, but when Su-grīva returned he escaped to Ṛishyamūka), MBh.; R. &c.; (*inī*), f. the constellation Aśvinī, L.

वाल 2. *vāla*, n. (said to be) = *parvan*, Nir. xi, 31.

वालखिल्य *vālakhilya*, n. (also written *bāl°*, of doubtful derivation) N. of a collection of 11 (accord. to some only 6 or 8) hymns of the Ṛig-veda (commonly inserted after viii, 48, but numbered separately as a supplement by some editors; they are also called *vālakhilyāḥ*, with or scil. *mantrāḥ* or *ṛicaḥ*, and *daśatī vālakhilyakā*), Br.; ŚrS. &c.; (*°lyā́*), pl. N. of a class of Ṛishis of the size of a thumb (sixty thousand were produced from Brahmā's body and surround the chariot of the sun), TĀr.; MBh.; Kāv. &c.; (*vā́lakhilyā*), f. N. of a partic. kind of brick, ŚBr. — **grantha**, m., **-śastra**, n. N. of wks. — **saṃhitā**, f. the collection of the V° hymns, Bh.

Vālakhilyâśrama, m. N. of a hermitage, Cat.

Vālakhilyêśvara-tīrtha, n. N. of a Tīrtha, ib.

वालन *vālana*, mfn. (fr. 1. *valana*) relating to the variation of the ecliptic, Gol.

वालम्मदेश *vālamma-deśa*, m. N. of a country, Cat.

वालव *vālava*, n. (in astron.) N. of the second Karaṇa (q. v.), VarBṛS.

वालावितु *vālāvitu*, m. N. of a man, Rājat.

वालाह *vālāha*, *°haka*. See *bālāha*.

वालिकाज्य *vālikājya*, m., g. *bhauriky-ādi*. — **vidha**, mfn. inhabited by Vālikājya, ib. (v. l. *vāṇikājya*; Kāś. *vālija*, *vālijyaka*).

वालिकायन *vālikāyana*, mfn. (fr. *valika*), g. *pakshâdi*.

वालिखिल्य *vālikhilya*, w. r. for *vālakh°*.

वालिखिल्ल *vālikhilla*, m. N. of a son of Draviḍa, Śatr.

वालु *vālu*, m. = *elavālu*, L.

Vāluka, mfn. (fr. next); containing or resembling sand, L.; made of salt, R.; m. a kind of poison, L.; (*ī*), f. a sandbank, L.; camphor, L.; Cucumis Utilissimus, L.; = *ela-v°* or *hari-vāluka*, L.

Vālukā, f., sg. and pl. (more commonly written *bālukā*; of doubtful derivation) sand, gravel, ŚvetUp.; Mn.; MBh. &c. — **gaḍa**, m. a species of fish, L. — **caitya-krīḍā**, f. 'playing at heaps of sand,' a kind of child's game, HPariś. — **°tmikā** (*°kâtm°*), f. brown-sugar, L. — **tva**, n. 'the being mere sand,' nothingness, vanity, Kautukas. — **°di** (*°kâdi*), m. pl. sand and other things, Subh. — **prabhā**, f. (with Jainas) a partic. hell, L. — **°bdhi** (*°kâbdhi*), m. 'sand-sea,' a desert, Vcar. — **maya**, mf(*ī*)n. consisting or made of sand, Bhpr.; Hcat. — **°mbudhi** (*°kâmb°*) = *vālukâbdhi*, Rājat. — **°mbhas** (*°kâmbhas*), n., id.; N. of a sea or lake, Kālac. — **yantra**, n. a sand-bath, Bhpr. — **°rṇava** (*°kârṇ°*), m. = *vālukâbdhi*, MBh.; Rājat. **Vālukêśvara**, m. 'sand-lord,' N. of Śiva, RTL. 90; *-tīrtha*, n. N. of a well-known sacred tank (called Walkeśvar) near Bombay, Cat.

Vāluki or **°kin**, m. N. of a preceptor, Cat.

Vālukela, n. a species of salt (cf. *elavāluka*).

Vāluṅka, (prob.) n. a kind of cucumber, HPariś.; (*ī*), f. Cucumis Utilissimus, L.

Vālūka, m. a kind of poison, L. (cf. *vāluka*); (*ā*), f. = *vālukā*, sand, R.

वालेय *vāleya*. See 2. *bāleya*.

वालौयपथक *vālauya-pathaka*, m. or n. N. of a place, Inscr.

वाल्क *vālka*, mf(*ī*)n. (fr. *valka*) made of the bark of trees, L.; n. cloth or a garment made of bark, MārkP.

Vālkala, mfn. (fr. *valkala*) made of bark, L.; (*ī*), f. intoxicating liquor, L.; n. a bark dress worn by ascetics, W.

वाल्गव्य *vālgavya*, m. patr. fr. *valgu*, g. *gargâdi*.

Vālgavyāyanī, f. of prec., g. *lohitâdi*.

Vālguka, mf(*ī*)n. very handsome or beautiful, g. *aṅguly-ādi*.

वाल्गुद *vālguda*, m. a kind of bat, Vishṇ. (cf. *vāg-guda*).

वाल्मीक *vālmīka*, m. (fr. *valmīka*) = *vālmīki*, MBh.; Hariv.; R.; N. of a son of Citra-gupta, Cat.; mfn. composed by Vālmīki, BrahmavP. — **bhauma**, n. an ant-hill, AdbhBr. (v. l. *valmīka-bh°*).

Vālmīki, m. (incorrectly *vālmiki*) N. of the celebrated author of the Rāmâyaṇa (so called, according to some, because when immersed in thought he allowed himself to be overrun with ants like an ant-hill; he was no doubt a Brāhman by birth and closely connected with the kings of Ayodhyā; he collected the different songs and legendary tales relating to Rāma-candra and welded them into one continuous poem, to which later additions may have been made; he is said to have invented the Śloka metre, and probably the language and style of Indian epic poetry owe their definite form to him; according to one tradition he began life as a robber, but repenting betook himself to a hermitage on a hill in the district of Banda in Bundelkund, where he eventually received Sītā, the wife of Rāma, when banished by her husband; cf. IW. 314; 315 &c.), MBh.; R. &c.; of a son of Garuḍa, MBh.; of a grammarian, TPrāt.; of the authors of various wks. (the Yoga-vāsishṭha, the Adbhuta-rāmâyaṇa, and the Gaṅgâshṭaka), Cat.; (with *kavi*) of the son of Rudra-maṇi Tri-pāṭhin and author of the Ramalêndu-prakāśa, ib. — **carita**, n., **-tātparya-taraṇi**, f., **-śikshā**, f., **-sūtra**, n., **-hṛidaya**, n. N. of wks.

Vālmīkīya, mfn. relating to Vālmīki, composed by him &c., R.; Ragh.

वाल्लभ्य *vāllabhya*, n. (fr. *vallabha*) the state of being beloved or a favourite, popularity, favour, MBh.; Kāv.; VarBṛS.; love, tenderness, Rājat.

वाल्वङ्गिरि *vālvaṅgiri*, m. Cucumis Utilissimus, L. (cf. *vāluka*).

वाव *vā́vá*, ind. (a particle laying stress on the word preceding it, esp. in relative clauses; also *ha vā́vá*, *ha* [*khálu*] *vāvá*, *u ha vāva*, *ha tvā́vá* [q. v.]) just, indeed, even, TS.; Br. (in ŚBr. only from book vi); Up.; BhP.

वावदूक *vāvadūka*, mfn. (fr. Intens. of √*vad*) talking much, eloquent, garrulous, disputatious, MBh.; Śaṃk.; m. N. of a man, g. *kurv-ādi*. — **tā**, f. garrulity, loquaciousness, MW. — **tva**, n. id., eloquence, Pañcar.

Vāvadūkya, m. patr. fr. *vāvadūka*.

वावय *vāvaya*, m. a sort of basil, Ocymum Sanctum, L.

वावर *vāvara*, m. a partic. Pañca-rātra, ĀśvŚr.

वावल *vāvala* (?), m. a kind of plant, L.

वावल्ल *vāvalla*, m. a kind of arrow, L.

वावशत् *vāvaśat*. See √*vāś*.

वावशान *vāvaśāná*. See √*vaś* and *vāś*.

वावसान *vāvasāná*. See √5. *vas*.

वावहि *vā́vahi*, mfn. (fr. Intens. of √*vah*) carrying or conducting well, RV.

वावात *vāvā́ta*, mfn. (Padap. *vavā́ta*; fr. √*van*) beloved, dear, RV.; (*ā*), f. a king's favourite wife (accord. to Sch. inferior to the *mahishī*, but superior to the *pari-vṛiktī*), Br.; GṛŚrS.; R.

Vāvā́tṛi, m. an adherent, follower, RV.

वावुट *vāvuṭa*, m. (cf. *vārbaṭa*) a raft, boat, vessel, L.

वावृत् *vāvṛit*, cl. 4. Ā. (Dhātup. xxvi, 51, rather Intens. fr. a lost √3. *vṛit*) *vāvṛityate* (only pr. p. *vāvṛityamāna*), to choose, select, Bhaṭṭ.

Vāvṛitta, mfn. chosen, selected, appointed, L.

वावृद्ध *vāvṛiddha*, v.l. for *vācā-vṛiddha*, q.v.

वावृधध्यै *vāvṛidhadhyai*. See √*vṛidh*.

Vāvṛidhénya, mfn. (Padap. *vav°*) to be increased or comforted, RV.

वाश् *vāś*, cl. 4. Ā. (Dhātup. xxvi, 54) *vāśyate* (ep. also *vāśyati*, Ved. and ep. also *vā́śati*, °*te*; pf. *vavāśe*, °*śire*; in RV. also *vāvaśre* and p. *vāvaśāná*; aor. *avāśishṭa*, Br.; fut. *vāśitā*, *vāśishyate*, Gr.; ind. *vāśitum*, ib.; ind. p. *vāśitvā*, *-vāśya*, VarBṛS.), to roar, howl, bellow, bleat, low (as a cow), cry, shriek, sing (like a bird), sound, resound, RV. &c. &c.: Caus. *vāśayati* (aor. *avavāśat*, in RV. also *avīvaśat*, *ávīvaśanta*), to cause to roar or low or resound or thunder, RV.; (Ā.) to roar or sound aloud, ib.: Desid. *vivāśishate*, Gr.: Intens. *vāvāśyate* (v.l. *rārāśyate*, MBh.), *vāvashṭi* (impf. aor. *ávāvaśanta*, *vāvaśanta*, *avāvaśītām*; p. *vā́vaśat*), to roar or scream or sound aloud, RV. [*Vāś* is sometimes wrongly written *vās*.]

1. **Vāśá**, mfn. roaring, sounding, RV. viii, 19, 31; (*vā́śa*). id. (only *ā* and *ī*, f. pl. applied to water), VS.; TS.

1. **Vāśaka**, mfn. (for 2. see below) croaking, screaming, warbling (said of birds), Mṛicch.

Vāśana, mfn. id., Bhaṭṭ.; m. (*saṃjñāyām*), g. *nandy-ādi*; n. the act of roaring, bleating &c., TBr., Sch. (cf. *ghora-v°*).

Vāśi, m. 'roaring,' fire or the god of fire, Uṇ. iv, 124, Sch.

1. **Vāśita**, mfn. roared, cried, sung, MBh. &c.; n. roaring, croaking, yelling, howl, cry, scream, MBh.; R.; VarBṛS.; Kathās.

Vāśin, mfn. (also written *vāsin*) howling, croaking &c., Kām. (cf. *ghora-v°*).

Vāśrá, mf(*ā́*)n. roaring, lowing, howling, thundering, sounding, whistling &c., RV.; BhP. (compar. *-tara*, Kāṭh.); m. a day, L.; (*ā*), f. (scil. *dhenú*) a lowing cow, any cow, RV.; AV. (also written *vāsrā*); a mother, MW.; n. (only L.) a building; a place where four roads meet; dung.

वाश 2. *vāśa*, m. patr. fr. *vaśa*, ŚāṅkhŚr.; n. N. of a Sāman, ĀrshBr.

वाशक 2. *vāśaka*, m. (and °*ikā*, f.) Gendarussa Vulgaris, L. (cf. 1. *vāsa*, *vāsaka*).

वाशव *vāśava*, m. = *vāsava*, L.

वाशा *vāśā*, f. a species of plant, Kauś.

वाशित 2. *vāśita* = 1. *vāsita*, L.

वाशिता *vāśitā*, f. (also written *vāsitā*, prob. fr. √*vaś*) a cow desiring the bull (also applied to other animals desiring the male, esp. to a female elephant), AV. &c. &c.; a woman, wife, MBh. — **gṛishṭi**, f. a young female elephant, MBh. xi, 642 (cf. Pāṇ. ii, 1, 65).

वाशिष्ठ *vāśishṭha*, incorrect for *vāsishṭha*.

वाशी *vā́śī*, f. (also written *vāsī*; accord. to some connected with √*vraśc*) a sharp or pointed knife or a kind of axe, adze, chisel (esp. as the weapon of Agni or the Maruts, and the instrument of the Ṛibhus, while the paraśu or axe is that of Tvashṭṛi), RV.; AV.; MBh.; sound, voice, Naigh. (cf. under 1. *vāśa*). — **mat** (*vā́śī-*), mfn. having a sharp knife, armed with an axe, RV.

वाशुरा *vāśurā*, f. (said to be fr. √*vāś*) night, Uṇ. i, 39, Sch. (cf. *vāsurā*).

वाष्कल *vāshkala*. See *bāshkala*.

वाष्टुका *vāshṭukā*, f. N. of a village, Rājat.

वाष्प *vāshpa* &c. See *bāshpa*.

वास् 1. *vās*. See *ni-*√5. *vas*.

वास् 2. *vās*, cl. 10. P. (Dhātup. xxxv, 32; perhaps only Nom. fr. next) *vāsayati* (ep. also °*te*; aor. *avavāsat*), to perfume, make fragrant, scent, fumigate, incense, steep, MBh.; Kāv. &c.

1. **Vāsa**, m. perfuming, perfume, Vikr.; Mālatīm.; Car.; Gendarussa Vulgaris, L. (also *ā*, f.) — **tāmbūla**, n. perfumed betel, Daś. — **dhūpi**, m. patr., Saṃskārak. — **yoga**, m. a powder formed of various fragrant substances (esp. the red powder scattered about and sprinkled on the clothes at the Holī festival, RTL. 430), L. **Vāsā-khaṇḍa-kushmāṇḍaka**, m. a partic. mixture or compound, L.

1. **Vāsaka**, m. scent, Pañcar.; (also *akā* and *ikā*, f.) Gendarussa Vulgaris or Adhatoda Vasica, VarBṛS.; Suśr. &c.; mfn. perfuming, fumigating, MW.

1. **Vāsana**, n. the act of perfuming or fumigating, infusing, steeping, Gīt., Sch.; (*ā*), f. id., Śiś., Sch.

Vāsikā. See 1. *vāsaka* above.

1. **Vāsita**, mfn. infused, steeped, perfumed, scented, MBh.; Kāv. &c.; affected with, influenced by (instr. or comp.), Śaṃk.; spiced, seasoned (as sauces), W.; (*ā*), f., see *vāśitā*.

1. **Vāsin**, mfn. fragrant; (*inī*), f. a Barleria with white flowers, L.

वास 2. *vāsa*, m. (fr. √4. *vas*) a garment, dress, clothes (m. c. for *vāsas*), MBh. (cf. *kṛishṇa-vāsa*). — **dhṛik**, mfn. wearing a garment, Hariv.

Vāsaḥ, in comp. for 1. *vāsas*. — **kuṭi**, f. a tent, L. — **khaṇḍa**, m. n. a piece of cloth, a rag, ŚārṅgP. — **palpūlī**, m. a washer of clothes, VS. — **śatá**, n. a hundred garments, ŚBr.

2. **Vāsaka** (ifc.) = 2. *vāsa*, clothing, clothes, Yājñ.; MBh. &c. (cf. *aśuddha-v°*).

2. **Vāsana**, n. covering, clothing, garment, dress, Kāv.; an envelope, box, casket, Yājñ. — **stha**, mfn. being in a box or casket, ib.

Vāsayitṛi, m. one who clothes or supports or preserves, MBh. iv, 420 (used also by Comm. to explain *vasu* and *vasuka*).

1. **Vā́sas**, n. (for 2. see col. 2) cloth, clothes, dress, a garment (du. an upper and under garment; cf. *vāso-yuga*), RV. &c. &c.; the 'clothing' or feathers of an arrow, MBh.; R. &c. (only ifc.; cf. *barhiṇa-v°*); cotton, L.; a pall, MW.; a screen, ib.; (with *markaṭasya*) a cobweb, L.; du. (with *samudrasya*) N. of two Sāmans, ĀrshBr.

2. **Vāsita**, mfn. clothed, dressed, L.; (*ā*), f., see *vāśitā*.

2. **Vāsin**, mfn. having or wearing clothes, (esp. ifc.) clothed or dressed in, wearing, AitBr.; MBh. &c.

Vāso, in comp. for 1. *vāsas*. — **da**, mfn. giving clothes, Mn. iv, 231. — **dā́**, mfn. id., RV. — **bhṛit**, mfn. wearing clothes, Bhartṛ.; (gender unknown) the hip, VarBṛS. — **yuga**, n. a pair of garments, suit of clothes (the dress of the Hindūs usually consisting of two pieces of cloth, viz. a lower garment fastened round the waist, and an upper one thrown loosely over the shoulders), MBh. — **vāyá**, mfn. weaving cloth, RV.

1. **Vāsya**, mfn. to be (or being) covered or enveloped, ĪśUp.; being worn (see *prathama-vāsyà*).

वास 3. *vāsá*, m. (fr. √5. *vas*) staying, remaining (esp. 'overnight'), abiding, dwelling, residence, living in (loc. or comp.; cf. Pāṇ. vi, 3, 18, Sch.), abode, habitation, RV. &c. &c.; ifc. = having one's abode in, dwelling or living in; *vāsaṃ* √*vas*, to take up one's abode, abide, dwell; place or seat of (gen.), R.; a day's journey, ib.; state, situation, condition, Hariv.; = *vāsa-gṛiha*, bed-chamber (see *-sajjā*); = *vāsanā*, imagination, idea, semblance of, MBh. — **karṇī**, f. = *yajña-śālā*, a sacrificial hall, L.; a place where public exhibitions (as Nāches &c.) are held, W. — **gṛiha** or **-geha**, n. 'dwelling-house,' the inner part of a house, sleeping-room, bed-chamber, MBh.; Kāv. &c. — **paryaya**, m. change of residence, VarBṛS. — **pushpā**, f. a kind of cress growing in gardens, L. — **pushpi**, m. patr. (also pl.), Saṃskārak. — **prāsāda**, m. a palace, Kathās. — **bhavana**, n. = *-gṛiha*, Kād. — **bhūmi**, f. dwelling-place, homestead, Hit. — **yashṭi**, f. a pole or stick serving as a perch for tame birds to rest upon, a roosting perch, Megh. — **veśman**, n. = *-gṛiha*, Kathās., Sch. — **sajjā**, f. 'ready in her chamber,' a woman ready to receive her lover (cf. *vāsaka-s°*), L. **Vāsâgāra**, n. = *vāsa-gṛiha*, Vās.; Prab. **Vāsâukas**, n. id., L.

3. **Vāsaka**, mf(*ikā*)n. causing to dwell or inhabit, populating, MW.; (ifc.) abode, habitation, Yājñ.; n. (ifc. f. *ā*) a sleeping-room, bed-chamber, Kathās. — **sajjā** or **-sajjikā**, f. a woman ready to receive her lover (cf. *vāsa-sajjā*), Kāv., Sch.

Vāsatīvara, mfn. (fr. *vasatī-vari*) relating to water left standing overnight, Bṛih.

Vā́sateya, mfn. (fr. *vasati*) to be lodged or sheltered, AV.; affording shelter, Bhaṭṭ.; (*ī*), f. night, Hcar.

3. **Vāsana**, mfn. belonging to an abode, fit for a dwelling, W.; n. causing to abide or dwell, Bālar.; abiding, abode, L.; a receptacle for water, L.; knowledge, L.; a partic. posture (practised by ascetics during abstract meditation, and by others; described as sitting on the ground with the knees bent and the feet turned backwards), W.; (*ā*), f., see next.

Vāsanā, f. the impression of anything remaining unconsciously in the mind, the present consciousness of past perceptions, knowledge derived from memory, Śaṃk.; Kāv.; Kathās.; fancy, imagination, idea, notion, false notion, mistake (ifc., e.g. *bheda-v°*, the mistake that there is a difference), ib.; Rājat.; Sarvad. &c.; thinking of, longing for, expectation, desire, inclination, Kathās.; liking, respectful regard, Bhām.; trust, confidence, W.; (in math.) proof, demonstration (= *upapatti*), Gol.; a kind of metre, Col.; N. of Durgā, BhP.; of the wife of Arka, ib.; of a Comm. on the Siddhânta-śiromaṇi. — **tattva-bodhikā**, f. N. of a Tantric wk. (= *tārā-rahasya-vṛittikā*). — **bhāshya**, n. N. of various wks. — **maya**, mf(*ī*)n. consisting in notions or ideas or in impressions of (comp.), Vedântas. (*-tva*, n.) — **vārttika**, n., **-vāsudevasyêtipadya-vyākhyā**, f. N. of wks.

Vāsanīya, mfn. intelligible only by much reflection, Vām.

Vāsayitavya, mfn. to be taken in or lodged, MBh.

2. **Vāsas**, n. lodging for the night, night-quarters, PraśnUp.

Vāsâyanika, mfn. (fr. 3. *vāsa* + *ayana*) going from house to house, making visits, MBh.

Vāsi, m. abiding, dwelling, W.; (*ī*), f., see *vāśī*.

3. **Vāsita**, mfn. caused to stop or stay (esp. 'overnight'), caused to dwell or live in (loc.), MBh.; Kāv. &c.; peopled, populous (as a country), W.; n. the art of rendering populous or causing to be inhabited, W.; knowledge (esp. derived from memory, = *vāsanā*, ib.)

3. **Vāsin**, mfn. staying, abiding, dwelling, living, inhabiting (often ifc. = living in or among or in a partic. manner or condition), TS. &c. &c.

2. **Vāsya**, mfn. to be caused to dwell or settle down, VarBṛS.

वासक 4. *vāsaka*, m. (in music) a species of *dhruvaka* (q.v.), Saṃgīt.

वासक 5. *vāsaka*, m. N. of a serpent-demon, MBh.; pl. N. of a people, MārkP.

वासत *vāsata*, m. an ass, L.; Terminalia Bellerica, L.

वासन्त *vāsantá*, mf(*ī*)n. (fr. *vasanta*) relating to or produced in the spring season, vernal, AV. &c. &c.; being in the spring of life, young, W.; = *avahita* or *vihita*, L.; m. (only L.) a camel; the Indian cuckoo; a young elephant, any young animal;

the southern or western wind (= *malayânila*, q.v.); Phaseolus Mungo or a black species of this kind of bean; a purple species of Barleria Cristata; Vangueria Spinosa; a dissolute man; (*ī*), f., see below.

Vāsantaka, mf(*ikā*)n. relating to or grown in spring, vernal, L.; (*ikā*), f. Gærtnera Racemosa, Pañcad.; N. of a forest deity, Cat.; of a drama (also *vāsantikā-pariṇaya*, m.), ib.

Vā́santika, mf(*ā*)n. relating to spring, vernal, VS. &c. &c.; = *vasantam adhīte veda vā*, Pāṇ. iv, 2, 63; m. the spring festival, Āpast.; an actor, dancer, the buffoon in a drama (= *vidūshaka*, q.v.), L.

Vāsantī, f. (see *vāsanta* above) N. of various plants (Gærtnera Racemosa, a kind of jasmine, Bignonia Suaveolens &c.), L.; = *nava-mālikā*, Bhpr.; a spring festival (held in the month Caitra in honour of Kāma-deva or in some places of Durgā), L.; a kind of metre, Col.; (in music) a partic. Rāgiṇī, Saṃgīt.; N. of a sylvan goddess, Uttarar.; of a daughter of king Bhūmi-śukla, Buddh. **-kusuma**, n. the flower Vāsantī, Gīt. **-pūjā**, f. the worship of Durgā in the month Caitra, MW.

वासमुलि *vāsamuli*, m. pl. patr., Saṃskārak. (prob. w.r. for *vāsamūli*).

वासर *vāsará*, mf(ī)n. (fr. *vasar*, √2. *vas*) relating to or appearing in the morning, matutinal, early, RV.; m. n. day (as opp. to 'night'), a day (in general), a week-day, GṛS.; Kāv.; Kathās. &c.; m. time, turn, succession, Hit. (v.l. *vāra*); N. of a serpent-demon, L.; (*ā*), f., w.r. for *vāsurā*, q.v.; (*ī*), f. a god of the day, Kālac.; N. of a cow, MW. **-kanyakā**, f. 'daughter of day,' night, L. **-kṛit**, m. 'day-maker,' the sun, L. **-kṛitya**, n. 'day-work,' the daily observances to be performed at fixed hours, Kathās. **-maṇi**, m. 'day-jewel,' the sun, Kāv. **-saṅga**, m. 'day-junction,' the morning, Bhaṭṭ. **Vāsarâdhiśa**, m. 'lord of the day,' the sun, Sāh. **Vāsarêśa**, m. id., Kathās.; the regent of a week-day (e.g. a planet, the sun, or the moon), L.

वासव *vāsavá*, mf(ī)n. (fr. 1. *vasu*) relating or belonging to the Vasus, derived or descended from them &c., AV.; TS.; Kāṭh.; ĀśvŚr.; relating or belonging to (king) Vasu, MBh.; containing the word *vasu*, g. *vimuktâdi*; m. N. of Indra (as chief of the Vasus), MBh.; Kāv. &c.; a son of (king) Vasu, MBh.; (with *Indrasya*) N. of a Sāman, L.; of a poet, Cat.; m. n. N. of the Nakshatra Dhanishṭhā (presided over by the Vasus), Sūryas.; (*ī*), f. patr. of the mother of Vyāsa (she was the offspring of the Apsaras Adrikā, who as a fish had swallowed the seed of king Vasu), MBh.; BhP.; Indra's energy, Cat.; (with or scil. *diś*) Indra's region or quarter, the east, Kād.; n. N. of a Sāman, ĀrshBr.; mf(*ī*)n. relating or belonging to Indra, Kād. **-grāma** or °**maka**, m. N. of a village, Divyāv. **-cāpa**, m. 'Indra's bow,' a rainbow, Vcar. **-ja**, m. 'Indra's son,' patr. of Arjuna, MBh. **-datta**, m. 'given by Indra,' N. of a man, Buddh.; (*ā*), f. N. of various women (esp. of the wife of Udayana, king of Vatsa and daughter of king Caṇḍa-mahā-sena of Ujjayinī [Kathās.] or of king Pradyota [Ratnâv.], to whom she offered herself after having been betrothed by her father to Saṃjaya [Mālatīm.]; and of the heroine of Subandhu's novel, who is represented to have been betrothed by her father to Pushpa-ketu, but carried off by Kandarpa-ketu); the story of Vāsava-dattā, Pāṇ. iv, 3, 87, Vārtt. 1, Pat. (esp. as narrated in Subandhu's tale); °*ttika*, mfn. acquainted with the story of V° or studying it, Pat. on Pāṇ. iv, 2, 60; °*ttâkhyāyikā*, f. the story of V°, Cat.; °*tteya*, m. metron. of *vāsava-dattā*, Pāṇ. iv, 1, 113, Sch. **-diś**, f. 'Indra's quarter,' the east, Kathās. **Vāsavâvaraja**, m. 'I°'s younger brother,' N. of Vishṇu, L. **Vāsavâvāsa**, m. I°'s abode or heaven, the sky, L. **Vāsavâśā**, f. = *vāsava-diś*, Śiś. **Vāsavêśvara-tīrtha**, n. N. of a Tīrtha, Cat. **Vāsavôpama**, mfn. resembling or like Indra, MW.

Vāsavi, m. 'Indra's son,' N. of Arjuna, MBh.; of the monkey Vālin, R.

Vāsaveya, mfn. (fr. *vāsava*), g. *sakhy-ādi*; (fr. *vāsavī*) metron. of Vyāsa, MBh.

वासवत *vāsavata*, m. pl. N. of a partic. grammatical school, Bhaṭṭ., Sch. (prob. w.r. for *rāsavata*, 'follower of the Rasa-vatī,' q.v.)

वासस्तेवि *vāsastevi* (?), m. pl., patr., Saṃskārak.

वासात *vāsāta* or °*taka*, mfn. (fr. *vasāti*) inhabited by the Vasātis, Pāṇ. iv, 2, 52, Vārtt. 2; 3, Pat.

Vā́sātya, mfn. relating to the dawn, dim, dusky, TĀr.; m. pl. N. of a people (= *vasāti*), MBh.

वासि *vāsi* or *vāsī*, f. a carpenter's adze, L. (cf. *vāśī*).

वासिक *vāsika*. See *kashāya-*, *rūpa-*, and *vana-v°*; (*ikā*), f., see under 1. *vāsaka*, p. 947, col. 2.

वासित 1. 2. 3. *vāsita* and *vāsin*. See p. 947.

वासिनायनि *vāsināyani*, m. patr. fr. *vāsin*, Pāṇ. vi, 4, 174.

वासिल *vāsila*, mfn. (fr. *vāsa*), g. *kāśâdi*; m. endearing form of *vāsishṭha*, Vām. v, 2, 63.

वासिशुम्फ *vāsishumpha* (?), m. or n. N. of a place, Cat.

वासिष्ट *vāsishṭa*, n. blood, L. (prob. w.r. for *vāsishṭha*; see next).

वासिष्ठ *vāsishṭhá*, mf(ī)n. (also written *vāśishṭha*) relating or belonging to Vasishṭha, composed or revealed by him (as the 7th Maṇḍala of the Ṛig-veda); with *śata*, n. the hundred sons of V°, AitBr.; MBh.; R. &c.; m. a son or descendant of V° (applied as a patr. to various Ṛishis), TS.; Br.; ŚrS. &c.; (*ī*), f. a female descendant of V°, Pāṇ. iv, 1, 78, Sch.; N. of a river (= *go-matī*), MBh.; (also with *śānti*) N. of various wks.; n. N. of various Sāmans, ĀrshBr.; = *yoga-vāsishṭha*, q.v.; blood, L.; N. of a Tīrtha, MBh. **-tātparya-prakāśa**, m., **-nava-graha-paddhati**, f. N. of wks. **-rāmâyaṇa**, n. = *yoga-vāsishṭha*. **-laiṅga** or **-laiṅgya**, n. = *vasishṭhôpapurāṇa*. **-vivaraṇa**, n., **-śikshā**, f., **-sāra**, m., **-siddhânta**, m., **-sūtra**, n., **-smṛiti**, f. N. of wks. **Vāsishṭhôttara-rāmâyaṇa**, n. N. of wk.

Vāsishṭhāyani, mfn. (fr. *vasishṭha*), g. *karṇâdi*.

Vāsishṭhika, mfn. (fr. id.), Pāṇ. iv, 3, 69, Sch. **-vācaspati** (?), N. of wk.

वासी *vāsī*. See *vāsi*.

वासीफल *vāsī-phala*, n. a kind of fruit, VarBṛS.

वासु *vāsu*, m. (said to be fr. √5. *vas*) N. of Vishṇu (as dwelling in all beings), Uṇ. i, 1, Sch.; the spirit or soul considered as the Supreme Being or Soul of the universe, W. (also Vṛiddhi form of *vasu* in comp.) **-devá**, see below. **-m-dhareya**, m. (fr. *vasum-dharā*) metron. of Naraka, Bālar.; (*ī*), f. metron. of Sītā, ib. **-pura**, n. N. of a town, W. **-pūjya**, m. (with Jainas) N. of the 12th Arhat of the present Avasarpiṇī (son of Vasu-pūjya-rāj), L. **-bha**, m. or n. (?) N. of a place, Virac. (cf. *vasubha*). **-bhadra**, m. N. of Kṛishṇa, L. **-mata**, mfn. containing the word *vasu-mat*, g. *vimuktâdi*. **-manda**, n. N. of two Sāmans, ĀrshBr.

Vāsudeva, m. (fr. *vasu-d°*) patr. of Kṛishṇa, TĀr. &c. (RTL. 111); of a king of the Puṇḍras, Hariv.; N. of a class of beings peculiar to the Jainas, L.; a horse, L.; N. of various kings and authors (also with *ācārya*, *dīkshita*, *śarman*, *śāstrin* &c.), Inscr.; Cat.; (*ī*), f. Asparagus Racemosus, L.; n. N. of an Upanishad; mf(*ī*)n. relating to (the god) Kṛishṇa, NṛisUp.; written or composed by V°, Cat.; *-jñāna*, n. N. of wk.; *-jyotis*, m. N. of a poet, Cat.; *-tīrtha*, m. N. of a man, ib.; *-dvādaśâksharī*, f., *-puṇyâha*, n., *-pūjā*, f. N. of wks.; *-priya*, m. 'friend of V°,' N. of Kārttikeya, MBh.; *-priyaṃ-karī*, f. Asparagus Racemosus, L.; *-manana*, n. N. of a Vedânta wk.; *-maya*, mf(*ī*)n. consisting of Kṛishṇa, representing him, AgP.; *-mahârādhana*, n., *-rahasya*, n. N. of wks.; *-vargīṇa* or *-vargya*, mfn. taking V°'s side, partial to him, Pāṇ. iv, 2, 104, Vārtt. 11, Pat.; *-vijaya*, m., *-sahasra-nāman*, n. N. of wks.; *-suta*, m., *-sena*, m. N. of authors, Cat.; *-stotra*, n. N. of a Stotra; °*vânandī-campū*, f. N. of a poem; °*vânubhava*, m. N. of a medical wk.; °*vâśrama*, m., °*vêndra*, m., °*vêndra-śishya*, m. N. of authors, Cat.; -°*vôpanishad*, f. N. of one of the more recent Upanishads of the Atharva-veda.

Vāsudevaka, m. = Vāsudeva (Kṛishṇa), AgP.; an adherent or worshipper of V°, Pāṇ. iv, 3, 98; one who disgraces the name V°, Hariv. (cf. 4. *ka*, p. 240); a second V°, Mṛicch. (in Prākṛit).

वासुक *vāsuka*, mfn. (fr. 1. *vasu*), g. *aśvâdi*; (*ī*), f. N. of a woman, HPariś.

वासुकि *vāsuki*, m. (fr. *vasuka*) N. of a divine being, Gobh.; Kauś.; of a serpent-king (one of the three chief kings of the Nāgas, the other two being Śesha and Takshaka; the gods and demons used the serpent Vāsuki as a rope for twisting round the mountain Mandara when they churned the ocean, RTL. 108, 233), MBh.; R. &c.; of an author, Pratāp., Sch.; of another man, Pravar. **-ja**, mfn. descended from Vāsuki, MBh. **-hrada**, m. N. of a lake, MW.

Vāsukeya, m. the serpent Vāsuki, L. **-svasṛi**, f. 'sister of Vāsuki,' N. of the goddess Manasā (presiding over serpents and regarded as wife of Jaratkāru), W.

वासुक्र *vāsukra*, mfn. composed by Vasukra, ŚāṅkhŚr.

वासुरा *vāsurā*, f. (fr. √5. *vas* or *vas*) night, L. (cf. *vāśurā*); the earth, L.; a woman, L.; a female elephant, L.

वासुरायणीय *vāsurāyaṇīya* (!), m. pl. N. of a school, L.

वासू *vāsū*, f. (of doubtful derivation) a young girl, maiden (voc. *vāsu*), Daś.

वासोद *vāso-da*, *vāso-bhṛit* &c. See p. 947, col. 2.

वासौकस् *vāsâukas*. See p. 947, col. 3.

वास्कल *vāskala*. See *bāshkala*.

वास्त *vāsta*, *vāstāyana*, *vāstika*. See *bāsta* &c.

वास्तव *vāstava*, mf(ī)n. (fr. 2. *vastu*, √5. *vas*) substantial, real, true, genuine, being anything in the true sense of the word, Gol.; BhP.; Pañcar.; fixed, determined, demonstrated, W.; n. an appointment, ib.; (*e*), ind. = *vastu-tas*, really, truly, Nalac., Sch. **-tva**, n. reality, substantiality, Sarvad. **Vāstavôshā**, prob. w.r. for *vāsurā* + *ushā*, L.

Vāstavika, mfn. = *vāstava*, real, substantial &c., L.; m. a realist, Vās.; a gardener, ib.

Vāstavyà, mfn. left on any spot (as a worthless remainder; also applied to Rudra, to whom the leavings of the sacrifice belong), TS.; VS.; Br.; settled, resident, an inhabitant, MBh.; R. &c.

Vā́stu, n. (m. only in BhP.) the site or foundation of a house, site, ground, building or dwelling-place, habitation, homestead, house, RV. &c. &c.; an apartment, chamber, VarBṛS.; m. N. of one of the 8 Vasus, BhP.; of a Rākshasa, Cat.; (prob.) f. N. of a river, MBh.; n. the pot-herb Chenopodium Album, L.; a kind of grain, ĀpŚr., Sch. (cf. *-maya*). **-ṛicaka**, m. or n. (?) N. of wk. **-karman**, n. house-building, architecture, R.; VarBṛS. **-kalpa**, m. N. of wk. **-kāla**, m. the time suited for building a house, Cat. **-kīrṇa**, m. a kind of pavilion, Vāstuv. **-cakra**, n., **-candrikā**, f. N. of wks. **-ja**, mfn. home-bred, MBh. **-jñāna**, n. knowledge of building, architecture, VarBṛS. **-tattva**, n. N. of wk. **-deva**, m. (W.), **-devatā**, f. (ĀśvGṛ.) the deity presiding over a house. **-nara**, m. the archetype or ideal pattern of a house personified as a deity, VarBṛS. **-nirmāṇa**, n. N. of wk. **-pá**, mfn. keeping the ground or homestead (when quitted by its owner), VS.; the tutelary deity of a h°, Vāstuv. **-paddhati**, f., **-parīkshā**, f. N. of wks. **-paśya**, (prob.) n. a partic. Brāhmaṇa, L. **-pāla**, m. the tutelary deity of a h°, Vāstuv. **-purusha**, m. = *-nara*, AgP.; *-vidhi*, m. N. of wk. **-pūjana**, n., **-pūjana-paddhati**, f., **-pūjā-vidhi**, m., **-prakaraṇa**, n., **-prakāśa**, m., **-pradīpa**, m., **-prayoga**, m., **-praveśa-paddhati**, f. N. of wks. **-praśamana**, n. the lustration or purification of a h°, SāmavBr. **-bandhana**, n. the building of a h°, VarBṛS. **-mañjarī**, f., **-maṇḍana**, n. N. of wks. **-madhya**, n. the centre of a h°, Mn. iii, 89. **-maya**, mf(*ī*)n. (prob.) domestic, AgP.; consisting of the grain called Vāstu, ĀpŚr. (Sch.) **-yāga**, m. a sacrifice performed before the building of a h°; *-vidhes tattva* or *-vidhi-tattva*, n. N. of a wk. (giving the rules for the above sacrifice). **-lakshaṇa**, n., **-vicāra**, m., **-vijñāna-phalâdeśa**, m. N. of wks. **-vidya**, mfn. (fr. next) relating to architecture, g. *ṛig-ayanâdi*. **-vidyā**, f. 'science in building,' architecture, MBh.; VarBṛS.; *-kuśala*, mfn. versed in arch°, Car. **– vidhāna**, n. house-building, R. **– vidhi**, m., **-vyākhyāna**, n. N. of wks. **– śamana** (or *-saṃśamana*, MW.), n. the purificatory ceremony performed on laying a foundation or on entering a new house, SāmavBr. **– śāka**, n. a kind of vegetable, Car. **– śānti**, f. = *-śamana* (also N. of various wks.); *-paddhati*, f., *-prayoga*, m.; °*ty-ādi*, m. N. of wks. **– śāstra**, n., **-śiromaṇi**, m. N. of wks. **– saṃśamanīya**, mfn. relating to the lustration of a h°, R. **– saṃhitā**, f., **-saṃgraha**, m., **-sanatkumāra**, m., **-samuccaya**, m. N. of wks. **– sampādana**, n. the preparation of a h°, Mn. iii, 255. **– sāra**, m., **-saukhya**, n. of wks. **– sthāpana**, n. the erection of a h°, Cat. **– ha**, mfn. left remaining on a (sacred) spot, remainder, AitBr. v, 14. **– homa**, m. N. of wk. (cf. *-yāga*). **Vāstûpaśama**, m., °**śamana**, n. = *vāstu-śamana*, Cat.; °*ma-paddhati*, f. N. of wk.

Vāstuka, mfn. left remaining on the sacrificial ground, BhP. (cf. prec. and *vāstu-ha*); m. n. Chenopodium Album, Suśr.; (*ī*), f. a kind of vegetable, L. **– śākaṭa** or **-śākina**, m. n. and (*ā*), f. a field producing Chenopodium, L.

Vāstūka, m. n. Chenopodium Album, L.

Vā́stosh-páti, m. (fr. *vāstos*, gen. of *vāstu* + *p*°) 'house-protector,' N. of a deity who presides over the foundation of a house or homestead (addressed in RV. vii, 54), RV.; AV.; PārGṛ.; Mn.; BhP.; N. of Rudra, TS.; of Indra, L. **– sûkta**, n. N. of a hymn (prob. RV. vii, 54), Cat. **Vāstoshpatīya** (TS.) or °**tya** (Kauś.), relating or belonging to Vāstosh-pati.

Vāstvà, mfn. = *vāstavyà*, left remaining; n. remainder, leavings, MaitrS. **– máya**, mf(*ī*)n. consisting of leavings, ib.

Vāstvya, mfn. = *vāstva*, Pāṇ. vi, 4, 175.

वास्तेय *vā́steya*, mf(*ī*)n. (fr. *vasti*; see *basti*) being in the bladder, AV.; ChUp. (cf. Pāṇ. iv, 3, 56); resembling the bladder, Pāṇ. v, 3, 101.

वास्त्र *vāstra*, mfn. (fr. *vastra*) covered with cloth, Pāṇ. iv, 2, 10, Sch.

वास्प *vāspa*. See *bāshpa*.

Vāspeya, m. the tree Nāga-kesara (commonly called Nāgesar), MW.

वास्य 3. *vāsya*, m. or n. (for 1. and 2. see p. 947) = *vāsi* or *vāśī*, an axe, Nilak. on MBh. i, 4605; v, 5250.

वास्र *vāsra*, m. (cf. *vāsara*) a day; (*ā*), f., see *vāśrā*.

वाह् 1. *vāh*, cl. 1. Ā. (Dhātup. xvi, 44) *vāhate*, to bear down, Car. (cf. *pra-√vāh*); to endeavour, make effort, try, Dhātup.: Caus. *vāhayati* (cf. under √1. *vah*), to cause to labour or work, use, employ, Bhaṭṭ.

1. **Vāhana**, n. (for 2. see col. 2) the act of making effort, endeavouring, exertion, W.

1. **Vāhita**, mfn. (for 2. see col. 2) exerted, endeavoured, ib.; removed, destroyed, Divyâv.

वाह् 2. *vāh* (nom. *vāṭ*; strong form of 2. *vah*, p. 933, col. 3), bearing, carrying.

Vāha, mf(*ā*)n. (ifc.) bearing, drawing, conveying, carrying, Kathās.; BhP.; flowing, BhP.; undergoing, MBh.; m. the act of drawing &c., MBh.; Hit.; riding, driving, ŚārṅgP.; flowing, current, Kathās.; a draught-animal, horse, bull, ass, RV. &c. &c.; any vehicle, carriage, conveyance, car (ifc. = having anything as a vehicle, riding or driving on or in), ŚvetUp.; MBh.; Kāv. &c.; a bearer, porter, carrier of burdens &c., W.; air, wind, L.; a measure of capacity (containing 10 Kumbhas or 2 Prasthas), L.; the arm, W.; a figurative N. of the Veda, Kuval. **– tva**, w.r. for *grāha-tva*, MBh. i, 399. **– dvishat**, m. 'horse-hater,' a buffalo, L. **– bhraṅś** (nom. *bhraṭ*) or **-bhraṅs** (nom. *bhraṭ*), falling from a vehicle &c., W. **– ripu**, m. 'horse-foe,' a buffalo, L. **– vāraṇa**, m. 'elephant among draught-animals,' Bos Gavæus, L. **– śreshṭha**, m. 'best of draught-animals,' a horse, L. **Vāhâvalī**, f. (prob.) = *vāhyâvalī*, Siṅhâs.

Vāhaka, mf(*ikā*)n. one who bears or carries, bearer, carrier, conveyer, Yājñ.; MBh.; R. &c.; (ifc.) causing to flow, carrying along, MārkP.; setting in motion, Prab.; stroking (in *aṅga-v*°), MatsyaP.; m. a partic. venomous insect, Suśr. (cf. *vāhyakī*); a driver or rider, W.; w.r. for *bārhataka*, q.v. **– tva**, n. the business of a carrier or porter, BhP.

2. **Vā́hana**, mfn. (for 1. see col. 1) drawing, bearing, carrying, conveying, bringing &c., Kathās.; Rājat.; m. N. of a Muni, Cat.; (*ā*), f. an army, Śiś. xix, 33; n. the act of drawing, bearing, carrying, conveying, MBh.; R. &c.; driving, Suśr.; riding, Kathās.; guiding (horses), MBh.; any vehicle or conveyance or draught-animal, carriage, chariot, waggon, horse, elephant (cf. Pāṇ. viii, 4, 8), AitBr. &c. &c. (ifc. [f. *ā*] riding or driving on or in); any animal, Kathās. xxi, 30; 'oar' or 'sail,' R. ii, 52, 5. **– kāra**, m. (prob.) a carriage-maker, waggon-maker, wheelwright; *-śālā*, f. a wheelwright's workshop, Lalit. **– tā**, f., **-tva**, n. the condition of a vehicle or of a draught-animal, Kād.; Kathās. **– pa**, m. a keeper of animals used in riding or draught, groom, R. **– prajñapti**, f. N. of a partic. method of reckoning, Lalit. **– śreshṭha**, m. 'best of draught-animals,' a horse, L.

Vāhanika, mfn. (fr. 2. *vāhana*) living by (tending or dealing in &c.) draught-animals, g. *vetanâdi*.

Vāhanī, in comp. for 2. *vāhana*. **– √kṛi**, P. *-karoti*, to make into a vehicle, Kathās. **– √bhū**, P. *-bhavati*, to become a vehicle, ib.

Vāhanīya, (prob.) m. a beast of burden, Kull. on Mn. vii, 151.

Vāhalā, f. a stream, current, L.

Vā́has, mfn. carrying, conveying, bringing, offering (cf. *uktha-*, *nṛi-yajña-v*° &c.); n. an offering, worship, invocation, RV.; VS.; ŚāṅkhŚr.

Vāhasá, m. the Boa Constrictor, TS.; VS.; a spring from which water flows (= *vāri-niryāṇa*), L.; fire, L.; a species of plant, L.

1. **Vāhi**, m. carrying, bearing, L.

2. **Vāhi**, in comp. for *vāhin*. **– tā**, f. flowing, flow, current, Cat. **– ttha**, see *vāhittha*. **– tva**, n., see *yoga-vāhitva*.

Vāhika, m. (fr. *vāha*) a car or vehicle drawn by oxen, L.; a large drum, L.; a carrier, Divyâv.; (pl.) N. of a people, MBh.; n. Asa Foetida, L. (in the two last meanings prob. w. r. for *bālhika* or *bālhīka*).

2. **Vāhita**, mfn. (for 1. see col. 1) caused to be borne or conveyed, R.; (ifc.) urged on, driven, actuated by, Ragh.; given, administered (as medicine), Bhpr.; taken in, deceived, Pañcat.

Vāhitṛi, m. a conductor, leader, guide, MBh. xiii, 1227 (= *voḍhṛi*, Nilak.)

Vāhittha, n. (*ttha* prob. for *stha*; cf. *aśvattha*, *kapittha*) the middle of an elephant's face, L.

Vāhin, mfn. conveying along, driving along (as a car), MBh.; (ifc.) drawing, R.; flowing, streaming, Hariv.; Pur.; Kathās.; causing to flow, shedding, MBh.; Kāv. &c.; bearing along (said of rivers), ib.; wafting (said of the wind), ib.; bringing, causing, producing, effecting, Hariv.; Kathās.; BhP.; carrying, bearing, wearing, having, possessing, Kāv.; Kathās.; Rājat.; undergoing, performing, practising, MBh.; m. a chariot, MBh.; (*inī*), f., see next.

Vāhinī, f. an army, host, body of forces, AV.; MBh. &c.; a partic. division of an army (consisting of 3 Gaṇas, i.e. 81 elephants, 81 cars, 243 horse, 405 foot; cf. *akshauhiṇī*), MBh.; a river, ib.; R. &c.; a channel, KātyŚr., Sch.; N. of the wife of Kuru, MBh. **– niveśa**, m. the camp of an army, W. **– pati**, m. 'chief of an army,' a general, MBh.; R.; BhP.; 'lord of rivers,' N. of the ocean, W.; N. of a poet, Cat.; (with *mahā-pātra bhaṭṭâcārya*) N. of a Commentator, ib. **– °śa** (°*nīśa*), m. 'lord of an army,' a general, MBh.; N. of a man, Cat.

Vāhinīka, ifc. for *vāhinī*, Ragh.

Vā́hishṭha, mf(*ā*)n. bearing or carrying best or most, RV.; flowing most, ib.

Vāhīka. See *bāhīka*.

Vāhīvah. See *prāsaṅga-v*°, p. 702, col. 3.

Vāheyika, mf(*ā*)n. perhaps connected with *bāhika*, MBh.

Vāhya, mfn. (cf. *bāhya*) to be (or being) drawn or driven or ridden or borne ('by or on,' comp.), Hariv.; Pañcat.; BhP.; (*ā*), f. N. of a river, MārkP.; n. any vehicle or beast of burden, an ox, horse &c., Mn.; MBh. &c. **– tva**, n. the being a vehicle, L. **– naya**, m. = *vāhīka-nīti*, MBh. (Nilak.) **Vāhyâlī**, f. a road for horses (also °*lī-bhū*, f.), Rājat.; HPariś. **Vāhyâśva**, m. (also written *bāhy*°) N. of a man, Hariv.

Vāhyaka, n. a chariot, L.; (*ī*), f. a partic. venomous insect, Suśr. (cf. *vāhaka*).

Vāhyakāyani, m. metron. fr. *vahyakā*, g. *tikâdi*.

Vāhyāyani, m. patr. fr. *vahya*, Uṇ. iv, 111, Sch.

वाहट *vāhaṭa*, m. N. of a medical writer, Cat. (cf. *bāhaṭa*).

वाहतक *vāhataka*, w.r. for *bārhataka*, q.v.

वाहादुर *vāhādura*, *vāhirvedika*, *vāhuka*. See *bāhādura* &c.

वाहुलि *vāhuli*, m. N. of a son of Viśvāmitra, MBh. (v.l. *vāduli*).

वाहूक *vāhūka*, m. N. of a man, Cat.

वाह्न *vāhna*, mfn. (fr. *vahni*) relating or belonging to Agni, addressed to him &c., VarBṛS.; BhP.

Vāhneya, m. patr. (fr. id.), Cat.

वाह्यस्क *vāhyaska*, m. patr. fr. *vahyaska*, g. *bidâdi*.

Vāhyaskāyana, m. patr. fr. *vāhyaska*, g. *haritâdi*.

वाह्लायन *vāhlāyana*, *vāhli*, *vāhlīka*. See *bālhāyana* &c.

वि 1. *ví*, m. (nom. *vís* or *vés*, acc. *vím*, gen. abl. *vés*; pl. nom. acc. *váyas* [acc. *vīn*, Bhaṭṭ.]; *vibhis*, *vibhyas*, *vīnā́m*) a bird (also applied to horses, arrows, and the Maruts), RV.; VS.; PañcavBr. (also occurring in later language). [Cf. 1. *váyas*; Gk. οἰωνός for ὀϝιωνος; Lat. *a-vis*; accord. to some Germ. *Ei*; Angl. Sax. *ǽg*; Eng. *egg*.] **– 1. -gata**, n. (for 2. see under *vi-√gam*) the flight of birds, MW. **– 1. -cchāya**, n. (for 2. see p. 950, col. 2) the shadow of a flock of b°, L. (also *ā*, f., BhP.) **– patman** (*ví-*), mfn. having the flight of (i.e. flying as fast as) a bird, RV. i, 180, 2. **– 1. -rāj**, m. (for 2. see s.v.) king of birds, BhP. **– va**, mfn. (said to be fr. √*vā*, *vāti* = *gacchati*) riding on a bird, Śiś. xix, 86.

वि 2. *vi*, n. an artificial word said to be = *anna*, ŚBr.

वि 3. *ví*, ind. (prob. for an original *dvi*, meaning 'in two parts;' and opp. to *sam*, q.v.) apart, asunder, in different directions, to and fro, about, away, away from, off, without, RV. &c. &c. In RV. it appears also as a prep. with acc. denoting 'through' or 'between' (with ellipse of the verb, e.g. i, 181, 5; x, 86, 20 &c.) It is esp. used as a prefix to verbs or nouns and other parts of speech derived from verbs, to express 'division,' 'distinction,' 'distribution,' 'arrangement,' 'order,' 'opposition,' or 'deliberation' (cf. *vi-√bhid*, *-śish*, *-dhā*, *-rudh*, *-car*, with their nominal derivatives); sometimes it gives a meaning opposite to the idea contained in the simple root (e.g. √*krī*, 'to buy;' *vi-√krī*, 'to sell'), or it intensifies that idea (e.g. √*hiṅs*, 'to injure;' *vi-√hiṅs*, 'to injure severely').

The above 3. *ví* may also be used in forming compounds not immediately referable to verbs, in which cases it may express 'difference' (cf. 1. *vi-lakshaṇa*), 'change' or 'variety' (cf. *vi-citra*), 'intensity' (cf. *vi-karāla*), 'manifoldness' (cf. *vi-vidha*), 'contrariety' (cf. *vi-loma*), 'deviation from right' (cf. *vi-śīla*), 'negation' or 'privation' (cf. *vi kaccha*, being often used like 3. *a*, *nir*, and *nis* [qq. vv.], and like the Latin *dis*, *se*, and the English *a*, *dis*, *in*, *un* &c.); in some cases it does not seem to modify the meaning of the simple word at all (cf. *vi-jāmi*, *vi-jāmātṛi*); it is also used to form proper names out of other proper names (e.g. *vi-koka*, *vi-prithu*, *vi-viṅśa*). To save space such words are here mostly collected under one article; but words having several subordinate compounds will be found s.v. **– kaṅsā**, f. N. of a woman, g. *śubhrâdi* (v.l.) **– kakara** (*ví-*), m. a kind of bird, VS. (cf. *-kakara*). **– kaṅkaṭa**, m. Asteracantha Longifolia, L.; °*ṭika*, mfn. (fr. prec.), g. *kumudâdi*. **– kaṅkata** (*ví-*), m. Flacourtia Sapida (from which sacrificial vessels are made), TS. &c. &c.; (*ā*), f. Sida Cordifolia and Rhombifolia, L.; °*tī-mukha*, mfn. thorny-mouthed, AV. **– 1. -kaca**, mfn. (for 2. see p. 953, col. 2) hairless, bald, MBh.; m. a Buddhist mendicant, L.; a species of comet (65 enumerated), MBh.; VarBṛS.; N. of a Dānava, Hariv.; (*ā*), f. a kind of shrub, L.; °*ca-śrī*, mfn. having the beauty of the hair gone, Kāv. **– kaccha**, mfn. having no marshy banks, L. **– kacchapa**, mfn. deprived of tortoises, Kathās. **– 1. -kaṭa**, mfn. (for 2. see s.v.) having no mat, without a mat, MW. **– kaṇṭaka**, m. 'having no thorns or having spreading thorns,' Alhagi Maurorum or Asteracantha Longifolia, L.; *-pura*, n. N. of a town, Pañcat. **– kadru**,

m. N. of a Yādava, Hariv. **-kapāla**, mfn. deprived of skull, ib. **-1. -kara**, mfn. (for 2. see *vi-√1. kṛi*) deprived of hands (as a punishment), Vishṇ. **-1. -karaṇa**, mfn. (for 2. see ib.) deprived of organs of sense (*-tva*, n.), Bādar., Sch. **-karāla**, mf(*ā*)n. very formidable or dreadful, MBh.; Kāv. &c.; (*ā*), f. N. of Durgā, Kathās.; of a courtezan, Kuṭṭanim.; *-tā*, f. formidableness, dreadfulness, Pañcat.; *-mukha*, m. N. of a Makara, ib. **-karālin**, mfn. hot, L.; m. heat, ib. **-karṇá**, mfn. (prob.) having large or divergent ears, AV.; having no ears, earless, deaf, Pañcat.; m. a kind of arrow, MBh.; N. of a son of Karṇa, Hariv.; of a son of Dhṛita-rāshṭra, MBh.; (pl.) of a people, ib.; (*ī*), f. a kind of brick, TS.; n. N. of a Sāman, ĀrshBr.; °*ṇaka*, m. N. of one of Śiva's attendants, L.; (*ikā*), f. (see *bala-karṇikā*); °*ṇika*, m. pl. N. of a people, L.; °*ṇin*, m. a kind of arrow, MBh. (also °*ṇi*, L.) **-1. -karman**, n. (for 2. see *vi-√1. kṛi*) prohibited or unlawful act, fraud, Mn.; MBh. &c.; various business or duty, W.; (with *Vāyoḥ*) N. of a Sāman, ĀrshBr.; mfn. acting wrongly or unlawfully, MBh.; not acting, free from action, ib.; °*ma-kṛit*, mfn. following unlawful occupation, Mn. viii, 66; active or busy in various ways, W.; °*ma-kriyā*, f. an illegal or immoral act, vicious conduct, Mn. ix, 226; °*ma-nirata* (BhP.), °*ma-stha* (Mn.), mfn. = °*ma-kṛit*; °*mika*, mfn. id., W.; m. a clerk or superintendent of markets and fairs, ib.; °*min*, mfn. acting wrongly or unlawfully, MBh. **-kala**, see s. v. **-kalaṅka**, mfn. spotless, bright (as the moon), Vām.; *-tā*, f., Harav. **-1. -kalpa**, m. (for 2. see under *vi-√kḷip*) an intermediate Kalpa, the interval between two Kalpas (q. v.), BhP. **-kalmasha**, mf(*ā*)n. spotless, sinless, guiltless, R. **-kavaca**, mfn. armourless, MBh.; R. **-kaśyapa**, mfn. (a sacrifice) performed without the Kaśyapas, AitBr. **-kākud**, mfn. having a badly formed palate, Pāṇ. v, 4, 148. **-kāṅksha** (MBh.), °**kshin** (Hariv.), mfn. free from desire; (°*kshā*) f., see *vi-√kāṅksh*. **-kāma**, mfn. free from d°, VarBṛS. **-1. -kāra**, m. (for 2. see *vi-√1. kṛi*) the syllable *vi*, BhP. **-kāraṇa**, mfn. causeless, Pañcat. (v. l.) **-kāla**, m. twilight, evening, afternoon (*am*, ind. in the evening, late), ĀpŚr.; MBh. &c.; °*laka*, m. id.; °*likā*, f. a sort of clepsydra or water-clock, L. **-1. -kāśa**, m. (for 2. see *vi-√kāś*) absence of manifestation or display, loneliness, privacy, L.; *-tva*, n. id., ib. **-kishku**, m. a carpenter's measure of 42 inches, L. **-kukshi**, mfn. having a prominent belly (*-tva*, n.), MBh.; Hariv. (also °*kshika*); m. N. of a son or grandson of Ikshvāku, ib. **-kuja**, mfn. without the planet Mars, Laghuj.; (with *dina*) any day except Tuesday, VarBṛS.; *-ravīndu*, mfn. without Mars and sun and moon, Laghuj. **-kuñja**, m. pl. N. of a people, MBh. **-kuṇṭha**, mfn. sharp, keen, penetrating, irresistible, BhP.; very blunt (*a-v°*, sharp &c.), ib.; m. N. of Vishṇu, MBh.; BhP.; N. of Vishṇu's heaven, BhP.; °*ṭhana*, m. N. of a son of Hastin, MBh.; (*ā*), f. inward glance, mental concentration, L.; °*ṭhita*, mfn., see *vi-√kuṇṭh*. **-kuṇḍala**, mfn. having no earrings, Hariv.; m. N. of a man, Cat. **-kumbhāṇḍa**, m. N. of a Dānava, Hariv. **-kūṭa**, m. or n. (?) N. of a place, Cat. (v. l. *tri-k°*). **-kūbara**, mfn. deprived of the shaft or pole, MBh. **-ketu**, mfn. deprived of the flag or banner, MBh. **-keśá**, mf(*ī*)n. having loose or dishevelled hair, AV.; hairless, bald, L.; m. N. of a Muni, Cat.; (*ī*), f. N. of a class of demoniacal beings, AV.; (with *tārakā*) 'a hair-like star,' comet, ib.; lint, L.; a small braid or tress of hair (first tied up separately and then collected into the Veṇī or larger braid), L.; a woman without hair, L.; N. of the wife of Śiva (manifested in the form of Mahī or 'the Earth,' one of his eight Tanus or visible forms), Pur.; °*śikā*, f. a kind of compress, lint, Suśr. **-koka**, m. N. of a son of the Asura Vṛika and younger brother of Koka, KalkiP. **-kośa**, mf(*ā*)n. uncovered, denuded, unsheathed, drawn (as a sword), MBh.; Kāv. &c.; having no prepuce, Suśr.; containing no passage from a dictionary, Cat. **-kautuka**, mfn. showing no curiosity or interest, indifferent, Śiś. **-1. -krama**, m. (for 2. see *vi-√kram*) the absence of the Krama-pāṭha (q. v.), ṚPrāt. **-krodha**, mfn. free from anger or wrath, ĀpGṛ. **-klava**, see under *vi-√klav*. **-kshaṇam**, ind. momentarily, for a moment, W. **-kshīra**, m. Calotropis Gigantea, L. **-kshudra**, mfn. comparatively smaller, each smaller than another, AitBr. **-kshubhā**, f. N. of Chāyā, L. **-khura**, m. 'hoofless,' a goblin, demon, Rākshasa, L. **-kheda**, mfn. free from weariness, fresh, alert, BhP. **-gaṇḍīra**, n. a kind of small amaranth, L. **-1. -gada**, mf(*ā*)n. (for 2. see under *vi-√gad*) free from disease, healthy, well, Śiś. **-gandha**, mfn. having a bad smell, VarBṛS.; Suśr.; odourless, Car.; °*dhaka*, m. Terminalia Catappa, L.; (*ikā*), f. = *hapushā*, L.; °*dhi*, mfn. ill-smelling, stinking, Bhartṛ. **-gara**, m. 'not swallowing,' an abstemious man, W.; a naked ascetic, ib.; a mountain, ib. **-garbhā**, f. delivered of a living child or fetus, MBh. **-gāthā** and **1. -gīti** (for 2. see *vi-√gai*), f. two kinds of the Āryā metre, Col. **-guṇa**, mfn. without a string (see below); deficient, imperfect, destitute of (comp.), KātyŚr.; MBh. &c.; unsuccessful, ineffective, Rājat.; adverse (as fortune), Pañcat. (v. l.); void of qualities, BhP.; destitute of merits, wicked, bad, MBh.; R. &c.; disordered, corrupted (as the humours of the body), Suśr.; *-tā*, f. disordered condition, corruption, ib.; °*ṇī-√kṛi*, P. *-karoti*, to detach the string of a bow, Mudr. **-1. -graha**, mfn. (for 2. see *vi-√grah*) freed from 'the Seizer' i. e. Rāhu (said of the moon), R. **-grīva** (*ví-*), mfn. having the neck twisted or cut off, RV. **-ghaṭikā**, f. a partic. measure of time (= $\frac{1}{60}$ Ghaṭikā), Rājat. **-1. -ghana**, mfn. (for 2. see s. v.) not stiff or very stiff (see *pūrṇa-vighana*); cloudless (loc. 'under a cloudless sky'), MBh.; °*nendu*, m. a cloudless moon, MW. **-cakra**, mfn. wheelless, AitBr.; MBh.; having no discus, Kāv.; m. N. of a Dānava, Hariv.; °*krôpaskarôpastha*, mfn. (a chariot) without wheels and implements and seat, MBh. **-cakshus**, mfn. eyeless, blind, MBh.; = 2. *vi-manas*, L.; m. N. of a prince, Hariv.; n. (in a formula, with *cakshus*), ĀpŚr.; °*shush-karaṇa*, n. rendering hostile, alienation, Buddh. **-catura**, mfn. containing various quarters (or half-verses), ŚāṅkhŚr. (cf. Pāṇ. v, 4, 77). **-candra**, mf(*ā*)n. moonless (as a night), R. **-1. -caraṇa**, mfn. (for 2. see *vi-√car*) footless, MBh. **-carman**, mfn. shieldless, MBh. **-carshaṇa** (prob. w. r.) and **-carshaṇi** (*ví-*), mfn. very active or busy, RV.; TĀr. **-cāru**, m. N. of a son of Kṛishṇa, BhP. **-1. -citta**, mfn. (for 2. see under *vi-√cit*) unconscious, Suśr.; not knowing what to do, helpless, Hcar.; *-tā*, f. unconsciousness, Sāh. **-citti**, f. perturbation (= *vi-bhrama*), Gal. **-citra**, see s. v. **-cūlin**, mfn. having no crest, Hariv. **-1. -cetana**, mf(*ā*)n. (for 2. see under *vi-√cit*) senseless, unconscious, absent-minded, MBh.; R. &c.; inanimate, dead, Hit.; foolish, stupid, Kum.; (f. *ī*), rendering unconscious, Pañcar. **-1. -cetas** (*ví-*), mfn. (for 2. see *vi-√cit*) absent-minded, confounded, perplexed, Hariv.; R.; BhP.; ignorant, stupid, MBh. **-cetī**, ind., with *√kṛi*, *bhū*, and *as*, Pāṇ. v, 4, 51, Sch. **-ceshṭa**, mfn. motionless, R. **-cchanda** (*ví-*), mfn. consisting of various metres, VS.; m. = next, L. **-cchandaka**, m. a building consisting of several stories and surrounded by a portico, a palace or temple, L. **-cchandas** (*ví-*), mfn. = *vi-cchanda*, Br.; ŚrS.; f. (scil. *ṛic*) a verse containing various metres, AitBr.; n. a kind of metre, L. **-cchardaka**, m. = *vi-cchandaka*, L.; (*ikā*), f. (see *vi-√chṛid*). **-2. -cchāya**, mf(*ā*)n. (for 1. see 1. *vi*, p. 949) destitute of shadow, shadowless, MW.; lacking colour or lustre or distinction, pale (*-tā*, f.), Kāv.; Kathās.; BhP.; m. a jewel, gem, L. **-cchāyaya**, Nom. P. °*yayati*, to free from shadow, deprive of colour or lustre (*-cchāyita*, colourless, pale), Kāv.; *-cchāyī-√kṛi*, P. *-karoti*, id., Kathās. **-jaṅgha**, mfn. having no legs i. e. wheels (said of a chariot), MBh.; °*ghā-kūbara*, mfn. having no wheels and no pole, ib. (v. l. °*ghâṅghrivara*). **-jaṭa**, mfn. unplaited (hair), ŚāṅkhGṛ.; °*ṭī-√kṛi*, to unplait, Pāṇ. iii, 1, 21, Sch. **-jana**, mfn. free from people, destitute of men, deserted, solitary, lonely, Mn.; MBh. &c.; n. a deserted or solitary place, absence of witnesses (*e*, rarely *eshu*, ind. in private, in a lonely spot where there are no witnesses; °*nam √kṛi*, to remove all w°s), MBh.; Kāv. &c.; *-tā*, f. solitude, Sāh.; °*nī-√kṛi*, to remove all w°s, R.; Ratnâv.; Kathās.; °*nī-kṛita*, mfn. separated from a (loved) person, R. **-janman**, n. a separate birth, birth in general, W.; m. a bastard, illegitimate child, the son of an out-caste or degraded Vaiśya, Mn. x, 23. **-japila**, mfn. = *picchila*, L. (v. l. *vi-javala*). **-jayina** (?), mfn. = *-jila*, L. **-jará**, mfn. not growing old, ŚBr. &c. &c.; m. a stalk, W.; (*ā*), f. N. of a river in Brahmā's world, KaushUp. **-jarjara** (*ví-*), mfn. decrepit, infirm, MBh.; rotten (as wood), Car.; °*rī-√kṛi*, to weaken, make old or infirm, MBh. **-jala**, mfn. waterless, dry, Hariv.; VarBṛS.; n. drought, AdbhBr.; m. n. and (*ā*), f. sauce &c. mixed with rice-water or gruel, W. **-javala** (?), mfn. = *picchila*, L. **-jāti**, mfn. belonging to another caste or tribe, dissimilar, heterogeneous, Kull.; m. N. of a prince, VP.; f. different origin or caste or tribe, W.; °*tīya*, mfn. = *-jāti*, Sarvad.; Kull. **-jāni** (*ví-*), mfn. 'strange, foreign' or 'having no wife,' AV. v, 17, 18. **-jānu**, n. a partic. mode of fighting, Hariv. **-jāman**, mfn. related, corresponding. **-jāmātṛi** (*ví-*), m. (prob.) = *jāmātṛi*, a son-in-law, RV. i, 109, 2 (accord. to Nir. 'a defective son-in-law, one who has not all the necessary qualifications'). **-jāmi** (*ví-*), mfn. (prob.) = *jāmi*, consanguineous, related (opp. to *á-jāmi*), RV. x, 69, 12. **-jighatsá**, mfn. not liable to hunger, not becoming hungry, ŚBr.; ChUp. **-jina**, **-jipila** (?), mfn. = *picchala*, L. **-jila**, mfn. id.; *-bindu*, N. of a town, Śaṃkar. **-jivila**, mfn. = *picchila*, L. **-jihma**, mfn. crooked, curved, bent, Kir.; sidelong (as a glance), Ragh.; dishonest, W.; *-tā*, f., *-tva*, n. crookedness, dishonesty, craftiness, ib. **-jihva**, mfn. deprived or destitute of tongue, tongueless, Vishṇ. **-jīvita**, mf(*ā*)n. lifeless, dead, R. **-jenyà**, mfn. (fr. *vi-jana*?) lonely, solitary, RV. i, 119, 4 (Sāy.) **-joshas** (*ví-*), mfn. (opp. to *sa-j°*) deserted, alone, RV. viii, 22, 10 (Sāy. 'delighting the gods'). **-jya** (*ví-*), mfn. stringless (as a bow), VS.; R.; BhP. **-jvara**, mf(*ā*)n. free from fever or pain, Kathās.; free from distress or anxiety, cheerful, MBh.; R. &c.; exempt from decay, W. **-jharjhara**, mfn. discordant, disagreeable, Śiś. **-tatkaraṇa** and **-tadbhāshaṇa**, see *a-vi-t°*. **-tatha**, see s. v. **-tanu** (*ví-*), mf(*vī*)n. extremely thin or slender, MBh.; bodiless, Kāvyâd.; having no essence or reality, TS.; m. the god of love (cf. *anaṅga*), Gīt. **-tantu**, m. a good horse, W.; f. a widow, ib. **-tantrī**, f. (nom. *īs*) a string out of tune, Kum. **-tamas**, mfn. free from darkness, light, MBh.; Ragh. **-tamaska**, mfn. id., MBh.; VarBṛS.; *-tā*, f., Jātak.; exempt from the quality of ignorance, MW. **-taram**, see s. v. **-tala**, n. N. of one of the seven hells, ĀruṇUp.; BhP. (cf. *pātāla*); depth of hell, Bālar.; *-loka*, m. the world or lower region of Vitala, MW. **-1. -tāna**, mfn. (for 2. see under *vi-√tan*) 'out of tune,' dejected, sad, Ragh. vi, 86; empty, Harav. (also in *a-v°*, Śiś. iii, 50); dull, stupid, W.; wicked, abandoned, ib.; °*nī-bhūta*, mfn. being sad or dejected, Jātakam. **-tāmasa**, mfn. = *-tamas*, Kathās. **-tāra**, mfn. starless, Ghaṭ.; without a nucleus (as a comet), VarBṛS. **-tāla**, mfn. (in music) breaking time, Saṃgīt.; m. wrong time or measure, Nalac.; (*ī*), f. an instrument for beating time. L. **-timira**, mfn. = *-tamas*, MBh.; R. &c. **-tilaka**, mfn. having no sectarian mark (on the forehead), BhP. **-tuṅga-bhāga**, mfn. not being on the highest point, VarBṛS. **-tusha**, mfn. unhusked, Gobh.; °*shī-karaṇa*, n. unhusking, Nyāyam., Sch.; °*shī-√kṛi*, P. *-karoti*, to unhusk, ŚBr. **-tushṭa**, mfn. displeased, dissatisfied, Pañcar. **-tṛiṇa**, mfn. grassless, Bhaṭṭ. **-tṛitīyá**, mfn. intermittent on the third day (said of a kind of fever), AV.; n. a third, ŚBr. **-tṛish** or **-tṛisha**, mfn. free from thirst, BhP. **-tṛishṇa**, mf(*ā*)n. id., MBh.; free from desire, not desirous of (comp.), BhP.; (*ā*), f. = next, BhP. (cf. under *vi-√tṛish*); *-tā*, f., *-tva*, n. freedom from desire, satiety, Kāv. **-toya**, mf(*ā*)n. waterless, Hariv. **-trapa**, m. 'shameless,' N. of a man, Rājat. **-dakshiṇa**, mfn. directed to another quarter than the south, Kām. **-1. -dagdha**, mfn. (for 2. see *vi-√dah*) undigested, W. **-daṇḍa**, m. a door-key, L.; N. of a king, MBh. **-danta**, mfn. toothless, deprived of his tusks (said of an elephant), Hariv. **-1. -dara**, mf(*ā*)n. (for 2. see under *vi-√dṛi*) free from cracks or holes, Kām. **-darbha**, see s. v. **-darvya**, mfn. (fr. *darvi*) hoodless (said of a serpent), ŚāṅkhGṛ. **-1. -dala**, mfn. (for 2. see *vi-√dal*) leafless, MW. **-daśa**, mfn. having no fringe or border (as a garment), MārkP. **-dārva** or **-dārvya**, m. N. of a serpent-demon, ŚāṅkhGṛ. (cf. *vi-darvya*). **-diś**, f. an intermediate point of the compass (as south-east), VS. &c. &c.; mfn. going into different quarters or regions, KātyŚr.; *-(dik-)caṅga*, m. a sort of yellow bird, L. **-diśā**, f. an intermediate quarter or region, MBh.; Hariv.; N. of a river and the town situated on it (the capital of the district of Daśārṇā now called Bilsa), MBh.; Kālid. &c.; of a town situated on the Vetravatī, Kād. **-dīdhiti**, mfn. rayless, VarBṛS. **-dushkṛita**, mfn. free from sins or faults or transgressions, KaushUp. **-dūra**, see s. v. **-dṛiś**, mfn. eyeless, blind, VarBṛS. **-deghá**, m. (older form of *vi-deha*, q. v.) N. of a man, ŚBr. **-deva** (*ví-*), mfn. godless, hostile to gods (as demons), AV.; performed without gods (as a sacrifice), Kāṭh. — **deśa,** see s.v. — **deha,** see s.v. — **dohá,** m. 'wrong or excessive milking,' taking too much profit out of anything, Br. — 1. **-dyut,** mfn. (for 2. see under *vi-√dyut*) devoid of splendour, lustreless, L. — 1. **-druma,** mfn. treeless, Naish. — 2. **-druma,** n. (accord. to L. m.) 'peculiar tree,' coral, MBh.; Kāv. &c.; m. a young sprout or shoot, L.; = *vṛiksha,* L.; N. of a mountain, VP.; *-cchavi,* m. 'coral-coloured,' N. of Śiva, Śivag.; *-cchāya,* mfn. 'coral-coloured' and 'affording no tree-shade,' Kuval. (cf. 1. *vi-druma*); *-taṭa,* mfn. having banks of coral, MW.; *-daṇḍa,* m. a branch of coral; *-tā,* f. the condition of a [fivefold] branch of c° [said of the hand], Kathās.; *-dehalī,* f. a threshold of c°, MW.; *-maya,* mf(*ī*)n. consisting of c°, Kād.; *-latā,* f. = *-daṇḍa,* Cat. (also *-latikā,* L.); a kind of fragrant substance, Bhpr.; N. of a woman, Vṛishabhân.; *-vana,* n. = *-daṇḍa,* Subh. — **dhana,** mfn. devoid of wealth, poor, VarBṛS.; *-tā,* f. poverty, Mṛicch.; Hit.; °*nī-√kṛi,* P. *-karoti,* to impoverish, Kathās. — **dhanushka, -dhanus,** or **-dhanvan,** mfn. having no bow, MBh. — 1. **-dharma,** mfn. (for 2. see *vi-√dhṛi*) wrong, unjust, unlawful (also °*maka*), MBh.; devoid of attributes or qualities (= *nir-guṇa,* said of Kṛishṇa), ib. (Nīlak.); m. wrong, injustice, MBh.; VarBṛS.; MārkP.; *-tas,* ind. wrongly, unlawfully, MBh.; *-stha,* mfn. 'abiding in wrong,' unjust, ib. — 1. **-dharman,** mfn. (for 2. see *vi-√dhṛi*) acting wrongly or unlawfully, ib. — **dharmika,** v.l. for *-dharmaka* (see above). — **dharmin,** mfn. transgressing the law (as speech), MBh.; of a different kind, Car. — 1. **-dhura,** mf(*ā*)n. destitute of a shaft (as a carriage), MBh. vi, 1890 (perhaps 'damaged' = 2. *vidhura,* see s.v.) — **dhūpa,** mfn. without perfume or incense, MārkP. — **dhūma,** mf(*ā*)n. smokeless, not smoking (said of fire), MBh.; R. &c. (*e,* ind. when no smoke is seen, Mn. vi, 56); m. N. of a Vasu, Kathās. — **dhūmra,** mfn. quite grey, BhP. — **dhūsara,** mfn. 'dust-coloured,' grey, Bhaṭṭ. — **nagna,** mfn. quite naked, Lalit. — **nadī,** f. N. of a river, MBh. (v.l. *vainadī*). — **namra,** mf(*ā*)n. bent down, stooping, submissive, humble, modest, Kāv.; VarBṛS.; Pur.; *-kaṃdhara,* mfn. having the neck bent, BhP. — **namraka,** n. the flower of Tabernæmontana Coronaria, L. — **nasa,** mf(*ā*)n. without a nose, noseless, Bhaṭṭ. — **nāda,** m. (prob.) a leather bag, Baudh. — **nāḍikā** or °**ḍī,** f. a period of 24 seconds (the 60th part of a Nāḍī or Indian hour), VarBṛS.; Yājñ., Sch. — **nātha,** mf(*ā*)n. having no lord or master, unprotected, deserted, R. — **nārāśaṇsa,** mf(*ā*)n. without the formulas called Nārāśaṇsa, TāṇḍBr. — **nāla,** mfn. without a stalk, MBh. — **nāsa,** mf(*ā*)n. noseless, AgP.; *-daśana,* mfn. bereft of nose and teeth, MBh. (B. *vi-nemi-d*°). — **nāsaka** or **-nāsika,** mfn. = *-nāsa,* L.; (*ikā*), f. a partic. venomous insect, Suśr. — **niḥkampa,** see *nishk*°. — **niketa,** mfn. having no fixed abode, Kāśīkh. — **nigaḍa,** mfn. free from foot-fetters (°*ḍī-√kṛi,* to unfetter), Daś. — **nighna,** see s.v. — **nidra,** mf(*ā*)n. sleepless, awake, MBh.; Kāv. &c. (also *-ka,* Kathās.); occurring in the waking condition, Kathās.; passed sleeplessly, Kāv.; expanded, blown, Śiś.; opened (as the eyes), Vikr.; m. a partic. formula recited over weapons, R.; *-tā,* f. (Bhpr.), *-tva,* n. (L.) sleeplessness, wakefulness, vigilance. — **nimitta,** mfn. having no real cause, not caused by anything, Car. — **nirodha,** mfn. uninfluenced, inactive, Harav. — **nirbāhu,** m. a partic. mode of fighting with a sword, Hariv. — **nirbhaya,** m. N. of a Sādhya, VahniP. — **nirbhoga,** m. N. of a cosmic period, Buddh. — **nirmala,** mfn. extremely pure, Hariv. — **nirmūḍha,** mfn. not stultified, not made void or vain, MārkP.; *-pratijña,* mfn. one who is faithful to a promise or agreement, ib. — **niścala,** mfn. immovable, firm, steady, Vikr.; Kathās. — **nishkampa,** mfn. id., AmṛitUp. — **nishkriya,** mfn. abstaining from ceremonial rites, MW. — **nīla,** mfn. dark-blue, blue, L.; *-bandhana,* mfn. having dark-blue stalks, MW. — **nīlaka,** n. a corpse that has become blue, Buddh. — **nīvaraṇa,** mfn. without hindrance, ib. — **nīvi,** mfn. deprived of a skirt or covering, denuded, BhP. — 1. **-netra,** mfn. (for 2. see under *vi-√nī*) eyeless, blind, Subh. — **nemi-daśana,** see *vi-nāsa-d*°. — **paktrima,** mfn. thoroughly matured, fulfilled, developed, Bhaṭṭ. — **pakva** (*ví-*), mf(*ā*)n. well cooked, well done, AV.; VarBṛS.; Suśr.; matured, ripe (as fruit), Kum.; fully developed, perfect, MBh.; BhP.; thoroughly burnt i.e. destroyed, BhP.; not burnt (= *pāka-hīna*), MBh. (Nīlak.) — **paksha,** see s.v. — **pakshapāta,** mfn. free from partisanship, impartial, indifferent, W.; m. impartiality, indifference, MW. — **pakshas** (*ví-*), mfn. going on both sides (of a chariot), RV. — **pañcikā,** f. = next, L.; N. of wk. — **pañcī,** f. the Indian lute, Kād.; Naish. (ifc. °*cīka,* mfn., R.); sport, amusement, L. — 1. **-paṇa,** m. (for 2. see *vi-√paṇ*) low or petty traffic, MW. — **patāka,** mfn. deprived of a flag or banner, MBh. — **patna** (?), m. or n. a kind of disease, Cat. — **patman** (*ví-*), mfn., see under 1. *vi,* p. 949. — **patha,** see s.v. — **padma,** mfn. deprived of a lotus-flower, Jātakam. — **pannaga,** mfn. destitute of serpents, Śiś. iv, 15. — **payas,** mfn. destitute of water, waterless, MW. — **parākrama,** mfn. destitute of courage or energy, MBh. — **parivatsara,** m. a year, L. — **parus** (*ví-*), mfn. without knots or joints, AV. — **parṇa,** (prob.) w.r. for *dvi-p*°, 'two-leaved,' ĀpGṛ., Sch. — **parṇaka,** m. the Palāśa tree, Butea Frondosa, L. — **paryak,** ind. (fr. *-paryañc*) invertedly, BhP. — **paryāṇa,** mfn. unsaddled, Kathās.; °*nī-kṛita,* mfn. id., ib. — **parva** (*ví-*), mfn. without joints or vulnerable points, RV. — **parvan** (*ví-*), mfn. id. (used to explain the prec.), Nir. ix, 25. — **pala,** n., see s.v. — **palāśa,** mfn. leafless, Hariv. — **pavana,** mf(*ā*)n. windless, VarBṛS. — **paśu,** mfn. deprived of cattle, ib. — **pāṇsula,** mf(*ā*)n. free from dust, dustless, MBh. — **pāṭala,** mfn. very red, Ratnâv.; *-netra,* mfn. red-eyed, Ṛitus. — **pāṇḍava,** w.r. for *-pāṇḍura,* Ṛitus. — **pāṇḍu,** mfn. pale, pallid, Kāv.; Suśr. (*-tā,* f.); painted with different yellow colours, MW.; °*ḍura,* mf(*ā*)n. pale, pallid, Kāv.; Sāh. — **pādikā,** f. (fr. *-pāda*) a disease of the foot, a sore tumour on the foot, Suśr.; Rājat.; a riddle, enigma, L. — **pāpá,** mf(*ā*)n. faultless, sinless, ŚBr.; Gaut.; (*ā*), f. N. of various rivers, MBh.; VP. — **pāpman** (*ví-*), mfn. = prec.; TBr.; Gaut. &c.; free from suffering, MBh.; m. N. of a being reckoned among the Viśve Devāḥ, ib. — **pārśva,** (only instr.) close by, R. — **pāla,** mfn. having no keeper or attendant, unguarded, Mn. viii, 240 &c. — **pāś** and **-pāśa,** see s.v. — **pīḍam,** ind. without harm or injury, Ragh. — **puṇsaka,** mfn. not quite manly, unmanly, Kathās. — **puṇsī,** f. a masculine woman, PārGṛ. (v.l. °*sā* and °*shī*). — **puṭa,** mf(*ā*)n. (prob.) without (large) apertures (said of a nose), VarBṛS. — **putra,** mf(*ā*)n. bereft of a son (calf), R. — 1. **-pura,** n. the intellect, VP. (cf. 3. *pur*). — 2. **-pura,** mfn. having no fixed abode or home; °*rī-√bhū, -bhavati,* to become homeless (*-bhāva,* m. homelessness), VāyuP. — **purīshá,** mfn. freed from ordure, ŚBr. — **purusha,** mfn. void of men, empty, MBh. — **pula,** see s.v. — **pulināmburuha,** mfn. having no sandbanks nor lotus-flowers (as a river), Śiś. — **pushṭa,** mfn. ill-fed, underfed, Pañcat. — **pushṭi,** f. perfect welfare or prosperity, Vait. — **pushpa,** mf(*ā*)n. flowerless (as a tree), R. — **pṛithu,** m., v.l. for *vi-pathá,* ŚāṅkhŚr.; N. of a prince belonging to the Vṛishṇis, MBh.; of a son of Citraka and younger brother of Pṛithu, VP. (w.r. *pṛitha*). — **pṛishṭhī-√bhū,** P. *-bhavati,* to be depressed or dejected, L. (prob. w.r. for *-pishṭī-bhū*). — **prakāśa,** mfn. (ifc.) = *prakāśa,* resembling, similar to, Hariv. — **pratikūla,** mfn. obstinate, refractory, BhP. — **pratipratyanīka,** mfn. = *-pratyanīka,* Lalit. — **pratīpa,** mfn. = *-pratikūla,* MBh.; reversed, inverted, Ratnâv. — **pratyanīka,** mfn. hostile, SaddhP. — **pratyanīyaka,** mfn. id., Lalit. — **pratyaya,** m. distrust, MBh.; Kāv. &c. — **pramatta,** mfn. (prob.) not neglected, Kathās. xxxiv, 255. — **pramanas,** mfn. dejected, low-spirited, MBh. vi, 2860 (B. *nâtipramanaso* for *te vipr*°; cf. *nâtipr*°). — 1. **-pralāpa,** mfn. (for 2. see under *vi-pra-√lap*) free from mere chatter (as truth), MBh. — **praśastaka,** m. pl. N. of a people, MārkP. — **priya** (*ví-*), mfn. disaffected, estranged, TS. (cf. *-preman*); disagreeable, unpleasant to (gen. or comp.), MBh.; Kāv. &c.; n. (also pl.) anything unpleasant or hateful, offence, transgression, ib.; *-kara* (Kathās.), *-kārin* and *-m-kara* (MBh.), mfn. doing what is displeasing, acting unkindly, offensive; *-tva,* n. unpleasantness, BhP., Sch. — **preman,** n. estrangement, AitBr. (cf. *-priya*). — 1. **-plava,** mfn. (for 2. see *vi-√plu*) having no ship or boat, MBh. — **pha,** mfn. without the sound or letter *pha,* TāṇḍBr. — **phala,** see s.v. — **phāṇṭa,** mf(*ā*)n. decocted or distilled with (comp.), Gobh. — **bandhu** (*ví-*), mfn. having no relations, AV.; BhP. — 1. **-barha,** mfn. (for 2. see under *vi-√1. bṛih*) having no tail-feathers, MBh. — **bala,** mfn. having no strength, weak, VarBṛS. — **balāka,** mfn. not filled with cranes (as a cloud), Hariv. (Sch.) — **bāṇa,** mfn. without an arrow (as a bow), Hariv.; *-jya,* mfn. without an arrow and a string, ib.; *-dhi,* mfn. without a quiver, MBh. — **bāhu,** mfn. deprived of arms, armless, MBh. — **bila,** mfn. having no hole or aperture (as a sheath), Kauś. — 1. **-buddha,** mfn. (for 2. see *vi-√budh*) without consciousness, W. — **buddhi,** mfn. unreasonable, Kautukas. — 1. **-budha,** mfn. (for 2. see *vi-√budh*) destitute of learned men, Kāvyâd. — 1. **-bodha,** m. (for 2. see ib.) inattention, absence of mind, L. — **bhaṅgi,** f. mere appearance or semblance (cf. *bhaṅgi*), Dharmaś. — **bhaya,** n. freedom from danger, BhP.; mfn. not exposed to danger, ib. — **bhasman,** mfn. free from ashes or dust; *mī-karaṇa,* n. freeing from ashes, dusting, KātyŚr. — **bhāṇḍa,** m. N. of a man, MBh.; = *-māṇḍavya,* Kāśīkh.; (*ī*), f. the senna plant, L.; = *nīla-gokarṇī,* L. — **bhāṇḍaka,** m. N. of a Muni, MBh.; Hariv.; R.; (*ikā*), f. Senna Obtusa, L. — 1. **-bhāshā,** f. (for 2. see *vi-√bhāsh*) a class of Prākṛit languages, Cat.; (in music) a partic. Rāgiṇī, Saṃgīt.; (with Buddhists) a great Commentary. — **bhāskara,** mfn. having no sun, without the sun, Laghuj. — **bhī,** mfn. fearless, MBh. — 1. **-bhīta,** mfn. (for 2. see s.v.), id., W. — **bhītaka,** see s.v. — **bhūma,** mfn. distant from the ground, AitĀr. — **bhrātṛivya** (*ví-*), n. rivalry, hostility, ŚBr. — **majjântra,** mfn. deprived of marrow and intestines (said of the body), MBh. — **maṇḍala,** n. the orbit of the planets and of the moon, Gaṇit. — 1. **-mati,** mfn. (for 2. see *vi-√man*) of different opinion (*-man,* m. difference of opinion, disagreement), g. *dṛiḍhâdi*; stupid, silly (*-tā,* f. stupidity, silliness), Bhartṛ. — **matsara,** mfn. free from envy or jealousy, unenvious, unselfish, MBh.; Kāv. &c.; °*rin,* mfn. id., Hcat. — **mada,** mfn. free from intoxication, grown sober, R.; Pañcat.; free from rut, Kāv.; free from pride or arrogance, MBh.; Hariv. &c.; joyless, MW.; (*á*), m. N. of a man protected by Indra (he gained his wife with the assistance of the Aśvins), RV.; (with Aindra or Prājāpatya) of the author of RV. x, 20–26, Anukr.; °*dī-√kṛi,* P. *-karoti,* to free an elephant from rut, MBh. — **madya,** mfn. one who has abstained from intoxicating drinks for a time, Car. — **madhya** (*ví-*), n. the midst, middle, RV.; *-bhāva,* m. mediocrity, Jātakam. — **madhyama,** mfn. middling, indifferent, ib. — **mana,** mfn. (m. c.) = *vi-manas,* dejected, downcast, R. — 1. **-manas** (*ví-*), mfn. having a keen or penetrating mind or understanding, sagacious, RV. x, 82, 2. — 2. **-manas,** mfn. destitute of mind, foolish, silly, RV. viii, 86, 2; out of one's mind or senses, discomposed, perplexed, dejected, downcast, heart-broken, Yājñ.; MBh. &c.; changed in mind or feeling, averse, hostile, R.; m. N. of the author of a hymn (v.l. for *viśva-manas,* q.v.) — **manaska,** mfn. perplexed in mind, distressed, disconsolate, MBh.; R. &c. — **manāya,** Nom. Ā. °*yate,* to be out of one's mind, be disconsolate or downcast, Naish.; Sāh. — **maniman,** m. depression of mind, dejectedness, g. *dṛiḍhâdi.* — **manī-kṛita,** mfn. offended, angry, Śiś. — **manī-bhūta,** mfn. changed or depressed in mind, W. — **manthara,** mfn. rather slow or dull, Hāsy. — 1. **-manyu** (*ví-*), m. longing, desire, RV. — 2. **-manyu,** mfn. free from anger or fury, Kum.; BhP. — **manyuka** (*ví-*), mfn. not angry, allaying anger or wrath, AV. — **mala,** see s.v. — **mastakita,** mfn. beheaded, decapitated, Naish. — **mahat,** mfn. very great, immense, MBh. — **mahas** (*ví-*), mfn. merry, joyous (said of the Maruts), RV. — **mahī** (*ví-*), mfn. (prob.) exhilarating, inspiring (plur. = spirituous liquors), RV. viii, 6, 44 (Sāy. and others, 'very great'). — **māṇsa,** n. unclean meat (e.g. the flesh of dogs &c.), Vishṇ.; Yājñ.; 'without meat' in °*sī-√kṛi, -karoti,* to deprive of meat, Jātakam. — **māṇḍavya,** mfn. N. of a people, MārkP. — **mātṛi,** f. a stepmother (g. *śubhrâdi*); *-ja,* m. a stepmother's son, Kull. on Mn. ix, 118. — **mātra,** mfn. unequal in measure (*-tā,* f.), Lalit. — 1. **-māna,** mfn. (for 2. see *vi-√man*) devoid of honour, disgraced, BhP. — **mānusha,** mfn. without or except men, VarBṛS. — **māya** (*ví-*), mfn. devoid of magic, free from illusion, RV. — 1. **-mārga,** m. (for 2. see *vi-√1. mṛij*) a wrong road, evil course, MBh.; R. &c.; mfn. being on a w° r°, MārkP.; *-ga* (Suśr.), *-gāmin* (MW.), mfn. going on a wrong r°; *-dṛishṭi,* mfn. looking in a wrong direction, Suśr.; *-prasthita* (Śak.), *-stha* (MBh.), mfn. following a wrong road. — **mithuna,** mfn. excluding the sign Gemini, VarBṛS. — **miśra,** see under *vi-√miśr.* — **mukha,** see s.v. — **muñja** (*ví-*), mf(*ā*)n. without a sheath, ŚBr. — **mudra,** mfn. 'unsealed,' opened, blown, L.; abundant, Vcar.; °*draṇa,* n. causing to blow, Naish.

— 1. **-mūḍha,** mfn. (for 2. see *vi-√muh*) not foolish; m. a kind of divine being, MW. — **mūrchana,** n. = *mūrchana*, modulation, melody, &c., Hariv. — **mūrdha-ja,** mfn. hairless (on the head), MBh. — **mūla,** mfn. uprooted (lit. and fig.), Hariv.; °*lana*, n. the act of uprooting, Śatr. — **mṛiga,** mfn. containing no deer (as a forest), R. — **mṛityu,** mfn. not liable to death, immortal, Up. — **megha,** mfn. cloudless, Vishṇ. — **mogha,** mfn. quite fruitless, idle, vain, BhP. — **mauna,** mfn. breaking silence, Kathās. — **mauli,** mfn. having no crest or diadem, Hariv. — 1. **-mlāna,** mfn. (for 2. see *vi-√mlai*) unfaded, MW. — **yantṛi,** mfn. deprived of a guide, MBh. — **yava,** m. a kind of intestinal worm, Suśr. — **yugala,** mfn. not fitting together, Nalac. — **yūtha,** mfn. separated from its herd, MBh. — **yodha,** mfn. deprived of combatants, ib. — **yoni,** f. the womb of animals, debased (or 'manifold') birth (of plants and animals), Mn.; MBh. &c. (also °*nī*); mfn. contrary to one's own nature, PañcavBr.; Kāṭh.; destitute of vulva, Suśr.; of low origin, MBh. (Nīlak.); *-ja*, m. or n. 'sprung from a low origin,' an animal, MBh.; *-janman*, n. the birth of animals and plants; mfn. having an animal for mother, MārkP.; °*mâdhyāya*, m. N. of ch. of VarBṛS. — **rakshas** (*ví-*), mfn. free from Rākshasas, ŚBr. (*-tama*, superl.; °*kshás-tā*, f., ib.) — 1. **-raṅga,** n. (for 2. see *vi-√rañj*) a partic. kind of earth (= *kaṅkushṭha*), L. — **raja,** see s. v. — **ratha,** mfn. chariotless, deprived of a chariot, MBh.; R.; Kathās.; °*thī-karaṇa*, n. the depriving any one of a ch°, R.; °*thī-√kṛi*, P. *-karoti*, to deprive a person of a chariot, BhP.; °*thī-kṛita*, mfn. deprived of a ch°, MBh.; Kathās.; °*thī-√bhū*, P. *-bhavati*, to be deprived of a chariot, Kathās.; °*thī-bhūta*, mfn. deprived of a chariot, ib. — **rathya,** m. 'delighting in by-roads (?),' N. of Śiva, MBh. — **rathyā,** f. (prob.) a bad road or a by-road, MārkP. — **raśmi,** mfn. rayless, MBh.; R.; VarBṛS. — **rasa,** mfn. juiceless, sapless, unseasoned, Āpast.; flavourless, tasteless, insipid (lit. and fig.), unpleasant, disagreeable, MBh.; Kāv. &c.; painful, MW.; (ifc.) having no taste for, Kull. on Mn. ii, 95; m. pain, MW.; N. of a serpent-demon, MBh.; (*am*), ind. unpleasantly, Mṛicch.; *-tva*, n. bad taste, nauseousness, Prab.; Śāntiś.; °*sânana-tva* (Suśr.), °*sâsya-tva* (ŚārṅgS.), n. a bad taste in the mouth; °*sī-√kṛi*, P. *-karoti*, to affect unpleasantly, Vās.; °*sī-bhāva*, m. the becoming sapless (said of the earth), Car.; °*sī-√bhū*, P. *-bhavati*, to become sapless or insipid, Jātakam.; to be unpleasantly affected, Kām. — 1. **-rāga,** mf(*ā*)n. passionless, without feeling, dispassionate, indifferent (*sarvatas*, 'to everything'), R.; BhP.; *-tā*, f. indifference to everything, stoicism, MBh. — **rātra,** m. or n. (fr. *rātri*) the end of night, MBh. — **riphita,** mfn. pronounced without an *r*, AitBr. — **rúkmat,** mfn. shining, RV.; m. a brilliant ornament, bright armour, ib. — 1. **-ruj,** f. violent pain, a great disease, BhP. — 2. **-ruj,** mfn. free from pain, well, healthy, VarBṛS. — 1. **-ruja,** mfn. (for 2. see under *vi-√1. ruj*) id., PārGṛS. — **rudra** (*ví-*), mfn. not accompanied by Rudra or the Rudras (others 'shining, brilliant'), RV. i, 180, 8. — **rūksha,** mf(*ā*)n. rough, harsh (as speech), VarBṛS.; Bhar.; *-kodrava*, m. a kind of inferior grain, L. — **rūpa,** see s. v. — **repas,** mfn. faultless, blameless, L. — **repha,** m. the absence of an *r*, W.; a river, L. — **rephas,** mfn. = *-repas*, Harav. — **roga,** m. absence of illness, L.; mfn. healthy, Hariv. — **rosha,** mfn. free from anger, MBh.; very angry, ib. (v. l. *sa-rosha*). — **rohita,** m. N. of a man, g. *gargâdi*. — **laksha,** mf(*ā*)n. having no fixed aim, Vāgbh.; Amar. (v. l.); missing its mark (as an arrow), Śiś.; having no characteristic mark or property, W.; having a different m° or a character different to what is usual or natural, strange, extraordinary, ib.; embarrassed, abashed, ashamed, astonished, surprised (*-tā*, f.), Kāv.; Pañcat.; Kathās. &c.; *-tva*, n. absence of mark or aim, absence of distinguishing property, W.; the missing of the mark (of an arrow), Śiś.; confusion, shame, ib.; °*kshī-√kṛi*, P. *-karoti*, to cause to miss the mark, disappoint, HPariś.; to disconcert, abash, Kathās.; °*kshī-kṛita*, mfn. disconcerted, abashed, ib.; scoffed at, insulted, MW. — 1. **-lakshaṇa,** mf(*ā*)n. (for 2. see *vi-√laksh*) having different marks, varying in character, different, differing from (abl. or comp.; *-tā*, f.; *-tva*, n.), NṛisUp.; Suśr.; Sāh. &c.; various, manifold, BhP.; not admitting of exact definition, BhP.; Kāvyâd., Sch.; n. any state or condition which is without distinctive mark or for which no cause can be assigned, vain or causeless state, L.; *-catur-daśaka*, n., *-janma-prakāśikā*, f., *-mokshâdhikāra*, m. N. of wks. — 1. **-lakshita,** mfn. (for 2. see *vi-√laksh*) undistinguished, undiscriminated, unmarked, W. — **lakshya,** mfn. having no fixed aim, Amar. (v. l.); missing its mark (as an arrow), MārkP. — **lajja,** mfn. shameless, BhP. — **liṅga,** n. absence of marks; mfn. of a different gender, Pat.; *-stha*, mfn. not to be understood, MBh. ii, 845. — 1. **-liptā** or °**tikā,** f. a second (= $\frac{1}{3600}$ of a degree), Gaṇit. — 1. **-loka,** (prob.) n. (for 2. see *vi-√lok*) absence of man (*-stha*, mfn. living apart from the world), MBh.; mfn. apart from the world, solitary, W. — 1. **-locana,** mfn. (for 2. see *vi-√loc*) distorting the eyes, MBh.; m. N. of a poet, Vās., Introd.; of a mythical person, Kathās.; of an antelope, Hariv. — **loma,** see s. v. — **lolupa,** mf(*ā*)n. free from all desires, Vishṇ. (v. l.; *a-vil°* with the same meaning, ib.) — 1. **-lohitá,** m. a kind of disease, (perhaps) bleeding of the nose, AV. — 2. **-lohita** (*ví-*), mfn. deep-red, VS.; Hariv. &c.; m. N. of Śiva, MBh.; of Rudra and Fire (as identified with R°), MW.; a kind of onion, L.; N. of a hell, VP.; (*ā*), f. N. of one of the 7 tongues of fire (v. l. *su-lohitā*), MuṇḍUp. — **lohitaka,** n. a dead body that has become red, L. — **vaṅśa,** m. pl., w. r. for *-viṅśa*, m. pl. below. — **vat,** mfn. containing the word *vi*, AitBr. — **vatsa,** mf(*ā*)n. deprived of a calf or young ones or children, Mn.; MBh. &c. — **varuṇá,** mfn. keeping off Varuṇa i. e. death, AV. viii, 7, 10. — **varūtha,** mfn. deprived of a chariot-guard i. e. of the wooden ledge fixed on a chariot (to ward off collision), MBh. — **varcas,** mfn. without splendour, R. — **varṇa,** mf(*ā*)n. colourless, bad-coloured, pale, wan, MBh.; Hariv.; R. &c.; low, vile, W.; belonging to a mixed caste, VarBṛS.; MārkP.; unlettered, stupid, L.; m. a man of low caste or of degrading occupation, an out-caste, W.; *-tā*, f. loss of colour, paleness, MBh.; Hariv.; R. &c.; a low condition of life, Dharmaśarm.; *-bhāva*, m. loss of colour, paleness, Ragh.; *-maṇi-kṛita*, mfn. (a bracelet) having its jewels discoloured, Śak.; *-vadana*, mfn. pale-faced, MBh. — **vartman,** n. a wrong road (fig.), Kām. — **varman,** mfn. deprived of armour, having no armour, MBh.; °*ma-dhvaja-jīvita*, m. (a warrior) who has been deprived of armour and banner and life, ib.; °*mâyudha-vāhana*, m. deprived of armour and weapons and chariot, ib. — **vavri** (*ví-*), mfn. unveiled, bare, RV. x, 99, 5. — **vaśa,** mf(*ā*)n. deprived or destitute of will, powerless, helpless ('through,' comp.), unwilling, involuntary, spontaneous (ibc. 'involuntarily'), Mn. &c. &c.; (only W.) unrestrained; independent; subject; apprehensive of death; desirous of death (as being free from worldly cares); m. a town, suburb (?), Gal.; pl., v. l. for *viviṅśa* below, VP.; *-tā*, f. absence of will, helplessness, Rājat.; °*śī-√kṛi*, to render helpless; °*śī-kṛita*, checked (as a carriage in motion), MBh.; Rājat.; Kathās. — **vasana,** mf(*ā*)n. unclothed, naked, MBh.; MārkP. &c.; m. a naked Jaina mendicant, Sarvad.; Bādar., Sch. — **vastra,** mf(*ā*)n. without clothes, unclothed, naked, MBh.; Pur. &c.; *-tā*, f. nakedness, MBh.; Kām. — **vāc,** see *vi-√vac*. — **vācas** (*ví-*), mfn. speaking in various ways, AV. xii, 1, 45. — **vāta,** m. a vehement wind, ShaḍvBr. — **vāśa,** m. pl., v. l. for *-viṅśa* below, VP. — 1. **-vāsa,** mfn. without clothes, naked, W. — 2. **-vāsa,** m. pl. (for 3. and 4. see under *vi-√4.* and *5. vas*) v. l. for *-viṅśa* below, VP. — **vāsas,** mfn. unclothed, naked, MBh.; BhP. — **viṅśa,** m. N. of various kings, MBh.; Pur.; pl. N. of a mythical caste in Plaksha-dvīpa (corresponding to the Vaiśyas), VP. — **viṅśati,** m. N. of various men, MBh.; Pur. — **vidyut,** mfn. without lightning, Hariv. — **vidha,** see s. v. — **vindhya,** m. N. of a Dānava, MBh. — **vibhaktika,** mfn. lacking case-terminations (*-tva*, n.), Pat. — **vivadha** (*ví-*), mfn. not counterpoising, TS. — **viśa,** m. pl., w. r. for *-viṅśa* above, VP. — **vishā,** f. Kyllingia Monocephala, L. — **vīvadha,** mfn. = *-vivadha*, PañcavBr. — **vrata** (*ví-*), mfn. reluctant, refractory, RV.; AV.; performing various actions or ceremonies, MW. — **śakala,** mfn. fallen into pieces, MBh. (°*lī-√kṛi*, to break into pieces, ib.); °*lita*, mfn. separated, divided, different, Sāh.; discriminated, sifted, Śiś. — **śaṅka,** mfn. fearless, not afraid of (ifc.), Kāv.; causing no fear, free from danger, safe, Kām.; (*am*), ind. fearlessly, Daś.; Śiś.; (*ā*), f., see below. — **śaṅkaṭa,** mf(*ā* or [L.] *ī*)n. (cf. *saṃkaṭa*) extensive, large, big, Kāv.; Pañcat. &c.; strong, vehement, MW.; ghastly, hideous, Mālatim.; Pañcat.; Kathās.; (*am*), ind. vehemently, MW. — 1. **-śaṅkā,** f. (for 2. see *vi-√śaṅk*) absence of fear; (*ayā*), ind. fearlessly, without hesitation, BhP. — **śaphá,** mfn. having no hoofs or inverted hoofs (said of a demon), AV. iii, 9, 1. — **śabda,** (ibc.) words of various kinds, Cat. — 1. **-śaraṇa,** mfn. (for 2. see *vi-√śrī*) destitute of protection, ib. — **śarada,** w. r. for *-śārada*, Kathās. xv, 148. — **śalabha-marut,** mfn. not exposed to grasshoppers (moths) or to the wind (as a lamp), VarBṛS. — **śalya,** see s. v. — **śastra,** mfn. weaponless, MBh.; *-tva*, n. an unarmed or defenceless condition, MW. — **śākha** (*ví-*; once *vi-śākha*, AV. xix, 7, 3), mf(*ā*)n. branched, forked, AV.; TS.; GṛŚrS.; branchless, Hariv.; handless, ib.; born under the constellation Viśākhā, Pāṇ. iv, 3, 34; m. a beggar, L.; a spindle, L.; a partic. attitude in shooting, L.; Bœrhavia Procumbens, L.; N. of Skanda, MBh.; a manifestation of Skanda (regarded as his son), ib.; Hariv.; VarBṛS. &c.; N. of a demon dangerous to children (held to be a manifestation of Sk°), Suśr.; ŚārṅgS.; Hcat.; of Śiva, MBh.; of a Devarshi, ib.; of a Dānava, Kathās.; of a Daśa-pūrvin and other persons, Bhadrab.; Rājat. &c.; = *viśākha-datta* below, L.; (*ā*), f. a species of plant, KātyŚr. (Dūrvā grass, Comm.; = *kaṭhillaka*, L.); (also du. or pl.) the 14th (later 16th) lunar asterism (figured by a decorated arch and containing four or originally two stars under the regency of a dual divinity, Indra and Agni; it is probably to be connected with the quadrangle of stars ι, α, β, γ Libræ; see *nakshatra*), AV. &c. &c.; N. of a woman, Buddh.; (*ī*), f. a forked stick, ŚrS.; n. a fork, ramification, Gobh.; *-ja*, m. the orange-tree, L.; *-datta*, m. N. of the author of the Mudrā-rākshasa (he was the son of Pṛithu and lived probably in the 9th century), IW. 507; *-deva*, m. N. of a poet, Subh.; of another man, Buddh.; *-māhātmya*, n. N. of wk.; *-yūpa*, m. N. of a king, Pur.; m. or n. (?) N. of a place, MBh.; *-vat*, m. N. of a mountain, MārkP. — **śākhaka,** mf(*ikā*)n. branched, forked, Hcat.; (*ikā*), f. a forked pole, Kād.; °*khikā-daṇḍa*, m. id., Hcar. — **śākhala,** n. a partic. attitude in shooting, L. (cf. *viśākha*). — **śākhila,** m. N. of an author, Vām.; Kāv.; of a merchant, Kathās. — **śāpa,** mfn. freed from a curse, BhP.; m. N. of a Muni, Cat. — **śārada,** mf(*ā*)n. experienced, skilled or proficient in, conversant with (loc. or comp.; *-tva*, n., Pañcad.), Mn.; MBh. &c.; learned, wise, W.; clever (as a speech), BhP.; of a clear or serene mind, Lalit.; famous, celebrated, W.; beautifully autumnal, Vās.; lacking the gift of speech, ib.; bold, impudent, ib.; = *śreshṭha*, L.; m. Mimusops Elengi, Kir., Sch.; N. of an author and of another person, Cat.; (*ā*), f. a kind of Alhagi, L.; °*di-man*, m. skill, proficiency, conversancy, Harav. — **śikhá** (or *ví-ś°*), mfn. devoid of the top-knot or tuft of hair (left on the head after tonsure), VS.; AV.; Hcat.; bald, unfeathered (as an arrow), RV.; pointless, blunt (as an arrow), R.; flameless (as fire), R.; tailless (as a comet), VarBṛS.; weak (?), MW.; m. an arrow (in general), MBh.; Kāv. &c.; a spear, javelin, L.; an iron crow, W.; a versed sine (= *śara*), Gaṇit.; a sort of Śara or reed, MW.; (*ā*), f. a little shovel, spade, hoe, W.; a small arrow, ib.; a sort of pin or needle, ib.; a spindle, ib.; a passage, road, street, Suśr.; Hcar.; a barber's wife, L.; = *nalikā* or *nālikā*, L.; a sick-room or the dwelling of the sick, W.; *-śreṇī*, f. a line of arrows, MW.; °*khânupraveśana*, n. entrance into a sick-room (= ent° into medical practice; °*śanīya*, mfn. treating of it), Suśr.; °*khântara*, n. the interior of a street (°*ram anu-√car*, to go through a st°; °*rāṇy ati-√pat*, to traverse streets), Car.; Śiś.; the vagina, Suśr.; °*khâvalī*, f. a line of arrows, MW.; °*khâśraya*, m. a quiver, L. — **śipriya** (*ví-*), mfn. (variously interpreted by the Commentators), VS.; TS. — **śira,** mfn., w. r. for *-śira* below. — **śiras,** mfn. headless, MBh.; Hariv.; freed from a (foreign) head, MBh.; topless, Hariv. — **śiraska,** mfn. headless, MBh. — **śiśnā** (*ví-*; MaitrS.) or **-śiśnyā** (Kāṭh.), f. (prob.) tailless. — **śishya,** mfn. without pupils. — **śīrshan** (*ví-*), mf(*shṇī*)n. headless, Br.; TĀr. — **śīla,** mfn. ill-behaved, ill-mannered, badly conducted, Mn.; MBh. — **śushka,** mfn. dried up, withered, parched (*-tva*, n., Car.), MBh.; Kāv.; Kathās.; thirsty, MW. — **śūnya,** mf(*ā*)n. perfectly empty, MBh.; R. — **śūla,** mfn. without a spear, Ragh. — **śṛiṅkhala,** mfn. unfettered, unrestrained, unbounded (*am*, ind., Śiś.), Kāv.; Rājat.; Kathās.; dissolute, MW.; sounding or tinkling excessively, Kāv.; Kathās.; (ifc.) abounding excessively in, Rājat. — **śṛiṅga,** mfn. deprived of a horn or horns, Hariv.; peakless, deprived of a peak (said of a hill), MBh. — **śoka,** m. cessation of sorrow, BhP.;

mf(*ā*)n. free from sorrow; removing sor°, AitBr.; Up. &c.; containing no description of any sor°, Sāh.; m. Jonesia Asoka, L.; N. of a spiritual son of Brahmā, VP.; of a Ṛishi, SV.; of the charioteer of Bhīma, MBh.; of a Dānava, Kathās.; of a mountain-chain, MārkP.; (*ā*), f. N. of one of the perfections which are obtained by Yoga, Sarvad.; VP.; exemption from grief (one of the original properties of man), MW.; N. of one of the Mātṛis attending on Skanda, MBh.; n. N. of a Sāman, SV.; *-koṭa*, N. of a mountain, MW.; *-tā*, f. freedom from sorrow, MBh.; MārkP.; *-deva*, m. N. of a man, Cat.; *-dvādaśī*, f. a partic. 12th day, ib.; *-parvan*, n. N. of a section of the Mahā-bhārata; *-shashṭhī*, f. a partic. 6th day, Cat.; *-saptamī*, f. a partic. 7th day, ib.; *°kī-√kṛi*, to free from sorrow, ib. **—śoṇita**, mfn. bloodless, Jātakam. **—śyāparṇa**, mfn. (a sacrifice) performed without the Śyāparṇas, AitBr. **—śravaṇa**, m. N. of a man, g. *śivâdi*. **—śrávas**, n. great fame, ŚBr.; KātyŚr.; Vait.; (*ví-*), mfn. famous, Br.; KātyŚr.; m. N. of a Ṛishi (son of Pulastya and father of Kubera, Rāvaṇa, Kumbha-karṇa and Vibhīshaṇa), MBh.; Hariv.; R.; BhP. **—śrī-√kṛi**, P. *karoti*, to rob of (i.e. surpass in) beauty, Dhūrtan. **—ślatha**, mfn. relaxed, loose, Ragh.; Pratāp.; *°thâṅga*, mfn. having languid limbs; (*am*), ind. with lang° limbs, Amar. **—śloka**, mfn. destitute of fame, Piṅg.; m. a kind of metre, ib.; Col. **—shama**, see s.v. **—shkandha** (*ví-*), n. (fr. *vi* + *skandha*) a partic. disease, AV.; TS. (cf. *sám-skandha*); *-dūshaṇa*, mfn. destroying it, AV. **—shṭāva**, m. (fr. *vi* + *stāva*) a subdivision of the periods of a Stoma, Lāṭ.; PañcavBr., Sch. **—shṭhala**, n. (fr. *vi* + *sthala*, Pāṇ. viii, 3, 96) a remote place, a spot situated apart or at a distance, W. **—saṃśaya**, mfn. free from doubt, certain, Pañcat. (v.l.); (*am*), ind. without doubt, MW. **—saṃshṭhula** (Kpr.; Rājat. &c.) or **—saṃsthula** (HYog.; Śatr.), mfn. (fr. Prākṛit *vi-saṃthula*, prob. derived from *√śrath*) unsteady, infirm, tottering; confused, frightened, HPariś.; *°shṭhula-gamana*, mfn. going unsteadily, tottering, MW. **—saṃsarpin**, mfn., see *tiryag-vi-s°*. **—saṃsthita**, mfn. not finished, unachieved, ŚrS.; *-saṃcara*, m. the place taken as long as the Savana is not completed, ib. **—saṃsthula**, see *-saṃshṭhula*. **—saṃkaṭa**, mfn. = *-śaṅkaṭa*, q.v.; m. a lion, W.; the Iṅgudī tree, MW. **—saṃkula**, mf(*ā*)n. not confused, self-possessed, Kum.; n. absence of confusion, composure (*sa-visaṃkulam*, ind.), Viddh. **—saṃgata**, mfn. unconnected, inconsistent, not in harmony, MW. **—saṃjña**, mf(*ā*)n. unconscious, MBh.; R. &c.; bereft of sense, lifeless, W.; *°jñāgati* and (prob. more correct) *°jñā-vatī*, f. a partic. high number, Buddh. **—saṃjñita**, mfn. deprived of consciousness, Hariv. **—sadṛiś**, mfn. (in *a-visadṛiś*, 'not dissimilar, correspondent'), L. **—sadṛiśa** (*ví-*), mf(*ā* or *ī*)n. unlike, dissimilar, different, not corresponding, unequal, RV.; KātyŚr., Sch. &c.; *-phala*, mfn. having dissimilar consequences (*-tā*, f.), Vās. **—1. -saṃdhi**, m. a secondary joint, SaddhP.; absence of Saṃdhi, Kpr. **—2. -saṃdhi**, mfn. jointless, MBh.; unallied with, Kām.; without (grammatical) Saṃdhi, Pratāp. **—saṃdhika**, mfn. without (grammatical) Saṃdhi, Kāvyâd. **—saṃnāha**, mfn. without a coat of mail, Mn. vii, 12; unclothed, naked, MW. **—sabhāga**, mfn. having no share (*-tā*, f.), Harav. **—samāpti**, f. non-completion, Pāṇ. ii, 1, 60, Vārtt. 5. **—salyá** or **-sályaka**, m. a partic. disease, AV. **—sāmagrī**, f. the absence of means; (in phil.) the absence of causes calculated to produce an effect, MW. **—sārathi**, mfn. being without a charioteer, R.; *-haya-dhvaja*, mfn. without char° and horses and banner, MBh. **—sira**, mf(*ī*)n. having no (prominent) veins, VarBṛS. **—sukalpa**, m. N. of a king, Buddh. **—sukṛit**, mfn. doing no good work, ŚBr. **—sukṛita**, mfn. without good works, KaushUp. **—sukha**, mfn. joyless, VarBṛ. **—suta**, mf(*ā*)n. childless, ib.; Kāv. **—suhṛid**, mfn. friendless, VarBṛ. **—sūta**, mfn. deprived of a charioteer, MBh. **—sūtra** &c., see *vi-√sūtr*. **—sūrya**, mfn. deprived of the sun, Hariv.; R. **—secaka**, mfn. = *vigataḥ secako yasmāt*, Pat. **—somá**, mf(*ā*)n. being without Soma, ŚBr.; moonless, MBh. **—saukhya**, n. absence of ease, pain, R. **—saurabha**, mfn. lacking fragrance, Kathās. **—sthāna**, mfn. belonging to another place or organ (as a sound), RPrāt. **—1. -spardhā**, f. (for 2. see under *vi-√spardh*) absence of envy or emulation, MW. **—spṛikka**, mfn. (applied to a partic. taste), VarBṛS. **—1. -smaya**, mfn. (for 2. see *vi-√smi*) free from pride or arrogance, BhP.; Śiś. **—srotas**, n. a partic. high number, Buddh. **—svapna**, **-svapnaj**, Pat. **—svara**, m. discord, Pañcar.; mfn. having no sound, CūlUp.; dissonant, discordant (*am*, ind.), MBh.; Hariv. &c.; pronounced with a wrong accent (*am*, ind.), Mn.; MBh.; Śiksh. **—svāda**, mfn. tasteless, W. **—1. -harsha**, m. excessive joy or gladness, MW. **—2. -harsha**, mfn. joyless, sad, BhP. **—hasta**, mfn. without a hand or trunk, handless, Naish. (*-tā*, f., Śiś.); unhandy, inexperienced (see *a-vih°*); confounded, perplexed, helpless, Kād.; Naish. (*-tā*, f., Śiś.; Hcar.); (ifc.) completely absorbed in, Ragh.; adroit, skilled, experienced (in; comp.), Hariv.; wise, learned, W.; m. a eunuch, L. **—hastita**, mfn. confused, embarrassed, Kathās. **—1. -hāyas** (*ví-*), mfn. (for 2., from which perhaps it is scarcely separable, see *vi-√hā*) vigorous, active, mighty, RV.; AV.; TĀr. (accord. to Sch. = *mahat, vañcana-vat, vyāptṛi, vividha-gamana-yukta*). **—hiṅsra**, see s.v. **—1. -hita**, mfn. (for 2. see under *vi-√dhā*) improper, unfit, not good, W. **—hút-mat**, mfn. presenting no offerings, RV. i, 134, 6; (Sāy. 'offering, invoking'); (*atī*), f. a special oblation, MW. **—hṛidaya** (*ví-*), n. want of courage, AV. **—hradin**, mfn. (perhaps) making pools, Kāṭh. xxiii, 6.

विंश 1. *viṅśa* (for 2. see below). See *pad-viṅśa*.

विंशति *viṅśati*, f. (prob. for *dvi-daśati*, 'two decades') twenty, a score (with a noun either in genitive or in apposition, e.g. *viṅśatir ghaṭānām*, '20 jars;' *viṅśatyā háribhiḥ*, 'with 20 horses'), RV. &c. &c.; a partic. form of military array (= *vyūha*), MBh. (Nīlak.); m. N. of a son of Ikshvāku, VP. [Cf. Gk. ϝίκατι, εἴκοσι; Lat. *viginti*.] **—tama**, mf(*ī*)n. twentieth, Pāṇ. v, 2, 56 (with *bhāga*, m. $\frac{1}{20}$), Yājñ., Sch.) **—taulika**, mfn. containing 20 Tulās, Hcat. **—dvija**, mfn. (a festival) to which 20 Brāhmans are invited, Mn. viii, 392. **—pa**, m. the chief of 20 (villages), MBh. **—bāhu**, m. '20-armed,' N. of Rāvaṇa, Bhaṭṭ. **—bhāga**, m. the twentieth part, Gaut.; Hcat. **—bhuja**, m. = *-bāhu*, R. **—varsha-deśīya**, mfn. about 20 years old, MW. **—vārshika**, mf(*ī*)n. lasting 20 years, ĀpŚr., Sch.; occurring after 20 years, Yājñ. **—vidha**, mfn. of 20 kinds, Car. **—śata** (*viṅśati-*), n. 120, ŚBr.; Lāṭy. **—sāhasra**, mf(*ā*)n. 20,000, Hariv.; R. **—stotra**, n., **-smṛiti**, f. N. of wks. **Viṅśatīśa** or **°tīśin**, m. = *viṅśati-pa*, Mn. vii, 115, 116.

2. **Viṅśá**, mf(*ī*)n. twentieth, Mn.; Yājñ.; BhP.; accompanied or increased by 20, VarBṛS. (with *śata*, n. 120, Pāṇ. v, 2, 46); consisting of 20 parts, TS. &c. &c.; (ifc.) = *viṅśati*, 20, Hcat.; m. (with or without *aṅśa* or *bhāga*) the 20th part, Mn.; VarBṛS.; N. of a king, MBh.; VP.; n. a decade, 20, MBh.; R. &c. **—ja**, m. N. of a king, VP. **Viṅśâṅśa**, m. the 20th part, Hcat.

Viṅśaka, mfn. accompanied or increased by twenty, BhP.; consisting of 20 parts, MBh.; n. a decade, 20, Hariv.; (with *śata*) 20 per cent., Yājñ.

Viṅśac-chlokī, f. (fr. *viṅśat* + *śl°*) N. of wk.

Viṅśat, in some comp. = *viṅśati* (see *eka-* and *pari-viṅśat*; *viṅśac-chlokī* and *viṅśad-bāhu*).

Viṅśatikīna. See *adhyardha-* and *dvi-v°*.

Viṅśatima, mfn. = *viṅśati-tama*, twentieth (with *bhāga*, m. $\frac{1}{20}$), Yājñ., Sch.

Viṅśaty, in comp. for *viṅśati*. **—akshara**, mfn. twenty-syllabled, ŚBr. **—aṅguli**, mfn. twenty-fingered, ib. **—adhipati**, m. = *viṅśati-pa*, MBh.

Viṅśad-bāhu, m. (fr. *viṅśat* + *b°*) 'twenty-armed,' N. of Rāvaṇa, R.

Viṅśin, mfn. consisting of twenty, PañcavBr. (cf. Pat. on Pāṇ. v, 237); = *viṅśati-pa*, Mn. vii, 119; = *viṅśati*, twenty, L.

विःकृन्धिका *viḥ-krindhikā*, f. a croaking sound, croaking, MaitrUp. (Sch.)

विक *vika*, m. N. of a man, Kshitīś.; n. the milk of a cow that has just calved, L.; (with *Prajā-pateḥ*) N. of a Sāman, Ārsh.

विकच 2. *vi-kaca*, mfn. (*√kac*; for 1. see p. 949, col. 3) opened, blown, Hariv.; Kāv. &c.; shining, resplendent, brilliant, radiant with (comp.), MBh.; Kāv. &c.; *-śrī*, mfn. having radiant beauty, Kāv.; *°cânana*, mf(*ā*)n. with a radiant face, Kathās.; *°câmbā*, f. N. of Durgā, L.

Vi-kacaya, Nom. P. *°yati*, to open, expand (a blossom), BhP. **°kacita**, mfn. opened, expanded, blown, Bhartṛ. (v.l.)

Vikacī-√kṛi, P. *-karoti*, to open, expand, Bhartṛ.

विकट 2. *ví-kaṭa*, mf(*ā* or *ī*)n. (prob. Prākṛit for *vi-kṛita*, cf. *ut-*, *pra-k°* &c.; for 1. *vi-kaṭa* see p. 949, col. 3) having an unusual size or aspect, horrible, dreadful, monstrous, huge, large, great, RV. &c. &c. (*am*, ind. terribly); unusually handsome, R.; Chandom.; large-toothed, L.; knitted (as brows), frowning, Prab.; obscure, obsolete, W.; m. a kind of plant or fruit, L.; N. of a son of Dhṛita-rāshṭra, MBh.; of one of the attendants of Skanda, ib.; of a Rākshasa, L.; of a mythical person, Kathās.; of a goose, ib.; Pañcat.; (*ā*), f. a bandy-legged girl (unfit for marriage), ĀpGṛ.; N. of the mother of Gautama Buddha, L.; of a female divinity peculiar to Buddhists, W.; of a Rākshasī, R.; n. (only L.) white arsenic; sandal; a peculiar attitude in sitting, a boil, tumour; *-grāma*, m. N. of a village, Cat.; *-tva*, n. (in rhet.) a sound of words reminding of a dance, Sāh.; *-nitambā*, f. N. of a poetess, Cat.; *-mūrti*, mfn. having a hideous or distorted shape, deformed, ugly, MW.; *-vadana*, m. 'hideous-faced,' N. of an attendant of Durgā, Kathās.; *-varman*, m. N. of a king, Daś.; *-vishāṇa* or *-śṛiṅga*, m. 'large-horned,' a stag, L.; *°ṭâkṛiti*, mfn. of dreadful appearance, Kathās.; *°ṭâksha*, mf(*ī*)n. having dreadful eyes, Pañcat.; m. N. of an Asura, Kathās.; *°ṭânana*, mfn. ugly-faced, Kathās.; m. N. of a son of Dhṛita-rāshṭra, MBh.; *°ṭâbha*, m. 'of terrible appearance,' N. of an Asura, Hariv. **°kaṭaka**, mfn. suffering from a partic. deformity, Buddh. **°kaṭī-√kṛi**, P. *-karoti*, to make wide, extend, Śiś.

विकत्थ् *vi-√katth*, Ā. *-katthate* (ep. also P. *°ti*), to boast, vaunt, brag, boast of or about (instr.), MBh.; R.; to praise, extol, commend (also ironically), R.; to mock or blame, disparage, humiliate by (instr.), MBh.: Caus. *-katthayati*, to humiliate, humble, MBh.; to boast, Śiś. **°katthana**, mfn. boasting, a boaster, braggart, MBh.; R. &c.; praising ironically, W.; n. and (*ā*), f. the act of boasting or vaunting or praising, MBh.; Daś.; Kathās. &c.; irony, W.; *-tva*, n. boastfulness, Rājat. **°katthanīya**, mfn. to be praised (also ironically), W. **°katthā**, f., **°katthita**, n. boast, vaunt, (ironical) praise, MBh. **°katthin**, mfn. boasting, vaunting, proclaiming, MBh.; Bhaṭṭ.

विकथा *vi-kathā*, f. (*√kath*) useless or irrelevant talk, Āpast.

विकम्प् *vi-√kamp*, cl. 1. Ā. *-kampate*, to tremble greatly, quiver, move about, MBh.; R. &c.; to become changed or deformed, change a position or place, shrink from, ib.: Caus. *-kampayati*, to cause to tremble, agitate, Kālid. **°kapita**, mfn. changed, altered, deformed, Pāṇ. vi, 4, 24, Vārtt. 1, Pat. **°kampa**, mfn. trembling, heaving, unsteady, shrinking from, W. **°kampana**, n. trembling, motion (of the sun), L.; m. N. of a Rākshasa, BhP. **°kampita**, mfn. trembling, shaking, tremulous, agitated, unsteady, Ṛitus.; n. a kind of sinking of the tone of the voice, APrāt.; a partic. faulty pronunciation of the vowels, Pat. **°kampin**, mfn. trembling, shaking, MārkP.; (*ī*), f. (in music) a partic. Śruti, Saṃgīt.

विकर 1. *vi-kara*, *vi-karaṇa*. See p. 950.

विकर 2. *vi-kara* &c. See *vi-√1. kṛi*.

विकर्त *vi-karta*, *°kartana*. See p. 955.

विकल *vi-kala*, mf(*ā* or *ī*)n. deprived of a part or a limb or a member, mutilated, maimed, crippled, impaired, imperfect, deficient in or destitute of (instr. or comp.; cf. Pāṇ. ii, 1, 31, Sch.), Up.; Mn.; MBh. &c.; confused, agitated, exhausted, unwell, depressed, sorrowful, MBh.; Kāv.; Kathās.; m. N. of a son of Śambara, Hariv.; of a son of Lambôdara, BhP.; of a son of Jīmūta, VP.; of another man, Cat.; (*ā* or *ī*), f. a woman in whom menstruation has begun, L.; (*ā*), f. the 60th part of a Kalā, the second of a degree, Sūryas.; a partic. stage in the revolution of the planet Mercury, VarBṛS.; *-tā*, f., *-tva*, n. deficiency, infirmity, imperfection, MBh.; Kāv. &c.; *-pāṇika*, m. one who has a mutilated or withered hand, a cripple, L.; *-vadha*, 'death of Vikala,' N. of a ch. in GaṇP.; *°lâṅga*, mf(*ī*)n. having mutilated or imperfect limbs, deformed, crippled, lamed, MBh.; VarBṛS.; *°lêndriya*, mfn. having impaired or defective organs of sense, Mn. viii, 66.

Vi-kalaya, Nom. P. *°yati*, to afflict, mutilate, injure, ill-treat, Bhām.

Vikalī-√kṛi, P. *-karoti*, to injure, impair, inflict

great injury upon, harm, distress, perplex (*kṛita-* or *-bhūta*, mfn. mutilated, injured, harmed), Śiś.; Gīt. &c.

विकल्प *vi-kalpa* &c. See under *vi-√klṛip*.

विकल्य *vi-kalya*, m. pl. N. of a people, MBh. (v.l. *vi-kalpa*).

विकश्वर *vi-kaśvara*, *vi-kashā*, *vi-kashvara*, incorrect for *vi-kasvara* &c.

विकस् *vi-√kas* (also incorrectly written *vi-kaś*), cl. 1. P. *-kasati*, to burst, become split or divided or rent asunder, Suśr. (cf. *vi-kasta*); to open, expand, blossom, bloom, MBh.; Kāv. &c. (cf. *vi-kasita*); to shine, be bright, beam (with joy &c.), Kāv.; VarBṛS.; to spread out, extend, increase, MBh.; Kāv.; Suśr.: Caus. *-kāsayati*, to cause to open or blow or expand or shine, Kāv.; Kathās.

Vi-kasa, m. the moon, L.; (*ā*), f. Bengal madder (also written *vikashā*), L.; = *mānsa-rohiṇī*, L. °**kasat**, mfn. opening, blown, expanding, shining, bright, Kāv.; Pur. °**kasana**, n. (°*ne-√kṛi*), g. *sākshād-ādi*. °**kasita**, mfn. (Pāṇ. vii, 2, 54) opened, open, expanded, budded, blown, MBh.; Kāv. &c.; *-kumudêndīvarâlokin*, mfn. looking like the expanded white and blue lotus, MW.; *-nayana-vadana-kamala*, mfn. opening (her) lotus-like eyes and mouth, Pañcat.; *-vadana*, mfn. with opened mouth, BhP. °**kasuka** (*ví-*), m. a partic. Agni, AgP. °**kasta** (*ví-*), mfn. (Pāṇ. vii, 2, 34) burst, split, rent asunder, RV.; VS.; Kauś. °**kasti** (*ví-*), f. the act of bursting, TS. °**kasvara**, mfn. opened (as eyes), Kathās.; expanded, blown, Śiś.; clear (as sound), Daś.; candid, L.

Vi-kāsa, m. expanding, budding, blowing (of flowers), Kum.; Śiś.; opening (of the mouth or eyes), VarBṛS.; Pañcat.; opening (of the heart), cheerfulness, serenity, Daś.; Śiś.; expansion, development, growth, Śiś.; Pur.; Sarvad.; *-bhāj* or *-bhṛit*, mfn. expanded, blown, Kāv. °**kāsaka**, mfn. opening, expanding (the mind i.e. making wise), Dhūrtas. °**kāsana**, mfn. causing to blow or expand, Kāv.; n. developing, Śaṃk. °**kāsita**, mfn. caused to expand, expanded, blown, Amar. °**kāsin**, mfn. blossoming, blooming, Śiś.; opened, open (as the eyes or nose), Daśar.; Sāh.; open = candid, sincere, L.; expanding, developing, Śiś.; extensive, great, Kāv.; Kām.; (ifc.) rich or abounding in, Rājat.; dissolving, relaxing, paralysing, Suśr.; °*si-tā*, f. expansion, development, Saṃk.; *-si-nilôtpala*, Nom. P. °*lati*, to resemble a blossoming blue lotus-flower, Sāh.

विकस्वरूप *vikasva-rūpa* (?), m. N. of a man, Saṃskārak.

विकाङ्क्ष् *vi-√kāṅksh*, P. Ā. *-kāṅkshati*, °*te*, to have anything in view, aim at (acc.), Hariv.; to tarry, linger, hesitate, TāṇḍBr. °**kāṅkshā**, f. (cf. *vi-kāṅksha*, p. 950, col. 1) hesitation, irresolution, indecision as to (inf. or gen.), MBh.; R.

विकार 1. *vi-kāra*. See p. 950, col. 1.

विकार 2. *vi-kāra* &c. See under *vi-√1. kṛi*.

विकाल *vi-kāla* &c. See p. 950, col. 1.

विकाश् *vi-√kāś* (in derivatives sometimes confounded with *vi-√kas*), cl. 1. Ā. *-kāśate*, to appear, become visible, shine forth, R.: Caus. *-kāśayati*, to cause to appear or shine forth, illuminate, make clear, publish, MBh.: Intens., see *vi-cākaśat* below. 2. °**kāśa**, m. (for 1. see p. 950, col. 1) brightness, radiance, Inscr.; appearance, display, manifestation, L.; = *prasāra* and *vishama-gati*, Kir. xv, 52 (Sch.); *-tā*, f., *-tva*, n. appearance, display, MW. °**kāśaka**, °**kāśana**, °**kāśita**, incorrectly for *vi-kāsana* &c. above. °**kāśin**, mfn. shining, radiant, (ifc.) illumining, illustrating, explaining, Kāv.; (*inī*), f. N. of one of the Mātṛis attending on Skanda, MBh.

Vi-cákaśat, mfn. (fr. Intens.) shining, radiant, RV.; looking on, seeing, beholding, perceiving, ib.

विकाषिन् *vi-kāshin* for *vi-kāśin* and *vi-kāsin*.

विकास *vi-kāsa* &c. See above.

विकिर *vi-kira*, *vi-kiraṇa*, *vi-kīrṇa* &c., see under *vi-√kṛī*.

विकिरिड *vikiriḍa* (Kāṭh.), °*rida* (TS.), °*ridra* (VS.), mfn. applied to Rudra (accord. to Sch. 'averting wounds' or 'sending off arrows').

विकुक्षि *vi-kukshi*, *vi-kuja* &c. See p. 950, col. 1.

विकुघास *vikughāsa*, g. *kṛiśāśvâdi* (v.l. *vi-kutyāsa*).

विकुचित *vi-kucita*, n. (*√kuc*) a partic. mode of fighting, Hariv.

विकुञ्च् *vi-√kuñc*, Caus. *-kuñcayati*, to contract, draw back (the ears), R. °**kuñcita**, mfn. contracted, crisped, curled, knitted (as the brow), MBh.; Kāv.; *-bhrū-latam*, ind. with contracted eyebrows, frowning, Kum.; *-lalāṭa-bhṛit*, mfn. having a scowling brow, MBh.

विकुत्यास *vikutyāsa*. See *vikughāsa*.

विकुण्ठित *vi-kuṇṭhita*, mfn. (*√kuṇṭh*) blunted, obtuse, Ragh.

विकुत्सा *vi-kutsā*, f. (*√kuts*) violent abuse or reviling, MBh.

विकुप् *vi-√kup*, only Caus. *-kopayati*, to disturb, Divyâv.

विकुर्वण *vi-kurvaṇa*, °*vāṇa*. See col. 3.

विकुसुक *vikusuka*, m. a partic. Agni, ĀpŚr. (cf. *ví-kasuka*).

विकुस्र *vikusra* or *vikrasra*, m. the moon, Uṇ. ii, 15 (prob. for *vi-kasra*).

विकूज् *vi-√kūj*, cl. 1. P. *-kūjati*, to chirp, sing, hum, warble (as birds), R. °**kūjana**, n. rumbling (see *antra-vik°*). °**kūjita**, n. humming, chirping, singing (of birds), MBh.; Ragh.

विकूण् *vi-√kūṇ*, to contract, wrinkle (the face), VarBṛS. °**kūṇana**, n. contraction (*mukha-v°*, wrinkling the face), L.; a side-glance, leer, wink, W. °**kūṇikā**, f. the nose, L.

विकृ *vi-√1. kṛi*, P. Ā. *-karoti*, *-kurute*, to make different, transform, change the shape (or the mind), cause to alter or change (esp. for the worse), deprave, pervert, spoil, impair, RV. &c. &c.; (Pass. and Ā., rarely P.) to become different, be altered, change one's state or opinions, Mn.; MBh. &c. (cf. Pāṇ. i, 3, 35); to develop, produce (esp. variously), RV.; MBh.; to embellish, decorate (in various manners), MBh.; to distribute, divide, RV.; ŚBr.; to destroy, annihilate, RV.; MBh.; to represent, fill the place of (acc.), KātyŚr., Sch.; (Ā.; cf. above) to move to and fro, wave, shake (hands or feet), R.; Suśr.; to be or become restless (with *netrābhyām*, 'to roll the eyes'), Suśr.; to utter (sounds), Pāṇ. i, 3, 34; to become unfaithful to (loc.), Mn. ix, 15; to act in a hostile or unfriendly way towards (gen. or loc.), MBh.; Kāv. &c.; to contend together, AV.; MBh.; to act in various ways, Bhaṭṭ.; Pass. *-kriyate*, to be changed &c. (cf. above): Caus. *-kārayati*, to cause to change or be changed, Hit.

2. **Vi-kara**, m. (for 1. see p. 950, col. 1; for 3. see *vi-√kṛī*) disease, sickness, L.; a partic. mode of fighting, Hariv. (v.l. *vishkara*).

2. **Vi-karaṇa**, m. (for 1. see p. 950, col. 1) 'producing a change,' (in gram.) a term for the affix or conjugational characteristic which is placed between the root and terminations, the inserted conjugational affix (according to Pāṇini these affixes are *śap*, *śapo luk*, *ślu*, *śyan*, *śnu*, *śa*, *śnam*, *u*, *śnā*, *yak*, and *cli* [with its substitutes], *tāsi*, *sya*, *sip*, the first nine of which are added in the Pres., Impf., Imperative, and Potential, and before a Kṛit which contains a mute palatal *ś*, in the case of Active verbs; *yak* is added in the case of the Karman or Bhāva, i.e. Passives or Neuters; *cli* is added in the Aorist, *tāsi* in the 1st Future, *sya* in the 2nd Future and Conditional, and *sip* before Leṭ.; *lug-vikaraṇa*, 'having *luk* for its Vik°' [said of rts. of cl. 2]; *ākhyāta-pada-vikaraṇāḥ*, 'words which modify the finite verb,' i.e. make it accented); (*ī*), f. a partic. Śakti, Hcat.; n. change, modification, Nir.; a disturbing influence, Sarvad. °**kartṛi**, m. a transformer, ŚBr. &c. &c.; an insulter, offender, R.; MBh. (v.l. *ni-kartṛi*). °**karman** &c., see p. 950, col. 1.

2. **Vi-kāra**, m. (for 1. see p. 950, col. 1) change of form or nature, alteration or deviation from any natural state, transformation, modification, change (esp. for the worse) of bodily or mental condition, disease, sickness, hurt, injury, (or) perturbation, emotion, agitation, passion, ŚrS.; MBh. &c.; an apparition, spectre, Kathās.; extravagance, ib.; a product, Gaut.; (in Sāṃkhya) a production or derivative from Prakṛiti (there are 7 Vikāras, viz. *buddhi*, 'intellect,' *ahaṃ-kāra*, 'the sense of individuality,' and the 5 *tan-mātras*, q.v.; these are also producers, inasmuch as from them come the 16 Vikāras which are only productions, viz. the 5 *mahā-bhūtāni*, q.v., and the 11 organs, viz. the 5 *buddhîndriyāṇi* or organs of sense, the 5 *karmêndriyāṇi* or organs of action, and *manas*, 'the mind'), IW. 82 &c.; the derivative of a word, Nir.; contortion of the face, grimace, Kathās.; change of sentiment, hostility, defection, MBh.; Rājat.; *-tas*, ind. from or through change, MW.; *-tva*, n. the state of change, transformation, Vedântas.; *-maya*, mf(*ī*)n. consisting of derivatives (from Prakṛiti), Up.; *-vat*, mfn. undergoing changes, Kām.; *-hetu*, m. 'cause of perturbation,' temptation, seduction, Kum. °**kārita**, mfn. changed, rendered unfavourable or unfriendly, Hit. °**kārin**, mfn. liable to change, changeable, variable, VPrāt.; MBh.; Suśr.; undergoing a change, changed into (comp.), Bhag.; feeling emotion, falling in love, Mālatīm.; inconstant, disloyal, rebellious (see *a-v°*); altered or changed for the worse, spoiled, corrupted, Suśr.; producing a change for the worse, corrupting (the mind), Hit.; m. n. the 33rd year in Jupiter's cycle of 60 years, VarBṛS.; °*ri-tā*, f. (Kām.), °*ri-tva*, n. (Vedântas.) change, alteration. °**kārya**, mfn. to be changed, liable to change, Bhag.; m. N. of Ahaṃ-kāra (the sense of individuality), BhP.

Vi-kurvaṇa, m. (prob. for *vi-kurvāṇa*) N. of Śiva, MBh. xiii, 1244; n. and (*ā*), f. the ability to assume various shapes, Buddh. °**kurvā**, f. id., ib. °**kurvāṇa**, mfn. undergoing a change, modifying one's self, Mn. i, 77; rejoicing, being glad, L. °**kurvita**, n. the assuming of various shapes, ib.

Ví-kṛita, mfn. transformed, altered, changed &c.; (esp.) deformed, disfigured, mutilated, maimed, unnatural, strange, extraordinary, Mn.; MBh. &c.; unaccomplished, incomplete, RV. ii, 33, 6; ugly (as a face), MBh.; estranged, rebellious, disloyal, hostile, ib.; decorated, embellished, set with (comp.), ib.; (with *vadha*, m.) capital punishment with mutilation, Mn. ix, 291; sick, diseased. L.; m. the 24th year in Jupiter's cycle of 60 years, VarBṛS.; N. of a Prajā-pati, R. (v.l. *vi-krīta* and *vi-krānta*); of a demon (the son of Pari-varta), MārkP.; (*ā*), f. N. of a Yoginī, Hcat.; n. change, alteration, Vop.; disgust, aversion, W.; misshaped offspring, abortion, Mn. ix, 247; untimely silence caused by embarrassment, Sāh. (v.l. *vi-hṛita*); *-janana-śānti-vidhāna*, n. N. of a ch. of the Padma-purāṇa; *-tva*, n. the state of being changed, transformation, Śaṃk.; *-daṇshṭra*, m. N. of a Vidyā-dhara, Kathās.; *-darśana*, mfn. changed in appearance, MBh.; R.; *-buddhi*, mfn. changed in mind, estranged, made unfriendly or ill-disposed, MW.; *-rakta*, mfn. dyed red, red-stained (as a garment), Bhpr.; *-locana*, mfn. having troubled eyes, MW.; *-vadana*, mfn. having a distorted face, ugly-faced, W.; *-veshin*, mfn. having an unusual dress, BhP.; °*tâkāra*, mfn. changed in form or appearance, misshaped, distorted in form, MBh.; °*tâkṛiti*, mfn. having a deformed shape or aspect, Mn. xi, 52; °*tâksha*, mfn. blind, Pāṇ. vi, 3, 3, Vārtt. 2, Pat.; °*tâṅga*, mfn. changed in form, having misshaped limbs, deformed, W.; °*tânana*, mfn. = °*ta-vadana* above, MBh.; *-mūrdhuja*, mfn. having a disturbed face and dishevelled hair, ib.; °*tôdara*, m. N. of a Rākshasa, R.

Ví-kṛiti, f. change, alteration, modification, variation, changed condition (of body or mind; acc. with *√gam*, *yā*, *vraj*, or *pra-√pad*, to undergo a change, be changed), MBh.; Kāv. &c.; sickness, disease, L.; perturbation, agitation, emotion, MBh.; Kathās. &c.; alienation, hostility, defection, Kām.; Pañcat.; a verse changed in a partic. manner, ŚBr.; KātyŚr.; an apparition, phantom, spectre, Kathās.; any production (ifc. anything made of), MBh.; Suśr.; (in Sāṃkhya) = 2. *vi-kāra*; (in gram.) a derivative, Nir.; formation, growth, development, AitBr.; abortion, Suśr. (v.l. *vaikṛita*); = *ḍimba*, L.; = *pralāpa*, Harav., Sch.; N. of a class of metres, Piṅg.; m. N. of a son of Jīmūta, VP.; *-kaumudī*, f., *-pradīpikā*, f. N. of wks.; *-mat*, mfn. liable to change, Śak.; indisposed, ill, Nalôd.; *-hautra*, n. N. of wk.

Vi-kriyā, f. transformation, change, modification, altered or unnatural condition, Kāv.; Pur.; Suśr.; change for the worse, deterioration, disfigurement, deformity, R.; ailment, indisposition, affection, R.;

Daś.; Suśr.; perturbation, agitation, perplexity, MBh.; Kāv. &c.; hostile feeling, rebellion, defection, alienation, Hariv.; Kāv.; Kathās.; injury, harm, failure, misadventure (acc. with *√yā*, to suffer injury, undergo failure), ib.; extinction (of a lamp), Kathās.; a strange or unwonted phenomenon, ib.; any product or preparation, Mn.; Yājñ.; MārkP.; contraction, knitting (of the brows; see *bhrū-v°*); bristling (of the hair; see *roma-v°*); °*yôpamā*, f. a kind of simile (in which the object of comparison is represented as produced from that to which it is compared, e.g. 'thy face, O fair one, seems to be cut out from the disc of the moon'), Kāvyâd. ii, 41.

विकृत् *vi-√2. kṛit*, P. *-kṛintati* (rarely *-kartati*), to cut into or through, divide by cutting, tear or rend asunder, RV.; AV.; ŚBr.; MBh.: Caus. *-kartayati*, id. (see *-kartita*).

Vi-karta, see *go-vikarta*. °**kartana**, mfn. cutting asunder, dividing, Nir.; m. the sun (prob. as the 'divider of clouds'), Uttarar.; Rājat.; a son who has usurped his father's kingdom, L.; n. the act of cutting asunder or dividing, L. °**kartita**, mfn. (fr. Caus.) cut or torn asunder, Pañcat. °**kartṛi**, see *go-vikarttṛi*.

Vi-kṛittikā, f. (perhaps w.r. for °*kṛintikā*) acute and violent pain in the limbs, Car. °**kṛintá**, m. one who cuts through or rends asunder, VS. (TS. *pra-kṛintá*).

विकृश् *vi-√kṛiś*, Caus. *-karśayati* (only p. p. *-karśita*), to emaciate, distort, deform, BhP.

विकृष् *vi-√kṛish*, P. *-karshati*, *-kṛishati* (°*te*), to draw apart or asunder, tear to pieces, destroy, TS.; ŚBr.; KātyŚr.; to bend (a bow), draw (a bow-string), MBh.; R.; to widen, extend, KātyŚr.; to draw along or after, MBh.; Kāv.; BhP.; to lead (an army), BhP.; to pull out, Bhartṛ.; Rājat.; to deprive, TS.; AitBr.; to withdraw, keep back, MBh.; (*-kṛishati*), to draw a furrow, plough, RV.; Lāṭy.

Vi-karsha, m. the drawing (a bow-string), R.; parting or dragging or drawing asunder (as in the separation of semivowel-combinations &c.), RPrāt.; Nid.; distance, Gobh.; Nir.; an arrow, L. °**karshaṇa**, mfn. drawing (a bow-string), MBh.; taking away, removing, destroying, BhP.; n. the act of drawing or dragging asunder, MBh.; Suśr.; the drawing (a bow-string), MBh.; Hariv.; Śiś.; putting apart, distributing, MBh.; BhP.; putting off eating, abstinence from food, MBh.; searching, investigation, Kām.; a cross-throw (in wrestling), MW.; m. 'distractor,' one of the five arrows of Kāma-deva, ib. °**karshin**, mfn. causing violent and acute pain in the limbs, Bhpr.; ear-distracting, shrill (as a sound), AV.Pariś.

Vi-kṛishṭa, mfn. drawn apart or asunder &c.; separated, isolated (as vowels), Prāt. (also *-kṛishita*); extended, protracted, long, R.; robbed, plundered, AitBr.; sounded, making a noise, W.; (*ā*), f. a partic. method of beating a drum, Saṃgīt.; *-kāla*, m. a long period, MW.; *-sīmânta*, mfn. (a village) having extended boundaries, R.

विकृ *vi-√kṛī*, P. *-kirati*, to scatter, throw or toss about, disperse, Mn.; MBh. &c.; to dishevel, BhP.; to pour out, utter, heave (sighs), Gīt.; to tear asunder, cleave, split, rend, burst, MuṇḍUp.; MBh. &c.; to scatter over, bestrew, cover, fill with (instr.), Mn.; MBh. &c.; to revile (?), MBh.

3. **Vi-kara**, m. (for 1. see p. 950, col. 1; for 2. p. 954, col. 2) an earth-pit, TS., Sch.; °*ryà*, mf(*â*)n. being in earth-pits, ib.

Vi-kira, m. scattering or anything scattered, L.; a scattered portion of rice (offered to conciliate beings hostile to sacrifice), Mn. iii, 245; 'scatterer,' a kind of gallinaceous bird, Āpast.; a partic. Agni, ib.; water trickled through, Suśr. (*cikira*, Bhpr.) °**kiraṇa**, n. scattering, strewing, Kull. on Mn. iii, 245; m. a partic. Samādhi, Buddh. (v.l. *vikiriṇa*). °**kīraṇa**, m. Calotropis Gigantea, L.

Vi-kīrṇa, mfn. scattered, thrown about, dispersed &c.; dishevelled (as hair), Kum. (cf. comp.); filled with, full of (comp.), MBh.; celebrated, famous, W.; n. a partic. fault in the pronunciation of vowels, Pat.; *-keśa* or *-mūrdhaja*, having dishevelled hair, MW. (cf. above); *-roman* or *-saṃjña*, n. a kind of fragrant plant, L.

विक्लृप् *vi-√klṛip*, Ā. *-kalpate*, to change or alternate, change with (instr.), AV.; MBh. &c.; to be undecided or questionable or optionable, Nyāyam.; Pañcat.; to be doubtful or irresolute, waver, hesitate, Hit.: Caus. *-kalpayati*, to prepare, arrange, contrive, form, fashion (in various ways), RV.; AV.; BhP.; to choose one of two alternatives, proceed eclectically, VarBṛS.; to call in question, prescribe variously, pronounce optional, Kāś.; Prab.; BhP.; to combine variously, vary, Car.; to state a dilemma, Śaṃk.; to consider with distrust (?), BhP.; to suppose, conjecture, imagine, presume, Kāv.; Pañcat.; to reflect upon, Bhaṭṭ.

2. **Vi-kalpa**, m. (for 1. see p. 950, col. 1) alternation, alternative, option, ŚrS.; Mn.; VarBṛS. &c. (*ena*, ind. 'optionally'); variation, combination, variety, diversity, manifoldness, KātyŚr.; MBh. &c.; contrivance, art, Ragh.; difference of perception, distinction, Nyāyas.; BhP.; indecision, irresolution, doubt, hesitation, MBh.; Kāv. &c.; admission, statement, BhP.; false notion, fancy, imagination, Yogas.; Gīt.; calculation, VarBṛS.; mental occupation, thinking, L.; = *kalpa-sthāna*, Car.; a god, BhP. (Sch.); (in rhet.) antithesis of opposites, Pratāp.; (in gram.) admission of an option or alternative, the allowing a rule to be observed or not at pleasure (*vêti vikalpaḥ*, Pāṇ. i, 1, 44, Sch.); a collateral form, VarBṛS.; pl. N. of a people, MBh. (C. *vikalya*); mfn. different, BhP.; *-jāla*, n. a number of possible cases, dilemma, Sarvad.; TPrāt., Sch.; *-tva*, n. manifoldness, variety, Suśr.; *-vat*, mfn. undecided, doubtful, Vedântas.; *-sama*, m. a partic. sophistical objection, Sarvad.; °*pânupapatti*, f. untenableness owing to a dilemma, Sarvad.; °*pâsaha*, mfn. not standing (the test of) a dilemma (*-tva*, n.), ib.; °*pôpahāra*, m. an optional offering, MW. °**kalpaka**, m. a distributer, apportioner, MBh.; a contriver, composer, Cat.; a transformer, changer, Car.; = 2. *vi-kalpa*, TejobUp. °**kalpana**, m. a contriver, composer, Cat.; n. and (*ā*), f. allowing an option or alternative, Pañcar.; Kār. on Pāṇ.; the use of a collateral form, VarBṛS., Sch.; distinction (pl. = different opinions), Sarvad.; false notion or assumption, fancy, imagination, BhP.; indecision, MW.; inconsideration, ib. °**kalpanīya**, mfn. to be calculated or ascertained, VarBṛS. °**kalpayitavya**, mfn. to be put as an alternative, Śaṃk. °**kalpita**, mfn. prepared, arranged &c.; divided, manifold (with *caturdaśa-dhā* = fourteenfold), BhP.; doubtful, undecided, ib.; Sarvad. (cf. *a-vikalpa*); optional (*-tva*, n.), Nyāyam.; Sāy. °**kalpin**, mfn. possessing doubt or indecision, liable to be mistaken for (comp.), Ṛitus.; versed in the Mīmāṇsā, Vas.; Baudh. °**kalpya**, mfn. to be distributed, VarBṛS.; to be calculated or ascertained, ib.; to be chosen according to circumstances, Car.

विकेतु *vi-ketu*, *vi-keśa* &c. See p. 950, col. 1.

विकोश *vi-kośa*, *vi-kautuka* &c. See ib.

विक्क *vikka*, m. an elephant twenty years old, L.

विक्त *vikta*. See under *√vic*, p. 958, col. 2.

विक्रम् *vi-√kram*, P. Ā. *-krāmati*, *-kramate* (cf. Pāṇ. i, 3, 41), to step beyond or aside, move away, depart from (abl.), RV.; AV.; ŚBr.; to move apart or asunder, become divided, RV.; AV.; TS.; to go or stride through, traverse, RV.; AV.; TBr.; to move on, walk, go, advance, RV. &c. &c.; to rise to (acc.), ŚBr.; MBh.; R.; to bestride, BhP.; to show valour or prowess, attack, assail, fight, MBh.; Kāv. &c.: Caus. *-kramayati*, to cause to step or stride over or through, KātyŚr.

2. **Vi-kramá**, m. (for 1. see p. 950, col. 1) a step, stride, pace, ŚBr. &c. &c.; going, proceeding, walking, motion, gait, MBh.; Kāś. &c.; course, way, manner (*anukrama-vikrameṇa* = *anukrameṇa*, in regular order), MBh.; valour, courage, heroism, power, strength, ib.; Kāv. &c. (°*maṃ √kṛi*, to display prowess, use one's strength); force, forcible means, ib. (°*māt*, ind. by force; *nâsti vikrameṇa*, it cannot be done by force); intensity, high degree, VarBṛS.; stability, duration (opp. to 'cessation'), BhP.; a kind of grave accent, TPrāt.; non-change of the Visarga into an Ūshman, RPrāt.; the 14th year in the 60 years cycle of Jupiter, VarBṛS.; the 3rd astrological house, ib.; a foot, L.; N. of Vishṇu, MBh.; of the son of Vasu, Kathās.; of a son of Vatsa-prī, MārkP.; of a son of Kanaka, Cat.; of various authors (also with *bhaṭṭa*), Cat.; = *candra-gupta*, ib.; = *vikramâditya*, Pañcad.; N. of a town, Cat.; *-karman*, n. an act of prowess, feat of valour, MW.; *-kesarin*, m. N. of a king of Pāṭali-putra, Kathās.; of a minister of Mṛigâṅka-datta, ib.; *-caṇḍa*, m. N. of a king of Vārāṇasī, ib.; *-candrikā*, f. N. of a drama; *-carita* or *-caritra*, n. N. of 32 stories describing the acts of Vikramâditya (also called *siṇhâsana-dvātriṇśat*, q.v.); *-tuṅga*, m. N. of a prince of Pāṭali-putra, Kathās.; of a prince of Vikrama-pura, ib.; *-deva*, m. N. of Candra-gupta, Inscr.; *-narêśvara*, m. = *vikramâditya*, Siṇhâs.; *-nava-ratna*, n. 'the 9 jewels (on the court) of Vikramâditya,' N. of wk.; *-nidhi*, m. N. of a warrior, Kathās.; *-paṭṭana*, n. 'V°'s town,' N. of Ujjayinī, Cat.; *-pati*, m. = *vikramâditya*, Cāṇ.; *-pura*, n. (Kathās.), *-purī*, f. (Buddh.) N. of a town (prob. = *-paṭṭana*); *-prabandha*, m. N. of wk.; *-bāhu*, m. N. of various princes, Ratnâv.; Cat.; *-bhārata*, a modern collection of legends about Vikramâditya and of Pauranic stories; *-rāja*, m. N. of a king, Rājat.; *-rājan*, m. = *vikramâditya*, Vcar.; *-rddhi* (for *ṛiddhi*), m. (with *kavi*) N. of a poet, Cat.; *-lāñchana*, m. id., ib.; *-śakti*, m. N. of various men of the warrior-caste, Kathās.; *-śīla*, m. N. of a king, MārkP.; of a monastery, Buddh.; *-sabhā*, f. V°'s court, Siṇhâs.; *-siṇha*, m. N. of a king of Ujjayinī, MārkP.; of a king of Ujjayinī, ib.; *-sena*, m. N. of a k° of Pratishṭhāna, Kathās. (°*na-campū*, f. N. of a poem); *-sthāna*, n. a walking-place, promenade, Kṛishṇaj.; °*mâṅka* (or *-deva*), m. N. of a king of Kalyāṇa (also called Tribhuvana-malla; of the 11th century A.D. and was celebrated by Bilhaṇa in the Vikramâṅka-deva-carita); °*mâditya*, m., see below; °*mârka*, m. = *vikramâditya* (*-carita*, *-caritra*, n. = *vikrama-c*); °*mârjita*, mfn. acquired by valour, W.; °*mêśa*, m. N. of a Buddhist saint, W.; °*mêśvara*, m. (with Buddh.) N. of one of the 8 Vita-rāgas, W.; of a temple built by Vikramâditya, Rājat.; °*môdaya*, n. N. of wk.; °*môpâkhyāna*, n. = *vikrama-carita*; °*môrvaśī*, f. 'valour-(won) Urvaśī,' N. of a celebrated drama by Kālidāsa. °**kramaka**, m. N. of one of Skanda's attendants, MBh. °**krámaṇa**, n. striding, a step, pace, stride (esp. of Vishṇu), RV. &c. &c.; bold advance, courage, heroism, strength, power, MBh.; (with Pāśupatas) supernatural power (*-dharmi-tva*, n. the being possessed of the above power), Sarvad.; the conforming to the rules of the Krama-pāṭha (q.v.), RPrāt. °**kramin**, mfn. striding (said of Vishṇu), MBh.; displaying valour, courageous, gallant, MBh.; Hariv.; m. a lion, L. °**kramīya**, N. of a Comm. on the Anangha-rāghava.

Vikramâditya, m. 'valour-sun,' N. of a celebrated Hindū king (of Ujjayinī and supposed founder of the [Mālava-] Vikrama era [cf. *saṃvat*], which begins 58 B.C. [but subtract 57–56 from an *expired* year of the V° era to convert it into A.D.]; he is said to have driven out the Śakas and to have reigned over almost the whole of Northern India; he is represented as a great patron of literature; nine celebrated men are said to have flourished at his court [see *nava-ratna*], and innumerable legends are related of him all teeming with exaggerations; according to some he fell in a battle with his rival Śāli-vāhana, king of the south country or Deccan, and the legendary date given for his death is Kali-yuga 3044 [which really is the epoch-year of the Vikrama era]; there are, however, other kings called Vikramâditya, and the name has been applied to king Bhoja and even to Śāli-vāhana), Inscr.; Kathās.; Vet. &c.; of a poet, Cat. (*-kośa*, m. N. of a dictionary; *-caritra*, n. N. of a poem = *vikrama-c°*; *-rāja*, m. N. of a king).

Ví-krānta, mfn. stepped beyond, taking wide strides &c.; courageous, bold, strong, mighty, victorious (with *dhanushi*, skilled in archery), MBh.; m. a warrior, L.; a lion, L.; 'passed over,' N. of a kind of Saṃdhi which leaves Visarga unchanged, RPrāt.; N. of a Prajā-pati, VP.; of a son of Kuvalayâśva and Madâlasā, MārkP.; (*ā*), f. N. of various plants (Cocculus Cordifolius, Clitoria Ternatea, Cissus Pedata &c.), L.; n. a step, stride, VS.; TBr.; manner of walking, gait, MBh.; R.; bold advance, courage, might, ib.; a sham diamond, L.; a kind of intoxicating drink, L.; *-gati*, m. a man with a portly gait, MW.; *-bhīma*, N. of a drama; *-yodhin*, m. an excellent warrior, MBh.; *-śūdraka*, N. of a drama, Sarasv.

Ví-krānti, f. stepping or striding through, striding everywhere i.e. all-pervading power, TS.; TBr.; ŚBr.; a horse's gallop, L.; heroism, prowess, courage, strength, might, Rājat.; *-varman*, m. (with *lubdhaka*) N. of a poet, Cat. (cf. *viśrānti-v°*). °**krāntṛi**, m. 'valiant,' a hero, W. °**krāmá**, m. a step's width, TBr.

Vi-cakramāṇa, mfn. (fr. Intens.) striding, traversing, MW.

विक्रय *vi-kraya* &c. See below.

विक्रस्र *vikrasra.* See *vikusra.*

विक्रान्त *vi-krānta* &c. See p. 955, col. 3.

विक्रिड *vikriḍa,* mfn. (applied to Rudra), MaitrS.

विक्रिया *vi-kriyā* &c. See p. 954, col. 3.

विक्री *vi-√krī,* Ā. *-krīṇīte* (Pāṇ. i, 3, 18), to buy and sell, barter, trade, VS.; AV.; to sell, vend, sell or exchange for (instr.), Mn.; MBh. &c.: Desid. *-cikrīshate,* to wish to sell, desire to exchange for (instr.), Daś.

Vi-krayá, m. sale, selling, vending, AV. &c. &c.; *-pattra,* n. a bill of sale, Rājat.; °*yânuśaya,* m. rescission of sale, Mn. viii, 5; °*yârtham,* ind. for sale, MW. °**krayaka,** m. a seller, MBh. (B. °*krayika*). °**krayaṇa,** n. the act of selling, Campak. °**krayika,** see °*krayaka.* °**krayin,** m. a seller, vender, Yājñ.; MBh. &c. °**krayya,** mfn. to be sold, MBh. °**krāyika,** m. a seller, L. °**krīta,** mfn. sold, Mn.; MBh. &c.; m. N. of a Prajā-pati, R. (v. l. *vi-krita* and *vi-krānta*); n. sale, Mn. viii, 165.

Vi-kretavya, mfn. to be sold, saleable, Campak.; Kull. °**kretṛi,** m. a seller, Yājñ.; Hariv. &c. °**kreya,** mfn. to be sold, vendible, Mn.; MBh. &c.; (prob.) n. selling price, Yājñ. ii, 246.

विक्रीड् *vi-√krīḍ,* P. *-krīḍati,* to play, jest, sport with (*saha*), MBh.; R.; Pur. °**krīḍa,** m. a play-ground, Hariv.; a plaything, toy, HPariś.; (*ā*), f. play, sport, BhP. °**krīḍita,** mfn. played, played with, made a plaything of, BhP.; n. play, sport, SaddhP.; a child's play (i. e. 'easy work'), Lalit.

विक्रुश् *vi-√kruś,* P. *-krośati* (ep. also °*te*), to cry out, exclaim, Mn.; MBh. &c.; to raise or utter (a cry), MBh.; R.; to call to, invoke (acc.), ib.; to sound, R.; to revile, MW. °**krushṭa,** mfn. called out &c.; harsh, abusive, cruel (as speech), W.; ifc. offensive to (e. g. *loka-v*°, offensive to men), Mn. iv, 176; n. a cry of alarm or help, Yājñ.; R.; abasing, reviling, L. °**krośa,** m. a cry of alarm or help, MBh.

Vi-krośana, m. N. a mythical being, Suparṇ.; of a king, Kathās.; n. the act of calling out, W.; abasing, reviling, ib. °**krośayitṛi,** m. a word used to explain *kuśika,* Nir. ii, 25. °**kroshṭṛi,** m. one who calls out or cries for help, Yājñ. ii, 234; a reviler, W.

विक्लम् *vi-√klam* (only in pf. *-caklame*), to become faint or weak, despond, despair, Śiś. xv, 127. °**klānta,** mfn. dispirited, fatigued, wearied, MW.

विक्लव् *vi-√klav,* Ā. *-klavate,* to become agitated or confused, Dhātup. xxxv, 84. °**klava,** mf(*ā*)n. overcome with fear or agitation, confused, perplexed, bewildered, alarmed, distressed, MBh.; Kāv. &c.; timid, shy, Megh.; Śiś.; (ifc.) disgusted with, averse from, Śak.; faltering (as speech), R.; unsteady (as gait), Śak.; impaired (as senses), Kāśīkh.; exhausted, Kathās.; n. agitation, bewilderment, R.; BhP.; *-tā,* f., *-tva,* n. agitation, confusion, alarm, fear, timidity, irresolution, MBh.; Kāv. &c.; °*vadana,* mfn. one whose face is troubled or sorrowful, R. °**klavaya,** Nom. P. °*yati,* to render despondent, depress, Bālar. °**klavita,** n. timid or despondent language, BhP.

Vi-klavī, in comp. for *viklava* (g. *ūry-ādi*). **-√kṛi,** P. *-karoti,* to depress, trouble, Vās. **-√bhū,** P. *-bhavati,* to grow despondent, despair, Kād.

विक्लित्ति *vi-klitti,* f. (√*klid*) becoming soft or moist, Car. °**klidhá,** mfn. moist with perspiration (others 'having projecting teeth' or 'leprous'), Br.; ŚrS. (Sch.)

Vi-klíndu, m. a kind of disease, AV.

Vi-klinna, mfn. softened (by cooking), L.; dissolved, decayed, MBh.; *-hṛidaya,* mfn. soft-hearted, one whose heart is easily moved with pity, MW.

Vi-kleda, m. getting wet, MBh.; R.; wetness, moisture, Suśr.; dissolution, decay, BhP. °**kledana,** n. the act of softening (by cooking or boiling), Nyāyam., Sch. °**kledīyas** (*ví-*), mfn. moistening more, AV.

विक्लिष्ट *vi-klishṭa,* mfn. (√*kliś*) hurt, harassed, destroyed, R.; n. a partic. fault in pronunciation, RPrāt. (prob. = next).

Vi-kleśa, m. 'indistinctness,' incorrect pronunciation of the dentals, ib.

विक्ली *viklī,* ind. (with √*kṛi, bhū,* or *as*), Gaṇar.

विक्षणम् *vi-kshaṇam.* See p. 950, col. 1.

विक्षत *vi-kshata,* mfn. (√*kshan* or *kshaṇ*) hurt severely, wounded, MBh.; n. a wound, ib.

विक्षय *vi-kshaya.* See under *vi-√4. kshi.*

विक्षर् *vi-√kshar,* P. *-ksharati,* to flow away or into, ŚBr.; ChUp.; MBh. °**kshará,** mf(*ā*)n. pouring out, Hariv.; m. effluence, AV.; N. of Vishṇu-Kṛishṇa, MBh.; of an Asura, ib. °**ksharaṇa,** n. flowing out, Daś. °**ksharā́,** m. a lucky hit, TBr. (Sch.)

विक्षा *vi-kshā,* f., g. *chattrâdi.*

विक्षाम *vi-kshāma,* mfn. (√*kshai*) burnt (as a cake), AV. Prâyaśc.; n. 'what has burnt out,' a dead coal, ŚāṅkhŚr.

विक्षालित *vi-kshālita,* mfn. (√2. *kshal*), washed off, bathed, Ragh.

विक्षाव *vi-kshāva,* m. (√*kshu*) sneezing, cough, L.; a sound, cry (pl.), Bhaṭṭ.

विक्षि *vi-√4. kshi,* P. *-kshiṇāti* (inf. *-kshetas,* TaṇḍBr.), to hurt, harm, waste, ruin, destroy, ŚBr.: Desid. *-cikshīshati,* to wish to hurt &c., ib.

Vi-kshaya, m. a partic. disease of drunkards, Car.

Vi-kshiṇatká, mfn. destroying (evil), VS. (Mahīdh.) °**kshita,** mfn. brought down, wretched, miserable, R. °**kshīṇa,** mfn. diminished, destroyed (*á-v*°), ŚBr. °**kshīṇaká,** v. l. for °*kshiṇatká;* m. 'destroyer,' N. of the chief of a class of demigods attendant on Śiva (described as causing destruction by pestilential diseases &c.), W.; a meeting or assembly of the gods, ib.; a place prohibited to eaters of meat, ib.

विक्षिप् *vi-√kship,* P. Ā. *-kshipati,* °*te,* to throw asunder or away or about, cast hither and thither, scatter, disperse, MBh.; Kāv. &c.; to remove, destroy (pain), Suśr.; to extend, stretch out, ib.; to bend (a bow), draw (a bow-string), MBh.; R.; to handle, manage, Kāś. on Pāṇ. ii, 3, 57; to separate, Sūryas.; to cause to deviate in latitude, ib.

Vi-kshipta, mfn. thrown asunder or away or about, scattered &c.; distorted, contracted (see comp.); agitated, bewildered, distraught, Sarvad.; frustrated (see *a-v*°); sent, dispatched, W.; refuted, falsified, ib.; projected, MW. (see *vi-kshepa*); n. the being dispersed in different places, RPrāt., Sch.; *-citta,* mfn. distraught in mind, Madhus.; *-bhrū,* mfn. having contracted eyebrows, BhP.; °*tendriya-dhī,* mfn. bewildered in senses and mind, BhP. °**kshiptaka,** n. a dead body which has been torn asunder or lacerated, Buddh.

Vi-kshepa, m. the act of throwing asunder or away or about, scattering, dispersion, MārkP.; Dhātup.; casting, throwing, discharging, Ragh.; VP.; moving about or to and fro, waving, shaking, tossing, MBh.; Kāv. &c.; drawing (a bow-string), Hariv.; letting loose, indulging (opp. to *saṃyama*), BhP.; letting slip, neglecting (time), L.; inattention, distraction, confusion, perplexity, MaitrUp.; Yogas.; Mālatīm.; extension, projection, Vedântas. (see *-śakti*); abusing, reviling, Bhar.; compassion, pity, Daśar.; celestial or polar latitude, Sūryas.; a kind of weapon, MBh. (Nīlak.); a camp, cantonment (?), Buddh.; a kind of disease, Cat.; sending, dispatching, W.; refuting an argument, ib.; *-dhruva,* m. (in astron.) the greatest inclination of a planet's orbit, W.; *-lipi,* m. a kind of writing, Lalit.; *-vṛitta,* n. = *kshepa-v*°, Gol.; *-śakti,* f. (in phil.) the projecting power (of Māyā or A-vidyā, i.e. that power of projection which raises upon the soul enveloped by it the appearance of an external world), Vedântas. (°*ti-mat,* mfn. endowed with the above power, ib.); °*pâdhipati,* m. the chief of a camp or cantonment (?), Buddh. °**kshepaṇa,** n. the act of throwing asunder or away &c.; moving to and fro, tossing about, Kuval.; Suśr.; confusion proceeding from error, Vedântas. (v. l. for *vi-kshepa*). °**kshepam,** ind. carrying to and fro, tossing, shaking (acc. or comp.), Pāṇ. iii, 4, 54, Sch. °**ksheptṛi,** m. a scatterer, disperser, MBh.

विक्षुण्ण *vi-kshuṇṇa,* mfn. (√*kshud*) trodden, pounded, Devīm.; (ifc.) urged on, actuated by, Pañcat.

विक्षुद्र *vi-kshudra.* See p. 950, col. 1.

विक्षुध् *vi-√kshudh,* P. *-kshudhyati,* to be hungry, TBr.

विक्षुभ् *vi-√kshubh,* Ā. *-kshobhate* &c. (Ved. inf. *vi-kshobdhos,* ŚBr.), to be shaken about or agitated or disturbed, AV.; BhP.; to confuse, disturb, ŚBr.: Caus. *-kshobhayati,* to agitate, disturb, throw into disorder or confusion, MBh.; R.; Suśr.

Vi-kshubdha, mfn. disturbed (see *á-v*°).

Vi-kshobha, m. shaking, agitation, motion, Hariv.; Ragh.; mental agitation, perturbation, distraction, alarm, MBh.; Kāv. &c. (cf. *á-v*°); tearing open or asunder, Śiś.; the side of an elephant's breast, L. °**kshobhaṇa,** m. N. of a Dānava, Hariv.; n. tossing about, violent motion, Buddh. °**kshobhita,** mfn. (fr. Caus.) shaken, tossed about, agitated, MBh. °**kshobhin,** mfn. agitating, disturbing (see *raksho-vikshobhiṇī*).

विख *vikha,* mfn. (prob. *vi-kha,* also *vikhu* and *vikhra*), noseless, L.

विखण्डित *vi-khaṇḍita,* mfn. (√*khaṇḍ*) cut into pieces, divided, lacerated, Pañcat.; BhP.; torn asunder, cleft in two, VarBṛS.; disturbed, interrupted, Pur.; refuted, W. °**khaṇḍin,** mfn. breaking, removing, destroying (enmity), Cat.

विखन् *vi-√khan,* P. *-khanati,* to dig up, AV. °**khanana,** n. digging up, Nir. °**khānasa,** m. (prob.) 'one who digs up (scil. roots),' N. of a Muni, Śak., Sch. (cf. *vaikhānasa*).

विखनस् *vikhanas,* m. N. of Brahmā, BhP.; of a Muni (cf. *vi-khānasa*).

विखाद *vi-khādá,* m. (√*khād*) devouring, destroying, RV. x, 38, 4 (= *saṃgrāma,* Naigh. ii, 17). °**khāditaka,** n. a dead body which has been devoured by animals, Buddh.

विखासा *vikhāsā,* f. the tongue, W.

विखिद् *vi-√khid,* P. *-khidati,* to tear asunder, rend apart, ŚāṅkhBr.

विखुर *vi-khura, vi-kheda.* See p. 950.

विख्या *vi-√khyā,* P. *-khyāti* (Ved. inf. *vi-khye,* Pāṇ. iii, 4, 11; *vi-khyai,* RV. x, 158, 4), to look about, look at, view, see, behold, RV.; ŚBr.; to shine, shine upon, lighten, illumine, RV.; AV.: Caus. *-khyāpayati,* to show, make visible, ŚBr.; to make known, announce, proclaim, declare, Mn.; MBh. °**khyāta,** mfn. generally known, notorious, famous, celebrated, Yājñ.; R. &c.; known as, called, named, MBh.; R.; Hit.; avowed, confessed, W. °**khyāti,** f. fame, celebrity, renown, R. °**khyāpana,** n. making known, announcing, publishing, Gaut.; explanation, exposition, W.; avowing, acknowledging, confessing, MW.

विख्रु *vikhra* or *vikhru.* See *vikha* above.

विगण् *vi-√gaṇ,* P. *-gaṇayati* (ind. p. *-gaṇayya*), to reckon, compute, calculate (Pass. to be reckoned i. e. amount to), Yājñ.; R.; to deliberate, consider, ponder, MBh.; Kāv. &c.; to regard as, take for (with double acc.), Ragh.; Kathās.; to esteem, regard (*a-vigaṇayya,* 'not taking notice of'), Kād.; BhP.; to disregard, take no notice of, Pañcat.; BhP. °**gaṇana,** n. paying off, discharge (of a debt), Pāṇ. i, 3, 36; reckoning, computing, W.; considering, deliberating, ib. °**gaṇita,** mfn. reckoned, calculated, W.; considered, weighed, ib.; reckoned off, discharged (as a debt), ib.

विगद 2. *vi-gadá,* m. (√*gad;* for 1. see p. 950, col. 2) talking or sounding variously, confused shouting, RV. x, 116, 5. °**gadita,** mfn. talked or spoken about, spread abroad (as a report), R.

विगम् *vi-√gam,* P. *-gacchati,* to go asunder, sever, separate, AV.; MBh.; to go away, depart, disappear, cease, die, AV. &c. &c.: Caus. *-gamayati,* to cause to go or pass away, speed (time), Śak.

2. **Vi-gata,** mfn. (for 1. see under 1. *vi*) gone asunder, dispersed, MBh.; gone away, departed, disappeared, ceased, gone (often ibc.), AV. &c. &c.; dead, deceased, Mn. v, 75; (ifc.) abstaining or desisting from, R.; come from (cf. *vidūra-vigata*), destitute of light, obscured, gloomy, dark, L.; (*ā*), f. a girl in love with another or unfit for marriage, L.;

-kalmasha, mfn. free from stain or soil or sin, sinless, pure, righteous, R.; *-klama*, mfn. one whose fatigues have ceased, relieved from fatigue, Mn. vii, 151; *-jñāna*, mfn. one who has lost his wits, MW.; *-jvara*, mfn. cured of fever, freed from feverishness or morbid feeling, freed from trouble or distress of mind, Nal.; exempt from decay, W.; *-tva*, n. the having disappeared, disappearance, TPrāt., Sch.; *-dvaṃdva*, m. 'free from pairs of opposites,' a Buddha (cf. *dvaṃdva*), L.; *-nayana*, mfn. eyeless, blind, Pañcat.; *-nāsika*, mf(*ī*)n. noseless, L.; *-puṉska*, mfn. castrated, ĀpŚr., Sch.; *-bhaya*, m. 'free from fear,' N. of a Brāhman, Kathās.; *-bhī*, mfn. fearless, MW.; *-manyu*, mfn. free from resentment, ib.; *-rāga*, mfn. devoid of passion or affection, MW. (*-dhvaja*, m. N. of a preceptor, Buddh.); *-lakshaṇa*, mf(*ā*)n. 'devoid of good or lucky marks,' unfortunate, Kathās.; *-śrīka*, mfn. destitute of fortune or splendour, unfortunate, Yājñ.; MBh.; *-saṃkalpa*, mfn. devoid of purpose or design, without resolution, Nal.; *-saṃtrāsa*, mfn. free from terror, intrepid, MBh.; *-sneha*, mfn. void of affection (*-sauhṛida*, mfn. one who has relinquished love and friendship), MBh.; *-spṛiha*, mfn. devoid of wish or desire, indifferent, W.; °*tārtavā*, f. a woman in whom the menstrual excretion has ceased, L.; °*tāśoka*, m. N. of a younger brother or a grandson of Aśoka, Buddh.; °*tāsu*, mfn. lifeless, dead, MBh.; °*tôddhava*, m. 'free from levity,' N. of Buddha, Divyâv.

Vi-gama, m. going away, departure, cessation, end, absence, Kāv.; Var. &c.; (ifc.) abstention from, avoidance, Yājñ.; *-candra*, m. N. of a prince, Buddh.

विगर्ज् *vi-√garj*, P. *-garjati*, to roar out, cry out, MBh. °**garjā**, f. pl. the roaring or thundering (of the ocean), Kāv.

विगर्ह् *vi-√garh*, Ā. *-garhate* (rarely °*ti*), to blame, abuse, revile, reproach, despise, contemn, Mn.; MBh. &c.: Caus. *-garhayati*, to revile, rail at, vituperate, MW. °**garha**, m., g. *pushkarâdi*. °**garhaṇa**, n. and (*ā*), f. the act of blaming, censure, reproach (°*naṃ √kṛi*, to blame), MBh.; R. °**garhaṇīya**, mfn. reprehensible, bad, wicked, Jātakam. °**garhā**, f. blame, censure, ib. °**garhita**, mfn. blamed, reprehensible, prohibited, forbidden by (instr., gen., or comp.) or on account of (comp.), Mn.; MBh. &c.; °*tâcāra*, mfn. of reprehensible conduct, Mn. iii, 167. °**garhin**, mfn. (ifc.) blaming, Hariv.; (*iṇī*), f. a place abounding in Vi-garha, g. *pushkarâdi*. °**garhya**, mfn. censurable, reprehensible, Mn.; BhP.; *-kathā*, f. reprehensible speech, censure, MW.; *-tā*, f. blame, reproach, censure (*-tām pra-√yā*, to incur censure), Rājat.

विगल् *vi-gal*, P. *-galati*, to flow or ooze away, drain off, dry up, melt or pass away, fall out or down, disappear, vanish, MBh.; Kāv. &c. °**galita**, mfn. flowed away, drained off, dried up, MBh.; Mṛicch.; Prab.; melted away, dissolved, Kathās.; Gīt.; fallen down or out, slipped out of (abl.), MBh.; Kāv.; Pañcat.; slackened, untied (see *-nīvi*); dishevelled (see *-keśa*); passed away, disappeared, vanished, Bhartṛ.; Kathās.; come forth, MBh.; *-keśa*, mfn. having dishevelled hair, W.; *-nīvi*, mfn. having the knot untied, MW.; *-bandha*, mfn. having the band loosened, Vikr.; *-lajja*, mfn. free from shame, bold, Gīt.; *-vasana*, mfn. destitute of garments, unclothed, ib.; *-śuc*, mfn. freed from sorrow, Megh.

विगा *vi-√gā* (only aor. *-gāt*), to go or pass away, disappear, PārGṛ.

Vi-gāman, n. a step, pace, stride (applied to the three strides of Vishṇu), RV. i, 155, 4.

विगान *vi-gāna*. See under *vi-√gai*.

विगाह् *vi-√gāh*, Ā. *-gāhate* (ep. also °*ti*), to plunge or dive into, bathe in, enter, penetrate, pervade, betake one's self into (acc. or loc.), RV. &c. &c.; to pierce, AV.; to agitate, disturb, Ragh.; to be engrossed by or intent upon, ponder, BhP.; to follow, practise, Kum.; to reach, obtain, Bhartṛ.; to approach, fall (as night), MBh.: Pass. *-gāhyate*, to be plunged into or penetrated, to be entered into or engaged upon, Kāv.; Pañcat. °**gāḍha**, mfn. plunged into, entered, R. (*ambhasi vigāḍha-mātre*, 'at the very moment of the water being plunged into'), one who has entered or plunged into, bathing in (loc.), ib.; (a weapon) that has deeply penetrated, MBh.; come on, advanced, begun, set in, taken place, MBh.; R. &c.; flowing copiously, W.; deep, excessive, ib.; *-manmatha*, mfn. one whose passion has become deep or ardent, Ragh. °**gāḍhṛi**, mfn. one who plunges or penetrates into (gen.), Bhaṭṭ.; one who agitates or disturbs, MW. °**gāhá**, mfn. one who plunges into or penetrates (said of Agni), RV. iii, 3, 5 (cf. *dur-vigāha*). °**gāhya**, mfn. to be plunged into or entered (as the Ganges), MBh.

विगुण *vi-guṇa* &c. See p. 950, col. 2.

विगुप् *vi-√2. gup*, Desid. *-jugupsate*, to shrink away from, wish to conceal from, ŚBr.; KaṭhUp. °**gopa**, m. exposure, commitment, HPariś.

विगुल्फ *vi-gulpha*, mfn. (cf. *vi-phalka*) abundant, plentiful, GṛŚrS.

विगूढ *vi-gūḍha*, mfn. (*√guh*) concealed, hidden, BhP.; blamed, censured, L.; *-cārin*, mfn. proceeding or acting secretly, Mn. ix, 260.

विगॄ *vi-√1. gṛī* (only *-gṛiṇīshe* in a very obscure passage, RV. vi, 35, 5, where others read *-vriṇīshe*).

विगै *vi-√gai*, P. *-gāyati* (only Pass. *-gīyate*), to decry, abuse, reproach, Naish.

Vi-gāna, n. inconsistency, contradiction, Śaṃk.; repugnance, Naish.; ill-report, detraction, L.

Vi-gīta, mfn. inconsistent, contradictory, Mn. viii, 53 (*-tva*, n., Śaṃk.); abused, reproached, W.; sung or said in various ways, ib.; sung badly, ib.

विग्न *vigna, vigra*. See under *√vij*.

विग्रथ् *vi-√1. grath* (or *granth*), P. *-grathnāti*, to connect, tie or bind together, wind round, ŚBr.; GṛŚrS. °**grathita** (*vi-*), mfn. tied together, ŚBr.; bound up (as a wound), Suśr.; having knots or tubercles, ib.; hindered, impeded, ib.

विग्रह् *vi-√grah*, P. Ā. *-gṛihṇāti*, °*ṇīte* (Ved. also *-gṛibhṇāti*, °*ṇīte*), to stretch out or apart, spread out, AV.; to distribute, divide (esp. to draw out fluids at several times), RV.; ŚBr.; TBr.; KātyŚr.; to hold apart, separate, isolate, ŚrS.; (in gram.) to analyse (cf. *vi-graha*); to wage war, fight against (acc.), MBh.; to quarrel, contend with (instr. with or without *saha* or *sârdham*), MBh.; Kāv. &c.; to seize, lay hold of (acc. or loc.), MBh.; Mṛicch.; to receive in a friendly manner, welcome, MBh.; to perceive, observe, BhP.: Caus. *-grāhayati*, to cause to fight, cause to wage war against, Daś.; Bhaṭṭ.: Desid. *-jighṛikshati*, to wish to fight against, Bhaṭṭ.

Vi-gṛihīta, mfn. stretched out or apart &c.; changed, BhP. 1. °**gṛihya**, ind. having stretched out or apart &c.; having warred against or contended with, aggressive, inimical (see comp.); *-gamana* or *-yāna*, n. aggressive movement, hostile advance, Daś.; *-vāda*, m. word-fight, discussion, disputation, Gaut.; *-sambhāshā*, f., id., Car.; °*hyâsana*, n. 'besieging' or 'sulkily encamping with' (instr.), Daś. 2. °**gṛihya**, mfn. to be (or being) separated or isolated, independent (in the Pada-pāṭha), APrāt.

2. **Vi-graha**, m. (for 1. see p. 950, col. 2) keeping apart or asunder, isolation, Nir.; BhP.; division, Bh.; distribution (esp. of fluids, cf. *vi-√grah*), KātyŚr.; (in gram.) independence (of a word, as opp. to composition), APrāt.; separation, resolution, analysis, resolution of a compound word into its constituent parts, the separation or analysis of any word capable of separation (such words are Kṛidantas, Taddhitas, all Samāsas or compound words, Ekaśeshas, and all derivative verbs like desideratives &c.; the only words incapable of resolution being the simple verb, the singular of the noun, and a few indeclinables not derived from roots; all compounds being called *nitya* or 'fixed,' when their meaning cannot be ascertained through an analysis of their component parts; cf. *jamad-agni*), Pāṇ., Sch.; Śaṃk. &c.; discord, quarrel, contest, strife, war with (instr. with or without *saha, sârdham* or *sākam*, loc., gen. with *upari*, or comp.), Mn.; MBh. &c.; (one of the 6 Guṇas or measures of policy, Mn. vii, 160 [cf. under *guṇa*], also applied to the conflict of hostile planets, in this sense also n., Sūryas.; R.; acc. with *√kṛi*, to make or wage war); separate i. e. individual form or shape, form, figure, the body, Up.; MBh. &c. (also applied to the shape of a rainbow; acc. with *√grah, pari-√grah, √kṛi, upâ-√dā*, to assume a form); an ornament, decoration, MBh.; R.; (in Sāṃkhya) an element; N. of Śiva, MBh.; of one of Skanda's attendants, ib.; *-grahaṇa*, n. the assumption of a form, Sarvad.; *-dhyāna*, n. N. of a Stotra; *-para*, mfn. intent on war, engaged in fighting, MW.; *-parigraha*, m. = *-grahaṇa*, Sarvad.; *-pāla-deva*, m. N. of a king, Col.; *-rāja*, m. N. of various kings, Rājat.; of a poet, Cat.; *-vat*, mfn. having form or figure, embodied, incarnate, MBh.; R. &c.; having a handsome form or shape, fine, beautiful, MW.; *-vyāvartanī*, f. N. of wk.; °*hâvara*, n. 'hinder part of the body,' the back, L.; °*hêcchu*, mfn. eager for combat, Mcar. °**gráhaṇa**, n. diffusion, distribution, TS.; TāṇḍBr.; taking hold of, seizure, MBh. °**grahaya**, Nom. P. °*yati*, to contend or fight with (*sârdham*), Hit. °**grahin**, mfn. waging war, Kām.; a minister of war, R.

Vi-grāha, m. a partic. kind of recitation, ĀśvŚr., Sch. °**grāham**, ind. in portions, successively, ĀśvŚr. °**grāhita**, mfn. 'taken hold of,' prejudiced, Divyâv. °**grāhya**, mfn. to be warred upon or contended with, Hit.

Vi-jigrāhayishu, mfn. (fr. Desid. of Caus.) to cause to fight or wage war, Bhaṭṭ. °**jighṛikshu**, mfn. (fr. Desid.) wishing to make war or fight, Rājat.

विग्लै *vi-√glai*, Caus. *-glāpayati*, to weary, distress, afflict, BhP. °**glāpana**, n. weariness, fatigue, ŚBr.

विघट् *vi-√ghaṭ* (often confounded with *vi-√ghaṭṭ*), Ā. *-ghaṭate*, to go or fly apart, become separate, disperse, Kāv.; to be broken or interrupted or marred or frustrated or destroyed, Rājat.; Hit.: Caus. *-ghaṭayati*, to tear or rend asunder, separate, disperse, Prab.; Hit.; to mar, frustrate, annihilate, destroy, Mṛicch.; Rājat. °**ghaṭana**, n. breaking up, separation, dispersion, destruction, ruin, Prab.; Sāh. °**ghaṭita**, mfn. broken, separated, divided, severed, Rājat.; Prab.

विघट्ट् *vi-√ghaṭṭ* (cf. *vi-√ghaṭ*), Ā. *-ghaṭṭate*, to smash or break to pieces, Prasannar.; P. *-ghaṭṭayati*, to strike or force asunder, open (a door), sever, disperse, MBh.; Kāv. &c.; to shake, stir, rub against, ib.; Suśr. °**ghaṭṭana**, mfn. opening, Hariv.; (*ā*), f. striking against, Śiś.; rubbing, friction, Bālar.; separation, Nalôd; n. rubbing, friction, Śiś.; moving to and fro, stirring, shaking (also pl.), Bālar.; Suśr.; striking against, Śiś.; striking asunder, forcing apart, hewing in pieces, Inscr.; Vcar.; Kād.; loosening, untying, Ragh. °**ghaṭṭanīya**, mfn. to be shaken or broken (*manaḥ°nīyam*, 'one should rack or cudgel one's brains about,' with loc.), Siṇhâs.; to be forced asunder or broken open, to be separated or set at variance, MW. °**ghaṭṭita**, mfn. broken, opened &c.; violated, betrayed, MBh.; untied, undone, W.; hurt, offended, MW. °**ghaṭṭin**, mfn. (ifc.) rubbing, Ragh.

विघन 2. *vi-ghaná*, mfn. (*√han*; for 1. see p. 950, col. 2) injuring, hurting, MantraBr.; m. an implement for striking, mallet, hammer, TS.; ĀpŚr.; N. of two Ekâhas, Br.; ŚrS. (*-tvá*, n., TBr.); N. of Indra, Kāṭh. °**ghanin**, mfn. slaying, killing, RV. vi, 60, 5 (Sāy.)

Vi-ghāta, m. a stroke, blow with (comp.), VarBṛS.; breaking off or in pieces, ib.; driving back, warding off, MBh.; R.; destruction, ruin, Kāv.; Var.; Pañcat.; removal, prohibition, prevention, interruption, impediment, obstacle, MBh.; Kāv. &c.; failure, want of success, Jātakam. °**ghātaka**, mfn. impeding, interrupting, MBh.; Bh. °**ghātana**, mfn. warding off, averting, MBh.; n. impeding, interrupting, disturbing, R.; Suśr.; *-siddhi*, f. the settling or removal of obstacles or impediments, W. °**ghātin**, mfn. fighting, slaying, MBh.; Hariv.; hurting, injuring, Vet.; opposing, impeding, preventing, interrupting, R.; Kathās.

Vi-ghna, m. a breaker, destroyer, MBh.; (ep. also n.) an obstacle, impediment, hindrance, opposition, prevention, interruption, any difficulty or trouble, Kauś.; Yājñ.; MBh. &c.; N. of Gaṇêśa, Up.; Carissa Carandas, L.; *-kara*, mfn. causing any obstacle or interruption, opposing, impeding, obstructing, RāmatUp.; VarBṛS.; *-kartṛi*, mfn. id., MBh.; Pañcar.; *-kārin*, mfn. id., R.; fearful or terrible to be looked at, L.; *-kṛit*, mfn. = *-kara*, RPrāt.; VarBṛS. &c.; *-jit*, m. 'conqueror of obstacles,' N. of the god Gaṇêśa (this deity being supposed capable of either causing or removing difficulties and being therefore worshipped at the commencement of all undertakings), Kathās.; *-tantrita*, mfn., g. *tāra-kâdi* (perhaps for *vighnita* and *tantrita*); *-dhvaṉsa*, m. the removal of obstacles, MW.; *-nāyaka*, m. 'obstacle-chief,' N. of Gaṇêśa, L.; *-nāśaka*, mfn. who or what removes obstacles or difficulties, W.; m. N. of Gaṇêśa, L.; *-nāśana*, n. destruction or removal of ob°, W.; m. N. of Gaṇêśa, L.; *-pati*, m. 'lord of ob°' N. of Gaṇ°, Kāraṇḍ.; *-pratikriyā*, f. counteraction or removal of an impediment, Ragh.; *-rāj*, m. 'ob°-king,' N. of Gaṇêśa, Caṇḍ.; *-rāja*, m. id., Kathās.; Pañcar.; N. of an author, Cat.; *-leśa*, m. a slight obstacle, W.; *-vat*, mfn. having obstacles, obstructed by difficulties or impediments, Śak.; *-vighāta*, m. removal of obstacles, MW.; *-vināyaka*, m. 'obstacle-remover,' N. of Gaṇêśa, Cat.; *-siddhi*, f. the settling or removal of obstacles, W.; *-hantṛi*, m. 'remover or destroyer of obstacles,' N. of Gaṇêśa, Cāṇ.; *-hārin*, mfn. removing ob°, MW.; m. N. of Gaṇ°, L.; °*nâdhipa*, m. = °*ghna-pati*, Cat.; °*nântaka*, m. = °*ghna-nāśaka*, Kathās.; °*nêśa*, m. = °*ghna-pati*, BhP.; Kathās.; pl. (with Śaivas) N. of those who have attained a partic. degree of emancipation, Hcat.; *-kāntā*, f. white-blossomed Dūrvā grass, L.; *-dāna-vidhi*, m. N. of wk.; *-vāhana*, m. 'vehicle of Gaṇ°,' a kind of rat, L.; °*nêśāna*, m. = *-ghna-pati*, L.; *-kāntā*, f. = °*ghnêśa-kāntā*, L.; °*nêśvara*, m. = °*ghna-pati*, Kathās.; N. of a teacher, Śaktir. (*-kavaca*, n., *-saṃhitā*, f., *-sahasra-nāman*, n., °*varâshṭôttara-śata*, n. N. of wks.) °**ghnaka** (ifc.) = *vi-ghna*, preventing, hindering, Vet. °**ghnaya**, Nom. P. °*yati*, to impede, check, obstruct, Kāv.; Rājat. °**ghnita**, mfn. impeded, stopped, prevented, obstructed, Kāv.; Var.; Kathās. &c.; *-karman*, mfn. one who is interrupted in his work, Pañcat.; *-dṛishṭi-pāta*, mfn. one whose sight is impeded, blinded, Kum.; *-pada*, mfn. one whose steps are impeded, VarBṛS.; *-samāgama-sukha*, mfn. having the joy of union frustrated, Vikr.; °*têccha*, mfn. one whose wishes are disappointed, frustrated in one's desires, Ragh.

विघर्षण *vi-gharshaṇa*, n. (√*ghṛish*) rubbing, Dhātup.

Vi-ghṛishṭa, mfn. excessively rubbed, sore, Suśr.

विघस *vi-ghasá*, m. or n. (√*ghas*) food, AV.; the residue of an oblation of food (offered to the gods, to deceased ancestors, to a guest, or to a spiritual preceptor), Mn.; MBh. &c. (°*sam bahu* √*kṛi*, to make an ample meal). **Vighasâśa** (MBh.) or °**śin** (Mn.), mfn. one who eats the remains of an offering.

विघुष् *vi-√ghush* (only ind. p. *-ghushya*), to cry or proclaim aloud, Mn. viii, 233. °**ghushṭa**, mfn. proclaimed loudly, cried, MBh.; made to resound, resounding, resonant, vocal, R.; VarBṛS.; BhP.

Vi-ghoshaṇa, n. the act of proclaiming aloud, proclamation, crying, W.

विघूणिका *vighūṇikā*, f. the nose, L.

विघूर्ण् *vi-√ghūrṇ*, P. Ā. *-ghūrṇati*, °*te*, to roll or whirl about, be agitated, MBh.; R. °**ghūrṇana**, n. (or *ā*, f.) swaying to and fro, Kād. °**ghūrṇita**, mfn. rolled about, rolling, shaken, agitated, MBh.; R. &c.

विघृत *ví-ghṛita*, mf(*ā*)n. (√1. *ghṛi*) besprinkled, dripping, RV. iii, 54, 6.

विघ्न *vi-ghna* &c. See p. 957, col. 3.

विघ्रा *vi-√ghrā*, P. *-jighrāti*, to smell or scent out, find out by smelling, BhP.; to smell, sniff, smell at, VarBṛS.

विङ्क *viṅka*, m. (with *bhāgavata*) N. of a poet, Cat.

विङ्ख *viṅkha*, m. a horse's hoof, L.

विच *vic* (cf. √*vij*), cl. 7. P. Ā. (Dhātup. xxix, 5) *vinákti*, *viṅkte* (2. sg. *vivekshi*, RV. vii, 3, 4; pf. *viveca*, AV., p. *vivikvás*, RV., aor. *avaikshīt*, Gr.; fut. *vektā*, *vekshyati*, ib.; inf. *vektum*, MBh.; ind. *-vicya*, *-vecam*, ŚrS., Kāv.), to sift, separate (esp. grain from chaff by winnowing), RV.; AV.; to separate from, deprive of (instr.), Bhaṭṭ.; to discriminate, discern, judge, RV. iii, 57, 1: Pass. *vicyáte* (aor. *aveci*), AV. &c.: Caus. *-vecayati* (aor. *avīvicat*), see *vi-√vic*: Desid. *vivikshati*, Gr.: Intens. (or cl. 3, see Dhātup. xxv, 12) *vevekti*, Kauś. [Cf. Gk. εἴκω; Lat. *vices* &c.]

Vikta, mfn. separated &c. (cf. *vi-vikta*); empty (prob. w.r. for *rikta*), MW.

विचकिल *vicakila*, m. a kind of jasmine (Jasminum Zambac), Vās.; Bālar.; Dhūrtan (L. also 'a species of Artemisia' and 'Vanguiera Spinosa'). **-maya**, mf(*ī*)n. made or consisting of Vicakila flowers, Viddh.

विचक्ष् *vi-√caksh*, Ā. *-cashṭe* (Ved. inf. *-cákshe*), to appear, shine, RV.; to see distinctly, view, look at, perceive, regard, RV.; AV.; BhP.; to make manifest, show, RV.; to proclaim, announce, tell, Br.; MBh.; BhP.: Caus. *-cakshayati*, to cause to see distinctly, make clear, RV.; to proclaim, tell, GopBr. °**cakshaṇá**, mfn. conspicuous, visible, bright, radiant, splendid, RV.; AV.; Br.; GṛŚrS.; distinct, perceptible, PārGṛ.; clear-sighted (lit. and fig.), sagacious, clever, wise, experienced or versed in, familiar with (loc. or comp.), RV. &c. &c.; m. N. of a preceptor (with the patr. Tāṇḍya), VBr.; (*ā*), f. Tiaridium Indicum, L.; N. of Brahmā's throne, KaushUp.; N. of a female servant, Viddh.; (*am*), ind., g. *gotrâdi*; *-canasita-vat*, mfn. accompanied by the word *vicakshaṇa* or *canasita*, KātyŚr.; *-tva*, n. sagaciousness, cleverness, discernment, judgment, wisdom, MBh.; *-m-manya*, mfn. considering one's self clever or wise, Sarvad.; *-vat*, mfn. connected with the word *vicakshaṇa*, AitBr. (cf. °*ṇânta*, Lāṭy., °*ṇôttara*, Vait.) °**cákshas**, m. a teacher, Uṇ. iv, 232, Sch.; n. seeing clear, clear-sightedness, MaitrS. (v.l. °*cakshus*). °**cákshya**, mfn. conspicuous, visible, RV.

विचक्षुस् *vi-cakshus*, *vi-catura*, *vi-candra* &c. See p. 950, col. 2.

विचख्नु *vicakhnu* or *vicakhyu*, m. N. of a king, MBh.

विचट् *vi-√caṭ*, P. *-caṭati*, to break (intr.), Bālar. °**caṭana**, n. breaking, Śil.

विचय *vi-caya*. See *vi-√*1. 2. *ci*, col. 3.

विचर् *vi-√car*, P. *-carati*, to move in different directions, spread, expand, be diffused, RV.; MBh.; VarBṛS.; to rove, ramble about or through, traverse, pervade, RV. &c. &c.; to sally forth, march against, make an attack or assault, Mn.; MBh. &c.; to wander from the right path, go astray, be dissolute, Mn. ix, 20; to commit a mistake or blunder (with words), BhP.; to run out, come to an end, RV.; to stand or be situated in (loc.; applied to heavenly bodies), VarBṛS.; to associate or have intercourse with (instr.), BhP.; to act, proceed, behave, live, MBh.; Pañcat.; to practise, perform, accomplish, make, do, Mn.; MBh. &c.; to graze upon, feed upon (a pasture), Bālar.: Caus. *-cārayati*, to cause to go or roam about, MBh.; R.; to cause to go astray, seduce, R.; to move hither and thither (in the mind), ponder, reflect, consider, Mn.; MBh. &c.; to doubt, hesitate, ib.; to examine, investigate, ascertain, ib. °**cara**, mfn. wandered or swerved from (abl.), MBh. v, 812. 2. °**caraṇa**, n. (for 1. see p. 950, col. 2) wandering, motion, Suśr. °**caraṇīya**, mfn. it is to be acted or proceeded, Pañcat. °**carita**, mfn. moved in different directions &c.; n. wandering, roaming about, MBh.

Vi-cāra, m. (ifc. f. *ā*) mode of acting or proceeding, procedure (also = a single or particular case), ŚrS.; change of place, Gobh.; pondering, deliberation, consideration, reflection, examination, investigation, RPrāt.; MBh. &c.; doubt, hesitation, R.; Kathās.; BhP.; a probable conjecture, Sāh.; dispute, discussion, W.; prudence, MW.; *-kartṛi*, m. one who makes investigation, a judge, investigator, W.; *-cintāmaṇi*, m. N. of wk.; *-jña*, mfn. knowing how to discriminate or judge, able to decide on the merits of a case, a judge, MW.; *-dṛiś*, mfn. 'employing no spies for eyes' (see *cāra*), and 'looking at a matter with consideration,' Naish.; *-nirṇaya*, m. N. of wk.; *-para*, m. N. of a king, Siṇhās.; *-bhū*, f. a tribunal, L.; the judgment-seat of Yama (judge of the dead), W.; *-mañjarī*, f., *-mālā*, f. N. of wks.; *-mūḍha*, mfn. foolish or mistaken in judgment, Ragh.; Hit.; *-vat*, mfn. proceeding with consideration, considerate, prudent, Śatr.; Kāv.; *-vid*, m. (prob.) 'knowing how to discriminate,' N. of Śiva, MBh.; *-śāstra*, n. N. of wk.; *-śīla*, disposed to deliberation or reflection, considerate, deliberative, MW.; *-sudhâkara*, m., °*dhârṇava*, m. N. of wks.; *-sthala*, n. a place for discussion or investigation, tribunal, MW.; a logical disputation, W.; °*rârka-saṃgraha*, m. N. of wk.; °*rârtha-samāgama*, m. assembly for the sake of trial or judgment, an assembly for investigation or discussion, MW.; °*rôkti*, f. discriminating speech, L. °**cāraka**, m. a leader, guide, R.; a spy, ib.; (ifc.) one who deliberates or considers, Sarvad.; (*ikā*), f. a female servant who looks after the garden and the various divisions of the house, L.; *-tā*, f., *-tva*, n. investigation, deliberation, discussion, W. °**cāraṇa**, n. (also *ā*, f.) consideration, reflexion, discussion, doubt, hesitation, MBh.; Kāv. &c.; changing a place (only n.), Suśr.; (*ā*), f. distinction, kind, Car.; N. of the Mīmāṇsā system of philosophy, W. °**cāraṇīya**, mfn. to be deliberated about, needing careful consideration, Mṛicch.; Ragh. °**cārita**, mfn. deliberated, considered, discussed, judged, Mn.; MBh. &c.; anything which is under discussion, dubious, doubtful, uncertain, ib.; anything which has been discussed or decided, ascertained, settled, Mn. xi, 28; n. (also pl.) deliberation, doubt, hesitation, MBh.; Mṛicch.; Pañcat. °**cārin**, mfn. having wide paths (as the earth), RV. v, 84, 2; moving about, wandering, traversing, MBh.; R. &c.; proceeding, acting, MBh.; changing, mutable, ĀśvŚr.; wanton, dissolute, lascivious, Cāṇ. (v.l.); (ifc.) deliberating, judging, discussing, MBh.; Mṛicch.; m. N. of a son of Kavandha, GopBr. °**cārya**, mfn. to be deliberated or discussed (n. impers.), dubious, doubtful, questionable, MBh.; Kathās. &c.

Vi-cīrṇa, mfn. gone or wandered through &c.; occupied by, W.; entered, ib.

विचर्चिका *vi-carcikā*, f. (√*carc*) 'coating, cover,' a form of cutaneous eruption, itch, scab, Suśr. °**carcita**, mfn. rubbed, smeared, anointed, applied (as an unguent), Ṛitus. °**carcī**, f. = °*carcikā*, Suśr.

विचर्मन् *vi-carman*, *vi-carshaṇi*. See p. 950, col. 2.

विचल् *vi-√cal*, P. *-calati*, to move about, shake, waver, R.; Kathās.; to move away, depart or swerve or deviate or desist from (abl.), AV.; Mn.; MBh. &c.; to fall off or down, Gīt.; Kathās.; to go astray, fail, be agitated or disturbed or destroyed, MBh.; Hariv.; Mṛicch.: Caus. *-cālayati*, to cause to move, loosen, shake, MBh.; Suśr.; to agitate, excite, stir up, trouble, MBh.; R.; to cause to turn off or swerve from (abl.), MBh.; BhP.; to destroy, rescind, Mn.; MBh. °**cala**, mfn. moving about, shaking, unsteady (see *a-v°*); conceited, W. °**calana**, n. wandering from place to place, roaming about, unsteadiness, BhP.; boastfulness, Bhar.; Daśar.; moving from, deviation, W. °**calita**, mfn. gone away, departed, deviated from (abl.), R.; troubled, obscured, blinded, Mṛicch.

Vi-cācala, °**cācalat**, °**cācali**, see *á-vicācala* &c.

Vi-cāla, m. putting apart, distributing, separating, Pāṇ. v, 3, 43; interval, L.; mfn. intervening, intermediate, W. °**cālana**, mf(*ī*)n. removing, destroying, R. °**cālita**, °**cālin**, °**cālya**, see *a-vicālita* &c.

विचाकशत् *vi-cākaśat*. See *vi-√kāś*.

विचार *vi-cāra* &c. See under *vi-√car*.

विचि *vici* or *vicī*, f. = *vīci*, a wave, L.

विचि *vi-√*1. *ci* (not always separable from *vi-√*2. *ci*), P. Ā. *-cinoti*, *-cinute* (Impv. *-citana*, *-ciyantu*, RV.), to segregate, select, pick out, cull, TS.; ŚBr.; MBh.; to divide, part (hair), VS.; to take away, remove, disperse, RV.; KātyŚr.; to clear, prepare (a road), RV.; to distribute, ib.; to gather, collect, ib.; Pañcat.; to pile or heap up in a wrong way, disarrange, ŚBr.

1. **Vi-caya**, m. gathering or putting together, arrangement, enumeration, Nidānas. °**cayishṭha** (*ví-*), mfn. removing most effectually, effacing, RV.

विचि *vi-√*2. *ci* (cf. prec.), P. *-ciketi*, *-cinoti* &c. (pr. p. *-cinvat* and *-cinvāna*), to discern, distinguish, RV.; TBr.; to make anything discernible or clear, cause to appear, illumine, R.; to search through, investigate, inspect, examine, MBh.; R. &c.; to look for, long for, strive after, ib.

2. **Vi-caya**, m. search, investigation, examination, Ragh.; Uttarar.; Car. °**cayana**, n. id., Cat.

Vi-cicīshā, f. (fr. Desid.) desire of searching,

Mcar. °**cit,** mfn. searching, sifting, VS. °**cita,** mfn. searched through, searched, MBh. °**citi,** f. = °*caya,* Nalôd. °**cítya,** mfn. to be sifted, TS. °**cinvatká,** mfn. (fr. pr. p. °*cinvat*) sifting, discriminating, ib.

Vi-cetavya, mfn. to be searched or examined or investigated or found out, MBh.; R. &c. °**cetṛi,** mfn. one who sifts, sifter (with gen.), ŚBr. °**ceya,** mfn. to be searched or searched through, R. (-*tā-raka,* mfn. having the stars distinguishable or separated by long intervals, Ragh.); n. investigation, R.

विचिकिल *vicikila,* v.l. for *vicakila,* L.

विचित् *vi-√4. cit,* P. Ā. -*cetati,* °*te,* to perceive, discern, understand, RV.; (Ā.) to be or become visible, appear, ib.; AV.: Caus. -*citayati,* to perceive, distinguish, RV. v, 19, 2: Desid. -*cikitsati,* to wish to distinguish, ib. iv, 16, 10; to reflect, consider, doubt, be uncertain, hesitate, TS.; Br.; KaṭhUp.; MBh.; BhP. °**cikitsana,** n. (fr. Desid.) the being uncertain, doubtfulness, Śamk. °**cikitsā,** f. doubt, uncertainty, question, inquiry, TBr.; ChUp.; BhP.; error, mistake, W., °*sârthīya,* mfn. expressing doubt or uncertainty, Nir. °**cikitsya,** n. (impers.) it is to be doubted, NṛisUp. 2. °**citta** (*ví-*), mfn. (for 1. see p. 950, col. 2) perceived, observed, perceivable, manifest, AV.; TBr.

2. **Vi-cetana,** see *a-vicetaná.* 2. °**cetas** (*ví-*), mfn. visible, clearly seen, RV.; discerning, wise, ib.

विचित्र *vi-citra,* mf(*ā*)n. variegated, many-coloured, motley, brilliant, MBh.; R. &c.; manifold, various, diverse, Mn.; MBh. &c.; strange, wonderful, surprising, MBh.; Kāv. &c.; charming, lovely, beautiful, R.; Ṛitus.; amusing, entertaining (as a story), Kathās.; painted, coloured, W.; (*am*), ind. manifoldly, variously, BhP.; charmingly, R.; m. the Aśoka tree, L.; N. of a king, MBh.; of a son of Manu Raucya or Deva-sāvarṇi, Hariv.; Pur.; of a heron, Hit.; (*ā*), f. a white deer, MW.; colocynth, L.; (in music) a partic. Mūrchanā, Saṃgīt.; N. of a river, VP.; n. variegated colour, party-colour, W.; wonder, surprise, Gīt.; a figure of speech (implying apparently the reverse of the meaning intended), Kuval.; Pratāp.; -*katha,* m. 'one whose stories are amusing,' N. of a man, Kathās.; -*caritra,* mfn. behaving in a wonderful manner, MW.; -*cīnâṇśuka,* n. variegated China cloth, shot or watered China silk, W.; -*tā,* f., -*tva,* n. variegation, variety, wonderfulness, Kāv.; Sāh.; -*deha,* mfn. having a painted body, W.; elegantly formed, ib.; m. a cloud, L.; -*pashu,* m. N. of a poet, Cat.; -*bhūshaṇa,* m. N. of a Kiṃ-nara, Buddh.; -*mālyâbharaṇa,* mfn. having variegated garlands and ornaments, Nal.; -*mauli-śrī-cūḍa,* m. N. of a prince, Buddh.; -*rūpa,* mfn. having various forms, various, diverse, MBh.; -*varshin,* mfn. raining here and there (not everywhere), VarBṛS.; -*vākya-paṭutā,* f. great eloquence, Prasaṅg.; -*vāgurôcchrāya-maya,* mf(*ī*)n. filled with various outspread nets, Kathās.; -*vīrya,* m. 'of marvellous heroism,' N. of a celebrated king of the lunar race (the son of Śāṃtanu by his wife Satya-vatī, and so half-brother of Bhīshma; when he died childless, his mother requested Vyāsa, whom she had borne before her marriage to the sage Parāśara, to raise up issue to Vicitra-vīrya; so Vyāsa married the two widows of his half-brother, Ambikā and Ambālikā, and by them became the father of Dhṛita-rāshṭra and Pāṇḍu; cf. IW. 375; 376), MBh.; Hariv.; Pur.; (-*sū,* f. 'mother of Vicitra-vīrya,' N. of Satya-vatī, L.); -*siṇha,* m. N. of a man, Rājat.; °*trâṅga,* m. 'having variegated limbs or a spotted body,' a peacock, L.; a tiger, L.; °*trâpīḍa,* m. N. of a Vidyā-dhara, Kathās.; °*trâlaṃkāra-svara,* m. N. of a serpent-demon, Buddh. —**citraka,** mfn. wonderful, surprising, Pañcar.; (ifc.) connected with (?), Hcat.; m. Betula Bhojpatra, L.; n. wonder, astonishment, L. —**citrita,** mfn. variegated, spotted, coloured, painted, MBh.; embellished by, adorned or decorated with (instr. or comp.), MBh.; BhP.; wonderful, W.

विचित्वारा *vicitvārā,* (prob.) w.r. for *vi-jitvarā.*

विचिन्त् *vi-√cint,* P. Ā. -*cintayati,* °*te,* to perceive, discern, observe, KenUp.; to think of, reflect upon, ponder, consider, regard, mind, care for, MBh.; R. &c.; to find out, devise, investigate, MBh.; Pañcat.; to fancy, imagine, BhP. °**cintana,** n. thinking, thought, MBh. °**cintanīya,** mfn. to be considered or observed, VarBṛS. °**cintā,** f. thought, reflection, care for anything, MBh.; R. °**cintita,** mfn. thought of, considered, imagined, BhP. °**cintitṛi,** mfn. one who thinks of (gen.), MBh. °**cintya,** mfn. to be considered or thought of or cared for, VarBṛS.; Prab.; BhP.; to be found out or devised, Daś.; doubtful, questionable, Vām.

विचिलक *vicilaka,* m. a kind of venomous insect, Suśr.

विचीरिन् *vicīrin,* w.r. for *vi-cārin,* Hariv.

विचीर्ण *vi-cīrṇa.* See under *vi-√car.*

विचुम्ब् *vi-√cumb,* P. -*cumbati,* to kiss eagerly, kiss, Sāh.

विचुल *vicula,* m. Vangueria Spinosa, L.

विचूर्ण् *vi-√cūrṇ,* P. -*cūrṇayati,* to grind to pieces, pound, smash, pulverize, MBh.; R.; Suśr. °**cūrṇana,** n. grinding to pieces, pulverizing, Suśr. °**cūrṇita,** mfn. ground, pounded &c.; m. N. of a man, Virac. °**cūrṇī-√bhū,** P. -*bhavati,* to become pulverized or smashed, become dust, Śaṃk.

विचृत् *vi-√cṛit,* P. -*cṛitati,* to loosen, detach, untie, open, set free, RV.; AV.; VS.; Kauś. °**cṛit,** f. the act of loosening or untying, RV. ix, 84, 2; du. N. of two stars, AV.; of the 17th Nakshatra, TS. °**cṛitta** (*ví-*), mfn. loosened, untied, opened, spread, RV.; AV. (°*cṛita,* w.r., VS. xxii, 7).

विचेतन *vi-cetana, vi-cetas* &c. See under *vi-√4. cit,* col. 1.

विचेष्ट् *vi-√cesht,* P. Ā. -*ceshṭati,* °*te,* to move the limbs about, writhe, wallow, struggle, MBh.; R.; Hariv.; to bestir or exert one's self, be active or busy, KaṭhUp.; R.; Suśr.; act or proceed against, deal with (loc.), Mn.; MBh. &c.: Caus. -*ceshṭayati,* to set in motion, rouse to action, Kathās. °**ceshṭana,** n. moving the limbs, MBh.; kicking or rolling (said of horses), Ragh. °**ceshṭā,** f. motion (see *nir-viceshṭa*); acting, proceeding, conduct, behaviour, MBh.; Kām.; BhP. (cf. *dur-viceshṭa*); effort, exertion, MW. °**ceshṭita,** mfn. struggled, striven, exerted &c.; effected, produced, Hit.; investigated, inquired into, W.; unconsidered, ill-judged, ib.; n. motion (of the body), gesture, Kāv.; Suśr.; action, exertion, conduct, behaviour, Yājñ.; MBh. &c.; evil or malicious act, machination, W. °**ceshṭitṛi,** mfn. moving the limbs, &c., L.

विच्छद् 1. *vi-cchad* (*√1. chad*), Caus. -*cchādayati,* to uncover, unclothe (only ChUp. viii, 10, 2, as v.l. for -*cchāyayati*).

विच्छद् 2. *vi-cchad* (*√3. chad*), Caus. -*chandayati,* to render or return homage (?), Buddh.

विच्छन्द *ví-cchanda, ví-cchandas, vi-cchardaka.* See p. 950, col. 2.

विच्छर्दन *vi-cchardana,* n. (*√chṛid*) the act of vomiting, W.; disregarding, ib.; wasting (?), ib. °**cchardikā,** f. the act of vomiting, L. °**cchardita,** mfn. vomited, ejected, W.; disregarded, neglected, ib.; diminished, impaired, ib.

विच्छाय् *vicchāy, vicchāyati.* See *vich.*

विच्छाय 1. 2. *vi-cchāya.* See pp. 949, 950.

विच्छिद् *vi-cchid* (*√chid*), P. -*chinatti,* -*chintte,* to cut or tear or cleave or break asunder, cut off, divide, separate, AV. &c. &c.; to interrupt (see *vi-cchidya*); to disturb, destroy, Bhaṭṭ.; to be divided, TS. °**cchitti** (*ví-*), f. cutting asunder or off, breaking off, prevention, interruption, cessation, TBr. &c. &c.; wanting, lack of (instr.), Śiś.; (in rhet.) a pointed or cutting or sharp style, Sāh.; Kuval.; irregularity or carelessness in dress and decoration, Vās.; Daśar.; colouring or marking the body with unguents, painting, Śak.; Śiś.; cæsura, pause in a verse, W. °**cchidya,** ind. having cut off &c.; separately, interruptedly, Prab.; Vedântas.

Ví-cchinna, mfn. cut or torn or split or cleft or broken asunder &c., AV.; Hariv.; BhP.; interrupted, disconnected (-*tā,* f. disconnectedness), incoherent, GṛS.; Kāv.; VarBṛS.; ended, ceased, no longer existing, Rājat.; crooked, L.; anointed, L.; -*dhūma-prasara,* mfn. having the free course of the smoke interrupted, Ragh.; -*prasara* (*vicchinna-prasara*), mfn. having its progress interrupted (said of science), Rājat.; -*bali-karman,* mfn. having sacrificial rites interrupted, ib.; -*madya,* mfn. one who has long abstained from spirituous liquor; -*śara-pātatva,* n. 'distance of an arrow's flight,' i. e. excessive nearness of combatants to each other, MBh.

Vi-ccheda, m. cutting asunder, cleaving, piercing, breaking, division, separation, Kāv.; Sāh.; interruption, discontinuance, cessation, end, MBh.; Kāv. &c.; removal, destruction, Rājat.; Kathās.; (ifc.) injury to, Kām.; distinction, difference (ifc. also 'variety,' i. e. different kinds of), MBh.; Śamk.; Sarvad.; division of a book, section, chapter, W.; space, interval, ib.; cæsura, pause in a verse, Piṅg., Sch. °**cchedaka,** mf(*ikā*)n. cutting off or asunder, dividing, separating, a cutter, divider, W. °**cchedana,** mfn. separating, interrupting, Suśr.; (*ā*), f. breaking off (pl.), Bālar.; n. cutting off, removal, annulment, destruction, Kāv.; VarBṛS.; distinguishing, MBh. °**cchedanīya,** mfn. to be separated, divisible, W. °**cchedin,** mfn. breaking, destroying, MBh.; Pañcar.; having breaks or intervals, VarBṛS.

विच्छुरण *vi-cchuraṇa,* n. (*√chur*) besprinkling, bestrewing, powdering, Kād. °**cchurita,** mfn. bestrewed or powdered or covered or inlaid with (instr. or comp.), Kum.; Vikr.; Caurap.; m. a partic. Samādhi, Kāraṇḍ.

विच्छो *vi-ccho* (*√cho*), Caus. -*cchāyayati,* to cut about, wound, MW. (cf. *√vich*).

विच्यु *vi-√cyu,* Caus. -*cyāvayati,* to cause to fall to pieces, throw down, destroy, PañcavBr. °**cyuta** (*ví-*), mfn. fallen asunder or to pieces, R.; fallen or departed or swerved or deviated from (abl.), Mn.; VarBṛS., Sch.; failed, perished, lost, Yājñ.; loosened, set free, RV. ii, 17, 3; (in surgery) separated from the living part, sloughed, W. °**cyuti,** f. falling from (lit. and fig.), Kathās.; severance, separation, MBh.; failure, miscarriage (see *garbha-v°*).

विच्छ् *vich,* cl. 10. P. (Dhātup. xxxiii, 109) *vicchayati,* to speak or to shine; *vicchāyáti* (xxviii, 129; cf. Pāṇ. iii, 1, 28), to go (with *ny-ā,* to press or rub one's self against): Caus. *vicchāyáyati,* to press, bring into straits, ŚBr. (perhaps ChUp. viii, 10, 2).

विज् 1. *vij* (cf. *√vic*), cl. 6. Ā. *vijáte* (m.c. also *vijati* and *vejate,* and accord. to Dhātup. xxix, 23 and xxv, 12 also cl. 1. P. *vinakti,* and cl. 3. P. Ā. *vevekti, vevikte;* pf. *vivije,* 3. pl. °*jre,* RV.; aor. *vikthās, vikta,* ib.; *avijit, vijishṭa,* Gr.; fut. *vijitā,* ib.; *vijishyati,* MBh.; *vejishyati,* Śatr.; inf. *vijitum,* Gr.), to move with a quick darting motion, speed, heave (said of waves), ŚBr.; to start back, recoil, flee from (abl.), RV.; AV.: Caus. *vejayati* (aor. *avīvijat*), to speed, accelerate, PañcavBr.; to increase (see *vejita*); to terrify (see id.): Desid. *vivijishati,* Gr.: Intens. *vevijyáte* (p. *vévijāna*), to tremble at (dat.), start or flee from (abl.), RV. [Cf. Germ. *wîchen, weichen;* Angl. Sax. *wîkan;* Eng. *vigorous; weak.*]

Vigna, mfn. shaken, agitated, terrified, alarmed, Ragh.; Kathās.

Vígra or **Vigrá,** mfn. (perhaps) strong, vigorous (according to Naigh. = *medhâvin*), RV.; noseless (prob. for *vi-ghra,* cf. *jighra*), L.

2. **Vij,** m. or f. (prob.) a stake at play, RV. ('a bird,' Sāy.)

1. **Vijita,** mfn. (for 2. see under *vi-√ji*) to be apprehended or feared, W.

Vijitṛi, mfn. who or what separates or divides, W.; m. a judge, discriminator, distinguisher, ib.

विजग्ध *vi-jagdha,* mfn. (*√jaksh*) eaten up, devoured, MBh. **Vijagdhaka,** g. *varāhâdi.*

विजङ्घ *vi-jaṅgha* &c. See p. 950, col. 2.

विजञ्जप *vi-jañjapa,* mfn. (fr. Intens. of *√jap*) whispering, Nir. v, 22.

विजन् *vi-√jan,* Ā. -*jāyate* (pf. p. *vi-jānivas,* gen. °*núshas,* RV.; inf. *ví-janitos,* TS.), to be born or produced, originate, arise, RV. &c. &c.; to be transformed, turn into, become (nom.), MBh.; to bear young, generate, bring forth, produce, AV.; TS.; Br.; MBh. °**janana,** n. the act of generating or bringing forth, birth, delivery, L. °**janita,** mfn. born, begotten, W. °**janyā,** f. a woman that is about to bring forth a child, pregnant, PārGṛ. °**jāta,** mfn. born, transformed &c.; born separately, W.; base-born, of mixed origin, ib.; (*ā*), f. a woman who has borne children, mother, matron, L. °**jāman,** mfn. related i. e. corresponding to each other, symmetrical, RV.; AV.; ŚBr. °**jāvatī** (*ví-*), f. (a woman) that has brought forth a child, AV. °**jávan**, mfn. bodily, own, RV.

विजन *vi-jana, vi-janman* &c. See p. 950, col. 2.

विजपिल *vi-japila, vi-jayina.* See ib.

विजल्प *vi-jalpa*, m. (√*jalp*) an unjust reproach, MārkP.; speech, talk, MW. °**jalpita**, mfn. spoken, uttered, Śak.

विजवल *vi-javala.* See p. 950, col. 2.

विजान *vi-jāna* &c. See under *vi-√jñā.*

विजि *vi-√ji*, Ā. *-jayate* (rarely °*ti*; cf. Pāṇ. i, 3, 19). to conquer, win or acquire by conquest, Br.; MBh. &c.; to vanquish, defeat, subdue, overpower, master, control, Mn.; MBh. &c.; to be victorious or superior, RV.; Br.; Up. &c.; (often in respectful salutation, e.g. *vi-jayasva rājan*, 'be victorious' or 'hail to thee, O king!') to contend victoriously with (instr.), AitBr.; to excel in (instr.), Bālar.; to be about to conquer, go to victory, Mn. vii, 107: Caus. (only aor. *vy-ajījayat*; but cf. *vi-jāpayitṛi*) to conquer, MBh.: Desid. *-jigīshate* (rarely °*ti*), to strive for victory, wish to conquer or vanquish, attack, assail, ŚBr. &c. &c.

Vi-jayá, m. contest for victory, victory, conquest, triumph, superiority, RV. &c. &c. (fig. applied to 'the sword' and to 'punishment,' MBh. xii, 6204; 4428); the prize of victory, booty, KātyŚr.; N. of a partic. hour of the day (esp. the 17th, and the hour of Kṛishṇa's birth, accord. to some the 11th Muhūrta), MBh.; Hariv. &c.; the third month, L.; the 27th (or first) year of Jupiter's cycle, VarBṛS.; a kind of military array, Kām.; a province, district, HParis.; (in music) a kind of flute, Saṃgīt.; a kind of measure, ib.; a kind of composition, ib.; a divine car, chariot of the gods (?), L.; N. of Yama, L.; of a son of Jayanta (son of Indra), Hariv.; of a son of Vasu-deva, ib.; of a son of Kṛishṇa, BhP.; of an attendant of Vishṇu, ib.; of an attendant of Padma-pāṇi, W.; of a son of Sva-rocis, MārkP.; of a Muni, Hariv.; of a prince, MBh.; of a son of Dhṛita-rāshṭra (?), ib.; of a warrior on the side of the Pāṇḍavas, ib.; of one of the eight councillors of Daśaratha, R.; of Arjuna, MBh.; BhP.; of a son of Jaya, Hariv.; Pur.; of a son of Cañcu or Cuñcu, ib.; of a son of Saṃjaya, VP.; of a son of Su-deva, BhP.; of a son of Purūravas, ib.; of a son (or grandson) of Bṛihan-manas, Hariv.; Pur.; of a son of Yajña-śrī, Pur.; of the founder of Buddhist civilisation in Ceylon, MW.; (with Jainas) N. of one of the 9 white Balas and of one of the 5 Anuttaras; of the 20th Arhat of the future and of the father of the 21st Arhat of the present Avasarpiṇī; of the attendant of the 8th Arhat of the same; of a son of Kalki, KalkiP.; of a son of Kalpa, KālP.; of a hare, Kathās.; of the lance of Rudra (personified), MBh.; (pl.) of a people, MBh.; (*ā*), f. N. of various plants (accord. to L. Terminalia Chebula; Sesbania Aegyptiaca; Vitex Negundo; Rubia Munjista; Premna Spinosa; a kind of hemp; a kind of *śamī*; = *vacā*), VarBṛS.; Suśr. &c.; of a partic. Tithi or lunar day (the 12th day in the light half of Śrāvaṇa, i.e. Kṛishṇa's birthday, the 10th in that of Āśvina, being a festival in honour of Durgā, and the 7th in that of Bhādrapada, if it falls on a Sunday; also the 7th night in the Karma-māsa), VarBṛS.; BhP. &c.; of a partic. magical formula, Bhaṭṭ.; N. of Durgā, MBh.; Hariv.; of a female friend of Durgā, Mudr.; of the wife of Yama, L.; of another goddess, Cat.; of a Yoginī, Hcat.; of a Surâṅganā, Siṇhâs.; of the mother of the 2nd Arhat of the present Avasarpiṇī, L.; of a daughter of Daksha, R.; of the mother of various Su-hotras, MBh.; of Kṛishṇa's garland, MBh.; of a Kumārī (i.e. small flag-staff) on Indra's banner, VarBṛS.; of a partic. spear, R.; n. the poisonous root of the plant Vijayā, Suśr.; a royal tent, Vāstuv.; a kind of pavilion, ib.; N. of a sacred district in Kaśmīra, Kathās. (cf. *-kshetra*); mfn. leading to victory, proclaiming victory, MBh.; victorious, triumphant, L. **–kaṇṭaka**, m. 'victory-thorn,' 'fighter for victory,' N. of a king, Inscr. **–kalpa-latā**, f. N. of wk. **–kuñjara**, m. a royal elephant, L. **–ketu**, m. N. of a Vidyā-dhara, Vās. **–kshetra**, n. N. of a sacred district in Kaśmīra (= *vi-jaya*, n.), Kathās.; Rājat.; *-bhaṭṭâgra-hāra*, m. pl., Vcar. **–gaṇi, -govinda-siṇha**, m. N. of authors, Cat. **–candra**, m. 'victory-moon,' N. of a king, Inscr. **–cchanda**, m. a necklace of pearls consisting of 504 rows or strings, VarBṛS. **–diṇḍima**, m. 'drum of victory,' a large military drum, Cat. **–tīrtha**, n. N. of a Tīrtha, ib. **–daṇḍa**, m. a triumphal staff, Pañcad.; a partic. detachment of an army, Mālav. **–datta**, m. N. of two men, Kathās.; Cat.; of the hare in the moon, Pañcat. **–daśamī**, f. the 10th day of the light half of the month Āśvina, the day of the Daśa-harā &c., MW.; *-nirṇaya*, m. N. of wk. **–dundubhi**, m. a triumphal drum (*tā*, f.), Ragh. **–devī**, f. N. of a woman, W. **–dvādaśī**, f. the 12th day in the light half of the month Śrāvaṇa; *-vrata*, n. a partic. ceremony, Cat. **–dvāra**, n. a gate leading to victory, VarYogay. **–dhvaja-tīrtha**, m. N. of an author, Cat. **–nagara**, n. N. of a town in Karṇāṭa, Cat. **–nandana**, m. N. of a Cakra-vartin, L. **–nandin, -nātha**, m. N. of authors, Cat. **–patākā**, f. a triumphal flag, Vās. **–pārijāta**, m. N. of a drama. **–pāla**, m. a kind of functionary, Mudr.; N. of various kings (also *-deva*), Siṇhâs.; Kathās.; Inscr.; (with prefixed *rājânaka*) of a poet, Subh. **–pura**, n. N. of various towns, Col.; *-kathā*, f. N. of wk. **–pūrṇimā**, f. a partic. full-moon night, Cat. **–prakoshṭha**, m. N. of an ancestor of Kshemîśvara, Caṇḍ. **–pratyarthin**, mfn. desirous of victory, Mālav. **–praśasti**, f. or °**ti-kāvya**, n. N. of a Kāvya. **–phala**, mfn. having victory for a result, MW. **–bhaṭṭārikā**, f. N. of a princess, Inscr. **–bhāga** (*vijayá-*), mfn. giving luck (in play), TBr. **–bhairava**, n., **-maṅgala-dīpikā**, f. N. of wks. **–mardala**, m. = *-ḍiṇḍima* above, L. **–malla**, m. N. of a man, Rājat. **–mahā-devī**, f. N. of a princess, Inscr. **–mādhava**, m. N. of a poet, Subh. **–mālikā**, f. N. of a woman, Pañcad. **–mālin**, m. N. of a merchant, Kathās. **–mitra**, m. N. of a man, Rājat. **–yantra-kalpa**, m. N. of a ch. of the Ādi-purāṇa. **–rakshita, -rāghava**, m. N. of authors, Cat. **–rāja**, m. N. of a king and of various other persons, Rājat.; Inscr. **–rāma**, m. N. of two authors, Cat. **–lakshmī**, f. N. of the mother of Veṅkaṭa, ib. **–vat**, mfn. possessing victory, triumphant, glorious, Inscr.; (*atī*), f. N. of a daughter of the serpent-demon Gandha-mālin, Kathās. **–varman**, m. N. of a poet, Subh.; of various other men, Ratnâv.; Kathās. **–vilāsa**, m. N. of sev. wks. **–vega**, m. N. of a Vidyā-dhara, Kathās. **–śrī**, f. the goddess of victory, Kāv.; N. of a Kiṃnara maiden, Kāraṇḍ.; of a woman, Cat. **–saptamī**, f. a partic. 7th day, Cat. **–siṇha**, m. N. of various kings, Rājat.; Inscr. **–siddhi**, f. accomplishment of victory, success, W. **–sena**, m. N. of various men, Kathās.; Siṇhâs.; (*ā*), f. N. of a woman, Lalit. **–stotra-baṭuka**, m. N. of wk. (prob. for *baṭuka-vijaya-stotra*). **–haṇsa-gaṇi**, m. N. of an author, Cat. **Vijayâkalpa**, m. N. of wk. **Vijayâṅkā**, f. N. of a poetess, ŚārṅgP. **Vijayā-daśamī**, f. the 10th day of the light half of the month Āśvina, Cat. **Vijayâditya**, m. N. of various kings, Inscr. **Vijayânanda**, m. a kind of measure, Saṃgīt.; N. of an author, Cat. **Vijayâparājitā-stotra**, n. N. of wk. **Vijayâbhinandana**, m. N. of a king, Vīrac.; of a great warrior yet to arise and to be the founder of an era, MW. **Vijayâbhyupāya**, m. means of victory, Kum. **Vijayā-rahasya**, n. N. of wk. **Vijayârtham**, ind. on account of victory, for vict°, MW. **Vijayârthin**, mfn. seeking victory, desirous of conquest, ib. **Vijayârdha**, m. N. of a mountain, Dharmaś. **Vijayā-saptamī**, f. the 7th day of the light half of a month falling on a Sunday, Tithyād. **Vijayêndra-parābhava**, m. N. of wk. **Vijayêśa**, m. 'lord of victory,' N. of the god Śiva, MW.; of a sacred place, Rājat.; *-sahasra-nāman*, n. pl. N. of wk. **Vijayêśvara**, m. N. of a sacred place (cf. prec.), Rājat.; *-māhātmya*, n. N. of wk. **Vijayâikādaśī**, f. the 11th day of the dark half of the month Phālguna, W. **Vijayôtsava**, m. 'vict°-festival,' N. of a festival in honour of Vishṇu celebrated on the 10th day of the light half of the month Āśvina, Cat. **Vijayôllāsa**, m. N. of a Kāvya.

Vi-jayaka, mfn. = *vijaye kuśalaḥ*, g. *ākarshâdi*. °**jayanta**, m. 'victorious,' N. of Indra, L.; (*ī*), f. N. of a Surâṅganā, Siṇhâs. °**jayantikā**, f. N. of a Yoginī, Hcat.

Vi-jayin, mfn. victorious, triumphant, Yājñ.; MBh. &c.; m. (ifc.) a conqueror, subduer, Kāv.; Pur.; °*yi-kshetra*, n. N. of a sacred district in Orissa, Inscr.; °*yîndra*, m. (with *yatîndra* or *bhikshu*), m. N. of an author (also *-svāmin*), Cat. °**jayishṭha**, mfn. conquering most, Pāṇ. vi, 4, 154, Sch.

Vi-jāpayitṛi, mfn. (fr. Caus.) causing or granting victory, Kāṭh.

Vi-jigīsha, mfn. (fr. Desid.) desirous of victory, emulous, W.; (*ā*), f. desire to conquer or overcome or subdue (acc., dat., or comp.), R.; Kām.; Kathās. (°*shā-vat* [Nīlak.] or °*shin* [MBh.], mfn. desirous to conquer or overcome; °*shā-vivarjita*, mfn. devoid of ambition, MW.; °*shīya*, mfn., g. *utkarâdi*). °**jigīshu**, mfn. desirous of victory or conquest, wishing to overcome or surpass (acc. or comp.), emulous, ambitious, Mn.; MBh. &c.; m. a warrior, invader, antagonist, MBh.; a disputant, opponent, Sarvad.; *-tā*, f. (Kathās.), *-tva*, n. (Kām.) desire of conquest, emulation, ambition.

2. **Ví-jita**, mfn. (for 1. see under √*vij*) conquered, subdued, defeated, won, gained, ŚBr. &c. &c.; m. or n. a conquered country, ŚBr.; any country or district, Lalit.; conquest, victory, ŚBr.; Lāṭy.; Gaut.; *-rūpa* (*vij*°), mfn. appearing as if conquered or won, ŚBr.; *-vat*, mfn. one who has conquered, victorious, W.; °*tâtman*, m. 'self-subdued,' N. of Siva, Śivag.; °*tâmitra*, mfn. one who has overcome his enemies, R.; °*tāri*, m. 'id.,' N. of a Rākshasa, ib.; °*tâśva*, m. N. of a son of Pṛithu, BhP.; °*tâsana*, mfn. one who has won a seat and is indifferent about sitting on it, BhP.; °*tâsu*, m. N. of a Muni, Kathās.; *têndriya*, mfn. one who has the organs of sense or passions subdued, Mn.; Yājñ.; R. °**jiti** (*ví-*), f. contest for victory, conquest, triumph, TS.; Br.; ŚrS.; (ifc.) gain or acquisition of, MaitrUp.; Kāvyâd.; N. of a goddess, MBh. °**jitin**, mfn. victorious, triumphant, AitBr. °**jitvara**, mf(*ā*)n. id. (*-tva*, n.), ChUp.; Kum.; (*ā*), f. N. of a goddess, Cat.

Vi-jetavya, mfn. to be subdued or overcome or restrained or controlled, MBh.; Kathās.; Sāh. °**jetṛi**, m. a vanquisher, conqueror (also in argument), MBh.; Hariv. &c. (with *purām*, 'conqueror of towns,' N. of Śiva, Kir.) °**jeya**, mfn. to be vanquished or overcome, Kathās.; *-vilāsa*(?), m. N. of wk.

Vi-jesha-kṛit, mfn. causing or bestowing victory (said of Indra), RV.

विजिगीत *vi-jigīta* (BṛĀrUp.) or *vi-jigīthá* (ŚBr.), mfn. (√*gai*) celebrated, famous.

विजिग्राहयिषु *vi-jigrāhayishu, vi-jighṛikshu.* See under *vi-√grah*, p. 957, col. 3.

विजिघांसु *vijighāṇsu*, mfn. (Desid. of √*han*) wishing to slay or to kill or to remove or to destroy, MBh.; BhP.

विजिज्ञासा *vi-jijñāsā* &c. See under *vi-√jñā.*

विजिन *vi-jina, vi-jila.* See p. 950, col. 3.

विजिहीर्षा *vi-jihīrshā*, f. (fr. Desid. of *vi-√hṛi*) wish or intention to roam about or take one's pleasure, Kir. °**jihīrshu**, mfn. wishing to walk about, Car.; wishing to sport or take one's pleasure, MBh.

विजिह्म *vi-jihma, vi-jihva.* See p. 950, col. 3.

विजीव् *vi-√jīv*, P. *-jīvati*, to revive, return to life, MBh.

विजु *viju*, m. that part of a bird's body on which the wings grow, AitĀr.

विजुल *vijula*, m. the root of Bombax Heptaphyllum, L. (prob. w. r. for *vijjala*).

विजृम्भ् *vi-√jṛimbh*, Ā. *-jṛimbhate*, to open the mouth, yawn, gape, VS. &c. &c.; to open (intr.), expand, become expanded or developed or exhibited, spread out, blossom, Kāv.; VarBṛS.; BhP.; to extend, become erect (said of the membrum virile), RV.; to arise, appear, awake (fig.), MBh.; R.; to begin to feel well or at ease, Hariv. °**jṛimbha**, m. bending or knitting (the brows), BhP.; (*ā*), f. yawning, L. °**jṛimbhaka**, m. N. of a Vidyā-dhara, Kathās.; (*ikā*), f. gasping for breath, Kād.; Suśr.; yawning, Suśr. °**jṛimbhaṇa**, n. yawning, Suśr.; opening, expanding, blossoming, budding, Ragh.; spreading, extension, Mālatīm.; bending, knitting (the brows), BhP. °**jṛimbhita**, mfn. yawned, gaped, opened, expanded, blown &c. (n. impers.); drawn, bent (said of a bow), MBh.; R.; sported, wantoned, W.; n. yawning, Gaut.; coming out, appearance, manifestation, consequences, Kāv.; Kathās.; Sarvad.;

exploit, Mālav. °**jṛimbhin,** mfn. breaking forth, appearing, Kāv.

विजेह् *vi-√jeh* (only pr. p. *-jéhamāna*), to open the mouth, show the tongue, RV.

विज्ज *vijja*, m. N. of a man, Rājat.; (*ā*), f. N. of a woman, ib. **-nāman,** m. N. of a Vihāra called after Vijjā, ib. **-rāja,** m. N. of a man, ib.

Vijjaka or **Vijjākā** or **Vijjikā,** f. N. of a poetess, Cat.

विज्जल *vijjala*, mfn. (L. also *vijjana* or *vijjila*) slimy, smeary, VarBṛS.; m. the root of Bombax Heptaphyllum, L.; (*ā*), f. N. of a woman, Rājat.; n. a kind of arrow, L.; sauce &c. mixed with rice-gruel, W. **-pura,** n. N. of a town, Cat. **-viḍa,** n. id. (cf. *vijila-bindu*).

विज्जुल *vijjula*, m. the bark of the Cassia tree, L.

Vijjūlikā, f. a species of Oldenlandia, L. (prob. w. r. for *vañjulikā*).

विज्ञा *vi-√jñā*, P. Ā. *-jānāti, -jānīte*, to distinguish, discern, observe, investigate, recognize, ascertain, know, understand, RV. &c. &c. (with *na* and inf. 'to know not how to'); to have right knowledge, KaṭhUp.; to become wise or learned, Mn. iv, 20; to hear or learn from (gen.), ChUp.; MBh.; to recognize in (loc.), Pañcat.; to look upon or regard or consider as (two acc.), Mn.; MBh. &c.; to learn or understand that (two acc. or *yat*), MBh.; Kāv. &c.; to explain, declare, BhP.: Pass. *-jñāyate*, to be distinguished or discerned &c.; (esp. 3. sg., 'it is known or understood,' ŚBr.; 'it is recognized or prescribed,' scil. by authorities, GṛŚrS; and in gram. *mā vi-jñāyi* with preceding nom., 'let this not be considered as'): Caus. *-jñapayati* or *-jñāpayati* (rarely °*te*; aor. *vy-ajijñapat*), to make known, declare, report, communicate, ŚBr. &c. &c.; to ask or request anything, Hariv.; to declare or tell that (two acc.), R.; to apprise, teach, instruct, ask, beg (with acc. of pers.; and dat. of thing, or with *artham* ifc., or *prati* and acc.), ŚBr. &c. &c.; to inform of or about (two acc.), Rājat.: Pass. (only Cond. *vy-ajñāpayishyata*, with v. l. °*shyat*), to become manifest, appear, ChUp. vii, 2, 1: Desid. of Caus., see *vi-jijñāpayisha* below (cf. also *vi-jñīpsu*): Desid. *-jijñāsati*, °*te*, to wish to understand or know &c., TS.; ChUp.

Vi-jāna, m. N. of a man, TāṇḍBr. °**jānaka,** mfn. knowing, familiar with (gen.), MBh. °**jānat,** mfn. understanding, knowing &c.; m. a wise man, sage, Mn.; MBh. &c. °**jānatā,** f. cleverness, shrewdness, Bālar.

Vi-jijñāpayishā, f. (fr. Desid. of Caus.) desire of teaching or instructing, Saṃk.

Vi-jijñāsā, f. (fr. Desid.) desire of knowing distinctly, wish to prove or try, inquiry about (comp.), ŚBr.; MBh.; BhP. °**jijñāsitavya,** mfn. wished or intended to be known or understood, ChUp. °**jijñāsu,** mfn. desirous of knowing or understanding, R.; wishing to learn from (gen.), MBh. °**jijñāsya** (or °*syà*), mfn. = °*jijñāsitavya*, ŚBr.; Yājñ.; Saṃk.

Vi-jña, mfn. knowing, intelligent, wise, clever; m. a wise man, sage, MBh.; Kāv. &c.; *-tā*, f., *-tva*, n. wisdom, skill, cleverness, W.; *-buddhi*, f. Indian spikenard, ib.; *-rāja*, m. a king or chief among sages, Karaṇḍ.; °*jñâbhimānin*, mfn. thinking one's self clever or wise, BhP.

Vi-jñapta, mfn. (fr. Caus.) made known, reported, informed, Kathās.; Hit. °**jñapti,** f. information, report, address (to a superior), request, entreaty of (gen.), Naish.; Kathās.; Rājat. (°*tiṃ √kṛi*, 'to announce anything, scil. to a superior;' with gen., 'to address a request to'); imparting, giving, L. °**jñaptikā,** f. a request, solicitation, Kāv. °**jñapya,** mfn. to be apprised or informed, Kathās.

Ví-jñāta, mfn. discerned, understood, known &c.; celebrated, famous, W.; *-vīrya* (*ví-*), mfn. of known strength, TBr.; *-sthālī*, f. (prob.) a vessel prepared in the known or usual manner, MaitrS.; °*tâtman*, m. N. of a poet, Cat.; °*târtha*, mfn. one who is acquainted with any matter on the true state of a case, MW. °**jñātavya,** mfn. to be recognized or known or understood, KaushUp.; to be found out, MBh.; to be regarded or considered as, VarBṛS.; to be inferred or conjectured with certainty, ib. °**jñāti** (*ví-*), f. knowledge, understanding, ŚBr.; N. of the 25th Kalpa (q. v.); m. N. of a deity, Cat. °**jñātṛí,** mfn. one who knows, a knower, understander, ŚBr.; MBh. &c.

Vi-jñāna, n. (ifc. f. *ā*) the act of distinguishing or discerning, understanding, comprehending, recognizing, intelligence, knowledge, AV. &c. &c.; skill, proficiency, art, Uttamac.; science, doctrine, Suśr.; worldly or profane knowledge (opp. to *jñāna*, 'kn° of the true nature of God'), Mn.; MBh. &c.; the faculty of discernment or of right judgment, MBh.; R. &c.; the organ of kn° (= *manas*), BhP.; (ifc.) the understanding of (a particular meaning), regarding as, Kāś. on Pāṇ. ii, 3, 17; 66 &c.; (with Buddhists) consciousness or thought-faculty (one of the 5 constituent elements or Skandhas, also considered as one of the 6 elements or Dhātus, and as one of the 12 links of the chain of causation), Dharmas. 22; 42; 58 (cf. MWB. 102; 109); *-kanda*, m. N. of a man, Cat.; *-kāya*, m. N. of a Buddhist wk.; *-kṛitsna*, n. one of the 10 mystical exercises called Kṛitsnas, Buddh.; *-kevala*, mfn. (with Śaivas) an individual soul to which only *mala* adheres, Sarvad.; *-kaumudī*, f. N. of a female Buddhist, Cat.; *-ghaná*, m. pure knowledge, nothing but intelligence, ŚBr.; Sarvad.; *-taraṃgiṇī*, f. N. of wk.; *-tā*, f. knowledge of (loc.), Cāṇ.; *-tārâvalī*, f. N. of wk.; *-taila-garbha*, m. Alangium Decapetalum, L.; *-deśana*, m. a Buddha, L.; *-naukā*, f. N. of sev. wks.; *-pati*, m. a lord of intelligence, TUp.; N. of one who has attained to a partic. degree of emancipation, Bādar., Sch.; *-pāda*, m. N. of Vyāsa, L.; *-bhaṭṭāraka*, m., *-bhārata*, m., *-bhikshu*, m. N. of scholars, Cat.; *-bhairava*, °*vôddyota-saṃgraha*, m. N. of wks.; *-máya*, mf(*ī*)n. consisting of knowledge or intelligence, all kn°, full of intell°, ŚBr.; Up. &c.; °*ya-kosha*, m. the sheath cons° of intell°, the intelligent sheath (of the soul, accord. to the Vedânta) or the sheath caused by the understanding being associated with the organs of perception, MW.; *-mātṛika*, m. 'whose mother is knowledge,' a Buddha, L.; *-yati*, m. = *-bhikshu*, Cat.; *-yogin*, m. = *vijñānêśvara*, Col.; *-latikā*, f., *-lalita* or °*ta-tantra*, n. N. of wks.; *-vat*, mfn. endowed with intelligence, Up.; ChUp., Sch.; Kathās.; *-vāda*, m. the doctrine (of the Yogâcāras) that only intelligence has reality (not the objects exterior to us), Bādar., Sch.; *-vādin*, mfn. one who affirms that only intelligence has reality; m. a Yogâcāra, Sarvad.; Buddh.; *-vinodinī-ṭīkā*, f., *-vilāsa*, m., *-śāstra*, n., *-śikshā*, f., *-saṃjñā-prakaraṇa*, n. N. of wks.; °*nâkala*, mfn. = °*na-kevala* above, Sarvad.; °*nâcārya*, m. N. of a teacher, Cat.; °*nâtman*, m. N. of an author, ib.; °*nântyâyatana*, n. (with Buddhists) N. of a world, Buddh.; °*nâmṛita*, n. N. of Comm.; °*nâśrama*, m. = °*nâtman*, Cat.; °*nâstitva-mātra-vādin*, mfn. = °*na-vādin*, Bādar., Sch.; °*nâhāra*, m. spiritual food as nourishment, L.; °*nêśvara*, m. N. of an author, Cat. (*-tantra*, n., *-vārttika*, n. N. of wks.); °*nêśvarīya*, n. a wk. of Vijñānêśvara, Cat.; °*nâika-skandha-vāda*, m. = °*na-vāda* above, Bādar., Sch. °**jñānanā,** f. (perhaps for °*jānanā* or °*jānatā*) perceiving, understanding, L. °**jñānika,** mfn. = *vi-jña* or *vaijñānika*, L. °**jñānin,** mfn. having intelligence or knowledge or science, clever, skilful, a specialist, Hcar.; Kathās.; MārkP.; °*ni-tā*, f. (ifc.) science or knowledge of, acquaintance with, Kām. °**jñānīya,** mfn. (ifc.) treating of the science or doctrine of, Suśr.

Vi-jñāpaka, mfn. (fr. Caus.) who or what makes known, W.; m. an informant, instructor, ib. °**jñāpana,** n. (or *ā*, f.) information, communication, address (esp. to a superior), request, entreaty, Kālid.; Mudr.; Kathās. °**jñāpanīya,** mfn. to be made known, to be communicated, BhP.; to be (respectfully) informed or apprised, Daś.; fit to be taught or instructed, L. °**jñāpita,** mfn. = °*jñapta*, Ragh.; Hit. °**jñāpin,** mfn. announcing, telling, Naish. °**jñāpti,** f. = °*jñapti*, MW. °**jñāpya,** mfn. = °*jñāpanīya*, MBh.; R. &c. °**jñāya,** mfn. recognizable (see *bala-v°*).

Vi-jñīpsu, mfn. (fr. Desid. of Caus.) wishing to inform, intending to address a request to, HPariś.

Vi-jñeya, mfn. to be perceived or known, knowable, cognizable, ŚBr.; MBh. &c.; to be understood or heard or learned, Mn.; R.; VarBṛS.; to be recognized or considered or regarded as (*-tva*, n.), TPrāt.; Up.; MBh. &c.

विज्य *vi-jya, vi-jvara* &c. See p. 950, col. 3.

विञ्जिलविन्दु *viñilavindu*, N. of a town, Cat.

विञ्जमर *viñjamara* or *viñjāmara*, n. the white of the eye, L.

विञ्जोली *viñjolī*, f. a line, row, range, L.

विट् *viṭ* (prob. artificial; cf. √*biṭ* and *viḍ*), cl. 1. P. *veṭati*, to sound, Dhātup. ix, 29.

Viṭa, m. (derivation doubtful) a voluptuary, sensualist, bon-vivant, boon-companion, rogue, knave, Kāv.; Rājat.; Kathās. &c. (in the drama, esp. in the Mṛicchakaṭika, he is the companion of a dissolute prince and resembles in some respects the Vidūshaka, being generally represented as a parasite on familiar terms with his associate, but at the same time accomplished in the arts of poetry, music, and singing; ifc. a term of reproach, g. *khasūcy-ādi*, Gaṇar.; L. also 'the keeper of a prostitute; a catamite; a mouse; Acacia Catechu; the orange tree; a kind of salt; = *prāñcalloha* [?]; = *viṭapa*, N. of a mountain'); n. a house, Gal. **-kāntā,** f. turmeric, L. **-1. -pa,** m. (for 2. see below) a keeper of catamites, L. **-putra,** m. N. of a writer on Kāmaśāstra, Kuṭṭanīm. **-peṭaka,** m. or n. a multitude of rogues, Rājat. **-priya,** m. a kind of jasmine, L. **-bhūta,** m. N. of an Asura, MBh. **-mākshika,** n. a sort of mineral, L. **-lavaṇa,** n. a kind of salt (= *viḍ-l°*), L. **-vallabhā,** f. Bignonia Suaveolens, L. **-vṛitta,** m. N. of a poet, Cat. **Viṭâṭikā** (?), f. a kind of small hog-weed, L.; a room where Viṭas meet, L. **Viṭâśraya,** m. a house occupied by a Viṭa, L.

Viṭaka, m. pl. N. of a people, VarBṛS.; = *piṭaka*, a boil, blister, Gal.; (*ā*), f. a room where Viṭas meet.

विटङ्क *vi-ṭaṅka*, m. n. (g. *ardharcâdi*; see √*ṭaṅk* and *ṭaṅka*) the loftiest point, top, pinnacle, MBh.; Kāv. &c. (also °*kaka*, L.); a dove-cot, aviary, L.; m. a big cucumber, L.; mfn. trim, nice, pretty, handsome, Pracaṇḍ.; BhP.; *-pura*, n. N. of a town, Kathās. °**ṭaṅkita,** mfn. stamped or marked or adorned with (instr. or comp.), BhP.

विटप 2. *viṭapa*, m. n. (g. *ardharcâdi*; of doubtful derivation, accord. to Uṇ. iii, 145 fr. √*viṭ*; for 1. *viṭa-pa* see under *viṭa*), the young branch of a tree or creeper, twig, sprout, shoot, bough, MBh.; Kāv. &c.; a bush, shrub, cluster, thicket, tuft, ib.; expansion, spreading, L.; the perinæum or the septum of the scrotum, Suśr.; m. N. of a man, g. *śivâdi* = *viṭa* or *viṭâdhipa*, L. **-śas,** ind. in branches or shoots, BhP.

Viṭapaka, m. a tree, Kād.; a rogue, voluptuary (= *viṭa*), ib.

Viṭapin, mfn. having branches or boughs (as a tree), MBh.; m. a tree, Kāv.; Kathās.; BhP. (m. c. also *viṭapi*, in gen. acc. pl. °*pīnām* and °*pīn*, R.); the Indian fig-tree, L. **Viṭapi-mṛiga,** m. 'tree-animal,' a monkey, ape, MW.

विटि *viṭi*, f. yellow sanders, L. **-kaṇṭhī-rava,** m. N. of Varada-rāja (the author of the Madhya-siddhânta-kaumudī), Cat.

विट्क *viṭka, viṭ-kārikā, viṭ-kṛimi* &c. See under 3. *vish*.

विट्कुल *viṭ-kula*. See under 2. *viś*.

विट्ठल *viṭṭhala*, m. (also written *viṭhala, viṭhṭhala*, and *viḍḍhala*) N. of a god worshipped at Pandharpur in the Deccan (he is commonly called Viṭho-bā, and stated to be an incarnation of Vishṇu or Kṛishṇa himself, who is believed to have visited this city and infused a large portion of his essence into a Brāhman named Puṇḍarīka or Puṇḍalīka, who had gained a great reputation for filial piety; his images represent him standing on a brick [cf. 2. *viḍ*] with his arms akimbo), RTL. 263; (also with *ācārya, dīkshita, bhaṭṭa* &c.) N. of various authors and teachers (esp. of a grammarian, disparaged by Bhaṭṭoji, and of a son of Vallabhâcārya and successor to his chair, also called Viṭṭhala-dīkshita or V°-nātha or Viṭṭhalêśa or °lêśvara, said to have been born in 1515), Cat. **-kavaca,** n. N. of a Kavaca (q. v.) **-miśra,** m. N. of a Commentator, Cat. **-sahasra-nāman,** n. N. of wk. **-sūnu,** m. N. of an author, Cat. **-stava-rāja,** m. N. of wk. **Viṭṭhalâcārya-sūnu,** m. N. of a Commentator, Cat. **Viṭṭha-lâshṭôttara-śata,** n. N. of a Stotra. **Viṭṭhalī-paddhati,** f. N. of an astron. wk. by Viṭṭhalâcārya.

Viṭṭhalêśa or °**lêśvara**, see above. **Viṭṭhalô-pâdhyāya-pattra**, n. N. of wk.

विट्पण्य *viṭ-paṇya*, *viṭ-pati* &c. See under 2. *viś*.

विठङ्क *viṭhaṅka*, mfn. bad, vile, W.

विठर *viṭhara*, mfn.=*vāgmin*, eloquent (applied to Bṛihas-pati), L.

विठल *viṭhala*, *viṭhṭhala*. See *viṭṭhala*.

विठोबा *viṭho-bā*. See *viṭṭhala*.

विड् 1. *viḍ* (cf. √*biṭ* and *viṭ*; prob. artificial and of doubtful connection with the following words), cl. 1. P. *veḍati*, to call, cry out, curse, swear, Dhātup. ix, 30, v.l.; to break, W.

2. **Viḍ**, f. a bit, fragment, W.

Viḍa, m. n. a kind of salt (either factitious salt, procured by boiling earth impregnated with saline particles, or a partic. kind of fetid salt used medicinally as a tonic aperient, commonly called Vit-lavan or Bit-noben, cf. *viḍ-lavaṇa*; it is black in colour and is prepared by fusing fossil salt with a small portion of Emblic Myrobalan, the product being muriate of soda with small quantities of muriate of lime, sulphur, and oxide of iron), Suśr.; m. N. of a country and its king, Inscr.; a fragment, bit, portion(?), W. — **gandha**, n. the medicinal salt described above, W. — **lavaṇa**, m. n. id., MBh.; Bhpr.

Viḍaṅga, mfn. clever, able, skilful, L.; m. and (*ā*), f. Embelia Ribes, L.; n. the fruit of the above plant (a vermifuge), L.

विडम्ब् *vi-√ḍamb*, Ā. *-ḍambate*, to imitate, vie with, BhP.; P. *-ḍambayati*, to imitate, copy, emulate, equal, be a match for any one or anything, Hariv.; Kāv.; Kāvyâd.; to mock, deride, ridicule, Hariv.; to impose upon, take in, cheat, deceive, Śak.; Bhartṛ.; Pañcat.; to afflict, MW. °**ḍamba**, mfn. imitating, representing, BhP.; m. mockery, derision, Kāv.; Sāh.; degradation, desecration, VarBṛS.; afflicting, distressing, annoyance, MW. °**ḍambaka**, mfn. imitating, strikingly resembling, Kād.; disgracing, profaning, Kāv.; BhP. °**ḍambana**, mfn. imitating, representing, acting like, BhP.; n. and (*ā*), f. imitation, copying, representing, playing the part of any one, imposture, disguise (esp. applied to a god assuming human form), Kāv.; Pur. (acc. with √*kṛi*, to imitate, copy, represent); derision, ridiculousness, mockery, scoff, scorn, vexation, mortification, MBh.; Kāv. &c. (acc. with √*kṛi*, to mock, deride); disgrace, degradation, profanation, BhP.; abuse, misusage, VarBṛS.; disappointing, frustrating, MW. °**ḍambanīya**, mfn. to be imitated &c.; to be distressed or annoyed, MW. °**ḍambita**, mfn. imitated, copied &c.; disguised, transformed, distorted, Hariv.; vexed, mortified, W.; low, poor, abject, ib.; deceived, disappointed, frustrated, MW.; n. an object of ridicule or contempt, despicable object, ib.; °*têśvara*, mfn. imitating or representing Śiva, Ragh. °**ḍambin**, mfn. imitating, copying, bearing a striking resemblance, Uttarar.; Kād.; mocking, deriding, vying with, surpassing, Śiś.; Kāvyâd.; disgracing, degrading, profaning, VarBṛS.; causing deception or error, MW. °**ḍambya**, n. an object of ridicule or contempt, BhP.

विडायतनीय *viḍ-āyatanīya*. See under 2. *viś*.

विडारक *viḍāraka*, *viḍāla*. See *biḍ°*.

विडिनाथकवि *viḍi-nātha-kavi*, m. (also written *vili-n°*) N. of an author, Cat.

विडीन *vi-ḍīna*, n. (√*ḍī*) the act of flying aslant or obliquely (one of the different modes of flight attributed to birds; others being *ava-*, *uḍ-*, *ni-*, *pari-*, *pra-*, *sam-ḍīna*, and *ḍīna-ḍīnaka*, q.v.), MBh.

Vi-ḍīnaka, n. flying apart, ib.

विडु *viḍu*, *viḍula*, w.r. for *viḍ°*.

विडूरज *viḍūra-ja* for *vi-dūra-ja*, p. 966, col. 1. (Cf. *vaiḍurya*.)

विडोजस् *viḍ-ojas* or *viḍ-aujas*, m. (also written *biḍ°*; said to be fr. *viḍ* = 2. *viś* + *ojas*) N. of Indra, Kālid.; Śatr. (in BhP. viii, 5, 41 as two words, meaning 'the Vaiśya and his trade').

विड्गन्ध *viḍ-gandha*, *viḍ-graha* &c. See under 3. *vish*.

विड्ड *viḍḍa*, n. bone, L. — **siṅha**, m. N. of a man, Rājat.

विड्ढल *viḍhḍhala*, v.l. for *viṭṭhala*, q.v.

विण्ट् *viṇṭ*, cl. 10. P. *viṇṭayati*, 'to kill' or 'to perish,' Dhātup. xxxii, 116 (v.l.)

विण्टक *viṇṭaka*, w.r. for *vi-ṭaṅka*, Vcar.

विण्मूत्र *viṇ-mūtra*. See under 3. *vish*.

वितंस *vi-taṅsa*, m. (√*taṅs*) any net or chain or apparatus for catching and confining beasts and birds, L. (cf. *vī-t°*; *ava-t°* and *ut-taṅsa*).

वितक्ष् *vi-√taksh*, P. *-takshati*, to cut off, cleave or split in pieces, RV.

Ví-tashṭa, mfn. hewn or carved out, planed, fashioned, ŚBr.

वितड् *vi-√taḍ*, P. *-tāḍayati* (Ved. Impv. *-tāḍhi*, *-tāḷhi*, for *-taḍḍhi*), to strike back, dash to pieces, RV.; to strike against (loc.), Pañcat.; to wound, MBh.

Vi-taṇḍa, m. (prob. connected with prec.) a sort of lock or bolt with three divisions or wards, W.; an elephant, ib.; (*ā*), f. cavil, captious objection, fallacious controversy, perverse or frivolous argument (esp. in Nyāya, 'idly carping at the arguments or assertions of another without attempting to prove the opposite side of the question,' cf. IW. 64), Nyāyas. (*-tva*, n., Sch.); Sarvad.; MBh. &c.; criticism, W.; a ladle, spoon, L.; Arum Colocasia, L.; = *karavīrī*, L.; = *śilâhvaya*, L.

Vi-taṇḍaka, m. N. of an author (*-smṛiti*, f. his wk.)

वितत *vi-tata* &c. See below.

वितथ *vi-tatha*, mf(*ā*)n. (fr. *vi* + *tathā*, not so) untrue, false, incorrect, unreal, vain, futile (instr. 'falsely;' °*thaṃ √kṛi*, 'to revoke, annul'), Mn.; MBh. &c.; free from (abl.), Āpast.; m. N. of Bharad-vāja, Hariv.; of a partic. class of domestic deities, VarBṛS.; Hcat.; *-tā*, f. untruth, falsehood (acc. with √*gam*, 'to become a lie'), Hariv.; *-prayatna*, mfn. one whose efforts are futile or in vain, Ragh.; *-maryāda*, mfn. incorrect in behaviour, MBh.; *-vāc* (Siṅhâs.), *-vādin* (Kathās.), mfn. speaking a falsehood, lying; °*thâbhiniveśa*, m. inclination to falsehood, Mn.; Yājñ. (*-vat*, mfn. prone to falsehood, Yājñ. iii, 135); °*thya*, mfn. untrue, MW.

Vitathaya, Nom. P. °*yati*, to render untrue, accuse of falsehood, Śiś.

Vitathī-√kṛi, P. *-karoti*, to render vain or futile, MBh.; Kum.; to remove, expel, Dharmaś.

वितद्भाषण *vi-tad-bhāshaṇa*. See *a-vit°*.

वितद्रु *vitadru*, f. N. of a river, Uṇ. iv, 102, Sch.

वितन् *vi-√tan*, P. Ā. *-tanoti*, *-tanute* (fut. *-tāyitā*, BhP.), to spread out or through or over, cover, pervade, fill, TUp.; MBh. &c.; to spread, stretch, extend (a net, snare, cord &c.), RV. &c. &c.; to draw or bend (a bow), MBh.; to spread out i.e. lay on, impose (a yoke), RV.; to apply (ointment), Kāv.; to extend, make wide (with *tanvàs*, the bodies, = to oppose or resist boldly, RV.; with *padāni*, steps, = to stride, Gīt.); to unfold, display, exhibit, manifest, RV. &c. &c.; to carry out, perform, accomplish (esp. a rite or ceremony), ib.; to sacrifice, Hariv.; to cause, effect, produce, Sāh.; to make, render (two acc.), Prasannar.

Ví-tata, mfn. spread out, extended &c.; diffused, drawn (as a bow-string), RV.; bent (as a bow), R.; covered, filled, Hariv.; prepared (as a road), AV.; extensive, far-spreading, broad, wide (*am*, ind.), VS. &c. &c.; n. any stringed instrument (such as a lute &c.), L.; *-tva*, n. extendedness, expansiveness, largeness, Hariv.; Pur.; *-dhanvan*, mfn. one who has drawn a bow to its full stretch, MBh.; *-vapus*, mfn. having an elongated body, MW.; °*tâdhvara* (*ví-*), mfn. one who has prepared a sacrifice, ŚBr.; °*tâyudha*, mfn. = *vitata-dhanvan*, MBh.; °*tôtsava*, mfn. one who has arranged a festival, Kathās.

Vi-tati, f. extent, length, BhP.; spreading, extension, expansion, diffusion, ib.; excess, Kāv.; quantity, collection, cluster, clump (of trees &c.), Kir.

Vitatī, in comp. for *vi-tata*. — **karaṇa**, f. spreading, W. — **√kṛi**, P. *-karoti* (pp. *-kṛita*), to stretch out, expand, Naish.

Vi-tatya, Nom. Ā. °*yate*, to stretch, expand, be diffused, ĀpŚr.

Vi-tana. See *āhara-vitanā*.

Vi-tanitṛi, mfn. one who spreads or extends, BhP.

2. **Vi-tāna**, m. n. (for 1. see p. 950, col. 3) extension, great extent or quantity, mass, heap, plenty, abundance, Kāv.; VarBṛS.; high degree, Bhartṛ.; manifoldness, variety, Gīt.; performance, accomplishment, development, growth, BhP.; an oblation, sacrifice, MBh.; Śiś.; BhP.; an awning, canopy, cover, MBh.; Kāv. &c.; the separate arrangement of the three sacred fires or the separate fires themselves, GṛŚrS.; m. or n.(?) a partic. bandage for the head, Suśr.; (*ā*), f. N. of the wife of Sattrāyaṇa, BhP.; n. N. of a partic. metre or of a class of metres, Piṅg., Sch.; Col.; leisure, opportunity, L.; *-kalpa*, m. N. of a Pariśishṭa belonging to the Atharva-veda, Caraṇ.; *-mūlaka*, n. the root of Andropogon Muricatus, L.; *-vat*, mfn. having a canopy or awning, Kum. °**tānaka**, m. n. an awning, canopy, covering, (esp.) a cloth spread over a large open hall or court (in which dancing, singing &c. are exhibited), R.; Kathās.; quantity, mass, Śiś.; an expanse, W.; Caryota Urens, L.

Vitānāya, Nom. (only Pass. °*yyate* impers.) to represent an awning or canopy, Mālatīm.

Vitānī, in comp. for *vi-tāna*. — **√kṛi**, P. *-karoti* (pp. *-kṛita*), to spread or extend over (as a canopy &c.), overshadow, MW. — **√bhū**, P. *-bhavati*, to represent a canopy, Bālar.

वितन्तसाय्य *vitantasâyya*, mfn. to be shaken or set in violent motion, RV.

वितप् *vi-√tap*, P. Ā. *-tapati*, °*te*, (P.) to give out heat, TBr.; to force asunder, tear, penetrate, RV.; AV.; (Ā.; cf. Pāṇ. i, 3, 27, Sch.) to burn (intr.), Bhaṭṭ.; to warm one's self or any member of the body, Pāṇ. i, 3, 27, Vārtt. 1, Pat.: Caus. *-tāpayati*, to heat, warm, VarBṛS.

वितमस् *vi-tamas*. See p. 950, col. 3.

वितरण *vi-taraṇa* &c. See under *vi-√tṝi*.

वितरम् *vi-tarám*, ind. (fr. 3. *vi* + *taram*) farther, farther off, more distant (either in space or time), more, RV. °**tarām**, id., ŚBr.; ĀpŚr.

वितर्क् *vi-√tark*, P. *-tarkayati*, to reflect, ponder, think, believe, suppose, conjecture, consider as or take for (acc.), MBh.; Kāv. &c.; to find out, ascertain, Kathās. °**tarka**, m. conjecture, supposition, guess, fancy, imagination, opinion, MBh.; Kāv. &c.; doubt, uncertainty, Yogas.; Sarvad.; a dubious or questionable matter, Yogas.; reasoning, deliberation, consideration, Kāv.; Sāh.; purpose, intention, Jātakam.; a teacher, instructor in divine knowledge, W.; a partic. class of Yogīs, Jātakam.; N. of a son of Dhṛita-rāshṭra, MBh.; pl. N. of the five principal sins, Jātakam.; *-padavī*, f. the path of conjecture or supposition, Prab.; *-vat*, mfn. (speech) containing a c° or s°, Daśar. °**tarkaṇa**, n. reasoning, conjecture, doubt, L. °**tarkita**, see *a-vitarkita*. °**tarkya**, mfn. to be considered, questionable, doubtful, BhP.

वितर्दि *vi-tardi* or °*dikā*, f. (said to be fr. √*tṛid*) a raised and covered piece of ground in the centre of a house or temple or in the middle of a court-yard, verandah, balcony &c., R.; Rājat. (L. also °*tardī*, °*tarddhī* and °*tarddhikā*).

वितष्ट *ví-tashṭa*. See col. 2.

वितस्त *vi-tasta*, mfn. (said to be fr. √*taṅs* or *tas*) = *upa-kshīṇa*, Nir. iii, 21, Sch.; (*ā*), f., see below; *-datta*, m. (for *vitastā-d°*, cf. Pāṇ. iv, 3, 63) N. of a merchant, Kathās.; °*tâdri*, m. N. of a mountain, Rājat. °**tastā**, f. N. of a river in the Panjāb (now called Jhelum or Bitasta or Bihat = the Hydaspes or Bidaspes [Ptolemy] of the Greeks; it rises in Kaśmīr; cf. *pañca-nada*), RV.; MBh. &c. (*-tva*, n., Rājat.); = *vi-tasti* (in *tri-vitastá*, q.v.); -°*khya* (°*tastâkhya*), n. N. of the habitation of the serpent-demon Takshaka in Kaśmīra, Rājat.; *-purī*, f. N. of a town, Cat.; *-māhātmya*, n. N. of wk.

वितस्ति *ví-tasti*, f. (once in Hcat. m.; prob. fr. √*tan*) a partic. measure of length (defined either as a long span between the extended thumb and little finger, or as the distance between the wrist and the tip of the fingers, and said to = 12 Aṅgulas or about 9 inches), ŚBr.; GṛŚrS. &c.; *-deśya*, mfn. almost a Vitasti long, Rājat.

वितान *vi-tāna* &c. See p. 962, col. 3.

वितामस *vi-tāmasa, vi-tāra*. See p. 950, col. 3.

विति *viti*, f. = *vīti*, in *gaurī-viti*, q. v.

वितिरे *vi-tire, vi-tīrṇa*. See *vi-√tṛī*.

वितुद् *vi-√tud*, P. Ā. *-tudati*, °*te*, to pierce, tear, strike, scourge, sting, prick, RV. &c. &c.; to strike i.e. play (a musical instrument), BhP.: Caus. *-tudāyati*, to prick, sting, AV. °**túda**, m. N. of a partic. spectral being, TĀr.

Vi-tunna, mfn. pierced, torn &c., MBh.; n. Marsilea Quadrifolia, L.; Blyxa Octandra, L.; (*ā*), f. Flacourtia Cataphracta, L. °**tunnaka**, m. n. and (*ikā*), f. Flacourtia Cataphracta, Car.; m. n. coriander, L.; blue vitriol, L.; m. or n.(?) a hole in the ear (for a ring), L.

वितुल *vitula*, m. N. of a prince of the Sauvīras, MBh. (B. *vipula*).

वितुष *vi-tusha* &c. See p. 950, col. 3.

वितूस्तय *vi-tūstaya*, Nom. (fr. *tūsta* with 3. *vi*) P. °*yati*, to comb out or smooth (hair), Pāṇ. iii, 1, 21, Sch.; to free from dust, Uṇ. iii, 86, Sch.

वितृण *vi-tṛiṇa, vi-tṛitīya* &c. See p. 950, col. 3.

वितृद् *vi-√tṛid*, P. Ā. *-tṛiṇatti, -tṛintte*, to pierce, bore, cleave, break asunder, excavate, AV.; KaṭhUp.: Caus. *-tardayati*, id., ŚāṅkhŚr.

Vi-tṛiṇṇa, mfn. pierced, cleft &c., ŚBr.

वितृप् *vi-√tṛip*, P. *-tṛipyati*, to be satisfied, become satiated with (loc.), BhP. °**tṛipta**, mfn. satisfied, satiated, R.; *-kāma* and *-dṛiś*, see *a-vitṛ*°. °**tṛiptaka**, mfn. satiated with (gen.), MBh. (in *a vitṛ*°).

वितृष् 1. *vi-√tṛish*, P. *-tṛishyati*, to be thirsty, VS.; TS.; Kāṭh.: Caus. *-tarshayati* (aor. *-tītṛishat*), to make thirsty, cause to thirst, TS.; Kāṭh. °**tṛishṇā**, f. (cf. p. 950, col. 3) thirst for, ardent desire, BhP.; N. of a river, VP.

2. **Vi-tṛish** &c. See p. 950, col. 3.

वितॄ *vi-√tṝī*, P. *-tarati, -tirati* (Ved. inf. *-tire*), to pass across or through, traverse, pervade, RV.; to bring away, carry off, remove, ib.; TS.; to cross, frustrate, disappoint (a wish), ib.; to extend, prolong, ib.; to give away (also in marriage), grant, afford, bestow, yield, MBh.; Kāv. &c. (with *āsanam*, to offer a seat; with *dvāram*, to grant admittance; with *uttaram*, to favour with an answer; with *darśanam* or *dṛishṭim*, to grant a sight, i. e. give an audience); to give (medicine), apply (a remedy), Suśr.; to produce, effect, perform, accomplish, Kāv.; Rājat.; BhP.: Caus. *-tārayati*, to pass (a comb) through, comb out, ŚBr.; to carry out, accomplish, ŚāṅkhŚr.: Intens. *-tartūryate* (p. *-tárturāṇa* or *-táritrat*), to pass over violently, labour or perform energetically, RV.

Ví-tara, mfn. leading further away (as a path), ŚBr. °**taraṇa**, mfn. one who crosses or passes over, MBh.; n. the act of crossing or passing over, MW.; leading over, transference, Suśr.; granting, bestowal, donation, gift, Inscr.; Kāv.; °*ṇâcārya*, m. N. of a preceptor, W. °**taritṛi**, m. a granter, bestower (with gen.), Bālar. °**tarturám**, ind. (fr. Intens.) alternately, RV. °**tārin**, see *a-vitārin*.

Vi-tīrṇa, mfn. one who has penetrated beyond or crossed or passed or gone over or through &c.; remote, distant (*-tara*, mfn. more distant), Nir. viii, 9; given, granted, afforded, bestowed, MBh.; Kāv. &c.; fought (as a battle), Rājat.; forgiven, pardoned, Bhartṛ.; performed, produced, accomplished, Rājat.; subdued, overcome, W.; effaced, id.

वितोला *vitolā*, f. N. of a river, Rājat.

वित्कोटिका *vitkoṭikā*(?), f. a kind of game, Divyâv.

वित्त् *vitt*, cl. 10. P. *vittayati*, to abandon, give away, Dhātup. xxxv, 78 (Vop.)

वित्त *vitta*. See under √1. *vid* &c.

वित्यज *vi-tyaja*. See *a-vityaja*.

वित्रस् *vi-√tras*, P. *-trasati, -trasyati*, to tremble, be frightened, MBh.; Kāv. &c.: Caus. *-trāsayati*, to cause to tremble, terrify, Mn.; MBh. &c. °**trasta**, mfn. frightened, alarmed, terrified, MBh.; Hariv. &c. °**trastaka**, mfn. a little affrighted or intimidated, R. °**trāsa**, m. fear, terror, alarm, Kathās.; Suśr.; mfn. = next, Hariv. °**trāsana**, mf(*ī*)n. terrifying, ib.; R.; n. the act of terrifying, Car. °**trāsayitu-kāma**, mfn. (inf. of Caus. + *k*°) wishing to frighten or terrify, R. °**trāsita**, mfn. (fr. Caus.) caused to tremble, terrified, affrighted, MBh.; R.; *-vihaṃgama*, mfn. having (its) birds frightened away, MW.

वित्रिभलग्नक *vi-tribha-lagnaka*, (prob.) n. = *tribhôna-l*°, the highest point of the ecliptic above the horizon, Gol.

वित्रुड् *vi-√truḍ* (for *truṭ*), P. *-truḍyati*, to scratch, excoriate, skin, KātyŚr., Sch.

वित्वक्षण *vi-tvákshaṇa*, mfn. (√*tvaksh*) very stout or strong or sturdy, RV. v, 34, 6 (Sāy. = *viśeshena tanū-kartṛi*).

वित्सन *vitsana*, m. an ox, bull (= *vrishabha*), L.

विथ् *vith* (cf. √*veth* and *vidh*), cl. 1. Ā. *vethate*, to ask, beg, Dhātup. ii, 32.

विथक् *vithak*, ind., g. *svar-ādi*.

विथुर *vithurá*, mf(*ā*)n. (√*vyath*) staggering, tottering, RV.; AV.; not solid, defective, precarious, AitBr.

Vithurya, Nom. P. °*yáti*, to stagger, totter, RV.

विथूतिस्तोत्र *vithūti-stotra*(?), n. N. of a Stotra, Cat.

विथ्या *vithyā*, f. a species of plant (= *go-jihvā*), L.

विद् 1. *vid*, cl. 2. P. (Dhātup. xxiv, 56) *vetti* (*vidmahe*, Br.; *vedati*, °*te*, Up.; MBh.; *vidáti*, °*te*, AV. &c.; *vindati*, °*te*, MBh. &c.; Impv. *vidām-karotu*, Pañcat. [cf. Pāṇ. iii, 1, 41]; 1. sg. impf. *avedam*, 2. sg. *avet* or *aves* [Pāṇ. viii, 2, 75], RV. &c. &c.; 3. pl. *avidus*, Br. [cf. Pāṇ. iii, 4, 109]; *avidan*, MBh. &c.; pf. *véda* [often substituted for pr. *vetti*, cf. Pāṇ. iii, 4, 83], 3. pl. *vidús* or *vidre*, RV.; *viveda*, MBh. &c.; *vidāṃ-cakāra*, Br. &c. [cf. Pāṇ. iii, 1, 38; accord. to Vop. also *vidām-babhūva*]; aor. *avedīt*, ib.; *vidām-akran*, TBr.; fut. *veditā*, ŚBr.; *vettā*, MBh.; fut. *vedishyati*, °*te*, Br.; Up.; *vetsyati*, °*te*, MBh. &c.; inf. *véditum*, °*tos*, Br.; *vettum*, MBh. &c.; ind. p. *viditvā́*, Br. &c.), to know, understand, perceive, learn, become or be acquainted with, be conscious of, have a correct notion of (with acc., in older language also with gen.; with inf. = to know how to), RV. &c. &c. (*viddhi yathā*, 'know that;' *vidyāt*, 'one should know,' 'it should be understood;' *ya evam veda* [in Br.], 'who knows thus,' 'who has this knowledge'); to know or regard or consider as, take for, declare to be, call (esp. in 3. pl. *vidus*, with two acc. or with acc. and nom. with *iti*, e.g. *taṃ sthaviraṃ viduḥ*, 'they consider or call him aged;' *rājarshir iti māṃ viduḥ*, 'they consider me a Rājarshi'), Up.; Mn.; MBh. &c.; to mind, notice, observe, remember (with gen. or acc.), RV.; AV.; Br.; to experience, feel (acc. or gen.), RV. &c. &c.; to wish to know, inquire about (acc.), ŚBr.; MBh.: Caus. *vedáyate* (rarely °*ti*; aor. *avīvidat*; Pass. *vedyate*), to make known, announce, report, tell, ŚBr. &c. &c.; to teach, explain, ŚāṅkhŚr.; Nir.; to recognize or regard as, take for (two acc.), MBh.; Kāv. &c.; to feel, experience, ŚBr.; Mn. &c.: Desid. of Caus. in *vivedayishu*, q. v.: Desid. *vividishati* or *vivitsati*, to wish to know or learn, inquire about (acc.), ŚBr. &c. &c.: Intens. *vevidyate, vevetti*, Gr. [Cf. Gk. εἶδον for ἔϝιδον, οἶδα for ϝοιδα = *veda*; Lat. *videre*; Slav. *věděti*; Goth. *witan, wait*; Germ. *wizzan, wissen*; Angl.Sax. *wât*; Eng. *wot*.]

1. **Vitta**, mfn. (for 2. see under √3. *vid*) known, understood (see comp.); celebrated, notorious, famous for (comp.), Daś. (cf. Pāṇ. viii, 2, 58). **Vittârtha**, m. 'one who knows the matter,' an expert, L.

1. **Vittaka**, mfn. very famous or renowned, Daś.

1. **Vitti**, f. consciousness, Sarvad.; understanding, intelligence, SaṃhitUp.

2. **Víd**, mfn. knowing, understanding, a knower (mostly ifc.; superl. *vit-tama*), KaṭhUp.; Mn.; MBh. &c.; m. the planet Mercury, VarBṛS. (cf. 2. *jña*); f. knowledge, understanding, RV.; KaushUp.; (pl.), Bhām.

Vida, mfn. = prec. (cf. *ko-, trayī-, dvi-v*°); m. knowledge, discovery (cf. *dur-v*°); m. N. of a man (cf. *bida*). **-gaṇá**(?), AV. xix, 22, 18. **-bhṛit**, m. N. of a man, g. *gargâdi* (cf. *vaidabhṛita*, °*tya*).

Vidatra. See *dur-* and *su-vidátra*.

Vidatriya. See *su-vidatriya*.

Vidátha, n. knowledge, wisdom; (esp.) 'knowledge given to others,' i.e. instruction, direction, order, arrangement, disposition, rule, command (also pl.), RV.; AV.; VS. (*vidatham ā-√vad*, to impart knowledge, give instruction, rule, govern); a meeting, assembly (either for deliberating or for the observance of festive or religious rites, i.e.) council, community, association, congregation, ib. (also applied to partic. associations or communities of gods, which in RV. viii, 39, 1 &c. are opposed to those of men; in RV. ii, 27, 8; vi, 51, 2 &c. three associations of gods are mentioned); a host, army, body of warriors (esp. applied to the Maruts), RV.; war, fight, ib.; a sage, scholar, L.; a saint, devotee, ascetic (= *yogin*), L.; = *kṛitin*, L.; N. of a man, Sāy. on RV. v, 33, 9. °**thin**, m. N. of a man, Pāṇ. vi, 4, 165 (cf. *vaidathina*). °**thyà**, mfn. fit for an assembly or council or any religious observance, festive, solemn, RV.

Vidāna. See under √3. *vid*.

Viditá, mfn. known, understood, learnt, perceived, known as (nom.), AV. &c. &c. (*viditam astu vaḥ* or *astu vo viditam*, 'let it be understood by you,' 'know that'); promised, agreed, L.; represented, W.; apprised, informed, ib.; m. a learned man, sage, W.; (*ā*), f. N. of a Jaina goddess, L.; n. information, representation, W.

Vidu, mfn. intelligent, wise, Gal.; m. the hollow between the frontal globes of an elephant, L.; N. of a man, Buddh.; m. or f. N. of a deity of the Bodhi tree, ib. **-pa**, m. N. of a king, VP.

Vidura, mfn. knowing, wise, intelligent, skilled in (comp.), Uttamac.; m. a learned or clever man, W.; an intriguer, ib.; N. of the younger brother of Dhṛita-rāshṭra and Pāṇḍu (they were all three sons of Vyāsa, but only the latter two by the two widows of Vicitra-vīrya; when Vyāsa wanted a third son, the elder widow sent him one of her slave-girls, dressed in her own clothes, and this girl became the mother of Vidura, who is sometimes called Kshattṛi, as if he were the son of a Kshatriya man and Śūdra woman; Vidura is described as *sarva-buddhimatām varaḥ*, and is one of the wisest characters in the Mahā-bhārata, always ready with good advice both for his nephews, the Pāṇḍavas, and for his brother Dhṛita-rāshṭra), MBh.; Hariv.; Pur. (cf. IW. 376; 385 &c.) **-tā**, f. the state or condition of (being) Vidura, MBh. xv, 752. **-nīti**, f. or **-prajāgara**, m. N. of chs. 32-39 of MBh. v. **Vidurâkrūra-varada**, m. N. of Kṛishṇa, Pañcar. **Vidurâgamana-parvan**, n. N. of chs. 200–206 of MBh. i.

Vidula, m. Calamus Rotang or Fasciculatus, Vās.; Car.; of a prince, VP.; (*ā*), f. a species of Euphorbia, Bhpr.; N. of a woman, MBh.

Vidush, weak form of *vidvas*, in comp. **-ṭara**, mfn. (compar. for *vidvat-tara*, fr. id.) wiser or very wise, RV. **-mat**, mfn. full of learned men, Vop.

Vidushī, f. (compar. °*shī-tarā*, Vop.; fr. *vidvas*) a wise woman, L.

Vidús, mfn. wise, attentive, heedful, RV.

Vidmán, n. knowledge, intelligence, wisdom (dat. *vidmáne* as Ved. inf. to know, to learn), RV.

Vidmana, mfn. (fr. prec.), Sāy.

Vidmanâpas, mfn. (fr. instr. of *vidman*, + *apas*) working skilfully or carefully, RV.; AV.

1. **Vidya** (for 2. see p. 965, col. 1) = *vidyā* (ifc.; see *a-v*°, °*kṛita-vidya, samāna-vidya-tā*).

Vidyā́, f. knowledge (cf. *kāla-jāta-v*°), science, learning, scholarship, philosophy, RV. &c. &c. (according to some there are four Vidyās or sciences, 1. *trayī*, the triple Veda; 2. *ānvīkshikī*, logic and metaphysics; 3. *daṇḍa-nīti*, the science of government; 4. *vārttā*, practical arts, such as agriculture, commerce, medicine &c.; and Manu vii, 43 adds a fifth, viz. *ātma-vidyā*, knowledge of soul or of spiritual truth; according to others, Vidyā has fourteen divisions, viz. the four Vedas, the six Vedāṅgas, the Purāṇas, the Mīmāṃsā, Nyāya, and Dharma or law; or with the four Upa-vedas, eighteen divisions; others reckon 33 and even 64 sciences [= *kalās* or arts]; Knowledge is also personified and identified with Durgā; she is even said to have composed prayers and magical formulas); any knowledge whether true or false (with Pāśupatas), Sarvad.; a spell, incantation, MBh.; Ragh.; Kathās.; magical skill, MW.; a kind of magical pill (which placed in the mouth is supposed to give the power of ascending to heaven), W.; Premna Spinosa, L.; a mystical N. of the letter *i*, Up.; a small bell, L. (cf. *vidyā-maṇi*). — 1. **-kara**, mfn. causing wisdom, giving knowledge or science, W. — 2. **-°kara** (°*yâk*°), m. 'mine of learning,' a learned man, W.; N. of a teacher, Cat.; (also °*ra-vājapeyin*) N. of an author, ib.; *-miśra-maithila*, m. N. of an author, ib. — **karmán**, n. the study of sacred science, Āpast.; (du.) kn° and action, ŚBr. — **kalpa-sūtra**, n. N. of wk. — **kośa-gṛiha**, n. or °**śa-samāśraya**, m. a library, Hcat. — **gaṇa**, m. pl. N. of a partic. Buddhist wk. — °**gama** (°*yâg*°), m. acquirement of kn°, proficiency in science, Kāv. — **gītā**, f. N. of wk. — **guru**, m. an instructor in science (esp. in sacred science), Gaut. — **grahaṇa**, n. acquisition of science, Kāś. — **cakravartin**, m. N. of an author, Cat. — **caṇa**, mfn. famous for learning, learned, Pāṇ. v, 2, 26, Sch. (cf. *-cuñcu*; *caṇa* and *cuñcu* are regarded by Pāṇ. as Taddhita affixes). — **caraṇa-sampanna**, mfn. perfect in kn° and of good moral conduct, Kāraṇḍ. — **cit**, mfn. puffed up by science, ŚBr. — **cuñcu**, mfn. = *-caṇa* above, Pāṇ. v, 2, 26, Sch. — **jambhaka-vārttika**, mfn. exercising magic of various kinds, MBh. — **tas**, ind. in consequence or by virtue of kn°, Āpast.; Nir.; also = abl. of *vidyā*. — **tīrtha**, n. knowledge compared to a sacred bathing-place, Prasaṅg.; N. of a b°-pl°, MBh.; of Śiva, Sāy.; of an author, Cat.; *-śishya*, m. N. of Sāyaṇa, Cat. — **tva**, n. the state or idea of *vidyā*, Kām. — **dala**, m. Betula Bhojpatra (whose leaves are used for writing), L. — **daśaka**, n. N. of wk. — **dātṛi**, mfn. one who gives or imparts knowledge, a teacher, MW. — **dāna**, n. the imparting of kn°, instruction in sc° (esp. sacred sc°), Hcat. — **dāyâda**, m. the inheritor of a sc°, Pāṇ. vi, 2, 5, Sch. — **devī**, f. 'goddess of learning,' a female divinity peculiar to the Jainas (16 are named), Campak. — **dhana**, n. the treasure of kn°, wealth consisting in learning, Mn. ix, 206. — **dhara**, mfn. possessed of science or spells, L.; m. a kind of supernatural being (dwelling in the Himâlaya, attending upon Śiva, and possessed of magical power), fairy (*-tva*, n.), Hariv.; Kāv. &c.; (also *-kavi*, °*râcārya*) N. of various scholars, Kir., Sch.; Vās., Introd.; Cat.; a kind of metre, Col.; (in music) a kind of measure, Saṃgīt.; (*ā* and *ī*), f. N. of a Surâṅganā, Siṃhâs.; (*ī*), f. a female of the above class of supernatural beings, fairy, sylph, MBh.; Kāv. &c.; N. of a daughter of Śūra-sena, Kathās.; *-cakravartin*, m. a supreme lord of the Vidyā-dharas, Vās.; *-tāla*, m. (in music) a kind of measure (= *vidyā-dhara*), Cat.; *-piṭaka* (?), N. of wk.; *-mahā-cakravartin*, m. the paramount lord of all fairy-like beings (°*ti-tā*, f.), Kathās.; *-yantra*, n. an apparatus for sublimating quicksilver, Bhpr.; *-rasa*, m. a partic. mixture, Cat.; °*râdhīśa*, m. = °*ra-cakra-vartin* (*-tā*, f.), Kathās.; °*râbhra*, m. a partic. mixture, L.; °*rī-parijana*, mfn. attended by Vidyā-dharīs, MW.; °*rī-√bhū*, to become a Vidyā-dhara, Kathās.; °*rī-vilāsa*, m. N. of wk.; °*rêndra*, m. a prince of the Vidyā-dharas (*-tā*, f., *-tva*, n.), Rājat.; Kathās.; N. of Jāmbavat, MBh. — **dhāma-muni-śishya**, m. N. of an author, Cat. — °**dhāra** (°*yâdh*°), m. 'receptacle of kn°,' a great scholar, Mālatim. — °**dhigama** (°*yâdh*°), m. acquisition of knowledge, study, ib. — °**dhidevatā** (°*yâdh*°), f. the tutelary deity of sc°, Sarasvatī, Pañcar. — °**dhipa** (°*yâdh*°), m. 'lord of knowledge,' (prob.) N. of Śiva, RāmatUp. — °**dhipati** (°*yâdh*°), m. N. of two poets, Kshem.; Subh. — °**dhirāja** or **-°dhirāya** (°*yâdh*°), m., °**ja-tīrtha**, n., **-°dhīśa-tīrtha** (°*yâdh*°), n., °**śa-nātha**, m., °**śa-muni**, m., °**śa-vaderu**, m., °**śa-svāmin**, m. N. of scholars, Cat. — **dhra**, m. = *-dhara*, a fairy, BhP. — **nagara**, n. (Buddh.; Col.) or (*ī*), f. (Inscr.) N. of a city. — °**nanda** (°*yân*°), m. 'delight in kn°,' Cat.; N. of ch. of the Pañca-daśī; of various authors, Kshem.; Cat.; *-nātha*, m. N. of an author, ib.; *-nibandha*, m. N. of wk. — **nātha**, m. (Pratāp.; Cat.), °**tha-bhaṭṭa**, m. (Col.), **-nidhi**, m. (Cat.), °**dhi-tīrtha**, m. (Cat.) N. of various authors or scholars. — **nivāsa**, °**sa-bhaṭṭâcārya**, m. N. of various men, Cat. — °**nupālana** (°*yân*°), n. encouragement or cultivation of science, W.; acquiring learning, studying, ib. — °**nupālin** (°*yân*°), mfn. cherishing or encouraging sc°, acquiring learning, W.; faithfully preserving (traditional) learning, Mn. ix, 204. — °**nulomalipi** (!), f. (°*yân*°) a partic. manner of writing, Lalit. — °**nusevana** (°*yân*°), n. the cultivation of science, W. — °**nusevin** (°*yân*°), mfn. cultivating learning, engaged in study, W. — °**nta** (°*yân*°), m. the end of an apprenticeship, ĀśvGṛ.; Gaut.; the end of knowledge, MW.; *-ga*, mfn. one who has completely mastered his profession, VarBṛS. — **nyāsa**, m. N. of a Mantra. — **pati**, m. the chief scholar at a court (*-tva*, n.), Rājat.; Vcar.; (also °*ti-svāmin*) N. of various authors or scholars, Kāv. &c. — **paddhati**, f. N. of sev. wks. — **pariṇaya**, m. N. of sev. dramas. — **pīṭha**, n. seat of kn°, Hcat. — **prakāśa-cikitsā**, f. N. of wk. — **pradāna**, n. = *-dāna* above, Cat.; N. of a ch. of the PSarv. — **pravāda**, n. N. of one of the Pūrvas or oldest writings of the Jainas. — **prâpti**, f. acquirement of kn°, W.; any acquisition made by learning, W. — **phala**, n. the fruit of learning, MW. — **bala**, n. the power of magic, MBh. — **bhaṭṭa**, m. N. of an author, Cat.; *-paddhati*, f. N. of wk. — °**bharaṇa** (°*yâbh*°), m. N. of an author, Cat.; (*ī*), f. N. of his wk. — **bhāj**, mfn. learned, VarBṛS. — °**bhimāna** (°*yâbh*°), m. the fancy or idea that one possesses learning, MW.; *-vat*, mfn. imagining one's self learned, Kathās. — °**bhīpsin** (°*yâbh*°), mfn. desiring kn°, KaṭhUp. — **bhūshaṇa**, m. N. of an author, Cat. — **bhṛit**, m. = *-dhara*, a fairy, Śatr. — °**bhyāsa** (°*yâbh*°), m. practice or pursuit of learning, application to books, study, Śaṃk. — **maṭha**, m. a college, monastic school, Pañcat. — **maṇi**, m. a small bell, L. — **maṇḍalaka**, n. 'circle of knowledge,' a library, Hcat. — **mada**, m. pride in one's learning, MBh. — **mandira**, n. a school-house, college, Kād. — **maya**, mf(*ī*)n. consisting of or absorbed in kn°, MBh.; BhP. — **mahêśvara**, m. 'lord of science,' N. of Śiva, Śivag. — **mātra-siddhi**, f., °**dhi-tri-daśa-śāstra-kārikā**, f. N. of Buddhist wks. — **mādhava**, m. N. of two authors. — **mādhavīya**, n., **-māhātmya**, n., **-°mṛita-varshiṇī** (°*yâm*°), f. N. of wks. — °**raṇya** (°*yâr*°), m. (also °*ya-tīrtha*, °*ya-yati*, °*ya-yogin*, °*ya-svāmin*, *bhāratī-tīrtha-vidyâraṇya*) N. of various scholars, Col.; W. &c.; *-jātaka*, n., *-nārāyaṇīya* (?), n., *-pañca-daśī*, f., *-bhāshya*, n., *-mūla*, n., *-saṃgraha*, m. N. of wks. — **ratna**, n. the jewel of learning, Cāṇ.; valuable knowledge, MW.; N. of wk.; °*nâkara*, m. N. of wk. — °**rambha** (°*yâr*°), m. beginning of study, Mall.; N. of a ch. of the PSarv. — **rāja**, m. a king of kn°, lord of spells, Buddh.; N. of Vishṇu, Pañcar.; of a saint, Buddh. — **rāma**, m. N. of an author, Cat. — **rāśi**, m. N. of Śiva, Śivag. — °**rcana-mañjarī** (°*yâr*°), f. N. of wk. — °**rjana** (°*yâr*°), n. acquirement of kn°, W.; acquiring anything by kn° or by teaching, W. — °**rjita** (°*yâr*°), mfn. acquired or gained by kn°, W. — °**rṇava** (°*yâr*°), m. N. of wk. — °**rtha** (°*yâr*°), m. the seeking for kn°, W.; mfn. desirous of kn°, Āpast.; *-dīpikā*, f., *-prakāśikā*, f. N. of wks. — °**rthin** (°*yâr*°), mfn. desirous of kn°, Cāṇ.; KaṭhUp., Sch.; m. a student, pupil, W. — °**laṃkāra** (°*yâl*°), °**ra-bhaṭṭâcārya**, m. N. of authors, Cat. — **labdha**, mfn. acquired or gained by learning, W. — °**laya** (°*yâl*°), m. abode or seat of learning, a school, college, W.; N. of a place, Cat. — **laharī**, f. N. of wk. — **lābha**, m. acquisition of l°, W.; any acquirement gained by l°, W. — **vaṃśa**, m. a chronological list of teachers in any branch of science, Pāṇ. ii, 1, 19, Sch. — **vat**, mfn. possessed of learning, learned, MBh.; Pañcat. &c.; (*atī*), f. N. of an Apsaras, VP.; of a Surâṅganā, Siṃhâs. — °**vataṃsa** (°*yâv*°), m. N. of a Vidyā-dhara, Bālar. — **vadhū**, f. a goddess thought to preside over learning, Vcar. (cf. *vidyâdhidevatā*). — **vayo-vṛiddha**, mfn. advanced in learning and years, MW. — **vallabha**, m. a partic. mixture, Rasêndrac. — **vāgīśa** ('master in sc° and speech') or °**śa-bhaṭṭâcārya**, m. N. of a scholar, Cat. — **vikraya**, m. 'sale of knowledge,' instruction in return for payment, Pañcat. — **vid**, mfn. learned, ĀpŚr. — **vinoda**, m. (also °*dâcārya*) N. of various scholars, Cat. &c.; of various wks. — **viruddha**, mfn. conflicting with science, Vām.; *-tā*, f., Sāh. — **vilāsa**, m. (prob.) N. of a king, L.; of wk. — **viśārada**, m. N. of a scholar, Cat.; of a minister, Vīrac. — **viśishṭa**, mfn. distinguished for learning, possessed of science, W. — **vishaye homa-vidhi**, m. N. of wk. — **vihīna**, mfn. destitute of kn°, ignorant, Siṃhâs. — **vṛiddha**, mfn. old in knowledge, increased in learning, Hit.; Sarvad. — **veda-vrata-vat** or **-veda-vrata-snāta**, mfn. one completely versed in religious observances and the Veda and the sciences, MBh. (cf. *vidyā-vrata-sn*°, *veda-vidyā-vrata-sn*°). — **veśman**, n. a school-house, college, Rājat. — **vyavasāya**, m. the pursuit of science, MW. — **vyasana**, n. id., A. — **vyākhyāna-maṇḍapa**, m. n. a hall where the sc°s are explained, college, Hcat. — **vrata**, n. a partic. religious observance, Cat.; m. (prob.) a kind of magician, Buddh.; *-snāta* (Mn. iv, 21) or °*taka* (GṛS.), mfn. one who is completely versed in the Veda and religious observances; (°*taka*), m. a Brāhman who has finished his studentship, W. — **śruta-sampanna**, mfn. well equipped with secular and sacred science, BhP. — **sadman**, n. 'abode of learning,' a school, Bhām. — **sampradāna**, n. = *-dāna*, Āpast. — **sāgara**, m. 'ocean of knowledge,' N. of various scholars, Cat. &c.; *-pāra*, N. of wk. — **sādhana**, n. N. of wk. — **sthāna**, n. a branch of kn°, Nir.; Bālar. — **snāta** (MBh.; R.) or **-snātaka** (PārGṛ.), mfn. one who has finished his studentship and completed his study of the Vedas. — **hīna**, mfn. destitute of knowledge, unlearned, uninstructed, Gaut.; Mn.; Pañcat. **Vidyêndra-sarasvatī**, m. N. of an author, Cat. **Vidyêśa**, m. 'lord of kn°,' N. of Śiva, Śivag.; = *vidyêśvara* (*-tva*, n.), Hcat.; Sarvad. **Vidyêśvara**, m. (with Śaivas) N. of a class of emancipated beings, Sarvad.; N. of a magician, Daś. **Vidyôttara-tāpinī**, f., **Vidyôtpatti**, f. N. of wks. **Vidyôpayoga**, m. acquisition of learning from (abl.), Gaut. **Vidyôpârjana**, n. (MW.) or °**nā**, f. (Ml.) acquisition of knowledge. **Vidyôpârjita**, mfn. acquired by learning, MW.

Vidyika. See *vāyov*°.

Vidvac, in comp. for *vidvat*. — **cakora**, m. (with *bhaṭṭa*) N. of a lexicographer, L. — **citta-prasādinī**, f. N. of wk.

Vidvaj, in comp. for *vidvat*. — **jana**, m. a wise man, sage, seer, Bhartṛ.; Hit.; *-parisevitā*, f. N. of a Kiṃ-narī, Kāraṇḍ.; *-mada-bhañjana*, n., *-manoharā*, f., *-vallabha*, m., *-vallabhīya*, n. N. of wks.

Vidvat, in comp. for *vidvas*. — **kaṇṭha-pāśa**, m. N. of a poem. — **kalpa**, mfn. a little learned, slightly learned, W. — **tama**, m. 'wisest, very wise,' N. of Śiva, Śivag. — **tara**, mfn. wiser, very wise, Vop. (cf. *vidush-ṭara*). — **tā**, f. (Hariv.), **-tva**, n. (Cāṇ.) scholarship, science, wisdom. — **prabodhinī**, f., **-saṃnyāsa-lakshaṇa**, n. N. of wks.

Vidvad, in comp. for *vidvat*. — **deśīya** or **-deśya**, mfn. = *vidvat-kalpa*, MW. — **bhūshaṇa-padya-saṃgraha**, m., **-vallabha**, m., **-vinoda-kāvya**, n., **-vinoda-mañjūshā**, f., **-vivāda**, m. N. of wks.

1. **Vidván**, mfn. = *vidvás*, AV. ix, 9, 7.

2. **Vidvan**, in comp. for *vidvat*. — **maṇḍana**, n., **-manorañjinī**, f., **-manoramā**, f., **-manoharā**, f. N. of wks. — **moda-taraṃgiṇī**, f. N. of a survey of philosophical and religious systems. — **modinī**, f. N. of a Comm. on Ragh. by Rāmabhadra.

Vidvalá, mf(*ā*)n. clever, artful, RV.

Vidvás, mf(*ushī*)n. one who knows, knowing, understanding, learned, intelligent, wise, mindful of, familiar with, skilled in (acc., loc., or comp.), RV. &c. &c. (cf. *vidvat-tara*, *vidvat-tama*, *vidush-ṭara*, *vidushī-tara*); m. a wise man, sage, seer, W.; N. of a Brāhman, Hariv.

1. **Vinna**, mfn. known, understood (= *jñāta*), L.

Vivitsā, f. (fr. Desid.) desire of knowing, MBh.

Vivitsu, mfn. desirous of knowing or learning (with acc.), MBh.; BhP.; m. N. of a son of Dhṛita-rāshṭra, MBh.

Vividishā, f., °**shu**, mfn. = *vivitsā*, °*tsu*, Śaṃk.

विद् 3. **vid** (originally identical with √1. *vid*), cl. 6. P. Ā. (Dhātup. xxviii, 138) *vindáti*, °*te* (Ved. also *vitté*, *vidé*; p. *vidāná* or *vidāna* [q. v.]; ep. 3. pl. *vindate*, Pot. *vindyāt*, often = *vidyāt*; pf. *vivéda* [3. pl. *vividus*, Subj. *vividat*], *vividé*, 3. pl. *vividre*, *vidré*, RV. &c. &c.; p. *vividvás*, RV.; *vividivas*, Pāṇ. vii, 2, 68; aor. *ávidat*, °*data*, ib. [Ved. Subj. *vidási*, °*dât*; Pot. *vidét*, *deta*, VS.; AV.; Br.; 3. sg. *videshṭa*, AV. ii, 36, 3]; Ā. 1. sg. *avitsi*, RV.; Br.; fut. *vettā*, *vedishyati*, Gr.; *vetsyati*, °*te*, Br. &c.; inf. *vidé*, RV.; *vettum*, MBh. &c.; *véttave*, AV.; °*ttavaí* [?] and °*tos*, Br.; ind. p. *vittvā*, AV.; Br.; *-vidya*, Br. &c.), to find, discover, meet or fall in with, obtain, get, acquire, partake of, possess, RV. &c. &c. (with *diśas*, to find out the quarters of the sky,

MBh.); to get or procure for (dat.), RV.; ChUp.; to seek out, look for, attend to, RV. &c. &c.; to feel, experience, Cāṇ.; to consider as, take for (two acc.), Kāv.; to come upon, befall, seize, visit, RV.; AV.; Br.; to contrive, accomplish, perform, effect, produce, RV.; ŚBr.; (Ā., m.c. also P.) to take to wife, marry (with or scil. *bhāryām*), RV.; Mn.; MBh. &c.; to find (a husband), marry (said of a woman), AV.; Mn.; MBh.; to obtain (a son, with or scil. *sutam*), BhP.: Pass. or Ā. *vidyáte* (ep. also °*ti*; p. *vidyamāna* [q.v.]; aor. *avedi*), to be found, exist, be, RV. &c. &c.; (esp. in later language) *vidyate*, 'there is, there exists,' often with *na*, 'there is not;' with *bhoktum*, 'there is something to eat;' followed by a fut., 'is it possible that?' Pāṇ. iii, 3, 146, Sch.; *yathā-vidé*, 'as it happens,' i.e. 'as usual,' 'as well as possible,' RV. i, 127, 4 &c.: Caus. *vedayati*, to cause to find &c., MBh.: Desid. *vividishati* or *vivitsati*, °*te*, Gr. (cf. *vivitsita*): Intens. *vevidyate*, *vevetti*, ib. (for p. *vévidat* and °*dāna* see *vi-* and *sam-√3. vid*).

2. **Vittá**, mfn. (for 1. see p. 963) found, acquired, gained, obtained, possessed, AV.; Br.; caught or seized by (instr. or comp.), Br.; Kauś.; (*ā*), f. taken, married (as a woman), ŚBr.; n. anything found, a find, AitBr.; (in later language also pl.) acquisition, wealth, property, goods, substance, money, power, RV. &c. &c.; the second astrological mansion, VarYogay. **–kāma**, mfn. desirous of wealth, covetous, avaricious, MBh.; °*myā́*, ind. (instr. f.) from avarice, AV. **–goptṛi**, m. 'guardian of w°,' N. of Kubera, MBh. **–ja**, mfn. produced by w°, Pañcat. **–jāni** (*vittá-*), mfn. one who has taken a wife, married, RV. **–da**, m. 'wealth-giver,' benefactor, W.; (*ā*), f. N. of one of the Mātṛis attendant on Skanda, MBh. **–dugdha**, n. 'milk-wealth,' wealth compared to milk, Hit. **–dhá**, mfn. 'w°-possessing,' rich, VS. **–nātha**, m. 'lord of wealth,' N. of Kubera, Kathās. **–nicaya**, m. pl. great wealth, opulence, MārkP. **–pa**, mf(*ā*)n. guarding w°, BhP.; m. N. of Kubera, R.; Hariv. **–pati**, m. = *-nātha*, Mn.; MBh. &c. **–pāla**, m. id., R.; N. of a poet, Cat. **–purī**, f. N. of a town, Kathās. **–peṭā** or **-peṭī**, f. money-receptacle, a purse, Pañcat. **–maya**, mf(*ī*)n. consisting in w°, KaṭhUp. **–mātrā**, f. a sum of money, Pañcat. **–rakshin**, m. a wealthy man, MBh. **–rddhi** (for *ṛiddhi*), f. increase or abundance of w°, MārkP. **–vat**, mfn. possessing w°, opulent, rich, ĀśvŚr.; MBh. &c. **–vardhana**, mf(*ī*)n. increasing w°, lucrative, MW. **–vivardhin**, mfn. increasing property or capital, bearing interest, Mn. viii, 140. **–śāṭhya**, n. cheating in money matters, Hcat. **–saṃcaya**, m. accumulation of w° or riches, R. **–hīna**, mfn. destitute of w°, poor, Pañcat. (v.l.) **Vittâgama**, m. acquisition of w°, means of making money, Mn.; Pañcat. **Vittâḍhya**, mfn. abounding in wealth, rich, Var. **Vittâpti**, f. = *vittâgama*, ib. **Vittâp-pati**, n. du. the lords of wealth and water (i.e. Kubera and Varuṇa), Mn. v, 96. **Vittêśa**, m. 'wealth-lord,' Kubera, Mn.; Hariv. &c.; *-patana*, n. Kubera's town, Rājat. **Vittêśvara**, m. a lord of w°, VarBṛS.; MārkP.; N. of Kubera, Kathās. **Vittêhā**, f. desire of wealth, cupidity, avarice, MBh. **Vittâishaṇā́**, f. id., ŚBr.

2. **Vittaka.** See *prasāda-v°* (for 1. see p. 963).

Vittāyana, mf(*ī*)n. (prob.) procuring wealth or riches, TS.; MaitrS.

2. **Vitti**, f. finding, acquisition, gain, ŚBr.; ChUp.; GṛŚrS.; a find, AitBr.; the being found, existence, L.; (ifc.) a term of praise, g. *matallikâdi*.

Vittoka, m. N. of a poet, Cat.

4. **Vid**, (ifc.) finding, acquiring, procuring (see *anna-*, *aśva-*, *ahar-vid* &c.)

Vidad (for *vidat*, pr. p. of √3. *vid*), in comp. **–aśva**, m. 'granting horses,' N. of a man (cf. *vaidadaśvi*). **–vasu** (*vidád-*), mfn. possessing or granting wealth, RV.; Br.

Vídāna or **vidāná**, mfn. (Ā. pr. p.) existing, being, real, RV.; AV.; common, usual, ib.; forming, making (?), RV.

Vidā́yya, mfn. to be found, RV. x, 22, 5.

2. **Vidya**, n. finding, acquiring, gaining (see *pati-v°* and *putra-v°*).

Vidyamāna, mfn. (Pass. pr. p.) 'being found,' existent, existing, present, real, Pat.; Kāv.; Pur. (cf. *a-vid°*). **–keśa**, mfn. one who possesses hair, MW. **–tā**, f., **-tva**, n. existence, presence, Saṃk. **–mati**, mfn. possessing understanding, wise, Pañcat.

2. **Vinna**, mfn. found, acquired &c.; existent, real, L.; (*ā*), f. a married woman, Yājñ. i, 85. **–pa**, m. N. of a king, Rājat.; of the saint Agastya, MW. (perhaps w.r. for *vitta-pa*).

Vividivas, vividvás. See under √3. *vid.*

विद् 5. *vid*, cl. 7. Ā. (Dhātup. xxix, 13) *vintte*, to consider as, take for (two acc.), Bhaṭṭ.

3. **Vitta** or **vinna**, mfn. = *vicārita*, L.

विदंश् *vi-√daṃś*, P. *-daśati*, to bite to pieces, bite asunder, PārGṛ.; Yājñ.; BhP. °**daṅśa**, m. biting, Kir.; any pungent food which excites thirst, Śiś. °**dadaṅkshu** (?), mfn. (fr. Desid.) wishing to bite or to eat, Śiś. x, 9.

Vi-dashṭa, mfn. crushed or forced asunder, Suśr.

विदग्ध *ví-dagdha.* See *vi-√dah* below.

विदन्वत् *vidanvat*, m. N. of a Bhārgava, PañcavBr.

विदय् *vi-√day*, Ā. *-dayate*, to divide, sever, destroy, RV.; to distribute, bestow, be liberal with (instr.), ib.

विदर *vi-dara*, *vi-daraṇa*. See under *vi √dṛī*, p. 966, col. 1.

विदर्भ *vi-darbha*, m. 'destitute of Darbha grass,' N. of a country south of the Vindhya hills (now called Berar; it was the country of Damayantī, wife of Nala; the soil was probably grassless and arid, but the absence of Darbha is said to be due to the fact that the son of a saint died of the prick of a sharp blade of that grass), MBh.; Kāv. &c.; a king of Vidarbha, MBh.; Naish.; a partic. disease of the gums (= *vaidarbha*), ŚārṅgS.; N. of a man, Hariv.; of a son of Jyā-magha, ib.; of a son of Ṛishabha, BhP.; (*ās*), m. pl. the inhabitants of V° and also the country itself; the interior of anything, Harav.; (*ā*), f. N. of the capital city of V° (= Kuṇḍina), MBh.; of a river, Hariv.; of a daughter of Ugra and wife of Manu Cākshusha, MārkP.; °*bha-jā*, f. 'V°-born,' N. of the wife of the saint Agastya, of Damayantī, and of Rukmiṇī, L.; °*bha-tanayā*, f. 'daughter of the Vidarbha king,' N. of Damayantī, MBh.; °*bha-nagarī*, f. the city of V°, MBh.; °*bha-pati*, m. the king of V°, Mālav.; °*bha-bhū*, f. the country of V°, Naish.; °*bha-rāj*, m. the king of V°, MW.; °*bha-rāja* (or °*jan*), m. id., R. (°*ja-dhānī*, f. the capital of V°, Cat.; °*ja-putrī*, f. patr. of Rukmiṇī, Śiś.); °*bhâdhipa*, m. the Vidarbha king, MBh. (*-rāja-dhānī*, f. his residence, Ragh.); °*bhâdhipati*, m. id., BhP.; °*bhâbhimukha*, mfn. facing V°, MW.; °*bhi*, m. N. of a Ṛishi, Saṃk.; °*bhī-kauṇḍinyá*, m. N. of a preceptor, ŚBr.

विदर्शना *vi-darśanā*, °*śin*. See under 2. *vi-√dṛiś*, p. 966.

विदल् *vi-√dal*, P. *-dalati*, to break or burst asunder, be rent or split asunder, Naish.; to open, rend or tear asunder, R. (Pass. fut. p. *-dalishyamāṇa*, Daś.)

2. **Vi-dala**, mf(*ā*)n. (cf. *bidala*; for 1. see p. 950, col. 3) rent asunder, split, Gṛihyas.; expanded, blown, Śiś.; m. rending, dividing, separating, W.; sweetmeats, a cake, L.; Bauhinia Variegata, L.; (*ā*), f. Ipomœa Turpethum, L.; n. anything split or pared, a chip, piece, fragment, Gaut.; MārkP.; Suśr. &c.; split bamboo, a cane, Mn. ix, 230; wicker-work, Yājñ. i, 85; a split pea, Suśr.; pomegranate bark, L. °**dalana**, n. the act of tearing or rending asunder, splitting, Kāv.; Sarvad.; bursting (intrans.), Kathās. °**dalita**, mfn. burst or rent asunder &c.; expanded, blown, Gīt. °**dalī-karaṇa**, n. the act of rending asunder or dividing, W. °**dalī-kṛita**, mfn. rent asunder, torn, cut, divided, separated, MBh.; R. &c.

विदस् *vi-√das*, P. *-dasyati* or *-dasati*, to waste away, become exhausted, come to an end, RV.; VS.; Kāṭh.; to be wanting, fail (with abl. of pers.), RV. °**dasta**, mfn. wasted away, exhausted (= *upakshīṇa*), Nir. i, 9, Sch. °**dasya**, see *a-vidasyá*. °**dāsin**, see *a-vidāsin*.

विदह् *vi-√dah*, P. *-dahati*, to burn up, scorch, consume or destroy by fire, RV.; MBh.; to cauterize (a wound), Suśr.; to decompose, corrupt, Car.: Pass. *-dahyate*, to be burnt &c.; to burn, be inflamed (as a wound), Suśr.; to suffer from internal heat, ib.; to be consumed by grief, waste, pine, MBh.; to be puffed up, boast, R. (v.l. *vi-katthase* for *vi-dahyase*).

Ví-dagdha, mfn. burnt up, consumed, ŚBr.; Kauś.; inflamed, Suśr.; cooked by internal heat as by the fire of digestion, digested, ib.; decomposed, corrupted, spoiled, turned sour, ib.; mature (as a tumour), Bhpr.; tawny or reddish brown (like impure blood), L.; clever, shrewd, knowing, sharp, crafty, sly, artful, intriguing, MBh.; Kāv. &c.; m. tawny (the colour), L.; a clever man, scholar, Paṇḍit, W.; a libertine, intriguer, ib.; N. of a teacher of the Vājasaneyins, ŚBr.; (*ā*), f. a sharp or knowing woman, W.; *-cuḍāmaṇi*, m. N. of an enchanted parrot, Kathās.; Vet.; *-tā*, f., *-tva*, n. cleverness, sharpness, skill in (loc.), Kāv.; *-toshiṇī*, f. N. of an astron. wk.; *-parivṛiddhatā*, f. the turning acid and swelling (of food in the stomach), Suśr.; *-parishad*, f. an assembly or company of clever people, Bhartṛ.; *-bodha*, m. N. of a grammar (by Rāma-candra Miśra); *-mādhava*, n. N. of a Nāṭaka or drama (by Rūpa Go-svāmin, in 7 acts, written A.D. 1549; it is a dramatic version of the Gita-govinda on the loves of Kṛishṇa and Rādhā); *-mukha-maṇḍana*, n. N. of a wk. on enigmas (by the Buddhist Dharmadāsa); *-vacana*, mfn. clever or skilful in speech, Pañcat.; *-vaidya*, m. N. of a medical writer; °*dhâjīrṇa*, n. a partic. form of indigestion, Bhpr.; °*dhâlāpa*, mfn. clever in language, elegant, witty, Bhartṛ.

Vi-dagdhaka, m. a burning corpse, Buddh.

Vi-dāha, m. burning, heat, inflammation (also applied to the action or to a diseased condition of the bile), Suśr.; ŚārṅgS.; the turning acid (of food in the stomach), Car.; *-vat*, mfn. burning, hot, Suśr. °**dāhaka**, n. caustic potash, L. °**dāhin**, mfn. burning, scorching, hot (°*hi-tva*, n.), Lāṭy.; Suśr.; Bhpr.; pungent, acrid, W.

विदा *vi-√1. dā*, P. *-dadāti*, to give out, distribute, grant, R.

Vi-datta, mfn. given out, distributed, Kār. on Pāṇ. vii, 4, 47.

Vi-dāyin, mfn. granting, causing, effecting, Śatr.

Vi-deya, mfn. to be given or granted, Āpast.

विदा *vi-√3. dā* (or *do*, not separable fr. √4. *dā*), P. *-dāti* or *-dyati* (ind. p. *-ditya*), to cut up, cut to pieces, bruise, pound, VS.; to untie, release, deliver from (abl.), ŚBr.; to destroy, Hariv. °**dāna**, n. cutting to pieces, dividing, ŚBr. °**dāya**, m. division, distribution, Pañcav. (v.l.); permission to go away, dismissal with good wishes (in this sense perhaps not a Sanskrit word; cf. وداع).

विदान्त *vidānta*, m. N. of a prince, Hariv.

विदार *vi-dāra*, °*raka*, °*raṇa*. See under *vi-√dṛī*, p. 966, col. 1.

विदाश् *vi-√dāś*, P. *-dāśati*, to reject, deny, RV. vii, 19, 9.

विदिव् *vi-√2. div*, P. Ā. *-dīvyati*, °*te*, to lose at play, Kāṭh.; MBh.; to play, ŚBr.

2. **Vi-devá**, m. (for 1. see p. 950, col. 3) game at dice, ŚBr. °**devana**, n. dicing, Vait.

विदिश् *vi-diś* &c. See p. 950, col. 3.

विदीगय *vidīgáya*, m. a species of gallinaceous bird, TS.; TBr. (= *śveta-baka*, Sch.)

विदीधयु *vidīdhayu*. See *a-v°*.

विदीप् *vi-√dīp* (only Ā. impf. *vy-adīpanta*), to shine forth, shine very brightly, MBh. vii, 7322: Caus. *-dīpayati*, to shine upon, illuminate, MBh.; R. &c. °**dīpaka**, m. a lantern, MBh. (C. *ikā*, f.) °**dīpita**, mfn. (fr. Caus.) illuminated, bright, MBh.; inflamed, incensed, BhP. °**dīpta**, mfn. shining, bright; *-tejas*, mfn. of bright splendour, MBh.

विदीर्ण *vi-dīrṇa*. See under *vi-√dṛī*.

विदु *vi-√2. du* (or *dū*), P. *-dunoti*, to consume or destroy by burning, AV.; Ā. *-dunute*, *-dūyate* (ep. also °*ti*), to be agitated or afflicted or distressed, MBh.; BhP.

Vi-dūna, mfn. distressed, afflicted, W.

विदु *vidu*, *vidura*, *vidula*. See under √1. *vid*, p. 963, col. 3.

विदुद् *vidud*, (prob.) = Vendidad, BhavP.

विदुष् *vi-√dush*, P. *-dushyati*, to be defiled, commit a fault or sin, transgress, Vishṇ.: Caus. *-dūshayati*, to defile, corrupt, disgrace, RV.; BhP.; (with *upahāsaiḥ*) to deride, ridicule, MārkP.

Vi-dūshaka, mfn. defiling, disgracing, BhP.;

facetious, witty, W.; m. a jester, wag, buffoon (esp. in dram.) the jocose companion and confidential friend of the hero of a play (he acts the same confidential part towards the king or hero, that her female companions do towards the heroine; his business is to excite mirth in person and attire, and to make himself the universal butt; a curious regulation requires him to be a Brāhman, or higher in caste than the king himself; cf. IW. 474), Hariv.; Kāv.; Sāh. &c.; a libertine, catamite, L.; N. of a Brāhman, Kathās. °**dūshaṇa**, mf(*ā*)n. defiling, detracting, corrupting, R.; n. censuring, reviling, abuse, satire, W. °**dūshaṇaka**, mfn. = prec., Sāy. °**dūshita**, mfn. soiled, defiled, disgraced, R.

Vi-dosha, m. a fault, sin, offence, Lāṭy., Sch.

विदुषितर *vidushi-tara*, *vidush-ṭara* &c. See p. 963, col. 3.

विदुह् *vi-√duh*, P. *-dogdhi*, to milk out, drain, exploit, RV.; AV.; ŚBr.

Vi-dohá, mfn. false or excessive milking out or exploiting, TBr.

विदूर *vi-dūra*, mf(*ā*)n. very remote or distant, ŚāṅkhŚr.; Kāv. &c. (acc. with √*kṛi*, to remove; *vi-dūram*, ind. far distant, far away, TBr.; *vi-dūrāt* or °*ra-tas*, from afar, far away; °*re*, far distant; °*ra*, ibc. far, from afar); far removed from, not attainable by (gen.), BhP.; (ifc.) not caring for, ib.; m. N. of a son of Kuru, MBh. (B.); of a mountain or town or any locality, Śiś., Sch. (cf. Pāṇ. iv, 3, 84); *-kramaṇa-kshama*, mfn. able to run far away, Kām.; *-ga*, mfn. going far away, Cat.; far-spreading (as scent), L.; *-gamana*, n. the going far away, Kathās.; *-ja*, n. cat's eye (a sort of jewel), Harav.; *-jāta*, mfn. grown a long way off, MBh.; *-tā*, f. = next, Mṛicch.; *-tva*, n. a great distance (abl. 'from afar'), Hariv.; *-bhūmi*, f. N. of a locality (= *vidūra*), Kum.; *-ratna*, n. = *-ja*, L.; *-vigata*, mfn. 'come from afar,' of lowest origin, BhP.; *-saṃśrava*, mfn. audible a long way off, R.; °*râdri*, m. N. of a mountain, W.; °*rī-√bhū*, P. *-bhavati*, to become far distant, Ragh.; °*rôdbhāvita*, n. = °*ra-ja*, L.

Vi-dūraya, Nom. P. °*yati*, to drive far away, Kāv. (v. l.)

विदूरथ *vidūratha*, m. (perhaps for *vidūra-ratha*) N. of a Muni, VarBṛS.; of a son of the 12th Manu, Hariv.; of a king, ib.; of a descendant of Vṛishṇi, MBh.; of a son of Kuru, ib.; of a son of Bhajamāna and father of Śūra, Hariv.; Pur.; of a son of Su-ratha and father of Ṛiksha (Sārvabhauma), ib.; of a son of Citra-ratha, BhP.; of the father of Su-nīti and Su-mati, MārkP. &c.; of a man who was killed by his wife; cf. Kām. vii, 54; Vās., Introd., p. 53.

विदृश् 1. *vi-dṛiś*, see under 3. *ví*, p. 950, col. 3.

विदृश् 2. *vi-√dṛiś* (only Pass. and Ā. *-dṛiśyate*; aor. *vy-adarśi*; cf. *vi-√paś*), to be clearly visible, become apparent, appear, RV.; MBh. &c.: Caus. *-darśayati*, to cause to see, show, MBh.; Hariv.; R.; to teach, R.

Vi-darśanā, f. (right) knowledge, Lalit. °**darśin**, w. r. for *ni-darśin*, R.

Vi-drashṭṛi, mfn. seeing clearly or distinctly, Pat.

विदृ *vi-√dṛī*, P. *-driṇāti*, to tear asunder or to pieces, lacerate, MBh.; R. &c.; to cleave, open (aor. Subj. *-darshasi*), RV. viii, 32, 5: Pass. *-dīryate* (ep. also °*ti*), to be torn or rent asunder, split open, ŚBr. &c. &c.; to be torn with grief or anguish, MBh.; R.: Caus. *-dārayati*, to cause to burst asunder, rend or tear to pieces, lacerate, MBh.; Kāv. &c.; to open, AitUp.; Hariv.; Ṛitus.; to scatter, disperse, R.; Rājat.; to push away, Kathās.: Intens. *-dardarīti*, to tear or split in pieces, burst asunder, open, RV.

2. **Vi-dara**, m. (for 1. see p. 950, col. 3) tearing asunder, rending, L.; a crevice, fissure, Naish.; n. Cactus Indicus (prob. the flower), L. °**daraṇa**, n. tearing asunder, reading, L.; = *vidradhi*, L.

Vi-dāra, m. tearing or rending asunder, cutting, splitting, Kāv.; Vop.; war, battle, L.; an inundation, overflow, L.; (*ī*), f., see below; a swelling in the groin, L. °**dāraka**, mfn. tearing asunder, cutting, splitting, lacerating, Subh.; ChUp., Sch.; a hole or pit for water in the bed of a dry river, L.; a tree or rock in the middle of a stream dividing its course, W.; (*ikā*), f. Hedysarum Gangeticum, VarBṛS.; Suśr.; Batatas Paniculata, L.; a swelling in the groin, Car.; N. of a female demon, AgP.; Hcat. (also *akī*, PārGṛ.) °**dāraṇa**, mf(*ī*)n. tearing or rending asunder, breaking, splitting, cleaving, piercing, crushing, lacerating, MBh.; R. &c.; m. Pterospermum Acerifolium, L.; a tree or rock in the middle of a stream to which a boat is fastened, MW.; n. the act of tearing asunder &c., MBh.; Kāv. &c.; hewing down, wasting (of a forest), Inscr.; opening wide (the mouth), Śaṃk.; repelling, rejecting, Kathās.; killing, L.; = *viḍamba* or °*bana*, L.; (also *ā*), f. war, battle, L. °**dāri** (m. c.), f. = °*dārī*, Hedysarum Gangeticum, Suśr. (also *-gandhā*, Car.); N. of a female demon, VarBṛS. °**dārita**, mfn. torn asunder, rent, split, broken open, Vet.; Suśr. °**dārin**, mfn. tearing asunder, breaking, cutting &c., MBh.; Kathās.; (*ī*), f. Gmelina Arborea, L. °**dārī**, f. Batatas Paniculata, L.; Hedysarum Gangeticum, L.; *-gandhā* (Suśr.) or *-gandhikā* (Bhpr.), id.

Vi-dīrṇa, mfn. rent asunder, torn, split, broken, wounded, burst open, ripped up, expanded, opened, MBh.; Kāv. &c.; *-mukha*, mfn. open-mouthed, Ragh.; *-hṛidaya*, mfn. broken-hearted, ib.

Vi-dṛiti, f. a suture in the skull, AitUp.

Vi-driya. See *a-vidriyá*.

विदेय *vi-deya*. See under *vi-√1. dā*.

विदेश *vi-deśa*, m. another country, foreign c°, abroad, Kauś.; Mn.; MBh. &c.; a partic. place (cf. *-stha*); *-ga*, mfn. going abroad, VarBṛS.; *-gata*, mfn. gone abroad, W.; *-gamana*, n. the act of going abroad or on a journey, Kathās.; Pañcat.; *-ja*, mfn. 'born or produced abroad,' foreign, exotic, W.; *-nirata*, mfn. taking delight in going abroad, VarBṛS.; *-vāsa*, m. staying ab°, absence, Vet.; *-vāsin*, mfn. dwelling ab°, VarBṛS.; *-stha*, mfn. remaining ab°, living in a foreign country, ĀśvGṛ.; MBh. &c.; standing apart or in a partic. place, Pat.; occurring elsewhere, Pāṇ. vi, 1, 37, Sch.; °*śin* or °*śīya*, mfn. belonging to another country, foreign, MW.; °*śyà*, mfn. foreign (opp. to *saṃ-deśya*), AV.

विदेह *vi-deha*, mfn. bodiless, incorporeal; deceased, dead (also *videha-prâpta*), MBh.; R.; BhP. &c.; (*á*), m. (cf. *vi-deghá*) N. of a country (= the modern Tirhut), ŚBr. &c. &c.; a king of V° (esp. applied to Janaka), Up.; BhP. Rājat.; N. of a medical author (also called *-pati* or °*hâdhipa*), Cat.; (*ā*), f. the capital city of V°, i. e. Mithilā, L.; (*ās*), m. pl. the people of V°; *-kaivalya-prâpti*, f. the attainment of emancipation after death, Madhus.; *-jā*, f. 'daughter of Janaka,' N. of Sītā, R.; *-tva*, n. bodilessness (acc. with *gataḥ* = deceased, dead), R.; *-nagara*, n. (Cat.), °*rī*, f. (Ragh.) the city of Mithilā; *-pati*, lord of M°; *-mukti*, f. deliverance through release from the body, RāmatUp. (°*ti-kathana* and °*ty-ādi-kathana*, n. N. of two treatises); *-rāja*, m. a king of V°, R.; °*hâdhipa*, see *viheha*; °*hâdhipati*, m. = °*ha-rāja*, Hariv.

Vi-dehaka, m. (fr. *vi-deha*) N. of a mountain, Buddh.; n. N. of a Varsha, Śatr.

विदोष *vi-dosha*. See col. 1.

विदोह *vi-dohá*. See p. 951, col. 1.

विद्दणाचार्य *viddaṇācārya*, m. N. of an author.

विद्ध *viddhá*, mfn. (p. p. of √*vyadh*) pierced, perforated, penetrated, stabbed, struck, wounded, beaten, torn, hurt, injured, AV. &c. &c.; cleft, split, burst asunder, MBh.; (with *śūlāyām*) impaled, Kathās.; opposed, impeded, L.; thrown, sent, L.; stung, incited, set in motion, BhP.; filled or affected or provided or joined or mixed with (instr. or comp.), Hariv.; VarBṛS.; BhP.; like, resembling, Śrutab.; m. Echites Scholaris, L.; n. a wound, MW. — **karṇa**, mf(*ī*)n. having the ears pierced or slit, W.; m. and (*ā*, *ī*, or *ikā*), f. Clypea Hernandifolia, L. — **tva**, n. the being penetrated or affected with, ChUp., Sch. — **parkaṭī**, f. Pongamia Glabra, L. — **prajanana**, m. N. of Saṇḍila, Gal. — **śāla-bhañjikā**, f. N. of a drama by Rāja-śekhara. **Viddhâyudha**, n. a bow of a partic. length, L.

Viddhaka, m. a kind of harrow, Kṛishis.

Viddhi, f. the act of piercing, perforating &c., Pāṇ. vi, 4, 2, Sch.

विद्मन् *vidman* &c. See p. 963, col. 3.

विद्य 1. *vidya*, *vidyā* &c. See p. 963, col. 3.

विद्य 2. *vidya*, *vidyamāna* &c. See p. 965.

विद्युत् 1. *vi-√dyut*, Ā. *-dyotate* (Ved. also P.), to flash forth, lighten, shine forth (as the rising sun), RV. &c. &c. (*vi-dyotate*, 'it lightens'; *vi-dyótamāne*, 'when it lightens'); to hurl away by a stroke of lightning, RV.; to illuminate, MBh.: Caus. *-dyotayati*, to illuminate, irradiate, enlighten, make brilliant, MBh.; R. &c.: Intens. (only p. *vi-dávidyutat*) to shine brightly, RV.

Vidyuc, in comp. for 2. *vidyut*. — **chatru** (for *śatru*), m. N. of a Rākshasa, BhP. — **chikhā** (for *śikhā*), f. a kind of plant with a poisonous root, Suśr.; N. of a Rākshasī, Kathās.

Vidyuj, in comp. for 2. *vidyut*. — **jihva**, mfn. having a lightning-like tongue, R.; m. N. of a Rākshasa, MBh.; R.; of a Yaksha, Kathās.; (*ā*), f. N. of one of the Mātṛis attending on Skanda, MBh. — **jvāla**, m. N. of a serpent-demon, Buddh.; (*ā*), f. the flashing of lightning, MW.; Methonica Superba, L.

2. **Vidyút**, mfn. flashing, shining, glittering, RV.; VS.; ĀśvGṛ.; m. a partic. Samādhi, Karaṇḍ.; N. of an Asura, Cat.; of a Rākshasa, VP.; f. lightning (rarely n.), a flashing thunderbolt (as the weapon of the Maruts), RV. &c. &c.; the dawn, L.; pl. N. of the four daughters of Prajā-pati Bahuputra, Hariv.; a species of the Ati-jagatī metre, Col. — **kampa**, m. the quivering or flashing of lightning, Megh. — **keśa** (R.) or **-keśin** (Cat.), m. N. of a Rākshasa; (°*śin*) of a king of the Rākshasas, MW. — **patāka**, m. 'having l° for its banner,' N. of one of the seven clouds at the destruction of the world, Cat. — **parṇā**, f. N. of an Apsaras, MBh.; Hariv. — **pāta**, m. a stroke of l°, Prab. — **puñja**, m. N. of a Vidyā-dhara, Kathās.; (*ā*), f. N. of his daughter, ib. — **prapatana**, n. a stroke of l°, Hariv. — **prabha**, mfn. flashing like lightning, L.; m. N. of a Ṛishi, MBh.; of a king of the Daityas, Kathās.; (*ā*), f. N. of a granddaughter of the Daitya Bali, ib.; of the daughter of a king of the Rākshasas, ib.; of the d° of a king of the Yakshas, ib.; of a Surâṅganā, Siṇhās.; of a serpent-maiden, Kāraṇḍ.; pl. N. of a class of Apsarases, MBh. — **priya**, n. 'l°-loved,' brass, bell-metal, L. — **vat**, mfn. containing or charged with l° (a cloud), MBh.; Megh.; m. a thunder-cloud, Kum.; N. of a mountain, Hariv.; R. — **sáni**, mfn. bringing l°, MaitrS. — **sampâtam**, ind. like a flash of lightning, i. e. in an instant, in a trice, MBh.

Vidyutaya, Nom. Ā. °*yate*, to flash or gleam (like lightning), be radiant, MW.

Vidyutā, f. = 2. *vidyut*, lightning (see comp.); a partic. Śakti, Hcat.; N. of an Apsaras, MBh. — °**ksha** (°*tâksha*), m. 'lightning-eyed,' N. of one of Skanda's attendants, MBh.

Vidyutyà, mfn. being or existing in lightning, VS. (cf. Pāṇ. iv, 4, 110, Sch.)

Vidyud, in comp. for 2. *vidyut*. — **aksha**, m. N. of a Daitya, Hariv. — **ambhas**, f. N. of a river, VP. — **unmesha**, m. a flash of lightning, Megh. — **dāman**, n. 'garland or mass of l°,' a flash or streak of forked lightning, ib. — **dyota**, m. the brightness of l°, Hariv.; (*ā*), f. N. of a princess, Kathās. — **dhasta** (*vidyúd-*), mfn. (for *v°* + *hasta*) holding a glittering weapon in the hand, RV. viii, 7, 25. — **dhvaja**, m. N. of an Asura, Kathās. — **ratha** (*vidyúd-*), mfn. 'borne on a glittering car' or 'having l° for a vehicle,' RV. — **vat**, w. r. for *vidyut-vat* (q. v.), R. — **varcas**, m. N. of a divine being, MBh. — **varṇā**, f. N. of an Apsaras, VP. (cf. *vidyut-parṇā*). — **vallī**, f. a flash of lightning, Bhartṛ.

Vidyun, in comp. for 2. *vidyut*. — **maṇḍala-vat**, mfn. wreathed with lightning (a cloud), R. — **mat** (*vidyún-*), mfn. 'containing l°,' gleaming, glittering, RV. i, 88, 1. — **mahas** (*vidyún-*), mfn. 'rejoicing in lightning' or 'brilliant with l°,' RV. v, 54, 1. — **māla**, m. N. of a monkey, R.; (*ā*), f. a wreath of l°, R.; VarBṛS.; Kathās. &c.; a kind of metre, Śrutab. &c.; N. of a Yakshī, Kathās.; of a daughter of Su-roha, ib. — **mālin**, mfn. wreathed with l°, R.; m. N. of an Asura, MBh.; of a Rākshasa, R.; of a god, HPariś.; of a Vidyā-dhara, ib. — **mukha**, n. a partic. phenomenon in the sky, L.

Vidyul, in comp. for 2. *vidyut*. — **lakshaṇa**, n. N. of the 59th Pariśishṭa of the AV. — **latā**, f. 'lightning-creeper,' forked l°, Kathās.; N. of Comm. — **lekhā**, f. a streak of l°, Kāv.; a kind of metre, Ked.; N. of a certain merchant's wife, Kathās. — **locana**, m. a partic. Samādhi, Kāraṇḍ.; (*ā*), f. N. of a Nāga maid, ib.

Vidyót, irreg. abl. of 2. *vidyut*, VS. (in TS. and TBr. *didyót*).

Vi-dyota, mfn. flashing, glittering, BhP.; m. a flash of light, lightning, Hariv.; N. of a son of Dharma and Lambā (father of Stanayitnu, 'the Thunder'), BhP.; (*ā*), f. N. of an Apsaras, MBh. °**dyotaka,** mfn. irradiating, illuminating, illustrating, Cat. °**dyotana,** mfn. id., Dhūrtas.; n. lightning, Saṃk. °**dyotamāna,** see *vi-√dyut.* °**dyotayitavya,** mfn. (fr. Caus.) to be illustrated or illuminated, PraśnUp. °**dyotin,** mfn. irradiating, illustrating, Cat.

विद्र *vidra,* n. (prob. invented to explain *vi-dradhi*) = *chidra,* a hole, chasm, L.

Vi-dradhi, f. (said to be fr. *vi* + *√dṛī*; accord. to others fr. *vidra* + *√dhā*) an abscess (esp. when deep-seated or internal), VarBṛS.; Suśr. &c. (°*dhī,* Car.); *-nāśana,* m. 'abscess-destroyer,' Hyperanthera Moringa, L. °**dradhikā,** f. a kind of abscess (which accompanies diabetes), Suśr.

विद्रध *vidradhá,* mf(*ā*)n. (of doubtful origin and meaning), RV. iv, 32, 23 (Nir. = *viddha;* Durga = *vikushitádho-bhāga;* Sāy. = *vi-dṛiḍha;* others = undressed, naked, fr. *vi* + *dradha* = *dradhas*); m. a kind of disease (= *vi-dradhi*), AV.

विद्रु *vi-√dru,* P. *-dravati,* to run apart or in different directions, disperse, run away, escape, RV. &c. &c.; to part asunder, become divided, burst, MBh.: Caus. *-drāvayati,* to cause to disperse, drive or scare away, put to flight, MBh.; R. &c.

Vi-drava, m. running asunder or away, flight, MBh.; R. &c.; panic, agitation, Bhar.; Sāh. &c.; flowing out, oozing, L.; melting, liquefaction, L.; censure, reproach, L.; intellect, understanding, L. °**dravaṇa,** n. running away, Āpast.

Vi-drāva, m. flight, retreat, W.; liquefaction, ib. °**drāvaka,** mfn. driving away, W.; causing to melt, liquefying, ib. °**drāvaṇa,** mfn. putting to flight, Kāv.; agitating, perplexing, Dhūrtan.; m. N. of a Dānava, Hariv.; n. the act of putting to flight, Chandom.; fleeing, flight, MBh. °**drāvita,** mfn. caused to disperse, driven away, defeated, routed, R.; BhP.; liquefied, fused, W. °**drāvin,** mfn. running away, fleeing, escaping, MBh.; (?) putting to flight, defeating (see *vajra-vidrāviṇī*). °**drāvya,** mfn. to be put to flight or driven away, R.; Sarvad.

Vi-druta, mfn. run away or asunder, running to and fro, flown, fled (n. impers.), MBh.; Kāv. &c.; burst asunder, destroyed, BhP.; agitated, perplexed, distraught, R.; Pañcat.; liquefied, fluid (as an oily or metallic substance when heated), L.; (prob.) n. a partic. manner of fighting (in which flight is simulated?), Hariv.; (*ā*), f. (scil. *sirā*) unsuccessful blood-letting (caused by a patient's moving his limbs hither and thither), Suśr. °**druti,** f. running, course, Mcar.; flight, L.

विद्रुम *vi-druma* &c. See p. 951, col. 1.

विद्रुह् *vi-√druh* (only Ā. pf. *-dudruhe*), to injure, do wrong (with dat.), BhP.

विद्रै *vi-√drai* (or *drā,* only Ā. pr. p. *-drāṇa*), to awake from sleep, Kaṭh.

विद्वत् *vidvat, vidvas* &c. See p. 964.

विद्विष् 1. *vi-√dvish,* P. Ā. *-dveshṭi, -dvishṭe,* to dislike, hate, be hostile to (acc.), KātyŚr.; MBh.; Hariv.; (Ā.) to hate each other mutually, dislike one another, AV.; KaṭhUp.; GṛŚrS.: Caus. *-dveshayati,* to cause to dislike, render an enemy, make hostile towards one another, Bhaṭṭ.

2. **Vi-dvish,** mfn. hating, hostile, an enemy to (mostly ifc.), MBh.; Kāv. &c. °**dvisha,** mfn. id., W. °**dvishat,** mfn. id., BhP. °**dvishāṇa,** mfn. id., Gaut. °**dvishṭa,** mfn. hated, disliked, odious, Mn.; Yājñ.; R.; hostile to (loc.), MBh.; (ifc.) opposite or contrary, R.; *-tā,* f. hatred, dislike, MBh.

Vi-dvesha, m. hatred, dislike, contempt, aversion to (loc. or gen.), AV. &c. &c. (°*shaṃ √gam,* to make one's self odious; °*shaṃ √kṛi,* with loc., to show hostility towards; °*shaṃ √grah,* with loc., to conceive hatred against); a magical act or formula used for exciting hatred or enmity (also *-karman,* n.), Cat.; proud indifference (even for desired objects), Bhar.; a class of evil demons, Hariv.; *-vīra,* m. N. of a chief of the Śaivas, Cat. °**dveshaka,** mfn. hating, adverse to (comp.), MBh. °**dvéshaṇa,** mfn. causing to hate, rendering hostile, RV.; m. one who hates, a hater, MW.; (*ī*), f. a woman of resentful disposition, ib.; N. of a female demon (daughter of Duḥ-saha), MārkP. (v.l. for °*shiṇī*); n. hating, disliking, having an aversion to (gen. or comp.), MBh.; Hariv.; the being hated or disliked, a means for making one's self hateful, MBh.; VarBṛS.; exciting hatred or enmity, Gaut.; a magical act performed to excite hatred, Cat. °**dveshas** (*ví-*), mfn. opposing or resisting enmity, RV. °**dveshin,** mf(*iṇī*)n. hating, hostile, inimical to (gen. or comp.), MBh.; Kāv. &c.; (ifc.) rivalling or vying with, Śrutab.; (*iṇī*), f. N. of a female demon, MārkP. (cf. °*shaṇī*); °*shi-tā,* f. hatred, enmity, Rājat.; °*shi-prabhava,* mfn. proceeding from an enemy, MW. °**dveshṭṛi,** mfn. one who hates, an enemy, Kāvyâd. °**dveshya,** mfn. hated, disliked, hateful to (comp.), Rājat.

विध् 1. *vidh,* cl. 6. P. *-vidhati* (in RV. also °*te*), to worship, honour a god (dat., loc., or acc.) with (instr.), RV.; AV.; TBr.; BhP.; to present reverentially, offer, dedicate, RV.; AV.; to be gracious or kind, befriend (said of Indra), RV. viii, 78, 7.

1. **Vidhi,** m. (for 2. see p. 968, col. 1) a worshipper, one who does homage, AitBr.

विध् 2. *vidh* (or *vindh*), cl. 6. Ā. *vindháte,* to be destitute or bereft of, lack, want (instr. or acc.), RV. i, 7, 7; viii, 9, 6; 51, 3.

Vidhava, in comp. for °*vā* below. **-tā,** f. widowhood, VarBṛS. **-yoshit,** f. a widow, ib.

Vidhavā, f. (accord. to some fr. *vi* + *dhava,* see 2. *dhavá,* p. 513) a husbandless woman, widow (also with *nārī, yoshit, strī* &c.), RV. &c. &c.; bereft of a king (a country), R. [Cf. Gk. ἠΐθεος; Lat. *vidua;* Goth. *widuwô;* Germ. *wituwa, witewe, Witwe;* Angl. Sax. *wuduwe, widewe;* Eng. *widow.*] **-gāmin,** m. one who has intercourse with a widow, Yājñ. ii, 234. **-dharma,** m. 'duty of a widow,' N. of ch. of the PSarv. **-vivāha,** m. 'marrying a widow,' N. of wk.; *-khaṇḍana,* n., *-vicāra,* m. N. of wks. **-°vedana** (°*vāv*°), n. marrying a widow, Mn. viii, 65. **-strī,** f. a widow, Pañcat.

Vidhas, m. = *vedhas* or *brahman,* L.

Vidhu, vidhura. See p. 968, col. 2.

विध् 3. *vidh,* weak form of *√vyadh.*

4. **Vidh,** mfn. (ifc.) piercing, penetrating (cf. *marmā-, mṛigā-, śvā-, hṛidayā-vidh*).

1. **Vidha,** m. piercing, perforating, L. (for other meanings see 2. *vidha,* col. 3).

विध् 5. *vidh,* cl. 1. Ā. *vedhate,* to ask, beg (v.l. for *√vith,* q.v.)

विधन *vi-dhana, vi-dhanushka* &c. See p. 951, col. 1.

विधम् *vi-√dham* (or *-√dhmā*), P. *-dhamati* (ep. also °*te*), to blow away, scatter, disperse, destroy, RV. &c. &c.: Caus. *-dhmāpayati,* to extinguish, HYogay.

Vi-dhama (2. sg. Impv.), **-cūḍā,** f., g. *mayūra-vyaṇsakâdi.* °**dhamana,** mfn. blowing out, extinguishing, Suśr.; blowing away, destroying (*-tā,* f.), Car.; n. the act of blowing away or asunder, Nir. °**dhamā,** f. N. of a female demon, AV.

Vi-dhmāpana, mfn. (fr. Caus.) scattering, dispersing, Vāgbh.

विधरण *vi-dharaṇa, vi-dhartṛi* &c. See *vi-√dhṛi.*

विधव *vidhava,* Nom. (fr. 1. *vidhu*) P. °*vati,* to resemble the moon, Kāvyâd.

विधवन *vi-dhavana.* See under **vi-√dhū.**

विधा *vi-√*1. *dhā,* P. Ā. *-dadhāti, -dhatte,* to distribute, apportion, grant, bestow, RV. &c. &c. (with *kāmam,* to fulfil a wish); to furnish, supply, procure (with *ātmanaḥ,* 'for one's self'), MBh.; to spread, diffuse, RV.; AV.; to put in order, arrange, dispose, prepare, make ready, RV.; AV.; Br.; Up.; to divide, parcel out, Śukas.; to ordain, direct, enjoin, fix, settle, appoint, GṛŚrS.; Mn.; MBh. &c.; to form, create, build, establish, found, ŚvetUp.; MBh. &c.; to perform, effect, produce, cause, occasion, make, do, Mn.; MBh. &c. (like *√kṛi* to be translated variously in connection with various nouns, e.g. with *siṇhatvam,* to change into a lion; with *saciva-tām,* to assume the office of a minister; with *vesham,* to put on a garment; with *vṛittim,* to secure a maintenance; with *upāyam,* to devise a means; with *mantram,* to hold a consultation; with *rājyam,* to carry on government, rule; with *saṃdhim,* to conclude peace; with *kalaham,* to pick up a quarrel; with *vairam,* to declare war; with *lajjām,* to display bashfulness; with *kolāhalam,* to raise a clamour; with *cumbanaṃ,* to give a kiss); to make, render (with two acc.), Kāv.; Kathās. &c.; to contrive or manage that (*yathā*), MBh.; R.; to put or lay on or in, direct towards (loc.), MBh.; Kāv. &c. (with *hṛidaye,* to take to heart; with *agrataḥ* or *adhaḥ,* to place before or below); to send out, despatch (spies), Mn. vii, 184; to take trouble with (dat.), Kir. i, 3; to treat, deal with (acc.), R. ii, 38, 17: Pass. *-dhīyate,* to be distributed &c.; to be allotted or intended for (gen.), Mn. ix, 119; to be accounted, pass for (nom.), ib. iii, 118: Caus. *-dhāpayati,* to cause to put, cause to be laid, R.; cause to put in order or arrange or fix, MW.: Desid. *-dhitsati,* °*te,* to wish to distribute or bestow, BhP.; to wish to decide or determine or fix or establish, Śaṃk.; to wish to find out or devise (a means), BhP.; to wish to procure or acquire, MBh.; to wish to perform or accomplish anything, intend, purpose, MBh.; Hariv.; BhP.; to wish to make or render (two acc.), BhP.

2. **Vidha** (for 1. see col. 2), m. n. of *vidhā* (ifc.); m. measure, form, kind, L.; food for an elephant, L. (cf. *vi-dhāna*); = *ṛiddhi,* L. (cf. next).

Vi-dhá, f. division, part, portion, ŚBr.; Śulbas. (often ifc. = 'fold;' cf. *eka-, bahu-vidha* &c.; also adv. in *tri-* and *dvi-vidhā,* q.v.); form, manner, kind, sort, TS. &c. &c. (*yayā kayā-cid vidhayā,* in whatsoever way, anyhow; often ifc.; cf. *asmad-, evaṃ-, nānā-vidha* &c.); fodder, Pat.; increase (= *ṛiddhi*), L.; wages, hire, L.; pronunciation, L.; = *vedhana,* L. (cf. 1. *vidha*). °**dhātavya,** mfn. to be fixed or settled, Hariv.; to be got or procured, MBh.; to be performed or accomplished or exhibited, MBh.; Kāv. &c.; to be striven after or cared for, ib.; n. impers. with *yathā,* 'care must be taken that,' R.; to be used or employed or appointed, Sāh.; Sarv. °**dhātā,** f. = *madya,* L. °**dhātṛi,** mf(*trī*)n. distributing, arranging, disposing &c.; m. a distributer, disposer, arranger, accomplisher, maker, author, creator, RV. &c. &c.; a granter, giver, bestower, Kum.; N. of Brahmā (as the creator of the world and disposer of men's fate, sometimes in pl. = *prajā-pati,* e.g. Śak. vii, $\frac{3}{2}\frac{3}{7}$; sometimes Vi-dhātṛi is mentioned together with Dhātṛi, e.g. MBh. iii, 10419 &c.; both are supposed to be the sons of Brahmā [MBh.] or of Bhṛigu [Pur.]; in VarBṛS. Vidhātṛi is the regent of the 2nd Tithi, while Brahmā presides over the first), MBh.; Kāv. &c.; Fate or Destiny (personified), Kāv.; Hit.; N. of Vishṇu, BhP.; of Śiva, Śivag.; of Kāma (god of love), L.; of Viśva-karman, MW.; (*trī*), f., see below; *-bhū,* m. 'son of Brahmā,' N. of Nārada, L.; *-vaśāt,* ind. from the will of Br°, through the power of destiny, MW.; °*tr-āyus,* m. the sunflower, L. °**dhātṛikā,** f. (used to explain *vidhavā*), Nir. iii, 15. °**dhātrī,** f. a female creator, mother of (comp.), Pañcav.

Vi-dhāna, mf(*ī*)n. disposing, arranging, regulating, Vait.; acting, performing, possessing, having, MW.; m. N. of a Sādhya, Hariv.; n. order, measure, disposition, arrangement, regulation, rule, precept, method, manner, RV. &c. &c. (instr. sg. and pl., and *-tas,* ind. according to rule or precept; *saṃkhyā-vidhānāt,* according to mathematical method, mathematically; *deśa-kāla-vidhānena,* in the right place and at the right time); medical prescription or regulation, diet, Suśr.; fate, destiny, MBh.; Kāv.; taking measures, contriving, managing, Mn.; MBh. &c.; a means, expedient, Pañcat.; setting up (machines), Yājñ.; creating, creation, Kum.; Ragh.; performance (esp. of prescribed acts or rites), execution, making, doing, accomplishing, Mn.; MBh. &c.; enumeration, statement of particulars, Suśr.; (in dram.) conflict of different feelings, occasion for joy and sorrow, Sāh.; Pratāp.; (in gram.) affixing, prefixing, taking as an affix &c., W.; an elephant's fodder &c., Śiś. v, 51 (only L. worship; wealth; wages; sending; act of hostility &c.); *-kalpa,* m., *-khaṇḍa,* m. or n. (?) N. of wks.; *-ga,* m. 'rule-goer,' a Paṇḍit, teacher, L.; *-gumpha,* m. N. of wk.; *-jña,* mfn. one who knows rules or precepts, MBh.; Suśr.; m. a teacher, Paṇḍit, W.; *-tilaka,* n., *-pārijāta,* m., *-mālā,* f. N. of wks.; *-yukta,* mfn. agreeable to rule or precept, MBh.; *-ratna,* n., *-ratnamālā,* f., *-rahasya,* n. N. of wks.; *-saptamī,* f. N. of the 7th day in the light half of Māgha, W.; *-sārasaṃgraha,* m. N. of wk.; °*nôkta,* mfn. proclaimed or enjoined according to rule or (sacred) precept, Bhag. °**dhānaka,** mfn. disposing, arranging, one who knows how to arrange, MW.; n. ordinance, regulation, rule, AgP.; distress, pain (= *vyathā*), L. °**dhāyaka**, mfn. enjoining, containing an injunction, Śaṃk.; KātyŚr., Sch.; performing, exhibiting, Rājat.; consigning, delivering, one who entrusts or deposits anything (*-tva*, n.), W.; m. a founder, builder, establisher, Pañcar.; Rājat. °**dhāyin**, mfn. regulating, prescribing, containing an injunction or ordinance with regard to (comp.), Nyāyas.; Rājat.; performing, accomplishing, Hariv.; Kathās.; causing, occasioning, Hariv.; Rājat.; placing, fixing, securing, W.; delivering, entrusting, ib.; m. a founder, builder, establisher, Rājat.

2. **Vidhi**, m. (for 1. see p. 967, col. 2) a rule, formula, injunction, ordinance, statute, precept, law, direction (esp. for the performance of a rite as given in the Brāhmaṇa portion of the Veda, which accord. to Sāy. consists of two parts, 1. Vidhi, 'precepts or commandments,' e. g. *yajeta*, 'he ought to sacrifice,' *kuryāt*, 'he ought to perform;' 2. Artha-vāda, 'explanatory statements' as to the origin of rites and use of the Mantras, mixed up with legends and illustrations), GṛŚrS.; Mn.; MBh. &c. (cf. IW. 24); a grammatical rule or precept, Pāṇ. i, 1, 57; 72; any prescribed act or rite or ceremony, Mn.; Kālid.; Pañcat.; use, employment, application, Car.; method, manner or way of acting, mode of life, conduct, behaviour, Mn.; MBh. &c.; a means, expedient for (dat., loc., or comp.; *adhvavidhinā*, by means of i. e. along the road), Hariv.; Kāv.; Pur.; Hit.; any act or action, performance, accomplishment, contrivance, work, business (ifc. often pleonastically, e. g. *mathana-vidhi*, the [act of] disturbing), Yājñ.; Śak. &c.; creation (also pl.), Kum.; Kir.; fate, destiny, MBh.; Kāv. &c.; the creator, Pañcar.; N. of Brahmā, Śak.; Naish.; of Vishṇu, L.; of Agni at the Prāyaścitta, Gṛihyas.; a physician, L.; time, L.; fodder, food for elephants or horses, L.; f. N. of a goddess, Cat. **-kara**, mf(*ī*)n. executing commands; m. a servant, BhP. **-kṛit**, mfn. or m. id., ib. **-ghna**, mfn. 'rule-destroying,' one who deviates from or disregards rules or disturbs modes of proceeding, W. **-jña**, mfn. 'rule-knowing,' one who knows the prescribed mode or form, ib.; learned in ritual, ib.; m. a Brāhman who knows the ritual, ib. **-tas**, ind. according to rule, ib. **-traya-paritrāṇa**, n. N. of wk. **-tva**, n. the state of being a rule, Sarvad. **-darśaka** or °**śin**, m. 'rule-shower,' a priest who sees that a sacrifice is conducted according to prescribed rules and corrects any derivation from them, L. **-drishṭa**, mfn. prescribed by rule, MBh.; R. **-deśaka**, m. = *-darśaka*, L. **-dvaidha**, n. diversity of rule, variance of rite, Lāṭy. **-nirūpaṇa**, n. N. of wk. **-nishedha-tā**, f. the being precept and prohibition, BhP. **-paryāgata**, mfn. come into possession through destiny, MBh. **-putra**, m. N. of Nārada, Pañcar. **-pūrvakam** (Mn.; R.; Suśr.) or **-pūrvam** (Gaut.; MBh.), ind. according to rule, duly. **-prayukta**, mfn. performed according to rule, MW. **-prayoga**, m. the application of a rule, acting according to rule, W. **-prasaṅga**, m. id., ib. **-bhūshaṇa**, n. N. of wk. **-mantra-puraskṛitam**, ind. in accordance with rule and with the due recitation of Mantras or mystical texts, MBh. **-yajña**, m. a sacrifice performed according to rule, Mn. ii, 85, 86; a ceremonial act of worship, W. **-yoga**, m. the observance of a rule, Mn. viii, 211; dispensation of fate (= *āt* or *-tas*, ind. according to the ruling of fate), Hit.; Kathās.; combining for any act or rite, W. **-ratna**, n. N. of various wks.; *-kṛit*, m. N. of an author, Hcat.; *-mālā*, f. N. of wk. **-rasâyana**, n., °**na-dūshaṇa**, n., °**na-vyākhyā**, f., °**na-sukhôpajīvinī**, f., °**payoginī**, f., **-rūpa-nirūpaṇa**, n. N. of wks. **-lopa**, m. transgression of a commandment, MBh. **-lopaka**, mfn. transgressing com°, ib. **-vat**, ind. according to rule, duly, MuṇḍUp.; Mn.; MBh. &c. **-vadhū**, f. 'wife of Brahmā,' Sarasvatī, Cat. **-vaśāt**, ind. through the power of fate or destiny, Megh. **-vāda**, m. N. of wk.; °*da-vicāra*, m. id.; °*dârtha*, m. id. **-vicāra**, m. N. of wk. **-viparyaya**, m. contrariety of fate, misfortune, Vikr. **-viveka**, m. N. of wk. **-vihita**, mfn. established by rule, MW. **-śoṇitīya**, mfn. treating of the blood in its normal state, Cat. **-shedha** (only *-tas*, ind.), commandment and prohibition, BhP. **-sāra**, m. N. of a king, ib. (w.r. for *bimbi-s*°). **-sudhâkara**, m., **-svarūpa-vādârtha**, m., °**pa-vicāra**, m. N. of wks. **-hīna**, mfn. destitute of rule, unauthorised, irregular, W.

Vi-dhitsamāna, mfn. (fr. Desid.) wishing to distribute or bestow &c.; intending to do, scheming, planning, interested, selfish, MBh. °**dhitsā**, f. intention to do, intention, design, purpose, desire for (comp.), MBh.; Kāv. &c.; the wish to make or turn into (comp.), Rājat. °**dhitsita**, mfn. intended; n. intention, purpose, BhP. °**dhitsu**, mfn. wishing to do or make, purposing to perform (acc.), MBh.; Kāv. &c.

Vi-dheya, mfn. to be bestowed or procured, BhP.; to be used or employed (*a-vidh*°), MBh.; to be (or being) enjoined (as a rule), PārGṛ.; to be stated or settled or established, VarBṛS.; Kām.; to be performed or practised or done, MBh.; Kāv. &c.; to be drawn (as a line), Gol.; to be kindled (as fire), MBh.; to be exhibited or displayed or shown or betrayed, Kāv.; Rājat.; Hit.; docile, compliant, submissive, liable to be ruled or governed or influenced by, subject or obedient to (gen. or comp.), MBh.; Kāv. &c.; (ifc.) subdued or overcome by, Ragh.; Prab.; Rājat.; n. what is to be done, duty, necessity, Rājat.; *-jña*, mfn. knowing what ought to be done, Pañcat.; *-tā*, f. fitness to be (or 'state of being') prescribed or enjoined, Prāyaśc. (opp. to *nishiddha-tā*); docility, submission, Car.; *-tva*, n. applicability, usefulness, MBh.; dependency, submission, Rājat.; necessity of being established or stated, Sāh.; *-pada*, n. an object to be accomplished, W.; *-mārga*, m. the seeking to do a necessary act, ib.; *-vartin*, mfn. submissive to another's will, obedient, Śiś.; °*yâtman*, mfn. having the soul (well) subdued or controlled, Bhag.

Vidheyī, in comp. for °*dheya*. **-kṛita**, mfn. subdued or subject to another's will, dependent, Mālatīm. **-bhūya**, ind. (ifc.) submissive or subject to, Inscr.

Vidhy, in comp. before vowels for 2. *vidhi*. **-anta**, m. a concluding act, Nyāyam.; KātyŚr., Sch.; *-tva*, n., Nyāyam. **-aparādha**, m. transgression of a rule, ŚrS.; Jaim.; *-prâyaścitta*, n.; °*tta-prayoga*, m., °*tta-sūtra*, n. N. of wks. **-apâśraya**, m. adherence to a rule, Bhar. **-alaṃ-kāra**, m. or **-alaṃ-kriyā**, f. a kind of rhetorical figure, Vās., Sch. **-ātmaka**, mfn. consisting of a positive injunction (opp. to *pratishedhâtm*°), Yājñ., Sch. **-ādi**, m. the commencement of an action, Nyāyam.

Vi-hita. See s. v.

विधाव् *vi-√1. dhāv*, P. *-dhāvati*, to run or flow off, trickle through, RV.; to flow away, disappear, Kāṭh.; to run away, be scattered or dispersed, RV; AV.; Br.; to run between (*antar*, said of a road), Kāṭh.; to run through, perambulate, R.; to rush upon, Bhaṭṭ. (aor. *vy-adhāvishṭa*, v.l. *vy-abādhishṭa*). °**dhāvana**, n. running hither and thither, Nir. iii, 15. °**dhāvita**, mfn. run in different directions, dispersed, MBh.

विधाव् *vi-√2. dhāv* (only Pass. pf. *-dadhāvire*), to wash off, Śiś.

Vi-dhauta, mfn. cleansed by washing, ib.

विधी *vi-√1. dhī* (or *didhi*, only Subj. *-dīdhayaḥ* and *-dīdhyaḥ*), to be uncertain, hesitate, RV.; AV.

विधु 1. *vidhú*, mfn. (prob. fr. √2. *vidh*; for 2. *vi-dhú* see *vi-√dhū*, col. 3) lonely, solitary, RV. x, 55, 5 (applied to the moon; accord. to Sāy. = *vi-dhātṛi*, *vi-dhārayitṛi*); m. the moon, Mn.; Bhartṛ.; Gīt.; (L. also 'camphor; N. of Brahmā and of Vishṇu; a Rākshasa; wind; an expiatory oblation; time; = *āyudha*'); N. of a prince, VP. (v.l. *vipra*). **-krānta**, m. (in music) a kind of measure, Saṃgīt. **-kshaya**, m. the wane of the moon, the dark nights of the month, Mn. iii, 127. **-gupti**, m. N. of a man, Bhadrab. **-tva**, n. the state or condition of (being) the moon, Naish. **-dina**, n. a lunar day, Gaṇit. **-m-tuda**, m. 'moon-troubler,' N. of Rāhu or the personified ascending node (causing the m°'s eclipses), Kāv. **-pañjara**, m. a scimitar, sabre, L. **-paridhvaṃsa**, m. distress i. e. eclipse of the m°, Śṛiṅgār. **-priyā**, f. 'dear to the moon,' a lunar mansion or Nakshatra (personified as a nymph, the daughter of Daksha and wife of the M°), W. **-maṇḍala**, n. the moon's disc, Kāv. **-maya**, mf(*ī*)n. consisting of moons, Hcar. **-māsa**, m. a lunar month, Gaṇit. **-mukhī** or **-vadanā**, f. a moon-faced woman, Kāv.

2. **Vidhura**, mf(*ā*)n. (for 1. see p. 951, col. 1) bereft, bereaved (esp. of any loved person), alone, solitary, Kāv.; Rājat.; (ifc.) separated from, destitute of, wanting, BhP.; Sarvad.; suffering from want, miserable, helpless, distressed, MBh.; Kāv. &c.; perplexed, troubled, depressed, dejected (*am*, ind.), Kāv.; Kathās.; Rājat.; adverse, unfavourable, hostile, ib.; m. a Rākshasa, L.; a widower, MW.; (*ā*), f. curds mixed with sugar and spices, L.; n. adversity, calamity, distress, Kathās. (L. also = *viślesha*, *praviślesha* or *pariślesha*); du. N. of two partic. joints of the body, Bhpr. **-tā**, f., **-tva**, n. want, trouble, distress, Kāv.; Sarvad. **-darśana**, n. the sight of anything alarming, agitation, uneasiness, MW.

Vidhuraya, Nom. P. °*yati*, to put in a miserable condition, deject, depress, Hcar.; Gīt.; Subh. °**rita**, mfn. dejected, depressed, Śiś.; n. pl. adversities, calamities, Rājat.

Vidhurī-kṛita, mfn. dejected, distressed, ib.

विधू *vi-√dhū*, P. Ā. *-dhūnoti*, *-dhūnute* (later also *-dhunoti*, *-dhunute*; inf. *-dhavitum* or *-dhotum*), to shake about, move to and fro, agitate, toss about (Ā. also 'one's self'), RV. &c. &c.; to fan, kindle (fire), MBh.; to shake off, drive away, scatter, disperse, remove, destroy, R.; Kathās.; BhP. &c.; (Ā.) to shake off from one's self, relinquish, abandon, give up, AV.; Mn.; MBh. &c.: Pass. *-dhūyate* (ep. also °*ti*), to be shaken or agitated, MBh.: Caus. *-dhūnayati*, to cause to shake about &c.; to shake violently, agitate, harass, annoy, MBh.; R. &c.

Vi-dhavana, n. shaking off, Nir. iii, 15; agitation, trembling, W. °**dhavya**, n. agitation, trembling, tremor, ib. °**dhāvya**, n. shaking, agitation, ib.

2. **Vi-dhú**, m. (for 1. see col. 2) palpitation, throbbing (of the heart), AV. ix, 8, 22. °**dhuta**, mfn. shaken about or off, dispersed, removed, abandoned, relinquished, Inscr.; VarBṛS.; BhP.; *-triliṅga*, mfn. liberated from the three qualities, BhP.; *-paksha*, mfn. shaking one's wings, VarBṛS.; *-bandhana*, mfn. released from bonds, Rājat.; *-mārtya*, mfn. one who has shaken off what is human or corporeal, BhP. °**dhuti**, f. shaking, agitating, tossing about, Kāv.; BhP.; removal, destruction, BhP. °**dhunana**, n. = °*dhūnana*, L. °**dhuvana**, n. trembling, tremor, W.

Vi-dhūta, mfn. shaken or tossed about &c.; shaken off, dispelled, removed, discarded, abandoned, relinquished, MBh.; Kāv. &c.; trembling, tremulous, W.; unsteady, ib.; n. the repelling of affection, repugnance, Bhar.; Daśar.; *-kalmasha*, mfn. having sin dispelled or removed, delivered from sin, MW.; *-keśa*, mfn. having hair tossed about or dishevelled, Kir.; *-nidra*, mfn. roused from sleep, awakened, Ragh. (v.l. *vinīta-n*°); *-pāpman*, mfn. delivered from evil or sin, MBh.; *-veśa*, mfn. shaking one's garment, R. °**dhūti**, f. shaking or tossing about, Śiś.; tremor, agitation, W. °**dhūnana**, mf(*ī*)n. (fr. Caus.) causing to move to and fro, Naish.; n. shaking, agitation, Sāh.; waving, undulating, Cat.; repugnance, repulsion (as of love), Daśar., Sch. °**dhūnita**, mfn. shaken, agitated, harassed, annoyed, W.

विधूप् *vi-√dhūp*, P. *-dhūpāyati*, to emit vapour, smoke, AV.; Pass. *-dhūpyate*, id., Suśr.

विधृ *vi-√dhṛi*, P. Ā. *-dharati*, °*te* (only pf. *-dadhāra*), to hold, bear, carry, BhP.: Caus. *-dhārayati* (rarely °*te*; Ved. inf. *-dhartári*), to keep asunder or apart, separate, divide, distribute, RV.; ŚBr.; Kauś.; to arrange, manage, contrive, MBh.; to keep off, withhold from (abl.), TĀr.; Hariv.; R.; to lay hold of, seize, hold fast, Hariv.; to check, restrain, Suśr.; to support, maintain, PraśnUp.; (with *vapūṃshi*) to possess or have bodies, MBh.; (with *manas*) to keep the mind fixed upon (loc.), BhP.; to preserve, take care of, BhP.: Intens. (only impf. *vy-âdardhar*) to divide, separate, RV.

Ví-dharaṇa, mf(*ī*)n. checking, restraining, ŚBr.; (*ī*), f. maintaining, supporting, ib. °**dhartṛi**, m. a distributer, arranger, supporter, RV.; VS.; AV.

2. **Ví-dharman**, m. (for 1. see p. 951, col. 1) a maintainer, arranger, disposer, RV.; AV.; n. that which encircles or surrounds, receptacle, boundaries, circumference, RV.; AV.; PañcavBr.; disposition, arrangement, order, rule, RV.; AV.; N. of a Sāman, ĀrshBr. °**dhāra**, m. (prob.) a receptacle, RV. ix, 110, 4 (others 'running through,' fr. √1. *dhāv*). °**dhāraṇa**, mf(*ī*)n. dividing, separating, Vas.; BhP.; n. stopping, detaining (a carriage), Kathās.; checking, restraining, retention, suppression, APrāt.; MBh. &c.; bearing, carrying, MBh.; Hariv. &c.;

maintaining, supporting, MBh. °**dhārayá,** mfn. (prob.) disposing, arranging, VS. °**dhārayitavya,** mfn. to be (or being) supported or maintained, PraśnUp. °**dhārayitṛi,** mfn. = °*dhāraya* (used to explain *vi-dhartṛi*), Nir. xii, 14. °**dhārin,** mfn. checking, restraining, Vāgbh.

Vi-dhṛita, mfn. kept asunder, divided, separated, TS. &c. &c.; kept off, avoided, Hariv.; stopped, checked, suppressed, restrained, MBh.; Kāv. &c.; held, borne (with *śirasā, mūrdhnā* or °*dhni,* borne on the head, i.e. highly esteemed; with *svôdareṇa,* borne in one's own body), ib.; held, possessed, Bhartṛ.; saved, preserved, BhP.; (with *antare*) pledged, Pañcat.; n., w.r. for *vi-dhūta* (q.v.), Sāh.; °*tâyudha,* mfn. holding weapons, MW. °**dhṛiti** (*ví-*), f. separation, division, partition, arrangement, regulation, AV.; VS.; TBr.; keeping away, Br.; anything that separates or divides, a boundary-line, barrier, TS.; N. of two blades of grass which indicate a boundary-line between Barhis and Prastara, TBr.; ŚBr.; KātyŚr.; m. a partic. Sattra, ŚrS.; N. of a partic. divine being, BhP.; of a king, ib.

विधृष् *vi-√dhṛish,* Caus. *-dharshayati,* to violate, spoil, injure, annoy, trouble, MBh. °**dhṛishṭi,** f. (in a formula), ŚāṅkhŚr.

विधेय *vi-dheya* &c. See p. 968, col. 2.

विध्मा *vi-√dhmā.* See *vi-√dham,* p. 967.

विध्यन्त *vidhy-anta,* &c. See p. 968, col. 2.

विध्वंस् *vi-√dhvaṅs* (or *dhvas*), Ā. *-dhvaṅsate* (rarely °*ti*), to fall to pieces, crumble into dust or powder, be scattered or dispersed or destroyed, perish, ŚBr. &c. &c.: Caus. *-dhvaṅsayati* (ind. p. *-dhvaṅsya* or *-dhvasya*), to cause to fall to pieces or crumble, dash to pieces, crush, destroy, annihilate, MBh.; Kāv. &c.; to hurt, injure, R.

Vi-dhvaṅsa, m. ruin, destruction, hurt, injury, MBh.; Kāv. &c.; cessation (of a disease), Suśr.; insult, offence, Kir.; violation (of a woman), Kathās. °**dhvaṅsaka,** m. a debaucher, violator (of a woman), ib. °**dhvaṅsana,** mfn. causing to fall, ruining, destroying, removing, MBh.; R.; n. the act of causing to fall &c., ib.; insulting, violating (a woman), Kathās. °**dhvaṅsita,** mfn. (fr. Caus.) dashed or broken to pieces, destroyed, R.; BhP. °**dhvaṅsin,** mfn. falling to pieces, perishing, Ragh.; causing to fall, ruining, destroying, Kāv.; VarBṛS. &c.; insulting, violating (a woman), Kathās.; hostile, adverse, W.; (*inī*), f. a partic. magical formula, ib.

Vi-dhvasta, mfn. fallen asunder, fallen to pieces, dispersed, ruined, destroyed, MBh.; Kāv. &c.; whirled up (as dust), R.; (in astron.) darkened, obscured, eclipsed, Sūryas.; *-kavaca,* mfn. one whose armour is destroyed, R.; *-tā,* f. ruin, destruction, Kathās.; *-nagarâśrama,* mfn. containing ruined cities and hermitages, MBh.; *-para-guṇa,* mfn. one who detracts from the merits of another, Vās.; *-vipaṇâpaṇa,* mfn. (a town) whose market and trade are ruined, R.

विनङ्गृस *vinaṅgṛisa,* m. (of unknown origin and meaning), RV. ix, 72, 3 (*kamanīyaṃ stotram gṛihṇāti yaḥ,* Sāy.; du. 'the two arms,' Naigh. ii, 4).

विनटन *vi-naṭana,* n. (√*naṭ*) moving to and fro, going hither and thither, Vās.

विनद् *vi-√nad,* P. *-nadati,* to sound forth, cry out, roar, bellow, thunder, MBh.; R. &c. (with *ravam mahā-svanam,* to roar aloud); to roar or scream at or about (acc.), MBh.; to fill with cries, Hariv.: Caus. *-nādayati* (Pass. *-nādyate*), to cause to sound or resound, fill with noise or cries, MBh.; Kāv. &c.; to sound aloud, R. °**nada,** m. sound, noise, R.; Alstonia Scholaris, L.; (*ā*), f. a partic. Śakti, Pañcar.; (*ī*), f. N. of a river, MBh.; VP. (v.l. *vainadī*). °**nadin,** mfn. roaring, thundering, grumbling, MBh. °**nādita,** mfn. (fr. Caus.) made to resound, caused to sound aloud, ib. °**nādin,** mfn. sounding forth, crying out, ib.

विनद्ध *ví-naddha,* mfn. (√*nah*) untied, unfastened, set free, AV.

Vi-nāha, m. a top or cover for the mouth of a well, L. (cf. *vī-nāha*).

विनन्द् *vi-√nand,* P. Ā. *-nandati,* °*te,* to rejoice, be glad or joyful, MBh.

विनम् *vi-√nam,* P. Ā. *-namati,* °*te,* to bend down, bow down, stoop, MBh.; Kāv. &c.: Caus. *-nāmayati* or *-namayati* (ind. p. *-nāmya* and *-namayya*), to bend down, incline, bend (a bow), MBh.; Hariv.; (in gram.) to cerebralize or change into a cerebral letter (cf. *-nāmita*).

Vi-nata, mfn. bent, curved, bent down, bowed, stooping, inclined, sunk down, depressed, deepened (*am,* ind.), MBh.; Kāv.; VarBṛS.; bowing to (gen.), Ghaṭ.; humble, modest, Bhaṭṭ.; Kathās.; dejected, dispirited, MW.; (in gram.) changed into a cerebral letter, Pāṇ., Sch. (cf. *-nāma*); accentuated in a partic. manner, Sāy.; m. a kind of ant, Kauś.; N. of a son of Su-dyumna, VP.; of a monkey, R.; (perhaps) n. N. of a place situated on the Go-matī, R.; (*ā*), f., see below; *-kāya,* mfn. one who has the body bent, stooping, SaddhP.; *-tā,* f. inclination, TPrāt., Sch.; °*tânana,* mfn. one who has his face bent or cast down, dejected, dispirited, MBh.; °*tâśva,* m. N. of a son of Su-dyumna, Hariv.; VP.; °*tôdara,* mfn. with bending waist, bending at the waist, MW. °**nataka,** m. N. of a mountain, Buddh.

Vi-natā, f. a girl with bandy legs or a hunchback, GṛS.; an abscess on the back or abdomen accompanying diabetes, Suśr.; Car.; a sort of basket, W.; N. of one of Kaśyapa's wives (and mother of Suparṇa, Aruṇa and Garuḍa &c.; in MBh. i, 2520, Vinatā is enumerated among the thirteen daughters of Daksha; the Bhāgavata-Purāṇa makes her the wife of Tārksha; the Vāyu describes the metres of the Veda as her daughters, while the Padma gives her only one daughter, Saudāminī), Suparṇ.; MBh. &c.; N. of a female demon of illness, MBh.; of a Rākshasī, R.; *-tanayā,* f. 'daughter of V°,' metr. of Su-mati, VP.; *-°nanda* (°*tân°*), m. N. of a drama by Go-vinda; *-suta* (Śiś.), *-sūnu* (L.), m. 'son of V°,' N. of Aruṇa, Garuḍa &c. °**nati,** f. bowing, obeisance to (loc.), Bhartṛ.; Kathās.; humility, modesty, W.

Vi-namana, n. the act of bending down (opp. to *un-n°*), Suśr. °**namita,** mfn. (fr. Caus.) bent or turned towards (*abhimukham*), Amar. °**namra,** see p. 951, col. 1.

Vi-nāma, m. crookedness (of the body, caused by pain), Bhpr.; Car. (also °*maka,* m., °*mikā,* f.); conversion into a cerebral letter, the substitution of *sh* for *s* and *ṇ* for *n,* Prāt. °**nāmita,** mfn. (fr. Caus.) bent down, inclined, MBh.

विनय 1. *vi-naya* (said to be artificially formed fr. *vi + nṛi;* for 2. see under *vi-√nī*), Nom. P. °*yati* (with prefix 3. *vi;* ind. p. *vi-vinayya*), Pāṇ. i, 4, 1, Vārtt. 7, Pat.

विनर्द् *vi-√nard,* P. Ā. *-nardati,* °*te,* to cry out, roar, thunder, MBh.; R. &c. °**nardin,** mfn. roaring (applied to a partic. method of chanting the Sāma-veda), ChUp.

विनश् *vi-√1. naś,* P. *-naśati,* to reach, attain, RV.

विनश् *vi-√2. naś,* P. *-naśati* or *-naśyati* (fut. *-naśishyati* or *-naṅkshyati;* inf. *-naśitum* or *-naṅshṭum*), to be utterly lost, perish, disappear, vanish, RV. &c. &c.; to come to nothing, be frustrated or foiled, ib.; to be deprived of (abl.), RV. ix, 79, 1; to destroy, annihilate, Hariv.: Caus. *-nāśayati* (aor. *vy-anīnaśat*), to cause to be utterly lost or ruined or to disappear or vanish, RV. &c. &c. (once in Sūryas. with gen. for acc.); to frustrate, disappoint, render ineffective (a weapon), AV.; to suffer to be lost or ruined, Ragh. ii, 56; (aor.) to be lost, perish, MBh.; R.

Vi-naṅśin, mfn. disappearing, vanishing, VS.

Vi-naśana, n. utter loss, perishing, disappearance (with *sarasvatyāḥ,* N. of a district north-west of Delhi [said to be the same as Kuru-kshetra and adjacent to the modern Paniput] where the river Sarasvatī is lost in the sand; also *sarasvatī-vin°*), PañcavBr.; ŚrS.; *-kshetra,* n. the district of Vinaśana, MW. °**naśvara,** mf(*ī*)n. liable to be destroyed or lost, perishable, Kāv.; Rājat. &c.; *-tā,* f., *-tva,* n. perishableness, transitoriness, Sarvad.

Vi-nashṭa, mfn. utterly lost or ruined, destroyed, perished, disappeared, MBh.; Kāv. &c.; spoilt, corrupted, Mn.; Yājñ.; (prob.) n. a dead carcass, carrion (see below); *-cakshus,* mfn. one who has lost his eyes, MBh.; *-tejas* (*ví-n°*), mfn. one whose energy is lost, weak, feeble, AV.; *-drishṭi,* mfn. one who has lost his sight, BhP.; *-dharma,* mfn. (a country) whose laws are corrupted, Rājat.; °*tôpajīvin,* mfn. living on dead carcasses or carrion, GopBr. °**nashṭaka,** see *bāla-vinashṭaka.* °**nashṭi** (*ví-*), f. loss, ruin, destruction, ŚBr.; KenUp.; BhP.

Vi-nāśa, m. utter loss, annihilation, perdition, destruction, decay, death, removal, TPrāt.; Up.; MBh. &c.; *-krit,* mfn. (ifc.) causing destruction of, destroying, Yājñ.; *-dharman,* mfn. subject to the law of decay, Ragh. viii, 10 (v.l. °*min;* but cf. Pāṇ. v, 4, 124); *-sambhava,* m. a source of destruction, cause of the subsequent non-existence of a composite body (*avayavin*), MW.; *-hetu,* mfn. being the cause of death, Suśr.; °*śânta,* m. 'end (caused by) destruction,' death, MBh.; mfn. ending in death, ib.; °*śônmukha,* mfn. ready to perish, fully ripe or mature, L. °**nāśaka,** mfn. (fr. Caus.) annihilating, destroying, a destroyer, MBh.; R. &c. °**nāśana,** mf(*ī*)n. (fr. id.) id., Yājñ.; MBh. &c.; m. N. of an Asura (son of Kalā), MBh.; n. causing to disappear, removal, destruction, annihilation, MBh.; Kāv. &c. °**nāśayitṛi,** mfn. (fr. id.) one who destroys, a destroyer, MW. °**nāśita,** mfn. (fr. id.) utterly destroyed, ruined, Pañcat. °**nāśin,** mfn. perishing, perishable (°*śi-tva,* n.), Mn.; MBh. &c.; undergoing transformation, W.; (mostly ifc.) destructive, destroying, MBh.; Kāv.; VarBṛS. &c.; (a tale) treating of the destruction of (gen.), MBh. °**nāśya,** mfn. to be destroyed or annihilated (*-tva,* n.), MBh.; Kathās.; Sarvad.

विना *vínā* or *vinā́,* ind. (prob. a kind of instr. of 3. *vi*) without, except, short or exclusive of (preceded or followed by an acc., instr., rarely abl.; cf. Pāṇ. ii, 3, 32; exceptionally ifc., e.g. *śuci-vinā,* without honesty, *satya-v°,* without faith, Subh.), AV. xx, 136, 13 (not in manuscript), Mn.; MBh. &c. (sometimes *vinā* is used pleonastically, e.g. *na tad asti vinā deva yat te virahitam Hare,* 'there is nothing, O god Hari, that is without thee,' Hariv. 14966). **–krita,** mfn. 'made without,' deprived or bereft of, separated from, left or relinquished by, lacking, destitute of, free from (instr., abl., or comp.), MBh.; Kāv. &c.; standing alone, solitary, R. °**kritya,** ind. setting aside, without (instr.), Subh. **–°nyonyam** (°*nân°*), ind. (perhaps two separate words) without each other, one without the other, MBh. **–bhava,** m. the being separated, separation from (abl.), R. **–bhāva,** m. id., ib. **–bhāvam,** ind. (√*bhū*) separately, Pāṇ. iii, 4, 62, Sch. **–bhāvin,** see *a-vinābh°.* **–bhāvya,** mfn. separable (in *a-vinābh°*), RāmatUp. **–bhūta,** mfn. separated from, bereaved of (instr.), MBh. **–bhūya** or **-bhūtvā,** ind. = *-bhāvam,* Pāṇ. iii, 4, 62, Sch. **–vāsa,** m. abiding separate from a beloved person, R. **Vinôkti,** f. (in rhet.) a figure of speech (using) *vinā* (e.g. *kā niśā śaśinā vinā,* 'what is the night without the moon?'), Kpr.

विनाट *vínāṭa,* m. (cf. *nāḍa*) a leather-bag, ŚBr.

विनायक *vi-nāyaka* &c. See under *vi-√nī.*

विनारुहा *vināruhā,* f. a kind of plant, L.

विनाल *vi-nāla, vi-nāsa* &c. See p. 951, col. 1.

विनिःश्वस् *vi-niḥ-√śvas* (cf. *vi-ni-√śvas*), P. *-śvasiti,* to breathe hard, heave a deep sigh, MBh.; R.; Kathās.; to hiss (as a serpent), R.; to snort (as an elephant), ib.

विनिःसृ *vi-niḥ-√sṛi,* P. Ā. *-sarati,* °*te,* to go forth, issue out, spring from (abl.), MBh.; R. &c. °**niḥsaraṇa,** n. the act of going forth or out, issuing forth, MW. °**niḥsṛita,** mfn. (often *vi-nisṛita*) gone forth or out, issued forth, sprung from (comp.), MBh.; Kāv. &c.; escaped, Hariv. °**niḥsṛiti,** f. escaping, flight, Lalit.

विनिःसृप्ताहुति *vi-niḥsṛiptâhuti,* f. (√*sṛip*) a kind of sacrifice, ĀśvŚr.

विनिःसृष्ट *vi-niḥ-√sṛishṭa,* mfn. (√*sṛij*) discharged, shot off, thrown, hurled, R.

विनिकषण *vi-ni-kashaṇa,* n. (√*kash*) scratching, scraping, Daśar.

विनिकृ *vi-ni-√1. kṛi,* P. Ā. *-karoti, -kurute,* to act badly towards, ill-treat, offend, Mn. ix, 213. °**nikāra,** m. offence, injury, MBh. °**nikṛita,** mfn. ill-treated, injured, damaged, MBh.; R.

विनिकृत् *vi-ni-√2. kṛit,* P. *-kṛintati,* to cut

or hew in pieces, cut away, tear off, destroy, MBh. °**nikarttavya**, mfn. to be cut down, ib. °**nikṛitta**, mfn. cut away, torn off, R. °**nikṛintana**, mfn. cutting in pieces, hewing down, ib.

विनिकॄ *vi-ni-√kṝi* (only ind. p. *-kīrya*), to cast off, abandon, Kum. °**nikīrṇa**, mfn. thrown asunder, scattered, dispersed, broken, MBh.; R.; covered, filled, crowded with (instr. or comp.), R.; Ragh.

विनिकोचन *vi-ni-kocana*, n. (√*kuc*) contraction (of the brows), Bhpr.

विनिक्ष् *vi-√niksh*, P. *-nikshati* (Ved. inf. *-nikshe*), to pierce, penetrate, RV.; AV. °**nikshaṇa**, n. the act of piercing, Nir. iv, 18.

विनिक्षिप् *vi-ni-√kship*, P. Ā. *-kshipati*, °*te*, to throw or put down, infix, insert, fasten, Yājñ.; R.; (with *manas*) to fix the mind upon (loc.), MBh.; to deposit, entrust with, ib.; to charge with, appoint to (loc.), ib. °**nikshipta**, mfn. thrown or put down &c.; (ifc.) placed in or under, ŚārṅgP. °**nikshepa**, m. tossing, throwing, sending, W.; separation, isolation (*guṇa-vinikshepa-tas*, with regard to the qualities singly or separately), Car. °**nikshepya**, mfn. to be thrown into (loc.), MBh.

विनिगद् *vi-ni-√gad*, P. *-gadati*, to speak to, address, Sāh.: Pass. *-gadyate*, to be called or named, ib.

विनिगमक *vi-ni-gamaka*, mfn. (√*gam*) deciding between two alternatives, Kap., Sch. °**nigamanā**, f. decision between two alternatives, Śaṃk.

विनिगुह् *vi-ni-√guh*, P. *-gūhati*, to cover over, conceal, hide, MBh.; R. °**nigūhita**, mfn. (fr. Caus.) covered, concealed, hidden, VarBṛS. °**nigūhitṛi**, m. one who conceals, keeper (of a secret), MBh.

विनिग्रह् *vi-ni-√grah* (only ind. p. *-gṛihya*), to lay hold of, seize, keep back, restrain, impede, MBh. °**nigraha**, m. separation, division, Nir.; restraining, checking, stopping, subduing, controlling, MBh.; Kāv. &c.; restriction, limitation, L.; disjunction, mutual opposition, an antithesis which implies that when two propositions are antithetically stated peculiar stress is laid on one of them, MW.; °*hârtha*, m. the sense of the above antithesis, ib.; °*hârthīya*, mfn. standing in the sense of the above antithesis, ib. °**nigrāhya**, mfn. to be stopped or restrained, MBh.

विनिघूर्णित *vi-ni-ghūrṇita*, mfn. (√*ghūrṇ*) moving to and fro, agitated, MBh. viii, 4665 (w.r. *vi-nicūrṇita*).

विनिघ्न *vi-nighna*, mfn. (√*han*) multiplied, Gaṇit. (cf. *ni-ghna*).

Vi-nighnat. See under *vi-ni-√han*.

विनिज् *vi-√nij* (only aor. *vy-ànijam*), to wipe off, AV. x, 4, 19.

विनिद्र *vi-nidra* &c. See p. 951, col. 1.

विनिधा *vi-ni-√dhā*, P. Ā. *-dadhāti*, *-dhatte*, to put or place or lay down in different places, distribute, TS.; ŚBr.; to put off, lay down or aside, MBh.; Suśr.; to put by, store up, VarBṛS.; to put or place on, fix upon, direct (mind, eyes &c.), Kāv.; Rājat.; (with *hṛidi*) to fix in the heart, bear in mind, Gīt.

Vi-nihita, mfn. put or laid down, placed or fixed upon, directed towards (loc. or comp.), Bhartṛ.; Gīt.; appointed to (loc.), Hariv.; separated, turned off (see °*tâtman*); *-dṛishṭi*, mfn. one who has the eyes fixed upon, eagerly looking at, Mṛicch.; *-manas*, mfn. one who has the mind fixed upon, intent upon, devoted to, Gīt.; °*tâtman*, mfn. disagreeing (in mind), not assenting, Āpast.

विनिधृ *vi-ni-√dhṛi*, P. *-dhārayati*, to fix (the eyes) upon, AmṛitUp.

विनिध्वंस् *vi-ni-√dhvaṇs* (or *dhvas*), P. Ā. *-dhvaṇsati*, °*te*, to fall to pieces, disappear, vanish (2. sg. Impv. *-dhvaṇsa*, begone, take thyself off), R. °**nidhvasta**, mfn. destroyed, ruined, struck down, ib.

विनिन्द् *vi-√nind* (or *nid*), P. *-nindati*, to reproach, revile, abuse, MBh.; Pur. °**ninda**, mfn. mocking (= surpassing, exceeding), Pañcar.; (*ā*), f. reproach, abuse, VP. °**nindaka**, mfn. blaming, censuring, Subh.; scoffing, deriding, MārkP.; mocking, i.e. surpassing, Gīt.

विनिपद् *vi-ni-√pad* (only ind. p. *-pādya*), to split open, cleave, sever, BhP.

विनिपत् *vi-ni-√pat*, P. *-patati*, to fall down, fall in or into (loc.), Hariv.; Sāh.; to flow down, alight upon (loc.), Hariv.; to fall upon, attack, assail, Kathās.: Caus. *-pātayati* (Pass. *-pātyate*), to cause to fall down, strike off (a man's head), MBh.; to throw down, kill, destroy, annihilate, Mn.; MBh. &c. °**nipatita**, mfn. fallen or flown down &c., Hariv.; Kāv. &c. °**nipāta**, m. falling down, falling, L.; a great fall, ruin, loss, calamity, Mn.; MBh. &c.; death, Hcar.; frustration, Subh.; failure (see *a-vin*°); *-gata*, mfn. fallen into misfortune, R.; *-pratikriyā*, f. (Kathās.), *-pratīkāra*, m. (Pañcat.) a remedy against m°; *-śaṇsin*, mfn. announcing m° or destruction, portentous, W. °**nipātaka**, mfn. throwing down, causing to fall, destroying, MBh. °**nipātana**, n. causing miscarriage, Harav. °**nipātita**, mfn. thrown down, killed, destroyed, R. °**nipātin**, see *a-vin*°.

विनिपीड् *vi-ni-√pīḍ*, Caus. *-pīḍayati*, to torment, harass, annoy, MBh. vi, 3515 (ind. p. *vi-nipīḍya*, with v. l. *ca nipīḍya*).

विनिबन्ध *vi-ni-bandha*, m. (√*bandh*) the being attached or attachment to anything, Buddh.

विनिबर्हण *vi-ni-barhaṇa*, mfn. (√1. *bṛih*) throwing down, crushing, MBh. °**nibarhin**, mfn. id., ib.

विनिमग्न *vi-ni-magna*, mfn. (√*majj*) dived under, bathed or immersed in (loc.), BhP.

विनिमय *vi-ni-maya*, m. (√*me*) exchange, barter (*ena*, alternately), Āpast.; MBh.; Kāv. &c.; mutual engagement, reciprocity (see *kārya-vin*°); a pledge, deposit, security, L.; transmutation (of letters), MW.

विनिमीलन *vi-ni-mīlana*, n. (√*mīl*) shutting, closure (of a flower, of the eyes &c.), Ratnâv.; Dharmaś. °**nimīlita**, mfn. closed, shut; °*têkshaṇa*, mfn. having the eyes closed, Bhaṭṭ.; Kathās.

विनिमेष *vi-ni-mesha*, m. (√*mish*) winking or twinkling of the eyes, a wink, sign, Kir. °**nimeshaṇa**, n. id., ib.

विनियम् *vi-ni-√yam*, P. *-yacchati*, to restrain, check, control, keep in check, regulate, Mn.; MBh. &c.; to draw in, withdraw, MBh.; to keep off, ib.; Kir.

Vi-niyata, mfn. restrained, checked, regulated, Bhag.; retrenched, limited, R. (see comp.); *-cetas*, mfn. one who has a controlled or regulated mind, MārkP.; °*tâhāra*, mfn. moderate in food or diet, abstemious, R.

Vi-niyama, m. limitation, restriction to (loc.), MBh.; restraint, government, W. °**niyamya**, mfn. to be restricted or limited, Pat.

विनियुज् *vi-ni-√yuj*, Ā. *-yuṅkte* (rarely P. *-yunakti*; cf. Pat. on Pāṇ. i, 3, 64), to unyoke, disjoin, loose, detach, separate, MBh.; to discharge (an arrow) at (loc.), R.; to assign, commit, appoint to, charge or entrust with, destine for (dat., loc., or *artham*), MBh.; R. &c. (with *sakhye*, to chose for a friend); to apply, use, employ, Kāv.; Kathās.; Car.; to eat, Dhūrtas.: Pass. *-yujyate*, to be unyoked &c.; to fall to pieces, decay, MBh.: Caus. *-yojayati*, to appoint or assign to, commit to (loc., or *arthāya* or *ártham*), Yājñ.; Hariv. &c.; to entrust anything (acc.) to (loc.), Mn. vii, 226; to offer or present anything (acc.) to (dat.), Pañcar.; to use, employ, ŚvetUp.; Car.; to perform, Pañcar. °**niyukta**, mfn. unyoked, disjoined &c.; appointed to, destined for (loc.), Sarvad.; enjoined, commanded, MW.; °*tâtman*, mfn. one who has his mind fixed on or directed towards, Kum.

Vi-niyoktavya, mfn. to be appointed to or employed in, W.; to be enjoined or commanded, MW. °**niyoktṛi**, mfn. one who appoints &c.; appointer to (loc.), employer, MBh.; Kām.; mf(*trī*)n. containing the special disposition of anything, KātyŚr., Sch.

Vi-niyoga, m. apportionment, distribution, division, Nir.; appointment to (loc.), commission, charge, duty, task, occupation, MBh.; R. &c.; employment, use, application (esp. of a verse in ritual), TĀr.; Hariv. &c.; relation, correlation, VPrāt.; Pāṇ. viii, 1, 61 &c.; = *adhikāra*, 'governing rule,' Kāś. on Pāṇ. i, 3, 11; separation, abandonment, W.; impediment, ib.; *-mālā*, f., *-saṃgraha*, m., *-sat-kriyā*, f. N. of wks. °**niyojita**, mfn. (fr. Caus.) appointed or directed or applied to, destined for, chosen as (with loc., *artham* or *arthāya*), R.; Hariv. &c. (*paśu-tve*, destined for a sacrificial victim; *adhipati-tve*, appointed to the sovereignty); commissioned, charged, deputed, R. °**niyojya**, mfn. to be applied or used or employed, Kāv.; Pur.

विनिरोधिन् *vi-ni-rodhin*, mfn. (√*rudh*) checking, obstructing, Harav.

विनिर्गम् *vi-nir-√gam*, P. *-gacchati*, to go out or away, depart or escape from (abl.), MBh.; R. &c.; to be beside one's self, BhP.

Vi-nirgata, mfn. gone out, come forth, issued, R.; VarBṛS. &c.; liberated or freed from (abl.), Mn. viii, 65. °**nirgati**, f. coming forth, issuing, Car.

Vi-nirgama, m. going out, departure from (abl.), Mn.; MBh. &c.; being spread or divulged, spreading abroad, MārkP.; the last of the three divisions of an astrological house, VarBṛS.

विनिर्घोष *vi-nir-ghosha*, m. (√*ghush*) sound, MBh.

विनिर्जि *vi-nir-√ji*, P. *-jayati*, to conquer completely, win, MBh.; R.; to vanquish, defeat, overpower, subdue, Mn.; MBh. &c.

Vi-nirjaya, m. complete victory, conquest, MBh.

Vi-nirjita, mfn. entirely conquered, subdued, won, ib.; R.; BhP.

विनिर्ज्ञा *vi-nir-√jñā* (only Pass. *-jñāyate*), to distinguish, discern, find out, ŚBr.

विनिर्णी *vi-nir-ṇī* (√*nī*; only ind. p. *-ṇīya*), to decide or determine clearly, BhP.

Vi-nirṇaya, m. complete settlement or decision, certainty, a settled rule, Mn.; MBh. &c.

Vi-nirṇīta, mfn. determined clearly, ascertained, certain, W.

विनिर्दह् *vi-nir-√dah*, P. *-dahati*, to burn completely, consume by fire, destroy, MBh.; BhP.

Vi-nirdagdha, mfn. completely burned up or consumed, utterly destroyed, MBh.; R.; Hariv.

Vi-nirdahana, n. the act of burning or destroying utterly, MW.; (*ī*), f. a partic. remedy, Suśr.

विनिर्दिश् *vi-nir-√diś*, P. *-diśati*, to assign, destine for (loc.), BhP.; to point out, indicate, state, declare, designate as (two acc.), MBh.; BhP.; Suśr.; to announce, proclaim, Yājñ.; VarBṛS.; to determine, resolve, fix upon, MBh. °**nirdishṭa**, mfn. pointed out &c.; charged or entrusted with (loc.), R. °**nirdeśya**, mfn. to be announced or reported, VarBṛS.

विनिर्धू *vi-nir-√dhū* (only ind. p. *-dhūya*), to shake off, drive or blow away, scatter, R.; to shake about, agitate, ib.; to reject, repudiate, Vcar. °**nirdhuta**, mfn. shaken off or about, tossed, agitated, ib. °**nirdhūta**, mfn. shaken off, BhP.; driven away, MBh.

विनिर्बन्ध *vi-nir-bandha*, m. (√*bandh*) persistence or perseverance in (comp.), MBh.; MārkP.

विनिर्बाहु *vi-nirbāhu*, *vi-nirbhaya* &c. See p. 951, col. 1.

विनिर्भग्न *vi-nir-bhagna*, mfn. (√*bhañj*) broken asunder, broken down, MBh.; *-nayana*, mfn. one who has his eyes dashed out, R.

विनिर्भर्त्स् *vi-nir-√bharts* (only ind. p. *-bhartsya*), to threaten or revile, R.; BhP.

विनिर्भिद् *vi-nir-√bhid* (only ind. p. *-bhidya*), to split asunder, pierce, shoot through, MBh.; Hariv. °**nirbhinna**, mfn. split asunder, cleft, opened, pierced, MBh.; Daś.; BhP.

विनिर्भुज् *vi-nir-√1. bhuj* (only ind. p. *-bhujya*), to bend or turn on one side, Suśr.

विनिर्भोग *vi-nir-bhoga*, m. (prob. fr. √3. *bhuj*) N. of a partic. cosmic period, Buddh.

विनिर्मथ् *vi-nir-√math* (or *manth*; only

ind. p. -*mathya*), to churn out, Suśr.; to crush, annihilate, Kathās.

विनिर्मा *vi-nir-√3. mā* (only pf. *-mame*, with act. and pass. meaning), to fabricate, create, fashion, form, build, construct out of (instr. or abl.), Bhaṭṭ.; Kathās. °**nirmāṇa**, n. meting out, measuring, MBh.; building, forming, creating (ifc. made of, formed according to), Kathās.; Rājat.; Pañcar. °**nirmātṛi**, m. a maker, builder, creator, MBh.

Vi-nirmita, mfn. formed, created, constructed, built, prepared, made from or fashioned out of (abl. or comp.), MBh.; R. &c.; laid out (as a garden), Kathās.; fixed, appointed, destined to be (nom.), Hariv.; Kāv.; kept, celebrated, observed (as a feast), R. °**nirmiti**, f. formation, building, creation, Hcat. °**nirmitsu**, mfn. (fr. Desid.) wishing to form or create, Kpr.

विनिर्मुच *vi-nir-√muc*, P. *-muñcati* (only ind. p. *-mucya*), to abandon, relinquish (the body, i. e. to die), Hariv.: Pass. *-mucyate*, to be liberated or set free, be delivered from, be rid of (instr.), PraśnUp. °**nirmukta**, mfn. liberated, escaped, free or exempt from (instr. or comp.), MBh.; VarBṛS.; Suśr. &c.; discharged, shot off, hurled, R. °**nirmukti**, f. (ifc.) liberation, W.

विनिर्मोक्ष *vi-nir-moksha*, m. (√*moksh*) emancipation, liberation, release from (comp.), MBh.; R.; exclusion, exemption, L.

विनिर्यत् *vi-nir-yat*, mfn. (√5. *i*) going forth, issuing, W.

विनिर्या *vi-nir-√yā*, P. *-yāti*, to go forth, go out, issue, set out, MBh.; Kāv. &c. °**niryāṇa**, n. the act of going forth, setting out, R. °**niryāta**, mfn. gone forth or out, set out, W.

विनिर्युज् *vi-nir-√yuj* (only fut. *-yokshyāmi*), to discharge, shoot off, R. ii, 23, 37 (B. *vi-ni-yokshyāmi*).

विनिर्लिख् *vi-nir-√likh*, P. *-likhati*, to make incisions in, scarify, Suśr.; to scratch or scrape off, free from dirt, Car.

विनिर्वम् *vi-nir-√vam*, P. *-vamati*, to vomit or spit out, R.

विनिर्वर्ण् *vi-nir-√varṇ* (only ind. p. *-varṇya*), to look closely at, contemplate, Śak. v, 11/12 (v.l. for *nir-varṇya*).

विनिर्वृत्त *vi-nir-vṛitta*, mfn. (√*vṛit*) proceeded, come forth, issued from (abl.), R.; completed, finished, Yājñ. ii, 31.

विनिर्हत *vi-nir-hata*, mfn. (√*han*) completely destroyed, AV.

विनिर्हृ *vi-nir-√hṛi*, P. Ā. *-harati*, °*te*, to take out, extract, Suśr.; to remove, destroy, MBh.

विनिविद् *vi-ni-√1. vid*, Caus. *-vedayati*, to make known, announce, inform, report, MBh.; R.; Kathās.; to offer, present, Hcat.

Vi-nivedana, n. the act of announcing, announcement, Kathās. °**vedita**, mfn. made known, announced, MBh.

विनिविश् *vi-ni-√viś*, Caus. *-veśayati*, to cause to enter into, set down or place in, put on, Hariv.; Kāv.; Rājat.; to apply, Kāv.; to appoint to, institute or instal in (loc.), MBh.; to fix (the eyes or thoughts) upon (loc.), MBh.; Hariv.; to fix or erect (a statue), Rājat.; to establish or found (a city), Kum.; to draw up in array (as troops), MBh.; (with *kare*) to place in tribute, make tributary, MBh.; (with *hṛidaye*) to impress on the heart, Rājat. °**nivishṭa**, mfn. dwelling or residing in (comp.), VarBṛS.; occurring in (loc.), Sāh.; placed on or in (loc.), Kām.; drawn on (loc.), R.; laid out (as tanks), MBh.; divided i.e. various or different, Laṭy., Sch.

Vi-niveśa, m. putting down, placing upon, Śiś.; Gīt.; an impression (as of the fingers &c.), Śak.; putting down (in a book), i.e. mentioning, Sarvad.; suitable apportionment or disposition, ŚrS., Sch.; entrance, settling down, MW. °**niveśana**, n. setting down, Dharmaś.; raising, erection, building, Rājat.; arrangement, disposition, ĀpŚr., Sch.; impressing, Yogas., Sch. °**niveśita**, mfn. raised, erected, built, Rājat.; placed or fixed in or on (loc.), MBh.; Kāv. &c. °**niveśin**, mfn. situated in or on (comp.), Kathās.

विनिवृ *vi-ni-√1. vṛi*, Caus. *-vārayati* (Pass. *-vāryate*), to keep or ward off, check, prevent, suppress, MBh.; Kāv. &c.; to prohibit, forbid, Rājat.; to remove, destroy, MBh.; R. &c.; to dismiss (a minister), depose (a king), Rājat.

Vi-nivāraṇa, n. keeping off, restraining, R.; Kathās. °**nivārita**, mfn. kept off, prevented, hindered, opposed, W.; screened, covered, ib. °**nivārya**, mfn. to be removed or supplanted, Rājat.

विनिवृत् *vi-ni-√vṛit*, Ā. *-vartate*, to turn back, return, MBh.; Kāv. &c.; to turn away, desist or cease from (abl.), ib.; to cease, end, disappear, Mn.; MBh. &c.; to be extinguished (as fire), Yājñ.; to be omitted, Laṭy.: Caus. *-vartayati*, to cause to return, call or lead back from (abl.), MBh.; Kāv. &c.; to cause to cease or desist from (abl.), R.; MārkP.; to draw back (a missile), MBh.; to avert, divert (the gaze), R.; Mālav.; to give up, abandon, MBh.; R.; to cause to cease, remove, R.; to render ineffective, annul (a curse, fraudulent transactions &c.), ŚvetUp.; Mn.; MBh. &c.

Vi-nivartaka, mfn. reversing, annulling, TPrāt.

Vi-nivartana, n. turning back, return, MBh.; R. &c.; coming to an end, cessation, Daśar., Sch.

Vi-nivarti, f. ceasing, cessation, Divyâv.

Vi-nivartita, mfn. caused to turn back or to desist from anything, MBh.; turned away, averted, Mālav. °**nivartin**, see *a-vinivartin*. °**nivṛitta**, mfn. turned back, returned, retired, withdrawn, Yājñ.; R.; turned away or averted or adverse from (abl. or comp.), R.; MārkP.; (ifc.) freed from, MBh.; desisting from (abl.), having abandoned or given up, R., disappeared, ended, ceased to be, Hariv.; Kāv.; Kathās.; *-kāma*, mfn. one whose desires have ceased, foiled in one's wishes, Bhag.; *-śāpa*, mfn. freed from (the evil effects of) a curse, Kathās. °**nivṛitti**, f. cessation, coming to an end, Mn.; Hariv. &c.; omission, discontinuance, PārGṛ.; Car.

विनिशम् *vi-ni-√śam* (only ind. p. *-śamya*), to hear, learn, MBh.

विनिश्चर् *vi-niś-√car*, P. *-carati*, to go forth in all directions, ŚBr.; MBh.

विनिश्चि *vi-niś-√2. ci* (only ind. p. *-citya*), to debate about, deliberate, consider, Mn.; MBh. &c.; to determine, resolve, decide, BhP.

Vi-niścaya, m. deciding, settling, ascertainment, settled opinion, decision, firm resolve regarding (gen. or comp.), Mn.; MBh. &c. (*aṅga-v*°, the fixing or settling of a horoscope, MW.); *-jña*, mfn. knowing the certainty of anything, MBh. °**niścāyin**, mfn. settling finally, deciding, Sarvad.

Vi-niścita, mfn. firmly resolved upon (comp.), MBh.; ascertained, determined, settled, certain, ib.; R. &c.; (*am*), ind. most certainly, decidedly, Amar.; °*tārtha*, mfn. having a decided meaning, Bhartṛ.

विनिश्वस् *vi-ni-√śvas* (cf. *vi-niḥ-√śvas*), P. *-śvasita*, to breathe hard, snort, hiss, R.; Bhaṭṭ.; to sigh deeply, MBh.; R. °**niśvasita**, n. exhalation, Jātakam. °**niśvāsa**, m. breathing hard, sighing, a sigh, W.

विनिषद् *vi-ni-shad* (√*sad*), P. *-shīdati*, to sit down separately.

विनिषूदित *vi-ni-shūdita*, mfn. (√*sūd*) destroyed utterly, MBh. (C. *-sūdita*).

विनिष्कम्प *vi-nishkampa*, *vi-nishkriya* &c. See p. 951, col. 1.

विनिष्कृ *vi-nish-√1. kṛi*, Caus. *-kārayati*, to cause to be mended or repaired, Kauś.

विनिष्क्रम् *vi-nish-√kram*, P. Ā. *-krāmati*, *-kramate* (ind. p. *-kramya*), to step forth, go out, issue from (abl.), MBh.; R. &c. °**nishkrānta**, mfn. gone forth, come out, MBh.

विनिष्टन् *vi-ni-shṭan* (prob. for *vi-niḥ-shṭan*; *shṭan* = √*stan*), P. *-shṭanati*, to groan loudly, Car.

विनिष्टप्त *vi-nish-ṭapta*, mfn. (√*tap*; cf. Pāṇ. viii, 3, 102) well roasted or fried, R.

विनिष्ठिव् *vi-ni-√shṭhiv*, P. *-shṭhīvati* or °*vyati*, to spit out, Suśr.

विनिष्पट् *vi-nish-√paṭ*, P. *-pāṭayati*, to split or cleave asunder, BhP.

विनिष्पत् *vi-nish-√pat*, P. *-patati*, to fall out of, fly forth from, rush forth, issue, MBh.; R. &c.; to fly or run away, Mn. vii, 106 (Kull. 'to double or flee or move crookedly, as a hare'). °**nishpatita**, mfn. rushed forth, lept out, MBh.; R. °**nishpāta**, m. rushing forth or out, pushing on (*mushṭi-vi-nish*°, a blow with the fist), BhP.

विनिष्पाद्य *vi-nish-pādya*, mfn. (√*pad*) to be accomplished or effected, MārkP.

विनिष्पिष् *vi-nish-√pish*, P. *-pinashṭi*, to grind to pieces, crush, bruise, MBh.; Kāv. &c.; (*pāṇau pāṇim*), to rub the hands together, MBh. °**nishpishṭa**, mfn. ground down, crushed into powder, smashed, MBh.; BhP.

Vi-nishpesha, m. grinding to pieces, rubbing together, friction, MBh.

विनिष्पीड् *vi-nish-√pīḍ*, P. *-pīḍayati*, to squeeze out, Suśr.

विनिसूद् *vi-ni-√sūd*. See *vi-ni-shūdita*.

विनिसृत *vi-ni-sṛita*. See *vi-niḥ-sṛita*.

विनिस्तप् *vi-nis-tap*. See *vi-nish-ṭapta*.

विनिस्मृत *vi-ni-smṛita*, mfn. (√*smṛi*) recorded, mentioned, Pañcar.

विनिहन् *vi-ni-√han*, P. *-hanti*, to strike down, slay, slaughter, kill, destroy, MBh.; Kāv. &c.

Vi-nighnat, mfn. striking down, destroying, R.

Vi-nihata, mfn. struck down &c.; dispelled (as darkness), MBh.; disregarded (as a command), R.; afflicted, distressed (as the mind), MBh.; m. a great or unavoidable calamity, infliction caused by fate or heaven, W.; a portent, comet, meteor, ib.

विनिह्नु *vi-ni-√hnu*, P. *-hnauti*, to deny, disown, MBh. xiii, 5521 (w.r. *hnoti*). °**nihnuta**, mfn. denied, disowned, hidden, concealed, Kāv.; Kathās.

विनी *vi-√nī*, P. Ā. *-nayati*, °*te*, to lead or take away, remove, avert, RV.; AV.; to throw off, drive away, dispel, expel (a disease), Car.; (Ā.) to elicit, draw from (abl.), RV.; to stir up (the Soma), RV.; to part (the hair), GṛŚrS.; to stretch, extend, ŚāṅkhBr.; R.; to train, tame, guide (horses), MBh.; Kāv. &c.; to educate, instruct, direct, MBh.; R. &c.; to chastise, punish, Yājñ.; Kum.; to induce, lead or cause to (inf.), RV. i, 1, 64, 6; to spend, pass (time), Gīt.; to perform, accomplish, MBh.; (Ā.) to pay off, restore (a debt), Pāṇ. i, 3, 36; to expand (esp. for religious purposes), ib., Sch.; to get rid of, give up, cease from (anger), Pāṇ. i, 3, 37: Desid. A. *-ninīshate*, to wish to get rid of or give up (egoism), ŚāṅkhŚr.

2. **Vi-nayá**, mfn. (for 1. see p. 969) leading away or asunder, separating, RV. ii, 24, 9; cast, thrown, L.; secret, L.; m. taking away, removal, withdrawal, Śiś. x, 42; leading, guidance, training (esp. moral tr°), education, discipline, control, MBh.; Kāv. &c.; (with Buddhists) the rules of discipline for monks, MWB. 55 &c.; good breeding, propriety of conduct, decency, modesty, mildness, ib. (in the Purāṇas sometimes personified as son of Kriyā or of Lajjā); an office, business, Śiś. xi, 36; N. of a son of Sudyumna, MārkP.; a man of subdued senses, L.; a merchant, trader, L.; (*ā*), f. Sida Cordifolia, L.; *-karman*, n. instruction, Ragh.; *-kshudraka* or °*ka-vastu*, n. N. of a Buddhist wk.; *-grāhin*, mfn. conforming to rules of discipline, compliant, tractable, L.; m. an elephant which obeys orders, L.; *-jyotis* (?), m. N. of a Muni, Kathās.; *-tā*, f. good behaviour; modesty, Cāṇ.; *-datta*, m. N. of a man, Mṛicch.; *-deva*, m. N. of a teacher, Buddh.; of a poet, Sadukt.; *-nandin*, m. N. of the leader of a Jaina sect, Inscr.; *-m-dhara*, m. N. of a chamberlain, Veṇis.; *-pattra*, n. = *-sūtra* (below), Buddh.; *-piṭaka*, 'basket of discipline,' (with Buddhists) the collection of treatises on discipline (cf. above); *-pradhāna*, mfn. having humility pre-eminent, of which modesty is chief, MW.; *-pramāthin*, mfn. violating propriety, behaving ill or improperly, W.; *-bhāj*, mfn. possessing propriety or modesty, ib.; *-maya*, mf(*ī*)n. consisting of propriety, Kād.; *-yogin*, mfn. possessing humility, MW.; *-rāma*, m. = *-sundara*, Cat.; *-vat*, mfn. well-behaved (in *a-vin*°), Vet.; (*atī*), f. N. of a woman, Kathās.; Daś.; Pañcat.; *-vallī*, f. N. of wk.; *-vastu*, n. (with Buddhists) N. of a section of the works which treat of Vinaya

(q.v.); *-vāc*, mfn. speaking modestly, W.; f. modest speech, ib.; *-vijaya*, m. N. of an author, Cat.; *-vibhaṅga*, m. N. of wk.; *-vibhāshā-śāstra*, n. N. of a Buddhist wk.; *-śrī*, f. N. of a woman, HPariś.; *-sāgara*, *-sundara*, m. N. of authors, Cat.; *-sūtra*, n. (with Buddhists) the Sūtra treating of discipline (cf. above); *-stha*, mfn. conforming to discipline, compliant, tractable, L.; *-svāminī*, f. N. of a woman, Kathās.; °*yâditya*, m. N. of Jayâpīḍa, Rājat.; of a king of the race of the Cālukyas, Inscr.; (*-pura*, n. N. of a town built by Jayâpīḍa, Rājat.); °*yâdidhara* (i.e. *vinaya-dh*°), m. N. of a man, Kāv.; °*yânvita*, mfn. endowed with modesty, humble, L.; °*yâvanata*, mfn. bending down modestly, bowing low with modesty, MBh.; Kathās.; °*yôkti*, f. pl. modest speech, Bālar. °**nayana**, mfn. taking away, removing, MBh.; Megh.; n. the act of taming or training, education, instruction, Daś.

Vi-nāyaka, mf(*ikā*)n. taking away, removing, MW.; m. 'Remover (of obstacles),' N. of Gaṇeśa, Yājñ.; VarBṛS. &c.; a leader, guide, MBh.; R.; a Guru or spiritual preceptor, L.; a Buddha, L.; N. of Garuḍa, L.; an obstacle, impediment, L.; = *a-nātha* (?), L.; N. of various authors &c., Cat.; pl. a partic. class of demons, MānGṛ.; MBh. &c.; N. of partic. formulas recited over weapons, R.; (*ikā*), f. the wife of Gaṇeśa or Garuḍa, L.; *-caturthī*, f. the fourth day of the festival in honour of Gaṇeśa, Cat.; (°*thī-vrata*, n. N. of wk.); *-carita*, n. N. of the 73rd ch. of the Krīḍā-khaṇḍa or 2nd part of the Gaṇeśa-Purāṇa.; *-dvādaśa-nāma-stotra*, n. N. of wk.; *-paṇḍita*, m. N. of a poet, ŚārṅgP.; = *nanda-paṇḍ*°, Cat.; *-purāṇa*, n., *-pūjā-vidhi*, m. N. of wks.; *-bhaṭṭa*, m. N. of various authors, Cat.; *-bhojana-varṇanā*, f., *-māhātmya*, n., *-vrata-kalpa*, m., *-vrata-pūjā*, f., *-śānti*, f., *-śānti-paddhati*, f., *-śānti-prayoga*, m., *-śānti-saṃgraha*, m., *-saṃhitā*, f., *-sahasra-nāman*, n., *-stava-rāja*, m. N. of wks. or chs. from wks.; *-snapana-caturthī*, f. the fourth day of the Gaṇeśa festival (when his image is bathed), Cat.; °*kâvatāra-varṇana*, n., °*kâvir-bhāva*, m., °*kôtpatti*, f. N. of parts of wks.

Vi-nīta, mfn. led or taken away, removed &c.; stretched, extended, R.; tamed, trained, educated, well-behaved, humble, modest, Mn.; MBh. &c.; versed in, acquainted or familiar with (loc. or comp.), Yājñ.; R. &c.; performed, accomplished, MBh.; one who has subdued his passions, L.; lovely, handsome, W.; plain, neat (in dress &c.), A.; m. a trained horse, L.; a merchant, trader, L.; N. of a son of Pulastya, VP.; *-tā*, f. (Kām.), *-tva*, n. (Ragh.) modesty, decency, decorum; *-datta* or *-deva*, m. N. of a poet, Cat.; *-prabha*, m. N. of a Buddhist scholar; *-mati*, m. N. of two men, Kathās.; *-vesha*, m. modest or plain attire, Śak.; °*shâbharaṇa*, mfn. humble or modest in dress and ornaments, Mn. viii, 2; *-sattva*, mfn. (a grove) containing tame animals, Ragh.; *-sena*, m. N. of a man, Buddh.; °*tâtman*, mfn. having a well-controlled mind, well-behaved, modest, Mn. vii, 39; °*tâśva*, m. N. of a man, Hcat.; °*têśvara*, m. N. of a divine being, Buddh. °**nītaka**, m. n. = *vainītaka*. °**nīti**, f. training, good behaviour, modesty, Hit. °**nīya**, m. = *kalka*, L.

Vi-netṛi, m. a leader, guide, instructor, teacher, MBh.; Kāv. &c.; a chastiser, punisher, Ragh.; Mcar.; a tamer, trainer, Kull. on Mn. iii, 162; a prince, king, L.

2. **Vi-netra**, m. (for 1. see p. 951, col. 1) a teacher, preceptor, Hariv.

Vi-neya, mfn. to be taken away or removed, Hariv.; to be trained or educated or instructed, Sāh.; Sarvad.; to be chastised, L.; m. a pupil, disciple, L.

विनील *vi-nīla*, *vi-nīvi* &c. See p. 951, col. 1.

विनु *vi-√3. nu*, Ā. *-navate*, to go or spread in different directions, RV. x, 22, 9.

विनुद् *vi-√nud*, P. Ā. *-nudati*, °*te*, to drive away or asunder, scare away, dispel, remove, RV.; ŚāṅkhŚr.; to strike (cords), play (on a musical instrument), BhP. (v. l. *vi-tud*): Caus. *-nodayati*, to drive asunder or away, dispel, Śiś.; Gīt.; to spend (time), MBh.; to divert, amuse, entertain, Hariv.; Kāv.; Kathās.; to amuse one's self with, delight in (instr.), Ragh. v, 67. °**nutti**, f. dispelling, removal, Kāṭh.; N. of an Ekâha, ŚrS. °**núd**, f. a stroke, thrust, blow, RV. ii, 13, 3. °**nunna**, mfn. driven asunder &c.; stricken, hurt, wounded, MBh.

Vi-noda, m. driving away, removal, VarBṛS.; Kathās.; diversion, sport, pastime, pleasure, playing or amusing one's self with (comp.), Kāv.; Kathās.; Pañcat. &c. (°*dāya*, ind. for pleasure); eagerness, vehemence, L.; a kind of embrace, L.; a kind of palace, L.; N. of a wk. on music; *-kallola*, m., *-mañjarī*, f., *-raṅga*, m. N. of wks.; *-rasika*, mfn. given or addicted to pleasure, Kathās.; *-vat*, mfn. amusing, delightful, ib.; *-sthāna*, n. ground (lit. and fig.) for pleasure or enjoyment, Śak.; °*dârtham*, ind. for the sake of sport or pl°, Kathās.; °*dôpapādin*, mfn. causing pl° or delight, ib. °**nodana**, n. diversion, play, amusement, pastime (*-tā*, f.), Kāv.; Kathās.; *-śata*, n. pl. hundreds of amusements, Vikr. °**nodita**, mfn. (fr. Caus.) driven away, dispelled, Śiś.; Gīt.; diverted, amused, delighted, R.; Hariv.; allayed, soothed, W.

Vi-nodin, mfn. driving away, dispelling, Śak.; Kathās.; amusing, diverting, Kathās.; Pañcar.

विनृत् *vi-√nṛit*, P. *-nṛityati*, to begin to dance, TBr.

विनोक्ति *vinôkti*. See under *vinā*, p. 969.

विन्त *vinta*, m. N. of a partic. divine being, MārkP.

विन्द् *vind*, P. *vindati*. See √3. *vid*.

Vinda, mfn. finding, getting, gaining (ifc.; see *go-*, *cāru-v*° &c.); m. a partic. hour of the day, R.; N. of a son of Dhṛita-rāshṭra, MBh.; of a king of Avanti, ib.

Vindaka, m. N. of a man, Rājat.

Vindát-vat, mfn. containing a form of √3. *vid*; (*atī*), f. a verse of this kind, MaitrS.

1. **Vindu**, mfn. finding, getting, acquiring, procuring, PañcavBr. (cf. *go-*, *loka-v*°).

विन्दु 2. *vindu*, mfn. (fr. √1. *vid*) knowing, acquainted or familiar with (ifc.), Vās.; = *veditavya*, L.

विन्दु 3. *vindu*, °*duka*, °*dula*. See *bindu*.

विन्ध् *vindh*, Ā. *vindhate*. See √2. *vidh*.

विन्ध *vindha*, *vindha-culaka*, w. r. for *vindhya*, *vindhya-culika*.

विन्धपत्त्र *vindha-pattra*, m. (or *ī*, f.) a plant (commonly called Bel Suṇṭh), L.

विन्धस *vindhasa* (?), m. the moon, L.

विन्ध्य *vindhya*, *as*, m. (of doubtful derivation) N. of a low range of hills connecting the Northern extremities of the Western and Eastern Ghauts, and separating Hindūstān proper from the Dekhan (the Vindhya range is reckoned among the seven principal ranges of Bhārata-varsha [see *kula-giri*, p. 294, col. 3], and according to Manu ii, 21, forms the Southern limit of Madhya-deśa or the middle region; according to a legend related in MBh. iii, 8782 &c., the personified Vindhya, jealous of Himâlaya, demanded that the sun should revolve round him in the same way as about Meru, which the sun declining to do, the Vindhya then began to elevate himself that he might bar the progress of both sun and moon; the gods alarmed, asked the aid of the saint Agastya, who approached the Vindhya and requested that by bending down he would afford him an easy passage to the South country, begging at the same time that he would retain a low position till his return; this he promised to do, but Agastya never returned, and the Vindhya range consequently never attained the elevation of the Himâlaya), Mn.; MBh. &c.; N. of a prince, HPariś.; a hunter, L.; (*ā*), f. Averrhoa Acida, L.; small cardamoms, L. **-kandara**, n. N. of a place, Cat. **-kūṭa**, °**ṭaka** or °**ṭana**, m. N. of the saint Agastya, L. **-ketu**, m. N. of a king of the Pulindas, Kathās. **-kailāsa-vāsinī**, f. a form of Durgā, Hariv. **-giri**, m. the Vindhya range of hills, Vās. **-culika**, m. pl. N. of a people, MBh. (v. l. *-pulika*). **-nilayā**, f. a form of Durgā, L. **-nivāsin**, m. N. of Vyāḍi, L. (cf. *-vāsin*). **-para**, m. N. of a king of the Vidyādharas, Kathās. **-parvata**, m. = *-giri*, Virac. **-pālaka**, m. pl. N. of a people, VP. **-pulika**, m. pl. id., MBh. (cf. *-culika*). **-mūlika** (VP.) or **-mauleya** (MārkP.), m. pl. id. **-vat**, m. N. of a man, MārkP. **-vana**, n. a forest in the Vindhya, R. **-varman**, m. N. of a king, Inscr. **-vāsin**, mfn. dwelling in the V°, L.; m. N. of Vyāḍi, Cat.; Vās., Introd.; of a medical writer, Cat.; (*inī*), f. (with or without *devī*) a form of Durgā, Kathās.; Daś.; N. of a place, VP.; °*nī-daśaka*, n. N. of wk. **-śakti**, m. N. of a king, VP.; Inscr. **-śaila**, m. the V° hills, MW. **-sena**, m. N. of a king, VP. (v. l. *bimbi-sāra*). **-stha**, mfn. residing in the V°, L.; m. N. of Vyāḍi, Cat. **Vindhyâcala**, m. = °*ya-giri*, Var.; *-vāsinī*, f. a form of Durgā, RTL. 575. **Vindhyâṭavī**, f. a forest in the Vindhya, VarBṛS.; Kathās. &c. **Vindhyâdri**, m. = °*ya-giri*, Ragh.; VarBṛS. &c.; *-vāsinī*, f. = *vindhya-vās*°, MW. **Vindhyâdhivāsinī**, f. a form of Durgā, Cat. **Vindhyânta-vāsin**, m. pl. the inhabitants of the inner V°, VarBṛS. **Vindhyâri**, m. N. of Agastya, Kāśīkh. **Vindhyâvali** or **-lī**, f. N. of the wife of the Asura Bali and mother of Bāṇa, Pur.; °*lī-putra* (C.) or *-suta* (W.), m. N. of the Asura Bāṇa. **Vindhyêśvarī-prasāda**, m. N. of an author, Cat.

Vindhyaka, m. pl. N. of a dynasty, VP.

Vindhyāya, Nom. Ā. °*yate*, to represent or act the part of the Vindhya mountains, Śiś.

विन्न *vinna*. See pp. 964, 965.

विन्निभट्ट *vinni-bhaṭṭa*, m. N. of an author, Cat.

विन्यय *vi-ny-aya*, m. (√5. *i*) position, situation, TPrāt.

विन्यस् *vi-ny-√2. as*, P. *-asyati* (rarely *-asati*), to put or place down in different places, spread out, distribute, arrange, Mn.; MBh. &c.; to put down, deposit, place or lay on, fix in, turn or direct towards, apply to (loc.), MBh.; Kāv. &c.; to mark or designate by (instr.), Megh.; to entrust or make over to (loc.), Vikr. °**nyasana**, n. putting down (*pada-vinyasanam* √*kṛi*, to put down the feet, step, stride), Vcar. °**nyasta**, mfn. put or placed down &c.; directed to (as the mind, eyes), R.; entrusted, delivered, Yājñ. °**nyasya**, mfn. to be put or placed upon (*upari*), VarBṛS. °**nyāsa**, m. putting or placing down &c.; a deposit, W.; putting on (ornaments), Kāvyâd.; movement, position (of limbs), attitude, TPrāt.; Kāv.; arrangement, disposition, order, Pur.; scattering, spreading out, MBh.; Hariv.; establishment, foundation, MārkP.; putting together, connecting (words &c.), composition (of literary works), Vās.; Sāh. &c.; exhibition, display (ifc. = showing, displaying), MBh.; the utterance of words of despair, Sāh.; assemblage, collection, W.; any site or receptacle on or in which anything is deposited, ib.; *-rekhā*, f. a line drawn, Bālar.

विन्याक *vinyāka*, m. the tree Echites Scholaris, L.

विप् 1. *vip* (or *vep*), cl. 1. Ā. (Dhātup. x, 6) *vepate* (ep. also °*ti*; p. *vipānā*, RV.; pf. *vivepe*, Gr.; *vivipre*, RV.; aor. *avepishṭa*, Br.; fut. *vepitā*, *vepishyate*, Gr.; inf. *vepitum*, ib.), to tremble, shake, shiver, vibrate, quiver, be stirred, RV. &c. &c.; to start back through fear, Pañcar.; Kathās.: Caus. *vipáyati* or *vepayati* (aor. *avīvipat*), to cause to tremble or move, shake, agitate, RV. &c. &c. [Cf. Lat. *vibrare*; Goth. *weipan*; Germ. *wîfen*, *weifen*, *Wipfel*; Eng. *whiffle*.]

2. **Vip**, mfn. inwardly stirred or excited, inspired, RV.; f. 'easily moved or bent, flexible (?),' a switch, rod &c., the shaft (of an arrow), the rods (which form the bottom of the Soma filter, and support the straining cloth), RV.; a finger, Naigh. ii, 5.

Vipá, m. a learned man (= *medhāvin*), Naigh. iii, 15; (*ā*), f. speech (= *vāc*), ib. i, 11.

Vipaś, in comp. for *vipas*. **-ci**, mfn. = next, TBr. **-cít**, mfn. inspired, wise, learned, versed in or acquainted with (comp.), RV. &c. &c.; m. N. of Indra under Manu Svārocisha, Pur.; of the Supreme Spirit, Sarvad.; of a Buddha (prob. w. r. for *vipaśyin*), Lalit. **-cita**, mfn. = prec., Hariv.

Vipina, n. 'stirring or waving (scil. in the wind),' a wood, forest, thicket, grove, MBh.; Kāv. &c.; a multitude, quantity, Bālar.; *-tilaka*, n. a kind of metre, Col.; °*nâukas*, m. 'wood-dweller,' an ape, monkey, Mcar.

Vipināya, Nom. Ā. °*yate*, to become or be like a forest, Gīt.

Vipo-dhā, mfn. (fr. *vipas* + 2. *dhā*) bestowing inspiration, RV. x, 46, 5.

Vipra, mf(*ā*)n. stirred or excited (inwardly), inspired, wise (said of men and gods, esp. of Agni, Indra, the Aśvins, Maruts &c.; cf. *paṇḍita*), RV.;

AV.; VS.; ŚBr.; learned (esp. in theology), TS.; ŚBr.; a sage, seer, singer, poet, learned theologian, RV.; VS.; ŚBr.; a Brāhman (*ī*, f. a Br° woman), Mn.; MBh. &c.; a priest, domestic priest, R.; the moon, L.; the month Bhādrapada, L.; Ficus Religiosa, L.; Acacia Sirissa, L.; (in prosody) a proceleusmatic, Col.; N. of a son of Ślishṭi, VP. (v.l. *ripra*); of a son of Śrutam-jaya (or Śṛitam-jaya), BhP.; of a son of Dhruva, ib.; pl. a class of demi-gods (mentioned with the Sādhyas, Yakshas and Rākshasas), ĀśvGṛ. **–kanyā**, f. a Brāhman girl, MW. **–kāshṭha**, n. Thespesia Populneoides, L. **–kuṇḍa**, m. adulterous offspring of Br° parents, L. **–cit**, m. N. of a Dānava (father of Rāhu), BhP. (cf. *-citti*). **–cita**, g. *sutaṃ-gamâdi*. **–citta**, w.r. for next. **–citti** (*vípra-*), mfn. sagacious, TBr.; m. N. of a preceptor, BṛĀrUp.; of a Dānava (father of Rāhu), Suparṇ.; MBh. &c. (cf. *-cit*); f. N. of an Apsaras, VP. **–cūḍāmaṇi**, m. 'Br°-jewel,' an excellent Br°, MW. **–jana**, m. a Br° or a priest (also collectively), MBh.; N. of a man (with the patr. Saurāki), Kāṭh. **–jūta** (*vípra-*), mfn. impelled or urged by the wise, RV. **–jūti**, m. N. of a man (with the patr. Vātaraśana, author of RV. x, 136, 3), Anukr. **–tama** (*vípra-*), mfn. most wise, wisest, RV. **–tā**, f. the rank or condition of a Br° (*-tām upa-√gam*, to become a Br°), VP. **–tāpasa**, m. a Br° ascetic, Kathās. **–tva**, n. the rank of a Br° or a scholar, Yājñ.; BhP. **–damana**, m. 'Br°-tamer,' N. of a man (in a farce), Kautukas. **–daha**, m. (possibly *vi + pra + daha*) dried fruit or roots &c., L. **–deva**, m. N. of a prince, Inscr.; of a chief of the Bhāgavatas, Cat. **–putra**, m. a Br°'s son, Kathās. **–priya**, mfn. dear to Br°s, R.; m. the Palāśa tree, L.; n. thick sour milk, L. **–bandhu**, m. 'Br°'s friend,' N. of the author of RV. v, 24, 4; x, 57–60 (having the patr. Gaupāyana and Laupāyana), Anukr. **–bhāva**, m. the rank or dignity of a Br°, Daś. **–maṭha**, m. a Br° monastery, Kathās. **–manman** (*vípra-*), mfn. having an inspired mind, RV. **–rājya**, n. the reign of the wise or pious, RV.; the kingdom or sovereignty of the Br°s or priests, Pañcar. **–rshabha** (for *ṛish°*), m. bull i.e. chief among Br°s, MBh. **–rshi** (for *ṛishi*), m. a Br° Ṛishi, priestly sage (e.g. Vasishṭha), MBh.; R.; Pur. **–lobhin**, m. 'Br°-enticing,' N. of the Kiṅkirāta tree, L. **–vacas** (*vípra-*), mfn. one whose words are inspired, RV. **–vat**, ind. like a Br°, Mn. iii, 220. **–vācana**, n. = *brāhmaṇa-v°*, Hcat. **–vāhas**, mfn. receiving the homage and offerings of the wise, RV. **–vitti**, v.l. for *-citti*. **–vīra**, m. a heroic Br°, Kathās.; (*vípra-*), mfn. having inspired men or inspiring men, RV. **–śeshita**, n. the remainder of a Br°s food, L. **–samāgama**, m. a concourse of Br°s, MW. **–sāt-√kṛi**, P. *-karoti*, to present anything (acc.) to Br°s, Ragh. **–sevā**, f. service of a Br° master, Mn. x, 123. **–sva**, n. the property of a Br°, Mṛicch. **Viprâdhipa**, m. the moon; *-mukhā*, f. a moon-faced woman, Hcat. **Viprânumadita**, mfn. rejoiced at by seer or poets, TBr.; ŚBr. **Viprâpavāda**, m. abuse of a Brāhman, W. **Viprâvamanyaka**, mfn. despising Brāhmans, VP. **Viprêndra**, m. chief of Brāhmans, MBh.

Vipraka, m. a contemptible Brāhman, Kautukas.

विपक्त्रिम *vi-paktrima*, *vi-pakva*. See p. 951, col. 1.

विपक्ष *vi-paksha*, mfn. deprived of wings, R.; m. 'being on a different side,' an opponent, adversary, enemy (mfn. 'counteracting,' Jātak.), Inscr.; Kāv.; Kathās.; a disputant, Kir.; a female rival, Ragh.; Śiś.; the day of transition from one half of a lunar month to another, KātyŚr.; (in gram.) an exception, MW.; (in logic) a counter-statement, counter-instance, argument proving the contrary (e.g. 'there cannot be fire in a lake, because there is no smoke there'), Tarkas.; Bhāshāp.; Sāh.; *-tas*, ind. from or after a rival, Kir.; hostilely, inimically, W.; *-tā*, f., *-tva*, n. hostility, enmity, opposition, R.; *-bhāva*, m. hostile disposition, state of hostility, Ragh.; *-ramaṇī*, f. a female rival, Amar.; *-śūla*, m. N. of a chief of a sect called Ārādhya, Cat.; °*kshâkrānta*, mfn. seized by an enemy, MW.; °*kshī-√kṛi*, P. *-karoti*, to deprive of wings, Kathās.; °*kshīya*, mfn. hostile, inimical, BhP.

Vipakshaya, Nom. P. °*yati*, to make enemies (p. p. *vi-pakshita*), MBh.

विपच् *vi-√pac*, P. *-pacati*, to cook thoroughly, dissolve by cooking or boiling, KātyŚr.; Suśr.; Pass. *-pacyáte*, to be cooked or baked or roasted, MBh.; to be digested, ib.; to be completely matured or ripened or developed, Ragh.; Suśr.; to bear fruit, develop consequences, VarBṛS.: Caus. *-pācayati*, to cook thoroughly, dissolve by cooking, melt, liquefy, Suśr. °**paktavya**, mfn. to be cooked or boiled, Car.

Ví-pāka, mf(*ā*)n. ripe, mature, RV.; m. cooking, dressing (= *pacana*), L.; ripening, maturing (esp. of the fruit of actions), effect, result, consequence (of actions in the present or former births pursuing those who commit them through subsequent existences), Yājñ.; MBh. &c.; maturing of food (in the stomach), digestion, conversion of food into a state for assimilation, MBh.; Hariv.; Suśr.; bad digestion, Car.; any change of form or state, Uttarar.; calamity, distress, misfortune, Yājñ.; Uttarar.; withering, fading, Śiś.; 'sweat' or 'flavour' (*sveda* or *svāda*), L.; (ibc.) subsequently, afterwards (see comp.); *-kaṭuka*, mfn. sharp or bitter in its consequences, Kathās.; *-kāla*, m. the time of ripening or maturing, Rājat.; *-tīvra*, mfn. sharp or terrible in consequence of (comp.), BhP.; *-dāruṇa*, mfn. terrible or dangerous in results, Prab.; *-dosha*, m. morbid affection of the digestive powers, Suśr.; *-visphūrjathu*, m. the consequences (of sins committed in a former birth) compared to a thunderstroke, Ragh.; *-śruta*, n. N. of a sacred book of the Jainas, W. °**pākin**, mfn. ripening, maturing, bearing fruits or having consequences, Mālatīm.; difficult to be digested (in *a-vip°*), Car.

विपञ्चय *vi-√pañcaya*, P. *-pañcayati*, to divulge, proclaim, HPariś. (cf. *pra-pañcaya*).

Vi-pañcanaka or °**cika**, m. a soothsayer, Divyâv.

विपञ्चिका *vi-pañcikā*, *vi-paṭāka* &c. See p. 951, col. 2.

विपट् *vi-√paṭ*, P. *-pāṭayati*, to split in two, tear open, tear out, destroy, MBh.; Kāv. &c.; to drive asunder, scare away, Kād.; Rājat.

Vi-pāṭa, m. a kind of arrow, MBh.; Śiś.; N. of a man, MBh. °**pāṭaka**, mfn. (prob.) opening, unfolding, bringing, MārkP. °**pāṭana**, n. the act of splitting in two, tearing open, Nir.; eradication, destruction, Rājat.; acute pain, Car. °**pāṭita**, mfn. split in two, torn asunder, uprooted, eradicated, destroyed, Hariv.; Pur. &c.; separated, divided, Shaḍguruś.

विपठ् *vi-√paṭh*, P. *-paṭhati*, to read through, peruse, BhP.

विपण् *vi-√paṇ*, P. *-paṇati*, to sell, Hariv.; Pañcat.; Ā. *-paṇate*, to bet, wager for (gen.), MBh.

2. **Vi-paṇa**, m. (for 1. see p. 951, col. 2) selling, sale, Mn.; MBh. &c.; a wager, MBh.; a trading-place, shop, market-place, MBh.; MārkP.; 'market' (fig. applied to speech, the organ of speech, or the energy of activity), MārkP.; N. of Śiva, MBh. (= *nir-vyavahāra* or *daṇḍâdi-rahita*); °*ṇâpaṇa-vat*, mfn. furnished with shops and markets, MBh. **–paṇana**, n. selling, traffic, Śiś., Sch. °**paṇi**, f. sale, traffic, Mn.; MBh.; Hariv.; a place where things are sold, shop, stall, fair, market-place, MBh.; Kāv. &c. (also *ī*, f.); any article or commodity for sale, L.; a street of shops, L.; *-gata*, mfn. being on the market, Mālav.; *-jīvikā*, f. subsistence by traffic, MBh.; *-jīvin*, mfn. subsisting by traffic, Hariv.; *-patha* m. a shop-street, Kād.; *-madhya-ga*, mfn. being in the midst of a market, Kathās.; *-stha-paṇya*, mfn. (a town) containing commodities exposed for sale, Ragh. °**paṇin**, m. a trader, shopkeeper, merchant, Śiś.

विपत् *vi-√pat*, P. *-patati*, to fly or dash or rush through, RV. i, 168, 6; to fly apart, fall off, burst asunder, be divided or separated, ŚBr.; ChUp.; to fly along, RV. x, 96, 9: Caus. *-patayati*, to fly in various directions, RV. iii, 55, 3; to fall asunder, be opened, ib. vi, 9, 6; *-pātayati*, to cause to fly away, shoot off (arrows), AV.; to cause to fly asunder or off, split or strike off (a head), ib.; to strike down, kill, MBh. °**patita** (*ví-*), mfn. flown away, fallen off &c.; *-loman*, mfn. one whose hair has fallen out, ŚBr.

Ví-patman. See under 1. *vi*, p. 949, col. 3.

Vi-pāta, g. *brāhmaṇâdi*. °**pātaka**, mfn. (fr. prec.), g. *yāvâdi*. °**pātana**, n. (fr. Caus.) melting, liquefying, Pāṇ. vii, 3, 39.

विपथ *vi-patha*, m. n. a different path, wrong road, evil course, L.; a partic. high number, Buddh.; (*á*), m. n. a kind of chariot (fit for untrodden paths), AV.; PañcavBr.; ŚrS.; *-gāmin*, mfn. going in a wrong way or evil course, MW.; *-gati*, f. the going in a wrong way, MBh.; *-yamaka*, n. a kind of Yamaka (q.v.) in which the paronomasia is only at the beginning and end of the verse (e.g. Bhaṭṭ. x, 16); *-yuga*, n. a yoke fit for bad roads, ĀpŚr.; *-vāhá*, m. drawing a chariot called Vipatha (see above), AV.; °*thâvapāta-paratā*, f. the inclination to go in wrong ways (or pursue evil courses), Rājat. **–pathaya**, Nom. P. °*yati*, to lead upon the wrong way, Lalit. **–pathi** (*ví-*), mfn. going in wrong ways, RV.; going on paths that spread in different directions, MW.

विपद् *vi-√pad*, Ā. *-padyate*, to fall or burst asunder, MBh. xi, 95; to come between, intervene, prevent, hinder, Kauś.; to go wrongly, fail, miscarry, come to nought, perish, die, ShaḍvBr.; MBh. &c.: Caus. *-pādayati*, to cause to perish, destroy, kill, Rājat.

Vi-pat, in comp. for *vi-pad*; *-kara*, mf(*ī*)n. causing misfortune, Harav.; (*ī*), f. N. of a goddess, ib.; *-kāla*, m. season of m° or calamity, Hit.; *-phala*, mfn. resulting in m°, calamitous, MW.; *-sāgara*, m. 'ocean of misfortune,' heavy calamity, W.

Vi-patti, f. going wrongly, adversity, misfortune, failure, disaster (opp. to *sam-patti*), MBh.; Kāv. &c.; unfavourableness (of time), Kām.; ruin, destruction, death, MBh.; R. &c.; cessation, end, MBh. xii, 9140; agony, torment (= *yātanā*), L.; *-kara*, mfn. causing misfortune or calamity, VarBṛS.; *-kāla*, m. a season of adversity or m°, Pañcat.; *-yukta*, mfn. attended with m°, unfortunate, W.; *-rahita*, mfn. free from misfortune, prosperous, happy, ib.

Vi-pad, f. going wrongly, misfortune, adversity, calamity, failure, ruin, death, MBh.; Kāv. &c.; *-ākrānta* and *-gata*, mfn. fallen into misfortune, L.; *-uddharaṇa*, n., *-uddhāra*, m. extrication from misfortune, W.; *-grasta*, mfn. seized by m°, unfortunate, ib.; *-daśā*, f. a state of m°, calamitous position, MW.; *-yukta*, mfn. attended with m°, unfortunate, W.; *-rahita*, mfn. free from m°, prosperous, ib. °**padā**, f. misfortune, adversity, calamity, L. °**padi**, f., g. *kumbha-pady-ādi*.

Vi-panna, mfn. gone wrong, failed, miscarried (opp. to *sam-panna*), MBh.; afflicted, distressed, Hit.; ruined, destroyed, decayed, dead, gone, MBh.; Kāv. &c.; m. a snake, L.; *-kṛitya*, mfn. (a deity) whose rites have been disturbed or neglected, VarBṛS.; *-tā*, f. misfortune, ruin, destruction, VarBṛS. (*-tām gataḥ*, ruined, R.); *-dīdhiti*, mfn. one whose splendour or glory is gone, Bhartṛ.; *-deha*, mfn. 'having a decomposed body,' dead, defunct, Mṛicch. i, 30; °*nnâpatyā*, f. a woman who has lost her child by abortion, MW.; °*nnârtha*, mfn. one whose property or fortune is ruined, R. (v.l. °*nnâtman*). °**pannaka**, mfn. unfortunate, dead, destroyed, MW.

Vi-pādana, n. the act of destroying, killing, destruction, W. °**pādanīya**, °**pāditavya**, or °**pādya**, mfn. to be killed, destructible, ib. °**pādita**, mfn. destroyed, killed, ib.

विपदुमक *vipadumaka* (?), n. a dead body gnawed by worms, Buddh.

विपन् *vi-√pan* (only 1. pl. pr. Pass. *-panyāmahe*), to pride one's self, boast, RV. i, 180, 7. °**panyā́** or °**panyáyā**, ind. joyfully, wonderfully, RV.; ŚāṅkhŚr. °**panyú**, mfn. praising, admiring, rejoicing, exulting, RV.; wonderful, admirable (said of the Aśvins and Maruts), ib.

विपरिक्रम् *vi-pari-√kram*, P. Ā. *-krāmati*, *-kramate*, to step or walk round, circumambulate, ŚBr. °**parikrānta**, mfn. one who has shown valour (in battle), courageous, powerful, R. °**parikrā́mam**, ind. having walked round, going all about, ŚBr.

विपरिगा *vi-pari-√gā*, P. *-jigāti*, to go over, be upset (as a cart), BhP.

विपरिच्छिन्न *vi-pari-cchinna*, mfn. (√*chid*) cut off on all sides, utterly destroyed; *-mūla*, mfn. having the roots cut completely round or off, entirely uprooted, MBh.

विपरिणम् *vi-pari-ṇam* (√*nam*), Pass. *-ṇamyate*, to undergo change or alteration, be changed into (instr.), Pāṇ. iii, 1, 87, Sch.: Caus. *-ṇamayati*, to alter, change into (instr.), Pat.; ĀpŚr., Sch.

°pariṇata, mfn. altered, changed, ib. °pariṇamana, n. changing, change, alteration, MW. °pariṇamayitavya, mfn. to be changed or altered, Pat. °pariṇāma, m. change, exchange, transformation, Pat.; Śaṃk. &c.; ripening, maturing, Naigh., Sch. °pariṇāmin, mfn. undergoing a change of state or form, turning into (instr.), Kull. on Mn. i, 27.

विपरिणीत vi-pari-ṇīta, mfn. (√nī) having one's place changed for that of another, ShaḍvBr.

विपरितप् vi-pari-√tap, Pass. -tapyate, to be greatly distressed, suffer great pain, R.

विपरिद्रु vi-pari-√dru, P. -dravati, to run round about, Kāṭh.

विपरिधा vi-pari-√1. dhā, Ā. -dhatte, to exchange, alter, TS.; Kaus.; (ind. p. -dhāya, with or scil. vāsas, having shifted one's clothes), Gobh.; Yājñ. °paridhāna, n. change, exchange, Kauś.

विपरिधाव् vi-pari-√dhāv, P. -dhāvati, to run about or through, overrun, MBh.; Hariv.; R.

Vi-paridhāvaka, mfn. running about or in all directions, R.

विपरिपत् vi-pari-√pat, P. -patati, to fly round or back, ŚBr.; Saṃk.

विपरिभ्रंश vi-pari-bhraṇśa, m. (√bhraṇś) failure, miscarriage, MBh.; (ifc.) being deprived of, loss, ib.

विपरिमुच् vi-pari-√muc, Pass. -mucyate, to be freed or released from (abl.), MBh.

विपरिम्लान vi-pari-mlāna, mfn. (√mlai) entirely faded or withered, R.

विपरिलुप्त vi-pari-lupta, mfn. (√lup) broken or destroyed utterly, broken up, Śaṃk. °parilopá, m. destruction, loss, ruin, ŚBr.; Śaṃk.

विपरिवृत् vi-pari-√vṛit, Ā. -vartate, to turn round, revolve, Bhag.; to roll (on the ground), Mn. vi, 22; to move about, roam, wander, MBh.; R. &c.; to turn round or back, return, MBh.; to be transformed, change, alter, ib.; to visit or afflict continually, ib.: Caus. -vartayati, to cause to turn round or revolve, turn round or away, Lāṭy.; MBh. &c.

Vi-parivartana, mf(ī)n. causing to turn round or to return; (ī), f. (with or scil. vidyā) a partic. magical formula supposed to be efficacious in causing the return of an absent person, Kathās.; n. turning round, ĀpŚr., Sch.; rolling about, wallowing, R. °parivartita, mfn. (fr. Caus.) turned away; °tâdhara, mfn. having the lips turned away, Ragh.

Vi-parivṛitti, f. turning round or back, return, Prab.

विपरिहृ vi-pari-√hṛi, P. Ā. -harati, °te, to transpose, exchange, Br.; GṛŚrS.

Vi-pariharaṇa, n. transposition, exchange, ĀpŚr., Sch. °parihāra, m. id., Sāy.

विपरी vi-parī (pari+√5. i), P. -pary-eti, to turn round or back, return, ŚBr.; to turn out badly or wrongly, fail, Mālatīm.

Vi-parīta, mfn. turned round, reversed, inverted, ĀśvŚr.; Nir. &c.; being the reverse of anything, acting in a contrary manner, opposite, contrary to (abl.), Kāv.; Kathās. &c.; going asunder or in different directions, various, different, KaṭhUp.; perverse, wrong, contrary to rule, MBh.; Kāv. &c.; adverse, inauspicious, unfavourable, ib.; false, untrue, Bhām.; (ā), f. a perverse or unchaste woman, L.; N. of two metres, RPrāt.; -kara or -kartṛi, mfn. acting in a contrary manner or perversely, MW.; -kārin, mfn. id., Gīt.; -krīḍā, f. N. of a ch. of ŚārṅgP.; -gati, mfn. going backwards or in a reverse direction, W.; f. inverse or reverse motion, ib.; -graha-prakaraṇa, n. N. of wk.; -citta (MBh.), -cetas (R.), mfn. contrary-minded, having a perverted mind or impaired mental faculties; -tā, f., -tva, n. contrariety, inversion, counterpart, Kāv.; Pañcat.; -pathyā, f. a kind of metre, Col.; -pratyaṅgirā, f. N. of a Tantric wk.; -buddhi (Pañcat.), -bodha (MW.), -mati (Yājñ.), mfn. = -citta; -malla-taila, n. a kind of preparation made of oil, Bhpr.; -rata, n. inverted sexual intercourse, Caurap.; -lakshaṇā, f. ironical description of an object by mentioning its contrary properties, MW.; -vat, ind. invertedly, R.; -vṛitti, mfn. acting or behaving in a contrary manner, Ragh.; °tâkhyānakī, f. 'inverted Ākhyānakī,' a kind of metre, Col.; °tâdi, n. (with vakra) a kind of metre, Ked.; °tânta, m. (with pragātha) a kind of metre, RPrāt.; °tâyana, n. a contrary Ayana or progress of the sun from solstice to solstice (-gata, mfn. situated in contrary Ayanas), MW.; °tôttara, n. (with pragātha) a kind of metre, RPrāt.

Vi-parītaka, mfn. reversed, inverted, Kāv.; m. (with bandha) inverted coitus, L.

Vi-paryaya, mfn. reversed, inverted, perverse, contrary to (gen.), BhP.; m. turning round, revolution, Jyot.; running off, coming to an end, R.; transposition, change, alteration, inverted order or succession, opposite of, ĀśvŚr.; Nir.; MBh. &c. (e. g. buddhi-v°, the opposite opinion; svapna-v°, the opp° of sleep, state of being awake; saṃdhi-viparyayau, peace and its opposite i. e. war; viparyaye, °yena and °yāt, ind. in the opp° case, otherwise); exchange, barter (e. g. dravya-v°, exchange of goods, buying and selling, trade), MW.; change for the worse, reverse of fortune, calamity, misfortune, Mn.; MBh. &c.; perverseness, R.; Kathās.; BhP.; overthrow, ruin, loss, destruction (esp. of the world), Kāv.; change of opinion, Sāh.; change of purpose or conduct, enmity, hostility, W.; misapprehension, error, mistake, Mn.; BhP.; Sarvad.; mistaking anything to be the reverse or opposite of what it is, MW.; shunning, avoiding, R. vii, 63, 31 (Sch.); N. of partic. forms of intermittent fever, Suśr. °paryāya, m. = vi-paryaya, reverse, contrariety, L.

विपरे vi-parê (parā-+√5. i; only Impv. -pârêtana), to go back again, return, RV. x, 85, 33.

विपर्य viparya, m. or n. (?) a partic. high number, Buddh.

विपर्यस् vi-pary-√2. as, Ā. -asyate, to turn over, turn round, overturn, reverse, invert, ŚBr.; Gaut.; to change, interchange, exchange, KātyŚr.; to have a wrong notion, be in error, Bhartṛ.: Caus. -āsayati, to cause to turn round or to change, Bālar. °páryasta, mfn. turned over, reversed, opposite, contrary, AitBr.; MBh. &c.; (in gram.) interchanged, inverted, Pāṇ. ii, 3, 56, Sch.; standing round, Kathās.; erroneously conceived to be real, W.; -tā, f. perverseness, Siṇhās.; -putrā, f. a woman bearing no male children, MW.; -manaś-ceshṭa, mfn. having mind and actions perverted or inverted, Mṛicch.

Vi-paryāsa, m. overturning, overthrow, upsetting (of a car), GṛS.; transposition, transportation, MBh.; expiration, lapse (of time), MBh.; exchange, inversion, change, interchange, ŚrS.; MBh. &c.; reverse, contrariety, opposition, opposite of (e. g. stuti-v°, the opposite of praise, i. e. blame), MBh.; Kāv. &c.; change for the worse, deterioration, MBh.; death, R.; perverseness, Rājat.; error, mistake, delusion, imagining what is unreal or false to be real or true, Kāv.; Bhāshāp.; Pañcat.; °sôpamā, f. an inverted comparison (in which the relation between the Upamāna and Upameya is inverted), Kāvyâd. °paryâsam, ind. alternately, AitBr.; ŚBr.; Śulbas.

विपर्यावृत् vi-pary-ā-√vṛit, Ā. -vartate, to be turned back, Kauś.: Caus. -vartayati, to cause to turn away from, cause to be overturned, TS.

विपर्यूह् vi-pary-√1. ūh, P. -ūhati, to place or fix separately, TS.

विपल vi-pala, n. (fr. pala) a moment, instant, ⅙ or $\frac{1}{10}$ of a breathing, Siddhântas.

विपलाय् vi-palây (fr. palā = parā + ay = √5. i; only impf. vy-apalâyata), to run away in different directions, R. °palâyana, n. running away or asunder, W. °palâyita, mfn. run away, routed, put to flight, ib. °palâyin, mfn. running away, fleeing, Yājñ.

विपलाश vi-palāśa, vi-pavana &c. See p. 951, col. 2.

विपल्यङ्ग् vi-paly-√aṅg (paly = pari; only Caus. vi-palyâṅgayanta), to envelop, surround, ŚBr.

विपल्यय् vi-paly-√ay (paly = pari + ay = √5. i), Ā. -ayate, to go back, turn round, return, ŚBr.

विपव्य vi-pavya. See vi-√pū, p. 975.

विपश् vi-√paś, P. -paśyati (rarely °te), to see in different places or in detail, discern, distinguish, RV.; AV.; AitBr.; KaṭhUp.; to observe, perceive, learn, know, R.; BhP. °paśyana, n. (or ā, f.) right knowledge, Buddh. °paśyin, m. N. of a Buddha (sometimes mentioned as the first of the 7 Tathāgatas or principal Buddhas, the other six being Śikhin, Viśva-bhū, Kraku-cchanda, Kanaka-muni, Kāśyapa, and Śākya-siṇha), Dharmas. 6 (cf. MWB. 136). °paśvin, m. N. of a Buddha, Kāraṇḍ.

विपश्चि vipaś-ci, vipaś-cit. See √vip.

विपा vi-√1. pā, P. Ā. -pibati, °te (rarely -pip°), to drink at different times, drink deep, RV.; AitBr.; to drink up from (abl.), VS.

Vi-pāna, n. drinking up, VS.; Br.

Vi-pipāna, mfn. one who drinks much or variously, RV.; AV.

Vi-pīta, mfn. drunk up, Sāy.; -vat, mfn. one who has drunk up, ib.

विपाक vi-pāka, vi-pākin. See under vi-√pac, p. 973.

विपाटल vi-pāṭala, vi-pāṇḍu &c. See p. 951, col. 2.

विपाठ vipāṭha, m. (cf. vi-pāṭa under vi-√paṭ) a kind of large arrow (described by Nīlak. as viśālo vaiśākhī-mukha-vat), MBh.; R.; (ā), f. N. of a woman, MārkP.

विपाप vi-pāpa, vi-pāpman &c. See p. 951.

विपाश् ví-pāś, f. (nom. -pâṭ) 'fetterless' (cf. next), the Vipāś or Vipāśā river (see below), RV. (ifc. °śam, ind., g. śarad-ādi); (-pāṭ)-chutudrī, f. du. the river V° and Śutudrī, RV. iii, 33, 1.

Vi-pāśa, mfn. having no noose, Hariv.; R.; unnoosed, untied, freed from fetters, AitBr.; MBh.; (ā), f. the Vipāśā or Beas river (one of the 5 rivers of the Panjāb, said to be so called as having destroyed the cord with which Vasishṭha had tried to hang himself through grief for his son slain by Viśvāmitra; it rises in the Kullu range of the Himālaya, and after a course of 290 miles joins the Sutlej at the southern boundary of Kapurthala; it is considered identical with the Ὕφασις of Arrian, the Hyphasis of Pliny, and Βίπασις of Ptolemy), MBh.; Hariv.; Var.; Pur.

Vi-pāśana, n. unbinding, unfettering, Nir. °pāśaya, Nom. (fr. vi-pāśa; only Pass. vyapāśyanta), to unbind, loose, ib.

Vi-pāśin (ví-), mfn. without fastenings, without a trace (as a chariot), RV. iv, 30, 11 (Nir.; but ví-pāśi is prob. loc. of ví-pāś).

विपिन vipina &c. See under √vip.

विपिश् vi-√piś, P. -piṇśati = vi-pushyati, Nir. vi, 11, Sch. °piśita, mfn. = vi-kasita or vinihita, placed or laid on (as an ornament), ib. viii, 11, Sch.

विपिष्टी vi-pishṭī. See vi-pṛishṭhī, p. 951.

विपुथ् vi-√puth, Caus. -pothayati, °te, to crush, dash to pieces, MBh.; Hariv.; R.; to grind down, pulverise, Car. °pothita, mfn. crushed, shattered, MBh.; Hariv.; MārkP.

विपुल vi-pula, mf(ā)n. (prob. fr. pula = pura; cf. under √pul) large, extensive, wide, great, thick, long (also of time), abundant, numerous, important, loud (as a noise), noble (as a race), PārGṛ.; MBh. &c.; m. a respectable man, W.; N. of a prince of the Sauvīras, MBh.; of a pupil of Deva-śarman (who guarded the virtue of Ruci, his preceptor's wife, when tempted by Indra during her husband's absence), MBh.; of a son of Vasu-deva, BhP.; of a mountain (either Meru or the Himâlaya), Pur.; (ā), f. the earth, L.; a form of the Āryā metre (in which the cæsura is irregular; divided into 3 species, Ādi-, Antya-, and Ubhaya-vipulā), Col.; (in music) a kind of measure, Saṃgīt.; n. a sort of building, Gal.; -grīva, mfn. long-necked, R.; -cchāya, mfn. having ample shade, shady, umbrageous, MW.; -jaghanā, f. a woman with large hips, ib.; -tara, mfn. larger or very large, Śiś.; -tā, f. (Śak.), -tva, n. (MBh.) largeness, greatness, extent, width, magnitude; -dravya, mfn. having great wealth, wealthy, Car.; -pārśva, m. N. of a mountain, Buddh.; -prajña (MBh.), -buddhi (Suśr.), mfn. endowed with great understanding; -mati, mfn. id., Bhartṛ.; m. N. of a Bodhi-sattva, Buddh.; -rasa, m. 'having abundant juice,' the sugar-cane, L.; -vrata, mfn. one who has undertaken great duties, MBh.; -śroṇi, mf(ī)n. having swelling hips, MW.; (°ṇī-bhara, mf[ā]n.id., Amar.); *-skandha*, m. 'broad-shouldered,' N. of Arjuna, L.; *-sravā*, f. = °*lâsravā*, L.; *-hṛidaya*, mfn. large-hearted, l°-minded, Bhartṛ. (v.l.); °*lâyatâksha*, mfn. having large and long eyes, MW.; °*lârtha-bhoga-vat*, mfn. having great wealth and many enjoyments, VarBṛS.; °*lâsravā*, f. Aloe Perfoliata, L.; °*lêkshaṇa*, mfn. large-eyed, MW.; *-lôraska*, mfn. broad-chested, ib.; °*lâujas*, mfn. having great strength, very strong, R.

Vi-pulaka, mfn. 'very extensive' and 'without bristling hair,' Śiś. (cf. *pulaka*).

Vipulaya, Nom. P. °*yati*, to lengthen, make longer, Subh.

Vipulī-√kṛi, P. *-karoti*, to extend, BhP.

Vipulī-bhāva, m. spaciousness, extensiveness, VP.

विपू *vi-√pū*, P. *-punāti*, to cleanse thoroughly, purify effectually, MBh.; = *vi-dārayati*, Nir. xii, 30, Sch.

Vi-pavya, mfn. to be thoroughly cleansed or purified, Pāṇ. iii, 1, 117, Sch.

Vi-pūya, mfn. cleansing, purifying, Bhaṭṭ.; m. Saccharum Munjia, Pāṇ. iii, 1, 117.

विपूजन *vi-pújana*, m. (√*pūj*) N. of a man, MaitrS.

विपूयक *vi-pūyaka*, n. (√*pūy*) suppuration or an offensive smell, Suśr.; a decomposed corpse, Buddh.

विपृच् *vi-√pṛic*, P. *-pṛiṇakti* (Impv. *-pṛiṅktam*, Pot. *-papṛicyāt*, inf. *-pṛíce*), to isolate, separate from (instr.), VS.; to scatter, dispel, RV. iv, 13, 3; to fill, satiate, ib. iv, 24, 5. °**pṛikta** (*ví-*), mfn. separated, divided, ib. i, 163, 3. °**pṛíkvat**, mfn. unmixed, pure, ib. v, 2, 3 (= *sarvato vyāpta*, Sāy.)

Vi-pṛic, mfn. isolated, separate, VS.

विपृच्छम् *vi-pṛiccham*. See *vi-√prach*.

विपृथ *vi-pṛitha, vi-pṛithu*. See p. 951.

विपोधा *vipo-dhā*. See √*vip*, p. 972.

विप्र *vipra* &c. See √*vip*, p. 972.

विप्रकीर्ण *vi-pra-kīrṇa*, mfn. (√*kṝī*) scattered or thrown about, dispersed, dashed to pieces, MBh.; R. &c.; dishevelled, loose (see comp.), extended, wide, spacious, R.; *-śiroruha*, mfn. having dishevelled or flowing hair, MBh. iii, 401; °*ṇâika-pārśva*, mfn. having one side stretched out, Megh. 87 (v.l. for *saṃ-ni-kīrṇ°*).

विप्रकृ *vi-pra-√1. kṛi*, P. *-karoti*, to treat with disrespect, hurt, injure, offend, oppress, MBh.; R. &c.; to appoint, admit (*sākshye*, as a witness), MBh. v, 1225 (prob. w.r. for *adhi-√kṛi*): Pass. of Caus. *-kāryate*, to be slighted or injured or treated disrespectfully, MW. °**prakartṛi**, mfn. injuring, an injurer, offender, ib.

Vi-prakāra, m. treating with disrespect, hurt, injury, wickedness, MBh.; Kāv. &c.; retaliation, W.; various manner, MW. (rather fr. *vi-pra-√kṛi*). °**prakārin**, mfn. treating with contempt, opposing, retaliating, W.

Vi-prakṛit, mfn. hurting, injuring, offending (with gen.), BhP. °**prakṛita**, mfn. hurt, injured, offended &c.; MBh.; Kāv. &c.; thwarted, frustrated, MBh. °**prakṛiti**, f. change, variation, Yājñ. ii, 9; injury, offence, opposition, retaliation, W.

विप्रकृष् *vi-pra-√kṛish*, P. *-karshati*, to drag or draw apart, lead away or home, MBh.; to remove from (abl.), Naish.

Vi-prakarsha, m. dragging away, carrying off, MBh.; remoteness, distance (in space or time), Gobh.; Kāv.; difference, contrast, MBh.; (in gram.) the separation of two consonants by the insertion of a vowel.

Vi-prakṛishṭa, mfn. dragged or drawn apart &c.; remote, distant, a long way off, R.: Pañcat.; Suśr. (with gen. or abl.; Pāṇ. ii, 3, 34; °*ṭâd āgataḥ*, come from afar, ib. ii, 1, 39, Sch.); remote in rank, see *a-vip°*; protracted, lengthened, MW.; *-tva*, n. remoteness, distance, MBh.; °*ṭântara*, mfn. separated by a long distance, Śak. °**prakṛishṭaka**, mfn. remote, distant, L.

विप्रकॢप्ति *vi-pra-klṛipti*, f. (√*klṛip*) separate or special arrangement or preparation, KātyŚr.

विप्रगम् *vi-pra-√gam*, *-gacchati*, to go apart or asunder, be dispersed or scattered, MBh.

विप्रगीत *vi-pra-gīta*, mfn. (√*gai*) that about which opinions differ, not agreed upon, Jaim., Sch.

विप्रचिन्त् *vi-pra-√cint* (only ind. p. *-cintya*), to meditate on, think about, MBh.

विप्रच्छन्न *vi-pra-cchanna*, mfn. (√*chad*) concealed, hidden, secret, Kathās.

विप्रछ् *vi-√prach*, P. *-pṛicchati* (rarely °*te*; Ved. inf. *-pṛiccham*), to ask various questions, make various inquiries, RV.; BhP.

Vi-pṛishṭa, m. N. of a son of Vasu-deva, BhP.

Vi-praśna, m. interrogation of fate, Pāṇ. i, 4, 39 (cf. *vaipraśnika*). °**praśnika**, m. a fortune-teller, Kath.; (*ā*), f. L.

विप्राजित्ति *viprájitti*, m. N. of a preceptor, ŚBr. (cf. *vipra-citti*).

विप्रणश् *vi-pra-ṇaś* (√*2. naś*), P. *-ṇaśyati*, *-ṇaśati*, to be lost, perish, disappear, Yājñ.; MBh.; to have no effect or result, bear no fruit, MBh.: Caus. *-ṇāśayati*, to cause to be lost or perish, SaddhP. °**praṇāśa**, see *a-v°*. °**praṇashṭa**, mfn. (not °*praṇashṭa*, cf. Pāṇ. viii, 4, 36) lost, disappeared, gone, fruitless, vain, MBh.; *-viśeshaka*, mfn. one who has lost his discriminative faculty, R.

विप्रणी *vi-pra-ṇī* (√*nī*), to turn (the mind) to (loc.), MBh.; to let elapse or pass away (time), ib.

विप्रतारक *vi-pra-tāraka*, m. (√*tṝī*) an impostor, deceiver, L. °**pratārita**, mfn. (fr. Caus.) imposed upon, deceived, Śatr.

विप्रतिकृ *vi-prati-√1. kṛi*, P. *-karoti*, to counteract, oppose, MW. °**pratikāra**, m. counteraction, opposition, reverse, retaliation, ib. °**pratikṛita**, mfn. counteracted, opposed, requited, ib.

विप्रतिपद् *vi-prati-√pad*, Ā. *-padyate*, to go in different or opposite directions, turn here and there, ŚBr.; to roam, wander (said of the senses), Kād.; to be perplexed or confounded, be uncertain how to act, waver, hesitate, MBh.; to differ or diverge in opinion, be mutually opposed, Śaṃk.; to be mistaken, have a false opinion about (loc.), Car.; to reply falsely or erroneously, Nyāyas., Sch.

Vi-pratipatti, f. divergence, difference or opposition (of opinion or interests), contrariety, contradiction, ŚrS.; Gaut.; VarBṛS. &c.; incompatibility of two conceptions, opposition of one rule to another, Sarvad.; erroneous perception or notion, error, mistake, Suśr.; Car.; suspicion about (loc.), Jātakam.; aversion, hostile feeling or treatment, ib.; false reply or objection (in argument), Nyāyas.; various acquirement, conversancy, W.; mutual connection or relation, ib.

Vi-pratipadya, mfn. to be opposed or contested, W.; to be variously acquired, ib.

Vi-pratipanna, mfn. gone in different directions &c.; perplexed, confounded, uncertain, Āpast.; of opposite opinion, dissentient, Śaṃk.; Sarvad.; wrong, false (as an opinion), Pat.; having a false opinion, being mistaken about or in (loc.), Car.; forbidden, prohibited, Āpast.; conversant or acquainted with in various ways, W.; mutually connected, ib.; *-buddhi*, mfn. having a false opinion, being mistaken or in error, Pat.

विप्रतिभा *vi-prati-√bhā*, P. *-bhāti*, to appear as, seem to be (nom.), MBh.

विप्रतिषिद्ध *vi-prati-shiddha*, mfn. (√*2. sidh*) prohibited, forbidden, KātyŚr.; contradicted, opposed (*am*, ind.), Nir.; Āpast. &c.; of opposed meaning, Pāṇ. ii, 4, 13.

Vi-pratishedha, m. restraining, keeping in check, MBh.; opposition, contradiction, contrariety, conflict (of two statements), ŚrS.; Śaṃk. &c. (esp. in gram., *pratishedhe*, where there is a conflict between two rules, Pāṇ. i, 4, 2; °*dhena*, in consequence of a conflict of two rules, iv, 1, 170, Vārtt. 1; *pūrva-vipratishedha*, a conflict of two rules of which the former prohibits the latter, iv, 2, 39, Vārtt. 1; *para-v°*, a conflict of two rules of which the latter prohibits the former, ii, 2, 35, Vārtt. 1, Pat.); prohibition, negation, annulment, Nyāyas.

विप्रतिसार *vi-prati-sāra*, n. (L. m., fr. √*sṛi*) repentance, Kāraṇḍ.; evil, wickedness, L.; anger, wrath, L.; *-vat*, mfn. = next, Jātakam. °**pratisārin**, mfn. full of repentance, Lalit.; afflicted, dejected, ib. °**pratisāra**, m. = °*pratisāra*, L.

विप्रथ् *vi-√prath*, P. Ā. *-prathati*, °*te*, (P.) to spread (trans.), RV. vi, 72, 2; (Ā.) to spread out, extend (intrans.), be wide, RV.; TS.; Hcar.: Caus. *-prathayati*, spread out or abroad, celebrate, RV.; MBh.; to unfold, display, exhibit, MBh. °**prathita**, mfn. spread out or abroad, celebrated, MBh.

विप्रदुष्ट *vi-pra-dushṭa*, mfn. (√*dush*) very corrupt or corrupted, very sensual or dissolute, very bad, Mn. ix, 72 &c.; *-bhāva*, mfn. having a very wicked or vicious disposition, ib. ii, 97.

विप्रदुह् *vi-pra-√duh*, P. *-dogdhi* (cf. *pra-vi-√duh*), to milk out, drain, exploit, RV. iv, 24, 9 (Sāy. 'to take').

विप्रद्रु *vi-pra-√dru*, P. *-dravati*, to run asunder or away, disperse, flee, PañcavBr.; MBh.; R. °**pradruta**, mfn. fled, escaped, MBh.; R.

विप्रधर्ष *vi-pra-dharsha*, m. (√*dhṛish*) harassing, annoyance (in *ati-v°*), R.

विप्रधाव् *vi-pra-√1. dhāv*, P. *-dhāvati*, to run in different directions, MBh.

विप्रनष्ट *vi-pranashṭa*. See *vi-pra-ṇaś*.

विप्रपात *vi-pra-pāta*, m. (√*pat*) a partic. method of flying, Pañcat.; a precipice, abyss, MBh.

विप्रबुद्ध *vi-pra-buddha*, mfn. (√*budh*) awakened, awake, Megh. °**prabodhita**, mfn. (fr. Caus.) mentioned, discussed, MBh.

विप्रमाथिन् *vi-pra-māthin*, mfn. (√*math*) destroying everything, destructive, Kām.

विप्रमादिन् *vi-pra-mādin*, mfn. (√*mad*) heeding nothing, thoroughly heedless, ib. (v.l.)

विप्रमुच् *vi-pra-√muc*, P. *-muñcati*, to loosen, unfasten, take off, MBh.; to liberate, set free, ib.; to discharge, hurl, shoot, R.: Pass. *-mucyate*, to be liberated or released from (abl.), get off free, MBh.; Kāv.; Pur.

Vi-pramukta, mfn. loosened &c.; discharged, shot, hurled, R.; delivered or freed from (instr. or comp.), MBh.; BhP.; v.l. for *vi-prayukta* (below); *-bhaya*, mfn. removed from danger, free from fear, Hariv. °**pramocya**, mfn. to be liberated or freed from (abl.), R.

विप्रमुह् *vi-pra-√muh*, Caus. *-mohayati*, to throw into confusion, render confused, MBh.

Vi-pramoha, m. committing a fault, transgression (in *a-vipr°*), ĀśvŚr. °**pramohita**, mfn. confused, perplexed, bewildered, MBh.

विप्रमोक्ष *vi-pra-moksha*, m. (√*moksh*) loosening, release, ChUp.; Sarvad.; deliverance from (abl. or gen.), MBh.; Hcat. °**pramokshaṇa**, n. (ifc.) deliverance from, Hariv.; Sarvad.

विप्रयाण *vi-pra-yāṇa*, n. (√*yā*) going away, flight, L. °**prayāta**, mfn. gone apart or asunder, fled in all directions, MBh.

विप्रयुज् *vi-pra-√yuj*, P. *-yunakti*, to separate from, deprive of (instr.), MBh.: Pass. *-yujyate*, to be separated from (instr.), R.: Caus. *-yojayati*, to cause to be separated from, deprive of (instr.), R.; to release from (instr.), Hariv.

Vi-prayukta, mfn. separated or removed or absent from, destitute of, free from, without (instr. or comp.), MBh.; Kāv. &c.; not being in conjunction with, VarBṛS. (v.l. °*pramukta*).

Vi-prayoga, m. disjunction, dissociation, separation from (instr. with or without *saha*, gen., or comp.), Mn.; MBh. &c.; absence, want, Sāh.; quarrel, disagreement, W.; the being fit or deserving, ib. °**prayogin**, mfn. separated (from a beloved object), Kathās. °**prayojita**, mfn. (fr. Caus.) freed from (instr.), Hariv.

विप्रलप् *vi-pra-√lap*, P. *-lapati*, to discourse or speak about variously, be at variance, disagree, Pāṇ. i, 3, 50 (also Ā.); to complain, lament, bewail, MBh. °**pralapita**, mfn. discussed, debated about, MW. °**pralapta**, n. discussion, debate, disquisition, MBh. 2. °**pralāpa**, m. (for 1. see p. 951, col. 2) discussion, explanation, MBh.; talking idly, prattle, Suśr.; mutual contradiction, Pāṇ. i, 3, 50; breaking of a promise or engagement, deception, L. °**pralāpin**, mfn. prattling, a prattler, Kāv.

विप्रलभ् *vi-pra-√labh*, Ā. *-labhate*, to insult, violate, to mock at, take in, cheat, deceive, MBh.; Kāv. &c.; to regain, recover, MBh. (B.) xiv, 1732 (C. *pra-vi-l°*, prob. w. r. for *prati-l°*): Caus. *-lambhayati*, to mock, insult, violate, BhP.

Vi-pralabdha, mfn. insulted, violated &c., MBh.; (*ā*), f. a female disappointed by her lover's breaking his appointment (one of the incidental characters in a drama), W.; (*am*), ind. deceitfully, falsely (in *a-v°*), BhP. °**pralabdhṛi**, mfn. deceiving, a deceiver, MW. °**pralabhya**, mfn. to be mocked at or imposed upon, Naish.

Vi-pralambha, m. (fr. Caus.) deception, deceit, disappointment, MBh.; Kāv. &c.; the being disappointed or deceived through (abl.), MBh. xiv, 133; separation of lovers, Ragh.; Uttarar. &c.; disunion, disjunction, W.; quarrel, disagreement, ib. °**pralambhaka**, mfn. deceiving, fallacious, a cheat or deceiver, Kathās.; Prab.; *-tva*, n. deceptiveness, fallaciousness, Saṃk. °**pralambhana**, n. pl. deception, fraud, trick, Daś. °**pralambhin**, mfn. deceiving, fallacious, Pañcat.

विप्रलम्बक *vi-pra-lambaka*, w. r. for °*lambhaka*, Prab.

विप्रलय *vi-pra-laya*, m. (√*lī*) extinction, annihilation, absorption in (loc.), R.; Uttarar. °**pralīna**, mfn. dispersed or scattered in all directions, routed (said of a defeated army), MBh.

विप्रलुप् *vi-pra-√lup*, P. *-lumpati*, to tear or snatch away, rob, plunder, Mn.; MBh.; to visit, afflict, disturb, MBh. °**pralupta**, mfn. robbed, plundered, MBh.; interrupted, disturbed, BhP.

Vi-pralumpaka, mfn. rapacious, exacting, avaricious, Mn. viii, 309.

Vi-pralopa, m. destruction, annihilation, Vajracch. °**pralopin**, mfn. plucking off, Jātakam.

विप्रलुभ् *vi-pra-√lubh*, Caus. Ā. *-lobhayate*, to allure, try to seduce or deceive, MBh. °**pralobhin**, m. a species of plant (= *kiṃkirāta*), L.

विप्रलून *vi-pra-lūna*, mfn. (√*lū*) cut off, plucked off, gathered, Sāh.

विप्रलोक *vi-pra-loka*, m. (√*lok*) a bird-catcher, Nalac.

विप्रलोडित *vi-pra-loḍita*, mfn. (fr. Caus. of √*luḍ*) disarranged, spoiled, MBh. vii, 6624.

विप्रवद् *vi-pra-√vad*, P. Ā. *-vadati*, °*te*, to speak variously, be at variance, disagree, Bhaṭṭ. (cf. Pāṇ. i, 3, 50). °**pravāda**, m. disagreement, MBh.

विप्रवस् *vi-pra-√5. vas*, P. *-vasati*, to set out on a journey, go or dwell abroad, GṛŚrS.; Mn.; MBh.: Caus. *-vāsayati*, to cause to dwell away, banish, expel from (abl.), Mn.; Yājñ.; MBh.; to take away, remove, R. °**pravasita**, mfn. withdrawn, departed (n. impers.), BhP. — 1. °**pravāsa**, m. going or dwelling abroad, staying away from (abl. or comp.), MBh.; R. &c. °**pravāsana**, n. expulsion, banishment, R.; residence abroad, W. °**pravāsita**, mfn. removed, destroyed (as sin), R.

Vi-prôshita, mfn. (*vi-pra + ushita*) dwelling abroad, set out or gone away to (acc.), absent from (abl.), MBh.; R.; Hariv.; banished (see next); *-kumāra*, m. (a kingdom) whose hereditary prince is banished, Ragh.; *-bhartṛikā*, f. (a woman) whose husband or lover is absent, W. °**prôshya**, ind. having dwelt abroad, having been absent, (returning) after a journey, Gobh.; Gaut.; Āpast.

विप्रवास 2. *vi-pra-vāsa*, m. (√*4. vas*) the offence committed by a monk in giving away his garment, Buddh.

विप्रविद्ध *vi-pra-viddha*, mfn. (√*vyadh*) dispersed, scattered, MBh.; violently struck or shaken, Ragh.

विप्रव्रज् *vi-pra-√vraj*, P. *-vrajati*, to go away in different directions, KātyŚr.; to depart from (abl.), Āpast. °**pravrājinī**, f. a woman who consorts with two men, ĀśvGṛ. (= *dvi-pr°*, Sch.)

विप्रश्न *vi-praśna*, *vi-praśnika*. See under *vi-√prach*, p. 975, col. 2.

विप्रसृ *vi-pra-√sṛi*, P. *-sarati* (Ved. inf. *-sartave*), to spread, be expanded or extended, RV.; MBh. &c.

Vi-prasāraṇa, n. (fr. Caus.) stretching out (the limbs), Suśr.

Vi-prasṛita, mfn. spread, extended, diffused, ib.

विप्रसृप् *vi-pra-√sṛip*, P. *-sarpati*, to wind about or round, meander (said of a river), Hariv.

विप्रस्था *vi-pra-√sthā*, Ā. *-tishṭhate* (m. c. also °*ti*), to spread in different directions, go apart or asunder, be diffused or dispersed, GṛS.; MBh.; to set out, depart, MBh.

Vi-prasthita, mfn. set out on a journey, departed, Hariv.

विप्रहत *vi-pra-hata*, mfn. (√*han*) struck down, beaten, defeated (as an army), MBh.; Hariv.; trodden (see *a-v°*).

विप्रहा *vi-pra-√3. hā*, P. *-jahāti*, to give up, abandon, MBh. °**prahāṇa**, n. disappearance, cessation, MBh. °**prahīṇa** (also written °*hīna*), mfn. excluded from (abl.), MBh.; disappeared, vanished, gone, ib.; deprived or destitute of, without, lacking (instr.), ib.

विप्रा *vi-√prā* (only 2. sg. pf. *-papråtha*), to fill completely, RV. vi, 17, 7.

विप्रापण *vi-prâpaṇa*, n. (√*āp*), Nir. vii, 13; ix, 26. °**prâpta**, mfn. (to explain *vi-shpitá*), ib. vi, 20 (= *vi-stīrṇa*, Sch.)

विप्राषिक *viprāshika* (?), m. a kind of culinary herb, MārkP.

विप्रिय *vi-priya* &c. See p. 951, col. 2.

विप्रु *vi-√pru* (cf. *vi-plu*), Ā. *-pravate*, to sprinkle about, scatter, MaitrS. °**pruta** (*ví-*), mfn. borne away, cast or carried away, vagrant, RV.

विप्रुष् 1. *vi-prush*, *-prushyati*, to ooze out, drip away, ŚBr.

Vi-pruḍ-ḍhoma, m. (for 2. *viprush + homa*) an expiatory offering designed to atone for the drops of Soma let fall at a sacrifice, ŚrS.

2. **Vi-prúsh**, f. (nom. °*prúṭ*) a drop (of water), spark (of fire), speck, spark, small bit, atom, AV. &c. &c.; pl. (with or scil. *mukhyāḥ*) drops falling from the mouth while speaking, Mn.; Yājñ.; MārkP.; a phenomenon (= *āścarya-v°*), Rājat.; *-mat*, mfn. having or covered with drops, BhP. °**prusha**, m. or n. a drop, Pañcat.; MārkP.; m. a bird, L.

विप्रे *vi-prê* (*pra + √5. i*), P. *-prâiti* (Impv. *-prâhi* for *-prehi*, MBh. i, 6392), to go forth in different directions, disperse, RV.; to go away, depart, MBh. °**prêta**, mfn. gone asunder or away, dispersed, ŚBr.

विप्रेक्ष् *vi-prêksh* (*pra + √īksh*), Ā. *-prêkshate*, to look here and there, regard, consider, MBh.; Kathās. °**prêkshaṇa**, n. looking round, R. °**prêkshita**, n. a look, glance, Kum. °**prêkshitṛi**, mfn. one who looks round, Rājat.

विप्रोषित *vi-prôshita*, *vi-prôshya*. See under *vi-pra-√5. vas*, col. 1.

विप्लु *vi-√plu*, Ā. *-plavate* (m. c. also P.), to float asunder, drift about, be dispersed or scattered, TS.; MBh.; to fall into disorder or confusion, go astray, be lost or ruined, perish, MBh.; Kāv. &c.: Caus. *-plāvayati*, to cause to swim or float about, Kauś.; to spread abroad, make known, divulge, Mn. xi, 198; to bring to ruin or calamity, waste, destroy, Śiś.; Bālar.; (*-plav°*), to perplex, confuse, confound, Kpr.

1. **Vi-plava**, m. (for 2. see p. 951, col. 2) confusion, trouble, disaster, evil, calamity, misery, distress, Mn.; MBh. &c.; tumult, affray, revolt, Kāv.; Rājat.; destruction, ruin, MBh.; Kāv. &c.; loss, damage, Yājñ.; violation (of a woman), Kathās.; profanation of the Veda by unseasonable study, Yājñ.; Sch.; shipwreck, Hariv.; rust (on a mirror), Kir. ii, 26; portent, evil omen, L.; terrifying an enemy by shouts and gestures, W.; spreading abroad, divulging (°*vaṃ √gam*, to become widely known), MW.; mfn. confused (as words), BhP.; *-tas*, ind. in consequence of misfortune, MW.; °*vâṭṭahāsa*, m. malicious laughter, Dharmaś. °**plavin**, mfn. fugitive, transitory, Kathās. °**plāva**, m. a horse's canter or gallop, L.; deluging, W.; devastating, ib.; causing tumult or public disturbance, ib. °**plāvaka** (Gaut.), °**plāvin** (Frâyaśc.), mfn. spreading abroad, divulging. °**plāvana**, n. abusing, reviling, Yājñ., Sch. °**plāvita** (fr. Caus.), mfn. made to float or drift about, divulged, confused, &c.; confounded, ruined, lost, BhP.

Vi-pluta, mfn. drifted apart or asunder, scattered, dispersed &c.; confused, disordered, gone astray, lost, perished, Mn.; MBh. &c.; suffused, dimmed (as the eyes), R.; agitated, excited, troubled (as speech or reason), MBh.; broken, violated (as chastity, a vow &c.), Mn.; Yājñ.; BhP.; vicious, immoral, Kathās.; committing adultery with (*saha*), Mn. viii, 377; (with *karmaṇā*) wrongly treated, mismanaged (in med.) Car.; (with *plava*) drawn out of the water, landed (?), Hariv.; depraved, wicked, W.; contrary, adverse, ib.; inundated, immersed, ib.; *am*, n. springing or bursting asunder, Hariv.; *-netra* or *-locana*, mfn. having the eyes suffused or bathed (with tears, joy &c.), R.; Hariv.; BhP.; *-bhāshin*, mf(*inī*)n. speaking confusedly, stammering, stuttering, R.; *-yoni*, f. (in med.) a partic. painful condition of the *vagina*, Suśr. °**pluti**, f. destruction, ruin, loss, Suśr.

विप्लुष् *vi-plush*, m. f. = 2. *vi-prush*, a drop of water, R.; Śiś.; pl. drops falling from the mouth while speaking, L.

विप्लुष्ट *vi-plushṭa*, mfn. (√*plush*) burned, scorched, R.

विप्सा *vipsā*, f. = *vîpsā*, repetition, succession, W.

विफल् *vi-√phal* (only pf. *-paphāla*, 3. pl. *-phelire*, v. l. *-pecire*), to burst or split asunder, MBh.; to bear or produce fruit, become fruitful, Ragh. (C.) xvii, 52.

विफल *vi-phala*, mf(*ā*)n. bearing no fruit (as a tree), Kāv.; VarBṛS.; fruitless, useless, ineffectual, futile, vain, idle, Yājñ.; Hariv. &c.; having no testicles, R.; m. Pandanus Odoratissimus, L.; *-tā*, f., *-tva*, n. fruitlessness, uselessness, unprofitableness, Kāv.; Pañcat.; *-prêraṇa*, mfn. flung in vain, Hit.; *-śrama*, mfn. exerting one's self in vain (*-tva*, n.), Rājat.; °*lârambha*, mfn. one whose efforts are vain or idle, Yājñ.; °*lâśa*, mfn. one whose hopes are disappointed, Hariv. (v. l. *nishphal°*).

Viphalaya, Nom. P. °*yati*, to render fruitless, frustrate, disappoint, prevent any one (gen.) from (inf.), Mudr.

Viphalī, in comp. for *vi-phala*. — **karaṇa**, n. making fruitless, frustrating, foiling, defeating, W.; doing anything in vain, ib. — **√kṛi**, P. Ā. *-karoti*, *-kurute*, to make fruitless or useless, frustrate, thwart, foil, Inscr.; Kāv.; to emasculate, R. — **kṛita**, mfn. rendered fruitless, frustrated, MBh.; Hariv.; R.; done in vain, W. (°*la-yatna*, mfn making fruitless efforts, MW.) — **bhavishṇu**, mfn. becoming or become useless or unprofitable (*-tā*, f., *-tva*, n.), Kāv. — **√bhū**, P. *-bhavati*, to become useless, be unprofitable, Kāv.; Pañcat. — **bhūta**, mfn. become useless, R.

विफल्फ *vi-phalpha*, mfn. (cf. *vi-gulpha*) abundant, plentiful, KātyŚr. (? w. r. for *vi-phalka*).

विबन्ध् *vi-√bandh*, P. Ā. *-badhnāti*, *-badhnīte*, to bind or fasten on different sides, stretch out, extend, RV.; AV.; ŚrS.; to seize or hold by (instr.), Kauś.; to obstruct (faeces), Car.

Vi-baddha, mfn. bound or fastened &c.; obstructed, constipated (as the bowels), Suśr. °**baddhaka**, mfn., g. *ṛiśyâdi*.

Vi-bandha, m. encircling, encompassing, MBh. vii, 5923; = *ākalana*, L.; a circular bandage, Suśr.; obstruction, constipation, ib.; a remedy for promoting obstr°, Car.; *-hṛit*, mfn. destroying or curing obstr°, Vāgbh. °**bandhana**, mfn. obstructing, constipating, Suśr.; n. the act of fastening or binding on both sides (*paraspara-v°*, mfn. mutually bound, depending on each other), MW.

विबन्धु *vi-bandhu*, *vi-bala*, *vi-bāṇa* &c. See p. 951, col. 2.

विबाध् *vi-√bādh*, Ā. *-bādhate*, to press or drive asunder in different directions, drive or scare away, RV.; AV.; Kāṭh.; to oppress, harass, annoy, molest, afflict, injure, violate, Kāv.; Pur.: Intens. *-bābadhe*, to release, set free, RV. vii, 36, 5.

Vi-bādhá, m. an expeller, remover, RV. x, 133, 4 (AV. *ví-b°*); expulsion, removal (in *°dhá-vat*, mfn. expelling, removing), TS.; Kāṭh.; (*ā*), f. pressure, pain, agony, anguish, L.

विबाली *vibālī*, f. (of doubtful derivation) N. of a river, RV. iv, 30, 12.

विबाहु *vi-bāhu*, *vi-bila* &c. See p. 951, col. 3.

विबुक *vibuka*, m. the son of a Vaiśya and a Mallī, L.

विबुध् *vi-√budh*, Ā. *-budhyate*, to awake, be awake or awakened, MBh.; Kāv. &c.; to become conscious or aware of, perceive, learn, BhP.: Caus. *-bodhayati*, to awaken, RV. &c. &c.; to restore to consciousness, Daś.

2. **Vi-buddha**, mfn. (for 1. see p. 951, col. 3) awakened, wide awake, MBh.; Kāv. &c.; expanded, blown, ib.; clever, experienced, skilful in (loc.), MBh. xiv, 1015; *-kamala*, mfn. having expanded lotuses, MBh.; *-cūta*, m. a mango-tree in blossom, Mālav.

2. **Vi-budha**, mfn. (for 1. see p. 951, col. 3) very wise or learned, Kāv.; Kathās.; Pañcat. &c.; m. a wise or learned man, teacher, Paṇḍit, ib.; a god, MBh.; Kāv. &c.; the moon, L.; N. of a prince (son of Deva-mīḍha), R.; of Kṛita, VP.; of the author of the Janma-pradīpa; *-guru*, m. 'teacher of the gods,' Bṛihas-pati or the planet Jupiter, VarBṛS.; *-taṭinī*, f. 'river of the gods,' the Gaṅgā, Prasaṅg.; *-tva*, n. wisdom, learning, Cat.; *-nadī*, f. = *-taṭinī*, Viddh.; *-pati*, m. 'king of the gods,' N. of Indra, Car.; *-priyā*, f. 'favourite of the gods,' N. of a metre, Piṅg.; *-mati*, mfn. of wise understanding, Kām.; *-rañjanī*, f. N. of wk.; *-rāja*, m. = *-pati*, R.; *-ripu*, m. an enemy of the gods, Prab.; *-rshabha* (for *-rish°*), m. chief of the gods, BhP.; *-vijaya*, m. a victory won by the gods, MW.; *-vidvish* (MBh.) or *-śatru* (Vikr.), m. 'foe of the gods,' a demon; *-sakha*, m. a friend of the gods, Bhaṭṭ.; *-sadman*, n. 'abode of the gods,' heaven or the sky, Kād.; *-strī*, f. 'divine female,' an Apsaras, Śak.; *°dhâcārya*, m. 'teacher of the gods,' N. of Bṛihas-pati, Daś.; *°dhâdhipa* (MBh.), *°dhâdhipati* (VarBṛS.), m. sovereign of the gods (*°tya*, n. sovereignty of the gods, BhP.); *°dhânucara*, m. a god's attendant, Mn. xii, 47; *°dhâvāsa*, m. 'god's abode,' a temple, Rājat.; *°dhêtara*, m. 'other than a god,' an Asura, BhP.; *°dhêndra*, m. 'best of the wise,' (with *ācārya* or *āśrama*) N. of a teacher, Cat.; *°dhêśvara*, m. lord of the gods, MBh.; *°dhôpadeśa*, m. N. of a vocabulary. **°budhāna**, m. a wise man, teacher, preceptor, MW.

2. **Vi-bodha**, m. (for 1. see p. 951, col. 3) awaking, MaitrUp.; Kāv. &c.; perception, intelligence, BhP.; (in dram.) the unfolding of the faculties in carrying out an object, Bhar.; Daśar. &c.; N. of a bird (a son of Droṇa), MārkP. **°bódhana**, m. an arouser, promoter of (gen.), RV. viii, 3, 22; n. awaking, awakening (trans. and intrans.), MBh.; MārkP. **°bodhayitavya**, mfn. (fr. Caus.) to be awakened, Bālar. **°bodhita**, mfn. (fr. id.) awakened, W.; instructed, ib.

विबुभूषा *vi-bubhūshā*. See under *vi-√bhū*.

विबृह् *vi-√1. bṛih* (or *vṛih*), P. *-bṛihati*, to tear in pieces, break or pluck off, tear away, RV.; Br.; GṛŚrS.

2. **Vi-barha**, m. (for 1. see p. 951, col. 2) scattering, dispersing (in *a-v°*), ŚāṅkhBr.

विबृह् *vi-√2. bṛih* (or *bṛiṇh*), P. *-bṛihati* (only 1. du. Pot. *-bṛiheva*), to embrace closely or passionately, RV. x, 10, 7; 8.

विब्बोक *vibboka*. See *bibboka*.

विब्रू *vi-√brū*, P. Ā. *-bravīti*, *-brūte*, to speak out, express one's self, state, depose, declare, Mn.; MBh. &c.; to explain, propound, teach, RV.; TS.; Br. &c.; to interpret, decide (a law), Mn. viii, 390; to answer (a question), Āpast.; MBh.; to make a false statement, Mn. viii, 13; 194; to be at variance, disagree, Kathās.; to dispute, contend about, RV. vi, 25, 4.

विभज् *vi-√bhaj*, P. Ā. *-bhajati*, *°te*, to divide, distribute, apportion, assign (with two acc., or with acc. of thing and dat. or loc. of pers., or with acc. of pers. and instr. of thing), RV. &c. &c. (Ā. also = 'to share together or with each other' or 'to share with [instr.];' with *samam*, to divide into equal parts; with *ardham* and gen., to divide in halves); to separate, part, cut, Mn.; MBh. &c.; to divide (arithmetically), Sūryas.; VarBṛS.; to open (a box or chest), Kathās.; to worship, MārkP.: Pass. *-bhajyate*, to receive one's share from (instr.), MBh. i, 2344: Caus. *-bhājayati*, to cause to distribute or divide or share, AV.; to divide, Kathās.; Sūryas. &c.

Ví-bhakta, mfn. divided, distributed among (instr.), AV. &c. &c. (*e*, ind. after a partition, Yājñ. ii, 126); one who has received his share, Mn. ix, 210; 215; one who has caused a partition to be made, BhP. (Sch.); parted, separated by (instr. or comp.), MBh.; Kāv. &c.; separated from, i.e. without (instr.), Yājñ. iii, 103; isolated, secluded, R.; distinct, different, various, manifold, MBh.; Kāv. &c.; divided into regular parts, harmonious, symmetrical, ib.; ornamented, decorated, Hariv.; Kathās.; divided (arithmetically), Sūryas.; m. N. of Skanda, MBh.; n. isolation, seclusion, solitude, Pāṇ. ii, 3, 42; *-gātra*, mfn. one whose limbs are embellished with (comp.), Hariv.; *-ja*, m. a son born after the partition of the family property between his parents and brothers, Gaut.; *-tva*, n. manifoldness, variety, Vām. iv, 1, 7 (quot.); *°tâtman*, mfn. divided (in his essence), Ragh. x, 66; *°tâvibhakta-nirṇaya*, m. N. of wk.

Ví-bhakti, f. separation, partition, division, distinction, modification, Br.; Mn.; MBh.; part, portion, share of inheritance &c., W.; (in gram.) inflection of nouns, declension, an affix of declension, case (accord. to Pāṇ. 'a termination or inflection either of a case or of the persons of a tense;' certain Taddhita affixes which are used like case terminations have also the name Vi-bhakti; in the Yājyā formulas esp. the cases of *agni* are so called), TS.; Br. &c.; a partic. division of a Sāman (= *bhakti*), ŚāṅkhBr., Sch.; a partic. high number, Buddh.; *-tattva*, n., *-vivaraṇa*, n.; *°ty-artha-kāraka-prakriyā*, f., *°ty-artha-nirṇaya*, m., *°ty-artha-vicāra*, m. N. of wks. **°bhaktika** (ifc.) = *°bhakti* (in *āpta-v°*, complete as to case terminations), TāṇḍBr. **°bhaktin**, see *a-vibhaktin*.

Vi-bhaktṛí (with gen., or *ví-bhaktṛi*, with acc.), mfn. one who distributes, distributer, apportioner, RV.; ŚBr.; (ifc.) an arranger, Pañcar.

Vi-bhaja, m. a partic. high number, Buddh. **°bhajana**, n. separation, distinction, L. **°bhajanīya**, mfn. to be apportioned or partitioned or distributed or divided &c., Pāṇ., Sch.; Kull. 1. **°bhajya**, mfn. to be divided, Hariv.; to be (or being) distinguished, Pāṇ. v, 3, 57. 2. **°bhajya**, ind. having distributed or separated or divided, by dividing or distinguishing &c.; *-pāṭha*, m. the distinct pronunciation (of every sound), Piṅg., Sch.; *-vāda*, m. a partic. Buddhist doctrine; *-vādin*, m. an adherent of the above doctrine, SaddhP.

Vi-bhāga, m. distribution, apportionment, RV.; AitBr.; partition of patrimony, law of inheritance (one of the 18 titles or branches of law), Mn.; Yājñ. &c. (cf. IW. 261); a share, portion, section, constituent part of anything, Yājñ.; MBh. &c.; division, separation, distinction, difference, Nir.; GṛŚrS. &c. (*ena*, separately, singly, in detail; cf. also *yoga-v°*); disjunction (opp. to *saṃ-yoga* and regarded in Nyāya as one of the 24 Guṇas), IW. 68; (in arithm.) the numerator of a fraction, Col.; N. of Śiva, R.; *-kalpanā*, f. apportioning or allotment of shares or portions, W.; *-jña*, mfn. (ifc.) knowing the difference between, ŚāṅkhGṛ.; MBh.; *-tas*, ind. according to a part or share, proportionately, Sarvad.; W.; *-tattva-vicāra*, m. N. of wk.; *-tva*, n. state of separation or distinction, Sarvad.; *-dharma*, m. the law of division, rule of inheritance, Mn. i, 115; *-pattrikā*, f. a deed of partition, MW.; *-bhāj*, mfn. one who shares in a portion of property already distributed (applied esp. to a son by a father and mother of the same tribe, born subsequently to a distribution of property amongst his parents and brethren, in which case he inherits the portion allotted or reserved to the parents), Yājñ.; Pañcat.; *-bhinna*, n. = *takra*, buttermilk mixed with water, L.; *-rekhā*, f. partition-line, boundary between (gen.), Bālar.; *-vat*, mfn. divided, separated, distinguished (*-tā*, f.), Sarvad.; *-śas*, ind. according to a part or share, separately, proportionately, Mn.; MBh. &c.; (ifc.) according to, BhP.; *-sāra*, m. N. of wk.; *°gêcchu*, mfn. wishing for a partition or distribution, MW. **°bhāgaka**, m. a distributer, arranger, Pañcar. (perhaps w.r. for *°bhājaka*). **°bhāgin**, see *a-vibhāgin*. **°bhāgī-√kṛi**, P. *-karoti*, to divide, parcel out, Pañcad. **°bhāgya**, mfn. to be separated or divided, Lāṭy.

Vi-bhāj, mfn. separating, dividing, Āpast. **°bhājaka**, mfn. id., Nīlak.; distributing, apportioning, Hariv.; (*°kī-bhūta*, mfn. being a distributer or divider, Cat.) **°bhājana**, n. division, distinction, L.; the act of causing to share or distribute, participation, MW. **°bhājayitṛi**, mfn. one who causes to divide or distribute, Pāṇ. iv, 4, 49, Vārtt. 3. **°bhājita**, mfn. caused to be divided, distributed, apportioned, partitioned, VarBṛS.; Kathās. **°bhājya**, mfn. to be divided or apportioned, divisible, Mn. ix, 219.

विभञ्ज् *vi-√bhañj*, P. *-bhanakti*, to break asunder, break to pieces, R.; VarBṛS. &c.; to frustrate, disappoint, VP.

Vi-bhagna, mfn. broken asunder, shattered, crushed, PañcavBr.; SaṃhitUp. &c.

Vi-bhaṅga, m. bending, contraction (esp. of the eyebrows), Ragh.; Vās.; a furrow, wrinkle, MBh.; Vās.; Gīt.; interruption, stoppage, frustration, disturbance, Kāv.; Pur.; fraud, deception, Vās.; a wave, Vās.; breaking, fracture, W.; division, ib.; N. of a class of Buddhist wks., MWB. 64, n. 1. **°bhaṅgi**, f. the mere semblance of anything (= *bhaṅgi*), Dharmaś. **°bhaṅgin**, mfn. wavy, undulating, wrinkled, MW. **°bhaṅgura**, mfn. unsteady (as a look), Śiś.

विभण्डक *vibhaṇḍaka*, w.r. for *vi-bhāṇḍaka* (see p. 951, col. 3).

विभरट्ट *vibharaṭṭa*, m. N. of a king, Buddh. (v.l. *vi-bharata*).

विभव *vi-bhava* &c. See under *vi-√bhū*.

विभा 1. *vi-√bhā*, P. *-bhāti*, to shine or gleam forth, come to light, become visible, appear, RV. &c. &c.; to shine upon, illumine, RV.; AV.; MBh.; to procure light, i.e. to kindle (fire, dat.), RV. i, 71, 6; to shine brightly, glitter, be resplendent or beautiful, strike or catch the eye, excel by (instr.), RV. &c. &c.; to strike the ear, be heard (as sound), MBh.; to seem or appear as, look like (nom. with or without *iva*, or adv. in *-vat*), RV. &c. &c.

2. **Vi-bhā́**, mfn. shining, bright, RV.; ŚāṅkhŚr.; f. light, lustre, splendour, beauty, Śiś.; Sāh.; N. of the city of Soma, VP.; *-kara*, m. 'light-maker,' the sun, Sāh.; fire, L.; that portion of the moon which is illumined by the sun, Gaṇit.; a king, prince (and 'the sun'), Sāh.; (*°ra-śarman*, m. N. of a poet, Cat.); *-vasu* (*vibhā́-*), mfn. abounding in light (applied to Agni, Soma, and Kṛishṇa), RV.; VS.; Hariv.; m. fire or the god of fire, MBh.; Kāv. &c.; the sun, APariś.; MBh.; BhP.; the moon, L.; a sort of necklace or garland, L.; N. of one of the 8 Vasus, BhP.; of a son of Naraka, ib.; of a Dānava, ib.; of a Ṛishi, MBh.; of a mythical prince dwelling on the mountain Gaja-pura, Kathās.; of a Gandharva (who is said to have stolen the Soma from Gāyatrī as she was carrying it to the gods), MW. **°bhā́t**, mfn. shining, splendid (applied to Ushas), RV.; m. the world of Prajā-pati, AitBr.; TS. **°bhāta**, mfn. shone forth, grown light &c. (*°tā vibhāvarī*, the morning has dawned, Kathās.); become visible, appeared, ChUp.; BhP.; n. dawn, day-break, morning, Kālid. **°bhānu**, mfn. shining, beaming, radiant, RV. 1. **°bhāva** (for 2. see p. 978, col. 3) and **°bhā́van**, mf(*arī*, see next)n. (voc. *ví-bhāvas*), id., ib. **°bhāvarī**, f. (see prec.) brilliant, bright (in RV. often applied to Ushas, 'Dawn;' accord. to Nīlak. on MBh. v, 4495 also = *kupitā*); the (starry) night, MBh.; Kāv. &c.; turmeric, L.; = *haridrā* and *°drā-dāru*, Bhpr.; a kind of ginger, L.; a procuress, L.; a deceitful woman, L.; a loquacious woman, L.; (?) the shreds of a garment torn in a scuffle (= *vivāda-vastra-gunṭhī* or *°tra-muṇḍī*), L.; a kind of metre, Ked.; N. of a daughter of the Vidyādhara Mandāra, MārkP.; of the city of Soma, BhP.; of the city of the Pracetas, ib.; *-kānta*, m. 'husband of night,' the moon, Kpr.; *-mukha*, n. 'beginning of night,' evening, MBh.; *-°śa* (*°rīśa*), m. 'lord of night,' the moon, VarBṛS.

विभाव 1. and 2. *vi-bhāva*. See above and p. 978, col. 3.

विभाष् *vi-√bhāsh*, Ā. *-bhāshate*, to speak

variously, speak against, abuse, revile, MBh.; (in gram.) to admit an alternative, be optional, Kāt.

2. **Vi-bhāshā**, f. (for 1. see p. 951, col. 3) an alternative, option, optionality (*vi-bhāshayā*, optionally), one of two ways (cf. *vi-kalpa*), APrāt.; (in gram.) the allowing a rule to be optional (of two kinds, viz. *prâpta-v°* or *prâpte v°*, an option allowed in a partic. operation which another rule makes necessary; *aprâpta-v°* or *aprâpte v°*, an option allowed in a partic. operation which another rule makes impossible), Pāṇ. i, 1, 44 &c.; *-vṛitti*, f. N. of wk. °**bhāshita**, mfn. admitting an alternative (esp. in gram. = optional), Nir.; Kauś.; Pāṇ.

विभास् *vi-√bhās*, Ā. *-bhāsate* (in Ved. also P.), to shine brightly or pleasantly, be bright, AV.; R.; Śatr.: Caus. *-bhāsayati*, to cause to shine, illuminate, brighten, MBh. °**bhās**, f. brightness, splendour, Kir. ix, 9; *-vat*, mfn. very brilliant or resplendent, Cat. °**bhāsá**, m. N. of one of the 7 suns, TĀr.; a partic. Rāga, Vās.; Gīt.; N. of a deity, MārkP.; (*ā*), f. shining brightly, light, lustre, W. °**bhāsita**, mfn. (fr. Caus.) made bright, illuminated, MBh.

विभिद् *vi-√bhid*, P. Ā. *-bhinatti*, *-bhintte*, to split or break in two, break in pieces, cleave asunder, divide, separate, open, RV. &c. &c.; to pierce, sting, ŚBr.; MārkP.; to loosen, untie, Hariv.; BhP.; to break, infringe, violate, R.; Bālar.; BhP.; to scatter, disperse, dispel, destroy, MBh.; Kāv. &c.; to alter, change (the mind), MBh.; BhP.: Pass. to be split or broken, burst asunder &c. (also P. Cond. *vyabhetsyat*, ChUp.); to be changed or altered, R.; BhP.: Caus. *-bhedayati*, to cause to split &c.; to divide, alienate, estrange, MBh.; R.

Vi-bibhitsu, mfn. (fr. Desid.) wishing to break asunder, purposing to cleave or pierce, MW.

Vi-bhitti, f. cleaving, splitting, Kāṭh.; ShaḍvBr.

Ví-bhida, m. N. of a demon, Suparṇ.; (*ā*), f. 'perforation' and 'falling away,' 'apostasy,' Śiś. xx, 23.

Vi-bhindú, mfn. splitting or cleaving asunder, RV.; m. N. of a man, ib. °**bhinduka**, m. N. of an Asura, PañcavBr.

Vi-bhinna, mfn. split or broken in two &c.; passed across or through (as by a heavenly body), VarBṛS.; opened blown, Ragh.; cleft (said of the temples of an elephant which exude during rut), Bhartṛ.; broken, destroyed, BhP.; altered, changed (also in one's feelings), Kāv.; Kathās.; alienated, estranged, become faithless, Rājat.; separated, divided, Kathās.; disunited, living at variance, R.; (a place) filled with dissensions, Kathās.; disappointed (see *āśā-v°*); contradictory, Subh.; various, manifold, Kathās.; MārkP.; mingled with (instr.), Kir.; m. N. of Śiva, MBh.; *-tamisra*, mfn. having darkness expelled or destroyed, MW.; *-tā*, f., *-tva*, n. the state of being broken or split asunder or scattered &c., ib.; *-darśin*, mfn. seeing different things, discerning differences, discerning well, MārkP.; *-dhairya*, mfn. having firmness or constancy shaken, BhP.; *-vesha*, mfn. dressed in various garments, Pañcar.; °*nnâṅga*, mfn. one who has his body pierced or transfixed, R.

Vibhinni-√kṛi, P. *-karoti*, to separate, divide, HYog.

Vi-bhettṛi, mfn. one who splits or breaks asunder, a destroyer of (gen.), Śak.

Vi-bheda, m. breaking asunder, splitting, piercing, division, separation, MBh.; R. &c.; knitting, contraction (of the brows), Sāh.; interruption, disturbance, Bālar.; change, alteration, Car.; diverging (in opinion), dissension, disagreeing with (*samam*), MBh.; Kāv. &c.; distinction, variety, VarBṛS.; Kathās.; BhP.

Vi-bhedaka, mfn. distinguishing anything (gen.) from (abl.), Cat.; m. = *vibhīdaka*, L. °**bhedana**, mfn. splitting, cleaving, piercing, VarBṛS.; n. the act of splitting &c., Nir.; MBh.; setting at variance, disuniting, MBh.; R. &c. °**bhedika**, mfn. separating, dividing (ifc.), Kāraṇḍ. °**bhedin**, mfn. piercing, rending (see *marma-bh°*); dispelling, destroying (with gen.), Hariv. °**bhedya**, mfn. to be split or cleft or broken, MBh.

विभी *vi-√bhī*, P. *-bibheti*, to be afraid of, fear, MBh.; MārkP.: Caus. *-bhīshayati*, °*te*, to frighten, terrify, intimidate, RV.; TS.; MBh.

1. **Vi-bhīta**, mfn. (for 2. see col. 2) afraid, intimidated, MārkP.

Vi-bhīshaka, mf(*ikā*)n. frightening, terrifying, MW.; (*ikā*), f. the act of terrifying, means of terrifying, terror, MBh.; Kāv. &c.; °*shikā-sthāna*, n. an object or means of terrifying, MW.

Vi-bhíshaṇa, mf(*ā*)n. terrifying, fearful, horrible, RV. &c. &c.; bullying or blustering (as language), MW.; m. miscarriage, abortion, MBh.; Amphidonax Karka, L.; N. of a brother of Rāvaṇa (his other brothers were Kubera [by a different mother] and Kumbha-karṇa; both Rāvaṇa and Vibhīshaṇa are said to have propitiated Brahmā by their penances, so that the god granted them both boons, and the boon chosen by V° was that he should never, even in the greatest calamity, stoop to any mean action; hence he is represented in the Rāmāyaṇa as endeavouring to counteract the malice of his brother Rāvaṇa, in consequence of which he was so ill-treated by him that, leaving Laṅkā, he joined Rāma, by whom, after the death of Rāvaṇa, V° was placed on the throne of Laṅkā), MBh.; Hariv.; R. &c.; N. of two kings of Kaśmīra (the sons of Go-narda and Rāvaṇa), Rājat. i, 192 &c. (in later times V° appears to have been used as a general N. of the kings of Laṅkā); N. of an author, Cat.; (*ā*), f. N. of one of the Mātṛis attending on Skanda, MBh.; n. the act or a means of terrifying, terror, intimidation, MBh.; N. of the 11th Muhūrta, Cat.; °*ṇâbhisheka*, m. 'V°'s inauguration,' N. of R. v, 91 (accord. to one recension).

Vi-bhīshā, f. the wish or intention of terrifying, MBh. °**bhīshikā**, f., see under *vi-bhīshaka* above.

Vi-bhetavya, n. (impers.) it is to be feared, Pañcat.; Hit. (v.l.)

विभीत 2. *vibhīta*, m. n. = next, ŚārṅgS.

Vibhítaka, m. (or *ī*, f.) the tree Terminalia Bellerica; n. its berry (used as a die), ŚBr.; MBh. &c.

Vibhídaka, m. n. id., RV.; GṛŚrS. (cf. *vi-bhedaka* under *vi-√bhid*).

विभु *vi-bhu* &c. See col. 3.

विभुक्त *vi-bhukta* (√3. *bhuj*), in *bhukta-v°*, g. *śāka-pārthivâdi* (Siddh. on Pāṇ. ii, 1, 69).

विभुग्न *vi-bhugna*, mfn. (√1. *bhuj*) bent, bowed, crooked, L.

Vi-bhuja, mfn., in *mūla-v°* (q. v.)

विभू *vi-√bhū*, P. *-bhavati*, to arise, be developed or manifested, expand, appear, RV.; TS.; MuṇḍUp.; to suffice, be adequate or equal to or a match for (dat. or acc.), ŚBr.; to pervade, fill, PañcavBr.; to be able to or capable of (inf.), BhP.; to exist (in *a-vibhavat*, 'not existing'), KātyŚr.: Caus. *-bhāvayati*, to cause to arise or appear, develop, manifest, reveal, show forth, display, ŚāṅkhBr.; MBh. &c.; to pretend, feign, Kull. on Mn. viii, 362; to divide, separate, BhP.; to perceive distinctly, find out, discover, ascertain, know, acknowledge, recognise as (acc.), MBh.; Kāv. &c.; to regard or consider as, take for (two acc.), Kuval.; to suppose, fancy, imagine, BhP.; Pañcar.; to think, reflect, Kathās.; Pañcat.; to suppose anything of or about (loc.), BhP.; to make clear, establish, prove, decide, Mn.; Yājñ.; to convict, convince, Yājñ.; Daś.: Pass. of Caus. *-bhāvyate*, to be considered or regarded as, appear, seem (nom.), MBh.; Kāv. &c.: Desid., see *-bubhūshā*: Intens., see *-bobhuvat*.

Vi-bubhūshā, f. (fr. Desid.) the wish or intention to manifest one's self, BhP. °**bubhūshu**, mfn. wishing to develop or expand one's self, ib.

Vi-bobhuvat, mfn. (fr. Intens.) spreading or expanding exceedingly over (loc.), MaitrS.

Vi-bhava, mfn. powerful, rich, MBh. xiii, 802; m. being everywhere, omnipresence, Kaṇ.; development, evolution (with Vaishṇavas 'the evolution of the Supreme Being into secondary forms'), Sarvad.; power, might, greatness, exalted position, rank, dignity, majesty, dominion, R.; Kālid.; VarBṛS. &c. (ifc. with loc., 'one whose power consists in,' Gīt.); influence upon (loc.), ŚāṅkhŚr.; (also pl.) wealth, money, property, fortune, MBh.; Kāv. &c.; luxury, anything sumptuary or superfluous, Hcar.; magnanimity, lofty-mindedness, W.; emancipation from existence, Inscr.; BhP.; N. of the 2nd year in Jupiter's cycle of 60 years, VarBṛS.; destruction (of the world), Buddh.; (in music) a kind of measure; *-kshaya*, m. loss of fortune or property, Cāṇ.; *-tas*, ind. according to rank or fortune or dignity, Kālid.; Prab.; *-mati*, f. N. of a princess, Rājat.; *-mada*, m. the pride of power, MW.; *-vat*, mfn. possessed of power, wealthy, Mṛicch. °**bhavin**, mfn. rich, wealthy, Śiś.

2. **Vi-bhāva**, m. (for 1. see under *vi-√bhā*) any condition which excites or develops a partic. state of mind or body, any cause of emotion (e.g. the persons and circumstances represented in a drama, as opp. to the *anu-bhāva* or external signs or effects of emotion), Bhar.; Daśar.; Sāh. (*-tva*, n.); a friend, acquaintance, L.; N. of Śiva, Pañcar. °**bhāvaka**, mfn. causing to appear, procuring or intending to procure (ifc.), MBh. iii, 1347 (Nīlak.); discussing, W. °**bhāvana**, mfn. causing to appear, developing, manifesting, Hariv.; (*ā*), f. (in rhet.) description of effects the causes of which are left to be conjectured (or, accord. to some, 'description by negatives, bringing out the qualities of any object more clearly than by positive description'), Vām.; Kāvyâd. &c.; n. causing to appear or become visible, development, creation, BhP. (Sch. = *pālana*); showing, manifesting, Kull. on Mn. ix, 76; clear perception, examination, judgment, clear ascertainment, Mn.; Vikr.; (ifc.) reflection on, Kathās.; the act of producing a partic. emotion by a work of art, Sāh.; °*nâlaṃkāra*, m. the rhetorical figure described above, MW. °**bhāvanīya**, mfn. (fr. Caus.) to be clearly perceived or ascertained, MārkP.; to be convicted (= *bhāvya*), Kull. on Mn. viii, 60. °**bhāvita**, mfn. (fr. Caus.) caused to arise or appear &c.; *-tva*, n. the state of being perceived or judged, W. °**bhāvin**, mfn. mighty, powerful, Śiś.; (ifc.) causing to appear (*varṇa-v°*, m. N. of Śiva), MBh. xiii, 1219; arousing a partic. emotion (esp. of love), Nalod. °**bhāvya**, mfn. to be clearly perceived or observed, distinguishable, comprehensible, MBh.; Kāv. &c.; to be attended to or heeded (n. impers. 'it should be heeded'), MBh.; Kāvyâd.

Vi-bhú or (Ved.) **vi-bhū́**, mf(*ū́* or *vī́*)n. being everywhere, far-extending, all-pervading, omnipresent, eternal, RV.; VS.; Up.; MBh. &c.; abundant, plentiful, RV.; VS.; Br.; mighty, powerful, excellent, great, strong, effective, able to or capable of (inf.), RV. &c. &c.; firm, solid, hard, L.; m. a lord, ruler, sovereign, king (also applied to Brahmā, Vishṇu, and Śiva), MBh.; Kāv. &c.; (ifc.) chief of or among, VarBṛS.; a servant, L.; the sun, L.; the moon, L.; N. of Kubera, L. (W. also 'ether; space; time; the soul'); N. of a god (son of Veda-śiras and Tushitā), BhP.; of a class of gods under Manu Sāvarṇi, MārkP.; of Indra under Manu Raivata and under the 7th Manu, ib.; BhP.; of a son of Vishṇu and Dakshiṇā, BhP.; of a son of Bhaga and Siddhi, ib.; of Buddha, L.; of a brother of Śakuni, MBh.; of a son of Śambara, Hariv.; of a son of Satya-ketu and father of Su-vibhu, VP.; of a son of Dharma-ketu and father of Su-kumāra, ib.; of a son of Varsha-ketu or Satya-ketu and father of Ānarta, Hariv.; of a son of Prastāva and Niyutsā, BhP.; of a son of Bhṛigu, MW.; pl. N. of the Ṛibhus, RV.; *-krátu*, mfn. strong, heroic, RV.; *-tā*, f. power, supremacy, W.; *-tva*, n. being everywhere, omnipresence, ŚvetUp.; Sarvad.; omnipotence, sovereignty, PraśnUp.; Śak.; Bālar.; *-tva-samarthana*, n. N. of wk.; *-pramita*, n. the hall of Brahmā, KaushUp.; *-mát*, mfn. extending everywhere, RV.; joined with the Vibhus or Ṛibhus, VS.; AitBr.; ŚrS.; *-varman*, m. N. of a man, Inscr. °**bhuvarī**, f. (prob. f. of *vi-bhvan*) far-reaching, Kāṭh.

Vi-bhū, in comp. for **vi-bhu**; *-dávan*, mfn. bestowing richly, liberal, TS.; *-mát*, mfn. joined with the Vibhus or Ṛibhus, MaitrS.; *-vasu* (*vibhū́-*), mfn. possessing mighty treasures or wealth, RV.

Vi-bhūta, mfn. arisen, produced &c.; great, mighty (see comp.); m. = next, Buddh.; *-m-gamā*, f. a partic. high number, Buddh.; *-dyumna* (*vi°*), mfn. abounding in splendour or glory, RV.; *-manas*, mfn. (used to explain *vi-manas*), Nir. x, 26; *-rāti* (*vi°*), mfn. bestowing rich gifts.

Ví-bhūti, mfn. penetrating, pervading, Nir.; abundant, plentiful, RV.; mighty, powerful, ib.; presiding over (gen.), ib. viii, 50, 6; m. N. of a Sādhya, Hariv.; of a son of Viśvāmitra, MBh.; of a king, VP.; f. development, multiplication, expansion, plenty, abundance, Kāv.; Kathās. &c.; manifestation of might, great power, superhuman power (consisting of eight faculties, especially attributed to Śiva, but supposed also to be attainable by human beings through worship of that deity, viz. *aṇiman*, the power of becoming as minute as an atom; *laghiman*, extreme lightness; *prâpti*, attaining or reaching anything [e.g. the moon with the tip of the finger]; *prākāmya*, irresistible will; *mahiman*, illimitable bulk; *īśitā*, supreme dominion; *vaśitā*, subjugating by magic; and *kāmâvasāyitā*, the suppressing all desires), ib.; a partic. Śakti, Hcat.; the might of a king or great lord, sovereign power, greatness, Kālid.; Pañcat.; Kathās. &c.; successful issue (of a sacrifice), MBh.; R.; splendour, glory, magnificence, Hariv.; Ragh.; VarBṛS.; fortune, welfare, prosperity, PraśnUp.; MBh. &c.; (also pl.) riches, wealth, opulence, Kām.; Kāv.; Kathās.; N. of Lakshmī (the goddess of fortune and welfare), BhP.; the ashes of cow-dung &c. (with which Śiva is said to smear his body, and hence used in imitation of him by devotees), Pañcar.; Sāh.; (in music) a partic. Śruti, Saṃgīt.; *-grahaṇa*, n. taking up ashes (at the Vaiśvadeva ceremony), RTL. 420; *-candra*, m. N. of an author, Cat.; *-dvādaśī*, f. a Vrata or religious observance on a partic. twelfth day (in honour of Vishṇu), ib.; *-dhāraṇa-vidhi*, m. N. of wk.; *-bala*, m. N. of a poet, Cat.; *-mat*, mfn. mighty, powerful, superhuman, Bhag.; BhP.; smeared with ashes, W.; *-mādhava*, m. N. of a poet, Cat.; *-māhātmya*, n. N. of a ch. of the PadmaP.; *-yoga*, m. N. of the 6th canto of the Śiva-gītā.

Vi-bhūman, m. extension, greatness, might, TS.; N. of Kṛishṇa, BhP. (prob. = 'appearing in manifold form' or 'omnipotent').

Vi-bhūr-asi, m. (lit. 'thou art mighty') a form of Agni or the god of fire, MBh.

Vi-bhūvas, mfn. (prob.) powerful, MaitrS.; m. N. of a man, Sāy.

Vibhva, in comp. for *vi-bhvan* below. **-tashṭá,** mfn. cut out or furnished by a skilful artificer, very perfect or handsome, RV.

Ví-bhvan, mfn. far-reaching, penetrating, pervading, RV.; m. N. of one of the Ṛibhus, ib.; (*án*), mfn. skilful, ib.; m. an artificer, ib.

Vibhvā-sáh, mfn. (*vibhvā* for *vi-bhvan*) conquering or overcoming the rich, RV.

विभूष् *vi-√bhūsh*, P. *-bhūshati*, to be brilliant, appear (?), RV. i, 112, 4 (Sāy. *vyāpto bhavati*); to adorn, decorate, ib. vi, 15, 9: Caus. *-bhūshayati*, to adorn, decorate, MBh.; Kāv. &c.

Vi-bhūshaṇa, mfn. adorning, R.; m. N. of Mañju-śrī, L.; n. (ifc. f. *ā*) decoration, ornament, MBh.; Kāv. &c.; splendour, beauty, Daśar.; *-kalā*, f. a partic. Samādhi, Kāraṇḍ.; *-vat*, mfn. adorned, decorated, Mṛicch.; °*nôdbhāsin*, mfn. glittering with ornaments, Kum. °**bhūshā,** f. ornament, decoration, VarBṛS.; Kām.; light, splendour, beauty, L. °**bhūshita,** mfn. adorned, decorated, MBh.; Kāv. &c.; n. an ornament, decoration, R.; °*tâṅga*, mfn. decorated about the body, MW.; °*tâlaṃkārā*, f. N. of a Gandharvī and of a Kiṃ-narī, Kāraṇḍ. °**bhūshin,** mfn. adorned, decorated (ifc.), MBh.; adorning, MW. °**bhūshṇu,** mfn. (prob.) 'omnipresent' or 'omnipotent' (said of Śiva; cf. *vi-bhū*), Śivag.

विभृ *vi-√bhṛi*, P. Ā. *-bharati*, °*te*, to spread out, spread asunder, RV.; AV.; (Ā.) to distribute, diffuse, ib.; VS.; to bear, endure, MBh.: Intens. (only *-bháribhrat* and *-jarbhṛitás*), to move hither and thither or from side to side (as the tongue), RV. ii, 4, 4; to open the mouth, gape, ib. i, 28, 7.

Ví-bhṛita, mfn. spread out, distributed, RV. x, 45, 2 &c.; upheld, supported, maintained, W. °**bhṛitra** (*ví-*), mf(*ā*)n. to be (or being) borne about or in various directions, RV. °**bhṛitvan,** mfn. bearing hither and thither, ib.

विभोक *vibhoka*, m. N. of a poet, Cat.

विभ्रंश् *vi-√bhraṇś* (sometimes written *bhraṇs*), Ā. *-bhraṇśate*, to fall off (fig.), be unfortunate, fail or be unsuccessful in (loc.), PañcavBr.; to be separated from, desert (abl.), KātyŚr.: Caus. *-bhraṇśayati*, to cause to fall, MBh.; to strike or break off, R.; to cause to disappear or vanish, destroy, annihilate, BhP.; to divert from, deprive of (abl.), MBh.; BhP. °**bhraṇśa,** m. diarrhœa, laxity of the bowels (see *manda-v*°); decline, cessation, end, MBh.; Kathās.; Pur.; disturbance, perturbation (see *citta-v*°); fall, decay, ruin, MBh.; VarBṛS.; BhP.; (ifc.) being deprived of, loss, Pur.; Rājat.; a precipice, MW.; *-yajña*, m. a partic. Ekâha, Vait. °**bhraṇśita,** mfn. (fr. Caus.) caused to fall &c.; *-jñāna*, mfn. deprived of reason or consciousness, BhP.; *-pushpa-pattra*, mfn. having the flowers and leaves knocked off, R. °**bhraṇśin,** mfn. crumbling to pieces (see *a-v*°); falling down, dropping from (ifc.), Megh.

Vi-bhrashṭa, mfn. fallen, sunk, MBh.; disappeared, vanished, gone, lost, R.; MārkP.; useless, vain, PañcavBr.; (ifc.) strayed from, Kathās.; deprived of, MBh.; R.; unsuccessful in, TS.; *-timira*, mfn. freed from darkness (as the sky), R.; *-harsha*, mf(*ā*)n. deprived of joy, ib.; °*ṭêshṭi-prayoga*, m. N. of wk.

विभ्रम् *vi-√bhram*, P. *-bhramati*, *-bhrāmyati*, to wander or roam or fly about, roll, hover, whirl, MBh.; Kāv. &c.; to reel, quiver, shake, BhP.; to roam over, wander through (acc.), MBh.; to fall into disorder or confusion, be disarranged or bewildered, MBh.; Hariv. &c.; to drive asunder, disperse, scare away, MBh.; to move about (the tail), R.: Caus. *-bhramayati* or *-bhrāmayati* (Pass. *-bhrāmyate*), to confuse, perplex, MārkP.; Hcat.

Vi-bhrama, m. (ifc. f. *ā*) moving to and fro, rolling or whirling about, restlessness, unsteadiness, Kāv.; VarBṛS.; Rājat.; violence, excess, intensity, high degree (also pl.), Kāv.; Kathās. &c.; hurry, rapture, agitation, disturbance, perturbation, confusion, flurry, MBh.; Kāv. &c.; doubt, error, mistake, blunder (with *daṇḍasya*, 'erroneous application of punishment'), Mn.; MBh. &c.; illusion, illusive appearance or mere semblance of anything, Kāv.; Kathās. &c. (cf. *-bhāshita*); beauty, grace, Kālid.; Mālatīm.; feminine coquetry, amorous gestures or action of any kind (esp. play of the eyes), perturbation, flurry (as when a woman in her confusion puts her ornaments in the wrong places), Bhar.; Daśar.; Sāh.; caprice, whim, MW.; (*ā*), f. old age, L.; *-tantra*, n. (= *-sūtra*); *-bhāshita*, n. pl. language in appearance, Subh.; *-vatī*, f. a girl, Harav.; N. of a female servant, Prab.; *-sūtra*, n. N. of a treatise on grammar (attributed to Hema-candra); °*mârka*, m. N. of a man, Rājat.

Vi-bhramin, mfn. moving hither and thither, Chandom.

Vi-bhrānta, mfn. wandered or wandering about &c. (n. impers. 'it has been roamed,' Nalôd.); rolling or ogling (as the eyes; see below); spread abroad (as fame), Prab.; confused, bewildered, MBh.; *-nayana*, mfn. one who rolls the eyes or casts side glances, R.; *-manas*, mfn. bewildered or confused in mind, MBh.; *-śīla*, mfn. confused in mind or disposition, intoxicated or insane, W.; m. a monkey, ib.; the disc of the sun or moon, ib. °**bhrānti,** f. whirling, going round, W.; hurry, agitation, ib.; error, delusion, Prab.

विभ्राज् 1. *vi-√bhrāj*, Ā. *-bhrājate* (ep. also P.), to shine forth, be bright or radiant, RV. &c. &c.; to shine through (acc.), RV.; AV.; Caus. *-bhrājayati*, to cause to shine or beam, MBh.; Hariv.; BhP.

2. **Vi-bhrāj,** mfn. (nom. *ṭ*) shining, splendid, luminous, RV.; m. (with *Saurya*) N. of the author of RV. x, 170, Anukr. °**bhrāja,** m. N. of a king, Hariv. °**bhrājita,** mfn. (fr. Caus.) made splendid or bright, caused to shine, MBh.

Ví-bhrāshṭi, f. radiance, flame, blaze, RV.

विभ्रु *vibhru*, m. (perhaps w. r. for *vi-bhu*) a prince, king, MBh. iii, 12705 (B. *-babhru*).

विभ्रेष *vi-bhresha*, m. (√*bhresh*) commission of an offence, transgression (used to explain *vi-pramoha*), ĀśvŚr., Sch.

विभ्वन् *vi-bhvan* &c. See col. 1.

विमंह् *vi-√maṇh*, Ā. *-maṇhate*, to distribute, bestow, RV.

विमज्ज् *vi-√majj*, P. *-majjati*, to plunge or dive into, enter into, MBh. vii, 9223 (perhaps w. r. for *ni-majj*): Caus. *-majjayati*, to submerge, cause to plunge, lead into (loc.), ib. vi, 538. °**majjita,** mfn. (fr. Caus.) submerged, drowned, ib. iii, 10612.

विमत *vi-mata*. See under vi-√man, col. 3.

विमति 1. *vi-mati*, *vi-matsara* &c. See p. 951, col. 3. For 2. *vi-mati*, see col. 3.

विमथ् *vi-√math* (or *manth*), P. Ā. *-mathati*, °*te*, *-mathnāti*, °*nīte* &c. (in Veda generally Ā.; inf. *-mathitos*, AitBr.; °*tum*, BhP.), to tear off, snatch away, TS.; ŚBr.; to tear or break in pieces, rend asunder, bruise, ib.; AitBr.; Kāṭh.; to cut in pieces, disperse, scatter, MBh.; R.; to confuse, perplex, bewilder, BhP. °**mathita,** mfn. crushed or dashed to pieces, scattered, dispersed, destroyed, ŚāṅkhŚr.; MBh. &c. °**mathitṛi,** m. a crusher, destroyer, ŚāṅkhŚr.

Vi-manthana, n. churning, R.

Vi-māthá, m. the act of crushing or destroying utterly, TBr.; ŚBr. °**māthin,** mfn. crushing down, destroying, Kathās.

विमद् 1. *vi-√mad*, P. *-mādyati* (Ved. also *-madati*), to be joyful or merry (only p. *-mádat*), AV.; to become perplexed or discomposed, AitBr.; to confound, embarrass, disturb, ŚāṅkhBr.: Caus. (only aor. *vy-amīmadam*), to confuse, perplex, bewilder, AV.

Vi-matta, mfn. discomposed, perplexed, AitBr.; being in rut, ruttish, ib.; Kir.; intoxicated, MW.

2. **Vi-mad,** f. pl. N. of partic. verses or formulas, ŚāṅkhBr.

Vi-mada &c. See p. 951, col. 3.

Vi-madita, mfn. (fr. Caus.) discomposed, bewildered, confused, AitBr.

विमध्य *vi-madhya*, *vi-madhyama*. See p. 951, col. 3.

विमन् *vi-√man* (only 1. pl. pr. Ā. *-manmahe*), to distinguish, RV. x, 92, 3: Caus. *-mānayati*, to dishonour, slight, treat with disrespect, SaṃhitUp.; MBh.; Kāv. &c.

Vi-mata, mfn. disagreed, at variance, of a different mind or disposition, hostile, ĀśvŚr.; slighted, offended, BhP.; any that may please (= 'every'), Sarvad.; m. an enemy, W.; m. or n. (?) N. of a place on the river Go-matī, R. 2. °**mati,** mfn. of different opinion, g. *dṛiḍhâdi*; f. difference of opinion, dissent, disagreement about (loc.), Pāṇ.; Naish.; Sāh.; dislike, aversion, R.; doubt, uncertainty, error, Lalit.; Saddh.; *-tā*, f. (MW.), *-man*, m. (g. *dṛiḍhâdi*) difference of opinion; *-vikīraṇa*, m. a partic. Samādhi, Buddh.; *-samudghātin*, m. N. of a prince, ib.

2. **Vi-māna,** m. (for 1. see p. 951, col. 3; for 3. under *vi-√mā*) disrespect, dishonour (see *a-vimāna*). °**mānana,** n. (and *ā*, f.) disrespect, contempt, slight, humiliation, MBh.; Kāv. &c.; refusal, denial, Suśr. °**mānita,** mfn. (fr. Caus.) dishonoured, slighted, treated with disrespect, MBh.; R. &c. °**mānya,** mfn. to be dishonoured or offended, Śak.

विमनस् 1. 2. *vi-manas*, *vi-manthara*, *vi-manyu* &c. See p. 951, col. 3.

विमभूपाल *vima-bhūpāla* (?), m. N. of a Scholiast, Cat.

विमय *vi-maya*. See under vi-√me, p. 981.

विमर्द *vi-marda*, *vi-marśa*. See under vi-√mṛid and vi-√mṛiś, p. 981, col. 1.

विमर्ष *vi-marsha*, °*shaṇa*, °*shin*, w. r. for *vi-marśa* &c.

विमल *vi-mala*, mf(*ā*)n. stainless, spotless, clean, bright, pure (lit. and fig.), MBh.; Kāv. &c. (*e*, ind. at daybreak, MBh. v, 7247); clear, transparent, Sarvad.; white (see °*lêbha*); m. a magical formula recited over weapons, R.; a partic. Samādhi, Buddh.; a partic. world, ib.; a lunar year, L.; N. of an Asura, Kathās.; of a Deva-putra and Bodhimaṇḍa-pratipāla, Lalit.; of a Bhikshu, ib.; of a brother of Yaśas, Buddh.; (with Jainas) N. of the 5th Arhat in the past Utsarpiṇī and of the 13th in the present Avasarpiṇī, L.; of a son of Su-dyumna, BhP.; of the father of Padma-pāda, Cat.; of various authors (also with *sarasvatī*), ib.; (*ā*), f. a species of Opuntia, L.; a partic. Śakti, Hcat.; N. of Dākshāyaṇī in Purushôttama, Cat.; of a Yoginī, Hcat.; of a daughter of Gandharvī, MBh.; (with Buddhists) N. of one of the 10 Bhūmis or stages of perfection, Dharmas. 64; n. silver gilt, L.; N. of a town (see *-pura*); of a Tantra; *-kirīṭa-hāra-vat*, mfn. having a bright crest and pearl-necklace, R.; *-kīrti*, m. 'of spotless fame,' N. of a Buddhist scholar; *-nirdeśa*, m. N. of a Mahāyāna-sūtra; *-garbha*, m. a partic. Samādhi, Buddh.; of a Bodhi-sattva and a prince, ib.; *-candra*, m. N. of a king, Buddh.; *-tā*, f., *-tva*, n. stainlessness, cleanliness, brightness, clearness, purity, MBh.; Kāv. &c.; *-datta*, m. a partic. Samādhi, Buddh.; N. of a prince, ib.; (*ā*), f. N. of a princess, ib.; *-dāna*, n. a gift or offering to a deity, MW.; *-nātha-purāṇa*, n. N. of a Jaina wk.; *-nirbhāsa*, m. a partic. Samādhi, SaddhP.; *-netra*, m. N. of a Buddha, ib.; of a prince, ib.; *-piṇḍaka*, m. N. of a serpent-demon, MBh.; *-pura*, n. N. of a city,

Kathās.; *-pradīpa*, m. a partic. Samādhi, Buddh.; *-prabha*, m. a partic. Samādhi, Buddh. (also *ā*, f., Dharmas. 136); N. of a Buddha, ib.; of a Deva-putra, ib. (v. l. *a-vimala-p°*); (*ā*), f. N. of a princess, Rājat.; *-prabhāsa-śrī-tejo-rāja-garbha*, m. N. of a Bodhi-sattva, Buddh.; *-praśnôttara-mālā*, f. N. of wk.; *-buddhi*, m. N. of a man, Kathās.; *-bodha*, m. N. of a Commentator, Cat.; *-brahma-varya*, m. N. of an author, ib.; *-bhadra*, m. N. of a man, Buddh.; *-bhāsa*, m. a partic. Samādhi, ib.; *-bhū-dhara*, m. N. of a Commentator, Cat.; *-maṇi*, m. crystal, L.; (*°ṇi-kara*, m. N. of a Buddhist deity, K-ṇḍ.); *-mati*, mfn. pure-minded, pure in heart, VP.; *-mitra*, m. N. of a scholar, Buddh.; *-vāhana*, m. N. of two princes, Śatr.; *-vega-śrī*, m. N. of a prince of the Gandharvas, Buddh.; *-vyūha*, m. N. of a garden, ib.; *-śrī-garbha*, m. N. of a Bodhi-sattva, ib.; *-sambhava*, m. N. of a mountain, ib.; *-svabhāva*, m. N. of a mountain, ib.; *°lâkara*, m. N. of a prince, Kathās.; *°lâgra-netra*, m. N. of a future Buddha, SaddhP.; *°lâtmaka*, mfn. pure-minded, clean, pure, L.; *°lâtman*, mfn. id., R.; *°lâditya*, m. a partic. form of the sun, Cat.; *°lâdri*, m. N. of the mountain Vimala or Girnar in Gujarāt (celebrated for its inscriptions; it is also called Śatrum-jaya), L.; *°lânana*, mfn. bright-faced, Kāv.; *°lânanda* (with *yogîndra*), m. N. of a teacher, Cat. (*°da-nātha*, m. N. of an author; *°da-bhāshya*, n. N. of wk.); *°lâpa*, mfn. having pure water, Laghuk.; *°lârthaka*, mfn. (said to be) = *vimalâtmaka*, L.; *°lâśoka*, m. or n. (?) N. of a place of pilgrimage, MBh.; *°lâśvā*, f. N. of a village, Rājat.; *°lêśvara-tīrtha*, n. and *°lêśvara-pushkariṇī-saṃgama-tīrtha*, n. N. of two Tīrthas, Cat.; *°lôdakā* or *°lôdā*, f. N. of a river, MBh.; *°lôrja* or *°logya* (?), n. N. of a Tantra.

Vi-malaya, Nom. P. *°yati*, to make clear or pure, Ragh.; Kuval.; *°lita*, mfn. clear, pure, Inscr. **°maliman**, m. clearness, purity, Daś. **°malī-karaṇa**, n. the act of clearing, purification, Sarvad.

विमस्तकित *vi-mastakita, vi-mahat* &c. See p. 951, col. 3.

विमा *vi-√3. mā*, P. Ā. *-māti, -mimīte*, to measure, mete out, pass over, traverse, RV.; Br.; Kauś.; to enumerate, BhP.; to ordain, fix, set right, arrange, make ready, prepare, RV.

3. **Vi-māna**, mf(*ī*)n. (for 1. see p. 951, col. 3; for 2. under *vi-√man*) measuring out, traversing, RV.; AV.; MBh.; m. n. a car or chariot of the gods, any mythical self-moving aerial car (sometimes serving as a seat or throne, sometimes self-moving and carrying its occupant through the air; other descriptions make the Vimāna more like a house or palace, and one kind is said to be 7 stories high; that of Rāvaṇa was called *pushpaka*, q. v.; the *nau-v°* [Ragh. xvi, 68] is thought to resemble a ship), MBh.; Kāv. &c.; any car or vehicle (esp. a bier), Rājat. vii, 446; the palace of an emperor or supreme monarch (esp. one with 7 stories), MBh.; Kāv. &c.; a temple or shrine of a partic. form, VarBṛS.; a kind of tower (?), R. v, 52, 8; a grove, Jātakam.; a ship, boat, L.; a horse, L.; n. measure, RV.; extension, ib.; (in med.) the science of (right) measure or proportion (e. g. of the right relation between the humours of the body, of medicines and remedies &c.), Car.; *-gamana*, n. 'going in a car,' N. of a ch. of the GaṇP.; *-cārin*, mfn. travelling in a celestial car, MW.; *-cyuta*, mfn. fallen from a cel° car, Rājat.; *-tā*, f., *-tva*, n. the state or condition of a cel° car, Kāv.; Kathās.; *-nirvyūha*, m. a partic. Samādhi, Kāraṇḍ.; *-pāla*, m. the guardian of a cel° car, MBh.; *-pratima*, mfn. resembling a cel° car, MBh.; *-prabhu-tā*, f. the ownership of a cel° car, MW.; *-māhâtmya*, n. N. of a ch. of the VP.; *-yāna*, mf(*ā*)n. going or driving in a cel° car, BhP.; *-rāja*, m. the driver of a celestial car, MW.; *-lakshaṇa*, n. N. of a wk. on architecture; *-vat*, ind. like a self-moving car, Kir.; *-vidyā*, f., *-śuddhi-pūjā*, f. N. of wks.; *-stha*, mfn. standing on a cel° car, MW.; *-sthāna*, n. N. of a wk. on medicine. **°mānaka** (ifc.) = *vi-māna*, a celestial car, Kathās.; a seven-storied palace or tower, R.

Vimānī-√kṛi, P. *-karoti*, to turn into a celestial car, Kād.

विमांस *vi-māṃsa, vi-mātṛi* &c. See p. 951.

विमातव्य *vi-mātavya.* See under *vi-√me.*

विमार्ग *1. vi-mārga* &c. See p. 951, col. 3.

विमार्ग *2. vi-mārga.* See under *vi-√mṛij.*

विमार्गण *vi-mārgaṇa*, n. (*√mārg*) the act of seeking for (gen.), Kir.

विमि *vi-√1. mi*, P. Ā. *-minoti, -minute*, to fix, build, erect, RV.; Br.; GṛŚrS.

Ví-mita, mfn. fixed, built &c.; n. a square shed or large building resting on four posts (ifc. any hall or building), ŚBr.; ŚrS.; ChUp.

विमिश्र *vi-√miśr*, P. *-miśrayati*, to mix or mingle together, MBh.

Vi-miśra, mf(*ā*)n. mixed, mingled, miscellaneous, MBh.; Hariv.; VarBṛS.; mixed or mingled with, attended or accompanied by (instr. or comp.), ib.; Suśr. &c.; applied to one of the 7 divisions into which the course of Mercury, accord. to Parāśara, is divided, VarBṛS.; n. capital and interest &c., Līl. **°miśraka**, mfn. mixed, miscellaneous, VarBṛS.; n. a kind of salt, L. **°miśrita**, mfn. mixed, mingled (with *lipi*, f. a partic. mode of writing), Lalit.

विमुक्त *vi-mukta.* See under 1. *vi-√muc.*

विमुख *vi-mukha*, mf(*ā*)n. having the face averted, turned backwards (acc. with *√kṛi*, 'to cause to fly,' 'put to flight'), MBh.; Kāv. &c.; turning away from (gen.), disappointed, downcast, Kāv.; Kathās.; Pur.; averse or opposed to, abstaining or desisting from (loc., abl., gen. with *upari*, or comp.), MBh.; Kāv. &c.; (ifc.) indifferent to, Vcar.; adverse, hostile (as fate), Veṇis.; (ifc.) wanting, lacking, Śāntiś.; (*vi* priv.) without the mouth or opening, ŚārṅgS.; deprived of the face or head, Hariv.; m. N. of a text (VS. xvii, 86; xxxix, 7), KātyŚr.; of a Muni (v. l. *vimuca*), R.; *-tā*, f., *-tva*, n. aversion, disinclination to (loc., acc. with *prati*, or comp.), Kāv.; Sāh.

Vimukhaya, Nom. P. *°yati*, to render averse; *°khita*, mfn. averse, hostile, Kād.

Vimukhin, mfn. having the face averted, averse from, hostile, W.; *°khi-tā*, f. (or *-tva*, n.) turning away, aversion, enmity, ib.

Vimukhī, in comp. for *vimukha*. **— karaṇa**, n. (ifc.) the rendering averse to, Śaṃk. **— √kṛi**, P. *-karoti*, to put to flight, MBh.; Hariv.; to render averse or indifferent to (abl. or comp.), Śaṃk.; *-kṛita*, mfn. turned away, averse, indifferent, ib.; Caurap.; frustrated, R. **— bhāva**, m. aversion, Gīt. **— √bhū**, P. *-bhavati*, to turn the back, flee, Ragh.; to turn away from (abl.), Mṛicch.

विमुग्ध *vi-mugdha.* See under *vi-√muh.*

विमुच 1. *vi-√muc*, P. Ā. *-muñcati, °te* (Impv. *-mumoktu*, RV. i, 24, 13), to unloose, unharness (Ā. 'one's own horses'), unyoke (i. e. 'make to halt, cause to stop or rest'), RV. &c. &c.; to take off (clothes, ornaments &c.), MBh.; Kāv. &c.; to release, set free, liberate, ib.; to leave, abandon, quit, desert, give up, relinquish, ib.; to shun, avoid, MuṇḍUp.; Bhag. &c.; to lose (consciousness), Hariv.; to pardon, forgive, Gīt.; BhP.; to emit, discharge, shed, pour or send forth, MBh.; R.; Pañcat. (with *grastam*, to set free a seized planet i. e. 'free it from eclipse,' Sūryas.); to throw, hurl, cast (with *ātmānam* and loc., 'to cast one's self into,' Uttarar.), MBh.; R. &c.; to utter (a sound), MBh.; to assume (a shape), Mn. i, 56; to lay (eggs), Pañcat. i, ३६३: Pass. *-mucyate*, to be unloosed or detached &c.; to be slackened (as reins), Śak.; to drop or be expelled (prematurely, as a fetus), Suśr.; to be freed or delivered or released (esp. from the bonds of existence), get rid of, escape from (abl., adv. in *-tas*, gen., or instr.), Mn.; MBh. &c.; to be deprived of (instr.), Hit.: Caus. *-mocayati*, to loosen, detach, Śak.; to unyoke, Kauś.; to set free, deliver from (abl.), Mn.; MBh. &c.; to keep off, avoid, R.: Desid. *-mumukshati, °te*, to wish to liberate (Ā. 'one's self'), BhP.

Vi-mukta, mfn. unloosed, unharnessed &c.; set free, liberated (esp. from mundane existence), freed or delivered or escaped from (abl., instr., or ifc.; rarely ibc.; cf. *-śāpa*), Mn.; MBh. &c.; deprived of (instr.), MBh.; launched (as a ship), R.; given up, abandoned, relinquished, deserted, ib.; BhP.; hurled, thrown, MBh.; emitted or discharged by, flowing from (comp.), Ratnâv.; shed or bestowed on (loc.), Rājat.; (a snake) which has recently cast its skin, MBh. viii, 740; dispassionate, R. iv, 32, 18; *-kaṇṭha*, mfn. having the throat or voice unloosed, raising a loud cry (*am*, ind. aloud, at the top of one's voice), Amar.; *-keśa*, mfn. having flowing or dishevelled hair, BhP.; *-tā*, f. loss of (gen.), Kām.; *-pragraha*, mfn. with slackened reins, Bhaṭṭ.; *-maunam*, ind. breaking silence, Kathās.; *-śāpa*, mfn. released from the (consequences) of a curse, VP.; *-sena*, m. N. of a teacher, Buddh.; *°tâcārya*, m. N. of an author, Cat. **°mukti**, f. disjunction (opp. to *yukti*), AitBr.; (ifc.) giving up, Kum.; release, deliverance, liberation, Kāv.; Kathās.; Pur.; release from the bonds of existence, final emancipation, Kap.; VP.; *-candra*, m. N. of a Bodhi-sattva, Buddh.; *-patha*, m. the way of final emancipation, MW.; *-mahiman*, m. N. of wk.

2. **Vi-múc**, f. unyoking, alighting, stopping, putting up, RV. (*vimuco napāt*, 'son of unyoking,' N. of Pūshan as 'conductor on the way to the next world,' ib.) **°muca**, m. N. of a Ṛishi, MBh.

Vi-moká, m. unyoking, unbending, cessation, termination, TS.; AV.; letting go, abandoning, giving up, AgP.; deliverance from (abl. or comp.), Nyāyam., Sch.; liberation from sensuality or worldly objects, Sarvad. **°mókam**, ind. so that the horses are unharnessed or changed, TS.; Br. **°moktavya**, mfn. to be let loose or set at liberty, MBh.; to be given up or abandoned, R.; to be discharged or hurled or cast at (dat. or loc.), MBh. **°moktṛi**, mf(*trī*)n. one who unyokes or unharnesses, VS.; TBr. **°mokya**, see *a-vimokyá*.

Vi-mocaka, mfn. releasing, delivering from (ifc.), Cat. **°mócana**, mf(*ī*)n. unyoking, loosening, RV.; &c. &c.; m. N. of Śiva, MBh.; (*ī*), f. N. of a river, VP.; n. unharnessing, alighting, stopping for rest, relief, RV.; TS.; ŚBr.; deliverance, liberation (esp. from sin), MBh.; MārkP.; giving up, abandoning, MBh.; N. of a place of pilgrimage, ib. **°mocanīya**, mfn. (ifc.) relating to the unharnessing of, ŚBr.; KātyŚr. (cf. *dundubhi-* and *ratha-v°*). **°mocita**, mfn. (fr. Caus.) loosened, liberated; m. N. of Śiva, Śivag. **°mocya**, mfn. to be released or delivered, MBh.

विमुद *vimuda*, m. or n. (?) a partic. high number, Buddh.

विमुह् *vi-√muh*, P. Ā. *-muhyati, °te*, to be confused, become bewildered or stupefied, faint away, Yājñ.; MBh. &c.: Caus. *-mohayati*, to confuse, bewilder, infatuate, MBh.; Kāv. &c.; to confound, efface, Sāy.

Vi-mugdha, mfn. confused, bewildered, infatuated, Hit.

Vi-mūḍha, id., MBh.; Kāv. &c.; (ifc.) perplexed as to, uncertain about, Kathās.; foolish, stupid, Prab.; *-cetas* (R.), *-dhī* (MārkP.), mfn. foolish-minded, simple; *-bhāva*, m. bewildered state, confusion, MW.; *-samjña*, mfn. bewildered in mind, senseless, unconscious, W.; *°ḍhâtman*, mfn. foolish-minded, perplexed in mind, senseless, Bhag. **°mūḍhaka**, n. a kind of farce, Bhar. (perhaps w. r. for *dvi-gūḍhaka*).

Vi-moha, m. confusion of the mind, perplexity (also *mati-v°*), Kathās.; BhP.; a kind of hell, VP.; *-da*, mfn. causing perplexity, bewildering, Kathās. **°mohaka**, mf(*ikā*)n. bewildering the mind, bewitching, Naish. **°mohana**, mfn. id., BhP.; m. a kind of hell, VP. (cf. *naraka*); n. confusion, perplexity, Rājat.; Prab.; the art of confusing or bewildering (= *ākulī-karaṇa*), Pāṇ. vii, 2, 54, Sch. **°mohita**, mfn. confused, infatuated, bewitched, beguiled, R.; Kathās. &c. **°mohin**, mfn. perplexing, bewildering, Kathās.; BhP.

विमूर्छित *vi-mūrchita*, mfn. (*√murch*) thickened, coagulated, become solid, Yājñ.; Vāgbh.; (ifc.) full of, mixed with, Bh.; Car.; resounding with, BhP.; n. 'becoming stiff,' fainting, a swoon, Divyâv.

Vi-mūrta, mfn. coagulated, become hard or solid, ŚāṅkhBr.

विमृज् *vi-√mṛij*, P. Ā. *-mārshṭi, -mṛishṭe* (pf. Pot. *-māmṛijīta*, RV.), to rub off or out, purify, cleanse, Br.; ŚrS.; to rub dry, TS.; to rub on or in, anoint, smear with (instr.), GṛŚrS.; to wipe off, MBh.; Mṛicch.; to rub, stroke, caress, MBh.; R. &c.; Ā. (with *tanvàm*), to adorn or arm one's self, RV. vii, 95, 3.

2. **Vi-mārga**, m. (for 1. see p. 951, col. 3) wiping off, ĀpŚr., Sch.; a broom, brush, L.

Vi-mārjana, n. wiping off, cleansing, purifying, ŚāṅkhŚr.

1. **Vi-mṛishṭa**, mfn. (for 2. see under *vi-√mṛiś*) rubbed off &c.; depressed (see below); *-rāga*, mfn. having the colour refined or purified, Kum.; *°ṭântarâṃsa*, mfn. having the space between the shoulders a little depressed (*nyūna*, Sch.), ŚBr.

विमृद् *vi-√mṛid*, P. *-mṛidnāti, -mardati*, to

crush or press to pieces, bruise, pound, grind down, lay waste, destroy, Mn.; MBh. &c.; to rub together, Suśr.: Caus. *-mardayati*, to crush to pieces, bruise, Kāv.; Pur.; to rub, Suśr.

Vi-marda, m. crushing, bruising, grinding, pounding, rubbing, friction, MBh.; Kāv. &c.; trampling, Ratnâv.; hostile encounter, conflict, scuffle, fight, war, tumult, MBh.; Kāv. &c.; laying waste, devastation, destruction, ib.; interruption, disturbance, Mṛicch.; Hit.; touch, contact, Sāṃkhyak.; refusal, rejection, R.; complete obscuration, total eclipse, Sūryas.; VarBṛS.; weariness, tediousness, MW.; the trituration of perfumes, W.; Cassia Sophora, L.; N. of a prince, MārkP.; *-kshama*, mfn. patient of being trampled on (in wars or tumults, said of the earth), Uttarar.; °*dârdha*, n. the time from the apparent conjunction to the end of an eclipse, W.; °*dôttha*, m. fragrance arising from the trituration of perfumes, ib. °**mardaka**, mfn. crushing, pounding, destroying, Hariv.; m. the act of pounding, grinding, destroying, MW.; rolling, ib.; the trituration of perfumes, ib.; the conjunction of the sun and moon, eclipse, ib.; Cassia Tora, L.; N. of a man, Daś. °**mardana**, mfn. pressing, squeezing, Sāh.; crushing, destroying, MBh.; R. &c.; fragrance, perfume, Gal.; N. of a Rākshasa, R.; of a prince of the Vidyādharas, Kathās.; n. (and *ā*, f.) the act of rubbing or grinding, or pounding or crushing, Gaut.; Āpast.; hostile encounter, fight, battle, war, Prab.; BhP.; devastation, destruction, MBh.; the trituration of perfumes, W.; an eclipse, ib. °**mardita**, mfn. (fr. Caus.) crushed, bruised, &c., R.; BhP.; rubbed, anointed, Suśr. °**mardin**, mfn. crushing to pieces, destroying, removing, MBh.; VarBṛS. &c.

Vi-mṛidita, mfn. bruised, pounded, broken, rubbed, Yājñ.; R.; Suśr.; *-dhvaja*, mfn. having a crushed or broken banner, R.

विमृध् *vi-mṛidh*, m. (√*mṛidh*) a despiser, foe, enemy, Vait.; 'averter of enemies,' N. of Indra, RV.; °*mṛid-vat*, mf(*atī*)n. belonging to Indra, ŚāṅkhBr. °**mṛidhá**, mf(*ā*)n. warding off an enemy, TS.

विमृश् *vi-√mṛiś* (often confounded with *vi-√mṛish*), P. *-mṛiśati*, to touch (with the hands), stroke, feel, MBh.; R.; to touch (mentally), be sensible or aware of, perceive, consider, reflect on, deliberate about, RV. &c. &c.; to investigate, examine, try, test, MBh.; Kāv. &c.; (with inf.) to hesitate about doing anything, Sāh.: Caus. *-marśayati*, to ponder, reflect on, consider, Kāv.; Pañcat.; BhP.

Vi-marśa, m. consideration, deliberation, trial, critical test, examination, PañcavBr.; MBh. &c.; reasoning, discussion, Prab.; knowledge, intelligence, Sarvad.; N. of Śiva, MBh.; (in dram.) critical juncture or crisis (one of the 5 Saṃdhis or junctures of the plot, intervening between the *garbha* or germ and the *nirvahana* or catastrophe, e.g. in the Śakuntalā the removal of her veil in the 5th act), Bhar.; Daśar. &c.; *-vat*, mfn. reflecting, meditative, doubtful, Jātakam.; *vādin*, mfn. uttering discussions, one who reasons, a reasoner, Prab.; °*śâṅga*, n. a division of the dramatic Vimarśa (of which there are said to be 13), Bhar. °**marśana**, m. (written °*marshaṇa*) N. of a king of the Kirātas, Cat.; n. discussing, investigation, BhP. °**marśita**, mfn. (fr. Caus.) reflected on, considered, Pañcat. °**marśin**, mfn. considering, trying, examining, Kathās.; Sarvad.

Vi-mṛiśa, m. reflection, consideration, deliberation, ib. °**mṛiśita**, mfn. reflected on, considered, BhP. 1. °**mṛiśya**, mfn. to be tried or examined, ib. 2. °**mṛiśya**, ind. having deliberated or considered (*-kārin*, mfn. acting after due deliberation), Hit.

2. **Vi-mṛishṭa**, mfn. (for 1. see under *vi-√mṛij*) reflected on, considered, weighed, MW.

विमृष् *vi-√mṛish*, P. Ā. *-mṛishyati*, °*te*, or *-marshati*, °*te* (cf. *vi-√mṛiś*), to be distressed, bear hardly, W.

Vi-marsha, m. irritation, impatience, displeasure, W. °**marshin**, mfn. impatient, intolerant, averse, disliking, ib.

विमे *vi-√me*, Ā. *-mayate*, to change places, alternate (?), RV. x, 40, 10.

Vi-maya, m. exchange, barter, L.

Vi-mātavya, mfn. to be bartered with (instr.), Vās.

विमेघ *vi-megha*, *vi-mogha*, &c. See p. 952.

विमोक्ष् *vi-√moksh*, P. *-mokshayati*, to set free, let loose, liberate, MBh. °**mokshá**, m. the being loosened or undone, PārGṛ.; release, deliverance from (abl. or comp.), MBh.; R. &c.; liberation of the soul, i.e. final emancipation (sometimes 8, sometimes 3 kinds are enumerated, cf. Dharmas. 59 and 73), ŚBr.; Bhag. &c.; letting loose, setting at liberty (a thief), Mn. viii, 3, 16; giving up, abandoning, VPrāt.; MBh.; letting flow, shedding (of tears), MBh.; gift, bestowal (of wealth), R.; discharge (of arrows), MBh.; *-karā*, f. N. of a Kiṃ-narī, Kāraṇḍ. °**mokshaka**, mfn. one who releases from (ifc.), R. °**mokshaṇa**, mfn. liberating from (ifc.), BhP.; n. untying, loosening, VarBṛS.; liberation, deliverance from (abl. or comp.), Mn.; MBh. &c. (also 'from an embryo,' MBh. i, 2369; *aṇḍa-v*°, 'laying eggs,' Pañcat.; *asṛig-v*°, 'letting blood,' Suśr.); taking off, casting away, Śṛiṅgār.; giving up (the ghost), MBh.; discharging (arrows), R. °**mokshin**, mfn. one who has attained to final emancipation, MBh.

विमोचक *vi-mocaka*, °*cana* &c. See p. 980.

विम्ब *vimba* &c. See *bimba*.

विम्रद् *vi-√mrad* (only Impv. *-mradā*), to make soft or tender, soften, RV. vi, 53, 3.

विम्रित् *vi-√mrit*, P. *-mrityati*, to fall to pieces, crumble away, decay, ŚBr.

विम्लै *vi-√mlai*, P. Ā. *-mlāyati*, °*te*, to wither away, languish, become weak or weary, ChUp.: Caus. *-mlāpayati*, to cause to wither or languish, weary, enfeeble, Suśr.

2. **Vi-mlāna**, mfn. (for 1. see p. 952, col. 1) faded or withered away, bereft of lustre or beauty, fresh, pure, W.

Vi-mlāpana, n. causing to wither or languish, softening, Suśr.

वियङ्ग *viyaṅga*. See 2. *avyaṅga*.

वियत् *vi-√yat*, Ā. *-yatate*, to dispose in various rows, AV.: Caus. *-yātayati*, to place in rows, arrange, TS.; to do penance, AV.; to torment, pain, punish, MBh.

वियत् *vi-yát*, mfn. (pr. p. of *vi-√5. i*) going apart or asunder, RV. i, 164, 38; being dissolved, passing away, vanishing, BhP.; n. the sky, heaven, air, atmosphere (prob. as 'that which parts asunder or forms the intermediate region between heaven and earth'), VS. &c. &c.; ether (as an element), BhP.; Sarvad.; N. of the 10th mansion, VarBṛS.; a kind of metre, VS. — **patākā**, f. 'sky-banner,' lightning, Ṛit. iii, 12. — **patha**, m. 'sky-path,' the atmosphere, Dharmaś. — **stha**, mfn. standing or being in the air, MBh.

Viyac, in comp. for *vi-yat*. — **cara**, mfn. flying through the air, MBh. — **cārin**, m. 'sky-goer,' Falco Cheela (= *cilla*), L.

Viyad, in comp. for *vi-yat*. — **gaṅgā**, f. the heavenly Ganges, i.e. the galaxy, L. — **gata**, mfn. moving or flying in the air, MBh.; Śiś. — **gati**, f. motion in the air, W. — **bhūti**, f. 'sky-power,' darkness, ib. — **vyāpin**, mfn. filling the air, Vṛishabhān.

Viyan, in comp. for *vi-yat*. — **maṇi**, m. 'sky-jewel,' the sun, L. — **madhya-haṅsa**, m. 'the flamingo in the middle of the sky,' the sun, Daś. — **maya**, mf(*ī*)n. consisting of air, Hcar.

वियति *viyati*, m. N. of one of the six sons of Nahusha, Pur.; a bird, L.

वियम् *vi-√yam*, P. *-yacchati* (3. pl. pf. Ā. *-yemire*, RV. iv, 54, 5), to spread out, extend, RV.; to stretch out the legs, step out (as a running horse), ib.; to hold apart or asunder, ib.: Caus. *-yāmayati*, to stretch out, extend, AV.

Ví-yata, mfn. stretched out, extended, kept apart, RV.; AV.; (*am*), ind. separately, at intervals, intermittingly, ŚrS.

Vi-yama, m. (only L.) = next, Pāṇ. iii, 3, 63.

Vi-yāma, m. (only L.) a partic. measure of length (= a fathom measured by the two extended arms); forbearance, restraint; rest, stop, cessation, pain, distress.

विया *vi-√yā*, P. *-yāti*, to go or pass through, traverse, cross, drive through (with a car), cut through (with wheels), destroy, RV.; MaitrS.; ŚBr.; to depart, turn away, MaitrS.; BhP. °**yāta**, mfn. 'gone apart or from the right path,' shameless, impudent, ill-behaved, L.; *-tā*, f. = next, Śiś. °**yātiman**, m. shamelessness, impudence, L.

वियाङ्ग *viyāṅga*. See 2. *avyaṅga*.

वियास *vi-yāsá*, m. (√*yas*) N. of a partic. demon who inflicts torment in Yama's world, VS.; TS.

वियु *vi-√yu*, P. *-yuyoti*, *-yauti*, to separate, part (intr.), RV.; AV.; to be separated from or deprived of (instr.), RV.; VS.; to separate (trans.), divide, detach or exclude from, deprive of (instr.), RV.; to keep off, avert, Śiś.; to spread, scatter, TS.; to open, RV.

Ví-yuta, mfn. separated from, deprived of (instr. or comp.), RV. &c. &c.; not being in conjunction with (comp.), VarBṛS.; diminished, that from which something has been subtracted, Sūryas.; (*ā*), f. du. 'the two separated ones,' heaven and earth, RV. iii, 54, 7; °*târthaka*, mfn. void of meaning, L. °**yuti**, f. the difference between two quantities, Bijag.

Vi-yotṛi, mfn. one who divides or separates, RV. iv, 55, 5.

वियुज् *vi-√yuj*, P. Ā. *-yunakti*, *-yuṅkte*, to disjoin, detach, divide, separate from or deprive of (instr., rarely abl.), AV. &c. &c.; to part from (instr.), Śaṃk.; (Ā.) to forsake, abandon (acc.), Kir.; to relax, abate, yield, BhP.: Pass. *-yujyate*, to be separated from or deprived of, lose (instr.), MBh.; Kāv. &c.; to break (a vow, instr.), Mn. v, 91; to be relaxed, yield, give way, R.: Caus. *-yojayati*, °*te*, to cause to be disjoined, separate or deliver from, deprive of (instr. or abl.), MBh.; Kāv. &c.; to rob, MBh.; to subtract, Līl.

Vi-yukta, mfn. disjoined, detached, separated or delivered from, deprived or destitute of, deserted by (instr. or comp.), Mn.; MBh. &c.; disunited (as husband and wife), Mn. ix, 102; failing, deficient, MW.; *-tā*, f. (ifc.) the being free from, L.

Vi-yoga, m. disjunction, separation (esp. of lovers), loss or absence or want of (instr. with or without *saha*, abl., or comp.), Mn.; MBh. &c. (°*gam* √*gam*, to be lost, Mṛicch. ix, 33/34); giving up, getting rid of, abstention from (comp.), Gaut.; subtraction, Gaṇit.; = *vi-yuti*, Bijag.; a partic. astrological Yoga, Cat.; *-tas*, ind. (ifc.) from want of, in consequence of any one's absence, Kathās.; *-tā*, w.r. for °*gi-tā* (q.v.), Kathās.; *-pura*, n. N. of a town, ib.; *-bāhya*, mfn. excluded from separation, not separated, MW.; *-bhāj*, mfn. suffering from s°, W.; °*gâvasāna*, mfn. ending in s° (*-tva*, n.), MW.; °*gâvaha*, mfn. bringing or causing separation, Śantiś.

Vi-yogāya, Ā. °*yate*, to be like or resemble a separation, Subh.

Vi-yogin, mfn. separated or absent from (instr. or comp.), Kathās.; MārkP.; Dhūrtas.; liable to separation (see *a-v*°); m. the ruddy goose, Anas Casarca (cf. *cakravāka*), L.; (*inī*), f. a woman separated from her husband or lover, MW.; a kind of metre (commonly called *vaitālīya*, q.v.); °*gi-tā*, f. the being separated, separation, Kathās.

Viyogi-karaṇa, n. causing separation, = *hiṅsā*, Śil.

Vi-yojana, n. detaching or liberating from (comp.), Sarvad.; separation from (comp.), Kāv.; Kathās.; subtraction, Līl. °**yojanīya**, mfn. to be separated from or deprived of (instr.), Kull. on Mn. viii, 374. °**yojita**, mfn. (fr. Caus.) disjoined, disunited, separated from or deprived of (instr. or comp.), MBh.; Kāv. &c. °**yojya**, mfn. to be separated from (abl.), Pañcat.

वियोतृ *vi-yotṛi*. See under *vi-√yu*.

वियोध *vi-yodha*, *vi-yoni* &c. See p. 952, col. 1.

विरक्त *vi-rakta* &c. See under *vi-√rañj*.

विरक्ष् *vi-√raksh*, P. *-rakshati*, to watch over, guard, protect, AV.; MBh.

विरग *viraga*, m. or n.(?) a partic. high number, Buddh.

विरच् *vi-√rac*, P. *-racayati* (rarely Ā.; aor. *vy-araracat*, once *-arīracat*; ind. p. *vi-racayya*; Pass. *vi-racyate*; aor. *vy-araci*), to construct, contrive, form, fashion, make, arrange, Kāv.; Kathās. &c.; to build, erect, Rājat.; to invent, produce, compose, write, Kāv.; VarBṛS. &c.; to put on, don, wear, Kāv.; BhP. °**racana**, n. (and *ā*, f.) arrangement, disposition, embellishment, Kāv. (with *alakānām*, beautifully arranged locks, Bālar.); putting on, wearing (ornaments &c.), Vikr.; Mālatim.; composition, compilation, W. °**racayitavya**, mfn. to be formed or made, Śaṃk. °**racita**, mfn. constructed, arranged &c.; performed, BhP.; composed, written, Kālid.; Pañcat.; put together, spoken, uttered (see comp.); put on, worn, Ragh.; furnished with (instr.), Megh.; put in, inlaid, set, MW.; (*ā*), f. N. of a woman, Kathās.; *-pada*, mfn. (a speech or song &c.) the words of which are artificially composed or arranged, rhythmic, poetic, Kālid.; *-vapus*, mfn. one who has his body formed or arranged, MW.; *-vāc*, mfn. one who has composed a speech or who has spoken, Ragh.; °*tôkti*, mfn. id., Kathās.

विरज *ví-raja* (3. *vi* + *raja* for *rajas*), mf(*ā*)n. free from dust, clean, pure (also fig. 'free from passion'), ŚBr.; MBh. &c.; free from the menstrual excretion, L.; m. N. of a Marut-vat, Hariv.; of a son of Tvashṭri, BhP.; of a son of Pūrṇiman, ib.; of a pupil of Jātūkarṇya, ib.; of the world of Buddha Padma-prabha, SaddhP.; (pl.) of a class of gods under Manu Sāvarṇi, BhP.; (*ā*), f. Panicum Dactylon (= *dūrvā*), MBh. (= *kapitthānī*, L.); of the wife of Nahusha (spiritual daughter of a class of Pitṛis called Su-svadhas or Sva-svadhas), Hariv.; of a mistress of Kṛishṇa (who was changed into a river), Pañcar.; of a Rākshasī, Cat.; n. N. of a place of pilgrimage, MBh.; *-prabha*, m. N. of a Buddha, Buddh.; *-loka*, m. N. of a partic. world, VB.; °*jâksha*, m. N. of a mountain (to the north of Meru), MārkP.; °*jā-kshetra*, n. N. of a sacred district, Cat.; °*jêsvarī*, f. N. of Rādhā, Pañcar.

Vi-rajas, mfn. = *-raja*, free from dust &c., MBh.; Kāv. &c.; m. N. of a serpent-demon, MBh.; of a Ṛishi, Hariv.; of a sage under Manu Cākshusha, ib.; of a son of Manu Sāvarṇi, MārkP.; of a son of Nārāyaṇa, MBh.; of a son of Kavi, ib.; of a son of Vasishṭha, BhP.; of a son of Paurṇamāsa, MārkP.; of a son of Dhṛita-rāshṭra, MBh.; f. a woman who has ceased to menstruate, L.; N. of Durgā, L.; *-karaṇa*, n. freeing from dust, cleansing, KātySr., Sch.; *-tamas*, mfn. free from (the qualities of) passion and ignorance, L.; *-tejaḥ-svara*, m. N. of a serpent-demon, Buddh.; *-tejo'mbara-bhūshaṇa*, mfn. having apparel and ornaments free from dust, MW.

Vi-rajaska, mfn. = *-rajas*, MBh.; Hariv.; BhP.; m. N. of a son of Manu Sāvarṇi, BhP.

Virajī, in comp. for *vi-raja* or *vi-rajas*. — √**kṛi**, P. Ā. *-karoti*, *-kurute*, to render free from dust or passion, ib.; *-kṛita*, mfn. freed from dust, cleansed, Śiś. xiii, 49. — √**bhū**, P. *-bhavati*, to be or become free from dust or p° (also with √*as*), Pāṇ. v, 4, 51, Sch.; *-bhūta*, mfn. free from dust or p°, pure, MW.

विरञ्च *virañca*, m. (perhaps fr. √*rac*) N. of Brahmā, BhP., Sch.

Virañcana (L.), °**ci** (Kāv.), °**cya** (BhP.), m. id.

विरञ्ज् *vi-√rañj*, P. Ā. *-rajyati*, °*te*, to be changed in colour, be discoloured, lose one's natural colour, Kāv.; VarBṛS. &c.; to become changed in disposition or affection, become indifferent to, take no interest in (abl. or loc.), MBh.; Kāv. &c.: Caus. *-rañjayati*, to discolour, stain, Suśr.

Vi-rakta, mfn. discoloured, changed in colour, Ragh.; changed in disposition, disaffected, estranged, averse, indifferent to, i. e. having no interest in (abl., loc., acc. with *prati*, or comp.), MBh.; Kāv. &c.; become indifferent, i. e. arousing no interest, Rājat.; impassioned, feeling excessive passion, W.; *-citta*, mfn. disaffected at heart, estranged, MW.; *-prakṛiti*, mfn. having disaffected subjects, Kām.; *-bhāva* (Pañcat.), *-hṛidaya* (Kathās.), mfn. = *-citta*; °*tâsarvasva*, n. N. of wk. °**rakti**, f. change of disposition or feeling, alienation of mind, want of interest, freedom of passion, indifference to (loc., gen. with *upari*, or acc. with *prati*), Rājat.; Pañcat.; BhP.; indifference to worldly objects, weanedness from the world, BhP.; *-mat*, mfn. indifferent to (loc.), Kathās.; connected with freedom from worldly attachment, BhP.; *-ratnâvali*, f. N. of a Stotra.

2. **Vi-raṅga**, m. (for 1. see p. 952, col. 1) = 2. *virāga*, L. (cf. *vairaṅgika*).

Vi-rajana, mfn. useful for or causing change of colour, Car.

Vi-rañjanīya. See *purīsha-virañjanīya*. °**rañjita**, mfn. estranged, cooled in affection, R.

2. **Vi-rāga**, m. (for 1. see p. 952, col. 1) change or loss of colour, Naish.; excitement, irritation, Pāṇ. vi, 4, 91; aversion, dislike or indifference to (loc., abl., or comp.), Kāv.; Rājat.; BhP.; indifference to external things or worldly objects, Sāṃkhyak.; the faulty suppression of a sound in pronunciation, RPrāt.; a partic. high number, Buddh.; *-vat*, mfn. indifferent (*sarvatra*, 'to everything'), Cat.; *-visha-bhṛit*, mfn. cherishing the poison of dislike or aversion, MW.; °*gârha*, mfn. qualified for freedom from passion (= *vairaṅgika*), L. °**rāgaya**, Nom. P. °*yati*, to estrange, alienate, Vishṇ.; to displease, Divyâv.; °*gita*, mfn. exasperated, irritated, Vajracch.; ifc., feeling aversion or dislike to, MBh. °**rāgin**, mfn. indifferent to (loc.), MBh.; R. &c.

विरट *viraṭa*, m. the shoulder, W.; a kind of black Agallochum, ib.; N. of a king, ib.

विरण् *vi-√2. raṇ*, Caus. *-raṇayati*, to cause to sound, make to resound, play upon (a musical instrument), BhP.

Vi-rāṇin, m. an elephant, L.

विरण 1. *vi-raṇa*. See *á-v°*.

विरण 2. *viraṇa*, n. = *vīraṇa*, Andropogon Muricatus, L.

विरत *vi-rata*, *vi-rati* &c. See under *vi-√ram* below.

विरथ *vi-ratha* &c. See p. 952, col. 1.

विरद् *vi-√rad*, P. *-radati*, to rend asunder, sever, RV. i, 61, 12; to open to, bestow on, vii, 62, 3.

विरद *virada*. See *viruda*.

विरप्श् *vi-√rapś*, Ā. *-rapśate*, to be full to overflowing, abound in (gen.), have too much of (instr.), RV.; AV. °**rapśá**, mf(*ī*)n. copious, abundant, RV. i, 8, 8; m. superabundance, ib. iv, 50, 3 &c. °**rapśin**, mfn. copious, exuberant, powerful, mighty, RV.; AV.; VS.

विरम् *vi-√ram*, P. *-ramati* (rarely Ā.; cf. Pāṇ. i, 3, 83), to stop (esp. speaking), pause, cease, come to an end, TS. &c. &c.; to give up, abandon, abstain or desist from (abl.), KātySr.; MBh. &c.: Caus. *-rāmayati*, to cause to stop or rest &c., bring to an end, finish, R.; BhP.: Desid., see *vi-riraṅsā*.

Vi-rata, mfn. stopped, ceased, ended, R.; Kālid. &c. (n. impers., e.g. *viratam vācā*, 'the speech ended,' Kathās.); one who has given up or resigned or ceased or desisted from (abl., loc., or comp.), MBh.; Kāv. &c.; *-tva*, n. the having come to an end, cessation, Sāh.; *-prasaṅga*, mfn. one who has ceased from being occupied in (loc.), Kum. iii, 47; °*tâśaya*, mfn. one whose desires have ceased or who has resigned worldly intentions, MW. °**rati**, f. cessation, pause, stop, end (ibc. = finally), Kāv.; Kathās. &c.; end of or cæsura within a Pāda, Śrutab.; resignation, desistence or abstention from (abl., loc., or comp.), Kāv.; Vedântas.; ŚārṅgS.

Vi-rama, m. cessation, end, MBh.; BhP.; sunset, Śiś. ix, 11; (ifc.) desistence or abstention from, MBh. °**ramaṇa**, n. ceasing, cessation, KātySr.; (ifc.) desistence from, Subh. °**ramita**, mfn. (fr. Caus.) made to cease, stopped, BhP.

Vi-rāma, m. cessation, termination, end, Śāṅkh-Gṛ.; Mn. &c. (acc. with √*yā* or *pra-√yā*, to come to an end, rest); end of a word or sentence, stop, pause (ifc. = ending with), APrāt.; Pāṇ. &c.; end of or cæsura within a Pāda, Śrutab.; (in gram.) 'the stop,' N. of a small oblique stroke placed under a consonant to denote that it is quiescent, i. e. that it has no vowel inherent or otherwise pronounced after it (this mark is sometimes used in the middle of conjunctions of consonants; but its proper use, according to native grammarians, is only as a stop at the end of a sentence ending in a consonant); desistence, abstention, Kāś.; Vop.; exhaustion, languor, Car.; N. of Vishṇu, MBh.; of Śiva, Śivag.; *-tā*, f. cessation, abatement, Pañcar. °**rāmaka**, mfn. ending in (ifc.), L. °**rāmaṇa**, n. a pause, Hcat.

Vi-riraṅsā, f. (fr. Desid.) the wish to cease or desist from, Subh.

विरल *virala*, mf(*ā*)n. (perhaps from *vira* = *vila* for *bila* + *la*, 'possessing holes') having interstices, separated by intervals (whether of space or time), not thick or compact, loose, thin, sparse, wide apart, MBh.; Kāv. &c.; rare, scarcely found, unfrequent, scanty, few, Kāv.; Kathās. &c. (ibc. and *am*, ind. sparsely, rarely, seldom; *viralaḥ* with or without *ko 'pi*, one here and there); n. sour curds (= *dadhi*), L. — **jānuka**, m. 'having knees wide apart,' a bandy-legged man, L. — **tā**, f. rareness, scarcity, Veṇis. — **dravā**, f. gruel made of rice or other grain with the addition of ghee &c., Suśr. — **druma**, mfn. (a wood) consisting of trees planted sparsely, Hariv. — **pātaka**, mfn. rarely committing crimes, sinning rarely, Vet. — **pārśvaga**, mfn. having a scanty retinue, Rājat. — **bhakti**, mfn. of little variety, monotonous, Ragh. — **sasya-yuta**, mfn. scantily furnished with grain, VarBṛS. **Viralâgata**, mfn. happening rarely, rare, MW. **Viralâṅguli**, mfn. (feet) having the toes wide apart, VarBṛS. **Viralâtapa-cchavi**, mfn. (a day) having little sunshine, Śiś. **Viralêtara**, mfn. 'other than wide apart,' dense, thick, close, L.

Viralāya, Nom. P. °*yate*, to be thin or rare, to become clearer (as a wood), Kād.

Viralikā, f. a kind of thin cloth, L.

Viralita, mfn. not dense or close (in *a-v°*), Uttarar.

Viralī-√kṛi, P. *-karoti*, to scatter, disperse, Siṅhâs. (*-kṛita*, mfn., Hariv.); to make clearer (a wood), Kād.

विरव *vi-rava*. See under *vi-√1. ru*.

विरस् *vi-√1. ras*, P. *-rasati*, to cry out, yell, shriek, Hariv.; Bhaṭṭ.

विरस *vi-rasa* &c. See p. 952, col. 1.

विरह् *vi-√rah*, P. *-rahayati* (inf. *-rahitum*; ind. p. *-rahayya*), to abandon, desert, relinquish, leave, SāṅkhGṛ.; R.; BhP.

Vi-raha, m. abandonment, desertion, parting, separation (esp. of lovers), absence from (instr. or comp.), MBh.; Kāv. &c.; lack, want (ifc. = lacking, with the exception of), Kāv.; Kathās. &c.; *-guṇita*, mfn. increased by separation, Megh.; *-ja*, mfn. arising from s°, Śak.; *-janita*, mfn. id., MW.; *-jvara*, m. the anguish of s°, ib.; *-virasa*, mfn. painful through (the idea of) separation, Śāntiś.; *-vyāpad*, mfn. decreased by s°, Megh.; *-śayana*, n. a solitary couch or bed, Megh.; °*hâdhigama*, m. experiencing s°, ib.; °*hânala*, m. the fire of s°, ib.; °*hârta*, mfn. pained by s°, W.; °*hâvasthā*, f. state of s°, MW.; °*hôtkaṇṭhikā*, f. (in dram.) a woman who longs after her absent lover or husband, Sāh.; °*hôtsuka*, mfn. suffering from s°, A. °**rahita**, mfn. abandoned, deserted, solitary, lonely, separated or free from, deprived of (instr., gen., or comp.), MBh.; Kāv. &c.; (*āt*), ind. with the exception of (gen.), Karaṇḍ. °**rahin**, mfn. separated, parted (esp. from a beloved person), lonely, solitary, Kāv.; Kathās. &c.; absent, Bhartṛ.; (ifc.) abstaining from, Sarvad.; (*iṇī*), f. a woman separated from her husband or lover, W.; wages, hire, ib.; °*ṇī-mano-vinoda*, m. N. of wk. °**rahī-√kṛi**, P. *-karoti*, to separate from (instr.), R.

विराज् *vi-√rāj*, P. Ā. *-rājati*, °*te*, to reign, rule, govern, master (gen. or acc.), excel (abl.), RV.; AV.; Br.; to be illustrious or eminent, shine forth, shine out (abl.), glitter, ChUp.; Mn.; MBh. &c.; to appear as (nom.), MBh.: Caus. *-rājayati*, (rarely °*te*) cause to shine forth, give radiance or lustre, brighten, illuminate, MBh.; R. &c.

2. **Vi-rā́j**, mfn. (for 1. see p. 949, col. 3) ruling far and wide, sovereign, excellent, splendid, RV.; mfn. a ruler, chief, king or queen (applied to Agni, Sarasvatī, the Sun &c.), ib.; AV.; VS.; Br.; MBh.; f. excellence, pre-eminence, high rank, dignity, majesty, TS.; Br.; ŚrS.; m. or f. the first progeny of Brahmā (according to Mn. i, 32 &c., Brahmā having divided his own substance into male and female, produced from the female the male power Virāj, who then produced the first Manu or Manu Svāyambhuva, who then created the ten Prajā-patis; the BhP. states that the male half of Brahmā was Manu, and the other half Śata-rūpā, and does not allude to the intervention of V°; other Purāṇas describe the union of Śata-rūpā with V° or Purusha in the first instance, and with Manu in the second; Virāj as a sort of secondary creator, is sometimes identified with Prajā-pati, Brahmā, Agni, Purusha, and later with Vishṇu or Kṛishṇa, while in RV. x, 90, 5 he is represented as born from Purusha, and Purusha from him; in the AV. viii, 10, 24; xi, 8, 30, V° is spoken of as a female, and regarded as a cow; being elsewhere, however, identified with Prāṇa), IW. 22 &c.; (in Vedânta) N. of the Supreme Intellect located in a supposed aggregate of gross bodies (= *vaiśvānara*, q. v.), Vedântas.; m. a warrior (= *kshatriya*), MBh.; BhP.; the body, MW.; a partic. Ekāha, PañcavBr.; Vait.; N. of a son of Priya-vrata and Kāmyā, Hariv.; of a son of Nara, VP.; of Buddha,

L.; of a son of Rādhā, MW.; of a district, ib.; f. a particular Vedic metre consisting of four Pādas of ten syllables each (and therefore also a symbolical N. of the number 'ten;' in RV. x, 130, 5 this metre is represented as attaching itself to Mitra and Varuṇa, and in AitBr. i, 4 Virāj is mystically regarded as 'food,' and invocations are directed to be made in this metre when food is the especial object of prayer; in prosody V° is applied to any metre defective by two syllables, RPrāt.); pl. N. of partic. bricks (40 in number), VS.; ŚBr.

Vi-rāja, mfn. shining, brilliant, Pañcar.; m. a partic. form of a temple, Hcat.; a part. Ekāha, Vait.; a species of plant, L.; N. of a Prajā-pati, Hariv.; of a son of A-vikshit, MBh. **°rājana,** mfn. embellishing, beautifying (ifc.), Car.; n. ruling, being eminent or illustrious, &c.; Nir. **°rājita,** mfn. eminent, illustrious, brilliant, splendid, glorious, MBh.; Kāv. etc. **°rājin,** mfn. splendid, brilliant, MBh. **°rājñī,** f. a female ruler, queen, TBr. **°rājya,** n. reign, dominion, MaitrUp.

Virāṭ, in comp. for 2. *vi-rāj.* **—kāmā,** f. a kind of Vedic metre, RPrāt. **—krama,** m. pl. a partic. religious observance, ĀpŚr. **—kshetra,** n. N. of a district, Cat. **—tva,** n. the being ten or tenfold (from the metre Virāj containing 10 syllables), AitBr. **—pūrvā,** f. N. of a metre, RPrāt. **—su,** n. (with *Vāmadevya*) N. of a Sāman, L. **—suta,** m. 'son of Virāj,' N. of a class of deceased ancestors (also called Soma-sads), Mn. iii, 195. **—sthānā,** f. a partic. Vedic form of the Trishṭubh metre, RPrāt. **—svarāja,** m. a partic. Ekāha, ŚāṅkhŚr. **—svarūpa,** mfn. consisting of Virāj (applied to the supreme Being), MW.

Virāṭa, m. N. of one of the midland or northwest districts of India (perhaps Berar), VarBṛS.; N. of an ancient king of a particular district in India, (the Pāṇḍavas being obliged to live in concealment during the thirteenth year of their exile, journeyed to the court of this king and entered his service in various disguises), MBh.; Hariv. &c.; N. of Buddha, L. **—ja,** m. = *rāja-paṭṭa,* a sort of inferior diamond (said to be found in the country Virāṭa), L.; (*ā*), f. N. of a daughter of king Virāṭa, MBh. **—nagara,** n. the city of the Virāṭas, MBh. (cf. Pāṇ. vi, 2, 89, Sch.) **—parvan,** n. N. of the fourth book of the Mahābhārata (describing the adventures of the Pāṇḍu princes when living in the service of king Virāṭa).

Virāṭaka, m. a diamond of inferior quality, MW.

Virāḍ, in comp. for 2. *vi-rāj.* **—ashṭama** (*virāḍ-*), mfn. having the metre Virāj in the eighth place, ŚBr. **—deha,** m. 'having the body of Virāj,' N. of the Universe, MW. **—rūpā,** f. a Vedic form of the Trishṭubh metre, RPrāt. **—varṇa,** mf(*ā*)n. having the form of the metre Virāj, ŚāṅkhBr.

विराणिन् *vi-rāṇin.* See under *vi-√2. raṇ.*

विरातक *virātaka,* m. Terminalia Arunja, L.; the fruit of Semecarpus Anacardium, L.

विराध् *vi-√rādh,* P. *-rādhyati,* to hurt, injure, Śiś.; (only aor. Ā. *-rādhishi*), to lose, be deprived of (instr.), AV.; ChUp.: Caus. *-rādhayati,* to become disunited, be at variance, disagree, PañcavBr. (cf. *a-virādhayat*).

Vi-rāddha, mfn. opposed, thwarted, offended, reviled, abused, W. **°rāddhṛi,** mfn. opposing, thwarting; an injurer, offender, Śiś.

Vi-rādha, m. thwarting, opposition, vexation, W.; N. of a Rākshasa, Hariv.; R. &c.; of a Dānava, Hariv.; *-gupta,* m. N. of a man, Mudr.; *-han,* m. 'slayer of Virādha,' N. of Indra or Vishṇu, Pañcar. **°rādhana,** n. failure, want of success, AV.; injury, offence, L.; (*ā*), f. hurt, injury, Śil. **°rādhaya** (fr. Caus.), g. *brāhmaṇâdi.* **°rādhāna** (?), n. hurt, pain, L. **°rādhya,** mfn. to be lost, anything of which one is to be deprived, Jātakam.

विराल *virāla,* m. = *viḍāla,* a cat, W.

विराव *vi-rāva* &c. See under *vi-√1. ru.*

विरावृत्त *virāvṛitta* (?), n. black pepper, L.

विराषह् *virā-shāh,* mfn. (nom. *-shāṭ; vira* prob. for *vīrā*) subduing or confining or harbouring men (applied to Yama's heaven), RV. i, 35, 6.

विरिच् *vi-√ric,* Pass. *-ricyate,* to reach or extend beyond (aor. *-reci*), RV. iv, 16, 5; to be emptied or purged, Lāṭy.: Caus. *-recayati,* to empty, drain, MBh.; to purge, Suśr.; to emit, Nīlak.

Vi-rikta, mfn. evacuated, emptied, purged, Mn.; Suśr. **°rikti,** f. purging, Car.

Vi-reka, m. purging, evacuation of the bowels, Suśr.; making the head clear, Car.; a purgative, cathartic, Suśr.

Vi-recaka, mfn. purgative; not accompanied by breath-exhalation (in this sense *vi* is priv.), Vām. ii, 2, 8 (in a quotation). **°recana,** mfn. opening, Suśr.; m. Careya Arborea or Salvadora Persica, L.; n. purging or any purging substance, Suśr.; a means for making the head clear, Car.; *-dravya,* n. any purging substance or medicine, Suśr. **°recita,** mfn. (fr. Caus.) purged, emptied, evacuated, W. **°recin,** mfn. purgative, L. **°recya,** mfn. to be purged.

विरिञ्च *viriñca,* m. (perhaps fr. *√ric;* but cf. *virañca*) N. of Brahmā (but also applied to Vishṇu and Śiva), MBh.; Kathās.; Pur. (*-tā,* f., BhP.)

Viriñcana, m. N. of Brahmā, L.

Viriñci, m. = *viriñca,* MBh.; BhP.; Sarvad.; N. of a poet, Cat. **—gola,** m. or n. (?) N. of a mythical place, Virac. **—nātha,** m. N. of an author (*°thīya,* n. his wk.), Cat. **—pāda-śuddha,** m. N. of a pupil of Śaṃkarâcārya, Cat.

Viriñcya, m. N. of Brahmā, BhP. (accord. to Sch. also 'N. of Brahmā's world').

विरिभ *vi-ribdha,* m. (*√ribh*) a note, tone, sound, Śiś. xi, 41 (cf. Pāṇ. vii, 2, 18).

Vi-ribhita and **vi-rebhita,** mfn., Pāṇ. vii, 2, 18, Sch.

विरिरंसा *vi-riraṃsā.* See under *vi-√ram.*

विरिष्ट *vi-rishṭa,* mfn. (*√riś;* cf. *vi-lishṭa*) rent asunder, broken, disordered, AV.; TS.

विरु *vi-√1. ru,* P. *-ruvati, -ravati, -rauti,* to roar aloud, cry, buzz, hum, yell, sing, lament, &c., Kāv.; Kathās. &c.; cry or call to, invoke, Bhaṭṭ.: Caus. *-rāvayati,* to roar or scream aloud, Mn. iv, 64.

Vi-ravá, m. roaring, thundering, RV. **°rāva,** m. crying, clamour, sound, noise, buzzing, humming, MBh.; Kāv. &c.; N. of a horse, MBh. **°rāvaṇa,** mfn. (fr. Caus.) causing clamour or roar, R. **°rāvita,** mfn. (fr. id.) made to resound, filled with noise, VarBṛS. **°rāvin,** mfn. shouting, roaring, crying, singing, lamenting, MBh.; R. &c.; sounding, resounding, R.; VarBṛS.; m. N. of a son of Dhṛitarāshṭra, MBh.; (*iṇī*), f. weeping, crying, W.; a broom, ib.; N. of a river, ib.

Vi-ruta, mfn. roared, cried, &c.; invoked, VarBṛS.; made to resound, filled with the cries &c. of (instr. or comp.), R.; BhP.; n. shrieking, howling, yelling, humming, chirping, &c., any noise or sound, Mn.; R. &c. **°ruti,** f. screaming, howling, Kād.; Mudr.

विरुच् *vi-√ruc,* Ā. *-rocate* (pf. *-rurucuḥ,* RV.; aor. *vy-arucat,* Ragh.; Kathās.; Bhaṭṭ.), to shine forth, be bright or radiant or conspicuous or visible, RV. &c. &c.; to appear as or like (nom.), MBh.; to outshine, excel (acc.), ib.; to please, delight (gen.), R.; (only pf. P.) to cause to shine, illuminate, RV. iv, 7, 1; x, 122, 5: Caus. *-rocayati,* to cause to shine, brighten, illuminate, RV.; BhP.; to find pleasure in, delight in (acc.), R.; Hariv.

Vi-rúkmat, mfn. shining, brilliant, bright, RV.; m. a bright weapon or ornament, ib.

Vi-ruca, m. a magic formula recited over weapons, R.

Vi-roká, m. shining, gleaming, effulgence, RV.; a ray of light, L.; (also n.) a hole, aperture, cavity, chasm, L. (cf. *nāsā-viroka*). **°rokin,** mfn. shining, radiant, RV.

Vi-rócana, mfn. shining upon, brightening, illuminating, MBh.; m. the sun or the god of the sun (also applied to Vishṇu), MBh.; Rājat.; the moon, MBh. ix, 2025; fire, L.; a species of Karañja, L.; a species of Śyonāka, L.; N. of an Asura (son of Prahrāda or Prahlāda and father of Bali and Mantharā or Dīrgha-jihvā), AV. &c. &c.; (*ā*), f. N. of one of the Mātṛis attendant on Skanda, MBh.; of the wife of Tvashṭṛi (and mother of Viraja), BhP.; n. (?) light, lustre, W.; *-vadha,* m. N. of a ch. of the GaṇP.; *-suta,* m. 'son of Virocana,' N. of Bali (sovereign of Mahābali-pura), W. **°rocishṇu,** mfn. shining, bright, Mn. i, 77; illuminating, making visible, W.

विरुज् *vi-√1. ruj,* P. *-rujati,* to break to pieces, tear asunder, crush, destroy, RV. &c. &c.

Vi-rugṇa, mfn. (less correctly *vi-rugna*) broken to pieces, torn asunder &c., Bhaṭṭ.

2. **Vi-ruja,** mfn. (for 1. see p. 952, col. 1) breaking, rending, causing pain, PārGṛ. **°rojana,** n. the act of breaking or tearing asunder, ĀpŚr., Sch.

विरुद् *vi-√rud,* P. *-roditi,* to weep or cry aloud, sob, lament, bewail, MBh.; BhP. **°rudita,** n. loud lamentation, wailing, grief, Uttarar.

विरुद *viruda,* m. (also written *biruda* and *birada*) a laudatory poem, panegyric (on a prince, in prose or verse), Sāh.; Pratāp.; crying, proclaiming, W. **—dhvaja,** m. a royal banner, R. (B.) **—maṇi-mālā,** f. N. of a poem (quoted in Sāh.)

Virudâvali (or **°lī**), f. a detailed panegyric, Vcar.; N. of a poem by Raghu-deva (celebrating the praises of a certain king of Mithilā).

विरुध् *vi-√1. rudh* (only in *-ródhat,* RV. i, 67, 9), to shoot forth.

विरुध् *vi-√2. rudh,* P. Ā. *-ruṇaddhi, -runddhe,* (P.) to hinder, obstruct, invest, besiege, R.; to close, Ṛitus.; (Ā.) to encounter opposition from (instr.), TS.: Pass. *-rudhyate* (m.c. also *°ti*), to be impeded or checked or kept back or withheld, R.; Kathās. &c.; to be opposed, to contend with (instr. with or without *saha,* gen., loc., or acc. with *prati*), MBh.; Kāv. &c.; to be at variance with or contradictory to (instr.), MBh.; BhP.; to fail, MBh.: Caus. *-rodhayati* (rarely *°te*), to set at variance, disunite, MBh.; R.; to oppose, encounter, fight against or contend, with (acc., rarely gen.); to object to (acc.), MBh. x, 180: Desid. *-rurutsati,* to wish to commence hostility, MBh.

Vi-ruddha, mfn. opposed, hindered, restrained, arrested, kept back, R.; Kalid. &c.; surrounded, blockaded, W.; forbidden, prohibited, Mn.; MBh. &c.; doubtful, uncertain, precarious, dangerous, MBh.; R.; hostile, adverse, at variance or at enmity with (instr., gen., or comp.), MBh.; Kāv. &c.; unpleasant, disagreeable, odious or hateful to (comp.), R.; Kathās.; disagreeing (as food), Bhpr.; contrary, repugnant, contrasted, reverse, inconsistent or incompatible with, excluded from (gen., instr., or comp.), KātyŚr.; Mn.; MBh. &c.; (*am*), ind. perversely, incongruously, MW.; m. pl. N. of a class of gods under the tenth Manu, Pur.; n. opposition, hostility, repugnance, MW.; (scil. *rūpaka*) a figure of speech in which an object compared to another object is said to lack its functions and to possess others not properly belonging to it (e.g. 'the moon of thy face does not rise in the sky, but only takes away my life'), Kāvyâd. ii, 84; N. of a wk. on Nyāya; *-grantha-pūrva-paksha-rahasya,* n., *-grantha-rahasya,* n. N. of wks.; *-tā,* f.; *-tva,* n. hostility, enmity, opposition, contrariety, incompatibility, Rājat.; Pañcat.; Sarvad.; *-dhī,* mfn. malevolently disposed, malignant, Rājat.; *-pūrva-paksha-grantha-ṭīkā,* f., *-pūrva-paksha-granthâloka,* m. N. of wks.; *-prasaṅga,* m. prohibited or unlawful occupation, Yājñ.; *-bhuj,* mfn. eating incompatible or unsuitable food, W.; *-bhojana,* n. incompatible food, ib.; *-mati-kārin,* mfn. suggesting contradictory notions, Sāh.; *°ri-tā,* f. a figure of speech which (by using ambiguous words) suggests contradictory notions (e.g. *vidadhāti galagraham,* 'she gives an embrace,' where the word *gala-graha* means also 'a disease of the throat'), Sāh.; Kpr.; *-mati-kṛit,* mfn. (= *-kārin*), Kpr.; Pratāp.; n. (= *-kāri-tā*), ib.; *-lakshaṇa,* n. N. of a ch. of the PSarv.; *-śaṃsana,* n. malignant or abusive language (= *gāli*), L.; *-sambandhanīya,* mfn. (in law) allied or kin in a forbidden degree; *-siddhânta-grantha-ṭīkā,* f., *-siddhânta-grantha-rahasya,* n., *-siddhânta-granthâloka,* m. N. of wks.; *°ddhârtha,* mfn. containing a contradiction (*-tā,* f.), Kāvyâd.; (*°tha-dīpika,* n. a partic. figure of speech in which seemingly contradictory functions are attributed to one and the same object, Kāvyâd. ii, 109); *°ddhâcarana,* n. wrong or improper course of conduct, MW.; *°ddhânna* or *°ddhâśana,* n. incompatible or forbidden food, Suśr.; *°ddhôkti,* f. adverse or contradictory speech, quarrel, dispute, L.; *°ddhôpakrama,* mfn. (in medicine) applying incompatible remedies (*-tva,* n.), Suśr.

Vi-roddhavya, mfn. to be opposed or contended with, Pañcat.; n. (impers.) it is to be contended or fought, Kathās. **°roddhṛi,** mfn. contending, fighting (in *a-vir°*), MBh.

Vi-rodha, m. opposition, hostility, quarrel, strife between (gen., rarely instr., or comp.) or with (instr. with or without *saha,* or comp.), MBh.; Kāv. &c.; hostile contact of inanimate objects (as of planets &c.), VarBṛS.; (logical) contradiction, contrariety, antithesis, inconsistency, incompatibility, KātyŚr.; Kaṇ.; Kap. &c.; (ifc.) conflict with, injury of (instr. = at the cost or to the detriment of), Yājñ.; MBh. &c.; hindrance, prevention, Gaut.; blockade, siege, W.; adversity, calamity, misfortune, Sāh.; perversity, Kathās.; (in rhet.) an apparent contradiction or incongruity (e.g. *bharato 'pi śatru-ghnaḥ*), Kpr.; (in dram.) impediment to the successful progress of a plot, W.; (*ī*), f. fixed rule, ordinance (?), W.; *-kāraka*, mfn. causing opposition or disagreement, fomenting quarrels, MW.; *-krit*, mfn. causing dissension or revolt, Yājñ., Sch.; m. an enemy, MW.; the 45th year in Jupiter's cycle of 60 years, Cat.; *-kriyā*, f. quarrel, strife, Ragh.; *-parihāra*, m. removal of incompatibility, reconciliation, Kull. on Mn. vii, 152; N. of a wk. on Bhakti (by Lakshmaṇâcārya); of another wk. on the reconciliation of the different Vaishṇava-systems (by Varadâcārya); *-phala*, n. the fruit or result of perverseness, Kathās.; *-bhañjanī*, f. N. of a commentary on the Rāmâyaṇa; *-bhāj*, mfn. contradictory, opposed to (instr.), Sāh.; *-vat*, mfn. containing a contradiction, Kāvyâd.; *-varūthinī*, f., *-varūthinī-nirodha*, m., *-varūthinī-bhañjinī*, f., *-vāda*, m. N. of wks.; *-śamana*, n. making up a quarrel, Daśar.; °*dhâcarana*, n. hostile conduct, L.; °*dhâbhāsa*, m. (in rhet.) apparent contradiction, the semblance of opposite qualities, Pratāp.; °*dhâlaṃkāra*, m. (in rhet.) a figure of speech implying incongruity (cf. under *vi-rodha*), MW.; °*dhôkti*, f. dispute, mutual contradiction, Pāṇ. i, 3, 50, Sch.; °*dhôddhāra*, m. N. of wk.; °*dhôpamā*, f. (in rhet.) a comparison founded on opposition (e.g. 'the lotus flower and thy face are opposed [as rivals] to each other,' i.e. resemble each other), Kāvyâd. ii, 33. °**rodhaka**, mfn. disuniting, causing dissension or revolt, Yājñ., Sch.; opposed to, incompatible with (gen. or comp.), MBh.; (ifc.) preventing, an obstacle to, ib. °**rodhana**, mfn. opposing, fighting, MBh.; n. checking, restraining, Nir. vi, 1 (Sch.); quarrel, contest, resistence, opposition to (gen.), Kām.; Kathās. &c.; harming, injuring, R.; (in dram.) either 'angry altercation' (e.g. in Śak. the dialogue between the king and Śārṅgarava), Bhar.; or 'consciousness of the risk of an enterprise' (e.g. Veṇīs. 6, 1), Sāh.; incongruity, inconsistency, W.; investing, blockading, ib.

Vi-rodhi, in comp. for **vi-rodhin**; *-grantha*, m. N. of wk.; *-tā*, f. enmity, hatred, strife, quarrel between (comp.) or with (*saha*), Kāv.; Kathās. &c.; obstinacy, restiveness (of a horse), VarBṛS.; contradictoriness, Sāh.; *-tva*, n. withdrawal, removal, Kap., Sch.; *-nirodha*, m., *-purusha-kāra*, m. N. of wks.; *-yodha*, m. a hostile warrior, Rājat.; *-vicāra*, m. N. of wk. °**rodhita**, mfn. (fr. Caus.) opposed, contended against or fought with, Mṛicch.; injured, impaired, R.; refused (see *a-virodhita*).

Vi-rodhin, mfn. opposing, hindering, preventing, obstructing, excluding, disturbing, Gobh.; Mn. &c.; obstructive (see *a-v*°), besieging, blockading, W.; dispelling, removing, Śak. (v.l.); adverse, hostile, inimical (often ifc. = foe or enemy of), MBh.; Kāv. &c.; disagree[ing] (as food), Bhpr.; opposed, contradictory, incon[sist]ent, Kaṇ.; MBh.; Rājat.; rivalling with, equalling, Kāvyâd.; contentious, quarrelsome, W.; m. N. of the 25th year of Jupiter's cycle of 60 years, VarBṛS.; (*inī*), f. a woman who causes enmity or promotes quarrel (between husband and wife &c.), MW.; N. of a female demon (daughter of Duḥsaha), MārkP.

Vi-rodhya, mfn. to be disunited or set at variance, MBh.; to be opposed or contended against, MW.

विरुष् *vi-√rush* (only pr. p. Ā. *-rushyamāṇa*), to be much irritated, be very angry with (gen.), Hariv. °**rushṭa**, mfn. very angry, wrathful, Caurap.

विरुह् *vi-√ruh*, P. *-rohati*, to grow out, shoot forth, sprout, bud, RV.; AV.; TBr.: Caus. *-rohayati* or *-ropayati*, to cause to grow, RV. viii, 91, 5; to thrust out, remove, expel, MBh.: Pass. *-ropyate*, to be planted, R.; to be caused to grow over, healed (see *vi-ropita*).

Vi-rūḍha, mfn. shot out, sprouted, budded, grown, ŚBr. &c. &c.; come forth, formed, produced, born, arisen, Āpast.; BhP.; ascended, mounted, ridden, MBh.; *-tṛiṇâṅkura*, mf(*ā*)n. overgrown with young grass, Mṛicch.; *-bodha*, mfn. one whose intelligence has increased or is matured, BhP. °**rūḍhaka**, m. n. grain that has begun to sprout, Suśr.; m. N. of a prince of the Kumbhâṇḍas, Lalit. (cf. MWB. 206; 220); N. of a Loka-pāla, Buddh.; of a son of Prasenajit (enemy of the Śākyas), ib.; of a son of Ikshvāku, ib. °**rūḍhi**, f. shooting forth, sprouting, L.

Vi-ropaṇa, mfn. (fr. Caus.) causing to grow, planting, MW.; causing to grow over, healing, Śak.; n. the act of planting, VarBṛS.; the act of healing (cf. *vraṇa-viropaṇa*). °**ropita**, mfn. caused to grow, planted, MW.; caused to grow over, healed; *-vraṇa*, mfn. one whose wound is healed or cicatrized, Daś.

Vi-rohá, m. growing out, shooting forth, MaitrS.; VarBṛS.; BhP.; 'place of growth,' source, origin, ib. °**rohaṇa**, mfn. causing to grow over or heal, Śak. (v.l. for *vi-ropaṇa*); m. N. of a serpent-demon, MBh.; growing out, shooting forth, budding, ŚrS.; MBh.; VarBṛS. °**rohin**, mfn. shooting forth, sprouting, budding, Suśr.

विरूक्षण *vi-rūkshaṇa*, mf(*ī*)n. (√*rūksh*) making rough or dry, drying, astringent, Suśr.; the act of making rough &c., acting as an astringent, ib.; censure, blame, imprecation, L. °**rūkshaṇīya**, mfn. fit for making rough, astringent, Car.; to be blamed or reviled, Vcar. °**rūkshita**, mfn. made rough &c.; smeared over, covered, VarBṛS.

विरुज *virūja*, m. N. of an Agni supposed to be in water, MantraBr.

विरूप *ví-rūpa*, mf(*ā*)n. many-coloured, variegated, multiform, manifold, various, RV.; TS.; Br.; Kauś.; varied, altered, changed, AitBr.; different, Pāṇ., Vārtt. (with *ekârtha*, 'different in form but the same in meaning;' ifc. 'different from,' Sāṃkhyak.); deformed, misshapen, ugly, monstrous, unnatural, ChUp.; MBh. &c.; less by one, minus one, VarBṛS.; m. jaundice, Gal.; N. of Śiva, MBh. (cf. *virūpa-cakshus* and *virūpâksha*); N. of an Asura, MBh.; Hariv.; of a son of the demon Parivarta, MārkP.; of an Āṅgirasa (author of RV. viii, 43; 44; 75; father of Pṛishad-aśva and son of Ambarisha; pl. the family of the Virūpas), RV.; MBh.; Pur.; of a son of Kṛishṇa, BhP.; of one of the descendants of Manu Vaivasvata, MW.; of a prince, W.; of two teachers, Buddh.; (*ā*), f. Alhagi Maurorum, L.; Aconitum Ferox, L.; N. of the wife of Yama, W.; (with Buddhists) N. of a Tantra deity, Kālac.; n. deformity, irregular or monstrous shape, W.; difference of form, variety of nature or character, ib.; the root of Piper Longum, L.; *-karaṇa*, mf(*ī*)n. disfiguring, BhP.; n. the act of disfiguring, R.; BhP.; inflicting an injury, Pañcat.; *-cakshus*, mfn. 'diversely-eyed,' N. of Śiva, MBh.; *-tas*, ind. like Virūpa or the Virūpas, RV.; *-tā*, f. manifoldness, variety, Sarvad.; deformity, ugliness, MBh.; R.; *-rūpa*, mfn. of deformed or monstrous shape, misshapen, MBh.; R.; *-śakti*, m. N. of a Vidyā-dhara, Kathās.; *-śarman*, m. N. of a Brāhman, ib.; °*pâksha*, mf(*ī*)n. 'diversely-eyed,' having deformed eyes (compar. *-tara*), PārGṛ.; R.; Kum.; having various occupations, Vās. (Sch.); m. N. of a partic. divine being, MānGṛ. (also *ī*, f. N. of a tutelary deity, Cat.); of Śiva (as represented with an odd number of eyes, one being in his forehead; cf. *tri-locana*), Vās.; of one of Śiva's attendants, Hariv.; of a Rudra, MBh.; of a Yaksha, Kathās.; of a Dānava, MBh.; of a Rākshasa, ib.; R.; of a serpent-demon, Lalit.; of a Loka-pāla, L.; of the author of VS. xii, 30, Ānukr.; of a teacher of Yoga, Cat.; (with *śarman kavi-kaṇṭhâbharana ācārya*) of a philos. author (who wrote in the 16th cent. A.D.), ib.; °*pâksha-pañcâksharī*, f. N. of a Mantra; °*pâksha-pañcāśat*, f. N. of a Stotra; °*pâśva*, m. N. of a prince, MBh.

Vi-rūpaka, mf(*ikā*)n. deformed, ugly, frightful, hideous, Vet.; unseemly, improper, Kād.; m. 'Ugly,' N. of a man, Daś.; N. of an Asura, MBh.

Vi-rūpin, m. 'changing various colours,' a chameleon, L.

विरेक *vi-reka* &c. See under *vi-√ric*.

विरेपस् *vi-repas*, *vi-roga* &c. See p. 952, col. 1.

विरोलित *vi-rolita*, mfn. (prob. for *vi-lolita*, p. 986, col. 1) disordered, disturbed, L.

विल् *vil*, cl. 6. P. *vilati*, to cover, conceal, clothe, Dhātup. xxviii, 66; cl. 10. P. *velayati*, to throw, cast, send, ib. xxxii, 65 (cf. √*pil*); to break or divide (cf. √*bil*).

Vila &c. See *bila*.

विलक्ष् *vi-√laksh*, P. Ā. *-lakshayati*, °*te*, to distinguish, discern, observe, perceive, mark, notice, MBh.; BhP.; to lose sight of one's aim or object, become bewildered or perplexed or embarrassed, MBh.; Pañcat. 2. °**lakshaṇa**, n. (for 1. see p. 952, col. 1) the act of distinguishing, perceiving, seeing, observing, W. 2. °**lakshita**, mfn. (for 1. see ib., col. 2) distinguished, marked by (instr. or comp.), BhP.; perceived, observed, noticed, MBh.; confused, bewildered, ib.; Kathās.; vexed, annoyed, Uttarar.

विलग् *vi-√lag*, P. *-lagati*, to hang to, cling to, hold on to (loc.), Cat. 1. °**lagita**, mfn. attached to &c., MW. °**lagna**, mfn. clung or fastened or attached to, resting or hanging on, connected with (loc. or comp.), MBh.; Kāv. &c. (*tīra-vilagna*, come ashore, landed, Kathās.); pendulous, flaccid (as breasts), R.; hanging in a cage, caged (as a bird), ib.; gone by, passed away, Pañcat.; thin, slender, MBh.; Kum.; m. or n. the waist, middle (as connecting the upper and lower parts of the body), L.; n. the rising of constellations, a horoscope &c. (= *lagna*), Var.; *-madhyā*, f. a woman with a slender waist.

विलगित 2. *vi-lagita* or *vi-laṅgita*, mfn. (√*lāṅg*), Pāṇ. vi, 4, 24, Vārtt. 1, Pat. (*upatāpe*).

विलङ्घ् *vi-laṅgh*, P. Ā. *-laṅghati*, °*te* (aor. *vy-alaghishuḥ*, Śiś. xvii, 55), to leap, jump, rise up to (acc.), Śiś.; BhP.: Caus. *-laṅghayati*, to leap or jump over, cross, pass (time), traverse (a distance), overstep (bounds), MBh.; Kāv. &c.; to transgress, contemn, neglect, violate (commands &c.), Kāv.; Kathās.; to rise up, ascend to (acc.), MBh.; Kir.; to rise beyond, overcome, subdue, Kāv.; Kathās.; to excel, surpass, Kāvyâd.; to pass over, set aside, abandon, Ragh.; Kathās.; to act wrongly towards, offend, Śiś.; to cause to pass over (the right time for eating), cause to fast, Suśr. °**laṅghana**, n. leaping over, crossing, MBh.; striking against, Kir.; offence, injury, ib.; Kathās.; (also pl.) fasting, abstention from food, Suśr.; (*ā*), f. passing beyond, overcoming, surmounting, Rājat. °**laṅghanīya**, mfn. to be overstepped or passed over or transgressed, W. °**laṅghayitvā**, ind. having transgressed or missed (the proper time), having waited, MBh. °**laṅghita**, mfn. overleaped, overstepped, &c.; baffled, defied (as efforts), Ragh. v, 48; °*tâkāśa*, mfn. passing or rising beyond the sky, MW.; n. fasting, abstention from food, Suśr. °**laṅghin**, mfn. passing beyond, overstepping, transgressing, Ragh.; Kāvyâd.; ascending to, striking against, Kathās. °**laṅghya**, mfn. to be passed over or crossed (as a river), Kāv.; to be overcome or subdued, tolerable, Kathās.; N. of wk. (cf. *-lakshaṇa*); *-tā*, f. tolerableness, Rājat.; *-lakshaṇa*, n. N. of a treatise on the changes of *e* and *ai* before a following vowel.

विलज्ज् *vi-√lajj*, Ā. *-lajjate* (rarely P.), to become ashamed or abashed, blush, MBh.; Kāv. &c. °**lajjita**, mfn. ashamed, abashed, ib.

विलप् *vi-√lap*, P. *-lapati* (rarely Ā. inf. *-lapitum* or *-laptum*; pr. p. *-lapyat*, MBh. vii, 2681), to utter moaning sounds, wail, lament, bewail (acc. with or without *prati*), AV. &c. &c.; to speak variously, talk, chatter, MBh.; Hariv.: Caus. *-lāpayati*, °*te*, to cause to mourn or lament, AV. (cf. Pāṇ. i, 4, 52, Vartt. 3, Sch.); to cause to speak much (Ā.), Bhaṭṭ.: Intens. (only p. *-lālapat*), to talk idly, MaitrS. °**lapana**, n. wailing, lamenting, Uttarar.; Hit.; talking idly or wildly, W.; the dirt or sediment of any oily substance (as of clarified butter, &c.), Yājñ., Sch.; *-vinoda*, m. removing grief by weeping, Uttarar. °**lapita**, mfn. wailed, lamented, &c.; n. lamentation, wailing, MBh.; R. °**lāpa**, m. = prec. n., ib.; *-kusumâñjali*, m. N. of a poem. 1. °**lāpana**, mfn. (for 2. see under *vi-√lī*) causing moaning or lamentation (as a weapon), R.; Hariv.; m. N. of one of Śiva's attendants, Hariv.; n. the act of causing moaning or l°, MBh. xii, 6113 (= *nāśa*, Nilak.); m. c. = *vi-lapana*, wail, l°, BhP. °**lāpin**, mfn. wailing, lamenting, uttering moaning or inarticulate sounds, Śiś.

विलभ् *vi-√labh*, Ā. *-labhate*, to part asunder, separate, KātyŚr.; to take away, remove (dung from a stable), Kṛishis.; to procure, bestow, grant, consign, hand over, deliver up, Inscr.; Kathās.; Rājat. &c.; to choose, elect, HPariś.: Caus. *-lambhayati*, to cause to receive or fall to the share of (two acc.), Kathās.: Desid. *-lipsate*, to desire to divide or distribute, ŚBr. °**labdha**, mfn. parted asunder, &c.; given, bestowed, consigned, Kathās. °**labdhi**, f. taking away, removing, Krishis. °**lambha**, m. gift, donation, liberality, L. °**lābha**, mfn., °**lābhiman**, m., g. *dṛiḍhâdi* (Kāś.)

विलम्ब् *vi-√lamb*, Ā. *-lambate* (rarely P.), to hang on both sides to (acc.), PañcavBr.; to hang down, hang on, be attached to (loc.), MBh.; R. &c.; to sink, set, decline, MBh.; to continue hanging, linger, delay, tarry, hesitate ('with' or 'to,' *prati*), Gaut.; MBh. &c.: Caus. *-lambayati*, to hang on (loc.), Pañcat. ii, $\frac{9}{3}\frac{3}{3}$ (read *-lambya* with B.); to cause to linger or loiter, detain, delay, Kathās.; to spend (time) unprofitably, waste, lose, Hariv.; to put off, procrastinate, Yājñ.; R.; Pañcat.

Vi-lamba, mfn. hanging down, pendulous (as arms), R.; m. hanging or falling down, pendulousness, W.; hanging for support, Śiś. iv, 25; slowness, tardiness, delay, procrastination (*āt*, 'with delay,' 'late;' *ena*, id., 'too late;' ibc. 'slowly'), Kāv.; Rājat. &c.; N. of the 32nd year in the 60 years' cycle of Jupiter, Cat.; *-sauparṇa*, n. N. of various Sāmans, PañcavBr. °**lambaka**, m. N. of a king, Kathās.; (*ikā*), f. a partic. form of indigestion (with retardation of the feces; accord. to some 'the last stage of exhaustion in cholera'), Suśr. °**lambana**, n. hanging down or from, depending, W.; (also *ā*, f.) slowness, delay, procrastination, MBh.; Kāv. &c. °**lambita**, mfn. hanging down, pendulous, Hariv.; Kāv.; (ifc.) dependent on, closely connected with, BhP.; delayed, retarded, loitering, tardy, slow, measured (in music opp. to *druta*, q. v.), MBh.; Kāv. &c.; (*am*), ind. slowly, tardily, ib.; m. a partic. class of heavy animals, L.; n. slowness, delay, procrastination (also impers. 'it has been delayed'), MBh.; Kāv. &c.; *-gati*, f. 'slow or tardy in motion,' N. of a metre, VarBṛS.; *-phala*, mfn. having the fruit or fulfilment delayed, MW. °**lambin**, mfn. hanging down, pendulous, hanging to or from, leaning against (loc. or comp.), Kāv.; VarBṛS.; Suśr. &c.; (ifc.) hung with, that from which anything hangs or falls down, MBh.; Pur.; tarrying, delaying, slow, reluctant, Śak. (v. l.); Gīt.; m. n. the 32nd year in the 60 years' cycle of Jupiter, VarBṛS.; (°*bi*)*-tā*, f. slowness, measuredness, L. °**lambya**, ind. having lingered or loitered, slowly, tardily, Rājat.; Kathās. (*a-vilambya*, 'without delay,' ib.)

विलय *vi-laya* &c. See *vi-√lī*, col. 3.

विलला *vilalā*, f. a sort of plant (=*śveta-balā*), L.

विलस् *vi-√las*, P. *-lasati*, to gleam, flash, glitter (only pr. p. *-lasat*, q. v., and pf. *-lalāsa*, Bhaṭṭ.); to shine forth, appear, arise, become visible, Śiś.; to sound forth, echo (see *vi-lasan*); to play, sport, dally, be amused or delighted, Kāv.; Kathās.; to vibrate, coruscate (see *vi-lasat*): Caus. *-lāsayati*, to cause to dance, Vās.

Vi-lasat, mf(*antī*)n. flashing, shining, glittering &c.; *-patāka*, mfn. having a gleaming or waving flag, MW.; *-saudāminī*, f. a flash of lightning, Bhartṛ.

Vi-lasan, in comp. for **vi-lasat**; *-marīci*, mfn. having rays of light gleaming or playing, MW.; *-megha-śabda*, m. the echoing sound of clouds (i. e. thunder), Kathās.

Vi-lasana, n. gleaming, flashing (of lightning), Megh.; play, sport, ib.; Daś. °**lasita**, mfn. gleaming, glittering, shining forth, appearing, BhP.; played, sported (n. also impers.), Kāv.; Kathās.; moving to and fro, BhP.; n. flashing, quivering (of lightning), Vikr.; Prab.; appearing, manifestation (*vidyā-v*°, manifestation of knowledge), Cat.; sport, play, pastime, dalliance, Kāv.; Kathās.; any action or gesture, Ragh.

Vi-lāsa, m. (ifc. f. *ā*) shining forth, appearance, manifestation, Ṛit.; Gīt.; sport, play, pastime, pleasure, diversion (esp. with women &c.; but also applied to any playful action or gesture), MBh.; Kāv. &c. (°*sāya*, 'for sport'); coquetry, affectation of coyness, wantonness (a form of feminine gesture considered as indicative of amorous sentiments), Hariv.; Kāv.; Daśar.; Sāh.; liveliness, joviality (considered as a masculine virtue), Daśar. ii, 9; wantonness, lust, Daśar.; Sāh.; grace, charm, beauty, BhP.; N. of a gram. wk.; (with *ācārya*) of a preceptor, Cat.; n. (and *ā*, f.) N. of a metre, VarBṛS.; *-kānana*, n. a pleasure-grove, L.; *-kodaṇḍa*, m. N. of the god of love, Vcar.; *-gṛiha*, n. a pl°-house, ib.; *-cāpa*, m. (=*-kodaṇḍa*), ib.; *-dolā*, f. a pl°-swing, Pañcat.; *-dhanvan*, m. (=*-kodaṇḍa*), Vcar.; *-pura*, n. N. of a town, Kathās.; *-bāṇa*, m. (=*-kodaṇḍa*), Vcar.; *-bhavana*, n. (=*-gṛiha*), Rājat.; *-bhitti*, f. a wall (only) in appearance, Vcar.; *-maṇi-darpaṇa*, m. a mirror set with jewels to play with, Rājat.; *-mandira*, n. (=*-gṛiha*), L.; *-maya*, mf(*ī*)n. full of grace, charming, Vcar.; *-mekhalā*, f. a toy-girdle (not a real one), Ragh.; *-rasikā*, f. N. of a Suraṅganā, Siṅhās.; *-vat*, mfn. sportive, playful, Sāh.; (*atī*), f. a wanton or coquettish woman, Kālid.; N. of various women, Vās.; Kād.; of a drama (quoted in Sāh.); *-vasati*, f. a pleasure resort, Kathās.; ŚārṅgP. (v. l.); *-vātāyana*, n. a pl°-balcony or terrace, Vcar.; *-vipina*, n. a pl°-grove, Prab.; *-vibhavānasa* (?), mfn. =*lubdha*, L.; *-vihāra*, m. a pl°-walk, promenading, Bhartṛ. (v. l.); *-veśman*, n. =*-gṛiha*, Kathās.; *-śayyā*, f. a pl°-couch, ib.; *-śīla*, m. N. of a king, ib.; *-sadman*, n. =*-gṛiha*, Vcar.; *-svāmin*, m. N. of a man, Inscr.; °*sêndra-gāminī*, f. N. of a Gandharvī, Kāraṇḍ. °**lāsaka**, mf(*ikā*)n. moving to and fro, dancing, fluttering, MBh.; (*ikā*), f. a kind of drama (in one act on any light subject or adventure), Sāh. °**lāsana**, n. (m. c. for *vi-lasana*) play, sport, dalliance, MBh. iii, 1829; fascination, W. °**lāsin**, mfn. shining, beaming, radiant, MBh.; moving to and fro, fluttering, ib.; wanton, sportive, playful, dallying with or fond of (comp.), R.; Ragh.; Dhūrtas.; coquettish, Ragh.; Gīt.; m. 'sporter,' a lover, husband, Kum.; Sāh. (L. also 'a sensualist; a serpent; fire; the moon; N. of Kṛishṇa, of Śiva, and of Kāma-deva'); (*inī*), f. a charming or lively or wanton or coquettish woman, wife, mistress (also °*nikā*, Pañcar.; °*nī-jana*, m., Śiś.); a kind of metre, VarBṛS.; N. of a woman, Kathās.; (°*si*)*-tā*, f., *-tva*, n. wantonness, playfulness, cheerfulness, Hariv.; Mālav.; Rājat.

विलात *vilāta*, mfn., g. *dṛiḍhâdi* (v. l. *vi-lābha*), Kāś.; (*ā*), f. a kind of bird, ib.

Vilātiman, m. (fr. prec.), ib.

विलातव्य *vi-lātavya*, *vi-lātṛi* &c. See *vi-√lī*, col. 3.

विलाल *vilāla*, m. (perhaps fr. √*lal*) = *yantra*, a machine, L.; =*bilāla*, a cat, W.

विलाषिन् *vi-lāshin*, mfn. (fr. √*lash*), Pāṇ. iii, 2, 144.

विलिख् *vi-√likh*, P. *-likhati* (Ved. inf. *-likhas*; cf. Pāṇ. iii, 4, 13, Sch.), to scratch, scrape, tear up, lacerate, Lāṭy.; MBh. &c.; to rub against, reach to, touch, Hariv.; to wound (the heart), i. e. vex, offend, ŚBr.; to scratch in or on, make a furrow or mark, write, delineate, paint, Gol.; MBh. &c.; (in medicine) to tear up, i. e. stir up (phlegm &c.), Car.: Caus. *-lekhayati* or *-likhāpayati*, to cause to scratch or write, Kṛishnaj.

Vi-likha, see *a-vilikha*. °**likhana**, n. the act of scraping, scratching &c., Bālar. °**likhita**, mfn. scratched, scraped, scarified, Pañcat.

Vi-lekha, m. scratching, tearing up, wounding, Śiś.; KātyŚr., Sch.; (*ā*), f. a scratch, furrow, mark, MBh.; Suśr.; a written contract, Nār. °**lekhana**, mfn. scratching, lacerating, Suśr.; n. the act of making an incision or mark or furrow, Dhātup.; scratching, wounding, lacerating, Gaut.; MBh.; the course (of a river), Hariv.; dividing, splitting, W.; digging, delving, rooting up, ib. °**lekhin**, mfn. scratching i. e. rubbing against, touching, reaching up to (ifc.), MBh.

विलिगी *viligī*, f. a kind of serpent, AV.

विलिनाथ *vili-nātha*, m. (with *kavi*) N. of a poet (author of the drama Madana-mañjarī), Cat.

विलिप् *vi-√lip*, P. Ā. *-limpati*, °*te*, to smear or spread over, anoint (also 'to anoint one's self,' P.), ŚBr. &c. &c.; to smear or spread with (instr.), Kum.: Caus. *-lepayati*, to smear or anoint with (instr.), Hcat.; *-limpayati*, see *-limpita*.

Vi-lipta, mf(*ā*)n. smeared over, anointed &c.; (*ā*), f., see p. 952, col. 2; (*ī*), f. a cow in a partic. period after calving, AV.

Vi-limpita, mfn. (fr. Caus.) smeared, anointed, L.

Vi-lepa, m. ointment, unguent (esp. the fragrant u° of sandal &c.), BhP.; anointing, plastering, W.; mortar, plaster, ib.; (*ī*), f. rice-gruel, Bhpr.; Car. °**lepana**, n. smearing, anointing (esp. with fragrant oils &c.), VarBṛS.; Kathās.; Suśr.; (ifc. f. *ā*), unguent, ointment, perfume for the person (as saffron, camphor &c.), MBh.; Kāv. &c.; a partic. mythical weapon, R.; (*ī*), f. a woman scented with perfumes &c., L.; rice-gruel, L.; °*nin*, mfn. smeared, anointed (in *a-vil*°), R. °**lepikā**, f. a female anointer, L.; rice-gruel, L. °**lepin**, mfn. smearing or plastering over, one who anoints &c., Kathās.; viscous, sticky (in *a-vil*°), Suśr.; (ifc.) stuck or clung to, accompanied by, Bhpr. °**lepya**, mfn. to be (or being) spread over or plastered, made of mortar or clay, BhP.; m. n. and (*ā*), f. rice-gruel, L.

विलिश् *vi-√liś*, Ā. *-liśate*, to become out of joint, be disarranged or disordered, break off, become rent or torn, TS.; ŚBr.

Vi-lishṭa, mfn. (cf. *vi-rishṭa*) broken off, out of due order, VS.; KātyŚr.; *-bheshaja*, n. a remedy for fractures or dislocation, AV. Paipp.

विलिस्तेङ्गा *vilisteṅgā*, f. N. of a Dānavī, Kāṭh.

विलिह् *vi-√lih*, P. Ā. *-leḍhi*, *-līḍhe*, to lick, lick up, lap, MBh.; BhP.; Suśr.: Intens. (only p. *-lelihat* and °*hāna*), to lick continually or repeatedly, MBh.

विली *vi-√lī*, Ā. *-līyate* (pf. *-lilyuḥ*, MBh.; fut. *-letā* or *-lātā*; ind. p. *-līya* or *-lāya*, Pāṇ. vi, 1, 51, Sch.), to cling or cleave or adhere to, MBh.; Ratnāv.; Śiś.; to hide or conceal one's self, disappear, MBh.; Kāv. &c.; to be dissolved, melt, AV. &c. &c.: Caus. *-lāpayati* or *-lāyayati* or *-lālayati* or *-līnayati* (Pāṇ. vii, 3, 39, Sch.), to cause to disappear, destroy, Śaṃk.; to cause to be dissolved or absorbed in (loc.), BhP., Sch.; to make liquid, dissolve, melt, Suśr.

Vi-laya, m. dissolution, liquefaction, disappearance, death, destruction (esp. d° of the world), MBh.; Kāv. &c. (acc. with √*gam*, *yā*, *vraj* &c. to be dissolved, end; with Caus. of √*gam*, to dissolve, destroy). °**layana**, mfn. dissolving, liquefying, Suśr.; n. dissolution, liquefaction, ib.; melting (intrans.), Kaṇ.; a partic. product of milk, Gaut.; Gobh.; corroding, eating away, W.; removing, taking away, ib.; attenuating or 'an attenuant, escharotic' (in medicine), ib.

Vi-lātavya and °**tṛi**, mfn., Pāṇ. vi, 1, 51, Sch.

2. **Vi-lāpana**, mf(*ī*)n. (fr. Caus.; for 1. see under *vi-√lap*) dissolving, destroying, removing, Suśr.; melting, liquefying (see *ājya-vilāpanī*); n. destruction, death, BhP.; a means of destruction, VP.; melting or a means of melting, ib.; a partic. product of milk, VarYog. (cf. *vi-layana*). °**lāpayitṛi**, m. a dissolver, Bālar. °**lāpita**, mfn. =next, BhP., Sch.

Vi-lāyita, mfn. dissolved, liquefied, Prab.; Suśr.

Vi-līna, mfn. clinging or sticking or attached to, fixed on, immersed in (loc. or comp.), Kāv.; Pañcar.; (ifc.) alighted or perched on (said of birds), Kathās.; sticking (see comp.); hidden, disappeared, perished, absorbed in (loc.), MaitrUp.; MBh. &c.; dissolved, melted, liquefied, ChUp.; Kathās.; Suśr.; contiguous to, united or blended with, W.; infused into the mind, imagined, ib.; *-shaṭpada*, mfn. having bees clinging or attached, MW.; °*nâksharam*, ind. so that the sound sticks (in the throat), Bhartṛ.

Vi-līyana, n. melting (intrans.), ĀpŚr., Sch.

विलुञ्च् *vi-√luñc*, P. *-luñcati*, to tear or pull out (hair), Bhaṭṭ. °**luñcana**, n. the act of tearing off, MW.

विलुठ् *vi-√2. luṭh* (cf. *vi-√luḍ* below), P. *-luṭhati*, to roll, move to and fro, quiver, flicker, Inscr.; Bālar.; Rājat.; Sāh. °**luṭhita**, mfn. agitated, excited, Cat.; n. rolling, wallowing, Vās. °**loṭhin**, mfn. moving to and fro, dangling, Pracaṇḍ.

विलुड् *vi-√luḍ* (cf. prec. and *vi-lulita*), Caus. *-loḍayati*, to stir about, stir up, mingle, Suśr.; Hcat.; to move to and fro, toss about, upset, disorder, confuse, MBh.; Hariv.; to betake one's self into (acc.), Naish., Sch.

Vi-loḍa, m. (prob. =*vi-loṭa*, q. v.) rolling, wallowing, Dhāt. ix, 27. °**loḍaka**, m. a thief (see *varṇa-v*°). °**loḍana**, n. stirring up, churning, Śiś.; splashing (in water), Daś. (v. l. °*nā*, f.); agitating, alarming, Pratāp. °**loḍayitṛi**, m. an agitator, disturber (used to explain *vi-gāḍhṛi*), Bhaṭṭ., Sch. °**loḍita**, mfn. agitated, churned &c.; n. =*takra* or *dadhi*, L.

विलुण्ट् *vi-√lunṭ* (only ind. p. *-luṇṭya*), to unhusk, Pañcat. iii, 83/84 (v.l. for *luñcitvā*).

विलुण्ठ *vi-√lunṭh* (cf. *vi-√luṭh*), P. *-luṇṭhati* (fut. *-luṇṭhishyati*, inf. *-luṇṭhitum*; Pass. *-luṇṭhyate*), to carry off, plunder, steal, ravage, Kāv.; Kathās. °**luṇṭhaka** (f. *ikā*), see *mukha-viluṇṭhikā*). °**luṇṭhana**, n. the act of plundering or robbing or stealing, R.; Sāh.; hanging down, dangling, Subh. (v.l.) °**luṇṭhita**, mfn. robbed, plundered &c.; = *vi-luṭhita*, rolling, wallowing, Rājat.

विलुप् *vi-√lup*, P. *-lumpati* (rarely Ā.), to tear or break off or to pieces, wound, lacerate, pull out or up, MBh.; Kāv. &c.; to tear away, carry off, ravish, seize, rob, plunder, AitBr. &c. &c.; to destroy, confound, ruin, MBh.; R. &c.; (Ā.) to fall to pieces, be ruined, disappear, Kauś.; ChUp.: Pass. *-lupyate*, to be torn away or carried off, be impaired or destroyed, perish, be lost, disappear, fail, AitBr. &c. &c.: Caus. *-lopayati* (°*te*), to tear or carry away, withhold, keep back, suppress, extinguish, destroy, MBh.; Kām.; MārkP. °**lupta**, mfn. torn or broken off, carried away &c.; impaired, destroyed, ruined, lost, MBh.; Kāv. &c.; *-pūrva*, mfn. torn off or carried away before, Mṛicch.; *-vitta*, mfn. one whose goods are robbed or plundered, VarBṛS.; *-sāvitrīka*, mfn. deprived of the Sāvitrī (cf. *patita-s*°), ĀpŚr., Sch. °**lupya**, mfn. destructible, perishable (in *a-vil*°), Prasaṅg. °**lumpaka**, mf(*ikā*)n. one who breaks or tears off &c.; m. a robber, ravisher, BhP.; a destroyer, MBh.

Vi-lopa, m. carrying off, taking away, Hariv.; a break, interruption, disturbance, injury, MBh.; Kāv. &c. (cf. *a-vil*°); ruin, loss, R. °**lopaka**, mfn. (and m.) = *-lumpaka*, MBh.; Hariv.; Pañcar. °**lopana**, n. the act of tearing or breaking to pieces, destroying, destruction, R.; cutting or plucking off, Subh.; leaving out, omission, Sāh.; robbing, stealing, Hariv. °**lopita**, mfn. (fr. Caus.) broken, destroyed, extinguished, MBh. °**lopin**, mfn. breaking, destroying, Śaṃk. °**loptṛi**, m. a robber, thief, MBh. °**lopya**, mfn. to be broken or destroyed, Inscr.

विलुभ् *vi-√lubh*, Caus. *-lobhayati*, to lead astray, perplex, confuse, Daśar.; to allure, entice, tempt, MBh.; Kāv. &c.; to divert, amuse, delight, R.; Śak. (v.l.)

Vi-lubhita, mfn. disordered, disarranged, agitated, Pāṇ. vii, 2, 54, Sch.; *-plava*, mfn. going in an agitated manner, Bhaṭṭ.

Vi-lobha, m. attraction, delusion, seduction, W. °**lobhana**, n. the act of leading astray, perplexing, beguiling, seduction, temptation, Ragh.; Kir.; Vās.; (in dram.) flattery, praise, commendation (e.g. Śak. i, 17–21, the stanzas containing the king's description of Śakuntalā's beauty), Bhar.; Daśar. &c. °**lobhanīya**, mfn. enticing, alluring, Vās.; Kād. °**lobhita**, mfn. (fr. Caus.) allured, beguiled, deceived, flattered, praised, W.

विलुलित *vi-lulita*, mfn. (√*lul*; cf. *vi-luḍ*) moved hither and thither, Vikr.; shaken down, falling down, shed, Uttarar.; BhP.; shaken, agitated, disordered, disarranged, MBh.; Kāv. &c.; °*tâlaka*, mfn. having dishevelled hair, Ṛitus.

Vi-lola, mf(*ā*)n. moving to and fro or from side to side, rolling, waving, tremulous, unsteady, Kāv.; Kathās. &c.; unsteadier than (abl.), Subh.; *-tā*, f., *-tva*, n. tremulousness, unsteadiness, rolling (of the eyes), W.; *-tāraka*, mfn. (a face) with rolling (pupils of the) eyes, ŚārṅgP.; *-locana*, mfn. having eyes swelling (with tears), BhP.; *-hāra*, mfn. having necklaces tossed about, MW. °**lolana**, n. the act of shaking, stirring, agitating, Naish. °**lolita**, mfn. (fr. Caus.) moved hither and thither, shaken, agitated, tossed about, MBh.; *-dṛiś*, mfn. rolling the eyes, having tremulous eyes, MārkP.

विलू *vi-√lū* (only ind. p. *-lūya*), to cut off, Bālar. °**lūna**, mfn. cut off, severed, ib.

विलोक् *vi-√lok* (only inf. *-lokitum* and ind. p. *-lokya*), to look at or upon, regard, examine, test, study, MBh.; Kāv. &c.: Caus. *-lokayati*, to look at, consider, observe, regard, examine, try, inspect, Gobh.; MBh. &c.; to be able to see, possess the faculty of seeing, Bhartṛ. (v.l.); to have regard to (acc.), Prab.; to look over or beyond (acc.), Mn. viii, 239: Pass. *-lokyate* (aor. *vy-aloki*), to be seen, be visible, Kathās.; BhP.

2. **Vi-loka**, m. (for 1. see p. 952, col. 2) a glance, view, BhP. °**lokana**, n. the act of looking or seeing, Kāv.; Pur.; Suśr.; looking at, regarding, observing, contemplating, Kāv.; Kathās.; looking for, finding out, ŚārṅgP.; Campak.; (ifc.) perceiving, noticing, becoming aware of, Kāv.; Kathās.; Pañcar.; paying attention to, studying (also pl., with gen.), Subh. °**lokanīya**, mfn. to be looked at or perceived or noticed or learnt (n. also impers.), Hcat.; Campak.; worthy to be looked at, lovely, beautiful (*-tā*, f., *-tva*, n.), W. °**lokita**, mfn. looked at, seen, beheld &c.; m. (in music) a kind of measure, Saṃgīt.; n. a look, glance, Śak.; observation, examination, Lalit. °**lokin**, mfn. looking at, looking, seeing, beholding, perceiving, noticing, becoming aware of (ifc.), Kathās.; Śatr. °**lokya**, mfn. to be (or being) looked at, visible, MārkP.

विलोचन 2. *vi-locana*, mfn. (√*loc*; for 1. see p. 952, col. 2) 'causing to see' or 'seeing' (ifc.), Hariv. 14943; n. (ifc. f. *ā*) the eye, sight, Hariv.; Kāv. &c.; *-patha*, m. the range of vision, Sāh.; *-pāta*, m. 'eye-fall,' a glance, look, Śiś.; °*nâmbu*, n. 'eye-water,' tears, W.

विलोट *vi-loṭa*, m. (used to explain √2. *luṭ*; cf. *vi-loḍa*), rolling, wallowing, Dhātup. ix, 27. °**loṭaka**, m. a sort of fish, Clupea Cultrata, L. °**loṭana**, n. = °*loṭa*, Dhātup. ix, 27.

विलोड *vi-loḍa*, *vi-loḍana* &c. See under *vi-√luḍ*, p. 985, col. 3.

विलोप *vi-lopa* &c. See *vi-√lup*, col. 1.

विलोभ *vi-lobha* &c. See *vi-√lubh*, ib.

विलोम *vi-loma*, mf(*ā*)n. (fr. 3. *vi* + *loman*) against the hair or grain, turned the wrong way, inverted, contrary to the usual or proper course, opposed (*pavana-vil*°, 'turned against the wind;' *am*, ind. 'backwards'), GopBr.; Var.; Rājat.; produced in reverse order, MW.; refractory, VarBṛS.; hairless (see *-tā* below); m. reverse order, opposite course, reverse, W.; a snake, L.; a dog, L.; N. of Varuṇa, L.; (*ī*), f. Emblic Myrobalan, L.; n. a water-wheel or machine for raising water from a well, L.; *-kāvya*, n. = *vilomâkshara-k*° below; *-kriyā*, f. reverse action, doing anything in reverse order or backwards, W.; (in arithm.) rule of inversion, ib.; *-ja* (VP.) or *-jāta* (BhP.), mfn. 'born in reverse order,' born of a mother belonging to a higher caste than the father; *-jihva*, m. an elephant, L.; *-tā*, f. the being hairless, (and) perverseness, Dharmaś.; *-trairāśika*, n. rule of three inverse, Col.; *-pāṭha*, m. recitation in reverse order (i.e. from the end to the beginning), Cat.; *-rasana*, m. an elephant, L.; *-varṇa*, mfn. = *viloma-ja* above, L.; m. a man of mixed or inferior birth, W.; *-vidhi*, m. an inverted rite, reversed ceremony, ib.; (in arithm.) rule of inversion, ib.; °*mâkshara-kāvya*, n. N. of a poem which may be read syllable by syllable either backwards or forwards, = *rāma-krishṇa-kāvya*, q.v.; °*mōtpanna*, mfn. = *viloma-ja* above, MW.

Vi-lomaka, mfn. inverted, reversed, L.

Vi-loman, mfn. against the hair or grain, turned in the opposite direction, inverted, TS.; Br.; VarBṛ.; hairless, Kathās.; m. N. of a king, Pur.

Vi-lomita, mfn. reversed, inverted, Naish.

विलोल *vi-lola*, *vi-lolana*, *vi-lolita*. See col. 1.

विलोलुप *vi-lolupa*, 1. 2. *vi-lohita*. See p. 952, col. 2.

विल्ल *villa*, *vilva*. See *billa*, *bilva*.

विवक्तृ *vi-vaktṛi*, *vi-vakvát*. See under *vi-√vac*, col. 3.

विवक्षण *vi-vákshaṇa*, mfn. (√*vaksh*) swelling, exuberant (applied to the Soma), RV. (Sāy. 'gushing,' 'spurting' or 'bringing to heaven' = *svarga-prâpaṇa-śīla*).

विवक्षसे *ví-vakshase* (fr. √*vaksh* or *vac* or *vah*, either 2. sg. Ā. or Ved. inf.), occurring only as refrain and without connection with other words in the hymns of Vi-mada, RV. x, 24 &c. (accord. to Naigh. iii, 3 = *mahat*).

विवक्षा *vivakshā*, f. (fr. Desid. of √*vac*) the wish or desire to speak or declare or teach or express, Saṃk; Sarvad. &c.; meaning, signification, sense, sense of (loc. or comp.), BhP.; Pāṇ., Sch.; the (mere) wish or intention to speak, uncertainty, doubt, hesitation ('as to,' comp.), MBh.; R.; wish, desire, W.; a question, MW.; *-°rtham* (°*kshâr*°), ind. (ifc.) in order to point out or lay stress upon, Pāṇ., Sch.; *-vaśāt*, ind. according to the meaning (of a speaker or writer), MW. °**vakshita**, mfn. wished or intended to be spoken or said, meant, intended, MBh.; R.; Śaṃk.; expressly meant, to be urged, essential (in *a-viv*°), Śaṃk.; chief, favourite, Kām.; literal (not figurative), W.; n. what is wished or intended to be spoken &c.; any desired object or aim, ib.; (*ā*), f. meaning, purpose, wish (?), ib.; *-tva*, n. the being intended or meant to be said, Nīlak. °**vakshitavya**, mfn. to be intended or meant to be said, necessarily meant, Nyāyam., Sch. °**vakshú**, mfn. calling or crying aloud, AV.; wishing to speak, intending to say or announce or tell or ask anything (acc., rarely gen., or comp.), MBh.; Hariv. &c.; wishing to speak to (acc.), MBh.

विवच् *vi-√vac*, P. *-vakti* (rarely Ā.), to declare, announce, explain, solve (a question), RV.; ŚBr.; to decide, Yājñ., Sch. (in explaining *vivāka*); to discuss, impugn, MBh.; (Ā.) to speak variously or differently, dispute with one another about (loc.), RV.

Vi-vaktṛi, mfn. one who declares or explains or sets right or corrects, AitBr.; *-tva*, n. eloquence, Rājat. °**vakvát**, mfn. eloquent, RV.

Vi-vāka, m. one who decides causes or pronounces judgment (cf. *prāḍ-v*°), Yājñ., Sch. °**vākya**, see *a-vivākyá*.

Ví-vāc, mfn. crying aloud, screaming, yelling, roaring, RV.; f. opposing shout, contest, battle, war, fight, ib. °**vācana**, m. one who decides, arbitrator (*ī*, f.), RV.; n. arbitration, authority, AitBr. °**vācas**, see p. 952, col. 2. °**vācya**, mfn. to be corrected or set right, ĀśvŚr.

विवञ्चिषु *vivañcishu*, mfn. (fr. Desid. of √*vañc*) wishing to deceive, deceitful, W.

विवत्सु *vivatsu* (Kāv.) or *vivadishu* (Sāy.), mfn. (fr. Desid. of √*vad*) wishing to speak or tell.

विवद् *vi-√vad*, P. Ā. (cf. Pāṇ. i, 3, 47, Sch.) *-vadati*, °*te*, (P.) to contradict, oppose (acc.), AV.; (P. Ā.) to be at variance, contest, litigate, dispute with (instr., rarely acc.) or about (loc., rarely acc.), TBr. &c. &c. (Ved. inf. *-vade* with √*yā*, 'to be about to quarrel;' pr. p. Ā. *-vadamāna*, 'disputing,' 'disputed,' 'questionable'); (P.) to talk, converse, Hariv.; (Ā.) to raise the voice, sing (said of birds), R.: Caus. *-vādayati*, to dispute or litigate, commence an action or lawsuit, Yājñ.: Intens. (only p. *-vâvadat*), to roar aloud, AV. °**vadana**, n. contest, quarrel, litigation, MBh. °**vadita**, mfn. disputing, quarrelling, MBh. xiii, 356; disputed, controverted, litigated, MW. °**vaditavya**, n. (impers.) it is to be disputed about (loc.), Śaṃk. °**vadishṇu**, see *a-vivadishṇu*.

Vi-vāda, m. (exceptionally n.) a dispute, quarrel, contest between (gen. or comp.) or with (instr. with or without *saha*, or comp.) or about, regarding (loc., gen., acc. with *prati*, or comp.), ShaḍvBr.; MBh.; Kāv. &c.; contest at law, legal dispute, litigation, lawsuit, Mn.; Yājñ. &c. (with *svāmi-pālayoḥ*, disputes between the owner and tender of cattle or between master and servant, IW. 261); an argument, Sarvad.; 'sound' or 'command,' Ragh. xviii, 42; *-kalpataru*, m. N. of wk.; *-kaumudī*, f. N. of a treatise on disputed points of grammar (by Līlā-maṇi); *-candra*, m., *-candrikā*, f., *-cintāmaṇi*, m., *-tattva-dīpa*, m., *-tāṇḍava*, n.(?), *-nirṇaya*, m. N. of wks. (cf. IW. 304, 305); *-pada*, n. the subject of a dispute or lawsuit, Yājñ., Sch.; *-pariccheda*, m. N. of wk.; *-bhaṅgârṇava*, m. N. of a compendium of civil law by Jagan-nātha (compiled at the close of the last century); *-bhīru*, mfn. afraid of a quarrel or contest, Mālav.; *-ratnâkara*, m. (IW. 305), *-vāridhi*, m. N. of wks. on law; *-śamana*, n. the allaying or settling of a dispute, pacification, LiṅgaP.; *-saṃvāda-bhū*, f. a matter or subject of controversy or discussion, BhP.; *-sārârṇava*, m. N. of a compendium of law by Sarvôru Trivedin (compiled by order of Sir William Jones); *-sindhu*, m., *-setu*, m., *-saukhya*, n. N. of wks.; °*dâdhyāsita*, mfn. subject to dispute, disputed, discussed, Sarvad.; °*dânavasara*, m. not an occasion for dispute or contest, BhP.; °*dânugata*, mfn. subject to dispute or litigation, Yājñ., Sch.; °*dârṇava-bhaṅga*, m. (or *-bhañjana*, n.) N. of a wk. on law (compiled by a number of Paṇḍits); °*dârṇava-setu*, m. N. of a legal digest by Bāṇeśvara and others (compiled by order of Warren Hastings); °*dârthin*, m. 'seeking for litigation,' a litigant, prosecutor, plaintiff, Yājñ., Sch.; °*dâspada*, n. the subject of a lawsuit (°*dī-bhūta*, mfn. become the subject of a lawsuit, litigated, contested at law), ib. °**vādin**, mfn. disputing, contending; a litigant, party in a lawsuit, Mn.; MBh.; Kathās.

विवध् *vi-√vadh* (only aor. *vy-ávadhīt*, Subj. *vi-vadhishaḥ*), to destroy utterly, RV.

विवध *vi-vadhá* or *vī-vadha*, m. (prob. fr. *√vadh = vah*; cf. *vadhū*) a shoulder-yoke for carrying burdens, TĀr.; ĀśvGṛ. &c. (cf. *vi-* and *sa-v*°); a store of grain or hay, provisions &c., Kāv.; Kām.; Pañcat.; a partic. Ekâha, Vaitān.; a road, highway, L. (*vīv*°, Pat. on Pāṇ. ii, 3, 12, Vārtt. 1); a ewer, pitcher, W.; the income which a king obtains from his subjects, L.; (*vīvadhā*), f. a yoke (fig.), i.e. chain, fetters (cf. *vṛiddha-v*°).

Vi-vadhika or **vī-vadhika**, mf(*ī*)n. one who carries a burden on a shoulder-yoke, Pāṇ. iv, 4, 17; m. a dealer, pedlar, hawker, W.

विवन्दिषा *vivandishā*, f. (fr. Desid. of *√vand*) the wish to salute or worship, HPariś.

Vivandishu, mfn. wishing to salute, intending to praise, MārkP.

विवयन *vi-vayana*. See under *vi-√ve*.

विवर *vi-vara*, *vi-varaṇa* &c. See under *vi-√1. vṛi*, p. 988.

विवरुण *vi-varuṇa* &c. See p. 952, col. 2.

विवर्जक *vi-varjaka*, *vi-varjana* &c. See under *vi-√vṛij*, p. 988.

विवर्ण् *vi-√varṇ* (also written *vi-√vṛiṇ*), q.v.), P. *-varṇayati* (aor. *vyavīvṛiṇat*), to excel in painting or description, Uttarar.; to discolour, Jātakam.; to dispraise, Divyâv. °**varṇayitavya**, mfn. to be disapproved, ib. °**varṇita**, mfn. dispraised, disapproved, Lalit.

विवर्ण *vi-varṇa* &c. See p. 952, col. 2.

विवर्त *vi-varta*, *vi-vartana* &c. See under *vi-√vṛit*, p. 988.

विवर्ध् *vi-√vardh*, P. *-vardhayati*, to cut off, sever, MW.

1. **Vi-vardhana**, n. (for 2. see under *vi-√vṛidh*) the act of cutting off, cutting, dividing, W.

1. **Vi-vardhita**, mfn. (for 2. see ib.) cut off, cut, divided, ib.

विवर्मन् *vi-varman* &c. See p. 952, col. 2.

विवर्षण *vi-varshaṇa* &c. See *vi-√vṛish*.

विवल् *vi-√val*, P. *-valati*, to turn away or aside (intr.), Kpr. °**valá**, mfn. (applied to a metre), VS. °**valita**, mfn. turned away, averted, Amar.

विवल्ग् *vi-√valg*, P. *-valgati*, to leap, jump, spring, Mṛicch.; to burst asunder, MW.

विवव्रि *vi-vavri*, *vi-vaśa* &c. See p. 952, col. 2.

विवस् *vi-√2. vas* (cf. *vyush*), P. *vy-ucchati*, to shine forth, shine, dawn, RV. &c. &c.; (*vi-váste*), to illumine, ŚBr.: Caus. *-vāsayati*, to cause to shine, RV.; TS.; Br.

Ví-vasvat or **vi-vásvat**, mfn. shining forth, diffusing light, matutinal (applied to Ushas, Agni &c.; *sadane vivasvataḥ*, 'at the seat of Fire'), RV.; VS.; Kāṭh.; m. 'the Brilliant one,' N. of the Sun (sometimes regarded as one of the eight Ādityas or sons of Aditi, his father being Kaśyapa; elsewhere he is said to be a son of Dākshāyaṇī and Kaśyapa; in epic poetry he is held to be the father of Manu Vaivasvata or, according to another legend, of Manu Sāvarṇi by Sa-varṇā; in RV. x, 17, 1 he is described as the father of Yama Vaivasvata, and in RV. x, 17, 2 as father of the Aśvins by Saraṇyū, and elsewhere as father of both Yama and Yamī, and therefore a kind of parent of the human race), RV. &c. &c.; the Soma priest, RV. ix, 14, 5 &c.; N. of Aruṇa (charioteer of the Sun), W.; of the seventh or present Manu (more properly called Vaivasvata, as son of Vivasvat), RV. viii, 52, 1; N. of a Daitya, MBh.; a god, L.; N. of the author of the hymn RV. x, 13 (having the patronymic Āditya), Anukr.; N. of the author of a Dharma-śāstra (cf. *-smṛiti*); (*atī*), f. N. of the city of the Sun, L.; *-suta*, m. 'son of Vivasvat,' N. of Manu Vaivasvata, Mn. i, 62; *-smṛiti*, f. the law-book of Vivasvat; (°*vad*)-*vāta*, mf(*ā*)n. (prob.) loved by Vivasvat, TS. °**vásvan**, only in instr. pl. (prob. = 'to shine forth'), RV. i, 187, 7.

3. **Vi-vāsa**, m. (for 1. and 2. see p. 952, col. 2) shining forth, dawning, ĀśvŚr.; *-kāle*, ind. at the time of daybreak, ib. 1. °**vāsana**, mfn. (for 2. see under *vi-√4. vas*) illumining, Nir.; n. illumination, ib.; *-vat*, mfn. (used to explain *vi-vasvat*), ib.

Vy-ushṭa, vy-ushṭi. See 2. *vy-√ush*.

विवस् *vi-√4. vas*, Ā. *-vaste*, to change clothes, TS.; ĀśvŚr.; to put on, don, Bhaṭṭ.: Caus. *-vāsayati* (Pass. *-vāsyate*), to put on, don, MBh.

2. **Vi-vāsana**, n. (for 1. see *vi-√2. vas*) being clothed in or covered with (instr.), MBh.

विवस् *vi-√5. vas*, P. *-vasati*, to change an abode, depart from (abl.), BhP.; (with *brahmacaryam*), to enter upon an apprenticeship, become a pupil, ChUp.; to abide, dwell, live, MBh.; R.; to pass, spend (time), ib. &c.: Caus. *-vāsayati*, to cause to dwell apart, banish, expel, MBh.; Kāv. &c.; to send forth, dismiss, MBh.

4. **Vi-vāsa**, m. (for 3. see under *vi-√2. vas*) leaving home, banishment, MBh.; R. &c.; separation from (instr.), MBh.; *-karaṇa*, n. causing banishment, banishing, transporting, W. 3. °**vāsana**, n. the act of banishing, banishment, exile, R.; Uttarar. °**vāsayitṛi**, m. an expeller, TBr., Sch. °**vāsita**, mfn. banished, exiled, transported, W. °**vāsya**, mfn. to be expelled or exiled, Mn.; Yājñ.; R.

Vy-ushita, vy-ushṭa. See 2. *vy-ushita*.

विवह् *vi-√vah*, P. *-vahati* (rarely Ā.), to bear or carry off, remove, RV.; MBh.; to lead away (the bride from her father's house), take in marriage, marry, AV. &c. &c.; (also Ā., with or without *mithas*) to marry or form a matrimonial alliance together, Gobh.; Āpast.; BhP.: Caus. *-vāhayati*, to marry (a girl) to (gen. or *saha*), MBh.; Pañcat.; (Ā.) to lead home, take to wife, Kathās.; Vet.; Pañcat.

Vi-vaha, m. 'carrying away,' N. of one of the seven winds, MBh.; Hariv.; of one of the seven tongues of fire, Col.

Vi-vāhá, m. leading away (of the bride from her father's house), taking a wife, marriage with (instr. with or without *saha*), AV. &c. &c. (eight kinds of marriage are enumerated in Mn. iii, 21, viz. Brāhma, Daiva, Ārsha, Prājāpatya, Āsura, Gāndharva, Rākshasa, and Paiśāca; cf. Yājñ. i, 58–61 and IW. 190 &c.); a partic. wind, Śak., Sch. (prob. w. r. for *vi-vaha*); a vehicle (and 'marriage'), AitBr. vii, 13; n. a partic. high number, Buddh.; *-karman*, n., °*ma-paddhati*, f. N. of wks.; *-kāma*, mfn. desirous of marriage, MW.; *-kārikā*, f. pl. N. of wk.; *-kāla*, m. the (right) time for m°, VarBṛS.; *-gṛiha*, n. 'm° house,' the house in which a wedding is celebrated, Kathās.; *-caturthika*, n. or *-caturthī-karman*, n. N. of wks.; *-catushṭaya*, n. a quadruple m°, the marrying of four wives, MW.; *-tattva* (or *udvāha-t*°), n., *-tattva-dīpikā*, f. N. of wks.; *-dīkshā*, f. the m° rite, m° ceremony, Ragh.; (°*kshā-tilaka*, m. n. a Tilaka mark made on the forehead during a m° cer°, MW.; °*kshā-vidhi*, m. the preparatory rites of m°, ib.); *-dvir-āgamana-paddhati*, f. N. of a wk. (containing rules to be observed on a bride's coming for the second time from her father's to her husband's house); *-nepathya*, n. a m°-dress, Mālav.; *-paṭala*, m. n. N. of various wks. (or of that section in an astrological wk. that treats of the times fit for m°); *-paṭaha*, m. a m°-drum, Mṛicch.; *-paddhati*, f., *-prakaraṇa*, n. (and °*ṇa-ṭīkā*, f.), *-prayoga*, m., *-bhūshaṇa*, n., *-mela-vāṇī-vidhi*, m. N. of wks.; *-yajña*, m. a m°-sacrifice, MW.; *-ratna*, n. N. of wk.; *-vidhi*, m. the law of m°, Mn. ix, 65 (also N. of wk.); *-vṛindāvana*, n. N. of an astrol. wk. by Keśavârka; *-vesha*, m. (ifc. f. *ā*) a m°-dress, Ragh.; *-samaya*, m. = *-kāla*, Pañcat.; *-sambandha*, m. relation or connection by m°, Pracaṇḍ.; *-siddhânta-rahasya*, n., *-saukhya*, n. N. of wks.; *-sthāna*, n. the place for a m°-ceremony (before a house), ĀpGṛ., Sch.; *-homa*, m. = m°-sacrifice; (°*ma-vidhi*, m. and °*mōpayuktā mantrāḥ*, m. pl. N. of wks.); °*hâgni*, m. a m°-fire, ĀśvGṛ.; °*hâdi-karmaṇām prayoga*, m. N. of wk.; °*hârtha*, m. purpose of m°, a m° suit, MW.; °*hêcchu*, mfn. desirous of m°, ib.; °*hôtsava*, m. 'marriage feast,' N. of wk. °**vāhanīyā**, f. to be led away (as a bride), to be married, Daś. °**vāhayitavya**, mfn. = *vi-vāhya*, Gobh., Sch. °**vāhita**, mfn. caused to marry, married (said of men and women), Pañcat.; Kathās. °**vāhin**, see *a-* and *dvi-vivāhin*. °**vāhya**, mfn. to be married, marriageable, Kathās.; connected by marriage, Yājñ. i, 110 (cf. *a-viv*°); m. a son-in-law, MānGṛ.; Gobh. &c.; a bridegroom, W.

Vi-voḍhṛi, m. a husband, L.

1. **Vy-ūḍha**, mfn. (for 2. see under *vy-√ūh*) led home, married, Kathās.; BhP.

विवा *vi-√vā*, P. *-vāti*, to blow on all sides or in every direction, blow through, blow, RV. &c. &c.

विवाक *vi-vāka*, *vi-vāc*. See under *vi-√vac*.

विवात *vi-vāta*, *vi-vāsa* &c. See p. 952.

विवान *vi-vāna*. See *vi-√ve*, p. 989.

विवारयिषु *vivārayishu*, mfn. (fr. Desid. of Caus. of *√1. vṛi*) wishing to keep back or ward off (an army), MBh.

विवालयिषु *vivālayishu*, mfn. (fr. Desid. of Caus. of *√val*) wishing to recover, HPariś.

विविक्त *vi-vikta*, *vi-vikvás* &c. See belo

विविक्ष् *viviksh*, *vivikshu*. See p. 989.

विविग्न *vi-vigna*, mfn. (*√vij*) very agitat d or alarmed, Kālid.; Kathās. &c.

Vi-vejita, mfn. (fr. Caus.) terrified, frightened, Hariv. 568 (v. l. *pratodita* and *virejita*).

विविच् *vi-√vic*, P. *-vinakti*, to sift (esp. grain by tossing or blowing), divide asunder, separate from (instr. or abl.), ŚBr.; ŚrS.; BhP.; to shake through (acc.), RV. i, 39, 5; to cause to lose, deprive of (abl.), Bhaṭṭ.; to distinguish, discern, discriminate, KaṭhUp.; BhP.; to decide (a question), MBh.; to investigate, examine, ponder, deliberate, Kāv.; Kathās.; BhP.; to show, manifest, declare, MBh.: Pass. *-vicyate*, to go asunder, separate (intrans.), AV.: Caus. *-vecayati*, to separate, distinguish, Mn.; Suśr.; to ponder, investigate, examine, Pañcar.; Sāh.

Vi-vikta, mfn. separated, kept apart, distinguished, discriminated, Kap.; MBh.; BhP.; isolated, alone, solitary, Mn.; MBh. &c.; (ifc.) alone with i. e. intent upon (e. g. *cintā-v*°), MBh.; free from (instr. or comp.), Hariv.; Kum.; pure, clean, neat, trim, Mn.; MBh. &c.; clear, distinct, Hariv.; Kām.; discriminative, judicious (= *vi-vekin*), L.; profound (as judgment or thought), W.; m. = *vasu-nandana* or *vasu-nanda*, L.; n. separation, solitude, a lonely place (see comp.); clearness, purity, MārkP.; *-ga*, mfn. going to a lonely place, seeking solitude, Kathās.; *-carita*, mfn. faultless in conduct or behaviour, BhP.; *-cetas*, mfn. pure-minded, ib.; *-tarka*, mfn. clear in reasoning, MW.; *-tā*, f. separation, isolation, Rājat.; clearness, purity, Suśr.; being well, good health, ib.; distinction, discrimination, L.; an empty or free place, loneliness, MW.; *-tva*, n. solitude, Mṛicch.; *-dṛishṭi*, mfn. clear-sighted, BhP.; *-nāman*, m. N. of one of the 7 sons of Hiraṇyaretas and of the Varsha ruled by him, ib.; *-bhāva*, mfn. having a mind separated or abstracted (from other pursuits), intent on any object, W.; *-varṇa*, mfn. containing letters or syllables distinctly enunciated, MW.; *-śaraṇa* (BhP.), *-sevin* (Bhag.), mfn. resorting to or seeking solitude; °*ktâsana*, mfn. having a secluded seat, sitting at a sequestered place, Mn. ii, 215; °*ktī-kṛita*, mfn. emptied, cleared, Kathās.; left, deserted, Ragh.

Vi-vikti (*ví-*), f. separation, division, VS.; discrimination, discernment, Sarvad.

Vi-vikvás, mfn. discriminating, discerning (applied to Indra), RV. iii, 57, 1.

Ví-vici, id. (applied to Agni or Indra), RV.; Br.; ĀśvŚr.; °*cīshṭi*, f. an oblation made to Agni Vivici, TS., Sch.

Vi-veka, m. discrimination, distinction, Mn.; Sarvad.; Suśr.; consideration, discussion, investigation, Gīt.; MārkP.; Sarvad.; true knowledge, discretion, right judgment, the faculty of distinguishing and classifying things according to their real properties, ChUp.; Kap. &c.; (in Vedânta) the power of separating the invisible Spirit from the visible world (or spirit from matter, truth from untruth, reality from mere semblance or illusion); a water-trough (=*jala-droṇī*), L.; N. of wk.; *-kaumudī*, f. N. of wk.; *-khyāti*, f. right knowledge, Sarvad.; *-candrôdaya*, m., *-cūḍāmaṇi*, m. N. of wks.; *-ja*, mfn. produced or arising from discrimination, Dharmas. 72; *-jña*, mfn. skilled in discr°, intelligent, well acquainted with (comp.), R. &c.; *-jñāna*, n. knowledge arising from discr°, the faculty of discr°, Sarvad.; *-tā*, w.r. for *viveki-tā* (q.v.); *-tilaka*, m., *-dīpaka*, m. (or *ikā*, f.) N. of wks.; *-dṛiśvan*, mfn. one who sees or is conversant with true knowledge (°*śva-tva*, n.), Bhaṭṭ.; *-dhairyâśraya*, m. N. of a wk. on Bhakti (by Vallabhâcārya); *-padavī*, f. 'path of discr°,' reflection, Kathās.; *-paripanthin*, mfn. obstructing right judgment, Kathās.; *-phala*, n. N. of wk.; *-bhāj*, mfn. 'possessed of discr°,' discerning, wise, Bhām.; *-bhrashṭa*, mfn. one who has lost the faculty of discr°, foolish, unwise, Bhartṛ.; *-makaranda*, m., *-mañjarī*, f. N. of wks.; *-mantharatā*, f. feebleness of judgment, Ml.; *-mārtaṇḍa*, m. N. of various wks.; *-rahita*, mfn. 'not separated' (applied to breasts) and 'wanting discernment,' Śṛiṅgār.; *-vat*, mfn. 'possessing discr°,' judicious, discerning, Kathās.; *-viguṇa*, mfn. 'wanting discr°,' unwise, foolish, Rājat.; *-viraha*, m. 'want of discr°,' ignorance, folly, Śāntiś.; *-vilāsa*, m. N. of wk.; *-viśada*, mfn. distinct, clear, intelligible, Rājat.; *-viśrânta*, mfn. void of discr°, foolish, unwise, Mālav.; *-śataka*, n., *-śloka*, m., *-saṃgraha*, m., *-sāra*, m., *-sāra-varṇana*, n., *-sāra-sindhu*, m., *-sindhu*, m.; °*kâñjana*, n., °*kâmṛita*, n., °*kârṇava*, m. N. of wks.; °*kârtham*, ind. in order to distinguish, Mn. i, 26; °*kâśrama*, m. N. of a man, Cat.; °*kôdaya*, m. the rise of true knowledge or wisdom, Bhartṛ. °**vekin**, mfn. discriminating, distinguishing, Rājat.; separated, kept asunder (in *a-viv°*), Kuval.; examining, investigating, Cat.; discriminative, judicious, prudent, discreet, wise, Kāv.; Kathās. &c.; m. N. of a king (son of Deva-sena), KālP.; °*ki-tā*, f., *-tva*, n. discriminativeness, discernment, judgment, Yājñ.; Bhartṛ. °**vektavya**, mfn. to be judged correctly (n. impers.), Sarvad. °**vektṛi**, mfn. one who discriminates or distinguishes, a discriminator, Rājat.; judicious, discerning, prudent, wise, ib.; Bālar.; *-tva*, n. discriminativeness, discernment, Rājat.

Vi-vecaka, mfn. discriminating, distinguishing, Nīlak.; discriminative, judicious, wise, Kap.; Śāntiś.; *-tā*, f., *-tva*, n. discernment, correct judgment, wisdom, Rājat.; Sāh.; Sarvad. °**vecana**, mf(*ī*)n. discriminating, distinguishing, BhP.; investigating, examining, treating critically, Sāh.; n. the act of discriminating or distinguishing (as truth from falsehood, reality from semblance), the making a distinction, Hariv.; Bālar.; Sarvad. (also *ā*, f.); investigation, examination, discussion, critical treatment, Mn.; MBh. &c.; right judgment, Pañcar.; °*nīkroḍa-pattra*, n. N. of wk. °**vecanīya**, mfn. to be distinguished or discussed, W. °**vecita**, mfn. discriminated, distinguished, investigated, MW. °**vecya**, mfn. =°*vecanīya*, ib.

विवित्ति *vi-vitti*, f. (√3. *vid*) gain, acquisition, TBr. (VS. *vi-vikti*).

विवित्सा *vivitsā*, *vivitsu*, *vividishu*. See p. 964, col. 3.

विविद् *vi-√*1. *vid* (only pf. *-veda*), to discern, know, RV.

विविध *vi-vidha*, mf(*ā*)n. of various sorts, manifold, divers, Mn.; MBh. &c.; m. a partic. Ekâha, ŚāṅkhŚr.; n. variety of action or gesture, MW.; (*am*), ind. variously, R.; Vedântas.; *-citra*, mfn. coloured variously, changing from one colour into another, Kāraṇḍ.; *-bhaṅgīka*, mfn. =*vi-vidha* above, HPariś.; *-rūpa-dhṛit*, mfn. having various forms, MW.; *-vidhi-prayoga-saṃgraha*, m. N. of wk.; *-śāstra-goshṭhī*, f. discourse about various sciences, L.; °*dhâgama*, mfn. comprising various sacred (or traditional) works, Mn. xii, 105; °*dhâtman*, mfn. (=*vi-vidha* above), Car.; °*dhôpala-bhūshita*, mfn. decorated with various jewels, MW.; °*dhôpêta*, mfn. (=*vi-vidha* above), R.

विविप् *vi-√vip*, Ā. *-vepate*, to quiver, tremble, Kauś.

विविश् *vi-√viś*, P. *-viśati*, to enter, penetrate (*abhyantaram*), MaitrUp.

विविष्टि *ví-vishṭi*, f. (√*vish*) = *viśesheṇa vishṭir vyāptir yasya brahmaṇas tat*, TĀr. (Sch.)

विवीत *vi-vīta*, m. (√*vye*) an enclosed spot of ground (esp. pasture ground), paddock, Yājñ.; *-bhartṛi*, m. the owner of a preserved or enclosed pasture, ib.

विवृ *vi-√*1. *vṛi* (cf. *vy-√ūrṇu*), P. Ā. *-vṛiṇoti*, *-vṛiṇute* &c. (in later language Ā. only intrans. or m. c.; in Veda aor. often *vy-āvar*, *-āvo*, *-āvaḥ*; inf. *-varitum* or *-varītum*), to uncover, spread out, open, display, show, reveal, manifest, RV. &c. &c.; to illumine (darkness), RV.; to unsheath (a sword), VarBṛS.; to part, comb (hair), HPariś.; to explain, describe, comment upon, MBh.; Kāv. &c.; to cover, cover up, stop up, MBh.; Hariv. (perhaps always w. r. for *pi-vṛi* = *api-√vṛi*, q. v.); pf. *vi-vavāra* (Śiś. xix, 100) = *vivārayām-āsa*, *jaghāna* (Sch.)

Vi-vará, m. n. a fissure, hole, chasm, slit, cleft, hollow, vacuity (also applied to the apertures of the body and to gaping wounds), RV. &c. &c.; intermediate space, interstice, MBh.; Kāv. &c.; difference, VarBṛS.; Gaṇit.; a breach, fault, flaw, vulnerable or weak point, MBh.; Kāv.; harm, injury, MārkP.; expansion, opening, widening, BhP.; N. of the number 'nine' (cf. above and under *randhra*), MW.; a partic. high number, Buddh.; *-darśaka*, mfn. showing one's weak points, MBh.; *-nālika*, f. a fife, flute, L.; °*rânuga*, mfn. seeking after (another's) weak points, MBh.; °*re-sad*, mfn. abiding in intermediate space, an inhabitant of the sky, Kir. °**varaṇa**, mfn. the act of uncovering, spreading out, opening, laying bare or open, TPrāt.; MBh.; Suśr.; explanation, exposition, interpretation, gloss, comment, translation, interpretation, specification &c., Pur.; Śaṃk.; Sarvad.; a sentence, MW.; N. of a wk. on Vedânta; *-kārikā-bhāshya*, n., *-catuḥsūtrī*, f., *-tattva-dīpana*, n., *-darpaṇa*, m., *-prameya-saṃgraha*, m., *-prasthāna*, n., *-bhāva-prakāśikā*, f., *-ratna*, n., *-vraṇa*(?), m., *-saṃgraha*, m., *-sāra-saṃgraha*, m.; °*ṇôpanyāsa*, m. N. of wks. °**varishu**, mfn. (fr. Desid. and prob. for *vivivarishu*) wishing to make manifest or explain or declare, Bhaṭṭ.

Vi-vāra, m. dilation, expansion, W.; (in gram.) open or expanded state of the organs of speech, expansion of the throat in articulation (one of the Ābhyantara-prayatnas or efforts of articulate utterance which take place within the mouth, opp. to *saṃ-vāra*, q. v.), Pāṇ. i, 1, 9, Sch. °**vārin**, mfn. keeping back, warding off, Śiś.

Vi-vṛit(?), in a formula, VS. xv, 9.

Vi-vṛita, mfn. uncovered, unconcealed, exposed, naked, bare, MBh.; Kāv. &c.; unhurt, woundless, MBh. iv, 2027; unclosed, open, ĀśvGṛ.; Up.; Prāt.; MBh. &c. (also applied to the organs in speaking and to the articulation of partic. sounds, =*vivṛita-prayatnôpêta*, Śaṃk. on ChUp. ii, 22, 5; superl. *-tama*, APrāt.); extensive, large, wide, W.; (also *vī-vṛita*) unfolded, exposed, revealed, explained, divulged, public, manifest, evident, known, MBh.; VarBṛS. &c.; opened i.e. presented, offered (as an opportunity), BhP.; (*am*), ind. openly, publicly, in the sight of every one, MBh.; (*ā*), f. a partic. disease, an ulcer attended with much pain and heat, Suśr.; a species of plant, ib.; n. the bare ground, MBh.; Hariv.; publicity (loc. 'in public' or 'straight out'), MBh. iv, 34, 4; (in gram.) open articulation, approach of the tongue towards the organ of speech but without contact; *-tā*, f. the being known, publicity (acc. with √*gam*, to become known or public), R.; *-dvāra*, mfn. 'open-gated,' unchecked, unbounded (sorrow), Kum.; *-paurusha*, mfn. one whose prowess is displayed, displaying valour, Mn. vii, 102; *-bhāva*, mfn. open-hearted, candid, sincere, Mālatīm.; *-vat*, mfn. one who has opened, Kathās.; *-snāna*, n. bathing publicly, PārGṛ.; *-smayana*, n. an open smile (i.e. one in which the mouth is sufficiently open to show the teeth), ĀśvŚr.; °*tâksha*, m. 'open-eyed,' a cock, L. (cf. *vi-vṛittâksha*); °*tânana*, mfn. open-mouthed (*-tva*, n.), Ragh.; °*tâsya*, mfn. id., MW.; °*tôkti*, f. open or explicit expression (opp. to *gūḍhôkti*), Kuval. °**vṛiti**, f. making clear or manifest, explanation, exposition, gloss, comment, interpretation, Sarvad.; exposure, discovery, W.; *-vimarśinī*, f. N. of wk.

विवृक्ण *vi-vṛikṇa*. See under *vi-√vraśc*.

विवृज् *vi-√vṛij*, Caus. *-varjayati*, to exclude, avoid, shun, abandon, leave, Mn.; MBh. &c.; to distribute, give (see below).

Vi-varjaka, mfn. avoiding, shunning, leaving, MBh. °**varjana**, n. the act of avoiding, shunning, leaving, giving up or desisting from (gen., abl., or comp.), Yājñ.; MBh. &c. °**varjanīya**, mfn. to be avoided or abandoned, R.; to be given up (as incurable), Car. °**varjita**, mfn. avoided, left, abandoned by, destitute or deprived of, free or exempt from (instr. or comp.), Up.; Yājñ.; MBh. &c.; (ifc.) that from which anything is excluded, excepting, excluding, Kāv.; VarBṛS.; that from which anything is subtracted, diminished by, Gaṇit.; distributed, given, MārkP.

Vi-vṛikta, mfn. abandoned, left; (*ā*), f. a woman disliked or deserted by her husband (=*dur-bhagā*), L. (v. l. *vi-viktā* and *vi-riktā*).

विवृण् *vi-√vṛiṇ*. See *vi-√varṇ*, p. 987.

विवृत् *vi-√vṛit*, Ā. *-vartate* (rarely P.), to turn round, revolve, RV.; to roll, wallow, MBh.; Hariv.; to writhe in convulsions, struggle, R.; Uttarar.; to turn hither and thither, move about (as clouds), Hariv. 3822 (v. l. *vi-vardhante*); to turn back or away, depart, part, sever, RV. &c. &c.; to go astray, MBh. v, 2861 (v. l. *ni-vartantam*); to be parted (as hair), TUp.; to change one's place, Suśr.; to go down, set (as the sun), MBh.; to come forth from (abl.), ŚBr.; to expand, develop, ŚvetUp.; (with *antikam*), to turn upon, set upon, attack, MBh. iii, 8438: Caus. *-vartayati*, to turn round (trans.), turn, roll, RV.; MBh.; to turn, make or produce by turning ('out of,' instr.), VP.; to cause to turn away, remove, withdraw, RV.; AV.; to keep asunder, RV.; to leave behind, ib.; to cast off (a garment), Divyâv.; to accomplish, execute, AitĀr.

Vi-vartá, m. 'the revolving one,' N. of the sky, VS.; TS.; a whirlpool, SV.; turning round, rolling onwards, moving about, Mcar.; turning away, L.; dance, L.; changing from one state to another, modification, alteration, transformation, altered form or condition, Kāv.; Kathās.; (in Vedânta) error, illusion, an apparent or illusory form, unreality (caused by A-vidyā, 'ignorance,' and removed by Vidyā, 'true knowledge'), Vedântas.; collection, multitude, L.; (with *Atreḥ*) N. of two Sāmans, ĀrshBr.; *-kalpa*, m. (with Buddhists) one of the 4 cosmic periods, Dharmaś. 87; *-vāda*, m. a method of asserting the Vedânta doctrine (maintaining the development of the Universe from Brahma as the sole real entity, the phenomenal world being held to be a mere illusion or Māyā; cf. *pariṇāma-vāda*), Madhus. °**vártana**, mfn. turning round, revolving, MBh.; changing, transforming, Kathās.; n. (ifc. f. *ā*) rolling (of a horse), RV. i, 162, 14; rolling or tossing about, struggling, Kāv.; Kathās. (also *ā*, f., Harav.); moving or wandering to and fro, Mn. xii, 75; turning round, Suśr.; turning, turn, change, TBr.; Mālatīm.; turning away or back, MBh.; Kālid.; returning, return, Kir.; a kind of dance (also *-nṛitya*, n.), Saṃgīt.; transformation, RPrāt.; existing, being, abiding, W.; going round, circumambulating (an altar &c.), ib.; reverential salutation, MW.; causing to turn or to change, overturning, ib. °**vartita**, mfn. (fr. Caus.) turned round &c.; MBh.; Kāv. &c.; turned away or back, averted, Kum.; distorted, Suśr.; knitted (as the brows), Śak.; whirled round (as dust), Kir.; removed from one's place, Śiś. °**vartin**, mfn. turning round, rolling, revolving, Kāv.; Kathās.; (ifc.) turning towards, Śak.; changing, undergoing a change, Kathās.; dwelling, abiding, ib.; MārkP.

Ví-vṛitta, mfn. turned or twisted round &c.; whirling round, flying in different directions (as a thunderbolt), RV.; opened (see comp.); uncovered, shown, displayed, Lalit.; (*ā*), f. a kind of eruption, Bhpr. (cf. *vi-vṛitā*); *-daṇshṭra*, mfn. with opened jaws, showing the teeth, Hariv. (m. c. for *vi-vṛita-d°*; v. l. *vi-vṛiddha-d°*); *-vadana*, mf(*ā*)n. bending or turning the face, Śak.; °*ttâksha*, mfn. distorting the eyes, R.; m. a cock, L. (cf. *vivṛitâksha*); °*ttâṅga*, mfn. distorting the limbs (in agony), R.; °*ttâsya*, mfn. open-mouthed (m. c. for *vivṛitâsya*), Hariv. °**vṛitti**, f. going asunder, opening, expansion, development, Kir.; BhP.; turning round, revolution, rolling, whirling, tumbling, Kir.; (in gram.) the opening of two vowels upon each other without blending, hiatus, Prāt.; *-pūrva*, mfn. preceded by a hiatus, ib.; °*tty-abhiprâya*, m. an intended or apparent hiatus, RPrāt.

विवृध् *vi-√vṛidh*, Ā. *-vardhate*, to grow, increase, swell, become large or powerful, thrive, prosper, RV. &c. &c.; to be lengthened, ŚāṅkhŚr.;

to be lucky or fortunate (cf. under *dishṭi*), MBh.; Kāv. &c.; to spring up, arise, MBh.: Caus. *-vardhayati*, to cause to grow or increase or prosper, nourish, rear, enlarge, augment, advance, further, promote, MBh.; Kāv. &c.; to gratify, exhilarate, gladden, MBh.; R.

2. **Vi-vardhana**, mf(*ī*, rarely *ā*)n. (for 1. see under *vi-√vardh*) augmenting, increasing, furthering, promoting (gen. or comp.), MBh.; Kāv. &c.; m. N. of a warrior, MBh.; n. growth, increase, prosperity, MBh.; R. &c. **°vardhanīya**, mfn. to be increased or furthered, Pañcat.

Vi-vardhayishu, mfn. (fr. Desid. of Caus.) wishing to increase or augment, MBh.; Hariv.; BhP.

2. **Vi-vardhita**, mfn. (for 1. see under *vi-√vardh*) increased, augmented, furthered, promoted, gratified, delighted, MBh.; Kāv. &c.; caused to increase (in instr.), R.

Vi-vardhin, mfn. increasing, augmenting, furthering, enhancing (only in f. *inī*, and at the end of a Śloka), Mn.; MBh. &c.

Vi-vṛiddha, mfn. grown, increased, enhanced, grown up, fully developed, large, numerous, abundant, mighty, powerful, ŚvetUp.; MBh. &c.; *-matsara*, mfn. one whose anger or resentment is increased, MW. **°vṛiddhi**, f. growth, increase, augmentation, enlargement, furthering, promotion, ŚrS.; MBh. &c. (acc. with *√gam, yā* &c., 'to be augmented or increased'); prosperity, Mn. i, 31; lengthening (of a vowel), Pāṇ. viii, 2, 106, Vārtt. 1; *-kara* or *-da*, mfn. causing increase or prosperity, VarBṛS.; *-bhāj*, mfn. growing, increasing, Kathās.

Vi-vṛidhat, mfn. (prob. w. r.) augmenting, increasing, Pañcad.

विवृष् *vi-√vṛish*, Caus. *-varshati* (aor. *vy-avīvṛishat*), to rain, rain upon, besprinkle or cover with (instr.), MBh. viii, 801.

Vi-varshaṇa, n. abundant flow (of milk from the female breast), Pañcar.

विवृह् *vi-√vṛih* (Ved. inf. *-vṛihas*, Kāṭh.), see *vi-√1.* and *2. bṛih*.

Vi-vṛiha, m. breaking loose, separating one's self (from others), Kauś.

Vi-vṛihat, m. (with *Kāśyapa*) N. of the author of RV. x, 163, Anukr.

विवे *vi-√ve*, P. Ā. *-vayati*, °*te*, to interweave, Lāṭy.

Vi-vayana, n. plaited work, Br.; Lāṭy.

Vi-vāna, n. plaiting, twisting, ŚrS.

Vy-uta, vy-ūta. See s. v.

विवेक *vi-veka* &c. See under *vi-√vic*.

विवेदयिषु *vivedayishu*, mfn. (fr. Desid. of Caus. of *√1. vid*) wishing to tell or communicate ('that &c.,' two acc.), MBh.

विवेन् *vi-√ven*, P. *-venati*, to be hostile or ill-disposed, RV.; TBr. (cf. *á-vivenat*).

Vi-vena. See *a-vivenam*.

विवेल्ल् *vi-√vell*, P. *-vellati*, to quiver, tremble, Kathās.

विवेविदत् *vi-vévidat*, mfn. (pr. p. of Intens. of *√3. vid*) seeking for, striving after, RV.

विवेष्ट् *vi-√vesht*, Caus. *-veshṭayati*, to strip off (the skin), AV.; to wind round (see next); to surround, invest (a stronghold), Rājat. **°veshṭita**, mfn. wound round, Hariv. (v. l. °*ceshṭ°*); Kathās.

विवोढृ *vi-voḍhṛi*. See under *vi-√vah*.

विव्यथित *vi-vyathita*, mfn. (*√vyath*) greatly troubled or alarmed, MBh.

विव्यध् *vi-√vyadh*, P. *-vidhyati*, to pierce through, transfix, VS.

Vi-vyādhin, mfn. piercing, transfixing, AV.

विव्रत *ví-vrata*. See p. 952, col. 2.

विव्रश्च् *vi-√vraśc*, P. *-vṛiścati*, to cut or hew in pieces, cut off, sever, RV.; AV.; BhP.

Vi-vṛikṇa, mfn. cut in pieces, entirely severed or cut asunder, RV.; BhP.

विव्वोक *vivvoka*. See *bibboka*.

विश् 1. *viś*, cl. 6. P. (Dhātup. xxviii, 130) *viśáti* (rarely, in later language mostly m. c. also Ā. *viśate*; pf. *viveśa, viviśe*, RV. &c. &c. [*viveśitha, viveśuḥ*, RV.; *viviśyās*, ib.; p. *-viśivás*, AV.; *viviśivas* or *viviśvas*, Pāṇ. vii, 2, 68; *aviveśīs*, RV.]; aor. *áviśran, ávikshmahi, veśīt*, RV.; *avikshat*, Br. &c.; *avikshata*, Gr.; Prec. *viśyāt*, ib.; fut. *veshṭā*, MBh.; *vekshyati*, °*te*, Br. &c.; inf. *veshṭum*, MBh. &c.; *veshṭavai*, Br.; *víśam*, RV.; ind. p. *-víśya*, AV. &c. &c.), to enter, enter in or settle down on, go into (acc., loc., or *antar* with gen.), pervade, RV. &c. &c. (with *punar* or *bhūyas*, to re-enter, return, come back); to be absorbed into (acc.), Bhag.; (in astron.) to come into conjunction with (acc.), VarBṛS.; (with *agnim, jvalanam* &c.) to enter the fire i. e. ascend the funeral pyre, MBh.; R. &c.; (with *apas*) to sink or be immersed in the water, BhP.; to enter (a house &c.), Hariv.; to appear (on the stage), R.; Kām.; to go home or to rest, RV.; ŚāṅkhBr.; to sit down upon (acc. or loc.), R.; Hariv.; to resort or betake one's self to (*agratas, agre*, or acc.), Ragh.; Pur.; to flow into (and 'join with;' applied to rivers and armies), Rājat. v, 140; to flow or redound to, fall to the share of (acc.), Hariv.; Ragh. &c.; to occur to (as a thought, with acc.), R.; to befall, come to (as death, with acc.), BhP.; to belong to, exist for (loc.), ib.; to fall or get into any state or condition (acc.), R.; Śāntiś.; to enter upon, undertake, begin, R.; PhP.; to mind (any business), attend to (dat.), MBh. xii, 6955: Caus. *veśáyati*, °*te* (aor. *avīviśat*; Pass. *veśyate*), to cause to enter into (acc.), AV.; to cause to sit down on (loc.), BhP.: Desid. *vivikshati*, to wish to enter (acc.), BhP.; (with *agnim* or *vahnim*) to wish to enter the fire i. e. to ascend the funeral pyre, Kathās.: Intens. *veviśyate, veveshṭi*, Gr. [Cf. Gk. οἶκος; Lat. *vicus*; Lith. *vėsz̃ėti*; Slav. *vĭsĭ*; Goth. *weihs*; Angl.-Sax. *wíc*; Germ. *wích, Weich-bild*.]

1. **Viṭ** (for 2. see p. 995, col. 2), in comp. for 2. *viś*. **-kula**, n. the house of a Vaiśya, ĀśvŚr. **-paṇya**, n. the wares or commodities of a man of the mercantile class, Mn. x, 85. **-pati**, m. 'chief of men,' a king, prince, MBh.; a chief of Vaiśyas, BhP.; a daughter's husband, son-in-law, Mn. iii, 148; a head-merchant, W. **-śūdra**, n. sg. Vaiśyas and Śūdras, R.

Viviksh, mfn. (fr. Desid.; nom. *viviṭ*) one who wishes to enter, Vop.

Vivikshu, mfn. (fr. id.) wishing or intending to enter (acc., rarely loc.), Kāv.; Kathās. &c.

2. **Viś**, f. (m. only L.; nom. sg. *viṭ*; loc. pl. *vikshú*) a settlement, homestead, house, dwelling (*viśás páti*, 'lord of the house' applied to Agni and Indra), RV.; (also pl.) a community, tribe, race (pl. also 'subjects,' 'people,' 'troops'), RV.; AV.; VS.; Br.; MBh.; BhP.; (sg. and pl.) the people κατ' ἐξοχήν (in the sense of those who settle on the soil; sg. also 'a man of the third caste,' 'a Vaiśya;' *viśām* with *patiḥ* or *nāthaḥ* or *īśvaraḥ* &c., 'lord of the people,' a king, sovereign); ŚBr. &c. &c.; with *sāma*, N. of a Sāman; (pl.) property, wealth, BhP.; entrance, L.; m. or f. a man in general, person, L.; f. or n. feces, L. (w. r. for *vish*). **-páti**, m. the chief of a settlement or tribe, lord of the house or of the people (also applied to Agni and Indra; du. 'master and mistress of the house'), RV.; AV.; TS.; pl. 'kings' or 'head-merchants,' BhP., Sch. [Cf. Zd. *vîs-paiti*; Lith. *vėsz-patis*.] **-pátnī**, f. the mistress or protectress of a house (also applied to the fire of attrition), RV.; AV.; TBr.

Viśa, mfn., see *dur-viśa*; w. r. for *bisa*, q. v.; m. N. of a man, g. *śubhrâdi*; n. and (*ā*), f. = 2. *viś*, a tribe, class, people (see *manushya-v°*); (*am*), ind. (ifc.), g. *śarad-ādi*.

Viśana, n. (ifc.) entering, entrance into, MBh.; VarBṛS.

Viśam-pa, mfn. (acc. of 2. *viś* + *pa*) 'people-protecting,' N. of a man (?), g. *aśvâdi* (cf. *vaiśampāyana*).

Viśam-bhala, n. (acc. of 2. *viś* + *bhala* = *bhara*?) supporting or nourishing the people, TBr., Sch. (to explain *vaiśambhalyā*).

Viś-aujas, mfn. (incorrectly for *viḍ-ojas*, p. 962) ruling the people (?), VS.

Viśyà, mfn. forming or belonging to a community &c., RV.; m. a man of the people or of the third caste, AV.; VS.

1. **Vishṭá**, mfn. (for 2. see under *√vish*) entered into, contained in (acc. or loc.), ŚBr.; BhP.; filled or accompanied with (instr.), TS. **-karṇa**, mfn. marked on the ear in a partic. manner, Pāṇ. vi, 3, 115. **-tva**, n. the being connected or accompanied with, Nyāyas., Sch. **-pura**, m. N. of a man, g. *śubhrâdi*.

विशंस् *vi-√śaṅs*, P. *-śaṅsati* (Ved. inf. *-śáse*), to recite, comprise in words, RV.; to divide in parts for recitation, AitBr.

1. **Vi-śasta**, mfn. (for 2. see under *vi-√śas*) praised, celebrated, W.

Vi-śasti, Gaṇar. 399.

विशङ्क् *vi-√śaṅk*, Ā. *-śaṅkate*, to be apprehensive or distrustful or uneasy, MBh.; to be afraid of (abl.), Kathās.; BhP.; to fear, apprehend (acc.), Śak.; to mistrust (acc.), R.; to doubt, suspect, MBh.; R.; to believe a person to have or to be (two acc.), Gīt.; (with *anyathā*) to judge wrongly, misjudge, Śak. v, 17. **°śaṅkanīya**, mfn. to be suspected or distrusted, doubtful, questionable, R.

2. **Vi-śaṅkā**, f. (for 1. see p. 952, col. 2) suspicion, doubt in (loc.), MBh.; R.; BhP.; apprehension, fear of (gen. or comp.), MārkP.; hesitation (acc. with *√kṛi*, Ā. *-kurute*, to hesitate), MBh. **°śaṅkita**, mfn. apprehensive, distrustful, suspicious, uncertain of (*prati* or comp.), MBh.; Kāv. &c. **°śaṅkin**, mfn. (ifc.) supposing, presuming, surmising, Śiś.; apprehending, fearing, afraid of, afraid that (comp. or Pot. with *iti*), Kathās. **°śaṅkya**, mfn. to be distrusted or suspected, R.; to be feared, Mālatīm.

विशङ्कट *vi-śaṅkaṭa*. See p. 952, col. 2.

विशद *vi-śada*, mf(*ā*)n. (prob. fr. *√1. śad*) 'conspicuous,' bright, brilliant, shining, splendid, beautiful, white, spotless, pure (lit. and fig.; *am*, ind.), MBh.; Kāv. &c.; calm, easy, cheerful (as the mind, the eye, a smile), Kālid.; Śiś.; Rājat.; clear, evident, manifest, intelligible (compar. *-tara*), Hariv.; Mṛicch.; Rājat.; tender, soft (to the touch; as food, wind, odour), MBh.; Suśr.; (ifc.) skilled or dexterous in, fit for, Mṛicch. i, 9; endowed with, Suśr.; m. white (the colour), L.; N. of a king (the son of Jayad-ratha), BhP.; n. yellowish sulphurate of iron, L.; *-tā*, f. clearness, distinctness, Pañcat. (v. l.); *-nara-karaṅkāya* (Ā. °*yate*), to resemble a white human skull, Caṇḍ.; *-prajña*, mfn. of clear understanding, keen-witted, sagacious, Rājat.; *-prabha*, mfn. of pure effulgence, shedding pure light, MW.; °*dâtman*, mfn. pure-hearted, Kām.; °*dânana*, mfn. (ifc.) one whose face is radiant with, Rājat.

Vi-śadaya, Nom. P. °*yati*, to clean, purify, Bālar.; Vāgbh.; to make clear, explain, Jaim., Sch.

Vi-śadāya, Nom. Ā. °*yate*, to become clear or evident, Cat. **°śadita**, mfn. purified, Bālar.

Viśadī-√kṛi, P. *-karoti*, to make clear, explain, illustrate, Pañcar.

विशप्त *vi-śápta*, n. (*√śap*) forswearing, abjuring, taking an oath against, MaitrS.

विशब्द *vi-śabda*. See p. 952, col. 3.

Vi-śabdana, n. (*√śabd*) = *prati-jñāna*, Kāś. on Pāṇ. vii, 2, 23. **°śabdita**, mfn. mentioned, indicated, R.

विशय *vi-śaya* &c. See under *vi-√śī*.

विशर *vi-śará*, 2. *vi-śaraṇa* &c. See under *vi-√śṛī*.

विशल *vi-śala*, m. (for *viśāla*?) N. of the son of Abja, MW.; (*ā*), f. N. of a town, ib. (cf. *vaiśālī*).

विशल्य *ví-śalya*, mfn. pointless (as an arrow), VS.; freed from an arrow-head, healed of an arrow-wound, MBh.; R.; free from thorns or darts, W.; freed from an extraneous substance in the body (*ā viśalya-bhāvāt*, 'until freed from the embryo'), Suśr.; freed from pain, MBh.; without trouble or care or pain, W.; (*ā*), f. N. of various plants (also of a specific for arrow-wounds), Suśr.; MBh.; R.; Cocculus Cordifolius, L.; Croton Polyandrum, L.; Convolvulus Turpethum, L.; Methonica Superba, Bhpr.; = *agni-śikhā*, L.; = *aja-modā*, L.; Menispermum Cordifolium, W.; a sort of pot-herb, ib.; a sort of fruit, Langaliya, ib.; N. of the wife of Lakshmaṇa, L.; of a river, MBh.; *-karaṇa*, mf(*ī*)n. healing wounds inflicted by arrows; (*ī*), f. a partic. herb with wonder-working properties, MBh.; R.; Kathās.; *-kṛit*, mfn. freeing from pain or distress, MW.; m. Echites Dichotoma, L.; *-ghna* or *-prâṇa-hara*, mfn. (prob. said of those spots of the body, such as the temples and space between the eye-brows a blow on which is fatal even without any point entering the surface, but commonly applied to those spots a wound on which becomes fatal as soon as a pointed weapon is extracted), Suśr.; °*yā-saṃgama*, m., °*yā-sambhava*, m. N. of chapters of the Revā-māhātmya.

Vi-śalyaya, Nom. P. °*yati*, to free from a pointed weapon or from pain, Kathās.

विशस् *vi-√śas*, P. *-śasati*, *-śasti*, *-śāsti* (2. pl. *-śasta*, RV.; 3. pl. Impv. *-śāsatu*, VS.; impf. *vy-aśāt*, ib.), to cut up, dissect, cut down, slaughter, immolate, kill, destroy, RV. &c. &c.: Desid., see *vi-śiśāsishat*. °**śásana**, mf(*ī*)n. causing death, deadly, MBh.; Mṛicch.; m. a sabre, crooked sword, MBh. (also fig. 'punishment'); m. n. a partic. hell, Pur.; n. cutting up, dissecting, MBh.; Suśr.; slaughter, havoc, fight, battle, MBh.; R.; cruel treatment, Uttarar. °**śasi**, g. *brāhmaṇâdi* (Kāś.) °**śasita**, mfn. cut up, dissected, Pāṇ. vii, 2, 19. °**śasitṛi**, m. one who cuts up, a dissector, Mn. v, 51.

2. **Vi-śasta**, mfn. (for 1. see under *vi-√śaṇs*) cut up, dissected, MBh.; R.; rude, ill-mannered, Pāṇ. vii, 2, 19. °**śastṛi**, m. = *-śasitṛi*, RV.; MBh. °**śāstṛi**, m. id., PañcavBr.

Vi-śiśāsishat, mfn. (fr. Desid.) wishing to cut up or dissect, ŚāṅkhŚr. °**shu**, mfn. id., AitBr.

विशस्त्र *vi-śastra*, *vi-śākha* &c. See p. 952.

विशातन *vi-śātana*, mf(*ī*)n. (√2. *śad*, Caus.) causing to fall to pieces, destroying, MBh.; BhP.; setting free, delivering, MW.; m. N. of Vishṇu, MBh. (= *saṃhartṛi*, Nīlak.); n. cutting off, VP.; hewing in pieces, destroying, MBh.

Vi-śātaya, Nom. P. °*yati*, to hew in pieces, cut down or off, MBh.; R.; to knock out (an eye), R.; to scatter, dispel, remove, destroy, MBh.; R.

विशायक *viśāyaka*. See *bisāyaka*.

विशारद *vi-śārada*. See p. 952, col. 3.

विशाल *viśālá*, mf(*ā*, accord. to g. *bahv-ādi* also *ī*)n. (prob. fr. √*viś*; accord. to others, fr. *vi-√śri*) spacious, extensive, broad, wide, large, TS. &c. &c. (*am*, ind. extensively, PañcavBr.); great, important, powerful, mighty, illustrious, eminent, MBh.; Kāv. &c.; (ifc.) abundant in, full of, Kap.; m. a kind of beast or bird or plant, L.; a partic. Shaḍ-aha, ŚrS.; N. of the father of Takshaka, ŚāṅkhGṛ.; of an Asura, Kathās.; of a son of Ikshvāku (founder of the city Viśālā), R.; of a son of Tṛiṇa-bindu, Pur.; of a king of Vaidiśa, MārkP.; of a mountain, ib.; (*ā*), f. colocynth, Suśr.; Basella Cordifolia, L.; Portulaca Quadrifida, L.; = *mahêndra-vāruṇī*, L.; (in music) a partic. Mūrchanā, Saṃgīt.; N. of the city Ujjayinī or Ougein, R.; Megh.; Kathās.; of another town (see *vaiśālī*, *vaiśalī*); of a river and a hermitage situated on it, MBh.; R.; BhP.; = *sarasvatī*, L.; N. of an Apsaras, VP.; of the wife of Aja-mīḍha, MBh.; of the wife of A-rishṭa-nemi (and daughter of Daksha), GāruḍaP.; (*ī*), f. a kind of plant, L.; n. N. of a place of pilgrimage, Bh.; du. (with *Vishṇoḥ*) N. of two Sāmans, ĀrshBr. **-kula**, n. a great or illustrious family, MW.; mfn. of noble family, ib.; *-sambhava*, mfn. sprung from an illustrious race, ib. **-grāma**, m. N. of a village, MārkP. **-tā**, great extent, greatness, Śiś.; eminence, distinction, W. **-taila-garbha**, m. Alangium Hexapetalum, L. **-tva**, n. = *-tā*, MW. **-tvac**, m. Bauhinia Variegata or Alstonia Scholaris, L. **-datta**, m. N. of a man, Pāṇ. v, 3, 84, Sch. **-dā**, f. Alhagi Maurorum, L. **-nagara**, n. N. of a town, Cat. **-nayana-tā**, f. having large eyes (one of the minor marks of a Buddha), Dharmaś. 84. **-netra**, m. 'large-eyed,' N. of a Bodhi-sattva, Buddh.; (*ī*), f. of a supernatural being, ib.; °*trī-sādhana*, n. N. of wk. **-pattra**, m. a species of bulbous plant, L.; a tree resembling the wine-palm, L. **-purī**, f. N. of a town, Cat. **-phalaka**, mf(*ikā*)n. bearing large fruits, L. **-locanā**, f. a large-eyed woman, Daś. **-varman**, m. N. of a man, ib. **-vijaya**, m. a kind of military array, Kām. **Viśālâksha**, mf(*ī*)n. large-eyed, MBh.; R.; m. a screech-owl, L.; N. of Śiva (also as author of a Śāstra), MBh.; Kām.; Daś.; of Garuḍa, L.; of a son of Garuḍa, MBh.; of a serpent-demon, Hariv.; of a son of Dhṛita-rāshṭra, ib.; (*ī*), f. Tiaridium Indicum, L.; a form of Durgā, Cat. (°*kshī-māhātmya*, n. N. of wk.); N. of one of the Mātṛis attendant on Skanda, MBh.; of a Yoginī, Hcat.; of a daughter of Śāṇḍilya, Cat.; n. N. of the Śāstra composed by Śiva Viśālâksha, MBh. xii, 2203.

Viśālaka, m. Feronia Elephantum, L.; N. of Garuḍa, L.; of a Yaksha, MBh.; (*ikā*), f. Odina Pinnata, L.

Viśālaya, Nom. P. °*yati*, to enlarge, magnify, Subh.

Viśālika, °**liya**, °**lila**, m. endearing forms of names beginning with *viśāla*, Pāṇ. v, 3, 84.

Viśāliya, mfn. (fr. *viśāla*), g. *utkarâdi*.

विशास् *vi-√śās*, P. *-śāsti*, to give different directions ('concerning,' acc.), ĀpŚr.

Vi-śís, f. (prob.) explanation, AV.

विशिका *viśikā*, f., g. *chattrâdi* (v. l. *śibikā*).

विशिक्ष् *vi-√śiksh* (properly Desid. of √*śak*; only Impv. *-śiksha*), to impart, share out, RV. iv, 35, 3. °**śikshu**, mfn. imparting willingly or readily, ib. ii, 1, 10.

विशिख *vi-śikha* &c. See p. 952, col. 3.

विशिञ्ज् *vi-√śiñj*, Ā. *-śiṅkte* (only pr. p. *-śiñjāna*), to sound, warble, Bhaṭṭ.

विशित *vi-śita*, mfn. (√*śi* or *śo*) sharpened, sharp, W.

विशिप *viśipa*, n. (said to be fr. √*viś*) a house, palace, temple, Uṇ. iii, 145, Sch.

विशिशासिषत् *vi-śiśāsishat*, °*shu*. See col. 1.

विशिशिप्र *viśi-śiprá*, m. (so divided in Padap.; accord. to Sāy. = *vigata-hanu*) N. of a demoniacal being, RV. v, 45, 6.

विशिश्रमिषु *vi-śiśramishu*, mfn. (fr. Desid. of *vi-√śram*, p. 991) wishing to rest, Daś.

विशिष् *vi-√śish*, P. *-śinashṭi*, to distinguish, make distinct or different, particularize, specify, define, Sāṃkhyak.; Sarvad.; to distinguish (from others), prefer to (instr.), MBh.; to augment, enhance, MBh.: Pass. *-śishyate*, to be distinguished or particularized by (instr.), differ from (abl. or instr.), Prāt.; Ragh.; to be pre-eminent, excel, be better than (abl. or instr.) or best among (gen. or loc.), Mn.; MBh. &c.: Caus. *-śeshayati*, to distinguish, define, specify, Pat.; Kāś.; to prefer, Kām.; to enhance the worth or value of (acc.), Bhartṛ.; to surpass, excel, MBh.; Kāv. &c.: Pass. *-śeshyate*, to be of much account, MBh. i, 3174 (v. l.)

Vi-śishṭa, mfn. distinguished, distinct, particular, peculiar, MBh.; Rājat.; Sarvad.; characterized by (instr. or comp.), MārkP.; Vedântas.; pre-eminent, excellent, excelling in or distinguished by (loc., instr., adv. in *tas*, or comp.), chief or best among (gen.), better or worse than (abl. or comp.), Mn.; MBh. &c.; m. N. of Vishṇu, MBh.; (*ī*), f. N. of the mother of Śaṃkarâcārya, Cat.; *-kula*, mfn. descended from an excellent race, Subh.; *-cāritra* or *-cārin*, m. N. of a Bodhi-sattva, SaddhP.; *-tama* and *-tara*, mfn. distinguished, chief, best, better than (abl.), MBh.; Mṛicch.; Śaṃk.; *-tā*, f. (Hit.), *-tva*, n. (Śaṃk.; Vedântas.) difference, speciality, peculiarity, distinction, excellence, superiority; *-buddhi*, f. differenced or distinguishing knowledge (e. g. the kn° of 'a man carrying a staff' which distinguishes him from an ordinary man), MW.; *-liṅga*, mfn. different in gender, Pāṇ. ii, 4, 7; *-varṇa*, mfn. having a distinguished colour, MBh.; *-vaiśishṭya*, (ibc.) 'what is different' and 'difference;' (*-jñāna-vādârtha*, m., *-bodha*, m., *-bodha-rahasya*, n., *-bodha-vicāra*, m., *-bodha-vicāra-rahasya*, n.; °*tyâvagāhi-vādârtha*, m. N. of wks.); °*tâdvaita*, n., see below; °*tôpamā*, f. a partic. comparison, MW.; *-yukta*, n. (scil. *rūpaka*) a metaphor which contains a partic. comp° (said to be a variety of the general Rūpaka), ib.

Viśishṭâdvaita, n. 'qualified non-duality,' the doctrine that the spirits of men have a qualified identity with the one Spirit (see Rāmânuja), RTL. 119 &c.; *-candrikā*, f., *-bhāshya*, n., *-vādârtha*, m. N. of wks.; *-vādin*, m. one who asserts the doctrine of qualified non-duality, L.; *-vijaya-vāda*, m., *-samarthana*, n., *-siddhânta*, m. N. of wks.

Vi-śesha, m. (once in Pañcat. n.; ifc. f. *ā*) distinction, difference between (two gen., two loc., or gen. and instr.), GṛŚrS.; MBh. &c.; characteristic difference, peculiar mark, special property, speciality, peculiarity, Mn.; MBh. &c.; a kind, species, individual (e. g. *vṛiksha-v°*, a species of tree, in comp. often also = special, peculiar, particular, different, e. g. *chando-v°*, 'a particular metre,' *v°-maṇḍana*, 'a peculiar ornament;' *argha-viśeshāḥ*, 'different prices'), MBh.; Kāv. &c.; (pl.) various objects, Megh.; distinction, peculiar merit, excellence, superiority (in comp. often = excellent, superior, choice, distinguished, e. g. *ākṛiti-v°*, 'an excellent form;' cf. *v°-pratipatti*), Mn.; MBh. &c.; (in gram.) a word which defines or limits the meaning of another word (cf. *vi-śeshaka* and *vi-śeshaṇa*); (in phil.) particularity, individuality, essential difference or individual essence (with the Vaiśeshikas the 5th category or Padârtha, belonging to the 9 eternal substances or Dravyas, viz. soul, time, place, ether, and the 5 atoms of earth, water, light, air, and mind, which are said to be so essentially different that one can never be the other), IW. 66 &c.; (in medicine) a favourable turn or crisis of a sickness, Suśr.; (in rhet.) statement of difference or distinction, individualization, variation, Kuval. (cf. *viśeshôkti*); a sectarian mark, any mark on the forehead (= *tilaka*), L.; (in geom.) the hypotenuse, Śulbas.; N. of the primary elements or Mahā-bhūtas (q. v.), MaitrUp.; the earth as an element, BhP.; the mundane egg, ib.; = *vi-rāj*, ib.; (ibc., *ena* or *āt*, ind. exceedingly, especially, particularly, even more, Mn.; MBh. &c.; *āt*, ifc., by reason or in consequence of, VarBṛS.; *yena yena viśesheṇa*, in any way whatever, MBh.); mf(*ā*)n. extraordinary, abundant, Ragh. ii, 14 (B. *viśeshāt* for *viśeshā*); *-karaṇa*, n. making better, improvement, Mālav.; *-kṛit*, mfn. making a distinction, distinguishing, RPrāt.; *-garhaṇīya*, mfn. especially reprehensible, even more blamable, Kuval.; *-guṇa*, m. a special or distinct quality, Nīlak.; (in phil.) a substance of a distinct kind (as soul, time, space, ether, and the five atoms enumerated above), W.; *-jña*, mfn. knowing distinctions, judicious, Kāv.; Kathās.; (ifc.) knowing various kinds of, R.; *-jñāna-vādârtha*, m. N. of wk.; *-tas*, ind. according to the difference of, in proportion to (comp.), Mn. xi, 2; especially, particularly, above all, Mn.; MBh. &c.; individually, singly, Vedântas.; *-tva*, n. distinction, notion of the particular, L.; *-dṛiśya*, mfn. of splendid aspect or appearance, Ragh.; *-dharma*, m. a peculiar or different duty, W.; a special law, MW.; *-niyama*, m. a partic. observance, MBh.; *-nirukti*, f. (ibc.) 'explanation of differences;' N. of wk. (*-kroḍa*, m., *-ṭīkā*, f., *-prakāśa*, m.; °*ty-āloka*, m. N. of wks.); *-pataniya*, n. a partic. crime or sin, Yājñ. iii, 298; *-padârtha*, m. (in Nyāya) the category of particularity (cf. above under *vi-śesha*); *-pratipatti*, f. a special mark of honour or respect, Ragh.; *-pratishedha*, m. a special exception, MW.; *-pramāṇa*, n. sp° authority, ib.; *-bhāga*, m. a partic. part of an elephant's fore-foot, L.; *-bhāvanā*, f. reflecting on or perceiving difference, W.; (in arithm.) a partic. operation in extracting roots, composition by the difference of the products, ib.; *-bhūta-pariśishṭa*, n. N. of wk.; *-maṇḍana*, n. a peculiar ornament, Śak.; *-mati*, m. N. of a Bodhi-sattva and of another man, Buddh.; *-mitra*, m. N. of a man, Buddh.; *-ramaṇīya*, mfn. especially delightful, particularly pleasant, Vikr.; *-lakshaṇa*, n. any specific or characteristic mark or sign, W.; (°*ṇā-ṭīkā*, f. N. of wk.); *-liṅga*, n. a partic. mark, specific property, attribute of a subordinate class, Kap.; *-vacana*, n. 'distinguishing or defining word,' an adjective, apposition, Pāṇ. viii, 1, 74; a special text, special rule or precept, W.; *-vat*, mfn. pursuing something particular, MBh. ii, 849; possessed of some distinguishing property or specific quality, BhP.; excellent, superior, better than (abl.), MBh.; Hariv.; making a difference (see *a-v°*); *-vāda*, m. the above doctrine of the Vaiśeshikas; (*-ṭīkā*, f. N. of wk.; °*din*, m. an adherent of that doctrine, Sāṃkhyak., Sch.); *-vikrama-ruci*, mfn. taking delight in splendid heroism, Bhartṛ.; *-vid*, mfn. = *-jña*, MBh.; *-vidvas*, m. 'eminently learned,' a sage, philosopher, W.; *-vidhi*, m. a special rule or observance, W.; *-vyāpti*, f. (in logic) a form of Vyāpti or pervasion, L.; N. of wk. (also *-rahasya*, n.); *-śārṅgadhara*, m. N. of wk.; *-śālin*, mfn. possessing peculiar merit or excellence, Kir.; *-śāstra*, n. (in gram.) a special rule (= *apavāda*), MW.; *-stha*, mfn. being (found only) in excellent persons or things, Kāvyâd. ii, 170; °*shâtideśa*, m. a sp° supplementary rule, ib.; °*shâmṛita*, n. N. of wk.; °*shârtha*, m. the sense or essence of distinction, difference (*am*, ind. for the sake of d°, MW.); *-prakāśikā*, f., *-bodhikā*, f. N. of wks.; °*shârthin*, mfn. seeking for excellence or distinction, MBh.; particular in searching for anything, MW.; (°*thi*)-*tā*, f. the searching for something better, Pañcat.; °*shâvasyaka-niryukti*, f. N. of wk.; *-shôkti*, f. 'mention of difference,' N. of a figure of speech (in which the excellence of a thing is implied by comparing it to some highly prized object, yet mentioning the difference, e.g. *dyūtaṃ nāma purushasyâsiṇhâsanaṃ rājyam*, 'truly gambling is a man's throneless kingdom,' Mṛicch. ii, 7/8), Vām. iv, 3, 23 (cf. Kāvyâd. ii, 323 &c.); enumeration of merits, panegyric, W.; °*shôcchvasita*, n. the peculiar breath or life, cherished object), a peculiar treasure (applied to an object especially dear), MW.; °*shôddeśa*, m. (in Nyāya) a partic. kind of enunciation, ib.

Vi-śeshaka (ifc.) = *vi-śesha*, distinction, difference, Bhāshāp.; mfn. distinguishing, qualifying, specifying, L.; m. n. a mark on the forehead (made with sandal &c.), R.; Mālav.; Kathās. (cf. *pattra-v°*); an attribute, predicate, W.; m. a partic. figure of speech (in which the difference of two objects otherwise said to be similar is dwelt upon; cf. *vi-śeshôkti*), Kuval.; N. of a scholar, Buddh.; of a country, Nalac.; (*ikā*), f. a kind of metre, Col.; n. a series of three stanzas forming one grammatical sentence; cf. *yugma* and *kalāpaka*), Śatr.; *-cchedya*, n. N. of one of the 64 Kalās (prob. the art of painting sectarian marks on the forehead), Cat.

Vi-śeshaṇa, mfn. distinguishing, discriminative, specifying, qualifying, L.; distinctive (as a property), W.; n. the act of distinguishing &c., distinction, discrimination, particularization, BhP.; Sarvad.; Sāh.; a distinguishing mark or attribute, MBh.; (in gram.) 'differencer,' a word which particularizes or defines (another word which is called *vi-śeshya*, q.v.), attribute, adjective, adverb, apposition, predicate, Pāṇ.; Tarkas.; Sāh. &c.; a species, kind, MBh. vii, 1124; surpassing, excelling, ib. i, 73; (in rhet.) = *viśeshôkti*, Sāh.; *-khaṇḍana*, n., *-jñāna-vādârtha*, m. N. of wks.; *-tā*, f. the state of a distinguisher or of distinguishing, Bhāshāp.; individuality, MW. (*-sambandha*, m. the relation of predicate to subject, ib.); *-traya-vaiyarthya*, n. N. of wk.; *-tva*, n. = *-tā*, MW.; adjectival nature, Sāy.; *-dvaya-vaiyarthya*, n. N. of wk.; *-pada*, n. a title of honour, Mudr.; *-mātra-prayoga*, m. the use of an adjective for a substantive (e.g. *sāgarâmbarā*, 'the sea-girt,' for *pṛithivī*, 'the earth'), Vām. v, 1, 10; *-viśeshya-tā*, f., *-viśeshya-bhāva*, m. the relation of predicate and subject, Vedântas.; *-vat*, mfn. endowed with discrimination, MW.; having a distinguishing attribute, ib.; *-varga*, m. N. of a ch. of the Śabda-ratnâvalī lexicon. °**śeshaṇī-√kṛi**, P. *-karoti*, to predicate, Kusum. **-śeshaṇīya**, mfn. to be distinguished or discriminated, W.; to be marked as different or distinct, ib.; to be particularized, MW.

Vi-śeshita, mfn. (fr. Caus.) distinguished, defined, characterized, Śaṃk.; preferred, Kām.; superior to, better than (abl.), MBh.; surpassed, exceeded, Hariv.; Mālav.; predicated, attributed, W. °**śeshin**, mfn. distinct, individual, BhP.; (ifc.) vying with, rivalling, Hariv.

Vi-śeshya, mfn. to be (or being) distinguished or qualified or particularized (see comp.); n. (in gram.) the word to be 'differenced' or distinguished (from another word which is called *vi-śeshaṇa*, q.v.), a substantive, noun, the object or subject of a predicate, Pāṇ.; Tarkas.; Vedântas.; *-tā*, f. the being defined or qualified, substantival nature, Kusum. (*-vāda*, m. N. of wk.); *-tva*, n. = *-tā*, f., KātyŚr., Sch. °**śeshyaka** (ifc.) = °*śeshya*, Bhāshāp.

विशिस् *vi-śís*. See *vi-√śās*, p. 990, col. 2.

विशी *vi-√śī*, Ā. *-śete*, to lie outstretched, BhP.; to remain lying or sitting, R.; to be subject to doubt, Śaṃk.

Vi-śaya, m. the middle, centre, Śulbas.; doubt, uncertainty, Jaim.; Śaṃk.; = *āśraya*, L.; *-vat*, mfn. = next, Nir. °**śayin**, mfn. doubtful, uncertain (°*yi-tva*, n. doubt, uncertainty), ĀpŚr., Sch.

Vi-śāya, m. sleeping and watching alternately, W. (cf. Pāṇ. iii, 3, 39). °**śāyin**, mfn., g. *grahâdi*.

विशीत *viśīta*, m. N. of a man (cf. *vaiśīti*).

विशीर्ण *vi-śīrṇa* &c. See under *vi-√śṝ*.

विशुक *viśuka*, m. Calotropis Gigantea Alba, L.

विशुण्डि *viśuṇḍi*, m. N. of a son of Kaśyapa, MBh.

विशुध् *vi-√śudh*, P. Ā. *-śudhyati*, °*te*, to become perfectly pure (esp. in ritual sense), Mn.; Yājñ. &c.; to become clear (said of the senses), R.; (in alg.) to remain naught, Bījag.: Caus. *-śodhayati*, to purify (esp. ritually), MBh.; Pañcar.; Suśr.; to improve, correct, Yājñ., Sch.; to free from suspicion, exculpate, Yājñ.; MBh.; R.; to justify, MBh.; to set clear, fix or determine accurately, Yājñ.; VarBṛS.; (in alg.) to subtract, VarBṛS.

Vi-śuddha, mfn. completely cleansed or purified (also in a ritual sense), clean, clear, pure (lit. and fig.), Mn.; MBh. &c.; free from vice, virtuous, honest, MBh.; Kāv. &c.; brilliantly white (as teeth), Ṛitus.; thoroughly settled or established or fixed or determined or ascertained, ib.; (ifc.) one who has gone through or thoroughly completed (*upadeśa-v°*), Mālav.; cleared i.e. exhausted, empty (as a treasury), Rājat.; (in alg.) subtracted, Gol.; n. a kind of mystical circle in the body (cf. *cakra* and *vi-śuddhi-c°*); *-karaṇa*, mfn. one whose acts are pure or virtuous, BhP.; *-gātra-tā*, f. the having bright or pure limbs (a minor mark of a Buddha), Dharmaś. 84; *-cāritra*, m. 'of virtuous conduct,' N. of a Bodhi-sattva, SaddhP.; *-tā*, f. (Kāv.), *-tva*, n. (Śaṃk.) purity; *-dhishaṇa* mfn. having the mind purified, BhP.; *-dhī*, mfn. id., Rājat.; *-dhīra*, mfn. pure and grave, Kathās.; *-netra-tā*, f. having the eyes bright (one of the minor marks of a Buddha), Dharmaś. 84; *-pārshṇi*, mfn. having the rear or back protected or covered, Kām.; *-prakṛiti*, mfn. of pure or virtuous disposition, Rājat.; *-bhāva* (R.), *-manas* (Bhartṛ.), mfn. pure-minded; *-mugdha*, mfn. p° and innocent, Mālatīm.; *-rasa-dīpikā*, f. N. of wk.; *-vaṇśya*, mfn. of a p° or virtuous family, Rājat.; *-sattva*, mfn. of a pure character, MuṇḍUp.; *-sattva-pradhāna*, mfn. chiefly characterized by pure goodness, MW.; *-sattva-vijñāna*, mfn. of pure character and understanding, R.; *-siṇha*, m. N. of a man, Buddh.; *-svara-nirghoshā*, f. a partic. Dhāraṇī, Buddh.; °*ddhâtman*, mfn. of a p° nature or character, MBh.; R. &c.; °*ddhêśvara-tantra*, n. N. of a Tantra.

Vi-śuddhi, f. complete purification, purity (also fig.), holiness, virtue, Mn.; MBh. &c.; rectification, removal of error or doubt, W.; settlement (of a debt), Sāṃkhyak., Sch.; retribution, retaliation (see *vaira-v°*); perfect knowledge, BhP.; (in alg.) a subtractive quantity, Bījag.; = *sama*, L.; *-cakra*, n. a kind of mystical circle or mark in the body (said to be in the region of the throat), Cat.; *-darpaṇa*, m. N. of wk.; *-mat*, mfn. possessing purity, free from sin or vice, pure, Mcar.

Vi-śodhana, mf(*ī*)n. cleansing, purging, washing away, R.; Suśr. &c.; m. N. of Vishṇu, MBh.; (*ī*), f. Croton Polyandrum or Tiglium, L.; N. of the capital of Brahmā, L.; n. cleansing, Suśr.; lopping (of trees), VarBṛS.; purification (in the ritual sense), Mn.; Yājñ.; a laxative, Suśr.; the becoming decided or certain (*a-v°*), Vishṇ.; subtraction, VarBṛS. °**śodhanīya**, mfn. to be purified or cleansed &c.; to be treated with laxatives, Car.; purging, ib.; to be rectified or corrected, MW. °**śodhita**, mfn. (fr. Caus.) purified, cleansed, freed from soil or taint, Yājñ.; VarBṛS. °**śodhin**, mfn. purifying, cleaning, clearing (°*dhi-tva*, n.), Hit.; (*inī*), f. Tiaridium Indicum, L.; °*dhinī-bīja*, n. Croton Jamalgota, ib. °**śodhya**, n. to be cleansed or purified &c.; to be subtracted from (abl.); n. debt, L.

विशुन्थलवण *viśuntha-lavaṇa*, n. rock salt, L.

विशुभ् *vi-√śubh*, Ā. *-śobhate*, to shine brightly, be beautiful, MBh.

Vi-śobhita, mfn. (fr. Caus.) beautified or adorned with (instr. or comp.), MBh.; R.

विशुष् *vi-√1. śush*, cl. 4. P. Ā. *-śushyati*, °*te*, to become very dry, dry up, wither away, MBh.; R. &c.: Caus. *-śoshayati*, to make dry, dry up, desiccate, ib.

Vi-śosha, m. dryness, drought, Vcar. °**śoshaṇa**, mfn. drying, desiccative, MBh.; Bh.; healing (a wound; cf. *vraṇa-viś°*); n. the act of drying up, desiccation, Rājat.; Suśr. °**śoshita**, mfn. (fr. Caus.) completely dried up or withered, Kum. °**śoshin**, mfn. drying up, withering, Ragh.; making dry, desiccating, Suśr.

विशून्य *vi-śūnya*, *vi-śūla*, *vi-śṛiṅkhala* &c. See p. 952, col. 3.

विशृध् *vi-√śṛidh*, Ā. *-śardhate*, to break wind, Suśr.

Vi-śardhita, n. the act of breaking wind, ib.

विशॄ *vi-√śṝ*, Pass. *-śīryate* (aor. *-śāri*, RV.), to be broken or shattered or dissolved, crumble or fall to pieces, waste away, decay, RV. &c. &c.; to be scattered or dispersed, Hariv.; to be severed from (abl.), R.; to be damaged or destroyed, perish, Mn.; MBh. &c.

Vi-śará, mfn. tearing asunder, rending, TS.; m. a kind of disease, AV.; killing, slaughter, L.

2. **Vi-śaraṇa**, n. (for 1. see p. 952, col. 3) dissolution, Dhātup.; killing, slaughter, L. °**śarāru**, mfn. falling to pieces, being scattered or dispersed, Vcar.; Hcar.; frail, perishable, Śil.; Hcar.; *-tā*, f. dissolution, decay, Kpr.; frailty, perishableness, Rājat. °**śarīka** (*ví-*), m. a kind of disease, AV. °**śāraṇa**, n. killing, slaughter, L.

Vi-śīrṇa, mfn. broken, shattered &c.; scattered, dispersed (as an army), R.; fallen out (as teeth), Kāv.; squandered (as a treasure), MBh.; rubbed off (as unguent), GāruḍaP.; frustrated (as an enterprise), Śāntiś.; destroyed (as a town), R.; *-jīrṇa-vasana*, n. pl. worn and shattered garments, Bhartṛ.; *-tā*, f. crumbling or falling to pieces, Kām.; *-dhāra*, mfn. intermittent (as urine), BhPr.; *-paṅkti*, mfn. having broken ranks or lines, Ragh.; *-parṇa*, m. Azadirachta Indica, L.; *-mūrti*, mfn. having the body destroyed (said of Kāma-deva), Kum. °**śīrya**, mfn. to be broken to pieces or dissolved, W.

विशेष *vi-śesha* &c. See p. 990, col. 2.

विशोक *vi-śoka*. See p. 952, col. 3.

विशोभगीन *viśobhagīna*, mf(*ā*)n. an adj. or epithet applied to Sarasvatī, ĀpŚr. (cf. *veśa-bhagīna* and *veśo-bhagīna*).

विशोविशीय *viśoviśīya*, n. N. of various Sāmans, TāṇḍyaBr. (also *Agner viś°*, ĀrshBr.)

विशौजस् *viś-aujas*. See p. 989, col. 2.

विश्वकद्रु *viś-cakadra*, m. (said to be fr. 2. *viś* = 3. *vi* + *c°*) 'a dog-keeper' (regarded as a low man) or 'a dog,' Nir. ii, 3, Sch.; °*drâkarsha*, m. the chastiser of a dog-keeper or of a dog, ib.

विश्न *viśna*, m. (fr. √*vich*), Pāṇ. iii, 3, 90.

विश्पति *viś-páti*, *viś-pátnī*. See under 2. *viś*, p. 989, col. 2.

विश्पला *viśpálā*, f. (accord. to some fr. 2. *viś* and *palā* = *pālā*) N. of a woman (whose lost leg was replaced by the Aśvins), RV. **-vasu** (*viś-pálā-*), mfn. (prob.) kind or friendly to Viśpalā (said of the Aśvins), ib.

विश्रण् *vi-√śraṇ*, Caus. *-śrāṇayati*, to give away, distribute, present, Gobh.; MBh. &c. °**śraṇana**, n. gift, donation, L. °**śrāṇana**, n. id., R.; Naish. °**śrāṇika**, mfn. (ifc.) treating of the gift or bestowal of, R. (v. l.) °**śrāṇita**, mfn. given away, distributed, bestowed, Gobh.; R. &c.

विश्रथ् *vi-√śrath* (only 3. sg. pf. Ā. *-śaśrathe*), to open for one's self, RV. ix, 70, 2: Caus. *-śrathayati* (2. sg. Impv. *-śrathāya*, Subj. aor. *śiśrathaḥ*), to loosen, untie, RV.; AV.; to remit, pardon (a sin), RV. iv, 12, 4; to destroy, ib. ii, 28, 7.

विश्रम् *vi-√śram*, P. *-śrāmyati* (ep. also *-śramati*, °*te*; ind. p. *-śrāmya* or *-śramya*), to rest, repose, recreate one's self, ŚBr.; MBh. &c.; to rest from labour, cease, stop, desist, Kāv.; Kathās.; Rājat.; to rest or depend on (loc.), Kāv.; to rest i.e. trust or confide in, rely on, R.; Cāṇ.; to feel at ease or comfortable, R.; Bhaṭṭ.: Pass. *-śrāmyate* (aor. *vy-aśrāmi*, Vop.; esp. 3. sg. Impv.; *-śrāmyatām*, 'you may rest,' 'enough of this'), Bhartṛ.; Ratnâv.: Caus. *-śrāmayati*, to cause to rest, make to cease, stop, ŚāṅkhGṛ.; MBh.; Kāv. &c.; to cause to rest or settle down on (loc.), Ragh.: Desid., see *vi-śiśramishu*.

Vi-śrama, m. rest, repose, quiet, relaxation, Kālid.; Śiś.; Vās.; N. of a scribe, MW. °**śramaṇa**, n. resting, relaxation, MBh.; Kathās.; BhP. °**śramita**, mfn. made to rest, allayed, Gīt.

Vi-śrānta, mfn. reposed, rested or ceased from (comp.), MBh.; Kāv. &c.; reposing, taking rest, VarBṛS.; Pañcat.; abated, ceased, stopped, Kāv.; Kathās.; coming to rest or to an end, reaching to (acc. or comp.), Kāv.; Rājat.; feeling at ease in or with (loc.), R.; (in comp.) destitute of (see *viveka-v°* and comp. below); m. N. of a king, VP.; *-katha*, mfn. speechless, dumb, mute, Ragh.; *-karṇa-yugala*, mfn. (for *k°-y-°v°*) reaching to the ears, Caurap.; *-nyāsa*, m. N. of wk.; *-pushpôdgama*, mfn. ceased from shooting forth blossoms, Vikr.; *-vigraha-katha*, mfn. one in whom 'war' or 'a body' (cf. *vi-graha*) is out of the question, i.e. 'unwarlike' and 'bodiless' (applied to king Udayana and to the god of love), Ratnâv. i, 8; *-vidyādhara*, m. N. of a grammar; *-vidyā-vinoda*, m. N. of a medical wk.; *-vilāsa*, mfn. one who has given up sporting or dallying, Kathās.; *-vaira*, mfn. one who has ceased from enmity, ib.

Vi-śrānti, f. rest, repose, Kāv.; Kathās.; abatement, cessation, coming to an end, Kathās.; Sāh.; N. of a Tīrtha, VarP.; *-kṛit*, mfn. causing or giving rest, Kathās.; *-bhūmi*, f. means of relaxation, Subh.; *-mat*, mfn. possessing rest, feeling at ease, Kāv.; *-varman*, m. N. of a poet, Subh.

Vi-śrāma, m. rest, repose, relaxation, calm, tranquillity, MBh.; Kāv. &c.; deep breathing (after exertion), VarBṛS.; resting-place, Hariv.; BhP.; cessation, abatement, R.; Śak.; Uttarar.; a pause, cæsura, Śrutab.; a house, Gal.; N. of various men, Cat.; (with *śukla*) N. of an author, ib.; *-bhū*, f. a resting-place, Veṇis.; *-veśman*, n. a resting-chamber, Hariv.; *-sthāna*, n. a place (i. e. means) of rest or recreation (said of a friend), Ratnâv.; °*mâtmaja*, m. N. of an author, Cat. °**śrāmaṇa**, n. causing to rest, Kauś., Sch.

विश्रम्भ् *vi-√śrambh* (accord. to some, more correctly *-srambh*), Ā. *-śrambhate*, to confide, be confident, trust in or rely on (loc.), BhP. (ind.p. *-śrabhya* = trustfully, with confidence): Caus. *-śrambhayati*, to relax, loosen, untie, Lāṭy.; to inspire with confidence, encourage, MBh.

Vi-śrabdha, mfn. confiding, confident, fearless, tranquil, calm, MBh.; Kāv. &c.; trusting in, relying on (*prati*), Mālav.; showing or inspiring confidence, Kāv.; BhP.; (only L.) 'trusted;' 'excessive;' 'firm;' 'mean' &c.; (*am*), ind. confidingly, quietly, without fear or reserve, Mn.; MBh. &c.; *-kārya*, mfn. one who has confidential business to transact, Śak.; *-tā*, f., *-tva*, n. trustiness, trustworthiness, W.; *-navôḍhā*, f. a confiding bride (one of the several classes into which brides are divided), MW.; *-pralāpin*, mfn. talking confidingly or confidentially, Śak.; *-supta*, mfn. sleeping peacefully, Mṛicch.

Vi-śrambha, m. (ifc. f. *ā*) slackening, loosening, relaxation (of the organs of utterance), cessation, RPrāt.; trust, confidence in (loc., gen., or comp.); absence of restraint, familiarity, intimacy, MBh.; Kāv. &c. (ibc. or *āt*, *eṇa*, ind. 'confidingly, confidentially;' °*bhaṃ √kṛi* with gen., 'to win the confidence of;' *kasmai* °*bhaṃ kathayāmi*, 'in whom shall I trust?'); a playful or amorous quarrel, L.; killing(?), L.; *-kathā*, f. (Vās.), *-kathita*, n. pl. (Śak.), *-garbha-kathā*, f. (Mālatīm.) confidential talk, affectionate conversation; *-tā*, f. trust, confidence (acc. with *√gam*, to win c°), R.; *-bhṛitya*, m. a confidential servant, Rājat.; *-vat*, mfn. trustful, certain, at ease, Jātakam.; *-saṃsupta*, mfn. quietly asleep, Kām.; *-saṃkathā*, f. = *-kathā*, Kathās.; °*bhâlāpa*, m. id., Hit. °**śrambhaṇa**, n. confidence (°*ṇaṃ √gam*, to win c°); gaining a person's c°, Daś. °**śrambhaṇīya**, mfn. inspiring a person (gen.) with c°, BhP. °**śrambhitavya**, n. (impers.) it should be trusted in (loc.), Jātakam. °**śrambhin**, mfn. trusting in, relying on (comp.), BhP.; Sāh.; enjoying c°, MBh.; confidential (as talk), Kathās.

विश्रवण *vi-śravaṇa*, *vi-śravas*. See p. 953, col. 1.

विश्राव 1. *vi-śrāva*, m. (fr. *√2. śru* = *sru*; for 2. see col. 2) flowing forth, dropping, W.

Vi-śrāvaṇa, n. (fr. Caus.) causing to flow forth, bleeding, ib.

1. **Vi-śruta**, mfn. (for 2. see col. 2) flowed away, flowing forth, W.

1. **Vi-śruti**, f. oozing, flowing, ib.; 'flowing asunder,' ramification of a channel or road, ŚāṅkhŚr.; 'flowing (scil. with milk),' N. of the cow, VS.; PañcavBr. (Sch. 'the celebrated one;' cf. 2. *vi-śruti*).

Vi-śrotasikā, f. = *pramāda*, Śil.

विश्रि *vi-√śri*, P. Ā. *-śrayati*, °*te*, to set or put asunder, separate, throw open, open, RV.; (mostly Ā.) to go asunder, be opened or separated or expanded or spread or diffused, ib.; to have recourse to, rely on, W.

Vi-śraya, m. having recourse to, dependance on, asylum, W. °**śrayin**, mfn., Pāṇ. iii, 2, 157.

Vi-śrita, mfn. (prob. = resounded), RV. i, 117, 1.

विश्रि *viśri*, m. (of doubtful derivation) death, L.; N. of a man (pl. his descendants), g. *grishṭy-ādi* and *yaskâdi* (cf. *visri*).

विश्रीकृ *vi-śrī-√kṛi*. See p. 953, col. 1.

विश्रु *vi-√1. śru*, P. *-śṛiṇoti*, to hear distinctly, TUp.; Hariv.; BhP.: Pass. *-śrūyate* (Ved. also Ā. *-śṛiṇute*), to be heard or be heard of far and wide, become known or famous, RV.; TBr.; MBh. &c.: Caus. *-śrāvayati*, to cause to be heard everywhere, narrate, communicate, MBh.; Kāv. &c.; to mention (one's name), MBh.; to tell (with acc. of pers. and acc. [v.l. loc.] of thing), ib.; to make famous, R.; Hariv.; to cause to resound, MBh.

2. **Vi-śrāva**, m. (for 1. see s.v., col. 1) noise, sound, Bhaṭṭ.; great fame or celebrity, L. °**śrāvaṇa**, n. causing to hear, narrating, apprising, W.

2. **Vi-śruta**, mfn. heard of far and wide, heard, noted, notorious, famous, celebrated, RV. &c. &c.; known as, passing for, named (nom.), Hariv.; pleased, delighted, happy, L.; m. N. of a man, Daś.; of a son of Vasu-deva, BhP.; *-of Bhava-bhūti*, Gal.; n. fame, celebrity, BhP.; learning (see comp.); *-deva*, m. N. of a king, Buddh.; *-vat*, mfn. possessing much learning, very learned, Hariv.; m. N. of Maru (the father of Bṛihad-bala), VP.; °*tâbhijana*, mfn. of a renowned family, of noted birth, MW.

2. **Vi-śruti**, f. celebrity, fame, notoriety, MBh.; BhP. (°*tiṃ √gam*, to become famous or celebrated); N. of a partic. Śruti, Saṃgīt.

विश्लथ *vi-√ślath* (only pr. p. *-ślathat* and *-ślathamāna*), to become loose or relaxed, BhP.; Pañcar.

Vi-ślatha &c. See p. 953, col. 1.

Vi-ślathita, mfn. loose, relaxed, BhP.

विश्लिष् *vi-√ślish*, P. Ā. *-ślishyati*, °*te*, to be loosened or dissolved or relaxed, Bhaṭṭ.; Kathās.; to be divided or separated (*mithaḥ*, 'from each other'), Kathās.; to fall wide of a mark, fail to strike, miss the aim, Ratnâv.; to divide, separate from (abl.), Kathās.: Caus. *-śleshayati*, to cause to be disunited, separate from (abl.), Kāv.; Pañcat.; to deprive of (instr.), Pañcat.

Vi-ślishṭa, mfn. loosened, Ragh.; disunited, disjoined, separated, AitBr.; Kathās.; severed from one's party, Kām.; dislocated (as limbs), Suśr.; *-tara*, mfn. standing far apart, Cat.

Vi-ślesha, m. loosening, separation, dissolution, disjunction, falling asunder, Kathās.; Suśr. (*saṃdhau v°* or *saṃdhi-v°*, non-union of letters, hiatus, Sāh.); separation (esp. of lovers), Kāv.; Kathās.; a chasm, MW.; (in arithm.) the converse of addition, Gaṇit.; *-jāti*, f. (in arithm.) the assimilation of difference, reduction of fractional d°, Līl.; *-sūtra*, n. a rule for (an operation which is) the converse of addition, Col. °**śleshaṇa**, mfn. dissolving, Suśr.; n. separation, BhP.; dissolution, Car. °**śleshita**, mfn. (fr. Caus.) separated, Megh.; Kathās.; torn, rent asunder, Mṛicch.; dissolved, Kum. iii, 38, Sch.; severed, Suśr.; *-vakshas*, mfn. one whose breast is torn or lacerated, Suśr. °**śleshin**, mfn. falling asunder, loosened, Ragh.; separated (from a beloved object), Kathās.

विश्लोक *vi-śloka*. See p. 953, col. 1.

विश्व *víśva*, mf(*ā*)n. (prob. fr. *√1. viś*, to pervade, cf. Uṇ. i, 151; declined as a pron. like *sarva*, by which it is superseded in the Brāhmaṇas and later language) all, every, every one; whole, entire, universal, RV. &c. &c.; all-pervading or all-containing, omnipresent (applied to Vishṇu-Kṛishṇa, the soul, intellect &c.), Up.; MBh. &c.; m. (in phil.) the intellectual faculty or (accord. to some) the faculty which perceives individuality or the individual underlying the gross body (*sthūla-śarīra-vyashṭy-upahita*), Vedântas.; N. of a class of gods, cf. below; N. of the number 'thirteen,' Gol.; of a class of deceased ancestors, MārkP.; of a king, MBh.; of a well-known dictionary = *viśva-prakāśa*; pl. (*víśve*, with or scil. *devâs*, cf. *Viśve-deva*, p. 995) 'all the gods collectively' or the 'All-gods' (a partic. class of gods, forming one of the 9 Gaṇas enumerated under *gaṇa-devatā*, q.v.; accord. to the Vishṇu and other Purāṇas they were sons of Viśvā, daughter of Daksha, and their names are as follow, 1. Vasu, 2. Satya, 3. Kratu, 4. Daksha, 5. Kāla, 6. Kāma, 7. Dhṛiti, 8. Kuru, 9. Purū-ravas, 10. Mādravas [?]; two others are added by some, viz. 11. Rocaka or Locana, 12. Dhvani [or Dhūri; or this may make 13]: they are particularly worshipped at Śrāddhas and at the Vaiśvadeva ceremony [RTL. 416]; moreover, accord. to Manu [iii, 90, 121], offerings should be made to them daily—these privileges having been bestowed on them by Brahmā and the Pitṛis, as a reward for severe austerities they had performed on the Himālaya: sometimes it is difficult to decide whether the expression *viśve devāḥ* refers to all the gods or to the particular troop of deities described above), RV. &c. &c.; (*ā*), f. the earth, L. (loc. pl. 'in all places, everywhere,' RV. viii, 106, 2); dry ginger, L.; Piper Longum, L.; Asparagus Racemosus, L.; = *ati-vishā* or *vishā*, L.; N. of one of the tongues of Agni, MārkP.; a partic. weight, L.; N. of a daughter of Daksha (the wife of Dharma and mother of the Viśve Devāḥ), MBh.; Hariv.; Pur.; of a river, BhP.; n. the whole world, universe, AV. &c. &c.; dry ginger, Suśr.; myrrh, L.; a mystical N. of the sound *o*, Up. **-kathā**, f., g. *kathâdi*. **-kadrākarsha**, w. r. for *viś-cakadr°*, q. v. **-kadru**, mfn. wicked, vile, L.; m. a dog trained for the chase, L.; sound, noise, L. **-kartṛi**, m. the creator of the world (°*tṛi-tva*, n.), Kāv.; Pur. &c.; N. of an author, Cat. **-karma** and **-karman**, see p. 994, col. 2. **-kāya**, mfn. whose body is the universe, BhP.; (*ā*), f. a form of Dākshāyaṇī, Cat. **-kāraka**, m. the creator of the universe (said of Śiva), Śivag. **-kāru**, m. the architect of the Universe, Viśva-karman, Pañcar. **-kārya**, m. N. of one of the seven principal rays of the sun, VP. (cf. *-karman*). **-kṛit**, mfn. or m. making or creating all, the creator of all things, AV.; ŚBr. &c.; m. the architect and artificer of the gods, Viśva-karman, MBh.; R.; MārkP.; N. of a son of Gādhi, Hariv. **-kṛita**, mfn. made by Viśva-karman (?), MBh. **-kṛishṭi** (*viśvá-*), mfn. dwelling among all men, universally known, kind to all men, RV. **-ketu**, m. 'whose banner is the universe,' N. of the god of love, L.; of Aniruddha (a son of the god of love), L. **-kośa**, m. N. of various wks. **-kshaya**, m. destruction of the world, Rājat. **-kshiti** (*viśvá-*), mfn. = *-kṛishṭi*, TBr. **-ga**, m. 'going everywhere,' N. of Brahmā, L.; of a son of Pūrṇiman, BhP. **-gata**, mfn. omnipresent, LiṅgaP. **-gandha** (only L.), mfn. diffusing odour everywhere; m. an onion; (*ā*), f. the earth; n. myrrh. **-gandhi**, m. N. of a son of Pṛithu, BhP. **-garbha** (*viśvá-*), mf(*ā*)n. bearing or containing all things, AV.; Śivag.; m. N. of a son of Raivata, Hariv. **-guṇâdarśa**, m. N. of wk. **-gudh**, mfn. (nom. *-ghuṭ*) all-enveloping, MW. **-guru**, m. the father of the universe, Kāv.; BhP. **-gūrṇa** (?), N. of wk. **-gūrta** (*viśvá-*), mfn. approved by or welcome to everybody, RV. **-gūrti**, mfn. id., ib. **-gocara**, mfn. accessible to all men, VP. **-gotra** (*viśvá-*), mfn. belonging to all families, ŚBr. **-gotrya** (*viśvá-*), mfn. (perhaps) bringing all kinsmen together (said of a drum), AV. **-goptṛi**, m. 'preserver of the universe,' N. of Vishṇu, Hariv.; of Śiva, Śivag.; of Indra, L. **-granthi**, m. a kind of plant (= *haṅsa-padī*), L. **-m-kara**, mfn. all-creating, making all, W.; m. the eye, L. **-cakra**, n. 'world-wheel,' a wheel made of gold representing the universe (or the gift of such a wheel offered to Brāhmans), Hcat.; *-dāna-vidhi*, m. N. of wk.; °*râtman*, m. N. of Vishṇu, Hcat.; MatsyaP. **-cakshа**, mfn. all-seeing, MW. **-cakshaṇa** (*viśvá-*), mfn. id., AV. **-cakshas** (*viśvá-*), mfn. id., RV. **-cakshus**, mfn. id. (or) n. an eye for all things, MaitrUp. **-candra**, mfn. all-radiant, all-brilliant, MW. **-camat-kṛiti**, f. N. of Comm. **-carshaṇi** (*viśvá-*), mfn. = *-kṛishṭi*, RV.; Naigh. **-cyavas**, m. one of the seven principal rays of the sun, VP., Sch. **-janá**, m. all men, mankind, VS.; TBr. (*-janasya cchattra* or *chattra*, n., Pāṇ. iv, 1, 76, Vārtt. 1, Sch.) **-janīna**, mfn. containing all kinds of people, AV.; ruling all people, ib.; good for or benefiting all men, MaitrS.; Kāv.; Pāṇ.; *-vṛitti*, mfn. one whose conduct or actions are for the benefit of the whole world, MW. **-janīya**, mfn. suitable to all men, benefiting all men, Pat. **-janman** (*viśvá-*), mfn. of all or various kinds, AV. **-janya** (*viśvá-*), mf(*ā*)n. containing all men; existing everywhere, universal, dear to all men, RV.; VS.; Mn.; universally beneficial, W. **-jayin**, mfn. conquering the universe, BhP. **-jit**, mfn. all-conquering, all-subduing, RV.; AV.; BhP.; m. N. of an Ekâha in the Gavām-ayana rite (the 4th day after the Vishuvat), AV. &c. &c.; a partic. form of Fire, MBh.; the cord or noose of Varuṇa, W.; N. of a Dānava, MBh.; of a son of Gādhi, Hariv.; of various other persons, ib.; Pur.; *-jic-chilpa*, m. (for *-jit* + *śilpa*)

N. of an Ekâha, PañcavBr.; ŚrS.; (*-jid*)*-atirātra-paddhati*, f. N. of wk. **-jinva**, mfn. all-refreshing, RV. **-jīva**, m. the universal Soul, BhP. **-jū**, mfn. all-impelling, RV. **-jyotisha**, m. N. of a man (pl. his descendants), Cat. **-jyotis** (*viśvá-*), mfn. all-brilliant, L.; m. N. of an Ekâha, PañcavBr.; KātyŚr.; of a man, Saṃskārak.; f. N. of partic. bricks (supposed to represent fire, the wind, and the sun), TS.; ŚBr.; ŚrS.; n. N. of a Sāman, SV. **-tanu**, mfn. whose body is the universe, BhP. **-tas** &c., see p. 994. **-túr**, mfn. all-surpassing, all-subduing, RV. **-turā-shah**, mfn. (nom. °*shāṭ*) all-surpassing, Hariv. **-tūrti** (*viśvá-*), mfn. id., RV. **-tṛipta**, mfn. satisfied with everything, Pañcar. **-toya**, mf(*ā*)n. having water for all, MBh. **-traya**, n. sg. the three worlds (viz. heaven, earth, and atmosphere; or h°, e°, and the lower world), MārkP. **-try-arcas**, m. one of the seven principal rays of the sun, VP. **-daṇshṭra**, m. N. of an Asura, MBh. **-datta**, m. N. of a Brāhman, Kathās. **-darśata** (*viśvá-*), mfn. visible to all, RV.; ĀpŚr.; to be honoured by all, MW. **-dáni**, mfn. all-giving, TBr. **-dāvá**, mfn. all-scorching, TS. **-dāvan**, mfn. all-distributing, AV. **-dāvyà**, mfn. all-scorching, AV.; MaitrS. **-dāsā**, f. one of the seven tongues of fire, TĀr., Sch. **-dīpa**, m. N. of wk. **-dṛiś**, mfn. all-seeing, BhP. **-drishṭa** (*viśvá-*), mfn. seen by all, RV. **-deva** (*viśvá-*), mfn. all-divine, RV.; Hariv.; m. N. of a god, Hariv.; of a teacher, Cat.; pl. a partic. class of deities, the Viśve Devāḥ (see *viśva* above), RV.; VS.; Hariv.; VarBṛS.; (*ā*), f. Uraria Lagopodioides, Suśr.; Hedysarum Lagop°, W.; a species of red-flowering Daṇḍotpala, L.; *-tā*, f. pl. the Viśve Devāḥ, L.; *-dīkshitīya*, n. N. of wk.; *-netra* (*viśvá-deva-*), mfn. led by the V° D°, VS.; *-bhakta*, mfn. (prob.) inhabited by worshippers of the V° D° (g. *aishukāry-ādi*); *-vat* (*viśvá-deva-*), mfn. united with all gods, AV. **-devya** (*viśvá-*), mfn. relating or sacred or dear &c. to all gods, RV.; distinguished by all divine attributes, MW.; °*vyā-vat*, mfn. relating or dear to all gods, RV.; VS. &c.; accompanied by the Viśve Devāḥ, AitBr.; ŚrS. **-daiva** or **-daivata**, n. the lunar mansion or asterism Uttarâshāḍhā (presided over by the V° D°), VarBṛS. **-dohas** (*viśvá-*), mfn. milking or yielding all things, RV. **-dhara**, mfn. preserving all things (N. of Vishṇu), Vishṇ.; N. of a man, Cat. **-dharaṇa**, n. preservation of the universe, Rājat. **-dhā** (*viśvá-*), mfn. (cf. *viśvádha*, p. 994) all-preserving, VS.; f. preservation of the universe, g. *chattrâdi*. **-dhātṛi**, mfn. all-sustainer, Hariv. **-dhāman**, n. a universal home, ŚvetUp. **-dhāyas** (*viśvá-*), mfn. all-sustaining, all-nourishing, RV.; AV. **-dhāra**, m. N. of a son of Medhâtithi, BhP.; n. N. of the Varsha ruled by him, ib. **-dhārin**, mfn. all-maintaining, W.; m. a deity, W.; (*iṇī*), f. the earth, L. **-dhṛik** or **-dhṛit**, mfn. sustaining everything, Sāy. **-dhena** (*viśvá-*), mf(*ā*)n. all-feeding, RV.; (*ā*), f. N. of the earth, MW. **-dhenu**, see *vaiśva-dhenava* and *vaiśva-dhainava*. **-nagara**, m. N. of a man, Dhūrtas. **-nanda**, n. N. of a spiritual son of Brahmā, VP. **-nara**, mfn. = *viśve narā yasya saḥ*, Pāṇ. vi, 3, 129. **-nātha**, m. 'lord of the universe,' N. of Śiva (esp. as the object of adoration at Benares, cf. *viśvêśa*), Inscr.; of various authors and other men (also with *kavi*, *cakravartin*, *dīkshita*, *daivajña*, *paṇḍita*, *miśra*, *rāja*, *vājapeyin* &c.), Kshitīś.; Cat.; Col.; *-kavi-rāja*, m. N. of the author of the Sāhitya-darpaṇa, IW. 457; *-caritra*, n., *-tājaka*, n. N. of wks.; *-tīrtha* and *-deva*, m. N. of various authors &c., Cat.; (°*va-prakāśa*, m. N. of wk.); *-nagarī*, f. the town of Viśva-nātha i.e. Kāśī, Cat.; (°*rī-stotra*, n. N. of wk.); *-nārāyaṇa*, *-nyāyâlaṃkāra*, m. N. of authors; *-pañcânana* (also with *bhaṭṭâcārya*), m. N. of the author of the Bhāshā-paricceda and of a Comm. on the Nyāya-sūtra of Gotama; *-purī*, f. (= *-nagarī*), MW.; *-bhaṭṭa*, m. N. of the author of the Sāhitya-darpaṇa (cf. *-kavi-rāja*), Cat.; *-siṇha* (or °*ha-deva*), *-sūri*, *-sena*, m. N. of authors; *-stotra*, n. N. of various wks.; °*thâcārya*, °*thâśrama*, m. N. of authors, Cat.; °*thâshṭaka*, n. N. of wk.; °*thôpādhyāya*, m. N. of an author, Cat. **-nāthiya**, mfn. composed by Viśva-nātha, Cat.; n. N. of wk. **-nābha**, m. N. of Vishṇu, Cat. **-nābhi**, f. the navel of the universe, BhP. **-nāman** (*viśvá-*), mf(*mnī*)n. having all names, AV. **-nighaṇṭu**, m. N. of wk. **-m-tara**, mfn. all-subduing (Buddha), Buddh.; m. N. of a king, AitBr.; of a former state of existence of the Buddha, Jātakam. **-paksha**, m. N. of an author of mystical prayers, Cat. **-pati**, m. 'lord of the universe,' N. of Mahāpurusha and of Kṛishṇa, Hariv.; N. of a partic. fire, MBh.; of various authors, Cat. **-pad** (*-pād*), w. r. for *-pā*, Hariv. **-parṇī**, f. Flacourtia Cataphracta, L. **-pā**, mfn. all-protecting, Hariv.; m. the sun, W.; the moon, ib.; fire, ib. **-pācaka**, mfn. cooking everything (fire), MārkP. **-pāṇi**, m. N. of a Dhyāni-bodhi-sattva, MWB. 203. **-pātṛi**, m. a partic. class of deceased ancestors, MārkP. **-pāda-śiro-grīva**, mfn. one whose feet and head and neck are formed of the universe, ib. **-pāla**, m. 'all-protector,' N. of a merchant, Cat. **-pāvana**, mf(*ī*)n. all-purifying, BhP.; Pañcar.; (*ī*), f. holy basil, Cat. **-piś**, mfn. all-adorned, having all sorts of ornaments, RV. **-púsh**, mfn. all-nourishing, ib. **-pūjita**, mfn. all-honoured, L.; (*ā*), f. holy basil, Cat. **-pūjya**, mfn. all-venerable, Kāv. **-peśas** (*viśvá-*), mfn. containing all adornment, RV. **-prakāśa**, m. N. of a lexicon by Mahêśvara (also °*kāśikā*, °*kāśin*); of sev. other wks.; *-paddhati*, f. N. of wk. **-pradīpa**, m. N. of wk. **-prabodha**, mfn. all-wakening, all-enlightening, BhP. **-prí**, N. of the section TBr. iii, 11, 5. **-psan**, m. (accord. to some corrupted fr. *viśva* + *bhasan*, cf. *bhasad*) = *deva*, Up. i, 158, Sch.; = *vahni*, *candra*, *samīraṇa*, *kṛitânta*, *sūrya*, L.; = *viśva-karman*, Uṇvṛ. **-psā**, m. fire, L. **-psu** (*viśvá-*), mfn. having all forms, RV. (cf. *viśvá-psu*). **-psnya** (*viśvá-*), mfn. (*psnya* said to be for *psanya* fr. √*psā*) either 'having all forms' or 'all-nourishing,' RV.; VS. (*-psnyā*, instr. f.); (*āya*), ind. (prob.) to the satiation of all, RV. **-bandhu**, m. a friend of the whole world, BhP. **-bīja**, n. the seed of everything, Pañcar. **-budbuda**, m. the world compared to a bubble, Śāntiś. **-bodha**, m. a Buddha, L. **-bhaṇḍa**, m. N. of a man, Hāsy. **-bhadra**, mfn. altogether agreeable &c., Kālac. **-bharas** (*viśvá-*), mfn. all-supporting, all-nourishing, RV.; ŚrS. **-bhartṛi**, m. an all-sustainer, BhP.; Kālac. **-bhava**, mfn. one from whom all things arise, BhP. **-bhānu** (*viśvá-*), mfn. all-illumining, RV. **-bhāva**, mfn. all-creating, BhP. **-bhāvana**, mfn. id., RāmatUp.; Pur.; m. N. of Vishṇu, MW.; of a spiritual son of Brahmā, VP. **-bhuj**, mfn. all-enjoying, all-possessing, W.; eating all things, MaitrUp.; Hariv.; m. N. of Indra, MW.; of a son of I°, MBh.; of a fire, ib.; of a class of deceased ancestors, MārkP. **-bhujā**, f. N. of a goddess, Cat. **-bhū**, m. N. of a Buddha, Dharmas. 6. **-bhūta**, mfn. being everything, Hariv. **-bhṛit**, mfn. = *-bharas*, AV.; MaitrUp.; f. pl. a hundred heat-making sun-rays, L. **-bheshaja** (*viśvá-*), mf(*ī*)n. containing all remedies, all-healing, RV.; VS.; AV.; m. a universal remedy, MW.; n. dry ginger, Suśr. **-bhojana**, n. the eating of all sorts of food, W. **-bhojas** (*viśvá-*), mfn. all-nourishing, granting all enjoyment, RV.; AV. **-bhrāj**, mfn. all-illuminating, RV. **-madā** or **-m-adā**, f. 'all-delighting' or 'all-consuming,' N. of one of the seven tongues of fire, L. **-manas** (*viśvá-*), mfn. perceiving everything, RV.; m. N. of the author of the hymns RV. viii, 23–26, RV.; PañcavBr. **-manus** (*viśvá-*), mfn. = *-krishṭi*, RV. **-maya**, mf(*ī*)n. containing the universe, Hcat.; Kathās. **-maha**, m. N. of a kind of personification, ŚāṅkhGṛ. (also *maha-viśva*). **-mahat**, m. N. of a son of Viśva-śarman, VP. **-mahas** (*viśvá-*), mfn. 'all-powerful' or 'all-pleasant,' RV.; ŚāṅkhŚr. **-mahêśvara**, m. the great lord of the universe (Śiva), Cat.; *-matâcāra*, m. N. of wk. (w. r. °*cara*). **-mātṛi**, f. all-mother, Kālac. **-mātṛikā**, f. N. of wk. **-mānava** (see *vaiśva-mānava*). **-mānusha** (*viśvá-*), mfn. (prob.) known to all men, MW. (cf. *viśvá-manus*); m. every mortal, RV. viii, 45, 42. **-mitra**, m. pl. (prob.) = *viśvā-mitra*, pl. the family of Viśvāmitra, AV. **-m-invá**, mf(*ā*)n. all-moving, all-pervading, all-embracing, RV.; all-containing, ib. **-mukhī**, f. N. of Dākshāyaṇī (as worshipped in Jālaṃdhara), Cat. **-mūrti**, mfn. having all forms (or one 'whose body is the universe'), MBh.; Hariv. &c. (applied to the Supreme Spirit); m. a kind of mixture, Rasêndrac.; *-mat*, mfn. having or taking all forms, MBh. **-m-ejaya**, mfn. all-shaking, all-exciting, RV. **-medinī**, f. N. of a lexicon. **-mohana**, mfn. all-confusing, Pañcar. **-m-bhará**, mf(*ā*)n. all-bearing, all-sustaining, AV.; ŚBr.; Caṇ. (also applied to the Supreme Being); fire, ŚBr.; KaushUp.; a kind of scorpion or similar animal, Suśr.; Car.; N. of Vishṇu, Pañcar.; Chandom.; of Indra, L.; of a king, Kshitīś.; of an author, Cat.; (*ā*), f. the earth, Kāv.; Rājat. &c.; *-kulāyá*, m. a fire-receptacle, ŚBr.; KaushUp.; *-maithilôpādhyāya*, m. N. of an author, Cat.; *-vāstu-śāstra*, n., *-śāstra*, n. N. of wks.; °*bharâdhipa* (MW.) or °*râdhīśvara* (Bhām.), m. 'lord of the earth,' a king; °*bharā-putra*, m. N. of the planet Mars, Vāstuv.; °*bharā-bhuj*, m. a king, Rājat.; °*bharôpanishad*, f. N. of wk. **-m-bharaka**, m. a kind of scorpion or similar animal, VarBṛS. **-m-bhari**, f. the earth, Dharmaśarm. **-yaśas**, m. N. of a man, Pāṇ. v, 4, 155, Sch. **-yoni**, m. or f. the source or creator of the universe, ŚvetUp.; MBh. &c.; N. of Brahmā, MW.; of Vishṇu, ib. **-ratha**, m. N. of a son of Gādhi, Hariv.; of an author, Col. **-rāj**, m. for *viśvā-rāj* (in the weakest cases); m. a universal sovereign, W. (also *-rāja*, A.) **-rādhas** (*viśvá-*), mfn. all-granting, AV. **-ruci**, m. N. of a divine being, MBh.; of a Dānava, Kathās.; = next, L. **-rucī**, f. 'all-glittering,' N. of one of the seven tongues of fire, MuṇḍUp. **-rūpa**, n. sg. various forms, Mn.; Pañcar.; RāmatUp.; (*viśvá-*), mf(*ā* or *ī*)n. many-coloured, variegated, RV.; AV. &c.; wearing all forms, manifold, various, RV.; AV.; TS. &c.; m. N. of partic. comets, VarBṛS.; of Śiva, MBh.; of Vishṇu-Kṛishṇa, Cat.; of a son of Tvashṭṛi (whose three heads were struck off by Indra), RV.; TS.; Br. &c.; of an Asura, MBh.; Hariv.; of various scholars &c. (esp. of a Sch. on Yājñ.), Kull.; Cat. &c.; (*ā*), f. a dappled cow, RV.; VS.; TBr.; N. of partic. verses (e.g. RV. v, 81, 2), Br.; Lāṭy.; pl. the yoked horses of Bṛihas-pati, Naigh.; (*ī*), f. N. of one of the seven tongues of fire, MuṇḍUp.; n. Agallochum, W.; (prob.) n. N. of wk.; *-keśava*, m., *-gaṇaka-munîśvara*, m. N. of authors, Cat.; *-tama*, mfn. having the greatest variety of forms or colours, MW.; *-tīrtha*, n. N. of a Tīrtha, Cat.; m. N. of a scholar, ib.; *-darśana*, n. N. of two chs. in the Krīḍā-khaṇḍa of the GaṇP.; *-deva*, m. N. of an author, Cat.; *-dhara*, mfn. wearing various forms, VP.; *-nibandha*, m. N. of a ch. of the BhavP.; *-maya*, mf(*ī*)n. representing Viśva-rūpa (i.e. prob. Vishṇu-Kṛishṇa), AgP.; *-vat*, mfn. appearing in various forms, R.; *-samuccaya*, m. N. of wk.; °*pâcārya*, m. N. of an author, Cat. **-rūpaka**, m. a kind of black aloe wood, L.; (*ikā*), f. N. of a Yoginī, Hcat. **-rūpin**, mfn. appearing in various forms, Hariv.; MārkP.; (*iṇī*), f. N. of a goddess, Cat. **-retas**, m. (?) 'seed of all things,' N. of Brahmā, L.; of Vishṇu, Pañcar. **-rocana**, m. Colocasia Antiquorum, L. **-liṅga**, mfn. containing the distinguishing word *viśva*, Nir. **-locana**, n. N. of a lexicon. **-lopa**, m. a species of tree, TS. **-vat** (*víśva-*), mfn. containing the word *víśva*, ŚBr. **-vada**, m. (prob.) = the Visparad, Cat. **-váni**, mfn. all-granting, TS. **-vápari**, mfn. = *viśvasmiñ jagati raśmīn āvaptā vistārayitā*, TBr. (Sch.) **-vayas** (*viśvá-*), mfn., AV. xix, 56, 2; m. a N., see *bamba-viś°* and *bambā-viś°*. **-vasu**, m. 'wealth of all,' N. of a son of Purū-ravas, MW. (cf. *viśvá-vasu*). **-vah** (in the strong cases *-vāh*, in the weak cases *viśvaúh*), mf(*viśvaúhī*)n., Pāṇ. vi, 4, 132, Sch. **-vāc**, f. 'all-speech,' N. of Mahāpurusha, Hariv. **-vājin**, Hariv. 11253 (doubtful, prob. *dṛiśya vā°* is better reading). **-vāra** (*viśvá-*), mf(*ā*)n. containing all good things, bestowing all treasures &c., RV.; VS.; ŚBr.; adored or cherished by all, RV. (Sāy.); (*ā*), f. N. of the authoress of the hymn RV. v, 28. **-vārya** (*viśvá-*), mfn. containing all good things, bestowing all treasures &c., RV. (Sāy. 'all-desired'). **-vāsa**, m. the receptacle of all things, MBh. **-vikhyāta**, mfn. known in the whole world, Sarvad. **-vijayin**, mfn. all-conquering, Pañcar. **-1. -víd**, mfn. knowing everything, omniscient, RV.; TS.; ŚvetUp. &c. **-2. -víd**, mfn. all-possessing, RV. **-vidvas**, mfn. all-knowing, Cat. **-vidhāyin**, m. 'all-making, all-arranging,' a creator, deity, W. **-vinna**, mfn., see *á-viśva-v°*. **-vibhāvana**, n. creation of the universe, BhP. **-viśruta**, mfn. = *-vikhyāta*, Kathās. **-viśva**, mfn. (perhaps) constituting all things (said of Vishṇu), Pañcar. **-visārin**, mfn. spreading everywhere, Inscr. **-vistā**, f. N. of the 15th day of the light half of the month Vaiśākha, L. **-vṛiksha**, m. 'tree of the universe,' N. of Vishṇu, Pañcar. **-vṛitti**, f. universal practice, L. **-veda**, m. N. of an author, Cat. **-1. -vedas** (*viśvá-*), mfn. = 1. *-vid*, RV.; VS.; AV.; a sage, saint, W. **-2. -vedas** (*viśvá-*), mfn. = 2. *-vid*, RV.; VS., BhP. **-vyacas** (*viśvá-*), mfn. embracing or absorbing all things, RV.; AV.; VS. &c.; f. N. of Aditi, MW. **-vyāpaka**, mfn. all-pervading, everywhere diffused, W. **-vyāpin**, mfn. filling the universe, all-diffused, RāmatUp.

— vyāpti, f. universal diffusion or permeation, W. **— śambhu** or **°bhu-rūni,** m. N. of a lexicographer, Cat. **— śambhū** (*viśvá-*), mfn. beneficial to all, RV.; VS.; MaitrS.; m. he who is the source of all prosperity, MW.; N. of Viśva-karman, ib. **— śardhas** (*viśvá-*), mfn. being in a complete troop, complete in number, RV.; displaying great power, making gr° exertion (Sāy.) **— śarman,** m. N. of the father of Viśva-mahat, VP.; of an author, Cat. **— śārada** (*viśvá-*), mfn. annual (or 'lasting a whole year'), AV. (applied to the disease called Takman as likely to occur every autumn). **— śúc,** mfn. all-enlightening, RV. **— śuci,** mfn. id., MW. **— ścandra** (*viśvá-*), mf(*ā*)n. all-glittering, RV. **— śraddhā-jñāna-bala,** n. N. of one of the ten faculties of a Buddha, Buddh. **— śrí,** mfn. useful to all (said of Agni), MaitrS. **— śrushṭi** (*viśvá-*), mfn. compliant to all, RV. **— saṃvanana,** n. means of bewitching all, Rājat.; Vcar. **— saṃhāra,** m. general destruction, Kathās. **— sakha,** m. a universal friend, Ragh. **— sattama,** mfn. the best of all (said of Kṛishṇa), MBh. **— samplava,** m. the destruction of the world, BhP. **— sambhava,** mfn. one from whom all things arise, Hariv. **— saha,** mfn. all-bearing, all-enduring, W.; m. N. of sev. men, Ragh.; Pur.; (*ā*), f. the earth, W.; N. of one of the seven tongues of fire, L. **— sahâya,** mfn. joined with the Viśve Devāḥ, Hariv. **— sâkshin,** mfn. all-seeing, Prab. **— sāman** (*viśvá-*), m. N. of a kind of personification, VS.; of the author of RV. v, 22, 1. **— sāra,** m. N. of a son of Kshatraujas, Cat.; n. (also *°ra-tantra*) N. of a Tantra, RTL. 207. **— sāraka,** m. Cactus Indicus, L. **— sâhva** or **-sāhvan,** m. N. of a son of Mahas-vat, BhP. **— siṇha,** m. N. of a king, Inscr. **— su-víd,** mfn. granting everything well, RV. **— sū,** f. all-generating, AV. **— sūtra-dhṛik,** m. 'architect of the universe,' N. of Vishṇu, Pañcar. **— sṛij** (nom. *-sṛik* or incorrectly *-sṛiṭ*), mfn. all-creating; m. creator of the universe (of whom there are ten accord. to some), AV. &c. &c. (*-sṛijām ayana,* n. a partic. festival, ĀpŚr.); N. of Brahmā, L.; of Nārāyaṇa, Kād. **— sṛit,** m. = *viśvasya srashṭā* (cf. prec.) or = *viśvasya pātā,* TBr. (Sch.) **— sṛishṭi,** f. creation of the universe, MārkP. **— sena,** m. N. of the 18th Muhūrta, Sūryapr.; of a preceptor, W.; *-rāj,* m. N. of the father of the 16th Arhat of the present Avasarpiṇī, L. **— saubhaga** (*viśvá-*), mfn. bringing all prosperity, RV. **— sthā,** f. Asparagus Racemosus, L.; a widow (w.r. for *viśvastā*), L. **— spṛiś,** mfn. all-touching, all-reaching (applied to Mahā-purusha), Hariv. (v.l. *diva-sp°*). **— sphaṭika, -sphāṭi, -sphāṇi, -sphārṇi, -sphiṇi, -sphūrji** or **-sphūrti,** m. N. of a king of Magadhā, Pur. **— srashṭṛi,** m. creator of the universe, W. **— svāmin,** m. N. of an author, Cat. **— hartṛi,** m. the world-destroyer (N. of Śiva), Śivag. **— haryaka** or (v.l.) **-haryata,** m. a sacrifice, L. **— hetu,** m. the cause of all things (applied to Vishṇu), Pañcar. **Viśvâksha,** mfn. having eyes everywhere, Hariv. **Viśvâṅgá,** mfn. all-membered, AV. **Viśvâṅgya,** mfn. being in all members, AV. **Viśvâcārya,** m. N. of a teacher, Cat. **Viśvâjina,** m. a N., Pāṇ. vi, 2, 106, Vārtt. 1. **Viśvâṇḍa,** n. the world-egg, Hcat. **Viśvâtithi,** m. a universal guest i.e. going everywhere, Bālar. **Viśvâtīta,** mfn. all-surpassing, Cat. **Viśvâtmaka,** mfn. constituting the essence of all things, Prab. **Viśvâtman,** m. the Soul of the Universe, the Universal Spirit, MaitrUp.; MBh.; Kum. &c.; the sun, L.; N. of Brahmā, L.; of Śiva, Kum.; of Vishṇu, Cat.; (*°nas*), ind. (knowing any one) in his whole nature, thoroughly, Hariv. **Viśvâd,** mfn. all-consuming, RV.; AV.; ŚBr. **Viśvâdarśa,** m. or **°śa-smṛiti,** f. N. of wk. **Viśvâdhāra,** m. support of the universe, Pañcar.; RāmatUp.; HYog. **Viśvâdhipa,** m. lord of the universe, ŚvetUp. **Viśvâdhishṭhāna, Viśvânanda-nātha,** m. N. of authors, Cat. **Viśvântara,** m. N. of a king, Kathās.; of a son of Su-shadman, MW. **Viśvânná,** n. 'food for all' or 'all-eating,' AV. **Viśvâmṛita,** mfn. (perhaps) immortal for all times, MaitrUp. **Viśvâyana,** mfn. penetrating everywhere, all-knowing, Hariv. **Viśvâyu,** mfn. = *viśvá-kṛishṭi,* RV.; VS.; m. N. of a son of Purū-ravas, MBh.; Hariv. (*viśvâyus?*); n. all people, RV.; *-poshas* (*viśvâyu-*), mfn. causing prosperity to all men, RV.; *-vepas,* mfn. exciting or terrifying all men, ib. **Viśvâyus,** m., see *viśvâyu;* n. universal life, un° health (in a formula), TS.; ŚāṅkhŚr. **Viśvâvarta,** m. N. of a man, Cat. **Viśvâvāsa,** m. a receptacle for everything, MBh.; MārkP. **Viśvêkshitṛi,** mfn. all-seeing, Prab. (v.l. *viśvêśitṛi*). **Viśvêśa,** m. lord of the universe (N. of Brahmā, Vishṇu or Śiva), MBh.; Hariv.; R. &c.; the Supreme Spirit, MW.; N. of a man, Cat.; (*ā*), f. N. of a daughter of Daksha and wife of Dharma, VP.; n. N. of a Liṅga, Cat.; the Nakshatra Uttarâshāḍhā (presided over by the Viśve Devāḥ), VarBṛS. **Viśvêśitṛi,** m. the lord of the universe, Bhartṛ. (cf. *viśvêkshitṛi*). **Viśvêśvara,** m. id., Up.; MBh.; Kāv. &c.; N. of a form of Śiva (esp. worshipped in Benares), RTL. 50; 437 &c.; of various authors and other persons, Cat.; (*ī*), f. the mistress of the universe, Cat.; a species of plant, VarBṛS.; N. of wk.; (prob. n.) N. of a place, Cat.; n. the Nakshatra Uttarâshāḍhā, VarBṛS.; *-kālī,* m. N. of a poet, Cat.; *-tantra,* n. N. of a Tantra; *-tīrtha,* m. N. of sev. authors, Cat.; n. N. of a sacred place, MW.; *-datta, -datta-miśra, -daiva-jña, -nātha,* m. N. of authors, Cat.; *-nīrājana,* n. N. of wk.; *-paṇḍita,* m. N. of sev. authors, Cat.; *-pattana,* n. N. of Benares, Śak., Sch.; *-paddhati,* f. N. of wk.; *-pūjya-pāda, -bhaṭṭa* (also with *gāgā-bhaṭṭa* and *maunin*), m. N. of authors &c., Cat.; *-māhātmya,* n. N. of wk.; *-miśra,* m. N. of a man, Cat.; *-liṅga,* n. N. of a Liṅga, Cat.; *-veda-pāda-stava,* m. N. of a Stotra; *-saṃhitā,* f. N. of a ch. of the Śiva-purāṇa; *-sarasvatī, -sūnu,* m. N. of sev. authors or learned men, Cat.; *-stuti-pārijāta,* m. N. of wk.; *-sthāna,* n. N. of a place, MBh.; *-smṛiti,* f. N. of wk.; *°rācārya, °rânanda-sarasvatī, °râmbu-muni, °râśrama,* m. N. of authors, Cat.; *°rī-paddhati,* f. N. of wk. **Viśvêśvarīya,** n. N. of wk. **Viśvâika-sāra,** n. 'one heart of the universe,' N. of a sacred region, Rājat. **Viśvôddhāra-tantra,** n. N. of a Tantra. **Viśvâujas,** mfn. all-powerful, RV.; ŚāṅkhŚr. **Viśvâushadha,** n. dry ginger, L. **Viśvâuhī,** see *viśva-vah.*

Viśvaka, mfn. all-pervading, all-containing, RāmatUp.; m. N. of a man (also called Kṛishṇiya, the Aśvins restored to him his lost son Vishṇāpū), RV.; (with the patr. *Karshṇi*) N. of the author of RV. viii, 86, Anukr.; of a son of Pṛithu, VP.

1. **Viśvá-karma,** mfn. accomplishing everything, all-working, RV. x, 166, 4.

2. **Viśva-karma,** in comp. for **°man;** *-jā,* f. 'daughter of Viśva-karman,' N. of Saṃjñā (one of the wives of the Sun), L.; *-purāṇa,* n., *°ṇa-saṃgraha,* m., *-prakāśa,* m., *-māhātmya,* n. N. of wks.; *-śāstrin,* m. N. of an author, Cat.; *-siddhânta,* m. N. of wk.; *-sutā,* f. = *viśva-karma-jā,* L.; *°mêśa* or *°mêśvara-liṅga,* n. N. of a Liṅga, Cat.

Viśva-karman, n. (only ibc.) every action, MaitrUp.; Vās.; (*viśvá-*), mfn. accomplishing or creating everything, RV.; AV.; Br.; MBh.; Hariv.; m. 'all-doer, all-creator, all-maker,' N. of the divine creative architect or artist (said to be son of Brahmā, and in the later mythology sometimes identified with Tvashṭṛi, q.v., he is said to have revealed the Sthāpatya-veda, q.v., or fourth Upa-veda, and to preside over all manual labours as well as the sixty-four mechanical arts [whence he is worshipped by Kārus or artisans]; in the Vedic mythology, however, the office of Indian Vulcan is assigned to Tvashṭṛi as a distinct deity, Viśva-karman being rather identified with Prajā-pati [Brahmā] himself as the creator of all things and architect of the universe; in the hymns RV. x, 81; 82 he is represented as the universal Father and Generator, the one all-seeing God, who has on every side eyes, faces, arms, and feet; in Nir. x, 26 and elsewhere in the Brāhmaṇas he is called a son of Bhuvana, and Viśva-karman Bhauvana is described as the author of the two hymns mentioned above; in the MBh. and Hariv. he is a son of the Vasu Prabhāsa and Yoga-siddhā; in the Purāṇas a son of Vāstu, and the father of Barhishmatī and Saṃjñā; accord. to other authorities he is the husband of Ghṛitācī; moreover, a doubtful legend is told of his having offered up all beings, including himself, in sacrifice; the Rāmâyaṇa represents him as having built the city of Laṅkā for the Rākshasas, and as having generated the ape Nala, who made Rāma's bridge from the continent to the island; the name Viśva-karman, meaning 'doing all acts,' appears to be sometimes applicable as an epithet to any great divinity), RV. &c. &c.; N. of Sūrya or the Sun, Vās.; MārkP.; of one of the seven principal rays of the sun (supposed to supply heat to the planet Mercury), VP.; of the wind, VS. xv, 16 (Mahīdh.); N. of a Muni, L.; (also with *śāstrin*) N. of various authors, Cat.

Viśvakarmīya, n. any work of Viśva-karman, Cat.; *-śilpa,* n. N. of work.

Viśvak-sena, w.r. for *vishvak-s°.*

Viśvag-aśva, viśvag-gati, viśvag-jyotis &c., w.r. for *vishvag-aśva* &c.

Viśvañc, &c., w.r. for *vishvañc.*

Viśva-taś, in comp. for *viśva-tas.* **— cakshus** (*°śvátaś-*), mfn. one who has eyes on all sides, RV.; MaitrS.

Viśvá-tas, ind. from or on all sides, everywhere, all around, universally, RV. &c. &c. (*°to bhayāt,* 'from all danger,' BhP.); = abl. of *viśva,* n. the universe, TĀr. **— pad** (*°śvátas-;* strong form *-pād*), mfn. one who has feet on every side, RV.; MaitrS. **— pāṇi** (*°śvátas-*), mfn. one who has hands on every side, AV. **— pṛitha** (*°śvátas-*), mfn. one who has his hands spread out everywhere, AV.

Viśva-to, in comp. for *viśva-tas.* **— dāvan,** mfn. granting from all sides, SV. **— dhī** (*°śváto-*), mfn. heedful of all, RV. **— bāhu** (*°śváto-*), mfn. one who has arms on every side, ib. **— mukha** (*°śváto-*), mfn. facing all sides, one whose face is turned everywhere, RV.; AV.; MBh. &c.; (*am*), ind. in every direction, BhP.; m. N. of the sun, MBh. **— vīrya** (*°śváto-*), mfn. powerful or effective everywhere, MantraBr. **— hasta** (*°śváto-*), mfn. one who has hands on all sides, MaitrS.

Viśvâtra, ind. everywhere, always, RV.; Kathās.

Viśvatha (ŚāṅkhŚr.) or **viśváthā** (RV. &c.), ind. in every way, at all times.

Viśvadānīm, ind. (cf. *tadānīm, id°*) at all times, at all seasons, RV.; AV.; ĀśvŚr.

Viśvadryañc, w.r. for *vishvadryañc.*

Viśvádha or **viśvádhā,** ind. in every way, at all times, on every occasion, RV.

Viśvayu, m. air, wind, L.

Viśváha or **viśváhā,** ind. always, at all times, RV.; AV.

Viśvā, in comp. for *viśva.* **— dhāyas,** m. a god, L. (cf. *viśva-dh°*). **— nara** (*viśvā́-*), mfn. relating to or existing among or dear to all men (applied to Savitṛi, Indra &c.), RV.; N. of a man, g. *bidâdi;* of the father of Agni, Cat.; = *vallabhâcārya,* ib. **— púsh,** mfn. all-sustaining, RV. **— psu** (*viśvā́-*), mfn. having all forms, ib. (cf. *viśvá-psu*). **— bhū,** mfn. being in everything or everywhere, ib. **— mitra,** see below. **— rāj,** mfn. all-ruling, TS. (cf. *viśva-rāj* and Pāṇ. vi, 3, 128). **— vaṭva** (?), m. N. of a man, Rājat. **— vat** (*viśvā-*), mfn. (perhaps) universal, TS.; (*atī*), f. N. of the Gaṅgā, MBh. (= *viśvam avantī pālayantī,* Nilak.) **— vasu** (*viśvā́-*), mfn. beneficent to all (said of Vishṇu), MBh.; m. N. of a Gandharva (regarded as the author of the hymn RV. x, 139), RV.; AV.; VS. &c.; of a Sādhya, Hariv.; of a Marut-vat, ib.; of a son of Purū-ravas (said to be one of the Viśve Devāḥ), ib.; VP.; of a prince of the Siddhas, Kathās.; Nāg.; of a son of Jamad-agni, MBh.; of one of the Manus, Uṇ., Sch.; of a poet, Cat.; of the 39th year in Jupiter's cycle of 60 years, VarBṛS.; of the 7th Muhūrta, AV.Jyot.; f. night, L.; N. of a partic. night, W.; *-mantra,* m. N. of wk. **— sáh** (strong form *sā́h*), mfn. all-conquering, RV.; AV.; TS.

Viśvâcī, f. (fr. *viśva* + 2. *añc*) universal, RV.; f. paralysis of the arms and the back, Suśr.; a partic. personification, VS.; N. of an Apsaras, MBh.

Viśvā́-mitra, m. (prob.) 'friend of all,' N. of a celebrated Ṛishi or Sage (having the patr. Gāthina, Gādheya, and Jāhnava; he was at first a functionary, together with Vasishṭha, of Su-dās, king of the Tṛitsus; seeing V° preferred by the king, he went over to the Bharatas, but could not prevent their being defeated by Su-dās, although he caused the waters of the rivers Vipāś and Śutudri to retire and so give the Bharatas free passage, RV. iii, 33; he was born as a Kshatriya, deriving his lineage from an ancestor of Kuśika, named Purū-ravas, of the lunar race of kings, and himself sovereign of Kanyā-kubja or Kanoj; his fame rests chiefly on his contests with the great Brāhman Vasishṭha, and his success in elevating himself, though a Kshatriya, to the rank of a Brāhman, see Manu vii, 42: the Rāmâyaṇa, which makes him a companion and counsellor of the young Rāma-candra, records [i, 51–65] how Viśvāmitra, on his accession to the throne, visited Vasishṭha's hermitage, and seeing there the cow of plenty [probably typical of *go,* 'the earth'], offered him untold treasures in exchange for it, but being refused, prepared to take it by force; a long contest ensued between the king and the saint [symbolical of the struggles between the Kshatriya and Brāhmanical classes], which ended in the defeat of Viśvāmitra, whose vexation was such that, in order to become a Brāhman and thus conquer his rival, he devoted himself to intense austerities [during which he was seduced by the nymph Menakā and had by her a daughter, Śakuntalā], gradually increasing the rigour of his mortification through thousands of years, till he successively earned the titles of Rājarshi, Ṛishi, Maharshi, and finally Brahmarshi; he is supposed to be the author of nearly the whole of RV. iii, and of ix, 67, 13–15; x, 137, 5; 167; moreover, a law-book, a Dhanur-veda, and a medical wk. are attributed to him), RV. &c. &c.; a partic. Catur-aha (= *Viśvāmitrasya saṃjayaḥ*), PañcavBr.; KātyŚr.; a partic. Anuvāka (= *Viśvāmitrasyânuvākaḥ*), Pat.; pl. the family of Viśvāmitra, RV.; AV.; (*ā*), f. N. of a river, MBh.; *-kalpa*, m., °*pa-taru*, m. N. of wks.; *-jamad-agni*, m. du. Viśvāmitra and Jamad-agni, RV.; *-nadī*, f. N. of a river, MBh.; *-pura*, n. or *-purī*, f. N. of a town (°*rīya*, mfn.), PratijñāS.; *-priya*, m. 'dear to Viśvāmitra,' the cocoa-nut tree, L.; N. of Kārttikeya, MBh.; *-rāśi*, m. N. of a man, Inscr.; *-saṃhitā*, f. N. of sev. wks.; *-sṛishṭi*, f. Viśvāmitra's creation (in allusion to several things fabled to have been created by this saint in rivalry of Brahmā, e.g. the fruit of the Palmyra in imitation of the human skull, the buffalo in imitation of the cow, the ass of the horse &c.), MW.; *-smṛiti*, f. N. of wk.

Viśvâhā, ind. = *viśvāhā*, at all times, RV.; AV.

Viśve-deva, m. pl. the Viśve Devāḥ (see under *viśva*), Pur.; sg. N. of the number 'thirteen' (at the end of the Saṃdeha-vishâushadhi); of Mahā-purusha, Hariv.; of an Asura, ib.; or another divine being, Kāṭh.; (*ā*), f. Uraria Lagopodioides, L.

Viśve-devṛi, m. the clitoris, L.

Viśve-bhojas, m. N. of Indra, Uṇ. iv, 237, Sch. (cf. *viśva-bh°*).

Viśve-vedas, m. N. of Agni, ib. (cf. *viśva-bh°*).

Viśvyā, ind. anywhere, RV.

विश्वस् *vi-√śvas*, P. *-śvasiti* (ep. also *-śvasati*, °*te*), to draw breath freely, be free from fear or apprehension, be trustful or confident, trust or confide in, rely or depend on (acc., gen., or loc.), MBh.; Kāv. &c.: Caus. *-śvāsayati*, to cause to trust, inspire with confidence, console, comfort, encourage, Kāv.; Kathās.; Pañcat. &c.: Desid. of Caus. *-śiśvāsayishati*, to wish to inspire confidence or to encourage, Bhaṭṭ. °**śvasana**, n. trusting, confiding in, W. °**śvasanīya**, mfn. to be trusted or relied on, reliable, trustworthy, credible, Kāv.; Pañcat. (n. impers. with loc., 'it should be trusted or relied on'); *-tā*, f., *-tva*, n. trustworthiness, credibleness, Kālid. °**śvasita**, mfn. full of confidence, fearless, unsuspecting, BhP.; trusted, believed or confided in, W. °**śvasitavya**, mfn. = °*śvasanīya*, MBh.; Prab.

Vi-śvasta, mfn. full of confidence, fearless, bold, unsuspecting, MBh.; Kāv. &c.; trusted, confided in, faithful, W.; (*am*), ind. confidingly, without fear or apprehension, Kāv.; (*ā*), f. a widow, Hcar.; *-ghātaka* (Pañcat.; HPariś.), *-ghātin* (Kathās.), mfn. ruining the trustful; *-vañcaka*, mfn. deceiving the trustful, Kathās.; *-vat*, ind. as if trustful, MW.

Vi-śvāsa, m. confidence, trust, reliance, faith or belief in (loc., gen., instr. with or without *saha*, or comp.), MBh.; Kāv. &c.; a confidential communication, secret, Daś.; Hit.; *-kāraka*, mf(*ikā*)n. inspiring confidence, causing trust, MBh.; *-kāraṇa*, n. reason for c°, Hit.; *-kārya*, n. a confidential matter of business, Hit.; *-kṛit*, mfn. = *-kāraka*, W.; *-ghāta*, m. destruction of confidence, violation of trust, treachery, RāmatUp.; *-ghātaka* or *-ghātin*, mfn. one who destroys c°, a traitor, MBh.; R. &c.; *-janman*, mfn. produced from c°, MW.; *-devī*, f. N. of the patroness of Vidyā-pati (to whom he dedicated his Gaṅgā-vākyâvalī, a wk. on the worship of the waters of the Ganges), Cat.; *-parama*, mfn. wholly possessed of c°, thoroughly trustful, R.; *-pātra*, n. 'receptacle of confidence,' a trustworthy person, Hit.; *-pratipanna*, mfn. possessed of c°, trustful, Hit.; *-prada*, mfn. inspiring c°, W.; *-bhaṅga*, m. violation of c°, breach of faith, Mālatīm.; *-bhūmi*, f. 'ground for c°,' a trustworthy person, Hit.; *-maya*, mf(*ī*)n. consisting in c°, Jātakam.; *-rāya*, m. N. of a minister, Cat.; *-sthāna*, n. 'place for or object of c°,' a hostage, surety, Pañcat.; *-hantṛi* (MārkP.) or *-hartṛi* (MBh.), m. 'destroyer or stealer of c°,' a traitor; °*sâika-bhū*, f. 'sole ground for c°,' sole trustworthy person, Kusum.; °*sâika-sāra*, m. 'one whose sole essence is c°,' N. of a man, MW.; °*sôjjhita-dhī*, mfn. 'one whose mind has abandoned c°,' distrustful, suspicious, Rājat.; °*sôpagama*, m. access of c°, Śak. °**śvāsana**, n. inspiring confidence (°*nârtham*, ind. for the sake of insp° c°), Pañcat. °**śvāsika**, mfn. trusty, confidential (*-tara*, mfn. more trusty), MBh. °**śvāsita**, mfn. (fr. Caus.) made to trust, inspired with confidence, W. °**śvāsin**, mfn. confiding, trustful, Megh.; Kathās.; trusty, confidential, trustworthy, honest, Kām. °**śvāsya**, mfn. to be trusted or confided in, trustworthy, MBh.; Kāv. &c. (*-tara*, mfn. more trustworthy, Daś.); to be inspired with confidence, liable to be consoled or encouraged or comforted, MBh.

विश्वि *vi-√śvi*, P. *-śvayati* (only pr. p. *-śvâyat*), to swell, RV.

विश्वित् *vi-√śvit*, Ā. *-śvetate* (only 3. pl. aor. *vy-àśvitan*), to shine, be bright, RV.

विष् 1. *vish*, cl. 3. P. *viveshṭi* (only RV., cf. Intens.; here and ep. also cl. 1. P. *véshati*, cf. below; Subj. *vivéḥ*, *viveshaḥ*, RV.; pf. *vivesha*, *vivishuḥ*, ib. [*áviveshīḥ*, iv, 22, 5 &c.]; aor. *avishat*, *avikshat*, Gr.; Impv. *viḍḍhi*, AV.; fut. *vekshyati*, °*te*, Br.; *veshṭā*, Gr.; inf. *veshṭum*, Gr.; *-vishe*, RV.; ind. p. *vishṭvī*, ib.; *-vishya*, AV.), to be active, act, work, do, perform, RV.; ŚBr.; (cl. 1. P. *véshati*, cf. Dhātup. xvii, 47) to be quick, speed, run, flow (as water), ib.; to work as a servant, serve, ib.; to have done with i.e. overcome, subdue, rule, ib.; (Naigh. ii, 8) to be contained in (acc.), Tattvak.: Caus. *veshayati*, to clothe, BhP.: Intens. (or cl. 3. accord. to Dhātup. xxv, 13) *véveshṭi*, *vevishṭe*, to be active or busy in various ways &c., RV.; AV.; (p. *vévishat*) to consume, eat, ib. (cf. Naigh. ii, 8); (p. *vévishāṇa*) aided or supported by (instr.), RV. vii, 18, 15.

2. **Viṭ** (for 1. see p. 989, col. 2) in comp. for 3. *vish*. **-kārikā**, f. 'ordure maker,' a kind of bird (prob. a variety of Turdus Salica), L. **-kṛimi**, m. a worm bred in the bowels, HPariś. **-khadira**, m. Vachellia Farnesiana, L. **-cara**, m. 'filth-goer,' a tame or village hog, L. **-śūla**, m. a partic. form of colic, Suśr. **-saṅga**, m. coherence or obstruction of the feces, constipation, ib. **-sārikā** or **-sārī**, f. a sort of thrush or variety of the bird inaccurately called 'Maina' in Bengal, L.

Viṭka (ifc.) = 3. *vish*, feces (cf. *karṇa-* and *bhinna-viṭka*).

Viḍ, in comp. for 3. *vish*. **-gandha**, n. = *-lavaṇa*, L. **-graha**, m. stoppage or obstruction of the feces, constipation, Bhpr. **-ghāta**, m. a partic. urinary disease, Car. **-ja**, mfn. produced from ordure, Yājñ.; n. a fungus, W. **-bandha**, m. constipation, Suśr. **-bhaṅga**, m. diarrhœa, ib. **-bhava**, mfn. = *-ja*, W. **-bhid**, f. = *-bhaṅga*, Bhpr. **-bhuj**, mfn. feeding on ordure, Mn. xii, 56; m. a dung-beetle or a similar insect, BhP. **-bheda**, m. = *-bhaṅga*, Car. **-bhedin**, mfn. laxative, Suśr.; (prob.) n. = *-lavaṇa*, L. **-bhojin**, mfn. = *-bhuj*, Pañcar. **-lavaṇa**, n. a medicinal salt (commonly called Vitlaban or Bitnoben), L. **-varāha**, m. a tame or village hog, BhP. **-vighāta**, m. = *-ghāta*, Car.

Viṇ, in comp. for 3. *vish*. **-mūtra**, n. (sg. or du.) feces and urine, Mn. iv, 48 &c.

2. **Vish**, mfn. consuming (cf. *jarad-vish*); = *vyāpana*, pervasion, L.

3. **Vish**, f. (nom. *viṭ*) feces, ordure, excrement, impure excretion, dirt, Mn.; Yājñ.; VarBṛS. &c.

Visha, m. a servant, attendant, RV.; N. of a Sādhya, Hariv. (cf. *dur-v°*); (*vishá*), n. (also m., Siddh.; ifc. f. *ā*) 'anything active,' poison, venom, bane, anything actively pernicious, RV. &c. &c.; a partic. vegetable poison (= *vatsa-nābha*), L.; water, Naigh. i, 12; a mystical N. of the sound *m*, Up.; gum-myrrh, L.; the fibres attached to the stalk of the lotus, W. (see *bisa*); (*ā*), f. a kind of aconite, L.; a tree (commonly called Atis, its bark is used as a red dye), W.; = 3. *vish*, feces (cf. *vīta-visha*); mf(*ā*)n. poisonous, AV. vii, 113, 2. [Cf. Gk. ἰός for ϝισος; Lat. *virus*.] **-kaṇṭakinī**, f. a kind of plant (= *bandhya-karkoṭakī*), L. **-kaṇṭha**, m. 'poison-necked,' N. of Śiva, A. (cf. *vishâgni-pā*). **-kanda**, m. a species of bulbous plant (= *nīla-kanda*), L. **-kanyakā** or **-kanyā**, f. a girl supposed to cause the death of a man who has had intercourse with her, Mudr.; Kathās. **-kāshṭha**, n. Thespesia Populnea, L. **-kumbha**, m. a jar of poison, Hit. **-kṛita**, mfn. poisoned, Kāv. **-kṛimi**, m. 'poison-worm,' a worm bred in poison, Cāṇ.; *-nyāya*, m. the rule of the poison-worm (denoting that what may be fatal to others, is not so to those who are bred in it), A. **-khā**, see *bisa-khā*. **-giri**, m. 'p°-mountain,' a mountain producing p°, AV. **-granthi**, N. of a plant (?), MW. **-ghaṭikā**, f. N. of a solar month; *-janana-śānti*, f. N. of a ch. of the Vṛiddha-gārgya-saṃhitā (describing rites for averting the evil consequences of being born at one of the 4 periods of the month V°-gh°). **-ghā**, f. a kind of twining shrub, Menispermum Cordifolium or Cocculus Cordifolius (= *guḍūcī*), L. **-ghāta**, m. 'p°-destroying,' a physician who applies antidotes, R. **-ghātaka**, mfn. one who kills with poison, VarBṛS. **-ghātin**, mfn. p°-destroying, antidotal, an antidote; m. Mimosa Sirissa (= *śirīsha*), L. **-ghna**, mf(*ī*)n. (cf. *-han*) destroying or counteracting p°, antidotal, an antidote, Mn.; Kathās.; Suśr.; m. (only L.) Mimosa Sirissa; Hedysarum Alhagi; Beleric Myrobalan; Terminalia Belerica; (*ī*), f. (only L.) Hingtsha Repens; another plant (commonly called Bicchati); turmeric; bitter apple or colocynth. **-ghnikā**, f. a species of strychnos, L. **-ja**, mfn. produced by p°, MBh. **-jala**, n. poisoned water, BhP. **-jit**, n. 'conquering or destroying p°,' a kind of honey, L. **-jihva** (*vishá-*), venom-tongued, ŚBr.; m. Lipeocercis Serrata, L. **-jushṭa**, mfn. possessed of poison, poisonous, W.; poisoned, Suśr. **-jvara**, m. a buffalo, L. (v.l. *-tvara*). **-tantra**, n. 'toxicology,' a ch. of most medical Saṃhitās. **-taru**, m. a p°-tree, Vās. **-tā**, f., or **-tva**, n. the state of poison, poisonousness, Vishṇ.; Kāv. &c. **-tindu**, m. Strychnos Nux Vomica, L.; a kind of ebony tree with poisonous fruit, Bhpr. **-tinduka**, m. a species of poisonous plant, Bhpr. **-tulya**, mfn. resembling poison, fatal, deadly, W. **-da**, mfn. yielding p°, poisonous, W.; m. 'shedding water,' a cloud, Śiś.; n. green vitriol, W. **-daṃshṭrā**, f. a medicinal plant and antidote (= *sarpa-kaṅkālī*), L. **-daṇḍa**, m. = *vishâpahāra-daṇḍa*, Pañcad. **-dantaka**, m. 'having poisonous teeth,' a snake, L. **-darśana-mṛityuka**, m. 'dying at the sight of p°,' a kind of pheasant, L. (cf. *visha-mṛityu*). **-dāyaka**, mf(*ikā*)n. or **-dāyin**, mfn. giving p°, poisoning, a poisoner, Kām.; R. **-digdha**, mfn. smeared with p°, empoisoned, poisoned, MBh. **-dûshaṇa**, mf(*ī*)n. destroying p°, AV.; n. corrupting by admixture of p°, poisoning (of food), Kām. **-dosha-hara**, mfn. taking away the ill effects of p°, MW. **-druma**, m. a kind of p°-tree, the Upas tree, Kāv.; Rājat. **-dvishā**, f. a kind of Guḍūcī, L. **-dhara**, mfn. holding or containing p°, venomous, poisonous; m. or (*ī*), f. a snake, Git.; Subh.; *-nilaya*, m. abode of snakes, Pātāla or one of the lower regions, MW.; m. (ifc. f. *ā*) 'containing water,' a receptacle of water, Vās. **-dharmā**, f. cowach, Carpopogon Pruriens or Mucuna Pruritus, L. **-dhātrī**, f. 'venom-preserver,' N. of a goddess who protects men from snakes (she was wife of the Ṛishi Jarat-kāru and sister of Vāsuki; cf. *manasā*), L. **-dhâna**, m. a receptacle of poison, AV. **-nāḍī**, f. a partic. inauspicious period of time (the evil consequences of being born in which are to be averted by religious rites), Saṃskārak.; *-janana-śānti*, f. N. of work (= *visha-ghaṭikā-j°*). **-nāśaka**, mf(*ikā*)n. p°-destroying, MW. **-nāśana**, m. 'id.,' Mimosa Sirissa, L.; n. removing or curing p°, W. **-nāśin**, mfn. p°-destroying, any antidote, W.; (*inī*), f. a kind of plant (= *visha-daṃshṭrā*), BhP. **-nimitta**, mfn. caused by p°, MW. **-nud**, m. 'p°-expeller,' Bignonia Indica, L. **-pattrikā**, f. a partic. plant with poisonous leaves, Suśr. **-pannaga**, m. a venomous serpent, Kām. **-parṇī**, f. = *nyag-rodha*, L. **-parvan**, m. N. of a Daitya, Kathās. **-pādapa**, m. a p°-tree, Kām. **-pīta**, mfn. one who has drunk p°, Hariv. **-puccha**, mf(*ī*)n. having a venomous tail, L. **-puṭa**, m. N. of a man (pl. 'his descendants'), g. *yaskâdi*. **-pushpa**, n. a poisonous flower, Kathās.; the blue lotus, L.; m. 'having poisonous flowers,' Vanguieria Spinosa, L. **-pushpaka**, mfn. (sickness or disease) caused by eating poisonous flowers, Pāṇ. v, 2, 81; m. Vanguieria Spinosa, L. **-pradigdha**, mfn. smeared with p°, empoisoned, VarBṛS. **-prayoga**, m. the use or employment of p°, administering p° as a medicine (also as N. of wk. or ch. of wk.), W. **-prastha**, m. N. of a mountain, MBh. **-bhakshaṇa**, n. the act of eating p°, taking p°, W. **-bhadrā**, f. N. of a plant (= *bṛihad-dantī*), L. (v.l. *bhishag-bh°*). **-bhadrikā**, f. N. of a plant (= *laghu-dantī*), L. **-bhishaj**, m. a poison-doctor, a dealer in antidotes, one who pretends to cure snake-bites, L. **-bhujaṃga**, m. a poisonous snake, L. **-bhṛit**, mfn. bearing or containing p°, venomous, poisonous; m. a snake, W. **-mañjarī**, f. N. of a medical wk. **-mantra**, m. a snake-charmer, one who pretends to charm snakes or cures the bite of snakes, L.; n. a charm for curing snake-bites, MW. **-maya**, mf(*ī* or *ā*)n. consisting of p°, poisonous, Kāv. **-mardanikā**, **-mardanī** or **-mardinī**, f. 'destroying p°,' a species of plant, L. **-muc**, mfn. 'discharging venom,' venomous (as speech), Śāntiś.; m. a serpent, Hcar.; Priy. **-mushṭi**, f. a kind of shrub possessing medicinal properties (commonly called Bishdori or Karsinh), Bhpr. **-mushṭika**, m. Melia Sempervirens, ib. **-mṛityu**, m. 'to whom poison is death,' a kind of pheasant (cf. *visha-darśana-mṛityuka*), L. **-rasa**, m. 'poison-juice,' a poisoned draught or potion, MBh. **-rūpā**, f. a species of plant, L. **-roga**, m. sickness arising from being poisoned, Cat. **-laḍḍuka**, mfn. poisoned, Vet. **-latā**, f. 'poisonous creeper,' the colocynth plant, L. **-lāṅgala**, m. or n. a species of plant, Suśr. **-lāṭā** or **-lāṇṭā**, f. N. of a place, Rājat. **-vat** (*vishá-*), mfn. poisonous, RV. &c. &c.; poisoned, Cat. **-vallarī**, **-vallī**, or **-vallī**, f. a poisonous creeper, Kāv.; Kathās. **-viṭapin**, m. = *-taru*, Veṇis. **-vidyā**, f. 'p°-science,' the administration of antidotes, cure of p°s by drugs or charms, ĀśvŚr. **-vidhāna**, n. administering poison judicially or by way of ordeal, W. **-vimuktâtman**, mfn. one whose soul or nature is released from poison, MBh. **-vṛiksha**, m. a poison-tree, the Upas tree, Rājat.; *-nyāya*, m. the rule of the p°-tree (denoting that as a tree ought not to be cut down by the rearer of it so a noxious object should not be destroyed by the producer of it; cf. Kum. ii, 55, *visha-vṛiksho 'pi saṃvardhya svayaṃ chettum asāmpratam*), A. **-vega**, m. 'poison-force,' the effect of p° (shown by various bodily effects or changes), Mālav. **-vaidya**, m. 'poison-doctor,' a dealer in antidotes or one professing to cure the bites of snakes, ib.; N. of wk. **-vairiṇī**, f. 'p°-enemy,' a kind of grass used as an antidote (= *nir-vishā*, q.v.), L. **-vyavasthā**, f. the state of being poisoned, Daś. **-śālūka**, see *bisa-ś°*. **-śūka** (Suśr.) or **-śṛiṅgin** (L.), m. 'having a poison-ous sting,' a wasp. **-saṃyoga**, m. vermilion, L. **-sūcaka**, m. 'p°-indicator,' the Greek partridge, Perdix Rufa (= *cakora*). **-sṛikvan**, m. 'poison-mouthed,' a wasp, L. **-secana**, mfn. emitting p°, Nidānas. **-ha**, mfn. removing p°, L.; (*ā*), f. Kyllingia Monocephala, L.; a kind of gourd, L. **-han**, mf(*ghnī*)n. destroying poison; (*-ghnī cikitsā*, the science of antidotes), Car.; m. a kind of Kadamba, L.; (*ghnī*), f. N. of various plants (see under *visha-ghna*). **-hantṛi**, mfn. destroying or counteracting p°; (*trī*), f. N. of various plants (= *a-parājitā* or *nir-vishā*), L. **-hara**, mf(*ā* or *ī*)n. removing venom, antidotal, MBh.; m. N. of a son of Dhṛita-rāshṭra, ib.; (*ā* or *ī*), f. the goddess who protects from the venom of snakes (see *visha-dhātrī*, *manasā*), L.; *-cikitsā*, f., *-mantra-prayoga*, m., *-mantrâushadha*, n. N. of wks. **-hīna**, mfn. free from poison (as a serpent), ŚārṅgP. **-hṛidaya**, mfn. poison-hearted, cherishing hatred or hostility, malicious, malignant, Hit. **-heti**, m. 'whose weapon is poison,' a serpent, Harav. **Vishâkta**, mfn. smeared with p°, poisoned, L. **Vishâgni**, m. the fire of p°, burning p°, Ṛitus.; *-pā*, m. 'drinker of burning p°,' N. of Śiva, MBh. (cf. *visha-kaṇṭha* and *vishântaka*). **Vishâgraja**, m. 'elder brother of p°,' a sword, L. **Vishâṅkura**, m. a poisoned sprout, Bhartṛ.; 'having a poisoned point,' a spear, dart, L. **Vishâṅganā**, f. = *visha-kanyakā*, Mudr. **Vishâd**, mfn. eating p°, Kāṭh. **Vishâdanī**, f. 'p°-destroying,' a kind of creeper (= *palāśī*), L. 1. **Vishâdin**, mfn. (for 2. see under *vi-√shad*, col. 3) swallowing p°, Vcar. **Vishânana**, m. 'p-mouthed,' a snake, L. **Vishânala**, m. = *vi-shâgni*, VarBṛS. **Vishântaka**, mfn. 'p°-destroying, antidotal;' m. N. of Śiva (so called because he swallowed the p° produced at the churning of the ocean), L. **Vishânna**, n. poisoned food, Daś. **Vishâpavādin**, mfn. curing poison by charms; (*inī*), f. a magical formula curing p°, ŚāṅkhBr. **Vishâpaha**, mfn. p°-repelling, antidotal, an antidote (*mantrair vishâpahaiḥ*, with texts or charms which have the power of repelling poison), Mn.; Suśr.; m. a kind of tree (= *mushkaka*), L.; N. of Garuḍa, L.; (*ā*), f. (only L.) a kind of birth-wort, Aristolochia Indica (= *arka-mūlā*); N. of various other plants (= *indra-vāruṇī*; *nir-vishā*; *nāga-damanī*; *sarpa-kaṅkālikā*). **Vishâpaharaṇa**, n. removing or destroying p°, Cat. **Vishâpahāra**, m. id.; *-stotra*, n. N. of a Stotra; *-daṇḍa*, m. a magical wand for destroying p°, Pañcad. **Vishâbhāvā**, f. 'having no p°,' a species of plant (= *krishṇa-dhattūraka*), L. **Vishâmṛita**, n. p° and nectar (also N. of wk.); *-maya*, mf(*ī*)n. consisting of p° and n°, having the nature of both, Kathās. **Vishâyudha**, m. = *visha-heti*, L.; °*dhīya*, m. a venomous animal, VarBṛS. **Vishârāti**, m. 'enemy of poison,' a kind of thorn-apple, L. **Vishâri**, m. 'p°-enemy,' a kind of plant or tree (L. = *mahā-cañcu* or *ghṛita-karañja*), Suśr. **Vishâstra**, n. a poisoned arrow, L. **Vishâsya**, m. 'p°-mouthed,' a snake, L.; (*ā*), f. the marking-nut plant, Semecarpus Anacardium, L. **Vishâsvāda**, mfn. tasting p°, Mn. xi, 9 (cf. *madhv-āpāta*). **Vishôddhāra**, m. N. of a wk. on toxicology. **Vishôlbaṇa**, mfn. full of p°, MBh. **Vishâushadhī**, f. Tiaridium Indicum, L.

Vishaṇi, m. a kind of snake, L.

Vishala, n. poison, venom, L.

Vishāya, Nom. Ā. °*yate* (m. c. also P. °*yati*), to become poison, turn into poison, Bhartṛ.; Subh.

Vishāra, m. a venomous snake, L.

Vishālu, mfn. venomous, poisonous, L.

Vishin, mfn. poisoned, Pañcar.

Vishī-bhūta, mfn. become poison (as food), Kathās.

2. **Vishṭa**, mfn. (for 1. see p. 989, col. 2) only in *pari-* and *saṃ-v°*, q.v.; (*ā*), f. the feces, excrement (w. r. for *vishṭhā*).

1. **Vishṭi**, f. (for 2. see p. 999, col. 1) service, (esp.) forced s°, compulsory work, drudgery (also collectively 'servants, slaves, bondsmen'), MBh.; R.; Inscr. (ifc. also °*ṭika*); m. N. of one of the seven Ṛishis in the 11th Manv-antara, MārkP.; (*ī* or *ibhis*), ind. changing, alternatively, by turns, RV. (in this sense accord. to some from *vi* + √1. *as*; cf. *abhi-*, *pari-shṭi*). **-kara**, m. the lord of bondsmen or slaves, MBh. (Nīlak.); = next, VarBṛS. **-kṛit**, m. a servant, slave, bondsman, ib.

1. **Vishṭhā**, f. (for 2. 3. see p. 999, col. 1) = 3. *vish*, feces, excrement (acc. with √*kṛi* or *vi-*√*dhā*, to void excr°), Mn.; MBh. &c. (often w. r. *vishṭā*). **-karaṇa**, n. voiding excrement, VarBṛS. **-bhū**, m. a worm living in ordure, BhP. **-bhūdāraka**, m. a tame or village hog, L. (cf. *viḍ-varāha*). **-sāt**, ind. into excrement or ordure (with √*as*, to be turned into excrement or ordure), HYog.

Vishya, mfn. worthy of poison, deserving death by poison, Pāṇ. iv, 4, 91.

विष् 4. **vish**, cl. 9. P. *vishṇāti*, to separate, disjoin, Dhātup. xxxi, 54.

विषञ्ज् **vi-shañj** (√*sañj*), P. *-shajati*, to hang on, hang to, attach, TS.; Kāṭh.; (*-shajjate*), to be attached or devoted to, BhP. (pr. p. *-shajjat*, addicted to worldly objects, ib.; *-shajjantī*, f. devoted to a man, ib.); to be stuck to or clung to, i. e. be followed at the heels by (instr.), ib.

Vi-shakta, mfn. hung to or on or upon, hung or suspended to, hanging or sticking on or in, firmly fixed or fastened or adhering to (loc.), AV. &c. &c.; turned or directed towards (loc. or comp.), MBh.; Kāv. &c.; spread or extended over (loc.), Jātakam.; (ifc.) dependent on, Daś.; produced, implanted, Uttarar.; stopped, interrupted (said of a cow that has ceased to give milk), RV. i, 117, 20; *-tva*, n. the being occupied with (loc.), MBh.

Vi-shaṅga, m. the hanging on or being attached to (see *nir-v°*). °**shaṅgin**, mfn. adhering, clinging or crowded together, Śiś.; (ifc.) smeared or anointed with, Pañcar.

Vi-shajjita, mfn. clinging or sticking or adhering to, BhP.

विषण्ड **vishaṇḍa**, n. = *mṛiṇāla*, the fibres of the stalk of the water-lily, L.

विषत्वर **vishatvara**, v. l. for *visha-jvara* (see p. 995, col. 3).

विषद् **vi-shad** (√*sad*), P. *-shīdati* (impf. Class. *vy-ashīdat*, Ved. *vya-shīdat* or *vy-asīdat*, Pāṇ. viii, 3, 119; pf. *vi-shasāda*, ib. 118; inf. *-shattum* or *-shīditum*, MBh.), to be exhausted or dejected, despond, despair, MBh.; Kāv. &c.; to sink down, be immersed in (loc.), R. v, 95, 15 (perhaps *vi-sheduḥ* w. r. for *ni-sh°*): Caus. *-shādayati*, to cause to despond or despair, vex, grieve, afflict, MBh.; R. &c.

Vi-shaṇṇa, mfn. dejected, sad, desponding, sorrowful, downcast, out of spirits or temper, Kāv.; Kathās.; BhP.; *-cetas*, mfn. dejected in mind, low-spirited, downcast, R.; *-tā*, f., *-tva*, n. dejection, sadness, languor, lassitude (esp. as one of the effects of unsuccessful love), L.; *-bhāva*, m. id., Daś.; *-manas*, mfn. = *-cetas*, BhP.; *-mukha*, mf(*ī*)n. dejected in countenance, looking sad or dejected, R.; *-rūpa*, mf(*ā*)n. having a sorrowful aspect, being in a dejected mood, R.; *-vadana*, mfn. = *-mukha*, ib.; °*ṇṇâtman*, mfn. low-spirited, desponding, downcast, BhP.

Vi-shāda, m. (ifc. f. *ā*) drooping state, languor, lassitude, Mālatīm.; dejection, depression, despondency (esp. as the result of unrequited love), MaitrUp.; MBh.; Kāv. &c.; disappointment, despair (one of the Vyabhicāras, q. v.), Daśar.; Sāh.; aversion, disgust, Bhartṛ.; fear, weakness, MW.; dulness, stupidity, insensibility (= *moha*), ib.; *-kṛit*, mfn. causing depression or grief, R.; *-janaka*, mfn. id., Prab., Sch.; *-vat*, mfn. dejected, downcast, sad, Kathās.; °*dârta-vadana*, mfn. looking depressed with care or sorrow, R. °**shādana**, mfn. causing depression or grief, R.; (*ī*), f., see *vishâdanī*, col. 1; n. the causing despondency or sadness, Car.; affliction, grief, despair, BhP.; a distressing experience, Kuval. °**shādita**, mfn. (fr. Caus.) caused to sink down, made sorrowful, dejected, MW.

2. **Vi-shādin**, mfn. (for 1. see col. 1) dejected, dismayed, disconsolate, sad, Mn.; MBh. &c.; (°*di*)-*tā*, f. (Kāv.; Kathās.), *-tva*, n. (Suśr.) dejection, despondency, grief, despair.

विषम **ví-shama**, mf(*ā*)n. (fr. *vi* + *sama*) uneven, rugged, rough, MBh.; Hariv.; Kāv. &c.; unequal, irregular, dissimilar, different, inconstant, Br.; ŚāṅkhGṛ.; Mn. &c.; odd, not even (in numbers &c.), Var.; Kāvyâd.; that which cannot be equally divided (as a living sheep among three or four persons), Mn. ix, 119; hard to traverse, difficult, inconvenient, painful, dangerous, adverse, vexatious, disagreeable, terrible, bad, wicked (ibc. 'terribly,' Śiś.), Mn.; MBh. &c.; hard to be understood, Gol.; Kāv.; unsuitable, wrong, Suśr.; Sarvad.; unfair, dishonest, partial, Mn.; MBh.; rough, coarse, rude, cross, MW.; odd, unusual, unequalled, W.; m. a kind of measure, Saṃgīt.; N. of Vishṇu, MW.; (*ī*), f. N. of various wks.; n. unevenness, uneven or rough ground or place (*sama-vishameshu*, 'on even and uneven ground,' Śiś.), bad road, VS.; TS.; ŚBr. &c.; oddness (of numbers), W.; a pit, precipice, Mn.; MBh. &c.; difficulty, distress, misfortune, MBh.; R. &c.; unevenness, inequality (*eṇa*, ind. 'unequally'), Kāś.; (in rhet.) incongruity, incompatibility, Kāvyâd.; Pratāp.; Kuval.; pl. (with *Bharad-vājasya*), N. of Sāmans, SV.; ĀrshBr.; (*am*), ind. unequally, unfairly, MW.; *-karṇa*, mfn. having unequal diagonals, Col.; m. or n. (?) any four-sided figure with un° di°, MW.; the hypotenuse of a right-angled triangle (esp. as formed between the gnomon of a dial and the extremities of the shadow), W.; *-karman*, n. an odd or unequalled act, W.; a dissimilar operation; the finding of two quantities when the difference of their squares is given and either the sum or the difference of the quantities, Col.; *-kāla*, m. an unfavourable time, inauspicious season, MW.; *-kriya*, mfn. undergoing unequal (medical) treatment (*-tva*, n.), Suśr.; *-khāta*, n. an irregular cavity or a solid with unequal sides, Col.; *-gata*, mfn. situated or placed on an uneven place (higher or lower), Āpast.; fallen into distress, ib.; *-cakra-vāla*, n. (in math.) an ellipse, Sūryapr.; *-catur-aśra* or *-catur-bhuja* or *-catush-koṇa*, m. an unequal four-sided figure, trapezium, Sūryapr.; *-chada*, m. = *sapta-cch°*, Alstonia Scholaris, L.; Echites Scholaris, W.; *-cchāyā*, f. 'uneven-shadow,' the shadow of the gnomon at noon when the sun is on the equinoctial line, W.; *-jvara*, m. irregular (chronic) fever, Suśr.; (°*râṅkuśa-lauha*, m. a partic. ferruginous preparation, Rasêndrac.; °*rântaka-lauha*, m. id., L.); *-tri-bhuja*, m. a scalene triangle, Col.; *-tva*, n. inequality, difference, MaitrUp.; dangerousness, terribleness, Vishṇ.; *-drishṭi*, mfn. looking obliquely, squint-eyed, ĀpGṛ., Sch.; *-dhātu*, mfn. having the bodily humors unequally proportioned, unhealthy, MW.; *-nayana* or *-netra*, mfn. 'having an odd number of eyes,' 'three-eyed,' N. of Śiva, L.; *-pada*, mf(*ā*)n. having unequal steps (as a path), Kir.; having un° Pādas (a stanza), RPrāt.; RAnukr.; VS. Anukr.; °*da-vritti*, f. N. of various commentaries; *-palāśa*, m. Alstonia Scholaris

(=*sapta-pal*°), L.; *-pāda*, mf(*ā*)n. consisting of unequal Pādas, Nidānas.; *-bāṇa*, m. 'five-arrowed,' N. of the god of love, L.; (°*ṇa-līlā*, f. N. of a poem); *-bhojana*, n. eating at irregular hours, MW.; *-maya*, mf(*ī*)n. = *vishamād āgataḥ*, L.; *-rāga*, mfn. differently nasalized (*-tā*, f.), RPrāt.; *-rūpya*, mfn. = *vishama-maya*, L.; produced by or resulting from unequal quantities or qualities, W.; *-rca*, mfn. (fr. *vishama + ṛic*) having an unequal number of verses, ŚāṅkhŚr.; *-lakshmī*, f. adverse fortune, bad luck, VarBṛS.; *-vibhāga*, m. unequal division of property amongst co-heirs, W.; *-vilocana*, m. 'three-eyed,' N. of Śiva (cf. *-nayana* above), Siddh.; *-viśikha*, m. 'five-arrowed,' N. of the god of love, Cat.; *-vṛitta*, n. a kind of metre with unequal Pādas, Piṅg.; *-vyākhyā*, f. N. of Comm.; *-vyāptika*, mfn. furnishing an example of partial or one-sided invariable concomitance, Sāṃkhyas., Sch.; *-śara*, m. 'five-arrowed,' N. of the god of love, Daś.; *-śāyin*, mfn. sleeping irregularly, W.; *-śishṭa*, mfn. inaccurately prescribed (*-tva*, n.), L.; left unfairly, unjustly divided (as property &c. at death), W.; *-śīla*, mfn. having an unequable disposition, cross-tempered, rough, difficult, W.; m. N. of Vikramâditya, Kathās.; of the 18th Lambaka of the Kathā-sarit-sāgara called after him; (w.r. for *vishama-śilā*, 'an uneven rock,' Pañcat. iii, 3 1/2 1/4); *-śloka-ṭīkā*, f., *-śloka-vyākhyā*, f. N. of wks.; *-sāhasa*, n. irregular boldness, temerity, W.; *-stha*, mf(*ā*)n. standing unevenly, W.; being in an inaccessible position, ib.; standing on a precipice, st° in a dangerous place, Pañcat.; being in difficulty or misfortune, MBh.; R. &c.; *-spṛihā*, f. coveting wrongly another's property, L.; °*mâksha*, m. 'three-eyed,' N. of Śiva, Śivag.; °*mâditya*, m. N. of a poet, Subh.; °*mânna*, n. irregular or unusual food, MW.; °*mâyudha*, m. 'five-arrowed,' N. of the god of love, Siṇhās.; °*mârtha-dīpikā*, f. N. of wk.; °*mâvatāra*, m. descending on uneven ground, MW.; °*mâśana*, n. eating irregularly (either as to quantity or time), Vāgbh.; Siṇhās.; Bhpr.; °*mâśaya*, mfn. having an unfair disposition, dishonest, crafty, W.; °*mêkshaṇa*, m. 'three-eyed,' N. of Śiva, Śiś.; °*mêshu*, m. 'five-arrowed,' N. of the god of love, Śiś.; Hit.; °*mônnata*, mfn. raised unevenly, L.; °*môpala*, mfn. having rough stones or rocks, MW.

Vishamaka, mfn. rather uneven, not properly polished (as pearls), VarBṛS.

Vishamāya, Nom. Ā. °*yate*, to become or appear uneven, Cāṇ.

Vishamita, mfn. made uneven or impassable, Kir.; made crooked, disarranged, ib.; Śiś.; Vās.; become dangerous or hostile, BhP.

Vishamī, in comp. for *vi-shama*. **— √kṛi**, P. *-karoti*, to make uneven, MBh.; to make unequal or crooked, Śiś., Sch.; to make hostile, BhP. **— bhāva**, m. derangement of equilibrium, MBh. **— √bhū**, P. *-bhavati*, to become uneven or irregular, Śak.

Vishamīya, mfn. connected with or produced by unevenness or inequality, uneven, unequal, g. *gahâdi*.

विषय *vishaya*, m. (ifc. f. *ā*; prob. either fr. √1. *vish*, 'to act,' or fr. *vi* + √*si*, 'to extend,' cf. Pāṇ. viii, 3, 70, Sch.) sphere (of influence or activity), dominion, kingdom, territory, region, district, country, abode (pl. = lands, possessions), Mn.; MBh. &c.; scope, compass, horizon, range, reach (of eyes, ears, mind &c.), ŚāṅkhŚr.; MBh. &c.; period or duration (of life), Pañcat.; special sphere or department, peculiar province or field of action, peculiar element, concern (ifc. = 'concerned with, belonging to, intently engaged on;' *vishaye*, with gen. or ifc. = 'in the sphere of, with regard or reference to;' *atra vishaye*, 'with regard to this object'), MBh.; Kāv. &c.; space or room (sometimes = fitness) for (gen.), Kāv.; Pañcat.; an object of sense (these are five in number, the five *indriya* or organs of sense having each their proper *vishaya* or object, viz. 1. *śabda*, 'sound,' for the ear, cf. *śruti-vishaya*; 2. *sparśa*, 'tangibility,' for the skin; 3. *rūpa*, 'form' or 'colour,' for the eye; 4. *rasa*, 'savour,' for the tongue; 5. *gandha*, 'odour,' for the nose: and these five Vishayas are sometimes called the Guṇas or 'properties' of the five elements, ether, air, fire, water, earth, respectively; cf. *śruti-vishaya-guṇa*), Yājñ.; Sāṃk.; Sarvad.; IW. 83; a symbolical N. of the number 'five,' VarBṛS.; anything perceptible by the senses, any object of affection or concern or attention, any special worldly object or aim or matter or business, (pl.) sensual enjoyments, sensuality, KaṭhUp.; Mn.; MBh. &c.; any subject or topic, subject-matter, MBh.; Kāv. &c.; an object (as opp. to 'a subject'), Sarvad.; a fit or suitable object ('for,' dat., gen., or comp.), MBh.; Kāv. &c.; (in phil.) the subject of an argument, category, general head (one of the 5 members of an Adhikaraṇa [q.v.], the other 4 being *viśaya* or *saṃśaya*, *pūrva-paksha*, *uttara-paksha* or *siddhânta*, and *saṃgati* or *nirṇaya*), Sarvad.; un-organic matter, IW. 73; (in gram.) limited or restricted sphere (e.g. *chandasi vishaye*, 'only in the Veda'), Kāś. (ifc. = restricted or exclusively belonging to); (in rhet.) the subject of a comparison (e.g. in the comp. 'lotus-eye' the second member is the *vishaya*, and the first the *vishayin*), Kuval.; Pratāp.; a country with more than 100 villages, L.; a refuge, asylum, W.; a religious obligation or observance, ib.; a lover, husband, ib.; semen virile, ib. **— karman**, n. worldly business or act, W. **— kāma**, m. desire of worldly goods or pleasures, ib. **— grāma**, m. the multitude or aggregate of objects of sense, Sāh. **— candrikā**, f. N. of wk. **— jña**, m. one who has a partic. domain of knowledge, a specialist, Rājat. **— jñāna**, n. acquaintance with worldly affairs, MW. **— tā**, f. the character or condition of being an object or having anything for an object, the relation between an object and the knowledge of it, Sāh.; Vedântas.; Sarvad.; *-rahasya*, n., *-vāda* (or *-vicāra*), m., *-vāda-ṭippaṇa*, n., *-vādârtha*, m. N. of wks. **— tva**, n. = *-tā*, Sarvad.; Yājñ., Sch.; (ifc.) the being restricted to, occurring only in, Pat. **— nirati**, f. attachment to sensual objects, A. **— nihnuti**, f. negation with regard to an object (not as to one's self), Kāvyâd. ii, 306. **— pati**, m. the governor of a province, Inscr. **— pathaka**, m. or n. (?) N. of a district, ib. **— parāṅmukha**, mfn. averted or averse from mundane affairs, Śak. **— pratyabhijñāna**, n. (in phil.) the recognition of objects, MW. **— pravaṇa**, mfn. attached to objects of sense, Kull. on Mn. ii, 99. **— prasaṅga**, m. = *-nirati*, A. **— lolupa**, mfn. eager for sensual enjoyment, Kathās. **— laukika-pratyaksha-kārya-kāraṇa-bhāva-rahasya**, n. N. of wk. **— vat**, mfn. directed to objects of sense, MBh.; objective, Yogas. **— vartin**, mfn. directed to anything (gen.) as an object, R. **— vākya-dīpikā** (also *-vāg-d*°), f., **-vākya-saṃgraha**, m., **-vāda**, m. N. of wks. **— vāsin**, mfn. inhabiting a country (*anya-vishaya-v*°, the inhabitant of another c°), Kāv.; Pañcat.; engaged in the affairs of life, W. **— vicāra**, m. N. of a treatise by Gadādhara (also called *vishayatā-vic*°, see *-tā* above). **— vishayin**, m. du. object and subject, Bādar. **— saṅga**, m. addiction to sensual objects, sensual; *-ja*, mfn. sprung from add° to s° objects, Mn. xii. 18. **— saptamī**, f. the locative case in the sense of 'with regard to,' Kāś. on Pāṇ. i, 1, 57. **— sukha**, n. the pleasures of sense, MW. **— sneha**, m. desire for sensual objects, Ragh. **— spṛihā**, f. id., MW. **Vishayâjñāna**, n. 'non-recognition of objects,' exhaustion, lassitude, L. **Vishayâtmaka**, mfn. consisting of or identified with worldly objects, sensual, carnal, Mn.; BhP. **Vishayâdhikṛita**, m. the governor of a province, Kathās. **Vishayâdhipati**, m. id., ib.; 'lord of a country,' a king, sovereign, R. **Vishayânantara**, mfn. immediately adjacent or adjoining, next neighbour, L. **Vishayânanda**, m. N. of various wks. **Vishayânta**, m. the boundary of a country, MBh.; R.; Kathās. **Vishayâbhimukhī-kṛiti**, f. directing (the senses) towards sensual objects, Cat. **Vishayâbhirati**, f. and °**bhilāsha**, m. the enjoyment of s° pleasures, Kir. **Vishayârha**, mfn. entitled to s° pl° (as youth), HPariś. **Vishayâsakta**, mfn. attached to s° pl°; *-manas*, mfn. one whose mind is devoted to the world, Śukas. **Vishayâsakti**, f. attachment to s° pl°, ib. **Vishayâsiddha-dīpikā**, f. N. of wk. **Vishayâishin**, mfn. addicted to s° pl°, devoted to worldly pursuits, L. **Vishayôparama**, m. cessation or abandonment of s° pl°, Sāṃkhyak. **Vishayôpasevā**, f. addiction to s° pl°, sensuality, Ragh.

Vishayaka (ifc.) = *vishaya*, having anything for an object or subject, relating to, concerning (*-tva*, n.), Siddh.; Nyāyas.; Nīlak.

Vishayāyin, m. (only L.) a prince; an organ of sense; a man of the world, sensualist, materialist; N. of the god of love.

Vishayika. See *dārshṭi-* and *samasta-v*°.

Vishayin, mfn. relating or attached to worldly objects, sensual, carnal, Yājñ.; Kāv. &c.; m. a sensualist, materialist, voluptuary (= *vaishayika* or *kāmin*), L.; a prince, king, L.; a subject of (gen.), Pañcar.; (in phil.) the subject, the 'Ego,' MBh.; Sāṃk. (*-tva*, n.); the god of love, L.; (in rhetor.) the object of a comparison (cf. under *vishaya*); n. an organ of sense, L.

Vishayī, in comp. for *vishaya*. **— karaṇa**, n. the making anything an object of perception or thought, Sāṃk. **— √kṛi**, P. *-karoti*, to make anything an object, Sāṃk.; TPrāt., Sch.; to make anything one's own, take possession of (acc.), Hcar. **— kṛita**, mfn. spread abroad, Cat.; made an object of sense or thought, perceived, Sāṃk.; Vedântas.; (ifc.) made an object of or for (*karṇa-vishayī-kṛita*, 'heard'), Cat. **— √bhū**, P. *-bhavati*, to become an object of sense or perception, Sāṃk. **— bhūta**, mfn. become the dominion of (gen.), Pañcat.

Vishayīya, m. or n. = *vishaya*, an object, Kusum.; mfn. relating to an object, MW.

विषह् *vi-shah* (√*sah*), Ā. *-shahate* (impf. *vy-ashahata* or *vy-asahata*, Pāṇ. viii, 3, 71; inf. *-shahitum* or *-soḍhum*, not *-shoḍhum*, ib., 115), to conquer, subdue, overpower, be a match for (acc.), RV.; AV.; MBh.; Hariv.; to be able to or capable of (inf.), MBh.; R.; to bear, withstand, resist, MBh.; Kāv. &c.; to endure, suffer, put up with (acc. also with inf.), R.; Gīt.; BhP.: Caus. (only aor. *vy-asīshahat*), Pāṇ. viii, 3, 116: Intens., see *vi-shāsahi*.

Vi-shahya, mfn. bearable, tolerable (see *a-v*°), conquerable, resistible, MBh.; R.; (also with *kartum*) possible, practicable, MBh.; ascertainable, determinable (see *a-v*°).

Vi-shāsahi, mfn. victorious, RV.; AV.; ŚBr.; *-vrata*, n. N. of a partic. observance, AV. Paddh. on Kauś. 57.

Vi-soḍha, mfn. (Pāṇ. viii, 3, 115) endured, Kathās.

विषा *vishā*, ind. = *buddhi*, Uṇ. iv, 36, Sch. (for *vishā*, f., see under *visha*, p. 995, col. 2).

विषाक्त *vishâkta*, &c. See p. 996, col. 1.

विषाण 1. *vishāṇa*, n. (for 2. see under *vi-√sho*, fr. which 1. may perhaps also come; in older language also *ā*, f., and accord. to g. *ardharcâdi*, also m.; ifc. *ā* or *ī*) a horn, the horn of any animal, AV. &c. &c. (cf. *kharī-*, *śaśa-v*°); a horn (wind-instrument), BhP.; the tusk (of an elephant or of a boar or of Gaṇêśa), MBh.; Hariv. &c.; the claws (of a crab), Pañcat.; a peak, top, point, summit, ShaḍvBr.; VarBṛS.; the horn-like tuft on Śiva's head, MBh.; the tip of the breast, nipple, BhP.; the chief or best of a class or kind (cf. *-bhūta*; *dhī-v*° = 'acuteness of intellect, sagacity'), MBh.; VarBṛS.; a sword or knife, R. (v.l. *kṛipāṇa*); (*ī*), f. N. of various plants (Odina Pinnata; the Indian tamarind; Tragia Involucrata; = *ṛishabha*, *karkaṭa-śṛiṅgī* and *kshīra-kākolī*), L.; Costus Speciosus or Arabicus, L. **— kośa**, m. the hollow of a horn, MW. **— bhūta**, mfn. being the chief or best, MBh. i, 3735. **— vat**, mfn. horned, Kathās.; m. 'having tusks,' a boar, Hariv. **Vishāṇânta**, m. N. of Gaṇêśa, Gal. **Vishāṇônnāmita-skandha**, mfn. one whose shoulders are raised up towards (or high enough to meet) the horns, MW. **Vishāṇôllikhita-skandha**, mfn. one whose shoulders are grazed or scratched by his horns (said of the leader of a herd of cattle to mark superiority), ib.

Vishāṇaka (ifc.) = 1. *vishāṇa*, a horn, L.; m. an elephant, Gal.; (*akā*), f. a species of plant, AV.; (*ikā*), f. N. of various plants (Odina Pinnata; the Senna plant; Asclepias Geminata; = *karkaṭa-śṛiṅgī* and *sātalā*), L.

Vishāṇin, mfn. having horns, horned, MBh.; Hariv. (°*ṇi-tva*, n.); having tusks, MBh.; m. an elephant, Hariv.; Śiś.; any horned animal, W.; Trapa Bispinosa, L.; a partic. plant growing on the Himavat (= *ṛishabha*), L.; pl. N. of a people, RV. vii, 18, 7 ('holding horns in the hand,' Sāy.)

विषातकी *vishātakī*, f. (meaning unknown), AV. vii, 113, 2.

विषाद *vi-shāda* &c. See under *vi-√shad*.

विषानन *vishânana*, *vishânala* &c. See p. 996, col. 1.

विषिच् *vi-shic* (√*sic*), P. *-shiñcati*, to spill, shed, ĀpŚr.: Intens. *-sesicyate*, Vop.

Vi-shikta, mfn. discharged, emitted (semen), ŚBr.

विषित *vi-shita*. See under *vi-√sho*.

विषिव् *vi-shiv* (√*siv*), P. *-shīvyati*, to sew or sew on in different places, Kāṭh.; TS.

विषु 1. *vishu*, ind. (only in comp. and derivatives, prob. connected with *viśva*, accord. to Pāṇ. vi, 4, 77, Vārtt. 1, Pat. a Ved. acc. *vishvam* = *vishuvam*) on both sides, in both directions; in various directions; similarly, equally. **—drúh** or **-drúha**, mfn. injuring or hurting in various parts(?), RV. viii, 26, 15 (Sāy. 'an arrow'). **—pada**, n. the autumnal equinox (?), MW. **—rūpa** (*víshu-*), mf(*ā*)n. different in shape or colour, manifold, various, RV.; TS.; VS. **—vát**, see below.

Víshuṇa, mfn. different, various, manifold, RV.; changing (as the moon), ib.; averse from (abl.), ib.; (*e*), ind. aside, apart, ib.; m. the equinox, L.

Vishuṇák, ind. to different parts or sides, RV.

Víshupa, m. or n. = *vishuva*, the equinox, L.

Vishuva, m. or n. (cf. *vishuvát*; acc. *vishuvam* or *vishvam*, cf. 1. *vishu* above) the equinox, MBh.; Pur. **—cchāyā**, f. the shadow of the gnomon or index of a dial at noon when the sun is on the equinoctial points, MW. **—dina**, n. the day of the equinox, ib. **—rekhā**, f. the equinoctial line, ib. **—saṃkrānti**, f. = *vishuvat-s°*, ib. **—samaya**, m. the equinoctial season, Hit.

Vishuvát, mfn. having or sharing both sides equally, being in the middle, middlemost, central, RV.; AitBr.; TS.; m. the central day in a Sattra or sacrificial session, AV.; Br.; ŚrS.; a partic. Ekâha, PañcavBr.; top, summit, vertex, AV.; m. n. equinoctial point or equinox, Yājñ.; MBh. &c.; *-pūrṇa-śītāṅśu*, m. the equinoctial full moon, Rājat.; *-prabhā*, f. the equinoctial shadow, Sūryas.; *-saṃkrānti*, f. the sun's equinoctial passage, the passing of the sun into the next sign at either equinox, Hit.; *-stoma*, m. a partic. Ekâha, ĀśvŚr.

Vishuvatka for °**vát** (in *a-vishuvatka*, having no central day), Lāṭy.

Vishuvad, in comp. for °*vat*. **—dina**, n., **-divasa**, m. the equinoctial day, Gaṇit. **—deśa**, m. a country situated under the equator, Āryav., Sch. **—bhā**, f. the equinoctial shadow, Sūryas. **—valaya** or **-vṛitta**, n. the equinoctial circle, equator, Gol.

Vishuvan, in comp. for °*vat*. **—maṇḍala**, n. the equator, Sūryas.

Vishū = 1. *vishu* above. **—vát** = *vishuvát* above. **—vṛít**, mfn. rolling in various directions (as a chariot), RV. (others 'balancing'); equally divided, AV.; indifferent to, not partaking of (gen.), RV. x, 43, 3 (others 'averter').

Vishū-kuh, mfn. (√2. *kuh*) split on both sides, divided in two, ĀśvŚr.; Lāṭy.

Vishūcaka (only in loc. m. c.) = *víshūcikā*, MBh.

Vishūci, m. or f. = *manas*, BhP.

Víshūcikā, f. (fr. *vishūcī*; incorrectly *visūcikā*) a partic. disease (indigestion attended with evacuation in both directions, accord. to some 'cholera in its sporadic form'), VS.; TBr.; Suśr.

Vishūcī, f. See under *vishvañc*, col. 2.

Vishūcīna, mfn. going apart or in different directions, spreading everywhere, RV.; AV.; VS.; TS.; BhP.; n. = *manas*, BhP. **—karaṇa**, n. causing to go asunder, separating, ĀpŚr., Sch. **Vishūcīnâgra**, mfn. with tops or points diverging in all directions, ĀpGṛ.

Vishvak, in comp. for °*vañc*. **—kaca**, mfn. 'one whose hair flies in all directions,' having dishevelled hair, BhP. **—sama**, mfn. equal on all sides or in all parts, L. **—sena**, m. (sometimes written *viśvak-s°*) 'whose hosts or powers go everywhere,' N. of Vishṇu-Kṛishṇa (or of a partic. form of that deity to whom the fragments of a sacrifice are offered), MBh.; Kāv. &c.; of Śiva, MBh. xiii, 1168; of an attendant of Vishṇu, Pur.; of a Sādhya, Hariv.; of the 14th (or 13th) Manu, VP.; of a Ṛishi, MBh.; of a king, R.; of a son of Brahma-datta, Hariv.; Pur.; of a son of Śambara, Hariv.; (*ā*), f. a kind of plant (= *priyaṅgu* or *phalinī*), L.; *-kāntā*, f. a kind of plant (= *priyaṅgu* or a Diascorea), Car.; *-priyā*, f. 'beloved of Vishṇu,' N. of Lakshmī, L.; a Diascorea, L.; *-saṃhitā*, f. N. of wk.

Vishvag, in comp. for °*vañc*. **—añcana**, mfn. turned or directed everywhere, Sāy. on RV. viii, 29, 1. **—avêkshaṇa**, mfn. looking in every direction, Sāh. **—aśva**, m. N. of a king (the son of Pṛithu), MBh. **—āyat**, mfn. spreading or going in every direction, MW. **—aida**, n. N. of a Sāman, PañcavBr. **—gata**, mfn. gone all about, spread, extended, W. **—gati**, mfn. going all about or everywhere, entering into every (topic), ib. **—gamana-vat**, mfn. moving in every direction, going everywhere, Vedântas. **—jyotis**, m. N. of the eldest of the 100 sons of Śata-jit, VP. **—yuj**, mfn., Pāṇ. vi, 3, 92, Sch. **—lopa**, m. general disturbance or confusion, MBh. **—vātá**, m. a kind of noxious wind which blows from all quarters, TS.; MBh. &c. **—vāyu**, m. id., L. **—vilupta-cchada**, mfn. having leaves torn off on all sides (said of a tree), ŚārṅgP. **—vṛita**, mfn. surrounded on all sides, VarBṛS.

Vishvañc, mf(°*shūcī*)n. (fr. 1. *vishu* + 2. *añc*) going in or turned to both (or all) directions, all-pervading, ubiquitous, general, RV. &c. &c.; going asunder or apart, separated or different from (instr. or abl.), RV.; TS.; Up.; getting into conditions of every kind, Gaut.; following in inverted order, ŚāṅkhŚr.; (°*shūcī*), f. the cholera (= *vishūcikā*, q. v.), Suśr.; ŚārṅgS.; n. the equinox, W.; (*víshvak*), ind. on both (or all) sides, sideways, RV.; AV.; in two, AV. iii, 6, 6; in all directions, all around, everywhere, RV. &c. &c.

Vishvadrīcīna, mfn. (fr. next) being everywhere, general, Cat.

Vishvadryañc, mf(°*drīcī*)n. (cf. *tadryañc*, *madryañc*) going everywhere or in all directions, all-pervading, Śiś.; (°*dryàk*), ind. forth on both or all sides or all directions, RV. vii, 25, 1.

Vishvam. See *vishuva*, col. 1.

Vishvâc, m. N. of an Asura, RV. i, 117, 16 (Sāy.)

विषु 2. *vi-shu* (√3. *su*; only pf. p. Ā. *-sushvāṇa* with pass. meaning, RV. ix, 101, 11; accord. to Vop. also aor. *vy-ashāvīt*; fut. *vi-soshyati* and *vi-savishyati*), to press or squeeze out (the Soma plant for obtaining its juice).

विषू *vi-shū* (√2. *sū*; only impf. Ā. *vy-asūyata*), to bring forth (a child), Bālar.

विषेव् *vi-shev* (√*sev*), Ā. *-shevate* (impf. *vy-ashevata*, pf. *vi-shisheva* &c.), Pāṇ. viii, 3, 63.

विषो *vi-sho* (√*so*), P. *-shyati* (aor. subj. *-shāt*; Pot. *-shīmahi*; Impv. *-shāhi*), to let loose, release, set free, flow, shed, cause to flow, RV.; AV.; ŚBr.; Kauś.; to unharness, unbridle, RV.; to open, ib.; to relax, mollify, ib.

2. **Vi-shâṇa**, n. (for 1. see p. 997, col. 3) discharging (a fluid), RV. v, 44, 11. °**shâyin**, mfn., g. *grahâdi*.

Ví-shita, mfn. let loose, released &c.; relieved (applied to the sun at the moment immediately before its setting), Lāṭy.; *-stuka*, mf(*ā*)n. one who has loose or dishevelled hair, RV.; *-stupa*, mfn. one whose tuft of hair has been untied or loosened, AV. (Paipp. *-stuga*).

विष्क् *vishk*, cl. 10. P. *vishkayati*, to see, perceive, Dhātup. xxxv, 34, v.l.

विष्क *vishka*, m. (cf. *vikka*) an elephant twenty years old, Śiś. xviii, 27 (Sch.)

विष्कन्तृ *vi-shkanttṛi* or *vi-skanttṛi*, mfn. (*vi* + √*skand*; cf. Pāṇ. viii, 3, 73) moving hither and thither, restless, Bhaṭṭ. °**shkanda**, m. dispersing, going away, W. °**skanna** (not °*shkaṇṇa*, cf. Pāṇ. viii, 3, 73), mfn. gone in different directions, dispersed, gone away, ib.

विष्कन्ध *vi-shkandha*. See p. 953, col. 1.

विष्कम्भ् *vi-shkambh* (√*skambh*; cf. Pāṇ. viii, 3, 77), P. *-skabhnoti* or *-skabhnāti* (inf. *-shkábhe*, RV.; *-shkambhitum*, Bhaṭṭ.), to fix, support, prop, RV.; to hurl, cast, ib.; to come forth, escape, Bhaṭṭ.: Caus. *-shkabhāyati*, to fix firmly, RV.; AV.

Vi-shkabdha, mfn. fixed, supported &c., Pāṇ. vii, 2, 34, Sch. °**shkabhita** (*ví-*), mfn. fixed or held asunder (heaven and earth), RV.

Vi-shkambha, m. a prop, support, Lāṭy.; Suśr.; the bolt or bar of a door, Ragh., Sch.; the supporting beam or pillar of a house, W.; a post (round which the string of a churning-stick is wound), L.; width, extension, MBh.; VarBṛS.; MārkP.; the diameter of a circle, Āryabh.; a mountain-range (= *-parvata*), MārkP.; an obstacle, impediment, L.; the first of the twenty-seven astronomical periods called Yogas or the leading star of the first lunar mansion, Col.; (in dram.) an interlude or introductory scene (coming between the acts [*aṅkayor madhya-vartī*] and performed by an inferior actor or actors [*nīca-pātra-prayojitaḥ*], who explain to the audience the progress of the plot, and inform them of what is supposed to have happened in the intervals of the acts, cf. *praveśaka*), Bhar.; Daśar. &c.; a partic. Yoga-posture, L.; a tree, L.; action, doing anything, W.; = *pratibimba*, L.; N. of a divine being reckoned among the Viśve Devāḥ, Hariv. (v. l. *viskumbhu*, *nikumba*, and *vishṭara*); *-parvata*, m. a mountain-range, MārkP.; *-vat*, mfn. (prob.) wealthy, opulent, Hcat.; °*bhârdha*, m. or n. the radius of a circle, Āryav. °**shkambhaka**, mfn. propping, supporting, KātyŚr., Sch.; m. (in dram.) an interlude (= *vishkambha*), Ratnâv.; Bhar. &c.; a partic. astron. Yoga (= id.), W.; (*ikā*), f. a piece of wood for supporting the pole of a carriage, KātyŚr., Sch.; °*bhaka-kāshṭha*, n. = id., ib. °**shkambhaṇa**, n. the act of obstructing or impeding &c., L.; a means of tearing open, Divyâv. °**shkambhita**, mfn. richly furnished with (comp.), Lalit.; driven away, rejected, Pañcat. °**shkambhin**, mfn. obstructing, impeding, W.; m. the bolt or bar of a door, ib.; N. of Śiva, MBh.; of a Bodhisattva, Buddh.; of a Tāntric deity, Kālac.

विष्कर *vi-sh-kara*, m. (√*kṛi* or *kṛī*?) the bolt of a door, L.; N. of a Dānava, MBh.; n. a partic. manner of fighting, Hariv.

विष्किर *vi-sh-kira*, m. (√*kṛī*) 'scatterer,' a gallinaceous bird (such as a domestic fowl, partridge, quail &c.), Gaut.; Yājñ. &c.; a partic. Agni, ĀpŚr.; any bird, W.; pulling or tearing to pieces, ib.; *-rasa*, m. chicken-broth, Suśr.

विष्कुम्भ् *vi-shkumbh* (√*skumbh*), P. *-shkubhnāti* or *-shkubhnoti*, Vop.

विष्ट् *vishṭ*. See √*veshṭ*.

विष्ट 1. 2. *vishṭa*. See under √*viś* and √1. *vish*.

विष्टन् *vi-shṭan*, w.r. for *vi-√stan*, q.v.

विष्टम्भ् *vi-shṭambh* (√*stambh*), P. *-shṭabhnoti* or °*nāti* (impf. *vy-ashṭabhnot* or °*nāt*, pf. *vi-tashṭambha*, Pāṇ. viii, 3, 63 &c.; ind. p. *-shṭabhya* or *-shṭambhitvā*), to fix asunder, hold or keep apart, prop, fix, fasten, support, RV.; AV.; Br.; to strengthen, encourage, MBh.; BhP.; to settle, ascertain, MBh. xii, 5429; to make stiff or rigid, MBh.; R.; MārkP.; to stop, check, restrain, suppress, Bhp.; to press close against (the mouth), Yājñ.; to plant (the feet) firmly, Hit.; to lean on or against (acc.), MBh.; R.; Bhaṭṭ.; to stiffen, i.e. fill through and through, pervade, permeate, MBh.; R.; to stuff (intr.), swell, remain undigested (in the stomach), Suśr.: Caus. *-shṭambhayati*, °*te* (aor. *vy-atastambhat*, Pāṇ. viii, 3, 116), to cause to stop, check, arrest, obstruct, MBh.; R. &c.; to cause or produce (illness) by obstruction, Cat.; to paralyse, MW.

Vi-shṭáp, f. top, summit, surface, highest part, height (esp. of heaven), RV.; VS.; PañcavBr.; ĀśvŚr. °**shṭápa**, n. (rarely m.) id., RV.; VS.; Br. (with *ṛishabhasya*, 'a hump,' ŚBr.; °*pe*, ind. in heaven, Āpast.); forking or bifurcation (of an Udumbara branch), VS., Sch.; a world, Mn.; MBh. &c.; *-traya*, n. the three worlds (cf. *loka-tr°*), Ragh.; *-hārin*, mfn. world-ravishing, Bhartṛ.

Ví-shṭabdha, mfn. firmly set or bound, ŚBr.; Mn.; MBh.; rigid, stiff, MBh.; Hariv.; Suśr.; checked, stopped, restrained, arrested, obstructed, paralysed, MBh.; R.; Suśr.; propped, supported, MBh.; Suśr.; filled, stuffed, PañcavBr.; undigested, Suśr.; *-gātra*, mfn. with rigid limbs, Hariv.; *-caraṇa*, mfn. with r° feet, MBh.; *-tā*, f. firmness, confidence, MW.; °*dhâksha*, mfn. with r° eyes, Suśr.; °*dhâjīrṇa*, n. indigestion arising from obstruction, ib. °**shṭabdhi**, f. fixing firmly, propping, supporting, Anup.

Vi-shṭabha, m. 'fixed or planted firmly,' the world, W. °**shṭabhita** (*ví-*), mfn. fixed firmly, well founded, AV.

Vi-shṭambhá, m. fixing, planting firmly (*pada-v°*), Kir.; prop, support, RV.; AV.; MBh.; Śaṃk.; 'supporters,' N. of partic. syllables inserted in sacred texts, PañcavBr.; checking, stopping, restraint, impediment, suppression, Kām.; BhP.; endurance, resistance, MBh.; obstruction of the urine or feces, ischury, constipation, Suśr.; a partic. disease of the fetus, ŚārṅgS.; paralysis, loss of motion, W.; *-kara*, mfn. stopping, restraining, obstructing, Suśr. °**shṭambhana**, mf(*ī*)n. propping, supporting, VS.; n. checking, restraining, suppressing, MaitrUp. °**shṭambhayishu**, mfn. wishing to stop or cause to stand still (a fleeing army), MBh. vii, 1746 (B. *saṃstambhayishu*). °**shṭambhita,** mfn. fixed firmly &c.; entirely filled or covered with (instr.), Hariv. °**shṭambhin,** mfn. supporting (lit. and fig.), Hcat.; checking, stopping, obstructing, Suśr.; chilling, W.; making motionless, ib.

विष्टर *vi-shṭara,* m. (√*stṛi*) anything spread out, a handful of rushes or grass for sitting on (esp. the seat of the presiding Brāhman at a sacrifice), GṛŚrS.; MBh.; a seat made of 25 shoots of Kuśa grass tied up in a sheaf, W.; a tree, L.; N. of a divine being reckoned among the Viśve Devāḥ, Hariv.; m. n. any seat or couch, chair, stool &c., MBh.; Kāv. &c.; mfn. = *vi-stara,* extensive, wide (?), see comp.; *-bhāj,* mfn. occupying a seat, seated, Ragh.; *-śrava,* m. = next, Hcat.; *-śravas,* m. 'broad-eared' or 'far-famed,' N. of Vishṇu-Kṛishṇa, MBh.; Hariv.; Śiś.; of Śiva, Śivag.; *-stha,* mfn. sitting on a seat, reclining on a bed (of leaves &c.), W.; °*râśva,* m. N. of a son of Pṛithu, Hariv.; °*rôttara,* mfn. covered with Kuśa grass, MW.

Vi-shṭārā, m. a layer of grass (?), RV. v, 52, 10 (others 'the far spread host, scil. of the Maruts'); a kind of metre (cf. next and Pāṇ. iii, 3, 34; viii, 3, 94); *-paṅkti* (°*tārā-*), f. a partic. form of Paṅkti metre (consisting of 8 × 12 × 12 × 8 syllables), VS.; RPrāt.; *-bṛihatī,* f. a species of Bṛihatī (8 × 10 × 10 × 8 syllables), RPrāt. °**shṭārin,** mfn. (prob.) spread, extended (applied to a partic. oblation), AV.

Vi-shṭír, f. expansion (opp. to *saṃ-stir*), RV.

विष्टि 2. *vishṭi,* f. (for 1. see p. 996, col. 2) = *vṛishṭi,* rain, L.

विष्टु *vi-shṭu* (√*stu*), P. *-shṭauti* or *-shṭavīti* (impf. *vy-astaut* or *vy-ashṭaut,* Pāṇ. viii, 3, 70), to praise very much, extol with praises, MBh.

Vi-shṭuta, mfn. praised highly, extolled, TBr.

Vi-shṭuti, f. a variety of arrangement for reciting the verses of the Tri-vṛit Stoma (3 such varieties are enumerated, viz. *udyatī, parivartinī,* and *kulāyinī*), Br.; Lāṭy.; pl. N. of a treatise on Vedic ritual.

विष्टुभ् *vi-shṭubh* (√*stubh*), Ā. *-shṭobhate* (aor. *vy-ashṭobhishṭa*), Vop.

विष्ठल *vi-shṭhala.* See p. 953, col. 1.

विष्ठा 2. *vi-shṭhā* (√*sthā;* for 1. *vishṭhā,* see p. 996, col. 2), Ā. *-tishṭhate* (cf. Pāṇ. i, 3, 22; Ved. and ep. also P.), to stand or go apart, be spread or diffused or scattered over or through (acc. or *adhi* with loc.), RV.; VS.; AV.; to be removed or separated from (instr.), TS.; AV.; to stand, be stationary, stand still, remain firm, abide, dwell, stop, RV. &c. &c.; to keep ground, not to budge, R.; to be present or near, MBh.; to be engaged in (loc.), Hariv.: Caus. (only aor. *-tishṭhipaḥ*) to spread, expand, RV. i, 56, 5.

3. **Vi-shṭhā́,** f. place, position, station, form, kind, RV.; AV.; TBr.; ŚrS.; a rope (?), Divyâv.; *-vrājin,* mfn. remaining in one place, stationary, ŚBr.

Vi-shṭhita, mfn. standing apart, RV.; scattered, spread, diffused, ib.; TBr.; AV.; standing, fixed, stationary (opp. to *jagat*), RV.; AV.; standing or being on or in (loc. or comp.), MBh.; R. &c.; being present or near, R.; Hariv.

विष्ण *vishṇa* (dat. *vishṇāya* = *vishṇave*), Pañcar. (wrong form used by uneducated persons).

विष्णापू *vishṇāpū́,* m. N. of a son of Viśvaka, RV.

विष्णु *víshṇu,* m. (prob. fr. √*vish,* 'All-pervader' or 'Worker') N. of one of the principal Hindū deities (in the later mythology regarded as 'the preserver,' and with Brahmā 'the creator' and Śiva 'the destroyer,' constituting the well-known Tri-mūrti or triad; although Vishṇu comes second in the triad he is identified with the supreme deity by his worshippers; in the Vedic period, however, he is not placed in the foremost rank, although he is frequently invoked with other gods [esp. with Indra, whom he assists in killing Vṛitra and with whom he drinks the Soma juice; cf. his later names Indrânuja and Upêndra]; as distinguished from the other Vedic deities, he is a personification of the light and of the sun, esp. in his striding over the heavens, which he is said to do in three paces [see *tri-vikrama* and cf. *bali, vāmana*], explained as denoting the threefold manifestations of light in the form of fire, lightning, and the sun, or as designating the three daily stations of the sun in his rising, culminating, and setting; Vishṇu does not appear to have been included at first among the Ādityas [q.v.], although in later times he is accorded the foremost place among them; in the Brāhmaṇas he is identified with sacrifice, and in one described as a dwarf; in the Mahā-bhārata and Rāmâyaṇa he rises to the supremacy which in some places he now enjoys as the most popular deity of modern Hindū worship; the great rivalry between him and Śiva [cf. *Vaishṇava* and *Śaiva*] is not fully developed till the period of the Purāṇas: the distinguishing feature in the character of the Post-vedic Vishṇu is his condescending to become incarnate in a portion of his essence on ten principal occasions, to deliver mankind from certain great dangers [cf. *avatāra* and IW. 327]; some of the Purāṇas make 22 incarnations, or even 24, instead of 10; the Vaishṇavas regard Vishṇu as the supreme being, and often identify him with Nārāyaṇa, the personified Purusha or primeval living spirit [described as moving on the waters, reclining on Śesha, the serpent of infinity, while the god Brahmā emerges from a lotus growing from his navel; cf. Manu i, 10]; the wives of Vishṇu are Aditi and Sinīvālī, later Lakshmī or Śrī and even Sarasvatī; his son is Kāma-deva, god of love, and his paradise is called Vaikuṇṭha; he is usually represented with a peculiar mark on his breast called Śrī-vatsa, and as holding a *śaṅkha* or conch-shell called Pāñcajanya, a *cakra* or quoit-like missile-weapon called Su-darśana, a *gadā* or club called Kaumodakī, and a *padma* or lotus; he has also a bow called Śārṅga, and a sword called Nandaka; his *vāhana* or vehicle is Garuḍa, q. v.; he has a jewel on his wrist called Syamantaka, another on his breast called Kaustubha, and the river Ganges is said to issue from his foot; the demons slain by him in his character of 'preserver from evil,' or by Kṛishṇa as identified with him, are Madhu, Dhenuka, Cāṇūra, Yamala, and Arjuna [see *yamalârjuna*], Kāla-nemi, Haya-grīva, Śakaṭa, Arishṭa, Kaiṭabha, Kaṅsa, Keśin, Mura, Śālva, Mainda, Dvi-vida, Rāhu, Hiraṇya-kaśipu, Bāṇa, Kāliya, Naraka, Bali; he is worshipped under a thousand names, which are all enumerated in MBh. xiii, 6950–7056; he is sometimes regarded as the divinity of the lunar mansion called Śravaṇa), RV. &c. &c. (cf. RTL. 44; IW. 324); N. of the month Caitra, VarBṛS.; (with *Prājāpatya*) of the author of RV. x, 84; of a son of Manu Sāvarṇa and Bhautya, MārkP.; of the writer of a law-book, Yājñ.; of the father of the 11th Arhat of the present Avasarpiṇī, L.; (also with *gaṇaka, kavi, daivajña, paṇḍita, bhaṭṭa, miśra, yatîndra, vājapeyin, śāstrin* &c.) of various authors and others, Inscr.; Cat.; = *agni,* L.; = *vasu-devatā,* L.; = *śuddha,* L.; f. N. of the mother of the 11th Arhat of the present Avasarpiṇī, L.; n. pl. (in a formula), ĀpŚr.; (*Vishṇor* with *apamārnam, ājya-doham, vratam*; [*oḥ*] *sāma, svarīyaḥ,* N. of Sāmans; with *shoḍaśa-nāma-stotram, anusmṛitiḥ, ashṭâviṅśati-nāma-stotram,* and *mahā-stutiḥ,* N. of wks.) **-ṛiksha,** n. the lunar mansion Śravaṇa (presided over by Vishṇu), Tithyād. **-kanda,** m. a species of bulbous plant, L. **-karaṇa,** n., **-kavaca,** n. N. of wks. **-kāñcī,** f. N. of a town, Cat. **-kāntī,** f. or °*ti-tīrtha,* n. N. of a Tīrtha, ib. **-kutūhala,** n., **-kośala,** N. of wks. **-kramá,** m. the step of Vishṇu, MW.; pl. N. of the three steps to be taken by the sacrificer between the Vedi and the Āhavanīya, TS.; ŚBr.; GṛS.; ŚrS. **-kramī́ya,** mfn. relating to the prec., ŚBr. **-krānta,** mf(*ā*)n. bestridden by Vishṇu, TĀr.; m. a kind of measure, Saṃgīt.; (*ā*), f. N. of various plants (accord. to L. Clitoria Ternatea; Evolvulus Alsinoides; a kind of dark Śaṅkha-pushpī), Pañcar.; ŚārṅgS. &c. **-krānti,** f. Evolvulus Alsinoides, L. **-kshetra,** n. N. of a sacred district, L. **-gaṅgā,** f. N. of a river, L. **-gāthā,** f. pl. a song in honour of Vishṇu, BhP. **-gāyatrī,** f. N. of a Gāyatrī celebrating V°, Hcat. **-gupta,** m. 'hidden by V°,' N. of the Muni Vātsyāyana, MW.; of the saint Kauṇḍinya (said to have been concealed by Vishṇu when pursued by Śiva, whom he had incensed), L.; of the minister and sage Cāṇakya, Kām.; VarBṛS. &c.; of a follower of Śaṃkarâcārya, Cat.; of an astronomer, Cat.; of a Buddhist, Kathās.; a species of bulbous plant, L.; *-siddhânta,* m. N. of wk. **-guptaka,** n. a kind of radish, L. **-gūḍha,** m. N. of wk.; *-svāmin,* m. N. of an author, Cat.; °*ḍhârtha,* m. N. of wk. **-gṛiha,** n. 'Vishṇu's abode,' N. of Tāmra-lipta, L. **-gopa-varman,** m. N. of a king, Inscr. **-gola,** m. the equator, Vīrac. **-granthi,** m. a partic. joint of the body, Cat. **-cakra,** n. Vishṇu's discus, R.; a partic. mystical circle (formed from the lines in the hand), VP. **-candra,** m. N. of various authors, VarBṛ., Sch.; Cat. **-citta,** m. N. of an author, Cat.; °*tīya,* n. N. of wk. **-ja,** mfn. born under Vishṇu (i. e. in the first lustrum of Jupiter's cycle of 60 years), VarBṛS.; m. N. of the 18th Kalpa or day of Brahmā, L. **-jāmala,** n., w. r. for *-yāmala.* **-jāmātṛi,** m. (prob.) Vishṇu-Kṛishṇa's brother-in-law (see *Kṛishṇa-svasṛi*). **-tattva,** n. V°'s real essence, Sarvad.; N. of wk.; *-nirṇaya,* m., *-rahasya,* n., °*ya-khaṇḍana,* n., *-saṃhitā,* f. N. of wks. **-tantra,** n., **-tarpaṇa,** n., °*ṇa-vidhi,* m., **-tātparya-nirṇaya,** m. N. of wks. **-tithi,** m. f. N. of the 11th and 12th lunar day of each fortnight, Inscr. **-tīrtha,** m. N. of an author, Cat.; n. N. of a Tīrtha, ib. **-tīrthīya-vyākhyāna,** n. N. of wk. **-tulya-parākrama,** mfn. having prowess equal to that of V°, MW. **-taila,** n. a kind of oil, BrahmavP. **-toshiṇī,** f., **-triśatī,** f. N. of wks. **-tva,** n. V°'s nature, R.; NṛisUp. &c. **-datta,** mfn. given by V°, BhP.; m. N. of Parīkshit, ib.; of various men, Kathās.; Sāh.; Cat.; °*tâgni-hotrin,* m. N. of an author, Cat. **-dattaka,** m. N. of a scribe, MW. **-dāsa,** m. 'Vishṇu's slave,' N. of a king, Cat.; of another man, ib. **-deva,** m. N. of an author, ib.; °*vârādhya,* m. N. of a man, ib. **-devatya,** mfn. having V° for a deity, ShaḍvBr. **-daivata,** mfn. = *-devatya,* L. **-daivatya,** mfn. id., ib.; (*ā*), f. = *-tithi,* ib. **-dvādaśa-nāma-stotra,** n. N. of a ch. of the Āraṇya-parvan (q.v.) **-dvish,** m. foe of V° (nine in number, accord. to Jainas), L. **-dvīpa,** m. N. of an island, W. **-dharma,** m. a kind of Śrāddha, MW.; N. of various wks.; *-mīmāṅsā,* f., °*môttara,* n. N. of wks. **-dharman,** m. N. of a son of Garuḍa, MBh. **-dhārā,** f. N. of a Tīrtha, Cat. **-dhyāna-stotrâdi,** N. of wk. **-nadī,** f. N. of a river, Cat. **-nāma-māhātmya-saṃgraha,** m., °*ma-ratna-stotra,* n., **-nīrājana,** n. N. of wks. **-nyaṅga,** mfn. containing incidental mention of Vishṇu, AitBr.; ŚāṅkhŚr. **-pañcaka,** n., °**ka-vrata-kathā,** f. N. of wks. **-pañjara,** n. a kind of mystical prayer or charm for securing V°'s favour, MW.; N. of wk.; *-yantra-vidhi,* m., *-stotra,* n. N. of wks. **-pati,** m. N. of an author, Cat. **-patnī** (*víshṇu-*), f. 'V°'s wife,' N. of Aditi, VS.; TS.; TBr.; ĀśvŚr. **-pada,** n. 'station or footmark of V°,' the zenith, Nir.; BhP.; the sky, MBh.; Ragh. &c.; the mark of V°'s foot worshipped at Gayā, RTL. 309; N. of a sacred hill (also called °*da-giri,* m.), MBh.; Hariv. &c.; a lotus, L.; m. n. the sea of milk, L.; (*ī*), f. the sun's passage (into the zodiacal signs of Taurus, Leo, Scorpio and Aquarius), Tithyād.; N. of the Ganges (as issuing from V°'s foot), MBh.; Hariv.; R. &c.; of the town Dvārikā, L.; *-tīrtha,* n. the sacred place called Gayā (= *vishṇu-pada*), Cat.; *-śrāddha,* n. N. of a partic. Śrāddha (performed in the temple containing Vishṇu's footprint), RTL. 312; °*dī-cakra,* n. a partic. astrological circle or diagram, MW.; °*dy-utpatti,* f. N. of ch. in the Padma-Purāṇa. **-paddhati,** f. N. of wk. **-parâyaṇa,** m. N. of an author of mystical prayers (with Tāntrikas), Cat. **-parṇikā,** f. Hedysarum Lagopodioides, L. **-pādâdi-keśânta-stuti,** f. N. of sev. wks. **-putra,** m. N. of a man, Cat. **-pur,** f. N. of a city, L. **-pura,** n. V°'s city, Vop.; N. of a c° (= *-pur*), L.; (*ī*), f. N. of a c°, MW.; of a mountain in the Himâlaya, L.; (*ī*), m. N. of a scholar, Cat. **-purāṇa** or °**ṇaka,** n. N. of one of the most celebrated of the 18 Purāṇas (it conforms more than any other to the definition *pañca-lakshaṇa* [q. v.]; and consists of 6 books, the 1st treating of the creation of the universe from Prakṛiti, and the peopling of the world by the Prajā-patis; the 2nd giving a list of kings with many curious geographical and astronomical details; the 3rd treating of the Vedas and caste; the 4th continuing the chronicle of dynasties; the 5th giving the life of Kṛishṇa; the 6th describing the dissolution of the world), IW. 517. **-pūjana,** n. 'worship of V°,' N. of wk. **-pūjā,** f. N. of wk.; *-krama,* m., *-dīpikā,* f., *-paddhati,* f., *-mantra,* m., *-vidhāna,* n., *-vidhi,* m. N. of wks. **-pratimā-sampròkshaṇa-vidhi,** m., **-pratishṭhā,** f., °**ṭhā-paddhati,** f. N. of wks. **-priyā,** f. basil, Dhanv. **-prīti,** f. land granted rent-free to Brahmans for the worship of V°, MW.; *-vāda,* m. N. of wk. **-brahma-mahêśvara-dāna-prayoga,** m. N. of wk. **-bha,** n. = *-ṛiksha,* VP. **-bhakta,** m. a worshipper of V°, RāmatUp.; *-lakshaṇa,* n. N. of a part of the Mahā-bhārata. **-bhakti,** f. the worship of V° (personified as a Yoginī), Prab.; *-kalpa-latā*, f., *-candrôdaya*, m., *-prabandha*, m., *-māhātmya*, n., *-rahasya*, n., *-latā*, f., *-stuti*, f. N. of wks. **-bhāgavata-purāṇa**, n. N. of wk. **-bhujam-ga**, °**ga-stotra**, n., °**gī**, f. N. of Stotras. **-mat**, mfn. containing the word 'Vishṇu,' PañcavBr.; (*atī*), f. N. of a princess, Kathās. **-mantra**, m. a hymn addressed to V°, Cat.; *-vidhānâdi*, *-viśesha*, m. N. of wks. **-mandira**, n. V°'s temple, Cat.; = *-gṛiha*, MW. **-maya**, mf(*ī*)n. emanating from V°, belonging to V°, having the nature of V° &c., MBh.; Hariv.; R.; VP. **-mahiman**, m. the glory or majesty of V°, Cat.; N. of wk.; °*himnaḥ stava*, m. N. of a Stotra in praise of V°. **-mānasa**, n. N. of a Stotra. **-māyā**, f. 'V°'s illusion,' a form of Durgā, KālP. **-māhātmya**, n., °**ya-paddhati**, f. N. of wks. **-mitra**, m. a common name (used like the Latin Caius), Kaṇ.; BhP.; N. of a priest, Cat.; (with *kumāra*) N. of a Scholiast, RPrāt., Introd. **-mukha** (*víshṇu-*), mfn. pl. having V° as chief, TS.; MaitrS. **-yantra-prakaraṇa**, n. N. of wk. **-yaśas**, m. N. of Kalkin or Kalki, MBh.; Hariv.; of the father of Kalkin, Pur.; Pañcar.; of a teacher, Cat. **-yāga**, m., °**ga-prayoga**, m., **-yāmala** or °**la-tantra**, n., or °**yāmila**, n. N. of wks. **-ratha**, m. 'V°'s chariot,' N. of Garuḍa (the bird and vehicle of Vishṇu), Cat. **-rahasya**, n. N. of various wks. **-rāja**, m. N. of a king, Buddh. **-rāta**, m. 'Vishṇu-given,' N. of Parikshit, BhP. (cf. *-datta*). **-rāma**, **-rāma-siddhânta-vāg-īśa**, m. N. of authors, Cat. **-laharī**, f. N. of wk. **-liṅgī**, f. a quail, L. **-loka**, m. V°'s world, Rājat.; VP.; Pañcar. (accord. to some = *brahma-l°*, or accord. to others, 'placed above it,' MW.) **-1. -vat** (*víshṇu-*), mfn. attended by V°, RV.; n. (with *ahar*) a partic. 11th or 12th day, Cat. **-2. -vat**, ind. as with Vishṇu, ĀpŚr. **-varṇanadhyānâdi**, N. of wk. **-vardhana**, m. N. of various kings (also *kali-vishṇu-va°*, *kubja-vishṇu-va°*), Inscr. **-varman**, m. N. of a king, ib. **-vallabha**, mfn. beloved by V°, W.; (*ā*), f. N. of Lakshmī, Tantras.; basil, L.; = *agni-śikhā* (a kind of plant), L.; Echites Caryophyllata, W.; Ocymum Sanctum, ib.; N. of wk. **-vāhana**, n. (Siṇhâs.) or **-vāhya**, m. (L.) 'V°'s vehicle,' N. of Garuḍa. **-vigraha-śaṅsana-stotra**, n., **-vijaya**, m. N. of wks. **-vṛiddha**, m. N. of a man; (pl.) his descendants, ĀśvŚr.; Inscr.; *-sahasra-nāma-stotra*, n. N. of ch. of the Padma-purāṇa. **-vrata-kalpa**, m. N. of wk. **-śakti**, f. 'V°'s energy,' Lakshmī, Rājat.; m. N. of a king, Kathās. **-śata-nāma-stotra**, n. N. of a Stotra. **-śayana-bodha-dina**, n. (ifc.) the day of Vishṇu's lying down and of his awaking, ŚāṅkhGṛ., Sch. **-śarman**, m. N. of various authors and other persons (esp. of the narrator of the Pañcatantra and the Hitôpadeśa), IW. 531; °*ma-dīkshita*, °*ma-miśra*, m. N. of authors, Cat. **-śilā**, f. the sacred stone of V° which contains an ammonite (= *śāla-grāma*, q. v.), L. **-śṛiṅkhala**, m. a partic. astrological Yoga, L. **-śrāddha**, n., °**dha-paddhati**, f. N. of wks. **-śruta**, m. N. of a man, Pāṇ. vi, 2, 148, Sch. **-shaṭpadī**, f., **-saṃhitā**, f., **-samuccaya**, m. N. of wks. **-saras** (Cat.) or °**ras-tīrtha** (MW.), n. N. of a Tīrtha. **-sarva-jana**, w. r. for next, Cat. **-sarva-jña**, m. N. of a teacher (also *sarvajña-vishṇu*), Cat. **-sahasra-nāman**, n. the thousand names of Vishṇu, Cat.; N. of a portion of the Anuśāsana-parvan (ii, 6936–7078) of the Mahā-bhārata (also °*ma-kathana* or °*ma-stotra*, n.) and of a ch. of the PadmaP.; °*ma-bhāshya*, n. N. of Śaṃkara's Comm. on the thousand names of V°. **-siṅha**, m. N. of a man, Cat. **-siddhânta**, m., °**ta-līlā-vatī**, f. N. of wks. **-sūkta**, n. a hymn addressed to V°, Cat. **-sūtra**, n. = *-smṛiti*. **-stava**, m., °**va-rāja**, m., **-stuti**, f., **-stotra**, n., **-smṛiti**, f., **-sva-rūpa-dhyānâdi-varṇana**, n. N. of wks. **-svāmin**, m. a temple or statue of V°, Rājat.; N. of various men, Kathās.; Sarvad. &c. (esp. of a celebrated Vaishṇava teacher, predecessor of Vallabhâcārya, RTL. 134). **-hari**, m. N. of a poet, Sadukt. **-hāra-deva**, m. N. of a man, Inscr. **-hitā**, f. basil, L. **-hṛidaya** or °**ya-stotra**, n. N. of a Stotra. **Vishṇûttara**, a grant of land rent-free for the worship of V°, MW. **Vishṇûtsava**, m. a festival in honour of V°, Vop.; a partic. day sacred to V°, MW. **Vishṇûpâdhyāya**, m. N. of a teacher, Cat. **Vishṇū-varuṇa**, m. du. Vishṇu and Varuṇa, TBr.

Vishṇūya, Nom. P. °*yati*, to act towards any one (loc.) as towards Vishṇu, Vop.

Vishṇv, in comp. before vowels for *vishṇu*. **-aṅgiras**, m. N. of an author, Cat. **-atikrama**, m. pl. N. of partic. texts of the Taittirīya-saṃhitā (iii, 5, 3), ĀpŚr. **-anushṭhita** (*vishṇv-*, MaitrS.) or **-anusthita** (*vishṇv-*, TS.), mfn. attended by Vishṇu. **-avatāra**, m. a descent or incarnation of V°, MW. **-ashṭôttara-śata-nāman**, n., **-ādi-devatā-pūjā-prakāra**, m., **-āvaraṇa-pūjā**, f. N. of wks.

विष्पन्द *vi-shpanda*, m. (see *vi-√spand*; prob. w. r. for *vi-spanda*) throbbing, beating, W.; a partic. dish (prepared from wheat-flour, Ghṛita, and milk), L. (prob. w. r. for *vi-shyanda*).

विष्पर्धस् *ví-shpardhas*, mfn. (*√spardh*; cf. *vi-√spardh*) emulating, vying, envious, RV. (Sāy. 'free from emulation'); VS.; m. N. of a Ṛishi, Br.; n. N. of a Sāman, ib. °**shpardhā**, f. (cf. *vi-spardhā*) contest for superiority, Vait.

विष्पश् *vi-shpáś*, m. (nom. *vi-shpáṭ*; fr. *√spaś*) one who espies, a spy, RV. i, 189, 6.

विष्पित *vi-shpitá*, n. (*√sphāy?*) straits, peril, difficulty, RV.

विष्पुलिङ्गक *vi-shpuliṅgaká*, mfn. (cf. *vi-shphuliṅga* below) sparkling, RV. i, 191, 12 (Sāy. 'a tongue of fire' or 'a sparrow').

विष्पॄ *vi-shpṝ* (for *vi-√spṝ*; only aor. Subj. *-shparat*), to tear asunder, separate, AV.

विष्फर् *vi-shphar*, *vi-shphāra*. See *vi-√sphar*.

विष्फाल *vi-shphāla*. See *vi-√sphal*.

विष्फुर् *vi-shphur*, *vi-shphul*. See *vi-√sphur* and *vi-√sphul*.

विष्फुलिङ्ग *vi-shphulíṅga* (*√sphul*; see *vi-√sphul* and *vi-sphuliṅga*), a spark of fire, RV.; ŚBr. &c.

Vi-shphuliṅgaka, m. id., AV.Pariś.

विष्य *vishya*. See p. 996, col. 2.

विष्यन्द् *vi-shyand* (for *vi-√syand*, q. v.), Ā. *-shyandate* (accord. to Pāṇ. viii, 3, 72, *vi-syandate* is the only correct form when the reference is to living beings), to overflow, flow out (of a vessel; pr. p. *vi-shyandamāna*), VS.; Br.; ŚrS.; to flow in streams or abundantly, Hariv.; Bhaṭṭ.; to dissolve, melt (intr.), Car.; to cause to flow, MBh.: Caus. *-shyandayati*, to cause to overflow (in *a-vishyandayat*), ĀpŚr.; to pour out, sprinkle, ŚBr.; Kauś.; to dissolve, melt (trans.), Car.

Vi-shyaṇṇa, mfn. overflowed, overflowing, TBr.

Vi-shyanda, m. (also written *vi-syanda* and *vi-spanda*, cf. also *vi-shpanda*) a drop, MBh.; R.; flowing, trickling, issuing forth, W. °**shyandaka** (or °*sy°*), m. or n. (?) N. of a place, Pañcar. °**shyandana** (or °*sy°*), m. a kind of sweetmeat, Madanav. (cf. *vi-shpanda*); dripping, liquid state, MBh.; Suśr.; overflowing, ĀpŚr., Sch.; dissolving, melting (trans.), Car. °**shyandin** (or °*sy°*), mfn. liquid, Suśr.

विष्व *vishva*, mfn. injurious, hurtful, mischievous (= *hiṅsra*), L.

विष्वक् *vishvak*, *vishvañc* &c. See p. 998.

विष्वञ्ज् *vi-shvañj* (*√svañj*), Ā. *-shvajate* (impf. *vy-ashvajata* or *vy-asvajata*, Pāṇ. viii, 3, 70; pf. *vi-shasvaje* or *vi-shasvañje*, Vop.), to embrace, R.

विष्वन् *vi-shvan* (for *vi-√svan*, q. v.), P. *-shvaṇati* (impf. *vy-ashvaṇat*), to make a sound in eating, smack the lips (in any other sense the dental *s* must be used, accord. to Pāṇ. viii, 3, 68 &c.), Śiś. xviii, 77. °**shvaṇa**, see *nara-vishvaṇa*. °**shvaṇana**, n. smacking the lips in eating, L. °**shvāṇa**, m. noisy eating, L. (cf. *ava-shvāṇa*).

विस् *vis*, *visa* &c. See *bis*, *bisa*.

विसंयुक्त *vi-saṃ-yukta*, mfn. (*√yuj*) disjoined, detached or separated from, omitting, neglecting (instr.), Mn. ii, 80.

Vi-saṃyoga, m. liberation from worldly fetters, Buddh.; disjunction, separation, omission, W.

विसंवद् *vi-saṃ-√vad*, P. *-vadati*, to break one's word or promise, Mn. viii, 219; to fail in an agreement, contradict, raise objections, Kathās.; Kull.: Caus., see *-saṃvādita*. °**saṃvāda**, m. false assertion, breaking one's word, disappointing, MBh.; contradiction, disagreement with (instr. with or without *saha*, loc., or comp.), MBh.; Kāv. &c. °**saṃvādaka**, mfn. breaking one's word (in *a-vis°*), MBh. °**saṃvādana**, n. the breaking one's word or promise, ib.; Jātakam. °**saṃvādita**, mfn. (fr. Caus.) disappointed, dissatisfied, R.; not generally proved, objectionable, Śak.; MārkP. °**saṃvādin**, mfn. breaking one's word, disappointing, deceiving (see °*di-tā*); contradicting, disagreeing, Ragh.; Rājat.; (°*di*)-*tā*, f. the breaking one's word, breach of promise (in *a-vis°*), Kām.; contradiction, disagreement with (instr.), Sāh.

विसंशय *vi-saṃśaya*, *vi-saṃshṭhula*, *vi-saṃsthita* &c. See p. 953, col. 1.

विसंसर्पिन् *vi-saṃ-sarpin*. See *tiryag-vis°*.

विसंहत *vi-saṃ-hata*, mfn. (*√han*) disjoined, loosened, Suśr. (v. l. °*hita*).

विसंचारिन् *vi-saṃ-cārin*, mfn. (*√car*) moving hither and thither, MBh.

विसपर्य *vi-saparya* (see *saparya*), P. °*yati*, to worship at different places, RV. i, 70, 10.

विसम्भरा *vi-sam-bharā*, f. (*√bhṛi*) the domestic lizard, L.

विसम्भोग *vi-sam-bhoga*, m. (*√3. bhuj*) separation, HPariś.

विसम्मूढ *vi-sam-mūḍha*, mfn. (*√muh*) utterly bewildered, Hariv.

विसर *vi-sara*, *vi-sāra*. See below.

विसर्ग *vi-sarga*, *vi-sarjana*. See p. 1001.

विसल्य *vi-salya*, *vi-sāmagrī*, *vi-sārathi* &c. See p. 953, col. 1.

विसिच् *visic*, m. a Jaina, Bādar., Sch.

विसिध् *vi-√1. sidh*, P. *-sedhati*, to resort to (acc.), Pāṇ. viii, 3, 113, Sch.

विसिस्मापयिषु *vi-sismāpayishu*, mfn. (fr. Desid. of Caus. of *vi-√smi*) wishing to astonish or surprise, MBh.

विसिस्मारयिषु *vi-sismārayishu*, mfn. (fr. Desid. of Caus. of *vi-√smṛi*) wishing to make forget, HPariś.

विसुकल्प *vi-sukalpa*, *vi-sukṛit*, *vi-sukha*, *vi-suta*, *vi-suhṛid* &c. See p. 953, col. 1.

विसूचन *vi-sūcana*, n. (*√sūc*) making known, MW. **Vi-sūcikā**, **vi-sūcī**, w. r. for *vi-sh°*.

विसूत्र् *vi-√sūtr*, P. *-sūtrayati*, to drive away, remove, Vās.; Bālar.; to throw into confusion, Rājat. °**sūtra**, mfn. confused, disordered, disconcerted, Rājat.; *-tā*, f. confusion, disorder, ib.; confusion of the mind, perplexity, ib. °**sūtraṇa**, n. driving away, Vcar.; throwing into confusion or disorder, Rājat.

विसूरण *vi-sūraṇa*, n. (*√sūr*) sorrow, distress, Vikr. iv, 19 (see the Prākṛit). °**sūrita**, n. id., L.; (*ā*), f. fever, L.

विसूर्य *vi-sūrya*. See p. 953, col. 1.

विसृ *vi-√sṛi*, P. *-sarati*, *-sisarti* (Ved. and ep. also Ā. perf. *vi-sasre*, RV.), to run or flow through, RV.; to spread out in various directions, extend (intr.), R.; Śiś.; (Ā.) to open or unfold one's self (with *tanvàm*), RV. x, 71, 4; to be separated, part from (instr.), AV.; to go forth in various directions, disperse, MBh.; to come forth, issue from (abl. or *-tas*), ib.; to rush upon (acc.), MBh.: Caus. *-sārayati*, to send forth, R.; to stretch forth, extend, MW.

Vi-sara, m. going forth or in various directions, spreading, extension, L.; a multitude, quantity, plenty, abundance, Kāv.; Kathās.; a partic. high number, Buddh.; bitterness, L.; mfn. bitter, L. °**saraṇa**, n. the act of going forth or out; spreading (of a cutaneous eruption), Suśr.; becoming loose or slackened or relaxed, ib. °**sarmán**, m. flowing asunder, dissolving, melting (acc. with *√kṛi*, to dissolve), RV. v, 42, 9.

Vi-sārá, m. spreading, extension, diffusion, RV.; Nalôd.; a fish, L.; n. a wood, timber, W.; (*ī*), f. the region of the winds, ib. °**sārita**, mfn. (fr. Caus.) made to go forth or spread, set on foot, occasioned, effected, performed, W.; °*tāṅga*, mfn. one who has an expanded or extended body, MW. °**sārin**, mfn. coming forth, issuing from (comp.), Ragh.; Śiś.; walking about, Pāṇ. v, 4, 16, Sch.; stretching over or through, spreading, diffusing (°*ri-tā*, f.), Kāv.; Kathās. &c.; m. a fish, W.; (*iṇī*), f. Glycine Debilis, L.

Vi-sṛit, f. the act of flowing asunder, RV. iv, 19, 5. °**sṛita**, mfn., Kir.; gone in various directions, dispersed, MBh.; come forth, issuing or proceeding from (comp.), VarBṛS.; Daś.; stretched out, spread, extended, R.; sent forth, despatched, ib.; fallen off or down, Hariv.; projecting, prominent, Hariv.; uttered, MW.; -*guṇa*, mfn. one who has the string (of a bow &c.) stretched out, Kir.; -*bhūshaṇa*, mfn. (a limb) from which the ornaments have fallen down, Hariv. °**sṛitvara**, mf(*ī*)n. spreading about, becoming diffused, Kum.; Śiś.; gliding along, flowing, W. °**sṛimara**, mf(*ā*)n. spreading about, Hcar.; flowing, gliding, W.

विसृज् *vi-√sṛij*, P. -*sṛijati* (ep. also Ā.), to send or pour forth, let go or run or flow, discharge, emit, shoot, cast, hurl (lit. and fig.; 'at,' loc., dat., or acc. with *prati*), RV. &c. &c.; to turn (the eye) upon (loc.), ŚāṅkhŚr.; to shed (tears), R.; Kālid.; Daś.; (Ā.) to evacuate the bowels, PraśnUp.; to utter (sounds or words), Br.; MBh. &c.; to set free, release (Ā. 'one's self') from (abl.), ChUp.; Hariv. &c.; to send away, dismiss, repudiate, reject, throw or cast off, Mn.; MBh. &c.; to despatch (a messenger), R.; to pass over, overlook, MārkP.; (in older language, Ā.) to abandon, desert, give up, renounce, MBh.; Kāv. &c.; to open, TS.; (Ā.) to stretch out, extend, ŚBr.; to spread about, diffuse, RV.; AV.; to remove, TS.; to remit, exempt from (acc.), Rājat.; to hand over, deliver, bestow, grant, MaitrS. &c. &c.; to produce, create (esp. 'in detail'), Up.; Mn.; MBh. &c.: Caus. -*sarjayati*, to discharge, emit, cast, hurl, throw (lit. and fig.), ĀśvGṛ.; MBh. &c.; to utter (a sound), ŚBr.; to set free, release, let go, dismiss, MBh.; Hariv.; Kālid.; to banish, exile, R.; to send out, despatch, Mn.; MBh. &c.; to abandon, desert, relinquish, give up, renounce, avoid, MBh.; R. &c.; to spare, save, MBh.; to commit, entrust, Kālid.; to lay aside, remove, VarBṛS.; to divulge, publish (news), Rājat.; to give away, MBh.; to hand over, deliver, grant, bestow, MBh.; Hariv. &c.; to produce, create, BhP.; to answer questions, Divyâv.

Vi-sargá, m. sending forth, letting go, liberation, emission, discharge, GṛŚrS.; MBh. &c.; voiding, evacuation (of excrement), ŚBr.; MBh.; Suśr.; opening (of the closed hand), KātyŚr.; getting rid of, sending away, dismissal, rejection, Mn.; MBh. &c.; letting loose i.e. driving out (cows; see *go-vis*°); final emancipation, exemption from worldly existence, BhP.; cessation, end, RV.; GṛS.; end of the annual course of the sun, Car.; destruction of the world, BhP.; giving, granting, bestowal, Mn.; MBh. &c.; scattering, hurling, throwing, shooting, casting (also of glances), MBh.; Ragh.; BhP.; producing, creating (esp. secondary creation or creation in detail by Purusha; see under *sarga*), Bhag.; BhP.; creation (in the concrete sense), product, offspring, Hariv.; BhP.; 'producer,' cause, BhP.; membrum virile, ib.; the sun's southern course, L.; separation, parting, W. (cf. -*cumbana*); light, splendour, ib.; N. of a symbol in grammar (= *vi-sarjanīya*, which is the older term, see below), Pāṇ., Sch.; Śrutab.; MBh.; BhP.; N. of Śiva, MBh. xiii, 1241; -*cumbana*, n. a parting kiss, Ragh.; -*lupta*, n. elision of the Visarga, Prātap. °**sargika**, see *loka-visargika*. °**sargin**, mfn. granting, bestowing, MBh. (cf. also *loka-vis*°).

Vi-sarjana, m. pl. N. of a family, BhP.; (*ī*), f. 'evacuating,' N. of one of the 3 folds of skin at the anus, Suśr.; (*vi-sárjana*), n. cessation, end, RV.; ŚrS.; Hariv.; relaxation (of the voice), VS.; ŚBr.; evacuation, RV.; abandoning, deserting, giving up, MBh.; Ragh.; discharge, emission, Mn.; Ragh.; sending forth, dismissal, Yājñ.; MBh. &c.; driving out (cows to pasture), Vās., Introd.; throwing (the image of a deity into holy water, as the concluding rite of a festival), Cat.; setting (a bull) at liberty (on partic. occasions), MW.; giving, bestowing, Kāv.; hurting, casting, shooting, R.; creating, RV.; product, creation, BhP.; answering a question, L.

Vi-sarjanīya, mfn. (fr. *vi-√sṛij*) to be sent forth or emitted &c., W.; (fr. *vi-sarjana*), see *vrata-visarjanīya*; m. (cf. *vi-sarga* above) N. of a symbol in grammar (usually marked by two perpendicular dots [:] representing a hard and distinctly audible aspiration; it generally, but not always, occurs at the end of a word, often taking the place of final *s* and *r*; it is called Visarjanīya either from its liability to be 'rejected' or from its being pronounced with a full 'emission' of breath, or from its usually appearing at the 'end' of a word or sentence; Paṇḍits in some parts of India seem to pronounce a vowel after it, e.g. *naraḥ* like *naraha*, *agniḥ* like *agnihi*), Prāt.; Pāṇ. &c. °**sarjayitavya**, mfn. (fr. Caus.) to be (or being) discharged (into the anus), PraśnUp. °**sarjayitṛi**, mfn. giving up, renouncing, Jātakam.

Vi-sarjikā (?), f. N. of the Tretā-yuga, L.

Vi-sarjita, mfn. (fr. Caus.) sent forth, emitted, dismissed, abandoned, left &c.; exposed (in a forest), Pañcat. °**sarjya**, mfn. (fr. id.) to be dismissed or sent away, MBh.

Vi-sṛijya, mfn. to be sent out or let go &c.; to be (or being) produced or effected (as subst. = 'effect'), BhP.

Ví-sṛishṭa, mfn. sent or poured forth, let go, allowed to flow or run, discharged, emitted, shed, cast, thrown, hurled, RV. &c. &c.; spat out, VP.; removed, TS.; turned, directed, Mṛicch.; deprived or destitute of (instr.), BhP.; spread, diffused, AV.; opened, Vait.; (ifc.) bestowed on, MārkP.; produced, created, founded, R.; Ragh.; n. (in gram.) = *vi-sarjanīya*, Kāt.; -*dhena* (*ví*°), mfn. streaming or yielding milk, RV.; -*bhūmi*, mfn. one who has space or room given (to sit down &c.), MW.; -*rāti* (*ví*-), mfn. munificent in gifts, RV.; -*vat*, mfn. one who has sent out or despatched (messengers), Kathās.; -*vāc*, mfn. uttering words i.e. breaking silence, ĀśvŚr.; °*tâtman*, mfn. one who has cast off (i.e. does not care for) his own self, unselfish, R. °**sṛishṭi** (*ví*-), f. letting go, allowing to flow, discharge, Kāṭh.; emission (of semen), L.; leaving, quitting, W.; giving, offering, ib.; creation, production, RV.; ŚBr. &c.; secondary creation or creation in detail, Pur.; offspring, Hariv.

विसृप् *vi-√sṛip*, P. -*sarpati* (m.c. also Ā.; Ved. inf. -*sṛipas*), to glide, move along or about, sneak, steal, VS. &c. &c.; to fly about (as arrows), MBh.; to be scattered or dispersed, RV.; to be spread or diffused over (acc.), VS.; MBh. &c.; to spread, diffuse, divulge, BhP.: Caus. -*sarpayati*, to spread, extend, Hariv.

Vi-sarpa, m. creeping along or about, spreading, diffusion, Uttarar.; Śāntiś. (v.l.); a partic. disease (erysipelas or any similar spreading eruption), Suśr.; (in dram.) an action which leads to an unhappy or undesired issue (e.g. Veṇis. iii, 10), Sāh.; -*khinna-vigraha*, mfn. one whose body is moist with the exudation caused by the Visarpa disease, Rājat.; -*ghna*, n. bees' wax (prob. as removing that disease), W.; -*cikitsā*, f. the cure of the above disease, MW. °**sarpaṇa**, mfn. creeping along, spreading, increasing, Car.; (*ī*), f. a species of plant, L.; n. leaving one's place, shifting, MBh.; R.; spreading, diffusion, increase, growth, Suśr. °**sarpi**, m., °**sarpikā**, f. the disease Visarpa, VarBṛS. °**sarpin** (*ví*-), mfn. creeping or shooting forth, issuing from or against (comp.), MBh.; Kālid.; gliding or roaming or swimming or winding about, MBh.; R. &c.; spreading, increasing, growing, Kāv.; Suśr.; suffering from the disease Visarpa; Hcat.; m. the above disease, Suśr.; a kind of hell, TĀr.: (*ī*), f. Ptychotis Ajowan, L.

विसोढ *vi-soḍha*, *vi-soḍhum*. See under *vi-shah*, p. 997, col. 1.

विसोम *vi-soma*. See p. 953, col. 1.

विस्कन्तृ *vi-skanttṛi*, *vi-skanna*. See p. 998, col. 2.

विस्कम्भ् *vi-√skambh*. See *vi-shkambh*.

विस्कुम्भु *viskumbhu*. See *vi-shkambha*.

विस्खल् *vi-√skhal* (only pf. -*caskhale*), to stumble, trip, Śiś. xv, 57. °**skhalita**, mfn. stumbling, stopping, faltering (as words), Kathās.; (ifc.) mistaken or blundering in, Ragh.; gone astray, Jātakam.

विस्त *vista*, m. (ifc. f. *ā*) a partic. weight of gold (= 80 Raktikās or a Karsha of 16 Māshas, about half an ounce troy), Prâyaśc.

विस्तन् *vi-√stan*, P. -*stanati*, to groan aloud, sound, Bhaṭṭ.; Jātakam.

विस्तृ *vi-√stṛi* (or *stṝ*), P. Ā. -*stṛiṇoti*, -*stṛiṇute*; -*stṛiṇāti*, -*stṛiṇīte* (ep. also -*starati*; ind. p. -*stīrya* or -*stṛitya*), to spread out, scatter, strew (sacrificial grass), R.; to expand, extend (wings), R.; to spread abroad, diffuse, divulge, BhP.; to enlarge or expatiate upon, speak diffusely about (acc.), MBh.; Kāv. (*vi-stīrya*, ind. copiously, at large); (with *vacanam*) to exchange words, converse with (instr.), ib.: Pass. -*stīryate* or -*staryate* (fut. -*starishyate*), to be spread abroad or widely diffused, Mn.; Pañcat.; BhP.; to be explained, Divyâv.: Caus. -*stārayati*, to spread, extend, diffuse, display, Mn.; MBh. &c. (-*stārya*, fully, copiously, at length); to discuss in detail, Kull.; to expose (wares for sale), Daś.

Vi-stara, mfn. extensive, long (as a story), Sāh.; m. (ifc. f. *ā*; cf. *vi-stāra* and Pāṇ. iii, 3, 31; Vām. v, 2, 41) spreading, extension, expansion, prolixity, diffuseness, MBh.; Kāv. &c.; a multitude, number, quantity, assemblage, large company, Mn.; R.; VarBṛS. &c.; becoming large or great (met. applied to the heart), Daś.; high degree, intensity, MBh.; Hariv.; BhP.; (pl.) great wealth or riches, MBh.; detail, particulars, full or detailed description, amplification (also as direction to a narrator = *vistareṇa kāryam*, 'give full particulars;' *eṇa* or *āt*, ind. diffusely, at length, fully, in detail; °*rī-√kṛi*, to spread, divulge, expand), MBh.; R. &c.; (ifc.) an extensive treatise, CūlUp.; affectionate solicitation, L.; a layer, bed, couch (= *vi-shṭara*), L.; (*ā*), f. a partic. Śakti, Hcat.; -*tas*, ind. diffusely, at length, Kāv.; Pur. &c.; -*tā*, f. extension, spreading, Ṛitus.; -*bhīru*, mfn. afraid of diffuseness, Sarvad.; -*śaṅkā*, f. fear of diff°, Sāh.; -*śas*, ind. = -*tas*, Mn.; MBh. &c. °**starakeṇa** (or °*staratarakeṇa*), ind. very diffusely, at full length, Pat. °**staraṇī**, f. N. of a goddess, MārkP. °**staraṇīya**, mfn. to be spread or extended, capable of being extended or expanded, MW.

Vi-stāra, m. (ifc. f. *ā*; cf. *vi-stara*) spreading, expansion, extent, width, MBh.; Kāv. &c.; becoming large or great (met. said of the heart), Sāh.; the breadth of a circle i.e. its diameter, Col.; specification, detailed enumeration or description, Yājñ.; Suśr. (*eṇa*, diffusely, at length, prob. w. r. for *vi-stareṇa*, R. iii, 4, 4); the branch of a tree with its new shoots, L.; a shrub, L.; the diameter of a circle, L. °**stāraṇa**, n. (fr. Caus.) outstretching (of the feet), Kāv. °**stārikā**, f. N. of a Comm. on the Kāvya-prakāśa. °**stārita**, mfn. (fr. id.) spread, extended, Ragh.; fully stated, amplified, MW. °**stārin**, mfn. extending, large, great, mighty, Hariv.; Kāv.; Pur.; (*iṇī*), f. (in music) a partic. Śruti, Saṃgīt.

Vi-stīrṇa, mfn. strewn or covered or studded with (instr. or comp.), Kāv.; Kathās.; spread out, expanded, broad, large, great, copious, numerous, MBh.; Kāv. &c.; extensive, long (as a tale), MBh.; far-sounding, R.; -*karṇa*, mfn. 'extending the ears' and 'broad-eared' (applied to an elephant), Bhartṛ.; -*jānu*, f. a bandy-legged girl (unfit for marriage), L.; -*tā*, f., -*tva*, n. breadth, diffusion, vastness, largeness, amplitude, MBh.; Kāv. &c.; -*bheda*, m. N. of a Buddha, Lalit.; -*lalāṭā*, f. 'having a large forehead,' N. of a Kiṃ-narī, Kāraṇḍ.; -*vatī*, f. N. of a partic. world, Buddh.

Vi-stṛita, mfn. strewn or covered or furnished with (comp.), Rājat.; BhP.; outstretched, expanded, opened wide, MBh.; Kāv.; BhP.; displayed, developed, Bhartṛ.; BhP.; extensive, broad, ample, wide, MBh.; R. &c.; far-sounding, Hariv.; spread, diffused, L.; (*am*), ind. fully, at length, Śatr.; BhP. °**stṛiti**, f. extent, width, breadth, Āryabh.; the diameter of a circle, Col.; spreading, expansion, W.

विस्थान *vi-sthāna*. See p. 953, col. 1.

विस्पन्द् *vi-√spand*, Ā. -*spandate*, to quiver, throb, tremble, start, MBh.; Hariv.; to struggle, strive, exert one's self, Jātakam.; to come forth, appear, ib. °**spanda**, see *vi-shpanda* and *vi-shyanda*. °**spandita**, see *a-vispandita*.

विस्पर्ध् *vi-√spardh*, Ā. -*spardhate* (m. c. also P.), to emulate, vie with (acc.; instr. with or without *saha* or *sârdham*), MBh.; R.; Jātakam. 2. °**spardhā**, f. (for 1. see p. 953, col. 1) emulation, rivalry, MBh. (Cf. *vi-shpardhas* and °*dhā*, p. 1000, col. 2.)

विस्पष्ट *vi-spashṭa*, mfn. (√*spaś*; cf. *vi*-

shpáś) very clear or apparent, manifest, evident, plain, intelligible (*am*, ind. clearly &c.), Mn.; MBh. &c.; *-tā*, f. great clearness or perspicuity, Sāh.; °*ṭârtha*, mfn. having a very clear or obvious sense, Mn. ii, 33.

Vispashṭī, in comp. for °*shṭa*. **-karaṇa**, n. the making clear or evident, L. **-√kṛi**, P. *-karoti*, to make clear or evident, Sāy.

विस्पृ *vi-√spṛi*. See *vi-shpṛi*, p. 1000, col. 2.

विस्फर् *vi-√sphar* (cf. *vi-√sphur*), Caus. *-sphārayati* (Pass. °*ryate*), to open wide (eyes), MBh.; Kāv. &c.; to draw, discharge (a bow), MBh.

Vi-sphāra, m. (also written *vi-shphāra*) opening wide, Sāh.; discharging a bow, the twang of a bow-string, MBh.; R.; trembling, agitation, W. °**sphāraka**, m. a kind of dangerous fever, Bhpr. (also °*sphuraka* and °*sphoraka*). °**sphāraṇa**, n. spreading (wings), Jātakam. °**sphārita**, mfn. opened wide, torn or rent asunder, MBh.; Kāv. &c.; exhibited, manifested, displayed, Śiś.; Jātakam.; n. drawing or discharging (a bow), MBh.

विस्फल् *vi-√sphal*. See next.

Vi-sphāla, m. (also written *vi-shphāla*, Pāṇ., Sch.), Kāś. on Pāṇ. vi, 1, 47.

विस्फाय् *vi-√sphāy*, Ā. *-sphāyate*, to swell, Sadukt.

Vi-sphita, mfn. abundant, plentiful, L.

विस्फुट् *vi-√sphuṭ*, P. *-sphuṭati*, *-sphoṭati* (fut. *-sphuṭishyati*), to burst open, be split or cleft or rent asunder, R.; MārkP.

Vi-sphuṭa, mfn. burst open, gaping (°*ṭī-kṛita*, mfn. = next), Suśr. °**sphuṭita**, mfn. opened, burst, MBh.

Vi-sphoṭa, m. cracking, crashing, MBh.; a blister, boil, Kāv.; Kathās.; Suśr.; mfn. open, Divyâv. °**sphoṭaka**, m. a blister, boil, Suśr.; a kind of leprosy, AgP.; ŚārṅgS.; small-pox, W.; N. of a serpent-demon, L.; (*ikā*), f. a blister, boil, Śak., Sch. °**sphoṭana**, n. the appearance of blisters, Kaṇ.; loud roaring, BhP.

विस्फुर् *vi-√sphur* (cf. *vi-√sphar*), P. *-sphurati* or *-shphurati* (Pāṇ. viii, 3, 76), to dart asunder (intr.), RV.; ŚBr.; to quiver, tremble, writhe, struggle, MBh.; Kāv. &c.; to vibrate, flash, glitter, ib.; to break forth, appear, Subh.; ŚārṅgS.

Vi-sphura, mfn. opening the eyes wide, R. °**sphuraṇa**, n. quivering (of lightning), Harav. (cf. also *buddhi-visphuraṇa*). °**sphurita**, mfn. trembling, quivering, palpitating (°*tâdhara*, mfn. having quivering lips, BhP.; °*têkshaṇa*, mfn. having trembling eyes, R.); flashing, glittering (*-śastra*, mfn. with glittering weapons, Uttarar.); swollen, enlarged, W.; n. = °*sphuraṇa*, Jātakam. °**sphuritavya**, mfn. to be opened wide (as the eyes), Kāraṇḍ.

Vi-sphoraka, see *vi-sphāraka*. °**sphorya**, mfn. (fut. p. p. of *vi-√sphur*), Pat.

विस्फुर्ज् *vi-sphurj* &c. See *vi-√sphūrj*.

विस्फुल् *vi-√sphul*, P. *-sphulati* or *-shphulati* (Pāṇ. viii, 3, 76), to wave or flicker to and fro, move hither and thither, Bhaṭṭ. °**sphuliṅga**, m. (cf. *vi-shphuliṅga*) a spark of fire, Up.; MBh. &c. (°*gī-√bhū*, P. *-bhavati*, to become a mere spark, Inscr.); a sort of poison, L.; (*ā*), f. a spark (= m.), Harav. °**sphuliṅgaka**, mf(*ikā*)n. sparkling, glittering, AgP.

विस्फूर्ज् *vi-√sphūrj* (incorrectly *-sphurj*), P. *-sphūrjati*, to resound, thunder, roar, BhP.; to snort, MBh.; to break forth, appear, Kāv.: Caus. *-sphūrjayati*, to cause to resound or twang (a bow), BhP. °**sphūrja**, m. roaring, thundering, breaking forth like thunder, Kaṇ.; Ragh. °**sphūrjathu**, m. thundering, roaring (as of waves), a thunder-clap, MW.; *-prakhya*, mfn. resembling a clap of thunder, ib. °**sphūrjana**, n. gaping, opening wide, Sarvad. °**sphūrjita**, mfn. resounded, resounding &c.; broken forth, appeared, Kāv.; outstretched, Suśr.; shaken, agitated, BhP.; m. N. of a serpent-demon, Buddh.; n. the act of rumbling, resounding, roaring, thundering, MBh.; R.; BhP.; breaking forth, sudden manifestation of (comp.), Ragh.; Prab.; knitting, contraction (of the brows), BhP.

विस्फोट *vi-sphoṭa* &c. See above under *vi-√sphuṭ*.

विस्मि *vi-√smi*, Ā. *-smayate* (m.c. also P.), to wonder, be surprised or astonished at (instr., loc., or abl.), ŚBr. &c. &c.; to be proud of (instr.), Mn. iv, 236: Caus. *-smāyayati* or *-smāpayati*, °*te* (cf. Pāṇ. i, 3, 68; vi, 1, 57), to astonish, surprise, MBh.; Kāv. &c.: Desid. of Caus., see *vi-sismāpayishu*.

1. **Vi-smaya**, m. (for 2. see p. 953, col. 1) wonder, surprise, amazement, bewilderment, perplexity (in rhet. one of the *sthāyi-bhāvas*, q. v.), MBh.; Kāv.; Daśar.; pride, arrogance, Mn.; BhP.; doubt, uncertainty, W.; *-kara*, *-kārin*, *-ṃ-kara*, *-ṃ-gama*, mfn. causing astonishment or admiration, astonishing, wonderful, MBh.; Kāv. &c.; *-vat*, mfn. manifesting pride or arrogance, Hcat.; *-vishāda-vat*, mfn. filled with astonishment and perplexity, Kathās.; *-harsha-mūla*, mfn. caused by astonishment and joy, MW.; °*yâkula*, °*yânvita* or °*yâvishṭa*, mfn. filled with astonishment or wonder, MBh.; °*yôt-phulla-nayana* (or *-locana*), mfn. having eyes wide open or staring with astonishment, MW. °**smayana**, n. astonishment, wonder, Cat. °**smayanīya**, mfn. astonishing, wonderful, MBh. °**smayin**, mfn. amazed, surprised, Śiś.

Vi-smāpaka, mfn. (fr. Caus.) causing astonishment or surprise, wonderful, Kāv. °**smāpana**, mf(*ī*)n. id., MBh.; VarBṛS.; BhP.; m. a juggler, conjurer, L.; illusion, deceit, L.; = *gandharva-nagara* (q. v.), L.; the god of love, L.; n. the act of astonishing or surprising, Hariv.; a means of surprising, Car.; Bhpr.; a surprising or miraculous sign or phenomenon, VarBṛS. °**smāpanīya**, mfn. causing astonishment ('in' or 'to,' gen.), Hariv. °**smāpayanīya**, mfn. id., MBh. °**smāpin**, mfn. = °*smāpana*, Harav.

Vi-smita, mfn. amazed, surprised, perplexed, MaitrUp.; MBh. &c.; wondered at, surprising, R.; BhP.; proud, arrogant, BhP.; n. and (*ā*), f. a kind of metre, Col.; *-mānasa*, mfn. surprised or perplexed in mind, MW.; °*tânana*, mfn. having a surprised face, ib. °**smiti**, f. astonishment, wonder, surprise, ib.

Vi-smera, mfn. wondering, astonished, surprised, Śiś.

विस्मृ *vi-√smṛi*, P. *-smarati* (m.c. also Ā.), to forget, be unmindful of (acc. or gen.), MBh.; Kāv. &c.: Pass. *-smaryate* (aor. *vy-asmāri*), to be forgotten, Rājat.: Caus. *-smārayati* (fut. *-smārayishyate*), to cause to forget, Vikr. iii, 18: Desid. of Caus., see *vi-sismārayishu*.

Vi-smaraṇa, n. the act of forgetting, oblivion, Kap.; Śak. °**smaraṇīya**, °**smartavya**, °**smarya**, mfn. to be forgotten, Kāv.; Kathās. &c.

Vi-smārita, mfn. (fr. Caus.) caused to forget anything (acc.), Rājat.; caused to be forgotten, lost to memory, BhP.

Vi-smṛita, mfn. one who has forgotten anything, forgetful of (acc. or comp.), Kāv.; forgetful of all, R. ii, 58, 30; forgotten by (instr. or gen.), R.; Kālid.; Rājat. &c.; *-pūrva-saṃskāra*, mfn. forgetting a former promise or resolution, MW.; m. N. of Bhava-bhūti, L.; *-vat*, mfn. one who has forgotten, Śak.; *-saṃskāra*, mfn. one who forgets an agreement, MW. °**smṛiti**, f. forgetfulness, loss of memory, oblivion, Kāv.; VarBṛS.; Kathās.

विस्यन्द् *vi-√syand*, *vi-syanda* &c. See *vi-shyand*, p. 1000, col. 2.

विस्र *visra*, mfn. (fr. √*vis* for *bis*?) musty, smelling of raw meat, VarBṛS.; Kathās.; Suśr. &c.; (*ā*), f. a species of plant (= *hapushā*), L.; n. (only L.) a smell like that of raw meat; blood; fat. **-gandha**, m. a musty smell, VarBṛS.; mfn. smelling musty or of raw meat, L.; (*ā*), f. = *visrā*, L. **-gandhi**, mfn. smelling of raw meat, Kād.; n. orpiment, L. **-tā**, f., **-tva**, n. mustiness, Suśr.

Visraka, mfn. = *visra*, smelling of raw meat, ŚārṅgS.

विस्रंस् *vi-√sraṇs*, Ā. *-sraṇsate* (ep. also P.; Ved. inf. *-srásaḥ*, cf. *vi-srás*), to fall asunder, break down, collapse, be broken (as limbs), fall off, become loose or unfastened (as hair), RV.; Br.; Up.; Hariv.; Pañcar.: Caus. *-sraṇsayati*, to cause to fall asunder &c., let fall, loosen, untie, AV. &c. &c.; to betray, publish, MBh.

Vi-sraṇsa, m. falling asunder, dropping down, relaxation, weakness, Br.; Suśr.; *-jā*, f. decrepitude, L. °**sraṇsana**, mfn. causing to fall down or away, casting off, MBh.; Sāh.; n. falling down, Gaut.; slackening, relaxation, Suśr.; loosening, unfastening, casting off, Gīt.; a laxative, aperient, W. °**sráṇsikā**, f. (of doubtful meaning), MaitrS.; Kāṭh.; ĀpŚr. (cf. Pāṇ. viii, 3, 110, Sch.) °**sraṇsita**, mfn. (fr. Caus.) caused to fall down or asunder, dropped, loosened, untied, Kāv.; Kathās. &c.; *-keśa-bandhana*, mfn. one whose hair-band has become loose, BhP.; *-sitâṇśuka*, mfn. one whose white garment has slipped down, Kathās. °**sraṇsin**, mfn. falling or slipping down (as a garland), Ragh.

Vi-srás, (prob.) f. dropping down, debility, decay (abl. °*srásaḥ* also as inf.), RV.; AV.; Br. °**srasā**, f. decrepitude, infirmity, senility, Bālar.

Vi-srasta, mfn. fallen asunder or down, unfastened, untied, loosened, detached, AV. &c. &c.; dishevelled (as hair), HPariś.; slackened, relaxed, MBh.; *-kusuma-sraj*, mfn. one whose garland of flowers has fallen off, Kathās.; *-cetas*, mfn. one whose spirit is dejected, MBh. (B. *vi-dhvasta-c*°); *-pauṇsna*, mfn. one whose manhood is broken or impaired, BhP.; *-bandhana*, mfn. having bonds or fetters unfastened, Kathās.; *-vasana*, mfn. having loosened garments, ib.; *-śiroruhâmbara*, mfn. having dishevelled hair and loosened garments, BhP.; *-srag-vibhūshaṇa*, mfn. one whose garland and ornaments have fallen off, MBh.; *-hāra*, mfn. one whose necklace has slipped off, MW.; °*tâṅga*, mfn. having a languid body or relaxed limbs, MBh.

Vi-srásya, mfn. to be loosened or untied, TS.

विस्रम्भ् *vi-√srambh*, *vi-srambha* &c. See *vi-√śrambh*, p. 992, col. 1.

विस्रि *visri*, m. N. of a man, g. *śubhrâdi* (v.l. *viśri*).

विस्रु *vi-√sru*, P. *-sravati*, to flow forth or away, issue from (abl.), ŚBr.; MBh.; to discharge or emit (any fluid), MBh.; R.; to flow asunder (fig.), melt, dissolve, come to nothing, MBh.: Caus. *-srāvayati*, to cause to flow forth or away, MBh.; to wash away, Car.; to let blood (with gen. or acc. of pers.), Suśr.

Vi-srava, m. a flow, stream, MBh.; efflux, issuing moisture, Jātakam. °**sravaṇa**, n. flowing asunder, Nir.

Vi-sravan-miśrá, mfn. (pr. p. of *vi-√sru* + *m*°) having blood streaming forth (on it), ŚBr.

Vi-srāva, m. (also written *-śrāva*) flowing forth, issuing, Hariv. °**srāvaṇa**, n. (fr. Caus.) causing to flow (blood, matter &c.), bleeding, Suśr. °**srāvita**, mfn. (fr. id.) wasted away, caused to flow out, bled, ib. °**srāvitavya**, mfn. (fr. id.) = next, MW. °**srāvya**, mfn. (fr. id.) to be made to flow, MBh. (cf. *a-visr*°); dissolving, melting, becoming liquid (*-tā*, f.), Cat.; to be bled, requiring bleeding, Suśr.

Vi-sruta, mfn. flowed forth, dropped, flowing, W.; spread, diffused, stretched, ib. °**sruti**, f. (also written *-śruti*) flowing forth, issuing from (abl.), VarBṛS.

विस्रुह् *vi-srúh*, f. (prob. fr. √*sruh* = *rudh*, to grow; cf. *vī-rudh*) a plant, shoot (?), RV. v, 44, 3 (read *vi-sruhām*); vi, 7, 6 (Nir. *āpaḥ*; Sāy. *nadyaḥ*).

विस्वन् *vi-√svan* (cf. *vi-shvan*), P. *-svanati*, to sound forth, roar, yell, Śiś. xviii, 77 (cf. Pāṇ. viii, 3, 69, Sch.)

विस्वप् *vi-√svap*, P. *-svapiti* (pf. *-sushvāpa*), Vop.

Vi-shupta, mfn. fallen asleep, sleeping, Kāṭh.; ĀpŚr. (cf. Pāṇ. viii, 3, 88, Sch.)

विस्वर *vi-svara*, *vi-svāda*. See p. 953, col. 2.

विहग *viha-ga*, *vihaṃ-ga* &c. See under *vi-√1. hā* below.

विहत् *vihat*, f. = *vehat*, L.

विहन् *vi-√han* (often w.r. for *ni-han*), P. *-hanti*, to strike apart or asunder, disperse, shatter, break, destroy, RV.; AV.; Br.; to beat asunder, extend (a skin), RV.; ŚBr.; to tear off, TBr.; to unbind, loosen (hair), Pāṇ. iii, 1, 21, Sch.; to ward off, repel, MBh.; R.; to keep back, withhold, refuse, MBh.; to hinder, interrupt, disturb, prevent, frustrate, annihilate, ib.; R. &c.: Pass. *-hanyate*, to be frustrated or disappointed, exert one's self in vain, MBh.; R.; Hariv.: Caus. *-ghātayati*, °*te*, to beat, vanquish, defeat, Hit.; (Ā.) to afflict, distress, annoy, MBh.; to interrupt, disturb, Kull. on Mn. v, 84:

Desid. *-jighāṇsati*, to wish to interrupt or disturb, BhP.: Intens. (*-jījahi?*), to harm, injure, MBh. vii, 2383.

Vi-hata, mfn. torn up, furrowed, TBr.; ŚBr.; struck or beaten away or dashed out (of a person's hand), BhP.; struck or touched or visited by (instr. or comp.), Kāv.; Pur.; warded off, repelled, MBh.; R.; rejected, repulsed, BhP.; disturbed, impeded, Kāv.; Pur. °**hati**, f. a stroke, blow, Bālar.; striking, killing, W.; prevention, removal, Bālar.; repulse, defeat, Ml.; m. a friend, companion, W. °**hanana**, n. (only L.) killing, slaying; hurting, injury; opposition, obstruction; a bow-like instrument for carding cotton. °**hantavya**, mfn. to be destroyed, Prab. °**hantṛi**, mfn. one who destroys or frustrates or disappoints (with gen. or ifc.), RV.; Up.

विहर *vi-hara* &c. See *vi-√hṛi*, col. 2.

विहर्य् *vi-√hary*, P. *-haryati*, to scorn, repudiate, Nir. vii, 17 (cf. *a-viharyata-kratu*).

विहर्ष *vi-harsha*, *vi-hasta* &c. See p. 953, col. 2.

विहल्ह *vihálha*, m. (of unknown meaning), AV. vi, 16, 1.

विहव *vi-hava* &c. See *vi-√hve*, p. 1004.

विहस् *vi-√has*, P. *-hasati*, to laugh loudly, burst out laughing, MBh.; Kāv. &c.; to laugh at (acc., rarely gen.), Kāv.; BhP.; Pañcat.

Vi-hasatikā, f. gentle laughter, smiling, Hcar. (v.l. °*sitikā*). °**hasana**, n. id., W. °**hasita**, mfn. laughing, smiling, Hariv.; Caurap.; laughed, smiled at, Kathās.; n. laughter, laughing, smiling, Kāv.; Sāh. °**hasitikā**, see °*hasatikā*.

Vi-hāsa, m. laughing, laughter, Hariv.; Pañcar.; mfn. opened, L.

विहा *vi-√1. hā*, Ā. *-jihīte*, to go apart, become expanded, start asunder, open, fly open, gape, yawn, RV.; AV.; TS.; ŚBr.: Caus. *-hāpayati*, to cause to gape, open, AV.; AitBr.; ŚBr.

Viha, (only ibc.) the sky, air. **–ga**, m. 'sky-goer,' a bird, MBh.; Kāv. &c.; an arrow, MBh. vii, 9021; the sun, L.; the moon, L.; a planet, L.; a partic. configuration of stars (when all the planets are situated in the 4th and 10th houses), VarBṛS.; *-pati*, m. 'king of birds,' N. of Garuḍa, Kāv.; *-vega*, m. 'having the swiftness of a bird,' N. of a Vidyā-dhara, Bālar.; *-gâdhipa*, m. (= *-pati*), L.; *-gâlaya*, m. 'abode of birds,' the air, sky, R.; *-gêndra* (*vihá-*), m. (= *-pati*), Suparṇ.; (°*dra-saṃhitā*, f., *-sampāta*, m. N. of Tāntric wks.); *-gôpaghushṭa*, mfn. resonant with birds, MW. **–ṃ-ga**, mfn. sky-going, flying, W.; m. = *vihaga*, a bird, Mn.; R. &c.; an arrow, MBh. viii, 3343; a cloud, L.; the sun, L.; the moon, L.; N. of a serpent-demon, MBh.; *-rāja*, m. (= *vihaga-pati*), L.; *-han*, m. a bird-killer, bird-catcher, MBh.; °*gârāti*, m. 'bird-enemy,' a falcon or hawk. **–ṃ-gaka**, m. a little bird, any bird, Hcar.; (*ikā*), f. a sort of pole or yoke for carrying burdens, L.; N. of a woman, Veṇīs. **–ṃ-gama**, mfn. moving in the sky, flying, MBh.; Hariv.; R.; m. (ifc. f. *ā*) a bird, Mn.; MBh. &c.; the sun, MBh.; N. of a class of gods under the 11th Manu, Pur.; (*ā*), f. a female bird, MBh.; = next, L. **–ṃ-gamikā**, f. a sort of yoke (= *vihaṃgikā*), L.

Vihā, ind. = *svarga*, heaven, Uṇ. iv, 36, Sch.

2. **Vi-hāyas**, m. n. (for 1. see p. 953, col. 2) the open space (cf. *vi-yat*), air, sky, atmosphere, Mn.; MBh. &c. (also °*saḥ-sthalī*, f. or °*sas-tala*, n.; instr. °*sā*, 'through the sky'); m. a bird, Kautukas.; °*sā-gāmin*, mfn. able to move through the sky, L.

Vi-hāyása, m. n. heaven, sky, atmosphere, TĀr.; MBh.; Hariv.; m. a bird, L.

विहा *vi-√3. hā*, P. *-jahāti* (ind. p. *-hāya*, see below), to leave behind, relinquish, quit, abandon, RV. &c. &c. (with *śarīram*, *prāṇān* &c., 'to abandon the body or life,' to die); to give up, cast off, renounce, resign, MBh.; Kāv. &c.; to be deprived of, lose, Ragh.; Sarvad.; to get rid of or free from (acc.), MBh.; R.; BhP.: to desist from (abl.), Subh.; to stop, pause, VarBṛS.: Pass. *-hīyate* (aor. *-hāyi*), to be left behind, ŚBr.; to be inferior to (abl.), MBh.; to be lost, AV.: Caus. *-hāpayati*, see next: Desid. *-jihāsati*, to wish to leave or abandon, HParis.

Vi-hāpita, mfn. (fr. Caus.) caused to abandon or give up &c.; given, W.; extorted, ib.; n. a gift, donation, Pārśvan. °**hāya**, ind. leaving behind, i.e. at a distance from (acc.), VarBṛS.; disregarding, overlooking, setting aside = more than (acc.), Kāv.; Kathās. &c.; in spite of, notwithstanding (acc.), Pañcat.; excepting, with the exception of (acc.), Hariv.; VarBṛS.

Vi-hīna, mfn. entirely abandoned or left &c.; low, vulgar, MBh.; (ibc.) wanting, missing, absent, R.; VarBṛS.; destitute or deprived of, free from (instr., abl., or comp.), MBh.; Kāv. &c.; *-tā*, f. abandonment, MW.; (ifc.) absence or want of, Hariv.; Pañcat.; *-tilaka*, mf(*ā*)n. having no coloured sectarian mark (see *tilaka*) on the forehead, R.; *-yoni*, mfn. of low origin, MBh.; *-varṇa*, mfn. of low caste, Gaut. °**hīnita**, mfn. deprived of (with inst.), Hariv.

विहान *vihāna* (?), m. n. morning, dawn, L.

विहारुहा *vihāruhā*, f. a species of plant, L.

विहिंस् *vi-√hiṇs*, P. *-hiṇsati*, to injure severely, hurt, damage, Mn.; MBh. &c.: Caus. *-hiṇsayati*, id., MBh. °**hiṇsaka**, mfn. injuring, hurting, harming (with gen. or ifc.), MBh.; R. &c. °**hiṇsa-tā**, f. the act of harming or injuring (with loc.), MBh. °**hiṇsana**, n. (BhP.), °**hiṇsā**, f. (MBh.; R.) id. (with gen. or ifc.) °**hiṇsita**, mfn. injured, hurt, damaged &c., MBh.; R. °**hiṇsra**, see *a-vihiṇsra*.

विहित 2. *ví-hita*, mfn. (fr. *vi-√1. dhā*, p. 967; for 1. *vi-hita*, see p. 953, col. 2) distributed, divided, apportioned, bestowed, supplied &c.; put in order, arranged, determined, fixed, ordained, ordered, RV. &c. &c.; prescribed, decreed, enjoined, GṛŚrS.; Mn.; MBh. &c.; destined or meant for (nom.), MBh.; contrived, performed, made, accomplished, done, Mn.; MBh. &c.; supplied, endowed, furnished with or possessed of (instr.), MBh.; R. (cf. *su-vihita*); n. an order, command, decree, Pañcat.; *-kshaṇa*, mfn. eager for the right moment, intent upon (*artham*), Vcar. (cf. *kṛita-ksh°*); *-tva*, n. the being enjoined or prescribed, prescription, direction, Hcat.; *-durga-racana*, mfn. one who has enjoined the building of a fortress, MW.; *-pratishiddha*, mfn. enjoined and prohibited (*-tva*, n.), KātyŚr., Sch.; *-yajña*, mfn. performing sacrifices, Śak. (v.l. for *vitata-y°*); *-vat*, mfn. one who has performed or undertaken, W.; *-vṛitti*, mfn. one who is maintained or nourished by (instr.), Rājat.; *-sena*, m. N. of a prince, Kathās.; °*tâgas*, mfn. one who has committed a fault, faulty, wicked, W.; °*tâñjali*, mfn. making a respectful obeisance, Śiś.; °*têndriya*, mfn. possessed of one's senses, Bhaṭṭ. °**hiti**, f. procedure, way of acting, AitBr.; action, performance, accomplishment, Kāvyâd.; Bālar. °**hitrima**, mfn. done according to rule, Bhaṭṭ.

विहीन *vi-hīna* &c. See above.

विहुण्डन *vi-huṇḍana*, m. (√*huṇḍ*) N. of one of Śiva's attendants, L.

विहुर्छ् *vi-√hurch* (or *-hūrch*), P. *-hūrchati*, to waddle, toddle, sway from one side to another (applied to a corpulent person's gait), ŚBr.; to stagger, totter, stumble, Kāṭh.

विहृ *vi-√hṛi*, P. *-harati* (rarely Ā.), to put asunder, keep apart, separate, open, RV.; AV.; Br.; ŚrS.; to distribute and transpose (verses or parts of verses), Br.; ŚrS.; to disperse (clouds, opp. to *sam-√hṛi*), Hariv.; (with *talāt talam*) to shift, let pass from hand to hand, MBh.; to divide (also arithmetically), KātyŚr.; Gol.; to construct (in geom.), Śulbas.; to cut off, sever, MBh.; to extract from (abl.), ib.; to carry away, remove, Kāv.; Rājat.; to tear in pieces, lacerate, RV.; to move on, walk, ĀśvŚr.; to spend or pass (time), Gobh.; Mn.; MBh. &c.; to roam, wander through (acc.), MBh.; (esp.) to walk or roam about for pleasure, divert one's self, Gaut.; Mn.; MBh. &c. (with *mṛigayām*, 'to go about hunting,' R.); to shed (tears), Śak.: Desid., see *vi-jihīrshā*, °*shu* (p. 960, col. 3).

Vi-hara, m. taking away, removing, shifting, changing, Bhartṛ.; separation, disunion, absence, W. °**haraṇa**, n. the act of taking away or removing or changing or transposing, Lāṭy.; MārkP.; opening, expanding, Pāṇ. i, 3, 20; stepping out, ib. i, 3, 41; going about for pleasure or exercise, roaming, strolling, Kāv.; Pur.; Suśr.; taking out for a walk or for airing, Gobh.; moving to and fro, brandishing, MBh. °**haraṇīya**, mfn. to be taken away, W.; to be rambled or sported, ib. °**hartṛi**, m. one who takes away, a robber, Yājñ.; MBh.; one who rambles about or enjoys himself, Ragh.

Vi-hāra, m. (once in BhP., n.) distribution, transposition (of words), AitBr.; Lāṭy.; arrangement or disposition (of the 3 sacred fires; also applied to the fires themselves or the space between them), ŚrS.; too great expansion of the organs of speech (consisting in too great lengthening or drawling in pronunciation, opp. to *saṃ-hāra*, q. v.), RPrāt.; walking for pleasure or amusement, wandering, roaming, MBh.; Kāv. &c.; sport, play, pastime, diversion, enjoyment, pleasure ('in' or 'with,' comp.; ifc. also = taking delight in), Yājñ.; MBh.; R. &c.; a place of recreation, pleasure-ground, MBh.; Kāv. &c.; (with Buddhists or Jainas) a monastery or temple (originally a hall where the monks met or walked about; afterwards these halls were used as temples), Lalit.; Mṛicch.; Kathās. &c. (cf. MWB. 68; 81 &c.); consecration for a sacrifice, Āpast.; N. of the country of Magadha (called Bihār or Behār from the number of Buddhist monasteries, see MWB. 68), Cat.; the shoulder, L.; a partic. bird (= *bindurekaka*), L.; = *vaijayanta*, L.; *-kārikā*, f. pl. N. of wk.; *-krīḍā-mṛiga*, m. a toy-antelope to play with, BhP.; *-gṛiha*, n. a pleasure-house, play-house, theatre, MW.; *-dāsī*, f. a female attendant of a convent or temple, Mālatīm.; *-deśa*, m. a place of recreation, pleasure-ground, MBh.; R.; MārkP.; *-bhadra*, m. N. of a man, Daś.; *-bhūmi*, f. = *-deśa*, Hariv.; a grazing-ground, pasturage, Kir.; *-yātrā*, f. a pleasure-walk, MBh.; *-vat*, mfn. possessing a place of recreation, Mn.; MBh.; (ifc.) delighting in, Mn. x, 9; *-vana*, n. a pleasure-grove, Daś.; *-vāpī*, f. 'pl°-pond,' N. of wk.; *-vāri*, n. water for sporting or playing about in, Ragh.; *-śayana*, n. a pl°-couch, R.; *-śaila*, m. a pl°-mountain, R.; *-sthalī*, f. (Vās.), *-sthāna*, n. (BhP.); °*râjira*, n. (= °*ra-deśa*); °*râvasatha*, m. (= °*ra-gṛiha*), MBh. °**hāraka**, mf(*ikā*)n. delighting in (comp.), Pañcar.; serving for the amusement of (comp.), Mālatīm.; roaming or walking about, a roamer, MW.; belonging to a Buddhist temple or convent, ib. °**hāraṇa**, n. pleasure, delight (ifc. = delighting in), Pañcar. °**hārin**, mfn. wandering about for pleasure, roaming, strolling, MBh.; Kāv. &c.; going as far as, extending to (comp.), R.; Rājat.; dependent on (comp.), MBh.; enjoying one's self with, delighting in, given or addicted to, fond of (comp.), Yājñ.; MBh. &c.; charming, beautiful, Bhartṛ. (v.l.); (*iṇī*), f. a girl too fond of gadding about (unfit for marriage), L.; °*ri-siṇha*, m. N. of a king, Inscr.

Vi-hṛita, mfn. set or put asunder, distributed, disposed &c.; transposed, varied (as words or Pādas), ŚrS.; n. a walk, R.; hesitation, reluctance, bashful silence (one of the 10 Hāvas or feminine modes of indicating love), Daśar.; Sāh.; *-shoḍaśī*, f. N. of wk. °**hṛiti**, f. expansion, increase, growth, Kir.; sport, pastime, pleasure, Nalôd.; taking away, MW.

विहेठ् *vi-√heṭh*, Caus. P. *-heṭhayati*, to hurt, injure, Lalit. °**heṭha**, m. hurt, injury, ib. °**heṭhaka**, mfn. hurting, injuring, an injurer, MBh.; a reviler, W. °**heṭhana**, n. the act of hurting, injuring, distressing, afflicting &c., L.

विहेल् *vi-√hel*, Caus. Ā. *-helayate*, to vex, annoy, MBh. xiii, 6720 (B. *-ghātayate*).

विह्नु *vi-√hnu*, Ā. *-hnute*, Sch. on APrāt. i, 100.

विह्मल् *vi-√hmal*, Caus. *-hmalayati*, ib.

विह्रु *vi-√hru* (cf. *vi-√hvṛi* below), P. *-hruṇāti*, to cause to deviate, turn aside, frustrate, spoil, RV. °**hrút**, f. a serpent-like animal, worm &c., VS. °**hruta** (*ví-*), mfn. crooked, dislocated, hurt, injured, RV.; AV.

विह्लण *vihlaṇa* &c. See *bilhaṇa*.

विह्वरित *vi-hvarita*. See *vi-√hvṛi*.

विह्वल् *vi-√hval*, P. *-hvalati*, to shake or sway to and fro, tremble, be agitated or unsteady, stagger, MantraBr.; MBh.; Kāv. &c.

Vi-hvala, mf(*ā*)n. agitated, perturbed, distressed, afflicted, annoyed (*am*, ind.), MBh.; Kāv. &c.; m. myrrh, L.; *-cetana* (MBh.), *-cetas* (Kathās.), mfn. distressed in mind, low-spirited; *-tanu*, mfn. one whose body is exhausted by (comp.), Pañcat.; *-tā*, f., *-tva*, n. agitation, perturbation, consternation, anxiety, MBh.; *-locana*, mfn. one who has unsteady or rolling eyes, MBh.; BhP.; *-sâlasâṅga*, mf(*ī*)n. one whose body is exhausted and languid, Caurap.; *-hṛidaya*, mfn. (= *-cetana*), BhP.; °*lâksha*, mf(*ī*)n. (= °*la-locana*), ib.; °*lâṅga*, mfn. (= °*la-tanu*), MārkP.; Pañcat.; °*lâtman*, mfn. (= °*la-cetana*), BhP. °**hvalita**, mfn. = °*hvala*, MBh.; Kāv. &c.; *-sarvâṅga*, mfn. trembling with the whole body, MBh.

Vihvalī-kṛita, mfn. made confused or agitated, MW.; fused, liquid, ib.

विह्वृ *vi-√hvṛi* (cf. *vi-√hru*), to stagger, stumble, fall, TĀr. (cf. *a-vihvarat*): Caus. (only aor. Subj. *-jihvaraḥ*), to cause to fall, overthrow, RV.

Vi-hvarita, mfn. staggered, fallen (Vedic, accord. to Kāś. on Pāṇ. vii, 2, 33).

Vi-hvâruka, mfn. tumbling, falling, MaitrS.

विह्वे *vi-√hve*, Ā. *-hvayate* (cf. Pāṇ. i, 3, 30), to call in different places, call, invoke, vie in calling, contend for anything, RV.; TS.; Br.

Vi-havá, m. invocation, RV.; AitBr. °**havīya**, n. 'containing the word *vihava*,' N. of the hymn RV. x, 128. °**hávya** or °**havyà**, mfn. to be invoked or invited or desired, RV.; AV.; VS.; m. (with *Āṅgirasa*) N. of the supposed author of RV. x, 128, Anukr.; of a son of Varcas, MBh.; (*ā*), f. N. of partic. bricks, TS.; (scil. *sûkta*) N. of RV. x, 128 (cf. °*havīya*), TS.; Kāṭh.; Lāṭy.

वी 1. *vī*, cl. 2. P. (Dhātup. xxiv, 39) *veti* (accord. to some in the conjug. tenses substituted for *√aj*; 2. sg. *véshi* also as Impv., RV.; 3. pl. *vyánti*, RV.; AV.; Br.; Subj. 2. 3. sg. *ves*, RV.; Impv. *vīhí*, *vītāt*, ib.; 3. pl. *viyantu*, TS.; p. Ā. *vyāná*, RV.; pf. *vivāya*, *vivye*, ib.; aor. *avaishīt*, Gr.; 3. pl. *aveshan*, Subj. *veshat*, RV.; fut. *vetā*, *veshyati*, inf. *vetum*, Gr.), to go, approach (either as a friend, i. e. 'seek or take eagerly, grasp, seize, accept, enjoy,' or as an enemy, i. e. 'fall upon, attack, assail, visit, punish, avenge'), RV.; AV.; TS.; Br.; to set in motion, arouse, excite, impel, RV.; to further, promote, lead or bring or help any one to (two acc.), ib.; to get, procure, ib.: Pass. *-vīyáte* &c., AV.; Br.: Caus. *vāyayati* or *vāpayati* (aor. *avīvayat*), to cause to go or approach &c.; to impregnate, Pāṇ. vi, 1, 55: Desid. *vivīshati*, Gr.: Intens., see *ā-√vī* and *√vevī*. [Cf., accord. to some, Lat. *ve-nari*; Germ. *weida*, *Weide*, *weiden*.]

2. **Vī**, mfn. going to, eager for, desirous or fond of (gen.), RV. i, 143, 5 (cf. *deva-ví*, *pada-ví*); set in motion (see *parṇa-ví*); m. the act of going, motion, L.

1. **Vītá**, mfn. gone, approached &c.; desired, liked, loved, pleasant, RV.; ŚāṅkhŚr.; straight, smooth, RV. iv, 2, 11; ix, 97, 17; trained, quiet, Rājat.; (*ā*), f. a line, row (= *rāji*), ĀśvGṛ.; n. a wish, desire, TĀr.; the driving or guiding of an elephant (with a goad) &c., Śiś. v, 47. **-tama** (*vītá-*), mfn. most acceptable or pleasant, RV. **-prishṭha** (*vītá-*), mf(*ā*)n. straight-backed (as a horse), ib. **-vat**, mfn. containing the word *vīta* or other forms fr. *√vī*, ĀśvŚr. **-vāra** (*vītá-*), mfn. straight-tailed (as a horse), ib. **-havya** (*vītá-*), mfn. one whose offerings are acceptable, ib.; m. N. of a man with the patr. *Āṅgirasa* (author of RV. vi, 15), Anukr.; of a man with the patr. *Śrāyasa*, TS.; PañcavBr.; of a king who obtained the rank of a Brāhman, MBh.; of a son of Śunaka and father of Dhṛiti, Pur.; of Krishṇa, Pañcar.; pl. the sons of Vīta-havya, MBh.; °*vyôpâkhyāna*, n. N. of a ch. of the Vāsishṭha-rāmāyaṇa.

1. **Vīti**, f. (dat. *vītáye* often used as inf.) enjoyment, feast, dainty meal, full draught &c., RV.; advantage, profit, ib. (L. also light, lustre, = *gati*, *prajana*, *dhāvana*); m. a partic. Agni, AitBr. **-rādhas** (*vīti-*), mfn. affording enjoyment, RV. **-hotra** (*vīti-*), mfn. inviting to enjoyment or to a feast, ib.; invited to a feast (as gods), VS.; m. fire or the god of fire, Rājat.; BhP. (pl. the worshippers of fire in any form, Cat.); the sun, L.; N. of a king, MBh.; of a son of Priya-vrata, BhP.; of a son of Indra-sena, ib.; of a son of Su-kumāra, ib.; of a son of Tāla-jaṅgha, ib.; VP. (pl. his descendants); of a priest, Cat.; *-dayitā* or *-priyā*, f. 'beloved of Vīti-hotra i. e. Agni,' N. of a Svāhā, Pañcar.

वी 3. *vī* (*vi-√5. i*), P. *vy-eti* (3. pl. *vi-yanti*; impf. *vy-ait*; pf. *vīyāya*; inf. *vy-etum*; for *vyayati*, *vyayayati*, see *√vyay*), to go apart or in different directions, diverge, be diffused or scattered or distributed or divided or extended, RV. &c. &c.; to be lost, perish, disappear, Up.; MBh. &c.; to go through, traverse, RV.; VS.; AitBr.: Intens. (or cl. 4) Ā. *vīyate*, to pass through, traverse, RV.

2. **Vīta**, mfn. gone away, departed, disappeared, vanished, lost (often ibc. = free or exempt from, without, -less), Up.; Mn.; MBh. &c. **-kalmasha**, mfn. freed from taint or sin, Mn. xii, 22. **-kāma**, mfn. free from desire, W. **-ghṛiṇa**, mfn. one from whom mercy has departed, merciless, MW.; *-tā*, f. mercilessness, ib. **-cinta**, mfn. free from anxiety about (loc.), Śak. **-janma-jarasa**, mfn. not subject to birth or old age, Kir. **-trasareṇu**, mfn. = *-rāga*, free from passions or affections, Bālar. iv, 1½ (printed *-trās*°). **-trishṇa**, mfn. free from all passions or desires, L. **-dambha**, mfn. free from pride, humble, L. **-bhaya**, m. 'fearless, undaunted,' N. of Śiva, Śivag.; of Vishṇu, L. **-bhī**, mfn. free from fear, intrepid, Mn. vii, 64. **-bhīti**, mfn. id., Śiś. xviii, 84; m. N. of an Asura, Kathās. **-matsara**, mfn. free from envy or passion, Mn. xi, 111. **-manyu**, mfn. free from resentment or anger, KaṭhUp.; exempt or free from sorrow, MBh. **-mala**, mfn. free from obscurity or darkness, clear, pure, MW. **-moha**, mfn. freed from illusion, MW.; °*hôpâkhyāna*, n. N. of wk. **-rāga**, mfn. free from passions or affections, dispassionate, desireless, calm, tranquil, MBh.; Kāv. &c. (also applied to 8 partic. Bodhi-sattvas and their attributes); not attached to (loc.), HPariś.; colourless, bleached, W.; m. a sage with subdued passions (esp. applied to a Buddhist or Jaina saint), L.; *-bhaya-krodha*, mfn. free from passions and fear and anger, Bhag.; *-bhūmi*, f. one of the 7 stages in the life of a Śrāvaka, Buddh.; *-stuti*, f. N. of a Jaina wk. **-viruddha-buddhi**, mfn. one whose hostile feelings have passed away, peaceable, W. **-visha**, mfn. free from impurities, clear (as water), Dhanaṃj. **-vrīḍa**, mfn. shameless, Bhartṛ. **-śaṅka**, mfn. fearless, intrepid (*am*, ind.), Śiś. **-śoka**, mfn. free from sorrow, ŚvetUp.; MBh.; m. the Aśoka tree, Jonesia Asoka, MBh.; (*ā*), f. N. of a town, HPariś.; °*ka-tā*, f. freedom from sorrow, Yājñ.; °*ka-bhaya*, mfn. free from sorrow and fear, Mn. vi, 32; °*ka-bhayâbādha*, mfn. free from the disturbance of sorrow and fear, MW. **-spṛiha**, mfn. free from wish or desire, W. **-hiraṇmaya**, mfn. one who does not possess any golden vessels (*-tva*, n.), Ragh. v, 2. **Vītârci** (or °*cis*), mfn. one whose flame is extinguished, ĀpŚr. **Vītâśoka**, m. a proper N. (= *vigatâśoka*), Buddh. **Vītôccaya-bandha**, mfn. having the fastening of the knot gone, Kir. **Vītôttara**, mfn. having no answer, unable to reply (*am*, ind.), Amar.

2. **Vīti**, f. separation, TS.

वी 4. *vī*, mfn. (weak form of *√vye*) covered (cf. *hiraṇya-ví*).

3. **Vītá**, mfn. covered, hidden, concealed, RV. (cf. *kṛitsna-v*°); covered or wrapped in, girt with (instr.), ib.; BhP. **-sūtra**, n. the sacred thread or cord, Vikr. v, 19 (cf. *ni-* and *upa-vīta*).

Vītaka, n. a vessel for camphor and sandal powder, L.; (in *a-v*°) = *vi-vīta*, an inclosed spot of ground, Yājñ. ii, 291.

Vītin, m. N. of a man (pl. his family), Saṃskārak.

वी 5. *vī*, m. = 1. *vi*, a bird (see *takva-ví*); f. a female bird, L.

Vīka, m. a 'bird' or 'wind,' Uṇ. iii, 47, Sch.; = *manas*, L.

वी 6. *vī*, in comp. = 3. *vi* (in *vī-kāśa*, *-cayana*, *-taṅsa*, *-nāha*, *-barha*, *-mārga*, *-rudh*, *-vadha*, *-vāha*, *-vidha*, *-vṛita*, *-sarpa*, *-hāra*, qq. vv.)

वीकाश *vī-kāśa*, m. = 1. *vi-k*°, L.; = 2. *vi-k*°, brightness, light, lustre, Daś.

वीकृड *vīkṛiḍa*, mfn. (applied to Rudra), MaitrS. (v. l.)

वीक्ष् *vīksh* (*vi-√īksh*), Ā. *vīkshate* (ep. also P.), to look at, see, behold, ŚBr. &c. &c.; to look upon, regard (*pitṛi-vat*, as a father), R.; (with *hṛidi*) to see in the heart, ponder, R.; to consider, observe, discern, ascertain, understand, Mn.; MBh. &c.; to think fit or proper, Suśr.; to look over, peruse, study, VarBṛS.: Pass. *vīkshyate*, to be looked at &c.; to look like, appear, Vikr.

Vīksha, m. sight, seeing, W.; (*ā*), f. id., R.; investigation, Cat.; knowledge, intelligence, BhP.; unconsciousness, fainting, L.; n. surprise, astonishment, W.; any visible object, ib.; °*kshâpanna* (or °*kshâp*°), mfn. astonished, surprised, ib.; °*kshâraṇya-māhātmya*, n. N. of wk. **Vīkshaṇa**, n. (ifc. f. *ā*) looking at, seeing, inspection, investigation, ŚrS.; MBh. &c.; a glance, gaze, Kāv.; VarBṛS.; BhP.; the eye, Śiś. xviii, 30; (in astrol.) aspect of the planets, VarBṛS. **Vīkshaṇīya**, mfn. to be looked at or regarded or considered, visible, observable, Kāv.; Kathās. **Vīkshita**, mfn. looked at, seen, beheld, regarded, VS. &c. &c.; n. a look, glance, Kālid.; Bhartṛ. **Vīkshitavya**, mfn. = *vīkshaṇīya* (n. impers. it should be looked &c.), Kathās. **Vīkshitṛi**, mfn. one who looks at or sees (ifc.), BhP. **Vīkshya**, mfn. = *vīkshaṇīya*, L.; astonishing, wonderful, W.; m. a dancer, actor, L.; a horse, L.; n. wonder, surprise, wonderful object, L.

वीखा *vīkhā*, f. (cf. *vīṅkhā*) a partic. motion, Siṇhâs.

वीङ्क *vīṅka*, n. N. of various Sāmans, ĀrshBr.

वीङ्ख् *vīṅkh* (*vi-√iṅkh*), Caus. *vīṅkhayati* (only 3. du. impf. *vy-aiṅkhayatām*), to toss to and fro, swing, PañcavBr.

Vīṅkhā, f. a partic. mode of moving, dancing &c. (also 'one of a horse's paces'), L.; = *saṃdhi*, L.; Carpopogon Pruriens, L.

वीङ्गित *vīṅgita*, mfn. (fr. *vi-√iṅg*) tossed, moved to and fro, TBr. (w. r. *vīṅkita*).

वीच *vīca*. See under *vīci*.

वीचयन *vī-cayana*, n. = *vi-c*° (see *vi-√2. ci*), research, inquiry, W.

वीचि *vīci*, f. (prob. fr. *vi* + 2. *añc*) going or leading aside or astray, aberration, deceit, seduction, RV. x, 10, 6; also m. (L.) and (*ī*), f. (ifc. °*ci* or °*cika*) a wave, ripple, Kāv.; VarBṛS. &c.; 'wave' as N. of a subdivision of a chapter (called *pravāha*, 'river'), Sadukt.; (prob. for *a-vīci*) a partic. hell, R. (L. also = *sukha*, *avakāśa*, *svalpa*, *alpa*, *āli*, *kiraṇa*). **-kshobha**, m. agitation or roughness of waves, Megh. **-taraṃga-nyāya**, m. wave-undulation-method (or the rule by which sound reaches the ear, a term used to denote successive operation), Bhāshāp. **-mālin**, m. 'wave-garlanded,' the ocean, L.

Vīca, prob. for *vīci* (in *ambu-vīca*, N. of a king, MBh. i, 7476).

Vīci-kāka, m. a partic. bird, MārkP.

वीज् *vīj* (cf. *√1. vij*), cl. 1. P. Ā. *vījati*, °*te* (pf. *vivyajuḥ*), to fan, cool by blowing upon or fanning, Hariv.; to sprinkle with water, MBh. (according to Dhātup. vi, 24 only Ā. 'to go'): Caus. or cl. 10 (Dhātup. xxxv, 84), *vījayati* (Pass. *vījyate*), to fan, blow, kindle (fire), MBh.; R. &c.; to stroke, caress, Suśr.

Vījana, m. N. of two kinds of bird (= *koka* and *jīvaṃ-jīva*), L.; n. fanning, wafting, Kāv.; Kathās. &c.; a fan, Bhpr.; = *vastu*, L.

Vījita, mfn. fanned, cooled &c.; sprinkled with water, wetted, Hariv. (v. l. *vejita*).

Vījya. See *sukha-v*°.

वीज *vīja* &c. See *bīja*.

वीट *vīṭa*, n. (only in Siddh.) or *vīṭā*, f. a small piece of wood shaped like a barley-corn and about a span long (it was struck with a stick or bat in a kind of game, like tip-cat, played by boys; accord. to some it was a kind of metal ball; others say it was held in the mouth as a form of penance), MBh. i, 5050 (Sch.) &c. **-mukha** (*vīṭā-*), mfn. holding the Vīṭā in the mouth, VP.

वीटक *vīṭaka*, n. (also written *bīṭaka*) a preparation of the Areca nut with spices and lime rolled up together in a leaf of the betel plant (commonly called betel or Pān), Pañcad.; (*ikā*), f. id., Daś.; Kathās. &c.; a tie or fastening (of a garment), Amar.

Vīṭi or **vīṭī**, f. the betel plant, Piper Betel, L.

वीड् *vīḍ* (accord. to some connected with *√vish*), only Caus. *vīḍayati* or *vīḷayati*, °*te*, (P.) to make strong or firm, strengthen, fasten, RV. viii, 45, 6; (Ā.) to be strong or firm or hard, ib. ii, 37, 3 &c.

Vīḍita or **vīḷita**, mfn. made strong, strengthened, firm, hard, RV.

Vīḍú or **vīlú**, mf(°*ḍvī*)n. strong, firm, hard, RV.; VS.; n. anything firmly fixed or strong, stronghold, RV. **-jambha** (*vīḍú-*), mfn. strong-jawed, RV. **-dvéshas**, mfn. hating the strong or hating strongly, ib. **-pátman**, mfn. flying strongly or incessantly, ib. **-paví**, mfn. having strong tires (as the Maruts), ib. **-pāṇi** (or *vīḍú-p°*), mfn. strong-handed, strong-hoofed, ib. **-haras** (*vīḍú-*), mfn. seizing firmly, holding fast, ib. **-harshin**, mfn. (prob.) fiercely passionate, refractory, ib. **Vīḍv-áṅga**, mfn. strong-limbed, firm in body, ib.

वीणा *vīṇā*, f. (of doubtful derivation) the Vīṇā or Indian lute (an instrument of the guitar kind, supposed to have been invented by Nārada, q. v., usually having seven wires or strings raised upon nineteen frets or supports fixed on a long rounded board, towards the ends of which are two large gourds; its compass is said to be two octaves, but it has many varieties according to the number of strings &c.), TS.; ŚBr. &c. &c.; (in astrol.) a partic. configuration of the stars (when all planets are situated in 7 houses), VarBṛS.; lightning, L.; N. of a Yoginī, Cat.; of a river, MBh. **-karṇa**, m. 'Lute-ear,' N. of a man, Hit. **-gaṇakin**, m. a music-master, the leader of a musical band, ĀpŚr. **-gaṇagin** (*vīṇā-*), m. id., ŚBr.; ŚāṅkhŚr.; KātyŚr. **-gāthin**, m. a lute-player, TBr.; ŚBr.; GṛŚrS. **-tantra**, n. N. of a Tantra. **-tūṇava**, n. sg. lutes and flutes, ĀpŚr. **-daṇḍa**, m. 'lute-stick,' the neck or long rounded board of a lute, L. **-datta**, m. N. of a Gandharva, Kathās. **-°nubandha** (*vīṇân°*), m. the tie of a lute (or lower part of one of its ends where the wires are fixed), L. **-paṇava-tūṇa-vat**, mfn. (*tūṇa* for *tūṇava*) furnished with a lute and a drum and a flute, R. **-pāṇi**, m. 'Lute-hand,' N. of Nārada, Pañcar. **-praseva**, m. the damper on a lute, L. **-bhid**, f. a kind of lute, MW. **-rava**, m. (ifc. f. *ā*) the sound of a lute, Kathās.; mfn. humming like a lute (*ā*, f. N. of a fly), Pañcat. **-vaṇsa-śalākā**, f. a round-headed peg round which the string of a l° is bound, L. **-vat**, mfn. possessed of a lute (*atī*, f. N. of a woman), Pāṇ. vi, 1, 219, Sch. **-vatsa-rāja**, m. N. of a king, Pañcat. **-vādá**, m. a lute-player, lutanist, VS.; ŚBr.; ĀpŚr.; playing on a lute, Bhartṛ. **-vādaka**, m. a lutanist, L. **-vādana**, n. a plectrum for sounding a lute, L. **-vādya**, n. playing on a lute, L. **-vinoda**, m. N. of a Vidyādhara, Bālar. **-śilpa**, n. the art of playing on the lute, Pañcar. **-°sya** (*vīṇâsya*), m. 'Lute-faced,' N. of Nārada, L. **-hasta**, mfn. holding a lute in his hand (Śiva), Śivag.

Vīṇāla, mfn. (fr. *vīṇā*), g. *sidhmâdi*.

Vīṇin, mfn. (fr. id.; g. *vrīhy-ādi*) furnished with a lute, playing on a lute, Megh.; Kathās.

वीत 4. *vīta*, mfn. (prob. fr. √*vai*; for 1. 2. 3. *vīta* see under √1. 3. 4. *vī*) worn out, useless, L.; n. a useless horse or elephant, L.

वीतंस *vī-taṇsa*, m. (fr. 1. *vi*+*t°*; cf. *vi-t°*) a cage or net or any enclosure for catching or confining or keeping birds or beasts, Hcar.

वीतन *vītana*, m. du. (possibly fr. *vi*+√*tan*) the sides or cartilages of the larynx or throat, L.

वीति 3. *vīti*, m. = 1. *pīti*, a horse, Rājat.

वीत्त *vī-tta*, mfn. (for *vi-datta*, √1. *dā*), APrāt., Sch. (cf. *parī-tta*).

वीथि *vīthi* or *vīthī*, f. (perhaps fr. √*vī*; cf. 1. *vīta*) a row, line, Kāv.; Rājat.; a road, way, street, MBh.; Kāv. &c.; a race-course, Śiś. v, 60; a market, stall, shop, ib. ix. 32; a row of pictures, p°-gallery, Uttarar. (v.l. *vīthikā*); a partic. division of the planetary sphere (comprising 3 asterisms), VarBṛS.; a terrace in front of a house, L.; a sort of drama (having an amatory intrigue for its plot and said to be in one act and performed by one or two players), Bhar.; Daśar. &c.

Vīthika, m. or n. (only m. c.) or **°kā**, f. a row, line, Ratnâv.; Kathās.; a road, street, R.; a terrace in front of a house, Hariv.; VarBṛS.; a picture-gallery, Uttarar. (v.l. for *vīthi*); a sort of drama (see under *vīthi*), Bhar.

Vīthī, in comp. for *vīthi*. **-kṛita**, mfn. placed or arranged in rows, MBh. **-mārga**, m. one of an elephant's paces, L.

Vīthīka (ifc.) = *vīthī*, Bhar.

Vīthy, in comp. for *vīthi*. **-aṅga**, n. a division of the Vīthi drama (described as a kind of dialogue consisting in quibble, equivoque, jest, abuse, and the like), W.

वीध्र *vīdhra*, mfn. (accord. to Uṇ. ii, 26 fr. *vi* + √*indh*) clean, clear, pure, L.; n. (only in loc.) a clear sky, sunshine, AV.; Kāṭh.; wind, L.; fire, L. **-bindu**, m. a rain-drop fallen in sunshine, Kāṭh. **-samṛiddha**, mfn. said to = *nabhas, vāyu, agni*, ib.

Vídhrya, mfn. relating to the clear sky, VS.

वीन् *vīn* (*vi-*√*in* or *inv*), P. *vīnoti*, to drive away, scatter, disperse, RV.; to send forth in various ways, bestow, ib.

वीना *vīnā*, f. N. of a river, MW. (cf. *vīṇā*).

वीनाह *vī-nāha*, m. (for 3. *vi*+*n°*; √*nah*) the top or cover of a well, MBh.; a kind of small sacrificial grass, L.

Vī-nāhin, m. (fr. prec.) a well, L.

वीन्द्र *vīndra*, mfn. (for 3. *vi*+*indra*) that from which Indra is excluded, TS. (cf. *apêndra*).

वीन्द्वर्क *vīndv-arka*, mfn. (fr. 3. *vi*+*indu*+*arka*) without or exclusive of the moon and the sun, Laghuj.

वीप *vīpa*, mfn. (fr. 3. *vi*+*ap*) destitute of water, waterless, Pat.

वीप्स् *vīps* (Desid. of *vy-*√*āp*), P. *vīpsati*, to wish to pervade, Pat.

Vīpsā, f. 'the desire of pervading' (with any property or quality simultaneously or continuously), several or successive order or series, distributiveness, repetition (esp. repetition of words to imply continuous or successive action; e. g. *vriksham vrikshaṃ siñcati*, he waters tree after tree; *mandam mandaṃ nudati pavanaḥ*, 'gently, gently breathes the wind,' cf. Pāṇ. viii, 1, 4; Vām. v, 2, 87), APrāt.; Pāṇ.; Śaṃk. **-vicāra**, m. N. of wk.

वीबर्ह *vī-barhá*, m. (for 3. *vi*+*b°*; √1. *bṛih*) scattering, dispersing, AV.

वीबुकोश *vībukośa* (?), m. = *cāmara*, a chowrie, W.

वीभ् *vībh*. See √*bibh*.

वीमार्ग *vī-mārga*, m. (for 3. *vi*+*m°*; √*mṛij*), Pāṇ. vi, 3, 122, Sch.

वीर् 1. *vīr* (*vi-*√*īr*; only aor. *vy-airat*), to split, break into pieces, tear open, divide asunder, RV.: Caus. *vīrayati* (impf. *vy-airayat*), id., ib.

वीर् 2. *vīr*, cl. 10. Ā. (Dhātup. xxxv, 49; rather Nom. fr. *vīrá* below) *vīrâyate*, to be powerful or valiant, display heroism, RV.; VS.; TBr.; (P. *vīrayati*) to overpower, subdue, Nir. i, 7.

Vīrá, m. a man, (esp.) a brave or eminent man, hero, chief (sometimes applied to gods, as to Indra, Vishṇu &c.; pl. men, people, mankind, followers, retainers), RV. &c. &c.; a hero (as opp. to a god), RTL. 272, n.; a husband, MBh.; R.; Pur.; a male child, son (collect. male progeny), RV.; AV.; Br.; GṛŚrS.; the male of an animal, AV.; ŚāṅkhŚr.; (with Tāntrikas) an adept (who is between the *divya* and the *paśu*, RTL. 191), Rudray.; (in dram.) heroism (as one of the 8 Rasas [q.v.]; the Vīra-carita [q.v.] exhibits an example), Bhar.; Daśar.; Sāh.&c.; an actor, W.; a partic. Agni (son of Tapas), MBh.; fire, (esp.) sacred or sacrificial fire, L.; N. of various plants (Terminalia Arunja; Nerium Odorum; Guilandina Bonduc, manioc-root), L.; N. of an Asura, MBh.; of a son of Dhṛita-rāshṭra, ib.; of a son of Bharad-vāja, ib.; of a son of Purusha Vairāja and father of Priya-vrata and Uttāna-pāda, Hariv.; of a son of Gṛiñjima, ib.; of two sons of Kṛishṇa, BhP.; of a son of Kshupa and father of Viviṇśa, MārkP.; of the father of Līlāvatī, ib.; of a teacher of Vinaya, Buddh.; of the last Arhat of the present Avasarpiṇī, L.; (also with *bhaṭṭa, ācārya* &c.) of various authors &c., Cat.; (pl.) of a class of gods under Manu Tāmasa, BhP.; (*ā*), f. a wife, matron (whose husband and sons are still alive), L.; an intoxicating beverage, ib.; N. of various plants and drugs (Flacourtia Cataphracta; Convolvulus Paniculatus; Gmelina Arborea; the drug Ela-vāluka &c.), L.; (in music) a partic. Śruti, Saṃgīt.; N. of the wife of Bharad-vāja, L.; of the wife of Karaṃ-dhama, MārkP.; of a river, MBh. (B. *vāṇī*); n. (only L.) a reed (Arundo Tibialis); the root of ginger(?); pepper; rice-gruel; the root of Costus Speciosus, of Andropogon Muricatus &c.; mf(*ā*)n. heroic, powerful, strong, excellent, eminent, L. [Cf. Lat. *vir*; Lith. *výras*; Goth. *wair*; Angl. Sax. *wër, wëre-wulf*; Eng. *were-wolf*; Germ. *Werwolf, Wergeld*.] **-karā**, f. 'hero-forming,' N. of a river, MBh. (B. *vīraṃ-k°*). **-kárma**, n. 'performing virile acts,' the membrum virile, RV. **-karman**, n. manly deed, Nir. **-kāṭī**, f. N. of a village, Kshitîś. **-kāma**, mfn. desirous of male offspring, ŚāṅkhBr.; ŚrS. **-kīṭa**, m. 'worm of a hero,' a pitiful warrior, MW. **-kukshi** (*vīrá-*), f. (a woman) bearing sons in the womb, RV. **-ketu**, m. N. of a man with the patr. Pāñcāla-putra, MBh.; of a king of Ayodhyā, Kathās.; of a king of Pāṭalī, Daś. **-kesarin** (or *-keś°*), m. N. of a king, Cat. **-kshurikā**, f. a dagger, Kathās. **-gati**, f. 'a hero's resort,' Indra's heaven, MBh.; BhP. **-gotra**, n. a family of heroes, MārkP. **-goshṭhī**, f. conversation between heroes, Hcar. **-ghnī**, see *vīra-han*. **-ṃ-karā**, see *vīra-k°*. **-cakra**, n. (with Tāntrikas) N. of a mystic diagram, RTL. 196; an army of heroes (see next); **°kreśvara**, m. 'lord of an army of heroes,' N. of Vishṇu, Pañcar. **-cakshushmat**, mfn. having the eye of a hero (said of Vishṇu), R. **-carita** or **-caritra**, n. 'exploits of the hero,' N. of a celebrated drama by Bhava-bhūti (= *mahāvīra-carita*, q.v.) and of a legendary history of Śāli-vāhana. **-carya**, m. N. of a king, Buddh.; (*ā*), f. the deeds of a hero, adventurous exploits, Kathās.; Rājat. **-cintāmaṇi**, m. N. of an extract from the Śārṅgadhara Paddhati. **-jánana**, mfn. generating h°s, MaitrS. **-jayantikā**, f. a kind of dance performed by soldiers after a victory or on going to battle, war-dance, war, battle, L. **-jāta** (*vīrá-*), mfn. (wealth) consisting in men or sons, RV. **-jita**, m. N. of a man, Kathās. **-taṇḍula**, n. Amaranthus Polygonoides, L. **-tantra**, n. N. of a Tantra wk. (also *-yāmala*), RTL. 204. **-tama** (*vīrá-*), m. (ifc. f. *ā*) a very strong or powerful man, an eminent hero, RV.; AV.; MBh. **-tara** (*vīrá-*), mfn. stronger, bolder; m. a great or a greater hero, RV.; MBh.; an arrow, L.; a corpse (?), L.; n. = *vīraṇa*, Andropogon Muricatus; **°râsana**, n. a partic. posture, L. **-taru**, m. N. of various trees and other plants (Pentaptera Arjuna; Andropogon Muricatus, Barleria Longifolia &c.), L. **-tā** (*vīrá-*), f. or **-tva**, n. heroism, manliness, VS.; MBh. &c. **-tāpiny-upanishad**, f. N. of an Upanishad. **-tṛiṇa**, n. Andropogon Muricatus, L. **-datta**, m. N. of a poet; *-gṛihapati-paripṛicchā*, f. N. of wk. **-dāman**, m. N. of a king, Inscr. **-deya**, w. r. for *vaira-d°*. **-deva**, m. N. of various men, Kathās.; Rājat.; of a poet, Cat. **-dyumna**, m. N. of a king, MBh. **-dru**, m. Terminalia Arunja, L. **-dhanvan**, m. 'having a powerful bow,' N. of Kāma-deva (god of love), L. **-dhara**, m. N. of a wheelwright, Pañcat. **-nagara**, n. N. of a town, VP. **-nātha**, m. N. of a man, Rājat.; mf(*ā*)n. having a hero as protector, R. **-nārāyaṇa**, m. N. of a king and a poet, Cat.; *-carita*, n., and **°yaṇīya**, n. N. of wks. **-ṃ-dhara**, m. (only L.) a peacock; fighting with wild beasts; a leather cuirass or jacket; N. of a river. **-paṭṭa**, m. a kind of military dress or accoutrement (worn round the forehead), Rājat. **-pattrī**, f. a kind of bulbous plant, L. **-patnī** (*vīrá-*), f. the wife of a hero, RV.; MBh. &c.; *-vrata*, n. a partic. observance, Hariv.; Kāv.; Pur. **-parākrama**, m. N. of two wks. **-parṇa**, n. a partic. drug (= *sura-parṇa*), L. **-pāṇa** or **-pāṇaka**, n. the drink of warriors or heroes (taken before or during a battle, for refreshment or to raise the courage), L. **-pāṇḍya**, m. N. of a king, Cat. **-pāna**, n. = *-pāṇa*, R. **-pura**, n. N. of a town in the district of Kānyakubja, Hit.; of a mythical town in the Himālaya mountains, Kathās. **-purusha**, m. (ifc. f. *ā*) a heroic man, hero, R.; Hariv. &c. (cf. Pāṇ. ii, 1, 58, Sch.); **°shaka**, mfn. (a village) the men of which are heroes, Pat. **-pushpa**, m. a kind of plant, L.; (*ī*), f. = *sindūra-pushpī*, L. **-peśas** (*vīrá-*), m. forming the ornament of heroes, RV. **-poshá**, m. thriving or prosperous condition of men or of sons, AV. **-prajāyinī** (MBh.), **-prajāvatī** (MārkP.), f. the mother of a hero. **-prabha**, m. N. of a man, Kathās. **-pramoksha**, N. of a Tīrtha, MBh. **-prasavā** (Kum.), **-prasavinī** (Mcar.), **-prasū** (Bālar.), f. a woman who brings forth heroes. **-bali**, m. N. of wk. **-bāhu**, m. 'strong-armed,' N. of Vishṇu, L.; of one of the sons of Dhṛita-rāshṭra and various kings and other men, MBh.; of a monkey, R. **-bukka**, m. N. of the founder of Vidyā-nagara, BhP., Introd.

(see *bukka*). **— bhaṭa,** m. a warrior, hero, Daś.; N. of a king of Tāmra-lipta, Kathās. **— bhadra,** m. a distinguished hero, L.; a horse fit for the Aśva-medha sacrifice, L.; Andropogon Muricatus, L.; N. of a Rudra, Yājñ., Sch.; of an incarnation or form of Śiva (sometimes regarded as his son, and worshipped esp. in the Marāṭha country; in the Vāyu-Purāṇa he is said to have been created from Śiva's mouth in order to spoil the sacrifice of Daksha, and is described as having a thousand heads, a thousand eyes, a thousand feet, and wielding a thousand clubs; his appearance is fierce and terrific, he is clothed in a tiger's skin dripping with blood, and he bears a blazing bow and battle-axe; in another Purāṇa he is described as produced from a drop of Śiva's sweat), MBh.; Pur.; Kathās. &c. (RTL. 79; 82); of a warrior on the side of the Pāṇḍavas, MBh.; of a king and various authors, Cat.; *-kālikā-vacana,* n. N. of a ch. of the Vīra-bhadra-tantra; *-campū,* f. N. of a poem; *-jit,* m. 'conqueror of V°,' N. of Vishṇu, Pañcar.; *-tantra,* n. N. of a Tantra; *-deva,* m. N. of a king and author (16th century; *-campū,* f. N. of a poem written in his praise); *-mantra,* m., *-vijaya,* m. N. of wks.; *-vijṛimbhaṇa,* n. N. of a drama, Daśar., Introd.; *-sutā,* f. a daughter of Vīra-bhadra; *-stotra,* n. N. of a Stotra. **— bhadraka,** n. Andropogon Muricatus, L. **— bhavat,** m. 'your heroic worship' (in reverential address), Kathās. **— bhānu,** m. N. of a king and an author, Cat. **— bhāryā,** f. the wife of a hero, L. **— bhāva,** m. heroic nature, heroism, Veṇis. **— bhukti,** f. N. of a place, Cat. (prob. for *tīra-bhukti*). **— bhuja,** m. N. of two kings, Kathās. **— bhūpati,** m. N. of a king of Vijaya-nagara (patron of Cauṇḍappâcārya), Cat. **— mati,** f. N. of a woman, HPariś. **— matsya,** m. pl. N. of a people, R. **— maya,** mf(*ī*)n. (with Tāntrikas) relating or belonging to an initiated person, L. **— mardana,** m. N. of a Dānava, Hariv. **— mardanaka,** w. r. for *mardalaka.* **— mardala** or °**laka,** m. a war-drum, L. **— malla,** m. N. of a man, Cat. **— mahêśvara,** m. (with *ācārya*) N. of an author, ib.; °*râcāra-saṃgraha,* m., °*rīya* and °*rīya-tantra,* n. N. of wks. **— māṇikya,** m. N. of a king, Prasannar. **— mātṛi,** f. the mother of a male child or of a hero, MBh.; BhP. **— mānin,** mfn. thinking one's self a hero, Kathās.; m. N. of a hero, Vcar. **— mārga,** m. the course or career of a hero, MBh.; Hariv. **— māhendra-kāṇḍa,** n. N. of wk. **— mitrôdaya,** m. N. of a short Comm. on the Mitâksharā, IW. 304. **— miśra,** m. N. of the author of the Vīra-mitrôdaya (commonly called Mitra-miśra), Cat. **— mukunda-deva,** m. N. of a king of Utkala (the patron of Mārkaṇḍeya-kavîndra), ib. **— mudrikā,** f. an ornament or ring worn on the middle toe, W. **— m-manya,** mfn. = *vīra-manya,* Bālar., Prasannar. **— yoga-vaha,** mfn. promoting men or heroes, MBh. xiii, 6526. **— yoga-saha,** mfn. resisting men or h°s, ib. (B.) **— rajas,** n. red lead, minium (= *sindūra*), L. **— ratha,** m. N. of a king, VP. **— rasa,** m. the Rasa of heroism (see *rasa*), MW. **— rāghava,** m. N. of various authors and teachers (also with *ācārya* and *śāstrin*), Cat.; *-stava,* m. N. of wk.; °*vīya,* n. N. of a poem (abridgment of the Rāmâyaṇa). **— reṇu,** m. N. of Bhīma-sena, L. **— lalita,** n. a hero's natural way of acting, VarBṛS.; N. of a metre, ib. **— loka,** m. 'hero-world,' Indra's heaven, MBh.; R.; pl. brave warriors or champions, heroes, MBh. **— vakshaṇa** (*vīrá-*), mfn. strengthening or refreshing heroes, RV. **— vat** (*vīrá-*), mfn. abounding in men or heroes, having followers or sons, RV.; consisting in men (as wealth or property), ib.; manly, heroic, ib.; (*atī*), f. a woman whose husband is living, BhP.; a partic. fragrant plant (= *māṉsa-rohiṇī*), Bhpr.; N. of a river, MBh.; of a woman, Kathās.; n. wealth consisting in men or sons, RV. **— vatsā,** f. the mother of a hero, L. **— vara,** m. 'best of heroes,' N. of various men, Kathās.; Hit.; *-pratāpa,* m. N. of a king, Cat. **— varman,** m. N. of various men, Inscr. **— váh** (strong form *vā́h*), mfn. conveying men, RV. **— vākya,** n. a heroic word, MārkP.; *-maya,* mf(*ī*)n. consisting in heroic words, Kathās. **— vāda,** m. heroic fame, glory, Mcar. **— vāmana,** m. N. of an author, Cat. **— vikrama,** m. (in music) a kind of measure, Saṃgīt.; N. of a king, Hit. **— vijaya,** m. N. of a drama. **— vid,** mfn. procuring men or heroes, AV. **— viplāvaka,** m. 'disturber of the sacrificial fire,' a Brāhman who performs oblations with money procured from the lowest or Śūdra caste, L. **— viruda,** N. of a kind of artificial verse, L. (cf. *śūra-śloka*). **— vṛiksha,** m. the marking-nut plant, Semecarpus Anacardium, Bhpr.; Pentaptera or Terminalia Arunja, L.; a sort of grain, Andropogon or Holcus Sorghum, L. **— vṛinda-bhaṭṭa,** m. N. of a medical author, Cat. **— vetasa,** m. Rumex Vesicarius, L. **— vyūha,** m. an heroic or bold military array, R. **— vrata,** mfn. acting like a man, adhering to one's purpose, BhP.; m. N. of a man (son of Madhu and Sumanas), ib.; n. heroism, Bālar.; *-caryā,* f. heroic duty or deed, ib. **— śaṅku,** m. an arrow, L. **— śaya,** m. (BhP.), **-śayana,** n. (MBh.) the couch of a dead or wounded hero (formed of arrows). **— śayyā,** f. id., MBh.; Rājat.; BhP.; a partic. posture, MBh. (cf. *vīra-sthāna*). **— śarman,** m. N. of a warrior, Kathās. **— śāka,** m. a kind of pot-herb, L. **— śāyin,** mfn. lying as a dead or wounded warrior on a couch of arrows (cf. *-śaya* &c.), MBh. **— śushma** (*vīrá-*), mfn. having heroic strength or courage, RV. **— śekhara,** m. N. of a Vidyā-dhara, Daś. **— śaiva,** m. pl. a partic. Śaiva sect, W.; N. of a wk. by Appaya Dīkshita; *-tattva-vivaraṇa,* n., *-dīkshā-vidhāna,* n., *-purāṇa,* n., *-pradīpikā,* f., *-liṅgârcana-vidhi,* m., *-siddhânta,* m., *-siddhânta-śikhāmaṇi,* m.; °*vâgama,* m., °*vâcāra-pradīpikā,* f., °*vânanda-candrikā,* f., °*vâmṛita-purāṇa,* n., °*vôtkarsha-pradīpa,* m. N. of wks. **— śrī,** f. (in music) a kind of composition, Saṃgīt. **— śreshṭha,** m. a matchless hero, MBh. **— samanvita,** mfn. attended or accompanied by heroes. **— sarasvatī,** m. N. of a poet, Cat. **— siṉha,** m. N. of various kings and authors, Cat.; *-deva,* m. N. of the patron of Mitra-miśra, ib.; *-mitrôdaye saṃskāra-prakaraṇa,* n., *-śivêndra-pūjā-kārikā,* f.; °*hâvaloka,* m. (or °*kana,* n.) N. of wks. **— sū,** f. 'hero-bearing,' the mother of a hero (*-tva,* n.), RV. &c. &c.; the mother of a male child, L. **— sena,** m. 'having an army of heroes,' N. of a Dānava, Kathās.; of a king of Nishadha (father of Nala), MBh.; Kāv. &c.; of a king of Siṉhala, Kathās.; of a king of Murala, Daś.; of a king of Kānyakubja, Hit.; of a k° of Kaliṅga (the murderer of his brother), Vās., Introd.; of a general of Agni-mitra, Mālav.; of a son of Vigatâśoka, Buddh.; of an author, Cat.; n. N. of a partic. plant (= *āruka*), L.; *-ja* or *-suta,* m. 'son of Vīra-sena,' N. of Nala (the hero of several well-known poems, e.g. the Nalôpâkhyāna, Naishadha, Nalôdaya), MBh.; Kāv. &c. **— sainya,** n. garlic, W. **— soma,** m. N. of the author of the Hasti-vaidyaka, Cat. (others call him Vīra-sena). **— skandha,** m. 'having powerful shoulders,' a buffalo, W. **— sthá,** mfn. abiding with a man, MaitrS. **— sthāna,** n. place or condition of a hero, ShaḍvBr.; a partic. posture (practised by ascetics), MBh. (cf. *vīrâsana*); N. of a place sacred to Śiva, MBh. **— sthāyin,** mfn. practising the Vīra-sthāna posture, MBh. **— snākā** (?), f. a stand for books &c. made of reeds or cane, L. **— svāmin,** m. N. of a Dānava, Kathās.; (with *bhaṭṭa*) of the father of Medhâtithi, Cat. **— haṇa,** mf(*ī*)n. hero-killing, MW. (cf. *-han*). **— hatyā,** f. the killing of a man, murder of a son, Mn. xi, 41. **— hán,** mf(*ghnī* or *haṇī*)n. slaying men or enemies, TS.; Br.; MBh.; R.; m. destroyer of sacrificial fire, a Brāhman who has suffered his sacred domestic fire to become extinct (either from carelessness, impiety, or absence), Vas.; N. of Vishṇu, MW. **— hari-pralāpa,** m. N. of a poem. **— hotra,** m. pl. N. of a people, MārkP. **Vîrâkshara-mālā-viruda,** n. N. of an artificial stanza in the Panegyric called Virudâvalī (in which the qualities of the hero are enumerated singly in alphabetical order), Cat. **Vîrâkhya,** m. Guilandina Bonduc, L. **Vîrâgama,** n. (?) N. of wk. **Vîrâcārya,** m. N. of an author, Gaṇar. **Vîrâdhvan,** m. = *vīra-mārga,* MBh.; an heroic death, VP. **Vîrânanda,** m. N. of a drama. **Vīrā-pura,** n. N. of a town, Cat. **Vîrâmla,** m. a kind of dock or sorrel (= *amla-vetasa*), L. **Vîrâruka,** n. a medicinal plant (= *āruka*), L. **Vîrâśaṉsana,** n. 'place wished for by heroes,' the post of danger in battle, L.; a field of battle, Śiś. xix, 79 (v. l. *vairâś°*); keeping watch, W.; a forlorn hope, MW. **Vîrâshṭaka,** m. 'consisting of eight men,' N. of one of Skanda's attendants, MBh. **Vîrâsana,** n. 'hero-sitting,' W.; sleeping out in the open air, the station of a guard or sentinel, BhP., Sch.; standing on an elevated spot (= *ūrdhvâvasthāna*), ib.; a bivouac, W.; a partic. sitting posture practised by ascetics (squatting on the thighs, the lower legs being crossed over each other, = *paryaṅka,* q. v.; cf. also 1. *āsana,* p. 159), Mn.; MBh. &c.; a field of battle, W.; kneeling on one knee, W. **Vîrêndra,** m. a chief of heroes, Kathās.; (*ī*), f. N. of a Yoginī, Inscr. **Vîrêśa,** m. 'chief of heroes,' N. of Śiva or Vīra-bhadra, L.; one who is emancipated in a certain degree, Sarvad.; n. a Liṅga of Śiva Vīrêśa, L. **Vîrêśvara,** m. 'chief of heroes,' N. of Śiva or Vīra-bhadra, Kāśīkh.; N. of various authors &c. (also with *bhaṭṭa, paṇḍita, ṭhakkura, dīkshita, maudgalya* &c.), Cat.; any great hero, W.; *-liṅga,* n. N. of a sacred Liṅga (= *vīrêśa,* n.); *-sūnu,* m. N. of an author, Cat.; *-stotra,* n. N. of a Stotra, ib.; °*rânanda,* m. N. of an author, ib. **Vîrôjjha,** m. a Brāhman who omits to offer burnt offerings or neglects his sacrificial fire, L. **Vîrôpajīvaka,** m. 'subsisting by a sacrificial fire,' a Brāhman who claims alms under pretence of maintaining a sacrificial fire, L.

Vīraká, m. a little man, manikin, RV. viii, 91, 2; a pitiable hero, Bālar. ix, ½; Nerium Odorum, L.; N. of one of the seven sages under Manu Cākshusha, BhP.; of a police-master, Mṛicch.; (pl.) of a people, MBh.; (*ikā*), f. N. of a wife of Harsha, Cat.

Vīraṇa, m. N. of a Prajā-pati (father of Vīraṇī or Asiknī), MBh.; Hariv.; of a teacher, Cat. (prob. w. r. for *vīraṇin*); (*ī*), f. a side-glance, leer, W.; a deep place, ib.; N. of a daughter of Vīraṇa and mother of Cākshusha, Hariv.; = n., L.; n. a fragrant grass, Andropogon Muricatus, MBh. **— stamba** or **-stambaka,** m. a tuft or bunch of (fragrant) grass, ib.

Vīraṇaka, m. (g. *ṛiśyâdi*) N. of a serpent-demon, MBh.

Vīraṇin, m. N. of a teacher, Cat.

Vīrayā́, ind. (instr.) with heroism, courageously, boldly, RV.

Vīrayú, mfn. heroic, valiant, bold, ib.

Vīrāya, Nom. Ā. °*yate,* to act like a hero, show heroism, Uttarar. (°*yita,* n. impers.)

Vīriṇa, m. n. (cf. *bīriṇa*) Andropogon Muricatus, ŚBr.; GṛŚrS.; (*iṇī*), f., see s. v. **— tūla,** n. a tuft of A° M°, Kauś. **— miśrá,** mfn. mixed with A° M°, ŚBr. **— vat** (in *karshū-vīriṇa-vat,* mfn. furnished with furrows or trenches and with the V° plant), KātyŚr.

Vīriṇī, f. a mother of sons, RV. x, 86, 9; N. of a wife of Daksha (also called Asiknī, daughter of Vīraṇa and mother of a thousand sons; cf. *vīraṇī*), MBh.; w. r. for *īriṇī,* MatsyaP.

Vīréṇya, mfn. manly, heroic, RV.

Vīryà, n. (ifc. f. *ā*) manliness, valour, strength, power, energy, RV. &c. &c.; heroism, heroic deed, ib.; manly vigour, virility, semen virile, MBh.; Kāv. &c.; efficacy (of medicine), Kum.; Kir.; poison, BhP.; splendour, lustre, W.; dignity, consequence, ib.; (*ā*), f. vigour, energy, virility, L.; N. of a serpent-maid, Kāraṇḍ. **— kara,** m. 'giving strength,' marrow, L. **— kāma,** mfn. wishing manly vigour or virility, AitBr.; BhP. **— kṛít,** mfn. performing manly deeds, VS.; TBr. **— kṛita** (*vīrya-*), mfn. performed with energy, TBr. (Sch.) **— ga,** mfn. taking up a position which gives (a planet) great power or influence, VarBṛS. **— candra,** m. N. of the father of Vīrā (wife of Karaṃ-dhama), MārkP. **— ja,** mfn. 'produced from manliness,' a son, BhP. **— tama,** mfn. most potent or powerful or effective, ib. **— dhara,** m. pl. 'bearing strength,' N. of the Kshatriyas in Plaksha-dvīpa, ib. **— paṇa,** mf(*ā*)n, purchased by heroism, ib. **— parihāṇi,** f. (with Buddhists) loss or want of energy, Dharmas. 79. **— pāramitā,** f. (with Buddhists) highest degree of fortitude or energy (one of the 6 perfections), Kāraṇḍ.; Dharmas. 17 (MWB. 128). **— prapāta,** m. discharge of semen virile, VP. **— pravāda,** n. N. of a Pūrva of the Jainas, L. **— bhadra,** m. N. of a man, Buddh. **— matta,** mfn. intoxicated by power, MBh. **— mitra,** m. N. of a poet, Cat. **— vat** (*vīryà-*), mfn. possessing vigour or might, strong, powerful, efficacious, victorious, AV. &c. &c.; requiring strength or power, ChUp.; m. N. of a divine being reckoned among the Viśve Devāḥ, MBh.; of a son of the tenth Manu, Hariv.; MārkP.; (*atī*), f. N. of one of the Mātṛis attendant on Skanda, MBh.; *-tama,* mfn. most powerful or efficacious, ŚBr.; *-tara,* mfn. more p° or eff°, AV.; ChUp. (°*ra-tva,* n., Śaṃk.); *-tā,* f. (GopBr.), *-tva,* n. (MBh.) power, strength, efficacy. **— vāhin,** mfn. bearing or producing seed, ŚārṅgS. **— vibhūti,** f. manifestation of power or strength, Kum. **— virahita,** mfn. devoid of prowess or vigour, W. **— viśishṭa,** mfn. distinguished by courage or vigour, ib. **— vṛiddhi-kara,** mfn. causing an increase of virile energy; n. an aphrodisiac, L. **— śālin,** mfn. possessing vigour or heroism, strong, heroic, MBh. **— śulka,** n. valour or heroism (reckoned) as purchase-money, Ragh.; BhP.; mf(*ā*)n. having prowess as its price, purchased by valour, MBh.; R. **— śṛiṅga,**

n. (met.) the horn of strength, Ragh. **-sattva-vat,** mfn. possessed of valour and courage, MBh. **-sampanna,** mfn. possessed of power or strength, MBh. **-saha,** m. N. of a son of Saudāsa, R. **-sena,** m. N. of a man, Buddh. **-hāni,** f. loss of vigour or virile energy, impotence, W. **-hārin,** m. 'stealing vigour,' N. of an evil demon, MārkP. **-hīna,** mfn. deprived of valour, cowardly, W.; seedless, ib. **Vīryâdhāna,** n. 'depositing of manly essence,' impregnation, Pañcar. **Vīryânvita,** mfn. possessed of strength, powerful, VarBṛS. **Vīryā-vat,** mfn. = *vīryà-vat,* TS.; TBr.; Kāṭh. **Vīryâvadāna,** n. effecting anything by prowess, W.; pl. valour and achievements, MW. **Vīryâvadhūta,** mfn. overcome or surpassed in prowess, W.

वीराणक *vīrāṇaka* (Inscr.) or *vīrānaka* (Rājat.), N. of a place.

वीरुध् *vī-rúdh,* f. (once in MBh. m.; fr. 3. *vi* + √1. *rudh* = *ruh,* cf. *vi-sruh*) a plant, herb (esp. a creeping plant or a low shrub), RV. &c. &c. (*vīrúdhām pátiḥ,* 'lord of plants,' in RV. applied to Soma, in MBh. to the moon); a branch, shoot, W.; a plant which grows again after being cut, MW.; the snare or noose of Indra, PārGṛ.

Ví-rudha, n. (AV.), **vī-rudhā,** f. (MārkP.), **vī-rudhi,** (prob.) f. (VarBṛS.) a plant, herb, shrub.

वीर्त्सा *vīrtsā́,* f. (fr. *vi* + *īrts,* Des. of √*ṛidh*) the wish to frustrate, want of success, failure, AV.

वीळु *vīḷu.* See *vīḍu.*

वीलक *vīlaka,* m. the son of a Śūdra and a Gholī, L.

वीवध *vī-vadha, vī-vadhika, vī-vidha, vī-vṛita* = *vi-vadha* &c., qq. vv.

वीवाह *vī-vāha,* m. = *vi-vāha,* taking a wife, marriage ('with,' *saha*), HPariś.; Pañcad.

वीश 1. *vīśa,* m. a kind of weight (= 20 Palas = ½ Tulā), Hcat.

वीश 2. *vīśa.* See *pád-vīśa.*

वीष् 1. *vīsh* (*vi-√ish*), P. *vīshati,* to go in various directions, spread, extend, Kāṭh.

Vīshita, mfn. spread, extended, ib.

वीष् 2. *vīsh* (*vi-√3. ish*), P. *vīcchati,* to seek for, TBr.

वीस *vīsa,* n. a kind of dance, Saṃgīt.

वीसर्प *vī-sarpa,* m. = *vi-s°,* Car.

वीसलदेव *vīsala-deva,* m. N. of a king, Inscr.

वीहार *vī-hāra,* m. = *vi-h°,* a temple, sanctuary, (esp.) a Jaina or Buddhist convent or temple, W.

वुक *vuka.* See *buka.*

वुङ्ग् *vuṅg.* See √*buṅg.*

वुड् *vuḍ,* cf. √*vruḍ.*

Vuḍita, mfn. submersed, submerged, KātyŚr., Sch.

वुण्ट् *vuṇṭ* (= √*viṇṭ*), cl. 10. P. *vuṇṭayati,* 'to hurt, kill,' or 'to perish,' Dhātup. xxxii, 116.

वुन्ध् *vundh, vus* &c. See √*bundh, bus.*

वुह्ना *vuhnā.* See *buhnā.*

वूर्ण *vūrṇa, vūrya.* See under √2. *vṛi.*

वूवशर्मन् *vūva-śarman.* See *būba-ś°.*

वूस् *vūs* (only in *vūsyet,* said to be = *pṛithak kuryāt*), Priy.

वृ 1. *vṛi,* cl. 5. 9. 1. P. Ā. (Dhātup. xxvii, 8; xxxi, 16, 20; xxxiv, 8) *vṛiṇóti, vṛiṇuté; vṛiṇā́ti, vṛiṇīte; várati, várate* (mostly cl. 5 and with the prep. *apa* or *vi;* of cl. 9. only *avṛiṇīdhvam,* AV. vi, 7, 3; cl. 1. only in RV. [cf. also √*ūrṇu*]; pf. *vavā́ra, vavré,* RV. &c. &c. [2. sg. *vavártha,* RV.; *vavaritha, vavrima* &c., Gr.; p. *vavrivás,* gen. *vavavrúshas,* RV.]; aor. *ávar* or *ā́var, avṛita,* RV. [1. sg. *vam,* 2. du. *vartam,* 3. pl. *avran,* p. Ā. *vrāṇá,* q. v., Impv. *vṛidhi,* ib.]; *avārīt,* Br.; *avarīshṭa,* Gr.; Subj. *varshathas,* RV.; Pot. *vriyāt, vūryāt, varishīshṭa,* Gr.; fut. *varītā, varīshyati,* ib.; inf. *vartum,* MBh., *varitum,* Bhaṭṭ., *varītum,* Sāh.; ind. p. *vṛitvā́,* RV.; AV.; Br.; *vṛitvī́,* RV.; *vṛitvā́ya,* Br.; *-vṛítya,* AV.), to cover, screen, veil, conceal, hide, surround, obstruct, RV. &c. &c.; to close (a door), AitBr.; to ward off, check, keep back, prevent, hinder, restrain, RV.; AV.; Bhaṭṭ.: Pass. *vriyate* (aor. *ávāri*), to be covered or surrounded or obstructed or hindered, RV.; MBh.: Caus. *vāráyati, °te* (aor. *avīvarat, ávīvarata,* AV.; *ávāvarīt,* RV.; Pass. *vāryate,* MBh. &c.), to cover, conceal, hide, keep back, hold captive, RV. &c. &c.; to stop, check, restrain, suppress, hinder, prevent from (abl. or inf.; rarely two acc.), MBh.; Kāv. &c.; to exclude, Siddh.; to prohibit, forbid, MBh.; to withhold, R.; Kathās. &c.: Desid. of Caus. *vivārayishate,* Br.: Desid. *vivarīshati, vuvūrshati, °te,* Gr.: Intens. *vevrīyate, vovūryate, varvarti,* ib. [Cf. Goth. *warjan;* Germ. *wehren, Wehr;* Eng. *weir.*]

1. **Vara, varaka, varaṇa** &c. See p. 921, col. 1.

Vārita, mfn. (fr. Caus.) concealed, hidden, covered, surrounded, obstructed, MBh.; Kāv. &c.; prevented, prohibited, forbidden, Kathās.; Rājat.

1. **Vṛit** (ifc.; for 2. see p. 1009, col. 2) surrounding, enclosing, obstructing (see *arṇo-* and *nadī-vṛit*); a troop of followers or soldiers, army, host, RV.

1. **Vṛitá,** mfn. concealed, screened, hidden, enveloped, surrounded by, covered with (instr. or comp.), RV. &c. &c.; stopped, checked, held back, pent up (as rivers), RV.; filled or endowed or provided or affected with (instr. or comp.), Mn.; MBh. &c. **-pattrā,** f. a kind of plant, L. (prob. w. r. for *vṛitta-p°*). **Vṛitârcis,** f. night, L.

Vṛitam-cayá, mfn. (acc. of *vṛit* + *c°*) collecting an army (said of Indra), RV.

1. **Vṛiti,** f. (for 2. see col. 3) surrounding, covering, W.; a hedge, fence, an enclosed piece of ground or place enclosed for partic. cultivation (esp. that of the Piper Betel, which in many parts of India is surrounded and screened by mats), Mn.; MBh. &c. **-druma,** m. a boundary tree, L. **-dvāra,** n. a gate in a hedge, Pañcat. **-bhaṅga,** m. a breach or fissure in a hedge, ib. **-ṃ-kara,** m. 'hedge-forming,' Flacourtia Sapida, L. **-mārga,** m. a fenced road, L.

1. **Vṛitya,** mfn. (for 2. see p. 1010, col. 2) to be surrounded or encompassed, Pāṇ. iii, 1, 109.

Vṛitrá, m. (only once in TS.) or n. (mostly in pl.) 'coverer, investor, restrainer,' an enemy, foe, hostile host, RV.; TS.; m. N. of the Vedic personification of an imaginary malignant influence or demon of darkness and drought (supposed to take possession of the clouds, causing them to obstruct the clearness of the sky and keep back the waters; Indra is represented as battling with this evil influence in the pent up clouds poetically pictured as mountains or castles which are shattered by his thunderbolt and made to open their receptacles [cf. esp. RV. i, 31]; as a Dānava, Vṛitra is a son of Tvashṭṛi, or of Danu, q. v., and is often identified with Ahi, the serpent of the sky, and associated with other evil spirits, such as Śushṇa, Namuci, Pipru, Sambara, Uraṇa, whose malignant influences are generally exercised in producing darkness or drought), RV. &c. &c.; a thunder-cloud, RV. iv, 10, 5 (cf. Naigh. i, 10); darkness, L.; a wheel, L.; a mountain, L.; N. of a partic. mountain, L.; a stone, KātyŚr., Sch.; N. of Indra (?), L.; n. wealth (= *dhana*) L. (v. l. *vitta*); sound, noise (= *dhvani*), L. **-khādá,** mfn. consuming or destroying (others 'plaguing,' fr. √*khid*) Vṛitra, RV.; m. 'devourer of enemies,' N. of Bṛihas-pati, MW. **-ghnī,** see *-hán.* **-tára,** m. a worse V°, RV. **-túr,** m. conquering enemies or V°, victorious, RV.; TS. &c. **-tū́r,** mfn. (dat. *tū́re*), id., MaitrS. **-tūrya,** n. conquest of enemies or V°, battle, victory, RV. **-tvá,** n. the state or condition of being V°, V°-ship, TS. **-druh,** m. 'V°'s foe,' N. of Indra, Mcar. **-dvish** (L.), **-nāśana** (Hariv.), m. id. **-putrā** (*vṛitrá-*), f. 'having V° as son,' V°'s mother, RV. **-bhojana,** m. a kind of pot-herb (commonly called Samaṭh; described by some as a kind of cucumber, = *gandīra*), L. **-ripu,** m. = *-druh,* VP. **-vadha,** m. the killing of V°, Nir.; Hariv. (also N. of a drama and of partic. chapters of the R. and the PadmaP.) **-vidvish** (Śiś.), **-vairin** (Kathās.), m. = *-druh.* **-śaṅkú,** m. a stone post, ŚBr. (Sch. on KātyŚr.) **-śatru,** m. = *-druh,* MBh.; R. &c. **-há,** mfn. slaying enemies, victorious, RV. **-hátya,** n. the slaying of V° or of enemies, victorious fight, RV.; ŚBr.; ŚāṅkhŚr.; (*ā*), f. id., BhP. **-hatha** (*vṛitrá-*), m. id., RV. iii, 16, 1. **-hán,** mf(*ghnī*)n. killing enemies or V°, victorious, RV. &c. &c. (mostly applied to Indra, but also to Agni and even to Sarasvatī); (*ghnī*), f. N. of a river, MārkP.; (*-hán*)*-tama,* mfn. most victorious, bestowing abundant victory, RV.; AV.; ŚāṅkhŚr. **-hantṛi,** m. 'slayer of V°,' N. of Indra, MBh. **-hāya,** Nom. (fr. *-ha* or *-han*) Ā. *°yate,* to act like Indra, Pat. **Vṛitrâri,** m. 'enemy of Vṛitra,' N. of Indra, Kathās.

Vrāṇá, mfn. held back, pent up (as rivers), RV.

वृ 2. *vṛi,* cl. 5. 9. P. Ā. (Dhātup. xxvii, 8; xxxi, 16, 20) *vṛiṇoti, vṛiṇute; vṛiṇā́ti,* (mostly) *vṛiṇīté* (in RV. also *váras, °rat, °ranta,* but these may be Subj. aor.; pf. *vavāra,* Bhaṭṭ.; *vavre,* RV. [2. sg. *vavṛishé,* 1. pl. *vavṛimáhe*] &c. &c.; aor. *avri, avṛita,* RV. [Pot. *vurīta,* p. *urāṇá*] &c. &c.; *avṛishi, °shata,* AV.; Br. [2. pl. *avṛiḍhvam*], Up.; *avarīshṭa,* Gr.; Prec. *varishīshṭa,* ib.; fut. *varītā,* ib.; *varishyate,* Br.; *varīshyate,* Gr.; inf. *varītum,* Bhaṭṭ.; Rājat.; *varitum,* Gr.; ind. p. *varitvā* or *vṛitvā,* GṛŚrS. &c.; *varītvā,* Gr.), to choose, select, choose for one's self, choose as (*-arthe* or acc. of pers.) or for (*-artham* or dat., loc., instr. of thing), RV. &c. &c.; to choose in marriage, woo, MBh.; Kāv. &c.; to ask a person (acc.) for (acc.) or on behalf of (*kṛite*), R.; Kathās.; to solicit anything (acc.) from (abl. or *-tas*), Kāv.; Pur.; to ask or request that (Pot. with or without *iti*), R.; MBh.; to like better than, prefer to (abl., rarely instr.), RV.; AitBr.; MBh.; R.; to like, love (as opp. to 'hate'), MBh. v, 4149; to choose or pick out a person (for a boon), grant (a boon) to (acc.), Rājat. iii, 421: Caus. (Dhātup. xxxv, 2) *varayati, °te* (ep. also *vārayati;* Pass. *varyáte,* Br.); to choose, choose for one's self, choose as (acc. of pers.) or for (*-artham,* dat. or loc. of thing), ask or sue for (acc.) or on behalf of (dat. or *-arthe*), choose as a wife (acc. with or without *patnīm, dārān,* or *patnyartham*), Br.; MBh.; Kāv. &c.; to like, love well, R. [Cf. Lat. *velle;* Slav. *voliti;* Got. *wiljian;* Germ. *wollan, wollen, Wahl, wohl;* Angl. Sax. *willan;* Eng. *will.*]

2. **Vara, varaka** &c. See p. 922, col. 1, and p. 923.

Vūrṇa, mfn. chosen, selected, MW.

Vūrya, n. 'choice,' in *hotṛi-vūrya,* q. v.

2. **Vṛitá,** mfn. chosen, selected, preferred, loved, liked, asked in marriage &c., RV. &c. &c.; n. a treasure, wealth (= *dhana*), L. **-kshaya,** m. a preferred abode, Nir. xii, 29 (to explain *vṛiksha*).

2. **Vṛiti,** f. selecting, choosing, a choice or boon, L. **-vallabha,** m. N. of a drama.

Vṛithak, ind. (prob.) = *vṛithā,* RV. viii, 43, 4; 5 (Sāy. = *pṛithak*).

Vṛithā, ind. (prob. connected with √2. *vṛi*) at will, at pleasure, at random, easily, lightly, wantonly, frivolously, RV.; Br.; Gobh.; Mn.; Yājñ.; MBh.; in vain, vainly, uselessly, fruitlessly, idly, TBr. &c. &c. (with √*kṛi,* 'to make useless,' disappoint, frustrate; with √*bhū,* 'to be useless,' be disappointed or frustrated); wrongly, falsely, incorrectly, unduly, MBh., Kāv. &c. **-kathā,** f. idle talk, nonsense, W. **-karman,** n. an action done uselessly or for pleasure, non-religious act, Āpast. **-kāra** (*°thâk°*), m. a false form, empty show, Pañcat. i, 62 (others 'one whose form is vain or illusory'). **-kula-samācāra,** mfn. one whose family and practices (or 'family-practices') are idle or low, MBh. **-kṛisara-saṃyāva,** m. a kind of food, (consisting of wheat-flour, rice and sesamum and prepared for no religious purpose), Mn. v, 7. **-°gni** (*°thâgni*), m. common fire, any fire, AV. Prâyaśc. **-°ghāta** (*°thâgh°*), m. striking uselessly, killing unnecessarily, W. **-°cāra** (*°thâc°*), mfn. frivolous or lawless in conduct, MBh. **-cheda,** m. useless or frivolous cutting, Yājñ. **-janman,** n. useless or unprofitable birth, MW. **-jāta,** mfn. born in vain (i.e. 'one who neglects the prescribed rites'), Mn. v, 89. **-°ṭyā** (*°thâṭyā*), f. strolling about in an idle manner, travelling for pleasure (regarded as a vice in a king), Mn. vii, 47. **-°tmāyāsa** (*°thâtm°*), m. useless self-mortification, Nāg. **-tva,** n. fruitlessness, futility, Sāh. **-dāna,** n. a useless or improper gift (as a gift promised to courtesans, wrestlers &c.; accord. to some there are 16 kinds of these gifts), Mn. viii, 139. **-°nna** (*°thânna*), n. food for one's own use only, Kauś.; Gaut. **-pakva,** mfn. cooked at random (i.e. only for one's own use), Gobh. **-palita,** mfn. grown gray in vain, Śiś. (cf. *-vṛiddha*). **-paśu-ghna,** mfn. one who kills cattle wrongly or unnecessarily (i. e. not for sacrifice), Mn. v, 38. — **prajā**, f. a woman who has borne children in vain, MārkP. — **pratijña**, mfn. one who makes a promise rashly, MW. — **bhoga**, mfn. enjoying in vain or to no purpose, ib. — **mati**, mfn. foolish-minded, wrong-minded, MBh. — **māṅsa**, n. 'flesh taken at random' or 'useless flesh' (i.e. flesh not destined for the gods or Pitṛis but for one's own use only; the eater of such flesh is said to be born as a demon), ŚBr.; Mn.; Gaut. &c.; m. one who eats 'useless' flesh, MW. — **°rtavā** (°*thârt*°), f. 'one whose menstrual discharge is fruitless,' a barren woman, Gal. — **°lambha** (°*thâl*°), m. cutting or plucking unnecessarily, Mn. xi, 144. — **liṅga**, mf(*ā*)n. having no true cause, unsubstantiated, MBh. — **liṅgin**, mfn. one who wears a sectarian mark without any right to it, Vishṇ. — **vāc**, f. frivolous or untrue speech, AitĀr.; Gobh. — **vādin**, mfn. speaking falsely or untruly, Pañcad. — **vṛiddha**, mfn. grown old in vain (i. e. without growing wise), Bālar. (cf. *-palita*). — **vrata**, n. a false religious observance, MBh.; mfn. one who performs false r° ob°s, Hariv. — **śrama**, m. vain exertion, useless labour, Pañcat. — **sháh** (strong *sháh*), mfn. one who easily overcomes or conquers, RV. — **saṃkara-jāta**, mfn. born in vain through the mixture of different castes (and hence neglectful in the performance of duties), MW. — **suta**, mfn. pressed out in vain, Nir. xi, 4. **Vṛithôkta**, mfn. spoken in vain, MārkP. **Vṛithôtpanna**, mfn. born or produced in vain, Mn. ix, 147. **Vṛithôdaká**, n. pl. water flowing at random (not in a channel), ŚBr. **Vṛithôdyama**, mfn. exerting one's self in vain, BhP.

वृंह् **vṛiṅh**, *vṛiṅhana* &c. See √2. *bṛih*.

वृक् **vṛik** (prob. artificial), cl. 1. Ā. *varkate*, to take, seize, Dhātup. iv, 18.

Vṛika, m. (prob. 'the tearer' connected with √*vrasc*, cf. *vṛikṇa*), a wolf, RV. &c. &c. (L. also 'a dog; a jackal; a crow; an owl; a thief; a Kshatriya'); a plough, RV. i, 117, 21; viii, 22, 6; a thunderbolt, Naigh. ii, 20; the moon, Nir. v, 20; the sun, ib. 21; a kind of plant (= *baka*), L.; the resin of Pinus Longifolia, L.; N. of an Asura, BhP.; of a son of Kṛishṇa, ib.; of a king, MBh.; of a son of Ruruka (or Bharuka), Hariv.; BhP.; of a son of Pṛithu, BhP.; of a son of Śūra, ib.; of a son of Vatsaka, ib.; (pl.) N. of a people and a country (belonging to Madhya-deśa), MBh.; Pur. (cf. *vārkenya*); (*ā*), f. a kind of plant (= *ambashṭhā*), L.; (*ī*), f. a she-wolf, RV. &c. &c.; a female jackal, Nir. v, 21; Clypea Hernandifolia, L. [Cf. Gk. λύκος; Lat. *lupus*; Slav. *vlŭkŭ*; Lith. *vìlkas*; Goth. *wulfs*; Germ. Eng. *wolf*.] — **karman**, mfn. acting like a wolf, wolfish, Veṇis.; m. N. of an Asura, Cat. — **khaṇḍa**, m. N. of a man (see *vārka-khaṇḍi*). — **garta**, m. or n. (?) N. of a place (°*tīya*, mfn.), Pāṇ. iv, 2, 137, Sch. — **grāha**, m. N. of a man, g. *revaty-ādi*. — **jambha**, m. N. of a man (see *vārka-j*°). — **tāt** or **-tāti** (*vṛiká-*), f. wolfishness, rapacity, RV. ii, 34, 9. — **tejas**, m. N. of a son of Ślishṭi and grandson of Dhruva, Hariv.; VP. — **daṅśa**, m. 'wolf-biter,' a dog, L. (v.l. for *mṛiga-d*°). — **dīpti**, m. N. of a son of Kṛishṇa, Hariv. — **deva**, m. N. of a son of Vasudeva, ib.; (*ā* or *ī*), f. N. of a wife of V° (daughter of Devaka), ib.; VP. — **dvaras** (*vṛ́ika-*), mfn., RV. ii, 30, 4 (= *saṃvṛita-dvāra*, Sāy.) — **dhūpa**, m. compounded perfume, L.; turpentine, L. — **dhūmaka**, m. a kind of plant, Car. — **dhūrta**, m. 'wolf-deceiver,' a jackal, W. — **dhūrtaka**, m. 'id.,' a bear, L.; a jackal, L. — **dhoraṇa**, m. a kind of animal, L. — **nirvṛiti**, m. N. of a son of Kṛishṇa, Hariv. — **prastha**, m. or n. (?) N. of a village, Veṇis. — **prêkshin**, mfn. looking at (anything) like a w°, MW. — **bandhu**, m. N. of a man, g. *revaty-ādi*. — **bhaya**, n. fear of or danger from wolves, Pāṇ. i, 2, 43, Sch. — **ratha**, m. N. of a brother of Karṇa, MBh. — **rūpya**, (prob.) N. of a place (see *vārka-r*°). — **lomán**, n. wolf's hair, ŚBr. — **vañcika**, m. N. of a man, g. *revaty-ādi*. — **vālā**, f. a piece of timber at the side of a door, L. — **sthala**, n. N. of a village, MBh.; (*ī*), f. N. of the town Māhishmatī, L. **Vṛikâkshī**, f. Ipomœa Turpethum, L. **Vṛikâjina**, m. 'wolf-skin,' N. of a man, Pāṇ. vi, 2, 165. **Vṛikâmlikā**, f. a kind of acid citron, L. **Vṛikârāti** or **vṛikâri**, m. 'wolf-enemy,' a dog, L. **Vṛikâvalupta**, n., Pāṇ. vi, 2, 145, Sch. **Vṛikâśva**, m. 'wolf-horse,' N. of a man (pl. his descendants), Saṃskārak.; v.l. for *vṛikâsya*, Hariv. **Vṛikâśvaki**, m. (perhaps w. r. for *vārk*°), N. of a man (pl. his descendants), Saṃskārak. **Vṛikâsura-vadha**, m. 'killing of the Asura Vṛika,' N. of a ch. of GaṇP. **Vṛikâsya**, m. 'wolf-mouthed,' N. of a son of Kṛishṇa, Hariv. (v.l. *vṛikâśva*). **Vṛikôdara**, m. 'wolf-bellied,' N. of Bhīma (the second son of Pāṇḍu, so called from his enormous appetite, cf. IW. 381), MBh.; BhP.; of Brahmā, W.; pl. a class of demons attendant on Śiva, ŚivaP.; *-maya*, mf(*ī*)n. (danger) arising from Bhīma, MBh.

Vṛikáti, m. a murderer, robber, RV. iv, 41, 4; N. of a son of Jīmūta, Hariv.; of a son of Kṛishṇa (?), ib.

Vṛikala, m. = (or w.r. for) *valkala*, a garment made of bark, Baudh.; N. of a son of Ślishṭi, MBh.; VP.; (*ā́*), f. a partic. intestine, ŚBr.; N. of a woman, g. *bāhv-ādi* (cf. *vārkali*, *vārkaleya*).

Vṛikāya, Nom. Ā. °*yate*, to resemble or act like a wolf, Car.

Vṛikāyú, mfn. wolfish, rapacious, murderous, RV.

वृक्क **vṛikká**, m. du. the kidneys, AV.; ŚBr.; GṛŚrS. &c. (*vṛ́ikya*, TS.; ĀpŚr.); sg. 'averter of disease' (?), RV. i, 187, 10 (*vyādher varjayitṛi*, Sāy.); (*ā*), f. = *bukkā*, the heart, L.

Vṛikkāvati (?), f. N. of a partic. verse, Vait.

वृक्ण **vṛikṇá**. See under √*vrasc*.

वृक्त **vṛiktá**, *vṛikti* &c. See under √*vṛij*, p. 1009, col. 1.

वृक्ष् **vṛiksh** (prob. artificial), cl. 1. Ā. *vṛikshate*, to select, accept, Dhātup. xvi, 3; to cover, ib.; to keep off, ib.

वृक्ष **vṛikshá**, m. (ifc. f. *ā*; prob. connected with √2. *bṛih*, 'to grow,' or with √1. *bṛih*, 'to root up,' or with √*vrasc*, as 'that which is felled') a tree, (esp.) any tree bearing visible flowers and fruit (see Mn. i, 47; but also applied to any tree and other plants, often = wood, see comp.), RV. &c. &c.; the trunk of a tree, RV. i, 130, 4; a coffin, AV. xviii, 2, 25; the staff of a bow, RV.; AV.; a frame (see comp.); Wrightia Antidysenterica, Suśr.; a stimulant, L. — **kanda**, m. the bulb of Batatas Paniculata, L. — **kukkuṭa**, m. 'tree-fowl,' a wild cock, L. — **keśa** (*vṛikshá-*), mfn. 'having trees for hair,' wooded (as a mountain), RV. — **khaṇḍa**, n. 'a party, i.e. number of trees,' a grove, Kāś. on Pāṇ. iv, 3, 38 (cf. *-shaṇḍa*). — **gulma**, m. pl. trees and shrubs, VarBṛS.; °*mâvṛita*, mfn. covered with trees and shrubs, Mn. vii, 192. — **gṛiha**, m. 'having a tree for a house,' a bird, L. — **ghaṭa**, m. N. of an Agra-hāra, Kathās. — **candra**, m. N. of a king, Buddh. — **cara**, mfn. going or living in trees; m. 'tree-goer,' a monkey, L. — **cikitsā-ropaṇâdi**, m. N. of a work. — **cūḍāmaṇika**, m. (prob.) a kind of animal (used to explain *pūti-ghāsa*), Suśr., Sch. — **cchāya**, n. the shade of many trees, a grove, L.; (*ā*), f. the shade of a tree, Hit. (accord. to L. 'the shade of a single tree or of two trees'). — **ja**, mf(*ā*)n. made of a tree, wooden, Hcat. — **jātīya**, mfn. belonging to the genus tree, MW. — **takshaká**, m. a wood-feller, R. — **tala**, n. the foot of a tree or the ground about it, W. — **taila**, n. tree oil, oil prepared from a tree, KātyŚr., Sch. — **traya**, n. three trees, Ml. — **tva**, n. the state or notion of 'tree,' Sarvad. — **da**, mfn. giving trees, MBh. — **dala**, n. the leaf of a tree, R. — **devatā**, f. a tree-divinity, dryad, Pañcat. — **dohada** (prob.), n. N. of wk. — **dhūpa** or **-dhūpaka**, m. 'tree-resin,' turpentine, L. — **nātha** or **-nāthaka**, m. 'lord of trees,' the Indian fig-tree, L. — **niryāsa**, m. the exudation of trees, gum, resin, Mn. v, 6. — **nivāsa**, m. dwelling or living in a tree, W. — **parṇa**, n. the leaf of a tree, R. — **pāka**, m. the Indian fig-tree, L. — **pāla**, m. a wood-keeper, R. — **puri**, f. N. of a town, Buddh. — **bandha**, m. a stanza shaped like a tree, IW. 456. — **bhakshā**, f. a kind of parasitical plant (= *vandāka*), L. — **bhavana**, n. 'tree-abode,' the hollow of a tree, L. — **bhid**, f. 'tree-splitter,' an axe, L. — **bhūmi**, f. the ground on which a tree grows, Kauś. — **bhedin**, m. 'tree-splitting,' a carpenter's chisel, hatchet, L. — **maya**, mf(*ī*)n. made of wood, wooden, Śāntik.; abounding with trees, consisting of trees, W. — **markaṭikā**, f. 'tree-monkey,' a squirrel, Bhpr. — **mārjāra**, m. a kind of animal, ib. — **mūla**, n. the root of a tree, Mn.; R.; *-tā*, f. lying or sleeping on roots of trees (as a hermit), Kām.; *-niketana*, mfn. dwelling at the roots of trees, MW. — **mūlika**, mfn. id. (with Buddhists one of the 12 Dhūta-guṇas or ascetic practices), Dharmas. 63. — **mṛid-bhū**, m. 'tree-earth-born,' a sort of cane or reed, Calamus Fascicularis or Rotang, L. — **yuddha**, n. a fight with trees (or branches, used as clubs), MW. — **rāj**, m. = *-nātha*, Yājñ., Sch. — **rāja**, m. N. of the Pārijāta tree, Hariv. — **ruhā**, f. 'tree-grower,' a parasitical plant whose roots attach themselves to another plant (as Cymbidium Thessaloides), Vanda Roxburghii &c.), L. — **ropaka**, m. a planter of trees, R. — **ropaṇa**, n. tree-planting, Cat. — **ropayitṛi**, m. = *-ropaka*, Kull. on Mn. iii, 163. — **ropin**, mf(*iṇī*)n. planting trees, MBh. — **vat**, m. 'abounding in trees,' a mountain, L. — **vāṭikā** or **-vāṭī**, f. a grove of trees or garden near the residence of a minister of state, L. — **vāsya-niketa**, m. N. of a Yaksha, MBh. — **śa**, m. (*śa* said to be fr. √*śī*, 'to sleep'), a lizard, a chameleon, L. — **śākhā**, f. the branch of a tree, Hit. — **śāyikā**, f. 'tree-residing,' a squirrel, Suśr. — **śūnya**, mfn. destitute of trees, Hariv. — **shaṇḍa**, m. = *-khaṇḍa*, R. — **saṃkaṭa**, n. a forest-thicket, Kām. — **sarpí**, f. (prob.) a female tree-serpent, AV. — **sāraka**, m. Phlomis Zeylanica, L. — **secana**, n. the watering of trees, Śak. — **stha**, **-sthāyin**, or **-sthita**, mfn. staying in or on a tree, MBh.; Kāv. &c. — **sneha**, m. = *-taila*, KātyŚr., Sch. **Vṛikshâgra**, n. the top of a tree, R. **Vṛikshâṅghri**, m. the foot or root of a tree, Hit. **Vṛikshâdana**, m. a carpenter's chisel or adze, hatchet, chopper &c., MBh.; the Indian fig-tree, L.; the Piyāl-tree, Buchanania Latifolia, L.; (*ī*), f. a parasitical plant (Vanda Roxburghii, Hedysarum Gangeticum &c.), L. **Vṛikshâdinī**, f. Vanda Roxburghii, L. **Vṛikshâdiruhaka**, °**rūḍha**, or **-rūḍhaka**, w. r. for *vṛikshâdhi-r*° &c. **Vṛikshâdi-vidyā**, f. the science of trees &c., botany, MW. **Vṛikshâdhirūḍhaka**, n. (cf. *vṛikshârūḍha*) a kind of embrace, Harav. **Vṛikshâdhirūḍhi**, f. id., Naish.; the growth or increase of a tree from the root upwards, ib.; the entwining (of a creeper) round a tree, L.; a kind of embrace, Naish. **Vṛikshâmaya**, m. 'tree-disease,' resin, lac, Bhpr. **Vṛikshâmla**, m. the hog-plum, Spondias Mangifera; n. the fruit of the tamarind used as an acid seasoning, Car. **Vṛikshâyurveda**, m. N. of a short treatise by Sura-pāla (on the planting and cultivation of trees) and of VarBṛS. lv. **Vṛikshârūḍha**, n. = *vṛikshâdhirūḍhaka*, Naish., Sch. **Vṛikshâropaka**, m. the planter of a tree, Mn. iii, 163. **Vṛikshâropaṇa**, n. the act of planting trees, W. **Vṛikshârohaṇa**, n. the climbing of a tree, GṛS. **Vṛikshârhā**, f. = *mahā-medā*, L. **Vṛikshâlaya**, m. = °*sha-gṛiha*, L. **Vṛikshâvāsa**, m. an ascetic, one who lives in the hollows of trees, W.; a bird, ib. **Vṛikshâśrayin**, m. 'tree-dweller,' a kind of small owl, L. **Vṛikshôttha**, mfn. growing on a tree, W. **Vṛikshôtpala**, m. Pterospermum Acerifolium (= *karṇi-kāra*), L. **Vṛikshôdaya**, m., **Vṛikshôdyāpana**, n. N. of wks. **Vṛikshâṅkas**, m. 'tree-dweller,' an ape, Mcar.

Vṛikshaka, m. a little tree (also *bāla-v*°), Kum.; Vcar.; (esp. ifc., f. *ā*) any tree, R.; Kālid. &c. (cf. *gandha-* and *phala-v*°); Wrightia Antidysenterica, Car.; n. the fruit of W° A°, Suśr.; a stimulant, L.

Vṛikshiya. See *eka-v*°.

Vṛikshe-śaya, mfn. (loc. of *vṛiksha* + *ś*°) abiding or roosting in trees (as birds), Ragh.; m. a kind of serpent, Suśr.

Vṛikshya, n. tree-fruit, ŚBr.

वृगल **vṛigala**. See *bṛigala*.

वृचया **vṛicayā**, f. N. of a woman (said to have been given by Indra to Kakshīvat), RV. i, 51, 13.

वृचीवत् **vṛicīvat**, m. pl. N. of a family (the descendants of Vara-śikha, slain by Indra), RV.

वृज् 1. **vṛij**, cl. 1. 7. P. (Dhātup. xxxiv, 7; xxix, 24) *varjati*, *vṛiṇákti*; cl. 2. Ā. (Dhātup. xxiv, 19) *vṛikte* (Ved. and BhP. also *várjate* and *vṛiṅkté*; Impv. *vṛiṅktām* [v.l. *vṛiktām*], Mn. ix, 20; *vṛiṅgdhvam*, BhP. xi, 4, 14; pf. *vavarja*, *vavṛije* [Gr. also *vavṛiñje*; RV. *vāvṛije*; *vavṛijyuḥ*, *vavṛiktam*; AV. p. f. *-varjúshī*]; aor. *avṛik*, AV.; *vark* [2. 3. sg.], *varktam*, *avṛijan*, Pot. *vṛijyām*, RV.; *ávṛikta*, ib.; *avṛiksham*, °*shi*, ib.; *avārkshīs*, Br.; *avarjīt*, *avarjishṭa*, Gr.; fut. *varjitā*, Br.; *varjishyati*, ib.; *varkshyati*, °*te*, Br.; inf. *vṛ́ije*, *vṛiñjáse*, *vṛijádhyai*, RV.; *varjitum* or *vṛiñjitum*, Gr.; ind. p. *vṛiktvī́*, RV.; *-vṛíjya*, *-vargam*, Br. &c.), to bend, turn, RV. iv, 7, 10; to twist off, pull up, pluck, gather (esp. sacrificial grass), RV.; TBr.; to wring off or break a person's (acc.) neck, RV. vi, 18, 8; 26, 3; to avert, remove, RV.; (Ā.) to keep anything from (abl. or gen.), divert, withhold, exclude, abalienate, RV.; TS.; Br.; Mn.; BhP.; (Ā.) to choose for one's self, select, appropriate, BhP.: Pass. *vṛijyáte*, to be bent or turned or twisted, RV. &c.: Caus. *varjayati* (Dhātup. xxxiv, 7; m. c. also °*te*; Pot. *varjayīta*, MBh.; aor. *avavarjat*), to remove, avoid, shun, relinquish, abandon, give up, renounce, ChUp.; GṛŚrS.; MBh. &c.; to spare, let live, MBh.; to exclude, omit, exempt, except (°*yitvā* with acc. = excepting, with the exception of), Mn.; MBh. &c.: Pass. of Caus. *varjyate*, to be deprived of, lose (instr.), Hariv. (cf. *varjita*): Desid. *vivṛikshâte* (Br.), *vivarjishati*, °*te* (Gr.), to wish to bend or turn &c.: Intens. *varīvṛijyate*, *varvarkti* (Gr.; p. *várīvṛijat*, RV.), to turn aside, divert: Caus. of Intens. *varīvarjáyati* (p. f. °*yantī*), to turn hither and thither (the ears), AV.

Varja, varjita &c. See p. 924, col. 1.

Vṛiktá, mfn. bent, turned, twisted &c. (see *apa-*, *parā-*, *pari-v°* &c.) **–barhis** (*vṛiktá-*), mfn. one who has gathered and spread the sacrificial grass (and so is prepared to receive the gods), sacrificing or loving to sacrifice, RV.; m. a priest, L.

Vṛikti. See *námo-* and *su-vṛikti*.

2. **Vṛij** = *bala*, strength, Naigh. ii, 9.

Vṛijána (once *vṛij°*), n. an enclosure, cleared or fenced or fortified place (esp. 'sacrificial enclosure;' but also 'pasture or camping ground, settlement, town or village and its inhabitants'), RV.; crookedness, wickedness, deceit, wile, intrigue, ib.; = *bala*, strength, Naigh. ii, 9; the sky, atmosphere, L.; = *nirākaraṇa*, L.; (*ī*), f. an enclosure, fold, RV. i, 164, 9 ('a cloud,' Sāy.); wile, intrigue, AV. vii, 30, 7.

Vṛijanyà, mfn. dwelling in villages &c.; (prob.) n. a community, people, RV. ix, 97, 23.

Vṛiji, m. N. of a man, L.; pl. N. of a people, Buddh. (cf. Pāṇ. iv, 2, 131); f. N. of a country, = *vraja* (the modern Braj, to the west of Delhi and Agra), W. **–gārhapata**, n., Pāṇ. vi, 242, Vārtt. 1, Pat.

Vṛijika, mfn. (fr. *vṛiji*), Pāṇ. iv, 2, 131.

Vṛijiná, mf(*ā*)n. bent, crooked (lit. and fig.), deceitful, false, wicked, RV. &c. &c.; disastrous, calamitous, MBh. ii, 857; m. curled hair, hair, L.; (*á*), f. deceit, intrigue, guile, AV.; n. id., RV.; AV.; TBr.; sin, vice, wickedness, MBh.; Kāv. &c.; distress, misery, affliction, BhP.; red leather, L. **–vat**, m. N. of a son of Kroshṭu (son of Yadu), BhP. **–vartani** (*vṛijiná-*), mfn. following evil courses, wicked, RV.

Vṛijināya, Nom. P. (only p. *-yát*) to be crooked or deceitful or wicked, RV.

Vṛijinī-vat, m. = *vṛijina-vat*, MBh.; Hariv.

Vṛijya, mfn. to be bent or turned away, MW.

वृञ्ज् *vṛiñj*. See √1. *vṛij*.

वृढ *vṛidha*. See under √1. 2. *bṛih*.

वृण् *vṛiṇ*, cl. 8. P. Ā. *vṛiṇoti*, *vṛiṇute*, to consume, eat, Dhātup. xxx, 6 (Vop.); cl. 6. P. *vṛiṇati*, to please, gratify, exhilarate, ib. xxviii, 40.

वृत् 1. *vṛit*, cl. 1. Ā. (Dhātup. xviii, 19) *vártate* (rarely °*ti*; in Veda also *vavartti* and [once in RV] *vartti*; Subj. *vavártat*, *vavartati*, *vavṛitat*; Pot. *vavṛityāt*, *vavṛitīya*; Impv. *vavṛitsva*; impf. *ávavṛitran*, °*tranta*; pf. *vavárta*, *vavṛitús*, *vavṛité*, RV. [here also *vāvṛité*] &c. &c.; aor. *avart*, *avṛitran*, Subj. *vártat*, *vartta*, RV.; *avṛitat*, AV. &c. &c.; *avartishṭa*, Gr.; 3. pl. *avṛitsata*, RV.; 2. sg. *vartithās*, MBh.; Prec. *vartishīshṭa*, Gr.; fut. *vartitā*, Gr.; *vartsyáti*, °*te*, AV. &c.; *vartishyati*, °*te*, MBh. &c.; Cond. *avartsyat*, Br.; *avartishyata*, Gr.; inf. *-vṛite*, RV.; *-vṛitas*, Br.; *vartitum*, MBh. &c.; ind. p. *vartitvā* and *vṛittvā*, Gr.; *-vṛitya*, RV. &c. &c.; *-vártam*, Br. &c.), to turn, turn round, revolve, roll (also applied to the rolling down of tears), RV. &c. &c.; to move or go on, get along, advance, proceed (with instr. 'in a partic. way or manner'), take place, occur, be performed, come off, Mn.; MBh. &c.; to be, live, exist, be found, remain, stay, abide, dwell (with *ātmani na*, 'to be not in one's right mind;' with *manasi* or *hṛidaye*, 'to dwell or be turned or thought over in the mind;' with *mūrdhni*, 'to be at the head of,' 'to be of most importance;' *kathaṃ vartate* with nom. or *kiṃ vartate* with gen., 'how is it with?'), ib.; to live on, subsist by (instr. or ind. p.), ĀśvGṛS.; MBh. &c.; to pass away (as time, *ciraṃ vartate gatānām*, 'it is long since we went'), BhP.; to depend on (loc.), R.; to be in a partic. condition, be engaged in or occupied with (loc.), Āpast.; MBh. &c.; to be intent on, attend to (dat.), R.; to stand or be used in the sense of (loc.), Kāś.; to act, conduct one's self, behave towards (loc., dat., or acc.; also with *itarêtaram* or *parasparam*, 'mutually'), Mn.; MBh. &c.; to act or deal with, follow a course of conduct (also with *vṛittim*), show, display, employ, use, act in any way (instr. or acc.) towards (loc. with *parâjñayā*, 'to act under another's command;' with *prajā-rūpeṇa*, 'to assume the form of a son;' with *priyám*, 'to act kindly;' with *svāni*, 'to mind one's own business;' *kim idam vartase*, 'what are you doing there?'), ŚBr.; Mn.; MBh. &c.; to tend or turn to, prove as (dat.), Śukas.; to be or exist or live at a partic. time, be alive or present (cf. *vartamāna*, *vartishyamāṇa*, and *vartsyat*, p. 925), MBh. &c. &c.; to continue (with an ind. p., *atītya vartante*, 'they continue to excel;' *iti vartate me buddhiḥ*, 'such continues my opinion'), MBh.; Kāv. &c.; to hold good, continue in force, be supplied from what precedes, Pat.; Kāś.; to originate, arise from (abl.) or in (loc.), BhP.; to become, TBr.; to associate with (*saha*), Pañcat.; to have illicit intercourse with (loc.), R.: Caus. *vartáyati* (aor. *avīvṛitat* or *avavartat*; in TBr. also Ā. *avavarti*; inf. *vartayádhyai*, RV.; Pass. *vartyate*, Br.), to cause to turn or revolve, whirl, wave, brandish, hurl, RV. &c. &c.; to produce with a turning-lathe, make anything round (as a thunderbolt, a pill &c.), RV.; R.; Suśr.; to cause to proceed or take place or be or exist, do, perform, accomplish, display, exhibit (feelings), raise or utter (a cry), shed (tears), MBh.; Kāv. &c.; to cause to pass (as time), spend, pass, lead a life, live, subsist on or by (instr.), enter upon a course of conduct &c. (also with *vṛittim* or *vṛittyā* or *vṛittena*; with *bhaikshеṇa*, 'to live by begging'), conduct one's self, behave, Mn.; MBh. &c.; to set forth, relate, recount, explain, declare, MBh.; Hariv.; R.; to begin to instruct (dat.), ŚāṅkhGṛ.; to understand, know, learn, BhP.; to treat, Car.; (in law, with *śiras* or *śīrsham*) to offer one's self to be punished if another is proved innocent by an ordeal, Vishṇ.; Yājñ.; 'to speak' or 'to shine' (*bhāshârthe* or *bhāsârthe*), Dhātup. xxxiii, 108: Desid. *vivṛitsati*, °*te* (RV.; Br.), *vivartishate* (Pāṇ. i, 3, 92), to wish to turn &c.: Intens. (Ved., rarely in later language) *várvartti*, *varīvartti*, *varīvartyáte*, *varīvartate*, p. *várvṛitat* and *várvṛitāna*, impf. 3. sg. *avarīvar*, 3. pl. *avarīvur* (Gr. also *varivartti*, *varīvṛitīti*, *varvṛitīti*, *varīvṛityate*), to turn, roll, revolve, be, exist, prevail, RV.; ŚBr.; Kāv. [Cf. Lat. *vertere*; Slav. *vrŭtĕti*, *vratiti*; Lith. *vartýti*; Goth. *wairthan*; Germ. *werden*; Eng. *-ward*.]

Varta, vartaka &c. See p. 925, col. 2.

Vivṛitsitṛi, mfn. (fr. Desid.) one who wishes to be, W. (cf. Pāṇ. vii, 2, 59, Vārtt. 4, Pat.)

2. **Vṛit**, mfn. (only ifc., for 1. see p. 1007, col. 2) turning, moving, existing; (after numerals) = 'fold' (see *eka-*, *tri-*, *su-vṛit*); ind. finished, ended (a gram. term used only in the Dhātup. and signifying that a series of roots acted on by a rule and beginning with a root followed by *ādi* or *prabhṛiti*, ends with the word preceding *vṛit*).

Vṛittá, mfn. turned, set in motion (as a wheel), RV.; round, rounded, circular, ŚBr. &c. &c.; occurred, happened (cf. *kiṃ-v°*), Āpast.; R. &c.; (ifc.) continued, lasted for a certain time, MBh. vii, 6147; completed, finished, absolved, MaitrUp.; past, elapsed, gone, KaushUp.; Mn.; MBh. &c.; quite exhausted, TBr. (= *śrānta*, Sch.); deceased, dead, Mn.; R.; studied, mastered, Pāṇ. vii, 2, 26; existing, effective, unimpaired (see *vṛittâujas*); become (e.g. with *mukta*, become free), Kathās. xviii, 306; acted or behaved towards (loc.), MBh.; R.; fixed, firm, L.; chosen (= *vṛita*), L.; m. a tortoise, L.; a kind of grass, L.; a round temple, VarBṛS.; N. of a serpent-demon, MBh.; (*ā*), f. N. of various plants (= *jhiñjarishṭā*, *māṇsa-rohiṇī*, *mahā-kośātakī*, and *priyaṅgu*), L.; a kind of drug (= *reṇukā*), L.; a kind of metre, Col.; n. (ifc. f. *ā*) a circle, Gaṇit.; the epicycle, Sūryas.; occurrence, use, Nir.; (ifc.) transformation, change into, RPrāt.; appearance, Vcar.; (ifc.) formed of or derived from (see *kiṃ-v°*); an event, adventure, R.; Kathās.; a matter, affair, business, ib.; (also pl.) procedure, practice, action, mode of life, conduct, behaviour (esp. virtuous conduct, good behaviour), ŚBr. &c. &c.; means of life, subsistence, Hariv. 335 (more correct *vṛitti*); 'turn of a line,' the rhythm at the end of a verse, final rhythm, RPrāt.; a metre containing a fixed number of syllables, any metre, Kāvyâd.; VarBṛS. &c.; a metre consisting of 10 trochees, Col. **–karkaṭī**, f. a water-melon (= *shaḍ-bhujā*), L. **–karshita**, v.l. for *vṛitti-k°*. **–kalpadruma**, m. N. of a metrical wk. **–kāya**, mf(*ā*)n. having a round body, Suśr. **–kautuka**, n., **-kaumudī**, f. N. of two metrical treatises. **–khaṇḍa**, n. a portion or segment of a circle, Col. **–gandhi** or **-gandhin**, n. 'having the smell of rhythm,' N. of a partic. kind of artificial prose containing metrical passages (°*dhi-tva*, n.), Vām.; Sāh. **–guṇḍa**, m. a kind of grass (= *dīrgha-nāla*), L. **–candrikā**, f., **-candrôdaya**, m. N. of two wks. **–cūḍa** (C. *-caula*), mfn. one whose tonsure has been performed, tonsured (accord. to Mn. ii, 35 this should be performed at the age of one or three years), Ragh. iii, 28. **–ceshṭā**, f. conduct, behaviour, MBh. **–caula**, see *-cūḍa*. **–jña**, mfn. knowing actions or established practices, W. **–taṇḍula**, m. Andropogon Bicolor, L. **–taraṃgiṇī**, f. N. of wk. **–tas**, ind. according to the practice or observance of caste, according to usage or customary procedure (*vṛittataḥ pāpam*, a sin according to usage), W. **–tuṇḍa**, mfn. round-mouthed, L. **–tumbī**, v.l. for *vṛinta-t°* (q.v.) **–tva**, n. roundness, Naish., Sch. **–darpaṇa**, m., **-dīpa-vyākhyāna**, n., **-dīpikā**, f., **-dyumaṇi**, m. N. of wks. **–nishpāvikā**, f. the round Nishpāvikā (a kind of leguminous plant), L. **–pattrā**, f. a species of creeper, L. **–pariṇāha**, m. the circumference of a circle, Āryabh. **–parṇī**, f. Clypea Hernandifolia, L.; = *mahā-śana-pushpikā*, L. **–pīna**, mfn. round and full (as arms), MBh. **–pushpa**, m. Nauclea Cadamba, L.; Acacia Sirissa, L.; Rosa Moschata, L.; = *mudgara*, L. **–pūraṇa**, n. filling out or completing a metre, Kshem. **–pratyabhijña**, mfn. well versed in sacred rites, Rājat. **–pratyaya**, m., **-pratyaya-kaumudī**, f., **-pradīpa**, m. N. of wks. **–phala**, m. the pomegranate, L.; the jujube, L.; (*ā*), f. the Myrobolan tree, L.; Solanum Melongena, L.; a kind of gourd &c., L.; n. black pepper, L. **–bandha**, m. metrical composition; °*dhôjjhita*, mfn. (prose) free from metrical passages, Sāh. **–bīja**, m. Abelmoschus Esculentus, L.; (*ā*), f. Cajanus Indicus, L. **–bījakā**, f. a kind of shrub, L. **–bhaṅga**, m. violation of good conduct and of metre, Kāv. **–bhūya** (MBh. i, 728), prob. a corrupted word. **–maṇikośa**, m. N. of wk. **–mallikā**, f. Jasminum Sambac, L.; Calotropis Gigantea Alba, L. **–māṇikya-mālā**, f., **-mālā**, f. (also with *vṛitta-muktā-phalānām*), **-muktâvalī** (and °*lī-ṭīkā*), f., **-mauktika**, n. N. of wks. on metre. **–yamaka**, n. a kind of verse containing a play on words (see *yamaka*), MW. **–yukta**, mfn. of good moral conduct, virtuous, Hcat. **–ratnâkara**, m. 'mine of jewels of metres,' N. of a short treatise on post-Vedic metres by Kedāra; *-ṭīkā*, f.; *-pañcikā*, f., *-vyākhyā*, f., *-setu*, m.; °*râdarśa*, m. N. of Comms. on the above wk. **–ratnâvali** or °**lī**, f., **-rāmâyaṇa**, n., **-lakshaṇa**, n. N. of wks. **–vaktra**, mfn. round-mouthed, L. **–vat**, mfn. round, MBh.; of virtuous or moral conduct, Yājñ.; MBh. &c. **–vārttika**, n., **-vinoda**, m., **-vivecana**, n., **-śata** or **-śataka**, n. N. of wks. on metre. **–śastra**, mfn. one who has studied (the science of) arms or warfare (= *adhīta-śastra-vidya*), Bhaṭṭ. **–śālin**, mfn. = *-yukta*, R. **–ślāghin**, mfn. praised for virtuous conduct, MBh. **–saṃketa**, mfn. one who has given his consent, Rājat. **–sampanna**, mfn. = *-yukta*, Mn. viii, 179. **–sādin**, mfn. destroying established usage, worthless, mean, vile, R. **–sārâvalī**, f., **-sudhôdaya**, m. N. of two wks. **–stha**, = *-yukta*, Mn.; MBh. &c. **–svâdhyāya-vat**, mfn. leading a virtuous life and devoted to repetition of the Veda, Bṛihasp. **–hīna**, mfn. without good conduct, ill-conducted, MBh. **Vṛittâkshepa**, m. denying or non-acceptance of any past occurrence, Kāvyâd. (cf. *bhavishyad-âkshepa* and *vartamānâkshepa*). **Vṛittâṅgī**, f. the Priyaṅgu plant, L. **Vṛittâdhyayana**, n. moral conduct and repetition (of Veda); *-rddhi* (for *ṛiddhi*) f., and *-sampatti*, f. welfare resulting from the above, L. **Vṛittânupūrva**, mfn. round and symmetrical (as legs; others 'taperingly round'), Kum. i, 35. **Vṛittânuvartin**, mfn. conforming to rule, obedient, virtuous, R. **Vṛittânusāra**, m. conforming to prescribed practice, W.; conformity to metre, MW.; (*āt*), ind. according to the metre or measure of a verse, for the sake of the metre, ib. **Vṛittânusārin**, mfn. conforming to established rule or practice, doing what is enjoined or proper, W. **Vṛittâyata-bhuja**, mfn. one who has round or long arms, R. **Vṛittârdha**, m. or n. a semicircle, Hcat. **Vṛit-**

têrvāru, m. a water-melon (=*shaḍ-bhujā*), L. **Vṛittôkti-ratna**, n. N. of a wk. on metre. **Vṛittôtsava**, mfn. one who has celebrated a festival, MBh. **Vṛittôru**, f. a round-thighed woman, Pāṇ. iv, 1, 69, Sch. **Vṛittâujas**, mfn. one who has effective power or energy, Mn. i, 6.

Vṛittaka (ifc.) = *vṛitta*, a metre, Sāh.; a Buddhist or Jaina layman, VarBṛS.; n. a kind of simple but rhythmical prose composition, Cat.

Vṛittânta, m. or (rarely) n. 'end or result of a course of action,' occurrence, incident, event, doings, life, ŚāṅkhBr. &c. &c.; course, manner, way (in which anything happens or is done), MBh.; Vikr.; (also pl.) tidings, rumour, report, account, tale, story, history, Mn.; MBh. &c.; a chapter or section of a book (*-śas*, ind. by chapters), Pat.; (only L.) a topic, subject; sort, kind; nature, property; leisure, opportunity; a whole, totality; mfn. alone, solitary, L.; *-darśin*, mfn. witnessing or being a spectator of any action, MW.; *°tânveshaka*, mfn. inquiring into what has taken place, ib.

Vṛitti, f. rolling, rolling down (of tears), Śak. iv, 5; 14; mode of life or conduct, course of action, behaviour, (esp.) moral conduct, kind or respectful behaviour or treatment (also v.l. for *vṛitta*), GṛŚrS.; Mn.; MBh. &c.; general usage, common practice, rule, Prāt.; mode of being, nature, kind, character, disposition, ib.; Kāv.; state, condition, Tattvas.; being, existing, occurring or appearing in (loc. or comp.), Lāṭy.; Hariv.; Kāv. &c.; practice, business, devotion or addiction to, occupation with (often ifc. = 'employed about,' 'engaged in,' 'practising'), MBh.; Kāv. &c.; profession, maintenance, subsistence, livelihood (often ifc.; cf. *uñcha-v°*; *vṛittim* √*kṛi* or √*klṛip* [Caus.] with instr., 'to live on or by;' with gen., 'to get or procure a maintenance for;' only certain means of subsistence are allowed to a Brāhman, see Mn. iv, 4–6), ŚrS.; Mn.; MBh. &c.; wages, hire, Pañcav.; working, activity, function, MaitrUp.; Kap.; Vedântas. &c.; mood (of the mind), Vedântas.; the use or occurrence of a word in a partic. sense (loc.), its function or force, Pāṇ.; Sāh.; Sch. on KātyŚr. &c.; mode or measure of pronunciation and recitation (said to be threefold, viz. *vilambitā*, *madhyamā*, and *drutā*, q. v.), Prāt.; (in gram.) a complex formation which requires explanation or separation into its parts (as distinguished from a simple or uncompounded form, e.g. any word formed with Kṛit or Taddhita affixes, any compound and even duals and plurals which are regarded as Dvandva compounds, of which only one member is left, and all derivative verbs such as desideratives &c.); style of composition (esp. dram. style, said to be of four kinds, viz. 1. Kaiśikī, 2. Bhāratī, 3. Sātvatī, 4. Ārabhaṭī, qq. vv.; the first three are described as suited to the Śṛiṅgāra, Vīra, and Raudra Rasas respectively, the last as common to all), Bhar.; Daśar. &c.; (in rhet.) alliteration, frequent repetition of the same consonant (five kinds enumerated, scil. *madhurā*, *prâuḍhā*, *purushā*, *lalitā*, and *bhadrā*), Daśar., Introd.; final rhythm of a verse (= or v.l. for *vṛitta*, q. v.); a commentary, comment, gloss, explanation (esp. on a Sūtra); N. of the wife of a Rudra, BhP. **-kara**, mf(*ī*)n. affording a livelihood, MBh.; Kathās.; Suśr. **-karshita**, mfn. distressed for (want of) a l°, Mn. viii, 411 (*bhṛity-abhāvena pīḍitaḥ*, Kull.); MBh. **-kāra** or **-kṛit**, m. the author of a Comm. on a Sūtra (esp. applied to Vāmana, the principal author of the Kāśikā-vṛitti). **-kshīṇa**, mfn. = *-karshita*, MBh. **-cakra**, n. conduct or mode of (mutual) treatment compared to a wheel, Pañcat. i, 81. **-candra-pradīpikā-nirukti**, f. N. of wk. **-ccheda**, m. deprivation of livelihood or subsistence, Kām. **-tā**, f., **-tva**, n. state of existence, mode of subsistence, profession, conduct, Mn.; MBh. &c. **-da** or **-dātṛi**, mfn. affording maintenance, a supporter, MBh.; R.; BhP. **-dāna**, n. the giving of m°, supporting, W. **-dīpikā**, f. N. of wk. **-nibandhana**, n. means of support, Kathās. **-nirodha**, m. obstruction or prevention of activity or function, Kām. **-pradīpa**, m., **-prabhā-kara**, m. N. of wks. **-bhaṅga**, m. loss of livelihood, Pañcat. **-bhāj**, mfn. 'performing sacrifices &c.' or 'doing good and evil,' Śiś. xiv, 19 (*homâdi-vyāpāraṃ kurvan* or *puṇya-pāpa-kārin*, Sch.) **-mat**, mfn. following the practice of (ifc.), BhP.; one who is engaged in a partic. matter or has a partic. way of thinking, Saṃkar.; having a means of subsistence (ifc. = 'living on or by'), Mn.; MBh.; BhP.; exercising a partic. function, active (ifc. having anything as its function), Sarvad.; Kap., Sch. **-mūla**, n. provision for maintenance, Gaut. **-lābha**, m. (in phil.) ascertainment of the concurrent, MW. **-vāda**, m., **-vārttika**, n. N. of wks. **-vaikalya**, n. lack of means of subsistence, want of a livelihood, Mn.; Pañcat **-saṃgraha**, m. N. of a concise Comm. on Pāṇini's Sūtras (by Rāma-candra, a pupil of Nāgoji). **-stha**, mfn. being in any state or condition or employment, MW.; m. a lizard, chameleon, L. **-han** (Up.), **-hantṛi** (MBh.), mfn. destroying a person's (gen.) means of subsistence. **-hetu**, m. = *-mūla*, Mn. iv, 11. **-hrāsa**, m. = *-bhaṅga*, Kusum.

Vṛittika and **vṛittin** (ifc.) = *vṛitti*, MBh.; Kāv. &c.

Vṛitty, in comp. for *vṛitti*. **-anuprāsa**, m. a kind of alliteration, frequent repetition of the same consonant, Sāh.; Pratāp. **-artha-bodhaka**, mf(*ikā*)n. indicating the meaning of a complex formation (see under *vṛitti*), MW. **-artham**, ind. for the sake of subsistence, in order to sustain life, Mn. ii, 141. **-uparodha**, m. a hindrance to maintenance or sustenance, MBh. **-upâya**, m. a means of subsistence, Mn. x, 2.

2. **Vṛitya**, mfn. (for 1. see p. 1007, col. 2) to be abided or stayed or remained &c., Pāṇ. iii, 1, 110, Sch.

वृत् 3. *vṛit*. See √*vāvṛit*, p. 947, col. 1.

वृथा *vṛithā* &c. See p. 1007, col. 3.

वृद्ध 1. *vṛiddha*, mfn. (fr. √*vardh*, p. 926, col. 1) cut, cut off, destroyed, MBh.; n. what is cut off, a piece, Śulbas. (v.l. *vṛidhra*).

1. **Vṛiddhi**, f. cutting off, abscission, W.; (in law) forfeiture, deduction, ib.

Vṛidhu, m. N. of a carpenter (prob. w.r. for *bṛibu*), Mn. x, 107.

Vṛidhra. See 1. *vṛiddha*.

वृध् *vṛidh*, cl. 1. Ā. (Dhātup. xviii, 20) *várdhate* (Ved. and ep. also *°ti*; pf. *vavárdha*, *vavṛidhe*, RV. &c. &c. [Ved. also *vāvṛ°*; *vavṛidhāti*, *°dhītās*, *°dhásva*, RV.; *vāvṛidhéte*, RV.; p. *vāvṛidhát*, RV.; AV.; aor. Ved. *avṛidhat*, *vṛidhātas*, *°dhātu*; p. *vṛidhát*, *°dhāná*]; *avardhishṭa*, MBh. &c.; Prec. *vardhishīmáhi*, VS.; fut. *vardhitā*, Gr.; *vartsyati*, Kāv.; *vardhishyate*, Gr.; inf. Ved. *vṛidhe* ['for increase,' 'to make glad'], *vṛidháse*, *vāvṛidhádhyai*; Class. *vardhitum*; ind. p. *vṛiddhvā* or *vardhitvā*, Gr.; in MBh. √*vṛidh* is sometimes confounded with √1. *vṛit*), trans. P., to increase, augment, strengthen, cause to prosper or thrive, RV.; AV.; ŚBr.; MBh.; to elevate, exalt, gladden, cheer, exhilarate (esp. the gods, with praise or sacrifice), RV.; (intrans. Ā.; in Ved. P. in pf. and aor.; in Class. P. in aor. fut. and cond.; also P. m. c. in other forms), to grow, grow up, increase, be filled or extended, become longer or stronger, thrive, prosper, succeed, RV. &c. &c.; to rise, ascend (as the scale in ordeals), Yājñ., Sch.; to be exalted or elevated, feel animated or inspired or excited by (instr., loc., gen.) or in regard to (dat.), become joyful, have cause for congratulation (*vṛidhaḥ*, *°dhat* in sacrificial formulas = 'mayest thou or may he prosper;' in later language often with *dishṭyā*), RV. &c. &c.: Caus. *vardháyati*, *°te* (in later language also *vardhāpayati*; aor. Ved. *avīvṛidhat*, *°dhata*), to cause to increase or grow, augment, increase, make larger or longer, heighten, strengthen, further, promote (Ā. 'for one's self'), RV. &c. &c.; to rear, cherish, foster, bring up, ib.; to elevate, raise to power, cause to prosper or thrive, AV.; ŚBr.; MBh. &c.; to exalt, magnify, glorify (esp. the gods), make joyful, gladden (Ā. in Ved. also = to rejoice, be joyful, take delight in [instr.], enjoy, RV. &c. &c.; (with or scil. *dishṭyā*) to congratulate, Kād.; (cl. 10. accord. to Dhātup. xxxiii, 109) 'to speak' or 'to shine' (*bhāshârthe* or *bhāsârthe*): Desid. of Caus., see *vivardhayishu*: Desid. *vivardhishate* or *vivṛitsati*, Gr.: Intens. *varivṛidhyate*, *varivṛidhīti*, ib.

2. **Vardha**, **vardhana** &c. See p. 926, col. 1.

2. **Vṛiddhá**, mfn. grown, become larger or longer or stronger, increased, augmented, great, large, RV. &c. &c.; grown up, full-grown, advanced in years, aged, old, senior (often in comp. with the names of authors, esp. of authors of law-books [cf. IW. 300, 302], to denote either an older recension of their wks. or the wk. of some older authors of the same name; cf. *vṛiddha-kātyāyana*, *-garga* &c.), TS.; Mn.; MBh. &c.; (ifc.) older by, Gaut. vi, 15; experienced, wise, learned, MBh.; Kām.; eminent in, distinguished by (instr. or comp.), Mn.; MBh. &c.; important, VPrāt.; exalted, joyful, glad (also applied to hymns), RV.; (in gram., a vowel) increased (by Vṛiddhi, q. v.) to *ā* or *ai* or *au*, APrāt.; Lāṭy.; containing (or treated as containing) *ā* or *ai* or *au* in the first syllable, Pāṇ. i, 73 &c.; m. an old man (ifc. 'eldest among'), Mn.; MBh. &c. (cf. comp.); a religious mendicant, VarBṛS.; an elephant eighty years old, Gal.; Argyreia Speciosa or Argentea, L.; (*ā*), f. an old woman, MBh.; Kāv. &c.; m. and (*ā*), f. an elder male or female descendant, a patronymic or metron. designating an elder descendant (as opp. to *yuvan*, q. v.; e.g. *Gārgya* is *vṛiddha*, *Gārgyāyaṇa* is *yuvan*), Pāṇ. i, 2, 65 &c.; n. a nominal stem (and some other stems) whose first syllable contains an *ā* or *ai* or *au*, Pāṇ. i, 1, 73 &c.; the word *vṛiddha*, ib. v, 3, 62. **-karman**, m. N. of a king, VP. **-kāka**, m. 'large crow,' a sort of crow or raven, L. **-kātyāyana**, m. the older Kātyāyana or an older recension of K°'s law-book, Dāyabh. **-kāla**, m. old age, Cāṇ.; N. of a king, Cat. **-kāverī**, f. N. of a river; *-māhātmya*, n. N. of wk. **-kumārī-vākya-vara-nyāya**, m. the principle of the boon asked for by the old virgin (who chose, accord. to the Mahā-bhāshya, *putrā me bahukshīra-ghṛitam odanaṃ kāñcana-pātryām bhuñjīran*, 'May my sons eat rice with much milk and ghee from a golden vessel,' which, if granted, would have covered all other wishes), A. **-kṛicchra**, n. a partic. penance (performed) by old people, Cat. **-keśava**, m. a partic. form of the sun, ib. **-koṭara-pushpī**, f. a kind of plant, L. **-kola**, m. an old boar, Mṛicch. **-kośa**, m. possessing a rich treasure, Kathās. **-kauśika**, m. the old or an old recension of Kauśika, Hcat. **-krama**, m. the rank due to old age, MBh. **-kshatra**, m. N. of a man (see *vārddhakshatri*). **-kshetra-vara-locana** (w.r. *-kshatra-v°*), n. a partic. Samādhi, Kāraṇḍ. **-kshema**, m. N. of a man (see *vārddhakshemi*). **-gaṅgā**, f. N. of a river (commonly called the Buḍi Gaṅgā), KālikāP.; *-dhara*, n. (scil. *cūrṇa*) a medicinal powder for diarrhœa, ŚārṅgP. **-garga**, m. the older Garga or the older recension of his wk., AV. Pariś. **-garbhā**, f. far advanced in pregnancy, MānGṛ. **-gārga**, mf(*ī*)n. = *-gārgīya*, Cat. **-gārgīya**, mfn. composed by Vṛiddha-garga, VarBṛS., Introd. **-gārgya**, m. the old Gārgya or an older recension of his law-book, Cat. **-giri-māhātmya**, n. N. of wk. **-gonasa**, m. a kind of snake, Suśr. **-gautama**, m. the older Gautama or an older recension of G°'s law-book; *-saṃhitā*, f. V°-G°'s law-book. **-cāṇakya**, m. the older Cāṇakya or an older recension of his wk., Cat. (cf. *laghu-cāṇakya-rāja-nīti*). **-jātaka**, n. N. of wk. **-tama**, mfn. oldest, most venerable, R. **-tā**, f. = *-tva*, MBh.; (ifc.) pre-eminence in (e.g. *jñāna-v°*, 'in knowledge'), Prab. **-tva**, n. old age, MBh. **-dāra** or **-dāraka**, m., **-dāru**, n. Argyreia Speciosa or Argentea, L. **-dyumna**, m. N. of a man (with the patr. Ābhipratāriṇa), AitBr.; ŚāṅkhŚr. **-dvija-rūpin**, mfn. bearing the form of an old Brāhman, MW. **-dhūpa**, m. Acacia Sirissa, L.; turpentine, L. **-nagara**, n. N. of a town, Cat. **-nābhi**, mfn. 'large-naveled,' having a prominent navel, L. **-nyāsa**, m. N. of wk. **-parāśara**, m. the older Parāśara or an older recension of P°'s law-book, Cat. **-pārāśarīya** or **°śarya**, n. the work of Vṛiddha-Parāśara, ib. **-pradhāna**, m. a paternal great-grandfather, MW. **-prapitāmaha**, m. id. (others 'a great-grandfather's father'), L.; (*ī*), f. a paternal great-grandmother, W. **-pramātāmaha**, m. a maternal great-grandfather, Gobh.; (*ī*), f. a maternal great-grandmother, W. **-balā**, f. a species of plant, L. **-bāla**, n. sg. old men and children, MBh. **-bālaka**, see *ā-vṛiddha-bālakam*. **-bṛihaspati**, m. the older Bṛihaspati or an older recension of B°'s law-book, Kull. **-baudhāyana**, m. the old Baudhāyana or an older recension of B°'s law-book, Cat. **-brahma-saṃhitā**, f., **-brāhmaṇôpanishad-bhāshya**, n. N. of wks. **-bhāva**, m. the state of being old, senility, R.; Pañcat. **-bhoja**, m. the elder Bhoja (i.e. Bhoja-deva), Vās., Introd. **-mata**, n. an ancient precept, MW. **-manu**, m. the older Manu or an older recension of Manu's law-book, Kull. (cf. *bṛihan-manu*). **-mahas** (*vṛiddhá-*), mfn. of great power or might, RV. **-yavana**, m. the older Yavana (also called *Yavanâcārya*); *-jātaka*, n.; *°nêśvara*, m. N. of wks. **-yājñavalkya**, m. the older Yājñavalkya or an older recension of Y°'s law-book (cf. *bṛihad-y°*). **-yuvati**, f. a procuress, Divyâv.; a midwife, ib. **-yoga-taraṃ-**

ginī, f., **-yoga-śataka**, n. N. of wks. — **yoshit**, f. an old woman, Kathās. — **raṅka**, m. an old beggar, Mṛicch. — **rāja**, m. Rumex Vesicarius, L. — **vayas** (*vṛiddhá-*), mfn. of great strength or power, RV.; advanced in age, old, Pañcad. — **vasishṭha**, m. the older Vasishṭha or an older recension of V°'s law-book, Cat. — **vāg-bhaṭa**, m. the older Vāgbhaṭa, Cat. — **vāda-sūri** (prob. w. r. for *vādi-sūri*), m. the older Vāda-sūri, Cat. — **vādin**, m. a Jina, Gal.; N. of a man, Cat. — **vāśinī**, f. a jackal, Nir. v, 21. — **vāhana**, m. the mango tree, L. — **viṭa**, m. an old voluptuary, Mṛicch. — **vibhītaka**, m. Spondias Mangifera, L. — **vishṇu**, m. the older Vishṇu or an older recension of Vishṇu's law-book, Yājñ., Sch. — **vīvadhā**, f. 'yoke of the ancients,' the bonds of traditional usage, Sarvad. — **vṛishṇa** (*vṛiddhá-*), mfn. (prob.) = next, AV. — **vṛishṇiya** (*vṛiddhá-*), mfn. of great manliness or strength, TS. — **vega**, mfn. of great intensity, violent, strong, VarBṛS. — **vaiyākaraṇa-bhūshaṇa**, n. N. of wk. — **śaṅkha**, m. the older Śaṅkha or an older recension of Śaṅkha's law-book; *-smṛiti*, f. the law-book of V°-Ś°, Cat. — **śabda-ratnaśekhara**, m. N. of a gram. wk. — **śavas** (*vṛiddhá-*), mfn. of great power or strength, RV. — **śākalya**, m. the older Śākalya, Cat. — **śātātapa**, m. the older Śātātapa or an older recension of Ś°'s law-book, Cat.; *-smṛiti*, f. the law-book of V°-Śāt°. — **śīlin**, mfn. having the nature or disposition of an old man, Gobh.; weak from age, decrepit, MBh. — **śocis** (*vṛiddhá-*), mfn. increased in lustre, very bright, RV. — **śaunakī**, f. N. of wk. — **śravas** (*vṛiddhá-*), mfn. possessed of great swiftness, RV.; m. N. of Indra, Vās.; of a Muni, Cat. — **śrāvaka**, m. an old Śaiva mendicant, VarBṛS., Sch. — **saṃgha**, m. an assembly of old men, council or meeting of elders, L. — **suśruta**, m. the older Suśruta or an older recension of S°'s wk., Cat. — **sūtraka**, n. a flock of cotton, flocculent seeds flying in the air, L. — **sṛigāla**, m. an old jackal, Hit. — **sena** (*vṛiddhá-*), mfn. bearing large missiles (others 'forming mighty hosts'), RV.; (*ā*), f. N. of the wife of Sumati (and mother of Devatā-jit), BhP. — **sevā**, f. reverence for the aged, Kām. — **sevin**, mfn. reverencing one's elders, Mn. vii, 38; °*vi-tva*, n. = *-sevā*, ib. viii, 7. — **hārīta**, m. the older Hārīta or an older recension of H°'s law-book, Cat. **Vṛiddhâṅguli**, f. the great finger, the thumb, W.; the great toe, MW. **Vṛiddhâṅgushṭha**, m. the great toe, ib.; the thumb, ib. **Vṛiddhâcala**, n. N. of a Tīrtha; *-māhātmya*, n. N. of wk. **Vṛiddhâtri**, m. the older Atri or an older recension of Atri's law-book, Cat. **Vṛiddhâtreya**, m. the older Ātreya, Cat. **Vṛiddhâditya**, m. a partic. form of the sun, ib. **Vṛiddhânuśāsana**, n. direction or ordinance of the aged, an old man's advice, Nal. **Vṛiddhânta**, (prob.) m. 'senior's limit,' the place of honour, Divyâv. **Vṛiddhâyu**, mfn. full of vigour or life, RV. **Vṛiddhâraṇya**, n. 'seer's grove,' a place where the Purāṇas &c. are read and expounded, W. **Vṛiddhârka**, m. 'old or declining sun,' evening hour, Kāv. **Vṛiddhâryabhaṭa**, m. the older or an ancient recension of Ārya-bhaṭa, Cat. **Vṛiddhâvasthā**, f. the condition or period of old age, senility, W. **Vṛiddhâśrama**, m. the old period or last stage in a Brāhman's life (see *āśrama*), ib. **Vṛiddhôksha**, m. an old bull, Kum. **Vṛiddhôpasevin**, mfn. honouring the aged, Mn.; MBh. &c.

Vṛiddhaka, mfn. aged, old; m. an old man, MBh.; Hariv.; n. a tale, Divyâv.

2. **Vṛiddhi**, f. (for 1. see p. 1010) growth, increase, augmentation, rise, advancement, extension, welfare, prosperity, success, fortune, happiness, RV. &c. &c.; elevation (of ground), VarBṛS.; prolongation (of life), Pañcat.; swelling (of the body), Suśr.; enlargement of the scrotum (either from swelled testicle or hydrocele), ib.; swelling or rising (of the sea or of the waters), waxing (of the moon), MBh.; gain, profit, R.; Subh.; profit from lending money &c., usury, interest, Mn.; Yājñ.; MBh. (the various kinds of interest recognized by Hindū lawyers are, 1. *kāyikā vṛiddhi*, 'body-interest,' i.e. either the advantage arising from the body of an animal pledged as security for a loan, or interest paid repeatedly without reducing the body or principal; 2. *kālikā v°*, 'time-interest,' i.e. payable weekly, monthly, annually, &c., but most usually computed by the month; 3. *çakra-v°*, 'wheel-interest,' i.e. interest upon interest, compound interest; 4. *kāritā v°*, 'stipulated interest,' at a rate higher than the usual legal rate; 5. *śikhā-v°*, 'interest growing like a lock of hair,' i.e. at a usurious rate payable daily; 6. *bhoga-lābha*, 'advantage [accruing to a creditor] from the use' of objects handed over to him as security, e.g. of lands, gardens, animals, &c.: 'lawful interest' is called *dharma-v°*, 'usurious interest' *a-nyāya-v°*, 'interest at the highest legal rate' *parama-v°*), IW. 264; the second modification or increase of vowels (to which they are subject under certain conditions, e.g. *ā* is the Vṛiddhi of the vowel *a*; *ai* of *i*, *ī*, and *e*; *au* of *u*, *ū*, and *o*; cf. 2. *vṛiddha* and *kṛita-vṛiddhi*), VPrāt.; Pāṇ.; Rājat.; Sarvad.; one of the 8 principal drugs (described as mild, cooling &c.; and a remedy for phlegm, leprosy, and worms), Suśr.; Bhpr.; N. of the 11th of the astrological Yogas (or the Yoga star of the 11th lunar mansion), L.; = *vṛiddhi-śrāddha*, GṛS.; m. (with *bhaṭṭa*) N. of a poet, Cat. — **kara**, mf(*ī*)n. yielding or causing increase, promoting growth or prosperity, augmenting (ifc.), Mn.; VarBṛS.; Rājat. — **jīvaka**, mfn. living by usury, MBh. — **jīvana**, mfn. id., ib.; n. = next, L. — **jīvikā**, f. livelihood gained by usury, L. — **da**, mf(*ā*)n. giving increase, causing advancement or prosperity, VarBṛS.; m. a kind of shrub (= *-jīvaka*), L.; Batatas Edulis, ib. — **datta**, m. N. of a merchant, Campak. — **dātrī**, f. a kind of plant, L. — **pattra**, n. a kind of lancet, Suśr.; Vāgbh. — **mat**, mfn. having increase, growing, increasing, Yājñ.; Bhartṛ.; become powerful or prosperous, Bhaṭṭ.; (in gram.) causing the vowel-modification called Vṛiddhi (q.v.), APrāt. — **r-ād-aic-sūtra-vicāra**, m. (see Pāṇ. i, 1, 1) N. of a gram. treatise. — **śrāddha**, n. a Śrāddha or offering to progenitors on any prosperous occasion (as on the birth of a son &c.), RTL. 305; *-dīpikā*, f., *-prayoga*, m., *-vidhi*, m. N. of wks.

Vṛiddhy, in comp. for *vṛiddhi*. — **ājīva** or °**vin** (L.), **-upajīvin** (R.), mfn. one who lives by money-lending or usury, a money-lender, usurer.

वृध्न *vṛidhna* (?), m. a bubo in the groin, W.

वृध्र *vṛidhra*. See 1. *vṛiddha*, p. 1010, col. 2.

वृन्त *vṛínta*, m. a kind of small crawling animal, caterpillar, AV. viii, 6, 22; the egg-plant, Suśr.; (*ā*), f. a species of plant, L.; a kind of metre (v. l. *vṛittā*), Cat.; n. the footstalk of a leaf or flower or fruit, any stalk, ŚrS.; MBh. &c.; the stand of a water-jar, KātyŚr.; a nipple, L. — **tumbī**, f. a kind of round gourd, L. (v. l. for *vṛitta-t°*). — **phala**, n. the fruit of the egg-plant, Suśr. — **yamaka**, n. a kind of Yamaka (e.g. Bhaṭṭ. x, 13).

Vṛintaka (ifc., f. *ikā*) = *vṛinta*, a stalk (see *kṛishṇa-*, *dīrgha-*, *nīla-vṛ°*); (*ikā*), f. a small stalk (in *palāśa-vṛ°*), MBh.

Vṛintāka, m. (or *ī*, f.) the egg-plant; n. its fruit, Bhpr. — **vidhi**, m. N. of a ch. of BhavP. ii.

Vṛintitā, f. the medicinal plant Wrightea Antidysenterica, L.

वृन्द *vṛindá*, n. (fr. √1. *vṛi*?) a heap, multitude, host, flock, swarm, number, quantity, aggregation (*vṛindam vṛindam*, *vṛindais*, or *vṛinda-vṛindais*, in separate groups, in flocks or crowds), Naigh.; MBh. &c.; a bunch, cluster (of flowers or berries &c.), BhP.; a chorus of singers and musicians, Saṃgīt.; a partic. high number (100,000 millions), L.; m. a tumour in the throat, Suśr.; a partic. high number (1,000 millions), Āryabh.; (with Jainas) a partic. Śakti, L. (prob. *vṛindā*); N. of a medical author, Bhpr.; (*ā*), f. sacred basil (= *tulasī*), Cat.; N. of Rādhā (Kṛishṇa's mistress), Pañcar.; Vṛishabhān.; of the wife of Jalam-dhara (daughter of king Kedāra), L.; mfn. numerous, many, much, all, W. — **gāyaka**, m. a chorus-singer, chorister, Saṃgīt. — **maya**, mf(*ī*)n. (ifc.) appearing as a multitude of, Śiś. — **mādhava**, N. of a medical wk. — **śas**, ind. in groups or crowds or herds, R.; Hariv.; BhP. — **saṃhitā**, f., **-sindhu**, m. N. of medical wks.

Vṛindara, mfn. (fr. *vṛinda*), g. *aśmâdi*.

Vṛindā, f. of *vṛinda*, in comp. — °**raṇya** (*vṛindâr°*), n. = *vṛindā-vana*, Pañcar.; Bhām.; *-māhātmya*, n. N. of wk. — **vana**, n. 'Rādhā's forest,' a wood near the town Go-kula in the district of Mathurā on the left bank of the Jumnā (celebrated as the place where Kṛishṇa in the character of Go-pāla, or cowherd, passed his youth, associating with the cowherds and milkmaids employed in tending the cattle grazing in the forest), Hariv.; Kāv. &c.; a raised platform or mound of earth on which the worshippers of Kṛishṇa plant and preserve the Tulasī, MW.; m. N. of various authors and others (also with *go-svāmin* and *śukla*), Cat.; (*ī*), f. holy basil (= *tulasī*), ib.; *-kāvya*, n. N. of a poem (°*vya-ṭīkā*, f. of the Comm. on it); *-khaṇḍe garga-saṃhitā*, f. N. of wk.; *-candra*, m. (with *tarkâlaṃkāra cakravartin*), N. of an author; *-campū*, f. N. of a poem; *-dāsa* and *-deva*, m. N. of authors, Cat.; *-nagara*, n. N. of a town, ib.; *-nirṇaya*, m., *-paddhati*, f., *-pratishṭhā*, f., *-mañjarī*, f., *-māhātmya*, n., *-yamaka*, n., *-rahasya*, n., *-līlāmṛita*, n., *-varṇana*, n., *-vinoda*, m. N. of wks.; *-vipina*, n. the Vṛindā-vana wood, Cat.; *-śataka*, n. and °*nâkhyāna*, n. N. of wks.; °*nêśa*, m. 'lord of V°,' N. of Kṛishṇa, Pañcar.; °*nêśvara*, m. id., ib.; (*ī*), f. N. of Rādhā, L.

Vṛindāra, mfn. = *vṛindāraka*, L.; m. a god, deity, Kum.

Vṛindāraka, mf(*akā* or *ikā*)n. being at the head of a host, chief, eminent, best or most beautiful of (loc. or comp.), Nir.; MBh. &c.; m. a god, MBh.; Pur.; a chief, the leader of a crowd or herd, W.; N. of a son of Dhṛita-rāshṭra, MBh.

Vṛindārakāya, Nom. P. (only inf. °*yitum*, ifc.) to represent the best of or best among, Cat.

Vṛindin, mfn. containing a multitude of (in *aśva-vṛ°*), MBh.

Vṛindishṭha and **vṛindīyas**, mfn. (superl. and compar. of *vṛindāraka*) most or more eminent or excellent, best, better, Pāṇ. vi, 4, 157; Vop.

वृश् *vṛiś*, cl. 4. P. *vṛiśati*, to choose, select, Dhātup. xxvi, 116.

वृश *vṛíśa*, m. a partic. small animal (L. 'a mouse or rat;' cf. 1. *vṛisha*), MaitrS.; N. of a man (with the patr. *Jāra*, *Jāna*, or *Vaijāna*, supposed author of RV. v, 2), PañcavBr.; Anukr. &c. (also written *vṛisha*); Gendarussa Vulgaris, L.; (*ā*), f. a partic. drug, L.; (*ī*), f., see *bṛisī*; n. ginger, W.

वृश्चद्वन *vṛiścád-vana*. See under √*vraśc*.

वृश्चन *vṛiścana*, m. (fr. √*vraśc*) a scorpion, L.

Vṛiścika, m. a scorpion, &c. &c.; the zodiacal sign Scorpio, VarBṛS.; Pur.; the month when the sun is in Scorpio, W.; a kind of caterpillar covered with bristles, L.; a sort of beetle found in cow-dung, W.; a centipede, ib.; N. of various plants (Bœrhavia Procumbens, = *madana* &c.), L.; (*ā*), f. Bœrhavia Procumbens, L.; (*ī*), f. a female scorpion, L.; (*ā* or *ī*), f. an ornament for the toes, Gal. — **cchadā**, f. Tragia Involucrata, L. — **pattrikā**, f. Basella Cordifolia, L. — **priyā**, f. Basella Rubra or Lucida, W. — **rāśi**, m. the zodiacal sign Scorpio, Vās. **Vṛiścikâli**, f. a line of scorpions, ib.; Tragia Involucrata, L. **Vṛiścikêśa**, m. 'ruler of the (zodiacal sign) Scorpio,' N. of the planet Mercury, VarBṛS.

Vṛiścikarṇī, f. (prob. for *vṛiścika-k°*) Salvinia Cucullata, L.

Vṛiścipattrī, f. (prob. for *vṛiścika-p°*) Tragia Involucrata, L.

Vṛiścīka, m. a species of plant, Suśr.

Vṛiścira (L.), **vṛiścīva** (Car.; Bhpr.), m. a Punar-navā with white flowers.

वृष् *vṛish*, cl. 1. P. (Dhātup. xvii, 56) *várshati* (ep. also Ā. *varshate* and Ved. *varshate*; pf. *vavarsha*, *vavṛishe*, MBh. &c.; 3. pl. P. ep. *vavṛishus* or *vavarshus*; p. P. *vavarshvás*, MaitrS.; Ā. *vāvṛishāṇá*, RV.; Impv. *vāvṛishasva*, ib.; aor. *ávarshīt*, RV. &c. &c.; fut. *vrashṭā*, MaitrS.; *varshitā*, Gr.; *varshishyati*, °*te*, Br. &c.; inf. *varshitum*, MBh. &c.; *varshṭos*, Br.; ind. p. *vṛishṭvā*, ib.; °*ṭvī*, RV.; *varshitvā*, Gr.), to rain (either impers., or with Parjanya, Indra, the clouds &c., in nom.), RV. &c. &c.; to rain down, shower down, pour forth, effuse, shed (Ā. = 'to bestow or distribute abundantly;' also with instr. = 'to rain upon, or overwhelm with,' e.g. with arrows; *várshati*, 'while it rains, during rain'), ib.; to strike, hurt, vex, harass, Dhātup.: Caus. *varshâyati* (aor. *avīvṛishat* or *avavarshat*), to cause to rain (Parjanya &c.) or to fall down as rain (flowers &c.), RV.; TS.; MBh.; (without acc.) to cause or produce rain, ChUp. ii, 3, 2; to rain upon (= overwhelm) with (a shower of arrows, instr.), MBh.; Ā. to have manly power, have generative vigour, Dhātup. xxxiii, 30: Desid. *vivarshishati*, Gr. (cf. *vivarshishu*): Intens. *varīvṛishyate*, *varīvarshṭi* &c., ib. [For cognates see under *varshā* and 1. *vṛisha*.]

Varsha, varshaṇa, varshita. See p. 926 &c.

1. **Vṛisha**, m. (prob. later form of *vṛishan*) a man, male, husband, Kāśikh.; the male of any animal (see *aśva-v°*); a bull (in older language only ifc.),

Mn.; MBh. &c.; the zodiacal sign Taurus, VarBṛS.; a strong or potent man (one of the four classes into which men are divided in erotic wks.), L.; the chief of a class or anything the most excellent or pre-eminent or best of its kind (e.g. *vrisho 'ṅgulīnām,* the chief among fingers, the thumb; *vrisho gavām* or simply *vṛishaḥ,* the bull among cows, the principal die in a game at dice; often ifc., e.g. *kapi-vṛishāḥ,* the chief monkeys), MBh.; Kāv. &c.; Justice or Virtue personified as a bull or as Śiva's bull, Mn. viii, 16; Pur.; Kāvyâd.; just or virtuous act, virtue, moral merit, Śiś.; Vās.; N. of Śiva, MBh.; semen virile, Vās.; water, ib., Sch.; a mouse or rat (cf. *vṛiśa* and *-daṅśa*), L.; an enemy, L.; a partic. form of a temple, VarBṛS.; a piece of ground suitable for the foundation of a house, L.; N. of Vishṇu-Kṛishṇa, MBh.; of Indra, MārkP.; of the Sun, ib.; of Kāma-deva, L.; of the regent of the Karaṇa Catush-pada, VarBṛS.; of Indra in the 11th Manv-antara, Pur.; of a Sādhya, Hariv.; of one of Skanda's attendants, MBh.; of an Asura (=*vṛishabha*), Kāvyâd.; of two sons of Kṛishṇa, BhP.; of Karṇa, MBh.; of a son of Vṛisha-sena and grandson of Karṇa, Hariv.; of a Yādava and son of Madhu, ib.; of a son of Sṛiñjaya, BhP.; of an ancient king, MBh.; of one of the 10 horses of the Moon, L.; N. of various plants (L. Gendarussa Vulgaris or Adhatoda; Bœrhavia Procumbens or Variegata; a species of bulbous plant growing on the Himavat &c.), Kāṭh.; Suśr.; (*ā*), f. Gendarussa Vulgaris or Adhatoda, L.; Salvinia Cucullata, L.; Mucuna Pruritus, L.; N. of a Sāman, ĀrshBr.; (*ī*), f., see *bṛisī;* n. a woman's apartment, L.; myrobolan, L.; a peacock's plumage or tail, L. [Cf. Lat. *verres* for *verses;* Lith. *vèrszis.*] **-karṇikā** (Car.) or **-karṇī** (L.), f. Cocculus Tomentosus. **-kṛita,** mfn., g. *pravṛiddhâdi.* **-ketana,** m. 'having a bull for a sign,' N. of Śiva, MBh. **-ketu,** m. id., R.; N. of a warrior, Cat.; *-śishya,* m. N. of Paraśu-rāma, Bālar. **-ga,** m. 'going on a bull,' N. of Śiva, Kāv. **-gandhā,** f. Argyreia Speciosa or Argentea, L. **-gāyatrī,** f. a partic. Gāyatrī (recited in honour of a bull), Hcat. **-cakra,** n. a partic. astrological diagram (shaped like a bull and having reference to agriculture), L. **-tā,** f. virility, generative power, Car. **-tva,** n., see under 2. *vṛisha.* **-daṅśa, -daṅśaka, -dat, -danta,** see above, line 13. **-darbha,** m. N. of a prince of Kāśi (pl. his family), MBh.; Hariv.; of a son of Śibi, Hariv. **-dāna,** n. N. of wk. **-deva,** m. N. of a king, Inscr.; (*ā*), f. of a wife of Vasu-deva, VP. **-dvīpa,** m. N. of a Dvīpa, VarBṛS. **-dhara,** m. 'bull-bearer,' N. of Śiva, Bālar. **-dhvaja,** m. =*-ketana,* MBh.; Kāv. &c.; 'having a rat for a sign,' N. of Gaṇêśa, W.; 'having virtue for a mark,' a virtuous man, ib.; N. of a king, Cat.; (with Tāntrikas) N. of an author of mystical prayers, ib.; of a mountain, MārkP.; (*ā*), f. N. of Durgā, Hariv. **-dhvāṅkshī,** f. a species of Cyperus, L. **-nādin,** mfn. roaring like a bull, Śiś. **-nāśana,** m. Embelia Ribes, L. **-pati,** m. 'lord of the bull,' N. of Śiva, L.; a bull set at liberty, L. (cf. *vṛishôtsarga*). **-pattrikā,** f. =*-gandhā,* L. **-parṇī,** f. Salvinia Cucullata, L.; Cocculus Tomentosus, L. **-parvan,** see under 2. *vṛisha.* **-pushpa,** n. a kind of pot-herb, Car. **-pūtana**(?), m. letting loose a black bull, L. (cf. *vṛishôtsarga*). **-bhānu,** m. (also written *-bhānu* or *-bhāna*) N. of a Vaiśya (the son of Sūra-bhāna and father of Rādhā; cf. *vārshabhānavī*), Cat.; *-jā,* f. patr. of Rādhā (also N. of a drama by Mathurā-dāsa; *-nandinī,* f. patr. of Rādhā, Vṛishabhān. **-bhāsā,** f. the residence of Indra and of the immortals (=*amarāvatī*), L. **-rāja**(?), m. N. of a medical author, Cat. **-rāja-ketana,** m. 'having the king of bulls for a sign,' N. of Śiva, Kum. **-lakshaṇā,** f. a masculine (lit. 'bullish-looking') girl (unfit for marriage), L. **-lāñchana,** m. =*-ketana,* Bālar. **-locana,** m. 'having the eyes of a bull,' a rat, L. **-vat,** m. N. of a mountain, MārkP. **-vāha,** m. riding on a bull, Pañcar. **-vāhana,** m. 'whose vehicle is a bull,' N. of Śiva, Hariv. **-vivāha,** m. = *vṛishôtsarga,* ib. **-vṛisha,** n. N. of a Sāman, ĀrshBr. **-śatru,** m. 'enemy of Vṛisha or Karṇa,' N. of Kṛishṇa or Vishṇu, L. **-śīla,** mfn. (used to explain *vṛishala*), Nir. iii, 16. **-śushṇa,** see *vṛisha-śushma* under 2. *vṛisha*). **-shaṇḍa,** m. N. of a man, Pravar. (cf. *vṛika-khaṇḍa*). **-sānu,** m. a man, L.; death, L. **-sâhvayā** (MBh.), **-sâhvā** (VP.), f. N. of two rivers. **-sṛikkin,** m. a wasp, L. (cf. *visha-śṛiṅgin* and *-sṛikkan*). **-sena,** see under 2. *vṛisha.* **-skandha,** mfn. 'bull-shouldered,' having the shoulders of a bull, Ragh.; N. of Śiva, MBh. **Vṛishâkara,** m. a kind of bean, Phaseolus Radiatus, L. **Vṛishâkṛiti,** mfn. bull-shaped (applied to Vishṇu), MBh. **Vṛishâkrāntā,** f. (a cow) covered by a bull, L. **Vṛishâksha,** mfn. bull-eyed (applied to Vishṇu), Hariv. **Vṛishâkhya,** n. N. of a partic. magical formula recited over weapons, R. **Vṛishâṅka,** m. 'bull-marked,' N. of Śiva, MBh.; Kāv. &c.; 'marked by virtue,' a pious man, L.; the marking-nut plant, L.; a eunuch, L.; *-ja,* m. 'Śiva-produced,' a kind of small drum (held in one hand and played by means of a string attached to it, =*ḍamaru*), L. **Vṛishâñcana,** m. 'bull-going,' 'borne on a bull,' N. of Śiva, L. **Vṛishâṇḍa,** m. 'having a bull's testicles,' N. of an Asura, MBh. **Vṛishâdri,** m. N. of a mountain, Cat. **Vṛishântaka,** m. 'destroyer of Vṛisha,' N. of Kṛishṇa or Vishṇu, L. (cf. *vṛisha-śatru,* col. 1). **Vṛishâmitra,** m. N. of a Brāhman, MBh. **Vṛishâvāha,** m. a kind of wild grain or rice, L. **Vṛishâhāra,** m. 'feeding on rats,' a cat, L. **Vṛishêndra,** m. an excellent bull, BhP. **Vṛishôtsarga,** m. letting loose a bull (or, accord. to some, a bull and four heifers, as a work of merit esp. on the occasion of a Śrāddha in honour of deceased ancestors), GṛS.; Pañcat.; RTL. 319; giving up virtuous acts, Vās.; N. of the 18th Pariśishṭa of the Atharva-veda; *-kaumudī,* f., *-tattva,* n., *-paddhati,* f., *-pariśishṭa,* n., *-prayoga,* m., *-vidhi,* m. N. of wks. **Vṛishôtsāha,** m. 'having the strength of a bull,' N. of Vishṇu, L. **Vṛishôdara,** m. 'bull-bellied,' id., MBh.

2. **Vṛisha** (not always separable from 1. *vṛisha*), in comp. for *vṛishan.* **-karman,** mfn. doing manly deeds (as Indra), RV.; acting like a bull (as Vishṇu), MBh.; m. a partic. magical formula recited over weapons, R. **-kāma,** mfn. desirous of the male, Kauś. **-kratu** (*vṛisha-*), mfn. manly-minded (as Indra), RV. **-khādi** (*vṛisha-*), mfn. having large bracelets or rings (as the Maruts; others 'ornamented with ear-rings'), ib. **-gaṇa** (*vṛisha-*), m. N. of a Ṛishi (pl. his descendants), ib. **-cyuta** (*vṛisha-*), mfn. excited by (drinking) the strong Soma, ib. **-jūti** (*vṛisha-*), mfn. having manly impulse or speed, ib. **-tvá** and **-tvaná,** n. (instr. °*nā*) manliness, virility, ib., TS. **-daṅśá,** m. 'having strong teeth,' a cat, VS. &c. &c.; a kind of animal living in holes, Suśr.; N. of a mountain, MBh.; *-mukha,* mfn. cat-mouthed, ib. **-daṅśaka** (Sāh.), **-daṅśakaka** (L.), m. =*-daṅśa,* a cat. **-dat** (*vṛisha-*), mf(*atī*)n. strong-toothed, AV. **-danta,** mfn. id., Pāṇ. v, 4, 145. **-dhūta** (*vṛisha-*), mfn. shaken i. e. pressed out by men, RV. **-nābhi** (*vṛisha-*), mfn. having a strong nave (as a chariot), ib. **-nāman** (of unknown meaning), RV. ix, 97, 54 (accord. to Sāy. *vṛisha*=*varshaṇa,* and *nāman*=*namana*). **-patnī** (*vṛisha-*), f. having a strong lord or husband, ruled by the strong (applied to the waters), RV. **-parvan** (*vṛisha-*), mfn. strong-jointed (Indra), ib.; m. the root of Scirpus Kysoor, L.; the areca-nut tree, L.; N. of Vishṇu, MBh.; of Śiva, L.; of a Dānava (father of Śarmishṭhā), MBh.; Hariv. &c.; of a Rājarshi, MBh.; MārkP.; of a monkey, R. **-pāṇa,** mfn. drunk by men, RV. **-pāṇi** (*vṛisha-*), mfn. strong-hoofed, ib. **-prabharman** (*vṛisha-*), mfn. to whom the strong (i. e. Soma) is presented or offered (Indra), ib. **-prayāvan** (*vṛisha-*), mfn. going with stallions (Maruts), ib. **-psu** (*vṛisha-*), mfn. of strong appearance (applied to the Maruts and their chariot), ib. **-bhará,** mfn. 'seizing strongly, holding fast' or 'crying aloud' (cf. √*bhṛi*), RV. (others 'supporting men'). **-maṇas** and **-manyu** (*vṛisha-*), mfn. manly-spirited, brave, courageous, ib. **-ratha** (*vṛisha-*), mfn. having a strong or mighty car, ib. **-raśmi** (*vṛisha-*), mfn. having strong reins or thongs, ib. **-vrata** (*vṛisha-*), mfn. 'bearing strong sway' or 'ruling over men,' ib. **-vrāta** (*vṛisha-*), mfn. forming strong troops (or 'troops of men'), ib. **-śiprá,** m. 'bull-cheeked,' N. of a demon, ib. **-śushma** (*vṛisha-*), mfn. of manly courage or strength, RV.; m. (also read *-śushṇa*) N. of a man with the patr. Vātāvata, AitBr.; KaushBr. **-savá,** mfn. 'pressed out by men' or 'impelling men' (Soma), RV. **-sená,** mfn. (prob.) having an army of men, VS.; m. N. of a son of the 10th Manu, Hariv.; of Karṇa, MBh.; Pur.; of a great-grandson of Aśoka, Buddh. **-stubh,** mfn. calling aloud, RV. (others 'praising the mighty i. e. the gods'). **Vṛishânna,** n. strong or nourishing food, Kauś. (cf. *vṛishabhânna*).

Vṛishaka, m. a species of plant, Suśr.; N. of a king (son of Su-bala), MBh.; n. (with *Indrasya*) N of various Sāmans, ĀrshBr.

Vṛishaṇ, in comp. for *vṛishan.* **-aśvá,** mfn. drawn by stallions (as a chariot), RV.; m. N. of a man (the father of Menā), ib.; MaitrS.; of a Gandharva, L. (w.r. °*ṇāśva*); of a horse of Indra, L. **-vat** (*vṛishaṇ-*), mfn. yoked with or drawn by or going with stallions, RV.; being among stallions, ib.; containing the word *vṛishan,* TS.; AitBr. **-vasu** (*vṛishaṇ-*), mfn. possessing or bringing great wealth, RV.; n. the treasure of Indra, L.

Vṛishaṇa, mf(*ī*)n. sprinkling, fertilizing, MW.; m. (or n., Siddh.) the scrotum, (du.) the testicles, VS. &c. &c.; m. N. of Śiva, MBh.; of a son of Madhu, Hariv.; of a son of Kārtavīrya, VP. **-kacchū,** f. ulceration of the scrotum, Suśr.

1. **Vṛishad,** in comp. for *vṛishat* (pr. p. of √*vṛish*). **-añji** (only in pl.), RV. viii, 20, 9 (=*vṛishatā somena añjantas,* Sāy.) **-gu,** m. N. of a king, MBh. ii, 324 (B. *rushadru;* cf. *ṛishad-gu*).

Vṛishan, mfn. (acc. *vṛishāṇam,* nom. pl. °*shāṇas;* prob. originally 'raining, sprinkling, impregnating') manly, vigorous, powerful, strong, mighty, great (applied to animate and inanimate objects), RV.; AV.; VS.; Br. (superl. *-tama*); m. a man, male, any male animal, a bull, stallion &c. (also N. of various gods, as implying strength, esp. of Indra and the Maruts), ib.; (ifc.) chief, lord (e.g. *kshiti-, kshmā-v*°, lord of the earth, prince), Rājat.; a kind of metre, RPrāt.; N. of a man, RV.; of Karṇa, L.; (*vṛishṇī*), f. a mare, Lāṭy., Sch.; n. N. of a Sāman, Lāṭy.

Vṛisham-dhi, m. (perhaps) lightning, RV. iv, 24, 2 (a 'cloud,' Naigh. i, 10).

Vṛishabhá, mfn. (cf. *ṛishabha*) manly, mighty, vigorous, strong (applied like *vṛishan* to animate and inanimate objects), RV.; AV.; m. (ifc., f. *ā*) a bull (in Veda epithet of various gods, as of Indra, Bṛihas-pati, Parjanya &c.; according to Sāy. =*varshayitṛi,* 'a showerer of bounties, benefactor'), RV. &c.; the chief, most excellent or eminent, lord or best among (in later language mostly ifc., or with gen.), ib.; the zodiacal sign Taurus, VarBṛS.; a partic. drug (described as a root brought from the Himâlaya mountains, resembling the horn of a bull, of cooling and tonic properties, and serviceable in catarrh and consumption), Bhpr.; the hollow or orifice of the ear, L.; N. of Daśad-yu, RV.; of an Asura slain by Vishṇu, Hariv. (v.l. *ṛish*°); of one of the sons of the 10th Manu, MārkP.; of a warrior, MBh.; of a son of Kuśâgra, Hariv. (v.l. *ṛish*°); of a son of Kārtavīrya, BhP.; (with Jainas) of the first Arhat of the present Avasarpiṇī, Col.; of a mountain in Giri-vraja, MBh.; Hariv. &c.; (in astron.) of the 28th Muhūrta; (*ā*), f. N. of the three lunar mansions (viz. of Maghā, Pūrva-phalgunī, and Uttara-phalgunī), VP. (cf. *vīthi*); of a river, MBh.; (*ī*), f. a widow, L.; Mucuna Pruriens, L. **-ketu,** m. 'having a bull for an emblem,' N. of Śiva, L. **-gati,** m. 'going on a bull,' N. of Śiva, L. **-carita,** mfn. done by bulls, VarBṛS.; n. N. of a metre (commonly called Hāriṇī), ib. **-tīrtha-māhātmya,** n. N. of wk. **-tva,** n. the state or condition of (being) a bull, Kathās. **-dāna,** n. N. of wk. **-dhvaja,** m. =*-ketu,* MBh.; R. &c.; N. of one of Śiva's attendants, MBh.; of a mountain, VarBṛS.; °*jêśvara-māhātmya,* n. N. of wk. **-yāna,** n. a car drawn by oxen, Mṛicch. **-lakshaṇa,** n. N. of wk. **-vīthi,** f. N. of the ninth division of the course of the planet Venus (comprising the lunar mansions Maghā, Pūrva-phalgunī, and Uttara-phalgunī), VarBṛS. **-shodaśa,** mfn. 'having a bull as sixteenth;' (*ā*), f. pl. (with or scil. *gāvaḥ*) fifteen cows and a bull, Mn. ix, 124; xi, 116 &c. **-skandha,** mfn. having shoulders like a bull, broad-shouldered, R. **-svarga-vidhāna,** n. N. of wk. **-svāmin,** m. N. of a king (founder of the family of Ikshvāku and father of Draviḍa), Śatr. **Vṛishabhâksha,** mfn. bull-eyed, MBh.; R.; (*ī*), f. colocynth, L. **Vṛishabhâṅka,** m. =°*bha-ketu,* MBh.; R. **Vṛishabhâdri,** m. N. of a mountain (cf. under *vṛishabha*); *-māhātmya,* n. N. of wk. **Vṛishabhânna,** mfn. eating nourishing food, RV. (cf. *vṛishânna*). **Vṛishabhâsura-vidhvaṅsin,** m. 'slayer of the Asura Vṛishabha,' N. of Vishṇu, Pañcar. **Vṛishabhêkshaṇa,** m. 'bull-eyed,' N. of Vishṇu, MW. **Vṛishabhâika-sahasrā,** f. pl. (with *gāvaḥ*) a thousand cows and a bull, Mn. xi, 127. **Vṛishabhâikādaśā,** f. pl. (with *gāvaḥ*) ten cows and a bull, Hcat. **Vṛishabhôtsarga,** m. 'letting loose a bull,' N. of wk. (cf. *vṛishôtsarga*).

1. Vrishaya. See *vrishāya.*

Vrishayú, mfn. ruttish, in heat, excitable, high-spirited (as a horse), RV.

Vrishalá or **vríshala,** m. (fr. *vrishan*) a little or contemptible man, low or mean or wicked fellow (in later language 'a Śūdra'), RV. &c. &c.; a dancer, L.; N. of king Candra-gupta (who was by birth a Śūdra), Mudr.; a norse, L.; an ox, L.; a kind of garlic, L.; (*ī*), f., see below; n. long pepper, L. — **tā,** f., **-tva,** n. the condition of a Śūdra, state of an out-caste, Mn.; MBh. — **pācaka,** mfn. one who cooks for a Ś°, MBh. (v.l. *yājaka*). — **yājaka,** mfn. one who sacrifices for a Ś°, ib. **Vrishalâtmaja,** m. the son of a Vrishala or of a reprobate, W.

Vrishalaka, m. a poor or contemptible Śūdra, Uttarar.

Vríshalī, f. a woman of low caste, Śūdra woman, ŚBr. &c. &c. (L. also 'an unmarried girl twelve years old in whom menstruation has commenced; a woman during menstruation; a barren woman; the mother of a still-born child'). — **pati,** m. the husband of a Śūdra woman or a Brāhman who owns such a w° as his mistress, Mn. iii, 155. — **putra** (or °*lyāḥ p°*), m. the son of a Ś° w°, Pāṇ. vi, 3, 22, Sch. — **phena-pīta,** mfn. one who has drunk the moisture (i. e. kissed the lips) of a Ś° woman, Mn. iii, 19. — **sevana,** n. respect to or intercourse with a Śūdra woman, W.

Vrishasya, Nom. P. °*yati,* to desire the male, be in heat (said of human beings and animals), Mn.; Bhaṭṭ.; Kathās.

Vrishasyantī, f. an amorous or lustful woman, L.; a cow in heat, L.

Vrishā, in comp. for *vrisha* or *vrishan.* — **ka-pāyī,** f. the wife of Vrishā-kapi (see next), RV. (by the Comm. identified with Dawn); = *śrī; gaurī; svāhā; śacī,* L.; Asparagus Racemosus and = *jīvantī,* L. — **kapi** (*vrishā́-*), m. 'man-ape,' N. of a semi-divine being standing in a partic. relation to Indra and Indrāṇī, RV. x, 86 (by the Comm. identified with the Sun; also supposed to be the son of Indra and the author of the above hymn; cf. RTL. 222, n. 1); the sun, MBh.; fire, Hariv.; N. of Śiva, MBh.; Kathās.; of Indra, BhP.; of Vishṇu, MBh.; of one of the 11 Rudras, ib.; of the hymn attributed to Vrishā-kapi, AitBr.; *-śastra,* n. N. of wk. — **gir,** m. 'strong-voiced,' N. of a man (cf. *varshāgiri*). — **darbha** (BhP.), **-darbhi** (MBh.), m. N. of a son of Śibi (cf. *vrisha-d°*). — **modinī,** f. enjoying the male, Kāṭh. — **yúdh,** mfn. combating men, RV. — **rava,** m. 'roaring like a bull,' a kind of animal, ib.; a kind of mallet or drumstick, TBr.; ŚBr. — **śīla,** mfn. (used to explain *vrishala*), Nir. iii, 16 (cf. *vrisha-ś°*).

Vrishāṇa, m. N. of Bāṇa (an attendant of Śiva), L.

Vrishāṇaka, m. N. of the author of RV. x, 136, 4 (having the part. Vātaraśana), Anukr.; of Śiva, L.; of one of Śiva's attendants, L.

Vrishāya (in Padap. °*shaya*), Nom. P. °*yati,* to cause any object (acc.) to rain, RV. x, 98, 1; Ā. °*yáte,* to burn with sexual desire, be ruttish, RV.; Car.; to long or be eager for, advance upon (acc., dat., or loc.), RV.; to roar like a bull, BhP.

Vrishāyaṇa, m. a sparrow, L.; N. of Śiva, MW.

Vrishin, m. (prob.) 'fond of rain,' a peacock, L.

Vrishiman, m. (fr. *vrisha*), g. *prithv-ādi.*

Vrishīya, Nom. P. °*yati* (fr. *vrisha*), Pāṇ. vii, 1, 51, Sch.

Vrishṭá, mfn. rained &c. (n. impers., e. g. *yadi na vrishṭam,* if it has not rained, VarBṛS.; °*shṭe,* ind. when it has rained, AV.); fallen or dropped as rain, KaṭhUp.; one who has rained, Pāṇ. i, 4, 88, Sch.; m. N. of a son of Kukura (cf. *vrishṭi*), VP. — **dharma,** m. N. of a king, VP. — **vat,** mfn. that has rained (as a cloud), Kathās.

Vrishṭi or **vrishṭí,** f. (sg. and pl.) rain, RV. &c. &c. (ifc. often = a shower of, cf. *pushpa-, śara-vṛ°*); (in Sāṃkhya) one of the four forms of internal acquiescence (cf. *salila*), MW.; m. a partic. Ekâha, ŚāṅkhŚr.; N. of a son of Kukura (cf. *vrishṭa*), VP. — **kara,** mf(*ī*)n. producing rain, sprinkling, raining, VarBṛS.; °*rêndra-prakaraṇa,* n. N. of wk. — **kāma** (*vrishṭi-*), mfn. desirous of rain, MaitrS. — **kāmanā,** n. f. desire of rain, Jaim., Sch. — **kāla,** m. the rainy season, W. — **ghnī,** f. small cardamoms, L. — **jīvana,** mfn. 'living by rain,' (land) nourished or watered by rain (= *deva-mātṛika*), W. — **tā,** f. the condition of rain, Naish. — **dyā́van** (*vrishṭí-*), mfn. (prob.) = next, MaitrS. — **dyo** (*vrishṭí-*), mfn. (only du. *-dyāvā* and pl. °*vas*), dwelling in the rain-sky, RV.; ĀśvŚr. — **pāta,** m. a shower of rain, Rājat. — **bhū,** m. 'rain-born,' a frog, L. — **mát** (or *vrishṭi-mat*), mfn. rainy, raining, RV.; ŚBr.; MBh.; m. N. of a son of Kavi-ratha, BhP. — **maya,** mf(*ī*)n. consisting of rain, Hcar. — **māruta,** m. rain and wind, Hariv. — **váni,** mfn. obtaining or causing rain, RV.; TS.; Br. — **vāta,** m. = *-māruta,* Hariv. — **sáni,** mfn. = *-váni,* MaitrS.; TS.; Kāṭh.; pl. N. of partic. bricks (*-tva,* n.), TS.; Kāṭh.; ĀpŚr. — **sampāta,** m. a shower of rain, Rājat. — **hávya,** m. N. of a man, RV. **Vrishṭy-ambu,** n. rain-water, L.

Vrishṇa, m. N. of a man (cf. *vriddhá-vrishṇa*).

Vrishṇí or **vríshṇi,** mfn. manly, strong, powerful, mighty, RV.; angry, passionate, L.; heretical, heterodox, L.; m. a ram, VS.; TS.; ŚBr.; a bull, L.; a ray of light, L.; air, wind, L.; N. of Śiva, MBh.; of Vishṇu-Kṛishṇa, L.; of Indra, L.; of Agni, L.; of various kings, Hariv.; Pur.; pl. N. of a tribe or family (from which Kṛishṇa is descended, = *yādava* or *mādhava*; often mentioned together with the Andhakas), MBh.; Hariv. &c.; n. N. of a Sāman, ĀrshBr. — **garbha,** m. 'born in the family of the Vrishṇis,' N. of Kṛishṇa, L. — **pāla,** m. a shepherd, Daś. — **pura,** n. the city of V°, MBh. — **mat,** m. N. of a king, VP. — **vareṇya,** m. 'best of the Vrishṇis,' N. of Kṛishṇa, Bhām. — **vriddha,** m. the eldest or best among the Vrishṇis, L.

Vrishṇika, m. N. of a man, g. *śivâdi.*

Vrishṇiya. See *vriddha-vrishṇiya.*

Vríshṇya, mfn. manly, vigorous, mighty, RV.; n. manliness, virility, RV.; AV.; Kauś. **Vríshṇyā-vat,** mfn. possessed of manly power, vigorous, strong, mighty (applied to Parjanya), RV. v, 83, 2.

Vrishya, mfn. = *varshya,* Pāṇ. iii, 1, 120; productive of sexual vigour, stimulating, VarBṛS.; Suśr.; m. N. of Śiva, MBh. 10372 (Nīlak. 'increasing merit;' rather 'most manly or vigorous'); Phaseolus Radiatus, L.; (*ā*), f. Asparagus Racemosus, L.; the myrobolan-tree, L.; a kind of bulbous plant, L.; n. an aphrodisiac, L. — **kandā,** f. Batatas Paniculata, L. — **gandhā,** f. Argyreia Speciosa or Argentea, L. — **gandhikā,** f. Sida Cordifolia or Rhombifolia, L. — **tā,** f. manly vigour or potency, virility, Cat. — **vallikā,** f. Batatas Paniculata, L.

वृषद् **2. vrishad,** m. (for 1. see p. 1012, col. 3) N. of a man, Uṇ. v, 21, Sch.

वृषदञ्जि *vrishad-añji, vrishad-gu.* See under 1. *vrishad,* p. 1012, col. 3.

वृषय **2. vrishaya,** m. = *āśraya,* refuge, shelter, Uṇ. iv, 100, Sch.

वृसय *vrisaya, vrisī.* See *brisaya, brisī.*

वृह् *vrih.* See √1. 2. *bṛih* &c.

वृह *vriha.* See *a-vriha.*

वृहत् *vrihat.* See *brihat* under √2. *bṛih.*

वॄ *vṝi* (Dhātup. xxxi, 16; 20). See √2. *vṛi.*

वे 1. *ve* (cf. √*ūy*), cl. 1. P. Ā. (Dhātup. xxiii, 37) *váyati,* °*te* (pf. p. *vavau* or *uvāya;* 2. sg. *uvayitha,* Gr.; 3. pl. *vavuḥ,* ib.; *ūvuḥ,* RV.; *ūyuḥ,* Bhaṭṭ.; Ā. *vave, ūve, ūye,* Gr.; aor. *avāsīt, avāsta,* Gr.; Prec. *ūyāt, vāsīshṭa,* ib.; fut. *vātā,* ib.; *vāsyati,* °*te,* ib.; *vayishyáti,* RV.; inf. *ótum, ótave, ótavaí,* ib.; *vā́tave,* AV.), to weave, interweave, braid, plait (fig. to string or join together artificially, make, compose, e. g. speeches, hymns), RV. &c. &c.; to make into a cover, into a web or web-like covering, overspread as with a web (said of a cloud-like mass of arrows filling the air), Bhaṭṭ.: Pass. *ūyate* (aor. *avāyi*), Gr.: Caus. *vāyayati,* ib.: Desid. *vivāsati,* °*te,* ib.: Intens. *vāvāyate, vāveti, vāvāti,* ib.

Uta, mfn. woven &c. See 1. *uta,* p. 175, col. 2.

Ūta, ūtí. See 1. *ūta* &c., p. 221, col. 1.

Vātavya, mfn. to be woven or sewn, Pat.

Vāna &c. See 3. *vāna,* p. 940, col. 2.

Vema, m. a loom (in *su-v°*), MBh. — **citra** or **-citrin,** m. N. of an Asura king, Buddh. — **bhū-pāla** or **-rāja,** m. N. of a king and author, Cat.

Vemaka, m. a weaver, Hariv.; (*ī*), f. the wife of a weaver, ib.

Véman, n. (L. also m.) a loom, VS.; a slay, TBr., Sch.

Vemana, mfn. (fr. prec.), g. *pāmâdi.*

Vemanya, mfn. skilful in weaving, Pat.

Veya, mfn. to be woven &c. — **gāna,** n. a partic. song-book or manual of singing (giving, with the Āraṇya-gāna, the various modifications of intonation for the Ārcika division of the Sāma-veda). — **cchalā,** f. N. of a ch. of the Sāma-veda-cchalā.

वे 2. *vé,* m. a bird (strong stem of 1. *ví,* q. v.)

वेकट *vekaṭa,* m. (cf. *vaikaṭika,* only L.) a youth; a jeweller; a sort of fish; a buffoon (= *vi-dūshaka*); ind. = *adbhuta* (cf. 2. *vi-kaṭa*).

वेकुरि *vekuri.* See *bekuri.*

वेक्ष् *veksh* (prob. for *avêksh,* q. v.), cl. 10. P. *vekshayati,* to see, Dhātup. xxxv, 84, 6 (v.l. *vleksh*).

Vekshaṇa, n. looking after, care about (gen.), Mn. ix, 11 (v.l. for *cêkshaṇe*).

वेग *véga,* m. (fr. √*vij*) violent agitation, shock, jerk, AV.; R.; a stream, flood, current (of water, tears &c.), AV.; ŚvetUp.; MBh. &c.; rush, dash, impetus, momentum, onset, MBh.; BhP.; impetuosity, vehemence, haste, speed, rapidity, quickness, velocity (*vegād vegaṃ* √*gam,* to go from speed to speed, increase one's speed), MBh.; Kāv. &c.; the flight (of an arrow), Kir.; outbreak, outburst (of passion), excitement, agitation, emotion, ib.; attack, paroxysm (of a disease), Suśr.; circulation, working, effect (of poison; in Suśr. seven stages or symptoms are mentioned), Yājñ.; Kāv. &c.; expulsion of the feces, Suśr.; semen virile, L.; impetus, Kaṇ.; Sarvad.; the fruit of Trichosanthes Palmata, L.; N. of a class of evil demons, Hariv. — **ga,** mf(*ā*)n. going or streaming fast, Hariv. — **ghna,** mfn. killing swiftly, MBh. — **javā,** f. N. of a Kiṃ-narī, Kāraṇḍ. — **tara,** m. greater swiftness (*vegād vegataraṃ* √*gam,* to run faster and faster; cf. *vega*), Pañcat. (B.) — **tas,** ind. with a sudden impetus, R.; with speed, quickly, hastily, impetuously, Kathās. — **daṇḍa,** m. (= *vetaṇḍa*) an elephant, Hcar. — **darśin,** m. N. of a monkey, R. — **nāśana,** m. 'preventing speed or activity,' phlegm, the phlegmatic humour, L. — **nā-śya-nāśaka-bhāvârtha-rahasya,** n. N. of wk. — **parikshaya,** m. cessation of the paroxysm of a disease, Suśr. — **rāja,** m. N. of an author; *-saṃhitā,* f. N. of his wk. (composed A. D. 1494). — **rodha,** m. obstruction of speed or activity, retardation, check, W.; obstruction of the movement or evacuation of the bowels, ib. — **vat,** mfn. agitated (as the ocean), R.; impetuous, rapid, hasty, swift, violent, MBh.; Kāv. &c.; m. a leopard, L.; N. of an Asura, MBh.; of a Vidyādhara, Kathās.; of a son of Kṛishṇa, BhP.; of a king (son of Bandhu-mat), ib.; of a monkey, R.; (*vatī*), f. N. of a river, R.; a partic. drug, Suśr.; a kind of metre, Piṅg.; N. of a Vidyādharī, Kathās.; (pl.) N. of a class of Apsarases or celestial nymphs, VP.; *-tama,* mfn. speediest, quickest, very quick or swift, MW.; *-tara,* mfn. more speedy, quicker, very quick, ib.; *-tā,* f. swiftness, velocity, ib.; *-stotra,* n. N. of a Stotra. — **vāhin,** mfn. going or flowing or flying swiftly, R.; Rājat.; (*inī*), f. an arrow, MBh.; MārkP. — **vidhāraṇa,** n. retardation of velocity, stopping, retarding, W.; obstruction of the natural excretions, constipation, Suśr. — **virodhin,** mfn. obstructing the movement or evacuation of the bowels, ŚārṅgS. — **vrishṭi,** f. a violent rain, L. — **sampanna,** mfn. endowed with swiftness, swift (said of horses), R. — **sara,** m. (cf. *vesara*) a mule, L.; (*ī*), f. a female mule, Kathās. — **sāra,** m. pl. N. of a people, VP. **Vegâghāta,** m. = *vega-vidhāraṇa,* W. **Vegânila,** m. a violent wind, Vikr. **Vegâvataraṇa,** n. swift descent, Śak. **Vegôdagra,** mfn. having rapid or intense effect (as venom), Vikr.

Vegi, in comp. for *vegin.* — **tā,** f., **-tva,** n. impetus, velocity, quickness, speed, W. — **hariṇa,** m. a kind of antelope, L.

Vegita, mfn. agitated, rough (as the sea), MBh.; impetuous, hasty, rapid, swift, fleet, MBh.; Kāv. &c.

Vegin, mfn. having velocity, swift, rapid, impetuous, MBh.; Kāv. &c.; m. a hawk, falcon, L.; an express, courier, W.; N. of Vāyu, L.; (*inī*), f. a river, MW.

Vegila, m. N. of a man, Kathās.

Vejana-vat, mfn. (fr. Caus. of √*vij*) used to explain *vājin,* Nir.

Vejita, mfn. (fr. id.) agitated, frightened, terrified, Hariv.; Ragh.; enhanced, increased, MBh.

वेङ्क *veṅka,* m. pl. N. of a people in the south of India, BhP.

Veṅkaṭa, m. (Prākṛit for *vyaṅkaṭa*) N. of a very sacred hill in the Drāviḍa country (in the district of North Arcot, about 80 miles from Madras; it reaches an elevation of about 2,500 feet above the sea-level, and on the summit is the celebrated temple dedicated to Kṛishṇa or Vishṇu in his character of 'Lord of Veṅkaṭa,' also called Śrī-pati or Tirupati, whence the hill is sometimes popularly known as Tri-pati; it is annually thronged with thousands of pilgrims, RTL. 267), BhP.; of a king of Vijaya-nagara (the patron. of Appaya Dīkshita), Cat.; (also with *adhvarin, ācārya, kavi, bhaṭṭa, yajvan, yogin* &c.) N. of various authors and teachers, ib. **—kavīya**, n. N. of a poem. **—kṛishṇa**, m. N. of an author, Cat.; °*ṇīya*, n. N. of his wk. **—giri**, m. the Veṅkaṭa hill, Cat.; *-nātha*, m. N. of a preceptor, Cat.; *-māhātmya*, n. N. of wk. **—nātha**, m. N. of various authors, Cat. **—pati**, m. king Veṅkaṭa, Kuval. **—bheṭ**, N. of wk. **—rāma, -rāya**, and **-subhā-śāstrin**, m. N. of authors, Cat. **Veṅkaṭâcala**, m., °*la-māhātmya*, n. = °*ṭa-giri*, °*ri-māhātmya*, Cat.; *-sūri*, m. N. of an author, ib.; °*lêśa*, m. Vishṇu as worshipped on the hill Veṅkaṭa, ib.; °*lêśvara-maṅgalâśāsana*, n. N. of wk. **Veṅkaṭâdri**, m. = °*ṭa-giri*, Cat.; (with *bhaṭṭa, yajvan, rāyasa*) N. of authors, ib.; *-nāthīya-graha-tantra*, n., *-māhātmya*, n. N. of wks. **Veṅkaṭêśa**, m. 'lord of Veṅkaṭa,' N. of Kṛishṇa, RTL. 267; N. of various authors (also *-kavi, -dīkshita, -paṇḍita* &c.), Cat.; *-kavaca*, n., *-dvādaśa-nāman*, n., *-namaskārâshṭaka*, n., *-pañcāśat*, f., *-prahasana*, n., *-maṅgala*, n., *-maṅgalâśāsana*, n., *-mālā-mantra*, m., *-māhātmya*, n., *-rahasya*, n., *-śataka*, n., *-sahasra-nāman*, n., *-su-prabhāta*, n., *-stotra*, n.; °*śâshṭaka*, n., °*śâshṭôttara-śata-nāman*, n. N. of wks. **Veṅkaṭêśvara**, m. 'lord of V°,' N. of Kṛishṇa or Vishṇu (see above), Cat.; N. of various authors (also *-kavi, -dīkshita* &c.), ib.; *-cātur-bhadrikā*, f., *-maṅgala-stotra*, n., *-māhātmya*, n., *-sahasra-nāman*, n., *-stotra*, n.; °*śvarīya*, n. N. of wks.

वेङ्कप्प *veṅkappa*, m. N. of a dramatic poet, Cat.

वेङ्कप्पय्य *veṅkappayya*, m. N. of an author, ib.

वेङ्कय्य *veṅkayya*, m. (with *prabhu*) N. of a poet, ib.

वेङ्गि *veṅgi* or *veṅgī*, f. N. of a town, Vcar.

वेङ्घर *veṅghara*, m. pride of beauty, L.

वेचा *vecā*, f. (said to be fr. √*vic*) hire, wages, L.

Vecā-rāma and **Vecu-rāma**, m. N. of two authors, Cat.

वेजानी *vejānī*, f. Vernonia Anthelmintica, L.

वेट् *veṭ*, ind. an exclamation used in sacrificial ceremonies, VS. **—kārá**, m. the exclamation *veṭ*, ŚBr.

वेट *veṭa*, m. a kind of tree (= *pīlu-vṛiksha*), Gaṇar.; (*ā*), f. the abode of the Vaiśya tribe (?), W.; (*ī*), f. a boat, L.

Veṭaka, m. N. of a man, Naigh., Introd.

Veṭā-vat, mfn. (fr. *veṭa*), Gaṇar.

वेट्य् *veṭy* (v. l. *vedy*), cl. 1. P. *veṭyati*, 'to be wicked' or 'to sleep' (*dhaurtye svapne ca*), g. *kaṇḍv-ādi*.

वेड *veḍa*, n. a kind of coarse sandal (= *sāndra-vicchinna-candana*), L.; (*ā*), f. (also written *beḍā*) a boat, L. (cf. *veṭī*).

वेढमिका *veḍhamikā*, f. a kind of bread or cake, L.

वेण् *veṇ* (prob. artificial; cf. √*ven*), to go, move; to know; to think; to discern; to play on an instrument; to hold or take, Dhātup. xxi, 13.

Veṇa, m. (cf. *veṇu* and *vīṇā*) a worker in reed, Vishṇ., Sch.; a musician (by caste, the son of a Vaideha and an Ambashṭhī), Mn. x, 19; 49 (cf. *vaiṇa*); the son of an Ugra and a Kshatriyā (who lives as a necromancer and conjuror), L.; v. l. for *vena*, q. v.; (*ā*), f., see next.

Veṇā, f. N. of a woman, HParis.; of a river, MBh.; Kāv. &c. **—taṭa**, m. the bank of the river Veṇā, Mṛicch.; m. pl. N. of a people, MBh. (AV. Pariś. *veṇa-taṭa*).

वेणि *veṇi*, f. (fr. √1. *ve*) weaving, braiding, L.; braided hair or a braid of hair, hair twisted into a single unornamented braid and allowed to fall on the back (so worn by widows and women who mourn for absent husbands, cf. *eka-veṇi*; the water of a river is often compared to such a braid, but in these meanings the form *veṇī* is more common, see below), MBh.; Kāv. &c.; the confluence or meeting of two or more rivers or streams in a common point of union (as at Prayāga or Allāhābād, cf. *tri-v°*), W.; property re-united after it has been before divided, Vas.; a cascade, L. **—mādhava**, m. a partic. square-shaped stone idol having four hands at Prayāga, L. (cf. *veṇī-mādhava-bandhu*). **—rāma**, m. N. of an author, Cat. **—vedhanī**, f. 'hair-penetrating,' a leech, L. **—vedhinī**, f. 'hair-piercer,' a comb, MW.

Veṇika, m. pl. N. of a people, MBh. (B. *vetrika*); (*ā*), f. = *veṇi*, a braid of hair &c., L.; (met.) a continuous line, uninterrupted stream, Hcar.; Kād.; a twisted stripe or band, Hcat.; Suśr. **—vāhin**, mfn. flowing or causing to flow in an uninterrupted stream, Kād.

Veṇin, m. 'having a hood like braided hair,' N. of a serpent-demon, MBh.; (*inī*), f. a woman with braided hair, L.

Veṇī, f. = *veṇi*, a braid of hair &c., MBh.; Kāv. &c.; a stream, current, L.; an abridgement of the title *veṇī-saṃhāra* (see below), Sāh.; Lipeocercis Serrata, Car.; a dam, bridge, L.; a ewe, L.; N. of a river, Hariv.; N. of wk., Cat. **—ga-mūlaka**, n. the root of Andropogon Muricatus, L. **—datta**, m. (also with *bhaṭṭa, śarman* &c.) N. of various authors and other men, Cat. **—dāna**, n. a ceremony performed at Prayāga (cutting off a braid of hair and offering it to the Ganges with gifts to the priests), RTL. 375. **—dāsa**, m. N. of a man, Cat. **—bhūta**, mfn. (hair) forming a braid, BhP. **—mādhava**, m. N. of an author, ib.; *-bandhu*, m. N. of the father of Raṅga-nātha, ib. **—rāma** (with *śāka-dvīpin* and *dharmâdhikārin*), m. N. of authors, ib. **—rūpa**, n., **-vilāsa**, m. N. of two poems. **—saṃvaraṇa** or **-saṃharaṇa**, n. = next. **—saṃhāra**, m. 'binding up of the braided hair,' N. of a well-known drama by Bhaṭṭa-nārāyaṇa (who probably lived in the 9th century; its subject is taken from an incident narrated in the 2nd and 8th books of the Mahā-bhārata, in which is described how Yudhishṭhira gambled away all his possessions, including Draupadī, and how Duḥ-śāsana then insulted Draupadī by loosening her braided hair and dragging her away by her dishevelled locks, and how Bhīma, who witnessed the insult, swore that he would one day kill Duḥ-śāsana and drink his blood; this threat he fulfilled, and Draupadī's hair was then bound up again; cf. MBh. ii, 2229–2235, viii, 4235). **—skandha**, m. N. of a serpent-demon, MBh.

वेणीर *veṇīra*, m. Sapindus Detergens (= *arishṭa*), L.

वेणु *veṇú* or *véṇu*, m. (prob. connected with √1. *ve*) a bamboo, reed, cane, RV. &c. &c.; a flute, fife, pipe, MBh.; Kāv. &c.; N. of a deity of the Bodhi tree, Lalit.; of a king of the Yādavas, MBh.; of a son of Śata-jit, VP.; of a mountain, MārkP.; of a river, L.; (pl.) the descendants of Veṇu, ĀśvŚr. (*Veṇor visāle*, N. of two Sāmans, ĀrshBr.) **—karkara**, m. Capparis Aphylla (a species of thorny plant = *karīra*, commonly called Karir or Karil), L. **—kāra**, m. a flute-maker, Lalit. **—gīta**, n. N. of wk. **—gulma**, m. n. a bamboo-thicket, BhP. **—gopāla-pratishṭhā**, f. N. of wk. **—ja**, mfn. 'reed-born,' produced in or from a reed (as fire), BhP.; m. b° seed or fruit, L.; n. pepper, L. **—jaṅgha**, m. N. of a Muni, MBh. **—jāla**, n. = *-gulma*, Vet. (v. l.) **—datta**, m. N. of a man, Cat. (v. l. *vainya-d°*). **—dala**, n. a split b°, Mn. viii, 299. **—dāri**, m. N. of a king, MBh.; Hariv. &c. **—dārin**, mfn. b°-splitting, Śiś.; m. N. of a demon, ib. **—dhma**, m. a flute-player, piper, L. **—nisruti**, m. the sugar-cane, W. **—nṛityā**, f. N. of a Tantra deity, Kālac. **—pa**, m. N. of a people, MBh. (v. l. *reṇu-pa*). **—pattra**, n. a bamboo leaf, Cat.; (*ī*), f. a kind of grass, L. **—pattraka**, m. a kind of snake, Suśr.; (*ikā*), f. = *-pattrī*, ib. **—bīja**, n. b° seed, L. **—bhārá**, m. a load of bamboo, ŚBr. **—maṇḍala**, n. N. of a Varsha in Kuśa-dvīpa, MBh. **—mat**, mfn. provided with bamboo, Yājñ.; m. N. of a mountain, Hariv.; of a son of Jyotish-mat, VP.; (*atī*), f. N. of a river, VarBṛS.; n. N. of a mountain, Hariv.; of the Varsha ruled by Veṇu-mat, VP. **—maya**, mf(*ī*)n. made or consisting of bamboo, VarBṛS.; Hcat. **—mudrā**, f. a partic. position of the fingers, Pañcar. **—yava**, m. pl. b° seed, GṛŚrS.; Suśr.; (*ī*), f. an oblation of b° s°, ŚāṅkhŚr. **—yashṭí**, f. a b° staff, ŚBr. **—vana**, n. a forest of b°, Rājat.; N. of a forest, Divyâv. **—vāda** or **-vādaka**, m. a flute-player, piper, L. **—vādana**, n. playing on the flute, Hcat. **—vādya**, n. id.; *-viśārada*, mfn. skilful in playing the flute (said of Kṛishṇa), Pañcar. **—vidala**, n. split b°, Gaut. **—vīṇā-dharā**, f. N. of one of the Mātṛis attendant on Skanda, MBh. **—vaidala**, mfn. made of split bamboo, Mn. viii, 327. **—śayyā**, f. a couch of reed, R. **—haya**, m. N. of a descendant of Yadu, Hariv.; BhP. **—hotra**, m. N. of a son of Dhṛishṭa-ketu, Hariv.; VP.

Veṇavin, mfn. furnished with a flute (said of Śiva), MBh. (v. l. *vaiṇavin*).

Veṇuká, m. a flute, pipe, Hariv.; amomum, L.; N. of a mythical being, Suparṇ.; pl. N. of a people, MārkP. (cf. *veṇu-pa*); (*ā*), f. a kind of plant with poisonous fruit, Suśr.; amomum, BhP., Sch.; n. a goad with a bamboo handle (used for driving an elephant), L.

Veṇukīya, mfn. (fr. *veṇu*), g. *naḍâdi*; (*ā*), f. a place where bamboos grow, Pāṇ. vi, 4, 153, Sch.

Veṇugradha (?), m. a species of plant, MārkP.

Veṇuna, n. black pepper, L.

वेण्ठ *veṇṭha*, n. a place where Viṭas congregate (*viṭâśraya*), L.

वेण्णा *veṇṇā, veṇyā, veṇvā*. See *kṛishṇa-v°*.

वेत *veta*, m. (prob. corrupted fr. *vetra*; but see Uṇ. iii, 118) a cane, reed, L.; (*ā*), f. = *vetana*, L.

वेतण्ड *vetaṇḍa*, m. (cf. *vitaṇḍa, vedaṇḍa, vega-daṇḍa*) an elephant, Hcar.; Kād.; Bhām.; (*ā*), f. a form of Durgā, Vās. (v. l. for *vetālā*).

वेतन *vetana*, n. (accord. to Uṇ. iii, 150 fr. √*vī*, but rather connected with √*vṛit*; cf. *vartana*) wages, hire, salary, subsistence, livelihood, Mn.; MBh. &c.; price, Rājat.; silver, L. **—jīvin**, mfn. subsisting by wages, stipendiary, MW. **—dāna**, n. the paying of wages, hiring, Pāṇ. i, 3, 36, Sch. **—bhuj**, m. 'earning wages,' a servant, Pañcar. **Vetanâdāna**, n. non-payment of wages, Mn. viii, 218.

Vetanin, mfn. receiving wages, stipendiary (mostly ifc., e. g. *kupya-v°*, receiving bad pay), MBh.

वेतस *vetasá*, m. (cf. *veta* and *vetra*) the ratan (Calamus Rotang) or a similar kind of cane, a reed, rod, stick, RV. &c. &c.; the citron (Citrus Medica), MW.; N. of Agni, ib.; (*ī*), f. the ratan, cane, reed, Kathās. (°*sī-taru*, Sāh.); n. a lancet shaped like a pointed leaf of the ratan, Vāgbh.; N. of a city, Kathās. [Cf., accord. to some, Gk. ἰτέα; Lat. *vitis*; Germ. *wîda, Weide*; Eng. *withy*.] **—gṛiha**, n. an arbour formed of reeds, Śak. **—pattra**, n. the leaf of the ratan, MārkP.; a lancet, W. **—parikshipta**, mfn. (an arbour) fenced or enclosed by reeds, Śak. **—pushpa**, n. the blossom of the ratan, VarBṛS. **—maya**, mf(*ī*)n. consisting of reeds, Hcar. **—mālin**, mfn. wreathed with reeds, Ml. **—vṛitti**, mfn. acting or pliant as a reed, Pañcat. **—śākhā**, f. a branch of reed, ŚBr. **Vetasâmla**, m. Rumex Vesicarius, L.

Vetasaka, m. pl. N. of a people, MBh. (v. l. *cet°*); (*ikā*), f. N. of a place, ib.

Vetasinī, f. N. of a river, VP. (cf. *vedasinī*).

Vetasú, m. N. of a man or of an Asura (pl. his descendants), RV.

Vetas-vat, mfn. abounding in reeds, Pāṇ. iv, 2, 87; N. of a place, PañcavBr.

वेताल *vetāla*, m. (of doubtful derivation) a kind of demon, ghost, spirit, goblin, vampire (esp. one occupying a dead body), Hariv.; Kāv.; Kathās. &c.; N. of one of Śiva's attendants, KālikāP.; of a teacher, BhP.; of a poet, Cat.; a door-keeper (?), L.; (*ā*), f. a form of Durgā, Vās.; (*ī*), f. N. of Durgā, Hariv. **—karma-jña**, mfn. knowing the doings of a Vetāla, VarBṛS. **—kavaca**, n. N. of a Kavaca (q. v.), Cat. **—jananī**, f. N. of one of the Mātṛis attendant on Skanda, MBh. **—pañca-viṉśati** or °**tikā**, f. a collection of 25 tales or fables told by a

Vetāla or demon to king Vikramâditya (of which there are 5 recensions extant, one by Kshemêndra in his Bṛihat-kathā-mañjarī, one by Soma-deva in the Kathā-sarit-sāgara, and the other three by Jambhala-datta, Vallabha, and Śiva-dāsa; versions of these popular tales exist in Hindī, Tamil and Telugu, and almost every Hindū vernacular). **-pura**, n. N. of a town, Siṃhās. **-bhaṭṭa**, m. N. of a poet (the author of the Nīti-pradīpa, and one of the 9 men of letters said to have flourished at the court of Vikramâditya; cf. *nava-ratna*), Cat. **-rasa**, m. a partic. mixture, L. **-viṅśati**, f. N. of a collection of 20 Vetāla tales by Veṅkaṭa-bhaṭṭa. **-sādhana**, n. winning or securing (the favour of) a Vetāla, Kathās. **-siddhi**, f. the supernatural power of a Vetāla, Buddh. **-stotra**, n. N. of a Stotra. **Vetālâkhyāyikā**, f. N. of wk. **Vetālâsana**, n. a kind of posture (in which the right hand holds the toe of the left foot, and the left hand holds the toe of the right foot), L. **Vetālôtthāpana**, n. the act of raising a Vetāla, Mālatim.

वेत्तृ 1. *vettṛi*, mfn. (fr. √1. *vid*) one who knows or feels or witnesses or experiences, a knower, experiencer, witness, ŚvetUp.; MBh. &c.; m. a sage, one who knows the nature of the soul and God, W. **-tva**, n. knowledge, MW.

वेत्तृ 2. *vettṛi*, m. (fr. √3. *vid*) one who obtains in marriage, an espouser, husband, Āpast.

वेत्र *vetra*, m. n. (accord. to Uṇ. iv, 166, fr. √1. *vī*; prob. connected with √1. *ve*, cf. *veṇu*) a kind of large reed (used for making sticks, prob. Calamus Rotang or Fasciculatus), Kauś.; MBh. &c.; n. a cane, staff, VarBṛS.; BhP.; MaitrUp.; Sch.; the rod or mace of an officer, staff of a door-keeper (see comp.); the tube of a flute, Saṃgīt. **-karīra**, m. n. the shoot or fresh sprout of a reed, Suśr. **-kāra**, m. a worker in reed, R. **-kīcaka-veṇu**, m. pl. different sorts of reed, BhP. **-grahaṇa**, n. 'grasping the staff,' the office of a door-keeper, Ragh. **-daṇḍika**, m. 'reed-staff bearer,' a door-keeper, L. **-dhara**, m. 'staff-bearer,' a door-keeper, L.; (*ā*), f. a female door-keeper, Ragh. **-dhāraka**, m. = *-dhara*, L. **-dhārin**, m. 'staff-bearer,' the servant of a great man, Pañcad. **-nadī**, f. N. of a river, Divyâv. **-pāṇi**, m. 'staff-handed,' a mace-bearer, Hariv. **-phala**, n. the fruit of Vetra, Suśr. **-bhṛit**, m. = *-dhara*, Dharmaś. **-yashṭi**, f. a staff of reed or cane, Śak. **-latā**, f. 'reed-branch,' a staff or stick, Pañcat.; *-caya*, m. a heap of sticks, R.; *-maya*, mf(*ī*)n. made of sticks, Hcar. **-vat**, mfn. containing or consisting of reeds, BhP.; m. N. of a mythical being (a son of Pūshan), Kathās.; (*atī*), f. a female door-keeper, Śak.; Prab.; a form of Durgā, Hariv. (v. l. *citra-rathī*); N. of a river (now called the Betwā, which, rising among the Vindhya hills in the Bhopāl State and following a north-easterly direction for about 360 miles, falls into the Jumnā below Hamīrpur), MBh.; R. &c.; of the mother of Vetrâsura, VarP. **-vana-māhātmya**, n. N. of wk. **-vyāsakta-hasta**, mfn. one whose hands cling to a reed or reeds, MBh. **-han**, m. N. of Indra, L. (prob. w. r. for *vṛitra-han*). **-hasta**, m. = *-pāṇi*, Kathās. **Vetrâgra**, n. the point of a reed, Suśr. **Vetrâghāta**, m. a blow with a cane, a caning, MW. **Vetrâbhighāta**, m. id., Kautukas. **Vetrâmla**, m. (prob.) = *vetasâmla*, Suśr. **Vetrā-vatī**, f. N. of a river, Cat. (cf. *vetra-vatī* and Vām. v, 2, 75). **Vetrâsana**, n. 'cane-seat,' a small oblong low couch of cane-work (used as a dooly or litter); °*nâsīna*, mfn. seated on such a seat, Kum. **Vetrâsava**, m. the juice or decoction of Vetra, Suśr. **Vetrâsura**, m. N. of an Asura, VarP. (v. l. *vaitr*°).

Vetrakīya, mfn. reedy, abounding with reeds or canes, g. *naḍâdi*; (*ā*), f. a reedy place, Pāṇ. vi, 4, 153, Sch. **-gṛiha**, n., **-vana**, n. N. of places, MBh.

Vetrika, m. pl. N. of a people, MBh. (v.l. *venika*).

Vetrin, mfn. (ifc.) having a cane, having anything for a cane, MaitrUp.; m. a staff-bearer, door-keeper, Rājat.

Vetrīya, mfn. (fr. *vetra*), g. *utkarâdi*.

वेद **1. veda**, m. (fr. √1. *vid*, q. v.) knowledge, true or sacred knowledge or lore, knowledge of ritual, RV.; AitBr.; N. of certain celebrated works which constitute the basis of the first period of the Hindū religion (these works were primarily three, viz. 1. the Ṛig-veda, 2. the Yajur-veda [of which there are, however, two divisions, see *taittirīya-saṃhitā*, *vājasaneyi-saṃhitā*], 3. the Sāma-veda; these three works are sometimes called collectively *trayī*, 'the triple Vidyā' or 'threefold knowledge,' but the Ṛig-veda is really the only original work of the three, and much the most ancient [the oldest of its hymns being assigned by some who rely on certain astronomical calculations to a period between 4000 and 2500 B.C., before the settlement of the Āryans in India; and by others who adopt a different reckoning to a period between 1400 and 1000 B.C., when the Āryans had settled down in the Panjāb]; subsequently a fourth Veda was added, called the Atharva-veda, which was probably not completely accepted till after Manu, as his law-book often speaks of the three Vedas—calling them *trayam brahma sanātanam*, 'the triple eternal Veda,' but only once [xi, 33] mentions the revelation made to Atharvan and Aṅgiras, without, however, calling it by the later name of Atharva-veda; each of the four Vedas has two distinct parts, viz. 1. Mantra, i.e. words of prayer and adoration often addressed either to fire or to some form of the sun or to some form of the air, sky, wind &c., and praying for health, wealth, long life, cattle, offspring, victory, and even forgiveness of sins, and 2. Brāhmaṇa, consisting of Vidhi and Artha-vāda, i.e. directions for the detail of the ceremonies at which the Mantras were to be used and explanations of the legends &c. connected with the Mantras [see *brāhmaṇa*, *vidhi*], both these portions being termed *Śruti*, revelation orally communicated by the Deity, and heard but not composed or written down by men [cf. I. W. 24 &c.], although it is certain that both Mantras and Brāhmaṇas were compositions spread over a considerable period, much of the latter being comparatively modern; as the Vedas are properly three, so the Mantras are properly of three forms, 1. Ṛic, which are verses of praise in metre, and intended for loud recitation; 2. Yajus, which are in prose, and intended for recitation in a lower tone at sacrifices; 3. Sāman, which are in metre, and intended for chanting at the Soma or Moon-plant ceremonies, the Mantras of the fourth or Atharva-veda having no special name; but it must be borne in mind that the Yajur and Sāma-veda hymns, especially the latter, besides their own Mantras, borrow largely from the Ṛig-veda; the Yajur-veda and Sāma-veda being in fact not so much collections of prayers and hymns as special prayer- and hymn-books intended as manuals for the Adhvaryu and Udgātṛi priests respectively [see *yajur-veda*, *sāma-veda*]; the Atharva-veda, on the other hand, is, like the Ṛig-veda, a real collection of original hymns mixed up with incantations, borrowing little from the Ṛig and having no direct relation to sacrifices, but supposed by mere recitation to produce long life, to cure diseases, to effect the ruin of enemies &c.; each of the four Vedas seems to have passed through numerous Śākhās or schools, giving rise to various recensions of the text, though the Ṛig-veda is only preserved in the Śākala recension, while a second recension, that of the Bhāshkalas, is only known by name; a tradition makes Vyāsa the compiler and arranger of the Vedas in their present form: they each have an Index or Anukramaṇī [q. v.], the principal work of this kind being the general Index or Sarvânukramaṇī [q.v.]; out of the Brāhmaṇa portion of the Veda grew two other departments of Vedic literature, sometimes included under the general name Veda, viz. the strings of aphoristic rules, called Sūtras [q. v.], and the mystical treatises on the nature of God and the relation of soul and matter, called Upanishad [q. v.], which were appended to the Āraṇyakas [q. v.], and became the real Veda of thinking Hindūs, leading to the Darśanas or systems of philosophy; in the later literature the name of 'fifth Veda' is accorded to the Itihāsas or legendary epic poems and to the Purāṇas, and certain secondary Vedas or Upa-vedas [q. v.] are enumerated; the Vedâṅgas or works serving as limbs [for preserving the integrity] of the Veda are explained under *vedâṅga* below: the only other works included under the head of Veda being the Pariśishṭas, which supply rules for the ritual omitted in the Sūtras; in the Bṛihad-āraṇyaka Upanishad the Vedas are represented as the breathings of Brahmā, while in some of the Purāṇas the four Vedas are said to have issued out of the four mouths of the four-faced Brahmā and in the Vishṇu-Purāṇa the Veda and Vishṇu are identified), RTL. 7 &c.; IW. 5; 24 &c.; N. of the number 'four,' VarBṛS.; Srutabh.; feeling, perception, ŚBr.; = *vṛitta* (v.l. *vitta*), L. (cf. 2. *veda*). **-kartṛi**, m. 'author of Veda,' N. of the Sun, MBh.; of Śiva, Pañcar.; of Vishṇu, ib. **-kavi-svāmin**, m. N. of a poet, Cat. **-kāra**, m. the composer of the Veda, Kusum. **-kāraṇa-kāraṇa**, n. 'cause of the cause of the V°,' N. of Kṛishṇa, Pañcar. **-kumbha**, m. N. of a preceptor, Kathās. **-kuśala**, mfn. versed in the V°, MW. **-kauleyaka**, m. 'belonging to the family of the V°,' N. of Śiva, L. **-gata**, mfn. standing at the fourth place, Śrutab. **-garbha**, mf(*ā*)n. full of the Veda, Cat.; m. N. of Brahmā (also transferred to Vishṇu), BhP.; a Brāhman, L.; N. of a Brāhman, Kshitîś. (v. l. *-garva*); of a treatise on the sacred syllable Om, Cat.; (*ā*), f. N. of the Sarasvatī, BhP.; °*bha-rāśi*, m. N. of a man, Inscr.; °*bhāpurī-māhātmya* or °*bhā-māhātmya*, n. N. of wk. **-garva**, see *-garbha*. **-gātha**, m. N. of a Ṛishi, Hariv. **-gāmbhīrya**, n. the deep or recondite sense of the V°, MW. **-gupta**, mfn. 'one who has preserved the Veda,' N. of Kṛishṇa (a son of Parāśara), BhP. **-gupti**, f. the preservation of the V° (by the Brāhmanical caste), W. **-guhya**, mfn. concealed in the V° (said of Vishṇu), Pañcar. (°*hyôpanishad*, f., ŚvetUp.) **-ghosha**, m. the sound caused by the recitation of the V°, L. **-cakshus**, n. the V° compared to an eye, MBh.; the eye for seeing (or discerning the sense of) the V°, Cat. **-jananī**, f. 'mother of the Veda,' N. of the Gāyatrī, KūrmaP. **-jña**, mfn. knowing the Veda, Mn. xii, 101. **-tattva**, n. 'Veda-truth,' the true doctrine of the Veda, Cāṇ. **-tattvârtha**, m. the true doctrine and meaning of the Veda, Mn. iv, 92; *-vid* or *-vidvas*, mfn. knowing the true meaning of the V°, ib., v, 42; iii, 96. **-tātparya**, n. the real object or true meaning of the V°, MW. **-taijasa**, n. N. of wk. **-traya**, n. (Mn.), **-trayī**, f. (Prab.) the three V°s. **-1. -tva**, n. (for 2. see p. 1017, col. 3) the nature of the V°, Hariv. **-dakshiṇā**, f. the fee for instruction in the V°, Āpast. **-darśana**, n. the occurring or being mentioned in the V° (°*nāt*, 'in accordance with the V°,'), Sūryas. **-darśin**, mfn. 'V°-seeing,' one who discerns the sense of the V°, Mn. xi, 234. **-dala**, mfn. 'four-leaved,' Hcat. **-dāna**, n. the imparting or teaching of the Veda, Cat. **-dīpa**, m. 'lamp of knowledge or of the V°,' N. of Mahī-dhara's Comm. on the Vājasaneyi-saṃhitā. **-dīpikā**, f. N. of a Comm. on the Brahma-sūtras by Rāmânujâcārya (= *vedânta-dīpa*). **-dṛishṭa**, mfn. approved or sanctioned by the V° or Vedic ritual, MBh. **-dhara**, m. N. of a man (= *vedêśa*), Cat. **-dharma**, m. N. of a son of Paila, Cat. **-dhāraṇa**, n. keeping the V° (in the memory), MBh. **-dhvani**, m. = *-ghosha*, R., Sch. **-nāda**, m. = *-ghosha*, W. **-nighaṇṭu**, m. N. of a Vedic glossary (commonly called Nighaṇṭu, q. v.), Sch. **-nidhi**, m. 'Veda-treasure,' a Brāhman, MW.; N. of a man, Cat.; *-tīrtha*, m. N. of a preceptor of the Madhva or Ānanda-tīrtha school (who died A.D. 1576), ib. **-nindaka**, m. 'Veda-denier,' any one who disbelieves in the Veda, an unbeliever, atheist, Buddhist, Jaina, L. **-nindā**, f. denying the Veda, unbelief, heresy, Mn. xi, 56. **-nindin**, m. = *-nindaka*, Kāvyâd. **-nirghosha**, m. = *-ghosha*, VarBṛS. **-paṭhitṛi**, m. one who recites or repeats the Veda, L. **-patha** or **-pathin**, m. the path of the Veda, BhP. **-pada-darpaṇa**, m. N. of a treatise on the Pada-text of the Veda (cf. *pada-pāṭha*). **-pada-stava**, (prob.) w. r. for *-pāda-stava*. **-pāṭha**, m. a partic. text or recitation of the Veda, L. **-pāṭhaka** (Nīlak.), **-pāṭhin** (MānGṛ.), mfn. = *-paṭhitṛi*. **-pāda-rāmâyaṇa**, n. N. of a wk. on Bhakti. **-pāda-śiva-stotra**, n., **-pāda-stava**, m., **-pāda-stotra**, n. N. of Stotras. **-pāraga**, m. 'one who has gone to the further end of the Veda,' a Brāhman skilled in the Veda, Gaut.; Vas. &c. **-pārâyaṇa-vidhi**, m. N. of wk. **-puṇya**, n. merit (acquired) by (the reciting or repeating) the V°, Mn. ii, 78. **-purusha**, m. the V° personified, AitĀr. **-prakāśa**, m. N. of wk. **-pradāna**, n. = *-dāna*, Mn. ii, 171. **-prapad**, f. N. of partic. formulas (in which *pra-pad* occurs), Kauś. **-pravāda**, m. a statement or declaration of the V°, MBh. **-plāvin**, m. one who promulgates or publicly teaches the V°, Yājñ. **-phala**, n. the meritorious fruit or result of (reciting or repeating) the V°, Mn. i, 109. **-bāhu**, m. 'Veda-armed,' N. of one of the 7 Ṛishis under Manu Raivata, Hariv.; of a son of Pulastya, VP.; of a son of Kṛishṇa, BhP. **-bāhya**, m. 'outside the Veda,' an unbeliever, sceptic, Sāṃk., Sch.; mfn. not founded on, i.e. contrary to the Veda,

MBh. – **bīja,** n. 'seed of the V°,' N. of Kṛishṇa, Pañcar. – **brahmacarya,** n. studentship for acquiring the V°, GṛS. – **brāhmaṇa,** m. a Brāhman knowing the V°, a true or right Br°, Buddh. – **bhāga,** m. a fourth part, one fourth, Hcat.; °*gâdi*, m. N. of wk. – **bhāshya,** n. a commentary on the V° (esp. Sāyaṇa's commentary on RV.); *-kāra*, m. N. of Sāyaṇa, Cat. – **mantra,** m. a M° or verse of the V° (see comp.); pl. N. of a people, MārkP.; *-daṇḍaka* (with *karmô-payogin*), m. N. of an author; °*trânukramaṇikā*, f., °*trârtha-dīpikā*, f. N. of wks. – **maya,** mf(*ī*)n. consisting of i.e. containing the V° or sacred knowledge, AitBr.; MBh. &c. – **mātṛi,** f. 'mother of the V°,' N. of Sarasvatī and Sāvitrī and Gāyatrī, TĀr.; MBh. &c.; *-ṭīkā*, f. N. of wk. – **mātṛikā,** f. = '*-mātṛi*,' N. of Sāvitrī, Pañcar. – **māli,** m. N. of a Brāhman, Cat. – **māhātmya,** n. N. of wk. – **mitra,** m. 'V°-friend,' N. of various preceptors and authors, Cat. – **mukha,** n. N. of wk. (cf. *-vadana*). – **muṇḍa,** m. (prob.) N. of an Asura; *-vadha*, m. N. of wk., Cat. – **mūrti,** f. 'embodiment of the V°' (applied to the sun), MārkP. (sometimes used as an honourable title before the names of learned Brāhmans). – **mūla,** mfn. 'Veda-rooted,' grounded on the Veda, Kām. – **yajña,** m. a Vedic sacrifice, Mn.; MBh.; *-maya*, mf(*ī*)n. formed or consisting of the above sacrifices, VP. – **rakshaṇa,** n. the preservation of the Veda (as a duty of the Brāhmanical class), W. – **rahasya,** n. 'secret doctrine of the Veda,' N. of the Upanishads, MBh. – **rāta,** w.r. for *deva-rāta*, Hariv. – **rāśi,** m. 'whole collection of the Veda,' the entire V°, Sāy.; *-kṛita-stotra*, n. N. of a Stotra. – **lakshaṇa,** n. or **-lakshaṇa-sūtra-vṛitti,** f. N. of wks. – **vacana,** n. a text of the Veda, W. – **vat,** mfn. having or familiar with the V°, Hariv.; (*atī*), f. N. of a river, MBh.; Pur. (cf. *vedasinī*, *vetasinī*); of a beautiful woman (daughter of Kuśa-dhvaja, whose story is told in the Rāmâyaṇa; she became an ascetic, and being insulted by Rāvaṇa in the wood where she was performing her penances, destroyed herself by entering fire, but was born again as Sītā or, accord. to other legends, as Draupadī or Lakshmī), R.; of an Apsaras, L. – **vadana,** n. 'Veda-mouth,' introduction to the V°, i.e. grammar, Gol. (cf. *-mukha*); N. of a place, Cat. – **vākya,** n. a text or statement of the V°, Sarvad. – **vāda,** m. id., MBh.; speaking about the V°, Vedic discussion, ib. &c.; *-rata*, mfn. delighting in such d°, Bhag. – **vādin,** mfn. versed in Vedic d° or in Vedic lore d°, Hcat. – **vāsa,** m. 'Veda-abode,' a Brāhman, L. – **vāha,** m. devoted to the Veda, MBh. (Nīlak.) – **vāhana,** mfn. carrying or bringing the V° (said of the sun), MBh. – **vāhya,** see *bāhya*. – **vikrayin,** mfn. selling i.e. teaching the Veda for money, MBh. – **vicāra,** m. N. of wk. – **vit-tva,** n. (fr. next) knowledge of the Veda, MārkP. – **vid,** mfn. knowing the V°, conversant with it (superl. *-vit-tama*, Mn. v, 107), ŚBr. &c. &c.; m. a Brāhman versed in the V°, W.; N. of Vishṇu, MW. – **vidyā,** f. knowledge of the V°; -°*tmaka* (°*dyâtm*°), mfn. one whose nature is kn° of the V°, thoroughly versed in Vedic lore, MārkP.; -°*dhigama* (°*dyâdh*°), m. acquisition of Vedic lore, MaitrUp.; -°*dhipa* (°*dyâdh*°), m. a master of Vedic lore, Pañcar.; *-vid*, mfn. versed in Vedic kn°, Kathās.; *-vrata-snāta*, mfn. one who has performed his ablutions after completing his knowledge of the Veda and his religious observances (cf. *snātaka*), Mn. iv, 31. – **vidvas,** mfn. = *-vid*, MBh. – **viplāvaka,** mfn. propagating the V°, Gaut. – **vilāsinī,** f. N. of wk. – **vihita,** mfn. taught or enjoined in the V°, W. – **vṛitta,** n. the doctrine of the V°, MW. – **vṛiddha,** m. N. of a V° teacher, Cat. – **vedâṅga** (ibc.) the V° and Vedâṅga (see col. 3); *-tattva-jña*, mfn. one who knows the nature or truth of the V° and Vedâṅga, Cāṇ.; *-pāra-ga*, mfn. one who has gone through the V° and Vedâṅga, MBh.; *-vigrahin*, mfn. one whose body consists of the V° and Vedâṅga (said of Vishṇu), Vishṇ.; *-vid*, mfn. knowing the V° and the Vedâṅga, R. – **vedânta-tattva-sāre sālagrāma-māhātmya,** n. N. of wk. – **vaināśikā,** f. N. of a river, R. (v. l. °*nāsikā*). – **vyāsa,** m. 'arranger of the V°,' N. of Vyāsa or Bādarāyaṇa, MBh.; Hariv. &c.; *-tīrtha* and *-svāmin*, m. N. of two teachers, Cat. – **vrata,** n. any religious observance performed during the acquirement of the Veda, Gaut.; Hcat.; mfn. one who has undertaken the vow of acquiring the V°, Gṛihyas., Sch.; *-pārâyaṇa*, mfn. one who is devoted to the V° and performs the necessary observances, VarBṛS.; *-vidhi* (or *-vratānāṃ vidhi*), m. N. of a Pariśishṭa of Kātyāyana. – **vratin,** mfn. id., Hcat. – **śabda,** m. the word 'Veda,' Āpast.; a statement or delaration of the V°, Mn. i, 21. – **śākhā,** f. a branch or school of the V°, BhP.; *-praṇayana*, n. establishing or founding a Vedic school, ib. – **śāstra,** n. the doctrine of the V°, Mn. iv, 260 &c.; pl. the V° and Śāstras, Cat.; *-purāṇa*, n. pl. the V° and Śāstras and Purāṇas, Subh.; *-vid*, mfn. knowing the V° and Śāstras, MBh.; *-sampanna*, mfn. versed in the V° and Śāstras, MW. – **śira,** m. N. of a son of Kṛiśâśva, BhP. – 1. **śiras,** n. (for 2. see under 3. *veda*) 'head of the Veda,' N. of a mythical weapon, Cat.; m. N. of a Ṛishi (son of Mārkaṇḍeya and Mūrdhanyā, progenitor of the Bhārgava Brāhmans), MBh.; Hariv.; Pur.; of a son of Prâṇa, MW.; of a son of Kṛiśâśva (cf. *-śira*), BhP. (B.) – **śīrsha,** m. N. of a mountain, Cat. – **śravas,** m. N. of a Ṛishi, MW. – **śrī,** m. N. of a Ṛishi, MārkP. – **śruta,** m. pl. N. of a class of gods under the third Manu, BhP. – **śruti,** f. the hearing or reciting of the V°, R.; Vedic revelation (also °*tī*), MBh.; N. of a river, R. – **saṃsthita,** mfn. contained in the V°, MārkP. – **saṃhitā,** f. a Vedic Saṃhitā, the S° text of the Veda, an entire V° in any recension, Mn. xi, 258. – **saṃnyāsa,** m. discontinuance of Vedic rites, W. – **saṃnyāsika** (Mn. vi, 86) or °**sin** (Kull. on ib. 95), m. a Brāhman in the fourth period of his life who has discontinued all recitation of the V° and performance of Vedic rites. – **samarthana,** n. N. of wk. – **samāpti,** f. complete acquisition of the V°, ĀśvGṛ. – **sammata,** mfn. conformable to the V°, W. – **sammita,** mfn. of equal measure with or conformable to the V°, MBh. – **sāra,** m. 'Essence of the Veda,' N. of Vishṇu, Pañcar.; *-rahasya*, n., *-śiva-sahasra-nāman*, n., *-śiva-stava*, m., *-śiva-stotra*, n., *-sahasra-nāman*, n. N. of wks. – **sûkta-bhāshya,** n. N. of a Comm. by Nāgêśa. – **sūtra,** n. a Sūtra belonging to the Veda, MBh. – **stuti,** f. 'praise of the Veda,' N. of the 87th ch. of the 11th book of the Bhāgavata-Purāṇa (also called *śruti-stuti*); *-kārikā*, f. a metrical paraphrase of the prec. wk. by Vallabhâcārya (inculcating the doctrine of devotion as a means of salvation); *-laghûpâya*, m. N. of a Comm. on the Veda-stuti. – **sparśa,** m. N. of a preceptor, Cat. – **smṛitā** or **-smṛiti** (MBh.), **-smṛitī** (VarBṛS.), f. N. of a river. – **svāmin,** m. N. of a man, Inscr. – **hīna,** mfn. destitute of (knowledge of) the V°, L. **Vedâṅśa,** m. a fourth part, one fourth, Hcat. **Vedâgny-utsādin,** mfn. one who neglects (recitation of) the V° and (maintenance of) the sacred fire, Vishṇ. **Vedâgraṇī,** f. 'leader of the Veda,' N. of Sarasvatī, L. **Vedâṅga,** see below. **Vedâcārya,** m. 'V°-teacher,' (with *āvasathika*) N. of the author of the Smṛiti-ratnâkara, Cat. **Vedâtman,** m. 'Soul of the Veda,' N. of Vishṇu, R.; of the Sun, MārkP. **Vedâtmaná** (?), m. 'id.,' N. of Brahmā, TĀr. **Vedâdi,** m. the beginning of the V°, ib.; m. n. the sacred syllable Om, ŚāṅkhGṛ.; *-bīja*, n. id., L.; *-rūpa*, mfn. having the beginning of the V° for its form or substance (as the syllable Om), Up.; *-varṇa*, n. = *-bīja*, W. **Vedâdhigama,** m. the repetition or recitation of the V°, Mn. ii, 2. **Vedâdhideva,** m. 'tutelary deity of the V°,' N. of Brahmā, Pañcar. **Vedâdhipa** or °**pati,** m. 'one who presides over the Veda,' N. of certain planets (viz. of Jupiter or Bṛihaspati, Venus, Mars, and Mercury, who are supposed to preside respectively over the Ṛig-, Yajur-, Sāma-, and Atharva-veda), MW. **Vedâdhyaksha,** m. 'protector of the Veda,' N. of Kṛishṇa, Hariv. **Vedâdhyayana,** n. the repetition or recitation of the V°, Āpast.; R. &c. **Vedâdhyayin,** mfn. = °*dhyāyin*, W. **Vedâdhyāpaka,** m. a teacher of the V°, W. **Vedâdhyāpana,** n. teaching the V°, ib. **Vedâdhyāya** or °**yāyin,** mfn. one who repeats or is constantly repeating the V°, Āpast. **Vedânadhyayana,** n. remissness in repeating the V°, Mn. iii, 63. **Vedânadhyāya,** m., **Vedânukramaṇikā,** f. N. of wks. **Vedânuvacana,** n. repetition or recitation of the V°, ŚBr.; Gaut.; Yājñ.; sacred doctrine, TUp. **Vedânusmṛiti,** f. N. of wk. **Vedânta** &c., see p. 1017. **Vedâpti,** f. acquisition of the V°, BrahmaP. **Vedâbhyāsa,** m. constant repetition of the V°, Mn. ii, 166 &c.; the repetition of the mystical syllable Om, W. **Vedâraṇya-māhātmya,** n., **Vedârambha-prayoga,** m. N. of wk. **Vedârṇa,** N. of a Tīrtha, Cat. **Vedârtha,** m. the meaning or sense of the Veda, Mn.; MBh. &c.; *-candra* (or *-pradīpa*), m., *-tattva-nirṇaya*, m., *-dīpa*, m., *-dīpikā*, f. (by Shaḍ-guru-śishya), *-nighaṇṭu*, m., *-prakāśa*, m. (Sāyaṇa's Comms. on several Vedas), *-prakāśikā*, f., *-pradīpikā*, f. (by Kātyāyana-śishya), *-yatna*, m., *-ratna*, n., *-vicāra*, m. N. of wks.; *-vid*, mfn. knowing the sense of the V°, Mn. iii, 186; *-saṃgraha*, m. an abstract of the more important Upanishads by Rāmânuja. **Vedâvatāra,** m. 'descent of the V°,' the revelation or handing down of the V°, MW. **Vedâvâpti,** f. = *vedâpti*, Hcat. **Vedâśra,** mfn. quadrangular, Hcat. **Vedâśvā,** f. N. of a river, MBh. **Vedêśa,** m. 'lord of the V°,' N. of a man (= *veda-dhara*), Cat.; *-tīrtha* or *-bhikshu*, m. N. of an author, ib. **Vedêśvara,** m. N. of a man (= *vedêśa*), Vās., Introd. **Vedôkta,** mfn. taught or declared or contained in the V°, Mn.; R.; *-śiva-pūjana*, n. N. of wk. **Vedôdaya,** m. 'origin of the V°,' N. of Sūrya or the Sun (from whom the Sāma-veda is said to have proceeded; cf. Mn. i, 23), L. **Vedôdita,** mfn. mentioned or enjoined in the V°, Mn. iv, 14 &c. **Vedôpakaraṇa,** n. 'Veda-instrument,' a subordinate science for aiding or promoting a knowledge of the Veda (= *vedâṅga*), Madhus.; *-samūha*, m. N. of wk. **Vedôpagrahaṇa,** n. an addition or supplement to the V°, R. (B. °*pabṛiṅhaṇa*). **Vedôpanishad,** f. the Upanishad or secret doctrine of the V°, TUp. **Vedôpabṛiṅhaṇa,** see °*pagrahaṇa*. **Vedôpayāma,** m. a partic. implement, MānŚr. **Vedôpasthānika,** f. attendance on the Veda, Hariv.

Vedaka, mf(*ikā*)n. making known, announcing, proclaiming, Rājat.; restoring to consciousness, Sarvad.; (*ikā*), f., see s.v.; (*akā*), f. N. of an Apsaras, VP.

1. **Vedana,** mfn. (for 2. see p. 1017, col. 2) announcing, proclaiming (see *bhaga-v*°); n. perception, knowledge, Nir.; MBh.; Kāv. &c. (rarely *ā*, f.); making known, proclaiming, Rājat.; (*ā*), f. pain, torture, agony (also personified as a daughter of Anṛita), MBh.; R. &c. (exceptionally n.); feeling, sensation, Yājñ.; Śiś. (with Buddhists one of the 5 Skandhas, MWB. 109); (*ī*), f. the true skin or cutis, L. **Vedanā-vat,** mfn. possessed of knowledge, Sāy.; feeling pain, full of aches, MBh.; painful, aching, Suśr.

Vedanīya, mfn. to be denoted or expressed or meant by (ifc.; *-tā*, f.), Sarvad.; to be (or being) felt by or as (ifc.; *-tā*, f., *-tva*, n.), ib.; to be known or to be made known, W.

Vedam. See *brāhmaṇa-* and *yāvad-v*°.

Vedaya, mfn. (fr. Caus.), Pāṇ. iii, 1, 138.

Vedayāna. See *a-v*°.

Vedayitavya, mfn. to be made known or communicated, R.

Vedayitṛi, mfn. one who perceives or knows, Kum.

1. **Védas,** n. (for 2. see p. 1017, col. 3) knowledge, science, RV. (cf. *keta-*, *jāta-*, *viśva-v*°).

Vedâṅga, n. 'a limb (for preserving the body) of the Veda,' N. of certain works or classes of works regarded as auxiliary to and even in some sense as part of the Veda, (six are usually enumerated [and mostly written in the Sūtra or aphoristic style]; 1. *Śikshā*, 'the science of proper articulation and pronunciation,' comprising the knowledge of letters, accents, quantity, the use of the organs of pronunciation, and phonetics generally, but especially the laws of euphony peculiar to the Veda [many short treatises and a chapter of the Taittirīya-āraṇyaka are regarded as the representatives of this subject; but other works on Vedic phonetics may be included under it, see *prātiśākhya*]: 2. *Chandas*, 'metre' [represented by a treatise ascribed to Piṅgala-nāga, which, however, treats of Prākṛit as well as Saṇskṛit metres, and includes only a few of the leading Vedic metres]: 3. *Vyākaraṇa*, 'linguistic analysis or grammar' [represented by Pāṇini's celebrated Sūtras]: 4. *Nirukta*, 'explanation of difficult Vedic words' [cf. *yāska*]: 5. *Jyotisha*, 'astronomy,' or rather the Vedic calendar [represented by a small tract, the object of which is to fix the most auspicious days for sacrifices]: 6. *Kalpa*, 'ceremonial,' represented by a large number of Sūtra works [cf. *sūtra*]: the first and second of these Vedâṅgas are said to be intended to secure the correct reading or recitation of the Veda, the third and fourth the understanding of it, and the fifth and sixth its proper employment at sacrifices: the Vedâṅgas are alluded to by Manu, who calls them, in iii, 184, Pravacanas, 'expositions,' a term which is said to be also applied to the Brāhmaṇas), IW. 145 &c. – **tīrtha,** m. N. of an author, Cat. – **tva,** n. the nature or condition of a Vedâṅga, Sarvad. – **rāya,** m. N. of various authors (esp. of the son of Tigulā-bhaṭṭa and father of Nandikêśvara, who wrote for Shah Jehān the Pārasī-prakāśa and the Śrāddha-dīpikā, A.D. 1643). **-śāstra**, n. the doctrine of the Vedâṅgas, Jyot. **Vedâṅgin**, m. one who studies or teaches the Vedâṅgas, MW.

Vedânta, m. end of the Veda (= 'complete knowledge of the Veda,' cf. *vedânta-ga*), TĀr.; MBh.; N. of the second and most important part of the Mīmāṃsā or third of the three great divisions of Hindū philosophy (called Vedânta either as teaching the ultimate scope of the Veda or simply as explained in the Upanishads which come at the end of the Veda; this system, although belonging to the Mīmāṃsā [q. v.] and sometimes called Uttara-mīmāṃsā, 'examination of the later portion or *jñāna-kāṇḍa* [q. v.] of the Veda,' is really the one sole orthodox exponent of the pantheistic creed of the Hindūs of the present day—a creed which underlies all the polytheism and multiform mythology of the people; its chief doctrine [as expounded by Śaṃkara] is that of Advaita i. e. that nothing really exists but the One Self or Soul of the Universe called Brahman [neut.] or Paramâtman, and that the Jīvâtman or individual human soul and indeed all the phenomena of nature are really identical with the Paramâtman, and that their existence is only the result of Ajñāna [otherwise called Avidyā] or an assumed ignorance on the part of that one universal Soul which is described as both Creator and Creation; Actor and Act; Existence, Knowledge and Joy, and as devoid of the three qualities [see *guṇa*]; the liberation of the human soul, its deliverance from transmigrations, and re-union with the Paramâtman, with which it is really identified, is only to be effected by a removal of that ignorance through a proper understanding of the Vedânta; this system is also called Brahma-mīmāṃsā and Śārīraka-mīmāṃsā, 'inquiring into Spirit or embodied Spirit:' the founder of the school is said to have been Vyāsa, also called Bādarāyaṇa, and its most eminent teacher was Śaṃkarâcārya), Up.; MBh. &c.; (*ās*), m. pl. the Upanishads or works on the Vedânta philosophy, Kull. on Mn. vi, 83. **-kataka**, m., **-kathā-ratna**, n. N. of wks. **-kartṛi**, m. the author of the Vedânta, Pañcar. **-kalpataru**, m. (°*ru-ṭīkā*, f., *-parimala*, m., *-parimala-khaṇḍana*, n., *-mañjarī*, f.), **-kalpadruma**, m., **-kalpalatā** or °**tikā**, f., **-kārikâvali**, f. N. of wks. **-krit**, m. = *-kartṛi*, Bhag. **-kaumudī**, f., **-kaustubha**, m. (°*bha-prabhā*, f.) N. of wks. **-ga**, m. one who has gone to the end of the Veda or who has complete knowledge of the Veda (= *veda-pāra-ga*), MBh.; a follower of the Vedânta, W. **-gamya**, mfn. accessible or intelligible by the Vedânta, MārkP. **-grantha**, m., **-candrikā**, f., **-cintāmaṇi**, m. N. of wks. **-jña**, m. a knower of the V°, W. **-ḍiṇḍima**, m., **-tattva**, n. (°*tva-kaumudī*, f., *-dīpana*, n., *-bodha*, m., *-muktâvalī*, f., *-sāra*, m.; °*tvôdaya*, m.) N. of wks. **-tātparya**, n. the object or purport of the V°, Sarvad. **-dīpa**, m., **-dīpikā**, f. N. of wks. **-deśika**, m., **-nayanâcārya**, m. N. of authors, Cat. **-nayana-bhūshaṇa**, n., **-nāma-ratna-sahasra-vyākhyāna**, n., **-nirṇaya**, m. N. of wks. **-nishṭha**, mfn. founded or resting on the V°, MBh. **-nyāya-mālā**, f., **-nyāya-ratnâvalī brahmâdvaitâmṛita-prakāśikā**, f., **-padârtha-saṃgraha**, m., **-paribhāshā**, f., **-parimala**, m., **-pārijāta-saurabha**, n., **-prakaraṇa**, n. (°*ṇa-vākyâmṛita*, n.), **-prakriyā**, f. N. of wks. **-praṇihita-dhī**, mfn. one who has his mind fixed upon the V°, Bhartṛ. **-pradīpa**, m. (= *-sāra*, q. v.), **-bhāshya**, n., **-bhūshaṇa**, n., **-maṅgala-dīpikā**, f., **-manana**, n., **-mantra-viśrāma**, m., **-mālā**, f., **-muktâvalī**, f., **-rakshā**, f. N. of wks. **-ratna**, n. the jewel of the V°; *-kośa*, m., *-traya-parīkshā*, f., *-mañjūshā*, f., *-mālā*, f.; °*tnâkara*, m. N. of wks. **-rahasya**, n. 'secret doctrine of the V°,' N. of wk.; *-dīpikā*, f. N. of wk.; *vettṛi*, m. a knower of the secret d° of the V°. **-vākya**, n. a statement of the V°; *-cūḍāmaṇi*, m. N. of wk. **-vāgīśa**, m. (with *bhaṭṭâcārya*) N. of two authors, Cat. **-vāda**, m. assertion of the V° doctrine, Sarvad.; °*dârtha*, m., °*dâvali*, f. N. of wks. **-vādin**, mfn. one who asserts the V° doctrine, Tattvas. **-vārttika**, n., **-vijaya**, m. N. of wks. **-vijñāna**, n. knowledge of the V°, MuṇḍUp.; *-naukā*, f. N. of wk. **-vid**, mfn. knowing the V°, Vedântas. **-vidyā**, f. knowledge of the V°; *-vijaya*, m., *-sāgara*, m. N. of wks. **-vibhāvanā**, f., **-vilāsa**, m., **-vivaraṇa**, n., **-viveka**, m. (°*ka-cūḍāmaṇi*, m.), **-vṛitti** (?), f. N. of wks. **-vedin**, m. = *-vid*, Pañcar. **-śata-ślokī**, f., **-śāstra** (?), n. (°*tra-saṃkshipta-prakriyā*, f.; °*trâmbudhi-ratna*, n.), **-śikhāmaṇi**, m., **-śiromaṇi**, m., **-śruti-sāra-saṃgraha**, m., **-saṃgraha**, m., **-saṃjñā**, f. (°*jñā-nirūpaṇa*, n., *-prakriyā*, f.), **-sapta-sūtra**, n., **-sammata-karma-tattva**, n. N. of wks. **-sāra**, m. 'essence or epitome of the V°,' N. of various wks.; (esp.) of a treatise on the V° by Sadânanda Yogîndra and of a brief Comm. on the V°-sūtra by Rāmânujâcārya (cf. *-pradīpa*); *-padya-mālā*, f., *-viśrāmôpanishad*, f., *-saṃgraha*, m., *-sāra*, m. (or *-jñāna-bodhinī*, an abstract of Sadânanda's Vedânta-sāra), *-siddhânta-tātparya*, n.; °*rôpanishad*, f. N. of wks. **-siṇha**, m. (= *-śata-ślokī*), **-siddhânta**, m. (°*ta-kaumudī*, f., *-candrikā*, f., *-dīpikā*, f., *-pradīpa*, m., *-bheda*, m., *-muktâvalī*, f., *-ratnâñjali*, m., *-sūkti-mañjarī-prakāśa*, f.), **-sudhā-rahasya**, n. N. of wks. **-sūtra**, n. N. of the aphorisms of the V° philosophy (ascribed to Bādarāyaṇa or Vyāsa, also called Brahma-sūtra or Śārīraka-s°); *-muktâvalī*, f., *-vṛitti saṃkshiptā*, f. N. of wks. **-saurabha**, n., **-syamantaka**, m. N. of wks. **Vedântâcārya**, m. N. of various teachers (esp. of a follower of Rāmânuja, founder of a separate sect, RTL. 124); *-caritra* (with *vaibhava-prakāśikā*), *-tārā-hārâvalī*, f., *-dina-caryā*, f., *-prapadana*, n., *-maṅgala-dvādaśī*, f., *-vigraha-dhyāna-paddhati*, f., *-vijaya*, m., *-saptati*, f. N. of wks. **Vedântâdhikaraṇa-cintāmaṇi**, m., °**karaṇa-mālā**, n. N. of wks. **Vedântâbhihita**, mfn. declared in the Upanishads or in the Vedânta, Mn. vi, 83. **Vedântâmṛita**, n. (and °*mṛita-cid-ratna-cashaka*, m.) N. of wks. **Vedântârtha**, m. the meaning or sense of the V°; *-vivecana-mahābhāshya*, n., *-saṃgraha*, m., *-sāra-saṃgraha*, m. N. of wks. **Vedântâloka**, m. a collective N. of Vijñāna-bhikshu's dissertations on a number of Upanishads. **Vedântâvabhṛitha-pluta**, m. one who performs an ablution after acquiring complete knowledge of the Veda, MBh. ii, 1908. **Vedântôpagata**, mfn. derived from or produced by the V°, Mn. ii, 160. **Vedântôpadeśa**, m., °**tôpanishad**, f., °**tôpanyāsa**, m. N. of wks.

Vedântin, m. a follower of the Vedânta philosophy, Sarvad.; (°*ti-bruva*, mfn. one who calls himself a Vedântin, Kap., Sch.; °*ti-mahādeva*, m. N. of a lexicographer, Vās., Introd.)

Vedâpaya (fr. 1. *veda*), Nom. P. °*yati*, to cause to know, impart knowledge, Pāṇ. iii, 1, 25, Vārtt. 2, Pat.

Vedâpti, &c. See p. 1016, col. 2.

1. **Vedi**, m. a wise man, teacher, Paṇḍit, L.; f. knowledge, science (see *a-v°*); a seal-ring (also °*dikā*), L.; (*ī*), f. N. of Sarasvatī, L.

2. **Vedi**, in comp. for 1. *vedin*. **-tā**, f. and 1. **-tva**, n. acquaintance or familiarity with (see *karuṇa-* and *kāruṇya-v°*, and cf. under 3. *vedi*).

Vedîśa, m. 'lord of the wise,' N. of Brahmā, L.

Veditavyà, mfn. to be learnt or known or understood, ŚBr. &c. &c.; to be known or recognized as, to be taken for, to be meant, Kāś.

Véditṛi or **veditṛí**, mf(*trī*)n. knowing, a knower (with acc. or gen.), AV.; ŚBr.; MBh. &c. (cf. *sarva-v°*).

1. **Vedin**, mfn. (for 2. 3. see col. 3) knowing, acquainted with or versed in (ifc.), Mn.; MBh. &c. (cf. *sarva-v°*); feeling, perceiving, MBh.; Pur.; announcing, proclaiming, MBh.; R.; m. N. of Brahmā, L.; (*inī*), f. N. of a river, R.

Védīyas, mfn. knowing (others' 'finding,' 'acquiring,' fr. √3. *vid*) better than (abl.), RV. vii, 98, 1.

1. **Védya**, mfn. notorious, famous, celebrated, RV.; AV.; to be learnt or known or understood, that which is learnt, ŚvetUp.; MBh. &c.; to be recognized or regarded as, MBh.; Hariv.; BhP.; relating to the Veda, MBh. (cf. g. *gav-ādi*). **-tva**, n. knowableness, intelligibility, Śaṃk.

Vedyâ, f. knowledge, RV.; instr. sg. (= nom.) and pl. 'with kn°,' i. e. manifestly, actually, indeed, ib.

वेद 2. *veda*, m. (fr. √3. *vid*) finding, obtaining, acquisition (see *su-v°*); property, goods, ĀśvGṛ. **-tā** (*vedá-*), f. (prob.) wealth, riches, RV. x, 93, 11.

2. **Védana**, mfn. finding, procuring (see *nashṭa-* and *pati-v°*); n. the act of finding, falling in with (gen.), MBh.; the act of marrying (said of both sexes, esp. the marriage of a Śūdra woman with a man of a higher caste; cf. Mn. iii, 44, and *utkṛishṭa-v°*), Mn.; Yājñ.; the ceremony of holding the ends of a mantle (observed by a Śūdra female on her marriage with a man of a higher caste), W.; property, goods, RV.; AV.

2. **Védas**, n. property, wealth, RV.; AV.

Vedasa. See *sarva-v°*.

2. **Vedin**, mfn. marrying (see *śūdrā-v°*).

Védishṭha, mfn. getting or procuring most, RV. viii, 2, 24.

Véduka, mfn. acquiring, obtaining, TS.; TBr.

2. **Védya**, mfn. to be (or being) acquired, TS.; VS.; to be married (see *a-v°*).

वेद 3. *vedá*, m. (perhaps connected with √1. *ve*, to weave or bind together) a tuft or bunch of strong grass (Kuśa or Muñja) made into a broom (and used for sweeping, making up the sacrificial fire &c., in rites), AV.; MS.; Br.; ŚrS.; Mn. **-tṛiṇa**, n. pl. the bunch of grass used for the above, ĀśvŚr. **-** 2. **-tvá**, n. (for 1. see p. 1015) state of being a V°, MaitrS. **-pralava**, m. a bunch of grass taken from the V°, MānŚr. **-yashṭi**, f. the handle of the broom called V°, L. (v. l. *deva-y°*). **-** 2. **-śiras**, n. (for 1. see p. 1016, col. 2) the head or broom end of the V° (cf. prec.), ĀśvŚr.; °*ro-bhūshaṇa*, n. N. of wk. **-staraṇa**, n. the strewing or scattering of the bunch of grass called V°, Kāty.

3. **Vedi**, f. (later also *vedī*; for 1. 2. see col. 2) an elevated (or according to some excavated) piece of ground serving for a sacrificial altar (generally strewed with Kuśa grass, and having receptacles for the sacrificial fire; it is more or less raised and of various shapes, but usually narrow in the middle, on which account the female waist is often compared to it), RV. &c. &c.; the space between the supposed spokes of a wheel-shaped altar, Śulbas.; a kind of covered verandah or balcony in a court-yard (shaped like a Vedi and prepared for weddings &c., = *vitardi*), Kāv.; Kathās.; a stand, basis, pedestal, bench, MBh.; Kāv. &c.; N. of a Tīrtha, MBh. (only *ī*); n. a species of plant (= *ambashṭha*), L. **-karaṇa**, n. the preparation of the Vedi, LāṭyŚr.; pl. the implements used for it, ĀpŚr. **-jā**, f. 'altar-born,' epithet of Draupadī, wife of the Pāṇḍu princes (the fee which Droṇa required for instructing the Pāṇḍu princes was that they should conquer Drupada, king of Pañcāla, who had insulted him; they therefore took him prisoner, and he, burning with resentment, undertook a sacrifice to procure a son who might avenge his defeat; two children were then born to him from the midst of the altar, out of the sacrificial fire, viz. a son Dhṛishṭa-dyumna, and a daughter Draupadī or Kṛishṇā, afterwards wife of the Pāṇḍavas), L. **-** 2. **-tvá**, n. (for 1. see under 2. *vedi*) the state or condition of being a Vedi or altar, MaitrS. **-para**, m. pl. N. of a country and people, L. **-purīsha**, m. the loose earth of the sacrificial ground, ĀśvGṛ. **-pratishṭha**, mfn. erected on s° gr°, MW. **-bhājaná**, n. that which is substituted for the s° gr°, ŚBr. **-matī**, f. N. of a woman, Daś. **-madhya**, mf(*ā*)n. (a woman) having a waist resembling a Vedi (q. v.), Kād. **-māna**, n. the measuring out of a (place for the) s° gr°, L. **-mekhalā**, f. the cord which forms the boundary of the Uttara-vedi, BhP. **-lakshaṇa**, n. N. of the 24th Pariś. of the AV. **-loshṭa**, m. a clod of earth taken from the s° gr°, MānGṛ. **-vat**, ind. like a Vedi, MW. **-vimāná**, n. = *-māna*, ŚBr. **-śroṇi** or **-śroṇī**, f. (met.) the hip-like side of the Vedi, ŚrS. **-shád** (for *-sad*), mfn. sitting on or at the V°, VS.; TBr.; m. = *prācīna-barhis*, BhP. **-sambhavā**, f. = *-jā*, Veṇīs. **-sammāna**, n. = *-māna*, ĀpŚr. **-sādhana-prakāra**, m. N. of wk. **Vedîśa**, see under 2. *vedi*, col. 2.

Vedika, m. a seat, bench, R.; Hariv.; (*ā*), f. (cf. *vedaka* and 1. *vedi*) id., MBh.; Kāv. &c.; a sacrificial ground, altar, VarBṛS.; a balcony, pavilion (= *vitardi*), Naish.; Vās.; Pañcat.

Vedikā-krama, m. N. of a wk. on the construction of fire-altars.

3. **Vedin**, n. a species of plant (= *ambashṭha*), L. (cf. 2. *vedi*).

Vedī. See under 1. and 3. *vedi*.

Vedika (ifc.) = *vedī*, a pavilion, balcony, Kathās.

Vedy, in comp. for 3. *vedi*. **-agni**, m. the fire on the Vedi, Vait. **-antá**, m. the end or edge of the V°, ŚBr.; Lāṭy. **-antara**, n. the interior of the V°, KātyŚr. **-ardha**, m. 'half of a V°,' N. of two mythical districts held by the Vidyādharas (on the Himālaya, one to the north, and one to the south), Kathās. **-ākṛiti**, f. a kind of V°, MānGṛ. **-āstaraṇa**, n. covering the V° with Darbha grass, L. (cf.

veda-st°). **-upôshaṇa**, mfn. burning the Vedi, ĀpŚr., Sch.

वेद 4. veda, m. N. of a pupil of Āyoda, MBh.; (ā), f. N. of a river, VP.

वेदण्ड vedaṇḍa, m. (cf. vitaṇḍa and vetaṇḍa) an elephant, L.

वेदमुख्य veda-mukhya, m. (cf. vedha-m°) a sort of insect, the winged bug, L.

वेदरकर vedarakara, vedarkara, prob. w.r. for bedar°.

वेदसिनी vedasinī, f. N. of a river, VP. (v.l. vetasinī).

वेदायन vedāyana, w.r. for baidāyana.

वेदार vedāra, m. a chameleon, lizard, L.

वेद्य vedy. See √veṭy, p. 1014, col. 1.

वेध् vedh (= vyath), cl. 1. Ā. vedhate, to tremble, quake, Lalit.

वेध 1. védha, mfn. (√vidh) = vedhas, pious, faithful, AV. (v.l.)

Vedhás, mfn. (in some meanings prob. connected with vi-√dhā; nom. m. vedhā́s, acc. vedhásam or vedhā́m) pious, religious, virtuous, good, brave (also applied to gods), RV.; AV.; TS.; MBh.; Hariv.; wise, Kām.; performing, accomplishing (in gambhīra-v°), BhP.; m. a worshipper of the gods, RV.; an arranger, disposer, creator (esp. applied to Brahmā, but also to Prajāpati, Purusha, Śiva, Vishṇu, Dharma, the Sun &c.), MBh.; Kāv. &c.; an author, Rājat.; Sarvad.; a wise or learned man, L.; N. of the father of Hari-ścandra (see vaidasa). **-tama** (vedhás-), mfn. most pious or religious, best, wisest, RV.

Vedhasa, n. the part of the hand under the root of the thumb (considered as sacred to Brahmā; see tīrtha), L.; m. N. of a Vedic Ṛishi (said to belong to the family of Aṅgiras), MW.; (ī), f. N. of a place of pilgrimage, Cat.

Vedhasyā́, f. (instr.) worship, piety, RV. ix, 82, 2.

वेध 2. vedha, m. (√vyadh) penetration, piercing, breaking through, breach, opening, perforation, VarBṛS.; Rājat.; Sarvad.; hitting (a mark), MBh.; puncturing, wounding, a wound, Suśr.; a partic. disease of horses, L.; hole, excavation, VarBṛS.; the depth of an excavation, depth, Car. (also in measurement, Col.); intrusion, disturbance, Vāstuv.; fixing the position of the sun or of the stars, VarBṛS.; mixture of fluids, L.; a partic. process to which quicksilver is subjected, Sarvad.; a partic. measure or division of time (= 100 Truṭis = 1/8 Lava), Pur.; N. of a son of Ananta, VahniP.; (ā), f. a mystical N. of the letter m, Up. **-gupta**, m. (in music) a partic. Rāga, Saṃgīt. **-maya**, mf(ī)n. consisting in perforation or penetration, Cat. **-mukhya**, m. Curcuma Zerumbet, L.; (ā), f. musk, L.; a civet-cat, L. **-mukhyaka**, m. Curcuma Zerumbet, L.

Veddhavya, mfn. to be pierced or perforated or hit (as a mark), MārkP.; to be entered or penetrated into (with the mind), MuṇḍUp.

Veddhṛi, mfn. one who pierces or hits (a mark), MBh.

Vedhaka, m. a piercer, perforator (of gems &c.), MBh.; R.; camphor, L.; sandal, L.; Rumex Vesicarius, L.; N. of one of the divisions of Naraka (destined for arrow-makers), VP.; n. coriander, L.; rocksalt, L.; grain, rice in the ear, W.

Vedhana, n. piercing, hitting (with an arrow), MBh.; penetration, excavation, MW.; affecting with (instr.), Śaṃk.; depth (cf. 2. vedha), MBh.; puncturing, pricking, wounding, MW.; (ī), f. an auger, gimlet, any piercing instrument (esp. for piercing an elephant's ears), L.; Trigonella Fœnum Græcum, L.

Vedhanikā, f. a sharp-pointed perforating instrument (esp. for piercing jewels or shells), auger, awl, gimlet &c., L.

Vedhanīya, mfn. capable of being pierced, penetrable, vulnerable, MW.

Vedhita, mfn. = viddha, pierced, perforated, penetrated, L.; shaken, trembling (applied to the earth), Divyâv.

Vedhi-tva, n. (fr. next + tva) capacity of piercing (see śabda-v°).

Vedhin, mfn. piercing, perforating, hitting (a mark), MBh.; R.; m. Rumex Vesicarius, L.; (inī), f. a leech, L.; Trigonella Fœnum Græcum, L.

Vedhya, mfn. to be pierced or perforated, VarBṛS.; Kathās. &c.; to be cut open or punctured (as a vein; -tā, f.), Car.; to be fixed or observed (cf. 2. vedha), Gaṇit.; (ā), f. a kind of musical instrument, L.; n. a mark for shooting at, butt, target, MārkP.

वेन् ven (in Dhātup. xxi, 13, v.l. for veṇ, q.v.), cl. 1. P. vénati, to care or long for, be anxious, yearn for, RV.; ŚBr.; to tend outwards (said of the vital air), AitBr.; to be homesick, TBr.; to be envious or jealous, RV. (accord. to Naigh. ii, 6 and 14 also 'to go' and 'to worship').

Vená, mf(ī)n. yearning, longing, eager, anxious, loving, RV.; m. longing, desire, wish, care, ib.; N. of the hymn RV. x, 123 (beginning with ayam venaḥ), ŚāṅkhBr.; = yajña, Naigh. iii, 17; N. of a divine being of the middle region, Naigh. v, 4; Nir. x, 38 (also applied to Indra, the Sun, Prajā-pati, and a Gandharva; in AitBr. i, 20 connected with the navel); of various men, (esp.) of the author of RV. ix, 85; x, 123 (having the patr. Bhārgava); of a Rājarshi or royal Ṛishi (father of Pṛithu, and said to have perished through irreligious conduct and want of submissiveness to the Brāhmans; he is represented as having occasioned confusion of castes, see Mn. vii, 41; ix, 66; 67, and as founder of the race of Nishādas and Dhīvaras; according to the Vishṇu-Purāṇa, Vena was a son of Aṅga and a descendant of the first Manu; a Vena Rāja-śravas is enumerated among the Veda-vyāsas or arrangers of the Veda), MBh.; Hariv.; Pur.; v.l. for veṇa, q.v.; (ā), f. love, desire, RV.

Venyá, mfn. to be loved or adored, lovable, desirable, RV.; m. N. of a man, ib.

वेन्ना vennā, f. (cf. veṇā and veṇvā) N. of a river, Uṇ. iii, 8, Sch.

वेप् vep. See √1. vip, p. 972, col. 3.

Vépa, mf(ī)n. vibrating (voice), RV. vi, 22, 5; m. = next, Kauś.; BhP.

Vepáthu, m. quivering, trembling, tremor, AV. &c. &c.; mfn. trembling, quaking, VarBṛS. **-parita**, mfn. possessed of tremor, trembling, R.; Suśr. **-bhṛit**, mfn. possessing tremor, trembling, Śiś. **-mat**, mfn. possessed of tremor, trembling, Śak.

Vepaná, mfn. trembling, quivering, fluttering, TS.; ŚBr.; VarBṛS.; Suśr.; n. quivering, trembling, tremor, Gobh.; R. &c.; shaking, brandishing, R. **-kara**, mfn. manifesting tremor, trembling, quivering, R.

Vépas, n. quivering, quaking, struggling, RV.; stirring, agitation, ib.; = anavadya, L.

Vepita, n. trembling, agitation (in sa-vepitam), Śāntiś.

Vépishṭha, mfn. (superl. of vipra, q.v.) most inspired, RV.

वेम vema, vemaka &c. See √1. ve, p. 1013.

वेमानभैरवार्य vemāna-bhairavârya, m. N. of an author, Cat.

वेर vera, m. n. (only L.) the body; n. the egg-plant; saffron; the mouth.

Veraka, n. camphor, L.

वेरट veraṭa, m. a low man or one of mixed caste (nīca or miśrī-kṛita), L.; n. the fruit of the jujube, L.

वेराचार्य verâcārya (?), m. N. of a prince, Buddh.

वेल् 1. vel (v.l. for vell, q.v.), cl. 1. P. velati, to move, shake, Dhātup. xv, 33.

Vela, n. a garden, grove, L. (cf. vipina fr. √1. vip); a partic. high number, Buddh.; m. the mango tree, L. **-ja**, m. bitter and salt and pungent taste, L.; mfn. bitter and salt and pungent, L.

Velāna, m. astringent and salt and pungent taste; mfn. astringent and salt and pungent, L.

वेल् 2. vel (rather Nom. fr. velā below), cl. 10. P. velayati, to count or declare the time, Dhātup. xxxv, 28. (Cf. ud-vela &c.)

Velā, f. limit, boundary, end, ŚBr.; Kāvyâd.; distance, ŚBr.; KātyŚr.; boundary of sea and land (personified as the daughter of Meru and Dhāriṇī, and the wife of Samudra), coast, shore (velāyām, on the sea-shore, coast-wise), MBh.; Kāv. &c.; limit of time, period, season, time of day, hour (with paścimā, the evening hour; kā velā, 'what time of the day is it?' kā velā prâptāyāḥ, 'how long has she been here?' -velam ifc. after a numeral = times), ŚBr. &c. &c.; opportunity, occasion, interval, leisure (velām pra-√kṛi, to watch for an opportunity; velāyām, at the right moment or season; artha-velāyām, at the moment when the meaning is under consideration), MBh.; Kāv. &c.; meal-time, meal (as of a god = īśvarasya bhojanam, Śiva's meal), L.; the last hour, hour of death, BhP.; easy or painless death, L.; tide, flow (opp. to 'ebb'), stream, current, MaitrUp.; MBh. &c.; 'sickness' or 'passion' (rāga or roga), L.; the gums, L.; speech, L.; N. of the wife of Buddha, L.; of a princess found on the sea-shore (after whom the 11th Lambaka of the Kathā-sarit-sāgara is called). **-°kula** (velâk°), mfn. agitated by the tide, W. **-kūla**, n. the sea-shore, coast (rarely the bank of a river), Uttamac.; BhP.; mfn. situated on the sea-coast, BhP.; n. N. of a district (the modern Tāmalipta or Tamlūk [see tāma-lipta], said to be in the district of Midnapur or in the southern part of the present Hūgli district, forming the west bank of the Hūgli river at its union with the sea; a village having the name Beercool [Bīrkūl], said to be derived from Velā-kūla, still exists near the sea-shore; it is a hot-weather retreat from Calcutta and was formerly a favourite resort of Warren Hastings; see Hunter's Gazetteer). **-jala**, n. sg. and pl. flood-tide (opp. to 'ebb'), Uttamac. **-taṭa**, m. the sea-shore (also °tānta, m.), Kathās. **-°tikrama** (velât°), m. overstepping the (right) time, tardiness, Pañcat. **-°tiga** (velât°), mfn. overflowing the shore (as the ocean), MBh. **-°dri** (velâdri), m. a mountain situated on the coast, Kathās. **-dhara**, m. a kind of bird (= bhāraṇḍa), HPariś. **-°nila** (velân°), m. a coast wind, Ragh. **-bala**, w.r. for -vana, MBh. **-mūla**, n. the sea-shore, W. **-°mbhas** (velâmbhas), n. = velā-jala, Uttamac. **-vana**, n. a forest on the sea-shore, MBh. **-°vali** (velâv°), f. (in music) a partic. scale. **-vitta**, m. a kind of official, Rājat. **-vilāsinī**, f. a courtezan, Nalac. **-vīci**, m. a shore-wave, breaker; pl. surge, Kir. **-samudra**, m. (Mṛicch.), **-salila**, n. (Vikr.) = -jala. **-hīna**, mfn. untimely, occurring before the time (as an eclipse), VarBṛS. **Velôrmi**, f. = velā-vīci, Rājat.

Velāya, Nom. fr. velā, g. kaṇḍv-ādi.

Velikā, f. (with bhū) a country situated on the sea-shore, maritime country, Hariv.

वेलव velava, m. a secretly born son of a Śūdra and a Kshatriyā, L.

वेलायनि velāyani, m. (prob. w.r. for vail°) a patr., Pravar.

वेलिभुक्प्रिय velibhuk-priya, m. a kind of fragrant mango, L. (prob. w.r. for bali-bhuk-priya).

वेलुव veluva, m. or n. (cf. vela) a partic. high number, Buddh.

वेल्ल् vell (cf. 1. vel and vehl), cl. 1. P. (Dhātup. xv, 33) vellati (pr. p. vellat or vellamāna, Vām. v, 2, 9), to shake about, tremble, sway, be tossed or agitated, Kāv.; Kathās. &c.: Caus. vellayati, to cause to shake &c.; to knead (a dough), Bhpr.

Vella, mfn. going, moving, shaking, W.; n. Embelia Ribes, L.; N. of a town (the modern Vellore, see comp. and cf. vellūra). **-ja**, n. black pepper, L. **-puri-vishaya-gadya**, n. an account in prose of the city and district of Vellore and of its ruler Keśa-veśa-rāja.

Vellaka, m., see kāra-v°; (ikā), f. Trigonella Corniculata, L.

Vellana, n. going, moving about, shaking, W.; rolling (of a horse), Śiś.; surging (of waves), Rājat.; brushwood, Bhpr.; a sort of rolling-pin with which cakes &c. are prepared, W.; (ī), f. a species of Dūrvā grass, L.; n. black pepper, L.

Vellantara, m. a partic. tree (= vīra-taru), Bhpr.

Vellahala, m. a libertine (= keli-nāgara), L.

Velli, f. (cf. valli) a creeping plant, L.

Vellikâkhya, f. Trigonella Corniculata, L. (cf. under vellaka).

Vellita, mfn. shaken, trembling &c.; bent, curved, crooked, MBh.; Kāv. &c.; entwined (as arms), Śiś.; n. going, moving, shaking, W.; the rolling of a horse,

L. **Vellitâgra**, mfn. curly at the end or point (as hair), MBh.; m. hair, Gal.

Vellitaka, m a kind of serpent, Suśr.; n. crossing (instr. crosswise), ib.

Vellūra, m. or n. (cf. *vella*) N. of a town and district (the modern Vellore in North Arcot, 80 miles from Madras; it has a celebrated fortress), VarBṛS.

वेविज *vevijá*, mf(*ā*)n. (fr. Intens. of √*vij*) starting, quick, RV.

Vévijāna. See Intens. of √*vij*.

वेविदत् *vévidat, vévidāna.* See Intens. of √3. *vid*.

वेविषत् *vévishat, vévishāṇa.* See Intens. of √*vish*.

वेवी *vevī* (cf. Intens. of √1. *vī*), cl. 2. Ā. *vevīte* (3. pl. *vevyate*, Pāṇ. vi, 1, 6, Sch.), to go; to pervade; to conceive; to desire; to throw; to eat, Dhātup. xxiv, 69.

वेश् *veś*. See √*ves*.

वेश *veśá*, m. (√1. *viś*) 'a settler,' small farmer, tenant, neighbour, dependent, vassal, RV.; Kāṭh. (once in VS. *véśa*); entrance, ingress, W.; a tent (see *vastra-v°*); a house, dwelling (cf. *veśa-vāṭa*), L.; prostitution or a house of ill fame, brothel, Mn.; Daś.; Kathās.; the behaviour of a courtezan, Kathās.; trade, business (to explain *vaiśya*), L.; the son of a Vaiśya and an Ugrī, L.; often w. r. for *vesha*. [For cognate words see under √1. *viś*.] **-kula**, n. a number of courtezans, Daś.; *-strī*, f. a common woman, Bhar. **-tvá**, n. the state of a tenant or (dependent) neighbour, vassalage, MaitrS. **-dāna**, **-dhara** &c., see *vesha-d°*, *vesha-dh°*. **-nada** (or *veśana-da*?), m. N. of a river, Inscr. **-bhaginī**, f. N. of Sarasvatī, Kāṭh. (cf. next). **-bhagína**, mf(*ā*)n. (an expression applied to Sarasvatī), MaitrS. (*viśo-bh°*, ĀpŚr.; cf. *veśo-bh°*, Pāṇ. iv, 4, 132). **-bhāva**, m. the nature or condition of prostitutes, Mṛicch. **-bhṛit**, see *vesha-bhṛit*. **-yámana**, mfn. ruling or managing people, MaitrS.; Kāṭh.; n. the act of ruling &c., ib. **-yuvati** (Bhar.), **-yoshit** (Hariv.), f. a harlot, prostitute. **-vat**, m. the keeper of a house of ill fame, Kull. on Mn. iv, 84. **-vadhū** (Hariv.), **-vanitā** (Mudr.), f. a common woman, harlot. **-vāṭa**, n. house and court, Daś. **-vāsa**, m. a house of prostitutes, brothel, Mṛicch. **-strī** (MBh.), **-sthā** (SāmavBr.), f. a prostitute. **Veśânta**, m. (BṛĀrUp.), or **veśântā**, f. (ŚBr.) a pond.

Veśaka, mfn. who or what enters, entering, W.; m. a house, L.; (*ikā*), f. entrance, ingress, W.

Veśana, n. the act of entering, BhP.; a house, W.; (*ī*), f. an entrance, waiting room, L.

Veśantá, m. a pond, tank, AV.; Kāv. (cf. *veśânta*); fire, L.; (*véśantā*, TBr.; *veśantī*, AV.), f. id.

Veśás, m. a neighbour, vassal, AV. ii, 32, 5.

Veśasa. See *yajña-v°*.

Veśā-pura, n. N. of a town, Vcar.

Veśika, n. (cf. *vaiśika*) a partic. art, Lalit.

Veśin, mfn. entering, Hariv. (also w. r. for *veshin*).

Veśī, f. 'entering, piercing (?),' a pin, needle, RV. vii, 18, 7 (Sāy.)

Veśo-bhagīna and **veśo-bhagya**, mfn. (fr. *veśas* + *bhaga*) nourishing neighbours or retainers, Pāṇ. iv, 1, 131; 132 (cf. *veśa-bhaginī* and *-bhagína*).

Veśma, in comp. for *veśman*. **-karman**, n. house-building, MW. **-kaliṅga**, prob. = (or w. r. for) next, L. **-kuliṅga**, m. a kind of bird, Suśr. **-kūla**, m. a kind of creeper, L. **-caṭaka**, m. a kind of sparrow, Bhpr. **-dhūma**, m. a species of plant (prob. = *gṛiha-dh°*), Car. **-nakula**, m. the musk rat or shrew, L. **-bhū**, f. building-ground, the site of a habitation, L. **-vāsa**, m. a sleeping-room, Kathās. **-sthūṇā**, f. the main post or column of a house, L. **Veśmânta** (ifc. f. *ā*) the interior of a house, R.

Veśmaka, mfn. (fr. *veśman*), g. *ṛiśyâdi*; m. pl. N. of a people, MārkP.

Véśman, n. a house, dwelling, mansion, abode, apartment, RV. &c. &c.; a palace, Āpast.; an astrological house, VarBṛS.; N. of the 4th astr° house, ib.

Veśya, mfn. to be entered (ifc., g. *vargyâdi*); (*ā*), f., see below; (*veśyà*) n. neighbourhood, dependence, vassalage, RV.; an adjacent or dependent territory, ib.; a house of prostitutes, house of ill fame, L.; prostitution (*veśyam* with Caus. of √*vah*, to be a prostitute), Divyâv. **-kāminī** (VarBṛS.), **-strī** (MBh.), f. a prostitute, harlot (= *veśyā*, see next).

Veśyā, f. 'intranda,' a harlot, courtezan, prostitute, Mn.; MBh. &c. (in comp. also *veśya*; see prec.); Clypea Hernandifolia, L.; a kind of metre, Col. **-gaṇa**, m. a company of harlots, L. **-gamana**, n. going after harlots, licentiousness, MW. **-gāmin**, m. one who visits harlots, fornicator, ib. **-gṛiha**, n. h°-house, brothel, VarYogay. **-ghaṭaka**, m. a procurer of harlots, pander, Kāv. **-°ṅganā** (*veśyâṅg°*), f. a common woman; *-kalpa*, m., *-vṛitti*, f. N. of wks. **-°cārya** (*veśyâc°*), m. the master or keeper of h°s or dancing girls, L.; a catamite, W. **-jana**, m. a h° or h°s, Śiś.; *-samāśraya* or **°nâśraya**, m. a brothel, L. **-tva**, n. the condition of a h°, Mṛicch., Sch. **-paṇa**, m. wages of a h°, Mṛicch. **-pati**, m. a h°'s husband, paramour, Kāv. **-putra**, m. an illegitimate son, bastard, Mṛicch. **-°yatta** (*veśyây°*), mfn. dependent on h°s; *°ttī-√kṛi*, to make dep° on h°s, Rājat. **-vāra**, m. a number of harlots, W. **-vāsa**, m. = *-gṛiha*, L. **-veśman**, n. id., Rājat. **-vrata**, n. a partic. observance performed by harlots, Cat. **-°śraya** (*veśyâśr°*), m. = *-gṛiha*, Hāsy.

वेशर *veśara, veśavāra.* See *vesara, vesavāra*, col. 3.

वेशि *veśi*, f. (in astron.) = φάσις, N. of the second astrological house from that in which the sun is situated, VarBṛS.

वेशिजात *veśijāta* or *veśījāta*, m. a kind of creeper (= *putra-dātrī*), L.

वेश्वर *veśvara*, m. = *vesara*, L.

वेष *vésha*, m. (ifc. f. *ā* or *ī*, cf. *bhūta-veshī*; fr. √*vish*) work, activity, management, VS.; Kauś.; KātyŚr.; dress, apparel, ornament, artificial exterior, assumed appearance (often also = look, exterior, appearance in general), Mn.; MBh. &c. (acc. with √*kṛi* or *ā-√sthā*, 'to assume a dress,' with √*gam* or *vi-√dhā*, 'to assume an appearance;' with *ā-cchādya*, 'concealing one's appearance,' 'disguising one's self;' *pracchanna-veshena*, id.); often w. r. for *veśa*; (*veshá*), mfn. working, active, busy, VS. (cf. *prātar-v°*). **-kāra**, m. (used to explain *veshṭana*), L. **-dāna**, m. the sunflower (= *sūrya-śobhā*), L. **-dhara**, mfn. having only the appearance of, disguising one's self, acting a part, Siṃhâs.; (ifc.) disguised as, Divyâv. **-dhārin**, mfn. wearing the dress of (comp.), R.; m. a hypocrite, false devotee, L. **-vat**, mfn. well-dressed (for *su-v°*), Kām. **-śri** or **-śrī** (*vésha-*), mfn. beautifully adorned, TS.; ŚBr. **Veshâdhika**, mfn. very well clothed, too well dressed, VarYogay. **Veshânya-tva**, n. change of dress, VP.

Veshaṇa or **véshaṇa**, n. service, attendance, RV.; (*ā*), f. id., MānGṛ.; Flacourtia Cataphracta, L.

Veshin. See *chadma-v°* and *vikṛita-veshin*.

Veshya, mfn. dressed, disguised, masked (as an actor), Pāṇ. v, 1, 100, Sch.; (*veshyà*), m. (prob.) a head-band, VS.; n. (prob.) work, labour (see *hasta-veshya*).

वेषवार *veshavāra*, incorrect for *vesavāra*.

वेष्क *veshká*, m. (cf. *veshṭa* and *bleshka*) a noose for strangling a sacrificial victim, ŚBr.

वेष्ट् *vesht* (cf. *visht*), cl. 1. Ā. (Dhātup. viii, 2) *veshṭate* (pf. *viveshṭe*, fut. *veshṭitā* &c., Gr.), to wind or twist round, Sāh.; to adhere or cling to (loc.), AV.; to cast the skin (said of a snake), R.; to dress, MW.: Caus. *veshṭayati*, *°te* (aor. *aviveshṭat* or *avaveshṭat*; Pass. *veshṭyate*), to wrap up, envelop, enclose, surround, cover, invest, beset, TBr.; Mn.; MBh. &c.; to tie on, wrap round (a turban &c.), MBh.; Rājat.; to cause to shrink up, ŚvetUp.: Desid. *viveshṭishate*, Gr.: Intens. *veveshṭyate*, *veveshṭi*, ib.

Veshṭa, m. enclosing, an enclosure, L.; a band, noose, Kauś.; MBh.; a tooth-hole, Suśr.; gum, resin, L.; turpentine, L.; n. (that which surrounds) Brahman or the sky, L. **-pāla**, m. N. of a man, Buddh. **-vaṃśa**, m. Bambusa Spinosa, L. **-sāra**, m. turpentine, L. **Veshṭâvāra** (?) n. a kind of factitious salt, L. (cf. *vesavāra*).

Veshṭaka, m., see *aṅguli-v°*; a wall, fence, W.; (in gram.) putting a word before and after *iti*, VPrāt.; Beninkasa Cerifera, L.; m. or n. turpentine, L.; n. a head-band, turban, L.; resin, gum, L.; mfn. who or what encompasses or surrounds, W.

Veshṭana, n. the act of surrounding or encompassing or enclosing or encircling (*kṛita-veshṭana*, 'surrounded,' 'beset;' cf. also *aṅguli-v°*), GṛŚrS.; Kāv.; Kathās. &c.; anything that surrounds or wraps &c., a bandage, band, girdle (*°naṃ √kṛi*, 'to bandage'), MBh.; Pañcat.; a head-band, tiara, diadem, MBh.; Ragh.; Kathās.; an enclosure, wall, fence, Megh.; a covering, case, MW.; a span, MārkP.; the outer ear (i. e. the meatus auditorius and concha), L.; a kind of weapon, L.; a partic. attitude in dancing (either a disposition of the hands or crossing of the feet), W.; a rope round the sacrificial post, L.; Pongamia Glabra, L.; bdellium, L.; = *gati* (?), L. **-veshṭaka**, m. a kind of coitus, L.

Veshṭanaka, m. a kind of coitus, L.

Veshṭanika. See *pāda-v°*.

Veshṭanīya, mfn. to be surrounded or wound round, Nyāyam.

Veshṭayitavya, mfn. id., ib., Sch.

Veshṭitá, mfn. enveloped, bound round, wrapped up, enclosed, surrounded, invested, beset, ŚBr. &c. &c.; covered with, veiled in (instr.), Mn. i, 49; accompanied or attended by (instr.), MBh.; twisted (as a rope), Kathās.; stopped, secured from access, W.; n. encompassing, encircling, W.; one of the gestures or attitudes of dancing (= *veshṭana*), ib.; a kind of coitus, L.; a turban (see *veshṭitin*). **-śiras**, mfn. one who has his head covered, Āpast.

Veshṭitaka. See *latā-v°*.

Veshṭitavya, mfn. = *veshṭanīya*, MW.

Veshṭitin, mfn. wearing a turban, Āpast.

Véshṭuka, mfn. sticking to, adhering, MaitrS.

Veshṭya, mfn. = *veshṭanīya*, MW.

वेष्प *veshpa*, m. water, Uṇ. iii, 23, Sch.

वेष्य *veshya.* See under *vesha*, col. 2.

वेस् *ves*, cl. 1. P. *vesati*, to go, move, Dhātup. xvii, 70; to desire, love, Naigh. ii, 6. (Cf. also 1. *vi*, 2. *ve*, √1. *vī*.)

वेसन *vesana*, n. a kind of flour made from a partic. vegetable product, Bhpr.

वेसर *vesara*, m. (cf. *vega-sara*; also written *veśara*) a mule, VarBṛS.; Śiś.; (*ī*), f. a female mule, Divyâv.; n. (used to explain *vāsara*), Nir. iv, 7; 11.

वेसवार *vesavāra*, m. (also written *veśav°* or *veshav°*) a partic. condiment or kind of seasoning (consisting of ground coriander, mustard, pepper, ginger, spice &c.), Suśr.

वेह् *veh* (also written *beh*), cl. 1. Ā. *vehate*, to strive, make effort, Dhātup. xvi, 42; cl. 1. P. *vehati* = *vehāya*, Vop.

वेहत् *vehát*, f. a barren cow or a cow that miscarries, VS.; AV.; Br. (cf. Uṇ. ii, 85; accord. to L. also 'a cow that desires the bull' or 'a pregnant cow').

Vehāya, Nom. (fr. prec.) Ā. *°yate*, to miscarry, g. *bhṛiśâdi*.

वेहानस *vehānasa*, (with Jainas) a partic. forbidden mode of suicide, Śil.

वेहार *vehāra*, m. (cf. *vihāra*) N. of a country (Behār), L.

वेह्ल् *vehl*, cl. 1. P. *vehlati*, v.l. for √*vell*, Dhātup. xv, 33.

वै 1. *vai* (orig. identical with √2. *vā*), cl. 1. P. (Dhātup. xxii, 24) *vā́yati*, to become languid or weary or exhausted, RV. (*śoshaṇe*, Dhātup.); to be deprived of (gen.), RV. viii. 47, 6; P. and (ep. also Ā.), to blow, Āpast.; MBh.

3. **Vāta**, mfn. (for 1. and 2. see pp. 934, 939) dried up (see 1. *a-vātá*).

Vāna, mfn. dried &c. (see 2. *vāna*, p. 940, col. 2).

वै 2. *vaí*, ind. a particle of emphasis and affirmation, generally placed *after* a word and laying stress on it (it is usually translatable by 'indeed,' 'truly,' 'certainly,' 'verily,' 'just' &c.; it is very rare in the RV.; more frequent in the AV., and very common in the Brāhmaṇas and in works that imitate their style; in the Sūtras it is less frequent and almost restricted to the combination *yady u vai*; in Manu,

MBh. and the Kāvyas it mostly appears at the end of a line, and as a mere expletive. In RV. it is frequently followed by *u* in the combination *vā́ u* [both particles are separated, v, 18, 3]; it is also preceded by *u* and various other particles, e.g. by *íd, áha, utá;* in the Brāhmaṇas it often follows *ha, ha sma, eva;* in later language *api* and *tu.* Accord. to some it is also a vocative particle).

वैंशतिक *vaiṅśatika,* mf(ī)n. (fr. *viṅśatika*) purchased with twenty, Pāṇ. v, 1, 27.

वैकंसेय *vaikaṇseya,* m. metron. fr. *vi-kaṇsā,* g. *śubhrâdi.*

वैकक्ष *vaikaksha,* n. (fr. *vi-kaksha*) = *vaikakshaka,* Mudr. (v. l.); an upper garment, mantle, L.

Vaikakshaka (Kād.; Sadukt.) or **vaikakshika** (Mudr.) or **vaikakshya** (ib.; Jātakam.), n. a garland suspended over the shoulder.

Vaikakshyaka (ifc. f. *ā*) a wrapper, mantle, Hcar.

वैकङ्क *vaikaṅka,* m. N. of a mountain, Pur.

वैकङ्कत *vaikaṅkatá* or *vaík°,* mf(ī)n. (fr. *vi-kaṅkata*) belonging to or coming from or made of Flacourtia Sapida, AV.; TS., Br. &c.; m. Flacourtia Sapida, L.

वैकटिक *vaikaṭika,* m. (fr. 2. *vi-kaṭa,* but cf. *vekaṭa*) a jeweller, Vcar.; (*ku-vaikaṭika,* m. a bad jeweller, Hcar.)

Vaikaṭya, n. hugeness, horribleness, atrociousness, Sāh.

वैकथिक *vaikathika,* mfn. = *vi-kathāyāṃ sādhuḥ,* g. *kathâdi.*

वैकयत *vaikayata,* m., g. *bhauriky-ādi.* **-vidha,** mfn. inhabited by Vaikayatas, L.

वैकर *vaikara,* mfn. (fr. *vi-kara*), g. *utsâdi.*

वैकरञ्ज *vaikarañja,* m. (fr. *vi-karañja*) a species of snake, Suśr.

वैकर्ण *vaikarṇá,* m. (fr. *vi-karṇa*) N. of two tribes (du.), RV.; patr. fr. *vi-karṇa,* PārGṛ. (accord. to Sch. N. of Garuḍa or of the wind); a patr. (if a Vātsya be meant), Pāṇ. iv, 1, 117 (cf. *vaikarṇeya*).

Vaikarṇāyana (Cat.) or **vaikarṇi** (Saṃskārak.), m. patr. fr. *vi-karṇa.*

Vaikarṇeya, m. patr. fr. *vi-karṇa* (if a Kāśyapa be meant), Pāṇ. iv, 1, 124 (cf. *vaikarṇa*).

वैकर्त *vaikarta,* m. (fr. *vi-karta*) a partic. edible part of a sacrificial victim, (perhaps) the loin, AitBr. (Sāy.); one who cuts up a sacrificial victim, a butcher, MW.

Vaikartana, mfn. (fr. *vi-kartana*) relating or belonging to the sun, Rāghav.; m. N. of Karṇa (as son of the sun), MBh.; patr. of Su-grīva, Rāghav. **-kula,** n. the solar race, Uttarar.

वैकर्म *vaikarma,* m. N. of the Muni Vātsya, MW.

वैकर्य *vaikarya,* mfn. (fr. *vi-kara*), g. *saṃkāśâdi.*

वैकल्प *vaikalpa,* n. (fr. *vi-kalpa*) dubiousness, ambiguity, indecision, MW.; optionality, A.; w. r. for *vaikalya,* Mn.; MBh.; Rājat.

Vaikalpika, mf(ī)n. admitting of difference of opinion, optional, ĀrshBr.; ĀśvŚr. &c. **-tā,** f. (Mṛicch., Sch.) or **-tva,** n. (Siddh.) optionality.

वैकल्य *vaikalya,* n. (fr. *vi-kala*) imperfection, weakness, defectiveness, defect, frailty (also *-tā,* f., R.; w. r. *vaikalpa-tā*), Mn.; MBh. &c.; incompetency, insufficiency, W.; despondency, MBh.; MārkP. &c.; confusion, flurry, MBh. (v. l. *vaiklavya*).

वैकायन *vaikāyana,* m. a patr., Saṃskārak. (also pl.)

वैकारिक *vaikārika,* mf(ī)n. (fr. *vi-kāra*) based on or subject to modification, modifying or modified, MBh.; Suśr.; Pur. &c.; m. a class of deities, MW.; (with *kāla*) the time necessary for the formation of the fetus, Car.; n. emotion, flurry, R. **-bandha,** m. (in the Sāṃkhya phil.) one of the threefold forms of bondage, Tattvas.

Vaikāri-mata, n., g. *rāja-dantâdi.*

Vaikārya, n. transformation, change, modification, MBh.

वैकाल *vaikāla,* m. (fr. *vi-kāla*) evening, afternoon, W.

Vaikālika, mf(ī)n. occurring in or belonging to the evening, W.; n. evening devotion, (or) an ev° meal, Vet.; Campak.; (*am*), ind. in the afternoon, MW.

Vaikālina, mf(ī)n. = *vaikālika* above, W.

वैकासेय *vaikāseya,* m. patr. fr. *vi-kāsa,* g. *śubhrâdi.*

वैकि *vaiki,* m. a patr., g. *taulvaly-ādi,* Cat. (pl.)

वैकिर *vaikira,* mfn. (fr. *vi-kira*) percolated, trickled through; n. (with *vāri*) percolated water, Suśr.

वैकुघासीय *vaikughāsīya,* mfn. (fr. *vikughāsa*), g. *kṛiśâśvâdi* (v. l. *vaikuṭyāsīya*).

वैकुट्यासीय *vaikuṭyāsīya,* mfn. (fr. *vikuṭyāsa*), g. *kṛiśâśvâdi* (Kāś.; v. l. *vaikughāsīya*).

वैकुण्ठ *vaikuṇṭhá,* m. (fr. *vi-kuṇṭha*) N. of Indra, ŚBr.; KaushUp.; of Vishṇu (Kṛishṇa), MBh.; Hariv. &c.; a statue of Vishṇu, Rājat.; the 24th day in the month of Brahmā, L.; (in music) a kind of measure, Saṃgīt.; a kind of Ocimum, L.; N. of various men (esp. authors and teachers), Cat.; (with Indra) N. of the supposed author of RV. x, 48–50, Anukr.; pl. or sg. (scil. *gaṇa*) N. of a class of gods, Pur.; m. or n. Vishṇu's heaven (variously described as situated in the northern ocean or on the eastern peak of mount Meru), Pañcat.; BhP. &c.; n. talc, W.; (*ā*), f. Vaikuṇṭha's (Vishṇu's) Śakti, Pañcar. **-gati,** f. going to Vishṇu's heaven, Pañcat. **-gadya,** n. N. of wk. **-caturdaśī,** f. the 14th day of the light half of the month Kārttika (sacred to Vishṇu), MW. **-tva,** n. the being Vishṇu (Kṛishṇa), Hariv. **-dīkshita,** m. N. of an author, Cat.; °*tīya,* n. N. of his wk. **-dīpikā,** f. N. of wk.; *-nātha,* m. 'lord of Vaik°,' Vishṇu; *-nâthâcārya,* m. N. of an author, Cat. **-purī,** f. Vishṇu's city, Siṅhâs.; m. N. of an author, Cat.; W. **-bhuvana,** n. or **-loka,** m. Vaikuṇṭha's (Vishṇu's) heaven, Cat. **-varṇana,** n. a description of Vaikuṇṭha, MW. **-vijaya,** m. N. of wk. **-vishṇu, -śishya** or **-śishyâcārya,** m. N. of authors, Cat. **-stava,** m., **-stava-vyākhyā,** f. N. of wks. **-svarga,** m. = *-bhuvana,* Pañcat.

Vaikuṇṭhīya, mfn. relating to Vishṇu's heaven, Pañcat.

वैकृत *vaikṛita,* mf(ī)n. (fr. *vi-kṛiti*) modified, derivative, secondary (*-tva,* n., Lāṭy.), RPrāt.; TPrāt., Sch. &c.; undergoing change, subject to modification, Sāṃkhyak.; KapS.; disfigured, deformed, MBh.; not natural, perpetuated by adoption (as a family), Cat.; m. N. of the Ahaṃ-kāra or I-making faculty, MBh.; of a demon causing a partic. disease, Hariv.; n. (ifc. f. *ā*) change, modification, alteration, disfigurement, abnormal condition, changed state, MBh.; R.; Suśr. &c.; an unnatural phenomenon, portent, Ragh.; VarBṛS.; Rājat.; mental change, agitation, MBh.; R. &c.; aversion, hatred, enmity, hostility, MBh.; Hariv.; Kathās.; Rājat. **-rahasya,** n. N. of wk. **-vat,** mfn. morbidly affected by (comp.), Rājat. **-vivarta,** m. a woeful plight, miserable condition, piteous state, Mālatīm. **-sarga,** m. a form of creation (opp. to *prākṛita-s°*), VP. **Vaikṛitâpaha,** mfn. removing or preventing change, W.

Vaikṛiti, w. r. for *vaikṛita,* n., MBh.

Vaikṛitika, mf(ī)n. subject to change, Sāṃkhyak.; changed, incidental, MW.; (in Sāṃkhya) belonging to a Vikāra i. e. to a production or evolved principle (see *vi-kāra, pra-kṛiti*), ib.

Vaikṛitya, mfn. changed (in form or mind), W.; n. change, alteration, R.; change for the worse, deterioration, degeneration, Hariv.; ugliness, repulsiveness, Sadukt.; an unnatural phenomenon, portent, MBh.; VarBṛS.; aversion, disgust, W.; hostility, R.; woeful state, miserable plight, A.

वैकृन्त *vaikṛinta* (?), m. mercury, L.

वैक्रान्त *vaikrānta,* m. n. (fr. *vi-krānta*) a kind of gem resembling a diamond (also °*taka*), L.

वैक्रिय *vaikriya,* mfn. (fr. *vi-kriyā*) resulting from change, HPariś.; subject to change, Śatr.; Sūryapr.

वैक्लव *vaiklava,* n. (fr. *vi-klava*) bewilderment, despondency, Pur.

Vaiklavya, n. id., MBh.; Hariv.; Kāv. &c.; frailty, feebleness, mental weakness, Kād.; Śak., Sch. **-tā,** f. = *vaiklava,* R.

वैक्ष *vaiksha,* mfn. = *vīkshā śīlam asya,* g. *chattrâdi.*

वैक्षमाणि *vaikshamāṇi,* m. patr. fr. *vīkshamāṇa,* Pat.

वैखरी *vaikharī,* f. N. of a partic. sound, RāmatUp.; Pat.; speech in the fourth of its four stages from the first stirring of the air or breath, articulate utterance, that utterance of sounds or words which is complete as consisting of full and intelligible sentences, MW.; the faculty of speech or the divinity presiding over it, ib.; speech in general, A.

वैखान *vaikhāna,* m. N. of Vishṇu, MBh.

वैखानस *vaikhānasá,* m. (fr. *vi-khānasa*) a Brāhman in the third stage of his life, anchorite, hermit (= *vānaprastha,* q. v.), Kāv.; Gaut.; BhP.; a patr. of Vamra, RAnukr.; of Puru-hanman, PañcavBr.; N. of partic. stars, VarBṛS.; of a sect of Vaishṇavas, W.; Cat.; (*ī*), f. a female anchorite, Bālar.; a vessel used for cooking the meat offered in sacrifice, W.; mf(ī)n. relating or belonging to Vaikhānasas or anchorites (with *tantra,* n. the Tantra of the sect called Vaikhānasa, BhP.), TS.; PañcavBr.; Lāṭy. &c.; n. N. of a Sāman, ĀrshBr. **-tantra,** n. (cf. above), **-bhṛigu-saṃhitā,** f. N. of wks. **-mata,** n. the rules for anchorites, Mn. vi, 21 (Kull.) **-vaishṇavâgama,** m., **-śrauta-sūtra,** n., **-saṃhitā,** f., **-saṃprôkshaṇa,** n., **-sūtra,** n. N. of wks. **Vaikhānasâgama,** m. N. of wk. **Vaikhānasâcārya,** m. N. of a teacher, Cat. **Vaikhānasârādhana,** n., °**sârcanā-nava-nīta,** n. N. of wks. **Vaikhānasâśrama,** m. N. of a hermitage, MBh.

Vaikhānasi, m. a patr., Cat.

Vaikhānasīyôpanishad, f. N. of an Upanishad.

वैखारक *vaikhāraka* (?), m. pungent (cf. *khara*) and salt taste, L.; mfn. pungent and salt, L.

वैगन्धिका *vaigandhikā,* f. (fr. *vi-gandha*) a species of plant, Car. (prob. m. c. for *vig°*).

वैगलेय *vaigaleya,* m. (with *gaṇa*) N. of a class of evil spirits, Hariv.

वैगुण्य *vaiguṇya,* n. (fr. *vi-guṇa*) absence of or freedom from qualities, absence of attributes, W.; difference of qualities, contrariety of properties, diversity, W.; imperfection, defectiveness (with *janmanaḥ,* 'inferiority of birth'), ŚrS.; Mn. &c.; faultiness, badness, unskilfulness, Mn.; MBh. &c.

वैग्रहि *vaigrahi* (fr. *vi-graha*), g. *sutaṃgamâdi.*

Vaigrahika, mf(ī)n. belonging to the body, corporeal, bodily, MW.

वैग्रि *vaigri* (fr. *vigra*), g. *sutaṃ-gamâdi.*

Vaigreya, m. patr. fr. *vigra,* g. *śubhrâdi.*

वैघटिक *vaighaṭika,* m. (cf. *vaikaṭika*) a jeweller, L.

वैघस *vaighasa,* m. (fr. *vi-ghasa*) N. of a huntsman, Hariv.

Vaighasika, mfn. feeding on the residue or remains of food, MBh.

वैघात्य *vaighātya,* n. (fr. *vi-ghātin*), g. *brāhmaṇâdi.*

वैङ्कि *vaiṅki* (cf. *vaiki*), m. a patr., g. *taulvaly-ādi.*

वैङ्गि *vaiṅgi,* m. a patr., Pāṇ. iv, 2, 113, Sch.

Vaiṅgīya, m. (fr. prec.), ib.

Vaiṅgeya, N. of a partic. region, Inscr.

वैचकिल *vaicakila,* mf(ī)n. made of the plant Vicakila, Sadukt.

वैचक्षण्य *vaicakshaṇya,* n. (fr. *vi-cakshaṇa*) experience, proficiency, skill in (loc.), Bhar.; Daś.; Bālar.

वैचित्त्य *vaicittya*, n. (fr. *vi-citta*) mental confusion, absence of mind, a swoon, Suśr.; Car. &c.

वैचित्य *vaicitya*, w.r. for prec.

वैचित्र *vaicitra*, n. (fr. *vi-citra*) = *vaicitrya* below, Rājat.; (*ī*), f. strangeness, wonderfulness, marvellous beauty, Bālar.; Kathās. **-vīrya**, m. (fr. *vicitra-v°*) patr. of Dhṛita-rāshṭra, of Pāṇḍu and of Vidura, Kāṭh.; MBh.; Hariv.; BhP. **-vīryaka**, mfn. belonging to Vicitra-vīrya &c., Hariv. **-vīryin** (m. c.), m. = *-vīrya*, MBh.

Vaicitrya, n. variety, manifoldness, diversity, Kap.; Hit.; VarBṛS. &c.; = *vaicitrī* above, Kāv.; Sāh. &c.; w.r. for *vaicittya*, Mālatīm.; sorrow, despair, MW. **-vīrya**, w.r. for *vaicitra-vī°*, MBh.

वैच्छन्दस *vaicchandasa*, mfn. (fr. *vi-cchandas*) consisting of various metres, Lāṭy.; n. a Sāman consisting of various metres, ib.

वैच्युत *vaicyuta*, m. (fr. *vi-cyuta*) N. of a Muni, Cat.

वैजग्धक *vaijagdhaka*, mfn. (fr. *vi-jagdha*), g. *varāhâdi*.

वैजन *vaijana* or °*na-deva*, m. N. of a king and author, Cat.

वैजनन *vaijanana*, mfn. (fr. *vi-janana*) relating to childbirth; (with or scil. *mās*), m. the last month of pregnancy, Hcar.; Rājat.

वैजन्य *vaijanya*, n. (fr. *vi-jana*) desertedness, solitude, Rājat.

वैजयन्त *vaijayanta*, m. (fr. *vi-jayat* or °*yanta*) the banner of Indra, MBh.; a banner, flag, R.; the palace of Indra, Buddh.; a house, A.; N. of Skanda, L.; of a mountain, MBh.; Hariv.; pl. (with Jainas) N. of a class of deities, L.; (*ī*), f. a flag, banner, MBh.; Kāv. &c.; an ensign, W.; a kind of garland prognosticating victory, MBh.; Pur.; the necklace of Vishṇu, MW.; N. of the 8th night of the civil month, Sūryapr.; Premna Spinosa, Suśr.; Sesbania Aegyptiaca, L.; N. of a lexicon by Yādava-prakāśa; of a Comm. to Vishṇu's Dharmaśāstra (IW. 304, 305); of various other wks.; of a town or a river, AV. Pariś.; n. N. of a gate in Ayodhyā, R.; of a town (= *vana-vāsī*), R.; Inscr.

Vaijayantika, mf(*ā* or *ī*)n. bearing a flag, a flag-bearer, L.; (*ā*), f. a flag, banner, Mālatīm.; a kind of pearl necklace (in Prākṛit), Vikr.; Sesbania Aegyptiaca, L.; Premna Spinosa, Bhpr.

वैजयि *vaijayi*, m. (fr. *vi-jaya*) N. of the third Cakra-vartin in Bhārata, L.

Vaijayika, mf(*ī*)n. conferring or foretelling victory (°*kīnām* [v.l. °*kānām*] *vidyānām jñānam*, one of the 64 arts), VarBṛS.; Hariv. &c.

Vaijayin, mfn. id., MBh.

वैजर *vaijara*, m. pl. N. of a school, Caraṇ.

वैजलदेव *vaijala-deva* or °*la-bhūpati*. See *baijala-deva*.

वैजव *vaijava*, m. pl. N. of a school, Caraṇ. (v.l. *vaijara*); w.r. for *paijavana*.

Vaijavana, w.r. for *paijavana*.

वैजवाप *vaijavāpa* &c. See *baij°*.

वैजात्य *vaijātya*, n. (fr. *vi-jāti*) diverseness, heterogeneousness, Sarvad.; exclusion from caste, W.; difference of caste, A.; strangeness, A.; looseness, wantonness (cf. *vaiyatya*), W.

वैजान *vaijāna*, m. patr. of Vṛiśa, PañcavBr.

वैजापक *vaijāpaka* or °*pakaka*, mfn. (fr. *vijāpaka*), g. *kacchâdi*.

वैजि *vaiji*, m. N. of a man, Bhartṛ. (perhaps w.r. for *baiji*).

वैजिक *vaijika* &c. See *baij°*.

वैज्ञानशालिक *vaijñānaśālika* (?), m., Campak.

वैज्ञानिक *vaijñānika*, mf(*ī*)n. (fr. *vi-jñāna*) rich in knowledge, proficient, L.

वैटप *vaiṭapa*, m. patr. fr. *viṭapa*, g. *śivâdi*.

वैटुष्य *vaiṭushya*, w.r. for *vaidushya*, Rājat.

वैट्टालिक *vaiṭṭālika* (of obscure meaning; for *vaitālika*?), Cat.

वैडव *vaiḍava*, m. patr. fr. *viḍu*, PañcavBr.

वैडाल *vaiḍāla*. See *baiḍ°*.

वैडूर्य *vaiḍūrya*, n. (rarely m.; cf. *vidūra-ja*) a cat's-eye gem (ifc. 'a jewel,' = 'anything excellent of its kind'), AdbhBr.; MBh.; Kāv. &c.; m. N. of a mountain (also *-parvata*), MBh.; VarBṛS. &c.; mf(*ā*)n. made of cat's-eye gems, MBh.; R. &c. **-kānti**, mfn. having the colour of a cat's-eye gem, VarBṛS.; m. N. of a sword, Kathās. **-prabha**, m. N. of a serpent-demon, Buddh. **-maṇi**, m. a cat's-eye gem; *-vat*, mfn. containing cat's-eyes, R. **-maya**, mf(*ī*)n. consisting or made of or resembling cat's-eyes, MBh.; R. &c. **-śikhara**, m. N. of a mountain, MBh. **-śṛiṅga**, n. N. of a mythical town, Kathās.

वैण *vaiṇa*, m. (fr. *veṇu*) a maker of bamboo-work (a partic. mixed caste), Āpast.; Mn.; Yājñ.; n. N. of a Sāman, ĀrshBr.

Vaiṇavá, mf(*ī́*)n. consisting or made of or produced from bamboo (with *nicayāḥ*, 'supply of b°;' with *agni*, 'a b° fire;' with *yava*, 'b°-corn'), TS.; ŚBr.; GṛS. &c.; made of grains of barley, KātyŚr.; belonging to a flute, Cat.; m. a flute, MBh.; a student's staff cut from a b°, any b°-staff, W.; a worker in b°, W.; the son of a Māhishya and a Brāhman woman, L.; a patr., ĀśvŚr.; N. of a sacred place of pilgrimage, MW.; (*ī*), f. (said to be) = *vīṇā*, Hcat.; bamboo manna, Bhpr.; n. the fruit of Veṇu, L.; gold from the Veṇu river, L.; N. of two Sāmans, ĀrshBr.; of a Varsha in Kuśa-dvīpa, MārkP.; of a sacred place, Col.

Vaiṇavika, m. a flute-player, Nalac.

Vaiṇavin, mfn. possessing a flute, MBh. (v.l. *veṇ°*); m. N. of Śiva, MW.

Vaiṇahotra, w.r. for *vain°*.

Vaiṇāvata, m. or n. (?) a bow, Lāṭy.

Vaiṇu (!), mfn. (said of the sea), ŚāṅkhGṛ.

Vaiṇuka, mfn. = *veṇau sādhuḥ*, g. *guḍâdi*; (fr. *veṇukīya*), g. *bilvakâdi*; m. a flute-player, L.; n. a pointed goad made of bamboo (for driving elephants), L.

Vaiṇukīya, mfn. (fr. *vaiṇuka*), g. *gahâdi*.

Vaiṇukeya, mf(*ī*)n. relating or belonging to a bamboo &c., W.; w.r. for *vaiṇ°*, L.

वैणिक *vaiṇika*, m. (fr. *vīṇā*) a lute-player, Śiś.; Kathās.; the smell of fæces (mfn. having the smell of fæces), L.

वैणेय *vaiṇeya*, m. pl. N. of a school, Caraṇ.

वैण्य *vaiṇya*, w.r. for *vainya*. **-datta**, m. N. of a man, Cat.

वैतंसिक *vaitaṇsika*, m. (fr. *vi-taṇsa* or *vī-t°*) a bird-catcher, MBh.; a butcher, L.; n. the act of ensnaring or entrapping, catching insidiously, MBh. (cf. *dyūta-vait°*, *dharma-vait°*).

Vaitaṇsikāya, Nom. Ā. °*yate*, to act the part of a bird-catcher, ensnaring, inveigling, Jātakam.

वैतण्डिक *vaitaṇḍika*, mfn. (fr. *vi-taṇḍā*) skilled in the tricks or artifices of disputation, g. *kathâdi*; m. a disputatious or captious person, MW.

Vaitaṇḍin, m. N. of a Ṛishi, Hariv.

Vaitaṇḍya, m. N. of a son of the Vasu Āpa, VP.

वैतत्य *vaitatya*, n. (fr. *vi-tata*) great extension, Śukas.

वैतथ्य *vaitathya*, n. (fr. *vi-tatha*) falseness, MāṇḍUp., Sch.; BhP. **-prakaraṇa**, n. N. of ch. of a wk. **Vaitathyôpanishad**, f. N. of an Upanishad.

वैतधृत *vaitadhṛita*, m. pl. = *vainadhṛita*, *vainabhṛita*, AV. Pariś.

वैतनिक *vaitanika*, mf(*ī*)n. (fr. *vetana*) living on wages, serving for wages; m. a hireling, labourer, Pāṇ. iv, 4, 12.

वैतरण *vaitaraṇa*, mf(*ī*)n. (fr. *vi-taraṇa*) intending to cross a river, MBh.; transporting (a departed spirit) over the river that flows between earth and the lower regions (as a cow given to Brāhmans; see below and RTL. 296, 297), Hcat.; (°*ṇá*), m. a patr., RV.; N. of a physician, Hariv.; Suśr.; (*ī*), f., see below.

Vaitaraṇi, f. = next, Uṇ. ii, 103, Sch.

Vaitaraṇī, f. N. of the Hindū Styx i.e. the river that flows between earth and the lower regions or abode of departed spirits presided over by Yama (it is described as rushing with great impetuosity, hot, fetid, and filled with blood, hair and bones, see RTL. 290, 570), MBh.; Pur. &c.; a cow (given to Brāhmans) that transports a dead man over that river, Hcat.; N. of a sacred river in Kaliṅga or Orissa (usually called Baitaraṇī), MBh.; Hariv.; R.; Pur.; of a division of the lower regions, MW.; of the mother of the Rākshasas, L. **-dāna**, n., **-māhātmya**, n., **-vidhi**, m., **-vratôdyāpana-vidhi**, m. N. of wks.

वैतस *vaitasá*, mf(*ī*)n. (fr. *vetasa*) made of or peculiar to a reed (°*sī vṛitti*, 'reed-like action,' i.e. yielding to superior force, adapting one's self to circumstances), TS.; Br.; KātyŚr. &c.; m. or n. a basket made of reed, KātyŚr.; m. (met.) the penis, AV.; Rumex Vesicarius, L.; Calamus Fasciculatus, W.

Vaitasaka, mfn. (fr. *vetasakīya*), g. *bilvakâdi*.

वैतसेन *vaitasena*, m. (prob. derived fr. a misunderstanding of *vaitaséna*, instr., RV. x, 95, 4; cf. *vaitasá*), N. of Purū-ravas, BhP.

वैतस्त *vaitasta*, mfn. coming from or contained in the Vi-tastā (q.v.), Rājat.

Vaitastya, mfn. id., Vcar.

वैतस्तिक *vaitastika*, mfn. (fr. *vi-tasti*) a span long (an arrow), MBh.; Hariv.; R.

वैतहव्य *vaitahavyá*, m. (fr. *vīta-havya*) a patr., AV.; ĀrshBr.; GṛŚrS.; n. N. of various Sāmans, Br. &c.

वैतहोत्र *vaitahotrá*, m. a patr., MaitrS. iv, 2, 6 (perhaps w.r. for *vaitih°*).

वैताढ्य *vaitāḍhya*, m. N. of a mountain, Śatr.

वैतान *vaitāna*, mf(*ī*)n. (fr. 2. *vi-tāna*) relating to or performed with the three sacred fires, GṛŚrS.; Mn.; MBh.; m. (m. c.) = *vitāna*, a canopy, BhP. (accord. to Comm. = *vitāna-samūha*); a patr., Caraṇ. (v.l. *vaitāyana*); n. a rite performed with the three sacred fires, PārGṛ.; Mn. &c.; an oblation with fire, W. **-kuśala**, mfn. skilled in or conversant with the above rites, Mn. **-prâyaścitta-sūtra**, n., **-sūtra**, n. N. of wks. **-stha**, mfn. occupied in a sacrificial rite, MBh. **Vaitānôpāsanā**, f. the regular presentation of burnt-offerings morning and evening, W.

1. **Vaitānika**, mf(*ī*)n. = *vaitāna* (with *dvi-ja* or *vipra*, a Brāhman who observes the precepts relative to the three sacred fires), GṛŚrS.; Mn.; MBh. &c.; sacrificial, sacred (as fire), W.; n. a burnt-offering (esp. of clarified butter, as presented daily by the Brāhmans), W.

वैतानिक 2. *vaitānika*, mfn. (fr. 1. *vi-tāna*), see under 2. *vaitālika* below.

Vaitānya, n. despondency, Jātakam.

वैतायन *vaitāyana*, m. a patr., Caraṇ. (v.l. *vaitāna*).

वैताल *vaitāla*, mf(*ī*)n. (fr. *vetāla*) relating to the Vetālas, VarBṛS.; m. = *vetāla*, Siṅhās. **-pura**, n. N. of a town, Siṅhās. (v.l. *vetāla-p°*).

1. **Vaitālika**, m. one who is possessed by a Vetāla, the servant of a Vetāla, W.; the worshipper of a Vetāla, MW.; a magician, conjurer, ib.

Vaitālīya, mfn. relating to the Vetālas, VarBṛS.; n. a kind of metre, VarBṛS.

वैतालकि *vaitālaki*, m. N. of a teacher of the Ṛig-veda, VP.

वैतालिक 2. *vaitālika*, m. (fr. *vi-tāla*) a bard, panegyrist of a king (whose duty also is to proclaim the hour of day), MBh.; Kāv. &c.; = *kheḍḍatāla*, L.; one who sings out of tune (?), W. (prob. w.r. for 2. *vaitānika* above); n. knowledge of one of the 64 arts, BhP., Sch. **-vrata**, n. the duty of a bard, Bālar.

Vaitālin, m. N. of one of Skanda's attendants, MBh.

Vaitālī, f. (with *sundarī*) a kind of metre, Ghaṭ., Sch.

वैतालिकर्णि *vaitāli-karṇi*, m. (and °*ṇi-kantha*, n.), v.l. for *baiḍāli-k°*, q.v.

वैतुल *vaitula*, m. (and °*la-kantha*, n.), g. *cihaṇâdi*.

वैतुषिक *vaitushika*, m. (fr. *vi-tusha*) N. of partic. hermits, Baudh.

Vaitushya, n. the being husked, ĀpŚr., Sch.

वैतृष्ण्य *vaitṛishṇya*, n. (fr. *vi-tṛishṇa*) quenching of thirst, Mn. v, 128; freedom from desire, indifference to (ifc.), MBh.; BhP.; Yogas. &c.

वैत्तपाल्य *vaittapālya*, mfn. (fr. *vitta-pāla*) relating to Kubera, MBh.

वैत्रक *vaitraka*, mf(ī)n. (fr. *vetra*) cany, reedy, W.; (fr. *vetrakīyā*), g. *bilvakâdi*.

Vaitrakīya, mf(ī)n. relating to a stick or cane, W. **-vana**, n. N. of a place, MBh. (v.l. *vetrak°*).

Vaitrâsura, m. (cf. *vetrâs°*) N. of an Asura, Cat.

वैद 1. *vaida*. See *baida*.

वैद 2. *vaida*, mf(ī)n. (fr. *vida*) relating to or connected with a wise man, learned, knowing, W.; m. a wise man, MW.; (ī), f. a wise man's wife, ib.

वैदग्ध *vaidagdha*, n. (fr. *vi-dagdha*; prob.) w.r. for *vaidagdhya*, Bhartṛ. (v.l.)

Vaidagdhaka, mfn., g. *varāhâdi*.

Vaidagdhī, f. = *vaidagdhya*, Sāh.; KātyŚr., Sch. &c.; grace, beauty, Śiś.

Vaidagdhya, n. (ifc. f. *ā*) dexterity, intelligence, acuteness, cunning in (loc. or comp.), Mālatīm.; Daśar.; Sāh. &c. **-vat**, mfn. possessed of cleverness, clever, skilful, experienced, Prasannar.; Vcar.

वैदत *vaidata*, mfn. (fr. *vidat*, √1. *vid*) knowing, g. *prajñâdi*.

वैदथिन *vaidathiná*, m. (fr. *vidathin*) a patr., RV.

वैददश्वि *vaídadaśvi*, m. (fr. *vidad-aśva*) a patr., RV.; Br.

वैदनृत *vaidanṛita* (?), n. N. of a Sāman, SV.

वैदन्वत *vaidanvata*, n. (fr. *vidanvat*) N. of various Sāmans, Br. &c.

वैदभृती *vaidabhṛitī*, f. (fr. *vida-bhṛit*). **-putra** (*vaid°*), m. N. of a teacher, ŚBr.

Vaidabhṛitya, m. a patr. g. *gargâdi*.

वैदम्भ *vaidambha*, m. (fr. *vi-dambha*) N. of Śiva, MBh.

वैदर्भ *vaidarbha*, mf(ī)n. (fr. *vi-darbha*) relating to the Vidarbhas, coming from or belonging to Vidarbha &c., Col.; m. a king of the Vidarbhas, AitBr.; MBh.; Hariv.; Kāv.; a gum-boil, Bhpr.; W.; (pl. or ibc.) = *vidarbha* (the Vid° people), Hariv.; VarBṛS. &c.; (ī), f., see below. **-rīti**, f. the Vid° style of composition (cf. under *rīti*).

Vaidarbhaka, mfn. relating to the Vid° (with *rājan*, a king of the V°), R.; m. a man belonging to the Vid°, a native of Vid°, Cat.

Vaidarbhi, m. a patr., PraśnUp.; MBh.

Vaidarbhī, f. a princess of the Vidarbhas, MBh.; Hariv.; R.; BhP.; N. of the wife of Agastya, W.; of Damayantī (wife of Nala), W.; of Rukmiṇī (one of Kṛishṇa's wives), W.; = °*bha-rīti* (q.v.), Pratāp.; Sāh.; Kpr.; the law of Vidarbha (which allowed first cousins to intermarry), W.; n. the chief city of the Vid°, = *kuṇḍina*, L.; ambiguous speech, L. **-jananī**, f. the mother of Damayantī, MW. **-pariṇaya**, m. N. of sev. dramas.

वैदर्व्य *vaidarvya*, m. (fr. *vi-darvya* or *vi-darvi*) a patr., GṛS.

वैदल *vaidala*, mf(ī)n. (fr. *vi-dala*) made of split bamboo, Mn.; m. any leguminous vegetable or grain (such as peas, beans &c.), Suśr.; Bhpr.; a kind of poisonous insect, worm &c., Suśr.; a kind of cake, L.; n. a wicker basket, Suśr.; the shallow cup or platter belonging to a religious mendicant, MW.

Vaidalika, mfn. belonging to leguminous vegetables, Suśr.

Vaidalya, n. N. of wk.

वैदान्तिक *vaidāntika*, m. one who is learned in the Vedânta, Siṇhâs. (w.r. *ved°*).

वैदायन *vaidāyana*, m. a patr. See *baid°*.

वैदारव *vaidārava*. See *śveta*.

Vaidārva or **vaidārvya**, m., v.l. for *vaidarvya*. See ib.

वैदारिक *vaidārika*, mfn. N. of a kind of fever, Bhpr.

वैदि *vaidi*, m. a patr. See *baidi*.

वैदिक *vaidika*, mf(ī)n. (fr. *veda*) relating to the Veda, derived from or conformable to the V°, prescribed in the V°, Vedic, knowing the V°, Mn.; MBh.; Hariv. &c.; m. a Brāhman versed in the V°, W.; n. a Vedic passage, Mn. xi, 96; a Vedic precept, MBh.; Kaṇ.; (°*keshu*), ind. = *vede*, in the Veda, Pat. **-karman**, n. an action or rite enjoined by the V°, MW. **-cchandaḥ-prakāśa**, m. N. of wk. **-tva**, n. conformity to the Veda, the being founded on or derived from the V°, W. **-durgâdi-mantra-prayoga**, m., **-dharma-nirūpaṇa**, n. N. of wks. **-pāśa**, m. a bad Veda-knower, Pāṇ. v, 3, 47. **-prakriyā**, f., **-vijaya**, m., **-vyaya-dhvaja**, m., **-śikshā**, f., **-sarvasva**, n. N. of wks. **-sārvabhauma**, m. N. of various authors, Cat. **-siddhânta**, m., **-su-bodhinī**, f. N. of wks. **Vaidikâcāra-nirṇaya**, m., °**kâbharaṇa**, n., °**kârcana-mīmāṇsā**, f. N. of wks.

वैदिश *vaidiśa*, mf(ī)n. of or belonging to the city of Vidiśā, near Vid°, MW.; m. a king of Vid°, Hariv.; Mālav.; pl. the inhabitants of Vid°, n. (also *-pura*, n.) N. of a town situated on the river Vidiśā, R.; Mālav.; Pur.

Vaidiśya, n. N. of a city not far from Vidiśā, MW.

वैदुरिक *vaidurika*, n. a sentiment or maxim of Vidura, BhP.

वैदुर्य *vaidurya*, w.r. for *vaidūrya* (or *vaiḍūrya*), MārkP.

वैदुल *vaidula*, mfn. coming from or made of the reed called Vidula, Suśr.

वैदुष *vaidusha*, mfn. (fr. *vidvas*) learned, g. *prajñâdi*.

Vaidushī, f. science, skill, Śrikaṇṭh.; learning, W.

Vaidushya, n. learning, erudition, science, R., Sch.; Rājat.

वैदूरपति *vaidūra-pati*, m. pl. N. of a dynasty, BhP.

वैदूर्य 1. *vaidūrya*, mf(ī or rī)n. (fr. *vi-dūra*) brought from Vidūra, Pāṇ. iv, 3, 84.

2. **Vaidūrya**, w.r. for *vaiḍūrya*.

वैदेशिक *vaideśika*, mf(ī)n. (fr. *vi-deśa*) belonging to another country, foreign; m. a stranger, foreigner, MBh.; Kāv. &c. **-tva**, n. foreignness, Bālar. **-nivāsin**, mfn. (pl.) foreign and native, R.

Vaideśya, mfn. foreign, Mṛicch.; n. the being in separate countries, separation in space, ŚāṅkhŚr., Sch.; foreignness, MW.

वैदेह *vaidehá*, mf(ī)n. (fr. *vi-deha*) belonging to the country of the Videhas, TS.; MaitrS.; (accord. to Comm. on TS.) having a handsome frame or body, well-formed; (*vaíd°*), m. a king of the Ved° (also °*ho rājan*), Br.; ŚāṅkhŚr.; MBh. &c.; a dweller in Videha, MW.; a partic. mixed caste, the son of a Śūdra by a Vaiśyā (Gaut.), or of a Vaiśya by a Brāhman woman (Mn.); a trader, L.; an attendant on the woman's apartments, L.; pl. = *videha* (N. of a people), MBh.; VarBṛS. &c.; people of mixed castes, MW.; (ī), f., see below.

Vaidehaka, mfn. relating or belonging to the Videhas, MBh.; m. a man of the Vaideha caste (said to be the offspring of a Śūdra father and Brāhman mother), Mn.; MBh. &c.; a merchant, Hcar.; N. of a mountain, Buddh.; pl. = *videha* (the people called so), VarBṛS.; MārkP.

Vaidehi, m. a patr., Pat.

Vaidehika, m. a man of the Vaideha caste, Mn. x, 36; (accord. to Kull.) a merchant.

Vaidehī, f. a cow from the country of the Videhas, Kāṭh.; MaitrS.; a princess of the Vid°, (esp.) N. of Sītā, MBh.; Kāv.; Buddh.; a woman of the Vaideha caste, Mn. x, 37; a sort of pigment (= *rocanā*), L.; long pepper, L. (cf. °*hī-maya*); a cow, MW. **-pariṇaya**, m. N. of sev. wks. **-bandhu**, m. 'friend or husband of the princess of Videha (Sītā),' N. of Rāma, Ragh. **-maya**, mf(ī)n. 'engrossed with Sītā' and 'consisting of long pepper,' Vās.

वैद्य *vaidya*, mfn. (fr. *vidyā*, and in some meanings fr. *veda*) versed in science, learned, ĀśvGṛ.; Kāty.; Mn. &c.; relating or belonging to the Vedas, conformable to the V°, Vedic, W.; medical, medicinal, practising or relating to medicine, W.; w.r. for *vedya*, MBh.; m. a learned man, Pandit, W.; follower of the Vedas or one well versed in them, ib.; an expert (versed in his own profession, esp. in medical science), skilled in the art of healing, a physician (accounted a mixed caste), MBh.; Kāv. &c.; Gendarussa Vulgaris, L.; N. of a Ṛishi, MBh. (w.r. for *raibhya*); (ā), f. a kind of medicinal plant, L.; (ī), f. the wife of a physician, Pāṇ. vi, 4, 150, Sch. **-kalpa-taru**, m., **-kalpa-druma**, m., **-kutūhala**, n., **-kula-tattva**, n., **-kaustubha**, m. N. of wks. **-kriyā**, f. the business of a physician, MW. **-gaṅgā-dhara** or **-gadā-dhara**, m. N. of a poet, Cat. **-candrôdaya**, m., **-cikitsā**, f. N. of wks. **-cintāmaṇi**, m. N. of an author, Cat.; of various wks. **-jīva-dāsa**, m. N. of a poet, Cat. **-jīvana**, n. (or m.), **-triṇśat-ṭīkā**, f. N. of wks. **-trivikrama**, m. N. of a poet, Sadukt. **-darpaṇa**, m. N. of sev. wks. **-dhanya**, m. N. of a poet, Cat. **-naya-bodhikā**, f. N. of wk. **-nara-siṇhasena**, m. N. of a scholiast, Cat. **-nātha**, m. lord of physicians, Kāv.; a form of Śiva, Inscr.; N. of Dhanvantari, W.; of various authors &c., Cat.; n. N. of a celebrated Liṅga and of the surrounding district, W.; *-kavi*, *-gāḍagila*, m. N. of authors, Cat.; *-tīrtha*, n. N. of a Tīrtha, ib.; *-dīkshita*, m. N. of various authors, ib.; *-dīkshitīya*, n. N. of wk.; *-deva-śarman*, *-pāya-guṇḍe* (or °*ḍa*), *-bhaṭṭa*, m. N. of authors, Cat.; *-bhaiṭ*, *-māhātmya*, n. N. of wks.; *-miśra*, m. N. of a man, Cat.; *-maithila*, m. N. of an author, ib.; *-liṅga-māhātmya*, n. N. of wk.; *-vācaspati-bhaṭṭâcārya*, *-śāstrin*, *-śukla*, *-sūri*, m. N. of authors, Cat.; °*thīya*, n. N. of wk.; °*thêśvara*, n. N. of a Liṅga, Cat. **-nighaṇṭu**, m., **-paddhati**, f. N. of wks. **-prajñapta**, mfn. prescribed by doctors, Divyâv. **-pradīpa**, m. N. of wk. **-bandhu**, m. Cathartocarpus (Cassia) Fistula, L. **-bodha-saṃgraha**, m., **-bhūshaṇa**, n., **-manôtsava**, m., **-manoramā**, f., **-mahôdadhi**, m. N. of wks. **-mātṛi**, f. the mother of a physician, MW.; Gendarussa Vulgaris, L. **-mānin**, mfn. thinking one's self a physician, pretending to be a phys°, Car. **-mālikā**, f., **-yoga**, m. N. of wks. **-ratna**, (prob.) n. N. of a man, Cat.; n. of wk.; *-mālā*, f.; °*nâkara-bhāshya*, n. N. of wks. **-rasa-mañjarī**, f., **-rasa-ratna**, n., **-rasâyana**, n., **-rahasya-paddhati**, f. N. of wks. **-rāj**, m. 'king among physicians,' N. of Dhanvantari (transferred to Vishṇu), Pañcar. **-rāja**, m. 'id.,' N. of Dhanvantari, R.; of the father of Śārṅga-dhara, Cat.; of an author, ib.; *-tantra*, n. N. of wk. **-vallabha**, m., °**bhā**, f. N. of wks. **-vācas-pati**, m. N. of a physician, Cat. **-vidyā**, f. the science or a text-book of medicine, Kāv. **-vinoda**, m., **-vilāsa**, m., **-vṛinda**, n. N. of wks. **-śāstra**, n. a text-book for physicians, treatise on the preparation of medicines, Cat.; *-sāra-saṃgraha*, m. N. of wk. **-saṃkshipta-sāra**, **-saṃgraha**, m., **-saṃdeha-bhañjana**, n., **-sarva-sva**, n., **-sāra**, m., **-sāra-saṃgraha**, m., **-sārôddhāra**, m. N. of wks. **-siṇhī**, f. Gendarussa Vulgaris, L. **-sūtra-ṭīkā**, f., **-hitôpadeśa**, m. N. of wks. **Vaidyâmṛita**, n. (and °*ta-laharī*, f.), °**dyâlaṃkāra**, m., °**dyâvataṇsa**, m., °**dyêśvara-māhātmya**, n. N. of wks.

Vaidyaka, mfn. medical, MW.; m. a physician, Śṛiṅgār.; n. the science of medicine, Suśr. **-grantha-pattra**, n. pl., **-paribhāshā**, f., **-prayogâmṛita**, n., **-yoga-candrikā**, f., **ratnâvalī**, f. N. of wks. **-śāstra**, n. the science of medicine, MW.; *-vaishṇava*, n. N. of wk. **-saṃgraha**, m., **-sarva-sva**, n., **-sāra**, **-sāra-saṃgraha**, m. N. of wks. **Vaidyakânanta**, N. of a man or of a wk., Cat.

Vaidyāya, Nom. Ā. °*yate*, to become a physician, Kulârṇ.

वैद्यसिक *vaidyasika*, w.r. for *vaighasika*, MBh.

वैद्याधर *vaidyādhara*, mf(ī)n. (fr. *vidyādhara*) relating or belonging to the Vidyādharas, R.; K[illegible]

वैद्यानि *vaidyāni*, m. a patr., Kāṭh., Anukr.

वैद्युत *vaidyutá*, mfn. (fr. *vidyut*) belonging to or proceeding from lightning; flashing, brilliant (with *śikhin*, m. the fire of lightning, Vcar.; °*ta-kriśānu*, m. id., ib.), VS. &c. &c.; m. N. of a son of Vapush-mat, MārkP.; of a mountain, ib.; pl. N. of a school, Caraṇ.; (prob.) n. the fire of lightn°, Yājñ.; BhP.; n. N. of the Varsha ruled by Vaidyuta, VP.

Vaidyuddhatī, f. (fr. *vidyut + hatī*) N. of AV. vii, 31; 34; 59; 108.

Vaidyota, mf(*ā*)n. angry, L.

वैद्रुम *vaidruma*, mfn. (fr. *vi-druma*) consisting or made of coral, Suśr.; Hariv.; Kathās.; Śiś.

वैध *vaidha*, mf(*ī*)n. (fr. *vidhi*) enjoined by rule or precept, prescribed, legal (*-tva*, n.), TS., Sch.; KātyŚr., Sch. &c. **-hiṇsâgha-timira-mārtaṇḍôdaya**, m. N. of wk. (containing an apology for animal sacrifices as enjoined in the Śruti and Smṛiti, and composed A. D. 1854).

Vaidhika, mf(*ī*)n. in accordance with rule, preceptive, ritual, W.

वैधर्मिक *vaidharmika*, mfn. (fr. *vi-dharma*) unlawful, MBh. (v. l. *vidharmaka* or °*mika*).

Vaidharmya, n. unlawfulness, injustice, MBh.; R.; difference of duty or obligation, W.; difference, heterogeneity, Suśr.; Kaṇ. &c. **-sama**, m. (in log.) a fallacy based on dissimilarity, Nyāyad.

वैधव *vaidhava*, m. (fr. 1. *vidhu*) 'son of the Moon,' N. of Budha, Vikr.

वैधवेय *vaidhaveya*, m. (fr. *vidhavā*) the son of a widow, Śak.

Vaidhavya, n. widowhood, MBh.; Hariv.; Kāv. &c. **-nirṇaya**, m. N. of wk. **-lakshaṇôpêtā**, f. a girl who has the marks of widowhood (unfit for marriage), L. **-veṇī**, f. a widow's braid, Hcar.

वैधस *vaidhasa*, mf(*ī*)n. (fr. *vedhas*) derived from fate, Naish.; composed by Brahmā, Cat.; m. patr. of Hari-ścandra, AitBr.; ŚāṅkhŚr.

वैधातकि *vaidhātaki* (?), m. = next, L.

वैधात्र *vaidhātra*, mf(*ī*)n. (fr. *vi-dhātṛi*) derived from Brahmā or fate, Rājat.; m. patr. of Sanat-kumāra, L.; (*ī*), f. a species of plant (= *brāhmī*), L.

वैधारय *vaidhāraya*, m. a patr., ĀrshBr.

वैधुरी *vaidhurī*, f. (fr. *vi-dhura*) adversity, adverseness (*vidhi-vaidh*°, adv° of fate), Prasannar.

Vaidhurya, n. desolation, Kathās.; bereavement, deprivation, absence (°*yaṃ vi-√dhā*, 'to deprive of,' 'remove'), Bālar.; Sāh.; misery, wretchedness, desperate plight, Kathās.; Rājat.; agitation, tremulousness, MW.

वैधूमाग्नी *vaidhūmāgnī*, f. N. of a city in the country of the Śālvas, L.

वैधृत *vaidhṛita*, m. (fr. *vi-dhṛiti*) N. of a partic. Yoga (or conjunction of the sun and moon when they are on the same side of either solstitial point [i. e. in the same Ayana, whether Uttarâyaṇa or Dakshiṇâyana] and of equal declination, and when the sum of their longitude amounts to 360 degrees; this is considered a malignant aspect, cf. *vy-ati-pāta*), Var.; N. of Indra in the 11th Manv-antara, BhP.; (*ā*), f. N. of the wife of Āryaka (mother of Dharma-setu), ib.; n. (with *Vāsishṭha*) N. of a Sāman, L. **-vāsishṭha**, n. N. of a Sāman, ib.

Vaidhṛiti, f. the above position of the sun and moon, Saṃskārak.; Hcat.; the Yoga star of the 27th lunar mansion, MW.; m. N. of Indra in the 11th Manv-antara (= *vaidhṛita*), BhP.; pl. N. of a class of gods, ib. **-janana-śānti**, f., **-vyatīpāta-saṃkrānti-janana-śānti**, f., **-śānti**, f. N. of wks.

Vaidhṛitya, the above position of the sun and moon, Kauś.

वैधेय *vaidheya*, mfn. (fr. *vidhi*) 'afflicted by fate,' stupid, foolish; m. an idiot, fool, Kāv.; Rājat.; mfn. relating to rule or precept, prescribed, MW.; m. N. of a disciple of Yājñavalkya (the celebrated teacher of the White Yajur-veda), Pur.; pl. N. of a school of the White Yajur-veda, Caraṇ.; Āryav.

Vaidheya-tā, f. = *vidheya-tā*, dependence on, the being in the power of (ifc.), Daś.

वैध्यत *vaidhyata*, m. N. of Yama's door-keeper, L.

वैन *vaina*, mf(*ā*)n. (fr. *vena*) relating to Vena, ŚāṅkhBr.; m. patr. of Pṛithi, Sāy. on RV. i, 112, 15.

वैनंशिन *vainaṅśiná*, m. a patr., VS.

वैनतक *vainataka*, n. (prob. fr. *vi-nata*) a vessel for holding or pouring out ghee (used at sacrifices), W.

Vainatīya, mfn. (fr. id.), g. *kṛiśâśvâdi*.

Vainateyá, m. (fr. *vi-natā*) metron. fr. *vi-natā*, MaitrS.; MBh. (also pl.); N. of Garuḍa (MBh.; Kāv. &c.) and of Aruṇa (MatsyaP.); N. of a son of Garuḍa, MBh.; of a poet, Sadukt.; pl. N. of a school, Caraṇ.; (*ī*), f. metron. fr. *vi-natā*, Pāṇ. iv, 1, 15, Sch.

Vainatya, n. (fr. *vi-nata*) humble demeanour, MBh.

वैनद *vainada*, mfn. (fr. *vi-nada*), g. *utsâdi*; (*ī*), f. N. of a river, VP. (v. l. *vinadī*).

वैनधृत *vainadhṛita*, m. pl. = next, pl., Āryav. (cf. *vaitadhṛita*).

वैनभृत *vainabhṛita*, m. a patr., Saṃskārak.; pl. N. of a school of the Sāma-veda, Caraṇ. (cf. prec.)

वैनयिक *vainayika*, mf(*ī*)n. (fr. *vi-naya*) relating to moral conduct or discipline or good behaviour (*vainayikīnāṃ* [w. r. °*kānāṃ*] *vidyānāṃ jñānam*, 'knowledge of the sciences relating to such subjects,' reckoned among the 64 arts), MBh.; R.; BhP.; Sch.; enforcing proper behaviour, W.; performed by the officers of criminal justice, magisterial, MW.; used in military exercises (as a chariot), L.; m. n. (and *ī*, f.) a chariot used in military exercises, a war-chariot, L.

Vaināyaka, mf(*ī*)n. (fr. *vi-nāyaka*) belonging to or derived from Gaṇêśa, SāmavBr.; AgP.; Kāv.; m. pl. N. of a partic. class of demons, = *vināyaka*, BhP. **-saṃhitā**, f. N. of wk.

Vaināyika, m. = prec., mfn., MW.; m. a Buddhist, L. (w. r. for *vaināśika*); the doctrines of a Buddhist school of philosophy, A.; a follower of that school, ib.

वैनव *vainava*, n. N. of a Sāman, ĀrshBr.

वैनहोत्र *vainahotra*, m. N. of a king, VP.

वैनाश *vaināśa*, n. (fr. *vi-nāśa*) = next, n., VarYogay.

Vaināśika, mfn. perishable, L.; believing in complete annihilation, L.; causing destruction or ruin, L.; dependent, L.; m. a Buddhist, BṛĀrUp., Sch.; Bādar., Sch.; the doctrines of the B°, A.; a dependent, subject, W.; a spider, L.; an astrologer (?), W.; n. the 23rd Nakshatra from that under which any one is born, VarYogay. **-tantra**, n. the doctrines or system of the Buddhists, B. **-samaya**, m. id., ib.

वैनीतक *vainītaka*, m. n. (fr. *vi-nīta*) a kind of litter, a palanquin &c. (with bearers relieving one another), L.; any indirect means of conveyance (as a porter who carries a sedan-chair, a palanquin-bearer, horse dragging a carriage &c.), W.

वैनेय *vaineya*, mfn. (fr. *vineya*) to be taught, to be converted to the true religion; m. a catechumen, Kāraṇḍ.; m. pl. N. of a school of the White Yajur-veda, Caraṇ.

वैन्दव *vaindava* &c. See *baindava* &c.

वैन्ध्य *vaindhya*, mfn. belonging to the Vindhya range, Ragh.

वैन्य *vainyá*, m. (less correctly spelt *vaiṇya*) patr. fr. *vena* (also pl.), N. of Pṛithi or Pṛithī or Pṛithu, RV.; Br. &c.; N. of a deity (?), MW. **-datta**, m. N. of a man, Cat. **-svāmin**, m. N. of a temple, Rājat.

वैंर *vainra*, n. (said to be fr. 1. *vi*, 'a bird' + *nṛi*, 'man'), Pat.

वैपञ्चमिक *vaipañcamika* (fr. *vi-pañcamaka*, v. l. of *vi-pañcanaka*, q. v.) or *vaipañcika*, m. a diviner, soothsayer, Buddh.

वैपथक *vaipathaka*, mfn. (fr. *vi-patha*), g. *arīhaṇâdi*; relating to a wrong path, MW.

वैपरीत्य *vaiparītya*, n. (fr. *vi-parīta*) contrariety, opposition, reverse, Pañcat.; Hit.; MārkP. &c.; counterpart, MW.; inconsistency, A.; m. or (*ā*), f. a species of Mimosa, L. **-lajjālu**, m. f. a species of Mimosa Pudica, MW. **-sambandha**, m. the relation of contrariety or contradictoriness, ib.

वैपश्चित *vaipaścita*, m. (fr. *vipaś-cit*) patr. of Tārkshya, ĀśvŚr.

वैपश्यत *vaipaśyata*, mf(*ī*)n. (fr. *vi-paśyat*) belonging or peculiar to a wise man, Hcar.; (°*tá*), m. patr. of Tārkshya, ŚBr.; ŚāṅkhŚr.

वैपात्य *vaipātya*, n. (fr. *vi-pāta*), g. *brāhmaṇâdi*.

वैपादिक *vaipādika*, mfn. (fr. *vi-pādikā*) afflicted with blisters or pustules &c. on the feet, g. *jyotsnâdi*; n. (Car.) or (*ā*), f. (L.) a kind of leprosy (= *vipādikā*).

वैपार्ष्णि *vaipārshṇi*, m. f. (?), L.

वैपाश *vaipāśa*, m. metron. fr. *vi-pāś*, g. *śivâdi*.

Vaipāśaka, mfn. (fr. *vi-pāśa*), g. *arīhaṇâdi*.

Vaipāśāyana, m. pl. = *vaipāśa*, g. *kuñjâdi*.

Vaipāśāyanya, m. id., ib.

वैपुल्य *vaipulya*, n. (fr. *vi-pula*) largeness, spaciousness, breadth, thickness, VarBṛS.; Rājat.; Kāraṇḍ. &c.; a Sūtra of great extension, Buddh. (also *-sūtra*, n.; cf. *mahā-vaipulya-s*°); m. N. of a mountain, ib.

वैपुष्पित *vaipushpita*, mfn. (for *vi-p*°) smiled (n. impers.), Divyâv.

वैपोताख्य *vaipotâkhya*, n. a kind of dance, Saṃgīt.

वैप्रकर्षिक *vaiprakarshika*, mfn. (fr. *vi-prakarsha*), g. *chedâdi*.

वैप्रचिति *vaipraciti*, mfn. (fr. *vipra-cita*), g. *sutaṃgamâdi*.

वैप्रचित्त *vaipracitta*, m. patr. fr. *vipra-citti*, MārkP.

वैप्रयोगिक *vaiprayogika*, mfn. (fr. *vi-prayoga*), g. *chedâdi*.

वैप्रश्निक *vaipraśnika*, mfn. (fr. *vi-praśna*), ib.

वैप्रुष *vaiprusha*, mfn. (fr. *vi-prush*) directed to the Soma drops (*homa*), ŚrS.

वैप्लव *vaiplava*, m. a partic. month (= Śrāvaṇa), Hcat.

वैफल्य *vaiphalya*, n. (fr. *vi-phala*) fruitlessness, uselessness, Kāv.; Kathās. &c.; inability to help, MBh.

वैबाध *vaibādha*, m. (fr. *vi-bādha*) 'that which forces asunder,' N. of the Aśvattha tree, AV. **-praṇutta** (°*dhá-*), mfn. forced asunder by the Aśvattha tree, ib.

वैबुध *vaibudha*, mf(*ī*)n. (fr. *vi-budha*) belonging or peculiar to the gods, divine, Śiś.; Kathās.; Alaṃkārat.

Vaibodhika, m. (fr. *vi-bodha*) one who awakens (princes by announcing the time &c.), a bard, panegyrist, Kir.

वैभक्त *vaibhakta*, mfn. (fr. *vi-bhakti*) relating to a case-termination, Pat.

वैभग्नक *vaibhagnaka*, mfn. (fr. *vi-bhagna*), g. *varāhâdi*.

वैभडि *vaibhaḍi* (?), m. a patr., Cat.

वैभव *vaibhava*, n. (fr. *vi-bhava*) might, power (ifc. f. *ā*); high position, greatness, Kāv.; Kathās. &c.; superhuman power or might, MW.; grandeur, glory, magnificence, Kathās. **-prakāśikā**, f. N. of wk.

Vaibhavika. See *śakti-v*°.

वैभाजन *vaibhājana*, mfn. (fr. *vi-bhājana*) intersected with many streets, Āpast. (Sch.)

Vaibhājitra, mfn. (fr. *vi-bhājayitṛi*) = *vibhājayitur dharmyam*, Pāṇ. iv, 4, 49, Vārtt. 2; n. apportioning, dividing, W.; appointment, MW.

Vaibhājya-vādin, w.r. for *vibhajya-vādin,* Buddh.

वैभाण्डकि *vaibhāṇḍaki,* m. (fr. *vi-bhāṇḍaka*) patr. of Ṛisya-sṛiṅga, Hariv.; R.

वैभातिक *vaibhātika,* mfn. (fr. *vi-bhāta*) matutinal, pertaining to the dawn, Vṛishabhān.

वैभार *vaibhāra,* m. (cf. *vaihāra*) N. of a mountain, Śatr.; HPariś. **-giri,** m. or **-parvata,** m. id., ib.

वैभावर *vaibhāvara,* mfn. (fr. *vi-bhāvarī*) nocturnal, nightly, Harav.

वैभाषिक *vaibhāshika,* mfn. (fr. *vi-bhāshā*) optional, TPrāt.; m. a follower of the Vibhāshā, N. of a partic. Buddhist school, MWB. 157 &c.

Vaibhāshya, n. a copious commentary (= *vibhāshā*), Buddh.

वैभीत *vaibhīta,* mfn. (fr. *vi-bhīta*) derived from or made of Terminalia Bellerica, Car.

Vaibhītaka (Kāṭh.; ĀśvŚr.; Āpast.; Suśr.) or **vaibhīdaka** (TS.; ShaḍvBr.; ŚāṅkhŚr.), mfn. id.

वैभीषण *vaibhīshaṇa,* mfn. derived from or relating to Vi-bhīshaṇa, Kāv.

वैभुजाग्नक *vaibhujāgnaka,* mfn., Kāś. on Pāṇ. iv, 2, 126.

वैभूतिक *vaibhūtika,* mfn. (fr. *vi-bhūti*) generally current or prevalent (?), Mahāvy.

वैभूवस *vaibhūvasá,* m. (prob. fr. *vibhū-vasu*) patr. of Trita, RV.

वैभोज *vaibhoja,* m. pl. (said to be N. of a people, but in MBh. i, 85, 34 separable into two words: *vai bhojāḥ*).

वैभ्र *vaibhra,* n. (derivation doubtful; said to be fr. *vi-bhrāj*) the heaven of Vishṇu, W.

वैभ्राज *vaibhrāja,* m. (fr. *vi-bhrāj* or *vi-bhrāja*) patr. of Vishvak-sena, Hariv.; N. of a world (also pl.), ib.; of a mountain, Pur.; m. N. of a celestial grove, Hariv.; Pur.; of a lake in that grove, Hariv.; of a forest, MW. **-loka,** m. N. of a world (= *vaibhrāja*), ib.

Vaibhrājaka, n. N. of a celestial grove (= *vaibhrāja*), BhP.

वैम *vaima,* mfn. (fr. *veman*), g. *saṃkalâdi.*

वैमतायन *vaimatāyana* (fr. *vi-mata*), g. *arīhaṇâdi.*

Vaimatāyanaka, mfn., ib.

वैमतिक *vaimatika,* mfn. (fr. *vi-mati*) mistaken, in mistake (?), Divyāv.

Vaimatya, m. a patr., g. *kurv-ādi;* pl. N. of a school of the White Yajur-veda, MW.; n. difference of opinion, Rājat.; aversion, dislike, MW.

वैमत्तायन *vaimattāyana* (fr. *vi-matta*), °*naka,* mfn., g. *arīhaṇâdi* (v.l.)

वैमद *vaimada,* mf(*ī*)n. of or relating to Vi-mada, AitBr.; RPrāt.

वैमन *vaimana,* mfn. (fr. *veman*), Pāṇ. vi, 4, 167, Sch.

वैमनस्य *vaimanasyá,* n. (fr. *vi-manas*) dejection, depression, melancholy (also pl.), AV.; MBh. &c.; sickness, MW.

वैमन्य *vaimanya,* mfn. (fr. *veman*), Pāṇ. vi, 4, 168, Sch.

वैमल्य *vaimalya,* n. (fr. *vi-mala*) spotlessness, cleanness, clearness, pureness (also fig.), Suśr.; Car.; MārkP. &c.

वैमात्र *vaimātra,* mfn. (fr. *vi-mātṛi*) descended from another mother (with *bhrātṛi,* m. a step-brother), R.; ŚāṅkhŚr., Sch.; heterogeneous (*-tā,* f.), Buddh.; m. a step-mother's son, half brother, W.; (*ā* or *ī*), f. a step-mother's daughter, ib.; (prob.) n. gradation (?), Buddh.; a partic. high number, ib.

Vaimātraka, m. a step-brother, Mcar.

Vaimātreya, mfn. descended from another mother, Kull. on Mn. viii, 116; m. a step-mother's son, half brother, R., Sch.; (*ī*), f. a step-mother's daughter, half sister, W.

वैमानिक *vaimānika,* mf(*ī*)n. (fr. *vi-māna*) borne in a heavenly car, Mn.; MBh.; Ragh. &c.; relating to the gods (with *sarga,* m. the divine creation), LiṅgaP.; m. a partic. celestial being or deity (*-tva,* n., Bālar.; Jainas reckon two classes: Kalpa-bhavas and Kalpâtītas), Mcar.; Kathās.; BhP. &c.; an aeronaut, A.; (prob.) n. N. of a Tīrtha, MBh.

वैमित्रा *vaimitrā,* f. (fr. *vi-mitra*) N. of one of the 7 mothers of Skanda, MBh.

वैमुक्त *vaimukta,* mfn. containing the word *vi-mukta,* Pāṇ. v, 2, 61; liberated, emancipated, W.; n. liberation, emancipation, W.

वैमुख्य *vaimukhya,* n. (fr. *vi-mukha*) the act of averting the face, avertedness, flight, W.; aversion, repugnance to (loc. or comp.), Hariv.; Rājat.; Kuval.

वैमूढक *vaimūḍhaka,* n. (fr. *vi-mūḍha*) a dance performed by men in women's dress, Mālatīm.

वैमूल्य *vaimūlya,* n. (fr. *vi-mūlya*) difference of price (*-tas,* ind. at different prices), Mn. ix, 28.

वैमृध *vaimṛidhá,* mf(*ī*)n. (fr. *vi-mṛidh*) sacred or consecrated or dedicated to Indra, TS.; ŚBr.; ŚāṅkhŚr.; m. N. of Indra (= *vi-mṛidh*), TS.

Vaimṛidhya, mfn. = *vaimṛidhá,* ĀśvŚr.

वैमेय *vaimeya,* m. (fr. *vi-meya;* √*me*) barter, exchange, L.

वैम्बकि *vaimbaki.* See *baim*°.

वैम्य *vaimya,* m. a patr. (also pl.), Saṃskārak.

वैयग्र *vaiyagra,* n. (fr. *vy-agra*) distraction or agitation of mind, perplexity, MW.; the being totally absorbed or wholly engaged (in any occupation), ib.

Vaiyagrya, n. perplexity, ib.; devotion to, absorption in (ifc.), Śukas.

वैयथित *vaiyathita,* m. (fr. *vyathita?*) the 5th cubit (*aratni*) from the bottom or the 13th from the top of the sacrificial post, L.

वैयधिकरण्य *vaiyadhikaraṇya,* n. (fr. *vy-adhikaraṇa*) non-agreement in case, Sāh.; Pratāp.; relation to different subjects, KapS., Sch.; Nyāyad., Sch.

वैयमक *vaiyamaka,* m. pl. N. of a people, MBh.

वैयर्थ्य *vaiyarthya,* n. (fr. *vy-artha*) uselessness, Vikr.; TPrāt., Sch. &c.

वैयल्कश *vaiyalkaśa,* mfn. (fr. *vy-alkaśa*), g. *dvārâdi.*

वैयवहारिक *vaiyavahārika,* mfn. (fr. *vy-avahāra,* less correct than *vyāvahārika*) conventional, usual, of everyday occurrence, Veṇīs.

वैयशन *vaiyaśana* (rather *vaíyaśana* or *vaiyaśaná*), m. (fr. *vy-aśana*), MaitrS. (a word used in a partic. formula; other forms are *vy-aśana, vy-áśniya, vy-aśnuvín*).

वैयश्व *vaiyaśvá,* m. (fr. *vy-aśva*) patr. of Viśva-manas, RV.; n. N. of various Sāmans, Br. &c.

Vaiyaśvi, m. patr. fr. *vy-aśva,* Vop.

वैयसन *vaiyasana,* mfn. (fr. *vy-asana*), Pāṇ. vii, 3, 3, Sch.

वैयाकरण *vaiyākaraṇa,* mfn. (fr. *vy-ākaraṇa*) relating to grammar, grammatical, W.; m. a grammarian, MBh.; Sāh. &c.; (*ī*), f. a female grammarian, MW. **-kārikā,** f., **-koṭi-pattra,** n. N. of wks. **-kha-sūci,** m. a grammarian who merely pierces the air with a needle, a poor grammarian, Pāṇ. ii, 1, 53, Sch. **-jīvātu,** f., **-pada-mañjarī,** f., **-paribhāshā-rūpa-śabdârtha-tarkâmṛita,** n. N. of wks. **-pāśa,** m. a bad grammarian, Pāṇ. v, 3, 47. **-bhārya,** m. a man who has a female grammarian for a wife, Vop. **-bhūshaṇa,** n., **-bhūshaṇa-saṃgraha,** m., **-bhūshaṇa-sarvasva,** n., **-bhūshaṇa-sāra,** m., **-bhūshaṇôpanyāsa,** m., **-mañjūshā,** f., **-sarvasva,** n., **-siddhânta-kaumudī,** f., **-siddhânta-dīpikā,** f., **-siddhânta-bhūshaṇa,** n., **-siddhânta-bhūshaṇa-sāra,** m., **-siddhânta-mañjūshā,** f., **-siddhânta-mañjūshā-sāra, -siddhânta-ratnâkara,** m., **-siddhânta-rahasya,** n. N. of wks. **-hastin,** m. an elephant given to a grammarian as a reward, Pāṇ. vi, 2, 65, Sch.

वैयाकृत *vaiyākṛita,* mfn. = *vyākṛita,* g. *prajñâdi.*

वैयाख्य *vaiyākhya* (prob.) n. = *vyākhyā,* an explanation (*sa-vaiy*°, mfn. furnished with an explanation), MBh.

वैयाघ्र *vaíyāghra,* mfn. (fr. *vyāghra*) coming from or belonging to a tiger, made of or covered with a tiger's skin, AV.; GṛŚrS. &c.; derived from Vyāghra (*dharmāḥ*), Cat.; m. a car cov° with a t°'s skin, A.; n. a tiger's skin, AV.; ŚāṅkhŚr. &c. **-paricchada,** mfn. covered with a tiger's skin, ŚāṅkhŚr.

Vaiyāghrapadī, f. relating to Vyāghra-pad, L.; a patr. (*-putra,* m. N. of a teacher, BṛĀrUp.)

Vaíyāghrapadya, mfn. composed by Vyāghrapad, Cat.; m. patr. from *vyāghra-pad* (also pl.), ŚBr.; Lāṭy. &c.; N. of a Muni (the founder of a family called after him), MW.; of an author (also °*pād* or °*pāda*), Hcat.; Madanap.

Vaiyāghrapād, m. N. of an author (see prec.)

Vaiyāghrapāda, m. = prec.; w.r. for *vaiyāghrapadya,* MBh.

Vaiyāghrya, mfn. tiger-like (as a partic. sitting posture), Cat.; n. the state or condition of a tiger, MW.; a partic. sitting posture, ib.

वैयात *vaiyāta,* mfn. = *vi-yāta,* Pāṇ. v, 4, 36, Vārtt. 4, Pat.

Vaiyātya, n. boldness, immodesty, shamelessness, Hit.; Rājat. &c.; rudeness, A.

वैयापद *vaiyāpada,* mfn. (fr. *vyāpad*), Kaiy.

वैयापृत्यकर *vaiyāpṛitya-kara,* mfn. (fr. *vy-āpṛita*) = *bhogin,* L. (cf. *vaiyāvṛitti-kara* and *vaiyāvṛittya-k*°).

वैयावृत्ति *vaiyāvṛitti,* w.r. for *vaiyāvṛittya,* HYog. **-kara,** mfn. = *bhogin,* L. (v.l. *vaiyāvṛittya-k*°).

Vaiyāvṛittya, n. (more correctly *vaiyāpṛitya*) a commission, business (entrusted to any one and not to be interrupted), Kalpas.; HYog.; mfn. = *-kara,* Kalpas. **-kara,** mfn. one who has to execute a commission, Kalpas.; Nār.; m. (with Buddhists) an incorporeal servant, Buddh.

वैयावृत्य *vaiyāvṛitya,* °*tya-kara,* w.r. for *vaiyāvṛittya,* °*ttya-kara,* Buddh.

वैयास *vaiyāsa,* mfn. derived from Vyāsa, Śiś.

Vaiyāsaki, m. patr. fr. *vyāsa,* MBh.; Prab., Sch.; BhP.

Vaiyāsi, m. id., BhP.

Vaiyāsika, mf(*ī*)n. derived from or composed by Vyāsa (*-mata,* n.), MBh.; TBr., Sch.; Prab.; BhP.; m. a son of V°, A.; (*ī*), f. with *nyāya-mālā,* N. of wk. **-sūtrôpanyāsa,** m. N. of wk.

वैयासव *vaiyāsava,* n. (abstr. noun fr. *vy-asu*), Kaiy.

वैयास्क *vaiyāska,* m. N. of a teacher, RPrāt. (there could also be two words, *vai yāskaḥ*).

वैयुष्ट *vaiyushṭa,* mfn. (fr. *vy-ushṭa*) occurring at dawn or daybreak, early, Pāṇ. v, 1, 97.

वैय्य° *vaiyya*°, w.r. for *vaiya*°.

वैर *vaíra,* mfn. (fr. *vīra*) hostile, inimical, revengeful, AV.; n. (exceptionally, m.[?], ifc. f. *ā*) enmity, hostility, animosity, grudge, quarrel or feud with (instr. with or without *saha* or *sārdham,* or comp.; often pl.), AV.; PañcavBr.; MBh. &c.; heroism, prowess, W.; a hostile host, Śiś.; money paid as a fine for manslaughter, TāṇḍyaBr. **-kara,** mfn. causing hostility, Mn.; VarBṛS. **-karaṇa,** n. cause of hostility, R. **-kāra,** mfn. = *-kara,* Pāṇ. iii, 2, 23; m. an enemy, W. **-kāraka,** mf(*ikā*)n. = *-kara,* MBh. **-kāraṇa,** n. a cause of hostility, MW. **-kārin,** mfn. quarrelsome; °*ri-tā,* f. quarrelsomeness, Kām. **-kṛit**, mfn. quarrelsome, hostile, MBh.; Pañcat.; m. an enemy, MW. **-khaṇḍin**, mfn. breaking or destroying hostility, Cat. **-m-kara**, mfn. showing enmity to any one (gen.), BhP. **-tā**, f. enmity, hostility, MBh. **-tva**, n. id., R. **-deya** (*vaira-*), n. enmity, revenge or punishment, RV.; Kāṭh. (cf. *vīra-d°*). **-niryātana**, n. requital of enmity, revenge, Hariv.; Pañcat. **-purusha**, m. any hostile person or enemy, MBh. **-pratikriyā**, f. requital of hostile acts, revenge, L. **-pratimocana**, n. deliverance from enmity, Ragh. **-pratiyātana**, n. the requital of enm°, taking vengeance, MBh. **-pratīkāra**, m. id., A. **-bhāva**, m. hostility, BhP. **-yātanā**, f. = *-niryātana*, MBh.; Hariv.; Pañcat.; expiation, Āpast. (accord. to Sch. *-yātana*, n.) **-rakshin**, mfn. guarding against or warding off hostility, Kathās. **-vat**, mfn. hostile, living in enmity, MBh. **-viśuddhi**, f. requital of enm°, retaliation, revenge, Rājat. **-vrata**, n. vow of enmity, Bālar. **-śuddhi**, f. = *-viśuddhi*, L. **-sādhana**, n. cause or motive of enmity, Pañcat.; retaliation, A. **Vairâtaṅka**, m. (for *vairântaka*) Terminalia Arunja, L. **Vairânubandha**, m. lasting enmity, BhP.; beginning of hostilities, MW.; mfn. continuing in enm°, BhP. **Vairânubandhin**, mfn. leading to or resulting in enmity or hostility (*°dhi-tā*, f.), Kām.; m. the calorific or heating solar ray, W.; N. of Vishṇu, W. **Vairânṛiṇya**, n. retaliation, A. **Vairântaka**, m. Terminalia Arunja, L. **Vairâroha**, m. rise or increase of hostility, furious combat, W. **Vairâśaṅsana**, n. a battle, Śiś. (v. l. *virâś°*). **Vairôddhāra**, m. removal of a grudge, revenge, L.

Vairaka, (ifc.) enmity, hostility, BhP.

Vairaki, m. patr. fr. *vīraka*, g. *taulvaly-ādi*.

Vairaṇaka, mfn. (fr. *vīraṇa*), g. *ṛiśyâdi*.

Vairaṇī, f. patr. fr. *vīraṇa*, Hariv.

Vairahatya, n. (fr. *vīra-han*) the murder of men or heroes, VS.; TBr.

Vairāya, Nom. Ā. *°yate* (pr. p. *vairāyamāṇa*, 3. pl. 1st fut. *°yitāraḥ*), to become hostile, behave like an enemy, begin hostilities against (*prati* or instr.), Kāv.

Vairāyita, n. hostility, Prasannar.

1. **Vairi**, m. an enemy, Pañcar. (perhaps *vairiḥ* w. r. for *vairī*).

2. **Vairi**, in comp. for *vairin*. **-tā**, f. enmity, hostility ('to,' *saha*), Pañcat.; Kathās.; heroism, W. **-tva**, n. enmity, hostility, Kathās.; heroism, W. **-vīra**, m. N. of a son of Daśa-ratha, VP. (v. l. *iḍaviḍa*). **-siṅha**, m. N. of a king, Inscr.

1. **Vairiṇá**, mfn. (fr. *vīraṇa*, Andropogon Muricatus), RV. i, 191, 3.

2. **Vairiṇa**, n. enmity (in *nir-v°*), Tattvas.

Vairiṇi, m. a patr., Cat.

Vairin, mfn. hostile, inimical; m. an enemy, Mn.; MBh. &c.; a hero, W.; (*iṇī*), a female enemy, Cāṇ.; Kathās.

Vairī-√bhū, P. *-bhavati*, to change into enmity, become unfriendly, Śak.

Vaireya, mfn. (fr. *vīra*), g. *sakhy-ādi*.

वैरक्त *vairakta* (L.) or *°tya* (Kathās.), n. (fr. *vi-rakta*) freedom from affections or passions, absence of affection, indifference, aversion.

वैरङ्गिक *vairaṅgika*, mfn. (fr. 1. *vi-raṅga*) free from all passions and desires, Pārśvan.

वैरट *vairaṭa*, m. N. of a king, Inscr.

वैरट्टी *vairaṭṭī*, f. N. of a woman, Buddh.

वैरण्डेय *vairaṇḍeya*, m. a patr., Cat.

वैरत *vairata*, m. pl. (prob. fr. *vi-rata*) N. of a people, MārkP.

Vairatya, n., g. *saṃkāśâdi*; w. r. for *vairaktya*, Kathās.

वैरथ *vairatha*, m. (fr. *vi-ratha*) N. of a son of Jyotishmat, VP.; n. N. of the Varsha ruled by him, ib.

वैरन्ती *vairantī*, f. N. of a town, Hcar. (v. l. *vairantya*).

Vairantya, m. N. of a king, Kām.; (cf. prec.)

वैरमण *vairamaṇa*, n. (fr. *vi-ramaṇa*) conclusion of Vedic study, Āpast.

Vairamaṇya, n. (ifc.) the abstaining or desisting from, Lalit. (w. r. *vairam manya*).

वैरम्भ *vairambha*, mfn. = *°bhaka*, Divyâv.; m. N. of an ocean, ib.

Vairambhaka, mfn. N. of partic. winds (pl. sometimes with *vāyu*), ib.

वैरल्य *vairalya*, n. (fr. *virala*) looseness or openness (of texture), MW.; scarceness, fewness, Rājat.

वैरस *vairasa*, n. (fr. *vi-rasa*) tastelessness, disgust, Kathās.

Vairasya, n. insipidity, bad taste, VarBṛS.; Suśr.; disagreeableness, Kāvyâd.; repugnance, disgust of (gen., loc., or comp.), Suśr.; Kathās.; Rājat. &c.

वैरसेनि *vairaseni*, m. (fr. *vīra-sena*) patr. of Nala, Naish.

वैराग *vairāga*, n. (fr. *vi-rāga*) absence of worldly passion, freedom from all desires, W.

Vairāgika, mfn. = *vairaṅgika*, L.

Vairāgin, mfn. id., BrahmavP.; m. a partic. class of religious devotees or mendicants (generally Vaishṇavas) who have freed themselves from all worldly desires, RTL. 87.

Vairāgī, f. (in music) a partic. Rāginī, Saṃgīt.

Vairāgya, n. change or loss of colour, growing pale, Suśr.; Kām.; disgust, aversion, distaste for or loathing of (loc., abl., or comp.), Bhag.; Ragh. &c.; freedom from all worldly desires, indifference to worldly objects and to life, asceticism, Up.; MBh. &c. **-candrikā**, f. N. of wk. **-tā**, f. aversion to (*prati*), Pañcat. **-pañcaka**, n., **-pañcâśīti**, f., **-prakaraṇa**, n., **-pradīpa**, m., **-ratna**, n. N. of wks. **-śataka**, n. '100 verses on freedom from worldly desires,' N. of the third century of Bhartṛihari's moral sentiments and of sev. other wks.

वैराज *vairājá*, mfn. (fr. 2. *vi-rāj*) belonging to or derived from Virāj, MBh.; Hariv.; BṛĀrUp., Sch.; belonging or analogous to the metre Virāj, consisting of ten, decasyllabic, Br.; ŚrS.; RPrāt.; relating to or containing the Sāman Vairāja, VS.; TS.; ŚāṅkhŚr.; belonging to Brahmā, Uttarar.; m. patr. of Purusha, Hariv.; BhP.; of Manu or of the Manus, VP.; of the Vedic Ṛishi Ṛishabha, MW.; N. of the 27th Kalpa or period of time, VP.; of the father of Ajita, BhP.; pl. N. of a partic. class of deities, MW.; of a class of Pitṛis, MBh.; Hariv.; VP.; of partic. worlds, Uttarar.; n. N. of the Virāj metre, MW.; of various Sāmans, AV.; VS.; Br. &c. **-garbha**, mfn. containing the Sāman Vairāja, ŚāṅkhŚr. **-pṛishṭha**, mfn. having the Sāman V° for a Pṛishṭha (q. v.), ŚrS.

Vairājaka, m. N. of the 19th Kalpa, Cat.

Vairājya, n. extended sovereignty, AitBr.; Lāṭy.; BhP.

वैराट *vairāṭa*, mfn. (fr. *virāṭa*) relating or belonging to Virāṭa (king of the Matsyas), MBh.; Kathās.; m. patr. fr. *virāṭa*, MBh.; a kind of precious stone, L.; a lady-bird, L.; an earth-worm, W.; a partic. colour or an object of a partic. colour, MBh.; N. of a country, Cat.; (*ī*), f. patr. fr. *virāṭa*, MBh.; BhP. **-deśa**, m. the country Vairāṭa, Cat. **-rāja**, m. the king of Vairāṭa, ib.

Vairāṭaka, n. a kind of poisonous bulbous plant, Suśr.

Vairāṭi, m. patr. fr. *virāṭa*, MBh.

Vairāṭyā, w. r. for *vairoṭyā*, L.

वैराणक *vairāṇaka*, g. *utkarâdi*. **°kīya**, mfn., L.

वैराधय्य *vairādhayya*, n. (fr. *vi-rādhaya*), g. *brāhmaṇâdi*.

वैराम *vairāma*, m. pl. N. of a people, MBh. (possibly separable into *vai rāmāḥ*).

वैरामती *vairāmatī*, f. N. of a town, VP. (v. l. *vairāvatī*).

वैरिञ्च *vairiñca*, mf(*ī*)n. (fr. *vi-riñca*) relating or belonging to Brahmā, BhP.; Bālar.; Caṇḍ.

Vairiñcya, m. a son of Brahmā, BhP.

वैरुचनाचार्य *vairucanâcārya* (rather *vairoc°*), m. N. of an author, Ragh., Sch.

वैरूप *vairūpá*, m. (fr. *vi-rūpa*) a patr., PañcavBr.; ĀśvŚr. &c.; pl. a division of the Aṅgirases, RV.; N. of a race of Pitṛis, MW.; n. N. of various Sāmans, AV.; VS.; Br. &c.; mfn. relating or belonging to the Sāman Vairūpa, VS.; TS.; ŚāṅkhŚr. **-garbha**, mfn. containing the Sāman Vairūpa, ŚāṅkhŚr. **-pṛishṭha**, mfn. having the Sāman Vairūpa for a Pṛishṭha (q. v.), ŚrS.

Vairūpâksha, mfn. (fr. *virūpâksha*) a patr., g. *śivâdi*; N. of a partic. Mantra, Gobh.; Gṛihyās.

Vairūpya, n. multiplicity of form, diversity, difference, MBh.; MārkP.; BṛĀrUp., Sch.; deformity, ugliness, MBh.; Hariv.; Yājñ. &c. **-tā**, f. state of deformity, MBh.

वैरेकीय *vairekīya*, mfn. (fr. *vi-reka*) purgative, purging, Suśr.

Vairecana, mfn. (fr. *vi-recana*) id., Suśr.; ŚārṅgS.

Vairecanika, mfn. id., Suśr.; Car.

वैरोचन *vairocana*, mfn. (fr. *vi-rocana*) coming from or belonging to the sun, solar, Kir.; descended from Virocana &c., MW.; m. a son of the Sun, L.; a son of Vishṇu, L.; a son of Agni, L.; 'son of the Asura Virocana,' patr. of Bali, MBh.; R.; BhP.; a partic. Samādhi, Buddh.; N. of a king, AitBr.; of a Dhyāni-Buddha, MWB. 202; of a son of the class of gods called Nīla-kāyikas, Lalit.; of a class of Siddhas, L.; of a world of the Buddhists, W. **-niketana**, n. 'abode of Bali,' the lower regions, L. **-bhadra**, m. N. of a scholar, Buddh. **-muhūrta** n. a partic. hour of the day, Cat. **-raśmi-pratimaṇḍita**, m. N. of a world, Buddh.

Vairocani, m. a son of Sūrya, L.; a son of the Asura Virocana (patr. of Bali), MBh.; Hariv.; VarBṛS.; Pur.; patr. of the son of Agni, MW.; N. of a Buddha, L.

Vairoci (?), m. patr. of Bāṇa son of Bali, L.; N. of Bali, A.

वैरोट्या *vairoṭyā*, f. (with Jainas) N. of a Vidyā-devī, L.

वैरोधक *vairodhaka*, mfn. (fr. *vi-rodhaka*) disagreeing (as food; *-tva*, n.), Car.; m. N. of a man, Mudr.

Vairodhika, mfn. = *vairodhaka*, Car.

वैरोहित *vairohita*, m. pl. (fr. *vi-rohita*) a patr., g. *kaṇvâdi*.

Vairohitya, m. patr. fr. *vairohita*, g. *gargâdi*.

वैल *vaila*, mf(*ī*)n. (fr. *vila* = *bila*) relating or belonging to or living in a hole or pit, MW. (cf. *baila*). **-stha**, see *mahā́-vaila-stha*. **-sthā́na**, n. a place like a hole, lurking-place, covert, RV.; a burying-place, MW. **-sthānaká**, mfn. situated in a hole or lurking-place or covert, RV.; n. a pit, MW.

वैलकि *vailaki*, m. a patr., g. *taulvaly-ādi* (Kāś.)

वैलक्षण्य *vailakshaṇya*, n. (fr. *vi-lakshaṇa*) difference, disparity, diverseness (often ifc.; *pūrvôkta-vailakshaṇyena*, in opposition to what was before stated), Rājat.; BhP.; Sāh. &c.; indeterminableness, indescribableness, Kāvyâd., Sch.; strangeness, A.

वैलक्ष्य *vailakshya*, n. (fr. *vi-laksha*: ifc. f. *ā*) absence of mark, W.; contrariety, reverse, W.; the reverse of what is usual or natural, unnaturalness, affectation (cf. *sa-vailakshyam*), W.; feeling of shame, embarrassment, Hariv.; Kāv. &c. **-vat**, mfn. abashed, embarrassed, Bālar.

वैलात्य *vailātya*, n. (fr. *vilāta*), g. *dṛiḍhâdi* (v. l. *vailābhya*).

वैलाभ्य *vailābhya*, n. (fr. *vi-lābha*), g. *dṛiḍhâdi* (Kāś.)

वैलिङ्ग्य *vailiṅgya*, n. (fr. *vi-liṅga*) absence of distinctive marks, ĀpŚr., Sch.

वैलेपिक *vailepika*, mfn. (fr. *vi-lepikā*), g. *mahishy-ādi*.

वैलोम्य *vailomya*, n. (fr. *vi-loma*) inversion, invertedness, Hcat.; contrariety, reverseness, opposition, MW.

वैल्व *vailva*. See *bailva*.

वैवक्षिक *vaivakshika*, mfn. (fr. *vi-vakshā*) intended to be said, meant, had in view, Sāh.; Śiś., Sch.; Kir., Sch.

वैवधिक *vaivadhika*, m. (fr. *vi-vadha*) a carrier, burden-bearer, porter (*-tā*, f.), Hcar.; hawker who carries wares to sell, L.; (*ī*), f. a female hawker, Rājat.

वैवर्णिक *vaivarṇika*, m. (fr. *vi-varṇa*) one who has lost or been expelled from his caste, an outcaste, Divyâv.

Vaivarṇya, n. change of colour (also *varṇa-vaiv°*), MBh.; Hariv.; Yājñ. &c.; secession or expulsion from tribe or caste &c., W.; heterogeneousness, diversity, W.

वैवर्त *vaivarta*, n. (fr. *vi-varta*), *°taka*, n. See *brahma-v°*.

वैवश्य *vaivaśya*, n. (fr. *vi-vaśa*) want of self-control, Rājat.

वैवस्वत *vaivasvatá*, mf(ī)n. (fr. *vivasvat*) coming from or belonging to the sun, R.; relating or belonging to Yama Vaivasvata, Kauś.; MBh.; Kāv.; relating to Manu Vaivasvata, MBh.; Hariv.; Pur.; m. patr. of Yama, RV. &c. &c.; of a Manu, AV.; ŚBr. &c.; of the planet Saturn, L.; N. of one of the Rudras, VP.; (*ī*), f. a daughter of Sūrya, MBh.; patr. of Yamī, MW.; the south, L.; N. of Yamunā, A.; n. (scil. *antara*) N. of the 7th or present Manv-antara (as presided over by Manu Vaivasvata), MW. **–tīrtha**, n. N. of a Tīrtha, Cat. **–manv-antara**, n. N. of the 7th or present Manvantara (q. v.), MW.

Vaivasvatīya, mfn. relating to Manu Vaivasvata, Rājat.

वैवाह *vaivāha*, mfn. (fr. *vi-vāha*) nuptial, R.

Vaivāhika, mf(*ī*)n. nuptial (*-maṇḍapa*, Campak.), treating of nuptial rites (said of a chapter), Mn.; MBh.; Hariv. &c.; n. preparations for a wedding, nuptial festivities, MBh.; R.; a marriage, wedding, MW.; alliance by marriage, BhP.; m. a son's father-in-law or a daughter's father-in-l° i.e. the father of a son's wife or of a daughter's husband, MW.

Vaivāhya, mfn. nuptial, ŚāṅkhGṛ.; related by marriage, GṛS.; VP.; n. nuptial solemnity, R.

वैविक्त्य *vaiviktya*, n. (fr. *vi-vikta*) deliverance from (ifc.), Rājat.

वैवृत्त *vaivṛitta*, mfn. (fr. *vi-vṛitti*) connected with a hiatus, RPrāt.; m. a partic. modification of Vedic accent, MW.

वैशद्य *vaiśadya*, n. (fr. *vi-śada*) clearness, purity, brightness, freshness (with *manasi*, 'cheerfulness of mind'), Suśr.; VarBṛS.; Sarvad.; distinctness, intelligibleness, Sāy.; whiteness, MW.

वैशन्त *vaiśantá*, mf(ī)n. (fr. *veśanta*) contained in or forming a tank, RV.; VS.; TS.; Br.; belonging to a Soma ladle or cup, MW.; (*ā́*), f. = *véśantā*, a tank, VS.; n. a cup of Soma juice, MW.

वैशम्पायन *vaiśampāyana*, m. (patr. fr. *vi-śam-pa*) N. of an ancient sage (teacher of the Taittirīya-saṃhitā [q. v.]; in epic poetry a pupil of Vyāsa and also the narrator of the Mahā-bhārata to Janam-ejaya), GṛS.; TĀr. &c. (cf. IW. 371, n. 1); of an author, Cat.; of a son of Śuka-nāsa (transformed into a parrot), Kād. **–nīti-saṃgraha**, m., **-saṃhitā**, f., **-smṛiti**, f. N. of wks.

Vaiśampāyanīya, mfn. of or belonging to Vaiśampāyana, Cat.

वैशम्फल्या *vaiśamphalyā* (ĀpŚr.) or *vaiśambalyā* (ib.) or *vaiśambhalyā́* (TBr.), f. N. of Sarasvatī.

वैशली *vaiśalī*, f. N. of a wife of Vasudeva, VP. (v.l. *vaiśālī*); of a town, MW. (cf. *vi-śalā, vaiśālī*).

वैशल्य *vaiśalya*, n. (fr. *vi-śalya*) deliverance from a painful incumbrance (as that of the fetus), Car.

वैशस *vaiśasa*, mfn. (fr. a form *vi-śasa*, derived fr. *vi-√śas*; cf. *vi-śasana*) causing death or destruction, MBh.; n. (ifc. f. *ā*) rending in pieces, MW.; slaughter, butchery, war, strife, injury, hurt, outrage, distress, calamity, ruin (with *premṇaḥ*, ruin of affection), MBh.; Hariv.; Kāv. &c.; the hell, BhP.; N. of a hell, ib.

Vaiśastya, n. (fr. *vi-śasti*), Gaṇar.

वैशस्त्र 1. *vaiśastra*, mfn. (fr. *vi-śasitṛi* [*vi-śastṛi*]), Pāṇ. iv, 4, 49, Vārtt. 2; n. government, sway, rule, W.

2. **Vaiśastra**, n. (fr. *vi-śastra*) the state of being unarmed, L.

वैशस्य *vaiśasya*, n. an abstr. noun fr. *vi-śasi*, g. *brāhmaṇâdi* (Kāś.); w.r. for *vaishamya*, Kathās.

वैशाख *vaiśākhá*, m. (fr. *vi-śākhā*) one of the 12 months constituting the Hindū lunar year (answering to April–May and in some places, with Caitra, reckoned as beginning the year), ŚBr.; Lāṭy.; MBh. &c.; a churning-stick, Śiś. xi, 8; the seventh year in the 12 years' cycle of Jupiter, VarBṛS.; (*ā*), f. N. of a lioness, Cat.; (*ī*), f. (with or scil. *paurṇamāsī*) the day of full moon in the month Vaiśākha, GṛŚrS.; MBh. &c.; a kind of red-flowering Punarnavā, L.; N. of a wife of Vasu-deva, Hariv.; VP.; n. a partic. attitude in shooting, Hariv.; N. of a town (also *-pura*), Kathās.; mf(*ī*)n. relating to the month Vaiśākha, ŚāṅkhGṛ. **–purāṇa**, n., **-māsa-vrata**, n., **-māhātmya**, n. N. of wks. **–rajju**, f. the string on a churning-stick, L. **–vadi**, ind. in the dark half of the month Vaiś°, Inscr. (in giving dates).

Vaiśākhin, m. a partic. part of an elephant's forefoot, L.

Vaiśākhya, m. N. of a Muni, Cat.

वैशाय्य *vaiśāyya*, n. (fr. *vi-śaya*), Gaṇar.

वैशारद *vaiśārada*, mf(ī)n. (fr. *vi-śārada*) experienced, skilled, expert, unerring, BhP.; n. profound learning, R.

Vaiśāradya, n. experience, skill in (loc.), expertness, wisdom, MBh.; Bālar.; Sāh.; clearness of intellect, infallibility, Yogas.; BṛĀrUp., Sch.; Buddha's confidence in himself (of four kinds), Divyâv. (cf. Dharmas. 77).

वैशाल *vaiśāla*, mfn. descended from Viśāla, BhP.; m. N. of a Muni, Cat.; (*ī*), f. a daughter of the king of Viśālā, MBh.; N. of a wife of Vasudeva, VP. (v.l. *vaiśalī*); of a town founded by Viśāla, R.; Pur.; Buddh.

Vaiśālaka, mfn. relating to or ruling over Vaiśālī, VP.

Vaiśālâksha, n. N. of the Śāstra composed by Śiva as Viśālâksha, MBh.

Vaiśālāyana, m. patr. fr. *viśāla*, g. *aśvâdi*.

Vaiśāli, m. patr. of Su-śarman, MārkP.

Vaiśālika, mfn. relating to Viśālā (Vaiśālī), R.

Vaiśālinī, f. patr. fr. *viśāla*, MārkP.

Vaiśālīya, mfn. (fr. *viśāla*), g. *kṛiśâśvâdi*.

Vaiśāleyá, m. patr. of Takshaka and of other serpent-demons, AV.; ŚāṅkhGṛ. &c.

वैशिक *vaiśika*, mf(ī)n. (fr. 1. *veśa*) relating to or treating of prostitution, Mṛicch.; associating with courtezans, versed in the arts of courtezans, L.; n. harlotry, the arts of harlots, R.; VarBṛS.; Gaut.; Buddh.

वैशिक्य *vaiśikya*, m. pl. N. of a people, MārkP.

वैशिख *vaiśikha*, mfn. (fr. *vi-śikhā*), g. *chattrâdi*.

वैशिष्ट *vaiśishṭa*, n. (fr. *vi-śishṭa*) distinction, difference (= next), Sāh. (prob. w.r.)

Vaiśishṭya, n. endowment with some distinguishing property or attribute, distinction, peculiarity, difference, Caṇḍ.; Tarkas.; Sāh. &c.; pre-eminence, excellence, superiority, MBh.; Kām. &c.

वैशीति *vaiśīti*, m. patr. fr. *viśita*, g. *taulvaly-ādi*.

वैशीपुत्र *vaiśī-putrá*, m. (*vaiśī*=*vaiśyā*+*p°*) the son of a Vaiśya woman, Br.

वैशेय *vaiśeya*, m. patr. fr. *viśa*, g. *śubhrâdi*.

वैशेषिक *vaiśeshika*, mf(ī)n. (fr. *vi-śesha*, p. 990) special, peculiar, specific, characteristic, Āpast.; Suśr.; Bhāshāp.; Hcat.; distinguished, excellent, pre-eminent, MBh.; relating or belonging to or based on or dealing with the Vaiśeshika doctrine, Bhāshāp.; Madhus.; m. a follower of the V° doctrine, Kap.; Kusum.; Buddh.; n. peculiarity, distinction, Kaṇ.; N. of the later of the two great divisions of the Nyāya school of philosophy (it was founded by Kaṇâda, and differs from the 'Nyāya proper' founded by Gautama, in propounding only seven categories or topics instead of sixteen; and more especially in its doctrine of *viśesha*, or eternally distinct nature of the nine substances, air, fire, water, earth, mind, ether, time, space, and soul, of which the first five, including mind, are held to be atomic), IW. 65 &c. **–darśana**, n., **-ratna-mālā**, f. N. of wks. **–sūtra**, n. the aphorisms of the Vaiśeshika (branch of the Nyāya philosophy, which have been commented on by a triple set of commentaries, and expounded in various works, of which the best known are the Bhāshā-pariccheda with its commentary, called Siddhânta-muktâvalī, and the Tarka-saṃgraha), IW. 60, n. 1; *°trôpaskara*, n. N. of wk. **Vaiśeshikâdi-shaḍ-darśana-viśesha-varṇana**, n. 'description of the difference between the Vaiśeshika and other systems,' N. of a phil. wk.

Vaiśeshin, mfn. specific, individual, Sāṃkhyak., Sch.

Vaiśeshya, n. peculiarity, specific or generic distinction, TPrāt.; Suśr.; Vedântas.; difference, superiority, pre-eminence, Mn. ix, 296 &c.

वैश्मिक *vaiśmika*, mfn. (fr. *veśman*) living in a house, Car.

Vaiśmīya, mfn. (fr. id.), g. *kṛiśâśvâdi*.

वैश्य *vaiśya*, m. (fr. 2. *viś*) 'a man who settles on the soil,' a peasant, or 'working man,' agriculturist, man of the third class or caste (whose business was trade as well as agriculture), RV. &c. &c.; pl. N. of a people, VarBṛS.; (*ā*), f., see below; n. vassalage, dependance, TS.; mfn. belonging to a man of the third caste, MBh. **–kanyā**, f. a Vaiśya damsel, a girl of the agricultural class, Mn. x, 8. **–karman**, n. the business of a Vaiśya, agriculture, trade (*°ma-pustaka*, n. N. of wk.) **–kula**, n. the house of a V°, KātyŚr. **–ghna**, m. the slayer of a V°, VarBṛS. **–caritra**, n. N. of wk. **–jātīya**, m. a V° (by birth), man of the third caste, L. **–tā**, f. the state or condition of a V° (acc. with *√gam*, to become a V°), AitBr.; MBh. &c. **–tva**, n. = *-tā*, MārkP. **–dhvaṃsin**, mfn. destroying V°s, VarBṛS. **–putra**, m. the son of a Vaiśya, a Vaiśya, Siṃhâs. **–pura**, n. N. of a town, Virac. **–bhadrā**, f. N. of a deity, Buddh. **–bhāva**, m. = *-tā*, Mn. x, 93. **–yajña**, m. the sacrifice performed by a V°, KātyŚr. **–yoni**, f. a V°'s mode of existence, ChUp. **–rata**, mfn. living at the expense of the Vaiśyas, Cat. **–vṛitti**, f. a V°'s mode of life or occupation, agriculture, trade, Mn. x, 83. **–sava**, m. a partic. sacrificial rite, TBr. **–stoma**, m. N. of an Ekāha, ShaḍvBr.; ŚrS. **Vaiśyântara**, m. N. of Buddha in his last birth but one, MWB. 113.

Vaiśyā, f. a woman of the Vaiśya caste, Mn.; Yājñ. &c.; N. of a deity, Buddh. **–ja**, mfn. born of a Vaiśya woman, the child of a Vaiśya mother, Mn. ix, 151. **–putra**, m. 'son of a Vaiśya mother,' N. of Yuyutsu, MBh.

वैश्रमण *vaiśramaṇa*, w.r. for *vaiśravaṇa*.

वैश्रम्भक *vaiśrambhaka*, mfn. (fr. *vi-śrambha*) awakening or inspiring confidence, BhP.; n. N. of a celestial grove, ib.

वैश्रवण *vaiśravaṇá*, m. (fr. *vi-śravaṇa*; cf. g. *śivâdi*) a patr. (esp. of Kubera and Rāvaṇa), AV. &c. &c.; (in astron.) N. of the 14th Muhūrta; mf(*ī*)n. relating or belonging to Kubera, MBh. **Vaiśravaṇânuja**, m. 'younger brother of K°,' N. of Rāvaṇa, R. **Vaiśravaṇâlaya**, m. 'K°'s abode,' the Indian fig-tree, L.; N. of a place, Cat. **Vaiśravaṇâvâsa** and **Vaiśravaṇôdaya**, m. 'Kubera's glory,' the Indian fig-tree, L.

वैश्रेय *vaiśreya*, m. patr. fr. *viśri*, g. *gṛishṭy-ādi*.

वैश्लेषिक *vaiśleshika*, mf(ī)n. (fr. *vi-ślesha*), Cat.

वैश्व *vaiśva*, mf(ī)n. (fr. *viśva*, of which it is also the Vṛiddhi form in comp.), relating to or presided over by the Viśve Devāḥ; (*ī*), f. N. of the Nakshatra Uttarâshāḍha, L.; n. id., VarBṛS.; (with *yuga*) the 8th cycle of 5 years in the 60 years' cycle of Jupiter, VarYogay. **–kathika**, mfn. (fr. *viśva-kathā*), g. *kathâdi*. **–karmaṇá**, mf(*ī*)n. relating or sacred to or coming from Viśva-karman, AV.; VS.; Br. **–janīna**, mfn. (fr. *viśva-jana*) kind to everybody, g. *pratijanâdi*. **–jita**, mfn. relating to or connected with the Viśva-jit sacrifice, AitBr.; Lāṭy.; one who has performed the above sacrifice, Gaut. **–jyotisha**, n. (fr. *viśva-jyotis*) N. of various Sāmans, ĀrshBr. **–tari**, w.r. for *vaiśvam-tari*.

Vaiśvadevá, mf(ī)n. (fr. *viśva-deva*) relating or sacred to all the gods or to the Viśve Devāḥ, VS. &c. &c.; m. a partic. Graha or Soma-vessel, VS.; ŚBr.; a partic. Ekâha, ŚāṅkhŚr.; (ī), f. N. of partic. sacrificial bricks, TS.; ŚBr.; the 8th day of the 2nd half of the month Māgha, Col.; a kind of metre, Śrutab.; n. a partic. Śastra, AitBr.; the first Parvan of the Cāturmāsya, TBr.; ŚBr.; (exceptionally m.) N. of a partic. religious ceremony which ought to be performed morning and evening and especially before the midday meal (it consists in homage paid to the Viśve Devāḥ followed by the *bali-haraṇa* or offering of small portions of cooked food to all the gods who give the food and especially to the god of fire who cooks the food and bears the offering to heaven), Āpast.; Mn. &c. (cf. RTL. 417); N. of partic. verses or formulas, TBr.; ŚBr.; of various Sāmans, ĀrshBr.; the Nakshatra Uttarâshāḍhā (cf. under *vaiśva*), VarBṛS.; *-karman*, n. the above homage to the deities collectively, W.; *-khaṇḍana*, n., *-pūjā*, f., *-prayoga*, m., N. of wks.; *-bali-karman*, n. du. N. of the above two ceremonies, RTL. 417, n. 2; *-vidhi*, m. N. of wk.; *-stut*, m. a partic. Ekâha, ŚrS.; *-homa*, m. the offering made to all the gods and to Fire at the Vaiśvadeva ceremony, TBr., Sch.; °*vâgni*, m. the fire at the V°-d° ceremony, L.; °*vâgni-māruta*, mfn. consecrated to the Viśve Devāḥ and to Agni and to the Maruts, MaitrS.; °*vâdi-mantra-vyākhyā*, f. N. of wk. °**devaka**, n. (fr. *viśva-deva*), g. *manojñâdi*. °**devata**, n. the Nakshatra Uttarâshāḍha, VarBṛS. (v. l. *-daivata*). °**devika**, mfn. relating or sacred to the Viśve Devāḥ &c., R. (v. l. *-daivika*); belonging to the Vaiśvadeva Parvan, MānŚr.; corresponding to the V°-d° ceremony, Yājñ.; pl. N. of partic. texts, MārkP. °**devya**, mfn. sacred to the Viśve Devāḥ, Nir. °**daivata**, n. = °*devata*. °**daivika**, v. l. for °*devaka*.

Vaiśvadha, mfn. (fr. *viśva-dhā*), g. *chattrâdi*.

Vaiśvadhenava, m. (fr. *viśva-dhenu*), Pāṇ. vii, 3, 25, Sch.; *-bhakta*, mfn., g. *aishukāry-ādi*. °**dhainava**, °*va-bhakta*, v. l. for °*dhenava*, °*va-bh*°.

Vaiśvam-tari, m. (fr. *viśvam-tara*) a patr., Saṃskārak.

Vaiśvamanasa, n. (fr. *viśva-manas*) N. of a Sāman, ĀrshBr.

Vaiśvamānava, m. (fr. *viśva-mānava*), g. *aishu-kāry-ādi*; *-bhakta*, mfn. inhabited by V°.

Vaiśvarūpa, mfn. (fr. *viśva-rūpa*) multiform, manifold, diverse, Suśr.; n. the universe, Sāṃkhyak. °**rūpya**, mfn. = prec., Hariv.; n. manifoldness, multiplicity, diversity, Sāṃkhyak. (*ena*, in various manners, Hariv.)

Vaiśvalopa, mf(ī)n. coming from (the tree) Viśva-lopa, Kauś.

Vaiśvavyacasá, mfn. (fr. *viśvá-vyacas*), VS.

Vaiśvasṛijá (fr. *viśva-sṛij*), TĀr.; ĀpŚr.; *-cayana-prayoga*, m., *-prayoga*, m. N. of wks.

Vaiśvānará, mf(ī)n. (fr. *viśvā-nara*) relating or belonging to all men, omnipresent, known or worshipped everywhere, universal, general, common, RV. &c. &c.; consisting of all men, full in number, complete, RV.; AV.; ŚrS.; relating or belonging to the gods collectively, Lāṭy.; all-commanding, AV.; relating or sacred to Agni Vaiśvānara, TS.; ŚBr.; ŚrS.; composed by Viśvānara or Vaiśvānara, Cat.; m. N. of Agni or Fire, RV. &c. &c. (Agni Vaiśv° is regarded as the author of x, 79, 80); a partic. Agni, ĀrshBr.; the fire of digestion, MW.; the sun, sunlight, AV.; ŚāṅkhBr.; (in the Vedânta) N. of the Supreme Spirit or Intellect when located in a supposed collective aggregate of gross bodies (= Virāj, Prajā-pati, Purusha), Vedântas.; RTL. 35; N. of a Daitya, Hariv.; Pur.; of various men, Kathās.; (pl.) of a family of Ṛishis, MBh.; (ī), f. N. of a partic. division of the moon's path (comprising both Bhadrapadā and Revatī; cf. *-patha* and *-mārga*), VP.; a partic. sacrifice performed at the beginning of every year, W.; n. men collectively, mankind, TBr.; N. of a Sāman, ĀrshBr.; *-kshāra*, m. a partic. mixture, L.; *-jyeshṭha* (°*rá-*), mfn. having V° for the first, AV.; *-jyotiś* (°*rá-*), mfn. having V°'s light, VS.; *-datta*, m. N. of a Brāhman, Cat.; *-patha*, m. N. of a partic. division of the moon's path (cf. above), R.; Hariv.; *-pathi-kṛita-pūrvaka-darśa-sthālī-pāka-prayoga*, m., and *-pathi-kṛita-sthālī-pāka-prayoga*, m. N. of wks.; *-mukha*, mfn. having V° for a mouth (said of Śiva), MBh.; *-vat* (°*rá-*), mfn. attended or connected with fire, TBr.; *-vidyā*, f. N. of an Upanishad. °**narāyaṇa**, m. patr. fr. *viśvānara*, g. *aśvâdi*. °**narīya**, mfn. relating to or treating of Vaiśvānara, AitBr.; Nir.; n. du. N. of the Sûktas AV. vi, 35 &c., Kauś.

Vaiśvāmanasa (cf. *vaiśva-m*°), N. of various Sāmans, ĀrshBr.

Vaiśvāmitra, mf(ī)n. relating or belonging to Viśvāmitra; m. patr. of various Vedic Ṛishis (as of Ashṭaka, Ṛishabha &c.), Br.; ŚrS.; BhP. (also pl.); (ī), f. a female descendant of V°, Pāṇ. iv, 1, 78, Sch.; the Gāyatrī of V°, ŚāṅkhGṛ.; n. N. of various Sāmans, ĀrshBr. °**mitri**, m. patr. fr. *viśvā-mitra*, MBh. °**mitrika**, mfn. relating to V°, Pāṇ. iv, 3, 69, Sch.

Vaiśvāvasavá, n. (fr. *viśvā-vasu*) the Vasus collectively, TBr. °**vasavya** (*vaí*°), m. (fr. id.) a patr., ŚBr. (cf. g. *gargâdi*).

वैश्वासिक *vaiśvāsika*, mf(ī)n. (fr. *vi-śvāsa*) deserving or inspiring confidence, trustworthy, Daś.

वैषद्य *vaishadya*, w.r. for *vaiśadya*.

वैषम *vaishama*, n. (fr. *vi-shama*) inequality, change, Amar. (v. l.) **-sthya**, n. (fr. *vishama-stha*), g. *brāhmaṇâdi*.

Vaishamya, n. unevenness (of ground), MBh.; inequality, oddness (opp. to 'evenness'), diversity, disproportion, ŚrS.; MBh. &c.; difficulty, trouble, distress, calamity, MBh.; Kāv. &c.; injustice, unkindness, harshness, R.; Kathās.; Sarvad.; impropriety, incorrectness, wrongness, Sarvad.; an error, mistake in or about (loc. or comp.), BhP.; solitariness, singleness, W. **-kaumudī**, f. N. of wk. **Vaishamyôd-dhariṇī**, f. difficulty-removing, N. of a Comm. on the Kirātârjunīya by Vaṅkima-dāsa.

वैषय *vaishaya*, n. (fr. *vi-shaya*) = *vishayāṇām samūhaḥ*, g. *bhikshâdi*.

Vaishayika, mf(ī)n. relating to or denotative of a country or district (as a suffix), Pat.; having a partic. sphere or object or aim (in gram. the *ādhāra* is called *vaishayika* when it is the aim or object of the action, Siddh. on Pāṇ. ii, 3, 36); relating to, concerning (comp.), Car.; belonging or relating to an object of sense, sensual, carnal, mundane, Pañcar.; HPariś.; m. a sensualist, one addicted to the pleasures of sense or absorbed in worldly objects, L. (also *-jana*); (ī), f. a voluptuous or unchaste woman, L.

वैषुवत *vaishuvata*, mf(ī)n. (fr. *vishu-vat*) being in the middle of anything, middlemost, central, ŚBr.; Āpast.; relating to the equinox, equinoctial, Sūryas.; n. the middle of anything, centre, Āpast.; the equinox, BhP.; N. of a Brāhmaṇa, MānGṛ.

Vaishuvatīya, mfn. = *vaishuvata*, ŚāṅkhBr.

वैष्क *vaishka*. See *baishka*.

वैष्किर *vaishkira*, mfn. consisting of the birds called Vishkira (as a flock), Car.; prepared from chickens (as broth, cf. *vishkira-rasa*), Suśr.

वैष्टप *vaishṭapá*, mfn. (fr. *vi-shṭapa*), AV.

वैष्टपुरेय *vaishṭapureyá*, m. patr. fr. *vishṭa-pura*, ŚBr. (g. *śubhrâdi*).

वैष्टम्भ *vaishṭambha*, n. (fr. *vi-shṭambha*) N. of two Sāmans, ĀrshBr.

वैष्टिक *vaishṭika*, m. (fr. 1. *vishṭi*) one who does compulsory service, one compelled to labour for a landlord, SaddhP.

वैष्टुत *vaishṭuta*, mfn. relating to or used at the Vishṭuti (q. v.), L.; n. = next, L.

वैष्टुभ *vaishṭubha*, n. the ashes of a burnt offering (cf. *vaishṇava*, n., and *vaishṇuta*), L.

वैष्ट्र *vaishṭra*, n. the world, Uṇ. iv, 159, Sch. ('the sky,' 'the wind,' or 'Vishṇu,' Uṇvṛ.)

वैष्णव *vaishṇavá*, mf(ī)n. relating or belonging or devoted or consecrated to Vishṇu (q. v.), worshipping V°, TS. &c. &c.; m. patr. fr. *vishṇu*, g. *bidâdi*; 'a worshipper of V°,' N. of one of the three great divisions of modern Hindūism (the other two being the Śaivas and Śāktas; the Vaishṇavas identify Vishṇu—rather than Brahmā and Śiva—with the supreme Being, and are exclusively devoted to his worship; they have become separated into four principal and some minor sects, as follow: 1. the Rāmânujas, founded by Rāmânuja, who is said to have lived for 120 years [from 1017 till 1137 A. D.]; his chief doctrines are described at p. 878, col. 1, and in RTL. p. 119 &c.; one peculiarity of his sect is the scrupulous preparation and privacy of their meals; 2. the Mādhvas, founded by a Kanarese Brāhman named Madhva, whose chief doctrines are described at p. 782, col. 3, and in RTL. p. 130 &c.; 3. the Vallabhas, founded by Vallabhâcārya, whose chief doctrines are described at p. 928, col. 3, and in RTL. p. 134 &c.; 4. a sect in Bengal founded by Caitanya [q. v.] who was regarded by his followers as an incarnation of Kṛishṇa; his chief doctrine was the duty of *bhakti* or love for that god which was to be so strong that no caste-feelings could exist with it [see RTL. p. 140 &c.] Of the minor Vaishṇava sects those founded by Nimbârka or Nimbâditya [RTL. 146] and by Rāmânanda [RTL. 147] and by Svāmi-Nārāyaṇa [RTL. 148] are perhaps the most important, to which also may be added the reformed theistic sect founded by Kabīr [RTL. 158] and the Sikh theistic sect founded by Nānak [RTL. 161]); N. of Soma (lord of the Apsarases), ĀśvŚr.; (*śrī-*) of a poet, Cat.; the 13th cubit (*aratni*) from the bottom or the 5th from the top of the sacrificial post, L.; a kind of mineral, L.; (scil. *yajña*) a partic. sacrificial ceremony, ib.; (ī), f. patr. fr. *vishṇu*, MBh.; a female worshipper of Vishṇu, Pañcar.; the personified Śakti of Vishṇu (regarded as one of the Mātṛis, and identified with Durgā and Manasā), MBh.; Rājat. &c.; Asparagus Racemosus, L.; Ocymum Sanctum, L.; Clitoria Ternatea, L.; (in music) a partic. Mūrchanā, Saṃgīt.; n. a partic. Mahā-rasa (q. v.), Cat.; a partic. prodigy or omen (belonging to or occurring in the *paraṃ divam* or upper sky), MW.; the ashes of a burnt-offering, ib.; N. of the Nakshatra Śravaṇa (presided over by Vishṇu), VarBṛS.; of two Sāmans, ĀrshBr.; of various wks., esp. of the Vishṇu-Purāṇa. **-karaṇa**, n., **-karṇâbharaṇa-saṃgraha**, m., **-kutūhala**, n., **-jyotisha-śāstra**, n., **-tantra**, n. N. of wks. **-tīrtha**, n. a Tīrtha of the Vaishṇavas, Cat. **-toshiṇī**, f. = *vishṇu-t*° (q. v.) **-tva**, n. belief in or worship of Vishṇu, Rājat. **-dāsa**, m. N. of an author, Cat. **-dīkshā-paddhati**, f., **-dharma-mīmāṃsā**, f., **-dharma-sura-druma-mañjarī**, f., **-dharmânushṭhāna-paddhati**, f., **-dhyāna-prakāra**, m., **-nārāyaṇâshṭâkshara-nyāsa**, m., **-purāṇa**, n., **-pramāṇa-saṃgraha**, m., **-praśna-śāstra**, n., **-matâbja-bhāskara**, m., **-mahā-siddhânta**, m., **-lakshaṇa**, n., **-vandanā**, f., **-vardhana**, n. N. of wks. **-vāruṇa**, mf(ī)n. addressed to Vishṇu and Varuṇa (as a hymn), ŚBr. **-vaidyaka-śāstra**, n., **-vyākaraṇa**, n., **-śaraṇâgati**, f., **-śānti**, f., **-śāstra**, n. (also pl.), **-saṃhitā**, f., **-sadâcāra-nirṇaya**, m., **-siddhânta-tattva**, n., **-siddhânta-dīpikā**, f., **-siddhânta-vaijayantī**, f. N. of wks. **-sthānaka**, n. (in dram.) walking about the stage with great strides, Daśar., Sch. **Vaishṇavâkūta-candrikā**, f., °**vâgama**, m. N. of wks. **Vaishṇavâcamana**, n. sipping water three times in the worship of Vishṇu, MW. **Vaishṇavâcāra**, m. the rites or practices of the Vaishṇavas; *-paddhati*, f., *-saṃgraha*, m. N. of wks. **Vaishṇavâbhidhāna**, n. N. of a wk. (containing the names of the disciples of Caitanya). **Vaishṇavâmṛita**, n., °**vâshṭaka**, n., °**vôtsava**, m., °**vôtsava-vidhi**, m., °**vôpayoga-nirṇaya**, m. N. of wks.

Vaishṇavāyana, m. patr. fr. *vaishṇava*, g. *haritâdi*.

Vaishṇavī-tantra, n. N. of a Tantra.

Vaishṇavyà, mfn. relating or belonging to Vishṇu, VS.; Gobh.

Vaishṇāvaruṇá, mf(ī)n. (prob. for *vaishṇava-varuṇa*) belonging to Vishṇu and Varuṇa, TS.

Vaishṇugupta, mfn. taught by Vishṇu-gupta, L.

Vaishṇuta (?), n. sacrificial ashes (cf. *vaishṇava*, n., *vaishṭuta*), L.

Vaishṇuvāruṇa, mf(ī)n. = *vaishṇāvaruṇa*, AitBr.

Vaishṇuvṛiddhi, m. patr. fr. *vishṇu-vṛiddhi*, Pravar.

वैष्वक्सेन्य *vaishvaksenya*, m. patr. fr. *vishvak-sena*, Pāṇ. iv, 1, 114, Vārtt. 7, Pat.

वैसर्गिक *vaisargika*, mfn. (fr. *vi-sarga*), g. *saṃtāpâdi*.

Vaisarjana, n. pl. (fr. *vi-sarjana*) N. of partic. sacrificial rites, ĀpŚr. **-tvá**, n. the condition of (being a rite called) Vais°, MaitrS. **-homāya**, mfn. used at the Vais° rite, Nyāyam., Sch.

Vaisarjanīya (KātyŚr.) and **vaisarjiná** (ŚBr.), n. pl. = *vaisarjana*.

वैसर्प *vaisarpa*, mfn. suffering from (the disease called) Vi-sarpa, g. *jyotsnâdi* on Pāṇ. v, 2, 103, Vārtt. 2; = *vi-sarpa*, L.

Vaisarpika, mfn. caused by Vi-sarpa, Hcat.

वैसादृश्य *vaisādṛiśya*, n. (fr. *vi-sadṛiśa*) dissimilarity, difference, BhP.

वैसारिण *vaisāriṇa*, m. (fr. and = *vi-sārin*) a fish, Pāṇ. v, 4, 16.

वैसूचन *vaisūcana*, n. (fr. *vi-sūcana*) assumption of female attire by a man (in dram.), L.

वैसृप *vaisṛipa*, m. (fr. *vi-sṛipa*) N. of a Dānava, Hariv.

वैस्तारिक *vaistārika*, mfn. (fr. *vi-stāra*) extensive, wide, Buddh.

वैस्तिक *vaistika*. See *bahu-v°* (add.)

वैस्पष्ट्य *vaispashṭya*, n. (fr. *vi-spashṭa*) clearness, distinctness, Pāṇ. v, 3, 66, Vārtt. 4.

वैस्रेय *vaisreya*, m. patr. fr. *visri*, g. *śubhrâdi*.

वैस्वर्य *vaisvarya*, mfn. (fr. *vi-svara*) depriving of voice, Suśr.; n. loss of voice or language, Vāgbh.; Sāh.; different accentuation, ŚāṅkhŚr.

वैहग *vaihaga*, mf(ī)n. (fr. *viha-ga*) relating or belonging to a bird (with *tanu*, f. 'the body or form of a bird'), Kathās.

Vaihaṃga, mfn. (fr. *vihaṃ-ga*) id. (with *rasa*, m. 'broth made of bird's flesh'), Suśr.

वैहति *vaihati*, m. patr. fr. *vi-hata*, g. *taulvaly-ādi*; (*ī*), f., Pat.

वैहलि *vaihali*, m. (also pl.) a patr., Saṃskārak.

वैहायन *vaihāyana*, m. (also pl.) a patr., ib.

वैहायस *vaihāyasa*, mf(ī)n. (fr. 2. *vi-hāyas*) being or moving in the air, suspended in the air, aerial, GṛS.; MBh. &c.; (*am*), ind. in the open air, Āpast.; m. pl. 'sky-dwellers,' the gods &c., BhP.; N. of partic. Ṛishis (personified luminous phenomena), VarBṛS.; m. N. of a lake, MW.; (*ī*), f. N. of a river, BhP.; n. the air, atmosphere, MBh.; flying in the air, BhP. (*-gata*, n. id., R.); a partic. attitude in shooting, L.

वैहार *vaihāra*, m. (fr. *vi-hāra*) N. of a mountain in Magadha, MBh. (cf. *vaibhāra*).

Vaihārika, mfn. serving for sport or amusement, L.

Vaihārya, mfn. to be played or sported with, to be conciliated by playfulness or raillery (applied to a wife's brother or brother-in-law or other relations of a wife), MBh.; n. playfulness, sportiveness, fun, ib.

वैहाली *vaihālī*, f. hunting, chase, Siṇhâs.

वैहासिक *vaihāsika*, m. (fr. *vi-hāsa*) a comic actor, buffoon, actor in general, L.; a playfellow, L.

वैहीनरि *vaihīnari*. See *baih°*.

वैह्वल्य *vaihvalya*, n. (fr. *vi-hvala*) exhaustion, debility, Rājat.

वोक्काण *vokkāṇa*, m. or n. (?) N. of a place, Divyâv.; m. pl. N. of a people, VarBṛS. (cf. *bokaṇa*).

वोच् *voc*. See √*vac*, p. 912, col. 1.

वोटा *voṭā*, f. a female servant or slave, L.

वोड *voḍa*, w.r. for *jhoḍa*, L.

वोड्र *voḍra*, m. a kind of large snake, L.; a sort of fish, L.; (*ī*), f. the fourth part of a Paṇa, L.

वोढ *voḍha*, mfn. (fr. √1. *vah*) led home, married, MBh.

Vóḍhave or **vóḷhave**, Ved. inf. of √1. *vah*.

Voḍhavya, mfn. to be borne or carried or drawn or led &c. (n. impers.), MBh.; Hariv.; to be undertaken or accomplished, MBh.; (*ā*), f. (a woman) to be led home or married, ib.

Voḍhu, m. the son of a woman living in her father's house (whose husband is absent), W.

Voḍhṛi or **vóḍhṛi**, mfn. drawing, bearing, carrying, bringing, one who bears or carries &c., RV. &c. &c.; wafting (as wind), Kum.; m. a draught horse, RV. (*vóḷhā*); MBh. &c. (also with *rathasya*, L.); a bull, ox (also with *dhuraḥ* or *halasya*), MBh.; Pañcat.; Hcat.; an offerer, MBh.; a guide, Śaṃk.; a porter, carrier, BhP. (also *bhāra-*); a charioteer, L.; a bridegroom, husband, Mn.; MBh. &c. (also with acc., Pāṇ. iii, 3, 169, Sch.); = *mūḍha*, L.

वोण्ट *voṇṭa*, m. = *vṛinta*, L.

वोद *voda*, mfn. = *ārdra*, L.

वोदाल *vodāla*, m. a species of fish, L.

वोद्र *vodra*, m. (and ī, f.), w.r. for *voḍra*, °*ḍrī*.

वोन्थादेवी *vonthā-devī*, f. N. of a princess, Inscr.

वोपदेव *vopa-deva*, m. N. of the author of the Mugdha-bodha grammar (also of the Kavi-kalpadruma and various other works, including, according to some, the Bhāgavata-Purāṇa; he was a son of Keśava and pupil of Dhaneśvara, and is said to have flourished about the latter half of the thirteenth century at the court of Hemâdri, king of Deva-giri, now Dowlatābād). **-śataka**, n. N. of a Kāvya by Vopa-deva.

वोपालित *vopālita* or *vopālita-siṇha*, m. N. of a lexicographer, Cat.

वोपुल *vopula*, m. N. of a man, Vīrac.

वोर *vora*, m. (prob. not a Sanskrit word) a sort of pulse, Dolichos Catjang, W. **-paṭṭi**, f. a sort of mat or mattress for sleeping on (perhaps made of the straw of the Vora), L. **-siddhi**, see *bora-s°*.

वोरक *voraka*, m. (cf. *volaka*) a copyist, writer, L.

वोरट *voraṭa*, m. Jasminum Multiflorum or Pubescens, L.

वोरव *vorava*, m. a kind of rice (perhaps that called Boro, which is cut in March or April), L.

वोरुखान *vorukhāna*, m. a horse (described as one of a pale red colour), L.

वोरुवाण *voruvāṇa*, w.r. for *roruvāṇa*.

वोल *vola*, m. gum-myrrh, Bhpr.

वोलक *volaka*, m. a whirlpool, L.; (cf. *voraka*) a copyist, writer, L.

वोल्लासक *vollāsaka*, m. or n. (?) N. of a place, Rājat.

वोल्लाह *vollāha*, m. a chestnut-coloured horse (with a light mane and tail), L.

वोहित्थ *vohittha*, n. a vessel, ship, L.

वौक् *vaúk*, nom. sg. for *vā́k* (fr. *vā́c*), ŚBr.

वौझट् *vaujhaṭ*, for *vaushaṭ*, ŚBr.; KātyŚr., Sch.

वौदन्य *vaudanya*, n. N. of a city, MBh. (v. l.)

वौद्ध *vauddha*. See *bauddha*.

वौलि *vauli* (?), m. a patr., Pravar.

वौषट् *vaúshaṭ*, ind. (prob. a lengthened form of *vashaṭ*, q.v.) an exclamation or formula (used on offering an oblation to the gods or deceased ancestors with fire), Br.; Hariv. &c.

व्य् *vy*, in comp. before vowels for 3. *ví*. **-aṇsa**, m. N. of a son of Vipra-citti, Hariv.; VP. (v. l. *vy-aṇsa*). **-aṇsaka**, m. a mountain, W. **-aṇsuka**, mfn. unclothed, naked, ib. **-áṇsa**, mfn. having shoulders wide apart, broad-shouldered, MBh.; m. N. of a demon vanquished by Indra, RV. (= shoulderless, Sāy.); of a son of Vipra-citti (cf. *vy-aṇsa*). **-aksha**, m. (cf. *nir-aksha*) 'having no latitude,' the equator, Sūryas. **-agra**, see s. v. **-aṅkuśa**, mfn. unrestrained, unchecked, BhP. **-aṅga**, see p. 1029, cols. 1, 3. **-aṅgāra**, mfn. without charcoal, having no fire (*e*, ind. at the time when the burning charcoal is extinguished), MBh.; MārkP.; °*rin*, mfn. having the charcoal extinguished, Hcat. **-aṅgula**, n. the 60th part of an Aṅgula, MW.; °*lī*-√*kṛi*, P.; *-karoti*, to deprive of the fingers, MBh. **-aṅgushṭha**, a kind of plant, L. (w. r. for *kāṅgushṭha*). **-adhikaraṇa**, mfn. being in a different case-relation, relating to another subject, KapS., Sch.; Vām.; n. incongruity, Kusum.; Śiś., Sch.; the subsisting or inhering in different receptacles or subjects or substrata (sometimes applied to a loose or ambiguous argument; opp. to *samānâdhik°*, see *viśesha-vyāpti*), MW.; N. of sev. wks.; *-dharmâvacchinna-vāda*, m., °*cchinnâbhāva*, m. (°*va-kroḍa*, m., °*va-khaṇḍana*, n., °*va-ṭīkā*, f., °*va-parishkāra*, m., °*va-prakāśa*, m., °*va-rahasya*, n.), N. of wks.; *-pada*, mfn. containing words in different cases (as a Bahuvrīhi, e.g. *kanthe-kāla*, 'one who has black colour in the throat' [= *kāla-kaṇṭha*, 'black-throated']), Laghuk. 1036; °*ṇâbhāva*, m. N. of wk. **-adhva**, m. half the way (*vyadhvé* [AV.] or *vyàdhve* [ŚBr.], in the middle of the way), KātyŚr.; MBh.; a bad road, wrong road, L.; mf(*ā́*)n. being in the air between the zenith and the surface of the earth, AV. **-ádhvan**, mfn. being in the midst of the way (or) going astray, RV. i, 141, 7; m. 'having various paths,' N. of Agni, MW. **-ânta**, mfn. separated, remote, TBr.; ĀpŚr.; °*tī*-√*kṛi*, P.; *-karoti*, to keep off, remove, L.; °*tībhāva*, m. the being removed, L. **-antara**, n. (ifc. f. *ā*); absence of distinction, Hariv.; an interval, Gobh.; m. 'occupying an intermediate position,' (with Jainas) N. of a class of gods (including Piśācas, Bhūtas, Yakshas, Rākshasas, Kiṃ-naras, Kim-purushas, Mahôragas and Gandharvas), Śatr.; HPariś.; Pañcat. &c.; (*ī*), f. a deity of the above class, Campak.; HPariś.; (*ám*), ind. moderately, ŚBr.; °*ra-paṅkti* (?), f., Cat. **-apatrapa**, mfn. shameless, MW.; (*ā*), f., see under *vy-apa*-√*trap*. **-apamūrdhan**, mfn. headless, L. **-1. -apâśraya**, mfn. (for 2. see *vy-apâ*-√*śri*) devoid of reliance or support, self-centred, self-dependent, Kām. **-abhimāna**, see s. v. **-abhra**, mf(*ā*)n. cloudless, unclouded, MBh.; Hariv. &c.; (*e*), ind. when the sky is cloudless, ib.; *-ja*, mfn. appearing when the sky is cloudless, VarBṛS. **-amla**, mfn. free from acidity (*-tā*, f.), Car. **-arka**, mfn. with exception of the sun, VarBṛ. **-1. -arṇa**, mfn. (for 2. see *vy*-√*ard*) waterless, without water, PañcavBr.; ŚrS. **-artha**, see s. v. **-alīka**, mfn. very false or untruthful, lying, hypocritical (*am*, ind.), Amar.; BhP.; disagreeable, painful, offensive, strange, MW.; improper or unfit to be done, MW.; not false, Śiś.; = *vyaṅgya*, L.; m. = *nāgara*, L.; a catamite, MW.; n. anything displeasing, ib.; any cause of pain or uneasiness, ib.; pain, grief, MBh.; Kāv.; Pur. &c.; a falsehood, lie, fraud (also pl.), Kāv.; Pur. &c.; transgression, offence, misdeed, Ratnāv.; Jātakam.; = *vailakshya*, L.; reverse, contrariety, inversion, MW.; *-tā*, f. or *-tva*, n. disagreeableness, painfulness, MW.; impropriety, displeasure, ib.; *-niḥśvāsa*, m. a sigh of pain or sorrow, Kum. **-alkaśa**, mfn. (accord. to Sāy.) having various branches; (*ā*), f. a kind of plant, RV. x, 16, 13. **-avadhāraṇa**, n. a special definition or designation, Nyāyam, Sch.; Jaim., Sch. **-avânin**, mfn. not breathing between, AitĀr. **-1. -aśana**, mf(*ā*)n. (for 2. see p. 1034, col. 3) abstinence from eating, fasting, Hariv. **-aśva**, mfn. deprived of horses, horseless, ShaḍvBr.; MBh.; Ragh.; m. N. of a Ṛishi, RV.; of an ancient king (also pl.), ib.; MBh.; *-vat*, ind. like Vyaśva, MW.; *-sārathy-āyudha*, mfn. deprived of horses and charioteer and weapons, Gaut. **-ashṭakā**, f. the first day in the dark half of a month, TS.; TBr.; Kāṭh.; Lāṭy.; the dark half of a month, ĀpGṛ. (Sch.) **-asi**, mfn. swordless, VarYogay. **-asu**, mf(*u*)n. lifeless, dead, MBh.; BhP.; Śiś.; Rājat.; *-tva*, n. loss of life, VarBṛS. **-asthaka**, mfn. boneless, PañcavBṛ. **-ahan** or **-ahna** (loc. °*hni*, °*hani*, or °*hne*), Pāṇ. vi, 3, 110; Vop. iii, 42; (*-ahna*), mfn. done or happening on separate days, MW.; (accord. to some 'done or produced in two days'). **-ākula**, see s. v. **-āmarsha**, m. impatience, MW. **-āyudha**, mfn. weaponless, MBh.; MW. **-1. -āvṛita**, mfn. (for 2. see under *vy-ā*-√1. *vṛi*) uncovered, opened, open to (loc.), Ragh. i, 19 (v. l.) **-āśā**, f. an intermediate quarter (of the compass), RāmatUp. **-1. -āśraya**, mfn. (for 2. see under *vy-ā*-√*śri*) having a different support or refuge (opp. to *samānâśraya*), Pat. **-āhanasya**, mf(*ā*)n. extremely lewd or obscene, AitBr. **-āhāva**, m. the invocation *śoṇsāvōm*, ĀpŚr.; (*am*), ind. separating by interposing the Āhāva, AitBr.; ĀśvŚr. **-uda**, mfn. waterless, dry, BhP. **-udaka**, mf(*ā*)n. id., ŚāṅkhGr.; Āpast.; BhP. **-upadrava**, mfn. undisturbed by any misfortune, not liable to unlucky accidents, Suśr. **-upavīta**, mfn. devoid of the sacred thread, Prâyaśc. **-1. -upaśama**, m. (for 2. see *vy-upa-√śam*) non-cessation, not ceasing or desisting, Mālatīm.; Sāh.; inquietude, MW. **-upaskara**, mfn. without appurtenance, MBh. **-ūdhnī**, f. having a large udder, TāṇḍyaBr. **-ūrdhva-bhāj**, w.r. for *vy-ṛiddha-bhāj*, Jaim. **-eka**, mf(*ā*)n. deficient by one, VarBṛS. **-ènas**, mfn. guiltless, RV. iii, 33, 13. **-ènī**, f. (of *vy-eta*) variously-tinted (said of the dawn), RV. v, 80, 4. **-ailaba**, mfn. making various noises, AV. **-òkas**, mfn. dwelling apart, Br. **-òdana** (*e*, ind., accord. to Sāy. = *vividhe 'nne labdhe sati*), RV. viii, 52, 9. **-1. -oman**, mfn. (for 2. see s.v.) one who cannot be saved (?), Kāṭh.

व्य 1. *vya*, m. (√*vye*) a coverer, MW.

व्य 2. *vya* (said to be an abbreviated form of *a-vyaya*) a technical symbol for indeclinables such as *ni, cit, svar* &c., Vop. iii, 17.

व्यंश *vy-aṅśa, vy-aṅsaka.* See p. 1028, col. 2.

व्यंस् *vy-√aṅs*, P. *-aṅsayati*, to cheat, deceive, Divyâv. **-aṅsaka**, m. a cheat, rogue, juggler, L. **-aṅsana**, n. cheating, deceiving, MBh. **-aṅsanīya**, to be cheated or deceived, W. **-aṅsayitavya**, mfn. id., Pañcat. **-aṅsita**, mfn. cheated, deceived, disappointed, W.

व्यकृड *vyakṛiḍa*, mfn. (applied to Rudra), MaitrS.

व्यक्त *vy-akta, vy-akti.* See cols. 2, 3.

व्यक्ष् *vy-√aksh*, P. *-akshati* or *-akshṇoti* = *vy-√aś*, to pervade, &c., MW.

व्यक्ष *vy-aksha.* See p. 1028, col. 2.

व्यग्र *vy-agra*, mf(*ā*)n. not attending to any one partic. point (opp. to *ekâgra*), distracted, inattentive; bewildered, agitated, excited, alarmed, MaitrUp.; MBh.; Kāv. &c.; diverted from everything else, intent on, engrossed by, eagerly occupied with or employed in (instr., loc., or comp.; sometimes said of hands and fingers), MBh.; Hariv.; Kāv. &c.; tottering, unsteady, exposed to dangers (see *a-vy°*); being in motion (as a wheel), BhP.; m. N. of Vishṇu, MW.; (*am*), ind. in an agitated manner, with great excitement, VarBṛS.; *-tā*, f. intense occupation, eagerness, intentness (ifc.), Śak.; Pañcat. &c.; perplexity, confusion, MW.; *-tva*, n. distraction; confusion, agitation, MaitrUp.; Pañcat.; (ifc.) intentness on, Kull. on Mn. viii, 65; *-puraṃdhri-varga*, mfn. having companies of matrons zealously occupied, MW.; *-manas*, mfn. perplexed or bewildered in mind, ib.; *-hasta*, mfn. having the hands occupied with (comp.), Divyâv.

Vyagraya, Nom. P. °*yati*, to divert or distract any one's thoughts, Car.

व्यङ्कट *vyaṅkaṭa*, older form of *veṅkaṭa*.

व्यङ्कुश *vy-aṅkuśa.* See p. 1028, col. 2.

व्यङ्ग 1. *vy-àṅga*, mf(*ā*)n. (for 2. see col. 3) without limbs, limbless, deficient in limb, deformed, crippled, AV.; Mn.; MBh. &c.; having no wheels, BhP.; lamed, lame, MW.; bodiless, ib.; ill-arranged, ib.; m. a cripple, ib.; m. or n. a kind of cat's eye (a precious stone), L.; (n., w.r. for *try-aṅga*, tripartite army, MBh.); *-tā*, f., *-tva*, n. deficiency of limb, crippled condition, mutilation, MBh.; VarBṛS.; Pañcat.; °*gârtha*, m. (in rhet.) suggested sense or meaning, MW.

Vy-aṅgaya, Nom. P. °*yati*, to deprive of a limb, mutilate, ĀpŚr.; Pañcat. °**gita**, mfn. mutilated (*karṇayor vy°*, perforated in the ears, MBh. [Nīlak.]; °*tâkêkshaṇa*, mf[*ā*]n. defective in an eye, one-eyed, Śiś.)

Vyaṅgin, mfn. deficient in limb, deformed, crippled, MBh.; MārkP.

Vyaṅgī-√kṛi, P. *-karoti* = *vyaṅgaya*, MBh.; Hariv.

व्यङ्गार *vy-aṅgāra* &c. See p. 1028, col. 2.

व्यङ्ग्य *vy-aṅgya* &c. See col. 3.

व्यच् 1. *vyac* (cf. √*vic*; prob. orig. identical with 2. *vy-√ac*), cl. 6. P. (Dhātup. xxviii, 12) *vicati* (only in cl. 3. pr. *vivyakti*, 3. du. *viviktás*, Subj. *vivyácat*, RV.; impf. *avivyak*, 3. pl. *avivyacus*, ib.; pf. *vivyā́ca*, 2. sg. *vivyáktha*, ib.; Br.; Gr. also aor. *avyācīt*; Prec. *vicyāt*; fut. *vyacitā, vicitā*; *vyacishyati*; inf. *vyacitum*; ind. p. *vicitvā*), to encompass, embrace, comprehend, contain, RV.; AitBr.; (*vicati*), to cheat, trick, deceive, Dhātup.: Caus. *vyācayati* (aor. *avivyacat*), Gr.: Desid. *vivyacishati*, ib.: Intens. *vevicyate, vāvyacīti, vāvyakti*, ib.

Vyácas, n. expanse, capacity, compass, RV.; AV.; VS.; wide space, free scope, room, RV.; AV.; ŚBr. (*vyacas-√kṛi*, to dilate, expand, open, Kauś.) **-kāma**, mfn. desirous of wide space, Kauś. **-vat** (*vyácas-*), mfn. spacious, expansive, RV.; VS.

Vyácishṭha, mfn. (superl.) most spacious or expansive, RV.

व्यच् 2. *vy-√ac* (or *añc*), P. Ā. *-acati*, °*te*, to bend asunder, make wide, extend, RV.; AV.

व्यच्छ *vyacchu*. See *go-vyacchá*.

व्यज् 1. *vy-√aj*, P. *-ajati*, to drive away (Pass. *vy-ajyáte*), RV. x, 85, 28; to go through or across, furrow, ib. v, 54, 4.

1. **Vy-aja**, Pāṇ. iii, 3, 119.

व्यज् 2. *vyaj* (= √*vīj*, only in *vyajeta*, Suśr.; for *vivyajuḥ* see √*vīj*), to fan, ventilate.

2. **Vyaja**, m. a fan, W.

Vyajana, n. (ifc. f. *ā*) fanning, Kād.; a palm-leaf or other article used for fanning, fan, whisk (often du.), Mn.; MBh. &c. **-kriyā**, f. the act of fanning, Kād. **-cāmara**, n. the tail of the Bos Grunniens used as a whisk or fan, a chowry (cf. *vyajana-cāmara*).

Vyajanaka, n. = *vyajana*, a fan, VarBṛS.

Vyajanin, m. the Yak (Bos Grunniens), L.

Vyajanī, in comp. for *vyajana*. **-√kṛi**, P. *-karoti*, to make into (or use as) a fan, Kād. **-√bhū**, P. *-bhavati*, to become or be a fan, Ragh.

व्यञ्च् *vyañc*. See *uru-vyáñc*.

व्यञ्चन *vyañcana*, w.r. for *vy-añjana*, Hariv.

व्यञ्चनवत् *vyañcana-vat*, mfn. (a word used to explain *vyácas-vat*), Nir. viii, 10.

व्यञ्ज् *vy-√añj*, P. Ā. *-anakti*, *-aṅkte*, (Ā.) to anoint thoroughly, RV.; to decorate, adorn, beautify, ib.; (P. Ā.) to cause to appear, manifest, display, RV. &c. &c.: Pass. *-ajyate*, to be manifested or expressed, RV.; Ragh.; Pañcat.: Caus. *-añjayati*, to cause to appear, make clearly visible or manifest, Mn.; MBh. &c.

Vy-àkta, mfn. adorned, embellished, beautiful, RV.; caused to appear, manifested, apparent, visible, evident (*am*, ind. apparently, evidently, certainly), MBh.; Kāv. &c.; developed, evolved (see below); distinct, intelligible (see *-vāc*); perceptible by the senses (opp. to *a-vyakta*, transcendental), MBh.; BhP.; specified, distinguished, L.; specific, individual, L.; hot, L.; wise, learned, Lalit.; m. heat, L.; a learned man, L.; an initiated monk, Śīl.; 'the manifested One,' N. of Vishṇu, MW.; of one of the 11 Gaṇâdhipas (with Jainas); n. (in Sāṃkhya) 'the developed or evolved' (as the product of *a-vyakta*, q.v.), Sāṃkhyak. (cf. IW. 82); *-kṛitya*, n. a public action or deed, Rājat.; *-gaṇita*, n. calculation with known numbers, arithmetic, IW. 176, n. 3; *-gandhā*, f. (only L.) long pepper; jasmine; a species of Sanseviera; Clitoria Ternatea; *-tā*, f., or *-tva*, n. distinctness, manifestation (instr. 'clearly, distinctly;' acc. with √*gam*, 'to appear'), Up.; Kathās.; *-tāraka*, mfn. having clear stars, MW.; *-darśana*, mfn. one who has attained to right knowledge, R.; *-drishṭârtha*, mfn. perceiving or witnessing a transaction with one's own eyes, a witness, L.; *-bhuj*, mfn. consuming all manifested or visible things (said of time), MW.; *-maya*, mf(*ī*)n. relating to what is perceptible by the senses, MBh.; *-māricika*, mfn. much peppered, Car.; *-rasa*, mfn. having a perceptible taste (*-tā*, f.), Suśr.; *-rāśi*, m. (in arithm.) known or absolute quantity; *-rūpa*, m. 'having a manifested form,' N. of Vishṇu, MW.; *-rūpin*, mfn. having a discernible shape, ib.; *-lakshman*, mfn. having evident signs or marks, clearly characterized, W.; *-lavaṇa*, mfn. much salted, Car.; *-vāc*, f. a clear or distinct speech, Pāṇ. i, 3, 48; *-vikrama*, mfn. displaying valour, MW.; °*tâvadhūta*, mfn. one who has publicly shaken off worldly ties (opp. to *guptâv°*, q.v.), W.; °*tôdita*, mfn. spoken clearly or plainly, MW.

Vy-aktaya, Nom. P. °*yati*, to manifest, Dharmaś.

Vy-akti, f. visible appearance or manifestation, becoming evident or known or public (acc. with √*bhaj*, *ā-√gam*, and *ā-√yā*, to appear, become manifest), MBh.; Kāv. &c.; specific appearance, distinctness, individuality, ib.; an individual (opp. to *jāti*), Bhag.; VarBṛS. &c.; (in gram.) gender, Pāṇ. i, 2, 51; case, inflection, the proper form of any inflected word, W.; a vowel (?), MW.; *-tā*, f., *-tva*, n. distinctness, individuality, personality, ib.; *-viveka*, m. N. of wk.

Vyaktī, in comp. for *vy-akta*. **-karaṇa**, n. the act of making manifest or clear or distinct, Dhātup.; Jātakam. **-√kṛi**, P. *-karoti*, to make m° or clear or d° (*-kṛita*, mfn. made m° or clear or d°), Kathās. **-bhāva**, m. the becoming m° or clear or d°, Śaṃk. **-√bhū**, P. *-bhavati*, to become m° or clear or d° (*-bhūta*, mfn. become manifest or clear or distinct), MBh.; VarBṛS.; Rājat.

2. **Vy-àṅga**, mfn. (for 1. see col. 1) spotted, speckled, AV.; m. freckles in the face, Suśr.; a blot, blemish, stain, Hariv.; a frog, L.; steel, L.

Vy-aṅgya, mf(*ā*)n. that which is manifested or indicated or made perceptible, Śaṃk.; Sāh.; (in rhet.) indicated by allusion or insinuation, implied, suggestive, Kpr.; °*gyârtha-kaumudī*, f., °*gyârtha-dīpikā*, f., °*gyârtha-dīpinī*, f. N. of wks.; °*gyôkti*, f. covert language or insinuation, MW.

Vy-añjaka, mf(*ikā*)n. making clear, manifesting, indicating (gen. or comp.), Mn.; BhP.; (in rhet.) indicating by implication, suggesting (*-tva*, n.), Sāh.; Pratāp.; m. indication of passion or feeling, Mālatīm.; a sign, mark, symbol, W.; figurative expression or insinuation, ib.; °*kârtha*, m. (in rhet.) suggested or implied sense.

Vy-àñjana, mfn. manifesting, indicating, Hariv. (v.l. *vyañcana*); m. (once for n.; cf. below) a consonant, VPrāt.; Pandanus Odoratissimus, L.; = *vāditra-karman*, L.; (*ā*), f. (in rhet.) implied indication, allusion, suggestion, Sāh.; Pratāp.; a figurative expression (°*nā-vṛitti*, f. figurative style), W.; n. decoration, ornament, RV. viii, 78, 2; manifestation, indication, Suśr.; Rājat.; allusion, suggestion (= *ā*, f.), Sāh.; ĀśvŚr., Sch.; figurative expression, irony, sarcasm, W.; specification, Nir.; a mark, badge, spot, sign, token, ĀpŚr.; R.; Kathās. &c.; insignia, paraphernalia, Kāv.; symptom (of a disease), Cat.; mark of sex or gender (as the beard, breasts &c.), the private organs (male or female), GṛŚrS.; MBh. &c.; anything used in cooking or preparing food, seasoning, sauce, condiment, MBh.; R. &c.; a consonant, Prāt.; ŚrS. &c; a syllable, VPrāt. (cf. *hīna-vy°*); the letter (as opp. to *artha*, 'meaning'), Mahāv.; a limb, member, part, L.; a day, L.; purification of a sacrificial animal (also m. and *ā*, f.), L.; a fan, L. (w.r. for *vyajana*); *-kāra*, m. the preparer of a sauce or condiment, MBh.; *-guṇa* (?), m. N. of a wk. on condiments in cookery; *-saṃgama*, m. a collection or group of consonants, MW.; *-saṃdhi*, m. (in gram.) the junction of consonants, ib.; *-saṃnipāta*, m. a falling together or conjunction of consonants, ib.; *-sthāne*, ind. in the place of sauce or seasoning, ib.; *-hārtkā*, f. N. of a female demon supposed to remove the hair of a woman's pudenda, MārkP.; °*nôdaya*, mfn. followed by a consonant, MW.; °*nôpadha*, mfn. preceded by a c°, ib. °**ñjanika**, n. (with *svarāṇām*) N. of a Pariś. of the VS.

Vy-añjijishu, mfn. (fr. Desid.) wishing to make clear or manifest, W.

Vy-añjita, mfn. (fr. Caus.) clearly manifested or made visible; *-vṛitti-bheda*, mfn. having various actions manifested, MW.

व्यड *vyaḍa*, m. N. of a man, Vop. (cf. *vyāḍi*).

व्यडम्बक *vyaḍambaka* or °*bana*, n. the castor-oil plant, Ricinus Communis, L.

व्यड्ड *vyaḍḍa*, m. N. of a man, Rājat. (also *-maṇḍala*, ib.)

व्यति *vy-áti*, m. (fr. 3. *vi* and √2. *at*; but not dissolved in Padap.) a horse, RV.

व्यतिकृ *vy-ati-√1. kṛi*, only Pass. *-kriyate*, to be greatly changed or moved, BhP.

1. **Vy-atikara**, mfn. acting reciprocally, reciprocal, W.; m. reciprocity, reciprocal action or relation, ib.; contact, contiguity, union (ifc. = joined with, spreading through or over, pervading), MBh.; Kāv. &c.; (ifc.) taking to, accomplishing, performing, Amar.; Daś.; Rājat.; incident, opportunity, Nalac.; reverse,

misfortune, calamity, accident, fatality, Hcar.; Pañcat.; Kathās.; destruction, end, BhP. °**atikṛita**, mfn. pervaded, MW.

व्यतिकॄ *vy-ati-√kṛī*, Pass. *-kiryate*, to be mixed or blended together, Saṃk.

2. **Vy-atikara**, m. mixing or blending together, mixture, MBh.; BhP.; a confusing (or striking) resemblance, Jātakam.; *-vat*, mfn. mixed, of contrary kind or nature, Mcar.

Vy-atikarita, mfn. mixed or joined with (instr. or comp.), Mcar.; Mālatīm.

Vy-atikīrṇa, mfn. scattered about in different directions, MBh.; mixed together, confused, MW.

व्यतिक्रम् *vy-ati-√kram*, P. Ā. *-krāmati*, *-kramate* (ind. p. *-kramya*), to go or pass by, step over or beyond (lit. and fig.), MBh.; R.; Pañcat.; to pass away, elapse, be spent (as time), ib.; BhP.; to excel, surpass, conquer, R.; to neglect, omit, violate, ib. °**atikrama**, m. going or passing by, Suśr.; gaining the start, MBh.; passing away, lapse (of time), R.; leaping or passing over, avoiding, escaping, getting rid of (gen.), MBh.; Kāv. &c.; overstepping, transgressing, neglect, violation, non-performance, disregard of (gen. or comp.), Gaut.; Mn.; MBh. &c.; violation of established order, transgression, crime, vice, fault, sin against (gen. or comp.), Āpast.; Mn.; MBh. &c.; inverted order, reverse, contrary, ŚrS.; Daś. °**atikramaṇa**, n. (ifc.) committing a sin against, wronging, Kauś. °**atikramin**, mfn. (ifc.) sinning against, wronging, Āpast.; passing over, deviating, transgressing, MW. °**atikrānta**, mfn. passed over &c.; reversed, inverted, W.; one who has wrongly taken to (acc.), MBh. xii, 6492; n. transgression, sin, fault, R. °**atikrānti**, f. (ifc.) committing a sin against, harming, wronging, Sāh.

व्यतिक्षेप *vy-ati-kshepa*, m. (*√kship*) mutual exchange or permutation, Āpast.; mutual altercation, strife, contest, MBh. (v.l. *vy-adhi-kshepa*).

व्यतिगम् *vy-ati-√gam*, P. *-gacchati*, to go against each other, Pāṇ. i, 3, 15, Sch. °**atigata**, mfn. passed by, elapsed (as time), MBh.

व्यतिगा *vy-ati-√gā*, P. *-jigāti* (only aor. *vy-aty-agāt*), to pass by, Ragh.

व्यतिचर् *vy-ati-√car* (only 1. sg. pr. Ā. *-care*), to transgress against, offend (acc.), R. °**aticāra**, see *a-vyaticāra*.

व्यतिचुम्बित *vy-ati-cumbita*, mfn. (*√cumb*) touched closely, in immediate contact with, Naish.

व्यतिजल्प् *vy-ati-√jalp*, P. *-jalpati*, to chatter together, gossip, Pāṇ. i, 3, 15, Vārtt. 1, Pat.

व्यतिजि *vy-ati-√ji* (only 3. sg. pf. Ā. *-jigye*), to conquer, surpass, excel, Bhaṭṭ.

व्यतितन् *vy-ati-√tan* (only 3. du. impf. Ā. *vy-atanvātām*), to vie with each other in extending or spreading out, Bhaṭṭ.

व्यतितॄ *vy-ati-√tṛī* (only 3. sg. du. fut. P. *-tarishyati*), to pass completely across, overcome, Bhag.

व्यतिनी *vy-ati-√nī*, P. *-nayati*, to let pass (time), ĀśvŚr.

व्यतिपठ् *vy-ati-√paṭh*, P. *-paṭhati*, to recite mutually, Pāṇ. i, 3, 15, Vārtt. 1, Pat.

व्यतिपाक *vy-ati-pāka*, m. (*√pac*), Pāṇ. iii, 3, 43, Vārtt. 1.

व्यतिपात *vy-ati-pāta*, m. (*√pat*) N. of a partic. astronomical Yoga (when sun and moon are in the opposite Ayana and have the same declination, the sum of their longitudes being = 180°), Var.; Hcat. &c. (cf. *vy-atī-pāta*); *-janana-śānti*, f., *-prakaraṇa*, n., *-vrata-kalpa*, m. N. of wks.

व्यतिभा *vy-ati-√bhā*, Ā. *-bhāte* (pf. *-babhe*), to shine forth fully or brightly (used impers.), Viddh.

व्यतिभिन्न *vy-ati-bhinna*, mfn. (*√bhid*) inseparably joined or connected with, Nyāyas., Sch.

Vy-atibheda, m. bursting forth together or simultaneously, Sāh.; pervading, penetration, Nyāyas.

व्यतिभू *vy-ati-√bhū*, Ā. *-bhavate* (3. sg. prec. *-bhavishīshṭa*, Pāṇ. vii, 3, 88, Sch.), to vie with any one (acc.), contend for precedence or superiority, Vop.

व्यतिमर्श *vy-ati-marśa*, m. (*√mṛiś*) a partic. kind of Vihāra (mutual transposition of the several Pādas or half verses or whole verses of the first and second Vālakhilya hymns which are repeated in sets, two always taken together), MW. °**atimarśam**, ind. so as to encroach, ĀśvŚr.; so as to skip or take alternately, MW.

व्यतिमिश्र *vy-ati-miśra*, mfn. mixed or confounded with one another, MBh.; VarBṛS.

व्यतिमूढ *vy-ati-mūḍha*, mfn. (*√muh*) excessively perplexed or embarrassed, utterly distracted, Hariv. °**atimoha**, see *á-vyatimoha*.

व्यतिया *vy-ati-√yā*, P. *-yāti*, to go completely through, penetrate, pervade, R.; to pass by, flow on (as time), Hariv.

Vy-atiyāta, mfn. gone by, elapsed, ib.

व्यतियु *vy-ati-√2. yu*, P. *-yauti* (only 2. du. pr. *-yutas*), to unite mutually, mix together, mingle, Bhaṭṭ.

व्यतिरा *vy-ati-√rā*, Ā. *-rāte*, Siddh. (*vy-aty-are*, Pāṇ. vi, 4, 64, Sch.)

व्यतिरिच् *vy-ati-√ric*, Pass. *-ricyate*, to reach far beyond, leave behind, surpass, excel (acc. or abl.), Hariv.; Ragh.; to be separated from (abl.), BhP.; to differ from, ib.; Śaṃk.

Vy-atirikta, mfn. reaching beyond, excessive, immoderate (ifc. = abundantly furnished with), MBh.; separate, different or distinct from, other than (abl. or comp.), Mn.; MBh. &c.; (ifc.) free from, Sarvad.; left remaining from, Ragh., Sch. (v.l.); withdrawn, withheld, W.; excepted, ib.; (*am*), ind. with the exception of, except, without (e.g. *svara-v°*, 'except the accent'), MW.; *-tā*, f. (BhP.), *-tva*, n. (Sarvad.) distinction, difference. °**atiriktaka**, n. a partic. manner of flying, MBh.

Vy-atireka, m. distinction, difference, separateness, separation, exclusion, Lāṭy.; Kāv.; Pur. &c. (*bhāvo vyatireka-tas*, a separate or particular existence; *vīta-vyatireka*, not separate or particular; *eṇa* or *āt*, ind. [or *vyatireka* ibc.], with exception of, without); negation, Kap.; contrariety, contrast to (comp.), Kām. (*e*, ind., on the contrary supposition); logical discontinuance (opp. to *anvaya*, q.v.), Bhāshāp.; (in rhet.) a partic. figure of speech (the contrasting of things compared in some respects with each other), Kāvyâd.; Sāh. &c.; N. of wk.; *-tas*, ind., see above; *-vyāpti*, f. 'pervasion of difference or dissimilitude,' a comprehensive argument derived from negation or non-existence of certain qualities, MW.; °*kâlaṃkāra*, m. the rhetorical figure called Vyatireka, ib.; °*kâvalī*, f. N. of wk.

Vy-atireki, in comp. for °**atirekin**; *-pūrva-paksha-rahasya*, n., *-rahasya*, n. N. of wks.; *-liṅga*, n. an exclusive mark, negative property (excluding its subject from the class possessing the corresponding positive property), MW.; *-siddhânta-rahasya*, n. N. of wk.; °*ky-udāharaṇa*, n. illustration by contrast or negation (of certain properties), W.

Vy-atirekin, mfn. distinguishing, excluding, excepting, negative, Tarkas.; different, reverse, W.

Vy-atirecana, n. contrasting, pointing out a contrast or difference (in a comparison), Sāh.

व्यतिरुह् *vy-ati-√ruh*, P. *-rohati*, to grow, MBh.; to attain to (another state, acc.), ib.

Vy-atiropita, mfn. (fr. Caus.) ejected, expelled, dispossessed, ib.

व्यतिलङ्घिन् *vy-ati-laṅghin*, mfn. (*√laṅgh*) falling or slipping away, Ragh.

व्यतिलू *vy-ati-√lū*, Ā. *-lunīte* (or P. *-lunāti*, if joined with *itarêtarasya* or *anyo 'nyasya*), to cut mutually, Pāṇ. i, 3, 14; 16, Sch.

व्यतिवह् *vy-ati-√vah*, Ā. *-vahate*, to bear mutually or reciprocally, Vop.

व्यतिविद्ध *vy-ati-viddha*, mfn. (*√vyadh*) pierced, transfixed, MBh. (B.); put through, entwined, Śiś.

व्यतिवृत् *vy-ati-√vṛit*, Ā. *-vartate*, to go over, pass through, R.; to escape, avoid, MBh.; to glide or pass away, elapse, ib.; R.; Hariv.; to depart from (abl.), leave, quit, abandon, R.

व्यतिव्रज् *vy-ati-√vraj*, P. *-vrajati*, to go past, Āpast.; to stride over, overstep, Pañcat. (v.l.)

व्यतिशङ्कित *vy-ati-śaṅkita*, mfn. (*√śaṅk*) 'suspecting' or 'suspected' (in *mithyā-v°*), Hariv.

व्यतिशी *vy-ati-√śī*, Ā. *-śete*, to extend or pass beyond, surpass, Kāṭh.

व्यतिशॄ *vy-ati-√śṛī*, P. *-śīryate* (pr. p. *-śīryat*), to burst into many pieces, MBh.

व्यतिषञ्ज् *vy-ati-shañj* (*√sañj*), P. Ā. *-shajati*, °*te*, (P.) to join or unite in opposite places, connect mutually, intertwine, TBr.; Uttarar.; to implicate, involve in (a game), Daś.; (Ā.) to change, MW.: Pass. *-shajyate*, to be mutually connected, ib.

Vy-atishakta, mfn. mutually connected or joined or related, intertwined, mixed together, TBr. &c. &c.; intermarried, intermarrying, MW.

Vy-atishaṅga, m. mutual connection, reciprocal junction or relation, PañcavBr.; KātyŚr.; entanglement, Śiś. v, 61; hostile encounter, MBh.; exchange, barter, BhP.; absorption, MW.; *-vat*, mfn. having mutual connection, connected, united, mixed, ib.

Vy-atishaṅgam, ind. so as to join or connect mutually, ŚBr. °**atishaṅgin**, mfn. (ifc.) hanging or sitting on, Śiś. °**atishajya**, ind. seizing each other by the hand, PañcavBr.

Vy-atishañjita, mfn. = *vy-atishakta*, Śiś., Sch.

व्यतिसंदह् *vy-ati-saṃ-√dah*, P. *-dahati*, to burn up entirely, ChUp.

व्यतिसृ *vy-ati-√sṛi*, only ind. p. *-sṛitya*, prob. 'in each case,' 'on every occasion,' MBh. xii, 4402 (*gurum anu-sṛitya*, Nilak.): Caus. *-sārayati* (with *kathām*), to converse, Divyâv.

व्यतिसृप् *vy-ati-√sṛip*, P. *-sarpati* (Pāṇ. i, 3, 15), to move to and fro, fly in every direction (as arrows), MBh.

व्यतिसेव् *vy-ati-√sev*, Pass. *-sevyate*, to be well furnished or provided with (instr.), MBh. vii, 7297.

व्यतिहन् *vy-ati-√han*, P. *-hanti*, to strike back or in return, MBh.; Bhaṭṭ.; to strike each other, fight together, Pāṇ. i, 3, 15: to kill together, Pat.

व्यतिहस् *vy-ati-√has*, P. *-hasati*, to laugh at each other, Pāṇ. i, 3, 15, Vārtt. 1, Pat.

व्यतिहिंस् *vy-ati-√hiṇs*, P. *-hiṇsati*, to hurt or injure each other, Pāṇ. i, 3, 15, Sch.

व्यतिहृ *vy-ati-√hṛi*, Ā. *-harate* (Vop.), to transpose mutually, Gobh.

Vy-atihāra, m. interchange, alternation, reciprocity, Pāṇ.; Vop.; exchange, barter, Kāṭh.; exchange of blows or abuse, W.

व्यती *vy-atī* (*ati-√5. i*), P. *-atyeti*, to pass away, elapse, MBh.; R. &c.; to take an irregular course, PañcavBr.; to depart or deviate or swerve from (abl.), R.; Ragh.; to go past or beyond or through (acc.), MBh.; Kāv. &c.; to surpass, overcome, conquer, MBh.; to disregard, neglect, Bhag.

Vyatīta, mfn. passed away, gone, Mn.; MBh. &c.; departed, dead, MBh.; left, abandoned, Prab.; (ifc.) having disregarded or neglected, R.; tardy, negligent, ib.; *-kāla*, mfn. one whose time is past, unseasonable, inopportune, Ragh.

Vy-atyaya, m. transposition, transmutation, change, reverse, inverted order, contrariety (with *karmaṇām*, inverted or reverse occupation; *e*, in the opposite case; *am*, alternately; *āt* and *ena*, against the usual rule or order), Lāṭy.; Yājñ.; Kāv. &c.; *-ga*, mfn. moving in the opposite direction, VarBṛS.

व्यतीकार *vy-atī-kāra*, m. = 1. *vy-atikara*, contact, hostile encounter, Hariv.

व्यतीक्षा *vy-atîkshā*, f. (*vy-ati-īkshā*), Pāṇ. iii, 3, 43, Vārtt. 4.

व्यतीपात *vy-atī-pāta*, m. = *vy-ati-pāta*, Āryabh. (here also = *vaidhṛita*); Hcat.; a great calamity or any portent indicating it, L.; disrespect, contempt, W.; the day of new moon (when it falls on Ravi-vāra or Sunday, and when the moon is in certain Nakshatras), ib.

व्यतीहा *vy-atîhā*, f. (fr. *vy-ati-√īh*), Pāṇ. iii, 3, 43, Vārtt. 4.

व्यतीहार *vy-atīhāra*, m.=*vy-atihāra*, q. v.

व्यत्यस् *vy-aty-√1. as*, Ā. *-ati-ste* (1. sg. *-ati-he*, 2. sg. *-ati-se*, Pāṇ. vii, 4, 50; 52), to be above, excel, surpass, Bhaṭṭ.

व्यत्यस्त *vy-aty-asta*, mfn. (√2. *as*) thrown or placed in an inverted position, reversed, inverted, W.; placed across or crosswise, crossed (as the hands), Mn. ii, 72; perverse, preposterous, Bhām.

Vy-atyāsa, m. exchange, barter, Lāṭy.; MBh.; change, inverted order, reverse (*ena* and *āt*, 'invertedly, alternately'), VarBṛS.; Suśr. °**atyāsam**, ind. alternating, alternately, ŚBr.; ŚrS.; having inverted, having placed crosswise, MW.

व्यत्यूह् *vy-aty-√1. ūh*, P. *-ūhati*, to place or arrange differently, Kāṭh.

व्यथ् *vyath*, cl. 1. Ā. (Dhātup. xix, 2) *vyáthate* (ep. also °*ti*; pf. *vivyathe*, 3. pl. °*thuḥ*, MBh.; aor. *vyathishi*, AV.; Subj. *vyathishat*, Br.; fut. *vyathitā*, °*thishyate*, Gr.; inf. *vyathitum*, ib., Ved. inf. *vyathishyai*), to tremble, waver, go astray, come to naught, fail, RV. &c. &c. (with abl. = to be deprived of, lose; with *caritra-tas*, to abandon the path of virtue); to fall (on the ground), Mn. vii, 84 ('to be dried up,' Kull.); to cease, become ineffective (as poison), Kām.; to be agitated or disturbed in mind, be restless or sorrowful or unhappy, AV. &c. &c.; to be afraid of (gen.), R.: Caus. *vyatháyati* (aor. *vivyathas*, Br.; *vyathayīs*, AV.), to cause to tremble or fall, RV. &c. &c.; to cause to swerve from (abl.), Bhaṭṭ.; to disquiet, frighten, agitate, pain, afflict, MBh.; Kāv. &c.: Pass. of Caus. *vyathyate*, to be set in restless motion, Suśr.: Desid. *vivyathishate*, Gr.: Intens. *vāvyathyate*, *vāvyatti*, ib.

Vyatha. See *jala-vyatha*.

Vyathaka, mfn. agitating, frightening, afflicting, Kir.

Vyathana, mfn. greatly disturbing or perplexing, MBh.; n. tottering, wavering, Pāṇ. v, 4, 46; alteration, change (of a sound), RPrāt.; feeling pain, Suśr.; vexing, tormenting, Dharmaś.; piercing, perforating (= *vyadhana*), Āpast.

Vyathanīya, mfn. to be pained or afflicted or disturbed, W.

Vyathayitṛi, mfn. (fr. Caus.) one who inflicts torture or punishment, Mṛicch.

Vyathā, f. agitation, perturbation, alarm, uneasiness, pain, anguish, fear, MBh.; Kāv. &c. (*vyathām √kṛi*, either 'to cause pain' or 'to feel pain'); loss, damage, ill-luck, ŚBr.; VarBṛS.; (with *hṛidi* or *hṛidaye*), palpitation, throbbing of the heart, Suśr. **-kara**, mfn. causing pain (bodily or mental), painful, excruciating, W. -°**kula** (*vyathâk*°), mfn. agitated by fear or anguish, Pañcat. -°**krānta** (*vyathâkr*°), mfn. id., Kathās. -°**tura** (*vyathât*°), mfn. suffering pain, pained, R. -°**nvita** (*vyathânv*°), mfn. id., MW. **-rahita**, mfn. free from pain, W. **-vat**, mfn. full of pain, MW.

Vyathi. See *a-vyathi*.

Vyathitá, mfn. tottering, rocking, reeling, R.; troubled, changed (as colour), Daś.; disquieted, agitated, perturbed, distressed, afflicted, MBh.; Kāv. &c.; painful, causing pain, BhP.

Vyathitavya, mfn. to be pained or distressed, MW.

Vyathin. See *a-vyathin*.

Vyathisha. See *a-vyathisha*.

Vyáthis, mfn. tottering, wavering, sloping, RV.; secret, unobserved by (gen.), ib.; insidious, fallacious, deceitful, ib.; AV. (accord. to some always n. = 'way, course'); n. perturbation, anger, Naigh. ii, 13.

Vyathya. See *a-vyathyá*.

Vyathyayas, w. r. for *a-vyathyayas* (see *a-vyathi*), Naigh. i, 14.

व्यद् *vy-√ad*, P. *-atti*, to bite through or on all sides, gnaw, nibble, eat, R.

Vy-advará, m. (*vy-ádvarī*, f., AV.) a gnawing animal, ŚBr. (cf. *vyadhvará*).

व्यद्य *vyadya*, n. a partic. Sûkta, Kauś.

व्यध् *vyadh*, cl. 4. P. (Dhātup. xxvi, 72) *vídhyati* (ep. also °*te*; pf. p. *vivyādha*, Br. &c.; 3. pl. *vivyadhuḥ*, MBh., *vividhuḥ*, Up.; Ā. *vivyadhe*, MBh.; p. *vividhvás*, RV.; aor. *vyātsīḥ*, Br.; Prec. *vidhyāt*, Gr.; fut. *veddhā*, *vetsyati*, °*te*, MBh.; *vyaddhā*, *vyatsyati*, Gr.; inf. *veddhum*, MBh.; *-vidhe*, RV.; ind. p. *viddhvā*, *-vidhya*, MBh.), to pierce, transfix, hit, strike, wound, RV. &c. &c.; (with *sirām*) to open a vein, bleed, Suśr.; to pelt with (instr.), RV.; AV.; MBh.; to inflict, attach to, affect with (acc. of pers. and instr. of thing), RV.; AV.; Br.; Up.; to shake, wave, MBh.; (in astron.) to fix the position of a heavenly body, Gol.; to cling to (acc.), ŚBr.: Caus. *vyādhayati*, (ep. also *vedhayati*; aor. *avīvidhat* or *avivyadhat*), to pierce, open (a vein), MBh.; Suśr.; to cause to pierce or perforate, AitĀr.: Desid. *vivyatsati*, to wish to affect or taint with (instr.), ŚBr.: Intens. *vevidhyate* or *vāvyaddhi* (?), Gr.

Viddhá &c. See p. 966, col. 2.

Vedha, vedhaka &c. See 2. *vedha*, p. 1018, col. 1.

Vyadha, m. piercing, hitting, striking, a stroke, wound, Śiś.; cutting, opening (of a vein), Suśr.; (*ā*), f. bleeding, MW.

Vyadhana, mfn. piercing, perforating, Suśr.; n. the act of piercing or perforating or severing (a vein), ib.; (ifc.) chase, hunting, Hcar.

Vyadhya, mfn. to be pierced or perforated, Suśr. (*-sira*, mfn. one who is to be bled, ib.); a bowstring, L.; a butt, mark to shoot at, W.

Vyadhvará, mfn. piercing, perforating, boring (as a worm), AV. (cf. *vy-advará*).

Vyādha, m. 'one who pierces or wounds,' a hunter, one who lives by killing deer (said to be the son of a Kshatriya by a low-caste mother), Mn.; MBh. &c.; a low man, wicked person, L. **-gīti**, f. a hunter's cry (in calling animals), Kād. **-tā**, f. the state or business of a hunter, Vishṇ. **-bhīta**, m. 'afraid of hunters,' a deer, W.

Vyādhaka, m. a hunter, Kauś.

Vyādhāya, Nom. Ā. °*yate*, to become or be like a hunter, Śṛiṅgār.

Vyādhi. See *vy-ādhi*, p. 1037, col. 1.

1. **Vyādhin**, mfn. piercing, perforating, VS.

2. **Vyādhin**, mfn. (fr. *vyadha*) possessing (i. e. frequented by) hunters, Nalôd.

Vyādhya, mfn. to be pierced or cut (as a vein), Suśr.; m. N. of Śiva, MBh. vii, 2877 (v. l. *vyādha*).

व्यधिक *vyadhika* (prob. w. r. for *hy-adhika*), Kām.

व्यधिकरण *vy-adhikaraṇa*, *vy-adhva* &c. See p. 1028, col. 3.

व्यधिक्षेप *vy-adhi-kshepa*, m. (√*kship*) invective, harsh language, MBh.

व्यन् *vy-√an*, P. *-aniti*, to respire, breathe, inhale and exhale, RV.; to draw in the breath through the whole body, ŚBr.

Vy-āna, m. one of the five vital airs (that which circulates or is diffused through the body; personified as a son of Udāna and father of Apāna; cf. *prâṇa*), AV. &c. &c.; *-dā́*, mfn. giving breath, VS.; *-dṛih*, mfn. (nom. *-dhṛik*) making the Vyāna strong or durable, TS.; Kāṭh.; *-bhṛit*, mfn. maintaining the Vyāna, ŚBr.; °*nôdāná*, m. du. Vyāna and Udāna, AV.

व्यनुधा *vy-anu-√1. dhā* (only 3. pl. pf. Ā. *-dhire*), to unfold, display, RV. i, 166, 10.

व्यनुनद् *vy-anu-√nad*, Caus. *-nādayati*, to cause to resound, fill with noise or cries, Bhag. °**anunāda**, m. reverberation, loud and extending sound or noise, W.

व्यनुसृ *vy-anu-√sṛi*, P. *-sarati*, to roam or wander through (acc.), MBh.; to pervade, Suśr.

व्यन्त *vy-anta*, *vy-antara* &c. See p. 1028, col. 3.

व्यन्वारभ् *vy-anv-ā-√rabh*, Ā. *-rabhate*, to lay hold of or touch on both sides, AitBr. °**ārambhaṇa**, n. laying hold of or touching on both sides, Sāy.

व्यप् *vyap* (v. l. *vyay*, see 2. *vyay*), cl. 10. P. *vyāpayati*, to throw, Dhātup. xxxii, 95; to throw away, waste, diminish (cf. 1. *vyay*), L.

व्यपकृष् *vy-apa-√kṛish*, P. *-karshati*, to draw or drag away or off, MBh.; R.; to lead astray, seduce, MBh.; to take off (as clothes), undress, ib.; to take away, remove, give up, abandon, Mn.; MBh. &c. °**apakarsha**, m. exception (from a rule), Patr. °**apakṛishṭa**, mfn. drawn off, taken away, removed, MBh.

व्यपक्रम् *vy-apa-√kram*, P. *-krāmati*, to go off, retire, depart, R.

व्यपगम् *vy-apa-√gam*, P. *-gacchati*, to go away, retreat, escape, disappear, MBh.; Kāv. &c.; to move away from, be entirely removed or distant, VarBṛS. °**apagata**, mfn. gone away, disappeared (see comp.); fallen away from (abl.), R.; *-tilaka-gātra-tā*, f. the having limbs free from freckles (one of the 80 minor marks of a Buddha), Dharmas. 84; *-raśmi-vat*, mfn. whose rays have disappeared, rayless, Sūryas., Sch.; *-śuc*, mfn. whose sorrow has departed, free from grief, MW. °**apagama**, m. passing away, lapse (of time), Kull. on Mn. v, 66; disappearance, Amar.

व्यपत्रप् *vy-apa-√trap*, Ā. *-trapate* (rarely °*ti*), to turn away through shame, become shy or timid, MBh.; R. °**apatrapā**, f. (for *vy-apatrapa*, see p. 1028, col. 3) shame, embarrassment, R. °**apatrāpya** (?), n. id., Divyâv.

व्यपदिश् *vy-apa-√diś*, P. *-diśati*, to point out, indicate, intend, mean, designate, name, mention, MBh.; Kāv. &c. (often Pass. *-diśyate*, 'so it is represented or intended or signified'); to represent falsely, feign, pretend, MBh.; R.; Prasannar.

Vyapadishṭa, mfn. pointed out &c.; informed, W.; tricked, ib.; pleaded as an excuse, ib.

Vy-apadeśa, m. representation, designation, information, statement, RPrāt.; ŚrS. &c.: a name, title, Uttarar.; a family, race, Śak.; summons (of an army), R.; appeal to (gen.), Pañcat.; talk, speech, MBh. iii, 8665 (Nīlak.); a partic. form of speech, MW.; fame, renown (see comp.); fraud, stratagem, pretext, excuse (*ena*, under pretext or excuse [also *-tas*], ifc. = under the pretext of), MBh.; Kāv. &c.; *-vat*, mfn. having a partic. designation or name (with *pitṛi-tas*, designated by the name of the father), Pat.; °*śârtham*, ind. for the purpose of (acquiring) renown, Mn. vii, 168. °**apadeśaka**, mfn. designating, indicating, BhP. °**apadeśin**, mfn. having a name or designation, L.; (ifc.) denoting, indicating, Saṃk.; (ifc.) conforming to, following the advice of, R. °**apadeśya**, mfn. to be designated or indicated or named, R.; Pat.; Saṃk.; to be censured or blamed, Hariv. °**apadeshṭṛi**, mfn. one who represents or shows or names, W.; one who represents falsely, a cheat, impostor, ib.

व्यपदृश् *vy-apa-√dṛiś*, Pass. *-dṛiśyate*, to be clearly seen, be distinctly visible, MBh.

व्यपनश् *vy-apa-√2. naś*, Caus. *-nāśayati*, to cause to disappear or perish, drive away, remove, MBh.

व्यपनी *vy-apa-√nī*, P. *-nayati* (inf. *-netum* or *-nayitum*), to lead or take away, MBh.; R.; to drive away, remove, banish, ib. &c.; to pour out or away, AitBr.; to take off, lay aside, get rid of (acc.), MBh.; Kāv. &c.: Caus. *-nāyayati*, to cause to take away or remove, MBh.

Vy-apanaya, m. taking away, removal, MBh. (v. l. *vy-apayana*). °**apanayana**, n. tearing off, removing, Veṇīs.

Vy-apanīta, mfn. led off, taken away, removed, R. °**apaneya**, mfn. to be taken away or removed, MBh.

व्यपनुद् *vy-apa-√nud*, P. *-nudati*, to drive away, remove, MBh. °**apanutti**, f. driving away, removal, AitBr.

व्यपमुच् *vy-apa-√muc*, P. *-muñcati*, to loosen, take off, R.

व्यपया *vy-apa-√yā*, P. *-yāti*, to go away, retire, withdraw, MBh.; Hariv.; to pass away, vanish, R. °**apayāta**, mfn. gone away, retired, MBh. °**apayāna**, n. retreat, flight, ib.

व्यपरुध् *vy-apa-√2. rudh* (only 2. sg. Intens. *-rorudhaḥ*), to exclude from sovereignty, dethrone, R. (B.)

व्यपरुह् *vy-apa-√ruh*, Caus. *-ropayati*, to lay aside, remove, take off, R.; to deprive of, expel from (instr. or abl.), MBh.; to root up, eradicate, extirpate (see next).

Vy-aparopaṇa, n. rooting up, extirpating, removing, destroying, Kām.; Sarvad.; tearing out, pulling (cf. *keśa-vy*°). °**aparopita**, mfn. rooted up, extirpated, removed, expelled, W.

व्यपवह् *vy-apa-vah*. See *vy-apôh*.

व्यपविद्ध *vy-apa-viddha*, mfn. (√*vyadh*)

thrown about, broken to pieces (*-bṛisī-maṭha*, mfn. with abandoned seats and cells), MBh.; cast away, rejected, MBh.; pierced, transfixed, MBh.

व्यपवृज् *vy-apa-vṛij*, Caus. *-varjayati*, to give up entirely, relinquish, Ragh.

Vy-apavârga, m. separation, division, difference, Pat.; cessation, termination, Jaim.

Vy-apavṛikta, mfn. separated, divided, Pat.

व्यपवृत् *vy-apa-√vṛit*, Ā. *-vartate*, to turn away, desist from (abl.), Uttarar.

व्यपसंसृ *vy-apa-sam-√sṛi* (only ind. p. *-sṛitya*), to go through (a series of existences), Divyâv.

व्यपसृ *vy-apa-√sṛi*, P. *-sarati*, to go asunder or in different directions, MBh.; to depart from (abl.), Sarasv. °**apasaraṇa**, n. (fr. Caus.) driving away, dispelling, Rāghav.

व्यपसृज् *vy-apa-√sṛij*, P. *-sṛijati*, to hurl, cast, discharge (arrows &c.), MBh.; to take off, relinquish (a garment), ib.

व्यपसृप् *vy-apa-√sṛip*, P. *-sarpati*, to go or creep or run away, escape, MBh.

व्यपस्फुर् *vy-apa-√sphur*, Ā. *-sphurate*, to break (intr.) or burst asunder, KātyŚr., Sch. °**apasphuraṇa**, n. bursting asunder, KātyŚr.

व्यपहन् *vy-apa-√han*, P. *-hanti*, to strike off, R. (B.); to keep off, prevent, Sāh.

व्यपहा *vy-apa-√3. hā* (only ind. p. *-hāya*), to relinquish, abandon, Hariv.

व्यपहृ *vy-apa-√hṛi*, P. Ā. *-harati*, °*te*, to cut off, MBh.; to take away, remove, destroy, Rājat.

व्यपाकृत *vy-apâ-kṛita*, mfn. (√*1. kṛi*) free from (comp.), Naish. °**apâkṛiti**, f. driving away, repelling, denial, W.

व्यपाकृष् *vy-apâ-√kṛish* (only inf. *-krash-ṭum*), to drag or draw away, tear off, MBh.

व्यपानुद् *vy-apā-√nud* (*apā* m.c. for *apa*), P. *-nudati*, to drive away, remove, MBh.

व्यपाश्रि *vy-apâ-√śri*, P. Ā. *-śrayati*, °*te*, to go to for refuge, have recourse to (acc.), MBh.; to adhere to any doctrine, confess (acc.), Śaṃk.

2. **Vyapâśraya**, m. (for 1. see p. 1028, col. 3) going away, secession, MW.; seat, place (ifc. = being in or on), R.; Kām.; Suśr.; place of refuge, shelter, support (ifc. = having recourse to, trusting in), MBh.; R. &c.; expectation, W. °**apâśrita**, mfn. one who has taken refuge with (acc. or comp.), MBh.; Kathās.; having taken or assumed, MBh.; BhP.

व्यपाहृ *vy-apâ-√hṛi*, P. *-harati*, to withdraw from (abl.), MBh.

व्यपे *vy-apê* (*-apa-√5. i*), P. *-apâiti*, to go apart or asunder, separate, MBh.; to cease, disappear, Mn.; Prab.

Vy-apâya, m. cessation, stop, end, MBh.; R. &c.; absence, want, Kathās.

Vy-apêta, mfn. gone apart or asunder, separated, MBh.; passed away, disappeared, ceased, Mn.; MBh. &c.; (ifc.) opposed to, Yājñ.; *-kalmasha*, mfn. having taint or guilt removed, free from sin, Mn. iv, 260; *-ghṛiṇa*, mfn. devoid of compassion, pitiless, Amar.; *-dhairya*, mfn. one who has abandoned firmness, MBh.; *-bhaya* or *-bhī*, mfn. free from fear, ib.; *-mada-matsara*, mfn. free from infatuation and selfishness, Yājñ.; *-harsha*, mfn. devoid of joy, R.

व्यपेक्ष् *vy-apêksh* (*-apa-√īksh*), Ā. *-apêkshate*, to look about, look for, regard, mind, pay regard or attention to (acc.), R.; Ragh. °**apêksha** (ifc.), see °*apêkshā* below. °**apêkshaka**, mfn. mindful of (comp.), MBh. °**apêkshaṇa**, n. looking for, expectation, regard, consideration, W. °**apêkshaṇīya**, mfn. to be looked for or expected, ib. °**apêkshā**, f. regard, consideration (ifc. regarding, minding), MBh.; R. &c.; looking for, expectation (ifc. expectant of), BhP.; Kathās.; requisite, supposition (see *sa-vy*°); application, use, W.; (in gram.) rection, Pāṇ. ii, 1, 1, Sch.; the mutual application of two rules, W. °**apêkshita**, mfn. looked for, expected, MW.; mutually expected or looked to, ib.; mutually related; employed, applied, ib. °**apêkshya**, mfn. to be looked for or expected, ib.

व्यपोह् *vy-apôh* (*-apa-√1. ūh*), P. *-apôhati* (ep. also °*te*), to drive away, keep off, remove, destroy, TUp.; Mn.; MBh. &c.; to atone for, expiate (guilt), Mn. ii, 102 &c.; to heal, cure (sickness), Suśr. °**apôḍha**, mfn. driven away, removed, destroyed (°*ḍhâbhra*, mfn. having the clouds driven away), MBh.; manifested, displayed, exhibited, ib.; opposite, contrary, reverse, W. °**apôha**, m. driving away, keeping off, removal, destruction, MBh.; Suśr.; denial, negation, Sāh.; sweepings, rubbish, MBh.; *-stava*, m. N. of a ch. of the LiṅgaP. °**apôhaka**, mfn. driving away, removing, Car. °**apôhana-stotra**, n. N. of a Stotra (prob. = *vyapôha-stava*). °**apôhya**, mfn. deniable (see *a-vy*°).

व्यभिचर् *vy-abhi-√car*, P. Ā. *-carati*, to act in an unfriendly way towards (acc. or gen.), sin against, offend, injure, MBh.; Kathās.; to bewitch, practise sorcery (pl. 'against each other'), Lāṭy.; Kathās.; to come to naught, fail, Bījag.; BhP.; to go beyond, transgress, deviate from (acc.), Kir.; Pāṇ., Sch. °**abhicaraṇa**, n. uncertainty, doubt (see *sa-vyabhicaraṇa*).

Vy-abhicāra, m. going apart or astray, deviating, not falling or fitting together, being separated or isolated, Kap.; Bhāshāp. &c. (cf. *a-vy*°); trespass, transgression, crime, vice, sin (esp. infidelity of a wife), Mn.; MBh. &c.; violation, disturbance, confusion, Mn. x, 24 &c.; change, mutation (in *a-vy*°, mfn.), Bhag.; (in phil.) wandering from an argument, erroneous or fallacious reasoning, the presence of the *hetu* (q. v.) without the *sādhya* (q. v.), MW.; (in gram.) deviation from or exception to a rule, irregularity, anomaly, ib.; *-kṛit*, mfn. committing adultery, Rājat.; *-tas*, ind. in consequence of straying or erring, Sāh.; (in phil.) from the Vyabhicāra involved in the other supposition, MW.; *-tā*, f., *-tva*, n. error, ib.; *-nirūpaṇa-khaṇḍa*, N. of wk.; *-bhāva*, w.r. for *vyabhicāri-bh*°, Cat.; *-vat*, mfn., see *a-vyabhicāra-vat*; *-vivarjita*, mfn. free from extravagance or debauchery, Hit.; °*rârtham*, ind. for the sake of (committing) adultery, Pāṇ. iv, 1, 127, Sch.

Vy-abhicāri, in comp. for °*cārin*; *-tā*, f., *-tva*, n. the state of going apart or astray, deviation, alteration, change, variability, Śaṃk.; Bhāshāp.; (*-tva*, in gram.) the having a secondary meaning or several meanings, Pāṇ., Sch.; *-bhāva*, m. a transitory state (of mind or body, opp. to *sthāyi-bh*° [q. v.], and said to be thirty-four in number, viz. *nirveda, glāni, śaṅkā, asūyā, mada, śrama, ālasya, dainya, cintā, moha, smṛiti, dhṛiti, vrīḍā, capalatā, harsha, āvega, jaḍatā, garva, vishāda, autsukya, nidrā, apasmāra, supta, vibodha, amarsha, avahitthā, ugratā, mati, upâlambha, vyādhi, unmāda, maraṇa, trāsa, vitarka*, qq. vv.), Daśar.; Kpr. &c.

Vy-abhicārin, mfn. going astray, straying or deviating or diverging from (abl.), Hariv.; Kāv.; Kathās. &c.; following bad courses, doing what is improper, profligate, wanton, unchaste (esp. said of women), faithless towards (gen.), MBh.; Kāv. &c.; changeable, inconstant (opp. to *sthāyin*; cf. °*ri-bhāva* above), MBh.; Sāh.; Pratāp.; (ifc.) transgressing, violating, breaking (see *samaya-vy*°); irregular, anomalous, MW.; (a word) having a non-primitive or secondary meaning, having several meanings, ib.; (*iṇī*), f. a wanton woman, unchaste wife, adulteress, W.; n. anything transitory (as feelings &c.), ib.

Vy-abhīcāra, m. transgression, offence, MBh.; change, alteration, ib.

व्यभिमान *vy-abhi-māna*, m. (√*man*) a false apprehension or notion, erroneous view, Nyāyas.

व्यभिहास *vy-abhi-hāsa*, m. (√*has*) derision, ridicule, Āpast.

व्यभ्र *vy-abhra, vy-amla*. See p. 1028, col. 3.

व्यय् 1. *vyay*, cl. 1. P. Ā. *vyayati*, °*te* (rather Nom. fr. *vyaya* below), to expend, spend, waste, Bhaṭṭ.; Hit.; Subh.; cl. 10. P. *vyayayati*, id., Dhātup. xxxv, 78; to go, move, ib.

Vyaya, mfn. (or *vy-aya*, fr. 3. *vi* + √*5. i*) passing away, mutable, liable to change or decay (only as opp. to or connected with *a-vyaya*), Mn.; MBh.; Pur.; m. (ifc. f. *ā*) disappearance, decay, ruin, loss, MBh.; Kāv. &c.; spending, expense, outlay, disbursement (opp. to *āya*, 'income,' and often with *kośasya, vittasya, dhanasya* &c.; without a gen. = 'extravagance, waste, prodigality;' with loc. or ifc. = 'outlay for or in'), Mn.; MBh. &c.; cost, sacrifice of (gen. or comp.; *vyayena*, ifc. = 'at the cost of'), R.; Kālid.; wealth, money, Yājñ. ii, 276; (in gram.) inflection, declension, Nir.; N. of the 20th (or 54th) year of Jupiter's cycle, VarBṛS.; of a serpent-demon, MBh.; of Pradhāna, MW.; m. or n. = *-gṛiha*, VarBṛS. **-kara**, mf(*ī*)n. one who makes payments, Kām. **-karaṇa** or **-karaṇaka**, m. a paymaster, Pañcad. **-karman**, n. the business of a paymaster, Yājñ.; R. **-gata**, mfn. (v. l. for next). **-guṇa**, mfn. prodigal, spendthrift, one who spends all his money, impoverished, MBh. **-gṛiha**, n. (in astron.) N. of the 12th house from the Lagna, VarBṛS. **-parāṅmukha**, mf(*ī*)n. averse from expenditure, parsimonious, Yājñ. i, 83. **-bhavana**, n. = *-gṛiha*, VarBṛS. **-vat**, mfn. liable to change, not complete, RPrāt.; spending much, prodigal, Yājñ.; inflected, VPrāt. **-śālin** (Rājat.), **-śīla** (Kāv.), mfn. disposed to prodigality, wasteful, spendthrift. **-saha**, mfn. 'bearing waste,' inexhaustible (as a treasure), Kām. **-sahishṇu**, mfn. bearing loss of money patiently, ib. **-sthāna**, n. = *-gṛiha*, Cat.

Vyayaka, mfn. expending, making payments, Kām.

Vyáyana, n. going apart, separation, RV.

Vyayamāna, mfn. expending, wasting, W.

Vyayi, in comp. for *vyayin*. **-tā**, f., **-tva**, n. prodigality, wastefulness, MW.

Vyayita, mfn. expended, spent, dissipated, dispersed, Hit.; gone away, declined, fallen into decay, W.

Vyayitavya, mfn. to be expended or spent, Camp.

Vyayin, mfn. declining, decaying, falling (in *udaya-vy*°, 'rising and falling'), Hit.; expending, spending, prodigal (in *bahu-vy*°, q. v.)

Vyayī, in comp. for *vyaya*. **-karaṇa**, n. the act of expending or disbursing, wasting, W. **-√kṛi**, P. Ā. *-karoti, -kurute*, to waste, expend, Kathās. **-kṛita**, mfn. expended, spent, lavished, Kām.; Rājat. **-bhūta**, mfn. spent, squandered, wasted, W.

व्यय् 2. *vyay* (v. l. for *vyap*), cl. 10. P. *vyāyayati*, to throw, Dhātup. xxxii, 95.

व्यर्क *vy-arka*. See p. 1028, col. 3.

व्यर्ण 1. 2. *vy-arṇa*. See ib. and below under *vy-√ard*.

व्यर्थ *vy-artha*, mf(*ā*)n. (fr. 3. *vi* + *artha*) useless, unavailing, unprofitable, vain, MBh. &c. &c.; deprived or devoid of property or money, Pañcat.; excluded from, having no right (instr.), Āpast.; unmeaning, inconsistent, Hariv.; Kāvyâd.; = °*tha-nāmaka* below, MBh.; (*am*), ind. uselessly, in vain, without having effected one's object, Kāv.; Pañcat. &c.; *-tā*, f. uselessness (°*tām √yā* or *√gam*, to become useless), Pañcat.; Kusum.; absence of meaning, nonsense, R.; falseness, MBh.; inoffensiveness, MW.; *-tva*, n. absence of meaning, contradictoriness, Kāvyâd., Sch.; *-nāmaka* or *-nāman*, mfn. having a name inconsistent with one's character, MBh.; *-yatna*, mfn. useless in its efforts, Hit.; °*thī-√kṛi*, P. *-karoti*, to make useless or superfluous, Prab.; Kād.; °*thī-√bhū*, P. *-bhavati*, to become useless, Naish.; Kād. °**arthaka**, mfn. useless, vain, R.; *-tā*, f. (Śiś.) or *-tva*, n. (MW.) uselessness.

Vyarthaya, Nom. P. °*yati*, to make useless or superfluous, Campak.

व्यर्द् *vy-√ard*, P. *-ardati*, to flow away, ŚBr.; to oppress, harass, pain (see *a-vyarṇa*): Caus. *-ardayati*, to cause to be scattered or dissolved, destroy, annihilate, RV.

2. **Vy-arṇa** or **vy-arṇṇa**, mfn. (cf. Pāṇ. vii, 2, 24) oppressed, harassed (see *a-vyarṇa*).

व्यर्धुक *vy-árdhuka*, mfn. (√*ṛidh*) being deprived of (instr.), Maitr.; ĀpŚr.

व्यर्पणा *vy-arpaṇā*, f. (of unknown meaning), Mahāvy.

व्यलीक *vy-alīka* &c. See p. 1028, col. 3.

व्यवकलन *vy-ava-kalana*, n. (√*2. kal*) separation, subtraction, deduction, Col. °**avakalita**, mfn. subtracted, deducted, Līl.; n. subtraction, deduction, ib.

व्यवकृष् *vy-ava-√kṛish*, P. *-karshati*, to draw or tear away, alienate, MBh. (v. l. *vy-apa-k*°).

व्यवकृ *vy-ava-√kṛī*, P. *-kirati*, to scatter or pour down or on or about, BhP. °**avakiraṇa**, f. mixing together, mixture, L. °**avakīrṇa**, mfn. intermixed or filled or set with (instr.), Kām.

व्यवक्रोशन *vy-ava-krośana*, n. (*√kruś*) mutual altercation or abuse, W.; abuse, reviling (in general), ib.

व्यवगम् *vy-ava-√gam*, Ā. *-gacchate*, to go apart, separate, Kāṭh.

व्यवगाह् *vy-ava-√gāh*, Ā. *-gāhate* (rarely °*ti*), to dive or plunge into, penetrate, MBh.; to set in, begin (as night), ib. °**avagāḍha**, mfn. dived or plunged into, immersed (*-vat*, mfn.), ib.

व्यवगृहीत *vy-ava-gṛihīta*, mfn. (*√grah*) brought down, bent down, ŚBr. °**avagrāham**, ind. having taken separately, singly, ŚāṅkhBr.

व्यवचारयितव्य *vy-ava-cārayitavya*, mfn. (*√car*) to be pondered over or considered, Mahāvy.

व्यवच्छिद् *vy-ava-cchid* (*√chid*), P. *-cchinatti*, to cut off, separate, ŚBr.; MBh. &c.; to tear asunder, open, sunder, R.; BhP.; to limit, fix, settle, ascertain, BhP.; to resolve on (*prati*), ib.: Pass. *-cchidyate*, to be cut off or separated, ŚBr.

Vy-avacchid, f. limitation, Harav. °**avacchinna**, mfn. cut off, separated &c.; distinguished, distinct, Tarkas.; interrupted (see *a-vyavacchinna*).

Vy-avaccheda, m. cutting one's self off from, separation, interruption (see *á-vy*°); exclusion, Sāh.; (ifc.) getting rid of, BhP.; distinction, discrimination, Sāh.; a division, W.; letting fly (an arrow), R.; *-vidyā*, f. the science of anatomy, MW. °**avacchedaka**, mfn. distinguishing, discriminating (*-tva*, n.), Sāṃkhyak.; excluding (*-tva*, n.), Kull. °**avacchedya**, mfn. to be excluded, Sāh.

व्यवतिष्ठमान *vy-ava-tishṭhamāna*. See *vy-ava-√sthā*.

व्यवदा *vy-ava-√3. dā* (or *do*; only ind. p. *-dāya*), to cut in two, divide, Kauś.

व्यवदीर्ण *vy-ava-dīrṇa*, mfn. (*√dṛī*) burst asunder, broken to pieces, distracted, R.

व्यवदै *vy-ava-√dai*, Pass. *-dāyate* (p. *-dāyamāna*), to be clearly diffused, Daś. °**avadāta**, mfn. clean, clear, bright, TĀr.

Vy-avadāna, n. purification, Divyâv.

व्यवद्रु *vy-ava-√dru*, P. *-dravati*, to run away, Kāṭh.

व्यवधा *vy-ava-√1. dhā*, P. Ā. *-dadhāti*, *-dhatte*, to place apart or asunder, ŚāṅkhBr.; to put or place between, interpose, Ragh.; to leave out, omit, Kāṭh.; to separate, divide, interrupt, BhP.: Pass. *-dhīyate*, to be separated or divided or interrupted, R.; BhP.: Caus. *-dhāpayati*, to separate, Naish.

Vy-avadhā, f. covering or anything that covers, L. °**avadhātavya**, n. (impers.) it is to be separated or divided, MBh. °**avadhātṛi**, mfn. one who separates or interposes or screens, MW.

Vy-avadhāna, n. intervening, intervention (esp. in gram. 'the intervention of a syllable or letter'), Prāt.; ĀśvŚr. &c. (*ena*, ind. = 'indirectly,' Nīlak.); obstruction, hiding from view, Ragh.; covering, a cover, screen, Kum.; Śaṃk.; separation, division, BhP.; interruption, ib.; cessation, termination, ib.; interval, space, L.; *-vat*, mfn. (ifc.) covered with, Kum.

Vy-avadhāyaka, mf(*ikā*)n. intervening, interposing, separating, Prāt.; interrupting, disturbing, Rājat.; concealing, screening, hiding, W. °**avadhāyika**, w.r. for prec.

Vy-avadhi, m. covering, concealing, intervention, Śiś.

Vy-avadheya, mfn. to be put in between or interposed, MW.

Vy-avahita, mfn. placed apart or asunder &c.; separated, not contiguous or immediately connected, Prāt.; interrupted, obstructed, disturbed, Śak.; screened from view, concealed, covered, Śaṃk.; hostile, opposed, BhP.; remote, distant, BhP.; passed over, surpassed, excelled, put to shame, W.; done, acted, performed, ib.

व्यवधाव् *vy-ava-√dhāv*, P. *-dhāvati*, to run in different directions, separate, R.; to run away, flee from (abl.), MBh.

व्यवधू *vy-ava-√dhū*, P. Ā. *-dhūnoti*, °*nute*, to shake off, ward off, remove, Kāṭh.; Hariv.; R.; to shake about, treat roughly or rudely, MBh.; to reject, repel, ib. °**avadhūta**, mfn. one who has shaken off all worldly desires, indifferent in regard to life, resigned, MBh.

व्यवधृ *vy-ava-√dhṛi*, P. *-dhārayati*, to fix, settle, establish, ĀpŚr. °**avadhāraṇa**, n. accurate determination, Nyāyam., Sch.

व्यवन *vyavana* (a word used to explain *vyoman*), Nir. xi, 40.

व्यवनी *vy-ava-√nī* (only ind. p. *-nīya*), to pour in separately, ŚBr.

व्यवपद् *vy-ava-√pad*, Ā. *-padyate*, to fall down or asunder, ŚBr.

व्यवभक्ष् *vy-ava-√bhaksh*, P. *-bhakshayati*, to swallow down or eat (in the interval of certain religious rites), PañcavBr.

व्यवभास् *vy-ava-√bhās*, Caus. *-bhāsayati*, to cause to shine out brightly, to illuminate beautifully, Kathās. °**avabhāsita**, mfn. brightly illuminated, ib.

व्यवमुच् *vy-ava-√muc* (only ind. p. *-mucya*), to unloose, unfasten, take off, R.

व्यवरुह् *vy-ava-√ruh*, P. Ā. *-rohati*, °*te*, to ascend, mount, get upon (acc.), MBh.: Caus. *-ropayati* (Pass. *-ropyate*; p. p. *-ropita*), to displace, remove, deprive of (abl.), MBh.; Kāv. &c.

व्यवलम्बिन् *vy-ava-lambin*. See *a-vy*°.

व्यवली *vy-ava-√lī*, Ā. *-līyate*, to recline, lie or cower down, MBh.; Hariv.

व्यवलोकन *vy-ava-lokana*, n. (*√lok*) the act of taking a view of, Divyâv. °**avalokita**, mfn. looked upon, viewed, beheld, ib.

व्यववद् *vy-ava-√vad*, P. Ā. *-vadati*, °*te*, to speak ill of, decry, PañcavBr.; to begin to speak, break silence, ChUp. (Śaṃk.) °**avavadya**, mfn. to be spoken ill of or decried, PañcavBr.

व्यवविद् *vy-ava-√1. vid*, P. *-vetti*, to discern, discriminate, ŚBr.

व्यवव्ली *vy-ava-√vlī*, P. *-vlināti*, to sink down, collapse, MaitrS.

व्यवशद् *vy-ava-√śad* (only pf. *-śaśāda*, *-śeduḥ*), to fall off or down, ŚBr. °**avaśādá**, m. falling off or down, ib.

व्यवश्चुत् *vy-ava-√ścut*, P. *-ścotati*, to ooze, drip off, ŚBr.

व्यवसद् *vy-ava-√sad*, P. *-sīdati*, to sit down, sink or fall down, MBh.; to pine or waste away, perish, ib.

व्यवसाय *vy-avasāya*. See col. 3.

व्यवसृज् *vy-ava-√sṛij*, P. Ā. *-sṛijati*, °*te*, to throw, cast, hurl upon (gen.), MBh.; to put or lay down, ib.; to dismiss, send away, ŚBr.; to distribute, bestow (see *vy-avasarga*), to hang on, fasten to (loc.), MBh. viii, 959 (prob. w. r. for *vyava-√sañj*).

Vy-avasargá, m. setting free, liberation, ŚBr.; distributing, bestowing, Pāṇ. v, 4, 2; renunciation, resignation, L.

व्यवसृप् *vy-ava-√sṛip*, P. *-sarpati*, to creep or steal in, AV.; TS.; Br.

व्यवसो *vy-ava-√so*, P. *-syati* (ep. also *-syate* [with act. and pass. meaning]; 1. sg. pr. *-sāmi*; Pot. *-seyam*, *-set*; fut. *-sishyati*), to settle down or dwell separately, ŚBr.; to differ (in opinion), contest, quarrel, ib.; to separate, divide (opp. to *sam-√as*), RPrāt.; to determine, resolve, decide, be willing to (acc., dat., *artham*, ifc., or inf.), TBr. &c. &c.; to settle, ascertain, be convinced or persuaded of, take for (acc.), MBh.; Kāv. &c.; to ponder, reflect, consider, MBh.; Śak.; to make strenuous effort, labour or seek after, make an attempt upon (acc.), MW.: Pass. *-sīyate*, to be settled or ascertained or fixed on or determined or decided (often impers.), MBh.; Kāv. &c.: Caus. *-sāyayati*, to cause to resolve, encourage to undertake, embolden, VS.; TS.; to incite or instigate to (inf.), Kir.

Vy-avasāya, m. strenuous effort or exertion, Car.; settled determination, resolve, purpose, intention to (loc., acc. with *prati*, or comp.; °*yam-√kṛi*, to make up one's mind, resolve, determine), MBh.; Kāv. &c.; Resolution (personified), R.; Pur.; trade, business, Campak.; an act, action, performance, R.; first impression or perception, Nīlak.; state, condition, MBh.; artifice, stratagem, trick, W.; boasting, ib.; N. of Vishṇu, MW.; of Śiva, ib.; of a son of Dharma by Vapus (daughter of Daksha), ib.; *-dvitīya*, mfn. doubled or attended by (i.e. possessing) resolution, BhP.; *-buddhi*, mfn. having a resolute mind, ib.; *-vat*, mfn. full of resoluteness or perseverance, MBh.; Hariv.; *-vartin*, mfn. acting resolutely, resolute, Kām.; °*yâtmaka*, mfn. full of resolve or energy, energetic, laborious, MBh. °**avasāyin**, mfn. one who acts resolutely or energetically, resolute, energetic, enterprising, industrious, MBh.; Kāv. &c.; engaged in trade or business, MW.; m. a tradesman, handicraftsman, ib.

Vy-avasita, mfn. finished, ended, done, Kāṭh.; decided, determined, resolved, undertaken (also n. impers.; with dat. or inf.), MBh.; Kāv. &c.; one who has resolved upon or is determined or willing to (loc., dat., or inf.), Kāv.; Pur.; settled, ascertained, known (n. impers.), convinced or sure of anything (with *samyak*, 'one who has ascertained what is right;' with acc., 'one who has acknowledged anything as true'), MBh.; BhP.; deceived, tricked, cheated, disappointed, L.; energetic, persevering, making effort or exertion, W.; n. resolution, determination, Kāv.; Pur.; an artifice, contrivance, Mṛicch. °**avasiti**, f. ascertainment, determination, resolution, Subh. °**avaseya**, n. (impers.) it is to be settled or determined, Pat.

Vy-avasta, mfn. = *vy-avasita*, Divyâv.; bound(?), ĀśvŚr. (Sch.)

व्यवस्तुभ् *vy-ava-√stubh*, P. *-stobhati*, to interpose certain sounds or interjections in chanting the Sāma-veda, Lāṭy.

व्यवस्था *vy-ava-√sthā*, Ā. *-tishṭhate*, to go apart, separate from (abl.), ŚāṅkhŚr.; to differ respectively, Śaṃk.; to halt, stop, stay, R.; to prepare or make ready for (dat.), ib.; to be settled, be (logically) true or tenable, MBh.; Sarvad.; to appear as (nom.), Nir.; Sāṃkhyak.: Caus. *-sthāpayati*, to put down, place, VarBṛS.; Vās.; to fix on, direct towards (loc.), Kum.; to charge with, appoint to (*artham*), Hit.; to stop, hold up, prevent from falling, MBh.; Rājat.; to restore, re-establish, Kum.; Jātakam.; to settle, arrange, establish, determine, prove to be (logically) tenable, Daś.; Sarvad.; to give a name, Divyâv.; to perform, MW.

Vy-avatishṭhamāna, mfn. standing apart, W.

Vy-avasthā, f. respective difference (*āyām*, loc. in each single case), ŚrS.; Kap.; Śaṃk.; abiding in one place, steadiness, Kathās.; fixity, perseverance, constancy, MBh.; R. &c.; a fixed limit, Śiś.; settlement, establishment, decision, statute, law, rule (*ayā*, instr. according to a fixed rule), BhP.; Pāṇ., Sch.; Kull.; legal decision or opinion (applied to the written extracts from the codes of law or adjustment of contradictory passages in different codes), W.; conviction, persuasion, R.; fixed relation of time or place, Pāṇ. i, 1, 34; rate, proportion, Bhpr.; state, condition, Kāv.; Rājat.; case, occasion, opportunity, Rājat.; W.; an engagement, agreement, contract, ib.; -°*tikrama* (°*sthât*°), m. transgression or violation of the law or settled rule, breaking an agreement or contract, W.; -°*tivartana* (°*sthât*°), n. id., ib.; -°*tivartin* (°*sthât*°), mfn. transgressing the law, breaking an agreement or contract, ib.; *-darpaṇa*, m., *-prakāśa*, m. N. of wks.; *-pattra*, n. a written deed, document, L.; *-ratna-mālā*, f., -°*rṇava* (°*thârṇ*°), m., *-sāra-saṃgraha*, m., *-sāra-saṃcaya*, m., *-setu*, m. N. of wks. °**avasthātṛi**, mfn. one who settles or determines, Pañcar. °**avasthāna**, mfn. persistent (applied to Vishṇu), MBh. xiii, 6991; n. steadiness, perseverance, continuance in (loc.), MBh.; R.; firmness, constancy, MBh.; state, condition (pl. 'circumstances'), GopBr.; Rājat.; regular arrangement or distribution, MW.; *-prajñapti*, f. a partic. high number, Buddh.

Vy-avasthāpaka, mfn. (fr. Caus.) settling, arranging, deciding, establishing (*-tva*, n.), Hāsy.; Nyāyam., Sch. °**avasthāpana**, n. supporting, encouraging, R.; fixing, establishing, deciding (also in law), Kām.; Kull. °**avasthāpanīya**, mfn. to be settled or established, Kull. on Mn. ix, 242. °**avasthāpita**, mfn. arranged, settled, Kum.; caused to be placed or arranged, W. °**avasthāpya**, mfn. to be established or declared (in each single case), Vop.; n. the state of being established &c., MW.

Vy-avasthita, mfn. placed in order, drawn up (in battle), Bhag.; placed, laid, put, stationed, situated, standing or being in or on or at (loc. or comp.), Yājñ.; MBh. &c.; standing on the side of, taking part with (comp.), Dhūrtas.; contained in (loc.), Sarvad.; used in the meaning of (loc.), signifying (as a word), Cat.; one who has waited or stayed, MBh.; based or dependent on (loc.), Kām.; Mālatīm.; resolved upon (loc.), MBh.; persevering in, sticking or adhering to (loc. or comp.; with *vākye*, 'abiding in what is said,' 'obeying'), Yājñ.; MBh. &c.; intent upon, caring for (loc.), MBh.; settled, established, fixed, exactly determined, quite peculiar or restricted to (loc. or comp.), Mn.; MBh. &c.; constant, unchanging, Suśr.; existing, present, MBh.; Sarvad.; proving, turning out or appearing as (nom. or instr. or ind. p. or adv.), MBh.; Kāv. &c.; *-tva*, n. continuance, permanence, duration, Suśr.; *-vikalpa*, m., *-vibhāshā*, f. (in law, gram. &c.) an option fixed or determined in each particular case, applicable or omitted throughout (the operation being in one case carried out throughout and in the other omitted throughout), Dāyabh.; Kull.; APrāt.; Pāṇ., Sch.; *-vishaya*, mfn. limited in sphere or range, Uttarar. °**avasthiti**, f. the being placed apart or kept asunder or distinguished, separation, distinction, difference, Bhag.; Nyāyam.; Sarvad.; staying, abiding, perseverance in (instr. or loc.), BhP.; constancy, steadfastness, Kathās.; fixity, fixed rule or statute, decision, determination, Mn.; Hariv. &c.; extracting(?), W.

व्यवस्रंस् *vy-ava-√srans*, Ā. *-sransate*, to fall asunder, TBr. °**avasransa**, m., see *a-vy°*.

व्यवस्रु *vy-ava-√sru*, P. *-sravati*, to flow or trickle asunder, dissolve, fail, come to nothing, MaitrS.: Caus. *-srāvayati*, to cause to flow asunder &c., Kāṭh.

व्यवहरण *vy-avaharaṇa*. See below.

व्यवहास *vy-ava-hāsa* (√*has*), mutual laughter, W.

व्यवहित *vy-avahita*. See *vy-ava-√dhā*.

व्यवहृ *vy-ava-√hṛi*, P. Ā. *-harati*, °*te*, to transpose, exchange, Nir.; to have intercourse with (instr. or loc.), GṛS.; BhP.; to meet (as foes), fight with (instr. with or without *sârdham*), MBh.; to act, proceed, behave towards or deal with (loc.), ib.; Kāv. &c.; to be active or busy, work, Yājñ., Sch.; to carry on commerce, trade, deal in (loc., instr., or gen.), Āpast.; VarBṛS.; BhP.; to bet at, play for (gen.), Pāṇ. ii, 3, 57, Sch.; to manage, employ, make use of (acc.), ib.; to carry on legal proceedings, litigate, MW.; to be intent upon, care for, cherish (acc.), MBh.; to roam or stroll about, ib.; to recover, regain, obtain, ib.; to distinguish, ib.: Pass. *-hriyate*, to be named or termed or designated, Sarvad.; Vedântas.: Caus. *-hārayati*, to allow any one to do what he likes, Kull. on Mn. viii, 362; to deal with (acc.), SaddhP.: Pass. of Caus. *-hāryate*, to be named or designated, BhP.

Vy-avaharaṇa, n. a contest at law, litigation, L. °**avahartavya**, mfn. to be managed or used or employed, Kull. on Mn. x, 51; to be transacted or done (n. impers.), Hariv.; Pañcat.; to be litigated or decided judicially, W. °**avahartṛi**, mfn. one who acts or transacts business, engaged in or occupied with (instr.), Yājñ.; Sāṃkhyak.; observing or following established usages, W.; m. the manager of any business, conductor of any judicial procedure, judge, umpire, Yājñ., Sch.; one engaged in litigation, a litigant, plaintiff, any one who institutes an action at law, W.; an associate, partaker, ib.; a Vaiśya, L.

Vy-avahāra, m. doing, performing, action, practice, conduct, behaviour, MBh.; Kāv. &c. (*vyavahāraḥ kāryaḥ*, with instr., 'it should be acted according to'); commerce or intercourse with (*saha* or comp.), Nir.; Kām. &c.; affair, matter, Nīlak.; usage, custom, wont, ordinary life, common practice, Pat.; BhP.; Hit.; activity, action or practice of, occupation or business with (loc. or comp.), Inscr.; Kāv.; Kathās.; mercantile transaction, traffic, trade with, dealing in (comp.), Mn.; MBh. &c.; a contract, Mn. viii, 163; legal procedure, contest at law with (*saha*), litigation, lawsuit, legal process (see *-mātṛikā* below), Mn.; Yājñ. &c.; practices of law and kingly government, IW. 209; mathematical process, Col.; administration of justice, Gaut.; (fig.) punishment, L.; competency to manage one's own affairs, majority (in law), ib.; propriety, adherence to law or custom, ib.; the use of an expression, with regard to, speaking about (*tair eva vyavahāraḥ*, 'just about these is the question,' 'it is to these that the discussion has reference'), Kap.; Sāh.; Sarvad.; designation, Jaim., Sch.; compulsory work, L.; a sword, L.; a sort of tree, L.; N. of a ch. of the Agni-purāṇa. **—kamalâkara**, m., **-kalpataru**, m., **-kāṇḍa**, n. N. of wks. **—kāla**, m. the period of action, a mundane period, MW. **—candrôdaya**, m., **-camatkāra**, m., **-cintāmaṇi**, m. (IW. 305), N. of wks. **—jña**, mfn. knowing the ways of the world, acquainted with practice or legal procedure, one competent to manage his own affairs (i. e. one who has passed his 16th year and legally arrived at his majority), Nār. **—tattva**, n. N. of a ch. of the Smṛiti-tattva, IW. 304. **—tas**, ind. according to established practice, practically, conventionally, MW. **—tilaka**, m. N. of a wk. by Bhava-deva Bhaṭṭa. **—tva**, n. the state of being common practice or usage or of being the occasion of litigation or of a lawsuit, MBh. **—darpaṇa**, m. N. of various wks. **—darśana**, n. judicial investigation, trial, Yājñ., Sch. **—daśa-ślokī**, f. N. of a wk. on law by Śrī-dhara Bhaṭṭa. **—daśā**, f. the state of common everyday life or reality, Sarvad. **—dīdhiti**, f., **-dīpikā**, f. N. of wks. **—drashṭṛi**, m. 'examiner of a lawsuit,' a judge, ĀpGṛ., Sch. **—nirṇaya**, m. (also with *śiva-kathita*) N. of wk. **—pada**, n. a title or head of legal procedure, occasion or case of litigation (cf. *-mātṛikā* below, IW. 297), Yājñ. **—paribhāshā**, f., **-pariśishṭa**, n., **-prakāśa**, m., **-pradīpa**, m., **-pradīpikā**, f. N. of wks. **—pāda**, m. the fourth part of a legal process, one of the four stages of a regular lawsuit (these four are, *pūrva-paksha*, *uttara-paksha*, *kriyā-pāda*, *nirṇaya-pāda*, qq.vv.; cf. *vyavahārasya prathamaḥ pādaḥ*, Mṛicch. ix, $\frac{3}{2}$), L. **—prâpta**, m. one who has attained a knowledge of business or legal procedure, a youth of 16 years of age (cf. *-jña*), W. **—mayūkha**, m. (IW. 305), **-mahôdaya**, m. N. of wks. **—mātṛikā**, f. the material or matter of ordinary judicature, legal process in general, any act or subject relating to the formation of legal courts or the administration of justice (arranged under thirty heads in the beginning of the second book or Vyavahārâdhyāya of the Mitâksharā, e. g. 1. *vyavahāra-darśanam*, 2. *vyavahāra-lakshaṇam*, 3. *sabhā-sadaḥ*, 4. *prāḍ-vivākâdiḥ*, 5. *vyavahāra-vishayaḥ*, 6. *rājñaḥ kāryânutpādakatvam*, 7. *kāryârthini praśnaḥ*, 8. *āhvānânāhvāne*, 9. *āsedhaḥ*, 10. *pratyarthiny āgate lekhyâdi-kartavyatā*, 11. *pañca-vidho hīnaḥ*, 12. *kīdṛiśaṃ lekhyam*, 13. *pakshâbhāsāḥ*, 14. *anādeyāḥ*, 15. *ādeyaḥ*, and fifteen others), MW.; N. of a wk. on Dharma (also called *nyāya-m°*) by Jīmūta-vāhana. **—mādhava**, m. N. of a ch. of the Parāśara-smṛiti-vyākhyā by Mādhavâcārya. **—mārga**, m. a course or title of legal procedure, Yājñ., Sch. (= *vishaya*, q. v.) **—mālā**, f., **-mālikā**, f., **-ratna**, n., **-ratna-mālā**, f., **-ratnâkara**, m. N. of wks. **—lakshaṇa**, n. a characteristic of judicial investigation, MW. **—vat**, mfn. having occupation, occupied with (comp.), Mn. x, 37; m. a man of business, Kām. **—vidhi**, m. legal enactment, rule of law, the precepts or code by which judicature is regulated, any code of law, Yājñ., Sch. **—vishaya**, m. a subject or title of legal procedure, any act or matter which may become the subject of legal proceedings (according to Mn. viii, 4-7 eighteen in number, viz. *ṛiṇâdānam*, *nikshepaḥ*, *asvāmi-vikrayaḥ*, *sambhūya-samutthānam*, *dattasyânapakarma*, *vetanâdānam*, *saṃvid-vyatikramaḥ*, *kraya-vikrayânuśayaḥ*, *svāmi-pālayor vivādaḥ*, *sīmā vivādaḥ*, *vāk-pārushyam*, *daṇḍa-pārushyam*, *steyam*, *sāhasam*, *strī-saṃgrahaṇam*, *strī-puṃ-dharmaḥ*, *vibhāgaḥ*, *dyūtam*, *āhvayaḥ*, qq. vv.) **—śataka**, n. N. of a wk. (containing rules of good manners, by Trivikramâcārya). **—samuccaya**, m., **-sāra**, m., **-sârôddhāra**, m., **-saukhya**, n. N. of wks. **—sthāna**, n. = *-vishaya*, Yājñ., Sch. **—sthiti**, f. judicial procedure, ib. **Vyavahārâṅśa**, m. any part or division of legal procedure, MW. **Vyavahārâṅga**, n. the body of civil and criminal law, ib.; *-smṛiti-sarvasva*, n. N. of wk. **Vyavahārâbhiśasta**, mfn. prosecuted, accused, proceeded against legally, W. **Vyavahārâyogya**, mfn. unfitted for legal proceedings, ib.; m. one incompetent to conduct business, a minor, one not yet of age, ib. **Vyavahārârtha-sāra**, m., **Vyavahārârtha-smṛiti-sāra-samuccaya**, m. N. of wks. **Vyavahārârthin**, m. one who has a lawsuit, a plaintiff, accuser, Mṛicch. ix, $\frac{3}{2}$. **Vyavahārâloka**, m. N. of wk. **Vyavahārâsana**, n. a judgment-seat, tribunal, Ragh. **Vyavahārôccaya**, m. N. of wk.

Vy-avahāraka, m. a dealer, trader, Pañcat.; (*ikā*), f. a female slave, R. (B. *vyāv°*); common practice, the ways of the world, L.; a broom, L.; Terminalia Catappa, L.

Vy-avahāram, ind. alternately, Kāṭh.

Vy-avahārayitavya, mfn. (fr. Caus.) to be occupied (esp. with compulsory work), Kull.

Vy-avahārika, w. r. for *vyāvahārika*.

Vy-avahārin, mfn. acting, proceeding, dealing with (ifc.), Hit.; Kull.; transacting, practising (any business or trade), MBh.; Yājñ.; VarBṛS.; fit or competent for legal proceedings or for affairs, being of age (°*ri-tā*, f. majority in law), Kāty.; relating to a legal process or action, W.; customary, usual, ib.; m. a man of business, trader, merchant, MBh.; Kāv. &c.; N. of a Mohammedan sect, W.

Vy-avahārya, mfn. to be transacted or practised (see *an-av°*); one who may be associated with, Yājñ.; MBh.; customary, usual, W.; to be employed or used, MW.; actionable, liable to a legal process, ib.; n. a treasure, L.

Vy-avahṛit, mfn. dealing in (ifc.), Kathās.; (as subst.) usage, practice, Harav. °**avahṛita**, mfn. practised, employed, used, MW.; n. commerce, intercourse, BhP. °**avahṛiti**, f. practice, conduct, action, Rājat.; Sāh.; intercourse, Rājat.; business, trade, commerce, BhP.; litigation, lawsuit, Cat.; speech, talk, rumour (see *dur-vy°*); *-tattva*, n. N. of a ch. of the Smṛiti-tattva (cf. *vyavahāra-t°*).

Vy-avahriyamāṇa, mfn. being named or designated (*-tva*, n.), Kusum.

व्यवे *vy-avē* (*-ava-√5. i*), P. *-avâiti*, to go or pass between, separate, ŚBr.; Kauś.; (in gram.) to resolve or separate by inserting a vowel, Prāt.; to dissolve, decompose, MW.

Vy-avāya, m. intervention, interposition, separation by insertion, being separated by (instr. or comp.), ŚrS.; Prāt.; Pāṇ.; entering, pervading, penetration, MBh.; Suśr.; change, transmutation, BhP.; sexual intercourse, copulation, MBh.; VarBṛS.; Suśr.; wantonness, lasciviousness, BhP.; covering, disappearance, W.; interval, space, ib.; an obstacle, impediment, MW.; n. light, lustre, L. °**avâyin**, mfn. intervening, separating, Prāt.; Pāṇ.; pervading, diffusive, Suśr.; ŚārṅgS. (°*yi-tva*, n., Car.); lascivious, lustful, Suśr.; m. a libertine, W.; any drug possessing stimulating properties, an aphrodisiac, ib.

Vy-avēta, mfn. separated, divided (esp. by insertion of a letter), Prāt.; Pāṇ. (*-tva*, n.)

व्यश् *vy-√1. aś*, P. Ā. *-aśnoti*, *-aśnute*, to reach, attain, Bhaṭṭ.; to obtain, take possession of, RV.; AV.; ŚBr.; ĀśvŚr.; to fall to one's share, RV.; AV.; to pervade, interpenetrate, fill, occupy, Ragh.; Bhaṭṭ.

2. **Vy-aśana**, m. (for 1. see p. 1028, col. 3), Kāṭh. (a word used in a partic. formula; other forms are *vaiyâśana*; *vy-âśniya*, TS.; *vy-aśnuvin*, VS.)

Vy-ashṭi, f. attainment, success, TS.; ŚBr. &c.; (in Vedânta) singleness, individuality, a separated aggregate (such as man, viewed as a part of a whole [e. g. of the Universal Soul] while himself composed of individual parts; opp. to *sam-ashṭi*, q. v.), Śaṃk.; Vedântas.; m. N. of a preceptor, ŚBr.; *-samashṭitā*, f. the state of individuality and totality, Vedântas.; °*ty-abhiprâya*, m. regarding (a group of objects) singly or individually, MW.

व्यश् *vy-√2. aś*, P. Ā. *-aśnāti*, *-aśnīte*, to eat up, consume by eating, RV.; AV.

व्यश्व *vy-aśva* &c. See p. 1028, col. 3.

व्यष्टक *vyashṭaka*, n. (v. l. for *mushṭhaka*, q. v.) black mustard, L.; °*kā*, f., see p. 1028, col. 3.

व्यष्ठ *vyashṭha*, n. copper, L.

व्यस् *vy-√2. as*, P. *-asyati* (ep. pf. *vivyāsa* as if fr. a √*vyas*), to throw or cast asunder or about or away, throw (effort) into, divide, separate, dispose, arrange; scatter, disperse; expel, remove, RV.&c.&c.

Vy-asana, n. moving to and fro, wagging (of a tail), Pāṇ. iii, 1, 20, Vārtt. 3; throwing (effort) into, assiduity, industry, Bhartṛ.; Subh.; separation, individuality, W.; attachment or devotion or addiction to (loc. or comp.), passion, (esp.) evil passion, sin, crime, vice (said to arise either from love of pleasure or from anger; eight are enumerated under the first head, viz. *mṛigayā, dyūta* or *aksha, divā-svapna, parivāda, striyaḥ, mada, taurya-trika, vṛithâṭyā*; and eight under the second, viz. *paiśunya, sāhasa, droha, īrshyā, asūyā, artha-dūshaṇa, vāk-pārushya, daṇḍa-pārushya*, qq.vv.), Mn. vii, 47, 48; MBh. &c.; favourite pursuit or occupation, hobby, MBh.; Pañcat.; Rājat.; evil predicament or plight, disaster, accident, evil result, calamity, misfortune (*vyasanāni*, pl. misfortunes), ill-luck, distress, destruction, defeat, fall, ruin, Mn.; MBh. &c.; setting (of sun or moon), Mṛicch.; Śak.; fruitless effort, L.; punishment, execution (of criminals), MW.; incompetence, inability, W.; air, wind, ib.; tale-bearing, L.; *-kāla*, m. time of need, Subh.; *-prasārita-kara*, mfn. having the hand stretched forth for (inflicting) calamity, Hit.; *-prahārin*, mfn. inflicting calamity, giving trouble or pain, W.; *-prâpti*, f. occurrence of calamity, Sāh.; *-brahmacārin*, m. a companion of adversity, fellow-sufferer, Mudr.; *-mahârṇava*, m. a sea of troubles, Mṛicch.; *-rakshin*, mfn. preserving from calamity, R.; Kathās.; *-vat*, mfn. one who has had ill-luck with (comp.), Kām.; *-vāgurā*, f. the net or snare of adversity, R.; *-saṃsthita*, mfn. one who indulges in any whim or favourite fancy, Pañcat.; °*nâkrānta-tva*, n. distressful condition, grievous distress, MW.; °*nâgama*, m. approach of calamity, Śukas.; °*nâtibhāra*, mfn. weighed down or overburdened with misfortunes, MW.; °*nâtyaya*, m. the passing away of calamity or distress, BhP.; °*nânantaram*, ind. immediately after misfortune, Kāv.; °*nâpāta*, m. (=°*nâgama*), Rājat.; °*nâvāpa*, m. receptacle or abode of calamity, BhP.; °*nânvita* or °*nâpluta*, mfn. involved in or overwhelmed with c°, MW.; °*nârta*, mfn. afflicted by calamity, suffering pain, L.; °*nôtsava*, m. a feast for the (evil) passions, an orgy &c., VarBṛS.; °*nôdaya*, m. the rising or approaching of misfortune, Pañcat.; mfn. followed by or resulting in calamities, MBh.

Vyasani, in comp. for *vyasanin*. **—tā,** f. devotion or attachment to (loc. or comp.), fancy for, Kāv.; Hit.; an evil passion, Kathās. **—tva,** n. (ifc.) attachment or addiction to, Rājat.

Vyasanin, mfn. working hard, taking great pains, MBh.; (ifc.) passionately addicted to, fond of, Kāv.; Kathās.; addicted to any kind of vice or evil practice (as gaming, drinking &c.), vicious, dissolute, Yājñ.; Hariv.; Kāv.; having a favourite pursuit or occupation, Śaṃk.; calamitous, unfortunate, unlucky with, suffering through or from (comp.), MBh.; Kāv. &c.

Vyasanī-√kṛi, P. *-karoti*, to consider or characterize as a vice, Jātakam.

Vyasanīya, m. a vicious person, profligate, libertine, W.

Vy-àsta, mfn. cut in pieces, dismembered (said of Vṛitra), RV. i, 32, 7; torn asunder, gaping, TPrāt.; severed, separated, divided, distinct (*vy-aste kāle*, 'at different times,' 'now and then'), single, simple, Mn.; MBh. &c.; multiplied, various, manifold, Prab.; Kāvyâd.; opposed to, inverse, reverse (see comp.); disordered, disarranged, confused, bewildered (see comp.); scattered, dispersed, Jyot.; Uttarar.; expelled, removed, Megh.; spread, extended (see comp.); changed, altered (see comp.); inherent in or pervading all the several parts of anything (in phil. opp. to *sam-asta*), penetrated, pervaded; (*am*), ind. severally, separately, partially, MW.; *-keśā*, mf(*ī*)n. having dishevelled hair, AV.; *-tā*, f., *-tva*, n. severalty, individuality, W.; individual inherence, ib.; agitation, bewilderment, ib.; *-trairāśika*, n. the rule of three inverted, Col.; *-nyāsa*, mfn. 'having separate impressions,' rumpled (as a couch), Ratnâv. ii, 11; *-pada*, n. confused statement of a case (in a law-court; as, when a man is accused of debt, it is stated in defence that he has been assaulted), counter-plaint, Yājñ., Sch.; (in gram.) a simple or uncompounded word, W.; *-puccha*, mfn. having an extended tail, Śulbas.; *-rātriṃ-diva*, mfn. dividing or separating night and day, MW.; *-vidhi*, m. inverted rule, any rule for inversion, Col.; *-vṛitti*, mfn. (a word) whose proper force or meaning is changed or altered, Ragh. xi, 73.

Vyastāra, m. (said to be fr. *vyasta* + *āra* fr. √4. *ṛi*; but rather formed in analogy to *vi-stāra*, fr. √*stṛi*) the issue of the fluid from the temples of an elephant in rut, L.

Vy-astikā, ind. with arms or legs spread asunder, Mahāvy.; *-kṛita*, mfn. being in the above position, ib.

Vy-āsa, m. severing, separation, division, Sarvad.; a kind of drawl (as a fault in pronunciation), APrāt.; extension, diffusion, prolixity, detailed account (instr.; abl. and *-tas*, ind. in detail, at length, fully), MBh.; Suśr.; BhP.; width, breadth, the diameter of a circle, Śulbas.; VarBṛS.; 'distributing, disjoining,' N. of the Pada-pāṭha or 'disjoined text,' APrāt.; 'arranger, compiler,' N. of a celebrated mythical sage and author (often called Veda-vyāsa and regarded as the original compiler and arranger of the Vedas, Vedânta-sūtras &c.; he was the son of the sage Parāśara and Satyavatī, and half-brother of Vicitra-vīrya and Bhīshma; he was also called Vādarāyaṇa or Bādarāyaṇa, and Kṛishṇa from his dark complexion, and Dvaipāyana because he was brought forth by Satyavatī on a Dvīpa or island in the Jumnā; when grown up he retired to the wilderness to lead the life of a hermit, but at his mother's request returned to become the husband of Vicitra-vīrya's two childless widows, by whom he was the father of the blind Dhṛita-rāshṭra and of Pāṇḍu; he was also the father of Vidura [q.v.] by a slave girl, and of Śuka, the supposed narrator of the Bhāgavata-Purāṇa, he was also the supposed compiler of the Mahā-bhārata, the Purāṇas, and other portions of Hindū sacred literature; but the name Vyāsa seems to have been given to any great typical compiler or author), MBh.; Hariv.; Pur., cf. IW. 371, n. 2; 373 &c.; a Brāhman who recites or expounds the Purāṇas &c. in public (=*pāṭhaka-brāhmaṇa*), MW.; n. a bow weighing 100 Palas, L. **—kūṭa,** n. N. of a wk. (containing puzzles for the amusement of Rāma in his solitude on the Mālyavat and for the delectation of simple minds). **—keśava,** m., **-gaṇapati,** m. N. of authors, Cat. **—gadya,** n. N. of a Stotra. **—giri**(?), m. N. of an author, Cat. **—gītā,** f. pl. N. of a ch. of the Kūrma-Purāṇa. **—caritra,** n., **-tātparya-nirṇaya,** m. N. of wks. **—tīrtha,** n. N. of a Tīrtha, Cat.; m. (also *-tīrtha-bindu* or *-bhikshu, vyāsa-yati*, and *vyāsa-rāja*) N. of an author of various Comms. and founder of the Vyāsarāya-matha (who died A. D. 1339), Cat. **—tulasī,** m., **-try-ambaka,** m. N. of men, ib. **—tva,** n. the state or title of a compiler, MBh. **—datti,** m. N. of a son of Vara-ruci, Cat. **—darśana-prakāra,** m. N. of wk. **—dāsa,** m. N. of a man, Cat. (also surname of Kshemêndra); of a chief of the Vaikhānasa sect, MW. **—deva,** m. the divine sage Vyāsa, ib.; N. of an author, Cat. (also *-deva-miśra*). **—nārāyaṇa,** m., **-nābha,** m. N. of men, ib. **—paripṛicchā,** f., **-pūjana-saṃhitā,** f. N. of wks. **—pūjā,** f. 'honour paid to an expounder of the Purāṇas,' N. of a partic. observance; *-paddhati*, f., *-vidhi*, m. N. of wks. **—prabhākara**(?), N. of wk. **—bhāshya-vyākhyā,** f. N. of a Commentary. **—mātṛi,** f. 'mother of Vyāsa,' N. of Satyavatī, L. **—mūrti,** m. N. of Śiva, Śivag. **—yati** and **-rāja,** see *-tīrtha*. **—vatsa,** m. N. of an author, Cat. **—vana,** n. N. of a sacred forest, MBh. **—varya,** m. N. of a man (the father of Hanumad Ācārya), Cat. **—viṭṭhala,** m. (with *ācārya*) N. of an author, ib. **—śataka,** n., **-śikshā,** f., **-śuka-saṃvāda,** m. N. of wks. **—sadânandaji,** m. N. of a grammarian, Cat. **—samāsa,** m. du. diffuseness and conciseness (instr. or *-tas*, ind. 'in a diffuse and concise manner'); °*sin*, mfn. diffuse and concise, MBh. **—siddhânta,** m. N. of wk. **—sū,** f. =*-mātṛi*, L. **—sūtra,** n. =*brahma-s°* (q.v.); *-candrikā*, f., *-bhāshya*, n., *-vṛitti*, f., *-vyākhyā*, f., *-śaṃkara-bhāshya*, n., *-saṃgati*, f. N. of wks. on the above Sūtra. **—stuti,** f. N. of wk. **—sthalī,** f. N. of a place, MBh. **—smṛiti,** f. N. of a law-book (mentioned by Yājñ. and in the PadmaP.) **Vyāsâcala,** m. N. of a poet, Cat. **Vyāsâcārya,** m. N. of a teacher of the Mādhva school (later called Veda-vyāsa-tīrtha, died 1560 A.D.), ib. **Vyāsâdi-pañca-siddhânta,** m. pl., **Vyāsâdri-taraṃgiṇī,** f. N. of wks. **Vyāsâraṇya,** m. N. of the Guru of Viśvêśvara, Cat. **Vyāsâśrama,** m. N. of Amalânanda, ib. **Vyāsâshṭaka,** n. N. of a hymn (containing the praise of Śiva, from the Kāśī-khaṇḍa). **Vyāsêśvara,** n. N. of a Tīrtha, Cat. (also *-tīrtha*).

Vyāsīya, mfn. relating to Vyāsa; n. a work by Vyāsa, Cat.

व्यसि *vy-asi, vy-asu* &c. See p. 1028, col. 3.

व्यह् *vy-√ah* (only 3. pl. pf. *-āhuḥ*), to explain, assign a reason, AitBr.

व्याकरण *vy-ākaraṇa* &c. See *vy-ā-√1. kṛi*.

व्याकीर्ण *vy-ā-kīrṇa*, mfn. (√*kṛī*) scattered or tossed in every direction, confused, disturbed, troubled, VarBṛS.; Pañcat.; n. confusion (of the cases), Pratāp.; *-keśara*, mfn. having a disordered or rough mane, Pañcat.; *-mālya-kavara*, mfn. variegated with interspersed garlands, MW.; °*ṇârcis*, mfn. having scattered or dim flames, VarBṛS.

व्याकुञ्चित *vy-ā-kuñcita*, mfn. (√*kuñc*) distorted, crooked, contracted, curved, L.

व्याकुल *vy-ākula*, mf(*ā*)n. (fr. 3. *vi* + *ā-kula*) entirely filled with or full of (instr. or comp.), MBh.; Kāv. &c.; intently engaged in or occupied with (comp.), Kālid.; Prab.; bewildered, confounded, perplexed, troubled, MBh.; Kāv. &c.; confused, disordered (*am*, ind.), ib.; quivering (as lightning), Uttarar.; m. N. of a king, Buddh.; *-citta* (Suśr.), *-cetas* (MārkP.), mfn. agitated or perplexed in mind; *-tā*, f., *-tva*, n. perturbation, agitation, bewilderment, alarm, Kathās.; Pañcat.; MārkP.; *-dhruva*, m. N. of a king, Buddh.; *-manas*, *-mānasa*, MBh.; R., mfn. (=*-citta*); *-mūrdhaja*, mfn. (ifc.) having the hair disarranged or dishevelled, Kathās.; *-locana*, mfn. (ifc.) having the eyes dimmed, MBh.; *-hṛidaya*, mfn. (=*-citta*), Pañcat.; °*lâlāpa*, mfn. uttering confused or discordant sounds, Kathās.; °*lêndriya*, mfn. (=*-citta*), MBh.; R.

Vyākulaya, Nom. P. °*yati*, to agitate, confuse, flurry, distract, Pañcar.; Pañcat.; to disarrange, throw into confusion, Prab.

Vyākulita, mfn. filled with, full of, Hariv.; R.; Kathās.; perplexed, bewildered, distracted, alarmed; MBh.; R. &c.; confused, disarranged, disturbed, corrupted, R.; Suśr.; *-cetana*, *-manas*, *-hṛidaya*; °*tântarâtman*, °*têndriya*, mfn. agitated or perplexed in mind, alarmed, bewildered, frightened. **—ākulitin,** mfn. =*vyākulitam anena*, g. *ishṭâdi*.

Vyākulī, in comp. for *vy-ākula*. **—√kṛi,** P. *-karoti*, to confound, perplex, bewilder, Kāv.; Kathās. **—kṛita,** mfn. filled with, full of (instr. or comp.), VarBṛS.; Pañcat.; perplexed, bewildered, R.; Kathās.; confused, disarranged, R. **—√bhū,** P. *-bhavati*, to become perplexed or bewildered, Pañcat. **—bhūta,** mfn. put to confusion, ib.

व्याकूत *vy-ā-kūta*, m. or n. pain, sorrow, Nalac. °**ākūti,** f. wrong or evil intention, fraud, deception, L.

व्याकृ *vy-ā-√1. kṛi*, P. Ā. *-karoti, -kurute*, to undo, sever, divide, separate from (instr.), RV.; AV.; VS.; ŚBr.; to expound, explain, declare, MBh.; R.; (with Buddhists) to predict (esp. future births), Divyāv.; to prophesy anything (acc.) about any one (acc.), Lalit.; Kāraṇḍ.; Pass. *-kriyate*, to be divided or separated, ŚBr.

Vy-ākaraṇa, n. separation, distinction, discrimination, MBh.; explanation, detailed description, ib.; Suśr.; manifestation, revelation, MBh.; Hariv.; (with Buddhists) prediction, prophecy (one of the nine divisions of scriptures, Dharmas. 62), SaddhP. &c.; development, creation, Śaṃk.; BhP.; grammatical analysis, grammar, MuṇḍUp.; Pat.; MBh. &c.; grammatical correctness, polished or accurate language, Subh.; the sound of a bow-string, L.; *kauṇḍinya*, m. N. of a Brāhman, Buddh.; *-kaustubha*, m. or n., *-khaṇḍana*, n., *-ḍhuṇḍhikā*, f., *-traya*, n., *-dīpa*, m. (also *-dīpa-vyākaraṇa*, n.), *-dīpikā*, f., *-durghaṭôdghāṭa*, m. N. of gram. wks.; *-prakriyā*, f. grammatical formation of a word, etymology, MW.; *-mahā-bhāshya*, n. the Mahā-bhāshya of Patañjali; *-mūla*, n., *-vāda-grantha*, m., *-saṃgraha*, m., *-sāra*, m. N. of gram. wks.; *-siddha*, mfn. established by grammar, grammatical, MW.; °*ṇâgama*, m. traditional rules of grammar, ib.; °*ṇâtmaka*, mfn. having the nature or faculty of discrimination, MBh.; °*ṇôttara*, m. N. of Śiva, RTL. 84, n. 1. °**ākaraṇaka,** n. a bad grammar, Pat. °**ākartṛi,** m. one who develops or creates, creator (*-tva*, n.), Śaṃk.; an expounder, Divyâv. °**ākāra,** m. change of form, deformity, W. (cf. 2. *vi-kāra*); development, detailed description, Kull.; *-dīpikā*, f. N. of wk.

Vy-ākṛita, mfn. separated, divided, developed, unfolded; analyzed, expounded, explained (see *á-vy°*); transformed, disfigured, changed, W. °**ākṛiti,** f. separation, distinction, ŚBr.; detailed description, explanation, Suśr.

Vy-ākriyā, f. development, creation, Śaṃk.

व्याकृष् *vy-ā-√kṛish*, P. *-karshati*, to drag apart, separate, remove, alienate, Prab.

Vy-ākarshaṇa, n. drawing to one's self, attracting, alluring, Kuṭṭanīm. °**ākṛishṭa**, mfn. drawn or taken off, R.; drawn to one's self, attracted, Ratnâv.

व्याकोच *vy-ā-koca*, mfn. (√*kuc*) fully expanded, blown (as a flower), L.

व्याकोप *vy-ā-kopa*, m. (√*kup*) contradiction, opposition, Śaṃk.

व्याकोश *vy-ā-kośa*, mfn. (also written *-ākosha*) fully expanded or blown, opened, MBh.; R. &c.; fully developed, Bhartṛ.; *-kokanada*, mfn. having expanded red lotuses (*tā*, f.), Śiś.; °*śī-√kṛi*, P. *-karoti*, to open (the hand), Gobh., Sch.

व्याक्रुश् *vy-ā-√kruś*, P. *-krośati*, to cry out aloud, complain, lament, R.

Vy-ākrośa, m. abusing, reviling, Prab. (also *ī*, f., Cat.); screeching, Hcar. °**ākrośaka**, mfn. one who abuses or reviles, Pāṇ. iii, 2, 147, Sch.

व्याक्षिप् *vy-ā-√kship*, P. Ā. *-kshipati*, °*te*, to stretch out (the hand &c.), MBh.; to shoot off (an arrow), ib.; to carry away, captivate (the mind), R.; Pañcat.

Vy-ākshipta, mfn. stretched out &c.; (ifc.) filled with, full of, VarBṛS.; *-manas* (Pañcat.), *-hṛidaya* (R.), mfn. having the mind or heart carried away or captivated or distracted.

Vy-ākshepa, m. invective, abuse, MBh.; distraction (of mind), Hariv.; VarBṛS. &c. (cf. *a-vy*°; *mano-vyākshepârtham*, 'in order to distract the mind,' HPariś.); throwing or tossing about, MW.; obstruction, hindrance, delay, ib. °**ākshepin**, mfn. driving away, removing, Mcar.

व्याक्षोभ *vy-ā-kshobha*, m. (√*kshubh*) commotion, perturbation, disturbance, MW.

व्याख्या *vy-ā-√khyā*, P. *-khyāti*, to explain in detail, tell in full, discuss, ŚBr.; ŚrS.; to relate, communicate, MBh.; Bhaṭṭ.; to name, call, Śrutab.: Desid. *-cikhyāsati*, to wish to explain, Śaṃk.

Vy-ākhyā, f. explanation, exposition, gloss, comment, paraphrase, MaitrUp.; Hariv. &c.; *-kusumâvalī*, f. N. of wk.; *-kṛit*, m. the author of a Commentary, Cat.; *-°gamya* (°*khyâg*°), n. anything which can only be understood by explanation, a kind of *uttarâbhāsa* (q.v.), MW.; indistinct assertion or declaration (said to proceed from grammatical inaccuracy or faulty construction), any obscure statement or passage, W.; *-°nanda* (°*khyân*°), m. N. of a Comm. on the Bhaṭṭi-kāvya; *-parimala*, m., *-pradīpa*, m., *-°mṛita* (°*khyâm*°), n., *-yukti*, f., *-ratnâvalī*, f. N. of wks.; *-śloka*, m. (= *kārikā*), L.; *-sāra*, m., *-sudhā*, f. N. of wks.; *-sthāna*, n. 'place for explanation,' lecture-room, school-room, Vcar.; *-svara*, m. 'tone of exposition,' the middle tone (in speech), ĀśvŚr.

Vy-ākhyāta, mfn. explained, fully detailed, related, told, ŚBr. &c. &c.; conquered, overcome (?), W. °**ākhyātavya**, mfn. to be explained or commented upon, Nir.; Pāṇ.; MBh. °**ākhyātṛi**, m. an explainer, commentator, expounder, MBh.; Kathās.; &c. (°*trī*, f., Siddh.)

Vy-ākhyāna, mf(*ī*)n. explaining, expounding, commenting, Pāṇ. iv, 3, 66, Sch.; (with gen.) reminding of, i.e. resembling, Pāṇ. ib., Vārtt. 4, Pat.; n. explaining, exposition, interpretation, gloss, comment, ŚBr. &c. &c.; narration, ŚBr.; recitation, ib.; *-prakriyā*, f., *-mālā*, f. N. of wks.; *-yogya*, mfn. deserving exposition, MW.; *-ratnâvalī*, f., *-vivaraṇa*, n. N. of wks. — **śālā**, f. 'teaching-hall,' a school, Inscr. °**ākhyānaya**, Nom. P. °*yati*, to communicate, narrate, report, Ratnâv. ii, ⅘ (in Prākrit). °**ākhyāyikā**, f. N. of a Comm. on the Vāsavadattā by Vikramarddhi. °**ākhyeya**, mfn. to be explained or expounded, Śaṃk.

Vy-ācikhyāsita, mfn. (fr. Desid.) wishing to explain. — **grantha**, m. one who is about to explain a book, Śaṃk. °**ācikhyāsu**, mfn. intending to explain or comment upon (acc. or gen.), Śaṃk.; ĀpŚr., Sch.

व्याघट्टन *vy-ā-ghaṭṭana*, n. rubbing, friction, W.; churning, ib.; (*ā*), f. rubbing, friction, Śiś. °**āghaṭṭita**, mfn. rubbed together, rubbed, W.; churned, stirred, ib.

व्याघात *vy-ā-ghāta*, m. (√*han*) striking against, beating, wounding, a stroke, blow, MBh.; R.; Vās.; a defeat, Śiś.; commotion, agitation, disturbance, MBh.; Hariv.; an obstacle, impediment, hindrance, R.; VarBṛS.; (in phil.) contradiction, inconsistency of statement, Śaṃk.; Sarvad.; (in rhet.) a partic. figure of speech (in which different or opposite effects are shown to arise from the same cause or by the same agency, e.g. 'the god of love reduced to ashes by the eye [of Śiva] is brought to life again by the eye [of beautiful women]),' Kpr.; Kuval. &c.; (in astron.) N. of the 13th Yoga, Vās.; Cassia Fistula, L. °**āghātaka**, mfn. striking against, thwarting, opposing, resisting, W. °**āghātin**, mfn. id., ib. °**āghātima**, m. or n. (with Jainas) spontaneous death by abstinence from food after a mortal injury, Śīl.

व्याघुट् *vy-ā-√ghuṭ* (only ind. p *-ghuṭya*), to turn back, return, Pañcat. °**āghuṭana**, n. turning back, return, HPariś.

व्याघुष् *vy-ā-√ghush*, Caus. *-ghoshayati*, to call aloud, shout or proclaim aloud, Hariv. °**āghushṭa**, mfn. sounded aloud, loud-sounding, resounding, MBh.

व्याघूर्ण् *vy-ā-√ghūrṇ*, P. Ā. *-ghūrṇati*, °*te*, to whirl or wave about, shake to and fro, MBh. °**āghūrṇita**, mfn. whirled about, rolling about, tottering, reeling, ib.

व्याघृ *vy-ā-√ghṛi*, Caus. *-ghārayati*, to sprinkle round or over, besprinkle, TS.; ŚBr.

Vy-āghāraṇa, n. the act of sprinkling, GṛŚrS. (cf. *dig-vy*°); pl. the verses or formulas recited during the act of sprinkling, ĀpŚr. °**āghārita**, mfn. besprinkled, sprinkled with oil or ghee, W.

व्याघ्रा *vy-ā-√ghrā*, P. *-jighrati*, to scent out, scent or smell at (prob. to explain *vyāghra* below), Pat. on Pāṇ. iii, 1, 137, Vārtt. 1.

Vyāghrá, m. a tiger (not in RV., but in AV., often mentioned with the lion; accord. to R. iii, 30, 26, Śārdūlī is the mythical mother of tigers; but in Vahni-Purāṇa they are said to be the offspring of Kaśyapa's wife Daṃshṭrā; cf. *citra-vy*°), AV. &c. &c.; any pre-eminently strong or noble person, 'a tiger among men' (cf. *ṛishabha, siṃha*); Pongamia Glabra, L.; a red variety of the castor-oil plant, L.; N. of a Rākshasa, VP.; of a king, Rājat.; of various authors (also abridged fr. *vyāghra-pad*), Cat.; (*ī*), f., see col. 3. — **ketu**, m. N. of a man, MBh.; Hcar.; Vās., Introd. — **gaṇa**, m. N. of a poet, Subh. — **giri**, m. N. of a mythical mountain, Vīrac. — **grīva**, m. pl. N. of a people, MārkP. — **carman**, n. a tiger's skin, AitBr.; KātyŚr.; Pañcat.; °*mamaya*, w.r. for °*ma-cchada*, MBh. — **jámbhana**, mfn. killing or destroying tigers, AV. — **tala**, m. a red variety of the castor-oil plant, L. (cf. *-dala*). — **tā**, f., *-tva*, n. the state or condition of a tiger, MBh.; Hit. — **daṃshṭra**, m. Tribulus Lanuginosus, L. — **datta**, m. N. of a man, MBh. — **dala**, m. Ricinus Communis, L. — **nakha**, m. a tiger's claw, W.; Tithymalus or Euphorbia Antiquorum, L.; m. n. a root or a partic. root, L.; m. or n. a kind of perfume, Unguis Odoratus, Suśr.; VarBṛS.; Bhpr.; (in this sense also *ī*, f., W.); n. = next, L. — **nakhaka**, n. a kind of medicinal herb or vegetable perfume, L.; a scratch of a partic. form made with finger-nails, L. — **nāyaka**, m. 'tiger-leader,' a jackal, L. (cf. *-sevaka*). — **pad** (nom. *-pād*), mfn. tiger-footed, Laghuk.; m. Flacourtia Cataphracta, L.; N. of the author of RV. ix, 97, 16–18 (having the patr. Vāsishṭha); of various other authors, Cat. (*-pat-smṛiti*, f. = *vyāghra-sm*°). — **pada**, m. a species of plant, VarBṛS. — **padya**, w.r. for *vaiyāghrapadya*, m., ChUp. — **parākrama**, m. N. of a man, Kathās. — **pād**, see *-pad*. — **pāda**, m. 'tiger-footed,' Flacourtia Sapida, L.; Asteracantha Longifolia, L.; N. of various men, MBh. &c.; *-smṛiti*, f. = *vyāghra-sm*°; *-stotra*, n. N. of a Stotra. — **puccha**, m. a tiger's tail, MW.; the castor-oil tree, Ricinus Communis, Bhpr. — **pucchaka**, m. id., L.; Palma Christi, L. — **pura**, n. 'tiger's town,' N. of a town, Cat. — **pushpi**, m. N. of a man, Pravar. — **pratīka** (*vyāghrá-*), mfn. having a tiger-like appearance, AV. — **bala**, m. N. of a king, Kathās.; of a mythical person, Vīrac. — **bhaṭa**, m. N. of an Asura, Kathās.; of a warrior, ib. — **bhūti**, m. N. of various authors, Cat. — **mārin**, m. N. of a man, Inscr. — **mukha**, m. N. of a king, Jyot.; of a mountain, MārkP.; pl. N. of a people, VarBṛS. — **rāja**, m. N. of a king, Buddh. — **rūpā**, f. a kind of Momordica, Dhanv. — **lomán**, n. a tiger's hair, VS.; ŚBr.; KātyŚr. — **vaktra**, mfn. tiger-faced, L.; m. N. of one of Śiva's attendants, Hariv.; (*ā*), f. (with Buddhists) N. of a goddess, Kālac. — **vadhū**, f. a tigress, MBh. — **śvan**, m. a tiger-like dog, Vop. — **śveta**, m. N. of a Yātudhāna, VP. — **sena**, m. N. of a man, Kathās. — **sevaka**, m. 'tiger's servant,' a jackal (being said to lead the t° to the deer), L. — **smṛiti**, f. N. of wk. **Vyāghrâksha**, mfn. tiger-eyed, L.; m. N. of one of Skanda's attendants, MBh.; of an Asura, Hariv. **Vyāghrâjina**, m. N. of a man, Pāṇ. v, 3, 82, Sch. **Vyāghrâṭa**, m. a skylark, L. **Vyāghrâdanī** or °**dinī**, f. Ipomœa Turpethum, L. **Vyāghrâsya**, n. the mouth or face of a tiger, MW.; mfn. tiger-faced, L.; m. a cat, L.; (*ā*), f. (with Buddhists) N. of a goddess, Kālac. (cf. *vyāghra-vaktrā*). **Vyāghrêśvara**, n. N. of a Liṅga, Cat.

Vyāghraka, m. endearing form for *vyāghrâjina*, Pāṇ. v, 3, 82, Sch.

Vyāghrāṇa, n. the act of smelling at, Nir. (used to explain *vyāghra*).

Vyāghriṇī, f. (with Buddhists) N. of a being attendant on the Mātṛis, W.

Vyāghrī, f. of *vyāghra*, a tigress, Śiksh.; MBh.; Kāv. &c.; Solanum Jacquini, Bhpr.; (with Buddhists) N. of a goddess, Kālac.

Vyāghryá, mfn. relating or belonging to a tiger, AV.

व्याङ्गि *vyāṅgi*, patr. fr. *vy-aṅga*, g. *svāgatâdi*.

व्याचक्ष् *vy-ā-√caksh*, Ā. *-cashṭe*, to recite, rehearse, ŚBr.; to explain, comment upon, ib.; KenUp.; Kās.

व्याचिख्यासित *vy-ācikhyāsita* &c. See col. 1.

व्याचिन्त् *vy-ā-√cint* (only 3.sg. impf. *vyācintayat*, w.r. for *vy-a-c*°), Pañcat.

व्याज *vy-āja*, m. (rarely n., ifc. f. *ā*; fr. *vy-√añj*, to smear over; cf. √*ac*) deceit, fraud, deception, semblance, appearance, imitation, disguise, pretext, pretence (ibc. 'treacherously, falsely,' also = ifc. 'having only the appearance of, appearing as, simulated, deceitful, false;' instr. and abl. 'treacherously, deceitfully,' 'under the pretext or guise of'), MBh.; Kāv. &c.; an artifice, device, contrivance, means, Ragh.; wickedness, W. — **kheda**, m. feigned weariness, Kathās. — **guru**, m. only in appearance a teacher, ib. — **tapodhana**, m. a feigned or false ascetic, ib. — **nidrita**, mf(*ā*)n. feigning sleep, Rājat. — **nindā**, f. (in rhet.) artful or ironical censure, Kuval. — **pūrva**, mfn. having only the appearance of anything, Ragh. — **bhānu-jit**, m. N. of a man, Cat. — **maya**, mf(*ī*)n. simulated, hypocritical, Kathās. — **vishṇu**, m. a feigned or false Vishṇu, ib. — **vyavahāra**, m. artful conduct or behaviour, Dhūrtas. — **sakhī**, f. a feigned or false (female) friend, Kathās. — **supta**, mf(*ā*)n. feigning sleep, ib.; n. feigned sleep, ib. — **stuti**, f. (in rhet.) 'artful praise,' praise or censure conveyed in language that expresses the contrary, indirect eulogy, ironical commendation, Vām.; Sāh. &c. — **haṃsâvalī**, f. a false or feigned Haṃsâvalī (N. of a woman), Kathās. — **hata**, mfn. killed treacherously, R. **Vyājâbhiprāya**, m. a feigned intention or opinion, Kathās. **Vyājâhvaya**, m. a false name, BhP. **Vyājôkti**, f. (in rhet.) dissimulating statement (a figure of speech in which the effect of one cause is ascribed to another, or where a feeling is dissembled by being attributed to a different cause), Sāh.; Kpr. &c.

Vyājaya, Nom. P. *-yati*, to cheat, deceive, Kathās.

Vyājī, in comp. for *vy-āja*. — **karaṇa**, n. fraud, deception, Dhātup. — √**kṛi**, P. *-karoti*, to hold out as a pretence or pretext (ind. p. *-kṛitya* = *apadiśya*), MW.

व्याजिह्म *vy-ā-jihma*, mfn. bent crooked or awry, Nāg.

व्याजृम्भ् *vy-ā-√jṛimbh*, Ā. *-jṛimbhate*, to open wide, gape, Prasannar.

व्याड *vyāḍa*, mfn. (said to be fr. 3. *vi* + √*aḍ*; cf. *vyāla*) malicious, mischievous, L. (with loc., g. *śauṇḍâdi*); m. a beast of prey, MBh.; R.; MārkP.; a snake, L.; 'a rogue' or 'a jackal' (= *vañcaka*), L.; N. of Indra, L. — **yaksha** (?), Divyâv. **Vyāḍâyudha**, n. Unguis Odoratus, L.

व्याडि *vyāḍi* or *vyāli* or *vyāḷi*, m. (patr. fr. *vyaḍa*, g. *svāgatâdi*) N. of various men (esp. of a poet, a grammarian, and a lexicographer), RPrāt.; Kathās.&c. **— paribhāshā**, f. pl. N. of a gram.wk. **— śālā**, f., g. *chāttry-ādi*. **— śikshā**, f. N. of a wk. on Vaidic phonetics (also written *vyāla-ś°*).

Vyāḍīya, mfn. coming from or composed by Vyāḍi (pl. the adherents of V°), g. *gahâdi*. **— paribhāshā-vṛitti**, f. N. of wk.

Vyāḍyā, f. patr. fr. *vyāḍi*, g. *krauḍy-ādi*.

व्यातन् *vy-ā-√tan* (only Ā. pf. 3. sg. *-tene*, Śiś. viii, 56; and 3. pl. *-tenire*, Kir. xv, 42, both with pass. meaning), to spread about, display, produce.

व्यात्युक्षी *vy-âty-ukshī*, f. (*√uksh*; cf. *vy-âbhy-ukshī*) mutual sprinkling with water, Śiś.; Prasannar.

व्यादा *vy-ā-√1. dā*, P. Ā. *-dadāti*, *-datte*, to open wide, open (esp. the mouth, with or scil. *mukham*; Ā., 'to open the m° of another person, cause any one to open the m°,' Siddh.), ChUp.; MBh. &c.

Vy-ātta, mfn. opened (esp. applied to the mouth), MBh.; expanded, vast, W.; n. the opened mouth, open jaws, AV.; VS.; ŚBr.; *°ttânana* or *°ttâsya*, mfn. open-mouthed, MBh.

Vy-ādāna, n. opening wide, opening, Bālar.; Hit.

Vy-ādāya, mfn. having opened &c. (with *śṛiṇvat*, 'hearing with open mouth,' BhP.; with *svapiti*, 'he sleeps with open mouth,' Pāṇ. iii, 4, 21, Vārtt. 5); *-svāpin*, m. 'sleeping with open mouth,' N. of a demon, Suparṇ.

Vy-ādita, mfn. opened (= *vy-ātta*); *°tâsya*, mfn. open-mouthed, MBh.; Hariv.

व्यादिश् 1. *vy-ā-diś*, f. (cf. *vy-ā-√diś*) a partic. point of the compass (prob. the point between two *vi-diś*, see p. 950, col. 3), MBh.

व्यादिश् 2. *vy-ā-√diś*, P. *-diśati*, to point out separately, divide among, distribute, TS. &c. &c.; to point out, show, explain, teach, R.; Prab.; to prescribe, enjoin, MBh.; Kāv. &c.; to appoint, assign, despatch to any place or duty, direct, order, command (with dat., loc., or *prati*), ib.; to declare, foretell, Mālav. v, 1/2 (v. l. *ādishṭā* for *vy-ād°*).

Vy-ādiśa, m. N. of Vishṇu, L. **°ādishṭa**, mfn. distributed, pointed out, explained, prescribed, ordered, declared, indicated, foretold, MBh.; Kāv. &c.

Vy-ādeśa, m. detailed or special injunction, direction, order, command, R.

व्यादीर्घ *vy-ā-dīrgha*, mfn. stretched out longways to the full extent, Bhartṛ.; Var.

व्यादीर्ण *vy-ā-dīrṇa*, mfn. 'stretched open' (in *°dīrṇâsya*, m. 'open-jawed,' a lion), L.

व्यादीप् *vy-ā-√dīp*, Caus. *-dīpayati*, to inflame or illuminate thoroughly, MBh.

व्यादृश् *vy-ā-√dṛiś*, Pass. *-dṛiśyate*, to be clearly seen or visible, BhP.

व्याध *vyādha* &c. See *√vyadh*, p. 1031.

व्याधा *vy-ā-√1. dhā*, Pass. *-dhīyate*, to be separated or divided, Br.; to be out of health, feel unwell, ChUp.

Vy-ādhāma, m. (rather fr. *√dhā* than fr. *√dhmā*; accord. to some also *vy-ādhāva*, fr. *√dhū*) Indra's thunderbolt (= *vajra*), L.

Vy-ādhi, m. (less probably from *√vyadh*, p. 1031) disorder, disease, ailment, sickness, plague (esp. leprosy), ChUp.; Mn.; MBh. &c.; Disease personified (as a Child of Mṛityu or Death), VP.; any tormenting or vexatious person or thing (ifc., e.g. *strī-v°*, a plague of a woman, very troublesome woman), VarBṛS.; Costus Speciosus or Arabicus, L. **— kara**, mfn. causing sickness, VarBṛS. **— grasta**, mf(*ā*)n. seized or afflicted with disease, MW. **— ghāta**, m. 'illness-destroyer,' Cathartocarpus Fistula (also *°taka*), Suśr.; Bhpr.; Calamus Rotang, L. **— ghna**, mf(*ī*)n. removing or destroying disease, W.; m. Cathartocarpus Fistula, Dhanv. **— durbhiksha-pīḍita**, mf(*ā*)n. afflicted with sickness and famine, MW. **— nigraha**, m. suppression of disease, Suśr. **— nirjaya**, m. the subduing of a disease, ib. **— pīḍita**, mfn. afflicted with dis°, Mn.; Śukas.; Vet. **— bahula**, mfn. frequently visited with disease (as a village), Mn. iv, 60. **— bhaya**, n. fear of disease, VarBṛS. **— yukta**, mf(*ā*)n. suffering from illness, sick, W. **— rahita**, mf(*ā*)n. free from disease, convalescent, W. **— ripu**, m. 'foe of disease,' Webera Corymbosa or Pterospermum Acerifolium, L. **— vardhaka**, m. 'dis°-increaser,' nickname of a physician, Kautukar. **— saṃgha-vimardana**, n. N. of wks. **— samuddeśīya**, mfn. descriptive of the nature of diseases, Suśr. **— siddhâñjana**, n. N. of wk. **— sindhu**, m. 'sea of diseases,' nickname of a physician, Hāsy. **— sthāna**, n. 'station of dis°,' the body, L. **— hantṛi**, mfn. = *-ghna*, MW.; m. yam, L.

Vyādhita, mf(*ā*)n. afflicted with disease, diseased, sick, GṛŚrS.; Mn.; Yājñ. &c.

3. **Vyādhin**, mfn. (for 1. and 2. see p. 1031, col. 2), id., MW.

Vyādhy, in comp. for *vy-ādhi*. **— argala**, N. of wk. **— ārta**, mfn. pained with or suffering from disease, Mn. viii, 64. **— upaśama**, m. allaying or curing diseases, W.

व्याधी *vy-ā-dhī*, f. (*√1. dhi* or *dhyai*) care, sorrow, AV.

व्याधू *vy-ā-√dhū*, P. Ā. *-dhūnoti*, *°nute*, to shake off, shake to and fro, move or toss about, MBh.; R.; Kālid. **°ādhūta**, mfn. shaken about, agitated, tremulous, Kāv.

व्याध्मातक *vy-ā-dhmātaka*, n. (*√dhmā*) a swollen corpse, L.

व्यान *vy-āna* &c. See *vy-√an*, p. 1031.

व्यानद्ध *vy-ā-naddha*, mfn. (*√nah*) connected mutually, interspersed, Hariv.

व्यानम् *vy-ā-√nam*, P. Ā. *-namati*, *°te*, to bend or bow down, MW.

Vy-ānata, mfn. bent down, having the face bent towards the ground, ib.; n. a kind of coitus, ib.; *-karaṇa*, n. a partic. posture in coitus, ib.

Vy-ānamra, mfn. bowed or bent down, Alaṃkāras. **°rī-√kṛi**, P. *-karoti*, to bow down, humble, put to shame, Bhām.

व्यानशि *vy-ā-naśi*, mfn. (*√1. naś*) pervading, penetrating (with acc.), RV. (Naigh. iii, 1 among the *bahu-nāmāni*). **°ānaśin**, mfn. = *vyāpana-śīla*, Sāy.

व्यानी *vy-ā-√nī*, Ā. *-nayate*, to pour in separately, ŚBr.

व्याप् *vy-√āp*, P. *-āpnoti* (rarely Ā. *-āpnute*), to reach or spread through, pervade, permeate, cover, fill, AV. &c. &c.; to reach as far as, extend to, L. (cf. Pāṇ. v, 2, 8): Pass. *vy-āpyate* (see *vy-āpyamāna*): Caus. *vy-āpayati* (see *vy-āpita*): Desid. *vîpsati* (see *vîpsa*).

Vy-āpaka, mf(*ikā*)n. pervading, diffusive, comprehensive, widely spreading or extending, spreading everywhere (*vyāpakaṃ ny-√as* or *nyāsaṃ √kṛi*, to put or place or fix or make applicable everywhere, AgP.); KaṭhUp., MBh. &c.; (in logic) invariably pervading or inherent or concomitant (as an attribute which is always found [as smoke] where some other [as fire] is found), Bhāshāp.; IW. 62; (in law) comprehending all the points of an argument, pervading the whole plea, W.; (*ikā*), f. a woman who shows herself everywhere (?), MW.; *-tā*, f., *-tva*, n. pervasion, diffusion, comprehensiveness, invariable concomitance or inherence (in logic), BhP.; Bhāshāp. &c.; (*-tā-vādârtha*, m. N. of wk.); *-nyāsa*, m. (in the Tantra system) a partic. disposition or arrangement of mystical texts over the whole person, L.

Vy-āpana, n. spreading through, pervading, penetration, covering, filling, Sāh.; Sāy. on RV. i. 113, 14. **°āpanīya**, mfn. to be pervaded or penetrated, permeable, Nir.

Vyāpi, in comp. for *vy-āpin*. **— tva**, n. the state of pervading, pervasion, extensiveness, extent, universality, extension to (ifc.), ĀśvŚr.; MBh.; Vedântas.

Vy-āpita, mfn. (fr. Caus.) filled up, filled, Pañcat.

Vy-āpin, mfn. reaching through, pervading, covering, diffusive, comprehensive, spreading everywhere, spread over (ifc.), extending or reaching or continuing to or filling up or containing (ifc.), Nir.; ŚvetUp.; MBh. &c.; invariably inherent or concomitant (in logic), Bhāshāp.; m. 'pervader,' N. of Vishṇu, MW.; an invariably pervading property as characteristic, ib.

Vy-āpta, mfn. spread through, pervaded, extended, covered or filled with, thoroughly occupied or penetrated by (as the universe by spirit), filled up, full, ŚvetUp.; Bhag.; R. &c.; comprehended or included under (a general notion), having invariably inherent properties, invariably pervaded or attended or accompanied by (in logic; e.g. *dhūmo vahninā vyāptaḥ*, 'smoke is invariably attended by fire'), Bhāshāp.; occupied, obtained, taken possession of, MBh.; Prab.; Pañcat.; wealthy, rich, AitBr.; celebrated, famous, W.; placed, fixed, ib.; open, outspread, expanded, ib.; *-tama*, mfn. most diffused, NṛisUp.; *°tântara*, mfn. having intervals or apertures or recesses filled up, MW.

Vy-āpti, f. (ifc. *°tika*) acquisition, attainment, accomplishment, AV.; ŚBr.; pervasion, inherence, inherent and inseparable presence of any one thing in another (as of oil in sesamum seed, heat in fire &c.), universal pervasion, invariable concomitance, universal distribution or accompaniment (e.g. 'smoke is always pervaded by fire,' or 'fire is necessarily attended with smoke,' cf. IW. 62), Kap.; Nyāyam., Sch.; universality, universal rule without an exception, Sarvad.; Vedântas.; omnipresence, ubiquity (as a divine attribute), W. **— karman**, mfn. whose business or function is to acquire or attain, Naigh. ii, 18. **— graha**, m. apprehension of a general proposition or of universal concomitance, induction, MW.; N. of wk. (also *°hôpâya*, m., *°hôpâya-ṭippaṇī*, f., *°hôpâya-pūrva-paksha-prakāśa*, m., *°hôpâya-rahasya*, n.) **— jñāna**, n. knowledge of pervading inherence or of the presence of invariably concomitant properties, W. **— nirūpaṇa**, n. N. of wk. **— niścaya**, m. (in logic) the ascertainment of pervading inherence or universal concomitance, MW. **— pañcaka**, n. (and *°ka-ṭīkā*, f., *-rahasya*, n.), **-parishkāra**, m., **-pūrva-paksha-prakāśa**, m., **-pūrva-paksha-rahasya**, n. N. of wks. **— mat**, mfn. spreading, extending, Śaṃk.; possessing pervasion, universally diffused or pervading, Mn.; Tarkas.; pervaded, attended by, MW.; *-tva*, n. the capacity of extending or pervading, Nir. **— lakshaṇa**, n. a sign or proof of universal pervasion or of the invariable attendance of an inherent property or characteristic, W.; N. of wk. **— vāda**, m. statement or assertion of universal pervasion &c.; *-kroḍa*, m., *-kroḍa-pattra*, n., *-prakāśa*, m., *-rahasya*, n. N. of wks.

Vyāpty, in comp. for *vy-āpti*. **— anugama**, m., **-anugama-prakāśa**, m., **-anugama-rahasya**, n., **-anugama-vādârtha**, m., **-anugamâloka**, m. N. of wks.

Vy-āpya, mfn. permeable, penetrable, capable of being attended by any inherent characteristic, BhP.; Kap., Sch.; Tarkas.; n. that which may be the site or locality of universal pervasion or of an invariably concomitant cause or characteristic (e.g. 'smoke which is invariably pervaded by fire'), IW. 62; the sign or middle term of an inference, proof, reason, cause (= *sādhana*, *hetu*), L.; Costus Speciosus or Arabicus, L.; *-tā*, f., *-tva*, n. permeableness, the state of being pervaded or attended by, Tarkas.; the capacity of obtaining, MW.

Vy-āpyamāna, mfn. being pervaded or permeated or comprehended or included, Pāṇ. iii, 4, 56.

व्यापद् *vy-ā-√pad*, Ā. *-padyate*, to fall away, fall into misfortune, perish, be lost, fail, miscarry, MBh.; Suśr.; to disappear, be changed into another sound or symbol, RPrāt., Sch. (cf. *vy-āpanna*): Caus. *-pādayati*, to cause to perish, make worse, injure, hurt, spoil, kill, destroy, MBh.; Kāv. &c.

Vy-āpatti, f. falling into calamity or misfortune, suffering injury, failure, loss, ruin, death, ŚrS.; MBh. &c.; disappearance, substitution (of one sound or letter by another), RPrāt.

Vy-āpad, f. (cf. *vi-pad*) misfortune, calamity, derangement, disorder, failure, ruin, death, MBh.; Kāv. &c.

Vy-āpanna, mfn. fallen into misfortune, disordered, spoiled, corrupted, Suśr.; hurt, injured, destroyed, perished, MBh.; disappeared, changed by the substitution of another sound or symbol (esp. applied to the change of Visarga or Visarjanīya to its corresponding sibilants; when Visarga remains unchanged it is called *vi-krānta*, q. v.), RPrāt.; *-citta*, mfn. evil-minded, malicious, Divyâv.

Vy-āpāda, m. destruction, ruin, death, Rājat.; evil intent or design, malice, Buddh. (one of the ten sins, Dharmas. 56). **°āpādaka**, mfn. destructive, murderous, fatal (as a disease), Rājat. **°āpādana**, n. destruction, killing, slaughter, death by (comp.), MārkP.; Suśr.; Pañcat.; ill-will, malice, W. **°āpādanīya**, mfn. to be destroyed or killed (*-tā*, f.), Pañcat. **°āpādayitavya**, mfn. id., Hit. **°āpādita**, mfn. destroyed, killed, slain (*-vat*, mfn. one who has destroyed &c.), MBh.; Hit. **°āpādya**, mfn. to be killed or destroyed, MW.

व्यापलण्डिका *vyāpalaṇḍikā* (?), the neck, L.

व्यापात *vy-ā-pāta*, m. (√*pat*; a word of unknown meaning), ĀpŚr. xiv, 22, 13.

व्यापीत *vy-ā-pīta*, mfn. quite yellow, VarBṛS.

व्याप्ृ *vy-ā-√2. pṛi*, Ā. *-priyate* or *-priṇute*, to be occupied or engaged in, be busy about (loc.; or with *artham* or *hetos* ifc.), be employed (in any office), MBh.; Kāv. &c.: Caus. *-pārayati*, to cause to be employed, set to work, keep busy, employ with or in or for (instr., loc., or *artham* ifc.), ib. (with *karam*, to place or fix the hand, Ragh.; with *hastam*, to wave the hand, Bālar.; with *vilocanāni*, to fix the eyes upon, direct the glance towards, Kum.; with *vāṇīm*, to use or raise one's voice, Hcar.)

Vy-āpāra, m. (ifc. f. *ā*) occupation, employment, business, profession, function (*sāyakānāṃ vyāp°*, 'the business of arrows' i.e. 'hitting the mark;' often in comp., e.g. *mānasa-vy°*, 'occupation of mind,' Vedāntas.; *vāg-vy°*, 'employment of speech,' talk, Hit.; *gṛiha-vy°*, 'occ° with domestic affairs'), MBh.; Kāv. &c.; doing, performance, action, operation, transaction, exertion, concern (acc. with √*kṛi*, 'to perform any one's [gen.] business,' Kathās.; 'to render good offices in any affair,' Kum.; 'to meddle in' [loc.], Pañcat.; with √*vraj*, 'to engage in' [loc.], Vikr.; with √*yā*, 'to be concerned about,' 'care for' [gen.]), MBh.; Kāv. &c.; N. of the tenth astrol. mansion, VarBṛS.; *-kāraka*, mfn. (ifc.) engaging (in contest) with, Hariv.; *-kārin*, mfn. (ifc.) performing the function of, being occupied in, exercising or practising, MBh.; *-rodhin*, mfn. hindering the operation of, opposed to the ways of (gen.), Śak.; *-vat*, mfn. effective, L. (*-vat-tā*, f. the possession of a partic. function, Sāh.) **°āpāraka**, mfn. (ifc.) having an occupation or function, Kusum.

Vy-āpāraṇa, n. (fr. Caus.) causing to be busy, setting to work, Pāṇ. viii, 2, 104, Sch. **°āpārita**, mfn. (fr. id.) made to be busy, set to work, engaged, occupied, Kāv. **°āpārin**, mfn. occ°, busy, engaged in (comp.), BrahmavP.; m. a worker, agent, dealer, trader, ib.

Vy-āpṛita, mfn. occupied, busy, engaged, employed or concerned in or with (loc. or comp.), MBh.; Kāv. &c.; m. a minister, official, Yājñ. **°āpṛiti**, f. occupation, activity, Car.

व्याप्त *vy-āpta*, *vy-āpti*. See p. 1037.

व्याप्व *vy-ā-pva*, m. (√*pū*?) the moon, L.

व्याबाध् *vy-ā-√bādh*, Ā. *-bādhayate*, to hurt, injure, Divyâv.

Vy-ābādha, m. (or *vy-āvādha*) disease, illness, ib.

व्याभग्न *vy-ā-bhagna*, mfn. (√*bhañj*) broken to pieces, shattered, Prab. (v.l. *-bhugna*).

व्याभाष् *vy-ā-√bhāsh*, Ā. *-bhāshate*, to speak, declare, speak to, address, MBh.; to pronounce (see below). **°ābhāshaka**, mfn. one who speaks &c., Pāṇ. iii, 2, 146, Sch. **°ābhāshaṇa**, n. way or manner of speaking, R. **°ābhāshita**, mfn. spoken &c.; pronounced (see *duḥkha-vy°*); n. a speech, MBh.; way or manner of speaking, R.

व्याभुग्न *vy-ā-bhugna*, mfn. (√*1. bhuj*) bent down or awry, Hariv.; Prab. (v.l. for *-bhagna*).

व्याभ्युक्षी *vy-âbhy-ukshī*, f. (√*uksh*; cf. *vy-âty-ukshī*) splashing about in water, bathing for pleasure, W.

व्याम *vy-āma*, m. (prob. for *vi-yāma*, q.v.; cf. *vy-āyāma*, *sam-āma*) the measure of the two extended arms (= 5 Aratnis), a fathom, AV.; ŚBr.; GṛŚrS. &c.; diagonal direction, AV.; disregard, disrespect (?), W.; smoke (?), L.; pl. N. of a class of deceased ancestors, VP.; Costus Speciosus or Arabicus, VarBṛS. **–mātra**, mf(*ī*)n. measuring a fathom, ŚBr.

Vyāmana, n. a fathom (= *vy-āma*), L.

Vyāmyá, mfn. going across, AV.

व्यामर्श *vy-ā-marśa*, m. (√*mṛiś*) rubbing out, erasure, W. (wrongly written *vy-ā-marsha*).

व्यामिश्र *vy-ā-miśra*, mfn. mixed together, blended (*e*, ind. 'when both cases are combined,' Pat. on Pāṇ. iii, 2, 111); manifold, of various kinds, MBh.; R. &c.; mingled with, accompanied by, provided with (instr. or comp.; *-tā*, f.), MBh.; Hariv.; Suśr. &c.; troubled, distracted, inattentive, MBh.

Vy-ā-mṛishṭa. See col. 2.

व्यामील् *vy-ā-√mīl* (only ind. p. *-mīlya*), to close and open the eyes, twinkle, Amar.

व्यामुच् *vy-ā-√muc*, P. *-muñcati*, to emit, discharge, Pañcar.

Vy-āmoka, m. release or freeing from, getting rid of, MW.

व्यामुह् *vy-ā-muh*, Ā. *-muhyate*, to become stupefied or bewildered, become confused in (loc.), Kād.: Caus. *-mohayati*, to stupefy, bewilder, confuse, infatuate, bewitch, MBh.

Vy-āmūḍha, mfn. entirely stupefied or confused or infatuated, Rājat.

Vy-āmoha, m. loss of consciousness, mental confusion, bewilderment, embarrassment, MBh.; Kāv. &c.; (ifc.) error or uncertainty regarding, Kāvyâd.; Kull.; ĀpŚr., Sch.; *-vidrāvaṇa*, n. 'removal of error,' N. of a phil. wk. **°āmohita**, mfn. (fr. Caus.) bewildered, infatuated, Pañcat.; *-citta*, mfn. confused or perplexed in mind, ib. **°āmohin**, mfn. (ifc.) perplexing, bewildering, Hāsy.

व्यामृष्ट *vy-ā-mṛishṭa*, mfn. (√*mṛij*) rubbed out or off, erased (*-tilaka*, mfn. having the Tilaka mark rubbed off), R.

व्यायम् *vy-ā-√yam*, P. Ā. *-yacchati*, *°te*, (P.) to pull or drag or draw asunder, extend, Lāṭy.; to sport or dally with (loc.), Suśr.; Ā. (P. only m. c.) to struggle or contend about (loc.), fight together, make efforts, strive, endeavour, TS.; Br.; MBh. &c.: Caus. *-yāmayati*, to cause to stretch out or struggle, make great effort or exertion, take exercise (ind. p. *-yāmya*, having taken exercise), Mn. vii, 216.

Vy-āyacchana. See *prāṇa-vy°*.

Vy-āyata, mfn. drawn asunder, separated (in *a-vy°*), RPrāt.; opened, expanded (see comp.); long, wide, distant, far (see comp.); hard, firm, strong, R.; Kām. &c.; excessive, intense (see comp.; *am*, ind. excessively, in a high degree, R.); occupied, busy (= *vyāpṛita*), L.; *-tā*, f. the being open, openness, gaping (of the mouth), Mṛicch., Sch.; *-tva*, n. firmness, strength, Śak.; *-pātam*, ind. while flying from afar, Kum.; *-pātin*, mfn. running far and wide (as horses), Prab.

Vy-āyāmá, m. dragging different ways, contest, strife, struggle, AV.; MBh.; exertion, manly effort, athletic or gymnastic exercise (e.g. 'playing with heavy clubs,' 'drawing a bow with a chain' &c.), MBh.; Kāv. &c.; (ifc.) exercise or practise in, MBh.; R.; Suśr.; (with Buddhists) right exercise or training, MWB. 44 (cf. Dharmas. 119); 'drawing out, extending,' a partic. measure of length, fathom (= *vi-yāma* and *vy-āma*), Śulbas.; a difficult passage, any difficulty (?), L.; *-karśita*, mfn. emaciated through bodily exercise, MBh.; *-kalaha*, m. du. contest and strife, ib.; *-prayoga*, m. N. of wk.; *-bhūmi*, f. exercising ground, gymnasium, Kām.; *-vat*, mfn. taking bodily exercise, g. *balâdi*; *-vid*, mfn. skilled in gymnastics, Rājat.; *-vidyā*, f. the science of g°, ib.; *-śālā*, f. an exercising hall, Kād.; *-śīla*, mfn. accustomed to or fond of exercise, active, robust, athletic, W. **°āyāmika**, mf(*ī*)n. relating to exercise, active, athletic, BhP., Sch. **°āyāmin**, mfn. = *āyāma-vat*, VarBṛS.; Vāgbh.

व्यायुक *vy-ā́yuka*, mfn. (√5. *i*) running away, escaping, MaitrS.; Kapishṭh.

व्यायुज् *vy-ā-√yuj* (only ind. p. *-yujya*), to disjoin or separate, MārkP.

Vy-āyoga, m. a kind of dramatic representation or composition in one act (belonging to the Prakaraṇa class, and describing some military or heroic exploit from which the sentiment of love is excluded), Bhar.; Daśar. &c.

Vyā-yojima, mfn. separated, loose (applied to a faulty bandage), Suśr.

व्यारब्ध *vy-ā-rabdha*, mfn. (√*rabh*) held on every side, properly upheld or maintained, AitBr.

व्यारोष *vy-ā-rosha*, m. (√*rush*) anger, wrath, L.

व्यार्त *vy-ārta*, mfn. (√*ṛi*) pained, distressed, Divyâv.

व्याल *vyāla*, mfn. (prob. connected with *vyāḍa*, q.v.) mischievous, wicked, vicious, AV.; Kāv.; Kathās.; prodigal, extravagant, L.; m. (ifc. f. *ā*) a vicious elephant, Kāv.; a beast of prey, Gaut.; MBh. &c.; a snake, MBh.; Kāv. &c.; a lion, L.; a tiger, L.; a hunting leopard, L.; a prince, king, L.; Plumbago Ceylanica, L.; the second *dṛikāṇa* (q.v.) in Cancer, the first in Scorpio, and the third in Pisces, VarBṛS.; a kind of metre, Col.; N. of the number 'eight,' Gaṇit.; N. of a man (cf. *vyāḍa*), Cat.; (*ī*), f. a female snake, MBh.; R. &c.; n. N. of one of the three retrograde stages in the motion of the planet Mars, VarBṛS. **–kara-ja** (Npr.) or **-khaḍga** (L.), m. = *-nakha*. **–gandhā**, f. the ichneumon plant, L. **–grāha**, m. a snake-catcher, Mn.; MBh. **–grāhin**, m. id., Hit.; Mudr. (in Prākṛit) &c.; (*iṇī*), f. a female snake-c°, Kāśikh. **–grīva**, m. pl. N. of a people, VarBṛS. **–jihvā**, f. a kind of plant, L. **–tama**, mf(*ā*)n. very fierce or cruel, W. **–tva**, n. the state of a vicious elephant, Mudr. **–danshṭra** (L.) or **°ṭraka** (Dhanv.), m. Asteracantha Longifolia or Tribulus Lanuginosus. **–dreshkāṇa**, m. the second *dṛikāṇa* (q.v.) in Cancer &c. (= *vyāla*), VarBṛS., Sch. **–nakha**, m. a kind of herb (Unguis Odoratus), L. **–pattrā**, f. Cucumis Utilissimus, L. **–pāṇi-ja**, m. or **-praharaṇa**, n. = *-nakha*, Npr. **–bala**, m. id., MW. **–mṛiga**, m. a fierce animal, W.; a beast of prey, MBh.; R.; VarBṛS.; a partic. beast of prey, MBh. (a hunting leopard, MW.) **–rūpa**, m. N. of Śiva, ib. **–1. -vat**, mfn. inhabited by beasts of prey or by snakes, Hcat. **–2. -vat**, ind. like a serpent; like a b° of pr°, MW. **–varga**, m. (either = *vyāla*) the second *dṛikāṇa* (q.v.) in Cancer &c., (or) the two first in Cancer and in Scorpio and the third in Pisces, VarBṛ. (Sch.) **–vala**, m. = *-nakha*, L. **–śikshā**, f. N. of wk.

Vyālâyudha, m. (!) n. = *vyāla-nakha*, L.

Vyālaka, m. a vicious elephant, L.; a beast of prey, or a serpent, MBh.

Vyālī, in comp. for *vyāla*. **–bhūta**, mfn. become or being a snake, MBh.

Vyālīya, Nom. P. *°yati*, to be like a snake, Vās., Introd.

व्यालम्ब् *vy-ā-√lamb*, Ā. *-lambate*, to hang down, Megh.; to hang down on all sides, Hcar.

Vy-ālamba, mfn. hanging down, pendent, VarBṛS.; *-hasta*, mfn. (an elephant) having its trunk hanging down, MBh.; m. the red Ricinus or castor-oil plant, L. **°ālambin**, mfn. hanging down, pendulous, MBh.; Kāv. &c.

व्यालि *vyāli*. See *vyāḍi*.

व्यालिख् *vy-ā-√likh*, P. *-likhati*, to scratch at or upon, scrape against, touch, graze, Kir.; to draw lines, write, Cat.

व्यालीन *vy-ā-līna*, mfn. (√*lī*) clinging or sticking close together, clustering, dense, thick, W.

व्यालुप् *vy-ā-√lup*, P. *-lumpati*, to take away, remove, Megh.: Pass. *-lupyate*, to be broken asunder or destroyed or removed, disappear, MBh.

व्यालून *vy-ā-lūna*, mfn. (√*lū*) cut off, Hariv. 9539 (v.l. for *nyālūna*).

व्यालोडित *vy-ā-loḍita*, mfn. (fr. Caus. of √*luḍ*) = *mathita*, L. (*vy-ā-loḍayat*, Hariv. 9091, w.r. for *vy-a-loḍayat*; see *vi-√luḍ*).

व्यालोल *vy-ā-lola*, mfn. (√*lul*) rolling about, quivering, tremulous, shaking, waving, Kāv.; Kathās. &c.; *-kuntala-kalāpa-vat*, mfn. having dishevelled locks of hair, Caurap. **°ālolana**, n. moving to and fro, Veṇis.

व्याळि *vyāḷi*. See *vyāḍi*, p. 1036, col. 3.

व्यावकलन *vy-âva-kalana*, *°lita* = *vy-ava-k°*, W.

व्यावक्रोशी *vy-âva-krośī*, f. (√*kruś*) mutual abuse or vituperation or imprecation, Hcar. (cf. Pāṇ. iii, 3, 43, Sch.)

व्यावचर्ची *vy-âva-carcī*, f. (√*car*) mutual or general repetition, Pāṇ. iii, 3, 43, Vārtt. 3.

व्यावचोरी *vy-âva-corī*, f. (√*cur*) mutual or common theft, ib.

व्यावप् *vy-ā-√vap*, only in pr. Subj. *-vapāti*, w.r. in Pāṇ. iii, 1, 34, Sch. (Kāś. and TS. *cyāvayāti*).

व्यावभाषी *vy-âva-bhāshī*, f. (√*bhāsh*) mutual or general abuse, L. (accord. to some also *vy-âva-bhāsī*).

व्यावर्ग *vy-āvarga*. See *vy-ā-√vṛij*.

व्यावर्ण् *vy-ā-√varṇ* (only ind. p. *-varṇya*), to enumerate, narrate in detail, Kathās.

व्यावर्त *vy-āvarta* &c. See below.

व्यावल्ग् *vy-ā-√valg*, P. *-valgati*, to jump about, bound or leap from one place to another, Bālar.; to gallop, Uttarar.; to quiver, throb, be agitated (as a bosom), Kuval. °**āvalgita**, mfn. rushing or sweeping along in gusts (as the east wind), MBh.

व्यावहारिक *vyāvahārika*, mf(ī)n. (fr. *vy-ava-hāra*) relating to common life or practice or action, practical, usual, current, actual, real (as opp. to 'ideal'), Mn.; MBh. &c.; (in phil.) practical existence (opp. to *pāramārthika*, 'real,' and *prātibhāsika*, 'illusory'), IW. 108; sociable, affable, Kām.; belonging to judicial procedure, judicial, legal, Mn. viii, 78; m. a counsellor, minister, official, R.; N. of a Buddhist school; n. business, commerce, trade, BhP. **-tva**, n. practicalness, the state of belonging to procedure or action, MW.; *-khaṇḍana*, n., *-khaṇḍana-sāra*, m. N. of wks.

Vyāvahārya, mfn. able, capable, not worn-out, MBh. (*a-śrānta*, Nīlak.)

व्यावहारी *vy-áva-hārī*, f. (√*hṛi* with *vi-ā-ava*) mutual taking, interchange of intercourse, Vop.

व्यावहासी *vy-áva-hāsī*, f. (√*has*) mutual or universal laughter, Bhaṭṭ. (cf. Pāṇ. iii, 3, 43, Sch.)

व्यावाध *vy-āvādha*. See *vy-ābādha*.

व्याविध *vy-ā-vidha*, mfn. of various kinds, MW.

व्याविश् *vy-ā-√viś*, P. *-viśati*, to enter, penetrate, pervade (acc. or loc.), RV.; ŚBr.

व्यावृ *vy-ā-√1. vṛi*, only pr. p. Ā. *-vriṇvāna*, hiding one's self, BhP. i, 11, 38 (B. *vy-ā-priṇvāna*, which accord. to Sch. = *vy-ā-priyamāṇa*).

2. Vy-āvṛita, mfn. (for 1. see p. 1028, col. 3) covered, screened, W.; removed, excepted, ib. (cf. *vy-āvṛitta*). °**āvṛiti**, f. covering, screening, W.; exclusion, ib. (cf. *vy-āvṛitti*). °**āvṛitya**, see *vy-ā-√vṛit*.

व्यावृ *vy-ā-√2. vṛi*, only 3. pl. impf. P. *vy-ávṛinvan*, 'they chose,' MBh. (B.) i, 4413 (C. *vy-avṛiṇvan*).

व्यावृज् *vy-ā-√vṛij* (only ind. p. *-vṛijya*), to exclude from (abl.), separate, divide, Br.

Vy-āvarga, m. a division, section, Lāṭy.

व्यावृत् *vy-ā-√vṛit*, Ā. *-vartate* (rarely P.), to become separated or singled out from (instr.), RV.; AV.; Br.; to become separate or distinct, be distinguished as or in some partic. form of, MaitrUp.; to turn or wind in different directions, divide (as a road), MBh.; to be dispersed (as an army), Hariv.; to be opened, Suśr.; to turn away from, part with, get rid of (instr. or abl.), Ragh.; Kathās.; to diverge from, be inconsistent with (abl.), Sarvad.; to go away, depart, Śāntiś.; to come back, return, Ratnâv.; Rājat.; to turn round, revolve, R.; to sink (as the sun), MBh.; to come to an understanding or settlement, AitBr.; to come to an end, cease, perish, disappear, MBh.; Hariv. &c.: Caus. *-vartayati* (Pass. *-vartyate*), to divide, separate from (instr. or abl.; ind. p. *-vartya*, 'with the exception of,' Bālar.), TBr. &c. &c.; to free from (instr.), MaitrS.; to turn about or round, MBh.; Kād.; to keep back, avert, R.; to throw about, strew, MBh.; to exchange, substitute one for another, Hariv.; to lay aside (the staff), R.; (with *anyathā*) to retract (a word), MBh.; to remove (pain or distress), Vikr.; to destroy or annul (an enemy or a rule), Ragh. xv, 7: Desid. *-vivṛitsate*, to wish or intend to liberate one's self from or get rid of (abl.), ŚBr.

Vy-āvarta, m. revolving, W.; encompassing, surrounding, ib.; separating, selecting, appointing, ib.; ruptured navel (= *nābhi-kaṇṭaka*), L. °**āvartaka**, mf(*ikā*)n. separating, removing, excluding, excepting (*-tā*, f., *-tva*, n.), Śāntiś.; Tarkas.; Vedāntas. &c.; distinguishing, distinctive, MW.; turning away from, ib.; encircling, encompassing, ib. °**āvártana**, mf(ī)n. averting, removing (cf. *vigraha-vyāvartanī*); excluding, Śaṃk.; n. turn (of a road), AV.; ChUp.; coil (of a snake), Kir.; turning away, Sāh.; turning round, revolving, encompassing, surrounding, W. °**āvartanīya**, mfn. to be taken back (see *a-vyāvart*°). °**āvartita**, mfn. (fr. Caus.) made to turn away, made to desist, made to revolve, MW.; exchanged, ib. °**āvartya**, mfn. to be removed or excluded or excepted, Kusum.

Vy-āvivṛitsu, mfn. (fr. Desid.) wishing to get rid of (abl. or comp.), Sāy.

Vy-āvṛit, f. distinction, superiority, pre-eminence over (gen. or instr.), TS.; TBr.; Kāṭh.; cessation, TBr. **-kāma** (°*vṛit-*), mfn. desirous of superiority, TS.

Vy-ávṛitta, mfn. turned away from, freed from, rid of (instr., abl., or comp.), AV.; MaitrS.; Kālid. &c.; split asunder, opened, Hariv.; Suśr.; (ifc.) different from, Kap.; averted, R.; Kathās.; distorted, ShaḍvBr.; turned back, returned from (abl.), Campak.; (ifc.) incompatible or inconsistent with, Bhāshāp.; thoroughly liberated or emancipated (as the soul), Kap.; ceased, disappeared, gone, Kum.; 'chosen' or 'fenced' (= *vṛita*), L.; excepted, excluded, W.; praised, hymned(?), ib.; *-kautūhala*, mfn. one whose interest is diverted from (comp.), Vikr.; *-gati*, mfn. one whose movement has ceased, abated, subsided, lulled (as wind), Kum.; *-cetas*, mfn. one whose mind is turned away from (abl.), Kathās.; *-tva*, n. the being separated or excluded from, inconsistency or incompatibility with (comp.), Sāh.; (in phil.) the being separated from, the being non-extensive (= *alpa-deśa-vṛittitvam*, 'existing in few places,' i. e. 'comprising but few individuals,' said of a species, and opp. to *adhika-d°-vṛ°*, 'existing in many places,' said of a genus), MW.; *-deha*, mfn. having the body split or burst asunder (said of a mountain), Hariv.; *-buddhi*, f. 'limited conception,' the conception of a class containing few individuals (or of a class comprised in a higher class), MW.; *-śiras*, mfn. having the head turned round, R.; *-sarvêndriyârtha*, mfn. turned away from all objects of sense, indifferent to all worldly matters, Pañcat.; °*ttâtman*, mfn. = °*tta-cetas*, Ragh.; °*ttêndriya*, mfn. (ifc.) having the senses averted from, MaitrUp., Sch. °**ávṛitti**, f. turning away, turning the back (see *a-vyāvṛ°*); rolling (the eyes), Suśr.; deliverance from, getting rid of (abl.), TS.; Śāntiś.; being deprived of, separation or exclusion from, Śaṃk.; exclusion, rejection, removal, Kum.; Kāvyâd.; Sāh. (cf. *paras-para-vy°*); discrimination, distinction, TS.; ŚBr.; distinctness (of sound or voice), Kāṭh.; difference, AitBr.; Nyāyas., Sch.; cessation, end, ĀpŚr.; a kind of sacrifice, ŚBr.; screening (prob. for *vy-āvṛiti*), ib.; praise, eulogium(?), ib.; *-tva*, n., see under *vy-āvṛitta*. °**āvṛitsu**, w.r. for *vy-āvivṛitsu*.

व्याव्यध् *vy-ā-√vyadh*, P. *-vidhyati*, to throw or wave about, brandish, MBh.; R.

Vy-āviddha, mfn. thrown or tossed about, whirling round, Mṛicch.; displaced, distorted, MBh.; R.; Daś.; Suśr. (*am*, ind., Car.); interlaced, entwined, MW.

व्याशा *vy-āśā*. See p. 1028, col. 3.

व्याश्रय *2. vy-ā-śraya*, m. (for 1. see p. 1028, col. 3) assistance, taking the party of any one, Pāṇ. v, 4, 48.

व्यास *vy-āsa* &c. See p. 1035, col. 2.

व्यासञ्ज् *vy-ā-√sañj* (only 3. du. impf. Ā. *vy-â-sajetām*; and ind. p. *-sajya*), to adhere separately or severally (see comp.); to begin to fight hand to hand, Śiś. xviii, 12.

Vy-āsakta, mfn. attached, fastened or adhering or clinging to, fixed on (loc. or comp.), Kāv.; Kathās.; devoted to, dependent on, connected with, engaged in, occupied with (loc. or comp.), MBh.; Kāv. &c.; clasped, embraced, Amar.; detached, disjoined (in this sense *vi* is privative), W.; bewildered, confused, ib.

Vy-āsaṅga, m. excessive attachment, close adherence, Bhartṛ.; Mālatīm.; devotion or addiction to, wish or desire of, longing or passion for (loc. or comp.), MBh.; Kāv. &c.; connection, Kusum.; addition, W.; detachment, separation (in this and the next senses *vi* is privative), W.; separate attention, distraction (of thought), Nyāyas. °**āsaṅgin**, mfn. attaching one's self or applying closely to anything, MW.

Vy-āsajya, ind. having firmly attached or fastened on, having adhered or inhered separately or severally, MW.; *-ceta*, mfn. attached (in mind) to, Divyâv.; *-vṛitti*, mfn. inhering in more subjects than one (as a quality &c.), MW.

व्यासिच् *vy-ā-√sic*, P. *-siñcati*, to distribute in pouring out, ĀśvŚr.

Vy-āseka, m.(?), Mahāvy.

व्यासिध् *vy-ā-√2. sidh*, P. *-sedhati* (inf. *-seddhum*), to keep off, prevent, Śiś.

Vy-āsiddha, mfn. prohibited, forbidden (as contraband), Yājñ.

Vy-āsedha, m. prohibition, hindrance, interruption (loc. with √*vṛit*, to annoy, be troublesome), VP.

व्यासुकि *vyāsuki*, m. (prob.) patr. of Vyāḍi, Cat.

व्यासृ *vy-ā-√sṛi*, P. *-sarati*, to run through or over (acc.), RV. ix, 3, 8.

व्यासृज् *vy-ā-√sṛij*, only in *vy-âsṛijetām*, v.l. or w.r. for *vy-âsajetām* (see *vy-ā-√sañj*).

व्यास्था *vy-ā-√sthā*, Caus. *-sthāpayati*, to send away in different directions, TBr.

व्याहन् *vy-ā-√han*, P. *-hanti*, to strike at excessively, strike back, repel, Vas.; BhP.; to impede, obstruct, fail, disappoint, Kāv.; Sāh.; Suśr.: Caus. *-ghātayati*, to repel, obstruct, MBh.

Vy-āghāta &c. See p. 1036, col. 1.

Vy-āhata, mfn. struck at, hit, R.; obstructed, impeded, repelled, disappointed, MBh.; Kāv. &c.; conflicting with, contradictory, MBh.; Sarvad.; confused, alarmed, W.; *-tva*, n. contradictoriness, L. °**āhati**, f. contradiction (in logic), Kpr.

Vy-āhantavya, mfn. to be violated or transgressed, R.

व्याहनस्य *vy-āhanasya*. See p. 1028, col. 3.

व्याहाव *vy-āhāva*. See ib.

व्याहृ *vy-ā-√hṛi*, P. Ā. *-harati*, °*te*, to utter or pronounce a sound, speak, say to (acc.), converse with (*saha*), name (with *nāmabhis*, to call by name; with *praśnān*, to answer questions; with *udāharāṇi*, to state examples), TBr. &c. &c.; to begin to talk (said of a child), MBh.; to confess, avow to (gen.), ib.; to utter inarticulate sounds, cry, scream (said of animals), KātyŚr.; to sport, enjoy one's self (exceptionally for *vi-√hṛi*), BhP.; to cut off, sever, MBh. vi, 2757 (B. *vi-√hṛi*): Desid. *-jihīrshati*, to wish to pronounce or utter, ŚBr.

Vy-āharaṇa, n. the act of uttering or pronouncing, utterance, speech (*mama °ṇāt*, 'because I say so'), MBh.; BhP.

Vy-āhartavya, mfn. to be uttered or told or said to (loc.), MBh.

Vy-āhāra, m. utterance, language, speech, discourse, conversation, talk about (comp.), Kāv.; Pañcat.; Sāh.; song (of birds), Hariv.; Mālav.; (in dram.) a jest, joke, humorous speech, Bhar.; Daśar. &c.; *-maya*, mf(ī)n. consisting of speech or talk about (comp.), Kathās.

Vyāhārin, mfn. speaking, saying, Lāṭy.; MBh.; singing (as a bird), Hariv.; resounding with, Prab.

Vy-áhṛita, mfn. spoken, uttered, said, told, declared, stated, VS. &c. &c.; one who has uttered a sound, R.; eaten, devoured, Jātakam.; n. speaking, talking, conversation, Kāv.; BhP.; information, instruction, direction, Pāṇ. v, 4, 35; inarticulate speech or song (of animals and birds), MBh.; Hariv.; *-saṃdeśa*, mfn. one who tells news or communicates information, MW.

Vy-áhṛiti, f. utterance, speech, declaration, statement, MBh.; Kālid.; VarBṛS.; (also °*tī*; ifc. °*tikā*), the mystical utterance of the names of the seven worlds (viz. *bhūr*, *bhuvar* [or *bhuvaḥ*], *svar*, *mahar*, *janar*, *tapar*, *satya* [qq. vv.], the first three of which, called 'the great Vyāhṛitis,' are pronounced after *om* by every Brāhman in commencing his daily prayers and are personified as the daughters of Savitṛi and Pṛiśni), TS.; Br.; RTL. 403; Mn. ii, 76; MBh. &c.; N. of a Sāman, ĀrshBr.; *-traya*, n. the first three of the above mystical words, MW.; *-pūrvaka*, mfn. preceded by the above three mystical words, ib.

व्याहृति *vyāhruti*, w.r. for *vy-āhṛiti*.

व्याह्वे *vy-ā-√hve*, Ā. *-hvayate* (ind. p. *-hāvam*), to separate by inserting the Āhāva or invocation (see *2. ā-hāva*), AitBr.; ĀśvŚr.

Vy-āhāva. See p. 1028, col. 3.

व्यु *vy-√u*, P. *-unoti*, to urge on, incite, animate, RV. v, 31, 1.

व्युक्ष् *vy-√uksh*, P. Ā. *-ukshati*, °*te*, (P.) to sprinkle, pour out, ŚBr.; (Ā.) to besprinkle, wet, RV. x, 90, 3.

व्युच्चर् *vy-uc-car* (*-ud-√car*), P. Ā. *-carati*, °*te*, to go forth in different directions, ŚBr.; to go out of the right path, transgress or offend against, be faithless or disloyal towards (acc.), MBh.; to commit adultery with (instr.), ib.

व्युच्छत् *vy-ucchat* &c. See *vi-√2. vas*.

व्युच्छिद् *vy-uc-chid* (*-ud-√chid*), only Pass. (with act. terminations) *-chidyati*, to be cut off or interrupted or extirpated, become extinct, come to an end, cease, fail, MBh.

Vy-ucchitti, f. cutting off or short, interruption, disturbance, MBh.; MārkP. °**ucchinna**, mfn. cut off, extirpated, destroyed, interrupted, ceased, MBh.; Kāv. &c. °**ucchettṛi**, mfn. who or what cuts off or destroys (see *a-vyucchettṛi*). °**uccheda**, m. = °*ucchitti*, HPariś.

व्युच्य *vy-úcya*, mfn. (√*vac*) to be contradicted or contested (n. impers.), TāṇḍBr.

व्युत *vy-ùta*, mfn. (√*ve*) interwoven, woven, variegated (as a garment), RV.; ŚBr.; levelled (as a road), RV. iii, 54, 9. °**uti**, f. weaving, sewing, L. °**ūta**, mfn. = °*uta*, HPariś.; KātyŚr., Sch. °**ūti**, f. = °*uti*, L.

व्युत्क्रम् *vy-ut-√kram*, P. *-krāmati*, to go apart or in different directions, AitBr.; ŚBr.; to overstep, transgress, neglect, Ragh.; to go astray, MW.

Vy-utkrama, m. going astray or out of the right course, inverted order, Sāṇḍ.; Vedântas.; transgression, offence, VarBṛS.; BhP.; dying, death, L. °**utkramaṇa**, n. going apart, separation, Pāṇ. viii, 1, 15.

Vy-utkrānta, mfn. gone apart or in different directions &c. (pl. with *dvaṃdvam* = 'paired off'), Pāṇ. ib., Sch.; gone away, departed, removed, ceased (see comp.); transgressed, disregarded, ib.; (*ā*), f. (scil. *prahelikā*) a kind of riddle, Kāvyâd.; *-jīvita*, mfn. one whose life has departed, lifeless, dead, Daś.; *-dharma*, mfn. neglectful of duty, MBh.; *-rajas*, mfn. one whose impurity is removed, free from passion, ib.; *-vartman*, mfn. one who has gone beyond the right path, Bhaṭṭ.; °*taka-samāpatti*, f. a partic. stage of concentration, Buddh.

व्युत्तॄ *vy-ut-√tṝi*, Caus. *-tārayati*, to pour out in different directions, MānŚr.

व्युत्त्रस् *vy-ut-√tras*, Caus. *-trāsayati*, to scare or frighten away, disperse, ĀpŚr.

व्युत्था *vy-ut-thā* (*-ud-√sthā*), P. Ā. *-tishṭhati*, °*te*, to rise in different directions (as light), RV.; to turn away from (abl.), give up, abandon, ŚBr.; to swerve from duty, forget one's self, MBh.; R.; to come back (from sea, cf. *vy-ut-√pad*), Divyâv.: Caus. *-thāpayati*, to cause to rise up &c.; to call in question, disagree about (acc.), MBh.; to seduce, win over, ib.; to set aside, remove, depose (from a place), Kathās.; to abandon treacherously, ib.

Vy-utthātavya, n. (impers.) it is to be desisted from (abl.), Śaṃk.

Vy-utthāna, n. rising up, awakening (a partic. stage in Yoga), Vedântas.; yielding, giving way (in *a-vy*°), MBh.; swerving from the right course, neglect of duties, ib.; opposition, L.; independent action, L.; a kind of dancing or gesticulation, MW. °**utthāpita**, mfn. (fr. Caus.) made to rise up, roused, brought up, ib.

Vy-utthita, mfn. greatly divergent in opinion, MBh.; strongly excited or agitated (see comp.); swerving from duty (with or scil. *dharmāt*), Hariv.; Sarvad.; *-citta*, mfn. strongly excited in mind, Sarvad.; °*ttâśva*, m. N. of a prince, VP.; °*ttendriya*, mfn. greatly agitated in the senses or feelings, Hariv.

व्युत्पद् *vy-ut-√pad*, Ā. *-padyate* (aor. *vy-ud-apādi*), to proceed from, arise, originate, have origin or derivation (esp. in gram.), be derived (from a root &c.), Śiś. x. 23; (P.) to come back (from sea, cf. *vy-utthā*), Divyâv.; to resist (?), ib.: Caus. *-pādayati*, to cause to arise or come forth, produce, cause, BhP.; (in gram.) to derive, trace back to a root &c., Śaṃk.; to discuss in detail, Hcar.: Desid., see *vy-utpitsu*, col. 2.

Vy-utpatti, f. production, origin, derivation (esp. in gram.), etymology, Nyāyam.; Sāh.; Vop.; development, perfection, growth (esp. in knowledge), proficiency (esp. in literature or science), comprehensive learning or scholarship, Nyāyam.; Kap.; Bālar. &c.; difference of tone or sound (fr. 3. *vi* denoting variation), VarBṛS.; *-dīpikā*, f. N. of a wk. (also called *prākṛita-prakriyā-vṛitti*); *-pakshe*, ind. on the side of derivation or etymology (an expression used by Vedic commentators when the accentuation is settled by the affixes and not accord. to the meanings of the words); *-mat*, mfn. learned, cultured, Śaṃk.; *-ratnâkara*, m., *-rahasya*, n. N. of wks.; *-rahita*, mfn. destitute of (clear) derivation, not to be explained etymologically, Kusum.; *-vāda*, m., *-vāda-kroḍa-pattra*, n., *-vāda-ṭīkā*, f., *-vāda-pattra*, n., *vāda-paryāya-pattra*, n., *-vāda-rahasya*, n., *-vādârtha*, m. N. of wks.

Vy-utpanna, mfn. arisen, originated, derived (esp. in gram.), to be explained etymologically (see *a-vy*°); learned, accomplished, experienced, versed in (instr.), Bhartṛ.; BhP.; Nyāyam., Sch.

Vy-utpādaka, mfn. (fr. Caus.) giving rise to, producing, productive, MW.; tracing back (a word to its root &c.), explaining etymologically, L. °**utpādana**, n. etymological explanation, derivation from (abl.), Madhus.; teaching, instruction, VarBṛS., Sch. °**utpādya**, mfn. capable of being traced back to its root, derivable, Sāṃkhyak.; to be explained or discussed, Nyāyam.

Vy-utpitsu, mfn. (fr. Desid.) desirous of making proficiency (in any science), MW.

व्युत्सद् *vy-ut-√sad*, P. *-sīdati*, to go out or away, AitBr.; to be unsettled, MW.; to be upset or overthrown, ib.

व्युत्सिच् *vy-ut-√sic*, P. *-siñcati*, to pour out or sprinkle in different directions, ĀpŚr.

Vy-utseka, m. pouring out in different directions, ĀpŚr., Sch.

व्युत्सृज् *vy-ut-√sṛij*, P. *-sṛijati*, to give away, give up, leave, abandon, ĀpŚr.; BhP.

Vy-utsarga, m. renunciation, resignation, HYog.

व्युत्सृप् *vy-ut-√sṛip*, P. *-sarpati*, to go out (of a place), AitBr.

व्युद् *vy-√ud* (or *und*), P. *-unatti*, to spring or gush forth, RV.; to sprinkle thoroughly, wet, drench, ib.; AV.

Vy-ùtta, mfn. well sprinkled or wetted, drenched, TS.

Vy-úndana, n. the act of well moistening or wetting, VS.

व्युदस् *vy-ud-√2. as*, P. *-asyati*, to throw about, scatter, Kauś.; MBh.; to discharge, emit, Gaut.; to cast off, reject, give up, abandon, MBh.; Kāv. &c.

Vy-udasta, mfn. thrown or scattered about, cast off, thrown aside, MBh.; Kāv. &c.

Vy-udāsa, m. throwing away, giving up, abandonment, MBh.; rejection, exclusion, Sāh.; Kull.; disregard for, indifference to, W.; destruction (of an enemy), Śiś. xv, 37; cessation, end, Nalôd.

व्युदित *vy-udita*, mfn. (√*vad*) disputed, debated, discussed, contested, ŚāṅkhBr.

व्युदूह् *vy-ud-√1. ūh*, P. *-ūhati* (Pot. *-uhyāt*), to push apart or asunder, move away or out, TS.; to sweep out or away, ŚBr.; KātyŚr.

व्युद्ग्रन्थन *vy-ud-granthana*, n. (√*grath*) binding up with several strings, KātyŚr.

व्युद्धाव् *vy-ud-√2. dhāv*, Caus. *-dhāvayati*, to cause to be rubbed off or polished or cleansed, Lāṭy.

व्युद्धृ *vy-uddhṛi* (*-ud-√hṛi*), P. *-harati* (ind. p. *-uddhāram*), to distribute in drawing up or taking out, TS.; ŚrS.; Nyāyam.; to extract, draw out of (abl.), BhP.

व्युन्मिश्र *vy-un-miśra*, mfn. intermingled or mixed with, soiled or adulterated with (instr.), MBh. (v. l. *vi-miśra*).

व्युप *vyupa* (?), m. one who eats out of his own hands, L.

व्युपकार *vy-upa-kāra*, m. (√*1. kṛi*) completely observing or accomplishing or satisfying (duty &c.), R.

व्युपजाप *vy-upa-jāpa*, m. (√*jap*; less correct *vy-upa-jāva*) whispering aside or apart, telling in a whisper, Āpast.

व्युपतोद *vy-upa-toda*, m. (√*tud*) striking against, ib.

व्युपदेश *vy-upa-deśa*, m. (√*diś*) pretext, pretence, W. (prob. w. r. for *vy-apa-deśa*).

व्युपनी *vy-upa-√nī*, P. *-nayati*, to lead or bring (sacrificial victims) separately or one by one, ŚBr.

व्युपपत्ति *vy-upa-patti*, f. (√*pad*) re-birth, Divyâv.

व्युपयुज् *vy-upa-√yuj*, Ā. *-yuṅkte*, to be concerned about or intent upon (acc.), MBh. v, 992 (v.l.)

व्युपरम् *vy-upa-√ram*, Ā. *-ramate* (ep. also °*ti*; ind. p. *-ramam*; in augmented forms not separable from *vy-upâ-√ram* below), to leave off or pause variously, ĀśvŚr.; to come to an end, cease, MBh.; Hariv.; to desist from (abl.), MBh.

Vy-uparata, mfn. rested, stopped, ceased, desisted, MBh.; Mṛicch.

Vy-uparama, m. pause, cessation, interruption, MBh.; Hariv.; Kāv.; end, close (of day), Hariv.; (*am*), ind., see *vy-upa-√ram* above.

व्युपविश् *vy-upa-√viś*, P. *-viśati*, to sit down at different places, ŚBr.

व्युपवीत *vy-upavīta*. See p. 1029, col. 1.

व्युपशम् *vy-upa-√śam*, P. *-śāmyati* (ep. also °*te*), to become quiet, be allayed, cease, MBh.

2. **Vy-upaśama**, m. (for 1. see p. 1029, col. 1) cessation, end, Mālatīm. (v. l. for *vy-uparama*), Sāh.; relief, Divyâv.

Vy-upaśānta, mfn. calmed, allayed, ceased (as pain), Kāraṇḍ.; desisting, Divyâv.

व्युपारम् *vy-upâ-√ram*, P. *-ramati*, to desist from, leave off, cease, Hariv. (cf. *vy-upa-√ram* above).

व्युपास् *vy-upâs* (*-upa-√2. as*), P. *-upâsyati*, to throw about, distribute, ŚBr.

व्युपे *vy-upé* (*-upa-√3. i*), P. *-upâiti*, to extend or be distributed (intr.) in or over, Kath.

व्युप्त 1. *vy-ùpta*, mfn. (p.p. of *vi-√1. vap*) shaved, shorn; *-keśa*, mfn. one whose hair is shorn, MaitrS.

व्युप्त 2. *vy-upta*, mfn. (p.p. of *vi-√2. vap*) scattered about, disordered, dishevelled; *-keśa*, mfn. having dishevelled hair, BhP.; m. N. of Rudra and of Fire (as identified with R°), MW.; *-jaṭā-kalāpa*, mfn. having a dishevelled mass of hair, BhP.

व्युब्ज् *vy-√ubj*, P. *-ubjati*, to uncover, open, display, AV.

व्युष् 1. *vyush* (also read *pyush*), cl. 4. P. *vyushati*, to burn (in this sense perhaps = *vy-√1. ush*), Dhātup. xxvi, 7; to divide, distribute (in this sense also written *pyus*, *push*, *byus*, *bus*), ib. 108; cl. 10. P. *vyoshayati*, to reject, discharge, emit (in this sense also written *pus*), ib. xxxii, 92.

1. **Vyushṭa**, mfn. (perhaps rather *vy-ushṭa*, fr. √*1. ush*; cf. above) burnt, W.

Vyosha. See s. v.

व्युष् 2. *vy-úsh*, f. (fr. *vi-√2. vas*) dawn, daybreak, AV. xiii, 3, 21 (loc. *vy-ùshi*, as inf., RV. v, 35, 8 &c.; cf. also *ā-vyusham* and *upa-vyushám*).

Vy-ushasa. See *upa-vyushasam*.

1. **Vy-ushita**, n. daybreak (only in loc.), ŚāṅkhŚr.

2. **Vy-ùshṭa**, mfn. dawned, become daylight, grown bright or clear, ŚBr.; MBh. &c.; n. daybreak, L.; fruit, result (= *phala*), L.; m. Daybreak personified (as a son of Kalpa, or as a son of Pushpârṇa and Doshā, or as a son of Vibhā-vasu and Ushas), BhP.; *-trirātra*, m., g. *yuktârohy-ādi*, Kāś. (v. l. *vyushṭi-tr*°).

1. **Vy-ùshṭi**, f. the first gleam or breaking of dawn, daybreak, RV.; AV.; Br.; consequence, fruit, reward for (gen., loc., or comp.), requital (of good or evil), MBh.; Kāv. &c.; grace, beauty, ChUp. iii, 13, 4; increase, prosperity, felicity, W.; a hymn, praise (= *stuti*), L.; N. of partic. bricks, ĀpŚr.; of

a partic. Dvi-rātra, ib.; *-tri-rātra*, m., g. *yuktârohy-ādi* (cf. *vyushṭa-tr°*); *-mat*, mfn. bringing reward, MBh.; endowed with grace or beauty, ChUp.

व्युषित 2. *vy-ushita*, mfn. (fr. *vi-√5. vas*; for 1. see p. 1040, col. 3) absent from home, BhP.; 'one who has passed (e.g. *rātrim*, a night),' MBh. (n. impers.); inhabited by (comp.), R.; *°lâśva*, m. N. of a king descended from Daśa-ratha, MBh.; Hariv.

3. **Vy-ushṭa,** mfn. one who has passed or spent (*rajanīm*, a night), MBh. (= *pary-ushita*, L.)

2. **Vy-ushṭi,** f. taking food only every eighth day, L. (cf. *upa-√5. vas*).

व्यूक *vyūka*, m. N. of a people, MBh.

व्यूत *vy-ūta*, *vy-ūti.* See *vy-uta*, p. 1040, col. 1.

व्यूर्णु *vy-√ūrṇu* (cf. *vi-√1. vṛi*), P. Ā. *-ūr-ṇoti*, *-ūrṇute*, to uncover, open, display, RV.

व्यूह *vy-√1. ūh*, P. *-ūhati* (ep. also *°te*, impf. *avyūhata*, *°hanta* as if fr. a *√vyūh*), to push or move apart, place asunder, divide, distribute, TS.; ŚBr.; ŚrS.; ĪśUp.; to arrange, place in order, draw up in battle-array, Mn.; MBh. &c.; to shift, transpose, alter, AitBr.; ŚBr.; ĀśvŚr.; to separate, resolve (vowels, Saṃdhi &c.), RPrāt.

2. **Vy-ūḍha** or **vy-ūḷha** (for 1. *vy-ūḍha* see p. 987, col. 3), mfn. pushed or moved apart, divided, distributed, arranged, Mn.; MBh. &c.; transposed, altered (see comp.); expanded, developed, wide, broad, large, MBh.; Kāv. &c.; compact, firm, solid, L.; = *-cchandas* below, TāṇḍBr., Sch.; *-kaṅkaṭa*, mfn. one who has arranged or put on armour, accoutred, mailed, L.; *-cchandas* (*vyūḍha-* or *vyūḷha-*), mfn. having the metres transposed, ŚBr.; AitBr.; *-jānu*, mfn. having the knees separated, ŚāṅkhGṛ; *-nava-rātra*, m.; *°ḍhâhīna-dvādaśâha-pariśishṭa*, n., *°ḍhâhīna-dvādaśâha-prayoga*, m. N. of wks.; *°ḍhoras*, mfn. = next (cf. *°ḍhôru*); *°ḍhoraska*, mfn. broad-chested, MBh.; R. &c. (cf. Pat. on Pāṇ. i, 3, 2); *°ḍhôru*, mfn. having thick thighs, MBh. (B. *°ḍhoras*).

Vy-ūḍhi, f. orderly arrangement or disposition, array, W.

1. **Vy-ūhá,** m. placing apart, distribution, arrangement, R.; VarBṛS. &c.; orderly arrangement of the parts of a whole (cf. *caraṇa-vy°*), disposition, Nyāyas.; military array, an army, host, squadron (various arrays are *daṇḍa-*, 'staff-like array;' *śakaṭa-*, 'cart array;' *varāha-*, 'boar array;' *maṇḍala-*, 'circular ar°;' *a-saṃhata-*, 'loose ar°;' *ākheṭa-vyūha*, 'hunting array' &c.), Mn. vii, 187; MBh. &c.; shifting, transposition, displacement, ŚBr.; ŚrS.; separation, resolution (of vowels, syllables &c.), RPrāt.; detailed explanation or description, SaddhP.; a section, division, chapter, Sarvad.; form, manifestation (esp. the quadruple manifestation of Purushôttama as Vāsudeva, Saṃkarshaṇa, Pradyumna, and Aniruddha), appearance (often ifc. after numerals, cf. *catur-*, *trir-vy°*), MBh.; BhP.; Sarvad.; formation, structure, manufacture, L.; an aggregate, flock, multitude, Vās.; Śatr.; the body, W.; breathing, Nyāyas.; *-pārshṇi*, m. or f., *prishṭha*, n. the rear of an army, L.; *-bhaṅga*, m., *-bheda*, m. the breaking of an array, throwing into disorder, W.; *-racanā*, f. arrangement of troops (*°nām vi-√dhā*, 'to assume a warlike attitude'), Pañcat.; *-1. -rāja*, m. the chief or best form of military array, MBh.; *°hântara*, m. a different arrangement or position, MW.

Vy-ūhaka (ifc.), form, manifestation (= 1. *vy-ūha*), AgP. **°ūhana,** mfn. pushing apart, separating, displacing (said of Śiva), Hariv. (= *jagat-kshobhaka*, Nīlak.); n. shifting, displacement, separate disposition, KātyŚr.; Suśr.; development (of the fetus), Yājñ.; arrangement, array (of an army), MW.

Vy-ūhita, mfn. arranged in order of battle, Hariv.; Pañcat.

Vyūhī-√kṛi, P. *-karoti*, to draw up in battle-array, Kām.

व्यूह *vy-√2. ūh*, Ā. *-ohate*, to forebode, perceive (accord. to others 'despise'), RV. ii, 23, 16.

2. **Vy-ūha,** m. reasoning, logic (= *tarka*), L.; *-mati*, m. N. of a Deva-putra, Lalit.; *-2. -rāja*, m. a partic. Samādhi, SaddhP.; N. of a Bodhi-sattva, ib. (*°jêndrā*, f. N. of a Kiṃ-narī, Kāraṇḍ.)

व्यृ *vy-√ṛi*, P. *-ṛiṇoti*, *-ṛiṇvati* (3. pl. *vy-ṛiṇvire*; pf. *vy-āra*), to open (intr.), go apart or asunder, RV.; to open (trans.), spread abroad, display, ib.

व्यृछ् *vy-√ṛich*, P. *-ṛicchati* (only impf. *vy-ārchat*), to go apart or asunder, ŚBr.

व्यृध् *vy-√ṛidh*, Pass. *-ṛidhyate*, to be unfortunate or unsuccessful, be excluded or deprived of (instr.), ŚBr.: Caus. *-ardhayati* (Pass. *-ardhyate*), to exclude from, deprive of (instr.), AitBr.; ŚBr.: Desid. *vīrtsati*, to wish to nullify or render vain, AV. (cf. *vīrtsā*, p. 1007, col. 1).

Vy-ṛiddha, mfn. unsuccessful, failed, miscarried, defective, imperfect, ŚBr.; Nir. (cf. *a-vy°*); sinful, criminal, Āpast.; *-bhāj*, mfn. receiving a defective oblation as a share, ib.

Vy-ṛiddhi, f. ill-luck, want of success, loss, failure, miscarriage, exclusion, VS.; AV.; Br.; Gaut.; want of prosperity, scarcity (of grain &c.), Pāṇ. ii, 1, 6.

व्यृष् *vy-√1. ṛish*, P. *-arshati*, to flow through (acc.), RV.

व्यृष् *vy-√2. ṛish*, P. *-ṛishati*, to pierce, penetrate, RV.

व्ये *vye*, cl. 1. P. Ā. (Dhātup. xxiii, 38) *vyáyati*, *°te* (pf. P. *vivyāya*, 2. sg. *vivyaythá*, Gr.; 2. du. *vivyathus*, RV.; Ā. *vivyé*, ib.; *-vyayām cakāra*, ŚBr.; aor. *avyat*, *avyata*, RV.; *avyāsīt*, *avyāsta*, Gr.; Prec. *vīyāt*, *vyāsīshṭa*, ib.; fut. *vyātā*, ib.; *vyāsyati*, *°te*, ib.; *vyayishye*, GṛŚrS.; ind. p. *-vīya*, Br. &c.; *-vāya*, Gr.), to cover, clothe, wrap, envelop (Ā. also 'one's self'), RV.; TS.; TBr.: Pass. *vīyáte* (pr. p. *vīyámāna*), to be covered &c., TS.: Caus. *vyāyayati*, Gr.: Desid. *vivyāsati*, *°te*, ib.; Intens. *vevīyate*, *vāvyeti*, *vāvyâti*, ib.

Vīta. See 3. *vīta*, p. 1004, col. 2.

व्येक *vy-eka*, *vy-enas* &c. See p. 1029, col. 1.

व्येमान *vy-emāna*, pr. p. of *vy-√am*, Kāś. on Pāṇ. vi, 4, 120.

व्योकार *vyo-kāra*, m. (prob.) 'making the sound *vyo*,' a blacksmith, Hcar.

व्योमन् 2. *vyòman*, m. (for 1. see p. 1029, col. 1; accord. to Uṇ. iv, 150 fr. *√vye*, accord. to others fr. *vi-√av* or *√ve*) heaven, sky, atmosphere, air (*vyomnā*, *vyoma-mārgeṇa* or *-vartmanā*, 'through the air'), RV. &c. &c.; space, Kap.; ether (as an element), Kāv.; Pur.; Suśr.; wind or air (of the body), BhP.; water, L.; talc, mica, L.; a temple sacred to the sun, L.; a partic. high number, L.; the 10th astrol. mansion, VarBṛS.; preservation, welfare, TS. (= *rakshaṇa*, Sch.); m. a partic. Ekâha, ŚrS.; N. of Prajā-pati or the Year (personified), TS.; VS. (Mahīdh.); of Vishṇu, Vishṇ.; of a son of Daśârha, Hariv.; Pur. (v.l. *vyoma*).

1. **Vyoma** (for 2. see col. 3), in comp. for 2. *vyoman*. **–keśa** (ŚatarUp.; MBh.) or **-keśin** (L.), m. 'sky-haired,' N. of Śiva. **–ga,** mfn. moving through the air, flying, Kathās.; m. a being that moves in the air, a divine being, Śiś. **–gaṅgā,** f. the heavenly Ganges, MBh.; Kāv. **–gamanī,** f. (with *vidyā*) the magic art of flying, Kathās. **–gāmin,** mfn. = *-ga*, ib. **–guṇa,** m. 'quality of the air,' sound, L. **–cara,** mfn. id., Kāv.; m. a planet, Gol. **–cārin,** mfn. = *-ga*, VarBṛS.; Kathās.; a bird, L.; a divine being, god, Rājat.; = *cira-jīvin* and *dvi-jāta* (prob. 'a bird'), L.; a saint, W.; a Brāhman, W.; a heavenly body, A.; (*°ri*)*-pura*, n. 'sky-floating city,' the city of Hari-ścandra (supposed to be suspended between heaven and earth), L. **–deva,** m. N. of Śiva, MW. **–dhāraṇa,** m. mercury, L. **–dhūma,** m. 'sky-smoke,' smoke or a cloud, L. **–dhvani,** m. a sound coming from the sky (*°ni-pati*), Hcat. (cf. *-śabda*). **–nāsikā,** f. a quail, L.; a sort of quail, W. **–pañcaka,** n. (prob.) the five apertures in the body, Cat. **–pāda,** mfn. one whose foot stands in the air (Vishṇu), Pañcar. **–pushpa,** n. a flower in the air (i.e. any impossibility or absurdity), HPariś. (cf. *kha-p°*). **–mañjara,** n. ('sky-cluster') or **-maṇḍala,** n. ('sky-circle') a flag, banner, L. **–madhye,** ind. in the middle of the sky, in mid-air, Vikr. **–māya,** mf(*ā*)n. 'sky-measuring,' reaching to the sky, high as the heaven, W. **–mudgara,** m. 'sky-hammer,' a gust of wind, L. **–mṛiga,** (prob.) m. N. of one of the Moon's ten horses, L. (cf. *vyomin*). **–yāna,** n. 'sky-vehicle,' a celestial car, chariot of the gods, Cat. **–ratna,** n. 'sky-jewel,' the sun, L. **–vatī,** f. N. of a Comm. **–vartman,** n. the path of the sky (*°manā*, through the air or sky), Kathās. **–vallikā,** f. Cassyta Filiformis, L. **–vistṛita,** n. the expanse of heaven, the sky, firmament, W. **–vyāpin,** mfn. filling the sky, Śiś. **–śabda,** m. = *-dhvani*, Hcat. **–śivâcārya,** m. N. of an author, Cat. **–sád,** mfn. dwelling in the sky, RV.; VS.; m. a deity, W.; a Gandharva, MW.; a spirit, W. **–sambhavā,** f. a spotted cow, L. **–sarit,** f. = *-gaṅgā*, Kathās. **–stha,** mfn. being on or in the sky, Śiś. **–sthalī,** f. 'ground of the sky,' the earth (?), L. **–spṛiś,** mfn. sky-touching, reaching to the sky, Śiś. **Vyomâkhya,** n. talc, mica, L.; original germ (= *mūla-kāraṇa*), L. **Vyomâdhipa,** m. 'lord of the heaven,' N. of Śiva, Hcat. **Vyomâbha,** m. 'heaven-like,' a Buddha, L. **Vyomâri,** m. N. of a being reckoned among the Viśve Devāḥ, MBh. **Vyomâikânta-vihārin,** mfn. moving exclusively in the air (as a bird), Pañcat. ii, 21 (v.l.). **Vyomôdaka,** n. 'sky-water,' rain-water, L.

2. **Vyoma,** m. (for 1. see col. 2) N. of a son of Daśârha, Pur. (v.l. for *vyoman*).

Vyomaka, (gender doubtful) a kind of ornament, Buddh.

Vyomin, m. N. of one of the Moon's ten horses, VP. (cf. *vyoma-mṛiga*).

Vyomnika. See *parama vy°*.

व्योष *vy-òsha*, mf(*ā*)n. (fr. *vi+√1. ush*; cf. *√vyush*) burning, scorching, AV.; m. a species of elephant, L.; n. the three hot substances (viz. dry ginger, long pepper, and black pepper), Suśr.

व्र *vrá*, m. (a formula of unknown meaning), AV. xi, 7, 3. For the form *vrā*, see p. 1043, col. 1.

व्रक्षस् *vrakshas*, w. r. for *vakshas*, Cat.

व्रज् *vraj*, cl. 1. P. (Dhātup. viii, 79) *vrájati* (m.c. also *°te*; pf. *vavrája*, RV. &c. &c.; aor. *avrājīt*, Br.; Up.; fut. *vrajitā*, Gr.; *vrajishyati*, Br. &c.; inf. *vrajitum*, MBh.; ind. p. *vrajitvā*, *-vrájya*, *-vrājam*, Br. &c.), to go, walk, proceed, travel, wander, move (also applied to inanimate objects; with acc. or instr. of the road, acc. of the distance, and acc., rarely loc. or dat., of the place or object gone to; with or scil. *padbhyām*, 'to go on foot;' with *upānadbhyām*, id., lit. 'with shoes;' with *dhuryais*, 'to travel by means of beasts of burden;' with *paramām gatim*, 'to attain supreme bliss;' with *śaraṇam* and acc., 'to take refuge with;' with *mūrdhnā pādau* and gen., 'to prostrate one's self at any one's feet;' with *antam* and gen., 'to come to the end of;' with *anyena*, *anyatra* or *anyatas*, 'to go another way or elsewhere;' with *adhas*, either 'to sink down [to hell]' or 'to be digested [as food];' with *punar*, 'to return to life'), RV. &c. &c.; to go in order to, be going to (dat., inf. or an adj. ending in *aka* [e.g. *bhojako vrajati*, 'he is going to eat']), Pāṇ. ii, 3, 15; iii, 3, 10 &c.; to go to (a woman), have sexual intercourse with (acc.), Mn.; Suśr.; to go against, attack (an enemy; also with *vidvisham*, *dvishato 'bhimukham*, *abhy-ari* &c.), Mn.; Yājñ.; Kām.; to go away, depart from (abl.), go abroad, retire, withdraw, pass away (as time), MBh.; Kāv. &c.; to undergo, go to any state or condition, obtain, attain to, become (esp. with acc. of an abstract noun, e.g. with *vināśam*, 'to go to destruction, become destroyed;' with *chattratām*, 'to become a pupil;' with *nirvṛitim*, 'to grow happy' [cf. *√gam*, *yā* &c.]; with *sukham*, 'to feel well;' with *jīvan*, 'to escape alive'), ib.: Caus. or cl. 10. P. (Dhātup. xxxii, 74) *vrājayati*, to send, drive, AitĀr.; to prepare, decorate, Dhātup.: Desid. *vivrajishati*, Gr.: Intens. *vāvrajyate*, *vāvrakti*, to go crookedly, Pāṇ. iii, 1, 23, Sch.

1. **Vraja,** m. (for 2. see p. 1042, col. 1) a way, road, L.; n. wandering, roaming, W.

Vrajaka, m. a wandering religious mendicant, L.

Vrájana, n. going, travelling (*anyatra*, 'elsewhere'), Pañcat. ii, 68; going into exile, ib. iii, 268 (v.l. *pra-vrajana*); a road, way, RV. vii, 3, 2; m. N. of a son of Aja-mīḍha and brother of Jahnu (considered as one of the ancestors of Kuśika), MBh.

Vrajitá, mfn. gone, proceeded (*anyena*, by another road), ŚBr.; n. going, roaming, W.

1. **Vrajyā,** f. (for 2. see next page, col. 1) travelling, wandering, gait, Nir.; Pāṇ.; Nyāyas., Sch.; march, attack, invasion, L.; N. of a poem by Kavicandra. **–mālā,** f. N. of a poem by Sarvânanda. **–vat,** mfn. having a graceful gait, Bhaṭṭ.; addicted to wandering or roaming, wandering, roaming, W.

1. **Vrāja**, m. (for 2. see below) going, movement, motion, MW.

Vrāji, f. 'who or what moves (?),' a gale of wind, W. (cf. *dhrāji*).

Vrājika, n. a kind of fast (subsisting on milk; observed by religious mendicants), L.

व्रज 2. *vrajá*, m. (n. only RV. v, 6, 7; ifc. f. *ā*; fr. √*vrij*) a fold, stall, cow-pen, cattle-shed, enclosure or station of herdsmen, RV. &c. &c.; m. N. of the district around Agra and Mathurā (the abode of Nanda, of Kṛishṇa's foster-father, and scene of Kṛishṇa's juvenile adventures; commonly called Braj; cf. *vriji*), Inscr.; a herd, flock, swarm, troop, host, multitude, MBh.; Kāv. &c. (*saṃgrāmaḥ sa-vrajaḥ*, 'a fight with many,' MārkP.; *vrajo giri-mayaḥ*, prob. = *giri-vraja*, q.v., Hariv.); a cloud (= *megha*), Naigh. i, 10; N. of a son of Havir-dhāna, Hariv.; VP. — **kiśora**, m. 'young herdsman' or 'a young man of Vraja,' N. of Kṛishṇa, MatsyaP. — **kshit**, mfn. remaining in a (heavenly) station i.e. in the clouds, VS. — **tattva**, n., -**nava-nāgara-candrikā**, f. N. of wks. — **nātha**, m. 'lord of the herds,' N. of Kṛishṇa, MBh.; -*bhaṭṭa*, m. N. of an author, Cat. — **paddhati**, f., -**bhakti-vilāsa**, m. N. of wks. — **bhāshā**, f. the language current around Agra and Mathurā, Col. — **bhū**, mfn. being or produced in Vraja, MW.; m. a variety of the Kadamba, L.; f. the district of Vr°, MW. — **bhūshaṇa**, -**bhūshaṇa-kavi**, -**bhūshaṇa-miśra**, m. N. of authors, Cat. — **maṇḍala**, n. the district of Vraja, MatsyaP. — **mohana**, m. 'fascinator of Vraja,' N. of Kṛishṇa, L. — **yuvati**, f. a young cowherdess, young shepherdess, Chandom. — **rāja**, -**rāja-gosvāmin**, -**rāja-dīkshita**, -**rāja-śukla**, m. N. of various authors and other men, Cat. — **rāmā**, f. a cowherdess, shepherdess, Chandom. — **lāla**, m. N. of a king, Cat.; of an author, ib. — **vadhū** (ib.) or -**vanitā** (Chandom.), f. = -*rāmā*. — **vara**, m. 'best in Vraja,' N. of Kṛishṇa, MatsyaP. — **vallabha**, m. 'beloved in Vraja,' id., L. — **vilāsa**, m., -**vilāsa-stava**, m., -**vihāra**, m. N. of wks. — **sundarī** (Gīt.) or -**strī** (Rājat.; BhP.), f. = -*rāmā*. **Vrajâṅgana**, n. a cow-yard or station of cowherds, Pañcar.; (*ā*), f. a cowherdess, Chandom.; Vās. **Vrajâjira**, n. a cow-yard, cattle-fold, cow-pen, W. **Vrajâvāsa**, m. a settlement of herdsmen, BhP. **Vrajêndra**, m. 'lord of Vr°,' N. of Kṛishṇa, Pañcar.; -*carita*, n. N. of wk. **Vrajêśvara**, m. = *vrajêndra*, Pañcar. **Vrajôparodham**, ind. enclosing in a fold or stall, Pāṇ. iii, 4, 49, Sch. **Vrajâukas**, m. a herdsman, Pur.

Vrajas-pati, m. (formed ungrammatically according to the analogy of *bṛihas-pati*) 'lord of the cow-pen,' N. of Kṛishṇa, BhP.

Vrajin, mfn. being in the stall, RV. v, 45, 1; herded or grouped together, MW.

Vrájya, mfn. belonging to a fold or pen, VS.

2. **Vrajyā**, f. division, group (= *varga*), Sāh.

2. **Vrājá**, m. (for 1. see above) = 2. *vrajá*, a troop, host, band (*am*, ind. in troops), AV.; a domestic cock, L. — **pati** (or *vrājá-p°*), m. the lord of a troop or host, RV.; AV. — **bāhu**, m. du. outstretched arms (lit. 'arms that form an enclosure'), ŚāṅkhBr.

Vrājin. See *vishṭhā-vrājin*, p. 999, col. 1.

व्रढिमन् *vraḍhiman*, m. (fr. *vṛiḍha*, see under √1. 2. *bṛih*), g. *dṛiḍhâdi*.

व्रण् 1. *vraṇ* (also written *braṇ*), cl. 1. P. *vraṇati*, to sound, Dhātup. xiii, 8.

व्रण् 2. *vraṇ* (rather Nom. fr. *vraṇa* below), cl. 1. P. *vraṇati*, to wound, Suśr.; cl. 10. P. (Dhātup. xxxv, 82) *vraṇayati*, id., Kāv.; Kathās. &c.

Vraṇa, m. (exceptionally n.) a wound, sore, ulcer, abscess, tumour, cancer, boil, scar, cicatrix, crack, Mn.; MBh. &c.; a flaw, blemish (also in inanimate objects), MBh.; Hariv.; VarBṛS. — **kārin**, mfn. making or causing a sore, wounding, L. — **kṛit**, mfn. id., L.; corroding, W.; m. Semecarpus Anacardium, L. — **ketu-ghnī**, f. a kind of small shrub, L. — **granthi**, m. a scar, cicatrix, Mcar. — **ghna-gaja-dāna-vidhi** (with *vriddha-gautamôkta*), m., -**ghna-ratna-dāna-vidhi**, m. N. of wks. — **ghnī**, f. Erythræa Centaureoides or Pharmaceum Mollugo, L. — **cikitsā**, f. 'cure of sores,' N. of wk. — **cintaka**, m. 's°-curer,' a surgeon, Car. — **jitā**, f. Schœnanthus Indicus, Dhanv. — **tā**, f. the state of a sore, Suśr. — **dvish**, mfn. (nom. *dviṭ*) 'hating i.e. healing sores,' MW.; m. Clerodendrum Siphonanthus, L. — **dhūpana**, n. the fumigation of a sore (with vapour &c.), Suśr. — **paṭṭa**, m. (Bālar.; Rājat.) or °**ṭṭaka**, m. (Kathās.) or °**ṭṭikā**, f. (ib.) a bandage on a wound (ifc. f. *ikā*). — **bhṛit**, mfn. wounded, Śiś. — **maya**, mf(*ī*)n., see *śastra-vraṇa-m°*. — **yukta**, mfn. wounded (-*tva*, n.), R. — **vat**, mfn. sore, wounded, MBh.; Śiś. — **vastu**, n. the place or seat of a wound, Suśr.; a part liable to ulcerate (as skin, flesh &c.), W. — **viropaṇa**, mfn. cicatrizing sores, healing sores, Śak. (v.l. *viśoshaṇa*); n. the healing of a sore, Daś. — **vedanā**, f. the pain of a sore, Suśr. — **śodhana**, n. the cleansing or cicatrizing of a sore, W. — **śoshin**, mfn. pining away with wounds or ulcers, Suśr. — **saṃrohaṇa**, n. the cicatrization or healing of a wound, R. — **sāmānya-karma-prakāśa**, m. N. of a section of the Jñāna-bhāskara. — **ha**, mfn. destroying or removing sores, L.; m. the castor-oil tree, L.; (*ā*), f. Cocculus Cordifolius, L. — **hṛit**, mfn. removing sores, L.; m. Methonica Superba, L. **Vraṇâyāma**, m. the pain of a sore or ulcer, ŚārṅgS. **Vraṇâri**, m. 'enemy of sores,' Agati Grandiflora, L.; myrrh, L. **Vraṇâsrāva**, m. discharge from wounds or ulcers, Suśr.

Vraṇana, n. piercing, perforating, Bālar.

Vraṇayita, mfn. becoming sore or ulcerated, Hcat.

Vraṇita, mfn. wounded, sore, ulcerated, R.; Suśr.; Kathās. &c. — **hṛidaya**, mf(*ā*)n. heart-stricken, MW.

Vraṇin, mfn. having a sore or wound, ulcerated, Suśr.; Bhartṛ.; Hcat.

Vraṇila, mfn. wounded, injured (said of a tree), ShaḍvBr.

Vraṇīya. See *dvi-v°*.

Vraṇya, mfn. beneficial for wounds or sores, Suśr.

व्रत *vratá*, n. (ifc. f. *ā*; fr. √2. *vṛi*) will, command, law, ordinance, rule, RV.; obedience, service, ib.; AV.; ĀśvGṛ.; dominion, realm, RV.; sphere of action, function, mode or manner of life (e.g. *śuci-vr°*, 'pure manner of life,' Śak.), conduct, manner, usage, custom, RV. &c. &c.; a religious vow or practice, any pious observance, meritorious act of devotion or austerity, solemn vow, rule, holy practice (as fasting, continence &c.; *vratáṃ* √*car*, 'to observe a vow,' esp. 'to practise chastity'), ib.; any vow or firm purpose, resolve to (dat., loc., or comp.; *vratāt* or *vrata-vaśāt*, 'in consequence of a vow;' cf. *asi-dhārā-vrata* and *āsidhāraṃ vratam*), MBh.; Kāv. &c.; the practice of always eating the same food (cf. *madhu-vr°*), L.; the feeding only on milk (as a fast or observance according to rule; also the milk itself), VS.; Br.; KātyŚr.; any food (in *a-yācita-vr°*, q.v.); = *mahā-vrata* (i.e. a partic. Stotra, and the day for it), Br.; ŚrS.; (with gen. or ifc.) N. of Sāmans, ĀrshBr. (L. also 'month; season; year; fire;' '= Vishṇu;' 'N. of one of the seven islands of Antara-dvīpa'); (*vráta*), m. (of unknown meaning), AV. v, 1, 7; ĀpŚr. xiii, 16, 8; N. of a son of Manu and Naḍvalā, BhP.; (pl.) N. of a country belonging to Prācya, L.; mfn. = *veda-vrata*, one who has taken the vow of learning the Veda, Gṛihyās. ii, 3 (Sch.) — **kamalâkara**, m., -**kalpa**, m., -**kalpa-druma**, m., -**kāla-nirṇaya**, m., -**kāla-viveka**, m., -**kośa**, m., -**kaumudī**, f., -**khaṇḍa**, m. N. of wks. — **grahaṇa**, n. the taking upon one's self of a religious vow, becoming a monk, Pañcat.; HPariś. — **caryā**, f. the practice of any religious observance or vow, ŚBr.; Mn.; MBh. &c.; (°*rya*), m. a rel° student, MW. — **cārin**, mfn. vow-performing, engaged in any religious observance or practice ('in honour of,' with gen.; °*ri-tā*, f.), RV.; ĀśvGṛ.; MBh. &c. — **cūḍāmaṇi**, m. N. of wk. — **tattva**, n. N. of a ch. of the Smṛiti-tattva. — **daṇḍin**, mfn. bearing a staff in accordance with a vow, Hariv. — **dāna**, n. the imposing of a vow, Pañcat.; a donation made in consequence of a vow, AgP. — **dugdha**, n. Vrata-milk, KātyŚr., Sch. — **dúghā** (ŚBr.; KātyŚr.) or -**duh** (ĀpŚr.; ib., Sch.), f. a cow which gives the Vrata-milk. — **dhara** (ifc.), see *daṇḍa-*, *nagna-v°* &c. — **dhāraṇa**, n. the fulfilling of a religious observance, f° of duties towards (with gen. or comp.), Kām.; BṛĀrUp., Sch.; BhP. — **dhārin**, mfn. fulfilling a rel° obs° &c., Sāṃkhyak., Sch. (cf. *mauna-v°*). — **nimitta**, mf(*ā*)n. caused by a vow, MW. — **nirṇaya**, m. N. of wk. — **nī**, mfn. 'obedient' or 'bearing the Vrata-milk,' RV. x, 65, 6. — **paksha**, m. du. (with *prajā-pater*) N. of two Sāmans, ĀrshBr.; Lāṭy. — **pañjī**, f. N. of wk. — **pati** (*vratá-*), m. 'lord of religious observances' &c.; N. of Agni, AV.; VS.; TS. &c. — **patnī**, f. mistress of religious obs° &c., Kauś. — **pā**, mfn. upholding or observing religious ordinances or duties, RV.; VS.; Br. — **pāraṇa**, n. (Ragh.; Rājat. &c.) or °**ṇā**, f. (MW.) conclusion of a fast, the first eating or drinking after a fast. — **pustaka** (?), -**prakāśa**, m. N. of wks. — **pratishṭhā**, f. the performance of a voluntary religious act; -*prayoga*, m. N. of wk. — **pradá**, mfn. presenting the Vrata-milk, Br.; ŚrS. — **pradāna**, n. the vessel wherein the Vrata-m° is presented, ŚrS.; the imposing of a vow, Pañcat. — **bandha-paddhati**, f. N. of wk. — **bhakshaṇa**, n. the feeding on Vrata-milk (-*kāle*), KātyŚr., Sch. — **bhaṅga**, m. the breaking of a vow, Cat.; br° of a promise, A. — **bhikshā**, f. soliciting alms (as one of the ceremonies at investiture with the sacred thread), W. — **bhṛit**, mfn. bearing the ordinance or oblation &c. (said of Agni), TS.; Br.; ŚrS. (cf. *samāna-v°*). — **mayūkha**, m., -**mālā**, f. N. of wks. — **miśra**, mfn. mixed with Vrata-milk, KātyŚr. — **mīmāṃsā**, f. inquiry into or discussion about religious observances, ŚBr. — **ratnâvalī**, f., -**rāja**, m. N. of wks. — **ruci**, mfn. delighting in religious observances, devout, Bhartṛ. — **lupta**, mf(*ā*)n. one who has broken a vow, MW. — **lopa**, m. violation of a vow or rel° obligation, Vait.; Yājñ. (cf. *snātaka-v°*). — **lopana**, n. id., Mn.; Yājñ. — 1. -**vat** (*vratá-*), mfn. fulfilling or performing a rel° vow &c., Kauś.; MBh.; Hariv. &c.; connected with the Vrata called Mahā-vrata, ŚrS.; containing the word *vratá*, ŚBr. — 2. -**vat**, ind. like (in or with) the Vrata-milk, KātyŚr. — **vallī**, f., -**vidhi**, m., -**viveka-bhāskara**, m. N. of wks. — **visarga**, m. conclusion of any vow or observance, PañcavBr. (cf. *vratâdeśana*). — **visarjana**, mf(*ī*)n. concluding a religious observance, Kauś.; Vait. — **visarjanīyôpayoga**, mfn. belonging to the conclusion of an obs°, ŚBr. — **vaikalya**, n. imperfection or incompletion of a vow or religious obs°, Pañcat. — **śayyā-gṛiha**, n. a sleeping-room set apart for the fulfilling of a rel° vow or observance, Kathās. — **śānti**, f. (with *nānā-vidhā*) N. of wk. — **śesha**, m. the remainder of a rel° obs°, MW. — **śrapaṇa**, n. boiling Vrata-milk, ŚāṅkhBr.; ŚāṅkhŚr. — **saṃrakshaṇa**, n. the keeping of a vow or penance, MW. — **saṃgraha**, m. the undertaking of any rel° obligation, L.; N. of wk. — **samāpana**, mf(*ī*)n. concluding a religious observance, Kauś. — **samāyana**, w.r. for prec., Daś. — **sampāta**, m. N. of wk. — **sampādana**, n. fulfilling a rel° obligation or vow, Vikr. — **sahyâdri**, m., -**sāra**, m. N. of wks. — **stha**, mf(*ā*)n. engaged in a vow or rel° observance &c., Mn.; MBh.; Kathās.; BhP. (cf. *kanyā-vrata-sthā*). — **sthita**, mfn. engaged in religious observances (as a Brahma-cārin), VarBṛS. — **snāta**, mfn. one who has bathed after completing a religious vow, R.; MārkP. — **snātaka**, mfn. id., GṛS. — **snāna**, n. bathing after the completing of a vow, R.; Rājat.; BhP. — **hāni**, f. relinquishment of a rel° observance or vow, ŚāṅkhGṛ. **Vratâcaraṇa**, n. the act of observing a vow or rel° obligation (esp. that of continence), MW. **Vratâcāra**, m. N. of wk. **Vratâtipatti**, f. omission of a rel° observance, ĀśvŚr. **Vratâdāna**, n. undertaking a religious vow or obligation, HPariś. **Vratâdānīya**, mfn. relating to the undertaking of a rel° vow, Kauś. **Vratâdeśa**, m. direction for undertaking a Vrata, imposition of a vow &c. (esp. that of a Brahma-cārin), R.; Yājñ.; investiture with the sacred cord, MW. **Vratâdeśana**, n. imposing or undertaking a vow, GṛS.; Mn.; -*visarga*, m. pl. the undertaking and concluding of a vow, PārGṛ. **Vratârka**, m., °**tâvalī**, f., °**tâvalī-kalpa**, m. N. of wks. **Vratâśa**, mfn. = *mitaṃ hitam medhyaṃ câśnāti*, MBh. (Nīlak.) **Vratêśa**, m. 'lord of observances,' N. of Śiva, MBh. **Vratôddyota**, m., °**tôdyāpana**, n., °**tôdyāpana-kaumudī**, f., °**tôdyāpana-vidhi**, m. N. of wks. **Vratôpanáyana**, n. initiation into a rel° vow &c., TBr. **Vratôpavāsa**, m. fasting as a religious obligation, R.; BrahmaP.; -*saṃgraha*, m. N. of wk. **Vratôpasád**, f. pl. the Vrata-milk and the ceremony Upasad, ŚBr. **Vratôpaha**, w.r. for *vratôpôha*. **Vratôpâyaná**, n. entering on a religious observance &c. (-*vat*, ind.), ŚBr.; KātyŚr.; presents of cakes &c. (to be eaten during a religious feast = *vāyana*), MW. **Vratôpâyanīya**, mfn. belonging to the Vratôpâyana &c., ŚBr.; ŚrS.; ĀpŚr., Sch. **Vratôpôha**, m. (with *Aṅgirasām*) N. of a Sāman, ĀrshBr.

Vrataka, n. a religious observance &c. (= *vratá*), Hariv.

Vrataya, Nom. P. *vratáyati*, to drink the (hot) Vrata-milk (also with *payas* &c.), TS.; Kāṭh.; ŚBr.; to eat or drink after a fast, TāṇḍyaBr.; AitĀr., Sch.

(w.r. *avrajayat*); to observe a vow, MW.; to fast or practise any abstinence in consequence of a vow, ib.; to avoid certain kinds of food (as Śūdra food), Pāṇ. iii, 1, 21, Sch.; to eat together, MW.

Vratayitavya, mfn. to be consumed (as Vrata-milk), TS., Sch.

Vratika, in *a-*, *cāndra-vr°* &c. (*umā-vr°*, w.r. for *umā-vrataka*, Hariv.)

Vratin, mfn. observing a vow, engaged in a religious observance &c., TS.; ŚBr.; Kauś. &c.; (ifc.) engaged in, worshipping, behaving like, MBh.; BhP.; m. an ascetic, devotee, MW.; a religious student, ib.; one who institutes a sacrifice and employs priests (= *yajamāna*), ib.; N. of a Muni, Cat.; (*inī*), f. a nun, HPariś.

Vrateyu, m. N. of a son of Raudrāśva, Pur.

Vratyà, mfn. obedient, faithful (with gen.), RV.; (*vrátya*), suitable or belonging to or fit for a religious observance, engaged in a rel° obs°, TS.; Br.; ŚrS.; n. food suitable for a fast-day, KātyŚr.

Vrāta &c. See below.

व्रतति *vratáti*, f. (prob. fr. √*vṛit*) a creeping plant, creeper, RV. &c. &c. (also °*tī*); expansion, extension, spreading (= *pra-tati*), L. — **valaya**, m. n. a creeper winding round like a bracelet, Śak.

व्रद् *vrad* (or *vrand*), Ā. *-vradate* (only impf. *avradanta*), to soften, become soft, RV. ii, 24, 3 (cf. Nir. v, 16).

Vrandín, mfn. becoming soft, RV. i, 54, 4, 5.

व्रध्न *vradhna*. See *bradhna*.

व्रयस् *vráyas*, n. (perhaps fr. √*vṛī*) overwhelming or superior power, RV. ii, 23, 16.

व्रश्च् *vraśc* (cf. √*vṛik*), cl. 6. P. (Dhātup. xxviii, 11) *vṛiścáti* (pr. p. *vṛiknan* [?], BhP.; pf. *vavraśca*, °*citha*, Gr.; aor. *avraścīt*, *avrākshīt*, ib.; *vṛikshi*, Br.; fut. *vraścitā*, *vrashṭā*, Gr.; *vraścishyati*, *vrakshyati*, ib.; ind.p. *vraścitvā*, ib.; *vṛishṭvā*, AV.; *vṛiktvī*, RV.; *-vráścam*, *-vṛiścya*, Br. &c.), to cut down or off or asunder, cleave, hew, fell (a tree), RV. &c. &c.: Pass. *vṛiścyáte* (in AV. also *vṛiścáte*), to be cut down or off &c.: Caus. *vraścayati* (aor. *avavraścat*), Gr.: Desid. *vivraścishati*, *vivrakshati*, ib.: Intens. *varīvṛiścyate*, *varīvṛiściti*, ib.

Vṛikṇá, mfn. cut off or down, cleft, felled, torn, broken, RV. &c. &c.; n. a cut, incision, AV.; TS. — **vat**, mfn. one who has cut or severed, W.

Vṛiścád-vana, mfn. (pr. p. of √*vraśc* + *vana*) felling or destroying trees (said of Agni), RV.

Vṛiścana, vṛiścika &c. See p. 1011, col. 3.

Vṛiścita, mfn. cut off or down &c., Kauś., Sch.

Vráścana, mfn. who or what cuts, cutting or fit for cutting, Mcar.; a file or saw or chisel, L.; the juice flowing from an incision in a tree, Gaut.; Yājñ.; n. cutting, wounding, a cut, incision, ŚBr.; Kāṭh. &c. — **prabhava**, mfn. flowing from an incision (in a tree, as juices &c.), Mn. v, 6.

Vrashṭavya, mfn. to be cut off or down &c., Pāṇ. viii, 2, 36, Sch.

Vraska. See *yūpa-vraská*.

व्रह्मन् *vrahman*. See *brahman*.

व्रा *vrā́*, f. (fr. √1. *vṛi*, accord. to some fr. a masc. stem *vra*) a heap, host, multitude (mostly *vrā́s*, pl.), RV. (Sāy. i, 121, 2 'night,' 'dawn'); AV.

व्राचट *vrācaṭa* or *vrācaḍa*, m. a kind of Apabhraṇśa dialect, Cat.

व्राज 1. 2. *vrāja* &c. See p. 1042, col. 1.

व्रात *vrā́ta*, m (connected with √1. *vṛi* or with *vratá* and √2. *vṛi*) a multitude, flock, assemblage, troop, swarm, group, host (*vrā́taṃ vrā́tam*, in companies or troops; *páñca vrā́tās*, the five races of men), association, guild, RV. &c. &c.; the company or attendants at a marriage feast, W.; = *manushya*, Naigh. ii, 3; the descendant of an out-caste Brāhman &c. (= *vrātya*), L.; n. manual or bodily labour, day-labour, ib. — **jīvana**, mfn. living by manual or bodily labour, MW. — **pata**, mf(*ī*)n. relating or belonging or sacred to Vrata-pati, ŚrS.; Vas.; °*tīya*, mfn. id., KātyŚr., Sch.; °*tēshṭi-prayoga*, m. N. of wk. — **pati** (*vrā́ta-*), m. lord of an assemblage or association, VS. — **bhṛita**, mf(*ī*)n. addressed to Agni Vrata-bhṛit, ĀpŚr. — **maya**, mf(*ī*)n. consisting of a multitude of (comp.), BhP. — **sāhá** (Padap. *-sahá*), mfn. conquering hosts or in hosts, RV.

Vrātika, n. a partic. observance, Gobh.

Vrātīna, mfn. living by the profession of a Vrāta, Pāṇ. v, 21; having no fixed employment, belonging to a vagrant gang, Lāṭy.; Bhaṭṭ.

Vrā́tya, m. a man of the mendicant or vagrant class, a tramp, out-caste, low or vile person (either a man who has lost caste through non-observance of the ten principal Saṃskāras, or a man of a partic. low caste descended from a Śūdra and a Kshatriyā; accord. to some 'the illegitimate son of a Kshatriya who knows the habits and intentions of soldiers;' in AV. xv, 8, 1; 9, 1, the Rājanyas and even the Brāhmans are said to have sprung from the Vrātya who is identified with the Supreme Being, prob. in glorification of religious mendicancy; accord. to ĀpŚr. *vrātya* is used in addressing a guest), AV. &c. &c.; (*ā*), f. a female Vrātya, Mn. viii, 373; a vagrant life, PañcavBr.; mfn. belonging to the Vrata called Mahā-vrata (q. v.), PañcavBr., Sch. — **gaṇa**, m. the vagrant class, KātyŚr. — **caraṇa**, n. (ib.), *-caryā*, f. (Lāṭy.) the life and practice of a vagrant. — **tā**, f., **-tva**, n. the condition of a Vrātya, Vishṇ.; Mn. &c. (IW. 271). — **dhana**, n. the property of a Vr°, PañcavBr. — **bruvá**, m. one who calls himself a Vr°, AV. — **bhāva**, m. = *-tā*, Kāty. — **yajña**, m. a kind of sacrifice, PañcavBr. (cf. *-stoma*). — **yājaka**, m. one who sacrifices for a Vr°, MW. — **stoma**, m. N. of partic. Ekâhas, ŚrS.; Gaut.; Vas.; (with *kratu*) a partic. sacrifice (performed to recover the rights forfeited by a delay of the Saṃskāras), Yājñ. i, 38.

व्राध् *vrādh* (prob. connected with √*vṛidh*), only in *vrādhanta* and superl. of pr. p. *vrā́dhantama*, (prob.) to be great or mighty (accord. to others 'to urge, incite'), RV.

व्रिश् *vríś*, f. pl. the fingers, RV. i, 144, 5 (Naigh. ii, 5).

व्री *vrī* (cf. √*vṛi* and *vlī*), cl. 9. P. and 4. Ā. *vrīṇāti*, *vriṇāti*, or *vrīyate*, 'to choose' or 'to cover' (*varaṇe*), Dhātup. xxxi, 33; xxvi, 31: Caus. *vrāyayati* or *vrepayati*, Gr.: Desid. *vivrīshati*, °*te*: Intens. *vevrīyate*, *vevrayīti*, *vevreti*, ib.

Vrīṇa, mfn. chosen, elected, MW.

व्रीड् *vrīḍ*, cl. 1. Ā. *vrīḍate* (accord. to Dhātup. xxvi, 18 also cl. 4. P. *vrīḍyati*; pf. *vivrīḍa*, Gr.; aor. *avrīḍīt*, ib.; fut. *vrīḍitā*, *vrīḍishyati*, ib.), to be ashamed, feel shame, be bashful or modest, MBh.; Kāv. &c.; (cl. 4. P.) to throw, hurl, Vop., Sch.: Caus. (or cl. 10. P.) *vrīḍayati* = *vīḍayati*, to make firm, Nir. v, 16 (cf. √*viḍ*).

Vrīḍa, m. = *vrīḍā*, shame, Kāv.; Rājat.

Vrīḍana, n. lowering, depression, RPrāt.; shame, bashfulness, L.

Vrīḍā, f. shame, modesty, bashfulness (*vrīḍāṃ* √*kṛi*, to feel shame), MBh.; Kāv. &c. — **dāna**, n. a gift offered out of modesty, Hcat. — °**nata** (*vrīḍān°*), mfn. bowed down with shame, ashamed, W. — °**nvita** (*vrīḍânv°*), mfn. ashamed, bashful, modest, ib. — **yuj**, mfn. possessing shame, ashamed, R. — **vat**, mfn. ashamed, abashed, MBh.; Gīt.

Vrīḍita, mfn. ashamed, abashed, modest, MBh.; Kāv. &c.; n. shame, embarrassment, Kir.

Vrīlana, n., Ved. = *vrīḍana*.

Vrīlasa, mfn. ashamed, modest, L.

व्रीस् *vrīs*. See √*vrūs*.

व्रीहि *vrīhí*, m. (of doubtful derivation) rice, pl. grains of rice (not mentioned in RV., but in AV. named together with *yava*, *māsha*, and *tila*; eight principal sorts are enumerated by native authorities), RV. &c. &c.; a field of rice, KātyŚr.; rice ripening in the rainy season, W.; any grain, L. — **kaṅka**, m., *-kāñcana*, m. or n. a sort of pulse, Ervum Lens or Hirsutum, L. — **droṇa**, m. a Droṇa (q. v.) of rice, MBh. — **drauṇika**, mfn. relating to or treating of a Dr° of rice, ib. — **parṇī**, f. a partic. shrub, Desmodium Gangeticum, L. — **bheda**, m. a kind of grain, (accord. to some) Panicum Miliaceum, L. — **mat**, mfn. mixed with r°, ĀśvGṛ.; grown with r° (as a field), Śiś., Sch.; (*atī*), f., Pāṇ. vi, 3, 119, Sch. — **mata**, m. pl. N. of a people (not belonging to the Brāhmanical order), Pāṇ. v, 3, 113, Sch. (cf. *vraihi-matya*). — **maya**, mf(*ī*)n. made or consisting of rice, ŚBr.; MBh. — **mukha**, mfn. (a surgical instrument) which resembles a grain of rice, Suśr. — **yavá**, m. du. or pl. (AV.; ŚBr.), n. sg. (MBh.), rice and barley. — **rājika**, n. Panicum Italicum or Miliaceum, L. — **vāpa**, n. sowing rice, Pāṇ. viii, 4, 11, Sch. — **vāpin**, mfn. one who sows rice, ib. — **velā**, f. the time of reaping rice, Lāṭy. — **śreshṭha**, m. 'best of grains,' rice or a kind of rice, L.

Vrīhika, mfn. having or bearing rice, Pāṇ. v. 2, 116.

Vrīhin, mfn. (a field) grown with rice, Śiś.

Vrīhila, mfn. = *vrīhika*, g. *tundâdi*.

Vrīhy, in comp. for *vrīhi*. — **agāra**, n. 'rice-house,' a shed where rice or other grain is stored, granary, L. — **apūpa**, m. a rice-cake, KātyŚr. — **āgrayaṇa**, n. an offering of firstfruits of rice, KātyŚr., Sch. — **urvarā**, f. a rice-field, Lāṭy.

Vraiha, mfn. made of rice &c., g. *bilvâdi*.

Vraihika, mfn. grown with rice, Gal.

Vraihimatya, m. a king of the Vrīhi-matas, Pāṇ. v, 3, 113, Sch.

Vraiheya, mfn. fit for or sown with rice (as a field), Pāṇ. v, 2, 2; made or consisting of r°, MW.; n. a field of rice, L.

व्रुड् *vruḍ*, cl. 6. P. *-vruḍati*, to cover, Dhātup. xxviii, 99, to heap, ib., to sink, ib.

Vruḍita, mfn. plunged in, immersed, sunk, Rājat.; gone astray, lost (in a thicket), ib.

व्रूस् *vrūs* (also written *vrūsh* or *brūs*; v.l. *vrīs*), cl. 1. 10. P. *vrūsati*, *vrūsayati*, to hurt, kill, Dhātup. xxxii, 121.

व्रेशी *vréśī*, f. a N. applied to water, VS. (*réśī*, TS.)

व्लग् *vlag*, only ind. p. *abhi-vlagya* or °*yā*, catching, seizing, RV. (Sāy.; accord. to others 'pressing hard' or 'wringing the neck;' cf. *abhi-vlaṅgá*).

व्ली *vlī* (or *blī*; cf. √*vrī*), cl. 9. P. (Dhātup. xxxi, 32) *vlīnāti* or *vlināti* (pf. *vivlāya*, Gr.; aor. *avlaishīt*, ib.; fut. *vletā*, ib.; *vleshyati*, Br.; ind. p. *-vlīya*, ib.), to press down, crush, cause to fall, Br. (Dhātup. also, 'to choose, select;' 'to go, move;' 'to hold, maintain, support'): Pass. *vlīyate*, to sink down, collapse, succumb, PañcavBr.; MaitrUp.: Caus. *vlepayati* (aor. *avivlipat*), Pāṇ. vii, 3, 36; 86: Desid. *vivlīshati*, Gr.: Intens. *vevlīyate*, to sink down, MaitrS.; *vevlayīti*, *vevleti*, Gr.

Vlīna, mfn. crushed, sunk down, collapsed (see *pra-*, *saṃ-vlīna*); gone, MW.; held, supported, ib.

व्लेष् *vleksh*. See *veksh*, p. 1013, col. 3.

व्लेष्क *vleshká*, m. a snare, noose (= *bleshka*). — **hata** (*vleshká-*), mfn. strangled by a noose, MaitrS.

श ŚA.

श 1. *śa*, the first of the three sibilants (it belongs to the palatal class, but in sound as well as euphonic treatment often corresponds to *sh*, though in some words pronounced more like *s*). — 1. **-kāra**, m. (for 2. see p. 1045) the letter or sound *śa*, Prāt.; *-bheda*, m. = next. — **bheda**, m. N. of a treatise on the proper spelling of words beginning with *ś*, *sh*, or *s*. — **varga**, m. the sibilating class of letters, i.e. the three sibilants and the letter *h*.

श 2. *śa* (ifc.) = *śaya* (see *giri-*, *vāri-*, *vṛiksha-śa*).

श 3. *śa*, m. = *śastra*, L.; = *śiva*, L.; n., see 2. *śam*.

शंय *śaṃya*, *śaṃyu* &c. See p. 1054.

शंव *śaṃva*, *śaṃvara*, *śaṃvūka*. See *śamba*, *śambara*, *śambūka*, p. 1055.

शंशमम् *śaṅśamam*, *śaṅśāmam*. See √*śam*.

शंस् *śaṅs*, cl. 1. P. (Dhātup. xvii, 79) *śaṅsati* (m. c. also Ā.; pf. *śaśaṅsa*, °*se*, Br. &c.; *śaśaṅsuḥ*, °*sire*, MBh.; p. *śaṅsivas*, q. v.; aor. *aśaṅsīt*, RV. &c., &c.: Subj. *śaṅsishat*, RV.; Br.; 2. pl. *śasta*, RV.; *śastāt*, AitBr.; 1. sg. *śaṅsi*, RV.; Prec. *śasyāt*, Gr.; fut. *śaṅsitā*, ib.; *śaṅsishyati*, Br. &c.; inf. *śaṅsitum*, MBh.; *-śase*, RV.; inf. p. *śastvā*, *-śasya*, *-śaṅsam*, Br. &c.; *-śaṅsya*, MBh.), to recite, repeat (esp. applied to the recitation of texts in the invocations addressed by the Hotṛi to the Adhvaryu, when *śaṅs* is written *śoṅs* and the formulas *śoṅsāmas*, *śoṅsāvas*, *śoṅsāva* are used; see

2. *ā-hāva*), RV.; Br.; ŚrS.; to praise, extol, RV. &c. &c.; to praise, commend, approve, VarBṛS.; to vow, make a vow (?), RV. x, 85, 9; to wish anything (acc.) to (dat.), ib. 124, 3; to relate, say, tell, report, declare, announce to (gen. or dat.; 'who or where anybody is,' acc.; also with two acc., 'to declare anybody or anything to be—'), AV. &c. &c.; to foretell, predict, prognosticate, R.; Kum. &c.; to calumniate, revile, W.; to hurt, injure, Dhātup.; to be unhappy, ib.: Pass. *śasyáte*, to be recited or uttered or praised or approved, RV. &c. &c.: Caus. *śaṇsayati* (aor. *aśaśaṇsat*), to cause to repeat or recite, AitBr.; Lāṭy.; BhP.; to predict, foretell, R.: Desid. *śiśaṇsishati*, Gr.: Intens. *śāśasyate*, *śāśaṇsti*, ib. [Cf. Lat. *carmen* for *casmen*; *Casmēna*, *Camēna*; *censeo*.]

Śáṇsa, m. recitation, invocation, praise, RV.; wishing well or ill to, a blessing or a curse, ib.; a promise, vow, ib. (*narā́ṃ śáṇsa*, RV. ii, 34, 6, prob. = *narā-ś°*, q.v.; *ṛijúr íc cháṇsa*, ii, 26, 1 either, by tmesis, 'the right praiser,' or *ṛiju-śaṇsa* as adj. 'righteous, faithful'); a spell, MW.; calumny, ib.; (*ā*), f. praise, flattery, eulogium, Kāv.; wish, desire, W.; speech, utterance, announcement, R.; mfn. reciting, proclaiming, praising, wishing (see *agha-*, *duḥ-ś°* &c.)

Śaṇsatha, m. conversation, PārGṛ.

Śaṇsana, n. reciting, recitation, praise, L.; report, announcement, communication, R. (applied to Śiva, Hariv. 7425 = *veda-praśasya*, Nīlak.)

Śaṇsanīya, mfn. to be praised, praiseworthy, Nir.; Rājat.

Śaṇsita, mfn. (often confounded with *saṃ-śita*, see *saṃ-√śo*) said, told, praised, celebrated, Pañcat.; praiseworthy, ib.; wished, desired, longed for, W.; calumniated, falsely accused, ib.

Śaṇsitṛi, m. a reciter (= *śaṇstṛi* below), MBh.; VāyuP.; Yājñ., Sch.; = *hotṛi*, AitĀr.

Śaṇsin, mfn. (only ifc.) reciting, uttering, announcing, telling, relating, betraying, predicting, promising, Hariv.; Kāv.; Kathās. &c.

Śaṇsivas, mfn. announcing, proclaiming, R.

Śaṇstavya, mfn. to be recited, AitBr.

Śáṇstṛi, m. one who recites, a reciter, RV.; AitBr. (a priest identified with the Praśāstṛi and mentioned along with five others in RV. i, 162, 5; his sacrificial duties correspond with those of the Maitrā-varuṇa of the later ritual); a praiser, encomiast, panegyrist, W.

Śáṇsya, mfn. to be recited, RV.; to be praised, praiseworthy, ib.; N. of Agni (in a formula), VS.; TBr.; KātyŚr.; Sch. (m. the eastward sacrificial fire, L.); to be wished for, desirable, W.

1. **Śas**, **śasa**, mfn. reciting (see *uktha-śás*, *-śasá*).

Śasitvā, ind. having praised &c. (= *śastvā*, see *√śaṇs*), MW.

1. **Śastá**, mfn. (for 2. see under *√śas*) recited, repeated, RV.; praised, commended, approved, MBh.; Kāv. &c.; auspicious (cf. *á-ś°*), AV.; Rājat.; beautiful, R.; happy, fortunate, Kathās.; n. praise, eulogy, RV.; happiness, excellence, W. **—keśaka**, mfn. having excellent or beautiful hair, L. **—tā**, f. excellence, MārkP. **Śastôkta**, mfn. one to whom a recitation has been made, VS.

Śastavya, mfn. to be recited or praised, MW.

Śastí, f. praise, a hymn, RV.; a praiser, singer, ib.

1. **Śastrá**, n. (for 2. see under *√śas*) invocation, praise (applied to any hymn recited either audibly or inaudibly, as opp. to *stoma*, which is sung, but esp. the verses recited by the Hotṛi and his assistant as an accompaniment to the Grahas at the Soma libation), VS.; Br.; ŚrS.; ChUp.; reciting, recitation, ŚāṅkhBr. **—pūjā-vidhi**, m. N. of wk. **—** 1. **-vat**, mfn. (for 2. see p. 1061, col. 1) accompanied by a Śastra, KātyŚr., Sch.

1. **Śastraka**, n. = 1. *śastra*, KātyŚr.

1. **Śastrin**, mfn. (for 2. see p. 1061, col. 2) reciting, a reciter, ĀpŚr., Sch.

Śásman, n. invocation, praise, RV.

1. **Śásya**, mfn. (for 2. see p. 1061, col. 2) to be recited or treated as a Śastra, Br.; to be praised or celebrated, Kāv.; to be wished, desirable, excellent, W.; n. recitation, ŚāṅkhBr.; good quality, merit, W.

शक् *śak*, cl. 5. P. (Dhātup. xxvii, 15) *śaknoti* (pf. *śaśāka*, *śekúḥ*, RV. &c. &c.; aor. *áśakat*, AV. &c. [Ved. also Pot. *śakeyam* and *śakyām*; Impv. *śagdhí*, *śaktam*]; fut. *śaktā* or *śakitā*, Gr.; *śakshyati*, °*te*, Br. &c.; *śakishyate*, °*te*, Gr.; inf. *-śaktave*, RV.; *śaktum* or *śakitum*, Gr.), to be strong or powerful, be able to or capable of or competent for (with acc., dat. or loc., rarely acc. of a verbal noun, or with an inf. in *am* or *tum*; or with pr. p.; e.g. with *grahaṇāya* or *grahaṇe*, 'to be able to seize;' *vadha-nirṇekam a-śaknuvan*, 'unable to atone for slaughter;' *śakéma vājíno yámam*, 'may we be able to guide horses;' *vīkshituṃ na śaknoti*, 'he is not able to see;' *pūrayan na śaknoti*, 'he is not able to fill'), RV. &c. &c. (in these meanings ep. also *śakyati*, °*te*, with inf. in *tum*; cf. Dhātup. xxvi, 78); to be strong or exert one's self for another (dat.), aid, help, assist, RV. vii, 67, 5; 68, 8 &c.; to help to (dat. of thing), ib. ii, 2, 12; iv, 21, 10 &c.: Pass. *śakyate* (ep. also °*ti*), to be overcome or subdued, succumb, MBh.; to yield, give way, ib.; to be compelled or caused by any one (instr.) to (inf.), ib.; to be able or capable or possible or practicable (with an inf. in pass. sense, e.g. *tat kartuṃ śakyate*, 'that can be done;' sometimes with pass. p., e.g. *na śakyate vāryamāṇaḥ*, 'he cannot be restrained;' or used impers., with or without instr., e.g. *yadi*[*tvayā*] *śakyate*, 'if it can be done by thee,' 'if it is possible'), Mn.; MBh. &c.: Caus. *śākayati* (aor. *aśīśakat*), Gr.: Desid., see *√śiksh*. [Cf., accord. to some, Gk. ὄπις, ἀοσσητήρ; Germ. *Hag*, *Hecke*, *hegen*; *behagen*.]

1. **Śaka**. See *su-śáka*.

Śakita, mfn. (cf. Kāś. on Pāṇ. vii, 2, 17) able, capable (mostly used with *na*, and giving a pass. sense to the inf., e.g. *na śakitaṃ chettum*, it could not be cut; also impers., e.g. *na śakitaṃ tena*, he was not able), MBh.; R.; Kathās.

Śakta, mfn. able, competent for, equal to, capable of (instr., gen., dat., loc., acc. of person with *prati*, inf., or comp.), Mn.; MBh. &c.; = *śakita*, able to be (with inf. in a pass. sense), Kāś. on Pāṇ. vii, 2, 17; m. N. of a son of Manasyu, MBh.

Śákti or **śaktí**, f. power, ability, strength, might, effort, energy, capability (*śaktyā* or *ātma-ś°* or *sva-ś°*, 'according to ability;' *paraṃ śaktyā*, 'with all one's might;' *vitta-śaktyā*, 'according to the capability of one's property;' *śaktim a-hāpayitvā*, 'not relaxing one's efforts, exerting all one's strength'), faculty, skill, capacity for, power over (gen., loc., dat., or inf.), RV. &c. &c.; effectiveness or efficacy (of a remedy), ŚārṅgS.; regal power (consisting of three parts, *prabhutva*, personal pre-eminence; *mantra*, good counsel, and *utsāha*, energy), Kām. (cf. Ragh. iii, 13); the energy or active power of a deity personified as his wife and worshipped by the Śākta (q.v.) sect of Hindūs under various names (sometimes only three, sometimes eight Śakti goddesses are enumerated, as follow, Indrāṇī, Vaishṇavī, Śāntā, Brahmāṇī, Kaumārī, Nārasiṇhī, Vārāhī, and Māheśvarī, but some substitute Cāmuṇḍā and Caṇḍikā for the third and sixth of these: according to another reckoning there are nine, viz. Vaishṇavī, Brahmāṇī, Raudrī, Māheśvarī, Nārasiṇhī, Vārāhī, Indrāṇī, Kārttikī, and Pradhānā: others reckon fifty different forms of the Śakti of Vishṇu besides Lakshmī, some of these are Kīrtti, Kānti, Tushṭi, Pushṭā, Dhṛiti, Śānti, Kriyā, Dayā, Medhā &c.; and fifty forms of the Śakti of Śiva or Rudra besides Durgā or Gaurī, some of whom are Guṇôdarī, Virajā, Śālmalī, Lolâkshī, Vartulâkshī, Dīrgha-ghoṇā, Sudīrgha-mukhī, Go-mukhī, Dīrgha-jihvā, Kuṇḍôdarī, Ardha-keśī, Vikṛita-mukhī, Jvālā-mukhī, Ulkā-mukhī &c.; Sarasvatī is also named as a Śakti, both of Vishṇu and Rudra: according to the Vāyu-Purāṇa the female nature of Rudra became twofold, one half *asita* or white, and the other *sita* or black, each of these again becoming manifold, those of the white or mild nature included Lakshmī, Sarasvatī, Gaurī, Umā &c.; those of the dark and fierce nature, Durgā, Kālī &c.), Kāv.; Kathās.; Pur. (cf. RTL. 181 &c.; MWB. 216); the female organ (as worshipped by the Śākta sect either actually or symbolically), RTL. 140; the power or signification of a word (defined in the Nyāya as *padasya padârthe sambandhaḥ*, i.e. 'the relation of a word to the thing designated'), Bhāshāp.; Sāh.; (in Gram.) case-power, the idea conveyed by a case (= *kāraka*), Pāṇ. ii, 3, 7, Sch.; the power or force or most effective word of a sacred text or magic formula, Up.; Pañcar.; the creative power or imagination (of a poet), Kāvyâd.; help, aid, assistance, gift, bestowal, RV.; a spear, lance, pike, dart, RV. &c. (also *śaktī*, g. *bahv-ādi*); a sword, MW.; (prob.) a flag-staff (see *ratha-ś°*); a partic. configuration of stars and planets (when the latter are situated in the 7th, 8th, 9th, and 10th astrological house), VarBṛS.; m. N. of a Muni or sage (the eldest of Vasishṭha's hundred sons; accord. to VP. he was father of Parāśara, and was devoured by king Kalmāsha-pāda, when changed to a man-eating Rākshasa, in consequence of a curse pronounced upon him by the sage; he is represented as having overcome Viśvāmitra at the sacrifice of king Saudāsa; he is regarded as the author of RV. vii, 32, 26; ix, 97, 19–21; 108, 3; 14–16; Śakti is also identified with one of the Vyāsas, and with Avalokiteśvara, and has elsewhere the patr. Jātukarṇa and Sāṃkṛiti), Pravar.; MBh. &c. **—kara**, mfn. producing strength, Cāṇ. **—kuṇṭhana**, n. the deadening or blunting of a faculty, MW. **—kumāra**, m. N. of a prince, Inscr.; of a man, Daś.; of a poet, Cat.; (*ī*), f. N. of a woman, Vcar. **—kumāraka**, m. N. of a man, Inscr. **—gaṇa**, m. the company or assemblage of Śaktis (see col. 2), MW. **—graha** (only L.), mf(*ā*)n. (cf. Pāṇ. iii, 2, 9, Vārtt. 1, Pat.) holding a spear or lance; taking hold of the force or meaning (of a word or sentence &c.); m. a spearman, lancer; N. of Kārttikeya and Śiva; perception or apprehension of the force or sense (of a word &c.) **—grāhaka**, m. who or what causes to apprehend the force or signification (of a word or phrase), determining or establishing the meaning of words (as a dictionary, grammar &c.), MW.; = *-graha*, ib. **—ja**, mfn. born from Śakti, ib.; m. a son of Ś°, ib. **—jāgara**, m. N. of a Tāntric wk. **—jāmala**, w.r. for *-yāmala*. **—jña**, mfn. one who knows his powers, MBh. **—tantra**, n. N. of a Tantra. **—tas**, ind. in consequence or by reason of power or strength, Kap.; Sāṃkhyak.; according to power, to the best of one's ability, Mn.; MBh. &c. **—tā**, f. (ifc.) power, capacity, faculty, BhP. **—traya**, n. the three constituents of regal power (see col. 2), ib. **—tva**, n. (ifc.) = *-tā*, Suśr. **—datta**, m. N. of a man, Cat. **—dāsa**, m. N. of the author of the Māyā-bīja-kalpa, ib. **—deva**, m. N. of a Brāhman, Kathās.; of an author of Mantras, Cat. **—dvaya-vat**, mfn. endowed with two powers or faculties, Vedântas. **—dhara**, mfn. bearing or holding a spear, VarBṛS.; m. 'spearman,' N. of a warrior, Hit. (v.l. *śakti-vara*); of Skanda, Hariv.; BhP. (cf. *kanaka-śakti*); of an author of Mantras, Cat.; of a Tāntric teacher, ib. **—dhṛik**, mfn. bearing a spear, MW. **—dhvaja**, m. 'having a spear for emblem,' N. of Skanda, Daś. **—nātha**, m. 'lord of Śakti,' N. of Śiva, Mālatīm. **—nyāsa**, m. N. of a Tāntric wk. **—parṇa**, m. Alstonia Scholaris, L. **—pāṇi**, m. 'spear-handed,' N. of Skanda, Kālac. **—pāta**, m. prostration of strength, MW. **—putra**, m. 'son of Ś°,' N. of Skanda, L. **—pūjaka**, m. a Śakti-worshipper, a Śākta, Cat. **—pūjā**, f. Śakti-worship, MW.; N. of wk. **—pūrva**, m. 'having Śakti for a forefather,' patr. of Parāśara, VarBṛS. **—prakarsha**, mfn. possessing superior capacity or power, MW. **—prakāśa-bodhinī**, f., **-bodha**, m. N. of wks. **—bhadra**, m. N. of an author, Cat. **—bhṛit**, mfn. bearing power, powerful, VārBṛS.; 'spear-holder,' N. of Skanda, L.; a spearman, W. **—bheda**, m. difference of power, MW.; a special capacity, ib. **—bhairava-tantra**, n. N. of a Tantra. **—mat**, mfn. possessed of ability, powerful, mighty, able to (inf. or loc.), Mn.; MBh. &c.; possessing a competence, one who has gained a fortune, MW.; possessed of or united with his Śakti or energy (as a god), Kathās.; armed with a spear or lance, Hariv.; m. N. of a mountain (prob. w.r. for *śukti-mat*), MBh.; (*atī*), f. N. of a woman, Kathās.; (*-mat*)*-tva*, n. power, might, Ragh. **—maya**, mf(*ī*)n. consisting of or produced from a Śakti &c., Cat. **—moksha**, m. 'loss of strength' and 'hurling a spear,' Vās. **—yaśas**, f. N. of a Vidyādharī and of the 10th Lambaka of the Kathā-sarit-sāgara (named after her). **—yāmala**, n. N. of a Tantra. **—rakshita** or °**taka**, m. N. of a king of the Kirātas, Kathās. **—ratnâkara**, m. 'jewel-mine of Śakti,' N. of a wk. on the mystical worship of Śakti or Durgā. **—vana-māhātmya**, n. N. of a ch. of the BhavP. **—vara**, see *-dhara*. **—vallabha**, m. N. of an author, Cat. **—vāda**, m. 'assertion of Śakti-doctrine,' N. of a phil. wk. by Gadādhara-bhaṭṭâcārya; *-kalikā*, f., *-ṭīkā*, f., *-rahasya*, n., *-vivaraṇa*, n.; °*dârtha-dīpikā*, f. N. of wks. **—vādin**, m. one who asserts the Śakti-doctrine, an adherent of Ś°-doctrine, a Śākta, Cat. **—vicāra**, m. N. of a phil. wk. (= *-vāda*). **—vijaya-stuti**, f., **-vijaya-svāmi-stotra**, n. N. of wks. **—vīra**, m. (in Śakti worship) the man who has intercourse with the woman representing Śakti, W. **-vega**, m. N. of a Vidyādhara, Kathās. **-vaikalya**, n. deficiency of power or strength, incapacity, debility, W. **-vaibhavika**, mfn. endowed with power and efficacy, MārkP. **-śodhana**, n. 'purification of Ś°,' a ceremony performed with the woman representing Ś°, W. **-shṭha** (for *-stha*), mfn. potent, mighty, L. **-saṃgama-tantra**, n., **-saṃgamâmṛita**, n. N. of Tāntric wks. **-siṇha**, m. N. of a man, Cat. **-siddhânta**, m. N. of wk. **-sena**, m. N. of a man, Rājat. vi, 216. **-stotra**, n. N. of a Stotra. **-svāmin**, m. N. of a minister of Muktâpīḍa, Cat. **-hara**, mf(*ā*)n. depriving of strength, Cāṇ. **-hasta**, m. = *-pāṇi*, Kālac. **-hīna**, mfn. powerless, impotent, Hit. **-hetika**, mfn. armed with a spear or lance, L.

1. **Śaktin**, mfn. (prob.) furnished with a flag-staff, MBh. (cf. *ratha-śakti*).

2. **Śaktin**, m. N. of a man (= *śakti*, m.), MBh.

Śakti-vat, mfn. (cf. *śakti*) 'powerful' or 'helpful,' RV.; TBr.

Śakty, in comp. for *śakti*. **-apêksha**, mfn. having regard or reference to ability, according to power or capacity, MW. **-ardha**, m. 'half-strength,' a partic. stage of exhaustion (perspiring or panting with fatigue), L. **-avara**, mfn. junior to Śakti, MW.

Śakna or **śaknu**, mfn. kind or pleasant in speech (= *priyam-vada*), L.

Śaknuvāna. See *a-ś°*.

Śákman, n. power, strength, capacity, RV.; energy, action, ib.; m. N. of Indra, L.

Śakya, mf(*ā*)n. able, possible, practicable, capable of being (with inf. in pass. sense, e.g. *na sā śakyā netum balāt*, 'she cannot be conducted by force;' *tan mayā śakyam pratipattum*, 'that is able to be acquired by me;' the form *śakyam* may also be used with a nom. case which is in a different gender or number, e.g. *śakyaṃ śva-māṇsâdibhir api kshut pratihantum*, 'hunger can be appeased even by dog's flesh &c.;' cf. Vām. v, 2, 25), MBh.; Kāv. &c.; to be conquered or subdued, liable to be compelled to (inf.), MBh.; explicit, direct, literal (as the meaning of a word or sentence, opp. to *lakshya* and *vyaṅgya*), Alaṃkāraś. **-tama**, mfn. most possible, very practicable (with inf. in a pass. sense), Hit. iii, 115 (v.l.) **-tā**, f., **-tva**, n. possibility, practicability, capacity, capability, Sarvad. (*-tâvacchedaka*, n. = *śakyâṅśe bhāsamāna-dharmaḥ*, L.) **-pratikāra**, mfn. capable of being remedied, remediable, Kathās. (*a-pr°*); m. a possible remedy or counter-agent, W. **-rūpa**, mfn. possible to be (inf. in pass. sense), MBh. xii, 2613. **-śaṅka**, mfn. liable to be doubted, admitting of doubt, Sarvad. **-sāmantatā**, f. the state of being able to conquer neighbouring kings, Kām.

Śakrá, mf(*ā́*)n. strong, powerful, mighty (applied to various gods, but esp. to Indra), RV.; AV.; TBr.; Lāṭy.; m. N. of Indra, MBh.; Kāv. &c.; of an Āditya, MBh.; Hariv.; of the number 'fourteen,' Gaṇit.; Wrightia Antidysenterica, L.; Terminalia Arjuna, L. **-kārmuka**, n. 'Indra's bow,' the rainbow, VarBṛS. **-kāshṭhā**, f. 'Indra's quarter,' the east, Dhūrtan. **-kumārikā** (KālP.) or **°rī** (VarBṛS.), f. a small flag-staff used with I°'s banner, VarBṛS. **-ketu**, m. Indra's banner, ib. **-krīḍâcala**, m. 'Indra's pleasure-mountain,' N. of the m° Meru, L. **-gopa** or **-gopaka**, m. the cochineal insect (cf. *indra-g°*), MBh.; Kāv. &c. **-cāpa**, n. = *-kārmuka*, MBh.; Hariv. &c.; *-samudbhavā*, f. a kind of cucumber, L.; °*pāya*, Nom. Ā. °*yate*, to represent a rainbow, Hariv. **-ja**, m. 'Indra-born,' a crow, L. **-janitrī**, f. 'I°'s mother,' N. of the largest flag-staff used with Indra's banner, VarBṛS. **-jāta**, m. = *-ja*, L. **-jānu**, m. N. of a monkey, R. **-jāla**, n. magic, sorcery, Kālac. **-jit**, m. 'I°'s conqueror,' N. of the son of Rāvaṇa (his first name was Megha-nāda, but after his victory over I°, described in the Rāmāyaṇa, Uttara-k° xxxiv, it was changed by Brahmā to Śakra-jit = Indra-jit, q.v.; he was killed by Lakshmaṇa), R.; Ragh. &c.; of a king, VP. **-taru**, m. a species of plant (= *vijayā*), L. **-tejas**, mfn. glorious or vigorous like I°, Bhag. **-tva**, n. I°'s power or dignity, MBh. **-dantin**, m. I°'s elephant (called Airāvata), Śiś. **-diś**, f. = *-kāshṭhā*, Kāv.; VarBṛS. **-deva**, m. N. of a king of the Kaliṅgas, MBh.; of a son of Śṛigāla, Hariv.; of a poet, Cat. **-devatā**, f. N. of a partic. night of new moon, MBh. **-daivata**, n. 'having I° as deity,' N. of the Nakshatra Jyeshṭhā, VarBṛS. **-druma**, m. Pinus Deodora, L.; Mimusops Elengi, L.; Terminalia Arjuna, L. **-dhanus**, n. = *-kārmuka*, MBh.; R. &c. **-dhvaja**, m. I°'s banner, MBh.; R.; VarBṛS.; *-taru*, m. id., Hariv.; °*jôtsava*, m. = *śakrôtsava*, MW. **-nandana**, m. 'I°'s son,' patr. of Arjuna, L. **-paryāya**, m. Wrightia Antidysenterica, L. **-pāta**, m. the lowering of I°'s flag, Yājñ. **-pāda**, m. the foot of I°'s banner, VarYogay. **-pādapa**, m. Pinus Deodora, L.; Wrightia Antidysenterica, L. **-pura**, n. (Kull.), **-purī**, f. (Kathās.) I°'s town. **-pushpikā** or **-pushpī**, f. Menispermum Cordifolium, L. **-prastha**, n. N. of ancient Delhi (= *indra-prastha*), MBh.; BhP. **-bāṇâsana**, n. = *-kārmuka*, R. **-bīja**, n. the seed of Wrightia Antidysenterica, L. **-bhaksha**, m. or n. = *śakrâśana*, Kautukas.; *-bhakshaka*, m. an eater of I°'s food, ib.; *-makha* or *-makhôtsava*, m. a festival in honour of the plant called 'I°'s food,' ib. **-bhavana**, n. I°'s heaven, Svarga or paradise, L. **-bhid**, m. = *-jit*, L. **-bhuvana**, n. = *-bhavana*, W. **-bhūbhavā**, f. Cucumis Coloquintida, L. **-bhūruha**, m. = *-vriksha*, L. **-mātṛi**, f. Clerodendrum Siphonantus, L. **-mātṛikā**, f. = *-janitrī*, KālP. **-mūrdhan**, m. I°'s head, an ant-hill, L. **-yava**, m. = *-bīja*, Suśr. **-yaśo-vidhvaṇsana**, n. N. of a ch. of GaṇP. ii. **-rūpa**, mfn. having the form of I°, MW. **-loka**, m. = *-bhavana*, Mn.; R.; *-bhāj*, mfn. sharing I°'s heaven or paradise, MW. **-vallī**, f. colocynth, L. **-vāpin**, m. N. of a serpent-demon, MBh. **-vāhana**, m. 'Indra's vehicle,' a cloud, L. **-vṛiksha**, m. Wrightia Antidysenterica, L. **-śarâsana**, n. = *-kārmuka*, L.; °*nāya*, Nom. P. °*yate* (°*yita*, n., impers.), to represent a rainbow, Dhanamj. **-śākhin**, m. = *-vriksha*, Bhpr. **-śālā**, f. 'I°'s hall,' a place or room prepared for sacrifices, L. **-śiras**, n. = *-mūrdhan*, L. **-sadas**, n. I°'s seat or palace, MBh. **-sārathi**, m. I°'s charioteer Mātali, L. **-suta**, m. 'I°'s son,' N. of the monkey Vālin, L.; of Arjuna (cf. *-nandana*), W. **-sudhā**, f. 'I°'s nectar,' gum olibanum, L. **-sṛishṭā**, f. 'I°-created,' Terminalia Chebula or yellow myrobalan (fabled to have sprung from the ground on which I° spilt a drop of nectar), L. **-stuti**, f. N. of wk. **Śakrâkhya**, m. 'I°-named,' an owl (cf. *ulūka* and Vām. ii, 1, 13), L. **Śakrâgni**, m. du. I° and Agni (lords of the Nakshatra Viśākhā), VarBṛS. **Śakrâtmaja**, m. 'I°'s son,' N. of Arjuna, MBh. **Śakrâdana**, n. = *śakra-taru*, L. **Śakrâditya**, m. N. of a king, Buddh. **Śakrânalâkhya**, mfn. called I° and Agni (ibc.), VarBṛS. (cf. *śakrâgni*). **Śakrâbhilagna-ratna**, n. a partic. gem, L. **Śakrâyudha**, n. = *śakra-kārmuka*, R.; VarBṛS.; MārkP. **Śakrâri**, m. 'I°'s enemy,' N. of Kṛishṇa, Pañcar. **Śakrâvatāra-tīrtha**, n. N. of a place of pilgrimage, Siṇhās. **Śakrâvarta**, m. id., MBh. **Śakrâśana**, m. 'I°'s food,' the plant Wrightia Antidysenterica (fabled to have sprung from the drops of Amṛita which fell to the ground from the bodies of Rāma's monkeys restored to life by I°), L.; n. the seed of Wr° Ant°, L.; an intoxicating drink prepared from hemp (= *bhaṅgā*), Hāsy.; Kautukas. (cf. *indrâśana*); *-kānana*, n., *-vāṭikā*, f., *-vipina*, n. a wood or garden in which hemp grows, ib. **Śakrâsana**, n. I°'s throne, MBh.; Kāv. **Śakrâhva**, m. (?) the seed of Wrightia Antidysenterica, L. **Śakrêśvara-tīrtha**, n. N. of a Tīrtha, Cat. **Śakrôtthāna**, n. the raising up of I°'s banner, = next, Cat. (also °*nôtsava*, m., VP.) **Śakrôtsava**, m. 'I°-festival,' a festival in honour of I° on the twelfth day of the light half of Bhādra (when a flag or banner was set up; cf. *dhvajôtthāna* and *śakra-dhvajôtsava*), MBh.

Śakrāṇī, f. N. of Śacī (wife of Indra), MBh.

Śakri, m. (only L.) a cloud; a thunderbolt; an elephant; a mountain.

Śakru, m. N. of a man, VP.

1. **Śakla**, mfn. (for 2. see p. 1047, col. 1) speaking pleasantly or kindly, affable, L. (cf. *śakna*).

Śákvan, mf(*arī*)n. powerful, able, mighty, VS.; m. an artificer, ŚBr.; an elephant, L.; (*arī*), f., see below.

Śakvara, m. a bull, Hcar.; Kām., Sch.; (*ā*), f. gravel, L. (prob. w.r. for *śarkarā*).

Śákvarī, f. pl. (wrongly written *śakkarī* or *śarkarī*) N. of partic. verses or hymns (esp. of the Mahānāmnī verses belonging to the Śākvara-Sāman), RPrāt.; Gobh.; a partic. metre (in Vedic texts of 7 × 8 syllables, and therefore called *sapta-padā*, later any metre of 4 × 14 syllables, e.g. the Vasanta-tilaka, q.v.), TS.; Kāṭh.; ChUp. &c.; pl. water, AV.; VS.; Gobh.; du. the arms, Naigh. ii, 4; sg. a cow, AV.; PañcavBr. (cf. Naigh. ii, 11); a finger, L.; a river, Uṇ. iv, 112, Sch.; N. of a river, L.; a girdle, Kāvyâd. iii, 149. **-tvá**, n. the state or condition of being a Śakvarī verse, MaitrS. **-pṛishṭha**, mfn. having the Śakvarī verses for a Pṛishṭha (q.v.), Lāṭy.

Śagmá, mf(*ā́*)n. powerful, mighty, strong, effective (others 'helpful, kind, friendly'), RV.; AV.; VS.; Br.; Kauś.

Śágman, n., v.l. for *śákman*, Naigh. ii, 1.

Śagmyà, mf(*ā*)n. = *śagma*, RV.; AV.; ŚBr.

शक 2. *śáka*, n. excrement, ordure, dung (cf. *śakan*, *śakṛit*), AV.; water (v.l. for *kaśa*), Naigh. i, 12; m. a kind of animal, Pañcar. (v.l. *śala*); w.r. for *śuka*, MBh. xiii, 2835; (*ā*), f. a kind of bird or fly or long-eared animal, VS.; TS. (Sch.) **-dhūma**, m. the smoke of burnt or burning cow-dung, AV.; (prob.) N. of a Nakshatra, ib.; a priest who augurs by means of cow-dung, Kauś.; *-já* or *-jā́*, mfn. produced or born from cow-dung, AV. **-mdhi**, m. N. of a man, g. *śubhrâdi*. **-piṇḍa**, m. a lump of dung, VS. **-pūṇa**, m. (fr. √*pūṇ*?) N. of a man (cf. *śākapūṇi*). **-pūta** (*śáka-*), mfn. 'purified with cow-dung,' N. of the author of RV. x, 132 (having the patr. Nārmedha), Anukr. **-bali** (*śáka-*), m. an oblation of cow-dung, AV. **-máya**, mf(*ī*)n. consisting of or arising from excrement, RV. **-mbhará**, mfn. bearing dung or ordure, AV. **-loṭa**, m. (√*luṭ*?) = *śālūka*, a lotus-root, Gobh. (Sch.; accord. to some = *śaka-loshṭa*, 'a lump or ball of cow-dung'). **-hū**, mfn., Pat. **Śakâidha**, m. a fire (made) with the excrement of animals, ĀpŚr.

Śakandhu, n. (perhaps for *śakan-andhu*) a dung-well (?), Pāṇ. vi, 1, 94, Vārtt. 4.

शक 3. *śaka*, m. pl. N. of a partic. white-skinned tribe or race of people (in the legends which relate the contests between Vasishṭha and Viśvāmitra the Śakas are fabled to have been produced by the Cow of Vasishṭha, from her sweat, for the destruction of Viśvāmitra's army; in Mn. x, 44, they are mentioned together with the Pauṇḍrakas, Oḍras, Draviḍas, Kāmbojas, Javanas or Yavanas, Pāradas, Pahlavas, Cīnas, Kirātas, Daradas, and Khaśas, described by Kullūka as degraded tribes of Kshatriyas called after the districts in which they reside: according to the VP. iv, 3, king Sagara attempted to rid his kingdom of these tribes, but did not succeed in destroying them all: they are sometimes regarded as the followers of Śaka or Śāli-vāhana, and are probably to be identified with the Tartars or Indo-Scythians [Lat. *Sacæ*] who overran India before the Āryans, and were conquered by the great Vikramâditya [q.v.]; they really seem to have been dominant in the north-west of India in the last century before and the first two centuries after the beginning of our era), AVPariś.; Mn.; MBh. &c.; a king of the Śakas, g. *kambojâdi* (on Pāṇ. iv, 1, 175, Vārtt.); an era, epoch (cf. *-kāla*); a year (of any era), Inscr.; a partic. fragrant substance, Gal. **-kartṛi** or **-kāraka**, m. the founder of an era, L.; °*kôtpatti*, f. N. of wk. **-kāla**, m. the Śaka era (beginning A.D. 78, and founded by king Śāli-vāhana; an *expired* year of the Śaka era is converted into the corresponding year A.D. by adding to it 78–79; e.g. 654 *expired* = A.D. 732–733), VarBṛS.; Rājat. (RTL. 433). **-kṛit**, m. = *-kartṛi*, L. **-cella** (?), m. N. of a poet, Cat. **-deśa**, m. N. of a country, Cat. **-nṛipati-saṃvatsara**, m. a year of the Śaka era, Inscr. **-nṛipāla**, m. a Śaka king, Jyot. **-purusha-vivaraṇa**, n. N. of wk. **-bhūpa-kāla**, m. = *śaka-kāla*, VarBṛS. **-vatsara**, m. a year of the Śaka era, L. **-varṇa**, m. N. of a king, VP. **-varman**, m. N. of a poet, Cat. **-varsha**, m. or n. = *-vatsara*, Jyot. **-vṛiddhi**, m. N. of a poet, Cat. **-sthāna**, n. N. of a country (Σακαστήνη), Hcar. **Śakâditya**, m. 'sun of the Ś°s,' N. of king Śāli-vāhana, L. **Śakâdhipa-rājadhānī**, f. the capital or residence of the Ś° king, i.e. Ḍillī (Delhi), L. **Śakântaka**, m. 'destroyer of the Ś°s,' N. of king Vikramâditya, L. **Śakâbda**, m. a year of the Ś° era, W. **Śakâri**, m. 'enemy of the Śakas,' N. of king Vikramâditya, Rājat. **Śakêndra-kāla**, m. = *śaka-bhūpa-kāla*, VarBṛS.

2. **Śakāra**, m. (for 1. see under 1. *śa*) a descendant of the Śakas, a Śaka, Pat. on Pāṇ. iv, 1, 130; a king's brother-in-law through one of his inferior wives (esp. in the drama represented as a foolish,

frivolous, proud, low, and cruel man, such as is Saṃsthānaka in the Mṛicchakaṭikā, he speaks the dialect of the Śakas i. e. Śākārī, which employs the sibilant *ś* exclusively; hence Śakāra, accord. to some, is for 'Śa-kāra,' one who uses the letter Śa), Bhar.; Daś.; Sāh. &c.

Śakāri-lipi, f. a partic. kind of writing, Lalit.

शकच *śakaca*, m. a proper N., Rājat.

शकट *śakaṭa*, n. (rarely m., of doubtful derivation) a cart, waggon, car, carriage, Nir.; ŚāṅkhŚr. &c.; (with *prājāpatyam* or *rohiṇyāḥ*, cf. *rohiṇī-ś°*) the five stars forming the asterism Rohiṇī compared to a cart, Kāv.; VarBṛS. &c.; (only) n. a partic. configuration of stars and planets (when all the planets are in the 1st and 7th house), VarBṛS.; m. n. a form of military array resembling a wedge, Mn. vii, 187; m. Dalbergia Ougeinensis, L.; Arum Colacasia, L.; an implement for preparing grain, MW.; w.r. for *śākaṭa*, q.v.; N. of a man, g. *naḍâdi;* of a demon slain by the child Kṛishṇa, Śiś.; m. or n.(?) N. of a place, Cat.; (*ī*), f., see below. **–dāsa**, m. N. of a man, Mudr. **–nīḍa**, n. the interior of a cart, ĀpŚr. **–bhid**, m. 'slayer of Śakaṭa,' N. of Vishṇu-Kṛishṇa, Pañcar. **–bheda**, m. division of the Ś° asterism by the moon or a planet passing through it, Col. **–mantra**, m. pl. the verses addressed to the chariot of Soma, ĀpŚr. **–vila** (?), m. a gallinule, W. (cf. *śakaṭâvila*). **–vyūha**, m. a partic. form of military array, MBh. **–vrata**, n. a partic. observance, Cat. **–sârtha**, m. a multitude or train of carts, caravan, Pat. on Pāṇ. iii, 2, 115. **–han**, m. = *-bhid*, W. **Śakaṭâksha**, m. the axle of a cart, MW. **Śakaṭâṅgaja**, m. a patr. = *śākaṭāyana*, Gaṇar. **Śakaṭâpaṇa**, m. pl. carts and merchandise, R. (w.r. *śakaṭâyana*). **Śakaṭâri**, m. 'enemy of Ś°,' N. of Kṛishṇa, L. **Śakaṭâvila** (?), m. a kind of aquatic bird (= *plava*), Yājñ., Sch. **Śakaṭâsura-bhañjana**, m. 'crusher of the demon Ś°,' N. of Kṛishṇa, Pañcar. **Śakaṭâhvā**, f. 'cart-named,' the asterism Rohiṇī (cf. above), L. **Śakaṭôccāṭana**, n. the upsetting or overturning of a cart, BhP.

Śakaṭāya, Nom. P. °*yati*, to represent or be like a cart, BhP.

Śakaṭāra, m. a bird of prey (perhaps a kind of vulture), MW.; N. of a monkey, Hit.; = *śakaṭāla*, W. **Śakaṭārôpâkhyāna**, n. the episode or fable of the monkey Śakaṭāra, Cat.

Śakaṭāla, m. N. of a minister of king Nanda (in revenge for ill-treatment he conspired with the Brāhman Cāṇakya to effect his master's death), Hcar.; Kathās.

Śakaṭi, f. = *śakaṭī*, g. *bahv-ādi*.

Śakaṭika, mfn. (fr. *śākaṭa*), g. *kumudâdi*.

Śakaṭikā, f. a small cart, a child's cart, toy-cart, Mṛicch. ix, $\frac{2}{2}\frac{8}{9}$ (cf. *mṛic-chakaṭikā*).

Śakaṭin, mfn. possessing a cart or carriage; m. the owner of a cart, Kathās.

Śakaṭī, f. a waggon, cart, carriage, RV. x, 146, 3 (cf. g. *bahv-ādi*). **–karṇa**, g. *suvâstv-ādi* (Kāś. *śaṭī-karṇa*). **–mukha**, mf(*ī*)n. 'cart-mouthed,' having a mouth like a cart, ShaḍvBr. **–śakaṭa**, mfn. (prob.) consisting of (or produced by) carts or carriages of all kinds (as a noise), Hariv.

Śakaṭīya-śabara, m. N. of a poet, Cat.

Śakaṭyā, f. a multitude of carts, g. *pāśâdi*.

शकन् *śakán*. See *śákṛit*, col. 3.

शकम् *śakam*. See under *śám* (ind.)

शकर *śákara*. See next.

शकल *śákala*, m. n. (in ŚBr. also *śákara*, of doubtful derivation) a chip, fragment, splint, log, piece, bit, TS. &c. &c. (*śakalāni* √*kṛi*, with acc., 'to separate, divide, dissipate,' Ragh.); a potsherd, Mn. vi, 28; a spark (in *kṛiśānu-ś°*), Śiś. v, 9; n. a half, Sāh. (*candra-ś°*, the half-moon, Kād.); a half-verse, Ked.; the half of an egg-shell, Mn.; MBh. &c.; skin, bark, Divyâv.; the scales of a fish (cf. *śalka*, *śalkala*), ib.; the skull (in *kapāla-ś°*); cinnamon, L.; a kind of black pigment or dye, L.; m. N. of a man, g. *gargâdi*. **–jyotis**, m. a kind of venomless snake, L. **–vat**, mfn., g. *madhv-ādi*. **Śakalâṅgushṭhaka**, mfn. (Vedic), Pāṇ. iii, 1, 59, Sch. **Śakalêndu**, m. the half-moon, Hariv. (also w.r. for *śakal°*).

Śakalaya, Nom. P. °*yati*, to break into pieces, divide, Mcar.

Śakalā-√kṛi, P. *-karoti*, id., g. *ūry-ādi*.

Śakalita, mfn. broken into pieces, reduced to fragments, Hcar.; Śiś.; Bālar.

Śakalin, m. 'having scales,' a fish, Harav.

Śakalī, in comp. for *śakala*. **–karaṇa**, n. the act of breaking in pieces, W. **–√kṛi**, P. *-karoti*, to break in pieces, divide, bruise, Kād.; ĀpŚr., Sch. **–kṛita**, mfn. broken or cut in pieces, reduced to fragments, smashed, bruised, divided, MBh.; Kāv. &c. **–kṛiti**, f. = *-karaṇa*, Harav. **–√bhū**, P. *-bhavati*, to be broken in pieces, burst asunder, MBh.; R. **–bhūta**, mfn. broken in pieces, bruised, crushed, burst, MBh.

Śakaly'eshin, mfn. (accord. to Padap. from *śakalya + eshin*) 'desiring fragments of wood,' devouring or licking (as a flame of fire), AV. i, 25, 2.

शकव *śakava*, m. (doubtful) a goose, W.

शकशकाय *śakaśakāya*, P. °*yati* (onomat.), to make a rustling noise, rustle (as the leaves of a tree in the wind), Bhaṭṭ.

शकार 1. 2. *śakāra*. See under 1. *śa* and 3. *śaka*.

शकुटा *śakuṭā*, f. a partic. part of an elephant's hind leg, L.

शकुन *śakuná*, m. (said to be fr. √*śak*, Uṇ. iii, 49) a bird (esp. a large bird or one of good or bad omen), RV. &c. &c.; a partic. kind of bird (either = *gṛidhra*, a vulture, or = *cilla*, a common kite or Pondicherry eagle), L.; a kind of Brāhman (*vipra-bheda*), MW.; a sort of hymn or song (sung at festivals to secure good fortune), W.; (with *Vasishṭhasya*) N. of a Sāman, ĀrshBr.; N. of an Asura, BhP.; pl. N. of a people, MBh.; Buddh.; (*ī*), f., see col. 3; n. any auspicious object or lucky omen, an omen or prognostic (in general; rarely 'an inauspicious omen'), Kāv.; Kathās.; Pañcat.; mfn. indicating good luck, auspicious, MW. **–jña**, mfn. knowing omens, Kathās.; (*ā*), f. a small house-lizard, L. **–jñāna**, n. knowledge of birds or omens, augury, Yājñ.; N. of a chapter of the ŚārṅgP. **–dīpaka**, m. (or *ikā*, f.) N. of a wk. on augury. **–devatā**, f. a deity presiding over good omens, Kathās. **–dvāra**, n. 'door of omens,' a partic. term in augury, VarBṛS. **–pattra**, n., **-parîkshā**, f., **-pradīpa**, m., **-ratnâvalī**, f. N. of wks. **–ruta-jñāna**, n. knowledge of the notes of birds, VarBṛS.; Rājat. **–vidyā**, f. = prec., Buddh. **–śāstra**, n. 'doctrine or book of omens,' N. of wk. **–sārôddhāra**, m. N. of wk. **–sûkta**, n. the bird-hymn (perhaps RV. i, 164, 20 or x, 146, 2), VarBṛS. **Śakunâdhishṭhātrī**, f. (a goddess) presiding over good omens, Kathās. **Śakunârṇava**, m., °*nâvalī*, f. N. of wks. on augury. **Śakunāśā**, f. N. of a plant, Suśr. (perhaps w.r. for *śakulâśa;* cf. *śakulâdanī*). **Śakunâhṛit**, m. a kind of rice, L.; a kind of fish, L. **Śakunâhṛita**, mfn. brought by birds, L.; a kind of rice, Suśr. (cf. prec.) **Śakunôpadeśa**, m. the doctrine of omens, augury, VarBṛS.

Śakunaka, m. a bird, MBh.; (*ikā*), f. a female bird, ib.; N. of one of the Mātṛis attendant on Skanda, ib.; of various women, Vās.

Śakúni, m. a bird (esp. a large bird, L. = *gṛidhra* or *cilla*, accord. to some 'a cock'), RV. &c. &c.; (in astronomy) N. of the first fixed Karaṇa (q. v.), VarBṛS.; N. of a Nāga, MBh.; of an evil demon (son of Duḥ-saha), MārkP.; of an Asura (son of Hiraṇyâksha and father of Vṛika), Hariv.; Pur.; of the brother of queen Gāndhārī (and therefore the brother-in-law of Dhṛita-rāshṭra and the Mātula or maternal uncle of the Kuru princes; as son of Subala, king of Gāndhāra, he is called Saubala; he often acted as counsellor of Duryodhana, and hence his name is sometimes applied to an old officious relative whose counsels tend to misfortune), MBh.; Hariv. &c. (cf. IW. 380); of a son of Vikukshi and grandson of Ikshvāku), Hariv.; of a son of Daśa-ratha, ib.; BhP.; of the great-grandfather of Aśoka, Rājat.; du. N. of the Aśvins, MW.; (*i* or *ī*), f., see below. **–graha**, m. N. of a demon causing children's diseases, MBh. **–prapā**, f. a drinking-trough for birds, L. **–vāda**, m. the first song of birds (or of a partic. bird) at dawn (accord. to some 'the crowing of a cock'), AitBr. **–savana**, n., g. *savanâdi*. **–sādá**, m. a partic. part of the sacrificial horse, VS.

Śakunîśvara, m. 'lord of birds,' N. of Garuḍa, L.

Śakuny-upâkhyāna, n. N. of wk.

Śakunī, f. (of *śakuna* or °*ni*, col. 2) a female bird, MBh.; Hariv.; a hen-sparrow, L.; Turdus Macrourus, L.; N. of a female demon (sometimes identified with Durgā) causing a partic. child's-disease (sometimes = *pūtanā*, and in this sense also *śakuni*), MBh.; Hariv.

Śakúnta, m. a bird, MBh.; Kāv. &c.; a partic. bird of prey, BhP.; a blue jay, L.; a sort of insect, L.; N. of a son of Viśvāmitra, MBh.

Śakuntaká, m. a small bird, VS.; MBh.; (*ikā*), f. a female bird, RV.

Śakuntalā, f. (said to be fr. *śakunta*) N. of a daughter of the Apsaras Menakā by Viśvāmitra (she was supposed to have been born and left in a forest, where she was protected by birds till found by the sage Kaṇva, who took her to his hermitage and reared her as his daughter; she was there seen by king Dushyanta, when on a hunting expedition, and married by him, and became the mother of Bharata, sovereign of all India; the story of Dushyanta's accidental meeting with Śakuntalā, their marriage, separation, his repudiation of her through temporary loss of memory caused by a curse, his subsequent recognition of her by means of a ring which was lost but afterwards recovered, forms the subject of Kālidāsa's celebrated drama called Abhijñāna-śakuntala, q.v.). **–°tmaja** (°*lâtm°*), m. 'Ś°'s son,' metron. of Bharata (sovereign of India), L. **Śakuntalôpâkhyāna**, n. 'story of Ś°,' N. of MBh. i, 60–74 and of PadmaP., Svargakh. 1–5.

Śakúnti, m. a bird, RV.; Kāv.

Śakuntikā. See *śakuntaka*.

शकुन्द *śakunda*, m. Nerium Odorum, L. (cf. *śata-kunda*).

शकुर *śakura*, mfn. tame, quiet (as an animal), Hcar.

शकुल *śakulá*, m. a kind of fish (perhaps 'the gilt-head'), VS.; AV.; MBh. &c.; a kind of spur-like projection (behind the hoof of an ox or cow), VS.; (with *Vasishṭhasya*) N. of a Sāman (v. l. for *śakuna*); (*ī*), f., see below. **–gaṇḍa**, m. a kind of fish, L. **Śakulâkshaka**, m. 'fish-eyed,' white bent-grass, Panicum Dactylon (the blossoms are white and compared to the eye of a fish), L. **Śakulâkshī**, f. a kind of Dūrvā grass, L. (cf. prec.) **Śakulâda**, m. pl. 'eating Śakulas,' N. of a people, g. *kāśyādi*. **Śakulâdanī**, f. (cf. *śakunâśā*) a kind of potherb (accord. to L. Commelina Salicifolia, Scindapsus Officinalis &c.), Car.; Vāgbh.; an earthworm, W. **Śakulârbhaka**, m. a sort of fish, L.

Śakulin, m. a fish, L. (prob. w. r. for *śakalin*, q. v.)

शकृत् *śákṛit*, n. (the weak cases are optionally formed fr. a base *śakán*, cf. Pāṇ. vi, 1, 3; *śakṛit*, nom. acc. sg. and ibc.; gen. sg. *śaknás*, AV.; instr. *śaknā́*, VS., or *śakṛitā*, KātyŚr., instr. pl. *śákabhis*, TS.; acc. pl. *śakṛitas*, VarBṛS.), excrement, ordure, feces, dung (esp. cow-dung), RV. &c. &c. [Cf. Gk. σκώρ, σκατός; accord. to some, κόπρος and Lat. *cacare*.] **–kari**, m. 'dung-making,' a calf, L. (cf. Pāṇ. iii, 2, 24). **–kāra**, mfn. making ordure, W. **–kīṭa**, m. a dung-beetle, L. **–padī**, f. having ordure at the feet, g. *kumbha-pady-ādi*. **–piṇḍa**, m. a lump or ball of cow-dung, Kauś.; Āpast.

Śakrid, in comp. for *śakṛit*. **–graha**, w.r. for *śakṛid-gṛ°*, q.v. **–deśa**, m. (R.), **-dvāra**, n. (K.) 'door of the feces,' the anus. **–bheda**, m. 'loosening of the feces,' diarrhœa, Suśr.

Śakṛin, in comp. for *śakṛit*. **–mūtra**, n. feces and urine, BhP. (cf. *mūtra-śakṛit*).

शक्कर *śakkara*, °*rī*. See *śakvara*, °*rī*.

शक्करि *śakkari*, m. a bull, L. (cf. *śakvara*).

शक्कुलि *śakkuli*, prob. w.r. for *śashkuli*, Siddh.

शक्त *śakta*, *śakti* &c. See p. 1044, col. 2.

शक्तु *śaktu*, *śaktuka*, incorrect for *saktu*, *saktuka*, q. v.

शक्त्रि *śaktri*, *śaktrin*, w. r. for *śakti*, m.

शक्मन् śakman, śakya, śakra &c. See p. 1045, col. 1.

शक्ल 2. śakla, m. (for 1. see p. 1045, col. 2) prob. for śakala, śalka, TS.

Śaklī-karaṇa, n. = śakalī-k°, breaking or hewing in pieces, Bālar.

शक्वन् śakvan, śakvara, śakvarī. See p. 1045, col. 2.

शग्म śagmá, śagmyà. See p. 1045, col. 3.

शङ्क् śaṅk, cl. 1. Ā. (Dhātup. iv, 12) śáṅkate (ep. also P.; aor. 2. sg. aśaṅkīs, aśaṅkishṭa, śaṅkishṭhās, śaṅkithās, MBh. &c., inf. śaṅkitum, ib.; ind. p.; -śaṅkya, ib.; Gr. also pf. śaśaṅke, fut. śaṅkitā, śaṅkishyate), to be anxious or apprehensive, be afraid of (abl.), fear, dread, suspect, distrust (acc.), Br.; MBh.; to be in doubt or uncertain about (acc.), hesitate, MBh.; Kāv. &c.; to think probable, assume, believe, regard as (with two acc.), suppose to be (śaṅke, 'I think,' 'I suppose,' 'it seems to me'), ib.; (in argumentative works) to ponder over or propound a doubt or objection: Pass. śaṅkyate (aor. aśaṅki), to be feared or doubted &c.: Caus. śaṅkayati, to cause to fear or doubt, render anxious about (loc.), Mālav.

1. **Śaṅka**, m. (for 2. see below) fear, doubt (see comp.); N. of a king, Buddh. (cf. śaṅkana); (ā), f., see below. **-tva-nirukti**, f. N. of wk.

Śaṅkana, m. 'causing fear or awe (?),' N. of a king, MW.

Śaṅkanīya, mfn. to be distrusted or suspected or apprehended (n. impers.), doubtful, questionable, Kāv.; Hit.; Sarvad. &c.; to be supposed to be, to be regarded as (e.g. bādhakatvena, 'as hurting or injuring'), Kusum.

Śaṅkā, f. (ifc. f. ā) apprehension, care, alarm, fear, distrust, suspicion of (abl., loc., or prati with acc., or comp.; brahma-hatyā-kritā śaṅkā, 'the fear of having committed the murder of a Brāhman,' R.; pāpa-śaṅkā na kartavyā, 'no evil is to be suspected,' Kathās.), ŚBr. &c. &c.; doubt, uncertainty, hesitation, MBh.; Kāv. &c.; (ifc.) belief, supposition, presumption (of or that any person or thing is—), ib.; a subject started in disputation, MW.; a species of the Daṇḍaka metre, W. **-°kula** (śaṅkâk°), mfn. bewildered by doubt or fear, MW. **-°taṅkita** (śaṅkât°), mfn. overcome with fear and anxiety, Subh. **-°nvita** (śaṅkânv°), mfn. filled with doubt, apprehensive, afraid, R. **-°bhiyoga** (śaṅkâbh°), mfn. accusation or charge on suspicion, Yājñ., Sch. **-maya**, mf(ī)n. full of doubt or uncertainty, fearful, afraid, R. **-śaṅku**, m. the thorn or sting of doubt or fear, Rājat. **-śīla**, mfn. of hesitating or diffident disposition, prone to doubt, MW. **-°spada** (śaṅkâsp°), n. cause of doubt, ground or matter of suspicion, Hit. **-sprishṭa**, mfn. touched with fear, seized with alarm, Megh. **-hīna**, mfn. free from doubt or apprehension, W.

Śaṅkita, mfn. alarmed, apprehensive, distrustful, suspicious, afraid of (abl., gen., or comp.), anxious about (loc. or acc. with prati), MBh.; Kāv. &c.; assuming, supposing, Rājat.; feared, apprehended, R.; Śāntiś.; doubted, doubtful, uncertain, Mn.; Mṛicch. &c.; weak, unsteady, W. **-drishṭi**, mfn. looking afraid or shy, Pañcat. **-manas**, mfn. faint-hearted, timid, apprehensive, MBh. **-varṇaka**, m. 'of doubtful appearance,' a thief, L.

Śaṅkitavya, mfn. to be feared or suspected or distrusted (n. impers. 'it should be feared' &c.), MBh.; Prasannar.; to be doubted, doubtful, questionable, MBh.

Śaṅkin, mfn. afraid of, fearing (comp.), MBh.; Kāv. &c.; timid, suspicious, distrustful as (comp., e.g. kāka-ś°, 'distrustful as a crow'), MBh.; Kathās.; assuming, supposing, suspecting, imagining, Ragh.; Hit.; full of apprehension or danger, Pañcat.

1. **Śaṅku**, m. (for 2. see col. 2) fear, terror, W.

Śaṅkura, mfn. causing fear, frightful, formidable, L.; m. N. of a Dānava, VP. (v. l. for śaṃkara).

Śaṅkya, mfn. to be distrusted or suspected or feared (n. impers.; superl. -tama), MBh.; Kāv. &c.; to be assumed or expected or anticipated, Daś.; Rājat.

शङ्क 2. śaṅka, m. a bull, L.

शङ्कर śaṅkara. See saṃkara, p. 1054, col. 3.

शङ्कव्य śaṅkavya. See under 2. śaṅku below.

शङ्किल śaṅkila, m. (prob. w. r. for śaṅkhila; cf. śaṅkha) a conch-shell suspended on the ear of an elephant, L.

शङ्कु 2. śaṅkú, m. (of doubtful derivation) a peg, nail, spike, RV. &c. &c.; a stick, Hariv.; a stake, post, pillar, MBh.; an arrow, spear, dart (fig. applied to the 'sting' of sorrow, pain &c.; cf. śaṅkā-, śoka-ś° &c.), Hariv.; Kāv.; Rājat.; a partic. weapon or any weapon, L.; the pin or gnomon of a dial (usually twelve fingers long), Col.; a kind of forceps (used for the extraction of a dead fetus), Suśr.; the fibre or vein of a leaf, ChUp.; the measure of twelve fingers, L.; (in astron.) the sine of altitude, Sūryas.; a partic. high number, ten billions (compared to an innumerable collection of ants), MBh.; R.; the clapper of a bell, Govardh. (L. also 'the penis; poison; Unguis Odoratus; a partic. tree or the trunk of a lopped tree; a partic. fish [accord. to some "the skate fish"] or aquatic animal; a goose; a measuring rod; a Rākshasa; N. of Śiva; of a Gandharva attendant on Śiva; of Kāma; of a Nāga; = aṅśa'); N. of a man, g. gargâdi; of a Dānava, Hariv.; of a Vṛishṇi (son of Ugra-sena), MBh.; Hariv.; Pur.; of a son of Kṛishṇa, Hariv.; of a poet (= śaṅkuka, q. v.), Cat.; of a Brāhman, Buddh.; n. N. of a Sāman, ĀrshBr. **-karṇa**, mf(ī or ā)n. having pointed ears, MBh.; R. &c.; m. an ass, L.; N. of a Dānava, Hariv.; of one of Skanda's attendants, MBh.; of a serpent-demon, ib.; of a Rākshasa, R.; of a son of Janam-ejaya, MBh.; of a camel, Pañcat.; -mukha, mfn. having pointed ears and mouth, MBh.; °nin, mfn. having pointed ears, Hariv.; °ṇêsvara, m. a partic. form of Śiva, MBh.; n. N. of a Liṅga, Cat. **-cchāyā**, f. the shadow of a gnomon, Sūryas. **-jīvā**, f. the sine of a gnomon, ib. **-taru**, m. the tree Vatica Robusta, L. **-tala**, n. the base of a gnomon, Gol. **-dhāna**, n. 'peg-receptacle,' a hole for a pin (made in a skin to fasten it when used as an amulet), Kauś. **-patha**, m., Pāṇ. v, 1, 77, Vārtt. 2. **-puccha**, n. the sting (of a bee &c.), Rājat. **-phaṇin**, m. a kind of aquatic animal, L. **-phalā** or **-phalikā**, f. Prosopis Spicigera, Bhpr. **-mat**, mfn. filled with stakes or spikes, L.; (atī), f. N. of a metre, Col. **-mukha**, mf(ī)n. having a pointed or sharp mouth (as a mouse), Suśr.; m. a crocodile, L.; a kind of leech, Suśr. **-mūlī**, f. the 15th day of the light half of the month Mārga-śīrsha, L. **-vicāra**, m. N. of a wk. (containing rules for finding out the hours by the shadows of pegs driven into the earth in sunshine) by Lakshmī-pati, Cat. **-vṛiksha**, m. = -taru, L. **-śiras**, mfn. spear-headed, L.; m. N. of an Asura, Hariv.; Pur. **-śravaṇa**, mfn. = -karṇa, VarBṛS. **-shṭha** (for -stha), mfn. Pāṇ. viii, 3, 97.

Śaṅkavya, mfn. fit for a peg or serving as a peg, Hcar. (cf. Pāṇ. v, 1, 2, Sch.)

Śaṅkuka, m. a small peg or nail, KātyŚr., Sch.; N. of a poet (author of the Bhuvanâbhyudaya, son of Mayūra), Rājat.; of a writer on rhetoric, Cat.

Śaṅkuci, m. a skate fish (= 2. śaṅku), L. (cf. sāṃkuci).

Śaṅkulā, f. a kind of lancet or knife, Uṇ. i, 37, Sch.; a pair of nippers or scissors (used to cut the areca-nut into small pieces), W. (cf. danta-śaṅku). **-khaṇḍa**, n. a piece cut off with a pair of nippers, Pāṇ. vi, 1, 2, Sch.

Śaṅkoca or **°ci**, m. = śaṅkuci, W.

शङ्ख śaṅkhá, m. n. (ifc. f. ā) a shell, (esp.) the conch-shell (used for making libations of water or as an ornament for the arms or for the temples of an elephant; a conch-shell perforated at one end is also used as a wind instrument or horn; in the battles of epic poetry, each hero being represented as provided with a conch-shell which serves as his horn or trumpet and often has a name), AV. &c. &c.; IW. 403; a partic. high number (said to = a hundred billions or 100,000 krores), MBh.; m. the temporal bone, temple (accord. to some also 'the bone of the forehead' or 'frontal bone'), Yājñ.; MBh. &c.; an elephant's cheek or the part between the tusks (= hasti-danta-madhya), L.; N. of the teeth of an elephant 23 years old, VarBṛS.; Unguis Odoratus, L.; a partic. Mantra, Gobh.; a kind of metre, Ked.; N. of one of Kubera's treasures and of the being presiding over it, MBh.; Kāv. &c.; a military drum or other martial instrument, W.; N. of one of the 8 chiefs of the Nāgas (q. v.), MBh.; Hariv.; Pur.; of a Daitya (who conquered the gods, stole the Vedas, and carried them off to the bottom of the sea, from whence they were recovered by Vishṇu in the form of a fish), ib.; of a demon dangerous to children, ĀpGṛ., Sch.; of a mythical elephant, R.; N. of various men (pl. N. of a Gotra), AV. &c. &c.; of a son of Virāṭa, MBh.; of a son of Vajra-nābha, Hariv.; Pur.; of a law-giver (often mentioned together with his brother Likhita, q. v.), Yājñ.; MBh. &c. (cf. comp. below); of the author of RV. x, 15 (having the patr. Yāmāyana), Anukr.; of another poet, Cat.; of a country in the south of India (said to abound in shells), VarBṛS. (cf. g. śaṇḍikâdi); of a mountain, Hariv.; Pur.; of a forest, VP.; (ā), f. a kind of flute, Saṃgīt. [Cf. Gk. κόγχη; Lat. concha, congius.] **-karṇa**, m. 'shell-eared,' N. of one of Śiva's attendants, L.; of a dog, Vcar. **-kāra** or **-kāraka**, m. a worker in shells, shell-cutter (described as a kind of mixed caste, accord. to some 'the adulterous offspring of Vaiśya-parents whose mother is a widow;' cf. śaṅkhika), Col. **-kumbhaśravas**, f. N. of one of the Mātṛis attendant on Skanda, MBh. **-kusuma**, n. Andropogon Aciculatus, L. **-kūṭa**, m. N. of a serpent-demon, L.; of a mountain, Pur. **-kshīra**, n. 'the milk of a shell,' any impossibility or absurdity, W. **-cakra**, (ibc.) a conch and a discus; -gadā-dhara, mfn. holding a c° and a d° and a mace (as Vishṇu), Vishṇ.; -dhāraṇa-vāda, m. N. of a treatise (treating of the marking of the limbs with a c°, d° and other emblems of Vishṇu) by Purushôttama; -pāṇi, mfn. holding a conch and a discus, VP.; -vidhi, m., -vivaraṇa, n. N. of wks. **-carī** or **-carcī**, f. a mark made with sandal on the forehead, L. **-cilla**, m. Falco Cheela, L. **-cūḍa**, m. N. of an Asura, Pañcar.; of a Gandharva, Cat.; of one of Kubera's attendants, BhP.; of a serpent-demon, Nāg. (also °ḍaka, L.); °ḍêsvara-tīrtha, n. N. of a Tīrtha, Cat. **-cūrṇa**, n. shell-powder, p° produced from shells, L. **-ja**, m. 'shell-born,' a large pearl shaped like a pigeon's egg and said to be found in shells, W. **-jāti** (?), f. N. of a princess, Buddh. **-tīrtha**, n. N. of a Tīrtha, MBh. **-datta**, m. N. of a poet, Rājat.; of another man, Kathās. **-dāraka**, m. a shell-cutter, Col. **-drāva** or **-drāvaka**, m. a solvent for dissolving the conch or other shells (used in medicine), L. **-drāvin**, m. 'shell-dissolver,' Rumex Vesicarius, L. **-dvīpa**, m. N. of a Dvīpa, VP. (one of the 6 islands of Anudvīpa, which lie in the southern sea, L.) **-dhara**, m. N. of various authors (esp. of the author of the Laṭaka-melana-prahasana), Cat.; (ā), f. Hingcha Repens, Madanav. **-dhavalā**, f. Jasminum Auriculatum, L. **-dhmá**, m. a shell-blower, one who plays on the conch or horn, VS.; ŚBr. **-dhmá**, m. id., Vop. **-dhvani**, m. the sound of a conch or horn, Mālatīm. **-naka**, m. = next, L. (prob. w. r.) **-nakha**, m. a kind of snail, MBh.; Vās.; the shell of the Trochus Perspectivus, MW.; the perfume called Nakhī (Unguis Odoratus) or another kind of perfume. L. **-nābha**, m. N. of a king (son of Vajra-nābha), VP. **-nābhi**, f. a kind of shell, Suśr.; (ī), f. a kind of plant or drug, ib.; Divyâv. **-nāmnī**, f. Andropogon Aciculatus, L. **-nārī**, f. a kind of metre, Col. **-nūpuriṇī**, f. having shell-bracelets and anklets, Pāṇ. v, 2, 128, Sch. **-pad** (strong form -pād), m. N. of a being enumerated among the Viśve Devāḥ, Hariv.; of a son of Kardama (said to have been made regent of the south), VP. **-pada**, m. N. of a son of Manu Svārocisha, MBh.; = next, Hariv.; VP. **-pā**, m. N. of a son of Kardama, VP. **-pāṇi**, m. 'holding a conch in the hand,' N. of Vishṇu, L. **-pātra**, n. a vessel formed like a conch-shell, R. **-pāda**, m. N. of a son of Kardama, VP.; of the chief of a partic. sect, Cat. **-pāla**, m. a kind of snake, Suśr.; a kind of sweetmeat (fr. Pers. شکر پاره), L.; N. of a serpent-demon, Hariv.; BhP.; of a son of Kardama, VP.; n. a house with a partic. defect (also °laka), Vāstuv. **-piṇḍa**, m. N. of a serpent-demon, MBh. **-pura**, n. N. of a town, Kathās. **-pushpikā**, f. Andropogon Aciculatus, Saṃskārak. **-pushpī**, f. id., Vās.; Suśr. (-śrita, mfn. boiled with the above plant, Mn. xi, 148); Canscora Decussata, L. **-poṭalin**, m. a partic. mixture, Bhpr. **-praṇāda**, m. = -dhvani, MW. **-pravara**, m. an excellent or the best shell, ib. **-prastha**, m. a spot in the moon, L. **-bhasman**, n. the ashes of a burnt shell, L. **-bhinna**, mf(ī)n., Pāṇ. iv, 1, 52, Sch. **-bhṛit**, m. 'conch-bearer,' N. of Vishṇu, R.

-mālinī, f. Andropogon Aciculatus, L. **-mitra**, m. N. of a man, Pravar. **-muktā**, f. mother of pearl, R.; pl. shells and pearls, MW. **-mukha**, m. 'shell-faced,' an alligator, L.; N. of a serpent-demon, MBh. **-mudrā**, f. a partic. position of the fingers, Kālac. **-mūla**, n. a partic. esculent root, L. **-mekhala**, m. N. of an ancient sage, MBh. **-mauktika**, m. 'shell-pearl,' a kind of wheat (the husks of which resemble a shell and the grains a pearl), L. **-yūthikā**, f. Jasminum Auriculatum, L. **-rāj**, m. the best of shells, MW. **-rāja**, m. N. of a king, Rājat. **-rāvita**, n. a sound of conches, R. **-roman**, m. N. of a serpent-demon, Hariv. **-lakshaṇa**, n. N. of wk. **-likhita**, mfn. perfect in its kind, faultless, flawless (with *vṛitti*, f. faultless conduct), MBh.; m. a king who practises justice, a just king, MW.; du. the two Ṛishis Śaṅkha and Likhita (authors of a law-book), IW. 203; *-priya*, m. 'beloved by Ś° and L°,' a friend of strict justice, Kathās.; *-smṛiti*, f. the law-book of Ś° and L°. **-vaṭī-rasa**, m. a partic. mixture, Bhpr. **-vat**, mfn. possessing or having a shell or shells, L. **-valaya**, m. n. a shell-bracelet, Śiś. **-visha**, n. white arsenic, L. **-śiras**, m. N. of a serpent-demon, MBh. **-śilā**, f. (prob.) a kind of stone, Lalit.; Divyâv. **-śīrsha**, m. N. of a serpent-demon, MBh. **-śuktikā**, f. mother of pearl (= *śuktikā*), L. **-śrī-dhara**, m. N. of a writer on Dharma, Cat. **-snāna**, n. N. of a wk. (on bathing the images of gods with libations of water from conch-shells), ib. **-smṛiti**, f. Ś°'s law-book (mentioned by Yājñ. &c. and existing in a Bṛihat, Vṛiddha and Laghu recension). **-svana**, m. = *-dhvani*, MW. **-svara**, prob. w. r. for *saṃkasvara* = *saṃkasuka*, Mahāvy. **-hrada**, m. N. of a lake, Hariv.; Kathās. **Śaṅkhâkhya**, m. a kind of perfume, MW. **Śaṅkhântara**, n. 'the space between the temples,' the forehead; *-dyotin*, mfn. shining in the forehead, Kum. **Śaṅkhâlu** or °**luka**, n. Dolichos Bulbosus, L. **Śaṅkhā-vatī**, f. (for *śaṅkha-v°*) N. of a river, MārkP. **Śaṅkhâvarta**, m. the convolution of a shell, Bhpr.; a kind of fistula in the rectum, ŚārṅgP. **Śaṅkhâsura**, m. the Daitya Śaṅkha, MW. **Śaṅkhâhata**, n. a partic. rite in the Gavām-ayana, Lāṭy. **Śaṅkhâhvā**, f. Andropogon Aciculatus, L. **Śaṅkhôdaka**, n. the water poured from a conch-shell, MW. **Śaṅkhôddhāra** (or °*ra-tīrtha*), n. N. of a Tīrtha, Cat.; *-māhātmya*, n. N. of wk.

Śaṅkhaka, m. n. the conch-shell (also worn as a bracelet), MBh.; m. the temporal bone, forehead, Yājñ.; disease of the head (pain in the forehead with heat and puffiness of the temples), Suśr.; ŚārṅgS.; (with Jainas) one of the 9 treasures, L.; (*ikā*), f. Andropogon Aciculatus, L.; n. a bracelet (cf. above), W.

Śaṅkhaṇa, m. N. of various men, VP.

Śaṅkhalikā, f. N. of one of the Mātṛis attendant on Skanda, MBh.

Śaṅkhika, m. N. of a man, Buddh.

Śaṅkhin, mfn. possessing a conch (as Vishṇu), MBh.; Hariv.; bearing shells (as water), Āpast.; possessing the treasure called Śaṅkha, MārkP.; possessed by the demon Ś°, ĀpGṛ.; m. the ocean, L.; a worker in shells, L.; N. of Vishṇu, L.; (*inī*), f., see next.

Śaṅkhinī, f. of prec.; mother of pearl, Bālar.; a partic. plant, Suśr.; Car.; ŚārṅgS. (accord. to L. Andropogon Aciculatus, Cissampelos Hexandra, = *śveta-cukrā*, *śveta-puṃnāga*, and *śveta-vṛindā*); a partic. vein (*nāḍī*), Cat.; N. of one of the four classes into which females are divided (the other three being *citriṇī*, *padminī*, and *hastinī*), RTL. 389; N. of a Śakti worshipped by Buddhists, Kālac.; a kind of semidivine being or fairy (*upadevatā-viśesha*), W.; N. of a Tīrtha, MBh. **-phala**, m. Acacia Sirissa, L. **-vāsa**, m. Trophis Aspera, L.

शंग *śaṃ-ga*, *śaṃ-gaya* &c. See p. 1034, col. 3.

शच् *śac*, cl. 1. Ā. *śacate*, to be strong &c. (in this sense a collateral form of √*śak*); to speak out, speak, say, tell, Dhātup. vi, 4.

Śaci (L.), **Śacikā** (VarBṛS.), f. N. of the wife of Indra (= *śacī*).

Śácishṭha, mf(*ā*)n. most powerful or helpful, RV.

Śácī, f. the rendering of powerful or mighty help, assistance, aid (esp. said of the deeds of Indra and the Aśvins, instr. *śácyā* and *śácībhis*, often = 'mightily' or 'helpfully'), RV.; kindness, favour, grace, ib.; AV.; AitBr.; skill, dexterity, RV.; VS.; speech, power of speech, eloquence, Naigh.; N. of the wife of Indra (derived fr. *śacī-pati*, q.v.), ŚāṅkhGṛ.; MBh. &c.; of the authoress of RV. x, 159 (having the patr. Paulomī), Anukr.; Asparagus Racemosus, L.; a kind of coitus, L. **-tīrtha**, n. N. of a Tīrtha, Śak. **-nandana**, m. metron. of Vishṇu, Cat. **-nara**, m. N. of a king of Kaśmīra, Rājat. **-páti** (*śácī-*), m. lord of might or help (applied to Indra and the Aśvins), RV.; AV.; N. of Indra, MBh.; Kāv. &c. (cf. *kshiti-ś°*). **-bala**, m. an actor who dresses like Śakra, L. **-ramaṇa**, m. 'lover or husband of Śacī,' N. of Indra, Bālar. **-vat** (*śácī-*), mfn. mighty or helpful (often in voc. *-vas*), RV. **-vasu**, mfn. (only in voc.), id., ib. **Śacîśa**, m. 'lord of Śacī,' N. of Indra, L.

Śacoka, m. N. of a poet, Cat.

शञ्च् *śañc*, cl. 1. Ā. *śañcate*, to go, L.

शट् *śaṭ* (prob. artificial), cl. 1. P. *śaṭati*, to be sick; to divide, pierce; to be dissolved; to be weary or dejected; to go, Dhātup. ix, 12: cl. 10. Ā. *śāṭayate*, Dhātup. xxxiii, 18, v.l. for √1. *śaṭh*.

Śaṭa, mfn. sour, astringent, acid, L.; m. N. of a man, g. *gargâdi*; of a son of Vasu-deva, Hariv. (prob. w.r. for *śaṭha*); of a country, g. *saṇḍikâdi*.

Śaṭi, f. the plant Curcuma Zedoaria, L.; a partic. kind of ginger (the fresh root of which is scented like a green mango), W.

Śaṭī, f. Curcuma Zedoaria, Suśr. (often written *śaṭhī*). **-karṇa**, g. *suvāstv-ādi* (Kāś.; cf. *śakaṭī-k°*).

शटा *śaṭā*, f. (= *saṭā*, *jaṭā*) an ascetic's clotted hair, W.

शट्टक *śaṭṭaka*, n. flour of rice mixed with water and ghee, Bhpr.

शठ् 1. *śaṭh* (cf. √*śaṭ*, *śal*), cl. 10. Ā. *śāṭhayate*, to praise, flatter, Dhātup. xxxiii, 18.

शठ् 2. *śaṭh* (cf. √1. *śvaṭh*), cl. 10. P. *śaṭhayati*, to speak ill (according to others 'to speak well'); to be true, Dhātup. xxxv, 4.

शठ् 3. *śaṭh* (cf. √2. *śvaṭh*, *saṭh*, *svaṭh*), cl. 10. P. *śāṭhayati*, to accomplish, adorn (others 'to leave unfinished or unornamented'); to go, move, Dhātup. xxxii, 28.

शठ् 4. *śaṭh*, cl. 1. P. *śaṭhati*, to deceive; to hurt; to suffer pain, Dhātup. ix, 65; cl. 10. P. *śāṭhayati* (cf. √*śuṭh*), to be idle or lazy, ib.

Śaṭha, mf(*ā*)n. false, deceitful, fraudulent, malignant, wicked, Āpast.; Mn.; MBh. &c.; m. a cheat, rogue (esp. a false husband or lover, who pretends affection for one female while his heart is fixed on another; one of the four classes into which husbands are divided), W.; a fool, blockhead, ib.; an idler, ib.; a mediator, umpire, L.; the thorn-apple, L.; white mustard seed, L.; N. of an Asura, MBh.; of a son of Vasu-deva, Hariv. (v.l. *gada* and *suta*); (*ī*), f., w. r. for *śaṭī*, Car.; n. saffron, L.; Tabernæmontana Coronaria, L.; steel, L.; tin, L. **-kopa**, m. (with *ācārya*) N. of an author, Cat.; *-vishaya*, m., *-sahasra-nāman*, n. N. of wks. **-tā**, f. (L.). **-tva**, n. (Sāh.) roguery, depravity, malice, wickedness (*-tâcaraṇa*, n. wicked or roguish conduct, MW.) **-dhī** (Mṛicch.), **-buddhi** (Prasaṅg.; *-tā*, f., R.), **-mati** (VP.), mfn. wicked-minded, malicious. **-vairi-vaibhava-dīpikā**, f., **-vairi-vaibhava-prabhākara**, m. N. of wks. **Śaṭhâmbā**, f. Clypea Hernandifolia, L. **Śaṭhâri**, m. 'enemy of the wicked,' (with *muni*) N. of an author, Cat.; *-vyutpatti-dīpikā*, f. N. of a poem. **Śaṭhôdarka**, mfn. deceitful or wicked in the end, MBh.

शढी *śaḍhī*, f. (cf. *śaṭī*) a kind of plant, L.

शण् *śaṇ*, cl. 1. 10. P. *śaṇati*, *śaṇayati*, to give; to go, Dhātup. xix, 35.

शण *śaṇá*, m. (L. also n.) a kind of hemp, Cannabis Sativa or Crotolaria Juncea, AV. &c. &c., an arrow, L. **-kulāyá**, n. a texture of hemp, hempen cloth, ŚBr. **-gaura**, mfn. yellowish like h°, R. **-ghaṇṭikā**, f. Crotolaria of various species, L. **-cūrṇa**, n. the refuse of hemp (after it has been crushed), L. **-tantu**, m. thread or string made of the fibre of the Crotolaria Juncea, MW. **-tāntava**, mf(*ī*)n. made of hempen string, Mn. ii, 42. **-tūla**, n. fibres of h°, Suśr. **-paṭṭa**, m. a hempen bandage, R. **-parṇī**, f. Pentaptera Tomentosa, L. **-pushpikā** or **-pushpī**, f. Crotolaria Verrucosa, Car.; Bhpr. **-phalā**, f. (prob.) a species of plant, Pāṇ. iv, 1, 64, Vārtt. 2, Pat. **-maya**, mf(*ī*)n. made of hemp, hempen, KātyŚr., Sch. **-rajju**, f. a hempen cord or rope, Kauś. **-valka**, m.n. the bark of h°, R. **-śakala**, m. a piece of h°, Kauś. **-śāka**, m. pulse of h°, Cāṇ. **-śulba**, n. a hempen cord or string, Kauś. **-sūtra**, n. id., GṛŚrS.; a net made of h°, W.; *-maya*, mf(*ī*)n. consisting of hempen threads or cord, Mn. ii, 44. **Śaṇâlu** or °**luka**, m. Cathartocarpus or Cassia Fistula, L.

Śaṇaka, m. N. of a man; *-bābhrava*, pl., g. *kārta-kaujapâdi* (Kāś. *śanaka-b°*); (*ikā*), f. Crotolaria of various species, L.

शणीर *śaṇīra*, n. a bank or alluvial island in the middle of the river Śoṇā, L.; an island enclosed by the branches of the river Sarayū at the point where it falls into the Ganges above Chupra (this spot is also called Dardarī-taṭa, 'D°-bank'), L.

शण्ठ *śaṇṭha*, mfn. = *śaṭha*, L.; m. an unmarried or an impotent man, Uṇ. iv, 104, Sch. (cf. *shaṇḍha*).

शण्ड् *śaṇḍ*, cl. 1. Ā. *śaṇḍate*, 'to hurt' or 'to collect' (*rujāyām saṃghāte ca*), Dhātup. viii, 27.

Śaṇḍa, m. thick sour milk, curds, L.; N. of an Asura priest (son of Śukra), VS.; MaitrS. (later N. of a Yaksha); w. r. for *shaṇḍha*, q.v. **Śáṇḍā-márka**, du. Śaṇḍa and Marka (two demons), TS.; Br. &c. (cf. g. *vanas-paty-ādi*).

Śaṇḍika, m. a descendant of Śaṇḍa, RV. ii, 30, 8 (Sāy.); N. of a country, Pāṇ. iv, 3, 92; (*ikā*), f. = *yuddha* (in the language of the Draviḍas), Nīlak.

Śaṇḍilá, m. N. of a man (pl. his descendants), ĀśvŚr.; TĀr. (cf. *śāṇḍila*, °*lya*); (*ī*), f. N. of Parvatī, L.

शण्ढ *śaṇḍha*, w. r. for *shaṇḍha*.

शत् *śat*, *śātayati*. See √2. *śad*, p. 1051.

शत *śatá*, n. (rarely m.; ifc. f. *ī*) a hundred (used with other numerals thus, *ekâdhikam śatam* or *eka-ś°*, a h° + one, 101; *viṃśaty-adhikam śatam* or *viṃśam ś°*, a h° + twenty, 120; *śate* or *dve śate* or *dvi-śatam* or *śata-dvayam*, 200; *trīṇi śatāni* or *tri-śatāni* or *śata-trayam*, 300; *shaṭ-śatam*, 600; or the comp. becomes an ordinal, e.g. *dvi-śata*, the 200th; *dvikam*, *trikam śatam* = 2, 3 per cent; *śatāt para*, 'beyond a h°, exceeding 100;' the counted object is added either in the gen., or in the same case as *śata*, or ibc., e.g. *śatam pitaraḥ* or *śatam pitṝṇām* or *pitṛi-śatam*, 'a h° ancestors;' sometimes also ifc., see comp. below; rarely *śatam* is used as an indecl. with an instr., e.g. *śatám ráthebhiḥ*, 'with a h° chariots,' RV. i, 48, 7; rarely occurs a masc. form in pl., e.g. *pañca-śatān rathān*, MBh. iv, 1057; and *śata*, n. rarely in comp. of the following kind, *catur-varsha-śatam* or °*tāni*, '400 years'), RV. &c. &c.; any very large number (in comp. as *śata-pattra* &c. below). [Cf. Gk. ἑ-κατόν, 'one' hundred; Lat. *centum*; Lith. *szìmtas*; Got. (*twa*) *hunda*; Germ. *hund-ert*; Eng. *hund-red*.] **-himа** (*śatá-*), mfn. = *śatá-hima*, AV. xix, 55, 4 (MSS.) **-kaṇṭaka**, m. Zizyphus Xylopyrus, L. **-kapālêśa**, m. 'lord of a hundred skulls,' (prob.) a form of Śiva, Rājat. **-karṇâcarya**, m. N. of an author, Cat. (w.r. *-karaṇ°*). **-karman**, m. the planet Saturn, L. **-kāṇḍa** (*śatá-*), mfn. having a h° sections, AV. **-kiraṇa**, m. a kind of Samādhi, Kāraṇḍ. **-kīrti**, m. N. of the 10th Arhat of the future Utsarpiṇī, L. **-kunta** (Bhpr. [MS.]) or **-kunda** (L.), m. Nerium Odorum. **-kumbha**, m. Nerium Odorum, Bhpr.; N. of a mountain, L.; (*ā*), f. Phyalis Flexuosa, W.; N. of a river, MBh.; n. gold, W. **-kulīraka**, m. a kind of crustaceous animal, Suśr. **-kusumā**, f. Anethum Sowa, Car. **-kṛitvas**, ind. a h° times, Kāv.; Kathās.; BhP. **-kṛishṇala** (*śatá-*), mf(*ā*)n. rewarded with a h° gold pieces, TS.; Kāṭh. **-kesara**, m. N. of a mountain, BhP. **-koṭi**, f. pl. 100 krores, a thousand millions, Pañcar.; Vās.; mfn. having a h° edges, MW.; m. Indra's thunderbolt, Vās.; Bhām.; N. of wk.; n. a diamond, Dharmaśarm.; *-khaṇḍana*, n., *-maṇḍana*, n., *-vyākhyā*, f. N. of wks. **-kratu** (*śatá-*), mfn. having h°-fold insight or power or a h° counsels &c., RV.; AV.; VS. &c.; containing a h° sacrificial rites (*ekôna-śata-kr°*, one who has made 99 sacrifices), ŚBr.; BhP.; m. N. of Indra (a h° Aśva-medhas elevating the sacrificer to the rank of Indra; cf. Gk. ἑκατομβαῖος), MBh.; Kāv. &c.; (cf. *kshiti-śata-kr°*); *-prastha*, n. N. of the residence of the Yādavas, MBh. (cf. *indra-pr°*); *-smṛiti*, f. N. of wk. **— krī**, mfn. purchased with a h°, Lāṭy. **— khaṇḍa**, n. 'having a h° pieces,' gold, L.; mfn. = *-maya* (°*ḍaṃ* √*kṛi*, to break into a h° pieces), Mṛicch.; *-maya*, mf(*ī*)n. consisting of a h° pieces (in *su-jīrṇa-śata-khaṇḍa-m°*); made of gold, MW. **— ga**, mfn. being in the hundredth, VarYogay. **— gu**, mfn. possessed of a hundred cows, Mn.; Gaut. [cf. Gk. ἑκατόμβη]. **— guṇa**, mfn. a h°-fold, a h°-fold more valuable &c.; a h° times (*am*, ind. a h° t°, a h° t° more than [abl.]), Mn.; MBh.; R.; Pañcar.; a h°, Pañcar.; °*ṇâcārya*, m. N. of a man, Cat.; °*ṇâdhikam*, ind. more than a h° times, MBh. **— guṇita**, mfn. increased a h°-fold, a h° times longer (as a night), Vikr. **— guṇī-bhāva**, m. a h°-f° increase, Kathās. **— guṇī-√bhū**, P. *-bhavati*, to be multiplied a h° times, Vikr.; Kād. **— guṇī-bhūta**, mfn. mult° a h° times, Kathās. **— guptā**, f. Euphorbia Antiquorum, L. **— go-dāna-paddhati**, f. N. of wk. **— granthi**, f. 'having a h° knots,' Dūrvā grass, L. **— grīva**, m. N. of a goblin, Hariv. **— gva**, mf(*ī*)n. h°-fold, MW. (cf. *daśa-gva*, *nava-gva*). **— gvin**, mfn. h°-f°, consisting of h°s, RV. **— ghaṇṭā**, f. N. of a spear, MBh.; of one of the Mātṛis attending on Skanda, ib. **— ghāta**, w.r. for *śara-gh°*, Hariv. **— ghora**, m. a kind of sugar-cane, L. (prob. w.r. for *-pora*). **— ghni**, f., m.c. for *-ghnī*, Hariv.; VarYogay.; BhP. **— ghnin**, mfn. having the weapon Śata-ghnī, MBh. xiii, 1157 (or else perhaps to be taken as one word, *śata-ghnī-khaḍgin*). **— ghnī**, f. (cf. *-han*, p. 1050) a partic. deadly weapon (used as a missile, supposed by some to be a sort of fire-arms or rocket, but described by the Comm. on the Mahābhārata as a stone or cylindrical piece of wood studded with iron spikes), MBh.; Hariv.; Kāv. &c.; a deadly disease of the throat, Suśr.; ŚārṅgS.; Tragia Involucrata, L.; Pongamia Glabra, L.; a female scorpion, W.; N. of Śiva (m.), MW.; *-pāśa-śakti-mat*, mfn. having a Śata-ghnī and a noose and a spear, MBh. xiii, 17, 134 (but *śata-ghnī* may also be separate). **— ghnu** (for *-hanu*?), a kind of plant, Śil. **— cakra** (*śatá-*), mfn. hundred-wheeled, RV. **— caṇḍī**, f. a hundred repetitions of Caṇḍī's exploits, Cat.; *-paddhati*, f., *-pūjā-krama*, m., *-vidhāna*, n., *-vidhāna-paddhati*, f., *-vidhi*, m., *-sahasra-caṇḍī-prayoga*, m., *-sahasra-caṇḍī-vidhi*, m., °*ra-caṇḍy-ādi-vidhāna*, n. N. of wks. **— candra**, mfn. adorned with a h° moons (or moon-like spots), MBh.; BhP.; (scil. *asi* or *carman*) a sword or a shield adorned with a h° m°, BhP.; m. N. of a warrior, MBh. **— candrita**, mfn. = *-candra*, Cat. **— caraṇā**, f. a centipede, ĀpGṛ., Sch. **— carman**, mfn. made of a h° skins, MBh. **— cchada**, m. a sort of woodpecker, Picus Bengalensis, L. **— cchidra**, mf(*ā*)n. having a h° holes or openings, Nyāyam., Sch. **— jit**, m. a vanquisher of a h° (Vishṇu), R.; N. of a son of Raja or Rajas or Viraja, Pur.; of a son of Sahasra-jit, ib.; of a son of Bhajamāna, BhP. (v.l. *śatā-jit*); of a son of Kṛishṇa, VP.; of a Yaksha, BhP. **— jihva**, mfn. h°-tongued (Śiva), MBh. **— jīvin**, mfn. living a h° years, VarBṛS. **— jyoti** or °**tis**, m. N. of a son of Su-bhrāj, MBh. (accord. to Nīlak. 'the moon'). **— ṃ-jayā**, w.r. for *śatrum-jayā*, MBh. **— tanti**, mfn. h°-stringed, KātyŚr., Sch.; ŚBr., Sch. **— tantu**, mfn. id., Kāṭh.; KātyŚr.; AitĀr.; a h°-fold, Kāśikh. **— tantrī** (only f.; ŚāṅkhŚr.) or **-tantrīka**, mfn. (TāṇḍyaBr.) = *-tanti*. **— tamá**, mf(*ā́* or *ī*)n. the hundredth, RV.; MBh.; R. &c. **— tardma**, mfn. having a hundred openings, KātyŚr. **— tarhá**, m. pl. the piercing &c. of a h° (with gen.), TS. **— tárham**, ind. piercing a h° (with gen.), AV. **— tārā**, f. 'having a h° stars,' the constellation Śata-bhishaj (q.v.), L. **— tejas** (*śatá-*), mfn. having a h°-fold vital power &c., ŚBr.; m. N. of a Vyāsa, Cat. **— traya**, n. (MārkP.; Rājat.) or **-trayī**, f. (Rājat.) three h°. **— da**, mfn. giving a h°, MBh. **— dakshiṇa**, mfn. giving a h°-fold reward, AV. (cf. *á-śata-d°*). **— daṇḍârha**, mfn. deserving a fine of a h° (Paṇas), Mn. viii, 240. **— dat** (*śatá-*), mfn. having a h° teeth (said of a comb), AV. **— dantikā**, f. Tiaridium Indicum, L. **— dala**, n. a lotus-flower, Amar.; (*ā*), f. a kind of fl°, L.; the Indian white rose, MW. **— dā** (*śatá-*), mfn. giving or granting a h°, SV. **— dātu** (*śatá-*), mfn. h°-fold, RV. **— dāya** (*śatá-* [RV.; AV.; MaitrS.] or *-dāyá* [TBr.]), mfn. = *-dā*; having abundant wealth, MW.; a h°-fold, ib. **— dāruka**, m. a kind of venomous insect, Suśr. **— dā́van**, mfn. = *-dā*, RV. **— dura** (*śatá-*; prob.) n. a place secured by a h° doors, RV. **— dūshaṇī**, f., **-dūshaṇī-khaṇḍana**, n., **-dūshaṇī-yamata** (for *-yamana*?), **-dūshaṇī-vyākhyā**, f., **-dūshiṇī**, f. N. of wks. **— dyumna** (*śatá-*), m. N. of various men, TBr.; MBh.; Hariv.; Pur. **— dru**, f. 'flowing in a h° (or numerous) branches,' N. of a river now called the Sutlej (it is the most easterly of the five rivers of the Pañjāb, and rises in a lake [prob. Mānasa Sarovar] on the Himālaya mountains; flowing in a south-westerly direction for 550 miles, it unites with the Vipāśā or Beas south-east of Amritsar [see *vipâś*], afterwards joining the Chenāb and falling into the Indus below Multan; it is also called *śutu-dri*, *śu-tu-dru*, *śita-dru* &c.), MBh.; Hariv.; R. &c.; N. of the Ganges, MW.; *-ja*, m. pl. people that dwell near the Sutlej, MārkP. **— drukā**, f. = *-dru*, the Sutlej, MBh. **— druti**, f. N. of a daughter of the sea-god and wife of Barhi-shad, BhP. **— drū**, f. = *-dru*, the Sutlej, R.; VarBṛS. **— dvaya**, n. two h°, VarBṛS.; (*ī*), f. id., Rājat.; °*yī-prâyaścitta*, n. N. of wk. **— d-vasu** (*śatád-*), mfn. (accord. to Sāy.) = *śata-vasu*, having hundreds of treasures, containing much wealth, RV. **— dvāra**, n. a h° doors, MW.; mf(*ā*)n. h°-gated, having a h° outlets, MBh.; Hit.; m. N. of a man, g. *śubhrâdi*. **— dhanu** (BhP.) or °**nus** (Pur.; Pāṇ., Sch.), m. N. of various men. **— dhanyà**, mfn. worth the price of a hundred, RV. **— dhanvan** (*śatá-*), mfn. having a h° bows, VS.; m. N. of various kings, Hariv.; Pur. **— dhara**, m. N. of a king, VāyuP.; Kād. **— 1. -dhā**, f. Dūrvā grass, L. **— 2. -dhā́**, ind. in a h° ways, W.; a h°-fold, into a h° parts or pieces (with √*bhū*, to be divided into a h° parts), ŚBr.; Up. &c. **— dhāman**, m. 'having a h° forms,' N. of Vishṇu, L. **— dhāya**, v.l. for *-dāya*, Kāṭh. **— dhāra** (*śatá-*), mf(*ā*)n. having a h° streams, RV.; VS.; having a h° (i.e. numberless) points or edges, RV.; m. 'h°-edged,' the thunderbolt, Vās.; *-vana*, n. (prob.) N. of a hell, Pāṇ. viii, 4, 4, Sch. **— dhāraka**, m. 'h°-edged,' Indra's thunderbolt, L. **— dhṛiti**, m. 'having a h° sacrifices,' N. of Brahmā, BhP.; of Indra, ib.; = *svarga*, L. **— dhenu-tantra**, n. N. of wk. **— dhauta**, mfn. cleansed a h°-fold, perfectly clean, Suśr.; Car. **— nirhrāda**, mf(*ā*)n. emitting manifold sounds, MBh. **— nītha** (*śatá-*), mfn. having a hundred tricks, RV. **— netrikā**, f. Asparagus Racemosus, L. **— pati** (*śatá-*), m. a lord of a h°, TBr. **— pattra**, n. (ibc.) a h° leaves, DhyānabUp.; a h° vehicles, Śiś.; (*śatá-*), mfn. having a h° (i.e. numberless) feathers or leaves, RV.; having a h° wings, borne by numerous conveyances (said of Bṛihas-pati), MW.; m. a woodpecker, MBh.; Hariv.; R. &c.; a peacock, BhP.; Vās.; the Indian crane, Jātakam. (?); L.; a kind of parrot, L.; a kind of tree, VarBṛS.; (*ā*), f. a woman, W.; (*ī*), f. a kind of rose, Dhanv.; n. a lotus which opens by day, MBh.; Hariv.; R. &c.; *-nivāsa*, mfn. abiding in a lotus, MW.; m. N. of Brahmā, Kavik.; *-yoni*, m. 'lotus-born,' N. of Brahmā, Kum.; °*ttrâyatêkshaṇa*, mfn. having long lotus-like eyes, MBh. **— pattraka**, m. a woodpecker, Suśr.; a kind of venomous insect, ib.; N. of a mountain, Śatr.; (*ikā*), f. a kind of rose, L.; Anethum Sowa, L.; n. a lotus which opens by day, Cat. **— patha**, mfn. having a h° (i.e. numerous) paths, very many-sided, MBh.; Cat.; proceeding in a h° ways, Siṃhâs.; m. = next; *-brāhmaṇa*, n. 'the Brāhmaṇa with a h° paths or sections,' N. of a well-known Brāhmaṇa attached to the Vājasaneyi-saṃhitā or White Yajur-veda, (like the Saṃhitā, this Brāhmaṇa is ascribed to the Ṛishi Yājñavalkya; it is perhaps the most modern of the Brāhmaṇas, and is preserved in two Śākhās or schools, Mādhyaṃdina and Kāṇva; the version belonging to the former is best known, and is divided into fourteen Kāṇḍas or books which contain one hundred Adhyāyas or lectures [or according to another arrangement into sixty-eight Prapāṭhakas]; the whole work is regarded as the most systematic and interesting of all the Brāhmaṇas, and though intended mainly for ritual and sacrificial purposes, is full of curious mythological details and legends; cf. *yajur-veda*, *vājasaneyi-saṃhitā*, *brāhmaṇa*), IW. 25 &c.; *-śruti*, f. N. of wk. **— pathika**, mf(*ī*)n. (fr. *-patha*), Pāṇ. iv, 2, 60, Vārtt. 9; following numberless paths or doctrines, W. **— pathīya**, mfn. belonging to the Śata-patha-brāhmaṇa, Cat. **— pad** or (strong form) **-pād** (*śatá-*), mf(*adī*)n. having a h° feet, RV.; ShaḍvBr.; Lāṭy.; MaitrS. (accord. to Padap. *-pád*); having a h° wheels, MW.; m. a centipede, Tulus, Suśr.; (*adī*), f. id., ib.; Car.; Kathās.; Asparagus Racemosus, L.; a kind of disease peculiar to horses, MBh., Sch. **— pada**, n. (with *cakra*) an astronomical circle with a h° divisions for exhibiting the various div° of the Nakshatras, L.; *-cakra*, n. id., Gobh., Sch. **— padī**, see under *-pad* above. **— padma**, n. the flower of the white lotus, L.; a l° with a h° petals, A. **— payas** (*śatá-*), mfn. containing a h° fluids &c., VS. **— parivāra**, m. a kind of Samādhi, Kāraṇḍ.; (*ā*), f. N. of a Nāga female, ib. **— parṇa**, m. N. of a man (see *śātaparṇeya*). **— parva**, n. vegetable perfume, L.; (*ā*), f. 'h°-jointed,' Dūrvā grass, (or) white D° g°, L.; a kind of Helleborus, L.; a kind of root, = *vacā*, L.; the night of full moon in the month Āśvina, L.; N. of the wife of Śukra, MBh.; °*vêśa*, m. 'lord or husband of Śataparvā,' the planet Venus, L. **— parvaka**, m. or n. (?) white-flowering Dūrvā grass, Suśr.; (*ikā*), f. D° g°, L.; barley, L.; a kind of root (= *vacā*), Bhpr. **— parvan** (*śatá-*), mfn. having a hundred knots or joints, RV.; AV.; Hariv. &c.; m. a bamboo, Bhpr.; a kind of sugar-cane, ib.; the thunderbolt (see comp.); n. a hole, L.; °*va-dhṛik*, m. 'bearer of the th°,' N. of Indra, BhP. **— pavitra** (*śatá-*), mf(*ā*)n. purifying a h°-fold, RV. **— pāka**, mfn. boiled a h° times; n. (with or scil. *taila*) a partic. unguent, MBh.; Suśr. **— pākya**, mfn. = prec.; (with *sneha*), m. a kind of oil, Car. **— pātin**, mfn. (?), MBh. ii, 51, 25. **— pād**, see *-pad*. **— pādaka**, m. a centipede, Suśr.; (*ikā*), f. id., L.; a kind of medicinal plant, L. **— pādī**, f. a centipede, L.; a kind of plant (= *sita-kaṭabhī*), L. **— pāla**, m. an overseer of a h° (villages, gen.), MBh. **— puṭa**, m. a partic. part of the body (= *adhyūdhnī*), KātyŚr., Sch. **— putra**, mfn. having a h° sons, MBh.; *-tā*, f. the possession of a h° s°, ib. **— pushkara**, mf(*ā*)n. consisting of a h° blue lotus-flowers, ĀśvŚr.; R. **— pushpa**, mf(*ā*)n. having a h° flowers, many-flowered, MW.; m. Anethum Sowa, Suśr.; VarYogay.; N. of the poet Bhâravi, L.; of a mountain, Buddh.; (*ā*), f. Anethum Sowa, Suśr.; Var.; Andropogon Aciculatus, L.; = *adhaḥ-pushpī*, *priyaṅgu*, *śukla-vacā*, L.; N. of a Gandharva female, Kāraṇḍ. **— pushpikā**, f. Anethum Sowa, L. **— pona**, m. (for *pavana*?) a sieve, W. **— ponaka**, m. fistula in ano, Suśr.; ŚārṅgS. **— pora** or °**raka**, m. (prob. fr. *parvan*) a kind of sugar-cane, Suśr. (cf. *-ghora* and *nila-pora*). **— prada**, mfn. giving a h°, Nir. **— prabhedana**, m. N. of the author of the hymn Ṛig-veda x, 113 (having the patr. Vairūpa). **— prasava** or **-prasūti**, m. N. of a son of Kambala-barhis, Hariv. **— prasūnā**, f. Anethum Sowa, L. **— prâyaścitta-vājapeya**, N. of wk. **— prâsa**, m. Nerium Odorum, L. **— phalin**, m. a bamboo, Bhpr. **— baddha**, mfn. pl. united in a h°, Hariv. **— bala**, m. N. of a monkey, R.; (*ā*), f. N. of a river, MBh.; VP.; °*lâksha*, m. (with the patr. *maudgalya*) N. of a grammarian, Nir. **— balāka**, m. N. of a teacher, VāyuP. **— bali**, m. a kind of fish, Āpast.; N. of a monkey, R.; (prob. more correct *-vali*). **— balśa** (*śatá-*), mf(*ā*)n. = *śatá-valśa*, AV. **— bāhú** (?), mfn. having a h° arms (a boar), TĀr.; m. a partic. small animal of a noxious kind, Suśr.; N. of an Asura, BhP.; of an evil demon (*māra-putra*), Lalit.; (*u*), f. N. of a goddess, Cat.; of a Nāga female, Kāraṇḍ. **— buddhi**, mfn. h°-witted; m. N. of a fish, Pañcat. **— bradhna** (*śatá-*), mfn. h°-pointed, RV. **— brāhmaṇa-ghāta-ja**, mfn. resulting from (i.e. equal to the guilt of) the murder of a h° Brāhmans, Ml. **— bhaṅgī-√bhū**, P. *-bhavati*, to be varied in a h° ways, Bālar. **— bhāga**, m. the 100th part, ŚvetUp. **— bhisha**, m. = *śatá-bhishaj*, N. of a Nakshatra, L.; (*śatá-bhishaṃ nákshatram*, MaitrS. ii, 13, 20, w.r. for *śatá-bhishan nákshatram*). **— bhishaj** (*śatá-*), m. f. 'requiring a h° physicians,' N. of the 22nd or 24th Nakshatra (containing 100 stars, one of which is λ Aquarii; its name is said to denote that Dhanvantari himself cannot cure a person affected with disease whilst the moon is in this asterism), AV.; TS.; TBr.; m. N. of a man, Pāṇ. iv, 3, 36; °*shak-sena*, m. N. of a man, ib. viii, 3, 100, Sch. **— bhishā**, f. = *śatá-bhishaj*, N. of a Nakshatra, MBh.; Hariv. &c. **— bhīru**, f. Jasminum Sambac, L. (correct *sita-bh°*). **— bhuji** (*śatá-*), mf(*ī*)n. h°-fold, RV.; having a h° enclosures or fortifications, MW. **— bhṛishṭi** (*śatá-*), mfn. having a hundred points or spikes, TS. **— makha**, m. 'having a h° sacrifices,' N. of Indra, Kāv.; Kathās. &c. (cf. *-kratu*); an owl, A. **— manyu** (*śatá-*), mfn. having h°-fold wrath, RV.; VarBṛS.; Rājat.; receiving a h° sacrifices, MW.; very spirited, v° zealous, ib.; m. N. of Indra, Rājat.; BhP.; Bhaṭṭ.; an owl, A.; *-kanthi* or °*thin*, a kind of plant.

Pañcar.; *-cāpa*, m. or n.(?) a rainbow, Kād. **— maya**, in *kapaṭa-śata-maya*, mfn. consisting of h°-fold fraud, Bhartṛ. **— mayūkha**, m. 'h°-rayed,' the moon, VarBṛ. **— mānti**, v.l. for *mānti* (q.v.), Cat. **— māna** (*śatá-*), mfn. h°-fold, VS.; weighing a h° (Raktikās, Sch.), TS.; Kāṭh.; ŚBr. &c.; m. any object made of gold which weighs a h° Mānas, ŚBr.; KātyŚr.; m. n. a weight (or gift) of a h° Mānas in gold or silver (*-dakshiṇa*, mfn., KātyŚr.), ib.; Mn.; Yājñ. &c.; a Pala of silver, W.; an Āḍhaka (q.v.), W.; *-dāna-vidhi*, m. N. of wk. **— māya**, mfn. employing a h° artifices, MBh. **— mārin**, m. 'h°-killer,' a man who has killed a h°, W. **— mārja**, m. (prob. for *śastra-m°*) a sword-polisher, L. **— mukha**, n. a h° mouths or openings, MW.; a h° ways, ib.; mfn. having a h° apertures or outlets, Pañcat.; Hit.; Kathās.; proceeding or possible in a h° ways, Bhartṛ.; having a h° issues or ways, MW.; m. N. of an Asura, MBh.; of one of Śiva's attendants, Hariv.; of a king of the Kiṃ-naras, Kāraṇḍ.; (*ī*), f. N. of Durgā, L.; a brush, broom, A.; *-rāvaṇa-caritra*, n. N. of wk. **— mūti** (*śatá-*), mfn. granting a h° aids, RV. (cf. *śatôti*). **— mūrdhan**, mfn. h°-headed, VS.; m. an ant-hill, L. **— mūla** (*śatá-*), mf(*ā*)n. having a h° roots, TĀr.; (*ā*), f. Dūrvā grass, L.; a kind of root = *vacā*, L.; (*ī*), f. Asparagus Racemosus, L. **— mūlikā**, f. Asparagus Racemosus, L. (also °*lī*); Anthericum Tuberosum, L. **— yajña**, m. 'having a h° sacrifices,' N. of Indra, L.; *-cāpa*, m. or n. Indra's rainbow, Kād.; °*ñôpalakshaka* (?) or °*ñôpalakshita*, mfn. characterized by a h° sacrifices; m. Indra, MārkP. **— yajvan**, m. 'sacrificing with a h°,' N. of Indra, Kir. **— yashṭika**, m. a necklace of a h° strings, L. **— yājam**, ind. with a h° sacrifices, AV. **— yātu** (*śatá-*), m. N. of a man, RV.; Vas. **— yāman** (*śatá-*), mfn. having a h° paths, RV. **— yūpa**, m. N. of a Rājarshi, MBh. **— yoga-mañjarī**, f. N. of wk. **— yojana**, n. a distance of a h° Yojanas, ŚāṅkhBr.; *-parvata*, m. N. of a mountain, Cat.; *-yāyin*, mfn. travelling a h° Yojanas, MBh.; *-vat*, ind. as long as a h° Y°, MW. **— yoni** (*śatá-*), mfn. having a h° receptacles or nests or dwellings, AV. **— rañjinī**, f. N. of wk. **— ratha**, m. N. of a king, MBh.; VP. **— rā** (*śatá-*), mfn. = *-sukha*, RV. x, 106, 5 (Naigh.) **— rātra**, m. n. a festival of a h° days, PañcavBr.; ŚrS.; Maś. **— rudra**, m. pl. a h° Rudras, Cat.; (with Śaivas) N. of a class of emancipated souls, Sarvad.; (*ā*), f. N. of a river and Tīrtha, MatsyaP.; (prob.) n. (perhaps) = *-rudrīya*, MBh. xiii, 7092; *-saṃhitā*, f. N. of a part of the Śiva-purāṇa. **— rudrīya**, mfn. belonging or sacred to a h° Rudras, VS. ('much celebrated,' Mahīdh.); n. (with or scil. *brahman*) N. of a celebrated hymn and prayer of the Yajur-veda addressed to Rudra (Śiva) in his hundred aspects (occurring in VS. xvi, 1–66), ŚBr.; Kāṭh. &c. (cf. RTL. 76); N. of an Upanishad; *-bhāshya*, n. N. of wk.; *-vat*, ind. as in the Śata-rudriya oblation, KātyŚr.; *-śiva-stotra*, n. N. of a ch. of the Mahā-bhārata; *-homa*, m. a partic. oblation, KātyŚr.; N. of the 16th Adhyāya of the Vājasaneyi-saṃhitā. **— rudrīya**, mfn. having a h° Rudras as divinity, L.; n. a hymn of the Yajur-veda (= *-rudrīya*, q.v.), TS.; TBr.; MBh. **— rūpa**, mfn. having a h° forms, L.; m. N. of a Muni, Cat.; (*ā*), f. N. of the daughter and wife of Brahmā (her incestuous intercourse with her father produced Manu Svāyambhuva, but some Purāṇas make Śata-rūpā the wife not mother of the first Manu), Hariv.; BṛĀrUp., Sch.; Pur. **— rca** (fr. *śata + ṛic*), n. a h° Ṛic, L. **— rcas** (*śatá-*; fr. *ś° + ṛic*), mfn. (prob.) having a h° supports (accord. to Sāy. = *śatârcis* or = *śata-vidha-gati-yukta*), RV. **— rcin** (fr. °*ta + ṛic*), m. pl. N. of the authors of the first Maṇḍala of the Ṛig-veda, GṛS.; AitĀr. &c. **— laksha**, n. a h° lacs, ten millions, Pañcar. **— lumpa** or °**paka**, m. N. of the poet Bhāravi, L. (cf. *śatru-lumpa*). **— locana**, mfn. h°-eyed; m. N. of one of Skanda's attendants, MBh.; of an Asura, Hariv. **— vaktra**, m. 'having a h° mouths,' N. of an incantation recited over weapons, R. **— vat** (*śatá-*), mfn. containing a h°, possessed of or accompanied with a h°, RV. **— vadha** (*śatá-*), mf(*ā*)n. causing a h° deaths, AV. **— vani**, m. N. of a man (cf. *śātavaneya*). **— vapus**, m. N. of a son of Uśanas, VP. **— varsha**, n. a h° years, W.; mf(*ā*)n. possessing or lasting a h° y°s, Āpast.; PārGṛ. &c.; *-sahasrin*, mfn. living a h° thousand years, MBh.; *-sāriṇī*, f. N. of wk. **— varshin**, mfn. = *-varsha*, MBh. **— varshman**, mfn. having a h° bodies, Hariv. (v.l. *-śīrsha*). **— vala**, m. (*vala = vali*, accord. to Comm.) N. of a partic. object given as reward for a sacrifice, ŚāṅkhŚr. **— valiśa** (*śatá-*), v.l. for next, MaitrS. **— valśa** (*śatá-*), mfn. having a h° branches, RV.; VS.; AV.; BhP. (cf. *śatá-balśa*). **— vāja** (*śatá-*), mf(*ā*)n. having or yielding a h° energies, RV. **— vāra** (*śatá-*), mfn. consisting of a h° hairs, AV. **— vāra-kam** or **-vāram**, ind. a h° times, AgP. **— vārshika**, mf(*ī*)n. lasting a h° years, MārkP. **— vāhī**, f. bringing a h° as dowry, AV. **— vicakshaṇa** (*śatá-*), mfn. having a h°-fold appearance, RV. **— vitṛiṇṇa** (*śatá-*), mfn. pierced with a h° holes, ŚBr. **— vīra**, m. N. of Vishṇu, L. **— vīrya** (*śatá-*), mfn. having a h° energies, AV.; TS.; Kāṭh.; Br.; m. a partic. Samādhi, Kāraṇḍ.; (*ā*), f. white-flowering Dūrvā grass, Suśr.; Car.; Pañcar.; a vine with reddish grapes, L.; Asparagus Racemosus, L. **— vṛishabha**, m. N. of the 23rd Muhūrta, Sūryapr. **— vṛishṇya** (*śatá-*), mfn. having h°-fold manly strength, AV. **— vedhin**, m. Rumex Vesicarius, L. **— vraja** (*śatá-*), mf(*ā*)n. having a h° folds, RV. **— śakti**, mfn. being able to give a h°, MBh. **— śarkara**, n. a h° grains of gravel &c. (*-tā*, f.), Śiś. **— śala**, a distance of a h° Śalas, MaitrS.; Kāṭh. **— śalāka**, mfn. having a h° ribs (as an umbrella), MBh.; R.; (*ā*), f. a parasol (?), Divyâv. **— śalya** (*śatá-*), mf(*ā*)n. h°-pointed, AV. **— śás**, ind. by or in h°s, a h° times (in connexion with a nom., acc. or instr.; *catur-daśa varshāṇi yāsyanti śata-śaḥ*, '14 years will pass away like a h°'), AV.; Mn.; MBh. &c. **— śākha** (*śatá-*), mf(*ā* or *ī*)n. having a h° branches (also fig.), AV.; MBh.; Hariv. &c.; *-tva*, n. the state of hav° a h° br°, h°-foldness, Rājat. **— śārada** (*śatá-*), mfn. containing or bestowing &c. a h° autumns, RV.; AV.; TS.; n. a period or age of a h° years, RV.; AV.; (*āya*), ind. for a h° autumns or years, MW. **— śāstra**, n., **-śāstra-vaipulya**, n. N. of wks. **— śīrsha**, mfn. h°-headed, MBh.; Hariv.; R.; m. a partic. incantation recited over weapons, R.; N. of a king of the Nāgas, Kāraṇḍ.; (*ā*), f. N. of the wife of Vāsuki, MBh. **— śīrshan** (*śatá-*), mfn. h°-headed, ŚBr.; °*sha-rudra-śamanīya*, mfn. fit to appease the h°-headed Rudra, ŚBr. **— śṛiṅga**, mfn. h°-peaked, R.; m. N. of a mountain, MBh.; BhP.; Pañcar. &c.; *-māhātmya*, n. N. of wk. **— śloka-vyavahāraka**, m., **-ślokī rāmāyaṇa**, n., **-ślokī**, f., **-ślokī-candra-kalā**, f., **-ślokī-vyākhyā**, f. N. of wks. **— saṃvatsara**, mfn. lasting a h° years, Maś.; *-kāla-sūcikā*, f., *-phala*, n. N. of wks. **— saṃkhya**, mfn. numbering a h°, MBh.; Hit.; m. pl. N. of a class of deities in the tenth Manv-antara, Pur. **— saṃgha-śas**, ind. in collections of a h°, by h°s (in connexion with a nom. or acc.), MBh. **— sani**, mfn. gaining or procuring a h°, ShaḍvBr.; PārGṛ. **— saṃdhāna**, mfn. fixing an arrow a h° times, MBh. **— sahasra**, n. sg. or pl. a h° thousand (the counted object may be in gen. or in apposition or comp.), Hariv.; R. &c.; *-dhā*, ind. into a h° th° pieces, R.; *-pattra*, n. a kind of flower, L.; *-yāna*, n. a h° th° roads, MW.; *-śas*, ind. by h°s of th°s (in connexion with a nom., acc., or instr.), MBh.; R.; BhP.; °*rāṅśu*, mfn. having a h° th° rays (said of the moon), MBh.; °*rânta*, mfn. spreading in a h° th° directions (said of the moon), MBh. (v.l.) **— sahasraka**, mf(*ikā*)n. consisting of a h° thousand, Buddh.; n. N. of a Tīrtha, MBh. (v.l. *-sāhasraka*). **— sā́**, mfn. = *-sani*, RV. **— sāhasra**, mf(*ī*)n. amounting to a h° thousand, containing a h° th°, consisting of a h° th°, a h° th°-fold, Mn.; MBh.; Hariv.; MārkP.; n. sg. (m. c.; with gen. pl.) = *-sahasra*, R.; a h° thousandth part, DhyānabUp.; *-saṃkhya*, mfn. numbering a h° th°, R.; *-sammita*, mfn. id., VP. **— sāhasraka**, n. N. of a Tīrtha, MBh. (cf. *-sahasraka*). **— sāhasrika**, mfn. consisting of a h° th°, Hariv. **— sukha**, n. h°-fold happiness, endless delight, Bhartṛ. **— sū**, f. bringing forth a h°, Pāṇ. iii, 2, 61, Sch. **— sūtrī**, f. N. of wk. **— séya**, n. the obtaining of a h°, RV. **— spṛih**, mfn. wished for by h°s, MW. **— sphya** (*śatá-*), mf(*ā*)n. having a h° beams or spars, TS. **— svín**, mfn. possessing a h°, RV. **— hán**, mf(*ghnī*)n. slaying a h°, TS.; (*ghnī*), f., see p. 1049. **— haya**, m. N. of a son of Manu Tāmasa, VP. (v.l. *śānta-h°*). **— hali**, mfn. possessing a h° large ploughs, Daś. **— hasta**, mfn. h°-handed, AV. **— hāyana** (*śatá-*), mfn. containing or lasting for a h° years, ib. **— hima** (*śatá-*), mf(*ā*)n. lasting for or living for a h° winters or years, RV.; AV. **— huta**, mfn. offered a h°-fold, ShaḍvBr. **— hrada**, m. N. of an Asura, Hariv.; (*ā*), f. (ifc. f. *ā*) 'containing a h° rays of light,' lightning or a partic. kind of l°, MBh.; Hariv.; Kāv. &c.; a thunderbolt, L.; N. of one of the daughters of Daksha (the wife of Bāhu-putra), VahniP.; of the mother of the Rākshasa Virādha, R. **— hrādā**, f. 'possessing a h° sounds,' the thunderbolt, W. **Śatâṅśa**, m. a hundredth part, MW. **Śatâṅśaka**, m. the 100th part or division (esp. of a constellation), VarYogay. **Śatâkarā**, f. N. of a Kiṃ-nara female, Kāraṇḍ. **Śatâkārā**, f. N. of a female Gandharva, ib. **Śatâksha**, mf(*ī*)n. h°-eyed, L.; m. N. of a Dānava, Hariv.; (*ī*), f. night, L.; Anethum Sowa, L.; N. of Durgā, MārkP. **Śatâkshara**, mf(*ā*)n. of a h° syllables, ĀpŚr. **Śatâgni-shṭoma**, mfn. connected with a h° Agni-shṭomas, ŚBr. **Śatâgra**, mfn. h°-pointed, Sāy.; the first among a h° (in *-mahishī*, f. the first wife among a h°), MārkP. **Śatâṅkura**, mf(*ā*)n. having a h° shoots, TĀr. **Śatâṅga**, mfn. h°-membered, manifold (applied to musical instruments = 'played upon in numerous ways'), MBh.; m. a chariot, L.; Dalbergia Ougeinensis, L.; N. of a Dānava, Hariv. **Śatâtirātra**, mf(*ā*)n. connected with a h° Atirātras, ŚBr.; KātyŚr. **Śatâtṛiṇṇa**, mf(*ā*)n. having a h° holes, Br.; Kauś.; (*ā*), f. a jar or vessel hav° a h° holes, ŚBr.; Vait. **Śatâtṛishṇā**, w.r. for °*tṛiṇṇā*, TBr. **Śatâtman**, mfn. possessing or bestowing a h° lives, RV.; containing a h° forms, having numerous manifestations, MW. **Śatâdhika**, mf(*ā*)n. exceeding a h°, constituting 101, MBh. **Śatâdhipati**, m. a commander of a h°, ib. **Śatâdhyāya**, m. = *śata-rudriya*, Cat. **Śatânaka**, n. a burning-ground, cemetery, L. **Śatânana**, m. Aegle Marmelos, L.; (*ā*), f. 'hundred-faced,' N. of a goddess, Cat. **Śatânanda**, m. 'delighting h°s,' N. of Brahmā, L.; of Vishṇu or Kṛishṇa, L.; of a sage and other men, MBh.; Hariv.; R. &c.; the car of Vishṇu, L.; (*ā*), f. N. of one of the Mātṛis attending on Skanda, MBh.; °*da-saṃhitā*, f. N. of wk. **Śatânīka**, mf(*ā*)n. having a h° forms of array, RV.; containing or possessing a h° hosts, MW.; m. an old man, L.; a father-in-law, L.; N. of various men, AV.; VS.; Br. &c.; of an Asura, Kathās. **Śatâparādha-prâyaścitta**, n., °**dha-stotra**, n. N. of wks. **Śatâpâshṭha**, mf(*ā*)n. h°-barbed, AV.; TBr. **Śatâbja**, mfn. having a h° lotus-flowers, DhyānabUp. **Śatâbda**, mfn. (a life) consisting of a h° years, Mṛicch.; n. a h° years, century, MW. **Śatâyu**, mfn. = *śatâyus*, ŚBr.; °*tâyu-tā*, f. the state of having existed for a h° years, ib. **Śatâyudha**, mfn. wielding a h° weapons, TS.; Gobh.; m. N. of a king of Vasanta-pura, HPariś.; (*ā*), f. N. of a Kiṃ-nara female, Kāraṇḍ. **Śatâyus**, n. an age or life (consisting) of a h° years, BhP.; (°*tấy°*), mf(*ushī*)n. attaining the age of a h° y°, AV.; Kāṭh.; Lāṭy. &c.; m. a man a h° years old, a centenarian, W.; N. of various men, MBh.; Hariv.; VP.; Kathās. **Śatâra** (or °*târa*), m. n. 'h°-angled,' a thunderbolt, L.; (with Jainas) a partic. Kalpa, Dharmaśarm. **Śatâritra**, mf(*ā*)n. h°-oared, RV.; VS.; AV. **Śatâruka**, m. a kind of leprosy, ŚārṅgS. **Śatâruṇa**, m. N. of a king of the ants, Kauś. (v.l. *śatā-varuṇa*). **Śatârusha**, m. (Car.) or °**rushī**, f. (MW.) or °**rus**, n. (Car.; Bhpr.) = *śatâruka*. **Śatârghá**, mfn. worth a h°, ŚBr. **Śatârṇā**, f. Anethum Sowa, L. **Śatârdha**, n. half a h°, fifty, VarBṛS.; *-saṃkhya*, mfn. numbering f°, ib.; °*dhâra*, mfn. f°-spoked, ŚvetUp. **Śatârha**, mfn. = *śatârghá*, ŚrS. **Śatâvadhāna**, m. 'a man with such a good memory that he can attend to a h° things at once' (also °*nin*), N. of Rāghavêndra, Cat. **Śatâvaya**, mfn. comprising or numbering a h° sheep, RV. **Śatâvara**, m. a fine of a hundred (Paṇas &c.), W.; (*ī*), f. Asparagus Racemosus, Suśr.; ŚārṅgS.; VarBṛS.; Bhpr.; a kind of plant, zedoary (= *śaṭī*), MW.; N. of the wife of Indra, L. **Śatâvarta**, mfn. having a h° tufts or curls (on the head; said of Śiva), MBh.; m. N. of Vishṇu, L.; *-vana*, n. N. of a forest, Hariv. **Śatâvartin**, m. N. of Vishṇu, L. **Śatâśri**, mfn. having a h° angles or edges (said of the thunderbolt), RV. **Śatâśva**, mfn. numbering a h° horses (*sahásram śatâśvam*, a thousand cattle with a h° horses), RV.; ŚrS.; Vait.; *-ratha*, n. sg. a h° cattle and a car with horses, KātyŚr.; *-vijaya*, m. N. of part of wk. **Śatâshṭaka**, n. one h° and eight, Pañcar. **Śatâhvayā**, f. Anethum Sowa, Suśr.; Asparagus Racemosus, L. **Śatâhvā**, f. Anethum Sowa, Suśr. (w.r. °*hva*); Bhpr.; Asparagus Racemosus (°*hve dve*, du.), Car.; N. of a river and Tīrtha, MatsyaP. **Śatếdhma**, n. a h° logs, Kāṭh.; MaitrS. **Śatêndriya**, mfn. having a h° senses, TS.; Br.; (*ā*), f. a proper N., MW. **Śate-pañcāśan-nyāya**, m. the rule that fifty are contained in a h°, TPrāt., Sch. **Śatêśa**, m. the chief of a h° (villages; cf. *grāma-ś°*), Mn. vii, 115, 117. **Śatêshudhi**, mfn. h°-quivered, ŚBr. **Śatâika-śīrshan**, mfn. possessing a h° unique or excellent heads, BhP. (Sch.) **Śatâikīya**, mfn. one of a h°, Rājat. **Śatôkthya**, mfn. having a h° Ukthya-days, ŚBr.; KātyŚr. **Śatôti**, mfn. affording a h° aids &c., protecting h°s, RV.; TS. **Śatôdara**, mfn. having a h° bellies, MBh.; Hariv.; m. a partic. incantation recited over weapons, R.; N. of one of Śiva's attendants, Hariv.; (*ī*), f. N. of one of the Mātṛis attending on Skanda, MBh. **Śatôdyāma**, mfn. having a h° cords or ropes, TBr. **Śatônmāna**, mfn. h°-fold, ŚBr. **Śatôpanishad**, 'a h° Upanishads,' N. of wk. **Śatôlūkhala-mekhalā**, f. N. of one of the Mātṛis attending on Skanda, MBh. **Śatâudanā**, f. N. of a partic. ceremony and of the cow that gives the milk employed in it, AV.; Kauś.; APrāt., Sch.

Śataka, mf(*ikā*)n. consisting of a hundred, comprising or amounting to a h°, Hariv.; MārkP.; the hundredth, R.; m. N. of Vishṇu, L.; (*ikā*), f. an amount of a hundred or of several hundreds (according to the numeral prefixed in comp., e.g. *dvi-śatikām dadāti*, he gives an amount or a sum of 200), Pāṇ. v, 4, 1, Sch.; (*akam*), n. a hundred, a century (construed like *śata*), MBh. &c. (esp. in titles of wks. 'a cento' or 'a collection of 100 stanzas;' cf. *amaru-*, *nīti-ś°* &c.) **–ṭīkā** and **-vyākhyā**, f. N. of Commentaries.

Śatā, in comp. for *śata*. **–jit**, m. 'conquering hundreds,' N. of a son of Bhajamāna, Hariv.; Pur. **–padī**, f. (m.c. for *śata-p°*) a centipede, Car. **–magha** (*śatā-*), mfn. possessing or distributing a h° (i.e. numerous) bounties or rewards (said of Indra), RV. (cf. *magha-van*). **–vat**, mfn. (prob. = *śata-vat*), ib. (accord. to Padap. = *śata* + *avat* fr. √*av*) 'bestowing hundredfold help'). **–varuṇa**, w.r. for *śatâruṇa*.

Śatika, mfn. containing or amounting to a hundred (*-vṛiddhi*, mfn. one whose gain in gambling amounts to 100), Yājñ. ii. 199; the hundredth, VarBṛS.; (accord. to Gr. and L. also) bought with a h°; doing or effecting anything with a h°; bearing tax or interest per h°; changed with or for a h°; indicative of a hundred &c.; (*ikā*), f., see *śataka*.

Śatín, mfn. consisting of hundreds, hundredfold, RV. (*śatínībhis*, ind. 'in a h° manners,' i, 39, 7); possessing a h° (with *gavām*, 'cows'), MBh.; Kāv. &c. (cf. *go-śatin*).

Śatya, mfn. consisting of a hundred, Yājñ.; = *śatika*, bought with a hundred &c., Pāṇ., Sch.

शततिन् *śatatin*, m. N. of a son of Raja or Rajas, VP. (W. *śata-jit*).

शतन *śatana*, n. (for *śātana*, √2. *śad*) cutting down, felling, Divyâv.

शतृ *śatṛi*, (in gram.) a technical term for the Kṛit affix *at* used in forming present participles of the Parasmai-pada.

शतेर *śatera*, m. = *śatru*, an enemy, Uṇ. i, 61, Sch.; hurt, injury, L.

शत्त्रि *śattri*, m. an elephant, Uṇ. iv, 67.

शत्रंजय *śatram-jaya*, (prob.) w.r. for *śatrum-jaya*.

शत्रि *śátri*, m. N. of a man (having the patr. Āgniveśi), RV. v, 34, 9.

शत्रु *śátru*, m. (said to be for *śat-tru*, fr. √2. *śad*) 'overthrower,' an enemy, foe, rival, a hostile king (esp. a neighbouring king as a natural enemy), RV. &c. &c.; the 6th astrological mansion, VarYogay.; Asparagus Racemosus, L.; N. of an Asura, MBh. i, 2543 (perhaps *krodha-śatru* as one word). [Cf. Gk. κότος, κοτέω; Germ. *Hader, Hass, hassen*; Eng. *hate*.] **–ṃ-saha**, mfn. bearing or patient with an enemy (also a proper N.), Pāṇ. iii, 2, 46, Sch. **–karśana** or °**shaṇa**, mfn. harassing enemies, MBh. **–kula**, n. the house of an enemy, Mn. viii, 93. **–gṛiha**, n. N. of the 6th astrol. mansion, VarYogay. **–gha** or **-ghāta**, mfn. slaying enemies, ib. 49, Sch. **–ghātin**, m. 'id.,' N. of a son of Śatrughna (son of Daśa-ratha), R.; Raghuv. **–ghna**, mfn. foe-killing, destroying enemies, Pañcar.; m. N. of one of Rāma-candra's brothers (he was son of Sumitrā and twin brother of Lakshmaṇa, and was the chosen companion of Bharata, son of Kaikeyī, as L° was of Rāma, son of Kauśalyā), R.; Ragh. &c. (cf. IW. 345; 503); of a son of Śva-phalka, Hariv.; of a son of Deva-śravas, ib.; (*ī*), f., see *-han*; n. a weapon, L.; *-jananī*, f. 'mother of Śatru-ghna,' N. of Su-mitrā, L.; *-śarman*, m. N. of an author, Cat. **–jana**, m. an enemy (also coll. 'enemies'), VarBṛS. **–jaya**, mfn. conquering an en°, Kull. on Mn. vii, 164. **–jit**, mfn. id., Pāṇ. iii, 2, 61, Sch.; m. N. of Śiva, Śivag.; of a son of Rājâdhideva, Hariv.; of the father of Ṛita-dhvaja or Kuvalayâśva, Pur.; of various other princes, ib. **–ṃ-jaya**, m. 'foe-conquering,' N. of a divine being, Kauś.; of a king, MBh.; of a door-keeper, Kathās.; of an elephant, Hariv.; R.; of the mountain Vimala (cf. *vimalâdri*) or Girnar in Gujarāt (*-māhātmya*, n. [IW. 367], *-stava*, m., *-stotra*, n. N. of wks.); (*ā*), f. N. of one of the Mātṛis attendant on Skanda, MBh.; of a river, Śatr. **–tas**, ind. from an en° or en°s, MW. **–tā**, f. hostility, enmity (*-tām* √*i*, to become a foe), Kāv.; Kathās. **–tāpana**, mfn. tormenting en°s (said of Śiva), Śivag.; m. N. of a demon producing illness, Hariv. **–tūrya**, n. the overcoming of an adversary, RV. **–tvá**, n. = *-tā*, RV.; Kāv. **–damana**, mfn. subduing enemies, g. *nandy-ādi*. **–nandana**, mfn. gladdening en°s, Hit. **–nāśa-kṛit** or **nāśana**, mfn. destroying en°s, VarBṛS. **–nikāya**, m. a host of en°s, W. **–nibarhaṇa**, mfn. foe-destroying, R. **–nilaya**, m. the dwelling of a foe, W. **–ṃ-tapa**, mfn. harassing en°s, MBh. (also as a proper N., Pāṇ. iii, 2, 46, Sch.; cf. *śātruṃtapi*). **–ṃ-dama**, mfn. subduing en°s, MārkP. (applied to Śiva, Śivag.) **–paksha**, m. the side or part of an en°, MBh.; mfn. taking the side of an en°, an antagonist, opponent, VarBṛS. **–parājaya**, m. (with *svara-śāstra-sāra*) N. of wk. **–bādhaka** (MW.), **-bâdhana** (TS.), mfn. harassing or distressing enemies. **–bha**, n. = *-gṛiha*, VarYogay. **–bhaṅga**, m. Saccharum Munjia, L. **–bhaṭa**, m. N. of an Asura, Kathās. **–mardana**, mfn. crushing or destroying en°s, Kathās.; m. a kind of pavilion, Vāstuv.; N. of a son of Daśa-ratha (= *śatru-ghna*), L.; of a son of Kuvalayâśva, MārkP.; of a king of Videha, W.; of an elephant, Kathās. **–mitrôpaśānti**, f. N. of wk. **–rūpa**, mfn. appearing in the form of an enemy, Pañcat. **–lāva**, mfn. cutting an en° to pieces, killing foes, Bhaṭṭ. **–lumpa**, m. N. of Bhāravi, Gal. (cf. *śata-l°*). **–loka**, w.r. for *śakra-l°*, MārkP. **–vat**, ind. like an en°, MW. **–vala**, mfn. having en°s, Siddh. on Pāṇ. v, 2, 112. **–vigraha**, m. 'war of en°s,' hostile invasion, MW. **–vināśana**, m. 'destroyer of en°s,' N. of Śiva, MBh. **–vilodana**, n. alarming the enemy, Pratāp. **–śalya-carita**, n., **-saṃhanana-kavaca**, m. n. N. of wks. **–sammukham**, ind. facing the en°, in front of the en°, MW. **–saha**, mfn. = *-sāha*, ib. **–sāt**, ind. (with Caus. of √*gam*) to deliver into the hands of an en°, MBh. **–sāha**, mfn. sustaining (the shock of) an en°, ib. **–sevin**, mfn. serving an en°, being in the service of a hostile prince, Mn. vii, 186. **–há**, mfn. slaying enemies, AV. **–hatyā**, f. foe-destruction, hosticide, MW. **–hán**, mfn. = *-há*, RV; BhP.; m. N. of a son of Śva-phalka (cf. *śatru-ghna*), Hariv.; (*ghnī*), f. N. of wk. **–hantṛi**, m. 'foe-slayer,' N. of a minister of Śambara, ib. **Śatrûpajāpa**, m. the treacherous whisperings of an en° (*-dūshita*, mfn. corrupted by an en°'s treachery), Kull. on Mn. vii, 62. **Śatrū-sháh** (strong form *-sháh*), mfn. overpowering enemies, RV.; AV.

Śatruka, m. an enemy, Subh.

Śatrūya, Nom. P. °*yáti*, to be an enemy, be hostile, RV.; AV.; VS.

शत्वरी *śatvarī*, f. (said to be fr. √*śad* or *śam*) night (cf. *śarvarī*), L.

शद् 1. *śad* (only occurring in the forms *śāśadúḥ*, *śāśadmahe*, *śāśadré*, and *śāśadāna*), to distinguish one's self, be eminent or superior, prevail, triumph, RV.; AV. [Cf. Gk. καδ, κεκάσμεθα, κεκασμένος.]

शद् 2. *śad*, cl. 1. 6. Ā. (Dhātup. xx, 25; xxviii, 134) *śīyate* (cf. Pāṇ. vii, 3, 78; P. in non-conjugational tenses, i, 3, 60; pf. *śaśāda*, *śeduḥ*, Br.; fut. *śatsyati*, AV.; aor. *aśadat*, Gr.; fut. *śattā*, ib.; inf. *śattum*, ib.), to fall, fall off or out, AV.; Br.; Bhaṭṭ.: Caus. *śādayati*, to impel, drive on (cattle), Pāṇ. vii, 3, 42; *śātáyati*, °*te* (cf. ib.), to cause to fall off or out or asunder, hew or cut off, knock out, AV. &c. &c.; to fell, throw down, slay, kill, MBh.; Hariv.; R.; to disperse, dispel, remove, destroy, Gobh.; Śiś.; Suśr.: Desid. *śiśatsati*, Gr.: Intens. *śāśadyate*, *śāśatti*, ib. [Cf., accord. to some, Lat. *cedo*.]

Śada, m. falling (see *parṇa-ś°*); produce, revenue, Gaut.; a partic. Ekâha, ĀśvŚr.; any edible vegetable product (*phala-mûlâdi*), L.

Śadaka, m. or n. (?) unhusked corn, Bhadrab. (v.l. *sadaka*).

Śadri (only L.), m. a cloud; an elephant; f. lightning; clayed or candied sugar.

Śadru, mfn. falling, perishing &c., Pāṇ. iii, 2, 159; m. N. of Vishṇu, L.

Śanna, mfn. fallen, decayed, withered &c. (*-mala*, mfn., Nir. xi, 8); n. offal (see *havishya-ś°*).

शड्वला *śadvalā*, f. N. of a river, Śatr.

शन *śana* (prob. connected with √*śam*), quiet, calm, soft (only in instr. pl. *śanais*, q.v.)

Śanakaiś-cara, m. (fr. next + *cara*) = *śanaiścara*, MW.

Śanakais, ind. (dimin. of *śanais*) quietly, softly, gently, by degrees, in every case that arises, with alternations, alternately, RV. &c. &c.

Śani, m. (prob. 'slow-moving;' cf. *manda*) the planet Saturn or its regent (fabled as the offspring of the Sun; he is represented as of a black colour or dressed in dark-coloured clothes; cf. *nīla-vāsas*), R.; VarBṛS. &c.; N. of Śiva, MW.; of a son of Atri, VāyuP. **–cakra**, n. Saturn's diagram (a peculiar diagram used to foretell good or bad fortune; it is marked with 27 compartments to represent the Nakshatras passed through by the planet Saturn), MW. **–ja**, n. 'S°-produced,' black pepper, W. **–trayodaśī-vrata**, n., **-pratimādana**, n. N. of wks. **–pradosha**, m. 'Saturn-evening,' N. of the worship performed to Śiva on the 13th day of the waxing or waning moon when it falls on a Saturday, MW.; *-vrata*, n. N. of wk. **–prasū**, f. 'mother of S°,' N. of Chāyā (wife of the Sun), L. **–priya**, n. 'dear to S°,' a dark-coloured stone (the emerald or sapphire), L. **–vāra** or **-vāsara**, m. S°'s day, Saturday, L. **–śānti**, f., **-sūkta**, n., **-stotra**, n. N. of wks. **Śany-ashṭaka**, n. N. of wk.

Śanair, in comp. for *śanais*. **–gaṅgam**, ind. where the Gaṅgā flows slowly, Pāṇ. ii, 1, 21, Sch. **–dehin**, w.r. for *-mehin*, Car. **–bhāva**, m. slowness, graduality (ibc. before a pr. p. = slowly, by degrees), Kathās. **–meha**, m. slow or painful discharge of water from the bladder, dysuria, ŚārṅgS.; °*hin*, mfn. suffering from dysuria, Suśr.

Śanaiś, in comp. for *śanais*. **–cara**, mfn. walking or moving slowly, Bhartṛ.; m. the planet Saturn or its regent (cf. *śani*), MBh.; Kāv. &c. (in MBh. also applied to other planets and even the sun); Saturday, Vishṇ.; *-kavaca*, m. n., *-pūjā*, f. N. of wks.; *-vāra*, m. Saturday, Subh.; *-vidhāna*, n., *-vrata*, n. N. of wks.; *-saṃvatsara*, m. the year of Saturn (during which this planet completes his course through the 28 Nakshatras; in modern astron. = 30 of our years), MW.

Śánais (RV.) or **śanaís** (ŚBr.), ind. (originally instr. pl. of *śana*, q.v.; cf. *uccais*, *nīcais*) quietly, softly, gently, gradually, alternately, RV. &c. &c. **–tarām**, ind. more (or very) quietly, softly &c., AitBr.; ĀśvŚr.

शनक *śanaka*, m. (cf. *śanaka*) N. of a son of Śambara, Hariv. (v.l. *senaka*).

Śanakâvali or °**lī**, f. (perhaps for *śaṇak°*; cf. *śaṇa*) Scindapsus Officinalis, L.

Śana-parṇī, f. (for *śaṇa-p°*?) Wrightia Antidysenterica, L. (cf. *śana* and *asana-p°*).

शनोत्साह *śanôtsāha*, m. = *gaṇḍaka*, L. (v.l. *svanôtsāha*).

शन्त *śanta*, *śanti* &c. See p. 1055, col. 1.

Śantanu, **śantama** &c. See *śam-tanu*, *śám-tama*, p. 1054, col. 3.

शन्न *śanna*. See √2. *śad*.

शंनोदेवी *śam-no-devī* &c. See p. 1054, col. 3.

शप् 1. śap, (in gram.) a technical term used for the Vikaraṇa *a* (inserted between the root and terminations of the conjugational tenses in verbs of the 1st class; see *vi-karaṇa*, p. 954).

शप् 2. śap, ind. a prefix implying assent or acceptance (as in *śap-karoti*, he admits or accepts), W.

शप् 3. śap, cl. 1. 4. P. Ā. (Dhātup. xxiii, 31; xxvi, 59) *śapati*, °*te* or *śapyati*, °*te* (the latter only in Bhaṭṭ.); pf. *śaśāpa*, *śepé*, aor. *aśāpsīt*, *aśapta*, Gr. [2. pl. *śāpta* in TS. prob. w. r.]; fut. *śaptā*, ib.; *śapsyati*, °*te*, ib.; *śapishye*, MBh.; inf. *śaptum* or *śapitum*, ib.; ind. p. *śapitvā*, ib.; *śaptvā*, Gr.), to curse (mostly P. with acc.; in AV. v, 30, 3, Ā. with dat.), RV. &c. &c.; (P. Ā.) to swear an oath, utter an execration (sometimes with *śapatham* or °*thān*; also with *anṛitam*, to swear a false oath), RV. &c. &c.; (P. Ā.) to revile, scold, blame (acc., rarely dat.), Yājñ.; Kāv.; Pur.; (Ā.; m. c. also P.) to curse one's self (followed by *yadi*, 'if,' i. e. to promise with an oath, vow or swear 'that one will not' &c.; or followed by dat. and rarely acc. of the person to whom and instr. of the object by which one swears; or followed by *iti*, e. g. *varuṇéti*, 'to swear by the name of Varuṇa, VS.), RV. &c. &c.; (Ā.) to adjure, supplicate, conjure any one (acc.) by (instr.), R.; Hariv.: Caus. *śāpayati* (aor. *aśīśapat*), to adjure, conjure, exorcise (demons), AV.; AitBr.; to cause any one (acc.) to swear by (instr.), Mn. viii, 113 (cf. *śāpita*): Desid. *śiśapsati*, °*te*, Gr.: Intens. *śāśapyate*, *śāśapti*, or *śaṅśapyate*, *śaṅśapti*, ib.

Śapa, m. a curse, imprecation, oath (= *śapatha*), L.; a corpse (w. r. for *śava*, q. v.), W.; N. of a man, g. *aśvâdi*.

Śapatha, m. (and n., g. *ardharcâdi*, ifc. f. *ā*) a curse, imprecation, anathema, RV. &c. &c.; an oath, vow, Mn.; MBh. &c.; an ordeal, Nār.; scolding, reviling, L. **— karaṇa**, n. swearing or taking an oath, Dhūrtan. **— jambhana**, mf(*ī*)n. nullifying a curse, Āpast. **— pattra**, n. written testimony on oath or affidavit, MW. **— pūrvakam**, mfn. with oaths, Cat. **— yávana**, mf(*ī*)n. averting a curse, AV. **— yópana**, mf(*ī*)n. warding off or nullifying a curse, ib. **Śapathôttaram**, ind. with oaths, Kathās.

Śapathīya, Nom. P. *-yáti* (only pr. p. °*yát*, uttering curses), AV.

Śapatheyyà, m. a curser, swearer, AV.

Śapathyà, mfn. depending on a curse, (a sin) consisting in cursing or imprecation, RV.

Śápana, n. a curse, imprecation, AV.; reviling, abuse, W.; an oath, asseveration by oath or ordeal, ib. **— tara** (*śapaná-*), mfn. inclined to cursing, ŚBr.

Śapita, mfn. cursed, R. vii, 55, 21.

Śaptá, mfn. id., Suparn.; MBh. &c. (*-vat*, mfn. = pf. *śaśāpa*, MBh.); adjured, conjured, R.; sworn, taken as an oath, W.; m. Saccharum Cylindricum, L.; n. a curse, imprecation, TBr.; Kāṭh.; an oath, R.

Śaptṛí, m. a curser, swearer, AV.

Śapya, mfn. to be cursed &c., Pāṇ. iii, 1, 98, Sch.

Śapva, m. abuse, reviling, L.

शफ śaphá, m. (L. also n.; ifc. f. *ā*; of doubtful derivation) a hoof (esp. the hoof of a horse), RV. &c. &c.; an eighth (because of the divided hoofs of the cow; cf. *pāda*, a fourth), RV.; TS.; ŚBr.; a claw, VS. xii, 4; a wooden implement formed like a claw or hook (for lifting an iron pot or pan from the fire), Br.; Lāṭy.; Unguis Odoratus, L.; (du., with *Vasishṭhasya*) N. of two Sāmans, KātyŚr.; n. the root of a tree, L. [Cf., accord. to some, Germ. *huof*, *Huf*; Angl. Sax. *hôf*; Eng. *hoof*.] **— grahá**, m. the hoof or claw of an animal used as a kind of receptacle, ŚBr. **— cyuta** (*śaphá-*), mfn. tossed up by hoofs (as dust), RV. **— 1. -vat** (*śaphá-*), mfn. possessing hoofs or claws (n. a hoofed animal), ib. **— 2. -vat**, ind. like a hoof, MW. **— śas**, ind. by eighths (see *śapha* above), PañcavBr. **Saphâksha**, m. N. of a man (cf. *śāphākshi*). **Saphârúj**, mfn. destroying hoofs or d° with the hoofs (said of demons), RV. **Saphôru**, mf(*ū*)n. (a woman) whose thighs resemble the two divisions of a cow's hoof, Pāṇ. iv, 1, 70.

Śaphara, m. (ifc. f. *ā*; also written *saphara* and said to be connected with *śapha*) Cyprinus Saphore (a kind of bright little fish that glistens when darting about in shallow water), Kāv.; VarBṛS.; Kathās. &c.; a carp or kind of large fish (that preys on other fish), Kathās. cxxiii, 10; (*ī*), f. a fish or a kind of fish (see *pūti-ś°*); ebony, L. **— rūpa**, n. the form of a carp or large fish, BhP. **Śapharâdhipa**, m. the fish Clupea Alosa (= *illiśa*), L.

Śaphari, (prob.) m. a small fish, Gal.

Śapharīya, mfn. (fr. *śaphara*), g. *utkarâdi*.

Śapharuka, m. a box, box-like receptacle, pot, Hcar.

शबर śabara, mfn. (also written *savara*; cf. *śabala* below) variegated, brindled, L.; relating or belonging to a Śabara (prob. for *śābara*), MBh.; m. N. of a wild mountaineer tribe in the Deccan (in later language applied to any savage or barbarian = *kirāta*, *pulinda*, *bhilla*; accord. to L. 'the son of a Śūdra and a Bhillī'), AitBr.; MBh. &c.; a kind of Lodhra or Lodh tree, L. (cf. comp.); N. of Śiva, L.; (with *Kākshīvata*) N. of the author of RV. x, 169, Anukr.; of a poet, Cat.; of a Buddhist, ib.; = *śabara-svāmin* (in *śabara-bhāshya*, q. v.); = *hasta* and *śāstra-viśesha*, L.; (*ā*), f. N. of a Yoginī, Hcat.; (*ī*), f. a Śabara woman, R.; Kathās. &c.; n. water, L. (prob. w. r. for *śambara*). **— kanda**, m. a sweet potato, L. **— jambu**, N. of a place (see *śābarajambuka*). **— bhāshya**, n. Śabara's i. e. Śabara-svāmin's Comm. on the Mīmāṅsā-sūtra (also called *śābara-bh°*; it has been critically annotated by the great Mīmāṅsā authority Kumārila). **— lodhra**, m. a kind of Lodhra, L. **— siṅha**, m. N. of a king (mentioned in the Kathârṇava), Cat. **— svāmin**, m. N. of an author (cf. *śabara-bhāshya*), IW. 98, n. 1. **Śabarâlaya**, m. the abode of savage tribes, L. **Śabarâhāra**, m. 'the Śabaras' food,' a kind of jujube, L.

Śabaraka, m. a Śabara, savage or barbarian, Kāv.; (*ikā*), f. a Śabara woman, Nalac.

Śabarāla, m. a sort of Lodhra, W.

Śabarī-√bhū, P. *-bhavati*, to become a Śabara or savage, Harav.

शबल śabála, mf(*ā* or *ī*)n. (also written *savala*; cf. *śabara* above) variegated, brindled, dappled, spotted (in RV. x, 14, 10 applied to the two four-eyed watch-dogs of Yama), RV. &c. &c.; variegated by, i. e. mixed or provided or filled with (instr. or comp.), Kāv.; Sarvad.; disfigured, disturbed, BhP. (see comp.); m. a variegated colour, W.; N. of a serpent-demon, MBh.; of a man (v. l. for *śabara*), Cat.; (*ā*) or (*ī*), f., see below; n. water (cf. *śabara*), W.; a partic. religious observance of the Buddhists, ib. **— gu**, mfn. having mottled cows, MW. **— cetana**, mfn. disturbed in mind, BhP. **— tā**, f., **-tva**, n. mixedness, mixture, Kāv.; Sāh. **— hṛidaya**, mfn. = *-cetana*, BhP. **Śabalâksha**, m. 'spotted-eyed,' N. of a Ṛishi, MBh. **Śabalâśva**, m. 'having a dappled-horse,' N. of a man (son of Avikshit), MBh.; pl. N. of the children of Daksha and Vairaṇī, Hariv.; Pur. **Śabalôdara**, m. 'having a spotted-belly,' N. of a demon, MantraBr.

Śabalaka, mfn. spotted, brindled (in alg. applied to the 13th unknown quantity), Col.

Śabalā, f. a spotted cow, L.; N. of a cow (Kāmadhenu, the cow of plenty), R.

Śabalikā, f. a kind of bird, Cat. (incorrectly written *sab°*).

Śabalita, mfn. variegated, Vās.

Śabaliman, m. variegated state or condition, mottled look or appearance, Śiś. vi, 27.

Śabalī, f. a spotted cow, L.; (nom. *īs*) the cow of plenty, TS.; Br. **— homa**, m. an offering to the cow of plenty, Lāṭy.

Śabalī-kṛita, mfn. (*śabalī* for °*la*) variegated, Ragh.; VarBṛS.

शब्द् śabd (rather a Nom. *śabdaya* fr. *śabda*), cl. 10. P. (Dhātup. xxxiii, 40) *śabdayati*, to make any noise or sound, cry aloud, Śiś.; Pañcat.; BhP.; to call, invoke, Śaṃk.; Kathās.; (*śabdāpayati*, °*te*), to call, address, R.: Pass. *śábdyate*, to be sounded &c.; to be called, MBh.; (impers.) it is chattered, Nir. i, 18.

Śábda, m. (in DhyānabUp. also n.; ifc. f. *ā*; perhaps connected with √3. *śap*, cf. also 2. *śap*) sound, noise, voice, tone, note (*śabdaṃ* √*kṛi*, to utter a sound, raise the voice, cry aloud; sound is supposed to be sevenfold [MBh. xii, 6858] or eightfold [Dharmas. 35] or tenfold [MBh. xiv, 1418]; in the Mīmāṅsā it is taught to be eternal); a word (*śabdena*, by word, explicitly, expressly), ib.; Kāś. on Pāṇ. ii, 3, 19; speech, language, BhP.; the right word, correct expression (opp. to *apa-śabda*), Pat.; the sacred syllable Om, AmṛitUp.; (in gram.) a declinable word or a word-termination, affix, Pāṇ., Sch.; a name, appellation, title, Mn.; MBh. &c. (*tac-chabdāt*, 'because it is so called,' KātyŚr.); a technical term, TPrāt.; verbal communication or testimony, oral tradition, verbal authority or evidence (as one of the Pramāṇas, q. v.), Nyāyas.; Sarvad. **— karmaka**, mfn. (a root) meaning 'to sound,' Kāś. on Pāṇ. i, 4, 52. **— 1. -karman**, n. 'sound-making,' a sound, noise, Āpast. **— 2. -karman**, mfn. = *-karmaka*, Pāṇ. i, 4, 52. **— kalpa**, m., **-kalpa-taru**, m. N. of gram. wks. **— kalpa-dru**, m. N. of a lexicon by Keśava (also called *kalpa-dru*). **— kalpa-druma**, m. N. of a modern Encyclopædia by Rādha-kānta-deva. **— kāra** (Pāṇ.), **-kārin** (Nir.), mfn. making a noise or s°, sounding, sonorous. **— kośa**, m. 'word-repository,' N. of a dictionary. **— kaumudī**, f. N. of a grammar by Cokka-nātha. **— kaustubha**, m. N. of a gram. by Īśvari-prasāda and of a Comm. on Pāṇ. i, 1; *-dūshaṇa*, n. N. of a gram. wk. by Bhāskara-dikshita. **— kriya**, mfn. = *-karmaka*, Pāṇ. i, 4, 52, Vārtt. 1. **— khaṇḍa**, m. n. N. of a ch. of the Tattva-cintāmaṇi; *-prakāśa*, m., *-vyākhyā*, f. N. of Comms. on it. **— ga**, mfn. perceiving sounds, BhP.; uttering sounds, MBh. **— gata**, mfn. being or residing in a word (as a poetical or metaphorical meaning), MW. **— gati**, f. 'method of sounds,' music, song, VarBṛS.; mfn. uttering s°s, Hariv. **— guṇa**, m. the quality of s°, MW.; the excellence of the sound or form (of a poem, as opp. to *artha-g°*, q. v.; there are 10 *guṇâlaṃkāras*, viz. *ojas*, *prasāda*, *ślesha*, *samatā*, *samādhi*, *mādhurya*, *saukumārya*, *udāratā*, *artha-vyakti*, and *kānti*, qq. vv.), Vām. iii, 1, 4. **— gocara**, m. the aim or object of speech (e. g. any one who is spoken to or spoken about), BhP. **— graha**, m. 'receiver of s°,' the ear, L.; receiving or catching sound, ib.; N. of a fabulous arrow, ib. **— grāma**, m. the totality of sounds, L. **— ghoshā**, f. N. of a collection of paradigms to the Saṃkshipta-sāra grammar. **— candrikā**, f. N. of a lexicon by Bāṇa-kavi and of a dictionary on materia medica by Vaidya Cakrapāṇi-datta. **— cāturya**, n. skill in words, cleverness of diction, eloquence, MW. **— cāli**, f. a partic. movement in dancing, Saṃgīt.; *-nṛitya*, n. a kind of dance, ib. **— citra**, n. sound-variation, alliteration &c., Kpr.; Sāh.; mfn. having various or fanciful sounds, MW. **— cintāmaṇi**, m. N. of a Comm. on Pāṇini's Ashṭādhyāyī and of a lexicon by Vyāsa-viṭṭhalâcārya; *-vṛitti*, f. N. of a Prākṛit grammar by Śubha-candra. **— cora**, m. 'word-thief,' a plagiarist, W. **— cyuta**, n. (prob.) = *-hīna*, Bharat. **— ja**, mfn. arising from s°, produced by words, MW. **— tattva-prakāśa**, m. N. of wk. **— tanmātra**, n. the subtle element of s°, MW. **— taraṃga**, m., **-taraṃgiṇī**, f., **-tāṇḍava**, n. (?), **-triveṇikā**, f. N. of wks. **— tva**, n. the condition or nature of s°, Tarkas.; *-jāti-pramāṇa*, n. N. of wk. **— dīpikā**, f. N. of a grammar (on irregular nouns) and a lexicon by Kumbhīnasa-nātha; of a Comm. on the Mugda-bodha by Govinda-rāma. **— nityatā**, f. the eternity of sound (also *-tva*, MW.); *-vicāra*, m. N. of wk. **— nirūpaṇa**, n., **-nirṇaya**, m. N. of wks. **— nṛitya**, n. a kind of dance, Saṃgīt. **— netri**, m. 'word-chief,' N. of Pāṇini (as chief of grammarians), Buddh. **— pati**, m. 'word-lord,' a mere nominal leader, Ragh. **— pada-mañjarī**, m. N. of a grammar. **— pariccheda**, m. N. of various wks.; *-rahasya*, n., *-rahasye 'pūrva-vāda-rahasya*, n. N. of wks. **— pāṭha**, m. a collection of paradigms of declension, by Gaṅgā-dhara. **— pāta**, m. range or reach of sound; (*am*), ind. as far as s° reaches, Bhaṭṭ. (v. l.) **— pātin**, mfn. aiming or hitting at any object by the mere s° (without seeing it), Nir.; falling with a s°, MW. **— prakāśa**, m. N. of various wks. **— prabheda**, m. N. of a grammar and lexicon; *-nāmamālā*, f. = *śabda-bheda-prakāśa*. **— pramāṇa**, n. verbal testimony or proof, oral evidence, MW. **— prāmāṇya-khaṇḍana**, n., **-prāmāṇya-vāda**, m. N. of two phil. wks. **— prāś**, mfn. enquiring after (the meaning of) a word, Uṇ. ii, 57, Sch. (cf. Pāṇ. vi, 4, 19). **— bāṇâgra-vedhin**, mfn. hitting (an unseen object) with an arrow's point by (aiming at) the mere sound, R. (cf. *śabda-vedhin*). **— bṛihatī**, f. N. of a Comm. on the Mahā-bhāshya. **— bodha**, m. (in phil.) knowledge derived from verbal testimony; *-prakāra*, m., *-prakriyā*, f., *-vicāra*, m. N. of wks. **-brahman**, n. 'word-brahman,' the Veda considered as a revealed sound or word and identified with the Supreme, MaitrUp.; Pur.; °*ma-maya*, mf(*ī*)n. consisting in the Veda identified with Br°, Pañcar. **-bhāj**, mfn. (ifc.) bearing the title of, Ragh. **-bhid**, f. perversion of words, BhP. **-bhūshaṇa**, n. N. of a grammar and a Comm. on Pāṇini's Ashṭādhyāyī. **-bhṛit**, mfn. bearing only the name of anything, BhP. (v.l.; cf. *śabda-pati*). **-bheda**, m. 'difference or distinction of sounds or words,' N. of a glossary; *-nirūpaṇa*, n., *-nirdeśa*, m. N. of wks.; *-prakāśa*, m. N. of a glossary of nouns (which although identical in meaning differ more or less in their orthography; it is usually appended to the Viśva-prakāśa and also called *śabda-bheda-nāma-mālā* or *śabda-prabheda-n*°). **-bhedin**, mfn. = *-vedhin*, L.; m. an arrow, L.; N. of Arjuna, L.; the anus, L. **-mañjarī**, f. N. of a grammar by Nārāyaṇa. **-maṇi-paricchedâloka**, m., **-maṇi-vyākhyā**, f. N. of a Commentary. **-maya**, mf(*ī*)n. consisting of sound or of sounds, VPrāt.; Hcar.; sounding, uttering sounds, Hariv.; (ifc.) consisting or formed of a partic. word, Ragh. xviii, 5. **-mātra**, n. sound only, a mere sound, Pañcat. **-mālā**, f. N. of a lexicon and a collection of paradigms of declension (accord. to the Kā-tantra grammar). **-mālikā**, f., **-mīmāṇsā**, f. N. of wks. **-muktā-mahârṇava**, m. N. of a modern dictionary (compiled for Colebrooke by Tārā-maṇi, son of Rāma-candra). **-mūla**, n. N. of a gram. wk. **-yoni**, m. the source or origin of a word, BhP.; a radical word, root, L. **-ratna**, n. N. of a Comm. on the Prauḍha-manoramā (q.v.) and of a lexicon; *-mālā*, f., *-samanvaya*, m.; °*tnâkara*, m., °*tnâvalī*, f. N. of grammars and dictionaries. **-rahasya**, n. N. of two phil. wks. **-rahita**, mfn. 'destitute of sound,' noiseless, VarBṛS. **-rāśi**, m. (in phil.) a collection of sounds or words or infallible verbal teachings (said of the Veda); 'collection of sounds or letters,' the alphabet; *-maheśvara*, m. 'great lord of the alphabet,' N. of Śiva (as the revealer of grammar to Pāṇini), RTL. 84, 1; Cat. **-rūpa**, n. the nature or quality of a sound, a partic. sound, Pañcat.; the gram. form of a word, Kāś. on Pāṇ. ii, 3, 48; N. of a gram. wk.; mf(*ā*)n. appearing in the form of a sound, Pañcar.; *-prakāśikā*, f. a collection of paradigms of declension (accord. to the Mugda-bodha grammar); °*pâvali*, f. N. of a gram. wk. **-lakshaṇa**, n. and **-lakshaṇa-rahasya**, n. N. of wks. **-liṅgârtha-candrikā**, f. 'elucidation of the gender and meaning of words,' N. of a lexicon. **-vajrā**, f. N. of a deity, Kālac. **-vat**, mfn. uttering sounds, sounding, noisy, Nir.; Hariv.; crackling (as flame), VarBṛS.; endowed with sound (as wind), BhP.; (*at*), ind. noisily, MBh.; MārkP. **-vādârtha**, m. N. of a wk. on the Nyāya by Raghu-nātha. **-vāridhi**, m. 'ocean of words,' a vocabulary, Cat. **-vidyā**, f. 'science of sounds or words,' grammar, philology, Daś.; Śiś.; *-śāstra*, n. id., Buddh.; °*dyôpâdhyāya*, m. a teacher of grammar, Rājat. **-vidhi**, m. N. of a gram. wk. **-virodha**, m. contradiction in words (not in sense), seeming contradiction, Mālav., Sch. **-viśesha**, m. difference or variety of sound; pl. the varieties of sound (these the Sāṃkhya arranges accord. to the accents, *udātta*, *an-udātta*, *svarita*, and the notes of the gamut, *shaḍ-ja*, *ṛishabha*, *gāndhāra*, *madhyama*, *pañcama*, *daivata*, *nishāda* &c., qq. vv.), MW. **-viśeshaṇa**, n. (in gram.) the attribute of a word, an adjective, ib. **-vṛitti**, f. (in rhet.) the function of a word, ib. **-vedha**, mfn. = *vedhin* (applied to an arrow), Pañcad.; m. the act of shooting at or hitting an invisible object the sound of which is only heard, MBh.; R.; Divyâv. **-vedhin**, mfn. 'sound-piercing,' hitting an unseen (but heard) object, Nir.; R. (°*dhi-tva*, n., MBh.; R.); N. of Arjuna, L.; of king Daśa-ratha, MW. **-vedhya**, mfn. to be shot at without being seen (cf. prec.), R.; n. = *-vedha*, m., ib. **-vailakshaṇya**, n. difference in word, verbal difference (as opp. to *artha-v*°, difference of meaning), MW. **-vyāpāra-vicāra**, m. N. of a wk. on Alaṃkāra by Rājânaka Mammaṭa. **-śakti**, f. the force or signification of a word, Kpr.; Pratāp.; *-prakāśikā*, f. N. of a Nyāya wk.; *-prabodhinī*, f. N. of a Comm. on it. **-śabdârtha-mañjūshā**, f. 'collection of words and their meanings,' N. of a lexicon. **-śāsana**, n. 'science of sounds or words,' grammar; *-vid*, mfn. versed in gr°, Śiś. **-śāstra**, n. = *-śāsana*, Vcar. (also N. of a partic. grammar). **-śuddhi**, f. 'purity of language,' N. of the 5th ch. of Vāmana's Kāvyâlaṃkāra-vṛitti. **-śesha**, mfn. having only the name remaining, Kāvyâd. (cf. *prabhu-śabda-ś*°). **-śobhā**, f. N. of a grammar. **-ślesha**, m. a verbal quibble, pun (opp. to *artha-śl*°), Śiś., Sch. **-saṃkīrṇa-nirūpaṇa**, n., **-saṃgraha-nighaṇṭu**, m., **-saṃcaya** (cf. *śabdâmbhodhi*), m. N. of wks. **-saṃjña**, mfn. bearing the name of (comp.), BhP. **-saṃjñā**, f. (in gram.) a technical term, Pāṇ. i, 1, 68. **-sad-rūpa-saṃgraha**, m. N. of a Nyāya wk. **-saṃdarbha-sindhu**, m. (cf. *śabdârṇavâbhidhāna*), N. of a lexicon (compiled for Sir W. Jones by Kāśi-nātha Bhaṭṭâcārya). **-sambhava**, m. the source or origin of sound (applied to air or the wind), Hariv. **-sāgara**, m. 'sea of words,' N. of Comm. on the Siddhânta-kaumudī. **-sādhana**, mfn. hitting a mere sound (i.e. hitting an object perceived only by the ear; cf. *śabda-vedhin*), MBh. **-sādhya-prayoga**, m. N. of a grammar by Rāma-nātha Cakra-vartin. **-sāra**, m. N. of a grammar by Yatīśa; *-nighaṇṭu*, m. N. of a dictionary. **-sāha**, mfn. = *-sādhana*, MBh. **-siddhânta-mañjarī**, f. N. of a gram. wk. **-siddhi**, f. 'correct formation or use of words,' N. of various wks.; *-nibandha*, m. N. of a modern school-book. **-saukarya**, n. facility of expression, A. **-saushṭhava**, n. elegance of words, a graceful style, ib. **-stoma-mahānidhi**, m. N. of wk. **-sparśa-rasa**, m. pl. sound and touch and taste, R. **-sphoṭa**, m. the crackling (of fire), Kām. **-smṛiti**, f. science of words, grammar, philology, Vām. iii, 1, 4. **-svātantrya-vāda**, m. N. of a Nyāya wk. **-hīna**, n. the use of a word in a form or meaning not sanctioned by standard authors, Kāvyâd. (cf. *śabda-cyuta*). **Śabdâkara**, m. 'word-mine,' N. of a grammar. **Śabdâkshara**, n. the sacred syllable Om uttered aloud or audibly, AmṛitabUp. **Śabdâkhyeya**, mfn. that which may be said aloud, Megh. **Śabdâḍambara**, m. high-sounding words, verbosity, bombast, Sāh. **Śabdâtīta**, mfn. beyond the reach of sound (applied to the Supreme), MW. **Śabdâdi**, m. (scil. *vishaya*, q.v.) the objects of sense beginning with sound, W.; *-dharmin* (ib.), *-mat* (Śaṃk.), mfn. having the quality of sound &c. **Śabdâdhikāra**, m. N. of a gram. wk. **Śabdâdhishṭhāna**, n. 'sound-receptacle,' the ear, L. **Śabdâdhyāhāra**, m. the supplying of a word (to complete an ellipsis), MW. **Śabdânanta-sāgara-samuccaya**, m., **Śabdânityatā-rahasya**, n. N. of wks. **Śabdânukaraṇa**, mfn. imitating sounds, Nir. **Śabdânukṛiti**, f. imitation of s°s, onomatopœia, ib. **Śabdânurūpa**, n. conformity to or imitation of sound, W. **Śabdânuviddha-samādhi-pañcaka**, n. N. of a Yoga wk. **Śabdânuśāsana**, n. 'word-instruction or explanation,' N. of Pāṇini's grammar and similar wks. (by Śākaṭāyana, Hema-candra &c.); *-durga-padâvali*, f., *-sūtra-pāṭha*, m. N. of wks. **Śabdânuśishṭi**, f. teaching of words or sounds, grammatical knowledge, Sarvad. **Śabdânusāra**, m. following a sound; (*eṇa*), ind. in the direction of a sound, Śak. **Śabdântara-vāda**, m., **Śabdâprāmāṇya-rahasya**, n. N. of wks. **Śabdâbdhi**, m. 'ocean of words,' N. of a lexicon (compiled by order of Prāṇa-kṛishṇa); *-tari*, f. 'boat on the ocean of w°s,' a glossary (of words formed by Uṇâdi suffixes, by Rāma-govinda). **Śabdâbhivaha**, mf(*ā*)n. conducting sound (as the auditory passage), Suśr. **Śabdâmbhodhi**, m. (also called *śabda-saṃcaya*) 'word-ocean,' N. of a wk. on declension by a Jain author. **Śabdârṇava**, m. 'id.,' N. of a grammar and a lexicon; *-candrikā*, f. N. of Comm.; *-vācaspati*, m. N. of a poet, Cat.; *-sudhā-nidhi*, m. N. of a grammar; °*vâbhidhāna*, n. N. of a lexicon (= *śabda-saṃdarbha-sindhu*). **Śabdârtha**, m. (du.) sound (or word) and sense, Sāh. (cf. *artha-śabdau*, g. *rāja-dantâdi*); the nature or meaning of sounds, VPrāt.; the meaning of a word (see *śabda-śabdârtha-mañjūshā*); sense or meaning of oral tradition (as a source of knowledge; cf. comp.); *-kalpa-taru*, m. N. of a lexicon; *-garbha-vat*, mfn. containing (virtually) sound and meaning, RāmatUp.; *-candrikā*, f., (°*kôddhāra*, m.), *-cintāmaṇi*, m., *-tarkâmṛita*, n., *-nirvacana*, n., (°*na-khaṇḍana*, n.), *-mañjarī*, f., *-ratna*, n., *-ratnâkara*, m., *-ratnâvalī*, f., *-rahasya*, n., *-saṃdīpikā*, f., *-sāra-mañjarī*, f. N. of wks.; °*thârambhaṇa*, mfn. beginning with the meaning or force of oral tradition, Āpast.; N. of a ch. of the Tattva-cintāmaṇy-āloka. **Śabdâlaṃkāra**, m. embellishment of the sound (of a sentence by rhyme, alliteration &c., as opp. to *arthâl*°, q.v.), a figure of speech depending for its pleasingness on sound or words (such as the *yamaka* and *anuprâsa*, qq. vv.); *-mañjarī*, f. N. of wk.; *-vicāra*, m. N. of a ch. of Vāmana's Kāvyâlaṃkāra-vṛitti. **Śabdâloka**, m. N. of wk.; *-rahasya*, n., *-viveka*, m.; °*kôddyota*, m. N. of Comms. **Śabdâvali**, f. a collection of paradigms of declension (belonging to the Kā-tantra grammar). **Śabdâvaloka**, m. N. of wk. **Śabdêndu-śekhara**, m. (with *bṛihat*) N. of a Comm. on Nāgoji-bhaṭṭa's Siddhânta-kaumudī; (with *laghu*) an abridgment of the prec. wk. by the same; *-doshôddhāra*, m. N. of an index of the errors in the same wk. **Śabdêndriya**, n. 'sound-organ,' the ear, Suśr. **Śabdôtpatti**, f. production or origin of sound, TPrāt. **Śabdôdadhi**, m. ocean or treasury of words, Cat.

Śabdaka, m. = *śabda*, a sound, AgP.

Śabdana, mfn. sounding, sonorous, Pāṇ. iii, 2, 148, Sch.; n. sounding, a sound, noise, W.; (ifc.) speaking, talking about, Cat.

Śabdanīya, mfn. to be invoked, Sāy.

Śabdāya (cf. √*śabd*), Nom. Ā. °*yate* (Pāṇ. iii, 1, 17; exceptionally also °*yati*), to make a sound (acc.), cry, yell, bray, Nir.; MBh. &c.: Caus. *śabdāyayati*, to cause a sound to be made by (instr.), Pāṇ. i, 4, 52, Vārtt. 1, Pat.; to cause any one (acc.) to cry by (instr.), Vop. v, 5.

Śabdāla, mfn. sonorous, L.

Śabdita, mfn. sounded, cried, uttered &c.; invoked (as a deity), Śiś.; communicated, imparted, taught, BhP.; called, named, MBh.; Hariv. &c.; n. noise, cry, the braying (of an ass), Pañcat.

Śabdin, mfn. sounding, noisy, AV.; (ifc.) resounding with, Hariv. (v.l. *-nādin*).

शम् 1. *śam*, cl. 4. P. (Dhātup. xxvi, 92) *śāmyati* (rarely °*te*, and ep. also *śamati*, °*te*; Ved. *śamyati*, *śimyati*; and cl. 9. *śamnāti* [Naigh. ii, 9], *śamnishe*, *śamnīthās*, Impv. *śamnīshva*, *śamīshva*, *śamishva*, *śamīdhvam*; pf. *śaśāma*, *śemuḥ*, Br. &c.; *śaśamé*, Subj. *śaśámate*, RV.; p. *śaśamāná* [q.v.]; aor. *áśamishṭhās*, RV.; *aśamat*, Br. [cf. pres.]; Prec. *śamyāt*, Gr.; fut. *śamitā*, *śamishyati*, ib.; ind. p. *śamitvā*, *śāntvā*, *śāmam*, ib.), to toil at, fatigue or exert one's self (esp. in performing ritual acts), RV.; TBr.; to prepare, arrange, VS.; to become tired, finish, stop, come to an end, rest, be quiet or calm or satisfied or contented, TS.; ŚBr. &c.; to cease, be allayed or extinguished, MBh.; Kāv. &c.; cl. 9. (cf. above) to put an end to, hurt, injure, destroy, Kāṭh.: Pass. *śamyate* (aor. *aśami*), Pāṇ. vii, 3, 34: Caus. *śamáyati* (m.c. also *śāmayati*; aor. *aśīśamat*; Pass. *śāmyate*), to appease, allay, alleviate, pacify, calm, soothe, settle, RV. &c. &c.; to put to an end or to death, kill, slay, destroy, remove, extinguish, suppress, TS. &c. &c.; to leave off, desist, MBh.; to conquer, subdue, Kālid.; Bhaṭṭ.: Desid. *śiśamishati*, Gr.: Intens. *śaṇśamīti* (Bālar.), *śaṇśamyate*, *śanśanti* (Gr.), to be entirely appeased or extinguished (cf. *śaṇśamāṃ cakruḥ*, Bhaṭṭ.). [Cf. Gk. κάμνω.]

Śama, m. tranquillity, calmness, rest, equanimity, quietude or quietism, absence of passion, abstraction from eternal objects through intense meditation (*śamaṃ* √*kṛi*, 'to calm one's self,' 'be tranquil'), Mn.; MBh. &c.; peace, peace with (*sârdham*), MBh.; Quietism or Tranquillity (personified as a son of Dharma and husband of Prâpti), MBh.; tranquillization, pacification, allayment, alleviation, cessation, extinction, MBh.; Kāv. &c.; absence of sexual passion or excitement, impotence, TāṇḍBr.; alleviation or cure of disease, convalescence, W.; final happiness, emancipation from all the illusions of existence, L.; indifference, apathy, Rājat.; the hand (cf. *śaya*), L.; imprecation, malediction (w.r. for *śapa*), L.; N. of a king of the Nandi-vegas, MBh.; of a son of Andhaka, Hariv.; of a son of Dharma-sūtra, BhP.; (*ā*), f. N. of a divine female, PārGṛ.; (*śáma*), mfn. tame, domestic, RV. i, 32, 15; 33, 15. **-kṛit**, mfn. devoted to quietism, L. **-gir**, f. a tranquillizing word or speech, Prab. **-nīca-medhra**, m. one whose generative organ hangs down from absence of passion or impotence, TāṇḍBr. **-para**, mfn. devoted to quiet, tranquil, VarBṛS. **-pradhāna**, mfn. id., Śak. **-prâpta**, mfn. one who has attained, quiet, Vedântas. **-vat**, mfn.

tranquil, peaceful, Śiś.; Veṇis. **-vyasanin**, mfn. dissolute from indifference, Rājat. **-śama**, mfn. enjoying perpetual tranquillity (as Śiva), MBh. **-sukha**, n. the joy or happiness of tr°, Bhartṛ. **-sudhā**, f. the nectar of tr°, ib. **-setu-pradīpa**, m. N. of wk. **-saukhya**, n. = *-sukha*, Śāntiś. **-stha**, mfn. engaged in quietism, MW. **-sthalī**, f. = *antar-vedī*, Gal. **Śamāgāsa** (?) and **Śamâṅga**, N. of two places, Rājat. **Śamâtmaka**, mfn. calm or tranquil by nature, R. **Śamântaka**, m. 'destroyer of tranquillity,' N. of Kāma-deva (god of love), L. **Śamânvita**, mfn. devoted to quietism, MuṇḍUp. **Śamôpanyāsa**, m. overtures of peace, Veṇis.

Śamaka, mfn. (fr. Caus.) pacifying, a pacifier, peace-maker, Pāṇ. vii, 3, 34, Sch.; (*ā*), f. a kind of creeper (found in Nanda-pura), Kauś.

Śamaṭha, m. (cf. Uṇ. i, 102, Sch.) N. of a Brāhman, MBh.

Śamatha, m. quiet, tranquillity, absence of passion, Lalit.; a counsellor, minister, L. **-vipaśyanā-vihārin**, m. 'enjoying quietude and right knowledge,' N. of Buddha, Divyâv. **-sambhāra**, m. (with Buddhists) quietude as one of the equipments (one of the 4 Sambhāras, q.v.), Dharmas. 117.

Śamana, mf(*ī*)n. calming, tranquillizing, soothing, allaying, extinguishing, destroying, KātyŚr.; MBh. &c.; m. 'settler, destroyer,' N. of Yama, Daś.; a kind of antelope, L.; a kind of pea, L.; (*ī*), f., see below; n. the act of calming, appeasing, allaying, tranquillization, pacification, extinction, destruction, Kauś.; MBh. &c.; killing, slaying, immolation, Kauś.; chewing, swallowing, L.; a mode of sipping water (prob. for *camana*), MW.; malediction, reviling (w.r. for *śapana*), W. **-vidhi**, m. N. of the 46th Pariś. of the AV. **-svasṛi**, f. 'Yama's sister,' the river Yamunā or Jumnā, L.

Śamanī, f. 'the calming one,' night, L. **-pāra**, m. (prob.) a partic. mode of reciting the Ṛig-veda, Pat. on Pāṇ. iii, 2, 1, Vārtt. 1. **-shada**, m. 'night-goer,' a Rākshasa, evil spirit, demon, L.

Śamanīya, mfn. to be tranquillized, consolable, MW.; serving for tranquillization, soothing, Suśr.; n. a sedative, ib., Sāh.

Śamayitṛi, m. (fr. Caus.) an alleviator, tranquillizer, Kauś. (*śámayitrikā*, f., MaitrS.); an extinguisher, destroyer, killer, slayer, Nir.; Ragh.

Śámala, n. (Uṇ. i, 111) impurity, sin, blemish, fault, harm, AV.; TS.; Kāṭh.; Kauś.; BhP.; feces, ordure, L. **-gṛihīta**, m. affected with a taint, AitBr.

Śamāya, Nom. Ā. °*yáte*, to fatigue or exert one's self, RV.; to set at rest, put to death, kill, slay, MaitrS.; Āpast.; (P.) to strive after mental calm, TUp.

Śamāha, m. a quiet place, hermitage, L.

Śámi, n. labour, toil, work, effort, RV.; AV.; f. a legume, pod (v.l. *śimi*), L.; the Śamī tree (see below); m. N. of a son of Andhaka, Hariv.; of a son of Uśīnara, BhP. **-roha**, m. 'ascending the Śamī tree,' N. of Śiva, L. **-shṭhala**, n., Pāṇ. viii, 3, 96.

Śamika, m. N. of a man, g. *bidâdi*.

Śamitá, mfn. (cf. *śānta*) prepared, ready (as an oblation), VS.; (fr. Caus.) appeased, allayed &c.; kept in order, cut (as nails), Megh. 89 (v.l.); destroyed, killed, Ragh.; relieved, cured, W.; relaxed, intermitted, ib.; m. N. of a Sthavira of the Jainas, HPariś.; (*ā*), f. rice-powder, L. **-ruci**, mfn. whose lustre is moderated or dimmed, MW. **Śamitâyāma**, mfn. having the length diminished, ib.

Śamitavya, mfn. to be appeased, MW.

Śamitṛi, mfn. one who keeps his mind calm, Rāj.; (°*trí*), m. a killer, slaughterer, cutter up (of a slaughtered victim), preparer, dresser, RV.; Br.; MBh.

Śamin, mfn. tranquil, pacific, incapable of any emotion, Kāv.; Rājat. (cf. Pāṇ. iii, 2, 141; compar. of f. *śaminī-tarā* or *śamini-tarā*, Pat.); m. N. of a son of Rājâdhideva, Hariv.; of a son of Śūra, VP.; of a son of Andhaka, ib.

Śamira, m. (cf. *śamīra*) a small variety of the Śamī tree, L.

Śamishṭha, mfn. most active, busiest (applied to the Ṛibhus), ŚāṅkhŚr.

Śámī, f. (cf. *śámi*) effort, labour, toil, RV.; VS.; (*śamī*) the Śamī tree, Prosopis Spicigera or (accord. to others) Mimosa Suma (possessing a very tough hard wood supposed to contain fire, cf. Mn. viii, 247; Ragh. iii, 9; it was employed to kindle the sacred fire, and a legend relates that Purū-ravas generated primeval fire by the friction of two branches of the Śamī and Aśvattha trees), AV. &c.; a legume, pod (cf. *-jāti*); a partic. measure (see *catuḥ-ś°*) = *valgulī* or *vāguji*, L. **-kuṇa**, m. the time when the Śamī tree bears fruit, Pāṇ. v, 2, 24. **-garbhá**, m. 'born in the Ś°,' the Aśvattha tree or Ficus Religiosa (which strikes root in the fissures of other trees), Br.; ŚrS.; MBh. &c.; fire (supposed to be contained in the Ś°), Hariv.; a Brāhman, L. **-jāta**, mfn. produced in a Ś° tree (cf. prec.), Hariv. **-jāti**, f. a kind of legume or pod, VarBṛS. **-dṛishada**, n. sg. a Ś° tree and a mill-stone, Laghuk. **-taru**, n. the Ś° tree, Śak. i, 17 (v.l. for *-latā*). **-dhānya**, n. Ś° grain (one of the 5 classes of grain; but often = any pulse or grain growing in pods), ŚBr.; Car. **-nivātam**, ind. so as to be protected from the wind by a Ś° tree, Pāṇ. vi, 2, 8, Kāś. **-pattra**, n. or **-pattrī**, f. 'having Ś° leaves,' a kind of sensitive plant, Mimosa Pudica, L. **-parṇá**, n. a leaf of the Ś° tree, TBr. **-pūjā-vidhi**, m. N. of wk. **-prastha**, n., g. *karky-ādi*. **-phalā**, f. a sensitive plant (prob. = *-pattrā*), L. **-mandāra-māhātmya**, n. 'glorification of the Ś° and Mandāra trees,' N. of ch. of the GaṇP. **-máya**, mf(*ī*)n. consisting or made of Ś° wood, TS.; Br.; GṛŚrS. **-latā**, f. a branch of the Ś° tree, Śak. i, 17. **-lūna**, mfn. one (whose hair is) cut with (an instrument made of) Ś° wood, Kauś. **-vat**, mfn. N. of a man (cf. *śāmīvata*). **-vṛiksha**, m. = *-taru*, Pañcat. **Śamyosha**, m. the grains or seed of a legume or pod, Āpast.

Śamīka, m. N. of various men (esp. of a Muni, son of Śūra and brother of Vasu-deva), VP.

Śamīra, m. = *śamira*, Pāṇ. v, 3, 88.

Śamya, mfn. to be appeased or kept quiet &c., MW.; = *rūksha*, TS., Sch.; m. a partic. personification, SāmavBr.; (*ā*), f., see next.

Śámyā, f. a stick, staff, (esp.) a wooden pin or peg, wedge &c., RV.; AV.; Br.; GṛŚiS.; the pin of a yoke (see *yuga-ś°*); a partic. instrument used in the treatment of hemorrhoids, Vāgbh.; a sacrificial vessel, W.; a kind of cymbal or other musical instrument (= *tāla-viśesha*), MW.; a partic. measure of length = 36 Aṅgulas, VarBṛS. (or = 32 A°s, KātyŚr., Sch.; cf. *-kshepa*, *-nipāta* &c. below); du. (*dhuroḥ śamye*) N. of two Sāmans, ĀrshBr. **-kshepa**, m. the cast of a staff, distance that a staff can be thrown, MBh. **-garta**, m. n. a hole for the Śamyā, ŚāṅkhŚr. **-grāha**, m. (prob.) one who plays the cymbals, R. **-tāla**, m. a kind of cymbal, MBh.; Car. **-nipāta** (MBh.), **-parāvyādhá** (ŚBr.), **-parâsa** (ĀpŚr.), m. = *-kshepa*. **-parâsin**, mfn. measuring the distance of the cast of a Ś°, PañcavBr. **-pāta**, m. (MBh.), **-prâsa**, m. (Āpast.), **-prâsana**, n. (Lāṭy.) = *-kshepa* above. **-mātrá**, mfn. having the measure of a Śamyā, TBr.

शम् 2. **śám**, ind. (g. *cādi* and *svar-ādi*) auspiciously, fortunately, happily, well (frequently used in the Veda, rarely in later language; often to be translated by a subst., esp. in the frequent phrase *śáṃ yóḥ* or *śáṃ ca yóś ca*, 'happiness and welfare,' sometimes joined with the verbs *bhū*, *as*, *kṛi*, *dā*, *vah*, *yā*, sometimes occurring without any verb; with dat. or gen. [cf. Pāṇ. ii, 3, 73, Sch.]; in some cases corresponding to an adj., e.g. *śaṃ tad asmai*, that is pleasant to him), RV. &c. &c. **-pāka**, m. Cathartocarpus Fistula, MBh.; Suśr. &c. (perhaps w.r. for *śamyāka*, cf. *śamyā*); N. of a Brāhman, MBh.; (only L.) = *vipāka* and *yāvaka* (v.l. *viyāta* and *yācaka*); = *tarkaka* and *dhṛishṭa*. **-pāta**, m. Cassia Fistula, MW. **-bhara**, m. N. of a man (cf. *śāmbhara*). **-bhavá**, mfn. = *śambhu*, VS.; m. (with Jainas) N. of the third Arhat of the present Avasarpiṇī, L. **-bhavishṭha** (*śáṃ-*), mfn., superl. of *śambhu*. **-bhu**, see *śambhu*, p. 1055. **-mad**, N. of an Āṅgirasa, PañcavBr. (cf. *śāmmada*).

Śam, in comp. for 2. *śam*. **-yu**, see *śaṃyú*, col. 3. **-yu-vāka**, m. a sacred formula containing the words *śáṃ yóḥ* (= next), ĀśvŚr. (cf. Pāṇ. ii, 4, 29, Vārtt. 1, Pat.) **-yor-vāká**, m. the sacred formula beginning with the words *tác cháṃ yór ā vṛiṇīmahe*, Br.; ŚrS. **-yós**, ind. = *śaṃ yos* (see under 2. *śam*), VS.; = *śaṃ-yor-vākā*, Br.; KātyŚrS. **-yv-ânta**, mf(*ā*)n. ending with the formula *śaṃyós*, Vait. **-vat** (*śáṃ-*), mfn. auspicious, prosperous, ŚBr.; containing the word *śam*, Cat. **-vada**, m. Pāṇ. iii, 2, 14, Sch. **-stha** or **-sthā**, mfn. being in prosperity, happy, prosperous, Pāṇ. iii, 2, 77, Sch. **-kará**, see below. **-kṛit** (*śáṃ-*), mfn. causing prosperity, beneficent, TĀr. **-gá**, mfn., v.l. for *-gú*, TS. **-gayá**, mf(*gáyī*)n. blessing the household, RV.; ĀśvŚr. **-garā**, f. = *śaṃkarā*, Pat. **-gavī** (*śáṃ-*), f. blessing cattle, ŚBr. **-gú**, mfn. id., VS.; (gender doubtful) a kind of plant, Pañcar. **-tanu** (*śáṃ-*), mfn. wholesome for the body or the person (*-tvá*, n.), TS.; m. (also written *śāṃtanu*) N. of an ancient king with the patr. Kauravya (he was fourteenth descendant of Kuru, son of Pratīpa and younger brother of Devāpi, and usurped the sovereignty whilst the latter became a hermit; he married Gaṅgā and Satya-vatī; by the former he had a son named Bhishma, and by the latter Citrâṅgada and Vicitra-vīrya, cf. IW. 375), RV.; MBh.; Hariv. &c.; (with *cakra-vartin*) N. of an author (son of Uddharaṇa, of the Tomara race), Cat.; *-tanūja*, m. 'son of Śaṃtanu,' N. of Bhīshma, Śiś. xv, 20. **-tama** (*śáṃ-*), mfn. most beneficent or wholesome or salutary, RV.; AV.; VS.; BhP. **-tāti** (*śáṃ-*), mfn. beneficent, auspicious, RV.; f. pl. benefits, ib.; *-sūktāni catvāri*, N. of four hymns attributed to Śaunaka, Cat.; °*tīya*, n. N. of the hymn RV. vii, 35, GṛŚrS. **-tvá**, n. beneficialness, auspiciousness, TS.; TBr.; Kāṭh. **-no-devī**, f. N. of the verse RV. x, 9, 4, Yājñ.; °*vīya*, m. (scil. *anuvāka*) N. of AV. i, 6, Pat. on Pāṇ. i, 3, 2, Vārtt. 1.

Śaṃya, mfn., Pāṇ. v. 2, 138.

Śaṃyú, mfn. benevolent, beneficent, RV.; TS.; happy, fortunate, Bhaṭṭ.; N. of a son of Bṛihas-pati, TS.; Br.; MBh. **-dhāyas** (*śaṃyú-*), mfn. beneficent, refreshing, TĀr.

Śaṃva. See *śamba*, p. 1055, col. 2.

Śaṃkará, mf(*ī*)n. causing prosperity, auspicious, beneficent, Nir.; MBh.; BhP.; m. N. of Rudra or Śiva, VS.; ĀśvGṛ.; MBh. &c.; of a son of Kaśyapa and Danu, VP.; of Skanda, AVPariś.; of a serpent-demon, L.; of a Cakra-vartin, L.; N. of various authors and commentators, (esp.) of Śaṃkarâcārya (see next page, col. 1; also with *bhaṭṭa*, *paṇḍita*, *śarman*, *rājânaka*, &c.); (*ā*), f. (cf. *śaṃ-garā* under *śam* above) = *śakunikā*, Pāṇ. iii, 2, 14, Vārtt. 1, Pat.; N. of a female, ib.; a partic. Rāga or musical mode, MW.; (*ī*), f., see p. 1055. **-kathā**, f. N. of wk. **-kavaca**, f. N. of a Kavaca. **-kavi**, m. N. of a poet, Cat. **-kiṃkara**, m. a servant or worshipper of Śiva (°*rī-bhava*, m. the being or becoming a w° of Ś°), Siṃhâs.; N. of an author, Sarvad. **-kroḍa**, m. N. of a Nyāya Commentary. **-gaṇa**, m. N. of a poet, Subh. **-giri**, m. N. of a mountain, Daś. **-gītā**, f. N. of a wk., Hcat. **-gaurīśa**, m. N. of a temple, Rājat. **-caritra**, n. N. of wk. **-ceto-vilāsa**, m. 'the play of Śaṃkara's wit,' N. of an artificial poem by Śaṃkara-dīkshita (celebrating the glories of Vārāṇasī, esp. of its kings Yavanâri and Ceta-siṃha or Chet Singh). **-jaya**, see *saṃkshepá-śaṃkara-jaya*. **-jit**, m. N. of a man, Cat. **-jī**, m. N. of an author, ib. **-jīka**, m. N. of a scribe, MW. **-tīrtha**, n. N. of ch. of the ŚivaP. **-datta**, m., **-dayālu**, m., and **-dāsa**, m. N. of authors, Cat. **-dig-vijaya**, m. 'Śaṃkara's victory over every quarter (of the world),' N. of a fanciful account of the controversial exploits of Śaṃkarâcarya (q.v.) by Mādhavâcārya (also called *saṃkshepa-śaṃkara-jaya*); = *śaṃkara-vijaya* below; *-ḍiṇḍima* and *-sāra*, m. N. of wks. **-dīkshita**, m. N. of a writer of the last century (son of Dīkshita Bāla-kṛishṇa; author of the Gaṅgâvatāra-campū-prabandha, Pradyumna-vijaya, and Śaṃkara-ceto-vilāsa). **-deva**, m. N. of a form of Śiva, Cat.; of a king and a poet, ib. **-dhara**, m. N. of a poet, ib. **-nārāyaṇa**, m. Vishṇu-Śiva (= *hari-hara*), RTL. 65; *-māhātmya*, n., °*nâshṭôttara-śata*, n. N. of wks. **-pati**, m. N. of a man, Buddh. **-pattra**, n., **-pāda-bhūshaṇa**, n. N. of wks. **-pushpa**, m. a white Calotropis, L. (cf. *śarkarā-p°*). **-prādur-bhāva**, m. N. of wk. **-priya**, m. 'dear to Śaṃkara,' the Francoline partridge (= *tittiri*), L.; (*ā*), f. Śiva's wife, Kathās. **-bindu**, m., **-bhaṭṭa**, m. N. of authors, Cat. **-bhaṭṭī**, f., **-bhaṭṭīya**, n. N. of wks. (or of one wk.) **-bhāratī-tīrtha**, m. N. of an author, Cat. **-bhāshya-nyāya-saṃgraha**, n., **-mandāra-saurabha**, n. N. of wks. **-miśra**, m. N. of various authors (esp. of a poet and a philosopher, son of Bhava-nātha; cf. IW. 62, 68), Cat. **-rksha** (for *-ṛiksha*), m. N. of the Nakshatra Ārdrā (presided over by Śiva), L. **-lāla**, m. N. of the patron of Kshemêndra (son of Bhū-dhara), Cat. **-vardhana**, m. N. of a man, Rājat. **-varman**, m. N. of a poet, Cat. **-vijaya**, m. 'Śaṃkara's victory,' N. of Ānanda-giri's biography of Śaṃkarâcārya (recording his controversial victories, as a Vedântin, over numerous heretics); of a fanciful life of Śaṃkarâcārya (in the form of a dialogue between Cid-vilāsa and Vijñāna-kanda); of a poem by Vyāsa-giri (describing the adventures of Śiva); *-vilāsa*, m. N. of a poem. **-vilāsa**, m. N. of ch. of the SkandaP. and of another wk. by Vidyâraṇya; *-campū*, f. N. of a poem by Jagan-nātha. **-śikshā**, f. N. of a wk. on Vedic phonetics. **-śukra**, n. quicksilver, Bhpr. **-śukla**, m. N. of a learned man, Cat. **-śvaśura**, m. 'Śiva's father-in-law,' N. of the mountain Hima-vat, R. **-saṃhitā**, f., **-sambhava**, m. N. of chs. of the SkandaP. **-siddhi**, m. N. of a man, Kathās. **-sena**, m. N. of a writer on medicine, Cat. **-stuti**, f. N. of the 7th Adhyāya of MBh. x. **-stotra**, n. N. of a Stotra by Bāla-kṛishṇa. **-svāmin**, m. N. of a Brāhman, Kathās. **Śaṃkarâkhya**, N. of two medical wks. by Rāma and Śaṃkara. **Śaṃkarâcārya**, see below. **Śaṃkarânanda**, m. N. of a philosopher (son of Vāñchêśa and Veṅkaṭâmbā, pupil of Ānandâtman and guru of Sāyaṇa; author of the Ātma-purāṇa or Upanishad-ratna, containing the substance of a number of Upanishads in verse; and of many Commentaries on Upanishads and similar wks.); *-tīrtha*, m., *-nātha*, m. N. of authors. **Śaṃkarâbharaṇa**, m. (in music) a partic. Rāga, Saṃgīt. **Śaṃkarâbhyudaya**, m. N. of a poem by Rāma-kṛishṇa. **Śaṃkarâlaya**, m. 'Śiva's abode,' the mountain Kailāsa, Cat. **Śaṃkarâvāsa**, m. id., MW.; a kind of camphor, L. **Śaṃkarâshṭaka**, n. N. of a wk. by Lakshmī-nārāyaṇa.

Śaṃkarâcārya, m. N. of various teachers and authors, (esp.) of a celebrated teacher of the Vedânta philosophy and reviver of Brāhmanism (he is thought to have lived between A.D. 788 and 820, but according to tradition he flourished 200 B.C., and was a native of Kerala or Malabar; all accounts describe him as having led an erratic controversial life; his learning and sanctity were in such repute that he was held to have been an incarnation of Śiva, and to have worked various miracles; he is said to have died at the age of thirty-two, and to have had four principal disciples, called Padma-pāda, Hastâmalaka, Surêśvara or Mandana, and Troṭaka; another of his disciples, Ānanda-giri, wrote a history of his controversial exploits, called Śaṃkara-vijaya, q.v.; tradition makes him the founder of one of the principal Śaiva sects, the Daśa-nāmī-Daṇḍins or 'Ten-named Mendicants,' RTL. 87; he is the reputed author of a large number of original works, such as the Ātma-bodha, Ānanda-laharī, Jñāna-bodhinī, Maṇi-ratna-mālā, &c.; and commentaries on the Upanishads, and on the Brahma-mīmāṃsā or Vedânta-sūtra, Bhagavad-gītā, and Mahā-bhārata, &c.), IW. 46; RTL. 53; *-carita*, n., *-vijaya-ḍiṇḍima* (cf. *śaṃkara-dig-vijaya-ḍ°*); *°ryâvatāra-kathā*, f., *°ryôtpatti*, f. N. of wks.

Śaṃkarī, f. the wife of Śiva, L.; Rubia Munjista, L.; Prosopis Spicigera or Mimosa Suma, ib.; *-gīta*, n., *-gīti*, f. N. of musical wks. **Śaṃkarīya**, mfn. (fr. *śaṃkara*), g. *utkarâdi*; n. N. of wk.

Śanta, °**ti**, °**tu**, mfn., Pāṇ. v, 2, 138.

Śántāti (?), f. = *śam-tāti*, TBr.; ĀpŚr.

Śantivá, mf(*ā*)n. beneficent, friendly, kind, AV.

Śambha, mfn., Pāṇ. v, 2, 138.

Śambhú, mfn. being or existing for happiness or welfare, granting or causing happiness, beneficent, benevolent, helpful, kind, RV.; AV.; Br.; ŚrS.; m. N. of Śiva, MBh.; Kāv. &c.; of Brahmā, MBh.; Hariv.; of a partic. Agni, MBh.; of Vishṇu, L.; of a son of Vishṇu, MBh.; of Indra in the 10th Manvantara, BhP.; of one of the 11 Rudras, MBh.; Hariv.; VP.; of a king of the Daityas, R.; of an Arhat, L.; of a Siddha, L.; of a king, MBh. (v.l. *śaṅku*); of a son of Śuka, Hariv.; of a son of Ambarīsha, BhP.; (also with *bhaṭṭa*) of various authors and other men, Cat.; a kind of Asclepias, L.; a kind of metre, Col.; f. N. of the wife of Dhruva, Hariv.; VP. **-kāntā**, f. 'Śiva's wife,' N. of Durgā, Kāv. **-giri**, m. N. of a mountain; *-māhātmya*, n. N. of ch. of the SkandaP. **-candra**, m. N. of a Zamīndār (who wrote the Vikrama-bhārata in the beginning of this century), Cat. **-tattvânusaṃdhāna**, n. N. of a Śaiva wk. by Śambhu-nātha. **-tanaya**, m. 'Śiva's son,' N. of Skanda and Gaṇeśa, L. **-dāsa**, m., **-deva**, m. N. of authors. **-nandana**, m. = *-tanaya*, L. **-nātha**, m. N. of a temple of Śiva in Nepāl, W.; (also with *ācārya* and *siddhânta-vāgīśa*) N. of various authors &c., Cat.; *-rasa*, m. a partic. mixture, L.; *°thârcana*, n. N. of a Tāntric wk. **-nityā**, f. N. of a Tāntric wk. **-priyā**, f. 'dear to Śiva,' N. of Durgā, L.; Emblic Myrobolan, L. **-bhaṭṭīya**, n. N. of a Nyāya wk. **-bhairava**, m. a form of Śiva, Cat. **-mayo-bhū**, f. du. N. of the hymns AV. i, 5 and 6. **-mahādeva-kshetra-māhātmya**, n., **-rahasya**, n. N. of wks. **-rāja**, m. N. of the author of the Nyāya-mañjarī, Cat.; *-caritra*, n. N. of wk. **-rāma**, m. N. of various authors, Cat. **-vardhana**, m. N. of a man, Rājat. **-vallabha**, n. 'beloved by Śiva,' the white lotus, L. **-vākya-palāśā-ṭīkā**, f. N. of an astron. wk. **-śikshā**, f. N. of a wk. on Vedic phonetics. **-horā-prakāśa**, m. N. of an astron. wk.

Śambhū, mfn. (= *śambhú* above) beneficent, kind, RV.; m. N. of an author of Tāntric prayers, Cat. **-nātha**, m. N. of an author, ib. (cf. *śambhu-n°*). **-rāja-caritra**, n. N. of wk., ib. (cf. *śambhu-r°*). **-vartani**, f. N. of a town (= *eka-cakrā*), Gal.

शमन्तकस्तोत्र *śamantaka-stotra*, n. N. of a Stotra, Cat. (prob. w. r. for *śamântaka-* or *syamantaka-st°*).

शमर *śamara* (in *roma-ś°*), prob. = *vivara*, GopBr.

शमाला *śamālā*, f. N. of a place, Rājat.

शमोप्य *śamópya* (Padap. *śam-op°*), n. (of unknown meaning), AV. i, 14, 3.

शम्पक *śampaka*, m. N. of a Śākya, Buddh.

शम्पा *śampā*, f. lightning, Harav.; a girdle, ib. **-tala**, w. r. for *śamyā-t°*, MBh.; Kathās.

शम्फली *śamphalī*, f. (cf. *śambalī* and *śambhalī*) a procuress, L.

शम्ब् *śamb*, cl. 1. P. *śambati*, to go, Dhātup. xi, 29 (Vop.); cl. 10. P. *śambayati*, to collect, ib. xxxii, 21 (v. l.)

शम्ब *śámba*, m. (derivation doubtful) a weapon used by Indra (accord. to some 'Indra's thunderbolt,' but cf. *śambín*), RV. x, 42, 7 (= *vajra*, Naigh. iv, 2); the iron head of a pestle, L.; an iron chain worn round the loins, W.; a partic. measure of length, L.; ploughing in the regular direction (= *anuloma-karshaṇa*), L.; the second ploughing of a field, W.; N. of an Asura (cf. *śambara*), TBr., Sch.; mfn. happy, fortunate, L. (cf. *śaṃ-vat*, p. 1054, col. 2); poor (?), L.

Śámbara, m. N. of a demon (in RV. often mentioned with Sushṇa, Arbuda, Pipru &c.; he is the chief enemy of Divo-dāsa Atithigva, for whose deliverance he was thrown down a mountain and slain by Indra; in epic and later poetry he is also a foe of the god of love), RV. &c. &c.; a cloud, Naigh. i, 10; a weapon, Sāy. on RV. i, 112, 14; war, fight, L.; a kind of deer, Vās.; Bhpr.; a fish or a kind of fish, L.; Terminalia Arunja, L.; Symplocos Racemosa, L.; a mountain in general or a partic. mountain, L.; best, excellent, L.; = *citraka*, L.; N. of a Jina, L.; of a king, Vās. (v. l. for *śambaraṇa* and *saṃ-varaṇa*); of a juggler (also called *śambara-siddhi*), Ratnāv.; (*ī*), f. Salvinia Cucullata, L.; Croton Polyandrum, L.; = *māyā*, sorcery, magic (prob. w. r. for *śāmbarī*), L.; n. water, Naigh. i, 12 (but Sāh. censures the use of *śambara* in this sense); power, might, Naigh. ii, 9; sorcery, magic, Kathās. (printed *saṃ-vara*); any vow or a partic. vow (with Buddhists), L.; wealth, L.; = *citra*, L.; (pl.) the fastnesses of Śambara, RV. **-kanda**, m. a kind of bulbous plant, L. **-ghna**, m. 'Śambara-slayer,' N. of the god of love, Hariv. **-candana**, n. a variety of sandal, L. **-dāraṇa**, m. 'Ś°-destroyer,' the god of love, Gīt. **-ripu**, m. 'enemy of Ś°,' id., Bhām. **-vṛitra-han**, m. 'slayer of Ś° and Vṛitra,' N. of Indra, R. **-siddhi**, m., see above. **-sūdana**, m. 'destroyer of Ś°,' the god of love, L. **-hátya**, n. the killing of Ś°, RV.; TBr.; ŚāṅkhŚr. **-han**, m. 'Ś°-killer,' N. of Indra, MBh. **Śambarântakara**, m. 'Ś°-destroyer,' the god of love, Hariv. **Śambarāri**, m. enemy of Ś°, Hāsy. **Śambarâsura**, m. the Asura Ś°; *-vadhôpâkhyāna*, n. story of the killing of Śambara (told in BhP. x, 55).

Śambaraṇa, m. N. of a king, Vās. (more correctly *saṃ-varaṇa*; cf. under *śambara*).

Śambā-√kṛi, P. Ā. *-karoti*, *-kurute* (Pāṇ. v, 4, 58), to plough twice or in both directions, Bhām. **-kṛita**, mfn. twice ploughed, L.

Śambin, m. 'having a pole or oar,' a rower, boatman, AV.

शम्बट् *śambaṭ*, ind. = *chambáṭ*, Suparṇ.

शम्बटी *śambaṭī*, f. (*māsha-śambaṭyaḥ*), Pat. on Pāṇ. i, 64, Vārtt. 59.

शम्बल *śambala*, m. n. (also written *sambala* or *saṃ-vala*, q. v.) provender or provisions for a journey, stock for travelling, Kāv.; Kāraṇḍ.; 'a bank, shore' or 'a race, family' (*kūla* or *kula*), L.; envy, jealousy, L.; (*ī*), f. a procuress, L. (cf. *śambhalī* and *śamphalī*).

शम्बु *śambu*, m. a bivalve shell, L.; N. of a man, ĀśvŚr.; (*ū*), f. N. of a woman (see *śambū-putra*). **-vardhana**, m. N. of a man, MW.

Śambuka, m. (cf. below and *śāmbuka*) a bivalve shell, L.; a partic. noxious insect, Suśr.; N. of a Śūdra, MBh. (B. *jambuka*); Ragh. (v. l. *kañcuka*); of a poet, Subh.

Śambukka, m. a bivalve shell, L.

Śambūka, m. a bivalve shell, any shell or conch, Kāv.; Kathās.; Suśr. (also *ā*, f., L.); a snail, W.; a kind of animal (= *ghoṅgha*), L.; the edge of the frontal protuberance of an elephant, L.; N. of a Śūdra (who had become a devotee and was slain by Rāma-candra), R.; Uttarar. (cf. *śambuka*); of a Daitya, L. **-pushpī**, f. a species of plant (= *śaṅkha-p°*), Bhpr. **Śambūkâvarta**, m. (cf. *śaṅkhâv°*) the convolution of a shell, Suśr.; a fistula of that shape in the rectum, ib.

Śambū-putra, m. 'son of Śambū,' patr. of a man, Nid.

शम्भल *śambhala*, m. (also written *sambhala*) N. of a town (situated between the Rathaprā and Ganges, and identified by some with Sambhal in Moradābād; the town or district of Śambhala is fabled to be the place where Kalki, the last incarnation of Vishṇu, is to appear in the family of a Brāhman named Vishṇu-yaśas), MBh.; Hariv.; Pur.; (*ī*), f. a procuress, L. (cf. *śamphalī* and *śambalī*). **-grāma**, m. the town Śambhala, MBh.; Hariv.; Pur. (also *-grāmaka*); *-māhātmya* (or *śambhala-m°*), n. 'glory of Śambhala,' N. of part of the SkandaP. **Śambhalêśvara-liṅga**, n. N. of a Liṅga, Cat.

शम्भव *śam-bhava*, *śam-bhavishṭha*. See under 2. *śam*, p. 1054, col. 2.

शम्भु *śambhu* for *śam-bhú*, *śam-bhū́* &c. See cols. 1, 2.

शम्य *śamya*, *śamyā* &c. See p. 1054, col. 2.

शम्यु *śamyu*. See *śaṃyu*, p. 1054, col. 3.

शम्व *śamva*, *śamvat*, w. r. for *śamba* and *śaṃvat*.

शय *śaya*, mf(*ā*)n. (fr. √1. *śī*) lying, sleeping, resting, abiding (ifc. after adv. or subst. in loc. case or sense; see *adhaḥ-ś°*, *kuśe-ś*, *giri-ś°* &c.); m. sleep, sleeping, Dhātup. xxiv, 60 (cf. *divā-ś°*); a bed, couch (see *vīra-ś°*); a snake (accord. to some 'the boa constrictor'), L.; a lizard, chameleon, L.; the hand (= *hasta*, also as a measure of length), VarBṛS.; Naish.; KātyŚr., Sch.; = *paṇa*, L.; abuse, imprecation, L. (prob. w. r. for *śapa*); pl. N. of a people, MBh.; (*ā*), f. a place of rest or repose (cf. *śayyā*), RV. [Cf. Gk. ὀρέσ-κοιος.]

Śayaṇḍa, mfn. addicted to much sleep, sleepy, sleeping, L.; m. N. of a place, Uṇ. i, 128, Sch. **-bhakta**, mfn., g. *aishukāry-ādi*.

Śayáṇḍaka, m. (cf. *śayāṇḍaka*) a lizard, chameleon, TS. (Sch.)

Śayata, m. one who sleeps much, L.; the moon (?), L.

Śayátha, m. a lair, abode, RV.; one who sleeps much, L.; the boa constrictor, L.; a fish, L.; a boar, L.; death, L.

Śayádhyai, Ved. inf. of √1. *śī*, q. v.

Śáyana, mfn. lying down, resting, sleeping, Pañcar.; n. the act of lying down or sleeping, rest, repose, sleep, MBh.; Kāv. &c.; (ifc., f. *ā*) a bed, couch, sleeping-place (acc. with √*bhaj*, *ā*-√*ruh*, *sam*-√*viś* &c., 'to go to bed or to rest;' with Caus. of *ā*-√*ruh*, 'to take to bed, have sexual intercourse with [acc.];' *śayanaṃ śrita* or °*ne sthita*, mfn.

gone to bed, being in bed), ŚBr. &c. &c.; copulation, sexual intercourse, L.; N. of a Sāman, L. **-gṛiha**, n. 'sleeping-house,' a bed-chamber, Śak. v, 3/4 (v.l.) **-tala-gata**, mfn. gone to bed, lying in bed, Subh. **-pālikā**, f. the (female) keeper of a (royal) couch, Jātakam. **-bhūmi**, f. 'sleeping-place,' a bed-chamber, Śak. **-racana**, n. the preparation of a bed or couch (one of the 64 arts), Cat. **-vāsas**, n. a sleeping-garment, Ṛitus. **-vidha**, mfn. having the form of a bedstead, Kauś. **-sakhī**, f. the female bed-fellow (of a woman), Kathās. **-stha**, mfn. being or reclining on a couch, Mn. iv, 74. **-sthāna**, n. = *-bhūmi*, L. **Śayanâgāra**, m. (L.), °**nâvāsa**, m. (Rājat.) = °*na-gṛiha*, L. **Śayanâsana**, n. sleeping and sitting (see comp.); 'sleeping or resting place,' a dwelling, cell, Buddh.; *-vārika*, m. a partic. official in a convent, ib.; *-sevana*, n. the enjoyment of sleeping and sitting, VarBṛS. **Śayanâspada**, n. = °*na-bhūmi*, L. **Śayanâikadaśī**, f. the 11th day of the light half of the month Āshāḍha (on which Vishṇu's sleep begins), L.

Śayanī-√kṛi, P. *-karoti*, to make into a couch or resting-place, Kād.

Śayanīya, mfn. to be slept or lain on, fit or suitable for sleep or rest (*am*, ind. 'it should be slept or rested'), MBh.; Kāv. &c.; n. a bed, couch, ib. **-gṛiha**, n. 'sleeping-house,' a bed-chamber, Kathās. **-tala**, n. (the surface of) a bed or couch, R. **-vāsa**, m. = *-gṛiha*, Vet. **Śayanīyâśrita**, mfn. gone to bed, R.

Śayanīyaka, n. a bed, couch, Kathās.

Śayāṇḍa (cf. *śayaṇḍa*), g. *aishukāry-ādi* (*ī*, f., g. *varaṇâdi*). **-bhakta**, mfn. ib.

Śayāṇḍaka, m. (cf. *śayaṇḍaka*) a kind of bird, VS.

Śayāna, mfn. lying down, resting, sleeping, Mn.; MBh. &c.; m. a lizard, chameleon, L.

Śayānaka, mfn. lying, resting (see *prati-sūrya-ś°*); m. a lizard, chameleon, L.; a snake, L.

Śayālu, mfn. sleepy, inclined to sleep, sluggish, slothful, Pañcar.; Śiś.; m. a dog, L.; a jackal, L.; the boa snake, L.

Śayita, mfn. reposed, lying, sleeping, asleep, MBh.; Kāv. &c.; m. the plant Cordia Myxa, W.; n. the place where any one has lain or slept, Kāś. on Pāṇ. ii, 3, 68. **-vat**, mfn. one who has lain down, gone to sleep, sleeping, asleep, W.

Śayitavya, mfn. to be lain or slept, Pañcar.; Kathās. (n. impers.; *mayā hutavahe śayitavyam*, 'it must be lain down by me in the fire,' Vās.)

Śayitṛi, m. one who sleeps or rests, Pāṇ. iv, 2, 15.

Śayīci, m. N. of Indra, L.

Śayú, mfn. lying down, sleeping, resting, RV.; m. the boa snake, L.; N. of a person protected by the Aśvins, RV.

Śayutrá, ind. on or to a couch, RV.

Śayuna, m. the boa constrictor, L.

Śayyam-bhadra or **Śayyam-bhava**, m. N. of one of the 6 Śruta-kevalins (with Jainas), HPariś.

Śayyā, f. (ifc. f. *ā*) a bed, couch, sofa (acc. with *sam-√viś* or *adhi-shṭhā* [*√sthā*], 'to go to bed or to rest;' with Caus. of *ā-√ruh*, 'to take [a woman] to bed, have sexual intercourse with' [acc.]; *śayyām ā-rūḍha*, mfn. 'gone to bed, lying in bed'), ShaḍvBr. &c. &c.; lying, reposing, sleeping, KātyŚr.; Mn.; MBh. &c.; resort, refuge (see comp.); stringing together (esp. of words, = *gumphana* or *śabda-gumpha*), rhetorical composition or a partic. rhetor. figure, L. ('couch' and 'rhetor. composition,' Kād., Introd., v. 8). **-kāla**, m. sleeping-time, ĀpGṛ. **-gata**, mfn. gone to bed, lying on a couch, MW. **-gṛiha**, n. 'sleeping-house,' a bed-chamber, MBh.; Kāv.; Kathās. **-°cchādana** (*śayyâcch°*), n. a bed-covering, counterpane, sheet, MW. **-tara**, mf(*ī*)n. affording refuge, HPariś. **-dāna**, n. 'offering a couch or resting-place,' N. of wk.; *-paddhati*, f. N. of wk. **-°dhyaksha** (*śayyâdh°*), m. = *-pāla*, MW. **-°ntara** (*śayyânt°*), n. the interior or middle of a bed (°*re*, in bed), Kām. **-pāla** or **-pālaka**, m. the guardian of the (royal) couch, Pañcat.; °*la-tva*, n. the office of g° of the bed-chamber, ib. **-prayoga**, m. N. of wk. **-prânta-vivartana**, n. rolling from one side to another of a couch, Śak. **-mūtra**, n. wetting a bed with urine, ŚārṅgS. **-°vāsa-veśman** (*śayyâv°*), n. a bed-chamber, Kathās. **-veśman**, n. id., ib. **-°sana** (*śayyâs°*), n. du. a couch and a seat, Mn. ii, 119 (*-stha*, mfn. occupying a couch or seat, ib.); lying and sitting (*-bhoga*, m. enjoyment of l° and s°, Nal.; cf. *śayanâsana-sevana*). **Śayyôtthāyam**, ind. at the time of rising from bed, early in the morning, Kathās. (cf. Pāṇ. iii, 4, 52, Sch.) **Śayyôtsaṅga**, m. = *śayyântara*, Megh.

शर **śará**, m. (fr. √*śṝi*, 'to rend' or 'destroy') a sort of reed or grass, Saccharum Sara (used for arrows), RV. &c. &c.; an arrow, shaft, MuṇḍUp.; Mn.; MBh. &c.; N. of the number 'five' (from the 5 arrows of the god of love), VarBṛS.; (in astron.) the versed sine of an arc (accord. to Āryabh. also 'the whole diameter with subtraction of the versed sine'); a partic. configuration of stars (when all the planets are in the 4th, 5th, 6th, and 7th houses), VarBṛS.; the upper part of cream or slightly curdled milk (v.l. *sara*), ĀpŚr.; Car.; mischief, injury, hurt, a wound, W.; N. of a son of Ṛicatka, RV.; of an Asura, Hariv. (v.l. *śuka*); (*ī*), f. Typha Angustifolia, L.; n. water (see *śara-varsha* and °*shin*). **-kāṇḍa**, m. the stem of the Saccharum Sara, Suśr.; the shaft of an arrow, W. **-kāra**, m. a maker of arrows, Sāh. **-kunde-śaya**, mfn. lying in a hollow place covered with Śara grass, R. **-kūpa**, m. N. of a well, Buddh. **-ketu**, m. N. of a man, Hcar. **-kshepa**, m. the range of an arrow-shot, Daś. **-gulma**, m. a clump of reeds, MBh.; N. of a monkey, R. **-gocara**, m. the range of an ar°, Pañcat. **-ghāta**, m. an ar°-shot, MBh. **-ja**, mfn. born in a clump of reeds, Pāṇ. vi, 3, 16; m. = *-janman*, L.; n. 'produced from sour cream,' butter, L. **-janman**, m. 'reed-born,' N. of Kārttikeya, Ragh.; Kathās. **-jāla**, n. 'net-work of arrows,' a dense mass or multitude of ar°s, R. (pl.); *-maya*, mf(*ī*)n. consisting of a dense mass of ar°s, Śiś. **-jālaka**, m. (?) a multitude of ar°s, L. **-talpa**, m. a couch formed of ar°s (esp. for a dead or wounded warrior), MBh.; Vās.; Gīt. (cf. *-pañjara*, *-śayana*, *-śayyā*). **-tā**, f. the state of an ar°, R. **-tvá**, n. the state of a reed, TS. **-daksha**, m. (or *śarad-a°*?) N. of the author of a law-book, Cat. **-daṇḍa**, m. a stalk of reed, MBh.; (pl.) N. of a country belonging to Śālva in Madhyadeśa, L.; (*ā*), f. N. of a river, R. (v. l. *sara-d°*). **-dānava-rātra-pūjā**, f. N. of wk. **-durdina**, n. a shower of arrows, R. **-deva**, m. N. of a poet, Subh. **-dvīpa**, m. N. of an island, Hariv. **-dhāna**, m. pl. N. of a people, VarBṛS. (cf. *śava-dh°*). **-dhi**, m. an ar°-case, quiver, Vikr.; Kuval. **-nikara**, m. a multitude of ar°s, shower of ar°s, Vās. **-nivāsa**, m. and **-niveśa**, m., g. *-kshubhnâdi*. **-pañjara**, n. = *-talpa*, BhP. **-pattra**, m. Tectona Grandis, L. **-parṇikā** (L.) or **-parṇī** (Pāṇ. iv, 1, 64, Sch.), f. a kind of plant. **-pāta**, m. an ar°'s fall or flight, W.; the range of an arrow-shot, MBh.; *-sthāna*, n. the place of an ar°'s fall, an ar°'s flight or range, a bow-shot, W. **-puṅkha**, m. the shaft or feathered part of an ar° (see *puṅkha*), Suśr.; Vāgbh.; (*ā*), f. id., W.; Galega Purpurea, Bhpr. **-puccha**, mf(*ī*)n., Pāṇ. iv, 1, 55, Vārtt. 2. **-pravega**, m. the rush or rapid flight of an arrow, a swift ar°, MBh.; R. **-phala**, n. the iron point or barb of an arrow, W. **-bandha**, m. a continuous line of arrows, MBh.; R. **-barhis**, n. a layer of reed, ŚBr. **-bhaṅga**, m. N. of a Ṛishi, MBh.; Kāv. **-bhū**, m. = *-janman*, L. **-bhṛishṭi** (*śará-*), f. the point of a reed, ŚBr.; Kauś.; the point of an ar°, MW. **-bheda**, m. 'a wound made by an ar°,' and 'deficiency of cream,' Vās. **-máya**, mf(*ī*)n. consisting or made of reeds, Kāṭh.; TS. &c. **-marīci-mat**, mfn. having ar°s for rays, MBh. **-malla**, m. 'arrow-fighter,' an archer, MW.; a kind of bird, L. **-mukha**, n. the point of an ar°, L. **-yantraka**, n. the string on which the palm-leaves of a manuscript are filed, Vās. **-loma**, m. pl. the descendants of Śara-loman, Pat. on Pāṇ. iv, 1, 85, Vārtt. 8. **-loman**, m. N. of a Muni, Car.; Bhpr. **-vaṇa** (see *-vana*), n. a thicket or clump of reeds, MBh.; R.; Kathās.; Suśr.; *-bhava* (with *deva*, Megh.), °*ṇâlaya* (MBh.) or °*ṇôdbhava* (ib.), m. 'born in a th° of r°,' N. of Kārttikeya. **-vat**, mfn. filled with ar°s, Hariv.; (also used in explaining *śalmali* and said to be = *kaṇṭakair hinasti*, Nir.) **-vana**, w. r. for *-vaṇa*. **-varsha**, n. a shower of arrows, MBh.; R. (pl.); a sh° of water, rain, Śiś. (pl.) **-varshin**, mfn. raining or showering down ar°s, Śiś.; Kathās.; discharging water, Śiś. **-vāṇi**, m. (only L.) the head of an ar°; a maker of ar°s; an archer; a foot soldier; = *pāpishṭha* (prob. w. r. for *padāti*). **-vāraṇa**, n. 'warder off of ar°s,' a shield, MBh. (v. l. *śarâvara*). **-viddha**, mf(*ā*)n. pierced with ar°s, R. **-vṛishṭi**, m. N. of a Marutvat, Hariv.; f. a shower of ar°s, L. **-vega**, m. 'swift as an ar°,' N. of a steed, Kathās. **-vrāta**, m. a mass of arrows, MBh.; Hariv.; Kāv. **-śayana**, n. (Daś.) or **-śayyā**, f. (Kathās.) = *-talpa*. **-śāstra**, n. N. of wk. **-saṃdhāna**, n. taking aim with an ar°, Śak. **-sambādha**, mf(*ā*)n. covered with ar°s, MW. **-sāt**, ind. (with *√kṛi*) to hit with an ar°, Naish. **-stamba**, m. a clump or thicket of reeds, MBh.; Hariv. &c.; N. of a place, MBh.; of a man, Cat. **Śarâkshepa**, m. flight of ar°s, MW. **Śarâgni**, g. *kshubhnâdi*; *-parimāṇa*, n. an aggregate of thirty-five, MBh. **Śarâgrya**, m. an excellent ar°, MW. **Śarâghāta**, m. an ar°-shot, L. **Śarâṅkuśa-vyākhyā** (?), f. N. of wk. **Śarâdāna**, n. taking hold of an ar°, L. **Śarâbhyāsa**, m. practice with bow and arrow, L. **Śarâyudha**, n. 'arrow-weapon,' a bow, L. **Śarâropa**, m. 'that on which arrows are fixed,' a bow, L. **Śarârcis**, m. N. of a monkey, R. **Śarā-vatī**, f. (for *śara-v°*) 'full of reeds,' N. of a river, MBh.; VP.; of a town, Ragh. **Śarâvara**, m. a quiver, R.; n. a shield, MBh.; (accord. to Nīlak. also 'a coat of mail'). **Śarâvaraṇa**, n. 'warder off of ar°s,' a shield, MBh. **Śarâvāpa**, m. 'casting ar°s,' a bow, ib.; (prob.) a quiver, ib. **Śarâśani**, m. or f. an ar° like a thunderbolt, Śiś. **Śarā-śari**, ind. arrow to arrow, ar° against ar°, Campak.; Uttamac. **Śarâśraya**, m. 'ar°-receptacle,' a quiver, L. **Śarâsa**, m. a bow, BhP. **Śarâsana**, m. 'shooting ar°s,' N. of a son of Dhṛita-rāshṭra, MBh.; n. a bow, ib.; Kāv. &c.; *-jyā*, f. a bow-string, MW.; *-dhara*, m. 'arrow-holder,' an archer, Mudr.; *-vid*, mfn. skilled in archery, Pracaṇḍ. **Śarâsanin**, mfn. armed with a bow, MBh.; Hariv.; MārkP. **Śarā-sāra**, m. a shower of ar°s, Vās. **Śarâsya**, n. a bow, MārkP. **Śarâhata**, mf(*ā*)n. wounded by an ar°, W. **Śarêshīkā** (ŚBr.; R.) or **śarâishīkā** (R.), f. a stalk of reed; (°*rêshīkā*) an ar°, MW. **Śarêshṭa**, m. 'desired by ar°s,' the mango tree (the m° being one of the blossoms which tip the ar°s of Kāma-deva), W. **Śarôttama**, n. best of arrows, a very good arrow, MW. **Śarâugha**, m. a shower of arrows (pl.), Śiś.

Śaraka, mfn. (fr. *śara*), g. *ṛiśyâdi*.

1. **Śaraṇa**, m. (for 2. see p. 1057, col. 1) one of the arrows of Kāma-deva, Cat.; n. falling asunder, bursting, falling in, Vop.; killing, slaying, L.; what slays or injures, MW.

1. **Śaraṇi**, f. (for 2. see under 2. *śaraṇa*) refractoriness, obstinacy, RV.; AV. (others 'hurt, injury, offence').

1. **Śaraṇya**, n. (for 2. see ib.) injury, hurt, W.

Śaravya, mf(*ā*)n. (fr. *śaru* below) capable of wounding or injuring, MW.; (°*vyà*), f. 'an arrow-shot' or 'a shower of arrows,' RV.; AV. &c.; an ar°, missile, an ar° personified, MW.; n. a butt or mark for ar°s, aim, target, Kāv.; *-tā*, f. the condition of a target, Kād. **-vyadha**, mfn. hitting a mark, Śiś.

Śaravyaka, n. = *śaravya*, an aim, L.

Śaravyaya, Nom. P. °*vyayati*, to aim at a mark, take aim at (*ati-ś°*), Naish.

Śaravyāya, Nom. Ā. °*vyāyate*, to form a mark or object aimed at, Daś.

Śaravyī-karaṇa, n. the act of taking aim, Naish.

Śáras, n. cream, film on boiled milk, VS.; TS. &c. (°*ro-gṛihīta*, mfn. covered with a skin or film, AitBr.); a thin layer of ashes, TBr.; ĀpŚr.; w. r. for *saras*, BhP.

Śarāya, Nom. Ā. °*yate*, to become or represent an arrow, Śṛiṅgār.; Naish.

Śarā́ru, mfn. injurious, noxious, RV.; Nir.; Hcar.; Śiś.; m. any mischievous creature, MW.

Śarāśari, ind. See under *śara* above.

Śari, mfn. = *hiṅsra*, Uṇ. iv, 127, Sch.; m. a wild beast, beast of prey, L.

Śarin, mfn. provided with arrows, MBh.; R.

Śarī-√kṛi, P. *-karoti*, to make anything into an arrow, Kuval.

Śáru, m. or (more frequently) f. a missile, dart, arrow, AV.; m. any missile weapon (esp. the thunderbolt of Indra and weapon of the Maruts; f. also that weapon personified), RV.; a partridge, L.; anger, passion, L.; N. of Vishṇu, L.; of a Deva-gandharva, MBh.; of a son of Vasu-deva, MW. [Cf. Goth. *hairus*.] **-mat** (*śáru-*), mfn. armed with missiles, RV.

Śare-ja, mfn. = *śara-ja*. See col. 2.

Śárya, m. an arrow, missile, RV. (Sāy. 'a fighter,

warrior'); (*ā*), f. a cane, shaft, arrow, RV. (Nir.); membrum virile (?), RV. x, 178, 4; night, L.; a finger, Naigh.; Nir.; (accord. to some) a porcupine (cf. *śalya*), MW.; pl. wicker-work (of the Soma sieve), RV.; n. id., ib.; mf(*ā*)n. hostile, injurious, hurtful, MW. **-hán,** m. killing with arrows, an archer, warrior, RV.

Śaryaṇa, m. pl. 'thicket of reeds,' N. of a district in Kuru-kshetra, Sāy. on RV. viii, 6, 39.

Śaryaṇā-vat, m. 'reedy,' a pond (also fig. of a receptacle for Soma; accord. to Sāy. N. of a lake or district in Kurukshetra), RV. i. 84, 4; viii. 6, 93; 7, 29 &c.

Śaryāṇa, (prob.) w. r. for *śaryaṇā* (v. l. *śarpaṇā*), g. *madhv-ādi.* **-vat,** mfn. (prob.) w. r. for *śaryaṇā-vat*, ib.

Śarvá, m. (fr. *śáru*) N. of a god who kills people with arrows (mentioned together with Bhava and other names of Rudra-Śiva); N. of the god Śiva (often in the later language; esp. in the form Kshiti-mūrti; du. Śarva and Śarvāṇī, cf. Vām. v, 2, 21), AV. &c. &c.; of one of the 11 Rudras, VP.; of Vishṇu, MW.; of a son of Dhanusha, VP.; of a poet, Sadukt.; pl. N. of a people, MārkP. (w. r. *sarva*); (*ā*), f. N. of Umā, BhP. **-kośa,** m. N. of a dictionary. **-datta,** m. 'given by Śarva,' N. of a teacher, VBr. **-patnī,** f. the wife of Śiva, Pārvatī, Kathās. **-parvata,** m. Śiva's mountain, Kailāsa; *-vāsinī*, f. N. of Durgā, Kathās. **-varman,** m. N. of various authors and other men, Kathās.; ŚārṅgP. &c. (v. l. *sarva-v°*). **Śarvâksha,** n. the fruit of Ganitrus Sphærica, L. **Śarvâcala,** m. Śiva's mountain, Kailāsa, Kathās. **Śarvâvatāra-māhātmya,** n. N. of wk.

Śarvaka, m. N. of a Muni, Cat.; (*ikā*), f. leprosy, L.

Śarvaṭa, m. N. of a man, Rājat.; of a poet, Subh.

Śarvāṇī, f. Śiva's wife, GṛŚrS.; MBh.; Kathās.; Daś. **-ramaṇa,** m. 'Śarvāṇī's husband,' N. of Śiva, Cat.

Śarvilaka, m. N. of a man, Mṛicch.

शरण 2. *śaraṇá*, mfn. (fr. √*śṛi* for *śri*; for 1. see p. 1056) protecting, guarding, defending, RV.; AV.; m. N. of a serpent-demon, MBh.; of a poet, Gīt. (cf. *-deva*); of a king, Buddh.; (*ā* and *ī*), f. N. of various plants &c. (prob. w. r. for *saraṇā*, °*ṇī*, q. v.); n. (ifc. f. *ā*), shelter, place of shelter or refuge or rest, hut, house, habitation, abode, lair (of an animal), home, asylum, RV. &c. &c.; refuge, protection, refuge with (*śaraṇam* √*gam* or *yā* or *i* &c., 'to go to any one for protection, seek refuge with' [acc. or gen.]; often ifc.), Mn.; MBh. &c.; water, L.; (with *Indrasya*) N. of a Sāman, ĀrshBr. **-m-gata,** mfn. = *śaraṇâgata*, MW. **-da** (BhP.), **-prada** (R.), mfn. affording protection. **-deva,** m. N. of a poet, Cat. **Śaraṇâgata,** mfn. come for pr°, one who comes for refuge or pr°, a refugee, fugitive, Mn.; MBh. &c.; *-ghātaka* (Vcar.) or *-ghātin* (Pañcat.), m. the slayer of a suppliant for pr°; *-tā*, f. the state of a suppliant for pr°, Kathās.; *-hantṛi*, m. (= *-ghātaka*), Mn. xi, 191. **Śaraṇâgati,** f. approach for pr°; *-gadya*, n., *-tātparya-ślokôpanyāsa*, m., *-dīpikā*, f. N. of wks. **Śaraṇâdhikāra-mañjarī,** f. N. of a Stotra. **Śaraṇâpanna,** mfn. = *śaraṇâgata*, L. **Śaraṇârtham,** ind. for the sake of pr°, MW. **Śaraṇârthin,** mfn. seeking refuge or pr°, wretched, MBh.; MārkP. **Śaraṇârpaka,** mfn. 'requiring pr° to be given,' ruined, L. **Śaraṇâlaya,** m. (place of) refuge or shelter, asylum, MBh. **Śaraṇâishin,** mfn. = *śaraṇârthin*, R.

2. **Śaraṇi, śaraṇī.** See *saraṇi*, °*ṇī*.

Śaraṇī, in comp. for *śaraṇa*. **-√kṛi,** Ā. *-kurute*, to seek the protection of (acc.), Rājat. (cf. *a-śaraṇī-kṛita*).

2. **Śaraṇya,** mf(*ā*)n. affording shelter, yielding help or protection to (gen. or comp.), MBh.; Kāv. &c.; needing shelter or protection, seeking refuge with (comp.), ŚāṅkhGṛ.; R.; VarBṛS. &c.; n. who or what affords protection or defence, W.; m. N. of Śiva, MW.; (with *ācārya*) N. of a Tāntric teacher, Cat.; (*ā*), f. N. of Durga, MW. **-tā,** f. (the condition of) affording protection, R. **-puramāhātmya,** n. 'praise of a city of refuge,' N. of wk.

Śaraṇyu, m. a protector, defender, W.; wind, air (prob. for *saraṇyu*), L.; a cloud, L.

शरण्ड *śaraṇḍa*, m. (also written *sar°*; only L.) a bird (in general); a lizard, chameleon; a quadruped (in general); a kind of ornament; a rogue, cheat; a libertine.

शरद् *śarád*, f. (prob. fr. √*śrā, śrī*) autumn (as the 'time of ripening'), the autumnal season (the sultry season of two months succeeding the rains; in some parts of India comprising the months Bhādra and Āśvina, in other places Āśvina and Kārttika, fluctuating thus from August to November), RV. &c. &c.; a year (or pl. poetically for 'years,' cf. *varsha*), ib. **-aksha,** see *śara-daksha*, on p. 1056, col. 2. **-anta,** m. the end of autumn, winter, L. **-ambu-dhara,** m. an autumnal cloud, Subh. **-āgama,** m. 'approach of autumn,' N. of a Commentary (also *-vyākhyā*). **-udâśaya,** m. an autumnal pond (dry in the other seasons), Kāv. **-ṛitu-varṇana,** n. 'description of the autumnal season,' N. of wk. **-gata,** mfn. arising in autumn, autumnal (as clouds), R. **-ghana,** m. = *-ambu-dhara*, Dhūrtan. **-dhima-ruci** (for *-him°*), m. the autumnal moon, Kām. **-dhrada** (for *-hrada*), m. a pond in autumn, BhP. **-yāminī,** f. a night in autumn, Kautukas. **-vat** (*śarád-*), mfn. 'full of years,' aged, RV.; m. N. of a son or other descendant of Gotama and other men, MBh.; Hariv.; Pur. (cf. Pāṇ. iv, 1, 102). **-vadhū,** f. autumn compared to a woman, Vcar. **-varṇana,** n. 'description of autumn,' N. of ch. of BhP. **-vasu,** m. N. of a Muni, Cat. **-vihāra,** m. autumnal sport or amusement, ib.

Śarac, in comp. for *śarad*. **-candra,** m. the autumnal moon, Śak.; Vet.; °*drāya*, Nom. P. °*yate*, to resemble the aut° moon, Kāv. **-candrikā,** f. aut° moonshine (*pariṇata-candrikāsu kshapāsu*, cf. *pariṇata*), Megh. **-chaśa-dhara** (for *-śaśa-*, Hāsy.), **-chaśin** (BhP.), m. = *-candra*. **-chāli** (for *-śāli*), m. rice ripening in autumn, Rājat. **-chikhin** (for *-śikhin*), m. a peacock in autumn (supposed to cease its cries), MBh. **-chrī** (for *-śrī*), f. N. of the wife of Kuṇāla, HPariś.

Śaraj, in comp. for *śarad*. **-jyotsnā,** f. autumnal moonshine, Pañcat.

Śarat, in comp. for *śarad*. **-kānti-maya,** mf(*ī*)n. lovely like autumn, Jātakam. **-kāmin,** m. 'desirous of aut°,' a dog, L. **-kāla,** m. the time or season of aut°, Kāv.; Pur.; °*līna*, mfn. autumnal, W. **-triyāmā,** f. a night in aut°, MW. **-padma,** n. an autumnal lotus (others 'a white lotus'), BhP. **-parvan,** n. an autumnal full-moon night (°*va-śasin*, m. the moon in such a night), Śaṃkar. **-pushpa,** m. Tabernæmontana Coronaria, L. **-pratîksham,** ind. having expected the aut°, MW. **-prāvṛishika,** mfn. (with *ṛitu*, du.) autumn and the rainy season, BhP. **-samaya,** m. = *-kāla*, Vās. **-sasya,** n. autumnal corn, VarBṛS.

Śarada (ifc.) = *śarad*, autumn, Pāṇ. v, 4, 107; (*ā*), f. autumn, L.; a year, L.; N. of a woman, Rājat.

Śaradā-tilaka, w. r. for *śār°*.

Śaradi-ja, mfn. (loc. of *śarad* + *ja*) produced in autumn, autumnal, Kathās.

Śaran, in comp. for *śarad*. **-mukha,** n. the (face or front, i. e.) commencement of autumn, W. **-megha,** m. an autumnal cloud (*-vat*, ind. like an autumnal cloud), Hit.

शरदक्ष *śara-daksha, śara-daṇḍa, śara-dhi* &c. See p. 1056, col. 2.

शरभ *śarabhá*, m. a kind of deer or (in later times) a fabulous animal (supposed to have eight legs and to inhabit the snowy mountains; it is represented as stronger than the lion and the elephant; cf. *ashṭa-pad* and *mahā-skandhin*), AV. &c. &c.; a young elephant, L.; a camel, L.; a grasshopper (= *śalabha*), W.; a locust, ib.; a kind of metre, Col.; N. of Vishṇu, MW.; of an Upanishad (cf. *śarabhôpanishad*); of an Asura, MBh.; of two serpent-demons, ib.; of various men, RV.; MBh. &c.; of a son of Śiśu-pāla, MBh.; of a brother of Śakuni, ib.; of a prince of the Aśmakas, Hcar.; of a monkey in Rāma's army, R.; (pl.) N. of a people, MBh. (B. *śabara*); (*ā*), f. a girl with withered limbs and therefore unfit for marriage, GṛS.; (prob.) a kind of wooden machine. [Cf., accord. to some, Gk. κίραφος, κόραφος.] **-kalpa-tantra,** n., **-kavaca,** n. N. of wks. **-ketu,** m. N. of a man, Vās., Introd. **-tā,** f. the condition or nature of a Śarabha, MBh. **-pakshi-rāja-prakaraṇa,** n., **-paddhati,** f., **-mantra,** m., **-mālā-mantra,** m. N. of wks. **-rāja-vilāsa,** m. a history of Śarabhoji of Tanjore (1798–1833) by Jagan-nātha. **-līla,** m. (in music) a kind of measure, Saṃgīt. **-līlā-kathā,** f., **-vidhāna,** n., **-sahasra-nāman,** n., **-stotra,** n., **-hṛidaya,** n. N. of wks. **Śarabhânanā,** f. 'Ś°-faced,' N. of a sorceress, Kathās. **Śarabhârcana-candrikā,** f., °**bhârcana-paddhati,** f., °**bhârcā-pārijāta,** m., °**bhāshṭaka,** n. N. of wks. **Śarabhêśvara-kavaca,** n. N. of ch. of wk. **Śarabhôpanishad,** f. N. of an Upanishad (also called Paippalādôpanishad).

Śarabhoji, m. N. of a king of Tanjore (he was born in 1778, reigned from 1798–1833 and is the author of various wks.; cf. *śarabha-rāja-vilāsa*). **-rāja-caritra,** n. N. of wk.

शरयु *śarayu, śarayū.* See *sarayu*, °*yū*.

शरल *śarala* &c. See *sarala*.

शरलक *śaralaka*, n. water, L.

शरव *śarava*, m. pl. N. of a people, MBh. vi, 2084 (prob. w.r. for *śabara*, q. v.)

शरव्य *śaravya* &c. See p. 1056, col. 3.

शरशराय *śaraśarāya*, °*yati* (onomat.), to hiss, make a hissing sound, ĀśvŚr.

शराक *śarāka*, m. (prob.) N. of a mixed caste, Cat.

शराटि *śarāṭi*, f. a sort of bird (of the heron kind; more commonly called Śarāli), L.

Śarāṭikā, śarāḍi, or **śarāti,** f. id., L.

Śarāri, f. the Śarāli bird (= *śarāṭi*), Kāv.

Śarārī, f. id., Suśr. **-mukhī,** f. a kind of scissors or an instrument pointed like a heron's beak, ib.

Śarāry-āsya, n. a partic. surgical instrument (prob. = prec.), Vāgbh.

Śarāli, °**likā,** and °**lī,** f. = *śarāṭi* above, L.

शरारु *śarāru.* See p. 1056, col. 3.

शराव *śarāva*, m. n. (g. *ardharcâdi*) a shallow cup, dish, plate, platter, earthenware vessel (also the flat cover or lid of any such vessel), GṛŚrS.; Mn.; MBh. &c.; a measure equal to two Prasthas or one Kuḍava, TS.; Bṛ.; ŚrS. **-kurda,** m. 'creeping among dishes,' a kind of snake, Suśr. **-sampāta,** m. the arriving or bringing in of dishes (*vṛitte ś°-sampāte*, when the dishes have been removed, i. e. when the meal is over), Mn. vi, 56.

Śarāvaka, m. (ifc. f. *ikā*) a kind of vessel or the cover of a vessel (= *śarāva*), Suśr.; Kathās.; (*ikā*), f. a partic. abscess, Suśr.

Śarāvin. See *māsha-śarāvi*.

शरि *śari, śarin.* See p. 1056, col. 3.

शरिमन् *śariman* or *śarīman*, m. (said to be fr. √*śṛī*, 'to break forth'), bearing, birth, bringing forth (= *prasava*), Uṇ. iv, 147, Sch.

शरी *śarī.* See under *śara*, p. 1056, col. 2.

शरीर *śárīra*, n. (once in R. m.; ifc. f. *ā*; either fr. √*śri* and orig. = 'support or supporter,' cf. 2. *śaraṇa* and Mn. i, 7; or accord. to others, fr. √*śṛī*, and orig. = 'that which is easily destroyed or dissolved') the body, bodily frame, solid parts of the body (pl. the bones), RV. &c. &c.; any solid body (opp. to *udaka* &c.), MBh.; VarBṛS.; Pañcat.; one's body i. e. one's own person, Mn. xi, 229; bodily strength, MW.; a dead body, ib. **-kartṛi,** m. 'body-maker,' a father, MBh. **-karshaṇa,** n. emaciation of the b°, Mn. vii, 112. **-kṛit,** m. = *-kartṛi*, MBh. **-grahaṇa,** n. assumption of a bodily form, VP. **-cintā,** f. care of the body (washing one's self &c.), Pañcad. **-ja,** mf(*ā*)n. produced from or belonging to or performed with the body, bodily, Mn.; Śiś.; VP.; m. (ifc. f. *ā*) offspring, a son, MBh.; the god of love, love, MBh.; sickness, L.; lust, passion, MW. **-janman,** mfn. = *-ja*, Kir. **-tā,** f. the state or condition of a body, Sarvad. **-tulya,** mf(*ā*)n. equal to the body, dear as one's own person, MBh. **-tyāga,** m. abandonment of the b°, renunciation of life, Vās. **-tva,** n. = *-tā*, KaṭhUp. **-daṇḍa,** m. corporal punishment, BhP.; Inscr. **-deśa,** m. a part of the b°, ŚBr. **-dhātu,** m. a chief constituent of the b° (flesh, blood &c.), MBh.; a relic of Buddha's body (such as a bone, tooth, a hair, or nail), MWB. 495. **-dhṛik,** m. 'bearing a body,' a corporeal being, Baudh. **-nicaya,** m. (accord. to Nīlak. = *śarīrasya* *saṃcayaḥ, śar° avasthitiḥ;* prob. w. r. for *-niścaya*) certainty about the body, MBh. **—nipāta,** m. collapse of the b°, falling down dead, Gaut. **—nyāsa,** m. casting off the b°, death, Āpast. **—pakti,** f. purification of the b°, MBh. **—patana,** n. = *-pāta,* MW. **—pāka,** m. 'ripening of the b°,' decline of bodily strength, decay, MW. **—pāta,** m. collapse of the b°, death, VarBṛ.; Kum. &c. **—pīḍā,** f. bodily pain or suffering, VarYogay. **—purusha,** m. a soul possessed with a b°, AitĀr. **—pradhānatā,** f. the character or nature of the b° (*ayā,* ind. in virtue of the b°), Vedântas. **—prabhava,** m. a begetter, father, R. **—prahlādana,** m. N. of a king of the Gandharvas, Kāraṇḍ. **—baddha,** mf(*ā*)n. endowed or invested with a b°, Kum. **—bandha,** m. the fetters of the b°, being fettered by the b°, BhP.; assumption of a (new) body, rebirth, Ragh.; (*ena*), ind. in bodily form, bodily, ib. **—bandhaka,** m. 'personal pledge,' a hostage, W. **—bhāj,** mfn. having a body, embodied, L.; m. an embodied being, BhP. **—bhūta,** mf(*ā*)n. become or being a body, MW. **—bhṛit,** mfn. 'containing the (future) body' and 'endowed with a body' (said of seed and the soul), MBh. **—bheda,** m. dissolution of the body, death, AitUp.; Gaut. &c. **—mātra,** n. the mere body or person, the body only, MW. **—yashṭi,** f. 'stick-like body,' a slender b°, slim figure, Ragh. **—yātrā,** f. means of bodily subsistence, subs°, Bhag.; Kathās. **—yoga,** m. bodily union; *-ja,* mfn. produced from bod° contact, Ragh. **—rakshaka,** m. a body-guard, L. **—rakshā,** f. defence of the body, protection of the person, Ragh. **—ratna,** n. a jewel of a body, i. e. an excellent body, Mālatīm. **—reshaṇa,** n. hurting or injuring the b°, sickness and death, ĀpGṛ. **—lakshaṇa,** n. N. of wk. **—vat,** mfn. provided with a b°, Sarvad.; substantial, TBr.; m. an embodied being, MBh.; *-tva,* n. the being provided with a b°, Sarvad. **—vāda,** m., **-viniścayâdhikāra,** m. N. of wks. **—vimokshaṇa,** n. liberation from body, death, Baudh.; Mn. **—vṛitta,** mfn. occupied about bodily state, Kathās. **—vṛitti,** f. maintenance of the body, support of life, Ragh. **—vaikalya,** n. imperfection or indisposition of the body, Hit. **—śuśrūshā,** f. attendance on the b°, personal att°, Mn.; Pañcat. **—śoshaṇa,** n. drying up i. e. mortification of the b°, Sarvad.; Pañcat. **—saṃskāra,** m. purification of the body (by the ceremonies at conception, birth, initiation &c.; see *saṃsk°*), Mn. ii, 26; n. decoration or adorning of the person, W. **—saṃdhi,** m. a joint of the body, BhP. **—sampatti,** f. health or prosperity of body, MW. **—sambandha,** m. 'bodily connection,' relation by marriage, ib. **—sāda,** m. exhaustion of body, Ragh. **—stha,** mfn. existing in the b°, Bhartṛ. **—sthāna,** n. the doctrine about the human b°, Cat.; *-bhāshya,* n. N. of wk. **—sthiti,** f. = *-vritti,* Hcar.; Kād. **—homa,** m. pl. N. of partic. oblations, ĀpŚr. **Śarīrâkāra,** m. (Mālatīm.) or **śarīrâkṛiti,** f. (Pat.) bodily gesture or mien. **Śarīrâtman,** m. 'the bodily soul' (as distinguished from *antarâtman,* q. v.), Pat. **Śarīrânta,** m. (ifc. f. *ā*) the hairs on the body, Pañcat.; *-kara,* mfn. making an end of or destroying the b°, MBh.; R. **Śarīrântara,** n. another body; *-cārin,* mfn. acting in another b°, MBh. **Śarīrâbhyadhika,** mfn. dearer than one's own person, Kathās. **Śarīrârdha,** m. the half of the body, Kum. **Śarīrâvayava,** m. a part of the b°, member, limb, Pāṇ. v, 1, 6. **Śarīrâvaraṇa,** n. 'body-covering,' a shield, MBh.; the skin (?), L. **Śarīrâsthi,** n. bones of the body, a skeleton, L.

Śarīraka, n. a small or tiny body, Śiś.; a wretched b°, Pañcat.; Kād.; Kathās. &c.; (m. c. for *śarīra;* ifc. f. *ikā*) the body, Yājñ.; Hcat.; m. the soul, A.

Śarīrin, mfn. having a body, embodied, corporeal, Mn.; Kāv. &c.; (ifc.) having anything as a body, Mn. iv, 243 (cf. *kha-ś°*); covered with bodies, MBh.; (ifc.) exercising one's own b°, BhP.; living, MW.; m. an embodied being, creature, (esp.) a man, Mn.; Yājñ.; MBh. &c.; the soul, Bhag.; Ragh. &c. (n., W.); an embodied spirit, MW.

Śarīrī-√bhū, P. *-bhavati,* to become embodied, assume bodily shape (pp. *-bhūta*), Kathās.

शरेफ *śarepha,* m. N. of a poet, Subh.

शरोगृहीत *śaro-grihīta.* See *śaras,* p. 1056.

शर्कर *śarkara,* mf(*ā*)n. consisting of gravel or grit, gritty, ŚBr.; KātyŚr.; m. a pebble, small stone, Kauś.; (m. c.) = *śarkarā* (see comp.); a kind of drum, Saṃgīt.; N. of a fabulous aquatic being, PañcavBr.; (pl.) N. of a people, MārkP.; (*ā* and *ī*), f., see below. **—karshin,** mfn. = *śarkarā-k°,* Hariv. **—jā,** f. ground or candied sugar, MW. **—tvá,** n. the condition or nature of grit or gravel, TS. **—varshin,** mfn. = *śarkarā-v°,* MBh.

Śarkaraka, mfn. (fr. *śarkarā*), g. *ṛiśyâdi;* m. a species of sweet citron or lime, L.; (*ikā*), f. ground or candied sugar, Param.

Śárkarā, f. (ifc. f. *ā*) gravel, grit, pebbles, shingle, gravelly mould or soil (mostly pl.), AV. &c. &c.; gravel (as a disease), Suśr.; hardening of the flesh, ib.; hardening of the ear-wax, ib.; ground or candied sugar, Kāv.; VarBṛS.; Suśr.; a fragment or piece of broken earthenware, potsherd, Naish. **—karshin,** mfn. attracting or carrying along gravel, ŚāṅkhGṛ. **—°ksha** (*°râksha*), m. N. of a man, g. *gargâdi* (*°kshya* [prob. w. r.], Śaṃk. on ChUp. v, 11, 1). **—°cala** (*°râc°*), m. 'sugar-hill,' a sugar-loaf (shaped like a conical hill), Cat.; *-dāna,* n. the gift of the above, ib. **—dhenu,** f. a gift of sugar moulded in the shape of a cow, ib. **—pushpa,** m. a white Calotropis, L. (cf. *śaṃkara-p°*). **—prabhā,** f. 'gravel-resemblance,' N. of the second of the Jaina hells, L. **—°mbu** (*°râmbu*), n. sugared water, Suśr. **—°rbuda** (*°rârb°*), m. n. a kind of tumour, Suśr. **—vat,** mfn. full of stony particles, gritty, gravelly, L. **—°vartā** (*°râv°*), f. N. of a river, BhP. **—varshin,** mfn. raining gravel, ŚāṅkhGṛ. **—saptamī,** f. a partic. observance on the 7th day of the light half of the month Vaiśākha, Cat. **—°sava** (*°râs°*), m. spirituous liquor distilled from sugar, rum, R. **Śarkarôdaka,** n. sugared water, Bhpr.

Śarkarāla, mfn. impregnated with gritty or gravelly particles (as wind &c.), Veṇīs.

Śarkarika, mfn. (g. *kumudâdi*) gritty, stony, gravelly, W.

Śarkarin, mfn. suffering from the disease called 'gravel,' Car.

Śarkarila, mfn. gravelly (= *śarkarā-vat*), Pāṇ. v, 2, 105.

Śarkarī, f. (only L.) a river; a belt; = *lekhanī;* a kind of metre (cf. *śakvarī*). **—dhāna,** n. N. of a village, Kāś. on Pāṇ. iv, 2, 109.

Śarkarī-kṛita, mfn. made into gravel or grit, L.

Śarkarīya, mfn., Pāṇ. iv, 2, 84.

शर्कार *śarkāra* (and *ī,* f.), g. *gaurâdi.*

शर्कु *śarku,* m. N. of an evil demon, AV.

Śarkura, mfn. young, tender, L.

Śarkoṭá, m. N. of a partic. snake, ib. (cf. *śārkoṭa* and *karkoṭaka*).

शर्णचापिलि *śarṇacāpili* (?), m. N. of a man, Pravar.

शर्दिस् *śardís* or *śárdis* (of unknown meaning), AV. xviii, 3, 16.

शर्ध *śárdha,* mfn. (√*śṛidh*) defiant, bold (orig. 'breaking wind against another'), RV.; m. breaking wind, flatulence, Vop.; a (defiant or bold) host, troop (esp. the host of the Maruts), RV. **—mjaha,** mfn. (*jaha* fr. √3. *hā*) causing flatulence, Pāṇ. iii, 2, 28, Vārtt. 1, Pat.; m. beans or any leguminous grain, pulse, W. **—nīti** (*śárdha-*), mfn. 'acting boldly' or 'leading the host (of Maruts),' RV. **—vat,** mfn. containing (the word) *śardha,* ĀpŚr.

Śárdhat, mfn. (pr. p.) defiant, mocking, bold, daring, RV.

Śardhana, n. the act of breaking wind, Kull.

Śárdhas, mfn. = *śárdhat* (only in compar. *śárdhas-tara,* more daring or defiant), RV.; n. a troop, host, multitude (cf. *śárdha*), ib.

Śardhin. See *bāhu-ś°.*

Śárdhya, mfn. bold, strong, RV. i, 119, 5.

शर्पणा *śarpaṇā,* f., g. *madhv-ādi* (Kāś.) **—vat,** mfn., ib. (cf. *śaryaṇā-vat*).

शर्ब् *śarb* (cf. √*śarv, śamb, samb, sarb, sarv*), cl. 1. P. *śarbati,* 'to go' or 'to kill,' Dhātup. xi, 29.

शर्मन् *śárman,* n. (prob. fr. √*śri* and connected with 1. *śaraṇa, śarīra*) shelter, protection, refuge, safety, RV. &c. &c.; a house, Naigh. iii, 4; joy, bliss, comfort, delight, happiness (often at the end of names of Brāhmans, just as *varman* is added to the names of Kshatriyas, and *gupta* to those of Vaiśyas), Yājñ.; MBh.; Kāv. &c.; N. of partic. formulas, VarYogay.; identified with *śarva* (Kauś.) and with *vāc* (AitBr.); mfn. happy, prosperous, W.

1. **Śarma,** n. = *śarman,* L.

2. **Śarma,** in comp. for *śarman.* **—kāma,** mfn. desirous of happiness, Yājñ. iii, 328. **—kārin** (Dhūrtan.), **-krit** (BhP.), mfn. causing h°, blessing. **—da** (ŚārṅgP.), **-dātṛi** (BhP.), **-prada** (Bhartṛ.), mfn. conferring h°, making prosperous, propitious. **—lābha,** m. obtaining h° or joy, Suśr. **—vat,** mfn. containing the word *śarman,* Mn. ii, 32; possessed of h°, lucky, auspicious, W. **—varma-gaṇa,** m. N. of a partic. Gaṇa of verses in the Atharva-veda, AV. Pariś. **—sád,** mfn. sitting behind a shelter or screen, RV. **Śarmôpâya,** m. a means of obtaining happiness, Kathās.

Śarmaka, m. pl. N. of a people, MBh.

Śarmaṇya, mfn. sheltering, protecting, TS.

Śarmaya, Nom. P. *°yati* (only in pr. p. *°yát,* = prec.), RV.

Śarmara, m. a sort of garment or cloth, L.; Curcuma Aromatica or another species, L.

Śarmin, mfn. possessing happiness, lucky, auspicious, MBh.; m. N. of a Ṛishi, ib.

Śarmilā. See *pāṇḍu-ś°.*

Śarmishṭhā, f. 'most fortunate,' N. of one of the wives of Yayāti (she was the daughter of Vṛishaparvan and mother of Druhyu, Anu, and Puru; cf. under *yayāti* and *deva-yānī*), MBh.; Kāv. &c. **—yayāti,** n. N. of a Nāṭaka (mentioned in Sāh.)

शर्य *śarya, śaryaṇa, śaryāṇa.* See p. 1056, col. 3, and p. 1057, col. 1.

शर्यात *śaryāta,* m. N. of a man, RV.; ŚBr. (cf. next and *śāryāta*).

Śaryāti, m. N. of a son of Manu Vaivasvata, MaitrUp.; MBh. &c.; of a son of Nahusha, VP.

शर्व् *śarv* (cf. √*śarb, sarv*), cl. 1. P. *śarvati,* to hurt, injure, kill, Dhātup. xv, 76.

शर्व *śarva, śarvaka* &c. See p. 1057, col. 1.

शर्वर *śarvara,* mfn. variegated, spotted (= *karvara;* cf. also *śabara, śabala*), L.; (*ī*), f., see below; n. darkness, L.; the god of love (?), L.

Śarvarin, m. (fr. next) the 34th year in Jupiter's cycle of 60 years, VarBṛS. (cf. *śārvarin*).

Śárvarī, f. the (star-spangled) night, RV.; evening, twilight, L.; turmeric or Curcuma Longa, L.; a woman, L.; N. of the wife of Dosha and mother of Śiśu-māra, BhP.; pl. the spotted steeds of the Maruts, RV. **—pati,** m. 'lord of night,' the Moon, L.; N. of Śiva, Śivag. **Śarvarīśa** (Rājat.), **°rīśvara** (Dhūrtan.), m. the Moon.

शर्वरीक *śarvarīka,* w. r. for *śarśarīka.*

शर्वला *śarvalā, °lī.* See *sarv°.*

शर्शरीक *śarśarīka,* mfn. (fr. Intens. of √*śṛī*) hurtful, mischievous, Uṇ. iv, 19, Sch.

शर्षीका *śarshīkā,* f. (cf. *sarshīkā*) a kind of metre, Nidānas.

शल् 1. *śal,* cl. 1. Ā. *śalate,* 'to shake' or 'to cover,' Dhātup. xiv, 19; cl. 1. P. *śalati,* to go, move, ib. xix, 13 (only found in comp. with prep., cf. *uc-chal, prôc-chal, sam-uc-chal*); cl. 10. Ā. *śālayate,* to praise, Dhātup. xxxiii, 18, Vop.

Śalá, mfn. (connection with above very doubtful) = *dravaṇa-samartha,* Nir., Sch.; m. a staff, TBr.; a dart, spear, L.; a kind of animal, Pañcat. (accord. to L. 'a camel' or 'an ass'); = *kshetra-bhid,* L.; = *vidhi,* L.; N. of Bhṛiṅgi (one of Śiva's attendants), L.; of Brahmā, W.; of a serpent-demon, MBh.; of a son of Dhṛita-rāshṭra, ib.; of a son of Soma-datta, ib.; of a son of Parīkshit, ib.; of a son of Śuna-hotra, Hariv.; m. or n. the quill of a porcupine, L.; a partic. measure of length (cf. *tri-, pañca-ś°* &c.); (*ī*), f., see below. **—kara,** m. N. of a serpent-demon, MBh. **—dā,** f. N. of a daughter of Raudrāśva, L. **—putra,** N. of a place, Buddh. (v. l. *śali-p°*).

Śalaka, m. a spider, L.; a bird, L.; (*ā*), f., w. r. for *śalākā,* Pañcat.

Śalala, n. the quill of a porcupine (prob. also = a boar's bristle), MBh.; Bhartṛ.; m. a porcupine, L.; (*ī*), f., see below. **—cañcu,** m. or n. the quill of a porcupine (used for writing), L.

Śalalita, mfn. furnished with quills, MBh.

Śalalī́, f. the quill of a porcupine (used in the ceremony of hair-parting and for applying collyrium), TBr.; ŚBr.; GṛŚrS.; a small porcupine. **-pisaṅga**, m. 'variegated as the quills of a porcupine,' N. of a Nava-rātra, ĀśvŚr.

Śalāka, m. (rare) = *śalākā*, Kāṭh.; Nār.; MBh. **-dhūrta**, m. 'one who deceives by employing a *śalākā*,' (perhaps) a bird-catcher (who deceives birds with a twig, see below), MBh. v, 1225.

Śalākalā́, f. (fr. next) a small stake or peg or splint, AV. (MS. *śalokakā*).

Śalākā, f. any small stake or stick, rod (for stirring &c.), twig (smeared with lime for catching birds), rib (of an umbrella), bar (of a cage or window), chip, splinter, splint, pencil (for painting or applying collyrium), ŚBr. &c. &c.; a piece of bamboo (borne as a kind of credential by mendicants and marked with their name), Buddh.; the quill of a porcupine, KātyŚr., Sch.; an oblong quadrangular piece of ivory or bone (used in playing a partic. game), ib.; a peg, pin, arrow-head, needle, a probe (used in surgery and sometimes taken as the N. of this branch of surgery, Suśr.), any pointed instrument, MBh.; R.; ŚārṅgS.; a sprout, sprig, shoot of any kind (see *ratna-ś°*); a ruler, W.; a toothpick or tooth-brush, L.; a match or thin piece of wood (used for ignition by friction), W.; a bone, L.; a finger, toe, Vishṇ.; Yājñ.; a porcupine, L.; a partic. thorny shrub, Vanguieria Spinosa, L.; the Sārikā bird, Turdus Salica, L.; N. of a town, R.; of a woman, g. *śubhrâdi*. **-pari**, ind. a term applied to a partic. throw or movement (said to be unlucky) in the game of Śalākā, Pāṇ. ii, 1, 10. **-purusha**, m. pl. (with Jainas) N. of 63 divine personages (viz. the 24 Jainas, 12 Cakra-vartins, 9 Vāsudevas, 9 Bala-devas, and 9 Prati-vāsudevas), L. **-bhrū**, f. N. of a woman, g. *śubhrâdi*. **-yantra**, n. (in surgery) a pointed instrument or probe (cf. above), Suśr.; Vāgbh. **-vat**, mfn., g. *madhv-ādi*. **-vṛitti**, n. famine of a partic. kind, Divyâv. **-stha**, mfn. being at or on a peg, ĀpŚr.

Śalākikā, f. = *śalākakā*, Kpr.

Śalākin, mfn. furnished with awns (as barley), Suśr.; furnished with ribs (*śrīmac-chata-ś°*).

Śalāhaka, m. the wind, L.

Śalya, m. n. (ifc. f. *ā*) a dart, javelin, lance, spear, iron-headed weapon (cf. *upa-ś°*), pike, arrow, shaft (also the point of an arrow or spear and its socket), RV. &c. &c.; anything tormenting or causing pain (as a thorn, sting &c.), or (in med.) any extraneous substance lodged in the body and causing pain (e.g. a splinter, pin, stone in the bladder &c.; also applied to the fetus, and, as a branch of med°, to 'the extraction of splinters or extraneous substances'), MBh.; R. &c.; Suśr.; a fault, defect, Hariv. (cf. *karma-ś°*); m. a porcupine, BhP.; a kind of fish, L.; a fence, boundary, L.; Vanguieria Spinosa, L.; Aegle Marmelos, L.; N. of an Asura, Hariv.; VP.; of a king of Madra (maternal uncle of the sons of Pāṇḍu and esp. of Nakula and Saha-deva, Madrī the wife of Pāṇḍu being sister to Śalya), MBh.; Hariv. &c.; of another king, Rājat.; (*ā*), f. a kind of dance (mentioned together with *lāsya* and *calita*), Kāvyâd. i, 39 (v.l. *śamya*); n. an iron crow, L.; poison, L.; abuse, defamation, L. **-kaṇṭha**, m. 'quill-throated,' a porcupine, L. **-kartana**, N. of a place, R. **-kartṛi**, m. an arrow-maker, ib.; = next, ib. (cf. *kriyā*). **-karttṛi**, m. 'cutter or remover of splinters,' a surgeon, MBh. **-karshaṇa** and **-kīrtana**, N. of places, R. **-kṛinta**, m. = *-karttṛi*, Āpast. **-kriyā**, f. the extraction of thorns or other extraneous substances lodged in the body, W. **-jñāna**, n., **-tantra**, n. N. of chs. of medical wks. **-dā**, f. a kind of plant (= *medā*), L. **-parṇikā** or **-parṇī**, f. a kind of medicinal plant, Bhpr. **-parvan**, n. N. of the ninth book of the Mahā-bhārata (this book describes how, on the death of Karṇa, Śalya, king of Madra, was appointed to the command of the Kuru army, and how a combat with maces took place between Śalya and Bhīma, and another great battle between Śalya and Yudhi-shṭhira, in which the former was at last killed). **-pīḍita**, mfn. hurt by an arrow or thorn &c., R. **-prôta**, mfn. pierced or transfixed by an arrow, Ragh. **-bhūta**, mfn. being a thorn or sting (fig.), MBh. **-loman**, n. a porcupine's quill, L. **-vat**, mfn. possessing an arrow, having an arrow-head sticking in it (as a deer), MBh. xii, 4649; or owning the arrow-head (and so owning the animal killed by the arrow), Mn. ix, 44; set with stakes, hampered or harassed with difficulties, W. **-vāraṅga**, n. 'arrow-handle,' the part by which an arrow or other foreign substance lodged in the body is laid hold of during the operation of extraction, ib. **-śāstra**, n. 'splinter (-extraction) science,' N. of a part of surgery and ch. of medical wks. (cf. *āyur-veda*). **-sraṅsana**, n. the extraction or removal of a thorn, Kauś. **-hartṛi**, m. 'remover of thorns,' a weeder, W.; = next, R.; Kathās. **-hṛit**, m. 'extractor of splinters,' a surgeon, VarBṛS. **Śalyâtman**, mfn. of a prickly or thorny nature, TS. **Śalyâpanayanīya**, mfn. treating of the extraction of thorns &c., Suśr. **Śalyâri**, m. 'enemy of Śalya,' N. of Yudhi-shṭhira, L. **Śalyâharaṇa-vidhi**, m. 'method of extracting splinters &c.,' N. of a ch. of the Ashṭâṅga-hṛidaya-saṃhitā. **Śalyôd-dharaṇa**, n., **°ddhāra**, m., **°ddhṛiti**, f. the extraction of arrows and thorns &c. (also as N. of wks.)

Śályaka, m. an arrow, dart, spear, thorn &c. (= *śalya*); a porcupine, VS. &c. &c.; a scaly fish, Vajras. (cf. *sa-śalka*); Vanguieria Spinosa, L. **-vat**, mfn. having a pointed mouth; m. (with *ākhu*) a shrew-mouse, MBh.

Śalyaya, Nom. P. *°yati*, to pain, torment, injure, Anarghar.

Śalyāya, Nom. Ā. *°yate*, to become a thorn or sting, Harav.

Śalla, m. (prob. fr. *śalya*) a frog, L.; bark, L.; (*ā*), f. Boswellia Thurifera, L.

Śallaka, m. (fr. *śalyaka*) a porcupine, Baudh.; Yājñ.; MBh. &c.; Bignonia Indica, L.; (*ikā*), f. a kind of ship or boat (v.l. *jhillikā*), Hariv.; (*akī*), f., see below; n. bark, L. **Śallakâṅga-ja**, mfn. grown on the body of a porcupine, Suśr.

Śallaki, f. (m.c.) = next, Suśr.

Śallakī, f. (also written *sallakī*) a porcupine, R.; Pañcar.; Boswellia Thurifera, MBh.; R. &c.; incense, olibanum, Suśr. **-tvac**, f. the bark of Boswellia Thurifera, Suśr. **-drava**, m. 'Śallaki-essence,' a kind of incense, olibanum, L.

Śallakīya, m. = *śallakī-drava*, MBh. (B. and C. *sallakīya*).

शल् 2. *śál*, onomat. (an exclamation used to express anything sudden), AV. xx, 135, 2.

शलकटङ्कट *śalakaṭaṅkata*, m. N. of Skanda, AV.Pariś.

शलङ्कट *śalaṅkaṭa*, m. N. of a man (in *uttara-śalaṅkaṭāḥ*, the descendants of Uttara and Śalaṅkaṭa), g. *tika-kitavâdi*.

Śalaṅku, m. N. of a man, g. *naḍâdi*.

शलङ्ग *śalaṅga*, m. a king, sovereign, L.; a kind of salt, L.

शलभ *śalabha*, m. (cf. *śarabha*) a grasshopper, locust (fabled to be the children of Pulastya or of Tārkshya and Yāminī), a kind of moth (such as is attracted by a lighted candle?), MBh.; Kāv. &c.; N. of a Deva-gandharva, MBh.; of an Asura, ib.; (*ī*), f. N. of one of the Mātṛis attendant on Skanda, ib. **-tā**, f. (Mcar.), **-tva**, n. (Kum) the state or condition of a grasshopper or moth. **Śalabhâsura**, m. the Asura Salabha, MBh. **Śalabhâstra**, n. a bow decorated with golden locusts, MBh. iii, 11967 (cf. iv, 1329).

Śalabhāya, Nom. P. *°yate*, to be or act like a grasshopper or moth (i.e. to fly recklessly into fire, run into certain death), Kāv.; Kathās.

शलल *śalala*, *śalākā* &c. See p. 1058, col. 3, and col. 1 above.

शलाट *śalāṭa*, m. a cart-load (= 20 times 100 Palas), L. (cf. 2. *śākaṭa*).

शलाटु *śalāṭu*, m. n. (cf. *śalālu* and *saṭālu*) the unripe fruit of a tree (accord. to some 'mfn. unripe'), Gobh.; Suśr.; m. Aegle Marmelos, L.; a kind of root, L.

शलातुर *śalātura*, N. of the abode of the ancestors of Pāṇini (cf. *śālāturīya*).

शलाथल *śalāthala*, m. N. of a man (pl. his descendants), g. *upakâdi*.

शलाभोलि *śalābholi*, m. a camel, L. (prob. w. r.)

शलालु *śalālu*, n. a sort of perfume or fragrant substance (*°luka*, mf(*ī*)n. dealing in it), Pāṇ. iv, 4, 54 (Siddh.); = *śalāṭu*, ĀpGṛ.

शलावत् *śalāvat*, m. N. of a man, Śaṃk. (cf. *śālāvat*, *śālāvatya*).

शलिपुत्र *śali-putra*, v.l. for *śala-putra*, q.v.

शलुन *śalúna*, m. a kind of insect, AV.

शल्क *śálka*, m. n. (cf. *śakala*, *śakla*, *śalāka*) a chip, shaving, piece, bit, portion, TS.; Kāṭh.; Br.; m. meal, flour, L.; n. a fish-scale, Mn.; MBh. &c.; bark, L. **-maya**, mf(*ī*)n. scaly, flaky, MW. **-yuta**, mfn. id., L.

Śalkala, n. = *śalka*, n., W.

Śalkalin, mfn. having scales (see *mahā-ś°*); m. a fish, L.

Śalkin, m. 'having scales,' a fish, L.

शल्प *śalpa*, *°paka*, *°pa-dā* &c., w.r. *śalya* &c.

शल्भ् *śalbh*, cl. 1. Ā. *śalbhate*, to praise, boast, Dhātup. x, 30.

शल्मलि *śalmali*, m. (cf. *śālmali*) the silk cotton tree, Salmalia Malabarica, RV.; VS.; Br.; Gobh.

Śalmalī, f. id., VarBṛS. (v.l.); L.

शल्य *śalya* &c. See col. 1.

शल्ल *śalla*, *śallaka*. See col. 2.

शल्व *śalva*, m. pl. N. of a people, L. (cf. *śálva*); a kind of plant, L.

शव् *śav* (prob. artificial), cl. 1. P. to go, Dhātup. xvii, 76 (cf. Naigh. ii, 14); to alter, change, transform, Dhātup. ib. (Vop.)

शव *śava*, m. n. (ifc. f. *ā*; prob. fr. √ 1. *śū* or *śvi* and orig. = 'swollen') a corpse, dead body, ŚBr. &c. &c.; n. water, L. **-karman**, n. the burning of a corpse, obsequies, Baudh. **-kāmya**, m. 'fond of or feeding on corpses,' a dog, L. **-kṛit**, m. 'c°-maker,' N. of Kṛishṇa, Pañcar. **-gandhin**, mfn. smelling of c°s, Cat. **-dahyā́**, f. cremation of a corpse, ŚBr. **-dāha**, m. id., W. **-dāhaka** or **-dāhin**, m. a c°-burner, ib. **-dhara**, mfn. carrying a c°, MBh. **-dhāna**, m. pl. N. of a people, MārkP. (cf. *śara-dh°*). **-nabhya**, n. a piece of the nave of (a wheel of) a vehicle used as a bier, KātyŚr. **-pannaga**, m. a dead serpent, MBh. **-bhasman**, n. the ashes of a c°, MW. **-bhūta**, mfn. become a c° or like a c°, ib. **-mandira**, n. a place for cremating corpses, MārkP. **-yāna**, n., **-ratha**, m. 'c°-vehicle,' a bier, litter, L. **-rūpa**, n. 'corpse-like,' a kind of animal, ŚāṅkhGṛ. **-loka-dhātu**, w.r. for *saha-l°*. **-vāha** or **-vāhaka**, m. a c°-carrier, MBh. **-visha**, n. c°-poison, the poison of a dead body, Suśr. **-śata-maya**, mf(*ī*)n. covered with a hundred corpses, Daś. **-śayana**, n. place (prepared) for (the cremation of) corpses, BhP. (accord. to Sch. also 'a lotus-flower'). **-śibikā**, f. 'corpse-litter,' a bier, Hcar. **-śiras**, n. the head or skull of a c°, Mn. xi, 72; *°ro-dhvaja*, mfn. carrying the skull (of a slain enemy) as an ensign, Āpast. **-śīrshaka**, m. 'c°-head,' the 7th cubit from the bottom or the 11th from the top of the sacrificial post, L. **-sādhana**, n. 'c°-rite,' a magical ceremony performed with a c°, Cat. **-sparśa**, m. touching a c°, MW. **-spṛiś**, mfn. one who has touched a corpse (and is consequently defiled), Mn. v, 64. **Śavâgni**, m. a funereal fire, ĀpŚr. **Śavâcchādana**, n. 'c°-covering,' a shroud, MW. **Śavânna**, n. funereal food, PārGṛ. **Śavâśa**, m. a c°-eater, Bhaṭṭ. **Śavâsthi-mālika**, mfn. wearing a garland of bones, Jain. **Śavôd-vahá**, m. a corpse-carrier, ŚBr.

Śávas, n. (orig. 'swelling, increase') strength, power, might, superiority, prowess, valour, heroism (*°sā*, ind. mightily, with might), RV.; AV.; water, L.; a dead body (= *śava*), L.; m. N. of a teacher, Cat.

Śavasāná, mfn. strong, vigorous, powerful, violent, RV.; m. a road, Uṇ. ii, 86, Sch.

Śavasā-vat, mfn. mighty, powerful, RV.

Śavasin, mfn. id., ib.

Śavasī́, f. 'the strong one,' N. of Indra's mother, ib.

Śavya, n. cremation of a corpse, funeral, ChUp.

शवर *śavara*, *śavala*. See *śab°*.

शश् *śaś* (prob. invented as a root for *śaśa*

below), cl. 1. P. (Dhātup. xvii, 77) *śaśati* (only pr. p. *śaśat*, Kir. xv, 5), to leap, bound, dance.

Śaśá, m. a hare, rabbit, or antelope (the markings on the moon are supposed to resemble a hare or rabbit), RV. &c. &c. (for *śaśasya vrata* see under *karshū*, p. 260); a kind of meteor, AV. v, 17, 4; N. of a man born under a partic. constellation, VarBṛS.; a man of mild character and easily led (one of the four classes into which men are divided by erotic writers, the other three being *aśva*, *mṛiga*, and *vṛishan*), L.; the Lodhra tree, Symplocos Racemosa, Kād.; gum-myrrh, L.; N. of a part of Jambu-dvīpa, MW.; (*ī*), f. N. of an Apsaras, Kāraṇḍ. [Cf. accord. to some, Gk. κεκήν; accord. to others, *śaśa* is for *śasa* and is connected with Germ. *haso, Hase*; Eng. *hare*.] **–karṇa**, m. the ear of a hare, L.; du. N. of a Sāman, Lāṭy.; 'hare-eared,' N. of the author of RV. viii, 9 (having the patr. *Kāṇva*), Anukr. **–ketu**, w.r. for *śaśi-k°*, Lalit. **–ghātaka** (Bhpr.) or **-ghātin** (Suśr.), m. 'h°-killer,' a hawk. **–ghna**, m. id., VarBṛS.; (*ī*), f., see *-han*. **–dhara**, m. 'bearer of hare-marks,' the moon, Kāv.; camphor, MW.; N. of various authors, Cat.; *-prabhā*, f., *-mālā*, f. N. of wks.; *-mukhī*, f. a moon-faced woman, Kautukar.; *-mauli*, m. 'moon-crested,' N. of Śiva, MW.; *°rācārya*, m. N. of an author, Cat. **–dharīya**, n. a work composed by Śaśa-dhara, Cat. **–dharman**, m. N. of a king, VP. **–pada**, n. a hare's track (easily got over), Hcar.; *-śakti*, f. N. of wk. **–plutaka**, n. a scratch with a finger-nail, L. **–bindu**, m. 'h°-spotted,' the moon, W.; N. of a king (son of Citraratha; pl. his descendants), MaitrUp.; MBh.; Hariv. &c. **–bhṛit**, m. 'hare-bearer,' the moon, VarBṛ.; Sāh.; Śatr. &c.; *°bhṛid-bhṛit*, m. 'moon-bearer,' N. of Śiva, KālP. **–mātra**, mf(*ī*)n. 'having the measure of a hare,' as large as a hare, W. **–muṇḍa-rasa**, m. a kind of fluid medicine made from a hare's head, ŚārṅgS. **– 1. -yāna**, n. (for 2. see col. 3) N. of a place of pilgrimage, MBh. **–rajas**, n. 'dirt on a hare,' a partic. measure of length or capacity, L. **–lakshaṇa**, m. 'h°-marked,' the moon, MBh. **–lakshmaṇa**, w.r. for prec., ib. **–lakshman**, n. the mark of a hare (on the moon), ib.; m. 'h°-marked,' the moon, Kathās.; Sāh.; **–lāñchana**, m. id., Kāv.; Pañcat. &c.; camphor, A. **–lupta**, n. disappearing like a hare, Pāṇ. vi, 2, 145, Sch. **–loman**, m. h°'s hair, L.; m. N. of a king, MBh. **–vishāṇa**, n. a h°'s horn (a term for an impossibility), Bhartṛ.; Kathās. &c. **–vishāṇāya**, Nom. Ā. *°yate*, to resemble a h°'s horn, to be an impossibility, Sarvad. **–śimbikā**, f. a partic. plant, L. **–śṛiṅga**, n. = *-vishāṇa*, Kull. on Mn. viii, 53; m. N. of a man, Viddh. (in Prākṛit). **–sthalī**, f. the Doab or country between the Ganges and Jumnā rivers, L.; w.r. for *kuśa-sth°*, L. **–han**, mf(*ghnī*)n. killing hares, Pāṇ. iii, 2, 53, Sch.; (*-ghnī*), f. a hawk, Car. (w.r. *śama-ghnī*). **Śaśâkshá**, m. 'hare-eyed,' N. of a mythical being, Suparṇ. **Śaśâṅka**, see below. **Śaśâda**, mfn. eating hares, L.; m. a partic. bird of prey, L.; N. of Vikukshi, MBh.; Hariv.; Pur. **Śaśâdana**, m. 'h°-eater,' the brown hawk, L. **Śaśôrṇa**, n. the hair of a rabbit or hare, Siddh.; L.; Buddh. **Śaśôlūka-mukhī**, f. N. of one of the Mātṛis attending on Skanda, MBh.

Śaśaka, m. a (little) hare, AdbhBr.; MBh.; R. &c.; a man of a partic. character (= *śaśa*, q.v.), A.; pl. N. of a people, MBh. **–vishāṇa**, n. = *śaśa-vish°*, Bhartṛ. **–śiśu**, m. the young of a hare, Vās. **Śaśakâdhama**, m. a miserable little rabbit, Hit.

Śaśat, mfn. leaping, jumping, Kir.

Śaśayú, mfn. pursuing hares, AV.

Śaśâṅka, m. 'hare-marked,' the moon, MBh.; Kāv. &c.; camphor, L.; N. of a king, Hcar., Sch.; *-kānta*, mfn. lovely as the m°, Jain.; *-kiraṇa-prakhya*, mfn. resembling a ray of the moon, MBh.; *-kula*, n. the lunar race, Kathās.; *ja* or *-tanaya*, m. 'the moon's son,' the planet Mercury, VarBṛS.; *-dhara*, m. N. of a grammarian, Cat.; *-pura*, n. N. of a town (also *-pūrvam puram*), Kathās.; *-bimba*, n. the disk of the moon, Jain.; *-bhās*, mfn. shining like the moon, MW.; *-mukuṭa*, m. 'having the moon as diadem,' N. of Śiva, Kathās.; *-mūrti*, m. 'having a hare-marked form,' N. of the moon, MW.; *-lekhā*, f. 'm°-streak,' the lunar crescent, Śak.; *-vatī*, f. N. of a princess (after whom the 12th Lambaka of the Kathā-sarit-sāgara is called), Kathās.; *-vadanā*, f. a moon-faced woman, Kāvyād.; *-śatru*, m. 'moon's foe,' N. of Rāhu, VarYogay.; *-śṛiṅga*, n. a horn or point of the moon's crescent (?), MW.; *-śekhara*, m. 'moon-crested,' N. of Śiva, BhP.; *-suta*, m. (= *śaśâṅka-ja*), VarBṛ.; *°kârdha*, m. the half-m°; *°kârdha-mukha*, mfn. having a head shaped like a half-m° (said of an arrow), Ragh.; *°kârdha-śekhara*, m. N. of Śiva, Rājat.; *°kôpala*, m. a kind of precious stone (= *candra-kānta*), Sāh. **Śaśâṅkita**, mfn. hare-marked (the moon), Śiś.

Śaśāṇḍuli or **°lī**, f. a kind of cucumber, L.

Śaśi, in comp. for *śaśin*. **–kara**, m. a moon-beam, MW. **–kalā**, f. a digit of the m°, the m° (in general), Vikr.; Kathās.; Chandom.; a kind of metre, Chandom.; N. of various women, Kathās.; Cat.; *-pañcāśikā*, f. N. of wk.; *°lâbharaṇa*, m. 'ornamented with a digit of the moon,' N. of Śiva, MW. **–kānta**, m. 'm°-loved,' the m°-stone (= *candra-k°*), VarBṛS.; (*ā*), f. N. of a river, VP.; n. a white lotus-flower opening by night, L. **–kiraṇa**, m. = *-kara*, Suśr. **–ketu**, m. N. of a Buddh. **–koṭi**, f. a horn of the m°, MW. **–kshaya**, m. the new m°, Hcat. **–khaṇḍa**, m. or n. (?) the m°'s crescent (see comp.); m. N. of a Vidyā-dhara, Kathās.; *-pada*, m. N. of a Vidyā-dhara, ib.; *-śekhara*, m. 'having the moon's crescent as diadem,' N. of Śiva, Hariv. **–gaccha**, m. the lunar race, Śatr. **–gupta**, m. N. of a king, VP. **–guhyā**, f. the juice of the liquorice-root, L. **–graha**, m. 'moon-seizure,' an eclipse of the m°, Cat.; *-samāgama*, m. a conjunction of the m° with asterisms or planets, VarBṛS. **–ja** (MBh.; Var.) or **-tanaya** (Var.), m. 'moon's son,' the planet Mercury. **–tejas**, m. N. of a Vidyā-dhara, Kathās.; of a serpent-demon, L. **–divākara**, m. du. moon and sun, Ml. **–deva**, m. N. of a king (= *ranti-d°*), L.; of a grammarian, Cat.; n. = next, VarBṛS. (v. l.) **–daiva**, n. the lunar mansion Mṛiga-śiras (presided over by the moon), ib. **–dhara**, m N. of a man, Inscr.; *-maṅgala-mata*, n. N. of wk. **–dhāman**, n. the m°'s splendour, MW. **–dhvaja**, m. N. of an Asura, Hariv.; of a king of Bhallāṭa-nagara, KalkiP. **–pāda**, m. a m°-beam, W. **–putra**, m. = *-ja*, Var. **–prabha**, mfn. shining like the m°, radiant as the moon, Ragh.; (*ā*), f. N. of a woman, Kathās.; n. a lotus-flower opening by night, L.; the white esculent water-lily, W.; a pearl, L.; (*ā*), f. the moon's lustre, m°-light, L. **–priya**, n. a pearl, L.; (*ā*), f. 'loved of the m°,' a lunar mansion personified, L. **–bindu**, w.r. for *śaśa-b°*, R. **–bhās**, f. a moon-beam, MW. **–bhūshaṇa**, m. 'm°-decorated,' N. of Śiva, L. **–bhṛit**, m. 'm°-bearer,' id., VarBṛS. (cf. *nava-śaśi-bh°*). **–maṇi**, m. the moon-stone (= *candra-kānta*), Nāg.; Kād. **–maṇḍala**, n. the disk of the m°, HPariś. **–mat**, mfn. possessing the m°, Sāh. **–maya**, mf(*ī*)n. consisting of or relating to the m°, Naish. **–mayūkha**, m. a m°-beam, MW. **–mukha**, mfn. moon-faced; (*ī*), f. a moon-faced woman, Kāv. **–mauli**, m. 'having the moon as a diadem,' N. of Śiva, Kum.; Kathās.; MārkP. **–raśmi**, m. a m°-beam, MW. **–rekhā**, f. 'm°-streak,' digit of the m°, L.; N. of a woman, Kathās. **–lekhā**, f. a digit of the m°, Viddh.; Vernonia Anthelminthica, Bhpr.; Dhanv.; Cocculus Cordifolius, L.; a kind of metre, L.; N. of an Apsaras, BrahmaP.; of a princess, Kathās.; of a female slave, Vās. **–vaṇśa**, m. the lunar race (*-ja*, mfn. sprung from the lunar race), Hariv.; Kāv.; N. of wk. **–vadanā**, f. = *-mukhī*, Chandom.; two kinds of metre, ib.; Śrutab. &c. **–vardhana**, m. N. of a poet, Kāv. **–vāṭikā**, f. Bœrhavia Procumbens, L. **–vimala**, mfn. pure as the moon (with *giri*, m. 'the Kailāsa'), R. (Sch.) **–śikhā-maṇi**, m. 'having the moon as diadem,' N. of Śiva, Rājat. **–śekhara**, m. id., ib., Kathās.; Inscr.; N. of a Buddha, L.; of one of the Jaina pontiffs, W. **–saṃnibha**, mfn. = *-prabha*, MBh. **–suta**, m. = *-ja*, Var. **Śaśibha**, w.r. for *śaśâṅka*, Cat. **Śaśīśa**, m. 'lord of the m°,' N. of Śiva; *-śiśu*, m. 'son of Śiva,' N. of Skanda (*-śī*, m. wounding Śiva), Kir. xv, 5.

Śaśika, m. pl. N. of a people, MBh. (v.l. *śāśika*).

Śaśin, m. 'containing a hare,' the moon, ŚvetUp.; MBh.; Kāv. &c.; N. of the number one, VarBṛS.; camphor, Hcat.; a kind of metre, Col.; N. of a man, Kathās.; the emblem of a partic. Arhat or Jina, W.; (*inī*), f. N. of the 8th Kalā of the moon, Cat.

1. **Śaśī**, f., see under *śaśa*.

2. **Śaśī**, in comp. for *śaśa*. **–√bhū**, P. *-bhavati*, to become a hare, Hariv.

शशमान *śaśamāná*, mfn. (fr. √1. *śam*) exerting one's self, zealous, toiling, working, active (esp. in worship), RV.; VS.; AV.

शशय *śaśayá*, mf(*ā*)n. (either fr. √1. *śī* or connected with *śaśīyas*, *śaśvat*) ever-flowing, unfailing, abundant, RV.

शशयान 2. *śaśayāná*, mfn. (pf. p. of √1. *śī*; for 1. *śaśa-y°*, see col. 1) lying, reposing, sleeping (= *śiśyāna*), RV.

शशीयस् *śáśīyas*, mfn. (prob. compar. of *śaśvat* below; accord. to Sāy. fr. √*śaś*) more numerous, mightier, richer, RV.

शश्वचै *śaśvacai*. See √*śvac*.

शश्वत् *śáśvat*, mf(*śáśvatī* or *°tī́*)n. (accord. to some for *sasvat* and corresponding to Gk. ἅπας) perpetual, continual, endless, incessant, frequent, numerous, many (esp. applied to the ever-recurring dawns), RV.; all, every, RV.; AV.; TBr.; (*at*), ind. perpetually, continually, repeatedly, always, ever (*śáśvat purā́*, from immemorial time; *śaśvac-chaśvat*, again and again, constantly), RV. &c. &c.; at once, forthwith, directly (generally preceded or followed by *ha*; *śáśvat—śáśvat*, no sooner—than forthwith), ŚBr.; BhP.; it is true, certainly, indeed, Br. **–kāma**, mf(*ā*)n. always intent on love, Pañcar. **–tamá**, mfn. most constant or frequent or numerous, RV.; (*ám*), ind. once more, again, ib.

Śaśva, Nom. P. *°yati* = *śaśvāyate* below, Vop.

Śaśvac-chānti, f. (for *°vat-ś°*) everlasting peace or tranquillity, eternal rest, MW.

Śaśvadhā́, ind. again and again, ever and ever again, RV.

Śaśvāya, Nom. P. *°te*, to be or become eternal (g. *bhṛiśâdi*).

शष् *śash*, cl. 1. P. *śashati*, to hurt, injure, kill, Dhātup. xvii, 39.

शष्कण्डी *śashkaṇḍī*, f. a kind of plant and its fruit, Gaṇar.

शष्कुल *śashkula*, m. Pongamia Glabra, L.; (ifc.) = next, Pāṇ. i, 2, 49, Sch.

Śashkuli or **°lī**, f. the orifice of the ear, auditory passage, Yājñ.; Suśr.; a kind of disease of the ear, ŚārṅgS.; a large round cake (composed of ground rice, sugar, and sesamum, and cooked in oil; also written *śask°*), MBh.; Suśr.; BhP.; a sort of fish, L.; Pongamia Glabra, L.; rice-gruel or barley-water, W.

Śashkulikā, f. a sort of cake (= prec.), Suśr.; VarBṛS.

शष्प *śáshpa*, n. (ifc. f. *ā*; accord. to Uṇ. iii, 28 fr. √*śas*; often incorrectly *śaspa* and *śashya*) young or sprouting grass, any grass, VS. &c. &c.; loss of consciousness (= *pratibhā-kshaya*), L. **–tulya**, mfn. resembling young grass, Pañcat. (v.l.) **–bṛisī**, f. a seat of Kuśa grass, R.; Suśr. **–bhuj** or **-bhojana**, m. 'grass-eater,' any animal feeding on grass, Pañcat. **–vat**, mfn. containing young grass, L. **Śashpâda**, mfn. grass-eating, graminivorous, Ml.

Śashpiñjara, mfn. (for *śashpa-p°*) yellowish-red like young grass, MS.; VS. (TS. *śasp°*).

शस् 1. *śas*, cl. 1. P. (Dhātup. xvii, 78) *śásati* (Ved. also *-śasti* and *-śāsti*; pf. *śaśāsa*, MBh.; 3. pl. *śaśasuḥ*, Gr.; fut. *śasitā*, ib.; *śasishyati*, Br.; Ved. inf. *-śásas*, Br.; ind. p. *-śasya*, MBh.), to cut down, kill, slaughter (mostly *vi-√śas*, q.v.)

Śásana, n. slaughtering, killing, RV.

Śásā, f. id., RV. v, 41, 18 (Sāy. = *stutyā*, fr. √*śaṇs*).

Śasita, **°tṛi**. See *vi-ś°*.

Śasitvā, ind. having wounded or hurt, MW.

2. **Śasta**, mfn. (for 1. see p. 1044, col. 1) cut down, slaughtered, killed, MBh. iii, 1638.

Śastaka, n. = *loha*, L. (prob. w.r. for *śastraka*); a defence for the finger of an archer (= *aṅguli-trāṇa*), L.

Śastri, m. a cutter, dissecter, RV.; AV.

2. **Śástra**, m. (for 1. see p. 1044, col. 1) a sword, L.; (*ī*), f., see below; n. an instrument for cutting or wounding, knife, sword, dagger, any weapon (even applied to an arrow, Bhaṭṭ.; weapons are said to be of four kinds, *pāṇi-mukta*, *yantra-mukta*, *muktâmukta*, and *amukta*), ŚBr. &c. &c.; any instrument or tool (see comp.); iron, steel, L.; a razor, L. **–karman**, n. 'knife-operation,' any sur-

gical operation, Suśr.; °*ma-kṛit*, m. 'performing a surgical op°,' a surgeon, ib.; °*ma-vidhi*, m. N. of wk. — **kali**, m. a duel with swords, Kathās. — **kāra**, m. 'weapon-maker,' an armourer, W. — **kuśala**, mfn. skilled or expert in arms, MW. — **kopa**, m. 'sword-fury,' war, battle, VarBṛS. — **kośa**, m. the sheath of a weapon; *-taru*, m. a thorny Gardenia, L. — **kshata**, mfn. killed by w°s, MW. — **kshāra**, m. borax, L. — **graha**, m. taking arms, battle, fight, Mcar. — **grāhaka**, mfn. taking arms, armed, Kām. — **grāha-vat**, mfn. having sea-monsters for weapons (said of a river), R. — **grāhin**, mfn. taking arms; m. an armed man, W. — **ghāta**, m. the stroke of a sword, VarBṛS. — **ghushṭa-kara**, mfn. making a noise or clanging with arms, W. — **cikitsā**, f. 'curing by means of instruments,' surgery, Hāsy. — **cūrṇa**, n. iron-filings, L. — **jāla**, n. a quantity of w°s, W. — **jīvin**, mfn. living by arms; m. a professional soldier, VarBṛS.; MārkP. — **tyāga**, m. abandoning or throwing away a weapon, W. — **devatā**, f. 'weapon-deity,' a deified weapon or goddess of war (represented as the offspring of Kṛiśāśva, and, according to some, one hundred in number), Uttarar.; Rājat. — **dhara**, mfn. bearing w°s; m. a warrior, W. — **dhāraṇa**, n. bearing arms or a sword, Kām.; MārkP.; *-jīvaka*, m. 'one who lives by bearing arms,' a soldier, MW. — **dhārin**, mfn. bearing arms, ib. — **nitya**, mfn. one who is continually under arms, MBh. — **nidhana**, mfn. dying by the sword, VarBṛS. — **nipāta**, m. 'fall or stroke of a sword,' killing by w°s, war, fight, ib.; = next, Suśr. — **nipātana**, n. 'stroke of the knife,' a surgical operation, ib. — **niryāṇa**, mfn. = *-nidhana*, VarBṛS. — **nyāsa**, m. 'laying down of arms,' abstention from battle, Vikr. — **pada**, n. 'knife-mark,' incision, Suśr. — **pāṇi**, mfn. (m.c. also °*nin*) 'weapon-handed,' armed; m. an armed warrior, Hit.; Vet. — **pāta**, m. 'fall or stroke of a weapon or knife,' incision, Kāvyâd. — **pāna**, n. a mixture for saturating w°s (so as to temper or harden them), VarBṛS. — **pūjā-vidhi**, m. N. of wk. — **pūta**, mfn. 'purified by w°s,' absolved from guilt by dying on the field of battle, Mālatīm. — **prakopa**, m. = *-kopa*, VarBṛS. — **prahāra**, m. a sword-cut, Kāvyâd. — **bhaya**, n. fear or danger of arms, calamity of war, VarBṛS. — **bhṛit**, m. = *-dhara*, Gaut.; Mn.; MBh. &c. — **maya**, mf(*ī*)n. (rain) consisting in or formed by w°s, R. — **mārja**, m. 'w°-cleaner,' an armourer, L. — **mukha**, n. the edge of a w°, L. — **lakshaṇa**, n. N. of wk. — 2. -**vat**, mfn. (for 1. see p. 1044, col. 1) provided with a w°, MBh.; Hariv. &c. — **vadha**, m. killing with a w° (in *a-ś°*, 'killing without a w°'), Pañcat. — **vārtta**, mfn. = *-jīvin*, VarBṛS. — **vikrayin**, m. a dealer in w°s, Mn. iv, 215. — **vidyā**, f. = *dhanur-veda*, Anarghar. — **vidvas**, mfn. skilled in arms, MBh. — **vihita**, mfn. inflicted with a w°, Ml. — **vṛitti**, mfn. = *-jīvin*, Mn. xii, 45. — **vyavahāra**, m. practice of w°s, Ragh. — **vraṇa-maya**, mf(*ī*)n. consisting in wounds produced by w°s, Śiś. — **śāstra**, n. the science of arms, military science, MW. — **śikshā**, f. skill with w°s or with the sword, Kathās. — **śikhin**, mfn. proud of (the practice of) w°s, MW. — **saṃhati**, f., -**samūha**, m. 'collection of w°s,' an arsenal, armoury, W. — **sampāta**, m. 'descent of weapons,' discharge of missiles, battle, fight, Bhag.; Kathās. — **hata**, mfn. struck or killed by a sword; *-caturdaśī*, f. N. of a partic. fourteenth day sacred to the memory of fallen warriors, L. **Śastrâkhya**, mfn. called a sword (applied to a comet), VarBṛS.; n. iron, L. **Śastrâgni-sambhrama**, m. trouble or alarm (caused) by war or fire, VarBṛS. **Śastrâṅgā**, f. a kind of sorrel, L. **Śastrâjīva**, mf(*ī*)n. = *śastra-jīvin*; m. a soldier, L. **Śastrânta**, mfn. dying by the sword, VarBṛS. **Śastrâbhyāsa**, m. the practice of arms, military exercise, L. **Śastrâmayârti**, f. distress (caused) by war or disease, VarBṛS. **Śastrâyasa**, n. iron, steel, L. **Śastrâyudha**, mfn. having the sword for a weapon (and not the Veda, as a Brāhman should have), Vet. **Śastrârcis**, mfn. blazing or flaming with weapons, MW. **Śastrâvapāta**, m. injury by a w°, Yājñ. ii, 277. **Śastrā-śastri**, ind. sword against sword, Daś.; AgP. **Śastrâstra**, (ibc.) w°s both for striking and throwing; *-bhṛit*, mfn. bearing w°s, m. (*-tva*, n. the use of arms), Mn. x, 79. **Śastrôtthāpana**, n., °**trôdyama**, m. lifting up a weapon (so as to strike), W. **Śastrôdyoga**, m. the practice of arms, VarBṛS. **Śastrôpakaraṇa**, n. arms and instruments of warfare, military apparatus, MW. **Śastrôpajīvin**, m. 'living by arms,' a warrior, soldier, Hcar.; an armourer, R. (Sch.)

2. **Śastraka**, n. (for 1. see p. 1044, col. 1) a knife, L.; iron, L.; (*ikā*), f. a dagger, knife, Daś.

2. **Śastrin**, mfn. having weapons, bearing arms, armed with a sword, MBh.; Hariv.; Kām. &c.

Śastrī, f. a dagger, knife, Bhartṛ. — **śyāma**, mfn. bluish like the blade of a knife, Śiś.

2. **Śasya**, mfn. to be cut down or slaughtered or killed, Vop.; n. corn, grain (more correctly *sasya*, q.v.)

Śasyaka, n. powder (= *cūrṇa*), R. (Sch.); v.l. for *sasyaka*, q.v.

शस् 2. *śas.* See √*sas.*

शस् 3. *śas*, (in gram.) the technical case-termination of the accusative plural, Pāṇ. iv, 1, 2; the Taddhita affix *śas* (forming adverbs from nouns, esp. from numerals and words expressive of quantity), ib. v, 1, 42 &c. (cf. *alpa-śas*, *bahu-śas*, *śata-śas* &c.)

शस्कुली *śaskulī*, *śaspiñjara*. See *śashk°*, *śashp°*, p. 1060, col. 3.

शस्ति *śasti*, *śasman*. See p. 1044, col. 1.

शहेन्द्रवर्णनविलास *śahendra-varṇana-vilāsa* (for *śāh°?*), m. N. of a poem, Cat.

शांवत्य *śāṃvatya*, m. (fr. *śaṃ-vat*) N. of an ancient teacher, ĀśvGṛ.

शांशप *śāṅśapá*, mf(*ī*)n. (fr. *śiṅśapā*) derived from the Śiṅśapā (Dalbergia Sissoo, a large and beautiful tree), made of its wood &c., AV.

Śāṅśapaka, mfn. id., g. *arīhaṇâdi*.

Śāṅsapāyana, m. N. of an ancient teacher (also called *Su-śarman*), Pur.

Śāṅsapāyanaka, mf(*ikā*)n. written or composed by Śāṅsapāyana, Cat.

Śāṅsapāyani, m. = *śāṅśapāyana*.

Śāṅsapāsthala, mfn. (fr. *śiṅśapā-sthala*), Pāṇ. vii, 3, 1, Sch.

शाक 1. *śāka*, m. (fr. √*śak*) power, might, help, aid, RV.; (*śākā*), m. helpful, a helper, friend, ib.

Śākin (once *śākin*), mfn. helpful or powerful, RV.; m. N. of a man, g. *kurv-ādi*; (*inī*), f. a kind of female demon attendant on Durgā, Pañcat.; Kathās.

1. **Śākiná**, mfn. (for 2. see col. 3) mighty, RV.

Śākinikā, f. a kind of female demon (= *śākinī* under *śākin*), Cat.

Śākī, f. (prob.) = 1. *śāka*, Pāṇ. v, 2, 100, Vārtt. 1, Pat.

शाक 2. *śāka*, n. (or m., g. *ardharcâdi*; of doubtful derivation, and scarcely to be connected with 1. *śāka*) a potherb, vegetable, greens, GṛŚrS.; Mn.; MBh. &c.; any vegetable food, Gaut.; m. the Teak tree, Tectona Grandis, GṛŚrS.; MBh. &c.; Acacia Sirissa, L.; N. of a Dvīpa (the sixth of the seven Dvīpas, called after the Teak tree growing there, surrounded by the sea of milk or white sea, and inhabited by the Ṛita-vratas, Satya-vratas, Dāna-vratas, and Anu-vratas), MBh.; Pur.; (*ā*), f. Terminalia Chebula, L.; m. or n.(?) N. of a place, Col. — **kalambaka**, m. leek, garlic, L. — **kāla**, m. the Śāka era, Jyot. — **cukrikā**, f. the tamarind, L. — **jagdha**, mf(*ā* or *ī*)n., Pāṇ. iv, 1, 53, Sch. — **jambu**, N. of a place; °*buka*, mfn., Pāṇ. iv, 2, 119, Sch. — **taru**, m. the Teak tree, L.; Capparis Trifoliata, W. — **dāsa**, m. N. of a teacher, VBr. — **dīkshā**, f. (pl.) feeding only on vegetables, MBh. — **dvīpa**, m. N. of a Dvīpa (see above). — **dvīpīya**, mf(*ā*)n. belonging to Śāka-dvīpa, MW. — **nighaṇṭu**, m. N. of a glossary of plants by Sītā-rāma Śāstrin. — **paṇa**, m. a handful of vegetables &c., a measure equal to a h°, L. — **pattra**, n. a leaf of the Teak tree, Suśr.; (prob.) = *pattra-śāka*, vegetables consisting of leaves, MārkP.; m. Moringa Pterygosperma, L. — **pātra**, n. a vessel for vegetables, vegetable dish, MW. — **pārthiva**, m. a king who eats or enjoys vegetables (= *śāka-bhoji pārthivaḥ*), Pat. ('a king dear to the era,' accord. to Siddh. on Pāṇ. ii, 1, 69, see 4. *śāka*). — **piṇḍī**, f. a mass of vegetables, ŚāṅkhGṛ. — **pota**, m. pl. N. of a people, MārkP. — **prati**, ind. a little potherb (?), MW. — **bāleya**, m. a partic. plant (= *brahma-yashṭi*), L. — **bilva** or °**vaka**, m. the egg-plant, L. (cf. *-vindaka*). — **bhaksha**, mfn. vegetarian; *-tā*, f. vegetarianism, Gaut. — **bhava**, m. N. of a Varsha in Plaksha-dvīpa, MārkP. — **mṛisha** (?), m. or n. a species of plant, Kauś. (v.l. *śāka-m°* and *śāka-vṛisha*). — **m-bharī**, f. 'herb-nourishing,' N. of a lake in Rājputāna (the modern Sāmbhar), Vās., Introd.; Col.; a form of Durgā, MBh.; Pur.; N. of a place or town sacred to D°, MBh.; observances there in honour of D° (accord. to some), MW. — **m-bharīya**, mfn. coming from Śākam-bharī, Bhpr.; n. a kind of fossil salt from the above lake, W. — **yogya**, m. coriander, L. — **racita**, mf(*ā*)n. composed of vegetables &c., VarBṛS. — **rasa**, m. edible vegetable juice, MBh.; °*sī*-√*kṛi*, P. *-karoti*, to turn into veg° j°, Kathās. — **rāj** or -**rāja**, m. 'king of veg°,' Chenopodium, L. — **varṇa**, mfn. = *śyāva*, Bhpr.; m. N. of a king, VP. — **vāṭa**, °**ṭaka**, m. or °**ṭikā**, f. a veg° garden, Kathās. — **viḍambaka**, mfn. disgracing (the name) *śāka*, Kāv. — **vindaka**, m. = *-bilva*, L. — **vīra**, m. Chenopodium, L.; a species of purslain, L. — **vṛiksha**, m. the Teak tree, L. — **vṛisha**, see *-mṛisha*. — **vrata**, n. a partic. vow, abstinence from veg° &c., MW. — **śākaṭa** or -**śākina**, n. a bed or field of veg°, L. — **śreshṭha**, m. 'best of herbs,' the egg-plant, L.; a partic. medicinal plant used also as a potherb, L.; Hoya Viridifolia, L.; Chenopodium Album, MW.; (*ā*), f. the above medicinal pl°, Bhpr.; = *jīvantī*; = *ḍoḍī*; the egg-plant, MW. — **hāra**, w.r. for *śākâhāra* (q.v.) **Śākâkhya**, m. the Teak tree, L.; n. a vegetable, potherb, MW. **Śākâṅga**, n. pepper, L. **Śākâda**, m. 'eater of veg°,' N. of a man; pl. his family, Cat. **Śākâmla**, n. the fruit of Garcinia Cambogia, Kālac.; the hog-plum, L.; *-bhedaka*, n. vinegar made from fruit (esp. from the tamarind-fruit), L.; *-bhedana*, n. id., L.; sorrel, MW. **Śākâlābu**, m. a species of cucumber, L. **Śākâśana**, mfn. feeding on vegetables, Kathās. (w.r. *śākāsana*). **Śākâshṭakā** (Cat.) or °**ṭamī** (W.), f. the 8th day of the dark half of the month Phālguna (on which veg° are offered to the Pitṛis). **Śākāsana**, w.r. for *śākâśana*, Kathās. **Śākâhāra**, mfn. eating vegetables, living on vegetables, Bhartṛ. **Śākêkshu**, m. a species of sugar-cane, L.

1. **Śākaṭa**, n. (ifc.) = next (cf. *ikshu-ś°*).

2. **Śākina**, n. (ifc.; for 1. see col. 2) a field (cf. *ikshu-*, 'a field of sugar-cane,' *mūla-*, *śāka-ś°*).

Śākinī, f. (cf. under *śākin*) a field or land planted with vegetables or potherbs, L.

Śākiya, mfn., g. *utkarâdi*.

शाक 3. *śāka*, m. N. of a man, g. *kuñjâdi*.

Śākāyana. See *śākāyanya*.

Śākāyanin, m. pl. (prob.) the followers of Śākāyanya, ŚBr.

Śākāyanya, m. patr. fr. *śāka*, g. *kuñjâdi* (pl. °*yanāḥ*, ib.)

शाक 4. *śāka*, mfn. (fr. *śaka*) relating to the Śakas or Indoscythians; m. n. (scil. *saṃvatsara*, *abda* &c.) the Śaka era (also *śāka-kāla*; see *śaka-k°*), VarBṛS., Sch.; (also) a general N. for any era; (pl.) N. of a people (w.r. for *śaka*), Buddh. — **pārthiva**, see under 2. *śāka*. **Śākêndra**, mfn. (a year) of a king of the Śakas, Inscr.

Śākeya, m. pl. N. of a school, L.

शाकट 2. *śākaṭa*, mf(*ī*)n. (fr. *śakaṭa*) relating or belonging to a cart, going in a cart, drawing a cart, filling a cart &c., L.; m. a draught-animal, L.; a cart-load, L.; Cordia Latifolia, L. — **potikā**, f. Basella Rubra, L. **Śākaṭâkhya**, m. a kind of tree, MW.

Śākaṭāyana, m. (fr. *śakaṭa*) patr. of an ancient grammarian, Prāt.; Nir.; Pāṇ.; of a modern grammarian, Gaṇar.; Vop.; of the author of a law-book (see *-smṛiti*). — **vyākaraṇa**, n. N. of a grammar (adopted by the Jaina community in opposition to the orthodox Ashṭâdhyāyī). — **smṛiti**, f. the law-book of Ś°, Hcat. **Śākaṭāyanôpanishad-bhāshya** (?), n. N. of a Comm. by Śaṃkarâcārya.

Śākaṭāyani, m. a patr. (prob. = °*yana*), Cat.

Śākaṭika, mfn. belonging to a cart or going in a cart, W.; m. a carter, VarBṛS.; Pañcat.

Śākaṭīkarṇa, mfn. (fr. *śakaṭi-karṇa*), g. *suvāstv-ādi*.

Śākaṭīna, mfn. belonging or relating to a cart, W.; m. a cart-load (also as a measure of weight = 20 Tulās), L.

शाकन्धव्य *śākandhavya*, m. patr. fr. *śakandhu*, g. *kurv-ādi*.

शाकंधेय *śākaṃdheya*, m. patr. fr. *śakaṃdhi*, g. *śubhrâdi*.

शाकपूणि *śākapūṇi*, m. (w. r. *śākapūrṇi*; fr. *śakapūṇi*) patr. of an ancient grammarian, Nir. (cf. IW. 159).

शाकरी *śākarī*, w. r. for *śākārī* below.

शाकल *śākala*, mfn. (fr. *śakala*) dyed with the substance called Śakala, Kāś. on Pāṇ. iv, 2, 2; relating to a piece or portion, MW.; derived from or belonging or relating to the Śākalas, Mn. ix, 200 (cf. Pāṇ. iv, 3, 128); m. or n. a chip, piece, fragment, splinter, ŚBr.; ŚrS.; m. (scil. *maṇi*) an amulet made of chips of wood, Kauś.; N. of an ancient teacher, Cat.; a kind of serpent, AitBr.; (pl.) the Śākalas (i. e.) followers of Śākalya, RPrāt. (g. *kaṇvâdi*); the inhabitants of the town Śākala, MBh.; n. the text or ritual of Śākalya, AitBr.; ĀśvGṛ.; Pat.; N. of a Sāman, ĀrshBr.; of a town of the Madras, MBh.; Kathās.; of a village of the Bāhīkas, Pat. on Pāṇ. iv, 2, 104, Vārtt. 4. — **prātiśākhya**, n. N. of the Ṛig-veda Prātiśākhya (ascribed to Śaunaka and handed down for the use of the Śākala school). — **śākhā**, f. the Śākala branch or school of the RV. (the text of the Ṛig-veda as handed down by the Śākalas constituting the only extant version), IW. 150. — **saṃhitā**, f. the Śākala Saṃhitā. — **smṛiti**, f. N. of a law-book (also called *śākalya-smṛiti*), Cat. — **homa**, m. a partic. kind of oblation, ib.; °*mīya*, mfn. relating or belonging to the Śākala-homa, Mn. xi, 256.

Śākalaka, mf(*ikā*)n. derived from or relating to the Śākalas, Pāṇ. iv, 3, 128.

Śākali or °**lin**, m. (cf. *śakalin*) a fish, Car.

Śākalika, mf(*ī*)n. dyed with the substance called Śakala, Pāṇ. iv, 2, 2, Vārtt. 1; having a piece or portion, fragmentary, W.; relating to the town Śākala, ib. iv, 2, 117, Sch.

Śākalya, m. patr. fr. *śakala*, ŚBr.; N. of an ancient grammarian and teacher, Prāt.; Nir.; Pāṇ. &c. (who is held to be the arranger of the Pada text of the Ṛig-veda); of a poet, Subh. — **carita**, n. N. of wk. — **palya**, m. N. of a poet, Cat. — **pitṛi**, m. the father of Ś°, RPrāt. — **mata**, n., -**saṃhitā**, f., -**saṃhitā-pariśishṭa**, n. N. of wks.

Śākalyāyanī, f. of *śākalya*, g. *lohitâdi*.

शाकारी *śākārī* or *śākārikā*, f. the dialect spoken by the Śakas or Śakāras (see 2. *śakāra*), Sāh.; Mṛicch., Introd.

शाकुन 1. *śākuna*, mfn. = *parôttāpin*, L. ('repentant,' 'regretful,' W.)

शाकुन 2. *śākuna*, mf(ī)n. (fr. *śakuna*) derived from or relating to birds or omens, Mn.; MBh. &c.; having the nature of a bird, Car.; ominous, portentous, W.; m. a bird-catcher, VarBṛS.; augury, omen, ib.; R.; N. of a wk. by Vasanta-rāja (= *śakunârṇava*, q.v.) — **vicāra**, m., -**śāstra-sāra**, m., -**sārôddhāra**, m. N. of wks. — **sûkta**, n. N. of a partic. hymn of the Ṛig-veda (= *śakuna-s°*).

Śākuni, m. 'a bird-catcher' or 'an augur,' VP.

Śākunika, mfn. relating to birds or omens, ominous, W.; m. a fowler, bird-catcher, Mn.; MBh. &c.; a fisherman, MaitrUp. — **praśna**, m. N. of a wk. on augury.

Śākunikāyinī, f. a female poulterer (?), Divyâv.

Śākunin, m. a fisherman, VarBṛS. (v. l. *śākuna*); a partic. evil demon, L.

Śākuneya, mfn. relating to birds or omens, MW.; composed or written by Śakuni, Cat.; m. a small owl, L.; N. of a Muni, Cat.; patr. of the Asura Vṛika, BhP.

शाकुन्तकि *śākuntaki*, m. pl. (fr. *śakunta* or *śakuntaka*) N. of a warrior-tribe, g. *dāmany-ādi*.

Śākuntakīya, m. a king of the Śākuntakis, ib.

Śākuntika, m. a fowler, bird-catcher, Car.

Śākunteya, m. N. of a physician, ib.

शाकुन्तल *śākuntala*, m. (fr. *śakuntalā*) metron. of Bharata (sovereign of India as son of Śakuntalā and Dushyanta), MBh.; n. (accord. to some also *ā*, f.) = next or the drama commonly called Śakuntalā or Abhijñāna-śakuntalam, Mālatim. **Śākuntalôpâkhyāna**, n. the story of Śakuntalā and Dushyanta (constituting the episode in MBh. i, 2815-3125).

Śākuntaleya, m. metron. of Bharata (cf. above), L.

शाकुलादिक *śākulādika*, mf(*ā* or *ī*)n. (fr. *śakulâda*), g. *kāśy-ādi*.

Śākulika, mfn. belonging to fish; m. a fisherman, Pāṇ. iv, 4, 35, Sch.; n. a multitude of fish, L.

शाकृत्क *śākṛitka*, mfn. (fr. *śakṛit*), Pāṇ. vii, 3, 51, Sch.

शाकोट *śākoṭa*, °*ṭaka*, w. r. for *śākh°*.

शाकोल *śākola*, m. the Amaranth creeper, L.

शाक्कर *śākkara*. See *śākvara*, col. 3.

शाक्की *śākkī*, f. N. of one of the five Vibhāshās or corrupt dialects, Cat.

शाक्त *śākta*, mfn. (fr. *śakti*) relating to power or energy, relating to the Śakti or divine energy under its female personification, Sarvad.; m. a worshipper of that energy (especially as identified with Durgā, wife of Śiva; the Śāktas form one of the principal sects of the Hindūs, their tenets being contained in the Tantras, and the ritual enjoined being of two kinds, the impurer called *vāmâcāra*, q. v., and the purer *dakshiṇâcāra*, q. v.), RTL. 185 &c.; (°*tá*), m. a teacher, preceptor, RV. vii, 103, 5; patr. of Parāśara, MBh. (C. *śāktra*); n. N. of a Sāman (prob. = *śāktya*, q. v.) — **krama**, m., -**tantra**, n. N. of Tantra wks. — **bhāshya**, n. N. of a wk. by Abhinava-gupta. — **mata-ratna-sūtra-dīpikā**, f., -**sarvasva**, n. N. of wks. **Śāktâgama**, m. N. of a Tantra wk. **Śāktânanda-taraṃgiṇī**, f. N. of a wk. compiled for the use of the Śāktas from the Tantras and Purāṇas. **Śāktâbhisheka**, m. N. of wk.

Śāktika, mf(*ī*)n. = *śaktyā jīvati*, g. *vetanâdi*; peculiar to the Śāktas, Tantras.; m. a worshipper of the Śakti (see *śākta* above), MW.; a spearman, ib.

Śāktīka, mfn. belonging or relating to a spear, spearing, speared, W.; m. a spearman, lancer, Śiś.

Śākteya, m. a worshipper of the Śakti (see above), Vop.; patr. of Parāśara, MBh.

Śāktya, m. a worshipper of the Śakti, W.; (°*tyá*), m. patr. of Gaura-vīti, AitBr.; ŚBr.; ŚrS.; (also -*sāman*, n.) N. of two Sāmans, ĀrshBr.

Śāktyāyana, m. patr. fr. *śāktya* (also pl.), Saṃskārak.

Śāktra and **Śāktreya**, m. patr. of Parāśara, MBh. (C.; cf. *śākta*, *śānta*, °*teya*).

शाक्मन् *śākman*, n. (cf. *śakman*) 'power' or 'help,' RV.

शाक्य *śākya*, mfn. derived or descended from the Śakas (= *śakā abhijano 'sya*), g. *śaṇḍikâdi*; m. N. of a tribe of landowners and Kshatriyas in Kapila-vastu (from whom Gautama, the founder of Buddhism, was descended), Buddh.; MWB. 21, 22; N. of Gautama Buddha himself, Nyāyam.; of his father Śuddhodana (son of Saṃjaya), Pur.; a Buddhist mendicant, VarBṛS.; patr. fr. *śaka*, g. *gargâdi*; patr. fr. *śāka* or *śākin*, g. *kurv-ādi*. — **kīrti**, m. 'glory of the Śākyas,' N. of a teacher, Buddh. — **ketu**, m. 'star of the Ś°s,' N. of Gautama Buddha, ib. — **pāla**, m. N. of a king, Rājat. — **puṃgava**, m. 'Ś° bull,' N. of Gautama Buddha, Buddh. — **putrīya**, m. a Buddhist monk, Hcar. — **prabha**, m. N. of a scholar, Buddh. — **buddha**, m. = -*muni*, ib. — **buddhi**, m. N. of a scholar, ib. (w.r. -*bodhi*). — **bodhi-sattva**, m. = -*muni*, ib. — **bhikshu**, m. a Buddhist monk or mendicant, VarBṛS. — **bhikshuka**, m. id.; (*ī*), f. a Buddhist nun, Daś. — **mati**, m. N. of a scholar, Buddh. — **mahā-bala**, m. N. of a king, ib. — **mitra**, m. N. of a scholar, ib. — **muni**, m. 'Śākya sage,' N. of Gautama Buddha, ib.; Kād.; Hcar. &c. (also -*buddha*). — **rakshita**, m. N. of a poet, Cat. — **vaṇśa**, m. the Ś° family, Buddh.; °*śâvatīrṇa*, m. 'incarnate in the Ś° f°,' N. of Gautama Buddha, ib. — **vardha**, m. = (or w.r. for) -*vardhana*; n. N. of a temple, Divyâv. — **śāsana**, n. the doctrine or teaching of Gautama Buddha, Hcar. — **śramaṇa** or °**ṇaka**, m. a Buddhist monk, Mṛicch. (in Prākṛit). — **śravaṇa**, m. id., VarBṛS., Sch. (prob. w.r. for *śramaṇa*). — **śrī**, m. N. of a teacher, Buddh. — **siṇha**, m. 'Śākya lion,' N. of Gautama Buddha, ib.; Rājat.

Śākyāyanīya, m. pl. N. of a school, L. (prob. w.r. for *śākāy°*).

शाक्र *śākra*, mf(*ī*)n. (fr. *śakra*) relating or belonging or sacred to or addressed to Indra, MBh.; VarBṛS.; Kathās.; (*ī*), f. Indra's wife (also applied to Durgā), Pur.; n. the Nakshatra Jyeshṭhā (presided over by Indra), VarBṛS.

Śākrīya, mfn. = *śākra* (-*dis*, f. 'Indra's quarter,' the east), Śatr.

शाक्वर *śākvará*, mfn. (fr. *śakvara*) mighty, powerful, strong (applied to Indra, the thunderbolt &c.), VS.; AV.; TBr.; relating to the Sāman Śakvara (or to the Śakvarī verses), TS.; TBr.; an imaginary kind of Soma, Suśr. (w.r. *śāṃkara*); m. a bull, ox, Hcar.; n. a kind of observance or ceremony, ŚāṅkhGṛ.; N. of a Sāman (one of the six chief forms, based upon the Śakvarī verses), ĀrshBr. — **garbha**, mfn. containing the Sāman Śākvara, ŚāṅkhŚr. — **pathyā**, f. a kind of metre, Śiś., Sch. — **pṛishṭha**, mfn. having the Sāman Ś° for a Pṛishṭha (q. v.), ŚāṅkhŚr. — **varṇa**, n. N. of a Sāman (comprising the verses RV. ix, 61, 10–12), ĀrshBr.

Śākvarya, n. (fr. *śākvara*), g. *purohitâdi*.

शाख् *śākh* (prob. artificial; cf. √*ślākh*), cl. 1. P. *śākhati*, to embrace, pervade, Dhātup. v, 12.

Śākha, m. N. of a manifestation of Skanda or of his son, MBh.; Hariv.; Pur.; Pongamia Glabra, L.; m. or n. N. of a place, Cat.; (*ā*), f., see next.

Śākhā, f. (ifc. f. *ā* or *ī*) a branch (lit. and fig.), RV. &c. &c.; a limb of the body, arm or leg, Suśr.; a finger, Naigh. ii, 5; the surface of the body, Car.; a door-post, VarBṛS. (cf. *dvāra-ś°*); the wing of a building, MārkP.; a division, subdivision, MBh.; BhP.; the third part of an astrological Saṃhitā (also °*khā-skandha*, m.), VarBṛS.; a branch or school of the Veda (each school adhering to its own traditional text and interpretation; in the Caraṇa-vyūha, a work by Śaunaka treating of these various schools, five Śākhās are enumerated of the Ṛig-veda, viz. those of the Śākalas, Bāshkalas, Āśvalāyanas, Śāṅkhāyanas, and Māṇḍukāyanas; forty-two or forty-four out of eighty-six of the Yajur-veda, fifteen of which belong to the Vājasaneyins, including those of the Kāṇvas and Mādhyaṃdinas; twelve out of a thousand said to have once existed of the Sāma-veda and nine of the Atharva-veda; of all these, however, the Ṛig-veda is said to be now extant in one only, viz. the Śākala-śākhā, the Yajur-veda in five and partially in six, the Sāma-veda in one or perhaps two, and the Atharva-veda in one: although the words *caraṇa* and *śākhā* are sometimes used synonymously, yet *caraṇa* properly applies to the sect or collection of persons united in one school, and *śākhā* to the traditional text followed, as in the phrase *śākhām adhīte*, he recites a particular version of the Veda), Prāt.; Mn.; MBh. &c.; a branch of any science, Car.; a year, Śrīkaṇṭh.; = *pakshântara*, L.; = *antika*, L. — **kaṇṭa**, m. Euphorbia Nerifolia or Antiquorum, L. — °**ṅga** (°*khâṅ°*), n. a limb of the body, Yājñ. — **caṅkramaṇa**, n. skipping from branch to branch, desultory study, MW. — **candra-nyāya**, m. rule of the moon on a bough (a phrase denoting that an object seen or matter discussed has its position or relation assigned to it merely from the *appearance* of contiguity), ib. — °**da** (°*khâda*), mfn. branch-eating; m. N. of a class of animals (such as goats, elephants &c.), Car. — **daṇḍa**, m. = -*raṇḍa*, L. — °**dhyetṛi** (°*khâdh°*), m. the reciter of a Śākhā, follower of any partic. text of the Veda, MW. — **nagara** (MBh.; Hariv.) or °**raka** (MBh.; MārkP.), n. 'branch-town,' a suburb. — °**ntaga** (°*khân°*), mfn. one who has finished one Śākhā, Mn. iii, 145. — °**ntara** (°*khân°*), n. another Vedic school, Āpast.; R. &c. — °**ntarīya** (°*khân°*), mfn. belonging to another Vedic school, Bādar., Sch.; Madhus.; -*karman*, n. the (rule of) action bel° to another V° school, MW. — **pavitra**, n. a means or instrument of purification fastened to a branch, ĀpŚr.; KātyŚr., Sch. — **paśu**, m. a victim tied to a branch (instead of to a sacrificial post), ŚāṅkhGṛ. — **pitta**, n. inflammation of the extremities (i. e. the hands, feet &c.), L. — **pura**, n. or -**purī**, f. = -*nagara*, L. — **pushpa-palāśa-vat**, mfn. having branches and blossoms and leaves, MBh. — **prakṛiti**, f. pl. the eight remoter princes to be considered in time of war (opp. to *mūla-prakṛiti*), Kull. on Mn. vii, 157. — **bāhu**, m. a branch-like (i. e. slender) arm, Śak. — **bhṛit**, m. 'branch-bearer,' a tree, Kir. — **bheda**, m. difference of (Vedic) school, W. — **maya**, mf(*ī*)n. (ifc.) consisting of branches of, Daś. — **mṛiga**, m. 'branch-animal,' a monkey, MBh.; R.; VarBṛS. &c.; a squirrel, W.; *-gaṇḍyuta*, mfn. filled with or possessed of troops of monkeys, MW.; *-tva*, n. the condition or nature of a monkey, R.; *°gânīka-pati*, m. 'lord of troops of monkeys,' N. of Sugrīva, MW. **—°mlā** (*°khâm°*), f. a kind of plant (= *vṛikshâmlā*), MW. **—raṇḍa,** m. a man who is faithless or a traitor to his Śākhā, i.e. a Brāhman who has deserted his own Vedic school, L. (cf. *-daṇḍa*). **—rathyā,** f. a branch-road, side-road, DevīP. **—vāta,** m. pain in the limbs, Suśr. **—vilīna,** mfn. settled or sitting on branches (said of birds), Kathās. **—śiphā,** f. 'br°-root,' a root growing from a br° (as in the Indian Banyan tree, = *avaroha*), L.; a creeper growing upwards from the root of a tree (accord. to some), MW. **—°śraya** (*°khāś°*), m. attachment to a Śākhā, adherence to a partic. school, ib. **—samāna,** N. of wk. **—stha,** mfn. standing or being on br°s (of trees), R. **—°sthi** (*°khās°*), n. a bone of the arm or leg, a long bone, L.

Śākhāla, m. Calamus Rotang, L.

Śākhi, m. pl. N. of a people (= *turushka*; cf. next), L.

Śākhin, mfn. provided with branches, Yājñ.; MBh.; Hariv.; separated into schools (said of the Veda), BhP.; adhering to a partic. Vedic school, Kull.; TPrāt., Sch.; m. a tree, Suparṇ.; MBh.; Kāv. &c.; a Veda which exists in various schools, L.; the follower of any Vedic school, Bādar., Sch.; Salvadora Persica, L.; N. of a king, L.; pl. N. of a people (= *turushka*; cf. *śākhi*), L.

Śākhila, m. N. of a man, Kathās.

Śākhīya, mfn. (ifc.) belonging to a branch or school of the Veda, BṛĀrUp.

Śākhya, mfn. resembling a branch, Pāṇ. v, 3, 103; belonging to the branch of a tree, branching, ramifying (lit. and fig.), W.

शाखोट *śākhoṭa* or *°ṭaka*, m. Trophis Aspera (a small, crooked, ugly tree), Bhpr.

शांकर *śāṃkara*, mf(*ī*)n. (fr. *śam-kara*) relating or belonging to Śiva, Kathās.; relating to or derived from or composed by Śaṃkarâcārya, Sarvad.; Cat.; m. a bull, W.; a follower of Śaṃkarâcārya, MW.; (*ī*), f., see below; n. the Nakshatra Ārdrā (presided over by Śiva), VarYogay. **—brāhmaṇa,** n. N. of a Brāhmaṇa.

Śāṃkari, m. patr. of Skanda, Bālar.; of Gaṇeśa, L.; fire, W.; a Muni, ib.

Śāṃkarī, f. Śiva's arrangement of the letters, the Śiva-sūtra, Cat.; the commentary of Śaṃkara-miśra, ib. **—kroḍa,** m., **-ratnamālā,** f. N. of wks.

Śāṃkarīya, n. N. of wk.

शाङ्कव्य *śāṅkavya*, m. a patr. fr. *śaṅku*, g. *gargâdi* and *kurv-ādi*.

Śāṅkavyāyanī, f. of *śāṅkavya*, g. *lohitâdi*.

Śāṅkuka, m. N. of a poet, Rājat.

Śāṅkupathika, mfn. (fr. *śaṅku-patha*), Pāṇ. v, 1, 77, Vārtt. 2.

Śāṅkura, m. (applied to the penis), AV.

शाङ्कुची *śāṅkucī*, f. the skate fish (cf. *śaṅkuci*, *sāṃkuci*), W.

शाङ्ख *śāṅkha*, mf(*ī*)n. (fr. *śaṅkhá*) relating to or made of a conch or any shell; n. the sound of a conch-shell, L.

Śāṅkhamitra, m. patr. fr. *śaṅkha-mitra*, Pravar.

Śāṅkhamitri, m. (patr. fr. id.) N. of a grammarian, APrāt., Sch.

Śāṅkhalikhita, mfn. composed by Śaṅkha and Likhita (q.v.), Parāś.

Śāṅkhāyana, m. (patr. fr. *śaṅkha*), N. of a teacher (author of a Brāhmaṇa and two Sūtras, pl. his descendants or followers), TPrāt.; mfn. relating &c. to Śāṅkhāyana, Cat.; n. Ś°'s work, ĀśvGṛ. **—gṛihya-sūtra,** n. the Gṛihya-sūtras ascribed to Ś°. **—caraṇa,** m. or n. N. of a Caraṇa of the Ṛig-veda. **—brāhmaṇa,** n. the Brāhmaṇa of Ś° (also called Kaushītaki-br°). **—śrauta-sūtra,** n. the Śrauta-sūtra of Ś°. **Śāṅkhāyanâraṇyaka,** n., **°kôpanishad,** f. N. of wks. **Śāṅkhāyanâhnika,** n. N. of a wk. by Acala.

Śāṅkhāyanin, m. pl. the pupils of Śāṅkhāyana, MW.

Śāṅkhāyanya, m. patr. fr. *śāṅkhāyana*, g. *kuñjâdi*.

Śāṅkhika, mf(*ī*)n. made from or relating to a conch-shell or to any shell, shelly, W.; m. a shell-blower or player on the conch-shell, Śiś.; a shell-cutter, worker or dealer in shells (constituting a partic. caste called Śāṅkhāri), L.

Śāṅkhina, m. patr. fr. *śaṅkhin*, Pāṇ. vi, 4, 166, Sch.

Śāṅkhya, mfn. made or prepared from shells, Suśr.; born in Śaṅkha, g. *śaṇḍikâdi*; m. patr. fr. *śaṅkha*, g. *gargâdi*.

शाङ्गुष्ठा *śāṅgushṭhā*, v.l. for *sāṅgushṭhā*.

शाचि 1. *śāci*, m. pl. (perhaps connected with 2. *śāka*) barley or other grain which has the husk removed and is coarsely ground, VS. (Mahīdh.)

शाचि 2. *śāci* (prob. fr. √*śac* = *śak*), and having the sense of 'strong' in the following compounds. **—gu,** mfn. (prob.) going or advancing strongly (fr. *gu* = *ga* [cf. *adhri-gu*]; Sāy. 'having strong cattle or clearly manifested rays,' fr. *gu* = *go*), RV. viii, 17, 12. **—pūjana,** mfn. (prob.) having earnest worship, ib.

शाट *śāṭa*, m. (fr. √*śaṭ* ?) a strip of cloth, a kind of skirt or petticoat, a partic. sort of garment or gown, Vas.; Cāṇ.; (*ī*), f., see below.

Śāṭaka, m. n. = *śāṭa*, Kāv.; Kathās. &c.; (*ikā*), f. id., Divyâv.

Śāṭi, f. id., SaddhP.

Śāṭī, f. id., MBh.; Kāv. &c. **—paṭīra,** n., **-paṭṭika,** n., **-picchaka,** n., **-pracchada,** n., g. *gavâśvâdi*.

Śāṭīya. See *tāmra-ś°*.

शाट्य *śāṭya*, mfn. born in Śaṭa, g. *śaṇḍikâdi*; patr. fr. *śaṭa*, g. *gargâdi*.

Śāṭyāyana, m. (patr. fr. *śāṭya*) N. of a teacher and author of various wks. (see below); pl. 'the followers of Śāṭyāyana,' ĀśvGṛ.; R. &c.; (*ī*), f. N. of an Upanishad; n. an oblation for remedying anything wrong in the performance of an act or rite (cf. *-homa*); mf(*ī*)n. of or belonging to Ś° or the Ś°-brāhmaṇa, MW. **—gotra,** n. the family of Ś°, R. **—brāhmaṇa,** n. the Brāhmaṇa of Ś°, ŚrS. **—smṛiti,** f. the law-book of Ś°, Hcat. **—homa,** m. N. of a partic. oblation (cf. above), Tithyād.

Śāṭyāyanaka, n. the Brāhmaṇa of Śāṭyāyana or a passage from it, ŚrS.

Śāṭyāyani, m. patr. of the author of a law-book, ŚBr. (cf. g. *tikâdi*).

Śāṭyāyanin, m. pl. the followers of Śāṭyāyana (N. of a Śākhā of the Yajur-veda), Lāṭy.; Sāy.

Śāṭyāyanīyôpanishad, f. N. of an Upanishad.

Śāṭyāyany-upanishad, f. id.

शाठ *śāṭha*, m. (prob. patr. fr. *śaṭha*), see *kaṭha-ś°*.

Śāṭhāyana. See next.

Śāṭhāyanya, m. patr. fr. *śaṭha* (pl. *°yanāḥ*), g. *kuñjâdi*.

Śāṭhin. See *kāṭha-ś°*.

Śāṭhya, n. wickedness, deceit, guile, roguery, dishonesty, MBh.; Kāv. &c. **—vat,** mfn. deceitful, wicked, dishonest, VarBṛS.

Śāṭhyāyanīya, m. pl. N. of a Śākhā or school, MW. (prob. w.r. for *śāṭy°*).

शाठर *śāṭhara*, m. a patr., Saṃskārak.

शाड *śāḍ*, cl. 1. Ā. *śāḍate*, to praise, Dhātup. viii, 37.

शाडव *śāḍava*, m. = *shāḍava*, Harav. (cf. *phala-ś°*).

शाड्वल *śāḍbala* or *śāḍvala*. See *śāḍvala*.

शाण 1. *śāṇa*, m. (or *ā*, f.; fr. √*śo*, cf. *śāna*) a whetstone, grindstone, touchstone, Kāv.; Rājat.; a saw, L. **Śāṇâjīva,** m. 'living by a whetstone,' an armourer, L. **Śāṇâśmaka** or **śāṇâśman,** n. a whetstone, grindstone, touchstone, Kāv.; *°śma-gharshaṇa*, n. rubbing (anything) on a touchstone, ib. **Śāṇôpala,** m. a whetstone, ib.

Śāṇita, mfn. sharpened on a grindstone, whetted, ground, L.

शाण 2. *śāṇa*, m. (or *ā*, f.) a weight of four Māshas, Hariv.; Bhpr. **—pāda,** m. a quarter of a Śāṇa (i.e. a Māsha), Car. **—pramāṇa,** mfn. weighing a Śāṇa, Hariv.

Śāṇika, mfn. weighing a Śāṇa, Bhpr.

Śāṇya. See *dvi-ś°*.

शाण 3. *śāṇá*, mf(*ī*)n. (fr. *śaṇa*) made of hemp or Bengal flax, hempen, flaxen, ŚBr. &c. &c.; m. or n. a hempen garment, Gaut.; (*ī*), f., see below. **—vāsa** or **-vāsika,** m. N. of an Arhat, L.

Śāṇaka, m. or n. a hempen cloth or garment, Lalit. **—vāsa,** m. = *śāṇa-vāsa*, Buddh.

Śāṇavatya, m. pl. N. of a people, MBh.

Śāṇi, m. Corchorus Olitorius (a plant from the fibres of which a coarse cloth or cordage is prepared), L.

Śāṇī, f. a hempen cloth or garment, MBh.; ragged or torn raiment, the tattered clothes of a Jain ascetic, L.; a single breadth of cloth given to a student at his investiture, W.; a small tent or screen, ib.; gesture, gesticulation, ib.

शाणीर *śāṇīra*, n. = *śaṇīra*, L.

शाण्ड *śāṇḍa*, m. (patr. fr. *śaṇḍa*) N. of a man, RV.; of the father of Lakshmī-dhara, Cat. **—dūrvā,** f. a kind of plant, AV. (v.l. *pāka-dūrvā*).

शाण्डाकी *śāṇḍākī*, f. a kind of animal, Car.

Śāṇḍika, m. an animal living in holes, ib. (v.l. *śāṭuka*).

शाण्डिक्य *śāṇḍikya*, mfn. born in Śaṇḍika, Pāṇ. iv, 3, 92.

शाण्डिल *śāṇḍila*, mfn. derived from or enjoined by Śāṇḍilya &c., ŚBr.; Lāṭy.; m. pl. the descendants of Śaṇḍila, TĀr.; ĀśvŚr. (cf. g. *kaṇvâdi*); (sg.) w.r. for *śaṇḍila* or *śāṇḍilya*; (*ī*), f., see next.

Śāṇḍilī, f. N. of a Brāhmaṇī (worshipped as the mother of Agni), MBh.; Hariv. **—putra** (*śāṇḍilī-*), m. N. of a teacher, ŚBr.; (prob.) of Agni, Cat. **—mātṛi,** f. the mother of Śāṇḍilī, Pañcat.

Śāṇḍileya, m. metron. fr. *śāṇḍilī*, (prob.) N. of Agni, Cat.

Śāṇḍilya, mfn. derived from or composed by Śāṇḍilya &c., Cat.; m. patr. fr. *śaṇḍila*, g. *gargâdi*; N. of various teachers, authors &c. (esp. of a Muni or sage from whom one of the three principal families of the Kanouj or Kānyakubja Brāhmans is said to be descended; he is the author of a law-book and of the Bhakti-sūtra or aphorisms enjoining 'love or devotion to God' as one of the three means of salvation—a doctrine said to have been formulated in the 12th century; see *bhakti*, RTL. 63); of Agni, Hariv.; Aegle Marmelos, Bhpr.; n. N. of various wks. of Śāṇḍilya (esp. = *-sūtra* and = *°lyôpanishad*). **—gṛihya,** n. the Gṛihya-sūtra of Ś°, ĀpŚr., Sch. **—gotra,** n. the family of Ś°, MW. **—putra,** m. N. of a teacher, ĀrshBr. **—lakshmaṇa,** m. N. of a Commentator, Sch. **—vidyā,** f. the doctrine of Ś° (in the ChUp.) **—sūtra,** n. the aphorisms of Ś° (see above); *-pravacana*, n., *-bhāshya*, n., *-vyākhyā*, f.; *°trī-bhāshya*, n. N. of Comms. on the above wk.; *°trīya*, mfn. relating to it, Cat. **—smṛiti,** f. the law-book of Ś°. **Śāṇḍilyôpanishad,** f. N. of an Upanishad.

Śāṇḍilyāyana, m. (patr. fr. *śāṇḍilya*) N. of a teacher, ŚBr.; Lāṭy.

Śāṇḍilyāyanaka, mfn. (fr. prec.), g. *arīhaṇâdi*.

शात 1. *śātá*, mfn. (fr. √*śo*; cf. *śita*) sharpened, whetted, sharp, Kathās.; Rājat.; thin, feeble, slender, emaciated, Hariv.; Kāv.; VarBṛS.; n. the thorn-apple, MW. **—śikha,** mfn. sharp-pointed, W. **—śṛiṅgin,** m. N. of a mountain, MārkP. **Śātâtapa,** m. N. of a lawgiver (cf. *vṛiddha-ś°*); *-smṛiti*, f. Ś°'s law-book; *°pīya*, mfn. composed by Ś°, Cat. **Śātôdara,** mf(*ī*)n. thin-waisted, slender, Kāv.; VarBṛS.; *-tva*, n. thinness, slenderness, Hariv.

1. **Śātana,** n. the act of sharpening or wetting, MW.; sharpness, thinness, ib.

शात 2. *śāta*, m. (fr. √2. *śad*) falling out or decaying (of nails, hair &c.), Suśr.

2. **Śātana,** mf(*ī*)n. causing to fall or decay, felling, destroying, hewing or cutting off, Nir.; Kāv.; Kathās.; n. the act of causing to fall &c.; cutting or plucking off, L.; destroying, ruining, MārkP.; polishing, planing, MārkP.; a means of removing or destroying, Suśr.; ŚārṅgS. (cf. *garbha-ś°*).

Śātita, mfn. caused to fall, overthrown, destroyed, cut off &c., MBh.

Śātin, mfn. cut off (ifc.), Ragh.

शात 3. *śāta*, n. joy, pleasure, happiness, L.; mfn. handsome, bright, happy, W.

शात 4. *śāta*, Vṛiddhi form of *śata*, in comp. — **kumbha**, n. (fr. *śata-kumbhā*) gold, MBh.; R. &c.; mfn. golden, ib.; m. Nerium Odorum, L.; the thorn-apple, L.; *-drava*, n. melted gold, Ml.; *-maya*, mf(*ī*)n. made or consisting of gold, golden, MBh.; Hariv.; R. — **kaumbha**, mfn. (fr. *śātakumbha*) golden, ib.; n. gold, ib.; *-maya*, mf(*ī*)n. golden, BhP. — **kratava**, mf(*ī*)n. (fr. *śatá-kratu*) relating to Indra (with *śarâsana*, n. a rainbow, Vcar.; with *āśā*, f. the east, Kād.) — **dvāreya**, m. patr. fr. *śata-dvāra*, g. *śubhrâdi*. — **pata**, mfn. (fr. *śata-pati*), g. *aśvapaty-ādi*. — **pattra**, mfn. (fr. *śata-pattra*), g. *śarkarâdi*. — **pattraka**, m. or °**kī**, f. (fr. id.) moonlight, L. — **patha**, mf(*ī*)n. relating or belonging to or based upon the Śatapatha-brāhmaṇa, Kāś.; Śaṃk.; = *śatapatha-br°*, Hcat.; °*thika*, m. an adherent or teacher of the ŚBr., L. — **parṇeya**, m. patr. fr. *śata-parṇa*, ŚBr. — **putraka**, n. (fr. *śata-putra*) the possession of a hundred sons, g. *manojñâdi*. — **bhisha**, mf(*ī*)n. born under the Nakshatra Śata-bhishaj, Pāṇ. iv, 2, 7, Vārtt. 1, Pat. — **bhishaja**, mf(*ī*)n. id., ib. — **bhīru**, m. (fr. *śata-bhīru*) a kind of Mallikā or Arabian jasmine, L. — **manyava**, mf(*ī*)n. (fr. *śata-manyu*) relating or belonging to Indra, Kir. (with *āśā*, f. the eastern quarter, Hcar.) — **māna**, mf(*ī*)n. (fr. *śata-māna*) bought with the measure of one hundred, Pāṇ. v, 1, 27. — **rātrika**, mfn. (fr. *śata-rātra*) relating to the ceremony of a hundred nights (or days), KātyŚr., Sch. — **vaneyá**, m. patr. fr. *śata-vani*, RV. — **śūrpa**, m. (fr. *śata-śūrpa*) N. of a man, Nid. — **hrada**, mfn. (fr. *śata-hrada*) relating or belonging to lightning, Ragh.

शातक *śātaka*, m. pl. N. of a people, VarBṛS. (v.l.)

शातकर्णि *śātakarṇi* or °*ṇin*, m. (fr. *śata-karṇa* or *śāta-k°*) N. of various kings, Ragh.; Pur.; of an author, Cat.

शातपन्त *śātapanta* (only du. °*ntā*; prob. w.r.), RV. x, 106, 5.

शातला *śātalā*, f., v.l. for *sātalā*, q.v.

शातलेय *śātaleya*, m. patr. fr. *śatala*, g. *śubhrâdi*.

शातवाहन *śātavāhana*, m. N. of a king (= *śāli-vāhana*), Kathās.

शातातप *śātâtapa*. See under 1. *śāta*.

शाताहर *śātāhara*, m. N. of a man, g. *śubhrâdi*.

Śātāhareya, m. patr. fr. prec., ib.

शात्र *śātra*, n. N. of various Sāmans, ĀrshBr.

शात्रव *śātrava*, mf(ī)n. (fr. *śatru*) belonging to an enemy, hostile, inimical, R.; Ragh.; m. an enemy, MBh.; Kāv.; n. enmity, hostility, L.; a multitude of enemies, L. **Śātravêṅgita**, n. an enemy's intention, MW.

Śātravīya, mfn. relating to an enemy, inimical, Śiś.

Śātruṃtapi, m. pl. (fr. *śatruṃ-tapa*) N. of a people or community, g. *dāmany-ādi*.

Śātruṃtapīya, m. a king or chief of the Śātruṃtapis, ib.

शात्वल *śātvala*, m. pl. N. of a Śākhā or Vedic school, MW.

शाद *śāda*, m. (fr. √2. *śad*, cf. 2. *śāta*) falling off, dropping (see *parṇa-ś°*); young grass, RV.; VS.; mud, slime, L.; = *rakshas*, Sāy. on RV. ix, 15, 6; (*ā*), f. a brick, Gobh. — **harita**, mfn. green or fresh with young grass, L.

Śādvala, mfn. (often written *śāḍvala*; cf. Pāṇ. iv, 2, 88) abounding in fresh or green grass, grassy, verdant, green; n. sg. and pl. (L. also m.; ifc. f. *ā*) a place abounding in young grass, grassy spot, turf, GṛS.; Yājñ.; MBh. &c.; m. a bull, L. (written *śāḍvala*). — **vat**, mfn. covered with grass, grassy, PārGṛ. — **sthalī**, f. a grassy spot, grass-plot, MW.

Śāḍvalâbha, m. a partic. green insect, Suśr.

Śādvalita, n. the being covered with grass, BhP.

Śādvalin, mfn. covered with grass, grassy, green, R.

शान् *śān* (for √*śo*), only in Desid. Ā. *śīśāṃsate*, to whet, sharpen, Dhātup. xxiii, 26 (cf. Pāṇ. iii, 1, 6).

Śāna, m. (cf. 1. *śāṇa*) a whetstone, grindstone, touchstone, L.; (*ī*), f. a sort of cucumber or colocynth, L. — **pāda**, m. N. of the Pāripātra mountain, MW.; a stone for grinding sandal, ib.

Śāni, f., Siddh.

Śānita, mfn. (cf. *śāṇita*) whetted, sharpened (compar. *-tara*), Kāv.

Śānīya, mfn. to be whetted or sharpened, Pat.

1. **Śānta**, mfn. (perhaps always w. r. for 1. *śāta*, q.v.) = *śānita*, L.; thin, slender, Hariv.; R. (Sch.)

Śāntôdara, mfn. (for *śātodara*, q.v.) slender-waisted (*-tva*, n.), Hariv.; VarBṛS.

शानच् *śānac*, (in gram.) a technical term for the Kṛit affixes *āna* or *amāna* (used in forming present participles Ātmane-pada when the radical syllable is accentuated, or for *āna* substituted for *hi*, the affix of the 2. sg. Impv.)

शानिल *śānila*, m. N. of a man, Cat.

शानैश्चर *śānaiścara*, mfn. (fr. *śanaiś-cara*) relating to Saturn or to his day, falling on a Saturday, Vet.

शान्त 2. *śāntá*, mfn. (fr. √1. *śam*) appeased, pacified, tranquil, calm, free from passions, undisturbed, Up.; MBh. &c.; soft, pliant, Hariv.; gentle, mild, friendly, kind, auspicious (in augury; opp. to *dīpta*), AV. &c. &c.; abated, subsided, ceased, stopped, extinguished, averted (*śāntam* or *dhik śāntam* or *śāntam pāpam*, may evil or sin be averted! may God forfend! Heaven forbid! not so!), ŚBr.; MBh.; Kāv. &c.; rendered ineffective, innoxious, harmless (said of weapons), MBh.; R.; come to an end, gone to rest, deceased, departed, dead, died out, ib.; Ragh.; Rājat.; purified, cleansed, W.; m. an ascetic whose passions are subdued, W.; tranquillity, contentment (as one of the Rasas, q. v.); N. of a son of Day, MBh.; of a son of Manu Tāmasa, MārkP.; of a son of Śambara, Hariv.; of a son of Idhma-jihva, BhP.; of a son of Āpa, VP.; of a Deva-putra, Lalit.; (*ā*), f. (in music) a partic. Śruti, Saṃgīt.; Emblica Officinalis, L.; Prosopis Spicigera and another species, L.; a kind of Dūrvā grass, L.; a partic. drug (= *reṇukā*), L.; N. of a daughter of Daśa-ratha (adopted daughter of Loma-pāda or Roma-pāda and wife of Ṛishya-śṛiṅga), MBh.; Hariv.; R.; (with Jainas) of a goddess who executes the orders of the 7th Arhat, L.; of a Śakti, MW.; n. tranquillity, peace of mind, BhP.; N. of a Varsha in Jambu-dvīpa, ib.; N. of a Tīrtha, W. — **karṇa**, m. (with prefixed *śrī*) N. of a king, BhP. — **krodha**, mfn. one whose anger is appeased, MW. — **guṇa**, mfn. one whose virtues are destroyed, i. e. deceased, R. — **ghora-vimūḍhatva**, n. calmness and vehemence and infatuation, BhP. — **cetas**, mfn. tranquil-minded, Kāv.; composed in mind, calm, Pañcat.; Hit. &c. — **jvara**, mfn. one whose fever or grief is alleviated, MBh. — **tā**, f. quietness, calmness, freedom from passion, Kathās. — **toya**, mfn. having calm or still waters, gently flowing, MW. — **tva**, n. = *-tā*, MaitrUp.; BhP. — **devatya**, mfn. who or what appeases a god, that by which a divinity is appeased, MW. — **pura**, n. (W.) or °**rī**, f. (Buddh.) N. of a town. — **bhaya**, m. N. of a son of Medhâtithi, VP.; n. N. of the Varsha ruled by him, ib. (v.l. *śāṃta-nava*). — **mati**, m. 'composed in mind,' N. of a Deva-putra, Lalit. — **manas**, mfn. composed in mind, MBh.; Śak.; VarBṛS. — **mala**, mfn. having all defilement removed, W. — **moha**, n. 'having delusion dispelled,' (with Jainas) N. of the 11th of the 14 steps towards supreme happiness, Cat. — **yoni** (*śāntá-*), mfn. one whose birth-place is auspicious, TBr. — **rajas**, mfn. dustless or passionless (lit. 'having dust or passion allayed'), Bhag. — **raya**, mfn. slackened in speed, W.; m. N. of a son of Dharma-sārathi, BhP. — **rava**, mfn. uttering auspicious sounds, VarBṛS. — **raśmi**, mfn. one whose rays are extinguished or dimmed (as the sun), R. — **rasa**, m. the sentiment of quietism or tranquillity, MW.; *-nāṭaka*, n. N. of a drama. — **rūpa**, mfn. having a tranquil appearance, tr°, calm, Pañcat. — **lābha**, mfn. that which has ceased to bear interest, Bṛihasp. — **vivāda**, mfn. having disputes allayed, reconciled, appeased, W. — **vīra-deśikêndra**, m. N. of an author, Cat. — **śrī**, m. N. of Pracaṇḍa-deva, W. — **sumati**, m. N. of a Deva-putra, Lalit. (cf. *śānta-mati*). — **sūri**, m. N. of a scholiast, Cat. — **sena**, m. N. of a son of Subāhu, BhP. — **haya**, m. N. of a son of Manu Tāmasa, VP. — **hṛidaya**, mfn. tranquil-hearted, ChUp.

Śāntâtman, mfn. calm-minded, composed, MaitrUp.

Śāntântakara, m. N. of a son of Śambara, Hariv.

Śāntârcis, mfn. whose flame is extinguished, gone out (as fire), MBh.

Śāntaka, mfn. allaying, appeasing (see *roga-ś°*).

Śāntaya, Nom. P. °*yati*, to calm any one, Śak.

Śānti, f. tranquillity, peace, quiet, peace or calmness of mind, absence of passion, averting of pain (*śānti! śānti! śānti!* may the three kinds of pain be averted!), indifference to objects of pleasure or pain, KaṭhUp.; MBh. &c.; alleviation (of evil or pain), cessation, abatement, extinction (of fire &c.), AV. &c. &c.; a pause, breach, interruption, Hcat.; any expiatory or propitiatory rite for averting evil or calamity, Br. &c. (cf. RTL. 346); peace, welfare, prosperity, good fortune, ease, comfort, happiness, bliss, MBh.; R. &c.; destruction, end, eternal rest, death, Kāv.; Kathās.; BhP.; = *śānti-kalpa*, BhP.; Tranquillity &c. personified (as a daughter of Śraddhā, as the wife of Atharvan, as the daughter of Daksha and wife of Dharma), Hariv.; Prab.; Pur.; m. N. of a son of Indra, MBh.; of Indra in the tenth Manv-antara, Pur.; of a Tushita (son of Vishnu and Dakshiṇā), ib.; of a son of Kṛishṇa and Kālindī, ib.; of a Ṛishi, MBh.; of a son of Aṅgiras, ib.; of a disciple of Bhūti, MārkP.; of a son of Nīla and father of Su-śānti, VP.; (with Jainas) of an Arhat and Cakra-vartin, L.; of a teacher (also called *ratnâkara-ś°*), Buddh. — **kamalâkara**, m. N. of part of wk. — **kara**, mfn. causing peace or prosperity, VarBṛS.; m. N. of a man, Kathās. — **karaṇa**, n. the averting of evil, KātyŚr. — **kartṛi**, mfn. causing tranquillity, calming, allaying, MW.; m. any divinity who averts evil or suffering, ib. — **karman**, n. any action for averting evil, ĀśvGṛ.; N. of wk. — **kalpa**, m., **-kalpa-dīpikā**, f., **-kalpa-pradīpa**, m., **-kalpa-latā**, f., **-kalyāṇī**, f. N. of wks. — **kāma**, m. desire of tranquillity, W.; mfn. desirous of tr°, ib. — **kārin**, mfn. soothing, pacifying, A. — **kṛit**, mfn. removing evil or causing alleviation by reciting texts &c., MBh. — **khaṇḍa**, **-gaṇa-pati**, m. N. of wks. — **gupta** (Buddh.), **-guru** (Cat.), m. N. of men. — **gṛiha** (VarBṛS.) or °**haka** (L.), n. a room for the performance of propitiatory rites to avert evil. — **grantha**, m., **-candrikā**, f., **-caritra**, n., **-caritra-nāṭaka**, n., **-cintāmaṇi**, m. N. of wks. — **jala**, n. = *śānty-uda*, W. — **tattvâmṛita**, n. N. of wk. — **da**, mfn. causing tranquillity or prosperity, VarBṛS.; N. of Vishṇu, RTL. 106, n. 1. — **dīpikā**, f. N. of wk. — **deva**, m. N. of a man, Buddh.; (*ā* [Hariv.; Pur.], or *ī* [VP.]), f. N. of a daughter of Devaka (and one of Vasu-deva's wives). — **nātha**, m. N. of an Arhat (with Jainas; = *śānti*), Śatr.; *-caritra*, n., *-purāṇa*, n. N. of wks. — **nirṇaya**, m., **-paṭala**, **-paddhati**, f. N. of wks. — **parvan**, n. 'Tranquillizing-section,' N. of the 12th book of the Mahā-bhārata (the longest in the whole poem and consisting chiefly of stories, discourses and episodes narrated for the tranquillizing of the troubled spirit of Yudhi-shṭhira after the termination of the war and the slaughter of his relatives). — **pāṭha**, m. N. of wk. — **pātra**, n. a vessel for propitiatory water, ŚāṅkhGṛ. — **pārijāta**, m. N. of wk. — **pura**, n. N. of a town, Kshitîś. — **purāṇa**, n., **-pustaka**, m., **-prakaraṇa**, n., **-prakāra**, m., **-prakāśa**, m. N. of wks. — **prabha**, m. N. of a man, Buddh. — **prayoga**, m. N. of wk. — **bhājana**, n. = *-pātra*, ŚāṅkhGṛ. — **bhāshya**, n., **-mantra**, m., **-mayūkha**, m. N. of wks. — **yukta**, mfn. connected with welfare or prosperity, auspicious, R. — **rakshita**, m. N. of a man, Buddh. — **ratna**, n. or **-ratnâkara**, m. N. of wk. — **vara-varman**, m. or **-varman**, m. N. of a king, Inscr. — **vācana**, n. the reciting of a text for averting evil &c., g. *puṇyâha-vācanâdi* on Pāṇ. v, 1, 111, Vārtt. 3; mfn. = *śānti-vācanam prayojanam asya*, ib. — **vāda**, m. N. of wk. — **vāhana**, m. N. of a king, Buddh. — **vidhāna**, n., **-vidhi**, m., **-vilāsa**, m., **-viveka**, m. N. of wks. — **vrata**, n. N. of a partic. religious observance, RāmatUp. — **śataka**, n., **-śataka-saṃgraha** (?), m. N. of wks. — **śarman**, m. N. of a Brāhman, Inscr. — **śīla**, m. 'quiet-tempered,' N. of a man, Vet. — **sadman**, n. a room for performing any propitiatory rite for averting evil (=-*gṛiha*), VarBṛS. **-sarvasva**, n. N. of wk. **-salila**, n. propitiatory water, Hcar. **-sāra**, m., **-sāra-bhāshya**, n. N. of wks. **-sūkta**, n. N. of a hymn, Cat. **-sūri**, m. N. of an author, ib. **-soma**, m. N. of a man, Kathās. **-stava**, m. N. of sev. wks. (cf. *bṛihac-chānti-st°*). **-homa**, m. a propitiatory oblation, Mn.; MBh.; -*mantra*, m. N. of work.

Śāntika, mfn. propitiatory, expiatory, averting evil, Hcat.; producing or relating to ease or quiet, MW.; m. pl. N. of a people, VarBṛS.; MārkP.; n. a propitiatory rite for averting evil, MBh.; VarBṛS. &c. **-karman**, n. a magical rite performed for removing obstacles, MW. **Śāntikâdhyāya**, m. N. of work.

Śāntivā, f. N. of a deity, Kauś.

Śānty, in comp. for *śānti*. **-agni-parîkshâdi-grantha**, m. N. of wk. **-ākara**, **-ākara-gupta**, m. N. of poets, Sadukt. **-uda**, n. propitiatory water; -*kumbha*, m. a vessel for holding prop° water, W. **-udaka**, n. = -*uda*, Gaut.; Vait.; Kāv.; -*prayoga*, m. N. of wk. **-uddyota**, m. N. of wk.

Śāntvā, ind. = *śamitvā*, having become tranquil, Pāṇ.; Vop.

शांतनव *śāṃtanava*, mf(ī)n. written or composed by Śaṃtanu, Cat.; m. patr. of Bhīshma (as son of king Śaṃtanu, the reputed great uncle of the Pāṇḍavas), MBh.; N. of a son of Medhâtithi, VP.; of various writers (esp. of the author of the Phiṭ-sūtras; cf. °*vâcārya*); (*ī*), f. (scil. *ṭīkā*) the Comm. composed by Śaṃtanu, Cat.; n. N. of the Dvīpa ruled by Śāṃtanava, VP. **-shaṭ-sūtra**, n. N. of a Vedânta wk. **Śāṃtanavâcārya**, m. the author of the Phiṭ-sūtras (on accentuation).

Śāṃtanu, m. N. of the father of Bhīshma (in older language *Śā́ṃtanu*, q.v.), MBh.; Hariv. &c.; a partic. inferior kind of grain, Suśr. **-tva**, n. the state or condition of (being) Śāṃtanu, MBh. **-nandana**, m. 'Ś°'s son,' patr. of Bhīshma, Dhanaṃj.

Śāṃtanū-ja, m. (m.c. for °*tanu-ja*) id., MBh.

शान्त्व् *śāntv* &c. See √*sāntv*.

शान्त्वति *śāntvati*, f. Clerodendrum Siphonantus, L.

शाप 1. *śāpa*, m. (ifc. f. *ā*; fr. √*śap*) a curse, malediction, abuse, oath, imprecation, ban, interdiction (with √*vac*, √*dā*, *pra*-√*yam*, *ny*-√*as*, *vi*-√*sṛij*, *ā*-√*diś*, 'to pronounce or utter a curse on any one,' with dat., gen., loc., or acc. with *prati*), MBh.; Kāv. &c. **-grasta**, mfn. seized by or suffering from a curse, W. **-ja**, mfn. arising from a c°, ib. **-tā**, f. being under a c°, Kād. **-nāśana**, m. 'c°-destroyer,' N. of a Muni, Cat. **-parikshata**, mfn. = -*grasta*, R. **-prada**, mfn. uttering a curse, MW. **-pradāna**, n. utterance of a c°, VP. **-bhāj**, mfn. labouring under a c°, ib. **-mukta**, mfn. freed from a c°, W. **-mukti**, f. deliverance from a c°, Kathās. **-moksha**, m. id., MBh.; uttering of a c°, R. **-yantrita**, mfn. restrained by a curse, Ragh. **-vimocana**, n. N. of wk. **-samāyukta**, mfn. = -*grasta*, R. **Śāpânta**, m. the end of a curse or of the period of its effect, Megh. **Śāpâmbu**, n. water used in formularies of cursing, VP. **Śāpâvasāna**, n. = *śāpânta*, MW. **Śāpâstra**, m. 'having curses for weapons,' a saint (whose c°s are formidable even to deities), L. **Śāpôtsarga**, m. the utterance of a curse, MBh. **Śāpôdaka**, n. = *śāpâmbu*, Mcar. **Śāpôddhāra**, m. deliverance from a curse, R.

Śāpāyana, m. patr. fr. *śapa*, g. *aśvâdi*.

Śāpita, mfn. (fr. Caus. of √*śap*) made to take an oath, one to whom an oath has been administered, sworn, Mn.; MBh. &c.

Śāpīya, m. N. of a school, PratijñāS. (v.l. *śābīya*).

Śāpeya, m. N. of a teacher (pl. his school), g. *śaunakâdi*.

Śāpeyin, m. N. of a disciple of Yājñavalkya, VāyuP.; m. the followers of Śāpeya, g. *śaunakâdi*.

शाप 2. *śāpa*, m. (of doubtful derivation) floating wood or other substances, RV.; AV.

Śāpeṭa, m. or n. (?) floating reed &c., Kauś.

शापटिक *śāpaṭika* or *śāpaṭhika*, m. a peacock, L.

शाफरिक *śāpharika*, m. (fr. *śaphara*) a fisherman, Pāṇ. iv, 4, 35, Sch.

शाफाक्षि *śaphākshi*, m., patr. fr. *śaphâksha*, Pravar.

शाफेय *śāpheya*, m. N. of a school of the Yajur-veda (cf. *śāpeya*).

शाब *śāba*. See 1. *śāva*.

शाबर *śābara*, mfn. (fr. *śabara*) wicked, malicious, L.; m. injury, offence, L.; Symplocos Racemosa, Bhpr. (cf. *sāvara*); N. of a teacher and of various wks. (cf. below); (*ī*), f. the dialect of the Śabaras, Sāh.; Mṛicch., Introd.; Carpopogon Pruriens, L.; n. copper, L.; darkness, L.; a kind of sandal (cf. *śāmbara*), L. **-kaustubha**, m. or n., **-cintāmaṇi**, m., **-tantra**, n., **-tantra-sarvasva**, n. N. of wks. **-bhāshya**, n. N. of Śabara's commentary on the Mīmāṃsa-sūtras. **-bhedâkhya**, n. copper, L. **-mahā-tantra**, n. N. of a Tantra by Śrī-kaṇṭha-śiva Paṇḍita. **Śābarôtsava**, m. a partic. festival of the Mlecchas, KālP. **Śābarôpanishad**, f. N. of an Upanishad.

Śābaraka, m. (w.r. *śāv°*) Symplocos Racemosa, L.; (*ikā*), f. a kind of leech, Suśr.

Śābarajambuka, mfn. (fr. *śabara-jambu*), Pāṇ. iv, 2, 119, Sch.

Śābarāyaṇa, m. patr. fr. *śabara*, g. *haritâdi*.

Śābari, m. N. of a man, Buddh.

शाबलीय *śābalīya*, mfn. (fr. *śabala*), g. *kṛiśâśvâdi*.

Śābalya, n. a mixture, medley, BhP.; (*ā́*), f. (prob.) a female buffoon, VS. (TS. *śābulyā́*).

शाबस्त *śābasta*, m. N. of a son of Yuvanāśva (and founder of the city Śābastī), BhP.; (*ī*), f. N. of a city, ib.

Śābasti, m. patr. fr. *śābasta*, BhP.

शाबीय *śābīya*. See *śāpīya*.

शाबुल्या *śābulyā*. See *śābalyā*.

शाब्द *śābdá*, mf(ī)n. (fr. *śabda*) sonorous, sounding, W.; relating to sound (as opp. to *ārtha*, q.v.), Sāh.; based on sounds, expressed in words, oral, verbal, (esp.) resting on or enjoined by sacred sound (i.e. on the Veda; with *brahman*, n. = 'the Veda'), ŚBr. &c.; nominal (as inflection), W.; m. a philologist, grammarian, RPrāt.; pl. a partic. sect, Hcar.; (*ī*), f. Sarasvatī (as goddess of speech and eloquence), W. **-tva**, n. the being based on sounds or words &c., Sāh. **-bodha**, m. 'verbal knowledge,' apprehension of the meaning of words, perception of the verbal or literal sense (of a sentence &c.); -*taraṃgiṇī*, f. a modern grammar by Īśvaridatta. **-prakriyā**, f. a philosophical grammar by Rāma-krishṇa. **-vyañjanā**, f. (in rhet.) suggestion or insinuation founded on mere words (as opp. to *ārtha-v°* or suggestion dependent upon the meaning of words), MW.

Śābdika, mfn. sonorous, uttering a sound, Pāṇ. iv, 4, 34; relating to sounds or words, verbal, W.; m. 'conversant with words,' a grammarian, lexicographer, Siṇhās.; ĀpastŚr., Sch. **-cintāmaṇi**, m. N. of a gram. wk. **-narasiṇha**, m. N. of a grammarian, Cat. **-rakshā**, f. N. of a gram. wk. **-vidvatka-vipramodaka**, m. or n. a list of words formed by Uṇādi suffixes (by Veṅkaṭêśvara who lived at the end of the 17th century). **Śābdikâbharaṇa**, n. N. of a grammar by Dharma-kīrti.

शाम *śāma*, mfn. (√1. *śam*) appeasing, curing, having curative properties, MW. **-datta**, m. (with *paṇḍita*) N. of an author, Cat.

Śāman, n. (cf. *sāman*) appeasing, reconciling, conciliation, W.

Śāmana, mfn. extinguishing, destroying, Pañcat. iii, 31 (v.l. for *śamana*); m. N. of Yama (= *śamana*), W.; (*ī*), f. the southern quarter, L.; n. a sedative, Car.; tranquillity, peace, W.; killing, slaughter, ib.; end (°*naṃ* √*yā*, to go to an end, be destroyed), MW.

Śāmam. See √1. *śam*.

Śāmala-dāsa or **Śāmala-bhaṭṭa**, m. N. of a modern poet, MW.

Śāmāyana, m. a patr.; pl., Pravar.

Śāmāyanīya, m. pl. N. of a school, Cat.

Śāmika, m. patr. fr. *śamika*, g. *bidâdi*.

Śāmitra, mfn. (fr. *śamitṛi*) relating to the official who cuts up the sacrificial victim (see -*karman*), BhP.; m. (scil. *agni*) the fire for cooking the sacrificial flesh, GṛŚrS.; n. the place for the above fire, ŚrS.; any place of immolation, shambles, Vait.; Mṛicch.; = next, MBh. **-karman**, n. the office of the above official, BhP.

Śāmīla, mf(*ī*)n. made of the wood of the Śamī tree (Prosopis Spicigera), KātyŚr.; Gobh. (cf. Pāṇ. iv, 3, 142; 155, Sch.); n. ashes, MW.; (*ī*), f. a chaplet, garland, ib.

Śāmīvata, m. pl. (fr. *śamī-vat*) N. of a tribe or race, Pāṇ. v, 3, 118; (*ī*), f. a princess of the Śāmīvatas, ib.

Śāmīvatya, m. a prince of the Śāmīvatas, ib.

Śāmeya, m. a patr.; pl., Pravar.

Śāmya, mfn. relating to peace, peaceful, MBh.; n. peace, reconciliation, ib. **-tā**, f. id., ib. **-prāśa**, m. a kind of sacrifice, Divyâv. **-vākā**, f. N. of a plant, Kauś.

शामा *śāmā́*, f. (prob.) a kind of plant (used for curing leprosy), AV. i, 24, 4 (Paipp. *śyāmā́*).

शामाक *śāmāka*, incorr. for *śyāmāka*.

शामुपाल *śāmu-pāla* (?), m. N. of a king, Buddh.

शामुल्य *śāmulyà*, n. (perhaps connected with *śamala*) a woollen shirt, RV.

Śāmūla, n. id., Kauś.; Lāṭy.

शाम्ब *śāmba*, m. N. of a king, Daś. (also w.r. for *sāmba*, q.v.)

शाम्बर *śāmbará*, mf(*ī*)n. relating or belonging or peculiar to Śambara, RV.; Hariv. &c.; coming from the deer called Ś°, Bhpr.; (*ī*), f. jugglery, sorcery, illusion (as practised by the Daitya Ś°), Naish.; a sorceress, W.; n. the fight with Ś°, RV.; a kind of sandal, L. (cf. *śābara*). **-śilpa**, n. the art of jugglery, magic, Naish.

Śāmbarika, m. a juggler, Cat.

शाम्बलाम्बावर्मरत्न *śāmbalāmbā-varma-ratna*, n. N. of a ch. of the Saubhāgya-lakshmī-tantra.

शाम्बव *śāmbava*, m. (fr. *śambu*), see next.

Śāmbavânanda-kalpa, m. N. of wk.

Śāmbavika, m. a worker or dealer in shells, W.

Śāmbavya, m. N. of a teacher, Cat.

Śāmbu, m. N. of a man, AV.

Śāmbuka, m. a bivalve shell, W.

Śāmbuvi, m. pl. N. of a Śākhā or school, Anup.

Śāmbūka, m. = *śāmbuka*, L.

शाम्भर *śāmbhara*, m. patr. fr. *śambara*, Pravar.; (prob. n.) N. of a lake in Rājputāna (commonly called Sāmbhar, where a kind of fossil salt is found), MW. **-nagara**, n. a town near S°, ib.

Śāmbharāyiṇī, f. (patr. fr. *śāmbhara*) N. of a woman, Cat. (v.l. *sāmbh°*). **-vrata**, n. a partic. observance, ib.

शाम्भव *śāmbhava*, mf(ī)n. (fr. *śam-bhu*) coming or derived from Śiva, relating or belonging or sacred to him, Kāv.; Kathās.; m. (only L.) a worshipper of Śiva; a son of Śambhu; Sesbana Grandiflora; camphor; a sort of poison; bdellium; (*ī*), f., see below; n. Pinus Deodora, L. **-dīpikā**, f. N. of a Tantra. **-deva**, m. N. of a poet, Cat.

Śāmbhavāha, m. a patr., Pravar.

Śāmbhavī, f. N. of Durgā, Tantras.; a kind of blue-flowering Dūrvā grass, L. **-tantra**, n. N. of a Tantra.

Śāmbhavīya, mfn. relating or belonging to Śiva, Mcar.

Śāmbhavya, m. N. of a teacher, GopBr.

शाम्मद *śāmmada*, n. (fr. *śam-mada*) N. of two Sāmans, ĀrshBr.

शाम्य *śāmya*. See above.

शाम्याक *śāmyāka*, mf(ī)n. (fr. *śamyāka*) derived or made from (the wood of) Cathartocarpus Fistula, Kauś.

शाय *śāya*, mfn. (fr. √*śī*) lying, sleeping, abiding (see *kaṅka-ś°*).

Śāyaka, mf(*ikā*)n. id., Vishṇ. (cf. *kośa-*, *vṛiksha-śāyikā*); (*ikā*), f. sleeping, lying ('manner of lying' or 'one's turn to rest'), Pāṇ. iii, 3, 108, Vārtt. 1; ii, 2, 15, Sch.; w.r. for *sāyaka*, arrow.

Śāyayitavya, mfn. (fr. Caus.) to be made to lie upon (loc.), Kād.; to be made to sleep (with *dīr-*

gham, 'to be made to sleep the long or eternal sleep,' i. e. 'to be put to death'), Bālar.

Śāyi-tā, f. (fr. next) the state of lying or reposing or abiding in (ifc.), MBh.; Kathās.

Śāyin, mfn. lying down, reclining, resting, abiding, Br.&c. &c. (mostly ifc.; cf. *adhaḥ-, eka-ś°* &c.)

Śāyyika, mfn. = *śayyayā jīvati*, g. *vetanâdi*.

शायण्डायन *śāyaṇḍāyana*, m. pl. N. of a partic. association, g. *aishukāry-ādi*. — **bhakta**, mfn. inhabited by the Śāyaṇḍāyanas, ib.

शायन *śāyana*, n. N. of a Sāman, ĀrshBr.

शायस्थि *śāyasthi*, m. N. of a teacher, VBr.

शार् *śār* (also written *sār*; cf. √*śṛī*) to be weak or feeble, Dhātup. xxxv, 16.

शार 1. *śārá*, mf(*ā*)n. (in most meanings also written *sāra*; of doubtful derivation) variegated in colour, of different colours (as dark hair mixed with grey), motley, spotted, speckled, Pāṇ. iii, 3, 21, Vārt. 2; yellow, W.; m. variegating or a variegated colour, (esp.) a mixture of blue and yellow, green, ib.; (also *śāraka*) a kind of die or a piece used at chess or at backgammon, Bhartṛ.; Daś.; air, wind, L.; hurting, injuring (fr. √*śṛī*), L.; (*ī*), f. a chessman &c. (see m.), Naish.; a kind of bird (= *śāri*), ib.; Kuśa grass, L.; n. a variegated colour, MW. — **tā**, f., -**tva**, n. variety of colour, yellowness, ib. — **pada**, m. a kind of bird, Car. (v.l. for *sāra-p°*).

Śāraṅga. See *sāraṅga*.

Śā́ri, f. (L. also written *śārī* or *sāri*) a partic. bird (= *śārikā* below), TS.; VS.; an arrow, RV.; an elephant's housings or armour, Śiś.; = *vyavahārântara* and *kapaṭa*, L.; N. of a daughter of Māṭhara (wife of Tishya and mother of the first disciple of Gautama Buddha; cf. *śāri-putra*), Buddh.; m. a chessman, piece at chess (or at a kind of draughts), Kād. (written *sāri*); a little round ball (= *guṭikā*), MW.; a kind of die or small cube used in games with dice, ib. — **kuksha**, mfn. = *śārer iva kukshir asya*, Pāṇ. v, 4, 120, Sch. — **jā**, f., see *pūti-śārijā*. — **paṭṭa**, m. a chequered cloth or board for playing draughts &c., chess-board, MW. — **prastara**, m. N. of a gambler, Kathās. — **phala**, n., -**phalaka**, m. n. = *-paṭṭa*, L. — **putra**, m. N. of one of the two chief disciples (Agra-śrāvaka), of Gautama Buddha (the other being Maudgalyāyana), MWB. 47. — **śākā** (of unknown meaning), AV. iii, 14, 5. — **śṛiṅkhalā**, f. a chessman or a square on a chess-board, L. — **suta**, m. = *-putra*, Buddh.

Śārika, m. (prob.) a kind of bird (= next), Vas. xiv, 18; (*ā*), f., see next.

Śārikā, f. a kind of bird (commonly called Maina, either the Gracula Religiosa or the Turdus Salica, also written *sārikā*, q.v.); playing at chess or draughts, Uṇ. iv, 127, Sch.; a bow or stick used for playing the Vīṇā or any stringed instrument, L.; a form of Durgā, Kathās.; Rājat.; N. of a woman (= *śāri*), Buddh. — **kavaca**, n. N. of a ch. of Rudra-yāmala-tantra. — **kūṭa**, n. 'Durgā's peak,' N. of a place, Kathās. — **nātha**, m. N. of an author, Pratāp., Sch. — **pīṭha**, n. 'Durgā's seat,' N. of a place, Kathās. — **stotra**, n. N. of a Stotra.

Śārita, mfn. variegated, coloured, Hcar.

Śārī. See 1. *śāra*.

Śāru. See *kim-śāru*.

Śāruka, mfn. one who injures or destroys (with acc.), Vop.; mischievous, injurious, Pāṇ. iii, 2, 154.

शार 2. *śāra*, Vṛiddhi form of *śara*, in comp. — **talpika**, mfn. (spoken by a dying warrior) from a bed of arrows, MBh. — **daṇḍāyani**, m. patr. fr. *śara-daṇḍa*, ib. — **daṇḍāyanī** or °*yinī*, f. the wife of Śāra-daṇḍāyani, ib. (Nīlak.) — **lomī**, m. patr. fr. *śara-loman*, Pāṇ. iv, 1, 85, Vārtt. 8, Pat. — **lomyā**, f. a patr., Pāṇ. iv, 1, 75, Vārtt. 3, Pat.

शारणिक *śāraṇika*, mfn. in need of protection, going for protection or refuge, a refugee, MBh.

शारद *śāradá*, mf(*ī* or *śāradī*)n. (fr. *śarad*) produced or growing in autumn, autumnal, mature, AV. &c. &c.; (prob.) that which offers a shelter in autumn (against the overflowings of rivers; applied to *puras* or 'castles;' others 'rich in years,' 'old'), RV. i, 131, 4; 174, 2; vi, 20, 10; new, recent, L. (perhaps Bhartṛ. i, 47 in *salilam śāradam*; cf. also *rajju-śārada* and *dṛishac-chārada*); modest, shy, diffident, L.; m. a year, L.; a cloud, L.; N. of various plants (a yellow kind of Phaseolus Mungo; Mimusops Elengi &c.), L.; autumnal sickness, W.; autumnal sunshine, ib.; N. of a teacher of Yoga (v. l. *śābara*), Cat.; (*ā*), f., see below; (*ī*), f. (only L.) the day of full moon in the month Kārttika (or Āśvina); Jussiæa Repens; Alstonia Scholaris; n. corn, grain, fruit (as ripening in autumn), VarBṛS.; the white lotus, L. — **bhūruh**, m. Alstonia Scholaris, Dharmaś. — **śarvarī**, f. N. of a poem. **Śāradôllāsa**, m. N. of a Comm. on the Laghu-candrikā.

Śāratka, mfn. = *śaradam adhīte veda vā*, g. *vasantâdi*.

Śāradaka, m. a kind of Darbha grass, L.; (*ikā*), f. Mimusops Elengi, L.; Cucumis Utilissimus, L.

Śāradā, f. a kind of Vīṇā or lute, L.; N. of two plants (= *brāhmī* and *sārivā*), L.; N. of a Sarasvatī, Śukas.; of Durgā, BhP.; of a daughter of Devaratha, Cat.; = *śāradā-tilaka*, ib. — **kalpa**, m., -**kalpa-latā**, f. N. of wks. — °**kāra** (°*dâk°*), m. N. of a poet, Cat. — **krama-dīpikā**, f. N. of a Tāntric wk. — **tanaya**, m. N. of an author, Pratāp., Sch. — **tilaka**, n. N. of a Bhāṇa (q. v.) by Śaṃkara and of a mystical poem by Lakshmaṇâcārya (cf. RTL. 207); *-tantra*, n. the Tantra called Śāradā-tilaka. — °**di-kalpa** (°*dâd°*), m., -**devī-māhātmya-paṭala**, n. N. of wks. — °**nanda** (°*dân°*), m. N. of a teacher of Yoga, Cat.; (prob.) n. N. of a Stotra. — °**nandana** (°*dân°*), m. N. of a man, Siṇhâs. — **purāṇa**, n., -**pūjā**, f., -**māhātmya**, n. N. of wks. — °**mbā** (°*dâmbā*), f. the goddess Ś°, Cat. — **sahasra-nāman**, n., -**stava**, m., -**stotra**, n. N. of wks.

Śāradika, mfn. autumnal (only applied to certain substantives, as *śrāddha, ātapa, roga*), Pāṇ. iv, 3, 12; 13; (*ā*), f., see *śāradaka*.

Śāradin, mfn. autumnal, belonging to autumn, W.

Śāradīna, mfn. autumnal, kept or taking place in autumn, Nalac.

Śāradīya, mf(*ā*)n. id. — **mahā-pūjā**, f. the autumnal great worship (of Durgā), Tithyād. **Śāradīyâkhya-nāma-mālā**, f. N. of a glossary by Harsha-kīrti (printed in Benares A.D. 1874).

Śāradya, n. autumnal corn or grain, VarBṛS.

Śāradvata, m. patr. fr. *śarad-vat*, g. *bidâdi*; N. of Kṛipa, MBh.; BhP.; of Gautama, Hariv. (pl. = *gautamāḥ*, Pravar.); of a disciple of Kaṇva, Śak.; (*ī*), f., see below.

Śāradvatāyana, m. patr. fr. *śāradvata*, Pāṇ. iv, 1, 102 (also pl., Saṃskārak.)

Śāradvatī, f. patr. of Kṛipī, MBh.; N. of an Apsaras, ib.; Hariv. — **putra**, m. = *śāri-putra*, Buddh. — **suta**, m. a son of Kṛipī, MBh.

शाराव *śārāva*, mf(*ī*)n. (from *śarāva*) placed on a shallow dish (as rice), Pāṇ. iv, 2, 14, Sch.

शारिवा *śārivā*. See *sārivā*.

शारीटक *śārīṭaka*, m. N. of a village, Rājat.

शारीर *śārīrá*, mf(*ī*)n. (fr. *śarīra*) bodily, corporeal, relating or belonging to or being in or produced from or connected with the body (with *daṇḍa*, m. corporal punishment), ŚBr. &c. &c.; made of bone, Suśr.; n. bodily constitution, MBh.; VarBṛS.; (in med.) the science of the body and its parts, anatomy, Suśr.; Car.; the feces, excrement, Mn. xi, 202; the embodied soul or spirit, W.; = *vṛisha* (?), L. — **brāhmaṇa**, n. (= *bṛihad-āraṇyaka*), -**lakshaṇa**, n., -**vidyā**, f., -**vaidya**, n. N. of wks. — **vraṇa**, m. a bodily ulcer or tumour, Suśr. — **sthāna**, n., see *vāgbhaṭa-śārīra-sth°*. **Śārīrôpanishad**, f. N. of an Upanishad (cf. *śārīrakôp°*).

Śārīraka, mfn. bodily, corporeal &c. (= *śārīra*); n. the soul or embodied spirit or the doctrine inquiring into its nature, MW.; = *-sūtra*, Vedântas.; N. of an Upanishad (cf. °*kôpanishad*) and of a medical wk. by Śrī-mukha; du. bodily joy and pain, BhP. — **ṭīkā**, f. N. of wk. by Vācas-pati. — **nyāya**, m. N. of a Vedânta wk.; *-nirṇaya*, m. a Comm. on Śaṃkarâcārya's Śārīraka-bhāshya by Ānanda-tīrtha; *-maṇi-mālā*, f. N. of wk.; *-raksha-maṇi*, m. a Comm. on Śaṃkarâcārya's Śārīraka-bhāshya by Appaya Dīkshita; *-saṃgraha*, m. an abridgment in verse of Rāmânuja's Comm. on the Brahma-sūtra by Bādhūla Śrī-nivāsâcārya. — **pradīpikā**, f. N. of a Mīmāṅsā wk. — **bhāshya**, n. N. of Śaṃkara's Comm. on the Brahma-sūtra; *-ṭīkā*, f., *-nyāya-vārttika*, n., *-vārttika*, n., *-vibhāga*, m., *-vyākhyā*, f. N. of Comms. on it. — **mīmāṅsā**, f. 'inquiry into the embodied spirit,' N. of the Brahma-sūtra; *-nyāya-saṃgraha*, m., *-bhāshya*, n., *-vyākhyā*, f. N. of Comms. on it. — **śāstra-darpaṇa**, m. N. of wk. — **saṃkshepa**, m. = *saṃkshepa-śārīraka*, q. v. — **saṃgraha**, m., -**sambandhôkti-saṃkshepa**, m. N. of wks. — **sūtra**, n. the aphorisms on the Vedânta philosophy (= *brahma-sūtra*); *-sārârtha-candrikā*, f. N. of wk. **Śārīrakôpanishad**, f. N. of an Upanishad.

Śārīrakīya, mfn. corporeal, psychological (as a book treating of the embodied soul), MW.

Śārīrika, mfn. relating to the body, corporeal, personal, material, contained in the body, incorporate, psychological, ib.

शारु *śāru, śāruka*. See col. 1.

शार्क *śārka*, m. = *śarkarā*, ground or candied sugar, L.

Śārkaka, m. (only L.) id.; a lump of sugar; a lump or ball of meat; the froth of milk, cream.

Śārkara, mf(*ī*)n. (fr. *śarkarā*) gravelly, stony, Pāṇ. v, 2, 105; made of sugar, sugary, Suśr.; m. a stony or gravelly place, MW.; the froth or skim of milk, L.; n. N. of two Sāmans, ĀrshBr. (also w.r. for *śākvara*).

Śārkaraka, mfn. gravelly, stony, W. (cf. Pāṇ. iv, 2, 83); m. a place abounding in stones or gravel, ib.

Śārkarâksha, m. a patr., BhP., Sch.; pl., see °*kshya*.

Śārkarâkshasa (?), m. N. of a section of the Hāridravīyas, L.

Śārkarâkshi, m. patr. fr. *śarkarâksha*, ĀśvŚr.

Śārkarâkshya, m. (g. *gargâdi*) patr. fr. id., ŚBr.; ChUp.; TĀr. (pl. °*kshāḥ* or °*kshyāḥ*).

Śārkarâkshyāyaṇī, f. a patr., Pāṇ. iv, 1, 73, Vārtt. 2, Pat.

Śārkarika, mfn. (fr. *śarkara*), Pāṇ. iv, 2, 84.

Śārkarin, mfn. suffering from gravel or stone, Car. (prob. w.r. for *śarkarin*).

Śārkarīdhāna, mfn. (fr. *śarkarī-dhāna*), Kāś. on Pāṇ. iv, 2, 109.

Śārkarīya, w.r. for *śarkarīya*.

शार्कोट *śārkoṭa*, mfn. coming from the serpent Śarkoṭa, AV.

शार्ग *śārgá*, m. a kind of bird, Maitr.; n. N. of various Sāmans (prob. w.r. for *śārṅga*, q.v.)

शार्गाल *śārgāla*, more correctly *sārgāla*, q.v.

शार्ङ्खलतोदि *śārṅkhalatodi*, m. patr. fr. *śṛiṅkhala-todin*, g. *bāhv-ādi*.

शार्ङ्ग *śārṅga*, mf(*ī*)n. (fr. *śṛiṅga*) made of horn, horny, corneous, Suśr.; derived or taken from the plant Śṛiṅga (as poison), Yājñ.; armed with a bow, Bhaṭṭ.; m. a kind of bird, MBh. (cf. *śārga*); patr. of various Vedic Ṛishis, RAnukr.; (*ī*), f. the female of the bird Śārṅga, MBh.; n. a bow (esp. that of Vishṇu), MBh.; Hariv.; Pur.; fresh ginger, L.; N. of various Sāmans, ĀrshBr. — **jagdha**, mf(*ī*)n. one who has eaten Śārṅga birds, Pāṇ. ii, 2, 36, Vārtt. 1, Pat. — **datta**, m. N. of the author of the Dhanurveda, Cat. — **deva**, m. N. of the author of the Saṃgīta-ratnâkara, ib. — **dhanus**, m. 'armed with the bow Śārṅga,' N. of Vishṇu-Kṛishṇa, Nalac. (°*nur-dhara*, m. id., Vishṇ.) — **dhanvan**, m. = *-dhanus*, MBh.; Kāv. &c. — **dhanvin**, m. id., MārkP. — **dhara**, m. (also with *śesha* and *miśra*) N. of various authors; *-paddhati* or *-vrajyā*, f. N. of a poetical anthology; *-saṃhitā*, f. N. of a medical wk.; °*rīya*, n. N. of a Nāṭaka. — **pakshin**, m. the bird Ś°, MBh. — **pāṇi**, m. 'holding (the bow) Ś° in the hand,' N. of Vishṇu-Kṛishṇa, Kāv.; Kathās. &c.; of the father of Vishṇu Sarva-jña (who was Sāyaṇa's Guru), Sarvad.; of a Vaishṇava, Cat.; *-stotra*, n. N. of a Stotra. — **bhṛit**, m. 'carrying (the bow) Ś°,' N. of Vishṇu-Kṛishṇa, Kathās. **Śārṅgâyudha**, m. 'armed with (the bow) Ś°,' id., Hariv.

Śārṅgaka, m. a kind of bird (= *śārṅga*), MBh.; (*ikā*), f. the female of that bird.

Śārṅgavata, n. (fr. *śṛiṅga-vat*) N. of the country Kuru-varsha, L.

Śārṅgi, in comp. for *śārṅgin*. — **deva**, m. (in music) a kind of time or measure, Saṃgīt.; N. of an author, ib., Introd. (cf. *śārṅga-deva*).

Śārṅgika, m. = *śārṅgaka*, MBh.

Śārṅgin, m. 'bowman, archer,' N. of Vishṇu-Kṛishṇa, Śiś.; of Śiva, MW.

शार्ङ्गरव *śārṅgarava*, m. (fr. *śṛiṅga-rava?*)

N. of a disciple of Kaṇva, Śak. (pl., Pravar.); (*ī*), f. N. of a woman, Pāṇ. iv, 1, 73.

शार्ङ्गेष्टा *śārṅgashṭā*, f. a tree resembling the Pongamia Glabra, L.; a kind of potherb, Car.

Śārṅgeshṭā and °**goshṭhā**, v.l. for prec., L.

शार्दूल *śārdūlá*, m. (of unknown derivation) a tiger, VS. &c. &c.; a lion, L.; a panther, leopard, L.; the fabulous animal Śarabha, L.; a kind of bird, L.; any eminent person, best, excellent, pre-eminent (ifc.; cf. *vyāghra*), MBh.; Kāv. &c.; Plumbago Zeylanica, L.; N. of two metres (cf. below), Col.; of a Rākshasa, R.; pl. N. of a Śākhā or school of the Yajur-veda; (*ī*), f. a tigress (also the mythical mother of tigers and other beasts of prey), MBh.; R. **–karṇa**, m. N. of a son of Tri-śaṅku, Buddh. **–carmán**, n. a tiger's skin, TBr. **–jyeshṭha** (*śārdūlá-*), mfn. having a tiger as superior or chief, ŚBr. **–mṛiga-sevita**, mfn. frequented by tigers and deer, MBh. **–lalita**, n. 'tiger's sport,' N. of a metre (consisting of four Pādas of 19 syllables each), Col. **–lomán**, n. tiger's hair, ŚBr. **–varman**, m. N. of a king, Inscr. **–vāhana**, m. 'riding on a tiger,' N. of Mañju-śrī, L. **–vikrīḍita**, n. 'tiger's play,' N. of a metre (consisting of four Pādas of 19 syllables each), Git.; Śrutab.; Chandom. (also mfn. imitating a tiger's play). **–śataka**, n. N. of a poem. **–sama-vikrama**, mfn. having prowess equal to a tiger, as bold as a tiger, MW.

शार्मण *śārmaṇa*, mfn. (fr. *śarman*), Kāś. on Pāṇ. iv, 2, 75.

शार्मण्य *śārmaṇya* or °*ṇya-deśa*, m. the modern N. of Germany.

शार्यात *śāryātá*, m. patr. fr. *śaryāti* (also pl. and *ī*, f.), RV.; Br.; Hariv.; (with *Mānava*) N. of the author of RV. x, 92, AitBr.; Anukr.; n. N. of various Sāmans, ĀrshBr.

Śāryātaka, m. = prec., Br.

शार्व *śārva*, mf(ī)n. (fr. *śarva*) relating or belonging or sacred to or derived from Śiva, Kāv.; Kathās. (with *diś*, f. the east, VarBṛS.)

Śārvavarmika, mfn. written or composed by Śarva-varman, Cat.

शार्वरि *śārvari*, mf(ī)n. (fr. *śarvarī*) belonging to night, nocturnal, Kād.; Hcar.; Vās.; pernicious, murderous, L.; (*ī*), f. night, Vcar.; ŚārṅgP.; n. (L. also m.) darkness, gloom, BhP.

Śārvarika, mfn. nocturnal, Vām. v, 2, 52.

Śārvarin, m. (cf. *śarvarin*) N. of the 34th year of Jupiter's cycle of 60 years, Cat.

शाल् *śāl* (cf. √*śād*, which in one sense is v.l.), cl. 1. Ā. *śālate*, to shine, be distinguished for or endowed with (instr.), Siṇhâs.; Śiś., Sch.; cl. 1. 10. Ā. *śālate* or *śālayate*, to praise, Dhātup. viii, 37; xxxiii, 18 (Vop.)

Śālita, mfn. shining with, beautified by, distinguished for (with instr. or comp.), Siṇhâs.

शाल 1. *śālá*, mfn. (fr. *śri* for *śri*) being in a house &c., ŚBr. (*ám*, ind. 'at home,' ib.); m. (also written *sāla*), an enclosure, court, fence, rampart, wall, Inscr.; Kāv.; the Śāl tree, Vatica Robusta (a valuable timber tree), MBh.; Kāv. &c.; Artocarpus Locucha, L.; any tree, L.; a kind of fish, Ophiocephalus Wrahl, Vās.; N. of a son of Vṛika, BhP.; of king Śāli-vāhana, L.; of a river, W.; (*ā*), f., see below; n. (ifc.) = *śālā* (col. 2). **–kaṭaṅkaṭa** (also written *śālaṅkaṭaṅk°*), m. N. of a Rākshasa, MBh.; du. N. of two supernatural beings, Yājñ.; (*ī*), f. of a Rakshasī, MBh.; R.; mfn. belonging to Śāl°, R. **–gupta**, m. N. of a man, Pat.; °*tāyani*, m. patr. fr. prec., ib. **–grāma**, m. N. of a village situated on the river Gaṇḍakī and regarded as sacred by the Vaishṇavas (its name comes from the Śāl trees growing near it), Prab.; Pur.; N. of Vishṇu as worshipped at Śāla-grāma or as identified with the Śālgrām stone, MBh.; m. n. a sacred stone worshipped by the Vaishṇavas and supposed to be pervaded by the presence of Vishṇu (it is a black stone which contains a fossil ammonite and is chiefly found near the above village in the Gaṇḍakī), RTL. 69, 1412; (*ī*), f. N. of the river Gaṇḍakī; *-kalpa*, m. N. of wk.; *-kshetra*, n. the district of Ś°, Cat.; *-giri*, m. N. of a mountain producing the Ś° stone, VāmP.; *-tīrtha*, n. N. of a Tīrtha, Cat.; *-dāna-kalpa*, m., *-nirṇaya*, m., *-parīkshā*, f., *-māhātmya*, n., *-lakshaṇa*, n. N. of wks.; *-śilā*, f. the Ś° stone, Cat.; *-stotra*, n. N. of a Stotra. **–ja**, m. a kind of fish (= 1. *śāla*), L. **–niryāsa**, m. the resinous exudation of the Śāl tree, Ragh.; Suśr. **–pattrā**, f. Desmodium Gangeticum, L. **–parṇikā**, f. a kind of fragrant plant (prob. = next), L. **–parṇī**, f. Desmodium or Hedysarum Gangeticum, L. **–pushpa**, n. the flower of the Śāl tree, MBh.; Hibiscus Mutabilis, L.; *-nibha*, mfn. resembling the flowers of the Śāl tree (i.e. reddish-yellow), MBh.; *-bhañjikā*, f. a partic. game, Pāṇ. vi, 2, 74, Sch.; *-maya*, mf(*ī*)n. made of the flowers of the Śāl tree, MBh. **–pota**, m. a young Śāl tree, MBh. **–prâṅśu**, mfn. as high as a Śāl tree, Ragh. **–bhañjikā**, f. an image or figure made of Śāl wood, Kathās.; Rājat.; a kind of game played in the east of India, Uṇ. ii, 32, Sch.; a harlot, courtezan, L.; *-prakhya*, mfn. resembling the above game, MW.; °*kāya*, Nom. Ā. °*yate*, to be like a statue, Nalac. (v.l. *śāli-bh°*). **–bhañjī**, f. a statue (made of Śāl wood), Prab. **–maya**, mf(*ī*)n. made of Śāl wood, Pāṇ. iv, 3, 144, Sch. **–markaṭaka**, w.r. for *śālā-markaṭaka*. **–rasa**, m. = *-niryāsa*, L. **–vaṅśa-nṛipa-muktâvalī**, f. N. of wk. **–vadana**, m. N. of an Asura, Hariv. **–vana**, see *bhadra-śāla-vana*. **–valaya**, m. n. an encircling wall or rampart, Vās. **–vāṇaka**, m. pl. N. of a people, VP. **–vāha**, m. N. of a poet, Cat. **–vāhana**, m. N. of a man, Cat.; = *śāli-v°*, Vīrac. **–veshṭa**, m. = *-niryāsa*, L. **–śṛiṅga**, n. the top of a wall, L. **–saṃkāśa**, mfn. resembling the Śāl tree, MBh. **–sāra**, m. a tree, L.; Asa Fœtida, L. **–skandha** and **–stambha**, m. the trunk of the Śāl tree, MBh. **Śālâṅkī**, f. a doll, puppet, wooden figure (cf. *śāla-bhañjikā*), L. **Śālêndra-rāja**, m. N. of a Buddha, SaddhP.

Śālaka (ifc.) = 1. *śāla* or = *śālā* (see *tri-*, *pīta-*, *priya-ś°*); m. (prob.) a jester, buffoon, Pāṇ. i, 4, 106, Sch.

Śālana, n. (also written *sāl°*) the resin of Vatica Robusta, Pañcar.

Śálā, f. (ifc. also *śāla*, n.) a house, mansion, building, hall, large room, apartment, shed, workshop, stable, AV. &c. &c. [cf. Germ. *saal;* Eng. *hall*]; a large branch (cf. *śākhā*), L.; a kind of metre (cf. *śālinī*). **–karkaṭaka**, n. a kind of radish, L. (v.l. *-markaṭaka* and *-śarkaṭaka*). **–karman**, n. house-building, PārGṛ.; °*ma-paddhati*, f. N. of wk. **–°ksha** (*śālâksha*), m. (prob.) 'house-eyed i.e. large-eyed (?),' N. of a man, ĀśvŚr. **–°gni** (*śālâgni*), m. domestic fire, Gaut.; Gobh. (RTL. 365). **–°jira** (*śālâj°*), m. a kind of dish, Hcar. **–tva**, n. the state of (being) a house &c., MārkP. **–dvār**, f. or *-dvāra*, n. a house-door; °*rya*, mfn. being at the door or entrance of a h° (as fire), KātyŚr.; m. a kind of sacrificial fire, Vait. **–pati** (*śā́lā-*), m. the lord of a house, a house-holder, AV. **–markaṭaka**, see *-karkaṭaka*. **–mukha**, n. the front of a house, L.; m. a kind of rice, Suśr.; °*khīya*, mfn. being at the front of a h° (cf. *-dvārya*); m. a kind of sacrificial fire, ŚrS. **–mṛiga**, m. 'house-animal,' a dog, L.; a jackal (as prowling near h°s?), R. (v.l. *śākhā-mṛiga*). **–vaṅśa**, m. the chief part of a shed, AitĀr. **–vat**, m. N. of a man, Pāṇ. v, 3, 118; (*ī*), f. N. of a wife of Viśvāmitra, Hariv. **–vata**, m. pl. the descendants of Śālāvat, Pāṇ. v, 3, 118; (*ī*), f. a princess of the Śālāvatas, ib. **–vatya**, m. a king of the Śālāvatas, ib.; patr. fr. *śalāvat*, ChUp. (Śaṃk.) **–vṛika**, m. 'h°-wolf,' a dog, cat, jackal &c., L. (cf. *śālāvṛiká*). **–śarkaṭaka**, see *-karkaṭaka*. **–°śraya** (*śālâśr°*), mfn. dwelling in a h° (*-tva*, n.), Baudh. **–sad**, mfn. sitting or being in a h° or stable, AitBr. **–stambha**, m. a house-post, KātyŚr. **–stha**, mfn. standing in a stable (as elephants), MBh.

Śālānī, f. the shrub Hedysarum Gangeticum, L.

1. **Śāli** (for 2. see p. 1068, col. 1), in comp. for *śālin*. **–1. -tā**, f., **-tva**, n. (for 2. see under 2. *śāli*) being connected or furnished or endowed with (comp.), Sarvad.; Suśr.; trust or confidence in, relying upon, W.

1. **Śālika**, mfn. relating or belonging to a hall or room, g. *vrīhy-ādi;* relating or belonging to the Śāl tree, W.; (*ā*), f. a house, shop (see *nāpita-ś°*).

Śālin, mfn. possessing a house or room &c., g. *vrīhy-ādi;* (ifc.) possessing, abounding in, full of, possessed of, amply provided or furnished with, conversant with, distinguished for, MBh.; Kāv. &c.; praiseworthy, BhP. (cf. √*śāl*); m. N. of a teacher, VāyuP.; (*inī*), f. a kind of metre (four times – – – –, – ᴗ – – ᴗ – –), Piṅg.; Chandom.; N. of a woman, Sukas.

Śālī, f. a kind of plant (= *kṛishṇa-jīraka*), W.

Śālīna, mf(*ā*)n. having a fixed house or abode, settled, established, domestic, Āpast.; Baudh.; impotent (in a partic. manner), Nār.; shy, bashful, modest, Kāv.; Pur. (*am*, ind., Naish.); like, resembling, W.; m. an opulent householder, one who devotes himself to household or worldly affairs, ib.; (*ā*), f. Anethum Panmorium or another species, L.; n. bashfulness, modesty, humility, (esp.) taking alms without begging, BhP. **–tā**, f. bashfulness, embarrassment, shyness, modesty, Kāv. **–tva**, n. the having a fixed abode or homestead, Baudh.; bashfulness, Bhaṭṭ.; *-varjita*, mfn. devoid of modesty, immodest, W. **–śīla**, mfn. having a bashful disposition or retiring nature (*-tva*, n.), Uttarar.

Śālīnī, in comp. for *śālīna*. **–karaṇa**, n. the making humble, humiliation, Pāṇ. i, 3, 70; abuse, reproach, MW. **–√kṛi**, P. *-karoti*, to make humble, humiliate, ib.

Śālīnya, m. patr. fr. *śālīna*, g. *kurv-ādi*.

Śālīya, mfn. 'belonging to a house,' g. *utkarâdi;* m. N. of a teacher, Pur.

शाल 2. *śāla*, m. (for 1. see col. 1) = *śala*, g. *jval-ādi;* m. n. (also written *sāla*), g. *ardharcâdi*.

शालग्राम *śāla-grāma* &c. See 1. *śāla*, col. 1.

शालङ्क *śālaṅka*, m. pl. the disciples of Śālaṅki, Pat.

Śālaṅkāyana, m. (also written *sāl°*) patr. fr. *śalaṅka*, g. *nadâdi;* N. of a Ṛishi (son of Viśvāmitra; pl. = Ś°'s descendants), ĀśvŚr.; MBh.; Pañcat.; of one of Śiva's attendants, L. **–gotra**, n. the family of the Śālaṅkāyanas, MW. **–jā**, f. 'Ś°'s daughter,' N. of Satyavatī, L. **–bāshkala**, m. pl. the Ś°s and the Bāshkalas, Hariv. **–sauśrava**, m. pl. the Ś°s and the Sauśravas, ib.

Śālaṅkāyani, m. a patr. (perhaps w.r. for °*yana*), Pravar.

Śālaṅkāyanin, m. pl. the school of Śālaṅkāyana, Lāṭy.

Śālaṅkāyanī-pútra, m. N. of a teacher, ŚBr.

Śālaṅki, m. patr. of Pāṇini, L.

शालङ्कटङ्कट *śālaṅkaṭaṅkaṭa*. See *śāla-k°*, on col. 1.

शालङ्कृत्य *śālaṅkṛitya*, m. pl. N. of a family, VP.

शालभ *śālabha*, mfn. (fr. *śalabha*) belonging to a moth or grasshopper; m. (with *vidhi*) the way of the moth (to fly into fire, i.e. 'rushing inconsiderately into danger'), Mudr. (cf. *pataṃga-vṛitti*).

शालव *śālava*, m. Symplocos Racemosa, L.

शालाक *śālāká*, m. (fr. *śalāka*) a collection of chips or brush-wood, ŚBr.; KātyŚr.; m. (scil. *agni*) a fire of brush-wood, ĀśvŚr.

Śālākabhreya, m. patr. fr. *śalākā-bhrū*, g. *śubhrâdi*.

Śālākin, m. (prob. w.r. for *śalākin*) a surgeon, barber, W.; a spearman, ib.

Śālākeya, m. metron. fr. *śalākā*, g. *śubhrâdi*.

Śālākya, m. an oculist who uses sharp instruments, VarBṛS.; n. employment of pointed instruments as a branch of surgery (cf. *āyur-veda*), Suśr.; metron. fr. *śalākā*, g. *kurv-ādi*. **–śāstra**, n. the science of using sharp instruments for diseases of the eye &c., ib.

शालाञ्चि *śālāñci*, v.l. for next.

शालाञ्जि *śālāñji*, f. Achyranthes Triandra, L. (v.l. *śālañca*, °*lāñci*, °*liñca*).

शालातुरीय *śālāturīya*, mfn. born in Śālātura, Pāṇ. iv, 3, 94; m. N. of Pāṇini, Gaṇar. 2.

शालाथल *śālāthala*, m. patr. fr. *śalāthala*, Pravar.

Śālāthaleya, m. patr. fr. id., g. *śubhrâdi*.

शालार *śālāra*, n. (perhaps connected with *śālā;* only L.) a bird-cage; a ladder, flight of stairs; the claw of an elephant; (also written *sālāra*) a pin or peg projecting from a wall, bracket, shelf (cf. *śalāka*).

शालालुक *śālāluka,* mfn. dealing in *śalālu* (q. v.), Pāṇ. iv, 4, 54.

शालास्थलि *śālāsthali,* m. a patr., g. *krauḍy-ādi.*

Śālāsthalyā, f., ib.

शालि 2. *śāli,* m. (accord. to some also f.; for 1. see p. 1067, col. 2) rice (of ten varieties), any grain of a similar character to rice, Mn.; MBh. &c.; the civet-cat, pole-cat, Hcar. (?); L.; N. of a Yaksha (who was transformed into a lion; cf. *śāli-vāhana* below); pl. grains of rice, rice, R. **–kaṇa,** m. a grain of rice, Kathās. **–kūṭa,** n. a heap of rice, R. **–kedāra,** m. a rice-field, Vās. (v.l.) **–kshetra,** n. id., Yājñ., Sch. **–gotra,** m. N. of a teacher, Cat. (v.l. *śāli-hotra*). **–gopī,** f. the female watcher of a rice-field, Ragh. **–cūrṇa,** n. rice-flour, ground rice, Rājat. **–jāla,** n. a mass or dense field of rice, Ṛitus. **–jâudana,** m. n. (*ja + od°*) rice-pap, boiled rice, VarBṛS. **–2. tā,** f., **-tva,** n. (for 1. see p. 1067, col. 2) the state or condition of rice, MW. **–nātha,** m. (also with *miśra*) N. of various authors, Cat. **–parṇī,** f. Glycine Debilis, Car.; = *māsha-parṇī,* L. **–piṇḍa,** m. N. of a serpent-demon, MBh. **–pishṭa,** n. rice-flour, Suśr.; crystal, L. **–bhañjikāya,** see *śāla-bh°.* **–bhadra,** m. N. of a Jina, Siṇhâs.; *-caritra,* n. N. of wk. **–bhavana,** n. (MBh.), **-bhū,** f. (Rājat.) a rice-field. **–mañjari,** m. N. of a Ṛishi, Cat. (written *sāli-m°*). **–vah** (strong form *-vāh*), mf(*śāly-ūhī*)n. carrying rice, Vop. **–vāha,** m. an ox used for carrying rice, MBh.; R. (Sch.; accord. to Nīlak. 'the measure of rice called *śāli-vāha*'); a proper N., MW. **–vāhana,** m. N. of a celebrated sovereign of India (said to be so called either from having ridden on a Yaksha called Śāli, or from Śāli for Śāla, the Śāl tree, Śāli-vāhana being represented as borne on a cross made of that or other wood; he was the enemy of Vikramâditya and institutor of the era now called Śaka, q. v.; his capital was Pratishṭhāna on the Godāvarī), Siṇhâs.; Subh.; Buddh.; *-caritra,* n., *-śataka,* n., *-saptatī,* f. N. of wks. **–śiras,** m. N. of a Deva-gandharva, MBh.; Hariv. **–śūka,** m. n. an awn or beard of rice, R.; m. N. of a Maurya, Pur. **–saṃrakshikā,** f. a female watcher of a rice-field, Vās., Sch. **–sūrya,** m. or n. N. of a place, MBh. **–stambhaka** (?), N. of wk. **–hotra,** m. 'receiving offerings of rice,' a poetical N. for a horse, L.; N. of a Muni and writer on veterinary subjects, MBh.; n. Śāli-hotra's work on veterinary science; *-jña,* mfn. versed in that science, Pañcat.; *-sāra,* m. N. of wk.; *°trāyaṇa,* m. patr. fr. *śāli-hotra* (pl.), Prav.; *°trin,* m. a horse, L.; *°trīya,* n., *°trônnaya,* m. N. of medical wks. **Śālikshu-mat,** mfn. sown with rice and sugar-cane, VarBṛS.

2. **Śālika,** mfn. (for 1. see p. 1067, col. 2) derived or prepared from rice (with *pishṭa,* n. rice-flour), Hcat.; m. (with *ācārya*) N. of a teacher; (*ā*), f. N. of wk. **–nātha,** m. N. of a poet, Cat.; of the author of a Comm. on the Gita-govinda, ib.

Śāleya, mf(*ī*)n. sown with rice, Bālar.; m. or (*ā*), f. Anethum Panmori or Sowa (n. its grain), Car.; m. a kind of radish, L.; N. of a mountain, Virac.

Śāly, in comp. for 2. *śāli.* **–anna,** n., **-odana,** m. n. boiled rice, Kāv.; Suśr.

शालिञ्च *śāliñca,* m., *°cī,* f. = *śālāñji,* L.

शाली 1. *śālī,* f. Nigella Indica, L.

शाली 2. *śālī,* f. (prob. Prākṛit for *śyālī;* cf. *śyāla*) a wife's sister (see comp.) **–bhartṛi,** m. the husband of a wife's s°, Gal. **Śāly-ūḍha,** m. id., ib.

Śālūḍha, m. (prob. corrupted) = prec., ib.

शालीकि *śālīki,* m. N. of a teacher, Baudh.

शालीन *śālīna* &c. See p. 1067, col. 3.

शालीहोत्रमुनि *śālīhotra-muni,* m. N. of an author (prob. w. r. for *śāli-h°*), Cat.

शालु *śālu,* m. (fr. √*śal*) a frog, L.; a kind of astringent substance, L.; a sort of perfume (commonly called Chor), L.; n. a partic. fruit coming from the north, VarBṛS.; an esculent lotus-root, L. **–vesa-kavaca,** n. N. of a Kavaca (q. v.)

Śāluka, n. the esculent root of different kinds of lotus, L.

Śālūka, m. a frog, L.; N. of a man, g. *śubhrâdi;* n. (ifc. f. *ā*) = *śāluka,* AV. &c. &c. (also *-kanda,* Kād.); a tumour in the throat, Car.; a nutmeg, L.; N. of a poet, Cat.

Śālūkikā, f. a country rich in esculent lotus-roots, Pat., Sch.

Śālūkikīya, mfn. (fr. *śālūkikā*), Pat.

Śālūkinī, f. = *śālūkikā,* g. *pushkarâdi;* N. of a Tīrtha, MBh.; of a village, Pāṇ. ii, 4, 7, Sch.

Śālūkeya, m. patr. fr. *śālūka,* g. *śubhrâdi.*

Śālūra, m. a frog, Kāśikh.; a kind of metre, Col.

Śālūraka, m. a kind of worm infesting the intestines, Car.

शालुड *śāluḍa,* m. N. of an evil demon, AV.

शालोत्तरीय *śālottarīya* (prob. w. r. for *śālāturīya,* q.v.), m. N. of the grammarian Pāṇini, L.

शाल्मल *śālmala,* m. the silk-cotton tree (only ifc.; see *sa-ś°*); the gum or resin of the cotton tree, L.; N. of a Dvīpa (also *-dvīpa*), Pur.

Śālmali, m. f. (or *°lī,* f.; cf. *śalmali*) the Seemul or silk-cotton tree, Bombax Heptaphyllum or Salmalia Malabarica (a lofty and thorny tree with red flowers; its thorns are supposed to be used for torture in one of the hells [cf. *kūṭa-ś°*], or it may stand for the N. of that hell), Mn.; MBh. &c.; one of the 7 Dvīpas or great divisions of the known continent (so called from the above tree said to grow there; it is surrounded by the sea of ghee or clarified butter), MBh.; Pur.; patr. of a man (f. *°lyā*), g. *krauḍy-ādi;* N. of a son of Avikshit, MBh.; of another man descended from Agasti, Hcat.; (*ī*), f., see below. **–dvīpa,** m. the Śālmali-dvīpa (see above). **–pattraka,** m. Alstonia Scholaris, L. **–stha,** m. 'abiding in the Śālmali,' a vulture, L.; N. of Garuḍa, ib.

Śālmalika, mfn. (fr. *śālmali*), g. *kumudâdi* (with *dvīpa,* m. = *śālmali-dv°,* MBh.); m. the tree Andersonia Rohitaka, L.; n. an inferior kind of Śālmali tree, MW.

Śālmalin, m. N. of Garuḍa (cf. *śālmali-stha*), L.; (*inī*), f. the silk-cotton tree, L.

Śālmalī, f. = *śālmali* (above); N. of a river in the infernal regions, Mn. iv, 90; of another river, R.; of one of the Śaktis of Vishṇu, MW. **–kanda,** m. the root of the Śālmali tree, ib. **–phala,** m. a partic. fruit-tree, L. **–phalaka,** n. a smooth board of Ś° wood (used to wash clothes upon), Mn. viii, 396. **–veshṭa** or **-veshṭaka,** m. the gum or resin of the Śālmali tree, L.

Śālmalyā. See under *śālmali.*

शाल्यन्न *śāly-anna, śāly-odana.* See *śāly,* col. 1.

शाल्यपति *śālya-pati,* m. N. of a man, Saṃskārak.

शाल्व *śālva,* m. pl. (also written *sālva;* cf. *śalva*) N. of a people, GopBr.; MBh. &c. (mfn. 'relating to the Śālvas,' g. *kacchâdi*); sg. a king of the Śālvas (mentioned among the enemies of Vishṇu; cf. *śālvâri* below), MBh.; Hariv.; BhP.; (*ā*), f. (prob.) N. of a river, g. *nady-ādi;* n. the fruit of the Śālva plant, Pāṇ. iv, 3, 166, Vārtt. 2, Pat. (v.l.) **–nagara,** n. the city of the Śālvas, Hariv. **–pati, -rāja** or **-rājan,** m. a king of the Śālvas, MBh. **–seni,** m. pl. N. of a people, MBh. **Śālvā-giri,** m. N. of a mountain, g. *kiṃśulakâdi.* **Śālvâri,** m. 'enemy of Śālva,' N. of Vishṇu, L.

Śālvaka, mf(*ikā*)n. relating or belonging to or ruling over the Śālvas, MBh.; (*°kī*), f., g. *gaurâdi.*

Śālvakinī, f. N. of a river, R.

Śālvaṇa, n. a poultice, cataplasm, Suśr.

Śālvāyana, mfn. = *śālvaka,* MBh.

Śālvika, m. (also written *sāl°*) a kind of bird, L.

Śālveya, m. pl. (also written *sāl°*) N. of a people, MBh.; sg. one who belongs to or reigns over the Śālveyas, Pāṇ. iv, 1, 169.

Śālveyaka, m. pl. N. of a people, MBh.

शाव 1. *śāva,* m. (prob. fr. √1. *śū* for √*śvi;* cf. *śiśu*) the young of any animal (cf. *mṛiga-śāva*), MBh.; Kāv. &c. **–tva,** n. (*dvi-tri-catuḥ-ś°,* 'the having two, three, or four young'), VarBṛS.

Śāvaka, m. the young of any animal, Kāv. (rarely applied to human beings, e.g. in *muni-ś°,* a young Brāhman), VarBṛS.; Hit. &c.

शाव 2. *śāva,* mfn. (fr. *śava*) cadaverous, relating to a dead body, produced by or belonging to a corpse, Gaut.; Mn.; MBh. &c.; dead, Hariv.; of a cadaverous or dark yellowish colour, tawny, W.; n. defilement caused by contact with a corpse or the death of a relation, MārkP. **Śāvâśauca,** n. = 2. *śāva,* n., W.

शाव 3. *śāva,* w. r. for *śyāva.*

शावर *śāvara* &c. See *śābara,* p. 1065.

शावसायन *śāvasāyana,* m. patr. fr. *śavas,* L.

शावस्त *śāvasta, °sti, °stī.* See *śābasta.*

शाविरी *śāvirī,* f. (in music) a partic. Rāga, Saṃgīt.

शाश *śāśa,* mfn. (fr. *śaśa*) belonging to or coming from a hare, Yājñ.; Car.

Śāśaka, mfn. id., Hariv.

Śāśakarṇi, m. (also written *śāsak°*) patr. fr. *śaśa-karṇa,* Saṃskārak.

Śāśabindu, mf(*ī*)n. descended from Śaśa-bindu, MBh.

Śāśādanaka, mfn. (fr. *śaśâdana*), g. *dhūmâdi.*

Śāśika, m. pl. N. of a people, MBh. (B. *śaśika*).

शाशदान *śāśadāna.* See √1. *śad,* p. 1051.

शाश्वत *śāśvatá,* mf(*ī*)n. (fr. *śaśvat*) eternal, constant, perpetual, all (*śāśvatībhyaḥ sámābhyaḥ, śāśvatīḥ samāḥ,* or *śāśvatam,* for evermore, incessantly, eternally), VS. &c. &c.; about to happen, future, MW.; m. N. of Śiva, L.; of Vyāsa, L.; of a son of Śruta (and father of Su-dhanvan), VP.; of a poet and various other writers (esp. of a lexicographer, author of the Anekârtha-samuccaya); (*ī*), f. the earth, L.; n. continuity, eternity, MBh.; heaven, ether, W. **–tva,** n. constancy, eternity, MBh. **–mandira,** mfn. having a fixed dwelling or abode, VarBṛS. **Śāśvatânanda** and **Śāśvatêndra** (with *saras-vatī*), m. N. of two authors, Cat.

Śāśvatika, mfn. = *śāśvata,* eternal, constant, permanent, Nir.; Āpast.; Kād. **–tā,** f. the being eternal, eternity, Harav.

शाषसान *śāshasāna,* m. N. of a physician, Cat.

शाष्कुल *śāshkula,* mfn. (cf. *śushkala* and *śaushkala*) eating flesh or fish, L.

शाष्कुलिक *śāshkulika,* mfn. (fr. *śashkulī*), Pāṇ. v, 3, 108; iv, 3, 96, Sch.; n. a quantity of baked cakes or pastry, L.

शाष्पक *śāshpaka,* mfn. (fr. *śashpa*), g. *dhūmâdi.*

Śāshpeya, m. N. of a teacher, g. *śaunakâdi.*

Śāshpeyin, m. pl. the school of Śāshpeya, ib.

शास् 1. *śās* (cf. √*śaṇs*), cl. 2. P. (Dhātup. xxiv, 67) *śāsti* (Ved. and ep. also *śāste* and *śāsati, °te;* du. *śishṭhaḥ* &c., Pāṇ. vi, 4, 34; 3. pl. *śāsati,* ib. vi, 1, 6; impf. *aśāt,* Br. &c.; Impv. *śādhi, śāstána,* RV.; Pot. *śishyāt,* Up.; GṛŚrS.; pf. *śaśāsa, °suḥ* [in RV. also Impv. *śaśādhi* and Subj. *śaśās*], RV. &c. &c.; aor. *aśishat* [in RV. also 1. pl. *śishāmahi* and p. *śishát*], ib.; fut. *śāsitā,* Gr.; *śāsishyati, °te,* Br. &c.; inf. *śāstum,* GṛŚrS.; *śāsitum,* MBh. &c.; ind. p. *śāsitvā* or *śishṭvā,* ib.; *-śishya,* Br.; Up.; *-śāsya,* MBh. &c.), to chastise, correct, censure, punish, RV. &c. &c.; to restrain, control, rule, govern (also with *rājyam* or *aiśvaryam*), MBh.; Kāv. &c.; to administer the laws (with *dharmam,* 'to adm° justice'), MBh.; to direct, bid, order, command, enjoin, decree (with an inf. or a sentence followed by *iti*), ib.; to teach, instruct, inform (with two acc., or with acc. of pers. and dat. or loc. of thing), RV. &c. &c.; to confess (a crime), Mn. xi, 82; to announce, proclaim, Bhaṭṭ.; to predict, foretell, VarBṛS.; to blame, reject, disdain(?), RV. x, 32, 4; to praise, commend (= √*śaṇs*), Hit. iii, 102: Pass. *śāsyate* or *śishyate* (cf. √*śish*), to be chastised or corrected &c., MBh.; Kāv. &c.: Caus. *śāsayati* (aor. *aśaśāsat,* Pāṇ. vii, 4, 2), to recommend, Bālar. v, 33: Desid. *śiśāsishati,* Gr.: Intens. *śeśishyate, śāśāsti,* ib.

2. **Śás,** f. command; a commander, ruler, RV.

1. **Śása,** m. order, command, RV.; (*śāsá*) a commander, ruler, chastiser, RV.; N. of the hymn x, 152, AitBr.; of its author (having the patr. Bhāradvāja), Anukr.

Śāsaka, m. a chastiser, teacher, instructor, governor, ruler, Śiś. (cf. *mahī-ś°*).

Śásana, mf(*ī*)n. punishing, a punisher, chastiser

(see *pāka-*, *pura-*, *rukmi-*, *smara-ś°*); teaching, instructing, an instructor, BhP.; (*ī*), f. an instructress, RV. i, 31, 11; (*am*), n. (ifc. f. *ā*) punishment, chastisement, correction (*śāsanam* √*kṛi*, to inflict punishment), Baudh.; Mn.; MBh. &c.; government, dominion, rule over (comp.), MBh.; Kāv. &c.; an order, command, edict, enactment, decree, direction (*śāsanam* √*kṛi* [*kāṅksh*, Baudh.] or *śāsane* √*vṛit* or *sthā*, 'to obey orders;' *śāsanāt* with gen., 'by command of;' *śāsanā*, f., Sch. on Śiś. xiv, 36), RV. &c. &c.; a royal edict, grant, charter (usually a grant of land or of partic. privileges, and often inscribed on stone or copper), Yājñ.; Kāv.; Rājat. &c.; a writing, deed, written contract or agreement, W.; any written book or work of authority, scripture (= *śāstra*), ib.; teaching, instruction, discipline, doctrine (also = 'faith,' 'religion'), MBh.; Kām.; Kathās.; a message (see comp.); self-control, W. **-dūshaka**, mfn. disobeying a (royal) command, Mṛicch. **-devatā** or **-devī**, f. (with Jainas) the female messenger of an Arhat, HPariś. **-dhara**, mfn. one who bears a message or order, a messenger, envoy, Kuval. **-pattra**, n. 'edict-plate,' a plate of copper or of stone on which an edict or grant is inscribed, W. **-parāṅmukha**, mf(*ī*)n. disobedient to an order, BhP. **-laṅghana**, n. transgression of an order or command, Rājat. **-vartin**, mfn. obeying the orders of (gen.), Kathās. **-vāhaka**, mfn. = *-dhara*, Kām. **-śilā**, f. an edict (engraved on) stone, Sadukt. **-hara**, mfn. = *-dhara*, L. **-hāraka** (Kām.), **-hārin** (Ragh.), mfn. id. **Śāsanâtivṛitti**, f. the transgression of a command, MW.

Śāsanīya, mfn. to be chastised or corrected, deserving punishment, punishable, MW.; to be governed or directed or instructed, Śak. (v.l.)

Śāsita, mfn. governed, ruled, directed, instructed, MBh.; Kāv. &c.; restrained, controlled, R.; punished, chastised, Hit.

Śāsitavya, mfn. to be taught or prescribed, Pāṇ. iii, 3, 133, Vārtt. 3; to be governed or directed &c., W.

Śāsitṛi, m. a punisher, chastiser, Mn. vii, 17; a governor, commander, ruler over (acc. or comp.), Rājat.; Kathās.; Campak.; a teacher, instructor, Mn.; Ragh.; Sarvad.

Śāsin, mfn. (only ifc.) punishing, chastising, Hariv.; governing, ruling, Ragh.; teaching, instructing, Śiś.

Śā́sus, n. order, command, RV.

1. **Śāsti**, f. correction, punishment, MārkP.; direction, order, command, Prab., Sch.; governing, ruling, W.; a sceptre, ib.

2. **Śāsti**, m. N. of the root *śās*, Śiś. xiv, 66.

Śāstṛi, m. a chastiser, punisher, MBh.; Kāv. &c.; a ruler, commander, TS. &c. &c.; a teacher, instructor, Āpast.; MBh.; Hariv. &c. (also applied to Punishment and to the Sword personified); N. of Buddha, Rājat. (accord. to L. also 'a Jina or the deified teacher of either of these sects'); a father, MW. **-tva**, n. the state of being a ruler, ruling, governing, BhP.

Śāstṛika, mfn. coming from a teacher, Pāṇ. iv, 2, 104, Vārtt. 15, Pat.

Śāstrá, n. an order, command, precept, rule, RV.; Kāv.; Pur.; teaching, instruction, direction, advice, good counsel, MBh.; Kāv. &c.; any instrument of teaching, any manual or compendium of rules, any book or treatise, (esp.) any religious or scientific treatise, any sacred book or composition of divine authority (applicable even to the Veda, and said to be of fourteen or even eighteen kinds [see under *vidyā*]; the word *śāstra* is often found ifc. after the word denoting the subject of the book, or is applied collectively to whole departments of knowledge, e.g. *Vedânta-ś°*, a work on the Vedânta philosophy or the whole body of teaching on that subject; *dharma-ś°*, a law-book or whole body of written laws; *kāvya-ś°*, a poetical work or poetry in general; *śilpi-ś°*, works on the mechanical arts; *kāma-ś°*, erotic compositions; *alaṃkāra ś°*, rhetoric, &c.), Nir.; Prāt.; Mn.; MBh. &c.; a body of teaching (in general), scripture, science, Kāv.; Pur. **-kāra**, m. the author of a Śāstra, VarBṛS. **-kṛit**, m. id., BhP.; Vedântas.; a writer or author (in general), W.: a Ṛishi (as the author of sacred works), ib. **-kovida**, mfn. skilled in sacred works, MW. **-gañja**, m. N. of a parrot, Kathās. **-gaṇḍa**, m. = *praghaṭā-vid*, a superficial reader of books or a general reader (?), L. **-cakshus**, n. 'eye of science,' grammar, L.; mfn. having authoritative works as eyes, MBh.; Kām.; Car. **-cāraṇa**, mfn. = *-darśin*, L. **-cintaka**, m. a learned man, MBh. **-caura**, m. one who unlawfully promulgates another's system of teaching (as if it were his own), MārkP. **-jaladhi-ratna**, n. N. of wk. **-jña**, mfn. (or m.) acquainted with the Ś°s, learned, a specialist (*kevala-ś°*, 'a mere theorist'), VarBṛS.; Suśr.; Pañcat. &c.; a mere theorist, MW.; *-tā*, f. or *-tva*, n. acquaintance with the Ś°s, W. **-jñāna**, n. knowledge of the Ś°s, kn° derived from the study of the Ś°s, W. **-tattva**, n. the truth (taught) in the Ś°s, W.; *-jña*, mfn. knowing thoroughly a Ś°, understanding the truth of the Śāstras, L.; m. an astrologer, L. **-tas**, ind. accord. to the Ś°s or accord. to prescribed rules, Mn.; MBh.; R.; Suśr. **-tva**, n. the being a rule &c., Sarvad. **-darpaṇa**, m. N. of various wks. **-darśana**, n. mention in a Ś° or in any sacred or authoritative work; (*āt*), ind. = *śāstra-tas*, MBh. **-darśin**, mfn. = *-jña*, L. **-dasyu**, m. = *-caura*, MBh. **-dīpa**, m., **-dīpârtha-sāra**, m. N. of wks. **-dīpikā**, f. N. of two Comms. on the Mīmāṅsā-sūtra (by Pārtha-sārathi-miśra and Prabhā-kara); **-kroḍa**, m., **-ṭīkā**, f., **-prakāśa**, m., **-prabhā**, f., **-praveśa**, m., **-loka**, m., **-vyākhyā**, f. N. of wks. **-dṛishṭa**, mfn. 'seen in the Ś°s,' mentioned or prescribed in the Ś°s, according to precept or rule, scientific, Mn.; Kāv. &c. **-dṛishṭi**, f. scriptural point of view, A.; mfn. = *-cakshus*, MBh.; m. an astrologer, MārkP. (cf. *-tattva-jña*). **-nindā**, f. reviling or denying the authority of the Ś°s, W. **-netra**, mfn. = *-cakshus*, Śivag. **-pāṇin**, w.r. for *śastra-p°*, Hit. **-pūjana-prakaraṇa**, n., **-prakāśikā**, f. N. of wks. **-prasaṅga**, m. the subject of the Ś°s, W.; discussion of sacred works, W. **-buddhi**, f. learning (derived) from the Ś°s, R. **-mati**, mfn. having a well-informed mind, learned in the Ś°s, Kām. **-mālā**, f., **-mālā-vṛitti**, f. N. of wks. **-yoni**, m. the source of the Ś°s (*-tva*, n.), MW. **-vaktṛi**, m. an expounder of sacred books, ib. **-1. -vat**, ind. = *-tas*, MBh.; Hit. (v.l.) **-2. -vat**, mfn. having or following sacred books or precepts, skilled in sacred writings, W. **-varjita**, mfn. free from all rule or law, Kāv. **-vāda**, m. a precept or statement or maxim of the Ś°s, R. **-vādin**, m. a teacher of the Ś°s, Kāv. **-vid**, mfn. = *-jña*, Mn.; Gaut.; VarBṛ.; one who has studied the Āyur-veda, L. **-vidhāna**, n. a precept of the Ś°s, W.; °*nôkta*, mfn. prescribed by sacred precept, MW. **-vidhi**, m. = *-vidhāna*, W. **-vipratishiddha**, mfn. forbidden by or contrary to the Ś°s, W. **-vipratishedha**, m. opposition to the Ś°s, any act contrary to sacred precept, ib. **-vimukha**, mfn. disinclined to learning, averse from study, Bhartṛ. **-viruddha**, mfn. opposed or contrary to the Ś°s, W. **-virodha**, m. opposition to sacred precept, ib.; mutual contradiction of books, incompatibility of different works, ib. **-vyutpatti**, f. perfect conversancy with the Ś°s, MW. **-śilpin**, m. the country of Kaśmīra, ib.; pl. the people of K°, L. **-saṃgraha**, m., **-sāra**, m., **-sārâvali**, f., **-sārôddhāra**, m. N. of wks. **-siddha**, mfn. established by the Ś°, W.; °*dhânta-leśa-saṃgraha*, m., °*dhânta-leśa-saṃgraha-sāra*, m. N. of wks. **Śāstrâcaraṇa**, n. observance of sacred precepts, A.; the study of the Ś°s, MW.; m. one versed in the Ś°s, a Paṇḍit, W.; a student of the Vedas or one whose conduct is regulated by their precepts, ib. **Śāstrâtikrama**, m. transgressing the Ś°s, violation of sacred precepts, ib. **Śāstrâtiga**, mfn. offending against the Ś°s, Baudh. **Śāstrâdhyāpaka**, m. a teacher of the Śāstras, L. **Śāstrânanushṭhāna**, n. disregard of the Ś°s, Hit. **Śāstrânushṭhāna**, n. observance of the Ś°s, W.; applying one's self to books, MW. **Śāstrânushṭhita**, mfn. established by the Ś°s, obeying sacred precepts, W. **Śāstrânusāra**, m. conformity to the Ś°s, ib. **Śāstrânvita**, mfn. conformable to doctrine or rule, L. **Śāstrâbhijña**, mfn. versed in the Ś°s, Hit. **Śāstrârambha-vādârtha**, m., °*rambha-samarthana*, n. N. of wks. **Śāstrârtha**, m. the object or purport of a book, a precept of the Ś°s or of any partic. Ś°, MW. **Śāstrâvarta-lipi**, f. a partic. mode of writing, Lalit. **Śāstrôkta**, mfn. declared or enjoined by the Ś°s, W. **Śāstrôpadeśa-krama**, m. N. of wk. **Śāstrâugha**, m. a treatise of great extent, IndSt.

Śāstrika, mfn. versed in the Śāstras, ŚivaP.

Śāstrita, mfn. (fr. *śāstra*), g. *tārakâdi*; treated according to the Śāstras, MW. **Śāstritârtha**, m. a scientifically treated subject, ib.

Śāstrin, mfn. or m. versed in the Śāstras, learned (cf. *satata-ś°*), Cat.; m. a teacher of sacred books or science, a learned man, W.; a Buddha, Śiś., Sch.

Śāstrīya, mfn. taught in or agreeable to the Śāstras, belonging to the Ś°s, conformable to sacred precepts, legal, Sāh.; Saṃk. &c. **-tva**, n. the fact of being prescribed in the Śāstras, Mn., Sch.

Śā́sya, mfn. to be punished, punishable, Mn.; Gaut.; Bālar.; to be controlled or governed, MBh.; to be directed, RV.; to be corrected, MW.; w. r. for *sasya*, MBh. xii, 2691.

Śishṭa, śishya &c. See 1. *śishṭá*, p. 1076, col. 3, and p. 1077, col. 1.

शास् 3. *śās*, strong form of √1. *śas*.

2. **Śāsá**, m. (for 1. see p. 1068, col. 3) a butcher's knife, Br.; ŚrS. **-hasta**, mfn. holding a butcher's knife in the hand, AitBr.

शास् 4. *śās*, strong form for 3. *śas* (see *uktha-śás*).

शाह *śāha*, m. = شاه (see *nema-*, *phatiha-*, *bhūmi-ś°*); N. of a country belonging to Kaśmīra, Rājat. **-jī**, m. N. of a king of Tanjore (1684–1711; he is the supposed author of various wks), Cat. **Śāhêśa**, m. the lord of Śāha, ib.

Śāhi, m. N. of a dynasty, Rājat. **-makaranda**, m. N. of a king and author, Cat.

शाहेव *śāheva*, m. (prob.) = صاحب, Rājat.

शाह्नाम *śāhnāma* = شاه نامه, Cat.

शि 1. *śi* (accord. to some = √*śo*), cl. 3. P. *śiśāti* (Impv. *śiśīhi*, *śādhi*), to grant, bestow, RV. (cf. Nir. v, 23); to present or satisfy with (instr.), ib.; cl. 5. P. Ā. (Dhātup. xxvii, 3) *śinoti*, *śinute* (p. *śishāya*, *śiśye*; aor. *aśaishīt*, *aśeshṭa*, fut. *śeshyati*, °*te*), to sharpen.

1. **Śitá**, mfn. (for 2. see p. 1071, col. 2) satisfied, regaled, RV. viii, 23, 13.

शि 2. *śi*, m. N. of Śiva, W.; auspiciousness, good fortune, ib.; peace, composure, calm, ib.

शि 3. *śi*, (in gram.) a technical term for the case-ending *i* (substituted for *jas* and *śas* in neuters).

शिंश *śiṅśa*, m. a kind of fruit-tree, MBh.

शिंशपा *śiṅśápā*, f. (rarely and m. c. *śiṅśapa*, m.) the tree Dalbergia Sissoo, AV. &c. &c.; the Aśoka tree, W. **-sthala**, see *śāṅśapāsthala*.

Śiṅśapāyana, v.l. for *vaiśampāyana*, VP.

Śiṅśipā, w.r. for *śiṅśapā*.

शिंशुमार *śiṅśumāra*, m. a porpoise, Delphinus Gangeticus (= *śiśu-māra*, q.v.), RV.; TS. (= *grāha*, Sāy.) **-śānti**, f., **-stava**, m. N. of wks.

शिंह् *śiṅh* = √*śiṅgh* (cf. *uc-chiṅhana* and *upa-śiṅhana*).

Śiṅhāṇa, °*ṇaka*. See *śiṅghāṇa* &c.

शिकम् *śikam*, ind., g. *cādi*.

शिक्कु *śikku*, mfn. idle, lazy, following no business or profession, L.

शिक्थ *śiktha*, °*thaka*. See *siktha*.

शिक्मन् *śikman*. See *sú-śikman*.

शिक्य *śikyà*, n. (L. also *ā*, f.) a kind of loop or swing made of rope and suspended from either end of a pole or yoke to receive a load, carrying swing (also applied to the load so carried), AV. &c. &c.; the string of a balance, W.; = *vajra-vikāra* (?), Vop. **-pāśá**, m. the string by which a vessel is suspended, ŚBr. **-vat**, mfn. provided with a carrying sling, KātyŚr. **Śikyá-kṛita** (?), mfn. suspended by strings, AV. xiii, 4, 8. **Śikyâdhāra**, m. 'loop-holder,' the hook or eye at each end of a pole or beam which bears the above looped cord for holding the strings of a balance, W. **Śikyôduta**, mfn. suspended in a swing or loop, ŚBr.

Śikyaka, (prob.) n. = *śikya*, a loop or swing (see next). **-vastra**, n. a balance made of cloth and suspended by strings, VarBṛS.

Śikyita, mfn. suspended in a swing or loop made of cord &c., L.

शिक्व *śikvá*, mfn. (fr. √*śak*) skilful, clever, artistic, AV.

Śikvan, mfn. id., RV.; TS. (accord. to Sāy. = *rajju* and *tejas*).

Śikvas, mfn. mighty, powerful, able, RV.

शिक्ष् *śiksh* (properly Desid. of √*śak*; cf. Pāṇ. vii, 4, 54), cl. 1. P. Ā. *śikshati*, °*te* (in later language oftener Ā.; cf. Dhātup. xvi, 4; pr. p. *śikshat*, *śikshamāṇa*, RV.; *śikshāṇa*, MBh.; Impv. *śiśiksha*, Nir.; aor. *aśikshishṭa*, Bhaṭṭ.), 'to wish to be able,' (P.) try to effect, attempt, undertake, TS.; AV.; (Ā.; rarely P.) to learn, acquire knowledge, study, practise, learn from (abl. or *sakāśāt* with gen.), RV. &c. &c.; to practise one's self in (loc.), Kathās. (cf. Pāṇ. i, 3, 21, Vārtt. 3, Sch.); 'to wish to be able to effect for others,' (P.) wish to help, aid, befriend (dat.), RV.; (P.) to wish to give, bestow, ib.; (P.) to wish to present with (instr.), Nir.; ŚāṅkhBr.; (Ā.) to offer one's service to, enter the service of (acc.), MBh.: Pass. *śikshyate* (aor. *aśikshi*), to be learnt or practised, Kād.; Kathās.: Caus. *śikshayati* (rarely °*te*; aor. *aśiśikshat*), to cause to learn, impart knowledge, inform, instruct, teach (with acc. of pers. or thing; also with two acc., or with acc. of pers. and loc. of thing, or with acc. of pers. and inf., or with acc. of thing and gen. of pers.), Mn.; MBh. &c.

Śiksha, m. N. of a king of the Gandharvas, R.; (*ā*), f., see below.

Śikshaka, mfn. teaching, instructing, Śiś., Sch. (m. a teacher, Mālav.; a trainer, see *hasti-ś*°; a learner, W.); one who knows Śikshā (q. v.), g. *kramâdi*.

Śikshaṇa, n. the act of learning, acquiring knowledge, W.; teaching, instruction in (loc. or comp.), Kām.; BhP.

Śikshaṇīya, mfn. to be taught (with acc.), Kāv.; Kathās.; to be learnt, W.

Śikshayitṛi, m. an instructor, teacher, MW.

Śikshā, f. desire of being able to effect anything, wish to accomplish, Kir. xv, 37; learning, study, knowledge, art, skill in (loc. or comp.; *śikshayā* or °*kshābhis*, 'skilfully, artistically, correctly'), MBh.; Kāv. &c.; teaching, training (held by Buddhists to be of three kinds, viz. *adhicitta-śikshā*, training in the higher thought; *adhiśīla-ś*°, tr° in the higher morality; *adhiprajñā-ś*°, tr° in the higher learning, Dharmas. 140), instruction, lesson, precept, ŚāṅkhBr.; TUp. &c.; chastisement, punishment, Nyāyam., Sch.; the science which teaches proper articulation and pronunciation of Vedic texts (one of the six Vedâṅgas, q. v.), Prāt.; MuṇḍUp. &c.; modesty, humility, diffidence, W.; (?) helping, bestowing, imparting (see *śikshā-nará*); the plant Bignonia Indica, L. **–kara**, m. 'instruction-causing,' a teacher, W.; N. of Vyāsa, L.; *-gupta*, m. (prob.) N. of a Sch. on the Hariprabodha, Cat. **–kāra**, m. a singer capable of teaching others, Saṃgīt.; the author of a Śikshā, TPrāt., Sch. **–°kshara** (*śikshâksh*°), n. a sound pronounced according to the rules of Ś°, R.; mfn. correctly pronounced, MBh. **–guru**, m. a religious preceptor, MW. **–°cāra** (*śikshâc*°), mfn. conducting one's self according to precept, Rājat. **–daṇḍa**, m. punishment (serving for) a lesson, ib. **–daśaka**, n. N. of a wk. on Bhakti. **–nará**, mfn. helping men or liberal towards men, RV. (= *dānasya netā*, Sāy.) **–nīti**, f., **-pañcaka**, n., **-pattra**, n. or **-pattrī**, f. N. of wks. **–pada**, n. moral precept, Buddh.; *-prajñapti*, f. N. of a part of the Vinaya (q. v.), ib. **–prakāśa**, m., **-bodha**, m. N. of wks. **–rasa**, m. desire of acquiring skill in (loc.), Viddh. **–vat**, mfn. possessed of knowledge, learned, Hariv.; full of instruction, instructive (as a tale), Kathās. **–vallī**, f. N. of the 1st ch. of the Taittirīya Upanishad. **–vidhi**, m. N. of wk. **–śakti**, f. 'power of learning,' dexterity, skill, W. **–saṃvara**, m. the moral life of a monk, Kāraṇḍ. **–samuccaya**, m., **-sūtra**, n. pl. N. of wks. **–svara**, m. = *śikshâkshara*, n., R.

Śikshāṇa. See under √*śiksh*.

Śikshita, mfn. learnt, studied, practised, Baudh.; Kāv. &c.; taught, instructed or trained or exercised in (acc., loc., or comp.), MBh.; Kāv. &c.; docile, W.; skilful, clever, conversant, ib.; modest, diffident, ib.; (*ā*), f. N. of a woman (see *śaikshita*); n. teaching, instruction, BhP. **Śikshitâkshara**, mfn. one who has been taught letters or literature, Rājat.; m. a pupil, scholar, L. **Śikshitâyudha**, mfn. skilled in weapons, L.

Śikshitavya, mfn. to be learnt from (abl.), ĀśvŚr., Sch.; to be instructed or taught, W.

Śikshitu-kāma, mfn. (*śikshitu* for inf. °*tum*) one who is willing to learn, a beginner in his art, Mṛicch.

Śikshin, mfn. learning; instructing, MW.

Śikshú, mfn. helpful, liberal, RV.

Śikshuka, mfn. one who studies Śikshā, MāṇḍŚ.

Śiksheṇya, mfn. instructive, Vait.

Śikshya, mfn. to be learnt or taught, W.

शिख *śikha*, m. N. of a serpent-demon (mentioned together with *anu-śikha*, q. v.), Pañcav-Br.; (*ā*), f., see below; (*ī*), f. a kind of magic, Divyâv.; N. of a river, VP.

शिखक *śikhaka*, m. = *lekhaka*, a writer, scribe, L.

शिखण्ड *śikhaṇḍá*, m. (cf. *śikhā*) a tuft or lock of hair left on the crown or sides of the head at tonsure, TS.; ŚBr.; Daś.; any crest or plume or tuft, MW.; a peacock's tail, Vikr.; a kind of plant, L.; (*ī*), f., see below. **Śikhaṇḍâsthá**, n. du. N. of partic. bones, ŚBr. (cf. next).

Śikhaṇḍaka, m. a tuft or lock of hair (= *śikhaṇḍa*), Kālid.; three or five locks left on the side of the head (esp. in men of the military class, = *kākapaksha*, q. v.), W.; a curl or ringlet, MW.; a peacock's tail, Git.; du. (accord. to Sch. n.) the fleshy parts of the body below the buttocks, TS.; (with mystic Śaivas) one who attains a partic. degree of emancipation, Hcat.

Śikhaṇḍi, in comp. for °*ṇḍin*. **–ketu**, m. 'having a peacock for an emblem,' N. of Skanda, Bālar. **–mat**, mfn. rich in peacocks, Kum.

Śikhaṇḍika, m. a cock, L.; (prob.) one who attains a partic. stage of emancipation, Hcat.; (*ā*), f. a tuft or lock of hair on the crown of the head, W.; (prob.) n. a kind of ruby, L.

Śikhaṇḍita, n. N. of a metre, Kad.

Śikhaṇḍin, mfn. wearing a tuft or lock of hair, tufted, crested (applied to various gods), AV.; MBh.; R.; m. a peacock, Kāv.; Pur.; Kathās.; a peacock's tail, L.; a cock, L.; an arrow, L.; one who attains a partic. degree of emancipation, Hcat.; N. of Vishṇu-Kṛishṇa, MBh.; of a Ṛishi or Muni (one of the seven stars of the Great Bear; cf. *citra-ś*°), W.; of a son of Drupada (born as a female [see *śikhaṇḍinī*], but changed into a male by a Yaksha; in the great war between Kauravas and Pāṇḍavas he became instrumental in the killing of Bhīshma who declined to fight with a woman, but he was afterwards killed himself by Aśvatthāman; in the ŚāṅkhBr. he has the patr. Yājñasena), MBh.; of a Brāhman, Lalit.; of a mountain, Cat.; (*inī*), f. a pea-hen, MBh.; the shrub Abrus Precatorius, L.; N. of a daughter of Drupada (afterwards changed to a male; see above), MBh.; of the wife of Antardhāna, Hariv.; Pur.; of two Apsaras (daughters of Kaśyapa and regarded as the authoresses of RV. ix, 104), Anukr.

Śikhaṇḍī, f. (of *śikhaṇḍa*, g. *gaurâdi*) a lock on the crown of the head, L.; Abrus Precatorius, L.; yellow jasmine, L. **–vedânta-sāra** (?), m. N. of wk.

Śikhāṇḍaka, m. = *śikhaṇḍaka*, a tuft or lock of hair, L.

शिखर *śikhara* &c. See col. 3.

शिखलोहित *śikha-lohita*, m. (perhaps for *śikhā-l*°, 'red as a flame') N. of a plant (commonly called *kukura-muḍā*), W.

शिखा *śíkhā*, f. (of doubtful derivation; prob. connected with √1. *śi*, 'to sharpen') a tuft or lock of hair on the crown of the head, a crest, top-knot, plume, ŚBr. &c. &c.; a peacock's crest or comb, MBh.; Hariv. &c.; a pointed flame, any flame, ib.; a ray of light, Kum.; Kathās.; a sharp end, point, spike, peak, summit, pinnacle, projection, end or point (in general), MaitrUp.; Kāv.; VarBṛS.; the end or point or border of a garment, Śak.; the point or tip of the foot, L.; the nipple, L.; a branch which takes root, any branch, L.; a fibrous root, any root, L.; the plant Jussiæa Repens, L.; the head or chief or best of a class, L.; the fever or excitement of love, L.; a partic. part of a verse or formula (the crest of the verse compared to a king), RāmatUp.; = *śikhā-vṛiddhi*, Gaut.; N. of various metres, Col.; of a river (prob. w. r. for *śikhī*), VP. **–kanda**, n. a kind of onion or garlic, L. **–°gra-dat** or **-°gra-danta** (*śikhâg*°), mfn., Pāṇ. v, 4, 145, Sch. **–cala**, w. r. for *-vala*, L. **–jaṭa**, mfn. having a single lock of hair on the top of the head (the rest being shaved off), Gaut.; Āpast.; Mn.; (cf. *-muṇḍa*). **–taru**, m. 'flame-support,' a lamp-stand, L. **–dāman**, n. a wreath worn on the top of the head, Megh. (Sch.) **–dhara**, mfn. having a sharp end or point, having a top-knot, W.; m. a peacock, Kir.; N. of a Mañjuśri, L.; *-ja*, 'peacock-produced,' a peacock's feather, MW. **–dhāra**, m. 'crest-wearer,' a peacock, L. **–pati**, m. N. of a man, Saṃskārak. **–pāśa**, m. a tuft of hair, Bhar. **–pitta**, n. inflammation in the extremities (as in fingers or toes), L. **–bandha**, m. a tuft of hair, L. **–bandhana**, n. the binding together of locks of hair, Cat. **–°bharaṇa** (*śikhâbh*°), n. a crest-ornament, diadem, Vikr. **–maṇi**, m. a crest-jewel, jewel worn on the head, Kāv.; Kathās.; (ifc.) the head or chief or best of a class, BhP.; Rājat. **–mārjita**, mfn. one who has his top locks combed and cleansed, Śak. **–muṇḍa**, mfn. one who has only one lock on the crown of his head left unshaven, Baudh. (cf. *-jaṭa*). **–mūla**, n. any root which has a tuft of leaves, W.; = *-kanda*, L. (v. l. *śikhi-m*°); a carrot, W.; a turnip, W. **–lambin**, mfn. hanging down from the top of the head, Kāvyâd. **–1. -vat**, ind. like a crest, MW. **–2. -vat**, mfn. flaming, burning, Śiś.; pointed, Kull. on Mn. i, 38; m. fire, Kir.; a lamp, W.; a comet or the descending node, L.; a partic. plant or tree (= *citraka*), MW.; N. of a man, MBh.; (*atī*), f. Sanseviera Roxburghiana, L.; another plant, cock's comb, MW. **–vara**, m. the jack fruit tree, L. **–°varta** (*śikhâv*°), m. N. of a Yaksha, MBh. **–vala**, mfn. pointed, crested, W.; m. a peacock, Kāvyâd.; (*ā*), f. Celosia Cristata, W. **–vṛiksha**, m. = *-taru*, L. **–vriddhi**, f. 'high-interest,' a kind of usurious interest increasing daily, Bṛihasp. **–sūtra**, n. the lock of hair on the crown of the head and the sacred thread (regarded as distinguishing marks of a Brāhman), MW. **Śikhôpanishad**, f. N. of an Upanishad.

Śikhara, mfn. pointed, spiked, crested, Megh.; Kathās.; m. n. a point, peak (of a mountain), top or summit (of a tree), edge or point (of a sword), end, pinnacle, turret, spire, MBh.; Kāv. &c.; erection of the hair of the body, L.; the arm-pit, L.; a ruby-like gem (of a bright red colour said to resemble ripe pomegranate seed), L.; (?) the bud of the Arabian jasmine (cf. *-daśanā*); N. of a mythical weapon (*astra*), R.; m. a partic. position of the fingers of the hand, Cat.; N. of a man, Kathās.; (*ā*), f. Sanseviera Roxburghiana (a plant from the fibres of which bow-strings are made), L.; N. of a partic. mythical club (*gadā*), R.; (*ī*), f. id., R. (B.); = *karkaṭa-śṛiṅgī*, L.; n. cloves, L. **–datī**, f. having pointed teeth, Vām. (in a quotation). **–daśanā**, f. id., Megh. (Sch. 'having teeth resembling the buds of the Arabian jasmine'). **–nicaya**, m. a collection of mountain-peaks, MW. **–vāsinī**, f. 'dwelling on a peak (of the Himālaya),' N. of Durgā, L. **–sena**, m. N. of a man, Mudr. **Śikharâdri**, m. N. of a mountain, MārkP. **Śikharêśa-liṅga**, n. N. of a Liṅga on the Kailāsa mountain, Cat.

Śikhari, in comp. for °*rin*. **–pattrin**, m. a winged or flying mountain, Bhartṛ. **–sama**, mfn. mountain-like, MW. **Śikharîndra**, m. the chief of mountains (applied to Raivataka, Sch.), Śiś. vi, 73.

Śikharin, mfn. pointed, peaked, crested, tufted, MBh.; R. &c.; resembling the buds of the Arabian jasmine, MW.; m. a peaked mountain, any mountain, MBh.; Kāv. &c.; N. of a mountain, Śatr., Sch.; a hill-post, stronghold, L.; a tree, L.; Achyranthes Aspera, L.; Andropogon Bicolor, L.; a partic. parasitical plant, L.; the resin of Boswellia Thurifera, L.; Parra Jacana or Goensis, L.; a kind of antelope, L.; (*iṇī*), f. an eminent or excellent woman, L.; a dish of curds and sugar with spices, Bhpr.; a line of hair extending across the navel, L.; a kind of vine or grape, L.; Jasminum Sambac, L.; Sanseviera Roxburghiana, L.; Arabian jasmine, L.; a kind of Atyashṭi metre (four times ◡–––––, ◡◡◡◡◡––◡◡◡–), Gīt.; Śrutab.; Chandom.

1. Śikhi, m. (m. c. for *śikhin*) a peacock, Hariv.; N. of Indra under Manu Tāmasa, MārkP.; the god of love, L.

2. **Śikhi,** in comp. for *śikhin.* **–kaṇa,** m. 'fire-particle,' a spark, Harav. **–kaṇṭha** or **-grīva,** n. blue vitriol, L. **–tama,** m. a partic. Gaṇa of Śiva, Harav. **–tā,** f. the state of a peacock, Kathās. **–tīrtha,** n. N. of a Tīrtha, Cat. **–diś,** f. Agni's quarter of the sky, south-east, VarBṛS. **–dyut,** mfn. gleaming like fire, Śiś. **–dhvaja,** m. 'fire-marked,' smoke, L.; 'peacock-marked,' N. of Kārttikeya, L.; n. N. of a Tīrtha, Cat.; *-tīrtha,* n. id., MW. **–piccha** (MBh.) or **-puccha** (L.), n. a peacock's tail. **–priya,** m. a kind of jujube tree, L. **–bhū,** m. N. of Skanda, Harav. **–maṇḍala,** m. Cratæva Roxburghii, L. **–mūla,** see *śikhā-m°.* **–modā,** f. a kind of plant (=*aja-m°*), L. **–yūpa,** m. a kind of antelope (=*śrī-kārin*), L. **–vardhaka,** m. Benincasa Cerifera, L. **–vāsas,** m. N. of a mountain, VP. **–vāhana,** m. 'having a peacock for his vehicle,' N. of Kārttikeya, L. **–vrata,** n. a partic. religious observance, GāruḍaP. **–śikhā,** f. a peacock's crest, W.; 'fire-peak,' a flame, W. **–śṛiṅga,** m. a spotted antelope, L. **–śekhara,** n. a peacock's crest, W.

Śikhîndra, m. ebony, Diospyros Ebenaster, L.

Śikhin, mfn. having a tuft or lock of hair on the top of the head, Gaut.; MBh. &c.; one who has reached the summit of knowledge, BrahmUp.; proud, MW.; m. a peacock, RPrāt.; Yājñ.; MBh. &c.; a cock, L.; Ardea Nivea (a kind of heron or crane), L.; a bull, L.; a horse, L.; 'having flame,' fire or the fire-god, Gṛihyas.; Yājñ.; MBh. &c.; the number 'three' (from the three sacred fires), VarBṛS.; a lamp, L.; a comet, VarBṛS.; N. of Ketu (the personified descending node), VP.; a mountain, L.; a tree, L.; Carpopogon Pruriens, L.; Trigonella Fœnum Græcum, L.; a kind of potherb (=*sitâvara*), L.; an arrow, L.; a Brāhman, L.; a religious mendicant, W.; N. of a serpent-demon, MBh.; of Indra under Manu Tāmasa, Pur.; of the second Buddha, Lalit.; Kāraṇḍ (cf. MWB. 136, n. 1; 516); of a Brahmā (with Buddhists), Lalit.; *(inī),* f. a pea-hen, R.; cock's comb, Celosia Cristata, L.

Śikhina, m. a partic. Gaṇa of Śiva, Harav.

शिखी *śikhī.* See *śikha,* p. 1070, col. 2.

शिग्रु *śigrú,* m. (of unknown derivation) Moringa Pterygosperma (a kind of horse-radish = *śobhâñjana;* the root and leaves and flowers are eaten), Yājñ.; Suśr. &c.; N. of a man, g. *bidâdi;* pl. N. of a people, RV.; n. the seed of the above tree, Kauś.; Car.; any potherb or vegetable, L. **–ja,** n. 'growing on or produced by the M°,' = next, L. **–bīja,** n. the seed of the Moringa tree, L. **–mūla,** n. the pungent root of the Moringa, W.

Śigruka, m. = *śigru,* m., Mn. vi, 14; n. any potherb, L.

शिङ्ख् *śiṅkh,* cl. 1. P. *śiṅkhati,* to go, move, Dhātup. v, 31.

शिङ्खप *śiṅkhapa,* m. N. of a man, Buddh.

शिङ्ग *śiṅga,* m. a tree, L.; = *kiśora,* L.; N. applied to various men. **–dharaṇîśa** or **-dharaṇi-sena,** m. N. of an author, Cat. **–bhaṭṭa,* m. N. of an author, ib.; *°ṭṭīya,* n. his wk. **–bhūpāla,** m. N. of an author (prob. = *-dharaṇîśa*), Pratāp., Sch.; *°līya,* n. his wk. **–rāja,** m. N. of an author (= *-bhūpāla*), Cat.

Śiṅgaya, m. N. of a man, Cat.

शिङ्गि *śíṅgi,* n. or *śiṅgī,* f. (perhaps) a partic. part of the entrails of a sacrificial animal, VS. (cf. next).

शिङ्गिन् *śiṅgin,* n. a beard, L.

शिङ्घ् *śiṅgh* (also written *śiṅh,* prob. for orig. *śiṅkh*), cl. 1. P. *śiṅghati,* to smell, Dhātup. v, 57 (cf. *upa-√śiṅgh*).

Śiṅghaṇa, n. = *śiṅghāṇa,* the mucus of the nose, L.; a beard (cf. *śiṅgin*), L. **–deva,** m. N. of a man (the patron of Śārṅgadeva), Cat.

Śiṅghāṇa, m. (also written *śiṅhāṇa* or *śiṅhāna*) Os Sepiæ, L.; swollen testicles, L.; (also n. and *ā,* f.) the mucus of the nose, L.; n. rust of iron, L.; any glass vessel, L.; a beard, L.

Śiṅghāṇaka, m. n. the mucus of the nose, phlegm, L.; *(ikā),* f. (also written *siṅgh°*) id. (cf. *śṛiṅkhāṇikā*).

Śiṅghāṇin, m. (or *inī,* f.) 'having mucus,' the nose, L.

Śiṅghita, mfn. perceived by the nose, smelled, L.

Śiṅghinī, f. (also written *siṅgh°*) 'smelling,' the nose, L.

शिच् *śic,* f. (nom. *śik*) = *śikya,* the cord or strap of a yoke or pole for carrying burdens, BhP.; a net, ib.

शिञ्ज् *śiñj,* cl. 2. Ā. (Dhātup. xxiv, 17) *śiṅkte* (accord. to Vop. also cl. 1. 10. Ā. *śiñjate, śiñjayate;* pr. p. *śiñjāna* or *śiñjat* [see below], Kāv.; pf. *śiśiñje,* Gr.; aor. *aśiñjishṭa,* ib.; fut. *śiñjitā, śiñjishyate,* ib.), to utter a shrill sound, tinkle, rattle, jingle, whirr, buzz, hum, twang, bellow, roar, RV. &c. &c. [Cf. collateral √*siñj.*)

Śiñjañjikā, f. a chain worn round the loins, W.

Śiñjat, mfn. tinkling, rattling, sounding &c.

Śiñjad, in comp. for *°jat.* **–valaya-subhaga,** mfn. pleasant with tinkling bracelets or zones, Megh. **–shaḍaṅghri,** mfn. full of humming bees, BhP.

Śiñjā, f. (also written *siñjā*) tinkle, jingle, (esp.) the tinkling sound of silver ornaments on the ankles or wrist, Hcar. (accord. to some also *śiñja,* m.); a bow-string, Bālar. **–latā,** f. a bow-string, ib. **–°śvattha** (*śiñjâśv°*), g. *rāja-dantâdi* (Kāś. *siñjâstha*).

Śiñjāna, mfn. tinkling, sounding &c. (= *śiñjat*). **–bhramara,** mfn. = *śiñjat-shaḍaṅghri,* Bhaṭṭ.

Śiñjāra, m. N. of a man, RV.

Śiñjita, mfn. (also written *siñjita*) tinkled, tinkling, rattling, sounding, Hariv.; Kāv.; n. tinkling, rattling, (esp.) the tinkling of metallic ornaments, MBh.; R. &c.

Śiñjin, mfn. tinkling, rattling, sounding, L.; *(inī),* f. a bow-string, MBh. (also written *siñj°*); the sine of an arc, Gol.; tinkling rings worn round the toes or feet, L.

शिट् *śiṭ* (also written *siṭ*), cl. 1. P. *śeṭati,* to despise, Dhātup. ix, 17.

शिटा *śiṭā,* f. a rope(?), Divyâv.

शिण्डाकी *śiṇḍākī,* f. (also written *siṇḍ°*) a partic. edible substance (made with rice and mustard and said to possess stomachic properties), L.

शित् *śit,* (in gram.) having *ś* as an indicatory letter.

शित 2. *śita,* mfn. (for 1. and 4. see under √*śi* and *śo*) w.r. for *sita,* 'bright-coloured, white.'

शित 3. *śita,* m. N. of a son of Viśvāmitra, MBh.

शितद्रु *śita-dru,* f. (cf. *sita-dru*) = *śata-dru,* the river Sutlej, L.

शिताभ्र *śitâbhra,* w.r. for *sitâbhra,* q.v.

शितामन् *śítāman,* n. (of doubtful derivation; cf. *śitiman*) a partic. part of a sacrificial victim (accord. to Yāska 'the under fore-foot,' accord. to others 'the shoulder-blade, the liver &c.;' see Nir. iv, 13), VS.; TBr. (*°ma-tás,* ind.)

शितावर *śitâvara.* See *sitâvara.*

शिति *śiti,* mfn. (perhaps fr. √*śo*) white, L. (cf. *sita*); black, dark-blue, Śiś.; m. the Bhojpattra or birch tree, L.; = *sāra,* L. **–kakud** (*śiti-*), mfn. white-humped, MaitrS. **–kakuda,** mfn. id., L. **–káksha,** mfn. white-shouldered, MaitrS. **–kakshín,** m. a vulture with a white belly (= *pāṇḍarôdaro gṛidhraḥ*), TS. (Sch.) **–káṇṭha,** mfn. white-necked, Kāṭh.; dark-necked (as Rudra-Śiva; cf. *nīla-k°*), VS. &c. &c.; m. a partic. bird of prey, MBh.; a peacock, Śiś.; Bālar.; a gallinule (= *dātyūha*), L.; N. of Śiva, Kāv.; of a serpent-demon, MBh.; (also with *dīkshita* and often confounded with *śrī-kaṇṭha*); of various authors &c., Cat.; *-rāmâyaṇa,* n., *-stotra,* n.; *°ṭhīya,* n., *°ṭhīya-ṭippaṇī,* f. N. of wks. **–kaṇṭhaka,** mfn. blue-necked (as a peacock), Vikr. **–kumbha,** m. the oleander tree, Nerium Odorum, L. **–keśa,** m. 'white-haired,' N. of one of Skanda's attendants, MBh. **–candana,** n. musk, L. **–cāra,** m. a kind of potherb (apparently Marsilea Dentata), L. **–cchada,** m. 'white-feathered,' a goose, L. (cf. *sita-cch°*). **–nas,** mfn. wh°-nosed, Pāṇ. v, 4, 118, Pat. **–paksha,** mf(*ā*)n. wh°-winged, Hariv.; m. a goose, L. (cf. *sita-p°*). **–pád** (strong form *-pād*), mf(*padī*)n. wh°-footed, RV.; AV.; Kauś.; black-footed, MW. **–pāda,** mfn. white-footed, MBh. **–pṛishṭhá,** mf(*ā*)n. wh°-backed (accord. to others 'black-backed'), RV.; VS.; Br.; Hariv.; m. N. of a serpent-priest (fabled to have acted as Maitrā-varuṇa at a sacrifice), MW. **–prabha,** mfn. white-hued, whitish, MBh. **–bāhu** or **-bāhú,** mfn. having wh° fore-feet, MaitrS.; AV.; ŚBr. **–bhasad** (*śiti-*), mfn. having wh° hinder parts, Kāṭh.; TS. **–bhrū,** mfn. wh°-browed, VS.; TS. **–mānsa,** n. 'wh°-flesh,' fat, Nir. **–ratna,** n. 'blue-gem,' a sapphire, Śiś. **–rándhra,** mfn. having white ear-holes, MaitrS. **–lalāṭa,** mfn. having a white forehead, Pāṇ. vi, 2, 138, Sch. **–vara,** m. Marsilea Quadrifolia, Bhpr. **–vāra,** mfn. white-tailed, TS.; m. = *-vara,* L. **–vāla,** mfn. wh°-tailed, ŚBr. **–vāsas,** mfn. wearing a dark garment, BhP. **–sāraka,** m. 'having a dark essence,' Diospyros Embryopteris, L. **Śitikshu,** m. N. of a son of Uśanas, VP. (v.l. *śiteyu, śitêkshu, śineyu*).

Śitiṅgá, mfn. (prob.) whitish, AV.

Śity, in comp. for *śiti.* **–áṅsa,** mfn. white-shouldered, TS. **–óshṭha,** mfn. white-lipped, ib.

शितीमन् *śitīmán* or *°mat* (only du. *°mábhyām* or *°madbhyām*) = *śitāman,* TS., Kāṭh.

शित्पुट *śitpuṭá,* m. (v.l. *śityuṭá,* Sch.) a partic. animal resembling a cat, TS.; a large black bee, L.

शिथिर *śithirá,* mf(*ā*)n. (for *śrithira* fr. √*śrath*) loose, lax, slack, flexible, pliant, soft, RV.; AV.; Br.

Śithilá, mf(*ā*)n. (collateral form of prec.) loose, slack, lax, relaxed, untied, flaccid, not rigid or compact, TS. &c. &c.; soft, pliant, supple, Pañcat.; unsteady, tremulous, MBh.; languid, inert, unenergetic, weak, feeble, MBh.; Kāv. &c.; careless in (loc.), R.; indistinct (as sound), L.; not rigidly observed, W.; loosely retained or possessed, abandoned, shaken off, ib.; *(am),* ind. loosely, not firmly, Ragh.; *(ī),* f. a kind of tawny-coloured ant (said to be a variety of the white ant), L.; *(am),* n. a loose fastening, looseness, laxity, slowness, MW.; a partic. separation of the terms or members of a logical series, ib. **–tā,** f., **-tva,** n. looseness, laxity, relaxation, want of energy or care, indifference, languor (*-tām* √*gam* or *vraj,* 'to undergo indifference,' be neglected), Hariv.; Kāv.; Pañcat. **–pīḍita,** mfn. loosely pressed or compressed (*-tā,* f.), Suśr. **–prayatna,** mfn. one whose efforts are relaxed, MW. **–bala,** mfn. relaxed in strength, weakened, relaxed, ib. **–m-bhāva,** see *á-ś°.* **–vasu,** mfn. having diminished wealth, MW.; shining with diminished rays, ib. **–śakti,** mfn. impaired in strength or power, ib. **–samādhi,** mfn. having the attention drawn off or relaxed, Mālav.

Śithilaya, Nom. P. *°yati,* to loosen, make loose, relax, Śak.; Ā. *°yate,* to neglect, let pass, ib. (v.l.)

Śithilāya, Nom. Ā. *°yate,* to become relaxed, Bhartṛ.

Śithilita, mfn. loosed, loosened, slackened, relaxed, dissolved, made soft, Kāv. **–jya,** mfn. (a bow) whose string has been relaxed, Kathās. **–mṛiṇāla,** mfn. (an armlet formed) of lotus-fibres hanging loose, Śak.

Śithilī, in comp. for *śithila.* **–karaṇa,** n. the act of loosening, relaxing, impairing, weakening, Sarvad. **–√kṛi,** P. Ā. *-karoti, -kurute,* to make loose, loosen, relax, slacken, weaken, impair, remit, abandon, MBh.; Kāv. &c. **–kṛita,** mfn. made loose, loosened, relaxed &c., ib. **–√bhū,** P. *-bhavati,* to become loosened or slackened, be relaxed, slacken, Kāv.; Kathās.; to desist from (abl.), Mṛicch. **–bhūta,** mfn. loosened, relaxed, slackened, languid, Kathās.; Suśr.

Śithilī-śānti, f. N. of wk.

शिन *śina,* m. N. of a man, Pravar.

Śini, m. N. of various men (of a son of Su-mitra, of a son of Garga, of the father of Sātyaka, &c.; *śiner naptṛi,* 'grandson of Ś°,' N. of Sātyaki, one of the Pāṇḍu chiefs), MBh.; Hariv.; Pur.; (ibc.) the race of Śini (see below); pl. N. of a class of Kshatriyas, Uṇ. iv, 51. **–pravīra,** m. a chief or hero of the race of Ś°, MBh. **–bāhu,** m. N. of a river, VP. **–vāsa,** m. N. of a mountain, BhP. (B. *śinī-v°*). **–vāsudeva,** m. pl., Pāṇ. vi, 2, 34

Śinika, m. N. of a preceptor, VP.

Śinī-pati, m. (for *śini-p°?*) N. of a warrior, Hariv. (v.l. *sinī-pati*).

Śinī-vāsa. See *śini-vāsa.*

Śineyu, m. N. of a son of Uśat, Hariv.; of Uśanas, VP. (v.l. *śiteyu*).

शिनीवाली *śinīvālī*, w. r. for *sin°*.

शिपद *śipada*. See *a-śipadá*.

शिपवित्नुक *śipavitnuká*, m. a kind of worm, AV.

शिपविष्ट *śipavishṭa*, m. = *śipiv°*, L.

शिपाटक *śipāṭaka*, m. N. of a man, Rājat.

शिपि *śipí*, m. a ray of light, Nir. v, 8; = *paśu*, TS.; = *prâṇin*, L.; f. skin, leather, W. **–vishṭá**, mfn. (accord. to Sāy.) pervaded by rays (applied to Rudra-Śiva and Vishṇu; cf. RTL. 416), RV. &c. &c.; bald-headed, Āpast.; 'leprous' or 'having no prepuce,' L.; superfluous, Kāṭh.; *-vat*, mfn. containing the word *śipivishṭa*, TS.; Br.; (*vatī*), f. a verse containing the above word, Br.; ĀpŚr. **–vishṭaká**, mf(*ā*)n. (prob.) smooth, TS.

Śipitá, mfn. (prob.) superfluous, ŚBr.

शिप्र *śipra*, m., see *sipra*; (ibc.) = *śiprā*, f. (see below). **–vat** (*śípra-*), mfn. having full cheeks, full-cheeked, RV. vi, 17, 2.

Śipraka, m. N. of the murderer of Su-śarman, VP.; of the first king of the Āndhras, MW.

Śíprā, f. (du.) the cheeks, RV.; (pl.) the visors (of a helmet), ib.; (sg.) the nose, Nir. vi, 17.

Śipriṇī-vat and **śiprin**, mfn. full-cheeked, RV.

शिफ *śipha*, m. (derivation unknown) = *śiphā* (which is the more usual form; see below), L.

Śiphā, f. a fibrous or flexible root (used for making whips &c.), Mn. ix, 230; a lash or stroke with a whip or rod, ib. viii, 369; N. of a river, RV. (L. also 'a branch; a river; a mother; a tuft of hair on the crown of the head; the root of a water-lily; spikenard; turmeric; a sort of dill or fennel'). **–kanda**, m. n. the root of a water-lily, L. **–dhara**, m. 'possessing fibres,' a branch, L. **–ruha**, m. 'growing from fibres which descend to the ground,' the Banyan tree, L.

Śiphāka, m. the root of a water-lily, L.

शिबि *śibi*, m. (also written *śivi*) N. of a Ṛishi (having the patr. Auśīnara and supposed author of RV. x, 179), Anukr.; of a king (renowned for his liberality and unselfishness, and said to have saved Agni transformed into a dove from Indra transformed into a hawk by offering an equal quantity of his own flesh weighed in a balance), MBh.; Hariv.; Pur.; (pl.) a people descended from Śibi, MBh.; Hariv.; VarBṛS.; N. of a son of Indra, MBh.; of Indra in the fourth Manv-antara (v.l. *śikhin*), VP.; of a son of Manu Cākshusha, BhP.; of a Daitya (son of Saṃhrāda), MBh.; a king of the Śibis, VarBṛS.; a beast of prey, L.; the birch tree (= *bhūrja*), L.; Typha Angustifolia, L. **–kāla**, m. N. of a Daitya, Hariv. **–carita** or **-caritra**, n. the story of Śibi (occurring as an episode of the MBh. iii, 10560–10596 and 13275–13300).

Śibika, m. N. of a king (= *śibi*), Buddh.; pl. N. of a people in the south of India, VarBṛS.; (*ā*), f., see next.

Śibikā, f. (also written *śivikā*) a palanquin, palkee, litter, bier, MBh.; R. &c.; a partic. weapon of Kubera (god of wealth), VP.; a stage or platform erected for exhibitions, MW.; a proper N., ib. **–dāna**, n. or **-dāna-vidhi**, m. 'the gift of a litter &c.,' N. of a ch. of the VahniP.

Śibira, n. (also written *śivira*) a royal camp or residence, tent in a royal camp, any tent, MBh.; R. &c.; an entrenchment for the protection of an army, MW.; a sort of grain, L.; m. N. of a tribe (?), MW.; (prob.) w.r. for *divira*, Rājat. v, 176. **–giri**, m. N. of a mountain, VarBṛS.

Śibī-ratha, m. a palanquin, litter, L.

शिभ्र *śibhrá*, mfn. (prob.) desirous of sexual intercourse, AV.

शिम् *śim* (= √1. *śam*), cl. 4. P. *śímyati*, to cut up, prepare (a sacrificial victim), TS.; Kāṭh.

Śima, m. a cutter up or preparer (of sacrificial food), TS.

Śimi, f. = *śamī*, a legume, pod, L.; work, labour = *śimī* (see *a-śimi-dvish*). **–jāvarī**, f. growing wild, TĀr. (Sāy.) **–dā** (*śimi-*), f. N. of a female demon, AV.; ŚBr.

Śimī, f. = *śamī*, effort, labour, work, industry, TS.; Kāṭh. **–vat** (*śímī-*), mfn. effective, mighty, strong, RV.

Śimyu, mfn. (prob.) strenuous, vigorous, aggressive, RV. i, 100, 18; m. pl. N. of a people, ib. vii, 18, 5.

शिमिका *śimikā*, f. N. of a place, Rājat.

शिमिद्वत् *śímidvat*, mfn. (applied to a partic. wind), MaitrS.

शिमिशिमाय *śimiśimāya*, °*yati* (onomat.; cf. *simisim°*), to simmer, bubble or boil with a murmuring sound, VarYogay.

शिमिषीपद *śimishī-pada*, m. (cf. *śamanī-shada*) a Rākshasa, L.

शिमृडी *śimṛiḍī*, f. a kind of shrub, L.

शिम्ब *śimba*, m. (also written *simba*) a pod, legume, Suśr.; Cassia Tora, L.; (*ā*), f. (also written *simbā*) a pod, L.

Śimbalá, m. a small pod or kind of flower (accord. to Sāy. 'the flower of the Śālmali tree'), RV. iii, 53, 22; a kind of plant, Kauś.

Śimbi, f. (also written *simbi*) a pod, legume, Mālatim.; Car. **–jā**, f. 'pod-born,' any pulse or grain growing in pods, MW. **–parṇikā** or **-parṇī**, f. Phaseolus Trilobus, L.

Śimbika, m. a black variety of Phaseolus Mungo, L.; (*ā*), f. a pod, legume, L.

Śimbī, f. a pod, legume, Suśr.; Phaseolus Trilobus, L.; Mucuna Pruritus, L.; = *nishvāpī*, L. **–dhānya**, n. leguminous grain, Car.; Bhpr. **–phala**, n. Tabernæmontana Coronaria, L.

शिम्बात *śimbāta*, mfn. (accord. to Naigh. iii, 6) = *sukha*, RV. x, 106, 5.

शिम्यु *śimyu*. See above.

शिम्रीडी *śimrīḍī*, (prob.) w. r. for *śimṛiḍī*.

शिर् *śir* (nom. *śīr*; √*śrī*), hurting, injuring, wounding (only ifc., e.g. *śaśīśa-śiśu-śīḥ*), Kir. xv, 5.

शिरस् *śíras*, n. (prob. originally *śaras* = *karas*; and connected with *karaṅka*, q.v.) the head, skull (acc. with √*dā*, 'to give up one's head i.e. life;' with √*dhṛi* or √*vah*, 'to hold up one's head, be proud;' with Caus. of √*vṛit* or with *upa-*√*sthā*, 'to hold out the head,' 'acknowledge one's self guilty,' see *śirôpasthāyin*; instr. with √*grah*, √*dhā*, √*dhṛi*, *vi-*√*dhṛi*, √*bhṛi*, √*vah*, or √*kṛi*, 'to hold or carry or place on the head, receive deferentially;' instr. with √*gam*, *abhi-*√*gam*, *pra-*√*grah*, √*yā*, *pra-ṇam* [√*nam*], *ni-*√*pat*, *pra-ṇi-*√*pat*, 'to touch with the head, bow or fall down before;' loc. with √*kṛi* or *ni-*√*dhā*, 'to place on one's head;' loc. with √*sthā*, 'to be on or stand over a person's head, stand far above [gen.]),' RV. &c. &c.; the upper end or highest part of anything, top, peak, summit, pinnacle, acme, MBh.; Kāv. &c.; the forepart or van (of an army), Śiś.; the beginning (of a verse), VarBṛS.; (ifc.) the head, leader, chief, foremost, first (of a class), BhP.; N. of the verse *āpo jyotir āpo 'mṛitam*, Baudh.; Vishṇ. &c.; of a Sāman (also with *Indrasya*), ĀrshBr.; Lāṭy.; of a mountain, Buddh. [Cf. *śīrshan*; Gk. κέρας, κάρη &c.; Lat. *cerebrum* for *ceresrum*, *cornu*; Germ. *hirni*, *Hirn*; Eng. *horn*.] **–tas**, ind. out of or from or at the head, GṛS.; Kāv. **–tāpin**, m. 'hot in the head,' an elephant, W. **–tra**, n. 'head-protector,' a helmet, Ragh.; Rājat. &c., a cap, turban, head-dress, W. **–trāṇa**, n. = prec., MBh.; Hariv.; Kāv.; a skull, L. **–pada**, n. the upper part, Car. **–stha**, see *śiraḥ-stha*.

1. **Śira**, m. = *śiras*, the head, MBh.; Pañcar. &c.; the root of Piper Longum, L. (v.l. *sira*); Betula Bhojpatra, L.; a Boa, L.; a bed, couch, L. **Śirô-pasthāyin**, mfn. 'holding out the head' (scil. for punishment, as a man must do if the person accused by him has cleared himself by an ordeal), Nār.

2. **Śira**, in comp. for *śiras*. **–upanishad**, f. N. of an Upanishad. **–ja**, m. 'head-produced,' the hair of the head, L. **–snāta**, mfn. = *śiraḥ-sn°*, MBh.

Śiraḥ, in comp. for *śiras*. **–kapāla**, n. 'head-bowl,' the skull, MBh.; Hariv.; Suśr. **–kapālin**, mfn. carrying a skull, Yājñ.; m. a religious mendicant who carries about a human skull (as a symbol of having abandoned the world), W. **–kampa**, m. the act of shaking the head (also pl.), MBh.; Rājat. **–kampin**, mfn. shaking the h°, Śiksh. **–karṇa**, n. sg. the h° and the ear, Kauś. **–kṛintana**, n. cutting off the head, decapitation, Siṇhās. **–kriyā**, f. (ifc.) presentation of the head, R. **–paṭṭa**, m. a turban, Pañcar. **–pāka**, m. a partic. disease of the h°, ŚārṅgS. **–piṇḍa**, m. du. the two protuberances on the forehead of an elephant, L. **–pīṭha**, n. the back of the neck, L. **–pīḍā**, f. head-ache, W. **–praṇāma**, m. bowing or bending the head, Bhartṛ. **–pradāna**, n. giving up the head or life, Cat. **–prâvaraṇa**, n. 'h°-covering,' a head-dress, turban, MW. **–phala**, m. the cocoa-nut tree, L. **–śāṭaka**, n. a turban, L. **–śila**, n. N. of a fortress, Rājat. **–śūla**, n. violent head-ache, Suśr.; Kathās. &c. **–śesha**, m. 'having only the head left,' N. of Rāhu, Bhartṛ. **–śrit**, mfn. (ifc.) being at the head or top of, Śiś. **–śreṇi**, m. f. a line or number of heads, MW. **–stha**, mfn. being or borne on the h°; hanging over one's h°, imminent, Kāv.; m. a chief, leader, W.; a plaintiff, L. **–sthāna**, n. a chief place, MBh. **–sthita**, mfn. being in the head, cerebral (as a letter or sound), Śiksh. **–snāta**, mfn. one who has bathed or perfumed his head, Mn.; MBh. &c. **–snāna**, n. bathing or perfuming the head, VarBṛS.; Pur. **–snānīya**, n. pl. all the requisites for bathing or perfuming the h°, ĀpGṛ., Sch. **–sraj**, f. a wreath worn on the head, Hcat.

Śiraś, in comp. for *śiras*. **–cheda**, m. (Kāv.; Kathās. &c.) or **-chedana**, n. (Cat.) cutting off the head, decapitation.

Śirasa = *śiras* in *sahasra-śirasôdara*, q. v.

Śirasi, loc. of *śiras*, in comp. **–ja**, m. (ifc. f. *ā*) 'produced on the head,' the hair of the head, Śiś.; Kād.; Pañcat.; *-pāśa*, m. a tuft of hair, Śiś. **–ruh** (W.) or **-ruha** (L.), m. 'growing on the head,' the hair. **–sic**, f. a head-cloth, L.

Śirasita, mfn. exalted (?), Divyâv.

Śiraska (ifc.; *-tva*, n.) = *śiras*, Suśr.; VarBṛS. &c.; mfn. belonging to or being on the head, MW.; m. or (L.) n. a helmet, HPariś.; n. a cap, turban, W.; (*ā*), f. a palanquin, W.

1. **Śirasya**, Nom. P. °*yati*, = *śira icchati*, Pāṇ. vi, 1, 61, Sch.

2. **Śirasya**, mfn. = *śira iva*, g. *śākhâdi*; belonging to or being on the head (= *śīrshaṇya*), Pāṇ. vi, 1, 61, Vārtt. 2, Pat.; m. 'the hair of the head,' or 'clean hair,' L.

Śiro, in comp. for *śiras*. **–gata**, mfn. = *śiraḥ-sthita*, Śiksh. **–gada**, m. a disease of the head, Suśr. **–gṛiha** or **-geha**, n. a top-room, a room on the top of a house, L. **–gaurava**, n. heaviness of head, Suśr. **–graha**, m. 'head-seizure,' disease or affection of the h°, Suśr.; ŚārṅgS. **–grīvá**, n. sg. the head and neck, MaitrS.; AitBr. **–ghāta**, m. a blow on the head, Mṛicch.; VarBṛS. **–ja**, n. pl. 'h°-produced,' the hair of the head, Hariv. **–jānu**, n.; g. *rāja-dantâdi*. **–jvara**, m. fever with head-ache, MBh. **–dāman**, n. a turban, Pañcar. **–duḥkha**, n. head-ache, Suśr. **–dhara**, m. (R.; BhP.) or **-dharā**, f. (MBh.; Hariv.; Kāv. &c.; ifc. f. *ā*) 'h°-supporting,' the neck. **–dharaṇīya**, mfn. to be borne on the h°, to be greatly honoured, Dhūrtas. **–dhāman**, n. the head (of a bed), Kād. (v.l. *-bhāga*). **–dhārya**, mfn. = *-dharaṇīya*, Bhām. **–dhi**, m. = *-dhara*, Śiś. **–dhūnana**, n. shaking the head, Kpr. **–dhra**, m. = *-dhara*, BhP. **–nati**, f. bowing the head, Kāv. **–nyāsa**, m. hanging down the head, Car. **–pti**, w.r. for *-'rti*, MānGṛ. **–bīja**, n., g. *rāja-dantâdi* (Kāś.) **–bhava**, m. the hair of the head, L. **–bhāga**, m. the top (of a tree), Kathās.; the head-end (of a bed; also *śayanīya-śiro-bh°*), Kād. (v.l. °*ro-dhāman*); Hcar. **–'bhitāpa** (°*ras-abh°*), m. head-ache, MBh.; Suśr. **–bhūshaṇa**, n. a head-ornament; °*shaṇāya*, Nom. Ā. °*yate*, to form a head-ornament, Kāvyâd., Sch. **–maṇi**, m. 'crest-jewel,' a jewel worn on the h°, Ṛitus.; VarBṛS. &c.; the chief of (gen. or comp.; *-tā*, f.), Pañcar.; Kathās.; HPariś. &c.; a title of honour conferred on Paṇḍits, MW.; N. of the chief wk. on any subject and of various eminent scholars, Cat.; *-khaṇḍana*, n., *-nyāyânusāri-vivṛiti*, f. N. of wks.; *-bhaṭṭa*, *-bhaṭṭâcārya*, m. N. of various authors, Cat.; *-mathurā-nāthīya*, n., *-vyākhyā*, f. N. of wks. **–marman**, m. a boar, L. **–mātrâvaśesha**, mfn. having only the head left (Rāhu), ŚārṅgP. **–mālin**, m. 'garlanded with skulls,' N. of

Śiva, MW. **-mukha**, n. sg. the head and face, ĀśvGr. **-mauli**, m. 'crest-jewel,' an eminent or distinguished person, Cat. **-rakshin**, m. the body-guard of a prince, Hcar. **-ratna**, n. 'crest-gem,' jewel worn on the head, L. **-ruj**, f. h°-ache, Suśr.; VarBṛS.; Kathās. **-rujā**, f. id., MBh.; Alstonia Scholaris, L. **-ruh**, m. 'head-growing,' hair of the head, L. **-ruha**, m. (ifc. f. *ā*) id., MBh.; Hariv.; Kāv. &c.; a horn, VarBṛS.; (*ā*), f. Leea Hirta, L. **-roga**, m. any disease of the head, Suśr.; *-ghna-yajñôpavīta-dāna*, n. N. of wk. **-'rti** (°*ras-ar*°), f. head-ache, Kathās. **-vartin**, mfn. being at the h°, being on the top or summit, W.; = *śirôpasthāyin*, Nār.; m. a chief, W. **-vallī**, f. the crest or comb of a peacock, L. **-vasti**, m. or f.(?) pouring oil or other liquids on the head, L. **-vāhya**, mfn. to be borne or worn on the h°, Campak. **-vireka**, m. anything for cleansing or clearing the h°, ŚārṅgS. **-virecana**, mfn. cleansing the h°, Suśr.; n. = *-vireka*, ib. **-vṛitta**, n. pepper, L.; *-phala*, m. a kind of Achyranthes Aspera with red flowers, Bhpr. **-vedanā**, f. head-ache, Kād. **-veshṭa**, m. or °*ṭana*, n. a head-dress, turban, L. **-vrata**, n. a partic. religious observance, MuṇḍUp. **-'sthi** (°*ras-as*°), n. 'head-bone,' the skull, L. **-hārin**, m. N. of Śiva, MW. **-hṛit-kamala**, n. the lotus of head and heart, Kathās.

शिरा *śirā, śirāla*. See *sirā, sirāla*.

शिरि *śiri*, m. (only L.; cf. Uṇ. iv, 142) a murderer, killer; a sword; an arrow; a locust.

शिरिणा *śíriṇā*, f. (prob.) night, RV. ii, 10, 3 (cf. Naigh. i, 7; others 'a cell').

शिरिम्बिठ *śirímbiṭha*, m. (prob.) a cloud, RV. x, 155, 1 (cf. Naigh. iv, 3; accord. to Anukr. 'N. of a Ṛishi having the patr. Bhāradvāja and author of the above hymn').

शिरिशिरा *śiriśirā* (onomat.), with √*bhū*, P. *-bhavati*, to hiss, ĀpŚr., Sch.

Śiriśirāya (onom.), Ā. °*yate*, id., ĀpŚr.

शिरीष *śirīsha*, m. Acacia Sirissa (n. its flower), ShaḍvBr. &c. &c.; m. pl. N. of a village, Pat. on Pāṇ. i, 2, 51. **-kusuma**, n. the flower of the Ś° tree, Śak. **-pattrā** or **-pattrikā**, f. a kind of white Kiṇihī (q.v.), L. **-phala**, n. the fruit of Ś° tree, Suśr. **-bīja**, n. the seed of Ś° tree, ib. **-vaṇa** or **-vana**, n. a wood of Ś° trees, Pāṇ. viii, 4, 6, Sch.

Śirīshaka, m. Acacia Sirissa, R.; N. of a serpent-demon, MBh.; (*ikā*), f. a kind of tree, Bhpr. (cf. *ambu-śirīshikā*).

Śirīshika, mfn. (fr. *śirīsha*), g. *kumudâdi*.

Śirīshin, m. N. of a son of Viśvāmitra, MBh.; (*iṇī*), f. a country abounding in Śirīsha trees, g. *pushkarâdi*.

शिल् *śil* (also written *sil*), cl. 6. P. *śilati*, to glean, Dhātup. xxviii, 70.

1. **Śila**, m. (L. also n.; for 2. see col. 2) gleaning, gathering stalks or ears of corn (accord. to Kull. on Mn. x, 112 *śila* = *aneka-dhānyônnayana*, i.e. 'gleaning more than one ear of corn at a time,' opp. to *uñcha* = *ekâika-dhānyâdi-guḍakôccayana*), Mn.; MBh. &c.; m. N. of a son of Pāryātra, Ragh. **-m-dhara** or **-m-dhari**(?), m. N. of a man, Pravar. **-rati**, mfn. satisfied with gleaning, MBh. **-vṛitti**, mfn. subsisting by gleaning, ib. **Śilâda**, m. 'eating ears of corn,' N. of a man, Cat. **Śilândhas**, n. ears of corn left on a field, BhP. **Śilâhārin**, mfn. one who gathers stalks or ears of corn, MBh. **Śilôñcha**, m. gleaning ears of corn, Āpast.; m. du. or n. sg. (as a Dvandva) gleaning ears and picking up grains (hence 'following an irregular occupation'), Mn.; Yājñ.; BhP.; *-vṛitti*, f. subsistence by gleaning (or by unusual and irregular occupation), MBh.; BhP.; mfn. = *śila-vṛitti*, MBh.; Hariv. **Śilôñchana**, n. gleaning ears of corn, BhP. **Śilôñchin**, mfn. subsisting by gleaning, Bālar.

Śilamba, m. a sage, L.; a weaver, L.

शिलमानखान *śilamāna-khāna*, m. = سليمان خان, Cat.

शिला *śilā́*, f. (perhaps connected with √1. *śi*) a stone, rock, crag, AV. &c. &c.; red arsenic, Suśr.; camphor, L.; the lower mill-stone, L.; the lower timber of a door, L.; the top of the pillar supporting a house, L.; a vein, tendon (for *śira*, q.v.), L.; N. of a river, R.; of a woman, Cat. **-karṇī**, f. Boswellia Thurifera, L. **-kuṭṭa** or **-kuṭṭaka**, m. a stone-cutter's chisel or hatchet, L. **-kusuma**, n. storax, W. **-°kshara** (°*lâk*°), n. 'stone-letter,' writing on stone, lithography, Veṇīs. **-gṛiha**, n. 'rock-house,' a grotto, R.; Rājat. **-ghana**, mfn. firm or hard as a stone or rock, Ragh. **-cakra**, n. a diagram on a stone, Pañcar. **-caya**, m. 'rock-mass,' a mountain (*kanaka-śilā-c*°, a m° of gold), VarBṛS. **-ja**, mfn. produced in a rock or mountain, mineral, W.; n. bitumen, Suśr.; iron, L.; benzoin, storax, W.; petroleum, MW.; any fossil production, ib. (cf. *śila-ja* below). **-jatu**, n. 'rock-exudation,' bitumen, MBh.; Suśr. &c.; red chalk, W.; *-kalpa*, m. N. of wk. **-jit**, n. 'rock-overpowering,' bitumen, L. **-°ñjanī** (°*lâñ*°), f. a partic. plant, L. **-°ṭaka** (°*lâṭ*°), m. = *aṭṭa*, L.; = *tila*, L.; = *vilepa*, L.; = *bila*(?), L.; a fence, enclosure, W. **-tala**, n. a slab of rock, MBh.; Kāv. &c.; the surface of a r°, W. **-°tmaja** (°*lât*°), n. 'rock-born,' iron, L. **-°tmikā** (°*lât*°), f. a crucible, L. **-tva**, n. the state or nature of stone, Naish. **-tvac**, f. = *-valkā*, L. **-dadru**, m. 'rock-eruption,' bitumen, L. **-dana**, n. the gift of a stone (e.g. of a 'Śāla-grāma'), Pañcar. **-°ditya** (°*lâd*°), m. N. of a king, Śatr. (cf. *śilâditya*). **-dhara**, m. N. of the chamberlain of Hima-vat, Pārvat. **-dhātu**, m. 'rock-mineral,' chalk, L.; yellow ochre, L.; red chalk, W.; a white fossil substance, W.; an aluminous earth of a white or yellowish colour, W. **-nicaya**, m. a heap or mass of stones or rock, VarBṛS. **-niryāsa**, m. 'rock-exudation,' bitumen, L. **-nīḍa**, m. N. of Garuḍa, L. (w.r. *-nīha*; cf. *śilâukas*). **-°nta** (°*lânta*), m. Bauhinia Tomentosa, L. **-nyāsa-paddhati**, f. N. of wk. **-paṭṭa**, m. a stone slab (for sitting on or grinding), MBh.; Kāv.; Vās. **-paṭṭaka**, m. id., Viddh. **-putra**, m. 'a little rock,' a grindstone, L.; a torso, KapS. **-putraka**, m. a grindst°, MW.; a torso, BṛĀrUp., Sch. **-pushpa**, n. 'rock-efflorescence,' bitumen, L.; storax or benzoin, W. **-pesha**, m. a grindstone, MārkP.; grinding with a st°, MW. **-pratikṛiti**, f. a stone image or statue, Hariv. **-prasūna**, n. 'rock-produced,' bitumen, L. **-prāsāda**, m. a stone temple, Rājat. **-phalaka**, n. = *-paṭṭa*, Vishṇ. (Sch.) **-bandha**, m. a stone fence or wall, Rājat. **-bhava**, n. 'rock-produced,' bitumen, L.; storax or benzoin, W. **-bhāva**, m. = *-tva*, Kathās. **-bhid**, m. Plectranthus Scutellarioides, Bhpr. **-bheda**, m. id., L.; a stone-cutter's chisel, W. **-maya**, mf(*ī* or less correctly *ā*)n. made of st° (with *varsha*, 'a shower of stones'), Kāv.; BhP.; Vās. **-mala**, n. 'rock-impurity,' bitumen, L. **-māhātmya**, n. N. of wk. **-yūpa**, m. N. of a son of Viśvāmitra, MBh. **-°rambhā** (°*lâr*°), f. the wild plantain, L. **-rasa**, m. 'rock-exudation,' olibanum, benzoin, incense, W. **-varshin**, mfn. raining stones, Ragh. **-valkala**, m. n. (W.) or **-valkā**, f. (L.) a partic. medicinal substance. **-vaha**, m. pl. N. of a people, R.; (*ā*), f. N. of a river, ib. **-vitāna**, m. n. a spreading of stones, shower of st°s, MW. **-vṛishṭi**, f. 'st°-rain,' a shower of st°, A.; hail, W. **-veśman**, n. 'rock-abode,' a grotto, Megh. **-vyādhi**, m. 'rock-ailment,' bitumen, L. **-śastra**, n. a stone weapon, Kathās. **-śita**, mfn. sharpened on a st° (as an arrow), MBh.; R. **-°sana** (°*lâs*°), n. a st° seat, W.; mfn. seated on a st°, R.; n. bitumen, L.; benzoin or storax, W. **-sāra**, n. 'rock-essence,' iron, L. **-stambha**, m. a st°-column, Kathās. **-sthāpana-paddhati**, f. N. of wk. **-sveda**, m. 'rock-perspiration,' bitumen, L. **-°hva** or **-°hvaya** (°*lâh*°), n. 'st°-named,' bitumen, L. **Śilôccaya**, m. 'rock-accumulation,' a mountain, MBh.; Kāv. &c.; a high m°, W. **Śilôttha**, mfn. growing upon rocks, produced from r° or st°, W.; n. bitumen, L.; benzoin, storax, W. **Śilôdbhava**, mfn. produced from st° or on r°, W.; n. bitumen, L.; gold, L.; a kind of sandal-wood, L.; benzoin, W. **Śilôdbheda**, m. = *śilā-bhid*, Car. **Śilôraska**, mfn. having a rocky breast (said of the Himâlaya), Kum. **Śilâukas**, m. 'dwelling in rocks,' N. of Garuḍa, L.

2. **Śila** (for 1. see col. 1), in comp. for *śilā*. **-garbha-ja**, m. a partic. plant (= *pāshāṇa-bhedana*), L. **-ja**, n. bitumen, L. (cf. *śilā-ja*); (*ā*), f. a partic. medicinal substance, L. **-prastha**, n. a N., Kāś. on Pāṇ. vi, 3, 63. **-vaha**, n. a N., ib. **-vāhā**, f. (prob.) N. of a river, Pāṇ. vi, 3, 63, Sch.

Śili, m. Betula Bhojpatra, L.; f. the lower timber of a door, W.

Śilika, m., g. *puro-hitâdi*.

Śilikā-koshṭha, N. of a village among mountains, Rājat.

Śilin, m. N. of a serpent-demon, MBh.

Śilina, m. N. of a man, ŚBr., Sch.

1. **Śilī**, f. a kind of worm, L. (accord. to some, the female of *gaṇḍa-pada*); a female frog, MBh., Sch.; = *stambha-śīrsha*, L.; = *dvārâdhaḥ-sthita-kāshṭha*, L.; a spike, dart, W.; an arrow, MW. **-pṛishṭha**, mfn. (applied to a sword), MBh. (*śilī* = *bhekī*, Nīlak.) **-mukha**, mfn. N. of a sword, ib. (cf. prec.); = *jaḍī-bhūta*, L.; m. (ifc. f. *ā*) an arrow, MBh.; Hariv.; Kāv. &c.; (ifc. f. *ā*) a bee, Kāv.; a fool, W.; a battle, L.; war, W.; N. of a hare, Hit.; Kathās.

2. **Śilī**, in comp. for *śilā*. **-√bhū**, P. *-bhavati*, to become stone, turn to st°, become as hard as st°, Vcar. **-bhūta**, mfn. turned to stone, become as hard as stone, Kum.

Śileya, mfn. coming from rock, rocky, stony, MW.; as hard as rock or stone, Pāṇ. v, 3, 102; n. bitumen, L.; benzoin, W.

शिलालिन् *śilālin*, m. N. of the supposed author of partic. Naṭa-sūtras, Pāṇ. iv, 3, 110.

शिलाह्य *śilāhya*(?), m. N. of a man, Pravar.

शिलिन्द *śilinda*, m. a kind of fish, L.

शिलीन्ध्र *śilīndhra*, m. (perhaps fr. acc. of 1. *śilī* + *dhra* = *dhara*) the plantain tree, Musa Sapientum, L.; a kind of fish, Mystus Chitala, L.; (*ī*), f. a kind of bird, L.; a kind of worm, L.; earth, clay, L.; (*am*), n. a mushroom, Hariv.; Kāv. &c. (cf. *uc-chil*°); the flower of the plantain tree, Śiś.; a kind of jasmine, L.; a kind of tree, L.

Śilīndhraka, n. a mushroom (esp. one growing out of cow-dung), Bhpr.

शिलीपद *śilīpada*, m. (= *śilī-p*°) enlarged or swelled leg, elephantiasis, Dhūrtas.

शिलूष *śilūsha*, m. Aegle Marmelos, L.; N. of a Ṛishi (said to have been an early teacher of the art of dancing), L. (cf. *śailūsha*).

शिलोञ्छ *śilôñcha* &c. See col. 1.

शिल्गु *śilgú*, m. = *sukha*, Naigh. iii, 7.

शिल्प *śílpa*, n. (of doubtful derivation) the art of variegating, variegated or diversified appearance, decoration, ornament, artistic work, VS.; Br.; Hariv.; Kathās.; BhP.; any manual art or craft, any handicraft or mechanical or fine art (64 such arts or crafts, sometimes called *bāhya-kalā*, 'external or practical arts,' are enumerated, e.g. carpentering, architecture, jewellery, farriery, acting, dancing, music, medicine, poetry &c. [cf. IW. 185]; and 64 *abhyantara-kalā*, 'secret arts,' e.g. kissing, embracing, and various other arts of coquetry), ŚāṅkhBr.; Mn.; MBh. &c.; skill in any art or craft or work of art, ingenuity, contrivance, MBh.; Kāv. &c.; any act or work (also m.), BhP.; ceremonial act, ceremony, rite (also m.), MW.; form, shape, Naigh. iii, 7 (cf. *su-śilpa*); a partic. kind of Śastra or hymn (of a highly artificial character, recited on the 6th day of the Pṛishṭhya Shaḍ-aha, at the Viśvajit &c.), Br.; ŚrS.; a kind of sacrificial ladle (?), L.; (du. with *Jamad-agneḥ*) N. of two Sāmans, ĀrshBr.; m. N. of a teacher, ŚBr.; (*ā*), f. a barber's shop, L.; (*ī*), f. a female artisan or mechanic, Cat.; (*śilpá*), mfn. variegated, VS.; TS. **-kara**, m., °**rī**, f. = *-kāra*, °*rī*, MW. **-karman**, n. manual labour, handicraft, W. **-kalā-dīpikā**, f. N. of wk. **-kāra** or °**raka**, m. an artisan, mechanic, L.; (°*rī* or °*rikā*), f. a female artisan, Kālid. **-kārin**, m. (MārkP.), °**riṇī**, f. (Bhar.) = prec. **-gṛiha** (BrahmavP.) or **-geha** (Kull.), n. a workshop, workroom, manufactory. **-jīvikā**, f. subsistence by art or by a craft, MBh. **-jīvin**, m. 'living by art &c.,' an artisan, mechanic, craftsman, ĀpŚr., Sch. (v.l.); (*inī*), f. a female artisan, L. **-tva**, n. the state of being variegated or decorated, PañcavBr. **-prajāpati**, m. N. of Viśva-karman, MBh. **-lekha**, m. N. of wk. **-vat**, m. 'skilled in art,' an artisan, MBh.; Hariv. **-vidyā**, f. the science of arts or mechanics, Pañcar. **-vidhāna-drishṭa**, mfn. made according to the rules of art, VarYogay. **-vṛitti**, f. = *-jīvikā*, Gaut. **-śāla**, n. or °**lā**, f. = *-gṛiha*, L. **-śāstra**, n. = *-vidyā*, VarBṛS. (also N. of a partic. class of wks. on any mechanical or fine art, as architecture &c.; cf.

IW. 184). — **sarvasva-saṃgraha**, m. N. of wk. — **sthāna**, n. skill in art, mechanical or manual skill, Divyâv. **Śilpâjīva**, m. = *śilpa-jīvin*, Āpast. **Śilpârtha-sāra**, m. N. of wk. **Śilpâlaya**, m. = *śilpa-gṛiha*, VarBṛS. **Śilpôpajīvin**, m. = *śilpa-jīvin*, Gaut.

Śilpaka, n. a kind of drama, Sāh. (IW. 472); (*ikā*), f. = *śilpinī* (q.v.), MW.

Śilpi, in comp. for *śilpin*. — **karman**, n. the work of an artisan, Divyâv. — **jana** (VarBṛS.), m. an artisan, craftsman. — **śāla**, n. or °**lā**, f. a workshop, manufactory, L. — **śāstra**, n. = *śilpa-śāstra*, Cat. — **sāra**, m. olibanum, Gal.

Śilpika, mfn. skilled in art (applied to Śiva), MBh. (accord. to Nīlak. = little versed in art); n. any handicraft or mechanical art, W.; a kind of drama (= *śilpaka*), ib.; (*ā*), f., see *śilpakā*.

Śilpin, mfn. belonging to or skilled in art; m. an artificer, artisan, craftsman, artist, Gaut.; Mn.; MBh. &c.; (ifc.) fashioner of, Naish.; (*inī*), f. a female artisan or artist, Daś.; a kind of herb or grass (commonly called Lahānasipī, used medicinally; otherwise described as a perfume = *kola-dala*), L.

शिल्हण *śilhaṇa*, m. (also written *śilhana* and *śihlaṇa*) N. of a poet from Kaśmīra (author of the Śānti-śataka).

शिव *śivá*, mf(*ā*)n. (according to Uṇ. i, 153, fr. √1. *śī*, 'in whom all things lie;' perhaps connected with √*śvi*, cf. *śavas*, *śiśvi*) auspicious, propitious, gracious, favourable, benign, kind, benevolent, friendly, dear (*ám*, ind. kindly, tenderly), RV. &c. &c.; happy, fortunate, BhP.; m. happiness, welfare (cf. n.), R. v, 56, 36; liberation, final emancipation, L.; 'The Auspicious one,' N. of the disintegrating or destroying and reproducing deity (who constitutes the third god of the Hindū Trimūrti or Triad, the other two being Brahmā 'the creator' and Vishṇu 'the preserver;' in the Veda the only N. of the destroying deity was Rudra 'the terrible god,' but in later times it became usual to give that god the euphemistic N. Śiva 'the auspicious' [just as the Furies were called Εὐμενίδες 'the gracious ones'], and to assign him the office of creation and reproduction as well as dissolution; in fact the preferential worship of Śiva as developed in the Purāṇas and Epic poems led to his being identified with the Supreme Being by his exclusive worshippers [called Śaivas]; in his character of destroyer he is sometimes called Kāla 'black,' and is then also identified with 'Time,' although his active destroying function is then oftener assigned to his wife under her name Kālī, whose formidable character makes her a general object of propitiation by sacrifices; as presiding over reproduction consequent on destruction Śiva's symbol is the Liṅga [q. v.] or Phallus, under which form he is worshipped all over India at the present day; again one of his representations is as Ardha-nārī, 'half-female,' the other half being male to symbolize the unity of the generative principle [RTL. 85]; he has three eyes, one of which is in his forehead, and which are thought to denote his view of the three divisions of time, past, present, and future, while a moon's crescent, above the central eye, marks the measure of time by months, a serpent round his neck the measure by years, and a second necklace of skulls with other serpents about his person, the perpetual revolution of ages, and the successive extinction and generation of the races of mankind: his hair is thickly matted together, and gathered above his forehead into a coil; on the top of it he bears the Ganges, the rush of which in its descent from heaven he intercepted by his head that the earth might not be crushed by the weight of the falling stream; his throat is dark-blue from the stain of the deadly poison which would have destroyed the world had it not been swallowed by him on its production at the churning of the ocean by the gods for the nectar of immortality; he holds a *tri-śūla* or three-pronged trident [also called Pināka] in his hand to denote, as some think, his combination of the three attributes of Creator, Destroyer, and Regenerator; he also carries a kind of drum, shaped like an hour-glass, called Ḍamaru: his attendants or servants are called Pramatha [qq. vv.]; they are regarded as demons or supernatural beings of different kinds, and form various hosts or troops called Gaṇas; his wife Durgā [otherwise called Kālī, Pārvatī, Umā, Gaurī, Bhavānī &c.] is the chief object of worship with the Śāktas and Tāntrikas, and in this connection he is fond of dancing [see *tāṇḍava*] and wine-drinking; he is also worshipped as a great ascetic and is said to have scorched the god of love [Kāma-deva] to ashes by a glance from his central eye, that deity having attempted to inflame him with passion for Pārvatī whilst he was engaged in severe penance; in the exercise of his function of Universal Destroyer he is fabled to have burnt up the Universe and all the gods, including Brahmā and Vishṇu, by a similar scorching glance, and to have rubbed the resulting ashes upon his body, whence the use of ashes in his worship, while the use of the Rudrâksha berries originated, it is said, from the legend that Śiva, on his way to destroy the three cities, called Tri-pura, let fall some tears of rage which became converted into these beads: his residence or heaven is Kailāsa, one of the loftiest northern peaks of the Himālaya; he has strictly no incarnations like those of Vishṇu, though Vīra-bhadra and the eight Bhairavas and Khaṇḍo-bā &c. [RTL. 266] are sometimes regarded as forms of him; he is especially worshipped at Benares and has even more names than Vishṇu, one thousand and eight being specified in the 69th chapter of the Śiva-Purāṇa and in the 17th chapter of the Anuśāsana-parvan of the Mahā-bhārata, some of the most common being Mahā-deva, Śambhu, Śaṃkara, Īśa, Īśvara, Mahêśvara, Hara; his sons are Gaṇêśa and Kārttikeya), ĀśvŚrS.; MBh.; Kāv. &c.; RTL. 73; a kind of second Śiva (with Śaivas), a person who has attained a partic. stage of perfection or emancipation, MBh.; Sarvad.; *śiva-liṅga*, L.; any god, L.; a euphemistic N. of a jackal (generally *śivā*, f., q.v.); sacred writings, L.; (in astron.) N. of the sixth month; a post for cows (to which they are tied or for them to rub against), L.; bdellium, L.; the fragrant bark of Feronia Elephantum, L.; Marsilia Dentata, L.; a kind of thorn-apple or = *puṇḍarīka* (the tree), L.; quicksilver, L. (cf. *śiva-bīja*); a partic. auspicious constellation, L.; a demon who inflicts diseases, Hariv.; = *śukra*, m., *kāla*, m., *vasu*, m., L.; the swift antelope, L.; rum, spirit distilled from molasses, L.; buttermilk, L.; a ruby, L.; a peg, L.; time, L.; N. of a son of Medhâtithi, MārkP.; of a son of Idhma-jihva, BhP.; of a prince and various authors (also with *dīkshita*, *bhaṭṭa*, *paṇḍita*, *yajvan*, *sūri* &c.), Cat.; of a fraudulent person, Kathās.; (du.) the god Śiva and his wife, Kir. v, 40; Pracaṇḍ. i, 20 (cf. Vām. v, 2, 1); pl. N. of a class of gods in the third Manvantara, Pur.; of a class of Brāhmans who have attained a partic. degree of perfection like that of Śiva, MBh.; (*ā*), f. Śiva's wife (also *Śivī*), see *śivā* below; (*am*), n. welfare, prosperity, bliss (*āya*, *éna* or *ébhis*, 'auspiciously, fortunately, happily, luckily;' *śivāya gamyatām*, 'a prosperous journey to you!'), RV. &c. &c.; final emancipation, L.; water, L.; rock-salt, L.; sea-salt, L.; a kind of borax, L.; iron, L.; myrobolan, L.; Tabernæmontana Coronaria, L.; sandal, L.; N. of a Purāṇa (= *śiva-purāṇa* or *śaiva*), Cat.; of the house in which the Pāṇḍavas were to be burnt, MārkP.; of a Varsha in Plaksha-dvīpa and in Jambu-dvīpa, Pur. — **kaṇṭha-malikā**, f. N. of a Stotra. — **kara**, mf(*ī*)n. causing happiness or prosperity, auspicious, propitious, W.; m. (with Jainas) N. of one of the 24 Arhats of the past Utsarpiṇī, L. — **karṇâmṛita**, n. N. of wk. — **karṇī**, f. N. of one of the Mātṛis attendant on Skanda, MBh. — **kavaca**, n. N. of various Kavacas (q. v.), Cat. — **kāñcī**, f. N. of a town (said to have been founded by Śaṃkara; cf. *vishṇu-kāñcī*), Cat.; -*māhātmya*, n. N. of wk. — **kāntā**, f. 'beloved of Ś°,' N. of Durgā, L. — **kāntī**, f. N. of a Tīrtha, Cat. — **kāmadughā**, f. N. of a river, ib. — **kāriṇī**, f. N. of a form of Durgā, ib. — **kiṃkara**, m. 'Ś°'s servant,' N. of an author, ib. — **kīrtana**, m. 'Ś°-praiser,' N. of Bhṛiṅgi or Bhṛiṅgarīṭa (one of Ś°'s attendants), L.; N. of Vishṇu, L.; n. the act of praising or celebrating Ś°, W. — **kuṇḍa**, m. or n. (?) N. of a place, Cat. — **kusumâñjali**, m. N. of a Stotra. — **kṛishṇa** (?), m. N. of an author, Cat. — **keśâdi-pādânta-varṇana-stotra**, n. N. of a Stotra. — **kesara**, m. Mimusops Elengi, L. — **kopa-muni**, m. N. of an author, Cat. — **kośa**, m. N. of a dictionary of synonyms of trees and medicinal plants by Śiva-datta. — **kshetra**, n. a district sacred to Ś°, BhP.; N. of a partic. district, Kathās. — **khaṇḍa**, m. n. N. of a ch. of the Skanda Purāṇa. — **gaṅgā**, f. N. of a river; -*tīrtha*, n. N. of a Tīrtha, Cat.; -*māhātmya*, n. N. of wk. — **gaṇa**, m. N. of a king, Cat.; n. (or -*pura*, n.) N. of a town founded by the above king, ib.; (for the Gaṇas of Śiva see col. 1.) — **gati**, mfn. having a prosperous course, auspicious, happy, W.; worshipping Śiva, ib.; m. (with Jainas) N. of the 24 Arhats of the past Utsarpiṇī, L. — **gayā**, f. N. of a wk. on the pilgrimage to Gayā. — **gāyatrī**, f. N. of a Tantra wk. — **gītā**, f. N. of a ch. of the Padma Purāṇa (propounding the doctrines of Śaivas; it is regarded as a Vedânta treatise, and attributed to Veda-vyāsa) and of various other wks. (esp. of chs. of the Bhāgavata and Skanda Purāṇas); -*tātparya-bodhinī*, f., -*dīpikā*, f., -*bhāshya*, n., -*vyākhyā*, f. N. of Comms. — **gupta-deva**, m. N. of a king, Inscr. — **guru**, m. N. of the father of Śaṃkarâcarya (son of Vidyâdhirāja), Cat. — **gharma-ja**, m. 'born from the perspiration of Ś°,' N. of the planet Mars, L. — **ṃ-kara**, mf(*ī*)n. = *śiva-kara*, L. (in MBh. xii, 4430 applied to Punishment personified); m. a sword, L.; N. of a demon causing illness, Hariv.; of one of Śiva's attendants, L. — **cakra**, n. N. of a partic. mystical circle, MW. — **catuḥ-ślokī-vyākhyā**, f. N. of wk. — **caturdaśī**, f. the 14th day of the dark half of the month Māgha kept as a festival in honour of Ś° (= *śiva-rātri*, q. v.), Pañcar.; -*vrata*, n. a fast and other observances on that day, MW. — **candra**, m. N. of the great grandfather of the late Mahārāja Satīśa-candra Rāya (author of the Ashṭâdaśôttara-śata-ślokī), Cat.; (with *siddhânta*) N. of the author of the Siddhânta-candrikā, ib. — **campū**, f., -**caritra**, n. N. of wks. — **citta**, m. N. of a man, Cat. — **jī**, m. N. of a well-known Marāṭha king (= Śiva-rāja), RTL. 265; of the author of the Paramânanda-tantra-ṭīkā, Cat. — **jña**, mfn. knowing what is fortunate or propitious, W.; worshipping Śiva, ib.; (*ā*), f. a female devotee of the Śaiva sect, ib. — **jñāna**, n. knowledge of what is fortunate or of auspicious moment, L.; -*tārāvalī*, f., -*bodha*, m., -*bodha-sūtra*, n., -*vidyā*, f. N. of wks.; °*nêśvara*, m. (with *ācārya*) N. of the author of the Bhakti-mīmāṃsā-bhāshya, Cat. — **jyotir-vid**, m. N. of an author, ib. — **tattva**, n. N. of a wk. on Vedânta; -*prakāśikā*, f., -*bodha*, m., -*ratna-kalikā*, f., -*ratnâkara*, m., -*rahasya*, n., -*viveka*, m., -*viveka-khaṇḍana*, n., -*sudhā-nidhi*, m.; °*ttvârṇava*, m., °*ttvâvabodha*, m. (= -*tattva-bodha*), °*ttvôpanishad*, f. (= *parama-haṃsôp°*) N. of wks. — **tantra**, n. N. of a Tantra wk. — **tama** (*śivá-*), mfn. most prosperous or auspicious, very fortunate, RV.; MaitrUp.; BhP. — **tara**, mfn. more (or most) prosperous or fortunate, Uttarar.; very complacent, MW. — **tā**, f. the state or condition of (a person absorbed in) Śiva, Sarvad. — **tāṇḍava**, m. or n. 'Śiva's dance,' N. of a Tantra wk. (RTL. 85); -*stotra*, n. N. of a Stotra. — **tāti**, mfn. causing good fortune, conferring happiness, propitious, Mālatīm. (also °*tika*, W.); f. auspiciousness, happiness, welfare, Jātakam. (cf. Pāṇ. iv, 4, 143; 144). — **tāla**, m. (in music) a kind of measure, Saṃgīt. — **tīrtha**, n. N. of a Tīrtha, Cat. — **tva**, n. the condition or nature of Śiva, Sarvad.; = -*tā*, ib. — **daṇḍaka**, (prob.) m. (?) N. of an author, Cat. — **datta**, m. 'given by or presented to Ś°,' (with *śarman*, *miśra* and *sūri*) N. of three authors, Cat.; of various other men, Kathās.; n. the discus of Vishṇu, MW.; -*pura*, n. N. of a town in the east, Pāṇ. vi, 2, 99, Sch. — **dayālu**, m. N. of the author of a Comm. on the Bhagavad-gītā. — **dayā-sahasra**, n. N. of a Stotra. — **daśaka**, n. N. of two wks. — **dāyin**, mfn., v. l. for -*tāti*, Mālatīm. — **dāru**, n. the tree Pinus Deodora, L. — **dāsa**, m. 'Ś°'s servant,' N. of various writers and other men (esp. of the author of the Kathârṇava, the Vetāla-pañcaviṃśati, and the Śāli-vāhana-caritra), Cat.; (with *cakravartin*) N. of the author of a Comm. on the Uṇâdi-sūtra of the Kātantra grammar, ib.; -*deva*, m. N. of a poet, ib.; -*sena*, m. N. of the author of the Tattva-candrikā, ib. — **diś**, f. 'Śiva's quarter,' the north-east, VarBṛS. — **dīkshā**, f. N. of wk.; -*ṭīkā*, f. N. of a Comm. on it. — **dīna**, m. N. of a lexicographer, Cat.; -*dāsa*, m. N. of an astronomer, ib. — **dūtikā**, f. N. of one of the Mātṛis attending on Śiva, L. — **dūtī**, f. 'Śiva's messenger,' N. of a form of Durgā, MārkP.; of a Yoginī, MW.; -*tantra*, n. N. of a Tantra. — **drishṭi**, f. N. of a wk. (containing the Śaiva system, by Somânanda-nātha). — **deva**, m. N. of two kings and of a grammarian, Cat.; n. = (or v. l. for) next, VarBṛS. — **daiva**, n. N. of the lunar mansion Ārdrā (presided over by Śiva), ib. — **dyumaṇi-dīpikā**, f. N. of a wk. (also called *dina-karôddyota*). — **druma**, m. Aegle Marmelos, L. — **dvishṭā**, f. Pandanus

Odoratissimus, L. **— dhanur-veda,** m. N. of a wk. attributed to Vyāsa, Cat. **— dharma,** n. N. of a ch. of the Nandikêśvara-saṃhitā ; °*môttara,* n. N. of a sequel of the prec. wk.; °*môpapurāṇa,* n. N. of an Upapurāṇa, IW. 521. **— dhātu,** m. 'Śiva's essence,' quicksilver, L.; Śiva's mineral, milk-stone, opal or chalcedony, L. **— dhāra,** m. N. of a Tīrtha, MatsyaP. **— dhāriṇī,** v.l. for *-kāriṇī.* **— dhyāna-paddhati,** f. N. of wk. **— nakshatra-purusha-vrata,** n. a partic. observance or ceremony, Cat. **— nakshatra-mālikā,** f. N. of a Stotra. **— nātha,** m. N. of a man, ib. **— nābhi,** m. 'Śiva's navel,' a partic. form of Śiva-liṅga, L. **— nāmâvalī,** f., **-nāmâshṭôttara-śata,** n. N. of wks. **— nārāyaṇa,** m. N. of a god, Cat.; *-ghosha,* m. N. of a man, ib.; (with *sarasvatī-kaṇṭhâbharaṇa*) *-dāsa,* m., °*yanânanda-tīrtha,* m. N. of authors. **— nirmālya-bhakshaṇa,** n. N. of a poem. **— nirvāṇa-stotra,** n. N. of a Stotra ascribed to Vyāsa. **— pañca-mukha-dhyāna,** n., **-pañca-vadana-stotra,** n., **-pañcâkshara-stotra,** n. N. of wks. **— pañcâksharī,** f. N. of a Tantra wk.; *-nakshatra-mālikā,* f., *-māhātmya,* n., *-muktâvalī,* f. N. of wks. **— pañcâṅga,** n. N. of a Stotra. **— pañcāśikā,** f. N. of a wk. by Appaya Dīkshita (also called *ātmârpaṇa-stuti*). **— pattra,** n. a red lotus-flower, L.; *-muhūrta-prakaraṇa* (?), n. N. of wk. **— pada,** n. final liberation, emancipation, L. **— paddhati,** f. N. of wk. **— para,** n. (prob.) N. of a Stotra. **— pavitraka,** n. a partic. festival, L. **— pādâdi-keśânta-varṇana-stotra,** n., **-pāramparya-pratipādika-śruti-smṛity-udāharaṇa,** n., **-pārvatī-saṃvāda,** m. N. of wks. **— putra,** m. 'Ś°'s son,' patr. of Gaṇêśa, Gal. **— pur,** f. 'Ś°'s city,' N. of the city Benares, Gal. **— pura,** n. 'id.,' N. of various cities, MBh.; Kathās.; (*ī*), f. N. of a city, Śatr.; *= vārāṇasī,* L. **— purāṇa,** n. N. of one of the 18 Purāṇas (devoted to the praise of Śiva, and consisting of 12 Saṃhitās, viz. Vighnêśa, Rudra, Vināyaka, Bhauma, Mātṛikā, Rudrâikadaśa, Kailāsa, Śata-rudra, Koṭi-rudra, Sahasra-koṭi-rudra, Vāyavīya, and Dharma-saṃhitā); *-tāmasatva-khaṇḍana,* n. N. of wk. (cf. IW. 514). **— pushpaka,** m. Calotropis Gigantea, L. **— pūjana,** n. 'worship or adoration of Ś°,' N. of wk. **— pūjā,** f. id.; *-paddhati,* f., *-prakāśa,* m., *-mahiman,* m., *-vidhāna,* n., *-vidhi,* m., *-saṃgraha,* m. N. of wks. **— prakāśaka-siṅha** or **-prakāśa-deva,** m. N. of the author of the Bhāgavata-tattva-bhāskara. **— praṇāma-śikshā-stuti,** f. N. of wk. **— pratishṭhā,** f. and **-pratishṭhā-paddhati,** f. N. of wks. **— prasāda,** m. N. of various authors, Cat.; (with *tarka-pañcânana*) N. of the father of Gaṅgā-dhara, ib.; *-vikṛiti,* f., *-sundara-stava,* m. N. of wks. **— prâdur-bhāva,** m. the manifestation of Śiva, MW. **— prârthanā-stotra,** n. N. of a Stotra. **— priya,** mfn. dear to or esteemed by Ś°, W.; m. Agati Grandiflora, L.; the thorn-apple, L.; (*ā*), f. N. of the goddess Durgā, L.; n. the seeds of the Elæocarpus Ganitrus, L.; crystal, L. **— phalâbhisheka,** m. N. of a wk. on scattering various kinds of fruit on the Liṅga (as offerings). **— bīja,** n. 'Śiva's seed,' quicksilver, L. **— bhakta,** m. 'devoted to Ś°,' a Śaiva, Cat.; *-māhātmya,* n. N. of wk.; °*tânanda,* N. of a Nāṭaka; °*tânanda-kārikā,* f. N. of a Stotra by Śaṃkarâcārya. **— bhakti,** f. devotion to the worship of Śiva; *-māhātmya,* n., *-muktâbharaṇa,* n., *-vilāsa,* m., *-sudhā-nidhi,* m., *-sudhârṇava,* m., *-sudhôdaya,* m. N. of wks. **— bhaṭṭa,** m. N. of the father of Nāgêśa-bhaṭṭa, Cat. **— bhadra,** m. (also with *śukla*) N. of an author; *-kāvya,* n. N. of a poem. **— bhāgavata,** m. (prob.) a worshipper of Śiva, Col. **— bhārata,** (prob.) n. the history of Śiva-rāja or Śiva-jī (A.D. 1627–1680) by Kavīndra, Cat.; (°*tī*), m. N. of the author of the Siddhânta-mañjūshā, ib. **— bhāskara,** m. 'Śiva compared to the sun,' (prob.) N. of a teacher, ib. **— bhujaṃga,** (ibc.) 'Ś° compared to a serpent;' *-stotra,* n., °*gâshṭaka,* n. N. of wks. **— bhūti** or **-bhūtika,** m. N. of a minister, Kathās. **— maṅgalâshṭaka,** n. N. of wk. **— mantra,** m. Ś°'s Mantra, Pañcat.; *-vidhi,* m. N. of wk. **— maya,** mf(*ī* or *ā*)n. full of prosperity, BhP.; entirely devoted to Ś°, Kathās. **— mallaka,** m. Terminalia Arjuna, L.; (*ikā*), f. Agati Grandiflora, L. **— mallī,** f. *= -mallikā,* L.; Getonia Floribunda, L. **— mahiman,** m. Śiva's majesty; °*ma-prakhyāpana,* n., °*ma-vyākhyā,* f., °*mnaḥ stava,* m., °*mnaḥ stotra,* n. N. of wks. **— mātra,** m. or n. (?) a partic. high number, Buddh. **— mānasa-pūjā,** f., **-mānasika-snāna,** n. N. of wks. **— mārga,** m. 'Śiva's path,' final liberation, L. **— mālā,** f., **-māhātmya,** n. N. of wks.; (°*tmya*)*-khaṇḍa,* m. N. of a ch. of the SkandaP.; *-muktâvalī,* f. N. of wk. **— mauli** and **-yajvan,** m. N. of authors, Cat. **— yoga,** m. (prob.) N. of wk., ib. **— yogin,** m. a Śaiva ascetic, Hcat.; N. of one of the six Gurus of Shaḍ-guru-śishya, ib.; °*gi-bhikshu* (with *rāmêśvara*) and °*gîndra,* m. N. of authors. **— yoshit,** f. Śiva's wife, Cat. **— ratra-mālā,** f., **-ratnâvalī,** f., **-ratnâvalī-vyākhyā,** f. N. of wks. **— ratha,** m. N. of a man, Rājat. **— rasa,** m. the water of boiled rice or pulse three days old (undergoing spontaneous fermentation), L.; 'secret doctrine of Ś°,' N. of a ch. of the SkandaP. (also *-khaṇḍa*) and of a Tantra wk. **— rahasya,** n., **-pañca-ratna,** n. pl. N. of wks. **— rāghava-saṃvāda,** m. N. of a ch. of the PadmaP. **— rāja,** m. N. of various men (also *= śiva-jī,* q.v.), Cat.; *-caritra,* n. N. of a poetical life of Śiva-jī; *-dhānī,* f. 'Śiva's capital,' N. of the city Kāśī or Benares, Cat.; *-bhaṭṭa,* m. N. of a man, Vās., Introd. **— rātri,** f. 'Śiva's night,' N. of a popular fast and festival in honour of Siva (kept on the 14th of the dark half of the month Māgha or January–February with many solemn ceremonies, observed during the day and night, cf. *śiva-caturdaśī*), Rājat.; RTL. 90; 428; a form of Durgā (*= mahā-kālī*), Hcat.; *-kathā,* f., *-kalpa,* m., *-nirṇaya,* m., *-pūjā,* f., *-māhātmya,* n., *-vrata,* n., *-vrata-kathā,* f., *-vrata-kalpa,* m., *-vratôdyāpana,* n.; °*try-argha,* m. N. of wks. **— rāma,** m. (also with *ācārya, cakra-vartin, bhaṭṭa* &c.) N. of various authors and other men; *-gira,* m. N. of a person, MW.; *-gītā,* f. N. of a wk. on Yoga; *-tīrtha,* m. N. of a preceptor, Cat.; *-stotra,* n. N. of a Stotra; °*mânanda-tīrtha,* m. N. of a preceptor, Cat.; °*mêndra,* m. (also with *yati* and *sarasvatī*) N. of various authors. **— rūpa,** n. the form or image of Śiva, MW.; mfn. having the form of Ś°, ib. **— rūpya,** (prob.) N. of a place (cf. *śaiva-rūpya*). **— laharī,** f. N. of wk. **— lāla,** m. (also with *sukula, pāṭhaka,* and *śarman*) N. of various authors. **— liṅga,** n. Śiva's genital organ or Śiva worshipped in the form of the Liṅga, VarBṛS.; Kathās.; any temple or spot dedicated to the worship of Śiva's Liṅga, MW.; N. of the city Kāśī or Benares, Gal.; m. (with *cola-bhūpati*) N. of an author; *-dāna-vidhi,* m., *-parīkshā,* f., *-pratishṭhā-krama,* m., *-pratishṭhā-prayoga,* m., *-pratishṭhā-vidhi,* m., *-lakshaṇa,* n., *-sūryôdaya,* m.; °*gânanda-jñānôdaya,* m. N. of wks. **— liṅgin,** m. a worshipper of Ś°'s Liṅga or one who carries that symbol on his person, MW. **— līlâmṛita,** n., **-līlârṇava,** m. N. of wks. **— loka,** m. Śiva's heaven (on Kailāsa), Pañcar. **— varman,** m. N. of a minister, Kathās.; (°*ma*)*-kathana,* n. N. of a ch. of the SkandaP. **— vallabha,** mfn. loved by Ś°, W.; m. the mango tree, ib.; gigantic swallow-wort, ib.; (*ā*), f. the goddess Pārvatī, ib.; the Indian white rose (*= śata-pattrī*), MW. **— vallikā,** f. a kind of plant, L. **— vallī,** f. id., L.; Acacia Concinna, L. **— vāhana,** m. 'Śiva's vehicle,' a bull, L. **— vipra,** m. a Brāhman worshipper of Śiva, Hcat. **— vilāsa-campū,** f. N. of a poem. **— vivāha-prayoga,** m., **-vishṇu-stotra,** n. N. of wks. **— vīja,** see *-bīja.* **— vīrya,** n. quicksilver, L. **— vrata-kalpa,** m. N. of wk. **— vratin,** m. a Brāhman engaged in a vow of standing on one foot, L. **— śakti,** f. (du.) Ś° and his female energy, Cat.; (sg.) attachment or devotion to Ś°, MW.; m. N. of a man, Rājat.; *-pūjana-vidhi,* m. N. of wk.; *-maya,* mf(*ī*)n. produced by Ś° and his energy, Cat.; *-siddhi,* f. N. of wk. by Harsha. **— śaṃkara,** m. N. of an author; *-gītā,* f. N. of wk. **— śataka,** n., **-śata-nāma-stotra,** n., **-śabda-khaṇḍa,** m. N. of wks. **— śarman,** m. N. of a man, Cat. **— śāsana,** n. 'Ś°'s ordinance,' N. of a law-book. **— śāstra,** n. (prob. = prec.), and **-śikhariṇī-stuti,** f. N. of wks. **— śekhara,** m. Śiva's crest or head, MW.; the moon, ib.; Agati Grandiflora, L.; the thorn-apple, L. **— śrī,** m. N. of a king, VP. **— shaḍ-akshara-stotra,** n., **-saṃhitā,** f. N. of wk. **— saṃkalpa** (*śivá-*), m. 'auspicious in meaning,' N. of the text VS. xxxii, 1–6 (also °*pa-sūkta;* also °*pôpanishad;* cf. Mn. xi, 251). **— sama-rasa,** mfn. having the same sentiments as Śiva (*-tā,* f.), Siṅhâs. **— samudra,** m. 'Ś°'s sea,' N. of a waterfall, L. **— sarvasva,** n., **-sahasra-nāman,** n., °**māvali,** f. N. of wks. **— sahāya,** m. 'Ś°'s companion,' N. of two authors. **— sāyujya,** n. absorption into or identification with Śiva, final emancipation, MW. **— siṅha,** m. (also *-deva*) N. of various princes (esp. of a king of Mithilā, brother of Padma-siṅha, and patron of Vidyā-pati), Inscr.; Cat. **— siddhânta,** m. (also *-śāstra,* n.) N. of an astrol. wk. **— sundarī,** f. 'Ś°'s wife,' N. of Pārvatī, L. **— sûkta,** n. N. of a partic. Vedic hymn. **— sūtra,** n. (cf. *spanda-sūtra*) N. of the aphorisms of the Śaiva philosophy (attributed to the god Śiva), Sarvad.; N. of the 14 Sūtras with which Pāṇini opens his grammar (containing a peculiar method of arranging the alphabet or alphabetical sounds, said to have been communicated to him by the god Ś°); *-jāla-grantha,* m., *-vimarśinī,* f., *-vivṛiti,* f. N. of wks. **— sūnu,** m. N. of an author, Cat. **— skanda** or **-skandha,** m. N. of a king, Pur. **— stava-rāja,** m., **-stuti,** f., **-stotra,** n. N. of Stotras. **— sthala-mahima-varṇana,** n. N. of wks. **— sva,** n. 'Ś°'s property,' anything that has been offered to Ś°, MW. **— svarūpa-pūjā,** f., **-svarūpa-pūjā-vidhi,** m., **-svarūpa-mantra,** m. N. of wks. **— svāti,** m. N. of a king, Pur. **— svāmin,** m. N. of various authors and teachers, Cat. **Śivâksha,** n. the seed of Elæocarpus Ganitrus, L. **Śivâkhya,** mfn. called happy, termed lucky, MW. **Śivâgama,** m. Ś°'s doctrine (also as N. of a wk.), Hcat. **Śivâcala-māhātmya,** n., **Śivâcāra-saṃgraha,** m. N. of wks. **Śivâṭikā** (or °*vâṭī*?), f. Bœrhavia Procumbens, L.; a kind of grass, Bhpr. **Śivâṭī,** f. (prob.) = prec., Suśr. **Śivâṇḍa-kalpa,** m. N. of a Tantra wk. **Śivâtmaka,** mf(*ikā*)n. consisting of the essence of Śiva, MW.; n. rock-salt, L. **Śivâtharva-śīrshôpanishad,** f. N. of an Upanishad. **Śivâditya,** m. (with *miśra*) N. of an author (also called *nyāyâcārya*), Cat.; *-prakāśikā,* f., *-maṇi-dīpikā,* f., °*kā-khaṇḍana,* n. N. of wks. **Śivâdeśaka,** m. a fortune-teller, astrologer, Mālav. **Śivâdy-ashṭôttara-śata-nāman,** n. N. of wk. **Śivâdvaita** (ibc.); *-nirṇaya,* m., *-prakāśikā,* f., *-siddhânta-prakāśikā,* f. N. of wks. **Śivâdhikya-śikhāmaṇi,** m. N. of wk. **Śivânanda,** m. 'Śiva's joy;' (also with *bhaṭṭa, ācārya, gosvāmin,* and *sarasvatī*) N. of various authors and other men, Cat.; *-nātha,* m. N. of an author (also called Kāśī-nātha-bhaṭṭa), ib.; *-laharī* (or *śiva-laharī*), f. N. of a wk. of Śaṃkarâcārya; *-sena,* m. N. of the author of the Kṛishṇa-caitanyâmṛita, Cat. **Śivânubhava-sūtra,** n. N. of wk. **Śivâpará,** mfn. 'other than propitious,' cruel, AV. **Śivâparādha-kshamāpaṇa-stotra,** n., **Śivâpamārjana-mālā-mantra-stotra,** n. N. of Stotras. **Śivâpīḍa,** m. Getonia Floribunda, L. **Śivâbhimarśana,** mfn. one whose touch is auspicious or beneficial, RV. **Śivâmbudhi,** m. N. of a Stotra. **Śivâyatana,** n. a Śiva temple, Vet. **Śivârâdhana-dīpikā,** f. N. of wk. **Śivârka,** m. Getonia Floribunda, L.; *-candrikā,* f., *-maṇi-dīpikā,* f.; °*kôdaya,* m. N. of wks. **Śivârcana,** n. worship of Ś°; *-krama,* m., *-candrikā,* f., *-paddhati,* f., *-mahôdadhi,* m., *-ratna,* n. N. of wks. **Śivârti,** f., **Śivârti-prakāra,** m. (*ârti* for *ārati*) N. of wks. **Śivârya,** m. N. of a man, Inscr. **Śivâlaya,** m. 'Ś°'s abode,' Kailāsa, Rājat.; (accord. to some also n.) any temple or shrine dedicated to Ś° (generally containing a Liṅga), Kathās.; a cemetery, place where dead bodies are burnt, L.; N. of a place, Cat.; red Tulasī or basil, L.; *-pratishṭhā,* f. N. of wk. **Śivâshṭaka,** n., **Śivâshṭapadī,** f., **Śivâshṭa-mūrti-tattva-prakāśa,** m., **Śivâshṭôttara-bhāshya,** n., **Śivâshṭôttara-śata-nāman,** n. N. of wks. **Śivâhlāda,** m. 'Śiva's joy,' Getonia Floribunda, L. **Śivâhvā,** f. 'called after Ś°,' a species of creeper, L. **Śivêtara,** mfn. 'other than propitious,' malignant, inauspicious, BhP. **Śivêndra,** m. (with *sarasvatī*) N. of an author, Cat. **Śivêshṭa,** m. 'loved by Ś°,' Aegle Marmelos, L.; Getonia Floribunda, L.; (*ā*), f. Dūrvā grass, L. **Śivôtkarsha,** m. N. of a Vedânta wk.; *-prakāśa,* m., *-mañjarī,* f. N. of wks. **Śivôdbheda,** m. N. of a Tīrtha, MBh. **Śivôpanishad,** f. N. of an Upanishad (supposed to have been the work on which the Śiva-sūtras were founded), Cat. **Śivôpapurāṇa,** n. N. of an Upapurāṇa, Cat.

Śivaka, m. an idol or image of Śiva, Pāṇ. v, 3, 99, Sch.; a pillar or post to which cows are tied (to be milked or for rubbing against), L.

Śivā, f. the energy of Śiva personified as his wife (known as Durgā, Pārvatī &c.), Inscr.; Kāv.; Kathās.; Pur.; final emancipation (*= mukti*), Pur.; a euphemistic N. of a jackal (generally regarded as an animal of bad omen), GṛS.; Baudh.; MBh. &c.; N. of various plants (accord. to L. 'Prosopis Spicigera or Mimosa Suma; Terminalia Chebula or Citrina, Emblica Officinalis; Jasminum Auriculatum; turmeric; Dūrvā grass &c.'); the root of Piper longum, L.; a kind of yellow pigment (= *go-rocanā*), L.; a kind of metre, L.; (in music) a partic. Śruti, Saṃgīt.; N. of the wife of Anila, MBh.; of the wife of Aṅgiras, ib.; of a Brāhman woman, ib.; of the mother of Nemi (the 22nd Arhat of the present Avasarpiṇī), L.; of the mother of Rudra-bhaṭṭa, Cat.; of a river, MBh.; Hariv. (In the following comp. not always distinguishable from *śiva*, m. or n.) **–priyā**, f. 'dear to the jackals,' a goat, L. **–phalā**, f. Prosopis Spicigera or Mimosa Suma, L. **–bali**, m. an offering to Durgā (offered at night and consisting chiefly of flesh; also N. of a ch. of the Rudra-yāmala Tantra), Cat. **–°mbā-triśatī** (*śivâmb°*), f. N. of wk. **–°rāti** or **°ri** (*śivâr°*), m. 'jackal's enemy,' a dog, L. **–ruta**, n. the howling of a jackal, L. **–rudra**, m. N. of Śiva (as half male, half female, see under *Śiva*), Pañcar. **–likhita** (*śivā-l°* or *śivâl°*?), m. or n., and **-likhita-paribhāshā**, f. N. of wks. **–vidyā**, f. 'jackal-science,' divination by the cries of jackals, Divyâv. **–stuti**, f., **-stotra**, n. N. of Stotras. **–smṛiti**, f. 'Durgā-remembrance,' the plant Sesbania Aegyptiaca, L.

Śivāku, m. N. of a man, g. *bāhv-ādi*.

Śivānī, f. the wife of Śiva (= Durgā, Pārvatī &c.), L.; the plant Sesbania Aegyptiaca (or accord. to others Celtis Orientalis), L.

Śivālu, m. a jackal (cf. under *śiva* and *śivā*), L.

Śivīya, Nom. P. *°yati*, to treat any one (acc.) like Siva, Vop.

शिवि *śivi, śivikā* &c. See *śibi*, p. 1072.

शिविपिष्ट *śivipishṭa*, m. (cf. *śipivishṭa*) N. of Śiva, L.

शिविर *śivira* &c. See *śibira*, p. 1072.

शिवीरथ *śivī-ratha*. See *śibī-ratha*, p. 1072.

शिशन् *śiśan* (only instr. *śiśnā*), collateral form of *śiśna* (q.v.), Pañcar.

शिशपा *śiśapā*, f., m.c. for *siṅśapā* (q.v.)

शिशय *śiśayá*, mfn. (fr. √1. *śi*) liberal, munificent, RV.

शिशयिषा *śiśayishā*, f. (fr. Desid. of √1. *śī*) desire to lie down or to sleep, sleepiness, W.

Śiśayishu, mfn. wishing to lie down, sleepy, drowsy, BhP.

शिशव *śiśava* (once for *śiśu* in *śiśavasya*).

शिशिर *śiśira*, mf(*ā*)n. (prob. connected with √*śyai*, *śīta* &c.) cool, chilly, cold, frigid, freezing, R.; VarBṛS. &c.; m. n. cold, coolness, hoarfrost, dew, MBh.; Kāv. &c.; the cool or dewy season (comprising two months, Māgha and Phālguna, or from about the middle of January to that of March; cf. *ṛitu*), AV. &c. &c.; m. N. of the seventh month of the year (accord. to one reckoning); of a mountain, R.; Hariv.; Pur.; of a son of Dhara and Manoharā, MBh.; Hariv.; of a son of Medhâtithi, MārkP.; of a teacher (a pupil or descendant of Śākalya Vedamitra), Cat.; (*ā*), f. a partic. drug (= *reṇukā*), L.; a kind of Cyperus, L.; n. the root of Andropogon Muricatus, L.; a partic. mythical weapon, R.; Hariv.; N. of a Varsha in Plaksha-dvīpa, MārkP. **–kara**, m. 'cool-rayed,' the moon, VarBṛS. **–kāla**, m. the cool season, W. **–kiraṇa**, m. = *-kara*, VarBṛS.; *-vāsara*, m. Monday, ib. **–gabhasti**, m., **-gu**, m. = *-kara*, ib. **–ghna**, m. 'cold-destroying,' N. of Agni or fire, MW. **–tara**, mfn. more cool, very refreshing, Vās.; Gīt. **–tā**, f. coolness, cold (see *a-śiśiratā*). **–dīdhiti**, m. (Ṛitus.) and **-mayūkha**, m. (VarBṛS.) = *-kara*. **–mathita**, mfn. pinched by cold, Megh. **–māsa**, m. the cool month, Śiś. **–rtu** (for *-ṛitu*), m. the cool season; *-varṇana*, n. N. of a poem. **–śrī**, f. the beauty of the cool season, Pañcat. **–samaya**, m. = *-kāla*, Cat. **Śiśirâṅśu**, mfn. having cool rays (*-tva*, n.), R.; Hariv.; m. the moon, Vikr. (*tanu-bhavaḥ śiśirâṅśoḥ*, 'son of the Moon,' N. of the planet Mercury, VarBṛS.) **Śiśirâksha**, m. N. of a mountain, MārkP. **Śiśirâtyaya**, m. 'close of the cool season,' spring, R. **Śiśirâpagama**, m. 'departure of the cool season,' id., Ragh. **Śiśirôpacāra**, m. 'artificial cooling,' a refrigerator, Hcar. **Śiśirôshṇa-varshā**, f. pl. the cool, hot, and rainy seasons, MW.

Śiśiraya, Nom. P. *°yati*, to cool, Daś.

Śiśirāya, Nom. Ā. *°yate*, to become cool or cooler, Hcar.

Śiśirāyaṇa, w.r. for *śaiś°* (q.v.)

Śiśirita, mfn. cooled, Pañcar.

Śiśirī, in comp. for *śiśira*. **–√kṛi**, P. *-karoti*, to cool, refresh, Hcar. **–√bhū**, P. *-bhavati*, to become cool, MW.

शिशु *śíśu*, m. (fr. √1. *śū* = *śvi*) a child, infant, the young of any animal (as a calf, puppy &c.; also applied to young plants, and to the recently risen sun; often ifc.), RV. &c. &c.; a boy under eight years of age, W.; a lad under sixteen, ib.; a pupil, scholar, ib.; N. of Skanda, MBh.; R. (cf. *kumāra*); of a descendant of Aṅgiras (author of RV. ix, 112), Anukr.; of a son of Sāraṇa, VP.; of a king, Buddh.; mfn. young, infantine, L. **–kāla**, m. time of infancy, childhood, Pañcat. **–kṛicchra**, n. a form of austerity or penance, Vas.; *°rātikṛicchra*, n. another kind of p°, L. **–kranda**, m. the weeping or crying of a child or infant, Pāṇ. iv, 3, 88 (*°dīya*, mfn. treating of it, ib.) **–krandana**, n. = *-kranda*, W. **–krīḍā**, f. a child's play, Naish., Sch. **–gandhā**, f. double jasmine, L. **–cāndrāyaṇa**, n. the lunar penance of children (eating four mouthfuls at sunrise and four mouthfuls at sunset for a month), Baudh.; Mn. xi, 219. **–jana**, m. young people, children. **–tā**, f., **-tva**, n. childhood, childishness, Kāv.; VarBṛS.; Pañcat.; pupilage, the period before sixteen, W.; the period up to eight years of age, ib. **–deśya**, mfn. being in the place of a child, not far from or almost a child, Rājat. **–nandi**, m. N. of a king, BhP. **–nāka**, see next. **–nāga**, m. a young snake, R.; a young elephant, MW.; a kind of Rākshasa or demon, ib.; N. of a king of Magadhā (pl. his descendants), BhP.; VP. (v.l. *-nāka*). **–nāman**, m. a camel, L. **–pāla**, m. 'child-protector,' N. of the king of the Cedis inhabiting a country in central India, probably the same as Bundelkhand (see *cedi*; he was son of Dama-ghosha, and is also called Sunītha; his impiety in opposing the worship of Kṛishṇa is described in the Sabhā-parvan of the Mahā-bhārata; when Yudhi-shṭhira was about to perform a Rājasūya sacrifice, numerous princes attended, and Bhīshma proposed that especial honour should be paid to Kṛishṇa, who was also present, but Śiśu-pāla objected, and after denouncing Kṛishṇa as a contemptible person challenged him to fight, whereupon Kṛishṇa struck off his head with his discus; the Vishṇu-Purāṇa identifies this impious monarch with the demons Hiraṇya-kaśipu and Rāvaṇa; his death forms the subject of Māgha's celebrated poem called Śiśupāla-vadha); *-kathā*, f. N. of a tale; *-nishūdana*, m. destroyer of Śiśu-pāla, N. of Kṛishṇa, L.; *-vadha*, m. 'slaying of Ś°,' N. of a poem by Māgha (q.v.) on the above subject; *-vadha-parvan*, n. N. of a ch. of the Mahā-bhārata (ii, 1418–1627) on the same subject; *-śiraś-chettṛi* (Pañcar.) and *-han* (W.), m. N. of Kṛishṇa. **–pālaka**, m. 'protector of children,' N. of a king (= *śiśu-pāla*), L.; the plant Nauclea Cordifolia, L. **–prabhodhâlaṃkāra**, m. N. of wk. **–priya**, m. 'dear to children,' treacle, L.; n. the white water-lily, L. **–bodha**, m., **-bodhinī**, f. N. of various wks. **–bhāva**, m. state of childhood, infancy, L. **–bhūpati**, m. a young prince, Rājat. **–mat** (*śíśu-*), mfn. accompanied by or possessed of children or young, RV.; VS.; PañcavBr. **–māra**, m. 'child-killer,' the Gangetic porpoise or dolphin, Delphinus Gangeticus, VS. &c. &c.; an alligator, Suśr.; a collection of stars supposed to resemble a dolphin (and held to be a form of Vishṇu; also personified as a son of Dosha and Śarvarī, or as father of Bhramī, wife of Dhruva), MBh.; Pur.; (*ī*), f. a female porpoise, PañcavBr.; a kind of plant, VarBṛS.; *°ra-mukhī*, f. 'dolphin-faced,' N. of one of the Mātṛis attending on Skanda, L.; *°ra-ṛshi*, m. a Ṛishi having the form of a d°, TāṇḍyaBr.; *°ra-vasā*, f. the marrow or fat of the Delphinus Gangeticus, Suśr.; *°ra-śiras*, n. 'the dolphin's head,' a part of the heavens having stars of that shape, the north-east point, MBh.; *°râkṛiti*, mfn. d°-shaped, VP. **–rakshā-ratna**, n. N. of a medical wk. (also called *bāla-cikitsā*). **–roman**, m. 'having hair like a child,' N. of a serpent-demon, MBh. **–varjitā**, f. a woman without a child, L. **–vāhaka** or **-vāhyaka**, m. 'carrying young,' a wild goat, L. **–saukhya**, n. N. of wk. **–hatyā**, f. ch°-murder, MW. **–hariṇa-dṛiś**, f. a girl having the eyes of a young antelope, Amar. **–hitâishiṇī**, f. 'benefiting children,' N. of a Comm. on the Kumāra-sambhava and Raghu-vaṅśa by Cāritra-vardhana.

Śiśuká, m. a child, young, AV. &c. &c.; a kind of aquatic animal (accord. to L. a porpoise or Delphinus Gangeticus), MBh.; a kind of tree, L.; N. of a king, VP.

Śiśūla, m. a little child or infant, RV.

Śiśvan. See *saṃ-śiśvan*.

Śiśvi. See *sú-śiśvi*.

शिशोक *śiśoka*, m. N. of a poet, Cat.

शिशोदर *śiśodara*, m. (perhaps w.r. for *śiśnôdara*) N. of a man, Vīrac.

शिश्न *śiśná*, m. n. (cf. *śiśan*; said to be fr. √*śnath*, 'to pierce') a tail, (esp.) the male generative organ, RV. &c. &c. **–cchedana**, n. cutting off the tail (or) cutting off the gen° organ, Āpast. **–deva** (*śiśná-*), m. 'having the gen° organ for a god,' a phallus-worshipper, (or) a tailed or priapic demon (accord. to Sāy. 'one who sports with the generative organ;' accord. to Nir. iv, 19, 'mfn. unchaste, lustful'), RV. **–praṇejinī**, f. wiping or washing the gen° organ, Lāṭy. **Śiśnôdara**, n. the gen° organ and the belly, MBh.; *-tṛip* (BhP.), *-parâyaṇa* (MW.), *-m-bhara* (BhP.), mfn. addicted to lust and gluttony.

Śiśnatha, m. piercing, perforation, RV.

शिश्लिक्षु *śiślikshu*, mfn. (fr. Desid. of √*ślish*) wishing to cling to or adhere (in *á-ś°*), AV. xx, 134, 6 (not in MS.)

शिश्वि *śiśvi* in *sú-śiśvi*, q.v.

शिश्विदान *śiśvidāna*, mfn. (accord. to Uṇ. ii, 93, fr. √*śvit*) innocent, virtuous (= *śukla-karman*), L.; guilty, sinful, wicked (= *kṛishṇa-karman*), L.

शिष् 1. *śish*, cl. 1. P. *śeshati*, to hurt, injure, kill, Dhātup. xvii, 36.

शिष 2. *śish*, cl. 7. P. (Dhātup. xxix, 14) *śinashṭi* (in TBr. also *śiṅshati*, in later lang. pr. p. *śeshat*; Impv. *śiṇḍḍhi* or *śiṇḍhi*, Kāś., Pāṇ. viii, 4, 65; pf. *śiśesha*, Gr.; *śiśishe*, Br.; aor. *aśishat*, ib.; Prec. *śishyāt*, Gr.; fut. *śeshṭā*, ib.; *śekshyati*, *°te*, Br.; ind. p. *śishṭvā*, ĀśvŚr.; *śishya*, *-śesham*, Br. &c.), to leave, leave remaining, TBr.; ŚrS. (accord. to Dhātup. also 'to distinguish'): Pass. *śishyáte*, to be left, remain (with *na*, 'to be lacking'), AV. &c. &c.: Caus. (or cl. 10; see Dhātup. xxxiv, 11) *śeshayati*, *°te* (aor. *aśīśishat*), to cause or allow to remain, leave, spare, MBh.; Kāv. &c.: Desid. *śiśikshati*, Gr.: Intens. *śeśishyate*, *śeśeshṭi*, ib.

1. **Śishṭá**, mfn. left, remaining, escaped, residual (often ifc., e.g. *nala-ś°*, 'having only the stem left;' *hata-ś°*, 'escaped from slaughter or destruction'), AV. &c. &c.; n. anything that remains or is left, remains, remnant, ŚBr. &c. &c. **–1. -tā**, f., **-tva**, n. the being left, the being residual, MW. **–bhaksha**, m. the eating of remnants of food, KātyŚr. **Śishṭâśana** or **°śin**, mfn. feeding on remnants, MBh.; Kāv. &c.

Śesha &c. See p. 1088, col. 3.

शिष् 3. *śish*, weak form of √*śās*, q.v.

2. **Śishṭá**, mfn. taught, directed, ordered, commanded (applied to persons and things), AV. &c. &c.; disciplined, cultured, educated, learned, wise (m. a learned or well-educated or wise man), ŚBr.; eminent, superior, Mālav. i, 15 (v.l. for *ślishṭa*); m. (cf. above) a chief, W.; a courtier, counsellor, ib.; n. precept, rule, RPrāt.; instruction (see *śishṭârtham*). **–gītā**, f. N. of a wk. on ethics. **–2. -tā**, f., **-tva**, n. culture, learning, refinement, Kāv. **–prayoga**, m. the practice of the learned, Vām. **–sabhā**, f. assembly of chiefs, council of state, Hit.; *-°cāra* (*°bhâc°*), m. history or tradition of eminent persons, W. **–sammata**, mfn. approved or loved by the learned, Mn. iii, 39. **–smṛiti**, f. tradition of the l°, Baudh. **Śishṭâkaraṇa**, n. non-performance or neglect of what is prescribed, Gaut. **Śishṭâgama**, m. tradition of the learned, Baudh. **Śishṭâcāra**, m. practice or conduct of the learned or virtuous, good manners, proper behaviour, Vas.; mfn. acting like a

learned man, well-behaved, MBh.; *-viruddha*, mfn. opposed to the practice of the virtuous, MW.; *°râviruddha*, mfn. not opposed to the pr° of the v°, ib. **Śishṭâcīrṇa**, mfn. practised by the learned, ib. **Śishṭâdishṭa**, mfn. prescribed or approved by the learned, MBh. **Śishṭâdhyāya**, m. N. of wk. **Śishṭântaka**, m. 'destroyer of the learned,' N. of a man, Kautukas. **Śishṭârtham**, ind. for (the sake of) instruction, MBh. (v.l. *śikshârtham*).

1. **Śishṭi**, f. (for 2. see below) direction, instruction, Pat.; order, command, Bhadrab.; correction, punishment, Gaut. (*°ty-artham*, for the sake of correction, Mn. iv, 164).

Śishya, mfn. to be taught (see *a-ś°*; *a-nishpanne nishpanna-śabdaḥ śishyaḥ*, 'it must be taught that the word *nishpanna* has the meaning of *a-nishpanna*,' Vārtt. on Pāṇ. iii, 2, 132); to be instructed (see *a-ś°*); m. a pupil, scholar, disciple (*ā*, f. a female pupil), ShaḍvBr.; MBh. &c.; passion, anger, W.; violence, ib. **-tā**, f., **-tva**, n. the state or character of a pupil, pupilage, instruction, Kāv.; Kathās.; BhP. **-dhī-vṛiddhida-mahā-tantra**, n. N. of wk. **-paramparā**, f. a series or succession of pupils or disciples, Sāṃkhyak. **-putra**, m. a pupil equal to a son, MW. **-pradeya**, mfn. to be delivered or imparted to p°s, ib. **-praśnôpanishad**, f. N. of a Vedânta wk. **-rūpin**, mfn. having the form or appearance of a disciple, Kathās. **-śikshā-vāda**, m. N. of a Nyāya wk. **-śishṭi**, f. chastisement or correction of a pupil, W. **-sakha**, m. having a p° for a friend, MBh. **-hitā**, f. N. of Bhaṭṭôtpala's Comm. on the Laghu-jātaka; *-nyāsa*, m. N. of a gram. wk. by Ugra-bhūti. **-hitâishiṇī**, f. 'p°'s well-wisher,' N. of a Comm. on Megha-dūta. **Śishyôpanishad**, f. N. of an Upanishad.

Śishyaka, m. a pupil, scholar, Yaiñ.; N. of a man, Buddh.

Śishyāya, Nom. (fr. *śishya*, only p. p. *°yāyita*, n. impers.) to become the pupil of (gen.), Sāh.

Śishyī-√kṛi, P. *-karoti*, to make any one (acc.) a pupil of (gen.), Kathās.

शिष्टि 2. *śishṭi*, f. (fr. *√śiksh*, for 1. see above), help, aid (in *su-ś°*, q.v.)

शिह्ल *śihla*, *śihlaka* &c. See *sihla*.

शिह्लण *śihlaṇa*. See *silhaṇa*.

शी 1. *śī*, cl. 2. Ā. (Dhātup. xxiv, 22) *śéte* (with Guṇa throughout the pr. stem: thus, *śáye* [in RV. also 3. sg.], *śéshe* &c., 3. pl. *śérate* [in AV. also *śére* and Class. *śayire*]; Pot. *śáyīta*, RV. &c.; Impv. *śetām* and *śayām*, AV.; impf. *aśeta*, ŚBr. &c., 3. pl. *aśerata* [in RV. also *áśeran*], p. *śáyāna*, RV. &c.; Ved. and ep. also cl. 1. *śáyate*, *°ti*; impf. *áśayat* and *aśáyata*, RV.; pf. *śiśye*, *śiśyire*, Br.; p. Ved. *śaśayāná*, Class. *śiśyāna*; aor. *aśayishṭa*, Subj. *śéshan*, RV.; fut. *śayitā*, Up., 2. sg. *°tāse*, ŚBr.; *śayishyate*, *°ti*, Br.; *śeshyate*, *°ti*, MBh.; inf. *śayádhyai*, RV.; *śayitum*, MBh.; ind. p. *śayitvā*, Up. &c.; *-śayya*, Kāv.), to lie, lie down, recline, rest, repose, RV. &c. &c.; to remain unused (as Soma), TS.; to lie down to sleep, fall asleep, sleep, GṛŚrS.; MBh. &c.; (with *patye*) to lie down to a husband (for sexual intercourse), Pat.; (*madane na √śī* = 'to be impotent'), VarBṛS.: Pass. *śayyate*, Gr. (aor. *aśāyi*, ib., pr. p. once in MBh. *śīyat*): Caus. *śāyayati*, *°te* (aor. *aśīśayat*), to cause to lie down, lay down, put, throw, fix on or in (loc.), MBh.; Kāv. &c.; to cause to lie down, allow to rest or sleep, Bhaṭṭ.; Rājat.; BhP.: Desid. *śiśayishate*, to wish to rest or sleep, Daś.: Intens. *śāśayyate*, *śeśayīti*, *śeśeti*, Gr. [Cf. Gk. κεῖσθαι, 'to lie;' κοίτη, 'a bed.']

Śayana, **śayanīya** &c. See p. 1055, col. 3.

2. **Śī**, mfn. (ifc.) lying, resting (see *jihma-*, *madhyama-śī* &c.); f. sleep, repose, L.; devotion, tranquillity, L.

शी 3. *śī* (connected with *√2. śad*; cf. Pāṇ. vii, 3, 78), cl. 4. Ā. *śīyate*, to fall out or away, disappear, vanish, TBr.; Bhaṭṭ.

शीक् *śīk* (also written *sīk*), cl. 1. Ā. (Dhātup. iv, 1) *śīkate* (pf. *śiśīke*, aor. *aśīkishṭa* &c., Gr.), to rain in fine drops, drizzle, sprinkle, wet, moisten, Hcar.; Bhaṭṭ.; to go, move, Dhātup. iv, 11 (v.l.): Caus. *śīkayati*, to besprinkle, Hcar.; (cl. 10.) 'to speak' or 'to shine' (*bhāshârthe* or *bhāsârthe*), Dhātup. xxxiii, 116; *āmarshaṇe* or *marshaṇe*, xxxiv, 20. [Cf. Gk. κηκίω.]

Śīkara, m. (mostly pl.; also written *sīkara*) fine or drizzling rain, drizzle, spray, mist, MBh.; Kāv. &c.; a fine drop of rain or water, W.; coldness, L.; n. the resin of the Sarala pine or the tree itself, L.; mf(*ā*)n. cold, L. **-kaṇa**, m. a drop of rain or water, Ratnâv. **-varshin**, mfn. raining in fine drops, drizzling, Megh. **Śīkarâmbu** (BhP.), **°mbhas** (VarBṛS.), n. rain-water. **Śīkarârdra**, mfn. wet with rain or spray, Ragh. **Śīkarâugha**, mfn. abounding with mist, having much spray or fine rain, W.

Śīkarin, mfn. sprinkling, drizzling, scattering spray, Ragh.; Sāh.; spirting water (as the trunk of an elephant), Uttarar.

Śīkāya, P. *°yati* (accord. to Pāṇ. iii, 1, 17, Vārtt. 1, Ā. *°yate*; only p. *°yát* and *°yishyát*), to rain in fine drops, drizzle, sprinkle, drip, TS.; VS.

Śīkitá, mfn. rained in fine drops, sprinkled, TS.

शीकयत *śīkayata*, m. N. of a man, g. *tikâdi*.

शीक्षा *śīkshā*, f. incorrect form of *śikshā* (q.v.), TĀr.; ĀpŚr. &c. **Śīkshâdhyāyôpanishad** and **Śīkshôpanishad**, f. N. of wks.

शीघ्र *śīghra*, mf(*ā*)n. (of doubtful derivation) quick, speedy, swift, rapid (*ám* and *eṇa*, ind. quickly, rapidly, fast), VS.; MBh.; Kāv. &c.; m. N. of a son of Agni-varṇa, Hariv.; Pur.; N. of Vāyu, the wind, L.; (*ā*), f. Croton Polyandrum or Tiglium, L.; N. of a river, MBh.; n. (in astron.) conjunction (accord. to others 'parallax'); the root of Andropogon Muricatus, L.; = *cakrâṅga*, L. **-karman**, n. the calculation of the conjunction of a planet, Sūryas. **-kārin**, mfn. acting or operating speedily, Hariv.; Kathās.; acute (as a disease), Car. (applied to a kind of fever, Bhpr.); *°ri-tva*, n. acuteness, Car. **-kṛit**, mfn. acting speedily, MBh. **-kṛitya**, mfn. to be done quickly, Pañcat. **-kendra**, n. the distance from the conjunction (of a planet), Sūryas., Sch. **-kopin**, mfn. quickly angry, irritable, MW. **-ga**, mf(*ā*)n. going or moving or running quickly, MBh.; Hariv.; R. &c.; m. N. of the sun, MBh.; of a son of Agni-varṇa, R.; of a hare, Pañcat.; *-tva*, n. quick motion, Kām. **-gaṅga**, mfn. (a place) where the Ganges flows rapidly, Pāṇ. ii, 1, 21, Sch. **-gati**, f. the swiftest motion of a planet (i.e. when arrived at the conjunction), VarBṛS.; mfn. = *-ga*, VarYogay. **-gantṛi** or **-gamana** (MW.) or **-gāmin** (R.; Pañcar.), mfn. id. **-cāra**, mfn. id. (in *maṇḍala-ś°*, 'whirling around'), Vikr. **-cetana**, mfn. having quick intellect, very sagacious (as a dog), Cāṇ.; m. a dog, L. **-janman**, m. Guilandina Bonduc, L.; another plant (= *karañja*), MW. **-java**, mfn. moving or running rapidly, R. **-tara**, mfn. more quick, very swift; (*am*, ind. as swiftly as possible), Pañcat.; *-gati*, mfn. moving more swiftly, VarYogay. **-tā**, f. (MBh.; Śiś.) or **-tva**, n. (MBh.; R.; MārkP.) quickness, speed, rapidity. **-parâkrama**, mfn. having quick energy, going to work quickly, quickly resolved, R. **-paridhi**, m. the epicycle of the conjunction of a planet, Sūryas. **-pāṇi**, mfn. quick-handed (applied to the wind), ShaḍvBr. **-pātin**, mfn. flying or moving or acting quickly, Kām. **-pāyin**, mfn. drinking or sucking quickly, Suśr. **-pushpa**, m. Agati Grandiflora, L. **-phala**, n. the equation of the conjunction, Sūryas. **-bāhukāyana**, m. N. of a man, Cat. **-buddha**, m. N. of a teacher, Buddh. **-buddhi**, mfn. quick-witted, MW. **-bodha**, mfn. quickly understood; m. N. of various wks.; *-bhūshaṇa*, n. N. of wk. **-bodhinī**, f. (with *nāma-mālā*) N. of wk. **-yāna**, n. (also pl.) rapid motion, MBh.; mfn. moving rapidly, Kām. **-yāyin**, mfn. id., R. **-laṅghana**, mfn. springing or jumping quickly, moving rapidly, Ghaṭ. **-vaha**, mf(*ā*)n. flowing rap°, Suśr. **-vāhin**, mfn. moving rap°, R. **-vikrama**, mfn. = *-parâkrama*, R.; BhP. **-vega**, mfn. having a rapid course, R. **-vedhin**, mfn. shooting quickly, L.; m. a good archer, MW. **-saṃcārin**, mfn. moving quickly, R. **-srotas**, mfn. having a rapid current, R. **Śīghrâstra**, mfn. having fast-flying missiles (*-tva*, n.), MBh. **Śīghrôcca**, n. 'apsis of the swiftest motion (of a planet),' a conjunction, Sūryas., Sch. (cf. IW. 179).

Śīghrāya, Nom. Ā. *°yate*, to become quick or rapid, Bhaṭṭ.; to hasten, MW.

Śīghrin, mfn. quick, speedy, hasty, fleet, rapid, Śiksh.

Śīghriya, (only L.) mfn. quick, fleet; m. N. of Śiva; of Vishṇu; the fighting of cats.

Śīghrīya, mfn. quick, speedy, rapid, MW.

Śīghrya, mfn. hasty, VS.; n. quickness, speed, rapidity, MW.

शीत् *śīt*, onomat. (also written *sīt*) a sound made by drawing in the breath (to express any sudden thrill of pleasure or pain, and esp. pleasurable sensations during sexual enjoyment). **-kāra**, m. (also written *sīt-kāra*) the sound *śīt* (supposed to indicate pleasure, pain, or applause; also applied to the noise of spirting water &c.), Kāv.; Kathās. **-kārin**, mfn. uttering the sound *śīt*, Amar. **-√kṛi**, P. *-karoti*, to utter the sound *śīt*, Git. **-kṛita**, n. or **-kṛiti**, f. the utterance of the sound *śīt*, Kāv. **-kṛitin**, mfn. = *-kārin*, Nalod.

शीत *śītá*, mf(*ā́*)n. (fr. *śyai*; cf. *śīna*) cold, cool, chilly, frigid (with ind. p. of *√kṛi* either *śītaṃ kṛitya* or *kṛitvā*, g. *sâkshâdi*), RV. &c. &c.; dull, apathetic, sluggish, indolent, L.; boiled (= *kvathita*; *śita* prob. w.r. for *śṛita*), L.; m. Calamus Rotang, L.; Cordia Myxa and Latifolia, L.; Azadirachta Indica, L.; = *asana-parṇī* and *parpaṭā*, L.; camphor, L.; (*ā*), f. spirituous liquor, L.; a kind of Dūrvā grass, L.; another kind of grass (= *śilpikā*), L.; often w.r. for *sītā* (q.v.); n. cold, coldness, cold weather, L.; cold water, L.; Cassia bark, L. **-kara**, mfn. causing coolness, Suśr.; m. 'cool-rayed,' the moon (*ambhaḥ-śīta-k°*, the m° reflected in water, Prab.), Var.; Kathās.; camphor, L. **-kāla**, m. the cold season, Suśr.; Ṛitus.; VarBṛS. &c. **-kālīna**, mfn. belonging to or produced in the c° season, W. **-kiraṇa**, m. 'cold-rayed,' the moon, Var. **-kumbha**, m. the fragrant oleander, L.; (*ī*), f. Pistia Stratiotes, L. **-kṛicchra**, m. (or n., A.) a partic. religious penance (consisting in eating only cold food), Vishṇ. **-kṛicchraka**, n. id., L. **-kriyā**, f. the act of cooling, Mālav. **-kshāra**, n. refined borax, L. **-gandha**, n. 'having cool fragrance,' white sandal, L.; (*ā*), f. Minusops Elengi, L. **-gātra**, m. 'causing cool limbs,' a kind of fever, Bhpr. **-gu**, m. = *-kiraṇa*, Var.; Kathās.; camphor, A.; *-tanaya*, m. 'son of the moon,' the planet Mercury, VarBṛS., Sch. **-campaka**, m. = *dīpa*, *tarpaṇa* (*ātarpaṇa*), *darpaṇa*, L. **-jvara**, m. a fever with cold fits, Kathās.; Bhpr. **-tā**, f. (MBh.; R.; Cāṇ. &c.) or **-tva**, n. (R.; Sāh.) coldness, cold. **-dīdhiti**, m. = *-kiraṇa*, VarBṛS. **-dūrvā**, f. white Dūrvā grass, L. (w.r. for *sita-a°*). **-dyuti**, m. = *-kiraṇa*, Hāsy. **-paṅka**, m. rum, spirit distilled from molasses, L. **-parṇī** (m.c., Suśr.) or **-parṇī** (L.), f. Gynandropsis Pentaphylla; (*ī*), f. Cleome Pent°, W.; another plant (= *arka*), W. **-pallava**, m. Ardisea Solanacea, W.; (*ā*), f. another plant (= *bhūmi-jambu*), MW. **-pākinī**, f. = *kākolī*, *mahāsamaṅgā*, L. **-pākī**, f. a kind of potherb, MBh. (Sida Cordifolia, Abrus Precatorius, = *kākolī*, L.) **-pākya**, n. (prob.) a kind of plant or fruit, Suśr. **-pāṇi**, mfn. 'cold-handed,' cold rayed (as the moon), ShaḍvBr. **-pitta**, n. a tumour caused by a chill (attended with fever and sickness and compared to a swelling caused by a wasp sting), BhP.; ŚārṅgS.; increase of bile or phlegm caused by cold, MW. **-pushpa** (only L.), m. Acacia Sirissa; (*ā*), f. Sida Cordifolia; n. Cyperus Rotundus. **-pushpaka**, m. Calotropis Gigantea, L. (v.l. *śiva-p°*); n. bitumen, L. **-pūtanā**, f. a kind of female demon (causing illness in children), MBh.; Suśr. **-prada** or **-prabha**, m. camphor, L. **-priya**, m. = *parpaṭa*, L. **-phala** (only L.), m. Ficus Glomerata; Cordia Myxa; (*ā*), f. Emblica Officinalis. **-balā**, f. a kind of plant (= *mahā-samaṅgā*), L. **-budhna**, mfn. having a cold bottom (as a vessel), ĀpŚr. **-bhañjirasa**, m. a partic. mixture, Bhpr.; Rasar. **-bhānavīya**, mf(*ā*)n. lunar, Dhūrtan. **-bhānu**, m. 'cool-rayed,' the moon, ib. **-bhīta**, mfn. afraid of cold (held to be wrong with Brāhmans), MBh. **-bhīru**, m. sensitive to cold, Jasminum Zambac, L. **-bhīruka**, mfn. sensitive to c°; m. a kind of rice, Suśr.; Vāgbh. **-bhojin**, mfn. eating cold food, Pāṇ. iii, 2, 78, Sch. **-mañjarī**, f. Nyctanthes Arbor Tristis, L. **-maya**, mf(*ī*)n. having a cold nature, cool, Hariv. **-mayūkha**, m. = *-kiraṇa*, VarYogay.; camphor, L.; *-mālin*, m. the moon, VarBṛS. **-marīci**, m. = *-kiraṇa*, Kāv.; camphor, L. **-mūlaka**, mfn. having a cool root, MW.; n. the root of Andropogon Muricatus, L. **– meha,** m. diabetes caused by or attended with cold, ŚārṅgS.; Bhpr. **– mehin,** mfn. suffering from the prec. complaint, Car. **– ramya,** mfn. pleasant in c° weather, MW.; m. a lamp, L. **– raśmi,** mfn. cool-rayed (*-tva,* n.), Śak.; m. the moon, MBh.; Hariv.; Kāv.; Var.; camphor, MW.; *-ja,* m. 'son of the moon,' the planet Mercury, VarBṛS. **– rasa,** m. spirituous liquor made from the unboiled juice of the sugar-cane, Bhpr. **– rasika,** mfn. having or causing a cold flavour, Suśr. **– ruc,** m. = *-kiraṇa,* Śiś. **– ruci,** m. id., Bālar. **– rūrá,** m. or n. du. a fever marked by cold and burning heat (alternating), TS.; Vait. **– rocis,** m. = *-kiraṇa,* Śiś. **– vatī,** f., see *mahā-ś°.* **– vana,** n. N. of a place of pilgrimage, MBh. (v.l. *sīta-v°*); of a place (for receiving) corpses in Magadha, Buddh. **– valka,** m. having cool bark, MW.; m. Ficus Glomerata, L. **– vaha,** mf(*ā*)n. flowing with cold water (a river), R. **– vātôshṇa-vetālī,** f. a kind of female demon, Hariv. **– vīrya,** mfn. having a cooling effect, cooling, ib. **– vīryaka,** m. Ficus Infectoria, L. **– śiva,** m. Anethum Sowa or another kind of anise, Suśr.; Mimosa Suma, L.; m. or (*ā*), f. a kind of fennel (= *madhurikā, miśreyā*), MW.; (*ā*), f. dill, L.; Mimosa Suma, L.; n. bitumen, L.; rock-salt, L. **– śūka,** m. barley, L. (cf. *sita-śūka*). **– saṃsparśa,** mfn. cool to the touch, R. **– saha** (only L.), mfn. bearing or enduring cold; m. Careya Arborea or Salvadora Persica; (*ā*), f. Vitex Negundo; = *vāsantī.* **– sparśa,** mfn. = *-saṃsparśa,* MW.; m. a cold sensation, Kāv. **– hara,** mfn. removing c°, Śiś. **– hrada** (*śītá-*), mfn. cool as a pond, AV. **Śītâṅśu,** mfn. c°-rayed (*-tā,* f.; *-tva,* n.), MBh.; R.; m. the moon, MBh.; Kāv.; VarBṛS. &c.; camphor, L.; *-taila,* n. c° oil, L.; *-bhāj,* (n.?) a Nakshatra, Kāv.; *-mat,* m. the moon, R. **Śītâkula,** mfn. benumbed with cold, frozen, W. **Śītâṅga,** mf(*ī*)n. cold-bodied, benumbed, Suśr.; m. a kind of fever, Bhpr.; (*ī*), f. a kind of Mimosa, L. **Śītâtapatra,** n. an umbrella that protects from cold (or rain) and heat (sunshine), VarBṛS. **Śītâda,** m. scorbutic affection of the gums, Suśr.; Bhpr. **Śītâdri,** m. the snowy mountains, the Himālaya, Kālac. **Śītâdhivāsa,** mf(*ā*)n. living in cool places, (or) cooling, Suśr. **Śītânta,** m. 'cold-bordered,' N. of a mountain, Pur. **Śītâbalā,** f. a kind of plant (= *mahā-samaṅgā*), L. **Śītâri-rasa,** m. a partic. mixture, Rasêndrac. **Śītârta,** mfn. suffering from cold, Kathās.; w.r. for *śītânta,* MārkP. **Śītâśman,** m. a cold stone, MW.; the moon-gem, L. **Śītêtara,** mfn. other than cold, hot; *-raśmi* (L.) or °*tarâcis* (Rājat.), m. 'hot-rayed,' the sun. **Śītêshu,** m. 'cold-arrow,' N. of a mythical missile, R. **Śītôttama,** n. 'best of cold things,' water, L. **Śītôda,** n. 'having cool water,' N. of a lake, Pur.; (*ā*), f. N. of a mythical river, Kathās. **Śītôdaka,** (prob.) m. N. of a hell, Kāraṇḍ. (w.r. *sitôd°*). **Śītôpacāra,** m. curing with cold remedies, Pañcat. **Śītôshṇa,** mf(*ā*)n. cold and hot, GṛŚrS.; Kāv. &c.; (*ā*), f. N. of a female demon, W. (w.r. *śīlôshṇā*); n. (sg. or du.) cold and heat, MBh.; Kāv. &c.; *-kiraṇa,* m. du. the moon and the sun, Mālav. **Śītôshma** or °**man,** n. N. of various Sāmans, ĀrshBr.

Śītaka, mf(*ikā*)n. cool, AV.; sluggish, idle, lazy, Pāṇ. v, 2, 72; healthy, L.; m. feeling of cold, shivering, Car.; the cold season, g. *yāvâdi,* L.; any cold thing, A.; a lazy man, W.; a happy or contented man, ib.; = *asana-parṇī,* L.; Marsilea Dentata, MW.; a scorpion, L.; pl. N. of a people, VarBṛS.; n. a kind of sandal, L.

Śītaya, Nom. P. *yati,* to cool (trans.), Hariv.

Śītala, mf(*ā*)n. cold, cool, cooling, MBh.; Kāv. &c.; shivering, frosty, Cat.; cold i.e. free from passion, calm, gentle, Ashṭāv.; Prasannar.; not exciting emotion, not causing painful feelings, Vikr. iv, 37; m. (only L.) the wind; the moon; Cordia Myxa; Michelia Champaka; = *asana-parṇī;* a kind of camphor; the resin of Shorea Robusta; green sulphate of iron (also m.); bitumen (also m.); a religious ceremony observed on the sun's entering Aries; (with Jainas) N. of the 10th Arhat of the present Avasarpiṇī; (*ā*), f., see below; (*ī*), f. Pistia Stratiotes, L.; small-pox, W.; (*am*), n. cold, coldness, cold weather, Subh.; sandal, L.; a lotus, L.; Costus Speciosus or Arabicus, L.; the root of Andropogon Muricatus, L.; a pearl, L. **– cchada,** m. a white leaf, MW.; mfn. having wh° leaves, ib.; m. Michelia Champaka, L. **– jala,** n. cold water, MW; a lotus-flower, L. **– tara,** mfn. more cool, colder, Śiś. **– tā,** f. coldness, ŚārṅgP.; insensibility, MW. **– tva,** n. coldness, L.; indifference, apathy, Campak. **– dīkshita,** m. N. of an author, Cat. **– pattrikā,** f. Maranta Dichotoma, L. **– prada,** mfn. giving or producing coolness, MW.; m. (or n., A.) sandal, L. **– prasāda,** m. N. of a person, MW. **– vāta,** m. a cool breeze, cold wind, ib. **– vātaka,** mfn. having cool breezes, ib.; m. the plant Marsilea Quadrifolia, L. **– saptamī,** f. = *śītalā-s°,* MW. **– sparśa,** mfn. cold to the touch, R. **– svāmin,** m. N. of an Arhat with Jainas, Śatr.

Śītalaka, m. marjoram, L.; n. a white lotus, L.

Śītalaya, Nom. P. °*yati,* to cool (trans.), Prasannar.

Śītalā, f. (only L.) sand; Pistia Stratiotes; = *kuṭumbinī* and *ārāma-śītalā;* a red cow; small-pox; the goddess inflicting small-pox (cf. comp. and RTL. 227, 228). **– gaurī-pūjā-vidhi,** m. N. of wk. **– pūjā,** f. worship of the goddess Śītalā (a festival on the 8th day of the second half of the month Phālguna), MW.; N. of wk. **– prakaraṇa,** n. N. of wk. **– vrata,** n. a partic. religious observance, Cat.; N. of a ch. of the Skanda-purāṇa. **– saptamī,** f. a festival kept on the 7th day of the light half of the month Māgha (in honour of the small-pox goddess, when only cold food is eaten), RTL. 430. **– °shṭaka** (°*lâshṭ°*), n., °**lā-stotra,** n. N. of wks.

Śītalāya, Nom. Ā. °*yate,* to become cool, Mālatīm.

Śītalī, in comp. for *śītala.* **– √kṛi,** P. *-karoti,* to cool, make cold, Daś.; Lalit. **– jaṭā,** f. Villarsia Cristata, L. **– √bhū,** P. *-bhavati,* to become cold (also fig.), Kathās.

Śītāru, mfn. sensitive to cold, L.

Śītālu, mfn. suffering from cold, sensitive to cold, shivering with cold, VarBṛ.; Śiś.; Kathās.

Śītikā, f. coldness, MW. **– vat,** mf(*atī*)n. cool, AV.

Śītiman, m. coldness, g. *dṛiḍhâdi.*

Śītī, in comp. for *śīta.* **– karaṇa,** n. act of cooling, means of cooling, Suśr. **– √kṛi,** P. *-karoti,* to make cold, cool (trans.), R. **– bhāva,** m. the becoming cool, Nir.; Car.; Kāraṇḍ.; cold state, coldness, MW.; the growing cold or passionless, perfect tranquillity of mind, Lalit.; final emancipation, MW. **– √bhū,** P. *-bhavati,* to become cold (see next). **– bhūta,** mfn. become cold, Suśr.; tranquillized, emancipated, Śīl. **– m-bhāva,** w.r. for *śītī-bh°,* Lalit.

Śītya, mfn. to be cooled or chilled, MW.; ploughed, tilled (in this sense more usually *sītya*), ib.

शीत्कार *śīt-kāra* &c. See p. 1077, col. 3.

शीधु *śīdhu* &c. See *sīdhu.*

शीन *śīná,* mfn. (fr. √*śyai;* cf. *śīta* and *śyāna*) congealed, frozen, coagulated, thick, Car. (cf. Pāṇ. vi, 1, 24); m. a large snake, L.; a fool, blockhead (= *mūrkha,* which is perhaps a w.r. for *mūrta*), L.; n. ice, VS.

शीपल्य *śīpalya,* mf(*ā*)n. overgrown with Śīpāla plants, ShaḍvBr. (v.l. *śaivalya*).

Śīpāla, m. n. the plant Blyxa Octandra, RV.; ĀśvGṛ.; (*ā*), f. water or a pool abounding in the above plants, AV.

Śīpālila, mfn. (also written *sīp°*) overgrown with Śīpāla plants, g. *kāśâdi.*

शीपुद्रु *śīpúdru,* w.r. for *cīpú-dru* (q.v.)

शीफर *śīphara,* mfn. charming, delightful, Daś.; = *sphīta,* L.

शीफालिका *śīphālikā,* f. (also written *śephālī* or *śephālikā*) the plant Nyctanthes Tristis, L.

शीभ् *śībh,* cl. 1. Ā. *śībhate,* to boast, Dhātup. x, 20.

शीभम *śībham,* ind. quickly, swiftly, speedily, RV.; AV.; TS.; Kauś.

Śībhya, mfn. moving quickly, VS.; m. a bull, L.; N. of Śiva, L.

शीभर *śībhara,* m. = *śīkara,* fine rain, L. (w.r. *śībhava*); mfn. = *śīphara,* charming, delightful, Harav.; Jātakam.

शीम *śīma.* See *duḥ-* and *su-śīma.*

शीर 1. *śīrá,* mfn. (fr. √*śo*) pointed, sharp, RV.; m. a large snake, the Boa Constrictor, Pañcat. **– śocis** (*śīrá-*), mfn. sharp-rayed, burning, RV.

Śīrin, m. a kind of Kuśa grass, L.

शीर 2. *śīra, śīra-deva* &c. See *sīra.*

शीरि *śiri* or *śīri,* f. (cf. *sirā*) a vein, artery, MaitrS.

शीर्ण *śīrṇá,* mfn. (fr. √*śṝ*) broken or rent asunder, shivered, crushed, shattered, injured, ŚBr. &c. &c.; fallen away or out, MBh.; R.; Rājat.; broken away, burst or overflowed (as river-water that has burst its banks), Nir.; withered, faded, shrivelled, shrunk, decayed, rotten, Mn.; MBh. &c.; thin, small, slender, W.; n. a sort of perfume (= *sthauṇeyaka*), Bhpr. **– tā,** f. (W.), **-tva,** n. (Mṛicch.) withered condition, rottenness, decay. **– danta,** mfn. one whose teeth have fallen out, toothless, MBh. **– nālā,** f. Hemionitis Cordifolia, L. **– pattra,** n. a withered leaf, MW.; mfn. having w° leaves, ib.; m. Pterospermum Acerifolium, L.; a kind of Lodhra, L. **– parṇa,** n. = prec. n.; mfn. = prec., MW.; m. Azadirachta Indica, L.; (*ī*), f. a kind of plant, L.; °*ṇa-phala,* mfn. having withered leaves and fruits (as a tree), MBh.; °*ṇâśin,* mfn. one who eats w° l°s, ib. **– pāda,** m. a thin or shrunken foot, MW.; 'having shrivelled feet,' N. of Yama (said to have become so in consequence of his mother's curse), L. **– pushpa,** mf(*ā*)n. having w° flowers (as a branch), R. **– pushpikā,** f. Anethum Sowa, L. **– mālā,** w.r. for *-nālā.* **– mūla,** mfn. having w° roots, MW. **– vṛinta,** m. 'slender-stalked,' a water-melon (n. its fruit), Suśr.; Vāgbh. **– śīrshan,** mfn. one who has a broken or shattered head, BhP. **Śīrṇâṅhri** or °**ṇâṅghri,** m. N. of Yama (= *śīrṇa-pāda,* q.v.), L.

Śīrṇaka, mfn. one who eats withered leaves, L.

Śīrṇi, f. breaking, crushing, shattering, Vop.

Śīrṇī-√kṛi, P. *-karoti,* to hurt, injure, sting, Kād.

1. **Śīrta,** mfn. fragile, destructible (in *a-śīrta-tanu* and *duḥ-ś°-t°,* q.v.)

Śīrti, f. breaking, shattering, Kāṭh.; ShaḍvBr.

Śīrya, mfn. destructible, perishable (see *a-śīrya*); n. a kind of grass, Gobh.

Śīrvi, mfn. hurtful, injurious, savage, Uṇ. iv, 54, Sch.

शीर्त 2. *śīrta,* mfn. (fr. 1. √*śrī*) mixed (in *á-śīrta,* RV. viii, 2, 9; cf. *śritá,* p. 1098).

शीर्ष *śīrshá,* n. (connected with *śiras;* collateral of *śīrshán* below, from which it is not separable in comp.; m. only in *vasti-ś°,* q.v.; ifc. f. *ā* or *ī*), the head, skull (acc. with Caus. of √*vṛit* = *śiras* with id.), AV. &c.; the upper part, tip, top (of anything, as of a letter &c.), Hariv.; Kāv.; the fore-part, front (in *raṇa-ś°,* q.v.), R.; black Agallochum or aloe wood, L.; m. a kind of grass, Pat.; N. of a mountain, W.; (*ā*), f. a kind of metre, Col. **– kapālá,** n. a skull, AV.; ŚBr.; TUp. **– ghātin,** m. 'one who beheads,' an executioner, Pāṇ. iii, 2, 51. **– cchida,** m. a partic. Ekâha, ŚāṅkhŚr. **– cchinná,** mfn. having the head cut off, decapitated, ŚBr. **– ccheda,** m. (Subh.), **-cchedana,** n. (MW.) the act of cutting off the h°, decapitation. **– cchedika,** w.r. for *śairshacch°* (q.v.) **– cchedya,** mfn. deserving decapitation, Ragh.; Uttarar. (°*dyam* √*kṛi,* 'to behead, decapitate,' Bhaṭṭ.) **– tás,** ind. from or at the head or top, in front, RV.; AV.; ŚBr. (*pādau ś° kṛitvā,* 'putting the h° where the feet ought to be,' R.) **– trāṇa,** n. 'head-protector,' a helmet, MBh. **– paṭṭaka,** m. 'head-cloth,' a turban, Kathās. **– parṇī,** (prob.) w.r. for *śīrṇa-p°.* **– bandhanā,** f. a head-band, MBh. **– bhāra,** m. a head-load, g. *bhastrâdi;* °*rika,* mf(*ī*)n. carrying a head-load, ib. **– bhidya,** n. h°-splitting, AV. **– māya,** m. N. of a man (pl. his descendants), g. *yaskâdi.* **– raksha,** m., **-rakshaṇa,** n. = *-trāṇa,* L. **– rogin,** mfn. having or producing h°-ache, MBh. **– vana,** (prob.) w.r. for *śirīsha-v°,* Kāraṇḍ. **– vartana,** n. submission to punishment (if an accused person clears himself in an ordeal; see under *śiras*), Vishṇ. **– virecana,** n. a means or remedy for making the head clear (= *śiro-v°;* cf. *vir°*), Car. **– vedanā** (Ratnâv.), **-vyathā** (Pañcad.), f. head-ache. **– śoká,** m. pain in the head, AV. **– hārya,** mfn. to be borne on the h° (opp. to *ano-vāhya*), TS.; Kāṭh. **Śīrshânta,** m. neighbourhood of the h° (°*tāt,* 'from the h° of a bed,' °*te,* 'under the pillow'), Kathās. **Śīrshâ-**

mayá, m. disease or morbid affection of the head, AV. **Śirshâvaśeshī-kṛita**, mfn. one who has only the h° left (as Rāhu), Bhartṛ. **Śirshâhārya**, mfn. = *śirsha-h°*, MaitrS. **Śirshôdaya**, mfn. rising in front (said of the zodiacal signs Gemini, Leo, Virgo, Libra, Scorpio, Aquarius, and Pisces).

Śirshaka, mfn. familiar with the text called *śiras*, Baudh.; m. N. of a Rāhu (the personified ascending node; cf. *śirshâvaśeshī-kṛita*), L.; n. the head, skull, BhP.; Pañcar.; the top of anything, L.; a cap or helmet, L.; a garland worn on the head, Gal.; judgment, verdict, sentence, result of judicial investigation (cf. next). **-stha**, mfn. being in or on the head, W.; abiding by a verdict, submitting to punishment (if an accused person clears himself in an ordeal), Yājñ.

Śirshakti, f. (prob. for *śirsha-śakti*) 'head-seizure,' pain in the head, AV. **-mát**, mfn. suffering from head-ache, TS.

Śirshan, in comp. for *śirshan*. **-vát**, mfn. having a head (opp. to *a-śirshaka*), AV.; TS.; ŚBr.

Śirshaṇī, f. the head of a couch, VarBṛS.

Śirshaṇyà, mf(*ā*)n. being in or on the head, RV. &c. &c.; being at the head (fig.), first, Kāṭh.; BhP.; m. clean and unentangled hair, L.; n. the head of a couch, ĀpŚr.; a helmet, L.

Śirshán, n. (for *śiras + an*; rare in later language; Veda has all cases in sg. except nom. acc.; also has nom. acc. du. pl. loc. pl.; later language has only acc. pl. and remaining cases; cf. also *a-, tri-, sahasra-ś°*) the head (also 'an eminent or illustrious person,' cf. RV. vii, 18, 24), RV. &c. &c.

Śirshaya, n. N. of a partic. mythical being, Vīrac.

Śirshika and **śirshin**. See *a-ś°*.

Śirshe, loc. of *śirsha*, in comp. **-bhāra**, m. a load on the head, g. *bhastrâdi* (cf. *śirsha-bh°*). **-bhārika**, mfn. carrying a load on the head, ib.

शील् 1. *śil* (rather Nom. fr. *śila* below), cl. 1. P. *śilati* (pf. *śiśila* &c.), to meditate, contemplate, Dhātup. xv, 16; to serve, worship, ib.; to act, do, practise, make, ib.: Caus. (or cl. 10. P., Dhātup. xxxv, 26) *śilayati* (aor. *aśiśilat*), to do, make, practise repeatedly or exceedingly, be intent upon or engaged in (acc.), exercise, cultivate, Āpast.; MBh.; Kāv. &c.; to wear, put on, Gīt.; to visit, frequent, Bhām. (cf. *śilita*); to exceed, excel, Vop.

Śila, n. (and m., g. *ardharcâdi*; ifc. f. *ā*) habit, custom, usage, natural or acquired way of living or acting, practice, conduct, disposition, tendency, character, nature (often ifc. = 'habituated' or 'accustomed' or 'disposed' or 'addicted to,' 'practising;' cf. *guṇa-, dāna-, puṇya-ś°* &c.), VS. &c. &c.; good disposition or character, moral conduct, integrity, morality, piety, virtue, Mn.; MBh. &c.; cf. IW. 208; (with Buddhists *śila*, 'moral conduct,' is one of the 6 or 10 perfections or Pāramitās [q. v.] and is threefold, viz. *sambhāra, kuśala-saṃgrāha, sattvârtha-kriyā*, Dharmas. 106); a moral precept (with Buddh. there are 5 fundamental precepts or rules of moral conduct, cf. *pañca-śila*), MWB. 126; form, shape, beauty, W.; m. a large snake (in this sense prob. fr. √1. *śi*), L.; N. of a man, Buddh.; of a king, Rājat.; (*ā*), f., see below. **-kirti**, m. 'glory of virtue,' N. of a man, Buddh. **-khaṇḍana**, n. violation of morality or virtue, Pañcat. **-gupta**, mfn. hidden or crafty by character, cunning, Kathās. (cf. *gupta-śila*). **-jña**, mfn. knowing v° or morality, Kathās. **-jñāna-nidhi**, m. a treasury of v° and knowledge, MBh. **-taṭa**, mfn. (fig.) having v° for a bank or shore, MW. **-tas**, ind. according or in regard to moral character or conduct, Mn.; Daś.; MārkP. **-tā**, f., **-tva**, n. disposition, inclination, customary practice; morality, virtuousness, Kāv.; Suśr. **-tulya**, mfn. resembling or equivalent to virtue, MBh. **-tyāga**, m. abandonment of virtue or honour, Kathās. **-dhara**, mfn. maintaining or possessing v°, virtuous, honourable, BhP.; m. N. of a man, Kathās. **-dhārin**, m. 'virtue-possessor,' N. of Śiva, MBh. **-nidhi**, m. a treasury of virtue, ib. **-pāramitā**, f. (with Buddhists) the perfection (called) *śila* (one of the 6 transcendental perfections, cf. under *śila*), SaddhP.; Kāraṇḍ. **-pālita**, m. 'virtue-protected,' N. of a man, Buddh. **-bhaṅga**, m. = *-khaṇḍana*, Kāv. **-bhaṭṭārikā**, w. r. for *śilā-bh°*, q. v. **-bhadra**, m. 'eminent in virtue,' N. of a teacher (also called Dharma-kośa), Buddh. **-bhāj**, mfn. possessing v°, honourable, MBh. **-bhraṅśa**, m. loss of virtue or integrity, Kathās. **-maya**, mf(*ī*)n. consisting in moral character or good conduct, Buddh. **-vañcanā**, f. deception in regard to a person's character, Mṛicch. **-vat**, mfn. possessed of a good disposition or character, well-conducted, moral, Mn.; MBh. &c.; (ifc.) having the custom or practice of, VarBṛS.; (*atī*), f. N. of a woman, Kathās. **-varjita**, mfn. destitute of morality or virtue, ill-conducted, immoral, R. **-vighna-kṛit**, mfn. causing an obstacle to v°, Rājat. **-viplava** (ib.), **-vilaya** (Bhartṛ.), m. ruin of virtue. **-vilāsa**, m. N. of wk. **-viśuddha-netra**, m. N. of a Deva-putra, Lalit. **-vṛitta**, n. sg. or m. du. v° and good conduct (*-dhara* and *-vid*, mfn. holding or knowing v° and g° c°), MBh.; Kāv.; mfn. virtuous and well-conducted, MBh. **-vṛitti**, f. practice of virtue, good conduct or behaviour, MW. **-vṛiddha**, mfn. rich in virtue, honourable, moral, MBh. **-vela**, mfn. = *-taṭa*, Mṛicch. **-vrata**, n. (with Buddh.) ceremonial practices (one of the ten fetters), MWB. 127. **-śālin**, mfn. possessed of v° or good conduct, Hcat. **-saṃgha**, m. N. of an author, Cat. **-samādāna**, mfn. observance of v° or morality, Divyâv. **-sampanna**, mfn. = *-śālin*, MBh. **-hara**, m. 'destroying virtue,' N. of a man, Kathās. **Śilâṅka**, mf(*ā*)n. characterized by virtue, HPariś.; m. N. of an author, Cat. **Śilâṅga**, m. N. of an author, ib. **Śilâḍhya**, mfn. abounding in v°, most honourable, MBh. **Śilâditya**, m. 'sun of v°,' N. of various kings (esp. of a son of Vikramâditya, also called Pratāpa-śila), Buddh. **Śilêndra-bodhi**, m. N. of a man, ib. **Śilôpadeśa-mālā**, f. 'garland of instruction in v°,' N. of wk. **Śilôpasampanna**, mfn. = *śila-sampanna*, MBh. **Śilôshṇa**, prob. w. r. for *śitôshṇa* (q. v.)

Śilaka, m. N. of a poet, Cat.; n. the root of the ear, L.

Śilana, n. repeated practice, constant study (of the Śāstras &c.), MBh.; frequent mentioning, Pat.; wearing, putting on, possessing, MW.; serving, honouring, ib.

Śilaya. See under √1. *śil*, col. 1.

Śilā, f. N. of the wife of Kauṇḍinya, Vās., Introd.; (also *-bhaṭṭārikā*) N. of a poetess, ŚārṅgP.; Cat.

Śilāra-vaṅśa, m. N. of a royal family, Inscr.

Śilika, mfn. accustomed to act (in *anyathā-ś°*, accustomed to act in another manner), GopBr.

Śilita, mfn. practised, exercised &c.; inhabited, frequented, Gīt.; (ifc.) prepared or made of, ib.; n. practice, conduct, MW.

Śilin, mfn. virtuous, moral, honest, MBh.; (ifc.) having the custom of, habituated or used to, practising, ib.; Hariv. &c.

शील् 2. *śil*, m. N. of a man, Inscr.

शीवन् *śivan*, mfn. (fr. √1. *śi*) lying, resting (see *uttāna-, talpa-, vahya-ś°*); m. a large snake, the Boa Constrictor, Uṇ. iv, 113, Sch.; (*arī*), f. an iguana (= *godhā*), ib.

शीवल *śivala*, n. the aquatic plant Blyxa Octandra (= *śevāla*), L.; benzoin or storax (= *śaileya*), L.

शीष्ट *śishṭa*, m. pl. (accord. to some) N. of a people, RV. viii, 53, 5.

शीहर *śihara*, m. N. of a scribe, MW.

शु 1. *śu*, cl. 1. P. *śavati*, to go &c.; cf. √*śav*, p. 1059, col. 3.

शु 2. *śu*, ind. (g. *svar-ādi*) quickly, swiftly (= *kshipram*), Naigh. ii, 15.

Śukam, ind. (g. *câdi*), id. (accord. to some).

शुंशुमार *śunśumāra*, incorrect for *śiśu-māra*, q. v.

शुक् *śuk*, cl. 1. P. *śokati*, to go, move, Dhātup. v, 5.

शुक *śuka*, m. (prob. fr. √1. *śuc*, and orig. 'the bright one') a parrot, RV. &c. &c.; a poet (?), Rājat. v, 31; Acacia Sirissa, L.; Zizyphus Scandens, L.; N. of a son of Vyāsa (narrator of the Bhāgavata-Purāṇa to king Parikshit), MBh.; Pur.; of a warrior, MBh.; of an Asura, Hariv. (v. l. *śara*); of a king of the Gandharvas, R.; of a minister of Rāvaṇa, ib.; of a Brāhman ascetic, Buddh.; (*ī*), f. a female parrot (also the mythical mother of parrots, fabled as daughter or, accord. to some, wife of Kaśyapa), MBh.; Pur.; N. of the wife of Saptarshi (loved by Agni), BhP.; n. N. of various plants (Acacia Sirissa, Bignonia Indica &c.), L.; a partic. drug and perfume (= *granthi-parṇa*, commonly called Gaṇṭhiāla), L.; the hem of a garment, L.; cloth, clothes, L.; a helmet or turban, L.; N. of a mythical weapon, MBh. **-karṇī**, f. (perhaps) a kind of plant, Pāṇ. iv, 1, 64, Sch. **-kūṭa**, m. a garland fixed over two pillars, L. **-cchada**, m. a parrot's wing, Dhūrtan.; n. = *granthi-parṇa*, Bhpr.; Xanthochymus Pictorius, L. **-jātaka**, n. N. of wk. **-jihvā**, f. a parrot's tongue, Suśr.; a plant (commonly called Śuyā-ṭhoṇṭī or parrot's beak), W.; Bignonia Chelonioides, L. **-taru**, m. Acacia Sirissa, L. **-tā**, f. or **-tva**, n. the state of a parrot, Kathās.; Uttamac. **-tātparya-ratnâvali**, f. N. of wk. **-tuṇḍa**, m. 'p°'s-beak,' a partic. position of the hands, Cat. **-tuṇḍaka**, n. a kind of cinnabar, Bhpr. **-deva**, m. N. of Kṛishṇa, Pañcar.; of a son of Vyāsa, ib.; of a son of Hari-hara, Cat.; of various authors, ib.; (with *paṇḍita-śiromaṇi*) of a man, ib.; *-caritra*, n. N. of a ch. of the Mahā-bhārata. **-druma**, m. = *-taru*, L. **-nalikā-nyāya**, m. the rule of the parrot (who was causelessly frightened by) the Nalikā plant; (*ena*), ind. accord. to that rule, i. e. causelessly, Nīlak. **-naśā**, w. r. for next, Suśr. **-nasā**, f. = *-nāsā*, ib. **-nāmā**, w. r. for *-nāsā*, L. **-nāśa** (L.), °*śā* (Suśr.), w. r. for *-nāsa*, °*sā*. **-nāśana**, m. 'p°-destroying,' a partic. plant (= *dadru-ghna*), L. **-nāsa**, mfn. having a nose like a p°'s beak, MW.; m. a partic. ornament on a house, Vāstuv.; Calosanthes Indica, L.; Bignonia Chelonioides, Bhpr.; Agati Grandiflora, L.; Bignonia Indica, W.; Sesbana Grandiflora, ib.; N. of a Rākshasa, R.; of a minister of Tārāpīḍa, Kād.; (*ā*), f. a kind of plant (accord. to L., = m., *kāśmīrī, nalikā*), Suśr. **-nāsikā**, f. a p°'s nose, MW.; a nose like that of a p°, ib.; an aquiline n°, ib. **-pakshiya**, n. or (*ā*), f., °*ya-vyākhyā*, f. N. of wks. **-piṇḍi**, w. r. for *śūka-p°*. **-pitāmaha**, m. 'grandfather of Śuka,' N. of the sage Parāśara (father of Vyāsa), W. **-puccha**, m. a parrot's tail, ib.; 'coloured like a p°'s tail,' sulphur, L. **-pucchaka**, n. a partic. drug (= *granthi-parṇa*), L. **-pushpa**, m. 'p°-flowered,' Acacia Sirissa, L.; n. = *granthi-parṇa*, Bhpr. **-potra**, m. a kind of harmless snake, L. **-praśna-saṃhitā**, f. N. of wk. **-priya**, mfn. dear to p°s, MW.; m. Acacia Sirissa, Bhpr.; Azadirachta Indica, L.; (*ā*), f. Eugenia Jambolana, L.; N. of a Surâṅganā, Siṃhās. **-phala**, m. Calotropis Gigantea, L. **-babhru** (*śúka-*), mfn. reddish like a p°, VS.; MaitrS. **-barha**, n. N. of a kind of fragrant substance, Car.; Bhpr. **-bṛihat-kathā**, f., **-mahimnaḥ-stava**, m. N. of wks. **-yogin**, m. N. of an author, Cat. **-rahasya**, n. or °**yôpanishad**, f. N. of an Upanishad. **-rūpa** (*śúka-*), mfn. having the colour of a p°, VS. **-lāṅgala**, (prob.) w. r. for *-lāṅgula* and = *-barha*, Suśr. **-vat**, ind. like a p°, MW. **-vallabha**, m. 'beloved by p°s,' the pomegranate tree, L. **-vāc**, mfn. having a voice like the note of a p° (Kṛishṇa), Pañcar. **-vāha**, m. 'p°-borne,' N. of Kāma-deva (whose vehicle is a p°), L. **-śārika**, n. a p° and a Maina bird, MW. (cf. *-sārikā-pralāpana*). **-śimbā** or **-śimbi**, w. r. for *śūka-śim°*. **-saṃvāda**, m., **-saṃhitā**, f., **-saṃdeśa**, m., **-saṃdeśa-vyākhyā**, f. N. of wks. **-saptati**, f. N. of 70 stories related by a parrot (of which there are 2 recensions extant). **-sārikā-pralāpana**, n. instruction about p°s and Maina birds (one of the 64 arts), Cat. (cf. *-śārika*). **-sûkti-sudhākara**, m., **-sūtra**, n. N. of wks. **-harí**, mfn. green like a p°, MaitrS.; Vait. &c. **-harita**, mfn. id., ĀpŚr. **Śukâkhyā**, f. Bignonia Chelonioides, Suśr. **Śukâdana**, m. 'p°'s food,' the pomegranate tree, L. **Śukânana**, mfn. parrot-faced, R.; (*ā*), f. Bignonia Chelonioides, L. **Śukânuśāsana**, n. 'Śuka-narrative,' N. of an episode of the Śānti-parvan of the Mahā-bhārata, i, 12046 &c. **Śukâshṭaka**, n., °**ṭakavyākhyā**, f. N. of wks. **Śukêśvara-tīrtha**, n. N. of a Tīrtha, Cat. **Śukêshṭa**, m. Acacia Sirissa, L.; Mimusops Hexandra, L. **Śukôkti-jāla**, n. N. of a Kāvya. **Śukôtpatti**, f. 'birth of Śuka,' N. of a section of the Śānti-parvan of the Mahā-bhārata. **Śukôdara**, n. a parrot's belly, MW.; a kind of tree (= *tālīsa-pattra*), L. **Śukôrvaśī-saṃvāda**, m. N. of wk.

Śukāyana, m. N. of an Arhat, Buddh.

Śukī-√bhū, P. *-bhavati*, to become a parrot, Kathās.

शुक्त *śuktá*, mf(*ā*)n. (perhaps fr. √1. *śuc* and orig. 'fermented') become acid or sour, ŚBr. &c. &c.; astringent and sour, L.; putrid, stinking, L.; harsh, rough (as words), Gaut.; Baudh. &c.; void of men, lonely, deserted, L.; united, joined (= *ślish-ṭa*), L.; pure, clean (prob. w.r. for *śukra* or *śukla*), L.; m. sourness, L.; N. of a son of Vasishṭha, MārkP. (cf. *śukra*); (*ā*), f. Rumex Vesicarius, L.; n. anything fermented or become sour, any sour liquor or gruel (esp. a kind of acid beverage prepared from roots and fruits), Gaut.; Suśr.; flesh, L.; hard or harsh speech (?), Yājñ. i, 33. **-tikta-kashāyaka**, mfn. astringent and sour and bitter, L.; m. ast° and sour and b° taste, L. **-pāka**, m. acid digestion, acidity of stomach, Car. **-svara**, mfn. (said to be) = *a-vyakta-svara*, MaitrUp. (Sch.)

Śuktaka, mfn. sour, sourish, Gaut.; n. acid eructation, Mn. iv, 121.

Śukti, f. (prob. fr. √1. *śuc* and orig. 'shining, bright') a pearl-oyster or oyster shell (eight sources of pearls are enumerated by Sch. on Kir. xii, 40, viz. clouds, elephants, fish, serpents, bamboos, conch-shells, boars, and oyster shells), Kauś.; Kāv. &c.; a small shell or cockle, L.; a portion of a skull (used as a cup &c.), W.; a bone, BhP.; Tamarindus Indica, L.; Unguis Odoratus, L.; any perfume or fragrant substance, R.; a curl or feather on a horse's neck or breast, Śiś.; a measure of weight (= ½ Pala or 4 Karshas), ŚārṅgS.; a partic. disease of the cornea, Suśr.; hemorrhoids, L.; m. N. of an Āṅgirasa, PañcavBr.; of a mountain, MārkP. (w.r. *sukti*); pl. N. of a people, VarBṛS. **-karṇa**, mfn. shell-eared, MBh.; N. of a serpent-demon, Hariv. **-khalati**, mfn. bald like an oy°, completely bald, Hcar. **-ja**, n. 'oy°-born,' a pearl, VarBṛS. **-paṭṭa**, m. a partic. musical instrument, Saṃg. **-parṇa**, m. Alstonia Scholaris, L. **-puṭa**, n. the hollow in the shell (in which the pearl rests), Śiś.; a pearl-oyster shell, W. **-peśī**, f. 'pearl-envelope,' a pearl-oyster, W. **-bīja**, n. 'oy°-seed,' a pearl, L. **-maṇi**, m. 'oy°-gem,' id., L. **-mat**, m. N. of one of the seven principal mountains or mountainous ranges in India (cf. *kula-giri*), MBh.; Pur.; (*atī*), f. N. of a river, ib.; of the capital of the Cedis, ib. **-vadhū**, f. mother of pearl (or the p° oy° which produces the p°), L. **-sâhvayā**, f. N. of a city (= *śukti-matī*), MBh. **-sparśa**, m. a dark spot or flaw on a pearl, W.

Śuktika, m. a partic. disease of the cornea, ŚārṅgS.; (*ā*), f. id., Suśr.; mother of pearl, Saṃk.; Sarvad.; Rumex Vesicarius, L.

Śukty, in comp. for *śukti*. **-udbhava**, m. 'sprung from or produced in a pearl-oyster,' a pearl, MW.

शुक्र *śukrá*, mf(*ā*)n. (fr. √1. *śuc*, cf. *śukla*) bright, resplendent, RV.; AV.; VS.; Br.; MBh.; clear, pure, RV.; AV.; VS.; ŚBr.; light-coloured, white, RV.; AV.; ŚāṅkhBr.; pure, spotless, RV.; Br.; m. N. of Agni or fire, R.; of a month (Jyeshṭha = May–June, personified as the guardian of Kubera's treasure), MBh.; Suśr.; the planet Venus or its regent (regarded as the son of Bhṛigu and preceptor of the Daityas), MBh.; R. &c.; clear or pure Soma, RV.; (with or scil. *graha*) a partic. Graha or receptacle for Soma, VS.; ŚBr.; a partic. astrol. Yoga, L.; a N. of the Vyāhṛitis (*bhūr, bhuvaḥ, svar*), MW.; a kind of plant (= *citraka*), ib.; N. of a Marutvat, Hariv.; of a son of Vasishṭha, VP.; of the third Manu, Hariv.; of one of the seven sages under Manu Bhautya, MārkP.; of a son of Bhava, VP.; of a son of Havir-dhāna (cf. *śukla*), VP.; (with Jainas) of a partic. Kalpa (q.v.); n. brightness, clearness, light, RV.; Up.; MBh.; R.; (also pl.) any clear liquid (as water, Soma &c.), RV.; VS.; juice, the essence of anything, Br.; ŚrS. (also pl.); semen virile, seed of animals (male and female), sperm, RV. &c. &c.; a morbid affection of the iris (change of colour &c. accompanied by imperfect vision; cf. *śukla*), Suśr.; ŚārṅgS.; a good action, L.; gold, wealth, L.; N. of a Sāman, ĀrshBr.; of a Vedic metre, RPrāt. **-kara**, mfn. producing semen, Bhpr.; m. the marrow of the bones, L. **-kṛicchra**, n. a partic. urinary disease, ŚārṅgS. **-gṛiha**, n. house or mansion of the planet Venus, Siṇhâs. **-cāra**, m. course of the planet V°, MW. **-ja**, mfn. 'produced from (one's own) semen,' one's own son, MBh.; m. pl. (with Jainas) a partic. class of gods, L. **-jyotis** (*śukrá-*), mfn. having bright splendour, VS. **-tīrtha**, n. N. of a Tīrtha, Cat. **-danta**, m. 'white-toothed,' N. of a man, Rājat. **-dúgha**, mfn. emitting a clear fluid, RV. **-dosha**, m. defect of semen, impotence, L. **-nāḍi**, f., **-nālikôdāharaṇa**, n., **-nīti**, f. N. of wks. **-pā**, mfn. drinking pure Soma, VS.; TBr. **-pāṇi**, m. N. of an author, Cat. **-pātrá**, n. the vessel for the Graha Śukra, ŚBr. **-píś**, mfn. radiantly adorned, RV. x, 110, 6 (cf. *śúci-peśas*). **-pūjā**, f. N. of wk. **-pūta-pā**, mfn. one who drinks bright and purified Soma, RV. **-pṛishṭha** (*śukrá-*), mfn. having a bright-coloured back, AV. **-bhuj**, m. 'seed-eater,' a peacock, L. **-bhū**, mfn. semen-produced, MW.; m. 'semen-source,' the marrow of the bones, L. **-mūtrala**, mfn. producing semen and urine, Suśr. **-meha**, m. seminal diabetes, Bhpr.; Car. **-mehin**, mfn. suffering from sem° diab°, Suśr.; Car. **-yajús**, n. pl. N. of partic. texts belonging to the Pravargya, TĀr. **-rūpa**, mfn. bright-coloured, MārkP. **-rshabha** (*śukrá-*; *-rsh°* for *-ṛish°*), mf(*ā*)n. having bright-coloured bulls, TS. **-vat** (*śukrá-*), mf(*atī*)n. containing pure juice or Soma, TS.; ŚBr.; KātyŚr.; cont° the word *śukra*, AitBr. **-varcas** (*śukrá-*), mfn. having bright lustre, RV. **-varṇa** (*śukrá-*), mf(*ā*)n. bright-coloured, bright, ib. **-vardhinī**, f. = *-kara*, m., L. **-vaha**, mfn. bringing semen, Suśr. **-vāra**, m. Venus' day, Friday, Sūryas.; Inscr. **-vāsara**, m. id., A. **-vāsas** (*śukrá-*), mfn. bright-robed, RV. **-visṛishṭi**, f. emission of semen, L. **-śānti**, f. N. of wk. **-śishya**, m. 'pupil of Śukra,' an Asura, L. **-śoca**, mfn. brightly shining, Sāy. **-śoci**, mfn. = next, RV. **-śocis** (*śukrá-*), mfn. bright-rayed, ib.; VS.; TBr. **-sadman** (*śukrá-*), mfn. having a br° dwelling-place, RV. **-sāra**, mfn. having semen as essence (*-tā*, f.), VarBṛS. **-suta**, m. son of the planet Venus, ib. **-sûkta**, n. N. of wk. **-sṛishṭā**, f. yellow myrobolan, L. **-stoma**, m. a partic. Ekāha, ŚāṅkhŚr. **-haraṇa**, mf(*ī*)n. bringing semen, Suśr. **Śukrâṅga**, m. 'having a brilliant body,' a peacock, L. **Śukrâcārya**, m. the sage Ś° (regent of the planet Venus and preceptor of the Daityas), W. **Śukrā́-manthínau**, m. nom. du. pure and meal-like Soma, TS.; Br. **Śukrêśvara**, N. of a temple, Cat.; of a Liṅga, MW.; *-stuti*, f. N. of 8 verses from the Kāśī-khaṇḍa. **Śukrôttara**, m. (with Jainas) N. of a Kalpa (q.v.)

Śukrala, mfn. producing semen, Suśr.; ŚārṅgS.; Car. (cf. *māṅsa-ś°*); spermatic, seminal, W.; abounding in semen, lascivious, L.; (*ā*), f. a sort of Cyperus, L.

Śukriman, m. brightness, pureness, g. *dṛiḍhâdi*.

Śúkriya, mfn. containing pure juice, Kāṭh.; Br.; belonging or sacred to Śukra, W.; seminal, spermatic, MW.; n. brilliance, ŚāṅkhGṛ.; (pl.) N. of certain Sāmans belonging to the Pravargya, TĀr.; Lāṭy.; N. of the Pravargya section or VS. 36–40 (also *-kāṇḍa*), Yājñ.; Caraṇ.; a partic. observance, ŚāṅkhGṛ.

Śukrī-√bhū, P. *-bhavati*, to become semen or sperm, Suśr.

Śuklá, mf(*ā*)n. (later form of *śukra*, for which it is sometimes w.r.) bright, light (with *paksha* = *śukla-p°*, q.v.), KātyŚr.; Mn.; MBh. &c.; white, whitish, AitBr. &c. &c.; pure, spotless, unsullied, MBh.; Kāv. &c.; m. the bright half of a lunar month or any day in it, GṛŚrS.; Mn.; MBh. &c.; the month Vaiśākha, BhP. (Sch.); white (the colour), L.; mucus, saliva (*śuklám √kṛi*, to spit at), AV.; ricinus or white r°, L.; Mimusops Hexandra, L.; the 37th (or 3rd) year of Jupiter's cycle of 60 years, VarBṛS.; the 24th of the astronomical Yogas, L.; N. of Śiva, MBh.; of Vishṇu, BhP.; of a son of Havir-dhāna (cf. *śukra*), Hariv.; of a Muni, Cat.; of a king, Buddh.; of a mountain, BhP.; (*ā*), f. a white cow, KātyŚr.; white or candied sugar, L.; Euphorbia Antiquorum, L.; = *kākolī* and *vidārī*, L.; N. of Sarasvatī, L.; of a daughter of Siṇha-hanu, Buddh.; of a river, BhP.; n. brightness, light, MaitrUp.; a white spot, white substance, anything white, AV.; ŚBr.; ChUp.; the white of the eye, ŚBr.; R.; Suśr.; a disease of the cornea or white part of the eye (opacity, albugo; cf. *śukra*), L.; silver, L.; fresh butter, L. **-kaṇṭhaka**, m. 'white-throated,' a kind of gallinule, L. **-kanda**, m. a kind of bulbous plant (= *mahisha-k°*), L.; (*ā*), f. = *ativishā*, L. **-karṇa**, mfn. white-eared, Pāṇ. vi, 2, 112, Sch. **-karman**, mfn. pure in action or conduct, L. **-kāra**, n. a water plant, L. **-kushṭha**, n. white leprosy, GāruḍaP. **-kṛishṇa**, n. du. light and dark fortnight, TĀr. **-keśa**, mfn. white-haired, MBh. **-kshīra**, mfn. having white milk or juice, MW.; (*ā* [L.] or *ī* [MW.]), f. a kind of plant (= *kākolī*). **-kshetra**, n. N. of a sacred district, Cat. **-janârdana**, m. N. of a man, Cat. **-tā**, f., **-tva**, n. whiteness &c., Pāṇ. v, 1, 123, Sch. **-tīrtha**, n. N. of a Tīrtha, Cat.; *-māhātmya*, n. N. of wk. **-daṇshṭra-tā**, f. having white teeth (one of the 80 minor marks of a Buddha), Dharmas. 84. **-dat**, mfn. white-toothed, AitBr.; BhP. **-daśana**, mfn. id., MW. **-daśa-bhāshya** (?), N. of wk. **-dugdha**, m. 'having wh° juice,' Trapa Bispinosa, L. **-deha**, mfn. pure in body or person, MBh. **-druma**, m. Symplocos Racemosa, R. (Sch.) **-dhātu**, m. a white mineral, chalk, L. **-dhānya**, n. white grain or corn, Pañcar. **-dhyāna**, n. meditation on pure spirit, HPariś. **-dhvaja-patākin**, mfn. having a wh° banner and flag (Śiva), MBh. **-paksha**, m. the light half of a month, the 15 days of the moon's increase, KātyŚr.; Kauś.; Mn. &c.; the rightful side of two contending parties, Divyâv. **-pakshīya**, mfn. relating to the light half of the month, MW. **-pushpa**, mfn. having white flowers, Kauś.; m. N. of various plants (accord. to L., Asteracantha Longifolia; Nerium Odorum; = *maruvaka* &c.), Pañcar.; (*ā*), f. Pistia Stratiotes, L.; = *nāga-dantī*, L.; (*ī*), f. = *nāga-dantī*, L. **-pṛishṭhaka**, m. Vitex Paniculata, L.; V° Nigundo, W. **-bala**, m. a white Bala or Baladeva (accord. to the Jainas; nine are enumerated, corresponding to the nine Kṛishṇas or black Vāsudevas; see *bala*, *b°-deva*), W. **-bīja**, m. (prob.) a kind of ant, MBh. **-buddhi-kara**, see *b°-k°*. **-bhāga**, m. the white of the eye, Suśr. **-bhāsvara**, mfn. shining bright, Bhāshāp. **-bhū-deva**, m. N. of an author, Cat. **-maṇḍala**, n. a white circle or globe, MW.; = *-bhāga*, L. **-mathurā-nātha**, m. N. of an astronomer, Cat. **-mālyânulepana**, mfn. having a white garland and unguents (i.e. wearing a wh° g° and anointed with ung°), MW. **-meha**, m. whitish diabetes, Car. **-mehin**, mfn. suffering from wh° diab°, ib. **-yajur-vedâdhyetṛi-praśaṇsā**, f. N. of wk. **-yajñôpavīta-vat**, mfn. invested with a white sacred thread, MBh. **-rūpá**, mfn. white-coloured, ŚBr. **-rohita**, m. a kind of plant, L.; a kind of bright-looking Rohita fish, MW. **-vacā**, f. Terminalia Chebula, L. **-vat** (*śuklá-*), mfn. containing the word *śuklá*, ŚBr.; KātyŚr. **-vatsā** (*śuklá-*), f. a cow which has a white calf, ŚBr.; KātyŚr. **-varga**, m. a class of white objects (as the conch-shell, pearl-oyster, and cowry), W. **-vastra**, mf(*ā*)n. wearing a white robe, Mn. ix, 70. **-vāyasa**, m. Ardea Nivea, L.; a crane, W.; a white crow, MW. **-vāsas**, mfn. = *-vastra*, TĀr. **-vidarśanā**, f. a partic. stage in the life of a Śrāvaka, Mahāvy. **-viśrāma**, m., see *viś°*. **-vṛitta**, mfn. pure in conduct, MBh. **-vṛitti**, f. pure employment or subsistence, maintenance derived by a Brāhman from other Br°s only, MW. **-śāla**, m. a kind of tree related to Melia Bukayun, L. **-sūtra**, n. N. of wk. **-harita**, m. pale-greenness, L.; mf(*ā* or *iṇī*)n. pale-green, ib. **Śuklâguru**, n. white agallochum, Kum. **Śuklâṅga**, m. 'having a wh° or brilliant body,' a peacock, L.; (*ī*), f. Nyctanthes Arbor Tristis, L. **Śuklâcāra**, mf(*ā*)n. pure in conduct, R. **Śuklâdi-śrāvaṇa-kṛishṇa-saptamī**, °*kṛishṇâshṭamī*, f. N. of certain festivals or holy days, Cat. **Śuklâpara**, mfn. having a white hinder part (said of the body), KātyŚr. **Śuklâpâṅga**, m. 'having wh° eye-corners,' a peacock, Megh. **Śuklâbhijātīya**, mf(*ā*)n. of a pure race, MBh.; R. **Śuklâmbara**, mfn. having a wh° garment, Ml.; *-dhara*, mfn. wearing or arrayed in wh° g°s, MW. **Śuklâmla**, n. a sort of sorrel (= *amla-śāka*), ib. **Śuklârka**, m. a kind of Calotropis, L. **Śuklârman**, n. a partic. disease of the wh° of the eye, Suśr.; Bhpr. **Śuklâshṭamī**, f. N. of wk. **Śuklêtara**, mfn. other than wh°, black, dirty, R. **Śuklêśvara** (Daśar., Introd.), °*vara-nātha* (Cat.), m. N. of authors. **Śukl'odana** (fr. *śukla* + *od°*), m. N. of a brother of Śuddhodana, Buddh. **Śuklôpala**, m. a white stone, MW.; (*ā*), f. id., W.; white sugar, ib.

Śuklaka, mfn. white, MW.; m. a white colour, ib.; the light fortnight, Tithyād.

Śuklala, mfn. white, whitening, L.; (*ā*), f. a kind of Cyperus (v.l. *śukralā*), L.

Śuklāyana, m. N. of a Muni, Cat.

Śukliman, m. whiteness, white colour, Hcar.

Śuklī, in comp. for *śukla*. **-karaṇa**, n. making

white, whitening, MW. — **√kṛi**, P. *-karoti*, 'to make white, whiten (see next). — **kṛita**, mfn. made white, Ṛitus.; Hit. &c. — **√bhū**, P. *-bhavati* (or *-√as*, Pat.), to become white, Kāv.

Śukvan. See *su-śukvan*.

शुक्षि *śukshi*, m. (accord. to Uṇ. iii, 155 fr. *√śush*) air, wind, L.; (perhaps fr. *√1. śuc*) = *tejas* or = *citram*, L.

शुङ्ग *śuṅga*, m. (etymology doubtful) the Indian fig-tree (= *vaṭa*), L.; Ficus Infectoria, L.; Spondias Mangifera, L.; the awn of corn, L.; the sheath or calyx of a bud, L.; N. of a man (pl. his descendants), Pravar. (cf. Pāṇ. iv, 1, 117); pl. N. of a dynasty which succeeded the Mauryas (sg. a king of the Ś° dyn°), Pur.; (*ā́*), f., see below; (*ī*), f, Spondias Mangifera, L.; Ficus Infectoria, L.; N. of the mother of Garuḍa, Suparṇ.; n. the sheath or calyx of a bud, (fig.) effect (opp. to *mūla*, 'cause'), ChUp.; Ficus Infectoria, L. — **rājan**, m. a king of the Śuṅga dynasty, VP.

Śuṅgā́, f. the sheath or calyx of a young bud (esp. of a fig-tree), GṛS.; Suśr.; the awn of barley &c., a bristle, L.; the waved-leaf fig-tree, W.; N. of the mother of Garuḍa, Suparṇ. — **karman**, n. a ceremony connected with the Puṃ-savana (q.v.) at which the calyx of a young bud of the Ficus Indica is used, Gṛihyas.

Śuṅgin, mfn. having a sheath or calyx, MW.; furnished with an awn, ib.; m. Ficus Indica or Infectoria, L.

शुच् 1. *śuc*, cl. 1. P. (Dhātup. vii, 1) *śocati* (Ved. and ep. also °*te*; once in ŚBr. *-śucyati* [cf. *sam-√1. śuc*]; and in MBh. iii, 2372 *śocimi*; pf. *śuśoca* [Impv. *śuśugdhi*, Pot. *śuśucīta*, p. *śuśukvás* and *śuśucāná*, aor. *aśucat* [p. *śucát* and *śucámāna*], RV.; *aśocīt* [2. sg. *śocīḥ*], Br.; *aśocishṭa*, Gr.; Prec. *śucyāsam*, ib.; fut. *śoktā* or *śocitā*, ib.; *śucishyati*, °*te*, MBh. &c. &c.; inf. *śucádhyai*, RV.; *śoktum* or *śocitum*, MBh. &c.; ind. p. *śocitvā*, MBh.; *śucitvā*, Pāṇ. i, 2, 26), to shine, flame, gleam, glow, burn, RV.; Br.; ĀśvŚr.; to suffer violent heat or pain, be sorrowful or afflicted, grieve, mourn at or for (loc. or acc. with *prati*), TS. &c. &c.; to bewail, lament, regret (acc.), MBh.; Kāv. &c.; to be absorbed in deep meditation, MW.; (cl. 4. P. Ā. *śucyati*, °*te*) to be bright or pure, Dhātup. xxvi, 56 (cf. Caus. and *śuci*); to be wet, ib.; to decay, be putrid, stink, ib.: Pass. (only aor. *áśoci*) to be kindled, burn, flame, RV. vii, 67, 2: Caus. *śocáyati*, °*te* (p. *śucáyat* [q.v.], RV.; aor. *aśūśucat*, *śūśucat*, AV.; Br.), to set on fire, burn, RV.; TBr.; to cause to suffer pain, afflict, distress, AV.; ŚBr.; MBh.; to feel pain or sorrow, grieve, mourn, MBh.; to lament, regret, Ragh.; Rājat.; to purify, VarYogay.; Kathās.: Pass. of Caus. *śocyate*, Kāv.: Desid. *śuśucishati* or *śuśocishati*, Pāṇ. i, 2, 26: Intens. *śośucyate*, *śośokti*, to shine or flame brightly, Gr. (only *śóśucan*, RV. vi, 66, 3; cf. *śóśucat*, *śóśucāna*, *śośucyamāna*).

2. **Śúc**, mfn. shining, illumining (see *tri-* and *viśva-śuc*); f. flame, glow, heat, RV.; AV.; Br.; brightness, lustre, RV.; (also pl.) pain, sorrow, grief or regret for (comp.), AV. &c. &c.; pl. tears, BhP.

Śucá, mf(*ā́*)n. = *śuci*, pure, RV. x, 26, 6; (*ā*), f. grief, sorrow, BhP.

Śucád-ratha, mfn. (pr. p. of *√1. śuc* + *r*°) having a shining car, RV.

Śucádhyai. See under *√1. śuc*.

Śucantí, m. N. of a person under the especial protection of the Aśvins, RV.

Śucáyat, mfn. (cf. Caus. of *√1. śuc*) shining, bright, RV.

Śúci, mfn. (f. nom. pl. *śucyas*, Mn. viii, 77) shining, glowing, gleaming, radiant, bright, RV. &c. &c.; brilliantly white, white, Bhartṛ.; clear, clean, pure (lit. and fig.), holy, unsullied, undefiled, innocent, honest, virtuous, RV. &c. &c.; pure (in a ceremonial sense), ChUp.; Mn.; Bhag. &c.; (ifc.) one who has acquitted himself of or discharged (a duty, see *rahaḥ-ś*°); m. purification, purity, honesty, virtue, Kāv.; fire, L.; N. of a partic. fire (a son of Agni Abhimānin and Svāhā or a son of Antardhāna and Sikhaṇḍinī and brother of the fires Pavamāna and Pāvaka), Pur.; oblation to fire at the first feeding of an infant, W.; a partic. hot month (accord. to some = Āshāḍha or Jyeshṭha, accord. to others 'the hot season in general'), VS.; ŚBr.; MBh. &c.; the sun, MaitrUp. (Sch.); the moon, L.; the planet Venus or its regent (cf. *śukra*), L.; a ray of light, L.; wind, L.; sexual love (= *śṛiṅgāra*), L.; a Brāhman, L.; a faithful minister, true friend, L.; the condition of a religious student, L.; a fever that attacks pigs, L.; judicial acquittal, W.; white (the colour), ib.; a partic. plant (= *citraka*), MW.; N. of Śiva, L.; of a son of Bhṛigu, MBh.; of a son of Gada, Hariv.; of a son of the third Manu, ib.; of Indra in the 14th Manv-antara, Pur.; of one of the 7 sages in the 14th Manv-antara, ib.; of a Sârthavāha, MBh.; of a son of Śata-dyumna, Pur.; of a son of Śuddha (the son of Anenas), ib.; of a son of Andhaka, ib.; of a son of Vipra, ib.; of a son of Artha-pati, Vās., Introd.; (also *ī*), f. N. of a daughter of Tāmrā and wife of Kaśyapa (regarded as the parent of water-fowl), Hariv.; VP. — **karṇa**, g. *kumudâdi* (2.); °*ṇika*, n. white lotus, L. — **kāma**, mfn. loving purity, Baudh. — **kranda** (*śúci-*), mfn. calling aloud, clear-voiced, RV. — **gātra-tā**, f. the state of having bright limbs (one of the 80 minor marks of a Buddha), Dharmas. 84. — **carita**, mfn. virtuous or honest in conduct, VP. — **janman** (*śúci-*), mfn. of pure or radiant birth, RV. — **jihva** (*śúci-*), mfn. flame-tongued (as Agni), ib. — **tā**, f. (Mn.; Kāv.; Rājat.), **-tvá**, n. (RV.) clearness, purity (lit. and fig.), uprightness, honesty, virtue. — **dat** (*śúci-*), mfn. bright-toothed, RV. — **drava** or **-dravya** (?), m. N. of a king, VP. — **druma**, m. 'holy tree,' the sacred fig-tree, L. — **nāsa-tā**, f. having a bright nose (one of the 80 minor marks of a Buddha), Dharmas. 84. — **netra-rati-sambhava**, m. N. of a king of the Gandharvas, Buddh. — **pati**, m. 'lord of purity,' fire, Gal. — **padī**, f. clean-footed, g. *kumbha-pady-ādi*. — **pā́**, mfn. drinking the clear (Soma), RV. — **peśas** (*śúci-*), mfn. brightly adorned, ib. — **praṇī**, f. 'inducing purity,' sipping water, cleansing the mouth &c., L. — **pratīka** (*śúci-*), mfn. radiant-faced, RV. — **bandhu** (*śúci-*), mfn. having a brilliant relative (said of Soma as related to fire), ib. — **bāhya**, mfn. externally pure, MW. — **bhrājas** (*śúci-*), mfn. shining brightly, ib. — **maṇi**, m. 'pure jewel,' crystal, W.; a jewel worn on the head, MW. — **mallikā**, f. Arabian jasmine (= *nava-m*°), L. — **mānasa**, mfn. pure-hearted, Kir. — **mukhī**, f. N. of a female flamingo, Hariv.; the plant Sanseviera Zeylanica, MW. — **ratha**, m. 'having a bright chariot,' N. of a king, VP. — **rocis**, m. 'white-rayed,' the moon, L. — **vana**, n. = *śushka-v*°, BhP. (Sch.) — **varcas**, mfn. having pure splendour, g. *bhṛiśâdi*; °*cāya*, Nom. Ā. °*yate*, ib. — **varṇa** (*śúci-*), mfn. bright-coloured, RV. — **vāc**, m. 'clear-voiced,' N. of a bird, Hariv. — **vāsas**, mfn. clothed in pure or bright garments, ĀśvGṛ. — **vāhya**, see *-bāhya*. — **vṛikshá**, m. N. of a man (pl. his descendants), MaitrS.; Pravar. — **vrata** (*śúci-*), mf(*ā*)n. whose observances are pure or holy (said of gods), RV.; TBr.; virtuous in conduct, Mn.; R. — **śravas**, m. 'having bright renown,' N. of Vishṇu, Vishṇ.; MBh.; BhP.; of a Prajā-pati, VP. — **shád**, mfn. dwelling in light or in clear (water), RV.; VS.; BhP.; abiding on the path of virtue, BhP. — **shah**, m. (nom. *-shāṭ*) N. of Agni, RV. — **saṃkshaya**, m. end of the hot season, beginning of the rains, MBh. — **samācāra**, mfn. maintaining pure practices, R. — **samudācāra-tā**, f. the being of pure behaviour (one of the 80 minor marks of a Buddha), Dharmas. 84. — **smita**, mf(*ā*)n. smiling brightly, MBh.; R. &c.; accompanied by a bright smile, Śiś.

Śucikā, f. N. of an Apsaras, MBh.; Hariv.

Śucita, mfn. grieved, sad, lamenting, W.; purified, pure, clean, ib.

Śucidratha, m. N. of a king, Pur. (prob. w.r. for *śucad-* or *śuci-ratha*).

Śucin, mfn. = *śuci*, clear, pure, MārkP.

Śucish-mat, mfn. (fr. *śucis* = *śocis* + *mat*) shining, radiant, RV.; m. N. of a son of Kardama, Cat.; (*atī*), f. N. of the mother of Agni, ib.

Śucī, in comp. for *śuci*. — **√kṛi**, P. *-karoti*, to make clear or bright, purify, Kalpas. — **√bhū**, P. *-bhavati*, to be pure (in a ceremonial sense), Pañcat.

Śucīya, Nom. Ā. °*yate*, to become clear or pure or white, g. *bhṛiśâdi*.

Śucīvatī, f., g. *śarādi*.

1. **Śucy** (for 2. see col. 3), in comp. for *śuci*. — **aksha**, mf(*ī*)n. pure-eyed, ĀpŚr. — **ācāra**, mfn. pure in conduct, Pat. — **upacāra**, mfn. performing holy actions, MW.

Śucyadaksha (?), mf(*ī*)n. (prob.) = *śucy-aksha*, MaitrŚ.

Śuśukvaná or °**kváni**, mfn. shining, resplendent, brilliant, RV.

Śuśukvás, śuśucāná. See *√1. śuc*, col. 1.

Śoka &c. See p. 1091, col. 1.

शुच् 3. *śuc*, cl. 4. P. Ā. (Dhātup. xxvi, 56), see under *√1. śuc*.

शुच्य् 2. *śucy* (also written *cucy*), cl. 1. P. *śucyati*, to distil (= *abhishave*, q.v.; others 'to perform ablution'), Dhātup. xv, 6.

शुज् *śuj* (cf. *√śvaj*; only in p. *śū́śujāna*), to be puffed up, be audacious or insolent, RV.

शुटीर *śuṭīra*, m. (prob.) a hero (cf. comp. and *śauṭīra*, °*rya*). — **tā**, f., **-tva**, n. heroism, L.

Śuṭīrya, n. valour, heroism, L.

शुठ् *śuṭh*, cl. 1. P. *śoṭhati*, 'to limp' or 'to be obstructed or impeded' (*gati-pratighāte*), Dhātup. ix, 56 (cf. *√śuṇṭh*); cl. 10. P. *śoṭhayati*, to be dull or slow, ib. xxxii, 102 (cf. *√4. śaṭh*).

Śoṭha, mfn. (only L.) foolish; idle, lazy; wicked, low; m. a fool; an idler &c.

शुण्ट *śuṇṭa*, n. the hair under the arm-pit, Gal.

शुण्ठ् *śuṇṭh*, cl. 1. P. *śuṇṭhati*, to limp, be lame, Dhātup. ix, 56 (cf. *√śuṭh*); to dry, become dry (*śoshaṇe*), ib. 60; cl. 10. P. *śuṇṭhayati*, to dry, become dry (*śoshaṇe*), ib. xxxii, 103.

Śuṇṭhá, mf(*ā*)n. (applied to a bull or cow), TS.; MaitrS.; Kāṭh.; ŚrS. (accord. to Sch. either 'white-coloured' or 'of small stature' or = *āveshṭita-karṇa*); a kind of grass, Gobh. (v.l.); a piece of flesh or meat, L.; (*ī*), f., see next. **Śuṇṭhā-kárṇa**, mfn. short-eared, MaitrS.; VS. (Mahīdh.) **Śuṇṭhâcārya**, m. N. of a great Śaiva sage or teacher, Dhūrtan. **Śuṇṭhâdhī**, mfn. (prob. w.r.), KātyŚr.

Śuṇṭhi or **śuṇṭhī**, f. dry ginger, Kāv.; VarBṛS.; Suśr. &c.

Śuṇṭhya, n. id., L.

शुण्ड् *śuṇḍ*, cl. 1. P. *śuṇḍati*, to break, crush, disturb, vex, torment, Dhātup. ix, 40.

Śuṇḍa, m. the juice exuding from the temples of an elephant in rut, L.; an elephant's trunk, MW.; (*ā* and *ī*), f., see below. — **roha**, m. (cf. *śuṇṭha*) a kind of fragrant grass, L.

Śuṇḍaka, m. a military flute or fife, L.; a distiller or seller of spirituous liquors, L.; (*ikā*), f. the uvula (in the throat), L.; swelling of the uvula (= *gala-ś*°), Vāgbh.

Śuṇḍā, f. an elephant's trunk, MBh.; Suśr.; Kathās.; spirituous liquor, L.; a tavern, L.; a partic. kind of animal (prob. a female hippopotamus), L.; a harlot, prostitute, bawd, L.; Nelumbium Speciosum, L. — **daṇḍa**, m. an elephant's trunk, Pañcat. — **pāna**, n. a place where spirituous liquor is drunk or sold, tavern, dram-shop, L. — **rocanikā** or **-rocanī**, f. a kind of plant, L. (cf. *śuṇḍī-r*°).

Śuṇḍāra, m. the trunk of a young elephant, Mcar.; an elephant 60 years old, Gal.; a distiller or seller of spirituous liquor, L.

Śuṇḍāla, m. 'possessing a proboscis or trunk,' an elephant, L.

Śuṇḍika, m. or n. (prob.) a tavern, dram-shop, Pāṇ. iv, 3, 76; m. pl. N. of a people, MBh. (C. *maṇḍika*); (*ikā*), f., see under *śuṇḍaka*.

Śuṇḍin, m. 'possessing spirituous liquor,' a distiller, preparer or seller of spirituous liquors (constituting a partic. mixed caste), Cat.; 'having a proboscis,' an elephant, W.

Śuṇḍi-mūshikā, f. (fr. *śuṇḍi* = °*ḍin* + *m*°) a musk rat, L. (cf. *gandha-śuṇḍinī*).

Śuṇḍī, f. the swelling or enlargement of any gland (cf. *kaṇṭha-* and *gala-ś*°); the plant Heliotropium Indicum, L. — **rocanikā** or **-rocanī**, f. a kind of plant, L. (cf. *śuṇḍā-r*°).

शुतुद्री *śutudrī*, f. (accord. to L. also *śutudri* and °*dru*) the Śata-dru or Sutlej river, RV. (see *śata-dru*).

शुदि *śudi*, ind. (contracted fr. *śukla* or *śuddha* and *dina*, also written *sudi* as if for *su-dina*) in the light fortnight or light half of a lunar month, Inscr. (cf. *vadi*).

शुध् *śudh* or *śundh*, cl. 1. P. Ā. (Dhātup. iii, 37) *śundhati*, °*te* (Impv. *śunddhi*, ĀśvGṛ.; pf. *śuśundha*, aor. *aśundhīt*, fut. *śundhitā*, *śundhishyati*, Gr.), to purify (Ā. 'one's self,' become or be pure), RV.; VS.; TBr.; GṛŚrS.; cl. 4. P. Ā. (Dhātup. xxvi, 82) *śudhyati* (m. c. also °*te*; pf. *śuśodha*, aor. *aśudhat*, fut. *śoddhā*, *śotsyati*, inf. *śoddhum*, Gr.), to be cleared or cleansed or purified, become pure (esp. in a ceremonial sense), VS.; Mn.; MBh. &c.; to become clear or free from doubts, R.; Mṛicch.; to be cleared or excused from blame, to be excusable, Kathās.: Pass. *śudhyate* (aor. *aśodhi*), Gr.: Caus. *śundhayati*, to clear, purify, VS.; *śodhayati* (aor. *aśūśudhat*), to purify (esp. in a ceremonial sense), TS. &c. &c.; to correct, improve, Yājñ., Sch.; to remove (impurity or anything noxious), Mn.; MBh. &c.; to clear off, pay (debts), Rājat.; Kull.; to acquit, exculpate, justify, Mn.; Kām.; to put to test, Kathās.; to try, examine, Pañcat.; Yājñ., Sch.; to make clear, explain, Vedāntas.; Madhus.; to subtract, Gaṇit.: Desid. *śuśutsati*, Nidānas.: Intens. *śośudhyate*, *śośoddhi*, Gr.

Śuddhá, mfn. cleansed, cleared, clean, pure, clear, free from (with instr.), bright, white, RV. &c. &c.; cleared, acquitted, free from error, faultless, blameless, right, correct, accurate, exact, according to rule, Kāv.; VarBṛS.; Suśr.; upright (see comp.); pure, i.e. simple, mere, genuine, true, unmixed (opp. to *miśra*), Mn.; MBh. &c.; pure, i.e. unmodified (as a vowel not nasalized), ŚāṅkhBr.; Prāt.; complete, entire, Rājat.; unqualified, unmitigated (as capital punishment), Mn. ix, 279; (in phil.) veritable, unequalled (=*dvitīya-rahita*), MW.; tried, examined, Kām.; authorised, admitted, W.; whetted, sharp (as an arrow), ib.; m. the bright fortnight (in which the moon increases), Inscr.; N. of Śiva, MBh.; of one of the seven sages under the 14th Manu, BhP.; of a son of Anenas, ib.; (with *bhikshu*) of an author, Cat.; of a bird, Hariv.; (pl.) of a partic. class of gods, MBh.; (*ā*), f. N. of a daughter of Siṇha-hanu, Buddh.; (*am*), n. anything pure &c.; pure spirit, W.; rock-salt, L.; black pepper, L. **–karṇa**, m. 'pure-eared,' N. of a man (cf. *śauddhakarṇi*). **–karman**, mfn. pure in practice, honest, Kum. **–kāṇsya-maya**, mf(*ī*)n. made or consisting of p° brass, Hcat. **–kīrti**, m. 'having pure renown,' N. of a man, Kathās. **–koṭi**, f. 'upright side,' one of the sides of a right-angled triangle, W. **–gaṇa-pati**, m. (opp. to *ucchishṭa-g°*, q. v.) Gaṇeśa as worshipped by those who have cleansed their mouths (from remnants of food), Col. **–caitanya**, n. pure intelligence, Vedāntas. **–jaṅgha**, m. 'having clean legs or thighs,' an ass, L. **–jaḍa**, m. a quadruped, L. **–tattva-dāsa-vijñapti**, f. N. of wk. **–tā**, f. purity, correctness, faultlessness, Pañcat.; *-kośa*, m. 'treasure of correctness,' N. of a grammar by Bhava-deva. **–tva**, n. = *-tā*, Campak. **–dat**, mfn. white-toothed, Pāṇ. v, 4, 145. **–danta**, mfn. id., ib.; made of pure ivory, MBh. **–dhī**, mfn. pure-minded, Rājat. **–naṭṭā**, f. (in music) a partic. Rāgiṇī, Saṃgīt. **–neri**, m. a kind of dance, ib. **–paksha**, m. the light half of a month, ŚāṅkhŚr.; KaushUp. **–paṭa**, m. 'having clean garments,' N. of a man, Pañcat. **–pāda**, m. 'straight-footed (?),' N. of a teacher, Cat. (v. l. *siddha-p°*). **–pārshṇi**, mfn. having the rear protected, Ragh. (cf. *viśuddha-p°*). **–purī**, f. N. of a town (Tiruparur in the Tripoli district); *-māhātmya*, n. N. of a ch. of the SkandaP. **–pratibhāsa**, m. a partic. Samādhi, Buddh. **–baṭuka**, m. (in music) a kind of drummer, Saṃgīt. **–badha**, see *-vadha*. **–buddha**, w. r. for next. **–buddhi**, mfn. = *-dhī*; m. N. of a teacher, Cat. (v. l. *siddha-buddha*). **–bodha**, mfn. (in Vedānta) possessed of p° intelligence. **–bhāva**, m. purity of mind, BhP.; mfn. pure-minded, MBh.; R. &c. **–bhikshu**, m. N. of an author, Cat. **–bhairava**, m. (in music) a partic. Rāga, Saṃgīt. **–mati**, mfn. = *-dhī*, Kāv.; m. N. of the 21st Arhat of the past Utsarpiṇī, L. **–madhya-mārgī**, f. (in music) a partic. Mūrchanā, Saṃgīt. **–māṇsa**, n. a kind of condiment or strong seasoning (made with pieces of meat, Asa Fœtida, turmeric &c.), Bhpr. **–miśratva**, n. the being both unmixed and mixed, Kṛishṇaj. **–mukha**, m. a well-trained horse, MW. **–rūpin**, mfn. having the pure or true form, Ashṭāv. **–vaṇśya**, mf(*ā*)n. of a pure family or race, Ragh. **–vat**, mfn. containing the word *śuddha*; (*atī*), f. N. of the verses RV. viii, 95, 7–9, Baudh.; Vas. **–varṇa**, mfn. having a pure colour or caste, being of high caste &c., W.; well-lettered, having clear words, perspicuous (as a speech), MW. **–vallikā**, f. a kind of plant (Cocculus Cordifolius or Menispermum Glabrum), L. **–vāla** (*śuddhá-*), mfn. bright-tailed, MaitrS. **–vāsas**, mfn. dressed in clean garments, W. **–virāj**, f., **-virāḍ-ṛishabha**, n. N. of metres, Col. **–vishkambhaka**, m. (in dram.) a pure interlude (in which only speakers of Sanskṛit take part, such as that between the second and third act of the Śakuntalā; opp. to *saṃkīrṇa-v°*, q. v.), Bhar. **–vesha**, mfn. = *-vāsas*, Ragh. **–śīla**, mf(*ā*)n. having a pure character, innocent, guileless, Śak. **–śukra**, n. a morbid affection of the pupil of the eye, ŚārṅgS. **–shaḍjā**, f. (in music) a partic. Mūrchanā, Saṃgīt. **–saṃgama**, mf(*ā*)n. having pure intercourse or association, Śrutab. **–sattva**, mf(*ā*)n. = *-śīla*, R. **–sâdhyavasānā** and **-sâropā** (or °*pa-lakshaṇā*), f. N. of two kinds of ellipsis, Sarvad. **–sāra**, m. a partic. Samādhi, Buddh. **–sūḍa-nṛitya**, n. (in music) a kind of dance, Saṃgīt. **–saukhya**, n. N. of wk. **–snāna**, n. bathing in pure water (without unguents &c.), Megh. **–svabhāva**, mf(*ā*)n. = *-śīla*, R. **–hasta** (*śuddhá-*), mfn. having pure hands, AV. **–hṛidaya**, mf(*ā*)n. p°-hearted, Bhartṛ. **Śuddhâksha**, m. or n. (?) N. of a gate, Hariv. **Śuddhâkhya-sahasra-saṃhitā**, f. N. of a ch. of the Vātula-tantra. **Śuddhâtman**, mfn. pure-minded, VP.; m. 'pure soul or spirit,' N. of Śiva, MBh. **Śuddhâdvaita-mārtaṇḍa**, m. N. of a Vedānta wk. by Giri-dhara. **Śuddhânanda**, m. 'pure joy,' N. of the teacher of Ānanda-tīrtha (also with *yati*), Cat.; (with *sarasvatī*) N. of an author (= *śuddha-bhikshu*), ib. **Śuddhânumāna**, n. 'correct inference,' a partic. figure of rhetoric, L. **Śuddhânta**, m. 'sacred interior,' the private or women's apartments (esp. in the palace of a king; pl. a king's wives and concubines), MBh.; Kāv. &c.; (*ā*), f. (in music) a partic. Mūrchanā, Saṃgīt.; (°*ta*)-*kāntā*, f. pl. the women of the harem, Rājat.; *-cara* and *-cārin*, mfn. attending on the women's apartments, Kāv.; *-pālaka* or *-rakshaka*, m. a guardian of or attendant in the women's apartments, eunuch, L.; *-yuj*, prob. w. r. for *śuddhântara-yuj*; *-rakshī*, f. a female guardian of the women's apartments, Ragh.; *-vṛiddha*, m. (with *jana*) an old servant in a h°, Vikr. **Śuddhântaḥ-pura**, n. = *śuddhânta* above, R. **Śuddhântara-yuj**, f. change of mode or key in music, W. (w. r. *śuddhânta-yuj*). **Śuddhâpahnuti**, f. 'entire denial,' a partic. figure of rhetoric (e.g. 'this is not the moon, it is a lotus of the heavenly Ganges'), L. **Śuddhâbha**, mfn. consisting of pure light, Mn. xii, 27. **Śuddhâbhijana-karman**, mfn. pure in family and in conduct, R. **Śuddhâvarta**, mfn. (said to be) = *pradakshiṇâvarta* (q. v.), ShaḍvBr. **Śuddhâvāsa**, m. 'pure abode,' a partic. region of the sky, Lalit.; *-deva*, m. = next, ib.; *-kāyika*, m. (with *deva*) a god belonging to the class who dwell in that region, ib.; *-deva-putra*, m. a Deva-putra belonging to the above class, ib.; Kāraṇḍ. **Śuddhâśaya**, mfn. p°-minded, having a p° heart or conscience, Kathās.; Pañcat. **Śuddhâśuddhīya**, n. N. of two Sāmans, ĀrshBr. **Śuddhâśu-bodha**, m. N. of an elementary grammar. **Śuddhôda**, mfn. having p° water, BhP.; m. = next, ib. **Śuddh'odana**, m. 'having p° rice or food,' N. of a king of Kapila-vastu (of the tribe of the Śākyas and father of Gautama Buddha, Buddh.; MWB. 21 &c.); *-suta*, m. 'son of Ś°,' Gautama Buddha; °*dani*, w. r. for *śauddhodani*.

Śuddhāyú, mfn. striving after purity, TS.

Śúddhi, f. cleansing, purification, purity (lit. and fig.), holiness, freedom from defilement, purificatory rite (esp. a partic. Śrāddha performed at the cost of a person who needs purification), TBr. &c. &c.; setting free or securing (from any danger), rendering secure, Kām.; VarBṛS.; justification, exculpation, innocence (established by ordeal or trial), acquittal, Yājñ.; quittance, clearing off or paying off, discharge (of a debt &c.), MW.; retaliation, ib.; Kāv.; Kathās.; verification, correction, making true, correctness, accuracy, genuineness, truth, Yājñ.; Mālatīm.; clearness, certainty, accurate knowledge regarding (gen. or comp.; *śuddhiṃ* √*kṛi*, 'to ascertain for certain;' *ś°* √*labh*, 'to receive certain intelligence'), Mn.; Kathās.; Vet.; (in arithm.) leaving no remainder (*śuddhim* √*i*, 'to leave no remainder'), Bījag.; subtraction of a quantity or a q° to be subtracted, Līl.; N. of Durgā, Cat.; of one of the Śaktis of Vishṇu, MW.; of Dākshāyaṇī as worshipped at Kapāla-mocana, ib. **–kara**, mf(*ī*)n. causing purity, purifying, correcting, MW. **–kṛit**, m. one who makes clean, a washerman, L. **–kaumudī**, f., **-candrikā**, f., **-cintāmaṇi**, m. N. of wks. **–tattva**, n. N. of a ch. of Raghu-nandana's Smṛiti-tattva; *-kārikā*, f. pl.; °*ttvârṇava*, m. N. of wks. **–tama**, mfn. (= *śuddha-tama*) purest, MaitrUp. **–darpaṇa**, m., **-dīpa**, m. (= *-pradīpa*) N. of wks. **–dīpikā**, f. N. of a wk. by Srī-nivāsa (on the position of stars considered favourable for marriages, journeys &c.) **–nirūpaṇa**, n., **-nirṇaya**, m., **-pañjī**, f. N. of wks. **–pattra**, n. a sheet or paper of corrections, errata list (often at the end of works), MW.; a certificate of purification by penance, ib. **–prakāśa**, m., **-pradīpa**, m., **-prabhā**, f. N. of wks. **–bhūmi**, f. N. of a country, W. **–bhṛit**, mfn. possessing purity, pure, virtuous, ib. **–makaranda**, m. N. of wk. **–mat**, mfn. = *-bhṛit*, Kāv.; Kathās.; innocent, acquitted, Bālar. **–mayūkha**, m., **-ratna**, n., **-ratnâkara**, m., **-ratnâṅkura**, m., **-locana**, n., **-viveka**, m., **-vivekôddyota**, m., **-vyavasthā-saṃkshepa**, m. N. of wks. **–śrāddha**, n. a kind of Śrāddha (see above), VP. **–sāra**, m., **-setu**, m., **-smṛiti**, f. N. of wks.

Śúndhana, mf(*ī*)n. purifying, TBr.; n. removal of anything impure (gen.), Āpast.

Śundhā-vat, mfn. sacred, holy, pure, MW.

Śundhyú or **śundhyū́**, mfn. pure, bright, radiant, beautiful; purified or free from, unmolested by (gen.), RV.; VS.; TS.; m. fire or Agni, the god of fire, Uṇ. iii, 20, Sch.; n. (with Bharad-vājasya) N. of a Sāman, ĀrshBr.

Śoddhavya, śodha &c. See p. 1091, col. 3.

शुन् *śun*, cl. 6. P. *śunati*, to go, Dhātup. xxviii, 46.

शुन 1. *śuná*, m. (prob. fr. √*śū* or *śvi*, and connected with *śūra*, *śūsha* &c.) 'the Auspicious one,' N. of Vāyu, Nir.; of Indra, ĀśvŚr.; (*ā*), f. (?) a ploughshare (see *śunā-vat* and *śunā-sīra*); n. growth, success, prosperity, welfare, ŚBr.; ŚāṅkhGṛ.; (*ám*), ind. happily, auspiciously, for growth or prosperity, RV.; AV. **–m-huvīyā**, f. N. of the verse RV. iii, 30, 22 (beginning with the words *śunáṃ huvema*), AitBr. **–m-kuri** (for *kari* ?), m. 'causing growth or prosperity,' N. of a rural deity, PārGṛ. **–pṛishṭha** (*śuná-*), mfn. having a back fit for riding (as a horse), RV. vii, 70, 1 (accord. to others 'carrying food on his back'). **–vat** (*śuná-* or *śunā́-*), mfn. (prob.) furnished with a share (as a plough), TBr. **–hotra** (*śuná-*), m. 'offering auspicious sacrifices,' N. of a son of Bharad-vāja (and author of RV. vi, 33, 34; pl. his family), Anukr.; of a son of Kshatra-vṛiddha, Hariv. (written *suna-h°*).

Śúnā-sīra, m. du. N. of two rural deities favourable to the growth of grain (prob. personifications of 'share' and 'plough;' but identified by Yāska with Vāyu and Āditya, by others with Indra and Vāyu or Indra and Sūrya); sg. (also written *śun°*) N. of Indra (cf. *vasuṃdharā-śun°*), TS. &c. &c.; (pl.) a partic. class of gods (also written *sun°*), BhP.; *-śarâsana*, n. 'Indra's bow,' a rainbow, Hcar.; °*rin*, mfn. (applied to Indra), ŚāṅkhŚr.; °*rīya* or °*ryà*, mfn. belonging or relating to Śunā-sīra, VS.; ŚBr. (cf. Pāṇ. iv, 2, 32); n. or (*ā*), f. N. of partic. oblations, Br.; ŚrS.

शुन 2. *śuna*, m. = *śvan*, a dog, L. **Śúnêshita**, mfn. drawn along or carried by dogs, RV.

Śunaḥ, in comp. for *śunas*. **–puccha**, m. 'dog-tailed,' N. of one of the three sons of Ṛicīka (or accord. to AitBr. the eldest of the three sons of Ajīgarta), AitBr.; ŚāṅkhŚr.; Hariv.; of the author of a law-book (*-smṛiti*, f. his wk.)

Śúnaḥ-śépa, m. 'dog-tailed,' N. of a Vedic Ṛishi (having the patr. Ājīgarti, as son of Ajīgarta or Ajigarta, and regarded as the author of the hymns i, 24–30, ix, 3; accord. to AitBr. vii, 13–18, king Hariścandra, whose priest was Viśvā-mitra, being childless, made a vow that on obtaining a son he would sacrifice him to the god Varuṇa; a son was then born to him named Rohita, but Hariścandra put off on various pretexts the fulfilment of his vow, and when he at length consented to perform it, his son refused to be sacrificed, and retiring to the forest passed six years there until he met a poor Brāhman Ṛishi named Ajīgarta, who had three sons, the second of whom, Śunaḥ-śepa, was purchased by Rohita for a hundred cows to serve as a substitute for himself; Varuṇa having accepted him as a ransom, he was about to be sacrificed, Viśvā-mitra being Hotṛi priest, when he saved himself by reciting verses in praise of various deities, and was received into the family of Viśmā-mitra as one of his sons under the name of Deva-rāta, q.v.: the legend is different in the Rāmāyaṇa, which makes Ambarīsha, king of Ayodhya, perform a sacrifice, the victim of which is stolen by Indra; this king is described as wandering over the earth in search of either the real victim or a substitute until he meets with a Brāhman named Ṛicīka, from whom he purchases his middle son, Śunaḥ-śepa, who is about to be sacrificed, when Viśvā-mitra saves him by teaching him a prayer to Agni and two hymns to Indra and Vishṇu; see R. i, 61, 62), RV. &c. &c. (IW. 25–27); n. the genital organ of a dog, MW. **–śepha**, m. later and less correct form of *śunaḥ-śepa.* **–sakha**, m. 'dog's friend,' N. of a man, MBh.

Śunaka, m. a young or small dog, any dog, MBh. xiii, 6070 (cf. Uṇ. ii, 32, Sch.); N. of a Ṛishi, MBh.; of an Āṅgirasa and disciple of Pathya, BhP.; of a king, MBh.; of a son of Ruru, ib.; of a son of Ṛicīka, R.; of a son of Ṛita, BhP.; of a son of Gṛitsa-mada, Hariv.; of the slayer of Puram-jaya and father of Pradyota, BhP.; = *śaunaka*, Cat.; pl. the family or race of Śunaka, ŚrS. (cf. *śaunaka*); (*ī*), f. a bitch, L. **–kañcuka**, m. a kind of plant (= *kshudra-cañcu*), L. **–cillī**, f. a kind of culinary herb (= *śva-cillī*), L. **–putra**, m. 'Śunaka's son,' Śaunaka (also applied to Gṛitsa-mada, who is elsewhere described as the father of Śunaka), MW. **–suta**, m. = *-śaunaka*, Cat.

Śunas, gen. of *śvan* in comp. **–karṇa**, m. 'dog-eared,' N. of a man, PañcavBr. (cf. g. *kaskâdi*).

Śuni, m. (fr. *śvan*) a dog, L. **–ṃ-dhama**, mfn. (said to be for *śunīṃ-dh°*), Vop. xxvi, 54. **–ṃ-dhaya**, mfn. (for *śunīṃ-dh°*), Pāṇ. iii, 2, 28, Vārtt. 1, Pat.

Śunī. See under *śvan.*

Śunīra, m. a number of dogs, L.

Śuno, in comp. for *śunas.* **–lāṅgūla**, m. 'dog-tailed,' N. of the youngest of the three sons of Ṛicīka (or, accord. to AitBr., of Ajīgarta), AitBr.; Hariv. (cf. *śunaḥ-puccha* and *-śepa*).

1. **Śunya**, mfn. (fr. *śvan*), g. *gav-ādi*; n. and (*ā*), f. a number of dogs or female dogs, L.

शुन्ध् *śundh* &c. See √*śudh*, p. 1082.

शुन्य 2. *śunya*, mfn. = *śūnya*, empty, void, L.; n. a cypher, L.

शुप् *śup*, (in gram.) a technical term for the affix *u* (the characteristic sign of the eighth class of verbs).

शुप्ति *śúpti*, f. (prob.) the shoulder (accord. to Sāy. = *mukha*), RV. i, 51, 5. [Cf. Zd. *supti.*]

शुफालिह *suphāliha*, N. of a place, Cat.

शुभ् 1. *śubh* (or 1. *śumbh*), cl. 1. Ā. or 6. P. (Dhātup. xviii, 11; xxviii, 33) *śóbhate, śumbháti* or *śúmbhati* (ep. also *śobhati*, and Ved. *śúmbhate*; 3. sg. *śóbhe*, RV.; pf. *śuśobha, śuśubhe*, MBh. &c.; *śuśumbha*, Gr.; aor. *aśubhat, aśobhishṭa, aśumbhīt*, ib.; p. *śúmbhāna, śubhāná*, RV.; fut. *śobhitā* or *śumbhitā*, Gr.; *śobhishyati*, MBh.; *śumbhishyati*, Gr.; inf. *śubhé, śobháse*, RV.; *śobhitum*, Gr.), to beautify, embellish, adorn, beautify one's self, (Ā.) look beautiful or handsome, shine, be bright or splendid; (with *iva* or *yathā*, 'to shine or look like;' with *na*, 'to look bad, have a bad appearance, appear to disadvantage'), RV. &c. &c.; to prepare, make fit or ready, (Ā.) prepare one's self, RV.; AV.; (*śúmbhate*, accord. to some) to flash or flit i.e. glide rapidly past or along, RV. (cf. *śubhānā, śumbhámāna*, and *pra-√śumbh*); (*śumbhati*) wrongly for *śundhati* (to be connected with √*śudh*, to purify), AV. vi, 115, 3; xii, 2, 40 &c.; (*śumbhati*) to harm, injure, Dhātup. xi, 42 (in this sense rather to be regarded as a second √*śumbh*, cf. √2. *śumbh, ni-śumbh*): Pass. aor. *aśobhi-tarām*, Inscr.: Caus. *śobhayati* (aor. *aśūśubhat*; cf. *śobhita*), to cause to shine, beautify, ornament, decorate, AV. &c. &c.; (*śubháyati*, °*te*) to ornament, decorate, (Ā.) decorate one's self, RV.; TBr.; (only pr. p. *śubháyat*), to fly rapidly along, RV.: Desid. *śuśobhishate* (accord. to Gr. also °*ti*, and *śuśubhishati*, °*te*), to wish to prepare or make ready, Nir. viii, 10: Intens. *śośubhyate* (Gr. also *śośobdhi*), to shine brightly or intensely, be very splendid or beautiful, MBh.

2. **Śúbh**, f. (dat. *śubhé* as inf.) splendour, beauty, ornament, decoration, RV.; AV.; VS.; TBr.; flashing or flitting past, gliding along, rapid course or flight, RV.; AV.; TS.; readiness(?), RV.

Śubha, mf(*ā*)n. splendid, bright, beautiful, handsome (often f. voc. *śubhe*, 'fair one!' in addressing a beautiful woman), Mn.; MBh.; Kāv. &c.; pleasant, agreeable, suitable, fit, capable, useful, good (applied to persons and things), ib.; auspicious, fortunate, prosperous, ib.; good (in moral sense), righteous, virtuous, honest, ŚvetUp.; Mn. &c.; pure (as an action), Yājñ., Sch.; eminent, distinguished, W.; learned, versed in the Vedas, ib.; m. water, L.; the Phenila tree (Sapindus Detergens), L.; a he-goat, L. (prob. w.r. for *stubha*); the 23rd of the astrol. Yogas, L.; N. of a man (cf. g. *tikâdi*), Kathās.; of a son of Dharma, BhP.; of an author, Cat.; (also *ā*, f.) a city floating in the sky (cf. *śaubha* = *vyoma-cāri-pura*), MW.; (*ā*), f. (only L.) light, lustre, splendour, beauty; desire; Prosopis Spicigera or Mimosa Suma; white Dūrva grass; = *priyaṅgu*; bamboo manna; a cow; the yellow pigment Gorocanā; an assembly of the gods; a kind of metre; N. of a female friend and companion of the goddess Umā; (*am*), n. anything bright or beautiful &c.; beauty, charm, good fortune, auspiciousness, happiness, bliss, welfare, prosperity, Kauś.; Kāv.; Kathās.; benefit, service, good or virtuous action, Kāv.; VarBṛS.; Kathās.; the wood of Cerasus Puddum, L. **–katha**, mfn. talking well or agreeably, MBh. **–kara**, mfn. causing welfare, auspicious, fortunate, VarBṛS.; (*ī*), f. Prosopis Spicigera, L. **–karman**, n. a good or virtuous act, ausp° action, Rājat. (°*ma-nirṇaya*, m. N. of wk.); mfn. acting nobly, MBh.; m. N. of one of Skanda's attendants, ib. **–kāma**, mfn. desirous of welfare, Kauś. **–kāmyā**, f. desire of welfare, L. **–kūṭa**, m. 'auspicious peak,' N. of Adam's Peak (in Ceylon), Buddh. **–kṛit**, mfn. = *-kara*, VarBṛS.; N. of the 37th (or 36th) year of Jupiter's cycle of 60 years, ib. **–kṛitsna**, m. pl. (with Buddhists) N. of a class of gods, Dharmas. 128; MWB. 212. **–kshaṇa**, n. an auspicious or lucky moment, MW. **–ga** (prob. w.r. for *su-bhaga*), mfn. going well or beautifully, gracious, elegant, W.; ausp°, fortunate, ib.; (*ā*), f. N. of a Śakti, Hcat. **–gandhaka**, n. 'agreeably-scented,' gum-myrrh, L. **–garbha**, m. N. of a Bodhi-sattva, Buddh. **–gābhīrī**, f. (in music) a partic. Rāgiṇī, Saṃgīt. **–graha**, m. an auspicious planet, lucky star (such as Jupiter, Venus, Mercury, and the moon when more than half full), MW.; °*hôdaya*, m. the rising of an ausp° planet, ib. **–ṃ-kara**, mfn. = *śubha-k°*, L.; m. N. of an Asura, Kathās.; of a poet and various other writers, Cat.; (*ī*), f. N. of Pārvatī, L. **–candra**, m. N. of the author of the Śabda-cintā-maṇi-vṛitti, Cat. **–jāni**, mfn. having a beautiful wife, Pāṇ. v, 4, 134, Sch. **–ṃ-carā**, f. pl. N. of a class of Apsarases, VP. **–tara**, mfn. more (most) auspicious or fortunate, R.; Pañcat. **–tāti**, f. welfare, prosperity (*-kṛit*, mfn. causing welfare or pr°), Śatr. **–da**, mfn. = *-kara*, Var.; m. the sacred fig-tree, L. **–datta**, m. N. of a man, Kathās. **–danta**, mf(*ī*)n. having good teeth, L.; (*ī*), f. a woman with g° t°, L.; the female of Pushpa-danta (elephant of the north-west quarter), L. (v.l. *śubha-datī* and *śubhra-dantī*). **–darśa** or **–darśana**, mfn. of auspicious aspect, beautiful, R. **–dāyin**, mfn. = *-da*, VarBṛS. **–dāru-maya**, mf(*ī*)n. made of beautiful wood, Hcat. **–dina**, n. an ausp° or lucky day, Daś. **–dṛiḍha-vrata**, mfn. of virtuous and firm principles, R. **–dṛishṭi**, mfn. = *-darśa*, MW. **–dhara**, m. N. of a man, Rājat. **–dhāraṇa**, mfn. one whose soul is fixed upon true welfare, BhP. **–naya**, m. 'of virtuous conduct,' N. of a Muni, Kathās. **–nāmā**, f. (in astron.) 'of ausp° name,' N. of the 5th and 10th and 15th lunar night. **–pattrikā**, f. 'having auspicious leaves,' Desmodium Gangeticum (a kind of shrub), L. **–pushpita-śuddhi**, m. a partic. Samādhi, Buddh. **–prada**, mfn. = *-kara*, Var.; Kathās. **–phala**, n. auspicious result, good or happy consequence, VarBṛS.; *-kṛit*, mfn. yielding ausp° r°s &c., ib. **–bhāvanā**, f. the forming of good thoughts or opinions, Subh. **–maṅgala**, n. good luck, welfare (accord. to others mfn., 'lucky, fortunate'), R. ii, 25, 34. **–maya**, mf(*ī*)n. splendid, beautiful, Subh. **–mālā**, f. N. of a Gandharvī, Kāraṇḍ. **–mitra**, m. N. of a man, Buddh. **–ṃ-bhāvuka**, mfn. splendid, beautiful, Dhūrtan. (cf. Pāṇ. iii, 2, 57). **–yoga**, m. a partic. astron. Yoga (see *śubha*), Cat. **–lakshaṇa**, mf(*ā*)n. having auspicious marks, characterized by auspiciousness, Kāv.; Kathās. **–lagna**, m. n. the rising of an ausp° constellation, a lucky moment, Hit.; Kautukas. **–locana**, mfn. fair-eyed, R. **–vaktrā**, f. 'of ausp° face,' N. of one of the Mātṛis attending on Skanda, MBh. **–vastu**(?), N. of a river (= *su-vāstu*), Buddh. **–vārttā**, f. good news, MW. **–vāsana**, v.l. (or w.r.) for *mukha-v°*, q.v. **–vāsara**, m. n. = *-dina*, Hcat. **–vimala-garbha**, m. 'wearing bright and pure garments,' N. of a Bodhi-sattva, Buddh. **–veṇu-triveṇu-mat**, mfn. furnished with a Tri-veṇu (q.v.) of excellent reeds, MBh. **–vyūha**, m. N. of a king, Buddh. **–vrata**, n. N. of a partic. religious observance (kept on the 12th day in one of the halves of the month Kārttika), Cat.; mf(*ā*)n. virtuous or moral in conduct, R.; MārkP. **–śaṃsin**, mfn. indicative of good luck, auspicious, Ragh.; Rājat. **–śakuna**, m. an ausp° bird, bird of good omen, Daś. **–śīla**, mfn. having a good disposition or character, W.; *-gaṇi*, m. N. of an author, Cat. **–saṃyuta**, mfn. endowed with prosperity or happiness, blissful, L. **–saptamī-vrata**, n. N. of a partic. religious observance, Cat. **–samanvita**, mfn. endowed with beauty, charming, R. **–sāra**, m. N. of a king, Buddh. **–sūcanī**, f. 'indicating good,' N. of a female deity (worshipped by women in times of calamity; she is also called Su-vacanī), L. **–sthalī**, f. 'ausp° place,' a room or hall in which sacrifices are offered, L. **Śubhâkara-gupta**, m. 'protected by a multitude of good works,' N. of a man, Buddh. **Śubhâksha**, m. 'auspicious-eyed,' N. of Śiva, MW. **Śubhâgama**, n. N. of partic. Tāntric wks. (regarded as especially orthodox), Cat. **Śubhâṅka**, m. N. of various authors, Cat. (cf. next). **Śubhâṅga**, mfn. handsome-limbed (applied to Śiva), Śivag.; m. N. of a Tushita-kāyika Deva-putra, Lalit.; of a lexicographer (v.l. *śubhâṅka*), Cat.; (*ī*), f. a handsome woman, W.; N. of a Daśârhī (and wife of Kuru), MBh.; of a Vaidarbhī (the daughter of Rukmin and wife of Pradyumna), Hariv.; of Rati (wife of Kāma-deva), A.; of the wife of Kubera (god of wealth), L. **Śubhâṅgada**, m. N. of a king, MBh. **Śubhâṅgin**, mfn. = *śubhâṅga*, RāmatUp. **Śubhâcāra**, mfn. pure in practices or observances, virtuous, MBh.; Ragh.; MārkP.; (*ā*), f. N. of a female attendant on Umā, L. **Śubhâñjana**, m. = *śobhâñjana*, L. **Śubhâtmaka**, mf(*ikā*)n. pleasant, charming, L.; benevolent, kind (in *a-śubhâtmaka*), Kām. **Śubhânana**, mfn. handsome-faced, good-looking (*ā*, f. 'a handsome woman'), MBh. **Śubhânandā**, f. N. of a goddess (said to be a form of Dākshāyaṇī), Cat. **Śubhânvita**, mfn. endowed with prosperity or good fortune, happy, prosperous, L. **Śubhâpāṅgā**, f. 'having beautiful eye-corners,' a beautiful woman, R. **Śubhârcita**, mfn. worshipped in the right manner, Kṛishṇaj. **Śubhârthin**, mfn. desirous of prosperity or welfare, R.; Rājat. **Śubhâvaha**, mfn. causing prosperity, conferring happiness, VarBṛS.; Rājat. **Śubhâśaya**, mfn. of virtuous disposition, Kām.; Rājat. **Śubhâśis**, f. good wishes, benediction, blessing, congratulation, Pañcar. (°*śīrvacana*, n., *-vāda*, m. [Hāsy.], utterance of b° or c°); mfn. receiving b° or c° (°*śishaṃ* √*kṛi*, with acc. 'to bless, congratulate'), ib. **Śubhâśubha**, mf(*ā*)n. pleasant and unpleasant, agreeable and disagreeable, prosperous and unfortunate, good and evil, Mn.; MBh. &c.; n. weal and woe, good and evil, MaitrUp.; Bhag.; VarBṛS.; *-prakaraṇa-ṭīkā*, f. N. of wk.; *-phala*, mfn. producing good or evil results, Mn. xii, 3; *-yoga*, m. an auspicious or inauspicious Yoga, Cat.; *-lakshaṇa*, n. a mark or sign of good and bad fortune, good or evil omen, MW. **Śubhâshṭaka-ṭīkā**, f. N. of wk. **Śubhâsana**, m. N. of a Tāntric teacher, Cat. **Śubhêkshaṇa**, mfn. having auspicious or fair eyes, R. **Śubhêtara,** mfn. other than ausp°, unlucky, unfortunate, evil, bad, Śiś. **Śubhâika-dṛiś,** mfn. seeing only what is good or right, Pañcar. **Śubhôdaya,** m. the rising of an auspicious (planet), Cat. (in *a-śubh°*); N. of a Tāntric teacher, ib. **Śubhôdarka,** mf(*ā*)n. having a prosperous issue or consequence, auspicious, lucky (*-tā*, f.), Kāv.; Kathās.

Śubham, in comp. for *śubham* (acc. of 2. *śubh*). **-yā́,** mfn. flying swiftly along, RV. **-yā́van,** mfn. id., ib. **-yú,** mfn. loving adornment, RV.; splendid, beautiful, handsome, Kāv.; happy, L. **-kara, -carā** &c., see under *śubha*, p. 1083, col. 2.

Śubhaṃyikā, f., Kāś. on Pāṇ. vii, 3, 46.

Śubhaka, m. mustard seed, Sinapis Dichotoma, L.

Śubhás-páti, m. du. (fr. gen. of 2. *śubh + p°*) the two lords of splendour (or 'of the rapid course,' applied to the Aśvins), RV.

Śubhāná, mfn. shining bright, brilliant, RV.; gliding rapidly along, ib.

Śubhāya, Nom. P. °*yate*, to be bright or beautiful, become a blessing (see *bahu-ś°*).

Śubhikā, f. a garland formed of flowers, MW.

Śubhitá, mfn. (accord. to Pat. on Pāṇ. iii, 1, 85) = *su-hita*, TS.

Śubhī-√kṛi, P. *-karoti*, to illumine, beautify, Kautukas.

Śubhrá, mf(*ā́*)n. radiant, shining, beautiful, splendid, RV. &c. &c.; clear, spotless (as fame), Pañcat.; bright-coloured, white, Mn.; VarBṛS. &c.; m. white (the colour), L.; sandal, L.; heaven, L.; N. of a man, g. *kurv-ādi*; of the husband of Vikuṇṭhā and father of Vaikuṇṭha, BhP.; of a poet, Cat.; pl. N. of a people, MārkP.; (*ā*), f. (only L.) crystal; bamboo-manna; alum; N. of the Ganges; n. (only L.) silver; talc; green vitriol; rock or fossil salt; the root of Andropogon Muricatus. **-kṛit,** w.r. for *śubha-kṛit*, L. **-khādi,** mfn. wearing glittering bracelets or rings (applied to the Maruts), RV. **-tā,** f., **-tva,** n. whiteness, Kāv. **-dat,** mf(*ī*)n. having white teeth, Pāṇ. v, 4, 145. **-danta,** mf(*ī*)n. id., Mṛicch.; (*ī*), f. N. of the female of the elephants Pushpa-danta (cf. *śubha-dantī*) and Sārvabhauma, L. **-bhānu,** m. 'white-rayed,' the moon, Inscr. **-mati,** (prob.) w.r. for *-vatī*, q.v. **-yāma** (*śubhrá-*), mfn. having a radiant chariot (as Ushas), RV. **-yāvan,** mfn. going in a radiant chariot (as the Aśvins), ib. **-raśmi,** m. = *-bhānu*, L. **-vatī,** f. N. of a river (v.l. *śvabhra-v°*), Hariv. **-śastama** (*śubhrá-*; prob. for *-śasta-tama*, superl. of *śastá*, pp. of *√śaṇs*), mfn. highly celebrated for shining, i.e. shining very much, RV. ix, 66, 26 (Sāy.) **Śubhrâṇśu,** m. = *śubhra-bhānu*, L.; camphor, L. **Śubhrâlu,** m. a partic. bulbous plant, L. **Śubhrá-vat,** mfn. (Padap. *śubhrá-vat*) splendid, beautiful, RV. ix, 15, 3.

Śubhri, mfn. shining, bright, beautiful, RV.; m. the sun, L.; a Brāhman, L.

Śubhrikā, f., Vop. iv, 8.

Śubhrī-√bhū, P. *-bhavati* (pp. *-bhūta*), to become white, Rājat.

Śúbhvan, mfn. shining, bright (accord. to others 'swift,' 'fleet,' see *√1. śubh*), RV.

Śúmbhana, mf(*ī*)n. (prob.) purifying, AV.

Śúmbhamāna or **śumbhámāna,** mfn. shining, bright, splendid, beautiful, RV.; (accord. to some) flying rapidly along, ib.; (*śúmbh°*), m. (said to be) N. of a Muhūrta in the dark fortnight of a month, TBr.

Śúmbhāna. See *√1. śubh*, p. 1083, col. 1.

Śumbhita, mfn. purified, adorned (in *brahma-ś°*, q.v.)

Śumbhū́, m. (said to be) N. of a Muhūrta in the dark fortnight of a month (= *śumbhamāna*), TBr.

Śobha &c. See p. 1092, col. 1.

शुम्ब *śumba*, n. = *śulba*, L.

शुम्बल *śúmbala*, n. pl. any substance which easily catches fire (as straw), ŚBr.

शुम्भ् 2. *śumbh* (for 1. see *√1. śubh*), cl. 1. P. *śumbhati*, to kill, harm, injure (cf. *√1. śubh*, *ni-√śubh*).

Śumbha, m. N. of an Asura or demon (slain by Durgā; he was the son of Gaveshṭhin and grandson of Prahlāda), Hariv.; R.; Pur. **-ghātinī,** f. 'Śumbha-killing,' N. of Durgā, L. **-deśa,** m. N. of a country, Col. (cf. *sumbha*). **-niśumbha,** m. du. Śumbha and Niśumbha, Mṛicch. **-pura,** n., **-purī,** f. 'city of Ś°,' N. of a town and district (the modern Sambhalpūr in the district of Gondwāna; it is also called Eka-cakra and Hari-griha), L. **-mathanī** or **-mardinī,** f. 'Ś°-destroying,' N. of a Durgā, L. **-vadha,** m. 'killing of Ś°,' N. of a ch. of the Devīmāhātmya. **-hananī,** f. = *-ghātinī*, L.

शुर *śura*, m. a lion, L.; w.r. for *śūra*, a hero, MBh. i, 3708.

शुरुध् *śurúdh*, f. pl. (prob. connected with *√śṛidh*) invigorating draughts, healing herbs, any refreshment or comfort, RV.

शुल्क् *śulk* (prob. artificial), cl. 10. P. *śulkayati*, to pay, give, Dhātup. xxxii, 75; to gain, acquire, ib.; to leave, forsake, ib.; to narrate, tell (cf. *√śvalk*), xxxii, 34.

Śulká, m. n. (ifc. f. *ā*) price, value, purchase-money, RV.; the prize of a contest, MBh.; toll, tax, duty, customs (esp. money levied at ferries, passes, and roads), Gaut.; Āpast.; Mn. &c.; nuptial gift (orig. a price given to parents for the purchase of a bride, but in later times bestowed on the wife as her own property together with the profits of household labour, domestic utensils, ornaments &c.), dower, dowry, marriage settlement, Gaut.; Vishṇ.; Mn. &c. (cf. IW. 267); wages of prostitution, Kathās.; MārkP.; w.r. for *śukra* and *śukla*, MBh. **-khaṇḍana,** n. defrauding the revenue, MW. **-grāhaka** or **-grāhin,** mfn. receiving a toll or duty, ib. **-tva,** n. the being a nuptial gift or dowry (cf. above), Dhāyabh. **-da,** m. the giver of a nuptial present, an affianced suitor, Mn.; Yājñ.; MBh. **-moshaṇa,** n. stealing or defrauding the revenue, Kull. on Mn. viii, 400. **-śālā,** f. a custom-house, Pāṇ. iv, 3, 75, Sch. (cf. *śaulkaśālika*). **-saṃjña,** mfn. having (merely) the name of a nuptial gratuity, MW. **-sthāna,** n. a toll-house, tax-office, custom house, Mn.; Yājñ.; any object of taxation or duty, W. **-hāni,** f. loss or forfeiture of wages or dower &c., W. **Śulkâdhyaksha,** m. a superintendent of tolls or taxes or revenue, L. **Śulkâbhidhāna,** mfn. = *śulka-saṃjña*, MW. **Śulkâvâpta,** mfn. obtained as a dowry, MBh. **Śulkôpajīvin,** mfn. living by tolls or taxes or revenue, ib.

Śulkikā, f. N. of a country, L. (cf. *śaulkikeya*).

शुल्ब् *śulb* or *śulv* (prob. artificial or Nom. fr. next), cl. 10. P. *śulbayati*, to mete out, Dhātup. xxxii, 71; to create, ib.

Śulba or **śulva,** n. (accord. to some also m. and *ā* or *ī*, f.) a string, cord, rope, ŚrS.; Sūryas.; BhP.; a strip, Bhpr.; N. of a Pariśishṭa, Cat.; L. also 'copper;' 'sacrificial act;' 'conduct;' 'vicinity of water;' m. N. of a man, Śaṃk. **-kalpa,** m., or **-kārikā,** f. N. of wks. **-ja,** n. brass, L. **-dīpikā,** f., **-pariśishṭa,** n., **-bhāshya,** n., **-mīmāṇsā,** f., **-rahasya-prakāśa,** m., **-vārttika,** n., **-vṛitti-vivaraṇa,** n. N. of wks. **-sūtra,** n. N. of a Sūtra work (belonging to the Śrauta ritual and containing curious geometrical calculations and attempts at squaring the circle); *-bhāshya-vārttika-vyākhyā*, f. N. of wk. **Śulbâgni-nidhi-ṭīkā,** f. N. of wk. **Śulbâri,** m. 'enemy of copper,' sulphur, L. **Śulbôpadhāna,** n. N. of wk.

Śulbika, n. = *śulba-pariśishṭa*, Cat.

शुल्ल *śulla*, n. = *śulba*, 'a rope' or 'copper,' L.

शुशुक्वन *śuśukvaná*, °*kváni*. See p. 1081, col. 3.

शुशुक्वस् *śuśukvás*. See *√1. śuc*, p. 1081.

शुशुक्षणि *śuśukshaṇi*. See *ā-śuś°* under *ā-√śuc*.

शुशुमारगिरि *śuśumāra-giri*, m. (perhaps for *śiś°*) N. of a place, Divyâv. **Śuśumāra-girīya** or °**yaka,** mfn. living at Śuśumāra-giri, ib.

शुशुलूक *śuśulūka*, m. a small owl, owlet, Sāy. on RV. vii, 104, 22. **-yātu** (°*lū́ka-*), m. a demon in the shape of an owlet, RV. vii, 104, 22.

Śuśulū́kā, f. a partic. bird, MaitrS. (Padap. *sushilīkā*).

शुश्रुवस् *śuśruvás*. See *√1. śru*.

शुश्रू *śuśrū*, f. (fr. Desid. of *√1. śru*) 'one who waits on a child,' a mother, MBh. xii, 9513 (B.)

Śuśrūshaka, mfn. desirous of hearing, attentive, obedient, attending or waiting on (gen. or comp.), MBh.; Kāv. &c.; m. an attendant, servant (comprehending five descriptions of persons, viz. a pupil, a religious pupil, a hired servant, an officer, and a slave), W. °**shaṇa,** n. desire of hearing, BhP.; obedience, service, dutiful homage to (gen., dat., loc., or comp.), MBh.; R. &c.; (ifc.) attention to, maintenance of (fire), MBh.

Śuśrūshā, f. desire or wish to hear, Kām.; obsequiousness, reverence, obedience, service (said to be of five kinds (see *śuśrūshaka*), Mn.; MBh. &c.; saying, speaking, telling, L.; *-para*, mfn. diligent or attentive in service, Kathās. °**shitavya,** mfn. to be obeyed or attended to, R.; n. (impers.) it should be obeyed, Pat. °**shitṛi,** mfn. obedient, attending on (gen.), MBh. °**shin,** mfn. id. (ifc.), ib.

Śuśrūshu, mfn. desirous of hearing or learning, NṛisUp.; Bhag. &c.; eager to obey, obedient, attentive, serving, attending on (gen. or comp.), TBr. &c. &c. °**shéṇya,** mfn. to be willingly heard or attended to, TS.; ŚāṅkhŚr. °**shya,** mfn. to be heard or obeyed or served, R.; Kathās.

शुष् 1. *śush* (prob. for orig. *sush*, *sus*), cl. 4. P. (Dhātup. xxvi, 74) *śúshyati* (m. c. also °*te*; pf. *śuśosha*; aor. *aśushat*; fut. *śoshṭā*, *śokshyati*; inf. *śoshṭum*; ind. p. *-śúshya*, Br.), to dry, become dry or withered, fade, languish, decay, AV. &c. &c.: Caus. *śoshayati* (aor. *aśūśushat*), to make dry, dry up, wither, parch, AV. &c. &c.; to afflict, injure, hurt, extinguish, destroy, MBh.: Desid. *śuśukshati*, Gr.: Intens. *śośushyate*, *śośoshṭi*, ib. [Cf. Gk. αὔω for σαύσω; Lat. *siccus*; Slav. *sŭchati*; Lith. *susù*, *sausiù*, *sausas* &c.]

2. **Śush,** (ifc.) drying, withering, Pāṇ. iv, 3, 166, Vārtt. 1; drying up, parching (see *parṇa-śush*).

Śusha, mfn. drying, drying up, L.; m. a hole in the ground, L.; the son of a Vena and a Tīvarī, L. (*śushásya* in AV. v, 1, 4 prob. w.r.)

1. **Śushi,** f. (for 2. see p. 1085, col. 1) drying, L.; a hole, chasm, L. (also written *sushi*); the hollow or groove in the fang of a snake, W.

Śushikā, f. dryness, thirst, L.

Śushira. See *sushira*.

1. **Śúshka,** mf(*ā*)n. dried, dried up, dry, arid, parched, shrivelled, emaciated, shrunk, withered, sere, RV. &c. &c.; useless, fruitless, groundless, vain, unprofitable, empty, Mn.; MBh. &c.; mere, simple (see *-gāna*); m. N. of a man (a relative of Sukha-varman; cf. *śushkaṭa-varman*), Rājat.; n. (and m., g. *ardharcâdi*) anything dry (e.g. dry wood, dry cow-dung &c.), RV.; Vishṇ. **-kaṇṭhá,** n. a partic. part of the neck of a sacrificial animal, VS. (Sch.) **-kalahá,** m. a groundless quarrel, Mudr.; Pañcat. **-kāshṭha,** n. pl. dry wood, MBh. **-kāsa,** m. a dry cough, Bhpr. **-kshetra,** w.r. for *sushkaletra*, q.v. **-gāna,** n. mere singing (unaccompanied by dancing), Sāh. **-gomaya,** m. dry cow-dung, L. **-carcana,** n. 'dry anointing,' idle talk, chaff, Hāsy. **-jñāna-nirādara,** m. N. of wk. **-tarka,** m. dry or unprofitable argument, MW. **-tā,** f., **-tva,** n. dryness, aridity, Pañcar.; Kām. **-toya,** mf(*ā*)n. (a river) whose water is dried up, MBh. **-dṛití,** f. a dry or empty bag, MaitrS. **-nitambha-sthalī,** f. shrunk or shrivelled hip-region, Dhūrtas. **-pattra,** n. a dry or withered leaf, MW.; a dried potherb, ib. **-parṇa,** n. a dry leaf (*-vat*, ind. like a dry leaf), ib. **-pāka,** m. dry inflammation (of the eyes; cf. *śushkâkshi-p°*), Suśr. **-pesham,** ind. (with *√pish*) to grind anything in a dry state (i.e. without any fluid), Bhaṭṭ. **-phala,** n. dry fruit, MW. **-bhṛiṅgāra,** m. N. of a teacher, KaushUp.; °*rīya*, n. the doctrine of Śushka-bhṛiṅgāra, ŚāṅkhŚr. **-matsya,** n. dried fish, MW. **-māṇsa,** n. dry flesh or meat, L. **-mukha,** mfn. dry-mouthed, R. **-rudita,** n. weeping without tears, Sāh. **-revatī,** f. N. of a female demon inimical to children, MatsyaP. **-vat,** mfn. dried up, Mṛicch. (cf. Pāṇ. viii, 2, 51). **-vāda-vivāda,** m. idle or useless discussion, BhP. **-vigraha,** m. a useless contest, ib. **-virohaṇa,** n. the sprouting of a dry tree, VarBṛS. **-vṛiksha,** m. Grislea Tomentosa, L.; a dry tree, MW. **-vaira,** n. groundless enmity, Mn. iv, 139. **-vairin,** mfn. quarrelling

causelessly, BhP. **-vraṇa**, m. a dried-up wound, scar, Mṛicch., Sch. **-sambhava**, n. Costus Speciosus or Arabicus, L. **-srota** or **-srotas**, mfn. having the stream dried up (as a river), R. **Śushkâkshi-pāka**, m. dry inflammation of the eyes, infl° without efflux, Suśr.; Vāgbh. (cf. *śushka-pāka*). **Śúshkâgra**, mf(*ā*)n. having a dry tip or point, TS.; Br.; ŚrS. **Śushkâṅga**, mf(*ī*)n. having shrivelled limbs, emaciated, withered, W.; m. Grislea Tomentosa, L.; (*ā* or *ī*), f. a crane, L.; (*ī*), f. Lacerta Godica, L. **Śushkânna**, n. 'dry food,' rice in the husk, VarBṛS. **Śúshkâpa**, mfn. having the water dried up (as the sea), R.; a dried-up pond, mud &c., ŚBr. **Śushkârdra**, mf(*ā*)n. dry and wet, R.; n. dry ginger, L. **Śushkârśas**, n. dry swelling of the eyelids, Suśr. **Śushkâsthi**, n. mere bone, a fleshless bone, VarBṛS. **Śúshkâsya**, mfn. = *śushka-mukha*, AV.

2. **Śushka**, Nom. (only inf. *śushkitum*) to become dry, Divyâv.

Śushkaka, mf(*ikā*)n. dried up, emaciated, thin, R.

Śushkaṭa-varman, m. N. of the father of the poet Vidyādhara, Subh. (cf. under 1. *śúshka*).

Śushkala, m. a kind of fish, L.; (also n. and *ī*, f.) flesh (f. also dry flesh), L.; n. a fish-hook, TBr., Sch.; mfn. one who eats flesh, L. (cf. *śaushkala*).

Śushkaletra, m. (for °*lêtara*?) N. of a mountain or a place, Rājat.

1. **Śushṇa**, m. the sun, L.; fire, L.

1. **Śushma**, m. n. fire, flame, L.; the sun, L.

1. **Śushman**, m. fire, Śiś.; Bālar.; a partic. plant (= *citraka*), MW.

Śosha &c. See 1. *śosha*, p. 1092, col. 2.

शुष 3. *śush* (cf. √*śvas*), cl. 6. P. *śusháti* (1. sg. also *-śushé* and p. *-śushāṇa*; see *ā-√śush*), to hiss (as a serpent), RV. i, 61, 10.

2. **Śushi**, f. (for 1. see p. 1084, col. 3) strength, power (= *bala*), L.

Śushila, m. air, wind, Uṇ. i, 57, Sch.

2. **Śúshṇa**, m. 'Hisser,' N. of a demon slain by Indra, RV. (accord. to some a drought demon; cf. √1. *śush*); n. strength (= *bala*), Naigh. ii, 9. **-hátya**, n. the slaughter of Śushṇa, RV.

2. **Śúshma**, mf(*ā*)n. hissing, roaring (as water), RV.; fragrant, ib.; strong, bold, ib.; m. hissing, roaring, rushing (of water, fire, the wind &c.), RV.; AV.; exhalation, fragrance, odour (of plants, esp. of the Soma), RV.; VS.; strength, vigour, vital or sexual energy, impulse, courage, valour, ib.; AV.; TBr.; semen virile (?), AV. ix, 1, 10; 20; air, wind, L.; a bird, L.; w.r. for *śushṇa*, Pāṇ. iii, 1, 85, Sch.; n. strength (= *bala*), Naigh. ii, 9. **-dá**, mfn. bestowing strength or valour, AV. **-vat** (*śúshma-*), mfn. fiery, violent, excited (esp. sexually), AV.

2. **Śushman**, n. strength, vigour, energy, courage, valour, Kāśikh.

Śushmaya, mfn. strengthening, encouraging, TS.

Śushmāyaṇa, m. patr. of a Soma, VP.

Śushmi, m. wind or the god of wind, L.

Śushmiṇa, m. N. of a king of the Śibis, AitBr.

Śushmín, mfn. roaring, rushing, RV.; strong, fiery, mettlesome, vigorous, impetuous, courageous, bold, ib. &c. &c.; sexually excited, ruttish (applied to bulls and elephants), MBh.; BhP.; m. pl. N. of a caste living in Kuśa-dvīpa (corresponding to the Kshatriyas), Pur. **-tama** (*śushmín-*), mfn. most strong or mighty or fiery or bold, RV.

Śosha. See 2. *śosha*, p. 1092, col. 2.

शू 1. *śū*, a weak form of √*śvi*, q.v.

2. **Śū** (ifc.) See *surā-śū*.

Śūtha, m. a place for sacrifice, L.

Śūna, mfn. (Pāṇ. vii, 2, 14) swelled, swollen (esp. 'morbidly'), increased, grown, Suśr.; m. N. of a man, MBh.; (*śū́na*), n. emptiness (orig. 'swollen state,' 'hollowness,' cf. *śūnya* below), lack, want, absence, RV.; a partic. incorrect pronunciation (esp. of vowels), RPrāt. **-gātra**, mfn. having swollen limbs, Suśr. **-tva**, n. the state of being swollen, Suśr. **-vat**, mfn. one who has increased, Pāṇ. vii, 2, 14. **Śūnâksha**, mfn. having swollen eyes, Suśr. **Śūnâṇḍa-meḍhra-tā**, f. swollen condition of the testicles and penis, ib.

Śūnyá, mf(*ā*)n. empty, void (with *vājin* = 'a riderless horse;' with *rājya* = 'a kingless kingdom'), hollow, barren, desolate, deserted, Br. &c. &c.; empty, i. e. vacant (as a look or stare), absent, absent-minded, having no certain object or aim, distracted, MBh.; Kāv. &c.; empty i.e. possessing nothing, wholly destitute, MBh.; Kathās.; wholly alone or solitary, having no friends or companions, R.; BhP.; void of, free from, destitute of (instr. or comp.), wanting, lacking, Kāv.; Kathās.; Pur.; Sarvad.; non-existent, absent, missing, Kāv.; Pañcat.; vain, idle, unreal, nonsensical, R.; Rājat.; Sarvad.; void of results, ineffectual (*a-śūnyam √kṛi*, 'to effect,' 'accomplish'), Śak.; Ratnâv.; free from sensitiveness or sensation (said of the skin), insensible, Bhpr.; bare, naked, MW.; guileless, innocent, ib.; indifferent, ib.; (*ā*), f. a hollow reed, L.; a barren woman, L.; Cactus Indicus = *malī* (for *nalī*?), L.; n. a void, vacuum, empty or deserted place, desert (*śūnye*, in a lonely place), MBh.; R. &c.; (in phil.) vacuity, nonentity, absolute non-existence (esp. with Buddhists), IW. 83, n. 3; 105, n. 4; MWB. 7, n. 1; 142; N. of Brahma, MW.; (in arithm.) nought, a cypher, VarBṛS.; Gaṇit. (cf. IW. 183); space, heaven, atmosphere, L.; a partic. phenomenon in the sky, L.; an earring (see next). [Cf. Gk. κενός, κενεός; Æol. κέννος.] **-karṇa**, m. an ear adorned with an earring, Amar. (Sch.) **-geha**, n. an empty house, W. **-citta**, mfn. vacant-minded, absent-minded, thinking of nothing, Hāsy. **-tā**, f. emptiness, loneliness, desolateness, R.; VarBṛ. &c. (cf. *a-śūnyatā*); absence of mind, distraction, Suśr.; Sarvad.; vacancy (of gaze), Dhūrtas.; (ifc.) absence or want of, Cāṇ.; Kum.; nothingness, non-existence, non-reality, illusory nature (of all worldly phenomena), Śiś.; Sarvad.; *-samāpti*, f. N. of wk. **-tva**, n. = *-tā*, Kāv.; Rājat.; Sarvad. **-paksha**, m. = *-vāda*, Sāṃkhyas., Sch. **-padavī**, f. 'path to non-existence,' the way or passage of the soul (= *brahma-randhra*), Cat. **-pāla**, m. 'keeper of a vacant place,' a substitute, MBh. **-bandhu**, m. N. of a son of Triṇa-bindu, BhP. **-bindu**, m. the mark of a cypher or nought (cf. *bindu*), Vās.; Dhūrtan. **-bhāva**, m. state of being empty, emptiness, AmṛitUp. **-madhya**, m. 'having a hollow or empty centre,' a hollow reed, L. **-manas**, mfn. = *-citta*, Śāntiś. **-mūla**, mfn. empty or unprotected at the base (said of a badly placed army), Kām. **-vat**, ind. like a cypher, as if it were annihilated or vanished, Daś. **-vāda**, m. the (Buddhist) doctrine of the non-existence (of any Spirit either Supreme or human), Buddhism, atheism, Madhus. **-vādin**, m. the affirmer of a void (i. e. of the non-existence of any Spirit, divine or human), a Buddhist, atheist, W.; MWB. 7; 142. **-vyāpāra**, mfn. free from occupation, unoccupied (= *vyāpāra-śūnya*), Prab. **-śarīra**, mfn. 'empty-bodied,' having nothing in the body (*-tā*, f.), Vās. **-śālā**, f. an empty hall, Kauś. **-śūnya**, mf(*ā*)n. thoroughly empty or vain (as a speech), Śiś. **-sthāna**, n. an empty place, W. **-hara**, n. 'remover of emptiness,' gold, L. **-hasta**, mfn. empty-handed, W. **-hṛidaya**, mfn. = *-citta*; (*-tva*, n.), RV.; Śak.; Kathās.; heartless, Pañcat. **Śūnyâkṛiti**, mfn. 'empty-formed,' having a vacant aspect, MW. **Śūnyâgāra-kṛitâlaya**, mfn. making an abode in deserted houses, ib. **Śūnyâlaya**, m. an empty or deserted house (sleeping in such a house is forbidden), ib. **Śūnyâśaya**, mf(*ā*)n. = *śūnya-citta*, Kathās. **Śūnyâśūnya**, n. emancipation of the spirit even during a person's life (= *jīvan-mukti*), L. **Śūnyâisha**, mf(*ī*)n. desiring a desert or solitude, AV.

Śūnyaka, mfn. (= *śūnya*) empty, void, g. *yāvâdi*; n. absence, lack of (gen.), MBh.

Śūnyī, in comp. for *śūnya*. **-√kṛi**, Ā. *-kurute*, to turn into a desert, lay waste, VarBṛS.; to leave empty, quit, abandon, Pañcat. **-√bhū**, P. *-bhavati*, to become deserted or desolate, Kād.

शू 3. *śū* (onomat.), in comp. **-kara**, m. 'making the sound *śū*,' a boar, hog (more correctly *sū-kara*, q.v.) **-kārá**, m. the act of startling with the sound *śū*, VS. **-kṛita** (*śū́-*), mfn. startled by the sound *śū*, ib.; urging, spurring (of a horse), RV.

शूक *śūka*, m. n. (g. *ardharcâdi*; derivation doubtful) the awn of grain, R.; Sarvad.; KātyŚr., Sch.; a bristle, spicule, spike (esp. the bristle or sharp hair of insects &c.), W.; the sheath or calyx of a bud, L.; pity, compassion (in *niḥ-śūka*), L.; m. a species of grain (cf. *dīrgha-ś°*), Suśr.; Bhpr.; sorrow, grief, L.; = *abhi-shava*, L.; (*ā*), f. scruple, doubt, L.; Mucuna Pruritus, L.; the sting of an insect (cf. above), anything that stings or causes pain, Suśr.; Car.; a partic. insect (produced in water and applied externally as an aphrodisiac), ib.; Bhpr.; a kind of grass, L. **-kīṭa** or **-kīṭaka**, m. a kind of caterpillar covered with bristles or hairs (accord. to some 'a scorpion'), L. **-taru**, w.r. for *śuka-taru*. **-triṇa**, n. a kind of spiky grass, L. **-dosha**, m. the injurious effect of the above Śūka insect, Suśr.; Bhpr. **-dhānya**, n. any awned or bearded grain (one of the 5 kinds of grain, the others being *śāli-*, *vrīhi-*, *śamī-*, and *kshudra-dh°*), Car.; Bhpr. **-pattra**, m. a kind of snake, Suśr. **-piṇḍi** or **-piṇḍī**, f. Mucuna Pruritus, L. **-roga**, m. = *-dosha*, Suśr. **-vat**, mfn. awned, bearded; (*atī*), f. Mucuna Pruritus, L. **-vṛinta**, m. a partic. venomous insect, Suśr. **-śimbā**, **-śimbi**, **-śimbikā**, and **-śimbī**, f. Mucuna Pruritus, L. **Śūkâḍhya**, n. 'abounding with spikes,' a kind of grass (= *śūka-triṇa*), L. **Śūkâmaya**, m. = *śūka-dosha*, L.

Śūkaka, (ifc.) = *śūka*, awn of grain (see *dīrgha-śūkaka*); barley or a bearded kind of wheat resembling barley, L.; the sentiment of compassion or tenderness, L.

Śūkin, mfn. awned, bearded, W.

शूकर *śū-kara*. See 3. *śū*, col. 2.

शूकल *śūkala*, m. (perhaps connected with *śū-kara* above) a restive horse, L.

शूकापुट्ट *śūkāpuṭṭa* or *śūkāpūṭṭa*, m. a partic. gem (perhaps a kind of amber, = *tri-maṇi*), L.

शूकुल *śūkula*, m. a fish, W.; a partic. kind of fish, ib.; a fragrant grass (a kind of Cyperus), ib.

शूक्ष्म *śūkshma*, incorrect for *sūkshma*, q.v.

शूघन *śūghaná*, mf(*ā*)n. going quickly, swift, fleet (= *kshipra*), RV. iv, 58, 7 (cf. Naigh. ii, 15).

शूचि *śūci*, w.r. for *śuci* (also *śūci* and *śūcī* for *sūcī*).

शूतिपर्ण *śūtiparṇa*, m. Cathartocarpus Fistula, L.

शूत्कार *śūt-kāra*, m. 'the sound *śūt*,' hissing, whistling, whizzing &c.

शूद्र *śūdrá*, m. (of doubtful derivation) a Śūdra, a man of the fourth or lowest of the four original classes or castes (whose only business, accord. to Mn. i, 91, was to serve the three higher classes; in RV. ix, 20, 12, the Śūdra is said to have been born from the feet of Purusha, q.v.; in Mn. i, 87 he is fabled to have sprung from the same part of the body of Brahmā, and he is regarded as of higher rank than the present low and mixed castes so numerous throughout India; *kevala-ś°*, a pure Ś°), RV. &c. &c. (IW. 212 &c.); a man of mixed origin, L.; N. of a Brāhman, Buddh.; pl. N. of a people, MBh.; Pur.; (*ā* and *ī*), f., see below. **-kanyā**, f. a Śūdra girl, Mn. x, 8, 9. **-kamalâkara**, m. N. of wk. **-kalpa**, mfn. resembling a Ś°, AitBr. **-kula-dīpikā**, f. N. of wk. **-kṛita** (*śūdrá-*), mfn. made by a Ś°, AV. **-kṛitya**, mfn. to be done by a Ś°, proper for a Ś°, MW.; n. the duty of a Ś°; N. of wk.; *-vicāraṇa*, n., °*ṇa-tattva*, n., *-vicāra-tattva*, n. N. of wks. **-gamana**, n. sexual intercourse with a Ś°, Āp. **-ghna**, mfn. killing a Ś°, the slayer of a Ś°, Pañcar. **-jana**, m. a person of the Ś° class, Mn. iv, 99. **-janman**, mfn. Śūdra-born, descended from a Ś°, PārGṛ.; m. a Ś°, Yājñ. **-japa-vidhāna**, n. N. of wk. **-tā**, f. or **-tva**, n. the state of a Ś° or servant, servile condition, servitude, Mn.; MBh.; Pur. **-dharma**, m. the duty of a Ś°, Cat.; *-tattva*, n., *-bodhinī*, f. N. of wks. **-pañca-saṃskāra-vidhi**, m., *-paddhati*, f. N. of wks. **-priya**, mfn. dear to a Ś°, L.; m. an onion, L. **-prêshya**, m. a man of one of the three superior castes who has become a servant to a Ś°, W.; n. the being servant to a Ś°, MW. **-bhikshita**, mfn. (anything) begged or received as alms from a Ś°, Yājñ. **-bhūyishṭha**, mfn. inhabited mostly by Ś°s, abounding with Ś°s, Mn. viii, 22. **-bhojin**, mfn. eating food of a Ś°, MBh. **-yājaka**, mfn. one who sacrifices for a Ś°, Gaut.; *-prâyaścitta*, n. the penance incurred by sacrificing for a Ś°, MW. **-yoni**, f. the womb of a Ś° woman, MBh.; *-ja*, mfn. born from the womb of a Ś°, MW. **-rājya**, n. a country of which a Ś° is king, Mn. iv, 61. **—varga**, m. the Ś° class, MW. **—varjam**, ind. except Ś°s, KātyŚr. **—viveka**, m. N. of wk. **—vṛitti**, f. the occupation of a Ś°, Mn. x, 98. **—śāsana**, n. an edict addressed to Ś°s, L. **—saṃskāra**, m. any purificatory rite relating to Ś°s, MW. **—saṃsparśa**, m. the touch of a Ś°, Mn. v, 104. **—sevana**, n. attendance on a Ś° master, the being in the service of a Ś°, Mn. xi, 69. **—smṛiti**, f. N. of wk. **—hatyā**, f. the killing of a Ś°, Mn. xi, 131; 140. **—han**, mfn. = *-ghna*, ib. xi, 130. **Śūdrâcāra**, m. the conduct or occupation of a Ś°; *-cintāmaṇi*, m., *-śiromaṇi*, m., *-saṃgraha*, m. N. of wks. **Śūdrânna**, n. food belonging to or received from a Ś°, Āp.; Mn. **Śūdrârtā**, f. Panicum Italicum, L. **Śūdrârtha-yājaka**, mfn. sacrificing at the expense (lit. 'with the property') of a Ś°, Gaut. **Śūdrâryá**, m. du. (n. sg., g. *rāja-dantâdi*) a Ś° and a Vaiśya, VS. **Śūdrê-śauca**, n. the impurity of a Ś°, MW. **Śūdrâhnika**, n. the daily ceremonies of a Ś°, Cat.; °*kâcāra-tattva*, n. N. of wk. **Śūdrôcchishṭa**, mfn. left by a Ś° (as water), Mn. xi, 148. **Śūdrôtpatti**, f. N. of wk. **Śūdrôdaka**, n. water polluted by the touch of a Ś°, MW.; *-pāna-prâyaścitta*, n. a penance for drinking water given by a Ś°, ib. **Śūdrôddyota**, m. N. of wk.

Śūdraka, m. N. of various kings (esp. of the author of the drama called Mṛicchakaṭikā), Mṛicch.; Kathās.; Hit. &c. **—kathā**, f. N. of a tale (written by Rāmila and Somila), Cat.

Śūdrā́, f. a woman of the fourth class or caste, AV. &c. &c.; N. of a daughter of Raudrāśva, Hariv. **—pariṇayana**, n. the marrying a Śūdra female, W. **—putra**, m. the son of a Ś° woman, PañcavBr.; Gaut. **—bhārya**, m. one who has a Ś° woman for wife, MW. **—vedana**, n. = *-pariṇayana*, W. **—vedin**, mfn. marrying a Ś° woman, Mn. iii, 16. **—suta**, m. = *-putra*, Mn. ix, 151; 153.

Śūdrāṇī, f. the wife of a Śūdra, MW.

Śūdrika, m. N. of a mythical person, Vīrac.

Śūdrī, f. a woman of the fourth caste, a Śūdra woman, Yājñ.; KātyŚr., Sch.; the wife of a Śūdra, L.

Śūdrī-√bhū, P. *-bhavati*, to become a Śūdra, Mn.; Kathās.

शून *śūna*. See p. 1085, col. 1.

शूना *śūnā*. See *sūnā*.

शून्य *śūnya* &c. See p. 1085, col. 1.

शूपकार *śūpa-kāra*. See *sūpa-kāra*.

शूर *śūr* (also written *sūr*), cl. 4. Ā. (Dhātup. xxvi, 48) *śūryate*, to hurt, injure, kill (only in pf. *śuśūre*, 'he cut off [the head],' Śiś. xix, 108); to be or make firm, Dhātup. ib.; cl. 10. Ā. to be powerful or valiant (in this sense rather Nom. fr. next), Dhātup. xxxv, 48.

Śū́ra, mfn. (prob. fr. √1. *śū* = *śvi* and connected with *śavas*, *śuna*, *śūna*) strong, powerful, valiant, heroic, brave (cf. *-tama* and *-tara*), RV.; MBh.; m. a strong or mighty or valiant man, warrior, champion, hero, one who acts heroically towards any one (loc.) or with regard to anything (loc., instr., or comp.; ifc. f. *ā*), RV. &c. &c.; heroism (?, = or w. r. for *śaurya*), Kāv.; a lion, L.; a tiger or panther, L.; a boar, L.; a dog, L.; a cock, L.; white rice, L.; lentil, L.; Arthocarpus Locucha, L.; Vatica Robusta, L.; N. of a Yādava, the father of Vasu-deva and grandfather of Kṛishṇa, MBh.; of a Sauvīraka, ib.; of a son of Ilina, ib.; of a son of Kārtavīrya, Hariv.; Pur.; of a son of Vidūratha, ib.; of a son of Deva-mīḍhusha, ib.; of a son of Bhajamāna, Hariv.; of a son of Vasu-deva, BhP.; of a son of Vatsa-prī, MārkP.; of a poet, Cat.; of various other men, Buddh.; Rājat.; w. r. for *sūra*, L.; (pl.) N. of a people, MBh.; Hariv. [Cf. Gk. κῦρος in ἄ-κυρος.] **—kīṭa**, m. 'insect-like hero,' a feeble hero, Mcar. **—grāma** (*śū́ra-*), mfn. having a multitude of h°s, RV. **—ṃ-gama**, m. a partic. Samādhi, Buddh.; N. of a Bodhi-sattva, ib.; *-samādhi-nirdeśa*, m. N. of wk. **—ja**, m. a son of Śūra, Rājat.; N. of a man, ib. **—tama**, mfn. most heroic or valiant, MBh. **—tara** (*śū́ra-*), mfn. more heroic or valiant, RV. **—tā**, f., **-tva**, n. state or condition of a hero, heroism, valour, bravery, Kāv.; Sāh. **—danta**, m. N. of a Brāhman, Kathās. **—deva**, m. N. of a son of king Vīra-deva, ib.; (with Jainas) N. of the second of the 24 Arhats of the future Utsarpiṇī, L. **—patnī** (*śū́ra-*), f. having a heroic lord or husband, RV. **—putrā** (*śū́ra-*), f. 'having a heroic son,' the mother of a hero (applied to Aditi), ib. **—pura**, n. 'hero-town,' N. of a town, Kathās.; Rājat. **—bala**, m. 'having heroic strength,' N. of a Deva-putra, Lalit. **—bhū** or **-bhūmi**, f. N. of a daughter of Ugrasena, BhP. **—bhogêśvara**, m. N. of a Liṅga in Nepal, Cat. **—maṭha**, m. n. the monastery of Śūra, Rājat. **—māna**, n. thinking one's self a hero, arrogance, vaunting, W. **—mānin**, mfn. one who thinks himself a hero, a boaster, MBh.; R. **—mūrdhamaya**, mf(*ī*)n. consisting of the heads of h°s, Kathās. **—m-manya**, mfn. = *śūra-mānin*, W. **—varman**, m. N. of various men, Kathās.; Rājat.; of a poet (also written *sūra-v°*), Cat. **—vākya**, n. pl. the words of a hero, speech of a boaster, R. **—vidya**, mfn. understanding heroism, heroic, Kathās. **—vīra** (*śū́ra-*), mfn. having heroic men or followers, AV.; m. N. of a teacher (having the patr. Māṇḍūkeya), AitĀr.; (pl.) N. of a people, Hariv. **—śloka**, m. a kind of artificial verse, Cat. **—sāti** (*śū́ra-*), f. 'hero-occupation,' din of battle, fighting (only in loc. sg.), RV. **—siṇha**, m. N. of an author, Cat. **—sena**, m. N. of the country about Mathurā, Pañcar.; a king of Mathurā (and ruler of the Yadus, applied to Vishṇu and Ugra-sena), MBh.; Hariv.; N. of a son of Kārtavīrya, Hariv.; of a son of Śatru-ghna, VP.; of various other men, Kathās.; pl. N. of the people inhabiting the above country (also °*naka* and °*na-ja*), Mn.; MBh. &c.; (*ā*), f. N. of the city of Mathurā, R.; (*ī*), f. a princess of the Śūra-senas, MBh. (cf. Pāṇ. iv, 1, 177). **Śūrâcārya**, m. N. of an author, Gaṇar. (v. l. for *sūrâc°*). **Śūrâditya**, m. N. of a son of Guṇâditya, Cat. **Śūrêśvara**, m. N. of an image erected by Śūra, Rājat.

Śūraka, v. l. for *śūdraka*, VP.

Śūraṇa, mfn. high-spirited, fiery (said of horses), RV. i, 163, 10 (= *vikrama-śīla*, Sāy.); m. (also written *sūraṇa*) Amorphophallus Campanulatus (the Telinga potato), Hcar.; Suśr.; Bignonia Indica, L. **Śūraṇôdbhuja**, m. a kind of bird, L.

Śūrī-√kṛi, P. *-karoti*, to turn into a hero, Kathās.

Śūrṇa, mfn. fixed, firm, MW.

शूर्त *śūrtá*, mfn. (√*śṝ*) scattered, crushed, slain, RV. i, 174, 6 (accord. to Naigh. ii, 15 = *kshipra*).

शूर्प् *śūrp* (prob. Nom. fr. *śūrpa* below), cl. 10. P. *śūrpayati*, to measure, mete out, Dhātup. xxxii, 71.

Śū́rpa, n. (and m., g. *ardharcâdi*; also written *sūrpa*) a winnowing basket or fan (i. e. a kind of wicker receptacle which, when shaken about, serves as a fan for winnowing corn; also personified as a Gandharva), VS. &c. &c.; a measure of 2 Droṇas, ŚārṅgS.; (*ī*), f. (g. *gaurâdi*) a small winnowing basket or fan (used as a child's toy), L.; = *śūrpaṇakhā* (q. v.), L. **—karṇa**, mfn. having ears like winnowing fans (applied to Gaṇêśa), Kathās. (w. r. *śūrya-k°*); m. an elephant, L.; N. of a mountain, MārkP. (incorrectly *sūrpa-k°*); pl. N. of a people, VarBṛS.; *-puṭa*, mfn. having ear-orifices like w° fans, Kathās. **—khārī**, f. a partic. measure (= 16 Droṇas), Hcat. **—grāha**, mf(*ī*)n. holding a w° basket, AV. **—ṇakhā** (rarely *-ṇakhī*), f. (wrongly *-nakhā*, °*khī*; cf. Pāṇ. iv, 1; 58) 'having finger-nails like w° fans,' N. of the sister of Rāvaṇa (she fell in love with Rāma-candra and, being rejected by him and insulted by Sītā's laughter, assumed a hideous form and threatened to eat her up, but was beaten off by Lakshmaṇa, who cut off her ears and nose and thus doubly disfigured her; in revenge she incited her brother to carry off Sītā), MBh.; R. **—ṇāya**, m. (for *-nāya*) N. of a man, g. *kurv-ādi* (w. r. *-ṇāyya*); °*yīya*, mfn. (fr. prec.), g. *utkarâdi*. **—nakhā**, °*khī*, see *-ṇakhā*, °*khī*. **—nishpāva**, m. a basket full of winnowed corn, L. **—parṇī**, f. a sort of bean, Phaseolus Trilobus, L. **—puṭa**, m. n. the nozzle of a winnowing fan, ĀśvGṛ. **—vāta**, m. the wind raised by a w° fan, MārkP. **—vīṇā**, f. a kind of lute, LāṭyŚr., Sch. **—śruti**, m. an elephant (= *-karṇa*, q. v.), Vās. **Śūrpâkāra**, mfn. shaped like a w° fan, VarBṛS. **Śūrpâdri**, m. N. of a mountain in the south of India, ib. (cf. *sūryâdri*).

Śūrpaka, m. N. of a demon (an enemy of Kāma-deva), L. **Śūrpakârāti** or **Śūrpakâri**, m. 'enemy of Śūrpaka,' N. of Kāma (god of love), L.

Śūrpī. See col. 2 under *śūrpa*.

शूर्पारक *śūrpāraka*, m. N. of a country and (pl.) its inhabitants, MBh.; R.; Pur.; n. N. of a town (accord. to some of two different towns), Hariv.; Mārk.; Buddh.

शूर्म *śūrma*, m. an iron image, W.; an anvil, ib.

Śūrmi, m. f., *śūrmikā* or *śūrmī*, f. id., ib. (cf. *sūrmi*, *sūrmī*, *sūrmya*).

शूर्यकर्ण *śūrya-karṇa*, w. r. for *śūrpa-karṇa*, q. v.

शूल् *śūl* (rather Nom. fr. next), cl. 1. P. *śūlati*, to hurt, cause pain (Dhātup. xv, 19), (only occurring in Ā. *śūlate* and cl. 4. P. Ā. *śūlyati*, °*te*, Car.; accord. to Dhātup. also *saṃghoshe* or *saṃghāte*, 'to sound' or 'to collect').

Śūla, m. n. (ifc. f. *ā*) a sharp iron pin or stake, spike, spit (on which meat is roasted), RV. &c. &c.; any sharp instrument or pointed dart, lance, pike, spear (esp. the trident of Śiva), MBh.; Kāv. &c.; a stake for impaling criminals (*śūlam ā-√ruh*, 'to be fixed on a stake, suffer impalement;' with Caus. of *ā-√ruh*, 'to fix on a stake, have any one [acc.] impaled,' cf. *śūlâdhiropita* &c.), Mn.; MBh. &c.; any sharp or acute pain (esp. that of colic or gout), Kāv.; VarBṛS.; Suśr.; pain, grief, sorrow, MBh.; Hariv.; death, L.; a flag, banner, L.; = *-yoga* (q. v.), VarBṛS.; (*ā*), f. a stake (= *śūla*), L.; a harlot, prostitute, Vās.; Kriṭṭanīm.; (*ī*), f. a kind of grass, L. **—kāra**, m. pl. N. of a people, MārkP. **—gava**, m. an ox fit for a spit (presented as an offering to Rudra), GṛŚrS.; *-prayoga*, m. N. of wk. **—granthi**, m. or f. a kind of Dūrvā grass (w. r. for *mūla-g°*), L. **—graha** (Sāmkhyak., Sch.) or **-grāhin** (Śivag.), m. 'spear-bearer,' N. of Śiva. **—ghātana**, n. 'pain-destroying,' iron rust, L. **—ghna**, mfn. removing sharp pain, anodyne, Suśr.; m. a kind of plant (= *tumburu*), L.; (*ī*), f. a reed-like plant, sweet flag, L. **—dosha-harī**, f. a kind of plant, L. **—dvish**, m. 'hostile to colic,' Asa Fœtida, L. **—dhanvan**, m. 'having a trident for a bow,' N. of Śiva, L. **—dhara**, mfn. bearing a spear (applied to Rudra-Śiva), R.; Śivag.; (*ā*), f. N. of Durgā, L. **—dhārin**, mfn. spear-holding; (*iṇī*), f. N. of Durgā, Tantras. **—dhṛik**, mfn. sp°-holding (said of Śiva), R.; f. N. of Durgā, L. **—nāśaka** or **-nāśana**, n. 'removing pain in the stomach,' sochal salt, L. **—nāśinī**, f. 'id.,' Asa Fœtida, L. **—pattrī**, f. a kind of grass, L. **—padī**, f. having spear-like feet, g. *kumbhapady-ādi*. **—parṇī**, f. a kind of plant, L. **—pāṇi**, mfn. having a spear in hand, BhP.; m. N. of Rudra-Śiva, ShaḍvBr.; MBh.; Hariv. &c.; of various scholars and of a poet, Sadukt.; Cat. &c. **—pāṇin**, mfn. = prec.; m. N. of Śiva, Cat. **—pāla**, m. (more correct form *śālā-p°*) the keeper of a brothel, or frequenter of br°s (see *śūlā*), Vās. **—prôta**, mfn. fixed on a stake, impaled; m. N. of a hell, BhP. **—bhṛit**, m. 'spear-holder,' N. of Śiva, MBh.; Kāv. **—bheda**, m. N. of a place, Cat. **—mudgara-hasta**, mf(*ā*)n. having a lance and mace in hand, MBh. **—yoga**, m. a partic. grouping of stars in which all the planets are in three houses or asterisms, VarBṛS. **—vat**, mfn. having sharp pain, Suśr. **—vara**, n. a partic. mythical weapon, R. **—vedanā**, f. sharp pain, MW. **—śatru**, m. 'hostile to colic,' Ricinus Communis, L. **—stha**, mfn. fixed on a stake, impaled, MBh. **—hantrī**, f. 'colic-removing,' Ptychotis Ajowan, L. **—hasta**, mfn. = *-pāṇi*, MBh.; m. a man armed with a lance, lancer, W.; N. of Śiva, Pañcar. **—hṛit**, mfn. removing sharp pain or colic, Suśr.; m. Asa Fœtida, L. **Śūlâgra**, n. the point of a pike or stake, MBh.; R.; mfn. pointed like a pike, VarBṛS. **Śūlâṅka**, mfn. marked with Śiva's spear, MBh. **Śūlâdhiropita**, mfn. fixed on a stake, impaled, Kathās. **Śūlā-pāla**, m., see *śūla-p°*. **Śūlâri**, m. Terminalia Catappa, L. **Śūlâropaṇa**, n. 'stretching out on a stake,' impalement, Kathās. **Śūlâvataṇsita**, mfn. impaled, Daś. **Śūlêśvarī**, f. N. of Durgā, Inscr.; *-tīrtha*, n. N. of a Tīrtha, Cat. **Śūlôtkhā** (W.) or **śūlôtthā** (L.), f. Serratula Anthelminthica. **Śūlôdyata-kara**, mfn. with uplifted spear in hand, MW.

Śūlaka, m. (cf. *śūkala*) a restive horse, L.

Śūlavata, n. (cf. *śūla-vat* and *-vara*) N. of a partic. mythical weapon, R.

Śūlā-√kṛi, P. *-karoti* (Pāṇ. v, 4, 65), to roast on a spit, ŚBr.

Śūlā-kṛita, mfn. roasted on a spit, Daś.

Śūli, mfn. (m. c.) = *śūlin*, armed with a spear, MBh.

Śūlika, mfn. roasted on a spit, L.; having a spear or any sharp instrument, MW.; m. one who impales criminals, L.; a cock, L.; a hare, L.; the illegitimate son of a Brāhman and a Śūdra woman, L.; the son of a Kshatriya and an unmarried Śūdra woman, L.; a strict guardian of the treasure and the harem, L.; (pl.) N. of a people (cf. *śūlīka* below), VarBṛS.; MārkP.; (*ā*), f. a spit for roasting, Suśr.; a kind of factitious salt, L.; n. roast meat, W.

Śūlin, mfn. having a dart or pike, armed with a spear, MBh.; Kāv. &c.; one who suffers from sharp internal pain or from colic, Kauś.; Vcar.; Hcat.; m. a spearman, lancer, L.; N. of Rudra-Śiva (as holding a trident), MBh.; a hare, Bhpr.; N. of a Muni, Cat.; (*inī*), f., see below.

Śūlina, m. the Indian fig-tree (= *bhāṇḍīra*), L.

Śūlinī, f. N. of Durgā (see comp.) **-kalpa**, m., **-kavaca**, n., **-durgā-dig-bandhana**, n., **-mantra-kalpa**, m., **-vidhāna**, n. N. of wks.

Śūlī. See under *śūla*, p. 1086, col. 3.

Śūlīka, m. pl. N. of a people (v. l. *sūlīka*), Car.

Śūlya, mfn. belonging to a spit (for roasting), roasted on a spit &c., KātyŚr.; Hariv.; Suśr.; deserving impalement on a stake, W.; n. roasted meat, ib. **-pāka**, m. any meat or food roasted on a spit, MW. **-māṇsa**, n. roast meat, meat cooked on a spit, ib.

शूल्वाण *śūlvāṇa*, m. N. of a demon, Kauś.

शूशुजान *śūśujāna*. See √*śuj*, p. 1081, col. 3.

शूशुवस् *śūśuvas, śūśuvāna*. See √*śvi*.

शूष् *śūsh* (also written *sūsh*), cl. 1. P. *śūshati*, to bring forth, procreate (*prasave*), Dhātup. xvii, 28.

शूष *śūshá*, mfn. (prob. either fr. √1. *śū* = *śvi* or fr. √*śush* = *śvas*) resounding, shrill, loud, hissing, RV.; high-spirited, courageous, bold, fierce, impetuous, ib.; m. a loud or resounding note, song of praise or triumph, ib.; VS.; Kāṭh.; (also *śū́sha*) spirit, vital energy, strength, power, RV.; VS.; TBr.; ŚBr.; N. of a man, TBr.; n. = *bala*, Naigh. ii, 9; = *śukha*, ib.

Śūsháṇi. See √*śvi*.

Śūshyà, mfn. resounding, loud-sounding, hissing, RV.

शृगाल *śṛigāla* (also written *śṛikāla*), m. a jackal &c. See *sṛigāla*.

शृङ्खल *śṛiṅkhala*, m. n. (derivation doubtful) a chain, fetter (esp. for confining the feet of an elephant), Ragh.; Pur.; a man's belt, L.; a measuring chain, MW.; (*ā* and *ī*), f., see below. **-tā**, f., **-tva**, n. the being chained together, concatenation, connection, order, a series, W.; restraint, ib. **-todin**, m. N. of a man, g. *bāhv-ādi* (cf. *śārṅkhalatodi*). **-baddha**, m. bound by a chain or fetter, MārkP.

Śṛiṅkhalaka, m. a chain, MW.; a young camel or other young animal with wooden rings or clogs on his feet (to prevent his straying), Śiś. xii, 7 (cf. Pāṇ. v, 2, 79); any camel, MW.

Śṛiṅkhalaya, Nom. P. °*yati*, to chain, fetter, Daś.

Śṛiṅkhalā, f. a chain, fetter &c. (= *śṛiṅkhala*), Kāv.; VarBṛS. &c. **-kalāpa**, m. (Mṛicch.), **-dāman**, n. (Ratnâv.), **-pāśa**, m. (Kathās.) a chain (-band). **-bandha**, m. (MW.), **-bandhana**, n. (Daś.) confining by chains or fetters.

Śṛiṅkhalita, mfn. chained, fettered, bound, confined, Daś.

Śṛiṅkhalī, f. Asteracantha Longifolia, L.

शृङ्खाणिका *śṛiṅkhāṇikā*, f. (v. l. *śṛiṅghāṇikā*; cf. *śiṅghāṇikā* and *siṅgh*°) mucus, Āpast.

शृङ्ग *śṛiṅga*, n. (perhaps connected with *śiras, śīrshan*; ifc. f. *ā* or *ī*) the horn of an animal, a horn used for various purposes (as in drinking, for blowing, drawing blood from the skin &c.), RV. &c. &c.; the tusk of an elephant, R.; Kām.; the top or summit of a mountain, a peak, crag, MBh.; Kāv. &c.; the summit of a building, pinnacle, turret, ib.; any peak or projection or lofty object, elevation, point, end, extremity, AV.; Kum.; Gīt.; a cusp or horn of the moon, R.; Hariv.; VarBṛS.; highest point, acme, height or perfection of anything, Hariv. 6424; the horn as a symbol of self-reliance or strength or haughtiness, Ragh.; the rising of desire, excess of love or passion (cf. *śṛiṅgāra*), Sāh.; a partic. military array in the form of a horn or crescent, MBh. vi, 2413; a syringe, water-engine, Ragh.; Śiś.; the female breast, BhP.; a lotus, L.; agallochum, L.; a mark, token, sign, L.; = *śaśa-śṛiṅga*, 'hare's horn,' anything impossible or extraordinary, Kusum.; m. a kind of medicinal or poisonous plant, L.; N. of a Muni (of whom, in some parts of India, on occasions of drought, earthen images are said to be made and worshipped for rain), MW.; (*ī*), f., see s. v. [Cf. Lat. *cornu*; Goth. *háurn*; Germ., Eng. *horn*.] **-kanda**, m. Trapa Bispinosa, L. **-kūṭa**, m. N. of a mountain, Pañcar. **-kośa**, m. a horn as a receptacle (of liquids), SāmavBr. **-giri**, m. N. of a hill and town in Mysore (see *śṛiṅgeri*), Cat. **-grāhikā**, f. 'taking by the horns' i. e. in a direct manner (instr. 'directly,' 'without any intervening agent'); (in logic) taking singly (all the particulars included under a general term), Sch. on ŚāṅkhBr.; Sch. on KātyŚr. &c. **-ja**, mfn. horn-produced, made from horn, Saṃgīt.; m. an arrow, shaft, MW.; n. aloe wood, L. **-jāha**, n. the root of a horn, L. **-dhara**, m. N. of a man, Buddh. **-pura**, n. N. of a town (cf. *śṛiṅgeri-p*°), Cat. **-prahārin**, mfn. h°-striking, butting or fighting with the horns, MW. **-priya**, m. 'fond of horn-blowing,' N. of Śiva (cf. *śṛiṅga-vādya-priya*), MBh. **-bhuja**, m. N. of a man, Kathās. **-maya**, mf(*ī*)n. (in *kanaka-śṛiṅga-maya*) furnished with (golden) h°s, MBh. **-mūla**, m. Trapa Bispinosa, L. **-mohin**, m. Michelia Champaka, L. **-ruha**, m. Trapa Bispinosa, L. **-roha**, v. l. for *śuṇḍa-r*°, L. **-vat**, mfn. horned, MBh.; having (many) peaks, peaked (as a mountain), R.; m. N. of a mythical mountain forming one of the boundaries of the earth, MBh.; Pur. **-varjita**, m. a hornless quadruped, L. **-vādya**, n. a horn for blowing, L.; *-priya*, m. 'fond of blowing his horn,' N. of Kṛishṇa (cf. *śṛiṅga-priya*), Pañcar. **-vṛish**, m. N. of a man, RV. viii, 17, 13. **-vera**, m. N. of a serpent-demon, MBh.; ginger (undried or dry), Suśr. (also °*raka*, L.); N. of a town (see *-pura*); *-kalka*, m. sediment of ginger, Suśr.; *-cūrṇa*, n. g°-powder, ib.; *-pura*, n. N. of a town (situated on the Ganges), MBh.; R. &c. (*-māhātmya*, n. N. of a ch. of the SkandaP.); °*râbha-mūlaka*, m. 'having a root like that of ginger,' Typha Angustifolia, L. **-śata**, n. a hundred peaks, MW. **-sukha**, n. (prob.) horn-music, L. **Śṛiṅgâgra-praharaṇâbhimukha**, mfn. ready to strike with the points of the h°, Hit. **Śṛiṅgântara**, n. the space or interval between the h°s (of a cow &c.), Ragh. **Śṛiṅgâbhihitá**, mf(*ā́*)n. bound by the h°s, MaitrS. **Śṛiṅg'īśvara-tīrtha**, n. (cf. next) N. of a Tīrtha, Cat. **Śṛiṅgêśvara**, m. or n. (?) N. of a place, ib. **Śṛiṅgôcchrāya**, m. a lofty peak, Megh. **Śṛiṅgôtpādana**, mfn. producing or having the power to produce h°s; m. (with or scil. *mantra*) a spell producing h°s, Kathās. **Śṛiṅgôtpādinī**, f. N. of a Yakshiṇī (producing horns and changing men into animals), ib. **Śṛiṅgônnati**, f. elevation of a horn, rising (cf. *śīrshôdaya*), Gaṇit.; °*ty-adhikāra*, m. N. of wk. **Śṛiṅgônnamana**, n. id., Gaṇit. **Śṛiṅgôshṇīsha**, m. a lion, L.

Śṛiṅgaka, m. n. (ifc. f. *ikā*) a horn or anything pointed like a horn, MBh.; Kathās.; Hcat.; a syringe, Ratnâv.; a cusp or horn of the moon, Cat.; m. a kind of plant (= *jīvaka*), L.; (*ikā*), f. a kind of flute, Saṃgīt.; aconite, L.; a kind of gall-nut, L.; a kind of Betula or birch tree, L.

Śṛiṅgalā, f. Odina Pinnata, L.

Śṛiṅgāṭa, m. Trapa Bispinosa (also *ī*, f.), Suśr.; Asteracantha or Barleria Longifolia, L.; an instrument shaped like the thorny fruit of Barl° Long°, L.; N. of a mountain in Kāmâkhyā, KālP.; m. n. a triangle or a triangular place, Kām.; (in astron.) a partic. configuration of the planets, VarBṛS.; (in anat.) N. of partic. junctions of veins or blood-vessels (in nose, ear, eye, or tongue), Car.; n. the triangular nut of Trapa Bispinosa, Suśr.; a place where three (or four) roads meet, L.

Śṛiṅgāṭaka, m. N. of various plants (Trapa Bispinosa &c. = *śṛiṅgāṭa*), MBh.; ŚārṅgS.; Bhpr.; a mountain having three peaks, W.; N. of a mountain (= *śṛiṅgāṭa*), KālP.; m. n. (ifc. f. *akā* and *ikā*) a place where four (or several) roads meet, crossway, MBh.; R. &c.; (in anat.) = *śṛiṅgāṭa*, Suśr.; (in astron.) a partic. configuration of the planets (when all of them are in the 1st, 5th, and 9th asterisms), VarBṛS.; n. a kind of pastry or minced meat &c. (called Samūsā in Hindī), Bhpr.; a door, W.

Śṛiṅgāya, Nom. Ā. °*yáte*, to butt with the horns, TBr.

Śṛiṅgāra, m. (prob. connected with *śṛiṅga* as *vṛindāra* with *vṛinda*) love (as 'the horned' or 'the strong one'?), sexual passion or desire or enjoyment, Kāv.; Rājat. &c.; (in rhet.) the erotic sentiment (one of the 8 or 10 Rasas, q. v.; it has Vishṇu for its tutelary deity and black for its colour; accord. to most authorities it is of two kinds, viz. *sambhoga*, 'mutual enjoyment,' and *vipralambha*, 'deception, disappointment,' to which by some is added as third *a-yoga*, 'separation'), Bhar.; Daśar.; Sāh. &c.; a dress suitable for amorous purposes, elegant dress, fine garments, finery, Kāv.; Pañcat.; Kathās. &c.; the ornaments on an elephant (esp. red marks on its head and trunk), L. (cf. *-dhārin*); any mark, MW.; (also with *bhaṭṭa*) N. of various persons (esp. of a poet), Rājat.; Cat.; (*ā*), f. N. of a woman, Inscr.; (*am*), n. (only L.) gold; red-lead; fragrant powder for the dress or person; cloves; undried ginger; black aloe-wood; mfn. handsome, pretty, dainty, fine, MBh.; R. **-kalikā**, f. N. of a Surâṅganā, Siṇhâs.; of a poem by Kāma-rāja Dīkshita. **-kośa**, m. N. of a poem and of a drama (of the class called Bhāṇa). **-kaustubha**, m. N. of a rhet. wk. **-garva**, m. the pride of love, L. **-gupta**, m. N. of an author, Cat. **-candrôdaya**, m. N. of wk. **-ceshṭā**, f. (Ragh.), **-ceshṭita**, n. (Sāh.) love-gesture, any outward action indicating love. **-janman**, m. 'born from desire,' N. of Kāma (god of love), L. **-jīvana**, n. N. of a drama (of the class called Bhāṇa). **-taṭinī**, f. N. of a rhet. wk. **-taraṃginī**, f. N. of a Bhāṇa and other wks. **-tā**, f. the state of being ornamental or decorative, Priy. **-tilaka**, n. N. of various wks. (esp. of a Kāvya, attributed to Kālidāsa, and of a rhet. wk. by Rudraṭa or Rudra-bhaṭṭa [12th or 13th century A. D.] corresponding in its contents to the 3rd ch. of the Sāhitya-darpaṇa). **-dīpaka**, m., **-dīpikā**, f. N. of wks. **-dhārin**, mfn. wearing ornaments, ornamented (as an elephant), R. **-paddhati**, f., **-padya**, n., **-pāvana**, n. N. of wks. **-piṇḍaka**, m. N. of a serpent-demon, Hariv. **-prakāśa**, m., **-prabandha-dīpikā**, f. N. of wks. **-bhāshita**, n. a love-story, MW.; amorous talk, A. **-bhūshaṇa**, n. red-lead, L.; N. of a Bāṇa. **-bheda-pradīpa**, m. N. of wk. **-mañjarī**, f. N. of a woman, Vās.; of a rhet. wk. **-maṇḍapa**, m. or n. 'love-temple,' N. of a temple, SkandaP. **-yoni**, m. 'love-source,' N. of Kāma-deva, L. **-rasa**, m. the erotic sentiment; *-maṇḍana*, n., *-vilāsa*, m. N. of rhet. wks.; °*sâshṭaka*, n. eight stanzas attributed to Kālidāsa; °*sôdaya*, m. N. of a drama. **-rājīvana**, n. (prob. for *rājīva-vana*) N. of a rhet. wk. **-lajjā**, f. shame or modesty caused by love, Śak. **-latā**, f., **-laharī**, f. N. of wks. **-vat**, mfn. 'well dressed' or 'amorous' (see f.); amatory, erotic, Daśar., Sch.; (*atī*), f. N. of a woman, Kathās.; of a town, Cat. **-vāpikā**, f. N. of a Nāṭaka by Viśva-nātha. **-vidhi**, m. a dress suitable for amorous interviews, MW.; N. of a rhet. wk. **-vesha**, mfn. dressed suitably for amorous enterprises, MBh.; °*shâbharaṇa*, mfn. dressed and ornamented suitably for the above purpose, ib. **-vairāgya-taraṃgiṇī**, f. N. of a Jaina poem by Soma-prabhâcārya. **-śata** or **-śataka**, n. 'a hundred verses on love,' N. of various collections (esp. of the stanzas of Amaru and of the 2nd book of Bhartṛi-hari's poem). **-śūra**, m. a hero in love affairs, Pañcar. **-śekhara**, m. N. of a king, Vās., Introd. **-sapta-śatī**, f., **-sarasī**, f., **-sarvasva**, n. N. of wks. **-sahāya**, m. an assistant in affairs of love, confidant of a dramatic hero, MW. **-sāra**, m. N. of a Kāvya (by Kālidāsa). **-siṇha**, m. N. of a man, Rājat. **-sudhâkara**, m. N. of the author of a Comm. on the Rāmâyaṇa. **-sundarī**, f. N. of a princess, Virac. **-stabaka**, m. N. of a drama (of the class called Bhāṇa). **-hāra**, m. N. of a rhet. wk. by Bala-deva. **Śṛiṅgārâdi-rasa**, m. N. of a rhet. wk. **Śṛiṅgārâbhra**, n. a partic. mixture, Rasêndrac. **Śṛiṅgārâmṛita-laharī**, f. N. of a rhet. wk. by Sāma-rāja. **Śṛiṅgārâika-rasa**, mfn. one whose sole feeling is love, MW.

Śṛiṅgāraka, mfn. horned, having a horn or crest, L.; m. love &c. (= *śṛiṅgāra*), MW.; (*ikā*), f. N. of a Surâṅganā, Siṇhâs.; n. red-lead, L.

Śṛiṅgāraṇa, n. (with Pāśupatas) feigning love, amatory gesture or behaviour, Sarvad.

Śṛiṅgārita, mfn. affected by love, impassioned, MW.; stained with red-lead, reddened, ib.; adorned, decorated, embellished, Śiś.

Śṛiṅgārin, mfn. feeling love or amorous passion, enamoured, impassioned, Kāv., Sch.; erotic, relating to love, Daśar.; adorned, beautifully dressed, Vās.; stained with red-lead, W.; m. an impassioned lover, ib.; dress, decoration, ib.; an elephant, L.; the betel-nut tree, L.; a ruby (?), Pracaṇḍ.; (*iṇī*), f. a mistress, wife, Inscr.

Śṛiṅgārīya, Nom. P. °*yati,* to long for love, Śāntiś.

1. **Śṛiṅgi,** f. (= *śṛiṅgī*) a species of fish, L.; gold used for ornaments (also *-kanaka*), W.

2. **Śṛiṅgi,** in comp. for *śṛiṅgin.* **-putra,** m. N. of a preceptor, Cat. **-vara,** m. N. of a man, ib.

Śṛiṅgika, m. a partic. vegetable poison, L.; m. or f. (only ifc., f. *ikā*) a kind of missile or catapult, MBh. iii, 363 (Nīlak.); (*ikā*), f., see *śṛiṅgaka.*

Śṛiṅgiṇa, mfn. horned, W.; m. a wild ram, L.; (*ī*), f., see next.

Śṛiṅgin, mfn. horned, crested, peaked (ifc. having horns of –), RV. &c. &c.; tusked, MBh.; having a sting (see *visha-śṛ°*); breasted (in *cāru-śṛ°*, beautifully breasted), BhP.; m. 'a horned or tusked animal,' a bull, L.; elephant, L.; a mountain, L.; Ficus Infectoria, L.; Spondias Mangifera, L.; a partic. bulbous plant (= *vṛishabha*), L.; N. of a mythical mountain or mountain-range forming one of the boundaries of the earth (see *śaila*), VP.; of a Ṛishi, MBh.; Hariv.; (*iṇī*), f. a cow, L.; Cardiospermum Halicacabum, L.; Jasminum Sambac, L.

Śṛiṅgī, f. (g. *gaurâdi*) a sort of Silurus or sheat fish, Bhpr.; N. of various plants (Trapa Bispinosa, Ficus Infectoria or Indica &c.), ib.; Suśr.; a kind of vessel (?), Hcat.; = *-kanaka,* L. **-kanaka,** n. a kind of gold used for making ornaments, L. **-visha,** n. a kind of plant having a poisonous root, Suśr.

Śṛiṅgeri or **Śṛiṅgerī,** (prob.) f. (for *śṛiṅga-giri*) N. of a hill and town in Mysore, RTL. 55. **-pura,** n. id., ib. **-maṭha,** f. N. of a monastery (founded by Śaṃkara), ib.

Śṛiṅgya, mfn. horn-like, horny, g. *śākhâdi.*

शृङ्घाणिका *śṛiṅghāṇikā.* See *śṛiṅkhāṇikā.*

शृत *śṛitá,* mfn. (fr. √*śrā*; cf. *śrātá*) cooked, boiled (opp. to *āma,* 'raw,' and esp. said of water, milk, and ghee), RV. &c. &c.; n. cooked food, (esp.) boiled milk, Br.; ĀśvŚr.; (*ám*), ind., see below. **-kāma** (*śṛitá-*), mfn. liking boiled milk, TBr.; Kāṭh. **-tvá,** n. the being cooked or boiled, TS.; TBr.; Kāṭh. **-pá,** mfn. one who drinks boiled milk, RV. **-pāka,** mfn. thoroughly cooked or boiled, ib. **-śīta,** mfn. boiled and cooled again, ĀpŚr.; VarBṛS.; Suśr. **Śṛitâtaṅkya,** mfn. to be curdled or coagulated in boiled milk, TS.; ĀpŚr. **Śṛitâvadāna,** n. a wooden implement for distributing the Puroḍāśa (q.v.), KātyŚr. **Śṛitôshṇa,** mfn. cooked and (still) hot, Bhpr.

Śṛitám, in comp. for *śṛitám.* **-kartṛi,** mfn. one who cooks thoroughly, TS. **-kāra,** m. pl. N. of texts containing the word *śṛita,* ĀpŚr. **-kṛita** (*śṛitám-*), mfn. cooked thoroughly, TBr. **-kṛitya,** mfn. to be cooked thoroughly, TS.

शृध् *śṛidh,* cl. 1. P. Ā. (Dhātup. xviii, 21; xxiii, 61) *śardhati,* °*te* (pr. p. Ved. *śárdhat* and *śárdhamāna*; Gr. also pf. *śaśṛidhe*; aor. *aśṛidhat* or *aśardhishṭa*; fut. *śartsyati* or *śardhishyate*; inf. *śardhitum*; ind. p. *śardhitvā* or *śṛiddhvā*), to break wind downwards (in *ava-* and *vi-*√*śṛidh,* q.v.); to mock at, ridicule, defy (with gen.), RV.; VS.; to moisten, become moist or wet, Dhātup. xxi, 9: Caus. *śardhayati* (only in *ati-praśardháyat*), RV. viii, 13, 6: Desid. *śiśardhishate, śiśṛitsati,* Gr.: Intens. *śarīśṛidhyate, śarīśṛidhīti, śarīśarddhi,* ib.

Śardha, śardhana &c. See p. 1058, col. 2.

Śárdhat or **śárdhamāna,** mfn. mocking, defiant, bold, RV.; VS.

Śṛiddha, mfn. expelled from the body downwards (as wind), MW.; moistened, ib.

Śṛidhu, m. f. the anus, L.; = *buddhi,* L.

Śṛidhū, f. the anus, Uṇ. i, 93, Sch.

Śṛidhyā́, f. boldness, defiance, RV.

शॄ *śṝi,* cl. 9. P. (Dhātup. xxxi, 18) *śṛiṇā́ti* (pr. p. Ā. *śṛiṇāná,* RV.; Impv. *śṛiṇa,* AV.; pf. *śaśāra,* 2. sg. *śaśaritha,* 3. pl. *śaśaruḥ* or *śaśruḥ,* Gr.; *śaśre,* AV.; aor. *aśarīt, aśarait,* AV.; *aśārīt,* Gr.; Prec. *śīryāt,* ib.; fut. *śarītā, śarīshyati,* ib.; *śarishyate,* Br.; inf. *śarītum,* Gr.; *śárītos,* RV.; *śaritos,* AitĀr.; ind. p. *-śīrya,* Br.), to crush, rend, break (Ā. with reference to self, as 'to break one's own arm'), RV.; AV.; Br.; to kill (game), Kir. xiv, 13: Pass. *śīryate* (m.c. also °*ti*; aor. *aśāri, śāri*), to be crushed or broken or rent or shattered, RV. &c. &c.; to fall out or off, MBh.; Kāv. &c.; to be worn out, decay, wither, fade, ŚBr.; Hariv. &c.: Caus. *śārayati* (aor. *aśiśarat*), Gr.: Desid. *śiśarīshati, śiśīrshati,* ib.: Intens. *śeśīryate, śāśarti,* ib.

Śīrṇá, śīrta, śūrtá. See s.v.

शेकु *śeku, śeku-shṭha,* Pāṇ. viii, 3, 97.

शेखर *śekhara,* m. (fr. or connected with *śikhara*) the top or crown of the head, Kathās.; a chaplet or wreath of flowers worn on the top of the head, crown, diadem, crest, Hariv.; Kām.; Pur. &c.; a peak, summit, crest (of a mountain), ib.; Rājat.; (mostly ifc.) the highest part, chief or head or best or most beautiful of (*-tā,* f.), Ṛit.; Caurap.; Dhūrtas.; (in music) a partic. Dhruva or introductory verse of a song (recurring as a kind of refrain); N. of an author (with *bhaṭṭa*), Cat.; of a grammatical work, ib.; (*ī*), f. Vanda Roxburghii, L.; n. cloves, L.; the root of Moringa Pterygosperma, L. **-jyotis,** m. N. of a king, Kathās. **-vyākhyā,** f. N. of a grammatical wk. (see above). **Śekharâpīḍa-yojana,** n. N. of one of the 64 Kalās or arts, BhP., Sch.

Śekharaka, m. N. of the Viṭa (q.v.) in the drama Nāgânanda.

Śekharaya, Nom. P. °*yati,* to make into a chaplet or diadem, Kāv.

Śekharāya, Nom. Ā. °*yate,* to become a chaplet or diadem &c., Nalac.

Śekharita, mfn. made into or serving for a chaplet or diadem &c., BhP.; crested, peaked, tipped with (comp.), Śiś.

Śekharī, in comp. for *śekhara.* **-√kṛi,** P. *-karoti,* to make into a chaplet or diadem, Kād. **-bhāva,** m. the becoming a d°, Bālar. **-√bhū,** P. *-bhavati,* to become a diadem, VP.

शेड *śeḍa* or *śeḍḍa,* (prob.) N. of a place, Rājat.

शेणवी *śeṇavī* or *śeṇā,* f. (cf. *ratna-śeṇā*) N. of wk.

शेत्य *śetya,* mfn. = *śetavya,* TāṇḍyaBr. (Sch.)

शेप *śépa,* m. (said to be fr. √1. *śī,* and connected with *śiva* and √*śvi*) the male organ, penis, RV.; AV.; VS.; TS.; a tail (cf. *paru-cchepa, śunaḥ-śepa*), RV. [Cf. Lat. *cippus.*] **-hárshaṇa,** mf(*ī*)n. causing erection of the male organ, AV.

Śépas, n. the male organ, AV.; ŚāṅkhBr.; Car.; the scrotum or a testicle, Uṇ. iv, 200.

Śepya. See *mayūra-śepya.*

Śepyā́, f. the skin which covers the tail, Kauś. (Sch.) **-vat,** mfn. tailed, AV.

Śepha, m. (cf. *śaphá, śiphā́*) = *śepa,* the male organ, TS. (v.l.); MBh.; the scrotum (du. 'the testicles'), AitBr.

Śephaḥ-stambha, m. (fr. *śephas + st°*) morbid rigidity and erection of the male organ, Car.

Śephas, n. the male organ, Suśr.; VarBṛS.

शेपान *śepāna.* See √*śap,* p. 1052, col. 1.

शेपाल *śepāla,* m. n. Vitex Negundo, L.

Śephāli or °**lī,** f. id., L.

Śephālikā, f. id., Suśr.; Ṛitus. &c. (accord. to some also 'the fruit of the above tree;' accord. to others 'Nyctanthes Arbor Tristis').

शेमुषी *śemushī,* f. (fr. pf. p. of √1. *śam*) understanding, intellect, wisdom, Vās.; Rājat.; resolve, purpose, intention (ifc. °*shika*), Rājat.; BrahmaP. **-mush,** mfn. robbing wisdom, Hcar.

शेय *śeya,* n. impers. (fr. √1. *śī*) it is to be lain or slept, Pāṇ. vii, 4, 22, Sch.

Śeyya. See *saha-śeyya.*

शेरभ *śerabha* and °*bhaka,* m. (cf. *śarabha*) N. of serpents, AV.

शेल् *śel* (also written *sel*), cl. 1. P. *śelati,* to go, Dhātup. xv, 36.

Śelāya, Nom. P. °*yati,* g. *kaṇḍv-ādi.*

शेलग *śelaga,* m. (cf. *sélaga*) N. of a man, Pravar.

शेलु *śelu,* m. Cordia Myxa, Suśr.

शेव् *śev* (cf. √*sev*), cl. 1. Ā. *śevate,* to worship, serve, Dhātup. xiv, 36.

शेव *śéva,* mfn. (prob. fr. √*śvi,* and connected with *śavas* and *śiva*) dear, precious, RV.; AV.; m. (only L.) the male organ (cf. *śepa*); a serpent; a fish; height, elevation; treasure, wealth; N. of Agni; (*ā*), f. the form of the Liṅga, L.; n. prosperity, happiness, W.; hail, homage (an exclamation or salutation addressed to the deities), ib. **-dhí,** m. (L. also n.) 'treasure-receptacle,' wealth, treasure, jewel, RV. &c. &c.; treasury, an inexhaustible quantity (of good or evil), Siṇhâs.; one of the nine treasures of Kubera, MW.; *-pā́,* mfn. guarding treasure, RV.

Śevas. See *su-śevas.*

Śévāra, m. (prob. for *śeva-vāra*) a treasury, RV. viii, 1, 22.

Śévṛidha or **śevṛidhá,** mfn. (prob. for *śeva-vṛidha*) 'increasing felicity,' dear, precious, RV.; m. a kind of snake (also °*dhaka*), AV.

Śévya, mfn. dear (as a friend), RV.

शेवरक *śevaraka,* m. N. of an Asura, Kathās.

शेवल *śévala,* mfn. (√1. *śi*) slimy (?), AV. i, 11, 4; m. (?) in comp. forming proper names, Pāṇ. v, 3, 84; n. (cf. *śaivala*) Blyxa Octandra, L. **-datta,** m. N. of a man, Pāṇ. v, 3, 84, Sch. **Sevalêndra-datta,** m. N. of a man, Pāṇ. ib., Kāś.

Śevalika, m. (an endearing form) for *śevala-datta,* Pāṇ. v, 3, 84.

Śevalinī, f. (cf. *śaivalinī*) a river, L.

Śevaliya or °**lila,** m. = *śevalika,* Pāṇ. v, 3, 84.

Śevāla, m. n. Blyxa Octandra, Dharmaśarm. **-ghosha,** m. N. of a mountain, Siṇhâs.; (*ī*), f. spikenard, L.

Śevālī, ind. (with √*kṛi* &c.) g. *ūry-ādi.*

शेशियत *śeśyita,* °*ta-vat.* See √1. *śī.*

शेश्वीयमान *śeśvīyamāna.* See √*śvi.*

शेष *śesha,* m. n. (fr. √2. *śish*) remainder, that which remains or is left, leavings, residue (pl. 'all the others'), surplus, balance, the rest (*śeshe,* loc. 'for the rest,' 'in all other cases;' *śeshe rātrau,* 'during the rest of the night;' *mama śesham asti,* 'there remains something to happen to me'); that which has to be supplied (e.g. any word or words which have been omitted in a sentence; *iti śeshaḥ,* 'so it was left to be supplied,' a phrase commonly used by Comm. in supplying any words necessary to elucidate the text); that which is saved or spared or allowed to escape (nom. with √*as* or √*bhū,* 'to be spared;' *śesham* √*kṛi,* 'to spare,' 'allow to escape;' *śesham avâp,* 'to escape'), Mn.; MBh.; R. &c.; remaining (used as an adj. at the end of adj. comp. [f. *ā*], cf. *kathā-ś°, kṛitya-ś°*), AitBr. &c. &c.; remaining out of or from, left from (with abl. or loc., e.g. *prayātebhyo ye śeshāḥ,* 'the persons left out of those who had departed;' but mostly ifc. after a pp. in comp., e.g. *bhukta-śesha,* 'remaining from a meal,' 'remnant of food;' *hata-śeshāḥ,* 'those left out of the slain,' 'the survivors' &c.), Mn.; MBh. &c.; end, issue, conclusion, finish, result, RV. 77, 15; last, last-mentioned, Rājat.; a supplement, appendix, Nir. iii, 13; a keepsake, token of remembrance, Daś.; secondary matter, accident, KātyŚr., Sch.; death, destruction, W.; m. N. of a celebrated mythological thousand-headed serpent regarded as the emblem of eternity (whence he is also called An-anta, 'the infinite;' in the Vishṇu-Purāṇa he and the serpents Vāsuki and Takshaka are described as sons of Kadru, but in one place Śesha alone is called king of the Nāgas or snakes inhabiting Pātāla, while elsewhere Vāsuki is also described as king of the Nāgas and Takshaka of the serpents; the thousand-headed Śesha is sometimes represented as forming the couch and canopy of Vishṇu whilst sleeping during the intervals of creation, sometimes as supporting the seven Pātālas with the seven regions above them and therefore the entire world; he is said to have taught astronomy to Garga; according to some legends he became incarnate in Bala-rāma, q.v.), MBh.; Hariv.; Pur. &c. (RTL. 105; 112; 232, n. 1); N. of one of the Prajā-patis, R.; VP.; of a Muni, MW.; (also with *ācārya, dīkshita, śāstrin* &c.) of various authors (cf. below); of one of the mythical elephants that support the earth, L.; a kind of metre, L.; (*ā*), f. pl. the remains of flowers or other offerings made to an idol and afterwards distributed amongst the worshippers and attendants (sg. 'a garden made of the remains of flowers'), MBh.; R. &c.; (*ī*), f. N. of a woman, Cat.; n., see above. **-kamalâkara**, m. N. of an author, Cat. **-karaṇa**, n. the leaving a remnant of (comp.), PārGṛ.; the doing what remains to be done, MW. **-kārita**, mfn. unfinished, undone, MBh. **-kāla**, m. the time of end or death, W. **-krishṇa**, m. (also with *paṇḍita*) N. of various authors, Cat. **-kriyā**, f. the remainder of a ceremony, Baudh. **-govinda**, m. (with *paṇḍita*) N. of an astronomer, Cat. **-cakrapāṇi**, m. N. of a grammarian, ib. **-cintāmaṇi**, m. N. of a poem. **-jāti**, f. (in alg.) assimilation of residue, reduction of fractions of residues or successive fractional remainders, Līl. **-tas**, ind. otherwise, else, R. **-tā**, see *āyuḥ-* and *lāvaṇya-śeshatā*. **-tva**, n. the state of being a remainder (*ena*, 'by the remainder, in every other case'), Bhpr.; KātyŚr., Sch.; all that is left, residue, MW.; secondariness, Jaim.; Bādar.; *-vicāra*, m. N. of a Vedânta wk. **-deva**, m. the serpent Śesha (worshipped) as a god, Pañcar. **-dharma**, m. N. of a ch. of the Hari-vaṇśa. **-nāga**, m. the serpent Śesha (see above); N. of the mythical author of the Paramârtha-sāra, Cat. **-nārāyaṇa**, m. N. of the author of the Sûkti-ratnâkara (a Comm. on the Mahā-bhāshya; also with *-paṇḍita*). **-pati**, m. a superintendent, manager, L. **-bhāga**, m. the rest or remaining part, W. **-bhāva**, m. the being a remainder, KātyŚr. **-bhuj**, mfn. one who eats leavings, Mn.; BhP. **-bhūta**, mfn. being left, remaining, ŚāṅkhŚr.; being secondary or accidental, Jaim., Sch.; (m.c. for *śeshā-bh°*) being (i.e. 'as if being, as it were') a garland of flowers (cf. *śeshā*, f.), Mṛicch. x, 44. **-bhūshaṇa**, m. 'having the serpent-demon Śesha for ornament,' N. of Vishṇu, Cat. **-bhojana**, n. the eating of leavings, eating the remnant of food (after feeding the family-guests &c.), W. **-bhojin**, mfn. = *-bhuj*, Āpast. **-rakshaṇa**, n. taking care that an undertaking is brought to a conclusion, W. **-ratnâkara**, m. N. of the author of the Sāhitya-ratnâkara (a Comm. on the Gīta-govinda). **-rātri**, f. the last watch of the night, W. **-rāma-candra**, m. N. of a Scholiast on the Naishadhīya-carita, Cat. **-rūpin**, mfn. appearing to be secondary, Sarvad. **-vat**, mfn. left alive, spared, MBh.; characterized by an effect or result (sometimes applied in logic to *a posteriori* reasoning), Nyāyas. **-vākyârtha-candrikā**, f. N. of a Vedânta wk. **-vistāra-pāṇḍu**, mfn. pale in its remaining surface (said of a cloud), Megh. **-śarīra**, n. the remainder (i.e. all the other parts) of the body, MW. **-śārṅga-dhara**, m. N. of an author, Cat. **-śeshin** (ibc.), secondary and primary matter; (*°shi*)*-tva*, n., *-bhāva*, m. the being secondary and p° m°, secondariness and primariness, Madhus. **-saṃhitā**, f. N. of wk. **-saṃgraha-nāma-mālā**, f., **-saṃgraha-sārôddhāra**, m. N. of supplements to Hema-candra's Abhidhāna-cintāmaṇi. **-samuccaya-ṭīkā**, f., **-homa-prayoga**, m. N. of wks. **Śeshâṅka-gaṇanā**, f. N. of an astron. wk. by Kamalâkara. **Śeshâdri**, m. N. of a grammarian, Cat. **Śeshâdhikārīya**, mfn. belonging to the section *śesha*, Pāṇ. vii, 3, 48. **Śeshânanta**, m., **Śeshânanda**, m. N. of two authors, Cat. **Śeshânna**, n. leavings of a meal &c. W. **Śeshâryā**, f. N. of a metrical introduction to the Vedânta by Śesha-nāga; *-vyākhyāna*, n. N. of wk. **Śeshâvacayana**, n. gathering up remnants, collecting what remains, MW. **Śeshâvasthā**, f. the last state or condition of life, old age, W. **Śeshâhi**, m. the serpent Śesha (see above), Pañcad.; N. of a teacher (also called Nāgeśvara), Cat.

Śeshaka, m. the serpent Śesha, Pañcar.

Śéshaṇa, n. a partic. term (in gambling), AV.

Śéshas, n. offspring, RV.

Śeshin, mfn. having (little) remainder (i.e. constituting the 'chief matter' or 'main point'), Sarvad.

Śeshī-√bhū, P. *-bhavati*, to be left, remain over, Bālar.

Śeshya, mfn. to be left or ignored or neglected, Kathās.

शै **śai**, v.l. for √*śyai* and *śrai*.

शैकयतायनि **śaikayatāyani**, m. patr. fr. *śikayata*, g. *tikâdi*.

शैकि **śaiki**, m. (only pl.) a patron., Pravar.

शैक्य **śaikya**, mfn. (fr. *śikya*) suspended in the loop of a yoke (or m. 'a kind of sling,' MBh. ii, 1916), Un. v, 16, Sch.; damasked (?), MBh.; pointed (for *śaikhya*), MW. **Śaikyâyasa**, mfn. made of damasked steel, MBh.; *-maya*, mf(*ī*)n. id., ib.

शैक्ष **śaiksha**, mf(*ī*)n. (fr. *śikshā*) in accordance with right teaching or with rule, correct, MBh.; m. a young Brāhman pupil studying with his preceptor, one who has recently begun to repeat the Veda, L.

Śaikshika, mfn. familiar with the Śikshā (q.v.), L.

Śaikshya, mfn. (v.l. for *śaiksha*) conformable to right teaching or to rule, correct, MBh.; n. learning, skill, MW. **-guṇa-krama**, mfn. possessing skill and cleverness and dexterity, ib.

शैक्षित **śaikshita**, m. metr. fr. *śikshitā*, Pāṇ. iv, 1, 113, Sch.

शैख **śaikha**, m. (fr. *śikhā*) the offspring of an outcaste Brāhman, Mn. x, 21.

Śaikhāyani, m. metron. fr. *śikhā*, g. *tikâdi*.

Śaikhāvata, m. patr. fr. *śikhā-vat*, Pāṇ. v, 3, 118; pl. and (*ī*), f., ib.

Śaikhāvatya, m. a king of the Śaikhāvatas, ib.; N. of a Brāhman, MBh.

Śaikhya, mfn. (cf. *śaikya*) pointed, spiked, MW.

शैखण्ड **śaikhaṇḍa**, mfn. (fr. *śikhaṇḍin*), Pāṇ. vi, 4, 144, Vartt. 1.

Śaikhaṇḍi, m. patr. fr. *śikhaṇḍin*, MBh.

Śaikhaṇḍina (fr. *śikhaṇḍin*), g. *suvāstv-ādi*; n. N. of various Sāmans, ĀrshBr.

शैखरिक **śaikharika**, m. (fr. *śekhara*) Achyranthes Aspera, Car.

Śaikhareya, m. id., L.

शैखिन **śaikhina**, mfn. (fr. *śikhin*) relating to or coming from or produced by a peacock, Suśr.

शैग्रव **śaigrava**, m. (fr. *śigru*) a patr., g. *bidâdi*; n. the fruit of Moringa Pterygosperma, g. *plakshâdi*.

शैघ्र **śaighra**, n. (fr. *śīghra*) swiftness, velocity, R.; Kām.; mfn. (in astron.) relating to a conjunction; (with or scil. *phala*, n.) the equation of the second epicycle, Sūryas.

Śaighrya, n. swiftness, rapidity, velocity, MBh.; Hariv. &c.; (in astron.) = preceding.

शैतिकक्ष **śaitikaksha**, m. patr. fr. *śiti-kaksha* (*-pāñcāleyāḥ*, Kāś. on Pāṇ. vi, 2, 37).

Śaitibāheya, m. metron. fr. *śiti-bāhu*, Pāṇ. iv, 1, 135, Sch.

शैतोष्म **śaitoshma** or *°man*, n. pl. (fr. *śita* + *ūshman*) N. of various Sāmans, ĀrshBr.

शैत्य **śaitya**, n. (fr. *śīta*) coldness, frigidity, cold, Yājñ.; MBh. &c. **-maya**, mf(*ī*)n. consisting in coldness, causing frost (*-tva*, n.), Sāh.

Śaityāyana, m. N. of a grammarian, TPrāt.

शैथिलिक **śaithilika**, mfn. (fr. *śithila*) loose, lax, slack, idle, Lalit.

Śaithilya, n. looseness, laxity, Hariv.; R. &c.; flaccidity, Suśr.; decrease, diminution, smallness, weakness, relaxation, remission, depression (of the mind), unsteadiness, vacancy (of gaze), MBh.; Kāv. &c.; negligence in (comp.), Campak.; relaxation of rule or connection, W.; dilatoriness, inattention, MW.

शैनेय **śaineya**, m. (fr. *śini*) patr. of Satyaka or Sātyaki (the charioteer of Kṛishṇa, represented as having destroyed numerous Dasyus), MBh.; Hariv. &c.; pl. the descendants of Śini (a branch of the Yādavas), ib.; (*°yá*), w.r. for *śyaineyá*, MaitrS.

Śainya, m. a patr., ĀśvŚr.; pl. the descendants of Śini (who became Brāhmans, though originally of the Kshatriya race), Pur.

शैपथ **śaipatha**, m. a patr., Pravar.

शैफालिक **śaiphālika**, mfn. (fr. *śephāli* or *°likā*) made of the Vitex Negundo, Pat.

शैब **śaiba**, mfn. (also written *śaiva*) inhabited by Śibis, Kāś. on Pāṇ. iv, 2, 52; 69; (*ī*), f. (of *śaibya*), Kāś. on Pāṇ. iv, 1, 73.

Śaibika, mfn. (fr. *śibikā*), g. *chattrâdi* (Kāś.)

Śaibya, mfn. (often written *śaivya*) relating or belonging to the Śibis, AitBr.; m. a descendant of Śibi or a king of the Śibis, PraśnUp.; MBh. &c.; N. of one of the four horses of Vishṇu, MBh.; Hariv.; BhP.; (*ā*), f. (cf. under *śaiba*) N. of various princesses, MBh.; Caṇḍ.; of a river, MBh.

शैबल **śaibala**, *°bāla*. See *śaivala*, *°vāla*.

शैम्ब्य **śaimbya**, mfn. (fr. *śimba*) relating or belonging to leguminous plants (such as pulse &c.), KātyŚr., Sch.

शैरस **śairasa**, n. (fr. *śiras*) the head of a bedstead, Car.

Śairasi, m. patr. fr. *śiras*, g. *bāhv-ādi*.

शैरिक **śairika** (cf. *sairika*), m. N. of a man, Cat.

Śairin (?), m. N. of a man, Pravar.

शैरीयक **śairīyaka** or *śaireyaka*, m. Barleria Cristata (a kind of shrub), W.

शैरीष **śairīsha**, m. (fr. *śirīsha*) coming from the Acacia Sirissa, Suśr.; having the colour of Acacia Sirissa, VarBṛS.; n. N. of a Sāman, ĀrshBr.

Śairīshaka, mfn., g. *arīhaṇâdi*; (prob.) n. N. of a place, Divyâv.

Śairīshi, m. patr. of the Ṛishi Su-vedas (q.v.), RAnukr.

Śairīshika, mfn., g. *kumudâdi*.

शैर्षघात्य **śairshaghātya**, n. (fr. *śīrsha-ghātin*), g. *brāhmaṇâdi*.

शैर्षच्छेदिक **śairshacchedika**, mfn. (fr. *śīrsha-ccheda*) one who deserves to have his head cut off, Pāṇ. v, 1, 65.

शैर्षायण **śairshāyaṇa**, mfn. (fr. *śīrsha*), g. *pakshâdi*.

Śairshika. See *caraṇa-ś°*.

Śairshya, mfn. (fr. *śīrsha*), g. *saṃkāśâdi*.

शैल **śaila**, mf(*ī*)n. (fr. *śilā*) made of stone, stony, rocky, MBh.; Hariv. &c.; stone-like, rigid (with *āsana*, n. a partic. manner of sitting), Cat.; m. (ifc. f. *ā*) a rock, crag, hill, mountain (there are seven [or, accord. to some, eight] mythical mountain ranges separating the divisions of the earth, viz. *Nishadha, Hema-kūṭa, Nīla, Śveta, Śṛiṅgin, Mālyavat, Gandha-mādana*, VP.), Mn.; MBh. &c.; N. of the number 'seven,' Gaṇit.; a dike, MW.; (*ā*), f. N. of a nun, Divyâv.; (*ī*), f., see below; n. (only L.) benzoin or storax; bitumen; a sort of collyrium. **-kaṭaka**, m. the brow of a hill, slope of a mountain, W. **-kanyā**, f. 'daughter of the m° (Himâlaya),' N. of Pārvatī, Hariv. **-kampin**, mfn. shaking m°s; m. N. of one of Skanda's attendants, MBh.; of a Dānava, Hariv. **-kuñja**, m. a m°-cope, thicket on a hill, MW. **-kūṭa**, m. n. a m°-peak, VarBṛS. **-gandha**, n. a kind of sandal, L. **-garbhâhvā**, f. a kind of medicinal substance, L. **-gāthā**, f. pl. N. of a collection of hymns, Divyâv. **-guru**, mfn. as heavy as a mountain, Ragh.; m. 'chief of m°s,' N. of the Himâlaya, Kum. **-ja**, mfn. m°-born, R.; made of stone, Hcat.; m. or n. a kind of lichen, L.; (*ā*), f. N. of various plants (= *siṅha-pippalī, gaja-pipp°* &c.), L.; N. of Durgā, MW.; n. bitumen, L.; benzoin or storax, W.; (*-jā*)*-mantrin*, m. N. of an author, Cat. **-jana**, m. a person inhabiting m°s, a mountaineer, W. **-jātā**, f. a kind of pepper, L.; Scindapsus Officinalis, L. **-tanayā**, f. = *-kanyā*, Kathās.; *-tāta*, m. 'father of Pārvatī,' the Himâlaya, Dhūrtan. **-tas**, ind. (= *śailāt*) from or than a m°, MW. **-tā**, f. (ŚārṅgP.) or **-tva**, n. (MBh.) the condition of a m°. **-duhitṛi**, f. = *-kanyā*, Kathās. **-dhanvan**, m. 'having a bow of rock,' N. of Śiva, L. **-dhara**, m. 'mountain-holder,' N. of Kṛishṇa, Dhanaṃj. **-dhātu**, m. a mineral, Hariv.; *-ja*, n. a kind of mineral resin, L. **-niryāsa**, m. 'rock-exudation,' id., L.; storax, benzoin, L. **-pati**, m. 'mountain-lord,' the Himâlaya, W. **-pattra**, m.

Aegle Marmelos, L. **-patha,** m. a m° path, Rājat.; N. of a man, Cat. (w.r. *-yatha*). **-putrī,** f. = *-kanyā*, MBh.; Hariv.; R.; N. of the Ganges, R. **-pura,** n. N. of a town, Kathās. **-pushpa,** n. bitumen, Suśr. **-pūrṇârya,** m. N. of a man, Cat. **-pratimā,** f. a stone image, idol made of stone, Mṛicch. **-prastha,** m.n. a mountain-plain, plateau, R. **-bāhu,** m. N. of a serpent-demon, Buddh. **-bīja,** m. 'having stony seeds,' the marking-nut plant, L. **-bhitti,** f. an instrument for breaking or cutting stones, L. **-bheda,** m. Coleus Scutellaroides, Suśr. **-maya,** mf(ī)n. made or consisting of stone, Hariv.; R. &c. **-mallī,** f. a kind of plant (commonly called *Koraiyā*), Bhpr. **-mūla,** n. a kind of Zerumbet (= *kacora*), Suśr. **-mṛiga,** m. a wild goat, MBh. **-yatha,** w.r. for *-patha*. **-randhra,** n. 'mountain-hole,' a cavern, cave, Ragh. **-rāj,** m. 'king of m°s,' N. of the Himālaya, R. **-rāja,** m. id., Kāv.; N. of Indra-kīla, MW.; *-duhitṛi*, f. patr. of Pārvatī, Cat.; *-sutā*, f. id., R.; patr. of Gaṅgā, ib. **-rugṇa,** mfn. crushed by m°s, Ragh. **-vanôpapanna,** mfn. possessed of m°s and woods, MW. **-vara,** m. 'best of m°s,' N. of the Himālaya, R. **-valkalā,** f. a kind of medicinal substance, L. **-vālukā(h),** w.r. for *śailavāl°*, Hariv.; Bhpr. **-vāsa,** m. a m°-habitation, MW. **-śikhara,** m. n. the peak of a m°, Kāv.; Hit. **-śikhā,** f. the top of a m°; a kind of metre, Piṅg. **-śibira,** n. 'rock-entrenched,' the ocean, L. **-śṛiṅga,** n. a m°-peak, MBh. **-śekhara,** m. id., Kpr.; Kuval. **-saṃdhi,** m. a valley, L. **-sambhava,** n. 'rock-produced,' bitumen, L. **-sambhūta,** n. red chalk, L. **-sarvajña,** m. N. of a poet, Sadukt. **-sāra,** mfn. hard as a rock, Ragh.; Kusum. **-sutā,** f. = *-kanyā*, Kum.; Kathās.; a kind of plant (= *mahā-jyotishmatī*), L.; *-kānta*, m. 'husband of Pārvatī,' N. of Śiva, Kathās.; *-caraṇa-rāga-yoni*, mfn. produced by the colour of P°'s feet, MW.; *-pati*, m. = *-sutā-kānta*, VarBṛS. **-setu,** m. a stone embankment, stone bridge, Rājat. **Śailâṅga** or **°ga-deśa,** m. N. of a country, MW. **Śailâkhya,** n. 'having the name Śaila,' bitumen, L. **Śailâgra,** n. a mountain top, L. **Śailâṅga** or **°ga-deśa,** m. N. of a country, MW. **Śailā-ja,** n. bitumen, L. (w.r. for *śaila-ja*). **Śailâṭa,** m. a mountaineer, wild hill tribesman, W.; a lion, L.; a Kirāta, L.; = *devalaka*, L.; crystal, L. **Śailâdhārā,** f. 'm°-support,' the earth, L. **Śailâdhipa,** m. 'king of m°s,' N. of the Himālaya, MW. **Śailâdhirāja,** m. id.; *-tanayā*, f. 'daughter of Himālaya,' N. of Pārvatī, Kāv. **Śailâbha,** mfn. m°-like, high as a m°, MBh.; R.; m. N. of a being reckoned among the Viśve Devāḥ, MBh. **Śailâlaya,** m. N. of a king, ib. **Śailâsana,** mfn. = next, Car.; *°nôdbhava*, mfn. made of stone or of the wood of Terminalia Tomentosa, Suśr. **Śailâsā,** f. N. of Pārvatī, L. **Śailâhva,** n. 'having the name Śaila,' bitumen, L. **Śailêndra,** m. the chief or lord of m°s (esp. as N. of the Himālaya), R.; MārkP.; *-jā*, f. N. of the Gaṅgā, L.; *-duhitṛi*, f. 'daughter of Himālaya,' N. of Pārvatī and of Gaṅgā, ib.; *-sutā*, f. id., Siṅhās.; *-stha*, m. a birch tree, L. **Śailêśa,** m. 'lord of m°s,' N. of the Himālaya; *-liṅga*, n. N. of a Liṅga, Cat. **Śailêśy-avasthā,** f. (with Jainas) the last stage of an ascetic's life, Śīl. **Śailôdā,** f. N. of a river, MBh.; R. **Śailôdbhavā,** f. a species of small *pāshāṇa-bhedin*, MW.

Śailaka, n. bitumen, VarBṛS.; benzoin or storax, W.

Śailāvatya, m. a proper N., MW.

Śailika, m. N. of a people, MārkP.; n. bitumen &c., L.

1. **Śailī,** f. (for 2. see col. 2) hardness, stoniness, W. (cf. *śailya*).

Śaileya, mfn. rocky, stony, mountain-like, hard, Pāṇ. v, 3, 102; produced in mountains or rocks, W.; m.n. bitumen (of various kinds), Kāv.; VarBṛS.; Suśr.; benzoin, L.; a kind of lichen, L.; m. a bee, L.; a lion, L.; (ī), f. patr. of Pārvatī, L.; n. Anethum Graveolens, L.; rock-salt, L. **-gandhi,** mfn. smelling of bitumen, fragrant with benzoin &c., W.

Śaileyaka, n. bitumen, benzoin &c., Suśr.; VarBṛS.

Śaileyika, mfn. relating to bitumen &c., MW.

Śailya, mfn. rocky, stony, hard, ib.; n. (cf. 1. *śailī*) rockiness, stoniness, hardness, ib.

शैलाद *śailāda*, m. (fr. *śilâda*) a patr., Cat.

Śailādi, m. (fr. id.) patr. of Nandin (one of Śiva's attendants), VāmP.

शैलाल *śailāla*, n. a work composed by Śilālin, Pāṇ. iv, 3, 110, Sch.

1. **Śailāli,** m. (fr. *śilālin*) N. of a teacher, ŚBr.

2. **Śailāli,** in comp. for *śailālin*. **-brāhmaṇa,** n. N. of a Brāhmaṇa, ĀpŚr. **-yuvan,** m. a young actor or dancer, Hcar.

Śailālin, m. (pl.) the school of Śilālin, Pāṇ. iv, 3, 110; (sg.) an actor, dancer, L. (cf. *śailūsha*).

शैलिक्य *śailikya*, m. = *sarva-liṅgin*, L.; n. (fr. *śilika*), g. *purohitâdi*.

शैलिन *śailiná*, m. (fr. *śilina*) N. of a preceptor, ŚBr.

Śailini, m. id., BṛĀrUp.

शैली 2. *śailī*, f. (fr. *śīla*; for 1. see col. 1) habit, custom, manner of acting or living, practice, usage, Kāv.; Kathās.; a special or particular interpretation (esp. a concise explanation of a grammatical aphorism), L. **-jñāpaka,** n. N. of wk.

शैलूत *śailūta*, m. or n. (?) N. of a place, R. (v. l. for *kolūka*).

शैलूष *śailūshá*, m. (said to be fr. *śilūsha*) an actor, public dancer, tumbler &c., VS. &c. &c.; the leader of a band, one who beats time (= *tāla-dhāraka*), L.; a rogue, L.; Aegle Marmelos, Bhpr.; N. of a Gandharva king, MBh.; R.; (pl.) of a people, MārkP.; (ī), f. an actress, female dancer, MBh.

Śailūshaka, mfn. inhabited by actors &c., g. *rājanyâdi*; m. = *śailūsha*, MW.

Śailūshi, m. patr. of the Vedic Ṛishi Kulmala-barhisha, RAnukr.

Śailūshika, m. and (ī), f. = *śailūsha*, °*shī*, Prâyaśc.

शैलेश्चय *śaileścaya* (?), m. (prob. w.r. for *śaile-śaya*) N. of a man (pl. his family), Pravar.

शैव 1. *śaiva*, mf(ī)n. (fr. *śiva*) relating or belonging or sacred to the god Śiva, coming or derived from Śiva, R.; Kathās.; Pur. &c.; m. patr. fr. *śiva*, Pāṇ. iv, 1, 112; 'a worshipper or follower of Śiva,' N. of one of the three great divisions of modern Hindūism (the other two being the Vaishṇavas and Śāktas, qq.vv.; the Śaivas identify Śiva—rather than Brahmā and Vishṇu—with the Supreme Being and are exclusively devoted to his worship, regarding him as the source and essence of the universe as well as its disintegrator and destroyer; the temples dedicated to him in his reproducing and vivifying character [as denoted by the Liṅga, q.v.] are scattered all over India; the various sects of Śaivas are described in RTL. 86 &c.); a particular religious rite in honour of Durgā (consisting of devout meditation and prostration of the body), MW.; the thorn-apple, L.; a kind of plant (= *vasuka*), L.; (with Jainas), N. of the fifth black Vāsudeva, L.; (ī), f. N. of the goddess Mānasā, Cat.; n. auspiciousness, welfare, prosperity, BhP.; N. of a Śāstra and of a Tantra and of a Purāṇa (see below). **-kalpadruma,** m. N. of a wk. by Appaya Dīkshita. **-tattva-prakāśa,** m., **-tattvâmṛita,** n., **-tantra,** n. N. of wks. **-tā,** f. devotion to or worship of Śiva, Rājat. **-tātparya-saṃgraha,** m. N. of wk. **-darśana,** n. the Śaiva philosophy, RTL. 89; N. of the 7th ch. of the Sarva-darśana-saṃgraha. **-dharma-maṇḍana,** n. N. of a wk. on Dharma. **-nagara,** n. N. of a town, Cat. **-nava-daśa-prakaraṇa,** n., **-pañcaka,** n., **-paribhāshā,** f. N. of wks. **-purāṇa,** n. N. of a Purāṇa (= *śiva-p°*, q.v.) **-pūjā-vidhāna,** n., **-bhāshya,** n. N. of wks. **-vāyavīya-purāṇa,** n. N. of a Purāṇa. **-vaishṇava,** n. N. of a Vedānta wk.; *-pratishṭhā-prayoga*, m., *-mata-maṇḍana*, n., *-vāda*, m., *-vādârtha*, m. N. of wks. **-śāstra,** n., **-sarvasva,** n., **-sarvasva-sāra,** n., **-siddhânta-dīpikā,** f., **-siddhânta-śekhara,** m., **-siddhânta-saṃgraha,** m., **-siddhânta-sāra,** m., **-siddhânta-sārâvalī,** f. N. of wks. **Śaivâgama,** m., **Śaivâshṭaka,** n., **Śaivâhnika,** n. N. of wks.

2. **Śaiva,** Vṛiddhi form of *śiva* in comp. **-gava,** m. (fr. *śiva-gu*) N. of a Gotra or family, ĀśvŚr. **-pāśupata,** mfn. relating to Śiva Paśupati, Cat.; m. a worshipper of Ś° P°, Prab. **-pura,** mfn. (fr. *śiva-pura*), Pāṇ. iv, 2, 109, Sch. **-rūpya,** mfn. (fr. *śiva-rūpa*), Pāṇ. iv, 2, 106, Sch.

Śaivāyana, m. patr. fr. *śiva*, g. *aśvâdi*.

Śaivi, m. patr. fr. *śiva*, Pravar.

Śaivya, mfn. (cf. *śaibya*) relating or belonging to Śiva &c., W.

शैव 3. *śaiva*, n. a kind of aquatic plant, Blyxa Octandra, L.

Śaivala, m. n. (ifc. f. *ā*; cf. *śevala*), Blyxa Octandra (a kind of duck-weed or green moss-like plant growing in pools and often alluded to in poetry), MBh.; Hariv.; Kāv. &c.; m. N. of a mountain, R.; of a serpent-demon, Buddh.; (pl.) of a people, MBh. (C. *śaibāla*); n. the (fragrant) wood of Cerasus Puddum (used in medicine), L. **-vat,** mfn. = next, Ragh.

Śaivalita, mfn. covered with Śaivala plants, g. *tārakâdi*.

Śaivalin, mfn. id., Śiś.; (*inī*), f. a river, L.

Śaivalya, mf(ā)n. = prec. mfn., ShaḍvBr. (v.l. *śīpalya*).

Śaivāla, n. the Śaivala plant, MBh.; Hariv. &c.; m. N. of a mountain, MārkP.; (pl.) of a people, MBh.; VP. **-vajra,** n. a kind of steel, L.

Śaivālaka (ifc.) = the above plant, Śṛiṅgār.; m. N. of a mountain, Siṅhās.

Śaivālin, mfn. = *śaivalin*, Bhām.

Śaivālīya, Nom. P. °*yati*, to resemble the Śaivala plant, Vās., Introd.

शैव 4. *śaiva*, w.r. for *śaiba*.

शैवाकवि *śaivākavi*, m. patr. fr. *śivāku*, g. *bāhv-ādi*.

शैशव *śaiśava*, mfn. (fr. *śiśu*) childish, Viddh.; m. a patr., Prav.; (pl.) N. of a people, MBh.; n. childhood, infancy, pupilage, the period under age (i.e. under sixteen), Mn.; MBh. &c.; childishness, stupidity, Prasannar.; N. of various Sāmans, ĀrshBr. **-yauvanīya,** mfn. representing childhood and youth, Naish.

Śaiśavya, n. childhood, infancy, Sarvad. (prob. w.r. for *śaiśava*).

शैशिक *śaiśika*, m. pl. N. of a people, VP.

शैशिर *śaiśirá*, mf(ī)n. (see *śiśira*) relating or belonging to the Śiśira or cool season, AV. &c. &c.; composed by Śiśira, Cat.; m. N. of a teacher and founder of a supposed Śākhā of the Ṛig-veda, ib.; of a mountain, MBh.; of a dark kind of Cātaka bird, L. **-śākhā,** f. N. of a Śākhā of the Ṛig-veda, (perhaps only a subdivision of the Śākala), Cat. **Śaiśirâstra,** mfn. having cold weapons (as the moon in fighting with the Daityas), Hariv. (v.l. *śiśirâstra*).

Śaiśirāyaṇa, m. patr. fr. *śiśira*, Hariv. (v. l. *śiśirāyaṇa*).

Śaiśiri, m. (patr. fr. id.) N. of a teacher of the White Yajur-veda, ĀśvŚr.

Śaiśirika, mfn. one who studies or knows Śiśira, g. *vasantâdi*.

Śaiśiriya, mfn. relating or belonging to Śaiśiri, g. *gahâdi* (accord. to some 'to be performed in the cool season') N. of one of the seven Śākala texts, Cat. **-śākhā,** f. a subordinate branch of the Śākala-śākhā, ib.

Śaiśiriyaka, mfn. = *śaiśiriya*, ib.

Śaiśireya, m. patr. of a teacher, ib.

शैशुनाग *śaiśunāga*, m. patr. fr. *śiśu-nāga*; (pl.) Śiśunāga and his descendants, VP.

Śaiśunāri (Hcar.) and **Śaiśunāli** (Vās., Introd.), m. (prob.) w.r. for *śaiśupāli*.

Śaiśupāla or **Śaiśupāli,** m. patr. fr. *śiśu-pāla*, MBh.

Śaiśumāra, mfn. relating or belonging to Śiśumāra, BhP.

शैश्न्य *śaiśnya*, m. (fr. *śiśna*; scil. *bhoga*) sexual enjoyment, BhP.

शैष *śaisha*, m. (? for *śaiśa*; see *śaiśirá* above) the cool season, L.

शैषिक *śaishika*, mf(ī)n. (fr. *śesha*) relating to the remainder, holding good in the remaining cases (but only now and not in previous cases), Kār. on Pāṇ.; Śiś., Sch. &c.; (ī), f. (with *shashṭhī*) the genitive case taught in Pāṇ. ii, 3, 50 (in the rule *shashṭhī śeshe*), Nyāyas., Sch.

शैषिरि *śaishiri*, w.r. for *śaiśiri* (q.v.)

शैष्योपाध्यायिका *śaishyopādhyāyikā*, f. (fr. *śishya + upâdhyāya*) the relation between pupil and teacher, Pāṇ. v, 1, 133, Sch.

शैसीक *śaisīka* and *śaisīta*, m. pl. N. of a people, VP.

शो *śo* (cf. √1. *śi*), cl. 3. P. Ā. *śiśāti*, *śi-śīte* (accord to Dhātup. xxvi, 36 also cl. 4. P. *śyati*, cf. *ni-√śo*; pf. *śaśau*, Gr.; p. *śaśānā*, AV.; aor. *aśīta*, cf. *sam-√śo*; *aśāt* or *aśāsīt*, Gr.; Prec. *śāyāt*, ib.; fut. *śātā*, *śāsyati*, ib.; ind. *-śāya*, AV.), to whet, sharpen (Ā. 'one's own' weapons or horns), RV.; AV.; Hariv.: Pass. *śāyate*, Gr.: Caus. *śāyayati*, ib.; Desid. *śiśāsati*, ib.: Intens. *śāśāyate*, *śaśeti*, *śāśāti*, ib. [? Cf. Gk. ἀκή &c.]

Śāta, mfn. See 1. *śāta*, p. 1063, col. 3.

4. **Śitá**, mfn. (for 1. &c. see p. 1069, col. 3) whetted, sharp, RV. &c. &c.; thin, slender, weak, feeble, L.

शोंस् *śons* (substituted in certain formulas) for √*śaṅs*.

Śonsāmas, °**sāvas**, °**sāva** (substituted) for *śan-sāmas*, °*sāvas*, °*sāva* (cf. *śom*, *śośoṉsavas*), TS.

शोक *śoká*, mfn. (√*śuc*) burning, hot, AV.; (*śóka*), m. (ifc. f. *ā*) flame, glow, heat, RV.; AV.; ŚBr.; sorrow, affliction, anguish, pain, trouble, grief for (gen. or comp.), RV. &c. &c.; Sorrow personified (as a son of Death or of Droṇa and Abhimati), Pur.; (*ī*), f., see below. **-kara**, m. Semecarpus Anacardium, L. (w.r. for *śopha-k°*). **-karshita**, mfn. harassed by sorrow, agonized with grief, R. **-carcā**, f. 's°-repetition,' indulgence in grief, L. **-cchid**, mfn. sorrow-removing, W. **-ja**, mfn. produced by s°, MBh. **-tará**, mf(*ā*)n. conquering s°, ŚBr. **-duḥkha-samanvita**, mfn. affected by s° and pain, MW. **-nāśa**, m. 's°-destroying,' the Aśoka tree, L. **-nāśana**, mfn. s°-destroying, a remover of grief, R. **-nihata**, mfn. struck down or overcome with s°, Mṛicch.; Hit. **-paṅka**, m. n. a slough of sorrow, s° compared to a quagmire, MBh. **-parâyaṇa**, mfn. wholly given up to s°, MBh.; R. **-paripluta**, mfn. overwhelmed with s°, MBh. **-pātrâtman**, mfn. id. (lit. 'whose soul is a receptacle for s°'), Śak. **-bhaṅga**, m. 's°-break,' dissipation or removal of grief, MW. **-bhāra**, m. a weight or burden of s°, MārkP. **-maya**, mf(*ī*)n. consisting of or full of s°, Kathās. **-mūrchita**, mfn. stupefied or stunned by grief, W. **-rugṇa**, mfn. broken down with s°, in great distress, R. **-lālasa**, mfn. entirely given up to s°, MBh.; R. **-vat**, mfn. sorrowful, ib. **-vartavya**, mfn. (fr. √1. *vṛi*) to be involved in or exposed or obnoxious to sorrow, Śak. (v.l.) **-vikala**, mfn. overwhelmed with s°, A. **-vināśana** or °**śin**, mfn. destroying or removing sorrow, MBh. **-vivardhana**, mfn. increasing s°, ib. **-vihvala**, mfn. afflicted with s°, A. **-saṃvigna-mānasa**, mfn. having the heart distracted with s°, Bhag. **-saṃtapta**, mfn. consumed by s°, R.; *-mānasa*, mfn. one whose mind is c° by s°, MW. **-sāgara**, m. a sea of sorrow, ocean of trouble, R. **-sthāna**, n. any circumstance or occasion of sorrow, MBh.; Hit. **-hārī**, f. a kind of plant (= *vana-barbarikā*), L. (w.r. for *śopha-hārin*). **Śokâkula**, mfn. overwhelmed or overcome with s°, Nal. **Śokâgāra**, m. n. 'lamentation-room,' an apartment to which women retire for weeping, Divyâv. **Śokâgni**, m. the fire of s°, violent grief, Kāv.; Hit.; *-saṃtapta*, mfn. consumed by the fire of s° or grief, W. **Śokâtiga**, mfn. overcoming s°, KaṭhUp. **Śokâtisāra**, m. diarrhœa produced by s°, MW. **Śokânala**, m. = *śokâgni*, ib. **Śokânuśoka**, n. s° upon s°, continual sorrow, R. **Śokântara**, mfn. free from sorrow, BṛĀrUp. (*á-ś°*, ŚBr.) **Śokânvita**, mfn. filled with s°, MW. **Śokâpanuda**, mfn. removing or alleviating s°, Pāṇ. iii, 2, 5. **Śokâpanoda**, m. removal of s°, MW.; mfn. = °*kâpanuda*, Pāṇ. iii, 2, 5, Vārtt.; m. a remover of grief, teacher of wisdom, W. **Śokâpaha**, mfn. destroying or removing sorrow, Vop. **Śokâpahartṛi**, mfn. taking away or removing s°, W. **Śokâbhibhūta**, mfn. afflicted with s°, A. **Śokârāti-bhaya-trāṇa**, n. protection or a protector from s° and enemies and danger, Hit. **Śokâri**, m. 'sorrow-enemy,' Nauclea Cadamba, L. **Śokârta**, mfn. afflicted with s°, Hit. **Śokârti**, f. visitation or affliction by s°, Mālatīm. **Śokâvishṭa**, mfn. filled with s°, ib. **Śokâveśa**, m. a fit or paroxysm of s°, Śak. **Śokâika-maya**, mf(*ī*)n. consisting of s° only, MW. **Śokôtpādana**, mfn. causing sorrow, ib. **Śokôdbhava**, mfn. arising from s°, W. **Śokôn-mathita-cittâtman**, mfn. having the thoughts and mind agitated by sorrow, MBh. **Śokôpahata**, mfn. afflicted with sorrow, ib.

Śoca. See *a-śoca*.

Śocana, mfn., Pāṇ. iii, 2, 150; n. (L.) and (*ā*), f. (Hāsy.) grief, sorrow.

Śocanīya, mfn. lamentable, deplorable (n. impers. 'it should be lamented'), Kālid., Rājat. **-tā**, f. deplorableness, Kum.

Śocayat, mf(*antī*)n. (fr. Caus.) causing to burn or causing to grieve; (*śocáyantī*), f. pl. 'inflaming,' 'afflicting,' N. of the Apsarases of the Gandharva Kāma, TBr.

Śocayitṛi, m. a causer of grief or pain, ib.

Śocí, f. flame, glow, AV.; ĀpŚr.

Śocitavya, mfn. to be lamented or mourned (°*vye*, ind. 'when there is reason for lamentation or mourning'), deplorable, MBh.; R.; Pañcat.

Śocish, in comp. for *śocis*. **-keśa** (*śocish-*), mfn. 'flame-haired,' having flaming locks (applied to Agni and the sun), RV.; ŚBr.; m. fire, L. **-mat** (*śocish-*), mfn. flaming, shining, radiant, RV.

Śocishṭha, mfn. shining very much, most brilliant (said to be superl. of *śukra*), RV.

Śocis, n. flame, glow, radiance, light, RV.; AV.; Hariv.; colour, Kpr.; splendour, beauty, BhP.; mfn. shining, brilliant, ib.

Śocya, mfn. to be lamented (n. impers.), deplorable, miserable, MBh.; Kāv. &c.; *-tā*, f. deplorableness, miserable condition, Kathās.; = next, MW.

Śocyaka, m. a deplorable or miserable person, wretched man, L.

शोकी *śókī*, f. = *rātri*, night, Naigh. i, 7.

शोटीर्य *śoṭīrya*, n. = *śauṭīrya*, valour, heroism, L.

शोठ *śoṭha*. See p. 1081, col. 3.

शोढ *śoḍha*, w.r. for *soḍha*, Kathās.

शोण् *śoṇ* (rather Nom. fr. next), cl. 1. P. (Dhātup. xiii, 13) *śoṇati* (occurring only in pf. *śuśoṇa*), to be or become red, Hcar.; to go, move, approach, Dhātup.

Śóṇa, mf(*ā* or *ī*)n. red, crimson, purple, RV. &c. &c.; m. redness, BhP.; fire, L.; Bignonia Indica or a variety of it, L.; red sugar cane, L.; a chestnut or bay horse, L.; the river Śoṇa or Sone (also *ā*, f.; it rises in Gondwana in the district of Nagpore, on the table-land of Amara-kaṇṭaka, four or five miles east of the source of the Narmadā [Nerbudda], and running first northerly and then easterly for 500 miles falls into the Ganges above Pāṭali-putra or Patnā), MBh.; R. &c.; N. of a partic. ocean, L.; of a man, g. *naḍâdi*; of a prince of the Pañcālas, ŚBr.; (*ā*), f., see above; n. blood, L.; red-lead, L. **-karṇa**, mfn. having red ears, Kāṭh. **-jhiṇṭikā**, f. a kind of red-flowering Barleria Cristata, L. **-jhiṇṭī**, f. N. of two plants (= *kurabaka* and *kaṇṭakinī*), L. **-tā**, f. redness, Kathās. **-nada**, m. N. of a river, MW. **-pattra**, m. a kind of red-flowering hogweed, L. **-padma**, m. (Gīt.) or °**maka**, n. (L.) a red lotus. **-pura**, n. N. of a well-known town and place of pilgrimage. **-pushpaka**, m. Bauhinia Variegata, Bhpr. **-pushpī**, f. a kind of plant (= *sindūra-p°*), L. **-prastha**, v.l. for *śoṇā-pr°*. **-bhadra**, m. N. of a river, R. **-maṇi** (m.c.), f. a ruby, Sāh. **-ratna**, n. a red gem, ruby, L. **-vajra**, n. a kind of steel, L. **-śāli**, m. red rice, L. **-saṃgama**, m. 'Śoṇa-confluence,' N. of a celebrated place of pilgrimage, MW. **-sambhava**, n. the root of long pepper, L. **-haya**, mfn. having red horses (said of Droṇa), MBh. **Śoṇâdhara**, mf(*ā*)n. red-lipped, Bhām. **Śoṇā-prastha**, g. *mālâdi*. **Śoṇâmbu**, m. 'having crimson water,' N. of one of the seven clouds at the destruction of the world, Cat. **Śoṇâśman**, m. a red stone, ruby, Vcar. **Śoṇâśva**, mfn. = *śoṇa-haya*, MBh.; m. N. of a son of Rājâdhideva, Hariv. **Śoṇôttarā**, f. N. of a woman, Mudr. **Śoṇôpala**, m. a red stone, MW.; a ruby, Dharmaśarm.

Śoṇaka, m. Bignonia Indica, Bhpr.

Śoṇāka, m. id., VarBṛS.

Śoṇāya, Nom. Ā. °*yate*, to redden, become red, BhP. °**yita**, mfn. become red, ib.

Śoṇita, mfn. red, W.; n. (ifc. f. *ā*) blood (also pl.), GṛŚrS. &c. &c.; the sap of trees, resin, Suśr.; saffron, Bhpr. **-candana**, n. red sandal, L. **-tva**, n. the being blood, bloodiness, MBh. **-pa**, mfn. drinking bl°, W.; bl°-sucking, MW. **-pāraṇā**, f. a breakfast of bl°, Ragh. **-pitta**, n. hemorrhage, Suśr.; *-vat*, mfn. subject to h°, ib. **-pura**, n. N. of the city of the Asura Bāṇa, Hariv.; Pur. **-priyā**, f. N. of a goddess, Siṅhâs. **-bindu-varshin**, mfn. showering drops of blood, MW. **-māṇsa-sāra**, mfn. having blood and flesh for essence, VarBṛS. **-mehin**, mfn. discharging urine mixed with bl°, Suśr. **-varṇana**, n. description of the properties of blood; °*nīya*, mfn. relating to that subject, Suśr. **-varshin**, mfn. flowing with bl°, Rājat. **-śarkarā**, f. sugar of honey, L. **-sâhvaya**, mfn. named after bl°; (with *pura*), n. = *-pura*, Hariv. **-snāta**, mfn. bathed in bl°, MW. **Śoṇitâksha**, m. 'having blood-shot eyes,' N. of a Rākshasa, R. **Śoṇitâkhya**, mfn. = °*ta-sâhvaya*, BhP. **Śoṇitâdigdha**, mfn. blood-stained, MBh. **Śoṇitâbhishyanda**, m. congestion of bl°, Car. **Śoṇitâmaya**, m. a partic. disease of the bl°, L. **Śoṇitârbuda**, n. a bloody tumour, Suśr. **Śoṇitârśas**, n. 'bl°-pustules,' a partic. disease of the eyelid, Suśr.; °*śin*, mfn. suffering from the above disease, Uṇ. iv, 195, Sch. **Śoṇitâśin**, mfn. drinking blood (fig.), Veṇīs. **Śoṇitâhvaya**, n. 'having name of bl°,' saffron, L. **Śoṇitôkshita**, mfn. bl°-stained, MBh. **Śoṇitôtpala**, n. a red lotus, MW. **Śoṇitôtpādaka**, m. a spiller of blood, Mn. iv, 168. **Śoṇitôda**, m. N. of a Yaksha, MBh. **Śoṇitôpala**, m. 'blood-stone,' a ruby, L. **Śoṇitâugha**, m. a torrent of blood, MW.

Śoṇitin. See *vāta-ś°*.

Śoṇiman, m. redness, Kāv.; Kād.; BhP.

Śoṇī, f. N. of a town. **-pura-māhātmya**, n. N. of a ch. of the Padma-purāṇa.

Śoṇī-√kṛi, P. *-karoti*, to colour blood-red, Hcar.; Kād.

शोण्ड *śoṇḍa*, *śoṇḍī*, w.r. for *śauṇḍa*, °*ḍī*.

शोथ *śotha*, m. (ifc. f. *ā*; fr. √*śū* = *śvi*) a swelling, tumour, morbid intumescence, dropsy, Suśr. **-kṛit**, m. 'causing swellings (? w.r. for *-hṛit*),' Semecarpus Anacardium, L. **-ghnī**, f. 'removing tumours,' Bœrhavia Procumbens or Desmodium Gangeticum, L. **-jit**, m. id., Bœrhavia Procumbens, L. **-jihma**, m. hogweed, MW. **-roga**, m. 'swelling disease,' dropsy, Bhpr. **-śatra**, m. = *śothâri*, L. **-hṛit**, m. 'tumour-removing,' Semecarpus Anacardium, L. **Śothâri**, m. 'enemy of swellings,' Bœrhavia Procumbens, L.

Śothaka, m. = *śotha* above, L.

शोद्धव्य *śoddhavya*, mfn. (fut. p. p., see √*śudh*) to be cleansed or purified or corrected, MW.

Śodha, m. purification, cleansing, Vop.; correction, setting right, MW.; payment, ib.; retaliation, ib. **-pattra**, n. a sheet or paper of corrections (cf. *śuddhi-p°*), ib.

Śodhaka, mf(*ikā*)n. purificatory, m. a purifier, R.; corrective, MW.; (in arithm. or alg.) 'corrector,' the subtrahend, the quantity to be subtracted from a number (to render it capable of yielding an exact square root), Col.; (*ikā*), f. a red variety of Panicum Italicum, L.; n. a partic. kind of earth (= *kaṅkushṭha*), L.

Śodhana, mfn. cleaning, purifying, cleansing, refining, purgative, Mn.; MBh.; Suśr.; m. the citron tree, L.; Alangium Hexapetalum, L.; (*ī*), f., see below; (*am*), n. the act of cleaning, purifying, correcting, improving, Nir.; KātyŚr.; MBh. &c.; refining (as of metals for chemical or medicinal purposes), W.; a means of purification, Mn.; Suśr.; clearing up, sifting, investigation, examination, correction, Kām.; Hit.; Yājñ., Sch.; payment, acquittance, W.; justifying, exculpating, R.; expiation, MW.; retaliation, punishment, ib.; removal, eradication, Mn.; MBh. &c.; (in arithm.) subtraction, Bijag.; excrement, ordure, ib.; green vitriol, ib.

Śodhanaka, m. a kind of official or servant in a judge's court (charged with cleaning and keeping it in order), Mṛicch.

Śodhanī, f. a broom, brush, L.; the indigo plant or = *tāmra-vallī*, L. **-bīja**, n. the seed of Croton Jamalgota, L.

Śodhanīya, mfn. to be cleansed or purified, Kull.; to be discharged or paid, Kathās.; serving for purification, Suśr.; to be corrected, W.; to be subtracted, ib.; n. a means of cleansing or purifying, Suśr.

Śodhayitavya, mfn. (fr. Caus.) to be cleansed or purified, SaddhP.

Śodhayitṛi, mfn. (fr. id.) purifying, a purifier, L.

Śodhita, mfn. (fr. id.) cleansed, purified, refined, corrected &c.; removed, Kām.; justified, exculpated, Mn. viii, 202; discharged, liquidated (as a debt), W.

Śodhin, mfn. cleansing, purifying, Suśr.; requiting, settling, ib.

Śodhya, mfn. to be cleansed or purified or refined or corrected or improved, Mn.; Yājñ. &c.; to be discharged, payable, due, W.; to be subtracted, VarBṛS., Sch.; m. an accused person, one to be tried or cleared, W.; n. (in arith.) a constant number to be subtracted, ib.

शोनाय *śonāya*, *śonita*, incorrect for *śoṇāya*, °*ṇita*.

शोफ *śopha*, m. (connected with √*śvi*; ifc. f. *ā*; cf. *śotha*) intumescence, morbid swelling, tumour, Suśr.; Kathās. **-ghnī**, f. 'removing swellings,' Desmodium Gangeticum, L.; a Punar-navā with red flowers, L. **-nāśana**, m. id., a kind of plant (= *nīla*), L.; (*ī*), f. Bœrhavia Procumbens, L. **-hārin**, m. id., Ocimum Pilosum, L. **-hṛit**, m. id., Semecarpus Anacardium, L. **Śophâri**, m. 'enemy of swellings,' a kind of bulbous plant, L.

Śophita, mfn. afflicted with tumours or swellings, Bhadrab.

Śophin, mfn. having tumours, subject to swellings, id., Car.

शोभ *śobha*, mfn. (fr. √*śubh*) bright, brilliant, handsome, W.; m. N. of a man, Rājat.; (pl.) of a class of gods, L.; of a class of heretics, L.; lustre (in comp. for *śobhā*, q.v.) **-kṛit**, m. causing lustre, beautifying, W.; the 36th (or 37th) year of Jupiter's cycle of 60 years (cf. *śubha-kṛit*), VarBṛS.; w.r. for *śotha-kṛit*, L. **-jāta**, m. 'lustre-born,' N. of a prince, Buddh.

Śobhaka, mf(*ikā*)n. brilliant, beautiful, Naish.; m. N. of a man, Rājat.

Śobhátha, m. splendour, SV.

Śobhaná, mf(*ā* or *ī*)n. brilliant, splendid, beautiful (at end of comp. = 'beautiful by reason of'), ŚBr.; Kauś.; MBh. &c.; excellent, glorious, magnificent, distinguished in or by (instr. or comp.), MBh.; Kāv. &c.; (ifc.) superior to, better than, BhP.; propitious, auspicious, VarBṛS.; Rājat.; virtuous, moral (see comp.); correct, right, Sarvad.; m. N. of Agni at the Śuṅgā-karman, Gṛihyas.; of Śiva, MBh.; a burnt offering for auspicious results, W.; the fifth of the astron. Yogas, L.; a planet, L.; the eleventh year of Jupiter's cycle, MW.; (*ā*), f. a beautiful woman (often in voc.), MBh.; Kāv. &c.; turmeric, L.; the yellow pigment Go-rocanā, L.; N. of one of the Mātṛis attending on Skanda, MBh.; (*am*), n. the act of adorning, causing to look beautiful, MW.; an ornament (see *karṇa-ś°*); anything propitious or auspicious, welfare, prosperity, R.; Pur.; moral good, virtue, ib.; brilliance, MW.; a lotus, L.; tin, L.; (with *Kaśyapasya*) N. of a Sāman, ĀrshBr. **-vatī**, f. N. of a town, W. **-vāha**, mfn. having splendid carriers or horses, MW. **-vyūha** (?), m. N. of a scholar, Buddh. **Śobhanâcarita**, n. virtuous practice, ib.

Śobhanaka, m. Moringa Pterygosperma, L.

Śobhanika, m. a kind of actor (v. l. *śaubhika*), Pat. on Pāṇ. iii, 1, 26, Vārtt. 15.

Śobhanīya, mfn. to be beautified or adorned, MW.; beautiful, splendid, Kāraṇḍ.

Śobhayitṛi, mfn. adorning, beautifying, Nir.

Śobháse, Ved. inf. of √*śubh*, q. v.

Śobhā́, f. (ifc. f. *ā*) splendour, brilliance, lustre, beauty, grace, loveliness (*kā śobhā* with loc., 'what beauty is there [in that],' i.e. 'it has no beauty;' *śobhāṃ na* √*kṛi*, 'to look bad or ugly;' ifc. often = 'splendid,' 'excellent,' e.g. *śaurya-śobhā*, 'splendid heroism;' *karma-śobhā*, 'a masterpiece'), TS. &c. &c.; distinguished merit, W.; colour, hue, VarBṛS.; Mudr.; wish, desire, L.; a kind of metre, Col.; turmeric, L.; the yellow pigment Go-rocanā, L. **-kara**, mfn. causing lustre, beautifying, MBh.; *-bhaṭṭa* and *-mitra*, m. N. of two authors, Cat. **-°ñjana** or **°ñaka** (*śobhâñj°*), m. Moringa Pterygosperma (its leaves, flowers and root are edible and are used medicinally, = *śigru*, q.v.), MBh.; Suśr.; Bhpr. **-maya**, mf(*ī*)n. full of lustre or beauty, beautiful, MW. **-vatī**, f. a kind of metre, Col.; N. of a town (cf. *śobhana-vatī*), Kathās. **-siṇha**, m. N. of a king, Kshitīś.

Śobhāka, m. N. of a poet, Cat.

Śobhāya, Nom. Ā. °*yate*, to represent the beauty of anything, Nalac.

Śobhita, mfn. (mostly ifc.) splendid, beautiful, adorned or embellished by, MBh.; Kāv. &c.

Śobhin, mfn. brilliant, splendid, beautiful, MBh.; (ifc.) resplendent with, beautified by, MBh.; Kāv. &c. (also for *śobha* = *śobhā*; e.g. *anumeya-śobhin*, 'whose splendour may be inferred from,' Kum. i, 37).

Śóbhishṭha, mfn. most brilliant or splendid, RV.

Śobhuśubha or **śaubhuśubha**, mfn. shining intensely or repeatedly, Uṇādi-vṛ. 19.

Śośubhyamāna, mfn. (fr. Intens. of √*śubh*) shining very much, very brilliant, MBh.

शोम् *śom*, ind. an exclamation interposed in reciting sacred texts (cf. *śoṃs*, *śoṃsāmos*, *śośoṃsāvas*), TUp.

शोली *śolī*, f. yellow turmeric, L.

शोशुचत् *śóśucat*, mfn. (fr. Intens. of √*śuc*) shining very brightly, very splendid, RV.

Śóśucāna, mfn. id., ib.

Śośucyamāna, mfn. sorrowing intensely, grieving deeply, Bhaṭṭ.

शोशोंसावस् *śośoṃsāvas*. See √*śaṃs*, *śoṃs*.

शोष 1. *śosha*, mfn. (fr. √1. *śush*) drying up, desiccating (also fig. = 'removing, destroying'), BhP.; m the act of drying up, desiccation, dryness, MBh.; Suśr.; pulmonary consumption (also personified as an evil demon), Suśr.; VarBṛS.; Hcat.; (also w. r. for *śotha* or *śopha*.) **-sambhava**, m. the root of long pepper, L. **Śoshâpahā**, f. 'removing consumption,' a kind of plant (= *klītanaka*), L.

Śoshaka, mfn. drying up, absorbing, removing, destroying, BhP.

Śoshaṇa, mf(*ī*)n. drying up, draining, parching, withering Nir.; MBh.; Suśr.; (ifc.) removing, destroying, BhP.; m. N. of an Agni, Hariv.; of one of the arrows of Kāma-deva (god of love), Vet.; Gīt., Sch.; Bignonia Indica, L.; n. drying up (intr.), desiccation, MaitrUp.; VarBṛS.; making dry, draining, suction, MBh.; Pañcat.; Suśr.; dry ginger, L.

Śoshaṇīya, mfn. to be dried or sucked up or drained or absorbed, VarBṛS.

Śoshayitavya, mfn. to be dried up &c., MW.

Śoshayitṛi, m. one who dries up or parches, Sāy.

Śoshita, mfn. dried or sucked up, drained, desiccated, absorbed, exhausted, emptied, Hariv.; Kāv. &c. **-saras**, mfn. possessing dried-up ponds, drying up ponds (as summer), Pañcat.

Śoshin, mfn. drying up (intr.), wasting away, consumptive, Suśr.; VarBṛS.; (mostly ifc.) drying up (trans.), frying, desiccating, absorbing, exhausting, MBh.; R.; Suśr.; (*iṇī*), f. ether (one of the five Dhāraṇās), Cat.

Śoshu, m. drought, thirst, L.

Śoshya. See *a-śoshya*.

शोष 2. *śósha*, m. (fr. √*śū* = *śvi*; cf. *śūsha*) breath, vital energy, VS. (Mahīdh.)

शोष्यन्ती *śoshyantī*, (prob.) w.r. for *soshyantī*, ĀpGṛ.

शोस् *śos* (?), ind. a particle of reproach or contempt, L.

शौक *śauka*, n. (fr. *śuka*) a flight of parrots, g. *khaṇḍikâdi*; a kind of coitus, L.; sorrowfulness (perhaps w.r. for *śoka*), L.

Śauki, m. a patr., Pravar.

Śaukeya, m. patr. fr. *śuka*, g. *śubhrâdi*.

शौकर *śaukara*, °*rava*. See *sauk°*.

शौक्त 1. *śaukta*, mfn. (fr. *śukta*) acid, acetic, acetous, W.

1. **Śauktika**, mfn. id., ib.; relating to sour gruel, Car.

शौक्त 2. *śaukta*, mfn. (fr. *śukti*) made of mother-of-pearl, Hcat.; n. N. of various Sāmans, ĀrshBr.

2. **Śauktika**, mfn. relating to a pearl, W.; n. a pearl, L.

Śauktikeya, n. a pearl, L.

Śaukteya, mfn. relating to a pearl, W.; n. a pearl, L.

शौक्र *śaukra*, mf(*ī*)n. (fr. *śukra*) seminal, relating to semen or sperm &c., MW.; relating to the planet Venus, VarBṛS.; (*am*), n. (with *ahan*) Tuesday, Vishṇ.

Śaukrāyaṇa, m. patr. fr. *śukra* (also pl.), Saṃskārak.

Śaukri, mfn., g. *sutaṃgamâdi*.

Śaukreya, m. patr. fr. *śukra*, g. *śubhrâdi*; (pl.) N. of a warrior-tribe, Pāṇ. v, 3, 117; (sg.) a king of the Śaukreyas, ib. iv, 1, 178, Sch.

Śaukrya, n. (fr. *śukra*), g. *dṛiḍhâdi*.

शौक्ल *śaukla*, mfn. (fr. *śukla*) relating to what is clean or pure or undefiled (with *janman*, n. 'birth from pure or blameless parents'), BhP.; n. N. of a Sāman (w.r. for 2. *śaukta*).

Śauklya, n. whiteness, brightness, clearness, VarBṛS.; Vedântas.

शौक्लिकेय *śauklikeya*, m. a sort of poison, L. (prob. w.r. for *śaulkikeya*, q.v.)

शौङ्ग *śauṅga*, m. (patr. fr. *śuṅga*, Pāṇ. iv, 1, 117) N. of various men (pl. of a Gotra), ĀśvŚr.; Vās., Introd.; (*ā* and *ī*), f., see below.

Śauṅgāyani and **Śauṅgi**, m. patr. fr. *śuṅga*, Pāṇ. iv, 1, 117; 2, 138, &c.

Śauṅgī-pútra, m. N. of a teacher, ŚBr.

Śauṅgīya, mfn. (fr. *śauṅgi*), g. *gahâdi*.

Śauṅgeyá, m. (metron. fr. *śuṅgā*) N. of Garuḍa, Suparṇ.; a falcon or hawk, Daś.

Śauṅgya, m. patr. fr. *śuṅga*, Pravar.

शौच *śaucá*, m. (fr. *śuci*) N. of a man (also called Āhneya), TĀr.; n. cleanness, purity, purification (esp. from defilement caused by the death of a relation), ĀśvŚr.; Mn.; MBh. &c.; purity of mind, integrity, honesty (esp. in money-matters), MBh.; R. &c.; (with Buddhists) self-purification (both external and internal), MWB. 240; evacuation of excrement, MW. **-kalpa**, m. mode of purification, purificatory rite, ib. **-kūpa**, m. 'excretion-pit,' a privy, ib. **-tas**, n. by way of purification, Āpast. **-tva**, n. purity, Hit. (v. l.) **-vat**, mfn. clean, pure (lit. and fig.), Yājñ.; MBh. **-vidhi**, m. rule of purification (after defilement by the death of a relation), W. **-saṃgraha-vivṛiti**, f. N. of wk. **Śaucâcamana-vidhi**, m. N. of wk. **Śaucâcāra**, m. purificatory rite, mode of cleansing the person by ablution &c. (after voiding excrement or contracting any defilement), W.; *-paddhati*, f. N. of wk. **Śaucêpsu**, mfn. wishing or intending to obtain purification, MW.

Śaucaka, mfn. pure (in *a-ś°*), Hcat.; n. purity (in *a-ś°*), MBh.

Śaucakīya, n. N. of wk., Hcat.

Śaucika, m. a cleaner, cleanser, MW.; a partic. mixed caste (the son of a Śauṇḍika and a Kaivarta woman), ib.

Śaucikarṇika, mfn. (fr. *śuci-karṇa*), g. *kumudâdi*.

Śaucin, mfn. pure (in *a-ś°*), Kull. on Mn. v, 84.

Śaucivṛikshi, m. patr. fr. *śuci-vṛiksha*, Nidānas. (pl. °*kshās*, ib.; f. °*kshī* or °*kshyā*, Pāṇ. iv, 1, 81).

Śauceya, m. a washerman, L.; (°*yá*), m. a patr., TS.; ŚBr.

शौचद्रथ *śaucadrathá*, m. (fr. *śucad-ratha*) patr. of Su-nītha, RV.

शौचादिरेय *śaucādireya*, m. a patr., Nidānas.

शौट् *śauṭ* (also written *śauḍ*, prob. artificial), cl. 1. P. to be proud or haughty, Dhātup. ix, 1.

Śauṭa, m. (cf. *śauḍa*) N. of a country, Inscr.

Śauṭīra, mfn. haughty, arrogant, proud of (comp.), MBh.; R.; liberal, munificent, L.; m. a hero, L.; an ascetic (who has given up worldly pursuits), Uṇ. iv, 30, Sch.; n. pride, manliness, R. (perhaps w.r. for *śauṭīrya*). **-tā**, f. heroism (in *yuddha-ś°*), R.

Śauṭīrya, n. manliness, haughtiness; pride in (comp.), MBh.; Hariv.; R.

शौड् *śauḍ* = √*śauṭ*, q.v.

Śauḍa, m. (cf. *śauṭa*) N. of a country, Rājat.

Śauṇḍarya, n. = *śauṭīrya*, L.

Śauṇḍīra, mfn. (also written *śauṇḍira* and *śauḍīra*) proud, haughty, bold, arrogant, MBh.; R.; n. haughtiness, pride, BhP. **–tā**, f. id., MW.

Śauṇḍīrya, n. haughtiness, pride, MBh.; R.; Mṛicch.

शौण्ड śauṇḍa, mf(*ā* or *ī*)n. (fr. *śuṇḍā*) fond of spirituous liquor, addicted to drinking, MBh.; MārkP.; drunk, intoxicated, L.; (ifc.) passionately fond of or devoted to (*-tā*, f.), MBh.; R.&c.; skilled in, familiar with, BhP.; being the pride of, Bālar. x, ¼; m. a cock, L.; (*ā*), f. spirituous liquor (ifc. perhaps w.r. for *śuṇḍa*), R.; (*ī*), f. long pepper or Piper Chaba, Bhpr.; = *kaṭabhī* (a tree), L.; a line of clouds, L.

Śauṇḍaka. See *tṛiṇa-śauṇḍikā* and *mada-śauṇḍaka*.

Śauṇḍāyana, m. pl. N. of a warrior-tribe, g. *kuñjâdi*.

Śauṇḍāyanya, m. a king of the Śauṇḍāyanas, ib.

Śauṇḍi, mfn. fond of, devoted to, BhP. (B.)

Śauṇḍika, m. a distiller and vendor of spirituous liquors (considered as a mixed caste; accord. to some 'the son of a Kaivarta and a Gāndhika woman;' accord. to others 'the son of a Nishṭhya and a Śūdra woman'), Yājñ.; R.; VarBṛS.; pl. N. of a people, MBh. (C. *śauṇḍīka*); (*ī*), f. a female keeper of a liquor-shop (regarded as one of the eight Akulas, accord. to the Śāktas), MW. **Śauṇḍikâgāra**, m. n. a liquor-shop, Cat.

Śauṇḍikeya, m. N. of a demon hostile to children, PārGṛ.

Śauṇḍin, m. = *śauṇḍika*, L.; (*inī*), f. = *śauṇḍikī*, ŚārṅgP.

Śauṇḍīka. See *śauṇḍika*.

Śauṇḍeya, m. (only in pl.) a patr. or a metron., Saṃskārak.

शौण्ड्रिन् śauṇḍrin, m. N. of a man, Pravar. (perhaps w.r. for *śauṇḍin*).

शौद्धाक्षर śauddhākshara, mfn. (fr. *śuddha* + *akshara*) relating to a pure vowel (without consonant or Anusvāra), ṚPrāt.

शौद्धोदनि śauddhodani, m. (fr. *śuddhôdana*) patr. of Gautama Buddha, Buddh.

शौद्र śaúdra, mfn. relating or belonging to a Śūdra, ŚBr.; MBh.; m. the son of a man of either of the first three classes by a Śūdra woman (the last of the twelve kinds of sons acknowledged in the ancient Hindū law), Mn. ix, 160.

Śaudrāyaṇa, m. patr. fr. *śūdra*, g. *aishukāry-ādi*. **–bhakta**, mfn. inhabited by the Saudrāyaṇas, ib.

शौद्रकायण śaudrakāyaṇa, m. patr. fr. *śūdraka*, g. *aśvâdi*.

शौधिका śaudhikā, f., incorrect for *śodhikā* (see under *śodhaka*).

शौन śauna, mf(*ī*)n. (fr. *śvan*) relating or belonging to a dog, MBh.; w.r. for *sauna*, q.v.

Śaunaḥśepá, m. (fr. *śunaḥ-śepa*) patr. of Nicumpuṇa, Kāṭh., Anukr.; n. (scil. *ākhyāna*) the story of Śunaḥ-śepa, Br.; N. of various Sāmans, ĀrshBr.

Śaunaḥśepi, m. patr. fr. *śunaḥ-śepa*, ĀrshBr.

Śaunika, mfn. relating to dogs or hunting (see comp.); w.r. for *saunika*, q.v. **–śāstra**, n. N. of a wk. on dogs or hunting.

शौनक śaúnaka, m. (patr. fr. *śunaka*, g. *bidâdi*) N. of various authors and teachers (also with Indrôta and Svaidāyana; esp. of the celebrated grammarian, author of the Rig-veda Prātiśākhya, the Bṛihad-devatā, and various other wks.; he is described as the teacher of Kātyāyana and especially of Āśvalāyana; he is said to have united the Bāshkala and Śākala Śākhās, and is sometimes identified with the Vedic Ṛishi Gṛitsa-mada; but according to the Vishṇu-Purāṇa, Ś° was a son of Gṛitsamada, and originated the system of four castes; he is quoted in ĀśvŚr., APrāt. and VPrāt.; the various legends about him are very confused), ŚBr.; Up.; MBh. &c.; pl. the descendants and pupils of Ś°, Hariv.; (*ī*), f. a wk. of Ś° (cf. *laghu-* and *vṛiddha-śaunakī*). **–kalpa-sūtra**, n., **-kārikā**, f. pl., **-gṛihya-pariśishṭa**, n. and **-gṛihya-sūtra**, n., **-pañca-sūtra**, n. N. of wks. attributed to Śaunaka. **–yajña**, m. a kind of sacrifice, Vait. **–sūtra**, n., **-smṛiti**, f. N. of wks. **Śaunakâtharvaṇa-sūtra**, n., °**kâraṇyaka**, n., °**kôpanishad**, f. N. of wks.

Śaunakāyana, m. patr. fr. *śaunaka*, Pāṇ. iv, 1, 2.

Śaunaki, m. patr. fr. id., Siṇhâs.

Śaunakin, m. pl. the pupils or followers of Śaunaka, Pāṇ. iv, 3, 106.

Śaúnakī-pútra, m. N. of a teacher, ŚBr.

Śaunakīya, mfn. belonging to or composed by Śaunaka or the Śaunakīyas; n. a wk. of Ś° or the Śaunakīyas, Hcat. **–caturādhyāyikā**, f. 'Ś°'s treatise in four chapters,' N. of the Atharva-veda Prātiśākhya. **–caraṇa**, n. N. of a Caraṇa (q.v.) **–prayoga**, m., **-svarâshṭaka**, n. N. of wks.

शौनहोत्र śaunahotra (ĀśvŚr. &c.), °*hotri* (Hariv.), m. (fr. *śuna-hotra*) patr. of the Ṛishi Gṛitsa-mada.

शौनायन śaunāyana, m. (only pl.) a patr., Saṃskārak.

शौनासीर्य śaunāsīrya, mfn. (fr. *śunā-sīra*), Lāṭy.

शौभ śaubha, m. (fr. *śubha*) a god, divinity, L.; the Areca or betel-nut tree, L.; w.r. for *saubha*, q.v.

Śaubhāyana, m. (fr. id.) N. of a warrior-tribe, g. *kuñjâdi*.

Śaubhāyani, m. a patr. (fr. id.), g. *tikâdi*.

Śaubhāyanya, m. a king of the Śaubhāyanas, g. *kuñjâdi*.

शौभनेय śaubhaneya, m. (fr. *śobhanā*) the son of a handsome mother, Pāṇ. iv, 1, 113, Sch.; mfn. relating to anything handsome or brilliant, W.

शौभाञ्जन śaubhāñjana, m. = *śobhâñjana*, Hcar., Sch.

शौभिक śaubhika, m. (cf. *saubhika*) a kind of actor, Pat. (v.l. *śobhanika*); the sacrificial post at a Homa, L.

शौभ्रायण śaubhrāyaṇa, m. pl. (fr. *śubhra*) N. of a partic. association or company, g. *aishukāry-ādi*. **–bhakta**, mfn. inhabited by the Saubhrāyaṇas, ib.

Śaubhreya, mf(*ī*)n. relating or belonging to anything white or shining, MW.; m. patr. fr. *śubhra* or metron. fr. *śubhrā*, Pāṇ. iv, 1, 123; pl. N. of a warrior-tribe, g. *yaudheyâdi*; (sg.) a king of the Śaubhreyas, ib.; (*ī*), f. a princess of this tribe, ib.

Śaubhrya, m. patr. fr. *śubhra*, g. *kurv-ādi*.

शौर śaura, mf(*ī*)n. (fr. *śūra*; also as Vṛiddhi form in comp.) relating to a hero, heroic, MW. **–devyà**, m. patr. fr. *śūra-deva*, RV. viii, 70, 15. **–sena**, mf(*ī*)n. relating to the Śūra-senas, g. *palady-ādi*; (*ī*), f. (scil. *bhāshā*) the language of the Ś°s (a Prākṛit dialect supposed to have been spoken at Mathurā and sometimes substituted for Sanskṛit in the plays, esp. as representing the speech of women of high rank), Bhar.; Sāh. &c. **–senikā**, f. = *-senī*, MBh. **–senya**, mfn. (fr. *-sena*), g. *saṃkāśâdi*.

Śauri, m. patr. of Vasu-deva, MBh.; BhP.; of Vishṇu-Kṛishṇa (also among the names of the sun), ib.; of Prajāti, MārkP.; of Bala-deva, MW.; Terminalia Tomentosa, L. (v.l. *sauri*); the planet Saturn (w.r. for *sauri*). **–datta** and **-sūnu**, m. N. of two authors, Cat.

Śaúrya, n. heroism, valour, prowess, might, ŚBr. &c. &c.; the heroic branch of dramatic art (= *ārabhaṭī*), W.; N. of a village, Pat. on Pāṇ. ii, 4, 7, Vārtt. 2. **–karaṇa**, n. prowess, L. **–karman**, n. an heroic deed, Mn. ix, 268. **–nagara**, n. N. of a town, HPariś. **–rāśi**, m. a collection or aggregate (= paragon) of heroism, Veṇīs. **–vat**, mfn. heroic, courageous, valiant, Kāv.; VarBṛS.; Kathās. **–vardhana**, mfn. strengthening or increasing h°, BhP. **–vrata**, n. a partic. observance, Cat. **–sāgara**, m. 'ocean of h°,' a collection (= paragon) of h°, Veṇīs. **Śauryâdi-mat**, mfn. endowed with h° and other virtues, Sāh. **Śauryônmādin**, mfn. 'intoxicated by h°,' foolhardy, Daś. **Śauryôpārjita**, mfn. acquired by heroism, W. **Śauryâudarya-śṛiṅgāra-maya**, mf(*ī*)n. composed of heroism and generosity and love, Kathās.

शौरण śauraṇa. See *sauraṇa*.

शौर्प śaurpa, mf(*ī*)n. (fr. *śūrpa*) belonging to or measured by a winnowing basket, Pāṇ. v, 1, 26.

Śaurpaṇāyya, m. (fr. *śūrpa-ṇāya*, g. *kurv-ādi*) N. of a teacher, ŚBr.

Śaurpika, mfn. = *śaurpa* above, Pāṇ. v, 1, 26.

शौल śaula, m. (fr. *śūla*) a partic. part of a plough, Kṛishis.

शौलायन śaulāyana, m. (only pl.) a patr., Saṃskārak.

शौलिक śaulika, m. pl. N. of a people, VarBṛS. (v.l. *śūlika*, *sūlika*, *maulika*).

शौल्क śaulka, mf(*ī*)n. (fr. *śulka*) relating to tolls or customs or taxes, levied (as a tax &c.), W.; m. a superintendent of tolls or customs, custom-house officer, ib.; n. N. of various Sāmans, ĀrshBr.

Śaulkaśālika, mf(*ī*)n. (fr. *śulka-śālā*) belonging to or derived from a custom-house, Pāṇ. iv, 3, 50; 75, Sch.

Śaulkāyani, m. patr. of a teacher, Pur.

Śaulkika, mfn. relating to taxes or tolls, Pat. on Pāṇ. iv, 1, 104, Vārtt. 13; eating fish and flesh, L.; m. a superintendent of tolls or customs, Yājñ.

शौल्किकेय śaulkikeya, m. (fr. *śulkikā*) a kind of poison (said to be produced in a country called Śulkikā; accord. to some 'the venom of a kind of snake'), L. (v.l. *śauklikeya*).

शौल्फ śaulpha, n. Anethum Sowa, L.

शौल्ब śaulba, mfn. (fr. *śulba*), ĀpŚr., Sch.

Śaulbāyaná, m. patr. fr. *śulba*, TS.; ŚBr.

Śaulbika, m. a coppersmith, L.

शौव 1. śauva, mf(*ī*)n. (fr. *śvan*) relating or belonging to dogs, doggish, canine, Pāṇ., Sch.; Vop.; m. N. of a partic. Udgītha, MW.; n. a multitude or pack of dogs, g. *khaṇḍikâdi*; the nature or state of a dog, MW.

Śauvadaṇshṭra, v.l. for *śauvādaṇshṭra*.

Śauvana, mfn. relating or belonging to a dog, canine, Pāṇ., Sch.; Vop.; n. a pack of dogs, g. *khaṇḍikâdi*; the nature of a dog, MW.; the progeny of a dog, ib.

Śauvani, mfn. (fr. *śvan*), g. *sutaṃgamâdi*.

Śauvaneya, m. patr. fr. *śvan*, g. *śubhrâdi*.

Śauvahāna, n. (fr. *śva-hāna*) N. of a town, Pāṇ. vii, 3, 8, Vārtt. 1, Pat.

Śauvādaṇshṭra, mfn. (fr. *śvā-daṇshṭrā*), ib.

Śauvāpada, mfn. (fr. *śvā-pada*) relating to or coming from a wild beast, ferocious, savage, wild, Anarghar.

Śauvāvatāna, °*nika*, (prob.) w.r. for *saudhāv*°.

Śauvāvidha, mfn. (fr. *śvā-vidh*), Pat.

शौव 2. śauva, mfn. (fr. 2. *śvas*) relating to the morrow, occurring to-morrow, L.

Śauvastika, mf(*ī*)n. of or belonging to the morrow, lasting till to-morrow, ephemeral, Pāṇ. iv, 3, 15. **–tva**, n. the lasting or enduring till to-morrow, ephemeralness, Bhaṭṭ.

शौषिर śaushira. See *saushira*.

शौष्कल śaúshkala, mfn. (fr. *śushkala*) living on dried flesh or fish or by selling it (accord. to some catching fish), VS.; m. N. of the chief priest of Rāvaṇa, Anarghar.

Śaushkula, v.l. for prec.

शौष्कास्य śaushkāsya, n. (fr. *śushkâsya*) dryness of the mouth, AV.

श्चन्द् ścand (cf. √*cand*), only in Intens. p. *cániścadat*, 'shining brilliantly,' RV.

Ścandra, mfn. shining, radiant (only ifc.; see *aśva-ścandra*, *puru-ścandrá*, *viśvá-ścandra*, *su-ścandrá*, *śvá-ścandra*, and *hári-ścandra*).

श्चम् ścam (prob. to be connected with √*śam* rather than with √*cam*), only in *ścamnan*, 'they may quench or appease,' RV. i, 104, 2.

श्चर् ścar (for *car*) in *upa-*√*ścar*, to come near, approach (only in *upâścarat*), MaitrS.

श्चुत् 1. ścut (often in later language written *ścyut*; cf. √*cyut*), cl. 1. P.

(Dhātup. iii, 4) *ścótati* (pf. *cuścota*, Br.; aor. *aścotīt* or *aścutat*, Gr.; fut. *ścotitā*, *ścotishyati*, ib.), to ooze, trickle, exude, drop, distil, RV.; Br.; BhP.; Bhaṭṭ.; to shed, pour out, sprinkle, Kāv.; Kathās.: Caus. *ścotayati* (aor. *-acuścutat*, inf. *-ścotayitavai*; cf. *abhi-* and *ā-√ścut*), to cause to drop or flow, shed, ŚBr.: Desid. *cuścotishati*, Pāṇ. vii, 4, 61, Sch.

2. **Ścut** (ifc.) distilling, sprinkling, shedding (ifc. see *ghṛita-*, *madhu-ścut* &c.)

Ścutita, mfn. oozed, exuded, sprinkled, shed, Br. &c. &c.

Ścota, m. oozing, sprinkling, aspersion, L.

Ścotana, n. the act of oozing or flowing, exudation (see *pra-śc°*).

Ścotan-mayūkha, mfn. (pr. p. of *√ścut + m°*) diffusing light, MW.

Ścoti, f. id., L.

श्च्युत् *ścyut*. See *√ścut*, p. 1093, col. 3.

श्नथ् *śnath*, cl. 1. P. (Dhātup. xix, 37) *śnathati* (only occurring in pr. Subj. *śnathat*, Impv. *śnathihi*, and aor. *śnathishṭam*, *°ṭana*; Gr. also pf. *śaśnātha*; fut. *śnathitā*, *°thishyati* &c.), to pierce, strike, injure, kill, RV.: Caus. *śnatháyati*, *°te* (aor. *aśiśnat*, *śiśnáthat*), id., ib.: Desid. *śiśnathishati*, Gr.: Intens. *śāśnathyate*, *śāśnatti*, ib.

Śnáthana, mfn. piercing, transfixing, RV.

Śnathitá, mfn. pierced, transfixed, ib.

Śnáthitṛi, m. a piercer, killer, slayer, ib.

श्नप्त्र *śnáptra* (VS.) or *śnyáptra* (TS.), n. the corner of the mouth (Mahīdh.)

श्नम् *śnam*, (in gram.) a technical term for the verbal affix *na* (inserted in roots of the 7th class).

श्ना *śnā*, (in gram.) a technical term for the affix *nā* (the characteristic sign of the 9th class of verbs).

श्नाभाश्नौष्टीय *śnābhāśnaushṭīya*, n. du. N. of two Sāmans (cf. *śnaushṭa* below), ĀrshBr.

श्नु *śnu*, (in gram.) a technical term for the affix *nu* (added to the root in the 5th class of verbs).

श्नुष्टि *śnushṭi*, f. (prob.) either 'a little heap' or 'a small measure' (for measuring grain), Kāṭh.; m. N. of an Āṅgirasa, PañcavBr.

Śnaushṭa, n. (fr. prec.) N. of various Sāmans (cf. *śnabhāśnaushṭīya* above), ArshBr.

Śnaushṭī-gava, n. N. of a Sāman, ib.

श्न्यप्त्र *śnyáptra*. See *śnáptra* above.

श्मन् *śman*, n. the body, Nir.; the mouth, L. (both meanings prob. invented to explain *śmaśāna* and *śmaśru*). **Śma-śayana**, n. (a compound artificially formed to explain *śmaśāna*) place of repose for dead bodies or the bones of burnt corpses, cemetery, Nir. iii, 5.

Śmaśá (a word invented to serve as the source of *śmaśāna*).

Śmaśā́, f. (prob. connected with *aśman*) the elevated ridge or edge of a trench or ditch or channel for water or of a vessel, RV. x, 105, 1 (but in ŚBr. the m. pl. *śmaśā́ḥ* is said to mean those deceased ancestors who consume or eat the oblations [?], and a comp. *śmaśānná* is formed to explain *śmaśāna*).

Śmaśāna, n. (accord. to Kir. iii, 5 for *śma-śayana* above; but prob. for *aśma-śayana*) an elevated place for burning dead bodies, crematorium, cemetery or burial-place for the bones of cremated corpses, AV. &c. &c.; an oblation to deceased ancestors (=*pitṛi-medha*, see above), PārGṛ.; KātyŚr., Sch.; = *brahma-randhra*. **—karaṇá**, n. the laying out of a burning-ground, ShaḍvBr. **—kālikā**, f. a form of Durgā, Cat. **—kālī**, f. id., ib.; *-kavaca*, n., *-mantra*, m. N. of wks. **—gocara**, mfn. frequenting burning-grounds, going about in places for burning the dead, Mn. x, 39. **—cit**, mfn. piled up like a pyre or a b°-gr° (*a-śmaśāna-cit*, 'not piled up like a pyre,' MaitrS.; *á-śmaśāna-cit*, 'not piling up a pyre,' TS.), TS.; MaitrS.; Śulbas. **—nilaya**, mfn. dwelling in b°-gr°s (Śiva), Śivag. **—nivāsin**, mfn. dwelling in b°-gr°s, a ghost, spectre, MW. **—pati**, m. (prob.) N. of a magician, Buddh. **—pāla**, m. a guardian of a b°-gr°, Kathās. **—bhāj**, m. 'inhabiting b°-gr°s,' N. of Śiva, MW. **—bhairavī**, f. a form of Durgā, Cat. **—vartin**, mfn. abiding in b°-gr°s, a ghost, spectre, MW. **—vāṭa**, m. the enclosure of a b°-gr°, Mālatīm. **—vāsin**, mfn. dwelling in b°-gr°s, L.; m. N. of Śiva, L.; (*inī*), f. N. of Kālī, L. **—vīthī**, f. a row of trees in a cemetery, Mṛicch. **—vetāla**, m. N. of a gambler, Kathās. **—veśman**, m. 'inhabiting b°-gr°s,' N. of Śiva, L.; a ghost, W. **—vairāgya**, n. momentary abandonment of worldly desires at the sight of a b°-gr°, ib. **—śūla**, m. n. a stake used for impaling criminals in a b°-gr°, Kum. **—sādhana**, n. magical rites performed in a b°-gr° to obtain control over evil spirits, MW.; N. of wk. **—sumanas**, n. a flower from a b°-gr°, Mṛicch. **Śmaśānâgni**, m. the fire of a b°-gr°, MW. **Śmaśānâlaya**, m. a place for burning the dead, a b°-gr°; *-vāsin*, mfn. inhabiting b°-gr°s (N. of Śiva), Śivag.; (*inī*), f. N. of Kālī, Tantras.

Śmaśānika, mfn. (prob. w. r. for *śmāś°*) abiding in burning-grounds (as a bird), Car.

Śmāśānika, mfn. frequenting burning-grounds, Buddh.; =*śmaśāne 'dhīte*, Pāṇ. iv, 4, 71, Sch.

श्मशारु *śmaśāru*= next in *hári-śm°*, q.v.

श्मश्रु *śmáśru*, n. (of unknown derivation, but cf. *śman*); the beard, (esp.) moustache, the hairs of the beard (pl.), RV. &c. &c. [Cf. Lith. *smakrà*; accord. to some also Lat. *maxilla*.] **—kara**, m. 'beard-maker,' 'b°-cutter,' a barber, VarBṛS. **—karman**, n. 'b°-cutting,' shaving, MārkP. **—jāta**, mfn. one whose b° has grown (=*jāta-śmaśru*), g. *āhitâgny-ādi*. **—dhara**, mfn. wearing a beard, bearded, BhP.; pl. N. of a people, VarBṛS. **—dhārin**, mfn. wearing a beard, MBh.; pl. N. of a people, MārkP. **—pravṛiddhi**, f. the growth of a beard, Ragh. **—mukhī**, f. 'a beard-faced woman,' w° with a b°, L. **—yajñôpavītin**, mfn. wearing a b° and invested with the sacred thread, Hcat. **—vat**, mfn. having a b°, bearded, GopBr. **—vardhaka**, m. 'b°-cutter,' a barber, R. **—śekhara**, m. the cocoa-nut tree, L.

Śmaśruṇá, mfn. bearded (as a goat), TS.; Kāṭh.; ĀpŚr.

Śmaśrula, mfn. having a beard, bearded, Mn.; MBh. &c.

Śmaśrūya, Nom. Ā. *°yate* (only pr. p. *°yamāṇa*), to appear as if bearded, look like a beard, Śiś.

श्मसि *śmasi*, in RV. ii, 31, 6. See *√vaś*.

श्मील् *śmīl* (also written *smīl*; cf. *√mīl*), cl. 1. P. *śmīlati*, to wink, twinkle, Dhātup. xv, 12.

Śmīla, n. winking, blinking, twinkling, W.

Śmīlita, mfn. winked, blinked, W.; n. a wink, blink, winking, ib.

श्मे *śme*, ind. (used as an abbreviation) for *pārthuraśme* (q.v.)

श्मेत्र *śmetra*, m.=*śvetra*, L.

श्यन् *śyan*, (in gram.) a technical term for the syllable *ya* (inserted after the root in the 4th class of verbs).

श्यान *śyāna*. See under *√śyai*, p. 1095.

श्यापर्ण *śyā́parṇa*, m. (cf. g. *bidâdi*) N. of a man (pl. his family), MaitrS.; Br.

Śyāparṇīya, mfn. relating or belonging to the Śyāparṇas, AitBr.

Śyāparṇeya, m. (also pl.) patr. fr. *śyāparṇa*, g. *kārta-kaujapâdi*.

श्यापीय *śyāpīya* (?), m. pl. N. of a school.

श्याम *śyāmá*, mf(*ā*)n. (said to be connected with *√śyai*) black, dark-coloured, dark blue or brown or grey or green, sable, having a dark or swarthy complexion (considered a mark of beauty), AV. &c. &c.; m. black or blue or green (the colour), L.; a cloud, L.; the Kokila or Indian cuckoo, L.; a black bull, TS.; ĀśvŚr.; N. of various plants (fragrant grass; thorn-apple; Artemisia Indica; Careya Arborea &c.), L.; (in music) a partic. Rāga, Saṃgīt.; N. of a son of Śūra and brother of Vasudeva, Hariv.; VP.; of a modern prince, Cat.; of a mountain, MBh.; of a sacred fig-tree at Prayāga or Allahābād, R.; Ragh.; Uttarar.; pl. N. of a Vedic school (a subdivision of the Maitrāyaṇīyas); (*ā*), f. a woman with peculiar marks or characteristics (accord. to some 'a girl who has the marks of puberty;' accord. to others 'a woman who has not borne children;' also described as 'a female of slender shape' &c.), Śiś.; Siṉhâs.; a N. or form of Durgā (worshipped by the Tāntrikas), W.; N. of Yamunā, L.; of a daughter of Meru (an incarnation of Gaṅgā), BhP.; of a princess, Vāś., Introd.; of another woman, MBh.; of a goddess who executes the commands of the 6th Arhat or of the mother of the 13th Arhat (with Jainas); a kind of bird (either 'the female of the Indian cuckoo' or 'a hen-sparrow'), VarBṛS.; Pañcat.; N. of various plants (=*gundrā*, *priyaṅgu*, *sārivā* &c.), R.; Suśr.; night (see *śyāmā-cara*); the earth, Gal.; N. of a river, MārkP.; n. black pepper, L.; sea-salt, L. **—kaṅgu**, m. black Panic, L. **—kaṇṭha**, m. 'black-throated,' a peacock, L.; a kind of small bird, W.; N. of Śiva, ib. **—kandā**, f. Aconitum Ferox, L. **—karṇa**, mfn. black-eared, BhP.; m. a horse suitable for a horse-sacrifice, MW. **—kāṇḍā** or **-granthi**, f. a kind of Dūrvā grass, L. **—caṭaka**, m. a kind of sparrow, L. **—jit**, m. N. of a man, Cat. **—tā**, f. (MBh.; MārkP.; Kād.) or **-tva**, n. (MBh.; R.) blackness, dark colour. **—dāsa**, m. N. of various men, Cat. **—deva**, m. a proper N., MW. **—pattra**, m. Xanthochymus Pictorius, L. **—phena**, mfn. having black foam or froth (*-tā*, f.), Kām. **—bhaṭṭa**, m. N. of a man, Cat. **—bhās**, mfn. of a brilliant black, glossy bl°, W. **—mukha**, mfn. bl°-faced (as a cloud), Kāv.; having bl° nipples, Kathās. **—ruci**, mfn. = *-bhās*, A. **—latā**, f. a kind of climbing plant (=*sārivā* or Echites Frutescens, L.), Kālid. **—varṇa**, mfn. dark-coloured (*-tva*, n.), Kām. **—vallī**, f. black pepper, L. **—vrata**, n. a partic. ceremony, Hāl., Sch. **—śabalá**, m. du. 'bl° and spotted,' Yama's two watch-dogs (regarded as sons of Saramā, cf. RV. x, 14, 10–12), TS. (RTL. 283, 289, 329, 422). **—śiṉśapā**, f. Dalbergia Sissoo, L. **—sāra**, m. a kind of Acacia Catechu, L. **—sāh śaṃkara** (with preceding *mahā-rāja*), m. N. of a king and author, Cat. **—sundara**, m. 'dark and beautiful,' N. of Kṛishṇa, MW.; (also with *cakra-vartin*) N. of various men, Cat. **Śyāmâṅga**, mfn. black-bodied, W.; m. the planet Mercury, L.; N. of Buddha, L.; (*ī*), f. N. of Bāhu-dā (q.v.), L. **Śyāmâcārya**, m. N. of a man, Cat. **Śyāmâmlī**, f. a kind of shrub, L. **Śyāmâruṇa**, mfn. dark-red, VarBṛS.; Śiś. **Śyāmârya**, m. N. of a Jaina saint, Cat. **Śyāmâvadāta**, mf(*ā*)n. dazzling black or blackish white, R.; BhP. **Śyāmêkshu**, m. a kind of sugar-cane, L.

Śyāmaka, mfn. dark-coloured, dark, VarBṛS.; m. Panicum Frumentaceum (a kind of cultivated millet), L.; a gramineous plant, MW.; N. of a man, g. *bidâdi*; of a brother of Vasu-deva, BhP.; a patr., g. *bidâdi* (pl., g. *gopa-vanâdi*); pl. N. of a people, MārkP.; (*ikā*), f. blackness, Kum.; Kād.; Hcar.; impurity, Ragh.; Kād.; Hcar.; a white-spotted blackish deer, L.; n. a kind of grass, L.

Śyāmala, mf(*ā*)n. dark-coloured, Hariv.; Kāv. &c.; m. black (the colour), W.; a kind of bee, L.; Terminalia Arjuna, PañcavBr., Sch.; a species of plant serving as a substitute for the Soma pl° (=*pūtīka*), KātyŚr., Sch.; the sacred fig-tree, L.; black pepper, W.; N. of a poet, Sadukt.; Kshem.; of another man, Vāś., Introd.; (*ā*), f. N. of various plants (Physalis Flexuosa; =*kaṭa-ohī*; =*kastūrī*; =*jambū*), L.; a form of Durgā, L.; N. of a woman, Buddh. **—cūḍā**, f. a kind of shrub (=*guñjā*), MW. **—tā**, f. (Naish.) or **-tva**, n. (Sarvad.) blackness, dark colour. **—devī**, f. N. of a princess, Inscr. **Śyāmalâṅgī**, f. N. of a woman, Virac. **Śyāmalêkshu**, m. a sort of sugar-cane, L.

Śyāmalaka, mfn. dark-coloured, dark (as N. of the 14th unknown quantity), Col.; m. N. of a man, Pañcat.; Dhanaṃj.; (*ikā*), f. the indigo plant, L. **—cūḍa**, f. Abrus Precatorius, L.

Śyāmalā, f. (of *śyāmala*) in comp. **—gītā**, f. N. of a Stotra. **—daṇḍaka**, m., **-nava-ratna**, n., **-mantra-sādhana**, n., **-°mbā-stotra** (*°lâmb°*), n., **-rahasya**, n., **-°shṭaka** (*°lâshṭ°*), n., **-sahasra-nāman**, n. N. of wks.

Śyāmalita, mfn. darkened, obscured, Hariv.; Prab.; Kād.

Śyāmaliman, m. blackness, darkness, Kpr.; Vcar.; Śiś.

Śyāmalī, in comp. for *śyāmala*. **—√kṛi**, P. *-karoti*, to darken, obscure, Prab.; Kathās.

Śyāmā, f. (of *śyāma*) in comp. **—kalpa-latā**, f., **-kalpa-latikā**, f., **-kavaca**, n. N. of wks. **—cara**, m. 'night-goer,' a Rakshas, Bālar. **—cāra-tantra**, n., **-tāpany-upanishad**, f., **-dīpa-dāna**,

n. N. of wks. **-devī**, f. N. of a princess, Hcar. **-nitya-pūjā-paddhati**, f., **-paddhati**, f. N. of wks. **-pūjā**, f. the worship of Śyāmā or Durgā (on the new moon of the month Kārttika), W.; *-paddhati*, f. N. of wk. **-prakaraṇa**, n., **-pradīpa**, m., **-prayoga-vidhi**, m., **-mantra**, m. pl., **-mānasârcana**, n., **-ratna**, n., **-rahasya**, n. N. of wks. **-ruta**, n. the song of the bird Śyāmā, Cat. **-°rcana-candrikā** (°*mâr*°), f. N. of wk. **-latā**, f. (prob.) = *śyāma-l*°, VarBṛS. **-vatī**, f. N. of a woman, Divyâv. **-saparyā-krama**, m., **-saparyā-vidhi**, m., **-sahasra-nāman**, n., **-stotra**, n. N. of wks.

Śyāmāka, m. a kind of cultivated millet (Panicum Frumentaceum; pl. grains of it), VS. &c. &c.; N. of a man, Divyâv.; pl. N. of a people, VarBṛS.; (°*māká*), mf(*ī*)n. made of Pan° Frum°, TS.; ŚrS.; MBh.; m. a patr., g. *vidâdi; gopa-vanâdi* (pl.) **-taṇḍulá**, m. a grain of Panicum Frum°, ŚBr. **-mushṭim-paca**, mfn. cooking (a mere) handful of millet i. e. living very frugally, Bālar. **Śyāmākâgrayaṇa**, n. the firstlings of millet, °*ṇêshṭi*, f. an oblation of the firstlings of millet, KātyŚr. Paddh. **Śyāmākêshṭi**, f. an oblation of millet, ĀpŚr.; KātyŚr. Paddh. **Śyāmākâudana**, m. rice with millet, KātyŚr.

Śyāmāya, Nom. Ā. °*māyate*, to assume a dark colour (°*māyita*, mfn. become dark), Kāv.; Sāh.

Śyāmāyana, m. a patr., g. *aśvâdi*; N. of a son of Viśvā-mitra, MBh.

Śyāmāyani, m. patr. of a teacher, Cat.

Śyāmāyanin, m. pl. N. of a school, Pāṇ. iv, 3, 104, Sch.

Śyāmāyanīya, m. pl. N. of a school of the Black Yajus, Hcat.; Caraṇ.

Śyāmita, mfn. blackened, darkened, Kir.

Śyāmī, in comp. for *śyāma*. **-√kṛi**, P. *-karoti*, to darken, Kāv. **-√bhū**, P. *-bhavati*, to become dark-coloured, Kir.; Naish.; Hcar.

Śyāmeya, m. a patr., g. *śubhrâdi*.

Śyāvá, mf(*ā́*)n. (connected with *śyāma*) dark-brown, brown, dark-coloured, dark, RV.; AV.; Br. &c.; drawn by brown or bay horses (said of chariots, Ved.), MW.; pungent and sweet and sour, L.; m. a brown horse, RV.; brown (the colour), W.; a partic. disease of the outer ear, Suśr.; pungent and sweet and sour taste, L.; N. of a man, RV.; pl. the horses of the Sun, Naigh.; (*ī*), f. a brown or bay mare, RV.; night, ib. (Naigh. i, 7); (*śyā́va*) m. N. of a man, RV. **-tā**, f. brownness, Suśr.; ŚārṅgS. **-taila**, m. the mango-tree, L. **-da** (w.r.) = next, Āpast. **-dat** (*śyāvá-*, AV.; TS.; TBr. &c.) or **-danta** (Kāṭh.; MārkP.; *-tā*, f. Mn.; Suśr.), or **-dantaka** (Mn.; Yājñ.; Suśr.; ŚārṅgS.), mfn. having dark or discoloured teeth (accord. to some 'having a little tooth growing over the two front teeth'). **-nāya**, m. N. of a man, g. *kurv-ādi*. **-nāyīya**, mfn., g. *utkarâdi*. **-nāyya**, m. patr. fr. *-nāya*, g. *kurv-ādi*. **-putra**, m. N. of a man, g. *kurv-adi*; °*trya*, m. patr. fr. it, ib. **-ratha**, m. N. of a man, ib.; °*thya*, m. patr. fr. that N., ib. **-vartman**, n. a partic. disease of the eyelid, Suśr.; ŚārṅgS. **Śyāvâksha**, mfn. brown-eyed, VarBṛS. **Śyāvâśva**, mfn. having brown horses, AV.; ŚāṅkhŚr.; TĀr.; m. N. of a Vedic Ṛishi (having the patr. Ātreya; he was the supposed author of various hymns in the 5th, 8th, and 9th Maṇḍalas; °*vâśvasya prahitau*, N. of two Sāmans), RV.; AV. &c.; n. the story of Śyāvâśva, ŚāṅkhŚr.; N. of various Sāmans, SV.; Br.; Lāṭy.; (°*vâśvá*)*-stuta*, mfn. praised by Śyāvâśva, RV.; °*vâśvi*, m. patr. of the Vedic Ṛishi Andhīgu, RAnukr. **Śyāvâsya**, mfn. brown-faced (*-tā*, f., Suśr.), PārGṛ.

Śyāvaka, mfn. brown, dark-coloured, MW.; m. N. of a man, RV.; pl. the horses of the Sun, MW.

Śyāvaya, Nom. P. *śyāvayati*, to embrown, make brown, Car.

Śyāvala, m. patr. fr. next, g. *vidâdi*.

Śyāvali, m. N. of a man, ib.

Śyāvyā́, f. (prob.) darkness, RV. vi, 15, 17.

श्याल *śyāla*. See *syāla*.

श्याव *śyāva*. See above.

श्येत *śyetá*, mf(*śyénī* or *śyetā*)n. (prob. connected with *śveta*, q.v.) reddish white, white, AV.; ŚBr.; ŚrS.; m. white (the colour), L.; (*śyenī*), f. a white cow (see *śyaineya*); a woman with a lily-white complexion (= *kumuda-pattrâbhā*), L. **-kolaka**, m. the Saphara fish, Cyprinus Saphore (commonly called Punṭi), L. **Śyetâkshá**, mf(*ī*)n. having reddish-white eyes, VS.; ŚBr.; Kāṭh.

Śyetī-√kṛi, Ā. *-kurute*, to master, overcome, TS.; TBr. (Sch.)

Śyená, m. a hawk, falcon, eagle, any bird of prey (esp. the eagle that brings down Soma to man), RV. &c. &c.; firewood laid in the shape of an eagle, Śulbas.; a kind of array (in battle), MBh.; Kām.; a partic. part of the sacrificial victim, Kauś.; a partic. Ekâha, ShaḍvBr.; KātyŚr.; a horse, L.; N. of a Ṛishi (having the patr. Āgneya and author of RV. x, 188), Anukr.; (with or without *Indrasya*) N. of a Sāman, ĀrshBr.; Lāṭy.; (*ā*), f. a female hawk, L.; (*ī*), f. a female hawk, L.; N. of a daughter of Kaśyapa (regarded as the mother of hawks), MBh.; Hariv.; Pur.; a kind of metre, Piṅg.; mfn. eagle-like, AitBr.; coming from an eagle (as 'eagle's flesh'), Kṛishṇaj. (prob. w. r. for *śyaina*). **-kapotīya**, mfn. (the story) of the hawk and the pigeon (cf. *śibi*), MBh. **-karaṇa**, n. 'acting like a hawk,' acting with precipitation, W.; burning on a separate funeral pile, ib. **-gāmin**, m. 'flying like a hawk,' N. of a Rākshasa, R. **-ghaṇṭā**, f. a kind of plant, L. **-cit**, mfn. piled in the shape of a hawk, Śulbas. **-jīvin**, m. a hawk-feeder, falconer, W. **-cita**, mfn. = prec.; m. a partic. Agni, MBh. **-citra**, m. N. of a man, ib. **-jit**, m. N. of a man, ib.; (*-jid*)*-ākhyāna*, n. 'hawk-story,' N. of an episode in the Mahā-bhārata. **-jīvin**, m. one who lives by selling or training h°s, a falconer, Mn. iii, 164. **-jūta** (*śyená-*), mfn. swift as an eagle, RV. **-pattrá**, n. an eagle's feather, ŚBr.; KātyŚr. **-patvan** (*śyená-*), mfn. 'flying by means of eagles,' borne or drawn along by eagles, RV. **-pāta**, m. an eagle's flight (a favourite feat of jugglers), Daś. (cf. Pāṇ. vi, 3, 71); mfn. flying along like an eagle, MBh. **-bṛihat**, m. N. of a Sāman (cf. *-vṛishaka*). **-bhṛita**, mfn. brought by the eagle (Soma), RV. **-yāga**, m. a kind of sacrifice, Col. **-vṛishaka**, n. N. of a Sāman, ĀrshBr. **-hṛita** (*śyená-*), mfn. brought by the eagle (Soma or some similar plant), ŚBr.; KātyŚr. **Śyenâkhya**, m. Ardea Sibirica, L. **Śyenâbhṛita**, mfn. = *śyena-bhṛita*, RV. **Śyenâvapātam**, ind. swooping down like an eagle or hawk, Prab. **Śyenâśva-śyena** or **-śyaina**, n. N. of a Sāman, ĀrshBr. **Śyenâhṛita**, m. = *śyena-hṛita*, L. **Śyenôpadeśa**, m. injunction to women to burn on a separate funeral pile (cf. *śyena-karaṇa*), W.

Śyenikā, f. a female hawk or eagle (said to be a N. of two metres), Piṅg., Sch.; Ked.

Śyenī. See *śyeta* and *śyena* above.

Śyaitá, m. (also pl.), a patr., AV.; ĀśvŚr.; n. N. of a Sāman, ĀrshBr.

Śyaina, mfn. coming from a hawk &c. (see *śyena*).

Śyainampāta, mf(*ā*)n. (fr. *śyena-pāta*) any place fit for the flying of hawks (= *śyena-pāto 'syām vartate*; with *mṛigayā*, f. 'hawking, hunting with hawks'), Pāṇ. iv, 2, 58, Sch.

Śyainika, mfn. relating or belonging to the Ekâha Śyena, PañcavBr., Sch.

Śyaineyá, mfn. (fr. *śyenī*) descended from a white cow, MaitrS.; metron. of Jaṭāyu, Mcar.

श्यै *śyai*, cl. 1. P. *śyāyati*, to cause to congeal or freeze, ŚBr.; (Ā.) *śyāyate* (Gr. also pf. *śaśye*; aor. *aśyāsta*; fut. *śyātā*, *śyāsyate*), to go, move, Dhātup. xxii, 67: Pass. *śīyate*, to congeal, freeze, be cold, TS.; TBr.: Caus. *śyāpayati*, Gr.: Desid. *śiśyāsate*, ib.: Intens. *śāśyāyate*, *śāśyeti*, *śāśyāti*, ib.

Śīta. See p. 1077, col. 3.

Śīna. See p. 1078, col. 2.

Śyāna, mfn. shrunk, become dry (see below); viscous, sticky, adhesive (as clarified butter), W.; coagulated, congealed, W.; gone, ib. [Cf. accord. to some, Lith. *szénas*; Slav. *sěno*.] **-pulina**, mfn. having dry sandbanks (as a river in the hot season), Bhartṛ.

श्योणाक *śyoṇāka* or *śyonāka*, m. Bignonia Indica, Car.; Suśr.; VarBṛS.

श्रंश *śraṅś*, *śraṅs*, w.r. for √*sraṅs*.

श्रङ्क् *śraṅk* (also written *ślaṅk*, *sraṅk*), cl. 1. Ā. *śraṅkate* &c., to go, move, creep, Dhātup. iv, 9-11.

श्रङ्ग् *śraṅg* (also written *ślaṅg*, *śvaṅg*, *svaṅg*), cl. 1. P. *śraṅgati* &c., to go, move, Dhātup. v, 43-45.

श्रण् *śraṇ* (only in *vi-√śraṇ*, q. v.), cl. 1. P. (Dhātup. xix, 36) *śraṇati*, or cl. 10. P. (xxxii, 42) *śrāṇayati* (aor. *aśiśraṇat* or *aśaśrāṇat*, Siddh.; Vop.), to give, grant, present.

श्रत् *śrát* or श्रद् *śrád*, ind. (accord. to Naigh. iii, 10 = *satya*, 'truth, faithfulness;' prob. allied to Lat. *credo* for *cred-do*; *cor*, *cord-is*; Gk. *καρδία*, *κραδίη*, Eng. 'heart;' only in comp. with √*kṛi* and *dāna* and √*dhā* and its derivations, see below).

Śrat-√kṛi, P. *-karoti*, to make secure, guarantee, RV. viii, 75, 2 (cf. Pāṇ. v, 4, 57, Sch.)

Śrad-dádhāna, mfn. having faith, trustful, believing, RV. &c. &c. **-tā**, f. belief, faith, Mn. vii, 86. **-vat**, mfn. trustful, believing, VP.

Śrad-dāna, n. faith, belief, faithfulness, Sarvad.

Śrad-dha, mfn. having faith, believing in, trusting, faithful, having confidence, Kāṭh.; TS.; (*ā*), f., see below; n. = *śraddhā*, W.

Śrad-dhayat (?), mfn. = *śrad-dadhāna*, MuṇḍUp.

Śrad-dhayita, mfn. trustful, believing in (gen.), Divyâv.

Śrad-√dhā, P. Ā. *-dadhāti*, *-dhatte* (pr. p. *śraddadhat*, *śrad-dádhāna*; Ved. inf. *śraddhé*, cf. *śrát* above), to have faith or faithfulness, have belief or confidence, believe, be true or trustful (with *na*, 'to disbelieve' &c.), RV. &c. &c.; to credit, think anything true (two acc.), MBh.; Kāv. &c.; to believe or have faith in or be true to (with dat., and in later language with gen. of thing or person, or with loc. of thing), RV. &c. &c.; to expect anything (acc.) from (abl.), MBh.; to consent, assent to, approve, welcome (with acc.; with *na*, 'to disapprove'), Kathās.; to be desirous of (acc.), wish to (inf.), ib.; BhP.: Caus. *-dhāpayati*, to make faithful, render trustful, inspire confidence, RV. x, 151, 5.

Śraddhā́, f. faith, trust, confidence, trustfulness, faithfulness, belief in (loc. or comp.; *śraddhayā* √*gam*, 'to believe in,' with gen., Divyâv.), trust, confidence, loyalty (Faith or Faithfulness is often personified and in RV. x, 151 invoked as a deity; in TBr. she is the daughter of Prajā-pati, and in ŚBr. of the Sun; in MBh. she is the daughter of Daksha and wife of Dharma; in MārkP. she is the mother of Kāma, and in BhP. the daughter of Kardama and wife of Aṅgiras or Manu), RV. &c. &c.; wish, desire (*śraddhayā*, ind. 'willingly, gladly'), longing for (loc., acc. with *prati*, inf., or comp.), MBh.; Kāv. &c.; desire of eating, appetite, Suśr.; the longing of a pregnant woman, Car.; curiosity (*śraddhām ākhyāhi nas tāvat*, 'just satisfy our curiosity and tell us'), Kathās.; purity, L.; respect, reverence, W.; calmness or composure of mind, MW.; intimacy, ib.; a term for the fem. nouns in *ā*, Kāt.; (with *Kāmāyanī*) N. of the authoress of RV. x, 151 (cf. above); du. (with *Prajā-pateḥ*) N. of two Sāmans, ĀrshBr. **-kṛita**, mfn. done with faith or faithfulness, W. **-jāḍya**, n. blind or obstinate adherence to one's f°, MW. **-deya**, n. trust, confidence, Divyâv.; also w.r. for next. **-deva** (*śraddhā́-*), mfn. trusting in the deity, faithful, believing, TS.; Br.; ChUp. (cf. *śrāddha-d*°). **-°nusārin** (*śraddhân*°), m. 'a follower or observer of faith,' one who acts faithfully, a Śrāvaka at a partic. stage of his religious life, Divyâv. **-°nvita** (*śraddhânv*°), mfn. endowed with f°, believing, W. **-prakaraṇa**, n., **-balâdhāna**, n. N. of wks. **-manas** (*śraddhā́-*), mfn. true-hearted, faithful, RV. **-manasyā́**, ind. (instr.) faithfully, RV. **-maya**, mf(*ī*)n. full of faith, believing, Bhag. **-yukta**, mfn. having f°, believing, W. **-rahita**, mfn. deprived of faith, disbelieving, ib. **-vat**, mfn. = *-yukta*, Bhag.; MārkP.; consenting, assenting, Kathās.; (*vatī*), f. N. of a mythical town on mount Meru, BhP., Sch. **-vitta** (*śraddhā-*), mfn. possessed of faith or belief, faithful, believing, ŚBr. **-vimukta**, m. 'released from faith,' a Śrāvaka at a partic. stage of his religious life, Divyâv. **-virahita**, mfn. = *-rahita*, MW. **-samanvita**, mfn. = *śraddhânvita*, ib. **Śraddhêndriya**, mfn. the faculty of believing, Lalit.

Śraddhātavya, n. (impers.) it should be believed, MBh.

Śraddhātṛi, mfn. one who has belief or is faithful, MW.

Śraddhāpana, n. (fr. Caus. of *śrad-√dhā*) a means of inspiring faith or belief, Jātakam.

Śraddhālu, mfn. disposed to believe or trust, faithful, trustful, Śaṃk.; BhP.; (ifc.) vehemently longing for, Rājat.; f. a pregnant woman who longs for anything, L.

Śráddhita, mfn. believed, trusted in or relied on (n. impers., with dat.), RV. i, 104, 6; consented to, approved, BhP.; gladly accepted, welcomed, ib.; trustful, believing, confident, ib.

Śraddhin, mfn. faithful, trustful, believing, MBh.

Śraddhivá, mfn. to be believed, credible, RV. i, 125, 4.

Śraddhéya, mfn. to be trusted, trustworthy, faithful, AV. &c. &c. (*tadā-tva-mātra-śr°*, one who believes only in the present time, Hariv. 11,180, v.l. *°tre śr°*). **–tā,** f. (Jātakam.), **-tva,** n. (Pañcat.) credibility, trustworthiness.

श्रथ् *śrath* or *śranth* (cf. *√ślath*), cl. 9. P. (Dhātup. xxxi, 39) *śrathnāti* (Ved. also *śrathnīte* and *śrinthati*, and accord. to Dhātup. also *śrathati, śrāthayati, śranthati, °te*; pf. *śaśrātha* or *śaśrantha*, Gr.; 3. sg. *-śaśrathe*, RV.; 3. pl. *śrethuḥ* or *śaśranthuḥ*, Gr.; aor. *aśranthīt, °thishṭa*, ib.; fut. *śranthishyati*, ib.; inf. *śrathitum* or *śranthitum*, ib.; ind. p. *śrathitvā* or *śranthitvā*, ib.; *-śrathya*, Nir.), to be loosened or untied or unbent, become loose or slack, yield, give way, RV. (cf. Pāṇ. iii, 1, 89, Sch.); to make slack, disable, disarm, RV. i, 171, 3; (Ā.) to loosen one's own (bonds &c.), AV.; v.l. for *grath, granth*: Caus. *śratháyati, °te* (in Saṃhitāp. also *śrathāyati* and accord. to Gr. also *śrāthayati* and *śranthayati* [cf. below]; aor. *aśiśrathat* [3. sg. Subj. *śiśrathat* and 3. pl. Impv. *śiśrathantu*, RV.] or *aśaśranthat*), to loosen, untie, unbend, slacken, relax (Ā. 'to become loose, yield'), RV.; AitBr.; to remit, pardon (sin), RV.; (*śrāthayati*), to strive eagerly, endeavour, use exertion, Dhātup. xxxii, 13; to delight, gladden, ib.; (*śranthayati*), to bind, tie, connect, arrange, Dhātup. xxxiv, 31; to hurt, kill, ib.

Śratha. See *hima-śratha.*

Śrathana, n. (only L.) the act of untying, loosening; destroying, killing; tying, binding, connecting; making effort, exertion; delighting.

Śratharya, Nom. P. *°yáti*, to become loose or relaxed, RV.

Śrathāya. See Caus. of *√śrath.*

Śrantha, m. (only L.) loosening, looseness; tying, binding, stringing together; N. of Vishṇu.

Śranthana, n. (only L.; cf. also *hima-śr°*) the act of loosening, untying, relaxing &c.; tying, binding, stringing together (flowers &c.); composing (a book); killing, destroying.

Śranthita, mfn. (only L.) loosened, let loose &c. (see *√śrath*).

श्रद्धा *śraddhā, śrad-dadhāna* &c. See p. 1095, col. 3.

श्रप *śrapa, śrapaṇa* &c. See p. 1097, col. 3.

श्रम् 1. *śram*, cl. 4. P. (Dhātup. xxvi, 95) *śrāmyati* (in later language also *śramati, te*; pf. *śaśrama*, 3. pl. *śaśramuḥ* or [ŚāṅkhBr.] *śremuḥ*, p. *śaśramāṇá*, RV.; MBh.; aor. *áśramat*, AV., Subj. *śramat*, RV.; *śramishma*, ib.; Br.; fut. *śramitā*, MBh.; *śramishyati*, Gr.; inf. *śramitum*, ib.; ind. p. *-śrámya*, Br.), to be or become weary or tired, be tired of doing anything (with inf.; also impers. *ná mā śramat*, 'may I not become weary!'), RV. &c. &c.; to make effort, exert one's self (esp. in performing acts of austerity), labour in vain, ib.: Pass. *śramyate* (aor. *aśrāmi*, Gr.), MBh.; Kāv. &c. (cf. *vi-√śram*): Caus. *śrāmayati* (aor. *aśiśramat*), to make weary, fatigue, tire, Kām.; Hariv.; Subh.; to overcome, conquer, subdue, R.; (*śrāmayati*), to speak to, address, invite (*āmantraṇe*), Dhātup. xxxv, 40 (v.l. for *grām°*, cf. *grāmaya*): Desid., see *vi-śiśramishu.*

Śráma, m. (ifc. f. *ā*) fatigue, weariness, exhaustion, RV. &c. &c.; exertion, labour, toil, exercise, effort either bodily or mental, hard work of any kind (as in performing acts of bodily mortification, religious exercises and austerity; *śramaṃ √kṛi*, 'to work hard at one's studies'), pains or trouble bestowed on (loc. or comp.), AV. &c. &c.; military exercise, drill, W.; N. of a son of Āpa, Hariv.; of a son of Vasu-deva, BhP. **–kara,** mfn. causing fatigue or trouble, Subh. **–karśita** or **-karshita,** mfn. worn out with fatigue, MBh. **–klānta,** mfn. exhausted with f°, Śak. **–khinna,** mfn. distressed by f°, R. **–ghna,** mfn. dispelling f°, Suśr.; (*ī*), f. the fruit of Cucurbita Lagenaria, L. **–cchid,** mfn. destroying f°, Ragh. **–jala,** n. 'toil water,' perspiration, Daś.; Śiś. **–nud,** mfn. removing f°, Ragh. **–pīḍita,** mfn. distressed with f°, MBh. **–mohita,** mfn. bewildered or stupefied by fatigue, ib. **–vat,** mfn. one who has exerted himself or worked hard, Cat. **–vāri,** n. (= *-jala*); *-bindu*, m., *-leśa*, m. a drop of perspiration, Kāv. **–vinayana,** mfn. dispelling f° (in *adhva-śr°-v°*), Megh. **–vinoda,** m. the act of dispelling f°, VarBṛS. **–śīkara,** m. = *-jala*, Git. **–saṃtāpa-karshita,** mfn. worn out by fatigue and pain, MBh. **–sādhya,** mfn. to be accomplished by exertion, MW. **–siddha,** mfn. accomplished by exertion or labour, ib. **–sthāna,** n. a place for work or exercise, workshop, drilling-place, L. **Śramâdhāyin**(?), mfn. causing pain or trouble, Rājat. **Śramâpanayana,** n. dispelling fatigue (in *ati-śr°*), Śak. **Śramâmbu,** n. = *śrama-jala*, Uttarar. **Śramâyukta,** mfn. worn out with fatigue, R. **Śramârta,** mfn. oppressed by fatigue, wearied, Mn. viii, 67.

Śramaṇá, mf(*ā* or *ī*)n. making effort or exertion, toiling, labouring, (esp.) following a toilsome or menial business, W.; base, vile, bad, ib.; naked, L.; m. one who performs acts of mortification or austerity, an ascetic, monk, devotee, religious mendicant, ŚBr. &c. &c.; a Buddhist monk or mendicant (also applied to Buddha himself, cf. MWB. 23 &c.; also applied to a Jain ascetic now commonly called Yati), MBh.; R. &c.; N. of a serpent-demon, Buddh.; (*ā* or *ī*), a female mendicant or nun, L.; a hard-working woman, L.; (*ā*), f. a handsome woman, L.; = *śabarī-bhid, māṅsī, muṇḍīrī*, L.; n. toil, labour, exertion, ŚāṅkhŚr. **–datta,** m. N. of a man, HParis. **–śākya-putrīya,** m. a disciple of Buddha, Divyâv. **Śramaṇâcārya,** m. a Buddhist or Jain teacher, Hcar. **Śramaṇôddeśa,** m. (and *ikā*, f.) a male or female disciple of a Śramaṇa, Divyâv.

Śramaṇaka, m. (and *ikā*, f.) a Buddhist or Jain ascetic, Mṛicch.; Daś.

Śramaṇāya, Nom. Ā. *°yate*, to be or become a Śramaṇa or monk or ascetic, Hit.

Śramayú, mfn. toiling, exerting one's self, RV.

Śramin, mfn. (only L.; cf. Pāṇ. iii, 2, 141) making great efforts; undergoing fatigue or weariness.

Śrāntá, mfn. wearied, fatigued, tired, exhausted (*śrānta-klānta*, mfn. 'wearied and exhausted'), pained, distressed, RV. &c. &c.; hungry, L.; calmed, tranquil (= *śānta*), L.; m. N. of a son of Āpa, VP.; n. fatigue, exertion, self-mortification, religious austerity (or its fruit), RV.; TS.; AitBr.; KātyŚr. **–citta** (Cāṇ.), **-manas** (Śak.), mfn. wearied or distressed in mind. **–saṃvāhana,** n. soothing a weary person (by rubbing or shampooing his limbs), relieving or tending the wearied, W. **–sád,** mfn. lying down wearied, AV. **–hṛidaya,** mfn. = *-citta*, R. **Śrāntâgata,** mfn. one who has arrived weary, L.

Śrāma, m. a temporary shed (= *maṇḍapa*), L.; a month, L.; time, L.; w. r. for *śrama*, R.

Śrāmaṇa, n. (fr. *śramaṇa*), g. *yuvâdi*; (*ī*), f. N. of a plant, L.

Śrāmaṇaka, m. or n. (fr. id.) N. of a partic. contrivance for kindling fire, Gaut.; Baudh.; Vas. (v. l. *śrāvaṇaka*).

Śrāmaṇera, m. (among Buddhists) a pupil or disciple admitted to the first degree of monkhood, a novice, Buddh., MWB. 77.

Śrāmaṇeraka, m. id., Divyâv.

Śrāmaṇya, n. religious austerity or mendicancy, HParis.

श्रम् 2. *śram*, ind., g. *svar-ādi.*

श्रम्भ् *śrambh* (also written *srambh*; generally found with the prefix *vi*; see *vi-√śrambh*, and cf. also *ni-śrimbhá, pra-śrabdhi*), cl. 1. Ā. *śrambhate* (Gr. also pf. *śaśrambhe*, fut. *śrambhitā* &c.), to be careless or negligent, Dhātup. x, 33; to trust, confide, xviii, 18.

श्रय *śraya*, m. (fr. *√1. śri*; cf. *ā-śraya, pari-śr°, bhadra-śr°, uc-chraya*) approaching for protection, asylum, refuge, protection, W.

1. **Śrayaṇa,** n. the act of going to or approaching (esp. for protection), recourse to (comp.), asylum, refuge, protection, shelter, BhP.

Śrayaṇīya or **śrayitavya,** mfn. to be had recourse to, to be depended on, MW.; to be sheltered or protected, ib.

Śrayin. See *ā-śrayin* and *saṃ-śrayin.*

1. **Śrāyá,** mfn. possessing anything, furnished or provided with (loc.), RV. v, 53, 4; m. refuge, reliance, shelter, protection, W.; a house, dwelling, abode (cf. *uc-chrāya*), Bhaṭṭ.

Śrāyat, mfn. having recourse to (acc.), RV. viii, 99, 3 (Nir. vi, 8).

Śrāyantīya, n. (fr. prec.) N. of a Sāman, Br.; ĀśvŚr.

श्रयण 2. *śrayaṇa*, n. (fr. *√śri*) mixing up, mixture, KātyŚr.

श्रव 1. *śravá*, mfn. (*√1. śru*) sounding, VS.; m. hearing (*āt*, 'from hearsay,' *e*, with gen., 'within hearing of'), MBh.; Hariv.; the ear, VarBṛS.; Kathās.; the hypotenuse of a triangle, Sūryas.

2. **Śrava,** in comp. for 1. *śravas.* **–eshá,** m. desire of praising, RV.

1. **Śrávaṇa,** n. the act of hearing (also 'that which is heard' = *śruti*, q.v.; *iti śravaṇāt*, 'because it is so heard or revealed' i. e. 'according to a Vedic text'), ŚBr.; Mn.; MBh. &c.; acquiring knowledge by hearing, learning, study (cf. *a-śravaṇāt*), Kām.; Sarvad.; (in phil.) the determining by means of the six signs the true doctrine of the Vedânta (in regard to the only really existing Being), Vedântas.; fame, reputation, ĀśvŚr.; Nir.; wealth, MW.; m. (rarely n.) the ear, MaitrUp.; MBh. &c.; m. (= *śramaṇa*) a Buddhist or Jain monk (cf. *śrāvaka*), HParis.; the hypotenuse of a triangle or the diagonal of a tetragon &c., Gol.; (*ā*), f. a female monk or nun or ascetic, HParis. **–kātaratā,** f. anxiety for hearing, Śak. **–gocara,** m. range of hearing, Kathās.; mfn. being within h° (*-tā*, f.), Vīrac. **–patha,** m. the region of the ears (see comp.); the ear-passage, auditory p°, ear, Śiś.; range of hearing (see comp.); *-gata*, mfn. reaching to the ear-passage or ears, Bhartṛ.; *-paryanta-gamana*, n. reaching to the limit of hearing, Gīt.; *°âtithi*, m. coming to (lit. 'being a guest of') the ears of any one (*°thi-tvam √i*, with gen., 'to come to the ears of,' 'be heard by'), Ratnâv. **–parusha,** mfn. hard or cruel to the ear, hard to be listened to, Megh. **–pāli,** f. the tip of the ear, Gīt. **–pāśa,** m. a beautiful ear, A. (cf. Gaṇar. on Pāṇ. ii, 1, 66). **–puṭaka,** m. the auditory passage, L. **–pūraka,** m. 'ear-filler,' an earring or other ornament for the ear, Śiś. **–prāghuṇika,** m. coming to any one's ears, Naish., Sch.; *°ṇikī-kṛita*, mfn. brought to any one's (gen.) ears, Naish. **–bhūshaṇa,** n. 'ear-ornament,' N. of wk. **–bhṛita,** mfn. brought to any one's ears, spoken of, BhP. **–maya,** mf(*ī*)n. consisting of ears, being nothing but ears, Dharmaśarm. **–mūla,** n. the root of the ear, Kathās. **–ruj,** f. ear-ache, disease of the ear, VarBṛS. **–vidāraṇa,** mfn. ear-rending (said of speech), Mudr. **–vidhi,** m. a method or rule of hearing or studying; *-vicāra*, m. N. of a treatise on the study of the Upanishads. **–vishaya,** m. = *-gocara*, Megh.; *-prâpin*, mfn. reaching the range of the ear, Ragh. **–vyādhi,** m. = *-ruj*, VarBṛS. **–śīrshikā,** f. Sphæranthus Mollis, L. **–sukha** (Śiś.) or **-subhaga** (Megh.), mfn. pleasant to the ear. **–hārin,** mfn. charming the ear, Vās. **Śravaṇâdhikārin,** m. 'ear-ruler,' a speaker, addresser, W. **Śravaṇânanda,** m., *°ndinī*, f. N. of wks. **Śravaṇâvabhāsa,** m. range of hearing, Buddh. **Śravaṇâhvayā,** f. a kind of plant, Suśr. **Śravaṇêndriya,** n. 'organ or sense of hearing,' the ear, W. **Śravaṇôtpala,** n. 'ear-lotus,' a lotus fastened in the ear (as an ornament), MW. **Śravaṇôdara,** n. 'ear-hollow,' the auditory passage, ear, Śiś. **Śravaṇôdyāpana,** n. N. of wk.

Śravaṇaka, m. = *śramaṇaka*, a Buddhist or Jain ascetic, HParis.

Śravaṇas (?), mfn. accompanying a song, Saṃgīt.

Śravaṇasya, m. a proper N., MW.

Śravaṇīya, mfn. to be heard, worth hearing, ShaḍvBr.; MBh. &c.; to be celebrated, praiseworthy, MW. **–pāra,** m. N. of one of the eight Sthānas (q.v.) of the Ṛig-veda.

1. Śrávas, n. sound, shout, loud praise, RV.; VS.; BhP.; glory, fame, renown, RV.; AV.; BhP.; the ear, L.; m. N. of a son of Santa, MBh. [Cf. Gk. κλέος for κλεϝος.] **—kāma** (*śrávas-*), mfn. desirous of praise, RV.

1. Śravasya, Nom. P. °*yáti* (only pr. p. °*yát*), to wish to praise, RV. i, 128, 1.

2. Śravasyà, n. fame, glory, renown, RV.; a glorious deed, ib.

1. Śravasyú, mfn. willing to praise or celebrate, RV.

Śravā́yya, mfn. to be praised or celebrated, praiseworthy, notorious, RV.; m. an animal fit for sacrifice, Uṇ. iii, 96, Sch.

Śravishṭha, mfn. most famous, MW.; born or produced under the Nakshatra Śravishṭhā, Pāṇ. iv, 3, 34; m. N. of a man, g. *aśvādi;* (*ā*), f., see below.

Śravishṭhaka, m. N. of a man, Cat.

Śravishṭhā, f. pl. (in later language also sg. and du.) N. of the 24th (or 21st or 22nd) Nakshatra (also called Dhanishṭhā and regarded as having the shape of a drum), AV.; TS.; TBr.; Sūryas.; of a daughter of Citraka, Hariv.; of a d° of Rājâdhideva, ib.; of a d° of Paippalādi, ib. **—ja** or **-bhū**, m. 'son of Śravishṭhā,' N. of the planet Mercury, L. **—ramaṇa**, m. 'lover of Śravishṭhā,' N. of the moon, L.

Śravishṭhīya, mf(*ā*)n. relating or belonging to the Nakshatra Śravishṭhā, ŚāṅkhGṛ.

Śravo, in comp. for 1. *śravas.* **—jit**, mfn. winning renown, glorious, RV.

Śravya, mfn. audible, to be heard, worth hearing, praiseworthy, MBh.; Kāv. &c. **—tva**, n. praiseworthiness, Sāh.

Śrāva, m. hearing, listening, MW.; N. of a son of Yuvanāśva (and father of Śrāvastaka), MBh.

Śrāvaka, mf(*ikā*)n. hearing, listening to (comp.), Vās.; audible from afar, Śiś.; m. a pupil, disciple, Mālatīm.; a disciple of the Buddha (the disciples of the Hīna-yāna school are sometimes so called in contradistinction to the disciples of the Mahā-yāna school; properly only those who heard the law from the Buddha's own lips have the name *śrāvaka*, and of these two, viz. Sāriputta and Moggallāna, were Agra-śrāvakas, 'chief disciples,' while eighty, including Kāśyapa, Upāli, and Ānanda, were Mahā-śrāvakas or 'great disciples'), MWB. 47, 75; a Jaina disciple (regarded by orthodox Hindūs as a heretic), MW.; a crow, L.; a sound audible from afar, Śiś.; that faculty of the voice which makes a sound audible to a distance, L.; (*ikā*), f., see below. **—kṛitya**, n. N. of wk. **—tva**, n. the state or condition of a Śrāvaka, HYog. **—yāna**, n. the vehicle of the Śr° (cf. under *yāna*), Dharmas. 3. **—vrata**, n. N. of a Jaina treatise. **Śrāvakânushṭhāna-vidhi**, m., **Śrāvakârâdhana**, n. N. of Jaina wks.

1. Śrāvaṇa, mfn. relating to or perceived by the ear, audible, MārkP. (cf. Pāṇ. ii, 2, 92, Sch.); taught or enjoined in the Veda (cf. *srauta*), MBh. iii, 100, 75; m. a heretic, L.; N. of a Muni, Cat.; (*ā* and *ī*), f. N. of various plants, Suśr.; n. causing to be heard, announcing, proclaiming, MBh.; Pañcat.; knowledge derived from hearing, MW. **—tva**, n. audibleness, Tarkas.

1. Śrāvaṇikā. See *mahā-śr°.*

Śrāvaṇīya, mfn. (fr. Caus.) to be caused to be heard, to be read, MārkP.; to be heard, audible, MBh.

Śrāvayat (pr. p. of id.), in comp. **—pati** (°*yát-*), mfn. making the lord famous, RV. **—sakhi** (°*yát-*), mfn. making the friend famous, ib.

Śrāvayitavya, mfn. (fr. id.) to be caused to be heard, to be communicated, VarBṛS.; to be caused to hear, to be apprized or informed, Śak.

Śrāvikā, f. a female Śrāvaka (see above; two female disciples of the Buddha were called *Agra-śrāvikā*, 'chief female disciples'), Śatr.; MWB. 48. **—tva**, n. the state or condition of a Śrāvikā (cf. *śrāvaka-tva*), HPariś.

Śrāvitá, mfn. (fr. Caus. of √1. *śru*) caused to be heard, announced, proclaimed, communicated, Hariv.; R.; BhP.; called, named, R.; taught, informed of (acc.), Yājñ.; MBh. &c.; n. (in ritual) call, cry, exclamation, ŚBr.

Śrāvitṛi, m. one who hears, a hearer, MBh.

Śrāvin, mfn. hearing, a hearer, Sarvad.

Śrāvishṭha, mf(*ī*)n. relating or belonging to the Nakshatra Śravishṭhā, L.

Śrāvishṭhāyana, m. patr. fr. *śravishṭha* (also pl., Pravar.), g. *aśvādi.*

Śrāvishṭhīya, mfn. born under the Nakshatra Śravishṭhā, Pāṇ. iv, 3, 34, Vārtt. 3, Pat.

Śrāvya, mfn. audible, to be heard, worth hearing, R.; Kathās.; Sāh.; to be announced or proclaimed, MBh.; to be apprized or informed, ib.

श्रव 3. *śrava, śravaka* &c. See *srava* &c.

श्रवण 2. *śrávaṇa*, mfn. (fr. √2. *śru;* for 1. *śravaṇa*, see p. 1096; cf. *sravaṇa*) limping, lame, KātyŚr.; m. N. of the 20th (or 23rd) Nakshatra (presided over by Vishṇu, and containing the three stars α, β, and γ Aquilæ, supposed to represent three footsteps; cf. *tri-vikrama*), AV.; GṛS.; MBh. &c.; a sort of disease (= *śroṇa*), MW.; N. of a son of Naraka, BhP.; (with *bhaṭṭa*) N. of a teacher, Cat.; (*ā*), f., see below; n. = *śravaṇā-karman*, ŚāṅkhGṛ. **—datta**, m. N. of a teacher, Br. **—dvādaśī**, f. a partic. Tithi or lunar day (when certain religious observances of great efficacy are performed; it is said to fall on the twelfth of the light half of Bhādra, when that month is connected with the asterism Śravaṇa), BhP.; *-vrata*, n. N. of a ch. of the BrahmavP.; *-vrata-kathā*, f. N. of a ch. of the ĀdityaP. **—māhātmya**, n. N. of wk.

Śravaṇā, f. N. of a Nakshatra (= 2. *śravaṇa*), VarBṛS.; Pur.; the night of full-moon in the month Śrāvaṇa, GṛŚrS. (cf. Pāṇ. iv, 2, 5); N. of a daughter of Citraka or Rājâdhideva (cf. *śravishṭhā*), Hariv. **—karman**, n. the ceremony performed on the day of full moon in Śrāvaṇa, GṛS.

Śravaṇikā-vrata, n. N. of a partic. religious observance (prob. = *śravaṇā-karman*), Cat.

2. Śrávas, n. (= *sravas*) a stream, flow, gush, RV.; swift course, rapid motion, flight (instr. pl. in flight, while flying), ib.; a channel, ib. vii, 79, 3; x, 27, 21; = *anna* or *dhana*, Nir. [Cf., accord. to some, Gk. κρουνός.]

3. Śravasya, Nom. P. °*yáti*, to be swift, hasten, fly along, RV.; to snatch up, ib. ii, 13, 13.

4. Śravasyà, mfn. swift, rapid, RV.

Śravasyā́, ind. swiftly, rapidly, fast, ib.

2. Śravasyu, mfn. flowing, streaming, RV.; swift, nimble, ib.; AV.

2. Śrāvaṇa, mf(*ī*)n. relating to or produced under the Nakshatra Śravaṇa; m. (with or scil. *mās* or *māsa*) N. of one of the twelve Hindū months (generally rainy and corresponding to July–August), Suśr.; GṛS.; Yājñ. &c.; (*ī*), f., see below; n. = next, GṛS. **—karman**, n. = *śravaṇā-k°* above; °*masarpa-bali-prayoga*, m. N. of wk. **—dvādaśī**, f. the twelfth day of the month Śrāvaṇa; *-pāraṇa-vidhi*, m., *-māhātmya*, n., *-vrata*, n., *-vrata-kalpa*, m. N. of wks. **—nishedha-vacana**, n., **-māhātmya**, n., **-vidhi**, m., **-śanivāra-vrata**, n. N. of wks. **—śukla** (ibc.) the light half of Śr°; *-caturthī* and *-tṛitīyā*, f. the fourth and third day in the light half of Śr°, MW. **—homa-mantra**, m. N. of wk. **Śrāvaṇôtsarga-karman**, n. N. of wk.

Śrāvaṇika, mfn. = 2. *śrāvaṇa*, W.; (*ā*), f., see next.

2. Śrāvaṇikā, f. (for 1. see col. 1) = *śrāvaṇī* below. **—vrata**, n. a partic. observance, Cat.

Śrāvaṇī, f. (cf. under 1. *śrāvaṇa*) the day of full-moon in the month Śrāvaṇa, GṛŚrS.; Mn.; Rājñ. &c.; a partic. Pāka-yajña, Gaut. **—karman**, n., **-karma-vidhi**, m., **-paddhati**, f., **-prayoga**, m. N. of wks.

श्रवण 3. *śravaṇa*, m. a kind of plant used for colouring white, Suśr.; (*ā*), f. = *muṇḍīrikā*, L.

श्रवण 4. *śravaṇa*, n. = *śrapaṇa*, L.; (*ī*), f., see *vapā-śravaṇī.*

श्रवण 5. *śravaṇa*, w.r. for *sravaṇa.*

श्रवाप्य *śravāpya*, w.r. for *śravāyya.*

श्रविष्ठ *śravishṭha* &c. See col. 1.

श्रव्य *śravya.* See col. 1.

श्रा *śrā* or *śrai* (cf. √*śrī*), cl. 1. or 4. P. (Dhātup. xxii, 21) *śrāyati* (accord. to xxiv, 45 also cl. 2. P. *śrāti;* pf. *śaśrau;* aor. *aśrāsīt;* Prec. *śrāyāt* or *śreyāt*, inf. *śrātum*, Gr.), to cook, boil, seethe, mature, ripen (only in Dhātup.; accord. to Vop. also 'to sweat'): Pass. *śrāyate* (aor. *aśrāyi*), Gr.: Caus. *śrapáyati*, °*te* (aor. *aśiśrapat;* Pass. *śrapyáte*), to cause to cook or boil, roast, bake, AV. &c. &c.; to make hot, heat, bake (earthenware), VS.; Gaut.; Vait.; to cause to sweat, Vop. [for *śrāpaya*, see p. 1098, col. 1]: Desid. *śiśrāsati*, Gr.: Intens. *śāśrāyati, śāśrāti, śāśreti*, ib.

Śrita. See p. 1088, col. 1 (cf. *śrīta*, p. 1098).

Śrapa. See *su-śrapa.*

Śrápaṇa, n. (fr. Caus.) cooking, boiling, TS.; ŚBr.; MBh.; m. (scil. *agni*) cooking fire (applied to the Āhavanīya and Gārhapatya), KātyŚr.; (*ī*), f., see *vapā-śrapaṇī.*

Śrapaṇīya or **śrapayitavya**, mfn. (fr. id.) to be cooked or boiled, MW.

Śrapayitṛi, m. (fr. id.) a cook, ŚBr.

Śrapāyya, m. (fr. id.) a sacrificial animal, L.

Śrapita, mfn. (fr. id.) caused to be cooked or boiled, MBh. (cf. Pāṇ. vi, 1, 27, Vārtt. 2, Pat.); (*ā*), f. rice-gruel, L.; n. boiled meat &c., MW.

Śrāṇa, mfn. cooked, boiled, Pāṇ. vi, 1, 27, Vārtt. 1, Pat.; moist, wet, L.; (*ā*), f. rice gruel, L.; n. boiled meat &c., MW.

Śrātá, mfn. (cf. *śritá*) cooked, boiled, roasted, RV.; TS.; ĀśvŚr. [Cf. Gk. κρατος in ἄ-κρατος.]

Śrāpin, mfn. (fr. Caus.) cooking, boiling, Kāty.

श्राद्ध *śrāddha*, mf(*ī*)n. (fr. *śrad-dhā*) faithful, true, loyal, believing, HPariś.; SaddhP. (cf. Pāṇ. v, 2, 101); relating to a Śrāddha ceremony, Cat.; n. a ceremony in honour and for the benefit of dead relatives observed with great strictness at various fixed periods and on occasions of rejoicing as well as mourning by the surviving relatives (these ceremonies are performed by the daily offering of water and on stated occasions by the offering of Piṇḍas or balls of rice and meal [see *piṇḍa*] to three paternal and three maternal forefathers, i. e. to father, grandfather, and great grandfather; it should be borne in mind that a Śrāddha is not a funeral ceremony [*antyêshṭi*] but a supplement to such a ceremony; it is an act of reverential homage to a deceased person performed by relatives, and is moreover supposed to supply the dead with strengthening nutriment after the performance of the previous funeral ceremonies has endowed them with ethereal bodies; indeed until those *antyêshṭi* or 'funeral rites' have been performed, and until the succeeding first Śrāddha has been celebrated the deceased relative is a *prêta* or restless, wandering ghost, and has no real body [only a *liṅga-śarīra*, q. v.]; it is not until the first Śrāddha has taken place that he attains a position among the Pitṛis or Divine Fathers in their blissful abode called Pitṛi-loka, and the Śr° is most desirable and efficacious when performed by a son; for a full description of the Śrāddha ceremonies, see RTL. 276, 304 &c.), GṛŚrS.; Mn.; MBh. &c.; gifts or offerings at a Śrāddha, MW. **—kara** and **-kartṛi**, m. one who performs a Śrāddha or offers an oblation to the Pitṛis, W. **—karman**, n. a Śr° rite, Gaut.; Mn.; Hariv. &c.; °*ma-vidhi*, m. N. of wk. **—kalā**, f. N. of wk. **—kalpa**, m. = *-karman*, Āpast.; Mn.; MBh.; N. of various wks. (also *-dīpa*, m., *-druma*, m., *-bhāshya gobhilīya*, n., *-latā*, f., *-sūtra*, n.) **—kāṇḍa**, m. n., **-kāṇḍa-saṃgraha**, m., **-kārikā**, f., **-kārya-nirṇaya-saṃkshepa**, m. N. of wks. **—kāla**, m. the time for offering a Śr° (accord. to some the eighth hour of the day), KaṭhUp. **—kāśikā**, f. N. of a Comm. on the Śrāddha-kalpa-sūtra by Kṛishṇa-miśra. **—kṛit**, m. = *-kara*, W. **—kaumudī**, f. N. of wk. **—kriyā**, f. = *-karman*, MW. **—gaṇa-pati**, m., **-guṇa-saṃgraha**, m., **-candrikā**, f., **-cintāmaṇi**, m. N. of wks. **—tattva**, n. N. of two chs. of Raghu-nandana's Smṛiti-tattva (called Chandoga-śrāddha-tattva and Yajurvedi-śr°-t°); *-ṭīkā*, f. N. of a Comm. on the former by Kāśi-rāma. **—tilaka**, m. N. of wk. **—tva**, n. faithfulness, loyalty, L.; the being a Śr°, MW. **—da**, m. the offerer of a Śr°, W. **—darpaṇa**, m. N. of wk. **—dina**, n. the day of a Śr°, anniversary of the death of a near relative, Cat. **—dīdhiti**, f., **-dīpa**, m., **-dīpa-kalikā**, f., **-dīpikā**, f. N. of wks. **—deva**, m. any god presiding over Śr° rites (esp. applied to Yama, lord of the dead, but also to his brother Manu Vaivasvata, who in a former mundane age was Manu Satya-vrata; also applied to Vivasvat himself, and even to Brāhmans), Mn.; MBh.; Pur.; *-tva*, n., Hariv. **—devatā**, f. any deity presiding over Śr° rites, BhP. (cf. prec.); a Pitṛi or progenitor, W.; *-nirṇaya*, m. N. of wk. **—dvā-saptati-kalā**, f. (pl.), **-nava-kaṇḍikā-sūtra**, n., **-nirūpaṇa**, n., **-nirṇaya**, m., **-paṅkti**, f., **-paddhati**, f. (also with *pañca-triṇśac-chlokī*), **-pallava**, m. n., **-pārijāta**, m., **-prakāśa**, m., **-prakīrṇa-kārikā**, f., **-pradīpa**, m., **-prabhā**, f., **-prayoga**, m., **-prayoga-cintāmaṇi**, m., **-prayoga-paddhati**, f., **-praśaṇsā**, f., **-brāhmaṇa**, n., **-bhāskara-prayoga-paddhati**, f. N. of wks. **— bhuj**, mfn. eating food prepared at a Śr°, Mn. iii, 250. **— bhojana**, n. participation in a Śr°, ŚāṅkhGṛ. **— mañjarī**, f., **-mayūkha**, m. N. of wks. **— mitra**, mfn. making friends through a Śr°, Mn. iii, 140. **— mīmāṇsā**, f., **-ratna**, n., **-rahasya**, n., **-vacana-saṃgraha**, m., **-vamana-prâyaścitta**, n., **-varṇana**, n., **-vasishṭha**, m. or n. N. of wks. **— vāsara**, m. n. = *-dina*, Cat. **— vidhi**, m., **-viveka**, m., **-viveka-saṃgraha**, m., **-vṛitti-prakaraṇa**, n., and **-vyavasthā-saṃkshepa**, m. N. of wks. **— śāka**, n. a kind of pot-herb, Bhpr. **— śishṭa**, n. remainder of a Śr°, W. **-saṃkalpa**, m., **-saṃkalpa-vidhi**, m., **-saṃgraha**, m., **-samuccaya**, m., **-sāgara**, m., **-sāra**, m. N. of wks. **— sūtaka**, mfn. relating or belonging to a Śr° or a natal feast (as food), MBh.; *-bhojana*, n. participation in a Śr° or a natal f°, ŚāṅkhGṛ. **— sūtra**, n. (= *śrāddha-kalpa-sūtra*), **-saukhya**, n., **-stabaka**, m., **-hemâdri**, m. or n. N. of wks. **Śrāddhâdarśa**, m., **Śrāddhâdi-vidhi**, m., **Śrāddhâdhikāra**, m., °**kāri-nirṇaya**, m., **Śrāddhânukramaṇikā**, f., **Śrāddhâparârka**, m., **Śrāddhâśaucīya-darpaṇa**, m. N. of wks. **Śrāddhâha**, m. = *śrāddha-dina*, Kathās.; °*hnika*, mfn. one who daily performs a Śr°, Hariv. **Śrāddhêndu**, m. N. of wk. **Śrāddhôpayogin**, mfn. serviceable or appropriate for a Śr° (with *mantra*, m. pl. and °*gi-vacana*, n. N. of wks.)

Śrāddhika, mfn. relating to a Śrāddha or ceremony in honour of deceased ancestors, the recipient of Śrāddha oblations, Pāṇ. v, 2, 83; n. a present given at a Śrāddha, Mn.; Yājñ.

Śrāddhin, mfn. performing Śrāddhas, Mn.; Hariv. (cf. *a-śr°*); partaking of a Śrāddha, Gaut.

Śrāddhīya, mfn. relating or belonging to a Śrāddha, Kull.

Śrāddheya. See *a-śrāddheya*.

श्रान्त *śrānta* &c. See under √1. *śram*, p. 1096, col. 2.

श्रापय *śrāpaya*, Nom. P. °*yati* (cf. Caus. of √*śrā* and *śri*), artificially formed from *śra* and connected with *śreyas*, *śreshṭha*, Vop.

श्राम् *śrām*. See Caus. of √1. *śram*.

श्राम *śrāma*, *śrāmaṇaka* &c. See p. 1096, col. 2.

श्राय 2. *śrāya*, mfn. (for 1. see p. 1096, col. 3) relating or belonging to Śrī, Siddh.

Śrāyasa, mfn. = *śreyasi bhavam*, Pāṇ. vii, 3, 1, Sch.; m. patr. of Kaṇva, Kāṭh.; TS.; of Vita-havya, TS.; PañcavBr.

श्राव *śrāva*, *śrāvaka*, *śrāvaṇa* &c. See p. 1097, col. 1.

श्रावन्ती *śrāvantī*. See *śrāvasti* below.

श्रावष्ठीय *śrāvashṭhīya*, w.r. for *śrāvishṭhīya*.

श्रावस्त *śrāvasta*, m. (prob. connected with √1. *śru*) N. of a king (son of Śrāva and grandson of Yuvanāśva), Hariv.; VP.; (*ī*), f. N. of a city situated north of the Ganges and founded by king Śrāvasta (it was the ancient capital of Kosala and said to have been the place where the wealthy merchant Anātha-piṇḍika built the Buddha a residence in the Jeta-vana monastery which became his favourite retreat during the rainy seasons: other authorities derive the name from a Ṛishi called Sāvattha, who is said to have resided there; it has been identified by General Cunningham with a place now called Sāhet-Māhet, about 58 miles north of Ayodhyā in Oudh), MBh.; Hariv.; Buddh. (cf. MWB. 48; 407 &c.)

Śrāvastaka, m. = *śrāvasta*, MBh.; Hariv.

Śrāvasteya, mfn. (fr. *śrāvastī*), g. *nady-ādi*.

श्रावितृ *śrāvitṛi*, *śrāvin* &c. See p. 1097, col. 1.

श्रि 1. *śri*, cl. 1. P. Ā. (Dhātup. xxi, 31) *śrayati*, °*te* (pf. *śiśrāya*, *śiśriye*; aor. *áśret*, *áśriyan*, RV.; *aśrait*, AV.; *áśiśriyat*, ib. &c.; *aśrāyishṭa*, Gr. [Ved. forms belonging either to the pf. or aor. type are also *aśiśret*, °*śrema*, °*śrayuḥ*, *śiśritá*]; fut. *śrayitā*, Gr.; *śrayishyati*, °*te*, Br. &c.; inf. *śrayitum*, MBh.; *śrayitavai*, Br.; ind. p. *śrayitvā*, MBh. &c., *-śritya*, Br. &c.), P. to cause to lean or rest on, lay on or in, fix on, fasten to, direct or turn towards, (esp.) spread or diffuse (light or radiance or beauty) over (loc.), RV.; TS.; Br.; (Ā. or Pass., rarely P.) to lean on, rest on, recline against (acc.), cling to (loc.), be supported or fixed or depend on, abide in or on (acc., loc. or adv.), ib.; ĀśvGṛ.; ChUp.; MBh.; (Ā. P.) to go to, approach, resort or have recourse to (for help or refuge), tend towards (acc.), MBh.; Kāv. &c.; (Ā.) to go into, enter, fall to the lot or take possession of (acc. or loc.), Kāv.; Kathās.; (Ā. P.) to attain, undergo, get into any state or condition (acc.), ib. &c.; to assume (with *śrāvikā-tvam*, 'to assume the form of a Śrāvikā,' q. v.), Kathās.; HPariś.; to show, betray (heroism), R.; to honour, worship, Dhātup.: Pass. *śrīyate* (aor. *áśrāyi*: cf. above), RV. &c. &c.: Caus. *śrāpayati* (in *uc-chr°*), VS.; *śrāyayati* (aor. *aśiśrayat*; for *aśiśriyat*, see above), Gr.: Desid. *śiśrayishati*, °*te* or *śiśrīshati*, °*te*, Gr.: Intens. *śeśrīyate*, *śeśrayīti*, *śeśreti*, ib. [Cf. Gk. κλίνω, κλίνη, κλῖμαξ; Lat. *clino*, *clivus*; Lith. *szlýti*, *szlëti*, *szlaitas*; Goth. *hlains*; *hlaiw*; Germ. *hlinên*, *linên*, *lehnen*; Angl. Sax. *hlinian*; Eng. *lean*.]

Śiśrivas, mf(°*ryushī*)n. one who has leaned against or gone to or approached, Pāṇ. vii, 2, 67, Sch.

Śraya, **śrayaṇa** &c. See p. 1096, cols. 2, 3.

2. **Śri**, in *antáḥ-* and *bahiḥ-śri* (q. v.)

3. **Śri**, light, lustre (= 3. *śrī*, q. v.) at end of adj. comp.

Śrit, mfn. going to, having gone or attained to in *kṛicchre-śrit*, *divi-śrit*, *nabhaḥ-śrit* &c.

Śritá, mfn. clinging or attached to, standing or lying or being or fixed or situated in or on, contained in, connected with (loc., acc., or comp.), RV. &c. &c.; one who has gone or resorted to (acc.), Rājat.; Kathās.; BhP.; having attained or fallen or got into any condition (acc. or comp.; cf. *kashṭa-śr°*), ib.; having assumed (a form), Kathās.; gone to, approached, had recourse to, sought, occupied (as a place), Kāv.; Kathās.; taken, chosen, Rājat.; served, honoured, worshipped, W.; subservient, subordinate, auxiliary, MW. **— kshama**, mfn. one who has had recourse to patience, composed, tranquil, Śatr. **— vat**, mfn. one who has taken refuge with (acc.), Kuval. **— sattva**, mfn. one who has taken courage or resolution, BhP.

Śriti, f. approach, recourse, entering (see *uc-chriti*); (*ī*) = *śrityai*, *śrayaṇârtham* (?), RV. ix, 14, 6.

श्रिमन्य *śri-manya*, n. (fr. 2. *śrī* + *manya*, connected with *śriyam-manyā* below, Pāṇ. vi, 3, 68, Vārtt. 5, Pat.)

Śriyam-manya, mf(*ā*)n. fancying one's self Śrī, Bhaṭṭ. (cf. Pāṇ. vi, 3, 68, Vārtt. 1, Pat.); conceited, proud, arrogant, W.

श्रियध्यै *śriyadhyai*, *śriyáse*, *śriyā* &c. See p. 1100, col. 2.

श्रियपुत्र *śriya-putra*, w.r. for *priya-p°*.

श्रिव् *śriv*. See √*sriv*.

श्रिष् 1. *śrish* (cf. √1. *ślish*), cl. 1. P. *śreshati*, to burn, Dhātup. xvii, 51.

श्रिष् 2. *śrish* (prob. a collateral form of √2. *ślish*), in *śreshāma* (accord to Sāy.) = *śleshayema*, 'may we connect or compose,' RV. iv, 43, 1, and *ā-ślishat* = *ā-ślishṭaṃ mā bhūt*, 'let it not be left on the ground,' ib. i, 162, 11 (cf. *abhi-śrish*, *doshaṇi-śrish*, *hṛidaya-śrish*, *ā-śresha*, *sam-śreshaṇi*).

श्री 1. *śrī* (cf. √*śrā*), cl. 9. P. Ā. (Dhātup. xxxi, 3) *śrīṇāti*, *śrīṇīté* (Gr. also pf. *śiśrāya*, *śiśriye*; aor. *aśraishīt*, *aśreshṭa* &c.; for *aśiśrayuḥ* see 2. *abhi-√śrī*), to mix, mingle, cook (cf. *abhi-* and *ā-√śrī*), RV.; TS.; VS.; Br.; (= √1. *śri*), to burn, flame, diffuse light, RV. i, 68, 1.

2. **Śrī**, mfn. (ifc.) mixing, mingling, mixed with; f. mixing, cooking.

Śrīta, mfn. mixed, mixed with (instr.), cooked, RV.

श्री 3. *śrī*, f. (prob. to be connected with √1. *śri* and also with √1. *śrī* in the sense of 'diffusing light or radiance;' nom. *śrīs*, accord. to some also *śrī*) light, lustre, radiance, splendour, glory, beauty, grace, loveliness (*śriyé* and *śriyai*, 'for splendour or beauty,' 'beauteously,' gloriously,' cf. *śriyáse*; du. *śriyau*, 'beauty and prosperity;' *śriya ātmajāḥ*, 'sons of beauty,' i. e. horses [cf. *śrī-putra*]; *śriyaḥ putrāḥ*, 'goats with auspicious marks'), RV. &c. &c.; prosperity, welfare, good fortune, success, auspiciousness, wealth, treasure, riches (*śriyā*, 'accord° to fortune or wealth'), high rank, power, might, majesty, royal dignity (or 'Royal dignity' personified; *śriyo bhājaḥ*, 'possessors of dignity,' 'people of high rank'), AV. &c. &c.; symbol or insignia of royalty, Vikr. iv, 13; N. of Lakshmī (as goddess of prosperity or beauty and wife of Vishṇu, produced at the churning of the ocean, also as daughter of Bhṛigu and as mother of Darpa), ŚBr. &c. &c.; N. of Sarasvatī (see *-pañcamī*); of a daughter of king Su-śarman, Kathās.; of various metres, Col.; (the following only in L. 'a lotus-flower; intellect, understanding; speech; cloves; Pinus Longifolia; Aegle Marmelos; a kind of drug, = *vṛiddhi*; N. of a Buddhist goddess and of the mother of the 17th Arhat'); m. N. of the fifth musical Rāga (see *rāga*), Saṃgīt.; mfn. diffusing light or radiance, splendid, radiant, beautifying, adorning (ifc.; see *agni-*, *adhvara-*, *kshatra-*, *gaṇa-*, *jana-śrī* &c.), RV. iv, 41, 8. [The word *śrī* is frequently used as an honorific prefix (= 'sacred,' 'holy') to the names of deities (e. g. Śrī-Durgā, Śrī-Rāma), and may be repeated two, three, or even four times to express excessive veneration (e. g. Śrī-śrī-Durgā &c.); it is also used as a respectful title (like 'Reverend') to the names of eminent persons as well as of celebrated works and sacred objects (e. g. Śrī-Jayadeva, Śrī-Bhāgavata), and is often placed at the beginning or back of letters, manuscripts, important documents &c.; also before the words *caraṇa* and *pāda* 'feet,' and even at the end of personal names.] **— āhnika**, n. N. of a wk. on Dharma. **— kaṇṭha**, m. 'beautiful-throated,' a partic. bird, VarBṛS.; N. of Śiva (cf. *nīla-k°*), MBh.; Hariv. &c.; (with Śaivas) N. of partic. emancipated spirits, Hcat.; of the poet Bhava-bhūti, Mālatim.; of a partic. Rāga (in music), Saṃgīt.; of various authors and other men (also with *ācārya*, *dīkshita*, *paṇḍita* &c.), Cat.; of an arid district north-west of Delhi, Vās., Introd.; of a peak in the Himālayas, Inscr.; *-kaṇṭha*, m. Śiva's neck, Kāv. (*ī*, f. = *-kaṇṭhīya-saṃhitā*, q. v.); *-kaṇṭha-taṭinī*, f. Ś°'s throat, Siṇhās.; *-kaṇṭhīya*, Nom. P. °*yati*, to be like Ś°'s neck, Vās., Introd.; *-carita*, n. N. of a poem (written by Maṅkha who lived in Kaśmīra in the 12th century A. D.); *-tā*, f. the state or condition of being Ś°, MBh.; *-tīrtha*, m. N. of an author, Cat.; *-tri-śatī*, f. N. of a Stotra; *-datta*, m. N. of a medical author, Cat.; *-deva*, m. (prob.) N. of a Jina, Siṇhās.; *-deśa*, m. the country of Śrī-kaṇṭha, Kathās.; *-nāthīya*, n. N. of wk.; *-nilaya*, m. the district of Śrī-kaṇṭha, Kathās.; *-pada-lāñchana*, m. 'marked by the name Śrī-kaṇṭha,' N. of the poet Bhava-bhūti, Mālatim.; *-bhāshya*, n., *-māhātmya*, n. N. of wks.; *-miśra*, m. N. of a grammarian, Cat.; *-vishaya*, m. the country of Śrī-kaṇṭha, Kathās.; *-śambhu*, m., *-śarman*, m., *-śiva* (with *ācārya*), m. N. of authors &c., Cat.; *-sakha*, m. 'Śiva's friend,' N. of Kubera, L.; *-stava*, m. 'praise of the district of Śrī-kaṇṭha,' N. of a poem. **— kaṇṭhikā**, f. (in music) a partic. Rāga, Saṃgīt. **— kaṇṭhīya**, mfn. relating to Śiva, Bālar.; relating to the author Śrī-kaṇṭha; *-saṃhitā*, f. N. of his wk. (also called *śrī-kaṇṭhī*). **— kandā**, f. a kind of gourd, L. **— kayya-svāmin**, m. N. of a partic. shrine or temple, Rājat. **— kara**, mf(*ā* or *ī*)n. causing prosperity, giving good fortune, Hcat.; m. N. of Vishṇu, L.; (also with *miśra*, *bhaṭṭa*, *ācārya*) of various authors &c., Cat.; n. the red lotus, L. **— karaṇa**, mfn. causing glory or distinction, MaitrS.; 'making the word Śrī,' a pen, L.; N. of the capital of the Northern Kosalas (and residence of king Prasena-jit; it was in ruins when visited by Fa-Hian, not far from the modern Fyzabad), Buddh.; °*ṇâdi*, m. a chief secretary, Inscr.; °*ṇâdhyaksha*, m. a kind of official (prob. = prec.), Campak. **— karṇa**, m. a kind of bird, VarBṛS.; *-deva*, m. N. of a king, Inscr. **— karṇīyaka**, m. a kind of bird, ib. **— kallaṭa**, m. N. of a Siddha, Rājat. **— kavaca**, n. N. of a Kavaca (q. v.) **— kānta**, m. 'beloved by Śrī,' N. of Vishṇu, L.; (with *miśra*) N. of an author, Cat.; °*tā-kathā*, f. N. of a tale. **— kāma** (*śrī*), mfn. desirous of distinction or glory, MaitrS.; AitBr.; (*ā*),

f. N. of Rādhā, Pañcar. **—kāra**, m. the word Śrī (written at the top of a book or letter &c.), MW. **—kārin**, m. 'causing increase,' a kind of antelope (=*kuraṅga*; the flesh of it is considered highly nutritious; some make the word *śrī-kārī*, f.), L. **—kīrti**, f. (in music) a kind of measure, Saṃgīt. **—kuñja**, n. and **-kuṇḍa**, n. N. of Tīrthas, MBh.; **—kula** and **-kūrma-māhātmya**, n. N. of wks. **—kṛicchra**, m. a kind of penance (living for three days on nothing but the liquid and solid excreta of a cow and on the grains of barley found in the latter), Prâyaśc. **—kṛishṇa**, m. 'the divine Kṛishṇa,' N. of various authors (also with *bhaṭṭa* and *vaidika*), Cat.; *-tarkâlaṃkāra-bhaṭṭâcārya,-tīrtha,-nyāya-vāg-īśa-bhaṭṭâcārya, -rāya, -vidyā-vāg-īśa, -vipra, -sarasvatī*, m. N. of various men, ib.; *-saroja-bhramarī*, f. pl. N. of a poem; °*ṇâlaṃkāra*, m. N. of a Commentary. **—keśava** or **-keśavâcārya**, m. N. of a teacher, Cat. **—kośa-hṛidaya**, n., **-krama**, m., **-krama-candrikā**, f., **-krama-tantra**, n., **-krama-saṃhitā**, f. N. of wks. **—kriyā-rūpiṇī**, f. N. of Rādhā, Pañcar. **—kshatra** or **-kshetra**, n. N. of a country, Buddh. **—khaṇḍa**, m. or n. (?) the sandal-tree, sandal, Kāv.; Kathās. &c.; (*ī*), f., see comp.; *-khaṇḍa*, m. n. a quantity of s°, Subh.; *-carcā*, f. s° unguent, Gīt.; *-tamāla-pattra*, Nom. P. °*ttrati*, to represent a s° mark on the forehead, Prasannar.; *-dāsa*, m. N. of a man, Ratnâv.; *-druma*, m. the s°-tree, Rājat.; *-pṛithvī-dhara*, m. 'sandal-mountain,' the Malaya range, Vcar.; *-vilepana*, n. anointing with s°, Hit.; *-śītala*, mfn. cool as s°, Kathās.; *-śaila*, m. (=*pṛithvī-dhara*), Gīt.; °*ḍâṅga-rāga*, m. anointing the body with s°, Kathās.; °*ḍârdra-vilepana*, n. moist unguent of s°, ib.; °*ḍī-vedânta-sāra*, m. N. of wk. **—gaṇeśa**, m. the divine Gaṇêśa, MW.; (*ā*), f. N. of Rādhā, Pañcar. **—gadita**, n. a kind of Uparūpaka or minor drama (described as a composition in one act, founded upon a famous story, and dedicated chiefly to the goddess Śrī), Sāh. **—garbha**, mfn. having welfare for its inner nature (applied to the sword and punishment), MBh.; m. N. of Vishṇu, Hariv.; of a Bodhi-sattva, Buddh.; of a merchant, Kathās.; of a contemporary of Maṅkha, Cat.; (with *Kavîndra*) of a poet, ib.; (*ā*), f. N. of a Rādhā, Pañcar.; *-ratna*, n. a kind of gem, L. **—giri**, m. N. of a mountain, W. **—guṇa-ratna-kośa**, m. N. of wk. **—guṇa-lekhā**, f. N. of a princess, Rājat. **—guṇa-sahasra-nāman**, n. N. of wk. **—gunna**, m. N. of a Mīmāṇsaka (a contemporary of Maṅkha), Cat. **—gupta**, m. N. of a man, Buddh. **—guru-sahasra-nāma-stotra**, n., **-goshṭhi-māhātmya**, n. N. of wks. **—graha**, m. a trough or place for supplying birds with water (=*śakunī-prapā*), L. **—grāma**, m. 'village of Fortune,' N. of a place, Cat. **—grāmara**, m. (fr. prec.) N. of the astronomer Nārāyaṇa, ib. **—ghana**, n. coagulated milk, sour curds, L.; m. a Buddha or N. of a Buddha, Pañcar. **—cakra**, n. a magical diagram (supposed to represent the orb of the earth), RTL. 196; 203; an astrological division of the body (said to represent the uterine or pubic region), L.; a wheel of Indra's car, L.; *-nyāsa-kavaca*, n., *-pattra*, n., *-pūjā-vidhi*, m. N. of wks. **—caṅkuṇa-vihāra**, m. N. of a Buddhist monastery, Rājat. **—caṇḍa**, m. N. of a man (of passionate character), Kathās. **—candana**, n. a kind of sandal, HPariś. **—candra**, m. N. of various men, Rājat. (also *-deva*, Col.) **—cūrṇa-paripālana**, n. N. of wk. **—ja**, m. 'born from Śrī,' N. of Kāma (god of love), L.; =*sāmba*, L. **—jagad-rāma**, m. N. of a man, Kshitîś. **—jyotir-īśvara**, m. N. of the author of the Dhūrta-samāgama, Dhūrtas. **—ḍhakka**, N. of a place, Rājat. **—tattva-nidhi**, m., **-tattva-bodhinī**, f. N. of wks. **—tala**, n. a partic. hell, VP. **—tāḍa**, m. (prob.) =*-tāla*, Hcat. **—tāla**, m. a kind of tree resembling the wine-palm, L. **—tīrtha**, n. N. of a Tīrtha, MBh. **—tejas**, m. N. of a Buddha, Lalit.; of a serpent-demon, Buddh. **—tri-kaṭuka-vihāra**, m. N. of a Buddhist monastery, ib. **—da**, mfn. bestowing wealth or prosperity, Pañcar.; m. N. of Kubera, Kuval.; (*ā*), f. N. of Rādhā, Pañcar. **—datta**, m. 'Fortune-giver,' N. of various authors &c. (also with *bhaṭṭa* and *maithila*), Kathās.; Vet.; Cat. **—dayita**, m. 'husband of Śrī,' N. of Vishṇu, Vop. **—darpaṇa**, m. N. of a Commentary. **—darśana**, m. N. of a man, Kathās. **—daśâkshara**, m. (scil. *mantra*) a partic. prayer consisting of ten syllables, Pañcar. **—dākshi-nagara**, n. N. of a town, Buddh. **—dāman**, m. N. of a playfellow of Kṛishṇa, Hariv.; Pañcar.; (°*ma-*)*carita*, n. N. of a drama; *-nanda-dātrī* and °*mêśvara-vallabhā*, f. N. of Rādhā, Pañcar. **—durgā-yantra**, n. a partic. diagram, Cat. **—deva**, m. (also with *ācarya, paṇḍita* and *śarman*) N. of various authors &c., Rājat.; Cat.; (*ā*), f. N. of a wife of Vasu-deva, Hariv.; Pur. **—druma**, m. the tree called Śrī (cf. above), Kād. **—dhana**, N. of a place (*-kaṭaka*, of a Caitya), Buddh. **—dhanvi-purī-māhātmya**, n. N. of wk. **—dhara**, m. 'bearer or possessor of fortune,' N. and a form of Vishṇu, MBh.; Hariv.; Pur.; N. of the month Śrāvaṇa, VarBṛS.; of the seventh Arhat of the past Utsarpiṇī, L.; (also with *ācārya, kavi, dīkshita, bhoṭṭa, miśra* &c.) N. of various authors and other men, Sarvad.; Buddh.; Cat.; (*am*), n. an ammonite of a partic. form, BrahmavP.; *-dāsa*, m., *-nandin*, m., *-pati*, m. N. of authors; *-paddhati*, f. N. of wk.; *-mālava*, m. N. of a man (the father of Śiva-dāsa), Cat.; *-sena*, m. N. of a king, Bhaṭṭ.; *-svāmin*, m. (also °*mi-yati*) N. of a well-known scholar (the pupil of Paramânanda and author of various Commentaries), Cat.; °*rânanda*, m. (also with *yati*) N. of authors; °*rī-pañcadaśī*, f., °*rīya*, n., °*rīya-vyākhyā*, f., °*rīya-saṃhitā*, f. N. of wks.; °*rêndra*, m. N. of an author (also called Khaṇḍa-deva), Cat. **—dharola-nagara**, n. N. of a town, Cat. **—dhāman**, n. abode of Śrī (applied to the lotus), BhP. **—dhra**, m. =*-dhara*, L. **—nagara**, n. (or *ī*, f.) 'city of Fortune,' N. of two towns (one situated in the district of Caunpore, the other in Bundelcund), Rājat.; Hit. &c. **—nandana**, m. metron. of the god of love, L.; (in music) a kind of measure, Saṃgīt. **—nandīya**, n. N. of wk. **—narêndra-prabhā**, f. N. of a woman, Rājat. **—narêndrêśvara**, m. N. of a statue of Śiva erected by Śrī-narêndra-prabhā, ib. **—nātha**, m. 'husband of Śrī,' N. of Vishṇu, Cat.; of various authors (also with *ācārya, kavi, paṇḍita, bhaṭṭa* and *śarman*), ib. **—nārada-purāṇa**, n. N. of a Purāṇa. **—niketa**, m. 'abode of beauty,' a paragon of beauty, BhP.; a lotus-flower, ib.; n. the resin of Pinus Longifolia, Suśr. **—niketana**, m. 'dwelling with Śrī,' N. of Vishṇu, BhP.; n. =prec. n., Suśr. **—nitambā**, f. 'having beautiful hips,' N. of Rādhā, Pañcar. **—nidhi**, m. 'receptacle of beauty,' N. of Vishṇu, Pañcar. **—nivāsa**, m. abode of Śrī, Kāv.; N. of Vishṇu, Chandom.; BhP.; N. of various authors and other men (also with *ācārya, kavi, dīkshita, bhaṭṭa* &c.), Cat.; (*ā*), f. N. of Rādhā, Pañcar.; m. or n. (?) the resin of Pinus Longifolia, L. (also °*saka*, Car.); *-kavacânta-stotra*, n. pl. N. of various Stotras from the Agni-purāṇa; *-campū*, f. N. of a poem by Veṅkaṭa; *-tīrtha*, m. N. of various authors, Cat. (°*thīya*, n. N. of wk.); *-dāsa*, m. N. of various authors &c., Cat.; *-dīkshitīya*, n., *-dīpikā*, f., *-brahma-tantra-para-kāla-svāmy-ashṭôttara-śata*, n., *-māhātmya*, n. N. of wks.; *-rāghava*, m. (with *ācārya*), *-śishya*, m. N. of authors, Cat.; °*sīya*, n. N. of wk. **—nīla-kaṇṭha**, m. (prob.) N. of a Jina, Cat. **—pañcamī**, f. the fifth day of the light half of Māgha (a festival in honour of Sarasvatī, goddess of learning, when books and implements of writing are worshipped), MW.; *-vrata*, n. the above religious observance, ib. **—pati**, m. 'lord of fortune,' a king, prince, L.; 'husband of Śrī,' (*śriyaḥ pati*) N. of Vishṇu-Kṛishṇa (esp. as worshipped on the hill Veṅkaṭa, q. v.), VarBṛS.; Śiś.; BhP.; N. of the father of Kṛishṇajī, Cat.; (also with *dvi-vedin, bhaṭṭa*, and *śarman*) of various authors &c., ib.; *-govinda*, m. N. of a poet, ib.; *-grantha*, m. N. of wk.; *-datta*, m. N. of the author of the Kātantra-pariśishṭa; *-paddhati*, f., *-bhāshya*, n., *-vyavahāra-nirṇaya*, m., *-vyavahāra-samuccaya*, m. N. of wks.; *-śishya*, m. N. of an author, Cat.; *-saṃhitā*, f.; °*tīya*, n. N. of wks. **—pattana**, n. N. of a town, Virac. **—patha**, m. a royal road, highway, L. **—padī**, f. a kind of jasmine, L. **—paddhati**, f. N. of a wk. (on the worship of Rādhā, Kṛishṇa, and Caitanya); *-pradīpa*, m. N. of a Comm. on it. **—padma**, m. N. of Kṛishṇa, MBh. **—parāpūjana**, n. N. of a Tantra wk. **—parṇa**, n. Premna Spinosa or Longifolia, Hcat.; a lotus, L.; (*ī*), f. Gmelina Arborea, Hcat. (L. also 'Premna Spinosa or Longifolia, Pistia Stratiotes, Salmalia Malabarica, and a species of Solanum'). **—parṇi**, f., (m.c.) =*-parṇī*, Hcat. **—parṇikā**, f. Myristica Malabarica and Myrica Sapida, Bhpr. **—parvata**, m. N. of various mountains, MBh.; Suśr.; Pur.; of a Liṅga, MW. **—pā**, mfn. preserving fortune, Siddh. **—pāñcarātra**, n., **-pāñcarātrârādhana**, n. N. of wks. **—pāda**, m. N. of various men, Cat. **—pāla**, m. N. of a king, Śatr.; of an author, Cat.; (with *kavi-rāja*) N. of a poet, ib.; *-carita*, n. N. of wk. **—pālita**, m. N. of a poet, Cat. **—pishṭa**, m. the resin of Pinus Longifolia, L. (prob. w. r. for *śrī-veshṭa*). **—puṭa**, m. a kind of metre, Col.; °*ṭôshṭha*, mfn. having beautifully formed closed lips, VarBṛS. **—putra**, m. 'son of Śrī,' N. of Kāma (god of love), L.; a horse, L. **—pura**, n. N. of a town (also °*ra-nagara*), Vet. **—purushôttama-tattva**, n. N. of a ch. in the Smṛiti-tattva. **—pushpa**, n. cloves, L.; n. white lotus, L.; the wood of Cerasus Puddum, L. **—pūjā-mahā-paddhati**, f. N. of wk. **—prada**, mf(*ā*)n. bestowing happiness or prosperity, Pañcar. **—prabhāva**, m. N. of Kambala, Buddh. **—praśna**, m. N. of wk., Hcat. **—prasūna**, n. cloves, L. **—priya**, n. orpiment, L. **—phala**, m. the Bilva tree, Aegle Marmelos, L.; (*ā*), f. the Indigo plant, L.; (*ī*), f. id., L.; myrobalan, L.; (*am*), n. 'sacred fruit,' the Bilva fruit, Mn.; Yājñ.; Hariv.; a cocoa-nut, GaruḍaP.; the fruit i.e. result of splendour &c., Cat.; *-kṛicchra*, m. a kind of self-mortification (regarded as specially efficacious, eating no food except the Bilva fruit for a whole month), Vishṇ.; *-vardhinī*, f. N. of wk. **—phalikā**, f. a kind of gourd, L.; a kind of indigo, L. **—baka**, m. (with *paṇḍita*) N. of a poet, Subh.; another man, Rājat. **—bappa**, m. N. of a man, Inscr.; *-pādīya-vihāra*, m. N. of a Buddhist monastery, ib. **—babba**, m. =*-bappa*, ib. **—bali**, m. N. of a village, Cat. **—bāpa**, m. a kind of garment, Pañcad. **—bhaksha**, m. auspicious food (applied to the Madhu-parka), Gobh. **—bhaṭṭa**, m. N. of a teacher of the Nimbârka school, Cat. **—bhaḍa**, m. N. of a man, ib. **—bhadra**, m. Cyperus Rotundus (generally *ā*, f.), L.; m. N. of a serpent-demon, Buddh.; of an author, Col.; (*ā*), f. N. of a goddess, Kalac.; of the second wife of Bimbisāra, Buddh. **—bhartṛi**, m. 'husband of Śrī,' N. of Vishṇu, Śiś. **—bhāgavata**, n. 'the sacred Bhāgavata,' N. of the Bhāgavata-Purāṇa, MW. **—bhānu**, m. N. of a son of Kṛishṇa, BhP. **—bhāshya**, n. N. of a Comm. on the Brahma-sūtra by Rāmânuja; *-dīpa*, m., *-vṛitti*, f., *-vṛitty-upanyāsa*, m., *-saṃgraha*, m.; °*shyândhra-ṭīkā*, f., °*shyôdāhṛitô-panishad-vākya-vivaraṇa*, n. N. of Comms. on it. **—bhuja** (ibc.), the arms of a person of high rank, Das. **—bhrātṛi**, m. 'brother of Śrī,' the horse (fabled to have sprung with her from the ocean when churned by the gods; cf. *lakshmī*), L. **—makuṭa**, n. gold, L. **—maṅgala**, m. N. of a man, Cat.; n. N. of a Tīrtha, ib. **—mañju**, m. N. of a mountain, Buddh. **—manas**, mfn. =*śrī-manas*. **—maṇḍapa**, m. N. of a mountain, Cat. **—mat**, mfn., see p. 1100, col. 2. **—mati**, f. (for *matī*?) N. of Rādhā, MW. **—matôttara**, n. N. of wk. **—mada**, m. the intoxication produced by wealth or prosperity, BhP. **—manas** (*śrī́-*), mfn. (prob.) well-disposed, VS. **—manta**, mfn. (m.c.) =*-mat*, Hcat. **—maya**, mf(*ī*)n. consisting of (or quite absorbed into) Śri, Pañcar. **—malā** or **-malāpahā**, f. a kind of shrub, L. **—mallakarṇi**, m. N. of a king, VP. **—mastaka**, m. 'Lakshmī's head,' a kind of garlic, L. **—mahā-devī**, f. N. of the mother of Saṃkara, W. **—mahiman**, m. the majesty of Śiva; °*mnaḥ stava*, m. N. of a Stotra. **—māla**, m. or n. (?) N. of a district and the town situated in it; *-khaṇḍa*, m. n., *-purāṇa*, n., *-māhātmya*, n. N. of wks. **—mālā-devī-siṇha-nāda-sūtra**, n. N. of a Buddhist Sūtra. **—mālinī-vijayôttara**, n. N. of wk. **—mitra**, m. N. of a poet, Cat. **—mukha**, n. a beautiful face, MW.; m. the word Śrī written on the back of a letter, ib.; the 7th (or 41st) year of Jupiter's cycle of 60 years, VarBṛS.; N. of a medical author (cf. *śrī-sukha*), Cat.; (*ī*), f., see next. **—mukhī-sahasra-nāman**, n. N. of wk. **—mudrā**, f. a mark made on the forehead &c. by worshippers of Vishṇu, MW. **—mush**, mfn. stealing beauty (ifc. = 'surpassing in beauty'), Megh. **—mushṭi-māhātmya** and **-mushṇa-māhātmya**, n. N. of a ch. in various Purāṇas. **—mūrti**, f. 'any divine image,' an image or personification of Vishṇu or of the Supreme Being; any idol, MW. **—yaśas**, n. splendour and glory (in *-kāma*, mfn. 'desirous of splendour and gl°'), KātyŚr.; m. N. of a king, Kālac. **—yaśasā**, n. splendour and glory, ŚBr. **—yāmala**, n. N. of a Tantra. **—yukta** or **-yuta**, mfn. 'endowed with Śrī,' happy, fortunate, famous, illustrious, wealthy &c. (prefixed as an honorific title to the names of men, and in the common language written *śrī-yut*), W. **-raṅga**, m., see col. 3. **-ratna-giri**, m. N. of a sacred hill, Buddh. **-ratnâkara**, m. N. of a Tantra wk. **-rasa**, m. the resin of Pinus Longifolia, Suśr. **-rāga**, m. (in music) a partic. Rāga, Saṃgīt. **-rāghavīya**, n. N. of a poem by Ragu-nâthâcārya. **-rāja-cūḍā-maṇi-dīkshita**, m. N. of an author, Cat. **-rādhā-vallabha**, m. a form of Vishṇu, W. **-rāma**, m. the divine Rāma, i. e. Rāma-candra (whose name in this form is used as a salutation by those who worship Vishṇu in this Avatāra), W.; N. of an author, Cat.; *-kalpa-druma*, m. N. of wk.; *-navamī*, f. the ninth of the light half of the month Caitra (observed as a festival in honour of the birthday of Rāma-candra), MW. (*-nirṇaya*, m. N. of wk.); *-paddhati*, f. N. of a wk. on the proper mode of worshipping Rāma (attributed to Rāmânuja); *-maṅgala*, n., *-rakshā*, f., *-stuti*, f.; °*môdanta*, m. N. of wks. **-rāshṭra-mitrâyush-kāma**, mfn. wishing eminence and dominion and friends and long life, KātyŚr. **-rudra-hṛidayôpanishad**, f. N. of an Upanishad. **-rūpā**, f. having the form of Śrī (applied to Rādhā), Pañcar. **-lakshmaṇa**, mfn. characterized by Śrī, BhP. **-lakshman**, m. N. of a man (= *lakshmī-dhara*), Vās., Introd. **-latā**, f. (for *śrīla-tā* see col. 3) a kind of plant (= *mahā-jyotishmatī*), L. **-lābha**, m. N. of various men, Buddh. **-lekhā**, f. N. of a princess, Rājat. **-vacana-bhūshaṇa-mīmāṇsā**, f. N. of wk. **-vat**, mfn. containing the word *śrī*, Kāth. **-vatsa**, m. 'favourite of Śrī,' N. of Vishṇu, L.; a partic. mark or curl of hair on the breast of Vishṇu or Kṛishṇa (and of other divine beings; said to be white and represented in pictures by a symbol resembling a cruciform flower), MBh.; Kāv. &c.; the emblem of the tenth Jina (or Vishṇu's mark so used), L.; a hole of a partic. form made through a wall by a housebreaker, L.; (in astron.) one of the lunar asterisms, Col.; N. of the eighth Yoga, MW.; N. of various authors (also with *ācārya* and *śarman*), Cat.; *-dhārin* or *-bhṛit*, m. 'wearing the Śrī-vatsa mark,' N. of Vishṇu, L.; *-piṇyāka*, m. the resin of Pinus Longifolia, L.; *-muktika-nandy-āvarta-lakshita-pāṇi-pāda-tala-tā*, f. having the palms of the hands and soles of the feet marked with Śrī-vatsa and Muktika (for *muktikā*?) and Nandy-āvarta (one of the 80 minor marks of a Buddha), Dharmas. 84; *-lakshman*, m. 'marked with the Śrī-vatsa,' N. of Vishṇu, MW.; *-lāñchana*, m. id., L.; N. of Maheśvara, Vās., Introd.; of an author, Cat.; °*tsâṅka*, mfn. having the Śrī-vatsa as a mark, VarBṛS.; m. a wolf, L.; N. of Vishṇu, L.; of an author, Cat. **-vatsakin**, m. a horse having a curl of hair on his breast (resembling that of Vishṇu), L. **-vada**, m. a kind of bird, L. **-vara**, m. N. of the author of the Jaina-taraṃgiṇī (said to be a continuation of the Rāja-taraṃgiṇī up to the year A.D. 1477), Cat.; *-bodhi-bhagavat*, m. N. of a man, Buddh. **-varāha**, m. 'divine boar,' N. of Vishṇu (in his boar-incarnation), L. **-vardhana**, m. 'increase or increaser of fortune,' a kind of musical composition, Saṃgīt.; N. of Śiva, MW.; of a man, Rājat.; of a poet, Cat. **-vallabha**, m. a favourite of fortune, MW.; N. of various authors; (also with *utprabhātīya* and *vidyā-vāg-īśa bhaṭṭâcārya*), Cat. **-vallī**, f. Acacia Concinna, L.; a kind of jasmine, L. **-vasukra**, m. N. of a grammarian, Gaṇar. **-vaha**, m. 'bringing fortune,' N. of a serpent-demon, MBh. **-vāñchêsvara-māhātmya**, n. N. of wk. **-vāṭī**, f. a species of Nāga-vallī, L. **-vāraka**, m. Marsilea Quadrifolia, L. **-1. -vāsa**, m. 'having a pleasant scent,' the resin of Pinus Longifolia, Bhpr. **-2. -vāsa**, m. 'abode of Śrī or beauty,' N. of Vishṇu or Śiva, L.; a lotus, L. **-vāsaka**, m., **-vāsas**, m. = 1. *śrī-vāsa*, L. **-vidyā**, f. a form of Durgā, Cat.; exalted science (also N. of wk.), ib.; *-triśatī*, f., *-paddhati*, f., *-pūjā-paddhati*, f., -°*rcana-candrikā* and *-paddhati* (°*dyârc*°), f., *-vishaya*, m., °*dyôttara-tāpinī*, f. N. of wks. **-viśāla**, mf(*ā*)n. abounding in good fortune, Megh. **-vishṇu-padī**, f. clinging to the feet of the divine Vishṇu, BhP. **-vṛiksha**, m. the sacred fig-tree, L.; the Bilva tree, L.; = next (see *sa-śrī-vṛiksha*). **-vṛikshaka**, m. a ring or curl of hair on the chest of a horse (cf. *śrī-vatsa*), Sch. on Śiś.; *-navamī-vrata*, n. N. of a partic. religious observance, MW.; °*kshakin*, mfn. marked with a curl or lock of hair (as a horse, cf. *śrī-vatsakin*), Śiś. v, 56. **-vṛiddhi**, f. N. of a deity of the Bodhi tree, Lalit. **-veshṭa** or **-veshṭaka**, m. the resin of the Pinus Longifolia, L. **-vaidya-nātha-māhātmya**, n. N. of wk. **-vaishṇava**, m. a member of the Vaishṇava sect (esp. a follower of Rāmânuja, q. v.), W. 1; °*vâcāra-saṃgraha*, m. N. of wk., Cat. **-°śa** (*śrīśa*), m. 'lord or husband of Śrī,' N. of Vishṇu, Prasaṅg.; of Rāma-candra (whose wife Sītā is regarded as an incarnation of Śrī or Lakshmī), L.; (*ā*), f. N. of Rādhā, Pañcar. **-śataka**, n. N. of an astron. wk. **-śalmalī-bhāṇḍa-tīrtha**, n. N. of a Tīrtha, Cat. **-śānta**, m. N. of a man, W. **-śuka**, m. N. of a poet and an astronomer, Cat.; *-tīrtha*, n. N. of a Tīrtha, ib. **-śaila**, m. N. of various mountains, BhP.; (with *sūri*) N. of an author; *-khaṇḍa*, m. n. N. of ch. of the SkandaP.; *-tātâcārya*, m. N. of a preceptor, Cat.; *-māhātmya*, n.; °*lôpâkhyāna*, n. N. of wks. **-śyāmalâmbā-stotra**, n., **-śloka-paddhati**, f. N. of wks. **-°śvara** (*śrīśv*°), m. N. of a modern author (alive in 1884), Cat. **-shavāyaṇa**, n. N. of a part of the spurious Romaka-siddhânta. **-sheṇa** (or *-sena*), m. N. of a king, Kathās.; of the author of the Romaka-siddhânta (quoted by Brahma-gupta); (*ā*), f. N. of a woman, HPariś. **-saṃsthā**, f., **-saṃhitā**, f., N. of wks. **-saṃgrāma**, m. N. of a partic. Maṭha (q. v.), Rājat. **-saṃjña**, n. 'called after Śrī,' cloves (the various names of Śrī being applied to cloves), L. **-sambhūtā**, f. (in astron.) N. of the sixth night of the Karma-māsa (q. v.) **-sarasvatī**, f. du. Lakshmī and Sarasvatī, MW. **-sahasra**, n. N. of a Stotra. **-sahôdara**, m. 'brother of Śrī,' the moon (as produced together with Śrī at the churning of the ocean; cf. *śrī-putra*), L. **-siddhi**, f. (in astrol.) N. of the sixteenth Yoga. **-sukha**, m. N. of a medical author, Cat. **-sûkta**, n. N. of the hymn RV. i, 165, ŚāṅkhBr.; AgP.; *-nyāsa*, m., *-vidhāna*, n., *-vidhi*, m. N. of wks. **-sena**, see *-sheṇa*. **-stava**, m., **-stuti**, f. N. of wks. **-sthala**, n. N. of a temple of Śiva; *-prakāśa*, m., *-māhātmya*, n. N. of wks. **-smaraṇa-darpaṇa**, m. N. of wk. **-sraja**, n. Śrī (or fortune) and a garland, Pāṇ. v, 4, 106, Sch. **-svarūpa**, m. N. of a disciple of Caitanya, W. **-svarūpiṇī**, f. having the nature of Śrī (applied to Rādhā), Pañcar. **-svāmin**, m. N. of a king, Rājat.; of the father of Bhaṭṭi, Bhaṭṭ., Sch. **-haṭṭa**, N. of a town (= Silhet), W. **-hara**, mfn. robbing (i. e. excelling all in) beauty (applied to Rādhā), Pañcar. **-hari**, m. N. of Vishṇu (°*rer utthāna*, n. N. of a festival on the 14th day of the month Kārttika), Col.; *-stotra*, n. N. of wk. **-harsha**, m. N. of various authors &c. (esp. of a celebrated king and poet or patron of poets, also called Śrī-harsha-kavi or Śrī-harsha-deva, who lived probably in the first half of the seventh century A. D. and is the supposed author of three plays, viz. Nāgânanda, Priya-darśikā, and Ratnâvalī). **-hastinī**, f. the sunflower, Heliotropium Indicum (so called as held in the hand of Śrī or Lakshmī), L.

Śriyadhyai, Ved. inf., Pāṇ. iii, 4, 9, Sch.

Śriyáse (dat. and Ved. inf.), for beauty or splendour or glory, splendidly, gloriously, RV.

Śriyā, f. (collateral form of 3. *śrī*) prosperity, happiness (personified as the wife of Śrī-dhara i. e. Vishṇu), Kāv.; BhP. **-°ditya** (*śriyâd*°), m. N. of a man, Cat. **-nakula**, m. or n. N. of a place, ib. **-vāsa**, m. abode of fortune or prosperity, MBh. **-vāsin**, m. 'dwelling with Śrī,' N. of Śiva, ib.

Śrīka (ifc.; f. *ā*) = 2. *śrī*, fortune, prosperity, wealth, beauty &c. (cf. *gata-*, *niḥ-*, *puṇya-śrīka* &c.); m. a kind of bird, VarBṛS. (= *śrī-karṇa*, Sch.); a kind of resin, ib. (= *śrī-vāsaka*, Sch.)

Śrī-mat, mfn. beautiful, charming, lovely, pleasant, splendid, glorious, MBh.; Kāv. &c.; possessed of fortune, fortunate, auspicious, wealthy, prosperous, eminent, illustrious, venerable (used, like *śrī*, as a prefix before the names of eminent persons and celebrated works and sometimes corrupted into *śrīmant*), of high rank or dignity (m. 'a great or venerable person'), ChUp.; MBh.; R. &c.; decorated with the insignia of royalty (as a king), VarBṛS.; abounding in gold (as Meru), Bhartṛ.; m. N. of Vishṇu, L.; of Kubera, L.; of Śākya-mitra, Buddh.; of a son of Nimi, MBh.; of a poet, Cat.; Ficus Religiosa, L.; another tree (= *tilaka*), L.; a parrot, L.; a bull kept for breeding, L.; (*atī*), f. N. of one of the Mātṛis attendant on Skanda, MBh.; of various women (esp. of the mother of Mâdhavâcārya), Buddh.; Cat.; *-kumbha*, n. gold, L.; *-tama*, mfn. (superl.) most prosperous or eminent or illustrious, KaushUp.; *-tā*, f. prosperity, thriving condition, beauty, splendour, Kāv. **Śrīmac-chata-śalākin**, mfn. (fr. *śrīmat* + *śata* + *ś*°) furnished with a hundred beautiful ribs (as an umbrella), MBh. **Śrīmad-dattôpanishad**, f. N. of an Upanishad. **Śrīman-nṛipurī**, f. a royal residence, Viddh. **Śrīman-manya**, mfn. fancying one's self possessed of Śrī, Bhaṭṭ.

Śrīya, mfn. = *śriyai hitaḥ*, Pat.

Śrīyāka, m. N. of a son of Śakaṭāla, HPariś.

Śrīra. See *a-śrīrá*.

Śrī-raṅga, m. N. of Vishṇu (accord. to some 'of Śiva,' and according to others 'of an ancient king who founded the city of Seringapatam'), MW.; n. N. of a town and a celebrated Vaishṇava temple (established by Rāmânuja near Trichinopoly), RTL. 71, n.; 448. **-gadya**, n., **-guru-stotra**, n. N. of Stotras. **-deva**, m. N. of an author, Cat.; *-devâlaya-pradakshiṇa*, n. N. of wk. **-nātha**, m. N. of Vishṇu, W. (cf. comp.); of the author of a Comm. on the Bhāmatī (Cat.); *-kshamā-shoḍaśī*, f., *-prapatti*, f., *-maṅgalâśāsana*, n., *-suprabhāta*, n., *-stotra*, n.; °*thârādhana-krama*, m., °*thâshṭôttara-śata*, n. N. of wks. **-nāyakī**, f. (of *-nāyaka*) wife of the lord of Śrī-raṅga, L.; *-stuti*, f., *-stotra*, n. N. of wks. **-pattana**, n. 'Vishṇu's city,' the city of Seringapatam (situated in Mysore on an island in a channel of the Kāverī, said to have been founded by an ancient king who called it after himself, or by a devotee who dedicated it to Vishṇu; cf. above), MW. **-māhātmya**, n., **-rāja-catushṭaya**, n., **-rāja-stava**, m., **-rāja-stotra**, n., **-vimāna-stotra**, n., **-sapta-prākāra-pradakshiṇa-vidhi**, m. N. of wks. **Śrīraṅgêśa**, m. lord of Śrī-raṅga (°*śvarī*, f. wife of the lord of Śr°).

Śrīla, mf(*ā*)n. (g. *sidhmâdi*) prosperous, happy, wealthy, beautiful, eminent, Pañcar. (cf. *a-śrīla*). **-tā**, f. high rank (compared to a creeping plant; for *śrī-latā* see col. 1), Rājat. **-śrī-vopadeva**, m. the eminent and illustrious Vopadeva, Vop. **-hanumat**, m. the celebrated Hanumat, Cat.

Śry, in comp. for 2. *śrī*. **-āhva**, n. 'having the name of Śrī,' a lotus-flower (the goddess Śrī or Lakshmī having appeared with a lotus, the type of beauty, in her hand and being connected with it in many of her names, cf. *padmā*), L.; a kind of tree, Car.

श्रीकजाक *śrīkajāka* (?), n. a building of a partic. form, Hcat.

श्रीणा *śrīṇā*, f. night (v. l. for *śiriṇā*), Naigh. i, 7.

श्रीबेर *śrībera*, n. Andropogon Muricatus, L.

श्रीव् *śrīv*. See √*sriv*.

श्रीवभास *śrīvabhāsa* (?), m. N. of a man, Rājat.

श्रु 1. *śru*, cl. 5. P. (Dhātup. xxii, 44) *śṛiṇóti* (Ved. and ep. also Ā. *śṛiṇute*, and in RV. 3. sg. *śṛiṇvé*, 2. sg. °*vishé*, 3. pl. °*viré* [cf. below]; Impv. *śṛiṇu*, °*ṇudhí* and °*ṇuhí*, pl. *śṛiṇutá*, °*ṇota* and °*ṇotana*, RV.; pf. *śuśrā́va* [once in R. with pass. sense], *śuśruvé* [2. sg. *śuśrotha*, 1. pl. *śuśruma*, in Up. also °*mas*; *śuśravat*, *śuśrūyā́s*, RV., p. *śuśruvás*, q. v.]; aor. Ved. *áśravam*, *áśrot*, 2. sg. *śróshi*; Subj. *śrávat*, °*vathaḥ*; [?] *śruvam*, TĀr.; Impv. *śrudhí*, *śrótu*, RV.; *aśraushīt*, Br. &c.; Subj. *śroshan*, Impv. *śroshantu*, RV. [cf. *śróshamāṇa*]; Prec. *śrūyā́sam*, AV. &c.; fut. *śrotā́*, MBh.; *śroshyati*, °*te*, Br. &c.; inf. *śrotum*, MBh. &c.; ind. p. *śrutvā́*, RV. &c.; *-śrútya*, AV. &c.; *śrā́vam*, GṛŚrS. &c.), to hear, listen or attend to anything (acc.), give ear to any one (acc. or gen.), hear or learn anything about (acc.) or from (abl., gen., instr., *mukhāt* or *sakāśāt*), or that anything is (two acc.), RV. &c. &c.; to hear (from a teacher), study, learn, ŚrS.; MBh. &c.; to be attentive, be obedient, obey, MBh.; R. &c.: Pass. *śrūyáte* (ep. also °*ti*; and in RV. *śṛiṇve* &c. [cf. above] with pass. meaning; aor. *aśrāvi*, *śrā́vi*), to be heard or perceived or learnt about (acc.) or from (gen., abl. or *mukhāt*; in later language often 3. sg. *śrūyate*, impers. 'it is heard,' 'one hears or learns or reads in a book,' = 'it is said,' 'it is written in (with loc.);' Impv. *śrūyatām*, 'let it be heard' = 'listen!'), RV. &c. &c.; to be celebrated or renowned, be known as, pass for, be called (nom.), RV.; to be heard or learnt (from a teacher), Pañcat.; to be taught or stated (in a book), Sarvad.; to be heard i. e. pronounced or employed (as a sound or word), TPrāt., Sch.: Caus. *śrāvayati* (ep. also °*te*, in RV. also *śravayati*; aor. *aśuśravi*, °*vuḥ*, RV.; *aśuśruvat*, Br.; *aśiśravat*, Gr.; Pass. *śrāvyate*, see below), to cause to be heard or learnt, announce, proclaim, declare, RV. &c. &c.; to cause to hear, inform, instruct, communicate, relate, tell (with acc. of thing, and acc., gen., or dat. of pers., or with instr. in sense of 'through'), Mn.; MBh. &c.: Pass. of Caus. *śrāvyate*, to be informed of (acc.), MBh. &c.: Desid. *śúśrūshate* (Pāṇ. i, 3, 57; ep. or m. c. also °*ti*; Pass. *śuśrūshyate*), to wish or like to hear (acc.), desire to attend or listen to (dat.), RV. &c. &c.; to attend upon, serve, obey (acc., rarely gen.), Mn.; MBh. &c.: Caus. of Desid. *śuśrūshayati*, to wait upon, be at the service of (acc.), Kull. on Mn. ii, 243: Desid. of Caus. *śiśrāvayishati* or *śuśrāvayishati*, Gr.: Intens. *śośrūyate*, *śośravīti*, *śośroti*, Gr. [Cf. Gk. κλύω, κλῦθι = *śrudhi*, κλυτός = *śrutá* &c.; Lat. *cluo*, *in-clutus*; Slav. *sluti*; Germ. *laut*; Eng. *loud*.]

Śuśruvás, mfn. one who has heard &c. (with two acc., 'that anything is –;' also = *śuśrāva*, 'he has heard'), RV.; R.; Ragh. &c.; one who has learnt or studied, a scholar, TS.; ŚBr.

Śuśrū, śuśrūshaka &c. See p. 1084, col. 3.

Śrava, śravaṇa &c. See 1. *śrava*, p. 1096, col. 3.

Śrāva, śrāvaka &c. See p. 1097, col. 1.

Śruṇa. See *su-śruṇa*.

1. **Śrút**, mfn. hearing, listening (only in next and ifc.; cf. *karṇa-*, *dīrgha-śrut* &c.); that which is heard, sound, noise, Harav. – **karṇa** (*śrút-*), mfn. one who has hearing ears, quick to hear, RV.; AV.

Śrutá, mfn. heard, listened to, heard about or of, taught, mentioned, orally transmitted or communicated from age to age, ŚBr.; ChUp.; MBh. &c.; known, famous, celebrated, RV.; AV.; Br.; MBh.; known as, called (nom. with *iti*), MBh.; R. &c.; m. N. of a son of Bhagīratha, Hariv.; of a son of Kṛishṇa, BhP.; of a son of Su-bhāshaṇa, ib.; of a son of Upagu, VP.; (*ā*), f. N. of a daughter of Dīrgha-daṃshṭra, Kathās.; (*am*), n. anything heard, that which has been heard (esp. from the beginning), knowledge as heard by holy men and transmitted from generation to generation, oral tradition or revelation, sacred knowledge (in the Pur. personified as a child of Dharma and Medhā), the Veda, AV. &c. &c.; the act of hearing, MuṇḍUp.; Kāv.; Kathās.; learning or teaching, instruction (*śrutam* √*kṛi*, 'to learn'), Āpast.; memory, remembrance, AV. i, 1, 2. – **ṛishi** (*śrutá-*), mfn. (cf. *śruta-ṛshi*) having famous Ṛishis, RV. – **kaksha** (*śrutá-*), m. N. of a Ṛishi (author of RV. viii, 81), Anukr. – **karman**, m. N. of a son of Saha-deva, MBh.; of a son of Arjuna, ib.; of a son of Somâpi, VP.; of Śani, L. – **kāma**, mfn. desirous of sacred knowledge, ŚāṅkhŚr. – **kīrti**, m. 'one whose fame is heard about,' N. of a son of Arjuna, MBh.; of an astronomer, Cat.; of another man (also -*bhoja*), Inscr.; (*ā*), f. N. of a daughter of Kuśa-dhvaja (wife of Śatru-ghna), R.; of a daughter of Śūra (sister of Vasu-deva and wife of Dhṛishṭaketu), Pur. – **kevalin**, m. N. of a class of Jaina Arhats (of whom six are enumerated), L. – **ṃ-jaya**, m. N. of a son of Sena-jit, VP.; of a son of Satyâyu, BhP. – **tas**, ind. as if heard, Gobh.; with regard to orally transmitted knowledge or tradition, Nir. – **tva**, n. the being taught or learnt, Saṃk. – **dīpa**, m. N. of wk. – **deva**, m. a god in respect of knowledge, BhP.; N. of a son of Kṛishṇa, ib.; of a servant of Kṛishṇa, ib.; (*ā*), f. N. of a daughter of Śūra (sister of Vasu-deva and wife of Vṛiddha-śarman), Hariv.; Pur.; (*ī*), f. 'goddess of learning,' N. of Sarasvatī, L. – **dhara**, mfn. retaining what has been heard, having a good memory, Kāv.; Kathās.; BhP.; m. the ear, BhP.; N. of a king, Kathās.; of a poet, Git., Introd.; pl. N. of the Brāhmans in Śālmala-dvīpa, BhP. – **dharman**, m. N. of a son of Udâpi, Hariv. (v. l. *śruta-śravas*). – **dhāraṇa**, mfn. = -*dhara*, BhP. – **dhi**, m. 'receptacle of knowledge,' N. of a man, Kathās. – **dhvaja**, m. 'characterized by kn°,' N. of a warrior, MBh. – **nigadin**, mfn. able to recite what has once been heard, SāmavBr. (°*di-tva*, n., Sch.) – **nishkraya**, m. fee for instruction, Ragh. – **ṃ-dhara**, m. a kind of pavilion, Vāstuv. – **pāra-ga** (R.), -**pāra-dṛiśvan** (Ragh.), mfn. extremely learned, R. – **pāla**, m. 'guardian of kn°,' N. of a grammarian, Cat. – **pūrva**, mf(*ā*)n. heard or learnt before, known by hearsay, R.; Kālid. – **prakāśa**, mfn. renowned for kn° of the Vedas, Ragh. – **prakāśikā**, f. N. of various wks.; -*khaṇḍana* (with *siddhânta-siddhâñjana*), n.; -°*cārya-kṛita-rahasya-traya* (°*kâc*°), n., -*tātparya-dīpikā*, f., -*saṃgraha*, m. N. of Vedânta wks. – **pradīpa**, m., °**pikā**, f. N. of Vedânta wks. – **bandhu**, m. N. of a Ṛishi (having the patr. *Gaupāyana* or *Laupāyana* and author of RV. v, 24, 3; x, 57–60), Anukr. – **bodha**, m. a short treatise or compendium on the most common Sanskṛit metres (attributed either to Kālidāsa or to Vara-ruci). – **bhāva-prakāśikā**, f. N. of a Vedânta wk. – **bhṛit**, mfn. bearing kn°, learned, HPariś. – **maya**, mf(*ī*)n. consisting of kn°, Buddh. – **mahat**, see *śruti-m*°. – **mātra**, n. mere hearing or hearsay, Śrutab. – **yukta**, mfn. endowed with kn°, learned, VarBṛS. – **ratha** (*śrutá-*), mfn. possessing a renowned chariot (others 'N. of a man'), RV. – **rshi** (for -*ṛishi*), m. a Ṛishi distinguished by kn°, a very learned Ṛishi or a Ṛ° of a partic. order (such as the author of the Su-śruta), Āpast.; Nir., Sch.; (*śrutá-*), mfn. having distinguished Ṛ°s, TBr. – **vat**, mfn. one who has heard &c., Kāv.; Hit.; possessing (sacred) kn°, learned, pious, MBh.; Kāv. &c.; connected with or founded on kn°, BhP.; m. N. of a son of Somâpi, BhP. – **vadana**, mfn. one whose speech is (readily) heard, AitĀr. – **vardhana**, m. N. of a physician, Kathās. – **varman**, m. N. of a man, Vās., Introd. – **viṅśati-koṭi**, w. r. for *śroṇa-koṭi-viṅśa* (q. v.) – **vid**, m. 'knowing sacred revelation,' N. of a Ṛishi (having the patr. *Ātreya* and author of RV. v, 62), RV. v, 44, 12. – **vindā**, f. N. of a river, BhP. – **vismṛita**, mfn. heard and forgotten, Kathās. – **vṛitta**, n. du. kn° and virtue, Mn. vii, 135; °*ttâḍhya*, mfn. rich in kn° and v°, learned and virtuous, R.; °*ttôpapanna*, mfn. id., Mn. ix, 244. – **vṛiddha**, m. 'rich in kn°,' a learned man, scholar, Ragh. – **śabdârtha-samuccaya**, m. a vocabulary (by Somêśvara), Cat. – **śarman**, m. N. of a son of Udâyus, VP.; of a prince of the Vidyā-dharas, Kathās. – **śālin**, mfn. possessed of kn°, learned, Siṃhâs. – **śīla**, n. learning and virtuous conduct, Mn. xi, 22; m. N. of a man, Cat.; -*vat*, mfn. learned and virtuous, Mn. iii, 27, v. l.; -*sampanna* (Gaut.); °*lôpasampanna* (Kām.), mfn. id. – **śravas**, m. N. of various men, MBh.; Hariv.; Pur.; f. (also °*vā*) N. of a daughter of Śūra (mother of Śiśu-pāla and sister of Vasu-deva), ib.; °*vo'nuja*, m. the planet Saturn (said to be one of the sons of Sūrya), L. – **śrī**, m. N. of a Daitya, MBh. – **śruvas**, w. r. for -*śravas*. – **śroṇī**, f. Anthericum Tuberosum (prob. w. r. for *suta-śr*°). – **sád**, mfn. abiding in what is heard (i. e. in transmitted knowledge or tradition), TS. – **sená**, m. having a famous army, VS. (Sch.); (*śrutá-*), m. N. of a brother (or son) of Janam-ejaya, ŚBr.; MBh. &c.; of a son of Saha-deva, MBh.; of a son of Parikshit, ib.; of a son of Bhīma-sena, BhP.; of a son of Śatru-ghna, ib.; of a son of Śambara, Hariv.; of a prince of Go-karṇa, Kathās.; (*ā*), f. N. of a wife of Kṛishṇa, Hariv. – **soma**, m. N. of a son of Bhīma, VP.; (*ā*), f. N. of a wife of Kṛishṇa, Hariv. **Śrutâñjana-ṭīkā**, f. N. of wk. **Śrutâdāna**, n. 'Veda-acceptation,' citing or explaining the Veda (= *brahma-vāda*), L. **Śrutâdhyayana-sampanna**, mfn. conversant with repetition or recitation of the Veda, W. **Śrutânīka** and **Śrutânta**, m. N. of men, MBh. **Śrutânvita**, mfn. acquainted with or conforming to the Veda, Bhaṭṭ. **Śrutā-magha** (for *śrutá-m*°), mfn. having renowned treasures, RV. **Śrutâyu** or °**yus**, m. N. of a king of the solar race (descended from Kuśa, son of Rāma), R.; of a son of Purū-ravas, MBh.; of another king and various other men, ib.; Hariv.; Pur. **Śrutâyudha**, m. N. of a man, MBh. **Śrutârtha**, mfn. one who has heard anything (gen.), Hariv.; m. any matter ascertained by hearing, MW.; (*ā*), f. N. of a woman, Kathās. **Śrutā-vatī** (for *śruta-v*°), f. N. of a daughter of Bharad-vāja, MBh.

Śrutár (in a formula) = *śrutaḥ* (nom.), TS.

Śrutárya, m. N. of a man, RV. i, 112, 9 (Sāy.)

Śrutárvan, mfn. N. of a man (having the patr. Arksha), RV.; MBh.; Hariv. (cf. *śrautarvaṇa*).

1. **Śrúti**, f. hearing, listening (*śrutim abhinīya*, 'feigning to hear;' *śrutiṃ vaco 'nugām* √*kṛi*, 'to listen to a speech'), ŚBr. &c. &c.; the ear, organ or power of hearing, Kāv.; VarBṛS.; Kathās.; the diagonal of a tetragon or hypothenuse of a triangle, Gol.; that which is heard or perceived with the ear, sound, noise &c. RV.; AV.; Prāt.; Kathās.; BhP.; an aggregate of sounds (whether forming a word or any part of a word), TPrāt.; rumour, report, news, intelligence, hearsay (*śrutau* √*sthā*, 'to be known by hearsay'), MBh.; Kāv. &c.; a saying, saw, word, MBh.; R.; BhP.; that which has been heard or communicated from the beginning, sacred knowledge orally transmitted by the Brāhmans from generation to generation, the Veda (i. e. sacred eternal sounds or words as eternally heard by certain holy sages called Ṛishis, and so differing from *smṛiti* or what is only remembered and handed down in writing by human authors, see Mn. ii, 10; it is properly only applied to the Mantra and Brāhmaṇa portion of the Vedas, although afterwards extended to the Upanishads and other Vedic works including the Darśanas; *iti śruteḥ*, 'because it is so taught in the Veda, according to a *śruti* or Vedic text;' pl. 'sacred texts, the Vedas,' also 'rites prescribed by the Vedas'), AitBr.; ŚrS.; Mn.; MBh. &c.; IW. 144; (in music) a particular division of the octave, a quarter tone or interval (twenty-two of these are enumerated, four constituting a major tone, three a minor, and two a semitone; they are said to be personified as nymphs), Yājñ.; Śiś.; Pañcar.; a name, title, Kāvyâd. ii, 331; learning, scholarship, Śak.; VarBṛS. (prob. w. r. for *śruta*); = *buddhi*, L.; N. of a daughter of Atri and wife of Kardama, VP. – **kaṭa**, m. (only L.) penance, expiation; a snake; = *prāñca-loha* or *prāñcalloha*. – **kaṭu**, mfn. harsh to the ear, unmelodious; m. (in rhet.) a harsh or unm° sound, cacophony, Kpr. – **kaṇṭha**, w. r. for -*kaṭa*. – **kathita**, mfn. mentioned or taught, or prescribed in the Veda, W. – **kalpadruma**, m., -**kalpalatā**, f., -**kīrti**, f., -**gītā**, f. N. of wks. – **gocara**, mf(*ā*)n. perceptible by the ear, RāmatUp; permitted to be heard by (gen.), BhP. – **candrikā**, f., -**cikitsā**, f. N. of wks. – **codana**, n. a Vedic precept, sacred precept or injunction, Mn.; Yājñ. – **jāti-viśārada**, mfn. familiar with the origin or different kinds of the quarter tones, Yājñ. iii, 115. – **jīvikā**, f. a law-book or code of laws, L. – **tattva-nirṇaya**, m. N. of wk. – **tatpara**, mfn. having ears, hearing, L.; intent on hearing or studying the Veda, L. – **tas**, ind. according to sacred or revealed knowledge, in respect of or according to sacred precept, Āpast. – **tā**, f., see *udātta-śruti-tā*. – **tātparya-nirṇaya**, m. N. of a Vedânta wk. – **dushṭa**, n. = -*kaṭu*, Sāh. – **dūshaka**, mfn. offending the ear, Saṃkar. – **dvaidha**, n. disagreement or contradiction of any two passages in the Vedas or of two Vedas, Mn. ii, 14 &c. – **dhara**, m. = (and often v. l. for) *śruta-dh*°, Hariv.; Suśr.; Git.; holding or observing the Vedas, W. – **nigadin**, mfn. = *śruta-n*°, Suśr. – **nidarśana**, n. Veda-demonstration, testimony of the V°, Mn. xi, 45. – **patha**, m. the range of hearing (-*pathaṃ* √*gam* with gen., 'to come to any one's ears,' 'be heard by'), MBh.; R. &c.; the auditory passage, hearing, Śiś. (see comp.); pl. tradition, Suśr.; *gata* (MBh.); -*prâpta* (Rājat.), mfn. come to the ears of, heard by (gen.); -*madhura*, mfn. pleasant to the ear, Śiś.; °*thâyāta*, mfn. = °*thagata*, Kathās. – **pāda**, m., -**prapādikā**, f., -**purāṇa-saṃgraha**, m., -**prakāśikā**, f. N. of wks. – **prasādana**, n. gratifying the ear, engaging the attention, Śak. – **prāmāṇyatas**, ind. on the authority or with the sanction of the Veda, Mn. ii, 8. – **bhāskara**, m. N. of a wk. on music (by Bhīmadeva). – **maṇḍala**, n. 'ear-circle,' the outer ear, W.; the whole circle of the quarter-tones, Śiś. i, 10. – **mat**, mfn. having ears, ŚvetUp.; possessed of knowledge, learned (often v. l. for the more correct *śruta-vat*), Kāv.; VarBṛS.; Kathās.; having the Veda as source or authority, supported by a Vedic text (-*tva*, n.), Nyāyam. – **matânumāna**, n. N. of a Vedânta wk. (by Try-ambaka Śāstrin). – **maya**, mf(*ī*)n. based on or conformable to sacred tradition or the Veda, MBh. – **mayūra**, m. N. of a wk. on ornithology. – **mahat**, mfn. mighty in sacred knowledge (v. l. *śruta-m*°), Śak. – **mārga**, m. = -*patha* (°*gaṃ gata* or °*ga-pravishṭa*, 'having come or entered by way of the ears,' 'heard;' *mārga*, ibc. or °*geṇa*, 'by way of the ears,' 'by hearing'), Kāv.; Kathās. – **mita-prakāśikā**, f., -**mīmāṅsā**, f., -**muktā-phala**, n. N. of wks. – **mukha**, mfn. having the Veda or sacred tradition for a mouth, Pañcar. – **mukhara-mukha**, mfn. one whose mouth is talkative or eloquent with learning, Bhartṛ.

– mūla, n. the root of the ear, Gīt.; the text of the Vedas, W.; °*laka*, mfn. founded on or springing from the Veda, MW. **– mṛigya,** mfn. to be sought by hearing or by the Veda (not by sight), MW. **– rañjanī,** f., **-rañjinī,** f., **-lakshaṇa-prâyaścitta,** n. N. of wks. **– vacana,** n. a Vedic precept, Vās. **– varjita,** mfn. devoid of hearing, deaf, L.; ignorant or unread in the Veda, W. **– vāk-sāra-saṃgraha,** m. N. of a Vedânta wk. **– vi-krāyaka,** mfn. selling the Veda or sacred knowledge, MBh. **– vipratipanna,** mfn. dissenting from the Veda or sacred tradition, disregarding the doctrine of the Veda, Bhag. **– vivara,** n. the auditory passage, VarBṛS. **– vishaya,** m. the object of hearing (i. e. sound, see *vishaya*); subject-matter or doctrine of the Veda, any sacred matter or ordinance, W.; mfn. conversant with sacred knowledge, familiar with the Veda, MW.; *-guṇa*, mfn. having the quality (sound) which is the object of hearing or which is perceptible by the ear (said of ether), Śak. **– vedha,** m. the piercing or boring of the ear, L. **– śiras,** n. a leading text of the Veda, Sarvad. **– śīla,** mfn. able to distinguish the difference of the tones of a lute (= *tantrī-nāda-vibhājana-śīla*), R. (Sch.); *-vat*, w. r. for *śruta-śīla-vat* (q.v.) **– saṃkshipta-varṇana,** n., **-saṃgraha,** m. N. of two Vedânta wks. **– sāgara,** m. the ocean (i. e. the whole substance or essence) of sacred knowledge (Vishṇu), Pañcar. **– sāra,** m. N. of two wks.; *-pañca-ratna*, n., *-samuccaya*, m., *-samuddharaṇa-prakaraṇa*, n. N. of wks. **– sukha,** mfn. pleasant to the ear, BhP.; *-da* (VarBṛS.) and °*khâvaha* (Ṛitus), mfn. giving pleasure to the ear, pleasant to hear. **– sûkti-mālā,** f., **-sūtra-tātparyâmṛita,** n., **-stuti,** f. (= *veda-stuti*) N. of wks. **– sphoṭā,** f. Gynandropsis Pentaphylla, L. **– smṛiti,** f. du. the Veda and human tradition or law; *-viruddha*, mfn. opposed to the V° and h° tr°, MW.; *-vihita*, mfn. enjoined by the V° and h° tr°, W.; °*ty-āai-tātparya*, n. N. of a Vedânta wk.; °*ty-udita*, mfn. declared or enjoined by the Veda and human law, Mn. iv, 155. **– hārin,** mfn. captivating the ear, Ṛitus.

Śrutin, mfn. one who has heard, g. *ishṭâdi*; obeying, observing, W.; having or following the Vedas, ib.

Śrutika (ifc., fr. *śruti* = *śruti*), MBh.

Śruty, in comp. for 1. *śruti*. **– anuprâsa,** m. a kind of alliteration consisting in the repetition of consonants belonging to the same class or organ of utterance (e. g. the palatal letters *j* and *y* &c.), Sāh. **– anta-sura-druma,** m., **-artha-ratna-mālā,** f. N. of wks. **– arthâbhāva,** m., **-ānarthakya,** n. the uselessness of the Veda or of oral sacred tradition, KātyŚr. **– ukta,** mfn. said or enjoined in the Veda, Mn. i, 108. **– udita,** mfn. id., MW.

Śrútya, mfn. to be heard, famous, glorious, RV.; n. a glorious deed, ib.

1. **Śrū** (for 2. *śrū*, see col. 2). See *deva-śrū*.

Śrūyamāṇa, mfn. (Pass. pr. p. of √1. *śru*) being heard, heard (*-tva*, n.), Vedântas.

Śrotavya &c. See p. 1103, col. 1.

श्रु 2. *śru* (only in *śrúvat*; generally an incorrect form of √*sru*), to dissolve into parts, burst asunder, RV. i, 127, 3.

2. **Śrávaṇa** &c. See p. 1097, col. 2.

2. **Śrút,** f. (= *srut*) a river (?), RV. i, 53, 9.

2. **Śrúti,** f. (cf. *sruti*) course, path (?), RV. ii, 2, 7; x, 111, 3; the constellation Śravaṇā, L.

1. **Śrotas** &c. See *srotas*.

श्रुघ्निका *śrughnikā*, incorrect for *sr*°.

श्रुच् *śruc* &c., incorrect for *sruc*.

श्रुधीय *śrudhīya*, n. (perhaps fr. Impv. *śrudhi*) N. of two Sāmans, ĀrshBr.

Śrudhīyát, mfn. (prob.) willing, obedient, RV.

Śrudhya, n. N. of two Sāmans, ĀrshBr.

Śru-mat, m. N. of a man, Pāṇ. v, 3, 118 (cf. *śromata*, *śraumata*, °*tya*).

श्रुव *śruva* &c. See *sruva*.

श्रुष् *śrush*, a collateral form of √1. *śru*, and appearing in the verbal forms *śroshan*, *śroshantu*, *śroshamāṇa*, and in *śraushṭi* &c. [Cf. Lith. *klausti*; Slav. *sluchŭ*.]

Śrushṭi or **śrúshṭi,** f. obedience, complaisance, willing service (*śrushṭiṃ* √*kṛi*, 'to obey;' *śrushṭī*, ind. 'willingly, gladly, immediately, quickly, at once'), RV.; confidence in (with gen.), RV.; mfn. obedient, willing, ib.; m. N. of an Āṅgirasa (prob. w. r. for *śnushṭi*, q. v.) **– gu** (*śrúshṭi-*), mfn. N. of a Ṛishi (having the patr. Kāṇva and author of RV. viii, 51), Anukr. **– mát,** mfn. obedient, willing, RV.

Śrushṭī-ván, mf(*ári*)n. willing, obedient, ready to help, RV.

श्रू 2. *śrū* (nom. *śrūs*, fr. √*śriv* = *sriv*), Vop.

श्रूषा *śrūshā*, f. Cassia Esculenta, L.

श्रेक् *śrek*. See √*srek*.

श्रेटी *śreṭī* or *śreḍī* or *śreḍhī*, f. (in the vernaculars *śeḍī*; cf. *śreṇī*) a partic. numerical notation or progression of figures (in arithm.), Col.

श्रेणि *śreṇi*, f. (L. also m.; according to Uṇ. iv, 51, fr. √*śri*; connected with *śreṭī* above) a line, row, range, series, succession, troop, flock, multitude, number, RV. &c. &c.; a swarm (of bees), Śiś.; a company of artisans following the same business, a guild or association of traders dealing in the same articles, Mn.; MBh. &c.; a bucket, watering-pot, L.; the fore or upper part of anything, L.; Sanseviera Roxburghiana, L. **– kṛita,** mfn. = *śreṇī-kṛ*°, Pāṇ., Sch. **– dat** (*śréṇi-*), mfn. one whose teeth form a row, RV. **– baddha,** mfn. bound into a row, forming a row, MBh. **– mat,** mfn. having a number of followers, presiding over an association or guild, ib. **– śás,** ind. in rows or lines or troops or flocks, RV. **– sthāna,** n. 'social state,' N. of the first three stages in the life of an Ārya (cf. *āśrama*), MBh. xii, 8917.

Śreṇika, m. a front-tooth, Gal.; N. of a king (= *bimbisāra*), HParīś.; (*ā*), f., see next. **– purāṇa,** n. N. of wk.

Śreṇikā, f. a kind of metre (= *śyenikā*), Col.; a tent, W.

Śreṇī, f. a line, row &c. (= *śreṇi*), Mn.; MBh. &c. **– kṛita,** mfn. made into a row, forming rows or lines, MBh. (cf. *śreṇi-kṛ*°). **– dharma,** m. pl. the customs of trades or guilds, Mn. viii, 41. **– bandha,** m. the formation of a row or line, Ragh. **– bhūta,** mfn. being i. e. forming a row or rows, Megh.

Śreṇya, m. N. of a king (= *śreṇika*), Buddh.

Śreḍhī, f. (cf. *śreṭī* &c.) any set or succession of distinct things, W.; (in arithm.) progression; sequence, ib. **– phala,** n. the sum of a progression, MW. **– vyavahāra,** m. the ascertainment or determination of progressions, ib.

Śraiṇya, m. (cf. *śreṇya*) N. of Bimbisāra, Buddh.

श्रेतृ *śretṛi*, m. one who has recourse to (gen.), MBh. (v. l. *ā-śretṛi*).

श्रेमन् *śre-mán*, m. (fr. 2. *śrī*) distinction, superiority, MaitrS.; Br.

श्रेयस् *śréyas*, mfn. (either compar. of *śrī* or rather accord. to native authorities of *śrī-mat* or *praśasya*; cf. Gk. κρείων) more splendid or beautiful, more excellent or distinguished, superior, preferable, better, better than (with abl. or with *na*, see below), RV. &c. &c.; most excellent, best, MBh. iii, 1256; propitious, well disposed to (gen.), ib. i, 3020; auspicious, fortunate, conducive to welfare or prosperity, Kāv.; Hit.; MārkP.; m. (in astron.) N. of the second Muhūrta; of the third month (accord. to a partic. reckoning); (with Jainas) N. of the 11th Arhat of the present Avasarpiṇī, L.; (*śreyasī*), f. N. of various plants (accord. to L. Terminalia Chebula or Citrina; Clypea Hernandifolia; Scindapsus Officinalis; = *rāsnā*, *ambashṭhā* and *priyaṅgu*), Car.; Bhpr. &c.; N. of a deity of the Bodhi tree, Lalit.; (*as*), n. the better state, the better fortune or condition (sometimes used when the subject of a sentence would seem to require the masc. form), AV.; TS.; Br.; Kauś.; good (as opp. to 'evil'), welfare, bliss, fortune, happiness, KaṭhUp.; MBh. &c.; the bliss of final emancipation, felicity (see *śreyaḥ-pariśrāma*, col. 3); ind. better, rather, rather than (used like *varam* [q. v.] with *na*; e. g. *śreyo mṛitaṃ na jīvitam*, 'better is death and not life' or 'rather than life,' or 'death is better than life'), MBh.; R. &c.; = *dharma*, L.; N. of a Sāman, ĀrshBr. **– kara** (*śréyas-*), mf(*ī*)n. making better or superior, VS.; causing or securing fortune, conducive to happiness or prosperity, salutary, wholesome, Mn.; MBh. &c.; *-tara*, mfn. more efficacious for securing happiness, Mn. xii, 84; 86; *-bhāshya*, n. N. of wk. **– kāma,** mf(*ā*)n. desirous of welfare or prosperity, MBh.; BhP.; *-tā*, f. desirous of causing happiness or rendering happy, MBh. **– kṛit,** mfn. = *-kara*, BhP. **– tara,** mfn. very much better, MW. **– tva,** n. betterness, superiority, Mn. x, 66.

Śreyaḥ, in comp. for *śreyas*. **– keta** (*śréyaḥ-*), mfn. striving after excellence or superiority, AV. **– pariśrāma,** m. toiling after final emancipation, BhP.

Śreyasa, n. welfare, happiness, bliss (mostly ifc.; cf. *ahaṃ-*, *niḥ-*, *śvaḥ-śr*°).

Śreyasi-tarā or **śreyasī-tarā,** f. a more excellent woman, Pāṇ. vi, 2, 45.

Śreyāṅsa, m. N. of the 11th Arhat of the present Avasarpiṇī, L.

Śreyo, in comp. for *śreyas*. **– 'bhikāṅkshin,** mfn. desiring bliss or welfare, Mn. iv, 91. **– maya,** mf(*ī*)n. consisting of bliss, excellent, best, ŚārṅgS. **– 'rthin,** mfn. desiring felicity or bliss, Śāntaś.: desirous of good, ambitious, W.

Śréshṭha, mf(*ā*)n. most splendid or beautiful, most beautiful of or among (with gen.), RV.; AV.; R.; most excellent, best, first, chief (*am*, n. 'the best or chief thing'), best of or among or in respect of or in (with gen., loc., or comp.), RV. &c. &c.; better, more distinguished, superior, better than (abl. or gen.), Mn.; MBh. &c.; most auspicious or salutary, VarBṛS.; oldest, senior, W.; m. a king, L.; a Brāhman, L.; N. of Vishṇu or Kubera, L.; N. of a king, Buddh.; (*ā*), f. an excellent woman, MW.; Hibiscus Mutabilis, L. (prob. w. r. for *lakshmī-śr*°); a kind of root resembling ginger, L.; n. cow's milk, L.; copper, L. **– kāshṭha,** m. Tectona Grandis, L.; n. the main pillar of a house, W. **– tama** (*śréshṭha-*), mfn. the very best, most excellent, RV. &c. &c.; (*ā*), f. holy basil, L. **– tara,** mfn. more excellent, better than (abl.), MBh. **– tas,** ind. according to excellence or superiority, Lāṭy. **– tā,** f. (AitBr.; Mn. &c.), **-tva,** n. (Suśr.) betterness, eminence, excellence, superiority. **– pāla,** m. N. of a king, Buddh. **– bhāj,** mfn. 'possessing the best,' = *śreshṭha*, best, excellent, MBh. **– yajña,** m. the best or chief sacrifice, AitBr. **– yāna,** n. (with Buddhists) the best or chief vehicle, Vajracch. **– varcas** (*śréshṭha-*), mfn. having most excellent vigour or energy or glory, RV. **– vāc,** mfn. pre-eminent in speech, eloquent, R. **– śāka,** n. a kind of excellent pot-herb (cf. *vara-pota*), L. **– śocis** (*śréshṭha-*), mfn. having the best splendour, most brilliant, RV. **– sāman,** n. the best or chief Sāman, PañcavBr. **– sena,** m. N. of a king, Rājat. **– sthā,** mfn. (nom. *-sthās*) fit for or belonging to the best, TāṇḍBr. **Śreshṭhânvaya,** mfn. descended from an excellent family, Mālatīm. **Śreshṭhâmla,** n. the fruit of Garcinia Cambogia, L. **Śreshṭhâśrama,** m. the best period or stage of a Brāhman's life, one who is in the best period, a householder, L.

Śreshṭhaka, °**ṭhika.** See *bhūri-śr*°.

Śreshṭhin, mfn. having the best, best, chief, W.; m. a distinguished man, a person of rank or authority, AitBr.; ŚāṅkhBr.; KaushUp.; a warrior of high rank, Jātakam.; an eminent artisan, the head or chief of an association following the same trade or industry, the president or foreman of a guild (also *inī*, f. a female artisan &c.), Hariv.; Kāv.; VarBṛS. &c.

Śraishṭhya, n. (fr. *śreshṭha*) superiority, pre-eminence among (gen. or comp.), AV. &c. &c. **– tama** (?), mfn. = *śreshṭha-tama*, ŚāṅkhGṛ.

श्रेष्मन् *śreshman*. See *a-śreshmán*.

श्रै *śrai*. See √*śrā*, p. 1097, col. 2.

श्रोण् *śroṇ* (prob. artificial; cf. √*śloṇ*), cl. 1. P. *śroṇati*, to collect, accumulate, Dhātup. xiii, 14; to go, move, Nir. iv, 3.

श्रोण *śroṇá*, mf(*ā*)n. (= 2. *śravaṇa*) lame, limping, a cripple, RV.; cooked, dressed, matured (prob. w. r. for *śrāṇa*), L.; m. (m. c.) and (*ā*), f. the constellation Śravaṇā, TS.; Kāṭh.; Baudh.; BhP.; (*ā*), f. rice-gruel (cf. *śrāṇā*), L. **– koṭi-karṇa** and **-koṭi-viṅśa,** m. N. of two men, Buddh. **Śroṇâparânta,** N. of a town (°*ta-ka*, m. pl. its inhabitants), ib.

Śroṇi, f. (L. also m.; mostly du.; ifc. f. *ī* for *śroṇī*, see below) the hip and loins, buttocks, RV.

&c. &c.; the thighs or sides of the Vedi or of any square, Baudh.; Śulbas.; a road, way, L. [Cf. Lat. *clunis*; Lith. *szlaunìs*.] **-kapāla**, n. the thigh bone, AitBr. **-taṭa**, m. the slope of the hips, BhP. **-tás**, ind. from the hips, VS. **-deśa**, m. the region of the hips, BhP. **-pratodín**, mfn. kicking the hinder parts or posteriors, AV. **-phala** or **-phalaka**, n. the hip and loins, L.; the hip-bone (os ilium), MW. **-bimba**, n. round hips (see *bimba*), Kālid.; a waist-band (= *kaṭi-sūtra*), L. **-mat** (*śróṇi-*), mfn. having strong hips (*-tara*, compar.), MaitrS. **-yugma**, n. a pair of hips, both hips, Pañcar. **-varjam**, ind. except the hips, MW. **-vimba**, see *-bimba*. **-vedha**, m. N. of a man (pl. his descendants), Saṃskārak. **-sūtra**, n. a string worn round the loins, MBh.; a sword-belt, ib.

Śroṇikā, f. the hips, Pañcar.

Śroṇī, f. the hips and loins &c. (= *śroṇī*); the middle, Dharmaś.; N. of a river, VP. **-phala**, n. the hip, Col. **-bhāra**, m. the weight of the buttocks, Megh. **-sūtra**, n. a string worn round the loins, R.

Śroṇīkā, f. = *śroṇikā*, Pañcar.

Śroṇya, m. N. of a man (pl. his descendants), Saṃskārak.

श्रोत **śrota.** See *srota*.

श्रोतव्य **śrotavya**, mfn. (fut. p. of √1. *śru*) to be heard or listened to, audible, worth hearing, ŚBr. &c. &c.; n. the moment for hearing (impers. 'it must be heard'), MBh.; Kāv. &c.

2. **Śrotas**, n. (fr. √1. *śru*) the ear, L. (also w.r. for *srotas*).

Śrotu, (prob.) m. hearing (only in next and *su-śrótu*). **-rāti** (*śrótu-*), mfn. giving an ear, hearing, RV.

Śrótṛi (with acc.) or **śrotṛí** (with gen.), mfn. one who hears, hearing, a hearer, RV. &c. &c.; m. N. of a Yaksha, BhP. (Sch.)

Śrótra, n. the organ of hearing, ear, auricle, RV. &c. &c.; the act of hearing or listening to, AV. &c. &c.; conversancy with the Veda or sacred knowledge itself, MW. **-kāntā**, f. a kind of medicinal plant, L. **-cit**, mfn. accumulated by hearing, ŚBr. **-jña**, mfn. perceiving by the ear; *-tā*, f. perception by the ear, Yājñ. **-tás**, ind. by the ear, on the ear, ŚBr. **-tā**, f. the state of (being) an ear, Amar. (v. l.) **-dā**, mfn. giving an ear, listening to, hearing, ĀpŚr. **-netra-maya**, mf(*ī*)n. consisting of eyes and ears, Kathās. **-pati**, m. the lord of hearing, TUp.; a partic. form of Īśvara, Śaṃk. **-padavī**, f. the range of hearing (°*vīm upa-√yā*, 'to come within the range of h°'), Cat. **-padânuga**, mfn. agreeable to the ear, MW. **-paramparā**, f. successive oral report or hearsay (°*rayā*, 'by successive oral communication'), Ratnâv. **-pā́**, mfn. protecting the ear, VS. **-pāli**, f., **-puṭa**, m. the lobe of the ear, Rājat. **-peya**, mfn. to be drunk in by the ear or attentively heard, worth hearing, Megh.; Kathās. **-bhid**, mfn. splitting the ears, MW. **-bhṛit**, mfn. N. of partic. bricks, ŚBr. **-máya**, mf(*ī*)n. consisting in hearing, whose nature or quality is h°, ib. **-mārga**, m. path or range of the ear (°*gam √gam* with gen., 'to be heard by'), Pañcat. **-mūla**, n. the root of the ear, R. **-ramya**, mfn. pleasant to the ear, BrahmaP. **-vat** (*śrótra-*), mfn. endowed with (the power of) hearing, ŚBr. **-vartman**, n. = *-mārga*, Bhartṛ. (v. l.) **-vādin**, mfn. willing to hear, obedient, Hariv. **-śukti-puṭa**, m. the hollow of the ear or auricle, Rājat. **-saṃvāda**, m. agreement of the ear, Mālatīm. **-sukha**, mfn. sounding agreeably, melodious, musical, VarBṛS. **-sparśin**, mfn. touching i. e. entering or penetrating the ear, BhP. **-svín**, mfn. having a good or quick ear, TBr. (cf. *śata-svin*). **-hārin**, mfn. enrapturing the ear, MārkP. **-hīna**, mfn. destitute of hearing, deaf, VarBṛS. **Śrotrâdi**, n. 'the ear and the other senses,' the five senses (see *indriya*), MW. **Śrotrânukūla**, mfn. = *śrotra-ramya*, R. **Śrotrâpêta**, mfn. = *śrotra-hīna*, KaushUp. **Śrotrâbhirāma**, mfn. = *śrotra-ramya*, Ragh. **Śrotrâśaya-sukha**, mfn. pleasant to the seat of hearing or ear, melodious, R. **Śrotrêndriya**, n. the sense or organ of hearing, Suśr.

Śrótriya, mfn. learned in the Veda, conversant with sacred knowledge, AV. &c. &c.; docile, modest, well-behaved, W.; m. a Brāhman versed in the Veda, theologian, divine, Mn.; MBh. &c.; a Brāhman of the third degree (standing between the Brāhmaṇa and Anūcāna), Hcat. **-tā**, f. (L.), **-tva**, n. (MBh.) conversancy with the Veda, the being a learned Brāhman. **-sva**, n. the property of a learned Brāhman, Mn. viii, 149.

Śrotriya-sāt-√kṛi, P. *-karoti*, to give into the possession of Brāhmans versed in the Veda, Ragh.

Śrómata, n. (cf. *śru-mat*) renown, fame, celebrity, glory (instr. pl. 'gloriously'), RV. [Cf. Zd. *sraoman*; Germ. *liumunt*, *Leumund*.]

Śróshamāṇa, mfn. (cf. *śrushṭi*) willing, obedient, confident, RV.

Śrauta, mf(*ī* or *ā*)n. relating to the ear or hearing, W.; to be heard, audible, expressed in words or in plain language (as a simile, opp. to *ārtha*, 'implied'), Kpr.; relating to sacred tradition, prescribed by or founded on or conformable to the Veda (with *janman*, n. 'the second birth of a Brāhman produced by knowledge of the Veda'), Yājñ.; Kāv.; Kathās. &c.; sacrificial, MW.; n. relationship resulting from (common study of) the Veda, Hariv.; a fault (incurred in repeating the Veda), Hcat.; any observance ordained by the Veda (e. g. preservation of the sacred fire), W.; the three sacred fires collectively, ib.; N. of various Sāmans, ĀrshBr. **-ṛishi**, m. patr. of Deva-bhāga, AitBr. **-kaksha**, n. N. of various Sāmans, ĀrshBr. **-karman**, n. a Vedic rite; (°*ma*)*-padârtha-saṃgraha*, m., *-prâyaścitta*, n., and (°*many*)*-āśvalāyanôpayogi-prâyaścitta*, n. N. of wks. **-grantha**, m., **-candrikā**, f., **-nṛisiṇha-kārikā**, f. N. of wks. **-padârtha-nirvacana**, n. an explanation of technical terms occurring in Śrauta sacrifices (compiled about 1880 by Benares Paṇḍits). **-paddhati**, f., **-paribhāshā-saṃgraha-vṛitti**, f., **-prakriyā**, f., **-prayoga**, m., **-prayoga-sāman**, n. pl., **-pravāsa-vidhi**, m., **-praśna**, m. N. of wks. **-praśnôttara-vyavasthā**, f. rules for sacrificial rites in the form of question and answer. **-prâyaścitta**, n. N. of a Pariśishṭa of the Sāma-veda and of other wks.; *-candrikā*, f., *-prayoga*, m. N. of wks. **-mārga**, m. (the path of) hearing, Śiś. **-mīmāṇsā**, f., **-yajña-darśa-paurṇamāsika-prayoga**, m. N. of wks. **-rshá**, m. (fr. *śruta-rshi*) patr. of Deva-bhāga, TBr.; n. N. of various Sāmans, ĀrshBr. **-vājapeya**, n., **-vyākhyāna**, n. N. of wks. **-śrava**, m. (fr. *śruta-śravā*) metron. of Śiśupāla, MBh. **-sarvasva**, n., **-siddhânta**, m. N. of wks. **-sūtra**, n. N. of partic. Sūtras or Sūtra works based on Śruti or the Veda (ascribed to various authors, such as Āpastamba, Āśvalāyana, Kātyāyana, Drāhyāyaṇa &c.; cf. IW. 146); *-vidhi*, m., *-vyākhyā*, f. N. of wks. **-smārta-karma-paddhati**, f. N. of wk. (= *kātyāyana-sūtra-p°*). **-smārta-kriyā**, f. any act conformable to the Veda and Smṛiti, q. v., MW. **-smārta-dharma**, m. a duty enjoined by the V° and Sm°, ib. **-smārta-vidhi**, m. N. of a wk. by Bāla-kṛishṇa. **-homa**, m. N. of a Pariśishṭa of the Sāma-veda. **Śrautâṇḍa-bilā**, f., **Śrautâdhāna**, n., **Śrautâdhāna-paddhati**, f., **Śrautânukramaṇikā**, f., **Śrautân-tyêshṭi**, f., **Śrautâhnika**, n., **Śrautôllāsa**, m. N. of wks.

Śrauti, m. a patr. (prob. fr. *śruta*), g. *gahâdi*.

Śrautīya, mfn. (fr. prec.), ib.

Śrautrá, mf(*ī*)n. (fr. *śrotra*) relating to the ear, VS.; ŚBr.; n. the ear (= *śrotra*), g. *prajñâdi*; a multitude of ears, g. *bhikshâdi*; (fr. *śrotriya*) = next, g. *yuvâdi*.

Śrautriyaka, n. (fr. *śrotriya*) conversancy with the Vedas, g. *manojñâdi*.

Śraumata, m. pl., see next.

Śraumatya, m. patr. fr. *śru-mat*, ŚBr. (cf. Pāṇ. v, 3, 118); pl. °*matāḥ*, ĀśvŚr. (cf. Pāṇ. ib.)

Śraúshaṭ, ind. (prob. for *śroshat*, Subj. of √1. *śru*, 'may he, i. e. the god, hear us!') an exclamation used in making an offering with fire to the gods or departed spirits (cf. *vashaṭ*, *vaushaṭ*), RV.; TS.; ŚBr. (cf. Pāṇ. viii, 2, 91).

श्रौष्ट **śraushṭa**, n. N. of a Sāman (prob. w. r. for *śnaushṭa*, q. v.) **Śraushṭi-gava** and °**ṭīya**, n. N. of Sāmans (prob. w. r. for *śn°*, q. v.)

श्रौष्टि **śraúshṭi**, mfn. (fr. *śrushṭi*) willing, obedient, RV.

श्र्याह्व **śry-āhva.** See p. 1100, col. 3.

श्लक्ष्ण **ślakshṇá**, mf(*ā*)n. (in Uṇ. iii, 19 said to be fr. √*ślish*) slippery, smooth, polished, even, soft, tender, gentle, bland, AV. &c. &c.; small, minute, thin, slim, fine (cf. comp.), L.; honest, sincere, W.; (*am*), ind. softly, gently, MBh.; R.; m. N. of a mountain, Divyâv.; (*ā*), f. N. of a river, ib. **-tara**, mfn. more or most slippery or smooth &c., R. **-tā**, f. smoothness, Car. **-tīkshṇâgra**, mfn. having a thin and sharp point, L. **-tvac**, m. 'having a smooth bark,' Bauhinia Tomentosa, L. **-pattraka**, m. ebony, Diaspyros Ebenaster, L. **-pishṭa**, mfn. ground fine, Suśr. **-rūpa-samanvita**, mfn. having a smooth (or slender) form (applied to the sacrificial post), R. **-vāc**, f. kindly speaking, L. **-vādin**, mfn. speaking softly or gently, ib. **-śilā**, f. a smooth or slippery stone, Suśr.

Ślakshṇaka, mf(*ikā*)n. (= *ślakshṇa*) slippery, smooth, AV.

Ślakshṇana, n. making slippery, smoothing, polishing, KātyŚr.

Ślakshṇaya, Nom. P. °*yati*, to make slippery, smooth, polish, ib.; to make thin or small, MW.

Ślakshṇī, in comp. for *ślakshṇa*. **-karaṇa**, n. smoothing, Nyāyam., Sch.; a means or method of polishing, ĀpŚr. **-√kṛi**, P. *-karoti*, to smooth, polish, ĀpŚr.; TS., Sch.

Ślākshṇabhārika, m. (fr. *ślakshṇa* + *bhāra*) bearing a small load, g. *vaṇśâdi*.

Ślākshṇika, mfn. id., g. *vaṇśâdi*; = *ślakshṇam adhīte veda vā*, g. *ukthâdi*.

श्लख **ślakha.** See *uc-chlakhá*.

श्लङ्क् **ślaṅk** (cf. √*śraṅk*), cl. 1. Ā. *ślaṅkate*, to go, move, Dhātup. iv, 11.

श्लङ्ग् **ślaṅg** (cf. √*śraṅg*), cl. 1. P. *ślaṅgati*, to go, move, Dhātup. v, 45.

श्लथ् **ślath** (collateral form of √*śrath*), cl. 1. P. *ślathati* (only pr. p. *ślathat*), to be loose or relaxed or flaccid, BhP.: Caus. *ślathayati*, id., Dhātup xxxv, 18; to let loose, relax, loosen, Śiś.; to hurt, kill, W.

Ślatha, mfn. loose, relaxed, flaccid, weak, feeble, languid, MBh.; Kāv. &c.; untied, unfastened, Kāv.; Kathās.; dishevelled (as hair), W. **-tva**, n. looseness, laxity, Sāh. **-bandhana**, mfn. having the muscles relaxed, Ṛitus. **-lambin**, mfn. hanging loosely, Kum. **-śila**, mfn. covered with a loose stone (as a well), VarYogay. **-saṃdhi**, mfn. having weak joints (*-tā*, f.), Vāgbh. **Ślathâṅga**, mfn. having relaxed or languid limbs (*-tā*, f.), Bhartṛ. **Ślathâdara**, mfn. having feeble or slight regard to (loc.), Prab. **Ślathôdyama**, mfn. relaxing one's effort, Bhartṛ.

Ślathāya, Nom. Ā. °*yate*, to become loose or relaxed, MBh.

Ślathī-√kṛi, P. *-karoti* (p. p. *-kṛitá*), to make loose, relax, Amar.; to diminish, Kathās.

श्लनवास **ślanavāsa**, m. N. of an Arhat, Buddh.

श्लवन **ślavana**, m. (cf. 2. *śravaṇa*; *śroṇa*) lame, limping, PañcavBr.

श्लाख् **ślākh** (cf. √*śākh*), cl. 1. P. *ślākhati*, to pervade, penetrate, Dhātup. v, 13.

श्लाघ् **ślāgh**, cl. 1. Ā. (Dhātup. iv, 41) *ślāghate* (ep. also °*ti*; pf. *śaślāghe*, °*ghire*, Hariv.; Gr. also aor. *aślāghishṭa*; fut. *ślāghitā*, *ślāghishyate*; inf. *ślāghitum*), to trust or confide in (dat.), ŚBr.; to talk confidently, vaunt, boast or be proud of (instr. or loc.), Āpast.; Baudh.; MBh. &c.; to coax, flatter, wheedle (dat.), Pāṇ. i, 4, 34, Kāś.; to praise, commend, eulogise, celebrate, MBh.; Kāv. &c. (cf. Pāṇ. ib.): Pass. *ślāghyate* (aor. *aślāghi*), to be praised or celebrated or magnified, MBh.; Kāv. &c.: Caus. *ślāghayati* (aor. *aśaślāghat*), to encourage, comfort, console, R.; to praise, celebrate, Hit.; BhP.

Ślāghana, mfn. boasting, a boaster, MBh.; n. or (*ā*), f. the act of flattering, praise, eulogy, Sāh.

Ślāghanīya, mfn. to be praised, praiseworthy, laudable, commendable, MBh.; Kāv. &c. **-tara**, mfn. more (or most) praiseworthy &c., R. **-tā**, f. praiseworthiness, Kāv.

Ślāghā, f. vaunt, boasting, MBh. (cf. Pāṇ. v, 1, 134); flattery, praise, commendation, MBh.; Kāv. &c. (cf. Pāṇ. i, 4, 34, Kāś.); pleasure or delight in anything, Jātakam.; service, obedience, L.; wish, desire, L. **-vaha**, mfn. meriting praise.

Ślāghita, mfn. flattered, praised, commended, BhP.

Ślāghin, mfn. boasting or proud of (comp.), Hariv.; R.; haughty (as a lion), BhP.; celebrated, famous for (comp.), MBh.; Kāv. &c.; (ifc.) praising, celebrating, R. (cf. *ātma-śl°*); = *śālin*, Divyav.; desiring, MW.

Ślāghishṭha, mfn. highly praised or celebrated, BhP.

Ślāghya, mfn. = *ślāghanīya* (*am*, ind.), MBh.; Kāv. &c. **-tama** (BhP.), **-tara** (Ragh.), mfn. most or more praiseworthy or laudable &c. **-tā**, f. praiseworthiness, Kām. **-yauvanā**, f. (a woman) in the glorious bloom of youth, Ratnāv. **Ślāghyânvaya**, mfn. descended from a honourable family, Mālatīm.

श्लि *śli* = √*śri*, in *pra-ślita*, q. v.

श्लिकु *śliku*, m. (accord. to Uṇ. i, 33 fr. √2. *ślish*) a servant, slave, dependant, L.; a profligate or low person, L.; m. or n. astronomy, astrology, L.; f. or n. exhaustion, L.

श्लिष् 1. *ślish* (cf. √1. *śrish*), cl. 1. P. *śleshati*, to burn, Dhātup. xvii, 52.

1. **Ślesha**, m. burning, MW.

श्लिष् 2. *ślish* (cf. √2. *śrish*), cl. 4. P. (Dhātup. xxvi, 77) *ślishyati* (rarely °*te*; pf. *śiślesha*, Br. &c.; aor. *aślishat*, MBh. &c.; *aślikshat* [only in the sense of 'to embrace,' Pāṇ. iii, 1, 46] or *aślaikshīt* [?], Gr.; fut. *śleshṭā*, *ślekshyati*, ib.; inf. *śleshṭum*, Kāv.; ind. p. *śl ishṭvā*, ib.; *-ślishya*, MBh. &c.), to adhere, attach, cling to (loc., rarely acc.), Suśr.; ChUp.; MBh.; to clasp, embrace, Gaut.; Gīt.; BhP.; to unite, join (trans. or intrans.), Kāv.; Kathās.; (Ā.) to result, be the consequence of anything, Śaṃk.: Pass. *ślishyate* (aor. *aśleshi*), to be joined or connected, MBh.; Kāv. &c.; to be implied or intimated, MW.: Caus. (Dhātup. xxxii, 38) *śleshayati*, °*te* (aor. *aśiślishat*), to (cause to) connect or embrace (cf. *śleshita*): Desid. *śiślikshate* (Gr. also °*ti*), to wish to clasp, cling to, AV. (not in MS.): Intens. *śeślishyate*, *śeśleshṭi*, Gr.

Ślishā, f. clinging, embracing, L.

Ślishṭa, mfn. clinging or adhering to (loc. or comp.), Kāṭh.; KātyŚr.; MBh. &c.; (with *sarvataḥ*) adhering closely, fitting tight (as a coat of mail), MBh. vii, 5161; adhering to one's self, i. e. not affecting others, merely personal (as an art or science), Mālav. i, 15 (v. l. *śishṭa*); joined together, united, connected, MBh.; Kāv. &c.; clasped, embraced, Kāv.; Kathās.; (in rhet.) connected so as to be susceptible of a double interpretation, equivocal, Sāh. **-paramparita-rūpaka**, n. a continuous series of words having a double meaning (a kind of metaphor), Śiś., Sch. **-rūpaka**, n. ambiguity as a metaphor, Kāv. ii, 87. **-vartman**, n. the adhering together of the eyelids, ŚārṅgS. **Ślishṭâkshepa**, m. an objection expressed through using words containing a double meaning, Kāvyâd. ii, 159; 160. **Ślishṭârtha-dīpaka**, n. a Dīpaka (q. v.) containing a double meaning, ib. ii, 113; 114. **Ślishṭôkti**, f. an expression containing a d° m°, Kathās.

Ślishṭi, f. adherence, connection, MW.; an embrace, ib.; m. N. of a son of Dhruva, Hariv.; VP.

2. **Ślesha**, m adhering or clinging to (loc.), R.; connection, junction, union (also applied to sexual union), MBh.; embracing, an embrace, Kāv.; Sāh.; (in rhet.) 'connection,' 'combination' (one of the ten Guṇas or merits of composition, consisting either in a pleasing combination of words or of contrasted ideas, or of words having a double meaning), double meaning, equivoque, ambiguity, paranomasia, pun, hidden meaning, Vām.; Kāvyâd.; Sāh. &c.; a grammatical augment, Nyāyas.; (*ā*), f. an embrace, BhP. **-kavi**, m. f. a poet or poetess skilled in the use of words with double meanings, Naish. **-campū-rāmâyaṇa**, n., **-cūḍāmaṇi**, m. N. of poems. **-bhittika**, mfn. resting on or adhering to a wall (said to mean simply 'resting on'), MW. **-maya**, see *pratyakshara-ślesha-maya*. **Śleshârtha**, m. implied or hidden or second meaning, MW.; mfn. having an implied m° (as a word); *-pada-saṃgraha*, m. N. of a dictionary of ambiguous words (by Śrī-harsha-kavi). **Śleshôkti**, f. an expression having a double meaning, Siṇhās. **Śleshôpamā**, f. a comparison containing double meanings, Kāv. ii, 28.

Śleshaka, mfn. attaching, adhering, Vāgbh.

Śleshaṇa. See *antaḥ-* and *loha-śl°*.

Śleshaṇīya, mfn. to be embraced &c., MW.

Śleshita, mfn. (fr. Caus.) joined, united, connected with (instr.), MBh.

Śleshin, mfn. adhering, clinging to, embracing, MW.

Śleshma, in comp. for *śleshman*. **-kaṭāhaka**, m. or n. (?) a spitting-box, spittoon, L. **-kṛita**, mfn. caused by phlegm or mucus (said of a disease), VarBṛS. **-kshaya**, m. decrease of phlegm, Suśr. **-gulma**, m. a swelling in the abdomen caused by phl°, L. **-ghana**, m. Pandarus Odoratissimus, L.; Arabian jasmine, L. **-ghna**, mfn. removing phlegm, L.; (*ā*), f. a kind of jasmine, L.; (*ī*), f. Arabian jasmine, L.; Cardiospermum Halicacabum, L.; the three spices (= *tri-kaṭu*), L. **-ja**, mfn. produced or proceeding from phl°, Suśr. **-jvara**, m. a fever caused by phlegm, Cat.; *-nidāna*, n. 'phlegm-origin,' N. of wk. **-tyāga**, m. discharging mucus or phl°, VarBṛS. **-dushṭa**, mfn. corrupted or vitiated by phl°, Suśr. **-dhātu**, m. the phlegmatic humour, MW. **-pitta**, n. 'phl° and bile,' a kind of disease, Bhpr.; *-jvara*, m. fever caused by phl° and bile, Cat. **-purīsha**, n. mucus and feces, MBh. **-bhava**, mfn. produced by or becoming phl°, Suśr. **-bhū**, m. du 'seat of phlegm,' the lungs, Car. **-vat**, mfn. furnished with cords (as a cart), PañcavBr. **-vidagdha**, mfn. = *-dushṭa*, Suśr. **-vināśa-kṛit**, mfn. destroying phlegm, Hāsy. **-vṛiddhi**, f. increase of phl°, Suśr. **-śopha**, m. a tumour proceeding from phl°, ib. **-saṃghāta-ja**, mfn. produced by the compacting together of phlegm (said of the breasts), Yājñ. iii, 97. **-ha**, m. 'removing phl°,' Cordia Latifolia, L. **-hara**, mfn. destroying or removing phlegm, Kāv.; Suśr. **Śleshmâgāra**, n. a receptacle of mucus or phl°, Bhartṛ. **Śleshmâtisāra**, m. dysentery or diarrhœa produced by vitiated phl°, Suśr. **Śleshmâtura**, mf(*ā*)n. suffering from phlegm, Hāsy. **Śleshmântaka**, mfn. = *śleshma-hara*, ib.; m. = *śleshmātaka*, Yājñ., Sch. **Śleshmâpihita-locana**, mfn. having the eyes filled up with phl° or slime, blear-eyed, MBh. **Śleshmâśmarī**, f. stone (the disease) produced by mucus, Suśr. **Śleshmâśru**, n. mucus and tears, Yājñ.; Pañcat. **Śleshmâsrāva**, m., °**môpanāha**, m. N. of diseases, Suśr. **Śleshmaûjas**, n. the phlegmatic humour, MW.

Śleshmaka, m. phlegm, the phlegmatic humour, L.

Śleshmaṇá, mfn. phlegmatic, slimy, ŚBr.; producing phlegm or mucus, Car.; (*ā*), f. a kind of plant, L.

Śleshmán, m. phlegm, mucus, rheum, the phlegmatic humour (one of the three humours of the body = *kapha*; see *dhātu*), ŚBr.; Yājñ.; Suśr.; MBh. &c.; n. a band, cord, string, AitBr.; Kāṭh.; lime, glue &c.; Āpast.; the fruit of Cordia Latifolia, Vishṇ. (Sch.)

Śleshmala, mf(*ā*)n. phlegmatic, abounding with phlegm or mucus (with *yoni*, f. 'discharging mucus'), Suśr.; Car. &c.; m. the plant Cordia Myxa or Latifolia, L.

Śleshmāta, m. Cordia Latifolia, L.

Śleshmātaka, m. (cf. *śleshmântaka*) = prec. (also *ī*, f.), MBh.; Var.; Suśr. &c.; the fruit of C° L°, MBh. xii, 1313. **-tvac**, f. the bark of C° L°, Suśr. **-phala**, n. the fruit of C° L°, Mn. vi, 14. **-maya**, mf(*ī*)n. made of C° L°, MBh.; R. **-vana**, n. 'forest of Śleshmātaka trees,' N. of a forest around Go-karṇa (where Śiva is said to have been concealed in the form of a stag), R.

Śleshmin, m. bdellium, L.

Ślaishmika, mf(*ī* and *ā*)n. (Pāṇ. v, 1, 38, Vārtt. 1, Pat.) relating or belonging to phlegm, producing or diminishing phlegm, phlegmatic, Suśr.; VarBṛS. &c.

श्लीपद *ślī-pada*, n. (thought by some to be fr. √*ślish* + *pada*; others suppose *ślī* to have the meaning 'elephant') morbid enlargement of the leg, swelled leg, elephantiasis, Suśr.; Bhpr. &c. **-prabhava**, m. 'source of elephantiasis,' the Mango tree, L. **Ślīpadâpaha**, m. 'removing or curing elephantiasis,' the tree Putranjiva Roxburghii, L.

Ślīpadin, mfn. having a swelled leg, suffering from elephantiasis; m. a club-footed man, Mn. iii, 165.

श्लील *ślīla*, mfn. (= *śrīra*; cf. *a-ślīla*) prosperous, fortunate, affluent, happy, W.

श्लु *ślu*, (in gram.) N. of the Vikaraṇa [q. v.] of the 3rd class of roots in which there is elision of the conjugational affix *a* (*ślu* is one of the 3 technical terms [containing *lu*] for grammatical elision, see 2. *luk*), Pāṇ. i, 1, 61 &c. **-vat**, ind. as if there were *ślu*, ib. iii, 1, 39.

श्लोक् *ślok* (prob. Nom. fr. *śloka* below), cl. 1. Ā. *ślokate*, to compose or be composed (*saṃghāte*), Dhātup. iv, 3 (accord. to Vop. also *sarjane* and *varjane*).

Ślóka, m. (prob. connected with √1. *śru*; R. i, 2, 33 gives a fanciful derivation fr. *śoka*, 'sorrow,' the first *śloka* having been composed by Vālmīki grieved at seeing a bird killed) sound, noise (as of the wheels of a carriage or the grinding of stones &c.), RV.; a call or voice (of the gods), ib.; fame, renown, glory, praise, hymn of praise, ib.; AV.; TS.; Br.; BhP.; a proverb, maxim, MW.; a stanza, (esp.) a partic. kind of common epic metre (also called Anu-shṭubh, q. v.; consisting of 4 Pādas or quarter verses of 8 syllables each, or 2 lines of 16 syllables each, each line allowing great liberty except in the 5th, 13th, 14th and 15th syllables which should be unchangeable as in the following scheme, ... ⏑ . . . | . . . . ⏑ – ⏑ ., the dots denoting either long or short; but the 6th and 7th syllables should be long; or if the 6th is short the 7th should be short also), ŚBr.; KaushUp.; MBh. &c.; N. of a Sāman, ĀrshBr. **-kāra**, m. a composer of Ślokas, Pāṇ. iii, 2, 23. **-kāla-nirṇaya**, m. N. of wk. **-kṛít**, mfn. making a sound, sounding, calling, noisy, AV.; TUp. **-gautama**, m. Gautama (when speaking) in Śl°s or in metre, Cat. **-caraṇa**, m. a single stanza of a Śl°, Saṃgīt. **-tarpaṇa**, n., **-traya**, n. N. of wks. **-tva**, n. versification, celebration in verse, R.; Ragh. **-dīpikā**, f. N. of wk. **-dvaya**, n. a couple of Śl°s, two verses; *-vyākhyā*, f. N. of wk. **-pañcaka-vivaraṇa**, n. N. of wk. **-baddha**, mfn. composed in Śl°s, R. **-bhū**, mfn. being or appearing in sound, AitĀr. **-mātra**, n. a single Śl°, MW. **-yantra** (*ślóka-*), mfn. confining sound (within the limits of metre; accord. to others, 'having Śl°s for reins'), RV. ix, 73, 6. **-vārttika**, n. (also called *mīmāṇsā-śl°-v°*) a metrical paraphrase of Śabara's Mīmāṇsā-bhāshya by Kumārila. **-saṃgraha**, m. N. of various wks. **-sthāna**, n. = *sūtra-sth°*, Car. **Ślokâbhinayana**, n. a dramatic performance accompanied by recitation of Śl°s. **Ślokâvali**, f. a collection of stanzas, anthology, Cat.

Ślokaya, Nom. P. °*yati* (Pāṇ. iii, 1, 25), to make resound, cause to sound, VS.

Ślokin, mfn. sounding, noisy, RV.; having a good reputation or fair fame, ŚāṅkhBr.

Ślókya, mfn. sounding, noisy, VS.; praiseworthy, BhP.

श्लोण् *śloṇ* (also written *śroṇ*, q. v.), cl. 1. P. *śloṇati*, to heap, collect, Dhātup. xiii, 15 (only 3. sg. *áśloṇat*, used to explain *śroṇá*, TBr.)

श्लोण *śloṇá*, mf(*ā*)n. (= *śroṇa*) lame, limping, AV.; TBr. (= *dushṭa-tvac*, Sch.)

Ślóṇya, n. lameness, TBr. (= *tvag-dosha*, Sch.)

श्वघ्निन् *śvaghnin*. See p. 1105, col. 2.

श्वङ्क् *śvaṅk* (also written *śraṅk*, *svaṅk*), cl. 1. Ā. *śvaṅkate*, to go, move, Dhātup. iv, 22.

श्वङ्ग् *śvaṅg* (also written *śraṅg*, *svaṅg* &c.), cl. 1. P. *śvaṅgati*, to go, move, Dhātup. v, 44.

श्वच् *śvac* or *śvañc*, cl. 1. Ā. (Dhātup. vi, 5, 'to go') *śvacate*, *śvañcate*, to become open, open (intrans.), receive with open arms (only *śaśvacai*), RV. iii, 33, 10: Caus. *śvañcáyati*, to open (trans.), ib. x, 138, 2. (Cf. *uc-chvañc*.)

श्वज् *śvaj* or *śvañj*, cl. 1. Ā. *śvajate*, *śvañjate*, to go, move, Dhātup. vi, 7 (Kāś.)

श्वठ् 1. *śvaṭh*, cl. 10. P. *śvaṭhayati* (Dhātup. xxxv, 4) = √2. *śāṭh*, q. v.

श्वठ् 2. *śvaṭh* or *śvaṇṭh*, cl. 10. P. *śvāṭhayati*, *śvaṇṭhayati* (Dhātup. xxxii, 28) = √3. *śaṭh*, q. v.

Śvaṭha, Pāṇ. vi, 1, 216.

श्वन् 1. *śván*, m. (nom. sg. du. pl. *śvā*, *śvānau*, *śvānas*; weakest base *śun*, cf. 2. *śuna* &c., p. 1082; in some comp. *śvā* for *śva*, cf. below), a dog, hound, cur, RV. &c. &c.; (*śunī*), f. a female dog. [Cf. Zd. *spā*; Gr. κύων; Lat. *canis*; Lit. *szů*; Goth. *hunds*; Eng. *hound*; Germ. *Hund*.] **-vatī** (*śvàn-*), f. N. of a class of Apsarases, AV.

1. **Śva**, in comp. for 1. *śvan*. **-kaṇṭaka**, m. the son of a Vrātya and a Śūdra (accord. to others 'a servant of Śūdras'), L. **-karṇa**, m. a dog's ear, KātyŚr., Sch. (cf. *śvā-k°*). **-kishkin**, mfn. (said of demons; accord. to some 'having the tail of a dog'), AV. viii, 6, 6. **-krīḍin**, mfn. keeping dogs for pleasure, Mn. iii, 164; m. a breeder of sporting dogs, W. **-kharôshṭra**, n. sg. a dog and an ass and a camel, Mn. iv, 115. **-gaṇa**, m. a pack of hounds, Hariv. **-gaṇika**, mf(*ī*)n. accompanied by a pack of h°, Prâyaśc.; m. a hunter, W.; m. and (*ī*) f. a dog-feeder; one who is drawn by d°s, ib. **-gaṇin**, mfn. having packs of h°s, Ragh.; m. a leader of p°s of h°s, Caṇḍ. **-gardabha**, n. sg. dogs and asses, Mn. x, 15; *-pati*, m. one who possesses dogs and asses, BhP. **-graha**, m. 'dog-seizer,' N. of a demon hostile to children, ĀpGṛ. **-ghnī**, see under *-han*. **-cakra**, n. 'chapter on dogs,' N. of the 89th Adhyāya of VarBṛS. **-caṇḍāla**, m. one whose father is a Brāhman and mother a Caṇḍālī, L.; n. (g. *gavâśvâdi*) a dog and a Caṇḍāla (also *-cāṇḍāla*, MW.) **-caryā**, f. a dog's state of life, MBh. **-cillī**, f. a kind of vegetable (= *śunaka-c°*), L. **-jāghanī**, f. a dog's tail, Mn.; MBh.; KātyŚr., Sch. **-jīvana**, mfn. living by breeding d°s, Nir., Sch. **-jīvikā**, f. dog-life, servitude, L. **-jīvin**, m. a breeder of dogs, Vishṇ. **-daṇshṭraka**, m. Tribulus Lanuginosus, L. **-daṇshṭrā**, f. a dog's tooth, W.; Asteracantha Longifolia, Suśr.; Car.; = *go-kshura*, MW. **-daṇshṭrin**, m. a kind of animal, Car. **-dayita**, n. 'dear to d°s,' a bone, L. **-dṛiti**, m. a d°'s bladder, MBh. **-dhūrta**, m. 'dog-rogue,' a jackal, L. **-nakula**, n. sg. a d° and an ichneumon, Mn. xi, 159. **-nara**, m. a dog-like fellow, low f°, currish or snappish f°, MW. **-niśa**, n. or (*ā*), f. 'dog-night,' a n° on which d°s bark and howl, L.; Pāṇ., Sch. **-nī**, m. a dog-leader, MaitrS. **-pa**, m. 'keeper of d°s,' a possessor of d°s, Hariv. **-paka**, w. r. for *-paca*, Rājat. **-pac**, m. = next, Mn. iii, 92. **-paca**, m. and (*ā* or *ī*) f. 'one who cooks d°s,' a man or woman of a low and outcaste tribe (the son of a Caṇḍāla and a Brāhmaṇī, or of a Nishṭya and a previously unmarried Kirātī, or of an Ugra woman by a Kshatriya, or of a Ksh° woman by an Ugra, or of a Brāhmaṇī by an Ambashṭha, often = *caṇḍāla*; he acts as a public executioner and carries out the bodies of those who die without kindred), ŚāṅkhGṛ.; Mn.; MBh. &c.; a dog-feeder, dog-keeper, W.; (*ī*), f. (cf. above); a form of one of the Śaktis of Śiva, MW.; *-tā*, f. or *-tva*, n. the condition of a member of the above low caste, MBh. **-pati** (*śvá-*), m. a lord or possessor of dogs, VS.; MaitrS.; BhP. **-pad** (*śvá-*), m. a wild animal, AV.; ĀpŚr. **-pada**, n. a dog's foot (or its mark branded on the body), Mn. ix, 237. **-pāka**, m. one who cooks dogs, a man of an outcaste tribe (= *-paca* above), Baudh.; Mn.; MBh. &c.; (*ī*), f. a woman of the above outcaste tribe, Rājat. **-pāda**, m. = *-pada*, ib. **-pāmana**, m. Pavetta Indica, L. **-puccha**, n. the tail or hind part of a dog, Pañcat.; Hemionitis Cordifolia, L. (cf. *śvā-p°*). **-poshaka**, m. a d°-feeder, huntsman, Kâd. **-phala**, m. a citron-tree, L.; n. the lime or common citron, MW. **-phalka**, m. N. of a son of Vṛishṇi, Hariv.; Pur. **-bāla**, w. r. for *-vāla*. **-bhaksha** or **-bhakshya** (v. l.), mfn. eating dog's meat, MBh. **-bhīru**, m. 'dog-fearing,' a jackal, L. **-bhojana**, n. a meal for d°s (said of the body), BhP.; m. 'having d°s for food,' N. of a hell, VP. **-bhojin**, mfn. eating dog's flesh, R. **-māṇsa**, n. dog's flesh, Mn. x, 106. **-mukha**, m. pl. N. of a people, VarBṛS. **-yātu** (*śvá-*), m. a demon in the shape of a dog, RV. **-yūtha**, n. (see *śvā-yūthika*) or **-yūthya**, n. (MW.) a number or pack of d°s. **-rūpa-dhārin**, mfn. wearing or having the form of a dog, MW. **-lih**, mfn. (nom. *-liṭ*) licking up or lapping like a dog, Pāṇ. viii, 4, 42, Sch. **-lehya**, mfn. to be lapped by a dog (as a well with little water), Pāṇ. ii, 1, 33, Sch. **-** 1. **-vat**, mfn. keeping dogs, m. a dog-feeder, d°-trainer, Mn.; MBh.; Vas. **-** 2. **-vat**, ind. like a dog, cur-like, MW. **-vartá**, m. a kind of worm, AV. (v. l. for *śavartá*). **-vāla**, m. d°'s hair, Kathās. **-vishṭhā**, f. dog's excrement, Mn. x, 91. **-vṛitti**, f. 'dog-subsistence,' gaining a livelihood by menial service (forbidden to Brāhmans), Mn. iv, 4, 6; Rājat.; BhP. &c.; mfn. living on d°s, Prâyaśc.; a 'lick-spittle' or most contemptible toady, Yājñ.; Sch. **-vṛittin**, mfn. living on d°s, Yājñ. **-vyāghra**, m. a beast of prey, a tiger or hunting leopard, L. **-śīrsha**, mfn. having a dog's head, L. **-suta** or **-suna**, m. Conyza Lacera, L. **-sṛigāla**, n. sg. a dog and a jackal, Pat. on Pāṇ. ii, 4, 12, Vārtt. 2. **-spṛishṭa**, mfn. touched by a dog, defiled, W. **-hata**, mfn. killed by a dog or dogs, ib. **-han**, mf(*ghnī*)n. one killing by means of d°s, MW.; m. a hunter, ib.; (*ghnī*), f. a hunter's wife, ib. **-hāna**, see *śauvah°*. **Śvâgra**, n. a dog's tail, Kathās. **Śvâjina**, n. a d°'s skin, Āpast. **Śvâda**, m. = *śva-pāka*, BhP. **Śvânala**, m. N. of a form of Garuḍa, Virac. **Śvâśva**, m. 'having a dog for a horse,' N. of Bhairava (or Śiva mounted on a dog), L. **Śvâhi**, m. 'dog-serpent,' N. of a son of Vṛijina-vat, BhP.

2. **Śva** (ifc.) = 1. *śvan*, MW.

Śvaka, m. a wolf, Nalac.

Śvaghnín, m. (prob. fr. *śva-han*, 'a dog-killer' or low fellow, but accord. to some for *sva-ghnin*, 'one who destroys his own') a gamester, professional gambler, RV.; AV.

Śvanin, mfn. keeping dogs, VS.

Śvā, in comp. for 1. *śvan* above. **-karṇa**, **-kunda**, **-daṇshṭra**, **-danta**, mfn., Kāś. on Pāṇ. vi, 3, 137 (cf. *śva-k°* &c.) **-jani**, m. N. of a Vaiśya, JaimBr. **-pad** (*śvā́-*), m. a beast of prey, AV. **-pada** (*śvā́-*), m. n. a beast of prey, wild b°, RV. &c. &c.; a tiger, L.; pl. N. of a people, MārkP. (w. r. *svāp°*); mfn. relating or belonging to a wild beast (= *śauvāpada*), Pāṇ. vii, 3, 9; *-rājan*, m. a king of the beasts, Ml.; *-sevita*, mfn. frequented or infested by wild b°, MW.; *°dâcarita*, mfn. overrun or infested by w° b°, MBh.; *°dânusaraṇa*, n. the chase after wild b°, MW. **-puccha**, mfn. or m. = *śva-p°*, q. v. **-varāha**, mfn. or m., Kāś. on Pāṇ. vi, 3, 137. **-varāhikā**, f. the enmity between the dog and the boar, Pāṇ. iv, 2, 104, Vārtt. 21, Pat. **-vidh**, see below.

Śvāgaṇika, mf(*ī*)n. (fr. *śva-gaṇa*) = *śva-gaṇika*, Yājñ.; Sch. (cf. Pāṇ. iv, 4, 11).

Śvādaṇshṭri, m. a patr., Pāṇ. vii, 3, 8, Sch.

Śvāna, m. a dog, Kāv.; Pañcat.; the wind (?), Sāy. on RV. i, 161, 13; (*ī*), f. a female dog, bitch (= *śunī*), Hcar. **-cillikā**, f. a kind of vegetable, L. **-nidrā**, f. dog's sleep, light slumber, MW. **-vaikharī**, f. 'd°'s speech,' snarling like a dog on trifling occasions, ib. **Śvānôcchishṭa**, n. 'dog-remnant,' anything left by a dog, ib.

Śvāpākaka, mfn. (fr. *śva-pāka*), g. *kulālâdi*.

Śvāphalka, m. patr. fr. *śva-phalka*, Pāṇ. iv, 1, 114; ii, 4, 58, Sch. **-caitraka**, m. pl., ib. vi, 2, 34, Sch.

Śvāphalki, m. patr. fr. id. (= *a-krūra*), BhP.

Śvābhastra, mfn. (fr. next), Pāṇ. vii, 3, 8, Vārtt. 3, Pat.

Śvābhastri, m. a patr., Pāṇ. vii, 3, 8, Sch.

Śvāyūthika, mfn. (fr. *śva-yūtha*), Pāṇ. vii, 3, 8, Vārtt. 2, Pat.

Śvāvic, in comp. for *śvā-vidh* below. **-caraṇa** (for *°vit-śaraṇa*), the lair or hole of a porcupine (which generally has two or more entrances), MW. **-chalalita** (for *°vit-śalalita*), mfn. furnished with porcupine quills, MBh.

Śvāvid, in comp. for *śvā-vidh* below. **-garta**, m. the hole or lair of a porcupine; *°tīya*, mfn., Pat. **-roman**, n. the quill of a porcupine, KātyŚr., Sch.

Śvā-vídh, m. (nom. *-vit*) 'dog-piercer,' a porcupine, AV.; VS.; MaitrS. &c.

Śvāvidha, m. = *śvā-vidh* above (or *°dhaḥ* may be pl. of *śvā-vidh*), R.

Śvāvil, in comp. for *śvā-vidh* above. **-loman**, n. a porcupine's quill; *°mâpanayana*, n. N. of a Tīrtha, MBh.; *°mâpaha*, n. id., ib.

श्वन् 2. *śvan* (prob. fr. √*śvi*) in *ṛiji-*, *dur-gṛibhi-*, and *mātari-śvan*, qq. vv.

श्वभ् *śvabhr* (rather Nom. fr. *śvabhra* below), cl. 10. P. *śvabhrayati* (only Dhātup. xxxii, 79), to go, move; to live in misery; to pierce, bore.

Śvábhra, m. n. (of doubtful derivation) a chasm, gap, hole, pit, den, RV. &c. &c.; m. hell or a partic. hell, Kāv.; MārkP.; Sarvad.; N. of a son of Vasudeva, Hariv.; of a king of Kampanā, Rājat. **-tiryañc**, m. an animal living in holes, Subh. **-pati**, m. (prob.) the king of hell, Śatr. **-mukha**, n. the mouth or entrance of a hole, MBh. **-vat**, mfn. full of holes, hollow, perforated, Suśr.; MBh.; (*atī*), f. N. of a river, Hariv. (v. l. *śubhra-vatī*).

Śvabhrita, mfn. full of holes, g. *tārakâdi*.

Śvabhrīya, Nom. P. *°yati*, to regard as a hole or pit, VarYogay.

श्वय *śvaya*, *śvayatha* &c. See √*śvi* next p.

श्वर्त् *śvart* (or *svart*) = or for √*śvabhr* (accord. to some authorities in Dhātup. xxxii, 79).

श्वल् *śval* (or *śvall*), cl. 1. P. (Dhātup. xv, 42) *śvalati*, to go quickly, run, Suśr.

श्वल्क् *śvalk*, cl. 10. P. (only Dhātup. xxxii, 34) *śvalkayati*, to tell, narrate.

श्वल्ल् *śvall*. See √*śval* above.

श्वशुर *śváśura*, m. (prob. for orig. *svaśura*; cf. below) a father-in-law, husband's or wife's father (in the oldest language commonly the former, in the Sūtras the latter, in Class. lang° both meanings; also applied to a maternal uncle and to any venerable person), RV. &c. &c.; du. (cf. Pāṇ. i, 2, 72) a father and mother-in-law, Yājñ.; Kathās. (also pl., e. g. RV. x, 95, 12; AV. xiv, 2, 27 &c.); (prob. *ī*), f. = *brāhmī*, L.; for *śvaśrū* see below. [Cf. Gk. ἑκυρός; Lat. *socer*; Lith. *szészuras*; Slav. *svekrŭ*; Goth. *swaihra*; Angl. Sax. *sweór*; Germ. *swëher*, *Schwäher*.]

Śvaśuraka, m. a dear or poor father-in-law, Pañcat.; Vet.

Śvaśurīya, mf(*ā*)n. relating or belonging to a father-in-law, ĀśvŚr.

Śvaśurya, m. a brother-in-law, wife's or husband's brother (esp. 'a husband's younger br°'), Kathās.

Śvaśrū́, f. (of *śvaśura*) a mother-in-law (either the wife's or the husband's m°), RV. &c. &c.; pl. the mother-in-law and the other wives of the father-in-law, RV. [Cf. Lat. *socrus*; Slav. *svekry*; Angl. Sax. *swëger*; Germ. *swigar*, *swiger*, *Schwieger*.] **-śvaśura**, m. du. (L.) or pl. (Kathās.) mother and father-in-law, parents-in-law. **-snushā**, f. du. mother-in-law and daughter-in-law, Kāv.; Kathās.; *-dhana-saṃvāda*, m. 'agreement in respect of the property of m° and daughter-in-law,' N. of wk.

श्वस् 1. *śvas* (cf. √3. *śush*), cl. 2. P. (Dhātup. xxiv, 61) *śvasiti* (Ved. and ep. also *śvásati*, *°te*; Impv. *śvasihi*, AV., *śvasa*, MBh.; impf. [or aor.] *aśvasīt*, ep. also *aśvasat*; Pot. or Prec. *śvasyāt*, ep. also *śvaset*; pr. p. *śvasat*, ep. also *śvasamāna* [for *śvasāna*, see below]; pf. *śaśvāsa*, MBh.; fut. *śvasitā*, Gr.; *śvasishyati*, MBh.; inf. *śvasitum*, ib.; ind. p. *-śvasya*, ib.), to blow, hiss, pant, snort, RV. &c. &c.; to breathe, respire, draw breath (also = live), MBh.; Kāv. &c.; to sigh, groan, ib.; to strike, kill, Naigh. ii, 19: Caus. *śvāsayati* (aor. *aśiśvasat*), to cause to blow or breathe &c.; to cause heavy breathing, Suśr.: Desid. *śiśvasishati*, Gr.: Intens. *śāśvasyate*, *śāśvasti*, ib. (only p. *śāśvasat*, snorting, MaitrS.)

Śvasátha, m. the act of blowing, hissing, snorting, panting, breathing, breath, RV.; ŚBr.

Śvasaná, mfn. blowing, hissing, panting, breathing, RV.; ŚāṅkhBr.; VarBṛS.; breathing heavily, Suśr.; m. air, wind (also of the body) or the god of wind, MBh.; R.; Suśr.; N. of a Vasu (son of Śvāsā), MBh. i, 2583; (*śvás°*) N. of a serpent-demon, Suparṇ.; Vanguieria Spinosa, Car.; (*am*), n. breathing, respiration, breath, Kāv.; Pur.; Suśr.; heavy breathing, Suśr.; clearing the throat, ib.; hissing (of a serpent), Śiś.; sighing, a sigh, Ratnâv.; feeling or an object of feeling, BhP. (Sch.) **-mano-ga**, mfn. moving as (fast as) wind or thought, VarYogay. **-randhra**, n. 'breath-hole,' a nostril, BhP. **-vat**, mfn. hissing, snorting, Sāy. **-samīraṇa**, n. wind (caused) by breathing, breath, Śiś. **Śvasanâśana**, m. 'air-swallower,' a snake, serpent (cf. *pavanâśana*, *vāyu-bhaksha*), Rājat. **Śvasanêśvara**, m. 'wind-lord,' the tree Pentaptera Arjuna, L. **Śvasanôtsuka**, m. 'eager for (swallowing) air,' a serpent, L. **Śvasanôrmi**, m. f. a wave or gust of wind, MW.

Śvasaya (?), mfn., Kauś. 107.

Śvasāna, mfn. breathing, living, alive, BhP.

Śvasita, mfn. breathed, sighed &c.; possessed of

breath or life, vivified, revived, Kathās.; n. breathing, breath, respiration, sighing, a sigh, Kāv.; Pur.

Śvasī-vat, mfn. = *śvasana-vat*, hissing, snorting, RV. i, 140, 10 (Sāy.)

Śvāsa, m. hissing, snorting, panting, R.; Kathās.; BhP.; respiration, breath (also as a measure of time = *prāṇa, asu*), MBh.; Kāv. &c.; breathing or aspiration (in the pronunciation of consonants), RPrāt., Introd.; inspiration, Sarvad.; sighing, a sigh, Śak.; Sāh.; affection of the breath, hard breathing, asthma (of which there are five kinds, viz. *kshudra, tamaka, chinna, mahat*, and *ūrdhva*), Suśr.; (*ā*), f. N. of the mother of Śvasana (the god of wind), MBh.; Convolvulus Turpethum, L.; *-karma-prakāśa*, m. N. of wk. **-kāsa**, m. 'breath-cough,' asthma (°*sin*, mfn. suffering from it), Hcat. **-kuṭhāra**, m. N. of a drug used as a remedy for asthma, Bhpr. **-tā**, f. the being breath, the being aspirated (cf. above), RPrāt.; breathing, respiration, aspiration, MW. **-dhāraṇa**, n. suppression or suspension of breath, KātyŚr., Sch. **-praśvāsa-dhāraṇa**, n. suppression or suspension of inspiration and expiration (= *prāṇāyāma*, q. v.), MW. **-rodha**, m. obstruction of the breath, oppression of the chest, BhP. **-śesha**, mf(*ā*)n. having nothing left but breath, consisting only in breathing (as life), Rājat. **-hikkā**, f. a kind of hiccough (°*kkin*, mfn. suffering from it), Car. **-heti**, f. 'remedy for asthma,' sound sleep, L. **Śvāsâkula**, mfn. troubled in breathing, out of breath, Campak. **Śvāsânila**, m. wind (caused) by breathing, breath, BhP. **Śvāsâri**, m. 'breath-enemy,' Costus Speciosus or Arabicus, L. **Śvāsôcchvāsa**, m. du. inspiration and expiration, respiration, MW.

Śvāsika, mfn. occurring in or resulting from asthma, Car.

Śvāsita, mfn. (fr. Caus.) caused to breathe &c.; w. r. for *sv-āśita*, R. ii, 84, 18.

Śvāsin, mfn. hissing, breathing, ĀśvGṛ.; breathing hard, asthmatic, Suśr.; aspirated (as a sound or letter), Śiksh.; m. wind, L.

श्वस् 2. *śvás*, ind. to-morrow, on the following day (*śváḥ śvaḥ*, 'day by day;' *śvó bhūté*, 'on the morrow,' 'next day'), RV. &c. &c.; in the future (see comp.); a particle implying auspiciousness, W.

Śvaḥ, in comp. for 2. *śvás*. **-kāla**, m. to-morrow's time, the morrow; (*e*), loc. on the morrow, to-m°, MBh. **-kraya**, m. a purchase (to be made) on the morrow, Lāṭy. **-prabhṛiti**, ind. from to-m° onwards. **-śreyasá**, n. 'better state on the morrow,' progressive improvement, ŚBr.; happiness, prosperity, L.; the Supreme Spirit, L.; mfn. happy, progressively prosperous, L. **-śvá**, n. putting off to the morrow, procrastination, ŚBr. **-sutyā**, f. 'to-morrow's preparation of the Soma,' the eve of the Sutyā rite, AitBr.; ŚBr.; Lāṭy. **-stotriya**, n. to-morrow's Stotriya (q. v.), AitBr.

Śvástana, mf(*ī*)n. relating or belonging to the morrow (°*ne 'hani*, 'on the morrow'), Kāv.; Pur. [cf. Lat. *crastinus*]; (*ī*), f. the next day, the morrow, MaitrS.; (in gram.) the terminations of the first future, Pāṇ. iii, 3, 15, Vārtt. 1; (*am*), n. to-morrow, next day, the future, Mn.; MBh. &c. (cf. *a-śv*°). **-vat**, mfn. having a future, PañcavBr.

Śvastanika. See *a-śv*°.

Śvastya, mfn. = *śvastana*, Pāṇ. iv, 2, 105.

Śvo, in comp. for 2. *śvás*. **-bhāva**, m. to-morrow's state of affairs, KātyŚr.; pl. the affairs or occurrences of to-m°, KaṭhUp. **-bhāvin** (MBh.; R.), **-bhūta** (Gaut.), mfn. what may happen to-m°. **-bhūti**, m. N. of a man, Pat., Sch. **-maraṇa**, n. imminent death or the thought of it, MBh. **-vasīya**, n. future welfare or prosperity, Daś.; mfn. 'happy for all future time,' auspicious, fortunate, MW. **-vasīyas**, mfn. id., ib. **-vasīyasa**, mf(*ī*)n. bestowing future welfare, MaitrS.; n. future w°, auspiciousness, good fortune, L. **-vasyasá**, mfn. = prec., TBr. **-vijayin**, mfn. one who is about to conquer on the morrow, MaitrS.

श्वाकर्ण *śvā-karṇa, śvā-kunda* &c. See p. 1105, col. 2.

श्वात्र् *śvātr*, cl. 1. P. *śvātrati*, to go, move, Naigh. ii, 14.

श्वात्र *śvātrá*, mfn. (prob. fr. √*śvi* = *śū*) invigorating, strengthening, strong (as Soma, the waters &c.; accord. to native authorities = *kshipra* or *mitra*; accord. to others, 'savoury,' 'dainty,' fr. √*śvad* = *svad*), RV.; VS.; (*ám*), ind. = *kshipram*, Nir. v, 3; (*am*), n. strengthening or savoury food or drink, a dainty morsel, RV.; = *dhana*, Naigh. ii, 10. **-bhāj**, mfn. = next, RV. viii, 4, 9.

Śvātrya, mfn. 'strengthening' or 'savoury' (cf. *śvātra*), RV.

श्वान *śvāna* &c. See p. 1105, col. 2.

श्वान्त *śvāntá*, mfn. (fr. √*śvam* = *śam*?) tranquil, placid, RV. (Sāy. = *śānta* or *śrānta*).

श्वापद *śvā-pada, śvā-vidh* &c. See p. 1105, col. 2.

श्वाशुर *śvāśura*, mf(*ī*)n. relating or belonging to a father-in-law, Kathās.; m. pl. = *śvāśurer yūnaś chāttrāḥ*, Pat.

Śvāśuri, m. the son of the father-in-law, ib.

Śvāśurya, w. r. for *śvaśurya*, Kathās.

श्वि *śvi* (connected with √*śū*; sometimes written *śvā*), cl. 1. P. (Dhātup. xxiii, 41) *śváyati* (pf. *śiśvāya* or *śuśāva*, Gr.; aor. *áśvat*, ŚBr., *aśvayīt*, HPariś.; Prec. *śūyāt*, Gr.; fut. *śvayitā*, *śvayishyati*, ib.; inf. *śváyitum*, Br.), to swell, grow, increase, TS.; ŚBr. &c.: Pass. *śūyate* (aor. *aśvāyi*), id., Car.: Caus. *śvāyayati* (aor. *aśiśvayat* [Bhaṭṭ.] or *aśūśavat*), id., Gr.: Desid. of Caus. *śiśvāyayishati* or *śuśāvayishati*, ib.: Desid. *śiśvayishati*, ib.: Intens. *śeśvīyate* (Bhaṭṭ.), *śośūyate; śeśvayīti, śeśveti*, to swell much.

Śūtha, śūna &c. See p. 1085, col. 1.

Śvaya, m. swelling, increase, MW.

Śvayátha, m. swelling, ŚBr.

Śvayathu, m. swelling, intumescence, Suśr. **-kara**, mfn. causing int°, ib. **-cikitsā**, f. the cure or treatment of swelling &c., ib. **-mat**, mfn. suffering from swelling or intumescence, Car.

Śvayana, n. swelling, APrāt., Sch.

Śvayas, n. swelling, L.; power, strength, L.

Śvayīci, m. or f. a kind of illness, Uṇ. iv, 71, Sch.

श्विक्न *śvíkna*, m. pl. N. of a people, ŚBr.

श्वित् 1. *śvit*, cl. 1. Ā. (Dhātup. xviii, 2) *śvetate* (occurring only in pr. p. *śvetamāna*, Mālatīm., and in aor. *aśvait* or *aśvitat*, p. *śvitānd* [q. v.], RV.; Gr. also pf. *śiśvite*, fut. *śvetitā, śvetishyate*, and aor. *aśvetishṭa*), to be bright or white: Caus. (only aor. *aśiśvitat*; but cf. *śvetaya* and *śvetita*), id., RV. [Cf. Lith. *szvaitýti*; Goth. *hweits*; Germ. *weiss*; Engl. *white*.]

2. **Śvit**. See *uda-śvit* and *sūrya-śvit*.

Śvita, mfn. white, n. whiteness, Sāy.

Śvitāná, mfn. being white, white-coloured, RV. vi, 6, 2.

Śviti, (prob.) f. whiteness, a white colour, Sāy.

Śvitīcí, śvítna, and **śvitnyá**, mfn. whitish, RV.

Śvitya, mfn. white, white-coloured, MW.; m. (cf. *śvaitya*) N. of a man, MBh. vii, 2183 (Nilak.)

Śvityáñc, mf(°*tīcī*)n. whitish, RV.

Śvitrá, mfn. whitish, white, AV.; TS.; having white leprosy, PañcavBr.; m. a partic. wh° domestic animal or any wh° an°, VS.; m. n. morbid whiteness of the skin, white leprosy, vitiligo, Suśr.; BhP.; = *antariksha*, Sāy. on RV. v, 19, 3; (*ā*), f. N. of a woman, Sāy. on RV. i, 13, 14. **-ghnī**, f. 'removing white leprosy,' the plant Tragia Involucrata, L. **-hara**, mfn. removing or curing white leprosy, Suśr. **Śvitrôpakāśa**, mfn. looking whitish, ĀpŚr.

Śvitrin, mfn. affected with whiteness of the skin, leprous, a leper, Gaut.; Mn. &c.

Śvitrya, m. metron. fr. *śvitrā*, RV. i, 33, 15 (Sāy.)

Śvetá, mf(*ā́* or *śvenī*)n. white, dressed in white, bright (with *párvata*, m. 'snow-mountain,' ŚBr.; with *kaṭâksha*, m. 'a bright side-glance,' Saṃgīt.), RV. &c. &c.; m. white (the colour), L.; a white horse, ŚBr.; a small white shell, cowry, L.; a silver coin, L.; a white cloud, L.; the planet Venus or its regent Śukra, L.; a partic. comet (cf. *-ketu*), VarBṛS.; a partic. plant (= *jīvaka*), L.; cumin seed, W.; N. of a serpent-demon (with *vaidārva* or *vaidārvya* or *vaidarvya*; others give *śvaita-vaidārava* as signifying 'a partic. deity connected with the sun'), GṛS.; Pur.; N. of one of Skanda's attendants, MBh.; of a Daitya (son of Vipra-citti), Hariv.; of a Muni, MBh.; Kathās.; of a partic. Avatāra of Śiva, Cat.; of a pupil of Śiva, IW. 122, n. 3; of a manifestation of Vishṇu in his Varāha incarnation (worshipped in a partic. part of India), MW.; of a Rājarshi, MBh.; of a son of the king Sudeva, R.; of a general, MBh.; of a son of Vapushmat, MārkP.; of a preceptor, Cat.; of a mythical elephant, MBh.; of the sixth range of mountains dividing the known continent (the white or 'snowy' mountains separating the Varshas of Hiraṇmaya and Ramyaka), MBh.; Pur. (IW. 420, n. 1); of one of the minor Dvīpas or divisions of the world (cf. *-dvīpa*), MBh.; R.; (*ā*), f. one of the seven tongues of Fire, Gṛihyas.; a small white shell, cowry, L.; N. of various plants (accord. to L. the birch tree, a white bignonia, Bœrhavia Procumbens, Achyranthes Atropurpurea &c.), Suśr.; VarBṛS.; crystal, L.; alum, L.; white or candied sugar, L.; bamboo-manna, L.; a mystical term for the letter *s*, Up.; N. of one of the Mātṛis attendant on Skanda, MBh.; of the mother of the elephant Śveta (or Śaṅkha), MBh.; R.; of a princess, Rājat.; (*ī*), f. N. of a river, MW.; n. the white of the eye, Suśr.; the growing white (of the hair), ChUp.; silver, L.; butter-milk and water mixed half and half, L. **-kaṇṭakārī**, f. a species of plant (= *priyaṃkarī*), MW. **-kaṇṭhin**, mfn. white-necked (as a jar), Hariv. **-kanda**, m. Allium Cepa or Ascalonicum; (*ā*), f. Aconitum Ferox, L. **-kapota**, m. a kind of mouse, Cat.; a kind of snake, Suśr. **-kamala**, n. a white lotus, MW. **-karṇa**, m. N. of a son of Satya-karṇa, Hariv. **-kalpa**, m. a partic. Kalpa or world-period, Hcat. **-kāka**, m. a white crow, i. e. any very unusual thing, Kautukas. **-kākīya**, mfn. relating to a white crow, rare, unusual, unheard of, MBh.; Mṛicch. **-kāṇḍā**, f. wh° Dūrvā grass, L. **-kāpotī**, f. a kind of plant, Suśr. **-kāmbojī**, f. a white variety of Abrus Precatorius, L. **-kiṇihī**, f. a kind of tree, L. **-kukshi**, m. a kind of fish, L. **-kuñjara**, m. 'white-elephant,' Indra's el° Airāvata, L. **-kuśa**, m. wh° Kuśa grass, L. **-kushṭha**, n. wh° leprosy, Cat.; mfn. suffering from wh° l° (*-tva*, n.), Kull. on Mn. xi, 51. **-kṛishṇā**, f. a kind of venomous insect, Suśr. **-ketu** (*śvetá-*), m. N. of a comet (also called Uddālaka-śv°), VarBṛS.; a Jaina saint, L.; N. of Auddālaki, ŚBr.; of Āruṇeya, ib. &c.; of a son of Sena-jit, Hariv.; of Gautama Buddha as a Bodhi-sattva, Lalit. **-keśa**, m. white hair, ib.; a kind of red-flowering Moringa, L. **-kola** or **-kolaka**, m. the fish Cyprinus Sophore, L. **-kshāra**, m. wh° nitre, saltpetre, alkali, L. **-khadira**, m. a wh° variety of the Khadira tree, L. **-gaṅgā**, f. N. of a river, Kād. **-gaja**, m. a wh° elephant or the el° of Indra, ib. **-garut** (L.) or **-garuta** (MW.), m. 'wh°-winged,' a goose. **-giri**, m. a wh° mountain, snowy range of hills (see under *śveta* above), Cat.; *-māhātmya*, n. N. of chs. of two Purāṇas. **-guñjā**, f. a white variety of Abrus Precatorius, L. **-guṇavat**, mfn. possessed of the quality of whiteness, Sāh. **-gokarṇī**, f. Clitoria Ternatea, Dhanv. **-godhūma**, m. a kind of wheat, Vās. **-ghaṇṭā**, f. a kind of plant (= *nāgadantī*), L. **-ghaṇṭī**, f., see *mahā-śveta-gh*°. **-ghoshā**, f. a wh° Ghoshā plant, MW. **-candana**, n. white sandal, Pañcar. **-campaka**, m. a kind of Campaka, ib. **-caraṇa**, m. a kind of bird, Suśr. **-cintā-maṇi**, m. N. of wk. **-cillikā** or **-cillī**, f. a kind of vegetable, L. **-cchattra**, n. a wh° umbrella, BhP.; mfn. having a wh° umb°, MW. **-cchattrāya**, Nom. to resemble a wh° umbrella (°*yita*, mfn.), Vcar. **-cchattrin**, mfn. having a wh° umb°, ĀpŚr. **-cchada**, m. 'wh°-winged' or 'wh°-leaved,' a goose, L.; a kind of plant, L.; Ocymum Album, W. **-jala**, N. of a lake, VP. **-jīraka**, m. wh° cumin, L. **-ṭaṅkaka** or **-ṭaṅkaṇa**, n. a kind of borax, L. **-taṇḍula**, m. a kind of rice, L. **-tantrī**, f. a kind of stringed instrument, Saṃgīt. **-tapas**, m. N. of a man, Cat. **-tara**, m. pl. N. of a school, Caraṇ. **-tā**, f. whiteness, MW. **-dūrvā**, f. white Dūrvā grass, Bhpr. **-dyuti**, m. the moon, L. **-druma**, m. Cratæva Roxburghii, L. **-dvipa**, m. a white elephant or Indra's el° Airāvata, L. **-dvīpa**, m. n. 'wh° island,' N. of a mythical abode of the blessed, MBh.; Hariv.; Kāv. &c. (cf. IW. 126, n. 1); of a sacred place near Kāśī, Cat. **-dvīpāya**, Nom. Ā. °*yate*, to resemble the white isle, Hcar. **-dhātu**, m. chalk, L.; opal or chalcedony, W.; any wh° mineral, MW. **-dhāman**,

m. (only L.) 'having white lustre,' the moon; camphor; cuttle-fish bone; Achyranthes Atropurpurea; a wh°-flowering variety of Clitoria Ternatea. —**nāman**, m. Clitoria Ternatea, Car. —**nīla**, mfn. wh° and black, L.; m. a cloud, L. —**nyaṅga**, mfn. having a white mark, ĀpŚr. —**paksha**, mfn. white-winged, PārGṛ. —**paṭa**, m. N. of a Jaina teacher, Piṅg., Sch.; pl. N. of a Jaina sect, Hcar.; Inscr. —**pattra**, n. a white feather, MW.; m. 'white-feathered,' a goose (see comp.); (*ā*), f. a kind of tree, L.; (°*ra*)-*ratha*, m. 'whose vehicle is a goose,' N. of Brahmā, L. —**padma**, n. a wh° lotus, Pañcar.; Kālac. —**parṇa**, m. N. of a mountain, MārkP.; (*ā*), f. Pistia Stratiotes, L. —**parṇâsa**, m. white basil, L. —**parvata**, m. 'wh° mountain,' N. of a m°, MBh.; Hariv.; R. —**pākī**, f. a kind of plant or its fruit, g. *haritaky-ādi*. —**pāṭalā**, f. a white-flowering variety of Bignonia, L. —**pāda**, m. N. of one of Śiva's attendants, L. —**piṅga**, m. 'wh° and tawny,' a lion, L. —**piṅgala**, mfn. tawny, L.; m. a lion, L.; N. of Śiva, MW. —**piṅgalaka**, m. a lion, L. —**piṇḍītaka**, m. a kind of tree, L. —**pītala**, m. yellow-whiteness; mf(*ā*)n. yellow-white, L. —**puṅkhā**, f. a kind of shrub, L. —**punarnavā**, f. wh°-flowering hogweed, MW. —**pushpa**, n. a wh° flower, Suśr.; mf(*ī*)n. wh°-flowering, GṛŚrS.; m. Vitex Negundo, L.; (*ā*), f. N. of various plants (Cratæva Roxburghii; a white-flowering species of Clitoria Ternatea; Artemisia Vulgaris or Alpinia Nutans; colocynth; a white-fl° variety of Vitex Negundo; =*ghoshātakī* or *nāga-dantī*), L.; (*ī*), f. a wh°-fl° variety of Clitoria Ternatea, Npr. —**pushpaka**, mfn. having white flowers, MW.; m. white oleander, L.; Nerium Odorum (the wh° variety), W.; (*ikā*), f. two kinds of plant (=*putra-dātrī* or =*mahā-śaṇapushpikā*), L. —**prasūnaka**, mfn. having wh° flowers, MW.; m. Tapia Cratæva, L. —**phalā**, f. a kind of plant, Pāṇ. iv, 1, 64, Vārtt. 2, Pat. —**barbara**, n. a kind of sandal, L. —**balā**, f. the wh° Balā (a kind of plant), MW. —**bindukā**, f. a girl with wh° spots (and therefore unfit for marriage), L. —**buhnā**, f. a kind of pl°, L. —**bṛihatī**, f. a kind of wh° Vārtākī or egg-pl°, L. —**bhaṇḍā**, f. a white-flowering variety of Clitoria Ternatea, L. —**bhadra**, m. N. of a Guhyaka, MBh. —**bhasman**, n. a partic. preparation of quicksilver, L. —**bhānu**, mfn. wh°-rayed (as the moon), Hariv.; m. the moon, Hcar.; Kād. —**bhikshu**, m. a kind of mendicant, Pañcat. —**bhiṇḍā**, f. a kind of plant, Car. —**bhujaṃga**, m. N. of an incarnation of Brahmā, Virac. —**maṇḍala**, m. a kind of snake, Suśr. —**madhya**, m. Cyperus Rotundus, L. —**mandāra** (Cat.) or °**raka** (L.), m. a kind of tree. —**mayūkha**, m. 'white-rayed,' the moon, Vcar. —**marica**, m. a kind of Moringa Pterygosperma, Dhanv.; n. the seed of it, L.; the s° of the Hyperanthera Mor°, W.; wh° pepper, MW. —**mahoṭikā**, f. a kind of plant, L. —**māṇḍavya**, m. N. of an author, Cat. —**mādhava** (Cat.) or °**va-tīrtha** (MW.), n. N. of a Tīrtha. —**māla**, m. 'having wh° wreaths,' a cloud, L.; smoke, L. (prob. w. r. for *khatam*°). —**mūtra**, mfn. having white urine (-*tā*, f.), ŚārṅgS. —**mūla**, m. (Suśr.) or °**lā**, f. (Npr.) Bœrhavia Procumbens. —**mṛid**, f. wh° clay, VarYogay. (pl.) —**meha**, w. r. for *sita-m*°, q. v. —**moda**, m. N. of a demon who causes diseases, Hariv. —**yâvarī**, f. wh°-flowing, (or) N. of a river, RV. viii, 26, 18. —**rakta**, m. pale redness; mfn. pale-red, L. —**rañjana**, n. 'white-coloured,' lead, L. —**ratha**, m. a white chariot, MW.; 'having a white car,' the planet Venus, L. —**raśmi**, m. N. of a Gandharva transformed into a white elephant, Kathās. —**rasa**, m. butter-milk and water mixed in equal parts, L. —**rājī**, f. a kind of plant, L. —**rāvaka**, m. Vitex Negundo, L. —**rāsnā**, f. the wh° Rāsnā plant, W. —**rūpya**, n. tin, L. —**rocis**, m. 'having wh° light,' the moon, L. —**roman**, n. wh° hair, MW.; °**mâṅka**, m. a spot of wh° h°, ib. —**rohita**, m. 'wh° and red,' N. of Garuḍa, L.; a kind of plant, L. —**lodhra**, m. a kind of Lodhra, L. —**lohita**, m. N. of a Muni (a pupil of Śveta), VP. —**vaktra**, m. N. of one of Skanda's attendants, MBh. —**vacā**, f. N. of two kinds of plant (=*ativishā* or =*śukla-vacā*), L. —**vatsā** (*śvetá*-), f. (a cow) having a white calf, TS.; Kāṭh.; ŚBr. —**varṇa**, mfn. white-coloured, MW.; (*ā*), f. chalk, Divyâv. —**valkala**, m. white bark, MW.; Ficus Glomerata, L. —**vastrin**, mfn. white-clad, Kālac. —**vah**, mfn. (nom. -*vāḥ*; instr. -*vāhā* [?] or *śvetâuhā*; du. -*vobhyām*; f. -*vāhī* [?] or *śvetâuhī*) borne by white horses, Pāṇ. iii, 2, 71, Vārtt.; Vop. xxvi, 65 &c.; m. N. of Indra, ib.; (°*tâuhī* or -*vāhī*, f. the wife of I°, ib. —**vājin**, m. a wh° horse, MW.; 'having wh° horses,' the moon, L.; N. of Arjuna, L. —**vārāha**, m. a partic. Kalpa, the first day in the month of Brahmā (also °*ha-kalpa*, m.), Cat.; N. of ch. of the Vāyu-purāṇa; -*tīrtha*, n. N. of a Tīrtha, Cat. —**vārija**, n. a white lotus-flower, L. —**vārttākī**, f. a kind of plant, L. —**vāsas**, m. an ascetic who wears white garments, L. —**vāh**, see -*vah*. —**vāha**, mfn. driving wh° horses or drawn by wh° h°; m. N. of Indra, L.; of Arjuna, MBh. —**vāhana**, mfn. = prec.; m. the moon, L.; a marine monster (=*makara*), W.; a form of Śiva, Hariv.; N. of Arjuna, MBh.; of Bhadrâśva, Cat.; of a son of Rājâdhideva, Hariv.; of a son of Śūra, VP. —**vāhin**, m. 'borne by white horses,' N. of Arjuna, L. —**vṛiksha**, m. Cratæva Roxburghii, L. —**vrata**, m. pl. a partic. sect (prob. for -*paṭa*), Vās., Introd. —**śara-puṅkhā**, f. a kind of shrub, L. —**śāla**, m. white rice, L. —**śiṅśapā**, f. a kind of tree, L. —**śikha**, m. N. of a pupil of Śveta, IW. 122, n. 3. —**śigru**, m. a wh°-flowering variety of Moringa, Bhpr. —**śimbikā**, f. wh° bean, L. —**śīrsha**, m. N. of a Daitya, Hariv. —**śuṅga**, m. 'having wh° awns,' barley, L. —**śūraṇa**, m. a kind of bulbous plant (=*vana-ś*°), L. —**śṛiṅga**, m. 'having wh° awns,' barley, MW. —**śaila**, m. a snow-mountain (or N. of a range, see under *śveta*), Hariv.; Kathās.; -*maya*, mf(*ī*)n. made of wh° stone or marble, Rājat. —**śyāma**, mfn. wh° and black (applied to a side-glance), Samgīt. —**sarpa**, m. a wh° snake, W.; Cratæva Roxburghii, L.; Tapia Crat°, W. —**sarshapa**, m. wh° mustard, a grain of wh° m°, Suśr. —**sāra**, m. Acacia Catechu or a wh°-flowering species of it, L.; Mimosa Catechu, W.; sandal, L. —**siṅhī**, f. a kind of pot-herb, L. —**siddha**, m. N. of one of Skanda's attendants, MBh. —**surasā**, f. a wh°-flowering variety of the Vitex Negundo or Nyctanthes Arbor Tristis, L. —**spandā**, f. Clitoria Ternatea or a wh°-flowering variety of it, L. —**hanu**, m. a kind of snake, Suśr. —**haya**, m. a wh° horse (N. of the h° of Indra), L.; 'having wh° h°s,' N. of Arjuna, L. —**hastin**, m. a wh° elephant, W.; N. of Airāvata (el° of Indra), L. —**hūṇa**, m. pl. the wh° Huns, VarBṛS. **Śvetâṅśu**, m. 'white-rayed,' the moon, ŚārṅgP. **Śvetâṅśuka**, mfn. clad in wh°, Rājat. **Śvetâksha**, m. a kind of Soma plant, Suśr. **Śvetâñjana**, n. wh° paint, Pañcad. **Śvetâṇḍa**, mfn. having a wh° scrotum (as a kind of stallion), MBh. **Śvetâtapatra**, n. a wh° umbrella, Vās.; °*patrāya*, Nom. Ā. °*yate*, to resemble a wh° umbrella, Kād. **Śvetā-trivṛit**, f. the wh° Trivṛit plant, MW. **Śvetâtreya**, m. N. of a man, Cat. **Śvetâdri**, m. N. of a mountain or mountain range, Hariv.; BhP. (accord. to Sch. = *kailāsa*); -*vāsâshṭaka*, n. N. of wk. **Śvetânukāśa**, see *śvetânūkāśa*. **Śvetânulepana**, mfn. covered with wh° ointment; m. N. of Bala-rāma, MBh. **Śvetânūkāśa**, mfn. shining wh°, TS.; ŚāṅkhBr. **Śvetâparājita-kalpa**, m. N. of wk. **Śvetâmbara**, mfn. clad in wh°; m. N. of the second great Jaina sect (opp. to the Dig-ambara, q. v.), MWB. 532 &c.; a form of Śiva, Cat.; N. of an author, ib.; -*candra*, m. N. of a man, ib. **Śvetâmlī**, f. Tamarindus Indica, L. **Śvetâraṇya**, n. N. of a forest, R.; of a Tīrtha situated on the northern bank of the Kāverī (also -*tīrtha*), Cat.; -*māhātmya*, n. N. of wk. **Śvetârka**, m. Calotropis Gigantea Alba, L.; -*kalpa*, m. N. of wk. **Śvetârcis**, m. 'wh°-rayed,' the moon, Kāvyâd. **Śvetâvara**, m. a kind of vegetable, L. **Śvetâśva**, m. a wh° horse, ŚāṅkhŚr.; R.; mfn. yoked with wh° steeds (as a car), ib.; m. 'drawn by wh° st°,' N. of Arjuna, MBh.; of a pupil of Śiva, IW. 122, n. 3; of a pupil of Śveta, W. (v. l. *śvetâsya*); (*ā*), f. N. of a goddess, Cat.; (°*va*)-*dāna-vidhi*, m. N. of wk. **Śvetâśvatara**, m. 'having white mules,' N. of a teacher, ŚvetUp.; pl. his school, TĀr., Sch.; -*śākhā*, f. or -*śākhin*, pl. id., Cat.; °*rôpanishad*, f. N. of an Upanishad, IW. 43 &c. (°*shat-prakāśikā*, f., °*shaḍ-dīpikā*, f. N. of Comms.) **Śvetâsthi**, n. a partic. kind of famine, Divyâv. **Śvetâsya**, m. 'wh°-faced,' N. of a pupil of Śveta, Cat. **Śvetâhvā**, f. a wh°-flowering variety of Bignonia (=*śukla-pāṭalā*), L. **Śvetêkshu**, m. a species of sugar-cane, L. **Śvetâiraṇḍa**, m. wh° Ricinus, L. **Śvetôtpala**, m. N. of an astronomer, Col. **Śvetôdara**, m. 'having a white belly,' a kind of snake, Suśr.; N. of Kubera, L.; of a mountain, MārkP. **Śvetôpakāśa**, mf(*ā*)n. = *śvitrôp*°, MaitrS.

Śvetaka, mfn. whitish, white, VarBṛS. (applied to the 7th unknown quantity, Col.); m. a cowry, L.; N. of a serpent-demon, Buddh.; n. silver, L.

Śvetaki, m. N. of an ancient king, MBh.

Śvetanâ, f. dawn, RV. i, 122, 4.

Śvetaya, Nom. P. °*yati*, = *śvetâśvam ācashṭe* or *śvetâśvenâtikrāmati*, Dhātup.; Vop.

Śvetayat, mfn. making white, whitening, MW.

Śvetāya, Nom. Ā. °*yate*, to become white, Kād.

Śvetāyin, mfn. belonging to the race of Śveta, Cat.

Śvetika, m. N. of a man, Rājat.

Śvetita, mfn. (prob.) whitened, MW. (cf. Pāṇ. vii, 2, 16, 17).

Śvetiman, m. whiteness, white colour, Car.; Kād.

Śvetâuhī. See *śveta-vah*, cols. 1, 2.

Śvetyà, mf(*ā*)n. white, brilliant (as the dawn), RV.; Naigh.; Nir.; (*ā*), f. N. of a river, RV.

Śvetra, n. white leprosy, L.

Śvaita, n. N. of the country Hiraṇmaya, L.

Śvaitacchattrika, mfn. (fr. *śveta-cchattra*) having a claim to a white umbrella, Pāṇ. v, 1, 63, Sch.

Śvaitarī, f. (accord. to Sāy.) a cow abounding in milk, RV. iv, 33, 1.

Śvaita-vaidārava. See under *śveta*, p. 1106.

Śvaitâṇśava, mfn. (fr. *śvetâṅśu*) lunar, Bālar.

Śvaiti (fr. *śveta*), g. *sutaṃgamâdi*.

Śvaitya, m. patr. of Sṛiñjaya, MBh.; n. whiteness, Kāv.; Vāgbh.; Sāh.; white leprosy, vitiligo, W.

Śvaitra, n. (fr. *śvitra*) white leprosy, vitiligo, W.

Śvaitreyá, m. (fr. *śvitra*) the fire or brilliancy of lightning, RV. v, 19, 3 (Sāy.); metron. fr. *śvitrā*, RV. i, 33, 14 (Sāy.)

Śvaitrya, n. (fr. *śvitra*) wh° leprosy, Mn. xi, 51.

श्विन्द् *śvind* (connected with √*śvit*), cl. 1. Ā. (Dhātup. ii, 9) **śvindate** (only pf. *śiśvinde*), to be white, Hcar.; to be cold, Dhātup. [Cf. Lith. *szvintù*.]

श्वैक्न *śvaikna*, m. a king of the Śviknas, ŚBr.

श्वोभाव *śvo-bhāva*, *śvo-bhāvin* &c. See p. 1106, col. 1.

ष SHA.

ष 1. *sha*, the second of the three sibilants (it belongs to the cerebral class, and is sometimes substituted for *s*, and more rarely for *ś*, and occasionally interchangeable with *kh*; in sound it corresponds to *sh* in the English word *shun*; many roots which begin with *s* are written in the Dhātu-pātha with *sh*, prob. to show that their initial *s* is liable to be cerebralized after certain prepositions). —**kāra**, m. the letter or sound *sha*, Prāt. —**tva**, n. the state of the letter *sha*, the substitution of *sh* for *s*, ib.; -*ṇa-tva*, n. the substitution of *sh* for *s* and of *ṇ* for *n*, ib.

ष 2. *sha*, mfn. (only L.; for 3. *sha* see below) best, excellent; wise, learned; m. loss, destruction; loss of knowledge; end, term; rest, remainder; eternal happiness, final emancipation; heaven, paradise; sleep; a learned man, teacher; a nipple; =*kaca*; =*mānava*; =*sarva*; =*garbha-vimocana*; n. the embryo; (accord. to some) patience, endurance.

षग् *shag*, *shagh*, *shac* &c. See √*sag* &c.

षट् *shaṭ*, *shaḍ* (in comp. for *shash*), see below.

षट्कार *shaṭ-kāra*, m. the syllable *shaṭ* (in *vaushaṭ*), AitBr.; ŚāṅkhŚr.

षट्ट् *shaṭṭ*, cl. 10. P. *shaṭṭayati* (*niketane*, *hiṅse*, *dāne*, *bale*), cf. √*saṭṭ*.

षट्टक *shaṭṭaka*, m. (cf. *shāḍava*) a kind of sweetmeat, Suśr., Sch.

षडग *shaḍaga* (?), m. a kind of snake.

षण्ड *shaṇḍa*, m. n. (often written *khaṇḍa*, also v. l. or w. r. for *śaṇḍa*, *shaṇḍha*, and *saṇḍa*) a group of trees or plants, wood, thicket (always ifc.; cf. *vana* and *vṛiksha-sh°*); any group or multitude, heap, quantity, collection, BhP.; m. a bull set at liberty (*-tva*, n.), Uṇ. i, 101; 113, Sch. (cf. *nila-sh°*); a breeding bull, L.; N. of a serpent-demon, TāṇḍBr.; Lāṭy.; n. = *liṅga* (used in explaining *pāshaṇḍa*), BhP. **-kāpālika**, m. N. of a teacher (v. l. *caṇḍa-k°*), Cat. **-tā**, f. state of a bull, &c.; *-yogya*, m. a bull fit for breeding, L. **-tila, -tva**, w. r. for *shaṇḍha-t°*.

Shaṇḍaka, shaṇḍaya, w. r. for *shaṇḍh°*.

Shaṇḍā-maka (Kām.), **Sháṇḍā-márka** (MaitrS.), w. r. for *śáṇḍā-márka*.

Shaṇḍālī, f. (only L.) a wanton woman; a pond, pool; a partic. measure of oil (called Chatāk).

Sháṇḍika, m. N. of a man, MaitrS. (*khaṇḍ°*, ŚBr.)

Shaṇḍīya, w. r. *shaṇḍhīya*.

षण्ढ *shaṇḍha*, m. (often wrongly written *shaṇḍa, śaṇḍa, sandha*) a eunuch, hermaphrodite (14 or even 20 classes are enumerated by some writers), GṛŚrS.; Mn.; MBh. &c.; (*ī*), f. (with *yoni*) the vulva of a woman that has no menstrual periods and no breasts, Suśr.; m. or n. (in gram.) the neuter gender, L.; m. N. of Śiva, L.; of a son of Dhṛitarāshṭra, MBh. **-tā**, f., **-tva**, n. the state of being a eunuch, impotence, weakness, Kathās. **-tila**, m. barren sesamum (met. 'a useless person'), MBh. **-vesha**, mfn. clothed like a eunuch, MBh.

Shaṇḍhaya, Nom. P. *°yati*, to castrate, emasculate, unman, HYogay.

Shaṇḍhitā, f. (with *yoni*) = *shaṇḍhī yoniḥ* (see under *shaṇḍha*), ŚārṅgS.

Shaṇḍhīya, Nom. P. *°yati* (fr. *shaṇḍha*), Pat.

षराजिम *sharājima, sharāñjima*, and *shārija*, N. of places, Cat.

षर्जूर *sharjūra* (perhaps for *kharjūra*), N. of a place, Cat.

षलागु *shalāgru*, N. of a place, Cat.

षष् *shásh*, mfn. pl. (prob. for orig. *shaksh*; nom. acc. *shát*, instr. *shaḍbhís*, dat. abl. *shaḍbhyás*, gen. *shaṇṇā́m*, loc. *shaṭsú*; in comp. *shash* becomes *shaṭ* before hard letters, *shaḍ* before soft, *sho* before *d*, which is changed into *ḍ*, and *ṇ* before nasals) six (with the counted object in apposition or exceptionally in gen. or ifc., e. g. *shaḍ ṛitavaḥ* or *shaḍ ṛitūnām*, 'the six seasons,' *shaṭsu shaṭsu māseshu*, 'at periods of six months,' Mn. viii, 403; at the end of a Bahuvrīhi compound it is declined like other words ending in *sh*, e. g. *priya-shashas*, nom. pl., Pāṇ. vii, 1, 22 schol.; among the words used as expressions for the number six (esp. in giving dates) are *aṅga, darśana, tarka, rasa, ṛitu, vajra-koṇa, kārttikeya-mukha*), RV. &c. &c.; (in gram.) a tech. N. for numerals ending in *sh* and *n* and words like *kati*, Pāṇ. i, 1, 24, 25; (*shaṭ*), ind. six times, ŚBr. [Cf. Gk. ἕξ; Lat. *sex*; Goth. *saihs*; Germ. *sëhs, sechs*; Eng. *six*.]

3. **Sha**, mfn. = *shash*, ifc. (in *pañca-sha*, q. v.)

Shaṭ, in comp. for *shash*. **-kapāla** (*sháṭ-*), mfn. distributed in six cups (as an oblation), ŚBr. **-karṇa**, mfn. six-eared, MW.; heard by six ears (said of secret counsel which has been unfortunately heard by a third person), Pañcat.; Hit.; Vet. &c.; m. a sort of lute, W. **-karman**, n. the six duties of Brāhmans (viz. *adhyayana*, 'studying or repeating the Veda,' *adhyāpana*, 'teaching the V°,' *yajana*, 'offering sacrifices,' *yājana*, 'conducting them for others,' *dāna*, 'giving,' and *pratigraha*, 'accepting gifts'), ŚāṅkhGṛ.; Mn. &c. (the six daily duties, accord. to the later law-books, are, *snāna*, 'religious bathing,' *saṃdhyā-japa*, 'repetition of prayers at the three Saṃdhyās,' *brahma-yajña*, 'worship of the Supreme Being by repeating the first words of sacred books,' *tarpaṇa*, 'daily oblations of water to the gods, sages, and Pitṛis,' *homa*, 'oblations of fuel, rice &c. to fire,' *deva-pūjā*, 'worship of the secondary gods either in the domestic sanctuary or in temples'), Parāś.; RTL. 394; six acts any one of which is allowable to a Brāhman householder as a means of subsistence (viz. *ṛita*, 'gleaning,' *amṛita*, 'unsolicited alms,' *mṛita*, 'solicited alms,' *karshaṇa*, 'agriculture,' *satyânṛita*, 'commerce or trade,' *śva-vṛitti*, 'servitude,' the last being condemned), Mn. iv, 4, 5, 6, 9; six acts belonging to the practice of Yoga (viz. *dhautī, vastī, netī, trāṭaka, naulika, kapāla-bhātī*, these consist of suppressions of the breath and self-mortifications of various kinds), Cat.; six acts for inflicting various kinds of injury on enemies (viz. *śānti, vaśya, stambhana, vidvesha, uccāṭana, māraṇa*, qq.vv.; these acts consist in repeating certain magical spells and texts taught in the Tantras), ib.; m. a performer of the above six acts, a Brāhman who is an adept in the Tantra magical formularies, Mn.; MBh.; *°ma-kṛit*, m. a Brāhman, L.; *°ma-dīpikā*, f., *°ma-prayoga*, m. N. of wks.; *°ma-vat*, m. a Brāhman, Kād.; *°ma-vidhi*, m., *°ma-viveka*, m., *°ma-vyākhyāna-cintāmaṇi*, m. N. of wks. **-kala**, mfn. lasting for six Kalās, KātyŚr., Sch. **-kāraka**, n. N. of a wk. on the use of six cases (consisting of 14 Ślokas); *-praticchandaka*, m., *praticchandasa, -bheda*, m., *-vivecana*, n. N. of gram. wks. **-kukshi**, mfn. six-bellied, TĀr., Sch. **-kulīya**, mfn. belonging to six families or tribes, Cat. **-kūṭa-ślokānām arthāḥ**, N. of wk. **-kūṭā**, f. a form of Bhairavī, Cat. **-kṛitvas**, ind. six times, Kauś.; Lāṭy. **-koṇa**, mfn. six-angled; n. a s°-a° figure, RāmatUp.; Pañcar.; the thunderbolt of Indra, L.; a diamond, L.; the sixth astrological house, L. **-khaṇḍa**, mfn. consisting of six parts, Dharmaśarm. **-kheṭaka**, n. N. of a town, Cat. **-cakra**, n. sg. the six mystical circles of the body (*mūlâdhāra, svâdhishṭhāna, maṇi-pūra, an-āhata, viśuddha, ājñākhya*), Pañcar.; N. of wk.; *-krama*, m., *-dīpikā*, f., *-dhyāna-paddhati*, f., *-nirūpaṇa*, n., *-nilaya*, m., *-prabheda*, m., *-bheda*, m., *-bheda-ṭippaṇī* or *-bheda-vivṛiti-ṭīkā*, f., *-vivṛiti-ṭ°*, f., *-sva-rūpa*, n., *-cakrâdi-saṃgraha*, m., *-cakrôpanishad-dīpikā*, f. N. of wks. **-catvāriṅśa**, mf(*ī*)n. the 46th (ch. of MBh. and R.) **-catvāriṅśaka**, mfn. id., Yājñ. **-catvāriṅśat**, f. 46, Nir.; ŚāṅkhŚr. **-caraṇa**, mfn. six-footed; m. a bee, Kāv.; VarBṛS.; Vās.; a louse, L.; a locust, MW.; *-tā*, f. the state or nature of a bee, VarBṛS.; *°ṇāya*, Nom. A. *°ṇāyate*, to represent or act like a bee, Kathās. **-citi**, mfn. consisting of six layers or strata, Jaim. **-citika** (*sháṭ-*), mfn. id., ŚBr. **-takra-taila**, n. a partic. medicinal compound, Bhpr. **-tantrī**, f. N. of the six philosophical systems, Cat.; *-sāra*, m. N. of wk. **-tāla**, m. a kind of measure, Saṃgīt. **-tila-dāna**, n. a partic. ceremony, W. (cf. next). **-tilin**, mfn. one who on certain festivals performs six acts with Tila or sesamum, Hcat.; Tithyād. **-triṅśá**, mf(*ī*)n. consisting of 36, RV.; PañcavBr.; ŚāṅkhŚr.; provided with the Stoma of 36 parts, Br.; Lāṭy.; the 36th (f. du. 'the 35th and 36th,' ŚBr.), MBh.; R.; Rājat.; 36 (in *°śona*, 'diminished by 36'), Lāṭy.; Nidānas. **-triṅśacchatya** (for *°ṅśatśatya*), mf(*ā*)n. consisting of 36 hundreds, KātyŚr. **-triṅśat** (*sháṭ-*), f. sg. 36 (with pl. of the counted object in the same case or in gen.), TS.; Br. &c.; N. of wk.; *-tattva*, n., *-padaka-jñāna*, n. N. of wks.; *-saṃvatsara*, mfn. 36 years old, Maś.; KātyŚr.; *-sahasra*, mf(*ā*)n. consisting of 36 thousands, ŚāṅkhŚr. **-triṅśati**, f. 36, ĀpŚr. **-triṅśatka**, mfn. consisting of 36, Kām. **-triṅśad** (for *triṅśat*); *-akshara* (*sháṭ-*), mf(*ā*)n. having 36 syllables, Br.; *-aha*, mfn. lasting 36 days, AitBr.; *-aha-śas*, ind. always in 36 days, KātyŚr.; *-ābdika*, mfn. lasting 36 years, Mn. iii, 1; *-ishṭaka* (*sháṭ-*), mfn. consisting of 36 bricks, ŚBr.; *-ūna*, mfn. diminished by 36, Lāṭy.; *-dīpikā*, f. N. of wk.; *-rātra*, mfn. lasting 36 days, KātyŚr.; *-vikrama* (*sháṭ-*), mf(*ā*)n. 36 steps long, ŚBr. **-triṅśan** (for *triṅśat*); *-mata*, n. a collection of the precepts of 36 Munis (held to be authors of as many law-books), Hcat.; Saṃskārak. **-triṅśika**, mfn. consisting of 36 lengths or 36 long, Śulbas. **-tva**, n. a hexade, Vārtt. on Pāṇ. v, 2, 29. **-paksha** (*sháṭ-*), mf(*ā*)n. provided with six side-posts, AV. **-pañca-varsha**, mfn. six or five years old, BhP. **-pañcāśa**, mfn. the 56th, Rājat. **-pañcāśat** (*sháṭ-*), f. sg. 56, ŚBr.; *-tama*, mfn. the 56th, MW.; *°śad-dhorā-vṛitti*, f. N. of wk. **-pañcāśatika-horā**, f., **-pañcāśatikā**, f., **-pañcāśikā**, f., **-pañcāśikā-vṛitti**, f. N. of wks. **-pattra**, mfn. six-leafed, NṛisUp. **-pad** (*sháṭ-*; strong base *-pād*), mf(*padī*)n. six-footed, AV.; one who advances or has advanced six steps, TS.; ĀśvGṛ.; (a verse) consisting of six divisions or Pādas (nom. f. *-pāt*), AV. Anukr.; (*adī*), f. (cf. under *-pada*) a louse, L.; a kind of composition, Saṃgīt. **-pada** (*sháṭ-*), mf(*ā*)n. having six places or quarters (as a town), MBh.; six-footed, ib.; (a verse) consisting of six divisions or Pādas, VS.; Br. &c.; m. a six-footed animal, insect, Cat.; (ifc. f. *ā*) a bee, ŚāṅkhŚr.; MBh.; Kāv. &c.; a louse, L.; (*ā*), f. a class of Prākṛit metres, Col.; (*ī*), f. a female bee, MW.; a louse, ib.; the six states (scil. hunger, thirst, sorrow, disordered intellect, old age, death, or [accord. to Nīlak.] *kāma-krodhau, śoka-mohau, mada-mānau*), MBh.; N. of two wks. (*-stotra*, n. N. of a hymn); n. a partic. advantageous position in chess, L.; *-jya*, mfn. 'having bees for a string,' N. of Kāma-deva's bow, Megh.; *-priya*, m. 'beloved by bees,' Mesua Roxburghii, L.; *°dâtithi*, m. 'having bees as guests,' the Mango tree, L.; Michelia Champaka, L.; *°dânanda-vardhana*, m. 'increasing the joy of bees,' red and yellow amaranth, L.; Jonesia Asoka, L.; a kind of acacia, L.; *°dâbhi-dharma*, m., *°dârtha-vivaraṇa*, n. N. of wks.; *°dālī*, f. a line of bees, Ragh.; *°dêshṭa*, m. 'dear to bees,' Nauclea Cadamba, L. **-padikā**, f. a class of Prākṛit metres, Col. **-palaka**, n. a partic. ointment, Suśr. **-palika**, mfn. having the weight of six Palas, ib. **-pāda**, mfn. six-footed, GopBr.; m. a bee, Hariv. **-pāramitā-nirdeśa**, m. a partic. Samādhi, Kāraṇḍ. **-pāramitā-paripūrṇa**, m. 'endowed with the six transcendental virtues,' N. of Buddha, Divyâv. **-pārâyaṇa-vidhi**, m., **-piṇḍa-vidhi**, m. N. of wks. **-pitā-putraka**, m. a kind of time (in music), L. **-putra**, mfn. having six sons, JaimBr. **-pura**, n. N. of an Asura town, Hariv. **-pragātha**, n. a hymn consisting of six Pragāthas, ŚrS. **-prajña**, mfn. (only L.) acquainted with the six objects (viz. *dharma, artha, kāma, moksha, lokârtha*, and *tattvârtha*); m. a dissolute man; a good-hearted neighbour. **-praśnôpanishad**, f. N. of an Upanishad, = *praśn°*; *-bhāshya*, n. N. of Comm. on it. **-śata** (*sháṭ-*), n. 106, ŚBr.; Vait.; (sg. or pl.) 600, AmṛitabUp.; MBh.; (*ī*), f. 600, Jyot.; VarBṛ.; mfn. consisting of or numbering 600, Mn. viii, 198; 367. **-śamī**, f. having the length of six Śamyās, Kauś. **-śas**, ind. sixfold, six times, Pañcar. **-śāstra-vicāra**, m. N. of wk. **-śāstrin**, m. one who has studied the six Śāstras or six systems of philosophy, MW. **-shashṭa**, mfn. the 66th (ch. of MBh.); increased by 66, Lāṭy. **-shashṭi**, f. (sg. or pl.) 66, MBh.; Śatr.; *-tama*, mfn. the 66th (ch. of R.) **-shoḍaśin**, mfn. consisting of six Stomas each of which has 16 parts, PañcavBr. **-sapta**, mfn. pl. six or seven, Rājat. **-saptata**, mfn. the 76th (ch. of MBh.) **-saptati**, f. 76, ib.; *-tama*, mfn. 76th (ch. of R.) **-sahasrá**, mfn. pl. numbering 6000, AV.; (*ī*), f. N. of wk. (*°ra-kāra*, m., Pratāp., Sch.); *-śata*, (ibc.) 600,000, MBh. **-sāhasrī**, f., **-sūtra**, n., **-sthala-nirṇaya**, m., **-sthala-mahiman**, m., **-sthalânubhava**, m., **-sthānaka-vṛitti**, f. N. of wks.

Shaṭka, mfn. consisting of six, Lāṭy.; RPrāt.; Suśr. &c. (*dvi-shaṭka* = 12, MBh.); bought for six &c., Pāṇ. v, 1, 22; occurring for the sixth time, doing anything for the sixth time, ib. v, 2, 77; Vārtt.; m. six, Gaṇit.; n. a hexade or aggregate of six (ifc. after another numeral, e.g. *nava-shaṭka*, 'consisting of nine hexades'), Nir.; ĀśvŚr.; MBh. &c.; the six passions collectively (viz. *kāma, mada, māna, lobha, harsha*, and *rushā*), L. **-pañcāśikā**, f. N. of wk. **-māsika**, mfn. hired for six months, Pāṇ.; ib., Vārtt., Sch.

Shaṭṭaya, mfn. of six different sorts or kinds, in six ways, ŚāṅkhBr.; ĀpŚr.

Shaḍ, in comp. for *shash*. **-aṅśa**, m. a sixth part, Ragh.; mfn. consisting of six parts (*-tā*, f.), Sarvad. **-aṅhri**, m. = *-aṅghri*, Bhartṛ. (v. l.) **-akshá**, mfn. six-eyed, RV.; ŚBr. **-akshara** (*shaḍ-* or *sháḍ-*), mf(*ī*)n. consisting of six syllables (*°rī mahā-vidyā*, Pañcar.; Kāraṇḍ.), VS.; ŚāṅkhGṛ. &c.; *-maya*, mf(*ī*)n. id., Hcat.; *-stotra*, n. N. of wk.; *-aksharī-deva*, m. N. of an author, Cat. **-akshīṇa**, m. 'six-eyed,' a fish, L. **-aṅga**, n. sg. the six principal parts of the body (viz. the two arms, two legs, head, and waist), L.; six auspicious things, i. e. the six things obtained from a cow (*go-mūtram go-mayaṃ kshīram sarpir dadhi ca rocanā*), A.; pl. the six limbs or works auxiliary to the Veda, six Vedâṅgas, Gauṭ.; Mn. &c.; any set of six articles, MW.; = *-rudra* (q. v.); (*ī*), f. the six Vedâṅgas, L.; mfn. six-limbed, having six parts, Br.; AmṛitabUp.; Suśr.; VarBṛS.; having six Vedâṅgas, PārGṛ.; Āpast.; R.; m. a kind of Asteracantha, L.; *-guggulu*, m. a partic. mixture, L.; *-jit*, mfn. subduing the six members, MW.; m. N. of Vishṇu, L.; *-pānīya*, n. an infusion or decoction of six drugs, W.; *-rudra*, N. of partic. verses taken from the VS. and used at the bathing of an image of Śiva; *-vid*, mfn. knowing the six Vedâṅgas, Mn. iii, 185; *-samanvāgata*, m. 'provided with the six chief requisites,' N. of Buddha, Divyâv. **-aṅgaka**, n. the body consisting of six parts, L. — **aṅginī**, f. a six-limbed i. e. complete army, Mn.; Kāv.; Kām. — **aṅguli** (Pat. on Pāṇ. i, 4, 18, Vārtt. 1) or °**li-datta** (id. on Pāṇ. v, 3, 84, Vārtt. 4), N. of a man. — **aṅghri**, m. 'having six feet,' a bee, Kāv. &c. — **aṇḍa**, g. *dhūmâdi* (*khaṇḍa* and *khaḍaṇḍa*, Kāś.) — **adhika**, mfn. exceeded by six, Mālatīm.; *-daśan*, mfn. pl. 10 + 6, MW.; *-daśa-nāḍī-cakra*, n. 'circle of the 16 tubular vessels,' i. e. the heart, ib. — **anvaya-mahā-ratna**, n., **-anvaya-śāmbhava-raśmi-pūjā-krama**, m. N. of wks. — **abhijña**, m. 'possessed of the six Abhijñās,' a Buddha, L.; a Buddhist, Śaṃkar. — **abhijñāta**, mfn. possessed of the six Abhijñās, Divyâv. — **ara** (*shád-* or *sháḷ-*), mfn. having six spokes, RV.; NṛisUp. — **aratni** (*shád-*), mfn. six Aratnis in length, ŚBr.; MBh. — **arcá**, n. a collection of six verses, ŚāṅkhŚr.; (prob. m.) pl. a hymn of six verses, AV. — **artha-nirṇaya**, m., **-artha-saṃkshepa**, m. N. of wks. — **avatta**, n. a portion consisting of six pieces cut off and designed for the Agnîdh, KātyŚr.; Vait.; a double vessel designed for the above, ĀpŚr. — **aśīta**, mfn. 86th (ch. of MBh.) — **aśīti**, f. 86, Sūryas.; = *-aśīti-mukha*, Hcat.; N. of various wks.; *-cakra*, n. a mystical circle (shaped like a man [whose limbs are formed of the Nakshatras] for telling good or bad luck at the Shaḍ-aśīti-mukha), L.; *-tama*, mfn. 86th (ch. of R.); *-mukha*, n. (or *ā*, f., scil. *gati*) the sun's entrance into the four signs (Pisces, Gemini, Virgo, and Sagittarius), Sūryas.; Hcat. — **aśra** (Cat.), **-aśraka** (Hcat.), or **-aśri** (MBh.; VarBṛS.), mfn. hexagonal (w.r. *-asra* &c.) — **aśrā**, f. Leea Hirta or Phyllanthus Emblica, L. — **aśva**, mfn. provided with or drawn by six horses, RV.; MārkP. — **ashṭaka**, n. (in astron.) a partic. Yoga, MW. — **ahá** (or *shaḷ-ahá*), m. a period of six days, esp. a Soma festival of six days, TS.; AV.; Br. &c. — **aho-rātra** (only *am*, acc.), six days and six nights, R. — **ātman**, mfn. having six natures (said of Agni), MārkP. — **ānana**, (ibc.) six mouths or six faces, Ragh.; mfn. six-mouthed, six-faced; m. N. of Skanda, MBh.; R.; Kathās.; MārkP. — **āmnāya**, m. the sixfold sacred texts (fabled to have proceeded from the six mouths of Śiva), L.; N. of wk.; *-shaḍ-darśana-saṃkshepa-vāda*, m., *-saṃhitā*, f., *-stava*, m. N. of wks. — **āyatana**, n. the seats of the six organs (or senses), MW.; mfn. consisting of the six Āyatanas (viz. *vijñāna*, earth, air, fire, and water, and *rūpa*), Bādar., Sch.; *-bhedaka*, m. N. of a Buddha, Divyâv. — **āra**, mfn. hexagonal, L. — **āvali**, f. any row of six objects (applied to a set of six Śatakas in verse, of which the Sūrya-śataka is one), MW. — **āhuti**, f. a number of six oblations, KātyŚr., Sch.; mfn. serving for six ob°, ĀśvGṛ. — **āhutika**, mfn. id., KātyŚr., Sch. — **iḍa**, mfn. containing six times the word *iḍā*; m. (with *pada-stobha*) N. of a Sāman, SV. — **uttara**, mfn. larger by six, PañcavBr. — **udyāma** (*shád-*), mfn. provided with six ropes or traces, TS.; KapS. — **unnata**, mf(*ā*)n. having six prominent parts of the body, MBh. — **unnayana-mahā-tantra**, n. N. of wk. — **upasatka**, mfn. connected with six festivals called Upasad, Lāṭy. — **ūna**, mf(*ā*)n. less by six, Lāṭy. — **ūrmi**, f. the six waves of existence, Kāv. — **ūshaṇa**, n. the six hot substances (viz. pepper &c.), Bhpr. — **ṛiksha**, mfn. having six asterisms, VarYogay. — **ṛicá**, m. n. a collection of six verses, AV.; Br. — **ṛitu**, m. pl. the six seasons, W.; *-varṇana*, n., *-vinoda*, m., *-sūkta*, n. N. of wks. — **gaṇa**, (prob.) w.r. for *-guṇa*, Hariv. 7225 and 7432. — **gata**, mfn. arrived at six (in arith. applied to the sixth power), MW. — **gayā**, f. the six things beginning with *gayā* or *ga* (and bestowing final emancipation), VāyuP. — **garbha**, m. pl. a partic. class of Dānavas, Hariv. — **gavá**, m. n. a yoke of six oxen, TS.; Kāṭh.; ŚBr.; ŚrS.; n. six cows, KātyŚr., Sch.; (ifc.) a yoke of six animals of any kind, MBh. — **gavīya**, mfn. drawn by six oxen, MBh. — **guṇa**, m. pl. the qualities perceived by the five senses and Manas, GarbhUp.; BhP.; the six excellencies or advantages, Hariv.; the six acts or measures to be practised by a king in warfare (viz. *saṃdhi*, 'peace,' *vigraha*, 'war,' *yāna*, 'marching,' *āsana*, 'sitting encamped,' *dvaidhī-bhāva*, 'dividing his forces,' *saṃśraya*, 'seeking the protection of a more powerful king'), ib.; Daś.; n. an assemblage of six qualities or properties, MW.; mfn. sixfold, six times, Hit.; Kathās.; having six excellencies or advantages, Sarvad.; °*ṇī-√kṛi*, to make sixfold, Jyot. — **guru-bhāshya**, n. N. of a Comm. — **guru-śishya**, m. N. of a Commentator on Kātyāyana's Ṛig-veda-sarvânukramaṇī (who lived in the 12th century, A.D.) — **grantha**, m. a kind of Karañja, L.; a variety of the Cæsalpinia Bonducella, W.; (*ā*), f. a kind of aromatic root (= *vacā* or *śveta-v*°, L.), Suśr.; Car. (w.r. *-grandhā*); Galedupa Piscidia, L.; Curcuma Zedoaria, L.; (*ī*), f. = *vacā*, L. — **granthi**, mfn. six-knotted, MW.; n. the root of long pepper, L. — **granthikā**, f. Curcuma Zedoaria, L. — **graha-yoga-śānti**, f., **-graha-śānti**, f. N. of wks. — **ja**, m. 'six-born,' N. of the first or (accord. to some) of the fourth of the 7 Svaras or primary notes of music (so called because it is supposed to be produced by six organs, viz. tongue, teeth, palate, nose, throat, and chest; the other six Svaras are Ṛishabha, Gāndhāra, Madhyama, Pañcama, Dhaivata, and Nishāda, of which Nish° and Gāndh° are referred to the Udātta, Ṛish° and Dhaiv° to the An-udātta, while Shaḍ-ja and the other two are referred to the Svarita accent; the sound of the Shaḍ-ja is said to resemble the note of peacocks), MBh.; Ragh.; VarBṛS. &c.; N. of the 16th Kalpa or day of Brahmā, Cat.; *-grāma*, m. (in music) a partic. scale, Saṃgīt.; *-madhyā*, f. a partic. Mūrchanā, ib.; *-°jāmareśvara*, m. N. of wk. — **dhá**, ind. = *-dhā*, ŚBr. — **dhotṛi** (fr. *shash* + *hotṛi*; *shád-*), m. 'relating to six Hotṛis,' N. of the verses TĀr. iii, 4 (to be recited at an animal sacrifice, also *-ḍhotā-râhuti*, KātyŚr., Sch.), Br.; ŚrS.; Baudh. — **darśana**, n. the six systems of philosophy, Sarvad. (IW. 46); mfn. one who is versed in the six systems of ph°, Vet.; *-candrikā*, f., *-vicāra*, m., *-viveka*, m., *-vṛitti*, f., *-saṃkshepa*, m., *-saṃgraha-vṛitti*, f., *-samuccaya*, m., *-siddhânta-saṃgraha*, m. N. of wks. — **darśini-nighaṇṭu**, m., **-darśini-prakaraṇa**, n. N. of wks. — **daśana**, mfn. having six teeth, L. — **durga**, n. a collection of six fortresses (viz. *dhanva-durgā*, *mahī-d*°, *giri-d*°, *manushya-d*°, *mṛid-d*°, *vana-d*°), MW. — **devatya**, mfn. addressed to six deities, TāṇḍyaBr. — **dhā**, ind. sixfold, in six ways, PañcavBr. — **dhāra**, mfn. six-edged, L. — **bindu**, mfn. having six drops or spots, Rājat.; m. N. of Vishṇu, L.; a kind of insect, L.; (with *taila*), n. an oily mixture six drops of which are drawn up the nose (as a remedy for head-ache), Bhpr. — **bhāga**, m. a sixth part (esp. the amount of tax or of grain &c. taken in kind by a king; with gen. or abl.), Mn. vii, 131; viii, 308, Mn.; Yājñ.; Hariv. &c.; *-dala*, (prob.) n. the 12th part, VarBṛS.; *-bhāj*, mfn. receiving or entitled to a sixth part of (gen.), Mn. viii, 305; *-bhṛit*, mfn. one who pays a sixth part as a tribute, Baudh. — **bhāgīyā**, f. having the sixth part of a man's length (said of a brick), Śulbas. — **bhāva-vādin**, m. a maintainer of the theory of the six Bhāvas (viz. *dravya*, *guṇa*, *karman*, *sāmānya*, *viśesha*, *samavâya*), Cat. — **bhāshā-candrikā**, f., °**shā-mañjarī**, f., °**shā-vārttika**, n., °**shā-sub-anta-rūpâdarśa** or °**antâdarśa**, m. N. of wks. — **bhuja**, mf(*ā*)n. six-armed, Pañcar.; six-sided; m. or n. (?) a hexagon, Col.; (*ā*), f. N. of Durgā, L.; a water-melon, L. — **yoga**, m. the six ways or methods practised in Yoga, Cat.; (°*gá*), mfn. drawn by six (horses), AV.; ŚrS. — **ratna-kāvya**, n. N. of wk. — **ratha**, m. N. of a king, Hariv. — **rada**, mfn. having six teeth, L. — **rasa**, m. the six flavours or tastes, Cat.; mfn. having the six flavours, Kathās.; n. water, L.; *-nighaṇṭa*, m., *-nighaṇṭu*, m., *-ratna-mālā*, f. N. of wks.; °*sâsava*, m. the lymphatic humour, L. — **rāga-candrôdaya**, m. N. of wk. — **rātrá**, m. 'six nights,' a period of six days or festival lasting six days, AV.; TS.; GṛŚrS. &c. — **rekhā**, f. a water-melon, L. — **lavaṇa**, n. six kinds of salt, L. — **vaktra**, mfn. six-mouthed, six-faced, MBh.; Pañcar.; m. N. of Skanda, MBh.; VarBṛS.; MatsyaP.; (*ī*), f. six faces, Bālar.; °*trôpanishad-dīpikā*, f. N. of wk. — **vadana**, m. N. of Skanda, A. — **varga**, m. a class or aggregate of six, Cat.; six cows with calves, KātyŚr., Sch.; the five senses and Manas, BhP.; the six inner foes or faults of men (viz. *kāma*, *krodha*, *lobha*, *harsha*, *māna*, and *mada*; also with *ari* or *ripu* or *śatru* prefixed, e.g. *ari-shaḍ-v*°), MBh.; Bhaṭṭ.; Kām. &c.; *-phala*, n. N. of wk.; *-vaśya*, mfn. subject to the above six faults, MW. — **vargika** or **-vargīya**, mfn. belonging to a class of six, Divyâv. — **vārgika**, (prob.) w.r. for *-vargika*, L. — **vārshika-maha**, m. a partic. festival, L. — **vārshikā**, f. of six years, Cat. — **viṇśá**, mf(*ī*)n. 26th (du. 25th and 26th), Sūryas.; Rājat. &c.; consisting of 26, ŚBr.; VarBṛS.; Śaṃk.; plus or increased by 26, Jyot.; n. = next; °*śa-brāhmaṇa*, n. N. of a Brāhmaṇa belonging to the Sāma-veda (being a supplement to the Pañca-viṇśa-brāhmaṇa and regarded as the 26th section of it), IW. 25. — **viṇśaka**, mfn. consisting of 26, CūlUp.; Pañcar. — **viṇśat**, 26 (°*śat*, acc.), Hcat. — **viṇśati** (*shád-*), f. 26 (*-rātra*, n., KātyŚr.), Br.; ŚrS.; VarBṛS.; BhP.; *-tama*, mfn. the 26th R., MBh.; *-sūtra*, n. N. of wk. — **viṇśatika** (prob. w.r.) or **-viṇśatima** (v.l.), mfn. the 26th, VarBṛS. — **viṇśatka**, mfn. consisting of 26, Kām. — **vikāram**, ind. in six uncommon ways, Kāraṇḍ. — **vidik-saṃdhāna**, n., **-vidyâgama**, m., **-vidyâgama-sāṃkhyāyana-tantra**, n. N. of wks. — **vidha** (*shád-*), mf(*ā*)n. sixfold, of six sorts, Br.; ŚāṅkhŚr.; Mn. &c.; *-yoga-phala*, n., *-sāṃkhya*, n. N. of wks. — **vidhāna** (*shád-*), mf(*ā*)n. forming an order or series of six, RV. — **vindhyā**, f. a kind of insect, L. — **vṛishá**, mfn. having six bulls, AV.

Shaḍika, m. endearing form of *shaḍ-aṅguli* (Pat.) or °*li-datta* (Pāṇ. v, 3, 84, Vārtt. 4), Pat.

Shaṇ, in comp. for *shash*. — **ṇagarika**, m. pl. N. of a school, Buddh. — **ṇagarī**, f. a union of six towns, Pāṇ.; Vop. — **ṇavata**, mfn. the 96th R., MBh. — **ṇavati** (*shán-*), f. 96, TS.; Mn.; Yājñ. &c.; *-tama*, mfn. the 96th (ch. of R.); *-śrāddha-nirṇaya*, m., °*dha-prayoga*, m. N. of wks. — **ṇāḍī-cakra**, n. (in astrol.) a partic. circular diagram, L. — **ṇābhi**, mfn. having six navels, MW.; six-naved, MBh. — **ṇābhika**, mfn. six-naved, ib. — **ṇālika**, mfn. lasting six times 24 minutes, Sāh. — **ṇidhana**, n. N. of a Sāman, ĀrshBr. — **ṇivartanī**, f. a partic. mode of subsistence, Baudh. (v.l. *-niv*°). — **mata-sthāpaka**, m. 'establisher of six sects or forms of doctrines,' N. of Śaṃkarâcārya, RTL. 59. — **mayūkha** (*shán-*), mfn. having six pegs, AV.; TBr. — **mātra**, mfn. containing six prosodial instants, Piṅg. — **māsa**, m. a period of six months, half a year (*āt*, ind. after six months), VarBṛS.; Rājat.; (*ī*), f. id., Campak.; °*sa-nicaya*, mfn. one who has a store (of food sufficient) for six m°s, Mn. vi, 18; °*sâbhyantare*, ind. within the space of six m°s, Hit. — **māsika**, mfn. happening every six months, half yearly, Mn.; Pañcat. (cf. *shāṇmās*°). — **māsya** (*shán-*), mfn. six m°s old, of six m°s standing, Br.; Kāṭh.; ŚrS.; n. a period of six months, GṛŚrS. — **mukha**, mfn. having six mouths or faces (Śiva), MBh.; m. N. of Skanda or Kārttikeya, TĀr.; MBh.; Kāv. &c.; of a Bodhi-sattva, Buddh.; of a king and of various other persons, ib.; Rājat.; (*ā*), f. a water-melon, L.; (*ī*), f. = *kumārī*, Kālac.; (with *dhāraṇī*) N. of a Sūtra, Buddh.; (prob.) n. = *shaḍ-aśīti-mukha*, Hcat.; N. of a Sūtra, Buddh.; *-kumāra*, m. N. of a man, Buddh.; *-lakshaṇa*, n., *-vṛitti-nighaṇṭu*, m. N. of wks.; °*khâgra-ja*, m. N. of Gaṇeśa, L. — **muhūrtī**, f. six Muhūrtas, Jyot.

Shaḷ, in comp. for *shash*. See *shaḍ-akshara*, *shaḍ-ara* &c.

Shashṭa, mfn. the sixtieth, consisting of sixty (only used in comp. after another numeral, e.g. *eka-sh*°, 'the sixty-first,' cf. *dvā-sh*°, *dvi-sh*°, *tri-sh*° &c.)

Shashṭi, f. sixty (m.c. also °*ṭī*; with the counted object in apposition, or in gen. pl. or comp.; °*ṭi-tas* = abl., VarBṛS.), RV. &c. &c. — **ja**, m. = *shashṭika*. — **tantra**, n. the doctrine of 60 conceptions or ideas (peculiar to the Sāṃkhya phil.), Sāṃkhyak.; Tattvas. — **tama**, mfn. (accord. to Pāṇ. v, 2, 58 the only form when used alone; cf. *shashṭa* above) the 60th, MBh.; R. — **triśata**, mfn. consisting of 360, Nidānas. — **dakshiṇa**, mfn. having a sacrificial fee or gift of 60, ĀpŚr. — **dina**, mfn. relating to or lasting a period of 60 days, Jyot. — **dhā**, ind. sixtyfold, in 60 ways or parts, Car. — **patha**, m. '60 paths,' N. of the first 60 Adhyāyas of the Śatapatha-brāhmaṇa. — **pathika**, mf(*ī*)n. studying the Shashṭi-patha, Vārtt. on Pāṇ. iv, 2, 60 (cf. *shāshṭi-pathika*). — **pūrti-śānti**, f. N. of wk. — **bhāga**, m. N. of Śiva, MBh. — **matta**, m. an elephant which has reached the age of 60 years (or is in rut at that period), MW. — **yojana**, mfn. 60 Yojanas distant, Kathās.; (*ī*), f. an extent of 60 Y°s, ib. — **rātra**, m. a period of 60 days, Pāṇ. v, 1, 90. — **latā**, f. a kind of plant (= *bhramara-mārī*; w.r. for *yashṭi-l*°), L. — **varshin**, mfn. having 60 years, 60 years old, MBh. — **vāsara-ja**, m. = *shashṭika*, L. — **vidyā**, f. (perhaps) = *-tantra*, Ind. St. — **vrata**, m. a partic. religious observance, Cat. — **śata**, n. sg. 160, KātyŚr. (*trīṇi shashṭi-śatāni*, 360, ŚāṅkhBr.) — **śāli**, m. = *shashṭika*, L. — **saṃvatsara**, m. a period of 60 years or the 60th year (from birth

&c.), MW.; *-phala*, n. N. of wk. **-sahasra**, n. pl. 60 thousand, BhP. **-sahasrin**, mfn. pl. numbering 60 thousand, ib. **-sāṃvatsarī**, f. N. of various wks. **-sāhasra**, mfn. pl. = *-sahasrin*, R. **-hāyana**, m. a period of 60 years or the 60th year (from birth &c.), MW.; mfn. 60 years old (as an elephant), MBh.; R.; m. an elephant, L.; a kind of grain or corn, L. **-hrada**, N. of a Tīrtha, MBh.

Shashṭishṭaka, mfn. containing 60 bricks, ŚBr.

Shashṭika, mfn. bought with sixty, W.; m. or (*ā*), f. a kind of rice of quick growth (ripening in about 60 days), MBh.; Suśr.; VarBṛS. &c.; n. the number 60, VarBṛS.

Shashṭikya, mfn. sown with the above rice, Pāṇ. v, 2, 3; (a field &c.) fit for sowing with this rice, W.

Shashṭis, ind. sixty times, Sūryas.

Shashṭy, in comp. before vowels for *shashṭi*. **-adhika**, mfn. exceeded by 60, MW.; *-śata*, n. 160, ib. **-abda**, n. the 60 years' cycle of Jupiter, VarBṛS. (also N. of wk.)

Shashṭhá, mf(*ī*)n. sixth, the sixth (with *bhāga* or *aṇśa*, m. 'a sixth part;' with or scil. *kāla*, m. 'the sixth hour of the day, the sixth meal eaten at the end of a fast of three days;' *shashṭhaṃ* √*kṛi*, 'to eat such a meal'), AV. &c. &c.; m. (scil. *akshara*) the sixth letter i. e. the vowel *ī*, RPrāt.; N. of a man, = *-candra*, Rājat.; (*ī*), f., see below; n. a sixth part, Gaut. **-kāla**, m. the sixth meal-time (on the evening of the third day; °*lôpavāsa*, m. 'a kind of fasting, taking food only on the ev° of every third day'), MBh. **-candra**, m. N. of a man, Rājat. **-bhakta**, n. the sixth meal (instr. with Caus. of √*vṛit*, 'to live on the sixth m°' or 'eat only on the evening of every third day'), MBh.; mfn. taking only the sixth meal (i. e. only on the ev° of every th° d°), ib. **-vatī**, f. N. of a river, BhP. **Shashṭhâṇśa**, m. a sixth part, (esp.) the amount of tax or of grain &c. taken in kind by a king (cf. *shaḍ-bhāga*), Yājñ.; Ragh.; MārkP.; *-vṛitti*, m. a king who subsists on the 6th part of the produce of the soil (taken as a tax), Śak. 187, ed. MW. **Shashṭhâdi**, mfn. (in Vedic gram.) beginning with the sixth letter i. e. with the vowel *ī*.

Shashṭhânna, n. the sixth meal; *-kāla*, mfn. = °*tha-bhakta* above; n. or °*la-tā*, f. (Mn. xi, 200) eating only at the time of the sixth meal (i. e. on the evening of every third day); *-kālaka*, n. id., L. (w. r. *shashṭhālu-k*°); *-kālika*, mfn. = °*na-kāla*, Pañcat. **Shashṭhâhnika**, mfn. corresponding to the sixth day (of the Shaḍ-aha), ŚāṅkhŚr.

Shashṭhaka, mfn. the sixth, Pāṇ.; Śrutab.; (*ikā*), f. the sixth day after a child's birth personified, Saṃskārak.; Tithyād.; N. of one of the divine mothers (see *shashṭhī*), MW.

Shashṭhama, mfn. the sixth; (*ī*), f. the sixth day of a lunar fortnight, Cat.

Shashṭhin, mfn. having a sixth, having or being the sixth (year &c.), W.

Shashṭhī, f. the sixth day of a lunar fortnight, MBh.; Hariv. &c.; a partic. Tithi when homage is offered to the sixth lunar digit, MW.; the sixth or genitive case, ŚrS.; Nir. &c.; N. of a partic. brick the length of which equals the 6th part of a man, Śulbas.; the personification of a portion of Prakṛiti, Cat.; N. of a personification of the sixth day after the birth of a child (when the chief danger for mother and child is over); N. of a divine mother or goddess often regarded as a form of Durgā (supposed to protect children and worshipped on the sixth day after delivery), NṛisUp.; Saṃskārak.; = *indra-senā*, NṛisUp.; RTL. 229. **-jāgara** (Kād.) or °**raka**, m. (L.) or °**raṇa-maha**, m. (Campak.) the waking on the sixth day after the birth of a child (N. of a partic. ceremony; this is the day on which the creator is supposed to enter the mother's chamber and write the child's destiny on its forehead), RTL. 370. **-jāya**, mfn. or m. one who has a sixth wife, Vop. **-tat-purusha**, m. a Tatpurusha compound of which the first member would (if uncompounded) be in the genitive case, Sch. on Pāṇ. v, 1, 9 &c. **-darpaṇa**, m. N. of wk. **-dāsa**, m. N. of a man, Kshitīś. **-devī**, f. the goddess Shashṭhī, Kād.; RTL. 229. **-pūjana**, n. or *-pūjā*, f. worship of the goddess Shashṭhī (esp. performed by a woman on the sixth day after delivery), MW. **-pūjā-vidhi**, m. N. of wk. **-priya**, m. N. of Skanda, MBh. **-vrata**, n. pl. N. of partic. religious observances, Cat.; °*tôdyāpana-vidhi*, m. N. of wk. **-samāsa**, m. = *-tat-purusha*, Sarvad.; Pāṇ., Vārtt.

Shashṭhy, in comp. before vowels for *shashṭhī*. **-artha-darpaṇa**, m. N. of wk. **-ādi-kalpa-bodhana**, n. a festival in honour of Durgā on the 6th day of the month Āśvina (when she is supposed to be awakened), Col. **-upâkhyāna-stotra**, n. N. of a Stotra.

Shashṭhya, m. a sixth part, Gaut.

Sho, in comp. for *shash*. **-ḍa**, mfn. (prob.) = next, VPrāt., Sch. **-ḍat**, mfn. having six teeth (indicative of a partic. period of life), Pāṇ. vi, 3, 109, Vārtt. 3; m. a young ox with six teeth, W. **-ḍanta**, mfn. = *-ḍat*, VPrāt. **-ḍaśá** &c., see below. **-ḷaśan**, °**ḷâkshara**, = *sho-ḍaśan*, °*ḍâksh*°.

1. **Sho-ḍaśá**, mf(*ī*)n. (ifc. f. *ā*) the sixteenth, (with *aṇśa* or *bhāga*, m. a 16th part, Mn.; MārkP.; *ṛishabha-shoḍaśāḥ* [Gaut.] or *vṛishabha-sh*° [Mn. ix, 124], '15 cows and one bull'), Br.; GṛŚrS. &c.; + 16, ChUp.; consisting of 16, VS.; TS.; PañcavBr. &c.; pl. incorrectly for *sho-ḍaśan*, 16, RāmatUp.; (*ī*), f. having the length of the 16th of a man (said of a brick), Śulbas.; N. of one of the ten Mahā-vidyās (also pl.), Pañcar.; Cat.; one of the 12 forms of Durgā called Mahā-vidyā, MW.; n. $\frac{1}{16}$, AV.; VarBṛS. **-bhāga**, m. $\frac{1}{16}$, VarBṛS. **Shoḍaśâṇśa**, m. id., ib.; Pañcar. 1. **Shoḍaśâkshara**, n. (for 2. see under 2. *shoḍaśa*) the 16th syllable, Ind. St.

2. **Shoḍaśa**, in comp. for *shó-ḍaśan* below. **-karma-prayoga**, m., **-karma-vidhi**, m. N. of wks. **-kala** (*shóḍ*°), mfn. having 16 parts, sixteen-fold, Br.; PraśnUp. &c.; (*ās*), f. pl. the 16 digits of the moon (named, 1. A-mṛitā; 2. Māna-dā; 3. Pūshā; 4. Tushṭi; 5. Pushṭi; 6. Rati; 7. Dhṛiti; 8. Śaśinī; 9. Candrikā; 10. Kānti; 11. Jyotsnā; 12. Śrī; 13. Prīti; 14. Aṅga-dā; 15. Pūrṇā; 16. Pūrṇâmṛitā), MW.; (°*la*)-*vidyā*, f. the science of the sixteenfold (spirit or soul), Col. **-kāraṇa-jaya-mālā**, f., **-kāraṇa-pūjā**, f., **-kārikā**, f., **-kūrca**, **-gaṇa-pati-dhyāna**, n., **-gaṇa-pati-lakshaṇa**, n. N. of wks. **-gṛihītá**, mfn. taken up 16 times, ŚBr.; KātyŚr.; °*târdha*, m. n. the (first) half of the Graha (q. v.) taken up 16 times, Vait. **-tva**, n. an aggregate or collection of 16, Hcat. **-dala**, mfn. having 16 petals, RāmatUp. **-dāna**, n. the aggregate of 16 kinds of gifts given at a Śrāddha &c. (said to be 'room, a seat, water, clothes, a lamp, food, betel, a parasol, perfumes, a garland, fruit, a bed, shoes, cows, gold, and silver'), MW. **-dhā**, ind. in 16 ways, in 16 parts or divisions, TS. **-nitya-tantra**, n., **-nyāsa**, m. N. of wks. **-paksha-śāyin**, mfn. lying torpid during 16 half months of the year (said of a frog), Hariv. **-pada**, mf(*ā*)n. consisting of 16 Padas, AitBr. **-bhāga**, m. a 16th part. **-bhuja**, mfn. 16-armed; (*ā*), f. a form of Durgā, KālP.; (°*ja*) *-rāma-dhyāna*, n. N. of wk. **-bhedita**, mf(*ā*)n. divided into 16 kinds, Sāh. **-mātṛikā**, f. pl. the 16 divine mothers (see *mātṛi*), L. **-mudrā-lakshaṇa**, n. N. of wk. **-rājika**, mfn. treating of 16 kings, MBh. **-rātra**, m. n. a festival lasting 16 days, Lāṭy.; Maś. **-rcá** (°*śa-ṛica*), m. a text consisting of 16 verses, AV.; ŚBr. **-rtu-niśā** (°*śa-ṛit*°), f. any night out of 16 from the commencement of menstruation, W. **-rtvik-kratu** (°*śa-ṛit*°), m. a grand sacrifice performed by 16 priests (see *ṛitv-ij*), MW. **-lakshaṇa**, n. the Sūtra of Jaimini (consisting of 16 Adhyāyas), Sarvad. **-varsha**, mfn. lasting for 16 years, 16 years old, PārGṛ. **-vidha**, mfn. of 16 kinds, 16-fold, Kām.; Pañcar. **-vistṛita**, mfn. extended to 16, BhP. **-śata**, n. 116, JaimBr. **-sahasra** (BhP.) or **-sāhasra** (Pañcar.), n. 16 thousand. **Shoḍaśâṇśu**, m. '16-rayed,' the planet Venus, L. **Shoḍaśâṅhri**, m. '16-footed,' a crab, L. **Shoḍaśâksha**, mfn. 16-eyed (fig.), R. 2. **Shó-ḍaśâkshara**, mfn. (for 1. see under 1. *sho-ḍaśá*) having 16 syllables, VS.; PañcavBr.; ŚrS. **Shoḍaśâṅga**, mfn. having 16 parts or ingredients; m. a partic. perfume, Tantras. **Shoḍaśâṅgulaka**, mfn. 'having a breadth of 16 fingers,' Yājñ. **Shoḍaśâṅghri**, mfn. having 16 feet; m. a crab, L. **Shoḍaśâḍhaka-maya**, mf(*ī*)n. consisting of 16 Āḍhakas, Hcat. (w. r. °*śâṭaka-m*°). **Shoḍaśâtmaka** or °**tman**, m. the soul (consisting) of 16 (Guṇas), BhP. **Shoḍaśâdi-tantra**, n., °**śâyudha-stuti**, f. N. of wks. **Shoḍaśâra**, mfn. having 16 spokes, NṛisUp.; h° 16 petals, MW.; n. a kind of lotus, ib. **Shoḍaśârcis**, m. '16-rayed,' the planet Venus, VP. **Shoḍaśâvarta**, m. 'having 16 convolutions,' a conch-shell, L. **Shoḍaśâha**, m. a fast &c. observed for 16 days, L. **Shoḍaśôpacāra**, m. pl. 16 acts of homage, see RTL. 414, 415.

Shoḍaśaka, mfn. consisting of 16 (°*kaḥ kaccha-puṭaḥ*, 'a box with 16 compartments'), MBh.; VarBṛS. &c.; m. 16 (°*kās trayaḥ* = 48), Car.; (*ikā*), f. a partic. weight (= 16 Māshas = 1 Karsha, ŚārṅgS.; or = 64 Māshas, Car.); n. an aggregate of 16, VarBṛS. **Shoḍaśikâmra**, n. a kind of weight (= *pala*), L.

Shó-ḍaśan, mfn. pl. (nom. °*śa*) sixteen, VS. &c. &c.

Shoḍaśama, mfn. the sixteenth, Gṛihyās.; BhP.

Shoḍaśi, in comp. for °*ḍaśin*. **-graha**, m. a libation consisting of 16 Grahas, Vait. **-tvá**, n. the state of having 16 parts, TS.; AitBr. **-pātra**, n. the sacrificial vessel used at the Shoḍaśi ceremony, ĀpŚr. **-prayoga**, m. N. of wk. **-mat** (°*śi-* or *-mát*), mfn. connected with the Shoḍaśi-stotra, TS.; ŚBr.; ŚrS. **-śastra**, n. a hymn or liturgical formula recited during the Shoḍaśin ceremony, ib. **-sāman**, n. the Sāman contained in the 16-partite Stotra, Br.; Lāṭy. **-stotra**, n. a Stotra consisting of 16 parts, Vait.

Shoḍaśika, mfn., in *a-shoḍ*°, 'not connected with the 16-partite Stotra,' ŚrS.; see also *sa-shoḍ*°; (*ā*), f., see under *shoḍaśaka* above.

Shoḍaśin, mfn. consisting of 16, having 16 parts (esp. with or scil. *stoma* or *stotra* &c., 'a Stoma or Stotra &c. cons° of 16 parts'), VS.; TS.; AitBr. &c.; connected with a 16-partite formula &c., VS.; TS.; Br.; ĀśvŚr.; m. a Sutyā day with a 16-partite formula (or such a libation), one of the Saṃsthās of the Soma ceremony, AV.; TS.; Br. &c.; a partic. kind of Soma vessel, MW.

Shoḍaśī-bilva, n. a kind of weight (= *pala*), ŚārṅgS.

Shoḍīya, Nom. P. °*yati* (prob. fr. *sho-ḍat*), = *sho-ḍantam ācashṭe*, Pāṇ. vi, 1, 64, Vārtt. 1, Pat.

Shoḍhā, ind. in six ways, sixfold, RV.; MaitrS.; Yājñ. **-nyāsa**, m. 16 ways of disposing magical texts on the body (as practised by the Tāntrikas), Cat. **-mukha**, m. 'six-faced,' N. of Skanda, Kāv. **-vihitá**, mfn. having six parts, TS.

षष्क् *shashk* (cf. √*shvashk*), cl. 1. P. *shashkati*, to go, move, Naigh. ii, 14.

षस *shasa*, (prob.) = *khākhasa*, poppy, Cat.

षहसान *shahasāna*, *shāc*. See *sahasāna*, *sāc*.

षहजि *shahji*, m. N. of a king of Tanjore 1684–1711 A.D.), Cat.

षाट् *shāṭ*, ind. a vocative particle or interjection of calling, L.

षाट्कुल *shāṭkula*, mfn. = *shaṭsu kuleshu bhavaḥ*, Pat. on Pāṇ. iv, 1, 88.

षाट्कौशिक *shāṭkauśika*, mfn. (fr. *shash* + *kośa*) enveloped in six sheaths, Kauś.; Sarvad.

षाट्पौरुषिक *shāṭpaurushika*, mfn. (fr. *shash* + *purusha*) relating or belonging to six generations, MW.

षाडण्डक *shāḍaṇḍaka*, mfn. (fr. *shaḍ-aṇḍa*), g. *dhūmâdi* (Kāś. *khāḍaṇḍaka*).

षाडव *shāḍava*, m. (cf. *khāḍava* and *khāṇḍava*) confectionery, sweetmeats, Suśr.; N. of partic. Rāgas (also *-rāga*), Saṃgīt.

Shāḍavika, m. a confectioner, R.

षाडहिक *shāḍahika*, mfn. (fr. *shaḍ-aha*), Lāṭy.

षाड्गुण्य *shāḍguṇya*, n. (fr. *shaḍ-guṇa*, q. v.) the aggregate of the six qualities, Kathās.; the six good qualities or excellencies, Car.; Śiś.; the six measures or acts of royal policy, Mn.; MBh. &c.; six articles of any kind, multiplication of anything by six, W. **-guṇa-vedin**, mfn. acquainted with the virtues of the six measures, Mn. vii, 167. **-prayoga**, m. the application or practice of the six m°s, MW. **-vat**, mfn. endowed with six excellencies, Ml. **-saṃyuta**, mfn. connected or accompanied with the six measures, Mn. vii, 58.

षाड्रसिक *shāḍrasika*, mfn. (fr. *shaḍ-rasa*) having six tastes or flavours, Car.

षाड्वर्गिक *shāḍvargika*, mfn. (fr. *shaḍ-varga*) relating to the five senses and the Manas, BhP.

षाड्विध्य *shāḍvidhya*, n. (fr. *shaḍ-vidha*) sixfoldness, Kull. on Mn. viii, 76.

षाण्ड *shāṇḍa*, m. N. of Śiva, L.

षाण्डश shāṇḍaśa, m. (and °śī, f.), g. gaurâdi.

षाण्ढ्य shāṇḍhya, n. (fr. shaṇḍha) the state of being a eunuch, impotence, Car. (printed śāṭhya).

षाण्मातुर shāṇmātura, m. (fr. shash + mātṛi) 'having six mothers,' N. of Kārttikeya (q. v.), L.

षाण्मासिक shāṇmāsika, mf(ī)n. (fr. shaṇ-māsa) six-monthly, half-yearly, six months old, of six months' standing, lasting six months, Mn.; MBh. &c. (cf. shaṇ-māsika); m. N. of a poet, Cat.

Shāṇmāsya, mfn. = shāṇmāsika, ĀśvŚr. (cf. shaṇ-māsya); (ī), f. a six-monthly funeral ceremony (between the 170th and 180th day after a person's death), L.

षात्वणत्विक shātvaṇatvika, mfn. (fr. shatva-ṇatva) relating to or treating of the substitution of sh for s and ṇ for n, Pāṇ. iv, 3, 67, Sch.

षामिल shāmila, N. of a place, Cat.

षाष्टिक shāshṭika, mfn. (fr. shashṭi) sixty years old, Pāṇ. v, 1, 58, Vārtt. 3, Pat.; (fr. shashṭika), see kshīra-shāshṭika.

षाष्टिपथ shāshṭipatha, mfn. = shashṭi-pathika, Kāś. on Pāṇ. iv, 2, 60.

षाष्ठ shāshṭha, mfn. (fr. shashṭha) the sixth (part), Pāṇ. v, 3, 50; taught in the sixth (Adhyāya), ib. viii, 1, 19, Sch.

Shāshṭhika, mfn. belonging to the sixth, explained in the sixth (Adhyāya), MW.; n. taking food with milk every sixth day (a four-monthly fast), L.

षाहविलास shāha-vilāsa (or shahji-v°), m. N. of a musical work by Dhuṇḍi-vyāsa.

षिड्ग shiḍga, m. (also written khiḍga, khiṅga) a profligate man, libertine, gallant, L.; the keeper of a prostitute, L.

षु shu, m. or shū, f. (fr. √4. su) child-bearing, parturition, delivery, L. (w. r. for sū).

षुक्क् shukk, cl. 1. Ā. shukkate, to go, move, Dhātup. iv, 26 (v. l.)

षुराजिम shurājima (cf. shar°), N. of a place, Cat.

षुरासाण shurāsāṇa (cf. khur°), N. of a place, ib.

षोड sho-ḍa, sho-ḍat &c. See p. 1110, col. 2.

Sho-laśa &c. for shoḍaśa, q. v.

ष्टम्भ् shṭambh. See √stambh.

ष्ट्युम shṭyuma or shṭyūma, m. (perhaps w. r. for shṭhyūma fr. √shṭhiv, or syūma fr. √siv; only L.) the moon; light; water; thread; auspiciousness.

ष्ट्यै shṭyai. See √styai.

ष्ठा shṭhā. See √sthā.

ष्ठि shṭhi, shṭhita. See under ni-√shṭhiv.

ष्ठिव् shṭhiv or shṭhīv, cl. 1. 4. P. (Dhātup. xv, 52; xxvi, 4) shṭhīvati or shṭhīvyati (pf. tishṭheva, Br.; ṭishṭheva, Gr.; aor. ashṭhevīt, ib.; fut. shṭhevitā, shṭhevishyati, ib.; inf. shṭhevitum, ib.; ind. p. shṭhevitvā or shṭhyūtvā, ib.; -shṭhīvya, Mn.), to spit, spit out, expectorate, spit upon (loc.), Suśr.; VarBṛS.; Kathās.: Pass. shṭhīvyate (aor. ashṭhevi), Gr.: Caus. shṭhevayati (aor. atishṭhivat or atishṭhivat), ib.; Desid. tishṭhevishati or tishṭhevishati; tushṭhyūshati or tushṭhyūshati), ib.: Intens. teshṭhīvyate or teshṭhīvyate, ib. [Cf. Gk. πτύω; Lat. spuo: Lith. spiáuju; Goth. speiwan; Germ. spîwan, speien; Angl. Sax. spîwan; Eng. spew.]

Shṭhīva. See hiraṇya-shṭhīva.

Shṭhīvana, mfn. spitting frequently, sputtering, Car.; n. spitting, ejecting saliva, expectoration, spitting upon (loc.), PārGṛ.; MBh.; Suśr. &c.; n. saliva, spittle, Mn.; MBh. &c.

Shṭhīvi or **shṭhīvin**, mfn. (only ifc.; cf. suvarṇa-, hiraṇya-shṭh°) spitting, ejecting.

Shṭhīvī, f. spitting (see rakta-shṭhīvī).

Shṭheva, m. spitting, sputtering, MW.

Shṭhevana, n. = shṭhīvana, Vop.

Shṭhevitavya, mfn. to be spit or spit out, MW.

Shṭhevitṛi, mfn. one who spits, spitting, ib.

Shṭhevin, mfn. spitting, ejecting from the mouth, ib.

Shṭhevya, mfn. to be spit or expectorated &c., ib.

Shṭhyūta, mfn. spit, ejected from the mouth, expectorated (as saliva); n. spitting, sputtering, L.

Shṭhyūti, f. spitting, sputtering out, MW.

ष्ठु shṭhu (only ind. p. shṭhutvā) = √shṭhiv, to spit out, ĀpŚr.

ष्वक्क् shvakk (cf. next), cl. 1. Ā. shvakkate, to go, Vop.

ष्वष्क् shvashk, cl. 1. P. shvashkati (Naigh. ii, 14) or cl. 1. Ā. shvashkate (Dhātup. iv, 26; v. l. shvask, svask; cf. prec. and shukk, shashk), to go, move.

ष्वस्क् shvask. See preceding.

स SA.

स 1. sa, the last of the three sibilants (it belongs to the dental class and in sound corresponds to s in sin). — **1. -kāra**, m. the sound or letter s, Prāt.; -bheda, m. N. of a gram. treatise on the difference of the sibilants (cf. śa-kāra-bheda).

स 2. sa, (in prosody) an anapest (⏑⏑–). — **2. -kāra**, m. id.; -vipulā, f. a kind of metre, Piṅg., Sch.

स 3. sa, (in music) an abbreviated term for shaḍ-ja (see p. 1109, col. 2).

स 4. sa (only L.), m. a snake; air, wind; a bird; N. of Vishṇu or Śiva; (ā), f. N. of Lakshmī or Gaurī; n. knowledge; meditation; a carriage road; a fence.

स 5. sa, mfn. (fr. √san) procuring, bestowing (only ifc.; cf. paśu-shá and priya-sá).

स 6. sá, the actual base for the nom. case of the 3rd pers. pron. tád, q. v. (occurring only in the nom. sg. m. f. [sá or sás, sā], and in the Ved. loc. [sásmin, RV. i, 152, 6; i, 174, 4; x, 95, 11]; the final s of the nom. m. is dropped before all consonants [except before p in RV. v, 2, 4, and before t in RV. viii, 33, 16] and appears only at the end of a sentence in the form of Visarga; sa occasionally blends with another vowel [as in sáishaḥ]; and it is often for emphasis connected with another pron. as with aham, tvam, esha, ayam &c. [e. g. so 'ham, sa tvam, 'I (or thou) that very person;' cf. under tád, p. 434], the verb then following in the 1st and 2nd pers. even if aham or tvam be omitted [e. g. sa tvā pṛicchāmi, 'I that very person ask you,' BṛĀrUp.; sa vai no brūhi, 'do thou tell us,' ŚBr.]; similarly, to denote emphasis, with bhavān [e. g. sa bhavān vijayāya pratishṭhatām, 'let your Highness set out for victory,' Śak.]; it sometimes [and frequently in the Brāhmaṇas] stands as the first word of a sentence preceding a rel. pronoun or adv. such as ya, yad, yadi, yathā, céd; in this position sa may be used pleonastically or as a kind of ind., even where another gender or number is required [e. g. sa yadi sthāvarā āpo bhavanti, 'if those waters are stagnant,' ŚBr.]; in the Sāṃkhya sa, like esha, ka, and ya, is used to denote Purusha, 'the Universal Soul'), RV. &c. &c. [Cf. Zd. hō, hā; Gk. ὁ, ἡ.]

Saká, mf(ā)n. (cf. Pāṇ. vi, 1, 132, Sch.; vii, 3, 45) he that man, she that woman &c., RV.; AV.; n. applied to the Intellect, VP.

स 7. sa, ind. (connected with saha, sam, sama, and occasionally in BhP. standing for saha with instr.) an inseparable prefix expressing 'junction,' 'conjunction,' 'possession' (as opp. to a priv.), 'similarity,' 'equality'; and when compounded with nouns to form adjectives and adverbs it may be translated by 'with,' 'together or along with,' 'accompanied by,' 'added to,' 'having,' 'possessing,' 'containing,' 'having the same' [cf. sa-kopa, ságni, sa-bhārya, sa-droṇa, sa-dharman, sa-varṇa]; or it may = 'ly,' as in sa-kopam, 'angrily,' sópadhi, 'fraudulently'), RV. &c. &c. [Cf. Gk. ἁ in ἁπλοῦς; Lat. sim in simplex; sem in semel, semper; Eng. same.] — **ṛiksha**, mf(ā)n. connected with a lunar mansion, Kṛishṇaj. — **ṛiṇa**, mfn. having debts, indebted, Nār., Sch. — **ṛishika**, mfn. together with the Ṛishis, ĀśvGṛ. — **ṛishi-rājanya**, mfn. together with the royal Ṛishis, ib.

सं sam (in comp.) = 2. sam, q. v.

संय sam-ya, m. (fr. 2. sam and √yam or yat) a skeleton, L.

संयज् sam-√yaj, P. Ā. -yajati, °te, to worship together, offer sacrifices at the same time, RV.; Br.; ŚrS.; to sacrifice, worship, adore, honour, Hariv.; BhP.; to consecrate, dedicate, Bhaṭṭ.: Caus. -yājayati, to cause to sacrifice together, (esp.) to perform the Patnī-saṃyājas (q. v.), Br.; to perform a sacrifice for (acc.), MBh.

Sam-yāja, m., **sam-yājana**, n., in patnī-saṃy° (q. v.) °yājya, mfn. to be made or allowed to sacrifice (see a-saṃy°); n. joining or sharing in a sacrifice, sacrificing (see a-yājya-saṃy°); (ā), f. N. of the Yājyā and Anuvākyā Mantras (recited in the Svishṭa-kṛit ceremony), Br.; ŚrS.

Sam-ishṭa. See s. v.

संयत् sam-√yat, Ā. -yatate, to unite (intrans.), meet together, encounter (rarely 'as friends,' generally 'as enemies'), contend, engage in contest or strife, quarrel (with saṃgrāmam, 'to begin a combat'), RV.; Br.; ChUp.; (P. °ti) to unite, join together (trans.), RV. vi, 67, 3.

Sam-yát, mfn. (in some senses fr. sam-√yam below, Pāṇ. vi, 4, 40, Vop. 26, 78) coherent, contiguous, continuous, uninterrupted, RV.; ŚāṅkhŚr.; f. an agreement, covenant, stipulation, ŚBr.; a means of joining or uniting, TS.; an appointed place, RV. ix, 86, 15; contest, strife, battle, war (generally found in loc. or comp.), MBh.; Kāv. &c.; N. of partic. bricks (-tvá, n.), TS.

Sam-yatin. See under sam-√yam.

Sám-yatta, mfn. (pl.) come into conflict (saṃgrāmé sáṃ-yatte, 'at the outbreak of war'), TS.; prepared, ready, being on one's guard, Mn.; MBh. &c.

Sam-yad, in comp. for sam-yat. — **vara**, m. (cf. sampad-vara) 'chief in battle,' a prince, king, Uṇ. iii, 1. — **vasu** (°yád-v°), mfn. having continuous wealth, VS.; AitBr.; m. one of the seven rays of the sun, VP., Sch. — **vāma**, mfn. uniting all that is pleasant or dear, ChUp. — **vīra** (°yád-v°), mfn. abounding in heroes, RV.

संयती sam-yatī, n. du. of pr. p. of sam-√5. i (q. v.)

संयन्त्रित sam-yantrita, mfn. (√yantr) fastened with bands, held in, stopped, Śak.

संयम् sam-√yam, P. -yacchati (rarely Ā.), to hold together, hold in, hold fast, restrain, curb, suppress, control, govern, guide (horses, the senses, passions), RV. &c. &c.; to tie up, bind together (hair or a garment), MBh.; Kāv. &c.; to put together, heap up (Ā. 'for one's self'), Pāṇ. i, 3, 75, Sch.; to shut up, close (a door), Bhag.; to press close to or against, Suśr.; to present with, give to (Ā. with instr. of person, when the action is permitted, P. with dat., when the action is not permitted), Pāṇ. i, 3, 35: Caus. -yamayati (cf. -yamita), to cause to restrain &c.; to bind up (the hair), Veṇis.

Sam-ya, **sam-yát**. See above.

Sám-yata, mfn. held together, held in, held fast &c.; self-contained, self-controlled with regard to (loc., instr., or comp.), Gaut.; MBh. &c.; tied together, bound up, fettered, confined, imprisoned, captive, Mn.; MBh. &c.; shut up, closed (opp. to vy-ātta), AV.; kept in order (see comp.); suppressed, subdued, MBh.; = udyata, prepared, ready to (inf.), Hariv.; m. 'one who controls himself,' N. of Śiva, MBh.; -cetas, mfn. controlled in mind, MW.; -prāṇa, mfn. having the breath suppressed or having the organs restrained, ib.; -mānasa, mfn. (= -cetas), ib.; -mukha, mf(ī)n. (= -vāc), Mṛicch.; -maithuna, mfn. one who abstains from sexual intercourse, MBh.; -vat, mfn. self-controlled, self-possessed, Hariv.; -vastra, mfn. having the dress or clothes fastened or tied together, Bhartṛ.; -vāc, mfn. restrained in speech, taciturn, silent, MW.; °tâksha, mfn. having the eyes closed, BhP.; °tâñjali, mfn. having the hands joined together in entreaty (= baddhâñjali) MW.; °tâtman, mfn. (= °ta-cetas), Mn. xi, 236; °tâhāra, mfn. temperate in eating, MBh.; °tên-

driya, mfn. having the senses or passions controlled, ib.; °*tôpaskara,* mfn. having the household utensils kept in order, Yājñ. °**yataka,** m. N. of a man, Kathās. °**yati,** f. penance, self-castigation, Kuṭṭanīm.

Saṃ-yatin, mfn. controlling, restraining (the senses), MārkP. (prob. w. r. for *saṃ-yamin* below); °**yatvara,** m. = *vāg-yata* or *jantu-samūha,* L.

Saṃ-yantavya, mfn. to be restrained or controlled, MBh. °**yantṛi,** mfn. one who restrains or controls, restraining, controlling (also as fut. 'he will restrain'), ib.

Saṃ-yama, m. holding together, restraint, control, (esp.) control of the senses, self-control, Mn.; MBh. &c.; tying up (the hair), Sāh.; binding, fettering, VarBṛS.; closing (of the eyes), MārkP.; concentration of mind (comprising the performance of Dhāraṇā, Dhyāna, and Samādhi, or the last three stages in Yoga), Yogas.; Sarvad.; effort, exertion (*āt,* 'with great difficulty'), MBh.; suppression, i. e. destruction (of the world), Pur.; N. of a son of Dhūmrâksha (and father of Kṛiśâśva), BhP.; *-dhana,* mfn. rich in self-restraint, MBh.; *-puṇya-tīrtha,* mfn. having restraint for a holy place of pilgrimage, MBh.; *-vat,* mfn. self-controlled, parsimonious, economical, Kathās.; °*māgni,* m. the fire of abstinence, Bhag.; °*mâmbhas,* n. the flood of water at the end of the world, BhP. °**yamaka,** mfn. checking, restraining, VahniP. °**yamana,** mf(*ī*)n. id., MBh.; Pur.; bringing to rest, RV.; (*ī*), f. N. of the city or residence of Yama (fabled to be situated on Mount Meru), MBh.; BhP.; n. the act of curbing or checking or restraining, VP.; self-control, KaushUp.; binding together, tying up, Vikr.; Sāh.; drawing tight, tightening (reins &c.), Śak.; confinement, fetter, Mṛicch.; Yama's residence (cf. above), Bādar. °**yamita,** mfn. (fr. Caus.) restrained, checked, subdued, Ragh.; bound, confined, fettered, Mṛicch.; clasped (in the arms), held, detained, Gīt.; piously disposed, R.; n. subduing (the voice), Mṛicch.

Saṃ-yamin, mfn. who or what restrains or curbs or subdues, W.; one who subdues his passions, self-controlled (°*mi-tā,* f. self-control, Kād.), Hcat.; tied up (as hair), Bhartṛ.; m. a ruler, Divyâv.; an ascetic, saint, Ṛishi, L.; *saṃyami-nāma-mālikā,* f. N. of a wk. (containing synonyms of names of Ṛishis, by Śaṃkarâcārya), Cat.; (*inī*), f. N. of the city Kāśī, Kāśikh.; of Yama's residence (also written *saṃ-yamanī,* q. v.), Śaṃk.; *saṃyaminī-pati,* m. N. of Yama, Kāśikh.

Saṃ-yamya, mfn. to be checked or restrained or subdued, Car.

Saṃ-yāma, m. = *saṃ-yama,* Pāṇ. iii, 3, 63; *-vat,* mfn. self-controlled, Bhaṭṭ.

संयस् *saṃ-√yas,* cl. 4. 1. P. *-yasyati, -yasati,* to make effort &c., Pāṇ. iii, 1, 72.

Saṃ-yāsá, m. making effort, exertion, VS.

संया *saṃ-√yā,* P. *-yāti,* to go or proceed together, go, wander, travel, TS. &c. &c.; to come together, meet, encounter (as friends or foes), contend with (acc.), MBh.; Kāv. &c.; to come to or into, attain (any state or condition, e.g. *ekatāṃ saṃ-√yā,* 'to go to oneness, become one'), Mn.; MBh. &c.; to conform to (acc.), MBh.

Saṃ-yāta, mfn. gone together, proceeded together, approached, come, MBh.; Kāv. &c. °**yāti,** m. N. of a son of Nahusha, MBh.; BhP.; of a son of Pracinvat (Bahu-gava) and father of Ahaṃ-yāti, ib. (Hariv. *sampāti*). °**yātrā,** f. travelling together (esp. by sea), L. °**yātrika,** w. r. for *sāṃ-yātrika.*

Saṃ-yāna, m. a mould, L.; (°*yānī*), f. N. of partic. bricks, Kāṭh.; ŚBr.; (*am*), n. going together, going along with (comp.), Kathās.; going, travelling, a journey (with *uttama,* 'the last j°,' i. e. the carrying out of a dead body), MBh.; R.; Hariv.; setting out, departure, MBh.; a vehicle, waggon, car &c., R.; Mṛicch.; N. of partic. Sūktas, TS.

संयाच् *saṃ-√yāc,* Ā. *-yācate,* to ask, beg, implore, solicit, MBh.; BhP.

संयु *saṃ-√2. yu,* P. Ā. *-yauti, -yute; -yunāti,* °*nīte* (Ved. also *-yuvati,* °*te*), to join or unite with one's self, take into one's self, devour, RV.; to join to another, bestow on, impart, RV. v, 32, 10; to join together, connect with (instr.), unite, mix, mingle, VS.; TBr.; KātyŚr.; Bhaṭṭ.

Saṃ-yavana, n. mixing, mingling, Jaim.; VS., Sch.; a square of four houses (= or w. r. for *saṃjavana*), MW. °**yāva,** m. a sort of cake (of wheaten flour fried with ghee and milk and made up into an oblong form with sugar and spices), Mn.; MBh. &c.

Sáṃ-yuta, mfn. joined or bound together, tied, fettered, R.; Ragh.; put together, joined or connected with (instr. with and without *saha,* or comp.), AV. &c. &c.; increased by, added to (instr. or comp.), VarBṛS.; Rājat.; (ifc.) being in conjunction with, VarBṛS.; consisting of, containing (instr. or comp.), R.; (ifc.) relating to, implying (*praîshya-s*°, 'implying service'), Mn. ii, 32; accumulated (v. l. for *sam-bhṛita*), Śak. iv, $\frac{1}{1}\frac{2}{2}\frac{0}{1}$. **—**°**yuti,** f. the total of two numbers or quantities, Bījag.; the conjunction of planets, Gaṇit.

Saṃ-yuyūshu, mfn. (fr. Desid.) wishing to join together, wishing to unite with (instr.), Bhaṭṭ.

संयुज् *saṃ-√yuj,* P. Ā. *-yunakti, -yuṅkte,* to join or attach together, conjoin, connect, combine, unite, RV. &c. &c.; to bind, fetter, Vait.; to endow or furnish with (instr.), ŚvetUp.; MBh. &c.; to form an alliance, league together, RV. viii, 62, 11; to place in, fix on, direct towards (loc.), MBh.; BhP.: Pass. *-yujyate,* to be joined together, be united &c.; to meet or fall in with (instr.), Ragh.; to be married to (instr.), Mn. ix, 22; (with *ratyā* or *grāmya-dharmatayā*) to have sexual intercourse, PraśnUp.; Śaṃk. on ChUp.; to be supplied or furnished with (instr.), MBh.; R. &c.: Caus. *-yojayati,* to cause to join together, bring together, unite, MBh.; Kathās.; MārkP.; to put to (horses), yoke, harness, ib.; to hold together, check, control (the senses), MaitrUp. (v. l.); to furnish or endow or present with (instr.), Yājñ.; MBh. &c.; to give over to, entrust with (gen. of pers. and acc. of thing), R.; Pañcat.; to add to (loc.), Sūryas.; to fix on, direct towards (loc.), MaitrUp.; MBh.; BhP.; to shoot, discharge (a missile), MBh.; to equip (an army), ib.; to use, employ, appoint, ib.; to institute, perform, accomplish, Hariv.; BhP.; (Ā.) to be absorbed, meditate, MBh. v, 7260.

Sáṃ-yukta, mfn. conjoined, joined together, combined, united (pl. 'all together'), TS. &c. &c.; conjunct (as consonants), Pāṇ. vi, 3, 59, Sch.; connected, related (= *sambandhin*), PārGṛ.; married to (instr.), Mn. ix, 23; placed, put, fixed in (loc.), MBh.; accompanied or attended by, endowed or furnished with, full of (instr. or comp.), Mn.; MBh. &c.; (ifc.) connected with, relating to, concerning, KātyŚr.; MBh. &c.; (*am*), ind. jointly, together, at the same time, ŚvetUp.; (*ā,* f. a kind of metre, Col.); *-saṃcaya-piṭaka,* m. N. of wk.; *-saṃyoga,* m. connection with the connected (e. g. the connection of a trace with a horse), Kaṇ.; *-samavâya,* m. inherence in the connected (one of the six kinds of perception in Nyāya), Tarkas.; *-samavêta-samavâya,* m. inherence in that which inheres in the connected, ib.; °*tâgama,* m. N. of a Buddh. Āgama; °*tâbhidharma-śāstra,* n. N. of a Buddh. wk.

Saṃ-yuga, n. (in BhP. also m.) union, conjunction, MBh.; conflict, battle, war, MBh.; Kāv. &c. (cf. Naigh. ii, 17); *-goshpada,* n. a contest in a cow's footstep (met. 'an insignificant struggle'), MBh.; *-mūrdhan,* m. the van or front of battle, Ragh.

Saṃ-yuj, mfn. joined together, united, connected, related, MBh.; BhP.; m. a relation, Śiś.; f. union, connection (= *saṃ-yoga*), BhP., Sch.

Saṃ-yoga, m. conjunction, combination, connection (°*ge* or °*geshu,* ifc. 'in connection with, with regard to, concerning'), union or absorption with or in (gen., or instr. with and without *saha,* or loc., or ifc.), Āpast.; MBh. &c.; contact (esp. in phil. 'direct material contact,' as of sesamum seed with rice-grains [in contradistinction to contact by the fusion of particles, as of water with milk], enumerated among the 24 Guṇas of the Nyāya, cf. under *sam-bandha*), Yogas.; Kaṇ.; Bhāshāp.; carnal contact, sexual union, MBh. &c.; matrimonial connection or relationship by marriage with or between (gen., *saha* with instr., or comp.), Gaut.; Mn.; MBh. &c.; a kind of alliance or peace made between two kings with a common object, Kām.; Hit.; agreement of opinion, consensus (opposed to *bheda*), R.; applying one's self closely to, being engaged in, undertaking (°*gaṃ √kṛi,* 'to undertake, set about, begin;' *agnihotra-saṃyogam √kṛi,* 'to undertake the maintenance of a sacred fire'), Āpast.; Mn.; R.; (in gram.) a conjunct consonant, combination of two or more consonants, Prāt.; Pāṇ. &c.; dependence of one case upon another, syntax, Vop.; (in astron.) conjunction of two or more heavenly bodies, MW.; total amount, sum, VarBṛS.; N. of Śiva, MBh.; *-pṛithak-tva,* n. (in phil.) separateness with conjunction (a term applied to express the separateness of what is optional from what is a necessary constituent of anything), MW.; *-mantra,* m. a nuptial text or formula, Gaut.; *-viruddha,* n. food which causes disease through being mixed, MW. °**yogita,** mfn. = (or w. r. for) °*yojita,* L. °**yogin,** mfn. being in contact or connection, closely connected with (instr. or comp.), Kaṇ.; Śaṃk.; MārkP.; united (with a loved object; opp. to *virahin*), Kāvyâd., Sch.; married, W.; conjunct, one of the consonants in a combination of c°s, Pāṇ. i, 2, 27, Sch.; (°*gi*)*-tva,* n. close connection, Sarvad.

Saṃ-yojaka, mfn. joining together, connecting, uniting, MW.; bringing together or about, occasioning (comp.), Gaut. °**yójana,** n. the act of joining or uniting with (instr. or loc.), ŚBr. &c. &c.; all that binds to the world, cause of re-birth, Divyâv.; copulation, sexual union, L.; (with *Mitrā-varuṇa-yoḥ, Aśvinoḥ,* and *Prahitoḥ*) N. of Sāmans, ĀrshBr. °**yojayitavya,** mfn. to be joined or united, Kāraṇḍ. °**yojita,** mfn. (fr. Caus.) conjoined, attached &c., BhP.; *-kara-yugala,* mfn. one who has both his hands joined together, ib. °**yojya,** mfn. to be joined or brought together, to be fixed upon (loc.), MBh.

संयुध् *saṃ-√yudh,* Ā. *-yudhyate* (rarely P. °*ti*), to fight together, fight with, combat, oppose (instr. with or without *sârdham*), MBh.; R.; BhP.: Caus. *-yodhayati,* to cause to fight together, bring into collision, RV.; to fight, encounter, MBh.: Desid. *-yuyutsati,* to wish to fight, be eager for battle, MBh. (cf. next).

Saṃ-yuyutsu, mfn. (fr. Desid.) wishing to fight, eager for battle, Rājat.

Saṃ-yoddhavya, n. (impers.) it is to be fought, MBh.

Saṃ-yoddhṛi. See *prati-saṃy*°.

Saṃ-yodha, m. fight, battle; *-kaṇṭaka,* m. 'a thorn in battle,' N. of a Yaksha, R.

संयुप् *saṃ-√yup,* Caus. *-yopayati,* to efface, obliterate, remove, RV.

संरक्ष् *saṃ-√raksh,* P. Ā. *-rakshati,* °*te,* to protect, guard, watch over, defend, preserve, save from (abl.), Mn.; MBh. &c.; to keep, secure, MBh.; Kathās.

Saṃ-raksha, mfn. guarding, a guardian (cf. *sāṃrakshya*), g. *purohitâdi;* (*ā*), f. guard, care, protection, MBh.; Kathās. °**rakshaka,** m. (and *ikā,* f.), a keeper, guardian (cf. *śāli-saṃrakshikā*). °**rakshaṇa,** n. the act of guarding or watching, custody, preservation, protection of (gen. or comp.) or from (comp.), Mn.; MBh. &c.; prevention, Suśr.; *-vat,* mfn. taking care of, having regard for (comp.), Car. °**rakshaṇīya,** mfn. to be protected, to be guarded against, R. °**rakshita,** mfn. protected, preserved, taken care of, Mn.; MBh. &c. °**rakshitavya,** mfn. to be preserved or guarded or taken care of, MW. °**rakshitin,** mfn. one who has guarded &c. (with loc.), g. *ishṭâdi.* °**rakshin,** mfn. one who guards, a guardian, keeper (lit. and fig.), MBh.; Hariv. (cf. *satya-rakshin*). °**rakshya,** mfn. to be guarded or protected from (abl.), Yājñ.; MBh. &c.; to be guarded against or prevented, Car.; Kathās.

संरञ्ज् *saṃ-√rañj,* Ā. *-rajyate,* to be dyed or coloured, become red, MBh.; to be affected with any passion, MW.: Caus. *-rañjayati,* to colour, dye, redden (see *-rañjita*); to please, charm, gratify, BhP.

Saṃ-rakta, mfn. coloured, red, R.; inflamed, enamoured (in *a-saṃr*°), Hariv.; charming, beautiful, R.; Megh.; angry, W.; *-nayana* (R.), *-locana* (MW.), mfn. having the eyes reddened (with passion or fury).

Saṃ-rañjana, mf(*ī*)n. gratifying, charming, pleasant, SaddhP. °**rañjanīya,** mfn. to be rejoiced at, delightful, Divyâv. °**rañjita,** mfn. coloured, dyed, reddened, Hariv.

Saṃ-rāga, m. redness, R.; passion, vehemence, ib.; attachment to (loc.), Prâyaśc.

संरभ् *saṃ-√rabh,* Ā. *-rabhate* (pr. p. *-rambhamāṇa,* MW.; Impv. *-rambhasva,* Bālar.), to seize or take hold of, mutually grasp or lay hold of (for dancing &c.), grasp, grapple each other (in fighting &c.), RV.; AV.; ŚBr.; to get possession of (instr.), R.; to grow excited, fly into a passion, MBh.; Kāv. &c.

Sáṃ-rabdha, mfn. mutually grasped or laid hold

of, joined hand in hand, closely united with (instr.; *am*, ind.), AV.; ChUp.; MBh.; agitated, excited, R.; enraged, furious, exasperated against (*prati*; n. impers.), MBh.; Kāv. &c.; angry (as speech), Daś.; Sāh.; increased, augmented, MBh.; Rājat.; swelled, swelling, R.; Suśr.; overwhelmed, MW.; *-tara*, mfn. more or most excited or angry, R.; *-netra*, mfn. having swollen eyes, ib.; *-māna*, mfn. one whose pride is excited, MBh.

Sam-rambha, m. (ifc. f. *ā*) the act of grasping or taking hold of, MBh. iv, 1056 (C.); vehemence, impetuosity, agitation, flurry, MBh.; Kāv. &c.; excitement, zeal, eagerness, enthusiasm, ardent desire for or to (inf. or comp.), Kāv.; Rājat.; anger, fury, wrath against (loc. or *upari* with gen.), Mn.; MBh. &c.; angriness (i.e.) inflammation or irritation of a sore or wound, Suśr.; pride, arrogance, W.; intensity, high degree (ibc. = 'intensely'), Kāv.; Kathās.; the brunt (of battle), Rājat.; beginning (= *ā-rambha*), MW.; *-tāmra*, mfn. red with fury, ib.; *-dṛiś*, mfn. having inflamed or angry eyes, BhP.; *-parusha*, mfn. harsh from rage, intensely or exceedingly harsh or rough, W.; *-rasa*, mfn having angry or impetuous feelings, ib.; *-rūksha*, mfn. exceedingly harsh or cruel, Vikr. iii, 20; *-vat*, mfn. wrathful, angry, Harav.; *-vega*, m. the violence or impetuosity of wrath, MW. °**rambhaṇa**, mfn. stirring, exciting (applied to the hymns, AV. iv, 31 &c.), Kauś. °**rambhin**, mfn. angry (as a sore), inflamed, irritable, Suśr.; ardently devoted to (comp.), MBh.; wrathful, furious, angry, irascible, MBh.; R.; BhP.; proud, W.; (°*bhi*)-*tā*, f., *-tva*, n. agitation, wrath, fury, Kāv.; pride, MW.

संरम् *sam-√ram*, Ā. *-ramate*, to be delighted, find pleasure in (loc.), Bhaṭṭ.; to have carnal pleasure or sexual intercourse with (*sākam*), BhP.

संरा *sam-√rā* (only pr. p. *-rárāṇa*), to give liberally, bestow, grant, RV.; VS.; AV.

संराज् *sam-√rāj*, P. *-rājati* (inf. *-rājitum*, Pāṇ. viii, 3, 25, Sch.), to reign universally, reign over (gen.), RV. (cf. *sam-rāj*).

Sam-rājitṛi, mfn., Pāṇ. viii, 3, 25, Sch.

संराध् *sam-√rādh*, Caus. *-rādhayati* (pr. p. *-rādháyat*, q. v.), to agree together, agree about or upon (loc.), TS.; Kāṭh.; to conciliate, appease, satisfy, BhP.

Sam-rāddha, mfn. accomplished, acquired, obtained, BhP. °**rāddhi**, f. accomplishment, success, Dhātup.

Sam-rādhaka, mfn. practising complete concentration of mind, thoroughly concentrated, Bādar. °**rādhana** (*sáṃ-*), mfn. conciliating, satisfying, ŚBr.; ĀśvŚr.; n. the act of conciliating or pleasing by worship, W.; perfect concentration of mind, meditation, Bādar.; shouting, applause, Jātakam.

Sam-rādháyat, mfn. (fr. Caus.) agreeing together, being in harmony, AV. °**rādhita**, mfn. propitiated, appeased, conciliated, W. °**rādhya**, mfn. to be conciliated, BhP.; to be appropriated, ib.; to be acquired by perfect meditation, Śaṃk.

संराव *sam-rāva* &c. See *sam-√ru*.

संरिह् *sam-√rih* (Vedic form of *sam-√lih*, see *√rih*; only pr. p. *-rihāṇá*), to lick affectionately, caress (as a cow its calf), RV. iii, 33, 3.

संरी *sam-√rī*, P. *-riṇāti*, to join together, restore, repair, RV.; KātyŚr.; Lāṭy.; to wash, purify, VS.

संरु *sam-√ru*, P. *-rauti*, to cry together, shout, roar, Bhaṭṭ.

Sam-rāva, m. crying together, clamour, uproar, tumult, Rājat. °**rāvaṇa**, n. id., Caṇḍ. °**rāvin**, mfn. shouting together, clamouring, roaring, W.

संरुच् *sam-√ruc*, Ā. *-rocate*, to shine together or at the same time or in rivalry, RV.; VS.; ŚBr.; to shine, beam, glitter, BhP.: Caus. *-rocayati*, to find pleasure in (acc.), like, approve, choose anything for (two acc.), resolve on (inf.), MBh.; R.; Hariv.

संरुज् *sam-√ruj*, P. *-rujati*, to break to pieces, shatter, crush, RV.

Sam-rugṇa, mfn. broken to pieces, shattered, Rājat.

Sam-rujana, n. pain, ache, Car.

संरुध् *sam-√2. rudh*, P. Ā. *-ruṇaddhi*, *-runddhe*, to stop completely, detain, obstruct, check, confine, ŚBr. &c. &c.; to block up (a road), MBh.; to invest, besiege, Hariv.; R. &c.; to shut up (the mind from external objects), MBh.; to keep off, avert, impede, prevent, ib.; to withhold, refuse, ib.: Caus. *-rodhayati* (only ind. p. *-rodhya*), to cause to stop, obstruct, Rājat.

Sam-ruddha, mfn. stopped completely, detained, obstructed, hindered &c.; surrounded by (comp.), Mn.; BhP.; held, closed, Kathās.; invested, besieged, R.; covered, concealed, obscured, MBh.; R.; stopped up, filled with, R.; Kathās.; BhP.; withheld, refused, Nir.; *-ceshṭa*, mfn. one whose motion is impeded, Ragh.; *-prajanana*, mfn. one who is hindered from having offspring, Nir. v, 2.

Sam-rúdh, f. a term used in gambling (prob. 'a kind of stake'), AV.

Sam-rodha, m. complete obstruction or opposition, restraint, hindrance, stop, prevention, Yājñ.; MBh. &c.; limitation, restriction, Lāṭy.; shutting up, confinement, R.; Megh.; investment, siege, blockade, BhP.; Sāh.; injury, offence, harm, MBh.; Kām.; suppression, destruction, BhP.; throwing, sending (= *kshepa*), L. °**rodhana**, n. complete obstruction, the act of stopping, checking, restraining, suppressing, MBh.; Kāv. &c.; fettering, confining, BhP. °**rodhya**, mfn. to be restrained or confined, Car.

संरुष् *sam-√rush*, Caus. *-roshayati* (Pass. pr. p. *-roshyamāṇa*), to enrage, irritate, MBh.

Sam-rushita, mfn. enraged, irritated, angry, ib.

संरुह् *sam-√ruh*, P. *-rohati*, to grow together, grow up, increase, Kāv.; to grow over, be cicatrized, heal, TS. &c. &c.; to break forth, appear, Hariv.; Sāh.: Caus. *-ropayati*, to cause to grow or increase, plant, sow, Bhartṛ.; BhP.; to cause to grow over or cicatrize, Suśr.; *-rohayati*, see *sam-rohaṇa* below.

Sam-rūḍha, mfn. grown, sprung up, sprouted, Ragh.; grown over, cicatrized, healed, MBh.; R.; burst forth, appeared, Hariv.; growing fast or taking root firmly, MBh.; confident, bold (= *prâuḍha*), L.; *-vraṇa*, mfn. having a healed or cicatrized wound, R.

Sam-ropaṇa, mfn. (fr. Caus.) causing to grow over or heal, Suśr.; planting, sowing, Kāv.; VarBṛS. °**ropita**, mfn. (fr. id.) caused to grow, planted, implanted (fig. 'in the womb'), Śak. vi, 23.

Sam-rohá, m. growing over, TS.; curing, healing, Suśr.; growing up, bursting forth or into view, appearance, BhP. °**rohaṇa**, n. growing over, cicatrizing, healing, R.; (fr. Caus.) sowing, planting, Mālav. i, 8 (v. l.); mfn. healing, curing, Suśr. °**rohin**, mfn. growing up or in (comp.), Kāvyâd.

संरूष् *sam-√rūsh*, Caus. *-roshayati* (?), to spread over, smear, cover, Suśr.

Sam-roshita, mfn. spread over, covered, besmeared, ib.

संरेज् *sam-√rej*, Ā. *-rejate*, to be greatly agitated, tremble, quake, ŚBr.

संरोदन *sam-rodana*, n. weeping together or vehemently, wailing, lamenting, Suśr.

संलक्ष् *sam-√laksh*, P. Ā. *-lakshayati*, °*te*, to distinguish by a mark, characterize, mark distinctly (see °*lakshita* below); to observe, see, perceive, feel, hear, learn, MBh.; Kāv. &c.; to test, prove, try, ib.: Pass. *-lakshyate*, to be marked or observed or perceived, appear, ib.

Sam-lakshaṇa, n. the act of distinctly marking, distinguishing, characterizing, W. °**lakshita**, mfn. distinguished by a mark, marked, Pañcar.; observed, recognized, known, perceived, learnt, Kāv.; Kathās. °**lakshya**, mfn. to be distinctly marked, distinguishable, perceptible, visible, Kpr.

संलग् *sam-√lag*, Caus. *-lāgayati*, to attach to, put or place firmly upon, KātyŚr., Sch.

Sam-lagna, mfn. closely attached, adhering, being in contact with, sticking to or in, fallen into (loc. or comp.), MBh.; Kathās.; fighting hand to hand (du. said of two combatants), MBh.; (ifc.) proceeding from or out of, Pañcar.

संलङ्घ् *sam-√laṅgh*, P. Ā. *-laṅghati*, °*te*, to leap over or beyond, pass by or away (see below).

Sam-laṅghana, n. passing away (of time), Lāṭy., Sch. **laṅghita**, mfn. passed away, gone by, Lāṭy.

संलज्ज् *sam-√lajj*, Ā. *-lajjate* (only pr. p. *-lajjamāna*), to be thoroughly ashamed or embarrassed, R.

संलप् *sam-√lap*, P. *-lapati*, to talk together, chat, converse, Daś.; HPariś.: Pass. *-lapyate*, to be spoken of or to, be called or named, Sarvad.: Caus., see °*lāpita* below.

Sam-lapana, n. the act of talking or chattering together; °*nôshṇatā*, f. desire of talking much, Suśr.

Sam-laptaka, mfn. affable, gentle, civil, Buddh.

Sam-lāpa, m. (ifc. f. *ā*) talking together, familiar or friendly conversation, discourse with (instr. with and without *saha*, or gen.) or about (comp.), MBh.; Kāv. &c.; (in dram.) a kind of dialogue (passionless, but full of manly sentiments, e. g. Mcar. ii, 34), Bhar. °**lāpaka**, m. a kind of dialogue (= prec.), Bhar.; n. a species of minor drama (said to be of a controversial kind), Sāh. °**lāpita**, mfn. (fr. Caus.) spoken to, addressed, Hit. °**lāpin**, mfn. discoursing, conversing, ib.

संलभ् *sam-√labh*, Ā. *-labhate*, to take hold of one another, seize or lay hold of mutually, TBr.; to wrestle with (instr.), MaitrS.; to obtain, receive, BhP.: Desid., see *-lipsu* below.

Sam-labdha, mfn. taken hold of, obtained, Kathās.

Sam-lipsu, mfn. (fr. Desid.) desirous of seizing or taking hold of, MBh.

संलय *sam-laya*, °*yana*. See *sam-√lī*.

संलल् *sam-√lal*, Caus. *-lālayati*, to caress, fondle, treat tenderly, BhP. °**lālita**, mfn. caressed, fondled, MW.

संलिख् *sam-√likh*, P. *-likhati*, to scratch, scarify, Suśr.; to write, engrave, inscribe, Pañcar.; to touch, strike, play upon (a musical instrument), Lāṭy. °**likhita**, mfn. scratched &c. (used in AV. vii, 50, 5 to express some act in gambling).

Sam-lekha, m. strict abstinence, Buddh.

संलिह् *sam-√lih* (cf. *sam-√rih*), P. *-leḍhi*, *-lihati* (pr. p. Ā. *-lihāna*), to lick up, devour, enjoy, Kāṭh.; MBh.; Bhaṭṭ.

Sam-līḍha, mfn. licked up, licked, enjoyed, MW.

संली *sam-√lī*, Ā. *-liyate*, to cling or adhere to (acc.), MBh.; to go into, find room in (loc.), ib.; to lie down, hide, cower, lurk, be concealed, ib.; R.; to melt away, ib.

Sam-layá, m. settling or sitting down, alighting or settling (of a bird), ŚBr.; sleep, L.; melting away, dissolution (= *pra-laya*), MW. °**layana**, n. sitting or lying down, Cat.; the act of clinging or adhering to, MW.; dissolution, ib.

Sam-līna, mfn. clinging or joined together, adhering or clinging to (loc.), MBh.; Kāv. &c.; entered into (loc.), MBh.; hidden, concealed, covered, cowering down, lurking in (loc.), MBh.; R.; contracted, Suśr.; *-karṇa*, mfn. one whose ears are depressed or hang down, Pañcat.; *-mānasa*, mfn. drooping or depressed in mind, Hariv.

संलुड् *sam-√luḍ*, Caus. *loḍayati*, to stir about, move to and fro, MBh.; to disarrange, disturb, throw into disorder or confusion, ib.: Pass. *-loḍyate*, to be disturbed or destroyed, ib.

Sam-loḍana, mfn. disturbing, throwing into confusion (comp.), MBh.; n. the act of disturbing or agitating or confusing, MW.

संलुप् *sam-√lup*, P. *-lumpati*, *-lupyati*, to rend or tear to pieces, tear away, pull away, AV.; ŚBr.: Caus. *-lopayati*, to destroy, efface, MBh.

संलुभ् *sam-√lubh*, P. *-lubhyati*, to be perplexed or disturbed, fall into confusion, ŚBr.: Caus. *-lobhayati*, to disarrange, throw into confusion, mix up, Lāṭy.; to efface, obliterate, AV.; to allure, entice, seduce, MBh.; R.

संलुलित *sam-lulita*, mfn. (*√lul*) agitated, disordered, confused, R.; come into contact with (comp.), Caurap. ('smeared with,' Sch.)

संलेप *sam-lepa*, m. mud, dirt, Heat.

संलोक् *sam-√lok*, Ā. *-lokate*, to look together, look at each other (with *ubhayataḥ*), AitBr.

Sam-lokin, mfn. being in view of others, observed by others, Gobh.

संवंह् *sam-vanh*. See *sam-√banh*.

संवच् sam-√vac, P. -vakti (in the non-conj. tenses also Ā.), to proclaim, announce, publish, communicate, Pañcar.; to speak or tell or say to (acc. with or without prati), MBh.; Pañcat.; Kathās.; (Ā.) to converse, talk with, RV.

Sam-vāc, f. speaking together, colloquy, RV. °**vācya**, n. (prob.) the art of conversation (as one of the 64 Kalās), BhP., Sch.; mfn. to be conversed with &c., MW.

Sam-ukta, mfn. spoken to, addressed, remonstrated or expostulated with, BhP.

संवञ्च् sam-√vañc, P. -vañcati, to totter, stagger, waver, TS.

संवत् 1. sam-vát, f. (fr. 2. sam; cf. ni-vát, pra-vát) a side, region, tract, RV.; AV.; = saṃgrāma, Naigh. ii, 17.

संवत् 2. sam-vat, ind. (a contraction of saṃ-vatsara below) a year, in the year (in later times esp. of the Vikrama era [beginning in 58 B.C., see vikramâditya] as opp. to the Śaka era [in modern times supposed to be founded by Śāli-vāhana; see 3. śaka]; sometimes = 'in the year of the reign of'), Inscr. &c.; IW. 494.

Sam-vátsam, ind. for a year, RV. iv, 33, 4.

Sam-vatsará, m. (rarely n.; cf. pari-v°) a full year, a year (having 12 [TS.] or 13 [VS.] months or 360 days [ŚBr.; AitBr.; Suśr.]; am, 'for a year;' eṇa, 'after or in course of a y°;' e or asya, 'after or within a y°'), RV. &c. &c.; a year of the Vikrama era (see above; varsha is used for the Śaka); the first in a cycle of five or six years, TS.; PārGṛ.; VarBṛS.; BhP.; the Year personified (having the new and full moon for eyes and presiding over the seasons), TS.; Pur.; N. of Śiva, MBh. — **kara**, m. 'year-causer,' N. of Śiva, Śivag. — **kalpa-latā**, f., -**kṛitya**, n. (or -dīdhiti, f.), -**kṛitya-prakāśa**, m., -**kaumudī**, f., -**kaustubha**, m. N. of wks. — **tama**, mf(ī)n. completing a full year, happening after a y° (-tamīṃ rātrim, 'this day year'), ŚBr. — **dīksha**, mfn. having the Dīkshā (q.v.) maintained for a y°, KātyŚr. — **dīkshita**, mfn. maintaining the Dīkshā for a year, ib. — **dīdhiti**, f., see -kṛitya. — **dīpa-māhātmya**, n., -**dīpa-vrata-māhātmya**, n. N. of wks. — **nirodha**, m. imprisonment for a y° (-tas, ind.), Mn. viii, 375. — **parvan**, n. the period of a y°, Pat. on Pāṇ. iv, 2, 21, Vārtt. 2. — **prakaraṇa**, n., -**prakāśa**, m. N. of wks. — **pratimā** (°rá-), f. the image of a y°, TBr. — **pradīpa**, m. N. of wk. — **prabarha** and -**pravalha**, m. a variety of the Gavām-ayana (q.v.), Lāṭy. — **prabhṛiti**, mfn. lasting a y° and longer, KātyŚr. — **pravāta**, mfn. exposed to the wind or air for a y°, ĀpŚr. — **phala**, n. 'the fruit or result of a year,' N. of wk. — **brāhmaṇa**, n. the symbolical meaning of an annual sacrifice, TāṇḍBr. — **bhukti**, f. a y°'s course (of the sun), BhP. — **bhṛit**, mfn. = -dīksha, Śulbas. — **bhṛita** (°rá-), mfn. maintained for a year (cf. next), ŚBr.; KātyŚr.; °**tôkha**, m. one who has borne the ukhā (q.v.) for a year, ŚāṅkhŚr. — **bhṛitin**, mfn. one who has maintained (a sacrificial fire) for a year, KātyŚr. — **bhrami**, mfn. revolving or completing a revolution in a y° (as the sun), MārkP. — **maya**, mf(ī)n. consisting of (a partic. number of) y°s, Jyot. — **mukhī**, f. the tenth day in the light half of the month Jyaishṭha, Hcat. — **raya**, m. a year's course, MW. — **rūpá**, n. a form of the y°, ŚBr. — **vāsin**, mfn. dwelling (with a teacher) for a year, ib. — **vidha** (°rá-), mfn. (to be performed) according to the rules of an annual sacrifice, ib. — **velá**, f. the period of a year, ib. — **sattra**, n. a Soma sacrifice whose Sutyā days last a year, ŚāṅkhŚr.; -bhāshya, n. N. of wk.; -sád, mfn. one who performs the above S° sacr°, PS.; ŚBr. — **sammita** (°rá-), mfn. equal to a y°, ŚBr.; similar to the Sattra lasting a y°, ŚāṅkhŚr.; n. and (ā), f. N. of partic. sacrificial days (in the middle of which occurs the Vishuvat-day), ŚrS. — **sahasrá**, n. a thousand years, ŚBr. — **sāta** (°rá-), mf(ā)n. acquired within a y°, TS. — **svadita** (°rá-), mfn. well seasoned or prepared for a y°, ib. **Saṃvatsarâtyāsam**, ind. having skipped a y°, Lāṭy. **Saṃvatsarâdi-phala**, n. N. of wk. **Saṃvatsarâyusha**, mfn. a year old, MaitrS. **Saṃvatsarâvara**, mfn. lasting at least a year, KātyŚr. **Saṃvatsarôtsava-kalpa-latā**, f., °**va-kāla-nirṇaya**, m. N. of wks. **Saṃvatsarôpasatka**, mfn. whose Upasad (q.v.) lasts a year, KātyŚr. **Saṃvatsarôpâsita**, mfn. served or maintained for a year, ŚBr.

Saṃvatsarika, w.r. for sāṃv°.

Saṃvatsarīṇa, mf(ā)n. yearly, annual, recurring every year, RV. &c. &c.

Saṃvatsarīya, mfn. id., MaitrS.

संवत् 3. sam-vat, mfn. containing the word sam, ŚāṅkhBr.; n. N. of a Sāman, PañcavBr.

संवद् sam-√vad, P. Ā. -vadati, °te (ind. p. sam-udya, q.v.), (Ā.) to speak together or at the same time, AitBr.; ChUp.; (P.; Ā. only m.c.) to converse with (instr.) or about (loc.), RV.; AV.; TS.; Br.; (P.) to sound together or in concord (said of musical instruments), AV.; to agree, accord, consent, Hariv.; Mṛicch.; Kathās.; to coincide, fit together (so as to give one sense), Ratnâv.; to speak, speak to, address (acc.), BhP.; to designate, call, name (two acc.), Śrutab.: Caus. -vādayati, °te (ind. p. -vādya, q.v.), to cause to converse with (instr.) or about (loc.), ŚBr.; ŚāṅkhŚr.; to invite or call upon to speak, Hit. (v.l.); to cause to sound, play (a musical instrument), MBh.; Kathās.

Sam-vadana, n. the act of speaking together, conversation, Saṃk.; a message, L.; consideration, examination, L.; (also ā, f.) subduing by charms or by magic (= or w.r. for saṃ-vanana, q.v.), L.; a charm, amulet, W. °**vaditavyà**, mfn. to be talked over or agreed upon, ŚBr.; to be spoken to or addressed.

Sam-vādá, m. (ifc. f. ā) speaking together, conversation, colloquy with (instr. with and without saha, loc., or comp.), RV. &c. &c.; appointment, stipulation, KātyŚr.; Kāv.; VarBṛS.; a cause, lawsuit, ĀpGṛ.; Kathās.; assent, concurrence, agreement, conformity, similarity, W.; information, news, ib. °**vādaka**, mfn. (fr. Caus.) agreeing, consenting, Sāṃkhyak.; m. N. of a man, Hcar. °**vādana**, n. (fr. id.) assent, agreement, Kathās. °**vādita**, mfn. (fr. id.) caused to speak with &c.; agreed upon, MBh. °**vādin**, mfn. conversing, talking, Ragh.; agreeing or harmonizing with, corresponding to (gen. or comp.), Kāvyād.; °di-tā, f. likeness, resemblance, Harav. °**vādya**, ind. (fr. Caus.) having declared truly or accurately, Mn. viii, 31.

1. **Sam-udita**, mfn. (for 2. see under sam-ud-√i) spoken to or with, addressed, accosted, BhP.; agreed upon (see yathā-samuditam); consented, settled, customary, Kathās. °**udya**, ind. having spoken together &c.; having concluded or agreed upon, BhP.

संवन् sam-√van, Caus. -vānayati (or -vanayati, cf. under √van), to cause to like or love, make well-disposed, propitiate, AV.

Sam-vánana, mf(ī)n. propitiating, AV.; (ifc.) making well-disposed to (in dāna-s°), R.; m. N. of an Āṅgirasa (author of RV. x, 191), Anukr.; n. or (ā), f. (cf. saṃ-vadana) causing mutual fondness, propitiating, subduing (esp. by spell), charming, fascination, AV. &c. &c.; gaining, acquiring (in kośa-s°), MBh.

संवन्द् sam-√vand, Ā. -vandate, to salute respectfully, BhP.

संवप् sam-√2. vap, cl. 1. P. Ā. -vapati, °te, to throw together, mix, pour in, VS.; TS.; ŚrS.; to scatter, sow, MW.

Sam-vapana, n. throwing or pouring in, KātyŚr. °**vāpa**, m. throwing together, mixing, mingling, ĀpŚr., Sch.

संवर sam-vara &c. See sam-√1. 2. vṛi.

संवर्ग sam-varga &c. See sam-√vṛij.

संवर्ण् sam-√varṇ, P. -varṇayati, to communicate, narrate, tell, MBh.; Kathās.; BhP.; to praise, commend, approve, sanction, MBh.; SaddhP.; Divyâv.

Sam-varṇana, n. narrating, describing, Cat.; praise, commendation, Jātakam. °**varṇita**, mfn. communicated, narrated &c.; approved, sanctioned, Lalit.; resolute, ib.; -mānasa, mfn. one who has made up his mind, resolute, ib.

संवर्त sam-varta, °taka &c. See under sam-√vṛit.

संवर्धक sam-vardhaka, °dhana &c. See under sam-√vṛidh.

संवर्मय sam-varmaya, Nom. P. °yati, to provide any one (acc.) with a coat of mail, Pāṇ. iii, 1, 25, Sch.; to equip, arm fully (fig.), Subh.

Sam-varmita, mfn. fully armed, W.

संवर्य sam-varya, Nom. P. °yati (usually written sambarya), to bring together, g. khaṇḍv-ādi.

संवर्षण sam-varshaṇa, w.r. for a-v°, Vet.

संवल sam-vala. See śambala.

संवलन sam-valana, n. or °nā, f. meeting, encountering (of enemies), Bālar.; mixture, union, Mālatīm.; Gīt.

Sam-valita, mfn. met, united, joined or mixed with, surrounded by, possessed of (instr. or comp.), Kāv.; Sāh.; broken, diversified (= cūrṇita), Kir. vi, 4, Sch.

संवल्ग् sam-√valg, Ā. -valgate, to wallow, roll, AV.; TS.

Sam-valgana, n. jumping (with joy), exulting, Anargh. °**valgita**, mfn. overrun, MW.

संववृत्वस् sam-vavṛitvas. See sam-√vṛit.

संवस् sam-√4. vas, Ā. -vaste, to be clothed or clad in (instr.), RV. v, 85, 4.

Sam-vastraṇa, n. wearing the same or similar clothes, MānGṛ., Sch.

Sam-vastraya, Nom. (fr. prec.) P. °yati (ind. p. -vastrya), to wear the same or similar garments, MānGr.; to put on, wear, Bhaṭṭ.

1. **Sam-vāsin**, mfn. (ifc.) clothed in, MBh.

संवस् sam-√5. vas, P. Ā. -vasati, °te (inf. -vastum; pr.p. -vasat or -vásāna [q.v.]), to dwell together, live or associate with (instr. with and without saha, or acc.), RV. &c. &c.; to cohabit with (acc.), W.; to meet or assemble together, R.; to stay, abide, dwell in (loc.), MBh.; R.; to spend, pass (time), R.; BhP.: Caus. -vāsayati, to cause to live together, bring together with (instr. with or without saha), RV.; TBr.; Lāṭy.; to provide with a lodging or dwelling, MBh.

Sam-vasati, f. dwelling together, Subh. °**vasatha**, m. an inhabited place, settlement, village, dwelling, house, Kaśīkh. °**vásana**, n. a dwelling-place, house, RV. °**vásāna**, m. = next, RV.

Sám-vasu, m. one who dwells along with, a fellow-dweller, RV.; AV.

Sam-vāsa, m. dwelling together, living or associating with (instr. with and without saha, or comp.), Mn.; MBh. &c.; cohabitation, sexual connexion with (comp.), Car.; a common abode, Kām.; a settlement, dwelling, house, MBh.; R. &c.; an open place for meeting or recreation, L.; association, company, society, W.

2. **Sam-vāsin**, mfn. dwelling together, a fellow-dweller, Kām.; Rājat.; (ifc.) dwelling in, inhabiting, MBh.; R.

Sam-ushita, mfn. one who has passed or spent (time), BhP.; dwelled or lived together, stayed with, MW.; passed, spent (as time), ib.

संवह् sam-vah (cf. sam-√1. ūh), cl. 1. P. Ā. -vahati, °te (inf. -voḍhum), to bear or carry together or along or away, take, convey, bring, AV. &c.; to load (a cart or car), R.; to take a wife, marry, MW.; to carry or move or rub (the hand) along the body, stroke, soothe, MBh. (3. du. pf. saṃ-vavāhatuḥ, iii, 11005, accord. to some fr. sam-√vāh); to manifest, express, BhP.: Pass. -samuhyate, to be borne by (instr.), ride on (instr.), MBh.; BhP.: Caus. -vāhayati, °te (Pass. -vāhyate), to cause to be brought together, bring together, assemble, Hariv.; Rājat.; to guide, conduct, drive (a carriage), MBh.; R.; Kathās.; to chase, hunt, Pañcat. v, 14; to rub, stroke, Āpast., R.; Śak. &c.; to set in motion, Kād.; to take (a wife), marry, Vet. (v.l.)

Sam-vaha, m. 'bearing or carrying along,' N. of the wind of the third of the 7 Mārgas or paths of the sky (that which is above the ud-vaha and impels the moon; the other five winds being called ā-, pra-, vi-, pari-, and ni-vaha), MBh.; Hariv. &c.; N. of one of the 7 tongues of fire, Col. °**vahana**, n. guiding, conducting, Suśr.; showing, displaying, Kuval. °**vahitṛi**, see sāṃvahitra.

Sam-vāha, mfn. setting in motion, moving (see triṇa-s°); = sam-vāhaka, L.; m. bearing or carrying along, pressing together, MW.; rubbing the body, shampooing, MārkP.; a park for recreation (cf. sam-vāsa), MBh.; Hariv.; a market-place, Pat., Sch.; extortion, oppression, Rājat.; N. of one of the

7 winds (= or w.r. for *sam-vaha* above), L. °**vāhaka**, mf(*ikā*)n. (fr. Caus.) one who rubs or shampoos the limbs; m. a shampooer, R.; Mṛicch. &c. °**vāhana**, n. (fr. id.) bearing, carrying, driving &c., MBh.; the moving along or passage (of clouds), Mālatīm.; rubbing the person, shampooing, Suśr.; Kāv.; Kathās. °**vāhitavya**, mfn. (fr. id.) to be rubbed or stroked, MBh. °**vāhin**, mfn. leading, conducting; (*inī*), f. a partic. vessel of the body (leading from the fetus to the mother), Car. °**vāhya**, mfn. to be borne or carried &c., Pañcat.; to be rubbed or kneaded, W.; to be shown or betrayed (*a-s*°), Kpr.

Sam-vodhṛi. See Pāṇ. iv, 3, 120, Vārtt. 8, Pat.

Sam-uhya, sam-ūḍha. See under *sam-√1. ūh.*

संवा *sam-√2. vā*, P. *-vāti*, to blow at the same time, blow, TBr.; MBh.

संवाञ्छ् *sam-√vāñch*, P. *-vāñchati*, to long for, wish, desire, Bhaṭṭ.

संवाटिका *samvāṭikā*, f. the aquatic plant Trapa Bispinosa, L.

संवाध *sam-√vādha*, incorrect for *sambādha*, q.v.

संवार *sam-vāra*, °*raṇa* &c. See p. 1116, col. 1.

संवावदूक *sam-vāvadūka*, mfn. agreeing, consenting, Anarghar.

संवाश् *sam-√vāś* (only Intens. *-vāvaśanta*, *-avāvaśitām*, and *-vāvaśānā*), to roar or cry together or at the same time, bellow, low, bleat, RV.: Caus. *-vāśayati*, to cause to cry or low together, Lāṭy.

संवासित *sam-vāsita*, mfn. (√*vās*) made fragrant, perfumed, MW.; made fetid, having an offensive smell (said of the breath), Suśr.

संवाह *sam-vāha* &c. See *sam-√vah.*

संविक्त *sam-vikta*, w.r. for *sam-vitka*, NṛisUp.

संविघ्नित *sam-vighnita*, mfn. impeded, hindered, prevented, Amar.

संविचिन्त् *sam-vi-√cint*, P. *-cintayati*, to consider fully, meditate or reflect upon, BhP.

संविचेतव्य *sam-vi-cetavya*, mfn. (√*2. ci*, cf. *vi-cetavya*, p. 959) to be entirely separated or kept apart, R.

संविज् *sam-√vij*, Ā. *-vijate*, to tremble or start with fear, start up, run away, AV.; VS.; to fall to pieces, burst asunder, ĀpŚr.: Caus. *-vejayati*, to frighten, terrify, RV.

Sam-vigna, mfn. agitated, flurried, terrified, shy, MBh.; Kāv. &c.; moving to and fro, BhP.; (ifc.) fallen into, ib.; *-mānasa*, mfn. agitated or distracted in mind, MBh.

Sam-vega, m. violent agitation, excitement, flurry, MBh.; Kathās.; vehemence, intensity, high degree, Uttarar.; Rājat.; desire of emancipation, HPariś.; *-dhāriṇī*, f. N. of a Kim-narī, Kāraṇḍ.

Sam-vejana. See *netra-* and *roma-s*°.

Sam-vejanīya, mfn. to be agitated, tending to agitate the mind violently, Jātakam.

संविज्ञा *sam-vi-√jñā*, P. Ā. *-jānāti*, *-jānīte*, to agree with, recommend, advise (with gen. of pers.), MBh.; to understand, BrahmUp.: Caus. *-jñāpayati* (aor. *-ajijñapat*), to make known, proclaim, recite, repeat, Rājat.

Sam-vijñāta, mfn. generally known, agreeing with (in *a-s*°).

Sam-vijñāna, n. agreement, consent, Suśr.; thorough or complete understanding, Śaṃk.; Sarvad.; perception, knowledge, Uttarar.; *-bhūta*, mfn. become generally known or employed, Nir.

संवितर्क् *sam-vi-√tark*, P. *-tarkayati*, to deliberate about, reflect upon, MBh.

संवित्क *samvitka*. See under *sam-√1. vid*, col. 2.

संविद् *sam-√1. vid*, cl. 2. P. Ā. *-vetti*, *-vitte* (3. pl. *-vidate* or *-vidrate*, Pāṇ. vii, 1, 7), to know together, know thoroughly, know, recognize, RV. &c. &c.; to perceive, feel, taste, Suśr.; to come to an understanding, agree with, approve (acc.), MBh.; R.: Caus. *-vedayati*, to cause to know or perceive, PraśnUp.; to make known, declare, MBh.; to know, perceive, Bhaṭṭ.: Caus., see *sam-vedita.*

Samvitka, mfn. (ifc.) possessing *sam-vid* (see meanings below), NṛisUp. (w.r. *sam-vikta*).

Sam-vitti, f. knowledge, intellect, understanding, ib.; Kir.; perception, feeling, sense of (comp.), Kir.; Sarvad.; mutual agreement, harmony, L.; recognition, recollection, W.

1. **Sam-vid**, f. consciousness, intellect, knowledge, understanding (in phil. = *mahat*), VS. &c. &c.; perception, feeling, sense of (gen. or comp.), Rājat.; BhP.; Sarvad.; a partic. stage of Yoga to be attained by retention of the breath, MārkP.; a mutual understanding, agreement, contract, covenant (acc. with √*kṛi* or Caus. of √*sthā* or *vi-√dhā*, 'to make an agreement with,' instr. [with and without *saha*, or gen.] or 'to' [inf. or dat.]; with Caus. of √*laṅgh* or *vy-ati-√kram*, 'to break an agreement'), TUp.; Mn.; MBh. &c.; an appointment, rendezvous, BhP.; a plan, scheme, device, Rājat.; conversation, talk about (comp.), MBh.; Kāv. &c.; news, tidings, MBh.; prescribed custom, established usage, Śiś. xii, 35; a name, appellation, ib.; satisfying (= *toshana*), Śiś. xvi, 47 (Sch.); hemp, L.; war, battle, L.; a watch-word, war-cry, W.; a sign, signal, ib.; (°*vit*)-*prakāśa*, m., *-siddhi*, m. N. of wks.; (°*vid*)-*vyatikrama*, m. breach of promise, violation of contract, Cat. (cf. Mn. viii, 5 and IW. 261); (°*vin*)-*maya*, mf(*ī*)n. consisting of intellect, NṛisUp.

Sam-vida, mfn. having consciousness, conscious (in *a-s*°), ŚBr.; n. (?) stipulation, agreement, MBh. viii, 4512. °**vidita**, mfn. known, recognized, understood, MBh.; VarBṛS.; Inscr.; searched, explored, Hariv.; assented to, agreed upon, approved (*am*, ind. 'with the approval of'), MBh.; R.; Mālav.; admonished, advised, BhP.

Sam-vidvás, mfn. one who has known or knows, AV.

Sam-veda, m. perception, consciousness, Hariv. °**vedana**, n. the act of perceiving or feeling, perception, sensation, MBh.; Kāv.; Sarvad.; making known, communication, announcement, information, Kathās.; ŚārṅgS. °**vedanīya**, mfn. to be perceived or felt, Nyāyas., Sch. °**vedita**, mfn. (fr. Caus.) made known, informed, instructed, MW.

1. **Sam-vedya**, mfn. to be known or understood or learnt &c.; intelligible, Daś.; Sāh.; Rājat.; to be communicated to (loc.), MBh.; m. and n., see 2. *sam-vedya*; *-tā*, f. intelligibility, Sāh.; *-tva*, n. id., ib.; sensation, Nyāyas., Sch.

संविद् *sam-√2. vid*, Ā. (cf. Pāṇ. i, 3, 29) *-vindate* (p. *-vidānā*, q.v.), to find, obtain, acquire, RV.; ŚBr.; BhP.; to meet with (instr.), be joined or united to, AV.; AitBr.; ŚBr.: Pass. *-vidyate*, to be found or obtained, be there, exist, Buddh.: Intens., see *-vévidāna* below.

2. **Sam-vid**, f. acquisition, property, MaitrS. °**vidānā**, mfn. joined or united or associated with (instr.), agreeing in opinion, harmonious, RV.; AV.; ŚBr.; ChUp. °**vidya** (*sám-*), n. = 2. *sam-vid*, AV.

2. **Sam-vedya**, m. the junction of two rivers, L.; n. N. of a Tīrtha, MBh.

Sam-vévidāna, mfn. joined with (instr.), RV.

संविद्युत् *sam-vi-√dyut* (only *-didyutat* and *-adyaut*), to flash or shine together or in rivalry, RV.; VS.

संविधा *sam-vi-√dhā*, P. Ā. *-dadhāti*, *-dhatte*, to dispose, arrange, settle, fix, determine, prescribe, MBh.; R.; Suśr.; to direct, order, Hariv.; to carry on, conduct, manage, attend to, mind, Mn.; MBh. &c.; to use, employ, R.; to make use of, act or proceed with (instr.), Pañcat.; (with *mānasam*) to keep the mind fixed or composed, be in good spirits, Bhartṛ.; to make, render (two acc.), Naish.; to set, put, lay, place, MBh.: Pass. *-dhīyate*, to be disposed or arranged &c., MBh.: Caus. *-dhāpayati*, to cause to dispose or manage, Kād.

Sam-vidh, f. (for *sam-vidhā* below) arrangement, plan, preparation, MBh.; R.

Sam-vidhā, f. id., R.; Ragh.; mode of life, Ragh. °**vidhātavya**, mfn. to be disposed or arranged or managed or done, MBh.; Hariv.; n. (impers.) it is to be acted, MBh. °**vidhātṛi**, m. a disposer, arranger, creator, MBh. °**vidhāna**, n. arrangement, disposition, management, contrivance, MBh.; Kāv. &c.; mode, rite, W.; *-vat*, mfn. acting in the right way, Suśr. °**vidhānaka**, n. a peculiar mode of action, Mṛicch.; Uttarar.

Sam-vidhi, m. disposition, arrangement, preparation, MBh.; Hariv.; Kathās.

Sam-vidhitsu, mfn. (fr. Desid.) wishing to do or make, Harav.

Sam-vidheya, mfn. to be managed or contrived or performed, Śāntiś.

Sam-vihita, mfn. disposed, arranged, managed, taken care of, MBh.

संविनी *sam-vi-√nī* (only ind. p. *-nīya*), to remove entirely, suppress, MBh.

संविन्द् *sam-vind*. See *sam-√2. vid.*

संविप् *sam-vip* for *sam-√vep*, q.v.

संविभज् *sam-vi-√bhaj*, P. Ā. *-bhajati*, °*te*, to divide, separate, Suśr.; give a share or portion to, distribute, apportion, share with (instr. with and without *saha*, dat., or gen.), MBh.; Kāv. &c.; to furnish or provide or present with (instr.), ib.: Caus., see °*vibhājya* below.

Sam-vibhakta, mfn. divided, separated, distributed, Hit. iv, 50 (v.l.); presented with (instr.), MBh. °**vibhaktṛi**, mfn. one who shares with another (gen.), MBh.

Sam-vibhajana, n. the act of sharing with another, Bālar. °**vibhajanīya**, mfn. to be distributed among (dat.), Kull. on Mn. vii, 97. °**vibhajya**, mfn. one with whom anything must be shared, MBh.

Sam-vibhāga, m. dividing together, sharing with others, partition, distribution, bestowal of (comp.) or upon (dat. or loc.), causing to partake in (comp.), Āpast.; Gaut.; MBh. &c.; giving (*ājñā-s*°, 'giving orders'), Kād.; participation, share (acc. with Ā. of √*kṛi* and instr., 'to partake in'), MBh.; *-manas*, mfn. disposed to share with others, MBh.; *-ruci*, mfn. liking to share with others (°*ci-tā*, f.), Suśr.; *-śīla* (Daś.) or *-śīla-vat* (VarBṛS.), mfn. accustomed to share with others. °**vibhāgin**, mfn. used to share with others, accustomed to share with (gen.), MBh.; R.; Hariv.; receiving a share of (gen.), Pañcat.; (°*gi*)-*tā*, f. (MBh.), *-tva*, n. (Kām.) participation, co-partnership. °**vibhāgī-√kṛi**, P. *-karoti*, to divide in equal portions, Nalac. °**vibhāgya**, mfn. to be made to partake of, to be presented with anything, Rājat. °**vibhājya** (fr. Caus.), w.r. for °*vibhajya*, MBh.

संविभा *sam-vi-√bhā*, P. *-bhāti*, to form ideas about, meditate on (acc.), MuṇḍUp. (= *saṃkalpayati*, Śaṃk.)

संविभाव्य *sam-vi-bhāvya*, mfn. (fr. Caus. of √*bhū*) to be perceived or understood, BhP.

संविभाष् *sam-vi-√bhāsh* (only ind. p. *-bhāshya*), to speak to, address, MBh.

संविमर्द *sam-vi-marda*, m. (√*mṛid*) a sanguinary or deadly battle, internecine struggle, MBh.; R.

संविमृश् *sam-vi-√mṛiś* (only ind. p. *-mṛiśya*), to reflect upon, consider, Kathās.

संविराज् *sam-vi-√rāj*, P. Ā. *-rājati*, °*te*, to shine forth, be very illustrious, MBh.

संविलङ्घ् *sam-vi-√laṅgh*, Caus. *-laṅghayati*, to leap over, pass by, transgress, neglect, Pañcar.

संविवर्धयिषु *sam-vivardhayishu*. See *sam-√vṛidh.*

संविवृध् *sam-vi-√vṛidh*, Ā. *-vardhate*, to grow, increase, prosper, MBh.

संविव्यान *sam-vivyāna*. See *sam-√vye.*

संविश् *sam-√viś*, P. *-viśati* (ep. also Ā. °*te*), to approach near to, associate or attach one's self to (acc. or instr.), RV.; VS.; to enter together, enter into (acc., rarely loc.), Kauś.; MBh. &c.; to merge one's self into (acc.), MBh.; to lie down, rest, repose in or upon (loc. or *upari*, ifc.), sleep with (instr. with and without *saha*, or dat.), ŚBr. &c. &c.; to cohabit, have sexual intercourse with (acc.), Mn.; Yājñ.; MārkP.; to sit down with (acc.), Hariv.; to engage in, have to do with (acc.), BhP.: Caus. *-veśayati*, to cause to lie together or down or on, Yājñ., Sch.; to place or lay together or on, bring to (loc.), Kauś.; MBh. &c.

1. **Sam-vishṭa**, mfn. approached, entered &c.; one who has lain down or gone to rest, resting, re-

posing, sleeping, MBh.; Kāv. &c.; seated together with (instr.), BhP.

Sam-veśá, m. approaching near to, entrance, TS.; Br.; lying down, sleeping, Ragh.; dreaming, a dream, W.; a kind of sexual union, L.; a bed-chamber, BhP.; a chair, seat, stool, L.; *-pati* (°*śá-*), m. the lord of rest or sleep or sexual union (Agni), VS.; ĀśvŚr. °**veśaka**, m. one who lays together (e.g. the materials of a house, cf. *gṛiha-s*°); one who assists in going to bed, Car. °**véśana**, mf(*ī*)n. causing to lie down, TĀr.; n. lying down, sleeping, RV.; GṛŚrS.; BhP.; entering, going in, Śaṃk.; sexual union, coition, KātyŚr.; a seat, bench, L. °**veśanīya**, mfn., g. *anupravacanâdi*. °**veśin**, mfn. going to bed (in *adhaḥ-* and *jaghanya-s*°, q.v.) °**veśyà**, mfn. to be entered or occupied, AV.

संविष् *sam-√vish* (only aor. Subj. *-véshishaḥ*), to prepare, procure, bestow, RV. viii, 75, 11.

2. **Sam-vishṭa**, mfn. (for 1. see p. 1115, col. 3) clothed, dressed, Hariv.

Sam-vesha, m., g. *saṃtāpâdi*.

संविषा *sam-vishā*, f. Aconitum Ferox, L.

संविसृज् *sam-vi-√sṛij*, P. *-sṛijati*, to dismiss, R.

संविहस् *sam-vi-√has*, P. *-hasati*, to break out into a laugh, Mṛicch.

संविहृ *sam-vi-√hṛi*, P. *-harati*, to divert one's self, sport, play, BhP.

संविह्वल् *sam-vi-√hval*, P. *-hvalati*, to stagger or reel about, rock to and fro, MBh.

संवीक्ष् *sam-vîksh* (*vi-√îksh*), Ā. *-vîkshate*, to look about, look at attentively, see, perceive, R.; Pañcat.

Sam-vîkshaṇa, n. looking about or at, seeing, perceiving, Kāśîkh.; search, inquiry, L.

संवीज् *sam-√vîj*, Caus. *-vîjayati*, to fan, BhP.; to cause (the hair of the body) to stand erect, Car.

संवीत *sam-vîta*, °*tin*. See *sam-√vye*.

संवुवूर्षु *sam-vuvūrshu*. See col. 2.

संवृ *sam-√1. vṛi*, P. Ā. *-vṛiṇoti*, *-vṛiṇute* &c. (inf. *-varītum*, ep. also *-vartum*), to cover up, enclose, hide, conceal, MBh.; Kāv. &c.; to shut, close (a door), MBh.; to put together or in order, arrange, Kathās.; to gather up (snares), Hit. (v.l.); to ward off, keep back, restrain, check, stop, Bhaṭṭ.; Kathās.; (Ā. *-varate*) to gather (intr.), accumulate, augment, increase, RV. i, 121, 5: Caus. *-vārayati* (ind. p. *-vārya*), to ward off, keep or drive back, repel, MBh.; Hariv.; Desid., see *saṃ-vuvūrshu*, col. 2.

1. **Sam-vara**, mfn. keeping back, stopping (in *kāla-s*°, applied to Vishṇu), Pañcar.; m. (often written and confounded with *śambara*) a dam, mound, bridge, Bhaṭṭ.; provisions, Divyâv.; shutting out the external world (with Jainas one of the 7 or 9 Tattvas), Sarvad.; N. of two Arhats, L.; n. (with Buddhists) restraint, forbearance (or 'a partic. religious observance'), Kāraṇḍ.; *-viṃśaka*, n., *-vyākhyā*, f.; °*rodaya-tantra*, n. N. of wks. 1. °**váraṇa**, mf(*ī*)n. covering, containing, Pracaṇḍ.; shutting, closing (with *vali*, f. 'one of the three folds of skin which cover the anus'), Suśr.; m. N. of the author of the hymns RV. v, 33; 34 (having the patr. Prājāpatya), Anukr.; of a king (son of Ṛiksha, husband of Tapatī, and father of Kuru), MBh.; Hariv.; Pur.; of another man, Vās., Introd.; (*am*), n. the act of covering or enclosing or concealing, MBh.; Kāv. &c.; closing, shutting, RPrāt.; Suśr.; concealment, secrecy, Mālatim.; a cover, lid, BhP.; an enclosure, sanctuary (as place of sacrifice), RV.; AV.; a dam, mound, R. °**varaṇîya**, mfn. to be covered or concealed or hidden, Prasannar.

Sam-vāra, m. (ifc. f. *ā*) covering, concealing, closing up, MW.; compression or contraction of the throat or of the vocal chords (in pronunciation), obtuse articulation (opp. to the *vi-vāra*, q.v., and regarded as one of the Bāhya-prayatnas), Pāṇ. i, 1, 9, Sch.; an obstacle, impediment, Mṛicch. vii, 7 (v.l.) °**vāraṇa**, mfn. (ifc.) warding off, keeping back, MBh. °**vārayishṇu**, mfn. (fr. Caus.) intending to ward off, MBh. vi, 3762 (B.) °**vārya**, mfn. to be covered or concealed (see *saṃvṛitta-s*°); to be kept back or warded off (see *a-s*°).

Sam-vuvūrshu, mfn. (fr. Desid.) wishing to cover or conceal, Bhaṭṭ.

1. **Sam-vṛit**, mfn. covering, TS.

Sám-vṛita, mfn. covered, shut up, enclosed or enveloped in (loc.), surrounded or accompanied or protected by (instr. with or without *saha*, or comp.), well furnished or provided or occupied or filled with, full of (instr. or comp.), AV. &c. &c.; concealed, laid aside, kept, secured, MBh.; Kāv. &c.; restrained, suppressed, retired, withdrawn, Hariv.; Śak. ii, 12 (v.l. for *sam-hṛita*); well covered or guarded (see *su-s*°); contracted, compressed, closed (as the throat), articulated with the vocal chords contracted, Prāt.; subdued (as a tone), ib.; Pat.; (in rhet.) hidden, ambiguous (but not offensive, see Vām. ii, 1, 14); m. N. of Varuṇa, L.; n. a secret place, KaushUp.; close articulation (cf. above), Prāt.; *-tā*, f. (TPrāt., Sch.), *-tva*, n. (Veṇis.) closed condition; *-mantra*, mfn. one who keeps his counsels or plans secret (*-tā*, f.), Kām.; *-saṃvārya*, mfn. one who conceals what ought to be concealed, Mn. vii, 102; °*tâkāra*, mfn. one who conceals all signs of feeling, MW.

Sam-vṛiti, f. closure, Suśr.; ŚārṅgP.; covering, concealing, keeping secret, Śiś.; Sarvad.; dissimulation, hypocrisy, Amar.; obstruction, HYog.; *-mat*, mfn. able to dissimulate, Śiś.; Subh.

संवृ *sam-√2. vṛi* (Ā. only *-vṛiṇate* as 3. pl.), to choose, seek for, BhP.

2. **Sam-vara**, m. choosing, election, choice (of a husband; v.l. for *svayam-vara*), MBh. vii, 6033. 2. °**varaṇa**, n. id.; *-nāṭaka*, n. N. of a drama; *-sraj*, f. the garland given by a woman to her chosen husband, Ragh.; Naish.

संवृंह् *sam-√vṛiṇh*. See *sam-√1. 2. bṛih*.

संवृज् *sam-√vṛij*, Ā. *-vṛiṅkte* (rarely P.), to sweep together, lay hold of or seize for one's self, appropriate, own, RV.; ŚBr.; Up.: Desid. *-vívṛikshate*, to wish to appropriate, ŚBr.

Sam-vargá, mfn. rapacious, ravenous, RV.; ŚBr.; Up.; ŚrS.; m. snatching up or sweeping together for one's self, gathering for one's self, TS.; Kāṭh. (with *Agneḥ* and *Prajāpateḥ*, N. of Sāmans, ĀrshBr.); devouring, consumption, absorption, the resolution of one thing into another, MW.; (?) mixture, confusion (in *varṇa-s*°), Vas.; multiplication of two numbers together or the product of such m°, Āryabh.; *-jit*, m. N. of a teacher, VBr.; *-vidyā*, f. (in phil.) the science of resolution or absorption (cf. above). °**vargaṇa**, n. attracting, winning (friends), Daś. °**várgam**, ind. laying hold of or snatching up, sweeping together for one's self, gathering, RV. °**vargaya**, Nom. P. °*yati*, to gather or assemble round one's self, Bhaṭṭ. °**vargya**, mfn. to be multiplied, VarBṛS.; m. N. of an astronomer, Cat.

Sam-varjana, n. the act of snatching or seizing for one's self, Śaṃk.; devouring, consuming, W.

Sam-vṛikta, mfn. laid hold of or snatched up, seized; *-dhṛishṇu* (*sám-*), mfn. one who seizes or overpowers the strong, RV. °**vṛij**, mfn. seizing, overpowering, VS.

संवृत् *sam-√vṛit*, Ā. *-vartate* (pf. p. *-vavṛitvás*, q.v.; Ved. inf. *-vṛitas*; ind. p. *-vartam*), to turn or go towards, approach near to, arrive at, RV.; AV.; R.; to go against, attack (acc.), MBh.; to meet, encounter (as foes), RV. iv, 24, 4; to come together, be rolled together, be conglomerated, PañcavBr.; Kauś.; (also with *mithas*) to have sexual intercourse together, ŚBr.; Āpast.; to take shape, come into being, be produced, arise from (abl.), RV. &c. &c.; to come round or about, come to pass, happen, occur, take place, be fulfilled (as time), MBh.; Kāv. &c.; to begin, commence, R.; to be, exist, ChUp.; MBh. &c.; to become, grow, get (with nom.), R.; Ragh.; to be conducive to, serve for (dat.), Lalit.: Caus. *-vartayati*, to cause to turn or revolve, roll (lit. and fig.), RV. &c. &c.; to turn towards or hither, RV.; to clench (the fist), Hariv.; to wrap up, envelop, MBh.; to crumple up, crush, destroy, MBh.; R.; to bring about, accomplish, perform, execute, Hariv.; R.; BhP.; to fulfil, satisfy (a wish), R.; to think of, find out (a remedy), Car.: Desid. *-vivṛitsati*, to wish to have sexual intercourse with (acc.), AV.

Sam-vartá, m. meeting, encountering (an enemy), MBh.; rolling up, destruction, (esp.) the periodical destruction or dissolution of the world, MBh.; R.; BhP.; a partic. cosmic period or Kalpa (q.v.), Cat.; anything rolled or kneaded, a lump or ball (of cake), Kauś.; a young rolled-up leaf, ĀpGṛ.; a dense mass (of people), Mālatim.; a rain-cloud, R.; Hariv.; a partic. kind of cloud (abounding in water and so distinct from the Ā-varta which has no water; cf. *droṇa*, *pushkalâvartaka*), L.; N. of one of the 7 clouds at the dissolution of the universe (cf. *bhīma-nāda*), Cat.; a year, L.; a partic. mythical weapon, Hariv.; R.; a partic. comet, VarBṛS.; a partic. conjunction of planets, ib.; Terminalia Bellerica, L.; Cicer Arietinum, L.; N. of a Muni and legislator (cf. *-smṛiti* and *bṛihat-saṃv*°), Yājñ.; of an Āṅgirasa (and author of RV. x, 172), AitBr. &c.; n. du. (with *Indrasya*) N. of two Sāmans, ĀrshBr. (perhaps w.r. for *sāṃ-v*°, q.v.); *-kalpa*, m. a partic. period of universal destruction, Buddh.; *-maruttīya*, mfn. relating to the Munis Saṃvarta and Marutta, MBh.; *-smṛiti*, f. S°'s law-book, IW. 203; °*tâgni*, m. the fire at the destruction of the world, MBh.; °*tâmbhas*, n. the water at the d° of the world, BhP.; °*târka*, m. the sun at the d° of the world, ib. °**vartaka**, mfn. (cf. *sāṃ-v*°) rolling up, destroying (all things at the end of the world), NṛisUp.; MBh. &c.; m. the world-destroying fire (pl. 'the fires of hell'), Gṛihyās.; BhP.; submarine fire (= *bāḍava*), L.; (scil. *gaṇa*) a group or class of world-destroying clouds, VP.; the end or dissolution of the universe, R.; Hariv.; Terminalia Bellerica, L.; N. of Bala-deva (q.v.), L.; of a serpent-demon, MBh.; of an ancient sage (= *sam-varta*), VarBṛS.; of a mountain, Col.; (*ikā*), f. a young lotus-leaf (still rolled up), Bhpr.; Kād.; n. Bala-deva's ploughshare, Hariv.; °*kâgni*, m. the world-destroying fire, MW.; °*kâbhra*, n. pl. the clouds at the destruction of the world, Nāgân.; °*kin*, m. N. of Bala-deva (cf. above), L. °**vartana**, mf(*ī*)n. issuing in, leading to (comp.), Divyâv.; n. a partic. mythical weapon, Hariv.; (*ī*), f. destruction of the world, Buddh. °**vartanīya**, mfn. (ifc. leading or conducive to), SaddhP. °**vartam**, ind. rolling up, destroying, PañcavBr. °**varti**, f. = °*vartikā* (see °*vartaka*), W. °**vartita**, mfn. (fr. Caus.) rolled up, wrapped up, enveloped, MBh.; Kāv. &c.

Sam-vavṛitvás, mfn. (pf. p. of *sam-√vṛit*) rolled up or together, gathered, dense (as darkness), RV. v, 31, 3.

Sam-vṛitta, mfn. approached near to, arrived, Gaut.; happened, occurred, passed, Kāv.; Pañcat.; fulfilled (as a wish), R.; become, grown (with nom.), MBh.; Kāv. &c.; often w.r. for *sam-vṛita*; m. N. of Varuṇa, L.; of a serpent-demon, MBh. °**vṛitti**, f. common occupation, Āpast.; the right effect, Car.; Fulfilment (personified), MBh.; being, existing, becoming, happening, MW.; often w.r. for *sam-vṛiti*.

संवृध् *sam-√vṛidh*, Ā. *-vardhate* (rarely P.), to grow to perfection or completion, grow up, increase, RV. &c. &c.; to fulfil, satisfy, grant, R.: Caus. *-vardhayati*, to cause to grow, rear, bring up, foster, cherish, augment, enlarge, strengthen, beautify, make prosperous or happy, MBh.; Kāv. &c.; to present with (instr.), R.; Ragh.; to fulfil, grant (a wish), Mn.; R.: Desid. of Caus., see *sam-vivardhayishu* below.

Sam-vardhaka, mfn. augmenting, increasing, W. °**vardhana**, mfn. id., Subh.; m. N. of a man, Rājat.; n. growing up, complete growth, Kathās.; rearing up, fostering, R.; a means for causing growth (as of the hair), ŚārṅgS.; prospering, thriving, MBh.; Vikr.; causing to thrive, furthering, promoting, Kām.; Daś. °**vardhanīya**, mfn. to be reared or fostered, Pañcat.; to be fed or maintained, Kull. on Mn. iii, 72; to be augmented or strengthened, Pañcat. °**vardhita**, mfn. (fr. Caus.) brought to complete growth, brought up, reared, raised, cherished, MBh.; Kāv. &c.

Sam-vivardhayishu, mfn. (fr. Desid. of Caus.) wishing to increase or to make prosper, Hariv.

Sam-vṛiddha, mfn. full grown, grown up, increased, augmented, thriving, prospering, MBh.; Kāv. &c.; large, big (in *ati-s*°). °**vṛiddhi**, f. full growth, MaitrUp.; might, power, Śiś.

संवृष् *sam-√vṛish*, P. *-varshati*, to rain upon, shower down, TS.

Sam-varshaṇa, n. raining or showering down, MW.

संवृह् *sam-vṛih*. See *sam-√1. 2. bṛih*.

संवे *saṃ-√ve*, P. *-vayati*, to weave together, interweave, RV.; VS.

Saṃ-uta. See *tardma-s°*.

संवेग *saṃ-vega, saṃ-vejana.* See *saṃ-√vij.*

संवेद *saṃ-veda, °dana* &c. See *saṃ-√1. vid.*

संवेप *saṃ-√vep*, Ā. *-vepate*, to tremble, ŚāṅkhBr.; MBh.

संवेश *saṃ-veśa, °śana* &c. See *saṃ-√viś*, p. 1115, col. 3.

संवेष्ट *saṃ-√vesht*, Ā. *-veshṭate*, to be rolled up, shrink together, MBh. vi, 4069 (B. *sam-aceshṭanta*): Caus. *-veshṭayati*, to envelop, clasp, surround, wrap up, cover, MBh.; R. &c.; to wind round, KātyŚr.; to roll up, Śaṃk.; to cause to shrink together, MBh.

Saṃ-veshṭa, n. the being enveloped in or covered with (comp.), MBh.; a covering, cover (ifc. 'covered with'), Hariv. **°veshṭana**, n. rolling up, Śaṃk.; encompassing, surrounding, Dhātup. xxviii, 53 (in explaining *√mur*).

संवोढृ *saṃ-vodhṛi.* See *saṃ-√vah.*

संव्यच *saṃ-√vyac*, P. *-vivyakti*, to compress or collect together or into one's self, comprehend, RV.; to roll up or together, ib.

संव्यथ् *saṃ-√vyath*, Ā. *-vyathate* (only 2. du. pf. P. *-vivyathuḥ*), to be thoroughly afflicted or discouraged, MBh.

Saṃ-vyātha. See *a-s°*.

संव्यध् *saṃ-√vyadh*, P. *-vidhyati* (m. c. also *°te*), to shoot or pierce continuously, MBh.

Saṃ-viddha, mfn. (ifc.) contiguous to, coinciding with, Hariv.

Saṃ-vyādhá, m. combat, fight, ŚBr.

संव्यपाश्रित *saṃ-vy-apâ-śrita*, mfn. (*√śri*) relying on, resorting to (acc.), MBh. vii, 6085.

संव्यवस्य *saṃ-vy-ava-sya*, mfn. (*√so*) to be decided upon or decreed, MBh. xii, 4734.

संव्यवहित *saṃ-vy-ava-hita.* See *a-s°*.

संव्यवहृ *saṃ-vy-ava-√hṛi*, to have intercourse or business with (instr.), Kathās.

Saṃ-vyavaharaṇa, n. doing business well together, prospering in affairs, worldly business, Kull. on Mn. x, 4. **°vyavahāra**, m. id. (cf. *loka-s°*), Gaṇit.; MārkP.; mutual dealing, traffic, intercourse, dealing with (comp.), Āpast.; Pañcat.; occupation with, addiction to (comp.), MBh.; MārkP.; *-vat*, m. a man of business, Kām.; a usual or commonly current term, Śaṃk. **°vyavahārika**, w.r. for *sāṃv°*. **°vyavahārya**, see *a-saṃv°*.

संव्याप्य *saṃ-vy-āpya*, mfn. (*√āp*) to be pervaded, MW.

संव्यूढ *saṃ-vy-ūḍha*, mfn. (*√1. uh*) combined together, mixed, united, W.

Saṃ-vyūha, m. combination, arrangement, BhP. **°vyūhima**, mfn. (prob.) distributing, Suśr.

संव्ये *saṃ-√vye*, P. Ā. *-vyayati, °te* (pf. p. *-vivyāna*, q. v.), to roll or cover up, RV.; Bhaṭṭ.; to put on, wrap one's self in (acc.), RV.; BhP.; to supply or furnish or provide or equip with, RV.; AV.; PārGṛ.: Caus., see *°vyāyita.*

Saṃ-vivyāná, mfn. clothing one's self in (instr.), RV.

Saṃ-vīta, mfn. covered over, clothed, mailed, armoured, MBh.; Kāv. &c.; covered or surrounded or furnished with, concealed or obscured by (instr. or comp.), ib.; hidden, invisible, disappeared, Hariv.; wrapped round, Bālar.; unseen i. e. connived at, permitted by (comp.), Vām. ii, 1, 19; n. clothing, Śāntiś.; *-rāga*, mfn. one whose passions have disappeared, Hariv.; *°tâṅga*, mfn. one who has the body covered, properly clothed, Mn. iv, 49. **°vītin**, mfn. girt with the sacred thread, Siṉhās.

Saṃ-vyāna, n. a cover, wrapper, cloth, garment, (esp.) upper g°, Śiś.; Bhaṭṭ.; HPariś.; covering, L.

Saṃ-vyāya, m. a wrapper, cloth, ŚāṅkhBr. **°vyāyita**, mfn. (fr. Caus.) wrapped in (acc.), HPariś.

संव्रज् *saṃ-√vraj*, P. *-vrajati*, to walk or wander about, go, ŚBr.

संव्रश्च् *saṃ-√vraśc*, P. *-vṛiścati* (ind. p. *-vṛiścya* or *-vraścam*, q. v.), to cut or divide into small pieces, AV.; ŚBr. &c.

Saṃ-vráścam, ind. in pieces, piece by piece, ŚBr.; ŚrS.

संव्रात *saṃ-vrāta*, m. or n. (prob.) = *vrāta*, a multitude, troop, swarm, Pañcar.

संव्ली *saṃ-√vlī*, Pass. *-vlīyate*, to contract or shrink in together, fall in together, collapse, TBr.

Saṃ-vlaya. See *á-s°*.

Sáṃ-vlīna, mfn. sunk down, collapsed, TS.; ŚBr.; Kāṭh.

संशंस् *saṃ-√śaṉs*, P. *-śaṉsati*, to recite together, AitBr.; ŚāṅkhŚr.

Saṃ-śaṉsā, f. praise, commendation, ŚāṅkhBr.

संशक् *saṃ-√śak*, P. *-śaknoti*, to be capable, be able to (inf.), AV.; BhP.; (with *na*) not to succeed with, not to be a match for (instr. or loc.), TS.; AV.

संशकला *saṃ-śakalā*, ind. killing, slaughter, W.; with *-√kṛi*, P. *-karoti*, g. *ūry-ādi* (cf. *śakalā*).

संशङ्क् *saṃ-√śaṅk*, Ā. *-śaṅkate*, to be very suspicious of (acc.) or with regard to (loc.), MBh. iv, 568.

संशद् *saṃ-√2. śad*, Caus. *-śātayati*, to cause to fall down, crush, break to pieces, MBh. iii, 865.

संशप् *saṃ-√śap*, P. Ā. *-śapati, °te*, to take an oath together, swear, curse, imprecate, MBh.

Saṃ-śapta, mfn. 'sworn together,' cursed, Kād.; *-vat*, mfn. one who has sworn with others, one who has cursed (also as pf. 'he has sworn or cursed'), Kathās. **°śaptaka**, m. a soldier or warrior sworn with others not to fly or give up fighting (till some object is gained), one bound by an oath to kill others (pl. a band of conspirators or confederates such as Tri-garta and his brothers who had sworn to kill Arjuna but were killed themselves), MBh.; *-vadha-parvan*, n. N. of the section of the MBh. (vii, 17) describing the above.

संशब्द् *saṃ-√śabd* (only ind. p. *-śabdya* and Pass. pr. p. *-śabdyamāna*), to exclaim, MBh.; to speak about, mention, ib.

Saṃ-śabda, m. calling out, provocation, MBh.; speech, BhP.; mention, Vop. **°śabdana**, n. making a sound, calling out, MW.; mentioning, Dhātup.; praising, eulogizing, ib. **°śabdya**, see above and *a-saṃśabdya.*

संशम् *saṃ-√1. śam*, P. *-śāmyati*, to become thoroughly calm or pacified, be comforted, R.; to be appeased, make peace with (instr. with or without *saha*), MBh.; to be extinguished, ŚBr.; ChUp.; to be allayed, cease, MBh.; to be or become ineffective, BhP.; to calm, allay, ŚBr.: Caus. *-śamayati*, to tranquillize, calm, pacify, ŚāṅkhŚr.; MBh. &c.; to bring to an end, settle, arrange, Pañcat.; to extinguish, R; to bring to rest, remove, destroy, kill, MBh.

Saṃ-śamá, m. complete ease, comfort, satisfaction, ŚBr.; Bhaṭṭ. **°śamana**, mf(*ī*)n. allaying, tranquillizing, Suśr.; removing, destroying (see *pāpa-s°*); n. pacification, Kām.; a sedative, Suśr. **°śamanīya**, see *vāstu-* and *saṃśodhana-s°*.

Saṃ-śānta, mfn. thoroughly pacified or allayed, MBh.; extinguished, destroyed, dead, MBh.; R. &c. **°śānti**, f. extinction, VarBṛS.

संशय *saṃ-śaya* &c. See *saṃ-√śī.*

संशर *saṃ-śará, saṃ-śāruka.* See *saṃ-√śṛī*, p. 1118, col. 1.

संशरण *saṃ-śaraṇa*, n. resorting to, seeking refuge with (gen.), Kām.

संशान *saṃ-śāna, saṃ-śita* &c. See *saṃ-√śo.*

संशास् *saṃ-√śās*, P. *-śāsti*, to direct, instruct, summon, call upon, Br.; GṛS.; to arrange or put in order with (instr.), TS.

Saṃ-śās, see *sú-saṃśās.* **°śāsana**, n. direction, ŚāṅkhBr. **°śāsita**, mfn. directed, instructed, Cat.

Saṃ-śis, f. direction, invitation, AV.

संशिक्ष् *saṃ-√śiksh*, Caus. *-śikshayati*, to teach (two acc.), BhP.; to try, test, Dhanaṃj.

संशिञ्ज् *saṃ-√śiñj*, Ā. *-śiṅkte*, to utter a shrill sound, ŚBr.: Caus. *-śiñjayati*, to clash together (trans.), ib.

संशिशरिषु *saṃ-śiśarishu.* See *saṃ-√śṛī.*

संशिश्रीषु *saṃ-śiśrīshu.* See *saṃ-√śri.*

संशिश्वन् *saṃ-śíśvan*, mf(*arī*)n. having one calf in common (said of cows), RV. (= *eka-śiśuka*, Sāy.)

संशिष्ट *sáṃ-śishṭa*, mfn. (*√śish*) left remaining, TS.

संशी *saṃ-√śī*, Ā. *-śete* (pr. p. *-śayāna*; ind. p. *-śayya*), to grow languid, become feeble, MW.; to waver, be uncertain or irresolute or doubtful, hesitate, MBh.; Kāv. &c.; to despair of (loc.), Kathās.; to lie down for rest, MW.; (P. *-śayati*), to differ in opinion or disagree about (acc.), Yājñ., Sch.

Saṃ-śaya, m. (ifc. f. *ā*) lying down to rest or sleep, L.; uncertainty, irresolution, hesitation, doubt in or of (loc., acc. with *prati*, or comp.; *saṃśayaḥ* with Pot., 'there is doubt whether;' *na s°, nâsti s°, nâtra s°, na hi s°, nâsty atra s°* &c., 'there is no doubt,' 'without doubt'), ĀśvŚr.; Mn.; MBh. &c.; a doubtful matter, Car.; (in Nyāya) doubt about the point to be discussed (one of the 16 categories), IW. 64; difficulty, danger, risk of or in or to (gen., loc., or comp.), ĀśvGṛ.; MBh. &c.; *-kara*, mf(*ī*)n. causing doubt or risk, dangerous to (comp.), Śiś.; *-kāraṇârthâpatti-pūrva-paksha-rahasya*, n., *-kāraṇârthâpatti-rahasya*, n. N. of Nyāya wks.; *-gata*, mfn. fallen into danger, Śak.; *-ccheda*, m. the solution of doubt (*°dya*, mfn. relating to it), Ragh.; *-cchedin*, mfn. clearing all doubt, decisive, Śak.; *-tattva-nirūpaṇa*, n., *-pakshatā-rahasya*, n., *-pakshatā-vāda*, m., *-parīkshā*, f., *-vāda*, m., *-vādârtha*, m. N. of wks.; *-sama*, m. (in Nyāya) one of the 24 Jātis or self-confuting replies, Nyāyas.; Sarvad. (cf. IW. 64); *-sama-prakaraṇa*, n. N. of wk.; *-stha*, mfn. being in uncertainty, doubtful, W.; *°yâkshepa*, m. 'removal of doubt,' a partic. figure of speech, Kāvyâd. ii, 163; 164; *°yâtmaka*, mfn. consisting of doubt, dubious, uncertain, Pañcat.; *°yâtman*, mfn. having a doubtful mind, a sceptic, Bhag.; Sarvad.; *°yânumiti*, f., *°yânumiti-rahasya*, n. N. of wks.; *°yâpanna*, mfn. beset with doubt, dubious (*-mānasa*, mfn. irresolute in mind), W.; *°yâvaha*, mfn. causing danger, dangerous to (gen. or comp.), MBh.; *°yôcchedin*, mfn. resolving doubts, Hit., Introd.; *°yôpamā*, f. a comparison expressed in the form of a doubt, Kāvyâd. ii, 26; *°yôpêta*, mfn. possessed of uncertainty, doubtful, uncertain, MW. **°śayālu**, mfn. disposed to doubt, doubtful or sceptical about (loc.), Naish. **°śayita**, mfn. irresolute, doubtful about (comp.), KātyŚr.; R.; subject to doubt, uncertain, dubious, questionable, MBh.; Kām.; n. doubt, uncertainty, MBh. **°śayitavya**, mfn. to be called in doubt, dubious, problematical, Śaṃk. **°śayitṛi**, mfn. one who hesitates, a doubter, sceptic, L. **°śayin**, mfn. doubtful, dubious, questionable, MW.

Saṃ-śīti, f. = *saṃ-śaya*, doubt, uncertainty, Kād.; Hcar.

संशीत *saṃ-śīta, saṃ-śīna.* See *saṃ-√śyai.*

संशीलन *saṃ-śīlana*, n. regular practice, habitual performance, Sarvad.; frequent intercourse with (gen.), Kāv.

संशुच् *saṃ-śuc*, P. *-śocati*, to flame or blaze together, ŚBr.; to mourn, regret, bewail, MBh.; (*-śīcyati*), to cause pain to (gen.), ŚBr.: Caus. *-śocayati* (ind. p. *-śocya*), to mourn, lament, MBh.

Saṃ-śoka, (prob.) m. = *sveda*, 'sweat,' 'moist heat,' in next. **-ja**, mfn. produced from moist heat (cf. *sveda-ja*), Bādar.

संशुध् *saṃ-√śudh*, P. *-śudhyati*, to become completely pure or purified, MW.: Caus. *-śodhayati*, to purify or cleanse thoroughly, clear, MBh.; Rājat.; to clear (expenses), pay off, R.; Kathās.; to clear, secure (as a road against attack), Mn. vii, 185; to subtract, VarBṛS.; to divide, Gaṇit.

Saṃ-śuddha, mfn. completely purified or cleansed, pure, clean, Yājñ.; BhP.; removed, destroyed, expiated (see comp.); cleared off, defrayed, paid, Kathās.; searched, tried, examined, Mn. vii, 219; acquitted (of a crime), W.; *-kilbisha*, mfn. one whose offences are expiated, purified from sin, Bhag. **°śuddhi**, f. perfect purification or purity (also in a ritual sense), Bhag.; Kām.; cleaning (the body), W.; acquittal, acquittance, ib.; correction, rectification, ib.

Saṃ-śodhana, mf(*ī*)n. (fr. Caus.) completely purifying, destroying impurity (of the bodily humours), Suśr.; n. purification or a means of p°, Suśr.; refining, clearing, W.; paying off, correcting, ib.; *-śamanīya*, mfn. treating of purifying and calming remedies, Suśr. °**śodhita,** mfn. completely cleansed and purified &c.; cleared off, paid, Kathās. °**śodhya,** mfn. to be completely cleansed &c.; to be purged, Car.; to be paid or acquitted (as a debt), W.; to be corrected or rectified, ib.

संशुभ् *saṃ-√śubh*, Ā. *-śobhate*, to look beautiful, be radiant or splendid, TBr.; MBh.; to shine equally with (instr.), RV.: Caus. *-śobhayati*, to decorate, adorn, beautify, AV.

Saṃ-śobhita, mfn. (fr. Caus.) adorned or shining with (instr.), Ṛitus.

संशुष् *saṃ-√1. śush*, P. *-śushyati* (ep. also °*te*), to be completely dried or dried up, MBh.; Kāv. &c.: Caus. *-śoshayati*, to make dry, dry up, ib.

Saṃ-śushka, mf(*ā*)n. completely dried up or withered, MBh.; Kāv. &c.; *-māṅsa-tvak-snāyu*, mfn. one whose flesh and skin and sinews are completely dried up or withered, MBh.; °*kāsya*, mfn. having a withered face, ib.

Saṃ-śosha, m. complete drying, drying up, VarBṛS. °**śoshaṇa,** n. id., MBh.; Suśr.; mfn. making dry, drying up, Car. °**śoshita,** mfn. (fr. Caus.) made thoroughly dry, dried up, MW. °**śoshin,** mfn. drying up, making dry, Subh. (said of a partic. form of fever, Bhpr.)

संशून *saṃ-śūna*, mfn. (√*śvi*) much swelled, swollen, Bhaṭṭ.

संशृङ्गी *saṃ-śṛiṅgī*, f. (fr. *sam* and *śṛiṅga*) a cow whose horns are bent towards each other, MaitrS.

संशॄ *saṃ-√śṝi*, P. *-śṛiṇāti*, to smash to pieces, crush, Br.; ĀśvGṛ.: Pass. *-śīryate* (aor. *-śāri*; pf. *-śaśre*), to be crushed, break down, RV.; AV.; to be dissipated or routed, fly in different directions, MBh.: Desid., see *saṃ-śiśarishu*.

Saṃ-śará, m. crushing, breaking, rending, VS.; TBr. °**śaraṇa,** n. the commencement of a combat, charge, attack, L. (prob. w.r. for *saṃ-saraṇa*).

Saṃ-śāruka, mfn. breaking down (in *a-s*°), Kap.

Saṃ-śiśarishu, mfn. (fr. Desid.) wishing to rend or tear, Nir. vi, 31.

संशो *saṃ-√śo*, P. Ā. *-śiśāti*, *-śiśite* (once *-śyati*, RV. i, 130, 4), to whet or sharpen thoroughly (Ā. 'one's own weapons'), RV.; TS.; ŚBr.; to urge, excite, speed, make ready, prepare, RV.; AV.; Br.; KātyŚr.

Saṃ-śāna, n. N. of various Sāmans, ĀrshBr.

Sáṃ-śita, mfn. (often wrongly written *śaṅsita* or *saṃsita*) whetted, sharpened, ŚBr.; pointed, sharp (see comp.); ready, prepared for or resolved upon (loc.), AV.; MBh. &c.; made ready, well-prepared, all right (applied to things), VS.; AV.; fixed upon, decided, firmly adhered to, rigid (as a vow), Mn.; MBh. &c.; completing, effecting, diligent in accomplishing, W.; m. N. of a man, g. *gargādi* (cf. *sāṃśitya*); *-tapas*, mfn. exposed or subjected to painful austerities or mortifications (said of a Śūdra), MBh.; *-vāc*, mfn. using harsh or sharp language, MBh.; *-vrata*, mfn. (*sáṃ-ś*°) firmly adhering to a vow, faithful to an obligation, honest, virtuous, ŚBr.; Mn.; MBh. &c.; m. a Ṛishi, Gal.; °*tātman*, mfn. one who has completely made up his mind, firmly resolved, MBh.

Saṃ-śiti, f. excessive sharpening, AitBr.

संश्चत् *saṃ-ś-cat*, m. (prob. fr. √*cat*) a juggler, rogue (= *kuhaka*), Uṇ. ii, 85, Sch. (v.l. *saṃ-śvat*); n. deceit, trick, illusion, juggling, W.

Saṃ-ścāya, Nom. (fr. prec.) Ā. °*yate*, g. *bhṛiśādi*.

संश्यै *saṃ-√śyai*, cl. 1. P. Ā. *-śyāyati*, °*te*, only in the forms below.

Saṃ-śīta, mfn. congealed, frozen, cold, cool, ŚārṅgS.

Saṃ-śīna, mfn. id., Car.

Saṃ-śyāna, mfn. id.; contracted, shrunk or rolled up together, collapsed, Kāś. on Pāṇ. vi, 1, 24.

संश्रद्धा *saṃ-śrad-√dhā* (only ind. p. *-dhāya*), to have complete faith in, believe, BhP.

संश्रान्त *saṃ-śrānta*, mfn. (√*śram*) completely wearied, languid, exhausted, MBh.; BhP.

संश्राव *saṃ-śrāva* &c. See *saṃ-śrāva*.

संश्रि *saṃ-√śri*, P. Ā. *-śrayati*, °*te* (aor. *-aśret*, RV.), to join together with, furnish with (Ā. 'to join one's self or connect one's self with'), RV.; AV.; TāṇḍBr.; to join or attach one's self to, go for refuge or succour to, resort or betake one's self to, cling to for protection, seek the help of (acc.), Mn.; MBh. &c.; to approach, go to any one with (instr.), R.; to approach for sexual union, MBh.; to rest or depend on (acc.), Mālatīm.; to obtain, acquire, Mn. x, 60; to serve, MW.

Saṃ-śiśrīshu, mfn. (fr. Desid.) wishing to have recourse to (acc.), Bhaṭṭ.

Saṃ-śraya, m. (ifc. f. *ā*) conjunction, combination, connection, association (ifc. 'joined or connected with'), relationship or reference to (ifc. 'relating to,' 'referring to;' *āt*, ind. 'in consequence of'), MBh.; Kāv. &c.; going or resorting or betaking one's self to any person or place (loc. or comp.), going for refuge or protection, having recourse to (cf. *kali-s*°), MBh.; Pañcat. &c.; league, alliance, leaguing together for mutual protection (one of the 6 Guṇas of a king), Mn. vii, 160; Yājñ. &c.; a refuge, asylum, shelter, resting or dwelling-place, residence, home (ifc. 'residing with,' 'living or dwelling or resting in or on'), MBh.; Kāv. &c.; devotion to, attachment to (ifc. 'devoted or attached to;' *āt*, ind. 'by means or help of'), MBh.; R. &c.; an aim, object, MW.; a piece or portion belonging to anything, MBh.; N. of a Prajā-pati, R.; *-kārita*, mfn. caused by alliance, Mn. vii, 176. °**śrayaṇa,** n. (ifc.) clinging to, attachment, MBh. °**śrayaṇīya,** mfn. to be resorted to, to be sought for protection (*-tā*, f.), Kām.

Saṃ-śrayitavya, mfn. to be sought for refuge (as a fortress), Pañcat.

Saṃ-śrayin, mfn. having recourse to, seeking protection; m. a subject, servant, Kām.; (ifc.) dwelling or resting or being in, Ragh.; Rājat.; Kathās.

Sáṃ-śrita, mfn. joined or united with (instr. or comp.), AV. &c. &c.; leaning against, clinging to (acc.), MBh.; R.; clung to, embraced, Kum.; one who has gone or fled to any one for protection, one who has entered the service of (acc. or comp.), Mn.; MBh. &c.; one who has betaken himself to a place, living or dwelling or staying or situated or being in (loc. or comp.), MBh.; Kāv. &c.; resorted to, sought for refuge or protection, MBh.; one who is addicted to, indulging in (acc.), Bhag.; Pañcat.; one who has laid hold of or embraced or chosen, MBh.; inherent in, peculiar to (acc. or comp.), MBh.; R.; relating to, concerning (loc. or comp.), ib.; BhP.; suitable, fit, proper, MBh. xii, 4102; m. a servant, adherent, dependant, Mn.; MBh. &c.; *-vat*, mfn. one who has joined or united himself with (instr.), Śak.; °*tānurāga*, m. the affection of dependants, MW. °**śritavya,** w.r. for °*śrayitavya*, Pañcat.

संश्री *saṃ-√śrī*, P. *-śrīṇati*, to join or unite or connect with, cause to partake of (instr.), TāṇḍBr.

संश्रु *saṃ-√1. śru*, P. Ā. *-śṛiṇoti*, *-śṛiṇute*, to hear or learn from (e.g. *mukhāt*, 'from any one's mouth'), attend or listen attentively to (acc.), MBh.; Kāv. &c.; to assent, promise (loc. or dat.), ib.; (Ā.) to be distinctly heard or audible, ŚāṅkhBr. (cf. Pāṇ. i, 3, 29, Vārtt. 2, Pat.): Pass. *-śrūyate*, to be heard or talked about or read about (*yathā saṃśrūyate*, 'as people say' or 'as we read in books'), MBh.: Caus. *-śrāvayati*, to cause to hear or to be heard, proclaim, announce (*nāma*, 'one's name'), relate or report anything (acc.) to any one (acc. or dat.), Yājñ.; to read out (see *saṃ-śrāvita*); to make resound, MBh.

Saṃ-śrava, m. hearing, listening (loc., 'within hearing'), MBh.; Mālatīm.; assent, promise, agreement, L.; mfn. audible (see *vidūra-saṃśrava*). °**śravaṇa,** n. the act of hearing or listening, MBh.; Suśr.; Sarvad.; (ifc.) hearing about, Hariv.; range of hearing, earshot (loc., 'within hearing, aloud'), MBh.; R.; Car. °**śrávas,** n. perfect glory or renown, Vait.; (*sáṃ-*), m. N. of a man (having the patr. Sauvarcanasa), TS.; °*saḥ-sāma*, N. of a Sāman, ĀrshBr.

Saṃ-śrāva, m. (ifc.) hearing, listening to, Kauś.
°**śrāvaka,** m. a hearer, disciple, Kāraṇḍ. °**śrāvam,** see *a-saṃśrāvam*. °**śrāvayitṛi,** m. (fr. Caus.) an announcer, crier, proclaimer, KaushUp.; *-mat*, mfn. having an announcer, ib. °**śrāvita,** mfn. (fr. id.) read out or aloud, Kathās. °**śrāvya,** mfn. audible (in *a-saṃśrāvyam*, v.l. for °*śrāvam*, q.v.); not to be caused to hear anything, not to be informed of (acc.), R.

Saṃ-śruta, mfn. well heard, learnt, Yājñ.; MBh. &c.; read about in (loc.), MBh.; agreed, promised to (gen.), MBh.; R. &c.; m. N. of a man, Pāṇ. vi, 2, 148, Sch. °**śrutya,** m. N. of a son of Viśvāmitra, MBh.

संश्रेषिण *saṃ-śreshiṇá*, m. perhaps 'the N. of a combat in which Indra is said to have engaged on a certain occasion,' AV.

संश्लाघ् *saṃ-√ślāgh*, Ā. *-ślāghate*, to vaunt or boast of (instr.), MBh.

संश्लिष् *saṃ-√ślish*, P. Ā. *-ślishyati*, °*te*, to stick or attach one's self to (acc.), Baudh.; Kām.; R. (cf. Pāṇ. iii, 1, 46, Sch.); to clasp, embrace, MBh.; R. &c.; to bring into close contact or immediate connection with (instr.), MBh.: Caus. *-śleshayati*, to connect, join, put together, unite or bring into contact with (instr. or loc.), Āpast.; Hariv.; Kathās.; to transfer to (loc.), Kull. on Mn. viii, 317; to attract, Kām.

Sáṃ-ślishṭa, mfn. clasped or pressed together, contiguous, coherent, closely connected with (instr. with and without *saha*, acc., or comp.), ŚBr. &c. &c.; coalescent, blended together, Prāt.; confused, indeterminate (as an action which is neither good nor bad), MBh.; endowed with, possessed of (instr.; *kiṃcij jīvitāśayā*, 'having a slight hope of life'), Pañcat.; m. a kind of pavilion, Vāstuv.; n. a heap, mass, multitude, R.; *-karman*, mfn. not distinguishing between good and evil actions, MBh. xii, 4220 (v.l. *saṃ-klishṭa-k*°); *-śarīra-kārin*, mfn. (pl.) putting their bodies together, i.e. dwelling or living together, MBh.

Saṃ-ślesha, m. (ifc. f. *ā*) junction, union, connection, close contact with (instr. or comp.; °*shaṃ √labh*, 'to attain, participate in'), MBh.; Kāv. &c.; embracing, an embrace, Kālid.; a joint, SāmavBr.; a bond, thong, MBh. °**śleshaṇa,** mf(*ī*)n. joining, connecting, ŚāṅkhBr.; n. clinging or sticking to, Dhātup.; the act of putting together or joining, Suśr.; a means of binding together, bond, cement &c., ŚāṅkhBr.; ĀpŚr.; Uttarar. °**śleshita,** mfn. (fr. Caus.) joined together, united, attached, MBh. °**śleshin,** mfn. clasping, embracing, joining together, ŚāṅkhBr.

संश्लोक *saṃ-√ślok*, P. *-ślokayati*, to celebrate in Ślokas or hymns, praise, BhP.

संश्वत् *saṃ-śvat*. See *saṃ-ś-cat*, col. 1.

संश्वायिन् *saṃ-śvāyin*, mfn. (√*śvi*) swelling (see *ubhayataḥ-s*°).

संष्ठुल *saṃshṭhula*. See *vi-s*°, p. 953, col. 1.

संसंयु *saṃ-saṃ-√2. yu* (only Ā. 2. sg. pr. *-yuvase*), to unite completely with one's self, consume, devour, RV. x, 191, 1.

संसच् *saṃ-√sac*, Ā. *-sacate*, to be connected with (instr.), RV. vi, 55, 1.

संसञ्ज् *saṃ-√sañj*, Pass. *-sajyate*, *-sajjate* (°*ti*; pf. *saṃ-sajjatuḥ*, MBh.), to adhere, stick to (loc.), MBh.; to encounter, engage in close combat with (instr.; also 'to attack,' with acc.), ib.; BhP.; to hesitate, falter (in voice), MBh.; R.; to flow together, be joined, MBh.; to be occasioned, arise (as a battle), ib.; (P.) to attach to a yoke, harness, ib.; MBh. ix, 819 (B.)

Saṃ-sakta, mfn. adhered or stuck together, met, encountered (also as enemies), MBh.; Hariv. &c.; sticking fast, faltering (speech), Hariv.; closely connected, united, Pañcar.; VāyuP.; fixed on or directed towards, occupied with, devoted to, intent upon, fond of (loc. or comp.), MBh.; Kāv. &c.; given to the world or mundane pleasures, BhP.; enamoured, MārkP.; endowed or furnished with (comp.), Hariv.; HParis.; close, near, adjoining, contiguous, MBh.; Kāv.; VarBṛS.; compact, dense, uninterrupted, continuous, R.; Kālid.; Kathās.; dependent, conditional, R.; *-citta*, mfn. (pl., with *itaretaram*) having their hearts (mutually) joined, heartily devoted to each other, Rājat.; *-cetas,* mfn. (= *-manas*), Cat.; *-jala,* mf(*ā*)n. joining or mingling its waters with (comp.), Ragh.; *-tā,* f. close adherence, Daś.; *-manas,* mfn. having the mind attached or fixed, MBh.; *-yuga,* mfn. attached to a yoke, harnessed, yoked, MW.; *-vadanâśvāsa,* mfn. having the breath adhering to the mouth, with suppressed breath, MBh.; *-hasta,* mfn. having the hands joined with (comp.), Ṛitus. °**sakti,** f. close connection or contact with (comp.), Śiś.; Rājat.; tying or fastening together, W.; intercourse, intimacy, acquaintance, ib.; addiction or devotion to, ib.

Saṃ-saṅga, m. connection, conjunction, Nir.; Lāṭy. °**saṅgin,** mfn. clinging or adhering to, coming into close contact or near relation (°*ginī-tva,* n.), Bhartṛ.; Śiś.

Saṃ-sajjamāna, mfn. adhering or sticking close together &c.; hesitating, stammering, faltering, MBh.; being prepared or ready, W.

संसद् *saṃ-√sad,* P. *-sīdati* (Ved. also °*te* and *-sadati*), to sit down together with (instr.) or upon (acc.), sit down, RV.; VS.; to sink down, collapse, be discouraged or distressed, pine away (with *kshudhā,* 'to perish with hunger'), Mn.; MBh. &c.: Caus. *-sādayati,* to cause to sit down together, RV.; TS.; Br.; ŚrS.; to meet, encounter (acc.), BhP.; to weigh down, afflict, distress, R.

Saṃ-sád, f. 'sitting together,' an assembly, meeting, congress, session, court of justice or of a king, RV. &c. &c.; (*saṃsadām ayana,* n. a partic. ceremony or festival of 24 days, ŚrS.); a multitude, number, R.; mfn. one who sits together, one who sits at or takes part in a sacrifice, MW. °**sada,** m. = *saṃsadām ayana* (above), KātyŚr. °**sadana,** n. dejectedness, depression, Car.

Saṃ-sāda, m. a meeting, assembly, company, MW. (cf. *strī-shaṃsādá*). °**sādana,** n. (fr. Caus.) putting together, arranging, KātyŚr.

Saṃ-sīdana, n. sinking, Divyâv.

संसन् *saṃ-√san,* P. *-sanoti,* to obtain, ŚāṅkhBr.

Saṃ-sanana, n. obtaining, acquiring, acquisition (in *anna-saṃs*°, used for explaining *vāja-sāti*), Nir. xii, 45.

संसप्तक *saṃ-saptaka,* w. r. for *saṃ-śaptaka;* (*ī*), f. a girdle, Gal.

संसमक *sáṃ-samaka,* mfn. united together, joined together, AV.

संसरण *saṃ-saraṇa.* See *saṃ-√sṛi,* col. 2.

संसर्ग *saṃ-sarga, saṃ-sarjana* &c. See *saṃ-√sṛij,* col. 3.

संसर्प *saṃ-sarpa,* °*paṇa* &c. See *saṃ-√sṛip,* p. 1120, col. 1

संसर्या *saṃsaryā,* ind. (with *√kṛi* &c.), g. *sâkshād-ādi.*

संसव *saṃ-sava,* m. (*√3. su*) a simultaneous Soma sacrifice, commingling or confusion of libations (when two Brāhmans perform the Soma sacrifice on the same spot and at the same time; held to be sinful), AitBr.; ŚrS.

संसह् *saṃ-√sah,* Ā. *-sahate,* to cope with, be a match for (acc.), MBh.; to bear, resist, hold out, stand, ib.; R.

Saṃ-saha, mfn. (ifc.) equal to, a match for, Bhaṭṭ.

संसहस्र *sáṃ-sahasra,* mfn. accompanied by a thousand, RV.

संसहायक *saṃ-sahāyaka,* m. a comrade, companion, MatsyaP.

संसाध् *saṃ-√sādh,* Caus. *-sādhayati,* to cause to be completely finished, accomplish, perform (with *marum* [q. v.] 'to practice abstinence from drinking'), Mn.; MBh. &c.; to overpower, subdue, MBh.; Hariv.; R.; to prepare food, MBh. i, 2841; to procure, provide, Kathās.; to get, attain, ib.; BhP.; to be successful, MBh. iii, 1478; to enforce (payment or the fulfilment of a promise), recover (a debt), Mn. viii, 50; to dismiss (a guest), Āpast.; to promote to (dat.), MBh. vii, 8389; to destroy, kill, extinguish, MW.: Pass. of Caus. *-sādhyate,* to be completely accomplished, ib.; to be thoroughly provided or furnished with, ib.

Saṃ-sādhaka, mfn. wishing to conquer or win, BhP. °**sādhana,** n. performance, accomplishment, fulfilment, MBh.; preparation, Kull. on Mn. xi, 95. °**sādhya,** mfn. to be accomplished or performed, Bhar.; MārkP.; to be got or obtained, R.: to be overcome or subdued, conquerable, MBh.; Hariv.

संसार *saṃ-sāra* &c. See *saṃ-√sṛi* below.

संसिच् *saṃ-√sic,* P. Ā. *-siñcati,* °*te,* to pour together, pour upon, sprinkle over, RV.; AV.; Suśr.; to cast, form, AV.

Saṃ-sikta, mfn. well sprinkled or moistened, MBh.; Kāv. &c.; *-reṇu,* mfn. having the dust laid or well watered, MW.

Saṃ-sic, mfn. pouring, shedding together, AV.

Saṃ-seka, m. sprinkling over, moistening, watering, R.; Rājat.

संसिध् *saṃ-√3. sidh,* P. *-sidhyati* (ep. also °*te*), to be accomplished or performed thoroughly, succeed, Pañcat.; to attain beatitude or bliss, Mn.; MBh.; BhP.

Saṃ-siddha, mfn. fully or thoroughly performed or accomplished, R.; attained, won, VarYogay.; Pur.; dressed, prepared (as food), R.; Hariv.; made, done, Hariv.; Kathās.; healed, cured, restored, MBh.; Kathās.; ready for (dat.), R.; firmly resolved, ib.; satisfied, contented, ib.; clever, skilled in (loc.), MBh.; one who has attained beatitude, MBh.; R.; Pur.; *-rasa,* mfn. = *rasa-siddha* (q. v.), Caṇḍ.; *-rūpa,* mfn. one who has his form restored, MBh.; °*ddhârtha,* mfn. one who has attained his goal, successful, R. °**siddhi,** f. complete accomplishment or fulfilment, perfection, success, Gobh.; MBh. &c.; perfect state, beatitude, final emancipation, Mn.; MBh.; Pur.; the last consequence or result, BhP.; fixed or settled opinion, the last or decisive word, R. (L. also = 'nature;' 'natural state or quality;' 'a passionate or intoxicated woman').

संसिव् *saṃ-√siv,* P. *-sīvyati,* to sew together, AV.

Saṃ-syūta, mfn. sewn together, inseparably connected, MBh.; interwoven with (instr.), ib.

संसु *saṃ-√3. su,* P. *-sunoti,* to press out Soma together, TS.; TBr.; Kāṭh.

Saṃsuta-soma, m. = *saṃ-sava,* Lāṭy.

संसुखित *saṃ-sukhita,* mfn. perfectly delighted or gratified. Lalit.

संसुदे *saṃ-súde.* See *saṃ-√svad.*

संसुप्त *saṃ-supta,* mfn. (*√svap*) soundly asleep, fast asleep, sleeping, MBh.; Kāv. &c.

संसू *saṃ-√2. sū,* Ā. *-sūte, -sūyate,* to bring forth, give birth to (acc.), Hariv.; to cause, produce, Subh.

संसूच् *saṃ-√sūc,* P. *-sūcayati,* to indicate or show plainly, imply, betray, tell, Kāv.; Var.; Kathās.: Pass. *-sūcyate,* to be indicated &c., Ṛitus.

Saṃ-sūcaka, mfn. indicating plainly, showing, betraying, MārkP. °**sūcana,** n. the act of indicating or betraying, Daś.; manifesting, uttering, MBh.; reproving, reproaching, MW. °**sūcita,** mfn. indicated, displayed, manifested, shown, BhP.; Pañcat.; informed, told, apprised, MW.; reproved, ib. °**sūcin,** mfn. = °*sūcaka,* Subh. °**sūcya,** mfn. to be indicated or manifested or betrayed, Daśar.

संसृ *saṃ-√sṛi,* P. *-sarati* (m. c. also °*te*), to flow together with (instr.), RV. ix, 97, 45; to go about, wander or walk or roam through, MBh.; Kāv. &c.; to walk or pass through (a succession of states), undergo transmigration, enter or pass into (acc.), Mn.; MBh. &c.; to be diffused or spread into (acc.), MBh.; to come forth, BhP.: Caus. *-sārayati,* to cause to pass through a succession of states or to undergo transmigration, Mn.; BhP.; to introduce, push into (loc.), MBh. xii, 7878; to put off, defer, ib. v, 1004; to use, employ, ib. xii, 11,932.

Saṃ-saraṇa, n. going about, walking or wandering through, MBh.; passing through a succession of states, birth and rebirth of living beings, the world, BhP.; Sarvad.; the unobstructed march of an army, L.; the commencement of war or battle, L.; a highway, principal road, L.; a resting-place for passengers near the gates of a city, W.

Saṃ-sāra, m. going or wandering through, undergoing transmigration, MaitrUp.; course, passage, passing through a succession of states, circuit of mundane existence, transmigration, metempsychosis, the world, secular life, worldly illusion (*ā saṃsārāt,* 'from the beginning of the world'), Up.; Mn.; MBh. &c.; w. r. for *saṃ-cāra,* Bhartṛ. — **kānana,** n. the world compared to a forest, Sch. on Uṇ. i, 108 (in a quotation). — **kāntāra,** m. n., id., AshṭāvS. — **kārā-gṛiha,** n. the w° comp° to a prison, Siṃhâs. — **kūpa,** m. the world comp° to a well or pit, BhP. — **gamana,** n. passing from one state of existence to another, transmigration, Mn. i, 117. — **guru,** m. the world's Guru (applied to Kāma, god of love), L. — **cakra,** n. the world comp° to a wheel, MaitrUp. — **taraṇi** or °**ṇī,** f. N. of wk. — **taru,** m. the w° comp° to a tree, BhP. — **duḥkha,** n. the pain or sorrows of the w°, ib. — **nirṇaya,** m. N. of wk. — **patha,** m. 'the world's passage,' the female organ, Gal. — **padavī,** f. the road of the world, BhP.; = prec., L. — **paritāpa,** m. = *-duḥkha,* BhP. — **parivartana,** n. the turning round or revolution of the w°, MBh. — **pariśrama,** m. the toils or troubles of the w°, BhP. — **bandhana,** n. the bonds or fetters of the world, MārkP. — **bīja,** n. the seed or origin of the world, Sarvad. — **maṇḍala,** n. the circle or wheel of the world, Śiś.; Śaṃk. — **mārga,** m. = *-padavī,* Subh. — **mukti-kāraṇa-vāda,** m. N. of wk. — **moksha,** m. emancipation from the w°, ŚvetUp. — **mokshaṇa,** n. id., MW.; mf(*ī*)n. liberating from mundane existence, ib. — **vat,** mfn. possessing or liable to mundane ex°, AshṭāvS. — **vana,** n. = *-kānana,* Bhartṛ. (v. l.) — **varjita,** mfn. freed from m° ex°, Sarvad. — **vartman,** n. = *-mārga,* Subh. — **viṭapâṅkura,** m. a shoot or sprout on the tree of m° ex°, AshṭāvS. — **visha-vṛiksha,** m. the poison-tree of m° ex°, Cat. — **vṛiksha,** m. the tree of m° ex°, Cāṇ. — **śrānta-citta,** mfn. wearied in mind by (the miseries of) the world, ib. — **saṅga,** m. attachment to the w°, Bhartṛ. — **samudra,** m. the ocean-like w°, Pañcat. — **saraṇi,** f. = *-padavī,* Bhartṛ. — **sāgara,** m. = *-samudra,* Kṛishṇaj. — **sāra,** m. the quintessence of (the joys of) the world, Dhūrtas. — **sārathi,** m. the charioteer of m° ex° (applied to Śiva), Śivag. — **sukha,** n. the joys of the world, Caurap. **Saṃsārâṅgāra,** m. the fire of m° ex°, Sarvad. (cf. next). **Saṃsārânala,** m. the fire of m° ex°, Vedântas. **Saṃsārânta,** m. the end of m° ex° or of human life, Bhartṛ. **Saṃsārâbdhi** or °**rârṇava,** m. the ocean of the world, Pañcar. **Saṃsārâvarta,** m. N. of wk. **Saṃsārôdadhi,** m. the ocean-like world, Bhartṛ.

Saṃ-sāraṇa, n. (fr. Caus.) setting in motion, causing to move away (a car), KātyŚr.; w. r. for *-saraṇa,* AshṭāvS.

Saṃ-sārin, mfn. moving far and wide, extensive, comprehensive (as intellect), MBh.; transmigratory, attached to mundane existence (°*ri-tva,* n.), BhP.; Vedântas.; Sarvad.; worldly, mundane, mixing with society, W.; m. a living or sentient being, animal, creature, man (with *sva,* 'a relative'), Śāntiś.; Mālatīm.; HPariś.; (°*ry-ātman,* m. [perhaps rather two separate words] the transmigratory soul, the soul passing through various mundane states [opp. to *paramâtman*], MW.)

Saṃ-sṛiti, f. course, revolution, (esp.) passage through successive states of existence, course of mundane existence, transmigration, the world (*-cakra,* n., and *-cakra-vāla,* n. 'the wheel or circle of mundane existence'), AshṭāvS.; BhP.

संसृज् *saṃ-√sṛij,* P. Ā. *-sṛijati,* °*te* (2. sg. aor. *-srāḥ,* AV.), to hit with (instr.), RV. i, 33, 13; to visit or afflict with (instr.), AV. xi, 2, 26; to join or unite or mix or mingle or endow or present with (instr.), RV.; AV.; VS.; Br.; Āp.; MBh.; (with *yudhaḥ*) to engage in battle, AV. x, 10, 24; to create, ŚvetUp.; Pur.; (Ā.) to share anything with others, MaitrS.; (Ā. or Pass.) to join one's self, be joined or united or mingled or confused, come into contact with, meet (as friends or foes, also applied to sexual intercourse; with instr. with or without *saha*), RV. &c. &c.: Caus. *-sarjayati,* to attract, win over, conciliate, Baudh.; Kām.; to furnish with (instr.), provide any one with anything, Car.: Desid. *-sisṛikshati,* to wish to create together or to partake of creation, BhP.

Saṃ-sarga, mfn. commingling, combining (intr.), KātyŚr.; m. (ifc. f. *ā*) mixture or union together, commixture, blending, conjunction, connection, contact, association, society, sexual union, intercourse with (gen., instr. with and without *saha,* loc., or comp.), ŚrS.; Prāt.; MBh. &c.; confusion, MānGṛ.; Hariv.; indulging in, partaking of (comp.), R.; Daś.; BhP.; sensual attachment, Mn. vi, 72; a partic. conjunction of celestial bodies, AV.Pariś.; a partic. combination of two humours which produces diseases (cf. *saṃ-nipāta*), Suśr.; community of goods, Dāyabh.; duration, MBh. iii, 11,238; point of intersection, Śulbas.; acquaintance, familiarity, W.; co-existence (= *samavâya*), ib.; (*ī*), f., see below; *-ja*, mfn. produced by union or contact, Suśr.; *-tas*, ind. through union or connection, in consequence of intercourse or familiarity, MW.; *-dosha*, m. the fault or evil consequences of association (with bad people), ib.; *-vat*, mfn. being in contact, connected with (comp.; also *-tva*, n.), Kālid.; *-vidyā*, f. the art of intercourse with men, social science, MBh.; °*gâbhāva*, m. (in Nyāya) a partic. form of the category of non-existence (said to be of three kinds, prior, incidental, and final, or absence of birth, destruction of present being, and necessary cessation of existence); *-prakaraṇa*, n. N. of wk. °**sargaka** (ifc.) = *saṃsarga*, Kusum. °**sargaya**, Nom. P. °*yati*, to gather or assemble (trans.) together or round, Bhaṭṭ. °**sargin**, mfn. commingled, mixed together, joined or connected or in contact with (comp.), Kāv.; Pur.; partaking or possessed of (comp.), Śaṃk.; one who lives together with his relatives (after partition of the family inheritance), Dāyabh.; familiar, friendly, acquainted, W.; m. an associate, companion, MW.; (°*gi*)*-tā*, f. (Kull.), *-tva*, n. (ĀpŚr.) connection, contact, combination, association. °**sargī**, f. purification, purging (in med.), Car.

Saṃ-sarjana, n. meeting, mingling, mixture or combination with (instr.), ĀśvŚr.; AV.Pariś.; attracting, winning over, conciliating, Kām.; = *saṃsargī*, Car.; discharging, voiding, abandoning, leaving, W.

Saṃ-sisṛikshu, mfn. (fr. Desid.) wishing to mix together or unite, W.

Saṃ-sṛij, f. commingling, collision, RV. x, 84, 6.

Sáṃ-sṛishṭa, mfn. gathered together, collected, RV. x, 84, 7; brought forth or born together (as a litter of animals), VS.; associated or connected together (as partners or brothers who combine their property after division), Mn.; Yājñ.; united, combined, mingled or mixed with, involved in (instr.), VS.; ŚBr.; R. &c.; nearly related or acquainted, friendly, familiar, MBh.; R.; Hariv.; affected with (comp.), Suśr.; connected with, belonging to (comp.), Hariv.; mixed, of various kinds, both good and bad in quality &c., ŚBr.; Car.; accomplished, performed (cf. *-maithuna*); cleared through vomiting &c., L.; cleanly dressed, W.; created, MW.; m. N. of a fabulous mountain, Kāraṇḍ.; (*am*), n. near relationship, friendship, intimacy (°*ṭam* √*car*, with loc., 'to enter on intimate relations with'), AitBr.; MBh.; *-karman*, mfn. denoting mixed or various actions, Nir.; *-jit*, mfn. victorious in contest, RV.; *-tva*, n. commixture, union, association, Śaṃk.; (in law) voluntary reunion or co-residence of kinsmen (as of father and son or of brothers with each other, after partition of the family property), Dāyabh.; *-dhayá*, mfn. sucking (as a calf) and left with (the cow), TBr.; *-bhāva*, m. near relationship, friendship, R.; *-maithuna*, mf(*ā*)n. one who has performed sexual intercourse, Yājñ.; *-rūpa*, mfn. mixed in form or kind, adulterated, W.; *-homa*, m. a common oblation (to Agni and Sūrya), TBr. °**sṛishṭi** (*sáṃ-*), f. union, combination, association, intercourse, MaitrS.; living together in one family, W.; collection, collecting, assembling, ib.; (in rhet.) the association of two distinct metaphors in close proximity in one sentence (cf. *saṃkara*), Vām.; Sāh. °**sṛishṭin**, m. a re-united kinsman (said of relatives who, after partition of the family inheritance, again live together, annulling the previous partition), Gaut.; Yājñ. &c.; a co-partner, co-parcener, W.

Sáṃ-srashṭṛi, mfn. one who engages in battle or contest, RV. x, 103, 3; united or connected with or concerned in anything, a partaker (opp. to *pari-drashṭṛi*, 'a beholder'), MBh.; one who mixes together or commingles, MW.

संसृप् *saṃ-√sṛip*, P. Ā. *-sarpati*, °*te*, to creep along, glide into (acc.), VS.; to go together, AitBr.; to move, glide along, MBh.; Kāv. &c.; to go to, approach (acc.), MBh.; to go away, withdraw from (abl.), Āpast.

Saṃ-sárpa, mfn. creeping, gliding (in a partic. formula), TS. (*saṃ-sarpá*, VS.); m. a partic. Catur-aha, ŚrS.; the intercalary month (occurring in a year in which there is a Kshaya-māsa), TS. &c.; creeping or gliding along, any equable or gentle motion, W. °**sarpaṇa**, n. creeping along, gliding, sneaking, Kād.; an unexpected attack, surprise, VarYogay.; mounting, ascent of (gen.), MBh. °**sarpat**, mfn. creeping or moving along; (°*sarpad*)*-dhvajinī-vimarda-vilasad-dhūlī-maya*, mf(*ī*)n. filled with dust rising from the tramp of a marching army, Kathās. °**sarpamāṇaka**, mfn. creeping, crawling, MBh. °**sarpin**, mfn. creeping, moving gently along, Kād.; floating or swimming about, Śiś.; (ifc.) reaching, extending to (°*pi-tā*, f.), Ragh.

संसेक *saṃ-seka*. See *saṃ-√sic*.

संसेव् *saṃ-√sev*, Ā. *-sevate*, to be associated with (used in explaining √*1. sac*), Nir.; to frequent, inhabit, Subh.; Pañcat.; to wait upon, attend on, serve, honour, worship, salute deferentially, MBh.; Kāv. &c.; to refresh, fan (said of the wind), R.; to court, fondle (carnally), Kāv.; Pañcat.; to be addicted or devoted to, use or employ or practise or perform continually, Mn.; MBh. &c.

Saṃ-sevana, n. waiting on, serving, doing homage, MārkP.; (only ifc.) using, employing, MBh.; exposing one's self to, Kathās.; association or intercourse with (gen.), Jātakam. °**sevā**, f. visiting, frequenting, BhP.; use, employment, ib.; attendance, reverence, worship, ib.; (ifc.) inclination to, predilection for, Rājat. °**sevita**, mfn. frequented, served &c. (cf. *kṛitâdi*). °**sevitṛi**, mfn. one who uses or employs, VarBṛS. °**sevin**, mfn. (ifc.) serving, worshipping, Cat. °**sevya**, mfn. to be (or being) frequented, Kathās.; to be served or worshipped, Pañcat.; to be used or employed or practised or indulged in, MBh.; BhP.

संस्कन्द् *saṃ-√skand*, P. *-skandati*, to drip or trickle off, ŚBr.

संस्कन्ध *sáṃ-skandha*, n. a partic. disease, AV.

संस्कृ *saṃ-s-√1. kṛi* (cf. *saṃ-kṛi*; *upa-s-kṛi* and *pari-sh-kṛi*), P. Ā. *-skaroti*, *-skurute* (impf. *sam-askurvata*, TS.; pf. *saṃ-caskāra*, Nir.; aor. *sam-askṛita*; Prec. *saṃ-skriyāt*, *saṃ-skṛishīshṭa*; fut. *saṃ-skarishyati*, MBh.; inf. *saṃ-skaritum*, Divyâv.; ind. p. *saṃ-skṛitya*, ŚBr.; Pāṇ. vi, 1, 137), to put together, form well, join together, compose, RV. &c. &c.; (Ā.) to accumulate (*pāpāni*, 'to add evil to evil'), Mṛicch. ix, 4; to prepare, make ready, dress, cook (food), MBh.; R. &c.; to form or arrange according to sacred precept, consecrate, hallow (in various ways; cf. *saṃ-skāra*), Mn.; MBh. &c.; to adorn, embellish, refine, elaborate, make perfect, (esp.) form language according to strict rules (cf. *saṃ-skṛita*), Sarvad.; to correct (astronomically), Sūryas.: Pass. *saṃ-skriyate*, to be put together or arranged or prepared or consecrated or refined, Mn.; MBh. &c.: Caus. *saṃ-skārayati*, to cause to (be) put together &c.; to cause to be consecrated, MBh.: Desid. *saṃ-cishkīrshati*, Vop.: Intens. *saṃ-ceshkrīyate*, ib.

Saṃ-skaraṇa, n. the act of putting together, preparing, Gobh.; cremating (a corpse), MBh. °**skartavya**, mfn. to be arranged or prepared or made ready, Hariv.; Śaṃk.; KātyŚr., Sch. °**skartṛi**, mfn. one who prepares or dresses or cooks (food), Mn. v, 51; one who consecrates or performs a rite, Uttarar.; one who produces an impression, Jaim., Sch.

Saṃ-skāra, m. (ifc. f. *ā*) putting together, forming well, making perfect, accomplishment, embellishment, adornment, purification, cleansing, making ready, preparation, dressing (of food), refining (of metals), polishing (of gems), rearing (of animals or plants), GṛŚrS.; MBh.; Kāv., &c.; cleansing the body, toilet, attire, Hariv.; forming the mind, training, education, R.; Ragh.; correction (also in an astronomical sense, Sūryas.), correct formation or use of a word, Nir.; Sarvad.; correctness, purity (esp. of pronunciation or expression), MBh.; R. &c.; making sacred, hallowing, consecration, Mn.; MBh. &c.; a sacred or sanctifying ceremony, one which purifies from the taint of sin contracted in the womb and leading to regeneration (12 such ceremonies are enjoined on the first three or twice-born classes in Mn. ii, 27, viz. 1. *garbhâdhāna*, 2. *puṃ-savana*, 3. *sīmantônnayana*, 4. *jāta-karman*, 5. *nāma-karman*, 6. *nishkramaṇa*, 7. *anna-prāśana*, 8. *cūḍā-karman*, 9. *upanayana*, 10. *keśânta*, 11. *samāvartana*, 12. *vivāha*, qq. vv.; accord. to Gaut. viii, 8 &c. there are 40 Saṃskāras), GṛS.; Mn.; MBh. &c. (IW. 188; 192 &c.; RTL. 353); the ceremony performed on a dead body (i.e. cremation), R.; any purificatory ceremony, W.; the faculty of memory, mental impression or recollection, impression on the mind of acts done in a former state of existence (one of the 24 qualities of the Vaiśeshikas, including *bhāvanā*, 'the faculty of reproductive imagination'), Kaṇ.; Sarvad. (IW. 69); (pl., with Buddhists) a mental conformation or creation of the mind (such as that of the external world, regarded by it as real, though actually non-existent, and forming the second link in the twelvefold chain of causation or the fourth of the 5 Skandhas), Dharmas. 22; 42; a polishing stone, MW. **-kamalâkara**, m. N. of wk. **-kartṛi**, m. (the Brāhman) who is called in to perform a Saṃskāra ceremony, Gal. **-kaumudī**, f., **-kaustubha**, m. (or *-dīdhiti*, f.), **-gaṅgādhara**, m. N. of wks. **-gaṇa-pati**, m. N. of an author, Cat. **-ja**, mfn. produced by purificatory rites, W. **-tattva**, n. N. of a wk. by Raghu-nandana. **-tā**, f. the state of being a Saṃskāra &c., Vās. **-tva**, n. id. (*-tvaṃ cakshushāṃ sam-√āp*, 'to become a hallowed object to the eye'), KātyŚr.; Mcar.; *-jāti-khaṇḍana*, n. N. of wk. **-dīdhiti**, see *-kaustubha*. **-nāman**, n. the name given to a child at the name-giving ceremony (and corresponding to the name given at baptism), VarBṛS. **-nirṇaya**, m., **-nṛi-siṃha**, m., **-paddhati**, f., **-paddhati-rahasya**, n., **-pariśishṭa**, n. N. of wks. **-pūta**, mfn. purified by sacred rites or by refinement, Kum. **-prakaraṇa**, n., **-prakāśa**, m., **-pradīpa**, m., **-pradīpikā**, f., **-prayoga**, m., **-bhāskara**, m. N. of wks. **-bhūshaṇa**, n. (speech) adorned by correctness, MBh. **-maya**, mf(*ī*)n. consisting in consecration, Ragh. **-mayūkha**, m., **-muktâvalī**, f., **-ratna**, n., **-ratna-mālā**, f. N. of wks. **-rahita**, mfn. = *-hīna* below. **-vat**, mfn. possessed of refinement, possessing correctness, elegant (*-tva*, n.), Kālid.; one who has received an impression, Buddh. **-varjita**, mfn. = *-hīna* below. **-vādârtha**, m., **-vidhi**, m. (= *gṛihya-kārikā*, pl.) N. of wks. **-viśishṭa**, mfn. made excellent by preparation or by good cooking (as food), Gaut. **-sampanna**, mfn. one who has received a good education, well-educated, R. **-sāgara**, m., **-sāra**, m., **-siddhi-dīpikā**, f., **-saukhya**, n. N. of wks. **-hīna**, mfn. without purificatory rites; m. a man of one of the three classes who has not been a recipient of initiation with the sacred thread or of the other purificatory ceremonies (and hence becomes an outcaste), L. **Saṃskārâdi-mat**, mfn. one who has received consecration &c., BhP. **Saṃskārâdhikārin**, mfn. one who has a right to receive all the purificatory ceremonies, MW. **Saṃskārôddyota**, m. N. of wk.

Saṃ-skāraka, mfn. preparing, making ready, KātyŚr., Sch.; purifying, consecrating (*-tva*, n.), MBh.; Jaim.; producing or leaving an impression on the mind, Jaim., Sch.; serving as an article of food or for cooking, MW. °**skārya**, mfn. to be prepared or perfected &c.; to be consecrated or hallowed with the necessary ceremonies, Mn.; MBh. &c.; (in astron.) to be corrected, Gol.; receiving a mental impression, Sarvad.

Saṃ-skṛitá (or *sáṃ-skṛita*), mfn. put together, constructed, well or completely formed, perfected, Lalit.; made ready, prepared, completed, finished, RV. &c. &c.; dressed, cooked (as food), MBh.; R.; BhP.; purified, consecrated, sanctified, hallowed, initiated, ŚBr. &c. &c.; refined, adorned, ornamented, polished, highly elaborated (esp. applied to highly wrought speech, such as the Sanskṛit language as opp. to the vernaculars), Mn.; MBh. &c.; m. a man of one of the three classes who has been sanctified by the purificatory rites, W.; a learned man, MW.; a word formed according to accurate rules, a regular derivation, ib.; (*ám*), n. making ready, preparation or a prepared place, sacrifice, RV.; TS.; ŚBr.; GṛŚrS.; a sacred usage or custom, MW.; the Sanskṛit language (cf. above), Śiksh.; Bhar.; Daśar. &c.; *-tva*, n. the being prepared or made ready &c., Jaim.; *-mañjarī*, f. N. of wk.; *-maya*, mf(*ī*)n. consisting of Sanskṛit, Kāśikh.; *-mālā*, f., *-ratna-mālā*, f., *-vākya-ratnâvalī*, f. N. of wks.; *-vat*, mfn. one who has perfected or elaborated or finished, MW.; °*tâtman*, m. one who has received the purificatory rites, Mn. x, 110; a sage, W.; °*tôkti*, f. refined or polished language, a Sanskṛit word or expression, Hit.

Saṃskritatra, n. a bench used in sacrificing or slaughtering animals, RV. vi, 28, 4.

Sáṃ-skriti, f. making ready, preparation, perfection, VS. &c. &c.; formation, AitBr.; hallowing, consecration, BhP.; determination, effort, L.; m. N. of Kṛishṇa, MBh. (B. *saṃ-skṛita*); of a king, VP. (v.l. *saṃ-kṛiti*).

Saṃ-skṛitrima, mfn. highly polished, artificially adorned (in *a-saṃskṛ°*), Bhaṭṭ.

Saṃ-skriyā, f. making ready, preparation, Sarvad.; formation, Śaṃk.; any purificatory rite or consecration (including funeral ceremonies and burning of the dead &c.), L.

संस्खलित *saṃ-skhalita,* n. (√*skhal*) an error, mistake, Nāg.

संस्त *sanst* = √*sas,* q.v.

संस्तम्भ् *saṃ-√stambh,* P. *-stabhnoti* or *°nāti,* to make firm, Kauś.; to support, sustain, encourage, MBh.; R. &c.; to make rigid (said of water), MBh.; to restrain, check, stop (esp. by magical means), Kathās.; to suppress (tears or sorrow), R.; BhP.; Ā. (only Impv. *-stambhasva*) to be firm, take heart or courage, Nir. ix, 12 (in R. iv, 1, 115 [B.] *-stambha,* id.; cf. *-stabhya*): Caus. *-stambhayati,* to confirm, strengthen (*ātmānam ātmanā,* 'one's self by one's self'), encourage, MBh.; R. &c.; to take heart or courage, R.; to make rigid or solid (water), MBh.; Rājat.; to check, stop, arrest, MBh.; Kāv. &c.; to paralyze, Nalac.; to suppress, restrain (grief or tears), R.; Kālid. &c.: Desid. of Caus., see *saṃ-stambhayishu.*

Saṃ-stabdha, mfn. supported, confirmed &c., MBh.; firm, rigid, Hariv.

Saṃ-stabhya, ind. having supported or confirmed or strengthened or encouraged (*ātmānam ātmanā,* 'one's self by one's self'), MBh.; R.; having supported or composed the mind firmly (in affliction), having taken heart or courage, ib.

Saṃ-stambhá, m. obstinacy, pertinacity, firmness in resistance, MaitrS.; TaitBr.; Nir.; MBh.; support, prop, W.; fixing, making firm, ib.; stop, stay, ib.; paralysis, muscular rigidity, ib. **°stambhana,** mfn. (fr. Caus.) constipating, obstructive, Vāgbh.; n. an obstructive remedy, Suśr.; stopping, arresting, Cat. **°stambhanīya,** mfn. (fr. prec.) to be confirmed or encouraged, R.; to be stopped, W. **°stambhayitri,** mfn. (fr. Caus.) one who stops or restrains, a restrainer, Ragh.; one who supports, a supporter, MW. **°stambhayishu,** mfn. (fr. Desid. of Caus.) wishing to stop or cause to stand still (a retreating army), MBh. (C. *vi-shṭambh°*). **°stambhita,** mfn. (fr. Caus.) supported, propped, MBh.; Kāv. &c.; stupefied, paralyzed, ib. **°stambhin,** mfn. stopping, averting (danger), MBh.

संस्तर *saṃ-stara, °raṇa.* See *saṃ-√stṛi.*

संस्तु *saṃ-√1. stu,* P. *-stauti,* to praise together with (instr.), Nir. vii, 6; to praise all at once, ĀśvŚr.; to praise properly or well, laud, celebrate, MBh.; Kāv. &c.

Saṃ-stava, m. (ifc. f. *ā*) common or simultaneous praise, Nir.; ŚāṅkhŚr.; praise, commendation (also pl.), Vīrac.; mention, KātyŚr., Sch.; intimacy, familiarity, acquaintance with (instr. with and without *saha,* or comp.), Kāv.; Rājat.; Kathās. (cf. *a-saṃst°*); *-prīti,* f. love proceeding from acquaintance, Kathās.; *-sthira,* mfn. firm through acqu°, MW. **°stavana,** n. praising together or simultaneously, ĀśvŚr.; praising, hymning, BhP. **°stavāna,** mfn. praising eloquently, eloquent, Uṇ. ii, 89, Sch.; m. a singer, chanter, MW.; joy (= *harsha,* accord. to some), ib.

Saṃ-stāvá, m. hymning or praising in chorus, ChUp.; the place occupied at a sacrifice by the Brāhmans reciting hymns and prayers, ŚBr.; simultaneous or common praise, Bhaṭṭ.

Sáṃ-stuta, mfn. praised or hymned together, TS.; TBr.; Nir.; praised, celebrated, extolled, Hariv.; R.; Pur.; counted together (as one Stotra), reckoned together, TS.; Br.; KātyŚr.; equal to, passing for (instr. or comp.), Āpast.; Kathās.; BhP.; acquainted, familiar, intimate, Kāv.; VarBṛS.; Rājat.; *-tva,* n. the being praised together, ChUp.; *-prâya,* mfn. for the most part lauded or hymned together, associated in hymns, MW. **°stutaka,** mfn. affable, condescending, civil, Buddh. **°stuti,** f. praise, eulogy, MBh.; BhP.; figurative mode of expression, Āpast.

संस्तुभ् *saṃ-stúbh,* f. shout of joy (as N. of a metre), VS.

Saṃ-stobha, m. or n. (with or without *marutām*), 'id.,' N. of a Sāman, ĀrshBr.

संस्तूप *saṃ-stūpa,* m. a heap of sweepings, Gobh. (Sch.)

संस्तृ *saṃ-√stṛi* (or *-√stṝ*), P. Ā. *-stṛiṇoti, -stṛiṇute; -stṛiṇāti, -stṛiṇīte* (ep. also *-starati*), to spread out (side by side), extend, TS.; ŚBr.; to strew over, cover, KaushUp.; MBh.; Suśr.; to spread, make even, level, Kauś.

Saṃ-stara, m. (ifc. f. *ā*) a layer (of grass or leaves), bed, couch, MBh.; Kāv. &c.; a scattered mass (of flowers &c.), MBh.; R.; a covering, cover, Kāvyâd.; scattering, strewing (v.l. for *-starana*), Śak.; spreading, extension, propagation (of laws or customs), Hariv.; a sacrifice or the ritual arrangements for a s° (generally ifc., as in *yajña-s°*), MBh.; R. **°starana,** n. a layer (of leaves &c.), couch, R.; strewing, covering over (v.l. *-stara*), Śak.

Saṃ-stāra, m. a bed, couch (m. c. for *-stara*), MārkP.; a sacrifice, Gal.; spreading out, extension, MW.; *-paṅkti,* f. a partic. form of the Paṅkti metre (12 + 8 + 8 + 12 syllables), RPrāt. **°stāraka,** (prob.) m. a layer, bed, Śil.

Saṃ-stir, f. contraction (opp. to *vi-shṭir,* 'expansion,' *saṃstiro vishṭirah* [acc. pl.], prob. 'what is near and what is far'), RV. i, 140.

Saṃ-stīrṇa, mfn. strewn, scattered, Kauś.; Śak.; = next, MBh.; R.

Saṃ-stṛita, mfn. bestrewn, covered over, MBh.

संस्त्यान *saṃ-styāna,* mfn. (√*styai*) coagulated, condensed, Nir.; n. the becoming condensed or solid or compact (applied to the fetus), Pat.

Saṃ-styāya, m. assemblage, collection, multitude, Nir.; a habitation, house, Mālatīm.; spreading, expansion, L.; vicinity, proximity, L.

संस्था *saṃ-√sthā,* Ā. *-tishṭhate* (Pāṇ. i, 3, 22; ep. and m.c. also P. *-tishṭhati;* Ved. inf. *-sthātos,* ĀpŚr.), to stand together, hold together (pf. p. du. *-tasthāné,* said of heaven and earth), RV.; to come or stay near (loc.), ib.; VS.; ŚBr.; to meet (as enemies), come into conflict, RV.; to stand still, remain, stay, abide (lit. and fig.; with *vākye,* 'to obey'), MBh.; R. &c.; to be accomplished or completed (esp. applied to rites), Br.; ŚrS.; Mn.; MBh.; BhP.; to prosper, succeed, get on well, MBh.; to come to an end, perish, be lost, die, MBh.; Kāv.; BhP.; to become, be turned into or assume the form of (acc.), Lalit.: Caus. *-sthāpayati* (subj. aor. *-tishṭipah,* ŚBr.), to cause to stand up or firm, raise on their legs again (fallen horses), MBh.; to raise up, restore (dethroned kings), ib.; to confirm, encourage, comfort (*ātmānam* or *hṛidayam,* 'one's self,' i.e. 'take heart again'), Kāv.; Pañcat.; to fix or place upon or in (loc.), Kauś.; MBh. &c.; to put or add to (*upari*), Yājñ.; to build (a town), Hariv.; to heap, store up (goods), VarBṛS.; to found, establish, fix, settle, introduce, set afoot, MBh.; R.; Rājat.; to cause to stand still, stop, restrain, suppress (breath, semen &c.), AitBr.; to accomplish, conclude, complete (esp. a rite), Br.; Kauś.; MBh.; to put to death, kill, ŚBr.; MBh.; to perform the last office for, i.e. to burn, cremate (a dead body), ŚāṅkhBr.; to put to subjection, subject, MW.: Desid. of Caus. *-sthāpayishati,* to wish to finish or conclude, ŚāṅkhBr.

Saṃ-stha, mf(*ā*)n. standing together, standing or staying or resting or being in or on, contained in (loc. or comp.), MBh.; Kāv. &c.; being in or with, belonging to (loc. or comp.), Mn.; MBh. &c.; based or resting or dependent on (loc.), MBh.; partaking or possessed of (comp.), MBh.; Pañcat.; existing, lasting for a time (comp.), Vet.; ended, perished, dead, L.; (*saṃ-sthá*), m. presence (only loc. 'in the presence or midst of,' with *cid,* 'by one's mere presence'), RV.; a spy, secret emissary (cf. *saṃsthā* below), L.; a dweller, resident, inhabitant, W.; a fellow-countryman, neighbour, ib.; (*ā*), f., see next.

Saṃ-sthā́, f. (ifc. f. *ā*) staying or abiding with (comp.), MBh.; shape, form, manifestation, appearance (ifc. = 'appearing as'), Up.; MBh. &c.; established order, standard, rule, direction (acc. with √*kṛi* or Caus. of √*sthā,* 'to establish or fix a rule or obligation for one's self;' with *vyati-√kram* or *pari-√bhid,* 'to transgress or break an established rule or obligation'), MBh.; R. &c.; quality, property, nature, Kāv.; Pur.; conclusion, termination, completion, TS.; ŚBr. &c.; end, death, Pur.; destruction of the world (= *pralaya,* said to be of four kinds, viz. *naimittika, prākṛitika, nitya, ātyantika*), ib.; a complete liturgical course, the basis or essential form of a sacrifice (the Jyotiḥ-shṭoma, Havir-yajña, and Pāka-yajña consist of seven such forms), ŚrS.; killing (*paśu-s°,* 'killing of the sacrificial animal'), BhP.; cremation (of a body; also *prêta-s°*), ib.; (prob.) = *śrāddha,* MārkP.; a spy or secret emissary in a king's own country (= *cara,* m. prob. a group of five spies consisting of a *vaṇij,* 'merchant,' *bhikshu,* 'mendicant,' *chāttra,* 'pupil,' *liṅgin,* 'one who falsely wears the mark of a twice-born,' and *kṛishīvala,* 'husbandman,' cf. *pañca-varga,* and Mn. vii, 154, Kull.), Kām.; continuation in the right way, L.; occupation, business, profession, W.; an assembly, ib.; a royal ordinance, ib.; *-kṛita,* mfn. settled, determined, Hariv.; *-°gāra* (*°thâg°*), m. n. a meeting-house, Lalit.; *-japa,* m. a closing prayer, ĀśvŚr.; *-tva,* n. the being a form or shape, BhP.; *-paddhati,* f. N. of wk.; *-°vayava-vat* (*°thâv°*), mfn. having a shape and limbs, BhP.

Saṃ-sthā́na, mfn. standing together, MW.; like, resembling, W.; applied to Vishṇu, MBh.; m. (pl.) N. of a people, ib.; n. (ifc. f. *ā*) staying or abiding in (comp.), Hit. (cf. *dūra-s°*); standing still or firm (in a battle), Gaut.; being, existence, life, MBh.; Śaṃk.; BhP.; abiding by, strict adherence or obedience to (comp.), Kām.; abode, dwelling-place, habitation, Nir.; KaushUp.; MBh. &c.; a public place (in a town), Mn.; MBh. &c.; shape, form, appearance (often with *rūpa*), MBh.; R. &c.; beauty, splendour, MBh.; the symptom of a disease, Suśr.; nature, state, condition, BhP.; an aggregate, whole, totality, BhP.; termination, conclusion, MaitrS.; end, death, L.; formation, L.; vicinity, neighbourhood, L.; *-cārin,* w.r. for *sa-sthāsnu-c°; -bhukti,* f. (with *kālasya*) the passage through various periods of time, BhP.; *-vat,* mfn. being, existing, R.; having various forms, Kām. **°sthānaka,** m. N. of Śakāra (the king's brother-in-law) in the Mṛicchakaṭikā.

Saṃ-sthāpaka, mfn. (fr. Caus.) fixing firmly, settling, establishing, Pañcar.; forming into a shape or various shapes (*khaṇḍa-s°,* 'one who makes various figures out of sugar'), R. **°sthāpana,** n. fixing, setting up, raising, erecting, MBh.; VarBṛS.; Suśr.; establishment, regulation (cf. *argha-s°*), Mn.; MBh. &c.; (*ā*), f. comforting, encouraging, Mṛicch. **°sthāpanīya,** mfn. to be established or settled, MW. **°sthāpayitavya,** mfn. to be cheered up or comforted, Kād. **°sthāpita,** mfn. placed, fixed, deposited, W.; stopped, restrained, controlled, ib.; made to stand together, heaped up, accumulated, MW. 1. **°sthāpya,** ind. having placed together &c.; excepting, Divyâv. 2. **°sthāpya,** mfn. to be put or placed in (loc.; with *vaśe* and gen., 'to be placed in subjection to;' with *cetasi* and gen., 'to be called to or impressed on the mind of'), Mn.; Rājat.; to be completed or finished (as a sacrifice), TS.; to be treated with a calming clyster, Car.

Saṃ-sthāsnu. See *sa-sthāsnu-cārin.*

Sáṃ-sthita, mfn. standing (as opp. to 'lying' or 'sitting'), Yājñ.; one who has stood or held out (in fight), MārkP.; placed, resting, lying, sitting, being in or on (*upari,* loc., or comp.), Yājñ.; MBh. &c.; abiding, remaining, left standing (for a long time, as food; with *tathâiva,* 'remaining in the same condition'), Yājñ.; VarBṛS.; Ragh.; lasting, enduring, MBh.; imminent, future, Hariv.; shaped, formed (cf. *duḥ-* and *su-s°*), appearing in a partic. shape or form, formed like, resembling (often ifc.; with *navadhā,* 'ninefold;' with *masī-rūpeṇa,* 'appearing in the form of black ink'), MBh.; Kāv. &c.; being in a partic. state or condition, addicted or given to, intent upon (loc. or comp.), Hariv.; Kāv.; VarBṛS.; founded or based upon (loc.), MBh.; directed towards, fixed upon (comp.), BhP.; relating to, concerning (loc. or comp.), Kām.; MārkP.; skilled in, acquainted or familiar with (loc.), MBh.; R.; started, set out for (dat. or *abhimukham*), R.; frequented (as a place), Mn. viii, 371; finished, concluded, completed, ready, Br.; ŚrS.; perished, died (n. impers.), Mn.; MBh.; BhP.; near or contiguous to, W.; heaped, collected, ib.; n. conduct, Cat.; form, shape, MBh.; *-yajús,* n. the final sacrificial formula and the oblation connected with it, Br.; *-vat,* mfn. (pl. = 3. pl. pf.; pl. [with *sukhena*] 'they lived happily together'), Pañcat.; *-homa,* m. a final sacrifice, ŚrS.

Saṃ-sthiti, f. staying together, living in or with

or near, union with (loc.), Mn.; MBh. &c.; standing or sitting on (loc.), Yājñ. i, 139; duration, continuance in the same state or condition, Hariv.; Kām.; constancy, perseverance, Hariv.; BhP.; being bent upon, attaching importance to (loc.), Mn. ix, 14; existence, possibility of (gen. or comp.), MārkP.; form, shape, ib.; established order, Kām.; VāyuP.; nature, condition, quality, property, Yājñ.; MBh.; Pur.; conclusion, completion (of a sacrifice), TS.; TBr.; Vait.; end, death, Pur.; obstruction of the bowels, constipation, Suśr.; heap, accumulation, W.; restraint, ib. °**sthitika,** see *evam-saṃsthitika.*

संस्थुल *saṃsthula.* See *vi-saṃsthula* under 3. *vi*, p. 953, col. 1.

संस्ना *saṃ-√snā*, Caus. *-snapayati* or *-snāpayati*, to bathe, wash, BhP.

Saṃ-snāta, mfn. (used to explain *sásni* in RV. x, 139, 6), Nir. v, 1. °**snāna,** n. common or regular bathing, Kāśīkh.

संस्निह् *saṃ-√snih*, Caus. *-snehayati*, to treat with oil or unguents, ŚārṅgS.

Saṃ-snehana, n. medical treatment with oil or unguents, Car.

संस्पन्द् *saṃ-√spand*, Ā. *-spandate*, to throb, quiver, pulsate with life, come to life, BhP.

संस्पर्ध् *saṃ-√spardh*, Ā. *-spardhate*, to emulate, vie or cope with (*paras-param*), MBh.

Saṃ-spardhā, f. emulation, rivalry, jealousy, Rājat.; BhP. °**spardhin,** mfn. jealous, vying with (comp.), ŚārṅgP.; BhP.

संस्पष्ट *saṃ-spashṭa*, mfn. (√*spaś*) famous, celebrated, KaushUp.

संस्पृश् *saṃ-√spṛiś*, P. *-spṛiśati* (rarely Ā. °*te*), to touch, bring into contact with (Ā. 'touch one's self'), AV. &c. &c.; (with or without *salilam*, *apas* &c.) to touch water, sprinkle, wash, MBh.; R.; to touch, come into contact (in astrol. sense), VarBṛS.; to reach or penetrate to, attain, MBh.; Kathās.; BhP.; Jātakam.; to come into close relation with (acc.), Rājat.; to come upon, visit, afflict, R.; to take out of (abl.), MBh. viii, 788: Caus. *-sparśayati*, to bring into contact, TS.; Br.; ŚrS.

Saṃ-sparśá, m. (ifc. f. *ā*) close or mutual contact, touch, conjunction, mixture, AV. &c. &c.; perception, sense, W.; (*ā*), f. a kind of fragrant plant or perfume (= *janī*), L.; (°*śa*)*-ja*, mfn. produced by contact or sensible perception, BhP. °**sparśana,** mfn. touching, MBh; n. contact, mixture with (instr., gen., or comp.), ŚāṅkhŚr.; MBh. &c. °**sparśāna,** m. = *manaḥ*, L. °**sparśin,** mfn. touching, coming into contact with (comp.), Yājñ.; Rājat.

Saṃ-spṛiś, mfn. touching (comp.), Amar.

Sáṃ-spṛishṭa, mfn. touched, brought into contact, closely united with (instr. or comp.), mutually joined, mixed, combined, contiguous, adjacent, TS. &c. &c.; reached, attained (in *a-s*°), Kathās.; visited, affected or afflicted by (instr.), Kāv.; VarBṛS.; (ifc.) defiled by (in *a-s*°), Sarvad.; *-maithunā*, f. a seduced girl (unfit for marriage), L.

Saṃ-sprashṭṛi, mfn. (used for explaining *pṛiśni*), Nir. ii, 11.

संस्पृह् *saṃ-√spṛih*, P. *-spṛihayati*. to desire eagerly (acc.), BhP.

संस्फल् *saṃ-√sphal*, Caus. *-sphālayati*, to dash in pieces, TĀr.

Saṃ-sphāla, m. a ram (= *mesha*), L.

संस्फान *saṃ-sphā́na*, mfn. (√*sphāy*) becoming fat, feeding one's self up, AV.

Saṃ-sphāyana, mfn., Pat. on Pāṇ. vi, 1, 66, Vārtt. 7.

Saṃ-sphīya, g. *dhūmâdi*.

संस्फुट *saṃ-sphuṭa*, mfn. bursting open, blossomed, blown, L.

Saṃ-sphoṭa, m. clashing together, Bāl.; war, battle, Harav. (also °*ṭi*, L.)

संस्फुर् *saṃ-sphur*, Ā. *-sphurate*, to dash or strike together, TBr.; ŚBr.; to twinkle, glitter, MaitrUp.

संस्फेट *saṃ-spheṭa*, m. (cf. *saṃ-pheṭa* and *saṃ-sphoṭa*) war, battle, L.

संस्मि *saṃ-√smi*, Ā. *-smayate*, to smile at, L.; to be ashamed, blush, RV.; TBr.: Desid. *-sismayishate*, to wish to laugh at or deride, Bhaṭṭ.

Saṃ-smera, mfn. smiling at, smiling, Subh.

संस्मृ *saṃ-√smṛi*, P. *-smarati*, to remember fully, recollect (acc.; rarely gen.), Mn.; MBh. &c.: Caus. *-smārayati*, to cause to remember, remind of (acc.), MBh.; Kāv. &c.; to cause to be remembered, recall to the mind of (gen.), MBh.; BhP.

Saṃ-smaraṇa, n. the act of remembering, calling to mind, recollecting (gen.), Kum.; MBh. °**smaraṇīya,** mfn. to be remembered, living in remembrance only, past, gone (*-śobha*, mfn. 'no more beautiful'), Śak. °**smartavya,** mfn. to be remembered or thought upon by (gen.), MBh.

Saṃ-smāraka, mfn. (fr. Caus.) putting in mind, reminding of (comp.), Chandom. °**smāraṇa,** n. counting over (cattle), MBh. °**smārita,** mfn. caused to remember, reminded of (acc.), BhP.; recalled to the mind, Hariv.

Saṃ-smṛita, mfn. remembered, recollected, called to the mind, Hariv.; MārkP.; prescribed, enjoined, Hariv.; called, named, Sāh.; °*tôpasthita*, mfn. appeared when thought of, Kathās. °**smṛiti,** f. remembering, remembrance of (gen. or comp.; acc. with √*labh*, 'to remember'), Kāv.; VarBṛS. &c.

संस्यन्द् *saṃ-√syand*, Ā. *-syandate*, to run together, converge, meet, Car.: Caus. *-syandayati*, to cause to run together (in *a-saṃ-syandayat*), ĀpŚr.

संस्युत *saṃ-syuta.* See *saṃ-√siv.*

संस्रष्टृ *saṃ-srashṭṛi.* See *sam-√sṛij.*

संस्रु *saṃ-√sru*, P. *-sravati*, to flow or run together, RV.; AV.; ŚBr.: Caus. *-srāvayati*, to cause to run together, AV.; Kauś.

Saṃ-sravá, m. (ifc. f. *ā*) flowing together, conflux, Suśr.; that which flows together, (esp.) the blended remainder of liquids, RV.; AitBr.; GṛŚrS.; flowing water, R.; any remainder, remains, a chip or piece of anything, MBh.; a kind of offering or libation, MW.; *-bhāga* (°*vá-*), mfn. one to whom the remainder of any liquid belongs, VS. °**sravaṇa,** in *garbha-s*° (q. v.)

Saṃ-srāvá, m. flowing together, conflux, AV.; accumulation of matter &c., Suśr.; the remainder of any liquid, dregs, TS.; Kāṭh.; ŚāṅkhGṛ.; a kind of offering or libation, MW.; *-bhāga* (°*vá-*), m. = *saṃ-srava-bh*°, TS.; TBr. °**srāvaṇa,** mfn. flowing or running together, AV.; n. spitting out, Hcat. (Sch.; written *saṃ-śr*°). °**srāvya,** mfn. flowed together, mixed, ib.

संस्वञ्ज् *saṃ-√svañj*, Ā. *-svajate*, to clasp, embrace, Bhaṭṭ.

संस्वद् *saṃ-√svad* (only inf. *-súde*), to taste, enjoy, RV. viii, 17, 6.

संस्वप् *saṃ-√svap.* See *saṃ-supta.*

संस्विद् *saṃ-√svid*, Caus. *-svedayati*, to cause to sweat or perspire, treat with sudorifics, Suśr.

Saṃ-sveda, m. sweat, perspiration, MBh.; *-ja*, mfn. produced from moist heat (as vermin), ib. °**svedayu,** mfn., Pāṇ. vii, 4, 35, Vārtt. 1, Pat. °**svedin,** mfn. perspiring, Suśr.

संस्वृ *saṃ-√svṛi*, P. *-svarati*, to sound or sing together, sing with one accord, praise in chorus, RV.; ŚrS.: Caus. *-svarate* (only 2. sg. aor. *-svarishīshṭhāḥ*), to pain, afflict, torment, Bhaṭṭ. (Sch.)

Saṃ-svāra, m. sounding together, ŚāṅkhŚr.

संहन् *saṃ-√han*, P. *-hanti* (ind. p. *-hatya*, q. v.), to strike or put together, join, shut, close (eyes, wings, hands), RV. &c. &c.; to beat together, make solid, Suśr.; to put together i. e. frame, fabricate, ŚāṅkhŚr.; (Ā.) to rush together (in battle), meet, encounter (instr.), RV. vii, 56, 22; (*jighnate*), to meet as a friend (instr.), ib. ix, 14, 4; (P.) to break, crush, kill, destroy, ib.: Pass. *-hanyate*, to be put together or joined, join, unite (intr.), Saṃk.; to become compact or solid, ŚBr.: Caus. *-ghātayati*, to strike together, kill, destroy utterly, MW.

Saṃ-ha (prob. = *saṃ-gha*) in comp.; *-tala*, m. the two hands joined with the open palms brought together, L. (cf. *saṃhata-* and *saṃgha-t*°); *-tāpana*, m. N. of a serpent-demon, MBh.

Saṃ-hát, f. (prob.) a layer, pile, RV. iii, 1, 7.

Saṃ-hata, mfn. struck together, closely joined or united with (instr.), keeping together, contiguous, coherent, combined, compacted, forming one mass or body, ĀśvŚr.; Mn.; MBh. &c.; accompanied or attended by (instr.), Mn. vii, 165; become solid, compact, firm, hard, MBh.; Kāv. &c.; strong-limbed, athletic, MBh.; strong, intensive, VarBṛS.; (prob.) complex, composite, compound (said of a partic. tone and odour), MBh.; struck, hurt, wounded, killed, W.; n. a partic. position in dancing, Saṃgīt.; *-kulina*, mfn. belonging to a family closely allied or related, ĀpŚr., Sch.; *-jānu* or *-jānuka*, mfn. knock-kneed, L.; *-tala*, m. the two hands joined with the open palms brought together, W.; *-tā*, f. close contact or union, Śiś.; *-tva*, n. id., Pañcat. (v. l.); complexity, compactness, close combination, W.; *-pucchi*, ind. with contracted tail, g. *dvidandy-ādi*; *-bhrū*, mfn. knitting the brows, MBh.; *-bhrūkuṭi-mukha*, mfn. one on whose face the brows are contracted, ib.; *-mūrti*, mfn. of compact form or shape, strong, intensive, VarBṛS.; *-vāk-kala*, mfn. (du.) 'joining the tones of the voice,' singing a duet, MārkP.; *-vṛittôru*, mfn. one who has round and firm thighs, R.; *-stanī*, f. a woman whose breasts are very close to each other, MW.; *-hasta*, mfn. seizing or holding each other by the hand (*-tva*, n.), Gobh., Sch.; °*tâṅga*, mfn. strong-limbed, well-knit, Suśr.; in close contiguity (as hills), MBh.; °*tâñjali*, mfn. joining the hollowed hands (as a mark of supplication), Hariv.; °*tâśva*, m. N. of a king (son of Nikumbha), Hariv.; °*tôru*, mfn. firm-thighed, MBh.

Saṃhati, f. striking together, closure, Kāv.; ŚārṅgS.; compactness, solidity, MBh.; VarBṛS.; thickening, swelling, ŚārṅgS.; keeping together, saving, economy, Kāv.; firm union or alliance, junction, joint effort, close contact or connection with (instr.), Kāv.; Pur.; Rājat.; a seam, Kum.; a compact mass, bulk, heap, collection, multitude, Kāv.; Kathās. &c.; *-śālin*, mfn. thick, dense, Śiś. °**hatībhāva,** m. close union or connection, Car. °**hatya,** ind. having struck or put together &c.; joined, combined, together with (instr.), MBh.; Kāv. &c.; *-kārin*, mfn. working together or with joined effort, BhP.; (°*ri*)*-tā*, f., *-tva*, n. common work or endeavour, KātyŚr.

Saṃ-hanana, mfn. compact, solid, firm, MBh.; BhP.; making compact or solid, Suśr.; striking together, MW.; killing, destroying, a destroyer, ib.; m. N. of a son of Manasyu, MBh.; n. the act of striking together, Suśr.; hardening, ib.; solidity, compactness, robustness, strength, muscularity, MBh.; R. &c.; firmness, steadfastness, Śil.; junction, connection (in *a-s*°), Nilak.; agreement, harmony, MBh.; the body (as having the limbs well compacted), L.; a mail-coat (?), L.; rubbing the limbs, W.; *-balôpeta*, mfn. endowed with firmness and strength, BhP.; *-vat*, mfn. strongly built, muscular, robust, Jātakam.; °*nôpeta*, mfn. endowed with strength or muscularity, MBh. °**hananīya,** mfn. compact, solid, firm, strong, MBh.

Saṃ-hantṛi, mfn. one who joins or unites, Saṃk.; (°*trī*), f. a female destroyer, Pañcar. (perhaps w. r. for *saṃ-hartrī*).

Saṃ-hāta, m. (for *saṃ-ghāta*, which is often v. l.) conciseness (in *akshara-s*°), Sāh.; N. of a partic. hell, Mn. iv, 89; of one of Śiva's attendants, L.

Saṃ-hātya, n. (v. l. *saṃ-ghātya*) violation of an alliance (by means of persuasion or bribery, or by the operation of fate), Sāh.

Sáṃ-hāna, mfn. narrow, MaitrS.

Saṃ-gha, saṃ-ghāta &c. See s. v.

संहनु *sáṃ-hanu*, mfn. striking the jaws together, AV.; ind. (with √*kṛi*) to seize between the jaws, ib.

संहर *saṃ-hara*, °*raṇa*. See *saṃ-√hṛi.*

संहर्ष *saṃ-harsha*, °*shaṇa*. See *saṃ-√hṛish.*

संहवन *saṃ-havana.* See *saṃ-√hu.*

संहा *saṃ-√1. hā*, Ā. *-jihīte* (pr. p. *-jihāna*), to rise up, RV.; Br.; GṛŚrS.; to move about, BhP.; to obtain, Nalôd.

Saṃ-hāyyam, ind. being able to rise (in *a-s*°), PañcavBr.

संहा *saṃ-√2. hā*, P. *-jahāti*, to leave together, Āpast.; to give up, abandon, MBh.: Desid. *-jihāsati*, to wish to leave or desert, Car.

संहार *saṃ-hāra*, *-raka* &c. See *saṃ-√hṛi.*

संहि *saṃ-√hi*, P. *-hinoti*, to send forth, BhP.; to bring about, contrive, compose, RV.

संहित *sáṃ-hita*, mfn. (√1. *dhā*) put together, joined, attached, RV. &c. &c.; fixed, settled, AitBr.; composed of (comp.), ib.; placed together (*pārśva-s°*, 'placed side by side'), Lāṭy.; uninterrupted (as a series of words), RPrāt.; joined or connected or endowed or furnished with, abounding in, possessed of, accompanied by (comp.), Mn.; MBh. &c.; agreeing with, conformable to (*dharma-s°*, 'in accordance with justice'), R.; relating to, concerning (comp.), ib.; connected with, proceeding from (comp.), MBh.; being on friendly terms with (instr.), ib.; (°*tá*), mfn. mixed in colour, variegated, VS.; TS.; (*ā*), f., see next; n. N. of a Sāman, ĀrshBr. **-pushpikā**, f. dill (Anethum Panmori), L. **Sáṃhitânta**, mfn. joined at the ends, AV. **Saṃhitêshu**, mfn. one who has fitted or placed an arrow on a bow-string, MW. **Saṃhitôru**, mfn. having the thighs joined (through obesity), Pāṇ. iv, 1, 70 (cf. *saṃhatôru*).

Saṃ-hitā, f. conjunction, connection, union, TUp.; (in gram.) the junction or combination of letters according to euphonic rules (= *saṃdhi*, but sometimes considered rather as the state preparatory to the actual junction than the junction itself), Prāt.; a text treated according to euphonic rules (esp. the real continuous text of the Vedas as formed out of the Padas or separate words by proper phonetic changes [according to various schools; cf. IW. 152]: beside the Saṃhitās of the Ṛig-, Sāma-, and Atharva-veda there is the Vājasaneyi-S° belonging to the White Yajur-veda, and five other Saṃhitās belonging to the black Yajur-veda, viz. the Taittirīya-S°, the Saṃhitā of the Ātreyas [known only by its Anukramaṇī], the S° of the Kaṭhas, the Kapishṭhala-Kaṭha-S°, and the S° of the Maitrāyaṇīyas or Maitrāyaṇī-s°), Nir.; Prāt. &c.; any methodically arranged collection of texts or verses (e.g. the Rāmāyaṇa, the various law-books, the medical works of Caraka and Śārṅgadhara, the complete system of natural astrology &c. [cf. *bṛihat-s°*]; there is also a Saṃhitā of the Purāṇas said to have been compiled by Vyāsa, the substance of which is supposed to be represented by the Vishṇu-purāṇa), MBh.; VarBṛS.; Pur. &c.; science, L.; the force which holds together and supports the universe (a term applied to the Supreme Being, accord. to some), MW.; N. of various wks. **-kalpa**, m. N. of a Pariśishṭa of the Atharva-veda. **-kāra**, m. the author of a Saṃhitā, Rājat. **-japa**, m. the recitation of a S° (of the Veda), Mn. xi, 201. **-daṇḍaka**, m. or n., **-dīpaka**, n. N. of wks. **-pāṭha**, m. the continuous text of the Veda (as formed out of the Pada-pāṭha, q.v.), Pat., Sch. **-prakāra**, m. pl. (with *ekādaśa*) N. of a wk. (containing 11 modes of reciting Vedic texts, viz. *saṃhitā, pada, krama, jaṭā, mālā, śikhā, lekhā, dhvaja, daṇḍa, ratha, gaṇa*). **-pradīpa**, m., **-bhāshya**, n., **-ratnâkara**, m. N. of wks. **-°dhyayana** (°*tâdh°*), n. the repeating of the S° of a Veda, MBh. **-°dhyāyin** (°*tâdh°*), mfn. repeating the S° of a Veda, ib. **-°rṇava** (°*târṇ°*), m. N. of wk. **-vat**, ind. as in the Saṃhitā text, MW. **-vidhi**, m. the method of the S° text, RPrāt., Sch.; *-vivaraṇa*, n. N. of wk. **-samāna-lakshaṇa**, n. N. of a phonetic treatise. **-sāra**, m., **-sārâvalī**, f. N. of astrol. wks. **-sūtra**, n. a kind of Prātiśākhya to the Ṛig-veda. **-skandha**, m., **-homa-paddhati**, f. N. of wks. **Saṃhitôpanishad**, f. N. of an Upanishad; *-brāhmaṇa*, n. of a Brāhmaṇa.

Sáṃ-hiti, f. putting together, connection, MaitrS.

Saṃhitika, w.r. for *sāṃh°*, APrāt., Sch.

Saṃhitī-bhāva, m. connection, mixture, combination, Car.

संहु *saṃ-√hu*, P. *-juhoti*, to sacrifice together, VS.; to sacrifice, MBh.

Saṃ-havana, n. the act of sacrificing together or in a proper manner, MW.; a quadrangle, group of four houses, L.

Saṃ-hotrá, n. community of sacrifice, RV.

संहूति *saṃ-hūti*. See *saṃ-√hve*.

संहृ *saṃ-√hṛi*, P. Ā. *-harati*, °*te*, to bring or draw together, unite, compress, collect, contract, abridge, RV. &c. &c.; to throw together, mix up, ŚrS.; to close, clench (the fist), MBh.; to concentrate (the mind) on (loc.), ib.; to support, maintain, Jātakam.; to take or fetch from (abl.), R.; to lay hold of, attract, take for one's self, appropriate, Mn.; MBh. &c.; to take away, carry off, rob, AitBr.; MBh.; to lay or draw aside, withdraw, withhold from (abl.), MBh.; Kāv. &c.; to restrain, curb, check, suppress, ib.; to crush together, crumple up, destroy, annihilate (often opp. to √*sṛij*, 'to emit or create'), Up.; MBh. &c.; Pass. *-hriyate*, to be brought or put together &c., MBh.; Kāv. &c.: Caus. *-hārayati*, °*te*, to bind t° (Ā. 'one's own hair &c.,' also 'cut'), GṛŚrS.; Car.: *-jihīrshati*, to wish to bring together &c., ŚBr.: Intens. *-jarīharti*, to destroy repeatedly, Cat.

Saṃ-hara, m. drawing together, contracting, MW.; destroying, ib.; N. of an Asura, Hariv.; °*râkhya*, m. N. of Agni Pavamāna, MatsyaP.

Saṃ-haraṇa, n. drawing or bringing together, collecting, gathering, MBh.; binding together, arranging (accord. to others 'cutting,' of hair), Āpast.; taking hold of, seizure, MBh.; fetching back (arrows &c. discharged by magical arts), Uttarar.; destroying, destruction (opp. to 'creation'), MBh.; Hariv.; Kathās.

Saṃ-hartavya, mfn. to be drawn together or collected, Hariv.; to be re-arranged or restored, Sāh.; to be destroyed, Nilak. °**hartṛi**, mfn. one who draws together or contracts, MW.; one who destroys, a destroyer, MBh.; R. &c.

Saṃ-hāra, m. bringing together, collection, accumulation, MBh.; contraction (of the organs of speech, opp. to *vi-hāra*, q.v.), RPrāt.; drawing in (of an elephant's trunk), Ragh.; binding together (of hair; cf. *veṇī-s°*), MBh.; fetching back (an arrow after its discharge by magical means), MBh.; R.; Pur. (cf. IW. 402, n. 1); abridgment, comprehensive description, a compendium, manual, Lāṭy.; destruction (esp. the periodical des° of the universe at end of a Kalpa), Mn.; MBh. &c.; a destroyer (= *saṃhartṛi*), MBh. xiv, 1577; end, conclusion (of a drama or of an act of a drama), Bhar.; Sāh. &c.; a division of the infernal regions, L.; N. of an Asura (v.l. *saṃ-hrāda*), Hariv.; practice, skill, W.; *-kārin*, mfn. causing universal destruction, Pañcat.; *-kāla*, m. the time of the des° of the world, MBh.; *-kālāya*, Nom. Ā. °*yate*, to appear like the time of the des° of the w°, Śukas.; *-buddhi-mat*, mfn. intending to destroy the world, Hariv.; *-bhairava*, m. Bhairava as world-destroyer (one of the 8 forms of Bh°, q.v.), Cat.; *-mudrā*, f. N. of a partic. posture in the Tantra worship (= *visarjana-mudrā*), MW.; *-varman*, m. N. of a man, Daś.; *-vega-vat*, mfn. ardently wishing to destroy the world, MBh. °**hāraka**, mfn. (cf. *asthi-s°*) drawing together, compressing, closing, MW.; destructive, ruinous, ib.; a destroyer, ib. °**hārika**, mfn. all-destroying, Hcat. °**hārin**, mfn. destroying (ifc.), Kathās.

Saṃ-hārya, mfn. to be brought or drawn together or collected (from various places), ŚāṅkhBr.; ŚrS.; to be transported, transportable, PañcavBr.; ŚrS.; to be avoided, TĀr.; to be removed or checked or restrained (in *a-s°*), MBh.; R.; to be led astray or corrupted (in *a-s°*), ib.; to be made to partake of, one who has a claim on (abl.), MBh.

Saṃ-hṛita, mfn. drawn or brought together &c.; interrupted (in *a-s°*), Uttarar.; *-busam*, ind. after the chaff has been got in, g. *tishṭhadgu-prabhṛiti*; *-yavam*, ind. after the barley has been got in, ib. °**hṛiti**, f. the destruction of the universe, MārkP.; conclusion, end, Kathās.; Sāh.; the root *hṛi* with *sam*, Śiś.; contraction, abridgment, W.; restraint, ib.; taking, seizure, ib.; *-mat*, mfn. containing the end of (comp.), Sāh.

Saṃ-hriyamāṇa, mfn. (Pass. pr. p. of *saṃ-√hṛi*) being brought together or in &c.; *-busam*, ind. while the chaff is being got in, g. *tishṭhadgu-prabhṛiti*; *-yavam*, ind. while the barley is being got in, ib.

संहृष *saṃ-√hṛish*, P. *-hṛishyati* (m.c. also Ā. °*te*), to bristle, stand erect (as the hair of the body from joy or fright), MBh.; Kāv. &c.; to thrill with delight, be glad, rejoice, ib.: Caus. *-harshayati*, to gladden, delight, R.; Divyâv.

Saṃ-harsha, m. bristling or erection of the hair of the body, thrill of delight, joy, pleasure, MBh.; Śiś.; sexual excitement, Suśr.; ardour, emulation, rivalry, jealousy (cf. *saṃ-gharsha*), MBh.; R. &c.; air, wind, L.; rubbing together, trituration (for *saṃgharsha*), W.; *-yogin*, mfn. possessing joy, enraptured, W. °**harshaṇa**, mf(*ī*)n. causing (the hair of the body) to stand erect (see *loma-h°*); gladdening, delighting (with gen.), MBh.; n. emulation, rivalry, Kām. °**harshita**, mfn. (fr. Caus.) bristling, standing erect (as the hair of the body), SaddhP. °**harshin**, mfn. thrilling with joy, gladdening, delighting (comp.), R.; envious, jealous, Śis.

Saṃ-hṛishita, mfn. = °*harshita*, Jātakam.; stiff or motionless (with fright), Hariv.

Saṃ-hṛishṭa, mfn. bristling, shuddering, MBh.; one whose hair stands erect (with joy), R.; thrilled, delighted, glad, MBh.; Kāv. &c.; flaming briskly (as fire), R.; *-manas*, mfn. delighted in mind, Pañcat.; *-roman* or *-româṅga*, mfn. one who has the hair of the body bristling (with joy), thrilled, delighted, MBh.; *-vat*, mfn. joyfully, gladly, R.; *-vadana*, mfn. one whose face is beaming with joy, ib. °**hṛishṭin**, mfn. erect (as the male organ), Car.

संहोत्र *saṃ-hotra*. See *saṃ-√hu*, col. 1.

संह्राद् *saṃ-√hrād*, Ā. *-hrādate*, to sound or rattle together, MBh.; Hariv.: Caus. *-hrādayati*, to knock together (with a sound or noise), ĀśvGṛ.; to resound loudly, MBh.

Saṃ-hrāda, m. a loud noise, uproar, sound, MBh.; R. &c.; 'Shouter,' N. of an Asura (son of Hiraṇya-kaśipu), MBh.; Hariv.; Pur. (v.l. *-hlāda*). °**hrādana**, mfn. uttering loud sounds, MBh. °**hrādi**, m. 'id.,' N. of a Rākshasa, R. °**hrādin**, mfn. sounding together, tumultuous, noisy, MBh.; m. N. of a Rākshasa, R.; (°*di*)-*kaṇṭha*, m. n. a noisy voice, Kir. °**hrādīya**, mfn. relating or belonging to (the Asura) Saṃ-hrāda, Hariv.

संह्रीण *saṃ-hrīṇa*, mfn. (√*hrī*) altogether ashamed, bashful, modest, Bhaṭṭ.

संह्लाद *saṃ-hlāda*, v.l. (or w.r.) for *saṃ-hrāda*, MBh.

संह्लादिन् *saṃ-hlādin*, mfn. refreshing, cheering, MBh.; Kām.

संह्वारित *sáṃ-hvārita*, mfn. (fr. Caus. of √*hvṛi*) crooked, curved, bent in (with *madhye*, 'thinner or more slender in the middle'), ŚBr.

संह्वे *saṃ-√hve*, Ā. *-hvayate* (Pāṇ. i, 3, 30; Ved. inf. *sáṃ-hvayitavai*), to call out loudly, shout together, AV.; ŚBr.; to relate, make known, Bhaṭṭ.

Saṃ-hūti, f. shouting or calling out together, general shout or clamour, L.

सक *saka*. See 6. *sa*, p. 1111, col. 2.

सकङ्कट *sa-kaṅkaṭa*, mfn. (i.e. 7. *sa* + *k°*) furnished with armlets, Hariv.

Sa (to be similarly prefixed to the following): **-kacchapa**, mfn. with tortoises, Ml. **-kañcuka**, mfn. furnished with armour, L. **-kaṭa**, mfn. bad, vile, L.; m. Trophis Aspera or Angeissus Latifolia, L.; °*ṭâksha*, mfn. casting side glances (*am*, ind.), MBh.; °*ṭânna*, n. impure food, Yājñ. iii, 15, Sch. **-kaṭuka**, mfn. poignant, bitter, harsh (as speech), MBh. **-kaṇṭaka**, mf(*ā*)n. having thorns, thorny, prickly, Cāṇ.; troublesome, perilous, W.; having the hairs of the body erected, thrilled with joy or desire, Kathās.; having pointed splinters, MBh. (v.l.); accompanied with bones (said of fish), Pat.; m. Guilandina Bonduc, L.; Blyxa Octandra, L. **-kaṇṭha-rodham**, ind. in a suppressed or low voice, Bālar. **-kaṇḍu** or **-kaṇḍūka**, mfn. attended with itching, Suśr. **-kapaṭam**, mfn. fraudulently, deceitfully, Sāh. **-kamala**, mfn. abounding in lotuses, Ragh. ix, 19. **-kampa**, mfn. having tremor, tremulous, trembling (*am*, ind.), Ratnâv. **-kampana**, mfn. id., MW.; accompanied with earthquakes, MBh. (= *sa-vidyut*, Nīlak.) **-1. -kara**, mfn. having hands, MW.; possessing a trunk (as an elephant), ib. **-2. -kara**, mfn. having rays, full of rays, W.; bearing tax, liable to pay taxes, ib. **-karaṇaka**, mf(*ikā*)n. transmitted by means of an organ (of the body), Śāṇḍ., Sch. **-karuṇa**, mfn. lamentable, pitiable, piteous, full of pity (*am*, ind. 'piteously'), Mṛicch.; Ratnâv.; Hit.; tender, compassionate (*am*, ind. 'compassionately'), Śak.; BhP. **-karṇa**, mfn. having ears, hearing, Vedântas.; Siṃhâs.; accompanied by Karṇa, MW.; *-puccha*, mfn. with or having ears and tail, KātySr.; *-prâvṛita*, mfn. wrapped or covered up to the ears, ĀpŚr. **-karṇaka**, mf(*ā*)n. 'having ears,' and 'having a pilot or guide,' Śiś. i, 63; having a peg &c., KātySr. **-kartṛika**, mfn. having an agent (*-tā*, f., *-tva*, n.), Kusum.; Sarvad. **-karmaka**, mfn. effective, having consequences, BhP.; (in gram.) 'having an object,' transitive, Pāṇ. i, 3, 53. **-karman**, mfn. (in gram.) = prec. (°*ma-tā*, f.), Kull. on Mn. ix, 37; performing any act or rite, W.; following similar business, ib. **-1. -kala**, mfn. (for 2. see s.v.) having a soft or low sound, MW. **-kalaṅka**, mfn. having spots or stains, stained, contaminated, ib. **-kalatra,** mfn. accompanied by a wife, ib. **-kalaha,** mfn. having quarrels, quarrelsome, quarrelling, ib. **-kalahansa-gaṇa,** mfn. (for *sakala-h°* see col. 2) having flocks of Kala-haṅsas, ib. **-kalika,** mfn. provided with buds, Ragh. **-kalusha,** mf(*ā*)n. troubled, impure, MBh. **-kalevara,** mfn. possessing or including bodies, Bhām. **-kalpa,** mfn. along with the sacrificial ritual, Mn. ii, 140; having rites or ceremonies, MW.; m. N. of Śiva, ib. **-kavaca,** mfn. having armour or mail, mailed, ib. **-kaśmīra,** mf(*ā*)n. together with Kaśmīra, Kathās. **-kashāya,** mfn. dominated by passion (*-tva,* n.), Vedântas.; Sarvad. **-kashṭam,** ind. unhappily, unfortunately, Hāsy. **-kākola,** mfn. together with the hell Kākola, Mn. iv, 89. **-kātara,** mfn. cowardly, timid (*am,* ind.), MBh. **-kāma** (*sá-*), mf(*ā*)n. satisfying desires, VS.; R.; having one's wishes fulfilled, satisfied, contented, MBh.; Kāv. &c.; consenting, willing (said of a girl), Vishṇ.; Mn.; Yājñ.; (ifc.) wishing, desirous of, Śiś.; acting on purpose or with free will, Tithyād.; full of love, loving, a lover, MBh.; Kāv. &c.; betraying love (as speech), Pañcat.; (*am*), ind. with pleasure, for the pl° of (acc.), Divyâv.; °*mâri,* m. 'enemy of lovers,' N. of Śiva, MW. **-kāyikā,** f. a game (v.l. *saṃ-k°*), Divyâv. **-3. -kāra,** mfn. (for 1. and 2. see p. 1111) active, energetic, Śiś. xix, 27. **-kāraṇa,** mfn. provided with a legal instrument, MBh.; = next, W. **-kāraṇaka,** mf(*ikā*)n. having a cause, originating from a cause, Kull. on Mn. vi, 73. **-kārmuka,** mfn. having a bow, armed with a bow, MW. **-kāla,** mfn. seasonable, ib.; (*am*), ind. seasonably, betimes, early in the morning, ib.; (*ī*), f., see s.v. **-kāsa,** m., see s.v. **-kāshāya,** mfn. wearing a brownish-red garment, Rājat. **-kiṃkara,** mfn. attended by servants, MBh. **-kirīṭa-kaustubha,** mfn. having a diadem and breast-jewel, MW. **-kīṭa,** mf(*ā*)n. full of worms &c., Hcat. **-kīla,** m. one who from sexual weakness causes his wife to have intercourse with another man before cohabiting with her himself, L. **-kukshi,** mfn. born from the same womb, Vop. **-kuñjara,** mfn. together with elephants, R. **-kuṭumba,** mf(*ā*)n. together with one's family, Kāv. **-kuṇḍa,** mf(*ā*)n. together with a well, Pañcad. **-kuṇḍala,** mfn. decorated with ear-rings, MW. **-kutūhala,** mfn. full of curiosity (*am,* ind.), Kathās. **-kula,** mfn. having a family, together with one's f°, ŚārṅgP.; belonging to a noble f°, MW.; belonging to the same family, ib.; m. an ichneumon (for *nakula,* by a play on the sound), PārGṛ.; *-ja,* mfn. born from the same f° with (gen.), MBh. **-kulya,** m. one of the same family and name (= *sa-gotra*); a distant relation, remote kinsman (said to apply to a grandson's grandson or even sometimes extended to the tenth descendant), Mn.; Yājñ. &c. **-kuśa,** mfn. holding Kuśa grass in the hand, R. **-kushṭhika,** mfn. = *sagulpha* or *sâṅgushṭha,* Āpast. (Sch.) **-kusumâstaraṇa,** mfn. strewn with flowers, Śak. **-kūti** (*sá-*), mfn. full of desire, enamoured, TBr. **-kṛicchra,** mfn. having trouble or distress, painful, distressing, MW. **-kṛit,** see s.v. **-kṛipa,** mfn. compassionate (*am,* ind.), Śāntiś.; accompanied by Kṛipa, MW. **-kṛipaṇam,** ind. piteously, Śāntiś. **-keta** (*sá-*), mfn. having the same intention, RV.; m. N. of an Āditya, TS. **-ketu,** mfn. having a banner, together with a b°, MBh.; Naish. **-keśa,** mfn. along with the hair, PārGṛ.; containing h° (said of food), MBh.; *-nakha,* mfn. with hair and nails, Gobh. **-kaitava,** mfn. deceitful, fraudulent (*am,* ind.), MW.; a cheat, deceiver, Kathās. **-kopa,** mf(*ā*)n. full of anger, enraged, displeased (*am,* ind.), Kād.; Hit.; *-vikṛiti,* mfn. agitated with anger, Kathās. **-kośa,** mfn. containing passages from dictionaries (opp. to *vi-k°*), Cat.; along with the shell or husk, MārkP.; along with the membrane, ib. **-kautuka,** mf(*ā*)n. full of expectation, expectant of, eager for (comp.; *am,* ind.), Ratnâv.; Kathās. **-kautūhalam,** ind. eagerly, with curiosity, Śak. **-kaurava,** mfn. along with the Kauravas, VarBṛS. **-kratu** (*sá-*), mfn. being of one accord or one mind with (instr.), RV. **-kriya,** mfn. having action, active, mutable, movable, migratory (*-tva,* n.), Kap.; Sāṃkhyak.; one who performs his religious acts, MW. **-krīḍa,** prob. w.r. for *-kroḍa* (q.v.) **-krudh,** mfn. wrathful, angry, Rājat. **-kroḍa,** mfn. along with (i.e. up to) the breast, MārkP. (w.r. *-krīḍa*). **-krodha,** mfn. full of anger, angry, enraged (*am,* ind.), MBh.; R.; *-hāsam,* ind. with an angry laugh, Bālar. **-krodhana,** mfn. = *-krodha,* R. **-kvaṇa,** mfn. making a tinkling sound, Dharmaś. **-kshaṇa,** mfn. (for *sakshána* see col. 3) having leisure for (loc.), BhP. **-kshata,** mfn. having a crack or flaw (as a jewel), L. **-kshatram,** ind. according to the rule of warriors, Laghuk. 973. **-kshāra,** mfn. caustic, acrid, pungent, VarBṛS. **-kshit,** mfn. dwelling or lying together or side by side, RV. **-kshīra,** mfn. provided with milk, milky (as plants; with *yūpa,* m. 'a sacrificial post made of a tree containing milky juice'), ShaḍvBr.; GṛŚrS.; R.; Suśr.; *-dṛiti,* mfn. supplied with leather bags containing milk, TāṇḍBr.; Lāṭy. **-khaḍga,** mfn. armed with a sword, sword in hand, Mṛicch. **-khaṇḍa,** mfn. (opp. to *a-kh°*), Nyāyak. **-khura,** mfn. with the claws or having c°, Vishṇ. **-khila,** mfn. (for *sakh°* see p. 1130, col. 3) with the supplements, Hariv. **-kheda,** mfn. having grief (*am,* ind. sadly), Śak. **-khelam,** ind. with a gentle motion, MBh.

सकल 2. *sa-kala,* mf(*ā*)n. (fr. 7. *sa + kalā;* for 1. *sa-kala* see p. 1123, col. 3) consisting of parts, divisible, material (opp. to *a-* and *nish-k°*), MaitrUp.; MBh.; possessing all its component parts, complete, entire, whole, all (*pratijñām sakalām* √*kṛi,* 'to fulfil one's promise;' m. [sometimes with *api*] 'everybody;' n. 'everything' or 'one's whole property'), KātyŚr.; Mn.; MBh. &c.; whole = wholesome, sound (opp. to *vi-kala*), Nīlak.; affected by the elements of the material world (with Śaivas applied to a soul which has not advanced beyond the lowest stage of progress), Sarvad.; paying interest, Naish. **-karma-cintāmaṇi,** m. N. of wk. **-kalusha,** N. of a forest region, Vikr. **-kāma-dugha,** mf(*ā*)n. granting all wishes, Bhartṛ. **-grantha-dīpikā,** f. N. of a lexicon by Sanat-kumāra. **-jana,** m. every person, everybody, Ratnâv. **-jananī,** f. the mother of all; *-stava,* m. N. of a Tantra wk. **-devatā-pratishṭhā,** f. N. of wk. **-deha,** m. the whole body, Dhūrtas. **-dosha-maya,** mf(*ī*)n. full of all defects, Hcat. **-pāṭha,** m. recitation of the whole (text), KātyŚr., Sch. **-purāṇa-tātparya-sāra,** m., **-purāṇa-samuccaya,** m., **-prabandha-varṇa-sāra-saṃgraha,** m., **-pramāṇa-saṃgraha,** m. N. of wks. **-bhuvana-maya,** mf(*ī*)n. containing the whole world, Pañcar. **-yajña-maya,** mf(*ī*)n. containing the whole oblation, BhP. **-yūtha-parivṛita,** mfn. surrounded by the whole herd or troop, Pañcat. **-rūpaka,** n. a complete metaphor, Kāvyâd. **-loka,** m. 'all the world,' every one, Hit. **-vidyā-maya,** mf(*ī*)n. containing all knowledge, VP. **-vedâdhyāyin,** mfn. repeating all the Vedas, L. **-vedin,** mfn. all-knowing, Bhaṭṭ., Introd. **-vedôpanishat-sārôpadeśa-sāhasrī,** f. the Upadeśa-sāhasrī (by Śaṃkarâcārya) on the essence of all the Vedas and Upanishads. **-śānti-saṃgraha,** m. N. of wk. **-siddhi,** f. the success of all (*-da,* mfn. 'granting success to all'), Cat.; mfn. possessing all perfection, BhP. **-haṅsa-gaṇa,** mfn. (for *sa-kalahaṅsa-g°* see col. 1) having entire or unbroken flocks of geese, MW. **Sakalâgama-saṃgraha,** m. N. of a Tantra wk. **Sakalâgamâcārya,** m. N. of a preceptor, Cat. **Sakalâdhāra,** m. 'receptacle of all,' N. of Śiva, Śivag. **Sakalâdhikāra,** m. N. of a wk. on architecture (attributed to Agastya). **Sakalârṇa-maya,** mf(*ī*)n. containing all sounds, Pañcar. **Sakalârtha-śāstra-sāra,** mfn. containing the essence of precepts about all things, MW. **Sakalârthi-sârtha-kalpa-druma,** m. the wishing tree for the multitude of all supplicants, Pañcat. **Sakalêndu,** m. the full moon, Hariv.; *-mukha,* mf(*ī*)n. having a face like a full moon, Vikr. **Sakalêśvara,** m. lord of the universe, BhP.; N. of an author, Cat.

Sakalaya, Nom. P. °*yati,* to make full, Harav.

Sakalī, in comp. for 2. *sa-kala.* **-√kṛi,** P. *-karoti,* to make full, complete, Pañcar.; Hcat. **-vi-√dhā,** P. *-dadhāti,* id., Pañcar.

सकलकल *sakalakala* (?), m. N. of a family, Cat.

सकलवर्ण *sa-ka-la-varṇa,* mfn. containing the syllables *ka* and *la;* n. (with *sa-ha-kāra*) having the syllables *ka, la, ha* (i.e. the word *kalaha,* strife), Nalôd.

सकाली *sakālī,* f. N. of a place, Cat. **-samudra,** ib.

सकाश *sa-kāśa,* mfn. having appearance or visibility, visible, present, near, L.; m. presence, propinquity, vicinity, nearness (used in the sense of a preposition, esp. after verbs of motion, such as 'to go, come,' &c., with a gen. [or rarely abl.] of a person, or ifc.; e.g. *sakāśam,* 'to, towards, near;' *sakāśe,* 'in the presence of, before;' *sakāśāt* or °*śatas,* 'from the presence of, from;' *ā sakāśāt,* 'as far as, up to' [the fire]), ŚrS.; Up.; MBh. &c.

सकुरुण्ड *sakuruṇḍa,* m. yellow Amaranth or Barleria (= *sāk°*), L.

सकृत् 1. *sa-kṛít,* mfn. (fr. 7. *sa + 1. kṛit*) acting at once or simultaneously, AV. xi, 1, 10; ind. at once, suddenly, forthwith, immediately, RV.; Br.; ŚrS.; Mn.; MBh.; once (= semel, with *áhnaḥ,* 'once a day;' repeated = 'in each case only once'), RV. &c. &c.; once, formerly, ever (with *mā* = 'never,' Kāv.; VarYogay.; once for all, for ever, ChUp.; Kāv.; MārkP.; at once, together, W. [For cognate words see under 7. *sa.*] **-praja,** m. 'having offspring once (a year),' a crow, L.; a lion, L. **-prayogin,** mfn. being employed only once, KātyŚr. **-prasūtikā,** f. one who has borne one child (esp. a cow that has calved once), L. **-phalā,** f. 'bearing fruit once,' the tree Musa Sapientum, L. **-sū́,** mfn. bringing forth once or at once, RV. x, 74, 4. **-snāyin,** mfn. bathing once, Mn. xi, 215.

Sakṛic-chruta-dhara, mfn. (for *sakṛit-śr°*) keeping in memory what has once been heard, Kathās.

Sakṛid, in comp. for 1. *sakṛit.* **-abhishuta** (*sakṛíd-*), mfn. once pressed out, TS. **-āgāmin,** m. 'returning only once again i.e. being re-born,' N. of the second of the four orders of Buddhist Āryas, MWB. 132; (°*mi*)*-tva,* n., Vajracch.; (°*mi*)*-phala* and *-phala-pratipannaka,* Dharmaś. 102; 103. **-ācchinná,** mfn. severed with one cut, ĀśvŚr. **-ādīpana,** n. setting on fire at once, Kauś. **-āhṛita,** mfn. (interest) paid at one time (not by instalments), Mn. viii, 151. **-ukta-gṛihītârtha,** mfn. grasping the sense of what has once been said, Cāṇ. **-upamathitá,** mfn. stirred or churned once, ŚBr. **-gati,** f. only a possibility, Sch. on Pāṇ. vii, 1, 50. **-garbha,** m. 'having only one conception,' a mule, L.; (*ā*), f. a woman who is pregnant only once, MW. **-guha** (VP.), **-graha** or **-grāha** (MBh.), **-vaha** (VP.), m. pl. N. of peoples. **-vidyuttá,** mf(*ā*)n. flashing or gleaning once, ŚBr.; n. the act of flashing once, ib. **-vibhāta,** mfn. appeared at once, Vedântas. **-vīra,** m. the plant Helminthostachys Laciniata, L.

Sakṛin, in comp. for 1. *sakṛit.* **-nandā,** f. N. of a river, MBh. **-nārāśaṅsa,** mfn. provided once with the Soma vessels called Nārāśaṅsas, AitBr. **-madvat,** ind. once, one time, ŚBr.; ŚāṅkhBr.

Sakṛil, in comp. for 1. *sakṛit.* **-lū,** Pāṇ. viii, 2, 4, Sch. **-lūna,** mfn. cut off at once, ŚāṅkhŚr. **-lekha,** w.r. for *sa-hṛill°*, Vas.; R.

सकृत् 2. *sakṛit,* w.r. for *śakṛit,* q.v.

सकृत *sakṛita,* n. an edict addressed to the Śūdras (= *śūdra-śāsana*), L.

सक्त *sakta, sakti, saktu* &c. See √*sañj.*

सक्थि *sákthi,* n. (derivation doubtful; the base *sakthán* [fr. which acc. pl. *sakthāni,* RV. v, 61, 3] appears in later language only in the weakest cases, e.g. sg. instr. *sakthnā́,* gen. abl. *sakthnás,* loc. *saktháni* or *sakthní,* cf. Pāṇ. vii, 1, 75; there occurs also nom. acc. du. *sakthyaù* [RV. x, 86, 16; AV. vi, 9, 1] formed fr. a fem. base *sakthī*), the thigh, thigh-bone; the pole or shafts of a cart (du. euphemistically 'the female organ'), RV. &c. &c.

Saktha (ifc.) = prec. (cf. *añji-, apara-, uttara-s°* &c.)

Sakthī. See under *sakthi.*

सक्मन् *sákman, sákmya.* See √*sac.*

सक्ष् *saksh,* cl. 1. P. *sakshati,* to go, Naigh. ii, 14 (only in pr. p. *sakshat* [RV. i, 131, 3], which, accord. to Sāy. = *saṃ-bhajamāna;* others derive it fr. √*sac* or *sah*).

सक्ष *saksha,* mfn. (fr. √*sah*) overpowering, TS.; TBr.

Sakshaṇa, mfn. (for *sa-kshaṇa* see col. 2) conquering, victorious, RV.

1. **Sakshaṇi,** mfn. vanquishing (with acc.), RV.

सक्षणि 2. *sakshaṇi,* mfn. (fr. √*sac*) connected or united with (gen. or instr.), a comrade, companion, possessor, RV.

सक्षम *sakshama*, m. N. of a teacher of the Haṭha-vidyā (v.l. *allama* and *su-kshāma*), Cat.

सख् *sakh*, *sakhyati* (invented to serve as the source of *sakhi*, q.v. under √1. *sac*).

सखोल *sakhola*, N. of a place, Rājat.

सग् *sag* (cf. √*sthag*), cl. 1. *sagati*, to cover, Dhātup. xix, 27.

सगजारोह *sa-gajâroha*, mfn. (i.e. 7. *sa*+*g*°) attended by men riding on elephants, MW.

Sa (to be similarly prefixed to the following): **-gaṇa** (*sá-*), mfn. having troops or flocks, attended by followers, accompanied by (instr.), RV. &c. &c.; m. N. of Śiva, Śivag. **-gatika**, mfn. connected with a preposition &c. (see *gati*), Pat. **-gadgada**, mfn. with stammering (voice); (*am*), ind. stammeringly, Pañcat.; BhP.; *-gir*, mfn. with or having a faltering or stammering voice, Ratnâv.; *-svaram*, ind. id., Sāh. **-gandha**, mfn. having smell, smelling, Suśr.; odoriferous, fragrant, W.; having the same smell as (instr. or comp.), VarBṛS.; Vop. (also °*dhin*, MBh.); related, kin, Śak. (in Prākṛit); proud, arrogant, Megh. (v.l. *-garva*). **-gandharva**, mfn. together with the Gandharvas, MW.; °*vâpsaraska*, mfn. together with the G°s and Apsarases, MBh. **-1. -gara** (*sá-*), mfn. (for 2. &c. see below) accompanied by praise (fr. *gara*, √1. *gṛī*; said of the fires), VS. (Sch.; accord. to others, 'swallowing,' 'devouring,' fr. *gara*, √2. *gṛī*). **-garas**, mfn. accompanied by praise (applied to Agni; cf. prec.), PañcavBr. **-garbha**, mf(*ā*)n. pregnant, impregnated by (abl. or instr.), Hariv.; Kathās. &c.; (a plant) whose leaves are still undeveloped, Kāśikh.; m. = next, L.; (*ā*), f. a pregnant woman, MW. **-garbhya** (*sá-*), m. a brother of whole blood, one by the same father and mother, VS.; Kāṭh. **-garva**, mfn. having pride, arrogant, exulting, elated by, proud of (loc. or comp.; also *am*, ind. proudly), R.; Kālid. &c. **-gu**, mfn. along with cows, ĀpŚr. **-guḍa**, mf(*ā*)n. sugared (?), Mṛicch. viii, 10. **-guḍa-śriṅgaka**, mf(*ikā*)n. furnished with cupolas, MBh. **-guṇa**, mf(*ā*)n. furnished with (or together with) a string or cord, MBh.; Kāv. &c.; furnished with partic. attributes or properties, ŚrS.; having qualities, qualified, BhP.; Vedântas.; having good qualities or virtues, virtuous (*-tva*, n.), Kāv.; Kathās. &c.; worldly, MW.; *-nirguṇa-vāda*, m. N. of a Vedânta wk.; *-vati*, f. N. of a wk. (on the mystic power of the letters of the alphabet, ascribed to Śamkarâcārya), Cat.; °*ṇin*, mfn. having good qualities, virtuous, Bhartṛ. **-gulika**, mfn. along with a pill, Kathās. **-gūḍham**, ind. secretly, privately, MW. **-gṛiha** (*sá-*), mfn. together with one's house or family, with wife and children, ĀpŚr. **-gṛiha-patika**, mfn. with the householder, ŚāṅkhŚr. **-gotra**, mfn. being of the same family or kin, related to (gen. or comp.), Br.; Gaut. &c.; m. a kinsman of the same family (one sprung from a common ancestor or one connected by funeral oblations of food and water), Āp.; Mn.; MBh. &c.; a distant kinsman, L.; n. a family, race or lineage, W. **-gomaya**, mf(*ā*)n. having or mixed with cow-dung, ĀpŚr., Sch. **-goshṭhī**, f. (ifc.) fellowship with, BhP. **-gauravam**, ind. with dignity, Ratnâv. **-gdhi**, °**gdhiti**, see col. 2. **-graha**, mfn. filled with crocodiles (as a river), R.; taken up by means of ladles or other vessels (see *graha*), ĀpŚr.; seized by the demon Rāhu, eclipsed (as the moon), R. **-ghana**, mfn. thick (as hair), SārṅgS.; clouded, VarBṛS.; dense, solid, MW. **-ghṛiṇa**, mf(*ā*)n. full of pity, compassionate, BhP.; tender of feeling, delicate, scrupulous, Jātakam.; disliking, abhorring (loc.), Naish. **-ghṛita**, mfn. mixed with ghee, Vishṇ. **-ghosha**, mfn. (pl.) shouting together, TāṇḍyaBr.

सगर 2. *sa-gara*, mfn. (fr. 7. *sa*+*gara*, 'poison,' √2. *gṛī*; for 1. *sa-gara* see above) containing poison, poisonous (n. 'poisonous food'), R.; BhP.; m. 'provided with moisture,' the atmosphere, air, RV.; TS.; Kāṭh. (cf. Naigh. i, 3); N. of a king of the solar race, sovereign of Ayodhyā (son of Bāhu; he is said to have been called Sa-gara, as born together with a poison given to his mother by the other wife of his father; he was father of Asamañja by Keśinī and of sixty thousand sons by Su-mati; the latter were turned into a heap of ashes by the sage Kapila [see *bhagīratha*], and their funeral ceremonies could only be performed by the waters of Gaṅgā to be brought from heaven for the purpose of purifying their remains; this was finally accomplished by the devotion of Bhagīratha, who having led the river to the sea, called it Sāgara in honour of his ancestor: Sagara is described as having subdued the Śakas, Yavanas, and other barbarous tribes; pl. 'the sons of Sagara'), MBh.; R. &c. (IW. 361); N. of a partic. Arhat, MW. **Sagarôpâkhyāna**, n. 'the story of Sagara,' N. of a ch. of the Padma-purāṇa.

सगर *ságara*, m. and (*ā*) f. (for 1. 2. *sa-g*° see col. 1) night (?), TS.; ŚBr. (in a formula).

सगरी *sagarī*, f. N. of a town, Buddh.

सग्धि *sá-gdhi*, f. (fr. 7. *sa*+*gdhi*=*jagdhi*) a common meal, VS.; TS.

Ságdhiti, f. id., MaitrS.

सग्म *sa-gmá*, m. (? fr. 7. *sa*+*gma*, √*gam*) agreeing, coming to terms, bargaining, VS.; TS.

Sa-gman (prob. fr. the same) = *saṃgrāma*, Naigh. ii, 17.

सघ् *sagh* (cf. √*sah*), cl. 5. P. (Dhātup. xxvii, 20) *saghnoti* (occurring only in impf. *ásaghnoḥ* °*not*, Pot. *saghnuyāt*, Subj. *sághat*, Prec. *saghyāsam*, and inf. *sagdhyai*; Gr. also pf. *sasāgha*, aor. *asaghīt* or *asāghīt* &c.), to take upon one's self, be able to bear, be a match for (acc.), RV.; TS.; MaitrS.; TĀr.; to hurt, injure, kill, Dhātup.

Sagha, m. N. of a man, Buddh.

Sághan, m. a vulture, TBr.

संकक्ष *saṃ-kaksha*. See *niḥ-s*°.

Saṃ-kakshikā, f. a kind of garment, Buddh.

संकट *saṃ-kaṭa*, mf(*ā*)n. (prob. Prākṛit for *saṃ-kṛita*; cf. 2. *vi-kaṭa* &c.) 'brought together,' contracted, closed, narrow, strait, MBh.; Kāv. &c.; crowded together, dense, impervious, impassable, MBh.; MārkP.; dangerous, critical, MBh.; (ifc.) crowded with, full of, Kād.; m. N. of a partic. personification (a son of Kakubh), BhP.; of a man, Rājat.; of a gander or flamingo, Kathās.; Pañcat.; Hit.; (*ā*), f., see below; (*am*), n. a narrow passage, strait, defile, pass, MBh.; Kāv. &c., a strait, difficulty, critical condition, danger to or from (comp.; cf. *prâṇa-s*°), ib. **-caturthī**, f. N. of the fourth day in the dark half of Śrāvaṇa, Cat. **-nāśana**, mfn. removing difficulties, Kām. **-mukha**, mfn. narrow-mouthed, ib. **-muha** (for *-mukha*), 'id.,' a kind of vessel, Śīl. **-stotra**, n. N. of a ch. of the Kāśī-khaṇḍa. **-stha**, mfn. being in difficulties, Kathās. **-hara-caturthī-vrata**, n. N. of wk. **Saṃkaṭâksha**, w.r. for *sa-k*°. **Saṃkaṭâpanna**, mfn. beset with difficulties, MW. **Saṃkaṭôttīrṇa**, mfn. released from difficulties, Kathās.

Saṃkaṭā, f. N. of a Yoginī (seven others are named, viz. Maṅgalā, Piṅgalā, Dhanyā, Bhrāmarī, Bhadrikā, Ulkā, Siddhi), Jyot.; of a goddess worshipped in Benares, L. **-nāmâshṭaka**, n. N. of a ch. of the Padma-purāṇa.

Saṃkaṭāya, Nom. Ā. °*yate*, to become narrow or too n°, Kād.; to become contracted, grow less, ib.

Saṃkaṭika, mfn., g. *kumudâdi*.

Saṃkaṭin, mfn. being in danger or difficulties, MārkP.

संकथ् *saṃ-√kath*, P. *-kathayati*, to relate or narrate fully, tell, speak about (acc.), converse, MBh.; BhP.

Saṃ-kathana, n. the act of narrating fully, narration, conversation with (instr. with and without *saha*), MBh.; Naish. °**kathā**, f. (ifc. f. *ā*) talk or conversation with (instr. with or without *saha*) or about (comp.), MBh.; R. &c.; accordance, agreement, Cat.

Saṃ-kathita, mfn. related, narrated, communicated, MBh.; R.

संकन् *saṃ-√kan* (only p. *-cakānā*), to be pleased or satisfied, RV. v, 30, 17.

संकम्प् *saṃ-√kamp*, Ā. *-kampate*, to shake about, tremble, quake, MBh.; R.: Caus. *-kampayati*, to cause to shake or tremble, MBh.

संकर *saṃ-kara* &c. See *saṃ-√kṛī*.

संकर्तम् *saṃ-kartam*. See *saṃ-√2. kṛit*.

संकर्ष *saṃ-karsha* &c. See *saṃ-√kṛish*.

संकल् *saṃ-√2. kal*, P. *-kālayati*, to drive (cattle) together (for grazing), Hariv.; to put to flight, MBh.; to carry out, perform the last or funeral honours to a dead person, R.

Saṃ-kalā, ind. killing, slaughter (?), W.

Saṃ-kālana, n. the act of driving (cattle) together (for grazing), Cat.; carrying out or burning (a corpse), R. (v.l. *saṃ-kalana*).

संकल् *saṃ-√3. kal*, P. *-kalayati*, to heap together, accumulate, Suśr.; to add, Gaṇit.; to be of opinion, Kpr.

Saṃ-kala, m. (cf. Pāṇ. iv, 2, 75) collection, accumulation, quantity, W.; addition, ib. °**kalana**, n. (or *ā*, f.) joining or adding or holding together, Kād.; addition, Bījag.; the act of heaping together, W. °**kalikā-cūrṇa**, n. shavings, Divyâv.

Saṃ-kalita, mfn. heaped together, accumulated &c.; added, Līl.; blended, intermixed, W.; laid hold of, grasped, MW.; (*ā*), f. (in arithm.) the first sum in a progression, Col.; n. addition, Līl.; °*tâikya*, n. the sum of the sums or terms (of an arithm. progression), Col. °**kalitin**, mfn. one who has made an addition (with loc.), g. *ishṭâdi*.

संकलुष *saṃ-kalusha*, (prob.) n. defilement, impurity (*yoni-s*°, 'an illegitimate marriage'), MBh. (cf. *kalusha-yoni*).

संकल्प *saṃ-kalpa* &c. See *saṃ-√klṛip*.

संकष्ट *saṃ-kashṭa*, (prob.) distress, trouble, need (in the following comp.) **-caturthī-kathā**, f., **-caturthī-vrata-kathā**, f., **-nāśana-gaṇapati-stotra**, n., **-nāśana-vrata**, n., **-nāśana-stotra**, n., **-vrata**, n., **-hara-caturthī-vrata**, n., **-hara-caturthī-vrata-kāla-nirṇaya**, m., **-haraṇa-stotra**, n. N. of wks.

संकसुक *sáṃ-kasuka*, mfn. (fr. *sam*+√1. *kas*; often written *saṃkusuka* or *śaṃkusuka*) splitting, crumbling up (applied to Agni as the destroyer of the body), AV.; (*saṃkás*°), crumbling away, ŚBr.; unsteady, irresolute, MBh. xii, 1044 (accord. to L. also = *durbala*, *manda*, *saṃkīrṇa*, *apavāda-śīla*, *durjana* and *saṃśleshaka*); m. N. of the author of RV. x, 18 (having the patr. *Yāmāyana*), Anukr.

सङ्का *sáṅkā*, f. (prob. connected with √*sañj*) contest, strife, fight, RV.; TBr.

संकायिका *saṃkāyikā*. See *sa-kāyikā*, p. 1124, col. 1.

संकार *saṃ-kāra*. See *saṃ-√kṛī*.

संकाश् *saṃ-√kāś*, Ā. *-kāśate*, to appear together, appear in sight, become visible, R.: Caus. *-kāśayati*, to look at, see, behold, AV.

Sáṃ-kāśa, m. (ifc. f. *ā*) look, appearance (often ifc. = 'having the appearance of,' 'looking like,' 'resembling'), AV. &c. &c.; vicinity, neighbourhood (w.r. for *sa-k*°), L. °**kāśya**, w.r. for *sāṃ-kāśya*.

संकिल *saṃ-kila*, m. (said to be fr. *śam* + √*kil*) a burning torch, fire-brand, L.

संकीर्ण *saṃ-kīrṇa* &c. See *saṃ-√kṛī*.

संकीर्त् *saṃ-√kīrt*, P. *-kīrtayati*, to mention or relate fully, announce, proclaim, celebrate, praise, MBh.; Kāv. &c.

Saṃ-kīrtana, n. the act of mentioning fully &c.; praise, celebration, glorification, MBh.; Kāv. &c. °**kīrti**, m. N. of a Vaiśya (said to have been the author of partic. Vedic hymns), MW. °**kīrtita**, mfn. mentioned fully, celebrated, praised, ib.

संकील *saṃkīla*, m. N. of a man (v.l. *saṃkīrṇa*), Cat.

सङ्कु *saṅku* (?), m. a hole, W.

संकुच् *saṃ-√kuc* (or *-kuñc*), P. *-kucati*, to contract, shrink, close (as a flower), Kāv.; Kathās.; Suśr.; to contract, compress, absorb, destroy, Nir., Sch.: Pass. *-kucyate*, to shrink, be closed or contracted, Suśr.: Caus. *-kocayati*, to contract, draw in, MBh.; Suśr.; to narrow, make smaller, lessen, Bhartṛ.; (Ā.) to withdraw, withhold, Subh.

Saṃ-kucana, m. 'Shriveller,' N. of a demon causing disease (v.l. *saṃ-kuṭana*), Hariv.; n. contraction, shrinking, shrivelling, Car.

Saṃ-kucita, mfn. contracted, shrunk, shrivelled, narrowed, closed, shut, R.; Bhartṛ.; Suśr.; crouching, cowering, MW.; N. of a place, g. *takshaśilâdi*.

Sam-kuñcita, mfn. curved, bent, Divyâv.

Sam-koca, m. contraction, shrinking together, compression, MBh.; Kāv. &c.; shutting up, closing (of the eyes), Sāh.; crouching down, cowering, humbling one's self, shyness, fear (acc. with √*kṛi*, 'to become shy or modest'), Hariv.; abridgment, diminution, limitation, restriction, Śaṃk.; Sarvad.; drying up (of a lake), Kāv.; binding, tying, L.; a sort of skate fish, L.; N. of an Asura, MBh.; n. saffron, L.; *-kārin*, mfn. making contraction, crouching down, humble, modest, Rājat.; *-pattraka*, mfn. causing the withering of leaves (said of a partic. disease affecting trees), Hariv.; *-piśuna*, n. saffron, L.; *-rekhā*, f. 'line of contraction,' a wrinkle, fold, L. °**kocaka**, mfn. contracting, causing to shrink or shrivel up, Kāvyâd., Sch. °**kocana**, mf(*ī*)n. (see *gātra-saṃkocanī*) id.; astringent, MW.; m. N. of a mountain, R.; (*ī*), f. the sensitive plant (Mimosa Pudica), L.; n. the act of contracting or closing or astringing, MBh.; Suśr.; Sāh. °**kocanīya**, mfn. to be limited or restricted (*-tva*, n.), Nyāyam., Sch. °**kocita**, n. (fr. Caus.) 'contraction of the limbs,' a partic. manner of fighting, Hariv. °**kocin**, mfn. closing (as a flower), Rājat.; contracting (see *gātra-saṃk°*); diminishing, lessening, Vcar.; astringent, MW.

संकुप् *sam-√1. kup*, P. *-kupyati*, to become agitated or moved, ŚvetUp.; to become angry or enraged, MBh.: Caus. *-kopayati*, to make angry, excite, MBh.; to become agitated or excited, ŚBr.

Sam-kupita, mfn. enraged, aroused, excited, MBh.

संकुल *sam-kula*, mf(*ā*)n. (cf. *ā-kula*) crowded together, filled or thronged or mixed or mingled or affected with, abounding in, possessed of (instr. or comp.), MBh.; Kāv. &c.; thick, dense (as smoke), R.; violent, intense (*-kalusha*, mfn. 'intensely turbid'), VarBṛS.; disordered, disturbed, confused, perplexed, MBh.; impeded, hindered by (instr.), VarBṛS.; Hit.; m. N. of a poet, Cat.; (*am*), n. a crowd, throng, mob, Mālatīm.; a confused fight, battle, war, MBh.; Hariv. &c.; trouble, distress, BhP.; MārkP.; inconsistent or contradictory speech, MW.

Sam-kulita, mfn. crowded or filled with, abounding in (comp.), BhP.; confused, perplexed, R.

Samkulī-kṛita, mfn. thronged, crowded, gathered together, R.; disordered, thrown into confusion, Kām.

संकुसुक *saṃkusuka*. See *sáṃ-kasuka*.

संकुसुमित *sam-kusumita*, mfn. flowering, Lalit.; fully blown or budded, fully expanded or manifested (occurring in the names of various Buddhas).

संकूजित *sam-kūjita*, n. (√*kūj*) the cry of the Cakra-vāka, Śiksh.

संकूटन *sam-kūṭana*, n., Pat. on Pāṇ. iii, 3, 44, Vārtt. 3.

संकृ *sam-√1. kṛi*, P. Ā. *-karoti*, *-kurute* (3. pl. pr. *sam-kurvate*, Mṛicch.; impf. *sam-akriṇvan*, RV.; pf. *sam-cakruḥ*, ib.; aor. *sam-akran*, ib.), to put together, compose, arrange, prepare &c. (= *sam-skṛi*, q. v.): Pass. *-kriyate* (aor. *sam-akāri*), RV.: Caus. *-kārayati*, to cause to arrange or prepare, celebrate (a wedding), MBh.; to make, render (two acc.), ib.

Sám-kṛiti, mfn. putting together, arranging, preparing, making ready, TS.; TBr.; m. N. of various men (pl. 'the family of S°;' cf. g. *gargâdi*), ŚrS.; MBh. &c.; f. a kind of metre (consisting of 4 Pādas of 24 syllables each), RPrāt.; Col.; n. N. of a Sāman, ĀrshBr.

संकृत् *sam-√2. kṛit* (only ind. p. *-kṛitya* and *-kártam*), to cut to pieces, cut through, pierce, ŚBr.

Sam-kṛitta, mfn. cut to pieces, cut through, pierced, MBh.

संकृष् *sam-√kṛish*, P. Ā. *-karshati*, °*te*, to draw together, contract, tighten, AV.; TS.; KātyŚr.; to draw away, drag along, carry off, MBh.; R.

Sam-karsha, mfn. drawing near, vicinity, neighbourhood, Gobh.; *-kāṇḍa*, m. N. of wk. (= *saṃkarshaṇa-k°*; see col. 2); *-bhāṭṭa-dīpikā*, f. N. of wk. °**karshaṇa**, n. drawing out, extraction, Hariv.; BhP.; a means of joining or uniting, BhP.; drawing together, contracting, W.; making rows, ploughing, ib.; m. N. of Bala-deva or Bala-rāma (also called Halâyudha [q. v.], the elder brother of Kṛishṇa; he was drawn from the womb of Devakī and transferred to that of Rohiṇī; among Vaishṇavas he is considered as the second of the four forms of Purushôttama), MBh.; Hariv.; Pur.; Sarvad.; N. of the father of Nīlâsura, Cat.; (also with *sūri*) of various authors, ib.; *-kāṇḍa* (or *sam-karsha-k°*), m. N. of an appendix to the Mīmāṅsā-sūtra; *-maya*, mf(*ī*)n. representing Bala-deva, AgP.; *-vidyā*, f. the art of drawing a child from the womb of one woman and transferring it to that of another (applied to Bala-deva, cf. above), Prab.; *-śaraṇa*, m. N. of an author, Cat.; *-sūtra-vicāra*, m. N. of wk.; °*ṇeśvara-tīrtha*, n. N. of a Tīrtha, Cat. °**karshin**, mfn. drawing together, contracting, shortening (see *kāla-s°*).

Sam-kṛishṭa, mfn. drawn together, contracted (as two sounds), drawn near to one another, KātyŚr.

संकॄ *sam-√kṝi*, P. *-kirati*, to mix or pour together, commingle, MBh.; to pour out, bestow liberally or abundantly, RV.; AV.; TS.: Pass. *-kīryate*, to become mixed or confused, MBh.

Sam-kara, m. mixing together, commingling, intermixture, confusion (esp. of castes or races, proceeding from the intermarriage of a man with a woman of a higher caste or from the promiscuous intercourse of the four tribes, and again from the indiscriminate cohabitation of their descendants; cf. *yoni-s°*), Mn.; MBh. &c.; the offspring of a mixed marriage, R.; any action similar to the intermixture of castes (sometimes n.), MBh.; (in rhet.) the confusion or blending together of metaphors which ought to be kept distinct (opp. to *sam-sṛishṭi*, q.v.), Sāh.; Kpr.; anything that may be defiled by the touch of any unclean thing, MBh.; dung, Car.; dust, sweepings, L.; the crackling of flame, L.; N. of a man, Buddh.; *-ja*, mfn. born from a mixed caste, Cat.; *-jāta*, mfn. id., Mn. v, 89; *-jāti*, mfn. id., BhP.; *-jātīya*, mfn. id., MW.; *-tā*, f. (see *varṇa-s°*); *-mīmāṅsā*, f. N. of wk.; *-saṃkara*, m. the mixed offspring of mixed offspring, Vishṇ.; *-sveda*, m. a partic. sudorific treatment; °*rāpātra-krityā*, f. an action which degrades a man to a mixed caste or makes him unworthy to receive gifts, Mn. xi, 126; °*rāśva*, m. 'mongrel horse,' a mule, L. °**karaka**, mfn. mixing, mingling, confusing, MBh. °**karita**, in *garbha-s°* (q. v.) °**karin**, mfn. one who has illicit intercourse with (comp.), Baudh.; mingling, confusing (in *putra-s°*, q. v.), Vishṇ.; Mn., Sch. &c.

Samkarī in comp. for *saṃkara*. **-karaṇa**, n. mixing together, confusing (esp. illegal intermixture of castes or any similar illegality), Vishṇ. **-√kṛi**, P. *-karoti* (pp. *-kṛita*), to mix together, confuse, MW.

Sam-kāra, m. dust, sweepings (*-kūṭa*, n. a heap of rubbish), Divyâv.; the crackling of flame, L.; (*ī*), f. a girl recently deflowered, new bride, L.

Sam-kīrṇa, mfn. poured together, mixed, commingled &c.; crowded with, full of (comp.), MBh.; joined or combined with (comp.), Yājñ., Sch.; mingled, confused, disordered, adulterated, polluted, impure, Mn.; MBh. &c.; born of a mixed marriage, MBh.; mixed, miscellaneous, of various kinds, manifold, Bhar.; Daśar.; sprinkled (esp. with fluid-exudation, as a rutting elephant; but cf. *-nāga*), L.; contracted, narrow, W.; scattered, strewed, spread, diffused, ib.; m. a man of mixed caste, Bhar.; (in music) a mixed note or mode; = *-nāga*, L.; N. of an ancient sage (v. l. *sam-kīla*), L.; (*ā*), f. a kind of riddle (of a mixed character), Kāvyâd. iii, 105; (*am*), n. confusion (in *vākya-s°*, q. v.); *-cārin*, mfn. wandering about confusedly, going to various places, Suśr.; *-jāti*, mfn. (= *yoni*), Cat.; *-tā*, f. confusion, confused order (of words in a sentence), Sāh.; *-nāga*, m. an elephant with mixed characteristics, VarBṛS.; *-neri*, m. a kind of dance, Saṃgīt.; *-yuddha*, n. a fight with various weapons, MBh.; *-yoni*, mfn. of mixed birth or caste, impure through illegal intermarriage, Mn. x, 25; *-rāgâdhyāya*, m. N. of a wk. on music; *-vishkambhaka*, m. (in dram.) a mixed interlude, Bhar.; °*ṇāra* (?), m. N. of a serpent-demon, VP.; °*ṇī-karaṇa*, n. = *saṃkarī-k°*, L.

संकृत् *sam-kṛīt*. See *sam-√kīrt*.

संक्लृप् *sam-√klṛip*, Ā. *-kalpate*, to be brought about, come into existence, ChUp.; to be in order or ready, ib.; to wish, long for, be desirous of (see *sam-kalpanīya*): Caus. *-kalpayati*, °*te*, to put together, arrange, AV.; to produce, create, BhP.; to move or rock to and fro (the head), R.; to determine, fix, settle, MBh.; Kād.; to destine for (loc.), MBh.; (with or without *manasā*), to will, purpose, resolve, intend, aim at, strive after, AV. &c. &c., to imagine, fancy, take for, consider as (acc. with *iva*), Daś.; to think about, ponder, hesitate, R.; to perform obsequies, ib.

Sam-kalpá, m. (ifc. f. *ā*) conception or idea or notion formed in the mind or heart, (esp.) will, volition, desire, purpose, definite intention or determination or decision or wish for (with loc., dat., or ifc.), sentiment, conviction, persuasion; (ibc. often = 'intentionally,' 'purposely,' 'on purpose,' 'according to will,' &c.; acc. with √*kṛi*, 'to form a resolution, make up one's mind'); AV. &c. &c.; idea or expectation of any advantage, W.; a solemn vow or determination to perform any ritual observance, declaration of purpose (e. g. a declaration by a widow of her intention to burn herself with her deceased husband), W.; the Will personified (as a son of Saṃ-kalpā and Brahmā), Hariv.; MārkP.; (*ā*), f. N. of a daughter of Daksha (the wife of Dharma and mother of Saṃkalpa), Hariv.; of Manu's wife, Hariv. **-kulmala** (°*pá-*), mfn. (an arrow) whose neck (see *kúlmala*) is (formed by) desire, AV. **-kaumudī**, f., **-candrikā**, f. N. of wks. **-ja**, mfn. produced from self-will or desire or idea of advantage, Mn.; Yājñ.; produced from mere will, Kum., Sch.; m. 'mind-born, heart-born,' wish, desire, BhP.; love or the god of love, MBh. **-janman**, mfn. born from desire, Kathās.; love or the god of love, Vas.; Kād. **-jūti** (°*pá-*), mfn. urged or impelled by desires, TBr. **-durga-bhañjana**, n. N. of wk. (cf. *saṃkalpa-smṛiti-d°*). **-prabhava**, mfn. born from desire, MBh. **-bhava**, mfn. id., ib.; m. love or the god of love, L. **-mūla**, mfn. rooted or based on some idea or desire of advantage, Mn. ii, 3. **-yoni**, mfn. having source or origin in (mere) will or desire, Prabh.; m. love or the god of love, Kālid. **-rāma**, m. N. of a preceptor, Cat. **-rūpa**, mfn. formed or consisting of will, comformable to the will or purpose, W. **-vat**, mfn. possessing determination, one who decides, a decider, Vedântas. **-śrāddha-prayoga**, m. N. of wk. **-sampatti**, f. fulfilment of a wish, Kathās. **-sambhava**, mfn. = *-mūla*, Mn. ii, 3; m. love or the god of love, L. **-siddha**, mfn. accomplished by mental resolve or will, one who has gained supernatural power through strength of will, MBh. **-siddhi**, f. accomplishment of an object by (strength of) will, Āpast. **-sūryôdaya**, m. N. of a philosophical drama in ten acts (an imitation of the Prabodha-candrôdaya). **-smṛiti-durga-bhañjana**, n. N. of a wk. on law. **Samkalpâtmaka**, mfn. consisting of will or volition, having the nature of mental resolve, ChUp.; willing, resolving, W.

Sam-kalpaka, mfn. (fr. Caus.) determining, deciding, purposing, wishing, AmṛitUp.; well discriminating, Nīlak.; reflecting, pondering, MW. °**kalpana**, n. (or *ā*, f.) purpose, wish, desire, ŚvetUp.; BhP.; (°*nā*)*-maya*, mf(*ī*)n. proceeding from purpose or desire, BhP. °**kalpanīya**, mfn. to be wished or desired or intended, ChUp. °**kalpita**, mfn. (fr. Caus.) wished for, desired, intended, purposed, determined, resolved on, Up.; Mn.; MBh. &c.; conceived, imagined, thought, fancied, contrived, MBh.; Kāv. &c.

Sam-klṛipta, mfn. contrived, prepared, made ready, MBh.; desired, wished, intended, ChUp.; destined or meant for (comp.), Āpast. °**klṛipti**, f. will, volition, ChUp.; thought, fancy, contrivance, MW.

संकेत *sam-keta*, m. (fr. *sam-√cit*) agreement, compact, stipulation, assignation with (gen., esp. with a lover), engagement, appointment (acc. with √*kṛi* or *grah* or *dā* or Caus. of √*klṛip*, 'to make an agreement or appointment' or 'appoint a place of meeting with any person' [gen. or instr. or instr. with *saha*, *samam*, *mithaḥ*]; ibc. 'according to agreement,' 'by appointment'), MBh.; Kāv. &c.; convention, consent, MBh.; intimation, hint, allusion, preconcerted sign or signal or gesture (acc. with √*kṛi*, 'to give a signal'), Kathās.; Git.; a short explanation of a grammatical rule (= *2. śaili*, q. v.), MW.; condition, provision, ib.; N. of a Comm. on the Kāvya-prakāśa and on the Harsha-carita; pl. N. of a people (cf. *sāketa*), MārkP. **-ketana**, n. a place of assignation, place appointed for meeting (a lover &c.), rendezvous, Kathās. **-kaumudī**, f. N.

of wk. **-gṛihaka,** m. or n. (in Prākṛit) = *-ketana,* Mālav. **-graha,** m. (Kusum.), **-grahaṇa,** n. (Sarvad.) making an agreement. **-candrôdaya,** m., **-traya,** n. N. of Tantra wks. **-niketa,** m. (Naish.), **-niketana,** n. (Kathās.) = *-ketana.* **-paddhati,** f. N. of a Tantra wk. **-pūrvakam,** ind. by agreement or appointment, Pañcar. **-bhūmi,** f. = *-ketana,* Vās. **-mañjarī,** f. N. of wk. **-milita,** mfn. met by appointment, Kathās. **-yāmala,** n. N. of a Tantra wk. **-ruta-praveśa,** m. a partic. Samādhi, Buddh. **-vākya,** n. a preconcerted word, watchword, Kāv. **-śikshā,** f. N. of a Tantra wk. **-stava,** m. (with Śāktas) a partic. hymn of praise, Cat. **-stha,** mf(*ā*)n. appearing by appointment, Ratnâv. **-sthāna,** n. = *-ketana,* Vās.; an object agreed upon by signs, Vet.; a sign, signal, intimation, MW. **-hetu,** m. motive for an appointment or meeting, VarBṛS. **Saṃketôdyāna,** n. a park or garden appointed as a rendezvous, Kathās.

Saṃketaka, m. an agreement, appointment, rendezvous, Mṛicch.; Pañcat.; Kathās. °**ketana,** n. id., Vet.

Saṃketaya, Nom. P. °*yati,* to agree upon, appoint (a time &c.), Kāv.; to be informed, learn, Vās.; to invite, call, MW.; to counsel, advise, ib.

Saṃketita, mfn. agreed upon, fixed, settled, Prâyaśc.; Sāh.; invited, MW.

Saṃketī-√kṛi, P. *-karoti,* to appoint (as a place of meeting). **-kṛita,** mfn. assigned or appointed (as a place of meeting), Gīt.

संकोच *saṃ-koca* &c. See *saṃ-√kuc.*

संक्रन्द् *saṃ-√krand* (only aor. *sam-akrān*), to cry or bellow or cry out together with (instr.), RV.: Caus. (only aor. *sám-acikradaḥ*) to bring together by shouting or calling out, ib.

Saṃ-kranda, m. sounding together, sound (of the flowing Soma), MBh.; wailing, lamentation, R.; war, battle, MBh. °**krándana,** mfn. calling or shouting or roaring, RV.; AV.; MBh.; m. N. of Indra, Bhaṭṭ.; of a son of Manu Bhautya, Hariv.; of a king (the father of Vapushmat), MārkP.; n. war, battle, MBh.; *-nandana,* m. patr. of Arjuna, Dhanaṃj.; of the monkey Vālin, Mcar.; Bālar.

संक्रम् *saṃ-√kram,* P. Ā. *-krāmati, -kramate,* to come together, meet, encounter, AV.; ŚBr.; to come near, approach, appear, TS. &c. &c.; to enter a constellation (said of the sun), Jyot.; to go or pass over or through, pass from (abl.) into (loc. or acc.), MBh.; Kāv. &c.; to overstep, transgress, ŚāṅkhBr.; to go along, wander, roam, MBh.; R.: Caus. *-krāmayati* (ind. p. *-kramayya*), to cause to go, lead to (acc.), Ragh.; to transfer, transport, deliver over, consign (with acc. of thing and loc. of pers.), MBh.; Kāv. &c.; to bring two words together (in the Krama [q. v.], by omitting those between), VPrāt.; to agree, MBh. v, 7494.

Saṃ-kramá, m. going or coming together, VS.; progress, course, (esp.) transition, passage or transference to (loc.), Kusum.; the passage of the sun or a planet through the zodiacal signs, Yājñ.; VarBṛS. &c.; the falling or shooting of stars, Mṛicch.; the meeting of two words in the Krama text (caused by omitting those between), VPrāt.; a bridge or steps leading down to water, Mn.; MBh. &c.; N. of one of Skanda's attendants, MBh.; of a king of the Vidyā-dharas (the son of Vasu), Kathās.; m. or n.(?) a particular high number, Buddh.; m. n. difficult passage or progress (as over rocks or torrents or inaccessible passes), L.; a means or vehicle for effecting a difficult passage or of obtaining any object, Daś.; n. du. (with *Indrasya* or *Vasishṭhasya*) N. of two Sāmans, ĀrshBr.; *-dvādaśâha,* m. a partic. form of the Dvādaśâha (q. v.), KātyŚr.; *-yajña,* m. a kind of sacrifice, Vait. °**krámaṇa,** n. going or meeting together, union with, entrance into, transference to (loc., dat., or comp.), ĀśvŚr.; Hariv. &c.; entrance, appearance, commencement (esp. of old age), Hariv.; the sun's passage from one sign of the zodiac to another (also *ravi* or *sūrya-s°*), Jyot.; the day on which the sun's progress north of the equator begins, MW.; passage into another world, decease, death, MBh.; R.; a means of crossing, ŚBr.; (in alg.) concurrence (said to be a general designation of a partic. class of problems), Col. °**kramaṇakā,** f. a gallery, Divyâv. °**kramita,** mfn. (fr. Caus.) conducted, led to (acc.), Ragh.; transferred, changed (*arthântaram,* 'into another meaning'), Sāh. °**kramitṛi,** mfn. who or what passes from one place to another, passing, proceeding, going, W. °**kramī-√kṛi,** P. *-karoti,* to use as a vehicle or means of attaining (*-kṛitya,* ind. by means of), Daś.

Saṃ-krānta, mfn. gone or come together, met &c.; passed or transferred from (abl.) to (loc.), Kāv.; transferred to a picture, imaged, reflected, W.; (in astron.) having a Saṃkrānti (as a mouth, cf. *a-s°*), MW.; (*ā*), f. N. of a ch. of the Maitrāyaṇī-saṃhitā.

Saṃ-krānti, f. going from one place to another, course or passage or entry into, transference to (loc. or comp.), Kāv.; MārkP.; (in astron.) passage of the sun or a planet from one sign or position in the heavens into another (e.g. *uttarâyaṇa-s°,* 'passage of the sun to its northern course' [cf. *kūṭa-s°*]; a day on which a principal Saṃkrānti occurs is kept as a festival, see RTL. 428), Sūryas.; transference of an art (from a teacher to a pupil), Mālav. i, 15, 18; transferring to a picture, image, reflection, W.; = *-vādin,* Buddh.; *-kaumudī,* f. N. of an astron. wk.; *-cakra,* n. an astrological diagram marked with the Nakshatras and used for foretelling good or bad fortune, MW.; *nirṇaya,* m., *-paṭala,* m. n., *-prakaraṇa,* n., *-phala,* n., *-lakshaṇa,* n. N. of wks.; *-vādin,* m. pl. a partic. Buddhist school; *-viveka,* m., *-vyavasthā-nirṇaya,* m., *-śānti,* f.; (°*nty*)-*udyāpana,* n. N. of wks.

Saṃ-krāma, m. passing away, ĀpŚr.; m. n. difficult passage or progress, L. °**krāmaṇa,** n. (fr. Caus.) transferring, transporting (*-viropaṇa,* n. 'transplanting'), VarBṛS.; (*ī*), f. a kind of magic or spell, Divyâv. °**krāmayitavya,** mfn. (fr. id.) to be transported or transferred, Hariv. °**krāmita,** mfn. (fr. id.) transferred, handed over, delivered, communicated, MBh.; Kāv. &c. °**krāmin,** mfn. passing over or being transferred to others, Kull. on Mn. iii, 7 (cf. *bhūta-s°*).

संक्री *saṃ-√krī,* P. Ā. *-krīṇāti, -krīṇīte,* to buy, purchase, MBh.

संक्रीड् *saṃ-√krīḍ,* Ā. *-krīḍate* (Pāṇ. i, 3, 21; rarely P. °*ti*), to sport or play together, play with (with instr. of thing and instr. with or without *saha* of pers.), R.; Bhaṭṭ.; (P.) to make a rattling sound (as wheels), Pāṇ. i, 3, 21, Vārtt. 1, Pat.

Saṃ-krīḍa, m. sport, play; pl. (with *marutām*) N. of Sāmans, ĀrshBr. °**krīḍana,** n. sporting, playing, Hariv.

Saṃ-krīḍita, mfn. played, sported; rattled (n. impers. or 'the rattling of wheels'), MBh.; Kir.

संक्रुध् *saṃ-√krudh,* P. *-krudhyati,* to be enraged, be angry with (acc.), MBh.; Bhaṭṭ. (cf. Pāṇ. i, 4, 38).

Saṃ-kruddha, mfn. greatly enraged, incensed, wrathful, violent, MBh.; R. &c.

संक्रुश् *saṃ-√kruś,* P. *-krośati* (rarely Ā. °*te*), to cry out together, raise a clamour, R.; MBh.; to shout at angrily, AV.

Saṃ-krośá, m. crying out together, clamour, shout of anger or indignation (pl. with *Aṅgirasām,* N. of Sāmans), ĀrshBr.; n. pl. those parts of a horse's body which in moving produce a sound, VS. (Sch.)

संक्लिन्न *saṃ-√klinna,* mfn. (*√klid*) thoroughly wet or moistened, Gṛihyās.; Mṛicch.

Saṃ-kleda, mfn. excessive wetness or moisture, saturation with (comp.), R.; Hariv. &c.; moisture (supposed to be the first stage of putrefaction), Car.; a fluid secretion (supposed to form upon conception and become the rudiment of the fetus), Yājñ.

संक्लिश् *saṃ-√kliś,* P. *-kliśnāti* (only inf. *-kleshṭum* and ind. p. *-kliśya*), to press together, ŚBr.; to torment, pain, afflict, R.: Pass. *-kliśyate,* to get soiled, Divyâv. (cf. next).

Saṃ-klishṭa, mfn. pressed together &c.; contused or bruised (as the flesh without injury to the skin), Suśr.; covered with mould or mildew, tarnished (as a mirror), Car.; beset with difficulties (see next); *-karman,* mfn. one who does everything with trouble or difficulty, MBh.

Saṃ-kleśa, m. pain, suffering, affliction, MBh.; R. &c.; *-nirvāṇa,* n. cessation of afflictions, MW. °**kleśana,** n. causing pain, Car.

संक्षप् *saṃ-√1. kshap,* P. *-kshapati,* to emaciate the body by fasting or abstinence, do penance, MBh.

संक्षम् *saṃ-√1. ksham* (only inf. *-kshantum*), to put up with, bear, endure, MBh.

संक्षर् *saṃ-√kshar,* P. *-ksharati,* to flow together or down, RV.

Saṃ-kshára, m. flowing together, ŚBr.

Saṃ-ksharita, mfn. flowing, trickling, ib.

Saṃ-kshāra, m. flowing together (*iḍānām s°* or *iḍā-s°,* N. of a Sāman), Br.

संक्षालन *saṃ-kshālana,* n. cleansing-water, ĀpŚr.; (*ā*), f. washing, ablution, Prasannar.

संक्षि *saṃ-√2. kshi,* P. *-ksheti,* to dwell together, abide with (instr.), RV. ix, 72, 3.

संक्षि *saṃ-√4. kshi,* P. *-kshiṇāti,* to destroy completely, annihilate, AV.: Pass. *-kshīyate,* to be destroyed or exhausted, waste away, disappear, perish, MBh.; Suśr.; Bhartṛ.: Caus. *-kshapayati,* to cause to disappear, destroy, Suśr.; *-kshayayati,* see *-kshayita.*

Saṃ-kshaya, m. complete destruction or consumption, wasting, waning, decay, disappearance, MBh.; Kāv. &c.; the dissolution of all things, destruction of the world, MBh.; N. of a Marutvat, Hariv. °**kshayita,** mfn. (fr. Caus.) wasted, waned, disappeared, R.

संक्षिप् *saṃ-√kship,* P. Ā. *-kshipati,* °*te* (ind. p. *-kshepam,* q. v.), to throw or heap together, pile up, Ragh.; to concentrate (the mind), AmṛitUp.; to suppress, restrain, Bhaṭṭ.; to dash together, destroy, MBh.; Kāv. &c.; to condense, compress, contract, abridge, shorten, diminish, ib.: Pass. *-kshipyate,* to be thrown together or compressed or diminished, shrink up, Mn.; MBh. &c.

Saṃ-kshipta, mfn. thrown or dashed or heaped together &c.; abbreviated, contracted, condensed, MBh.; Sāṃkhyak. (*ena,* ind. 'concisely,' Divyâv.); narrow, short, small, Nir.; Mālav.; Suśr.; taken from or away, seized, W.; (*ā*), f. = *-gati,* VarBṛS.; *-kādambarī,* f. N. of a poem; *-gati,* f. one of the 7 parts in the circle of the Nakshatras (accord. to Parāśara's system), VarBṛS.; *-calârcā-vidhi,* m. N. of a ch. of the Rāja-dharma-kaustubha by Anantadeva; *-tva,* n. a state of contraction or narrowness, condensation, Suśr.; *-dairghya,* mfn. having the length diminished, MW.; *-nirṇaya-sindhu,* m., *-bhārata* (cf. *saṃ-kshepa-bh°*), *-bhāshya,* n., *-rāgânugā-pūjā-paddhati,* f., *-rāmâyaṇa-pāṭha-prayoga,* m., *-vedânta,* m., *-vedânta-śāstra-prakriyā* (or *vedânta-śāstra-saṃkshipta-pr°*), f., *-śāstrârtha-paddhati,* f., *-śyāmā-pūjā-paddhati,* f. N. of wks.; *-sāra,* m. N. of a grammar (in 8 chapters, by Kramadīśvara, with his own Comm.); *-sāra-saṃgraha,* m. N. of a grammar (by Pītāmbara-śarman); *-homa-prakāra,* m. N. of a wk. on Dharma (by Rāmabhaṭṭa). °**kshiptaka,** m. (in dram.) = next, Bhar. °**kshipti,** f. throwing together, compressing, abridgment, W.; throwing, sending, ib.; ambuscade, ib.; (in dram.) a sudden change of heroes or in the character of the same hero (accord. to some 'a simple expedient'), Bhar.; Daśar.; Sāh. °**kshiptikā,** f. (in dram.) = prec., Daśar., Sch.

Saṃ-kshepa, m. throwing together, destruction, MBh.; compression, comprehension, condensation, abridgment, conciseness, brief exposition, compendium, epitome, essence or quintessence (ibc., *āt, eṇa, am* or °*pa-tas,* 'briefly,' 'concisely,' 'in short'), MBh.; R. &c.; the whole thrown together, total, aggregate (*eṇa* and °*pa-tas,* 'in the aggregate'), Mn. vii, 167; Kull. on i, 68 &c.; Cat.; a means of compressing, Suśr.; (pl.) straits, poverty, MBh.; (in dram.) a brief declaration (of willingness to be at the service of another), Sāh.; throwing, W.; taking away, ib.; *-gāyatrī-nyāsa,* m. N. of wk.; *-tas,* see above; *-tithi-nirṇaya-sāra,* m., *-puraścaraṇa-vidhi,* m., *-pūjā-vidhi,* m., *-bhāgavatâmṛita,* n., *-bhārata* (cf. *saṃkshipta-bh°*), N. of wks.; *-mātra,* n. only an abridgment, MW.; *-yoga-vāsishṭha,* n., *-rāmâyaṇa,* n. (or *r°-s°,* m.) N. of wks.; *-lakshaṇa,* mfn. characterized by brevity, described briefly, MW.; *-vimarśâdhiroha,* m., *-śaṃkara-jaya* (= *ś°-dig-vijaya,* q. v.), m. N. of wks.; *-śārīraka,* a summary in verse of Śaṃkarâcārya's Brahma-sūtra-bhāshya by Sarvajñâtman Mahāmuni (*-ṭīkā,* f., *-phala-lakshaṇa,* n., *-bhāshya,* n., *-vyākhyāna,* n., *-sambandhôkti,* f. N. of wks. connected with prec.); *-siddhi-vyavasthā,* f. N. of a wk. on Dharma; °*pâdhyâtma-sāra,* m., °*pâmṛita,* n., °*pârcana-vi-*

dhi, m., °*pâhnika-candrikā*, f. N. of wks. °**kshepaka**, mfn. one who throws together, destroyer, MBh. °**kshepaṇa**, n. throwing or heaping together, compression, abridgment, brief exposition, L.; throwing, W.; taking away, ib. °**kshepaṇīya**, mfn. to be thrown together or abridged, MW. °**kshepam**, ind. briefly, concisely, Pañcar. °**kshepṭri**, mfn. = °*kshepaka*, MBh.

संक्षुद् *saṃ-√kshud*, P. *-kshodati*, to crush together, pound, bruise, MBh.; R. &c.

संक्षुभ् *saṃ-√kshubh*, Caus. *-kshobhayati*, to shake about violently, agitate, toss, excite, BrahmaP.

Saṃ-kshubdha (R.), **saṃkshubhita** (MBh.), mfn. tossed together, violently shaken or agitated.

Saṃ-kshobha, m. a violent shock or jolt, jerk, overturning, upsetting, MBh.; Kāv. &c.; commotion, disturbance, agitation, excitement, ib.; pride, arrogance, W. °**kshobhaṇa**, n. a violent shock or commotion (in *ati-s*°), Suśr. °**kshobhita**, mfn. (fr. Caus.) tossed or shaken about, MW. °**kshobhin**, mfn. shaking about, jolting, jerking (as a carriage), Car.

संक्ष्णु *saṃ-√kshṇu*, Ā. *-kshṇute* (Pāṇ. i, 3, 65; pr. p. *-kshṇuvāna*, ind. p. *-kshṇutya*), to sharpen well or thoroughly (lit. and fig.), whet, point, stimulate, excite, intensify, ShaḍvBr.; Bhaṭṭ.

संखाद् *saṃ-√khād*, P. *-khādati*, to chew thoroughly, eat up, devour, consume, ŚrS.; Mṛicch.

Saṃ-khādaka, m. 'chewer,' a tooth, Pat., Sch. °**khādakin**, mfn. toothed, fanged (in reproach), Pat.

संखिद् *saṃ-√khid*, P. *-khidati*, to press or force together, RV.; TS.; to drag or tear away, ChUp.

संख्या *saṃ-√khyā*, P. *-khyāti*, to reckon or count up, sum up, enumerate, calculate, ŚBr.; Mn.; MBh. &c.; to estimate by (instr.), MBh.; Ā. (only aor. *saṃ-akhyata*) to appear along with, be connected with, belong to (instr.), RV.; VS.: Caus. *-khyāpayati*, to cause to be looked at or observed by (instr.), TS.; ŚBr.

Saṃ-khya, mfn. counting up or over, reckoning or summing up, Pāṇ. iii, 2, 7, Sch. (ifc.; cf. *go-s*°); m. N. of a man, Cat.; (*ā*), f., see below; n. conflict, battle, war (only in loc.; cf. Naigh. ii, 17), MBh.; Kāv.; Rājat.; *-tā*, f., *-tva*, n. numerableness, numeration, MW. °**khyaka**, mfn. numbering, amounting to (ifc.; cf. *sahasra-s*°).

Saṃ-khyā, f. reckoning or summing up, numeration, calculation (ifc. = 'numbered or reckoned among'), R.; Ragh.; Rājat.; a number, sum, total (ifc. 'amounting to'), ŚBr. &c. &c.; a numeral, Prāt.; Pāṇ. &c.; (in gram.) number (as expressed by case-terminations or personal t°), Kāś. on Pāṇ. ii, 3, 1; deliberation, reasoning, reflection, reason, intellect, MBh.; Kāv.; name, appellation (= *ākhyā*), R.; a partic. high number, Buddh.; manner, MW.; (in geom.) a gnomon (for ascertaining the points of the compass), RāmRās. **-kaumudī**, f. N. of wk. **-°ṅka-bindu** (°*khyâṅk*°), m. a cipher, Kāv. **-tas**, ind. from a number, MW. **-°tiga** (°*khyât*°), mf(*ā*)n. 'going beyond numeration,' innumerable, Bhartṛ. **-nāman**, n. a numeral, Nir. **-nidāna-ṭīkā**, f. N. of wk. **-pada**, n. a numeral, VPrāt. (v. l.) **-parityakta**, mfn. 'deserted by numeration,' innumerable, Pañcat. **-parimāṇa-nibandha**, m. N. of a work on ceremonial law considered by number and measure (by Keśava Kavīndra). **-maṅgala-granthi**, m. the auspicious ceremony of tying knots in a thread corresponding to the number of the past years of one's life, Uttarar. **-mātra**, n. the amount of, MW.; mere numeration, ib. **-mushṭy-adhikaraṇa-kshepa**, m. N. of wk. **-yoga**, m. a partic. constellation (relating to the number of Nakshatras in which a planet is situated), VarBṛS. **-ratna**, n., *-ratna-kośa*, m. N. of wks. **-lipi**, f. a partic. mode of writing, Lalit. **-1. -vat**, mfn. having number, numbered, Vās.; possessing reason or intellect, intelligent, discriminating, ib.; Mcar. **-2. -vat**, ind. like number, MW. **-vācaka**, mf(*ikā*)n. expressive of number; m. a numeral, ib. **-vidhāna**, n. the making of a calculation, VarBṛS. **-°vṛitti-kara** (°*khyâvṛ*°), mfn. 'causing repetition of counting,' difficult to be counted, very numerous, Hariv. **-śabda**, m. a numeral, L. **-śas**, ind. in great numbers, BhP. **-samāpana**, m. N. of Śiva, MBh.

Saṃkhyāka, mfn. amounting to (ifc., e.g. *saptati-s*°, q. v.), Hariv.

Sáṃ-khyāta, mfn. reckoned up, enumerated, numbered, counted, measured, AV. &c. &c.; estimated by, R.; considered (see comp.); m. pl. N. of a people, VarBṛS.; (*ā*), f. (scil. *prahelikā*) a kind of riddle based on counting, Kāv. iii, 101; n. number, multitude, BhP.; *-saṃkhyeya*, mfn. one who has considered what is to be considered, Car.; °*tânudeśa*, m. a subsequent enumeration the members of which correspond successively to those of a previous one, Kāś. on Pāṇ. ii, 3, 7. °**khyāna**, n. becoming seen, appearance, BhP.; reckoning up, enumeration, calculation, Kāṭh.; ŚrS.; MBh. &c.; a number, multitude, Hcat.; measurement, Hariv.; MārkP.

Saṃ-khyeya, mfn. to be numbered or enumerated, definite in number, calculable, not numerous, Pāṇ.; MBh. (cf. *a-s*°); to be considered (see *saṃkhyāta-s*°).

संग *saṃ-ga* and *saṅga*. See below and √*sañj*.

सङ्कट *saṅgaṭa*. See p. 1133, col. 1.

संगणना *saṃ-gaṇanā*, f. counting together, enumeration, MBh.

Saṃ-gaṇikā, f. society, the world, Divyâv.

संगम् *saṃ-√gam*, Ā. *-gacchate* (rarely P. °*ti*, and accord. to Pāṇ. i, 3, 29 only with an object; pf. *-jagme*; Vedic forms &c. *-gamemahi*, *-gamāmahai*, *-ajagmiran*, *-agata* [3. sg.], *-aganmahi*, *-agasmahi* or *-agaṇsmahi*, *-gmishīya*, *-gasīshṭa* or *-gaṇsīshṭa*, *-gaṇsyate* &c.; cf. √1. *gam* and Pāṇ. i, 2, 13; vii, 2, 38), to go or come together, come into contact or collision, meet (either in a friendly or hostile manner), join or unite with (instr. with and without *saha* or *sârdham*), RV. &c. &c.; to unite sexually with (acc.), Bhaṭṭ.; to harmonize, agree, fit, correspond, suit, R.; Kathās.; Vedântas.; to go to or towards, meet (acc.), BhP.; to come together or assemble in (loc.), AV.; to undergo or get into any state or condition, become (e.g. with *viśrambham*, 'to become trustful, confide'), BhP.; (P.) to partake of (instr.), RV.; to go away, depart (this life), decease, die, Lāṭy.; (P.) to visit (acc.), Pāṇ. i, 3, 29, Sch.: Caus. *-gamayati* (ind. p. *-gamayya*), to cause to go together, bring together, connect or unite or endow or present with (instr. of pers. and acc. of thing), AV. &c. &c.; to lead any one to (two acc.), Hit., Introd.; to deliver or hand over to (loc.), transfer, bestow, give, MBh.; Ragh.; to connect, construe (words), Sāh.; to cause to go away or depart (this life), kill, MBh. (Nīlak.): Desid. *-jigaṇsate*, to wish to meet with (instr.), Pat.; *-jigāṇsati*, to wish to attain to (acc.), ib.

Saṃ-gá, m. (for *saṅga* see √*sañj*) 'coming together,' conflict, war, RV. (cf. Naigh. ii, 17).

Saṃ-gat, See Vop. xxvi, 78.

Sáṃ-gata, mfn. come together, met, encountered, joined, united, AV. &c. &c.; allied with, friendly to (instr. or comp.), Gaut.; Rājat.; fitted together, apposite, proper, suitable, according with or fit for (comp.), Kāv.; Kathās.; contracted, shrunk up, MBh. (cf. comp.), in conjunction (as planets), W.; m. (scil. *saṃdhi*) an alliance or peace based on mutual friendship, Kām.; Hit.; N. of a king (belonging to the Maurya dynasty), Pur.; (*am*), n. coming together, meeting with (instr., loc., gen., or comp.), MBh.; Kāv. &c.; frequent meeting, intercourse, alliance, association, friendship or intimacy with (instr., gen., or comp.), KaṭhUp.; Mn.; MBh. &c.; addiction or devotion to (gen.), Kāvyâd.; agreement, MBh.; *-gātra*, mfn. having contracted or shrivelled limbs, MBh.; *-saṃdhi*, m. a friendly alliance (see above), MW.; °*târtha*, mfn. containing a fit or proper meaning, KātyŚr. °**gataka**, m. contact (see *bhrū-s*°); N. of a story-teller, Kathās.

Sáṃ-gati, f. coming together, meeting with (gen. or comp.), RV. &c. &c.; going or resorting to (loc.), Cāṇ.; Hit.; association, intercourse, society, company (with instr. with and without *saha* or *samam*; loc., gen., or comp.), MBh.; Kāv. &c.; a league, alliance, Cāṇ.; sexual union, L.; meeting or coming to pass accidentally, chance, accident (°*tyā*, ind. 'by chance, haply'), MBh.; R. &c.; adaptation, fitness, appropriateness, applicability, Kathās.; Sarvad.; connection with, relation to (instr. or comp.), Kāvyâd.; becoming acquainted, knowledge, L.; questioning for further information, W.; (in the Pūrva-mīmāṇsā) one of the 5 members (Avayavas) of an Adhikaraṇa, Sarvad.; *-prakāśa*, m., *-mālā*, f., *-lakshaṇa*, n., *-vāda*, m., *-vicāra*, m.; (°*ty*)*-anumiti*, f., *-anumiti-vāda*, m. N. of wks. °**gatika** (ifc.) = *saṃ-gati*, Sarvad. °**gatin**, mfn. come together, met, assembled, MārkP.

Saṃ-gathá, m. meeting-place, centre, RV.; TBr.; conflict, war, Naigh.; (*ā*), f. confluence, MW.

Saṃ-gamá, m. (or n., g. *ardharcâdi*; ifc. f. *ā*) coming together, meeting (in a friendly or hostile manner), union, intercourse or association with (instr. with and without *saha*, gen., or comp.), RV. &c. &c.; connection or contact with (instr. or comp.; with *anarthena*, 'coming to harm,' 'injury'), R.; Kām.; sexual union, L.; confluence (of two rivers as of the Ganges and the Jumnā, or of a river, at its mouth, with the ocean; such confluences are always held sacred, RTL. 347), Yājñ.; MBh. &c.; conjunction (of planets), VarBṛS.; harmony, adaptation, W.; point of intersection, Gol.; an uninterrupted series of (comp.), RPrāt.; acquirement of (gen.), Pañcat.; *-jñāna*, m. N. of a scholar (cf. *-śrī-jñ*°), Buddh.; *-tantra-rāja*, N. of wk.; *-datta*, m. N. of a man, Kathās.; *-maṇi*, m. a jewel effecting union (of lovers), Vikr.; *-śrī-jñāna*, m. N. of a scholar (cf. *saṃgama-jñ*°), Buddh.; *-sādhvasa*, n. perturbation in regard to sexual union, Mālav.; *-svāmin*, m. N. of a man, Kathās.; °*mâditya*, m. N. of a man, Cat.; °*mêśa*, n. N. of a Liṅga, Kāśikh.; °*mêśvara*, m. a surname of Viśva-nātha (the author of the Vrata-rāja), Cat.; N. of a Liṅga, Kāśīkh.; (°*ra-māhātmya*, n., *-stotra*, n. N. of wks.; *-svāmin*, m. N. of a man, ib.) °**gamaka**, mfn. leading to, showing the way, Nīlak. on Hariv. 8992. °**gámana**, mf(*ī*)n. gathering together, a gatherer, RV.; AV.; m. N. of Yama (q.v.), MW.; n. coming together, coming into contact with, meeting with (comp.), AV.; TBr.; partaking of (instr.), MBh. °**gamanīya**, mfn. leading to union, effecting union, Vikr. °**gamita**, mfn. (fr. Caus.) brought together, united, ib.; *-vat*, mfn. one who has brought together or united, Daś. °**gamin**, mfn. associating with (comp.), MārkP.

Saṃgin, mfn. (for *saṅgin* see √*sañj*) going with or to, uniting with, meeting, W.

संगमनेर *saṃgamanera*, N. of a place, Cat.

संगर *saṃ-gara* &c. See *saṃ-*√1. 2. *gṛī*.

संगर्ज् *saṃ-√garj*, P. *-garjati*, to roar together, shout at or against (acc.), MBh.

संगव *saṃ-gava*, m. (fr. *sam* and *go*) the time when grazing cows are collected for milking or when they are together with their calves (the second of the five divisions of the day, three Muhūrtas after Prātastana, q. v.), RV.; AV.; Br.; ŚrS. **-kāla**, m. (JaimBr.), **-velā**, f. (ChUp.) the time when cows are collected for milking.

Saṃ-gavinī, f. the place where cows come together for milking, AitBr. (Sāy.)

संगा *saṃ-√gā*, P. *-jigāti*, to come together, AV.; to go to, approach (acc.), BhP.

संगायन *saṃ-gāyana*. See *saṃ-√gai*.

संगाह् *saṃ-√gāh*, Ā. *-gāhate* (only aor. *sam-agāhishṭa*), to plunge into, enter, go into (acc.), Bhaṭṭ.

संगिर् *saṃ-gir*, *saṃ-gira*. See *saṃ-*√1. 2. *gṛī*, p. 1129, col. 1.

संगीत *saṃ-gīta* &c. See *saṃ-√gai*.

संगुण *saṃ-guṇa*, mfn. multiplied with (comp.), VarBṛS.; Gaṇit.

Saṃguṇaya, Nom. (fr. prec.) P. °*yati*, to multiply, Sūryas.

Saṃguṇī-kṛita, mfn. multiplied, Gol.

संगुप्त *saṃ-gupta*, mfn. (√*gup*) well guarded or protected or preserved, MBh.; well hidden, concealed, kept secret, ib.; m. a partic. Buddha or Buddhist saint, L.; °*târtha*, m. a secret matter, hidden meaning; mfn. having a hidden meaning (*-lekha*, m. a letter having a hidden meaning), Kull. on Mn. vii, 153. °**gupti**, f. guarding, protection, MBh.; concealment, Pratâp.

Saṃ-gopana, mfn. hiding or concealing well, Pañcar.; n. the act of hiding or concealing well, complete concealment, Sāh. °**gopanīya**, mfn. to be completely hidden or concealed, Pañcar.

संगूढ *saṃ-gūḍha*, mfn. (√*guh*) completely concealed or hidden from view &c.; contracted, abridged, W.; heaped up, arranged, ib.

Sam-jughukshā, f. (fr. Desid.) the wish to conceal or cover well, desire of hiding, W. °**jughukshu**, mfn. wishing to conceal or hide, Bhaṭṭ.

संगृभाय *sam-gribhāya* (cf. *sam-√grah*), P. *-gribhāyati*, to grasp together, seize, snatch, RV.

Sam-gribhita, mfn. seized or held together, concentrated, BhP. °**gribhita** (*sám-*), mfn. seized or held together, grasped, griped, RV. °**gribhītri** (*sám-*), mfn. restraining, governing, ruling, ib. i, 109.

संगृ *sam-√1. grī*, P. Ā. *-grināti*, *-grinīte* &c., to agree together, assent, promise, RV.; AV.; (P.) to praise, celebrate, BhP.; (Ā. *-girate*), to recognize, acknowledge, aver, assert, Sarvad.; TPrāt., Sch.; to assent, agree with (Dat.), Daś.; to praise unanimously (acc.), Bhaṭṭ.; to promise or vow (to one's self), Daś.; to agree in calling or naming (two acc.), Śrutab.

1. **Sam-gara**, m. agreeing together, agreement, assent, AV. &c. &c.; conflict, combat, fight, battle with (instr.) or for (gen.), Mn.; MBh. &c.; a bargain, transaction of sale, L., knowledge, L.; *-kshama*, mfn. fit for combat or war, Kām.; *-stha*, mfn. engaged in combat or war, R. °**garana**, n. transaction together, agreement, Nir. iii, 9.

Sam-gir, f. assent, promise, RV.

Sam-gīrna, mfn. agreed, assented to, promised, L.

संगृ *sam-√2. grī*, P. *-girati* (once *-grināti*), to swallow up, devour, AV. (cf. Pāṇ. i, 3, 52, Sch.)

2. **Sam-gara**, m. swallowing up, devouring, MW.; n. poison, L.; misfortune, calamity, L.; n. the Śamī fruit, L.

Sam-girá, mfn. swallowing up, devouring, AV.

संगै *sam-√gai*, P. *-gāyati*, to sing together, celebrate by singing together, sing in chorus, chant, ŚBr. &c. &c.: Pass. *-gīyate*, to be sung or praised in chorus, BhP.

Sam-gāyana, n. singing or praising together, KātyŚr.

Sam-gīta, mfn. sung together, sung in chorus or harmony; n. a song sung by many voices or singing accompanied by instrumental music, chorus, a concert, any song or music, Kāv.; Kathās.; Pur.; the art or science of singing with music and dancing (= *-śāstra*), Cat.; *-kalā-nidhi*, m., *-kalikā*, f., *-kalpadruma*, m., *-kaumudī*, f., *-cintāmani*, m., *-tāla*, m., *-darpana*, m., *-dāmodara*, m., *-nārāyana*, m., *-nritta-ratnâkara*, m., *-nrityâkara*, m., *-pārijāta*, m., *-pushpâñjali*, m., *-makaranda*, m., *-mādhava*, m., *-mimāṃsā*, f., *-muktâvalī*, f., *-raghu-nandana*, m., *-ratna*, n., *-ratnamālā*, f., *-ratnâkara*, m., *-ratnâvalī*, f., *-rāga-lakshana*, n., *-rāghava*, m., *-rāja*, m., *-vinode nrityâdhyāya*, m. N. of wks.; *-vidyā*, f. the science of singing with music &c., Pañcat.; *-vritta-ratnâkara*, m. N. of wk.; *-veśman*, n. a concert-room, Kathās.; *-vyāprita*, mfn. engaged in singing or music, MW.; *-śālā*, f. a music hall, Mṛicch.; *-śāstra*, n. the science of singing &c. or any wk. on the above subject, Cat.; *-śiromani*, m., *-sarvasva*, n. N. of wks.; *-sahāyinī*, f. a female who accompanies another in singing, Mālav.; *-sāgara*, m., *-sāra*, m., *-sāra-saṃgraha*, m., *-sārâmrita*, n., *-sārôddhāra*, m., *-siddhânta*, m., *-sudhā*, f., *-sudhâkara*, m., *-sundara-setu*, m.; °*tâmrita*, n., °*târnava*, m. N. of wks.; °*târtha*, m. the apparatus or materials or subject of any musical performance, MW.; °*tâvasāna*, n. the close of a concert, ib.; °*tôpanishad*, f. and (°*shat*)-*sāra*, m. N. of wks. °**gītaka**, n. a concert, symphony, musical entertainment, Kāv.; Kathās.; *-griha*, n. a concert-room, Kathās.; *-pada*, n. a situation or office at a concert or theatre, Mālav.

Sam-gīti, f. singing together, concert, symphony, the art of s° combined with music and dancing, W.; conversation, L.; a species of the Āryā metre, Col.; *-paryāya*, m. N. of a Buddhist wk.; *-prāsāda*, m. a concert-hall and a council-hall, Buddh.

संगोपन *sam-gopana* &c. See p. 1128, col. 3.

संग्रथन *sam-grathana*, n. tying together, repairing or restoring by tying together, Kād.

Sám-grathita, mfn. strung or tied or knotted together, RV.

Sam-granthana, n. tying together &c.; (with *kalahasya*) beginning a quarrel, MBh.

संग्रभ् *sam-grabh*. See *sam-√grah*, col. 2.

संग्रस् *sam-√gras*, P. Ā. *-grasati*, °*te*, to swallow up, devour, consume, Bhaṭṭ.

Sam-grasana, n. eating up, devouring, BhP.

संग्रह् *sam-√grah* (or *√grabh*), P. Ā. *-grihnāti*, *-grihnīte* (Ved. generally *-gribhnāti*, *-gribhnīte*), to seize or hold together, take or lay hold of, grab, grasp, gripe, clasp, clench, snatch, RV. &c. &c.; to take, receive (kindly or hospitably), encourage, support, favour, protect, Hit.; BhP.; to seize on, attack (as an illness), MBh.; to apprehend, conceive, understand, BhP.; to carry off, ib.; to gather together, assemble, collect, compile, ib. &c.; to include, comprehend, contain, Gaut.; Pat.; to draw together, contract, make narrower, abridge, ŚBr.; to draw together (a bow in order to unstring it), MBh.; to hold in, restrain, check, govern, MBh.; to constrain, force, Mn. viii, 48; to keep together, close, shut (as the mouth), KātyŚr.; to concentrate (the mind), BhP.; to take in marriage, marry, ib.; to mention, name, ib.: Caus. *-grāhayati*, to cause to grasp or take hold of or receive or comprehend or understand, impart, communicate (with acc. of thing and acc. or dat. of person), Car.; BhP.: Desid. *-jighrikshati*, to wish to take hold of &c.; to wish to collect, MBh.; to wish to take in marriage, desire to marry, Daś.

Sam-gribhāya, °**bhita** &c. See col. 1.

Sam-grihīta, mfn. grasped, seized, caught, taken, received, collected, gathered, MBh.; Kāv. &c.; made narrower, contracted, abridged, ŚBr.; held in, restrained, ruled, governed, MBh.; received kindly, welcomed, BhP.; *-rāshtra*, mfn. (a king) who has a well-governed kingdom, Mn. vii, 113. °**grihīti**, f. curbing, taming, Vās. °**grihītri**, mfn. (often v.l. or w.r. for *sam-grah*°) one who holds in or restrains or rules, (esp.) a tamer of horses, charioteer, MBh.; R. &c. (cf. Pāṇ. iii, 2, 135, Vārtt. 7, Pat.)

Sam-graha, m. holding together, seizing, grasping, taking, reception, obtainment, MBh.; Kāv. &c.; taking (in the sense of eating or drinking food, medicine &c.), Ragh.; Bhartṛ.; the fetching back of discharged weapons by magical means, MBh.; Hariv.; bringing together, assembling (of men), R.; Ragh.; Siṇhâs.; collecting, gathering, conglomeration, accumulation (as of stores), Mn.; MBh. &c.; (in phil.) agglomeration (= *saṃyoga*, q.v.), MW.; a place where anything is kept, a store-room, receptacle, BhP.; complete enumeration or collection, sum, amount, totality (*ena*, 'completely,' 'entirely'), Yājñ.; MBh. &c.; drawing together, making narrower, narrowing, tightening, making thin or slender, the thin part of anything, Car.; Vāgbh.; KātyŚr., Sch.; a compendium, summary, catalogue, list, epitome, abridgment, short statement (*ena* or *āt*, 'shortly,' 'summarily,' 'in few words'), KaṭhUp.; MBh. &c.; inclusion, comprehension, Kusum.; Kull.; check, restraint, control, ib.; Vet.; keeping, guarding, protection, Mn.; MBh. &c.; a guardian, ruler, manager, arranger, R.; BhP.; obstruction, constipation (see *-grahanī*); attracting, winning, favouring, kind treatment, propitiation, entertaining, entertainment, Mn.; MBh. &c.; taking to wife, marriage (see *dāra-s*°); perception, notion, Kap.; BhP.; mention, mentioning, L.; elevation, loftiness, L.; velocity, L.; N. of Śiva, MBh.; of various wks. (esp. of a gram. wk. in 100,000 Ślokas by Vyāḍi; also often in comp.); *-kāra*, m. the composer or author of the Saṃgraha; *-grantha*, m. N. of wk.; *-grahanī*, f. a partic. form of diarrhœa (alternating with constipation), Bhpr.; *-cūdāmani*, m., *-parvan*, n. (IW. 370, n. 1), *-prakāśikā*, f., *-ratnamālā*, f., *-rāmâyana*, n. N. of wks.; *-vat*, mfn. provided with a short summary of a subject, Cat.; *-vastu*, n. an element of popularity, Divyâv.; *-vivarana*, n., *-vaidyanāthīya*, n. N. of wks.; *-śloka*, m. a verse recapitulating what has been explained before (in prose intermixed with Sūtras).

Sam-grahana, mf(*ī*)n. grasping, seizing, taking, AV.; Gobh.; (*ī*), f. = *saṃgraha-grahanī*, Bhpr.; n. the act of grasping or taking (see *pāni-s*°); receiving, obtaining, acquisition, R.; gathering, compiling, accumulating, Kāv.; Kathās.; encasing, inlaying (of a jewel), Pañcat.; complete enumeration, L.; stopping, restraining, suppressing, Suśr.; Vāgbh.; attraction, winning over, propitiation, TS.; MBh.; sexual intercourse with (comp.), adultery, Mn.; Yājñ.; VarBṛS.; (°*nī*)-*ratna*, n. N. of wk. °**grahanīya**, mfn. to be taken hold of; to be taken as a remedy against (any disease, e.g. diarrhœa), Car.; to be directed towards (loc.), Śaṃk.; to be drawn together or contracted or restrained, MW. °**grahin**, m. a collector, procurer, MBh.; Subh. (v.l.) °**grahītavya**, mfn. to be retained, Pat. on Pāṇ. iii, 1, 94, Vārtt. 6. °**grahītri**, mfn. one who lays hold of &c., one who wins over or propitiates, Āpast.; m. a charioteer, VS.; Br.

Sam-grāha, m. grasping, laying hold of, forcible seizure, W.; the fist or clenching the fist, L. (cf. Pāṇ. iii, 3, 36, Sch.); the handle of a shield, L. °**grāhaka**, mf(*ī*)n. putting together, summing up, Sarvad.; astringent, obstructing, constipating, Suśr.; drawing or attracting to one's self, Mahāvy.; m. a charioteer, Jātakam.; a gatherer, collector, compiler, MW. °**grāhita**, mfn. (fr. Caus.) caused to be grasped or received, bestowed, imparted, communicated, BhP. °**grāhin**, mfn. grasping, collecting, gathering, accumulating, Subh.; astringent, constipating, Suśr.; winning over, propitiating (see *loka-s*°); m. Wrightia Antidysenterica, L. °**grāhya**, mfn. to be grasped or seized or clasped or embraced, ŚBr.; to be stopped (as bleeding), Suśr.; to be appointed (to an office), MBh.; Hcat.; to be attracted or won or propitiated, Hit.; to be accepted or taken to heart (as words), BhP.

संग्राम् *samgrām* (rather Nom. fr. *sam-grāma* below), Ā. *samgrāmayate* (accord. to Vop. also P. °*ti*), to make war, fight, Dhātup. xxxv, 68: Desid., see *sishaṃgrāmayishu* and *sisaṃgrāmayishu*.

Sam-grāmá, m. (and n., Siddh.; cf. *grāma*) an assembly of people, host, troop, army, AV.; battle, war, fight, combat, conflict, hostile encounter with (instr. with and without *samam*, *saha*, *sârdham*, or comp.), ib. &c. &c.; N. of various men, Rājat.; Cat. **–karman**, n. the work or turmoil of battle, Rājat. **–gupta**, m. N. of a man, ib. **–candra**, m. 'excelling in b°,' N. of a man, Rājat. **–jit**, mfn. victorious in b° (*-tama*, superl.), ŚBr.; MBh.; MārkP.; m. N. of a man, MBh.; of a son of Kṛishṇa, Hariv.; Pur. **–tulā**, f. the ordeal of b°, Prasannar. **–tūrya**, n. a war-drum, Pañcat. **–datta**, m. N. of a Brāhman, Kathās. **–deva**, m. 'war-god,' N. of a king, Rājat. **–nagara**, n. N. of a city, ib. **–paṭaha**, m. a war-drum, L. **–pāla**, m. N. of a king, Rājat. **–bhūmi**, f. a field of battle, MBh.; Pañcat. **–mūrdhan**, m. the van or front of battle, MBh.; BhP. **–mrityu**, m. death in battle (v.l. °*me mr*°), Hit. **–rāja**, m. N. of two kings, Rājat. **–vardhana** and **-varsha**, m. N. of two men, Kathās. **–vijaya**, m. 'victory in battle,' N. of a poem. **–śiras**, n. = *-mūrdhan*, MBh. **–sāhi**, m. N. of a king, Inscr. **–siṇha**, m. 'lion in battle,' N. of an official in the lower regions, Kathās. **–siddhi**, m. N. of an elephant, ib. **Saṃgrāmâgra**, m. the van of b°, Śiś.; Rājat. **Saṃgrāmâṅgana**, n. battle-field, Bhām. **Saṃgrāmâpīḍa**, m. N. of two kings, Rājat. **Saṃgrāmârthin**, mfn. desirous of war or battle, pugnacious, Hāsy. **Saṃgrāmâśis**, f. a prayer for aid in battle (personified), Ind. St.

Saṃgrāmika, w.r. for *sāmgr*°.

Saṃgrāmin, mfn. engaged in war, MaitrS.

Saṃgrāmya, mfn. fit for war or battle, Nir. vi, 33; n. = (or w.r. for) *sam-grāma*, Kāṭh.

संघ *sam-gha*, m. (fr. *sam* + *√han*) 'close contact or combination,' any collection or assemblage, heap, multitude, quantity, crowd, host, number (generally with gen. pl. or ifc., e.g. *muni-s*°, 'a multitude of sages,' BhP.; *śatru-s*°, a host of enemies, Rājat.), MBh.; Kāv. &c.; any number of people living together for a certain purpose, a society, association, company, community; a clerical community, congregation, church, Mn.; Sāh. &c.; (esp.) the whole community or collective body or brotherhood of monks (with Buddhists; also applied to a monkish fraternity or sect among Jainas), Buddh.; Sarvad.; MWB. 176. **–gupta**, m. N. of the father of Vāg-bhaṭa, Cat. (cf. *saṃgha-pati*). **–guhya**, m. N. of a man, Buddh. **–cārin**, mfn. going in flocks or shoals, gregarious, MBh.; R.; m. a fish, L. **–jīvin**, mfn. living in company, belonging to a vagrant band, L.; m. a hired labourer, porter, cooly, W. **–tala**, m. = *saṃha-t*° (q.v.) **–dāsa**, m. N. of a man, Buddh. **–pati**, m. the chief of a brotherhood (*-tva*, n.), Śatr.; N. of the father of Vāg-bhaṭa, Cat. (cf. *saṃgha-gupta*). **–purusha**, m. an attendant on the Buddhist brotherhood, Siṇhâs. **–pushpī**, f. Grislea Tomentosa, L. **–bodhi**, m. N. of a king of Ceylon (also called Parākrama-bāhu), Buddh. **-bhadra**, m. N. of a man, Buddh. **-bheda**, mfn. causing division among the brotherhood (one of the 5 unpardonable sins), Dharmas. 60. **-bhedaka**, mfn. one who causes division &c., Buddh. **-mitra**, m. N. of a poet, Cat. **-rakshita** and **-vardhana**, m. N. of men, Buddh. **-vṛitti**, f. a league, alliance, Viddh.; *-tā*, f. combined action, MW. **-śas**, ind. by troops or numbers, collectively, all together, MBh.; R. &c. **Saṃghâdhipa**, m. (with Jainas) the chief of the brotherhood, Śatr. **Saṃghânanda**, m. N. of a patriarch, Buddh. **Saṃghânna**, n. food offered from a community, Āpast. **Saṃghârāma**, m. 'resting-place for a company (of monks),' a Buddhist convent or monastery (= *vihāra*), MWB. 428. **Saṃghâvaśesha**, m. N. of those sins which are punished with temporary excommunication, Buddh.

Saṃghaka, m. a number, multitude, Pañcar.

Saṃghatitha, mfn. numerous, abundant, Śiś. (cf. Pāṇ. v, 2, 52).

Saṃ-ghātá, m. (rarely n.; ifc. f. *ā*) striking or dashing together, killing, crushing, MBh.; Suśr.; closing (of a door &c.), VS.; TBr.; combat, war, battle, VS.; Kāṭh.; MBh.; compressing, condensation, compactness, hardening, Yājñ.; Hariv.; Suśr.; VarBṛS.; close union or combination, collection, cluster, heap, mass, multitude, TS.; MBh. &c.; a company of fellow-travellers, caravan, VP.; a collection of mucus, phlegm (cf. *saṃghāṇaka*), L.; a bone, L.; any aggregate of matter, body, Bhag.; Pur.; intensity, R.; Suśr.; a poem composed in one and the same metre, Kāvyâd.; (in gram.) a compound as a compact whole (opp. to its single parts), Kāś. on Pāṇ. ii, 3, 56; a vowel with its consonant (opp. to *varṇa*, 'a letter'), Kāty.; (in dram.) a partic. gait or mode of walking, W.; N. of a division of the infernal regions (cf. *saṃhāta*), Yājñ.; Buddh.; *-kaṭhina*, mfn. hard or firm or solid from compactness, Kum.; *-cārin*, mfn. living in herds, gregarious, Suśr.; *-ja*, mfn. produced by a complicated derangement of the three humours (= *sāṃnipātika*), Bhpr.; *-pattrikā*, f. Anethum Sowa, L.; *-parvata*, m. N. of two mountains in hell (which open and then close), Jātakam.; *-vat*, mfn. having close union, closely compacted, dense, Kām.; *-vihārin* (?), m. N. of Buddha, Divyâv.; *-śūla-vat*, mfn. suffering pain from bodily oppression, Suśr. °**ghātaka**, m. separation of such as keep together, Bhar.; (*ikā*), f. wood of the Ficus Religiosa used for kindling fire by rubbing, L. °**ghātana**, n. killing, destroying, HYog. °**ghātam**, ind. dashing together, Kāṭh. °**ghātya**, m. a kind of dramatic performance, = °*ghātaka*, Bhar.

Saṃghī, in comp. for *saṃgha*. **-√bhū**, P. *-bhavati*, to assemble in troops or herds, Kull.

संघट् *saṃ-√ghaṭ*, Ā. *-ghaṭate*, to assemble together, meet, Rājat.; to meet, encounter, Siṅhâs.: Caus. *-ghāṭayati*, to cause to assemble, collect, Kathās.; to join or fasten together, Sarvad.; to strike (a musical instrument), R.: Intens. *-jāghaṭīti*, to be well fitted or adapted for anything, ib.

Saṃ-ghaṭa, mf(*ā*)n. heaped, piled up, AgP. °**ghaṭaka** (used for explaining *saṃdhi*), TBr., Sch. °**ghaṭana**, n. (or *ā*, f.) union or junction with (comp.), Vcar.; Ratnâv.; Sāh.; (*ā*), f. combination of words or sounds, Sāh.

Saṃ-ghaṭita, mfn. assembled together, met &c.; struck (as a musical instrument), R.

Saṃ-ghāṭa, m. fitting and joining of timber, joinery, carpentry, R.; a pot (?), Divyâv.; (ifc.) = *saṃ-ghāta* (in *pada-* and *varṇa-s°*, qq. vv.); *-sūtra*, n. N. of a Buddhist Sūtra. °**ghāṭi** or °**ghāṭī**, f. a kind of garment, a monk's robe (cf. *bhikshu-s°*), Suśr.; Divyâv. °**ghāṭikā**, f. a pair, couple, L.; a woman's garment, Śil.; procuress, a bawd, L.; Trapa Bispinosa, L.; the nose, L.

संघट्ट *saṃ-√ghaṭṭ*, Ā. *-ghaṭṭate*, to strike or clasp or rub together, knead, crush to pieces, bruise, R.: Caus. *-ghaṭṭayati* (ind. p. *-ghaṭṭayya*), to cause to rub against (instr.), Ragh.; to stir, AgP.; to strike against, touch, MBh.; to cause to sound by striking, R.; to bring together, collect, assemble, MBh.; Rājat.; to meet, encounter, Naish.

Saṃ-ghaṭṭa, m. rubbing or clashing together, friction, collision, conflict, rivalry, MBh.; Kāv. &c.; a stroke (in *hṛidaya-s°*, q. v.); junction or union with (instr.), Naish.; embracing, W.; (*ā*), f. a large creeper (= *latā*), L.; *-cakra*, n. a partic. astrological diagram (for determining the proper season for war), Cat.; *-paṇita*, n. a wager, Hcar. °**ghaṭṭana**, m. a kind of spectral being or phantom, Hariv.; n. rubbing together, Prasannar.; friction, collision, Rājat.; meeting, encountering, close contact or union (as the intertwining of wrestlers, the embrace of lovers &c.), ib.; Vet.; Sāh.; Pratāp. (also *ā*, f.; often v. l. or w. r. for *saṃ-ghaṭana*).

Saṃ-ghaṭṭita, mfn. rubbed or struck together or against &c.; kneaded, Pañcat. iii, 236 (v. l.); collected, assembled, MBh.; m. du. (with *pāṇī*) the joined hands of bride and husband, Prasannar. (perhaps w. r. for *saṃ-ghaṭita*). °**ghaṭṭin**, m. (incorrect for *saṃ-ghaṭin*) an adherent, follower, BhP.

संघस *saṃ-ghasa*, m. food, victuals, Bhaṭṭ.

सङ्घाणक *saṅghāṇaka*, m. the mucus of the nose (cf. *siṅgh°* and *śiṅgh°*), KātyŚr., Sch. (v. l.)

संघात *saṃ-ghāta* &c. See col. 1.

संघुषित *saṃ-ghushita*, mfn. (√*ghush*) sounded, proclaimed, Pāṇ. vii, 2, 28, Sch.; n. sound, noise, cry, Bhaṭṭ. °**ghushṭa**, mfn. sounded, resonant, MBh.; Hariv.; proclaimed, Pāṇ. vii, 2, 28, Sch.; offered for sale, Yājñ. i, 168; m. sound, noise, W. °**ghushṭaka**, mfn. suited or accustomed to each other, Pat. on Pāṇ. i, 1, 50, Vārtt. 8.

Saṃ-ghosha, m. a station of herdsmen (= *ghosha*), MārkP. °**ghoshiṇī**, f. a partic. class of demons, Siṅhâs.

संघृष् *saṃ-√ghṛish*, P. *-gharshati*, to rub together or against each other, contend or vie with (instr.), MBh.; Ragh.: Pass. *-ghṛishyate*, to be rubbed or wetted (as a sword), Subh.; (pr. p. *-ghṛishyat*), to be brought or come into collision, vie or rival with (also with *paras-param*), MBh.

Saṃ-gharsha, m. rubbing together, friction, MBh.; Kāv. &c.; mutual attrition, rivalry, envy, jealousy in regard to (acc. with *prati* or comp.), ib.; sexual excitement, MBh. (B.) xv, 840 (C. *saṃharsha*); going gently, gliding (= *saṃ-sarpa*), L.; (*ā*), f. liquid lac, L.; *-śālin*, mfn. envious, jealous, Kathās. °**gharshaṇa**, n. rubbing together or against each other, Pur.; any substance used for rubbing in, ointment, unguent, MBh. °**gharshayitṛi**, m. a rival, Sāy. on RV. x, 18, 9. °**gharshin**, mfn. rubbing together, emulating, rivalling, vying with one another or with regard to (comp.), MBh.; jealous, envious, Śiś.

Saṃ-ghṛishṭa, mfn. rubbed with, rubbed together, MBh.

संघ्रा *saṃ-√ghrā*, Caus. *-ghrāpayati*, to bring into close connection or intimacy, make intimate, ŚBr.

सच् 1. *sac* (connected with √2. *sajj*, *sañj*, *sakh*; cf. √*sap*), cl. 1 Ā. (Dhātup. vi, 2) *sácate* (in RV. also P. *sacati* and *síshakti*, 2. sg. *sáśrasi*, 3. pl. *saścati*, 2. 3. pl. *saścata*, 1. sg. Ā. *saśce*; p. *sácamāna*, *sacāná* and *sáścat* or *saścát* [q. v.]; pf. Ved. *saścima*, *saścuḥ*; Ā. *saścire*, RV.; *secire*, AV.; aor. 3. pl. *asakshata*, RV.; *sakshat*, *sakshata*, *sakshante*, *sakshīmáhi*, ib.; *asacishṭa*, Gr.; fut. *sacitā*, *sacishyate*, ib.; inf. *sacádhyai*, RV.), to be associated or united with, have to do with, be familiar with, associate one's self with (instr.), RV.; AV.; be possessed of, enjoy (instr. or acc.), ib.; to take part or participate in, suffer, endure (instr.), RV.; to belong to, be attached or devoted to, serve, follow, seek, pursue, favour, assist (acc.), RV.; AV.; VS.; to be connected with (instr.), Pat. on Pāṇ. i, 4, 51; to fall to the lot of (acc.), ŚBr.; to be together, RV.; AV.; (*síshakti*), to go after, follow, accompany, adhere or be attached to (acc.), RV.; to help any one to anything (two dat.), ib.; to abide in (loc.), ib.; (3. pl. *saścati* and *saścata*), to follow, obey, RV.; to belong to (acc.), ib.; to be devoted to or fond of (acc.), ib. [Cf. Gk. ἕπομαι; Lat. *sequor*; Lith. *sekù*.]

Sákman, n. association, attendance, RV.

Sákmya, n. that which belongs to anything, peculiar nature, ib.

Sakha, m. (ifc. for *sákhi*, cf. Pāṇ. v, 4, 91) a friend, companion, R.; Kālid. &c.; attended or accompanied by (comp.), Kāv.; Kathās. &c.; the tree Mimosa Catechu, MW.

Sákhi, m. (strong cases, nom. *sákhā*, pl. *sákhāyaḥ*; acc. sg. *sákhāyam*; gen. abl. *sákhyus*; other cases regularly from *sakhi*) a friend, assistant, companion, RV. &c. &c.; the husband of the wife's sister, brother-in-law, Gal.; (*ī*), f., see below. [Cf. Lat. *socius*.] **-tā**, f. (MBh.; R.), **-tvá**, n. (RV. &c. &c.), **-tvaná**, n. (RV.) friendship, companionship, intimacy with (instr. with and without *saha*, gen., or comp.) **-datta**, m., g. *sakhy-ādi*. **-pūrva**, mfn. one who has been formerly a friend, MW.; n. = next, MBh. **-bhāva**, m. friendship, intimacy, Kathās. **-1. -vat** (*sákhi-*), mfn. having friends or adherents, RV. **-2. -vat**, ind. like a friend, as a friend, MW. **-vigraha**, m. war of friends, civil war, MW. **-víd**, mfn. winning friends, VS.

Sakhila, mfn. (for *sa-khila* see p. 1124, col. 2) friendly, L.

Sakhī, f. a female friend or companion, a woman's confidante, MBh.; Kāv. &c.; a mistress, VarBṛS.; (ifc.) a woman who shares in or sympathizes with, Kum. **-kadambaka**, n. a number of female friends, MW. **-gaṇa**, n. id.; *-samāvṛita*, mfn. surrounded by a company of f° fr°s, Nal. **-jana**, m. a f° fr° or f° fr°s (collectively), Śak. **-sahita**, mfn. attended by f° fr°s, MW. **-sneha**, m. the love for a f° fr°, Śak. **-hṛidayâbharaṇa**, m. N. of a man, Cat.

Sakhīya, Nom. P. °*yati* (only p. °*yát*), to seek the friendship of (instr.), attend or attach one's self as a friend, RV.

Sakhyá, n. friendship, intimacy with, relation to (loc. or instr. with and without *samam*, *saha* &c.), fellowship, community, RV. &c. &c. **-visarjana**, n. dissolution of partnership or association (in a ritual observance), GṛŚrS.

2. **Sac** (ifc., strong form *sāc*), in *apatya-*, *ayajña-sac*, *āyu-shak* &c. (qq. vv.)

Saca, mfn. attached to, worshipping, a worshipper (see *a-saca-dvish*).

Sacátha, m. companionship, assistance, RV.

Sacathyà, mfn. helpful, kind, RV.; n. assistance, help, ib.

Sacádhyai. See √*sac*.

Sacaná, mfn. ready to befriend or help, kindly disposed, doing kind offices (also °*nā-vat*), RV.

Sácanas. See *sá-canas* below.

Sacanīya, mfn. to be followed or honoured or served, MW.

Sacasya, Nom. Ā. °*syáte*, to receive assistance or care, RV.

Sácā, ind. near, at hand, along, together, together with, in the presence of, before, in, at, by (with loc. either preceding or following), RV.; VS.; TBr. **-bhū́**, m. a fellow, companion, friend, associate, RV.; mfn. attended or accompanied by (instr.), ib.

Sáci, ind. together, along with, ŚBr. **-vid**, mfn. belonging together, familiar, intimate, RV.

Saciva, m. an associate, companion, friend, (*ī*, f.); esp. a king's friend or attendant, counsellor, minister (ifc. = 'assisted by,' 'provided with'), Gaut.; Mn.; MBh. &c.; the dark thorn-apple, L. **-tā**, f. (Rājat.), **-tva**, n. (Kathās.) the position or rank of a minister. **Sacivâmaya**, m. a disease to which king's attendants are liable (said to be a kind of 'jaundice'), L.

Sacī &c. See *śacī*, p. 1048.

Saścát, m. a pursuer, enemy, RV.

सच् 3. *sac* = √*sañj* in *ā-√sac*, to adhere to, MaitrS.; Kāṭh.

सचकित *sa-cakita*, mfn. (i. e. 7. *sa* + *c°*) trembling, timid, startled (*am*, ind.), Ratnâv.; Amar.

Sa (to be similarly prefixed to the following): **-cakra**, mf(*ā*)n. having wheels, wheeled, MBh.; having a circle or discus, MW.; having troops (of soldiers), MBh.; (*am*), ind. together with a wheel or discus, Pāṇ. vi, 3, 81, Sch.; °*krin*, m. a charioteer, TBr. (Sch.); °*krôpaskara*, mfn. with wheels and appendages, MBh. **-cakshusha**, mfn. having eyes, seeing, MBh. **-cakshus** (*sá-*), mfn. id., ŚBr.; MBh.; Kāv. &c. **-canas** (*sá-*), mfn. being in harmony with, RV. i, 127, 11; °*cánas-tama*, mfn. (superl.), ib. viii, 27, 8; °*canasya*, Nom. Ā. °*yate*, to treat tenderly, cherish, foster, ib. x, 4, 3. **-candraka**, mf(*ikā*)n. having a moon-like spot, Suśr. **-candrikā-prakāśa**, m. N. of wk. **-camatkāram**, ind. with astonishment or surprise, Mcar.; Kathās. **-caraṇa-lākshā-rāga**, mfn. having the colour of lac or dye used for the feet, MW. **-carâcara**, mfn. comprehending everything moving and motionless, Mn. vii, 29; n. the universe, MW. **-carma**, mfn. along with the skin, Kauś. **-cala**, mfn. having moving things, moving, ib. **-cāmara**, mfn. furnished with chowries, Vishṇ. **-cāru**, mf(*vī*)n. very beautiful, MW. **-cit**, mfn. thinking, wise, RV. x, 64, 7 (others 'of the same mind'). **-citka**, m. thinking, BhP. **-citta** (*sá-*), mfn. of the same mind, AV.; endowed with reason, Pat. on Pāṇ. i, 3, 25, Vārtt. 1 (quot.) **-citra,** mfn. garnished with pictures, Hariv.; together with pictures, Megh.; painted, variegated, MW. **-cinta,** mf(*ā*)n. absorbed in thought, thoughtful (*am,* ind.), Kāv.; Kathās.; °*tâkulam,* ind. thoughtfully, Śak. **-cillaka,** mfn. having sore eyes, blear-eyed, L. **-cihna,** mfn. having marks, marked, branded (*am,* ind.), Yājñ. **-cīnaka,** mfn. together with Panicum Miliaceum, MārkP. **-cetana,** mfn. having reason or consciousness or feeling, sentient, sensible, animate, rational, PārGṛ.; R.; Kathās. &c. **-cetas** (*sá-*), mfn. having the same mind, unanimous, RV.; AV.; conscious, intelligent, rational, RV. &c. &c. **-cela,** mfn. having clothes, clothed, dressed, Gaut.; Mn.; Yājñ. **-ceshṭa,** mfn. making effort or exertion, active, W.; m. the mango tree, L. **-caitanya,** mfn. having consciousness, conscious, VP. **-caila,** mfn. = *-cela* (*am,* ind.), Yājñ.; MBh. &c. **-cchadis,** mfn. covered, hidden, ĀpŚr. **-cchanda** (*sá-*), mf(*ā*)n. consisting of the same metres (*ā,* f. [scil. *ric*] a verse cons° of the s° m°s), VS. **-cchandas** (*sá-*), mfn. = prec., VS.; ŚBr. **-cchandasya,** mfn. id., Lāṭy. **-cchandoma,** mfn. connected with the Chandoma (*-tva,* n.), Lāṭy. **-cchala,** mf(*ā*)n. deceitful, fraudulent, Kathās. **-cchala-jāti-nigraha-maya,** mf(*ī*)n. consisting of defeat (in disputation) accompanied by self-refuting objections and unfair arguments, Prab. **-cchāya,** mf(*ā*)n. giving shade, shady, Pañcad.; having beautiful colours, glittering, L.; (ifc.) having the same colour as, Śiś. **-cchidra,** mfn. having defects, faulty, MW. **-ccheda,** mfn. having cuttings or divisions, interrupted, Vet. **-cyuti** (*sá-*), mfn. (said to =) accompanied by seminal effusion, MaitrS.; TBr.; ĀśvŚr. **-janá,** mfn. together with men or people, Rājat.; having men, frequented or inhabited by men (*e,* ind. among men, in public), ŚBr.; MBh. &c.; m. a man of the same family, kinsman, MW.; °*nâmātya,* mfn. accompanied by men and ministers, ib. **-janapada,** mfn. having the same country, a fellow-countryman, Pāṇ. vi, 3, 83. **-janíya,** n. (scil. *sûkta*) N. of the hymn RV. ii, 12 (having the burden *sa janāsa indraḥ*), TS.; AitBr.; KātyŚr. (also *sa-janya,* Kāṭh.) **-janú,** mfn. born or produced together, ŚBr. **-janya** (*sá-*), mfn. belonging to a kinsman, RV. (cf. *-janiya*). **-japa,** mfn. together with the Tūshṇīm-japa (q. v.), ŚāṅkhŚr.; m. a partic. class of ascetics, R. **-jambāla,** mfn. having mud, muddy, clayey, L. **-jala,** mfn. possessing or containing water, watery, wet, humid, R.; Megh.; Śiś.; *-tva,* n. wateriness, MW.; *-nayana,* mfn. watery-eyed, Megh.; *-pṛishata,* mfn. containing water-drops, ib. **-jāgara,** mfn. waking, awake, Kathās. **-jāta,** °**ti** &c., see s. v. **-jāni,** mfn. together with a wife, Rājat. **-jāmi,** w.r. for prec. **-jāya,** mfn. having a wife, married, Kathārṇ. **-jāra,** mf(*ā*)n. accompanied by a lover, together with a paramour, Hit. **-jāla,** mfn. having a mane, maned, Kathās. (v.l. *saṭāla*). **-jítvan,** mf(*arī*)n. victorious, superior, RV.; MaitrS. **-jishṇu,** mfn. accompanied by Arjuna, MBh. **-jīva,** mf(*ā*)n. having life, alive (*-tā,* f.), MBh.; Kāv. &c.; having a bow-string (*-tā,* f.), Śiś. **-jush,** mfn. (Vop. iii, 150; 164) attached to or associated with, an associate, companion, W.; (*ūs* or *ūr*), ind. (Pāṇ. viii, 2, 66) at the same time, besides, moreover, RV.; AV.; ŚBr. (*sajūḥ-kritya,* 'together with,' Bhaṭṭ.; cf. g. *ūry-ādi*); with, along or together with (instr.), RV.; VS.; ŚāṅkhŚr.; BhP.; (*-jūr*)*-abdíya,* mfn. (fr. *sajūr-abda*), ŚBr. **-jṛimbhikam,** ind. with a yawn, yawning, Kathās. **-jósha,** mfn. = *-joshas,* RV.; AV.; VS. **-joshaṇa,** n. common enjoyment or pleasure, ŚāṅkhŚr. **-jóshas,** mfn. associated together, united, being or acting in harmony with (instr.), RV.; AV.; VS.; TBr.; ind. together, RV. **-jya,** see s.v., col. 2. **-jyotis,** mfn. having the same or a common light, Pāṇ. vi, 3, 85; ind. according to the light (i.e. either by day from the disappearance of the stars till sunset, or by night from sunset till the appearance of the stars), Mn. iv, 106; v, 82 (°*tishi,* id., Gaut. ii, 11); as long as the sun is in the sky, Gaut. xvi, 31. **-jyotsnā,** f. having moonlight; (scil. *rātri*) a moonlight night, MW. **-jvara,** mfn. having fever, feverish, Prasaṅg.

सचाङ्काचपुष्पी *sacāṅkāca-pushpī* (?), f. a kind of plant, SāmavBr.

सज् *saj.* See √*sañj,* p. 1132, col. 3.

सजन *sa-jana* &c. See col. 1.

सजात *sa-jātá,* mf(*ā*)n. born together or at the same time, related; m. a kinsman, countrymen, RV.; AV.; Br.; KātyŚr.; together with kinsmen or offspring, Gobh. **-kāma,** mfn. desirous of dominion over his kin, Kāṭh. **-vat** (°*tá-*), mfn. surrounded by his kin, TBr. **-vanasyā,** f. 'desire of dominion over kindred or countrymen,' N. of a partic. verse, TS.; ĀśvŚr. **-váni,** mfn. conciliating relations or countrymen, VS. **-śaṃsá,** m. a curse uttered by one's relatives, TBr.

Sa-jāti, mfn. belonging to the same tribe or caste or class or kind, similar, like, Mn.; Yājñ.; m. the son of a man and woman of the same caste, W.

Sa-jātīya, mfn. of the same caste or kind or species, homogeneous, like, similar, resembling, Yājñ.; Hariv. &c. **-viśishṭântarâghaṭita-tva,** n. N. of wk.

Sa-jātyà, mfn. being of the same race or family, RV.; Mn.; n. like origin or descent, brotherhood, relationship, RV.

सजानि *sa-jāni, sa-jami* &c. See col. 1.

सज् 1. *sajj,* cl. 1. P. *sajjati,* to go, move, Dhātup. vii, 22.

सज् 2. *sajj* (= √*sañj;* cf. *sajjaya*), Caus. *sajjayati,* to cling, adhere, fasten or fix or attach to (loc.), Kathās.; to fix (the mind) upon, BhP.; to cause one's self to be embraced (by other men) Mn. viii, 362.

Sajja, mf(*ā*)n. fixed, prepared, equipped, ready for (dat., loc., inf., or comp.), MBh.; Kāv. &c.; fit for everything (said of hands and feet), Pañcad.; dressed in armour, armed, fortified, L.; having a bow-string, strung, placed on a bow-string (in these senses often a mere v.l. for *sa-jya,* q. v.), MBh.; R.; (*ā*), f. equipment, armour, mail, L.; dress, decoration, L. **-karman,** n. the act of making ready or equipping, preparation &c.; stringing a bow, MBh. i, 7034 (cf. *sajya-karman*). **-tā,** f. the being equipped or prepared, readiness, Daś.

Sajjana, mfn. (for *saj-jana* see p. 1135, col. 1) hanging round (e.g. *kaṇṭha-s*°, 'h° r° the neck'), Mn. ii, 63; n. a flight of steps or Ghāt leading down to the water, ferry, L.; equipment, preparation &c., L.; caparisoning an elephant (also *ā,* f.); a guard, sentry, L.

Sajjaya, Nom. P. °*yati* (rarely Ā. °*te*), to equip, prepare, make ready (Ā. 'to prepare one's self'), MBh.; Kāv. &c.: Pass. *sajjyate,* to be equipped or prepared &c., HPariś.

Sajjita, mfn. fastened or attached to, fixed upon (in *a-sajjitâtman,* 'not having the mind fixed upon'), BhP.; equipped, prepared, ready to or for (comp. or *artham* ifc.), MBh.; R. &c.; dressed, ornamented, W.; strung (as a bow), Kathās.

Sajjī, in comp. for *sajja.* **-karaṇa,** n. the act of equipping, arraying, arming, preparing, W. **-√kṛi,** P. *-karoti,* to equip, prepare, arm, make ready, MBh.; Kāv. &c.; to string (a bow), Kathās.; BhP.; Hit. **-kṛita,** mfn. arrayed, armed, equipped, prepared, ib. **-√bhū,** P. *-bhavati,* to become equipped or prepared or made ready for (dat.), ib. **-bhūta,** mfn. equipped, prepared, made ready to or for, ib.

Sajjīya, Ā. °*yate,* to make one's self ready, MBh.

सज्जन *saj-jana.* See under *sat,* p. 1135, col. 1.

सज्जल *sajjala,* m. N. of a man, Rājat.

सज्जीक्षार *sajjīkshāra,* w.r. for *sarjī-ksh*° (q. v.)

सज्य *sa-jya,* mfn. (fr. 7. *sa* + 3. *jyā́,* q. v.) having a bow-string, strung (as a bow), placed on the bow-string (as an arrow), Kauś.; MBh.; R. &c. **-karman,** n. the act of stringing a bow, MBh. (B.) **-sāyaka,** mfn. having an arrow on the bow-string; MW.

Sajyī-√kṛi, P. *-karoti,* to string a bow, BhP.

सज्योतिस् *sa-jyotis* &c. See col. 1.

सञ्च् *sañc,* v.l. for √1. *sajj,* q. v.

सञ्च *sañca,* m. (perhaps fr. *sañcaya*) a collection of leaves for writing, a copy-book, L.

Sañcaka, m. or n. (?) a stamp or mould, Naish.; (*ikā*), f. in *darśa-* and *yajñôpavīta-pratishṭhā-s*° (q. v.)

संचकान *saṃ-cakāna.* See *saṃ-*√*kan.*

संचकास् *saṃ-cakās* (cf. √*kās*), P. *-cakāsti,* to light up, illuminate, BhP.

संचकित *saṃ-cakita,* mfn. (√*cak*) greatly startled, trembling, afraid, W.

संचक्ष् *saṃ-*√*caksh,* Ā. *-cashṭe* (pf. p. *cakshāṇa;* Ved. inf. *-cákshe* and *-cákshi*), to look attentively at, observe, notice, consider, survey, examine, reflect upon, RV.; AV.; R.; BhP.; to enumerate, ŚBr.; Lāṭy.; to report or relate fully, MBh.; to call, name, Car.; to avoid, shun (aor. *sam-acakshishṭa*), Vop. (cf. *ava-* and *pari-saṃcakshya*).

Saṃ-cakshas, m. a priest, sage, L.

सञ्चत् *sañcat,* m. a cheat, juggler (= *pratāraka*), L. (prob. w.r. for *saṃścat,* q. v.)

संचय *saṃ-caya* &c. See *saṃ-*√1. *ci.*

संचर् *saṃ-*√*car,* P. *-carati* (rarely Ā. °*te;* cf. Pāṇ. i, 3, 54, Sch.), to go or come together, meet, join, Gīt.; to come near, approach, appear, RV.; AV.; to go or wander about, walk about, roam, go or drive or ride in or on (instr.), AV. &c. &c.; to reach to (*ā*), Kum.; to go in or through, enter, traverse, pervade, AV. &c. &c.; to pass over to, pass from one to another (gen.), Pañcat.; to issue from (abl.), ŚBr.; to move, live, exist, be, ŚBr.; ŚrS.; Bhartṛ.; to practise, perform, BhP.: Caus. *-cārayati,* to cause to come together, make to meet, bring into contact, VS.; ŚBr.; Lāṭy.; to cause to go, set in motion, Kālid.; Hit.; to lead about, turn out (to graze), Śak.; BhP.; to cause to pass through, BhP.; to let pass, hand round, Car.

Saṃ-cara, mfn. going about, moving (see *divā-s*°); going or belonging together, simultaneous, VS.; ĀpŚr.; m. (ifc. f. *ā*) passage, a way, road, path, place for walking (esp. the space assigned to each person who takes part in a rite), TS.; ŚBr.; ŚrS.; Kālid.; Kathās.; a difficult passage, defile, bridge over a torrent &c., W.; (in Sāṃkhya) evolution, development, emanation, Tattvas.; the body, L.; killing, W.; *-bhāgin,* mfn. obtaining a share with difficulty (?), Vas. °**cárana,** mf(*ī*)n. fit or suitable for going or walking upon, accessible, practicable, RV.; ŚBr.; going or coming together, meeting, converging, MW.; (*am*), n. going together or through, passage, motion, passing over from (abl.) or in (loc. or comp.) or by means of (comp.), Kāv.; Pañcat.; (with *samudrám*) navigation, RV.; setting in motion, use, MW.; °**caritra,** n. coupling, procuring, L. °**carishṇu,** mfn. disposed to move or ramble about, Śiś. °**caréṇya,** mfn. suitable for going or walking on, practicable, RV.

Saṃ-cāra, m. (ifc. f. *ā*) walking about, wandering, roaming, driving or riding, any motion, MBh.; Kāv. &c.; transit, passage, ib.; the passage or entrance of the sun into a new sign, MW.; passing over, transition, transference to (comp.), Yājñ.; transmission (of disease), contagion, W.; course, path, way (also fig. = 'mode, manner'), MBh.; Hariv.; track (of wild animals), Śak., Sch.; course of life, career, Sāh.; a partic. class of spies, L.; difficult progress, difficulty, distress, W.; leading, guiding, ib.; inciting, impelling, ib.; a gem supposed to be in the head of a serpent, ib.; = *huṃ-kāra,* ChUp.; [w.r. for *saṃ-cara, saṃ-sāra,* and *sac-cāra*]; *-jīvin,* m. (prob.) a tramp, vagabond, L.; *-patha,* m. a walk, walking-place, Hariv.; (in dram.) a female attendant on a king (= *yavanī*), Bhar.; *-pūta,* mfn. purified by the course or passage (of anything), MW.; *-vyādhi,* m. a partic. (prob. infectious) disease, L. °**cāraka,** m. a leader, guide, Hit.; N. of one of Skanda's attendants, MBh.; (*ikā*), f. a procuress, go-between, L.; a female servant to whom is entrusted the principal care (of money matters &c.), L.; the nose, L. °**cāraṇa,** n. bringing near, conveying, mixing, adding, transmission, insertion, Kāv.; Sāh.; delivering (a message), Jātakam.; (*ī*), f. (with Buddhists) N. of one of the 6 goddesses of magic, Dharmas. 13. °**cāraṇīya,** mfn. to be walked or wandered through or circumambulated, Bālar.; to be transmitted or transferred to (loc.), Sāh. °**cārayitṛi,** m. (and °*trī,* f., fr. Caus.) a leader, guide, MaitrUp., Sch. °**cārita,** mfn. (fr. id.) caused to go, set in motion, impelled, driven, guided, Kālid.; Rājat.; transmitted, communicated (as a disease), W.; m. a person who carries out the intentions of his masters, L.

Saṃcāri for *sam-cārin* in comp. **-cuṇḍikā**, f. an easily propagated cutaneous eruption, smallpox, Gal. **-tā**, f. penetration into (comp.), Mcar. **-tva**, n. transitoriness, inconstancy (of feeling), Sāh. **-bhāva**, m. a transitory feeling (= *vyabhicāri-bh°*, q.v.), MW.

Saṃ-cārin, mfn. going together or about, going hither and thither, roaming, wandering, moving in (loc. or comp.), Kāv.; Rājat.; Kathās.; Inscr.; going or passing from one to another, transmitted, infectious, contagious, hereditary (as a disease), Yājñ.; Rājat.; ascending and descending (applied to a note or tone), Saṃgīt.; penetrating into (comp.), Mcar.; coming together, meeting, in contact with, adjacent or contiguous to (instr.), Kād.; taken or carried together with one (as an umbrella &c.), Rājat.; carrying with one (comp.), Kām.; being in (comp.), Suśr.; Mṛicch.; engaged in, occupied with (comp.), Pañcar.; passing away, transitory, adventitious, unsteady, inconstant, fickle (= *vy-abhicārin*, q.v.), Śiś.; Sāh.; influencing, impelling, setting in motion, MaitrUp.; difficult, inaccessible, W.; m. incense or the smoke rising from burnt incense, L.; air, wind, L.; (*iṇī*), f. a kind of Mimosa (= *haṃsa-padī*), L.; *-tva*, n. transitoriness, inconstancy (of feeling), Sāh.

Saṃ-cārya, mfn. to be walked upon, accessible (in *a-s°*, q.v.); brought about or produced by (comp.), Śaṃk.

संचर्वण *sam-carvaṇa*, n. (√*carv*) the act of chewing or masticating, Rājat.

संचल *saṃ-√cal*, P. *-calati*, to move about or to and fro, waver, oscillate, quiver, tremble, MBh.; R.; to move away, set out or depart from (abl.), Hariv.; Śak. (v.l.); to start or jump up from (a seat), R.: Caus. *-cālayati*, to cause to move about or to and fro, shake, agitate, Hariv.; Śak. (v.l.); to push away, remove, expel, MBh.

Saṃ-cala, mfn. moving about, trembling, quivering; *-nāḍi*, f. 'moving tube,' an artery, vein, pulse, R. °**calana**, n. moving about, agitation, trembling, shaking, Kāv.; Dhātup.

Saṃ-cāla, m. (of unknown meaning), BrahmavP.; (*ī*), f. the seed of Abrus Precatorius, L. °**cālaka**, m. a guide (perhaps w.r. for °*cāraka*), L.

संचस्कारयिषु *saṃ-caskārayishu*. See *saṃ-cishk°*, col. 2.

संचाकु *sam-cāku*, m. (said to be fr. √2. *ci*; but cf. *sam-cakshas*) a Ṛishi, L.

सञ्चाधर *sañcādhara*, m. N. of a poet, Cat. (v.l. *sāñc°*).

सञ्चान *sañcāna*, m. a kind of bird (= *mahāvīra*), L.

संचि *saṃ-√1. ci*, P. Ā. *-cinoti*, *-cinute*, to heap together, pile up, heap up, ŚBr.; ŚrS.; to arrange, put in order, ib.; Bhaṭṭ.; to accumulate, gather together, collect, acquire, Mn.; MBh. &c.

Saṃ-caya, m. (ifc. f. *ā*) collection, gathering, accumulation, heap, hoard, store, multitude, quantity (dat., 'in order to have more'), Nir.; MBh. &c.; collecting the bones of a burnt body (in *asthi-s°*), RTL. 284; 300; *-vat*, mfn. possessed of wealth, rich, opulent, MBh. °**cayana**, n. the act of piling or heaping together, heaping up, gathering, collecting (esp. the ashes or bones of a body lately burnt, see *asthi-s°*), GṛŚrS.; Mn. &c. °**cayanīya**, mfn. to be gathered or collected, MW. °**cayika**, mfn. having provisions (in *a-* and *māsa-saṃc°*, qq. vv.) °**cayin**, mfn. who or what collects, W.; possessed of riches, MBh.; (°*yi*)*-tva*, n. the being heaped up, Suśr.

Saṃ-cāyya, mfn. (scil. *kratu*, a ceremony) at which the Soma is accumulated, Pāṇ. iii, 1, 130.

Sám-cita, mfn. piled together, heaped up, gathered, collected, accumulated, ŚBr. &c. &c.; dense, thick (as a wood), R.; fitted or provided with, full of (comp.), MBh.; impeded, obstructed, VarBṛS.; frequently practised or exhibited, MBh.; *-karman*, n. the rites to be performed after arranging the sacrificial fire, ŚrS. °**citi**, f. N. of the 9th book of the Śatapatha-brāhmaṇa; heaping together, collecting, saving, Kāv.

Saṃ-cinvānaka, mfn. (fr. *-cinvāna*, pr. p. Ā. of *sam-√1. ci*) occupied with the accumulation of wealth or treasures, MBh.

Saṃ-ceya, mfn. to be gathered or collected or accumulated, R. (cf. Pāṇ. iii, 1, 130, Sch.)

संचि *sam-√2. ci* (only in ind. p. *-citya*, perhaps w.r. for *-cintya*), to reflect, ponder, Rājat.

संचिकीर्षु *sam-cikīrshu*, mfn. (fr. Desid. of *sam-√1. kṛi*) wishing to do or perform, Kull. on Mn. v, 86.

संचिक्षिप्सु *sam-cikshipsu*, mfn. (fr. Desid. of *sam-√kship*) wishing to give a short description, VarBṛS.

संचित् *saṃ-√4. cit* (only pf. p. P. *-cikitvás*, and 3. pl. pf. Ā. *-cikitre* and *-cikitrire*), to observe together, survey, notice, RV.; to agree together, be unanimous, ib.: Caus. *-cetayati* (pr. p. *-cetayamāna*), to observe, be aware of, perceive, MW.

संचित्रा *saṃ-citrā*, f. Salvinia Cucullata, L.

संचिन्त् *saṃ-√cint*, P. *-cintayati* (ind. p. *-cintya* or *-cintayitvā*), to think about, think over, consider carefully, reflect about (acc.), MBh.; Kāv. &c.; to design, intend, destine, BhP. °**cintana**, n. careful consideration or reflection, anxiety, Bhpr. °**cintita**, mfn. carefully considered or thought about, deliberated, weighed (*-vat*, mfn. 'one who has carefully considered' or 'he has carefully considered'), MBh.; Kāv. &c.; designed, appointed, BhP.

1. **Saṃ-cintya**, ind. intentionally, Divyâv.

2. **Saṃ-cintya**, mfn. to be thought over or considered, Yājñ.; MBh.; to be regarded as (*vat*, ifc.), R. (cf. *duḥ-saṃc°*).

संचिष्कारयिषु *saṃ-cishkārayishu*, mfn. (fr. Desid. of Caus. of *sam-√skṛi*) wishing any one (acc.) to perform a purificatory rite, MBh. xv, 706 (B. *sam-cask°*).

संचीवरय *saṃ-cīvaraya*, Nom. Ā. °*yate*, to assume the coarse dress or rags of an ascetic, Anarghar. (cf. Pāṇ. iii, 1, 20).

सञ्चु *sañcu*, m. or f. (with Jainas) a commentary, Cat. (cf. *sañca*).

संचुद् *saṃ-√cud*, Caus. *-codayati*, to impel, push on, drive, shoot off, MBh.; R.; to inflame, arouse, animate, instigate, further, ib.; BhP.; to brandish, wield, MBh.; to summon, challenge, ib.; to procure quickly, assist to obtain, RV.

Saṃ-codaka, m. 'impeller,' N. of a Devaputra, Lalit. °**codana**, m. (or *ā*, f.) urging, exciting, inflaming, arousing, MBh.; Jātakam.; (*ā*), f. a stimulant, MBh. °**codayitavya**, mfn. (fr. Caus.) to be urged on or impelled, Hariv. °**codita**, mfn. (fr. id.) impelled, ordered, commanded, BhP.

संचूर्ण् *saṃ-√cūrṇ*, P. *-cūrṇayati*, to grind to powder, comminute, pulverize, Suśr.

Saṃ-cūrṇana, n. the act of grinding to powder, comminution, crushing or breaking to pieces, Alaṃkārat. °**cūrṇita**, mfn. completely pulverized or comminuted, cut or broken to pieces, MBh.; Śaṃk.; Rājat.

संचूष् *saṃ-√cūsh*, Pass. *-cūshyate*, to be in a state of great heat, boil over, Suśr.

संचृत् *saṃ-√cṛit*, P. *-cṛitati*, to be joined with (instr.), AV. iii, 31, 1.

Saṃ-cṛit, f. junction, union, RV. ix, 84, 2.

संचेष्ट् *saṃ-√cesht*, Ā. *-ceshṭate*, to move about restlessly, be disturbed, MBh.; to exert one's self, strive, act, ib.

संच्यु *saṃ-√cyu*, Caus. *-cyāvayati*, to cause to fall off, strike off, remove, MBh.

संछद् *saṃ-√1. chad*, Caus. *-chādayati*, to cover over, envelop, conceal, hide, obscure, ŚBr.; MBh. &c.; to put on (as a garment), Vop.

Saṃ-channa, mfn. entirely covered or enveloped or clothed, MBh.; Hariv. &c.; concealed, hidden, obscure, unknown, MBh.

Saṃ-chādanī, f. 'that which covers,' the skin, L.

संछद् *saṃ-√2. chad* (or *chand*), Caus. *-chandayati* (only ind. p. *-chandya*), to present, offer (with acc. of pers. and instr. of thing), MBh.

संछर्दन *saṃ-chardana*, n. spitting out, vomiting forth, ejecting (one of the ten ways in which an eclipse is supposed to end, cf. *rāhu-grasana*), VarBṛS.

संछिद् *saṃ-√chid*, P. Ā. *-chinatti*, *-chintte*, to cut to pieces, cut through, pierce, split, destroy, AV. &c. &c.; to remove, resolve (a doubt), Bhag.; to decide, settle (a question), BhP.: Pass. *-chidyate*, to be cut to pieces &c., MBh.

Saṃ-chidā, f. destruction, Kāśikh.

Saṃ-chinna, mfn. cut to pieces, cut off &c., MBh.

Saṃ-chettavya, mfn. to be cut through or removed or resolved (as a doubt), MBh. °**chettṛi**, mfn. one who removes or resolves (a doubt), ib.

Saṃ-chedya, n. 'the flowing together of two rivers' or 'the mouth of a river entering the sea,' L.

सञ्ज् 1. *sañj* (or *sajj*), cl. 1. P. *sañjati*, *sajjati*, to go, move, Dhātup. vii, 22.

सञ्ज् 2. *sañj* (or *saj*), cl. 1. P. (Dhātup. xxiii, 18) *sájati* (rarely Ā. °*te*; pf. *sasañja*, Br. &c. [in some rare and doubtful cases in MBh. and Ragh. *sasajja*]; 3. pl. *sejuḥ*, ŚBr.; aor. *asāṅkshīt*, *sāṅkshīt*, Up. &c.; *asañji*, Br.; *ásakthās*, °*ta*, RV.; Br.; Prec. *sajyāt*, Gr.; fut. *saṅktā*, *saṅkshyati*, ib.; inf. *saktum*, MBh.; *saṅktos*, Br.; ind. p. *-sajya*, *-sáṅgam*, ib. &c.), to cling or stick or adhere to, be attached to or engaged in or occupied with (loc.), Br.; Ragh.; Naish.: Pass. *sajyáte* (generally *sajjate*, ep. also °*ti*), to be attached or fastened, adhere, cling, stick (with *na*, 'to fly through without sticking,' as an arrow), ŚBr. &c. &c.; to linger, hesitate, MBh.; R.; to be devoted to or intent on or occupied with (loc.), MBh.; Kāv. &c.: Caus. *sañjayati* (aor. *asasañjat*; for *sajjayati* see √*sajj*), to cause to stick or cling to, unite or connect with (loc.), Bhag.; Śaṃk.: Desid. *sisaṅkshati*, see *ā-√sañj*: Intens. *sāsajyate*, *sāsaṅkti*, Gr. [Cf., accord. to some, Lat. *segnis*; Lith. *segù*, 'I attach.']

Saktá, mfn. clinging or adhering to, sticking in (loc. or comp.; *saktaḥ* or *bhitti-s°* with √*sthā*, 'to stand as if nailed or as if rooted to the spot'), AV. &c. &c.; belonging to (gen.), Pañcad.; committed or intrusted to (comp.), Kām.; fixed or intent upon, directed towards, addicted or devoted to, fond of, engaged in, occupied with (loc., acc. with *prati*, or comp.), MBh.; Kāv. &c.; hindered, impeded (see *a-s°*); impending, near at hand, MW. **-tā**, f., **-tva**, n. attachment, addiction (esp. to worldly objects), MBh. **-dvish** (Hāsy.), **-vaira** (Śak.), mfn. being engaged in a feud with (instr.) **-mūtra**, mfn. making water slowly or with difficulty, Car. **-vat**, mfn. one who has attached himself to (= *sasañja*), R.

Saktavya, mfn. (fr. *saktu*) intended to serve for grit or to be coarsely ground (as grain), Pāṇ. v. 1, 2, Vārtt. 4, Pat.

Sakti, f. connexion, entwinement (of creepers), Kir.; clinging or adhering to (loc. or comp.), attachment, addiction (esp. to worldly objects), Śiś.; Rājat.; Sarvad. **-mat**, mfn. attached or devoted to, fond of (in *ati-s°*), Kām.

Sáktu, m. (or n., g. *ardharcâdi*; also written *śaktu*) coarsely ground meal, grit, groats (esp. of barley-meal), RV. &c. &c. **-kāra**, m. one who grinds barley-meal, R. **-kāraka**, m. (and *ika*, f.) id., Nir. **-ghaṭâkhyāyikā**, f. the story of the vessel of barley-meal (Pañcat. v, 59-74). **-dhānī**, f. a vessel of b°-m°, Pat. **-prasthīya**, mfn. relating to a Prastha of b°-m° (said of the episode of MBh. xiv, 2711 &c.) **-phalā** or **-phalī**, f. Prosopis Spicigera or Mimosa Suma, L. **-miśra**, mfn. mixed with b°-m°, Suśr. **-śrí**, mfn. id., VS. **-sindhu**, m., Pāṇ. vii, 3, 19, Sch. **-homa**, m. an oblation of barley-meal, Vait.

Saktuka, m. (also written *śak°*) a partic. vegetable poison, L.

Saktula, mfn., g. *sidhmâdi*.

Saṅga, m. (ifc. f. *ā* or *ī*) sticking, clinging to, touch, contact with (loc. or comp.), TS. &c. &c.; relation to, association or intercourse with (gen., instr. with and without *saha*, loc., or comp.), MBh.; Kāv. &c.; addiction or devotion to, propensity for, (esp.) worldly or selfish attachment or affection, desire, wish, cupidity, Mn.; MBh. &c.; (with *Atreḥ*) N. of a Sāman, Br. **-kara**, mfn. causing attachment or desire, Sarvad. **-gupta-sūnu**, m. N. of an author, Cat. **-tala**, m. N. of a man, Buddh. **-tyāga**, m. abandonment of attachment or desire, Bhartṛ. **-rahita** and **-varjita**, mfn. free from attachment, indifferent, unworldly, W. **-vicyuti**, f. separation from worldly attachment, ib.

Saṅgaṭa and **Saṅgika**, m. N. of men, Rājat.

Saṅgin, mfn. hanging on, sticking in, clinging or adhering to (comp.), Kāv.; Kathās.; coming into contact with, touching (comp.), MārkP.; attached or devoted or addicted to, fond of, intent on, connected with (gen., loc., or comp.), MBh.; Kāv. &c.; full of affection or desire, worldly, licentious, Pur.; Kathās.; continuous, uninterrupted, Kir.

Saṅgiya, m. N. of a man, Rājat.

Sañja. See *sam-ja* below.

Sañjaka, m. N. of a man, Rājat.

Sañjana, n. the act of attaching or fastening, Bālar.; joining, folding (the hands), Naish.; the act of clinging, adhering, sticking, MW.; (*ī*), f. that on which anything is hung, Nir.

Sañji, sañjimat, g. *yavâdi.*

सञ्जतर *sañjatara*, n. N. of a city, Pañcat. (prob. w.r.)

संजन् *sam-√jan*, Ā. *-jāyate*, to be born or produced together with (abl.), RV.; ŚvetUp.; to be born from (loc. or abl.), arise or come forth from (abl.), come into existence, take place, appear, happen, Mn.; MBh. &c.; to bring forth, R.; to become, be, Hariv.; R.; to elapse, pass (as time), Pañcat.: Caus. *-janayati*, to cause to be born, bring forth, generate, produce, create, cause, form, make, MBh.; R. &c.

Sam-ja, m. 'universal Creator,' N. of Brahmā or Śiva, L.; (*ā*), f. a she-goat, L.; *-pāla*, m. N. of a man, Rājat. °**janana**, mf(*ī*)n. producing, causing, effecting (comp.), MBh.; Kāv. &c.; n. production, creation, growth, development, ŚāṅkhŚr.; MBh. &c. °**janita**, mfn. (fr. Caus.) produced, caused, created, MBh.; Pañcat.

Sam-jāta, mfn. born, produced, grown, arisen, become, appeared (often in comp. = 'becoming, grown;' cf. below), MBh.; Kāv. &c.; passed, elapsed (as time), Pañcat.; m. pl. N. of a people, VP.; *-kopa*, mfn. growing angry, becoming enraged, R.; *-kautuka*, mfn. having curiosity roused, becoming curious, MW.; *-nidrā-pralaya*, mfn. one whose sleep has come to an end, L.; *-nirveda*, mfn. grown despondent, Kathās.; *-pāśa*, mfn. one who has become fettered by (comp.), Śak.; *-lajja*, mfn. one who has become ashamed or embarrassed, Ratnâv.; *-viśrambha*, mfn. having confidence excited, becoming confident, R.; *-vepathu*, mfn. trembling, BhP.; °*ṭérshya*, mfn. becoming envious, MW.

संजप् *sam-√jap*, P. *-japati*, to whisper or talk about, report, communicate, MBh.; MārkP.

संजय *sam-jaya* &c. See *sam-√ji.*

संजर्भुराण *sam-járbhurāṇa*, mfn. (fr. Intens. of *sam-√bhur*) quivering, flickering, RV.

संजल्प् *sam-√jalp*, P. *-jalpati* (pr. p. *-jalpat* or °*pamāna*); to speak or talk together, converse, chatter, MBh.; R.

Sam-jalpa, m. talking together, conversation, chattering, uproar, confusion, MBh.; Hariv. °**jalpita**, mfn. spoken together, spoken, uttered; n. spoken words, talk, BhP.

संजवन *sam-javana*, n. (fr. *sam-√ju*; perhaps for *sam-yavana* fr. *sam-√1. yu*) a group of four houses, quadrangle, L.; a way-mark, sign-post, Hariv. (Nilak.)

Sam-jāvana, n. (perhaps for *sam-yāvana*) pouring a little buttermilk into warm milk, L.

संजि *sam-√ji*, P. *-jayati* (pf. p. *-jigīvas*), to conquer together, RV.; AV.; TBr.; to conquer completely, gain or acquire by contest, ib.; to subdue completely, control (the senses), Hcat.: Pass. *-jīyate*, to be overpowered or subdued, Subh.

Sam-jayá, mf(*ā́*)n. completely victorious, triumphant, RV.; AV.; AitBr.; m. conquest, victory (with *Viśvāmitrasya*, N. of a Catur-aha), PañcavBr.; a kind of military array, Kām.; N. of a chief of the Yakshas, Buddh.; of a Sūta (the son of Gavalgaṇa and follower of Dhṛita-rāshṭra), MBh.; of a son of Dhṛita-rāshṭra, ib.; of a son of Su-pārśva, VP.; of a son of Prati or Pratikshatra, BhP.; of a son of Bharmyâśva, ib.; of a son of Raṇam-jaya, ib.; of a Vyāsa, Cat.; of a preceptor, Buddh.; n. N. of various Sāmans, ĀrshBr.; *-kavi-śekhara*, m. N. of a poet, Cat.

Sam-jáyat, mf(*antī*)n. conquering, winning, AV.; (*antī*), f. N. of a town, MBh.; Suśr. °**jayin**, m. 'victorious,' N. of a man, Buddh.

Sam-jít, m. a conqueror, winner, RV. °**jita**, mfn. entirely conquered or won, TBr. °**jiti**, f. complete victory, AitBr.; ŚrS.

संजिघृक्षु *sam-jighṛikshu*, mfn. (fr. Desid. of *sam-√grah*) wishing to gather or collect, Daś.; wishing to sum up or epitomise, Sarvad.

संजिहान *sam-jihāna.* See *sam-√1. hā.*

संजिहीर्षु *sam-jihīrshu*, mfn. (fr. Desid. of *sam-√hṛi*) wishing to destroy, R.; BhP.

संजीव् *sam-√jīv*, P. *-jīvati* (ep. also Ā. °*te*; pr. p. *-jīvat* or *-jīvamāna*), to live with or together, AV.; to live, exist, live by any business or occupation (instr.), ib.; TS.; MBh.; BhP.; to revive, be restored to life, ŚBr.; MBh.: Caus. *-jīvayati*, to make alive, vivify, animate, ĀśvŚr.; Mn.; MBh. &c.; to keep alive, maintain, nourish, Rājat.: Desid. of Caus. and Desid., see next.

Sam-jijīvayishu, mfn. (fr. Desid. of Caus.) wishing to bring to life or enliven, MBh. °**jijīvishu**, mfn. (fr. Desid.) wishing to live, loving life, ib.

Sam-jīvá, mf(*ā́*)n. living together, living, MW.; making alive, vivifying, AV.; ĀśvŚr.; m. the act of reviving, revival (see comp.); a particular hell, Divyâv.; *-karaṇa*, mf(*ī*)n. bringing to life, animating, R.; °*vârma*, n., Pāṇ. vi, 2, 91. °**jīvaka**, mf(*ikā*)n. living together, MW.; making alive, vivifying, animating, ŚrS.; BhP.; m. N. of a bull, Kathās.; Pañcat.; (*ī*), f. N. of a woman, Vās., Introd. °**jīvana**, mf(*ī*)n. making alive, animating, MBh.; Kāv. &c. (v. l. often °*jīvinī*); m. a kind of antidote, Suśr.; a partic. hell, Mn.; Yājñ.; (*ī*), f. a kind of plant (= *rudantī*), L. (v. l. °*jīvinī*); making alive, causing life, MW.; a kind of elixir, ib.; N. of a lexicon and of Mallinātha's Commentaries on the Kumāra-sambhava, Megha-dūta, and Raghu-vaṃśa; (*am*), n. the act of living or reviving, MBh.; Kāv. &c.; animating, bringing to life, W.; a cluster of four houses (= *sam-javana*), L. °**jīvita**, mfn. (fr. Caus.) vivified, enlivened, animated, MBh. °**jīvin**, mfn. rendering alive, enlivening, MBh.; BhP.; m. N. of a minister of Megha-varṇa (king of the crows), Pañcat.; (*ī*), f. N. of a plant, L. (see °*jīvanī*); of a Commentary, Cat.

संजुघुक्षु *sam-jughukshu*, mfn. (fr. Desid. of *sam-√guh*) wishing to completely conceal, Bhaṭṭ.

संजुष्ट *sam-jushṭa*, mfn. (*√jush*) visited or frequented or inhabited by, filled with (instr. or comp.), MBh.

संजूर्व् *sam-√jūrv*, P. *-jūrvati*, to burn up, consume (by fire), RV.

संजृम्भ् *sam-√jṛimbh*, Ā. *-jṛimbhate*, to gape open, be unfolded or displayed, appear, Rājat.

संजॄ *sam-√1. jṝ*, P. *-jīryati*, to become old together, MaitrS.

संजॄ *sam-√2. jṝ*, Ā. *-jarate*, to sound together, sound forth, RV.

संज्ञ 1. *sam-jña*, mfn. (fr. *sam* + 1. *jña* = *jñu*; cf. 1. *pra-jña*) knock-kneed, L.

Sam-jñu, mfn. id., L.

संज्ञा *sam-√jñā*, P. Ā. *-jānāti, -jānīte*, (Ā.) to agree together, be of the same opinion, be in harmony with (loc.; accord. to Pāṇ. ii, 3, 22, also instr. or acc.), RV.; AV.; VS.; ŚBr.; (Ā.) to obey (dat.), AitBr.; (Ā.) to appoint, assign, intend (for any purpose), destine, ib.; (only ind. p. *-jñāya*) to direct, order, command, Hariv.; to acknowledge, recognize, own, Pāṇ. i, 3, 46, Sch.; (P.) to acknowledge or claim as one's own, take possession of, SaddhP.; (P.) to think of, recollect sorrowfully (with acc. or gen.), Pāṇ.; Vop.; Ā. to know well, understand, R.; to watch for, Bhaṭṭ.: Caus. *-jñāpayati*, °*te*, to cause to be of the same opinion or agree together, AV.; AitBr.; to cause to acquiesce or agree in (euphemistically said of a sacrificial victim, which ought not to be led forcibly to its death but made to resign itself), ŚBr.; GṛŚrS.; MBh.; BhP.; to appease, satisfy, MBh.; Kālid.; to make to be understood or known, cause to understand, ŚBr.; to make signs to (acc.), communicate or make anything known by signs, Mṛicch.; Hcar.; to command, enjoin, instruct, Hariv.

2. **Sam-jña**, mfn. (ifc. for *sam-jñā*, e.g. *labdha-samjña*, 'one who has recovered consciousness,' MBh.; *-tā*, f. 'recovery of c°,' Veṇis.); (*ā*), f., see below; n. a yellow fragrant wood, yellow sanders, L. °**jñaka**, mf(*ikā*)n. (ifc.) = 2. *samjña* (e.g. *prāṇa-samjñako jīvaḥ*, 'life has the name breath,' MaitrUp.; cf. *naṭa-, ravi-s°*).

Sam-jñapana, n. (fr. Caus.) causing agreement or harmony, AV.; killing a sacrificial animal (by suffocation; cf. above), ŚBr.; ŚrS.; MBh.; BhP.; deception, defrauding, Prâyaśc. °**jñapita**, mfn. sacrificed, killed, Pāṇ. vi, 4, 52, Sch. °**jñapta**, mfn. informed, apprised, MW.; killed, suffocated, sacrificed, Hariv.; *-homa*, m. an oblation performed after killing a sacrificial animal, ĀpŚr. °**jñapti**, f. killing, slaying, sacrificing, ĀpŚr., Sch.; apprising, informing, W.

Sam-jñā́, f. (ifc. f. *ā*) agreement, mutual understanding, harmony, TBr.; ŚBr.; Kathās.; consciousness, clear knowledge or understanding or notion or conception, ŚBr. &c. &c.; a sign, token, signal, gesture (with the hand, eyes &c.; *samjñām √kṛi* or *dā*, 'to give a signal'), MBh.; Kāv. &c.; direction (in *a-kṛitas°*, 'one who has received no d°'), MBh.; a track, footstep, BhP.; a name, appellation, title, technical term (ifc. = 'called, named'), Nir.; Mn.; MBh. &c.; (in gram.) the name of anything thought of as standing by itself, any noun having a special meaning (*samjñāyām* therefore denotes '[used] in some peculiar sense rather than in its strictly etymological meaning,' e.g. as a proper name), Pāṇ. i, 1, 34; 2, 53 &c.; a technical expression in grammar (see *-sūtra*); (with Buddhists) perception (one of the 5 Skandhas, q. v.), Dharmas. 22; MWB. 109; N. of the Gāyatrī (q. v.), L.; of a partic. high number, Buddh.; N. of a daughter of Tvashṭṛi or Viśva-karman (the wife of the Sun and mother of Manu, Yama and Yamī), Hariv.; Pur. **-karaṇa**, n. giving a name, Nir. i, 2; *-parisishṭa*, n. N. of wk. **-karman**, n. (= *-karaṇa*), Kaṇ. **-tantra**, n. N. of an astron. wk. by Nila-kaṇṭha. **-tva**, n. the being a technical term, Cat. **-°dhikāra** (°*jñâdh°*), m. (in Pāṇ.) a heading or governing rule which gives a partic. name to the rules which fall under it and influences them all. **-paribhāshā**, f., **-pāṭī**, f., **-pāda-vyākhyā**, f., **-prakaraṇa**, n., **-prakriyā**, f. N. of wks. **-°rtham** (°*jñâr°*), ind. for the sake of a sign, Bhag. **-vat**, mfn. having consciousness, revived, recovered, R.; having a name or denomination, W. **-viveka**, m. N. of wk. **-vishaya**, m. 'having a name or noun for a subject,' an epithet, W. **-samuccaya**, m. N. of a medical wk. **-suta**, m. 'son of Saṃjñā,' N. of the planet Saturn, L. **-sūtra**, n. any Sūtra which teaches the meaning of a technical term, Pāṇ., Sch. **-°stra** (°*jñâstra*), n. N. of a mythical weapon of Pradyumna, Hariv. **Samjñôpasarjanī-√bhū**, P. *-bhavati*, to become a proper name or the subordinate member of a compound, Pat. on Pāṇ. i, 1, 27, Vārtt. 2.

Sam-jñāta, mfn. well known, understood (see comp.); intended or destined for (comp.), MBh.; *-rūpa* (*sám°*), mfn. one whose form or appearance is universally known, RV. °**jñāti**, f. agreement, harmony, AitBr. °**jñātṛi**, mfn. one who recollects sorrowfully (gen.), Pat.

Sam-jñāna, mf(*ī*)n. producing harmony, AitBr.; (*ī*), f. a ceremony for producing unanimity, TS.; ĀśvŚr.; n. unanimity, harmony with (loc. or instr.), RV.; AV.; VS.; TS.; consciousness, ŚBr.; AitUp.; BhP.; right conception, Pratijñās.; perception (= *sam-jñā*), Buddh. °**jñānanā** (?), f. consciousness, ib.

Sam-jñāpana, n. (fr. Caus.) apprising, informing, teaching, W.; killing, slaughter, ib. °**jñāpita**, mfn. (fr. id.) killed, suffocated (as a victim), BhP.

Sam-jñikā, f. a name, appellation, MBh. xii, 6825. °**jñita**, mfn. made known, communicated, R.; apprised by a sign or gesture, Rājat.; called, named, termed (generally ifc.), MaitrUp.; Mn.; MBh. &c. °**jñin**, mfn. having consciousness, conscious of (comp.), Vajracch.; SaddhP.; Sarvad.; having a name, named, termed, that which receives a name or has a term given to it in grammar (°*jñitva*, n.), Pat.; Kāś.; Kap.; Sarvad.

Samjñī-bhūtaka, mfn. that which has become a name, Pat. on Pāṇ. iv, 3, 68.

Sam-jñeya, m. N. of a king, VP.

संज्ञु *sam-jñu.* See col. 2.

संज्वर् *sam-√jvar*, P. *-jvarati*, to be in great

fever or heat, be greatly depressed or grieved, be afflicted or sorrowful, MBh.

Saṃ-jvara, m. great heat or fever (also applied to the heat of anger or any violent agitation; °*ram* √*kṛi*, 'to feel agitated'), Mn. (in *a-s°*, q.v.), Kāv.; Kathās. &c.; *-kara,* mfn. causing agitation, Vcar.; *-vat,* mfn. full of heat or fever (see *sneha-s°*); °*rât-tura,* mfn. afflicted with fever, fevered, MW.

Saṃ-jvārin, mfn. feeling the heat of fever &c., feverish, Bhaṭṭ. (cf. Pāṇ. iii, 2, 142).

संज्वल् *saṃ-√jval,* P. *-jvalati,* to blaze up or flame brightly, MBh.: Caus. *-jvālayati,* to cause to flame, illuminate, light, ib.

Saṃ-jvalana, n. that which illuminates, fuel, Anarghar.

Saṃ-jvālya, ind. having lighted or kindled.

सट् *saṭ,* cl. 1. P. *saṭati,* to be a part of, Dhātup. ix, 26: Caus. or cl. 10. *sāṭayati* (see √*sāṭ*).

सट *saṭa,* m. n. = next, L.; a person whose father is a Brāhman and whose mother is a Bhaṭi, L.

Saṭā, f. (cf. *śaṭā, chaṭā* and *jaṭā*) an ascetic's matted or clotted hair, a braid of hair (in general), MBh.; the mane (of a lion or horse) or the bristles (of a boar), MBh.; Kāv. &c.; a crest (= *śikhā*), L.; a multitude, number, VarBṛS.; light, lustre, BhP. **—°ṅka** (°*ṭâṅka*), mfn. 'mane-marked,' a lion, L. **—pāṭala,** m. the red mane of a lion.

Saṭāla, m. having a mane, maned (v. l. *sa-jāla*), Kathās.; (ifc.) richly provided with, full of, Inscr.

सटंकार *sa-ṭaṃkāra,* mfn. (fr. 7. *sa*+*ṭ°*) having notoriety or fame, famous, MW.

सटालु *saṭālu* = *śalāṭu,* an unripe fruit, PārGṛ.

सटि *saṭi* &c. See *śaṭi.*

सटीक *sa-ṭīka,* mfn. (fr. 7. *sa*+*ṭīkā*) accompanied or explained by a commentary, MW.

सट्ट् *saṭṭ,* cl. 10. P. *saṭṭayati,* to hurt, Dhātup. xxxii, 31; to be strong, ib.; to dwell, ib.; 'to take' or 'to give' (*dāne* v. l. for *ādāne*).

सट्ट *saṭṭa,* n. two pieces of timber at the side of a door, L.

सट्टक *saṭṭaka,* n. a sort of minor drama in Prākrit (e.g. the Karpūra-mañjarī of Rāja-śekhara), Sāh.; buttermilk mixed with the juice of cumin &c. (cf. *śaṭṭaka*), L. **—ṭīkā,** f. N. of wk.

Saṭṭaya, n. a kind of drama (= *saṭṭaka*), Cat. **—vyākhyā,** f. N. of wk.

सट्वा *saṭvā,* f. a kind of bird, L.; a musical instrument, L.

सठ् 1. *saṭh,* cl. 10. P. *sāṭhayati* = √*śaṭh,* Dhātup. xxxii, 28 (Vop.)

सठ् 2. *saṭh,* m. N. of a man, Inscr.

सठी *saṭhi.* See *śaṭhi.*

सड *sa-ḍa,* mfn. = *saha ḍena vartate,* Pāṇ. viii, 3, 56, Sch.

सडिण्डिमम् *sa-ḍiṇḍimam,* ind. by sound of drum, Kathās.

सड्ड *saḍḍa,* m. N. of two men, Rājat.

सणतूल *saṇa-tūla, saṇa-sūtra.* See *śaṇa-t°, śaṇa-s°.*

सणहाष *saṇahāsha,* N. of a place, Cat.

सणि *saṇi,* m. the smell of the breath of a cow, L.; mfn. smelling like the breath of a cow, ib.

संटङ्क *saṃ-ṭaṅka,* m. connection, Nalac., Sch.

सण्ड *saṇḍa,* m. pl. N. of a people, MBh. (C. *shaṇḍa*); a eunuch (= *śaṇḍa* and *shaṇḍha*), L.

संडिश *saṃḍiśa* (?), m. (= *saṃ-daṇśa*) a pair of tongs or nippers, L.

संडीन *saṃ-ḍīna,* n. (√*ḍī*) flying together (one of the modes of flight attributed to birds), MBh.

Saṃḍīnôḍḍīna, n. a partic. mode of flight (a combination of prec. and *ud-ḍīna,* 'flying up;' accord. to some 'flying well'), ib.

संडीविन् *saṃḍīvin,* m. (perhaps w. r. for *saṃ-jīvin,* q. v.) N. of a minister of the crow-king Megha-varṇa, Kathās.

सण्ढिका *saṇḍhikā,* f. a female camel, Pañcad.

सत् *sát,* mf(*satī́*)n. (pr. p. of √1. *as*) being, existing, occurring, happening, being present (*sato me,* 'when I was present;' often connected with other participles or with an adverb, e.g. *nāmni kṛite sati,* 'when the name has been given;' *tathā sati,* 'if it be so;' also ibc., where sometimes = 'possessed of,' cf. *sat-kalpavṛiksha*), RV. &c. &c.; abiding in (loc.), MBh.; belonging to (gen.), ŚBr.; living, MuṇḍUp.; lasting, enduring, Kāv.; RV. &c. &c.; real, actual, as any one or anything ought to be, true, good, right (*tan na sat,* 'that is not right'), beautiful, wise, venerable, honest (often in comp., see below), RV. &c. &c.; m. a being, (pl.) beings, creatures, RV. &c.; a good or wise man, a sage, MBh.; R.; good or honest or wise or respectable people, Mn.; MBh. &c.; (*ī́*), f., see *satī́* below; (*sat*), n. that which really is, entity or existence, essence, the true being or really existent (in the Vedânta, 'the self-existent or Universal Spirit, Brahma'), RV. &c. &c.; that which is good or real or true, good, advantage, reality, truth, ib.; water, Naigh. i, 12; (in gram.) the terminations of the present participle, Pāṇ. iii, 2, 127 &c.; (*sat*), ind. (cf. *sat-√kṛi* &c.) well, right, fitly. [Cf. Gk. ὤν, ἐών for ἐσων; Lat. *sens* in *ab-sens, præ-sens; sons,* 'guilty,' orig. 'the real doer;' Lith. *sąs, ěsąs;* Slav. *sy, sąšta.*] **—kathā,** f. (ifc. f. *ā*) a good conversation or tale, R.; BhP. **—kadamba,** m. a species of Kadamba, L. **—karaṇa,** n. doing (the last) honour (to the dead), cremation of a corpse, funeral obsequies, R. **—kara-tva,** see *a-sat-k°.* **—kartavya,** mfn. one who is to be honoured, MBh. **—kartṛi,** mfn. doing good, acting well, treating w° or kindly, a benefactor (*brāhmaṇa-sat-k°,* 'one who does good or honour to Brāhmans'), MBh.; Mṛicch.; m. N. of Vishṇu, L. **—karman,** n. a good work, virtuous act, Pur.; Rājat.; virtue, piety, W.; hospitality, ib.; funeral obsequies, ib.; expiation, ib.; mfn. performing good actions, Rājat.; m. N. of a son of Dhṛita-vrata, BhP.; (*sat-karma-kalpadruma,* m., °*ma-candrikā,* f., °*ma-cintāmaṇi,* m., °*ma-darpaṇa,* m., °*ma-dīpikā,* f. N. of wks.) **—kalā,** f. a fine art, Kāv. **—kalpavṛiksha,** mfn. (a grove) where Kalpa-trees are found, Śak. **—kavi,** m. a good or true poet, Kāv.; Rājat. &c.; *-tva,* n. 'a true poetic gift,' Vet.; *-miśra,* m. N. of a poet, ŚārṅgP. **—kāñcanāra,** m. Bauhinia Variegata, L. **—kāṇḍa,** m. a kite, hawk, falcon (Falco Cheela), L. **—kāya-dṛishṭi,** f. the (heretical) view (or doctrine) of the existence of a personality or individuality, Divyâv.; Mahāvy. **—kāra,** m. (sg. or pl.) kind treatment, honour, favour, reverence (with *paścima,* = *-karaṇa,* Hariv.; *rāja-sat-k°,* 'the favour of a king,' R.), Mn.; MBh. &c.; hospitable treatment, hospitality, ib.; feasting (or = 'a meal'), festival, religious observance, MW.; care, attention, consideration of or regard for a thing, Yogas.; w. r. for *saṃskāra,* Hariv.; °*râṛha,* mfn. worthy of hospitable treatment, Nal. **—kārya,** mfn. that which is effected, L.; deserving of honour or hospitality, R.; one to whom the last honours (i. e. cremation) are to be paid, ib.; n. (in Sāṃkhya phil.) the necessary existence of an effect (as inherent in a cause), Sāṃkhyak.; Tattvas.; Kap., Sch.; *-vāda,* m. (or *-siddhânta,* m., Kap.) the doctrine of the actual existence of an effect (in its cause), Bādar., Sch.; *-vādin,* m. an adherent of the above doctrine, ib. **—kāvya,** n. a good poem, Kāv.; *-kalpadruma* m. N. of wk. **—kishku,** m. the length of 48 inches, L. **—kīrti,** f. good reputation, BhP.; mfn. having a good r°, Cat.; *-candrôdaya,* m. N. of wk. **—kula,** n. a good or noble family, MārkP.; Kathās.; ŚārṅgP.; mfn. belonging to a g° or n° f° (*-tā,* f., Sāh.), Kām.; °*lôdbhava,* mfn. sprung from a n° f°, MW. **—kulīna,** mfn. = *-kula,* L. **—√kṛi,** P. Ā. *-karoti, -kurute* &c., to set right, put in order, arrange, prepare, adorn, garnish, Mn.; MBh.; R. &c.; to treat well or with respect, honour, treat or receive hospitably, MBh.; R.; Kāv. &c.; to pay the last honours to (acc.), cremate, R.: Caus. *-kārayati,* to cause to be treated with respect or reverence, show rev°, pay resp°, MW.; to cause to pay the last honours, MBh. **—kṛita,** mfn. done well, W.; adorned with (comp.), MBh.; Pur.; honoured, treated with respect or hospitality, entertained, MBh.; R.; VarBṛS. &c.; worshipped, adored, VarBṛS.; m. N. of Śiva, MW.; n. virtue, W.; respect, ib.; honourable reception, MārkP. **—kṛiti,** f. doing good, virtue, morality, W.; kind treatment, hospitable reception, hospitality, MBh.; BhP.; Kathās. &c. **—kṛitya,** ind. p. having treated with respect, having hospitably entertained, Yājñ.; R.; devotedly, piously, zealously, eagerly, Jātakam. **—kṛitya-muktâvalī,** f. N. of wk. **—kriya,** mfn. doing good, MBh.; (*ā*), f. putting in order, preparation, Kāv.; Kām.; explication, Cat.; a good action, charity, virtue, W.; (sg. or pl.) kind or respectful treatment, hospitable reception, hospitality (*vivāha-sat-kr°,* 'the celebration of a wedding,' Ragh.; *para-loka-sat-kr°,* 'honouring in regard to the other world,' funeral ceremonies, MBh.), Mn.; Yājñ.; Kāv. &c.; any purificatory ceremony, W.; funeral ceremonies, L.; N. of wk.; (*sat-kriyā-kalpa-mañjarī,* f. N. of wk.) **—kshetra,** n. a good field, Mudr.; Rājat. **—tattva,** n., **-tattva-bindu,** m., **-tattva-ratnamālā,** f. N. of wks. **—tama** (*sát-*), mfn. very good or right, the best, first, chief of (gen. or comp.), Br.; ŚāṅkhŚr.; ChUp. &c.; most virtuous, W.; very venerable or respectable, ib.; *-tā,* f. the first rank of all, BhP. **—tarka,** m. an orthodox system of philosophy (*a-sat-t°,* BhP.), Cat.; *-siddhâñjana,* n. N. of wk. **—tā,** f. existence, being, Up.; Kaṇ.; Tarkas. &c.; a partic. Jāti (in phil.), MW.; goodness, excellence, W.; *-jāti-prāmāṇya,* n. N. of wk.; *-mātra,* n. mere entity or existence (°*trât-man,* mfn. 'whose nature is entitled only to the predicate *being*'), VP.; *-vat,* mfn. entitled to the pred. 'being,' endowed with existence, Bhāshāp.; -°*vāpya* (°*tâv°*), mfn. included in (the notion of) ex°, MW. **—tāka,** (ifc.) = *-tā* (*-tva,* n.), Nīlak. **—tvá,** see below. **—pakshin,** m. a good or useful or innocuous bird, Śukas. **—pati** (*sát-*), m. a mighty lord, leader, champion, RV.; AV.; a good lord or ruler, PraśnUp.; BhP.; the lord of the g°, lord of real men, lord of heroes, MW.; a g° husband, Ragh.; Kathās.; N. of Indra, RV. **—pattra,** n. a new leaf (as of a water-lily), L. **—path,** (only instr. °*thā*) = next, R. **—patha,** m. a good or right way, correct or virtuous conduct, orthodox doctrine, MBh.; Hariv.; R. &c. **—pathīna,** mfn. going on the right way (fig.), Kāśīkh. **—paddhati,** f., **-padya-ratnâkara,** m. N. of wks. **—parigraha,** m. acceptance (of gifts) from a proper person, W. **—paśu,** m. a suitable animal, victim fit for a sacrifice, L. **—pātra,** n. a worthy recipient (of anything), worthy person, Pur.; Pañcat.; Kām. &c.; *-varsha,* m. raining down or bestowing favours on worthy objects, W.; *-varshin,* mfn. bountiful to w° o°, MW. **—putra,** m. a good or virtuous son, Cāṇ. (v. l.); ĀpŚr., Sch.; a son who performs all the prescribed rites in honour of his ancestors, MW.; mfn. one who has a son, Mn. ix, 154. **—purusha,** m. a good or wise man, Kāv.; Kām. &c.; °*shâshṭaka,* n. N. of wk. **—pushpa,** mf(*ā*)n. being in bloom, Pāṇ. iv, 1, 64, Vārtt. 1, Pat.; having good flowers, MW. **—prakriyā-vyākṛiti,** f. N. of wk. **—pratigraha,** m. acceptance of gifts from virtuous men, Mn.; Yājñ. **—pratijña,** mfn. one who has promised anything, L. **—pratipaksha,** mfn. liable to a valid opposite argument or objection; m. (with or scil. *hetu*) an argument liable to a valid obj° (*-tā,* f.), Tarkas.; Sarvad.; Kusum.; contrariety of arg°, existence of opposite premisses proving the existence or non-ex° of a thing, W.; N. of wk.; *-kroḍa,* m., *-grantha,* m., *-grantha-rahasya,* n., *-tā,* f., *-tā-vyavahāra-kroḍa,* m., *-deśaṇâbhāsa-prakaraṇa,* n., *-pattra,* n., *-pūrva-paksha-grantha-ṭīkā,* f., *-pūrva-paksha-grantha-dīdhiti-ṭīkā,* f., *-pūrva-paksha-grantha-prakāśa,* m., *-pūrva paksha-grantha-rahasya,* n., *-bādha-grantha,* m., *-vāda,* m., *-vicāra,* m., *-vibhāga,* m., *-vishayatā-śūnyatva-vicāra,* m., *-siddhânta-kroḍa,* m., *-siddhânta-grantha-ṭīkā,* f., *-siddhânta-grantha-dīdhiti-ṭīkā,* f., *-siddhânta-rahasya,* n., *-siddhântânugama,* m. N. of wks. **—pratipakshita,** mfn. (a reason) against which a valid objection has been raised, Kap., Sch. **—pratipakshin,** mfn. = *-pratipaksha* (°*shi-tā,* f.; *-tva,* n.), Bhāshāp.; ib., Sch.; containing opposite reasons or arguments, W. **—prabhā,** f. brilliant lustre, Kāv. **—pramuditā,** f. (in Sāṃkhya phil.) N. of one of the 8 perfections, Tattvas. (cf. *sadā-pramudita*). **—phala,** mfn. having good fruit, MW.; m. the pomegranate-tree, L.; n. the pomegranate, Cat. (*-phalānām,* w. v. l. for *-kalānām,* Subh.) **—phalin,** mfn. bearing good fruits, Śatr. **—saṃvin-maya** (fr. *-saṃvid* + *m°*), mfn. consisting of existence and consciousness (*-tva,* n.), NṛisUp. **—saṃsarga,** m. association with the good, the society of the good, W. **—saṃkalpa,** mfn. one who has good intentions, BhP. **—saṅga,** m. intercourse or association with the good, VarBṛS.; Pañcat.; Pur. &c.; *-vijaya*, m. N. of wk. **— saṃgati**, f. = *-saṅga*, Kāv. **— saṃgraha**, mfn. being understood by the good, BhP. **— saṃnidhāna**, n. association or intercourse with the g° or wise, Hit. **— samāgama**, m. association with the g°, W. **— sampradāya**, m. good tradition or traditional usage, Prasaṅg.; *-pradīpikā*, f. N. of wk. **— samprayoga**, m. right application, MW. **— sahāya**, m. a good companion, A.; mfn. one who has good or virtuous friends, W. **— sāra**, mfn. having good sap or essence, ib.; m. a kind of plant, L.; a painter, L.; a poet, L. **— siddhânta-mārtaṇḍa**, m. N. of wk. **— sukhânubhava**, m. 'fruition of real happiness,' N. of wk.

Sac, in comp. for *sat*. **— candrikā**, f. splendid moonlight, Kāv. **— carita**, n. good conduct, Śak.; Kathās.; BhP. &c.; history or account of the good, A.; mfn. well-conducted, virtuous, Kāv.; *-mīmāṅsā*, f. N. of wk. **— caritra**, n. good conduct, Rājat.; history of the good, A.; mfn. virtuous, W.; *-paritrāṇa*, n., *-rakshā*, f., *-sudhā-nidhi*, m. N. of wks. **— caryā**, f. = *-carita*, n., Kathās. **— cāra**, m. a good spy, Kām. (w.r. *saṃc*°). **— cit**, n. '(pure) existence and thought,' N. of Brahmā or the One self-existent Spirit (see *saccid-ānanda* below), MW. **— chāka** (*s*° + *śāka*), n. a leaf of the ginger, L. **— chāstra** (*s*° + *śā*°), n. a good or genuine doctrine or treatise, Mn.; Yājñ.; Pur. &c.; *-vat*, mfn. possessed of a good or genuine d°, Pañcat. **— chīla** (*s*° + *śī*°), n. a good character, VarBṛS.; mfn. of a virtuous disposition, benevolent, MW. **— chūdra** (*s*° + *śū*°), m. a good Śūdra, a Śūdra who has gone through the ceremonies customary in some places even for men of the lower caste, W.; °*râcāra*, m., °*râhnika*, n. N. of wks. **— chloka** (*s*° + *śl*°), mfn. having a good reputation, Kāv.

Saccid, in comp. for *sac-cit* above. **— aṅśa**, m. a portion of existence and thought, W. **— ātman**, m. the soul which consists of ex° and th°, ib. **— ānanda**, m. pl. existence and thought and joy; mfn. consisting of ex° and th° and joy; n. (pure) 'Existence and Thought and Joy,' N. of the One self-existing Spirit (= Brahmă), Up.; Pañcar. &c.; N. of Vishṇu as identified with Brahmā, MW.; *-cāṭu*, N. of wk.; *-tīrtha*, *-nātha*, *-bhāratī*, *-yogîndra*, *-śāstrin*, *-sarasvatī*, *-svāmin*; °*dâśrama*, m. N. of scholars and authors; *-bhujaṃga*, m. N. of wk.; *-maya*, mfn. consisting of ex° and thought and joy, NṛisUp.; °*dânubhava-dīpikā*, f., °*dânubhava-pradīpikā*, f. N. of wks.; *-stotra*, n. N. of a hymn.

Saccin, in comp. for *sac-cit*. **— maya**, mf(*ī*)n. consisting of existence and thought, ŚārṅgP.

Saj, in comp. for *sat*. **— jaṭā**, f. a kind of perfume, Pañcar. **— jana**, mfn. (for *sajjana* see p. 1131, col. 2) well-born, respectable, virtuous, Hariv.; m. a good or virtuous or wise man, Mn. &c. &c.; N. of various men, Rājat.; Buddh.; Cat.; *-garhita*, mfn. despised by the virtuous, Mn. x, 38; *-citta-vallabha*, *-maṇḍana*, n., *-manoratha*, m., *-rañjinī*, f., *-vallabha*, m. or n., °*bhā*, f. N. of wks.; °*nêshṭa*, mfn. desired or chosen by the good, MW.; °*nâika-vasati*, mfn. residing only in the g°, ib. **— jala**, m. N. of a man, Rājat. **— jushṭa**, mfn. liked by the good, R.

Satâsat (°*tâsatī́*), n. du. (= *sad-asatī*, formed in analogy to *sutâsutê*) the true and the false, TBr.

Sati-tarā. See next.

1. **Satī́**, f. (fem. of *sat*; for 2. see p. 1138, col. 2) her ladyship, your ladyship (= *bhavatī*, sometimes = 'you'), MBh.; a good and virtuous or faithful wife (esp. applied in later use to the faithful w° [popularly called Suttee] who burns herself with her husband's corpse, W.; compar. *satī-tarā*, *sati-t*° or *sat-t*°), Kāv.; VarBṛS.; Kathās. &c.; a wife, female (of an animal), BhP.; a female ascetic, MW.; a fragrant earth, L.; two kinds of metre, Col.; N. of the wife of Viśvāmitra, RV.; of the goddess Durgā or Umā (sometimes described as Truth personified or as a daughter of Daksha and wife of Bhava [Śiva], and sometimes represented as putting an end to herself by Yoga, or at a later period burning herself on the funeral pyre of her husband), Pur.; Kum.; of one of the wives of Aṅgiras, BhP.; of various women of modern times (also *-devī*), Cat. **— tā**, f. (MW.) or **-tva**, n. (Hariv.; Kathās.; MārkP. &c.) wifely fidelity (esp. as evinced by cremation with a husband's corpse, MW.) **— dehatyāga**, m. N. of ch. of the Brahma-vaivarta-purāṇa. **— putra**, m. the son of a virtuous woman, MW. **— pratishṭhā**, f. N. of ch. of the Matsya-purāṇa. **— vṛitti**, f. N. of Comm. **— vrata**, n. = *-tva*, Pañcad.; (*ā*), f. a faithful wife, Vās.; N. of a woman, ib., Introd. **— °śvara** (°*tīś*°) or °**ra-liṅga**, n. N. of a Liṅga, Cat. **— saras**, n. the lake of Satī (N. of a lake in Kaśmīra), Rājat.

Sâtīka, n. water, TS. (Naigh. i, 12).

Satīná, mfn. real, essential (see comp.); m. a kind of pease, Pisum Arvense, Kāṭh.; MaitrS.; Suśr. &c.; a bamboo, L.; n. water, Naigh. i, 12. **— kaṅkata** (°*ná-*), m. (accord. to Sāy.) an aquatic snake, RV. i, 191, 1. **— manyu** (°*ná-*), mfn. really angry or zealous, ib. x, 112, 8 ('eager to [shed] rain-water,' Sāy.) **— satvan** (°*ná-*), mfn. leading real warriors (applied to Indra), ib. i, 100, 1 ('a sender of water,' Sāy.)

Satīnaka, m. Pisum Arvense, L.

Satīya, n. = *satya* (formed by stretching *satya* for the purpose of mystical explication of this word), ChUp.; m. pl. N. of a people, VP. (v.l. *sanīya*).

Satīla (only L.), m. Pisum Arvense; a bamboo; wind; (*ā*), f. Pisum Arvense.

Satīlaka, m. Pisum Arvense, L.

Sat-tvá, n. (ifc. f. *ā*) being, existence, entity, reality (*īśvara-s*°, 'the existence of a Supreme Being'), TS &c. &c.; true essence, nature, disposition of mind, character, PañcavBr.; MBh. &c.; spiritual essence, spirit, mind, MuṇḍUp.; Yājñ.; MBh.; BhP.; vital breath, life, consciousness, strength of character, strength, firmness, energy, resolution, courage, self-command, good sense, wisdom, magnanimity, MBh.; R. &c.; the quality of purity or goodness (regarded in the Sāṃkhya phil. as the highest of the three Guṇas [q. v.] or constituents of Prakṛiti because it renders a person true, honest, wise &c., and a thing pure, clean &c.), MaitrUp.; Mn.; Yājñ. &c.; MBh.; R.; material or elementary substance, entity, matter, a thing, Nir.; Prāt.; a substantive, noun, W.; m. n. a living or sentient being, creature, animal, Mn.; MBh. &c.; embryo, fetus, rudiment of life (see *-lakshaṇā*); a ghost, demon, goblin, monster, R.; VarBṛS.; Kathās.; m. N. of a son of Dhṛita-rāshṭra, MBh. **— kartṛi**, m. the creator of living beings, R. **— kashāya**, m. decay of energy, one of the 5 signs of decay (see *kash*°), Buddh. **— guṇa**, m. the quality of purity or goodness (see above), W. **— guṇin**, mfn. having the above quality predominant, MW. **— tā**, f. purity, goodness, the existence of the Sattva-guṇa, W. **— dhātu**, m. the animal sphere, animated nature, Vajracch. **— dhāman**, n. 'abode of the quality Sattva,' N. of Vishṇu, BhP. **— pati**, m. the lord of creatures, ib. **— prakāśa**, m. the manifestation of the quality S° (personified as a king), Cat. **— pradhāna**, mfn. = *-guṇin*, MW. **— bhārata**, m. N. of Vyāsa, L. (cf. *satya-bh*°). **— maya**, mf(*ī*)n. formed or consisting of the quality S°, MBh. **— mūrti**, mfn. id., BhP. **— m-ejaya**, mfn. making animals tremble, Bhaṭṭ. **— rāśi**, m. quintessence of energy or courage, Kathās. **— lakshaṇā**, f. showing signs of pregnancy, pregnant, Śak. **— loka**, m. a world of living beings, MWB. 120. **— vat**, mfn. endowed with life, living, existent, a living being, W.; endowed with or possessed of the true essence, MW.; resolute, energetic, courageous, MBh.; R.; Suśr. &c.; abounding in the quality S°, Suśr.; (*atī*), f. pregnant, Divyâv.; N. of a Tantra deity, Buddh. **— vara**, m. N. of various men, Kathās. **— viplava**, m. loss of consciousness, Ragh. **— vihita**, mfn. effected by nature, natural, MW.; caused by goodness, ib.; virtuous, upright, W. **— vṛitti**, f. the condition or quality of goodness &c., ib. **— śālin**, mfn. energetic, courageous, Kathās.; Siṇhâs. **— śīla**, mfn. of a virtuous disposition, MW.; m. N. of a man, Kathās. **— saṃrambha**, m. extraordinary courage, (and) violence or fury of animals, ib. **— saṃśuddhi**, f. purity of nature or disposition, Bhag. **— samāvishṭa**, mfn. filled or thoroughly penetrated by the quality of goodness, ib. **— sampanna**, mfn. endowed with the quality of g°, good, excellent, W.; equable, even-minded, ib. **— samplava**, m. universal destruction of beings, ib.; loss of vigour, ib. **— sarga**, m. a creation of the quality Sattva, BhP. **— sāra**, m. essence of strength, MW.; extraordinary courage, Dhanaṃj.; Vās.; a very powerful person, MW. **— stha**, mf(*ā*)n. being in the nature (of anything), W.; adherent in firmness of character, resolute, energetic, MaitrUp.; CūlUp. &c.; clinging to or adherent in the quality of goodness, Bhag.; BhP.; Yogavās.; inherent in animals, W.; animate, ib. **— sthāna**, n. the standing in the quality of g°, Cat. **— hara**, mfn. taking away the quality of g°, BhP. **Sattvâtman**, mfn. having the nature of the quality of g°, ib. **Sattvâdhika**, mfn. having a noble disposition, Vet.; spirited, energetic, courageous (said of persons and actions), Siṇhâs.; Kathās. **Sattvâdhīna**, mf(*ī*)n. depending on courage, Siṇhâs. **Sattvânurūpa**, mfn. according to nature, acc° to one's innate disposition, Bhag.; acc° to one's substance or means, Ragh. **Sattvâvajaya**, m. self-command, strength of mind or character, Car. **Sattvôcchrita**, mfn. pre-eminent in courage, Ml. **Sattvôtkarsha**, m. excess of magnanimity, Hit. **Sattvôtsāha**, m. natural energy, W.; du. courage and en°, Kathās.; *-vat*, mfn. endowed with courage and en°, Pañcat. **Sattvôdrikta**, mfn. one in whom the quality of goodness predominates, Rājat. **Sattvôdreka**, m. excess or predominance of the quality of goodness, superabundance of energy, Sāh.

Sattvaka, m. the spirit of a departed person, L.; N. of a man, see *sāttvaki*.

Satyá, mf(*ā*)n. true, real, actual, genuine, sincere, honest, truthful, faithful, pure, virtuous, good, successful, effectual, valid (*satyaṃ* √*kṛi*, 'to make true, ratify, realise, fulfil'), RV. &c. &c.; m. the uppermost of the seven Lokas or worlds (the abode of Brahmā and heaven of truth; see *loka*), L.; N. of the ninth Kalpa (q. v.), Pur.; the Aśvattha tree, L.; N. of Vishṇu, L.; of Rāma-candra, L.; of a supernatural being, Gaut.; VarBṛS.; Hcat.; of a deity presiding over the Nāndī-mukha Śrāddha, L.; of one of the Viśve Devāḥ, Cat.; of a Vyāsa, Cat.; of a son of Havir-dhāna, BhP.; of a son of Vitatya, MBh.; of one of the 7 Ṛishis in various Manvantaras, Hariv.; Pur.; (with *ācārya*) N. of an astronomer (author of the Horā-śāstra), VarBṛS.; pl. N. of a class of gods in various Manvantaras, Hariv.; Pur.; (*ā*), f. speaking the truth, sincerity, veracity, W.; a partic. Śakti, Pañcar.; N. of Durgā, Cat.; of Sītā, L.; of Satyavatī (mother of Vyāsa), L.; = *satya-bhāmā*, MBh.; Hariv.; Śiś.; of the family deity of the Kutsas and Atharvans, Cat.; of a daughter of Dharma (and wife of Śaṃ-yu), MBh.; of the mother of Satya (= *tushita*), VP.; of the wife of Manthu (and mother of Bhauvana), BhP.; of a daughter of Nagna-jit (and wife of Kṛishṇa), ib.; (*am*), n. truth, reality (*satyena*, 'truly,' 'certainly,' 'really;' *kásmāt sátyāt*, 'for what reason, how is it that?' *téna satyéna*, 'for that reason, so truly;' *yathā—tena* [or *evaṃ*] *satyena*, 'as—so truly;' with Buddhists truth is of two kinds, viz. *saṃvṛiti-* and *paramârtha-satyam*, 'truth by general consent' and 'self-evident truth,' Dharmas. 95; for the four fundamental truths of Buddhists, see MWB. 43; 56), RV. &c. &c.; speaking the truth, sincerity, veracity, KenUp.; Mn.; R. &c.; a solemn asseveration, vow, promise, oath (*satyaṃ cikīrshamāṇa*, 'wishing to fulfil one's promise or keep one's word'), AV. &c. &c.; demonstrated conclusion, dogma, W.; the quality of goodness or purity or knowledge, MW.; the first of the four Yugas or ages (= 1. *kṛitá*, q. v.), L.; a partic. mythical weapon, R.; the uppermost of the 7 Lokas (see under m.), Vedântas.; BhP.; one of the 7 Vyāhṛitis, L.; a partic. Satya-formula, ĀśvŚr.; = *udaka*, water, Naigh. i, 12; (also with *Prajāpateḥ*) N. of Sāmans, ĀrshBr.; ŚrS.; (*ám*), ind. (g. *cādi* and *svar-ādi*) truly, indeed, certainly, verily, necessarily, yes, very well (*satyam—tu, kiṃ tu, tathâpi*, 'it is true—but, yet, however;' *yat satyam*, 'indeed, certainly'), RV. &c. &c. [Cf. accord. to some, Gk. ἐτεός.] **— karṇa**, m. N. of a son (or grandson) of Candrâpīḍa, Hariv.; VP. **— karman**, n. sincerity in action, truthfulness, Gaut.; mfn. one whose actions are true, RV.; m. Ægle Marmelos, Npr.; N. of a son of Dhṛita-vrata, Hariv.; VP. **— kāma** (*satyá-*), mfn. truth-loving, lover of truth, ChUp.; m. N. of various men, Br.; Up. &c.; *-tīrtha*, m. N. of a man, Cat. **— kāya**, m. N. of a man, Saṃskārak. (perhaps w.r. for *-kāma*). **— kāruṇya-vedin**, mfn. possessing truth and tenderness and the Veda, MW. **— kīrti**, m. N. of a spell spoken over weapons, R. **— kṛit**, mfn. performing what is real, one who does nothing in vain, BhP. **— ketu**, m. N. of a Buddha, Lalit.; of a son of Dharma-ketu, Hariv.; Pur.; of a son of Su-kumāra, Hariv.; of a son of Akrūra, ib. **— kriyā**, f. a promise, oath, Buddh. **— kshetra-māhātmya**, n. N. of wk. **— khāna**, m. N. of a Khān (also joined with *śrī-māna-datta*), Cat. **— ga**, mfn. (prob.) w.r. for *satyâṅga*, Cat. **— gir**, mfn. true to one's word, MBh.; Rājat. (Campak. 265; the correct reading is *satyā gīḥ*); *-vāhas* (*satyá-gir-*), mfn. getting true praise, RV. **— granthin**, mfn. binding or tying securely (with knots), MantraBr. **— ghna**, mfn. breaking one's word, Pañcar. **— ṃ-kāra**, m. a promise, Rājat.; Pracaṇḍ.; HPariś.; making true or good, ratification of a contract or bargain, L.; something given in advance as an earnest or security for the performance of a contract, earnest-money, Yājñ., Sch.; N. of a man, g. *kurv-ādi*; *-kṛita*, mfn. delivered as earn°-m°, Yājñ. **— cūḍāmaṇi**, m. N. of wk. **— jā**, mfn. of a true nature, AitBr. **— jít**, mfn. truly victorious, conquering by truth, VS.; AV.; m. N. of a Dānava, Hariv.; of a Yaksha, BhP. (Sch.); of Indra in the third Manvantara, ib.; of a king, MBh.; of various men (the sons of Bṛihad-dharman, Kṛishṇa, Su-nīta, Su-nītha, Ānaka and Amitra-jit), Hariv.; VP. &c. **— jiti**, f. a true victory, ŚrS. **— jña**, mfn. knowing what is true, Nir. **— jñānânanda-tīrtha** (also °*tha-yati*), m. N. of various scholars, Cat. **— jyotis** (*satyá-*), mfn. having real splendour, VS. **— tapas**, m. 'practising true austerity,' N. of a Muni (who was once a hunter, but after performing severe austerities obtained from Durvāsas the boon of great saintship), Cat. **— tama**, mfn. most or quite true, MW. **— tara**, mfn. more or very true, ib. **— tas**, ind. in truth, truly, really, Kathās. **— tā**, f. reality, truth (*agrya-satyatām* √*gam*, 'to become fully recognised in one's true character,' Rājat.), ŚBr.; Kathās.; love of truth, veracity, MBh.; R. &c. **— tāt** (*satyá-*), f. truth, reality, RV. **— tāti** (*satyá-*), f. reality (*ā*, loc., in reality), RV.; mfn. (perhaps) making true, ib. **— titikshā-vat**, mfn. truthful and patient, Kāv. **— tva**, n. reality, truth, Kathās.; Sarvad. &c.; veracity, MBh. **— darśin**, mfn. truth-seeing, t°-discerning, ib.; m. N. of a Ṛishi in the 13th Manvantara, Hariv. (v. l. *tattva-d°*); of a man, Lalit. **— dūta** (*satyá-*), m. a true messenger, MaitrS. **— dṛiś**, mfn. = *-darśin*, BhP. **— deva**, mfn. shining through truth, MW.; m. N. of a poet, Subh. **— dhana**, mfn. rich in truth, exceedingly truthful, Kir. **— dhara**, m. N. of a prince, Kathās.; of another man, Cat. **— dharma**, m. the law of truth, eternal t°, R.; mfn. one whose ordinances are true, Up.; m. N. of a son of the 13th Manu, BhP.; of a Brāhman, Sukas.; *-tīrtha*, m. N. of a scholar, Cat.; *-patha*, m. the path of eternal truth, R.; *-parâyaṇa*, mfn. devoted to truth and virtue, MBh.; *-vipula-kīrti*, m. N. of a Buddha, Lalit. **— dharman** (*satyá-*), mfn. one whose ordinances are true, RV.; TS.; AV.; TBr.; adhering to or speaking the truth, Gaut.; ruling by fixed ordinances, MW. **— dhāman** (*satyá-*), mfn. having truth for an abode (= *ṛitádh°*), ŚBr. **— dhṛita**, m. N. of a son of Pushpa-vat, VP. **— dhṛiti** (*satyá-*), mfn. sincere in purpose, ŚBr.; KaṭhUp.; R.; holding fast to truth, strictly truthful, MBh.; m. N. of a Ṛishi (author of the hymn RV. x, 185), RAnukr.; of several other persons, MBh.; Hariv.; Pur. **— dhvaja**, m. 'truth-bannered,' N. of a son of Ūrja-vaha, VP.; °*jâvatāra*, m. N. of wk. **— dhvṛít**, mfn. perverting truth, RV. **— nātha**, m. N. of various men, Cat.; *-tīrtha* or *-yati*, m. N. of an author, ib.; *-māhātmya-ratnâkara*, m., *-vilāsa*, m., *-stuti*, f., °*thâbhyudaya*, m. N. of wks. **— nāma**, mf(*ā*)n. = next, R. **— nāman**, mf(= m. or °*mnī*)n. having a true or correct name, rightly named (°*ma-tā*, f.), MBh.; R.; Kathās.; MārkP.; f. Polanisia Icosandra, Npr. **— nārāyaṇa**, m. N. of a partic. divinity (called Satyapīr in Bengālī), MW.; *-kathā*, f., *-vrata-kathā*, f. N. of wks. **— nidhi**, **-nidhi-tīrtha**, m. N. of authors, Cat. **— nidhi-vilāsa**, m. N. of wk. **— netra**, m. 'true-eyed,' N. of a Ṛishi (son of Atri), Hariv.; VP. **— pá**, mfn. truth-drinking, ŚBr. **— para**, mfn. given up to truth, thoroughly honest, Car. **— parākrama**, mfn. truly brave or mighty, MBh.; Kāv.; *-tīrtha*, m. N. of a man, Cat. **— parâyaṇa-tīrtha**, m. N. of a man, ib. **— pāramitā**, f. perfection in truth, Buddh. **— pāla**, m. N. of a Muni, MBh. **— pāśa**, m. truth compared to a fetter, R.; Pur. **— pura**, n. the city of Satya-nārāyaṇa, SkandaP.; the world of Vishṇu, MW. **— pushṭi**, f. true or permanent prosperity, ŚrS. **— pūta**, mfn. purified by truth (as a speech &c.), Mn.; Cāṇ. &c. **— pūrṇa-tīrtha**, m. N. of a man, Cat. **— pratijña**, mfn. (R.) or **-pratiśrava**, mf(*ā*)n. (R.; MārkP.) true or faithful to a promise. **— pratishṭhāna**, mfn. having truth for a foundation, grounded in truth, R. **— prabodha-bhaṭṭāraka**, m. N. of an author, Cat. **— pravāda**, n. N. of one of the Jaina Pūrvas, L. **— prasava** (*satyá-*), mfn. (TS.; VS.; ŚBr.) or °**vas**, mfn. (VS.) one whose stimulating impulse or inspiration is true or continues true to itself. **— prāśū** (*satyá-*), mfn. = *-parākrama*, TBr. (Sch.) **— priya-tīrtha**, m. N. of a man, Cat. **— phala**, m. Ægle Marmelos, L. **— bandha**, mfn. bound by truth, adhering to the truth, truthful, MW.; w.r. for *-saṃdha*, MBh. **— bodha**, m. N. of a poet, Sadukt.; *-tīrtha*, *-parama-haṇsa-parivrājaka*, m. N. of men, Cat.; *-vijaya-stotra*, n. N. of wk. **— bhāmā**, f. 'having true lustre,' N. of a daughter of Satrā-jit and one of the eight wives of Kṛishṇa (she is described as having promoted the quarrels of the Yādavas), MBh.; Hariv.; Pur. &c.; *-pariṇaya*, m., *-°bhyudaya* (°*mâbh°*), m., °*daya-kāvya*, n., *-daya-vyākhyāna*, n., *-vilāsa*, m. N. of wks. **— bhārata**, m. N. of the poet Vyāsa, L. (cf. *sattva-bh°*). **— bhāshaṇa**, n. the speaking of truth, Subh. **— bhūya** (*satyá-*), n. trueness, truth, ŚBr. **— bhedin**, mfn. violating truth, promise-breaking, Kām. **— madvan** (*satyá-*), mfn. really inspired or intoxicated, RV. **— mantra** (*satyá-*), mfn. one whose words are true or effective, RV. **— manman** (*satyá-*), mfn. having true thoughts, RV.; TBr.; ŚāṅkhŚr. **— maya**, mf(*ī*)n. consisting of truth, truthful, ŚāṅkhBr.; MBh.; Hariv. **— māna**, n. a true measure, BhP. **— m-ugra** (*satyá-*), mfn. truly powerful, RV. ix, 113, 5. **— mṛishā-viveka**, m. discrimination of truth and falsehood, Naish. **— medhas**, mfn. having true intelligence (said of Vishṇu), MBh. **— maudgala**, m. pl. N. of a school or system of teaching, Cat. **— m-bharā**, f. N. of a river, BhP. **— yáj**, mfn. worshipping or sacrificing truly or with success, RV. **— yajña** (*satyá-*), m. N. of a man, ŚBr.; ChUp. **— yuga**, n. the first or Kṛita age, Kāv.; °*gâdyā*, f. the third day of the light half of Vaiśākha (on which the commencement of the Kṛita-yuga is celebrated), MW. **— yoni** (*satyá-*), mfn. having a real or fixed abode, RV. **— yauvana**, m. 'having real youth,' a Vidyā-dhara, L. **— rata**, mfn. devoted to truth, honest; m. N. of Vyāsa, L.; of a son of Satya-vrata, MatsyaP. **— ratha**, m. N. of a king of Vidarbha, Cat.; of a son of Mīna-ratha, VP.; of a son of Sama-ratha, BhP.; (*ā*), f. N. of the wife of Tri-śaṅku, Hariv. **— rathi**, m. N. of a king, MW. **— rājan**, m. a true or perpetual king, VS. **— rādhas** (*satyá-*), mfn. bestowing real blessings, truly beneficent, RV. **— rūpa**, mfn. having a true appearance, KūrmaP.; probable, credible, R. **— loka**, m. 'world of truth,' N. of the highest of the 7 worlds, BhP.; Pañcar. &c. **— laukika**, n. the true and the worldly (or untrue), spiritual and worldly matters, BhP. **— vaktṛi**, mfn. a truth-speaker, W. **— vacana**, n. the speaking of truth, ChUp.; Gaut.; Āpast.; MBh.; a promise, solemn assurance, R.; Kathās.; claiming of merit or reward, Divyâv.; mfn. speaking the truth, VarBṛS.; °*nârtham*, ind. for the sake of telling the truth, MW. **— vacas**, n. veracity, truth, W.; mfn. true-speaking; m. a Ṛishi, L.; N. of a man, TUp. **— vat**, mfn. truthful, veracious, MBh.; R.; BhP.; Pañcar.; containing the word *satya*, AitBr.; w.r. for *sattva-vat*, Ragh.; m. N. of a spell spoken over weapons, R.; of a son of Manu Raivata, Hariv.; of a son of Manu Cākshusha, BhP.; of a son of Dyumat-sena (husband of Sāvitrī), MBh.; R.; (*atī*), f. N. of the wife of Parāśara (Śāṃtanu) and mother of Vyāsa, MBh.; Hariv.; Pur.; Pañcar.; of a daughter of Gādhi and wife of Ṛicīka (fabled to have become the Kauśikī river), MBh.; Hariv.; R.; Pur.; of the wife of Nārada, MBh.; of the wife of Śiva-rāja-bhaṭṭa, Vās., Introd.; of a river = *acchôdā*, Cat.; (°*tī*)*-suta*, m. 'son of Satyavatī,' N. of the poet, Vyāsa, MBh. **— vadana**, n. the speaking of truth, GṛŚrS.; *-śīla*, mfn. habitually truthful, Yājñ., Sch. **— vadya**, mfn. speaking truly, Bhaṭṭ.; n. truth, W. **— vara**, w.r. for *sattva-v°*, Kathās.; *-tīrtha*, m. N. of a man, Cat. **— vartman** (*satyá-*), mfn. following a true or fixed path or course (said of the chariot of Mitra-Varuṇa), AV.; m. N. of a man, Inscr. **— varman**, m. N. of a man, Daś. **— varyârya**, m. N. of an author, Cat. **— vasu**, m. N. of a class of the Viśve Devāḥ, Saṃskārak. **— vāka**, m. the speaking of truth, Kauś. **— vākya**, n. true speech, veracity, truth, Gaut.; mfn. true in speech (*-tā*, f.), MBh.; R.; MārkP. **— vâc**, f. true speech, Subh.; assurance, RV.; mfn. truth-speaking, veracious, RV.; TS.; AV. &c.; m. a Ṛishi, L.; a partic. spell spoken over weapons, R.; a crow, L.; N. of a Deva-gandharva, MBh.; of a Ṛishi, ib.; of a son of Manu Cākshusha, Hariv.; VP.; of a son of Manu Sāvarṇa, MārkP. **— vācaka**, mfn. speaking the truth, truthful, GāruḍaP. **— vāda**, m. the giving of a promise, a promise, R. **— vādín**, mfn. = *-vācaka*, AV.; Br.; Mn. &c.; m. N. of Kauśika, MBh.; (*inī*), f. a form of Dākshāyaṇī, Cat.; N. of a goddess of the Bodhi-tree, Lalit.; °*di-tā*, f. (Kām.) or °*di-tva*, n. (Hit.) veracity, truthfulness. **— vāha**, m. N. of a man, MuṇḍUp. **— vāhana**, mfn. conveying truth (said of a dream), Rājat. **— vikrama**, mfn. having real valour, truly valiant, MBh.; R. **— vijaya-tīrtha**, **-vijaya-śishya**, m. N. of scholars, Cat. **— vidyā**, f. N. of wk. **— vīra-tīrtha**, m. N. of a man, Cat. **— vṛitta**, n. true conduct, MBh.; mfn. practising truth, honest or upright in conduct, W. **— vṛitti**, mfn. devoting one's self to truth, R. **— vṛídh**, mfn. = *ṛitā-v°*, ŚBr. **— vyavasthā**, f. ascertainment of truth, Gaut. **— vrata**, n. a vow of truthfulness, Hariv.; Kāv.; mf(*ā*)n. devoted to a vow of t°, strictly truthful, ŚāṅkhŚr.; MBh.; Hariv. &c.; m. N. of an ancient king, Pañcat.; of a Rājarshi, BhP.; of Manu Vaivasvata, MW.; of a son of Dhṛita-rāshṭra, MBh.; of a son of Deva-datta, Cat.; of a son of Trayyāruṇa, Hariv.; Pur.; of the author of a Dharma-śāstra, Cat.; of other men, Kathās.; pl. N. of the Kshatriyas in Śāka-dvīpa, BhP.; of a class of supernatural beings attending on Satya-sena, ib.; *-tīrtha*, m. N. of a man, Cat.; *-parâyaṇa*, mfn. devoted to truth and religious observances, MW.; *-smṛiti*, f. N. of wk. **— śapatha**, mfn. one whose oaths are true or whose curses are fulfilled, MBh. **— śavas** (*satyá-*), mfn. truly vigorous, decidedly impetuous, RV. **— śīla** (Āpast.; R.) or **-śīlin** (MBh.; R.), mfn. addicted to truth. **— śushma** (*satyá-*), mfn. truly valiant, RV.; TS. **— śravas** (*satyá-*), n. true renown, ŚBr.; ŚrS.; m. 'having true r°' (cf. Gk. Ἐτεοκλῆς); N. of the author of the hymns RV. v, 79; 80 (having the patr. *Ātreya* or *Vāyya*), Anukr.; of various other men, ĀrshBr.; BhP. &c. **— śrāvaṇa**, n. the taking of an oath, Pañcat. **— śrī**, m. N. of a son of Satya-hita, Cat.; of a teacher of the Ṛig-veda, MW.; f. N. of a Śrāvikā, Śatr. **— śrut**, mfn. listening to the truth, RV. **— saṃrakshaṇa**, n. keeping one's word, MBh. **— saṃrakshin**, mfn. one who keeps his word, ib. (prob. w.r.) **— saṃśrava**, m. a promise, vow, solemn assurance, R. **— saṃhita**, mfn. true to one's agreement or promise, AitBr. **— saṃkalpa** (*satyá-*), mfn. true in purpose or resolve, one whose purpose is fulfilled (*-tva*, n., BṛĀrUp.), ŚBr.; Up. &c.; *-tīrtha*, m. N. of a man, Cat. **— saṃkāśa**, mfn. having the appearance of truth, likely, probable, W. **— saṃgara**, mfn. true to an agreement or promise, MBh.; Kāv. &c.; m. N. of Kubera, L.; of a Ṛishi, MBh. **— satī**, f. a truly faithful wife, Cat. **— satvan**, m. a true warrior (or mfn. 'having true warriors'), RV. **— sad**, mfn. = *ṛita-sad*, AitBr. **— saṃtushṭa-tīrtha**, m. N. of a man, Cat. **— saṃdha** (*satyá-*), mf(*ā*)n. true to engagements, keeping one's agreement or promise, faithful (*-tā*, f., MBh.; Rājat.), AV.; Mn.; MBh. &c.; m. N. of Bharata, L.; of Rāma-candra, L.; of Janam-ejaya, L.; of one of Skanda's attendants, MBh.; of a son of Dhṛita-rāshṭra, ib.; (*ā*), f. N. of Draupadī, L.; *-tīrtha*, m. N. of a man, Cat. **— saṃnibha**, mfn. = *-saṃkāśa*, MW. **— sava** mf(*ā*)n. (RV.; VS.; AV.) or **-savana** or **-savas** (MaitrS.; *satyá-*), mfn. one whose orders are true or valid; (*-sava*) really generating, MW.; possessing true energy, ib. **— sâh**, mfn. (nom. *-sâṭ*) = *ṛitā-sháh*, ŚBr. **— sahas**, m. N. of the father of Sva-dhāman, BhP. **— sâkshin**, m. a genuine or trustworthy witness, Mn. viii, 257. **— sādhana**, mfn. making true, Hariv. **— sāman**, n. N. of a Sāman, KātyŚr. **— sāra**, mf(*ā*)n. thoroughly true, BhP. **— sūtra**, n. N. of wk. **— sena**, m. N. of various men, MBh.; BhP. **— stha**, mfn. holding fast to the truth, keeping one's word, R. **— sravas**, m. N. of a teacher, VP. (prob. w.r. for *-śravas*). **— svapna**, mfn. one whose dream comes true (*-tā*, f.), Viddh. **— havis** (*satyá-*), m. N. of an Adhvaryu, MaitrS. **— havya**, m. N. of a man (see *sātya-h°*). **— hita**, mfn. really benevolent, R.; m. N. of a son of Pushpavat, Hariv.; of the father of P°, BhP.; of a teacher, Cat. **Satyâgni**, m. N. of Agastya, L. **Satyâṅga**, mfn. having parts or members formed of truth, Cat.; m. pl. N. of the Śūdras in Plaksha-dvīpa, BhP. **Satyâcārya**, m. N. of a preceptor, Kautukas. **Satyâtmaka**, mfn. having truth for essence, R. **Satyâtma-ja**, m. a son of Satyā or Satya-bhāmā, BhP. **Satyâtman**, mfn. = °*tmaka*, TUp.; R.; having a true soul, true, MW.; m. a virtuous and upright man, W. **Satyânanda**, m. true bliss, RāmatUp.; N. of a man, Cat.; *-cid-ātman*, m. true bliss and true intellect (°*ma-tā*, f., Prab.), RāmatUp.; *-tīrtha*, *-nātha*, *-parama-haṇsa-parivrājaka*, m. N. of scholars, Cat. **Satyânurakta**, mfn. devoted to truth, upright, true, W. **Satyânṛitá**, mfn. true and false, containing truth and falsehood, Hit.; apparently true (but really false), A.; n. du. truth and falsehood, RV.; VS.; Br.; Āpast.; sg. or du. practice of truth and f°, commerce, trade, Mn. iv, 6; BhP. **Satyā-pariṇaya**, m., °*naya-kāvya*, n. N. of wks. **Satyâbhidhāna**, mfn. truth-speaking, MW. **Satyâbhidhyāyin**, mfn. meditating upon truth, VP. **Satyâbhinava-tīrtha**, m. N. of an author, Cat. **Satyâbhinavôdaya**, m. N. of wk. **Satyâbhiyācana**, mfn. fulfilling or granting requests, R.; (*ā*), f. appeal to the truth (of one's faith), Divyâv. **Satyâbhisaṃdha**, mfn. true-speaking, faithful to a promise or agreement, ChUp.; R.; Car. **Satyâbhisaṃdhāna**, mf(*ā*)n. id., R. **Satyâbhisaṃdhin**, mfn. id., MBh. **Satyâyana**, w.r. for *satyāpana* (q.v.) **Satyâyu**, m. N. of a son of Purū-ravas, BhP. **Satyâlāpin**, mfn. truth-speaking, veracious, Mṛicch. **Satyā-van**, mfn. = *ṛitā-van*, ŚBr.; m. N. of a man, AV. **Satyâśis**, f. a realized wish or prayer, PañcavBr.; mfn. one whose wish or prayer is realized, ib.; BhP. **Satyâśraya**, m. N. of various kings, Inscr. **Satyâshāḍha**, m. N. of various men, GṛS.; Cat.; (*ī*), f. N. of a school of the Black Yajur-veda, Āryav.; (°*ḍha*)-*prayoga*, m. N. of wk.; -*hiraṇya-keśin*, see *hir*°. **Satyêtara**, n. untruth, falsehood, L. **Satyêpsu**, m. N. of an Asura, MBh. **Satyêśa-sthāpana-pūjā**, f. N. of wk. **Satyêshṭa-tīrtha**, m. N. of a man, Cat. **Satyôkti**, f. a true speech, RV.; Rājat. **Satyôtkarsha**, m. eminence or excellence in truth, W.; true exc°, MW. **Satyôttara**, n. admission of the truth, confession (in law); mf(*ā*)n. mainly or essentially true, AitBr. **Satyôdaka**, mfn. having truth for water, flowing with truth, MW. **Satyôdya**, mfn. speaking the truth, L. **Satyôpayācana**, mfn. = *satyâbhiyācana*, R. **Satyôpākhyāna**, n. N. of various wks. **Satyâùjas**, mfn. truly mighty, VS.; TS.; AV.

Satyaka, mfn. = *satya*, W.; m. N. of a son of Śini, MBh.; Hariv.; Pur.; of a son of Manu Raivata, MārkP.; of a son of Kṛishṇa and Bhadrā, BhP.; pl. N. of a class of deities under Manu Tāmasa, BhP.; n. ratification of a bargain, L.

Satyā, in comp. for *satya*. — **√kṛi**, P. -*karoti*, to make true, conclude an agreement or bargain, Pāṇ.; Vop. — **kṛiti**, f. conclusion or ratification of an agreement or bargain, L.

Satyāpana, n. (cf. *satyāpaya* below) verification, Bālar.; speaking or observing the truth, MW.; (also °*nā*, f.) ratification of a bargain, L.

Satyāpaya, Nom. P. °*payati*, to verify, Bālar.; HPariś.; Pañcad.; to speak the truth, MW.; to ratify (a bargain or contract), ib.

Satyeyu, m. N. of a son of Raudrāśva, MBh.; BhP.

Sátvan, mfn. living, breathing, RV.; strong, powerful, ib.; m. a living being, ib.; a warrior; pl. warriors, vassals, attendants, followers, RV.; VS.; AV. &c.; (sg.) = *udaka* or *karman*, Nir. vi, 30; N. of a Ṛishi, MBh. (v.l. *ṛitvan*).

Satvaná, m. a warrior (= prec.), RV.

Satvanāyát, mfn. behaving like a warrior, AV.

Satvī, f. N. of a daughter of Vainateya, wife of Bṛihan-manas, Hariv.

1. **Sad**, in comp. for *sat*. — **añjana**, n. calx of brass used as collyrium, L. — **anugraha**, m. favour towards the good, BhP. — **apadeśa**, mfn. possessing reality only in semblance, ib. — **ambha**, mfn. (for *sadambha* see p. 1139) having good water, Kāśīkh. — **artha**, m. a matter in question, Kām.; Hit.; mfn. wealthy, MārkP.; being, L.; -*sāra-mañjarī*, f. N. of wk. — **alaṃkāra-candrikā**, f. N. of wk. — **alaṃkriti**, f. a genuine ornament (-*tā*, f.), Kathās. — **aśva**, m. a good horse, KaṭhUp.; MBh.; Hariv. &c.; (*sád*-), mfn. possessing g° h°s, RV.; drawn by g° h°s, BhP.; m. N. of a son of Samara, Hariv.; VP.; -*vat*, ind. like a g° h°, MW.; -*sena*, m. N. of a man, Inscr.; °*vôrmi*, m. N. of a man, MBh. (v.l. *sadasyôrmi*). — **asat**, mfn. being and not being, real and unreal, BhP.; true and false (see n.); good and bad, VarBṛS.; m. pl. the g° and the b°, Rājat.; n. what is existent and non-ex° (also du.), BhP.; the true and the false, Kāv.; good and evil, Ragh.; du. existence and non-ex°, truth and falsehood, MW.; -*khyāti-vicāra*, m. N. of wk.; -*tva*, n. existence and non-ex°, BhP.; -*pati*, m. a lord of what is existent and non-ex°, Pañcar.; -*phala*, (ibc.) good and evil consequences, °*la-maya*, mf[*ī*]n. consisting of g° and e° c°, MaitrUp.; VarBṛS. — **asad** for -*asat* in comp.; -*ātmaka*, mf(*ikā*)n. having the nature both of entity and non-entity, Mn.; Hariv.; BhP.; n. original germ, L.; -*ātmatā*, f. the having the nature both of entity and non-entity, BhP.; -*bhāva*, m. reality and unreality, truth and falsehood, Śāntiś.; -*rūpa*, mf(*ā*)n. having the appearance of being and non-being, BhP.; -*viveka*, m. discrimination between true and false or bet° good and bad, W.; -*vyakti-hetu*, m. the cause of the discrim° between true and false or bet° good and bad, MW. — **asan** for -*asat* in comp.; -*maya*, mf(*ī*)n. formed or consisting of existent and non-ex°, Pur. — **asthi-mālā**, f. N. of Comm. — **ākārin**, mfn. (for *sadā-k*° see under *sadā*) having a good appearance, GāruḍaP. — **āgati**, m. (for *sadā-g*° see under *sadā*) = *nirvāṇa*, L.; = *sad-īśvara*, ib. — **āgama**, m. (for *sadā-g*° see p. 1139, col. 2) a good doctrine, Sāh.; Prab.; Dharmaśarm.; arrival of a good man, Sāh. — **ācaraṇa**, n. the manner of acting or behaviour of the good or wise, Cat. — **ācāra**, m. practice of good men, virtuous conduct, good manners, approved usage, Mn.; Yājñ.; Kāv. &c.; N. of wk.; mf(*ā*)n. well-conducted, virtuous, Kathās.; Rājat. &c.; -*krama*, m., -*candrôdaya*, m., -*cintana*, n., -*dharma*, m., -*nirṇaya*, m., -*paddhati*, f., -*prakaraṇa*, n. N. of wks.; -*vat*, mfn. well-conducted, well-behaved, having approved usages, Mn.; Pur.; -*varṇana*, n., -*vidhi*, m., -*vivaraṇa*, n., -*saṃgraha*, m., -*samṛiddhi*, f., -*sāra-saṃgraha*, m., -*stuti-stotra*, n., -*smṛiti*, f., -*smṛiti-vivaraṇa*, n., -*smṛiti-vyākhyā*, f.; °*rāhnika-vidhi*, m. N. of wks. — **ācārin**, mfn. (in *vimala-bhrājat-sad-āc*°, 'having pure and bright and good conduct'), Cat. — **ācārya**, m. N. of an author, ib. — **ātman**, mfn. possessing a good nature, good, virtuous, W.; m. (with *muni*) N. of an author, Cat. — **ānana**, mfn. fair-faced, Kir. — **ānanda-cid-ātmaka**, mfn. consisting of existence and joy and thought, RāmatUp. — **āpa**, mfn. provided with good water, Kāśīkh. — **ābhāsa**, mfn. reflecting the really existent, BhP.; having the appearance of r° ex°, ib. — **āśaya**, mfn. of a good or noble mind, HPariś. — **āśis**, f. a good wish or prayer, BhP. — **āśrita**, mfn. (for *sadāś*° see p. 1139, col. 3) having recourse or attaching one's self to the virtuous, belonging to the good, virtuous, W. — **īśvara**, m. = -*āgati*, L. — **ukti**, f. a good word, BhP.; mfn. accompanied with g° w°s, ib.; -*karṇâmṛita*, n. N. of an anthology. — **uttara**, n. a proper answer, good reply, W. — **uparāga-candrôdaya**, m., -**upahāra-ratnâkara**, m. N. of wks. — **gati**, f. good or happy state or fortune, MBh.; R.; BhP. &c.; the way of good men, Kāv. — **gava**, m. a good bull, MBh. — **guṇa**, m. a g° quality, virtue, R.; Kathās.; BhP. &c.; mf(*ā*)n. having g° qual°s, virtuous, Kathās.; -*nirguṇa-vāda*, m. N. of wk.; *sad-guṇâcārya*, m. N. of an author, Cat. — **guru**, m. a good teacher, Kāv.; BhP.; Siṇhās.; -*stotra*, n. N. of wk. — **goraksha**, m. N. of an author, Cat. — **graha**, m. a good or auspicious planet, VarBṛS.; mfn. clinging or attached to what is good or true (with *kṛishṇe*, 'att° to Kṛishṇa as to the really true'), BhP. — **ghana**, m. wholly existence, nothing but existence, NṛisUp. — **dhan** (for -*han*), m. N. of a Deva-gandharva, MBh. (v.l. *satvan*, *ṛitvan*). — **dhana**, n. good wealth or property, MW. — **dharma**, m. the good law, true justice, R.; Pur.; (with Buddhists and Jainas) designation of the Buddhist or Jaina doctrines, Buddh.; Inscr.; -*candrôdaya*, m., -*cintāmaṇi*, m., -*tattvâkhyâhnika*, -*puṇḍarīka*, n. (MWB. 69), -*laṅkâvatāra*, m., -*samparigraha*, m. N. of wks. — **dhī**, mfn. wise, sage, Kāśīkh. — **dhetu** (for -*hetu*), m. the existence of cause and effect, W. — **dhyāyin**, mfn. meditating on what is true, MaitrUp. — **brahman**, n. the true Brahman, ib. — **bhāgya**, n. good fortune, felicity, Pañcar. — **bhāva**, m. real being, existence, Bhag.; R.; MārkP. &c.; the being true, truth, real state of things (*śāstra-bh*°, 'the true purport of a work'), MBh.; VarBṛS.; BrahmaP. &c.; the quality of goodness, W.; uprightness, GāruḍaP.; goodness, kindness, affection for (*prati*), faithfulness, MBh.; Kāv.; Kathās. &c.; -*śrī*, f. N. of a goddess, Rājat. — **bhāshya**, n. N. of wk. — **bhūta**, mfn. who or what is really good or true (°*tôtpādaka*, mfn. 'producing what is t°'), MBh.; Hariv. — **bhūta-dakshiṇīya**, m. N. of Pratyeka-buddhi, Divyâv. — **bhṛitya**, m. a good servant, Kathās. — **yājin**, mfn. sacrificing what is true, MaitrUp. — **yukti**, f. good reasoning, Hit.; -*muktâvalī*, f. N. of wk. — **yuvatī**, f. a good young woman, virtuous maiden, W. — **yoga-muktâvalī**, f., -**yoga-ratnâvalī**, f. N. of wks. — **ratna**, n. a genuine gem or pearl, Kathās.; Pañcar.; -*mālā*, f. N. of wk. — **rasa**, (prob.) w.r. for *shaḍ-r*°, Kāv. — **ruci**, mfn. kindly disposed, L. — **rūpa-tva**, n. reality, KapS. — **vaṇśa**, m. a good bamboo, Sāh.; Prasaṅg.; a noble race, ib.; Pañcar.; mfn. 'having a fine hilt' (as a sword) and 'of noble race' (-*tva*, n.), Śiś.; -*jāta*, mf(*ā*)n. sprung from a n° r°, Kathās. — **vacas**, n. a fair speech, Ṛitus. — **vat** (*sád*-), mfn. containing or accompanied with a verse cont° some form of √*as* or *bhū*, TS.; Br.; ŚrS.; (*atī*), f. N. of a daughter of Pulastya and wife of Agni, VP. — **vatsala**, mfn. kind to the virtuous, Ragh. — **vartaka**, (prob.) w.r. for *saṃv*°, MārkP. — **vasatha**, m. a village, L. (w.r. for *saṃv*°). — **vastu**, n. an excellent work, MW.; a good thing, A.; a good plot or story, Vikr. — **vaha**, m. N. of a king, Buddh. (v.l. *vāha*). — **vājin**, m. a noble steed, Kāv. — **vādita**, mfn. well-spoken, MW. — **vādin**, mfn. true-speaking, MaitrUp. — **vārttā**, f. good news (°*tām* √*prach*, 'to enquire about any one's health'), Kāv. — **vigarhita**, mfn. censured by the good, Mn.; Kām. — **vicheda**, m. separation from the g°, Pañcar. — **vidya**, mfn. having true knowledge, well-informed, Kāv.; Rājat.; (*ā*), f. true kn°, Bhartṛ.; °*yā-vijaya*, m. N. of wk. — **vidhāna**, w.r. for *saṃv*°, Pañcar.; -*pariśishṭa*, n. N. of wk. — **viyoga**, m. = -*viccheda*, MW. — **vṛiksha**, m. a good or fine tree (-*ja*, mfn. 'made of the wood of a fine tree,' Hcat.), Kāv. — **vṛitta**, n. a well-rounded shape, ŚārṅgP.; the behaviour of good men, good conduct (-*śālin* or -*stha*, mfn. 'being of virtuous cond°'), KaushUp.; MBh.; R. &c.; mf(*ā*)n. well-conducted, MBh.; R. &c.; Gīt.; containing beautiful metres, Cat.; -*ratnamālā*, f., -*ratnâvalī*, f. N. of wks.; °*ttânta*, mfn. having good or beautiful stories, MW. — **vṛitti**, f. good conduct, Kām.; -*bhāj* (Malamāsat.) or -*viśishṭa* (MW.), mfn. possessing good habits, having a good character. — **velā**, f. the right moment, Pañcad. — **vesha-dhārin**, mfn. well-clothed, VP. — **vaidya**, m. a good physician, Kāv.; -*nātha*, m. N. of an author, Cat.; -*ratnâkara*, m. N. of wk. — **vrata**, w.r. for -*vṛitta*, n. (good conduct), Kām.

San, in comp. for *sat*. — **nāman**, n. a good or beautiful name, Nalôd. — **nimitta**, n. a good omen, R.; a g° cause; the cause of the g°, MW.; (*am*), ind. for a g° c°, Hit.; (*e*), ind. for the sake of the g°, MW. — **nivāsa**, mfn. (for *saṃ-n*° see *saṃ-ni-*√5. *vas*) staying with the g° (Vishṇu), MBh. — **nisarga**, m. g° nature, kindness, ib. — **maṅgala**, n. a g° and auspicious rite &c., Ragh. — **maṇi**, m. a genuine gem, Kathās. — **mati**, f., see *a-san-m*°; mfn. well-disposed, noble-minded, Kathās. — **mantra**, m. an excellent spell, Ragh. — **mātura**, prob. w.r. for *sān-m*°, of a virtuous mother, MW. — **mātṛi**, f. a v° m° (see *sānmātura*). — **mātra**, mfn. that of which only existence is predicable, RāmatUp.; Śivag.; m. N. of Ātman, MW. — **māna**, n. respect or esteem for the good, W. (frequently w.r. for *sanmāna*). — **mārga**, m. the right path (fig.), Mālav.; Kathās. &c.; -*maṇi-darpaṇa*, m. N. of wk.; -*yodhin*, mfn. fighting honourably, Ragh.; -*stha*, mfn. walking in the r° p°, Amar.; °*gâlokana*, n. the seeing or following of good paths (of morality &c.), MW. — **mitra**, n. a good or true friend, Bhartṛ. — **miśra-keśava**, m. N. of an author, Cat. — **muni**, see *daiva-jña-san-m*°. — **muhūrta**, m. n. a good moment, Pañcad. — **maulika**, m. N. of a class of Kāyasthas, Col.

सत 1. *sáta*, m. n. a kind of sacrificial vessel, VS.; ŚBr.; KātyŚr.

सत 2. *sata*. See *dvaya-* and *dve-s*°.

सतःपङ्क्ति *sataḥ-paṅkti*. See *satas*.

सतक्षन् *sa-takshan*, mfn. (i.e. 7. *sa* + *t*°) together with an artisan, KātyŚr.

Sa (to be similarly prefixed to the following): — **tata**, -**táti**, see s.v. — **tattva**, mfn. knowing the real truth, MW.; containing the words *tad*, 'that,' and *tva*, 'thou,' ib.; n. natural property, nature (-*tas*, ind. 'really, in reality'), BhP.; Vedântas.; -*ratnamālā-vyākhyāna*, n. N. of wk. — **tanu** (*sá*-), mfn. having a body, together with the body, TS.; TBr. — **tantra**, mfn. corresponding to a model or type, ĀśvŚr. — **tandra**, mf(*ā*)n. having lassitude, languid, exhausted, Caurap. — **tapas** (*sá*-), mfn. together with heat, TS.; ŚBr. — **tamasā**, f. N. of a river (or 'together with the river Tamasī'), MārkP. — **tamaska**, mfn. obscured, eclipsed, VarBṛS. — **tarka**, mfn. having argument or reasoning, skilled in speculation, MW.; cautious, considerate, ib. — **tarsha**, mfn. having thirst, thirsty (*am*, ind.), ib. — **tala**, mfn. having a bottom, ib. — **talatra**, mfn. having leather guards (used in archery), MBh. — **tas**, see s.v. — **tānūnaptrin** (*sá*-), m. a companion in the performance of the (ceremony called) Tānūnaptra, MaitrS.; Br.; KātyŚr.

— **tāpa**, mfn. full of pain or sorrow, Kād. — **tāra**, mfn. together with the stars (and 'with Tārā'), Hariv. — **tālavṛinta**, mfn. furnished with fans, Vishṇ. — **timira**, mf(*ā*)n. covered with darkness, obscured, overcast (as the sky), R. — **tila**, mfn. together with sesamum grains, Cat. — **tīrtha**, mfn. having sacred bathing-places, MW.; having the same bathing-place, ib.; m. 'having the same teacher,' a fellow-(religious) student, Vop.; N. of Śiva, MBh. (prob. w. r. for *su-t°*); pl. N. of a people, VP. (v.l. *sanīya*). — **tīrthya**, m. = *sa-tīrtha*, a fellow-student, Mālatim. (cf. Pāṇ. iv, 4, 107; vi, 3, 87). — **tuṅga**, m. N. of a place, MBh. (v. l. *su-t°*). — **tusha**, mfn. having husk or chaff, KātyŚr., Sch.; n. grain which has the husk remaining on it, L. — **tuhina**, mfn. accompanied by frost or ice, wintry, Śiś. — **tūrya**, mfn. accompanied by music (*am*, ind.), Hariv.; Kāv.; VarBṛS. — **tūla** (*sá-*), mf(*ā*)n. together with a tuft (of grass or reed &c.), ĀpŚr. — **tṛiṇa**, mfn. grown with grass, VarBṛS.; ibc. and (*am*), ind. with grass, grass and all, Pāṇ. ii, 1, 6, Sch.; °*'bhyavahārin*, mfn. eating grass and all (fig. = 'undiscerning'), Vām. i, 2, 1. — **tṛish** or **-tṛisha**, having thirst, thirsty, desirous, L. — **tṛishṇa**, mfn. id.; (*am*), ind. thirstily, yearningly, with longing, Kālid. — **tejas** (*sá-*), mfn. attended with splendour or energy or vital power &c. (*-tvá*, n.), TS.; AitBr.; Kāṭh. — **toka** (*sá-*), mfn. together with offspring, AV. — **toda**, mfn. attended with a pricking pain, Suśr. — **toraṇa**, mf(*ā*)n. furnished with arched doorways, MBh. — **trapa**, mf(*ā*)n. having shame or modesty, ashamed, modest, bashful (*am*, ind.), MBh.; Kathās. &c. — **trā** &c., see col. 2. — **trāsa**, mfn. having a partic. flaw (as a jewel), L.; (*am*), ind. with terror or fear, in a fright, Kathās.; Hit. — **trikūṭa**, mfn. 'having the mountain Trikūṭa' and 'practising threefold deceit,' Siṅhās. — **trijātaka**, n. a kind of dish (consisting of meat fried with three sorts of spices; it is then soaked and dried and again dressed with ghee and condiments), L. — **tvakka** (ĀpŚr.), **-tvac** (Mn.), **-tvaca** (Kāśikh.), mfn. having skin or bark. — **tvacas** (*sá-*), mfn. id., ŚBr. — **tvara**, mf(*ā*)n. having or making haste, speedy, expeditious, quick (*am* and compar. *-taram*, ind.), MBh.; Kāv. &c.; *-tā*, f., *-tva*, n. quickness, hastiness, speed, ib.; *-racanam*, ind. quickly, immediately, at once, Git. — **tvaritam**, ind. hastily, quickly, forthwith, R. — **tvā-siñcāmi-prayoga**, m. N. of wk.

सतत *sa-tata*, mfn. (fr. 7. *sa* + *t°*; accord. to Pāṇ. vi, 1, 144, Vārtt. 1 = *saṃ-tata* as *sa-hita* = *saṃ-h°*) constant, perpetual, continual, uninterrupted (only in comp. and *am*, ind. 'constantly, always, ever;' with *na*, 'never'), Mn.; MBh. &c. — **ga** (MBh.; Śiś.), **-gati** (Megh.), m. 'always moving,' the wind. — **jvara**, m. constant fever, one not intermitting, MW. — **durgata**, mfn. always miserable, Bhartṛ. — **dhṛiti**, mfn. ever resolute, Prab. — **parigraha-dharma-kāṅkshiṇī**, f. N. of a Kiṃnarī, Kāraṇḍ. — **parigraham**, ind. continually, incessantly, ib. — **mānasa**, mfn. always directing the mind towards anything, Hariv. — **yāyin**, mfn. constantly moving or going, always tending to decay, Mn. i, 50. — **yukta**, mfn. constantly devoted, Bhag. — **śāstrin**, mfn. studying incessantly, R. — **samitâbhiyukta**, m. N. of a Bodhi-sattva, Buddh. — **spandana**, mfn. continually or regularly throbbing, Car. **Satatâbhiyoga**, m. constant application or exertion, VarBṛS. **Satatôtthita**, mfn. always intent upon (loc.), MBh.

Satataka, mfn. recurring twice a day (as fever), Suśr.

Sa-táti, mfn. coherent, uninterrupted, TS.

सतत्त्व *sa-tattva* &c. See p. 1137, col. 3.

सतस् *satas*, ind. (fr. 7. *sa* + *tas*) equally, like (only in comp.)

Sataḥ, in comp. for *satas*. — **paṅkti**, f. a kind of metre consisting of two Pādas of 8 and of two Pādas of 12 syllables alternating with each other, Piṅg.

Sato, in comp. for *satas*. — **bṛihat** (*sató-*), mfn. equally large or high, TBr.; PañcavBr.; (*ī*), f. a kind of metre consisting of 12 + 8 + 12 + 8 syllables, ŚBr.; Kāṭh.; Piṅg. (cf. *sataḥ-paṅkti*). — **maghavan** (*sató-*), mfn. equally liberal, RV. x, 27, 4 (if one word). — **mahat** (*sató-*), mfn. equally great, RV. viii, 30, 1. — **mukhā**, see *mahā-satomukhā*. — **vīra** (*sató-*), mfn. equally brave or valiant, RV. vi, 75, 9.

सतानन्द *satānanda*, w.r. for *śatān°*, q. v.

सतारा *satārā*, f. N. of a country, Cat.

सति *sati*, f. = *sāti*, *santi*, Pāṇ.; Vop.; = *dāna*, *avasāna*, L.

सतितरा *sati-tarā*. See 1. *sati*, p. 1135.

सतिमिर *sa-timira* &c. See col. 1.

सती 2. *satī*, f. (for 1. see p. 1135, col. 1) = *sāti*, L.

सतीक *sátika*, *satīná*, *satīya*. See p. 1135.

सतूर्य *sa-tūrya*, *sa-tṛiṇa* &c. See col. 1.

सतेर *satera*, m. husk, chaff (= *tusha*), L.

Sateraka, n. a season of two months (= *ṛitu*), L.

सत्कथा *sat-kathā*, *sat-kāra*. See p. 1134.

सत्त्व *sat-tvá*. See p. 1135, col. 2.

सत्य *satya* &c. See p. 1135, col. 3.

सत्र् *satr*, cl. 10. Ā. *satrayate* and *satrāpayate*, to extend, Dhātup. xxxv, 52 (*sambandhe*, *saṃtatau*, Vop.)

सत्र *satra*, incorrect for *sattra*.

सत्रम् *satram*, ind., g. *svar-ādi* (= next, L.)

सत्रा *sa-trā́*, ind. (fr. 7. *sa* + *trā́*) together, together with (instr.), altogether, throughout; always, by all means, RV.; AV.; Br. — **kará**, mfn. always effective, RV. — °**ja** (prob. fr. *satrā* + 1. *aja*), m. complete victory, ŚāṅkhŚr. — **jit**, mfn. always victorious, RV.; m. N. of an Ekâha, ŚāṅkhŚr.; N. of a son of Nighna and father of Satya-bhāmā (he was father-in-law of Kṛishṇa and was killed by Śata-dhanvan), Hariv.; Pur. — **jita**, m. N. of a son of Nighna (see prec.), BhP. — **dāvan**, mfn. always granting, giving all at once, RV. — **sahá** (or *-sāhá*), mfn. always overcoming or conquering, irresistible, RV. ii, 21, 3. — **sáh**, mfn. (dat. *-sā́he*; Padap. *-sáhe*), id., RV. i, 79, 8; ii, 21, 2 &c. — **sāhīya**, n. N. of various Sāmans, ĀrshBr. — **há** or **-hán**, mfn. always destroying, destroyer of mighty foes, RV.

Satrā́c, mf(*ā́cī*)n. going together, united, joined, RV.; concentrated, whole (as the mind or heart), ib.

सत्वत् *satvát*, m. pl. N. of a people inhabiting the south of India (cf. *sātvata*), Br.; KaushUp.; MBh.; Hariv.; of a son of Madhu, Hariv.

Satvata, m. N. of a son of Mādhava (Māgadha) and Aṅśa, Hariv.; VP.

सत्वन् *sátvan* &c. See p. 1137, col. 1.

सथूत्कार *sa-thūtkāra*, mfn. (fr. 7. *sa* + *th°*) sputtering in speech (n. the act of sputtering; cf. *ambū-kṛita*), W.

सद् 2. *sad*, cl. 1. or 6. P. (Dhātup. xx, 24 and xxviii, 133) *sīdati* (ep. also °*te*; Ved. *sádati* or *sīdati*, °*te*; pf. *sasā́da*, *sasáttha*, *sedús*, *sedire*, RV.; *sīdatus*, MBh.; *sasadyāt*, AV.; aor. *asadat* [cf. pres. stem], Gr.; 2. 3. sg. *sátsi*, *sátsat*, RV.; *asādīt*, TĀr.; fut. *sattā*, Gr.; *satsyati*, Br.; *sīdishyati*, Pur.; inf. *sáde*, RV.; *sattum*, Br.; *sīditum*, MBh.; ind. p. *-sádya*, *-sádam*, RV.; *-sā́dam*, Br.), to sit down (esp. at a sacrifice), sit upon or in or at (acc. or loc.), RV.; AV.; VS.; ŚBr.; to sit down before, besiege, lie in wait for, watch (acc.), RV.; AitBr.; to sink down, sink into despondency or distress, become faint or wearied or dejected or low-spirited, despond, despair, pine or waste away, perish, Mn.; MBh. &c.: Pass. *sadyate* (aor. *asādi*, *sādi*, RV.): Caus. *sādáyati*, °*te* (aor. *asīshadat*), to cause to sit down or be seated, place down, put upon or in (loc.), RV. &c. &c.; to put in distress, afflict, weary, exhaust, ruin, destroy, MBh.; Kāv. &c.: Desid. *sishatsati*, Gr.: Intens. *sāsadyate* (Gr. also *sāsatti*), to sit down in an indecent posture, Bhaṭṭ. [Cf. Gk. ἵζω for σίσδω; Lat. *sidere*, *sedere*; Lith. *sėsti*, *sedėti*; Slav. *sěsti*; Goth. *sitan*; Germ. *sitzen*; Angl. Sax. *sittan*; Eng. *sit*.]

Sattá, mfn. (cf. *pra-satta* and *ni-shatta*) seated, RV.

Satti, f. sitting down, sitting (cf. *ni-shatti*), entrance, beginning, L.

Sáttri, mfn. sitting down (esp. at a sacrifice), RV.

Sattrá, n. 'session,' a great Soma sacrifice (lasting, accord. to some, from 13 to 100 days and performed by many officiating Brāhmans; also applied to any oblation or meritorious work equivalent to the performance of a Sattra; *sattrāsyárddhiḥ*, N. of a Sāman, ĀrshBr.), RV. &c. &c.; a house, asylum, hospital, Rājat.; Kathās.; an assumed form or disguise, illusive semblance, MBh.; Daś.; fraud, deception, L.; a wood, forest, Kir.; a tank, pond, L.; liberality, munificence, L.; wealth, L.; clothes, L. — **gṛiha**, n. hall of sacrifice, place of refuge, asylum, Kathās. — **tva**, n. the condition of (being) a Sattra or great Soma sacrifice, Kāṭh. — **pariveshaṇa**, n. a distribution of food or other gifts at a sacrifice, AitBr. — **phala-da**, mfn. yielding the fruit of a Soma sac°, Hariv. — **yāga**, m. a S° sac°, Kathās.; BhP. — **rā́j**, m. the king of a S° sac°, VS. — **vardhana**, mfn. increasing or promoting sac°, BhP. — **vasati**, f., **-śālā**, f. = *-gṛiha*, Kathās. — **sád**, m. a companion at a Soma sac°, AV.; VS.; ŚBr. — **sadman**, n. = *-gṛiha*, Kathās. — **sádya**, n. companionship at a Soma sac°, AV. **Sattrâgāra**, n. = *sattra-gṛiha*, Campak. **Sattrâpaśraya**, m. a place of refuge, asylum, MW. **Sattrâyaṇá**, n. a long course of sacrifices, Br.; ChUp.; m. 'moving in the Soma sac°,' N. of Śaunaka, BhP.; of the father of Bṛihad-bhānu, ib. **Sattrôtthāna**, n. rising from a Soma sacrifice, ŚBr.; KātyŚr.

Sattraya, Nom. Ā. °*yate*, Dhātup. xxxv, 52.

Sattrāpaya, Nom. Ā. °*yate*, = prec., Vop.

Sattrāya, Nom. Ā. °*yate*, Pāṇ. iii, 1, 14, Vārtt. 1, Pat.

Sattri, m. one who is accustomed to perform sacrifices, L.; an elephant, L.; a cloud, L.

Sattrin, m. the performer or partaker or companion of a Sattra sacrifice, TS. &c. &c.; an ambassador or agent in a foreign country, W.; one whose merits are equal to the performance of a S°, MBh.; disguised, ib.; Kām.

Sattriya, mf(*ā*)n. relating to the Sattra sacrifice, Br.

Sattri-√bhū, P. *-bhavati*, to feed others, MBh.

Sattrīya (ĀpŚr.), **sattryà** (ŚBr.), mfn. = *sattriya*.

3. **Sád**, mfn. (mostly ifc.; for 1. see p. 1137, col. 1) sitting or dwelling in (cf. *adma-*, *antariksha-*, *apsu-sad* &c.); m. covering (the female), AV.

Sada, mfn. = prec. (cf. *barhi-*, *samanī-shada*; *sabhā-sada*); m. fruit (cf. *śada*), Mn. viii, 151; 241; a partic. Ekâha, ŚāṅkhŚr.; N. of a son of Dhṛita-rāshṭra, MBh. i, 4548 (if *sadaḥ-suvāc* is not one word); n. a partic. part of the back of a sacrificial animal, AitBr.

Sadaḥ, in comp. for *sadas*. — **sada**, m. the partaker of a Sadas, TāṇḍBr. — **suvāc**, see *sada*. — **stha**, mfn. present at an assembly, BhP.

Sádana, mf(*ī*)n. causing to settle down or remain, RV.; n. a seat, dwelling, residence, house, home (often ifc. = 'abiding or dwelling in'), RV. &c. &c.; settling down, coming to rest, RV.; relaxation, exhaustion, Suśr.; water (= *udaka*), Naigh. i, 12; the abode of sacrifice, sacrificial hall, MW.; the abode of Yama, ib.

Sadanā-sád, mfn. sitting on a seat, RV.

Sadani, m. or f. water, L.

Sadanyà. See *sādanyà*.

Sádas, n. (accord. to some also f.) a seat, residence, abode, dwelling, place of meeting, assembly (esp. at a sacrifice; *sádasas-páti*, m. = *sádas-páti*; *sadasi*, 'in public'), RV. &c. &c.; a shed erected in the sacrificial enclosure to the east of the Prācīna-vaṅśa, AV.; VS.: Br.; MBh.; Hariv.; du. heaven and earth (= *dyāvā-pṛithivī*), Naigh. iii, 30. [Cf. Gk. ἕδος.] — **páti** (*sádas-*), m. du. 'lords of the seat or of the sacrificial assembly,' N. of Indra and Agni, RV.

Sadasa. See *antaḥ-* and *bahiḥ-sadasam*.

Sadasyà, m. 'present in the sacrificial enclosure,' an assessor, spectator, member of an assembly (at a sacrifice), a superintending priest, the seventeenth priest (whose duties, accord. to the Kushītakins, are merely to look on and correct mistakes), TS.; Br.; GṛŚrS.; MBh.; BhP.; a person belonging to a learned court-circle, Jātakam. — **paddhati**, f. N. of wk. **Sadasyôrmi**, m. N. of a man, MBh. (v.l. *sadaśvôrmi*).

Sadi. See *pathi-shādi*.

Sado, in comp. for *sadas*. — **gata**, mfn. gone to or present at an assembly, MBh. — **gṛiha**, n. 'assembly house,' the court of a prince, council-chamber &c., Ragh. — **'jira**, n. a vestibule, Kāśikh. — **bila**, n. the entrance into the Sadas, ĀpŚr. — **viśīya**, n. (also *Prajāpateḥ*) N. of a Sāman, ĀrshBr. — **havirdhāna**, n. du. and pl. the Sadas and the Havirdhāna, AV.; pl. (with *Prajāpateḥ*) N. of various Sāmans, ĀrshBr.; °*nin*, mfn. provided with Sadas and Havirdhāna, TS.

Sadma, in comp. for *sadman*. — **citi**, f. a collection of houses, W. **-nivāsin**, mfn. dwelling in houses, MBh. **-niveśita**, mfn. deposited in a shed (as a carriage), R. **-barhis** (*sádma-*), mfn. preparing the sacrificial grass, RV. **-makhas** (*sádma-*), mfn. performing a sacrifice in a sacred precinct, RV.

Sadmán, m. a sitter, assessor, spectator, R.; (*sá*°), n. a seat, abode, dwelling, house, place (esp. of sacrifice), temple, RV. &c. &c.; a stand, stable, RV. v, 11, 5; 67, 7; (?) an astrological house, Cat.; water, Naigh. i, 12; war, battle (= *sam-grāma*), ib. ii, 17; (du.) heaven and earth, ib. iii, 30; mfn. dwelling in, inhabiting (ifc.), L.

1. **Sadya**, n. in *upari-*, *talpa-*, *sattra-s*°, qq. vv. (for 2. 3. see p. 1140, col. 1).

Sadri, m. an elephant, L.; a mountain, L.; a ram, L.

Sadru, mfn. sitting, Bhaṭṭ.

Sanná, mfn. set down, VS.; ŚBr.; ŚrS.; sitting at, i.e. occupied with (comp.), Hariv.; sunk down in (loc.), BhP.; depressed, low (in spirits), languid, exhausted, decayed, perished, lost, dead, AV. &c. &c.; shrunk, contracted (see comp.); resting, motionless (see ib.); weak, low (see ib.); (= *prasanna*), appeased, satisfied (see *sannī-kṛita*); m. Buchanania Latifolia, L.; (prob.) n. destruction, loss (see *sanna-da*). **-kaṇṭha**, mf(*ī*)n. one who has a contracted throat, scarcely able to articulate, choking, choked, Kālid.; Kir. **-jihva**, mfn. one whose tongue is motionless or silent, BhP. **-tara**, mfn. more depressed, very weak or feeble; (in gram.) lower (in tone or accent), more depressed than the ordinary accentless tone (= *anudātta-tara*), Pāṇ. i, 2, 40. **-da**, mfn. destroying, Hariv. (Nilak.) **-dhī**, mfn. depressed in mind, dispirited, BhP. **-nauka**, mfn. one who has lost his ship, MBh. **-bhāva**, mfn. despondent, despairing (*-tva*, n.), MBh. **-maya**, mf(*ī*)n. caused by despair, Nalôd. **-musala**, n. a motionless pestle; (*e*), ind. at the time when the p° lies m°, Mn. vi, 56. **-vāc**, mfn. speaking with low or feeble voice, BhP. **-śarīra**, mfn. one whose body is wearied or exhausted, VarBṛS. **-harsha**, mfn. one whose joy has departed, depressed in spirits, desponding, W.

Sannaka, mfn. low, dwarfish, L.; m. = next, L. **-dru** or **-druma**, m. Buchanania Latifolia, L.

Sanni, f. depression of the mind, despondency, despair, BhP. **-mat**, mfn. desponding, despairing, ib.

Sannī-kṛita, mfn. appeased, satisfied, Kathās.

Sādá, m. sitting (on horseback), riding, RV. i, 162, 17; sinking in (of wheels), VarBṛS.; sinking down, exhaustion, weariness, Kāv.; Suśr.; perishing, decay, loss, ruin, Kālid. (cf. comp.); despondency, despair, Hariv.; Nalôd.; purity, clearness, cleanness (cf. *pra-sāda*), W.; going, motion, MW. **-da**, mfn. (ifc.) destroying, removing, Śiś. **-maya**, mf(*ī*)n. caused or produced by despair, Nalôd.

Sādaka, mfn. (fr. Caus.) exhausting, wearying, destroying, MW.

Sādád-yoni, mfn. sitting in one's place, RV.

Sā́dana, mfn. (fr. Caus.) = *sādaka*, Śiś.; m. a text recited when anything is being set down (cf. below), ĀpŚr.; (*ī*), f. a partic. plant (= *kaṭukī*), L.; exhaustion, decay, MW.; n. causing to sink, wearying, exhausting, destroying, W.; setting down, arranging (of vessels &c.), ŚBr.; KātyŚr.; sinking in (of wheels), VarBṛS.; (= *sadana*) a seat, house, dwelling, place, home, MBh.; R.; BhP.; a vessel, dish, BhP. **-spṛ́ś**, mfn. 'home-touching,' brought or coming into one's house, RV.

Sādanyà, mfn. belonging to a house, domestic, RV.

Sādayitavya, mfn. (fr. Caus.) to be destroyed, destructible, R.

Sādasa, mfn. being in the Sadas, Lāṭy.

1. **Sādi**, m. (for 2. see s.v.) a horseman, MBh.; a charioteer, L.; a warrior, L.; wind, L.; a dispirited or melancholy person, L.

Sādita, mfn. (fr. Caus.) made to sit down, set down, BhP.; depressed, broken, wasted, destroyed, MBh.; Kāv. &c.; made to go, drawn, dragged, W.

Sādin, mfn. any one sitting or riding on (comp.); m. a horseman, charioteer, AV. &c. &c.; (fr. Caus.) exhausting, wearying, destroying, R.

Sādya, mfn. (fr. *sādin*) fit for riding; m. a riding-horse, ĀśvŚr.

सदंश *sa-daṇśa*, mfn. (i.e. 7. *sa* + *d*°) having a sharp beak or bill; *-vadana*, m. 'having a mouth with a sharp beak,' a heron, L.

Sa (to be similarly prefixed to the following): **-daṇśaka**, mfn. having teeth; m. 'having nippers,' a crab, L. **-daksha** (*sá-*), mfn. endowed with reason, TS. **-dakshiṇa**, mf(*ā*)n. having presents, accompanied by gifts, Mn.; Rājat. **-daṇḍa**, mfn. punished, fined, L. **-dat**, mfn. having teeth, preserving one's teeth (*-tva*, n.), MaitrS. **-dadhan**, mfn. mixed with sour milk, Mṛicch. **-dambha**, mfn. (for *sad-ambha* see p. 1137, col. 1) with hypocrisy, hypocritical, Cāṇ. (cf. Pāṇ. v, 2, 76, Sch.) **-daya**, mf(*ā*)n. merciful, compassionate, kind, gentle (ibc. and *am*, ind. 'mercifully, kindly, gently, gradually'), Kāv.; Kathās.; *-tva*, n. kindness, gentleness, Jātakam.; *-hṛidaya*, mfn. having a compassionate heart, tender-hearted, MW. **-dara**, mfn. fearful, afraid, W.; m. N. of an Asura, Hariv. **-darpa**, mfn. having pride, haughty, arrogant (*am*, ind.), Hit. **-1. -daśa**, mfn. (fr. *daśan*) having decades (of Stomas), ŚāṅkhŚr.; *-bandhaka*, mfn. that to which a tenth part is added, Yājñ. ii, 76; *-ratha*, see below. **-2. -daśa**, mfn. (fr. *daśā*) having a fringe, fringed, MBh.; °*śā-pavitra*, mfn. having a fringed straining-cloth, ĀpŚr. **-daśana-jyotsna**, mf(*ā*)n. displaying the brightness of the teeth, having bright teeth, Ragh. **-daśanârcis**, mfn. id., ib. **-daśa-ratha**, mf(*ā*)n. having Daśa-ratha (q.v.), R. **-1. -dāna** (*sá-*), mfn. having gifts, with gifts, RV. **-2. -dāna**, mfn. having ichor (exuding from the temples), being in rut (as an elephant), Kir. **-dāma** (*sá-*), mfn. together with a band or ligament, ŚBr. **-dāra**, mfn. accompanied by a wife, ĀpŚr.; Ragh.; *-putra*, mfn. together with wife and son, MW. **-dāham**, ind. with a burning sensation, Suśr. **-divas**, ind. (= *sadyás*), RV. **-diś**, mfn. together with the quarters (of the sky), MW. **-dīkshôpasátka**, mfn. with Dīkshā and Upasad, ŚBr. **-dīnam**, ind. lamentably, Pañcat. **-dīpaka**, mfn. together with a lamp, Vishṇ. **-duḥkha**, mf(*ā*)n. having pain, distressed, afflicted, sad, Kathās.; Rājat. **-dugdha**, mf(*ā*)n. abounding in milk, Hcat. **-durdina**, mfn. enveloped in clouds, Hariv. **-dūrva**, mfn. covered with Dūrvā grass, ĀśvGṛ. **-dṛiksha**, **-dṛiś** &c., see s. v. **-dṛishṭi-kshepam**, ind. with a glance of the eye, with a sidelong glance, Śak. (v. l. °*ṭi-vikshepam*). **-deva** (*sá-*), mf(*ā*)n. accompanied or protected by gods (*-tvá*, n.), TS.; Br.; *-maṇi*, mfn. (see *deva-m*°) with curls or twists of hair on their necks, Vās.; *-manushya*, mfn. together with gods and men, ĀśvGṛ.; °*vâsura-rākshasa*, mfn. accompanied by gods and Asuras and Rākshasas, MBh. **-devaka**, mfn. together with the gods, MBh. **-devīka**, mfn. along with or accompanied by a queen, Kathās. **-deśa**, mfn. possessing a country or of the same c°, W.; proximate, neighbouring (ifc.; cf. Pāṇ. vi, 2, 23); m. neighbourhood, ĀpŚr., Sch.; *-tva*, n. proximity, neighbourhood, Lāṭy.; Gobh. **-daivata**, mfn. together with the deities, ŚāṅkhGṛ. **-1. -dosha**, mfn. together with the night, Kāvyâd. **-2. -dosha**, mfn. having faults, defective, wrong, objectionable, Kāvyâd.; Hcat.; *-vat*, mfn. containing anything defective, MW.; *-vikāśa*, m. a defective exhibition, ib. **-doshaka**, mfn. faulty, defective, L. **-dyas** &c., see s.v. **-dravya**, mfn. together with (or keeping one's) money, Mn. ix, 241; gold-coloured, R. **-droṇa**, mfn. with a Droṇa added to a Droṇa, L. **-dvaṃdva**, mfn. quarrelsome, contentious, litigious, Subh.; possessing opposite feelings, able to bear the opposites (see *dvaṃdva*), MW.

सदक *sadaka*, m. or n. (?) unhusked grain, Bhadrab.

सदम् *sádam*, ind. (prob. fr. *sadā* below and connected with 7. *sa*) always, ever, for ever, at any time, RV.; AV.; ŚBr.; Vait.

Sadadí, ind. (cf. next) generally, usually, MaitrS.

Sadaṃ-di, mfn. (prob. fr. *sadam* + *di* fr. √4. *dā*) binding or lasting for ever (applied to the disease called Takman), AV.

Sadā́, ind. always, ever, every time, continually, perpetually (with *na*, 'never'), RV. &c. &c. **-kān-tā**, f. N. of a river, MBh. **-kārin**, mfn. (for *sad-āk*° see under 1. *sad*) always active, GāruḍaP. **-kāla-vaha**, mf(*ā*)n. flowing at all seasons (opp. to *prāvṛiṭ-kāla-v*°), MārkP. **-gati**, f. (for *sad-āg*° see under 1. *sad*) constancy, MBh.; mfn. always in motion, ib.; Śivag.; m. wind (also in medical sense), the god of wind, ib.; MBh.; R.; Suśr.; VarBṛS.; the sun, L.; the Universal Spirit, W. **-gama**, m. (for *sad-āg*° see under 1. *sad*) 'always moving,' wind, Dharmaśarm. **-candra**, m. N. of a king, VP. **-toyā**, f. the plant Mimosa Octandra, W.; the Karatoyā river (cf. *sadā-nīrā*), W. **-1. -dīna**, n. (see 1. *dāna*) 'always giving,' liberality, L.; mfn. always liberal, Pañcat. **-2. -dāna**, mfn. (see 2. *dāna*) always exuding rut-fluid (as an elephant), ib.; an elephant in rut, L.; N. of Airāvata (the el° of Indra), L.; of Gaṇeśa, L. **-°nanda** (°*dân*°), m. perpetual bliss, Cat.; mfn. feeling or giving perp° bl°, NṛisUp.; Prab.; m. N. of Śiva, L.; of various writers (esp. of the author of the Vedānta-sāra, a modern Vedāntist), Cat.; (*-kāśmīra*, *-gaṇi*, *-giri*, *-nātha*, *-yogîndra*, *-vyāsa*, *-śukla*, *-sarasvatī*), m. N. of various authors, Cat.; *-girīya*, n. N. of wk.; *-maya*, mf(*ī*)n. consisting of perp° bl°, Cat.; *-ratna-mālā*, f.; °*dâkhya-dharmârṇava*, m.; °*dôpanishad*, f. N. of wks. **-narta**, mfn. always dancing; m. the wagtail, L. **-nirāmayā**, f. N. of a river, MBh. **-nīravahā**, f. = next, L. **-nīrā́**, f. N. of a river (= *kara-toyā*, L.), ŚBr.; MBh.; Pur. **-°nukāla-darśinī**, **-nuvṛitti** (°*dân*°), f. N. of Kiṃ-nārīs, Kāraṇḍ. **-nonuva**, mfn. (fr. Intens. of √*nu*) used to explain next, Nir. vi, 30. **-nva**, mfn. (fr. √*nu*) always crying out, RV.; Nir.; (°*dā́-nvā*), f. N. of a class of female demons, RV.; AV.; *-kshayaṇa*, mfn. destroying the Sadā-nvās, AV.; *-cā́tana*, mfn. scaring them away, ib. **-paribhūta**, m. N. of a Bodhisattva, Buddh. **-parṇa**, mfn. always leafed, MBh. **-pushpa**, mfn. alw° in flower, ib.; m. the cocoa-nut, L.; (*ī*), f. Calotropis Gigantea and another species, ŚāṅkhGṛ.; Car.; Suśr.; a kind of jasmine, L.; *-phala-druma*, mfn. provided with trees always in flower and bearing fruit, Kathās. **-pṛiṇá**, mfn. alw° munificent, RV.; m. N. of a Ṛishi (having the patr. Ātreya and author of the hymn, RV. v, 45), Anukr. **-pramudita**, n. 'perpetual gladness,' N. of one of the 8 Sāṃkhya perfections, Sāṃkhyak., Sch. **-prasūna** (only L.), mfn. alw° in flower; m. Andersonia Rohitaka; Calotropis Gigantea; = *kunda*. **-prasravaṇī**, f. (prob.) alw° menstruous, L. **-phala**, mf(*ā*)n. alw° bearing fruit, Pañcat.; m. a partic. kind of fruit tree (accord. to L. 'Ficus Glomerata; Aegle Marmelos; the cocoa-nut tree; Artocarpus Integrifolia'), Siṇhâs.; (*ā* or *ī*), f. Hibiscus Rosa Sinensis, L.; a kind of Solanum, L. **-bhadrā**, f. Gmelina Arborea, ib. **-bhava**, mf(*ā*)n. perpetual, continual, Bhaṭṭ., Sch. **-bhavya**, mfn. alw° present, MW.; attentive, W. **-bhrama**, mfn. always wandering, L. **-matta**, mfn. alw° excited with joy, R.; alw° in rut (as an elephant), Pañcat.; Kathās.; m. N. of a man (pl. of his family), g. *yaskâdi*; pl. N. of a class of divine beings, Divyâv. **-mattaka**, n. N. of a town, ib. **-mada**, mfn. alw° excited with joy, Hariv.; R.; alw° drunk, MārkP.; ever-furious, MW.; alw° proud, Śiś.; alw° in rut (said of an elephant), Pañcat.; m. N. of Gaṇeśa, L. **-°marsha** (°*dā́m*°), mfn. alw° impatient, very imp°, petulant, MW. **-mudita**, n. a partic. Siddhi, KapS., Sch. **-yogin**, mfn. alw° practising Yoga, Tithyâd.; m. N. of Vishṇu, L. **-rāma**, m. (also °*ma-tri-pāṭhin*) N. of various authors, Cat. **-°rjava** (*dâr*°), mfn. always honest, Cāṇ. **-vara-dāyaka**, m. a partic. Samādhi, Kāraṇḍ. **-vṛitti**, f. N. of wk. **-vṛidha** (*sadā́-*), mf(*ā*)n. always delighting, RV.; always increasing or prospering, MW. **-śaṃkara**, m. N. of an author, Cat. **-śiva**, mfn. alw° kind &c., TĀr.; NṛisUp.; alw° happy or prosperous, MW.; m. N. of Śiva (*-tā*, f.), Rājat.; BhP.; of various authors and other men (also *-kavi-rāja-go-svāmin*, *-tīrtha*, *-tri-pāṭhin*, *-dīkshita*, *-deva*, *-dvi-vedin*, *-brahmêndra*, *-bhaṭṭa*, *-muni-sārasvata*, *-mūlôpâkhya*, *-śukla*; °*vânanda-nātha*, °*vânanda-sarasvatī*, °*vêndra*, °*vêndra-sarasvatī*), Inscr.; Cat.; (*ā*), f. N. of Durgā, MBh.; *-kavaca*, n., *-gītā*, f., *-nāma-mantra*, m., *-pada*, n., *-brahman*, n., *-brahma-vṛitti*, f., *-brahmâryā*, f., *-bhaṭṭīya*, n., *-mālā*, f., *-shaṇ-mukha-saṃvāda*, m., *-saṃhitā*, f., *-sahasra-nāman*, n., *-stotra*, n.; °*vâryā*, f., °*vâshṭaka*, n. N. of wks. **-°śrita** (°*dâś*°), mfn. (for *sad-āś*° see under 1. *sad*) alw° resorting to or dependent on, W. **-sáh**, mfn. (acc. *-sáham*) always holding out or lasting, RV.; alw° conquering, MW. **-sā́**, mfn. (nom. pl. *-sā́ḥ*) alw° gaining (superl. *-tama*), RV.; alw° subsisting abundantly, ib. **-sukha**, n. perpetual welfare or happiness, R. **-huta**, mfn. always sacrificed, SāmarBr. **Sadâika-rasa**, mfn. having always only one object of desire, NṛisUp. **Sadâika-rūpa-rūpa**, mfn. alw° continuing the same, VP. **Sadôt-sava**, mfn. ever-festive, MW. **Sadôdyama**, mfn. one who alw° exerts himself, AgP. **Sadôpacāra-muktāvalī**, f. N. of wk. **Sadôpayoga**, m. constant use, MW. **Sadôpavāsin**, mfn. alw° fasting, MBh.

Sadātana, mfn. continual, perpetual (*-tva*, n.), Bhaṭṭ.; Kusum.; m. = *aja*, N. of Vishṇu, L.

सदम *sadama*, m. or n.(?) a partic. high number, Buddh.

सदर्थ *sad-artha, sad-aśva* &c. See p. 1137, col. 1.

सदाश्व *sadāśva*, m. N. of a man (v.l. for *sad-aśva*), VP.

सदिवस् *sa-dívas*, ind. (= *sa-dyas*) on the same day, at once, immediately, RV. ii, 19, 6.

सदृक *sadṛika*, m. a kind of sweetmeat, Suśr.

सदृक्ष *sa-dṛíksha*, mf(ī)n. (fr. 7. *sa* + *dṛ°*) like, resembling, corresponding or similar to (comp.), VS.; BhP.

Sadṛig, in comp. for *sadṛiś*. **-bhavam**, ind. on the same grade or degree with (instr.), ŚBr.

Sadṛiś, mfn. (nom. *sadṛíṅ* or *sadṛik*; n. pl. *sadṛiṇśi*) = *sadṛiksha* (with instr. or ifc.), RV. &c. &c.; fit, proper, just, right, MW.

Sadṛiśa, mf(ī, once in R. ā)n. like, resembling, similar to (gen., instr., loc., or comp.) or in (instr., loc., or comp.), RV. &c. &c. (accord. to Pat. on Pāṇ. vi, 2, 11, Vārtt. 2 also compounded with a gen., e.g. *dāsyāḥ-s°, vṛishalyāḥ-s°*); conformable, suitable, fit, proper, right, worthy, MBh.; Kāv. &c.; (*am*), ind. suitably, well, Uttarar. **-kshama**, mfn. of equal patience or forbearance, Mālav. **-tama**, mfn. most like or similar, Pāṇ. i, 1, 50, Sch. **-tā**, f. (W.), **-tva**, n. (KātyŚr., Sch.) likeness, similarity, sameness. **-vinimaya**, m. confusing or mistaking similar objects, Mālav. **-vṛitti**, mfn. behaving similarly (*-tā*, f.), Rājat. **-śveta**, mfn. equally white, Pāṇ. ii, 1, 68, Sch. **-strī**, f. a wife of equal caste, Mn. ix, 125. **-spandana**, n. any regular or even throbbing motion (= *ni-spanda*), MW. **Sadṛiśâsadṛiśa-yogyâyogya-tva**, n. similarity and dissim° and fitness and unf°, Vedântas.

सदोगत *sado-gata* &c. See p. 1138, col. 3.

सद्गति *sad-gati* &c. See p. 1137, col. 2.

सद्मन् *sadman* &c. See p. 1139, col. 1.

सद्यस् *sa-dyás*, ind. (fr. 7. *sa* + *dyu*; cf. *sa-divas*) on the same day, in the very moment (either 'at once,' 'immediately' or 'just,' 'recently'), RV. &c. &c.; daily, every day, RV.; AV.; AitBr.; MBh. **-kāra**, mf(ā)n. being performed on the same day, MBh. **-kāla**, m. the same day, KātyŚr., Sch.; present time, MW.; mf(ā)n. falling on the same day (*-tva*, n.), ĀpŚr.; ib., Sch.; KātyŚr., Sch. **-kālīna**, mfn. belonging to the present time, recent, modern, MW. **-krī**, mfn. = *sadyaḥ-k°*. **-tapta**, mfn. just heated, MW. **-tā**, f. (Lāṭy.) or **-tva**, n. (KātyŚr.) the falling on the same day.

2. **Sadya**, m. (for 1. see p. 1139, col. 1) a form of Śiva (= *sadyo-jāta*), L.

3. **Sadya**, in comp. for *sadyas*. **-ūti** (*sadyá-*), mfn. assisting quickly or daily, RV. **Sadyôtpanna**, mfn. newly born, MBh.

Sadyaḥ, in comp. for *sadyas*. **-kāla**, mfn. = *sadyas-k°*. **-kṛita**, mfn. done at the moment, done quickly or promptly, W.; n. a name, L. **-kṛitta**, mfn. recently cut, Megh. **-kṛittôta**, mfn. spun and woven on the very same day, ĀpGṛ. **-krī**, mfn. bought on the same day; m. a partic. Ekâha (during which an abridged form of the Dīkshā, Upasad, and Sutyā ceremonies is performed), AV.; ŚBr.; ŚrS.; N. of wk.; (also written *sadyas-k°*). **-kshata**, n. a fresh contusion or wound, Suśr. **-paryushita**, mfn. one day old, ib. **-pāka**, mf(ā)n. having immediate consequences, VarBṛS.; m. a dream during the fourth Yāma (between 3 and 6 a.m.), L. **-pātin**, mfn. quickly falling or dropping, Megh. **-prakshālaka**, mfn. one who cleans corn for immediate use (without storing it), Mn. vi, 18. **-prakshālitânnaka**, m. a person who has food cleansed for one day, L. **-prajñā-kara**, mf(ī)n. quickly causing intelligence, Cāṇ. **-prajñā-hara**, mf(ā)n. quickly taking away intelligence, ib. **-prasūtā**, f. a female that has just brought forth, BhavP.; Uttarar. **-prâṇa-kara**, mfn. quickly causing vitality or inspiriting, Cāṇ. **-prâṇa-hara**, mfn. qu° destroying vigour, ib. **-phala**, mf(ā)n. bearing fruit immediately or having immediate consequences (*-tva*, n.), VarBṛS.; Pañcat. &c. **-śakti-kara**, mfn. quickly causing strength, Cāṇ. **-śakti-hara**, mfn. qu° destroying strength, ib. **-śuddhi**, f. = *-śauca*, MW. **-śotha**, mfn. quickly swelling; (ā), f. Mucuna Pruritus, L.; Carpopogon Pruriens, W. **-śauca**, n. present or immediate purity, Gaut. **-śrāddhin**, mfn. one who has recently taken part in a Śrāddha, ib. **-sutyā**, f. pressing out the Soma on the same day, AitBr. **-snehana**, n. a quickly operating emollient, Suśr.

Sadyaś, in comp. for *sadyas*. **-chinna**, mfn. recently severed or cut or incised (said of a wound), Suśr.

Sadyaska, mfn. belonging to the present day, immediate, present, quick, MW.; new, recent, fresh, Suśr.; a kind of sacrifice, MBh. (v.l. *sād°*).

Sadyastana, mf(ī)n. fresh, instantaneous, L.

Sadyo, in comp. for *sadyas*. **-artha** (*sadyó-*), mfn. quickly attaining one's aim, RV. **-ja**, mfn. newly born, g. *saṃkalâdi* (for *sādyo-j°*?). **-jāta**, mf(ā)n. id., PañcavBr.; Hariv.; Pañcar.; addressed to Śiva Sadyojāta, Hcat.; m. a newly-born calf, L.; a calf, W.; a form of Śiva, Hcat.; (ā), f. a female that has just brought forth, BhavP.; *-pāda*, m. N. of one of the 5 forms of the god of the Śaivas, Sarvad. **-jū**, mfn. quickly excited, RV. **-jvara**, m. fresh fever, Bhpr. **-dugdha**, mfn. freshly milked, Lāṭy. **-'nugata**, mfn. just received (into the womb), Car. **-bala**, mfn. quickly causing vigour, Car.; *-kara*, mfn. id., GāruḍaP.; *-hara*, mfn. qu° depriving of v°, ib. **-bodhinī-prakriyā**, f. N. of wk. **-bhava**, mfn. recently arisen, Ragh. **-bhāvin**, mfn. newly born; m. a newly-b° calf, L.; any calf, W. **-'bhivarsha**, m. falling of rain on the same day, VarBṛS. **-bhṛit**, mfn. borne on the s° day, ŚBr. **-manyu**, mfn. causing immediate anger, BhP. **-maraṇa**, n. death happening on the same day, immediate death, Var. **-māṇsa**, n. fresh flesh, Cāṇ. **-mṛita**, mfn. just dead, R. **-yajña**, m. a sacrifice performed on the same day, ĀpŚr., Sch.; *-saṃsthā*, f. the performance of a sac° in one day, ShaḍvBr. **-varsha**, m. (VarBṛS.) or **-varshaṇa**, n. (Cat.) falling of rain on the same day. **-vṛídh**, mfn. enjoying one's self every day, RV. **-vṛishṭi**, f. = *-varsha*, Kṛishis.; ch. of VarBṛS.; *-lakshaṇa*, n. N. of the 65th Pariśishṭa of the AV. **-vraṇa**, m. a suddenly caused wound, Suśr.; ŚārṅgS.; Vāgbh. **-hata**, mfn. recently wounded or injured, Suśr.; rec° killed, Vāgbh.

सध 1. *sadha* (= 2. *saha*), with, together with, in the same manner (only in comp.; cf. Pāṇ. vi, 3, 96). **-ní**, m. (in Padap. *sa-dhanī*) a fellow, comrade, RV.; (*-ni*)*-tvá*, n. companionship, ib. **-mád** or **-mád**, m. (only in strong cases; n. sg. *-mád* or *-más*) a drink-companion, fellow-reveller, comrade or friend in general, RV. **-māda**, m. drinking together, drinking bout, convivial party, feast (*°dam* √*mad* with instr., 'to feast or revel with'), RV.; AV.; fellowship, companionship, RV. **-mādin**, mfn. = *-mad*, AitĀr. **-mādya**, mfn. relating to a convivial party or feast, convivial, festal, RV.; m. = *-mad*, ib.; n. a convivial feast, TBr. **-mitra**, m. N. of a man, g. *kāśy-ādi*. **-vīra**, mfn. joined with men or heroes (= *saha-v°*), RV. **-stuti** (*sadhá-*), f. joint praise (when used as instr. = 'with joint praise'), RV.; mfn. praised together (as Indra and Agni), ib. **-stutya** (*sadhá-*), n. joint praise or applause, ib. **-stha** (*sadhá-*), mfn. 'standing together,' present, RV.; AV.; n. 'place where people stand together,' place of meeting, any place, spot, abode, home, region, world, ib.; VS.

सध 2. *sadha*, n. or *sadhā*, f. (only in du., 'heaven and earth,' v.l. for *svadhe*), Naigh. iii, 30.

सधन *sa-dhána*, n. (i.e. 7. *sa* + *dh°*) common property, ŚBr.; mfn. possessing riches, wealthy, opulent, R.; VarBṛS.; together with riches, Kathās.; *-tā*, f. wealthiness, Prasaṅg.

Sa (to be similarly prefixed to the following): **-dhanus**, mfn. having or armed with a bow, Hariv.; *°nushka*, mfn. id., MBh.; together with a bow, Hariv.; *°nush-pāṇi*, mfn. bow in hand, RāmatUp. **-dharma**, m. the same nature or qualities, BhP.; mfn. having the same nature or qualities, Sāh.; subject to the same law, equal, like, BhP. (also *°maka*, ĀpŚr., Sch.); virtuous, honest, VarBṛS.; *-cāriṇī*, f. 'practising the same duties (with a husband),' a wife, (esp.) a legal or virtuous wife, MBh.; Kāv. &c.; *-tva*, n. the having a similar nature, homogeneousness, Suśr.; Pañcat. **-dharmaka**, mfn. = *-dharma* above. **-dharman**, mfn. having the same duties, L. (v.l. *°min*); having the same nature or similar properties, resembling, like, equal to (gen., instr., or comp.), Vas.; Mn.; MBh. &c. **-dharmin**, mfn. having the same duties, L. (cf. prec.); having the same properties, like, resembling (comp.), R.; (*iṇī*), f. a legal or virtuous wife, L. **-dhavastrī**, f. a wife whose husband is living, L. **-dhavā**, f. id. (cf. *vi-dhavā*). **-dhātu**, see *pada-sadhātu*. **-dhī** (*sá-*), mfn. endowed with reason or intellect, ŚBr. **-dhura** (*sá-*), mfn. harnessed to the same yoke, agreeing together, AV. **-dhūma** (*sá-*), mfn. enveloped in smoke, MaitrS.; R.; *-varṇā*, f. N. of one of the seven tongues of Agni, VS., Sch. **-dhūmaka**, mfn. smoky (*am*, ind.), Suśr. **-dhūmra**, mfn. dusky, dark, ib.; *-varṇā*, f. = *sa-dhūma-v°*, MārkP. **-dhairyam**, ind. with firmness, firmly, gravely, MW. **-dhvaṇsa**, m. N. of a Ṛishi (having the patr. Kāṇva, the supposed author of RV. viii, 8), Anukr. **-dhvaja**, mfn. having a banner, bannered, with a flag, MW.

सधि *sadhi*, m. (said to be fr. √*sadh* = *sah*) fire, L.; a bull, L.

सधिस् *sádhis*, n. (prob. fr. √*sadh* = *sādh*) the end or goal of any movement, the place where it comes to rest, RV.; Kāṭh.

सध्रि 1. *sádhri*, m. N. of a Ṛishi (having the patr. Vairūpa and author of RV. x, 114), Sāy.; N. of Agni, L.

सध्रि 2. *sadhri* (= 2. *saha*), with, along with, together with, Pāṇ. vi, 3, 95; (*ī*), ind. to the same goal or centre, RV. ii, 13, 2.

Sadhrīcīna, mf(ā)n. (fr. *sadhryañc*) directed to one aim, pursuing the same goal, united, RV.; furthered or promoted by (comp.), Nilak.; leading to the right goal, right, correct (instr. 'in the right way'), BhP.

Sadhryañc, mf(*sadhrīcī*)n. turned in the same direction or to one centre, converging, associated, RV.; AV.; PañcavBr.; Kauś.; leading in the right direction, right, correct, BhP.; tending towards, flowing into (comp.), HPariś.; m. a friend, companion, Śiś.; (*īcī*), f. a woman's companion or female friend, Bhaṭṭ.; n. = *manas*, BhP.; (*àk*), ind. together with, jointly, unitedly (as opp. to *pṛithak*), RV.; in the right way, BhP.

सन् 1. *san*, cl. 1. P., 8. P. Ā. (Dhātup. xiii, 21; xxx, 2) *sánati*, *°te* or *sanóti*, *sanute* (Ā. rare and only in non-conjugational tenses; pf. *sasāna*, RV.; p. *sasavás*, ib., f. *sasanúshī*, Br.; *sasanivas* or *senivas*, Gr.; *sene*, ib.; aor. *asānisham* [Subj. *sanishat*, Ā. *sanishāmahe*, *sánishanta*], RV.; Impv. *sánishantu*, SV.; *sesham*, *set*, MaitrS.; Br.; *asāta*, Gr.; Prec. *sanyāt*, *sāyāt*, ib.; fut. *sanitā*, ib.; *sanishyáti*, RV.; Br.; inf. *sanitum*, Gr.), to gain, acquire, obtain as a gift, possess, enjoy, RV.; AV.; Br.; ŚrS.; to gain for another, procure, bestow, give, distribute, RV.; (Ā.) to be successful, be granted or fulfilled, ib.: Pass. *sanyate* or *sāyate*, Pāṇ. vi, 4, 43: Caus. *sānayati* (aor. *asīshaṇat*), Gr.: Desid. of Caus. *sisānayishati*, ib.: Desid. *sisanishati* (Gr.) or *sīshāsati* (? *sīshatī*, AV. iv, 38, 2), to wish to acquire or obtain, RV.; TS.; AV.; to wish to procure or bestow, RV.; AV.: Intens. *saṇsanyate*, *sāsāyate*, *saṇsanti* (Gr.), to gain or acquire repeatedly (only 3. pl. *sanishṇata*, RV. i, 131, 5).

Sa. See 5. *sa*, p. 1111, col. 2.

Sati. See p. 1138, col. 2.

2. **San**, in *go-shán*, q.v.

1. **Sana**, m. (for 2. see p. 1141, col. 1) gain, acquisition (in *ahaṃ-sana* and *su-shaṇa*, qq.vv.); presenting, offering, BhP.

Sanad, in comp. for *sanat* (pr. p. of √1. *san*). **-rayi** (*sanád-*), mfn. bestowing wealth, RV. **-vāja** (*sanád-*), mfn. acquiring or bestowing wealth, ib.; N. of a son of Śuci, BhP.

Sanana, n. gaining, acquiring (used in explaining *sani*; cf. *su-shaṇana*), Nir. vi, 22.

Sanāyú, mfn. wishing for gain or reward, RV.; AV. Paipp.

1. **Saní**, m. f. (for 2. see p. 1141, col. 3) gain, acquisition, gift, reward (dat. with √*dhā*, 'to grant, fulfil;' acc. with √*i*, 'to go after gifts, go begging'), RV.; AV.; TS.; Br.; mfn. gaining, procuring, bestowing (cf. *aśva-*, *dhana-s°* &c.) **-kāma** (*saní-*), mfn. desirous of gain or reward, RV. **-mát**, mfn. rich in gifts, liberal, MaitrS.

Sániti, f. acquisition, obtainment, RV.

Sánitṛi or **sanitṛí**, mfn. gaining, obtaining, procuring, bestowing (with acc. or gen.), RV.; TS.; TBr.

Sanítra, n. a gift, oblation, RV.

Sánitva, mfn. to be gained or acquired, ib.

Sanítvan, n. a gift or reward, ib.

Sánishṭha, mf(*ā*)n. gaining or acquiring most, ib.

Sanishyú, mfn. wishing to gain or acquire, eager for booty, ib.

Sanī, f. = 1. *sani*, gift, L. — **hāra**, mfn. (cf. *sanīhāra*, col. 3) bringing or bestowing gifts, liberal, ĀpŚr.

Sanutri, mfn. (only in f. *sánutrī*) gaining, procuring, RV.

Sanéru, mfn. (prob.) distributing, RV. x, 106, 8 (= *sambhaktṛi*, Sāy.)

Santi. See *sati*, p. 1138, col. 2.

Santya, mfn. bestowing gifts, bountiful (only voc. in addressing Agni; accord. to others fr. *sat* = 'benevolent, kind'), RV.

सन् 3. *san*, (in gram.) a technical term for the syllable *sa* or sign of the desiderative.

सन् 4. *san*, N. of an era (current in Bengal and reckoned from 593 A.D.), RTL. 433.

सन 2. *sána*, mf(*ā*)n. (derivation doubtful; for 1. see p. 1140, col. 3) old, ancient (*am*, ind. 'of old, formerly'), RV.; AV.; lasting long, BhP.; m. N. of a Ṛishi (one of the four or seven spiritual sons of Brahmā; cf. *sanaka*), MBh.; Hariv. [Cf. Lat. *senex, senior*; Lith. *sénas*; Goth. *sinista*.] — **já** or **-jā́**, mfn. born or produced long ago, old, ancient, RV. — **vitta** (*sána-*), mfn. long since existing or obtained, RV. — **śruta** (*sána-*), mfn. famous of old, ib.; N. of a man, AitBr.

Sanaḥ, in comp. for *sanas*. — **śruta**, mfn. = *sana-śruta*.

Sanaká, mfn. former, old, ancient (*āt*, ind. 'from of old'), RV.; m. N. of a Ṛishi (one of the four mind-born sons of Brahmā, described as one of the counsellors or companions of Vishṇu and as inhabiting the Janar-loka; the other three are Sana, Sanat-kumāra, and Sa-nandana; some reckon seven of these mind-born sons), MBh.; Hariv.; BhP. (cf. RTL. 422); of an inspired legislator, W. [Cf. Lat. *Seneca*; Goth. *sineigs*.] — **saṃhitā**, f. N. of a Vedânta or Tantra wk. **Sanakânīka**, m. pl. N. of a people, Inscr.

Sanáj, mfn. ancient, old, RV. i, 62, 7.

Sanat, ind. (g. *svar-ādi*) from of old, always, ever, L.; m. N. of Brahmā (prob. inferred from *sanat-kumāra*), L. — **kumāra**, m. 'always a youth' or 'son of Brahmā,' N. of one of the four or seven sons of Brahmā (cf. *sanaka*; he is said to be the oldest of the progenitors of mankind [= *vaidhātra*, q. v.], and sometimes identified with Skanda and Pradyumna, he is also the supposed author of an Upapurāṇa and other wks.; with Jainas he is one of the 12 Sārvabhaumas or Cakravartins [emperors of India]; the N. of Sanat-k° is sometimes given to any great saint who retains youthful purity), ChUp.; MBh.; Hariv. &c.; *-kalpa*, m. N. of wk.; *-ja*, m. pl. (with Jainas) a partic. class of gods, L.; *-tantra*, n., *-pulastya-saṃvāda*, m., *-saṃhitā*, f., *-stava*, m.; °*rīya*, n., °*rôpapurāṇa*, n. N. of wks. — **sujāta**, m. 'always beautiful,' N. of one of the seven mind-born sons of Brahmā, MBh.; *-vedânta*, m. N. of wk.; °*tiya*, n. N. of MBh. v, 40–45.

Sanātá, ind. from of old (with *na*, 'never'), RV.

Sanātra, mf(*ī*)n. = *sanātana*, AV.

Sanáya or **sánaya**, mf(*ā*)n. old, ancient, RV.

Sanas, ind. = *sanā* (in *sanaḥ-śruta*, *sano-ja*, qq. vv.)

Sánā, ind. (g. *svar-ādi*) from of old, RV.; ŚBr. — **jū́**, mfn. nimble or active from of old, RV. — **jūr**, mfn. weak from age (or 'long since aged'), RV. — **liṅga**, m. the son of a Vaiśya and a Ratha-kārī, L.

Sanā́t, ind. (g. *svar-ādi*) from of old, always, for ever, RV.; ŚāṅkhŚr.

Sanātána, mf(*ī*, m.c. also *ā*)n. eternal, perpetual, permanent, everlasting, primeval, ancient, ŚBr. &c. &c.; m. N. of Brahmā, L.; of Vishṇu, Bhaṭṭ.; of Śiva, L.; a guest of deceased ancestors, one who must always be fed whenever he attends Śrāddhas, L.; N. of a Ṛishi (in MBh. and later 'a mind-born son of Brahmā'), TS. &c. &c.; of a king, Buddh.; (with *śarman* and *go-svāmin*) of two authors, Cat.; pl. N. of partic. worlds, Hariv.; (*ī*), f. N. of Durgā, Cat.; of Lakshmī or Sarasvatī, L. — **tama**, m. 'most eternal or ancient,' N. of Vishṇu, MBh. — **siddhânta**, m. N. of wk.

Sanāya, Nom. P. °*yati* (only in dat. sg. of pr. p. *sanāyaté* [accord. to some w. r. for *sánāya te*], RV. i, 62, 13) 'to be from of old' or 'linger, tarry.'

Sánīyas, mfn. being from of old, ancient, TS.

Sano, in comp. for *sanas*. — **jā́**, mfn. being from of old, eternal, RV.

Sányas, mfn. = *sánīyas*, RV.

सन 3. *sana*, m. the flapping of an elephant's ears, L.; Bignonia Suaveolens or Terminalia Tomentosa (cf. 2. *asana*), L. — **parṇī**, f. Marsilea Quadrifolia (= *asana-p*°), L.

सनख *sanakha*, w.r. for *saṃ-nakha*, q.v.

सनग *sánaga*, m. N. of a teacher (cf. *sanaka*), ŚBr.

सनङ्गु *sanaṅgu*, m. or f. (perhaps fr. *sanam* + *gu*, 'formerly a cow?') a partic. object or substance prepared from leather, Pāṇ. v, 1, 2, Vārtt. 1, Pat.

Sanaṅgavya, mfn. fit for Sanaṅgu, ib.

सनदीगिरिकानन *sa-nadī-giri-kānana*, mfn. (fr. 7. *sa* + *n*° &c.) together with rivers and mountains and forests, R.

सनन्द *sa-nanda*, m. (i. e. 7. *sa* + *n*°) = *sanandana*, BhP.; (*ī*), f., g. *gaurâdi*.

Sa (to be similarly prefixed to the following): — **nandaka**, w. r. for next, Hariv. — **nandana**, m. 'having joy,' N. of one of the 4 or 7 mind-born sons of Brahmā (said to have preceded Kapila as teachers of the Sāṃkhya phil.; cf. *sanaka*), MBh.; Hariv.; Pur.; of a pupil of Śaṃkarâcārya and another author, Cat.; *-saṃhitā*, f. N. of a Tantra wk. (one of the Śubhâgamas), MW. — **nara** (*sá-*), mfn. together with men, RV.; *-dvipa*, mfn. accompanied by men and elephants, MW. — **narma-hāsa**, mfn. attended with merry laughter (as a speech), Kathās. — **naladânala-da**, mfn. 'having the Nalada' (i. e. Uśīra plant) and 'removing heat' (cf. 3. *a*), Kir. v, 27. — **navanīta**, mfn. along with fresh butter, Pañcar. — **nāka-vanita**, mfn. having celestial women or Apsarases, MW. — **nātha**, mfn. having a master or protector, protected by (instr. or comp.), Kāv.; Pur.; having a lord or husband (*ā*, f. 'a woman whose husband is living'), L.; filled with persons, crowded (as an assembly), Śāntiś., Sch.; occupied by, possessed of, possessing, furnished or endowed with (instr. or comp.), Kāv.; Pur.; Pañcat. &c.; *-tā*, f. the state of having a protector or husband (acc. with √*i*, 'to take refuge with'), Vcar.; Pañcat.; °*thī-√kṛi*, P. *-karoti*, to cause to possess a master, afford shelter, protect, Śak.; Kathās.; Hit.; to occupy (a place), VarBṛS. — **nābha**, m. a near kinsman, uterine brother, BhP. — **nābhi** (*sá-*), mfn. having the same nave or centre (as the spokes of a wheel or the fingers of the hand), RV. (cf. Naigh. ii, 5); connected by the same navel or womb, uterine, of kindred blood, a blood-relation; m. or f. an uterine brother or sister (accord. to some = *sa-piṇḍa*, 'a kinsman as far as the seventh degree'), RV.; AV.; Mn.; BhP.; having a navel, naveled, TS.; resembling, like, equal to (gen. or comp.), Bālar.; Vcar.; Vās. — **nābhya**, m. a blood-relation (to the seventh degree), Mn. v, 84. — **nāma**, mf(*ā*)n. having the same name as (gen.), MBh. — **nāmaka**, mf(*ikā*)n. id., Hariv.; m. Hyperanthera Moringa, L. — **nāman** (*sá-*), mf(*mnī*)n. = *-nāma*, RV.; MBh.; similar, like, RV.; °*magrāha*, mf(*ā*)n. together with mention of the name, Lāṭy. — **nārāśaṇsa**, mfn. together with the Nārāśaṇsa verses, AitBr. — **nāla**, mfn. furnished with a stalk, MBh.; (*ī*), f. a procuress (?), Gal. — **niḥśvāsam**, ind. with a sigh, Śak. — **nikāra**, mfn. degrading (as punishment), Mṛicch. — **nigaḍa-caraṇa**, mfn. dragging a chain on the foot (*-tva*, n.), ib. — **nigraha**, mfn. furnished with a handle, Suśr. — **nidra**, mf(*ā*)n. sleeping, asleep, Kathās. — **ninda**, mfn accompanied with censure or reproach (*am*, ind.), Śak. (v. l.) — **nimesha**, mfn. winking (as an eye), Kathās. — **niyama**, mf(*ā*)n. restricted, limited (*-tva*, n.), Kap.; one who has undertaken a religious observance, Vikr.; Kir. — **nirghāta**, mfn. accompanied by a hurricane or whirlwind, MW. — **nirghṛiṇa**, mfn. having no pity, merciless, cruel, R. — **nirviśesha**, mfn. indifferent, Kād. — **nirveda**, mfn. having weariness or absence of liveliness, dull (as conversation), Kād.; (*am*), ind. with indifference, Dhūrtan.; in low spirits, despairingly, Daś.; Kathās. — **niśvāsam**, ind. with a sigh, Mṛicch. (v. l. *-niḥśv*°, q. v.) — **nishādika**, mfn. together with the Nishādī (q. v.), Suparṇ. — **nishṭhīva**, mfn. accompanied with emission of saliva or sputtering, sputtered (as speech), L. (accord. to W. also *-nishṭheva*). — **nishpesham**, ind. with a clashing sound, Hariv. — **nishyadá**, mf(*ā*)n. flowing, running, AV. — **nīḍa** (*sá-*), mfn. (in RV. *sá-nīḷa*) having the same nest, closely united or related, kindred, akin, RV.; AV.; near, proximate (also °*ḍaka*), L.; m. or n. vicinity, neighbourhood (*e*, ind. 'near, close to'), Bhaṭṭ. — **nīhāra**, mfn. (for *sanī-hāra* see col. 1) covered with mist or fog, R. — **nemi** (*sá-*), mfn. having a felly (as a wheel), RV.; complete, perfect, ib.; ind. completely, at all times, always, ib.

सनव *sanava*, m. or n. (?) N. of a desert, Buddh.

सनसय *sanasaya*, m. (w. r. for *śana-śaya*?) N. of a teacher, ib.

सना *sanā*, *sanāt* &c. See col. 1.

सनायु *sanāyu*. See p. 1140, col. 3.

सनारु *sanāru*, m. N. of a teacher, ŚBr.

सनि 2. *sani*, f. (for 1. see p. 1140, col. 3) a quarter of the sky, L.

सनितुर् *sanitúr*, ind. (accord. to Sāy. gen. of *sanitṛi* fr. √*san*?) besides, without (with preceding acc.), RV.

Sanutár, ind. (perhaps orig. identical with prec.) aside, away, off, far from (abl.; with √*yu* and *dhā*, 'to keep away, ward off'), ib.; secretly, clandestinely, Naigh. iii, 25.

Sánutara, mfn. furtive, clandestine, ib.

Sánutya, mfn. furtive, lying furtively in ambush, ib.

सनुतृ *sanutṛi*, *saneru*. See col. 1.

सनूदपर्वत *sanūda-parvata* (?), m. N. of a mountain, Hariv.

सनोजा *sano-jā*. See col. 2.

सन्त *santa*, m. = *saṃha-tala*, L.; N. of a son of Satya, MBh.

सन्तक *santaka*, mf(*ikā*)n. (fr. *sat*) belonging to (gen.), Divyâv.

संतक्ष् *saṃ-√taksh*, P. *-takshati* (rarely Ā. °*te*), to cut out together, cut out, form or fashion by cutting, ŚrS.; VarBṛS.; to compose, construct (hymns), RV. ii, 31, 7; to cut through, cut to pieces, wound, MBh.; to hurt with words, Pāṇ. iii, 1, 76, Sch.

Saṃ-takshaṇa, n. hurting with words (*vāk-s*°, pl. 'sarcasm'), Daś.

संतड् *saṃ-√taḍ*, P. *-tāḍayati*, to strike together or forcibly, hit hard, hit with (an arrow &c.), MBh.; Hariv.; R.; to beat or play a musical instrument, MBh.

Saṃ-tāḍana, n. striking or dashing to pieces, ŚārṅgP. °**tāḍya**, mfn. to be forcibly struck or beaten, MBh.

संतन् *saṃ-√tan*, P. *-tanoti* (ind. p. *-tānam*), to stretch along or over, cover, RV. &c. &c.; to unite or join one's self with (instr. or acc.), RV.; Lāṭy.; to join or connect or keep together, make continuous, TBr. &c. &c.; to add, annex, Vait.; to effect, accomplish, TS.; MuṇḍUp.; to exhibit, display, evince, Bhaṭṭ.: Caus. *-tānayati*, to cause to extend or accomplish, cause to be finished, BhP.

Sáṃ-tata, mfn. (cf. *sa-tata*) stretched or extended along, spread over (loc.), PraśnUp.; covered with (instr.), MBh.; Hariv.; R.; held or linked or woven or sewn or strung together, dense, continuous, uninterrupted, lasting, eternal (ibc. or *am*, ind. 'continually, uninterruptedly, incessantly'), ŚBr. &c. &c.; *-jvara*, m. continuous fever, Suśr.; *-druma*, mfn. (a wood) containing dense (rows of) trees, R.; *-varshin*, mfn. raining continuously, Dhūrtas.; *-vepathu*, mfn. trembling all over, MW.; °*tâpad*, mfn. one whose misfortunes are continuous, ib.; °*tâbhyāsa*, m. habitual practice, regular study or repetition (of the Vedas &c.), W.; °*tâśru-nipātana*, n. continuous shedding of tears, R.

Sáṃ-tati, f. stretching or extending along, expanse, continuity, uninterruptedness, TS. &c. &c.;

causal connection (of things), MBh. i, 291 (Nilak.); a continuous line or series or flow, heap, mass, multitude, MBh.; Kāv. &c.; density, intensity (of darkness), Rājat.; uninterrupted succession, lineage, race, progeny, offspring, Mn.; MBh. &c.; continued meditation (= *dhi-s°*), Prab.; disposition, feeling, Divyâv.; = *-homa*, ŚBr.; N. of a daughter of Daksha and wife of Kratu (cf. *sam-nati*), MārkP.; m. N. of a son of Alarka, BhP.; *-mat*, mfn. possessing offspring, MārkP.; *-homá*, m. N. of partic. sacrificial texts, TBr. °**tatika** (ifc.) = *saṃ-tati*, progeny, offspring, Kull. on Mn. iii, 15.

Sam-tateyu, m. (fr. *saṃ-tata*) N. of a son of Raudrāśva (cf. *saṃ-nateyu*), Pur.

Sam-tani, mfn. continuing, prolonging, forming an uninterrupted line or series, AitBr.; Lāṭy. &c.; (°*tani*), m. or f. sound, harmony, music, RV.; (°*tánī*), m. or f. a partic. oblation, ŚBr.; KātyŚr.; n. N. of a Sāman, ĀrshBr. °**tanika**, n. du. (with *Prajāpateḥ*) N. of a Sāman, ib. °**tanu**, m. N. of a youth attending on Rādhā, Pañcar.

Sam-tāná, m. (ifc. f. *ā*) continued succession, continuance, continuity, MBh.; Kāv. &c.; an uninterrupted series, continuous flow, Kālid.; ramification, Suśr.; a sinew or ligature (of an animal), TS.; coherence, connection, transition (in recitation &c.), ŚrS.; TUp.; a continuous train of thought, Sarvad.; = *saṃdhi*, Kām.; one of the five trees of Indra's heaven, the Kalpa tree or its flower, Hariv.; N. of a son of Rudra, MārkP.; of a place, Cat.; (pl.) N. of a partic. class of worlds, R.; m. n. continuous succession, lineage, race, family, offspring, son or daughter, Nir.; Mn.; MBh. &c.; n. a partic. mythical weapon, R.; *-karman*, n. the act of producing offspring, Nir.; *-kartṛi*, m. a producer of offspring, ib.; *-gaṇa-pati*, m. a form of Gaṇeśa (worshipped to obtain progeny), W.; *-go-pāla*, m. a form of Kṛishṇa (worshipped to obtain progeny, also N. of a Kāvya), Cat.; (°*la-vidhi*, m. N. of wk.); *-ja*, mfn. sprung from the race of (gen.; with *suta*, m. = 'the son of'), Hariv.; *-dīpikā*, f., *-prada-sūrya-stotra*, n., *-rāma-stotra*, n. N. of wks.; *-vat*, mfn. possessing offspring, MBh.; *-vardhana*, mfn. propagating a family, Yājñ.; *-vivekâvali*, f., *-saṃhitā*, f. N. of wks.; *-saṃdhi*, m. a peace cemented by family alliance (by giving a daughter in marriage &c.), Kām.; Hit.; °*nârtham*, ind. for the sake of (begetting) progeny, Mn. iii, 96. °**tānaka**, mf(*ikā*)n. stretching, spreading, who or what spreads, W.; m. one of the five trees of Indra's heaven, the Kalpa tree or its flower, MBh.; Kāv. &c.; pl. N. of partic. worlds, R.; (*ikā*), f. a cobweb, Suśr.; cream, coagulated milk, ib.; froth, foam, L.; the blade of a knife or sword, L.; N. of one of the Mātṛis attending on Skanda, MBh.; °*ka-maya*, mf(*ī*)n. consisting of flowers of the Kalpa tree, Ragh.; °*kâkīrṇa*, mfn. strewn with celestial flowers (cf. prec.), MW.; °*kâranya*, n. N. of a place, Bālar. °**tānika**, mf(*ī*)n. made from flowers of the Kalpa tree (as a garland), R.; m. pl. N. of partic. worlds (v. l. *sāṃt°*), R.; n. (with *Prajāpateḥ*) N. of a Sāman (v. l. *saṃ-tanika*), ĀrshBr. °**tānin**, m. the subject of an uninterrupted train of thought, Sarvad.; (*inī*), f. the upper part of milk, cream, L. °**tānīya** (?), Hcat.

संतप् **sam-√tap**, P. *-tapati*, to heat thoroughly, scorch, parch, dry up, R.; Suśr.; VarBṛS. &c.; to feel pain or remorse, Mn.; MBh.; to pain by heat, torture, oppress, afflict, harass, RV. &c. &c.: Pass. *-tapyate* (ep. also °*ti*), to be oppressed or afflicted, suffer pain, undergo penance (3. sg. impers. with gen. of pers.), ŚBr. &c. &c.: Caus. *-tāpayati* (Pass. *-tāpyate*), to cause to be heated, make very hot, burn, inflame, scorch, Kauś.; MBh. &c.; to pain by heat, torture, torment (*ātmānam*, 'one's self,' i. e. 'to afflict the body by austerities'), afflict, trouble, distress, MBh.; Kāv. &c.

Sam-tapana, mfn. heating, warming, ĀpŚr., Sch.; the act of becoming warm, Kauś.; inflaming, tormenting, MW.

Sam-tapta, mfn. greatly heated or inflamed, burnt up &c.; red-hot, molten, melted (see comp.); oppressed, pained, tormented, distressed, wearied, fatigued, MBh.; Kāv. &c.; n. pain, grief, sorrow, Mṛicch.; *-cāmīkara*, n. glowing or molten gold, MW.; *-rajata*, n. molten silver, ib.; *-vakshas*, mfn. oppressed in the chest or breathing, short-breathed, Suśr.; *-hṛidaya*, mfn. feeling great anguish of heart, R.; °*tâyas*, n. heated or red-hot iron, Bhartṛ. °**tapyamāna**, mfn. being inflamed or tormented or distressed, BhP.; *-manas*, mfn. one whose mind is in a state of torture, Vikr.

Sam-tāpá, m. (ifc. f. *ā*) becoming very hot, great or burning heat, glow, fire, ŚBr. &c. &c.; affliction, pain, sorrow, anguish, distress (acc. with √*kṛi*, 'to be distressed about [gen.],' or 'to cause pain'), MBh.; Kāv. &c.; self-mortification, remorse, repentance, penance, MBh.; Kir.; *-kara* (Suśr.), *-kārin* (Kathās.), mfn. causing pain or affliction; *-vat*, mfn. afflicted with pain, sorrowful, Kathās.; *-hara* (Daś.), *-hāraka* (Śak.), mfn. removing heat, cooling, comforting. °**tāpana**, mfn. burning, paining, afflicting (comp.), BhP.; m. N. of one of the arrows of Kāma-deva, L.; of a demon possessing children, Hariv.; of one of Śiva's attendants, L.; n. the act of burning, paining, afflicting, exciting passion, W.; N. of a partic. mythical weapon, R. °**tāpita**, mfn. (fr. Caus.) made very hot, burnt, scorched, tormented, pained, afflicted, wearied, MBh.; Kāv. &c. °**tāpyá**, mfn. to be inflamed or kindled, ŚBr.

संतम् **sam-√tam**, P. *-tāmyati*, to be distressed, pine away, Gīt.

Sam-tamaka, m. oppression or distress (in breathing; a form of asthma), Suśr.

Sam-tamas, n. great or universal darkness, W. °**tamasa**, n. id.; great delusion of mind, Kāv.; Kathās. &c.; mfn. darkened, clouded, W.

संतरण *saṃ-taraṇa* &c. See *saṃ-√tṛī*.

संतरम् *saṃ-tarám* or *saṃ-tarām*, ind. (fr. 2. *sám + t°*) more together, RV.; AV.; TS.; ŚBr.

संतर्क् *saṃ-√tark*, P. *-tarkayati*, to consider or regard as (two acc.), MBh.

संतर्ज् *saṃ-√tarj*, Caus. *-tarjayati*, to threaten, abuse, scold, terrify, MBh.; Kāv. &c.

Sam-tarjana, mfn. threatening, abusing, reviling, Car.; m. N. of one of Skanda's attendants, MBh.; n. and (*ā*), f. the act of threatening or reviling, MBh.; Kām.; BhP. °**tarjita**, mfn. threatened, abused, scolded, reproved, W.

संतर्पक *saṃ-tarpaka*, °*paṇa* &c. See *sam-√tṛip*, col. 3.

संतवीत्वत् *saṃ-távītvat*, mfn. (pr. p. of Intens. of *saṃ-√tu*) one who has great power to effect or accomplish, able, capable, RV.

संताय् *saṃ-√tāy*, Pass. *-tāyyate*, to be spread or stretched out, VS.

सन्ति *santi*, f. = *sati* or *sāti*, L.

संतिज् *saṃ-√tij*, Caus. *-tejayati*, to stir up, excite, arouse, MBh.; Bālar.

Sam-tejana, n. sharpening (fig.), exciting, Suśr.

संतुद् *saṃ-√tud*, P. *-tudati*, to strike at, goad, sting, MBh.; (with *prarohān*) to put forth new sprouts, i. e. recur again and again (as a disease), BhP.

Sam-todín, mfn. striking, stinging, AV.

संतुल् *saṃ-√tul*, P. *-tolayati*, to weigh one thing against another, balance together (also in the mind), MBh.

संतुष् *saṃ-√tush*, P. *-tushyati*, to feel quite satisfied or contented, be pleased or delighted with, have great pleasure in (instr.; *-tushya*, ind. 'with joy, joyfully'), MBh.; Kāv. &c.: Caus. *-toshayati* (m. c. also °*te*), to make well satisfied or contented, propitiate, please, rejoice or present with (instr.)

Sam-tushita or °**taka**, m. N. of a Deva-putra, Lalit.

Sam-tushṭa, mfn. quite satisfied or contented, well pleased or delighted with (instr. or comp.), MBh.; Kāv. &c.; *-tarṇaka-vatī*, f. (a cow) having an easily satisfied calf, Hcat. °**tushṭi**, f. complete satisfaction, contentment with (instr.), MBh.; BhP.

Sam-tosha, m. (ifc. f. *ā*) satisfaction, contentedness with (instr. or loc.; °*shaṃ √kṛi*, 'to be satisfied or contented'), MaitrUp.; MBh. &c.; Content (personified as a son of Dharma and Tushṭi and reckoned among the Tushitas, q. v.), Prab.; Pur.; (*ā*), f. N. of the mother of Gaṅgā-dāsa, Cat.; *-vat*, mfn. satisfied, contented (in *a-s°*), Pañcat.; °*shânanda*, m. N. of an author, Cat. °**toshaka**, mfn. satisfactory, gratifying, pleasing, MW. °**toshaṇa**, n. the act of satisfying, propitiating, comforting, MBh. °**toshaṇīya**, mfn. to be gratified or propitiated (*-rūpa*, mfn. 'one who has the semblance of being gr° or pr°'), MBh. °**toshita**, mfn. (fr. Caus.) satisfied, pleased, comforted, Bhartṛ.; Rājat. °**toshin**, mfn. satisfied, contented, pleased with (comp.), Yājñ.; Śāntiś.; ŚārṅgP. °**toshṭavya**, mfn. to be satisfied or gratified (n. impers.), Śaṃk.; Sarvad. °**toshya**, mfn. to be contented or gratified, MBh.

संतृद् *saṃ-√tṛid*, P. Ā. *-tṛiṇatti*, *-tṛintte*, to fasten or tie together by means of a perforation (through which a peg or pin is passed), ŚBr.; Kāṭh.; ChUp.; to hollow out, perforate (see below).

Sam-tardana, m. N. of a son of Dhṛishṭa-ketu, Pur.; n. the act of connecting or fastening together, Jaim.

Sam-tṛiṇṇa, mfn. joined or fastened together, ŚBr.; KātyŚr.; hollowed out, perforated, ŚBr.

Sam-tṛidya, mfn. to be joined together by pegs or fastenings (see above), ĀpŚr.

संतृप् *saṃ-√tṛip*, P. *-tṛipnoti* or *-tṛipyati*, to satiate or refresh one's self with (gen.), RV.; MBh.: Caus. *-tarpayati*, to satiate, refresh, invigorate, gladden, delight, ŚBr.; MBh. &c.; to feed on (instr.), Car.

Sam-tarpaka, mfn. satiating, refreshing, invigorating, Bhpr. °**tarpaṇa**, mfn. id., Kāv.; Suśr.; n. the act of satiating or refreshing, refreshment, R.; a means of strengthening, restorative, Suśr.; a partic. luscious dish (consisting of a mixture of grapes, pomegranates, dates, plantains, sugar, flour, and ghee), L. °**tarpaṇīya**, mfn. treating of restoratives, Car. °**tarpita**, mfn. (fr. Caus.) satiated, satisfied, Dhūrtas. °**tarpya**, mfn. to be satiated or refreshed or gladdened, MBh.

संतॄ *saṃ-√tṝ*, P. *-tarati* (Ved. also *-tirati*; rarely Ā.), to cross or traverse together, pass through (acc.), RV. &c. &c.; to escape or be rescued from (abl.), MBh.; Rājat.; to bring safely over, rescue, save, MBh.: Caus. *-tārayati* (Pass. *-tāryate*), to cause to pass over, save or preserve from (abl.), Mn.; MBh. &c.

Sam-táraṇa, mfn. conveying over or across, bringing out of (a danger), VS.; n. the act of crossing over or passing through (comp.), R.

Sám-tarutra, mfn. conveying across, effective, sufficient (as wealth), RV.

Sam-tāra, m. crossing, passing over or through (gen. or comp.), MBh.; R. &c. °**tāraka**, mfn. conveying or helping over; *-vidhi*, m. N. of wk. °**tārita**, mfn. (fr. Caus.) made to pass over, saved, rescued, delivered, R. °**tārya**, mfn. to be crossed over or passed through (lit. and fig.), R.; Hariv. (v. l. for *sam-dhārya*).

Sam-tīrṇa, mfn. crossed or passed over &c.; saved or escaped from (abl.), MBh.

सन्त्य *santya*. See p. 1141, col. 1.

संत्यज् *saṃ-√tyaj*, P. *-tyajati*, to relinquish altogether, abandon, leave, quit, desert, MBh.; Kāv. &c.; to avoid, shun (*dūreṇa*, 'from afar'), Bhartṛ.; to give up, renounce, resign, Mn.; MBh. &c.; to withdraw from (an obligation), Yājñ. ii, 198; to yield, deliver up, Kathās.; BhP.; to leave alone, disregard, omit (*-tyajya*, ind. 'excepting'), VarBṛS.; Rājat.: Caus. *-tyājayati*, to cause to abandon, deprive of (two acc.), MBh.; to rid of, free from (abl.), Bhaṭṭ.

Sam-tyakta, mfn. entirely relinquished or abandoned, left, R.; deprived or destitute of, wanting, lacking (instr. or comp.), VarBṛS.; Pañcat.

Sam-tyajana, n. the act of entirely deserting or abandoning, W. °**tyajya**, mfn. to be left or abandoned, MārkP.

Sam-tyāga, m. relinquishment, abandonment, renunciation, resignation, R.; MārkP. °**tyāgin**, mfn. relinquishing, leaving, abandoning, ib. °**tyājya**, mfn. to be left or abandoned or given up, MBh.; Kāv. &c.

संत्रस् *saṃ-√tras*, P. *-trasati* or *-trasyati*, to tremble all over, be greatly terrified or frightened, MBh.; Kāv. &c.: Caus. *-trāsayati*, to cause to tremble, frighten, terrify, ib.

Sam-trasta, mfn. trembling with fear, frightened, alarmed, MBh.; *-gocara*, mfn. one who is looked at with terror, Car.

Sam-trāsa, mfn. great trembling, terror, fear of (abl., *-tas*, or comp.), MBh.; R. &c. °**trāsana**,

n. (fr. Caus.) the act of terrifying, alarming, Chandom. °**trāsita**, mfn. (fr. id.) made to tremble with fear, frightened, terrified, Bhaṭṭ.; Pañcat.

संत्रै *sam-√trai* (only inf. *-trātum*, but cf. below), to protect well or effectually, preserve, defend, MBh.

Sam-trāṇa, n. saving, rescuing, MārkP.

Sam-trāyati, m. (used as a substantive to represent the above verb *sam-√trai*), MBh. viii, 1992.

संत्व *sam-tvá*, n. (fr. 2. *sam*), TBr. (also w. r. for *śantvá*).

संत्वर् *sam-√tvar*, Ā. *-tvarate*, to be in a great hurry, hasten, ŚBr. &c. &c.: Caus. *-tvarayati*, to cause to hurry or hasten, urge on, MBh.; R.

Sam-tvarā, f. great haste, hurry, ĀśvŚr. °**tvarita**, mfn. greatly hurried, hastening, MBh.; R.; (*am*), ind. in a hurry, in great haste, quickly, ib.

संदंश् *sam-√daṅś*, P. *-daśati*, to bite together, seize with the teeth, MBh.; R.; BhP.; to press together, compress, press closely on anything, indent by pressure, MBh.; Kālid.

Sam-daṅśá, m. compression (of the lips), MBh.; too great compression of the teeth in the pronunciation of vowels, RPrāt.; junction, connection, Subh.; a pair of tongs or pincers or nippers, AV.; Br.; Pur.; Suśr.; N. of those parts of the body which are used for grasping or seizing (as the thumb and forefinger together, the opposite eye-teeth, the nippers of a crab &c.), Yājñ.; VarBṛS.; Suśr.; Pañcat.; Kathās.; a partic. Naraka or hell (where the flesh of the wicked is tortured with pincers), Pur.; a chapter or section of a book, Dāyabh.; a partic. Ekâha, Vait.; the site of a village &c. (fixed according to the compass), L. °**daṅśaka**, m. (or *ikā*, f.) a pair of tongs or pincers or nippers, small shears or tongs, a vice, Daś.; Amar.; (*ikā*), f. biting, pecking (with the beak), Lalit. °**daṅśita**, mfn. armed, mailed, MBh. (B. *sa-d°*); m. a defendant, L.

Sam-dashṭa, mfn. bitten, compressed, pressed closely together, pinched, nipped, MBh.; Kāv. &c.; n. a partic. fault in pronunciation (arising from keeping the teeth too close together), RPrāt.; Pat.; *-kusuma-śayana*, mfn. indenting (by pressure of the limbs) a couch of flowers, Śak.; *-tā*, f. (= *saṃdashṭa*, n.), RPrāt.; *-danta-cchada*, mfn. biting or compressing the lips, MW.; °*ṭâdhara(-pallava)* or °*ṭâushṭha(-puṭa)*, mfn. id., MBh.; Amar. °**dashṭaka**, n. a kind of paronomasia, L.

संददस्वस् *sam-dadasvas*. See *sam-√das*.

संददि *sam-dadi*. See *sam-√1. dā*, col. 2.

संदर्प *sam-darpa*, m. pride, arrogance, boasting of (comp.), Kathās.

संदर्भ *sam-darbha*, m. (√2. *dṛibh*; ifc. f. *ā*) stringing or binding together (esp. into a wreath or chaplet), weaving, arranging, collecting, mixing, uniting, Kāv.; Kathās.; Sarvad.; a literary or musical composition, Mcar.; Pratāp.; Mṛicch., Sch.; *-grantha* (?), m. N. of a wk. on the worship of Kṛishṇa; *-cintāmaṇi*, m. N. of a Comm. on the Śiśupālavadha by Candra-śekhara; *-vat*, mfn. artificially connected or composed, Harav.; *-viruddha*, mfn. contrary to order or consistency, incoherent, unconnected, MW.; *-śuddha*, mfn. clearly arranged, coherent, connected, ib.; *-śuddhi*, f. clearness of connection or arrangement (as of the parts of a composition or narrative), regular coherence, Gīt.; °*bhâmṛita-toshiṇī*, f. N. of a Comm. on the Mugdhabodha. °**darbhita**, mfn. strung together, arranged, composed, L.

Sám-dṛibdha, mfn. strung together, interwoven, bound or collected into a tuft or bunch, ŚBr.; arranged, composed, Naish.; corroborated, confirmed (*-tva*, n.), Śaṃk.

संदर्श *sam-darśa*, °*śana* &c. See *sam-√dṛiś*, p. 1144, col. 1.

संदलित *sam-dalita*, mfn. (√*dal*) pierced through, pierced, Dhūrtas.

संदशस्य *sam-daśasya*, Nom. P. *-daśasyati*, to remit, pardon (a sin), RV. iii, 7, 10.

संदस् *sam-√das* (only pf. p. P. *-dadasvás*), to die out or become extinguished (as fire), RV. ii, 2, 6 (accord. to Sāy. *sam-dadasvas* = *samyak-prayacchat*).

संदह् *sam-√dah*, P. Ā. *-dahati*, °*te*, to burn together, burn up, consume by fire, destroy utterly, RV. &c. &c.; (Ā.) to be burnt up, be consumed, MW.: Pass. *-dahyate*, to be burnt up, TS.; to burn, glow, BhP.; to be distressed or grieved, pine away, Ragh.: Caus. *-dāhayati*, to cause to burn up, MBh.: Desid., see *sam-didhakshu*.

Sam-dagdha, mfn. burned up, consumed, TS. &c. &c.

Sam-dāha, m. burning up, consuming, MW.; inflammation of the mouth and lips, ib.

Sam-didhakshu, mfn. (fr. Desid.) wishing to burn up or to consume by fire, MBh.; VarBṛS.; BhP.

संदा *sam-√1. dā*, P. Ā. *-dadāti*, *-datte*, to give together, present, grant, bestow, RV.; AV.; to hold together, AV.; (Ā. or Pass.) to meet, RV. i, 139, 1; iv, 44, 5.

Sam-dadi, mfn. grasping, comprehending, RV.

1. **Sam-dāya**, mfn. giving, presenting (in *go-s°*, q. v.) °**dāyin**, mfn. id., Subh.

संदा *sam-√3. dā* (or *do*), P. *-dāti* or *-dyati*, to cut together, gather by or after cutting (as the sacrificial grass), KātyŚr.; to cut, divide, AV.

1. **Sam-dāna**, n. the act of cutting or dividing, MW.; that part of an elephant's temples whence the fluid called Mada issues (cf. 2. *dāna*), W.

1. **Sam-dita**, mfn. cut off, cut, MW.

संदा *sam-√4. dā*, P. *-dyati*, to bind together, fasten together, tie, RV.; AV.; VS.; KātyŚr.

Sam-dātṛi, mfn. one who ties up or fetters, Mn. viii, 342.

2. **Sam-dắna**, m. the part under the knee of an elephant where the fetter is fastened (also *-bhāga*), L.; a bond, halter, fetter, RV.; AV.; ŚBr.; *-tā*, f., Daś. °**dānikā**, f. a kind of tree, L. °**dānita**, mfn. bound together, tied, fettered, Kāv. °**dānitaka**, n. a collection of three Ślokas forming one sentence, Naish., Sch. °**dāninī**, f. a cow-house, L.

2. **Sam-dāya**, m. a rein, leash, Hariv.

2. **Sam-dita**, mfn. bound or fastened together, detained, caught, R.; Hariv.

संदामितक *saṃdāmitaka*, w. r. for *sam-dānitaka*.

संदाव *sam-dāva*, m. flight, retreat, L.

संदिश् *sam-√diś*, P. *-diśati* (ind. p. *-diśya*, q. v.), to point out, appoint, assign, R.; Bhaṭṭ.; to state, tell, direct, command, give an order or message to (gen. or dat., sometimes two acc.; with *abhi-dūti*, 'to a female messenger'), MBh.; Kāv. &c.; to despatch any one (acc.) on a message to (dat.), Kum.: Caus. *-deśayati*, to cause to point out or declare, invite or ask to speak about, MBh.

Sam-diśya, ind. bidding farewell, Divyâv.

Sam-dishṭa, mfn. pointed out, assigned &c.; stipulated, promised, Yājñ.; n. news, tidings, information, W.; *-vat*, mfn. one who has given an order or message to (gen.; also = pf. *sam-dideśa*, 'he has given &c.'), Kathās. °**ṭârtha**, m. one who communicates information or news, a messenger, herald, pursuivant, W.

Sam-deśa, m. (ifc. f. *ā*) communication of intelligence, message, information, errand, direction, command, order to (gen. or loc.; *-tas* with gen., 'by order of'), Kauś.; MBh. &c.; a present, gift, L.; a partic. kind of sweetmeat, L.; *-gir*, f. news, tidings, L.; *-pada*, n. pl. the words of a message, Ragh.; *-vāc*, f. (= *-gir*), L.; *-hara*, m. a news-bringer, messenger, envoy, ambassador, Kāv.; (*ā*), f. a female messenger, Gal.; *-hāra*, mfn. bringing news or tidings, Sāh.; *-hāraka* (Sāh.), *-hārin* (Śak.), m. (= *-hara*); °*śârtha*, m. the contents of a message, Megh.; °*śôkti*, f. (= *-gir*), L. °**deśaka**, m. or n. information, news, tidings, Pañcat. °**deśita**, mfn. (fr. Caus.) made to point out, asked to declare, MBh. °**deśyà**, mfn. to be directed or instructed, Kathās.; founded on direction or impulse, done on purpose, AV.; belonging to this place, domestic (as opp. to *vi-deśya*, 'foreign'), AV. °**deshṭavya**, mfn. to be informed or instructed, MBh.; to be pointed out or enjoined or communicated, Śak.; n. an injunction, direction, order, MW.

संदिह् *sam-√dih*, P. *-degdhi*, to smear, besmear, cover, Kauś.; MBh. &c.; to heap together, MW.; Ā. *-digdhe* (pr. p. *-dihāna* or *-dehamāna*), to be doubtful or uncertain (said of persons and things), Kāv.; Śaṃk.: Pass. *-dihyate*, to be smeared over or covered, be confused, confounded with (instr.), Nir. ii, 7; be indistinct or doubtful or uncertain, MBh.; Kāv. &c.: Caus. *-dehayati*, to make indistinct or uncertain, confuse, perplex, MBh.; (Ā.) to be doubtful or uncertain (in *sam-dehayāna*, v. l. *-dehamāna*), ib.

Sam-digdha, mfn. smeared over, besmeared or covered with (instr. or comp.), MBh.; Kāv. &c.; confused, confounded with, mistaken for (instr. or comp.), Nir.; Kum.; questioned, questionable, MBh.; Kāv. &c.; precarious, doubtful, dubious, uncertain, unsettled, doubtful about, despairing of (comp.), ib.; riskful, dangerous, unsafe (as a ship), Gaut.; (*am*) n. an ambiguous suggestion or expression, Kpr.; Pratāp.; *-tā*, f. (MW.), *-tva*, n. (Sāh.) uncertainty, hesitation, indistinctness; *-niścaya*, mfn. one who hesitates to hold a firm opinion, R.; *-punarukta-tva*, n. uncertainty and tautology, Sāh.; *-phala*, mfn. having arrows with poisoned tips (accord. to others 'of uncertain result or efficacy'), Daś.; *-buddhi* (Śak.), *-mati* (Yājñ.), mfn. having a doubtful mind, sceptical; *-lekhya*, n. a writing or document of doubtful meaning or authority, W.; °*dhâkshara*, mfn. having indistinct utterance, MW.; °*dhârtha*, mfn. having doubtful meaning, dubious in sense, ib.; m. a doubtful or disputed matter, Yājñ. ii, 12; °*dhī-krita*, mfn. made to present a doubtful resemblance, Bālar. vi, 31.

Sam-dih, f. a heap, mound, wall, RV.

Sam-degdhṛi, mfn. inclined to doubt, L.

Sam-deghá, m. (cf. next) a conglomeration of material elements (said contemptuously of the body), ŚBr.

Sam-dehá, m. (ifc. f. *ā*) a conglomeration or conglutination (of material elements; see above), ŚBr.; ChUp.; doubt, uncertainty about (gen., loc., or comp.; *na* or *nâsti saṃdehaḥ* or *saṃdeho nâsti* [used parenthetically], 'there is no doubt, without doubt'), Āpast.; MBh. &c.; (in rhet.) a figure of speech expressive of doubt (e. g. 'is this a lotus-flower or an eye?'), Vām. iv, 3, 11; risk, danger, Kāv.; Pañcat.; *-gandha*, m. a whiff or slight tinge of doubt, MW.; *-cchedana*, n. cutting i. e. removal of d°, Kām.; *-tva*, n. state of d° or uncertainty, Sāh.; *-dāyin*, mfn. raising d° or unc° concerning i. e. reminding of (comp.), Vās.; *-dolā*, f. the oscillation or perplexity (caused by) d°, MBh; (°*lā-stha*, mfn. 'one who is in a state of suspense,' Kām.); *-pada*, mfn. subject to d°, doubtful, Kālid.; *-bhañjana*, n. breaking or destroying d°, Kām.; *-bhañjikā*, f. N. of wk.; *-bhṛit*, mfn. having d° about (loc.), Mcar.; *-vishâushadhi*, f., *-samuccaya*, m. N. of wks.; °*hâpanodana*, n. (= *-cchedana*), APrāt., Sch.; °*hâlaṃkāra*, m. or °*hâlaṃkṛiti*, f. a partic. figure of speech (cf. above), Sāh.; Pratāp. °**dehayāna**, see *sam-√dih*. °**dehin**, mfn. doubtful, dubious, MW. °**dehya**, m. the body (= *sam-deha*), BṛĀrUp.

संदी *sam-√2. dī* (only Impv. *-dīdihi* or *-didīhi*), to shine together, VS.; to bestow by shining, RV.

सन्दी *sandī*, w. r. for *āsandī*.

संदीक्षित *sam-dīkshita*, mfn. (√*dīksh*) consecrated together, KātyŚr., Sch.

संदीन *sam-dīna*, mfn. (√3. *dī*) greatly depressed or afflicted, Hariv.

संदीप् *sam-√dīp*, Ā. *-dīpyate* (ep. also °*ti*), to blaze up, flame, burn, glow, Hariv.: Caus. *-dīpayati*, to set on fire, kindle, inflame, RV. &c. &c.; to fire, animate, MBh.; BhP.

Sam-dīpaka, mfn. inflaming, exciting, making envious or jealous, Gīt. °**dīpana**, mfn. kindling, inflaming, exciting, arousing, MBh.; Uttarar.; m. N. of one of Kāma-deva's 5 arrows, Vet.; (*ī*), f. (in music) a partic. Śruti, Saṃgīt.; n. the act of kindling or inflaming or exciting (envy &c.), Ṛitus.; Pañcar.; *-vat*, mfn. containing inflammable matter, KātyŚr. °**dīpita**, mfn. (fr. Caus.) lighted up, kindled, inflamed, excited, Pañcat.; BhP. °**dīpta**, mfn. inflamed, flaming, burning, being on fire, ŚBr. &c. &c.; *-locana*, mfn. one who has inflamed or flashing eyes, Hariv. °**dīpya**, m. Celosia Cristata, L.

संदुष् *sam-√dush*, P. *-dushyati*, to become utterly corrupt or polluted or unclean, MBh.: Caus. *-dūshayati* (ind. p. *-dūshya*), to corrupt, vitiate, defile, stain, spoil, R.; Suśr.; Rājat.; to revile, abuse, censure, expose to shame or infamy, MBh.; Kām.

Saṃ-dushṭa, mfn. corrupted, defiled &c.; depraved, wicked, bad, R.; ill-disposed, ill-affected towards (gen.), ib.

Saṃ-dūshaṇa, mfn. (fr. Caus.) corrupting, defiling, Mn. ix, 13; n. the act of vitiating or corrupting, any vice which causes defilement, Yājñ.; *-kara*, mf(*ī*)n. defiling, disgracing (gen.), Hariv. **°dūshita**, mfn. (fr. id.) utterly corrupted or vitiated or spoiled, Hariv.; made or grown worse (as a disease), Suśr.; exposed to shame, reviled, abused, MBh.

संदुह् *saṃ-√duh*, P. Ā. *-dogdhi, -dugdhe*, to milk together or at the same time, MBh.; (Ā.) to suck, imbibe, enjoy, RV. ix, 18, 5; (Ā.) to yield (as milk &c.), AV.: Caus. *-dohayati* (ind. p. *-dohya*), to cause to milk &c., ŚBr.

Saṃ-dugdha, mfn. milked at the same time, milked together, MW. **°duhyā**, see *sukha-saṃduhyā*.

Saṃ-doha, m. milking together, milking, Hariv.; BhP.; the whole milk (of a herd), Nār.; Hariv.; totality, multitude, heap, mass, abundance, Kāv.; Kathās. &c. **°dohana**, mfn. yielding (as milk), bestowing, Śukas. **°dohyā**, see *sukha-saṃdohyā*.

संदृब्ध *saṃ-dṛibdha*. See p. 1143, col. 1.

संदृश् *saṃ-√dṛiś*, P. Ā. (only in non-conj. tenses, e.g. pf. *-dadarśa, -dadṛiśe*, fut. *-drakshyati, °te*; ind. p. *-dṛiśya*; inf. *-drashṭum*, Ved. *-dṛiśe*; cf. *sam-√paś*), to see together or at the same time, see well or completely, behold, view, perceive, observe, consider, MBh.; Kāv. &c.; (Ā. and Pass. *-dṛiśyate*), to be seen at the same time, appear together with (instr.), RV.; ŚBr.; to look like, resemble, be similar or equal, RV.; to be observed, become visible, appear, MBh.; Kāv. &c.: Caus. *-darśayati*, to cause to be seen, display, show, feign (*ātmānam mṛita-vat saṃ-d°*, 'to feign one's self dead'), ib.; to represent, Gīt.; Rājat.; to expose, explain, Divyâv.; to show one's self to (acc.), MBh.; R.: Desid. of Caus., see *saṃ-didarśayishu*: Desid., see *saṃ-didṛikshu*.

Saṃ-darśa, m. sight, appearance, MBh.; BhP.

Saṃ-darśana, n. the act of looking steadfastly, gazing, viewing, beholding, seeing, sight, vision (*svapne °nam √gam*, 'to be seen by or appear to [gen.] in a dream;' *°nam pra-√yam*, 'to show one's self to [gen.];' *°ne*, 'in view or in the presence of [gen. or comp.]'), Nir.; KātyŚr.; MBh. &c.; a gaze, look, R.; Sāh.; surveying, inspection, consideration, MBh.; Vikr.; Hit.; appearance, manifestation, Kāv.; Sāh.; the rising of a heavenly body with the sun, VarBṛS.; meeting or falling in with (instr. with or without *saha*), Kathās.; Pañcat.; (fr. Caus.) the act of causing to see, showing, displaying, exhibition of or to (comp.), MBh.; R.; Pur.; (*ī*), f. (scil. *vṛitti*) a partic. manner of subsistence, Baudh. **-dvīpa**, m. N. of a Dvīpa, R. **-patha**, m. the range of sight, Hariv.

Saṃ-darśayitṛi, mfn. (fr. Caus.) causing to see, showing, pointing out, Nir. **°darśita**, mfn. shown, displayed, manifested, Mālav.; represented, Gīt.

Saṃ-didarśayishu, mfn. (fr. Desid. of Caus.) wishing to show, Bhaṭṭ.

Saṃ-didṛikshu, mfn. (fr. Desid.) wishing to see, MBh.

Saṃ-dṛíś, f. (*e*, dat. as inf.; cf. above) sight, appearance, RV. (*samyak paśyati yaḥ*, 'one who sees well or thoroughly,' Sāy.); AV.; VS.; KaṭhUp.; view, direction, RV. ii, 13, 10. **°dṛiśa**, see *madhu-saṃdṛiśa*. **°dṛiśya**, mfn. to be looked at i. e. appearing as (nom.), MBh.

Saṃ-dṛishṭa, mfn. completely seen or beheld (*pāpa-s°*, 'having an evil aspect'), VarBṛS.; foreseen, ordained, prescribed (in sacred books), R.

Saṃ-dṛishṭi, f. complete sight, full view, aspect, RV. **°dṛishṭika**, w.r. for *sāṃd°*, Divyâv.

Saṃ-drashṭavya, mfn. to be seen or sought for, MBh. **°drashṭṛi**, mfn. one who sees well or beholds, Nir.; BhP.

संदेश *saṃ-deśa*. See *sam-√diś*.

संदेह *saṃ-deha*. See *sam-√dih*.

संदोल *saṃ-dola*, m. (or *ā*, f.) a kind of pendulous ornament, Pañcar.

संदोह *saṃ-doha, °hana, °hyā*. See *sam-√duh*, col. 1.

संद्रु *saṃ-dru*, P. *-dravati*, to run together, RV.

Saṃ-drava, m. flight, L.

Saṃ-drāva, m. running together, a place where people run together, Pat. on Pāṇ. v, 1, 119, Vārtt. 5; flight, L.; gait, manner of walking, Bhaṭṭ.

संध *saṃ-dha, saṃ-dhaya* &c. See *sam-√1. dhā*.

संधनजित् *saṃ-dhana-jit*, mfn. (= *dhana-saṃ-jit*) winning booty together, accumulating booty by conquest, AV.

संधन्व् *saṃ-√dhanv* (only pf. Ā. *-dadhanve, °vire*), to run towards or together, RV.

संधम् *saṃ-√dham* (or *dhmā*), to blow together (into a flame), fuse or melt together, RV.; AV.; to proclaim aloud, TĀr.

संधर्तृ *saṃ-dhartṛi*. See *sam-√dhṛi*.

संधर्षित *saṃ-dharshita*, mfn. (from Caus. of *sam-√dhṛish*) greatly injured, violated, disgraced, Hariv.

संधा *saṃ-√1. dhā*, P. Ā. *-dadhāti, -dhatte* (ep. 1. pl. pr. *-dadhāmahe* = *-dadhmahe*; pr. p. *-dhāna* = *-dadhāna*; inf. *-dhitum* = *-dhātum*), to place or hold or put or draw or join or fasten or fix or sew together, unite (with *akshīṇi*, 'to close the eyes;' with *vraṇam*, 'to heal a wound;' with *manas*, 'to compose the mind;' with *mitrá-dhitāni*, 'to conclude an alliance;' with *vācam*, 'to hold or interchange conversation'), to combine, connect with (instr.), RV. &c. &c.; (Ā.) to bring together, reconcile, Mn.; MBh.; to be reconciled, agree with (instr., rarely acc.), Pañcav. Br. &c. &c.; to mend, restore, redress, AitBr.; ChUp. &c.; to lay down on or in (loc.), fix on (esp. an arrow on a bow, with instr. or with loc., e.g. *dhanuḥ śareṇa* or *śaraṃ dhanushi*, 'to take aim;' generally Ā.), MBh.; R.; Hariv.; (Ā.) to direct towards (*tataḥ*), Ragh.; to aim at (?), RV. v, 54, 2; to involve in (loc.), RV. i, 165, 6; to confer on (loc.), grant, yield, bestow (with *nāma* and gen., 'to give a name to;' Ā. with *śraddhām* and loc., 'to place credence in;' with *sāhāyyam*, 'to afford assistance'), MBh.; Kāv. &c.; to cause, inflict, MBh.; Kir.; (Ā.) to be a match for, hold out against (acc.), Pañcat.; to comprehend, MBh.; (Ā.) to use, employ (instr.), MBh. iv, 964: Pass. *-dhīyate*, to be put together or joined or connected &c.; to be placed or held in (loc.), RV. i, 168, 3; to become possessed of (instr.), AitBr.: Desid. *-dhitsati*, to wish to place or join together, desire to repair, ŚBr.

Saṃ-hita. See p. 1123, col. 1.

Saṃ-dha, mfn. holding, possessing, W.; joined, united, ib.; n. junction, connection, ŚBr.; (*ā*), f., see below.

Saṃ-dhanīya, w.r. for *saṃ-dhānīya*.

Saṃ-dhaya, Nom. (fr. *saṃ-dhi*; also with *anu* prefixed, Kāśīkh.) P. *°yati*, to put or join together, unite (esp. 'to join bow and arrow,' 'take aim;' with *ātmani*, 'to appropriate to one's self, assume, acquire'), MuṇḍUp.; MBh. &c.; to be reconciled, conclude peace (only in inf. *saṃ-dhitum*, which may also be referred to *sam-√dhā*), BhP.

Saṃ-dhā́, f. intimate union, compact, agreement, AV.; TS.; Gobh.; a promise, vow, Ragh.; intention, design, Daś.; mixture, preparation of a beverage &c., L.; a boundary, limit, Campak.; fixed state, condition (= *sthiti*), L.; often w.r. for *saṃdhyā* (q. v.); *-bhāshita, -bhāshya*, or *-vacana*, n. allusive speech (cf. *saṃ-dhāya*), SaddhP.; *-veṇikā*, f. a game, Divyâv. **°dhātavya**, mfn. to be joined together or added, Suśr.; to be allied with (n. impers.), MBh.; Hit. **°dhātṛi** (*sáṃ-*), mfn. one who puts together or joins, RV.; m. N. of Śiva and Vishṇu, MBh.

Saṃ-dhāna, mfn. joining, uniting, healing, Suśr.; m. a partic. spell recited over weapons, R.; N. of a minister, Kathās.; (*ī*), f. mixing, distilling, the manufacture of fermented or spirituous liquors, L.; a foundery or place where metals are wrought or stored, L.; the small egg-plant, L.; (*am*), n. the act of placing or joining together or uniting, junction, union, Vait.; MBh. &c.; assembling or meeting of men (*°nam ā-√yā*, 'to receive admission'), Hariv.; Kām. &c.; a joint, point of contact, boundary, TS.; Lāṭy.; Suśr.; a means of union, TUp.; growing together, re-uniting, healing (as a wound), Suśr.; fixing on (as an arrow on a bow-string), aiming at, MBh.; R.; BhP.; perceiving, perception, Nalac.; combination of words (also 'euphonic c°' = *saṃ-dhi*, q. v.), Prāt.; ŚāṅkhŚr.; bringing together, alliance, league, association, friendship, making peace with (instr. with or without *saha*), MBh.; Kāv. &c.; compounding, mixing, preparation (of a beverage &c.; cf. *nīla-saṃdhāna-bhāṇḍa*), ŚārṅgS.; Bhpr.; sour rice-gruel, L.; a kind of relish eaten to excite thirst, L.; spirituous liquor, L.; mixed or bell-metal (= *saurāshṭra*), MW.; *-karaṇa*, mf(*ī*)n. causing union or combination, who or what re-unites or heals or reconciles, W.; n. the act of uniting or healing, ib.; allying, making peace, ib.; *-kartṛi*, mfn. uniting, connecting, healing, ib.; *-kalpa-vallī*, f. N. of wk.; *-kārin* (MBh.; Vāgbh.), *-kṛit* (Suśr.), mfn. (= *-kartṛi*); *-tāla* or *-bhāva*, m. a kind of measure, Pañcar.; *°nāsana*, n. = *saṃ-dhāyāsana*, MBh. **°dhānikā**, f. a kind of pickle or sauce, MW. **°dhānita, °dhāninī**, w.r. for *saṃ-d°* (q. v.) **°dhānīya**, mfn. to be allied with, fit for an alliance, Pañcat. (B. *°dheya*); causing to grow together, healing, Car.

Saṃ-dhāya, ind. having placed together &c.; having formed an alliance or settled terms of peace with reference to, Buddh.; *-gamana*, n. a march after peace has been made, Kām.; *-sambhāshā*, f. a learned conversation among friends, Car.; *°yāsana*, n. a halt after terms of peace have been agreed upon (cf. *saṃ-dhānāsana*), ib. **°dhāyin**, mfn. joining or fixing together (as an arrow and a bow), Śiś.

Saṃ-dhí, mfn. containing a conjunction or transition from one to the other &c., TBr.; m. (exceptionally f.; once in MBh. loc. pl. *saṃdhīshu*) junction, connection, combination, union with (instr.), KaṭhUp.; Subh.; association, intercourse with (instr.), MBh.; comprehension, totality, the whole essence or scope of (comp.), Pañcat.; agreement, compact, TBr.; alliance, league, reconciliation, peace between (gen.) or with (instr. with or without *saha*), making a treaty of peace, negotiating alliances (one of a king's six courses of action, see *guṇa*; many kinds are specified, e.g. *adṛishṭa-purusha, ucchinna, kāñcana, kapāla, saṃtāna*, qq. vv.), Mn.; Yājñ.; Hit. &c.; euphonic junction of final and initial letters in grammar (every sentence in Sanskṛit being regarded as a euphonic chain, a break in which occurs at the end of a sentence and is denoted by a Virāma or Avasāna, 'stop;' this euphonic coalition causing modifications of the final and initial letters of the separate words of a sentence and in the final letters of roots and stems when combined with terminations to form such words), Prāt.; Kathās.; Sāh.; contrivance, management, Ragh.; Daś.; place or point of connection or contact, juncture, hinge, boundary, boundary line, TS.; Āpast.; MBh. &c.; critical juncture, crisis, opportune moment, MW.; a joint, articulation (of the body; esp. applied to the five junctures of the parts of the eye), RV. &c. &c.; interstice, crevice, interval, MBh.; the space between heaven and earth, horizon, ŚBr.; GṛŚrS.; the interval between day and night, twilight (= *saṃ-dhyā*), VS. &c. &c.; a seam, Amar.; a fold, Pañcat.; a wall or the hole or cavity or breach in a wall made by a housebreaker (acc. with *√chid* or *bhid* or Caus. of *ut-√pad*, 'to make a breach in a wall'), Mn.; Mṛicch.; Daś.; the vagina or vulva, L.; a juncture or division of a drama (reckoned to be five, viz. *mukha, pratimukha, garbha, vimarśa*, and *nirvahaṇa*, qq. vv.; or one of the 14 kinds of *nirvahaṇa* or catastrophe), Bhar.; Daśar. &c.; a period at the expiration of each Yuga or age (equivalent to one sixth of its duration and intervening before the commencement of the next; occurring also at the end of each Manv-antara and Kalpa), W.; a pause or rest, ib.; a part, portion, piece of anything, AitBr.; Hariv.; Naish., Sch.; a partic. Stotra, Br.; (in mensuration) the connecting link of a perpendicular, ib.; the common side of a double triangle, Śulbas.; = *sâvakāśa*, L.; N. of a son of Prasuśruta, BhP.; f. N. of a goddess presiding over junction or union, VS. **-kāshṭha**, n. the wood below the top of a gable, L. **-kuśala**, mfn. skilled in the art of making treaties or forming alliances, MW. **-gupta**, n. an artificial sentence in which (by euphonic changes of letters) the meaning is hidden, Cat. **-gṛiha**, m. a bee-hive, MBh., Sch. **-granthi**, m. a gland which connects (and lubricates) a joint, W. **—camasa,** m. N. of partic. schools, ĀpŚr.; Vait. **—cora,** m. = next, A. **—caura,** m. 'hole-thief,' a thief who enters a house by a hole made in the wall, L. **—cchidā,** f. dismemberment, Pracand. **—ccheda,** m. making holes or breaches (in a wall &c.), A. **—cchedaka,** m. = *-caura,* L. **—cchedana,** n. housebreaking, burglary, Mṛicch. **—ja,** mfn. produced by conjunction or by transition &c., GṛS.; produced by euphonic Saṃdhi, RPrāt., APrāt., Sch.; belonging to the junctures of the parts of the eye (see above), Suśr.; prod° by distillation, L.; (*ā*), f. Hibiscus Rosa Sinensis, L.; n. spirituous liquor, L. **—jīvaka,** mfn. one who lives by dishonest means, L. **—tas,** ind. from an alliance, MW. **—taskara,** m. = *-caura,* L. **—dūshaṇa,** n. the violation of a treaty, breaking of peace, Kir. (pl.) **—nāla,** m. or n. Unguis Odoratus, L. **—nirmocana,** n. N. of a Buddhist Sūtra. **—pāda,** m. N. of wk. **—pūjā,** f. N. of the third division of the great autumnal Durgā-pūjā, MW. **—prabandhana,** n. (in anat.) the ligament of a joint, Suśr. **—bandha,** m. the ligaments or sinews of the joints, Śak.; (perhaps) cement or lime, Inscr.; the plant Kæmpferia Rotunda, L.; = next, Śak. **—bandhana,** n. 'joint-binding,' a ligament, tendon, Śak. **—bhaṅga,** m. joint-fracture, dislocation of a joint, ŚārṅgS. **—mat,** mfn. containing a concurrence of two days or day periods or life periods (*vayaḥ-saṃdhi-matī = aprasūta-taruṇī,* L.), Jyot.; KātyŚr., Sch.; ĀpŚr., Sch.; being or existing in peace (said of Vishṇu), MBh.; having an alliance, allied, Kām.; m. N. of two ministers, Rājat. **—mati,** m. N. of a minister, ib. **—mukta,** mfn. 'joint-loosened,' dislocated, MW.; n. dislocation of a joint, Suśr. **—mukti,** f. dislocation, MW. **—randhrakā,** f. a hole or breach in a wall, L. **—rāga,** m. = *saṃdhyā-r°,* Cat. **—rūpa,** n. N. of wk. **—rodha,** m. obstruction of a point of junction (as of the hinge in the lid of any vessel), Bhpr. **—vigraha,** m. du. peace and war, MW.; *-kāyastha,* m. a secretary for managing (foreign) affairs in making peace and war, Kathās.; *-kāryâdhikārin,* m. du. the ministers presiding over the above affairs, Hit.; *-yāna-dvaidhī-bhāva-samāśraya-grantha,* m. N. of wk.; °*grahâdhikāra,* m. superintendence over the affairs of peace and war, MW.; °*grahâdhikārin,* m. superintendent over the affairs of p° and w°, a chief foreign minister, ib. **—vigrahaka,** m. a minister presiding over the above, Rājat. **—vigrahika,** m. id., MBh. **—vicakshaṇa,** m. one skilled in peacemaking, an able negotiator of treaties, W. **—vid,** mfn. skilled in alliances, MW.; m. a negotiator of treaties, minister, W. **—viparyaya,** m. du. peace and its opposite (i.e. war), Mn. vii, 65. **—velā,** f. the period of twilight, GṛŚrS.; Mn.; any period or time which connects parts of the day or night or fortnight (e.g. morning, noon, evening, new moon, the first or 13th day of the fortnight, full moon &c.), W. **—śūla,** n. a kind of painful indigestion (= *āma-vāta*), L. **—shāman** (for *-sām°*), n. a Sāman belonging to the Stotras called Saṃdhis, PañcavBr.; ŚrS. **—sambhava,** mfn. produced by grammatical Saṃdhi; m. a diphthong, Cat. **—sarpaṇa,** n. creeping through crevices, PārGṛ. **—sitâsita-roga,** m. a kind of disease of the eye, Cat. **—stotra,** n. N. of a partic. hymn. **—hāraka,** m. = *-caura,* L. **Saṃdhīraṇa,** m. N. of a man, HPariś. **Saṃdhîśvara,** m. N. of a sanctuary sacred to the putting together of the parts of the body of Saṃdhi-mati, Rājat.

Saṃdhika, (ifc.) = *saṃ-dhi,* a joint, Kathās.; m. a kind of fever, Cat.; (*ā*), f. distillation, L.

Saṃdhiga, m. a kind of fever, Bhpr. **—cikitsā,** f. its cure, ib.

Saṃdhita, mfn. joined or fastened together, MBh.; Hariv.; Rājat. &c.; put to or on, fixed (as an arrow), MBh.; BhP.; joined or united with (*mṛityu-s°,* 'united with or destined to death'), ib.; allied, one who has concluded an alliance, MBh.; Pañcat. &c.; concluded (as an alliance), see *sama-saṃdh°*; prepared, mixed together, Bhpr.; pickled, W.; w.r. for *saṃdita,* Mn. viii, 342; m. binding the parted hair, L.; n. pickles, W.; spirituous liquor, L. **Saṃdhitêshu,** mfn. having an arrow fitted on a bow-string, MW.

Saṃdhitavya, mfn. = *saṃdheya,* col. 2, MW.

Saṃdhitsu, mfn. (fr. Desid.) wishing to make peace or form an alliance with (*saha*), Śiś.; Kām.

Saṃdhin, m. a minister of alliances, R.; (*inī*), f., see next.

Saṃdhinī, f. a cow in heat, Gaut.; Āpast. &c.; (accord. to L.) a cow which has just taken the bull; a cow milked unseasonably or every second day. **—kshīra,** n. the milk of a cow in heat (prohibited as an article of food), Āpast.; Mn. &c.

Saṃdhilā, f. (only L.) a breach or hole made in a wall; a chasm, mine, pit; spirituous liquor; = *nāndī = dvādaśa-tūrya-nirghosha;* = *nadī,* a river (w.r. for *nāndī*).

Saṃdheya, mfn. to be joined or united (see *āśu-s°*); to be connected with &c., VPrāt.; to be reconciled, to be made peace or alliance with, MBh.; BhP.; to be made amends for (see *a-s°*), Pañcat. &c. (see also *a-s°, āśu-s°*); to be aimed at, MW.; to be subjected to grammatical Saṃdhi, Kāt.; n. (impers.) it is to be allied or reconciled with (instr. or loc.), MBh.; BhP.

Saṃdhy, in comp. for *saṃdhi.* **—akshara,** n. a compound vowel, diphthong, ŚrS.; RPrāt. &c. **—adhyāya,** m. an Adhyāya or chapter on Saṃdhi, MW. **—arksha** (for *-ṛiksha?*), MārkP.

1. **Saṃ-dhya,** mfn. (for 2. see col. 3) being on the point of junction &c., ŚBr.; Gobh.; Suśr.; based on Saṃdhi or euphonic combination, Prāt.; (*ā*), f., see next.

1. **Saṃ-dhyā́,** f. holding together, union, junction, juncture, (esp.) j° of day and night, morning or evening twilight, Br.; GṛŚrS.; MBh. &c.; juncture of the three divisions of the day (morning, noon, and evening), VarBṛS.; the religious acts performed by Brāhmans and twice-born men at the above three divisions of the day (acc. with √*ās* or *anv-√ās* or *upa-√ās,* 'to perform these Saṃdhyā services,' which consist of sipping water, repetition of prayers and mantras, especially of the Gāyatrī prayer; if regarded as an act of meditation the *saṃdhyā* may be connected with *saṃ-dhyai*), Mn.; R.; Pur.; RTL. 401; 407; Twilight (esp° evening Tw°, personified as a manifestation or daughter of Brahmā, and as the consort of Śiva, of the Sun, of Kāla, of Pulastya, of Pūshan &c., and as the mother-in-law of Vidyut-keśa), MBh.; R.; Pur. &c.; a girl one year old representing the goddess Saṃdhyā at the Durgā festival, L.; a deity presiding over the three divisions of the day, ĀśvPariś.; the period which precedes a Yuga or age of the world (see *yuga*), Hariv.; BhP.; a boundary, limit, L.; promise, agreement, assent, L.; = *saṃ-dhāna,* L.; a partic. flower, L.; N. of a river, MBh. **—°ṇśa** (°*dhyâṇ°*), m. (Mn.; Hariv.; Pur.) or **—°ṇśaka,** m. (Hariv.) 'portion of twilight,' the period at the end of each Yuga (see above). **—°ṇśu** (°*dhyâṇ°*), m. 'tw°-ray,' twilight, W. **—°ṇsa** (°*dhyâṇ°*), mfn. having the morning and evening tw° for shoulders, MBh. **—kalpa,** m., **-kārikā,** f. pl. N. of wks. **—kārya,** n. the morning or evening devotional acts &c., Vikr. **—kāla,** m. tw°-time, evening-time, R.; VarBṛS.; Hit.; Cāṇ.; the interval of a Yuga, W. **—kālika,** mfn. belonging to tw°-time, vespertine, Vās., Sch. **—krama-paddhati,** f. N. of a wk. treating of the Saṃdhyā ceremonial. **—°cala** (°*dhyâc°*), m. 'tw°-mountain,' N. of a m°, KālP.; *-tarpaṇa-vidhi,* m. N. of wk. **—traya,** n. the 3 divisions or periods of the day (morning, noon, and evening), VarBṛS.; *-prayoga,* m., *-vidhi,* m. N. of wks. **—tva,** n. the state of tw°, Daś.; the time for devotional exercises, MW. **—°di-brahma-karman** (°*dhyâd°*), n. N. of wk. **—nāṭin,** m. 'dancing at evening tw°,' N. of Śiva, L. (w.r. *-nādin*). **—nirṇaya,** m., **-nirṇaya-kalpa-vallī,** f., **-nyāsa,** m., **-pañcī-karaṇa-vārttika,** n., **-paddhati,** f. N. of wks. **—payoda,** m. a tw° rain-cloud, Śak. **—pātra,** n. a vessel used for pouring out water in performing the Saṃdhyā ceremonies, MW. **—pushpī,** f. Jasminum Grandiflorum, L.; nutmeg, MW. **—prayoga,** m. = *-kārya,* Cat.; N. of wk. **—prâyaścitta,** n. N. of wk. **—bala,** m. 'strong during tw°,' a Rākshasa, L. **—bali,** m. the evening or tw° oblation, Megh.; a bull (or its image) in a temple of Śiva, L. **—bhāshya,** n. N. of various wks. **—°bhra** (°*dhyâbh°*), n. = *-payoda,* Kāv.; BhP.; Pañcat.; a sort of red chalk, L. **—maṅgala,** n. the auspicious Saṃdhyā service, Vikr. **—mantra,** m. pl., **-mantra-vyākhya,** f., **-mantra-vyākhyāna,** n. N. of wks. **—maya,** mf(*ī*)n. consisting of twilight, Hcar. **—māhātmya,** n. N. of wk. **—rāga,** m. the red glow of tw°, VarBṛS.; Vās.; mfn. having the colour of tw°; n. red-lead, L. **—°rāma** (°*dhyâr°*), m. 'delighting in the Saṃdhyā,' N. of Brahmā, L. **—vandana,** n. the morning and evening hymns and acts of worship, Vedāntas.; Vās.; N. of wk.; *-guru-bhāshya,* n., *-bhāshya,* n., *-mantra,* m., *-laghu-bhāshya,* n., *-vidhi,* m., *-vivaraṇa,* n.; °*danôpâsana-krama,* m. N. of wks. **—vāsa,** m. N. of a village, Kathās. **—vidyā,** f. N. of Vara-dā, TĀr. **—vidhi,** m. = *-kārya,* Kathās.; N. of wk.; *-mantra-samūha-ṭīkā,* f. N. of wk. **—śaṅkha,** m. the evening conch-shell (of worship, used as an instrument to sound the evening hour); *-dhvani,* m. the sound made with it, Mālatīm. **—śata-sūtrī-bhāshya,** n. N. of wk. **—samaya,** m. tw°-period, Hit.; Vās.; a portion of each Yuga, MW. **—sūtra-pravacana,** n. N. of wk. **Saṃdhyôpanishad,** f. N. of an Upanishad. **Saṃdhyôpasthāna,** n. adoration (of the Sun) at the Saṃdhyā, TBr., Sch.; RTL. 406. **Saṃdhyôpâsana,** n. worship performed at the S°, Mn. ii, 69; *-vidhi,* m. N. of various wks.

Saṃdhyāya, Nom. Ā. °*dhyāyate,* to resemble twilight, Kād. (°*yāyita,* mfn., Subh.)

संधारण *saṃ-dhāraṇa* &c. See *saṃ-√dhṛi.*

संधाव् *saṃ-√1. dhāv,* P. Ā. *-dhāvati,* °*te* (ind. p. *-dhāvya*), to run together, AV.; MBh.; to run up to violently, assail, attack, Hariv.; to run to, arrive at (acc.), MBh.; to run through (births), Divyâv.

संधाव् *saṃ-√2. dhāv,* Ā. *-dhāvate* (ind. p. *-dhāvya*), to cleanse or wash one's self, ŚrS.

संधुक्ष् *saṃ-√dhuksh,* Ā. *-dhukshate,* to inflame, kindle, animate, revive, MBh.; Bhaṭṭ.: Caus. *-dhukshayati,* to set on fire, light up, inflame, animate, MBh.; Kāv. &c.

Saṃ-dhukshaṇa, mfn. inflaming, exciting (comp.), Uttarar.; n. the act of kindling, inflammation, MBh.; Suśr.; Daś. **°dhukshita,** mfn. kindled, inflamed, Kāv.; Suśr. **°dhukshya,** mfn. to be inflamed or kindled (as the fire of digestion), Car.

संधू *saṃ-√dhū,* P. Ā. *-dhūnoti,* °*nute,* (P.) to scatter or distribute liberally, bestow on (dat.), RV.; (Ā.) to seize or carry off, ib.

संधूमाय *saṃ-dhūmāya,* Nom. Ā. °*yate,* to smoke, Divyâv.

संधृ *saṃ-√dhṛi,* P. Ā. *-dhārayati,* °*te* (impf. ep. *sam-adhāram* = *-adhārayam;* pr. p. P. *saṃdhārayat;* Ā. *-dhārayamāna* or *-dhārayāṇa;* pf. *sam-dadhāra*), to hold together, bear, carry, MBh.; R.; BhP.; to hold up, support, preserve, observe, maintain, ib.; to keep in remembrance, Pañcat.; to hold back, restrain, withstand, MBh.; R.; to suffer, endure, ib.; to hold or fix the mind on (loc.), BhP.; to promise, MBh.; to hold out, live, exist, MārkP.; to be ready to serve any one (gen.) with (instr.), Kāraṇḍ.: Pass. *-dhriyate,* to resolve or fix upon (loc.), TS.; to be kept or observed, R.; *-dhāryate,* to be held together or borne or kept or maintained, MBh.; R. &c.

Saṃ-dhartṛi, m. one who holds together, AtharvaśUp.

Saṃ-dhāraṇa, mfn. holding together, supporting (life), MBh.; (*ā*), f. attitude, posture, position (e.g. *mukha-s°,* 'p° of the mouth'), VPrāt., Sch.; direction (of thoughts), BhP.; (*am*), n. the act of holding together, supporting, maintaining, MBh.; Kād.; bearing (*kukshi-s°,* 'bearing in the womb'), MBh.; holding in or back, checking, restraining, RPrāt.; Suśr.; Car.; Hcat.; refusal (of a request), Car. **°dhāraṇīya,** mfn. to be supported or kept alive, Kād. **°dhārya,** mfn. to be borne or carried, R.; to be kept (as a servant), Pañcat. (v.l.); to be held or maintained or observed, Mn. iii, 79; to be held back or restrained (v.l. *saṃ-tārya,* q.v.), Hariv.

Sáṃ-dhṛita, mfn. firmly held together, closely connected, AV. **°dhṛiti,** f. holding together, Subh.

संध्मा *saṃ-√dhmā.* See *saṃ-√dham.*

संध्यै *saṃ-√dhyai,* P. *-dhyāyati,* to reflect or meditate on, think about, MBh.

2. **Saṃ-dhya,** mfn. (for 1. see col. 2) thinking about, reflecting, Vās., Sch.

2. **Saṃdhyā,** f. thinking about, reflection, meditation, L.

Saṃ-dhyātṛi, mfn. one who reflects or meditates, W.; one who binds (w.r. for *saṃ-dātṛi*), Mn. viii, 342.

संध्वान *sáṃ-dhvāna,* mfn. sounding or whistling together (said of winds), MaitrS.

सन्न *sanna, sannaka.* See p. 1139, col. 1.

संनख *saṃ-nakha*, mfn. 'having the nails (of fingers and thumb) brought into contact,' tightly closed; m. (with *mushṭi*) as much as can be grasped, a handful, ĀpŚr.; Car.

संनत *saṃ-nata* &c. See *saṃ-√nam*.

संनद् *saṃ-√nad*, P. -*nadati*, to cry aloud, sound, roar, MBh.: Caus. -*nādayati*, to cause to resound, fill with noise or cries, MBh.; R.; Hariv.; to cry aloud, MBh.

Saṃ-nāda, m. (sg. and pl.) shouting together, a confused or tumultuous noise, uproar, din, clamour (also -*śabda*), MBh.; R. &c.; m. N. of a monkey, R. °**nādana**, mfn. (fr. Caus.) making to sound, filling with noise or clamour, MBh.; m. N. of a monkey, R. °**nādita**, mfn. (fr. id.) caused to resound, filled with noise or cries, MBh.; R.

संनद्ध *saṃ-naddha*. See *saṃ-√nah*.

संनम् *saṃ-√nam*, P. Ā. -*namati*, °*te*, to bend together, bend down, bow down before or to (dat., gen., or acc. of person), MBh.; R.; (Ā.) to submit or conform to, comply with, obey (dat.), RV.; TS.; VS.; to direct, bend in the right direction, put in order, arrange, prepare, make ready, RV.; AV.; VS.; Br. (Ā.) to be brought about or fulfilled, VS.; (P. Ā.): Caus. -*nāmayati*, to bend, cause to bow or sink, MBh.; Kum.; BhP.; to bend in a particular direction, make right, arrange, prepare, bring about, AV.; ŚBr.; GṛŚrS.; to subdue, Divyâv.

Saṃ-nata, mfn. bent together, curved, stooping or bowing to (gen.), MBh.; R. &c.; bowed before, revered, BhP.; deepened, sunk in, depressed, Śulbas.; MBh. &c.; bent down through sorrow, dispirited, downcast, R.; (*sáṃ-*), du. conforming to or harmonizing with each other, VS.; m. N. of a monkey, R.; -*tara*, mfn. more deepened, deeper, KātyŚr., Sch.; -*bhrū*, mfn. bending or contracting the brow, frowning, MBh.; °*tâṅga*, mf(*ī*)n. having the body bent, having rounded limbs, Kum. i, 34.

Sáṃ-nati, f. bending down, depression, lowness, Śiś.; inclination, leaning towards, favour, complaisance towards (gen.), ib.; N. of verses expressing favour or respect (e.g. AV. iv, 39, 1), Kauś.; subjection or submission to, humility towards (loc.), MBh.; Hariv.; R. &c.; Humility personified (as a daughter of Devala and wife of Brahma-datta or as a daughter of Daksha and wife of Kratu), Hariv.; Pur.; diminishing, lightening (of a burden), Hariv.; sound, noise, L.; m. N. of a son of Su-mati, Hariv.; of a son of Alarka, ib.; -*mat*, mfn. humble, modest towards (gen.), Hariv.; m. N. of a son of Su-mati, Pur.; -*homá*, m. N. of partic. oblations (cf. *saṃtati-h*°), TBr. °**nateyu**, m. N. of a son of Raudrāśva (cf. *saṃ-tateyu*), MBh.; Hariv.

Saṃ-nám, f. favour, kindness, AV. iv, 39, 1. °**namana**, n. bending together, narrowing, KātyŚr., Sch.

Saṃ-nāma, m. bowing down, submission, Nalôd.; changing, L. °**nāmayitavya**, mfn. (fr. Caus.) to be rendered submissive, Divyâv.

संनमस्य *saṃ-namasya*, Nom. P. °*syati*, to show respect or honour, worship, Hariv.

संनय *saṃ-naya* &c. See *saṃ-√nī*.

संनर्द् *saṃ-√nard*, P. -*nardati* (ep. also °*te*), to roar aloud, bellow, MBh.

संनश् *saṃ-√1. naś* (only in Ved. inf. *saṃnáśe*), to reach, attain, RV.; VS.

संनष्ट *saṃ-nashṭa*, mfn. (√2. *naś*) entirely disappeared, perished, R.

संनस् *saṃ-√nas*, Ā. -*nasate*, to come together, meet, be united, RV.

संनह् *saṃ-√nah*, P. Ā. -*nahyati*, °*te*, to bind or tie together, bind or fasten on, put or gird on (acc.), clothe or furnish with (instr.), AV. &c. &c.; (Ā.) to put anything (acc.) on one's self, dress or arm one's self with (e.g. *saṃnahyadhvaṃ cārūṇi daṃśanāni*, 'put ye on your beautiful armour'), ib.; to prepare for doing anything (inf.), Bhartṛ.: Pass. -*nahyate*, to be fastened on &c., be harnessed, MBh.; Hariv.: Caus. -*nāhayati*, to cause to gird or bind on, cause to equip or arm one's self, GṛŚrS.

Sáṃ-naddha, mfn. bound or fastened or tied together, girt, bound, RV. &c. &c.; armed, mailed, equipped, accoutred, RV. &c. &c.; harnessed, AitBr.; prepared, ready, Rājat.; ready to discharge water (said of a cloud), Megh.; Vikr.; ready to blossom (as a bud), Śak.; wearing amulets, provided with charms, W.; sticking or clinging or adhering to, pervading (loc.), Kālid.; adjoining, bordering, near, R.; -*kavaca*, mfn. one who has girded on his armour, clad in mail or accoutred, Kāṭh.

Saṃ-naddhavya, n. (impers.) it is to be girded or fastened or made ready, MBh.

Saṃ-náhana, n. tying or stringing together, Nir.; AśvGṛ.; preparing, making one's self ready, Hariv.; a band, cord, rope, TBr.; ŚrS.; MBh.; equipment, armour, mail, MBh.; R. °**nahanīya**, w.r. for *saṃ-hananīya*, MBh.

Saṃ-nāha, m. tying up, girding on (esp. armour), arming for battle, MBh.; R.; VarBṛS.; making one's self ready, preparation, Daś.; equipment, harness, ib.; Kathās.; accoutrements, armour, mail, a coat of mail (made of iron or quilted cotton), AitBr. &c. &c.; a cord, string, MBh. °**nāhya**, m. 'armed or ready for battle,' a war elephant, L.

सन्नामन् *san-nāman* &c. See p. 1137, col. 3.

सन्नि *sanni* &c. See p. 1139, col. 1.

संनिकाश् *saṃ-ni-√kāś*, Caus. -*kāśayati*, to make quite clear, manifest, reveal, announce, declare, make known, MBh.; Kir. xiii, 35.

Saṃ-nikāśa, mf(*ā*)n. having the appearance of, resembling (comp.), MBh.; R. &c.

संनिकुञ्च् *saṃ-ni-√kuñc* (only ind. p. -*kuñcya*), to draw together, contract, Siṃhâs.

संनिकीर्ण *saṃ-ni-kīrṇa*, mfn. (√*kṝ*) stretched out at full length, Megh.

संनिकृष् *saṃ-ni-√kṛish* (ind. p. -*kṛ hya*, see below), Pass. -*kṛishyate*, to come into close or immediate contact with (instr.), Nyāyas., Sch.

Saṃ-nikarsha, m. drawing near or together, approximation, close contact, nearness, neighbourhood, proximity, vicinity (*e*, 'in the vicinity of, near,' with gen. or comp.; *āt*, 'from the neighbourhood or proximity of'), Nir.; GṛŚrS.; MBh. &c. (-*tā*, f., Kusum.); connection with, relation to, (in phil.) the connection of an Indriya or organ of sense with its Vishaya or object (this, accord. to the Nyāya, is the source of *jñāna*, and is of two kinds, 1. *laukika*, which is sixfold, 2. *a-laukika*, which is threefold, MW.), Śaṃk.; Sarvad.; a receptacle, repository, BhP.; mfn. near, at hand, Hariv.; -*tattva-viveka*, m., -*tā-vāda*, m., -*vāda*, m., -*vādârtha*, m., -*vicāra*, m. N. of wks. °**nikarshaṇa**, n. drawing together, approximation, close contact with (instr.), BhP.

Saṃ-nikṛishṭa, mfn. drawn together or near, contiguous, proximate, near, imminent, MBh.; R. &c.; one who takes up the same or a similar position, Kathās.; n. nearness, vicinity (*e*, ind. 'in the neighbourhood of,' with gen. or comp.), MBh.; Kāv. &c. °**nikṛishya**, ind. approaching, coming near, Daś.

संनिक्षार *saṃ-nikshāra*, m. the Piyāla tree, W.

संनिक्षिप् *saṃ-ni-√kship*, P. -*kshipati*, to throw or lay down, R.

संनिगम् *saṃ-ni-√gam*, P. -*gacchati*, to go or come together, meet or unite with (instr.), ŚBr.

संनिग्रह् *saṃ-ni-√grah*, P. -*gṛihṇāti*, to hold down, keep under, overcome, subdue, MBh.; VarBṛS.; to lay hold of, seize, MBh.; to check, curb, restrain, suppress, ib.

Saṃ-nigraha, m. restraint, punishment, MBh.

संनिघृष् *saṃ-ni-√ghrish*, P. -*gharshati*, to rub or mix together, ŚāṅkhGṛ.

संनिचय *saṃ-ni-caya*, m. (√1. *ci*) piling or heaping together, gathering, collecting, MBh.; store, provision (see *alpa-s*°).

Saṃ-nicita, mfn. heaped together &c.; congested, constipated, stagnated, Suśr.

संनिताल *saṃ-nitāla*, m. (in music) a kind of time or measure, Saṃgīt.

संनिदर्शित *saṃ-nidarśita*, mfn. (fr. Caus. of √*dṛiś*) brought into view, shown, pointed out, R.

संनिदाघ *saṃ-nidāgha*, m. scorching heat (esp. of the sun), BhP.

संनिधा *saṃ-ni-√1. dhā*, P. Ā. -*dadhāti*, -*dhatte*, to put or place down near together, put down near or into, deposit in (loc.), place or put upon, direct towards (with or without *dṛishṭim*, 'to fix the eyes upon;' with *manas* or *hṛidayam*, 'to fix or direct the mind or thoughts'), TS. &c. &c.; to place together, collect, pile up, MBh.; (Ā.) to appoint to (loc.), PraśnUp.; (Ā.) to be present in, be found with (loc.), Daś.; (Ā. or Pass. -*dhīyate*) to be put together in the same place, be near or present or imminent, Kāv.; Kathās. &c.: Caus. -*dhāpayati*, to bring near, make present or manifest, represent, BhP.: Pass. of Caus. -*dhāpyate*, to appear or become manifested in the presence of (gen.), ib.

Saṃ-nidha, n. juxtapositiou, vicinity, L.

Saṃ-nidhātṛi, mfn. one who places down near, one who is near or close at hand (f. °*trī* = fut. 'she will be present'), Naish.; depositing, placing in deposit, W.; receiving in charge, MW.; m. a receiver of stolen goods, Mn. ix, 278; an officer who introduces people at court, Pañcat.; Rājat.; = *kshattṛi*, ŚBr., Sch.

Saṃ-nidhāna, n. juxtaposition, nearness, vicinity, presence (*e*, with gen. or ifc., 'in the presence of, near;' *āt*, with gen., 'from [one's presence];' °*na-tas*, ifc. 'towards'), R.; Hariv. &c.; presence = existence (cf. *a-s*°), Rājat.; placing down, depositing, W.; a place of deposit, receptacle, gathering-place, rallying-point, MBh.; Bhartṛ.; BhP.; receiving, taking charge of, ib. °**nidhānin**, mfn. (perhaps) gathering together or collecting (goods &c.), Divyâv.

Saṃ-nidhāyin, mfn. being near or close at hand, present, Mālatīm.

Saṃ-nidhi, m. depositing together or near, KātyŚr.; Sāh.; juxtaposition, nearness, vicinity, presence (*au*, with gen. or ifc., 'in the presence of, near;' *im*, 'near to, towards;' id., with √*kṛi*, *vi-*√1. *dhā* or √*bandh* and loc., 'to take one's seat or place or abode in'), ĀśvŚr.; Mn.; MBh. &c.; visibility, existence (cf. *a-s*°), Kusum.; receiving, taking charge of, W.; -*kāra*, m. laying aside (food for one's self), Buddh.; -*vartin*, mfn. being near, neighbouring, MW.; -*viyoga*, m. separation (of vicinity), Mālav.

Saṃ-nihita, mfn. deposited together or near, contiguous, proximate, present, close, near, at hand, MuṇḍUp.; MBh. &c.; deposited, fixed, laid up (see *hṛidaya-s*°); prepared to, ready for (dat.), Śak.; staying, being, W.; m. a partic. Agni, MBh.; -*taratva*, n. greater nearness, Gobh., Sch.; °*tâpāya*, mfn. having loss or destruction near at hand, transient, transitory, fleeting, Hit.

संनिनी *saṃ-ni-√nī* (only ind. p. -*nīya*), to bring or pour together, mix, ŚāṅkhGṛ.

संनिपत् *saṃ-ni-√pat*, P. -*patati*, to fly or fall down, alight, descend upon (loc.), MBh.; R.; Hariv.; to come together, meet, fall in with (instr. with or without *saha*), Āpast.; Megh.; to present one's self, arrive, appear among or in (loc.), Vajracch.; to perish, be destroyed, MBh.: Caus. -*pātayati*, to cause to fall down, shoot down or off, discharge, MBh.; R.; to cause to come together, join, unite, assemble, convoke, GṛŚrS.; MBh. &c.; to stretch out (a cord) to (loc.), Śulbas.

Saṃ-nipatita, mfn. flown or fallen down, descended &c.; met together, assembled, Kāraṇḍ.; appeared, arrived, MBh. °**nipatya**, ind. having flown or fallen down &c.; immediately, directly (see comp.); -*kārin*, mfn. acting immediately, Nyāyam.; °*tyôpakāraka*, mfn. directly effective, Madhus.

Saṃ-nipāta, m. falling in or down together, collapse, meeting, encounter, contact or collision with (instr.), MBh.; Kāv. &c.; conjunction, aggregation, combination, mixture, Prāt.; ŚrS.; MBh. &c.; (also with *maithune*) sexual intercourse with (loc.), Āpast.; MBh.; a complicated derangement of the three humours or an illness produced by it, Suśr.; a partic. manner of wrestling, VP.; falling down, descent (see *lakshaṇa-s*°); utter collapse, death, destruction, MBh.; (in astron.) a partic. conjunction of planets, VarBṛS.; (in music) a kind of measure, Saṃgīt.; -*kalikā*, f., -*kalikā-ṭīkā*, f., -*candrikā*, f., -*cikitsā*, f. N. of wks.; -*jvara*, m. a dangerous fever resulting from morbid condition of the three humours (one of the 8 kinds of fever), Suśr.; -*nāḍī-lakshaṇa*, n. N. of wk.; -*nidrā*, f. a swoon, trance,

Kād.; *-nud*, m. 'removing the above fever,' a species of Nimba tree, Suśr.; *-paṭa*, m. or n.(?), *-mañjarī*, f. N. of wks. °**nipātaka**, m. (in med.) =°*nipāta*, Suśr. °**nipātana**, n. (fr. Caus.) causing to fall together, ŚāṅkhŚr. °**nipātika**, w.r. for *sām-n*° (q.v.) °**nipātita**, mfn. (fr. Caus.) thrown or shot down, discharged, R.; brought or called together, assembled, MBh. °**nipātin**, mfn. falling together, meeting (°*ti-tva*, n.), ĀpŚr., Sch.; furthering or promoting immediately, Nyāyam., Sch. °**nipātya**, mfn. (fr. Caus.) to be caused to fall down, to be hurled upon (loc.), Śak.

संनिबद्ध *saṃ-ni-baddha*, mfn. (√*bandh*) firmly bound together or on, closely connected with or attached to, dependent on or engrossed by (loc.), R.; BrahmavP.; (ifc.) planted or covered with, MBh.

Saṃ-nibandha, m. binding firmly together or on, tying together, W.; attachment, connection, consequence, ib.; effectiveness, ib. °**nibandhana**, n. the act of lying firmly or binding fast, ib.

संनिबर्हण *saṃ-nibarhaṇa*, n. the act of overthrowing or subduing, Kām.

संनिबुध् *saṃ-ni-√budh*, P. *-bodhati*, to perceive completely or thoroughly, MārkP.

Saṃ-niboddhavya, mfn. to be thoroughly perceived or understood, VarBṛS.

संनिभ *saṃ-nibha*, mfn. like, similar, resembling (ifc.; often pleonastically with names of colours, e.g. *pītāruṇa-s*° = *pītāruṇa*), MBh.; Kāv. &c.

संनिभृत *saṃ-nibhṛita*, mfn. (√*bhṛi*) well kept secret, concealed, hidden, Hit. (v.l.); discreet, prudent, modest, BhP.

संनिमज्ज् *saṃ-ni-√majj*, P. *-majjati*, to sink entirely under, sink down, be immersed, MBh.

Saṃ-nimagna, mfn. sunk entirely under, immersed, W.; sleeping, asleep, ib.

संनिमन्त्र् *saṃ-ni-√mantr*, P. *-mantrayati*, to invite, MBh.

सन्निमित्त *san-nimitta* &c. See p. 1137.

संनिमील् *saṃ-ni-√mīl*, P. *-mīlati*, to entirely close, completely shut (the eyes), MBh.

संनियम् *saṃ-ni-√yam*, P. *-yacchati*, to hold together, keep back, restrain, subdue, suppress, Mn.; MBh. &c.; to annihilate, destroy, BhP.

Saṃ-niyacchana, n. (fr. pres. stem) checking, restraining, guiding (of horses), MBh. viii, 1654. °**niyata**, mfn. restrained, controlled, R.

Saṃ-niyantṛi, mfn. one who restrains or chastises, a chastiser (with gen.), Mn. ix, 320.

Saṃ-niyama, m. exactness, precision, Jaim.; Suśr.

संनियुज् *saṃ-ni-√yuj*, P. *-yunakti*, to connect with, place or put in (loc.), MārkP.; to appoint, employ, MBh.: Caus. *-yojayati*, to place in or on (loc.), Hariv.; MārkP.; to appoint to, intrust with (loc.; or *artham*, *arthāya*, ifc.), MBh.; R.

Saṃ-niyukta, mfn. attached to, connected with (comp.), Pat.; appointed, employed, Yājñ., Sch.

Saṃ-niyoga, m. connection with, attachment, application (to any pursuit &c.), W.; appointment, commission, Hariv.; R.; injunction, precept, Pāṇ. vii, 3, 118; 119, Vārtt. 3, Pat. °**niyojita**, mfn. (fr. Caus.) appointed, commissioned, Pañcat.; destined, assigned, ib. °**niyojya**, mfn. to be appointed or employed or commissioned, Baudh.

संनिरुध् *saṃ-ni-rudh*, P. *-ruṇaddhi*, to keep back, restrain, hinder, check, stop, obstruct, suppress, MBh.; Hariv.; to shut in, confine, ŚvetUp.; Hariv.; BhP.; to withdraw (the senses from the outer world), Yājñ.: Pass. *-rudhyate*, to be kept back &c., MBh.

Saṃ-niruddha, mfn. kept back, held fast, restrained, suppressed, MBh.; Hariv. &c.; raked together (as fire), R.; crowded, filled, covered over, MBh.; Hariv.; *-guda*, m. obstruction of the lower intestine, Suśr. °**niroddhavya**, mfn. to be shut up or confined, Mn. ix, 83. °**nirodha**, m. restraint, obstruction, suppression, Suśr.; MBh.; BhP.; confinement, imprisonment, BhP.; narrowness, a narrow pass (in *parvata-s*°), MBh.

संनिर्गम् *saṃ-nir-√gam*, P. *-gacchati*, to go out together, go away, start, depart, MBh.

संनिर्मथ् *saṃ-nir-√math* (only ind. p. *-mathya*), to churn out, stir or shake about together, crush together, Pañcar.

संनिर्मित *saṃ-nir-mita*, mfn. (√3. *mā*) constructed, composed of (abl.), AitBr.

संनिर्वप् *saṃ-nir-√2. vap*, P. *-vapati*, to scatter about, distribute, dispense, AitBr.

संनिली *saṃ-ni-√lī*, Ā. *-līyate*, to settle down, alight, MBh.; to cower down, hide or conceal one's self, disappear, R.

संनिवप् *saṃ-ni-√2. vap*, P. *-vapati*, to throw or heap together, heap up, AitBr.

Saṃ-nivapana, n. heaping together, piling up (see next). °**nivapanīya**, mfn. connected with the piling up (of the sacrificial fire), ŚāṅkhBr. °**nivāpa**, m. the heaping together or mingling (of fires), Āpast.

संनिवर्तन *saṃ-nivartana* &c. See *saṃ-ni-√vṛit*, col. 3.

संनिवस् *saṃ-ni-√4. vas*, Ā. *-vaste*, to clothe with, put on (clothes &c.), MBh.

संनिवस् *saṃ-ni-√5. vas*, P. *-vasati*, to dwell or live together with (instr.), MBh.; to live in, inhabit (loc.), ib.

Saṃ-nivāsa, m. (for *san-n*° see p. 1137, col. 3) dwelling or living together, BhP.; common habitation, a nest, MBh. °**nivāsin**, mfn. dwelling, inhabiting (see *vana-s*°).

संनिवाय *saṃ-ni-vāya*, m. (√*ve*) connection, combination, BhP.

संनिवारण *saṃ-nivāraṇa*, °*rya*. See col. 3.

संनिविद् *saṃ-ni-√1. vid*, Caus. *-vedayati*, to cause to know, make known, announce, inform, tell, MBh.; R.; to offer, present (*ātmānam*, 'one's self'), R.

संनिविश् *saṃ-ni-√viś*, Ā. *-viśate*, to sit or settle down together with, have intercourse or intimate connection with (instr.), MBh. (v.l.): Caus. *-veśayati*, to cause to enter or sit down together, introduce into or lodge in (loc.), Hariv.; R.; to set down, deposit, ib.; to draw up (an army), MBh.; to cause (troops) to encamp, R.; Kathās.; fasten or fix or establish in or on (loc.), Up.; Mn.; MBh. &c.; to cast or hurl upon (loc.), MBh.; to found (a city), Hariv.; to appoint to (loc.), MBh.; R. &c.; to intrust or commit anything to (loc.), MārkP.; to direct (the mind) towards (loc.), BhP.

Saṃ-nivishṭa, mfn. seated down together, encamped, assembled, MBh.; R.; Kathās.; fixed in or on, sticking or resting or contained in (loc. or comp.), Up.; MBh. &c.; being on (a road or path, loc.), MBh.; R.; dependent on (loc.), R.; entered deeply into, absorbed or engrossed in, MW.; contiguous, neighbouring, present, at hand, W.

Saṃ-niveśa, m. entering or sitting down together, entrance into, settlement (acc. with √*kṛi* or *vi-√dhā*, 'to take up a position, settle down'), Kāv.; Suśr.; seat, position, situation (ifc. 'situated in or on'), Suśr.; Kālid.; Vās.; station, encampment, abode, place, Kāv.; Kathās.; vicinity, W.; an open place or play-ground in or near a town (where people assemble for recreation), L.; assembling together, assembly, crowd, Prasannar.; causing to enter, putting down together, W.; insertion, inclusion, Hcat.; attachment to any pursuit, MW.; impression (of a mark; see *lakshaṇa-s*°); foundation (of a town), Cat.; putting together, fabrication, construction, composition, arrangement, Kāv.; Pur.; Sāh.; Construction personified (as son of Tvashṭṛi and Racanā), BhP.; form, figure, appearance, Ragh.; Uttarar.; BhP.; form of an asterism, W. °**niveśana**, n. (fr. Caus.) settlement, dwelling-place, abode, MBh.; R.; Kām.; erection (of a statue), VarBṛS.; insertion, arrangement, Sāh. °**niveśayitavya**, mfn. (fr. id.) to be placed or made to enter or inserted, Śaṃk. °**niveśita**, mfn. (fr. id.) made to enter in or settle, stationed, encamped, located, R.; entered, impressed, ib.; imposed, committed, intrusted, Śak. (v.l.) °**niveśin**, mfn. seated or fixed in (comp.), Suśr. °**niveśya**, mfn. to be put in (loc.), VarBṛS.; to be put on or drawn (with colours), Hcat.

संनिवृ *saṃ-ni-√1. vṛi*, Caus. *-vārayati*, to keep off or back, restrain, MBh.

Saṃ-nivāraṇa, n. keeping back, restrained, MBh. °**nivārya**, mfn. to be kept back or restrained, ib.

संनिवृत् *saṃ-ni-√vṛit*, Ā. *-vartate*, to turn back, return from (abl.), MBh.; R. &c.; to desist from (abl.), R.; Pur.; to leave off, cease, stop, BhP.; to pass away, MBh.: Caus. *-vartayati*, to cause to return or turn back, send back, MBh.; R.; to hinder, prevent or divert from (abl.), ib.; to cause to cease, suppress, stop, R.

Saṃ-nivartana, n. (also pl.) turning back, return, MBh.; R. °**nivartita**, mfn. (fr. Caus.) caused to return, sent back or away, MārkP.

Saṃ-nivṛitta, mfn. turned or come back, returned, MBh.; Kāv. &c.; withdrawn, Megh.; desisted, stopped, ceased, BhP.; Suśr. °**nivṛitti**, f. returning, coming back (in *a-s*° and *a-bhūyaḥ-s*°), Ragh.; desisting from, forbearance, avoiding, W.

संनिशम् *saṃ-ni-√śam* (only ind. p. *-śāmya*), to perceive, hear, learn, MBh.; Kathās.

संनिश्चय *saṃ-niścaya*, m. a settled opinion (acc. with √*yā*, 'to make up one's mind'), MBh.

संनिश्रय *saṃ-ni-śraya*, m. (√*śri*) support (see *kim-s*°).

Saṃ-niśrita, mfn. connected with, devoted to, Divyāv.

संनिषद् *saṃ-ni-shad* (√*sad*), to sink or sit down, AV.; MBh.

Saṃ-nishaṇṇa, mfn. settled down, seated, R.; halted, stationary, W.

संनिषिच् *saṃ-ni-shic* (√*sic*), P. *-shiñcati*, to pour into, MBh.

संनिषेवित *saṃ-ni-shevita*, mfn. (√*sev*) served, frequented, inhabited by (instr.), MBh.

Saṃ-nishevya, mfn. to be attended to or treated medically, MBh.

संनिसर्ग *saṃ-nisarga*, m. good-naturedness, gentleness, MBh.

संनिसूदित *saṃ-ni-sūdita*, mfn. (√*sūd*) altogether killed, destroyed, MBh. (B. *-shūdita*).

संनिसृष्ट *saṃ-ni-srishṭa*, mfn. (√*sṛij*) delivered up or over, intrusted, committed, MBh.

संनिहती *saṃ-nihatī*, f. N. of a river, Prāyaśc.; of a Tīrtha, MBh.

Saṃ-nihana, n. (used to explain *saṃ-nihatī*), MBh.

संनिहन् *saṃ-ni-√han*, P. *-hanti*, to strike at, strike, kill, MBh.

संनी *saṃ-√nī*, P. *-nayati*, to lead or bring or put together, join, connect, unite, conglomerate, RV.; TS.; Āpast.; BhP.; to mix together, mingle, mix (esp. with sweet or sour milk), ŚBr.; Kauś.; Mn. &c.; to lead or direct towards, bring, procure, bestow, TS.; Br.; MBh.; to present with (instr.), RV.; to bring back, restore, pay, RV.; AV.; Br.; Mn.; to direct (the mind) towards (loc.), BhP.

Saṃ-nayá, mfn. leading or bringing together, RV.; m. a collection, assembly, MBh.; the rear of an army, rear-guard, L. °**nayana**, n. leading or bringing together, Kauś.

Saṃ-nāyya, w.r. for *sāmn*°, q.v.

Saṃ-neya, mfn. to be led or brought together, Pāṇ. iii, 1, 129, Sch.

संनु *saṃ-√3. nu*, Ā. *-navate*, to come together, meet, RV. x, 120, 2.

संनु *saṃ-√4. nu*, Ā. *-navate*, to roar or sound together, bellow, bleat, RV.

संनुद् *saṃ-√nud*, P. *-nudati*, to impel or bring together, AV.; Kauś.: Caus. *-nodayati*, to bring together or near, procure, find, MBh.; R.; to push or urge on, impel, MBh.; to drive or scare away (?), MBh. xii, 5443 (Nīlak.)

Saṃ-nodana, mfn. driving away, Kāśikh. °**nodayitavya**, mfn. (fr. Caus.) to be impelled or stimulated, Harav.

संनृत् *saṃ-√nṛit*, P. *-nṛityati*, to dance together, AV.

संन्यस् saṃ-ny-√2. as, P. -asyati (rarely -asati), to throw down together, place or put or lay together, ŚBr.; to impose, put or lay upon, intrust or commit to (gen. or loc.), Mn.; MBh. &c.; to put or lay down, deposit, MBh.; Kāv. &c.; to lay aside, give up, abandon, resign (esp. the world, i.e. become an ascetic or Saṃnyāsin), Mn.; MBh. &c.

Saṃ-nyasana, n. throwing down, laying aside, giving up, resignation, renunciation of worldly concerns, Bhag.

Saṃ-nyasta, mfn. thrown down, laid aside, relinquished, abandoned, deserted, MBh.; Kāv. &c.; encamped, R.; deposited, intrusted, consigned, ib.; *-deha*, mfn. one who has given up his body, MW.; *-śastra*, mfn. one who has laid aside his weapons, Ragh.

Saṃ-nyāsa, m. (ifc. f. *ā*) putting or throwing down, laying aside, resignation, abandonment of (gen. or comp.), MBh.; R.; Sarvad.; renunciation of the world, profession of asceticism, Mn.; MBh. &c.; abstinence from food, L.; giving up the body, sudden death, W.; complete exhaustion, Suśr.; deposit, trust, R.; Mṛicch.; compact, agreement, Kathās.; stake, wager, MBh.; Indian spikenard, L.; *-karma-kārikā*, f. N. of wk.; *-grahaṇa*, n. assuming or practising asceticism, Pañcar.; *-grahaṇa-paddhati*, f., *-grahaṇa-ratnamālā*, f., *-grāhya-paddhati*, f., *-dīpikā*, f., *-dharma-saṃgraha*, m., *-nirṇaya*, m., *-pada-mañjarī*, f., *-paddhati*, f. N. of wks.; *-palli*, f. (for °*si-p*°?) an ascetic's hut, L.; *-bheda-nirṇaya*, m., *-rīti*, f. N. of wks.; *-vat*, mfn. connected with asceticism, L.; *-vidhi*, m.; °*sâśrama-vicāra*, m., °*sâhnika*, n., °*sôpanishad*, f. N. of wks. °**nyāsika**, in *veda-s*° (q.v.)

Saṃ-nyāsin, mfn. laying aside, giving up, abandoning, renouncing, AshṭāvS.; abstaining from food, Bhaṭṭ.; m. one who abandons or resigns worldly affairs, an ascetic, devotee (who has renounced all earthly concerns and devotes himself to meditation and the study of the Āraṇyakas or Upanishads, a Brāhman in the fourth Āśrama [q.v.] or stage of his life, a religious mendicant; cf. RTL. 53, 55 &c.), Up.; MBh.; Pur.; (°*si*)*-tā*, f., *-tva*, n. abandonment of worldly concerns, retirement from the world, MW.; *-darśana*, n. N. of a ch. of the PadmaP.; *-saṃdhyā*, f., *-samārādhana*, n. N. of wks.

सन्मङ्गल san-maṅgala, san-maṇi &c. See p. 1137, col. 3.

सप् 1. sap (cf. √sac), cl. 1. P. (Dhātup. xi, 6) *sapati* (and Ā. °*te*, pf. *sepuḥ*, RV.; fut. *sapitā*, *sapishyati*, Gr.), to follow or seek after, be devoted to, honour, serve, love, caress (also sexually), RV.; TS.; VS. (cf. Naigh. iii, 5; 14): Caus. *sāpayati* (Subj. aor. *sīshapanta*), to serve, honour, worship, do homage (others 'to receive homage'), RV. vii, 43, 4; to have sexual intercourse (?), TBr. [? cf. Gk. σέβομαι, σέβας].

2. Sap (ifc.), see *ṛita-* and *keta-sáp*.

Sápa, m. (cf. *śépa* and *pásas*) the male organ of generation, TBr.; ĀśvŚr.; MaitrS.

1. Saparya, Nom. P. °*yáti* (prob. fr. a lost noun *sapar*), to serve attentively, honour, worship, adore, RV.; AV.; to offer or dedicate reverentially, RV. x, 37, 1; to accept kindly, Kauś.

2. Saparyà, mfn. (of doubtful meaning), RV. x, 106, 5; (*ā*), f., see next.

Saparyā, f. (also pl.) worship, homage, adoration (acc. with √*kṛi* or √*dā*, *vi-* or *prati-vi-*√*dhā*, and Caus. of √*rac* or *ni-*√*vṛit*, 'to perform worship, do homage;' with √*labh* or *prati-*√*grah*, 'to receive w° or h°;' instr. with √*pūj*, *abhi-*√*gā*, *upa-*√*ās*, *praty-ud-*√*i*, 'to worship, adore, approach reverentially'), MBh.; Kāv. &c. **–saptaka**, n., **-sāra**, m. N. of wks.

Saparyú, mfn. serving, honouring, devoted, faithful, RV.

Saparyéṇya, mfn. to be worshipped or adored, RV.

Sapin. See *nish-shapin*.

सपक्ष sa-paksha, mfn. (7. *sa*+*p*°) having wings, winged, MBh.; Hariv. &c.; feathered (as an arrow), Śiś.; having partisans or friends, ib.; containing the major term or subject, MW.; m. 'taking the same side,' an adherent, friend (*-tā*, f., *-tva*, n.), Kāv.; Kathās.; partaker, one being in like or similar circumstances, Naish.; (in logic) an instance on the same side (e.g. the common illustration of 'the culinary hearth'), a similar instance or one in which the major term is found, MW.

Sa (to be similarly prefixed to the following): **–pakshaka**, mfn. having wings, winged, Kathās. **–pakshapātam**, ind. with partiality or devotion, devotedly, Rājat. **–paṅkaja**, mf(*ā*)n. provided with a lotus, ŚārṅgP. **–paṭaham**, ind. with the sound of a drum, Kathās. **–paṭṭī**, f. (du.) two pieces of timber at the side of a door, L. **–paṇa**, mfn. accompanied with a wager, Yājñ. **–patāka**, mfn. furnished with flags or banners, MBh.; Hariv. **–pattana**, mfn. possessing towns or cities, MW. **–pattra**, mfn. having feathers, feathered (as an arrow), ŚāṅkhŚr.; *-lekha*, mfn. having fragrant pigments, Ṛitus. **–pattraka**, mfn. together with Achyranthes Triandra, Pañcar. **–pattrā**, ind.; *-karaṇa*, n. wounding with an arrow or other feathered weapon so that the feathers enter the body (causing excessive pain), L.; *-*√*kṛi*, P. *-karoti*, to wound in the way described above, Daś. (cf. Pāṇ. v, 4, 61 and *nish-pattrā-*√*kṛi*), L.; *-kṛita*, mfn. (accord. to some also *sa-pattra-kṛita*) severely wounded (as above described), MW.; m. a deer or other animal severely wounded, ib.; *-kṛiti*, f. = *-karaṇa*, L. **–pattrita**, mfn. = *sa-pattrā-kṛita*, L. **–pátna**, °**tnī**, see s.v. **–padi**, ind. (*sa*+*pada*) at the same instant, on the spot, at once, immediately, quickly, Kāv.; VarBṛS.; Pur. &c. **–padma**, mfn. having a lotus, Ṛitus. **–padmaka**, mfn. having a l° and splendid (fr. *padmā* = *śrī*), Śiś. **–pannaga**, mfn. having serpents, MW. **–para**, n. a partic. high number, MBh. **–parākrama**, mfn. having valour, brave, bold, ib. **–parikara** and **-parikrama**, mfn. attended by a retinue, Pañcat. **–paricchada**, mf(*ā*)n. attended by a train, provided with necessaries, Mn.; MBh. &c. **–parijana**, mfn. = *-parikara*, Pañcad. **–paritosha**, mfn. possessing satisfaction, much pleased (*am*, ind.), Kāv.; Kathās. **–paribādha**, mfn. impeded, restricted, limited, Śak. **–paribṛiṇhaṇa**, mfn. (the Veda) together with (its) supplements (such as the Vedānta &c.), Mn. xii, 109. **–parivāra**, mfn. = *-parikara*, Pañcad. **–parivāha**, mfn. overflowing, brimful, Śak. **–parivyaya**, mfn. (food prepared) with condiments, Mn. vii, 127. **–pariśesha**, mfn. having a remainder, with the rest, MW. **–pariśraya** (*sá-*), mfn. with an enclosure, ŚBr. **–pariśritkam**, ind. up to the Pariśrits (q.v.), KātyŚr. **–parishatka**, mfn. surrounded by a college of disciples (as a teacher), Gobh. **–parihāram**, ind. with reserve or shyness, Śak. **–parihāsa**, mfn. with jesting, jocose, jocular, Kād. **–parṇa**, mf(*ā*)n. furnished with leaves, Hcat. **–paryāṇa**, mfn. provided with a saddle, saddled, Kād. **–parvata**, mfn. together with mountains; *-vana-druma*, mfn. with m° and forests and trees, MBh.; *-vanârṇava*, mfn. possessing m° and forests and seas (said of the earth), ib. **–parshatka**, mfn. (cf. *parishatka*) together with the court-circle, Jātakam. **–palāśa**, mf(*ā*)n. = *-parṇa*, AitBr.; GṛŚrS.; together with a Palāśa tree, MW. **–pallava**, mfn. together with shoots, having branches, ib. **–pavitra**, mf(*ā*)n. together with sacrificial grass (*-tā*, f.), KātyŚr.; Mn. **–pavitraka**, mfn. id., MW. **–paśu** (*sá-*), mfn. together with cattle, TS.; ŚBr.; connected with animal sacrifice, KātyŚr. (also °*śuka*, ib., Sch.) **–pātra**, mf(*ā*)n. together with the (necessary) vessels &c., KātyŚr.; holding the vessels &c. in the hands, ib. **–pāda**, mfn. having feet (see comp.); with a quarter, increased by one-fourth, Mn.; Rājat.; BhP.; *-pīṭha*, mfn. furnished with a footstool, MW.; *-matsya*, m. the shad-fish, Silurus, L.; *-laksha*, m. or n. one hundred thousand and a quarter of it, i.e. 125,000, Pañcat.; N. of a district (*-kshmā-pāla*, m. a king of the above district; *-śikharin*, m. N. of a mountain), Uttamac.; Inscr.; *-vandanam*, ind. 'saluting a person's feet,' respectfully, deferentially, Mālatīm. **–pāduka**, mfn. wearing shoes or sandals, R. **–pāla**, mfn. attended by a herdsman, Mn. viii, 240; together with a king or kings, BhP.; m. N. of a king, Buddh. **–piṇḍa** &c., see s.v. **–pitṛika**, mfn. along with a father or with Pitṛis (deceased ancestors), ĀśvGṛ. **–pitṛi-rājanya**, mfn. along with royal Pitṛis, ib. **–pitvá**, n. (cf. *apa-pitva* &c.) union, communion, RV. i, 109, 7. **–pidhāna**, mfn. provided with a cover or lid, MBh. **–piśāca**, mf(*ā*)n. connected with or proceeding from Piśācas (as a storm), Pāṇ. vi, 3, 80, Sch. **–pīḍa**, mfn. having pain or anguish, painful, MW. **–pītaka**, m. Luffa Foetida or another species, L.; (*ikā*), f. a large gourd or cucumber, L. **–pīti** (*sá-*), f. compotation, conviviality, drinking together, MaitrS.; VS.; m. a boon-companion, RV.; TS. **–puccha**, mfn. with the tail or extreme end, KātyŚr., Sch. **–putra**, mf(*ā*)n. having (or accompanied by) a son or children (also said of animals), ŚrS.; Mn.; MBh. &c.; adorned with child-like figures, Hariv.; *-jñāti-bāndhava*, mfn. with sons and kinsmen and relations, Nār.; *-dāra*, mfn. with son and wife, MBh. **–putraka**, mf(*ikā*)n. together with a little son, PārGṛ. **–putrin**, mfn. together with sons or children, Hariv. **–puraścaraṇa** (*sá-*), mfn. together with preparations, ŚBr. **–purīsha** (*sá-*), mf(*ā*)n. provided with stuffing or seasoning, KātyŚr.; containing fæces, ŚBr. **–purusha**, mfn. together with men or followers, PañcavBr. **–puro 'nuvākya**, mfn. together with the Puro 'nuvākyā (q.v.), ŚāṅkhŚr. **–purolāsa**, mfn. provided with the Purolāsa (applied to a partic. Ekâha), ŚāṅkhŚr. **–purohita**, mfn. accompanied by a family-priest, MBh. **–pulaka**, mfn. having bristling hairs, thrilled with joy or desire (*am*, ind.), Amar.; Gīt. **–pushpa**, mfn. having (or adorned with) flowers, flowering, Vishṇ.; Kāv.; *-bali*, mfn. filled with offerings of flowers, Ṛitus. **–pūrva**, mf(*ā*)n. along with the preceding (letter or sound), TPrāt.; having or possessed by ancestors, Rājat. **–pṛishata**, mfn. accompanied by rain, MBh. **–pṛishad-ājya**, mfn. with curdled or clotted butter, KātyŚr. **–pota**, mf(*ā*)n. having a ship or boat, Siṇhās. **–paura**, mfn. accompanied by citizens, MBh. **–paushṇa-maitra**, mfn. together with the Nakshatras Revatī and Anurādhā, VarBṛS. **–prakāraka**, mfn. containing a statement of particulars or specification, Tarkas. **–prakṛitika**, mfn. along with root or stem or base, Pat. **–pragātha**, mfn. together with the Pragātha (q.v.), ŚāṅkhŚr. **–praja**, mf(*ā*)n. = *-prajas*, Ragh.; together with the children or offspring, BhP. **–prajas**, mfn. possessing offspring, Kauś. **–prajāpatika**, mfn. together with Prajāpati, AitBr.; ĀśvGṛ. **–prajña**, mfn. endowed with understanding, MBh. **–praṇaya**, mfn. having affection, affectionate, confident, friendly, kind (*am*, ind.), MBh.; Kāv. &c. **–praṇava**, mf(*ā*)n. together with the sacred syllable Om, Vas.; Suśr. **–praṇāmam**, ind. with a bow, Śak.; Dhūrtas. **–pratigha**, mfn. having an opposite, Buddh. **–pratibandha**, mfn. attended with obstacles, Mālav. (in law said of a legacy which, if there are not direct male descendants, devolves on a collateral branch or the widow &c., Yājñ., Sch.) **–pratibha**, mfn. possessed of quick discernment or presence of mind, R.; Kathās. **–pratibhaya**, mfn. dangerous, uncertain (*-tā*, f.), Jātakam. **–pratishṭha** (*sá-*), mfn. together with the receptacle, ŚBr. **–pratikāśa**, mfn. together with the reflection, ĀśvGṛ. **–pratīksham**, ind. expectantly, R. **–pratīvāpa**, mfn. with an admixture, Suśr. **–pratīśa**, mfn. respectful, Divyâv. **–pratoda**, mfn. together with a goad, ŚāṅkhŚr. **–pratyabhijñam**, ind. with recognition, Mālatīm. **–pratyaya**, mf(*ā*)n. having trust or confidence, trusting in (loc.), Kāv.; Kathās.; certain, secure, sure (with *vṛitti*, f. 'sure means of subsistence'), MBh.; = next, MW. **–pratyayaka**, mfn. together with a suffix, Pat. **–pratyādhāna** (*sá-*), mfn. together with (its) repository, ŚBr. **–pratyāśam**, ind. hopefully, expectantly, Vikr. **–pratha**, mfn. (prob. for next) = *sabhya*, TBr. (Sch.); m. N. of the author of RV. x, 181, 2 (having the patr. Bhāradvāja). **–prathas** (*sá-* or *sa-práthas*), mfn. extensive, wide, RV.; VS.; effective or sounding or shining far and wide, ib.; m. N. of Vishṇu, MW.; *-tama*, mfn. (superl.) very extensive or large, ib. **–prapañca**, mfn. with all belonging thereto or connected therewith, BhP. **–prabha**, mfn. having the same lustre or appearance (*-tva*, n.), MBh.; VarBṛS.; possessing splendour, brilliant, MW. **–prabhāva**, mf(*ā*)n. possessing power or might, powerful, Kathās. **–prabhṛiti**, mfn. beginning in the same way; m. the same or a like beginning, PañcavBr.; ŚāṅkhBr. (cf. Pāṇ. vi, 3, 84). **–pramāṇa**, mf(*ā*)n. having proof or evidence, authentic, MW.; having the law on one's side, having a right or title, entitled, R. **–pramāda**, mfn. heedless, inattentive, off one's guard, Kāv. **–pramodanam** or °**dam**, ind. joyfully, Dhūrtas. **–prayoga-nivartana**, mfn. along with the (secret spells for) using and restraining (certain weapons), R. **–prayoga-rahasya**, mfn. possessing secret spells for (their) use (said of magical weapons which are not wielded manually but by repetition of spells), ib. **–pravargya**, mfn. together with the Pravargya (q.v.), KātyŚr. **–pravāda**, mfn. together with the derivative case forms, RPrāt. **—praśrayam**, ind. affectionately, respectfully, Kāv.; Kathās.; Pañcat. **—prasava**, mf(*ā*)n. having progeny (*-tva*, n.), Kāv.; Sāh.; pregnant, with child, Dhūrtas. **—prasāda**, mfn. accompanied with favour or kindness, propitious, gracious (*am*, ind.), Kād.; Pañcat.; Kathās.; *-rādhā-krishṇa-pratishṭhā-vidhi*, m. N. of wk. **—prasveda**, mfn. having perspiration, sweating, MBh. **—prahāsam**, ind. with laughter, bursting into a laugh, Mālav. **—prâṇa** (*sá-*), mfn. having breath, living, TS.; R.; BhP. **—prâya**, mfn. like, similar (ifc.), Lāṭy. **—pru** (*sá-*), mfn. (said to =) attended by lightning (cf. √*pru*), AitĀr. **—prema**, mf(*ā*)n. having love, affectionate, Kathās. **—preman**, mfn. rejoicing in (loc.), Rājat. **—prêshya**, mfn. attended by servants, MBh. **—praisha**, mfn. together with the Praisha (q. v.), ŚrS. **—psará**, mfn. (of doubtful meaning) either 'doing injury' (= *hiṇsaka*, Sāy.), or 'having the same form' (= *samāna-rūpa*, cf. 2. *psu*, p. 715), or (accord. to others) 'eating the same food' (cf. *psaras*), or 'inspiring awe' (said of the Maruts), RV. i, 68, 9.

सपत्न *sa-pátna*, m. (fr. 1. *sa-pátnī* below) a rival, adversary, enemy, RV. &c. &c. **—kárśana**, mfn. harassing rivals, AV. **—ksháyaṇa**, mf(*ī*)n. destroying rivals, AV.; TS.; Kauś. **—kshit**, mfn. id., VS. **—ghnī**, see *-hán*. **—cā́tana**, mfn. scaring away rivals, AV. **—ja**, mfn. produced by r°s, Ragh. **—jit**, mfn. conquering r°s, MBh.; m. N. of a son of Kṛishṇa and Su-dattā, Hariv. **—tā**, f. rivalry, enmity, MBh. **—túr**, mfn. (nom. *-tū́ḥ*) overcoming rivals, TBr. **—tva**, n. = *-tā*, Hariv. **—dámbhana**, mfn. injuring rivals, VS.; AV. **—dūshaṇa**, mfn. destroying r°s, ŚāṅkhGṛ. **—nāśa**, m. destruction of a rival, MBh. **—bala-sūdana**, mfn. destroying a rival's power, ib. **—vṛiddhi**, f. increase or power of rivals, R. **—śrī**, f. the fortune or triumph of a r°, MBh. **—sāda**, w. r. for next. **—sāhá**, mf(*ī*)n. = *-túr*, VS.; TS.; Hariv. **—hán**, mf(*ghnī*)n. slaying r°s, RV.; ŚBr.; MBh.

Sapatnâri, m. Bambusa Spinosa, L.

1. **Sa-pátnī**, f. (once in R. °*tni*) a woman who has the same husband with another woman (Pāṇ. iv, 1, 35) or whose husband has other wives, a fellow-wife or mistress, female rival, RV. &c. &c. **—jana**, m. fellow-wives (collectively), Śak. **—tas**, ind. from a rival wife, MW. **—tva**, n. the state of a woman whose husband has other wives, MBh. **—duhitṛi**, f. the daughter of a rival wife, MW. **—putra**, m. the son of a rival w°, ib. **—°śa** (°*nīśa*), m. N. of Śiva, Hariv. **—spardhā**, f. the rivalry among co-wives, Rājat.

2. **Sa-patnī**, mfn. = next, R.

Sa-patnīka, mfn. accompanied with a wife or wives, ŚrS.; Ragh.; Kathās.

Sapatnī-kṛita, mfn. made a rival, Cat.

Sapatnya, w. r. for *sāp*° (q. v.)

सपिण्ड *sa-piṇḍa*, m. 'having the same Piṇḍa,' a kinsman connected by the offering of the Piṇḍa (q. v.) to certain deceased ancestors at the Śrāddha (q. v.; the kinship is through six generations in an ascending and descending line, or through a man's father, father's father, father's grandfather; mother, mother's father, mother's grandfather; son, son's son, son's grandson; daughter, daughter's son &c.; and also includes father's mother, father's grandmother &c., also father's brothers and sisters, mother's brothers and sisters, and several others), GṛŚrS.; Gaut.; Mn. v, 60; MBh. &c. (RTL. 285; 286; IW. 248; 266). **—tā**, f. the condition of being a Sapiṇḍa, Sapiṇḍaship, Mn. v, 60. **—nirṇaya**, m. N. of wk.

Sapiṇḍana, n. investing with the relationship of a Sapiṇḍa, Cat. **—prayoga**, m. N. of wk.

Sapiṇḍaya, Nom. P. °*yati*, to invest a person with the rights of a Sapiṇḍa, L.; to perform the Śrāddha with Sapiṇḍas (at the end of a full year after the death of a relative), L.

Sapiṇḍī, in comp. for *sapiṇḍa*. **—karaṇa**, n. = *sapiṇḍana*, ŚāṅkhGṛ.; Yājñ. &c.; N. of wk. (also °*ṇa-khaṇḍana*, n., °*ṇānta-karman*, n., and °*ṇān-vashṭakā*, f.) **—√kṛi**, P. *-karoti* = *-piṇḍaya*, Dattakac. **—kṛita**, mfn. invested with the relationship of a Sapiṇḍa, W. **—kramaṇa**, w. r. for *-karaṇa*.

सप्तन् *saptán*, sg. and pl. (nom. acc. *saptá*; instr. °*tábhis*; dat. abl. °*tábhyas*; gen. °*tānā́m*; loc. °*tásu*) seven (a favourite number with the Hindūs, and regarded as sacred, often used to express an indefinite plurality [in the same manner as 'three,' by which it is sometimes multiplied]; hence 7 Mātṛis, 7 streams, 7 oceans, 7 cities [RV. i, 63, 7], 7 divisions of the world, 7 ranges of mountains, 7 Ṛishis, 7 Vipras [RV. i, 62, 4], 7 Ādityas, 7 Dānavas, 7 horses of the Sun, 7 flames of fire, 7 Yonis of fire, 7 steps round the fire at marriage, 7 Samidhs, 7 tones, 7 sacrificial rites, 7 Maryādās, thrice 7 Padāni or mystical steps to heaven [RV. i, 72, 6], thrice 7 cows &c.), RV. &c. &c. [Cf. Zend *hapta*; Gk. ἑπτά; Lat. *septem*; Lith. *septynì*; Slav. *sedmĭ*; Goth. *sibun*; Germ. *sieben*; Eng. *seven*.]

Sapta, ifc. (cf. *tri-shaptá*, *tri-saptá*) and in comp. for *saptán*, seven; mfn. = °*tamá*, L.; m. N. of Vishṇu, Vishṇ. iii, 44 (where *sapta mahā-bhāga* may be two words; cf. *sapta-mahā-bh*°). **—ṛishi**, m. pl. = *saptarshí*, RV.; ŚBr. &c.; N. of the authors of the hymn RV. ix, 107, Anukr.; *-vat* (°*shí-*), mfn. attended by the 7 Ṛishis, AV. **—ṛishīṇa**, mfn. (fr. *-ṛishi*), Nir. **—kathā-maya**, mf(*ī*)n. consisting of 7 tales, Kathās. **—kapāla** (*saptá-*), mfn. being in or on 7 dishes or receptacles, ŚBr. **—karṇa**, m. N. of a man, TĀr. **—kumārikâvadāna**, n. the legend of the 7 maids, Buddh. **—kṛit**, m. N. of a being reckoned among the Viśve Devāḥ, MBh.; (*-kṛid*)-*bhava-parama*, m. a Śrāvaka in a partic. stage of progress, L. **—kṛitvas**, ind. 7 times, Pur.; VarBṛS. **—koṇa**, mfn. septangular, MW. **—gaṅga**, n. N. of a place, MBh.; (*am*), ind., Pāṇ. ii, 1, 20, Sch. **—gaṇa** (°*tá-*), mfn. consisting of 7 troops, TS.; TBr. **—gu** (°*tá-*), mfn. possessing 7 oxen or cows, driving 7 oxen; m. N. of an Āṅgirasa (author of the hymn RV. x, 47), Anukr. **—guṇa**, mf(*ā*)n. sevenfold, Jyot.; Kathās. **—gṛidhrá**, m. pl. the 7 vultures (?), AV. viii, 9, 18. **—go-dāvara**, n. N. of a place (*am*, ind., Pāṇ. ii, 1, 20, Sch.), MBh.; (*ī*), f. N. of a river, BhP. **—grantha-nibarhaṇa śaiva-vaishṇava-vicāra**, m., **-granthī**, f. N. of wks. **—grahī**, f. the meeting of the 7 planets under one sign, MW. **—cakra** (°*tá-*), mfn. having 7 wheels, RV. **—catvāriṇśa**, mfn. the 47th, ch. of MBh. and R. **—catvāriṇśat** (°*tá-*), f. 47, ŚBr. **—caru**, n. (nom. °*rum*?) N. of a place, MBh. **—citika** (°*tá-*), mfn. piled up in 7 layers, ŚBr. **—cchada**, m. '7-leaved,' a kind of tree, MW.; Alstonia Scholaris, MBh.; Kāv.; Suśr.; (*ā*), f. id., MW. **—cchandas**, mfn. containing 7 metres, SaṃhUp. **—cchidra**, mf(*ā*)n. having 7 holes, Kauś. **—jana**, m. pl. a collective N. of 7 Munis, R. **—jāni** or **-jāmi**, mfn. (Ved.; prob.) having 7 brothers or sisters, MW. **—jihva**, mfn. 7-tongued, MBh.; m. N. of Agni or fire (the 7 tongues of fire have all names, e.g. *kālī*, *karālī*, *mano-javā*, *su-lohitā*, *su-dhūmra-varṇā*, *ugrā* or *sphuliṅginī*, *pradīptā*, and these names vary accord. to the partic. rite in which fire is used, see *hiraṇyā*, *su-varṇā*, *su-prabhā* &c.), VarBṛS.; BhP.; Śiś., Sch. **—jvāla**, m. '7-flamed,' fire, L. **—tanti**, mfn. 7-stringed, ŚBr., Sch.; KātyŚr., Sch. **—tantu** (°*tá-*), mfn. '7-threaded,' consisting of 7 parts (as a sacrifice), RV.; MBh.; m. a sacrifice, offering, MBh.; Śiś.; BhP. &c. **—tantra**, mf(*ī*)n. 7-stringed, MBh.; Mṛicch. **—triṇśa**, mfn. the 37th, ch. of MBh. and R. **—triṇśat**, f. 37 (with a noun in apposition), MBh.; Rājat.; Pañcar.; (°*śad*)-*rātra*, n. a partic. ceremony, ŚrS. **—triṇśati**, f. 37 (with the noun in apposition), Rājat. **—daśá**, mf(*ī*)n. the 17th, ŚBr.; ĀśvGṛ.; VarBṛS. &c.; connected with 17, plus 17, ŚBr.; consisting of 17, TS.; VS.; Br. &c.; connected with or analogous to a Stoma which has 17 parts, TBr.; VS.; ĀśvŚr.; having 17 attributes (said of a *kula* or family), MW.; pl. 17 (= *-daśan*), MBh.; m. (scil. *stoma*) a Stoma having 17 parts, VS.; TS.; Br.; ĀśvŚr.; N. of a collection of hymns, MW.; (*am*), n. a group or collection of 17, ŚrS.; N. of a Sāman, VP.; *-vat* (°*śá-*), mfn. connected with the above kind of Stoma, ŚBr.; *-vartani* (°*śá-*), mfn. forming the course for the above St°, TS.; *-stoma*, mfn. having the above St°, ŚāṅkhŚr.; °*śā́bhiklṛipta*, mfn. corresponding to the above St°, ŚBr. **—daśaka**, mfn. consisting of 17 (*saṃkhyāne* °*śaka*, 'supposing the number to be 17'), BhP. **—daśan** (°*tá-*), mfn. pl. (nom. acc. °*śa*) 17, TS.; VS.; Br. &c.; °*śa-cchadi* (°*tá-*), mfn. having 17 roofs, TS.; °*śa-tā*, f. the being 17 in number, KātyŚr.; °*śa-dhā*, ind. 17-fold, ŚBr.; Saṃkhyak.; °*śa-rātrá*, m. n. a partic. sacrificial performance lasting 17 days, TS.; Maś.; °*śa-rcá* (°*śa-ṛic*), mfn. consisting of 17 verses; n. a hymn c° of 17 verses, AV.; °*śa-vidha*, mfn. 17-fold, ŚāṅkhŚr.; °*śa-śarāva* (°*tá-*), mfn. having 17 Śarāvas (a partic. measure), Br.; °*śa-sāmidhenīka*, mfn. having 17 Sāmidhenī verses, ŚāṅkhBr.; ĀpŚr.; °*śâkshara* (°*tá-*), mfn. having 17 syllables, VS.; °*śāra*, mfn. having 17 spokes, Lāṭy.; °*śāratni* (°*tá-*), mfn. 17 cubits or ells in length (°*tni-tā*, f., Jaim., Sch.), ŚBr. **—daśama**, mfn. the 17th, Cat. **—daśin**, mfn. possessing 17, having 17 (Stotras), PañcavBr. **—dina** or **-divasa**, (ibc.) 7 days, a week, VarBṛS. **—dīdhiti**, m. 'having 7 rays of light,' fire, L. **—dvārâvakīrṇa**, mfn. scattered over or dominated or affected by the 7 gates (i. e. accord. to Kull., 'by the 5 organs of sense, the mind and the intellect,' or 'by this world and the 3 above and the 3 below it'), Mn. vi, 48. **—dvīpa**, (ibc.) the 7 divisions of the earth, the whole earth, Pur.; mf(*ā*)n. consisting of 7 Dvīpas (the earth), MBh.; Hariv.; Śak. &c.; (*ā*), f. N. of the earth, MW.; (°*pa*)-*dharā-pati*, m. the lord of the whole earth, Cat.; *-pati*, m. 'lord of the 7 Dv°,' id., MW.; *-vat*, mfn. consisting of 7 Dv° (the earth), NṛisUp.; Pur.; Siṃhās.; (*atī*), f. the whole earth (*-pati*, m. lord of the whole e°), BhP. **—dhātu** (°*tá-*), mf(*u*)n. consisting of 7, 7-fold, RV.; cons° of 7 constituent elements (as the body), GarbhUp.; m. N. of one of the ten horses of the Moon, L.; pl. the 7 constit° el° of the body (viz. chyle, blood, flesh, fat, bone, marrow, and semen), W.; *maya*, mf(*ī*)n made of 7 various metals or elements, Hcat.; *-varūthaka*, mfn. having the 7 constit° el° of the body for a chariot-guard, BhP. **—dhātuka**, mfn. consisting of 7 elements (see prec.), GarbhUp. **—dhānya**, n. sg. or pl. the 7 kinds of grain, Hcat.; *-maya*, mf(*ī*)n. made of the 7 kinds of grain, ib. **—dhāra**, n. (Cat.) or **-dhārā-tīrtha**, n. (MW.) N. of a Tīrtha. **—nalī**, f. bird-lime, Kāv. **—navata**, mfn. the 97th, Rājat.; ch. of MBh. **—navati**, f. 97, MBh.; *-tama*, mfn. the 97th, ch. of R. **—nāḍika**, n. (with *cakra*) = next, L. **—nāḍī-cakra**, n. an astrological diagram supposed to foretell rain (it consists of 7 serpentine lines marked with the names of the Nakshatras and planets), L. **—nāman** (°*tá-*), mfn. having 7 names, RV. **—nāmā**, f. Polanisia Icosandra, L. **—nidhana**, n. N. of a Sāman, ĀrshBr. **—pañcāśa**, mfn. the 57th, ch. of MBh. and R. **—pañcāśat**, f. 57, MBh.; Nir. **—pattra**, mfn. 7-leaved, L.; drawn by 7 horses, Vās.; m. Alstonia Scholaris, ib.; a kind of jasmine, L.; the sun, Harav. **—pad** (°*tá-*), mf(*adī*)n. making 7 steps (round the sacred fire for the conclusion of the marriage ceremony or for the ratification of a treaty), TS.; GṛS.; Mn., Sch.; ratified, sealed, MBh.; sufficient for all wants, RV. **—pada** (°*tá-*), mf(*ā*)n. making the 7 steps (described above), AV.; PārGṛ.; consisting of 7 Pādas, TS.; Br. &c.; (*ī*), f. the 7 steps (round the sacred fire at the marriage ceremony), Kṛishis.; RTL. 364, 380, 3; °*dârtha-candrikā*, f., °*dârtha-nirūpaṇa*, n., °*dârthī*, f., °*dârthī-ṭīkā*, f., °*dârthī-vyākhyā*, f. N. of wks.; °*dī-karaṇa*, n. (Mn. ix, 71, 72, Sch.) or *-gamana*, n. (MW.) the walking together round the nuptial fire in 7 steps (see above). **—parāka**, m. a kind of penance, RāmatUp. **—parṇa**, mfn. 7-leaved, W.; m. Alstonia Scholaris, MBh.; Hariv.; R. &c.; (*ī*), f. Mimosa Pudica, Suśr.; n. the flower of Alst° Sch°, ŚārṅgP.; a sort of sweetmeat, L. **—parṇaka**, m. Alstonia Scholaris, Pañcar. **—parvata-māhātmya**, n. N. of wk. **—palāśa**, mf(*ī*)n. consisting of 7 leaves, Kauś.; m. Alstonia Scholaris, L. **—pāka-yajña-bhāshya**, n., **-pāka-yajña-śesha**, **-pāka-saṃsthā-vidhi**, m. N. of wks. **—pātāla**, n. the 7 Pātālas or regions under the earth (viz. *Atala*, *Vit*°, *Sut*°, *Rasāt*°, *Talāt*°, *Mahāt*° and *Pātāla*, RTL. 102), Rājat. **—putra** (°*tá-*), mfn. having 7 sons or 7 children, RV.; *-sū*, f. the mother of 7 sons or ch°, L. **—purushá**, mfn. consisting of 7 Purushas or lengths of a man, ŚBr. **—prakṛiti**, f. pl. the 7 constituent parts of a kingdom (viz. the king, his ministers, ally, territory, fortress, army, and treasury, see *prak*°), W. **—bāhya**, n. N. of the kingdom of Bālhika, Hariv. **—buddha-stotra**, n. N. of a Stotra. **—budhna** (°*tá-*), mfn. having 7 floors or bases, RV. **—bodhy-aṅga-kusumâḍhya**, m. N. of Buddha, Divyâv. **—bhaṅgan**, m. N. of the Jainas, VP.; °*gi-naya*, m. (with Jainas) the method of the 7 formulas of sceptical reasoning (each beginning with the word *syāt*, 'perhaps,' cf. *bhaṅga*), Sarvad. **—bhaṅgī-taraṃgiṇī**, f. N. of wk. **—bhaṅgī-naya**, m. = °*gi-naya*, Bādar., Sch.; N. of wk. **—bhadra**, m. Acacia Sirissa, L. **—bhuvana**, n. pl. the 7 worlds (one above the other, see *loka*), MW. **—bhūma**, mfn. having 7 stories, 7 st° high, HPariś. **—bhūmi**, f. = *rasā-tala*, R. (Sch.); *-maya*, mf(*ī*)n. = *-bhūma*, Siṃhās. **—bhūmika**, mfn. id., Pañcat. (°*kā-prā-*

sāda, w.r.); °*kā-vicāra,* m. N. of wk. **-bhauma,** mfn. = *-bhūma,* MBh.; R. **-maṅgala-māhâtmya,** n., **-maṭhâmnāya-daśa-nāmâbhidhāna,** n., **-maṭhâmnāyika,** N. of wks. **-mantra,** m. fire, L. **-marīci,** mfn. 7-rayed; m. fire, VarBṛS. **-mahā-bhāga,** m. N. of Vishṇu, MBh. (accord. to Nīlak. *saptabhir gāyatry-ādibhir arpaṇīyāḥ saptâiva mahānto yajña-bhāgā yasya;* cf. *saptan*). **-mātṛi** (°*tá-*), mfn. having 7 mothers, RV.; f. collective N. of the 7 mothers, L. **-mānusha** (°*tá-*), mfn. dwelling among the 7 races of mankind, present among all, RV. **-mārga,** m. N. of a man, Virac. **-māsya,** mfn. (a child) of 7 months, Kāṭh. **-mushṭika,** m. a partic. mixture used as a remedy for fever, ŚārṅgS. **-mūrti-maya,** mf(*ī*)n. having 7 forms, Siṃhâs. **-mṛittikā,** f. pl. 7 earths collected from 7 places and used in certain solemn rites, MW. **-yama,** mfn. with or having 7 tones or pitches of the voice, RPrāt. **-yojanī,** f. a distance or extent of 7 Yojanas, Rājat. **-rakta,** n. sg. the 7 red-coloured parts of the body (viz. palms of hands, soles of feet, nails, eye-corners, tongue, palate, lips), L. **-ratna,** n. N. of various wks.; *-padma-vikārin,* m. N. of a Buddha, Buddh. (v.l. *-padma-vikrānta-gāmin*); *-maya,* mf(*ī*)n. consisting of 7 gems, Kāraṇḍ. **-raśmi** (°*tá-*), mfn. 7-roped, RV.; AV.; (perhaps) 7-tongued, ib.; 7-rayed, MW.; m. N. of Agni, RV. **-rātra,** n. a period of 7 nights (or days), a week, Mn.; MBh.; R. &c.; (°*trá*), m. a partic. Ahīna, AV.; ŚrS.; Maś.; n. pl. N. of various Vaishṇava sacred books. **-rātraka,** mf(*ikā*)n. lasting 7 days, Hariv. **-rātrika** (?), mfn. id., MW.; n. a period of 7 nights or days, IndSt. **-rāva,** m. N. of a son of Garuḍa, MBh. (v.l. *-vāra*). **-rāśika,** the rule of proportion with 7 terms, Col. **-ruci,** mfn. 7-rayed; m. fire, Śiś. **-rcá** (°*ta + ṛic*), mfn. having 7 verses; n. a hymn of 7 v°s, Vait. **-rshí** (°*ta-ṛishí*), m. pl. the 7 Ṛishis, q.v.; (in astron.) the 7 stars of the constellation Ursa Major (*-pūtā dik,* 'the northern quarter of the sky'); sg. one of the 7 Ṛishis, MBh.; *-kuṇḍa,* n. pl. N. of bathing-places sacred to the 7 Ṛishis, ib.; *-cāra,* m. N. of the 13th Adhyāya of VarBṛS. and of another astron. wk.; *-ja,* m. the planet Jupiter, L.; *-tā,* f. the condition of the 7 Ṛishis, Hariv.; *-mat,* mfn., Pat.; *-mata,* n. N. of various wks.; *-loka,* m. the world of the 7 Ṛishis, Cat.; *-stotra,* n., *-smṛiti,* f., *-smṛiti-saṃgraha,* m.; °*shîśvara-māhâtmya,* n. N. of wks. **-rshika** (°*ta-ṛish°*), = *-rshi* (ibc.), Hariv. **-lakshaṇa,** n. N. of various wks.; *-bhāshya,* n. N. of wk.; *-maya,* mf(*ī*)n. having 7 characteristic marks, Siṃhâs. **-loka,** m. pl. the 7 worlds; *-maya,* mf(*ī*)n. constituting the 7 worlds (said of Vishṇu), AgP. **-lokī,** f. the 7 divisions of the world, the whole earth, Prasannar. **-vat,** mfn. containing the word *saptan;* (*atī*), f. a verse c° the word *saptam,* ĀpŚr.; N. of a river, BhP. **-vadhri** (°*tá-*), mfn. fettered by 7 thongs (applied to the soul), BhP.; m. N. of an Ātreya (protected by the Aśvins and author of the hymns RV. v, 78, viii, 62), RV.; AV. **-varūtha,** mfn. having 7 guards (said of a chariot, see *var°*), BhP. **-varga,** m. a group of 7, Nidānas. **-varman,** m. N. of a grammarian, Buddh. **-varsha,** mf(*ā*)n. 7 years old, ŚāṅkhGṛ., Sch. **-vādin,** m. N. of the Jainas (cf. *-bhaṅgin*), VP. **-vāra,** m. N. of one of Garuḍa's sons, MBh. (v.l. *-rāva*). **-vārshika,** mf(*ī*)n. 7 years old, Pañcat.; Siṃhâs. **-viṇśá,** mfn. the 27th, Br.; consisting of 27, CūlUp. **-viṇśaka,** mfn. id., RPrāt. **-viṇśat** (acc. °*śat*), 27, VP. **-viṇśati** (°*tá-*), f. 27 (with a noun in apposition or gen. or comp.), VS.; ŚBr.; Mn. &c.; *-tama,* mfn. the 27th, KātyŚr., Sch.; *-rātra,* n. N. of a Sattra, KātyŚr.; *-śata,* n. pl. 127, ŚāṅkhBr.; AitĀr.; *-sādhu-lakshaṇa,* n. N. of wk. **-viṇśatika,** mfn. consisting of 27, MārkP. **-viṇśatima,** mfn. the 27th, Cat. **-viṇsin,** mfn. consisting of 27, Lāṭy.; Nidānas. **-vidāru,** m. a partic. kind of tree, Col. **-vidha** (°*tá-*), mf(*ā*)n. 7-fold, of 7 kinds, ŚBr.; MaitrUp.; Śulbas. &c. (°*dhā-tā,* f., ŚBr.) **-vibhakti-nirṇaya,** m. N. of wk. **-vṛishá,** mfn. possessing 7 bulls, AV. **-velam,** ind. 7 times, ŚārṅgS. **-vyasana-kathā,** f., **-śakti-stotra,** n. N. of wks. **-śata,** mfn. 700 (see *ardha-sapta-s°*); n. 700; 107 (= *saptâdhikam śatam*), MW.; (*ī*), f. 700, MBh.; the aggregate of 700, MW.; a collection of 700 verses, ib.; N. of various wks. (cf. *-śataka*); (°*tī*)*-kalpa,* m., *-kavaca-vivaraṇa,* n., *-kāvya,* n., *-guptavatī-vyākhyā,* f., *-chāyā,* f., *-japârtha-nyāsa-dhyāna,* n., *-daṇśôddhāra,* m., *-dhyāna,* n., *-nyāsa,* m., *-prayoga-paṭala,* *-bīja-mantra-vidhāna,* n., *-bhāshya,* n., *-mantra-vibhāga,* m., *-mantra-homa-vidhāna,* n., *-māhātmya,* n., *-mūla,* n., *-vidhāna,* n., *-vivṛiti,* f., *-vyākhyā,* f., *-stotra,* n.; °*ty-utkīlana,* n. N. of wks. **-śataka,** n. N. of a collection of 700 erotic verses in Prākrit by Hāla (q.v.); (*ikā*), f. the aggregate of 700, MW.; N. of wk.; °*tikā-vidhi,* m. N. of wk. **-śapha** (°*tá-*), mf(*ā*)n. 7-hoofed, MaitrS.; ĀpŚr. **-śalāka,** m. (MW.) or °**ka-cakra,** n. (L.) a kind of astrological diagram marked with twice 7 lines crossing each other at right angles (it is used for indicating auspicious days for marriages); °*kra-vidhi,* m. N. of wk. **-śāli-vaṭī,** f. a kind of mercurial pill used as a remedy for syphilis, Bhpr. **-śiras,** mfn. 7-headed, R. **-śirā,** see *-sirā.* **-śiva** (°*tá-*), mf(*ā*)n. blessing the 7 (worlds), RV. i, 141, 2 (Sāy.); (*ā*), f. a kind of plant (= *nāga-vallī*), ib. **-śīrsha,** mfn. 7-headed, MBh.; N. of Vishṇu (interpreted in different ways), Vishṇ. **-śīrshan** (°*tá-*), mf(*shṇī*)n. 7-headed, RV. **-śrotas,** w.r. for *-srotas.* **-ślokī,** f. (also with *gītā*), N. of wk.; *-bhāgavata,* n., *-rāmâyaṇa,* n., *-vivaraṇa,* n. N. of wks. or parts of wks. **-shashṭa,** mfn. the 67th, MBh. **-shashṭi,** f. 67 (*-śata,* n. pl.; *-sahasra,* n. pl.), Jyot.; MārkP.; *-tama,* mfn. the 67th, R.; *-bhāga,* m. the 67th part, IndSt. **-saṃsthā,** f., **-saṃsthā-prayoga,** m., **-saṃsthāna,** n., **-saṃkhyā,** f. N. of wks. **-saṃkhyāka,** mfn. 7 in number, amounting to 7, MW. **-saptaka,** mfn. consisting of seven times seven or 49, Cat.; n. 7 × 7 (= 49); *-vettṛi,* m. one who knows 7 × 7 sciences, R. **-saptata,** mfn. the 77th, Rājat. **-saptati,** f. 77 (*vatsare °ptatau,* 'in the 77th year,' Rājat.), Caraṇ.; VarBṛS.; *-tama,* mfn. the 77th, ch. of R. **-sapti,** mfn. having 7 horses; m. N. of the Sun (cf. *saptâśva*), MBh.; Kāv. &c. **-saptin,** mfn. each consisting of 7, TāṇḍyaBr. **-sama,** see *prācya-sapta-s°.* **-samādhi-parishkāra-dāyaka,** m. N. of Buddha, Divyâv. **-samudra-vat,** mfn. surrounded by the 7 oceans, BhP. **-samudrânta,** mf(*ā*)n. extending to the 7 oceans (the earth), R. **-sāgara,** n. N. of a Liṅga, Kāśīkh.; *-dāna,* n. 'gift of the 7 oceans,' a partic. valuable gift (represented by 7 vases with 7 different contents), Cat.; *-prādānikā,* f., *-mahādāna-prayoga,* m., *-māhātmya,* n. N. of wks. or chs. of wks.; *-mekhala,* mf(*ā*)n. girded by the 7 oceans (the earth), NṛisUp.; *-vidhi,* m. = °*ra-dāna,* Cat. **-sāgaraka,** n. = °*ra-dāna,* Hcat. **-sārasvata,** n. N. of a Tīrtha, MBh. **-sirā,** f. betel, L. (w.r. *-śirā*). **-sū,** f. the mother of 7 children, L. **-sūtra,** n., **-sūtra-saṃnyāsa-paddhati,** f., **-soma-saṃsthā-paddhati,** f., **-stava,** m., **-sthala-māhātmya,** n. N. of wks. **-spardhā,** f. N. of a river, R. **-srotas,** n. N. of a Tīrtha, BhP. (w.r. *-śrotas*); (°*to*)*-māhātmya,* n. N. of wk. **-svasṛi** (*saptá-*), mf(*ṛi*)n. having 7 sisters, RV.; Nir. **-ha,** n. N. of a Sāman (also with *Jamad-agnes*), Br. **-hán,** mfn. slaying 7, RV. **-haya,** m. = *saptâśva,* Kāśīkh. **-hasta,** mfn. having 7 hands, W.; measuring 7 cubits, ib. **-hotṛi** (°*tá-*), mfn. having 7 sacrificial priests, RV.; VS.; AV. &c.; m. pl. N. of partic. Mantras, TBr. **-hautra,** n., **-hautra-prayoga,** m., **-hautra-sūci,** f. N. of wks. **Saptâṇśu,** mfn. having 7 rays, MW.; *-puṃgava,* m. 'eminent with 7 rays of light,' the planet Saturn, L. **Saptâkshara,** mf(*ī*)n. containing 7 syllables, MaitrS.; Pañcar.; m. a word or a Pāda which contains 7 s°s, MW. **Saptâgāram,** ind. in 7 houses, Cat. **Saptâgārika,** mfn. taking place in 7 houses, Vishṇ. **Saptâṅga,** mfn. consisting of 7 members or parts, Up.; Mn. &c. **Saptâcala-dāna-paddhati,** f. N. of wk. **Saptâtman,** mfn. having 7 essences, NṛisUp.; m. N. of Brahman, MW. **Saptâdri,** m. '7 mountains,' N. of m°, Inscr. **Saptâmraka,** n. N. of a temple near Vaiśālī, Divyâv. **Saptârci,** m. fire (= next), R.; MārkP. **Saptârcis,** mfn. 7-rayed, 7-flamed, L.; evil-eyed, L.; m. N. of Agni or fire, MBh.; Ragh.; VarBṛS. &c.; of the planet Saturn, VP.; a partic. plant (= *citraka*), MW. **Saptârṇava,** (ibc.) the 7 oceans (*-jale-śaya,* mfn.), Ragh.; mf(*ā*)n. surrounded with 7 oceans, BhP. **Saptā-viṇśati,** f. (m.c. or incorrectly) = *sapta-v°* (acc. °*ti*), Hariv.; VarBṛS. **Saptâśīta,** mfn. the 87th, L. **Saptâśīti,** f. 87, L.; *-tama,* mfn. the 87th, L.; *-śloka-sūtra,* n. N. of wk. **Saptâśra,** mfn. septangular, Hcat. (w.r. °*tāsra*); m. n. a heptagon (also spelt °*tâsra*), MW. **Saptâśva,** mfn. having 7 horses, RV.; m. the sun (the 7 horses symbolizing the 7 days of the week), Kāśīkh.; *-vāhana,* m. 'borne by 7 horses,' ib. **Saptâshṭan,** mfn. pl. 7 or 8 (°*ṭa,* ibc., MBh.; R.), Hcat. **Saptâsthita,** mfn. furnished with 7 (spikes &c.), TāṇḍyaBr.; (*ā*), f. N. of a Vishṭuti, ib., Sch. **Saptâsya,** mfn. 7-mouthed, RV.; having 7 openings, ib. **Saptâsra,** see °*tâśra.* **Saptâhá,** m. (ifc. f. *ā*) 7 days; a sacrificial performance lasting 7 days, Br.; KātyŚr.; Mn. &c. **Saptâhvā,** f. a kind of plant (= *saptalā*), Suśr. **Saptôttara,** mfn. having 7 in addition (e.g. °*raṃ śatam,* 100 + 7 i.e. 107), Yājñ. **Saptôtsada,** mfn. N. of a village, Divyâv. **Saptôtsāda,** mfn. having 7 prominent parts on the body, Buddh.; *-tā,* f. (one of the 32 signs of perfection of a Buddha), Dharmas. 83. **Saptônā,** f. (scil. *viṇśati,* 20 being the normal number of verses in a Sûkta) '20 − 7 i.e. 13,' Sāy.

Saptaka, mfn. consisting of 7 (*catvāraḥ saptakāḥ,* 'cons° of 4 × 7 i.e. 28,' Hariv.; *sapta saptakāḥ* or *saptakāḥ sapta,* '7 × 7 i.e. 49,' ib.; R.), RPrāt.; Mn.; MBh. &c.; the 7th, W.; m. (Car.) or n. (Divyâv.) a week; (*ī*), f. a woman's girdle, L.; n. (ifc. f. *ikā*) a collection or aggregate of 7, Mn.; Suśr.; Kathās. &c.

Saptata, mfn. the 70th (only used after another numeral; see *eka-s°, dvā-s°, tri-s°* &c., and cf. Pāṇ. v, 2, 58).

Saptátaya, mf(*ī*)n. consisting of 7 parts, ŚBr.; ĀpŚr.

Saptatí, f. 70 (with the counted noun in apposition or in gen. pl. or ibc. or ifc.), RV.; AV.; ŚrS. &c.; 70 years, Mn.; Suśr.; N. of wk. (= *sāṃkhya-kārikā*); du. 2 seventies, W.; pl. many sev°, ib. **-tama,** mfn. the 70th, ch. of MBh. and R. **-ratna-mālikā,** f. N. of wk. **-saṃkhyāka,** mfn. amounting to 70, Hariv. **-sambandha,** m. a collection of 70 tales, Śukas. **-hāyana,** mfn. 70 years old, VarBṛ.

Saptatima, mfn. the 70th (with *bhāga,* m. 'a 70th part'), Hcat.

Saptátha, mf(*ī*)n. the 7th, RV.

Saptadhā́, ind. in 7 parts, 7-fold, TS. &c. &c.; 7 times, Ragh.

Saptamá, mf(*ī́*)n. the 7th, VS.; TS.; ŚBr. &c.; (*ī*), f., see below. [Cf. Zd. *haptatha;* Gk. ἕβδομος; Lat. *septimus;* Lith. *sèkma-s;* Slav. *sedmŭ* &c.] **-kalā,** f. the 7th digit of the moon, MW. **Saptamâshṭamá,** mfn. du. the 7th and the 8th, AV.

Saptamaka, mfn. the 7th, Śrutab.

Saptamī, f. (of *saptamá* above) the 7th Tithi or lunar day of the fortnight (on which day in the light fortnight there is a festival in honour of the 7th digit of the moon; often ifc., see *gaṅgā-s°, jayantī-s°*), ŚrS.; MBh.; VarBṛS. &c.; the 7th case, i.e. the locative or its terminations, Nir.; VPrāt. &c.; the potential or its terminations, Kāt.; a partic. Mūrchanā, Saṃgīt. **-pratirūpaka,** mfn. having the form of a locative case, Pāṇ. i, 4, 66, Sch.; g. *câdi.* **-vrata,** n. a religious observance to be performed on the 7th day of a month, Cat. **-samāsa,** m. a Tat-purusha compound of which the first member is supposed to be in a locative case, Kaiyy. on Pāṇ. viii, 4, 35. **-snapana,** n. 'bathing on the 7th day,' a partic. religious observance, Cat. **Saptamy-arka-vrata,** n. a partic. religious observance, ib.

Saptamīya, mfn. the 7th, MārkP.

Saptala, m. N. of a man, g. *naḍâdi;* (*ā*), f. N. of several plants (Arabian jasmine; a soap-tree; Mimosa Concinna; Abrus Precatorius; Bignonia Suaveolens), Suśr.; Pañcar.; Hcar.; = *nava-mālikā,* MW.; = *carma-kaśā,* ib.

Saptalikā, f. a kind of plant, Suśr.

Saptârsha, n. (? °*târ°*) N. of a Tīrtha, Vishṇ.

Saptika, mfn. having the length of 7, Śulbas.

1. **Saptin,** mfn. (for 2. see under *sapti* below) containing 7, RPrāt.; m. the 7-partite Stoma, PañcavBr.; Lāṭy.

सप्ति **sápti,** m. (possibly connected with √*sap*) a horse, steed, courser (cf. *sapta-s°*), RV.; VS.; Kāv.; Pañcar.; N. of the author of RV. x, 79 (having the patr. Vājambhara), Anukr. **-tā,** f. the condition of being a horse, MBh.

2. **Saptin** (only f. *saptinī,* formed in analogy to *vājinī*), Lāṭy.

Sápti-vat, mfn. moving with horses, RV.

Sáptya, n. (prob.) a riding-ground for horses, race-course, RV.

सप्रकारक **sa-prakāraka,** *sa-prakṛitika* &c. See p. 1148, col. 3.

सप्रतिपादन *sa-pratipādana*, w.r. for *sam-pratip°*.

सप्रस्तार *sa-prastāra*, w.r. for *sam-pr°*.

सफ *sa-pha*, mfn. (7. *sa* + *pha*) together with the sound or letter *ph* (*-tva*, n.), TāṇḍBr.; m. N. of various men, ĀrshBr.; n. N. of various Sāmans, (*-tva*, n.), ib. &c.

सफर *saphara*. See *śaphara*.

सफल *sa-phala*, mf(*ā*)n. together with fruits, having or bearing fruit or seed, fruitful (as a tree), PārGṛ.; MBh.; Kathās.; 'having seed,' i.e. possessing testicles, not emasculated, R.; having good results, productive, profitable, successful (with √*kṛi*, 'to fulfil,' 'keep a promise'), MBh.; Kāv. &c.; together with the result, VarBṛS.; *-tva*, n. profitableness, successfulness, Śiś.; Kathās.; Sāh.; *-prârthana*, mfn. one whose desire is fulfilled, Vikr.; *°lôdaya*, m. 'one whose appearance brings good results,' N. of Śiva, MBh.; *°lôdarka*, mfn. bearing fruit in the future, promising success, Mālatīm.

Saphalaka, mfn. furnished with a shield, MBh.

Saphalaya, Nom. P. *°yati*, to make profitable or successful, derive advantage from, enjoy, Kāv.; Kathās.

Saphalī, in comp. for *saphala*. **-karaṇa**, n. the act of making successful, Kāśikh. **-√kṛi**, P. *-karoti* = *saphalaya*, Pañcat.; Śatr. **-kṛita**, mfn. made profitable or useful, Kāv.; Kathās.; fulfilled, accomplished, R. **-√bhū**, P. *-bhavati*, to be successful, yield profit, Subh. **-bhūta**, mfn. become profitable or advantageous.

सफेन *sa-phena*, mfn. having foam, foamy, frothy, VarBṛS.; *-puñja*, mfn. covered with dense masses of foam (as the ocean), Kum.

सबन्ध *sa-bandha*, mfn. (i.e. 7. *sa* + *b°*) having a pledge, secured by a pledge, L.

Sa (to be similarly prefixed to the following): **-bandhaka**, mfn. = *sa-bandha* above, Yājñ. **-bandhu** (*sá-*), mfn. being of the same race or family, related, of kin, RV.; AV.; VS.; possessing a kinsman, having a friend, befriended, Hit. **-barhis**, mfn. furnished with sacrificial grass, Kauś. **-bala** (*sá-*), mfn. powerful, strong, RV. &c. &c.; together with strength or power, L.; accompanied by a force or army, MBh.; R.; together with Bala (Kṛishṇa's eldest brother), BhP.; m. N. of a son of Manu Bhautya, Hariv.; of a son of Vasishṭha (and one of the 7 Ṛishis), MārkP.; of one of the 7 Ṛishis under Manu Sāvarṇa, ib.; *-tā*, f. (ŚāṅkhBr.), *-tva*, n. (Śiś.) power, strength; *-vāhana*, mfn. with an army and followers, Yājñ., Sch.; *-siṅha*, m. N. of a king, Inscr.; *°lāt-kāram*, ind. with force, forcibly, Śak.; *°lânuga*, mfn. followed by an army, MBh.; R.; = *sa-bala-vāhana*, MW. **-bali**, mfn. endowed with royal revenue, ib.; accompanied with the Bali offering, ib.; m. evening twilight (when the offering is made), L. **-bahumānam**, ind. with great honour or reverence, very respectfully, Kālid.; Ratnāv. &c. **-bādh**, mfn. harassed, annoyed, afflicted, TS. **-bādha**, mfn. painful, detrimental to (gen.), Yājñ. **-bā́dhas**, mfn. = *-bā́dh*, RV. v, 10, 6; ind. urgently, eagerly, ib. vii, 8, 1; 26, 2 &c.; m. = *ṛitvij*, Naigh. iii, 15. **-bāndhava**, mfn. having kindred or relations, MW. **-bāla-vṛiddha**, mfn. with children and old men, ib. **-bāshpa**, mf(*ā*)n. tearful, weeping (*am*, ind.), Hariv.; Kāv.; Kathās.; *-gadgadam*, ind. with tears and in a faltering voice, Ragh. **-bāshpaka**, mfn. steaming, fuming, emitting vapour, Suśr. **-bāhyântaḥ-karaṇa**, mfn. with the external and internal organs (with *ātman*, m. 'the whole self'), Vikr. **-bindu**, m. N. of a mountain, MārkP. **-bīja**, mf(*ā*)n. with seed or germ (lit. and fig.), containing s° or g° (*-tva*, n.), MBh.; Kap.; VP. **-bībhatsam**, ind. with disgust or abhorrence, Mālatīm. **-búva**, mfn. accompanied by the sound *buvam* (v.l. *sabva*), TBr. (Sch.) **-brahmaka**, mfn. together with (the priest called) Brahman, AśvŚr.; tog° with (the god) Brahmā, MBh.; together with the world of Br°, Buddh. **-brahmacārika**, m. (prob.) = next, Yājñ. ii, 85. **-brahmacārin**, m. a fellow-student, one who studies the same Śākhā of the Veda (*iṇī*, f.), GṛS.; Mn.; Yājñ.; Kathās.; (ifc.) a fellow, companion (in *duḥkha-s°*), Kād.; mfn. rivalling, vying with, ib. **-brāhmaṇa** (*sá-*), mfn. together with Brāhmans, AV. **-brāhmaṇaspatya**, mfn. t° with the Pragāthas addressed to Brahmaṇas-pati, ŚāṅkhŚr.

सबर् *sabar*, (prob.) n. (accord. to Sāy. =) milk, nectar (only in comp. and prob. connected with Germ. *saf*, *Saft*; Angl.Sax. *sæp*; Eng. *sap*; perhaps also with Lat. *sapio*, *sapor*). **-dúgha**, mf(*ā*)n. yielding milk or nectar, RV. **-dúh**, mfn. (nom. *-dhúk*) id., ib. **-dhú**, mfn. id., ib.

सब्द *sabda*, m. (in a formula) = *sagara*, TS.; = *ahaḥ*, ŚBr.

सब्व *sabvà*, n. digested food (= *pakvâśaya-gatam annam*), VS.; Mahīdh. (*sabvàm* may perhaps be acc. of a f. *sabū́*; cf. *sa-búvam*).

सभ् *sabh* = √1. *sah* (cf. *pra-sabham*).

सभ *sabha*. See *sabhā* below.

सभक्तिकम् *sa-bhaktikam*, ind. (fr. 7. *sa* + *bhakti*) respectfully, Śukas.

Sa (to be similarly prefixed to the following): **-bhaksha**, m. a messmate (in *yathā-sabhaksham*, q.v.) **-bhaṅga**, mfn. with division (of a word into different parts); *-ślesha*, m. a Ślesha formed by the above division, Sāh. **-bhadra-musta**, mfn. full of the grass Cyperus Rotundus, Ṛitus. **-bhaya**, mf(*ā*)n. fearful, apprehensive (*am*, ind.), Kāv.; Kathās. &c.; riskful, dangerous, Lalit. **-bharas** (*sá-*), mfn. (perhaps) harmonizing with (instr.; others 'furnished with oblations or gifts'), RV. **-bhartṛikā**, f. (a woman) whose husband is alive, L. **-bhava**, m. together with Bhava (i.e. Śiva), BhP. **-bhasmaka**, mfn. tog° with ashes, GopBr. **-bhasman**, mfn. mixed or smeared with ashes, R.; (*°ma*)*-dvija*, m. pl. N. of Pāśupata or Śaiva mendicants, Buddh. **-bhāga**, mfn. (for *sabhā-ga* see under *sabhā*) having a share (see comp.); common, universal, Buddh.; corresponding, answering, ib.; *-tā*, f. participation, companionship, association, ib.; *°gaya*, Nom. *°yáti*, to impart, AV. **-bhāgya**, mf(*ā*)n. having good fortune, fortunate, Hariv.; R.; MārkP. **-bhājana**, mfn. (for *sabhājana* see under *sabhāj*, col. 3) furnished with vessels, MBh. (B. *mahājana*). **-bhāṇḍa**, mfn. being in a vessel or receptacle, BhP. **-bhāra-tā**, f. fulness, abundance, great prosperity, ŚāṅkhBr. **-bhārya** or **-bhāryaka**, mfn. with a wife, having a wife, MBh.; R.; Pañcar. **-bhāvana**, m. N. of Śiva, MBh. **-bhīti**, mfn. having fear, fearful, timid, MW. **-bhīma**, mfn. together with Bhīma, ib. **-bhūta**, mfn. attended by demons, Kum. **-bhūmi** (*sá-*), mfn. with landed property, including l° pr°, ŚBr.; KātyŚr. **-bhrikuṭī-mukha**, mfn. having a frowning face, frowning, MW. **-bhṛiti** (*sá-*), mfn. (prob.) offering or serving food, RV. **-bhṛitya**, mfn. attended by servants, with (the assistance of) servants, MW. **-bhrātṛi** or **-bhrātṛika**, mfn. with a brother, attended by brethren, ib. **-bhrū-kshepam**, ind. with a frown, Mṛicch. **-bhrū-bhaṅga**, mfn. with a frown, frowning, knitting the brows (*am*, ind.), Kāv.; Kathās. **-bhrū-bhedam**, ind. frowningly, Śak. (v.l.) **-bhrū-vilāsam**, ind. with play of the brows, Kathās.

सभा *sabhā́*, f. (of unknown derivation, but probably to be connected with 7. *sa*; ifc. also *sabha*, n.; cf. Pāṇ. ii, 4, 23 &c., and *eka-sabhá*) an assembly, congregation, meeting, council, public audience, RV. &c. &c.; social party, society, good society (see comp.); Society (personified as a daughter of Prajāpati), AV.; a place for public meetings, large assembly-room or hall, palace, court of a king or of justice, council-chamber, gambling-house &c., ib.; a house for lodging and accommodating travellers, Mn.; MBh. &c.; an eating-house (see *mahā-s°*). [Cf. Goth. *sibja*; Germ. *sippa*, *Sippe*; Angl.Sax. *sibb*; Eng. *god-sib*, *gossip*.] **-kāra**, m. the builder of a hall &c., MBh.; R. **-kaumudī**, f. N. of wk. **-°ksha** (*sabhâksha*), m. N. of a man, Hariv. **-gá**, mfn. (for *sa-bhāga* see above) going into an assembly or council, ŚBr.; ChUp. **-gata**, mfn. one who appears before or is present at a court of justice, Yājñ., Sch. **-gṛiha**, n. an assembly-hall, Cat. **-cará**, mfn. = *-gá*, VS. **-cāturya**, n. politeness in society, MW. **-°cāra** (*sabhâc°*), m. the customs or usages of society, court-manners, ib. **-taraṃga**, m. N. of a wk. on polite conversation in Sanskṛit (by Jagan-nātha-miśra). **-dhairya**, n. boldness in company, MW. **-nara**, m. N. of a son of Kaksheyu, Hariv.; of a son of Anu, Pur. **-nāṭaka**, n. N. of a drama (by Maheśvara). **-nāyaka**, m. the president of an assembly, chairman, MW.; the keeper of a gambling-house, ib. **-°ntare** (*sabhânt°*), ind. in society, Subh. **-páti**, m. the president of an assembly or council, VS.; Kathās. &c.; N. of Bhūta-karman, MBh.; of an author, Cat.; *-vilāsa*, m. N. of wk. **-parishad**, f. the session of an assembly or council, MBh. **-parvan**, n. N. of the second book of the Mahā-bhārata (describing the great assembly at Hastināpura and the gambling between Yudhi-shṭhira and Śakuni, in which the former staked all his possessions, including his wife Draupadī). **-pāla**, m. the keeper of a public building or assembly, TBr.; MBh. **-pūjā**, f. respectful words addressed to an audience (in the prelude of a drama), MW. **-prapādin**, mfn. frequenting assemblies, NilarUp. **-praveśana**, n. entering a court of justice, PārGṛ. **-°bharaṇa**, (prob.) w.r. for *sabhyâbh°*. **-maṇdana**, n. the adorning or arranging of an ass°-room, MW. **-maṇḍapa**, m. an assembly-hall, Vās. **-madhye**, ind. in society, Cāṇ. **-yogya**, mfn. suitable for (good) society, Prasaṅg. **-rañjana**, n. N. of a Kāvya (by Nīla-kaṇṭha Dīkshita). **-°raṇya-vitaṅka-vat** (*sabhâr°*), mfn. one to whom the Sabhā- and Araṇya-parvan (of the Mahā-bhārata) are the highest point, MBh. **-vat** (*sabhā́-*), mfn. fit for a council or assembly, RV. **-vaśa-kara**, mfn. controlling or influencing an ass°, Hit. **-°vasara** (*sabhâv°*), m. the occasion of an ass°, Vet. **-vín**, m. the keeper of a gambling-house, TBr. (Sch.) **-vinoda**, m. N. of a wk. (by Daiva-jña Dāmôdara) on proper conduct in assemblies. **-sád**, m. 'sitting at an ass°,' an assistant at a meeting or assessor in a court of justice, AV. &c. &c. **-sada**, m. id., R.; Pañcat. **-saṃnayana**, n., Pat. on Pāṇ. i, 1, 73, Vārtt. 2. **-sāhá**, m. one who is superior in an ass°, superior, eminent, RV. **-siṅha**, m. N. of a king of Bundelkhand (patron of Śaṃkara Dīkshita), Cat. **-°sīna** (*sabhâs°*), mfn. sitting in (or presiding at) a council or court of justice, Rājat. **-°stāra** (*sabhâst°*), m. an assistant at an ass°, assessor in a court of justice, Bhar.; a partaker of a game, MBh. **-stha**, mfn. being at an ass° or court; m. one who sits in an ass°, a courtier, MW. **-sthāṇú**, m. 'post at a gambling-house,' either 'a gambling-table' or 'a man who sits like a post at a g°-table,' a persistent gambler, VS. **-sthāna-stha**, mfn. being in the audience-hall (said of a king), Rājat. **Sabhêśvara-stotra**, n. N. of a hymn. **Sabhôcita**, mfn. fit for an assembly or for good society; m. a learned Brāhman or any educated person, W. **Sabhôddeśa**, m. the neighbourhood of any place of meeting, Nal. **Sabhôpavishṭa**, mfn. = *sabhâsīna*, Pañcat.

Sabhika, m. the keeper of a gambling-house, Yājñ.; Mṛicch.

Sabhīka, m. id., W.

Sabhéya, mfn. fit for an assembly or council, civilized, clever, well-behaved, decent, RV.; VS.; ŚāṅkhŚr.

Sábhya, mfn. being in an assembly-hall or meeting-room, belonging to or fit for an assembly or court, suitable to good society, courteous, polite, refined, civilized, not vulgar, decorous (as speech), AV. &c. &c.; being at the court of (gen.), Vās., Introd.; m. an assistant at an assembly or council, (esp.) an assessor, judge, Mn.; MBh. &c.; the keeper of a gambling-house, W.; a person of honourable parentage, ib.; N. of one of the five sacred fires (see *pañcâgni*), KātyŚr.; Mn. iii, 100, 185, Kull. **-kaṇṭhâbharaṇa**, n. N. of wk. **-tama**, mfn. very worthy of good society, very courteous or polite or refined; m. a very polite or refined person, an ornament of society, W. **-tā**, f., **-tva**, n. politeness, refinement, good manners or breeding, W. **Sabhyâbharaṇa**, n. N. of a poem by Rāma-candra. **Sabhyâbhinava-yati**, m. N. of an author, Cat. **Sabhyêtara**, mfn. 'other than refined,' vulgar, indecorous, opposite to good manners, Nir.; Kāv.; Śaṃk.

सभाज् *sabhāj*, cl. 10. P. (Dhātup. xxxv, 35; rather Nom. fr. 7. *sa* + *bhāj*) *sabhājayati* (rarely *°te*), to serve, honour, worship, MBh.; Kāv. &c.; to praise, celebrate, Kathās.; BhP.; to visit, frequent, Car.; Kathās.; to beautify, MW.; to show, ib.

Sabhājana, n. (for *sa-bhājana* see above, col. 2) service, honour, courtesy, politeness, civility (esp. in receiving or taking leave of a friend), R.; Kālid.; Śiś.

Sabhājita, mfn. served, honoured, gratified, pleased, MBh.; R. &c.; praised, celebrated, BhP.

Sabhājya, mfn. to be honoured or praised by (gen.), R.

सभाण्ड *sa-bhāṇḍa*, *sa-bhārya*, *sa-bhīti* &c. See col. 2.

सम् 1. *sam* or *stam*, cl. 1. P. *samati* or *stamati*, to be disturbed (accord. to some 'to be undisturbed;' cf. √*śam*), Dhātup. xix, 82; cl. 10. P. *samayati* or *stamayati*, to be agitated or disturbed, Vop.

सम् 2. *sám*, ind. (connected with 7. *sa* and 2. *sama*, and opp. to 3. *vi*, q.v.) with, together with, along with, together, altogether (used as a preposition or prefix to verbs and verbal derivatives, like Gk. σύν, Lat. *con*, and expressing 'conjunction,' 'union,' 'thoroughness,' 'intensity,' 'completeness,' e.g. *saṃ-√yuj*, 'to join together;' *saṃ-√dhā*, 'to place together;' *saṃ-dhi*, 'placing together;' *saṃ-√tap*, 'to consume utterly by burning;' *sam-uccheda*, 'destroying altogether, complete destruction;' in Ved. the verb connected with it has sometimes to be supplied, e.g. *āpo agnim yaśásaḥ sám hí pūrvīḥ*, 'for many glorious waters surrounded Agni;' it is sometimes prefixed to nouns in the sense of 2. *sama*, 'same;' cf. *samartha*), RV. &c. &c.

सम 1. *sama*, mfn. (connected with 7. *sa* and with 2. *samá* and *samāna;* cf. *samaha*, used as pron.: declined like *sarva*, e.g. *samasmai*, RV. vi, 51, 6) any, every, RV. [Cf. Gk. ἀμός, ἁμός; Goth. *suma;* Angl. Sax. *sum;* Eng. *some.*]

सम 2. *samá*, mf(*ā*)n. (prob. originally identical with prec.; cf. *samāna*) even, smooth, flat, plain, level, parallel (*karṇa-s°*, 'on a level with the ear;' *bhūmi-* or *bhūmeḥ samam-√kṛi*, 'to make level with the earth'), RV. &c. &c.; same, equal, similar, like, equivalent, like to or identical or homogeneous with (instr., e.g. *mayā sama*, 'like to me;' or gen., rarely abl.), like in or with regard to anything (instr., gen., loc., or *-tas*, or comp.; *samaṃ √kṛi*, 'to make equal, balance'), ib.; always the same, constant, unchanged, fair, impartial towards (loc. or gen.), ib.; even (not 'odd'), a pair, VarBṛS.; having the right measure, regular, normal, right, straight (*samaṃ √kṛi*, 'to put right or in order'), AitBr. &c. &c.; equable, neutral, indifferent, VarBṛS.; equally distant from extremes, ordinary, common, middling, Mn.; MBh. &c.; just, upright, good, straight, honest, ib.; easy, convenient, Pañcat.; full, complete, whole, entire, L.; m. peace (perhaps w. r. for *śama*), R.; Kām.; the point of intersection of the horizon and the meridian line, Gol.; N. of partic. zodiacal signs (esp. Vṛisha, Karkaṭa, Kanyā, Vṛiścika, Makara, and Mīna), MW.; a kind of straight line placed over a numerical figure to mark the process of extracting the square root, ib.; (in music) a kind of time, Saṃgīt.; a grass-conflagration, L.; a Jina, Gal.; N. of a son of Dharma, VP.; of a son of Dhṛitarāshṭra, MBh.; of a king of the Nandi-vegas (v. l. *śama*), ib.; (*ā*), f. a year, see *samā*, p. 1153; (*am*), n. level ground, a plain (*samé bhūmyāḥ*, 'on level ground'), AV.; ŚBr.; Mn.; MBh.; R.; equability, equanimity, imperturbability, MBh.; likeness, similarity, equality (*ena*, 'equally, in the same manner'), Kāś. on Pāṇ. ii, 3, 18; right measure or proportion (*ena*, 'exactly, precisely'), ŚBr.; settlement, compensation, Mn. viii, 177; good circumstances, Mṛicch.; (in rhet.) a partic. figure, sameness of objects compared to one another, Pratāp.; Kuval.; (in geom.) a mean proportional segment (described as a fourth proportional to the two perpendiculars and the link or segment, and used for solving problems in a trapezium), Col.; = *samā*, f. a year (see *pāpa-s°*, *puṇya-s°*, and *su-shama*); (*samám*), ind. in like manner, alike, equally, similarly, RV. &c. &c.; together with or at the same time with or in accordance with (instr. or comp.), ŚBr.; Mn.; MBh. &c.; just, exactly, precisely, Mn.; VarBṛS.; BhP.; honestly, fairly, R. [Cf. Gk. ἅμα, ὁμός, ὁμαλός; Lat. *similis;* Germ. *same, -sam;* Eng. *same.*] **–kaksha**, mfn having equal weight (*-tā*, f.; *-tva*, n.), Sāh.; (*ā*), f. equilibrium (°*kshāṃ √tul*, P. *tulayati*, 'to balance one another'), MBh. **–kanyā**, f. a suitable maiden, a girl fit to be married, Dhanaṃj. **–kara**, mfn. (for *sa-makara* see p. 1153, col. 2) levying regular or fair taxes, Siṇhâs. **–karṇa**, m. 'having equal ears,' N. of Śiva, MBh.; of Buddha (*-tā*, f. one of the 80 minor marks of a B°), Dharmas. 84; Buddh.; m. n. 'having two equal diagonals,' an equi-diagonal tetragon, Col. **–karman**, mfn. having equal occupation, MBh. **–kāla**, m. the same time or moment, W.; (ibc. or *am*, once also *e* [v. l.]), ind. simultaneously, Yājñ.; Kāv. &c.; *-bhava*, m. a contemporary of (comp.), Rājat. **–kālīna**, mfn. simultaneous with (comp.), Nyāyas., Sch. **–kola**, m. 'having an even breast,' a serpent, snake, L. **–koshṭha-miti**, f. the measure of compartments or number of equal squares of the same denomination (as cubit, fathom &c.) in which the dimension of the side is given; the area or superficial contents, Col. **–krama**, mfn. keeping pace with, Śiś.; *-tā*, f. having the steps equal (one of the 80 minor marks of a Buddha), Dharmas. 84. **–kriya**, mfn. acting uniformly in or towards (loc.), MBh.; Bhartṛ.; subject to the same medical treatment (*-tva*, n.), Suśr. **–kshetra**, n. (in astron.) 'having an even or complete figure,' N. of a partic. division or arrangement of the Nakshatras, MW. **–khāta**, n. a cavity having the figure of a regular solid with equal sides, a parallelepipedon, cylinder &c., Col. **–gandha**, m. constant odour (one of the 4 kinds of odours), Dharmas. 37; mfn. having the same odour, L. **–gandhaka**, m. a perfume compounded of similar ingredients, L. **–gandhika**, mfn. having equal or similar fragrance, MW.; n. the fragrant root of the Andropogon Muricatus, Bhpr. **–cakra-vāla**, n. a circle, IndSt. **–catur-aśra** (or *-asra*), mf(*ā*)n. having four equal angles, square, ĀśvGṛ.; VarBṛS.; BhP. &c.; m. n. a rectangular tetragon, square, Śulbas.; Āryabh.; Hcat.; an equilateral tetr°, MW.; (*ī*), ind. (with √*kṛi*) to transform into a square, Hcat. **–catur-bhuja**, mfn. having four equal sides; m. or n. (?) a square or rhombus, Col. **–catush-koṇa**, mfn. having four equal angles (distinguished from *sama-catur-aśra*), IndSt. **–catvāriṇśa-danta-tā**, f. the having 40 even teeth (one of the 32 signs of perfection in a Buddha), Dharmas. 83. **–citta**, mfn. even-minded, possessing equanimity, equable, Kāv.; BhP.; indifferent, W.; having the thoughts directed to the same subject, MW.; *-tā*, f. (L.) or *-tva*, n. (Bhag.) equanimity towards (loc.) **–cetas**, mfn. = *-citta*, Bhartṛ.; BhP. **–codita**, mfn. = *sam-c°*, driven or shot off, MBh. **–ccheda**, mfn. having an equal denominator, Āryabh., Sch.; °*dī-kṛi*, P. *-karoti*, to cause to have an equal den°, Bījag. **–cchedana**, mfn. having like divisions or denominators, MW. **–jāti**, mfn. equal in kind, homogeneous, MW. **–jātīya**, mfn. id., MBh. **–jñā**, f. fame, L. (v. l. for *samājñā*). **–taṭa**, N. of a country in eastern India, VarBṛS.; Buddh. **–tā** (*samá-*), f. sameness of level, VarBṛS.; equality, sameness, identity with (instr., gen., or comp.), ŚBr.; MBh.; Hariv. &c.; fairness, impartiality towards (loc. or comp.), Mn.; MBh.; Kāv. &c.; equableness, normal condition (°*tāṃ √nī*, 'to decide or settle equitably'), Mn.; MBh.; Suśr. &c.; equanimity, MW.; mediocrity, Hit.; benevolence, Pañcar.; *-jñāna*, n. (with Buddhists) one of the 5 kinds of knowledge, Dharmas. 94. **–tīrthaka**, mf(*ikā*)n. full to the brim, Lalit. **–tulā**, f. equal value, Kāv. **–tulita**, mfn. of equal weight, VarBṛS. **–tṛiṇa-maṇi-loshṭa-kāñcana**, mfn. one to whom grass and jewels and clods and gold are of equal value, Siṇhâs. **–traya**, n. an equal quantity of 3 ingredients (viz. yellow myrobalan, dry ginger, and sugar), L. **–tri-bhuja**, mfn. having 3 equal sides, Col.; m. n. any figure containing 3 equal s°, MW.; an equilateral triangle, ib. **–tryaṇśa**, mfn. consisting of 3 eq° parts; (*ā*), f. a partic. Vishṭuti, TāṇḍyaBr. **–tva**, n. equality with (instr. or gen.), KātyŚr.; VS.Prāt.; VarBṛ. &c.; equanimity, HYog.; uniform conduct towards (loc. or comp.), Bhag.; BhP.; equableness, normal condition, Suśr. **–tvish**, mfn. equally bright or lovely, W. **–daṇshṭra-tā**, f. the having equal eye-teeth (one of the 50 minor marks of a Buddha), Dharmas. 84. **–danta**, mfn. having even teeth; *-tā*, f. one of the 32 signs of perfection (of a Buddha), Dharmas. 83. **–darśana**, mfn. (ifc.) of similar appearance, like, R.; (also with *sarvatra* or *sarveshām*) looking on all (things or men) with equal or indifferent eyes, MBh.; Kāv.; Pur. **–darśin**, mfn. looking impartially on (loc.), regarding all things imp°, MBh.; R. &c. **–duḥkha**, mf(*ā*)n. feeling pain in common with another, compassionate, Kāv.; *-sukha*, mfn. sharing grief and joy with an°, MBh.; Śak.; indifferent to pain and pleasure, Bhag.; Ashṭāv. **–dṛiś**, mfn. looking indifferently or impartially upon, Bhartṛ.; BhP.; regarding all things imp°, BhP. **–dṛishṭi**, f. the act of looking on all equally or impartially, Kathās.; mfn. looking on all imp° (*-tva*, n.), BhP.; Rājat.; Vās.; even-eyed, Vās. **–deśa**, m. even ground, Śak. **–dyuti**, mfn. equal in radiance, MW. **–dvādaśāsra**, m. n. an equilateral dodecagon or dodecahedron, ib. **–dvi-dvibhuja**, mfn. having 2×2 equal sides; m. or n. (?) a rhomboid, Col. **–dvi-bhuja**, mfn. having 2 equal sides, ib.; m. n. a rhomboid hav° 2 s° eq°, MW. **–dharma**, mf(*ā*)n. (ifc.) of equal nature or character, resembling, BhP. **–dhā**, ind. equally with (instr.), Gaut. **–dhura**, mfn. (for *sa-madh°* see p. 1154) bearing an equal burden with (gen.), Ragh. **–dhṛita**, mfn. made eq° in weight, Mn.; Vishṇ.; equal or equivalent to, W. **–nara**, m. = *-śaṅku*, Gol.; Gaṇit. **–nindā-navana**, mf(*ā*)n. indifferent to blame and praise, Nalod. **–pakshapāta**, mf(*ā*)n. favouring both sides equally, impartial, Kir. **–paṭa-vāsa**, m. (prob.) = *-gandhaka*, L. **–pada**, m. 'holding the feet even,' a partic. posture in sexual union, L.; an attitude in shooting, ib. **–padāti**, ind., g. *tishṭhad-gu.* **–pāda**, n. 'holding the feet even,' a partic. posture in dancing, Saṃgīt.; a posture in shooting, L. **–prabha**, mfn. having equal splendour, Mn. i, 9. **–prādhānya-saṃkara**, m. (in rhet.) the artificial combination of two metaphors, Kuval. **–prêpsu**, mfn. eager for an equal position in regard to (loc.), Gaut. **–buddhi**, mfn. esteeming all things alike, indifferent; m. N. of a Muni, Cat. **–bhāga**, m. an equal share, MW.; mfn. (prob.) receiving an equal share, Pāṇ. vi, 2, 1, Sch. **–bhāva**, m. equability, homogeneousness, Bhām.; HPariś.; mfn. of like nature or property, W. **–bhūmi**, f. even ground (°*mi-tale*, 'on ev° gr°'), R.; ind. (prob.) = *-m-bhūmi* (below), g. *tishṭhad-gu.* **–maṇḍala**, n. 'even-circle,' the prime vertical circle (*-śaṅku*, m. prime vert° pin or gnomon), Sūryas.; Gol. &c. **–mati**, mfn. even-minded, equable, BhP. **–maya**, mf(*ī*)n. of like origin, Pāṇ. iv, 3, 82, Sch. **–mātra**, mfn. of the same size or measure, W.; of the same prosodial meas°, IndSt. **–miti**, f. mean measure, W. **–m-bila**, mf(*ī*)n. filled with (instr.) to the aperture or brim, KātyŚr. **–m-bhūmi**, ind. even with the ground, ŚBr.; KātyŚr.; Kauś. **–yuga**, g. *pratijanâdi.* **–yoga**, w. r. for *samāy°*, L. **–raṇhas**, mfn. having equal impetuosity or speed, MW. **–rajju**, f. equal or mean cord, mean or equated depth, Col. **–rañjita**, mfn. coloured equally, Hariv.; = *saṃ-r°*, tinged, coloured, MW. **–rata**, m. n. a partic. posture in sexual union, L. **–ratha**, m. N. of a king, BhP. **–rabha**, m. 'eq°-embrace,' a kind of coitus, MW. **–rasa**, mfn. having eq° feelings (*-tva*, n.), Kāśikh. **–rasī-karaṇa**, n. causing to have eq° feelings, ib. **–rūpa**, mfn. of the same form, MW. **–rūpya**, mfn. = *samād āgataḥ*, formerly in the possession of an honest man (cf. *rūpya*), Pāṇ. iv, 3, 81, Sch. **–rekha**, mfn. forming an even line, straight, Śak. **–°rca** (fr. *sama + ṛic*), mfn. having the same number of verses, ŚāṅkhŚr. **–lamba**, mfn. having equal perpendiculars; m. or n. (?) a trapezoid, Col. **–lepanī**, f. a bricklayer's instrument for levelling, a plane, L. **–loshṭa-kāñcana**, mfn. one to whom a clod and piece of gold are all the same, Ragh.; Divyâv. **–loshṭâśma-kāñcana**, mfn. one to whom a clod and stone and gold are all the same, Ashṭāv. **–loshṭra-kāñcana**, mfn. (prob. w. r.) = *-loshṭa-k°*, MārkP. **–vayaska**, mfn. of equal age, MW. **–varṇa**, mf(*ā*)n. of the same colour, L.; being of eq° caste, Mn. viii, 269; ix, 156; m. community of caste &c., W. **–vartin**, mfn. being eq°, being of a fair or impartial disposition, MW.; acting uniformly, L.; being equidistant (*bāṇa-pāta-s°*, 'b° equid° with an arrow-shot'), Śak.; m. N. of Yama, MBh.; Car. **–varshaṇa**, mfn. raining equally, Inscr. **–vibhakta**, mfn. divided equally, symmetrical (°*tâṅga*, mfn., R.), KātyŚr. **–vibhāga**, m. a division of property amongst sons in equal shares, MW. **–vishama**, n. pl. level and uneven ground, Pañcat.; Śiś.; *-kara*, mfn. producing what is smooth and rough (as time), Śukas. **–vīrya**, mfn. equal in strength, Hit. **–vṛitta**, mfn. uniformly round or equal and r°, BhP.; n. the prime vertical circle, Gol.; a uniform metre, a metre with 4 eq° Pādas, Piṅg.; *-karṇa*, m. the hypotenuse of the shadow of the time when the sun reaches the prime vertical circle, Gaṇit.; *-śaṅku*, m. = *sama-ś°*, ib. **–vṛitti**, f. even state or temper, equanimity, MW.; of an equal or even temper, equable, fair, moderate, W.; whose conduct is uniform, Kir.; *-sāra*, N. of wk. **–vegavaśa**, m. pl. N. of a people, MBh. **–vedha**, m. the mean depth, Col. **–vesha**, m. a similar dress (°*shaṃ √kṛi*, Ā. *-kurute*, 'to dress alike'), MBh. **–vyatha**, mfn. suffering eq° pain, ib. **–vyāptika**, mfn. furnishing an example of mutual perpetual pervasion or concomitance, KapS., Sch. **–śaṅku**, m. the sun's gnomon i. e. altitude when it reaches the prime vertical circle, Gaṇit.; Gol. **-śarkara,** mfn. containing the same quantity of sugar; n. (with *cūrṇa*) a partic. medicinal preparation, Bhpr. **-śaśin,** m. a moon with equal horns, VarBṛS. **-śas,** ind. (to divide) into equal parts, ĀpŚr. **-śīrshikā,** f. equality with (instr. or comp.), Rājat. **-śīla,** mf(*ā*)n. having the same customs or character, MBh.; BhP. **-śīlin,** mfn. id., MBh. **-śodhana,** n. equal subtraction, s° of the same quantity on both sides of the equation, Col. **-śruti,** mfn. having equal intervals, Saṃgīt. **-śreṇi,** f. a straight line (*-gata,* mfn. 'written in st° lines' [as letters]), MatsyaP. **-saṃsthāna,** n. (with Yogins) N. of one of the 10 sitting postures, Yogas., Sch. **-saṃsthita,** mfn. being in easy circumstances, Mṛicch. **-saṃkhyāta,** mfn. pl. equal in number with (instr.), BhP. **-saṃdhi,** m. equal alliance, peace on equal terms, W. **-saṃdhita,** mfn. allied on eq° terms, bound or connected equally, ib.; concluded on eq° terms (as an alliance), Kām.; Hit. (accord. to Kām., Sch. read *-saṃdhi-tas,* ind.) **-samaya-vartin,** mfn. simultaneous; (°*ti*)*-tā,* f. simultaneousness, Sarvad. **-sarva-guṇa,** mfn. pl. endowed equally with all virtues, Kathās. **-siddhānta,** mfn. pursuing eq° objects, ĀśvŚr. **-supti,** f. equal or general sleep (='the end of a Kalpa and dissolution of the universe'), L. **-sūtra-ga** or **sūtra-stha,** mfn. situated on the same diameter (i.e. situated on two opposite points of the globe), living at the antipodes, Sūryas. **-saurabha,** m. N. of a man, MBh. **-stha,** mf(*ā*)n. occurring with an even number, VarBṛS.; being in flourishing circumstances, MBh.; R.; being level or even, equal, level, uniform, W.; like, similar, ib. **-sthala,** n. even or level ground, ib.; (*ī*), f. id.; the Doab or country between the Ganges and Jumnā rivers (cf. *antar-vedī*), L.; °*lī-√kṛi,* to turn into level gr°, make level with the gr°, Śiś.; °*lī-krita,* mfn. made into level ground, levelled, filled up, W. **-sthāna,** n. a partic. posture in Yoga (in which the legs are closely contracted), L. **-sparśa,** mfn. having the same contact, equal in touch, having the same effect of cont°, equally defiling, MW. **-svara,** mfn. having the same or a similar tone or accent, RPrāt. **Samâṇśa,** m. an equal share (as in an inheritance; *ena,* ind. 'in eq° sh°s'), Kathās.; Vajracch.; mfn. containing equal parts, Suśr.; entitled to or obtaining an eq° sh°, Mn. ix, 157; (*ā*), f. Sida Cordifolia, L.; *-bhāgin,* mfn. sharing in equal portions, L.; *-hārin,* mfn. taking an eq° port°, sharing equally, a co-heir, Dāyat. **Samâṇśaka,** mf(*ikā*)n. obtaining an eq° share, ib.; Yājñ. **Samâṇśika,** mfn. consisting of equal parts, Suśr.; entitled to an equal share, MW. **Samâṇśin,** mfn. obtaining an equal sh°, Yājñ.; Dāyat. **Samâkara,** mfn. (ifc. or m.c.)=next, R. **Samâkāra,** mfn. (ifc.) of like appearance, similar, like, R.; Pañcat. **Samâkshara,** mfn. having the same number of syllables, R.; *-pada-krama,* mfn. containing a succession of Padas or metrical feet of the s° n° of syl°, MW.; °*ksharâvakara,* m. a partic. Samādhi, Buddh. **Samâṅghrika,** mfn. standing evenly on (all four) feet (as a lion), Kathās. **Samâcara,** m. (for *samâcāra* see *sam-ā-√car*) equal manners or customs, MBh.; eq° or virtuous conduct, ib.; mfn. eq° or similar in practice or in virtuous cond°, ib. **Samâñjana,** n. a partic. eye-ointment, Suśr. **Samâtmaka,** mfn. possessing equanimity, MBh. (v. l. *śamât*°). **Samâtman,** mfn. id., ib. (prob. w. r. for *mahât*°). **Samânana,** mfn. (for *sa-mānana* see s. v.) having a like face with (instr.), Nalôd. 1. **Sámânta,** m. (for 2. *samânta* see under *samā*) a borderer, neighbour, MaitrS. (cf. *sāmanta*). 1. **Samântara,** mfn. (for 2. *samânt*° see under *samā*) being a constant unit of difference (in measurement; e.g. 'if a man forms the unit, a horse is *tri-samântaraḥ,* i.e. = three men'), Kām.; parallel, A. **Samâ-priya,** mfn. = *saṃtatāni ā samantāt priyāṇi yasmin,* BhP. (Sch.) **Samâphala,** N. of wk. **Samârtha,** w.r. for *sam*°, MBh. **Samârthaka,** mfn. having the same sense, L. **Samârthin,** mfn. seeking or desiring equality, W.; seeking peace with (instr.), R. (perh. w. r. for *śam*°). **Samârdha-ga,** mfn. situated on the same side, VarYogay. **Samârsha,** mfn. descended from the same Ṛishi, MBh. **Samâvat** &c., see col. 2. **Samâ-vikarta,** mfn. symmetrically cut (without being notched), ĀpŚr. **Samâsana,** mfn. (for *sam-ās*° see *sam-√ās*) sitting on even ground, MārkP. **Samâsama,** mfn. du. equal and unequal, of eq° and uneq° rank, Gaut.; Sarvad. **Samâhva,** mfn. having the same name as (comp.), Śiś.; (*ā*), f. a kind of plant (= *go-jihvā*), L. **Samôttara-tas,** ind. directly northwards, Āryabh. **Samôdaka,** mfn. containing the same quantity of water, L.; n. a mixture of half buttermilk and half water, L. **Samôpamā,** f. = *upamā* (ifc. = 'like, resembling'), Divyâv.; (in rhet.) comparison expressed by *sama* in composition with the substantive to which an object is likened, MW.

Samâñjas, m. N. of a son of A-samañjas, VP.

Samaka, mfn. equal, alike, Kāv.; Divyâv.

1. **Samaya,** P. °*yati* (for 2. see *sam-√i*), to level, regulate, L.

1. **Samáyā,** ind. through, into the middle of or midst of anything (acc. or instr.), RV.; entirely, thoroughly, ib.; in the neighbourhood of (acc. or instr. or gen.), Śiś.; Daś.

2. **Samayā,** ind. See under *sam-aya,* p. 1164, col. 2.

Samayitavya, mfn. to be levelled, to be adjusted (as a dispute), Bhar. (prob. w. r. for *śam*°).

Samas. See *aishámas.*

Sámā, f. (of 2. *sama* above) a year, RV. &c. &c. (also *sama,* n. in *pāpa-sáma, puṇya-s*°, *su-shāma*); a half year, AV.; season, weather, AitBr.; Kauś.; Nir.; a day, MW. **-°tīta** (°*mât*°), mfn. more than one y° old, Car. **-nicaya,** mfn. one who has a store (of provisions) sufficient for a year, Mn. vi, 18. **-2. -°nta** (°*mân*°), m. (for 1. *samân*° see under 2. *sama,* col. 1) the end of a year, ib. iv, 26. **-2. -°ntara** (°*mân*°), n. (for 1. *samân*° see col. 1) the interval of a y°; (*e*), ind. within a y°, Car. **-°rbuda** (°*mâr*°), n. 100 millions of years, MBh.

Samāṃ-saminā, f. (fr. *samāṃ samām*) a cow bearing a calf every year, Pāṇ. v, 2, 12.

Samāti. See *ā-s*°.

Samālokya, n. (fr. *sama-loka,* m.c. for *sāmal*°) sharing the same world with (gen.), MārkP.

Samāvac, in comp. for *samávat* below. **-chás** (for *-śas*), ind. equally, similarly, in like manner, TS.; MaitrS.

Samāvaj, in comp. for next. **-jāmi,** mfn. uniform, AitBr.

Samávat, mfn. similar, equally great or much, TS.; Br.; ind. equally much, TS.; Kāṭh.; ĀśvŚr.

Samāvad, in comp. for prec. **-indriya,** mfn. = *-vīrya,* TāṇḍyaBr. **-bhāj,** mfn. obtaining an equal share, GopBr. **-vīrya** (*samávad-*), mfn. equally strong, ĀpŚr.

1. **Samika** (fr. *sámā*; for 2. see s. v.), see *dvai-s*°.

Samī, in comp. for *sama.* **-karaṇa,** n. the act of making even, levelling, Kull. on Mn. vii, 184 &c.; assimilation, Vedântas.; putting on a level with (instr.), Mn., Sch.; (in arithm.) equation, Bijag.; equalizing, setting to rights, ChUp., Sch.; a roller (to level a sown field), L. **-kāra,** m. equation, Col. **-√kṛi,** P. Ā. *-karoti, -kurute,* to make even, level, KātyŚr.; R.; MārkP. &c.; to equalize, Hcat.; to place on an equality with, declare to be equal to (instr.), Kāvyâd.; to adjust, settle, MBh.; R.; Mn., Sch.; to raze to the ground, annihilate, Kathās.; Jātakam. **-kṛita,** mfn. made even, levelled, equipoised, equalized, MW.; done in the same manner, imitated, ib.; summed up, added, ib. **-kṛiti,** f. levelling, L.; weighing, Naish. **-kriyā,** f. the act of equalizing, MW.; (in arithm.) equation, Col. **-bhāva,** m. the becoming in a normal state, Car. **-√bhū,** P. *-bhavati,* to be or become equal, be equalized, MW.; to place one's self on an equality, Āpast.; to be razed to the ground or destroyed, Jātakam. **-bhūta,** mfn. placed equally, Vet.; equalized, equipoised, Yājñ.; become indifferent, Bhartṛ.; identified, MW.

Samīna, mfn. (fr. *samā,* 'year'), Pāṇ. v, 1, 85; yearly, annual, A.; hired for a year, ib.; a year hence, ib.

Samīnikā, f. (a cow) bearing a calf every year, L.

1. **Samīya,** Nom. Ā. °*yate,* to be treated or accounted as equal by (instr.), Pañcat.

2. **Samīya,** mfn., g. *gahâdi*; similar, like, of like origin, MW.

सम 3. *sa-ma,* mfn. (fr. 7. *sa*+*mā*) 'together with Lakshmī,' happy, prosperous, Nalôd.

समकर *sa-makara,* mfn. (for *sama-kara* see p. 1152, col. 1) having marine monsters.

समक्त *sam-akta.* See *sam-√añj,* col. 3.

समक्न *sam-akna.* See *sam-√añc,* col. 3.

समक्ष *sam-aksha,* mfn. being within sight or before the eyes, present, visible, Śak.; BhP.; (*ám, ât, e,* and *a-tas*), ind. before the eyes, visibly, manifestly, in the sight or presence of (dat., gen., or comp.), RV. &c. &c. **-tā,** f. visibility, MW. **-darśana,** n. the act of seeing with the eyes, ocular evidence, Mn. viii, 74.

समग्र *sám-agra,* mf(*ā*)n. (see 2. *sam*) all, entire, whole, complete, each, every (ibc. = 'fully,' 'entirely;' n. 'all, everything'), AV. &c. &c.; fully provided with (instr. or comp.), Mālav.; Kāvyâd.; one who has everything or wants nothing, MBh.; R. **-ṇī,** mfn. the very first among (gen.), BhP. **-dhana,** mfn. possessing the whole of one's property, Mn. viii, 380. **-bhakshaṇa-śīla,** mfn. eating everything, Cat. **-mala-hāraka,** mfn. taking (upon one's self) all impurity, Mn. viii, 308. **-vartin,** mfn. entirely resting or fixed upon (loc.), Mālav. **-śakti,** mfn. possessing full force, Ragh. **-sampad,** mfn. one who has every happiness, ib. **-sauvarṇa,** mfn. entirely golden, Kathās. **Samagrâṅga,** mfn. one who has his body or limbs complete, MBh. **Samagrêndu,** m. the full moon; *-nibhânana,* mfn. having a face like the f° m°, MBh.

Samagraya, Nom. P. °*yati,* to make full or complete, restore, Cat.

समङ्क 1. *sam-aṅká,* mfn. (for 2. see *sam-√añc*) bearing the same mark or sign, ŚBr.

समङ्ग *sám-aṅga,* mf(*ā*)n. (see 2. *sam*) having all the limbs, complete, AV. (in MBh. applied to the mythical cow Bahulā); m. a kind of game, L.; N. of two men, MBh.; (pl.) of a people, ib.; (*ā*), f. N. of various plants (accord. to L. 'Rubia Munjista and Cordifolia, Mimosa Pudica, Aloe Indica, &c.'), VarBṛS.; Suśr.; of a river, MBh.

Sam-aṅgin, mfn. complete in all parts, furnished with all requisites, KātyŚr.; (*inī*), f. N. of a Bodhi-vṛiksha-devatā, Lalit.

समङ्गल *sa-maṅgala,* mfn. endowed with happiness, auspicious, MW.

समज् *sam-√aj,* P. *-ajati,* to bring or collect together, RV.; to bring into conflict, ib.; to subdue, overcome, ib.

Sám-aja, m. N. of Indra, AitĀr.; a multitude of animals, L.; a number of fools, L.; n. a forest, wood, L. °**ajyā,** f. place of meeting, Kauś.; meeting, assembly, L.; fame, celebrity (v. l. for *samājñā*), L.

Sam-āja, m. meeting with, falling in with (gen. or comp.), VarBṛS.; BhP.; a meeting, assembly, congregation, congress, conclave, society, company (cf. *dyūta-s*°), association, collection (accord. to L. not applied to animals), Āpast.; Mn.; MBh. &c.; a convivial meeting, party, club, W.; a quantity, plenty, abundance (in *sukha-s*°), Gīt. xi, 21; a partic. conjunction of planets, VarBṛS.; an elephant (prob. w. r. for *sāmaja*), L.; *-saṃniveśana,* n. a building or place suitable for an assembly, assembly-room, meeting-house, MW. °**ājika,** w. r. for *sāmājika.*

समज्ञा *samajñā,* w. r. for *sam-ājñā.*

समञ्च् *sam-√añc* (only ind. p. *-acya*), to bend together, ŚBr., Sch.: Pass. *-acyate,* to be pressed or thrown together, RV. v, 54, 12.

Sam-akna, mfn. bent together, Pāṇ. viii, 2, 48, Sch.; going or moving together or simultaneously, going, moving, W.

2. **Sam-aṅka,** m. (for 1. see above) a hook, crotchet (fig. = 'pain, ache'), AV.; a partic. animal destroying corn, ib.

Sam-áñcana, n. bending in, contracting, TBr.; ŚBr.

समञ्ज् *sam-√añj,* P. Ā. *-anakti, -aṅkte,* to smear over, anoint, adorn, beautify, VS.; ŚBr.; to prepare, make ready, RV.; to honour, worship, ib.; VS.; TBr.; to fit or put together, unite, compose, RV.; to devour (Ā. with instr., 'to feed on'), ib.

Sám-akta, mfn. prepared, made ready, RV.; furnished with (instr.), ib.; combined or united with (instr.), TBr.

Sam-áñjana, mfn. fitting together, AV.; n. smearing, anointing (see next); *-vat,* mfn. well smeared, SaṃhUp. °**añjanīya,** mfn. employed in anointing, ŚāṅkhGṛ.

Sam-añjasa, mfn. proper, right, fit, correct, sound, good, excellent (*am,* ind.), Mn.; MBh. &c.; m. N. of Śiva, Śivag.; (*ā*), f. (with *vṛitti*) N. of a Comm. on the Brahma-sūtra; n. propriety, fitness, truth, consistency, correct evidence, MW.; °*sārtha-dīpikā,* f. N. of a Comm. on the Rasa-mañjarī.

समण्ठ *samaṇṭha*, m. or n.(?) a kind of culinary herb, L.

समत् *sam-√at*, P. *-atati*, to resort to, approach, visit, RV.

समतिक्रम् *sam-ati-√kram*, P. Ā. *-krāmati*, *-kramate*, to go or pass by entirely, cross or step over, MBh.; to step out of (abl.), R.; to transgress, neglect, disregard, lose, ib.; to surpass, excel, exceed, MBh.; to pass away, elapse (as time), Vet.; to let pass by or elapse (*dvau māsau samatikramya*, 'after the lapse of two months'), R.

Sam-atikrama, m. going entirely over or beyond (see *duḥ-s°*); deviating from, transgressing, omission, Mn. xi, 203. °**atikrānta**, mfn. gone entirely over or beyond, gone through, fulfilled (as a promise), R.; passed away, elapsed, Vet.; surpassed, exceeded, MBh.; transgressed, neglected, ib.; n. omission, transgression, R.

समतिप्रशंस् *sam-ati-pra-√śaṅs*, P. *-śaṅsati*, to praise excessively, MBh.

समतिया *sam-ati-√yā*, P. *-yāti*, to go completely beyond, pass by, elapse, R.

समतिरिक्त *sam-ati-rikta*, mfn. (√*ric*) excessively redundant or abundant, exceeding, excessive, much, W.

समतिवह् *sam-ati-√vah*, Caus. *-vāhayati*, to cause to be spent, pass, spend (as time), Nāg.

समतिवृत् *sam-ati-√vṛit*, Ā. *-vartate*, to pass by (acc.), MBh.; to run away, escape from (acc.), avoid, R.; Hariv.

समतिसृष्ट *sam-ati-sṛishṭa*, mfn. (√*sṛij*) one who has taken leave, allowed to go, ChUp.

समतिस्रुत *sam-ati-sruta*, mfn. (√*sru*) entirely flowed asunder, become thoroughly liquid, Suśr.

समती *sam-atī* (*-ati-√5. i*), P. *-aty-eti*, to go or pass by entirely, go through or beyond, cross over, MBh.; Kāv. &c.; to surpass, excel, Bhag.

Sam-atīta, mfn. gone or passed by, MBh.; R. &c.

समत्सर *sa-matsara*, mfn. having envy or jealousy, envious, jealous of (*uddiśya*), Ragh.; Kathās.; indignant, angry, Rājat.

समथ *samatha*, w.r. for *śamatha*, Lalit.

समद् *sam-√ad*, P. *-atti*, to eat completely up, entirely devour, Bhaṭṭ.

समद् *samád*, f. (prob. fr. 7. *sa* + *mad*, 'raging together;' accord. to Yāska either fr. *sam-√ad* or fr. *sam-√mad*; accord. to others fr. 2. *sam* + suffix *ad*; cf. *sámana*) strife, battle (often in loc. pl.; acc. with √*kṛi* or √*dhā* and dat., 'to cause strife among or between'), RV.; AV.; Br.

Samádvan, mfn. fighting, warlike, RV.

समद *sa-mada*, mf(*ā*)n. intoxicated, excited with passion, Kāv.; ruttish, MBh.

Sa-mádana, n. conflict, strife, RV.; mf(*ā*)n. impassioned, enamoured, Mṛicch.; Vās.; furnished with thorn-apple trees, Vās.

समदु *samadu* (?), f. a daughter, L.

समधिक *sam-adhika*, mf(*ā*)n. superabundant, superfluous, excessive, exceeding (with *māsa*, m. 'more than a month, a month and more'), R.; VarBṛS.; Hit.; exceeding what is usual, extraordinary, intense, plentiful (*am*, ind.), Kāv.; Sāh. **–tara**, mfn. more abundant, exceeding, excessive; *-rūpa*, mfn. more beautiful than (abl.), Ragh.; °*rôcchvāsin*, mfn. breathing or sighing more heavily, Megh. **–lajjā-vatī**, f. excessively ashamed or bashful, Sāh. **–lāvaṇya**, n. excessive loveliness or charm, ib. **Samadhikârambha**, m. an extraordinary enterprise, Uttarar.

समधिकृत् *sam-adhi-√kṛit* (only ind. p. *-kṛitya*), to cut up in addition or completely, MBh.

समधिगम् *sam-adhi-√gam*, P. *-gacchati*, to go towards together, come quite near, approach, MBh.; BhP.; to acquire, obtain, Mn.; MBh. &c.; to go completely over, surpass, Ragh.; Kir.; to go over, study, read, Mn. iv, 20.

Sam-adhigata, mfn. gone quite near to, approached, BhP. °**adhigama**, m. thoroughly understanding, perceiving, ib. °**adhigamana**, n. going beyond or above, surpassing, overcoming, W. °**adhigamya**, mfn. to be understood or perceived, Śaṃk.

समधिरुह् *sam-adhi-√ruh*, P. *-rohati*, to rise up, mount, ascend, AitBr.; Hariv.; to rise up to (the knowledge of), be convinced of, MBh.

Sam-adhirūḍha, mfn. one who has risen up or mounted (with *tulām*, 'brought into a critical condition'), Bālar.; convinced of (acc.), MBh. °**adhirohaṇa**, n. mounting up, ascending, Car.

समधिशी *sam-adhi-√śī*, Caus. *-śāyayati*, to lay or put anything in the place of any other thing, Nid.

समधिश्रि *sam-adhi-√śri*, P. Ā. *-śrayati*, °*te*, to proceed or advance towards, approach, attack, MW.; to put in or on the fire, MBh.

समधिष्ठा *sam-adhi-shṭhā* (√*sthā*), P. Ā. *-tishṭhati*, °*te*, to stand over, preside, govern, guide, Kām.; to administer, manage, MBh.; to mount upon, ascend, MW.

Sam-adhishṭhāna, n. abiding, residing, Kāśīkh.

Sam-adhishṭhita, mfn. standing upon (acc.), MBh.; standing above or at the highest place, Pañcar.; filling, penetrating (acc.), Car.; ridden or guided by (instr.), MBh.

समधिसृप् *sam-adhi-√sṛip*, P. *-sarpati*, to glide or slide along, ŚāṅkhŚr.

समधी *sam-adhī* (*-adhi-√5. i*), Ā. *-adhīte*, to go over, repeat or read through or study thoroughly, Mn. vi, 93.

Sam-adhîta, mfn. gone over, read through, studied, MBh.

Sam-adhyayana, n. going over or studying together, (or) that which is gone over or repeated together, Āpast.

समधुर *sa-madhura*, mfn. (for *sama-dh°* see p. 1152, col. 3) sweet, L.; (*ā*), f. a grape, L.

समध्यम *sa-madhyama*, mfn. moderate, Kull. on Mn. vii, 155.

समध्यास् *sam-adhy-√ās*, Ā. *-āste*, to sit upon together, inhabit, occupy, R.; Ragh.: Desid. *-āsisishate*, to wish to occupy, Bhaṭṭ.

Sam-adhyāsita, mfn. sat upon or occupied together (as a seat), Ragh.

समध्व *sam-adhva*, mfn. being on the same road, travelling in company, Bhaṭṭ.

समन् *sam-√an*, P. *-aniti*, to breathe, live, RV.

Sam-anana, n. breathing together, Nir.

Sam-āná, m. (for *samāna* and *sa-māna* see p. 1160) one of the five vital airs (that which circulates about the navel and is essential to digestion; it is personified as a son of Sādhya), AV. &c. &c.

समन *sámana*, n. (prob. connected with 2. *sam*, or 2. *sama*) meeting (cf. *a-samaná*), assembly, concourse, festival, RV.; AV.; intercourse, commerce, pursuit, RV. i, 48, 6; amorous union, embrace, RV. vi, 75, 4 &c.; conflict, strife, ib. vi, 73, 3; 5 &c. (Naigh. ii, 17). **–gá**, mfn. going to an assembly, RV.

Samaná, ind. in one point, together, RV.; at a time, all at once, ib.; likewise, uniformly, ib.

Samanyà, mfn. fit for an assembly or for a festival (as a garment), RV.

समनन्तर *sam-anantara*, mf(*ā*)n. immediately contiguous to or following (abl. or gen.; *yac câtra sam-anantaram*, 'and what is immediately connected with it'), R.; BhP.; Sarvad.; (*am*), ind. immediately behind or after (gen. or abl. or comp.), MBh.; R. &c.

समनस् *sá-manas*, mfn. being of the same mind, unanimous, RV.; VS.; Kauś.; endowed with understanding, BhP.

Sa-manaska, mfn. unanimous, KaṭhUp.; Sarvad.

समनीक *sam-anīká*, n. battle, war, RV. (Naigh. ii, 17); Bālar. vii, ३१. **–tas**, ind. in battle-array, AitBr. **–mūrdhan**, m. the front of b°, Vcar.

समनुकम्प् *sam-anu-√kamp*, Ā. *-kampate*, to sympathise with, have pity on (acc.), Ragh.

समनुकीर्तन *sam-anukīrtana*, n. praising highly, high praise, MBh.

समनुक्लृप् *sam-anu-√klṛip*, Caus. *-kalpayati*, to make any one (acc.) attain to any state or condition (loc.), MBh.

समनुक्रम् *sam-anu-√kram* (only ind. p. *-kramya*), to go or pass through completely, run through (acc.), BhP.

समनुगम् *sam-anu-√gam*, P. *-gacchati*, to go after, follow, pursue (acc.), R.; to penetrate, pervade, MBh.

Sam-anugata, mfn. gone after or through, followed, pervaded, Śaṃk.; coherent or connected with (instr.), ib.

समनुगा *sam-anu-√gā* (only aor. *-anv-agāt*), to go after together, follow quite closely, follow, MBh.

समनुगै *sam-anu-√gai*, P. *-gāyati*, to repeat in verse or metre, Car.

समनुग्रह् *sam-anu-√grah*, P. Ā. *-gṛihṇāti*, *-gṛihṇīte*, to collect or gather together, arrange or put in order, MBh.; to show favour or grace to (acc.), Kām.

Sam-anugrāhya, mfn. to be favoured or treated graciously, Hariv.

समनुचिन्त् *sam-anu-√cint*, P. *-cintayati*, to reflect deeply about, meditate on, remember (acc.), MBh.

समनुज *sam-anuja*, mfn. together with a younger brother, BhP.

समनुजन् *sam-anu-√jan*, Ā. *-jāyate*, to be born similar to or resembling (acc.), MBh.

समनुज्ञा *sam-anu-√jñā*, P. Ā. *-jānāti*, *-jānīte*, to fully permit or allow or consent to, wholly acquiesce in or approve of (acc.), MBh.; Hariv.; to authorize, empower, ib.; to indulge, pardon, forgive, excuse (gen. of pers.), R.; to grant leave of absence, allow to go away, dismiss, MBh.; to favour, ib.: Caus. *-jñāpayati*, to beg or request any favour from (abl.), MBh.; to ask leave, beg permission from (abl.), ib.; R.; to take leave of, bid adieu (acc.), Mn.; MBh. &c.; to greet, salute, MBh.

Sam-anujñā, f. leave, permission, L. °**anujñāta**, mfn. entirely consented or agreed to &c.; authorized, empowered, MBh.; allowed to go away, dismissed, ib.; favoured, treated kindly, ib. °**anujñāna**, mfn. entirely acquiesced in, permitted, allowed, W.; assent, permission, ib.

समनुतप् *sam-anu-√tap*, Pass. *-tapyate*, to suffer great subsequent pain, be very penitent, repent, MBh.

समनुदिश् *sam-anu-√diś*, P. *-diśati*, to assign or apportion anything (acc.) to any one (dat.), AitBr.

समनुदृश् *sam-anu-√dṛiś*. See *sam-anu-√paś*.

समनुद्रु *sam-anu-√dru*, P. *-dravati* (ep. also Ā. °*te*), to run after together, follow, pursue, MBh.

समनुधाव् *sam-anu-√1. dhāv*, P. *-dhāvati*, to run after together, follow, pursue, MBh.

समनुध्यै *sam-anu-√dhyai*, P. *-dhyāyati*, to reflect upon, think of (acc.), MBh.

समनुनिशम् *sam-anu-ni-√śam* (only ind. p. *-śamya*), to perceive, learn, R.

समनुपद् *sam-anu-√pad*, Ā. *-padyate* (ep. also P. °*ti*), to enter into or upon, attain to, MBh.; Hariv. (v. l. *-vatsyati* for *-patsyati*).

समनुपश् *sam-anu-√paś*, P. Ā. *-paśyati*, °*te* (only pres. base), to look well after, look at or on, MBh.; BhP.; to perceive, observe, MBh.; SaddhP.; to regard as, consider, MBh.

समनुपाल् *sam-anu-√pāl*, P. *-pālayati*, to maintain or observe well, keep (a promise &c.), MBh.; R.

समनुप्रछ् *sam-anu-√prach*, P. *-pṛicchati*, to ask or inquire about (acc.), MBh.

समनुप्राप् *sam-anu-prâp* (*-pra-√āp*), P. *-prâpnoti*, to attain or reach or arrive at (acc.), MBh.

Sam-anuprâpta, mfn. come, arrived at, R.;

one who has attained to (acc.), MBh.; obtained, assumed, MW.; entirely covered or overspread, ib.

समनुबन्ध *sam-anubandha*, m. = *anubandha*, L.

समनुभू *sam-anu-√bhū*, P. *-bhavati*, to enjoy together, feel, perceive, Ragh.

समनुमन् *sam-anu-√man*, Ā. *-manyate*, to assent, consent to (see next); to recognize together as (acc.), Kām.

Sam-anumata, mfn. consented to, agreed upon; n. consent, AitBr.

समनुया *sam-anu-√yā*, P. *-yāti*, to go after, follow, MBh.; VarBṛS.

Sam-anuyāta, mfn. gone after, followed, MBh.

समनुयुज् *sam-anu-√yuj* (only ind. p. *-yujya* and Pass. *-yujyate*), to inquire after, ask about, Cat.; to appoint, order, enjoin, R.

Sam-anuyojya, mfn. to be combined or mixed with (instr.), VarBṛS.

समनुवर्णित *sam-anu-varṇita*, mfn. (√*varṇ*) well described or narrated, explained, MBh.; BhP.

समनुवस् *sam-anu-√5. vas*, P. *-vasati*, to abide by, follow, conform to (acc.), Hariv. (v.l. *-patsyati* for *-vatsyati*).

समनुविद् *sam-anu-√1. vid*, Caus. *-vedayati*, to cause to know or remember, remind, AitBr.

समनुवीक्ष् *sam-anu-vîksh* (*-vi-√īksh*), Ā. *-vîkshate*, to well observe, behold, Kāv.

समनुवृत् *sam-anu-√vṛit*, Ā. *-vartate*, to follow after, obey, conform to (acc.), MBh.; R. &c.; to ensue, be the result or consequence, BhP.: Caus. *-vartayati*, to cause to take place or happen, R.

Sam-anuvartin, mfn. obedient, willing, devoted to (gen.), R.

समनुव्रज् *sam-anu-√vraj*, P. *-vrajati*, to go after, follow or pursue with others, MBh.

समनुव्रत *sam-anuvrata*, mf(*ā*)n. entirely devoted or attached to (acc.)

समनुशास् *sam-anu-√śās*, P. *-śāsti*, to teach thoroughly, instruct (two acc.), BhP.; (with *rājyam* or *rājya-lakshmīm*) to rule or regulate well, govern, MBh.; Inscr.

Sam-anuśishṭa, mfn. well taught or instructed in (acc.), BhP.

समनुशुच् *sam-anu-√śuc*, P. *-śocati*, to mourn over, regret (acc.), MBh.

समनुष्ठित *sam-anu-shṭhita*, mfn. (√*sthā*) furnished or provided with, rich in (comp.), ĀśvŚr.

Sam-anushṭheya, mfn. to be accomplished or performed, MBh.

समनुष्य *sa-manushya*, mfn. together with men, ĀśvGṛ.; visited or frequented by men, Sāy. **-rājanya**, mfn. together with the princely among men, ĀśvGṛ.

समनुसृप् *sam-anu-√sṛip*, P. *-sarpati*, to come near together, approach, MBh.

समनुस्मृ *sam-anu-√smṛi*, P. *-smarati*, to remember together, recollect, Jātakam.

समनुस्वृ *sam-anu-√svṛi*, P. *-svarati*, to resound, leave a sound, Śiksh.

समन्त *sám-anta*, mf(*ā*)n. 'having the ends together,' contiguous, neighbouring, adjacent, RV.; AV.; PañcavBr.; 'being on every side,' universal, whole, entire, all (*sámantam*, ind. 'in contiguity or conjunction with,' 'together with;' *samantám* or °*tāt* or °*ta-tas*, ind. 'on all sides, around,' or 'wholly, completely;' °*tena*, ind. 'all round;' with *na* = 'nowhere'), AV. &c. &c.; (*ā*), f. (pl.) neighbourhood, ŚBr.; N. of a grammar, Col.; n. (also with *Agneḥ*, *Varuṇasya*, or *Vasishṭhasya*) N. of various Sāmans, Br.; n. or m. (?) N. of a country, Buddh. **-kusuma**, m. N. of a Deva-putra, Lalit. **-gandha**, m. a kind of flower, L.; N. of a Deva-putra, SaddhP. **-cāritra-mati**, m. N. of a Bodhi-sattva, Buddh. **-tas**, ind., see above. **-darśin**, m. N. of a Buddha, Lalit. **-dugdhā**, f. a species of Euphorbia, L.; (*ī*), f. = *snuhā*, Hcar., Sch. **-netra**, m. N. of a Bodhi-sattva, Buddh. **-pañcaka**, n. N. of the district Kuru-kshetra or of a Tīrtha in it (where Paraśu-rāma is said to have destroyed the Kshatriyas), MBh.; Pur. **-paryāyin**, mfn. all-embracing, AitBr. **-prabha**, m. a kind of flower, L.; N. of a Bodhi-sattva, Buddh. **-prabhāsa**, m. N. of a Buddha, SaddhP. **-prasādika**, m. N. of a Bodhi-sattva (v.l. *-prās°*), Buddh. **-prāsādika**, mfn. affording help or assistance on all sides (also v.l. for prec.), ib.; *-tā*, f. complete readiness to offer help (one of the 80 minor marks of a Buddha), Dharmas. 84. **-bhadra**, mfn. wholly auspicious, Harav.; m. a Buddha or a Jina, L.; N. of a Bodhi-sattva, Kāraṇḍ. (cf. Dharmas. 12); of a poet &c., Cat.; n. N. of a grammar. **-bhuj**, m. 'all-devouring,' N. of Agni or fire, L. **-mukha-dhāriṇī**, f. N. of a Buddhist Sūtra. **-raśmi**, m. N. of a Bodhi-sattva, Buddh. **-vilokitā**, f. N. of a partic. Buddhist world, Lalit. **-vyūha-sāgara-carya-vyavalokana**, m. N. of a Garuḍa-rāja, Buddh. **-śiti-bāhu** (*samantá-*), mfn. having both fore-feet white, VS.; MaitrS. **-śiti-randhra** (*samantá-*), mfn. having both ear-cavities white, ib.; Pat. on Pāṇ. ii, 1, 1, Vārtt. 27. **-sthūlâvalokana**, m. or n. (?) a kind of flower, Buddh. **-sphāraṇa-mukha-darśana**, m. N. of a Garuḍa-rāja, ib. **Samantâloka**, m. a partic. Samādhi, ib. **Samantâvalokita**, m. N. of a Bodhi-sattva, ib.

Sam-antara, m. pl. N. of a people, MBh.

Sám-antikam, ind. contiguously, near (compar. °*ka-taram*), ŚBr.

समन्त्र *sa-mantra*, mfn. accompanied with sacred verses or texts, ĀpŚr., Sch.

Sa-mantraka, mfn. id., ib.; possessing charms or spells, MW.

समन्त्रिन् *sa-mantrin*, mfn. together with or accompanied by counsellors (°*tri-tva*, n.), Rājat.

Sa-mantrika, mfn. id., MW.

समन्धकार *sam-andhakāra*, m. great or universal darkness, Pat. on Pāṇ. ii, 2, 6.

Samandhakārī-kṛita, mfn. made dark or inaccessible on all sides, Kir.

समन्मथ *sa-manmatha*, mfn. filled with love, enamoured, Ṛitus.

समन्य *samanyà*. See p. 1154, col. 2.

समन्यु *sá-manyu* or *sa-manyú*, mfn. having the same mind, unanimous (applied to the Maruts), RV.; wrathful, angry, ib.; filled with sorrow, sorrowful, MBh.; m. N. of Śiva, ib.

समन्वङ्गीभूत *sam-anvaṅgi-bhūta*, mfn. possessed by, provided with (instr.), Divyâv.

समन्वय *sam-anvaya* &c. See *sam-anv-√5.i*.

समन्वागत *sam-anv-ā-gata*, mfn. (√*gam*) attended by, furnished or provided with (comp.), Buddh.

समन्वारभ् *sam anv-ā-√rabh*, Ā. *-rabhate*, to take hold of or clasp together, take hold of one another, AitBr.; ŚBr.; ĀśvŚr.

Sam-anvārabdha, mfn. taken hold of, MBh.; holding, touching, ĀśvŚr.; (pl.) taking hold of one another, Vait. °**anvārambha**, m. taking hold of from behind, Śaṃkar. °**anvārambhaṇa**, n. id., Bādar.

समन्वारुह् *sam-anv-ā-√ruh*, P. *-rohati*, to ascend after (as a wife the funeral pyre after her husband), MBh.

समन्वि *sam-anv-√5 i*, P. *-eti*, to go together after, follow, MW.; to infer or ensue as a consequence, ib.

Sam-anvaya, m. regular succession or order, connected sequence or consequence, conjunction, mutual or immediate connection (*āt*, ind. 'in consequence of'), Kap.; Bādar.; MBh. &c.; *-pradīpa*, m., *-pradīpa-saṃketa*, m., *-sūtra-vivṛiti*, f. N. of wks.

Sam-anvita, mfn. connected or associated with, completely possessed of, fully endowed with, possessing, full of (instr. or comp.), ŚvetUp.; Mn.; MBh. &c.; corresponding or answering to (comp.), R.

समन्विष् *sam-anv-√1. ish*, P. *-ishyati*, to seek out, look for or after, Bālar.

समन्विष् *sam-anv-√3. ish*, P. *-icchati* (ind. p. *-ishya*), to search through, seek about everywhere, MBh.

Sam-anveshaṇa, n. searching or seeking everywhere, L.

समन्वीक्ष् *sam-anv-√īksh* (only ind. p. *-īkshya*), to look towards, look or gaze after, ŚBr.; to keep looking at, keep in view, ib.

समपच्छिद् *sam-apa-cchid* (√*chid*), P. *-cchinatti*, to cut off, Śulbas.

समपध्यै *sam-apa-√dhyai*, P. *-dhyāyati* (ep. also Ā. °*te*), to think ill or badly of, meditate evil or injury against, injure, MBh.

समपवृज् *sam-apa-√vṛij*, Caus. *-varjayati* (p. p. *varjita*), to deliver over, present with, offer to (dat.), MBh.

समपवृत् *sam-apa-√vṛit*, Caus. *-vartayati*, to cause to roll away, drive away, RV.

समपावृ *sam-apā-√1. vṛi*, P. *-vṛiṇoti*, to unfasten, open, MBh. (w.r. *sam-upā-√vṛi*).

समपिधा *sam-api-√1. dhā* (only ind. p. *-dhāya*), to cover completely, ŚBr.

समपिरुह् *sam-api-√ruh*, P. *-rohati*, to grow together, grow over, AV.

समपोह् *sam-apôh* (*-apa-√1. ūh*), P. *-apôhati*, to dispel completely, entirely exclude, Sarvad.

समभिकीर्त् *sam-abhi-√kīrt* (only ind. p. *-kīrtya*), to relate or tell fully, narrate, MBh.

समभिक्रम् *sam-abhi-√kram* (only ind. p. *-kramya*), to go near to, approach, MBh.

समभिक्रुद्ध *sam-abhi-kruddha*, mfn. (√*krudh*) greatly enraged, angry, MBh.

समभिगम् *sam-abhi-√gam*, P. *-gacchati*, to go towards together, approach, R.; to go to, have sexual intercourse with (instr.), Kathās.

समभिगर्ज् *sam-abhi-√garj*, P. *-garjati*, to shout or cry at defiantly, challenge with a shout (acc.), MBh.

समभिगुह् *sam-abhi-√guh*, Ā. *-gūhate*, to crouch down, cower, Hariv.

समभिच्छन्न *sam-abhi-cchanna*, mfn. (√*chad*) completely covered with (instr.), MBh.

समभिजन् *sam-abhi-√jan*, Ā. *-jāyate*, to spring up together, arise, R.

समभिज्ञा *sam-abhi-√jñā* (only ind. p. *-jñāya*), to recognize fully, entirely acknowledge or perceive, MBh.

समभितर्ज् *sam-abhi-√tarj*, P. *-tarjayati*, to threaten or menace greatly, abuse, blame, scold, Hariv.

समभितस् *sam-abhitas*, ind. towards, to (acc.), MBh.

समभित्यज् *sam-abhi-√tyaj*, P. *-tyajati*, to give up entirely, wholly renounce or resign, MBh.

Sam-abhityakta, mfn. wholly given up, renounced, risked, MBh.; *-jīvita*, mfn. one who has quite renounced his life, Hariv.

समभिद्रु *sam-abhi-√dru*, P. *-dravati* (ep. also Ā. °*te*), to run or hasten towards or against, rush full upon, attack, assail (acc.), Nir.; MBh. &c.

Sam-abhidruta, mfn. running towards or against, rushing upon, MBh.; rushed upon, attacked, infested, ib.; (*am*), ind. hurriedly, quickly, ib.

समभिधा *sam-abhi-√1. dhā*, P. *-dadhāti*, to speak to, address (acc.), Kathās.; to proclaim, announce, Kir.; to direct all one's thoughts to (acc.), MW.

Sam-abhidhā, f. (only ifc.) a name, appellation, Inscr.

Sam-abhihita, mfn. addressed, spoken to, BhP.

समभिधाव् *sam-abhi-√1. dhāv*, P. Ā. *-dhāvati*, °*te*, to run hastily up to or towards, fly or dart at, assail, MBh.; R.

समभिध्यै *sam-abhi-√dhyai*, P. *-dhyāyati* or *-dhyāti*, to reflect deeply on, meditate on, MBh.; to direct all the thoughts upon, long for (acc.), Suśr.

समभिनन्द् *sam-abhi-√nand*, P. *-nandati*, to rejoice together with (see next); to greet, salute, R.; Kathās.

Sam-abhinandita, mfn. rejoiced with, congratulated, Kathās.

समभिनिःसृत *sam-abhi-niḥ-sṛita*, mfn. (√*sṛi*) come forth, gushed forth (as blood from a wound), MBh.

समभिपत् *sam-abhi-√pat*, P. *-patati*, to fall upon, attack (acc.), R.

समभिपद् *sam-abhi-√pad*, Ā. *-padyate*, to come to, arrive at, attain (acc.), MBh.; to get one's reward, ib.; to reply, answer, ib.

समभिपाल् *sam-abhi-√pāl*, P. *-pālayati*, to protect, rule, govern (acc.), Hariv.

समभिपीड् *sam-abhi-√pīḍ*, P. *-pīḍayati*, to squeeze together, crush, Hariv.

समभिपूज् *sam-abhi-√pūj*, P. *-pūjayati*, to worship, honour, MBh.

समभिपृ *sam-abhi-√pṛī*, Caus. *-pūrayati*, to fill up, fill, MBh.

समभिप्रेक्ष् *sam-abhi-prêksh* (*-pra-√īksh*), Ā. *-prêkshate*, to look at, perceive, view, R.

समभिप्लु *sam-abhi-√plu*, Ā. *-plavate*, to inundate, wash (see next); to overwhelm, cover, MBh.; R.

Sam-abhipluta, mfn. inundated, flooded, washed, R.; overwhelmed, covered, MBh.; eclipsed (as the moon), R.; (with *rajasā*) covered with menstrual excretions, Mn. iv, 42.

समभिभाष् *sam-abhi-√bhāsh*, Ā. *-bhāshate* (ep. also P. °*ti*), to speak with or to, address (acc.), MBh.

Sam-abhibhāshaṇa, n. conversation, colloquy with (instr. or comp.), R.

समभिया *sam-abhi-√yā*, P. *-yāti*, to approach any one (acc.) together, go towards or near, advance, MBh.; Hariv.; MārkP.

समभियाच् *sam-abhi-√yāc*, P. Ā. *-yācati*, °*te*, to ask earnestly, implore, Hariv.

समभिरञ्ज् *sam-abhi-√rañj*, Ā. or Pass. *-rajyate*, to be reddened, appear red, flash, glitter, MBh.

समभिरुह् *sam-abhi-√ruh*, P. *-rohati*, to grow up together, ascend, Hariv. (v.l. *sam-adhi-r*°): Caus. *-rohayati* (Pass. *-ropyate*), to cause to grow up or ascend, place or impose on (as a burden &c.), ib.

समभिलष् *sam-abhi-√lash*, P. *-lashati*, to long for, be eager for, Hariv.

समभिवद् *sam-abhi-√vad*, Caus. *-vādayati*, to address or salute respectfully, MBh.; Hariv.

समभिवध् *sam-abhi-√vadh* (defective; see √*vadh*), to strike or hit at any one (acc.), MBh.

समभिवाञ्छ् *sam-abhi-√vāñch*, P. *-vāñchati*, to long for, be eager for, VarBṛS.

समभिवीक्ष् *sam-abhi-vīksh* (*-vi-√īksh*), P. *-vīkshate*, to perceive, become aware of (acc.), Śak. (v.l.)

समभिवृत् *sam-abhi-√vṛit*, Ā. *-vartate*, to go towards, advance, MBh.; to attack, assail, Hariv.; to come near, approach, MBh.; to turn back, return, recur, Suśr.; to remain, continue (*tūshṇīm*, 'silent'), R.; w.r. for *sam-ati-√vṛit*.

समभिवृध् *sam-abhi-√vṛidh*, Ā. *-vardhate*, to grow up, increase, Hariv.: Caus. *-vardhayati*, to make larger, enlarge, increase, augment, MBh.; R.

समभिवृष् *sam-abhi-√vṛish*, P. *-varshati*, to rain down upon, BhP.

समभिव्याहृ *sam-abhi-vy-ā-√hṛi*, P. Ā. *-harati*, °*te*, to mention together, Nyāyam.; to bring together, associate together, MW.

Sam-abhivyāhāra, m. mentioning together, KātyŚr.; bringing together, association, company, Kaṇ.; association with a word of well-known meaning (= *prasiddhârthakasya śabdasya saṃnidhiḥ*), MW. °**abhivyāhārin**, mfn. mentioning together, ib.; accompanying, ib. °**abhivyāhṛita**, mfn. mentioned or spoken of together, Kusum.; associated (= *sahita*), accompanied by, MW.

समभिशुभ् *sam-abhi-√śubh*, Ā. *-śobhate*, to be beautiful or shine with (instr.), R.

समभिश्यान *sam-abhi-śyāna*, mfn. (√*śyai*) thoroughly coagulated, Kāś. on Pāṇ. vi, 1, 26.

समभिषिच् *sam-abhi-shic* (√*sic*), P. *-shiñcati*, to sprinkle down upon, wet, Hariv.; to anoint, consecrate, Kathās.

समभिष्टु *sam-abhi-shṭu* (√*stu*), P. Ā. *-shṭauti*, *-shṭute*, to praise highly, extol, MBh.; R.

Sam-abhishṭuta, mfn. extolled, celebrated, BhP.

समभिष्ठा *sam-abhi-shṭhā* (√*sthā*), P. *-tishṭhati*, to mount upon (as upon an elephant), MBh.

समभिष्यन्द् *sam-abhi-shyand* (√*syand*), Caus. *-shyandayati*, to cause to flow towards (acc.), Car.

Sam-abhishyandin, mfn. causing hypertrophy, Car.

समभिसंवृत *sam-abhi-saṃ-vṛita*, mfn. (√1. *vṛi*) entirely surrounded, encompassed, MBh.

समभिसंधा *sam-abhi-saṃ-√1. dhā*, P. Ā. *-dadhāti*, *-dhatte*, to place or put into (loc.), MBh.; to aim at, strive after, determine on (acc.), ib.

समभिसृ *sam-abhi-√sṛi*, P. *-sarati* (ind. p. *-sṛitya*), to go towards, approach, advance, attack, MW.

Sam-abhisaraṇa, n. the act of going towards or against, approaching, seeking, wishing or endeavouring to gain, ib.

समभिहृ *sam-abhi-√hṛi*, P. Ā. *-harati*, °*te*, to seize upon or take together, MW.; to seize, take, take out, ib.

Sam-abhiharaṇa, n. the act of seizing upon, taking &c., ib.; repetition, Pat. on Pāṇ. iii, 1, 22. °**abhihāra**, m. seizing or taking together, MW.; repetition, reiteration (*kriyā-samabhihāreṇa*, 'by a repetition of acts,' 'by repeated acts'), Pāṇ.; Śiś.; excess, surplus, W.

समभिहृष् *sam-abhi-√hṛish*, Caus. *-harshayati*, to cause great joy or exultation, gladden, delight, MBh.

समभी *sam-abhî* (*-abhi-√5. i*), P. *-abhy-eti*, to go towards, come near, approach, RV.; R. &c.; to accrue to (acc.), MārkP.; to follow, attend, wait upon, Śiś.

समभ्यतिक्रम् *sam-abhy-ati-√kram*, P. *-krāmati*, to come upon or into, enter into, R.

समभ्यर्च् *sam-abhy-√arc*, P. *-arcati*, to pay great honour to, worship, greet, salute (acc.), Yājñ.; MBh.

Sam-abhyarcana, n. the act of paying great honour to, worshipping, reverencing, W. °**abhyarcita**, mfn. greatly honoured, worshipped, saluted, ib.

समभ्यर्थ् *sam-abhy-√arth*, Ā. *-arthayate*, to petition, solicit, request, MW.

Sam-abhyarthayitṛi, mfn. seeking, petitioning, a petitioner, Kum.

समभ्यवगा *sam-abhy-ava-√gā*, P. *-jigāti*, to go into (acc.), GopBr.

समभ्यवे *sam-abhy-avê* (*-ava-√5. i*), P. *-avâiti*, to penetrate entirely into (acc.), ŚBr.; to come to an agreement with (instr.), ib.

समभ्यस् *sam-abhy-√2. as*, P. *-asyati*, to practise, exercise, Subh.

Sam-abhyāsa, m. practice, exercise, study, Kāśikh.

समभ्यागम् *sam-abhy-ā-√gam*, P. *-gacchati*, to come near (see next); to meet, Prasannar.

Sam-abhyāgata, mfn. come near, approached, Pañcat.

समभ्यागा *sam-abhy-ā-√gā*, P. *-jigāti*, to come near, approach, MBh.; to come upon, seize, visit (with affliction), ib.

समभ्यादा *sam-abhy-ā-√1. dā*, Ā. *-datte*, to comprehend, ŚBr.

समभ्यानी *sam-abhy-ā-√nī*, P. *-nayati*, to lead near or towards, introduce, MBh.

समभ्याश *sam-abhyāśa*, m. nearness, presence, MBh.

Sam-abhyāśī-karaṇa, n. bringing near, Pat. on Pāṇ. ii, 1, 51.

समभ्याहार *sam-abhyāhāra*, m. bringing together, association, accompaniment, MW.

समभ्युच्चय *sam-abhyuccaya*, m. heaping, piling up (*-vat*, ind.), ĀpŚr.

समभ्युत्था *sam-abhy-ut-thā* (√*sthā*), Ā. *-tishṭhate*, to rise (said of a planet), Hariv.

समभ्युद्गम् *sam-abhy-ud-√gam* (only ind. p. *-gamya*), to come forth or spread from (abl.), Divyâv.

समभ्युद्धृ *sam-abhy-ud-dhṛi* (√*hṛi*), Ā. *-dharate*, to draw out, extract, Sarasv.; to draw out of danger or distress, rescue, raise, promote, further, MBh.

Sam-abhyuddharaṇa, n. drawing out, rescuing, MBh.

समभ्युद्यत *sam-abhy-ud-yata*, mfn. (√*yam*) striving, endeavouring, Divyâv.

समभ्युन्नत *sam-abhy-un-nata*, mfn. (√*nam*) raised, risen, towering high (as clouds), Mṛicch.

समभ्युपगमन *sam-abhyupagamana*, n. the act of approaching or going near, MW.; following, approving, agreeing with, RPrāt., Sch.

समभ्युपे *sam-abhy-upê* (*-upa-√5. i*), P. *upâiti*, to go very near, approach, MW.

Sam-abhyupeya, mfn. to be gone or approached or followed, ib.; n. = *sam-abhyupagamana*, RPrāt., Sch.

समभ्ये *sam-abhy-ê* (*-ā-√5. i*), P. *-âiti*, to come up to, approach, go near to (acc.), MBh.; Pañcat.

समम् *samam* &c. See 2. *sama*, p. 1152.

समम् *sam-√am*, Ā. *-amate*, to ask eagerly, solicit, win over, RV.; to fix or settle firmly, ib.; to ally or connect one's self with, AV.

समय *sam-aya* &c. See p. 1164, col. 1.

समर *sam-ara* &c. See *sam-√ṛi*, p. 1170.

समर्घ *sam-argha*, mfn. cheap, VarBṛS.; Vas.

समर्च् *sam-√arc*, P. *-arcati*, *-ṛicati* (pf. *-ānṛica*, R.; *-ānṛice*, RV.), to fix, establish, RV. i, 160, 4; to honour, worship, adore, R.; to adorn, decorate, VarBṛS.: Caus. *-arcayati*, to honour &c., MBh.

Sam-arcaka, mfn. worshipping, Kāśīkh. °**arcana**, n. (or *ā*, f.) the act of worshipping, adoration, Pañcar. °**arcā**, f. id., Kāśīkh. °**arcita**, mfn. worshipped, adored, honoured, W.

समर्ण *sam-arṇṇa*. See *sam-√ard*, p. 1157.

समर्ति *sam-arti*, f. suffering loss or damage or misfortune (in *á-s*°, perhaps w.r. for *a-samārti*), TS.

समर्थ *sam-√arth* (in some senses rather Nom. fr. *sam-artha* below), Ā. *-arthayate* (rarely P. °*ti*), to make fit or ready, prepare, RV.; to finish, close, L.; to connect with (instr.) in sense, construe (grammatically), Sāh.; Kull.; to judge, think, contemplate, consider, MBh.; Kāv. &c.; to suppose to be, take for (acc. with *prati*), Vikr. iv, 58; to notice, perceive, find out, Kām.; Kum.; Śaṃk.; to fix upon, determine, approve, R.; to cheer up, comfort, encourage, Kathās.; *samarthaya*, often w.r. for *samarpaya*, see *sam-√ṛi*.

Sam-artha, mf(*ā*)n. having a similar or suitable aim or object, having proper aim or force, very forcible or adequate, well answering or corresponding to, suitable or fit for (gen. or comp.), MBh.; Kāv. &c.; very strong or powerful, competent, capable of, able to, a match for (gen., dat., loc., inf., or comp.; rarely acc., abl., or pr. p.; with *varâṅganāsu* = 'sexually potent'), Mn.; MBh. &c.; having the same sense or meaning (= *tulyârtha*, *ekârtha*), Pāṇ. i, 3, 42 &c.; connected in sense, having the same grammatical construction (= *sambaddhârtha*), Pāṇ.; APrāt. &c.; m. a word which

has force or meaning, significant word, MW.; the construction or coherence of words in a significant sentence, ib.; n. ability, competence (see *-yukta*); conception, intelligibility (see *duḥ-s°*); *-tara*, mfn. more (or most) competent, capable &c., Pañcat.; *-tā*, f. (Sarvad.), *-tva*, n. (Rājat.) ability, capability, competence (*-tayā*, with gen., 'by virtue of'); sameness of meaning, force or signification (of words), MW.; *-pada-vidhi*, m. N. of a gram. wk.; *-yukta*, mfn. adequate to or qualified for (loc.), R. **°ar-thaka**, mfn. able to, capable of (inf.), Vet.; maintaining, establishing, proving, corroborating, Sāh.; n. Amyris Agallocha (?), W.

Sam-arthana, n. (or *ā*, f.) reflection, deliberation, contemplation (*°naṃ-√kṛi*, 'to reflect, consider'), MBh.; Kathās.; reconciling differences, reconciliation, W.; objecting, objection, ib.; (*ā*), f. persuasion, invitation, MBh.; insisting on what is impossible, Vop.; (*am*), n. establishing, maintaining, corroboration, vindication, justification, Pratāp.; Kuval.; energy, force, ability, competence (*āt*, with gen., 'by virtue of'), MBh. **°arthanīya**, mfn. to be determined or fixed or established, TPrāt., Sch.

Sam-arthita, mfn. taken into consideration, considered, judged, regarded, held, R.; Vikr.; resolved, determined, R.; maintained, established, TPrāt., Sch.; able, capable, Kāv.; *-vat*, mfn. one who has judged or considered &c., Pañcat.; Kathās.

Sam-arthya, mfn. to be established or corroborated or justified, Sāh.

समर्द् *sam-√ard*, Caus. *-ardayati*, to pain greatly, distress, wound, MBh.

Sam-arṇṇa, mfn. pained, wounded &c., Pāṇ.; Vop.; asked, solicited, W.

समर्धक *sam-ardhaka*, *°dhana* &c. See *sam-√ṛidh*, p. 1171, col. 1.

समर्पक *sam-arpaka*, *°paṇa* &c. See *sam-√ṛi*, p. 1170, col. 3.

समर्य *sa-maryà*, mfn. (for *sam-aryà* see *sam-√ṛi*) attended by many persons, frequented (as a sacrificial ceremony), RV.; attended by (his) followers (said of Indra), ib.

समर्याद *sa-maryāda*, **mfn. bounded, limited,** keeping within bounds or in the right course, correct, Vās.; respectful, MW.; contiguous, neighbouring, L.; (*am*), ind. decisively, exactly, Bhartṛ.; m. contiguity, vicinity, L.

समर्ह् *sam-√arh*, Caus. *-arhayati*, to show honour, pay respect to, BhP.

Sam-arhaṇa, n. respect, reverence, a respectful gift (acc. with *upa-√hṛi*, *ni-√dhā* and Caus. of *pra-√vṛit*, 'to show honour' or 'offer a gift of honour'), BhP.

समल *sa-mala*, **mfn. having stains or spots,** dirty, foul, impure, Vās.; Bhpr.; sinful, Uṇ. i, 109, Sch.; m. N. of an Asura (v. l. *sṛimara*), Hariv.; n. (cf. *śamala*) excrement, feculent matter, ordure, L.

Samalī-√kṛi, P. *-karoti*, to make dirty, stain, pollute, defile, Bhadrab.

समलंकृ *sam-alaṃ-√kṛi*, P. Ā. *-karoti*, *-kurute*, to decorate highly, embellish, adorn, MBh.; R.

Sam-alaṃkṛita, mfn. highly decorated, well adorned, ib.

समल्लिकाक्ष *sa-mallikāksha*, **mfn. with white spots on (their) eyes (said of horses), Vās.**

समव् *sam-√av*, **P. *-avati*, to drive or force** into (hostile) contact, RV. v, 34, 8; **to aid, refresh,** comfort, RV.; AV.

Sam-avana, n. helping, **protecting,** BhP.

समवकार *sam-ava-kāra*, **m. (√1. *kṛi*) a kind** of higher Rūpaka or drama **(in three acts, representing the heroic actions of gods or demons),** Bhar.; Daśar.; Sāh.

समवकॄ *sam-ava-√kṝi*, **P. *-kirati*, to scatter** completely over, cover **entirely, overwhelm** with, MBh.; R.; BhP.

समवक्षिप् *sam-ava-√kship*, **P. *-kshipati*,** to cast or thrust away, **repel, MBh.**

समवगम् *sam-ava-√gam*, P. *-gacchati*, to perceive or understand thoroughly, become thoroughly acquainted with, BhP.

समवगुण्ठित *sam-ava-gunṭhita*, mfn. (√*gunṭh*) completely wrapped up or enveloped in (acc.), R.

समवगुह् *sam-ava-√guh*, Ā. *-gūhate*, to crouch down, cower, Hariv.

समवच्छद् *sam-ava-cchad* (√*chad*), Caus. *-cchādayati* (Pass. *-cchādyate*), to cover completely over, conceal, obscure, MBh.; Hariv.

Sam-avacchanna, mfn. covered all over, ib.

समवतॄ *sam-ava-√tṝi*, Caus. *-tārayati*, to cause to descend, MBh.

Sam-avatāra, m. a sacred bathing-place (= *tīrtha*), Kir.

समवदिश् *sam-ava-√diś*, P. *-diśati*, to point or refer to, explain with reference to anything, Kāṭh.

समवदो *sam-ava-√do* (or √3. *dā*), P. *-dāti* or *-dyati* (3. pl. pf. Ā. *-dadire*), to divide and put together piece by piece, Br.

Sam-ávatta, mfn. cut up into bits, divided into fragments, ŚBr.; *-dhāna*, mfn. containing the gathered fragments, ĀśvGṛ.; (*ī*), f. a vessel containing the gathered fragments, ŚBr.; ŚrS.

समवद्रु *sam-ava-√dru*, P. *-dravati*, to run away together, ŚBr.

समवधा *sam-ava-√1. dhā*, P. Ā. *-dadhāti*, *-dhatte*, to lay or put together, ĀpŚr.

Sam-avadhāna, n. the being brought together, meeting, Kusum.; Sarvad.; Buddh.; great attention, MW.; preparation, ib.

Sam-avahita. See *á-sam-avahitam*.

समवधीरय *sam-avadhīraya*, Nom. P. *°yati*, to disregard, pay no heed to, Kād.

समवनत *sam-ava-nata*, mfn. (√*nam*) completely bent down, bowed, bending down, stooping (to drink water &c.), MW.

समवनी *sam-ava-√nī*, P. Ā. *-nayati*, *°te*, to lead together, unite, ŚBr.; to pour in together, ib.; AitBr.; ĀśvGṛ.

समवपीड् *sam-ava-√pīḍ*, P. *-pīḍayati*, to press together, Suśr.

समवप्लुत *sam-ava-pluta*, mfn. (√*plu*) lept down, jumped off, MBh.

समवबुध् *sam-ava-√budh*, Ā. *-budhyate*, to perceive clearly, understand fully, learn, know, MBh.; R.

Sam-avabodhana, n. thorough knowledge, intelligence, perception, MBh.

समवमृश् *sam-ava-√mṛiś*, P. *-mṛiśati*, to lay hold of, ŚBr.

समवरुध् *sam-ava-√2. rudh*, P. *-ruṇaddhi* (ep. also *-rundhati*), to shut up, enclose, confine, MBh.: Pass. *-rudhyate*, to be enclosed or contained in (loc.), PañcavBr.; to be shut out of, be deprived of, Hariv.

Sam-avaruddha, mfn. shut up, enclosed &c.; attained, obtained, BhP.

समवलम्ब् *sam-ava-√lamb*, Ā. *-lambate*, to take hold of, clasp, embrace, MBh.; VarBṛS.

समवली *sam-ava-√lī*, Ā. *-līyate*, to be dissolved, Vedāntas.

समवलोक् *sam-ava-√lok*, P. *-lokayati*, to look at or about, R.; to inspect, survey, ib.; Hit. (v.l.); to behold, perceive, R.; Śak.; Kathās.

समववृत् *sam-ava-√vṛit*, Caus. *-vartayati*, to turn towards, ŚBr.

Sam-ávavṛitta, mfn. turned towards, ib.

समवशेषित *sam-ava-śeshita*, mfn. (√*śish*) left, spared, remaining, MBh.

समवश्यान *sam-ava-śyāna*, mfn. (√*śyai*) wasted, destroyed, Kāś. on Pāṇ. vi, 1, 26.

समवष्टम्भ् *sam-ava-shṭambh* (√*stambh*; only ind. p. *-shṭabhya*), to raise or hold up, support, confirm, MBh.; to rest on for support (ind. p. = 'with the help of'), ib.; R.

समवसन्न *sam-ava-sanna*, mfn. (√*sad*) sunk down, depressed, low-spirited, MBh.

समवसृ *sam-ava-√sṛi*, P. *-sarati*, to come down, descend (from heaven to earth; said of a Jina), HPariś.

Sam-avasaraṇa, n. meeting, assembling, an assembly, Buddh.; descent (of a Jina from heaven to earth) or place of descent, HPariś.; aim, goal, Buddh.

Sam-avasṛita, mfn. descended (from heaven to earth), HPariś. **°avasṛiti**, f. = *sam-avasaraṇa*, ib.

समवसृज् *sam-ava-√sṛij*, P. *-sṛijati*, to let go, cast or hurl down upon (loc.), MBh.; to abandon, ib.; to leave out, AitBr.; to impose (a burden) upon (loc.), MBh.

Sam-avasarga (of unknown meaning), Mahāvy. **°avasargya**, mfn. to be let go or abandoned &c., Pāṇ. iii, 1, 124, Vārtt. 2, Pat.

Sam-avasṛijya, mfn. id., AitBr.

समवसो *sam-ava-√so*, P. *-syati*, to decide, be in agreement with another (upon the same place or time), ŚBr.; ĀpŚr.; to reach, attain, BhP.

समवस्कन्द् *sam-ava-√skand*, Caus. *-skandayati*, to attack, assail, Mn. vii, 196; to seize upon (acc.), Car.

Sam-avaskanda, m. a bulwark, rampart &c., Kām.

समवस्था *sam-ava-√sthā*, Caus. *-sthāpayati*, to cause to stand firm or still, stop, MBh.; to establish, found, ib.

Sam-avasthā, f. firm or fixed state or condition, Kālid.; (ifc. f. *ā*) similar condition or state, Ragh. **°avasthāna**, n. resting or abiding in (loc.), Nilak.; state, condition, BhP. **°avasthāpita**, mfn. (fr. Caus.) made to stand firmly, set up, MBh.; fully established, founded, ib. **°avasthita**, mfn. standing or remaining firm, remaining fixed, steady, MBh.; Kāv. &c.; being in any place or position, R.; VarBṛS.; Pur.; ready, prepared for (dat.), MBh.; Hariv.

समवस्रु *sam-ava-√sru* (only ind. p. *-srutya*), to flow off or away, flow out, MānGṛ.

Sam-avasrava, m. flowing off or away, flowing out, effluence, ĀśvGṛ. **°avasrāviṇī**, f. a partic. arrangement of 11 sacrificial posts (so that the middlemost is the lowest and the rest become lower and lower from both ends), ĀpŚr.

समवहा *sam-ava-√3. hā* (only ind. p. *-hāya*), to avoid, abandon, BhP.

समवहास्य *sam-ava-hāsya*, mfn. (√*has*) to be laughed at or derided (*°tāṃ √gam*, 'to become ridiculous'), MBh.

समवहित *sam-avahita.* See col. 2.

समवहृ *sam-ava-√hṛi* (only ind. p. *-hāram*), to collect, gather, ChUp.

Sam-avahāra, m. collection, quantity, abundance, MBh.; mixture, BhP.

समवाकार *sam-avākāra*, w. r. for *sam-ava-kāra* (see col. 1).

समवाप् *sam-avâp* (*-ava-√āp*), P. Ā. *-avâpnoti*, *°pnute*, to meet with, attain, reach, gain, obtain, incur, MBh.; R. &c.

Sam-avâpta, mfn. obtained, attained (*-kāma*, mfn. 'one who has obtained his desires'), MBh. **°avâpti**, f. attainment, obtaining, getting, W.

समवार्ज् *sam-avârj* (*-ava-√ṛij*), P. *-avârjati*, to abandon or leave off together, ŚBr.

समवे *sam-avé* (*-ava-√5. i*), P. *-avâiti*, to come or meet or mix or assemble together, be united in (acc.), ŚBr.; Śaṃk. (cf. Pāṇ. iv, 4, 43); to regard, consider (with *iva*, 'to regard as'), VP.

Sam-avâya, m. coming or meeting together, contact, concourse, congress, assemblage, collection, crowd, aggregate (*ena* or *āt*, 'in combination;' *°yaṃ √kṛi*, 'to meet, combine, flock together'), GṛS.; Gaut.; Mn. &c.; conjunction (of heavenly bodies), MBh.; VarBṛS.; collision, ŚrS.; Gaut.; Sarvad.; (in phil.) perpetual co-inherence, inner or intimate relation, constant and intimate union, inseparable concomitance (= *nitya-sambandha*, the sixth Padārtha or category of the Vaiśeshikas, expressing the relation which exists between a substance and its qualities, between a whole and its parts [e.g. between cloth and the yarn composing it], between a genus and its individuals &c.), Kap.; Jaim.;

IW. 66; 69; course, duration (*e*, with gen., 'during'), MBh. i, 556; *-khaṇḍana*, n. N. of wk.; *-tas*, ind. in consequence of constant and intimate connection or relation, MW.; *-tva*, n. the state of (being) intimate relation, Kusum.; *-pramāṇa-vādârtha*, m., *-vāda*, m. N. of wks.; *-sambandha*, m. intimate and constant connection, inseparable relation (as described above), connection by inseparable inherence, W. °**avâyana**, n. the act of coming or meeting together &c., L. °**avâyika**, mfn. being in connection with, Saṃskārak.

Samavâyi, in comp. for *samavâyin*. **-kāraṇa**, n. inseparable or inherent connection, material or substantial cause (in the Vedânta *upâdāna-k°* is more commonly used; also *-tva*, n.), Sarvad. **-tva**, n. intimate connection or relation, Bhāshāp.

Samavâyin, mfn. met together, closely connected or united, concomitant, inherent in (comp.), Kaṇ.; Suśr.; Vās.; Sarvad.; aggregated, multitudinous, W.; m. a partner, L.; (with *purusha*), the soul combined (with a body), the individual soul, Yājñ. iii, 125; having or consisting of a combination (of the humours), Suśr.

Samavâyī-kṛita, mfn. come together, combined, united, Hariv.; Pur.

Sam-avêta, mfn. come together, met, assembled, united, all, Mn.; MBh. &c.; closely connected with, contained or comprised or inherent in (comp.), Sāh.; Sarvad.; approached, come to (acc.), MārkP.; *-tva*, n. the state of being intimately related or connected, MW.; °*târtha*, mfn. containing a meaning, significant, instructive, BhP.

समवेक्ष् *sam-avêksh* (*-ava-√īksh*), Ā. *-avêkshate* (ep. also P. °*ti*), to look at, behold, observe, perceive, notice, MBh.; R.; to reflect or ponder on, consider, mind, heed, Mn.; MBh. &c.; to acknowledge, think fit or necessary, R.: Caus. *-avêkshayati*, to cause to look at or consider, Kauś.

Sam-avêkshita, mfn. observed, considered, R.

समश् *sam-√1. aś*, P. Ā. *-aśnoti*, *-aśnute* (in ŚBr. once fut. *-aśnuvishyāmahe*), to reach, attain, gain, obtain, RV. &c. &c.; to accomplish, fulfil (a wish), RV.; to pervade or penetrate thoroughly (see *sam-ashṭi*).

Sam-aśnuva, mf(*ī*)n. reaching, taking hold of, seizing, ĀśvGṛ.

Sám-ashṭi, f. reaching, attaining, attainment, TS.; Br.; receipt, reception, TS., Sch.; conclusion, end, TBr., Sch.; (in Vedânta) collective existence, collectiveness, an aggregate, totality (as opp. to *vyashṭi*, q.v.), Śaṃk.; Vedântas.; VP.; *-tā*, f. the state of (being) an aggregate &c., Vedântas.; (°*ty*)-*abhiprâya*, m. the regarding a group of objects collectively, MW.

समश् *sam-√2. aś*, P. *-aśnāti*, to eat, taste, enjoy (lit. and fig.), Mn.; MBh.

Sam-aśana, n. eating together, Kauś.; eating promiscuously, Car.; eating in general, Pāṇ. vi, 2, 71, Sch. °**aśanīya**, mfn. to be eaten together, Gobh.

समष्ठिल *sam-ashṭhila*, m. (cf. 3. *ashṭi*, *ashṭhi* &c.) a kind of shrub, L.; (*ā*), f. (also °*ṭhīlā*) a kind of culinary herb or cucumber, L.

समस् *sam-√1. as*, P. *-asti*, to be like, equal (acc.), RV.; to be united with (*saha*), AV.; to be (there), exist, Kāv.

समस् *sam-√2. as*, P. *-asyati* (Ved. inf. *sam-âsam*), to throw or put together, add, combine, compound, mix, mingle, connect, AV.; ŚBr.; KātyŚr.; Śulbas.: Pass. *-asyate*, to be put together or combined &c.; (in gram.) to be compounded, form a compound, Pāṇ. ii, 2, 1 &c.

Sam-asana, n. the act of throwing or putting together, combination, composition, contraction, L.; anything gathered or collected, TS., Sch.; °*nâd*, mfn. eating collected food, TS.

Sám-asta, mfn. thrown or put together, combined, united, whole, all, ŚBr. &c. &c.; (in gram.) compounded, compound; (in phil.) inherent in or pervading the whole of anything; abridged, contracted, W.; m. a whole, the aggregate of all the parts, ib.; *-kāla-nirṇayâdhikāra*, m., *-devatā-pūjā-vidhi*, m. N. of wks.; *-dhātṛi*, m. the bearer or supporter of all (applied to Vishṇu), VP.; *-bala*, n. a whole army, entire force, MW.; *-mantra-devatā-prakāśikā*, f. N. of wk.; *-loka*, m. the whole world, MW.; *-vastu-vishaya*, mfn. relating to the whole matter, Kpr.; *-vishayika*, mfn. inhabiting the whole country, Inscr.; *-vyasta-rūpaka*, n. a kind of Rūpaka (q.v.), Kāvyâd.; *-sâkshi*, m. witness of all, KaivUp.; °*tâgni-prayoga*, m. N. of wk.

Sam-asya, mfn. to be thrown or put together or compounded and combined, W.; to be made entire or complete, ib.; °*syârthā*, f. the part of a stanza to be completed (cf. next), L.; (*ā*), f., see next.

Sam-asyā, f. junction, union, the being or remaining together with (comp.), MBh.; Hariv.; Naish.; a part of a stanza given to another person to be completed, Siṇhâs.; *-pūraṇa-vidhi*, m., °*-rṇava* (°*syârṇ*°), m., *-saṃgraha*, m. N. of wks.

1. **Sam-āsa**, m. (for 2. see *sam-√ās*) throwing or putting together, aggregation, conjunction, combination, connection, union, totality (*ena*, 'fully, wholly, summarily'), Br.; ŚrS.; Mn. &c.; succinctness, conciseness, condensation (ibc. and *-tas*, 'concisely, succinctly, briefly'), KaushUp.; Mn.; MBh. &c.; (in gram.) composition of words, a compound word (of which there are, accord. to native grammarians, 6 kinds, viz. Dvaṃdva, Bahu-vrīhi, Karma-dhāraya, Tat-purusha, Dvigu, and Avyaya or Avyayī-bhāva [qq. vv.]; an improper compound is called *asthāna-samāsa*), Prāt.; Pāṇ. &c.; euphonic combination (= *saṃdhi*), VPrāt.; (in astron.) a partic. circle, Sūryas.; composition of differences, reconciliation (= *samarthana*), L.; the part of a Śloka given for completion (= *samasyā*), L. **-cakra**, n., **-candrikā**, f., **-cūḍāmaṇi**, m., **-tattva-nirūpaṇa**, n. N. of wks. **-tas**, ind. in a summary manner, succinctly, concisely, Mn.; R.; VarBṛS. &c. **-paṭala**, N. of wk. **-pāda**, m. N. of chs. of various wks. **-prakaraṇa**, n. N. of wk. **-prâya**, mfn. consisting chiefly of compound words, L. **-baddha-manoramā** (?), f. N. of wk. **-bahula**, mfn. abounding in compounds (as a poetical style), MW. **-bhāvanā**, f. composition of the sum of the products, Col.; the rule for finding the sine of sum of two arcs, Siddhântaś. **-mañjarī**, f. N. of wk. **-vat**, mfn. possessing compounds, compounded, MW.; contracted, abridged, ib.; m. Cedrela Toona, L. **-vāda**, m., **-vāda-sāra**, **-vidhi**, m. N. of wks. **-vyāsa-yoga-tas**, ind. succinctly and at large, BhP. **-śikshā**, f., **-śobhā**, f. N. of wks. **-saṃhitā**, f. a concise astronomical Saṃhitā, Cat. **-saṃgraha**, m. N. of wk. **-saṃjña**, mfn. called a compound, MW. **Samāsâṅga**, n. a member or part of a comp° word, RPrāt. **Samāsâdhyāhāra**, m. the supplying an ellipsis in a comp° &c., MW. **Samāsânta**, m. a suffix at the end of a compound belonging to the whole of it, Pāṇ.; Pat. **Samāsârṇava**, m. N. of wk. **Samāsârtha**, m. the sense of a comp°, MW.; (*ā*), f. the part of a stanza given for completion (= *sam-asyā*), L.; (°*tha*)-*prakāśikā*, f. N. of wk. **Samāsâvali**, f. N. of wk. **Samāsôkta**, mfn. concisely expressed, VarBṛS.; Sāh.; contained in a comp°, KātyŚr. **Samāsôkti**, f. concise speech (a figure of speech by which the proceedings of any object spoken of are indicated by describing the similar action or attributes of another object), Vām. iv, 3, 3.

Sam-āsita, mfn. formed into a collection, assembled, aggregated, MW. °**āsin**, see *vyāsa-s°*.

समस्थ *sama-stha* &c. See p. 1153, col. 1.

समह *samaha*, ind. (fr. 1. *sama*) anyhow, somehow, RV. (accord. to Sāy. voc. of an adj. = *praśasta*, *sadhana* &c.)

समहस् *samahas*, w. r. for *su-mahas*, q. v.

समहाव्रत *sa-mahāvrata*, mfn. having a Mahāvrata day, ApŚr.

समहीधर *sa-mahīdhara*, mfn. having mountains, mountainous, MW.

समह्या *samahyā* (?), f. fame, reputation (cf. *sam-ajyā*), L.

समा *samā*. See p. 1153, col. 2.

समांश *samâṅsa* &c. See p. 1153, col. 1.

समांस *sa-māṅsa*, mfn. connected or combined with meat, containing meat, fleshy, R.; VarBṛS. &c.

समाकर्ण् *sam-ā-√karṇ*, P. *-karṇayati*, to give ear to, listen to, hear, Pañcat.; Kathās.

Sam-ākarṇitaka, n. any gesture which expresses the act of listening (*ena* = 'with an attitude of listening;' as a stage direction), Bālar.

समाकाङ्क्ष् *sam-ā-√kāṅksh*, P. *-kāṅkshati*, to long or hope for, desire, MBh.

समाकुञ्चित *sam-ā-kuñcita*, mfn. (√*kuñc*) drawn in, brought to an end, stopped (as speech), Naish.

समाकुल *sam-ākula*, mf(*ā*)n. crowded together, crowded or filled with, full of, abounding in (instr. or comp.), MBh.; R. &c.; greatly agitated or confounded, troubled, confused, flurried, bewildered by (comp.), ib. **-tā**, f., **-tva**, n. great agitation or confusion, great bewilderment or trouble of mind, MW.

समाकृ *sam-ā-√1. kṛi*, P. Ā. *-karoti*, *-kurute*; *-kriṇoti*, *-kriṇute*, to bring together, unite, RV.; VS.; to gather, collect, RV.; AitBr.; to make ready, prepare, RV.; AV.: Caus. *-kārayati*, see next.

Sam-ākāraṇa, n. (fr. Caus.) calling, summoning, Pañcad.

Sam-ākṛita, mfn. brought or collected together, MW.

समाकृष् *sam-ā-√kṛish*, P. *-karshati*, to draw together, draw towards, attract, MBh.; to draw away or out, extract, take out, Pañcat.: Caus. *-karshayati*, to draw away, carry off, ib.

Sam-ākarsha, m. drawing near or towards, Bādar. °**ākarshaṇa**, n. id., Sāh. °**ākarshin**, mfn. (only L.) drawing together, attracting; spreading or extending far, diffusing fragrance; (*iṇī*), f. a far-spreading odour, MW.

Sam-ākṛishṭa, mfn. drawn together, attracted, Amar.

समाकॄ *sam-ā-√kṝi*, P. *-kirati*, to scatter or pour or strew over, cover or fill with anything, MBh.; R.

Sam-ākīrṇa, mfn. strewn over, bestrewed, completely covered, overspread, ib.

समाक्रन्द् *sam-ā-√krand*, P. Ā. *-krandati*, °*te*, to cry out together, cry or lament piteously, MBh.

Sam-ākrandana, n. crying, shouting, Bhartṛ.

समाक्रम् *sam-ā-√kram*, P. Ā. *-krāmati*, *-kramate*, to tread or step upon, MBh.; R.

Sam-ākramaṇa, n. treading upon, stepping in, entering, frequenting, PañcavBr.; Ragh. °**ākrānta**, mfn. trod or stepped upon, MBh.; MārkP.; pressed or borne down, R.; overrun, attacked, assailed, seized upon, Ragh.; Pañcat.; Kathās.; kept (as a promise), R.

समाक्रीड् *sam-ā-√krīḍ*, P. *-krīḍati*, to play or sport along with (another), MBh.

समाक्रुष्ट *sam-ā-krushṭa*, mfn. (√*kruś*) reviled, abused, R.

समाक्लिन्न *sam-ā-klinna*, mfn. (√*klid*) well moistened, wet (with *vasu*, n. prob. = 'food and drink'), MBh. iii, 13472.

समाक्षिक *sa-mākshika*, n. together with honey, Suśr.

समाक्षिप् *sam-ā-√kship*, P. Ā. *-kshipati*, °*te*, to throw together, heap or pile up, MBh.; to thrust or throw away, hurl, ib.; to move violently, toss about (lips, arms &c.), ib.; to send forth, utter (words), ib.; to drive away, expel, ib.; to throw down from, tear off, R.; to take away, withdraw, MBh.; to destroy, annihilate, ib.; to insult, mock, ridicule, ib.; to hint at, suggest, indicate, Mṛicch., Sch.

Sam-ākshipta, mfn. thrown or heaped together, thrown or cast off &c., MBh. °**ākshepa**, m. hinting at, suggestion of (comp.), Sāh.

समाख्या *sam-ā-√khyā*, P. *-khyāti*, to reckon up, count up, calculate, enumerate, Mn.; MBh.; R.; to relate fully, report, communicate, tell, declare, MBh.; Kāv. &c.

Sam-ākhyā, f. name, appellation, Nir.; Kaṇ.; BhP.; explanation, interpretation, Sarvad.; report, fame, celebrity, L.; *-bhaksha*, m. drinking the Soma while mentioning by name (the partic. receptacles for holding it), ĀśvŚr., Sch. °**ākhyāta**, mfn. reckoned up, enumerated, Mn. vii, 56; completely or fully related, MBh.; Sāṃkhyak.; proclaimed or declared to be (*iti*), Pañcat.; acknowledged as (comp.),

Car.; named, called, VP.; famed, celebrated, notorious, W. °ākhyāna, n. naming, mentioning, Āpast.; Kām.; report, narrative, MBh.; appellation, name, KātyŚr. °ākhyāya, mfn. to be addressed or exhorted, Āpast. (v.l.) °ākhyāyam, ind. while mentioning by name (in aṅga-s°), AitBr.

समागम sam-ā-√gam, P. -gacchati, to come together (in a friendly or hostile manner; also sexually), meet, be united with (instr. with and without saha or sârdham), ŚBr.; ChUp.; MBh. &c.; to come together (as heavenly bodies in conjunction or occultation), VarBṛS.; to come to, come near, approach, arrive at (acc. or loc.), MBh.; Kāv. &c.; to come back, return from (abl.), ib.; to meet with, come upon, find (acc.), MBh.: Caus. -gamayati, to cause to come together, bring together, unite one thing or person (acc.) with another (instr. or loc.), R.; Vikr.

Sam-āgata, mfn. come together, met, encountered, joined, assembled, Mn.; Yājñ.; MBh. &c.; being in conjunction with (instr.), VarBṛS.; come to, approached, arrived, returned, R.; Mṛicch. &c.; (ā), f. a kind of riddle or enigma (the meaning of which is hidden by the Saṃdhi, q.v.), Kāvyâd. °āgati, f. coming together, meeting, union, W.; approach, arrival, similar condition or progress, ib.

Sam-āgantavya, n. (impers.) it is to be met or approached, Vās.

Sam-āgama, m. (ifc. f. ā) coming together (either in a hostile or friendly manner), union (also sexual), junction, encounter or meeting with (instr. with or without saha, gen., [rarely] loc., or comp.), Mn.; MBh. &c.; association, assembly of (comp.), MBh.; R.; Kathās.; conjunction (of planets), VarBṛS.; approach, arrival, W.; -kārin, mfn. causing union, MW.; -kshaṇa, m. the moment of union, Rājat.; -prârthanā, f. the desire of association, MW.; -manoratha, m. the desire of union, Vikr.; °mộpâya, m. means of union, MW. °āgamana, n. coming together, meeting, union (also = sexual intercourse), MBh. °āgamin, mfn. coming together, meeting, Ind.Ant.; future, imminent, ib.

समागलित sam-ā-galita, mfn. (√gal) fallen down, fallen, MBh.

समागाढ sam-ā-gāḍha, mfn. (√gāh) intense, violent (only in -tara, 'more or most intense or violent'), Kāraṇḍ.

समागृभाय sam-ā-gṛibhāya, P. -gṛibhāyati (√grah), to seize together or at once, take hold of, RV.; AV.

समाघात sam-āghāta. See sam-ā-√han.

समाघ्रा sam-ā-√ghrā, P. -jighrati, to smell at, smell, R.; Mṛicch.; to kiss, MBh.; Ragh.

Sam-āghrāṇa, n. smelling at anything, Kād.

समाचक्ष् sam-ā-√caksh, Ā. -cashṭe, to relate fully, tell, report, MBh.; R.; BhP.

समाचम् sam-ā-√cam (only ind. p. -camya), to sip water (as a religious act in ceremonial observances, cf. ā-√cam), MBh.

समाचर् sam-ā-√car, P. -carati (ep. also Ā. °te), to act or behave or conduct one's self towards (loc.), MBh.; Pañcat.; to practise, perform thoroughly, do, accomplish (with āhāram and instr., 'to feed upon'), Mn.; MBh. &c.; to associate with (instr.), Gaut.; (with dūrāt) to remove, Mn. iv, 151.

Sam-ācara, mfn. practising, observing, W. °ācaraṇa, n. practising, performing, observing, behaving, performance, ib. °ācaraṇīya, mfn. to be practised or observed, Daś. °ācarita, mfn. practised, performed, done, committed, W.

Sam-ācāra, m. (for samâc° see p. 1153, col. 1) procedure, practice, conduct, behaviour in (comp.), MBh.; R. &c.; custom, usage, usual way or method, Pañcat.; KātyŚr., Sch.; (ifc.) the customary presentation of, Kathās.; 'doings,' news, report, information, tradition, W.

Sam-ācīrṇa, mfn. performed, done, practised, committed, MBh.

समाचि sam-ā-√1. ci, P. Ā. -cinoti, -cinute, to put together, heap up, accumulate, MBh.; Hariv.; Pāṇ., Sch.; to load or cover with (instr.), MBh.; R. &c.; to fill up (cavities in a road), AV.

Sam-ācayana, n. putting or heaping together, accumulation, aggregation, Pat. on Pāṇ. iii, 1, 19, Vārtt. 3. °ācita, mfn. heaped together, covered with, overspread, MBh.; Kāv. &c.

समाचेष्टित sam-ā-ceshṭita, n. (√cesht) gesture, procedure, behaviour, conduct, Kād.

समाच्छद् sam-ā-cchad (√chad), Caus. -cchādayati, to cover completely with, overspread, veil, cloud (also fig. to obscure or stupefy the mind), MBh.

Sam-ācchanna, mfn. completely covered with &c., W.

समाच्छिद् sam-ā-cchid (√chid; only ind. p. -cchidya), to cut or tear off, snatch away, R.

समाज sam-āja &c. See sam-√aj, p. 1153.

समाजुहूषमाण sam-ājuhūshamāṇa. See sam-ā-√hve, p. 1163, col. 3.

समाज्ञा sam-ā-√jñā, to know or understand thoroughly, become acquainted with, ascertain, perceive, observe, recognize, MBh.; Hariv.; Vet.: Caus. -jñāpayati (cf. next), to order, command, direct, authorize, MBh.; R. &c.

Sam-ājñapta, mfn. (fr. Caus.) ordered, commanded, directed, Hariv. °ājñā, f. appellation, name, Lāṭy.; TUp.; reputation, fame, L.

Sam-ājñāta, mfn. known, ascertained, acknowledged as (nom. or comp.), MBh.; Hariv. °ājñāna, n. the being acknowledged as (comp.), Nyāyas., Sch.

समातन् sam-ā-√tan, P. Ā. -tanoti, -tanute, to extend, stretch, bend (a bow), MBh.; Rājat.; to effect, produce, cause, MBh.

Sam-ātata, mfn. extended, stretched, strung (as a bow), MBh.; continuous, uninterrupted, W.

समाति samāti. See á-samāti.

समातृ sa-mātṛi, f. a stepmother, BhP.

Sa-mātṛika, mfn. together with a mother, BhP.

Sa-mātṛi-cakravāla, mfn. attended by the whole circle of divine Mātṛis, MW.

समादर sam-ā-dara, m. (√dṛi) great respect, veneration, MW. °ādaraṇīya, mfn. to be greatly respected or venerated, ib.

Sam-ādṛita, mfn. very respectful, showing great regard, BhP.

समादा sam-ā-√1. dā, P. Ā. -dadāti, -datte, (P.) to give, bestow, present, MBh.; Hariv.; to give back, restore, BhP.; (Ā.) to take away fully or entirely, take away with one, accept, receive, RV. &c. &c.; to take out or away, remove, withdraw, Mn.; MBh.; to take hold of, grasp, seize, MBh.; to gather, collect, MBh.; to apprehend, perceive, comprehend, find out, Daśar.; to take to heart, reflect on, BhP.; to undertake, begin (with vacanam or vākyam, 'a speech'), MBh.: Caus. -dāpayati, to establish, Divyâv.; to instigate (see sam-ādāpaka &c.)

Sam-ādatta, mfn. taken away, taken hold of, seized, received, BhP.

Sam-ādāna, n. taking fully or entirely, taking upon one's self, contracting, incurring, MBh.; beginning, undertaking, Lalit.; resolve, determination, ib. (L. also 'receiving suitable donations;' 'the daily observances of the Jaina sect;' 'the middle part of the sacrificial post'). °ādānika, mfn. (fr. prec.), Mahāvy. °ādāpaka, mfn. (fr. Caus.) exciting, instigating, Divyâv. °ādāpana, n. excitation, instigation, Lalit. °ādāya, ind. having undertaken, Divyâv.

Sam-ādeya, mfn. to be taken or received, Pañcat.

समादिश् sam-ā-√diś, P. -diśati, to assign, allot, Mn.; MBh.; R.; to point out, indicate, announce, communicate, declare, Kāv.; VarBṛS.; BhP.; to appoint, name, designate, MBh.; R. &c.; to foretell, foreshow, Kāv.; Kathās.; to direct, advise, order, command to (dat., inf., or -artham), ŚrS.; MBh. &c.: Caus. -deśayati, to order, command, Pañcat.

Sam-ādishṭa, mfn. assigned, indicated, directed, commanded, enjoined, MBh.; Kāv. &c.

Sam-ādeśa, m. direction, advice, instruction, order, command, Āpast.; R. &c. °ādeśana, n. information, instruction, Sāh.

समाद्रु sam-ā-√dru, P. -dravati (ep. also Ā. °te), to run together towards or against, rush at, attack, assail (acc.), MBh.; R.

समाधा sam-ā-√1. dhā, P. Ā. -dadhāti, -dhatte, to place or put or hold or fix together, ŚBr.; MBh. &c.; to compose, set right, repair, put in order, arrange, redress, restore, MBh.; Hit.; to put to, add, put on (esp. fuel on the fire), AV.; ŚBr.; R.; to kindle, stir (fire), ŚBr.; to place, set, lay, fix, direct, settle, adjust (with astram, 'to adjust an arrow;' with garbham, 'to impregnate;' with savituḥ, 'to lay in the sun;' with drishṭim, cittam, cetas, matim, manas, 'to direct or fix the eyes or mind upon [loc.];' with matim, 'to settle in one's mind, resolve,' 'make up one's mind' [followed by iti]; with ātmānam or manas, 'to collect the thoughts or concentrate the mind in meditation &c.;' without an acc. = 'to be absorbed in meditation or prayer'), RV. &c. &c.; to impose upon (loc.), MBh.; to entrust or commit to (loc.), ib.; to establish in (loc.), Ragh.; to effect, cause, produce, Hariv.; (in the following meanings only Ā.) to take to or upon one's self, conceive (in the womb), put on (a garment or dress), assume (a shape), undergo (effort), show, exhibit, display, MBh.; Kāv. &c.; to devote one's self entirely to, give one's self up to (acc.), R.; Hariv. &c. (once in Bhaṭṭ. P.); to lay down as settled, settle, establish, prove, declare, Kap., Sch.; to admit, grant, Kull. on Mn. viii, 54: Desid. -dhitsati, to wish to put together, desire to collect the thoughts, MBh. xii, 9586.

Sam-ādhā, m. (only L.) putting together, adjusting, settling, reconciling, clearing up difficulties &c.; completion, accomplishment. °ādhātavya, mfn. to be put in order or set right, Hit.

Sam-ādhāna, n. putting together, laying, adding (esp. fuel to fire), Gobh.; composing, adjusting, settling, R.; reconciliation, MBh.; intentness, attention (acc. with √kṛi, 'to attend'), eagerness, Śaṃk.; Pañcar.; fixing the mind in abstract contemplation (as on the true nature of spirit), religious meditation, profound absorption or contemplation, MBh.; Kāv.; Vedântas.; justification of a statement, proof (cf. -rūpaka), Sarvad.; (in logic) replying to the Pūrva-paksha, MW.; (in dram.) fixing the germ or leading incident (which gives rise to the whole plot, e.g. Śak. i, 27); -mātra, n. mere contemplation or meditation, MW.; -rūpaka, n. a kind of metaphor (used for the justification of a bold assertion), Kāvyâd. °ādhānīya, mfn. to be put together or joined, Uṇ. ii, 109, Sch. °ādhāyaka, mfn. composing, reconciling, Shaḍguruś.

Sam-ādhi, m. putting together, joining or combining with (instr.), Lāṭy.; a joint or a partic. position of the neck, Kir.; union, a whole, aggregate, set, R.; Hariv.; Ragh.; completion, accomplishment, conclusion, Kum.; setting to rights, adjustment, settlement, MBh.; justification of a statement, proof, Sarvad.; bringing into harmony, agreement, assent, W.; RPrāt.; intense application or fixing the mind on, intentness, attention (°dhiṃ √kṛi, 'to attend'), MBh.; R. &c.; concentration of the thoughts, profound or abstract meditation, intense contemplation of any particular object (so as to identify the contemplator with the object meditated upon; this is the eighth and last stage of Yoga [IW. 93]; with Buddhists Samādhi is the fourth and last stage of Dhyāna or intense abstract meditation [MWB. 209]; in the Kāraṇḍa-vyūha several S°s are enumerated), Up.; Buddh.; MBh. &c.; intense absorption or a kind of trance, MBh.; Kāv. &c.; a sanctuary or tomb of a saint, W.; RTL. 261; (in rhet.) N. of various figures of speech (defined as ārohâvaroha-krama, artha-drishṭi, anya-dharmāṇām anyatrâdhirohaṇa &c.), Kāvyâd.; Vām.; Kpr. &c.; N. of the 17th Kalpa (q.v.), of the 17th Arhat of the future Utsarpiṇī, L.; of a Vaiśya, Cat. (accord. to L. also 'silence; a religious vow of intense devotion or self-imposed abstraction; support, upholding; continuance; perseverance in difficulties; attempting impossibilities; collecting or laying up grain in times of dearth'); -garbha, m. N. of a Bodhi-sattva, Buddh.; -tva, n. the state of profound meditation or devotion, Sarvad.; -nishṭha, mfn. devoted to m°, Pañcat.; -parihāṇi, f. diminution of m°, Dharmas. 59; -prakaraṇa, n. N. of wk.; -bala, n. the force of m°, Dharmas. 75; -bhaṅga, m. the disturbing or interruption of m°, Pañcat.; -bhṛit, mfn. absorbed in m°, Śiś.; -bheda, m. (= -bhaṅga), Kum.; -bhedin, mfn. one who interrupts m°, Ragh.; -mat, mfn. absorbed in m°; Kum.; attentive, R.; making a promise or assent or permission, W.; -matikā, f. N. of a woman, Mālav. (v.l. for samāhitikā in B.); -yoga, m. employment of meditation, the efficacy of contemplation, MW.; *-yoga-rddhi-tapo-vidyā-virakti-mat*, mfn. possessing or accompanied with m° and self-abstraction and supernatural power and mortification and knowledge and indifference, BhP.; *-rāja*, m., N. of wk.; *-vigraha*, m. embodiment of m°; *-vidhi*, m. N. of wk.; *-samānatā*, f. N. of a Samādhi, Buddh.; *-stha*, mfn. absorbed in m°, Pañcat.; *-sthala*, n. N. of a place in Brahmā's world, Kathās. **°ādhita**, mfn. propitiated, reconciled, Kathās. **°ādhitsā**, f. (fr. Desid.) desire of settling or adjusting, KātyŚr., Sch. **°ādhitsu**, mfn. (fr. id.) wishing to set right or prove, Nyāyas., Sch. **°ādhin**, mfn. absorbed in contemplation, W.

Sam-ādheya, mfn. to be put in order or set right, R.; to be directed or informed or instructed, ib.; to be granted or admitted, Kull.; Siddh.

Sam-āhita, mfn. put or held together, joined, assembled, combined, united (pl. 'all taken together'), ŚBr.; MBh. &c.; joined or furnished or provided with (instr. or comp.), ib.; put to, added (as fuel to fire), AV.; put or placed in or upon, directed, applied, fixed, imposed, deposited, entrusted, delivered over, ib. &c. &c.; composed, collected, concentrated (as the thoughts upon, with loc.); one who has collected his thoughts or is fixed in abstract meditation, quite devoted to or intent upon (with loc.), devout, steadfast, firm, Up.; MBh. &c.; put in order, set right, adjusted, R.; suppressed, repressed, lowered (as speech), L.; made, rendered, Hariv.; completed, finished, ended, MBh.; concluded, inferred, demonstrated, established, L.; granted, admitted, recognised, approved, Āpast.; Hariv.; corresponding or equal to, like, resembling (comp.), R.; Hariv.; harmonious, sounding faultlessly, L.; m. a pure or holy man, MW.; n. great attention or intentness, MW.; (in rhet.) a partic. kind of comparison, Vām. iv, 3, 29; *-dhī*, mfn. one who has concentrated his thoughts in devotion, BhP.; *-mati*, mfn. one who has an attentive mind, Yājñ., Sch.; *-manas*, mfn. having the mind absorbed in (anything), MW.; *-mano-buddhi*, mfn. having the mind or thoughts collected or composed, R.; *°tâtman (samâh°)*, mfn. one whose spirit is united with (instr.), ŚBr.

Samāhitikā, f. N. of a woman (cf. *samādhi-matikā*), Mālav.

समाधाव् *sam-ā-√1. dhāv*, P. Ā. *-dhāvati*, *°te*, to run together towards, rush towards, run near to, MBh.; Hariv.

समाधूत *sam-ā-dhūta*, mfn. (√*dhū*) driven away, dispersed, scattered, R.

समाध्मा *sam-ā-√dhmā*, P. *-dhamati* (only pf. *-dadhmuḥ*), to cause (musical instruments) to sound forth together, blow (a horn &c.), Bhaṭṭ.

Sam-ādhmāta, mfn. made to sound forth together, blown into, MBh.; Hariv.; swelled up, puffed up, swollen, inflated, Suśr.

समाध्यै *sam-ā-√dhyai*, P. *-dhyāyati*, to meditate deeply upon, reflect upon, be lost in thought, Hariv.; R.

समान *samānā*, mf(*ī* or *ā*)n. (connected with 1. and 2. *sama*; in RV. v, 87, 4 abl. sg. *samānásmāt* for *samānāt*, see 1. *sama*; for *sam-āna* see *sam-√an*, for *sa-māna* see col. 3) same, identical, uniform, one (= *eka*, L.), RV. &c. &c.; alike, similar, equal (in size, age, rank, sense or meaning &c.), equal or like to (with instr., gen., or comp.), VS. &c. &c.; having the same place or organ of utterance, homogeneous (as a sound or letter), Vop.; holding the middle between two extremes, middling, moderate, BhP.; common, general, universal, all, RV.; Br.; ŚrS.; BhP.; whole (as a number, opp. to 'a fraction'), Pāṇ. v, 2, 47, Vārtt. 4; being (= *sat*, after an adj.), Divyâv.; virtuous, good, L.; = *varṇa-bhid*, L.; (*am*), ind. like, equally with (instr.), Kir.; m. an equal, friend, TBr.; Cāṇ.; BhP.; (*ī*), f. a kind of metre, Piṅg.; (prob.) n. N. of wk. (cf. *śākhā-s°*). **-karaṇa**, mfn. having the same organ of utterance (said of a sound), Prāt. **-kartṛika**, mfn. (in gram.) having the same subject (i.e. that which is spoken of) in a sentence (*-tā*, f.; *-tva*, n.), Pāṇ.; ĀpŚr., Sch.; KātyŚr., Sch. (see *kartṛi*). **-kartṛi-tva**, n. identity of subject, ĀpŚr., Sch. **-karmaka**, mfn. (in gram.) having the same object, Pāṇ. iii, 4, 48 (see *-karman*). **-karman**, n. the same object, (ibc.) the same action, KapS.; mfn. expressing the same a°, Nir. **-kāraka**, mfn. making all things equal or the same (said of time), Śukas. **-kāraṇa**, see *a-s°*. **-kāla**, mfn. simultaneous (*am*, ind.), RPrāt.; of equal length or quantity (as a vowel), TPrāt. **-kālīna**, mfn. simultaneous, contemporaneous (*-tva*, n.), L. **-kshema**, mfn. having the same or an equal basis, balancing each other (*-tva*, n.), KapS. **-khyāna**, mfn. = *sakhi*, Sāy. (cf. *samānâkhy°*). **-gati**, mfn. 'going together,' agreeing together (*-tva*, n.), Bādar., Sch. **-guṇa**, mfn. having equal virtues, Vet. **-gotra**, mfn. being of the same family, ŚāṅkhBr.; ĀśvŚr. **-grāma**, m. the same village, PārGṛ. **-grāmīya**, mfn. dwelling in the same village, ĀśvGṛ. **-jana**, m. a person of the same rank, PañcavBr.; ŚrS.; Anup.; a person of the same family or race, MW.; *-pada*, mfn. being of the same people, KātyŚr. **-janman** (*°nā-*), mfn. having the same origin, ŚBr.; of equal age, Mn. ii, 208. **-janya**, mfn. proceeding from or belonging to persons of the same rank, PañcavBr. **-jāti**, mfn. of the same kind, ĀśvŚr. **-jātīya**, mf(*ā*)n. of the same kind with (comp.; *-tva*, n.), ŚāṅkhŚr.; Sarvad. &c. **-jñātitva-maya**, mf(*ī*)n. based on equality of race, Jātakam. **-tantra**, mfn. having the same chief action, proceeding in one and the s° line of action, ŚrS. **-tas** (*°nā-*), ind. uniformly, RV.; (prob.) w.r. for *sa-nāma-tas*, 'with the s° name,' Gaut. **-tā** (*°nā-*), f. equality with (gen. or comp.), ŚBr.; RPrāt.; Śiś. &c.; community of kind or quality, W. **-tejas**, mfn. having equal splendour, equal in glory, MW. **-tra** (*°nā-*), ind. on the same spot, ŚBr.; GṛŚrS. **-tva**, n. equality with (instr.), KapS.; MārkP. &c.; community of quality, MW. **-daksha**, mfn. having the same will, agreeing, RV. **-dakshiṇa**, mfn. attended with an equal reward, ŚāṅkhŚr. **-duḥkha**, mfn. having the same griefs, sympathizing, MW. **-dṛiś**, looking at (loc.) equally, HPariś. **-devata**, mfn. relating to the same deity, Lāṭy. **-devatyà**, mf(*ā*)n. id., ŚBr. **-dharman**, mfn. having the same qualities, similar to (instr.), Kām.; a sympathiser, appreciator of merits, Mālatīm. **-dhishṇya** (*°nā-*), mfn. having the same Dhishṇya (q.v.), ŚBr. **-nāman**, mfn. having the same name, Vop. vi, 98. **-nidhana** (*°nā-*), mfn. having the same conclusion, ŚBr. **-pakshá**, m. the same half-month, TBr. **-pātra** (*°nā-*), mfn. having the same cup, MaitrS. **-pratipatti**, mfn. of equal intelligence, judicious, Ratnâv. **-prabhṛiti** (*°nā-*), mfn. beginning equally, TS.; Kāṭh.; ŚBr.; KapS. **°prayojana**, mfn. having the s° object, MW. **-pravara-grantha**, m. N. of wk. **-prasiddhi**, mfn. having eq° success, Sāy. **-preman**, mfn. equally loving, Mālatīm. **-bandhu** (*°nā-*), mf(*u*)n. having the same relatives, RV.; ŚBr. **-barhis** (*°nā-*), mfn. having the same sacrificial grass, ŚBr.; ŚrS. **-bala**, mfn. of eq° strength (*-tva*, n.), Nyāyam., Sch. **-brahma-cārin**, = *sa-b°*, L. **-brāhmaṇa**, mfn. having the same (directions given in the) Brāhmaṇa texts, ĀpŚr. **-brāhmaṇīya**, mfn. id. (*-tva*, n.), ĀpŚr., Sch. **-bhṛit**, f. N. of partic. bricks, ŚBr. **-māna**, mfn. equally honoured with (instr.), Kir. **-mūrdhan**, mf(*dhnī*)n. equal-headed, PārGṛ. **-yama**, m. the same pitch of voice, APrāt. **-yoga-kshema**, mf(*ā*)n. being under the same circumstances of security &c. with (instr.), Car.; (ifc.) having the same value with (*-tva*, n.), Sarvad. **-yojana** (*°nā-*), mfn. yoked in the same way, equally harnessed, RV. **-yoni** (*°nā-*), mfn. born from the same womb, ŚBr. **-ruci**, mfn. having the same taste (*-tā*, f.), Rājat. **-rūpa**, mf(*ā*)n. having the s° colour as (gen. or comp.), VarBṛS.; having the s° appearance as (comp.), L.; (*ā*), f. a kind of riddle in which the same words are to be understood in a literal and figurative sense, Kāvyâd. **-°rshi** (fr. *°na + ṛishi*), mf(*ī*)n. having the same Ṛishi (for ancestor), Gobh. **-loka** (*°nā-*), mfn. gaining the s° heaven, ŚBr. **-vacana**, mfn. = *sa-v°*, Pāṇ.; Vop. **-vayas** (BhP.) or **-vayaska** (Sāy.), mfn. of the same age. **-varcas** (*°nā-*), mfn. having equal vigour &c., RV.; Nir.; of eq° splendour, MW. **-varcasa**, mfn. having equal splendour with (comp.), MBh. **-varṇa**, mf(*ā*)n. having the same colour, VarBṛS.; having the s° vowels, RPrāt. **-vasana**, mfn. clothed in the same way, Kauś. **-vidya**, mfn. possessing equal knowledge (*-tā*, f.), Mālav. **-vrata-cārin**, mfn. having the same practices with any one (gen.; *°ri-tva*, n.), Vishṇ. **-vrata-bhṛit**, mfn. leading a similar life, Kāv. **-śabdā**, f. a kind of riddle, Kāvyâd. **-śayya**, mfn. having the same bed (*-tā*, f.), Lāṭy. **-śākhīya**, mfn. belonging to the same Śākhā, g. *gahâdi*. **-śīla**, mf(*ā*)n. of a similar disposition, BhP. **-saṃkhya**, mf(*ā*)n. of an equal number with (instr.), RPrāt. **-sambandhana** (*°nā-*), mf(*ā*)n. equally connected, ŚBr. **-salila**, mfn. = *samānôdaka*, VP. **-sukha-duḥkha**, mfn. having joys and sorrows in common (*-tā*, f.), Kām.; Hit. **-sūtra-nipāta**, m. 'falling of the same line;' (*e*), ind. on the diametrically opposite side, BhP. **-stotriya**, mfn. having the same Stotriya, ŚāṅkhŚr. **-sthāna**, n. interposition, BhP.; mfn. being in the same place, Sāy.; occupying the same position (in the month), VPrāt. **Samānâkshara**, n. a simple vowel (short or long; opp. to *saṃdhy-ak°* or 'diphthong'), RPrāt.; APrāt.; TPrāt. **Samānâkhyāna**, mfn. = *sakhi*, Nir. (cf. *samāna-khy°*). **Samānâcārya**, m. a common or universal teacher, Divyâv. **Samānâdhikaraṇa**, n. grammatical agreement in case with (comp.), Pāṇ. iii, 2, 124; common or same government or case-relation, MW.; s° predicament or category, common substratum, W.; mfn. being in the same case-relation with (instr. or comp.), relating to the s° subject (*-tā*, f.; *-tva*, n.), Tarkas.; Sarvad. &c.; being in the same category or predicament or government, MW.; having a common substratum (in the Vaiśeshika phil.), ib. **Samānâdhikāra**, m. the same rule or government or generic character, ib. **Samānâbhihāra**, m. intermixture of equal things, Sāṃkhyak. **Samānârtha**, m. equivalence, Lalit.; mf(*ā*)n. having the same object or end, ĀśvŚr.; R.; having the s° meaning as (instr. or comp.), Kāś.; *-tā*, f. equivalence, equality of birth or rank, Lalit.; *-tva*, n. having the s° object, KātyŚr.; identity of meaning, Kāś.; *-prayojana*, mfn. having a common object and purpose, MW. **Samānârthaka**, mfn. having the same meaning, Pāṇ. iii, 3, 152, Sch. **Samānârsha-pravara**, mf(*ā*)n. descended from the same Ṛishi and having the same Pravaras, Vishṇ. **Samānârsheya**, mfn. descended from the same Ṛishi, ŚāṅkhGṛ. **Samānâlaṃkāra**, mfn. wearing the same ornaments, MW. **Samānâsya-prayatna**, mfn. being pronounced with the same effort of the organs, VPrāt.; APrāt., Sch. **Samānôttama-madhyamâdhama**, mfn. one to whom the best and the middle and worst are all the same, BhP. **Samānôdaka**, mfn. having (only) libations of water (to ancestors) in common, distantly related (the relationship, accord. to some, extending to the 14th degree, the first 7 being both Sa-piṇḍas and Samānôdakas, while the remaining 7 are Sam° only), Mn. ix, 187; Kull., Sch.; VP.; RTL. 286; *-bhāva*, m. the above relationship, Mn. **Samānôdarka**, mfn. ending equally, TS.; ŚBr.; KapS. **Samānôdarya**, mfn. descended from the same mother, AitBr.; m. a brother of whole blood, Bhaṭṭ. **Samānôpamā**, f. a simile in which the common term is one in sound but yields two senses (e.g. *sâlakânana*, 'a face with curls,' and *sālakānana*, 'a wood with Sāla trees'), Kāvyâd. ii, 29. **Samānôpâdhyāya**, m. a common or general preceptor, Divyâv. **Samānôlba**, mfn. having equal or similar embryo-membranes, ŚBr.

Samānaya, Nom. P. *°yati*, to make equal or similar, equalise, R.; Ghaṭ.

Samānikā, f. a kind of metre, Col.

Samānyā́, ind. equally, jointly, together, RV.; MaitrS.

समान 1. *sa-māna*, mfn. (for *samāna* see col. 1; for *sam-āna* see p. 1154, col. 2) possessing honour or esteem, honoured by (gen.), Vet.; with anger, BhP.

Sa-mānana, mfn. (for *samānana* see p. 1153, col. 1) being in honour or respect, Nalôd.

Sa-mānitam, ind. honourably, respectfully, Kathās.

समान 2. *sa-māna*, mfn. (for 1. see above) having the same measure, L.

समानन्द् *sam-ā-√nand*, Caus. *-nandayati*, to gladden, rejoice, Subh.

समानास *samānāsa* (?), m. N. of a serpent-demon, L.

समानी *sam-ā-√nī*, P. Ā. *-nayati*, *°te*, to lead or conduct together, join, unite, collect, assemble, MBh.; Kāv. &c.; to lead any one to another, unite one person (acc.) with another (instr. with or without *saha*), ib.; to lead towards, bring near, ib.; to bring home, ib.; to pour together, mingle (liquids), ŚBr.; KātyŚr.; to bring or offer (an oblation), MBh.: Caus. *-nāyayati* (ind. p. *-nāyya*), to cause to be brought together or near, convoke, assemble, MBh.; Hariv.; R.

Sam-ānayana, n. bringing together or near, Bhar.; pouring together, Jaim.

Sam-ānīta, mfn. brought together or near, brought, conducted, convoked, assembled, MBh.; Kāv. &c.

समान्त *samânta, samântara.* See p. 1153, cols. 1 and 2.

समाप् *sam-√āp*, P. *-āpnoti*, to acquire or obtain completely, gain, AV.; MBh. &c.; to accomplish, fulfil, ŚBr.; KātyŚr.; to reach, AV.: Caus. *-āpayati*, to cause to gain or obtain completely, ŚBr.; to bring to an end, finish, complete, conclude, Mn.; MBh. &c.; to put an end to, put to death, destroy (with or scil. *ātmānam*, 'one's self'), Āpast.; Kathās.; BhP.: Desid. of Caus. *-āpipayishati*, to wish or try to accomplish, ŚBr.: Desid. *-īpsati*, to wish to obtain or reach or accomplish, wish for, desire, ib.

Sam-āpa, m. sacrificing, offering oblations to the gods (= *deva-yajana*), Vop. °**āpaka**, mf(*ikā*)n. (fr. Caus.) completing, finishing, supplying (*-tva*, n.), Śiś.; Bhar.; (*ikā*), f. a verb or any part of speech used as a verb to complete a sentence, MW.; (°*aka*)-*kriyā*, f. a finishing act, f° stroke, ib. °**āpana**, mfn. (in some meanings fr. Caus.) accomplishing, completing, concluding, Kauś.; MBh.; (*ā*), f. highest degree, perfection, MBh.; n. the act of causing to complete or completing, completion, conclusion, Br.; GṛŚrS.; Mn. &c.; coming to an end, dissolution, destruction (of the body), MBh.; section, chapter, division (of a book), MārkP.; profound meditation (= *samādhāna*), L. °**āpanīya**, mfn. relating to completion, Kauś. °**āpayitavya**, mfn. (fr. Caus.) to be furnished or provided with anything, KaushUp.

Sam-āpita, mfn. (fr. Caus.) accomplished, finished, concluded, done, Kāv.; Kathās.

Sam-āpin, mfn. concluding, forming the conclusion of anything, Kathās.

Sam-āpipayishu, mfn. (fr. Desid. of Caus.) wishing to cause to complete, desirous of accomplishing, MBh.

Sam-āpta, mfn. completely obtained or attained or reached, concluded, completed, finished, ended, KātyŚr.; Mn.; MBh. &c.; perfect, clever, MBh. xiv, 2561; *-cinta*(?), m. N. of a man, Buddh.; *-punar-ātta* or °*ttaka*, mfn. concluded and again resumed; n. a partic. kind of pleonasm (also °*tta-tva*, n.), Kpr.; Sāh.; Pratāp.; *-prayoga*, m. N. of wk.; *-prāya*, mfn. nearly finished, MW.; *-bhūyishṭha*, mfn. nearly completed or ended, ib.; *-lambha*, m. a partic. high number, Buddh.; *-śiksha*, mfn. one who has completed his studies, MW.

Sam-āptāla(?), m. a lord, master, L.

Sám-āpti, f. complete acquisition (as of knowledge or learning), Āpast.; accomplishment, completion, perfection, conclusion, ŚBr. &c. &c.; dissolution (of the body), Mn. ii, 244; reconciling differences, putting an end to disputes, L.; *-vāda*, m. N. of a Nyāya wk.; *-sādhana*, n. means of accomplishment or completion, MW.; °*ty-arthā*, v.l. for *samasyârthā* (q.v.) °**āptika**, mfn. one who has finished or completed (esp. a course of Vedic study), Mn. iii, 145; final, finite, Kathās.

Sam-āpyà, mfn. to be reached or attained, AV.; to be accomplished or concluded or completed (n. impers.), Sāh.

Sam-īpsita, mfn. (fr. Desid.) wished or longed for, desired, R.

समापत् *sam-ā-√pat*, P. *-patati*, to fly together towards, rush violently upon, attack, assail (acc.), MBh.; R. &c.; to descend, alight, VarBṛS.; to come together, be united sexually with (*saha*), MBh.; to come to, attain, ib.

Sam-āpatita, mfn. come, arrived, taken place, Kautukas.

समापद् *sam-ā-√pad*, Ā. *-padyate*, to fall upon, attack, assail, MBh.; to fall into any state or condition, attain to, undergo, incur, ib. &c.; to undertake, begin, Kāraṇḍ.; to take place, occur, appear, APrāt., Sch.: Caus. *-pādayati*, to cause to come to pass, MW.; to bring about, complete, accomplish, ib.; to restore, ib.

Sam-āpatti, f. coming together, meeting, encountering, Kālid.; accident, chance (see comp.); falling into any state or condition, getting, becoming (comp.), Yogas.; assuming an original form, APrāt.; completion, conclusion, Āpast. (v.l. *sam-āpti*); yielding, giving way (in *a-s°*), ib.; (with Buddhists) a subdivision of the fourth stage of abstract meditation (there are eight Samāpattis), MWB. 233; *-dṛishṭa*, mfn. seen by chance, Daś.

Sam-āpadyana, n. (? fr. *samāpadya* stem of pres. tense) the being absorbed, absorption into, SaddhP.

Sam-āpanna, mfn. fallen into (acc.), MBh.; meeting with (?), Divyâv.; having, ib.; one who has undertaken (instr.), Kāraṇḍ.; arrived, come, happened, occurred, Hit. (v.l. *sam-āsanna*); furnished or endowed with (comp.), MBh.; R. &c.; perfect, proficient (in any science), W.; accomplished, concluded, done, L.; distressed, afflicted, ib.; killed, ib.; n. death, L.

Sam-āpādana, n. (fr. Caus.) the act of bringing about, accomplishing &c., MW.; restoration, ib. °**āpādanīya**, mfn. to be brought together or in accordance with (comp.), ĀpŚr. °**āpādya**, mfn. to be restored to its original form, Prāt.; n. the change of Visarga to *s* or *sh* (= *upâ-carita*), ib.; the change to *sh* (in Vedic phonetics, = *sha-tva*), ib.

समापा *sam-ā-√1. pa*, P. *-pibati*, to drink in entirely, suck in, absorb, MBh.; Kām.

समापू *sam-ā-√pū*, P. *-punāti*, to purify thoroughly, purge, Siddh.

समापॄ *sam-ā-√pṝ*, Pass. *-pūryate*, to become completely full, be quite filled, MBh.: Caus. *-pūrayati*, to make quite full, fill out with (instr.), ŚBr.; to draw or bend (a bow), R.

Sam-āpūrṇa, mfn. completely full, whole, entire, R.

समाप्यै *sam-ā-√pyai*, Ā. *-pyāyate* (only in pf. *-pipye*), to grow larger, swell, grow, increase, Bhaṭṭ.: Caus. *-pyāyayati*, °*te*, to cause to increase or grow, refresh, reanimate, enliven, MārkP.

Sam-āpyāyita, mfn. nourished, invigorated, refreshed, MBh.

समाप्रछ् *sam-ā-√prach* (only ind. p. *-pricchya*), to take leave of, R.; Kathās.

समाप्लु *sam-ā-√plu*, Ā. *-plavate*, to immerse together, immerse in water, bathe, MBh.; Hariv.; to overflow, inundate, overwhelm, MBh.; to spring or rush upon (acc.), R.; to come into violent collision with, MBh.

Sam-āplava or **sam-āplāva**, m. immersion in water, bathing, a bath, MBh.

Sam-āpluta, mfn. immersed, flooded, overwhelmed, bathed, MBh.

समाबन्ध् *sam-ā-√bandh* (only in ind. p. *-badhya*), to bind or fasten on firmly, R.

समाभा *sam-ā-√bhā*, P. *-bhāti*, to appear like (*iva*), MBh.

समाभाष् *sam-ā-√bhāsh*, Ā. *-bhāshate*, to talk with, converse together, address, speak to, MBh.; R.; BhP.; to speak about, communicate, MBh.

Sam-ābhāshaṇa, n. talking together, conversation with (comp.), Ragh.

समाभुज् *sam-ā-√3. bhuj*, P. *-bhunakti*, to enjoy or possess entirely, rule over (acc.), BhP.

समाभृ *sam-ā-√bhṛi*, P. *-bharati* or *-bibharti*, to bring together, produce, procure, TS.

Sam-ābhṛita, mfn. brought together, procured, AV.

समाम *sam-āmá*, m. (cf. *vy-āma*) length, AV.

Sam-āmyà, mfn. stretching or extending in length, ib.

समामन्त्र् *sam-ā-√mantr*, Ā. *-mantrayate*, to call upon, invoke, Cat.; to bid farewell to (acc.), MBh.

समाम्ना *sam-ā-√mnā*, P. Ā. *-manati*, °*te*, to repeat or mention together, repeat memoriter, hand down from memory or by tradition (esp. collections of sacred words or texts), GṛŚrS.; MBh. &c.; to suppose to be, take for (acc.), Nir.

Sam-āmnāta, mfn. repeated or mentioned together, handed down by tradition or from memory, MBh.; BhP.; (ifc.) mentioned as, g. *kṛitâdi*; n. mentioning together, enumeration, Āpast. °**āmnātṛi**, m. a repeater memoriter, collector or editor of Vedic texts, Śaṃk.

Sam-āmnāna, n. mentioning together, enumeration, repetition from memory, Nir.

Sam-āmnāya, m. mention together, traditional collection, enumeration, list, Nir.; Prāt. &c.; handing down by tradition or from memory, MBh.; collection or compilation of sacred texts (esp. any special redaction of a Vedic text), ĀśvŚr.; the sacred texts in general, BhP.; the destruction of the world (= *saṃhāra*), ib.; totality, aggregate, W.; N. of Śiva, MBh.; *-maya*, mf(*ī*)n. consisting of (or containing) the sacred texts, BhP. °**āmnāyika**, see *paśu-samāmnāyika*.

समाय *sam-āya*, °*yin*. See p. 1164, col. 2.

समायत्त *sam-ā-yatta*, mfn. (√*yat*) resting or dependent on (loc.), MBh.; R.

समायम् *sam-ā-yam*, P. Ā. *-yacchati*, °*te*, to draw together, contract, TS.; ŚBr.; to draw, pull, stretch, RV.

Sam-āyata, mfn. drawn out, lengthened, extended, long, MBh.

समायस्त *sam-ā-yasta*, mfn. (√*yas*) distressed, troubled, oppressed, R.

समाया *sam-ā-√yā*, P. *-yāti*, to come together, meet, MBh.; Kāv. &c.; to come near, approach, come from (abl.) or to (acc. or loc.), go to or towards (acc.), ib.; to elapse, pass away, MBh.; to fall upon, get into any state or condition (acc.), Pañcat.; Rājat.

Sam-āyāta, mfn. come together or near &c.; returned, Hcat.

समायु *sam-ā√2. yu*, P. *-yauti*, to mingle, stir up, MaitrS.

Sam-āyuta, mfn. joined or brought together, gathered, collected, Nir.; made or consisting of (comp.), MBh.; united or connected with, possessed of (comp.), ib.; Suśr.

समायुज् *sam-ā-√yuj*, P. Ā. *-yunakti*, *-yuṅkte*, to join or fasten together, join, prepare, make ready, BhP.; to meet, encounter (in a hostile manner), MBh.; to surround, MW.: Caus. *-yojayati*, to furnish or supply with (instr.), MBh.

Sam-āyukta, mfn. joined, prepared, ready, R.; entrusted, committed, MBh.; met together, encountered, brought into contact, MBh.; R.; furnished or supplied or provided with (instr. or comp.), Mn.; MBh. &c.; intent upon, devoted to, MW.

Sam-āyoga, m. conjunction, union, connection, contact with (instr. with and without *saha*, or comp.; *āt* with gen. or ifc. = 'in consequence of' or 'by means of'), Mn.; MBh. &c.; making ready, preparation, Kād.; Hcar.; fitting (an arrow to a bow), aiming, MW.; heap, multitude, W.; cause, origin, motive, object, ib.

समारक *sa-māraka*, mfn. including the world of Māra, Buddh.

समारत *sam-ā-rata*, mfn. (√*ram*) ceased from, left off, desisted, ChUp.

समारभ् *sam-ā-√rabh*, Ā. *-rabhate* (rarely P. °*ti*), to take in hand, undertake, begin, commence (with acc. or inf.; ind. p. *-rabhya* with acc. = 'beginning from'), TS. &c. &c.; to try to get near to or propitiate, MBh.

Sam-ārabdha, mfn. taken in hand, undertaken, begun (also 'begun to be built'), MBh.; Kāv. &c.; one who has begun or commenced, MBh.; happened, occurred, R.; *-tara*, mfn. more frequent, Nidānas. °**ārabhya**, mfn. (cf. above) to be undertaken or begun (superl. *-tama*), MBh.

Sam-ārambha, m. undertaking, enterprise, MBh.; R. &c.; spirit of enterprise, MBh. v, 990; beginning, commencement, Śāntiś.; w.r. for *sam-ārambhaṇa*, an unguent, Śak., Sch. °**ārambhaṇa**, n. taking in hand, undertaking, grasping, Kāv.; anointing (= *sam-ālambhana*), Śak., Sch. °**ārambhin**, mfn. (prob.) hung with, Cat.

समाराण *sam-ārāṇá*. See *sam-√ṛi*, p. 1170.

समाराध् *sam-ā-√rādh*, Caus. *-rādhayati* (m. c. also Ā. °*te*), to conciliate, propitiate, win over, MBh.; Pur.

Sam-ārādhana, n. conciliation, propitiation,

gratification, Ragh.; Sarvad.; a means of propitiating or winning, Mālav.

समारुध् *sam-ā-√1. rudh* (only ind. p. *-rudhya*), to block up, obstruct, R.

समारुह् *sam-ā-√1. ruh*, P. *-rohati*, to ascend or rise to or upon (acc., loc., or *upari*), mount, enter (acc.), Mn.; MBh. &c.; to advance towards or against (acc.), MBh.; to enter upon, attain to, undertake, begin (with *tulām*, 'to become like or similar'), KaushUp.; Mn. &c.: Caus. *-rohayati* or *-ropayati*, to cause to mount or ascend (two acc. or acc. and loc.), AV. &c. &c.; to cause to rise (a star), MārkP.; to place upon, impose, MBh.; R.; Kathās.; to lift up, erect, raise (lit. and fig.), MBh.; Kāv. &c.; to place in or among (acc.), Kāv.; Kathās.; to deposit (the sacred fire) in (acc. or loc.), TS.; Br.; to string (a bow), R.; BhP.; to deliver over, entrust or commit to (loc.), MBh.; to ascribe, attribute, transfer to (loc.), BhP.; Sarvad.: Desid., see next.

Sam-ārurukshu, mfn. (fr. Desid.) wishing to mount or ascend (acc.), Ragh.

Sam-ārūḍha, mfn. mounted or ridden by (instr.), MBh.; R.; Kathās.; one who has mounted or ascended, riding upon (acc., loc., or *upari*), fallen upon, entered on or in (acc.), ib.; one who has agreed upon (acc.), Mn. viii, 156; grown, increased, Ratnâv.; grown over, healed, Hariv.

Sam-āropa, m. (fr. Caus.) placing in or upon (loc.), KātyŚr., Sch.; stringing (a bow), Bālar.; transference to (loc.), attribution, Daśar.; Sāh.; Pratāp. °**āropaka**, mf(*ikā*)n. making to grow or thrive, Divyâv. °**āropaṇa**, n. transference, transposition, change of position (esp. of the sacred fire), ĀśvŚr., Sch.; stringing (a bow), Bālar.

Sam-āropita, mfn. caused to mount or ascend &c.; placed in or on (acc.), Veṇis.; put forth, displayed, R.; *-kārmuka*, mfn. one who has strung a bow, ib.; *-bhāra*, mfn. one on whom a burden has been placed, ib.; *-vikrama*, mfn. one who has displayed valour, ib.

Sam-āroha, m. ascending, mounting, riding upon, W.; agreeing upon, ib. °**āróhaṇa**, n. the act of mounting or ascending, ascent to (gen.), ŚBr.; Nir. &c.; growing (of the hair), MārkP.; changing the position of the sacred fire (symbolically), Siṇhâs. °**ārohaṇiyā**, f. pl. N. of partic. verses, ŚāṅkhŚr.

समार्गण *sa-mārgaṇa*, mfn. furnished with arrows, MBh.; *-guṇa*, mfn. furnished with arrows and a bowstring, ib.

समार्दव *sa-mārdava*, mfn. having softness, with softness, together with leniency, Yājñ.

समालक्ष् *sam-ā-√laksh* (only ind. p. *-lakshya*), to look at, behold, observe, consider, watch, MBh.

Sam-ālakshya, mfn. visible, perceptible, Sāh.

समालग्न *sam-ā-lagna*, mfn. (√*lag*) adhering or clasped or united together, closely attached, MBh.

समालप् *sam-ā-√lap*, P. *-lapati*, to speak to, address (acc.), Sāh.

Sam-ālāpa, m. talk, conversation with (*saha* or *anyo 'nyam*, also *anyo 'nya-s°*), Kāv.; Kathās.

समालभ् *sam-ā-√labh*, Ā. *-labhate*, to take hold of, seize, touch, ŚBr. &c.; to stroke, handle, MBh.; to obtain, acquire, Hit. (v.l.); to rub, anoint, smear over, Kāv.; Kathās.; Suśr.

Sam-ālabdha, mfn. taken hold of &c.; (ifc.) come into contact with, Vās. °**ālabhana**, n. unguent, Śak. (v.l.)

Sam-ālambha, m. taking hold of, seizing a victim (for sacrifice), MBh.; unguent (ifc. = 'anointed with'), ib. °**ālambhana**, n. taking hold of, touching (in *a-s°*), Gobh.; anointing, unguent, R.; Śak. °**ālámbham**, ind. while taking hold of, ŚBr. °**ālambhin**, mfn. seizing (the sacrificial victim), killing, MBh.

समालम्ब् *sam-ā-√lamb*, Ā. *-lambate*, to hang on, cling to (acc.), MBh.; Rājat.; to lean on, depend on, trust to (acc.), Kathās.; to take to (acc.), Cat.; to take hold of, seize, grasp, Kum.; Kathās.; to have recourse to, assume, R.; Mṛicch.; Bhaṭṭ.; to acquire, obtain, appropriate, Hit. (v.l.); to fall to the lot of (loc.), ib.: Caus. *-lambayati*, to cause to hang or rest, suspend to (loc.), Pañcat.

Sam-ālambana, n. the act of clinging to, leaning on, support, W. °**ālambita**, mfn. suspended, MW.; clung to, ib.; rested on, supported, upheld, maintained, ib. °**ālambin**, mfn. clinging to, laying hold &c., ib.; m. a kind of fragrant grass, L.

समालिख् *sam-ā-√likh*, P. *-likhati*, to scratch or mark down, mark out, write down, delineate, paint, VarBṛS.; Kathās.; Sarvad.; Hcat.

समालिङ्ग् *sam-ā-√liṅg*, P. Ā. *-liṅgati*, °*te*, to embrace closely, clasp or hold in a firm embrace, MBh.; R. &c.

Sam-āliṅgana, n. a close embrace, VarBṛS. °**āliṅgita**, mfn. clasped firmly, embraced closely, Pañcat.

समालिप् *sam-ā-√lip*, P. Ā. *-limpati*, °*te*, to anoint all over (A. 'one's self'), Bhaṭṭ.: Caus. *-lepayati*, to anoint or smear over, anoint well, Sāh.

Sam-ālipta, mfn. well anointed or smeared, MW.

समाली *sa-mālī*, f. a collection of flowers, nosegay, L.

Sa-mālya, mfn. garlanded, crowned, Hariv.

समालुड् *sam-ā-√luḍ*, Caus. *-loḍayati*, to stir up, stir in, mix together, mingle with (instr.), MBh.; Suśr.; AgP.; to agitate, disturb, confuse, MBh.; to rummage, investigate, Cat.

समालोक् *sam-ā-√lok*, P. *-lokayati*, to look at attentively, inspect, view, behold, regard, MBh.; Kāv. &c.; to consider or acknowledge as (two acc.), Pañcat.

Sam-āloka, m. looking at, viewing, beholding, Gīt.; Sāh. °**ālokana**, n. id., contemplation, inspection, VarBṛS., Rājat. °**ālokin**, mfn. looking into, one who has considered or studied (comp.), Cāṇ.

समालोच् *sam-ā-√loc*, P. *-locayati*, to look at attentively, consider well or thoroughly, Pañcar.; Hit. (v.l.)

Sam-āloca, m. colloquy, conversation (= *saṃvadana*), L. °**ālocin**, v.l. for °*ālokin*.

समावच्छस् *samāvacchás* &c. See *samāvac*, p. 1153, col. 2.

समावद् *sam-ā-√vad*, P. *-vadati*, to speak with certainty, state, declare, MBh.

समावप् *sam-ā-√2. vap*, P. *-vapati*, to sow or scatter together, mix up together, throw in together, Br.; GṛŚrS.; Suśr.: Caus. *-vāpayati*, id., MBh.; Suśr.

Sam-āvāpa, m. mixing up (the sacred fires), a sacrifice in which the fires are mixed up or combined, ĀśvŚr.

Sam-ôpta, m. thrown in together, mixed, mingled, Lāṭy.

समावर्जन *sam-āvarjana*. See *sam-ā-√vṛij*.

समावर्त *sam-āvarta* &c. See *sam-ā-√vṛit*.

समावलोक्य *sam-āva-lokya*, mfn. (√*lok*; prob. m. c. for *sam-ava-l°*) to be perceived or observed, MW.

समावस् *sam-ā-√5. vas*, P. *-vasati*, to dwell or settle in, inhabit (acc.), R.; Kām.; BhP.; to halt, encamp (for the night), Kathās.: Caus. *-vāsayati*, to pitch a camp, halt, settle down, Hit.

Sam-āvāsa, m. dwelling-place, residence, abode, halting-place, encampment, MBh.; Pañcat. °**āvāsita**, mfn. (fr. Caus.) made to dwell or settle, lodged, encamped, sojourned, Hit.; *-kaṭaka*, mfn. one who has pitched a camp, ib.

समावह् *sam-ā-√vah*, P. Ā. *-vahati*, °*te*, to bear or bring together or near, collect, assemble, Br.; Hariv.; (Ā.) to procure means of subsistence, AitBr.

Sam-āvaha, mfn. bringing about, effecting, causing, producing, Suśr.

समावाप्ति *sam-āvâpti*, f. (m. c. for *sam-av°*, q.v. under *sam-avâp*, p. 1157), Hcat.

समावाय *sam-āvâya*, m. (m. c. for *sam-av°*, q.v. under *sam-avê*, p. 1157), MBh.; R.; BhP.

समाविग्न *sam-ā-vigna*, mfn. (√*vij*) agitated, terrified, trembling greatly, R.

समाविद् *sam-ā-√1. vid*, Caus. *-vedayati*, to cause to know or be known thoroughly, report fully, announce, tell, MBh.; Kām.

Sam-āvedya, mfn. to be told or communicated fully, W.

समाविश् *sam-ā-√viś*, P. *-viśati*, to enter together or at once, enter into, enter thoroughly, take possession of, occupy, penetrate, fill, MBh.; Hariv.; Pur.; to sit or settle down in or on (acc. or loc.), Mn.; MBh.; R.; to go or fall into any state or condition (acc.), MBh.; to apply one's self to, begin, undertake, R.: Caus. *-veśayati*, to cause to enter together or thoroughly, introduce, insert, Kauś.; to cause to sit down, Rājat.; to conduct, lead or bring to or into (acc.), BhP.; to place or fix (eyes or mind) upon, direct towards (loc.), MBh.; Kāv. &c.; (with *svasmin*) to insert in one's self, contain, Pāṇ. v, 1, 52, Sch.; (Ā.) to deliver over, consign or commit or entrust to (loc.), ib.

Sam-āvishṭa, mfn. entered together or at once, seized, occupied, possessed by or filled with (instr. or comp.), Mn.; MBh. &c.; provided or endowed or furnished with (comp.), MBh.; Vet.; Pañcar.; taught or instructed in (instr.) or by (instr.), MBh. xiii, 1971.

Sam-āveśa, m. entering together or at once, entering, Cat.; meeting, penetration, absorption into (comp.), RPrāt.; Hariv.; simultaneous occurrence, co-existence, MBh.; Daśar.; (in gram.) applying together, common applicability of a term, Vārtt. on Pāṇ.; Kāś.; agreeing with, agreement, Uṇ. i, 108, Sch. °**āveśana**, n. entering, taking possession, Saṃskārak.; consummation of marriage, ĀpGṛ. °**āveśita**, mfn. (fr. Caus.) made to enter together, brought together, caused to enter, inserted, placed, fixed, absorbed, engrossed, Kāv.; Pur.

समावृ *sam-ā-√1. vṛi*, P. Ā. *-vṛiṇoti*, *-vṛiṇute*, to cover all over, conceal, veil, envelop, encompass, surround, MBh.; R. &c.; to fill, pervade, MBh.; to obstruct, hinder, stop, ib.

Sam-āvṛita, mfn. covered all over, concealed, enveloped, wrapt in, surrounded or beset with (instr. or comp.), MBh.; R.; protected or guarded by (instr.), MBh.; filled or inhabited by (comp.), R.; closed to i.e. withdrawn from (gen.), MBh.

समावृज् *sam-ā-√vṛij*, Ā. *-vṛiṅkte*, to bend or turn towards one's self, appropriate, TS.: Caus. *-āvarjayati*, see °*āvarjita*.

Sam-āvarjana, n. attracting, winning, Daśar. °**āvarjita**, mfn. bent down, inclined, lowered; *-ketu*, mfn. one who has lowered his standard, Kum.; *-netra-śobha*, mfn. one who has the (lustre of) his eyes bent down, Ragh.

समावृत् *sam-ā-√vṛit*, Ā. *-vartate*, to turn back, come back, return, RV. &c. &c.; to return home (said esp. of a Brahma-cārin or young Brāhman student of the Veda who has returned home after completing his studies in the house of a preceptor), GṛŚrS.; MBh. &c.; to come near, approach, MBh.; to turn towards (acc.; *pradakshiṇam*, 'with one's right side'), R.; to turn out well, succeed, MBh. xii, 1155; to come to nought, perish, VS. (Mahīdh.): Caus. *-vartayati*, to cause to return, drive away or home, RV.; to dismiss (a pupil after the completion of his studies), ChUp.; to repeat, recite, VarYogay.; Hcar.

Sam-āvarta, m. turning back, return to (loc.), MBh.; N. of Vishṇu, ib.

Sam-āvartana, n. returning, (esp.) the return home of a Brāhman student as above (also 'the Saṃskāra ceremony performed on the above occasion;' cf. *saṃskāra*), Mn.; Saṃk.; BhP.; Sarvad. (RTL. 353 &c.); *-karman*, n., *-prayoga*, m., *-vidhi*, m.; °*nâdi-prayoga*, m. N. of wks. °**āvartanīya**, mfn. relating to a return, Kauś. °**āvartamāna**, mfn. (pr. p.) returning from the home of a preceptor, MW. °**āvartin**, mfn. id., Saṃskārak.

Sam-āvṛitta, mfn. turned back, returned (esp. as described above), Mn.; MBh. &c.; approached, come from (comp.), MBh.; Kāv. &c.; completed, finished, MBh. i, 3256; *-vrata*, mfn. one who has completed a religious vow, MBh. °**āvṛittaka**, m. a pupil who has returned home, L. °**āvṛitti**, f. = °*āvartana*, Gaut. °**āvṛittika**, see *a-samāvṛittika*.

समावे *sam-ā-√ve*, P. Ā. *-vayati*, °*te*, to weave or string together, ŚBr.

Sam-ôta, mfn. woven or strung together, AV.

समावेष्ट् *sam-ā-√veshṭ*, Caus. *-veshṭayati*, to cover with, Suśr.

समाव्यध् *sam-ā-√vyadh*, P. *-vidhyati*, to whirl, brandish, R.; Hariv.

Sam-āviddha, mfn. shaken, agitated (others 'wasted, destroyed'), MBh. xv, 1031.

समाव्रज् *sam-ā-√vraj*, P. *-vrajati*, to go back, return, MBh.

समाश *sam-āśa*, m. (√2. *aś*) a common meal, Pat.; eating, a meal, Pāṇ. vi, 2, 71, Sch.

समाशंस् *sam-ā-√śaṇs*, P. Ā. *-śaṇsati*, °*te*, (P.) to adjudge, assign anything to (dat.), RV.; (Ā.) to trust or confide in (acc.), MBh.; to wish or long for, desire, MW.

समाशङ्कित *sam-ā-śaṅkita*, mfn. (√*śaṅk*) very fearful or apprehensive, W.; doubted, doubtful, ib.

समाशिर् *sám-āśir*, mfn. mixed (as Soma), RV.

समाश्रि *sam-ā-√śri*, P. Ā. *-śrayati*, °*te*, to go or have recourse to together (esp. for protection), fly to for refuge, seek refuge with, lean on, trust to, confide in (acc.), Mn.; MBh. &c.; to resort to, approach, enter, occupy, obtain, assume, ib.; to follow, practise, MBh.; Kāv. &c.

Sam-āśraya, m. (ifc. f. *ā*) going together to any one (esp. for support or shelter), connection with, dependence on, relation to (ifc. = 'relating to, concerning;' *āt*, 'in consequence of, owing to'), MBh.; R.; VarBṛS. &c.; support, shelter, place of refuge, asylum, Kāv.; Pur.; Kathās.; dwelling-place, habitation, home (ifc. = 'living or dwelling or situated or being in'), R.; Pañcat.; Kathās. °**āśrayaṇa**, n. resorting or attaching one's self to, choosing, selecting (comp.), Bālar.; *-sampradāya*, m. N. of wk. °**āśrayaṇīya**, mfn. to be had recourse to or taken refuge with, Pañcat.; m. 'to be taken service with,' a master (as opp. to *sam-āśrita*, 'a servant'), Rājat. °**āśrayin**, mfn. assuming, occupying (a place), taking possession of (comp.), Rājat.

Sam-āśrita, mfn. come together, assembled, Nir.; going or resorting to, living or dwelling in, fixed or staying or standing in or on, flowing into (acc., loc., or comp.), MBh.; Kāv. &c.; (also *-vat*, 'one who has attained,' with acc.), Hariv.; Pañcat.; following or practising, leaning on, taking refuge with (acc.), ŚāṅkhGṛ.; R.; resting or dependent on (loc.), KaṭhUp.; relating to, concerning (comp.), R.; MBh.; Rājat.; stating, asserting, Sarvad.; (with pass. sense) leaned on (for support), resorted to, Rājat.; had recourse to, chosen, Kār. on Pāṇ. vii, 1, 1; endowed or provided or furnished with (instr.), Kathās.; visited or afflicted by (comp.), MBh.; m. a dependant, servant (cf. °*āśrayaṇīya*), Rājat.; *-tva*, n. resort to, seeking refuge with (comp.), Pañcat.

समाश्रु *sam-ā-√śru*, P. Ā. *-śriṇoti*, *-śriṇute*, to promise, MW.: Caus. *-śrāvayati*, to inform, apprise of (two acc.), BhP.

समाश्लिष् *sam-ā-√ślish*, P. *-ślishyati*, to cling to (acc.), MBh.; to embrace closely or firmly, ib. &c.: Caus. *-śleshayati*, to join together, TS.

Sam-āślishṭa, mfn. closely embraced, firmly attached (also with *anyo 'nyam*), MBh.; Sāh.

Sam-āślesha, m. a close or firm embrace, MBh.; Mālatīm. °**āśleshaṇa**, n. id., Pañcar.

समाश्वस् *sam-ā-√śvas*, P. *-śvasiti* or *-śvasati*, to breathe again, recover breath, revive, take courage (often in 2. sg. Impv. *-śvasihi*, 'take courage!'), MBh.; Kāv. &c.; to trust or confide in (loc.), MBh.: Caus. *-śvāsayati*, to cause to revive, reanimate, encourage, comfort, calm, console, MBh.; R. &c.

Sam-āśvasta, mfn. recovered, revived, reanimated, comforted, consoled, R.; Kathās.; trusting, confiding, full of confidence, Mn. vii, 59.

Samāśvāsa, m. recovering breath, relief, comfort, R.; trust, belief, confidence, MBh.; Kathās.

Sam-āśvāsana, n. (fr. Caus.) the act of causing to take breath, encouraging, cheering, comforting, consolation, R.; Vikr.; Pañcat. °**āśvāsita**, mfn. reanimated, revived, refreshed &c., MBh.; R. °**āśvāsya**, mfn. to be revived or cheered or comforted, R.; Kathās.

समास् *sam-√ās*, Ā. *-āste* (pr. p. *-āsīna*, q. v.), to sit together, sit or assemble round (acc.), RV.; AV.; MBh.; to sit, be seated, Mn.; R.; to sit or abide in (loc.), R.; to hold a council, deliberate, AV.; ŚBr.; to practise, observe (acc.), R.; to behave like (*iva*), resemble, MBh.; to be dejected or low-spirited, R.; to mind, attend to, acknowledge, R.; to be a match for, cope with (acc.), MBh.; R.

2. **Sam-āsa** (for 1. see under *sam-√2. as*), m. abiding together, connection, MW.

Sam-āsana, n. (for *samâs*° see p. 1153, col. 1) sitting down, s° together with (*saha*), MBh. °**āsīna**, mfn. sitting together with (instr.), ib. °**āsyā**, f. sitting together, session, colloquy, interview, MBh.; R.

समासञ्ज् *sam-ā-√sañj*, P. *-sajati*, to fasten or stick together, join or attach to, fix or place on, wrap or suspend round, MBh.; Hariv.; to impose, resign or deliver over to (loc.), Mn.; MBh. &c.: Pass. *-sajyate* or *-sajjate*, to cling or adhere closely together, cling or stick to, become attached to, MW.

Sam-āsakta, mfn. suspended, attached to or fixed upon (loc.), MaitrUp.; R.; harnessed with (instr.), R.; dependent on (loc.), ib.; concerning, relating to (loc.), MBh.; intent upon, devoted to, occupied with (loc. or comp.), MBh.; Pañcar.; stopped (in its effect, as poison), MBh.; committed or entrusted to (loc.), R.; affected by (comp.), Kathās.; joined, united, combined, MW.; reached, attained, ib. °**āsakti**, f. sticking or adhering closely to, attachment, devotion, MārkP.; Rājat.

Sam-āsaṅga, m. the committing or entrusting (of business) to any one (loc.), R. °**āsañjana**, n. (accord. to some also *-āsajjana*) joining, union, connection, contact, W.

समासद् *sam-ā-√sad*, P. *-sīdati*, to betake one's self to, come near to, approach or advance to, reach, arrive at (acc.), MBh.; R. &c.; to meet, encounter (either in a friendly or hostile manner), attack, assail, MBh.; to attain, obtain, meet with, find, recover, Rājat.; Kathās.: Caus. *-sādayati* (ind. p. *-sādya*, q. v.), to come to, to approach, advance to, arrive at, fall or get into, reach, attain, incur, MBh.; Kāv. &c.; meet, encounter (a friend or enemy), attack, assail, ib.; to hit (as an arrow), MBh.; to accrue to (acc.), Rājat.

Sam-āsatti, f. nearness, vicinity, Pāṇ. iii, 4, 50.

Sam-āsanna, mfn. reached, approached, attained &c.; near, proximate, close to (comp.), Yājñ.; Ragh.; Kathās.

Sam-āsādana, n. (fr. Caus.) the act of approaching, meeting with, attaining, Pat.; effecting, accomplishing, W. °**āsādita**, mfn. approached, met with &c., W. 1. °**āsādya**, ind. having approached &c.; according to, by means or on account of (acc.), MBh.; Kāv. &c. 2. °**āsādya**, mfn. attainable, practicable, L.

समासार्ध *sa-māsârdha*, mf(*ā*)n. (a year) with a half-month added, Rājat.

समासिच् *sam-ā-√sic*, P. *-siñcati*, to sprinkle or pour out together, ŚBr.; KātyŚr.; to instil (wisdom) into (acc.), MBh. xii, 4585.

Sam-āseka, m. pouring out together, Kauś., Sch.

Sam-āsecana, n. id., Kauś.

समासृज् *sam-ā-√sṛij*, P. *-sṛijati* (often v. l. *-sajati*), to attach or fasten to (loc.), MBh.; R.; to deliver over, consign to (loc.), Hariv.; Mn.

Sam-āsarjana, n. delivering over, consigning, abandoning, W.

Sam-āsṛishṭa, mfn. delivered over, consigned, abandoned, ib.

समासेव् *sam-ā-√sev*, Ā. *-sevate*, to practise, perform, pursue, enjoy, Mn.; Subh.; to serve, honour, gratify, MW.

Sam-āsevana, n. the act of practising, following, employing, serving, W. °**āsevita**, mfn. practised, followed, employed, served, ib.

समास्कन्द् *sam-ā-√skand*, P. *-skandati*, to assail, attack, Bhaṭṭ.; MārkP.

Sam-āskanna, mfn. attached or added to (loc.), Nir.; scattered over (= *viprakīrṇa*), ib., Sch.

समास्तृ *sam-ā-√stṛi*, P. Ā. *-stṛiṇoti*, °*ṇute* or *-stṛiṇāti*, °*ṇīte*, to spread entirely over, cover over, MBh.; R.; Jātakam.; to extinguish, MBh.

समास्था *sam-ā-√sthā*, P. Ā. *-tishṭhati*, °*te*, to mount, ascend, Hariv.; to go to, R.; to stop, halt, MBh.; to enter upon, undergo, undertake (a march), assume (a form), seek (a maintenance), apply (assiduity) to (loc.), MBh.; R. &c.; to perform, accomplish, BhP.: Caus. *-sthāpayati*, to cause to stop, make to halt, R.; to cause to be performed or practised, ib.

Sam-āstha, w. r. for *sama-stha*, MBh. v, 6029.

Sam-āsthita, mfn. standing or sitting upon (acc., loc., or comp.), MBh.; R.; persevering in (loc.), R.; one who has entered upon or submitted to (as slavery &c.), MBh.; one who has had recourse to, engaged in, occupied with, intent upon (acc.), MBh.; R.

समास्वद् *sam-ā-√svad*, Caus. *-svādayati*, to taste, enjoy, R.; Kām.

समाहन् *sam-ā-√han*, P. *-hanti*, to strike together, TS.; ŚBr.; to strike upon or against, MBh.; Hariv. &c.; to strike down, slay, kill, MBh.; to clash together, meet with (instr.), ib.; to beat (a drum), TBr.; MBh. &c.

Sam-āghāta, m. striking together, collision, Daśar.; Sāh.; conflict, war, battle, L.

Sam-āhata, mfn. struck together, MBh.; joined, united, Nir.; struck down, wounded, killed, MBh.; Kāv. &c.; beaten (as a drum), Amar.; Kathās.

Sam-āhanana, n. the act of striking upon or against, ĀpŚr., Sch.

समाहित *sam-āhita*. See p. 1160, col. 1.

समाहूत *sam-āhūta*. See *sam-ā-√hve*.

समाहृ *sam-ā-√hṛi*, P. Ā. *-harati*, °*te* (ind. p. *-hṛitya*, q. v.), to bring together, collect, assemble, contract, combine, unite, AV. &c. &c.; to bring back, restore to its place (loc.), Mn. viii, 319; to draw back, withdraw, Hariv.; to ravish, enrapture, ib.; to take off, put aside, BhP.; to crush together, destroy, annihilate, Bhag.; to perform, offer (a sacrifice), R.

Sam-āhara, mfn. crushing together, destroying, R. °**āharaṇa**, n. bringing together, collection, accumulation, combination, composition, W. °**āhartṛi**, m. a collector (in *artha-s*°), Mn. vii, 60.

Sam-āhāra, m. seizing, taking hold of, Gṛihyās.; aggregation, summing up, sum, totality, collection, assemblage, multitude, MBh.; Kāv. &c.; (in gram.) conjunction or connecting of words or sentences (as by the particle *ca*), Śaṃk.; Prāt., Sch.; Pāṇ., Sch.; compounding of words, a compound (esp. applied to a Dvaṃdva whose last member is in the neuter gender [e. g. *ahi-nakulam*, 'a snake and an ichneumon'], or to a Dvigu, when it expresses an aggregate; see *trilokī*), Pāṇ.; = *pratyāhāra*, Vop. (cf. IW. 169, n. 1); withdrawal (of the senses from the world), Kām.; contraction, abridgment, L.; *-varṇa*, m. N. of the diphthongs *ai* and *au*, Pat. °**āhārya**, mfn. to be collected or united or combined, ŚBr.; MBh.

Sam-āhṛita, mfn. brought together, collected, fetched, MBh.; Kāv. &c.; gathered, assembled, met, Hariv.; Ragh.; BhP.; taken together, contracted, combined, all, Kāś.; Kathās.; drawn (as a bowstring), Kathās., related, told, BhP.; accepted, received, taken, W. °**āhṛiti**, f. taking together, collecting (= *saṃgraha*), L.; withdrawal (of the senses) from (abl.), L. °**hṛitya**, ind. (taking) together, all at once, TBr.; Kauś.

समाह्वे *sam-ā-√hve*, P. Ā. *-hvayati*, °*te* (ind. p. *-hūya*), to call together, convoke, MBh.; R. &c.; to call near, invite, ib.; to summon, challenge, provoke (to battle or to a game of chance), ib.: Desid. *-juhūshate*, see next.

Sam-ājuhūshamāṇa, mfn. (fr. Desid.) challenging (e. g. *samarāya*, 'to battle'), MW.

Sam-āhūta, mfn. called or collected together, assembled, summoned, challenged (to fight or to a game of chance), MBh.; Kāv. &c.

Sam-āhva, m. calling out, mutual calling, challenge, defiance, W.; (*ī*), f. id., ib.; (*ā*), f. a partic. plant (= *go-jihvā*), L.; mfn. (fr. *sam* + *āhvā*) bearing the same name, Śiś. °**āhvaya**, m. challenge, conflict, MBh.; setting animals to fight for sport, betting (esp. betting on animals, as distinguished from gaming with dice &c.; see *dyūta*), Mn.; Yājñ.; an appellation, name (also n.), Pañcar.

Sam-āhvātṛi, m. one who summons, a challenger to (dat.), MBh.

Sam-āhvāna, n. calling upon or together, R.; Pañcat.; summons, challenge (to fight or to grumble), MBh.; R.; betting on the battles of animals, Susr.

समि *sam-* √5. *i*, P. *-eti*, to go or come together, meet at (acc.) or with (instr. or dat.), encounter (as friends or enemies), RV. &c. &c.; to come together in sexual union, cohabit (acc. or *sârdham*, *saha*), MBh.; R.; to come to, arrive at, approach, visit, seek, enter upon, begin, RV. &c. &c.; to lead to (acc.), RV. iii, 54, 5; to consent, agree with (instr. 'it is agreed between,' with gen. of pers. and loc. of thing), ŚBr.; MBh.: Pass. *-īyate*, to be united or met or resorted to &c.: Intens. *-īyate*, to visit, frequent, RV.; to appear, be manifested, BhP.

Sam-ayá, m. (ifc. f. *ā*) coming together, meeting or a place of meeting, AV.; ŚBr.; intercourse with (instr.), Mn. x, 53; coming to a mutual understanding, agreement, compact, covenant, treaty, contract, arrangement, engagement, stipulation, conditions of agreement, terms (*ena* or *āt* or *-tas*, 'according to agreement, conditionally;' *tena samayena*, 'in consequence of this agreement;' *samayaṃ*, acc. with √*kṛi*, 'to make an agreement or engagement,' 'agree with any one [instr. with or without *saha*],' 'settle,' 'stipulate;' with *sam-√vad*, id.; with √*dā*, 'to propose an agreement,' 'offer terms;' with √*brū* or √*vac* or *abhi-√dhā*, 'to state the terms of an agr°,' 'make a promise;' with √*grah* or *prati-√pad*, 'to enter into an agr°,' 'make or accept conditions of an agr°;' with √*pāl* or √*raksh* or *pari-√raksh* &c., 'to keep an agr°,' 'keep one's word;' with √*tyaj* or √*bhid* or *vy-abhi-√car* &c., 'to break an agr°;' abl. with √*bhraṃś*, id.; loc. with √*sthā*, 'to keep an engagement,' 'keep one's word;' acc. with Caus. of √*sthā* or of *ni-√viś*, 'to fix or settle terms,' 'impose conditions'), TS. &c. &c.; convention, conventional rule or usage, established custom, law, rule, practice, observance, MBh.; R.; BhP.; order, direction, precept, doctrine, Nir.; MBh.; Śaṃk.; Sarvad.; (in rhet.) the conventional meaning or scope of a word, Kusum.; appointed or proper time, right moment for doing anything (gen. or Pot., Pāṇ. iii, 3, 68), opportunity, occasion, time, season (ifc. or ibc. or *e*, ind., 'at the appointed time or at the right moment or in good time for,' or 'at the time of,' 'when there is;' *tena samayena*, 'at that time'), MBh.; Kāv. &c.; juncture, circumstances, case (*iha samaye*, 'under these circumstances,' 'in this case'), Pañcat.; Hit.; an ordeal, Vishṇ.; sign, hint, indication, W.; demonstrated conclusion, ib.; limit, boundary, ib.; solemn address, harangue, speech, declaration, Vishṇ.; (in gram.) a Vedic passage which is the repetition of another one, RPrāt.; (in dram.) end of trouble or distress, Bhar.; Daśar.; Sāh.; N. of a son of Dharma, VP.; (with Śāktas) N. of the author of a Mantra, Cat. **–kamalâkara**, m., **-kalpa-taru**, m. N. of wks. **–kāma** (*samayá-*), mfn. desiring an agreement, TS. **–kāra**, m. making an agr° or appointment or engagement, fixing a time, W.; =*śailī*, *saṃketa*, L. **–kriyā**, f. making an agr° or compact or engagement, MW.; enjoining certain duties or obligations, Mn. vii, 202; preparation of an ordeal, Vishṇ. **–cyuti**, f. neglect of the right time, Bhartṛ. **–jña**, mfn. knowing the right time (said of Vishṇu), MBh. **–dharma**, m. a duty based on agreement, covenant, stipulation, Pañcat.; Yājñ., Sch. **–naya**, m., **-nirṇaya**, m. N. of wks. **–pada**, n. pl. any matters or points agreed upon, Āpast. **–parirakshaṇa**, n. the observance of a compact, Kir. **–prakāśa**, m., **-pradīpa**, m. N. of wks. **–bandhana**, mfn. bound by an agreement, MārkP. **–bheda**, m. breaking an agr°; °*dôparacana-cakra*, n. N. of wk. **–bhedin**, mfn. breaking an agr°, Mn. viii, 218. **–mayūkha**, m., **-mātṛikā**, f., **-ratna**, n., **-rahasya**, n. N. of wks. **–vajra**, m. N. of a man, Buddh. **–vidyā**, f. 'science of right moments,' astrology, Daś. **–vidhāna**, n. N. of wk. **–viparîta**, mfn. contrary to agreement, not performing engagements, Bk. **–velā**, f. a period of time, Śṛiṅgār. **–vyabhicāra**, m. transgression or violation of a compact, MW. **–vyabhicārin**, mfn. breaking an agreement, Mn. viii, 220; 221. **–sāra**, N. of wk. **–sundara-gaṇi**, m. N. of an author, Cat. **–sûkta**, n. pl. N. of wk. **–setu-vārita**, mfn. restrained by the barrier of custom, MW. **Samayâcāra**, m. conventional or established practice, R.; (with Tāntrikas) N. of partic. orthodox wks.; *-tantra*, n., *-nirūpaṇa*, n. N. of wks. **Samayā-tantra**, n. N. of wk. **Samayâdhyushita**, mfn. half-risen (as the sun), Gṛihyās.; Mn. &c.; n. a time at which neither stars nor sun are visible, MW. **Samayânanda-saṃtosha**, m. N. of an author, Cat. **Samayânuvartin**, mfn. following established rules, observant of duties, MW. **Samayânusāreṇa**, ind. according to the occasion, suitably to the time or season, ib. **Samayârṇa-mātṛikā**, f., °**yâloka**, m., °**yâshṭa-nirūpaṇa**, n. N. of wk. **Samayôcita**, mfn. suited to the occasion or time or to an emergency, seasonable, opportune, BhP.; (*am*), ind. suitably to the occ°, MW.; *-śloka*, m. N. of wk. **Samayôddyota**, m. N. of wk. **Samayôllaṅghita-tva**, n. the violating of contracts or agreements, MW.

2. **Samayā** (for 1. *samayā* see p. 1153, col. 2), in comp. for *samaya*. **–√kṛi**, P. *-karoti*, to pass time, let time pass, lose time (=*kāla-kshepaṃ √kṛi*), Pāṇ. v, 4, 60.

Samayī-√kṛi, P. *-karoti*, to stipulate, make incumbent or necessary, R.

Sam-āya, m. a visit, arrival, W. °**āyín**, mfn. occurring together or simultaneously (cf. *a-s°*), ŚBr.

Sam-it, f. (for *samit* see below) hostile encounter, conflict, battle, war, MBh.; Kāv. &c.; *-sajja*, mfn. ready for war or battle, Rājat.

Sám-ita, mfn. (for *sa-mita* see below) come together, assembled, joined or united or combined with (instr. or comp.), RV.; MBh.; promised, agreed, assented to, MW.; finished, completed, ib.

1. **Sám-iti**, f. (for 2. see below) coming together, meeting, assembling, an assembly, council, RV.; AV.; MBh.; BhP.; a flock, herd, Kir.; association, society (personified as daughter of Prajā-pati), BhP.; a league, plot, RV.; AV.; encounter, hostile meeting, war, battle, Br.; MBh.; R.; sameness, likeness (cf. 2. *samá*), L.; (with Jainas) rule of life or conduct (five are enumerated, viz. *īryā-*, *bhāshā-*, *eshaṇā-*, *ādāna-*, and *utsarga-s°*), Sarvad. **–ṃgama** (°*tím-*), mfn. assisting a council, ŚBr. **–ṃjaya** (°*tíṃ-*), mfn. 'victorious in battle' or 'eminent in an assembly' (also N. of Yama and Vishṇu), MBh.; Hariv.; BhP.; m. N. of a warrior, MBh. **–mardana**, mfn. crushing or harassing in battle, ib. **–śālin**, mfn. warlike, brave, BhP. **–śobhana**, mfn. conspicuous in fight or battle, MBh.; R.

Sam-ithá, m. hostile encounter, conflict, collision, RV.; fire, L.; offering, oblation, ib.

समिक 2. *samika*, n. (for 1. see p. 1153, col. 2) a pike, javelin, dart, L.

समिङ्ग् *sam-√iṅg*, Caus. *-iṅgayati*, to cause to move or throb, agitate, shake about, RV.

समित *sa-mita*, mfn. (fr. 7. *sa* + 2. *mita*) measured, meted out (opp. to *a-mita*), Kpr.; (=*sam-mita*) commensurate, equal to (comp.), MBh.; Suśr.; (*am*), ind. continually, always, Kāraṇḍ.; (*ā*), f. wheat-flour, Bhpr.; Divyâv.

समिति 2. *sam-iti*, ind. (for 1. see above) a sacred verse beginning with *sam*, MW.

समितृ *samitṛi*, w. r. for *śamitṛi*, q. v.

समित्र *sa-mitra*, mfn. attended by a friend, along with friends, MBh.

समिथुन *sá-mithuna*, mf(*ā*)n. together with the pair or couple (or 'with the mate'), ŚBr.

समिद्ध 1. *sam-iddha*, mfn. (for 2. see col. 3), Prākrit for *sam-ṛiddha*, perfect, full, complete, HirGṛ.

समिन् *samin*, m. N. of a son of Rājâdhideva (v. l. *śamin*), Hariv.

समिनक्ष् *sam-inaksh* (see *inaksh*), *-inakshati*, to wish to attain, strive to reach, be desirous of, RV.

समिन्ध् *sam-√indh*, Ā. *-inddhe* or *-indhe* (once in Br. 3. pl. impf. *-aindhan*; cf. Nir. x, 8; Ved. inf. *-ídham* and *-ídhe*), to set fire to, set alight, light up, kindle, ignite, inflame (lit. and fig.), RV.; AV.; Br.; Mn.; to take fire, RV. vii, 8, 1; to swell, increase, exhibit, show, betray (skill), Bhaṭṭ.: Pass. *-idhyate*, to be kindled, take fire, break out into flame, RV. &c. &c.

Samit, in comp. for *samidh* (for *sam-it* see above). **–kalāpa**, m. a bundle of firewood, IndSt. **–kāshṭha**, n. pl. logs of wood, fuel, ŚBr. **–kuśa**, n. fuel and Kuśa grass, Ragh. **–tvá**, n. the state of (being) fuel, TBr.; Bālar. **–pāṇi** (*samít-*), mfn. holding fuel in the hands, ŚBr.; m. N. of a pupil of Śaṃkarâcārya, Cat. **–pāntha**, m. fire, Gal. **–pūla**, m. a bundle of firewood, MānGṛ. **–samāropaṇa-prātar-aupāsana-prayoga**, m., and **-samāropaṇa-vidhāna**, n. N. of wks.

Samid, in comp. for *samidh*. **–anta**, mfn. ending with the word *samidh*, KātyŚr. **–ādhāna**, n. the placing on of wood or fuel (for the oblation to fire), Mn. ii, 176. **–āharaṇa**, n. fetching fuel, Śak. **–idhma-vraścana**, n. splitting firewood of various kinds, Mcar. **–dṛishadá**, n. f° and a stone, Pāṇ. v, 4, 106, Sch. **–dhārá** (for *-hāra*), mfn. fetching f° (nom. with √*gam*, 'to go to fetch f°'), Āpast. **–dhoma** (for *-homa*), m. an oblation of f° (to fire), MW. **–vat** (*samíd-*), mfn. provided with f°, Śak.; containing the word *samidh* (*samid-vatī*, f. a verse containing the word *samidh*), TS.; Vait.

2. **Sám-iddha**, mfn. (for 1. see col. 2) set alight or on fire, lighted, kindled, ignited, inflamed, RV. &c. &c. **–darpa**, mfn. inflamed with pride, MW. **–vat**, mfn. containing the word *samiddha*, KātyŚr. **–śaraṇa**, mfn. having (its) habitations set on fire (as a town), MW. **–homá**, m. a libation poured out upon lighted wood, ŚBr. **Sámiddhâgni**, mfn. one who has kindled his fire, RV. **Samiddhârcis**, n. a blazing flame, MW. **Samiddhârthaka**, m. N. of a man, Mudr.

Samídh, mfn. igniting, flaming, burning, RV.; f. firewood, fuel, a log of wood, faggot, grass &c. employed as fuel (7 Samidhs, or sometimes 3 × 7 are mentioned, as well as 7 Yonis, 7 flames &c.), RV. &c. &c.; kindling, flaming, RV.; VS.; ŚBr.; =*samid-ādhāna*, ŚrS. °**idha** (ifc.) = *samidh*, fuel, wood, R.; m. fire, L.; (*ā*), f. an oblation to fuel or firewood, Gṛihyās.

Samídham, °**idhe**. See above under verb.

Sam-idhya, Nom. P. °*yati* (fut. *-idhyitā* or *-idhitā*), to wish for fuel, Pāṇ. vi, 4, 50, Sch.

Sam-idhyamāna, mfn. (pr. p. Pass.) being kindled or ignited; *-vat*, mfn. containing the word *samidhyamāna*, KātyŚr.

Sam-indhana, m. N. of a man, Cat.; n. the act of kindling, Nir.; fuel, firewood, Bhaṭṭ.; a means of swelling or increasing of (gen.), MBh. xii, 4385.

Sam-eddhṛí, mfn. one who kindles, kindling, RV.

समिन्व् *sam-√inv*, P. *-invati*, to impart, bestow, RV.; to put together, restore, ib.

समिर *sam-ira*, m.=*sam-īra*, wind, air (see *sam-√īr*), L.; N. of Śiva, L.

समिश्र *sa-miśra*, mfn. mixing, mingling, undergoing mixture or combination (in *a-sam°*), BhP.

समिष् *sam-ísh*, f. (√1. *ish*) a dart, javelin, RV.

Sam-ishaṇya, Nom. P. °*yati*, to drive together, RV.

समिष्ट *sam-ishṭa*, mfn. (√*yaj*) sacrificed together, sacrificed; n. sacrifice (see next); *-yajus*, n. sacrificial formula and sacrifice, VS.; ŚBr.; KātyŚr.

Sám-ishṭi, f. a complete sacrifice or oblation, TS.; TBr.

समीक *samīka*. See *samy-añc*, p. 1181.

समीकरण *samī-karaṇa*, *samī-√kṛi* &c. See p. 1153, col. 2.

समीक्ष् *sam-√īksh*, Ā. *-īkshate*, to look at or inspect thoroughly, investigate closely, view, perceive, see, VS. &c. &c.; to become aware of, ascertain, R.; to find out, contrive, invent, MBh.; to think of, aim at, have in view, bear in mind, MBh.; to consider well, inquire into, investigate, examine, contemplate, Mn.; MBh. &c.; to look closely at in order to choose or destine for (two acc.), R.: Caus. *-īkshayati*, °*te*, to cause to look at or view or perceive, AV.; KātyŚr.; to let one's self be seen, show one's self, appear, AV.

Sam-īksha, n. 'complete investigation,' N. of the Sāṃkhya system of philosophy, L.; (*ā*), f. thorough or close inspection, perceiving, beholding (dat. 'within the range of any one's [gen.] sight'), Āpast.; desire or wish to see, MBh.; a glance, BhP.; view, opinion in regard to (with *prati*), MBh.; deep insight, understanding, intellect, BhP.; investigation, search, W.; the Mīmāṅsā philosophy or any work examining or explaining Vedic ritual, ib.;

essential nature or truth or principle (= *tattva*, q.v.), ib.; effort, ib. °**īkshaṇa,** n. looking at or looking about thoroughly, ŚrS.; search, close investigation, W.; mfn. (fr. Caus.) causing to look at or perceive, BhP. °**īkshita,** mfn. well looked at, perceived, considered, investigated, PārGṛ.; R. °**īkshitavya,** mfn. to be well considered or investigated or ascertained, RPrāt., Sch. °**īkshya,** mfn. id., ib.; n. the Sāṃkhya philosophy, Śiś. ii, 59.

समीच *samīca* &c. See under *samy-añc.*

समीच्छा *samīcchā,* w. r. for *sam-īkshā* or *sam-īhā,* MBh. xii, 9363.

समीज् *sam-√ij,* Ā. *-ijate,* to drive together, collect, RV.

समीड् *sam-√īḍ* (only 3. pl. pf. *-īḍire*), to praise together, celebrate, BhP.

समीदा *samīdā,* m. fine wheat-flour (cf. *samitā*), L.

समीन *samīna* &c. See p. 1153, col. 2.

समीप *samīpa,* mfn. (prob. fr. *sam* + 2. *áp* and formed analogously to *pratīpa, dvīpa, anūpa;* accord. to some fr. *sam* + √*āp* and = 'easy to attain') near (in place or time), contiguous, proximate, adjacent, close by, at hand, approaching, imminent, Kāv.; VarBṛS. &c.; (*am*), n. nearness, proximity, vicinity, presence, imminence (with gen. or ifc., *am,* 'to, towards;' *āt,* 'from;' *e,* 'in the vicinity, near, close at hand, beside, in the presence of, at the time of, before, at, towards;' cf. *saṃdhi-velā-s°*), KātyŚr.; MBh.; Kāv. &c. **–kāla,** m. nearness in time, Pāṇ. viii, 1, 7, Sch. **–ga,** mf(*ā*)n. going near, accompanying, standing beside (gen. or comp.), MBh.; R. &c. **–gamana,** n. the act of going near, approach, R. **–ja,** mf(*ā*)n. growing close by (gen.), MBh.; relating to nearness, approaching, R. **–jala,** mfn. having water close by, being near the water, VarBṛS. **–tara,** mfn. nearer; *-vartin,* mfn. being nearer at hand, neighbouring, Mṛicch., Sch. **–tas,** ind. (with gen. or ifc.) from, from the presence of, Hariv.; Kathās.; near at hand, near, in the presence of, MBh.; R. &c.; (with gen.) towards, to, R.; Pañcat.; immediately, very soon, VarBṛS. **–tā,** f., **–tva,** n. nearness, contiguity, proximity, Kāv.; Sarvad. **–deśa,** m. a country or place close at hand, neighbourhood, Yājñ., Sch. **–nayana,** n. leading near to, bringing to (gen.), Śak. **–bhāj,** mfn. 'partaking of nearness,' neighbouring, Kautukar. **–maraṇa-cihna,** n. the signs of approaching death (a topic treated of in certain Purāṇas), Cat. **–vartin,** mfn. being near, living near &c., Ṛitus.; Pañcat. **–saptamī,** f. the locative case expressing nearness, ĀpGṛ., Sch. **–sahakāra,** m. a mango tree standing near, Śak. iv, 13 (v. l.) **–stha,** mfn. = *-vartin,* MBh.; Kāv. &c.; approaching, imminent (as death), Subh. **–sthāna,** n. the being near or in the vicinity, Sāy. **Samīpâvasita,** mfn. settled down in the neighbourhood, KātyŚr. **Samīpôpagata,** mfn. approached near, MW.

Samīpaka, n. nearness, vicinity (*e,* ifc., 'near, close by'), Hcat.

Samīpī, in comp. for *samīpa.* **– √kṛi,** P. *-karoti,* to make near, bring near. **– √bhū,** P. *-bhavati,* to become near, Pāṇ. v, 4, 50, Vārtt. 3 (also with √*as*).

समीभाव *samī-bhāva, samīya* &c. See p. 1153, col. 2.

समीर् *sam-√īr* (only impf. *-airat*), to join together, bring about, create, RV.; to effect, promote, ib.: Caus. *-īrayati,* °*te,* to cause to move, set in motion, impel, agitate, urge on, send forth, RV.; TBr.; Bhaṭṭ.; to bring about, accomplish, produce, create, RV.; AV.; to reanimate, revive, ŚBr.; to confer, bestow, endow with, AV.; ŚBr.

Sam-īra, m. air, breeze, wind (also of the body, see below), MBh.; Kāv. &c.; the god of wind, L.; the Śamī tree, MW.; pl. N. of a people, MBh.; *-gaja-kesarin,* m. a partic. mixture used as a remedy for disease of the nerves, L.; *-lakshman,* n. 'wind-sign,' dust, Śiś.; *-sāra,* m. Aegle Marmelos, L.

Sam-īraṇa, mfn. setting in motion, causing activity, stimulating, promoting, MBh.; R.; Car.; m. (ifc. f. *ā*) breeze, wind, air, breath (also 'the god of wind'), MBh.; Kāv. &c.; wind of the body (of which there are five, see *vāyu*), Suśr.; N. of the number 'five,' VarBṛS.; a traveller, L.; marjoram or a similar plant, L.; (*am*), n. setting in motion, TPrāt.; hurling, throwing, MBh.; *-sahāya,* mfn. accompanied or fanned by the wind (as a forest fire), MW. °**īrita,** mfn. stirred, moved, tossed, thrown, MBh.; Kāv. &c.; sent forth, uttered (as a sound), R.

Sam-īrṇa, mfn. (accord. to Pāṇ. vii, 1, 102, Sch., fr. *sam-√ṛi*) moved about, moved &c., MW.

समीष् *sam-√īsh,* Ā. *-īshate,* to become extended or lengthened out, Kāṭh.

Sam-īshantī, f. a partic. Vishṭuti, Lāṭy.

Sám-īshita, mfn. extended, stretched out, lengthened, TS.; Kāṭh.

समीह् *sam-√īh,* Ā. *-īhate* (pr. p. *-īhat*), to strive after, wish for, desire, endeavour to gain (acc.), VS. &c. &c.

Sam-īhana, mfn. zealous, eager (said of Vishṇu), MBh.

Sam-īhā, f. striving after, longing for, wish, desire, MBh.; Kāv. &c. °**īhita,** mfn. longed or wished for, desired, striven after, undertaken, R.; Bhartṛ.; Pañcat.; n. great effort to obtain anything, desire, longing, wish, Kāv.; Kathās.; Hit.

समु *samu,* a metre containing 76 syllables, Nidānas.

समुक्त *sam-ukta.* See *saṃ-√vac,* p. 1114.

समुक्ष् *sam-√1. uksh,* P. *-ukshati,* to sprinkle well or thoroughly, besprinkle, pour over or out, RV.; AV.; ŚBr.

Sam-ukshaṇa, n. the act of sprinkling or pouring over, shedding, effusion, Mālatīm.

Sám-ukshita, mfn. sprinkled, poured out, effused, RV.; AV.; MBh.; strengthened, increased, encouraged (cf. √*vaksh*), RV.

समुख *sa-mukha,* mfn. 'mouthy,' talkative, loquacious, eloquent, L.

समुच् *sam-√uc,* P. *-ucyati* (pf. *-uvoca*), to delight in, like to be together with (instr.), RV.

Sam-ucita, mfn. delighted in, liked, well suited, fit, right, proper, R.; Megh.; Inscr.; accustomed or used to (gen.), Megh.

समुच्च *sam-ucca,* mfn. lofty, high, Kāśīkh.

समुच्चर् *sam-uc-car* (*-ud-√car*), P. *-carati,* to go out together, Nir.; to go up, be borne upwards, ascend, MW.; to utter, pronounce, repeat, HPariś.: Caus. *-cārayati,* to utter sounds together, talk together, MW.

Sam-uccara, m. going or coming forth together, MW.; ascending, flying upwards, ib.; traversing, ib.

Sam-uccāra, m. utterance, pronunciation, Kāśīkh. °**uccāraṇa,** n. (fr. Caus.) simultaneous utterance or pronunciation, Pāṇ. i, 3, 48.

समुच्चल् *sam-uc-cal* (*-ud-√cal*), P. *-calati,* to start or set out together, Daś.; Mālatīm.

समुच्चि *sam-uc-ci* (*-ud-√1. ci*), P. Ā. *-cinoti, -cinute* (ind. p. *-cayitvā*), to heap or pile up together, accumulate, add together, MBh.; to collect, gather, arrange in order, Baudh.: Desid., see *sam-uccicīshā.*

Sam-uccaya, m. aggregation, accumulation, collection, assemblage, multitude, Kāv.; totality, aggregate, Kāv.; Suśr.; Kathās.; conjunction of words or sentences (as by the particle *ca,* 'and'), conjunctive sense (opp. to the disjunctive *vā,* 'or'), Nir.; GṛS.; Suśr. &c.; (in rhet.) a figure of speech (the joining together of two or more independent things associated in idea with some common action), Sāh.; Kpr.; °*yâlaṃkāra,* m. the above rhetorical figure; °*yôpamā,* f. a simile containing the above, Kāvyâd. ii, 21. °**uccayana,** n. collecting or heaping together, Pat.

Sam-uccicīshā, f. (fr. Desid.) the wish to accumulate or collect or combine or add together, VS., Sch.

Sam-uccita, mfn. accumulated, collected together, regularly arranged, Kār. on Pāṇ. vii, 2, 10 (°*tī-kṛita,* mfn. id., Naish.)

Sam-uccetavya, mfn. to be taken together or collectively (i. e. one equally with the other), Nyāyam. °**ucceya,** mfn. id., ib., Sch.

समुच्छद् *sam-uc-chad* (*-ud-√1. chad*), P. *-chādayati,* to uncover, undress, MW.

Sam-ucchanna, mfn. = *sam-utsanna,* uncovered, destroyed, annihilated, Prab. (v. l.)

समुच्छल् *sam-uc-chal* (*-ud-√śal*), only in *-ucchalat* and *-ucchalita,* mfn. jerking or jerked up, Cat.

समुच्छिद् *sam-uc-chid* (*-ud-√chid*), P. Ā. *-chinatti, -chintte,* to cut up or off completely, tear up, uproot, exterminate, destroy utterly, MBh.; Pañcat.

Sam-ucchitti, f. cutting off completely, utter destruction, Divyâv.

Sam-ucchinna, mfn. torn up, uprooted, eradicated, utterly destroyed, lost, Sūryas.; *-vāsana,* mfn. one whose dress is torn off (or 'one whose delusion is completely removed'), Prab.

Sam-uccheda, m. utter destruction, extermination, MBh.; Kāv. &c. °**ucchedana,** n. id., Subh.

समुच्छुष् *sam-uc-chush* (*-ud-√śush*), P. *-chushyati,* to be or become completely dried up, Bhaṭṭ.

समुच्छ्रि *sam-uc-chri* (*-ud-√śri*), P. Ā. *-chrayati,* °*te* (only 3. pl. pf. *-uc-chiśriyuḥ*), to raise well up, raise aloft, erect, elevate, Bhaṭṭ.

Sam-ucchraya, mfn. who or what rises or grows up (*sarvaṃ °rayam* = 'all living beings'), R.; m. raising aloft, erection, elevation, MBh.; SaddhP.; height, length, Hariv.; Ragh.; VarBṛS.; an eminence, hill, mountain, MBh.; rising, rise, exaltation, high position, MBh.; Kāv. &c.; increase, growth, high degree, Hariv.; Suśr.; stimulation, Suśr.; accumulation, multitude, Kāraṇḍ.; (with Buddh.) birth (according to others 'body'), Divyâv.; opposition, enmity, L. °**ucchrāya,** m. rising, increase, growth, height, high degree, Suśr.; Dhātup.

Sam-ucchrita, mfn. well raised or elevated, MBh.; Kāv. &c.; surging, high, ib.; exalted, powerful, Suśr.; *-dhvaja-vat,* mfn. having flags hoisted (in it, said of a town), R.; *-bhuja,* mf(*ā*)n. having arms well raised, ib. °**ucchriti,** f. augmentation, increase, growth, Suśr.

समुच्छ्वस् *sam-uc-chvas* (*-ud-√śvas*), P. *-chvasiti* or *-chvasati,* to breathe well or regularly, Suśr.; to breathe again, recover, revive, Kathās.; to spring or sprout up, Śiś.: Caus., see *sam-ucchvāsita.*

Sam-ucchvasita, mfn. breathed or sighed deeply (n. used impersonally), Amar.; n. breathing, Kād.; a heavy or deep sigh, W. °**ucchvāsa,** m. heavy expiration, sighing, ib. °**ucchvāsita,** mfn. raised, elevated, swelled, Kum. iii, 38 (= *vi-śleshita,* Sch.)

समुज्जिहीर्षु *sam-uj-jihīrshu,* mfn. (fr. Desid. of 2. *sam-ud-√hṛi*) desirous of drawing up, Kir.; desirous of taking away or removing, BhP.

समुज्जृम्भ् *sam-uj-jṛimbh* (*-ud-√jṛimbh*), Ā. *-jṛimbhate,* to gape wide open, be extended or spread out, Mṛicch.; to burst forth, become visible, arise, Prab., Sch.; to begin, be about to (inf.), Bhartṛ.

समुज्ज्वल् *sam-uj-jval* (*-ud-√jval*), P. *-jvalati,* to blaze up with great intensity, shine very brightly, MBh.: Caus. *-jvalayate,* to set on fire, kindle, GopBr.

Sam-ujjvala, mfn. shining, radiant, splendid in or with (comp.), Kāv.; Kathās. &c.

समुज्झ् *sam-√ujjh,* P. *-ujjhati,* to abandon, renounce, give up, Pañcat.

Sam-ujjhita, mfn. abandoned, renounced, resigned, Prab.; (ifc.) free from, rid of, ib.; n. that which is left, a remnant, leavings (see *bhukta-s°*).

समुञ्ज *sa-muñja,* mfn. having Muñja grass, Gobh.

समुत्क *sam-utka,* mfn. desirous of, longing for (comp.), Kathās.

समुत्कच *sam-utkaca,* mfn. beginning to bloom, blooming, expanded, Pañcar.

समुत्कट *sam-utkaṭa,* mfn. high, elevated, sublime, Kāśīkh.; (ifc.) richly furnished with, Jātakam.

समुत्कण्टकित *sam-utkaṇṭakita,* mfn. having the hair (of the body) bristling or thrilled with joy or passion, Kād.

समुत्कण्ठ *sam-utkaṇṭha,* Nom. Ā. *-utkaṇṭhate,* to think of regretfully, pine or long after, Sāh.

Sam-utkaṇṭhā, f. wish or longing for (comp.), Vās.

समुत्कम्पिन् *sam-utkampin,* mfn. trembling vehemently, Jātakam.

समुत्कीर्ण *sam-ut-kīrṇa,* mfn. (√*kṝi*) completely perforated or pierced, Ragh.

समुत्कृत् *sam-ut-√kṛit* (only ind. *-kṛitya*), to cut off or out completely, MBh.

समुत्कृष् *sam-ut-√kṛish*, P. *-karshati*, to draw or raise well up, elevate, MBh.; to draw tight (the bowstring), BhP.

Sam-utkarsha, m. self-elevation, setting one's self up (as belonging to a higher rank than one's own tribe), Mn. xi, 55; pre-eminence, excellence, MBh.; Bhar.; laying aside (a girdle), MBh.

समुत्क्रम् *sam-ut-√kram*, P. Ā. *-krāmati, -kramate*, to go upwards, depart (from life), NādabUp.; to overstep, transgress, violate, MBh.

Sam-utkrama, m. going upwards, rise, ascent, W.; transgressing proper bounds, MW.

समुत्क्रुष्ट *sam-ut-krushṭa*, mfn. (√*kruś*) cried out, called out, R.

Sam-utkrośa, m. crying out aloud, clamour, MW.; an osprey, L.

समुत्क्लिष्ट *sam-ut-klishṭa*, mfn. (√*kliś*) greatly distressed or disturbed, very uneasy or uncomfortable, Suśr.

Sam-utkleśa, m. great uneasiness or disturbance, Car.

समुत्क्षिप् *sam-ut-√kship*, P. Ā. *-kshipati*, °*te*, to throw or raise or lift up, MBh.; Pañcat.; MārkP.; to throw or scatter about, throw aside, loosen, R.; to liberate, Pañcat.; to waste, destroy, R.

Sam-utkshepa, m. throwing in (a word), allusion to (dat.), MBh. ii, 2513. °**utkshepaṇa,** n. the altitude above the horizon (opp. to *nāmana*), Gol.

समुत्खन् *sam-ut-√khan*, P. Ā. *-khanati*, °*te* (ind. p. *-khāya*), to dig up by the roots, Kauś.; to eradicate, exterminate or destroy utterly, Prab.; to draw forth, draw (a sword), Prasannar.

समुत्तर *sam-uttara*, n. = *uttara*, answer, reply, Sāh.

समुत्तान *sam-uttāna*, mfn. = *uttāna*, having the palms turned upwards (said of the hands), Cat.

समुत्तिज् *sam-ut-√tij*, Caus. *-tijayati*, to excite, fire with enthusiasm, Divyâv.

Sam-uttejaka, mfn. exciting, stimulating, SaddhP. °**uttejana,** n. the act of exciting or inflaming greatly, Mudr. °**uttejita,** mfn. (fr. Caus.) greatly excited or inflamed or irritated, W.

समुत्तुङ्ग *sam-uttuṅga*, mfn. = *uttuṅga*, lofty, high, L.

समुत्तॄ *sam-ut-√tṛī*, P. *-tarati* (ind. p. *-tīrya*), to pass or come out of (abl.; with or without *jalāt*, 'to step or emerge out of the water'), GṛS.; MBh. &c.; to escape from, get rid of (abl.), MBh.; R. &c.; to break through, pass over or beyond, cross over, cross, ib.

Sam-uttāra, m. passing over safely, deliverance from (comp.), Divyâv.

Sam-uttīrṇa, mfn. come forth from, escaped from, passed through, crossed, landed, Yājñ.; MBh. &c.; broken through, MBh. vii, 5219.

समुत्त्रस् *sam-ut-√tras*, Caus. *-trāsayati*, to frighten thoroughly, terrify, Sāh.

Sam-uttrasta, mfn. thoroughly frightened, greatly alarmed, ŚBr.

समुत्था *sam-ut-thā* (*-ud-√sthā*), P. Ā. *-tishṭhati*, °*te*, to rise up together, Jātakam.; to rise up (as from death), get up (from sleep &c.), ŚBr.; MBh. &c.; to recover (from sickness), Car.; to rise (in the sky), gather (as clouds), MBh.; Kathās.; to come forth, spring from (abl.), appear, become visible, ŚBr. &c. &c.; to arise for action, prepare for or to (loc. or inf.), MBh.; VarBṛS.: Caus. *-thāpayati*, to cause to rise together, lift or raise up, elevate, MBh.; R.; BhP.; to awaken, excite, arouse, R.; Jātakam.

Sam-uttha, mf(*ā*)n. rising up, risen, appearing, occurring in, occasioned by, sprung or produced or derived from (comp., rarely abl.), MBh.; Kāv. &c.

Sam-utthāna, n. (ifc. f. *ā*) the act of rising up together, rising, getting up, R.; hoisting (of a flag), Tithyād.; recovering from sickness or injury, MBh.; healing, cure, Mn.; Yājñ.; swelling (of the abdomen), R.; augmentation, increase, growth (of property), Yājñ.; rise, origin (ifc. = 'rising or springing from'), Suśr.; Hariv.; Kāv.; performance of work, active operation, effort, industry (*ekī-s*° or *sambhūya-s*°, 'common enterprise,' 'co-operation,' 'partnership,' Mn. viii, 4), Mn.; Kām.; MBh.; R.; indication or symptom of disease, L.; *-vyaya*, m. the expense of recovery or cure, Mn. viii, 287. °**utthāpaka,** mfn. (fr. Caus.) rousing up, awakening, stirring, Buddh. °**utthāpya,** mfn. (fr. id.) to be raised or elevated, VarBṛS.

Sam-utthita, mfn. risen up together, risen, raised (as dust), towering above (as a peak), surging (as waves), gathered (as clouds), MBh.; Kāv. &c.; appeared, grown, sprung or obtained or derived from (abl. or comp.; *dhanaṃ daṇḍa-samutthitam*, 'money derived from fines'), ŚvetUp.; Mn.; MBh. &c.; ready, prepared for (loc.), MBh.; R.; BhP.; one who withstands all (opponents), R.; cured, healed, W.; swollen up, MW. °**uttheya,** n. (impers.) it is to be risen (for action), MBh.

समुत्पट् *sam-ut-√paṭ*, P. *-pāṭayati*, to tear completely out or up, uproot, detach, sever, MBh.; R.; Kathās.; to expel, dethrone, Rājat.

Sam-utpāṭa, m. tearing out or away, severing, detaching, W. °**utpāṭita,** mfn. torn completely out or away, uprooted, detached, ib.

समुत्पत् *sam-ut-√pat*, P. *-patati*, to fly up together, spring up, ascend, rise (as the sun, clouds &c.), AV. &c. &c.; to rush upon, attack, assail, Kām.; to rush out of, burst forth, MBh.; to arise, appear, ib.; to fly away, depart, disappear, Pañcat.: Desid., see below.

Sam-utpatana, n. the act of flying up together, rising, ascending, Pañcat.; making effort, energy, exertion, W.

Sam-utpatita, mfn. flown up together, sprung up, risen, appeared, MBh.; Hariv.; BhP.; flown away, departed, gone, Pañcat.; exerted, vigorous, W. °**utpatishṇu,** mfn. desirous of standing or rising up, Harav.

Sam-utpāta, m. a portent (boding some calamity), MBh.; Ragh.

Sam-utpipatishu, mfn. (fr. Desid.) about to start or spring up, Kir.

समुत्पद् *sam-ut-√pad*, Ā. *-padyate* (ep. also °*ti*), to spring up together, be brought forth or born of (loc.), arise, appear, occur, take place, happen, MBh.; Kāv. &c.: Caus. *-pādayati*, to cause to arise, produce, effect, cause, MBh.; R.; Pur.

Sam-utpatti, f. rising together, rise, birth, origin, Mn.; MBh. &c.

Sam-utpanna, mfn. sprung up together, arisen, produced, begotten by (abl.) or on (loc.), occurred, happened, taking place, Mn.; MBh. &c.

Sam-utpāda, m. rise, origin, production, Sarvad. °**utpādana,** n. (fr. Caus.) the act of bringing forth, producing, effecting, W. °**utpādya,** mfn. to be produced or caused, Pañcat.

समुत्पिञ्ज *sam-utpiñja*, mfn. excessively confused or confounded, bewildered, disturbed, L.; m. complete confusion, MBh. vii, 8514.

Sam-utpiñjala (W.) and °**jalaka** (MBh.), m. id.

समुत्पिष्ट *sam-ut-pishṭa*, mfn. (√*pish*) crushed or squeezed together, greatly crushed, Suśr.

समुत्पीडन *sam-ut-pīḍana*, n. (√*pīḍ*) the act of pressing together, great pressure or distress, Dhūrtas.

समुत्पुंसन *sam-ut-puṇsana*, n. (see √*puṇs* and *utpuṇsaya*) wiping away, removing, destroying, Alaṃkārav.

समुत्पॄ *sam-ut-√1. pṛi*, Caus. *-pārayati*, to spread out, stretch forth, MW.

समुत्प्लु *sam-ut-√plu*, Ā. *-plavate*, to jump or leap up together, move by jumps, Bhaṭṭ.

समुत्फाल *sam-utphāla*, m. a jump, canter, gallop, L.

Sam-utphulla, mfn. (having the eyes) opened wide, Kād.

समुत्सद् *sam-ut-√sad*, Caus. *-sādayati*, to destroy utterly, overturn, overthrow, MBh.; R.

Sam-utsanna, mfn. utterly destroyed, see *samucchanna*.

समुत्सव *sam-utsava*, m. a great festival or festivity, R.

समुत्सह् *sam-ut-√sah*, Ā. *-sahate* (rarely P. °*ti*), to be able to or capable of, have energy to do anything (inf.), MBh.; R.; MārkP.: Caus. *-sāhayati*, to strengthen or encourage together, animate, incite, MBh.

Sam-utsāha, m. energy, force of will, MBh.; Suśr.; *-tā*, f. id. (with *dāne*, 'alacrity in giving, great liberality'), Cāṇ.

समुत्सिक्त *sam-ut-sikta*, mfn. (√*sic*) overflowing with, proud of (comp.), MBh.; R.

समुत्सुक *sam-utsuka*, mf(*ā*)n. very uneasy or anxious, anxiously desirous, longing for (comp.), eager to (inf.), MBh.; Kāv. &c. **-tā,** f. desire, longing, Daś. **-tva,** n. agitation, emotion, R.; = prec., Ṛitus.

Sam-utsukaya, Nom. P. °*yati*, to cause to long for or yearn after, Kir.

समुत्सृ *sam-ut-√sṛi*, Caus. *-sārayati*, to send away, dismiss, MBh.; to drive away, disperse, dispel, Kād.; Hcar.; Prab.

Sam-utsāraka, mfn. driving away, dispelling, Hcar. °**utsāraṇa,** n. the act of driving away &c., Kād.; Vās.

समुत्सृज् *sam-ut-√sṛij*, P. *-sṛijati*, to pour out or send forth together, hurl, throw, shoot off (arrows), R.; to give forth, emit, discharge (urine &c.), shed (tears), utter (a curse &c.), Mn.; MBh. &c.; to leave or abandon or completely put aside, put off or down, throw into (loc.), ib.; to let loose, release, ib.; to give up, renounce (together or at the same time), MBh.; Kāv. &c.; to deliver over, present to (dat.), give, R.; Hcat.

Sam-utsarga, m. pouring out or shedding forth together (of urine), Mn. iv, 50; emission (of semen; °*gaṃ √kṛi* with loc., 'to have sexual intercourse with'), Kull.

Sam-utsṛishṭa, mfn. altogether poured or shed forth, given away, wholly given up or abandoned, MBh.; Kāv. &c.

समुत्सृप् *sam-ut-√sṛip*, P. *-sarpati*, to glide or soar upwards together, to rise up to (acc.), Ragh.; to rise, set in, begin (as darkness), Amar. (v.l.)

Sam-utsarpaṇa, n. getting along, proceeding, being accomplished, Inscr.

समुत्सेध *sam-utsedha*, m. (ifc. f. *ā*) elevation, height, MBh.; R.; swelling up, intumescence, fatness, thickness, MW.

समुद् *sam-√ud* (or *und*), P. *-unatti* (ind. p. *-udya*, 'having well moistened'), to moisten thoroughly, sprinkle all over, water, wet, PārGr.; Nir.

Sam-udrá, m. (n. only RV. vi, 72, 3; ifc. f. *ā*; cf. *udrá*, *an-udrá*; for *sa-mudra* see p. 1168, col. 2) 'gathering together of waters,' the sea, ocean (in Veda also 'the aerial waters,' 'atmospheric ocean or sky' [cf. Naigh. i, 3]; in VP. ii, 4, seven circular concentric [elsewhere 3 or 4] oceans are named, viz. *lavaṇa*, 'salt-water;' *ikshu*, 'syrup;' *surā*, 'wine;' *ghṛita*, 'clarified butter;' *dadhi*, 'curds;' *dugdha*, 'milk;' *jala*, 'fresh water;' in later language the Ocean is often personified as king of the rivers), RV. &c. &c.; N. of the number 'four' (four principal oceans being reckoned by some, one for every quarter of the sky), Gaṇit.; a large Soma vessel, RV. vi, 69, 6; ix, 29, 3 &c.; N. of an immensely high number (1 with 14 cyphers), TS.; ŚāṅkhŚr.; MBh.; a partic. configuration of the stars and planets (when the 7 pl° are situated in the 2nd, 4th, 6th, 8th, 10th and 12th houses), VarBṛS.; = *rukma*, VS., Sch.; N. of Śiva, MBh.; of a Daitya, Hariv.; of various authors (also with *sūri*), Cat.; of the son of a merchant born on the sea, Buddh.; of other men, HPariś.; of a wk. quoted by Padmanābha, Cat.; of a place, ib.; (*ā*), f. N. of two plants (= *śaṭī* and *śamī*), L.; m. or n. N. of two Sāmans, ĀrshBr.; of various metres, TS.; Nidānas. &c. **-kaṭaka,** a ship, VarYogay., Sch. **-kapha,** m. = *-phena*, L. **-kara, -kara-bhāshya,** n. N. of wks. **-kallola,** m. 'ocean-wave,' N. of an elephant, Kathās. **-kāñcī,** f. 'sea-girdled,' the earth, L. **-kāntā,** f. 'sea-beloved,' a river, L.; Trigonella Corniculata, L. **-kukshi,** f. the sea-shore, MBh. **-ga,** mf(*ā*)n. ocean-going, seafaring, VarBṛS.; flowing towards the ocean, MārkP.; m. a seafarer, seaman, W.; (*ā*), f. a river, MBh.; Kāv.

-gamana, n. going or voyaging by sea, sea-roving, MW. **-gāmin**, mfn. sea-going, seafaring, ib. **-gupta**, m. N. of a king of Northern India (who reigned from about 345 till 380 A.D.), Inscr. **-gṛiha**, n. a bath-house, bath-room, L. **-culuka**, m. 'holding the ocean in his mouth,' N. of the sage Agastya (fabled to have drunk up the ocean), L. **-já**, mfn. produced or found in the sea, AV.; Suśr.; Pañcat. **-jyeshṭha** (°*drá-*), mf(*ā*)n. having the ocean as chief (said of waters), RV. **-taṭa**, n. the sea-coast, W. **-tatā**, f. a kind of metre, Col. **-tás**, ind. from the sea, RV. **-tīra**, n. the sea-shore, Hit. **-tīrīya**, mfn. dwelling on the sea-shore, Buddh. **-tva**, n. the state or condition of the ocean, Pat. **-datta**, m. N. of various persons, Kathās.; Hit. &c. **-dayitā**, f. 'sea-beloved,' a river, L. **-deva**, m. the god of the ocean, Siṅhās. **-devatā**, f. an oc°-deity, Uttamac. **-navanīta** or °**taka**, n. 'oc°-ghee,' the nectar (produced at the churning of the ocean), L.; the moon, ib. (cf. RTL. 108). **-nishkuṭa**, m. a pleasure-ground near the sea; N. of a pl°-gr°, MBh. **-nemi**, mf(*ī*)n. surrounded by the oc° (as the earth), MBh.; Ragh.; (also °*mī*), f. the earth, MBh.; °*mī-pati* or °*mīśvara*, m. 'earth-lord,' a king, MBh. **-patnī**, f. 'wife of the sea,' a river, Ragh. **-paryanta**, mf(*ā*)n. sea-bound (as the earth), AitBr.; Pañcat. **-priya**, m. N. of a man, HPariś. **-phala**, n. 'sea-fruit,' a partic. drug, L. **-pheṇa** (w. r.) or **-phena**, m. 'sea-foam,' the bone of the cuttle-fish (so light that it floats), Ragh.; Suśr.; Bhpr. **-bandha-yajvan**, m. N. of a man, Cat. **-bhava**, mfn. being in the oc°, produced from or in the sea, MW. **-mathana**, m. N. of a Daitya, Hariv.; n. the churning of the oc°, Nītiś.; N. of a drama. **-mahishī**, f. 'chief wife of the ocean,' N. of the Ganges, MBh. **-mātra**, n., Pāṇ. vi, 2, 14, Sch. **-mālin**, mfn. sea-wreathed (the earth), R. **-m-iṅkhaya**, mfn. causing the Soma-vessel to shake or move (as Soma), RV. **-mekhalā**, f. 'sea-girdled,' the earth, L. **-yātrā**, f. a sea-voyage, Hariv. **-yāna**, n. id., Mn. viii, 157; a vessel, ship, MW.; *-mīmāṅsā*, f. N. of wk. **-yāyin**, m. a seafarer, Mn.; VarP. **-yoshit**, f. 'wife of the sea,' a river, Vcar. **-rasana**, mf(*ā*)n. (also written *-ras°*) sea-girdled (said of the earth), Hariv.; Ragh.; VarBṛS.; (*ā*), f. the earth, L. **-lavaṇa**, n. sea-salt, L. **-varṇana**, n. N. of the 68th ch. of the Sundara-kāṇḍa of the Rāmāyaṇa. **-varman**, m. N. of a king, Kathās. **-vallabhā**, f. 'mistress of the sea,' a river, Vcar. **-vasana**, mf(*ā*)n. sea-clothed, sea-girt (the earth), Hariv.; (*ā*), f. the earth, L. **-vahni**, m. submarine fire, L. **-vākya**, n. N. of wk. **-vāsas** (°*drá-*), mfn. 'sea-clothed,' veiled or concealed in the waters (said of Agni), RV. **-vāsin**, mfn. dwelling near the sea, MBh. **-vijaya**, m. N. of the father of the 22nd Arhat of the present Avasarpiṇī, L. **-velā**, f. the flood-tide, MaitrUp.; Hit.; an ocean-wave, W. **-vyacas** (°*drá-*), mfn. whose capacity equals that of the sea or a Soma-vessel (said of Indra), VS. **-vyavahārin**, mfn. trading by sea, Śak. **-śukti**, f. a sea-shell, Mālav.; Siṅhās. **-śūra**, m. N. of a merchant, Kathās. **-śosha**, m. the creeping plant Convolvulus Argenteus, MW. **-śrī**, f. N. of a woman, HPariś. **-salile-śaya**, mfn. lying in sea-water (a kind of penance), Hariv. **-sāra**, n. 'quintessence of the sea,' a pearl, MBh. **-subhagā**, f. 'ocean's-favourite,' the Ganges, MW. **-sūri**, m. N. of an author, Cat. **-sena**, m. N. of a king, MBh.; of a merchant, Kathās. **-sthalī**, f., g. *dhūmâdi*. **-snāna**, n. ablution in the sea; *-vidhi*, m. N. of wk. **Samudrâdi**, the 4th or other syllable in a stanza when a cæsura follows, Piṅg., Sch. **Samudrânta**, m. the sea-shore, Cāṇ.; mf(*ā*)n. reaching to the sea (said of the earth), R.; Kathās.; falling into the sea (as a river), BhP.; (*ā*), f. the earth, MBh.; the shrub Alhagi Maurorum, Bhpr.; the cotton plant, ib.; Trigonella Corniculata, ib.; n. nutmeg, L. **Samudrâbhisāriṇī**, f. a maiden going to meet the god of the ocean, Vikr. **Samudrâmbarā**, f. 'sea-clothed,' the earth, L. **Samudrâmbhas**, n. sea-water, MW. **Samudrâyaṇa**, mf(*ā*)n. flowing to the sea, PraśnUp. **Samudrâru**, m. 'sea-torment,' a large fabulous fish (= *grāha-bheda*); also = *setu-bandha*, L. **Samudrârtha**, mf(*ā*)n. tending to the sea, RV. **Samudrâvagāhana**, m. a partic. Samādhi, Kāraṇḍ. **Samudrâvaraṇa**, mf(*ā*)n. sea-clothed (the earth), BhP. **Samudrâvarohaṇa**, m. a partic. Samādhi, Kāraṇḍ. **Samudre-shṭhá**, mf(*ā*)n. being in the waters, TS. **Samudrônmādana**, m. N. of one of Skanda's attendants, MBh. **Samudrôpapluta**, mfn. inundated or submerged by the ocean, BhP.

Samudrāya, Nom. Ā. °*yate*, to resemble the sea, appear like the ocean, Mṛicch.

Samudriya, mf(*ā*)n. belonging to or flowing into the sea, RV.; relating to or being in the Soma vessel, ib. ix, 107, 16; n. (prob.) a kind of metre, ŚBr.

Samudrīya, mfn. relating to the sea, marine, oceanic, MW.

Samudryà, mfn. id., SV.

Sam-undana, n. becoming thoroughly wet, moisture, wetness, L.

Sam-unna, mfn. well moistened or sprinkled, thoroughly wet, L.

समुद् **sa-mud**, mfn. joyful, glad, Śiś.

समुदञ्च् *sam-ud-√añc*, P. *-añcati*, to rise, draw up, come near, begin, Bhām.

Sam-udakta, mfn. lifted up, raised up, thrown up, L.

समुदन्त *sam-údanta*, mfn. rising above the edge, about to overflow, MaitrS.; Br.; ŚrS.

समुदस्त *sam-ud-asta*, mfn. (√2. *as*) drawn or raised from a deep place, L.

समुदागम् *sam-ud-ā-√gam*, P. *-gacchati*, to rise together, Divyâv.; to arrive at full knowledge (see next).

Sam-udāgata, mfn. one who has attained full knowledge, excelling in (comp.), Lalit.

Sam-udāgama, m. full or complete knowledge, Buddh.

समुदाचर् *sam-ud-ā-√car*, Ā. *-carate*, to move or travel about (e.g. *rathena*, 'in a chariot'), Siddh.; P. *-carati*, to act towards, treat, MBh.; to practise, accomplish, do, ib.; to speak to, address, Divyâv.

Sam-udācarita, mfn. addressed, Divyâv.

Sam-udācāra, m. presentation, offering, entertainment (of a guest &c.), MBh.; Hariv.; proper or right practice or usage or conduct or behaviour, MBh.; R. &c.; intercourse with (instr.), MBh.; address, Hariv.; Kāv. &c.; salutation, Divyâv.; intention, purpose, design, motive, L.; mfn. = next, BhP.; *-vat*, mfn. one who conducts himself well, MBh. °**udācārin**, mfn. accosting, addressing, Divyâv.

समुदानय 1. *sam-ud-ā-naya*, m. (√*nī*) bringing together, assembly, MBh.; bringing about, accomplishment, perfection, Lalit.; *-tā*, f. id., Divyâv.

2. **Sam-udānaya**, Nom. P. °*yati*, to collect, Divyâv.; to bring about, attain, ib. °**udānayana**, n. bringing near, Jātakam. °**udānayitavya**, mfn. to be mastered thoroughly, SaddhP. °**udānita**, mfn. attained (v.l. °*nīta*), Lalit.; Divyâv. °**udānitatva**, n. the being accomplished, Jātakam. °**udānetavya**, mfn. to be brought near, Divyâv.

समुदावह् *sam-ud-ā-√vah*, P. *-vahati*, to lead or conduct out, draw or carry away, Hariv.; to draw along (said of horses), R.; to conduct home, marry, MBh.

समुदाहृ *sam-ud-ā-√hṛi*, P. *-harati*, to utter together, pronounce, declare, Hariv.; R.; BhP.

Sam-udāharaṇa, n. declaring, uttering, W.; illustrating, illustration, ib. °**udāhāra**, m. (in *kathā-s°*) conversation, Divyâv.

Sam-udāhṛita, mfn. talked to, addressed, Hariv.; talked about, mentioned as, named, called, ĀśvŚr.; Mn.; R. &c.; stated, declared, Yājñ.; illustrated, W.

समुदि *sam-ud-√5. i*, P. *-eti*, to go upwards or rise up together, come together or prepare (for battle &c.), MBh.; to rise (as the sun), ib.

Sam-udaya, m. (rarely n.) coming together, union, junction, combination, collection, assemblage, multitude, aggregation, aggregate (acc. with √*kṛi*, 'to collect or assemble'), MaitrUp.; MBh. &c.; (with Buddhists) the aggregate of the constituent elements or factors of any being or existence (in later times equivalent to 'existence' itself), Buddh.; Sarvad.; a producing cause (e.g. *duḥkha-s°* = 'the cause of suffering'), Dharmas. 22; income, revenue, Mn.; MBh.; success, prosperity, Mṛicch.; war, battle, L.; a day, L.; = *udgama* or *samud-gama*, L.; rising (of the sun &c.), W.; n. an auspicious moment (= *lagna*), L.

Sam-udāya, m. combination, collection, multitude, mass, totality, a whole, Prāt.; Kāv.; Pañcat.; (with Buddhists) = *sam-udaya*, Sarvad.; a partic. Nakshatra, VarYogay.; war, battle, L.; the rear or reserve of an army, L.; *-prakaraṇa*, n. N. of wk. °**udāyin**, mfn. combining, forming an aggregate, Śaṃk.

2. **Sam-udita**, mfn. (for 1. see *saṃ-√vad*, p. 1114, col. 2) gone up, risen, elevated, lofty, R.; Kir.; collected, gathered together, united, assembled, R.; Daś.; Siddh.; possessed of, furnished with (instr. or comp.), MBh.; R.; furnished with everything, well supplied, wanting nothing, ib.

Sam-uditṛi, mfn. rising, surging (used to explain *samudrá*), Nir. x, 32.

Sam-uditvara, mfn. going up, rising, Kāśīkh.

समुदीक्ष् *sam-ud-√īksh*, Ā. *-īkshate*, to look up at, look at attentively, perceive, observe, R.; Amar.; to have regard or respect for (acc.), MBh.

समुदीर् *sam-ud-√īr*, Caus. *-īrayati*, to drive out, expel, MBh.; to raise (dust), MBh.; to hurl, throw, ib.; to utter, speak, declare, Kathās.

Sam-udīraṇa, n. setting in motion or getting into motion, MārkP.; raising the voice, uttering, pronouncing, reciting, W. °**udīrita**, mfn. (fr. Caus.) set in motion, raised, uttered, pronounced, MBh. °**udīrṇa**, mfn. greatly moved or agitated or excited, R.; Suśr.; *-khara*, mfn. agitated and sharp or pungent, Suśr.; *-mānasa*, mfn. agitated or excited in mind, R.

समुदीष् *sam-ud-√īsh*, P. *-īshati*, to rise well upwards, ChUp.

समुदेत *sam-udêta*, mfn. (cf. 2. *sam-udita* above) excelling in (comp.), Āpast.; possessed of all good qualities, ib.

समुद्ग **samudga**, m. (of doubtful derivation; for *sam-udga* see below) the point of a bud (in *arka-s°*, q.v.); a round box or casket (said to be also n.; ifc. f. *ā*), Yājñ.; VarBṛS.; Kathās.; a round form of a temple, VarBṛS.; (in rhet.) a kind of paronomasia (in which a verse or part of a verse identical in sound but different in meaning is repeated), Kāvyâd. iii, 54-56; *-yamaka*, n. id., Bhaṭṭ., Sch.

Samudgaka, m. n. a round box or casket, Daś.; Ratnâv. &c.; (in rhet.) = prec., L.

Samudgala. See *ratna-s°*.

समुद्गम् *sam-ud-√gam*, P. *-gacchati*, to go or rise up together, come or break forth, MW.

Sam-udga, mfn. (for *samudga* see above) going up or rising together, W. °**udgata**, mfn. risen up, come forth, appeared, begun, Ṛitus.; Lalit. °**udgama**, m. going up, rising, ascending, Kāv.; Kathās.

समुद्गार *sam-ud-gāra*, m. (√2. *gṛī*) vomiting or spitting out, ejection, Hariv.

Sam-udgīrṇa, mfn. vomited forth, ejected, raised; uttered, exclaimed (in these senses perhaps fr. √1. *gṛī*), L.

समुद्गीत *sam-ud-gīta*, mfn. (√*gai*) sung out loud, chanted loudly, MW.; n. a loud song, chant, ib.

समुद्गुञ्ज् *sam-ud-√guñj*, P. *-guñjati*, to begin to hum, Prasannar.

समुद्ग्रन्थ् *sam-ud-√granth* (only ind. p. *-grathya*), to bind up together, tie or fasten up, MBh.

समुद्ग्रह् *sam-ud-√grah*, P. *-gṛihṇāti*, to raise or lift up, take hold of, seize on, ŚBr.

समुद्घट् *sam-ud-√ghaṭ*, Caus. *-ghāṭayati*, to open, R.; to uncover (one's head, i.e. 'be able to show one's self in public'), Kād.

Sam-udghāṭa, m. taking away, removal (perhaps w.r. for °*ghāta*), Lalit.

समुद्घात *sam-udghāta*, m. destruction, extermination, Buddh.

Sam-udghātin. See *vimati-s°*, p. 979, col. 3.

समुद्घृष् *sam-ud-√ghṛish*, P. *-gharshati*, to rub together, grind, pound, Prasannar.

समुद्दण्ड *sam-uddaṇḍa*, mfn. uplifted (as an arm), Daś.

समुद्दिधीर्षु *sam-uddidhīrshu.* See below.

समुद्दिश् *sam-ud-√diś*, P. *-diśati* (ind. p. *-diśya*, q. v.), to point out or indicate fully, mention at full, state, declare, communicate, Mn.; MBh. &c.; to designate as, name (two acc.), VarBṛS.; to enter into discussion with (instr.), AitĀr.; to refer or relate to (see next).

Sam-uddiśya, ind. having fully pointed out &c.; (with acc.) with reference or regard to, on account or in behalf or in honour of, at, against, towards, to, MBh.; Kāv. &c. °**uddishṭa**, mfn. fully pointed out or declared or indicated, shown, explained, enumerated, particularized, Mn.; MBh. &c.; designated as, named, called, VarBṛS.

Sam-uddeśa, mfn. full exposition, accurate or complete description, theory, doctrine, MBh.; Sarvad.; a place, locality, abode of (gen.), MBh.; R.; Hariv. °**uddeśīya**, see *vyādhi-samuddeśīya*.

समुद्दीप् *sam-ud-√dīp*, Caus. *-dīpayati*, to light up, inflame, R.

समुद्दृप्त *sam-ud-dṛipta*, mfn. (√*dṛip*) haughty, arrogant, R.

समुद्दॄ *sam-ud-√dṝ*, Pass. *-dīryate*, to be completely rent or torn in pieces, burst asunder, MW.

समुद्द्युत् *sam-ud-√dyut*, Ā. *-dyotate*, to blaze up, shine very brilliantly, Prab.

समुद्द्रु *sam-ud-√dru*, P. *-dravati*, to run forth together, escape together, ŚBr.

समुद्धत *sam-ud-dhata*, mfn. (√*han*) raised well up, uplifted, elevated, whirled up (as dust), flowing (as a river) high up on (comp.), heaving, swelling (as waters), towering, lofty, high, MBh.; Kāv. &c.; increased, intense, violent, R.; Jātakam.; puffed up with pride, arrogant, impudent, L.; swelling with, abounding in, full of (comp.), R.; Śiś.; w.r. for *sam-ud-dhuta* and *-dhṛita*; *-taraṃgin*, mfn. (a river) whose waves are heaving or swelling, MBh.; *-lāṅgūla*, mfn. (an animal) whose tail is raised or cocked up (v.l. *sam-un-nata*), Hit.

समुद्धस्त *sam-ud-dhasta* (for *-ud-hasta*), mfn. wiped off with the hand, W.

समुद्धा *sam-ud-dhā* (*-ud-√2. hā*), Ā. *-ujjihīte*, to rise together, come forth, appear, BhP.; to burst forth, be heard, sound, Prasannar.

समुद्धुर *sam-uddhura*, mfn. lifted up, stretched out, Caurap.

समुद्धू *sam-ud-√dhū*, P. Ā. *-dhūnoti*, *-dhūnute*, to shake up, raise (dust), agitate, move hither and thither, MBh.; R.; Hariv.

Sam-uddhūta, mfn. shaken up, agitated, moved hither and thither, ib.; hurled or thrown near, MBh.

समुद्धूषर *sam-uddhūshara*, mfn. (prob.) dust-coloured, grey (= *dhūsara*), Pañcar.

समुद्धृ 1. *sam-ud-√dhṛi* (only in next).

Sam-uddidhīrshu, mfn. wishing to save, Cat.

समुद्धृ 2. *sam-ud dhṛi* (*-ud-√hṛi*), P. Ā. *-uddharati*, °*te*, to take quite out, draw well out, extract from (abl.), Kauś.; MBh.; Kāv. &c.; to root out, extirpate, exterminate, destroy utterly, MBh.; to rescue, save, deliver from (abl.), MBh.; Jātakam.; Pañcat.; to lift, hold up, MBh.; Mṛicch.; to pick up (a coin), Hit.; to raise up, strengthen, restore, MBh.; to divide, Bījag.; R. &c.: Desid., see *samujjihīrshu* (s. v.)

Sam-uddharaṇa, n. the act of drawing well out or up, extricating, raising, lifting, MBh.; Kāv. &c.; taking off or away, removal, Cat.; eradication, extirpation, W.; taking out from (as a part or share), deduction, ib.; food thrown up (from the stomach), vomit, L. °**uddhartṛi**, mfn. one who lifts up or raises or extricates from (abl.), MBh.; MārkP.; m. an uptearer, extirpator, Ragh.

Sam-uddhāra, m. drawing out, extraction from (abl.), MārkP.; extrication from any danger, rescue, delivery, Śatr.; removal, destruction, Kāv.; N. of a prince (for *hari-kṛishṇa-s*°), Kshitīś.

Sam-uddhṛita, mfn. well raised or drawn up or uplifted &c. &c.; taken out from (as a share), deducted (°*tôddhāre*, loc. 'if a deduction be made'), Mn. ix, 116.

समुद्धृष् *sam-ud-dhṛish* (*-ud-√hṛish*), Caus. *-uddharshayati*, to excite joyfully, gladden, delight, Kāṭh.

Sam-uddharsha, m. war, battle (perhaps w.r. for *sam-udgharsha*), MBh.

समुद्ध्वस्त *sam-ud-dhvasta*, mfn. (√*dhvaṇs*) completely overspread, sprinkled or covered with (comp.), R.

समुद्बन्ध् *sam-ud-√bandh* (only ind. p. *-badhya*), to bind up firmly, MBh.

Sam-udbandhana, n. hanging up (*ātmanaḥ*, 'one's self'), Kād.

समुद्बुध् *sam-ud-√budh*, Caus. *-bodhayati*, to rouse up thoroughly, awaken, animate, Nīlak.

Sam-udbodha, m. becoming consciousness, Sāh. °**udbodhana**, n. (fr. Caus.) thorough rousing up, awakening (from a swoon), resuscitation, Prasannar.

समुद्बृह् *sam-ud-√1. bṛih*, P. *-bṛihati*, to draw out together, pull out, MBh.

समुद्भासन *sam-udbhāsana*, n. lighting up, illuminating, Kād.

समुद्भू *sam-ud-√bhū*, P. *-bhavati*, to spring up from, arise, be produced, exist, Kāv.; to increase, augment, grow, Suśr.

Sam-udbhava, m. (ifc. f. *ā*) existence, production, origin (ifc. either 'arisen or produced from' or 'being the source of'), Mn.; MBh. &c.; coming to life again, revival, MBh.; N. of Agni at the Vratâdeśa, Gṛihyās.

Sam-udbhūta, mfn. sprung up, arisen, born, produced, derived, MBh.; R.; Pur.; existing, Pratāp.; v.l. or w.r. for *sam-uddhūta* or *sam-ud-dhata*, MBh. °**udbhūti**, f. arising, appearance, Sāh.

समुद्भेद *sam-udbheda*, m. bursting forth, appearance, development, growth, Daśar.; Sāh.; iii, 8522.

समुद्भ्रान्त *sam-ud-bhrānta*, mfn. (√*bhram*) roused up, excited, bewildered, MBh.; Kāv. &c.

समुद्य *sam-udya.* See *saṃ-√vad* and *sam-√ud*, pp. 1114, 1166.

समुद्यम् *sam-ud-√yam*, P. *-yacchati*, to raise up, lift up, MBh.; R. &c.; to rein in, curb, restrain, drive (horses &c.), MBh.

Sam-udyata, mfn. raised up, lifted up, MBh.; Kāv. &c.; offered, presented, R.; MārkP.; intended, prepared, begun, ib.; ready or eager for action, prepared to or about to (inf. or dat.), engaged in (loc.), R.; BhP.; Kathās.; ready to march against (*prati*), MBh. vi, 5166.

Sam-udyama, m. lifting up, raising, MBh.; great effort or exertion, setting about, readiness to or for (loc., dat., or comp.), Kāv.; Kathās. °**udyamin**, mfn. exerting one's self, strenuous, eager, zealous, Kām.

समुद्या *sam-ud-√yā*, P. *-yāti*, to rise up against (acc.), assail, MBh.

Sam-udyāta, mfn. risen up against (acc.)

समुद्युज् *sam-ud-√yuj*, Caus. *-yojayati*, to excite, animate, Mālav.; Prab.

Sam-udyoga, m. thorough preparation, making ready, setting about (acc. with Caus. of √*kṛi* and gen., 'to undertake anything against'), MBh.; R. &c.; employment, use, MBh.; concurrence (of many causes), Pratāp.

समुद्र *sa-mudra*, mf(*ā*)n. (for *sam-udra* see p. 1166, col. 3) having a stamp or seal, stamped, sealed, marked, Mn.; Yājñ.; Mudr.

Sa-mudra-lekhaka, mfn. marked with partic. inauspicious signs (perhaps w.r. for *sām*°), Buddh.

समुद्रिक्त *sam-ud-rikta*, mfn. (√*ric*) abundantly furnished with (instr.), VP.

समुद्वस् *sam-ud-√5. vas*, Caus. *-vāsayati*, to expel, remove, ŚBr.

समुद्वह् *sam-ud-√vah*, P. Ā. *-vahati*, °*te*, to lift out, carry forth, Bhaṭṭ.; to lead away, lead home, marry, Yājñ.; R.; BhP.; to lift up, raise, MBh.; to bear (with *manasā* or *hṛidayena*, 'in the heart'), tolerate, suffer, endure, MBh.; R.; Kathās.; to wear, possess, Ratnâv.; to exhibit, show, display, R.; VarBṛS.

Sam-udvaha, mfn. who or what lifts up, W.; moving up and down, ib. °**udvāha**, m. bearing up, MW.; leading away, marriage, MBh.

समुद्विज् *sam-ud-√vij*, Ā. *-vijate*, to tremble greatly, shrink or start back together, MBh.

Sam-udvigna, mfn. greatly agitated or disturbed, terrified, anxious, R.; Pur. °**udvega**, m. great agitation or perturbation, terror, alarm, fear, MBh.

समुद्वीक्ष् *sam-ud-vīksh* (*-vi-√īksh*), Ā. *-vīkshate*, to look at together, look at, perceive, MBh.; Pañcat.

समुद्वृत् *sam-ud-√vṛit*, Caus. *-vartayati*, to cause to rise or swell, R.

Sam-udvṛitta, mfn. risen up, swollen, MBh.

समुद्वृह् *sam-ud-√vṛih.* See *sam-ud-√1. bṛih.*

समुन्द् *sam-√und.* See *sam-√ud*, p. 1166.

समुन्नद् *sam-un-nad* (*-ud-√nad*), P. *-nadati*, to cry out together, shout out, roar out, MBh.; Hariv.

Sam-unnada, m. N. of a Rākshasa, R. °**unnāda**, m. simultaneous roaring or shouting, MBh.

समुन्नम् *sam-un-nam* (*-ud-√nam*), P. *-namati*, to rise up or ascend together, rise aloft, ascend, Bhaṭṭ.: Caus. *-nāmayati*, to raise well up, erect, lift completely up, elevate, MBh.; Śak.; Suśr.

Sam-unnata, mfn. risen up, lifted up, raised aloft, Kāv.; arched, vaulted, VarBṛS.; Rājat.; high, sublime, Kām.; proud, arrogant, W.; *-lāṅgula*, mfn. having the tail erect, Hit. (cf. *sam-uddhata-l*°). °**unnati**, f. rising, swelling, Subh.; exaltation, eminence, high position, MBh.; Kāv. &c.; elevation, increase, growth (with *manasaḥ*, 'elevation of mind;' *cittaṃ samunnatim aśnute*, 'the spirit experiences elevation'), Kālid.; Pañcat.

Sam-unnamana, n. raising, arching (as the brows), Sāh.

समुन्नस *sam-unnasa*, mfn. having a prominent nose, Hariv.

समुन्नह् *sam-un-nah* (*-ud-√nah*), P. Ā. *-nahyati*, °*te*, to bind or tie up &c. (see next).

Sam-unnaddha, mfn. tied or bound up (= *ūrdhva-baddha*), L.; swollen, pressed up or out, Suśr.; raised up, elevated, exalted, Kāv.; Pur.; full, excessive, BhP.; proud, arrogant, ib.; unfettered, loosened, ib.; produced, born, L.

Sam-unnāha, m. pressing up or out, Suśr.; height, elevation, BhP.

समुन्निद्र *sam-unnidra*, mfn. wide awake, opened wide (as eyes), Dharmaś.

समुन्नी *sam-un-nī* (*-ud-√nī*), P. Ā. *-nayati*, °*te*, to lead or conduct upwards together, raise completely up, elevate, increase, MBh.; BhP.; to instigate, stimulate, Kām.; to deduce, infer, Rājat.; Sāh.; to pay off (a debt), Kull. on Mn. ix, 107.

Sam-unnaya, m. bringing out, inference, deduction, Cat.; occurrence, event, advent, Bhaṭṭ. °**unnayana**, n. raising up, arching (as the brows), Daśar. °**unnīta**, mfn. raised up, elevated, increased, MBh. °**unneya**, mfn. to be brought out or deduced, Sāh.

समुन्मज्ज् *sam-un-majj* (*-ud-√majj*: only ind. p. *-majjya*), to dive under, bathe, MBh.

समुन्मिश्र *sam-unmiśra*, mfn. mixed or mingled with, accompanied by (instr.), MBh.; Hariv.

समुन्मिष् *sam-un-mish* (*-ud-√mish*), P. *-mishati*, to rise up, spring up from (abl.), Rājat.; to shine forth, shine bright, HYogay.

समुन्मील् *sam-un-mīl* (*-ud-√mīl*), P. *-mīlati*, to become fully expanded or unfolded or displayed, Amar.; Prab.: Caus. *-mīlayati*, to open (the eyes), MBh.; R.; to expand, display, exhibit, Uttarar.

Sam-unmīlita, mfn. opened, expanded, displayed, Prab.

समुन्मुख *sam-unmukha*, mfn. 'having the face erected,' upright, high (°*khī-√kṛi*, 'to lift up'), Naish.

समुन्मूल् *sam-un-mūl* (*-ud-√mūl*), P. *-mūlayati*, to uproot or eradicate completely, exterminate or destroy utterly, Rājat.; Hit.

Sam-unmūlana, n. the act of uprooting or eradicating completely, utter destruction, extermination, Uttarar.; Prab.

समुन्मृज् *sam-un-mṛij* (*-ud-√mṛij*), to rub up, MaitrS.; MānŚr.; to rub completely off or out, Kāṭh.

समुपकृष् *sam-upa-√kṛish*, P. *-karshati*, to draw towards at one time or together, draw near, R.

समुपकॢप् *sam-upa-√klṛip*, Ā. *-kalpate*, to be prepared or made ready together, MW.: Caus. *-kalpayati*, to make ready together, prepare, make ready, accomplish, MBh.

Sam-upakalpita, mfn. made ready, prepared, arranged, MBh.; R. °**upaklṛipta,** mfn. prepared or made ready together, ŚāṅkhŚr.

समुपक्रम् *sam-upa-√kram*, P. Ā. *-krāmati*, *-kramate*, to go up to, approach, MW.; to begin, commence to (inf.), MBh.; R.

Sam-upakrama, m. commencement, L.; com° of medical treatment, Car. °**upakramya,** mfn. to be treated medically, ib. °**upakrānta,** mfn. approached, MW.; one who has begun, R.

समुपगम् *sam-upa-√gam*, P. *-gacchati*, to go or proceed together towards, go or come near to (acc.), approach, have recourse to, MBh.; R.; to go to any state or condition, undergo, R.; Kathās.

Sam-upagata, mfn. approached, W.; undergone, Śak.

Sam-upagantavya, mfn. to be gone to &c.; n. it is to be gone to &c. (*asya viśvāse samupagantavyam*, 'one should place confidence in him'), Pañcat.

Sam-upagama, m. going near, approach, contact, W.

समुपगुह् *sam-upa-√guh*, P. Ā. *-gūhati*, °*te*, to embrace, surround, Caurap.

समुपघ्रा *sam-upa-√ghrā*, P. *-jighrati*, to smell at, kiss, R.

समुपचार *sam-upacāra*, m. attention, homage, Pañcar.

समुपचि *sam-upa-√1. ci*, P. *-cinoti*, to heap up, gather, Nāg.: Pass. *-cīyate*, to grow up, increase, Suśr.

Sam-upacita, mfn. collected, heaped, W.; abundant, Ratnâv.; thick, Car.; *-jala*, mfn. having accumulated waters (as the ocean), MW.

समुपच्छाद *sam-upa-cchāda*, m. (√1. *chad*), Pāṇ. vi, 4, 96, Sch.

समुपजन् *sam-upa-√jan*, Ā. *-jāyate*, to arise, spring up, take place, Kāv.; to be born again, MBh.: Caus. *-janayati*, to generate, cause, produce, Ṛitus.

Sam-upajanita, mfn. (fr. Caus.) generated, produced, caused, ib.

Sam-upajāta, mfn. arisen, produced, Prab.; aroused, MW.; *-kopa*, mfn. one whose anger is roused, provoked or moved to an°, ib.; °*tâbhiniveśam*, ind. after having formed a determined resolution, Prab.

समुपजोषम् *sam-upajosham*, ind. entirely according to wish or liking, quite contentedly (= *upaj*°, q. v.), L.

समुपज्ञा *sam-upa-√jñā*, P. Ā. *-jānāti*, *-jānīte*, to ascertain fully, find out, MBh.; to perceive, learn, W.

समुपतप् *sam-upa-√tap*, Pass. *-tapyate*, to feel pain, MBh.

समुपदिश् *sam-upa-√diś*, P. *-diśati*, to point out or indicate fully, show, MBh.; to assign (with acc. of person and of thing), R.

समुपदृश् *sam-upa-√dṛiś*, Caus. *-darśayati*, to cause to see or be seen, show, exhibit, Kāraṇḍ.

समुपद्रु *sam-upa-√dru*, P. *-dravati* (ep. also Ā. °*te*), to run together towards, rush upon (acc.), MBh.; R.; to run up to, assail, attack, VarBṛS.

Sam-upadruta, mfn. assailed, attacked, overrun, ib.

समुपधा *sam-upa-√dhā*, P. Ā. *-dadhāti*, *-dhatte*, to put together, construct, create, produce, MW.

समुपधाव् *sam-upa-√1. dhāv*, P. *-dhāvati*, to run near or towards (acc.), MBh.

समुपनी *sam-upa-√nī*, P. Ā. *-nayati*, °*te*, to lead up to together, bring or draw near to, lead to (acc.), MBh.; Kāv.; VarBṛS.; to take away, carry off, MBh.; to offer (a sacrifice), R.; to bring about, cause, Hariv.

Sam-upanayana, n. the act of leading near to, Dharmaśarm.

Sam-upanīta, mfn. brought or led to (acc.), R.

समुपन्यस् *sam-upa-ny-√2. as*, P. *-asyati*, to lay down fully, state at full length, Hit.

Sam-upanyasta, mfn. fully stated, ib.

समुपपद् *sam-upa-√pad*, Ā. *-padyate*, to come to pass, be brought about or accomplished, MBh.; to meet with (acc.), experience, ib.: Caus. *-pādayati*, to bring about, make ready, prepare, R.

Sam-upapādita, mfn. (fr. Caus.) made ready, prepared, ib.

समुपप्लुत *sam-upa-pluta*, mfn. (√*plu*) overwhelmed, assailed, distressed, R.

समुपबृह् *sam-upa-√2. bṛih*, Caus. *-bṛiṇhayati*, to cause to increase, augment, strengthen, complete, MBh.; VāyuP.

समुपभुज् *sam-upa-√1. bhuj*, Ā. *-bhuṅkte*, to enjoy sexually, have sexual union with (acc.), MBh.; R.

Sam-upabhoga, m. enjoying, eating, MBh.; cohabitation, sexual union, MW.

समुपया *sam-upa-√yā*, P. *-yāti*, to go up to or approach (with acc.), R.; to betake one's self to (acc.), MBh.; VarBṛS.; to go to any state or condition (with acc.), VarBṛS.

Sam-upayāta, mfn. gone up to, approached (with acc.), ib.

समुपयुज् *sam-upa-√yuj*, P. *-yunakti*, to make complete use of, consume, MBh.: Caus. *-yojayati*, id., ib.

Sam-upayukta, mfn. completely used up or consumed, eaten, MW. °**upayukta-vat,** mfn. one who has consumed, MBh.

समुपयोषम् *sam-upayosham*, ind.= *samupajosham*, col. 1.

समुपरुज् *sam-upa-√ruj*, P. *-rujati*, to break or cut up, MW.; to press hardly upon, Hariv.

समुपरुध् *sam-upa-√rudh*, P. *-ruṇaddhi*, to hinder greatly, disturb, obstruct: Pass. *-rudhyate*, to be hindered or interrupted, MBh.

समुपलक्ष् *sam-upa-√laksh*, P. Ā. *-lakshayati*, °*te*, to look at or observe attentively, Kām.; to see, perceive, MBh.

समुपलभ् *sam-upa-√labh*, Ā. *-labhate* (ep. also P. *-labhati*), to take or receive fully, obtain, MBh.; R.; to acquire by experience, learn, perceive, VarBṛS.

समुपवस् *sam-upa-√5. vas*, P. *-vasati*, to abide wholly in, engage in, devote one's self to (see below); to abide in a state of abstinence, fast, Hcat.

Sam-upôshaka, mfn. fasting, Kṛishṇaj. °**upôshita,** mf(*ā*)n. engaged in, devoted to (acc.), MārkP.; one who has fasted, MBh.; VarBṛS.; BhP.

समुपवह् *sam-upa-√vah*, P. *-vahati*, to bear or carry along with, flow with, MBh.: Pass. *-upôhyate*, to be borne near, approach, Hariv.

Sam-upôḍha. See p. 1170, col. 2.

समुपविश् *sam-upa-√viś*, P. *-viśati*, to sit down together or near, sit down on (loc., acc., or gen. with *upari*), ŚBr.; GṛŚrS.; ChUp. &c.; to lie down upon (acc.), ib.; to encamp, ib.; to oversleep (the right time for anything), R.: Caus. *-veśayati*, to cause to sit down, ask to be seated, Hit.; to cause to encamp, Rājat. °**upavishṭa,** mfn. seated, sat down, MBh.; Pañcat. &c.

Sam-upaveśa, m. sitting down together, MW.; inviting any one to sit down or rest, entertaining, W.; a seat, Uttarar. °**upaveśana,** n. the act of causing to sit down, MW.; a habitation, building, ib.; a seat, Uttarar. °**upaveśita,** mfn. made to sit down, invited to rest, W.

समुपवृत् *sam-upa-√vṛit*, Ā. *-vartate*, to go together towards, proceed together, MW.; to behave, R.

समुपशम् *sam-upa-√śam*, P. *-śāmyati*, to become quiet, cease, MBh.; Car.

समुपश्रु *sam-upa-√śru*, P. *-śṛiṇoti*, to listen to anything (acc.), hear, hear or perceive any one (gen.), hear from or be told by any one (abl.), MBh.; R.; BhP.

समुपष्टम्भ *sam-upashṭambha*, m.=*sam-upastambha* below, MBh.

समुपसंहृ *sam-upa-sam-√hṛi*, P. Ā. *-harati*, °*te*, to restrain, stop (see next).

Sam-upasaṃhṛita, mfn. restrained, stopped, Uttarar.

समुपसद् *sam-upa-√sad*, P. *-sīdati*, to go to, approach (acc.), MBh.; to get at, obtain (acc.), Śiś.

समुपसृ *sam-upa-√sṛi*, P. *-sarati*, to come near, approach, R.

समुपसृप् *sam-upa-√sṛip*, P. *-sarpati*, to go to (acc.), approach, MBh.; R.; Bālar.; to attack, MW.

समुपसेव् *sam-upa-√sev*, Ā. *-sevate*, to make use of together, MW.; to be addicted to, enjoy, R.

समुपस्तम्भ *sam-upastambha*, m. propping, supporting, MBh.; a support, Car.

समुपस्था *sam-upa-√sthā*, P. Ā. *-tishṭhati*, °*te*, to stand near (at any one's service), R.; to lean on (acc.), ib.; to go to, approach (acc.), MBh.; to occur, arise, befall, Śak.: Caus. *-sthāpayati*, to set up, Suśr.

Sam-upasthā, f. standing near, approximation, proximity, W.; happening, befalling, ib. °**upasthāna,** n. approximation, approach, ib.; nearness, ib.; happening, occurring, ib.

Sam-upasthita, mf(*ā*)n. approximated, approached, come to (*teshām agrato nadī samupasthitā*='they came upon a river'), MBh.; Hariv.; R. &c.; sitting or lying on (loc.), R.; arisen, Hariv.; appeared, begun, imminent, MBh.; Hariv.; R. &c.; seasonable, opportune, MBh.; come upon, fallen to, fallen to one's share (with acc. or gen.), Kāv.; Bhag. &c.; ready for (dat. or loc.), MBh.; BhP.; undertaken, resolved, R.; attained, acquired, W. °**upasthiti,** f.=°*upasthāna* above, ib.

समुपस्पृश् *sam-upa-√spṛiś*, P. *-spṛiśati*, to touch, R.; to touch (water for ablution), touch with water (instr.), bathe in (loc.), MBh.; Yājñ.; to sip water, MW.

समुपहत *sam-upa-hata*, mfn. (√*han*) stricken, impaired (as reason), VarYogay.

समुपहव *sam-upahava*. See *sam-upa-√hve* below.

समुपहृ *sam-upa-√hṛi*, P. Ā. *-harati*, °*te*, to bring towards, offer, R.; Jātakam.; to pay (honour), Jātakam.; to perform (a sacrifice), MW.

समुपह्वर *sam-upahvara*, m. a hidden place, hiding-place, MBh.

समुपह्वे *sam-upa-√hve*, P. Ā. *-hvayati*, °*te* (ind. p. *-hūya* or *-hāvam*), to call together, invite, TS.; Br.; ŚrS.; to challenge (to fight), MBh.; R.

Sam-upahavá, m. an invitation together with others, common invitation, Br.; Lāṭy.

समुपाकृ *sam-upâ-√1. kṛi*, P. Ā. *-karoti*, *-kurute*, to satisfy, pay off, MBh.

समुपाक्रान्त *sam-upâ-krānta*, mfn. (√*kram*) one who has approached or attained to or arrived at (acc.), R.

समुपागम् *sam-upâ-√gam*, P. *-gacchati*, to go up to together, go near to, resort to, approach, meet, MBh.; Kāv. &c.; to undergo, incur, get into any state or condition (acc.), R.

Sam-upâgata, mfn. gone near to, approached,

met, come, arrived, MBh.; Kāv. &c.; one who has attained, R.; one who has incurred or undergone, ib.

समुपाघ्रा *sam-upâ-√ghrā* (only ind. p. *-ghrāya*), to smell at, kiss, MBh.; R.

समुपाचर् *sam-upâ-√car*, P. *-carati*, to attend, wait on, treat (medically), Suśr.; to practise, attend to, be intent upon (acc.), MBh.

समुपादा *sam-upâ-√1. dā*, Ā. *-datte* (ind. p. *-dāya*, q.v.), to gain, receive, acquire, MBh.; MārkP.; to take away from, deprive of, MBh.; to collect, heap together, R.; to assume, put on, MBh.

Sam-upâtta, mfn. gained, acquired, taken, robbed, gathered, collected, MBh.; R. &c.

Sam-upâdāya, ind. having gained &c. &c.; having used or employed (with acc. = 'with the help of,' 'by means of'), R.

समुपानी *sam-upâ-√nī*, P. *-nayati*, to conduct or lead together towards, bring or gather together, assemble, R.

Sam-upânayana, n. bringing near, procuring, MBh.

Sam-upânīta, mfn. brought together, gathered, assembled, MBh.

समुपाभिच्छाद *sam-upâbhi-cchāda*, m. (fr. √1. *chad*), Pat. on Pāṇ. vi, 4, 96.

समुपाया *sam-upâ-√yā*, P. *-yāti*, to go up to together, go or resort to (acc.), approach, meet, MBh.; Kathās.

Sam-upâyāta, mfn. come near, approached, arrived, Kāv.

समुपायुक्त *sam-upâ-yukta*, mfn. (√*yuj*) furnished with, possessed of, surrounded by, full of (instr.), MBh.

समुपारब्ध *sam-upâ-rabdha*, mfn. (√*rabh*) begun, commenced, undertaken, MBh.

समुपारुज् *sam-upâ-√ruj* = *sam-upa-√ruj*.

समुपारुह् *sam-upâ-√1. ruh*, P. *-rohati*, to mount up, ascend, MBh.

Sam-upârūḍha, mfn. mounted upon, ascended, R.

समुपार्ज् *sam-upârj* (*-upa-√arj*), Caus. *-upârjayati*, to gain or acquire together, procure, Bhpr.

Sam-upârjana, n. the act of gaining or acquiring together, simultaneous acquisition, Mn. vii, 152. °**upârjita**, mfn. brought together, prepared, MW.; acquired, gained, ib.; stored up, ib.

समुपालम्भ *sam-upâlambha*, m. reproach, censure, MBh.

समुपाविश् *sam-upâ-√viś*, P. *-viśati*, to enter upon together, undertake, begin, commence, R.: Caus. *-veśayati*, to conceal, hide, HPariś.

समुपावृ *sam-upâ-√vṛi*, (prob.) w.r. for *sam-apâ-√1. vṛi* (q.v.)

समुपाश् *sam-upâś* (*-upa-√2. aś*), P. *-upâśnāti*, to taste fully or completely, enjoy, MBh.

समुपाश्रित *sam-upâ-śrita*, mfn. (√*śri*) leaning against, supported by, resting on (acc.), MBh.; R. &c.; resorted to, one who has recourse to (acc.), ib.; occupied by (instr.), Rājat.; visited or afflicted by (instr.), MBh.

समुपास् *sam-upâs* (*-upa-√ās*), Ā. *-upâste* (pr. p. *-upâsīna*), to sit near together or near each other, R.; to engage in or devote one's self to anything together, practise in common (or singly), Gṛihyas.; R.; to serve or honour together, revere, worship, adore, MBh.; Mṛicch.; Ragh.

समुपास्था *sam-upâ-√sthā*, P. Ā. *-tishṭhati*, °*te*, to stand near to, Hariv.; to practise, observe, MBh.

Sam-upâsthita, mfn. come near, approached, MBh.; R.

समुपाहृ *sam-upâ-√hṛi*, P. Ā. *-harati*, °*te*, to bring near, fetch, procure, MBh.; R. &c.; to offer, sacrifice, MBh.; R.; BhP.; to sacrifice one's self, Rājat.; to enter upon (initiation), R.

समुपे *sam-upê* (*-upa-√5. i*), *-upâiti*, to come together, meet (as friends or foes), MBh.; R.; Pañcat.; to have sexual intercourse, MBh.; to come near, approach, go to (acc.), ib.; to have recourse to, apply to, ŚārṅgP.; to attain, incur, partake of, VarBṛS.; Śiś.; to occur, happen, appear, MBh.; to come upon, befall, R.; to be absorbed in, RPrāt.

Sam-upêta, mfn. come together &c. &c.; come, arrived, MBh.; furnished or supplied with, abounding in (instr. or comp.), ib.

समुपेक्ष् *sam-upêksh* (*-upa-√īksh*), Ā. *-upêkshate* (ep. also °*ti*), to look completely over or beyond, take no notice of, disregard, neglect, abandon, MBh.; Mṛicch.; Amar.

Sam-upêkshaka, mfn. overlooking, not heeding, disregarding, neglecting (gen.), BhP.

समुपेप्सु *sam-upêpsu*, mfn. (fr. Desid. of *sam-upa-√āp*) wishing to obtain, striving after (acc.), Kāv.

समुपोढ *sam-upôḍha*, mfn. (√1. *ūh*) brought near, presented, offered, Mn. vi, 41; commenced, begun (as a battle), R. (also *-upôḻha*, ĀśvGṛ.); risen (as the moon), Uttarar.

समुपोपविष्ट *sam-upôpa-vishṭa*, mfn. (cf. *upôpa* [for *upa-upa*]-√*viś*) seated together, sitting down, Hariv. 7042.

समुपोष् *sam-upôsh* (*-upa-√ush*), P. *-upôshati*, to burn or consume together, burn up completely, ŚBr.

समुब्ज् *sam-√ubj*, P. *-ubjati*, to cover over, close up, press together, ŚBr.

Sám-ubjita, mfn. covered over, closed up, AV.

समुभ् *sam-√ubh*, P. *-ubhnāti*, *-unapti* (impf. *-unap*), to confine, shut up, keep closed, cover up, RV.

Sám-ubdha, mfn. confined, closed, covered up, ib.

समुल्बण *sam-ulbaṇa*, mfn. strong, big, brawny, VarBṛS.

समुल्लङ्घ् *sam-ul-laṅgh* (*-ud-√laṅgh*), P. *-laṅghayati*, to leap beyond, violate, transgress, neglect, MārkP.; to carry over, transport, Hcar.

समुल्लम्बित *sam-ul-lambita*, mfn. (fr. *sam-ud-√lamb*), hanging up, hanging, Mṛicch.

समुल्लस् *sam-ul-las* (*-ud-√las*), P. *-lasati*, to shine forth, gleam, glitter, Śiś.; to break forth, appear, Kir.; Pañcat.; to sound, resound, Prasannar.: Caus. *-lāsayati*, to cause to jump or sport, exhilarate, make glad, MW.

Sam-ullasita, mfn. shining forth, gleaming, brilliant, beautiful, Gīt.; sportive, sporting, W.

Sam-ullāsa, m. sporting, dancing, prancing (of a horse), L.; excessive brilliance, exhilaration, MW.

Sam-ullāsin, mfn. shining forth, glittering, Kpr.

समुल्लिख् *sam-ul-likh* (*-ud-√likh*), P. *-likhati*, to scratch up all round, dig up, ŚBr.; to scratch, furrow, Kum.; to rub against, graze, R.; to write down, mention (in a book), L.

Sam-ullekha, m. digging up all round, extermination (= *utsādana*), L.

समुल्लुप् *sam-ul-lup* (*-ud-√lup*), P. *-lumpati*, to seize upon, lay hold of, pick up, ŚBr.; KātyŚr.

समुष् *sam-√ush*, P. *-oshati*, to burn up, consume by fire, AV.; ŚBr.

समुषित *sam-ushita*. See *saṃ-√5. vas*, p. 1114, col. 3.

समुष्क *sa-mushka*, mfn. having testicles, uncastrated, Baudh.

समुष्यल *sam-ushyalá*, mf(*ā*)n. (fr. *sam* + √*ush* = *vaś*) desirous, loving or exciting love, AV.

समुहितृ *samuhitṛi*, v.l. for *sam-uditṛi* (q.v.)

समुह्य *sam-uhya*, *sam-ūḍha*. See *sam-√1. ūh*.

समूर *samūra* or *samūru*, m. a kind of deer (the skin of which may be used as a student's seat &c.; accord. to some it has a white mane; cf. *camūru*), L.

Samūruka, m. id., W.

समूर्तक *samūrtaka*, (prob.) w.r. for *sam-vartaka*, MārkP.

समूल *sá-mūla*, mfn. having roots, overgrown, grassy, green, verdant, ŚBr.; Kauś.; R.; together with the root, root and branch, entire or entirely (also ibc. and *am*, ind.), Br. &c. &c.; based upon, founded, Gobh., Sch. **— kāsham**, ind. with root and branch (with √*kash*, 'to exterminate completely'), Mcar.; Sarvad. **— ghātam**, ind. with utter extirpation (with √*han*, 'to destroy utterly'), Śiś.; Sarvad.

Sa-mūlaka, mfn. together with the roots, MBh.; together with radish-root, ib.

समूह् *sam-√1. ūh* (cf. *saṃ-√vah*), P. Ā. *-ūhati*, °*te* (ind. p. *-ôham*, q.v.), to sweep together, bring or gather together, collect, unite, RV.; AV.; Br.; Up.; BhP.: Caus. *-ūhayati*, to sweep together, heap up, Kauś.

Sam-uhya, mfn. in comp. for *sam-ūhya*. **— purīsha** (°*hyà-*), mfn. consisting of rubbish swept or heaped together, ŚBr.; KātyŚr.

Sám-ūḍha (or *-ūḻha*), mfn. swept or pressed together, brought together, collected, united, RV.; TS.; regularly arranged, restored to order (as opp. to *vy-ūḍha*, 'disarranged,' 'transposed'), Br.; ŚrS.; purified, L.; tamed, L.; *-cchandas*, mfn. having metres restored to their order, ŚBr.; *-dvādaśâha-paddhati*, f., *-puṇḍarīka-paddhati*, f. N. of wks.

Sam-ūhá, m. (ifc. f. *ā*) a collection, assemblage, aggregate, heap, number, multitude, AV. &c. &c.; an association, corporation, community, Mn.; Yājñ. &c.; sum, totality, essence, MBh.; N. of a divine being(?), MBh. xiii, 4355; (*ā*), f. (scil. *vritti*) a partic. mode of subsistence, Baudh.; (°*ha*)-*kārya*, n. the business or affairs of a community, MW.; *-kshāraka*, m. civet, L.; *-gandha*, m. civet, L. °**ūhaka**, m. collection, heap, multitude, ĀpŚr.; Pañcat. °**ūhana**, mfn. sweeping together, collecting, gathering, Mn. iv, 102; (*ī*), f. a broom, Āpast.; Baudh.; n. the act of sweeping together &c., ŚāṅkhGṛ.; placing an arrow on the bowstring, L. °**ūhin**, mfn. forming an aggregate or fit for the formation of an aggregate, Nyāyas., Sch.

1. **Sam-ūhyà**, mfn. to be swept together &c. (in Sulbas. = *samuhyà-purīsha* above), TS.; Kāṭh.; m. (scil. *agni*) a kind of sacrificial fire (to be brought or carried by the priest), Pāṇ. iii, 1, 131; a place prepared for the reception of the sacrificial fire, W.

2. **Sam-ūhya**, ind. having brought together.

Sam-ohá, m. hostile encounter, conflict, war, RV.

Sam-óham, ind. bringing or sweeping together, ib.

समूह् *sam-√2. ūh* (only Pot. *-uhyāt*), to perceive, understand, Vop.

समृ *sam-√ṛi*, P. *-iyarti*, *-ṛiṇoti*, *-ṛiṇvati*, or *-ṛicchati* (in some forms also Ā.; for *-ṛicchati*, °*te*, see Pāṇ. i, 3, 29), to join together, bring to pass, bring about, RV. iii, 2, 1; to bring together, drive together (3. sg. aor. *-ārata*; perf. p. *-ārāṇa*), ib. i, 54, 1; to be brought about, ib. iii, 11, 2; to run together, hasten together towards (acc. or loc.), meet with (instr.), come into collision or conflict, RV.; AV.; ŚBr.; Kauś.; Bhaṭṭ.: Caus. *-arpayati*, °*te*, to throw at, hurl at (acc.), strike, hit, AV.; MBh.; to cause to come into conflict or collision, ŚBr.; to fix or place or insert in, put in or on or down, ib. &c. &c.; to impose, enjoin, R.; to deliver over, consign, commit, Kāv.; Kathās.; Sāh.; to send off, despatch (a messenger), R.

Sam-ará, m. (or n., g. *ardharcâdi*) coming together, meeting, concourse, confluence, RV.; AV.; ŚBr.; (ifc. f. *ā*) hostile encounter, conflict, struggle, war, battle with (*saha*), ŚāṅkhBr.; MBh. &c.; N. of a king of the Vidyā-dharas, Kathās.; of a king of Kāmpilya, Hariv.; of a brother of king Avanti-varman, Rājat.; *-karman*, n. the action of battle or war, R.; *-kātara*, m. 'timid in battle,' N. of a general, Kautukas.; *-kāma-dīpikā*, f. N. of wk.; *-kshiti*, f. field of b°, R.; *-jambuka*, m. 'b°-jackal,' N. of a man, Kautukas.; *-jit* (Kathās.), *-m-jaya* (Cat.), m. 'victorious in b°,' N. of a king; *-tuṅga*, *-bala*, and *-bhaṭa*, m. 'eminent in b°,' and 'battle-force,' and 'battle-soldier,' N. of warriors, Kathās.; *-puṃgava*, m. (with *dīkshita*) N. of an author, Cat.; *-bhū* or *-bhūmi*, f. field of b°, Vās.; *-manoharī*, f. N. of an astron. wk.; *-mardana*, m. 'destroying in b°,' N. of Śiva, MBh.; *-mūrdhan*, m. the front or van of b°, R.; *-varman*, m. N. of a king, Rājat.; *-vasudhā*, f. (= *-bhū*), Inscr.; *-vijaya*, m. N. of a ch. of the Rudra-yāmala; *-vijayin*, mfn. victorious in b°, Bhartṛ.; *-vīra*, m. 'b°-hero,' N. of the father of Yaśo-dā, W.; *-vyasanin*, mfn. fond of war, Mṛicch., Introd.; *-śiras*, n. (= *-mūrdhan*), Kāv.; Kathās.; *-śūra*, m. a hero in battle, VarBṛS.; *-sāra*, m. n. N. of wk. (containing prognostics of success or defeat in warfare; also *-saṃgraha*, m.); *-siṇha*, m. 'b°-lion,' N. of an astronomer, Cat.; *-sīman*, m. or f. battle-field, Bālar.; *-svāmin*, m. N. of an image or idol set up by Samara-varman, Rājat.; °*râkhya*, m. (in music) a kind of time; °*râgama*, m. outbreak of war, VarBṛS.; °*râgra*, n. the front of b°, R.; °*râṅgaṇa* or °*râṅgana* (Kathās.), °*râjira* (Śiś.), n. b°-field; °*râtithi*, m. 'b°-comer,' any one encountered in battle, Hariv.; °*rôcita*, mfn. fit for b° (as an elephant), L.; °*rôtsava*, m. the festival or joy of b°, Kathās.; °*rôddeśa*, m. battle-field, MBh.; °*rôdyata*, mfn. prepared for battle or war, MW.; °*rôpâya*, m. stratagem of war, VarYogay.

Sam-áraṇa, n. coming together, meeting, Nir.; conflict, strife, battle, war, RV.

Sam-arpaka, mfn. (fr. Caus.) furnishing, yielding (*-tā*, f.), Saṃk.; Sarvad.

Sam-árpaṇa, n. the act of placing or throwing upon, ŚBr.; delivering or handing completely over, consigning, presenting, imparting, bestowing (cf. *ātma-s*°), R.; Kathās.; BhP.; making known, communicating, Śaṃk.; Sarvad.; (in dram.) angry invective between personages in a play (one of the 7 scenes which constitute a Bhāṇikā, q.v.), Sāh. °**arpaṇīya**, mfn. to be delivered or handed over or entrusted, Kād. °**arpayitavya**, mfn. id., Hit. °**arpayitṛi**, mfn. one who hands over or bestows or imparts (gen. or comp.), MBh.; Hariv. °**arpita**, mfn. thrown or hurled at &c. &c. (see Caus.); placed or fixed in or on, made over or consigned to (loc. or comp.), ŚBr. &c. &c.; restored, Hit.; filled with, Lalit.; *-vat*, mfn. one who has consigned or delivered over, MW. °**arpya**, mfn. to be handed over or consigned, Pañcar.

Sam-aryà, n. (for *sa-m*° see p. 1157, col. 1) concourse (of people assembled on festive occasions), crowd, multitude, RV.; an assembly, congregation, community, ib.; tumult of battle, ib.; *-jit*, mfn. victorious in war or b°, RV.; *-rājya*, n. the region occupied by a concourse (such as the above), ib.

Samarya, Nom. P. °*yáti*, to long for battle or war, RV.

Sam-īrṇa, mfn. (referred to *sam-ṛī* = *sam-√ṛi*, Sch. on Pāṇ. vii, 1, 102), see under *sam-√īr*.

Sám-ṛita, mfn. come together, met, RV.; come into conflict or collision (see next); *-yajña*, m. pl. coincident or concurrent sacrifices, TS.; *-somá*, m. pl. concurrent Soma-sacrifices, ib. °**ṛiti** (*sám-*), f. coming together, meeting, contact, RV.; conflict, war, fight, ib.

समृच् *sam-ṛic*. See *sam-√arc*, p. 1156.

समृछ् *sam-ṛich*. See *sam-√ṛi*, p. 1170.

समृध् *sam-√ṛidh*, P. *-ṛidhyati*, *-ṛidhnoti* (Ved. inf. *-ṛidhe*), to succeed well, prosper, flourish, increase or grow greatly, Mn.; MBh.: Pass. *-ṛidhyate*, to be completely successful, be fulfilled or accomplished, succeed, prosper, RV.; AV.; ChUp.; R.; to share in abundantly, be amply furnished with (instr.), ŚBr.: Caus. *-ardhayati*, to cause to succeed or prosper, accomplish, fulfil, VS.; ŚBr.; to cause to be abundantly furnished with (instr.), ib.; to bestow liberally on (dat.), BhP.

Sam-ardhaka, mfn. (fr. Caus.) causing to prosper &c., granting or bestowing any advantage, L. °**ardhana**, mf(*ī*)n. causing to prosper or succeed, ŚāṅkhŚr. °**ardhayitṛi**, mf(*trī*)n. one who fulfils, fulfiller, bestower, ĀśvGṛ.; ChUp.

Sam-ardhuka, mfn. prospering, succeeding, TS.; = *sam-ardhaka*, L.; (*ā*), f. a daughter, L.

Sám-ṛiddha, mfn. accomplished, succeeded, fulfilled, perfect, very successful or prosperous or flourishing, fortunate, AV.; Br.; ChUp.; MBh.; R.; full-grown (as trees), MBh.; complete, whole, entire, ib.; fully furnished or abundantly endowed with (instr., abl., or comp.), ŚBr.; Mn.; MBh. &c.; rich, wealthy, ib.; Kathās.; plenteous, abundant, much, Ratnâv.; m. N. of a serpent-demon, MBh.; *-tejas*, mfn. endowed with splendour or strength, R.; *-yaśas*, mfn. rich in fame, renowned, celebrated, MW.; *-vega*, mfn. increasing in speed, excessively swift, Bhag.; °*ddhârtha*, mfn. having increased substance or wealth, increasing in resources, R.

Sám-ṛiddhi, f. great prosperity or success, growth, increase, thriving, welfare, fortune, perfection, excellence (ifc. = 'increased by'), AV.; ŚBr.; Up.; MBh. &c.; abundance, plenty of (comp.), Kāv.; wealth, riches (also pl.), Yājñ.; MBh. &c.; N. of a partic. Vedic hymn (causing prosperity), VarBṛS.; *-karaṇa*, n. means of procuring prosperity, PārGṛ.; *-kāma* (*sám*°), mfn. desirous of pr°, ŚBr.; *-mat*, mfn. perfectly succeeding or successful or fortunate, MBh.; Naish.; MārkP.; richly furnished with (comp.), Kāvyâd.; *-vat*, mfn. (prob. w.r.), id., Śaṃk.; *-vriddhi-lābha*, m. acquisition of increase of prosperity, MBh.; *-samaya*, m. a season of great prosperity, MW.

Sam-ṛiddhin, mfn. possessing abundance of (comp.), MBh.; R.; prosperous, happy, blessed (said of Gaṅgā), MBh.

Samṛiddhī-√kṛi, P. *-karoti*, to make prosperous or wealthy, Daś.

Sam-ṛidh, f. success, welfare, RV. vi, 2, 10. °**ṛidha**, mfn. full, complete, perfect, ib. viii, 103, 5.

समृष् *sam-√1. ṛish*, P. *arshati*, to come together, meet with (instr.), RV.; to come together to (acc.), AV.

समे *sam-ē* (*-ā-√5. i*), P. *-âiti* (pr. p. *-ēyāna*, MBh.), to come together, approach together, meet at or in (acc. or loc.) or with (instr. with or without *samam*), go to or across, arrive at (acc.), RV. &c. &c.; to unite with (instr.) in marriage, R.; to enter, Hit.; to emulate, cope with (acc.), R.; (with *yogam*) to lead or join together, form an alliance between (gen.) and (instr.), ŚvetUp. (= *sam-gamayya*, Śaṃk.)

Sam-ēta, mfn. come together, assembled, joined, united, Mn.; MBh. &c.; connected or united or furnished with, possessed of (instr. or comp.), MBh.; Kāv. &c.; encountered, come into collision with (instr.), MBh.; come near or to, got into any state or condition (acc.), Pañcat.; *-māya*, mfn. affected by or possessing illusions, MW.

समेघलेख *sa-megha-lekha*, mfn. having streaks of cloud, MW.

समेज् *sam-√ej*, P. *-ejati*, to rise, get in motion, RV.; MBh.

समेडी *samedī*, f. N. of one of the Mātṛis attending on Skanda (cf. *bhedī*), MBh.

समेद्धृ *sam-eddhṛi*. See *sam-√indh*.

समेध् *sam-√edh*, Ā. *-edhate*, to prosper greatly, thrive, increase, AV.; BhP.: Caus. *-edhayati*, to cause to prosper or succeed, make happy or fortunate, increase, swell, strengthen, ĀśvGṛ.; MBh. &c.

Sam-edhana, n. thriving, prospering, growth, increase, R. °**edhita**, mfn. greatly increased or augmented, swelled, increased, strengthened, made happy or fortunate, MBh.; R.; BhP.

समेध *sá-medha*, mfn. full of strength or vitality, vigorous, TS.

समेर् *sam-ēr* (*-ā-√īr*, only in 3. pl. pf. Ā. *-ērire*), to put together, create, RV. x, 40, 4.

समैरय *samairaya* (of unknown meaning, in *vaiśvadevāḥ samairayāḥ*), ĀrshBr.

समोकस् *sám-okas*, mfn. living or dwelling together, closely united with (instr.), RV.; TBr.; Kauś.; furnished with, possessed of (instr.), RV.

समोत्तरतस् *samôttara-tas*, *samôdaka* &c. See p. 1153, col. 2.

समोपेत *sam-ôpeta*, mfn. (for *sam-ā-up*°, *√5. i*) furnished or endowed with, possessed of (comp.), MBh.; Pañcat.

समोप्त *sam-ôpta*. See *sam-ā-√2. vap*.

समोह *sam-oha*, °*ham*. See *sam-√1. ūh*.

समौजस् *samâujas*. See p. 1153, col. 2.

समौलिरत्न *sa-mauli-ratna*, mfn. with a crown-jewel, having a crest-jewel, MW.

सम्प *sampa*, m. = *patana*, L.; (*ā*), f. = *śampā*, lightning (for *sam-pā* see p. 1172, col. 3).

सम्पच् *sam-√pac*, Caus. *-pācayati*, to bake or cook thoroughly, burn, Suśr.

Sam-pakva, mfn. thoroughly boiled, made tender by boiling, Kull.; thoroughly matured or ripened, Hariv.; Suśr.; ripe for death, about to die, MBh.

Sam-pāka, m. cooking or ripening thoroughly, maturing, MW.; Cathartocarpus Fistula (prob. w.r. for *śamyāka*), Suśr. (L. also 'mfn. reasoning well; impudent; lustful, lewd; small, little').

Sam-pācana, n. (fr. Caus.) making ripe, maturing, making tender (by boiling), softening, fomenting (a tumour &c.), Suśr.

सम्पठ् *sam-√paṭh*, P. *-paṭhati*, to read aloud or recite or repeat (Vedic texts) thoroughly or continuously, Mn. iv, 98.

Sam-pāṭha, m. an arranged text, Pat. on Pāṇ. iv, 2, 59. °**pāṭhya**, mfn. to be read or recited together with (cf. *a-s*°).

सम्पत् *sam-√pat*, P. *-patati*, to fly or rush together (in a friendly or hostile manner), encounter, meet any one (acc.), meet with (instr.), RV. &c. &c.; to fly along, fly to, hasten towards, arrive at, reach (acc. or loc.), AitBr.; MBh. &c.; to fly or fall down, alight on (loc.), MBh.; to go or roam about, R.; VarBṛS.; to come to pass, take place, happen, occur, MBh.; Hariv.: Caus. *-pātayati*, to cause to fly or fall, throw or hurl down, R.; BhP.

Sám-patita, mfn. flown or rushed together &c. &c.; run together, coagulated, AV.

Sam-pāta, m. (ifc. f. *ā*) flying or rushing together, collision, concussion, encounter with (*saha*), MBh.; Kāv. &c.; confluence, VarBṛS.; place of contact, point of intersection, id.; Gol.; flight, swift descent, fall, MBh.; R. &c.; a partic. mode of flight (of birds), Pañcat.; a partic. manner of fighting, MBh.; Hariv.; taking place, happening, appearance, occurrence, Kauś.; MBh. &c.; that which falls or settles to the bottom, remnant (of fluid), residue (of an offering), Kāṭh.; GṛŚrS.; Suśr.; anything thrown in or added as an ingredient, MW.; = *-sûkta*, AitBr.; ŚrS.; N. of a son of Garuḍa (prob. w.r. for *sampāti*), RV.; *-pāṭava*, n. skill in jumping, L.; *-vat*, mfn. ready, at hand, the first the best, any one, Kauś.; containing Sampāta hymns (see next), ĀśvŚr.; containing ingredients, MW.; *-sûkta*, n. pl. certain hymns which are contiguous in the Saṃhitā and ritual, ŚrS.; °*tâyāta*, mfn. come or brought in without any obvious purpose, Sāṃkhyapr. °**pātaka**, mfn. relating to a remnant or residue, Saṃskārak. °**pātam**, ind., see *vidyut-s*°.

Sam-pātaya, Nom. P. °*yati*, to sprinkle with the remnant of a fluid, Kauś., Sch.

Sam-pāti, m. N. of a fabulous bird (the eldest son of Aruṇa or Garuḍa and brother of Jaṭāyu), MBh.; R. &c.; of a king, MBh.; of a son of Bahugava and father of Ahaṃ-yāti (cf. *saṃ-yāti*), Hariv.; of a monkey, R.; of a Rākshasa, ib. °**pātika**, m. the above bird, W.; pl. N. of partic. demons, Gobh. °**pātin**, mfn. flying together, MBh.; flying as rivals (= 'equally swift'), Nir.; falling down, Uttarar.; N. of a fabulous bird, R.; of a Rākshasa, ib.

सम्पत्नी *sám-patnī*, f. (a woman) together with her husband, AV.

Sampatnīya, m. a partic. libation, ĀpŚr.

सम्पद् *sam-√pad*, Ā. *-padyate* (in some forms also P.; ind. p. *-pādam*, q.v.), to fall or happen well, turn out well, succeed, prosper, accrue to (dat. or gen.), AV. &c. &c.; to become full or complete (as a number), amount to, Br.; ChUp.; Hariv.; to fall together, meet or unite with, obtain, get into, partake of (instr. or acc.), Br.; Mn.; MBh. &c.; to enter into, be absorbed in (acc. or loc.), ChUp.; BhP.; to be produced, be brought forth, be born, arise, MBh.; R.; to become, prove, turn into (nom.), MBh.; Kāv. &c.; to be conducive to, produce (dat.), Pañcat.; Vārtt. on Pāṇ. ii, 3, 13; (with adv. in *sāt*) to become thoroughly, Pāṇ. v, 4, 53; to fall into a person's power, ib. 54; (with adv. in *tra*) to fall to a person's share, ib. 55; to produce a partic. sound (as that expressed by an onomatopoetic word in *ā*), Vop. vii, 88: Caus. *-pādayati* (rarely °*te*), to cause to succeed, cause to arise, bring about, produce, effect, accomplish (with *śuśrūshām* and gen., 'to obey'), MBh.; Kāv. &c.; to make full, complete, ŚBr.; BhP.; to transform, make or turn into (acc.), Kathās; to provide or furnish with (instr.; with **kriyayā**, 'to charge or entrust a person with a business'), ŚBr.;

MBh.; SaddhP.; to afford to, procure for (dat. or gen.), AitBr.; MBh. &c.; to attain, obtain, acquire, AV.; R. &c.; to ponder on, deliberate, MBh.; to consent, agree, Br.; ChUp.: Desid. of Caus. *-pipādayishati* (see *sam-pipādayishā* &c., col. 2): Intens. *-panīpadyate*, to fit well, Sarvad.

Sampac, in comp. for *sampad*. **-chanivāra-pūjā** (*-śan°*), f., **-chukravāra-pūjā** (*-śukr°*), f. N. of wks.

Sampat, in comp. for *sampad*. **-kumāra**, m. N. of a form of Vishṇu; *-prapatti*, f., *-maṅgalâśāsana*, n., *-vijaya*, m., *-stotra*, n. N. of wks. **-pradā**, f. 'bestowing fortune,' N. of a form of Bhairavī, Cat.; of a Buddhist deity, W. (cf. Dharmas. 4). **-saṃtāna-candrikā**, f. N. of wk.

Sam-patti, f. prosperity, welfare, good fortune, success, accomplishment, fulfilment, turning out well (instr. = 'at random'), Nir.; R. &c.; concord, agreement, ŚrS.; attainment, acquisition, enjoyment, possession, AitBr. &c. &c.; becoming, turning into, Śaṃk.; being, existing, existence, Suśr.; Hcat.; good state or condition, excellence, MBh.; Suśr.; plenty, abundance, affluence, Kāv.; Kathās.; MārkP.; a sort of medicinal root, W.; a partic. Kalā (q.v.) of Prakṛiti and wife of Īśāna, Cat. **°pattika** (ifc.) = *°patti*, good condition, excellence, Kull.

Sampád, f. success, accomplishment, completion, fulfilment, perfection, Yājñ.; MBh. &c.; a condition or requisite of success &c., BhP.; concord, agreement, stipulation, bargain, TS.; ĀpŚr.; equalization of similar things, Śaṃk.; attainment, acquisition, possession, enjoyment, advantage, benefit, blessing, VarBṛS.; Sarvad.; Pur.; turning into, growing, becoming, Śaṃk.; being, existence (ifc. = 'possessed of'), R.; Kathās.; BhP.; right condition or method, correctness, RPrāt.; MBh.; excellence, glory, splendour, beauty, Mn.; MBh. &c.; excess, abundance, high degree, MBh.; Kāv. &c.; fate, destiny, Bhag. (also pl.); good fortune, prosperity, riches, wealth (personified = *lakshmī*), ŚBr.; ChUp.; MBh. &c.; a kind of medicinal plant (= *vṛiddhi*), L.; a necklace of pearls, L.; *-vara*, v.l. for *samyad-v°*, Uṇ. iii, 1, Sch.; *-vasu*, m. N. of one of the seven principal rays of the sun (supposed to supply heat to the planet Mars; cf. *saṃyad-v°*), VP.; *-vipada*, n. (prob.) good and ill-luck, Kāś. on Pāṇ. v, 4, 106; *-vinimaya*, m. an interchange of benefit or advantage, MW.

1. **Sam-pada** (for 2. see col. 2) = *sam-panna*, furnished with (ifc.), Car.

Sampadin, m. N. of a grandson of Aśoka, Buddh.

Sam-panna, mfn. fallen or turned out well, accomplished, effected, perfect, excellent (ifc. or with loc. = 'perfectly acquainted or conversant with'), AV. &c. &c.; of perfect or correct flavour, palatable, dainty, ĀśvGṛ.; MBh.; R.; endowed or furnished with, possessed of (instr., adv. in *-tas*, or comp. also with transposition of the members; cf. below), ŚBr.; MBh. &c.; (ifc.) become, turned into, R.; m. N. of Śiva, MBh.; (*am*), n. dainty food, a delicacy, MBh. xiii, 4567; *-krama*, m. a partic. Samādhi, Buddh.; *-kshīrā*, f. giving good milk (superl. *°ra-tamā*), Kāś. on Pāṇ. ii, 3, 41; *-ṃ-kāram*, ind. making dainty, seasoning, ib. iii, 4, 26; *-tama*, mfn. most complete or perfect, AitĀr.; *-tara*, mfn. more or most dainty or delicate, R.; *-tā*, f. the being endowed with or possessed of (comp.), Daś.; *-danta*, mfn. possessing teeth, ĀśvGṛ.; *-pānīya*, mfn. rich in water, Pat. on Pāṇ. i, 2, 52; *-rūpa*, mfn. of perfect form, complete, MW.; dainty, delicate, ib. **°pannaka**, mfn. = *°panna*, ib.

Sam-pāda, m. (in *duh-s°*, q.v.)

Sam-pādaka, mfn. (fr. Caus.) procuring, bestowing, Uttamac.; effecting, producing (*-tva*, n.), Vās.

Sam-pādana, mf(*ī*)n. (fr. id.) procuring, bestowing, MBh.; accomplishing, carrying out, Vcar.; n. the act of procuring or bestowing, Kathās.; Sarvad.; bringing about, carrying out, accomplishing, effecting, making, Kāv.; Pañcat.; Kathās.; putting in order, preparing, Mn. **°pādanīya**, mf(*ā*)n. to be procured, to be carried out or accomplished or effected, Hit.; Kull.; to be appeased (as a longing), Uttarar.

Sam-pādam, ind. making complete (in number), TBr. **°pādayitṛi**, mfn. a procurer, accomplisher, producer, Kum.; Sāh.; Kull.

Sam-pādita, mfn. brought about, accomplished, fulfilled (*-tva*, n.), Śak. **°pādin**, mfn. coinciding with, fit or suitable for (instr. or comp.), Nir.; effecting, accomplishing, procuring, Yājñ.; Kathās.; Sāy. **°pādya**, mfn. to be brought about or accomplished (*-tva*, n.), MBh.; Sarvad.; to be made complete (in number), TS.

Sam-pipādayishā, f. (fr. Desid.) the wish to bring about or accomplish, Yogas., Sch.; the desire to make fit or appropriate, Śaṃk. **°pipādayishita**, mfn. wished to be completed (*-tva*, n.), Śaṃk.

सम्पद 2. *sam-pada*, n. (for 1. see col. 1) standing with the feet together or even (= *samam pada-yugmam*), L.

सम्पर *sam-para*, g. *utkarâdi*.

Sampariya, mfn. (fr. prec.), ib.

सम्पराय *sam-parâya*, m. (fr. *sam-parā-√5. i*) decease, death, Vas.; BhP.; existence from eternity, Śāṇḍ.; conflict, war, battle, Suparṇ.; Daś.; calamity, adversity, L.; futurity, future time, L.; a son, W. **°parâyaka**, m. hostile encounter, war, battle, L.

Sam-paréta, mfn. liable to die, AitĀr.; deceased, dead, BhP.

सम्परिकम्प् *sam-pari-√kamp*, Caus. *-kampayati*, to cause to tremble, shake violently, agitate, BhP.

सम्परिकीर्त् *sam-pari-√kīrt*, P. *-kīrtayati*, to enumerate fully, VarBṛS.

Sam-parikīrtita, mfn. fully enumerated, Suśr.

सम्परिक्रम् *sam-pari-√kram*, P. Ā. *-krāmati*, *-kramate*, to go or walk round, visit in succession, MBh.; Pañcat.

सम्परिख्या *sam-pari-√khyā*, P. *-khyāti*, to communicate completely, relate in full, MBh.

सम्परिग्रह् *sam-pari-√grah*, P. Ā. *-gṛihṇāti*, *-gṛihṇīte*, to accept, receive, R.; to receive in a friendly manner, MBh.; to embrace, MW.; to undertake, accomplish, perform, MBh.; to take in or understand thoroughly, KaṭhUp.

Sam-parigraha, m. receiving with kindness, Ragh.; property, MBh.

सम्परिचर् *sam-pari-√car*, P. *-carati*, to attend on, serve, BhP.

सम्परिचिन्तित *sam-paricintita*, mfn. (√*cint*) thought out, devised, R.

सम्परितुष् *sam-pari-√tush*, P. *-tushyati*, to feel quite satisfied or content, MW.; Caus. *-toshayati*, to satisfy completely, appease, ib.

Sam-paritoshita, mfn. (fr. Caus.) fully satisfied, quite appeased, ib.

सम्परित्यज् *sam-pari-√tyaj*, P. *-tyajati*, to abandon, desert, leave, Hariv.; R.

Sam-parityakta, mfn. abandoned, given up; *-jīvita*, mfn. (a battle) in which expectation of life is abandoned, R.

सम्परिदह् *sam-pari-√dah*, Pass. *-dahyati*, to be burnt or consumed by fire, MBh.

सम्परिपालन *sam-pari-pālana*, n. (√*pāl*) guarding, protecting, R.

सम्परिपूज् *sam-pari-√pūj*, Caus. *-pūjayati*, to respect highly, revere, MBh.

सम्परिपूर्ण *sam-pari-pūrṇa*, mfn. (√*prī*) quite filled, fully satisfied, R.; perfected; *-vidya*, mfn. perfect in knowledge, MBh.

सम्परिपृष्ट *sam-pari-pṛishṭa*, mfn. (√*prach*) questioned, asked, MBh.

सम्परिप्रेप्सु *sam-pari-prêpsu*, mfn. (Desid. √*āp*) lying in wait to seize (acc.), MBh.

सम्परिप्लु *sam-pari-√plu*, Ā. *-plavate*, to flow quite over, overflow (see p. p.)

Sam-paripluta, mf(*ā*)n. overflowed, MBh.; overwhelmed (with misfortune), distressed, ib.

सम्परिभू *sam-pari-√bhū*, P. *-bhavati*, to despise, contemn: Pass. *-bhūyate*, to be despised, MBh.: Caus. *-bhāvayati*, to cause to keep together, fix firmly together, ib.

सम्परिभ्रष्ट *sam-pari-bhrashṭa*, mfn. (fr. √*bhraṃś*) deprived of (abl.), MBh.

सम्परिमार्गण *sam-pari-mārgaṇa*, n. (√*mārg*) searching about for, search, R.

सम्परिमुद् *sam-pari-√mud*, Ā. *-modate*, to rejoice or exult far and wide, Hariv.

सम्परिरक्ष् *sam-pari-√raksh*, P. *-rakshati*, to protect, defend, R.

सम्परिरभ् *sam-pari-√rabh*, Ā. *-rabhate*, to clasp or embrace together, R.; to take well hold of, MW.

सम्परिवृ *sam-pari-√1. vṛi*, P. *-vṛiṇoti*, *-vṛiṇute*, to surround, encompass (see below): Caus. *-vārayati*, id., MBh.; R.

Sam-parivārita, mf(*ā*)n. (fr. Caus.) surrounded, encompassed, ib.

Sam-parivṛita (R.) or **°pariv°** (AV.), mfn. id.

सम्परिवृज् *sam-pari-√vṛij*, Caus. *-varjayati*, to shun, avoid, MBh.

सम्परिवृत् *sam-pari-√vṛit*, Ā. *-vartate*, to turn round, roll round (with acc.), revolve, roll (as the eyes; with *hṛidi* or *manasi*, 'to turn over in the mind'), MBh.; Hariv.; R. &c.; to exist, MW.; to turn back, return, R.; to turn back or desist from (abl.), BhP.: Caus. *-vartayati*, to lead round, R.; to wring (the hands), Divyâv.

Sam-parivarta, m. moving to and fro, stirring, Dharmaśarm.

Sam-parivṛitta, mfn. turned round, Suśr.

सम्परिवेष्टित *sam-pari-veshṭita*, mfn. (fr. √*vesht*) wound round, Suśr.

सम्परिशोषण *sam-pari-śoshaṇa*, n. drying or withering up, R.

सम्परिश्रान्त *sam-pari-śrānta*, mfn. (√*śram*) exceedingly wearied or fatigued, R.

सम्परिश्रि *sam-pari-√śri*, P. Ā. *-śrayati*, *°te*, to cover over, AitBr.

Sam-pariśrita, mfn. covered over, ib.

सम्परिष्वञ्ज् *sam-pari-shvañj* (√*svañj*), P. Ā. *-shvajati*, *°te*, to clasp, embrace, MBh.; Hariv.; R. &c.

Sam-párishvakta, mfn. closely embraced, ŚBr.; MBh.

सम्परिहृ *sam-pari-√hṛi*, P. Ā. *-harati*, *°te*, to cause to turn round or back, MBh.

सम्परिहृष् *sam-pari-√hṛish*, Caus. *-harshayati*, to make completely happy, delight, MBh.

सम्परी *sam-parī* (*-pari-√5. i*), P. *-paryeti*, to go round, circumambulate, R.; to embrace, contain, AV.; to deliberate, ponder, KaṭhUp.

सम्परेत *sam-parêta*. See col. 2.

सम्पर्क *sam-parka* &c. See *sam-√pṛic*.

सम्पर्याप् *sam-pary-√āp* (only ind.p. *-āpya*), to take hold of together or simultaneously, Kauś.

सम्पर्यासन *sam-pary-āsana*, n. (Caus. of √*2. as*) the act of upsetting (as of a carriage), VarBṛS.

सम्पलाय् *sam-palây* (see *palây*; only aor. *-palâyishṭa*), to run away together, escape, Bhaṭṭ.

सम्पवन *sam-pavana* &c. See *sam-√pū*.

सम्पश् *sam-√paś*, P. Ā. *-paśyati*, *°te* (occurring only in present; cf. *sam-√dṛiś*), to see at the same time, survey (Ā. 'to look at each other,' also = 'to be together'), RV.; TS.; AV.; to see, behold, perceive, recognize (*yasya sam-paśyataḥ*, 'before whose eyes'), Mn.; MBh. &c.; to look at, inspect, review, ib.; to see, i.e. admit into one's presence, receive, MBh.; R.; to look upon as, regard as (two acc.), MBh.; to attend to, ponder, consider, Mn.; MBh. &c.; to count over or up, calculate, recapitulate, TS.; ŚBr.

सम्पा *sam-√1. pā*, P. Ā. *-pibati*, *°te*, to drink together, RV.; AV.; Br.; ŚāṅkhGṛ.: Caus. *-pāyayati*, to cause to drink together, make to drink, BhP.

Sam-pā, f. drinking together, TS.; ŚBr.; (with *Vasishṭhasya*) N. of a Sāman, ĀrshBr.

Sam-pibá, mfn. swallowing down, AV.

Sam-pīti, f. drinking in company, compotation, Pāṇ. iii, 3, 95, Sch.

सम्पाक *sam-pāka* &c. See *sam-√pac*.

सम्पाट *sam-pāṭa*, m. (= *pāṭa*) the intersection of the prolonged side of a triangle by a perpendicular, Col.; a spindle, L.

सम्पात *sam-pāta*, °*ti* &c. See *sam-√pat*.

सम्पाद *sam-pāda*, °*daka* &c. See *sam-√pad*.

सम्पार *sam-pāra*, °*raṇa* &c. See *sam-√1. pṛi*.

सम्पाल् *sam-√pāl*, P. *-pālayati*, to protect, guard, MBh.; MārkP.; to keep (a promise), MBh.

Sam-pālita, mfn. got over, overcome, MBh.

सम्पिण्ड् *sam-√piṇḍ*, P. *-piṇḍayati*, to heap together, accumulate, MBh.

Sam-piṇḍita, mfn. heaped together, drawn or brought together into one mass, R.; Kathās.; °*tāṅguli*, mfn. having the fingers clenched or closed, L.

सम्पिधान *sam-pidhāna*, n. covering, a cover (= *ācchādana*), L.

सम्पिष् *sam-√pish*, P. *-pinashṭi*, to grind or rub together, pound or crush to pieces, shatter, destroy, kill, RV. &c. &c.

Sam-pishṭá, mfn. crushed or broken to pieces, pounded, bruised, shattered, destroyed, MBh.; R.

Sam-pesha, m., g. *saṃtāpâdi* (cf. *sāmpeshika*). °**peshaṇa**, n. the act of grinding together, pounding, MW.

सम्पीड् *sam-√pīḍ*, P. *-pīḍayati*, to compress, press or squeeze together, torment, harass, force (ind. p. *-pīḍya* = 'by pressure or force,' 'forcibly'), MBh.; Kāv. &c.; to reckon up, calculate together, Sūryas.; Kull.; (in astron.) to obscure, eclipse (cf. below).

Sam-pīḍa, m. pressing or squeezing together, pressure, Kir.; (*ā*), f. pain, torture, Gobh.; Mn.; Hariv. °**pīḍana**, n. compression, pressing, squeezing (also as a partic. fault in pronunciation), MBh.; Kāv. &c. °**pīḍita**, mfn. pressed together, squeezed &c.; obscured, eclipsed, VarBṛS.; thoroughly filled with, Karaṇḍ.

सम्पीति *sam-pīti*. See above.

सम्पुञ्ज *sam-puñja*, m. a heap, multitude, Subh.

सम्पुट *sam-puṭa*, m. (ifc. f. *ā*; cf. *puṭa*) a hemispherical bowl or anything so shaped, Kāv.; Suśr.; Hcat.; the space between two bowls, Bhpr.; a round covered case or box or casket (for jewellery &c.), Nīlak.; a hemisphere, Gol.; the Kurabaka flower, L.; a kind of coitus, L.; credit, balance (°*ṭe √likh* with gen., 'to write down to the credit of'), Kathās.; N. of a work, Buddh.; = *eka-jātīyôbhaya-madhya-vartin*, Tantras.

Sam-puṭaka, m. (prob.) a wrapper, envelope, Hcat.; a round case or box or casket, L.; a kind of coitus, L.; (*ikā*), f. a box filled with ornaments, Pañcat.

Sampuṭī, in comp. for *sam-puṭa*. — **karaṇa**, n. the furnishing with a cover or lid, Saṃk. — **√kṛi**, P. *-karoti*, to furnish with a cover, cover up, Hcat.; AgP.

सम्पुथ् *sam-√puth*, Caus. *-pothayati*, to crush down, destroy, MBh.; Hariv.

सम्पुष् *sam-√push*, P. *-pushṇāti*, to become thoroughly nourished, increase, grow, Bhartṛ.

Sam-pushka, mfn. = *akshata*, unground (perhaps w. r. for *sam-śushka*), ĀpGṛ.

Sam-pushṭi, f. perfect prosperity, ŚrS.

Sam-poshya, mfn. to be well nourished or supported, MW.

सम्पू *sam-√pū*, P. Ā. *-punāti*, *-punīte*, to cleanse thoroughly, purify, RV.; ĀśvGṛ.: Caus. *-pāvayati*, to make thoroughly clean, cleanse, purify, ŚBr.

Sam-pavana, n. perfect purification, Gṛihyas.

Sam-pāvana, n. (fr. Caus.) id., KātyŚr.

Sam-pūyana, n. the being thoroughly purified, complete purification, Gṛihyas.

सम्पूज् *sam-√pūj*, Caus. *-pūjayati*, to salute deferentially, honour greatly, revere, Mn.; MBh. &c.; to present respectfully with (instr.), Hit.; to praise, commend, MBh.

Sam-pūjaka, mfn. honouring, revering, Car.

Sam-pūjana, n. the act of treating with great respect, Mn. iii, 137.

Sam-pūjā, f. honouring, reverence, esteem, MBh. °**pūjanīya** or °**pūjayitavya**, mfn. to be highly honoured or valued or respected, W. °**pūjita**, mfn. greatly honoured &c.; m. N. of a Buddha, Lalit. °**pūjya**, mfn. to be greatly honoured or respected, Mn.; MBh. &c.

सम्पूर्व *sam-pūrva*, mfn. preceded by or compounded with *sam*, MW.

सम्पृ *sam-√1. pṛi*, Caus. *-pārayati*, to bring or convey over to the further side, bring to an end, accomplish, perform, Br.; ŚrS.

Sam-pāra, m. N. of a king (son of Samara and brother of Pāra), VP. °**pāraṇa**, mfn. conveying to the further side, leading to a goal, furthering, promoting (any useful object), RV.; ŚBr.; (*am*), n. accomplishment, fulfilment, MaitrS. °**pārin**, mfn. conveying across (as a boat or ship), AitBr.

सम्पृच् *sam-√pṛic*, P. Ā. *-pṛiṇakti*, *-pṛiṅkte* (Ved. also Impv. *-pipṛigdhi*; Pot. *-pipṛicyāt*; inf. *-pṛicaḥ*), to mix together, commingle, bring into contact, connect, unite (Ā. and Pass., 'to be mixed &c.;' 'to be in contact or connected or united'), RV. &c.; to fill up, fill or satiate or endow or present with (instr.; Ā. and Pass., 'to be filled or presented with'), RV.; AV.; TBr.

Sam-parka, m. (ifc. f. *ā*) mixing together, mixture, commingling, conjunction, union, association, touch, contact between (comp.) or with (instr. with or without *saha*, gen., or comp.), MaitrUp.; MBh.; Kāv. &c.; bodily contact, sexual intercourse with (comp.), Kull.; addition, sum, Āryabh. °**parkin**, mfn. (cf. Pāṇ. iii, 2, 142) mixed, blended, W.; connected or united with, Bhaṭṭ.; Bālar. °**parkīya**, mfn. relating to contact or connection, liable to come in contact, W.

Sam-parcana, n. (used to explain *√kuc* and *ric*), Dhātup.

Sám-pṛikta, mfn. mixed together, blended, combined, connected, come into contact with (instr., loc., or comp.), MBh.; Kāv. &c.; filled with, TBr.; interspersed, inlaid, W.; *-tva*, n. the being connected or united, junction, union, Vām. iii, 1, 14.

Sam-pṛic, mfn. being in or coming into contact, VS.

सम्पृच्छम् *sam-pṛiccham*, *sam-pṛicche*. See *sam-√prach*, p. 1174, col. 1.

सम्पॄ *sam-√pṝī*, Pass. *-pūryate*, to be completely filled, become quite full, ŚBr.: Caus. *-pūrayati*, to fill completely, make full, Pañcat.; Kathās.; to complete (a number), Lāṭy.; to fill (with noise), MBh.; to fulfil (a desire), Kathās.

Sam-pūraka, mfn. filling completely, cramming or stuffing (as the stomach), Car. °**pūraṇa**, n. filling the stomach, eating one's fill (also 'nourishing food'), ib. °**pūraṇīya**, mfn. to be made complete (as a number), Hcat. °**pūrita**, mfn. filled quite full, filled with, Pañcat.

Sam-pūrṇa, mfn. completely filled or full (also said of the moon), full of, completely endowed or furnished with (instr., gen., or comp.), MBh.; Kāv. &c.; complete (also in number), whole, entire, Mn.; MBh. &c.; abundant, excessive, Bhartṛ.; possessed of plenty, ŚārṅgP.; fulfilled, accomplished, Mṛicch.; Śak.; m. (in music) a scale which comprehends all the notes of the gamut, W.; one of the four wagtails employed for augury, VarBṛS. xl, 2; (*ā*), f. a partic. Ekādaśī (q.v.); n. ether, the ethereal element or atmosphere, W.; *-kāma*, mfn. filled with desire, Kum.; *-kālīna*, mfn. occurring at the full or right time, Kull.; *-kumbha*, m. a full jar, Subh.; *-tara*, mfn. more filled, very full, R.; *-tā*, f. complete fulness, perfection, completeness, Rājat. (also *-tva*, W.); a full measure (*-yukta*, mfn. 'possessing abundance or one's fill'), Pañcat.; *-puccha*, mfn. spreading the tail (as a peacock), Mṛicch.; *-puṇya-mahiman*, mfn. one whose greatness is acquired by abundant meritorious acts, Rājat.; *-phala-bhāj*, mfn. obtaining a full reward, Mn. i, 109; *-mūrchā*, f. a partic. mode of fighting, MBh.; *-lakshaṇa*, mf(*ā*)n. complete in number, Kathās.; *-vidya*, mfn. replete with knowledge, MW.; *-vrata*, n. a partic. observance, Cat.; *-saṃhitā*, f. N. of wk.; *-spṛiha*, mfn. one whose desire is fulfilled (*-tā*, f.), Sāh.; °*ṇâṅga*, mfn. complete in limbs or parts, entire, Mudr.

Sam-pūrti, f. fulfilment, completion, Sāy.; Naish.

Sam-pṛiṇa, mfn. filling up, filling, ŚāṅkhŚr.

सम्पेष *sam-pesha*, °*shaṇa*, See *sam-√pish*.

सम्प्रकम्प् *sam-pra-√kamp*, Ā. *-kampate*, to tremble or be greatly agitated, shiver, Kāṭh.: Caus. *-kampayati*, to cause to tremble, agitate, R.

सम्प्रकाश् *sam-pra-√kāś*, Ā. *-kāśate*, to become manifest, be visible, appear; to shine, glitter, MBh.; R.: Caus. *-kāśayati*, to illuminate, make manifest, discover, Lalit.

Sam-prakāśa, m. bright appearance, Bhaṭṭ. °**prakāśaka**, mfn. manifesting, announcing, directing, Lalit. °**prakāśana**, n. manifestation, discovering, Kām.; *-tā*, f. the taking place of a manifestation, Buddh. °**prakāśita**, mfn. made manifest, displayed, MBh. °**prakāśya**, mfn. to be manifested or displayed, Pañcat.

सम्प्रकीर्ण *sam-pra-kīrṇa*, mfn. (*√kṝī*) mixed, mingled (*a-s*°), ŚāṅkhŚr.

सम्प्रकीर्तित *sam-prakīrtita*, mf(*ā*)n. mentioned, MBh.; designated, called, Bhag.; Pañcat.; Suśr.

सम्प्रकृ *sam-pra-√kṛi*, P. Ā. *-karoti*, *-kurute*, to produce or effect together, Car.; to perform, begin, MBh.; to effect, render, cause anything to become (with two acc.), R.

सम्प्रकृष् *sam-pra-kṛish*, P. *-karshati*, to drag along with, MBh.

सम्प्रक्लृप् *sam-pra-√klṛip*, Caus. *-kalpayati*, to install, MBh.; to regulate, appoint, settle, Kāty.

Sam-prakalpita, mfn. (fr. Caus.) installed, disposed, settled, MBh.

Sam-praklṛipta, mfn. prepared, arranged, Bhaṭṭ.; well provided with, MW.

सम्प्रक्रम् *sam-pra-√kram*, Ā. *-kramate*, to proceed to do or set about anything, to begin (with acc. or inf.), MBh.; R.

सम्प्रक्लिश् *sam-pra-√kliś*, P. *-kliśnāti*, to crush or press together, knead, squeeze, ĀpŚr.

सम्प्रक्षाल *sam-pra-kshāla*, mfn. (*√2. kshal*) performing the prescribed ablutions, MBh.; m. a kind of hermit or holy man, R.

Sam-prakshālana, n. the act of washing entirely away, destruction (of the world) by inundation, ib.; complete ablution, purification by water, MW.; bathing, ib.; (*ī*), f. (scil. *vṛitti*) a partic. kind of livelihood, Baudh.

सम्प्रक्षिप् *sam-pra-√kship*, P. Ā. *-kshipati*, °*te*, to throw or hurl at, cast, MBh.

सम्प्रक्षुभ् *sam-pra-√kshubh*, P. Ā. *-kshubhyati*, *-kshobhate*, to be shaken or agitated, become confused, R.

Sam-prakshubhita, mfn. shaken, tossed about; *-mānasa*, mfn. agitated or confused or perplexed in mind, R.

सम्प्रक्षै *sam-pra-√kshai*, Caus. *-kshāpayati*, to extinguish, TS.

सम्प्रख्यान *sam-prakhyāna*, n., Mahāvy.

सम्प्रगर्जित *sam-pra-garjita*, n. (*√garj*) loud roaring, Buddh.

सम्प्रगाह् *sam-pra-√gāh*, Ā. *-gāhate*, to dive or plunge into, enter (acc.), MBh.

सम्प्रगॄ *sam-pra-√1. gṝī*, P. *-gṛiṇāti*, to name, AitBr.; to recite or celebrate together, MW.

सम्प्रगै *sam-pra-√gai*, P. *-gāyati*, to begin to sing, sing, pronounce by singing, Lāṭy.; MBh.

सम्प्रग्रह् *sam-pra-√grah*, P. Ā. *-gṛihṇāti*, *-gṛihṇīte*, to hold forth or stretch forth together, ŚBr.; to seize or take hold of together, ib.; to take hold of, MBh.; VarBṛS.; to accept, receive (with *vacanam*, 'to receive any one's words well or kindly'), ib.; Yājñ.

सम्प्रघृष् *sam-pra-√ghṛish*, P. *-gharshati*, to rub into or on, Suśr.

सम्प्रचक्ष् *sam-pra-√caksh*, Ā. *-cashṭe*, to explain, expound, ib.; to suppose, assume, BhP.

सम्प्रचर् *sam-pra-√car*, P. *-carati*, to advance, begin to move, R.; to go on, be carried on, take place, MBh.; BhP.: Caus. *-cārayati*, to dismiss, Hcat.

सम्प्रचि *sam-pra-√1. ci*, P. Ā. *-cinoti*, *-cinute*, to gather, increase, MBh.

सम्प्रचुद् *sam-pra-√cud*, Caus. *-codayati*, to urge on or impel quickly, set in rapid motion, incite, drive on; to promote, encourage, MW.

Sam-pracodita, mf(*ā*)n. urged on, impelled, incited, MBh.; required, R.

सम्प्रच्छिद् *sam-pra-cchid* (*√chid*), P. Ā. *-cchinatti*, *-cchintte*, to cut or split to pieces, cut through, Hariv.

सम्प्रच्यु *sam-pra-√cyu*, Caus. *-cyāvayati*, to cause to proceed or come forth from different directions, bring together, TS.

सम्प्रछ् *sam-√prach*, P. Ā. *-pṛicchati*, °*te* (Ved. inf. *-pṛiccham* and *-pṛicche*), to ask, question about (with two acc.), inquire into the future, MBh.; Hariv.; BhP.; VarBṛ.; (Ā.) to make inquiries, consult about, salute or greet one another, RV.

Sam-pṛishṭa, mfn. asked, interrogated, inquired about, MBh.; R.; BhP.; Śukas.

Sam-praśná, m. asking, inquiring about (comp.), inquiry, question (°*praśno 'tra na vidyate*, 'there is here no question, it is a matter of course'), RV.; MBh.; Kāv. &c.; courteous inquiry, MW.; a refuge, asylum (Ved.), ib.

Sam-prashṭavya, mfn. to be inquired, MBh.

सम्प्रजन् *sam-pra-√jan*, Ā. *-jāyate*, to be produced, spring up, arise from (abl.), R.; Pañcat.; to exist, be existent, Pañcat.; to be born again, MBh.

Sam-prajāta, mfn. produced, arisen, MW.; (*ā*), f. (a cow) which has calved, Gobh.

सम्प्रज्ञा *sam-pra-√jñā*, P. Ā. *-jānāti*, *-jānīte*, to distinguish, discern, recognize, know accurately or perfectly, MBh.; Hariv.

Sam-prajanya (?), n. full consciousness, Divyâv. °**prajāna** (?), id., L.

Sam-prajñāta, mfn. distinguished, discerned, known accurately, Yogas.; *-yogin*, m. a Yogin who is still in a state of consciousness, KapS., Sch.; °*tâvasthā*, f. the above state, ib.

सम्प्रज्वल् *sam-pra-√jval*, P. *-jvalati*, to flame or blaze up, catch fire, MBh.; Hariv.; R.: Caus. *-jvālayati*, to light up, kindle, MBh.

Sam-prajvalita, mfn. flaming, blazing, ib.; lighted, kindled, MW.

सम्प्रणद् *sam-pra-ṇad* (*√nad*), P. Ā. *-ṇadati*, °*te*, to cry out, cry, R.: Caus., see *-nādita*.

Sam-praṇāda, m. sound, noise, Hariv. °**praṇādita**, mfn. (fr. Caus.) made to resound, R.

सम्प्रणम् *sam-pra-ṇam* (*√nam*), P. *-ṇamati*, to bow down or bend one's self before (acc.), ib.

सम्प्रणर्दित *sam-pra-ṇardita*, mfn. (*√nard*) roared out, bellowed, W.

सम्प्रणश् *sam-pra-ṇaś* (*√2. naś*), P. *-naśyati*, to be lost, vanish, disappear, MBh.

Sam-pranashṭa, mfn. (Pāṇ. viii, 4, 36) vanished, disappeared, ib.

सम्प्रणिधा *sam-pra-ṇi-√dhā*, P. Ā. *-dadhāti*, *-dhatte*, to leave behind in (loc.), MBh.; to put aside, disregard, ib.

सम्प्रणी *sam-pra-ṇī* (*√nī*), P. Ā. *-ṇayati*, °*te*, to bring together, collect, raise (taxes), MBh.; to compose, ib.; (with *daṇḍam*) to apply the rod, inflict punishment on (loc.), Mn. vii, 16.

Sam-praṇīta, mfn. brought together, MBh.; composed (as poetry), ib.

Sam-praṇetṛi, m. a leader, chief (of an army), MBh.; a ruler, judge, W.; (with *daṇḍasya*) 'applier of the rod,' an inflicter of punishment, Mn. vii, 26; a maintainer, sustainer, MBh.

सम्प्रणुद् *sam-pra-ṇud* (*√nud*), P. Ā. *-ṇudati*, °*te*, to drive or press forward, urge on, remove or move away from (abl.), MBh.

Sam-praṇudita, mfn. driven or urged on, ib.

सम्प्रतप् *sam-pra-√tap*, Caus. *-tāpayati*, to warm, TBr., Sch.

Sam-pratapta, mfn. excessively heated, MW.; greatly pained, tortured, ib.; suffering pain, distressed, Suśr.; Kām. °**pratāpana**, n. (fr. Caus.) the act of heating, Suśr.; inflicting great pain, afflicting, W.; N. of a hell, Mn.; Yājñ.; Vishṇ.

सम्प्रतर्क् *sam-pra-√tark*, P. *-tarkayati*, to form a clear conclusion or conjecture, MW.; to consider as, think, regard (with two acc.), Hariv.

सम्प्रतर्दन *sam-pratardana*, mfn. (prob.) cleaving, piercing (v. l. °*pramardana*), MBh.

सम्प्रति 1. *sam-pratí*, ind. directly over-against or opposite, close in front of (acc.), ŚBr.; PārGṛ.; rightly, in the right way, at the right time, Br.; ChUp.; exactly, just, TS.; ŚBr.; ChUp.; now, at this moment, at present, Kāv.; RāmatUp.; VarBṛS. &c.; (with impf.) immediately, at once, Kathās. **—vid**, mfn. knowing (only) the present (not what is beyond), having only common sense, KaushUp.

सम्प्रति 2. *sam-prati*, m. N. of the 24th Arhat of the past Utsarpiṇī, L.; of a son of Kuṇāla, HPariś.

सम्प्रतिग्रह् *sam-prati-√grah*, P. Ā. *-gṛihṇāti*, *-gṛihṇīte*, to receive hospitably, welcome, MBh.

Sam-pratigraha, m. kind reception, predilection for, Jātakam.

सम्प्रतिज्ञा *sam-prati-√jñā*, P. Ā. *-jānāti*, *-jānīte*, to promise, MBh.

Sam-pratijñāta, mfn. promised, ib.

सम्प्रतिनन्द् *sam-prati-√nand*, P. *-nandati*, to greet or welcome gladly (see next).

Sam-pratinandita, mfn. greeted joyfully, welcomed, MBh.

सम्प्रतिपद् *sam-prati-√pad*, Ā. *-padyate*, to go towards together, go near to, approach, arrive at (acc.), Gaut.; Suśr.; to addict one's self to, indulge in (acc.), Pañcat.; to attain to, obtain, recover, R.; Hariv.; to be fully agreed about, agree upon, assent to (acc. or loc.), MBh.; R.; to consider, regard as (two acc.), Kum.; to come to pass, arise, MW.; to bring about, perform, accomplish, MBh.: Caus. *-pādayati*, to cause to come to or receive, bestow, grant, give over to (gen. or loc.), MBh.; BhP.

Sam-pratipatti, f. going towards, approach, arrival, attaining to, obtaining, acquirement, MBh.; correct conception, right understanding, Kaṇ.; Pat.; MBh. &c.; presence of mind (see comp.); agreement, concurrence, acknowledgement, admission, assent, affirmation, MBh.; Kāv. &c.; going against, assault, W.; (in law) a partic. kind of reply or defence, confession or admission of a fact (cf. *pratyavaskanda*), Bṛihasp.; co-operation, W.; bringing about, performing, effecting, ib.; *-mat*, mfn. having presence of mind, MBh.

Sam-pratipanna, mfn. gone near, come up to, approached, attained, arrived, MBh.; Kāv. &c.; agreed upon or assented to, acknowledged, recognized, Yājñ., Sch.; Kull.; brought about, performed, W.

Sam-pratipādana, n. (fr. Caus.) the act of causing to receive, delivering or giving over to, granting, Kām.; appointing to (loc.), MBh.

Sam-pratipādita, mfn. (fr. id.) delivered over, bestowed, given, BhP.

सम्प्रतिपाल् *sam-prati-√pāl* (only Pass. *-pālyate*), to expect, wait for, Hariv.

सम्प्रतिपूज् *sam-prati-√pūj* (only ind. p. *-pūjya*), to honour greatly, revere, respect, R.

Sam-pratipūjā, f. great respect or reverence, Pat. on Pāṇ. v, 3, 99. °**pūjita**, mfn. greatly honoured, much respected, MBh.

सम्प्रतिप्राण *sam-prati-prāṇa*, m. the chief breath, AitĀr.

सम्प्रतिबुध् *sam-prati-√budh*, Caus. *-bodhayati*, to rouse up or awaken thoroughly, MBh.

सम्प्रतिभा *sam-prati-√bhā*, P. *-bhāti*, to shine out fully, appear, seem, MBh.; to appear clearly, be fully understood ib.

सम्प्रतिभाष् *sam-prati-√bhāsh*, Ā. *-bhāshate*, to speak in return, answer, MBh.

सम्प्रतिभास *sam-pratibhāsa*, m. perception which tends to combine or unite, Sāṃkhyas., Sch.

सम्प्रतिमुक्त *sam-prati-mukta*, mfn. (*√muc*) firmly or completely bound, fastened, BhP.

सम्प्रतिरोधक *sam-pratirodhaka*, m. complete restraint, confinement, imprisonment, obstruction, Yājñ.

सम्प्रतिलक्ष् *sam-prati-√laksh*, Pass. *-lakshyate*, to be seen or perceived clearly, MBh.

सम्प्रतिविद् *sam-prati-√1. vid*, Caus. *-vedayati*, to cause to be fully known, announce, report, relate, MBh.

सम्प्रतिवेधकी *sam-prati-vedhakī* or °*dhikī*, f. (*√vyadh*) opening, disclosing, Divyâv.

सम्प्रतिश्रु *sam-prati-√śru* (only ind. p. *-śrutya*), to listen attentively to, assent, promise, BhP.: Caus. *-śrāvayati*, to make to promise or repeat a promise, remind of a promise, R.

सम्प्रतिषिध् *sam-prati-shidh* (*√2. sidh*), P. *-shedhati*, to ward off, keep at a distance, MBh.

सम्प्रतिष्ठा *sam-prati-shṭhā* (*√sthā*), P. *-tishṭhati*, to stand firmly on, rely on (loc.), MBh.: Caus. *-shṭhāpayati*, to enclose, confine (as cows), MBh.; to concentrate in (loc.), ChUp.; to make firm, establish, MBh.; to found, introduce, BhP.

Sam-pratishṭhā, f. perseverance, BhP.; permanence, continuance (as opp. to 'beginning' or 'end'), Bhag.; high rank or position, MBh. °**pratishṭhāna**, n. a means for supporting (the frame) or keeping one's self upright, Car. °**pratishṭhita**, mfn. standing or resting firmly on (loc.), established, fixed, settled, Up.; MBh.; lasting, existing, being, Cat.

सम्प्रतिसंचर *sam-pratisaṃcara*, m. re-absorption or resolution (*brāhmaḥ s°*, 're-absorption into Brahma'), MBh.

सम्प्रतिहन् *sam-prati-√han*, Pass. *-hanyate*, to hurt one's self, strike (instr.) against, Car.

सम्प्रती *sam-pratī* (*-prati-√5. i*), P. *-pratyeti*, to go towards, arrive at, come to a firm conviction, believe firmly in, trust in (gen.), R.; Bhaṭṭ.: Pass. *-pratīyate*, to be meant or understood, Pat.: Caus. *-pratyāyayati*, to cause to be meant or understood by, ib.

Sam-pratīta, mfn. come back again, returned, BhP.; firmly believing in, fully convinced of, MBh.; firmly resolved, ib.; thoroughly ascertained or admitted, well known, renowned, ib.; respectful, compliant, MW.

Sam-pratīti, f. complete belief or trust, full knowledge, notoriety, fame, Kir.; respect for, compliance, MW.

Sam-pratyaya, m. assent, agreement (see *yathā-s°*); firm conviction, perfect trust or faith or belief, MBh.; Kāv. &c.; right conception, Pat.; KātyŚr., Sch.; notion, idea, VarBṛS. °**pratyāyaka**, mf(*ikā*)n. (fr. Caus.) causing any one to mean anything (gen.) by (*-tva*, n.), Pat.

सम्प्रतीक्ष् *sam-pratīksh* (*-prati-√īksh*), Ā. *-pratīkshate* (ind. p. *-pratīkshya*, q.v.), to look out for, wait for, await, expect, MBh.

Sam-pratīksha, mfn. expecting (ifc.), Śiś. °**pratīkshā**, f. expectation, W. 1. °**pratīkshya**, mfn. to be expected, Yājñ. 2. °**pratīkshya**, ind. while waiting for, i.e. a long time, MBh.

सम्प्रतीष् *sam-pratīsh-* (*-prati-√3. ish*), P. *-pratīcchati*, to wish together with, assent to, agree, promise, MW.

सम्प्रतुष् *sam-pra-√tush*, P. *-tushyati*, to be or become quite satisfied, be contented, MBh.

सम्प्रतॄ *sam-pra-√tṝi*, P. *-tarati*, to cross over (acc.), Naish.

सम्प्रतोली *sam-pratolī*, f. = *pratolī* (q.v.), MBh.

सम्प्रत्ति *sam-pratti*. See *sam-pra-√1. dā*.

सम्प्रत्यय *sam-pratyaya*. See *sam-prati*.

सम्प्रत्यवेक्षणता *sam-praty-avêkshaṇatā*, f. (√*īksh*) complete perception or comprehension.

सम्प्रत्यागत *sam-praty-ā-gata*, mfn. (√*gam*) come back, returned, MBh.

सम्प्रथा *sam-prathā*, (prob.) w.r. for *su-prathāḥ*, Rājat.

सम्प्रथित *sam-prathita*, mfn. (√*prath*) universally known or celebrated, MBh.

सम्प्रदह् *sam-pra-√dah*, P. -*dahati*, to burn quite up, consume, destroy, MBh.

सम्प्रदा *sam-pra-√1. dā*, P. Ā. -*dadāti*, -*datte* (ind. p. -*dāyam*), to give completely up or deliver wholly over, surrender, give (also in marriage), PañcavBr.; MBh. &c.; to transmit, hand down by tradition, impart, teach, MBh.; KātyŚr., Sch.; Cat.; to grant, bestow, MBh.: Caus. -*dāpayati*, to cause to give over or transmit, R.: Desid. -*ditsati*, to wish to give over, Nir.

Sam-prátti, f. (for *sam-pradatti*) giving entirely up, delivering over, ŚBr.; -*karman*, n. the act of delivering over, KaushUp., Sch.

Sam-prada, mfn. giving, liberal, Hcat. °**pradatta**, mfn. given over, imparted, transmitted, handed down, MBh.; given in marriage (in *a-s*°), Hariv. °**pradātavya**, mfn. to be given or delivered over or transmitted, MBh.; to be handed down, ib.; to give, administer (medicine), Car. °**pradātṛi**, m. one who gives or delivers over, Mn. ix, 186.

Sam-pradāna, n. the act of giving or handing over completely, presenting, bestowing (also in marriage), Mn.; MBh.; Kāv. &c.; handing down by tradition, imparting, teaching, VPrāt.; Gaut.; granting, allowing, R.; a gift, present, donation, KaushUp.; MBh. &c.; (in gram.) one of the six Kārakas, the idea expressed by the dative case, the recipient to which the agent causes anything to be given (see 1. *kāraka*), Pāṇ. i, 4, 32; 44 &c. °**pradānīya**, mfn. to be given or delivered over, Pañcat.; relating to the tradition (of any doctrine), Suśr.

Sam-pradāya, m. a bestower, presenter, ŚārṅgP.; tradition, established doctrine transmitted from one teacher to another, traditional belief or usage, GṛŚrS. &c. &c.; any peculiar or sectarian system of religious teaching, sect, RTL. 61; 62; -*candrikā*, f. N. of wk.; -*tas*, ind. according to tradition, MW.; -*nirūpaṇa*, n., -*paddhati*, f., -*pariśuddhi*, f., -*prakāśinī*, f., -*pradīpa*, m., -*pradīpa-paddhati*, f. N. of wks.; -*pradyotaka*, m. a revealer of the tradition of the Veda, Kusum.; -*prâpta*, mfn. obtained through tradition, MW.; -*vigama*, m. want or loss of tradition, Śiś.; -*vid*, m. one versed in traditional doctrines or usages, Sāy.

Sam-pradāyin, mfn. bringing about, causing, effecting, VarBṛS.; m. 'having a tradition,' a holder of any traditional doctrine, a member of a sect (e.g. Vaishṇavas are sometimes called Śrī-sampradāyins), W.

सम्प्रदिश् *sam-pra-√diś*, P. -*diśati*, to point out or indicate fully, appoint, designate, MBh.; BhP.

Sam-pradishṭa, mfn. clearly pointed out, indicated, designated, MBh.; VarBṛS.; known as, called (nom.), MBh.

सम्प्रदीप् *sam-pra-√dīp*, Caus. -*dīpayati*, to set fire to, inflame, kindle, MBh.

Sam-pradīpta, mfn. blazing or flaming up, shining very brightly, brilliant, ŚāṅkhŚr.; MBh.; Hariv.

सम्प्रदुत *sam-praduta* (?), m. N. of a man, Buddh.

सम्प्रदुष् *sam-pra-√dush*, P. -*dushyati*, to become thoroughly bad, deteriorate, MBh.; Suśr.

Sam-pradushṭa, mfn. wholly corrupted or polluted, VarBṛS.

Sam-pradūshaṇa, n. utter deterioration, corruption, Car.

सम्प्रदृश् *sam-pra-√dṛiś* (cf. *sam-pra-√paś*), Pass. -*dṛiśyate* (°*ti*), to be clearly seen or observed, appear, MBh.; R.; Hariv.: Caus. -*darśayati*, to cause to see, show, indicate, declare (*ātmānam mṛita-vat*, 'to feign one's self dead'), ib. &c.

Sam-pradarśita, mfn. (fr. Caus.) clearly shown, exhibited, manifested, declared, MBh.

सम्प्रद्रु *sam-pra-√dru*, P. -*dravati*, to run away together, run quite off, escape, MBh.; BhP.

Sam-pradruta, mfn. run away, escaped, MBh.

सम्प्रधान *sam-pra-dhāna*, n. (√1. *dhā*) consideration, ascertainment, W.

सम्प्रधाव् *sam-pra-√1. dhāv*, to run quite away, hurry off, escape, MBh.; to hasten towards, be attracted, BhP.

सम्प्रधृ *sam-pra-√dhṛi*, Caus. -*dhārayati*, to direct towards, deliver over to (dat.), MBh.; (with *buddhim*) to fix the mind or thoughts steadily upon (loc.), determine, resolve, settle, decide, ib.; Śiś.; (with or without *buddhyā*, *manasā*, or *hṛidaye*) to ponder, reflect, consider, deliberate or think about (acc.), Mn.; MBh.; Kāv. &c.: Pass. -*dhāryate*, to be fixed upon or determined, MBh.

Sam-pradhāraṇa, n. (and *ā*, f.) determination, deliberation, deciding on the propriety or impropriety of anything, Bhar.; Daśar.; Sāh. °**pradhārita**, mfn. fixed or determined upon, deliberated about, MW. °**pradhārya**, mfn. to be considered or deliberated about, R.

सम्प्रधृष् *sam-pra-√dhṛish*, Caus. -*dharshayati*, to offer violence to, outrage, insult, violate, hurt, MBh.

सम्प्रनृत्त *sam-pra-nṛitta*, mfn. (√*nṛit*) beginning to dance or move about, MBh.

सम्प्रपच् *sam-pra-√pac*, Pass. -*pacyate*, to become quite ripe or mature, come to a head (as a boil &c.), Suśr.

सम्प्रपद् *sam-pra-√pad*, Ā. -*padyate* (in some forms also P.), to go towards or enter together, approach, enter (acc.), AitBr.; BhP.; to set out (on a journey, acc.), Hariv.; to betake one's self or have recourse to (acc.), MBh.; Hariv.; BhP.; to succeed, be accomplished, Pañcat.; to become, be turned into (-*sāt*), Bhaṭṭ.; to set about, begin, MW.

Sam-prapanna, mfn. gone together towards, entered &c.; one who has recourse to (acc.), MBh.; (ifc.) endowed or filled with, Caurap.

सम्प्रपद *sam-prapada*, n. pl. standing on tiptoe, Yājñ. iii, 51 (cf. Mn. vi, 21).

सम्प्रपीड् *sam-pra-√pīḍ*, Caus. -*pīḍayati*, to press well together, Car.

Sam-prapīḍita, mfn. greatly afflicted or harassed, MBh.

सम्प्रपुष्पित *sam-prapushpita*, mfn. richly furnished with blossoms or flowers, R.

सम्प्रपूज् *sam-pra-√pūj*, Caus. -*pūjayati*, to honour greatly, revere, Hariv.

सम्प्रबाध् *sam-pra-√bādh*, Ā. -*bādhate*, to press or drive back, repel, resist, MBh.; to oppress, pain, torment, R.

सम्प्रबुध् *sam-pra-√budh*, Ā. -*budhyate*, to awake, i.e. begin to take effect (as a spell or incantation), Cat.: Caus. -*bodhayati*, to rouse up, awaken, ŚBr.

Sam-prabuddha, mfn. roused up, awakened, MBh. °**prabodhita**, mfn. (fr. Caus.) convinced, persuaded, Hariv.; consulted or deliberated about, ib.

सम्प्रभग्न *sam-pra-bhagna*, mfn. (√1. *bhañj*) entirely broken, broken up, dispersed, routed (as an army), MBh.: R.

सम्प्रभव *sam-prabhava*, m. coming forth, rising, appearance (only ifc.), VarBṛS.

सम्प्रभा *sam-pra-√bhā*, P. -*bhāti*, to shine forth clearly, be conspicuous, appear, MBh.

सम्प्रभाष् *sam-pra-√bhāsh*, Ā. -*bhāshate* (ep. also °*ti*), to speak to, accost, address (acc.), MBh.; to speak, say, proclaim, recite, repeat, ib.; Hariv.

सम्प्रभिन्न *sam-pra-bhinna*, mfn. (√*bhid*) split quite asunder, split open, cleft (said of an elephant whose temples are cleft during the rutting season; cf. *mada*), MBh.

सम्प्रमत्त *sam-pra-matta*, mfn. (√*mad*) very excited (said of an elephant in rut), Hariv.; very careless, thoughtless, neglectful, MBh.; very fond of (inf.), ib. viii, 3509 (B. *sam-pra-vṛitta*).

सम्प्रमथ् *sam-pra-√math* (or *manth*), P. -*mathati*, -*manthati*, or -*mathnāti* (ind. p. -*mathya*, q.v.), to stir about or agitate violently, violate, outrage, oppress, harass, annoy, MBh.; to tear out (the eyes), R.

Sam-pramathya, ind. violently, by force, R.

सम्प्रमर्दन *sam-pramardana*. See *sam-pra-√mṛid* below.

सम्प्रमाद *sam-pramāda*. See *a-s*°.

सम्प्रमापण *sam-pramāpaṇa*, n. (fr. *sam* + 2. *pr*°) killing, slaughter, Yājñ., Sch.

सम्प्रमार्ग *sam-pra-mārga*, m. (√*mṛij*) purification, Gobh., Sch.

सम्प्रमुखित *sam-pramukhita*, mfn. (see *pramukha*) placed at the head, foremost, first, chief, Lalit.

सम्प्रमुच् *sam-pra-√muc*, P. Ā. -*muñcati*, °*te* (ind. p. -*mucya*, q.v.), to loosen entirely, set quite free, deliberate, ŚāṅkhBr.: Pass. -*mucyate*, to free one's self from, get rid of (abl.), GopBr.

Sam-pramukti, f. letting loose (cattle), Kāṭh.

Sam-pramucya, ind. having abandoned or quitted, being quite free from (abl.), ŚBr.

सम्प्रमुषित *sam-pra-mushita*, mfn. (√*mush*) carried quite away, abstracted, distracted, L.

Sam-pramosha, m. carrying off, abstraction, loss (= *nāśa*), BhP.

सम्प्रमुह् *sam-pra-√muh*, P. Ā. -*muhyati*, °*te*, to become completely stupefied or embarrassed, be perplexed or unconscious, MBh.; to be obscured or darkened, R.: Caus. -*mohayati*, to completely perplex, confuse, embarrass, MBh.

Sam-pramugdha, mfn. completely confused; -*tva*, n. confusion, perturbation, Pat.

Sam-pramūḍha, mfn. utterly bewildered or confused, perplexed, embarrassed, MBh.

Sam-pramoha, m. utter bewilderment, embarrassment, infatuation, MBh.

सम्प्रमृद् *sam-pra-√mṛid* (only ind. p. -*mṛidya*), to trample or crush to pieces, destroy, MBh.

Sam-pramardana, mfn. crushing down, destroying, ib.

सम्प्रमेह *sam-prameha*, m. morbid flow of urine, Car.

सम्प्रमोक्ष् *sam-pra-√moksh*, P. Ā. -*mokshayati*, °*te*, to make free, clear away (Ā. 'to clear a way for one's self'), MBh.

सम्प्रमोद *sam-pramoda*, m. excessive joy or delight, MBh.

सम्प्रयत् *sam-pra-√yat*, Ā. -*yatate*, to strive eagerly for, exert one's self about, be intent upon (dat.), Kām.

सम्प्रयम् *sam-pra-√yam*, P. Ā. -*yacchati*, °*te*, to offer or present or bestow together (Ā. also 'mutually'), give or present to (dat., gen., accord. to Pāṇ. i, 3, 55 also instr.), RV. &c. &c.; to give in marriage, MBh.; to give back, restore, R.

सम्प्रया *sam-pra-√yā*, P. -*yāti*, to proceed or set off together, to advance towards, go to (acc. with or without *prati*), ŚāṅkhŚr.; MBh. &c.; to move, revolve (as the heavenly bodies), Sūryas.; to go (together) to any state or condition (acc.), VarBṛS.

Sam-prayāṇa, n. proceeding together towards, setting out, departure, MBh.; BhP. °**prayāta**, mfn. gone forth together &c.; proceeding with, i.e. making use of, employing (instr.), MBh.

सम्प्रयाच् *sam-pra-√yāc*, Ā. -*yācate*, to ask for together, solicit, beg, request (two acc.), MBh.

सम्प्रयास *sam-prayāsa*, m. great exertion, effort, exhaustion, BhP.

सम्प्रयुज् *sam-pra-√yuj*, P. Ā. -*yunakti*, -*yuṅkte*, to yoke or join together, yoke, harness, MBh.; R.; to employ, make use of, BhP.; to perform, execute (a song), L.; to instigate, incite, induce to (instr.), R.: Pass. -*yujyate*, to be joined or connected with (instr.), be added or attached, Nir.; Hariv. &c.; to be united sexually, Rājat.; to be implicated in (instr.), Yājñ.: Caus. *-yojayati*, to join together, connect with (instr.), MBh.; Sāh.; to equip, prepare, Hariv.

Sam-prayukta, mfn. yoked or joined together, yoked, harnessed &c.; united or connected or furnished or endowed with (instr. or comp.), RPrāt.; MBh. &c.; come into contact or having intercourse with (instr.), Mn. xi, 179; sexually united, MW.; encountering in a hostile manner, MBh.; engaged in or occupied with (comp.), Kām.; concentrated, wholly intent on one object, MBh.; bound to, dependent on (loc.), ib.; urged, impelled, incited, ib.

Sam-prayuktaka, mfn. co-operative, L.

Sam-prayuj, mfn. surrounded or encompassed by (comp.), Śiś.

Sam-prayoktavya, mfn. to be used or employed, Sāh. °**prayoga**, m. (ifc. f. *ā*) joining together, attaching, fastening, Mṛicch.; conjunction, union, connection, contact with (instr. with and without *saha*, or comp.), Āpast.; MBh. &c. (cf. MWB. 44); matrimonial or sexual union with (comp.), MBh.; VarBṛS.; (in astron.) conjunction (of the moon and the lunar mansions), VarBṛS.; mutual proportion, connected series or arrangement, W.; application, employment, Cat.; spell, L.; mfn. = *arthita*, L. °**prayogikā**, f. N. of wk. °**prayogin**, mfn. addicted to sexual intercourse, wanton = *kāmuka*, L.; = *su-prayoga*, L.

Sam-prayojita, mfn. (fr. Caus.) joined together, connected, Sāh.; produced, brought forward, MBh.; employed, used, MW.; well suited for anything, adapted, suitable, ib. °**prayojya**, mfn. to be executed or performed, Bhar.

सम्प्रयुध् *sam-pra-√yudh*, Ā. *-yudhyate*, to begin to fight together, commence a war or battle, fight, R.; Hariv.

Sam-prayuddha, mfn. engaged in war, fighting, MBh.; Hariv.

सम्प्ररुच् *sam-pra-√ruc*, Ā. *-rocate*, to appear very bright or beautiful, appear good or right, please, MBh.

सम्प्ररुध् *sam-pra-√2. rudh*, Pass. *-rudhyate*, to be completely debarred from, be deprived of (v.l. *sam-ava-r°*), Hariv.

सम्प्ररुष्ट *sam-pra-rushṭa*, mfn. (√*rush*) greatly enraged or irritated, furious, MBh.

सम्प्रलाप *sam-pralāpa*, m. talk, chatter, Sāh.

सम्प्रली *sam-pra-√lī*, Ā. *-līyate*, to be completely dissolved in (loc.), become absorbed, disappear, vanish, MBh.; BhP.

Sam-pralīna, mfn. wholly dissolved or melted away, disappeared, vanished, R.; absorbed i. e. contained in (loc.), MBh.

सम्प्रलुप् *sam-pra-√lup*, Pass. *-lupyate*, to be violated or injured, MBh.

सम्प्रलुभ् *sam-pra-√lubh*, Caus. *-lobhayati*, to allure or entice away, try to seduce or deceive, MBh.

सम्प्रवच् *sam-pra-√vac*, P. *-vakti*, to explain or declare together, ŚāṅkhBr.; to relate at full or comprehensively, declare, communicate, announce, Mn.; MBh. &c.

Sam-prôkta, mfn. spoken to, addressed, MBh.; declared, announced, proclaimed, Mn.; MBh. &c.

सम्प्रवद् *sam-pra-√vad*, P. Ā. *-vadati*, °*te* (Ved. inf. *-vaditos*), to pronounce aloud, PañcavBr.; (P.) to utter cries together, sing together, Pāṇ. i, 3, 48, Sch.; (Ā.) to talk or converse together, Bhaṭṭ.: Caus. *-vādayati*, see below.

Sam-pravadana, n. talking together, conversation, W.

Sam-pravāda, m. id., AitĀr. °**pravādana**, n. (fr. Caus.) the act of causing to sound together or at the same time, ĀpGṛ., Sch. °**pravādita**, n. causing to sound together, Lalit.

सम्प्रवाह *sam-pravāha*, m. continuous stream, uninterrupted continuity, Kād.; BhP.

सम्प्रविचर् *sam-pra-vi-√car*, Caus. *-cārayati*, to examine or consider carefully, R.

सम्प्रविप् *sam-pra-√vip*, Ā. *-vepate*, to tremble violently, MBh.

सम्प्रविलापन *sam-pravilāpana*, n. dissolving, causing to disappear, MBh., Sch.

सम्प्रविश् *sam-pra-√viś*, P. *-viśati* (ep. also °*te*), to enter into together or completely (with *mānasam* or *dhyānam*, 'to be lost in thought'), ĀśvGṛ.; MBh. &c.; to have commerce or intercourse with (acc.), MBh.; to be sexually united with (acc.), Mn.; MBh.: Caus. *-veśayati*, to cause to enter, introduce, lead into (acc. or loc.), R.; Hariv. &c.

Sam-pravishṭa, mfn. entered together or completely, gone into, R.; Kathās. &c.

Sam-praveśa, m. entering into together, complete entrance, going into (loc. or comp.), KātyŚr.; MBh.; R.; place of entrance, place entered by (gen.), MBh. °**praveśita**, mfn. (fr. Caus.) made or allowed to enter or return (opp. to *nir-vāsita*, 'exiled'), Rājat.

सम्प्रविहृ *sam-pra-vi-√hṛi* (only ind. p. *-hṛitya*), to roam or wander all over (acc.), MBh.

सम्प्रवृ *sam-pra-√2. vṛi*, Caus. *-vārayati*, to wait on, entertain, Divyâv.

सम्प्रवृत् *sam-pra-√vṛit*, Ā. *-vartate*, to come forth, arise, be produced from (abl.), MBh.; Kāv. &c.; (with *manasi*) to turn or think over in the mind, think deeply about, R.; to begin, commence (said of persons and things), set about, prepare for (dat., loc., or inf.), MBh.; R. &c.; to take place, happen, R.; to act, proceed, deal with (loc.), R.; MārkP.; Sāh.; to go against, assail, attack, MW.; to be present or near at hand, ib.: Caus. *-vartayati*, to cause to proceed or go forward, spread about, circulate, set in motion or action, MBh.; BhP.; Rājat.; to undertake, begin, MBh.; Hariv.

Sam-pravartaka, mfn. (fr. Caus.) setting in motion, promoting, furthering, Kām.; producing, creating (applied to Śiva), MBh. °**pravartana**, n. moving or hurrying about, Kām.; the act of setting in motion or action, undertaking, MW. °**pravartin**, mfn. putting in order, setting right, Car.

Sam-pravṛitta, mfn. gone forward, proceeded, set off, BhP.; arisen, existent, present, near at hand, ib.; commenced, begun, MBh.; R.; passed, gone by, W.; setting about anything (inf., dat., or loc.), MBh.; engaged in (loc. or comp.), ib.

Sam-pravṛitti, f. (only pl.) coming forth, appearance, occurrence, MBh.

सम्प्रवृध् *sam-pra-√vṛidh*, Ā. *-vardhate*, to grow well up, attain full growth, grow, increase, MBh.; Kāv. &c.: Caus. *-vardhayati*, to cause to grow or increase, R.

Sam-pravṛiddha, mfn. full grown, increased, swelled, enhanced, well advanced, MBh.; VarBṛS.; Kām.; rich in (instr.), MBh.

सम्प्रवृष्ट *sam-pra-vṛishṭa*, mfn. (√*vṛish*) begun to rain, MBh.; n. what has been completely rained, a whole rainfall, VarBṛS.

सम्प्रवे *sam-pra-√ve*, P. Ā. *-vayati*, °*te*, to interweave, sew or string together, connect, ŚāṅkhBr.

सम्प्रवेष्ट् *sam-pra-√veshṭ*, Caus. *-veshṭayati*, to wind round, Suśr.

सम्प्रव्यथित *sam-pra-vyathita*, mfn. (√*vyath*) greatly troubled or alarmed, R.

सम्प्रशान्त *sam-pra-śānta*, mfn. (√*śam*) ceased, disappeared, MBh.

सम्प्रशास् *sam-pra-√śās*, P. *-śāsti*, (with *rājyam*) to exercise government, bear sway, rule, reign, MBh.

सम्प्रश्न *sam-praśna*, *sam-prashṭavya*. See *sam-√prach*, p. 1174, col. 1.

सम्प्रश्रय *sam-praśraya*, m. respectful demeanour, modesty, humbleness, BhP.

Sam-praśrita, mfn. modest, humble, well-behaved, MW.

सम्प्रसञ्ज् *sam-pra-√sañj*, Pass. *-sajjate* (ep. also °*ti*), to cling to, be attached to or fond of (loc. or instr.), MBh.

Sam-prasakta, mfn. devoted to, intent upon, occupied with (*atra*), MBh.; lasting, continuous, permanent, R.

सम्प्रसद् *sam-pra-√sad*, P. *-sīdati*, to settle down quietly, be soothed, be kindly disposed or gracious towards (gen.), MBh.; R. &c.: Caus. *-sādayati*, to appease, propitiate, ib.

Sam-prasatti, f. = *sam-prasāda* (in Vedânta), Śaṃk.

Sam-prasanna, mfn. soothed, appeased, ChUp.; propitious, favourable, gracious, BhP.

Sam-prasāda, m. perfect quiet (esp. mental repose during deep sleep), ŚBr.; Lalit.; favour, grace, Uttarar.; serenity, Bhaṭṭ. (v.l.); (in Vedânta) the soul during deep sleep, ChUp.; MBh. &c.; trust, confidence, W. °**prasādana**, mfn. (fr. Caus.) calming, sedative, Car.

सम्प्रसव *sam-prasava*, m. (*sam* + 2. *pr°*) admission, Kull. on Mn. viii, 112 (v.l. *prati-pr°*).

सम्प्रसह् *sam-pra-√sah*, P. *-sahati* (fut. *-sahishyati* or *-sakshyati*, v.l. *-śakshyati*), to have power over, become a match for, withstand, check, curb, restrain, MBh.; to endure, tolerate, ib.; to overcome, ib.

Sam-prasahya, ind. thoroughly, by all means, MBh.

सम्प्रसाध् *sam-pra-√sādh*, Caus. *-sādhayati*, to accomplish, settle, set right (see below); to make one's own, acquire, MW.

Sam-prasādhana, n. accomplishing, arranging, decorating, Car.; Bhpr.; the act of effecting or accomplishing, W. °**prasādhya**, mfn. to be accomplished or set right, Kām.

सम्प्रसिच् *sam-pra-√sic*, Pass. *-sicyate*, to flow out, issue, Hariv.; Suśr.

सम्प्रसिद्ध *sam-pra-siddha*, mfn. (√3. *sidh*) well prepared, cooked, Suśr.

Sam-prasiddhi, f. success, good luck, Divyâv.

सम्प्रसुप्त *sam-pra-supta*, mfn. (√*svap*) fallen fast asleep, sleeping, MBh.; closed (not expanded, as a flower), ib.

सम्प्रसू *sam-pra-√2. sū*, Ā. *-sūte* or *-sūyate*, to bring forth, beget, generate, Mn.; MBh.: Pass. *-sūyate* (or °*ti*), to be born, MBh. iii, 12978.

Sam-prasūta, mfn. brought forth, begot, procreated, MuṇḍUp.; MBh. &c. °**prasūti**, f. bringing forth together or at the same time, VarBṛS.

सम्प्रसृ *sam-pra-√sṛi*, Caus. *-sārayati*, °*te*, to stretch or spread out, extend, VS.; TS.; MaitrS.; Hcat.; to draw asunder, ĀpŚr.

Sam-prasāra, m. one through whom all goes on well, BrahmUp. °**prasāraṇa**, n. drawing asunder, Anup.; (in gram.) the mutual interchange of the vowels *i*, *u*, *ṛi*, *ḷṛi*, and their corresponding semi-vowels *y*, *v*, *r*, *l*, Pāṇ. i, 1, 45 &c.

सम्प्रसृप् *sam-pra-√sṛip*, P. *-sarpati*, to approach or enter in a creeping way, ŚBr.

Sam-prasarpaṇa, n. moving along, ŚāṅkhŚr.

सम्प्रस्तार *sam-prastāra*, m. = *pra-stotṛi*, Hariv. (Nīlak.)

सम्प्रस्तुत *sam-pra-stuta*, mfn. (√*stu*) ready to, prepared for (inf.), Rājat.

सम्प्रस्था *sam-pra-√sthā*, Ā. *-tishṭhate*, to take up a position together (before the altar), ŚāṅkhBr.; to set out together, depart, proceed, advance, approach, go to (acc. or loc.), PraśnUp.; MBh. &c.: Caus. *-sthāpayati*, to dispatch, send out to (acc.), R.

Sam-prasthāna, n. the act of setting out together, setting out on a journey, departure, W.

Sam-prasthita, mfn. set out on a journey, departed, MBh.; R. &c.; advancing towards Buddhahood (?), Divyâv.

सम्प्रस्पृश् *sam-pra-√spṛiś*, P. *-spṛiśati*, to touch or sprinkle with water, wash, bathe, MW.

सम्प्रस्रु *sam-pra-√sru*, P. *-sravati*, to flow forth together, issue from (abl.), Up.; R.: Caus. *-srāvayati*, to cause to run together, mix, mingle, TBr.

सम्प्रहस् *sam-pra-√has*, P. *-hasati*, to laugh together, break into a laugh, MBh.; R.; BhP.: Caus. *-hāsayati*, to make sport of, deride, Vas.

Sam-prahāsa, m. laughing at, loud laughter, Bhaṭṭ.; mockery, derision, R.

सम्प्रहा *sam-pra-√3. hā*, P. *-jahāti*, to leave, abandon, MBh.; R.

सम्प्रहित *sam-pra-hita*, mfn. (√*hi*) thrown, hurled, MBh.

सम्प्रहृ *sam-pra-√hṛi*, P. Ā. *-harati*, °*te*, to hurl or throw together, hurl upon (dat. or loc.), MBh.; to attack, assail, strike at, rush upon (acc. or loc.); Ā. (m.c. also P.) to strike at mutually, come to blows, fight together (cf. Pāṇ. i, 3, 15, Vārtt. 2, Pat.), MBh.; R. &c.

Sam-prahāra, m. mutual striking or wounding, war, battle, fighting with (acc. or instr. with or without *saha*; with *madīya*, 'fighting with me'), MBh.; Kāv. &c.; a stroke, blow, R.; going, motion, gait, Vas. °**prahāri**, Uṇ. iv, 124, Sch. °**prahārin**, mfn. fighting together, combating, R.

सम्प्रहृष् *sam-pra-√hṛish*, P. Ā. *-hṛishyati*, °*te*, to rejoice greatly, be exceedingly glad, thrill with pleasure, MBh.; Kāv. &c.: Caus. *-harshayati*, to rejoice, make glad, comfort, ŚāṅkhBr.; MBh. &c.

Sam-praharsha, m. great joy, thrill of delight, MBh.; R. °**praharshaṇa**, mfn. exciting sexually, Car.; (also *ā*, f.) impelling, encouragement, Jātakam. °**praharshita**, mfn. (fr. Caus.) much pleased, thrilled with delight, MBh. °**praharshin**, mfn. rejoicing greatly, delighted, very glad, R.

Sam-prahṛishṭa, mfn. excessively rejoiced, rejoicing, joyful, MBh.; R. &c.; erect, bristling (or 'standing on end,' as the hair of the body), thrilling, ib.; *-tanūruha*, mfn. having the hairs of the body bristling with delight, MBh.; *-manas*, mfn. overjoyed in heart, R.; *-mukha*, mfn. having the face radiant with joy, MBh.

सम्प्राद्रु *sam-prâ-√dru* (only in pr. p. *-prâdravat*, with v.l. *-pra-dr*°), to run away together, MBh. ix, 1675.

सम्प्रान्त *sam-prânta*, m. ultimate or absolute end, Kāśikh.

सम्प्राप् *sam-prâp* (*-pra-√āp*), P. *-prâpnoti*, to reach or attain fully to, arrive at, effect, accomplish, ŚBr. &c. &c.; to get, obtain, acquire, partake of, incur, undergo, Mn.; MBh. &c.; to obtain as a wife or in matrimony, Kathās.: Caus. *-prâpayati* (aor. *-prâpipan*), to cause to get or obtain, ŚBr.: Desid., see *sam-prêpsu* below.

Sam-prâpta, mfn. well reached or attained, obtained, gained &c.; one who has reached or attained, arrived at, met with, fallen into (acc.), MBh.; Kāv. &c.; (ifc.) extending to, Suśr.; come, become, appeared, arrived (as a period of time), Mn.; MBh. &c.; sprung or descended from (*-tas*), Mn. ix, 141; *-yauvana*, mfn. one who has fully attained youth or manhood, come of age, MBh.; *-vidya*, mfn. one who has acquired all knowledge, ib. °**prâptavya**, mfn. to be got or obtained, MBh. °**prâpti**, f. arrival at (comp.), MBh.; R.; rise, appearance, Car.; Sāh.; attainment, gain, acquisition, MBh.; R. &c.; *-dvādaśī*, f. N. of a partic. twelfth day, Cat. °**prâpya**, mfn. to be fully attained to, attainable, obtainable, MW.

Sam-prêpsu, mfn. (fr. Desid.) wishing to attain, striving after (acc.), MBh.; wishing to get at, waylaying, ib.

सम्प्रार्थ् *sam-prârth* (*-pra-√arth*), P. *-prârthayati*, to ask for earnestly, request, entreat, MBh.; R.

Sam-prârthita, mfn. asked for, begged, requested, MBh.

सम्प्राव् *sam-prâv* (*-pra-√av*), P. *-prâvati*, to assist together, aid, help, AV.

सम्प्राश् *sam-prâś* (*-pra-√2. aś*), P. *-prâśnāti*, to eat, enjoy, Hcat.

सम्प्री *sam-√prī*, Ā. *-prīyate*, to be completely satisfied or contented, be greatly pleased with, delight in (loc. or abl.), MBh.; R. &c.: Caus. *-prīṇayati*, to make completely happy or pleased, Pur.; Hcat.

Sám-priya, mfn. mutually dear, being on friendly terms with (instr.), VS.; TS.; GṛS.; very dear or beloved, MW.; (*ā*), f. N. of the wife of Vidūratha (or Vidūra), MBh.; n. contentment, satisfaction, R.; *-tā*, f. dearness, the being very dear or dearer than (abl.), Kir.

Sam-prīṇana, n. (fr. Caus.) gladdening, delighting, BhP. °**prīṇita**, mfn. made completely happy, thoroughly satisfied, well pleased, MārkP.

Sam-prīta, mfn. completely satisfied or pleased, delighted, MBh.; *-mānasa*, mfn. delighted in mind, ib. °**prīti**, f. complete satisfaction, joy, delight in (loc. or comp.), MBh.; Kāv. &c.; attachment, affection, good will, friendship with (instr. with or without *saha*), love for (loc. or gen.), Mn.; MBh. &c.; *-mat*, mfn. satisfied, pleased, delighted, MBh.

सम्प्रे *sam-prê* (*-pra-√5. i*), P. *-praìti*, to go forth together, flow together, RV.; AV.

सम्प्रेक्ष् *sam-prêksh* (*-pra-√īksh*), to look well at, observe carefully, become aware of, perceive, MBh.; Kāv. &c.; to consider well, reflect on, examine, Mn.; MBh. &c.

Sam-prêkshaka, mfn. looking well at, a spectator, beholder, Hariv. °**prêkshaṇa**, n. the act of looking well at, beholding, seeing, W.; deliberating about, considering, investigating, ib. °**prêkshita**, mfn. well looked at or seen, beheld, ib.; considered, investigated, ib.

सम्प्रेद्ध *sam-prêddha* (*-pra + iddha*), mfn. kindled, lighted, AV.

सम्प्रेप्सु *sam-prêpsu*. See *sam-prâp*, col. 1.

सम्प्रेर् *sam-prêr* (*-pra-√īr*), Ā. *-prêrte*, to come forth together, rise together, RV.; TS.: Caus. *-prêrayati*, to drive or push forwards, Pañcat.

Sam-prêrṇa, mfn. risen up together, MW.

सम्प्रेष् *sam-prêsh* (*-pra-√1. ish*), P. *-prêshyati*, to send forth, throw, fling, cast, MW.; (in Vedic ritual) to summon, invite (cf. 2. *prêsh*), Br.; ŚrS.: Caus. *-prêshayati*, to send forth together, send away, despatch, send, dismiss, MBh.; R. &c.; to send a message to (gen.), MBh.; to direct (the thoughts) towards (loc.), Lalit.

Sam-prêsha, m. = *sam-praìsha*, L. °**prêshaṇa**, n. the act of sending forth together, sending away, despatching, Mn.; MBh. &c.; dismissal, R.; (*ī*), f. N. of a funeral ceremony (performed on the twelfth day after death), L. °**prêshita**, mfn. sent forth, despatched, ordered, MBh.; summoned, invited, ĀśvŚr.

Sam-praìshá, m. summons, invitation, direction (to an officiating priest), ŚBr.; ŚrS.; dismissing, sending away, W.

सम्प्रोक्त *sam-prôkta*. See *sam-pra-√vac*.

सम्प्रोक्ष् *sam-prôksh* (*-pra-√uksh*), P. Ā. *-prôkshati*, °*te*, to sprinkle well over (Ā. 'one's self'), consecrate by sprinkling, Kauś.; Yājñ.

Sam-prôkshaṇa, n. the act of sprinkling well over, consecration (of a temple &c.), Cat.; (*ī*), f. consecrated water, Kauś.; (°*ṇa*)-*krama*, m., *-vidhi*, m., *-saṃgraha*, m. N. of wks. °**prôkshita**, mfn. well sprinkled or wetted (esp. with holy water), consecrated, Kauś.

सम्प्रोर्णु *sam-prôrṇu* (*-pra-√ūrṇu*), P. Ā. *-prôrṇoti* or °*ṇauti*, *-prôrṇute*, to cover all over, cover completely, RV.; ŚBr.

सम्प्लु *sam-√plu*, Ā. *-plavate*, to flow or stream together, meet (as waters), MBh.; to be heaped or massed together (as clouds), ChUp.; to founder, go down (as a ship), GopBr.; to fluctuate, waver (as the mind), Uttarar.: Caus. *-plāvayati*, to cause to flow or mass together (as clouds), TS.; ŚBr.; to melt into, mingle or merge with (instr.), AgP.; to float over, inundate, submerge, MBh.; R.

Sam-plava, m. flowing together, meeting or swelling (of waters), flood, deluge, R.; Hariv.; BhP.; a dense mass, heap, multitude, Mn.; MBh. &c.; conglomeration, taking a form or shape, rise, origin, BhP.; noise, tumult (esp. of battle), Hariv.; R.; submersion by water, destruction, ruin, Yājñ.; MBh.; Kāv. &c.; end, close of (comp.), BhP.

Sam-pluta, mfn. flowed or streamed together, met, MBh.; one who has bathed in (comp.), BhP.; flooded over, overspread, covered or filled with (instr. or comp.), MBh.; BhP.; °*tôdaka*, mfn. flooded with water, Bhag.

सम्प्सा *sam-√psā* (only ind. p. *-psāya*), to chew thoroughly, bite in pieces, ŚBr.

सम्फल *sam-phala*, mf(*ā*)n. (√*phal*) rich in fruit or seed, fruitful, Pāṇ. iv, 1, 64, Vārtt. 2, Pat.; m. = *sam-phāla*, L.

Samphalīya, mfn. (fr. prec.), g. *utkarâdi*.

Sam-phāla, m. a ram, sheep, L.

Sam-phulla, mfn. full-blown, blossomed, fully opened or expanded (as a flower), Kāv.; Rājat.

सम्फेट *sam-pheṭa*, m. (prob. for *sam-spheṭa*, q.v.) mutual conflict or encounter of angry persons, angry or passionate contention (in dram. one of the 13 elements of the *vimarśa* [q.v.], illustrated by the altercation between Śakuntalā and the king in Śak.; or as one of the 4 elements of the *ārabhaṭī* [q.v.], illustrated by the encounter of Mādhava and Aghora-ghaṇṭa in Mālatīm.), Bhar.; Daśar.; Sāh.

सम्ब *samb*, *samba* &c. See √*śamb*, p. 1055.

सम्बंह् *sam-√baṇh*, Caus. *-baṇhayati*, to make firm or prosperous, establish firmly, increase, Bhaṭṭ.

Sam-bāḍha, mfn. firm, strong, TĀr. (Sch.)

सम्बत् *sambat*, ind. = *saṃ-vat*, L.

सम्बन्ध् *sam-√bandh*, P. *-badhnāti*, to bind or fasten or tie together, bind or fix on, attach, connect, join, construct, form, ŚBr. &c. &c.; to procure, furnish, supply, Ragh.: Pass. *-badhyate*, to be bound or fastened together &c.; to be connected with or supplied, belong to, Kāś. on Pāṇ. i, 4, 51 &c.: Caus. *-bandhayati*, to cause to bind or be bound together &c., R.; to cause to connect with or refer to (instr.), Kull. on Mn. v, 85.

Sam-baddha, mfn. bound or tied together, joined, connected, ŚBr.; KātyŚr.; connected in sense, coherent, having meaning (see *a-s*°); shut, closed, Kām.; connected or covered or filled with, belonging or relating to (instr. or comp.), Mn.; MBh. &c.; combined with, i.e. containing (comp.), Hariv.; attached to anything, i.e. existing, being, found in (loc.), Kālid.; (*am*), ind. jointly, moreover, MBh. ix, 3443; *-darpa*, mfn. one who has feelings of pride (existing in his heart), MBh.; *-sainyâugha*, mfn. one who has the main body of troops concentrated, Kām.; °*ddhânta* (*sám-*), mf(*ā*)n. joined with the ends, ŚBr. °**badhyamāna**, mfn. being bound together or connected, MW. °**badhyamānaka**, mfn. (ifc.) being in some degree related to, L.

Sam-bandha, m. (ifc. f. *ā*) binding or joining together, close connection or union or association, conjunction, inherence, connection with or relation to (instr. with or without *saha*, or comp.; in phil. relation or connexion is said to be of three kinds, viz. *samavāya*, *saṃyoga*, and *sva-rūpa*, q.v.), ŚrS.; Śaṃk.; Sarvad.; personal connection (by marriage), relationship, fellowship, friendship, intimacy with (instr. with and without *saha*, loc., or comp.), PārGṛ.; Mn.; MBh. &c.; a relation, relative, kinsman, fellow, friend, ally, Āpast.; MBh.; BhP.; a collection, volume, book, Śukas.; a partic. kind of calamity, VarBṛS.; prosperity, success, L.; fitness, propriety, L.; the application of authority to prove a theological doctrine, W.; mfn. able, capable, L.; fit, right, proper, L.; (ifc.) often w.r. for *sam-baddha* (q.v.); *-gaṇa-pati*, m., *-tattva*, n., *-nirṇaya*, m., *-pañcāśikā*, f., *-rahasya*, n. N. of wks.; *-varjita*, n. 'want of coherence,' a partic. fault of style, Pratāp.; *-vārttika*, n., *-viveka*, m., *-vyavasthāvikāśa*, m.; °*dhôddyota*, m., °*dhôpadeśa*, m. N. of wks. °**bandhaka**, n. connection by birth or marriage, relation, friendship, intimacy, MBh.; R.; a relation, friend, MW.; (scil. *saṃdhi*) a kind of alliance proceeding from relationship, ib.; mfn. relating to, concerning, W.; fit, suitable, MW. °**bandhayitṛi**, mfn. one who connects or puts together (v.l. for *sam-bodhayitṛi*), MaitrUp.

Sam-bandhi (m.c. and in comp. for °*bandhin*), mfn. joined or connected with (see *sukha-s*°); m. a relation, kinsman, Hariv.; *-tā*, f. belonging to (comp.), Yājñ., Sch.; connection with, relation to (instr. or comp.), Sarvad.; relationship, con° by marriage, MBh.; *-tva*, n. relation to or con° with (instr. or comp.), Sarvad.; kinship, relationship, MārkP.; *-bhinna*, mfn. divided or shared by relatives, MW.; *-śabda*, m. a word expressing relationship, Pāṇ. i, 1, 71, Vārtt. 3.

Sam-bandhikatva, n. connection, Saṃskārak.

Sam-bandhin, mfn. connected with, belonging or relating to (gen. or comp.), adjunct, inherent, Mn.; MBh. &c.; connected with = possessed of (comp.), Sarvad.; related, connected by marriage, a relative, Mn.; MBh. &c.

Sam-bandhu, m. a kinsman, relative, AV.Paipp.

सम्बर *sambara*, v.l. for *śambara*, *saṃ-vara*, and *sam-bhara* (qq.vv.)

सम्बर्य *sambarya*. See *saṃ-varya*, p. 1114.

सम्बल *sambala*. See *śambala*, p. 1055.

सम्बलन *sambalana*, w.r. for *saṃ-vanana*.

सम्बहुल *sam-bahula*, mfn. very much or many, very numerous, plentiful, abundant, Lalit.; Jātakam.

सम्बाध् *sam-√bādh*, Ā. -*bādhate*, to press together, compress, press down, AV.; to bind firmly together, ŚāṅkhŚr.; to oppress, afflict, torment, R.

Sam-bādhá, m. a throng, crowd; contracted space (ifc. [f. *ā*] = 'crowded with,' 'full of,' 'abounding with'), MBh.; Kāv. &c.; the female organ of generation, Vām. ii, 1, 17; pressure, affliction, distress, annoy, RV.; AV.; MBh.; the road to Naraka or hell, L.; mf(*ā*)n. contracted, narrow, Suśr.; crammed with, full of (instr.), Śiś.; -*tandrī*, f. pl. affliction and exhaustion, AV.; -*vartin* or (v.l.) -*vartman*, mfn. (pl.) moving in dense crowds, jostling or crowding together on a road, Ragh. °**bādhaka**, mfn. pressing together, contracting, Bhaṭṭ.; pressing upon, thronging, crowding, MW. °**bādhana**, n. (only L.) compressing, obstructing, opposing; a barrier, gate; the female organ; a door-keeper; the point of a stake or spit; (*ā*), f. rubbing, chafing, Siṇhās.

सम्बाळ्ह *sam-bāḷha*. See *sam-√baṇh*.

सम्बीज *sam-bīja*, n. universal seed, Kāśikh.

सम्बुध् *sam-√budh*, Ā. -*budhyate* (pr. p. -*budhyamāna*, q.v.), to wake up, MBh.; R.; to perceive or understand thoroughly, notice, observe, know, ib. &c.: Caus. -*bodhayati*, to cause to wake up, rouse, R.; to cause to know, inform, advise, instruct; teach (two acc.), MBh.; Kāv. &c.; to call to, MBh.; Kāś. on Pāṇ. i, 2, 33; to cause to agree, MW.: Desid. of Caus., see *sam-bubodhayishu*.

Sam-buddha, mfn. wide awake, clever, wise, prudent, R.; well perceived, perfectly known or understood, ib.; m. a Buddha or a Jaina deified sage, L. (cf. MWB. 133).

Sam-buddhi, f. perfect knowledge or perception, MW.; calling out to (a person in the distance), making one's self heard, KātyŚr.; Pāṇ. i, 2, 33; the vocative case or its termination, Pāṇ. i, 1, 16 &c.; an epithet, W.

Sam-budhyamāna, mfn. being quite aware, MBh.

Sam-bubodhayishu, mfn. (fr. Desid. of Caus.) wishing to arouse or make attentive, MBh.; wishing to convert, HPariś.

Sam-bodha, m. perfect knowledge or understanding, MBh.; Hariv. (sometimes w.r. for *saṃ-rodha*). °**bodhana**, mfn. (partly fr. Caus.) awaking, arousing, MBh.; perceiving, noticing, observing, MBh.; recognizing, MaitrUp.; the act of causing to know, reminding, MBh.; Hariv.; calling to, Pāṇ. ii, 3, 47; the vocative case or its termination, Siddh.; Subh. °**bodhayitṛi**, mfn. (fr. Caus.) causing to know, informing, MaitrUp. °**bodhi**, f. (with Buddhists) perfect knowledge or enlightenment, MWB. 43 (°*dhy-aṅga*, n. 'an integral part of perfect knowledge or enlightenment,' Lalit.) °**bodhita**, mfn. fully warned, duly apprised, MBh. °**bodhya**, mfn. to be enlightened or instructed, Pañcat.; Kathās.

सम्बृह् *sam-√1. bṛih* (or *vṛih*), P. -*bṛihati* (pf. -*babarha* or -*vavarha*), to tear out together, pluck out, extract, AV.; ŚBr.

सम्बृह् *sam-√2. bṛih* (or *bṛiṇh*), P. -*bṛihati* (pf. -*babarha*), to join firmly, AV.; ŚBr.: Caus. -*barhayati*, to join or unite with (dat.), RV.; -*bṛiṇhayati*, to strengthen, refresh, encourage, MBh.

Sam-bṛiṇhaṇa, n. (fr. Caus.) strengthening, refreshing, Car.

सम्ब्रू *sam-√brū*, P. Ā. -*bravīti*, -*brūte*, to speak well, converse, RV.; (Ā.) to talk together, agree, ib.; to say anything to (acc.), MBh.

सम्भक्ष् *sam-√bhaksh*, P. -*bhakshayati*, to eat together, ĀśvŚr.; to eat up, devour, consume, MBh.; R. &c.

Sam-bhaksha, mfn. feeding upon (comp.), one who eats or devours, MBh.; eating together, food in common, MW.

सम्भज् *sam-√bhaj*, P. Ā. -*bhajati*, °*te*, to distribute completely, share, bestow, grant, Sāy.; (Ā.) to cause to participate in, present with a gift, PārGṛ.; MBh.; to divide, Sūryas.

Sám-bhakta, mfn. distributed, divided, shared &c.; participating in, possessed of (gen.), AV.; devoted to, faithfully attached (v.l. *sam-sakta*), Hariv. °**bhakti**, f. distribution, allotment, bestowal, Dhātup.; possessing, enjoying, MW.; favouring, honouring, ib. °**bhaktṛi**, mfn. one who distributes or grants (-*tama*, superl.; -*tara*, compar.), Nir.; Sāy.; one who shares or participates, MW.; one who favours or honours or worships, ib.

Sam-bhaja (of unknown meaning), Sch. on Kauś. xli, 18. °**bhajana**, n. distributing, granting, bestowing, Sāy. °**bhajanīya**, mfn. to be shared in or enjoyed or liked, MW.; to be favoured or honoured, ib.

सम्भञ्ज् *sam-√bhañj*, P. -*bhanakti*, to break to pieces, shatter, shiver, MBh.; Kathās.

Sam-bhagna, mfn. broken to pieces, shattered, dispersed, routed, defeated, MBh.; baffled, frustrated, ib.; m. N. of Śiva, ib. (accord. to Nīlak. fr. *sam-√bhaj* = *samyak-sevita*).

सम्भर *sam-bhará* &c. See *sam-√bhṛi*.

सम्भर्त्सित *sam-bhartsita*, mfn. (√*bharts*) much censured, abused, reviled, R.

सम्भल् *sam-√bhal*, P. -*bhālayati*, to observe well, perceive, learn, Naish.

सम्भल *sam-bhalá*, m. (prob. originally = *sam-bhara*; often v.l. for *śambhala*, q.v.) 'one who brings together,' a match-maker, AV.; Kauś.; a suitor, wooer, MW.; a procurer, ib.; (*ī*), f. a procuress, ib.

Sambhalīya, mfn. relating to a procuress &c., Naish.

सम्भव *sam-bhavá* &c. See p. 1179, col. 1.

सम्भा *sam-√bhā*, P. -*bhāti*, to shine fully or brightly, be very bright, TBr.; to shine forth, be visible or conspicuous, MBh.; to appear, seem to be (nom. with and without *iva* or *yathā*), ib.; R. &c.

सम्भाण्डय *sam-bhāṇḍaya* (fr. *sam* + *bhāṇḍa*), Nom. P. Ā. °*yati*, °*te*, to collect vessels or utensils, Bhaṭṭ.; to gather provisions, Hcar.

सम्भावन *sam-bhāvana* &c. See p. 1179.

सम्भाष् *sam-√bhāsh*, Ā. -*bhāshate* (pr. p. in MBh. also -*bhāshat*), to speak together, converse with (instr. with or without *saha*), Gaut.; Mn.; MBh. &c.; to speak to (acc.), address, greet, salute, KaushUp.; MBh.; Kāv. &c.; to join in a conversation, Vait.; to agree, consent, enter into an engagement, R.; to talk over, persuade, Hit.; to speak, say, recite, Hariv.; to have sexual intercourse with, MW.: Caus. -*bhāshayati* (ind. p. -*bhāshitvā*, v.l. in B. for -*bhāshayitvā*), to converse with (instr.), Hariv.; to speak to, address (acc.), R.; to persuade, prevail upon (v.l. for -*bhāvayati*), MBh.

Sam-bhāsha, m. discourse, talk, conversation with (gen. or instr. with or without *saha*, or comp.), Gṛihyas.; R. &c.; (*ā*), f. id., MBh.; Kāv. &c.; engagement, contract, agreement, Subh.; watchword, W.; greeting, MW.; sexual connection, ib. °**bhāshaṇa**, n. conversation, discourse with (gen., instr., or comp.), MBh.; Kāv. &c.; watchword, MW.; sexual intercourse, ib.; -*nipuṇa*, mfn. skilled in conversation, Daś. °**bhāshaṇīya**, mfn. to be conversed with, BhP. °**bhāshita**, mfn. spoken or conversed with &c.; n. talk, conversation, Pañcat. °**bhāshin**, mfn. conversing, speaking, Amar. °**bhāshya**, mfn. to be conversed with, MBh.; BhP.; to be addressed, Sāh.; fit for conversation (see *a-s*°).

सम्भिद् *sam-√bhid*, P. Ā. -*bhinatti*, -*bhintte*, to break to pieces, split or break completely asunder, pierce, hurt, AV. &c. &c.; to bring into contact, combine, join, mingle, TS. &c. &c.; to associate with (acc.), SaddhP.

Sam-bhinna, mfn. completely broken or divided &c.; interrupted, abandoned (see -*vṛitta*); contracted (see -*sarvâṅga*); joined, combined, mingled, TS. &c. &c.; come into contact with (comp.), Bhaṭṭ.; close, tight, Pañcar.; solid, compact, MārkP.; -*tā*, f. the being joined or united with, Sarvad.; -*pralāpa*, m. idle talk (with Buddhists one of the 10 sins), Divyâv. (Dharmas. 56); -*pralāpika*, mfn. talking idly, ib.; -*buddhi*, mfn. one whose understanding is broken or impaired, Pat.; -*maryāda*, mfn. one who has broken through barriers or bounds, MBh.; -*vṛitta*, mfn. one who has abandoned good conduct, ib.; -*vyañjanā*, f. a kind of hermaphrodite (°*na*, n. 'the condition of a hermaphrodite'), Mahāvy.; -*sarvâṅga*, mfn. one who has contracted or compressed the whole body (as a tortoise), MBh.

Sam-bheda, m. breaking, piercing, Suśr.; becoming loose, falling off, ib.; disjunction, division, separation (of friends or allies), sowing dissension, Kām.; a kind, species, Cat.; union, junction, mixture, Kāv.; Sāh.; contact with (comp.), Sāh.; the confluence of two rivers, junction of a river with the sea, ŚBr. (cf. *á-s*°), TS. &c.; -*vat*, mfn. come into contact or collision with (*sârdham*), Git. °**bhedana**, n. breaking, splitting, Cat.; bringing into contact or collision, MW. °**bhedya**, mfn. to be broken through or pierced or perforated, Sarasv.; to be brought into contact (see *a-s*°).

सम्भीत *sam-bhīta*, mfn. (√*bhī*) greatly alarmed, afraid of (gen.), R.

सम्भुग्न *sam-bhugna*, mfn. (√*1. bhuj*) completely bent or curved, Bhaṭṭ.

1. **Sambhoga**. See *bhuja-s*°, p. 759, col. 1.

सम्भुज् *sam-√3. bhuj*, P. Ā. -*bhunakti*, -*bhuṅkte* (aor. Subj. -*bhujam*, RV.), to eat together, make a meal in common, AV.; Āpast.; to enjoy (esp. carnally), Rājat.; to partake of (gen.), RV. ii, 1, 4: Caus. -*bhojayati*, to cause to enjoy or eat, feed any one (acc.) with (instr.), Yājñ.; MBh.; BhP.

Sam-bhukta, mfn. eaten, enjoyed &c.; run through, traversed, VarBṛS., Sch.

Sam-bhoktṛi, m. an eater, enjoyer, Pañcar.

2. **Sam-bhogá**, m. (ifc. f. *ā*) complete enjoyment, pleasure, delight in (comp.), ŚBr. &c. &c.; carnal or sensual enjoyment, sexual union with (comp.), MBh.; Kāv. &c.; (in rhet.) a subdivision of the Śṛiṅgāra or sentiment of love (described as 'successful love leading to union,' and opp. to *vipralambha*, 'disappointed love, separation'), Daśar.; Sāh. &c. (only L., 'duration; joy; employment, use; a partic. part of an elephant's trunk; a Jaina or Buddhist edict; a libertine'); N. of a man, Buddh.; -*kāya*, m. 'body of enjoyment,' N. of one of the three bodies of a Buddha, MWB. 247; -*kshama*, mfn. suitable for enj°, MW.; -*yakshiṇī*, f. N. of a Yoginī (also called Vīṇā, w.r. °*kshaṇī*), Cat.; -*vat*, mfn. having enj°, leading a joyous life, VarBṛS.; -*veśman*, n. 'enjoyment-room,' the chamber of a concubine, Cat. °**bhogin**, mfn. enjoying together or enjoying each other mutually, AitBr.; ŚāṅkhŚr.; enjoying, using, possessing, Kāv.; VarBṛS.; m. a sensualist, libertine, L. °**bhogya**, mfn. to be (or being) enjoyed or used (-*tā*, f.), Kām.

Sam-bhoja, m. food, BhP. °**bhojaka**, m. one who serves food, attendant at a meal (perhaps 'a cook'), MBh.; an eater, taster, MW. °**bhojana**, n. eating together, a common meal, dinner party, MBh.; food, Suśr.; (*ī*), f. eating together, Āpast.; Mn.; MBh. °**bhojanīya**, mfn. to be fed, BhP. °**bhojya**, mfn. id., ib.; to be eaten, eatable, MBh.; one with whom one ought to eat (see *a-s*°).

सम्भू *sam-√bhū*, P. Ā. -*bhavati*, °*te* (ind. p. -*bhūya*, q.v.), to be or come together, assemble, meet, be joined or united with (instr. with or without *saha*, or loc.), RV. &c. &c.; to be united sexually with (instr. with or without *saha* or *sârdham*, or acc.), AV.; ŚBr.; MBh. &c.; to be born or produced from (abl.), arise, spring up, develop, ib.; to happen, occur, be, be found, exist, MBh.; Kāv. &c.; to be possible, Hit.; Vedântas.; to be or become anything (nom.), RV.; Br.; MBh.; to accrue to, fall to the share of (loc. or gen.), R.; Kathās.; to prevail, be effective, ŚBr.; to be able to or capable of (inf. or loc.), Śiś.; to enter into, partake of, attain to (acc.), Yājñ.; to find room in, be contained in or numbered among (loc.), RV.; MBh. &c.; to be adequate, MBh.; to be capable of holding, Pāṇ. v, 1, 52: Caus. -*bhāvayati*, to cause to be together, bring together, present or affect any one (acc.) with (instr.; with *dosheṇa*, 'to attach blame to,' with *annena*, 'to give food to'), Kāv.; Kathās.; BhP.; to cause to be born or produced, effect, accomplish, make, AitBr.; MBh. &c.; to foster, cherish, MBh.; to resort to (acc.), ib.; to meet with, find (*jīvantīm*, 'alive'), Hcar.; to honour, revere, salute, greet, MBh.; Kāv. &c.; to receive or accept graciously, Pañcat.; to imply, suggest a possibility, suppose anything possible in any one (loc. or gen.), MBh.; Kāv. &c.; to regard or consider as (two acc.), Kālid.; Pañcat.; to think it possible that (Pot. with and without *yad*, or fut.), Pāṇ. iii, 3, 155, Sch.; (with *na*) to think it impossible that (Pot. with and without *yad, yacca, yatra, yadā, yadi*, or *jātu*; fut. with and without *kiṃ kila*), Pāṇ. iii, 3, 145 &c., Sch.; (Ā.) to reach, arrive at (acc.), Pat.: Pass. of Caus. *-bhāvyate*, to be brought about or together &c. (see above); to be (thought) possible or probable or fitting or consistent, Mṛicch.; Kālid. &c.: Desid. *-bubhūshati*, to wish to thrive or prosper, ŚāṅkhŚr.

Sam-bhavá (or *sám-bhava*), m. (ifc. f. *ā*) being or coming together, meeting, union, intercourse (esp. sexual int°, cohabitation), Gobh.; finding room in, being contained in (ifc. = 'contained in'), MBh.; Suśr.; birth, production, origin, source, the being produced from (abl.; ifc. = 'arisen or produced from, made of, grown in'), Mn.; MBh. &c.; cause, reason, occasion (ifc. = 'caused or occasioned by'), ib.; being brought about, occurrence, appearance (ifc. = 'occurring' or 'appearing in'), ib.; being, existence, ŚvetUp.; MBh. &c.; capacity, ability, possibility (ifc. 'made possible by;' *ena*, 'according to possibility,' 'as possible'), MBh.; MārkP.; Sāh.; (in rhet.) a possible case, Kuval.; (in phil.) equivalence (regarded as one of the Pramāṇas, q. v.; illustrated by the equivalence between one shilling and twelve pence), MW.; agreement, conformity (esp. of the receptacle with the thing received), W.; compatibility, adequacy, ib.; acquaintance, intimacy, ib.; loss, destruction, ib.; (with Buddhists) N. of a world, SaddhP.; N. of a prince, VP.; of the third Arhat of the present Avasarpiṇī, L.; mf(*ā*)n. existing, being, Pañcar.; *-kāṇḍa*, m. n. N. of a Pauranic wk.; *-parvan*, n. 'the section about the origin (of the gods),' N. of ch. of the first book of the MBh. °**bhavana**, n. containing, Pāṇ. i, 4, 23, Vārtt. 9. °**bhavin**, mfn. possible, Sāh.; Sarvad. °**bhavishṇu**, m. a producer, creator, BhP. °**bhavya**, mfn. to be produced together, be capable &c. (cf. *a-s°*); m. Feronia Elephantum, L.

Sam-bhāvana, mfn. (fr. Caus.) having a high opinion of (comp.), BhP.; (*ā*), f. (rarely *am*, n.) bringing together, assembling, Pañcat.; bringing near, procuring, R.; coming together, meeting with (gen.), Ratnāv.; worship, honour, respect, esteem, regard for, high opinion of (loc.; *ātmani*, 'of one's self'), MBh.; Kāv. &c.; imagination, supposition, assumption (also as a rhet. figure, described by some as the use of the verb in the Imperative or Potential mood; acc. with √*bhaj*, 'to be supposed;' °*nôjjhita*, mfn. 'rejected as an assumption,' 'doubted'), Pāṇ.; Kāv.; Sarvad.; Kpr.; Vās., Sch.; fitness, adequacy, Kir.; competency, ability, W.; fame, celebrity, ib. °**bhāvanīya**, mfn. to be partaken of or assisted at (n. impers.), MBh.; to be honoured or respected or greeted, BhP.; to be assumed or supposed, possible, probable, Mṛicch. (cf. *a-s°*), Sāh. °**bhāvayitavya**, mfn. to be respected or honoured, Prab.; to be supposed, probable, Śaṃk. °**bhāvayitṛi**, mfn. one who honours or respects or reveres, Daś. °**bhāvita**, mfn. brought together, brought about &c.; seized, grasped, Kād.; thought highly of, esteemed, honoured, respected, MBh.; Kāv. &c.; honoured or presented with (instr.), BhP.; considered, supposed, conjectured, reflected, MBh.; R. &c.; suited, adequate, fit for, possible, probable, Śak.; Ragh.; n. conjecture, supposition, Ratnāv.; *-tama*, mfn. most honoured or respected, Śaṃk.; *-tara*, mfn. more honoured or esteemed, more confided in, R.; °*tâtman*, mfn. noble-minded, of respected character, ib. °**bhāvitavya**, mfn. = °*bhāvayitavya* (v.l. °*bhāvanīya*), BhP. °**bhāvin**, mfn. faithfully adhering or devoted to, Kathās.; suitable, conformable, MBh. °**bhāvya**, m. to be honoured or respected or well treated, Hariv.; MārkP.; to be (or being) honourably mentioned, MBh.; to be regarded or considered as (nom.), Pañcat.; to be supposed or expected, possible, probable, MBh.; Kāv. &c.; suited, fit, adequate, Sāy. (in a quotation); capable of, able to (loc.), Pañcat. (v.l.); m. N. of a son of Manu Raivata, VP.; n. adequacy, competency, fitness, MW.

Sam-bhu, mfn. produced from, made of (comp.), Yājñ.; m. a parent, progenitor, Pāṇ. iii, 2, 180, Kāś.; N. of a metre, Col.

Sam-bhūta, mfn. being or come together, united or combined with (see *-tva*); become, born, produced or arisen or proceeding from, made or composed of (abl. or comp.), Up.; Mn.; MBh. &c.; (ibc.) one in whom anything has arisen &c., i. e. provided with, possessed of &c. (see comp.); become or changed into anything (nom.), MBh.; capable, adequate, equal, W.; m. N. of a son of Trasa-dasyu, Hariv.; VP.; of a judge, Buddh.; *-tva*, n. state of union or combination with (loc.; *pañcasu bhūteshu sambhūta-tvaṃ ni-√gam*, 'to undergo union with the five elements,' i.e. 'to die'), MBh. xiv, 174; *-bhūri-gaja-vāji-padāti-sainya*, mfn. possessed of an army (consisting) of numerous elephants and horses and foot-soldiers, Kathās.; *-vijaya*, m. (= °*ti-vijaya*), HPariś.; *-saṃtrāsa*, mfn. seized with fear, afraid, alarmed, Rājat. °**bhūti** (*sám-*), f. birth, origin, production (ifc. = 'risen or produced or descended from'), VS. &c. &c.; growth, increase, ŚBr.; ŚāṅkhŚr.; manifestation of might, great or superhuman power (= *vi-bhūti*), BhP. (Sch.); suitability, fitness (also personified as the daughter of Daksha and wife of Marīci, or as the wife of Jayad-ratha and mother of Vijaya), Pur.; m. N. of a son of Duḥsaha, VP.; of a brother of Trasa-dasyu, ib.; of a judge, Buddh.; *-vijaya*, m. (with Jainas) N. of a Śruta-kevalin (also = *ta-vijaya*), HPariś.

Sam-bhūya, ind. being together, being united or combined with (in later language often used as an adv. = 'together, in common, in company,' and sometimes forming first member of a comp.; *sambhūya samutthānam*, 'engaging in business after joining partnership,' 'association in trade,' 'partnership'), Mn.; MBh. &c. (cf. IW. 261); *-kārin*, mfn. acting in concert or in company, a coadjutor, co-partner, colleague, W.; *-gamana*, n. or *-yāna*, n. going in company, Kām. °**bhūyas**, g. *bāhv-ādi*.

Sam-bhūyasya, Nom. P. °*syati*, g. *kaṇḍv-ādi*.

सम्भूष् *sam-√bhūsh*, P. *-bhūshati*, to procure or provide anything (acc.) for any one (loc.), RV.

सम्भृ *sam-√bhṛi*, P. Ā. *-bharati*, °*te* (Ved. pf. *-jabhāra*), to draw together, roll or fold up, RV. i, 115, 4; (Ā.) to close (the jaws), ib. x, 79, 1; to bring together, gather, collect, unite, compose, arrange, prepare, make ready, procure (materials or ingredients of any kind, esp. for a sacrifice; with *sam-bhārān*, 'to collect all requisites,' 'prepare what is necessary'), RV. &c. &c.; to pay back, MaitrS.; to maintain, cherish, R.; to offer, present, MW.: Caus. *-bhārayati*, to cause to bring together or prepare, R.

Sam-bhará, mfn. one who brings together, a supporter, bestower, RV.; m. N. of a district and lake in Rājputāna (the lake commonly called Sambhar, where the salt *gaḍa-lavaṇa* is found, lies between the Jaipur and Jodhpur states), L.; °*rôdbhava*, n. 'produced in S°,' the above salt, L. °**bháraṇa**, m. a kind of brick, TS.; (*ī*), f. a partic. Soma-vessel, KātyŚr.; n. putting together, composition, arrangement, preparation, ShaḍvBr.; KātyŚr.; collection, mass, multitude, RV. °**bharaṇīya**, mfn. to be brought together or collected or combined or united, TBr., Sch.; (ifc.) relating to the preparation of, ŚrS.

Sam-bhārá, m. (ifc. f. *ā*) bringing together, collecting (= *sam-bhṛiti*), ŚBr.; preparation, equipment, provision, necessaries, materials, requisite, collection of things required for any purpose (with Buddhists twofold, viz. 1. *puṇya-s°*, 'meritorious acts,' and 2. *jñāna-s°*, 'science;' others add 3. *śamatha-s°*, 'quietude,' and 4. *vidarśana-s°*, 'far-sightedness,' Dharmas. 117), AV. &c. &c.; = *-yajus*, TBr.; property, wealth, MBh.; fulness, completeness, ib.; multitude, number, quantity, Kāv.; Pur.; Sarvad.; high degree, excess of (love, anger &c.), Ratnāv.; Vās.; maintenance, support, nourishment, W.; *-tvá*, n. the state of (being) a requisite, ŚBr.; *-yajúṡ*, n. N. of partic. texts, ĀpŚr.; *-śīla*, n. (with Buddhists) the virtue of possessing the requisites (see above), Dharmas. 106. °**bhārin**, mfn. full of (comp.), Kāv. °**bhārya**, mfn. to be put together or composed of various parts, Br.; ŚrS.; to be prepared or made useful (compar. *-tara*), TS.; to be maintained or nourished, a dependant, W.; m. N. of an Ahīna, ĀśvŚr.

Sám-bhṛita, mfn. brought together, collected, assembled, accumulated, concentrated, RV. &c. &c.; provided, stored, laden, filled, covered, furnished or endowed with, possessed of (instr. or comp.), AV. &c. &c.; carried, borne (in the womb), MBh.; well maintained or nourished, RV.; R.; honoured, respected, BhP.; produced, effected, caused, made, prepared, ŚBr.; Kālid.; Suśr.; loud, shrill (as a sound), MBh. vii, 3911; *-kratu*, mfn. one in whom all knowledge is concentrated, intelligent, wise (said of Indra), RV.; *-tama*, mfn. fully concentrated, ŚāṅkhŚr.; *-bala*, mfn. one who has assembled an army, Rājat.; *-śrī* (*sám°*), mfn. one in whom all beauty is concentrated, lovely, charming, AV.; Megh.; *-śruta*, mfn. possessed of knowledge, learned, wise, Rājat.; *-sambhāra* (*sám°*), mfn. one who has brought together all requisite materials, quite ready or prepared for anything, TS.; MBh.; BhP.; *-sneha*, mfn. full of love for (loc.), Megh.; °*tâṅga* (*sám°*), mfn. one whose body is well nourished or fed, TBr.; (ifc.) one whose limbs are covered with, MBh. (B. *sam-vṛit°*); °*târtha*, mfn. one who has accumulated wealth, Ragh.; °*tâśva* (*sám°*), mfn. one who has well-fed horses, RV.; °*taushadha*, mfn. one who has collected many drugs, MBh. °**bhṛiti**, f. collection, L.; equipment, preparation, provision, ĀpŚr.; Kathās.; multitude, Harav.; plenitude, fulness, W.; complete maintenance, support, nourishment, ib. °**bhṛitya**, mfn. to be collected or arranged or prepared, TS.; TBr.; to be maintained or nourished, W. °**bhṛitvan**, mfn. collecting, accumulating, AV.

सम्भृष्ट *sam-bhṛishṭa*, mfn. (√*bhrajj*) thoroughly fried or roasted, parched, dried, dry, brittle, Suśr.

सम्भ्रंश् *sam-√bhraṅś* (or *bhraś*, only 3. sg. Pot. Ā. *-bhraśyeta*), to fall quite away, slip off, ŚāṅkhŚr.

सम्भ्रम् *sam-√bhram*, P. *-bhramati* or *-bhrāmyati*, to roam or wander all about, go quite astray, Kathās.; to be greatly confused, be perplexed or puzzled, MBh.; Kāv. &c.: Caus. *-bhrāmayati*, to lead astray, perplex, bewilder &c.: (only in) Pass. *-bhrāmyate*, to be perplexed about, despair of (abl.), MBh.

Sam-bhrama, m. (ifc. f. *ā*) whirling round, haste, hurry, flurry, confusion, agitation, bustling; activity, eagerness, zeal (*āt* and *ena*, 'excitedly, hurriedly;' acc. with √*kṛi* or √*gam*, and dat., 'to get into a flurry about, show great eagerness or zeal;' with √*tyaj* or *vi-√muc*, 'to compose one's self'), MBh.; Kāv. &c.; awe, deference, respect, Kāv.; Kathās.; error, mistake, delusion (ifc. = 'feigning or seeming to be'), Rājat.; Kathās.; grace, beauty (v.l. for *vi-bhrama*), Bhartṛ.; N. of a class of beings attending on Śiva, Cat.; mfn. agitated, excited, rolling about (as the eyes), BhP.; *-jvalita*, mfn. excited by flurry, MW.; *-bhṛit*, mfn. possessing bewilderment, embarrassed, agitated, ib.

Sam-bhrānta, mfn. whirled about, flurried, confused, perplexed, agitated, excited, MBh.; Kāv. &c.; quickened, brisk, lively (gait), R.; *-jana*, mfn. one whose people are bewildered, MW.; *-manas*, mfn. bewildered in mind, MBh. °**bhrānti**, f. agitation, bewilderment, Sāh.

सम्भ्राज् *sam-√bhrāj* (only pr. p. P. *-bhrājat*), to shine brightly, sparkle, BhP.

सम्मग्न *sam-magna*, mfn. (√*majj*) sunk down, immersed in or overwhelmed by (comp.), MBh.; R.

सम्मथ् *sam-√math* (or *manth*; only Pass. *-mathyate*), to bruise or pound together, crush to pieces, MBh.

Sam-mathita, mfn. bruised, pounded, dashed to pieces, destroyed, ib.

सम्मद् *sam-√mad*, P. Ā. *-madati*, °*te*, to rejoice together, rejoice with (instr.), RV.; to rejoice at, delight in (instr.), ib.; VS.: Caus. *-madayati*, °*te*, to intoxicate, exhilarate, AitBr.; (Ā.) to be completely intoxicated or exhilarated, AV.; AitBr.

Sam-matta, mfn. completely intoxicated (lit. and fig.), exhilarated, enraptured, enamoured, MBh.; Hariv.; rutting, in rut, ib.

Sam-mad, f. (used to explain *samád*), Nir. ix, 17. °**mada**, m. exhilaration, happiness, joy, delight at (comp.), Hariv.; Kathās.; Sāh.; N. of a Ṛishi, Br.; of a king of the fish, VP.; mfn. = next, W.; *-maya*, mf(*ī*)n. greatly exhilarated, happy, glad, Kathās.; *-vat*, mfn. 'being together in rut or sexual passion,' and 'feeling delight,' Bālar. °**madin**, mfn. gladdening, exhilarating, Bhām.

Sam-māda, m. great exhilaration, intoxication, frenzy, L.

सम्मन् *sam-√man*, Ā. *-manyate* (ep. also P. °*ti*), to think together, agree, assent to, approve (see *sam-mata* below); to think, fancy, MBh.; to regard or consider as (acc. or two acc.), ib. &c.; to mean, contemplate, intend, resolve, R.; to think highly of, esteem, value, honour, MBh.; R.: Caus. *-mānayati*, to honour, reverence, respect, Yājñ.; MBh. &c.; to regard, consider, Bhaṭṭ.; to assure any one (gen.) of (acc.), MārkP.: Desid. of Caus., see *sam-mimānayishu* below.

Sam-mata, mfn. thinking together, being of the same opinion, agreed, consented or assented to, concurred in, approved by (gen. or comp.), MBh.; Kāv. &c.; (ifc.) agreeing with, BhP.; thought, supposed, considered or regarded as (nom.), R.; thought highly of, esteemed, renowned, celebrated, highly honoured by (gen.), Mn.; MBh. &c.; allowed, authorized (see *a-sammata*); m. N. of a son of Manu Sāvarṇa, Hariv.; (pl.) of a school, Buddh.; (*ā*), f. N. of a daughter of Marutta, Hariv.; of a treatise on the Dhātu-pāṭha; (*am*), n. opinion, impression (*e* or *ena* with gen., 'in the opinion of,' 'under the idea of'), MBh.; consent, assent, approval, acquiescence, concurrence (*e*, 'with the consent or approval of'), MW. °**mati**, f. sameness of opinion, harmony, agreement, approval, approbation, ĀśvŚr.; Prab.; Hit.; opinion, view, Siddh.; respect, homage, R.; Kir.; wish, desire, L.; self-knowledge, L.; regard, affection, love, W.; order, command, ib.; N. of a river, VP.; mfn. being of the same opinion, agreeing, g. *dṛiḍhādi* (*-man*, m., ib.); m. N. of a son of Harsha, VP. °**matīya**, m. N. of one of the four divisions of the Vaibhāshika system of Buddhism (said to have been founded by Upāli, a disciple of Gautama Buddha), MWB. 157, n. 1 &c.

Sám-manas, mfn. unanimous, AV.; ŚBr. °**manìman**, m. unanimousness, harmony, g. *dṛiḍhādi*. °**mantavya**, mfn. to be highly valued, MBh.

1. **Sam-māna**, m. or (accord. to some) n. (for 2. see col. 2) honour, respect, homage, MBh.; Kāv. &c.; *-kara*, mfn. doing honour, honouring, RPrāt. °**mānana**, n. (or *ā*, f.; fr. Caus.) the act of honouring, worshipping, homage, Nir.; Pāṇ.; MBh. &c. °**mānanīya**, mfn. (fr. id.) to be honoured or respected, BhP. °**mānita**, mfn. (fr. id.) honoured, treated with reverence or respect, Kāv.; Kathās.; *-vimānita*, mfn. (first) honoured and (then) disgraced, Ml. °**mānin**, mfn. having a sense of honour, Kāv. °**mānya**, mfn. to be (or being) highly honoured by (gen.), R.

Sam-mimānayishu, mfn. (fr. Desid. of Caus.) wishing to honour or revere, MBh.

सम्मन्त्र् *sam-√mantr*, P. *-mantrayati* (ind. p. *-mantrya* or *-mantrayitvā*), to consult together, take council with (instr. with or without *saha* or *samam*), MBh.; R. &c.; to hold a council, deliberate, advise, express an opinion, R.; to salute, greet, address, MBh.

Sam-mantraṇīya, mfn. to be consulted, MW.; to be saluted, MBh.

Sam-mantrita, mfn. deliberated, considered, Kathās.

सम्मन्द् *sam-√mand*, Ā. *-mandate*, to rejoice at, delight in (instr.), RV. viii, 12, 16; (aor. *-amandishuḥ*), to intoxicate, exhilarate, ib. 52, 10.

सम्मय *sam-maya*, °*yana*. See *sam-√1. mi.*

सम्मर्द *sam-marda*, °*dana* &c. See *sam-√mṛid*, p. 1181, col. 1.

सम्मर्शन *sam-marśana*, °*śin*. See *sam-√mṛiś*, p. 1181, col. 1.

सम्मर्ष *sam-marsha*, m. = *marsha*, patience, endurance, BhP.

सम्महस् *sam-mahas*, n. (prob.) common or mutual joy (see *mahas*), ŚrS.

सम्मा *sam-√3. mā*, P. Ā. *-māti*, *-mimīte*, to measure out, measure, RV. &c. &c.; to make of the same measure, make equal, equalize (in size, number, quantity &c.), AV.; TS.; ŚBr.; to compare with (instr.), BhP.; to mete out, distribute, bestow, RV. iii, 1, 15; v, 4, 2; (with *śrávāṅsi*) to direct one's course or flight towards, ib. iii, 34, 22; to be of the same capacity with, be contained in (loc.), Kuval.: Pass. *-mīyate*, to be of the same measure, be contained in (loc.), Nīlak.

Sam-mā, f. equality in size or number, symmetry, AitBr.; PañcavBr.; a kind of metre, RPrāt.

1. **Sam-mātṛi**, mfn. (for 2. see below) one who measures &c., Pat. on Pāṇ. iv, 1, 115.

2. **Sam-māna**, n. (for 1. see *sam-√man*) the act of measuring out, equalizing, comparing, MW.; measure, ib.

Sám-mita, mfn. measured out, measured, meted, BhP.; measuring so much, just so much (no more nor less), MBh.; BhP.; of the same measure or extent, equal, like, same (in length, height, number, value &c.), corresponding to, resembling, passing for (instr., rarely gen.; or comp.), AV. &c. &c.; reaching up to (comp.), ŚBr.; ĀśvŚr.; symmetrical (?), Pañcar.; consisting of, furnished or provided with (instr. or comp.), MBh.; Pañcar.; destined for (comp.), MBh. v, 2462 (B. *saṃdhita*); (*am*), ind. perpetually, incessantly, Kāraṇḍ. (prob. w.r. for *samitam*); m. N. of a mythical being, Yājñ.; of a son of Vasishṭha, VP.; (*am*), n. distance (*e*, ifc. = 'at a distance from'), VarBṛS.; *-tva*, n. (in rhet.) universal analogy, Pratāp.; *-varṇā*, f. N. of a Commentary. °**miti**, f. equalization, comparison, Pāṇ. iv, 4, 35 (v.l. *sam-iti*).

सम्मातुर *sammātura*, w.r. for *sāmmātura*, q.v.

सम्मातृ 2. *sam-mātṛí* or *sám-mātṛi*, mfn. (for 1. see above) having the same mother, twin, RV.; AV.; Kāṭh.

सम्मान 1. 2. *sam-māna*. See *sam-√man* and *sam-√3. mā*, col. 1.

सम्मार्ग *sam-mārga*, *sam-mārjaka* &c. See *sam-√mṛij*, p. 1181, col. 1.

सम्मि *sam-√1. mi*, P. Ā. *-minoti*, *-minute*, to fasten at the same time or together, fix, erect, TS.; ŚBr.; ŚāṅkhGṛ.

Sam-maya, m. (of unknown meaning), Vop. xxvi, 171 (v.l.). °**mayana** (*sám-*), n. erection of a sacrificial post, ŚBr.

सम्मिक्ष् *sam-√1. miksh* (or *-mimiksh*; cf. √1. *miksh*; only Impv. *-mimikshvá* and 2. du. pf. *-mimikshátḥuḥ*, but accord. to some referable to *sam-√1. mih*, q.v.), to mix with, furnish or endow with (instr.), RV. i, 48, 16; to prepare (an oblation), ib. viii, 10, 2.

सम्मित *sam-mita* &c. See above.

सम्मिमर्दिषु *sam-mimardishu*. See *sam-√mṛid*, p. 1181, col. 1.

सम्मिमानयिषु *sam-mimānayishu*. See *sam-√man*, col. 1.

सम्मिल् *sam-√mil*, P. Ā. *-milati*, °*te*, to meet or assemble together, be present, associate with, Kathās.

Sam-milita, mfn. met together, assembled, collected, ib.; Pañcat.

Sam-melana, n. mingling or meeting together, mixture, union, Uttarar.; Sāh.

सम्मिश्र *sam-miśra*, mf(*ā*)n. commingled, mixed together, joined, connected, furnished or endowed with (instr. or comp.), MBh.; R. &c. °**miśraṇa**, n. the act of commingling or mixing together, Kull. on Mn. vii, 193. °**miśrita**, mfn. mixed together, mingled, intermixed with (instr.), MBh.

Sám-miśla, mf(*ā*)n. = *sam-miśra* above, RV.; m. 'universal mingler,' N. of Indra, MBh.

सम्मिह् *sam-√mih*. See *sam-√1. miksh* and √1. *miksh*, √1. *mih*.

सम्मील् *sam-√mīl*, P. *-mīlati*, to shut the eyes, RV.; Br.; GṛŚrS.; to close up (as a flower), Śak.; Suśr.: Caus. *-mīlayati* (with or without *netre*), to close the eyes, Kālid.; Kathās.; Suśr.; to cause to close the eyes, i.e. make insensible, kill, Uttarar.; Sāh.

Sam-mīlana, n. closing (of a flower, of the eyes &c.), Suśr.; cessation of activity, Daśar.; covering up, obscuring, a total eclipse, Sūryas. °**mīlita** (*sám-*), mfn. one who has closed the eyes, TS.; closed (as eyes &c.), asleep (opp. to *vi-buddha*, 'awake'), Suśr.; Ragh.; *-druma*, m. a Punarnavā with red flowers, L. 1. °**mīlya**, ind. having closed or shut or covered, RV. &c. &c. 2. °**mīlya**, n. N. of a Sāman, Br.

सम्मुख *sam-mukhá*, mf(*ī*, rarely *ā*)n. facing, fronting, confronting, being face to face or in front of or opposite to (gen. or ifc. or ibc.), present, before the eyes, ŚBr. &c. &c.; being about to begin or at the beginning of (comp.), Hariv.; directed or turned towards, ŚBr.; KātyŚr.; inclined or favourable to (gen. or comp.), propitious, Kāv.; Kathās.; Pañcat.; intent upon (loc. or comp.), Śatr.; Kathās.; adapted to circumstances, fit, suitable, Lalit.; with the mouth or face, ĀpŚr.; (*am*), ind. towards, near to (*atmanaḥ*, 'one's self'); opposite, in front or in presence of (gen.), MBh.; Kāv. &c.; (*e*), ind. opposite, before, face to face, in front or in presence or in the beginning of (gen. or comp.; with √*bhū*, 'to oppose, resist;' with √*sthā*, 'to look any one in the face'), ib. **-vinaya**, m. (prob.) reproving any one face to face (i.e. when he is alone and no one else present), Mahāvy.

Sam-mukhaya, Nom. P. °*yati*, to aim at (loc.), Bhām.

Sam-mukhin, m. a looking-glass, mirror, L.

Sammukhī, in comp. for °*kha*. **-√kṛi**, P. *-karoti*, to place facing, make one's chief aim (°*khī-kṛita*, mfn. 'aimed at'), Rāghav. **-√bhū**, P. *-bhavati*, to be or stand face to face or opposite, be opposed to, Bālar.

Sammukhīna, mf(*ā*)n. facing, confronting, opposite, Bhaṭṭ.; Hcar. &c.; propitious, favourable to (gen.), Ragh.; *-tva*, n. the being in front, Kull. on Mn. iv, 52; presence, Sāh.

सम्मुच् *sam-√muc*, P. *-muñcati*, to let loose together, pour out, discharge, shed (tears), MBh.: Caus. *-mocayati*, see next.

Sam-mocita, mfn. (fr. Caus.) set free, liberated, released, Ragh.

सम्मुद् *sam-√mud* (only in pr. p. *-modamāna*, q.v.)

Sam-múd, f. joy, delight (cf. *svādu-s°*), AV.

Sam-moda, m. id., L.; odour, fragrance, MBh. (v.l.); *-gandha*, m. id., Jātakam. °**modana**, mf(*ī*)n. friendly, kind (°*nī-kathā*, f. 'complimentary talk'), Divyâv. °**modanīya** (Mahāvy.), °**modamāna** (Divyâv.), mfn. friendly, ib. °**modika**, m. a kind or friendly person, comrade, companion, SaddhP.

सम्मुर्छ् *sam-√murch* (or *-mūrch*), P. *-mūrchati*, to congeal into a fixed form, become dense, thicken, coagulate, Kāv.; VarBṛS.; Suśr.; to become stupid or senseless (see *-mūrchita*); to acquire consistency or firmness or strength, increase, expand, become powerful, make a loud sound, Ragh.: Caus. *-mūrchayati*, to cause to assume consistency, form, fashion (see *-mūrchita-vat*); to stupefy, cause to faint, Uttarar.

Sam-mūrcha, m. (prob.) thickening, augmenting, increase, expansion, spreading, L.; *-ja*, m. grass or any gramineous plant, ib. °**mūrchana**, n. the act of congealing or thickening, increasing, spreading, accumulating, Kaṇ.; stupefaction, insensibility, fainting away, L.; height, elevation, W.; °*nódbhava*, m. a fish or other aquatic animal, L. °**mūrchita**, mfn. coagulated, congealed, thickened, strengthened, intensified (ifc. = 'filled with'), R.; Suśr.; stupefied, senseless, unconscious, MBh.; R.; reflected (as rays), VarBṛS.; modulated (as tone), Bhar.; *-vat*, mfn. one who has (or = he has) formed or shaped, Śaṃk.

सम्मुष् *sam-√mush*, P. *-mushṇāti*, to steal, rob, take away, Hariv.

सम्मुह् *sam-√muh*, P. *-muhyati* (pf. *-mumoha* or *-mumuhe*), to become quite stupefied or bewildered or unconscious, MBh.; R.; BhP.; to become confused or unrecognizable (as the quarters of the sky), MBh.: Caus. *-mohayati*, to stupefy, make unconscious, perplex, bewilder, lead astray, MBh.; Kāv. &c.

Sam-mugdha, mfn. gone astray (see *a-s°*); perplexed, bewildered, stupefied, Uttarar.; not clearly understood, Nīlak.; (*am*), ind. furtively, Git.

Sam-mūḍha, mfn. completely stupefied, astounded, perplexed, bewildered, unconscious, senseless, MBh.; Kāv. &c.; foolish, ignorant, Yājñ.; Rājat.; heaped, accumulated (as clouds; accord. to others, 'torn asunder'), Hariv.; produced rapidly, W.; broken, ib.; (*ā*), f. a kind of riddle or enigma, Cat.; (°*ḍha*)-*cetas*, mfn. troubled or infatuated in mind, Śāntiś.; -*tā*, f. (Kathās.), -*tva*, n. (MaitrUp.) stupefaction, infatuation, bewilderment, unconsciousness; -*piḍakā*, f. N. of partic. eruptions on the membrum virile, Suśr.; -*hṛidaya*, mfn. troubled in heart, MW.

Sam-mohá, m. stupefaction, bewilderment, confusion, insensibility, unconsciousness, ignorance, folly, illusion of mind (also with *manasaḥ; manaḥ-, mati-, citta-s°* &c.), ŚBr. &c. &c.; tumult, battle (= *saṃgrāma*), Naigh. ii, 17; (in astrol.) a partic. conjunction of planets, VarBṛS.; (*ā*), f. a kind of metre, Col.; (°*ha*)-*maulin*, mfn. having illusion for a diadem, MaitrUp. °**mohaka**, mfn. (fr. Caus.) stupefying, infatuating, bewitching, fascinating, MBh. °**mohana**, mf(*ī*)n. (fr. Caus.) id., MBh.; Hariv. &c.; m. N. of one of the five arrows of Kāma-deva, Kum.; Gīt., Sch. (cf. RTL. 200); (*ī*), f. a kind of fascination or illusion (*māyā*), Hariv.; n. deluding, infatuating, leading astray, MārkP.; a kind of mythical weapon, MBh.; Ragh.; Kathās.; -*tantra*, n. N. of a Tantra. °**mohita**, mfn. (fr. id.) stupefied, bewildered, fascinated, enraptured, R.; Gīt.; BhP.

सम्मूत्रण *sam-mūtraṇa*, n. making water upon (comp.), VarBṛS.

सम्मृज् *sam-√mṛij*, P. -*mṛijati*, -*mārshṭi*, -*mārjati*, -*mārjayati* (cf. √*mārj*), to sweep together, sweep clean, rub or wipe off, cleanse, strain, filter (Soma), purify (fire by removing ashes), RV. &c. &c.; to take away, remove, Rājat.; to stroke, caress, R.

Sam-mārga, m. wiping off, cleansing, Kum.; TBr., Sch.; a wisp of grass (for tying faggots together), ŚrS.

Sam-mārjaka, mfn. sweeping, cleansing, a sweeper, Kull. on Mn. vii, 126; = *bahu-dhānyârjaka*, L.; m. a broom, L. °**mārjana**, n. the act of sweeping or cleansing thoroughly, cleansing, scouring, purifying, brushing, ŚrS.; Mn.; MBh. &c.; the anointing and washing (of images &c.), MW.; a wisp (or bunch of Darbha grass for purifying ladles &c.), TBr.; KātyŚr.; remains of food wiped off from dishes &c., MārkP.; a wisp or broom (made of tough grass and stalks), Saṃskārak.; Kull. °**mārjita**, mfn. well swept or scoured, MBh.; Hariv.; removed, destroyed, Rājat.

Sam-mārshṭi, f. cleansing, purification, L.

Sam-mṛishṭa, mfn. well swept or scoured, cleaned, cleansed, ŚBr. &c. &c.; strained, filtered, L.

सम्मृण् *sam-√mṛiṇ*, P. -*mṛiṇati*, to kill, slay, destroy, RV.; Kāṭh.

सम्मृत *sam-mṛita*, mfn. quite dead, W.

सम्मृद् *sam-√mṛid*, P. -*mṛidnāti*, -*mardati* (Ved. inf. -*marditoḥ*), to press or squeeze together, rub or grind to pieces, crush, destroy, TS.: Caus. -*mardayati* (pr. p. -*mardayāna*), to cause to be rubbed together, crush, pound, bruise, R.; BhP.; to rub, Suśr.; to clean, MW.

Sam-marda, m. pressing or rubbing together, friction, pressure, Pratāp.; trampling, MBh.; R. &c.; impact (of waves), Rājat.; meeting, encounter (esp. with enemies), war, battle, MBh.; Kāv. &c. °**mardana**, m. N. of a son of Vasu-deva, BhP.; of a king of the Vidyā-dharas, Kathās.; n. rubbing, friction, Siṇhās. °**mardin**, mfn. pressing thoroughly, rubbing, crushing, Bhaṭṭ.

Sam-mimardishu, mfn. about to crush, MBh.

सम्मृश् *sam-√mṛiś*, P. Ā. -*mṛiśati*, °*te*, to take hold of, seize, grasp, touch, graze, stroke (Ā. 'each other'), ŚBr.; GṛŚrS.; to touch mentally, judge (see below).

Sam-márśana, n. stroking, ŚBr.; ŚrS. °**marśin**, mfn. able to judge, TUp.

सम्मेघ *sam-megha*, m. the cloudy season, TāṇḍBr.

सम्मेत *sammeta*, m. (cf. *samêta* and next) N. of a mountain, Śatr.

सम्मेद *sammeda*, m. N. of a mountain (-*māhātmya*, n. N. of wk.), Cat.

सम्मेलन *sam-melana*. See *sam-√mil.*

सम्मोक्ष् *sam-√moksh*, P. -*mokshayati*, to set quite free, liberate, MBh.

सम्मोद *sam-moda*, °*dana* &c. See *sam-√mud*, p. 1180, col. 3.

सम्मोह *sam-moha*, °*haka*, °*hana* &c. See col. 1.

सम्म्यक्ष् *sam-√myaksh* (only 3. pl. pf. -*mimikshuḥ* and -*mimikshire*), to be held together or united or associated, dwell together, RV.

सम्म्रक्षित *sam-mrakshita*, mfn. (√*mraksh*) rubbed in, anointed, Suśr.

सम्यञ्च् *samy-áñc*, mfn. (fr. *samī́* = 2. *sam* + 2. *añc*, cf. Pāṇ. vi, 3, 93; nom. *samyáṅ*, *samī́cī* or *samīcī*, *samyák*) going along with or together, turned together or in one direction, combined, united (acc. with √*dhā*, 'to unite or provide with' [acc. or dat. of pers. and instr. or acc. of thing]), entire, whole, complete, all (*samyañcaḥ sarve*, 'all together'), RV.; Br.; ŚāṅkhŚr.; turned towards each other, facing one another, RV.; VS.; Br.; lying in one direction, forming one line (as footsteps), ŚBr.; correct, accurate, proper, true, right, BhP.; uniform, same, identical, W.; pleasant, agreeable, ib.; (*īcī*), f. praise, eulogy, L.; a doe, Uṇ. iv, 92, Sch.; N. of a divine female, TBr.; of an Apsaras, MBh.; Hariv.; (*ák*), ind. in one or the same direction, in the same way, at the same time, together (with √*sthā*, 'to associate with'), RV.; MBh.; in one line, straight (opp. to *akshṇayā*, 'obliquely'), ŚBr.; KātyŚr.; completely, wholly, thoroughly, by all means (with *na*, 'by no means, not at all'), Mn.; MBh. &c.; correctly, truly, properly, fitly, in the right way or manner, well, duly (with √*kṛi*, 'to make good [a promise]'), Up.; Mn.; MBh. &c.; distinctly, clearly, MW.

Samīká, n. hostile encounter, conflict, fight, RV.; (sometimes written *śamīka*) N. of a Ṛishi, MBh.; Hariv.; Pur.; of a son of Śūra, ib.

Samīca, m. the sea, ocean, Uṇ. iv, 92, Sch.; (*ī*), f., see *samy-áñc* above.

Samīcaka, m. sexual union, copulation, W.

Samīcīná, mf(*ā*)n. tending in a common direction, going with or in company with, being or remaining together, connected, united, complete, all, whole, RV.; TS.; fit, proper, correct, true, just, right, KaushUp.; Pañcat.; BhP.; n. N. of a Sāman, ĀrshBr.; = next, W. — **tā**, f. (Rāghav.), -**tva**, n. (Nilak.), propriety, fitness, truth.

Samyak, in comp. for *samyañc*. — **karmânta**, m. (with Buddhists) right action or occupation (one division of the *āryâshṭâṅga-mārga*, 'holy eightfold path;' the other 7 are given below), Lalit.; Dharmas. 50; MWB. 44 &c. — **kārin**, see *a-s°*. — **cāritra**, n. (with Jainas) r° conduct (see *ratna-traya*). — **tā**, f. rightness, correct manner, Prab., Sch. — **tva**, n. id., MBh.; completeness, perfection, Śatr. (*kshāyika-s°*, 'that perfection in which material existence is destroyed,' W.); -*kaumudī*, f., -*prakāśa*, m.; °*tvâdhyayana* or °*dhyāpana*, n. N. of wks.; -*mithyā-tva-sarva-saṃgrasana*, m. a partic. Samādhi, Buddh. — **pāṭha**, m. r° pronunciation, VPrāt. — **pālana**, n. r° or due protection, Ratnâv. — **praṇidhāna**, n. true or profound meditation (as leading to Arhatship), Divyâv. — **prayoga**, m. r° use or employment, due practice (*ena*, 'by the use of proper means'), MBh.; Kum.; Car. — **pravṛitti**, f. r° action or function (of the senses), Col. — **prahāṇa**, n. (= Pāli *sammappadhāna*) right abandonment, r° effort, r° exertion (with Buddhists of four kinds, 1. to prevent demerit from arising; 2. get rid of it when arisen, 3. produce merit, 4. increase it), Divyâv.; Dharmas. 45; MWB. 50. — **śraddhāna**, n. (with Jainas) r° belief, Sarvad. — **saṃkalpa**, m. (with Buddh.) r° resolve. — **sattva**, n. N. of a Commentary. — **satya**, m. N. of a man, Buddh. — **samādhi**, m. right meditation (with Buddh.) — **sambuddha**, mfn. one who has attained to complete enlightenment (said of the Buddha), Kāraṇḍ. — **sambuddhi**, f., -**sambodha**, m. and °**dhi**, f. complete enlightenment, ib. — **sthiti**, f. remaining together, BhP., Sch. — **smṛiti**, f. (with Buddh.) right recollection.

Samyag, in comp. for *samyañc*. — **avabodha**, m. right understanding, Pāṇ. i, 3, 47, Sch. — **ājīva**, m. r° living. — **ājñā**, f. = -*avabodha*, Mahāv. — **ukta**, mfn. properly or accurately said, said in the same way, MW. — **gata**, mfn. behaving r°ly, holy, Divyâv. °**gamana**, n. the act of going with, accompanying, MW. — **guṇa**, n. r° or true virtue, Vet. — **goptṛi**, m. a true protector or guardian, MW. — **ghuta** (for -*huta*), mfn. properly kindled (fire), Ragh. — **jñāna**, n. r° knowledge (see *ratna-traya*); -*tva*, n., Śaṃk. — **dagdha**, n. (in surgery) r° burning or cauterizing, Suśr. — **daṇḍana**, n. the act of punishing rightly or legally, W. — **darśana**, n. right perception or insight (see *ratna-traya*); mf(*ā*)n. = next, BhP.; -*sampanna*, mfn. possessed of true insight, Mn. vi, 74. — **darśin** (Śaṃk.), -**dṛiś** (Cat.), mfn. id. — **dṛishṭi**, f. r° insight or belief (with Buddh.), Lalit.; mfn. possessed of r° belief, orthodox (-*tva*, n.), HPariś.; Divyâv. — **bodha**, m. right understanding, Pāṇ. i, 3, 47, Sch. — **yoga**, m. a true Yoga, MaitrUp.; BhP. — **varṇa-prayoga**, m. 'right use of sounds,' correct pronunciation, Śiksh. — **vartamāna**, mfn. continuing in the r° discharge of duty, W. — **vāc**, f. r° speech (with Buddh.) — **vānta**, mfn. that has well vomited (as a leech), Suśr. — **vijayin**, mfn. completely victorious, MBh. — **vṛitta**, mfn. well-conducted, MW.; wholly confiding in, ib. — **vṛitti**, f. regular or complete performance, right discharge of duties, MBh. — **vyavasita**, mfn. firmly resolved, Bhag. — **vyāyāma**, m. right exertion (with Buddhists).

Samyaṅ, in comp. for *samyañc*. — **mati**, f. correct opinion, Śaṃk.

सम्राज् *sam-rā́j*, m. (fr. *saṃ-√rāj*, Pāṇ. viii, 3, 25; nom. *samrā́ṭ*) a universal or supreme ruler (a N. of Varuṇa, the Ādityas, Indra, Manu &c.), RV.; VS.; ŚBr.; VP.; a sovereign lord, paramount sovereign (of men); one who rules over other princes and has performed the Rājasūya sacrifice, RV. &c. &c.; N. of a son or grandson of Kāmyā, Hariv.; of a son of Citra-ratha, BhP.; of various authors, Cat.; a kind of metre, RPrāt.; a partic. Ekâha, Vait.; (-*rāj*), f. N. of a daughter of Priya-vrata, VP.

Samrāja, Nom. P. (fr. prec.; cf. *saṃ-√rāj*) °*jati* (only pr. p. °*jat*), to reign over, rule (gen.), RV. i, 27, 1.

Samrājñī, f. a queen or any woman or mistress who is superior in rank, RV.; AV.; TBr.

Samrāṭ, in comp. for *samrāj*. — **siddhânta**, m. N. of wk.

Samrāḍ, in comp. for *samrāj*. — **āsandí**, f. a chair or stool used for the Pravargya-gharma (q.v.), ŚBr.; ŚrS. — **dúghā**, f. the cow that gives milk for the Pravargya, ŚBr. — **yantra**, n. N. of wk.

सय् *say*, cl. 1. Ā. *sayate*, to go, Dhātup. xiv, 8.

सय 1. *saya* (fr. *si*), only in the following. — **tvá**, n. binding, fastening, TS.; TBr.; Kāṭh.

Sayana, n. binding, Nir.; m. N. of a son of Viśvāmitra, MBh. (B. *seyana*).

सय 2. *sa-ya*, mfn. (i.e. 7. *sa* + *ya*) with the sound or letter *ya*, RPrāt.

Sa (to be similarly prefixed to the following): — **yakshman**, mfn. having consumption, suffering from c°, consumptive, MBh. — **yajña-pātra**, mfn. together with sacrificial vessels, Hcat. — **yati**, mfn. having a cæsura, with a cæsura, Ked. — **yatna**, mfn. making efforts, taking pains with, endeavouring to (inf.; *am*, ind. 'with effort'), Hit. — **yantra**, mfn. with or possessing machines, MW.; -*jala-śaila*, mfn. having engines and water and a rock, ib. — **yantrika**, mfn. together with a charioteer, KātyŚr. — **yava**, mfn. together with barley, Kauś. — **ya-va**, mfn. containing the sounds *ya* or *va*, VPrāt. — **yāvaka**, mfn. dyed with lac, Kir. — **yā́van**, mf(*arī*)n. going along with, associated with (instr.), accompanying, RV. — **yuktvá**, n. (fr. *sa-yuj*) the being united, ŚBr. — **yúgvan**, mfn. (fr. id.) united or associated with, a companion of (gen.), ib.; having a team of horses, ChUp. — **yúj**, mfn. united, a companion, comrade, RV.; AV.; Br.; ŚrS.; f. N. of partic. bricks, TS. — **yujya**, mfn. (fr. prec.) closely united with, MW.; -*tā*, f. intimate union or junction, ib. — **yudhi-shṭhira**, mfn. with or accompanied by Yudhi-shṭhira, MW. — **yūthya** (*sá-*), mfn. (cf. Pāṇ. iv, 4, 114) belonging to the same herd or tribe, VS.; AitBr. — **yoga**, mfn. possessed of Yoga, Ragh.; m. (m. c.) for *saṃ-yoga*, junction, union (opp. to *viyoga*), BhP.; n. (scil. *guṇa-sthāna*, with Jainas) N. of the last but one of the 14 stages leading to emancipation, Cat. **-yoni** (*sá-*), mfn. having a womb, female, L.; having the same womb, uterine, having a common origin with (instr.), RV.; AV.; connected with the womb or place of origin or birth-place &c., AV.; TS.; m. (only L.) 'one who is from the same womb,' a uterine brother; proximity to a wife (?); a pair of nippers for cutting areca-nut; N. of Indra; *-tā*, f. (AitBr.), *-tvá*, n. (TS.) identity of origin, the having the same birth-place. **-yoshaṇa**, mfn. attended by women, along with the women, MW. **-yauvana**, mfn. possessing youth, youthful, young, Ṛitus.

सर *sará*, mf(*ā*)n. (fr. √*sṛi*) fluid, liquid, VS.; cathartic, purgative, laxative, Suśr.; Vāgbh.; (ifc. f. *ī*, Pāṇ. iii, 2, 18) going, moving &c. (cf. *anu-*, *abhi-*, *puraḥ-s°*); m. going, motion, L.; a cord, string (cf. *prati-*, *maṇi-*, *muktā-maṇi-*, and *maukti-ka-s°*); a short vowel (in prosody), Col.; salt, L.; N. of Vāyu or the wind, L.; a waterfall, L.; often v.l. or w.r. for *śara* (also in comp. *sara-ja* &c. for *śara-ja* &c.); (*ā́*), f. moving or wandering about, Gal.; a brook, AV.; TS.; a cascade, waterfall, L.; Pæderia Fœtida, L.; (*ī*), f. a cascade (cf. *sarī*), L.; n. a lake, pool (also irregularly in comp. for *saras*), Uṇ. iv, 188, Sch.; milk, L. **-tva**, n. fluidity, laxity, the being a purgative, Suśr. **-vatī**, f. N. of the river Vitastā, MW. **Sarôtsava**, m. 'delighting in water,' the Indian crane, L. **Sarôdaka**, n. the water of a pond, Śiś. **Sarôdapāna**, n. pl. ponds and wells, MBh. **Sarôpânta**, n. the neighbourhood of a pond, Pañcat.

Saraḥ, in comp. for *saras*. **-kāka**, m. 'lake-bird,' a gander (*ī*, f. a goose), L. **-priya**, m. 'fond of water,' a partic. aquatic bird (v.l. *sura-pr°*), Hariv.

Saraka, mfn. going, moving, proceeding, L.; m. or n. a drinking vessel, goblet (esp. for spirituous liquors), R.; Suśr.; spirituous liquor (esp. that distilled from sugar), rum, Kathās.; drinking sp° l°, Śiś. xv, 114; distribution of sp° l°, L.; a caravan, L.; (*ikā*), f. a kind of plant (= *hiṅgu-pattrī*), L.; a string of pearls, L.; n. a pearl, jewel, L.; a pond, lake, L.; 'going' or 'the sky' (*gamana* or *gagana*), L.; N. of a Tīrtha, MBh.

Saraṇa, mfn. (for *sa-raṇa* see p. 1183) going, moving, running, GopBr.; m. a kind of tree, Col. (perhaps w.r. for *sarala*); N. of a king, Buddh.; (*ā* or *ī*), f. Pæderia Fœtida, L.; (*ā*), f. a sort of convolvulus, L.; n. running, quick motion (with *ājeḥ*, 'a foot-race,' 'running-match'), GṛŚrS.; ChUp.; MBh.; moving from one place to another, locomotion, VarBṛS.; running after, following, R.; iron rust or filings, L. **-jīvin**, mfn. living by running, ĀśvGṛ. **-deva**, m. N. of a grammarian, Col.

Saraṇi, f. a road, path, way (also *°ṇī*), Bhartṛ.; Daś.; a strait or continuous line, L.; a disease of the throat, L.

Saraṇya, Nom. P. *°yáti*, to run, hasten, speed, RV.

Saraṇyú, mfn. quick, fleet, nimble, RV.; m. (only L.) wind; a cloud; water; spring; (*ū́*), f. N. of a daughter of Tvashṭṛi (in RV. represented as the wife of Vivasvat and mother of the two Aśvins, and, accord. to some, of the twins Yama and Yamī, whom she brought forth in the form of a mare; accord. to some also N. of the Dawn), RV. x, 17, 2; cf. Naigh. v, 6; Nir. xii, 9. [Cf., accord. to some, Gk. Ἐριννύς.]

Sarat, mfn. going, flowing, proceeding &c. (see √*sṛi*); m. a thread, L.

Sárapas, (prob.) n. flowing water, RV. ii, 13, 12.

Sarámā, f. 'the fleet one,' N. of a female dog belonging to Indra and the gods (represented in RV. x, 14, 10 as the mother of the four-eyed brindled dogs of Yama [cf. IW. 470], and called in MBh. i, 671 *deva-śunī*; in the RV. said to have gone in search of and recovered the cows stolen by the Paṇis; elsewhere regarded as the mother of beasts of prey; Saramā Deva-śunī is also said to be the authoress of part of RV. x, 108), RV.; PārGṛ.; MBh. &c.; a female dog in general, bitch, L.; N. of a Rākshasī, R.; of a daughter of the Gandharva king Śailūsha and wife of Vibhīshaṇa, ib.; of a wife of Kaśyapa, VahniP. **-°tmaja** (*°mâtm°*), m. 'son of Saramā,' a dog, VarBṛS. **-putra** and **-suta**, m. id., Subh.

Saraya, Nom. Ā. *°ráyate*, to begin to flow, RV. iv, 17, 2.

Saráyu, m. air, wind, L.; f. N. of a well-known river (commonly called Surjoo; on which stood the ancient city Ayodhyā [cf. R. i, 5; 6]; it is a tributary of the Gogra [see *gharghara*], and in RV. is mentioned along with the rivers Sarasvatī, Sindhu, Gaṅgā, Yamunā, and Śutudri).

Sarayū, f. later N. of the river Sarayu (above), MBh.; Kāv. &c. **-taṭa**, m. n. the bank of the Sarayu, Ragh.; N. of a place, Cat. **-vana**, n. a forest on the river Sarayu, MW.

Sararūka (used in explaining *salalūka*), Nir. vi, 3.

Sarala, mf(*ā*)n. 'running on,' straight (not 'crooked'), Kāv.; Rājat.; outstretched, Kathās.; Rājat.; right, correct, Prasaṅg.; TPrāt., Sch.; upright, sincere, candid, honest, artless, simple, Kāv.; Kathās.; Rājat.; real (not 'sham'), Bālar.; = *vigīta*, L.; m. a species of pine tree, Pinus Longifolia, MBh.; Kāv. &c.; a kind of bird, Pavo Bicalcaratus, L.; fire, L.; a Buddha, L.; (*ā*), f. the above pine, Bhpr.; Ipomœa Turpethum, L.; N. of a river, L.; (*am*), n. resin of the pine, R.; Suśr.; a partic. high number, Buddh. **-kāshṭha**, n. the wood of the pine, MW. **-tā**, f. uprightness, honestly, simplicity, Prasannar. **-tva**, n. straightness, Cat. **-drava**, m. the above resin, L. **-yāyin**, mfn. going in a straight line, W.; upright, honest, ib.; (*inī*), f. a plant with an upright stem, ib. **-skandha-saṃghaṭṭa-janman**, mfn. arising from the friction of pine-branches, MW. **-syanda**, m. = *-drava*, Rājat. **Saralâṅga**, m. id., L. **Saralâṅguli-śobhin**, mfn. having beautiful straight fingers, Rājat.

Saralaya, Nom. P. *°yati*, to make straight, straighten, Nalac.

Saralā-bhāshya, n. N. of wk.

Saralāya, Nom. Ā. *°yate*, to advance well, L.

Saralita, mfn. straightened, straight, Vcar.

Saralī, in comp. for *sarala*. **-karaṇa**, n. making straight, Cat. **-√kṛi**, P. *-karoti*, to make straight, ib.

Sáras, n. 'anything flowing or fluid,' a lake, large sheet of water, pond, pool, tank, RV. &c. &c.; a trough, pail, RV.; water, Naigh. i, 2; speech (a meaning given to account for *saras-vatī*), ib. i, 11. **-tīra**, n. the shore or bank of a lake or pond, Pañcat. **-vat** (*sáras-*), mfn. abounding in or connected with ponds &c., BhP.; juicy, sapid, L.; elegant, ib.; sentimental, ib.; finding pleasure or delight in (loc.), Cat.; m. N. of a divinity belonging to the upper region (considered as offspring of the water and plants, as guardian of the waters and bestower of fertility), RV.; AV.; TS.; PañcavBr.; of a male deity corresponding to Sarasvatī, TS.; ŚBr.; the sea, Śiś.; a river, L.; N. of a river (= *sarasvatī*), BhP.; a buffalo, W.; (*atī*), f., see s.v.

Sarasa, n. (for *sa-rasa* see s.v.) = *saras*, a lake, pond, pool (see *jala-*, *deva-*, and *maṇḍūka-s°*).

Sarasara, mfn. moving hither and thither, L.

Sarasarāya, Nom. Ā. *°yate*, to move hither and thither, Kāraṇḍ.

Sarasi (loc. of *saras*), in comp. **-ja**, mfn. produced or living in lakes or ponds (as fish), Suśr.; n. a lotus, Kāv.; Kathās.; *-mukhī*, f. a lotus-faced woman, Dhūrtan.; *-°jākshī*, f. a lotus-eyed woman, Daśak. **-janman**, m. 'lotus-born,' N. of Brahmā, Śiś. **-ruha**, n. 'growing in a lake or pond,' a lotus, Kāv.; *-janman*, m. 'lotus-born,' N. of Brahmā, MW.; *-sūnu*, m. 'lotus-son,' id., Bhām.

Sarasika, m. the Indian crane (also *sarasīka*; cf. *sārasa*), L.

Sarasī, f. a pool, pond, lake, RV.; Kāv.; Rājat.; N. of a metre, Col. **-ja**, n. 'lake-born,' a lotus, Kāv.; *-locana*, *-°jâksha*, and *-°jêkshaṇa*, mfn. lotus-eyed, ib. **-ruh**, n. 'lake-growing,' a lotus, ib.; m. N. of a poet, Cat. **-ruha**, n. id., ib.; *-bandhu*, m. 'friend of the lotus,' the sun, Vcar.; *°hâksha* or *°hêkshaṇa*, mfn. lotus-eyed, Kāv.

Sarasyà, mfn. relating to ponds or lakes, VS.; TS.; KātyŚr.

Sarasvati, in comp. for *sarasvatī*. **-kṛita** (*sár°*), mfn. made by Sarasvatī, VS. **-vat**, mfn. accompanied by Sarasvatī, KātyŚr.

Sárasvatī, f. (of *sárasvat*, q.v. under *sáras*) a region abounding in pools and lakes, MBh. i, 7745; N. of a river (celebrated in RV. and held to be a goddess whose identity is much disputed; most authorities hold that the name S° is identical with the Avestan Haraquaiti river in Afghanistan, but that it usually means the Indus in the RV., and only occasionally the small sacred river in Madhya-deśa [see below]; the river-goddess has seven sisters and is herself sevenfold, she is called the mother of streams, the best of mothers, of rivers, and of goddesses; the Ṛishis always recognize the connection of the goddess with the river, and invoke her to descend from the sky, to bestow vitality, renown, and riches; elsewhere she is described as moving along a golden path and as destroying Vṛitra &c.; as a goddess she is often connected with other deities, e.g. with Pūshan, Indra, the Maruts and the Aśvins; in the Āprī hymns she forms a triad with the sacrificial goddesses Iḍā and Bhāratī; accord. to a myth told in the VS. xix, 12, S° through speech [*vācā*] communicated vigour to Indra; in the Brāhmaṇas she is identified with *Vāc*, 'Speech,' and in later times becomes goddess of eloquence, see below), RV. &c. &c.; N. of a well-known small river (held very sacred by the Hindūs; identified with the modern Sursooty, and formerly marking with the Dṛishadvatī one of the boundaries of the region Ārya-deśa and of the sacred district called Brahmâvarta [see Mn. ii, 17]; in RV. vii, 95, 2, this river is represented as flowing into the sea, although later legends make it disappear underground and join the Ganges and Jumnā at Allahābād; see *tri-veṇī*, *prayāga*), ib.; N. of various rivers (esp. of rivers which in sacredness are equal to S° and which are three accord. to AV. vi, 101, and seven accord. to MBh. ix, 2188); any river, Naigh. i, 13; N. of the goddess of eloquence and learning (cf. above; she is opposed to Śrī or Lakshmī [cf. Vikr. v, 24], and sometimes considered as the daughter and also wife of Brahmā, the proper wife of that god being rather Sāvitrī or Gāyatrī; she is also identified with Durgā, or even with the wife of Vishṇu and of Manu, and held to be the daughter of Daksha), Mn.; MBh. &c.; speech or the power of speech, eloquence, learning, wisdom, MBh.; Kāv. &c.; a celestial or oracular voice, Kālid.; Kathās.; Rājat.; a cow, VS. viii, 43; an excellent woman (= *strī-ratna*), L.; N. of various plants (Cardiospermum Halicacabum, Ægle Marmelos, Ruta Graveolens &c.), L.; N. of a two-year-old girl representing Durgā at her festival, L.; of a poetess, Cat.; of various other women (esp. of the wives of Dadhīca, Śaṃkarâcārya, Maṇḍana-miśra &c.), ib.; of one of the ten mendicant orders traced back to Śaṃkarâcārya (whose members add the word *Sarasvatī* to their names). **-kaṇṭhâbharaṇa**, n. the necklace of Sarasvatī (goddess of eloquence), Dhūrtas.; N. of a wk. on Alaṃkāra (generally ascribed to Bhoja-deva, but probably written by some Paṇḍit during or after the reign of that king, in the end of the 11th century A.D.) **-kuṭumba**, m. N. of a poet, Cat.; *-duhitṛi*, f. of a poetess, ib. **-kṛita**, mfn. made or composed by S°, ib. **-tantra**, n. N. of two wks. **-tīrtha**, n. N. of a Tīrtha (*-māhātmya*, n.), Cat.; m. N. of an author (also called *nara-hari*), ib. **-daṇḍaka**, n., **-daśa-ślokī**, f., **-dāna-vidhi**, m., **-dvādaśa-nāma-stotra**, n. N. of wks. **-nivāsa**, m. N. of a poet (author of the Rukmiṇī-nāṭaka), Cat. **-purāṇa**, n. N. of wk. **-pūjana**, n. or **-pūjā**, f. the worship of S° (observed as a holiday on the fifth of the light half of the month Māgha and therefore also called Vasanta-pañcamī, on which day books and writing implements are held sacred and not allowed to be used), RTL. 429; (*°jā*)*-vidhāna*, n. N. of wk. **-prakriyā**, f. N. of a Comm. on the S°-sūtra (by Anubhūti-svarūpa). **-prayoga**, m. a kind of mystical rite peculiar to the Tāntrikas, MW. **-bāla-vāṇī**, f. a partic. dialect, Col. **-mantra**, m., **-māhātmya**, n., **-rahasyôpanishad**, f. N. of wks. **-vat** (*sár°*), mfn. accompanied by S°, RV.; AitBr. **-vinaśana**, n. the place where the river S° disappears, PañcavBr. **-vilāsa**, m. N. of various wks. **-vrata**, n. N. of a partic. religious observance, Cat. **-shaṭ-ślokī**, f. N. of wk. **-saras**, n. N. of a sacred lake, MW. **-sûkta**, n. N. of a hymn. **-sūtra**, n. the aphorisms of the S° grammar (by an unknown author; cf. *-prakriyā*). **-stava**, m., **-stotra**, n. N. of hymns. **-svāmin**, m. N. of an author, Cat.

Sarasvaty-ashṭaka-stotra, n. N. of a Stotra.

Sarāsara, mfn. moving hither and thither, L.

Sari, f. a cascade, waterfall (cf. *sara*, *°rā*, *°rī*), L.; a quarter of the compass, L.

Sarika, mfn., see *agre-s°*; (*ā*), f., see *saraka*.

Sarit, f. a river, stream (*saritām varā*, 'best of rivers,' the Ganges; *°tāṃ nātha*, 'lord of rivers,' the ocean; *°tām pati*, id., an expression for the number 'four,' RV. &c. &c.; a metre of 72 syllables, Nidānas.; a thread, string, L.; N. of Durgā, L. **-kapha**, m. Os Sepiæ, Bhpr. **-pati**, m. 'lord of rivers,' the ocean, Kāv.; Kathās.; BhP. **-vat**, mfn. 'possessed of rivers,' the ocean, L. **-sāgara** (?), m. N. of wk. **-suta**, m. 'river-son,' N. of Bhīshma (son of Gaṅgā), L. **-suraṅgā**, f. a channel of water, Nalac.

Sarita, mfn. flowing, fluent (as speech), Māhāvy.

Sarid, in comp. for *sarit.* **—adhipati,** m. lord of rivers, the ocean, Śukas. **—āśrita,** see *arṇava-sarid-āśrita.* **—ubhaya,** (prob. n.) the bank of a river, VarYogay. **—dvīpa,** m. N. of a son of Garuḍa (v. l. *pari-dvīpa*), MBh. **—bhartṛi,** m. = *-adhipati;* N. for the number 'four,' Ked. **—vadhū,** f. a woman compared to a river, MW. **—varā,** f. 'best of rivers,' the Ganges, MBh.

1. **Sárin,** mfn. approaching, coming to aid, RV.

2. **Sarin,** in comp. for *sarit.* **—nātha,** m. 'river-lord,' the ocean, L. **—maru-vanâśraya,** mfn. protected by a river and a desert and wood, MW. **—mukha,** n. the mouth or source of a river, W.

Sariman, m. wind, air, Uṇ. iv, 147, Sch.; going, proceeding, W.

Sarirá, n. (cf. *salila*) the heaving sea, flood, tide, VS.; TBr.; = *bahu,* Naigh. iii, 1; the universe (= *loka* or *tri-loka*), VS., Sch.

Sarila, n. = *salila,* water, L.

Sárīman (only loc. °*mani*) the course or passage of the wind, RV.; = *sariman,* Uṇ. iv, 147, Sch.

Saro, in comp. for *saras.* **—ja,** mfn. produced or found in lakes or ponds, Tarkas.; n. a lotus, Kāv.; VarBṛS.; m. a prosodial foot containing 6 instants (accord. to some '6 long syllables'), Col.; *-kalikā,* f. N. of wk.; *-khaṇḍa,* n. a group of lotuses, Kāś. on Pāṇ. iv, 2, 51; *-tā,* f. the being a lotus, Naish.; *-dṛiś, -nayanā,* and *-netrā,* f. a lotus-eyed woman, Kāv.; *-rāga,* m. a ruby (cf. *padma-r°*), Hcat.; *-sundara,* m. or n. (?) N. of wk. **—janman,** n. 'lake-born,' a lotus, L. **—jala,** n. the water of a pond or lake, W. **—jin,** mfn. (fr. *saro-ja*) having lotuses; m. N. of Brahmā (connected with a lotus), L.; of a Buddha, L.; (*inī*), f. a pond abounding in l°s or a multitude of l°s (also incorrectly = 'a l°-flower'), Kāv.; Sāh. **—jīya,** Nom. (fr. *saro-ja*), P. °*yati,* to be like a l°, Kāv. **—bindu,** m. a kind of song (*gītaka*), Yājñ. **—raksha,** m. the guardian of a pool, MW. **—ruh,** n. 'lake-growing,' a lotus, L. **—ruha,** n. id.; Kāv.; Kathās. &c.; m. N. of a poet, Cat.; *-dṛiś,* f. a lotus-eyed woman, Bhām.; *-vajra,* m. N. of a man, Buddh.; °*hâkshī,* f. (= °*ha-dṛiś*), Uttarar.; °*hâsana,* m. 'sitting on a l°,' N. of Brahmā (as having appeared sitting on the lotus which grew from the navel of Vishṇu), L. **—ruhiṇī,** f. = *sarojinī,* Kir. **—vara,** n. (accord. to some also m.) a lake or large pond, any piece of water deep enough for the lotus, Kāv.; Pur. &c.

Sártave, sártavai. See √*sṛi.*

Sártṛi, m. a courser (horse), ŚBr.

Sárma, m. going, running, flowing, RV. i, 80, 5. [Cf. Gk. ὁρμή.]

सरक्त *sa-rakta,* mfn. (i. e. 7. *sa* + *r°*) bleeding, bloody, Suśr.

Sa (to be similarly prefixed to the following): **—rakta-gaura,** mfn. being of a red and whitish colour, Laghuj. **—ranga,** mfn. (for *saranga* see s. v.) having colour, Kāv.; having a nasal sound, Śiksh.; (also °*gaka*) a kind of metre, Col. **—raja,** mfn. dusty, dirty, BhP.; m. pl. N. of a people, MārkP. **—rajas,** mfn. having dust or pollen, Pāṇ. v, 4, 77, Sch.; f. a woman in her monthly period, L. **—rajasa,** mfn. dusty, dirty, PañcavBr. (*-tā,* f., Kir.); (*am*), ind. with the dust, i. e. with the last remnant, Pāṇ. v, 4, 77, Sch. **—rajaska,** mf(*ā*)n. 'having pollen' and 'having the menses,' Bhām. **—raṇa,** mfn. (for *saraṇa* see p. 1182, col. 1) connected with war or conflict, Lalit. **—raṇaraṇi-kam,** ind. (perhaps w. r. for °*ṇakam*) with longing, regretfully, Śukas. **—ratha** (*sá-*), mf(*ā*)n. together with the chariot, ŚBr.; MBh.; (*sa-rátham*), ind. on the same chariot with, (or simply) together with, accompanied by (instr.), RV.; m. a warrior or Kshatriya (as riding in a ch°), MW.; *-pādāta,* mfn. accompanied by or along with chariots and infantry, ib. **—rathin,** mfn. riding on the same chariot, VS. **—randhra,** mfn. having holes or openings or apertures, perforated, Ragh.; having a loop (for pulling anything through), ĀpastPray. **—rabhasa,** mfn. possessing speed or impetuosity, impetuous, speedy, quick, agitated, eager, passionate (*am,* ind. impetuously, hurriedly, passionately; also ibc.), Kāv.; Kathās.; Vet. **—rasana,** mfn. having a girdle or together with the g°, ĀpŚr. **—raśmi** (*sá-*), mfn. having rays, radiant, RV. **—rasa** &c., see s. v. **—rahasya,** mfn. along with the secret or mystical doctrine (i. e. with the Upanishads, Mn. ii, 140, 165); possessing anything secret or mystical, MW. **—rāga,** mfn. having colour (sometimes = 'not quite clean'), Kād.; reddened, MBh.; Kālid.; charming, lovely (*am,* ind.), Bhaṭṭ.; enamoured, impassioned, passionate (*am,* ind.), Kām.; Gīt.; *-tā,* f. (Pañcat.), *-tva,* n. the being coloured or flushed with passion, impassioned, redness, passion, love; *-netra,* mfn. red-eyed, MBh. **—rājaka** (MBh.; *ikā,* f., Jātakam.), **-rājan** (KātyŚr.), mfn. possessing a king, along with the king. **—rāti** (*sá-*), mfn. equal in (bestowing) gifts, equally kind, RV. **—rātri,** mfn. = *sa-māna-r°,* Pāṇ. vi, 3, 85. **—rāshṭra** or °**ṭraka,** mfn. possessing or along with a kingdom, MW. **—rāhu,** mfn. possessed or held by Rāhu (q. v.), eclipsed, BhP. **—rīḍham,** ind. with contempt or neglect, Kāśikh. **—ruc,** mfn. possessing splendour, splendid, magnificent, Śiś. **—ruj,** mfn. feeling the same pain, Sāh.; suffering pain, sick, ill, Hāsy. **—ruja,** mfn. having pain, causing it, Car.; suffering pain or sickness, ill, diseased, MBh.; R. &c.; *-tva,* n. sickness, illness, Mālav.; *-siddhâcarya,* m. N. of a teacher, Cat. **—rudhira,** mfn. bloody (*am,* ind.), Suśr.; *-mūtra,* mfn. discharging bloody urine (*-tā,* f.), ib. **—rush,** mfn. angry, enraged, Śiś.; Pañcat. **—rūpa** (*sá-*), mfn. having the same shape or form, uniform, similar, like, resembling (gen. or comp.), RV. &c. &c.; having the same sound, identical in s°, consonant, Kavyâd.; having shape or form, embodied, VP.; shapely formed, beautiful, handsome (prob. also w. r. for *su-r°*), PañcavBr.; Kāv.; m. a partic. mythical being, Suparṇ.; (*ā*), f. N. of the wife of Bhūta and mother of innumerable Rudras, BhP.; (°*pa*)*-kṛit,* mfn. producing the same form or colour, AV.; (°*paṃ*)*-káraṇa,* mf(*ī*)n. id., ib.; *-tā,* f., *-tva,* n. identity of form, likeness, resemblance to (comp.), AitBr.; MBh.; Kām. &c.; assimilation to the deity (one of the four stages in the progress towards final emancipation), RTL. &c.; *-vatsā,* f. a cow with a calf of the same colour, GṛŚrS.; °*pôpamā,* v. l. for *samāna-rūp°,* Kāvyâd. **—rūpaya,** Nom. (fr. *sa-rūpa*), P. °*yati,* to make equal in form, Sarvad. **—rūpin,** mfn. equally shaped or formed, Kāśikh. **—retas** (*sá-*), mfn. having semen, possessing seed, Br. **—repha,** mfn. together with the sound or letter *r,* RPrāt. **—roga,** mfn. affected with disease, sick, diseased; *-tā,* f. (v. l. °*gi-tā*) sickliness, Hit. °**rogin,** mfn. (and °*gi-tā,* f.) = prec., W. **—rodha,** mfn. having hindrance or obstruction or opposition, MW.; having destruction or loss, ib.; m. obstruction, opposition, W. **—roma,** mfn. having hair, hairy, VarBṛS.; *-kaṇṭaka,* mfn. having the hair bristling or thrilling with ecstacy, MW.; *-vikriya,* mfn. id., ib.; °*mâñca,* mfn. id. (*am,* ind.), Kathās.; Prab. **—rosha,** mfn. full of anger, angry, wrathful (*am,* id.), R.; Kālid.; Pur.; *-rāgôpahata,* mfn. suffused with a flush of anger, MW.; *-sambhrama,* mfn. wrathful and agitated, Śiś.; *-smitam,* ind. with an angry smile, Ratnâv. **—rksha, -rca** &c., see *sa-rksha, sa-rca,* s. v.

सरघ् *sarágh,* f. (of unknown derivation; only in nom. sg. *saráṭ,* dat. pl. *saráḍbhyaḥ,* and nom. pl. *sarághaḥ*) a bee, RV.; TS.; ŚBr.

Saraghā, f. id., TBr.; PañcavBr.; Ragh.; Pongamia Glabra, L.; N. of the wife of Bindumat and mother of Madhu, BhP.

Saráṭ, f., see *sarágh;* (prob.) m. 'wind' or 'a cloud,' Uṇ. i, 133, Sch.

Saraṭa, m. a lizard, chameleon, Mn.; VarBṛS.; wind, Uṇ. iv, 105, Sch. **—patana-praśānti,** f. N. of a wk. (on removing the evil consequences of a lizard falling on one's head). **—śāstra,** n. N. of a wk. (on prognostics derived from the movements of lizards).

Saraṭaka, m. N. of a Bharaṭaka, Cat.

Saraṭu, m. a lizard, chameleon, L.

Sarad, (prob.) m. a kind of tree, L.; a cloud, L.; a kind of camel, L.

Sarada, m. the crawling of a serpent, L.; a tree, L.

सरङ्ग *saraṅga,* m. (for *sa-r°* see col. 1) a kind of bird, L.; a kind of antelope (cf. *sāraṅga*), L.

सरजत् *sarájat,* mfn. (of unknown meaning; Sāy. = *saha-rajat;* others = *sṛijat;* accord. to others *saraj-* = Gk. ὀρεγ-), RV. x, 115, 3.

सरण *saraṇa,* °*ṇi* &c. See p. 1182, col. 1.

सरण्ड *saraṇḍa,* m. (cf. *śaraṇḍa*) a bird, Uṇ. i, 128, Sch.

सरत्नि *saratni,* mf. (cf. *ratni, aratni*) a partic. measure (from the elbow to the closed hand), L.

सरथ *sa-ratha,* °*thin.* See col. 1.

सरपत्त्रिका *sara-pattrikā,* f. a lotus-leaf (prob. w. r. for *śara-p°*), L.

सरपस् *sarapas.* See p. 1182, col. 1.

सरभ *sarabha,* m. N. of a monkey (prob. w. r. for *śarabha*), RāmatUp.

Sarabhaka, m. a kind of insect infesting grain, AdbhBr.

सरभस *sa-rabhasa* &c. See col. 1.

सरमा *saramā.* See p. 1182, col. 1.

सरषट्ट *sarashaṭṭa,* N. of a place, Cat.

सरस *sa-rasa,* mf(*ā*)n. (for *sarasa* see p. 1182, col. 2) containing sap, juicy, pithy, potent, powerful, TS.; Br.; GṛŚrS.; Megh.; moist, wet, Hariv.; Kāv.; Kathās.; fresh, new, Mālav.; Śiś.; Sāh.; tasty, tasting like (comp.), Kathās.; elegant, beautiful, charming, gracious, Kāv.; Kathās.; expressive of poetical sentiment (see *rasa*); passionate, impassioned, enamoured, full of love or desire, ib.; (*am*), ind. with rapture, Vikr.; (*ā*), f. = *saralā,* Ipomœa Turpethum, L. **—kavi-kulânanda,** m. N. of a Bhāṇa (q. v.) by Rāma-candra. **—tā,** f. juiciness, AitBr.; ŚāṅkhBr. **—tva,** n. id., Kāṭh.; freshness, novelty, Subh. **—bhāratī,** f. N. of a poem. **—vāṇī,** f. N. of the wife of Maṇḍana-miśra, Cat. **—śabda-saraṇi,** f. N. of a vocabulary. **Sarasâṅga-yashṭi,** mfn. one whose delicate body is moist with perspiration (cf. 2. *yashṭi*), MW.

Sarasi-√kṛi, P. *-karoti,* to moisten, refresh, comfort, Prasannar.

सरसम्प्रत *sarasamprata* (?), m. Asteracantha Longifolia, L.

सरसिक *sarasika, sarasi-ja* &c. See p. 1182.

सरस्वती *sarasvatī* &c. See p. 1182, col. 2.

सरह *saraha,* m. N. of a man, Buddh.

सराट *saräṭa,* N. of a place. Cat.

सरारी *sarārī.* See *kṛimi-s°.*

सराव *sarāva,* m. a kind of venomous insect, Suśr.; w. r. for *śarāva.*

सरि *sari, sarit* &c. See p. 1182, col. 3.

सरिण्यु *sariṇyu,* w. r. for *saraṇyu.*

सरिषप *sarishapa,* m. = *sarshapa,* mustard, a mustard seed, L.

सरिस्र *sarisrará* (?), m. (fr. Intens. of √*sṛi*) going or flowing apart, TBr.

सरिस्रुत् *sarisrut* (?), f. (fr. id. or √*sru* ?) = *surā,* Harav.

सरीसृप् *sarī-sṛip,* m. (fr. Intens. of √*sṛip*) = *sarīsṛipa,* any creeping animal, BhP.

Sarīsṛipá, mfn. crawling, creeping; m. or n. (ifc. f. *ā*) a creeping animal, reptile, snake, RV. &c. &c.; m. N. of Vishṇu, L.

सरु *sáru,* mfn. (for *śaru* fr. √*śrī,* p. 1056) minute, thin, fine; m. = *śáru,* m. an arrow = *tsaru,* the hilt or handle of a sword, L.

सरुच् *sa-ruc, sa-ruj* &c. See col. 2.

सरुद्भव *sarudbhava,* (prob.) w. r. for *sarôd-bhava,* a lotus.

सरोज *saro-ja* &c. See col. 1.

सर्क *sarka,* m. (of unknown derivation) the wind, air, L.; the mind, L.; N. of Prajā-pati, L.

सर्क्ष *sa-rksha,* mf(*ā*)n. (i. e. 7. *sa* + *ṛiksha*) joined or united with a Nakshatra, Kṛishṇaj.

सर्ग *sárga,* m. (ifc. f. *ā;* fr. √*sṛij*) letting go, discharging, voiding (as excrement), MBh.; R.; starting (a race-horse), racing, RV.; a herd let loose from a stable, any troop or host or swarm or multitude, ib.; Rājat.; a draught of air, gust of wind, RV.; a stream, gush, rush, downpour (of any fluid; acc. with

√*kṛi*, 'to cast or strike down,' RV.); a dart, shot, ib.; emission or creation of matter, primary creation (as opp. to *pratisarga*, 'secondary creation'), creation of the world (as opp. to its *pralaya*, 'dissolution,' and *sthiti*, 'maintenance in existence;' 9 different creations are enumerated in BhP. iii, 10, 13; *ā sargāt*, 'from the creation or beginning of the world;' *sarge*, 'in the created world'), Up.; Mn.; MBh. &c.; a created being, creature (with *daiva*, 'a divine creation,' 'a god'), Ragh.; begetting, procreation, MBh.; origin, BhP; offspring, a child, ib.; nature, natural property, disposition, tendency, Bhag. v, 19; effort, exertion, resolution, resolve, will, Ragh.; Śiś.; a section, chapter, book, canto (esp. in an epic poem); assent, agreement, L.; fainting (= *moha*), L.; implement of war, MBh. xi, 2165 (Nīlak.); = *visarga*, the aspiration at the end of a word, Cat.; N. of Śiva, MBh.; of a son of Rudra, Pur. **-kartṛi**, m. the creator (*-tva*, n.), Pañcar. **-kālīna**, mfn. relating to or happening at the time of creation, Sāṃkhyapr. **-kṛit**, m. = *-kartṛi*, Hariv. **-krama**, m. the order of creation, MW. **-takta** or **-pratakta** (*sárga-*), mfn. dashing along in rapid motion, hastening, RV. **-pralaya-kaṇṭakôddhāra**, m. N. of wk. **-bandha**, m. 'chapter-construction,' any poem or composition divided into sections or chapters (esp. a Mahā-kāvya or great poem), Kāvyâd.; Sāh.

Sargaka, mfn. producing, effecting, Sarvad.

Sargya. See *pāṇi-s°*.

Sarja, m. one who emits or lets go, one who creates or makes (see *rajju-s°*); Vatica Robusta, MBh.; Kāv. &c.; the resin of V° R°, VarBṛS.; Terminalia Tomentosa, L.; (*ī*), f., see s. v. **-gandhā**, f. the ichneumon plant, L. **-nāman**, n. the resin of Vatica Robusta, Suśr. **-niryāsaka**, m., **-maṇi**, m. id., L. **-rasa**, m., MBh.; Suśr.; a kind of tree, Hariv. (v.l.); a partic. musical instrument, L. **-vṛiksha**, m. Vatica Robusta, Hcat.

Sarjaka, m. Terminalia Tomentosa, L.; Vatica Robusta, L.; n. the first change in warm milk when mixed with Takra, L.; (*ikā*), f., see below.

Sarjana, n. abandoning, giving up or over, surrendering, ceding, MBh.; voiding (excrement &c.), L.; the act of creating, creation, Sarvad.; the rear of an army, L.; m. resin, L.; (*ī*), f. one of the three folds of the anus, ŚārṅgS.

Sarjayitavya, mfn. to be emitted or created, Up.

Sarji, f. natron, impure alkali or carbonate of soda, L. **-kshāra**, m. id., L.

Sarjikā, f. natron (cf. *sarjī*), Suśr. **-kshāra**, m. id., L.

Sarjī, f. natron, L. **-kshāra**, m. id., L.

Sarjya, m. the resin of Vatica Robusta, L.

सर्च *sa-rca*, m. (fr. 7. *sa* + *ṛic*) accompanied by a Ṛic, Gobh.

सर्ज् 1. *sarj*, cl. 1. P. *sárjati*, to rattle, creak, RV.

सर्ज् 2. *sarj* (cf. √*arj*), cl. 1. P. *sarjati*, to earn by labour, acquire, gain, Dhātup. vii, 50.

Sarju, m. a merchant, trader, L.; f. lightning, L.

Sarjū, m. a merchant, Uṇ. i, 82, Sch.; a necklace, L.; going, following, L.

Sarjūra, m. a day, L.

सर्णिक *sarṇika*, n. (perhaps connected with √*sṛi*) water, ŚBr. (Naigh. i, 12).

Sarṇṇa, m. a kind of serpent, L.

सर्दिगृदि *sárdigṛidi*, m. a facetious expression for the female organ, TS.

सर्प *sarpá*, mf(ī)n. creeping, crawling, stealing along, Gaut. (cf. *pīṭha-*, *vṛiksha-s°*); m. (ifc. f. *ā*) a snake, serpent, serpent-demon (cf. *nāga*; *sarpāṇām ayanam*, 'a partic. annual festival'), tortuous motion, RV. &c. &c.; a partic. constellation (when only the three unfavourable planets are situated in the three Kendras), VarBṛS.; Mesua Roxburghii, L.; N. of one of the 11 Rudras, MBh.; of a Rākshasa, VP.; (pl.) N. of a partic. tribe of Mlecchas (formerly Kshatriyas and described as wearing beards), Hariv.; (*ī*), f. a female snake, MBh.; N. of the wife of a Rudra, ib.; n. = *sarpa-sāman*, q.v. [Cf. Gk. ἑρπετόν; Lat. *serpens*; see also under √*sṛip*.] **-ṛishi**, m. 'serpent-Ṛishi,' N. of Arbuda, AitBr. **-kaṅkālikā** or **°lī**, f. N. of a partic. medicinal plant and antidote, L. **-koṭara**, n. a sn°'s hole, Pañcat. **-gati**, f. a snake's tortuous movement (in wrestling), R. **-gandhā**, f. the ichneumon plant, L. **-ghātinī**, f. a kind of plant, L. **-cīra-nivāsana**, m. 'clothed in a snake's skin,' N. of Śiva, MW. **-cchattra** (W.) or **°raka** (Car.), n. 'snake-umbrella,' a mushroom. **-jāti**, f. a species of sn° (of which there are 80 varieties), L. **-tanu**, f. a species of Solanum (*bṛihatī*), L. **-tā**, f. the being a sn°, Kathās. **-tṛiṇa**, m. = *nakula*, L. **-tva**, n. = *-tā*; *-sambhāvanā*, f. supposing anything to be a sn°, mistaking for a sn°, Vedântas. **-daṇshṭra**, m. a sn°'s fang, W.; Croton Polyandrum or Tiglium, L.; (*ā*), f. Tragia Involucrata, ib. **-daṇshṭrikā** or **°ṭrī**, f. Odina Pinnata or Tragia Involucrata, ib. **-daṇḍā**, f. a kind of pepper, ib.; (*ī*), f. a kind of plant (= *go-rakshī*), ib. **-danti**, f. Tiaridium Indicum, ib. **-damanī**, f. a kind of plant (= *vandhyā-karkoṭakī*), ib. **-dashṭa**, n. a sn°-bite, Suśr. **-deva-janá**, m. pl. the Sarpas and Deva-janas (*-vidyā*, f.), ChUp. **-devī**, f. N. of a Tīrtha, MBh. **-dvish**, m. 'snake-foe,' a peacock, Subh. **-dhāraka**, m. a snake-catcher or charmer, MW. **-nāmá**, n. pl. N. of partic. texts, ŚBr.; (*ā*), f. a kind of plant, L. **-nirmocana**, n. the cast-off skin of a sn°, Car. **-netrā**, f. an ichneumon plant (a bulb), L. **-pati**, m. a sn°-king, Hariv. **-puṃgava**, m. N. of a sn°-demon, VP. **-puṇya-jana**, m. pl. the Sarpas and Puṇya-janas, GopBr.; Vait. **-pura-kshetra-māhātmya**, n. N. of wk. **-pushpī**, f. Tiaridium Indicum, L. **-phaṇa**, m. a sn°'s hood, Suśr.; *-ja*, m. 'produced in a sn°'s hood,' the sn°-stone (a gem or pearl said to be found in a sn°'s head and to resemble the berry of the Abrus Precatorius), L. **-bandha**, m. 'sn°-fetter,' an artifice, subtle device, MBh. **-bala**, n. N. of a Pariśishṭa of the Sāma-veda. **-bali**, m. an offering to Serpents, PārGṛ.; N. of wk.; *-karman*, n. (= *-bali*), Cat.; *-vidhi*, m. N. of wk. **-bhuj**, m. 'sn°-eater,' a peacock, L.; a crane, W.; a large snake or a kind of snake, L. **-bhṛitā**, f. 'supported by sn°,' the earth, L. **-maṇi**, m. 'sn°-gem,' the sn°-stone, a kind of carbuncle (said to be found in a sn°'s head and to have the power of expelling poison), W. **-mālā**, f. a kind of plant, L. **-mālin**, m. N. of a Ṛishi, MBh. (v.l. *sarpi-m°*). **-mudraka**, n. a seal-ring with a sn°, Mālav. **-yāga**, m. a sn°-sacrifice, BhP. **-rāja**, m. a sn°-king, Gobh.; Hariv. &c.; N. of Vāsuki, R. **-rājñī**, f. a sn°-queen, Br.; pl. (or du.) N. of the verses RV. x, 189 (or TS. i, 5, 4), ĀpŚr. **-rūpin**, mfn. formed like a sn°, Mālav. **-latā**, f. Piper Betle, L. **-vallī**, f. id., ib. **-vid**, mfn. acquainted with sn°, ŚBr.; ĀśvŚr.; m. one who understands sn°, a sn°-charmer, MW. **-vidyā**, f. sn°-science, ŚBr.; ŚāṅkhŚr.; the charming of sn°, MW. **-vināśana**, n. destruction of sn°, MBh. **-vivara**, m. n. the hole of a sn°, Hit. **-visha-pratishedha**, m. the keeping off or expelling of sn°-poison, Cat. **-visha-hara-mantra**, m. N. of wk. **-vṛiścika-roma-vat**, mfn. having sn°s and scorpions for hair, R. **-veda**, m. sn°-science, GopBr.; N. of wk. **-vyāpādana**, n. the killing of a sn°, MW.; the being killed by a sn°, ib. **-śapharī**, f. a kind of sn°, L. **-śiras**, m. (scil. *hasta*) 'sn°-headed,' N. of a partic. position of the hands, Cat. **-śīrshá**, mfn. having a head like a sn°, Vas.; m. a partic. position of the hands, Cat.; n. a partic. brick, TS.; Kāṭh. **-śīrshan** or **°shin**, m. 'sn°-headed,' a kind of fish, Āpast. **-saṃskāra**, m. N. of wk. **-sattra**, n. a sn°-sacrifice (performed by Janam-ejaya), MBh.; (prob.) = *sarpāṇām ayanam* (see *sarpá*), PañcavBr.; ŚrS. **-sattrin**, m. 'performer of a sn°-sacrifice,' N. of king Janam-ejaya (a legend relates that to revenge the death of his father, who was killed by a sn°-bite, he employed Mantras to compel the whole serpent-race to be present at a sacrifice, where all except a few chief snakes were destroyed), L. **-sahā**, f. a kind of plant, L. **-sāt**, ind. to a sn°, to the state of a serpent, MW. **-sāman**, n. N. of various Sāmans, SV.; Br. **-sugandhā**, f. a kind of plant, SāmavBr. **-han**, m. 'sn°-killer,' an ichneumon, L. **-hṛidaya-candana**, m. a kind of sandal. **Sarpâksha**, m. the berry of the Elæocarpus Ganitrus, L.; Ophiorrhiza Mungos, ib.; (*ī*), f. a kind of plant, Suśr.; the pl° Sarpa-kaṅkālī, MW.; = *gandha-nākulī*, L.; = *gaṇḍālī*, Bhpr.; = *nāga-phaṇī*, ib.; = *nāḍī-kalāpaka*, MW. **Sarpâkhya**, m. Mesua Roxburghii, L.; a species of bulbous plant, ib. **Sarpâṅgâbhihata**, n. a tumour caused by the touch of a sn°, Suśr. **Sarpâṅgī**, f. a variety of pepper, L.; = *nākulī*, Bhpr.; another plant (= *-ghātinī*), L.; a variety of the Sarpa-kaṅkālī, W. **Sarpâdanī**, f. the ichneumon plant, L. **Sarpânta**, m. N. of one of the sons of Garuḍa, MBh. **Sarpâhārin**, m. N. of a robber, Vīrac. **Sarpâbha**, mfn. resembling a sn°, L. **Sarpârāti**, m. 'enemy of sn°,' N. of Garuḍa, L.; an ichneumon, W.; a peacock, ib. **Sarpâri**, m. 'id.,' a peacock, Subh.; an ichneumon, L.; N. of Garuḍa (in next); *-ketana*, m. N. of Kṛishṇa, Hariv. **Sarpâvali**, f. a row of sn°, MW. **Sarpâvāsa**, m. the abode of a sn°, Hariv.; an ant-hill, VarBṛS.; n. the Sandal tree or wood, L. **Sarpâśana**, m. 'sn°-eater,' a peacock, L. **Sarpâsya**, m. 'sn°-faced,' N. of a Rākshasa, R.; (*ā*), f. N. of a Yoginī, Kāśikh. **Sarpâhuti**, f. N. of the section TS. v, 5, 10. **Sarpêtara-jana**, m. pl. the serpent-race and the Itara-jana, GopBr.; ĀpŚr.; Vait. **Sarpêśvara**, m. 'serpent-king,' N. of Vāsuki, Hit.; *-tīrtha*, n. N. of a Tīrtha, Cat. **Sarpêshṭa**, n. 'loved by snakes,' the Sandal tree or wood, L. **Sarpâushadhi**, N. of a Buddhist monastery, Buddh.

Sarpaṇa, n. the act of creeping or gliding, stealing away, AitBr.; Nir.; MBh. &c.; (in ritual) moving softly &c., GṛŚrS.; going tortuously, MW.; the flight of an arrow nearly parallel with the ground, W.

Sárpat, n. the crawling creature, all that crawls, AV.

Sarpāya, Nom. Ā. *°yate*, to resemble a snake, Śṛiṅgār.

Sarpi, m. N. of a man, AitBr.; n. (m. c. for *sarpis*) clarified butter, VarYogay. **-maṇḍa**, m. = *sarpir-m°*, Divyâv.

Sarpiḥ, in comp. for *sarpis* below. **-samudra**, m. the sea of clarified butter, L.

Sarpikā, f. a little snake (see *toya-s°*); N. of a river, R.

Sarpita, n. a real snake-bite, Suśr.

Sarpin, mfn. (ifc.) creeping, gliding, moving slowly (*śītânila-s°*, 'exposed to currents of cold winds'), ŚBr.; Hariv.; Kir.; (*inī*), f. a female serpent, Kāśīkh.; a kind of shrub (= *bhujagī*), L.; w. r. for *sarpa-vāṇī*, a serpent's voice, Pañcat.

Sarpir, in comp. for *sarpis* below. **-anna** (*°pír-*), mfn. eating clarified butter, RV. **-abdhi**, m. the sea of cl° b°, MārkP. **-āsuti** (*°pír-*), mfn. sipping cl° b°, RV.; sacrificed or worshipped with cl° b°, MW.; m. N. of Agni, RV. **-ilā**, f. N. of the wife of a Rudra, BhP. **-grīvá**, mf(*ī*)n. having a neck composed of cl° b°, TS. **-dāna-ratna**, n. N. of wk. **-maṇḍa**, m. the scum of melted butter, Suśr. **-mālin**, m. N. of a Ṛishi, MBh. (v.l. *sarpa-m°*). **-mehin**, mfn. having urine like cl° butter, Suśr.

Sarpish, in comp. for *sarpis*. **-kāmya**, Nom. P. *°yati*, to like clarified butter, Pāṇ. viii, 3, 39, Sch. **-kuṇḍikā**, f. a butter-jar, g. *kaskâdi*. **-ṭama**, n. superl., Kāś. on Pāṇ. viii, 3, 101. **-ṭara**, n. more genuine cl° b°, more excellent ghee, ib.; APrāt., Sch. **-ṭas**, ind., Kāś. on Pāṇ. viii, 3, 101. **-ṭā**, f. (ib.) or **-ṭva**, n. (ib.; Kāṭh.) the being cl° b°. **-mat** (*sárpish-*), mfn. provided or prepared with cl° b°, ŚBr.; Uttarar. **-vat** (*sarpish-*), mfn. id., Kāṭh.; TS.; TBr.

Sarpishka (ifc.) = *sarpis*, g. *uraḥ-prabhṛiti*.

Sarpis, n. clarified butter (i. e. melted butter with the scum cleared off, commonly called 'ghee,' either fluid or solidified; also pl.), RV. &c. &c. **-samudra**, m. = *sarpiḥ-s°*, W. **-sāt**, ind., APrāt., Sch.

1. **Sarpī**, f., see under *sarpá*. **-°shṭa** (*°pīsh°*), n. = *sarpêshṭa*, L. (prob. w. r.)

2. **Sarpī**, in comp. for *sarpa*. **-√bhū**, P. *-bhavati*, to become a serpent, Kathās.

सर्ब् *sarb* (also written *samb*), cl. 1. P. *sarbati*, to go, move, Dhātup. xi, 30.

सर्म *sarma.* See p. 1183, col. 1.

सर्व् *sarv*, v.l. for √*śarv*, q.v.

सर्व *sárva*, mf(*ā*)n. (perhaps connected with *sāra*, q.v.; inflected as a pronoun except nom. acc. sg. n. *sarvam*, and serving as a model for a series of pronominals, cf. *sarva-nāman*) whole, entire, all, every (m. sg. 'every one;' pl. 'all;' n. sg. 'everything;' sometimes strengthened by *viśva* [which if alone in RV. appears in the meaning 'all,' 'every,' 'every one'] and *nikhila*; *sarve 'pi*, 'all together;' *sarvaḥ ko 'pi*, 'every one so ever;' *gavāṃ sarvam*, 'all that comes from cows;' *sarva* with a negation = 'not any,' 'no,' 'none' or 'not every one,' 'not everything'), RV. &c. &c.; of all sorts, manifold, various, different, MBh. &c.; (with another adjective or in comp.; cf. below) altogether, wholly, completely, in all parts, everywhere, RV.; ChUp. &c.; (*am*), ind. (with *sarveṇa*) completely, Divyâv.; m. (declined like a subst.) N. of Śiva, MBh.; of Kṛishṇa, Bhag.; of a Muni, Cat.; pl. N. of a people, MārkP.;

n. water, Naigh. i, 12. [Cf. Gk. ὅλος for ὀλϝος; Lat. *salvus.*] **-m-saha,** mfn. all-bearing, all-enduring, bearing everything patiently, MBh.; Pañcat.; Hit. &c.; (*ā*), f. the earth, Kāv.; Inscr.; a partic. Śruti, Saṃgīt. **-m-hara,** mfn. taking or carrying away everything, ŚāṅkhBr. **-kara,** m. 'maker of all,' N. of Śiva, MBh. **-kartṛi,** m. the maker or creator of all (*-tva,* n., Sarvad.), KapS.; Kālac.; N. of Brahmā, L. **-karman,** n. pl. all kinds of works or rites or occupations (°*ma-saha,* mfn. 'equal to all k° of w°;' °*ma-kārin,* mfn. 'performing all k° of w°'), ŚrS.; Mn. &c.; mfn. containing all works, ChUp.; m. one who performs all acts, MW.; N. of Śiva, ib.; of a son of Kalmāsha-pāda, MBh.; Hariv. **-karmiṇa,** mfn. doing every work, practising or understanding every occupation, Pāṇ.; Bhaṭṭ.; pervading ev° action &c., W. **-kāñcana,** mfn. wholly of gold, R.; MārkP. **-kāma,** m. pl. all kinds of desires, MBh.; RāmatUp. &c.; (*sarvá-*), mfn. wishing everything, ŚāṅkhBr.; ŚrS.; BhP.; fulfilling all wishes, Kauś.; MBh.; possessing everything wished for, ŚBr.; MBh.; m. N. of Śiva, MW.; of a son of Ṛitu-parṇa, Pur.; of an Arhat, Buddh.; *-gama,* mfn. going or moving wherever one wishes, MBh.; *-da,* m. 'granting all desires,' N. of Śiva, MBh.; *-dugha,* mf(*ā*)n. yielding everything wished for (like milk), MBh.; BhP.; *-duh,* mfn. id., Cat.; *-maya,* mf(*ī*)n. full of wishes, MaitrUp.; *-vara,* m. 'best of all objects of desire,' N. of Śiva, MBh.; *-samṛiddha,* mfn. amply stocked with all desired objects, fulfilling every desire, ib.; m., see *sārva-kāma-s°*. **-kāmika,** mfn. fulfilling all wishes, BhP.; obtaining all one's desires, MBh. **-kāmin,** mfn. fulfilling all wishes, ib.; acting entirely according to one's wish, ŚāṅkhŚr.; having all desired objects, MBh. **-1. -kāmya,** Nom. P. °*yati,* to wish for everything, Pat. **-2. -kāmya,** mfn. loved by all, Pañcar.; to be wished for by every one, having everything one can desire, MW.; w.r. for *-kāma,* MBh. **-kāraka,** mfn., Pāṇ. vi, 2, 105, Sch. **-kāraṇa,** n. the cause of everything, Madhus.; *-kāraṇa,* n. (incorrectly also m.) the c° of the c° of ev°, Pañcar. **-kārin,** mfn. making or doing all things, W.; able to do all things, R.; m. the maker of all things, MW. **-kāla** (ibc.), at all times, always, BhP.; (*am*), ind. id. (with *na,* 'never'), VarBṛS.; Kathās. &c.; (*e*), ind. id., Pañcat.; (°*la*)-*prasāda,* m. 'propitious at all seasons,' N. of Śiva, MBh.; *-mitra,* n. a friend at all times, Mṛicch.; *-vicārin,* mfn. always irresolute, Car. **-kālikâgama,** m. N. of wk. **-kālina,** mfn. belonging to all times or seasons, perpetual, W. **-kāsham,** ind. (with √*kash*) so as to rub away or destroy utterly, Prab. **-kṛicchra,** mfn. being in all kinds of difficulties, MBh. **-kṛit,** mfn. all-producing, Hariv. **-kṛishṇa,** mfn. quite black, Pāṇ. vi, 2, 93, Sch. **-keśa,** m. N. of a place, g. *saṇḍikâdi.* **-keśaká,** mfn. having the hair of the head entire, AV. **-keśin,** m. 'having all kinds of head-dress,' an actor, Pat.; L. (cf. *-veshin*). **-kesara,** m. Mimusops Elengi, Kir., Sch. **-kratu,** m. pl. sacrifices of any or every sort (*-tā,* f.), Lāṭy.; BhP.; *-maya,* mf(*ī*)n. containing all sorts, Pañcar. **-kshatriya-mardana,** m. the destroyer of all Kshatriyas, MBh. **-kshaya,** m. destruction of the universe, Kād. **-kshāra,** m. a kind of alkali, L. **-kshit,** mfn. abiding in all things, MaitrUp. **-kshiti-patitva,** n. lordship of the world, Jātakam. **-kshetra-tīrtha-māhātmya,** n. N. of wk. **-ga,** mfn. all-pervading, omnipresent (*-tva,* n.), Up.; MBh.; Yājñ. &c.; m. the universal soul, L.; spirit, soul, W.; N. of Brahman, L.; of Śiva, ib.; of a son of Bhīma-sena, MBh.; of a son of Paurṇamāsa, VP.; of a son of Manu Dharma-sāvarṇika, ib.; (*ā*), f. the Priyaṅgu plant, L.; n. water, ib. **-gaṇa,** m. the whole company, PārGṛ.; (*sárva-* or *sarvá-*), mfn. having or forming a complete company, RV.; AV.; TS. &c.; having all kinds or classes, of every kind, MW.; n. salt soil, L. (v.l. *sārvag°*). **-gata,** mfn. = *-ga* (*papracchânāmayaṃ tayoḥ sarva-gatam,* 'he asked whether they were in all respects well,' MBh.; *yacca kiṃ cit sarva-gataṃ bhūmau,* 'all whatever exists on the earth,' ib.), Up.; Yājñ. &c.; m. N. of a son of Bhīma-sena, BhP.; *-tva,* n. universal diffusion, omnipresence, Bhāshāp. **-gati,** f. the refuge of all, MBh.; Pañcar. **-gandha,** m. pl. all kinds of perfumes, Suśr.; VarBṛS.; Hcat.; (*sárva-*), mfn. containing all odours, ŚBr.; ChUp.; m. n. a partic. compound of various perf°s, Bhpr.; Hcat.; any perf°, W.; (*ā*), f. a partic. perf°, Suśr.; (°*dha*)-*maya,* mf(*ī*)n. including all perfumes, Hcat.; *-vaha,* mfn. wafting perfume of all kinds, Mn. i, 76. **-gandhika,** mfn. consisting of all perfumes, Suśr. **-gambhīra,** mfn. deepest of all, Buddh. **-gavī,** f. pl. all cows, ĀpŚr., Sch. **-gātra,** n. pl. all limbs, Ml. **-gāmin,** mfn. = *-ga,* A. **-gāyatra** (*sarvá-*), mfn. consisting wholly of the Gāyatrī, Br. **-gila,** mfn. all-swallowing; m. N. of a minister, Campak. **-gu** (*sárva-*), mfn. together with all cows, AV. **-guṇa,** mfn. valid through all parts, see *guṇa;* *-viśuddhi-garbha,* m. N. of a Bodhi-sattva, Buddh.; *-saṃcaya-gata,* m. a partic. Samādhi, ib.; *sampanna,* mfn. endowed with every excellence, gifted with ev° good quality, MW.; °*ṇâlaṃkāra-vyūha,* m. a partic. Samādhi, SaddhP.; °*ṇôpêta,* mfn. endowed with every good quality, MW. **-guṇin,** mfn. possessing all excellences, MBh. **-guru,** mfn. consisting of only long syllables, Piṅg., Sch. **-guhya-maya,** mf(*ī*)n. containing all mysteries, MBh. **-gṛihyá,** mfn. together with all domestics, ŚBr. **-granthi,** m. or **-granthika,** n. the root of long pepper, L. **-graha,** m. eating or swallowing all at once, Car.; *-rūpin,* mfn. (perhaps) having the form of (or pervading) all the planets (said of Kṛishṇa), Pañcar. **-grāsa,** mfn. swallowing all, NṛisUp.; (*am*), ind. (with √*gras*) so as to entirely devour, Prab. **-m-kasha,** mf(*ā*)n. oppressing or injuring all, cruel to all, Kāv.; Rājat. &c.; all-pervading, Bhaṭṭ.; m. a rogue, wicked man, W.; (*ā*), f. N. of Mallinātha's Comm. on the Śiśupāla-vadha. **-cakra-vicāra,** m. N. of wk. **-cakrā,** f. (with Buddhists) N. of a Tantra deity, Buddh. **-caṇḍāla,** m. 'wholly a Caṇḍāla,' N. of a Māra-putra, Lalit. **-candra,** m. N. of an author, Cat. **-carita,** n. N. of a drama. **-caru,** m. N. of a man, Br. **-carmiṇa,** mfn. wholly made of leather, Pāṇ. v, 2, 5; made of every kind of skin or l°, W. **-cārin,** m. 'all-pervading,' N. of Śiva, MW. **-cchandaka,** mfn. all-winning or all-captivating, MBh. ('fulfilling all wishes,' Nīlak.) **-ja,** mf(*ā*)n. wheresoever produced, ĀpŚr.; prod° from or suffering from all three humours, Suśr. **-jagat,** f. the whole world, the universe, W. **-jaṭa,** mfn. (prob.) wearing a whole braid of hair, MānGṛ. **-jana,** m. every person, VarBṛS.; BhP.; Pañcar. &c.; *-tā,* f. id., Pañcar.; *-priya,* mfn. dear to ev° one, ib.; (*ā*), f. a kind of medicinal plant (= *ṛiddhi*), L.; *-vaśya-hanuman-mantra,* m. N. of wk. **-janīna,** mfn. salutary to every one, Pāṇ. v, 1, 9, Vārtt. 4, Pat.; relating or belonging to every one, Sarvad.; peculiar to every one (*-tva,* n.), ib.; Sāy. **-janīya,** mfn. = *sarveshāṃ janāya hitaḥ,* Pāṇ. v, 1, 9, Vārtt. 5, Pat. **-janman** (*sarvá-*), mfn. of all kinds, AV. **-jaya,** m. a complete victory, Cat.; (*ā*), f. Canna Indica, L.; a partic. religious observance performed by women in the month Mārgaśīrsha, SkandaP. **-jāgata** (*sarvá-*), mfn. consisting wholly of Jagatī, ŚBr. **-jit,** mfn. all-conquering, L.; conqu° all (three) humours, Car.; all-surpassing, excellent, W.; m. death, Car.; a partic. Ekāha, PañcavBr.; KātyŚr.; Vait.; the 21st year of Jupiter's cycle of 60 years, VarBṛS.; N. of a man, KaushUp.; (*-jin*)-*mahā-vrata-prayoga,* m. N. of wk. **-jīva,** m. the soul of all, BhP.; Pañcar.; *-maya,* mf(*ī*)n. being the soul of all, R. **-jīvin,** mfn. one whose progenitors (i.e. father, grandfather, and great grandf°) are all alive, ĀśvŚr. **-jña,** mf(*ā*)n. all-knowing, omniscient (said of gods and men, esp. of ministers and philosophers), Up.; Kāv. &c.; a Buddha, L.; an Arhat (with Jainas), ib.; N. of Śiva, Pañcat.; Kāśikh.; of various men, R.; Hit.; Buddh.; (*ā*), f. N. of Durgā, DevīP.; of a Yoginī, Hcat.; *-jñāmin,* mfn. thinking one's self omniscient, Divyâv.; *-tā,* f. (MBh.; Kathās.) or *-tva,* n. (MBh.; R. &c.) omniscience; *-deva* (Buddh.), *-nārāyaṇa* (Cat.), m. N. of scholars; *-putra,* m. N. of Siddha-sena, Siṅhâs.; *-bhaṭṭa,* m. N. of a man, ib.; *-mānin,* mfn. (= *-jñānin*), Divyâv.; *-mitra,* m. N. of various persons, Rājat.; Buddh.; *-m-manya,* mfn. (= *-jñānin;* °*ya tā,* f.), Rājat.; *-rāmêśvara-bhaṭṭâraka,* m. N. of an author, Cat.; *-vāsudeva,* m. N. of a poet, ib.; *-vishṇu,* m. N. of a philosopher, Sarvad.; *-vyavasthāpaka,* N. of wk.; *-śrī-nārāyaṇa,* m. N. of an author, Cat.; *-sūnu,* m. patr. of Skanda, Kāśikh.; °*jñâtma-giri* (Col.) or °*ma-muni* (Cat.), m. N. of an author; °*jñârdha-śarīriṇī,* f. N. of Umā, Kāśikh. **-jñātṛi,** mfn. omniscient; *-tva,* n. omniscience, Cat. **-jñāna,** n. 'all-knowledge,' N. of a Tantra wk.; m. N. of a deity, Buddh.; *-tantra,* n. N. of a Tantra wk.; *-maya,* mf(*ī*)n. containing all knowledge, Mn.; R.; *-vid,* mfn. acquainted with all kn°, MW.; °*nôttama* or °*nôttama-tantra,* n., °*nôttara,* n., °*nôttara-vṛitti,* f. N. of wks. **-jñīya,** mfn., Kan., Sch. **-jyāni,** f. the complete loss of all one's property, AV.; Br.; ŚrS.; SaṃhUp. **-jyotisha-saṃgraha,** m. N. of wk. **-jyotis,** m. N. of an Ekâha, PañcavBr.; KātyŚr. **-jvara,** m. all kinds of fever, (or) fever arising from disturbances of all the humours; *-vipāka,* m. N. of ch. of the Rudray.; *-hara* (L.) or *-jvarâpaha* (Suśr.), mfn. removing such fever. **-tathāgata,** in comp.; *-dharma-vāṅ-nishprapañca-jñāna-mudrā, -prajñā-jñāna-m°, -bandhana-jñāna-m°, -vajrâbhisheka-jñāna-m°, -viśva-karma-jñāna-m°,* f. N. of partic. positions of the fingers, L.; *-vyavalokana,* m. a partic. Samādhi, Kāraṇḍ.; *-saṃtoshaṇī,* f. N. of a Tantra deity, L.; *-samājâdhishṭhāna-jñāna-mudrā,* f. a partic. position of the fingers, L.; *-su-rata-sukhā,* f., °*tâkarshaṇī,* f. N. of Tantra deities, L.; °*tânurāgaṇa-jñāna-mudrā,* f. a partic. position of the fingers, L.; °*tânurāgaṇī,* f. N. of a Tantra deity, L.; °*tâśā-paripūraṇa-jñāna-mudrā,* f. a partic. position of the fingers, L. **-tanu** or °**nū** (*sárva-*), mfn. complete in regard to the body or person, AV.; ŚBr.; TĀr.; ĀśvŚr.; (*ū*), m. one who is born again with his whole body, MW. **-tantra,** n. pl. all doctrines, Hcat.; mfn. = *sarvaṃ tantram adhīte veda vā,* Pat. on Pāṇ. iv, 2, 60; universally acknowledged, admitted by all schools (as a philosophical principle), W.; m. one who has studied all the Tantras, ib.; *-maya,* mf(*ī*)n. (prob.) containing all doctrines, Hcat.; *-śiromaṇi,* m. N. of wk.; *-siddhânta,* m. a dogma admitted by all systems (opp. to *prati-tantra-s°,* q.v.), Car.; Nyāyad. **-tapo-maya,** mf(*ī*)n. containing all penances, Pañcar. **-tamo-nuda,** mfn. driving away all darkness (as the sun), MBh. **-tara,** comp. of *sarva,* Pāṇ. vi, 1, 191, Sch. **-tas,** see s.v. **-tā,** f. wholeness, totality, Nyāyam. **-tāti** (*sarvá-*), f. totality, RV.; completeness, perfect happiness or prosperity, soundness, ib.; AV.; (*ā,* loc.), ind. all together, entirely, RV.; ŚāṅkhŚr.; (accord. to Sāy. 'everywhere' or 'at the sacrifice.') **-tāpana,** mfn. all-inflaming, W.; m. N. of Kāma, L. **-tiktā,** f. Solanum Indicum, L. **-tīkshṇa,** mfn. quite sharp, VPrāt. **-tīrtha,** N. of a village, R.; n. pl. all sacred bathing-places, MBh.; *-maya,* mf(*ī* or [m. c.] *ā*) n. containing all sacred b°-pl°, Hcat.; Pañcar.; *-yātrā-vidhi,* m. N. of wk.; °*thâtmaka,* mfn. (= °*tha-maya*), Pañcar.; °*thêśvara,* n. N. of a Liṅga in Benares, Kāśīkh. **-tūrya-ninādin,** m. 'playing all instruments,' Śiva, MW. **-tejas,** n. all splendour (see comp.); m. N. of a son of Vyushṭa, BhP.; °*jo-maya,* mf(*ī*)n. containing all spl°, all-glorious, Mn.; R.; Hit.; cont° all power, W. **-tyāga,** m. complete renunciation, Mcar.; loss of everything, Car. **-traishṭubha** (*sarvá-*), mfn. consisting wholly of Trishṭubh, ŚBr. **-tvá,** n. wholeness, totality, completeness, ib.; TS. **-thā,** see s.v. **-da,** mf(*ā*)n. all-bestowing, Siṅhâs.; Kuval.; Pañcat.; m. N. of Śiva, MW.; *-rāja,* m. N. of a king, Buddh. **-daṇḍa-dhara,** mfn. punishing every one (Śiva), MBh. **-damana,** mfn. all-subduing or all-taming; m. N. of Bharata (son of Śakuntalā), MBh.; Hariv.; Śak.; of an Asura, Kathās. **-darśana,** mfn. all-viewing, BhP.; Śivag.; *-śiromaṇi,* m. N. of wk.; *-saṃgraha,* m. 'compendium of all the Darśanas,' N. of a treatise on the various systems of philosophy (not including the Vedânta) by Mādhavâcārya or his brother Sāyaṇa, IW. 118; 119. **-darśin,** mfn. all-seeing, MBh.; R.; VarBṛS.; m. a Buddha, L.; an Arhat (with Jainas), ib. **-dā,** see s.v. **-dātṛi,** mfn. all-giver (*-tva,* n.), Sāy. **-dāna,** n. the gift of everything, gift of one's all, L.; *-vidhi,* m. N. of wk.; °*nâdhika,* mfn. better than every gift, Yājñ. **-dāsa,** m. N. of a poet, Cat. **-dāha,** m. complete combustion, ĀpŚr. **-digvijaya,** m. conquest of all regions, universal conq°, MW. **-diṅ-mukham,** ind. towards all regions, Śatr. **-duḥkha-kshaya,** m. destruction of all pain, final emancipation from all existence, L. **-dushṭânta-kṛit,** mfn. destroying all the wicked, Pañcar. **-dṛiś,** mfn. all-seeing, Hariv.; BhP.; Pañcar.; f. pl. all eyes, i.e. all organs of senses, BhP. **-deva,** m. pl. all the gods, Ml.; *-tā-pushpâdi-pūjana,* n., *-tā-pratishṭhā-sāra-saṃgraha,* m. N. of wks.; *-tā-maya,* mf(*ī*)n. containing all deities, BhP.; *-pūjana-prakāra,* m., *-pūjana-prayoga,* m., *-pratishṭhā,* f., *-pratishṭhā-karman,* n., *-pratishṭhā-krama-vidhi,* m., *-pratishṭhā-vidhi,* m. N. of wks.; *-maya,* mf(*ī*)n. comprising or representing all gods, R.; Rājat.; BhP. &c.; m. N. of Śiva, MW.; *-mu-*

kha, m. (?) 'mouth of all the gods,' N. of Agni, L.; *-mūrti-pratishṭhā-vidhi*, m., *-sādhāraṇa-nitya-pūjā-vidhi*, m., *-sūkta*, n. N. of wks.; *-sūri*, m. N. of an author, Cat.; *-hutâśana*, mfn. eating the sacrifice designed for all gods; m. N. of Agni, R.; °*vâtmaka* (Sāy.) or °*vâtman* (RāmatUp.), mfn. having the nature of all gods, containing all gods; °*vêśa*, m. lord of all gods (Śiva), MBh.; *sarva-devī-mayī*, f. containing or representing all goddesses, Hcat. — **devata**, mfn. relating to all the deities, MW. — **devatyà**, mfn. sacred to or representing all the gods, TS.; Br. — **deśa-vṛittânta-saṃgraha**, m. N. of wk. — **deśīya**, mfn. coming from or existing or found in every country, Kāśīkh.; Kull. on Mn. viii, 143. — **deśya**, mfn. being in all places, RPrāt. — **daivatya**, mfn. representing all the gods, BṛĀrUp., Sch.; = *sārvad*°, MW. — **dravya**, n. pl. all things, Ml. — **drashṭṛi**, mfn. all-viewer, all-seeing, NṛisUp. — **dvārika**, mfn. favourable to a warlike expedition towards all regions, VarYogay. — **dhana**, n. all one's property, W.; (in arithm.) a sum total, sum or total of a series (in progression), ib. — **dhanin**, mfn. possessed of all goods, Pat. on Pāṇ. ii, 1, 69, Vārtt. 5. — **dhanvin**, m. 'best archer,' the god of love, L. (w. r. *-dhanvan*). — **dhara**, m. N. of a lexicographer, Col.; Cat.; n. N. of wk. — **dharman**, m. N. of a king, VP.; (*sarva-dharma*, in comp.; *-pada-prabheda*, m. a partic. Samādhi, Buddh.; *-prakāśa*, m. N. of wk.; *-praveśana*, n., *-praveśa-mudra*, m. N. of a partic. Samādhi, Buddh.; *-maya*, mf(*ī*)n. containing all laws, Yājñ.; *-mudra*, m. a partic. Samādhi, Buddh.; *-vid*, mfn. knowing all laws, Mn.; Yājñ., Sch.; *-samatā*, f. N. of a Samādhi, Buddh.; *-samatā-jñāna-mudrā*, f. a partic. position of the fingers, ib.; *-samavasaraṇa-sāgara-mudrā*, f., *-samavasaraṇa-sāgara-mudra*, m.; °*rmâtikramaṇa*, m. N. of Samādhis, ib.; °*rmâpravṛitti-nirdeśa*, m. N. of wk.; °*rmôttara-ghosha*, m. N. of a Bodhisattva, Buddh.; °*rmôdgata*, m. N. of a Samādhi, ib.) — **dhā́**, mfn. all-refreshing, all-pleasing, RV.; all-containing, all-yielding, MW. — **dhāman**, n. the abode or home of all, Pañcar. — **dhārin**, m. 'all-holder,' N. of Śiva, MBh.; of the 22nd year of Jupiter's cycle of 60 years (also *-dhārī*, f. accord. to some), VarBṛS. — **dhārī**, the 22nd year of the cycle (accord. to some; cf. prec.), W. — **dhurā-vaha**, mfn. bearing all burdens, mfn., L.; m. = next, m., W. — **dhurīṇa**, mfn. fit for any kind of carriage or draught, Pāṇ. iv, 4, 78; m. a dr°ox or other animal, W. — **nakshatrêshṭi**, f. N. of wk. — **nara**, m. every man, Vedântas. — **nāman**, n. (in gram.) N. of a class of words beginning with *sarva* (comprising the real pronouns and a series of pronominal adjectives, such as *ubhaya, viśva, ekatara* &c.; cf. under *sarva*), Āpast.; Nir.; APrāt. &c.; mfn. having all names, Nir.; BhP.; °*ma-tā*, f. or °*ma-tva*, n. the being a pronoun or a pronominal; °*ma-śakti-vāda*, m. N. of wk.; °*ma-sthāna*, n. a case-termination before which the strong base of a noun is used, Pāṇ. — **nāśa**, m. complete loss, KātyŚr.; destruction of everything, complete ruin (°*śaṃ* √*kṛi*, 'to lose everything'), Mn.; Pañcat.; Hit. — **nāśin**, mfn. all-destroying, MW. — **nikshepā**, f. a partic. method of counting, Lalit. (cf. *-vikshepatā*). — **nidhana**, m. a partic. Ekâha, ŚāṅkhŚr. — **niyantṛi**, m. all-subduer (*-tva*, n.), Vedântas. — **niyojaka**, mfn. impelling or directing all (Vishṇu), Pañcar. — **nirākṛiti**, mfn. causing to forget everything, BhP. — **nilaya**, mfn. having one's abode everywhere, ib. — **nivaraṇa-vishkambhin**, m. N. of a Bodhisattva, Buddh. (w. r. *-ṇīv*°, Kāraṇḍ.) — **m-dada**, m. N. of a man, Buddh. — **m-dama** or °**mana**, m. 'all-subduing,' N. of Bharata (son of Śakuntalā), L. — **paṭṭa-maya**, mf(*ī*)n. made of cloth of all kinds, Vās. — **pati**, m. a lord of everything. — **pattrīṇa**, mfn. occupying the whole chariot, Pāṇ. v, 2, 7. — **patha**, m. every road or way, every direction, W. — **pathīna**, mf(*ā*)n. occupying the whole road, Pāṇ.; Bhaṭṭ.; Śiś.; going in every direction, propagated or celebrated everywhere (*-tā*, f.), Hcat.; Śiś., Sch. — **pad** (strong base *-pād*; *sárva-*), mfn. all-footed, AV. — **pada**, n. pl. (or ibc.) words of every kind, Naigh.; Nir. — **paddhati**, f. N. of wk. — **pariphulla**, mfn. full blown, L. — **parus** (*sárva-*), mfn. having all joints, AV. — **paro'ksha**, mf(*ā*)n. imperceptible by all, SaṃhUp. — **paśu**, m. 'all animal,' N. of a blockhead, Cat.; pl. all animal sacrifices, Lāṭy.; (*sarvá-*), mfn. fit for every animal or animal sacrifice, consisting entirely of animal sac°, ib.; TBr. — 1. **-pā**, mfn. drinking everything, MW.; f. N. of the wife of the Daitya Bali, L. — 2. **-pā**, mfn. all-preserving, MW. — **pāñcālaka**, mfn. consisting entirely of Pañcālas, Pāṇ. vi, 2, 105, Sch. — **pātrīṇa**, mfn. filling the whole dish, Pāṇ. v, 2, 7. — **pāda**, m. N. of a man, W. — **pāpa-roga-hara-śata-māna-dāna**, n. N. of wk. — **pāpa-hara**, mfn. removing all sin, MW. — **pāraśava**, mfn. made entirely of iron, MBh. — **pārśva-mukha**, m. 'having a face on all sides,' N. of Śiva, MW. — **pārshada**, n. a text-book received by all grammatical schools (*-tva*, n.), Sarvad. — **pālaka**, mfn. all-preserving or -protecting, Pañcar. — **pāvana**, m. 'all-purifying,' N. of Śiva, MBh. — **puṇya**, mfn. perfectly beautiful, MBh.; *-samuccaya*, m. N. of a Samādhi, Buddh. — **pura-kshetra-māhātmya**, n., *-purāṇa*, n., *-purāṇa-sāra*, *-purāṇârtha-saṃgraha*, m. N. of wks. — **purusha** or *-pūr*° (*sárva-*), mfn. having all men &c., AV.; ĀśvŚr.; Kauś. — **pūjita**, m. 'worshipped by all,' N. of Śiva, MBh. — **pūta**, mfn. completely pure, NṛisUp. — **pūraka**, mfn. all-filling, Pañcar. — **pūrṇa**, mfn. full of everything; *-tva*, n. entire fulness or completeness, complete preparation or provision, L. — **pūrti-kara-stava**, m. N. of wk. — **pūrva**, mfn. the first of all, Pat.; preceded by any (sound), RPrāt. — **pṛithvī-maya**, mf(*ī*)n. containing the whole earth, Hcat. — **pṛishṭha** (*sárva-*), mf(*ā*)n. provided with all the (6) Pṛishṭhas (q. v.), TS.; Kāṭh.; Br.; ĀśvŚr.; (*ā*), f. a partic. sacrifice, TS.; ŚāṅkhBr.; m. or n. (?) N. of various wks.; *-prayoga*, m., *-hautra-prayoga*, m.; °*ṭhâptor-yāma-pray*°, m., °*ṭhâptor-yāma-sāman*, n. pl., *-ṭhâptor-yāma-hautra-prayoga*, m., °*ṭhêshṭi*, f., *-ṭhêshṭi-prayoga*, m., °*ṭhêshṭi-hautra*, n., *-ṭhêshṭi-hautra-paddhati*, f. N. of wks. — **prakāra**, mfn. existing in all forms, Sarvad.; (*am*), ind. in every manner, in every respect, MārkP. — **pratyaksha**, mf(*ā*)n. being before the eyes of all, SaṃhUp. — **pratyaya-mālā**, f. N. of wk. — **prathamam**, ind. before all, first of all, Lalit. — **prada**, mf(*ā*)n. all-bestowing, Pañcar. — **prabhu**, m. the lord of all, Ragh. — **prayatna**, m. every effort; (*ena*), ind. with all one's might, to the best of one's ability, Hcat. — **prāṇa**, m.; (*ena*), ind. with all one's soul, R.; Kathās. — **prâpti**, f. attainment of all things, KapS. — **prâyaścittá**, mf(*ī*)n. atoning for everything, ŚBr.; n. expiation for everyth°, Gaut.; a partic. libation in the Āhavanīya, GṛŚrS.; N. of wk.; *-prayoga*, m., *-lakshaṇa*, n., *-vidhi*, m. N. of wks. — **prâyaścitti**, f. complete atonement, AitBr. — **prâyaścittīya**, mfn. relating or belonging to the Sarva-prâyaścitta libation, Kauś.; Vait. — **priya**, mfn. loving all or dear to all, W. — **phala-tyāga-caturdaśī**, f. N. of a partic. 14th day; *-vrata*, n. a partic. religious observance, Cat. — **bandha-vimocana**, m. 'delivering from every bond,' N. of Śiva, MBh. — **bala**, n. a partic. high number, Lalit. — **bāhu**, m. a partic. mode of fighting, Hariv. — **bāhya**, mfn. the outermost of all, IndSt. — **bīja**, n. the seed of everything, Pañcar.; °*jin*, mfn. containing all seed, Pāṇ. v, 2, 135, Vārtt. 2, Pat. — **buddha**, in comp.; *-kshetra-saṃdarśana*, m. a partic. Samādhi, Kāraṇḍ. (w. r. *-buddha-kshatra-s*°); *-vijayâvatāra*, m. N. of a Buddhist Sūtra wk.; *-saṃdarśana*, m. N. of a world, Buddh. — **bhaksha**, mf(*ā*)n. eating or devouring everything, omnivorous (*-tva*, n.), MBh.; R. &c.; being entirely eaten up, ŚrS.; (*ā*), f. a she-goat, L. — **bhakshin** (Kāv.; Pañcat.; Hit.) or **-bhakshya** (w. r. for *-bhaksha*), mfn. all-devouring, eating all things, omnivorous. — **bhaṭṭa**, m. N. of an author, Cat. — **bhayam-kara**, mfn. terrifying all, Pañcar. — **bhavâraṇi**, f. the Araṇi or cause of all welfare, MārkP. — **bhavôttaraṇa**, m. a partic. Samādhi, Kāraṇḍ. — **bhāj**, mfn. sharing in everything (*liṅgānāṃ na sarva-bhāk*, 'not being of every gender'), Pāṇ.; Kār. — **bhāva**, m. (ifc. f. *ā*) whole being or nature, MW.; the whole heart or soul, R.; complete satisfaction, Bālar.; pl. all objects, MaitrUp.; Mn.; *ena* (Bhag.; Hit.; BhP.) or *ais* (Pañcar.) or ibc. (R.), with all one's thoughts, with one's whole soul; *-kara*, m. 'causer of all being,' N. of Śiva, MBh.; °*vâdhishṭhātṛi*, m. the chief of all beings (*-tva*, n.), Cat. — **bhāvana**, mfn. all-creating or all-producing, R.; Pañcar.; m. N. of Śiva, MBh. — **bhāsa**, mfn., Pāṇ. vi, 2, 105, Sch. — **bhuj**, mfn. all-devouring, BhP. — **bhūtá**, mfn. being everywhere, Pur.; n. pl. (or ibc.) all beings, TĀr.; ŚāṅkhGṛ.; MBh. &c.; *-kṛit*, mfn. framing all beings, Mn. i, 18; m. n. the maker or cause of all things or beings, W.; *-guhā-śaya*, mfn. being in the heart of all beings, ŚvetUp.; *-damana* (*sárva-bh*°), mfn. subduing all beings, TĀr.; (°*nī*, f. a form of Durgā, Hcat.); *-pitāmaha*, m. 'grandfather of all beings,' N. of Brahmā, MBh.; *-maya*, mf(*ī*)n. containing or representing all b°, Mn.; R.; BhP.; m. the supreme pervading Spirit, W.; *-ruta-grahaṇī*, f. 'comprising the sounds of all b°,' a kind of writing (cf. *sarva-ruta-saṃgrahiṇi-lipi*), Lalit.; *-stha* or *-sthita*, mfn. present in all elements or b°, MBh.; *-hara*, m. N. of Śiva, ib. (RTL. 82); *-hita*, n. the welfare of all created b°, ib.; mfn. serviceable to all creatures, Kāv.; °*bhūtâtmaka*, mfn. comprising all beings, MārkP.; °*bhūtâtman*, m. the soul of all b° (°*ma-bhūta*, mfn. being the soul of all b°, BhP.), Mn. i, 54; the essence or nature of all creatures (°*ma-medhas*, mfn. 'having a knowledge of the essence of all cr°'), MW.; N. of Śiva, ib.; mfn. having the nature of all b°, containing all b°, ib.; °*bhūtâdhipati*, m. the supreme lord of all b° (Vishṇu), ShaḍvBr.; °*bhūtântaka*, mfn. destroying all b°, MBh.; °*bhūtântar-ātman*, m. the soul of all b°, RāmatUp.; MBh.; Śaṃk.; °*bhūtêpsita*, mfn. desired by all b°, MW. — **bhūmi**, f. the whole earth, Pāṇ. v, 1, 41; g. *anuśatikâdi*; mfn. owning the whole e°, AitBr. — **bhṛit**, mfn. all-sustaining or all-supporting, Bhag. — **bhogin**, mfn. enjoying all, W. — **bhogīṇa**, mfn. advantageous to all, to be enjoyed by all, Bhaṭṭ. — **bhogya**, mfn. id., Śak. — **bhauma**, w. r. for *sārvabh*°, Kathās. — **maṅgala**, mfn. universally auspicious, Pañcar.; (*ā*), f. N. of Durgā, RāmatUp.; Hit.; of Lakshmī, Pañcar.; of various wks.; n. pl. all that is auspicious, R.; *-mantra-paṭala*, N. of ch. of wk. — **maṇḍala-sâdhanī**, f. N. of wk. — **manorama**, mf(*ā*)n. delighting every one, MBh. — **mantra-śāpa-vimocana**, n., *-mantrôtkīlana*, n., *-mantrôtkīlana-śāpa-vimocana-stotra*, n., *-mantrôpayukta-paribhāshā*, f. N. of wks. — **máya**, mf(*ī*)n. all-containing, comprehending all, ŚBr.; Nir. &c. — **malâpagata**, m. a partic. Samādhi, Buddh. — **mahat**, mfn. greatest of all (*-tara*, 'greater than all the rest'), MBh.; Kathās.; completely great, Pāṇ. vi, 2, 93. — **mahī**, f. the whole earth, W. — **māṃsâda**, mfn. eating every kind of flesh, Mn. v, 15. — **māgadhaka**, mfn. consisting entirely of Magadhas, Pat. — **mātṛi**, f. the mother of all (du. with *rodasī*), MBh. — **mātṛikā-pushpâñjali**, m. N. of wk. — **mātrā**, f. a kind of metre, RPrāt.; Nidānas. — **mānya-campū**, f. N. of wk. — **māya**, m. N. of a Rākshasa, Mcar. — **māra-maṇḍala-vidhvaṇsana-karī**, f. 'destroying the whole company of Māras,' N. of a partic. ray, Lalit. — **māra-maṇḍala-vidhvaṇsana-jñāna-mudrā**, f. a partic. position of the fingers, Buddh. — **mitra**, m. a friend of every one, MBh.; N. of a man, Buddh. — **mukha**, mfn. facing in every direction (*-tva*, n.), BṛĀrUp., Sch. — **mūrti**, mfn. all-formed, VP. — **mūrdhanya**, m. (with Śāktas) N. of an author of mystical prayers, Cat. — **mūlya**, n. 'general token of value,' a cowry, L.; any small coin, MW. — **mūshaka**, m. 'all-stealing,' time, L. — **mṛityu**, m. universal death, Pañcar. — **medhá**, m. a universal sacrifice (a 10 days' Soma s°), ŚBr.; ŚrS. &c.; every sacrifice, BhP.; N. of an Upanishad. — **medhya**, mfn. universally or perfectly pure (*-tva*, n. 'universal purity'), Yājñ.; VarBṛS. &c. — **m-bhari**, mfn. all-supporting, ChUp., Sch. — **yajña**, m. every sacrifice (without Soma, accord. to Sch.), BhP.; pl. all sac°s, MBh. — **yatna**, m. ev° effort (*ena*, ind. 'with all one's might,' to the best of one's ability), MBh.; Cāṇ. &c.; *-vat*, mfn. making ev° possible eff°, Kām. — **yantrin**, mfn. provided with all implements, KātyŚr. — **yamaka**, n. congruity in sound of all the 4 Pādas (e. g. Bhaṭṭ. x, 19). — **yogin**, m. N. of Śiva, MW. — **yoni**, f. the source of all (*-tva*, n.), Ragh.; ChUp., Sch. — **yoshit**, f. pl. all women, Ml. — **rakshaṇa**, mfn. preserving from everything, BrahmavP.; *-kavaca*, n. an all-preserving amulet or charm, MW. — **rakshita**, m. N. of a grammarian, Cat. — **rakshin**, mfn. all-protecting, MW.; preserving from all (harm), R. — **ratna**, m. 'having all gems,' N. of a minister of king Yudhi-shṭhira, Rājat.; (*ā*), f. N. of a Śruti, Saṃgīt.; *-maya*, mf(*ī*)n. made up of all (kinds of) jewels, Kathās.; entirely studded with j°, MBh.; R.; *-samanvita*, mfn. possessed of all j°, MBh. — **ratnaka**, m. (with Jainas) N. of one of the 9 treasures and of the deity presiding over it, L. — **rathá**, ind. with the whole line of chariots, RV. — **rasa**, m. every taste or flavour, BhP.; the saline fl°, L.; the resinous exudation of the Vatica Robusta, Bhpr. (w. r. for *sarja-r*°); pl. (or ibc.) all kinds of juices or fluids, VarBṛS.; BhP.; all kinds of palatable food, ŚārṅgP.; mfn. (*sárva-*)

containing all juices, ŚBr.; ChUp.; wise, learned, L.; m. a sort of musical instrument, L.; a scholar, W.; °*sôttama*, m. 'best of all flavours,' the saline flavour, ib. — **rāj**, m. a king of all, VS.; MBh. — **rā-jêndra**, m. 'chief of all kings,' N. of a divine being, Cat.; (*ā*), f. a partic. position of the fingers, Kāraṇḍ. — **rājya**, n. universal sovereignty, MBh. — **rātra**, m. the whole night; ibc. or (*am*), ind. all through the night, KātyŚr.; Śiś.; Vās. — **rāsa**, m. (cf. *-rasa* above) the resinous exudation of the V° R°, L.; a sort of musical instrument, ib. — **ruta-kauśalya**, m. or n. (?) a partic. Samādhi, Buddh. — **ruta-saṃgrahiṇi-lipi** (?), f. a partic. mode of writing, Lalit. — **rūpa** (*sárva-* or *sarvá-*), mf(*ā*)n. having or assuming all forms (*-tā*, f.), Pañcar.; Jaim., Sch.; having all colours, ŚBr.; ŚrS.; of all kinds, AitBr.; PārGṛ.; MuṇḍUp.; *-bhāj*, mfn. assuming all forms, Ragh.; *-saṃdarśana*, m. a partic. Samādhi, SaddhP. — **rūpin**, mfn. having or assuming all forms, R. — **roga**, (ibc.) all kinds of diseases, Cat.; *-nidāna*, n., *-śānti*, f. N. of wks. — **rodha-virodha-sam-praśamana**, m. a partic. Samādhi, Buddh. — **ro-hita** (*sarvá-*), mfn. quite red, ŚBr.; KātyŚr. — **rtu** (°*va* + *ritu*), m. every season, MW.; 'containing all seasons,' a year, L.; *-parivarta*, m. 'revolution of all the s°s,' id., ib.; *-phala*, n. the fruit of all the s°, MW. — **rtuka** (°*va* + *ṛit*°), mfn. adapted to every season, habitable in every s°, existing in ev° s°, Mn.; R.; Hariv. &c.; *-vana*, n. N. of a forest, Hariv. — **lak-shaṇa**, (ibc.) all auspicious marks, R.; BhavP.; *-tāt-parya*, n., *-pustaka*, N. of wks.; *-lakshita*, m. 'characterized by all marks,' N. of Śiva, MBh. — **laghu**, mfn. entirely consisting of short syllables, Ked. — **lāla-sa**, m. N. of Śiva, MBh. — **liṅga**, mfn. having all genders, used as an adjective (*-tā*, f.), Pat.; *-pradātṛi*, mfn. liberal to adherents of every faith, MBh.; *-saṃ-nyāsa*, m., *-saṃnyāsa-nirṇaya*, m., *-sādhanī*, f.; °*gâdhyāya*, m. N. of wks. — **liṅgin**, m. 'having all kinds of external marks,' a heretic, L. — **luṇṭāka**, m. 'all-robbing,' N. of a fraudulent official, Campak. — **loká**, m. the whole world, VS.; Hariv.; R.; the whole people, VarBṛS.; every one, MBh.; R. &c.; pl. (or ibc.) all beings, VarBṛS.; ev° one, R.; Pañcar. &c.; *-kṛit*, m. 'Universe-maker,' N. of Śiva, MBh.; *-guru*, m. N. of Vishṇu, BhP.; *-dhātu-vyavalo-kana*, m. N. of a Samādhi, Kāraṇḍ.; *-dhatûpadra-vôdvega-pratyuttīrṇa*, m. N. of a Buddha, Buddh.; *-pitāmaha*, m. 'progenitor of all creatures,' N. of Brahmā, R.; *-prajāpati*, m. 'father of the Universe,' N. of Śiva, Śivag.; *-bhayam-kara*, mfn. appalling to the whole world, R.; *-bhayâstambhita-tva-vidhvaṇsana-kara*, m. N. of a Buddha, Buddh.; *-bhṛit*, mfn. supporting the whole w° (said of Śiva), Śivag.; *-maya*, mf(*ī*)n. containing the whole w°, R.; Hcat.; *-maheśvara*, m. N. of Śiva, R.; of Kṛishṇa, Bhag.; *-vid*, mfn. acquainted with all w°s, MBh.; °*kântarātman*, m. the soul of the whole w°, MBh.; °*kêśa*, m. 'lord of the whole world,' N. of Kṛishṇa, Kṛishṇaj.; °*kêśvara*, m. 'id.,' id., ib.; N. of Brahmā, R. — **lokin**, mfn. containing the whole world, RāmatUp. — **locanā**, f. the ichneumon plant, L. — **loha**, mfn. entirely red, Mn., Sch.; m. an iron arrow, L.; n. (ibc.) all kinds of metal, Cat.; *-maya*, mf(*ī*)n. entirely of iron, Pañcat. — **lohita**, mfn. entirely red, R. — **lauha**, m. 'entirely of iron,' an iron arrow, L. — **vat**, mfn. containing all, MānGṛ. — **vani**, mfn. all-acquiring or all-possessing, Kāv. — **varṇa**, mf(*ā*)n. all-coloured, TĀr. — **varṇikā**, f. the tree Gmelina Arborea, L. — **varṇin**, mfn. (prob.) of various kinds, MBh. — **vartikā**, v.l. for *-varṇikā*, L. — **varman**, m. N. of a grammarian (cf. *śarva-v*°), Buddh. — **vallabha**, mfn. dear to all, MW.; (*ā*), f. an unchaste woman, L. — **vāg-īśva-rêśvara**, m. N. of Vishṇu, Pañcar. — **vāṅ-ni-dhana**, m. N. of an Ekâha, ŚāṅkhŚr. — **vāṅ-maya**, mf(*ī*)n. containing all speech, entirely consisting of speech, BhP.; Cat. — **vāta-saha**, mfn. able to bear every wind (said of a ship), MW. — **vādin**, m. N. of Śiva, MBh.; (°*di*)*-sammata*, mfn. approved by all disputants, universally admitted, MW. — **vāram**, ind. all at once, simultaneously, Pañcat. — **vārshi-ka-parvan**, n. pl. all the junctures or special periods of a year, BhP. — **vāsa**, m. 'all-abiding,' Śiva, MBh. — **vāsaka**, mfn. completely clothed, MBh. — **vā-sin**, m. = *-vāsa*, MW. — **vikrayin**, mfn. selling all kinds of things, Mn. ii, 118. — **vikshepatā**, f. a partic. method of counting, Buddh. (cf. *-nikshe-pā*). — **vikhyāta**, m. 'celebrated by all,' N. of Śiva, MBh. — **vigraha**, m. 'all-shaped,' Śiva, ib. — **vi-jñāna**, n. knowledge of everything, Sarvad.; mfn. knowing everything (*-tā*, f.), R., Sch. — **vijñānin**, mfn. id.; (°*ñāni*)*-tā*, f. omniscience, ib. (v.l.); Kām. — **vid**, mfn. all-knowing, omniscient, AV.; MuṇḍUp.; MBh. &c.; m. the Supreme Being, MW.; f. the sacred syllable Om, L.; (*-vit*)*-tva*, n. omniscience, Cat. — **vidya**, mfn. possessing all science, omniscient, ŚvetUp.; (*ā*), f. all science, TBr.; every sc°, pl. all sc°s, TĀr.; °*yā-maya*, mf(*ī*)n. containing all sc°, Cat.; °*yâlaṃkāra*, °*yā-vinoda*, °*yā-vinoda-bhaṭṭâcārya*, m. N. of authors, ib.; °*yā-siddhânta-varṇana*, n. N. of wk. — **vināśa**, m. entire destruction, Gaut. — **vinda**, m. a partic. mythical being, ib. — **vibhūti**, f. dominion over all, MW. — **viśrambhin**, mfn. trusting all, Car. — **viśva**, n. the whole world, Pañcar. — **vishaya**, mfn. relating to everything, general, Vām. — **vishṭuti-prayoga**, m., **-vihārīya-yantra**, n. N. of wks. — **vīra** (*sárva-*), mf(*ā*)n. all-heroic, consisting of or relating to or accompanied by or leading all men or heroes, RV.; AV.; Kauś.; possessing numerous male descendants, MW.; *-jit*, mfn. conquering all heroes, Pañcar.; *-bhaṭṭāraka*, m. N. of an author, Cat. — **vīrya** (*sárva-*), mf(*ā*)n. endowed with all powers, ŚBr. — **vṛiddha**, mf(*ā*)n. recited entirely according to the quantity of the vowels, SaṃhUp. — **vega**, m. N. of a king, VP. — **vettṛi**, mfn. all-knower, omniscient (*-tva*, n.), L. — **veda**, mfn. having all knowledge, MW.; acquainted with all the Vedas, Pat. on Pāṇ. iv, 2, 60; m. a Brāhman who has read the four Vedas, W.; *-tri-rātra*, m. a partic. Ahīna, ŚāṅkhŚr.; *-maya*, mf(*ī*)n. containing all the Vedas, BhP.; °*dâtman*, w.r. for *sarva-devâtman*, RāmatUp.; °*dârtha*, m. N. of ch. of the BhP. — **vedas** (*sárva-*), mfn. having complete property, AV.; m. one who gives away all his prop° to the priests after a sacrifice, L. — **vedasá**, mfn. accompanied by a gift of all one's goods (as a sacrifice; also m. [scil. *kratu*] 'a sacrifice of the above kind'), MaitrS.; Br.; ŚrS.; giving all one's property to priests after a sac°, Mn. xi, 1 (v.l.); (*am*), n. all one's prop°, TS.; Br.; KaṭhUp.; ŚrS.; *-dakshiṇa*, mf(*ā*)n. attended with a gift of all one's prop° as a fee (at a sacrifice), ŚrS.; Mn. — **vedasin**, mfn. giving away all one's property, Kāṭh. — **veditṛi**, mfn. = *-vettṛi*, MBh. — **vedin**, mfn. omniscient, Śiś.; knowing all the Vedas, Hariv. — **veshin**, m. 'having all dresses,' an actor, L. (w.r. *-veśin*). — **vaidalya-saṃgra-ha**, m. N. of wk. — **vaināśika**, mfn. believing in complete annihilation, Col.; m. a Buddhist, ib.; N. of a class of Buddh° who hold the doctrine of total annih°, MW. — **vyāpad**, f. complete failure, AitBr. — **vyāpin**, mfn. all-pervading, Up.; MBh.; embracing all particulars, MW.; m. N. of Rudra, ib.; (°*pi*)*-tva*, n. universality, ib. — **vyūha-rati-sva-bhāva-naya-saṃdarśana**, m. N. of a king of the Gandharvas, Buddh. — **vrata**, n. a universal vow, ĀśvGṛ.; BhP.; mfn. all-vowing, ĀśvGṛ.; Kauś.; °*tôdyāpana*, n., °*tôdyāpana-prayoga*, m. N. of wks. — **śak**, mfn. all-powerful, omnipotent, MW. — **śakti**, f. entire strength (°*tyā*, ind. 'with all one's might'), MBh.; power of accomplishing all, Jam. — **śaṅkā**, f. suspicion of everybody, L. — **śabda-ga**, mfn. uttering various sounds, MBh. — **śarīra**, n. the body of all things (*-tā*, f.), Sarvad. — **śarīry-âtman**, m. the soul of all that has a body, BhP. — **śás**, see s.v., p. 1189, col. 2. — **śastrin**, mfn. provided with all kinds of weapons, MBh. — **śā-kuna**, n. the complete science of augury, VarBṛS. — **śānti**, f. universal tranquillity or calm, AV.; N. of wk.; *-kṛit*, m. 'causing univ° tr° or calm,' N. of Bharata (sovereign of all India and son of Śakuntalā), L. (cf. *-damana*); *-prayoga*, m. N. of wk. — **śāsá**, mfn. all-ruling, RV. — **śāstra**, mfn. knowing every science, MW.; *-pravetṛi*, m. 'charioteer of all science,' one well acquainted with all sc°, ib.; *-maya*, mf(*ī*)n. containing all treatises, Pañcar.; *-vid* or *-viśārada*, mfn. skilled in all sc°, MW.; °*trâr-tha-nirṇaya*, m. N. of wk. — **śishya**, mfn. to be taught by every one (*-tā*, f.), Kshem. — **śīghra**, mfn. swiftest of all, IndSt. — **śukla**, mf(*ā*)n. entirely light or white, ŚārṅgP. — **śuddha-vāla** (*sarvá-*), mfn. entirely white-tailed, VS.; MaitrS. — **śubhaṃ-kara**, mfn. auspicious to all, MBh.; m. N. of Śiva, MW. — **śūnya**, mf(*ā*)n. completely empty, Cāṇ.; Hit.; Vet. &c.; thinking everything non-existent, Pañcar.; *-tā*, f. complete void, KapS., Sch.; the theory that everything is non-ex°, nihilism, Sarvad.; *-tva*, n. id. (*-vādin*, m. 'an adherent of that theory, nihilist,' Bādar., Sch.), ib. — **śūra**, m. N. of a Bodhisattva, Kāraṇḍ. — **śesha**, mfn. remaining out of a whole, W. — **śaikyâyasa**, mf(*ī*)n. (prob.) entirely damaskeened, MBh. — **śoka-vināśin**, mfn. removing all sorrow or griefs, MW. — **śrāvya**, mfn. audible to all, ib. — **śruti-purāṇa-sāra-saṃ-graha**, m. N. of wk. — **śreshṭha**, mfn. the best of all (*-tama*, id., MBh.), R.; MārkP. — **śveta** (*sárva-*), mfn. entirely white, Suparṇ.; whitest of all, Pāṇ. vi, 2, 93, Sch.; (*ā*), f. a kind of venomous insect, Suśr.; a partic. mythical herb, Kāraṇḍ. — **saṃślishṭa**, mfn. contained in everything, MBh.; Pañcar. — **saṃsarga-lavaṇa**, n. salt soil, L.; a partic. kind of salt or salt soil (mixing with everything), MW. (v.l. *sārvasaṃ*°). — **saṃstha**, mfn. omnipresent, Hariv.; all-destroying, ŚvetUp.; (*ā*), f. pl. all the Soma-saṃsthās, ĀpŚr. — **saṃsthāna**, mfn. having all shapes, VarBṛS. — **saṃhāra**, mfn. all-destroying; m. time, R.; universal destruction, NṛisUp.; Hariv. — **saṃhārin**, mfn. all-destroying, Kathās. — **saguṇa**, mfn. possessing excellencies in everything, ib. — **saṃgata**, mfn. united with all, met with universally, W.; m. a sort of rice ripening in 60 days, L. — **saṅga-parityāga**, m. abandonment of all worldly affections or connections, MW. — **saṅgā**, f. N. of a river, MBh. — **saṃgra-ha**, m. a general or universal collection, W.; N. of various wks.; mfn. possessed of everything, R. — **saṃjñā**, f. (with Buddhists) a partic. high number, Lalit. — **sattva-trātṛi**, m. N. of a mythical being, SaddhP. — **sattva-pāpa-jahana**, m. N. of a Samādhi, Buddh. — **sattva-priya-darśana**, m. N. of a Buddha, ib.; of a Bodhi-sattva, ib.; of another person, ib. — **sattvâujo-hārī**, f. N. of a Rākshasī, ib. (v.l. *-sattvôj*°). — **satya**, mfn. truest of all, Pañcar. — **saṃnahana**, n. (L.) or °**hanârthaka**, m. (MW.) a complete armament or armour. — **saṃ-nāha**, m. id., W.; being completely armed or prepared for anything, going about anyth° zealously, L.; the universally-pervading spirit, W. — **samatā**, f. sameness or identity with all things, ib.; equality or impartiality towards everything, Mn. xii, 125. — **samarpaṇa-stotra**, n. N. of wk. — **samāsa**, m. complete union, all together, KātyŚr. — **samā-hara**, mfn. all-destroying, R. — **samṛiddha** (*sar-vá-*), mfn. entirely well arranged, ŚBr.; ĀśvGṛ. — **sampatti**, f. success in everything, R.; Hcat.; abundance of ev°, Kathās. — **sampád**, f. complete agreement, ŚBr. — **sampanna**, mfn. provided with everything, ĀśvGṛ.; *-sasya*, mf(*ā*)n. having grain or corn provided everywhere, Mṛicch. — **sam-pāta**, m. every residue, all that remains, Hariv. — **sampradāyâbheda-siddhânta**, m. N. of wk. — **sambhava**, m. the source of everything, MārkP. — **sammata-śiksha**, f. N. of wk. — **sara**, m. a kind of ulcer in the mouth, Suśr.; Bhpr. — **sasya**, (ibc.) all kinds of grain; mf(*ā*)n. yielding all kinds of grain, L.; *-bhū*, f. a field y° all k° of gr°, L.; *-vat*, mfn. (= *-sasya*, mfn.), Hcat. — **saha**, mf(*ā*)n. all-enduring, very patient, MBh.; BhP.; Śivag.; m. bdellium, L.; (*ā*), f. the earth, MW.; N. of a mythical cow, MBh. — **sâkshin**, m. the witness of everything, NṛisUp.; Pañcar.; N. of the Supreme Being, MW.; of the Wind, ib.; of Fire, ib. — **sāda**, mfn. that wherein everything is absorbed, Hariv. (Nīlak.). — **sādhana**, mfn. accomplishing everyth°, Pañcat.; m. Śiva, MBh. — **sādhāraṇa**, mf(*ā* or *ī*)n. common to all, NṛisUp.; R. &c.; *-prayoga*, m. N. of wk. — **sādhu**, ind. very good, very well! (used as an exclamation), Hit.; *-nishevita*, m. 'honoured by all good people,' Śiva, MBh. — **sāmānya**, mf(*ā*)n. common to all, Rājat. — **sāmprata**, n. omnipresence, Śatr. — **sāmya**, n. equality in all respects, ĀśvŚr. — **sāmrājya-medha-sahasra-nāman**, n. N. of wk. — **sāra**, n. the essence or cream of the whole (also *-tama*), Cat.; N. of various wks.; *-nir-ṇaya*, m., *-saṃgraha*, m. N. of wks.; *-saṃgra-haṇī*, f. a partic. mode of writing, Lalit.; °*sārô-panishad*, f. N. of an Upanishad. — **sāraṅga**, m. N. of a serpent-demon, MBh. — **sāha**, mfn. all-enduring, ib. — **siddhā**, f. N. of the 4th and 9th and 14th lunar nights, IndSt. — **siddhânta**, m., **-sid-dhânta-saṃgraha**, m. N. of wks. — **siddhâr-tha**, mfn. having every object accomplished, having ev° wish gratified, Mn.; R.; Pañcar. — **siddhi**, f. accomplishment of ev° object, universal success, W.; entire proof, complete result, KapS.; m. Ægle Marmelos, L. — **sukha-kṛit**, mfn. causing universal happiness, MBh. — **sukha-duḥkha-nira-bhinandin**, m. a partic. Samādhi, Buddh. — **su-khâya**, Nom. Ā. °*yate*, to feel every pleasure or delight, Hcat. — **surabhi**, n. everything fragrant, all perfumes, ŚBr. **– sulabha**, mfn. easy to be obtained by every one, Sarvad. **– sûkta**, n. N. of wk. **– sūkshma**, mfn. finest or most subtle of all, MBh. **– sūtra** (*sárva-*), mfn. made of all-coloured threads, MaitrS. (cf. *sārvas*°). **– sena** (*sárva-*), mfn. leading all the host, RV.; m. the lord of the whole host, MW.; N. of a son of Brahma-datta, Hariv.; of an author, Cat.; of a place, g. *śaṇḍikâdi*; °*nâdhinātha* (Viddh.) or °*nā-pati* (MBh.), m. a commander in chief. **– sauvarṇa**, mfn. entirely of gold, Pāṇ. vi, 2, 93, Sch. **– steya-kṛit**, mfn. one who steals everything, Mn. iv, 256. **– stoma** (*sárva-*), mf(*ā*)n. provided with all the (6) Stomas, TS.; Br.; ŚrS.; m. N. of an Ekâha, KātyŚr.; Lāṭy.; Vait. **– sthāna-gavāṭa**, m. N. of a Yaksha, Kathās. **– smṛit**, mfn. (prob.) w. r. for *-sprit*, all-obtaining or -procuring, MaitrUp. **– smṛiti**, f., **-smṛiti-saṃgraha**, m. N. of wks. **– sva**, n. (ifc. f. *ā*) the whole of a person's property or possessions, GṛŚrS.; Mn.; MBh. &c.; (ifc.) entirety, the whole, whole sum of, MBh.; Hariv.; Kāv. &c.; (*ā*), f. entire property, Kauś.; *-dakshiṇa*, mfn. (a sacrifice) at which the whole prop° is given away, Ragh.; *-daṇḍa*, mfn. fined or mulcted of all possessions, W.; n. confiscation of entire prop°, ib.; *-phalin*, mfn. with all one's possessions and fruits, Mṛicch.; *-rahasya*, n. N. of wk.; *-haraṇa*, n. or *-hāra*, m. the seizure or confiscation of all one's property, W. **– svara-lakshaṇa**, n. N. of wk. **– svarita**, mfn. having only the Svarita (q.v.), VPrāt., Sch. **– svarṇa-maya**, mf(*ī*)n. entirely golden, Kāv. **– svāmin**, m. the owner or master of all, W.; a universal monarch, ib.; (°*mi*)-*guṇôpêta*, mfn. endowed with all the qualities of a master, ib. **– svāya**, Nom. Ā. °*yate*, (ifc.) to regard as one's whole property, Kpr., Sch. **– svāra**, m. N. of an Ekâha, Lāṭy.; Maś.; Nyāyam. **– svin**, m. a kind of mixed caste (the offspring of a Gopa or cowherd female and a Nāpita or barber), BrahmavP. **– hatyā**, f. every kind of murder, NṛisUp. **– hara**, mfn. appropriating everything, MBh.; inheriting a person's whole property, Vishṇ.; all-destroying (as death), Bhag.; R.; VarBṛS.; Pañcar.; m. N. of Yama, Hariv. **– haraṇa**, n. confiscation of one's entire property, Mn., Sch. **– hari**, m. N. of the hymn RV. x, 96, ŚāṅkhBr.; ŚāṅkhŚr.; of the author of the same hymn (having the patr. *Aindra*), Anukr. **– harsha-kara**, mfn. causing universal joy, Pañcar. **– hāyas** (*sárva-*), mfn. having all strength or vigour, AV. **– hāra**, m. = *-haraṇa*, Mn. viii, 399; (*am*), ind. confiscating a person's whole property, Kathās. **– hārin**, m. 'all-seizing,' N. of an evil spirit, MārkP. **– hāsya**, mfn. derided by all, Rājat. **– hita**, mfn. useful or beneficial to all; m. N. of Śākya-muni, VarBṛS.; n. pepper, L. **– hút**, mfn. offered completely (as a sacrifice), RV.; TS.; Br.; Lāṭy.; (prob.) all-sacrificing or sacrificing all at once, MW. **– huta** (*sárva-*), mfn. offered entirely (*-tva*, n.), AV.; TS.; GṛŚrS. **– huti**, f. a complete sacrifice, AitBr. **– hṛid**, n. the whole heart or soul; (°*dā*), ind. with all one's heart, RV. **– hema-maya**, mf(*ī*)n. entirely golden, Hcat. **– homa**, m. a complete oblation, ib.; (*asarva-h*°, 'not a complete obl°,' KātyŚr.); *-paddhati*, f. N. of wk. **Sarvâkara-prabhā-kara**, m., °**kara-varôpêta**, m. N. of partic. Samādhis, Buddh. **Sarvâkāra** (ibc.) or °**kāram**, ind. in all forms, in every way, Ratnâv.; Mcar. **Sarvâksha**, mfn. (prob.) casting one's eyes everywhere, Pañcar. **Sarvâgamôpanishad**, f. N. of an Upanishad. **Sarvâgneya**, mfn. sacred only to Agni, ŚāṅkhŚr. **Sarvâgrayaṇa-kāla-nirṇaya**, m. N. of wk. **Sarvâṅka**, m. N. of an author (or of wk.), Cat. **Sarvâṅga**, n. (ifc. f. *ī*) the whole body, Vās.; Kathās. &c.; pl. all the limbs, R.; Kathās.; MaitrUp., Sch.; all the Vedâṅgas, KenUp.; (*sárv*°), mf(*ī*)n. entire or perfect in limb, RV.; AV.; complete, (*-bhaṅga*, m. 'entire collapse'), Kām.; Rājat.; m. N. of Śiva, MBh.; (*am*), ind. in all respects, exactly, Kathās.; *-nyāsa*, m., *-yoga-dīpikā*, f. N. of wks.; *-rūpa*, m. N. of Śiva, MBh.; *-vedanā-sāmānya-karma-prakāśa*, m. N. of ch. of wk.; *-sundara*, mfn. beautiful in every member, completely beautiful, MW.; m. (also *-rasa*, m. 'whose essence is good for all the limbs') a partic. drug or medicament, L.; (*ī*), f. N. of various Comms. **Sarvâṅgika**, mfn. (an ornament) destined for the whole body, Mālatīm. **Sarvâṅgiṇa**, mf(*ā*)n. (w. r. °*gīna*) covering or pervading or thrilling the whole body, Kāv.; Kāvyâd. &c.; relating or belonging to the Aṅgas or Vedâṅgas collectively, W. **Sarvâcāra**, m. N. of wk. **Sarvâcārya**, m. the teacher of all, Veṇīs. **Sarvâjīva**, mfn. bestowing a livelihood on all, ŚvetUp. **Sarvâñc**, see p. 1189, col. 2. **Sarvâtithi**, mfn. receiving every one as guest, Gaut.; MBh.; *-vrata*, mfn. devoted to all guests, W. **Sarvâtithya**, n. N. of a lake, Śukas. **Sarvâtiśāyin**, mfn. surpassing everything, Mcar. **Sarvâtisārin**, mfn. suffering from diarrhœa caused by all the humours, Suśr. **Sarvâtodya-parigraha**, m. 'comprehending every musical instrument,' N. of Śiva, MBh. **Sarvâtmaka**, the whole soul (*ena*, ind. 'with all one's s°'), BhP.; mfn. all-containing (*-tva*, n.), ib.; Saṃk.; contained in everything, NṛisUp.; R.; proceeding from all the Doshas (= *sarva-doshâtm*°), Bhpr.; m. a partic. form of the Aptor-yāma, ĀpŚr., Sch. **Sarvâtmán**, m. the whole person (°*nā*, ind. 'with all one's soul'), ŚBr.; Mn.; MBh. &c.; the universal Soul, Up.; MBh.; R. &c.; the wh° being or nature (°*nā*, ind. 'entirely, completely'), Kād.; Nyāyam., Sch.; a Jina, HYog.; N. of Śiva, MBh.; (*sárv*° or °*vât*°), mfn. entire in person or nature, AV.; Br.; ĀśvŚr.; °*ma-tva*, n. the state or condition of the univ° Soul, LiṅgaP. (*-darśana*, n. 'the doctrine of the oneness of everything with Spirit,' MW.); °*ma-dṛiś*, mfn. seeing one's self everywhere, Cat.; °*ma-bhūti*, f. welfare of the whole self, Mn. iii, 91; all beings collectively, W. **Sarvâdi**, m. the beginning or first of all things, Pañcar.; mfn. having any kind of commencement whatever, RPrāt. **Sarvā-dṛiśa**, mfn. like to all, MW. **Sarvâdbhuta-śānti**, f. N. of wk. **Sarvâdya**, mf(*ā*)n. the first of all, having existed the first, Pañcar. **Sarvâdhāra**, m. a receptacle of everything, ib. **Sarvâdhika**, mfn. superior to everything, Bhām. **Sarvâdhikaraṇa**, n. pl. all occasions (*eshu*, ind. 'on all oc°'), MatsyaP. **Sarvâdhikāra**, m. general superintendence, W.; a chapter on various objects, Cat.; a ch° on objects concerning all, ĀpŚr., Sch. **Sarvâdhikārin**, mfn. superintending everyth°, Rājat.; m. a general superintendent, W. **Sarvâdhikya**, n. superiority to all, ib. **Sarvâdhipatya**, n. universal sovereignty, ŚvetUp. **Sarvâdhyaksha**, m. a general superintendent, Pañcar. **Sarvânanda**, m. N. of various authors and other persons (also *-kavi*, *-nātha*, *-miśra*, *-vandya-ghaṭīya*), Cat.; of wk. **Sarvânavadya-kāriṇī**, f. N. of wk. **Sarvânavadyâṅga**, mf(*ī*)n. having an entirely faultless body, MBh. **Sarvânukārin**, mfn. all-imitating, MW.; (*iṇī*), f. Desmodium Gangeticum, L. **Sarvânukrama**, m. (Caraṇ.), °**maṇikā**, f. (Cat.) or °**maṇī**, f. (ib.) a complete index (esp. to the Veda); N. of wks.; °*ṇī-vṛitti*, f. N. of Comm. **Sarvânudātta**, mfn. entirely accentless (*-tva*, n.), RPrāt.; Sāy. **Sarvânunāsika**, mfn. speaking through the nose, Śiksh. **Sárvânubhū**, mfn. all-perceiving, ŚBr. **Sarvânubhūti**, f. universal experience, MW.; a white variety of the Tri-vṛit plant, ib.; Convolvulus Turpethum, Car.; m. 'all-perceiving,' (with Jainas) N. of two Arhats, L. **Sarvânumati**, f. the consent of all, MW. **Sarvânushṭubha**, mfn. entirely consisting of Anushṭubh, ŚBr. **Sarvânusyūta**, mfn. strung together with everything (*-tva*, n.), BhP. **Sarvânta**, m. the end of everything (*e*, ind. 'at the very end of [gen.]'), Divyâv.; *-kṛit*, mfn. making an end of everything, Pañcar. **Sarvântaka**, mfn. = prec., ib. **Sarvântará** (ŚBr.; NṛisUp.) or °**tarastha** (Cat.), mfn. being in everything. **Sarvântar-âtman** (Pañcar.) or °**tar-yāmin** (BhP., Sch.), m. the universal Soul. **Sarvânna-bhakshaka**, mfn. eating all sorts of food (whether pure or not), L. **Sarvânna-bhūti**, m. a kind of divine being, ŚāṅkhGṛ. (doubtful reading). **Sarvânna-bhojin** (L.) or °**vânnin** (Āpast.) or °**vânnīna** (Pāṇ.; L.), mfn. = °*vânna-bhakshaka*. **Sarvânya**, mfn. entirely different, Pāṇ. viii, 1, 51. **Sarvâpara-tva**, n. 'being beyond all things,' final emancipation, MaitrUp. **Sarvā-pushṭi-prayoga**, m. N. of wk. **Sarvâpêksha**, mfn. relating to every particular, ĀpŚr., Sch. **Sarvâpti**, f. attainment of all, AitBr.; KaushUp. **Sarvâbhayam-kara**, mfn. causing universal safety, R. **Sarvâbhaya-prada**, mfn. giving safety to all (said of Vishṇu), Vishṇ. **Sarvâbharaṇa-bhūshita**, mfn. adorned with all ornaments, Nal. **Sarvâbharaṇa-vat**, mfn. having all ornaments, Hcat. **Sarvâbhāva**, m. non-existence or failure of all, Āpast.; Mn. ix, 189; absolute non-existence, Sāṃkhyak. **Sarvâbhibhū**, m. N. of a Buddha, Buddh. **Sarvâbhiśaṅkin**, mfn. mistrusting all (°*ki-tva*, n.), MBh.; Car. **Sarvâbhisaṃdhaka**, mfn. deceiving every one, Mn. iv, 195. **Sarvâbhisaṃdhin**, mfn. id., L.; m. a cynic, calumniator, W. **Sarvâbhisāra**, m. an attack with a complete army, Pārśvan. **Sarvâbhyantara**, mfn. the innermost of all, IndSt. **Sarvâmara-tva**, n. absolute immortality, R. **Sarvâmātya**, m. pl. all who belong to a household or family, servants &c., MānGṛ. **Sarvâmbhonidhi**, m. the sea, ocean, MBh. **Sarvâyasa**, mf(*ī*)n. entirely made of iron, ib. **Sarvâyu**, mfn. having or bestowing &c. all life (*-tva*, n.), VS.; Br.; ŚāṅkhŚr. **Sarvâyudha**, m. 'armed with ev° weapon,' N. of Śiva, MBh.; °*dhôpêta*, mfn. possessing all weap°, ib. **Sarvâyusha** (TUp.) or °**vâyus** (TS.), n. whole life. **Sarvâraṇyaka**, mfn. living on whatever a forest affords, Baudh. **Sarvârambha**, m. entire energy in the beginning of a work (*eṇa*, ind. 'with all one's might'), Cāṇ. **Sarvârishṭa-śānti**, f. N. of wk. **Sarvârtha**, m. pl. (or ibc.) all things or objects, all manner of things, MaitrUp.; Madhus.; all matters (*eshu*, ind. 'in all m°, in all the subjects contained in any particular work'), MW.; (*am*), ind. for the sake of the whole, Jaim.; mfn. suitable for ev° purpose (*-tva*, n.), KātyŚr.; ib., Sch.; regarding or minding everything, Pañcar.; m. N. of the 29th Muhūrta (in astron.); *-kartṛi*, m. the creator of all things, Pañcar.; *-kuśala*, mfn. skilful in all matters, Nal.; *-cintaka*, mfn. thinking about everything; m. a general overseer, chief officer, Mn.; MBh.; *-cintāmaṇi*, m. N. of various wks.; *-tā*, f. the possessing of all obj°, MW.; 'attending to everything,' distraction (opp. to *ekâgra-tva*), Cat.; *-nāman*, m. N. of a Bodhi-sattva, Buddh.; *-sādhaka*, mf(*ikā*)n. effecting everything, fit for everything (*-stotra*, n. N. of wk.), MBh.; Kathās. &c.; (*ikā*), f. N. of Durgā, Devīm.; *-sādhana*, mfn. = *-sādhaka*; (or) n. a means of accomplishing everything, Pañcat.; Kāv.; *-sāra-saṃgraha*, m. N. of wk.; *-siddha*, mfn. one who has accomplished all aims, R.; m. N. of Gautama Buddha (so called, according to some, because his parents' wishes were all fulfilled by his birth), Lalit.; of a king, W.; *-siddhi*, f. accomplishment of all aims, Kathās.; N. of various wks.; m. pl. (with Jainas) a class of deities, L.; °*thânusādhin*, effecting all things; (*inī*), f. N. of Durgā, L. **Sarvârhaṇa**, mfn. deserving everything, having a claim to everything, Pañcar. **Sarvâloka-kara**, m. N. of a Samādhi, Kāraṇḍ. **Sarvá-vat**, mfn. containing everything, ŚBr.; entire, complete, Divyâv. **Sarvâvasara**, m. 'universal leisure,' midnight, L.; (*am*), ind. on ev° occasion, Vet. **Sarvā-vasu**, m. a partic. sun-beam, VP. **Sarvâvastham**, ind. 'in all positions,' from all sides, MBh. **Sarvâvasthā**, f. every condition (*āsu*, 'at all periods'), MW. **Sarvâvāsa** (MBh.; Śivag.) or °**sin** (Śivag.), mfn. having one's abode everywhere. **Sarvâvṛiddha**, mf(*ā*)n. entirely recited without giving the quantity of the vowels, SaṃhUp. **Sarvâśaya**, m. 'refuge of all,' N. of Śiva, MBh. **Sarvâśin**, mfn. eating all sorts of food, Mn. ii, 118. **Sarvâścarya-maya**, mf(*ī*)n. containing or consisting of all marvels, Bhag.; BhP.; Pañcar. **Sarvâśyā**, n. the eating of all things, ŚBr. **Sarvâśramin**, mfn. belonging to or being in ev° order of life, KaivUp. **Sarvâśraya**, mf(*ā*)n. common to all, Yājñ.; giving shelter or protection to all, W.; m. N. of Śiva, MBh. **Sarvâsambhava**, m. the not being possible everywhere, KapS. **Sarvâstitva-vādin**, m. = °*sti-vādin*, Bādar., Sch. **Sarvâsti-vāda**, m. the doctrine that all things are real (N. of one of the 4 divisions of the Vaibhāshika system of Buddhism, said to have been founded by Rāhula, son of the great Buddha), MWB. 157; = next, MW. **Sarvâsti-vādin**, mfn. or m. an adherent of the above doctrine, Buddh. **Sarvâstra**, mfn. having all weapons, MW.; (*ā*), f. N. of one of the 16 Jaina Vidyā-devīs, L.; *-mahā-jvālā*, f. N. of one of the 16 J° V°-d°, ib.; *-vid*, mfn. knowing or skilled in all w°s, MW. **Sarvâsya**, n. the whole mouth, Śiksh.; mfn. connected with the wh° m°, TS., Sch. **Sarvâham-mānin**, mfn. believing everything to be the Ego, NṛisUp. **Sarvâhṇá**, m. the whole day, MaitrS.; (*am*), ind. all the day, Āpast. **Sarvâhṇika**, mfn. daily, Pañcar. (w. r. °*hnika*). **Sarvâhna**, m. = °*hṇa*, MW. **Sarvêndriya-sambhava**, mfn. arising from ev° sense, ib. **Sarvêla**, mfn. connected with all Ilās (Iḍās), ŚāṅkhŚr. **Sarvêśa**, m. the lord of all, KaushUp.; Pañcar.; the Supreme Being, W.; a universal monarch, ib.; (*ā*), f. the mistress of all, Pañcar. **Sarvêśvara**, m. the lord of all, NṛisUp.; BhP.; Pañcar. &c.; a universal monarch, W.; a partic. medicinal preparation, Cat.; N. of Śiva, W.; of a Buddhist saint, W.; (also with *tīra-bhuktīya* or *soma-yājin*) of a teacher and various authors, Sadukt.; Cat.; *-tattva-nirṇaya*, m. N. of ch. of wk.; *-tva*, n. almightiness, RāmatUp.; Vedāntas.; *-stuti-ratna-mālā*, f. N. of wk. **Sarvêshṭa-da**, mf(*ā*)n. accomplishing all wishes, Cat. **Sarvâiśvarya**, n. the sovereignty of every one, KapS.; sov° over all, Pañcar. **Sarvôcchitti**, f. (KapS.) or °**cchedana**, n. (Pañcat.) complete extermination. **Sarvôtkarsha**, m. pre-eminence over all, KapS. **Sarvôttama**, mfn. best of all, Kāv.; *-stotra*, n. N. of a Stotra. **Sarvôttaratvâbhidhāna**, n. N. of wk. **Sarvôdātta**, mfn. having the acute accent everywhere, RPrāt.; VPrāt., Sch. **Sarvôdyukta**, mfn. exerting one's self to the utmost, R. **Sarvôpakārin**, mfn. assisting all, MW.; (*iṇī*), f. N. of various Comms. **Sarvôpadha**, mfn. having any kind of preceding vowel, having any penultimate letter, RPrāt. **Sarvôpanishat-sāra**, °**sāra-praśnôttara**, n., **Sarvôpanishad**, f., °**shad-arthânubhūti-prakāśa**, m. N. of wks. **Sarvôparama**, m. cessation of all things, absolute rest (*-tva*, n.), Vedāntas. **Sarvôpâdhi**, m. a general attribute, MW. **Sarvôpâya-kauśalya-praveśana**, m. a partic. Samādhi, Kāraṇḍ. (w. r. °*ya-koś*°). **Sarvôru-trivedin**, m. N. of an author, Cat. **Sarvôllāsa-tantra**, n. N. of wk. **Sarvâugha**, m. an army complete in all its accoutrements, L.; = *guru-bheda* or *guru-vega*, L.; n. a kind of honey, L. **Sarvâushadhá**, mfn. consisting of various herbs, TBr.; n. all herbs, ŚBr.; TUp.; Lāṭy.; a partic. compound of strong smelling herbs, L.; *-nidāna*, n. N. of wk. **Sarvâushadhi**, f. sg. or pl. all (kinds of) herbs, GṛŚrS. &c.; (*ī*), f. pl. N. of 10 different h°s, Hcat.; (*i*), m. a class of 10 partic. h°s, L.; *-gaṇa*, m. id., ib.; *-nishyandā*, f. a partic. kind of writing, Lalit.; *-rása*, m. the juice or infusion of the herb called the Sarvâushadhi, MW.; *-varga*, m. = *sarvâushadhi*, m. ib.

Sarvaká, mf(*ikā*)n. all, every, whole, entire, universal, AV.; (*e*), ind. everywhere, L.

Sárvata, mf(*ā*)n. (perhaps) all-sided, MaitrS.

Sarvataḥ, in comp. for *sarvatas*. **-pāṇi-pāda**, mfn. having hands and feet everywhere, ŚvetUp.; Vishṇ.; MBh. **-śubhā**, f. Panicum Italicum, L. **-śruti-mat**, mfn. having ears everywhere, ŚvetUp.; MBh. **-sarvêndriya-śakti**, mfn. having organs all of which operate everywhere, Vishṇ.

Sarvataś, in comp. for *sarvatas*. **-cakshus**, mfn. having eyes everywhere, MBh.

Sarvátas, ind. from all sides, in every direction, everywhere, RV. &c. &c.; around (acc.), Vop. v, 7; Pāṇ. ii, 3, 2, Sch.; entirely, completely, thoroughly, AV.; Mn.; MBh. &c.; = *sarvasmāt* or *sarvebhyas*, from all, from every one &c., ŚrS.; Mn.; Yājñ. &c.

Sárvati, m. N. of a man, MaitrS.

Sarvato, in comp. for *sarvatas*. **-'kshi-śiro-mukha**, mfn. having eyes and head and mouth everywhere, ŚvetUp.; Vishṇ.; MBh. **-gāmin**, mfn. going in all directions, Kum. **-dikka**, mfn. extending in every direction, Jaim., Sch.; (*am*), ind. = (or w.r. for) next, Rājat. **-diśam**, ind. from all sides, in all directions, MBh.; R.; Rājat.; BhP.; (*as*), ind. id., MW. **-dhāra**, mfn. having a sharp edge in ev° dir°, MBh. **-dhura**, mfn. being everywhere at the head, Baudh. **-bhadra**, mfn. in ev° dir° or on ev° side good, in ev° way auspicious &c., BhP.; Pañcar.; m. a temple of a square form and having an entrance opposite to ev° point of the compass, ib.; a form of military array, Kām.; a square mystical diagram (painted on a cloth, and used on partic. occasions to cover a sort of altar erected to Vishṇu; but cf. below), W.; an artificial stanza in which each half Pāda read backwards is identical with the other half (e.g. Kir. xv, 25; Śiś. xix, 40; also n., Kpr.); a kind of riddle or charade (in which each syllable of a word has a separate meaning?), Kāv.; the car of Vishṇu, L.; N. of a mountain, BhP.; of a forest, MW.; Azadirachta Indica, L.; a bamboo, ib.; a kind of perfume, VarBṛS.; (*ā*), f. the tree Gmelina Arborea, Bhpr.; a sort of Dioscorea, L.; an actress, ib.; (*am*), n. a building having continuous galleries around, VarBṛS.; a mystical diagram of a square shape but enclosing a circle (employed for astrological purposes or on special occasions to foretell good or bad fortune; perhaps identical with the above), Cat.; a partic. mode of sitting, ib.; N. of a garden of the gods, BhP.; (m. or n.?) N. of various works; *-cakra*, n. a partic. diagram (see above), Cat.; N. of various wks.; °*kra-vyākhyāna*, n. N. of wk.; *-devatā-sthāpana-prayoga*, m., *-prayoga*, m., *-phala-vicāra*, m., *-maṇḍala*, n., *-maṇḍala-krama*, m., *-maṇḍala-devatā-mantra*, m. pl., *-maṇḍalâdi-kārikā*, f., *-lakshaṇa*, n., *-liṅgato-bhadra*, *-homa*, °*bhadrâdi-cakrâvali*, f. N. of wks. **-bhadraka**, m. (with *cheda*) a fourfold incision in the anus for fistula, Suśr.; a partic. form of temple (= *-bhadra*), VarBṛS.; (*ikā*), f. Gmelina Arborea, L. **-bhāva**, m. the being all around, Nir. **-mārgam**, ind. in all ways or directions, BhP. **-mukha** (*sarváto-*), mf(*ī*)n. facing in all dir°, turned ev° where, VS.; TS.; ŚBr. &c.; complete, unlimited, Kāv.; m. a kind of military array, Kām.; soul, spirit, L.; N. of Brahmā ('having four faces'), ib.; of Śiva, ib.; a Brāhman, L.; of Agni, MBh.; the heaven, Svarga, ib.; N. of wk.; n. water, Cat.; sky, heaven, L.; *-kārikā*, f. pl., *-paddhati*, f., *-prakaraṇa*, n., *-prayoga*, m.; °*khôdgātṛi-tva*, n., °*khôdgātra-prayoga*, m. N. of wks. **-vilāsa**, m. N. of Comm. **-vṛitta**, mfn. omnipresent, MBh.

Sarvátra, ind. everywhere, in every case, always, at all times (often strengthened by *api*, *sarvadā* &c.; with *na*, 'in no case'), ŚBr. &c. &c.; = *sarvasmin* (with *na*, 'in no case,' 'not at all' &c.), MBh.; Kāv. &c. **-ga**, mf(*ā*)n. all-pervading, omnipresent, Mn.; MBh. &c.; m. air, wind, W.; N. of a son of a Manu, Hariv.; MārkP.; of a son of Bhīma-sena, VP. **-gata**, mfn. extending to ev°thing, universal, perfect, MBh. **-gāmin**, mfn. all-pervading, Lalit.; m. air, wind, L. **-gāminī-pratipatti-jñāna-bala**, n. the faculty of knowing the means of going everywhere (one of the 10 faculties of a Tathāgata), Dharmas. 76. **-sattva**, n. omnipresence, RāmatUp. **Sarvatrâpi**, mf(*ī*)n. reaching everywhere, PañcavBr. **Sarvatrâpratigha**, mfn. not kept back from i. e. penetrating everywhere, MW.

Sarváthā, ind. in every way, in ev° respect, by all means (often joined with *sarvatra* and *sarvadā*; also with *api*; with *na*, 'in no case,' 'not at all'), Mn. &c. &c.; in whatever way, however, MBh.; R.; RPrāt.; altogether, entirely, in the highest degree, exceedingly, MBh.; Kāv.; Hit.; at all times, MW. **-vishaya**, mfn. in whatever way appearing, Cat.

Sarvadā́, ind. always, at all times (often joined with *sarvatra* and *sarvathā*; with *na*, 'never'), AV. &c. &c. **Sarvadâiva-sattva**, n. being at all times, RāmatUp.

Sarvadry-añc, mfn. (see 2. *añc*) turned towards all, Vop.; honouring all, MW.

Sarvaśás, ind. wholly, completely, entirely, thoroughly, collectively, altogether, in general, universally (sometimes used to denote that a collective noun in sg. or the pl. may be in any case or ibc.), TBr.; ChUp.; ŚāṅkhŚr. &c.; in every or any way, Mn.; R.; universally, always, everywhere, TBr.; RPrāt.; on all sides, MW.

Sarvâñc, mfn. (°*va* + 2. *añc*) turned in all directions, ŚāṅkhGṛ.

Sarvāṇī, f. N. of Śiva's wife or Durgā, Cat. (cf. *śarvāṇī*).

Sarvīya, mfn. relating or belonging to all, suitable or fit for all, Pāṇ. v, 1, 10, Vārtt. 1, Pat.

सर्वरी *sarvarī*, w.r. for *śarvarī*, q.v.

सर्वला *sarvalā* or °*li*, f. an iron club or crow, L.

सर्षप *sarshapa*, m. mustard, mustard-seed, ShaḍvBr. &c. &c.; a mustard-seed used as a weight, any minute weight, Mn.; ŚārṅgS.; a kind of poison, L.; (*ī*), f. a kind of herb, L.; a partic. eruption of the body, Car.; a kind of small bird (said to be a species of wagtail, = *khañjanikā*), L. **-kaṇa**, m. a grain of mustard-seed, Kāv. **-kanda**, m. a kind of poisonous root, Suśr. **-taila**, n. mustard-oil, ib. **-śāka**, m. a kind of culinary herb, Car. **-sneha**, m. = *-taila*, Suśr. **Sarshapâruṇa**, m. N. of a demon that seizes on children, PārGṛ.

Sarshapaka, m. a kind of snake, Suśr.; (*ī*), f. a partic. venomous insect, ib.; a kind of eruption (= *sarshapī*), ib.

Sarshapāya, Nom. Ā. °*yate*, to appear as small as a grain of mustard-seed, BhP.

Sarshapika, m. a partic. venomous insect, Suśr.; (*ikā*), f., see *sarshapaka*.

सर्षिगण *sa-rshi-gaṇa*, mfn. (fr. 7. *sa* + *ṛishi-g*°) having or attended by a host of Ṛishis, MW.

Sarshi-marud-gaṇa, mfn. with a host of Ṛishis and Maruts, ib.

सर्षिका *sarshikā*, f. a kind of metre, RPrāt.

सर्ष्टिक *sa-rshṭika*, mf(*ā*)n. (fr. 7. *sa* + *ṛishṭ*°) furnished with spears, MBh. (v.l.)

सल् *sal* (for *sar*, a form of √*sṛi*), cl. 1. P. *salati*, to go, move, Dhātup. xv, 40.

Sala, m. (cf. *sara*) a dog, L.; water, L.

Salalūka, (prob.) n. aimless wandering (?), RV. iii, 30, 17.

Salasala, mfn. going, moving, L.

Salilá, mf(*ā*)n. (cf. *sarirá*) flowing, surging, fluctuating, unsteady, RV.; AV.; MaitrS.; (*ā*), f. (in Sāṃkhya) one of the four kinds of *ādhyātmikā tushṭi* or internal acquiescence (the other three being *ambhas*, *ogha*, and *vṛishṭi*; cf. *su-pārā*), Tattvas.; (*am*), n. (ifc. f. *ā*) flood, surge, waves, RV.; AV.; Br.; (also pl.) water (acc. with √*kṛi*, 'to offer a libation of water to [gen.]'), Kauś.; MBh. &c.; rain-water, rain, VarBṛS.; eye-water, tears, Megh.; a kind of wind (see *-vāta*); a partic. high number, ŚāṅkhŚr.; a kind of metre, Nidānas. **-karman**, n. 'water-rite,' a libation of w° offered to a deceased person, MBh. **-kukkuṭa**, m. a partic. aquatic bird, BhP. **-kuntala**, m. 'w°-hair,' Vallisneria or Blyxa Octandra, L. **-kriyā**, f. = *-karman*, R. **-gargarī**, f. a w°-jar, Mṛicch. **-guru**, mfn. heavy with tears, Megh. **-cara**, m. 'water-goer,' an aquatic animal, VarBṛS.; *-ketana*, m. 'fish-bannered,' the god of love, Daś. **-ja**, mfn. produced or living in w°, VarBṛS.; m. an aquatic animal, ib.; a shell, MBh.; n. = next, L. **-janman**, n. 'w°-born,' a lotus, L. **-tva**, n. the state of w°, MārkP. **-da**, m. 'presenter of w°,' a kind of official, R.; a cloud, VarBṛS. **-dāyin**, mfn. causing rain, ib. **-dhara**, m. 'w°-bearer,' a cloud, MBh. **-nidhi**, m. 'water-receptacle,' the ocean, Chandom.; a kind of metre, Col. **-nipāta**, m. fall of rain, VarBṛS. **-nisheka**, m. sprinkling with w°, Ṛitus. **-pati**, m. 'w°-lord,' N. of Varuṇa, VarBṛS. **-pavanâśin**, mfn. drinking only water and air, Kāv. **-pūra**, m. a large quantity of w° (*-vat*, ind.), Pañcat. **-priya**, m. 'fond of w°,' a hog, L. **-bhaya**, n. danger from w°, inundation, VarBṛS.; *-dāyin*, mfn. causing in°, ib. **-bhara**, m. 'mass of water,' a lake, Bhām. **-maya**, mf(*ī*)n. consisting of water, VarBṛS. **-muc**, m. 'discharging w°,' a rain-cloud, Bālar. **-yoni**, m. 'w°-born,' N. of Brahmā, Hariv. **-raya**, m. 'w°-flow,' a current, stream, W. **-rāja**, m. = *-pati*, MBh. **-rāśi**, m. 'heap of w°,' the ocean, Śiś.; any piece of w°, W. **-vat**, mfn. provided with w°, R. **-vāta** (*salilá-*), mfn. = *salilâkhyena vāta-viseshenânugrihītaḥ*, TS. (Sch.) **-saraka**, m. n. a bowl of w°, Suśr. **-stambhin**, mfn. stopping w°, Veṇis. **-sthala-cara**, m. 'living in w° and on land,' an amphibious animal, Pañcat. **Salilâkara**, m. a great mass of w°, MBh.; the ocean, Rājat. **Salilâñjali**, m. two handfuls of w° (as a libation), R. **Salilâdhipa**, m. = °*la-pati*, Hariv. **Salilârṇava**, m. the (heaving) ocean, R.; *-śāyaka*, mfn. reposing on w° (applied to Vishṇu), Vishṇ. **Salilârthin**, mfn. wishing for w°, thirsty, MW. **Salilâlaya**, m. 'w°-receptacle,' the ocean, R. **Salilâvagāha**, m. bathing in w°, Śak. **Salilā-vatī**, f. N. of a place, VP. **Salilâśana**, mfn. subsisting only on w°, BhP. **Salilâśaya**, m. 'w°-receptacle,' a pond, lake, R.; VarBṛS.; BhP. **Salilâhāra**, mfn. = °*lâśana*, R. **Salile-cara**, mfn. moving about in w°, MBh. **Salilêndra**, m. (= °*la-pati*); *-pura*, n. Varuṇa's city, R. **Salilêndhana**, m. 'w°-ignition,' the submarine fire (cf. *vaḍabâgni*), L. **Salilêśa**, m. = °*la-pati*, MBh. **Salile-śaya**, mfn. resting or lying in w° (also as a kind of penance), MBh.; Hariv.; Pur. **Salilêśvara**, m. (= °*la-pati*), MBh. **Salilôccaya**, mf(*ā*)n. abounding in w°, ib. **Salilôttha**, mfn. risen from the ocean, Mṛicch. **Salilôdbhava**, mfn. 'produced in water,' Hariv.; m. a shell, MBh.; n. a lotus-flower, R. **Salilôpajīvin**, mfn. subsisting by w° (as a fisherman), VarBṛS. **Salilôpaplava**, m. 'a flood of w°,' inundation, MW. **Salilâukas**, mfn. dwelling or living in w°, R.; BhP. **Salilâudana**, m. n. rice boiled in water, Hariv.

सलक्ष *sa-laksha*, mfn. (i.e. 7. *sa* + *l*°) having a lac or a hundred thousand, MW.

Sa (to be similarly prefixed to the following): **-lakshaṇa**, mfn. having the same marks or characteristics, homogeneous, similar, Daśar.; Kāvyâd. **-lakshman** (*sá-*), mfn. id., RV.; VS.; TS. **-lagnaka**, mfn. (a loan) secured by a surety, Vivâd. **-lajja**, mfn. feeling shame or modesty, bashful, embarrassed (*am*, ind.), Kāv.; Kathās. &c.; m. Artemisia Indica and Austriaca, L.; *-tva*, n. shame, bashfulness, Campak. **—lajjita**, mf(*ā*)n. ashamed, abashed, Pañcar.; *-sneha-karuṇam*, ind. with bashfulness and love and compassion, Uttarar. **—lalitam**, ind. with sport, wantonly, MW. **—lavaka**, mfn. together with the substance called Lavaka, Pañcar. **—lavaṇa**, mfn. with salt, VarYogay.; n. tin (?), L. **—lāja-kusuma**, mfn. accompanied with sprinkled grain and flowers, MW. **—liṅga**, mf(*ā*)n. having the same marks or attributes, ĀśvŚr.; Kauś.; (ifc.) corresponding i.e. directed to, MBh. **—liṅgin**, m. 'having the usual marks (as of an ascetic &c., without belonging to the order),' a religious impostor (applied to the 7 schisms), Jain. **—līla**, mf(*ā*)n. playing, sporting (not in earnest), MBh.; R.; mocking, sneering, R.; sportive, coquettish, Śak.; Kathās.; (*am*), ind. playfully, with ease (also with *iva*), R.; BhP.; sportively, coquettishly, Mṛicch.; Kālid.; Kir.; *-gaja-gāmin*, m. N. of a Buddha, Lalit.; *-parihāsa*, mfn. smiling coquettishly, Mālatīm.; *-haṅsa-gamanā*, f. having the wanton gait of a Haṅsa, Kathās. **—leka** (*sá-*), m. (said to be) N. of an Āditya (cf. *leka*), TS. **—lepa**, mfn. with oily substances, KātyŚr. **—leśa**, mfn. having parts or portions, with every part, entire; (*am*), ind. with every particle, entirely, wholly, MW. **—loka** (*sá-*), mfn. being in the same world with (gen. or loc.), AitBr.; ŚBr.; with the people or inhabitants, Cat. **—lokátā**, f. the being in the same world or sphere with (gen., instr., or comp.), residence in the same heaven with the personal Deity (one of the four states of final beatitude = *sālokya*, RTL. 41), AitBr. &c. &c. **—lokya**, mfn. = *-loka* (with gen.), MBh. **—lobha**, mfn. greedy, avaricious, Kathās. **—lomadhi**, m. N. of a king (cf. *lom°* and *su-l°*), BhP. **—loman** (*sá-*), mfn. with the grain, corresponding to or co-extensive with (instr.), TS.; Br.; *°ma-tvá*, n. the being with the grain &c., ŚBr.; PañcavBr. **—lohita**, mf(*ā*)n. having the same blood, Vop.; coloured blood-red, MBh.

सलखक *salakhaka*, m. N. of a man, Inscr.

सलद *salada*, (f. ī), g. *gaurâdi* (Kāś. *salanda*).

सलरिन् *salarin* (?), m. N. of author, Cat.

सलल्लूक *salalūka*. See p. 1189, col. 3.

सलवि *salavi*. See *apa-s°* and *pra-s°*.

सलावृकी *salā-vṛikī*, f. = *sālā-vṛ°* (q. v.), TS.; MaitrS.

सलिग *sáliga*, mfn. (said of the sea; v. l. *salīga*), MaitrS.; Kapishṭh.

सलून *salūna*, m. a kind of worm or parasite, SārṅgS.

सलैस् *salais*. See *apa-salaiḥ*.

सल्य *salya*, *salyaka*. See *vi-s°*.

सल्लकी *sallakī*, *sallakīya* = *śall°*, q. v.

सल्लक्षणतीर्थ *sal-lakshaṇa-tīrtha*, n. (fr. *sát* + *l°*, see p. 1134) N. of a Tīrtha, W. **Sal-lakshya**, n. a good aim, right aim or object, Cat. **Sal-loka**, m. pl. good people, excellent persons, Kāv.

सल्लद्र *salladra*, m. (with *bhaṭṭa*) N. of a poet, Cat.

सल्लय *sallayá*, *sallāpa*, w.r. for *sam-l°*.

सल्व *sálva*, m. pl. N. of a people (also written *śalva*), ŚBr. **—deśa**, m. N. of a country, MW.

सल्ह *salha*, m. N. of a man (also written *sahla*), Rājat.

Salhaṇa, m. N. of a man, ib.

सव 1. *savá*, m. (fr. √3. *su*) pressing out the juice of the Soma plant, RV.; ŚBr.; ŚāṅkhŚr.; pouring it out, L.; the moon, L.; n. the juice or honey of flowers, L. **—latā**, f. the plant yielding Soma-juice (cf. *soma-l°*), Sāy. on RV. viii, 29, 1. **—vidha** (*savá-*), mfn. = *savana-v°*, ŚBr.

1. **Sávana**, n. (for 2. see col. 2) the act of pressing out the Soma-juice (performed at the three periods of the day; cf. *tri-shavaṇa*; *prātaḥ-*, *mādhyam-dina-* and *tṛitīya-s°*), RV. &c. &c.; the pressed out Soma-juice and its libation, a Soma festival, any oblation or sacrificial rite, ib.; (with *puṅsaḥ*) = *puṃsavana*, Yājñ. i, 11; (pl.) the three periods of day (morning, noon, and evening), Gaut.; Mn.; BhP.; time (in general), BhP.; bathing, ablution, religious bathing (performed at m°, n°, and ev°), Kir. **—karman**, n. the sacred rite of libation, Śak. **—kāla**, m. the time for libation, ŚBr. **—kṛit**, mfn. performing a 1°, ŚBr. **—krama**, m. the order of 1° or sacr° rites, VPrāt. **—gata**, mfn. going to perform a 1°, Āpast. **—traya**, n. the three 1°s, ShaḍvBr. **—devatā**, f. the deity of a 1°, ŚāṅkhŚr. **—paṅkti**, mfn. accompanied by five 1°s, AitBr. **—prayoga**, m. N. of wk. **—bhāj**, mfn. partaking of a 1°, TS. **—mukhá**, n. the beginning of a 1°, TS.; *°khīya*, mf(*ā*)n. belonging to it, KātyŚr. **—vid**, mfn. knowing the times or periods of a 1°, BhP. **—vidha**, mfn. of the same value as a 1°, like a 1°, Lāṭy. **—śas**, ind. at each of the 1°s, ĀśvŚr.; BhP. **—saṃsthā**, f. the end of a 1°, Lāṭy. **—samīshanti**, f. a partic. Vishṭuti, ib. **—stha**, mfn. engaged in a 1° or sacrifice, Yājñ. **Savanânukalpam**, ind. according to the three periods of day, Āpast. **Savanânta**, m. the end of a 1° or sacrifice, KātyŚr.

Savanika. See *tṛitīya-s°*.

Savanīya, mfn. relating to the Soma libation or to any sacrificial rite, fit for it &c., Br.; ŚrS.; having access to a sacrifice, authorized to partake of it, Baudh. **—kāla**, m. the time for a Soma 1°, ŚāṅkhŚr. **—paśu**, m. an animal fit for sacrifice, BhP. **—pātra**, n. a Soma vessel, ĀpŚr.

सव 2. *savá*, m. (fr. √1. *sū*) one who sets in motion or impels, an instigator, stimulator, commander, VS.; ŚBr.; m. the sun (cf. *savitṛi*), L.; setting in motion, vivification, instigation, impulse, command, order (esp. applied to the activity of Savitṛi; dat. *savāya*, 'for setting in motion'); RV.; AV.; VS.; TBr.; N. of partic. initiatory rites, inauguration, consecration, Br.; a kind of sacrifice, Kauś.; any sacrifice, MBh.; a year (?), BhP. (see *bahu-s°*). **—kāṇḍa**, m. N. of the fifth book of the Śatapatha-brāhmaṇa. **—pati** (*savá-*), m. the lord of the Sava ceremony, MaitrS.

2. **Sávana**, n. (for 1. see col. 1; for 3. see p. 1191, col. 2; for *sa-vana* see col. 3) instigation, order, command (cf. *satyá-s°*), RV.; MaitrUp.

Savas, n. id. See *satyá-s°*.

Savitara, Nom. P. *°rati*, to be like the sun, resemble the sun (cf. next), Kpr.

Savitṛí, m. a stimulator, rouser, vivifier (applied to Tvashṭṛi), RV. iii, 55, 19; x, 10, 5; N. of a sun-deity (accord. to Naigh. belonging to the atmosphere as well as to heaven; and sometimes in the Veda identified with, at other times distinguished from Sūrya 'the Sun,' being conceived of and personified as the divine influence and vivifying power of the sun, while Sūrya is the more concrete conception; accord. to Sāy. the sun before rising is called Savitṛi, and after rising till its setting Sūrya; eleven whole hymns of the RV. and parts of others [e.g. i, 35; ii, 38; iii, 62, 10–12 &c.] are devoted to the praise of Savitṛi; he has golden hands, arms, hair &c.; he is also reckoned among the Ādityas [q.v.], and is even worshipped as 'lord of all creatures,' supporting the world and delivering his votaries from sin; the celebrated verse, RV. iii, 62, 10, called *gāyatrī* and *sāvitrī* [qq. vv.] is addressed to him), RV. &c. &c.; the orb of the sun (in its ordinary form) or its god (his wife is Pṛiśni), MBh.; Kāv. &c.; N. of one of the 28 Vyāsas, VP.; of Śiva or Indra, L.; Calotropis Gigantea, L.; (*°trī*), f., see below. **—tanaya**, m. N. of the planet Saturn, VarBṛS. **—datta**, m. N. of a man, Kāś. on Pāṇ. v, 3, 83. **—devata** or **-daivata**, n. the constellation Hastā or the 13th of the lunar mansions (presided over by the sun), L. **—putra**, m. the son of Savitṛi, IndSt. **—prasūta** (*savitṛi-*), mfn. stimulated or roused by S° (*°tá-tā*, f.), TS.; Br. **—suta**, m. = *-tanaya*, VarBṛS.; *-dina*, n. Saturday, ib.

Savitṛila, m. endearing form of *savitṛi-datta*, Kāś. on Pāṇ. v, 3, 83.

Savitriya, mfn. relating or belonging to the sun, solar, Siddh.

Sávīman, n. (only in loc,) setting in motion, instigation, direction, guidance, RV.; VS.; ŚāṅkhŚr.

सव 3. *sava*, m. (fr. √2. *sū*) offspring, progeny, L.

Sávitave. See √2. *sū*.

Savitra, n. (prob.) a cause of generation, instrument of production, Pāṇ. iii, 2, 184.

Savitrī, f. (accord. to some f. of *savitṛi* above) a mother, Kum.; a female producer, Kir. (w. r. for *sāvitrī*, q. v.)

सवंशा *sa-vaṇśā*, f. (i.e. 7. *sa* + *vaṇśa*) a kind of plant, Kauś.

Sa (to be similarly prefixed to the following): **—vacana**, mfn. = *samāna-v°*, Pāṇ. vi, 3, 85. **—vajra-saṃghāta**, mfn. with the stroke of a thunderbolt, MBh. **—vat**, mfn. containing (6.) *sa*, PañcavBr. **—vatsa**, mfn. together with a calf, having a calf, Kauś.; MBh.; having descendants, MW. **—vadhūka**, m. along with a wife, a man and his wife, Kathās. **—vana**, mf(*ā*)n. (for *savana* see col. 1 &c.) together with woods, MBh. **—vapusha**, mf(*ī*)n. having a body or form, embodied, W. **—vayas** (*sá-*), mfn. (Pāṇ. vi, 3, 85) being of the same vigour or age, MaitrS.; m. a co-eval, contemporary, comrade, friend, RV.; Ragh.; Kathās.; f. a woman's female friend or confidante, Śiś. **—vayasa** (BhP.), **-vayaska** (Kāśīkh.), mfn. equal in age. **—varūtha** (MBh.), *°thin* (Hariv.), mfn. furnished with a protecting ledge (see *varūtha*). **—vargīya**, mfn. belonging to the same group of consonants (as gutturals &c.), TPrāt. **—varṇa** (*sá-*), mf(*ā*)n. having the same colour or appearance, similar, like, equal to (gen. or comp.), RV. &c. &c.; of the same tribe or class, Mn.; MBh. &c.; belonging to the same class of sounds, homogeneous with (comp.), Prāt.; Pāṇ. (cf. *a-s°*); m. the son of a Brāhman and a Kshatriya woman, Gaut.; a Māhishya (q. v.) who lives by astrology, L.; (*ā*), f. a woman of the same caste, Gaut.; Āpast.; N. of the woman substituted by Saraṇyū for herself as a wife of the Sun (she is said to have given birth to Manu, and is called in later legends Chāyā; cf. *saraṇyū*), L.; of a daughter of the Ocean and wife of Prācīna-barhis, Hariv.; VP.; *°ṇa-tva*, n. identity of colour with (instr.), Suśr.; having the same denominator, Āryabh.; *°ṇa-varṇa*, n. the same colour, MBh.; *°ṇâbha*, mfn. similar in colour to (comp.), MārkP.; *°ṇâsavarṇa-vivāha*, m. the marriage of people of the same and of different castes, MW.; *°ṇôpāyin*, mfn. one who approaches a woman of the same caste, ib. **—varṇana**, n. reduction to the same denominator, Līl. **—varṇaya**, Nom. P. *°yati*, to reduce to the same denominator, ib. **—varṇi-liṅgin**, mfn. wearing the marks of a religious student, disguised as a Brahmacārin (see *varṇin*), MW. **—varṇī-karaṇa**, n. = *-varṇana*, Āryabh., Sch. **—varman**, mfn. having armour, along with armour, MW. **—várya**, mfn. endowed with excellent qualities, TBr. (Sch.) **—valga**, mfn. provided with a bridle, Śiś. **—vāk-chala**, mfn. untruthful in speech, mendacious, Kathās. **—vācas** (*sá-*), mfn. employing similar speech (v. l. *su-v°*), AV. **—vātṛí** (?), mfn. having the same calf, VS.; TBr. (Sch.) **—vārija**, mfn. abounding in lotus-flowers, Kir. **—vārttika**, mfn. (a Sūtra) with its Vārttikas, Pat. **—vālakhilya**, mfn. together with the Vālakhilya hymns, MW. **—1. -vāsa**, mfn. scented, perfumed, Jātakam. **—2. -vāsa**, mfn. having a dwelling, ib. **—vāsas** (*sá-*), mfn. with clothes, clothed, ŚBr.; Mn. v, 77 &c. **—vāsin**, mfn. dwelling together, AV. **—viṅśá**, mfn. that to which one-twentieth is added, Jyot.; m. a partic. Stoma, VS.; TS. **—vikalpa**, mfn. possessing variety or admitting of distinctions, differentiated, Vedântas. (also *°paka*, ib. &c.); admitting of an alternative or option or doubt, optional, doubtful, MW.; together with the intermediate Kalpas, BhP. **—vikāra**, mfn. with its developments or derivatives or products, Gaut.; Bhag.; BhP.; altered in feeling, growing fond of, Gīt.; undergoing modification or decomposition (as food), Siṅhâs. **—vikāśa**, mf(*ā*)n. shining, radiant, Kathās. **—vikrama**, mfn. vigorous, energetic, Śiś. **—vikrośam**, ind. with a cry of alarm, MBh. **—viklavam**, ind. piteously, dejectedly, Mālav. **—vigraha**, mfn. having body or form, embodied, Rājat.; having meaning or import, meaning, importing, W. **—vicāra**, mf(*ā*)n. that to which consideration is given, Lalit. **—vicikitsitam**, ind. having or causing doubt, doubtfully, Mcar. **—vijñāna** (*sá-*), mfn. endowed with right understanding, ŚBr.; *-tva*, n., Sāy. **—vitarkam**, mfn. accompanied with reason or thought, Lalit.; (*am*), ind. thoughtfully, Ratnâv. **—vitta**, mfn. together with the property, Lāṭy. **—vid**, mfn. (said to be) = *savita-rūpa* and = *vidvas*, MaitrUp. **—vidiś**, mfn. with the intermediate quarters, MW. **—vidya**, mfn. pursuing the same studies, Vop.; having learning, versed in science, Cāṇ.; Rājat. **—vidyut**, mfn. accompanied with lightning, MBh.; *-stanita*, mfn. acc° with 1° and thunder, MW. **—vidyutá**, n. a thunderstorm, AV. **—vidha**, mfn. of the same kind or sort, APrāt.; proximate, near, Mālatim.; n. proximity, Kāv.; Kathās.; (*am*), ind. according to rule or precept, BhP. **–vidhī-√kṛi,** P. *-karoti,* to bring near, Bālar.; *-√bhū,* P. *-bhavati,* to be or become near, ib. **–vinaya,** mfn. having good behaviour or propriety, well-conducted, well-behaved, modest (*am,* ind.), Kāv.; Kathās. **–vibhaktika,** mfn. having a case-termination, Pat. **–vibhāsa,** m. 'having great lustre,' N. of one of the seven suns (prob. w.r. for *vibhāsa*), VP. **–vibhrama,** mfn. employing amorous or coquettish glances, coquettish, wanton (*am,* ind.), Kāv. **–vimarśa,** mf(*ā*)n. reflecting, thoughtful, deliberate (*am,* ind.), Kāv.; Kathās. **–vilaksham,** ind. with shame or embarrassment, Pañcat.; °*ksha-smitam,* ind. with a bashful smile, Mṛicch.; Pañcat. **–vilambam,** ind. hesitatingly, dilatorily, Rājat. **–vilāsa,** mfn. acting coquettishly, wanton, amorous, playful (*am,* ind.), Kāv.; VarBṛS.; BhP. **–vivadha,** mfn. holding the equipoise (*-tvá,* n.), TS. **–viveka,** mfn. possessed of judgment, discerning, Kathās. **–viśaṅka,** mf(*ā*)n. having apprehension or anxiety, suspicious, R. **–viśesha,** mfn. possessing specific or characteristic qualities, Sarvad.; peculiar, singular, extraordinary, Kum.; Kathās.; having discrimination, discriminating, Hit.; (*am*), ind. with all particulars, in detail, Mcar.; Pañcat.; particularly, especially, exceedingly (*-kānta,* mfn. excessively beloved, Ragh.; *-kautūhalam,* ind. in a particularly festive or solemn manner, Mālav.; *-taram,* ind. more particularly, particularly), MBh.; Kāv. &c.; n. the number indicating the proportion of the diagonal of a square to its side, Śulbas. **–viśeshaka,** mfn. with particular characteristics or particularity, Bhāshāp.; having distinguishing properties or peculiar qualities, MW.; discriminated, ib.; n. any distinguishing peculiarity or characteristic, ib. **–viśeshaṇa,** mfn. possessing distinctions or peculiarities or attributes, L.; *-rūpaka,* n. a metaphor consisting of mere attributes, Kāvyād. **–viśeshatas,** ind. especially, particularly, singularly, excellently, W. **–viśrambha,** mf(*ā*)n. confidential, intimate (*am,* ind.), Kathās. **–viśvāsam,** ind. with confidence, Vās., Sch. **–visha,** mf(*ā*)n. poisonous, Suśr. (°*shâśis,* mfn. 'having venomous fangs,' Rājat.); poisoned, Śak.; m. a partic. hell, Yājñ. **–vishāṇa,** mfn. possessing horns or tusks, along with tusks, MBh. **–vishāda,** mf(*ā*)n. having despondency, despairing, dismayed (*am,* ind.), Kāv.; Pañcat. **–vishṭara,** mfn. having a bundle of rushes or grass spread out for sitting upon, Hcat. **–visaṃkulam,** see *vi-saṃkula,* p. 953, col. 1. **–vistara,** mf(*ā*)n. having diffuseness, diffuse, detained, complete (*am,* ind.), Pañcat.; Kathās.; with the texts belonging to it (i.e. to the Veda), Hariv.; BhP. **–vismaya,** mf(*ā*)n. having astonishment, surprised, perplexed, doubtful (*am,* ind.), Śiś.; Ratnâv. **–vihaṃga,** mfn. possessing birds, with birds, MW. **–vīra** (*sá-*), mfn. with retainers or followers, TBr. **–vīrya** (*sá-*), mfn. having equal power or strength with (instr.), VS.; ŚBr.; powerful, mighty (*-tvá,* n.), TS.; Kāṭh.; ŚāṅkhGṛ. **–vīvadha,** mfn. (*-tā,* f., *-tva,* n.) = *-viv*°, AitBr.; PañcavBr. **–vṛiksha-kshupa-lata,** mfn. having trees and bushes and creepers, MW. **–vṛit** (in a formula), VS. **–vṛita-yajña,** m. (prob.) an oblation offered at the same time, GopBr. **–vṛita-soma,** mfn. offering a Soma libation at the same time, ib.; Vait. **–vṛitta,** mfn. well-conducted, R.; (of unknown meaning), Nir. v, 4. **–vṛitti,** mfn. with a maintenance or salary, Mṛicch. **–vṛittika,** mfn. being in motion, active (*-tā,* f.), Sarvad. **–vṛiddhika,** mfn. bearing interest, along with the interest, Bṛihasp. **–vṛidh,** mfn. increasing together, RV.; having increase, growing, VS. **–vṛishaṇa,** mf(*ā*)n. having testicles, with the test°, R.; Gaut.; Āpast.; possessing two fruits or seeds resembling test°, ĀpGṛ. (Sch.) **–vṛishṭika,** mfn. accompanied by rain, Cat. **–vega,** mfn. equal in speed or velocity to (comp.), R.; violent, impetuous (*am,* ind.), Śiś.; Pañcat. **–veṇī,** f. = *samāna-v*°, Vop. **–veṇu-vīṇam,** ind. with flutes and lutes, VarBṛS.; °*ṇā-paṇavânunāda,* mfn. resounding with flutes and lutes and tabours, MW. **–vetāla,** mfn. occupied by a Vetāla (said of a dead body), Kathās. **–vedanam,** ind. with pain, painfully, Dhūrtas. **–vedas** (*sá-*), mfn. having the same or common property (Agni-Soma), RV. **–vedika,** mfn. along with a seat or bench, MBh. **–vedha,** mfn. = *sa-vidha,* proximate, near, L.; n. proximity, ib. **–vepathu,** mfn. having tremor, tremulous, MBh.; Kāv.; Suśr. **–vepitam,** ind. tremblingly. **–veśa,** mfn. neighbouring, near, Pāṇ. vi, 2, 23. **–veśīya,** n. (with *Marutām*), N. of a Sāman, ĀrshBr. **–vesha,** mfn. apparelled, dressed, ornamented, decorated, W. **–veshṭana,** mfn. having a turban, turbaned (as a head), Mṛicch. **–vaiklavyam,** ind. with bewilderment or despair, Mṛicch.; Mālatim. **–vaidika,** w.r. for *-vedika.* **–vaira,** mfn. hostile, inimical, Śiś. **–vairāgyam,** ind. with disgust or indifference, Pañcat.; Dhūrtas. **–vailakshya,** mf(*ā*)n. with shame, ashamed, pretended, forced (*am,* ind.), Ratnâv.; having contrary marks or characteristics, unnatural, MW.; *-smitam,* ind. with a pretended or forced smile, Ratnâv. **–vyajana,** mfn. with fanning, Suśr. **–vyañjana,** mfn. with consonants, joined with a c°, Prāt. **–vyatha,** mf(*ā*)n. feeling pain, afflicted, grieved, sorrowful, Kāv.; Kathās. **–vyadha,** mfn. having cuts or wounds, MW. **–vyapatrapa,** mf(*ā*)n. ashamed, bashful, abashed, R. **–vyapêksha,** mfn. requiring, presupposing, dependent on or connected with (comp.), Uttarar.; Kathās. **–vyabhicaraṇa,** mfn. liable to inaccuracy, possibly inexact or false, not absolutely exact or certain, Car. **–vyabhicāra,** mfn. id.; m. (in phil.) an argument wide of the mark or incompatible with the conclusion drawn from it, an allegation proving too much (one of the Hetv-ābhāsas, q.v.), a too general middle term (as 'fire' to prove smoke), Nyāyas.; Sarvad.; N. of various Nyāya wks.; *-kroḍa,* m., *-grantha-rahasya,* n., *-nirukti,* f., *-pūrva-paksha-kroḍa,* m., °*ksha-grantha-ṭīkā,* f., °*ksha-grantha-dīdhiti-ṭīkā,* f., °*ksha-grantha-loka,* m., *-vāda,* m., *-sāmānya-nirukti,* f., and °*ti-kroḍa,* m., *-siddhânta-grantha-ṭīkā,* f., °*tha-dīdhiti-ṭīkā,* f., °*tha-prakāśa,* m., °*tha-rahasya,* n., °*tha-loka,* m. N. of wks. **–vyāja,** mfn. artful, fraudulent, false, deceitful (*am,* ind.), Kālid.; Ratnâv. **–vyādhi,** mfn. seized with illness, sick, Kāv. **–vyāpāra,** mf(*ā*)n. having an employment, occupied, busily engaged, Megh. **–vyāhṛiti,** mfn. accompanied with the three Vyāhṛitis (q.v.), Amṛit-Up. (also °*tika,* Yājñ. i, 238); *-praṇavaka,* mfn. with the above and the syllable Om (see *praṇava*), Mn. xi, 248. **–vraṇa,** mfn. having a wound, wounded, sore, MBh. (with *śukra,* n. 'a partic. disease of the white in the eye,' Suśr.); having a fault or flaw, Hariv. **–vrata** (*sá-*), mf(*ā*)n. fitting together, harmonious (others 'following the same law or order'), RV.; bound by a rule or law, ĀśvŚr. **–vratin,** mfn. acting in like manner or having the same customs with (comp.), MBh. **–vrīḍa,** mfn. feeling shame, bashful, modest (*am,* ind.), MBh.; Kāv. &c.

सवत्य *savatyà,* mfn. = *savātya,* MaitrS.

सवथ *savatha,* m. (fr. √*su* or *sū*) N. of a man, Rājat.

सवन 3. *savana,* n. (fr. √*su* or *sū;* for 1. 2. see 1190, cols. 1. 2; for *sa-vana,* p. 1190, col. 3) fire, BhP.; a kind of hell, VP.; N. of a son of Bhṛigu, MBh.; of a son of Vasishṭha (one of the seven Ṛishis under Manu Rohita), VP.; of a son of Manu Svayambhuva, Hariv.; of a son of Priya-vrata (v.l. *savala*), Pur.

सवर *savara,* n. (cf. *śabara*) = *śiva* or *salila,* L.

सवल *savala.* See *śabala* and 3. *savana.*

सवहा *savahā,* f. = *saralā,* a kind of Convolvulus, L.

सवात्य *savātyà* or *savātyá,* mfn. (said to =) born from one mother, MaitrS.; VS.; TS.; TBr.; Kāṭh.

सविडालम्भ *saviḍālambha* (?), n. a partic. kind of jest (for exciting laughter), Bhar.

सवितृ *savitṛi, savīman.* See p. 1190, col. 2.

सव्य *savyá,* mf(*ā*)n. (accord. to Uṇ. iv, 109 fr. √*sū;* perhaps for *skavya,* cf. Gk., col. 3) left, left hand (*am, ena, ā, e,* and ibc., 'on the left'), RV. &c. &c.; opposite to left, right, right hand (*am, ena,* and ibc., 'on the right'); south, southern (*am* &c., 'to the south'), Sūryas.; VarBṛS.; reverse, contrary, backward, L.; m. the left arm or hand, RV.; Br.; KātyŚr.; Yājñ.; the left foot, KātyŚr.; Gobh.; one of the ten ways in which an eclipse takes place, VarBṛS.; a fire lighted at a person's death, L.; N. of Vishṇu, L.; (*sávya*) N. of a man befriended by the Aśvins, RV.; of an Āṅgirasa and author of RV. i, 51–57, Anukr.; n. (scil. *yajñôpavīta*) the sacred thread worn over the left shoulder (acc. with √*kṛi,* 'to put the sacred th° over the l° sh°'), KātyŚr., Sch. [accord. to some for *skavya,* cf. Gk. σκαιός; Lat. *scaevus;* accord. to others for *syavya,* cf. Slav. *šujĭ*]. **–cārin,** mfn. v.l. for *-sācin,* MBh. **–jānu,** n. a mode of fighting (by using the l° knee), Hariv. **–tas,** ind. from or on the l° (also 'contrary' or 'inauspicious') side (acc. with √*kṛi,* 'to place on the l° side'), RV.; MBh.; on the right side, VarBṛS. **–pāda-lekhā,** f. an outline or impression of the l° foot, Kir. **–bāhu,** n. a mode of fighting with the left arm, Hariv. **–shṭṛi,** m. (nom. *-shṭhā*) id., ŚBr.; *-sārathi,* du. (prob.) two warriors (or charioteers) standing on the left and right side, ib. **–shṭhā,** m. a warrior standing on the left side (in a chariot), AV. **–sācin** (*savyá-*), mfn. drawing (a bow) with the left hand, ambidexterous, MBh.; m. N. of Arjuna, ib.; of Kṛishṇa; Terminalia Arjuna, L. **Savyâdhara,** mfn. having the l° undermost, Lāṭy. **Savyânata,** n. 'bending to left,' a partic. mode of fighting, Hariv. **Savyâpagrahaṇa,** mfn. that which is laid aside or to rest on the left, MaitrS. **Savyâpasavya,** mfn. left and right, reverse and direct, wrong and right, MW. **Savyā-prashṭi,** m. the horse harnessed on the l° side of the yoke-horses (opp. to *dakshiṇā-pr*°), ŚBr. **Savyā-yugya,** m. the l° yoke-horse (opp. to *dakshiṇā-y*°), ib. **Savyâvṛit,** mfn. with a turn to the l°, GṛŚrS. **Savyâvṛitta,** mfn. turned to the l°, KātyŚr.; Kauś. **Savyâśūnya,** mfn. not loosened on the l°, KātyŚr. **Savyêtara,** mfn. 'other than l°,' right, MBh.; Kāv. &c.; n. a partic. mode of fighting, Hariv.; *-tas,* ind. l° and r°, BhP. **Savyôttāna,** mfn. holding the left hand with the palm uppermost, ŚāṅkhŚr. **Savyônnata,** n. 'uplifted towards the left,' a partic. mode of fighting, Hariv.

Savye (loc. of *savya*), in comp. **–shṭha,** m. (= *savya-shṭha*); *-sārathi,* du. two charioteers standing left and right, TBr. (Sch.) **–shṭhṛi,** m. a charioteer, Uṇ. ii, 102, Sch.

सशकल *sa-śakala,* mfn. (i.e. 7. *sa* + *ś*°) having scales, together with scales, IndSt.

Sa (to be similarly prefixed to the following): **–śaṅka,** mf(*ā*)n. fearful, doubtful, timid, shy (*am,* ind.), MBh.; Kāv. &c.; suspicious, Kathās. **–śaṅkha,** mfn. having a conch-shell, MW.; *-gosha,* mfn. resounding with conch-shells, ib. **–śatru,** mfn. having enemies, MBh. **–śapatham,** ind. with an oath, Mṛicch. **–śabda,** mf(*ā*)n. having sound or noise, full of cries, sounding, Kāv.; Kathās.; Rājat.; proclaimed, MW.; (*am*), ind. with noise, noisily, Gobh.; MBh. &c. **–śayana,** mf(*ī*)n. lying or standing together, contiguous, neighbouring, ShaḍvBr.; Lāṭy. **–śara,** mfn. furnished with an arrow, together with an arrow, R.; Kālid.; *-cāpa-hasta,* mfn. holding a bow with an arrow in the hand, Ml.; °*râsana,* mfn. with a bow, VarYogay.; °*rin,* mfn. furnished with an arrow, MBh. **–śarīra** (*sá-*), mf(*ā*)n. with the body, embodied, TBr.; PañcavBr.; R.; with the bones, KātyŚr. **–śarkara,** mf(*ā*)n. together with gravel or sand, VarBṛS.; with brown sugar, Suśr. **–śalka,** mfn. having bark or rind or scales, Gaut.; m. 'scaly,' a kind of fish, Mn. v, 16. **–śalya,** mf(*ā*)n. pierced by an arrow or dart, stung, wounded (also fig. = 'pained, afflicted'), R.; Kālid.; Kathās.; thorny, connected with pain or sorrow, troublesome, difficult, HPariś.; m. a bear, L. **–1. -śastra,** mf(*ā*)n. having or containing an invocation (see p. 1044, col. 1), MārkP.; *-marutvatīya,* m. the second Graha (q.v.) at the midday libation, VS., Sch. **–2. -śastra,** mfn. having arms, armed, Veṇīs. **–śasya,** mfn., w.r. for *-sasya,* Hariv.; (*ā*), f. Tiaridium Indicum, L. **–śādvala,** mf(*ā*)n. covered with grass, Vishṇ. **–śālmala,** mfn. possessing silk-cotton trees, MBh. **–śikhaṇḍin,** mfn. accompanied by Śikhaṇḍin, MBh. **–śikhara,** mfn. having a top (as a tree), R. **–śibira,** mfn. together with (his) camp, Śṛiṅgār. **–śiras,** mfn. along with the head, Āpast.; °*raḥ-kampam,* ind. shaking the head, Mṛicch.; °*raska,* mfn. (= *-śiras*), Gobh.; °*râvamajjana,* n. (fr. *śira* = *śiras* + *av*°) diving with the head foremost, ĀpŚr., Sch. **–śishya,** mfn. attended by pupils, Śak. **–śītkāra,** mfn. uttering a murmuring sound, Vikr.; (*am*), ind. with a m° s°, MW.; with a sigh, ib. **–śīrshan** (*sá-*), mfn. having a head (opp. to *apa-ś*°), TS.; TBr. **–śukra** (*sá-*), mfn. together with brightness or with what is bright (*-tvá,* n.), TS.; ŚBr. **–śuc,** mfn. grieved, afflicted, Amar. **–śūka,** mf(*ā*)n. furnished with awns, ĀpŚr.; m. a believer in the existence of God (= *āstika*), L. **–śūlam,** ind. with sharp pain (as of colic or gout), Suśr. **–śṛiṅgāra,**

mfn. having ornaments, adorned, decorated, Pañcat.; Kathās.; °*rakam*, ind. with love, passionately, tenderly, Mṛicch. **-śesha**, mfn. having a remainder, not entirely emptied or exhausted, incomplete, unfinished, KātyŚr.; *-tva*, n. the having a remainder (*-tvād āyushaḥ*, 'because life had not yet run out'), MBh.; °*shânna*, mfn. one who eats up the remnants of food (= 'having a good appetite'), Suśr. **-śaila-vana-kānana**, mfn. having mountains and woods and groves, MBh. **-śoka**, mf(*ā*)n. sorrowful, sad (*am*, ind.), R.; Kālid. &c.; *-tā*, f. sorrow, sadness, MBh. **-śmaśru**, mfn. having a beard, bearded, L.; f. a woman with a beard, L. **-śyāparṇa**, mfn. attended by the Śyāparṇas, AitBr. **-śraddha**, mf(*ā*)n. trustful, frank, confident, Kathās. **-śrama**, mf(*ā*)n. feeling fatigue, wearied, W. **-śrī**, mfn. like, similar to (comp.), Kāśikh. **-śrīka**, mf(*ā*)n. having beauty, lovely, splendid (*-tā*, f., *-tva*, n.), Vikr.; Ratnâv.; having prosperity, prosperous, fortunate, Śiś., Sch. **-śrī-vṛiksha**, mfn. marked with a circular tuft or curl of hair on the breast (as a horse), Kathās. **-ślāgham**, ind. boastfully, pompously, Vikr.; Prab.; with praise, eulogistically, MW. **-ślesha**, mfn. ambiguous, having a double meaning (*-tva*, n.), Kāvyâd. **-śvāsa**, mfn. having breath, breathing, living, Rājat.

सश्च् *saśc* (only *saścat*). See √*sac*.

सश्यान *saśyāna*, w. r. for *saṃ-śāna*, GopBr.

सषोडशिक *sa-shoḍaśika*, mfn. connected with the 16 partite Stotra, PañcavBr.

सष्कि *sashki* (?), g. *sidhmâdi* (Kāś. *sakthi*). **Sashkila**, mfn., ib.

सष्टुभ् *sa-shṭúbh*, f. a kind of metre (cf. *anu-*, *pari-shṭubh* &c.), TS.

सस् *sas*, cl. 2. P. (Dhātup. xxiv, 70) *sásti* (in TS. also *sasásti* and in VS. *sásasti*, pr. p. *sasát*, RV.; AV.; Gr. also pf. *sasāsa*; aor. *asāsīt*; fut. *sasitā*, *sasishyati*), to sleep, RV. &c. (cf. above); Naigh. iii, 22; to be inactive or idle, RV.: Caus. *sāsayati* (aor. *asīshasat*), Gr.: Desid. *sisasishati*, ib.: Intens. *sāsasyate*, *sāsasti*, ib.

Sasá, mfn. sleeping, Naigh. iv, 2; m. N. of an Ātreya (author of RV. v, 21); m. or n. (?) herb, grass, corn (cf. *sasyá*), RV.

ससंरम्भ *sa-saṃrambha*, mfn. (i. e. 7. *sa* + *s*°) enraged, angry, Kathās.; (*am*), ind. angrily, Prab.; hastily, hurriedly, very briefly, Sarvad.

Sa (to be similarly prefixed to the following). **-saṃvāda**, mf(*ā*)n. agreeing (*am*, ind.), Kathās. **-saṃvid**, mfn. one with whom an agreement has been made, ib. **-saṃśaya**, mf(*ā*)n. doubting, doubtful, uncertain, MBh.; Kathās.; dubious, R.; (in rhet.) ambiguity (regarded as a fault), Kāvyâd. **-saṃhāra**, mfn. having the means of restraint (said of magical weapons which can only be made to return to the owner by repeating certain Mantras), MW. **-sakhi**, ind. similar to a friend, Pāṇ. ii, 1, 6. **-sakhīkā**, f. together with female friends, Kathās. **-sakhī-gaṇā**, f. with all the company of f° fr°, ib. **-saṃkaṭa**, mfn. containing difficult passes or defiles (as a road), Śaṃkar. **-saṃketa**, mfn. one with whom an agreement has been made or who is privy to any secret compact, Kathās. **-saṅga**, mfn. adhering, attached (*-tva*, n. 'adhesion, contact'), Kap. **-saṃgraha**, mfn. one who studies the Saṃgraha (q. v.) together (i. e. subsidiarily), Pat. on Pāṇ. iv, 2, 60. **-saciva**, mfn. along with (his) minister or ministers, MBh. **-saṃjña**, mfn. having sense, sensible, conscious, R. **-saṭa**, mfn. very shaggy, VarBṛS. **-sattrín** (or *sá-s*°), m. a companion at a sacrifice or festival, ŚBr. **-sattva**, mf(*ā*)n. possessing energy or vigour, MBh.; containing living creatures or animals, Mn.; Ragh.; (*ā*), f. 'containing an embryo,' a pregnant woman, Ragh. iii, 9. **-satya** (*sá-*), mfn. accompanied with truth, MaitrS. **-sad-bhāva**, mfn. acc° with affection, Kād. **-saṃtatika** (Kull.), **-saṃtāna** (Mn. iii, 15), mfn. together with offspring. **-saṃdeha**, mfn. having doubt or hesitation, Kathās.; (in rhet.) a kind of indirect praise, Kāvyâd. ii, 358. **-saṃdhya**, mf(*ā*)n. having or relating to the period called Saṃdhyā, vespertine, R.; °*dhyâṇśa*, mfn. with the period called Saṃdhyâṇśa, Mn. i, 70. **-saṃnāma**, mfn. bending down, submissive, humble, Nalôd. **-saptaka**, mfn. containing a heptade, Jyot. **-sapta-dvīpa**, mf(*ā*)n. with the seven Dvīpas (q. v.), NṛisUp. **-sabhya**, mfn. along with assessors or judges, Yājñ., Sch. **-samid-gaṇa**, mfn. with a heap of fuel, R. **-sampad**, mfn. possessing happiness or prosperity, happy, Śiś. **-sampada**, mfn. happy, delighted, W. **-sampātin**, mfn. together with (the Rākshasa) Sampātin, R. **-sam-praîsha**, mfn. with a summons or invitation (to the officiating priest to commence a ceremony), Cat. **-sambhāra-yajushka**, mfn. with the Yajus called Sambhāra, ĀpŚr. **-sambhrama**, mf(*ā*)n. filled with confusion or bewilderment, bewildered, flurried, agitated (*am*, ind.), R.; Kālid. &c. **-sarpa**, mf(*ā*)n. having serpents, infested by s°, MBh. **-sasya**, mf(*ā*)n. grown with corn, Hariv. **-sahâya**, mfn. along with associates, having companions or accomplices, Mn. viii, 193. **-sâkshika**, mfn. (happening) before witnesses (*am*, ind.), Yājñ. **-sāgara**, mfn. together with the oceans, Ratnâv. **-sātyaka**, mfn. with Sātyaka, Hariv. **-sādi**, mfn. with charioteers, MBh. **-sādhana**, mfn. having means, MBh.; with materials or instruments (of war &c.), Kām.; °*nôpavarga-nirūpaṇa*, n. N. of ch. of a wk. **-sādhvasa**, mfn. dismayed, terrified, alarmed, timid (*am*, ind.), Śiś.; Ratnâv. **-sādhvīka**, mfn. with Arundhatī, VarBṛS. **-sāṃnāyyaka**, mfn. with the oblation called Sāṃnāyya, KātyŚr., Sch. **-sāra**, mfn. possessing strength or energy (*-tā*, f.), Kum.; Śiś.; with curds, Suśr.; *-vāṇa*, mfn. possessing both strength and sound, MW. **-sārathi**, mfn. with the charioteer, Kauś. **-sârtha**, mf(*ā*)n. with a caravan, Kathās.; containing goods, laden (as a ship), R. **-sāvarṇa**, mfn. with the Saṃhitā Sāvarṇikā, Cat. **-sita**, mfn. with sugar, Suśr.; °*tôpala*, mfn. id., Pañcar.; °*tôtpala-mālin*, mfn. wreathed with white lotus flowers, VarBṛS. **-sīta**, mfn. with Sītā, R. **-sīmaka**, mfn. with the limit or boundary, Pāṇ. i, 1, 7, Vārtt. 8, Pat. **-sīman**, mfn. having the same boundary, conterminous, near, L. **-sugandha**, mfn. having a pleasant smell, fragrant, VarBṛS.; °*dhi-gātra*, mfn. accompanied by perfumed men, Vishṇ. **-suta**, mf(*ā*)n. having a son, together with sons or children, MBh. **-sutvan**, mfn. accompanied by Soma-offering priests, MW. **-sudarśana**, mfn. armed with Vishṇu's discus (called Sud°), Hcat. **-sundarīka**, mfn. with a beautiful woman or wife, Siṇhās. **-suparṇa**, mfn. with the Sup° texts, IndSt. **-subrahmaṇya**, mfn. with the Subrahmaṇya, ĀpŚr., Sch. **-1. -sura**, mfn. along with the gods, Śiś.; *-cāpam*, ind. with Indra's bow, MW. **-2. -sura**, mfn. with liquor, having liquor, Śiś.; intoxicated, Cat. **-suvarṇa**, mfn. with gold, Vishṇ. **-suhṛid**, mfn. having friends or kinsfolk, MBh.; °*hṛij-jana*, mfn. id., MW.; °*hṛin-mitra-bāndhava*, mfn. with friends and companions and relatives, Pañcar. **-sūka** (of unknown meaning), HPariś. **-sūta**, mfn. with the charioteer, MBh. **-sūti** (*sá-*), w. r. for *sá-kūti*, MaitrS. **-sūnu** (*sá-*), w. r. in AV. v, 27, 1. **-sena**, mfn. with an army, commanding an army, MW. **-sainya**, mfn. id., R.; *-bala-vāhana*, mfn. with guards and armies and equipages, MW. **-soma** (*sá-*), mfn. with Soma, ŚBr. (*-tva*, n., TāṇḍBr.); *-pītha*, mfn. partaking of a draught of Soma equally with another (instr.), AitBr. **-saurabha**, mfn. having perfume, fragrant, Śiś. **-saurāshṭra**, mfn. with the Saur°, Kathās. **-stara**, m. having leaves strewn so as to form a bed, W. **-stuta-śastra**, mfn. joined with a Stotra and Śastra, ĀpŚr. **-strīka**, mfn. attended by a wife, ib.; having a wife, married, Kāv. **-sthaṇḍilaka**, mfn. with the sacrificial places, Pāṇ. i, 1, 7, Vārtt. 8, Pat. **-sthāṇu-jaṅgama**, mfn. along with immovables and movables, MBh. **-sthāna**, mfn. occupying the same position as (gen.), ĀrshBr.; produced in the same part of the mouth or with the same organ as (gen. or comp.), Prāt. **-sthâvan**, mfn. standing or fixed together, RV. viii, 37, 4. **-sthāsnu-cārin**, mfn. = *sthāṇu-jaṅgama*, MBh. vii, 372 (w. r. *saṃ-sth*° and *saṃ-sthāna-cārin*). **-sthūṇa** (*sá-*), mfn. together with the pillar, ŚBr.; *-cchinna*, mfn. hewn down with the stump, Kām. **-sneha**, mf(*ā*)n. oily, greasy, Mn.; MBh. &c.; affectionate (*am*, ind.), MBh.; Kāv. &c.; *-bahumāna*, mfn. with affection and esteem, Kathās. **-spṛiha**, mfn. filled with desire or longing, longing for, desirous of (loc. or inf.), Ratnâv.; expressing a desire, Kād.; (*am*), ind. lovingly, Śiś.; enviously, Ragh. **-sphura**, mfn. throbbing, i. e. living, Bhaṭṭ. **-sphuliṅga**, mfn. emitting sparks, Nār.; MBh.; R. **-smaya**, mf(*ā*)n. haughty, arrogant (*am*, ind.), Śiś. **-smita**, mf(*ā*)n. accompanied with smiles, smiling, laughing (*am*, ind.), Ratnâv.; Śiś. **-smeram**, ind. smilingly, Hāsy. **-syád** = *-srút*. **-sraj**, mfn. wreathed, garlanded, ŚāṅkhŚr. **-srút**, mfn. flowing, streaming, RV. **-srotas** (*sá-*), mfn. id., VS. **-svadha**, m. pl. 'having the Svadhā (q. v.),' a partic. class of deceased ancestors, MW. **-svana**, mf(*ā*)n. sounding, loud (*am*, ind.), MBh. **-svara**, mfn. sounding, having the same sound with (instr. or comp.), Prāt.; having accent, accentuated, IndSt.; (*am*), ind. loudly, VP. **-svāhā-kāra**, mfn. accompanied with the exclamation Svāhā, AitBr.; ĀpŚr. **-sveda**, mfn. moist with sweat, perspiring, exuding, MBh.; Kathās.; Rājat.; (*ā*), f. a girl who has been recently deflowered, L.

ससर्परी *sasarparī́*, f. (prob. fr. √*sṛip*, of unknown meaning, accord. to Sāy. = *vāc*; accord. to others = 'war-trumpet,' or 'N. of a mystical cow'), RV. iii, 53, 15; 16.

ससवस् *sasavas*. See √1. *san*, p. 1140.

सस्नि *sásni*, mfn. (fr. √1. *san*) procuring, bestowing; gaining, winning, RV.; = *saṃ-snāta*, Nir. v, 1. **-tama**, mfn. most bountiful (fr. √1. *san*), or cleanest, purest (fr. √*snā*), or most firmly joined (fr. √*snai*), ŚBr.

सस्पिञ्जर *saspiñjara*, mfn. = *śasp*°, TS.

सस्य 1. *sasyá*, n. (of unknown derivation; also written *śasya*; ifc. f. *ā*) corn, grain, fruit, a crop of corn (also pl.), AV. &c. &c. **-kreṇī**, f. buying corn, Uṇ. iv, 48, Sch. **-kshetra**, n. a corn-field, Hit. **-pāla**, m. a field-guarder, Rājat. **-pūrṇa**, mfn. full of or grown with corn, Hit. **-prada**, mfn. yielding c°, fertile, Mn. vii, 212. **-pravṛiddhi**, f. the growth of c°, VarBṛS. **-mañjarī**, f. an ear of c°, L. **-mārin**, m. 'corn-destroying,' a kind of rat or large mouse, L. **-mālin**, mfn. 'corn-wreathed,' abounding in corn or crops (as the earth), R. **-rakshaka**, m. = *-pāla*, Hit. **-rakshā**, f. guarding the fields, L. **-vat**, mfn. bearing a rich crop, Hariv.; R.; Mārk. **-veda**, m. the science of agriculture, Hcat. **-śālin**, mfn. = *-pūrṇa*, R.; Hcat. **-śīrshaka**, n. = *-mañjarī*, L. **-śūka**, n. an awn of grain, L. **-saṃvara** or **-saṃvaraṇa**, m. Vatica or Shorea Robusta, L. **-han**, mfn. destroying crops, MBh.; m. N. of an evil demon (the son of Duḥsaha), MārkP. **-hantṛi**, m. = prec., ib. **Sasyâkara-vat**, mfn. (prob.) producing abundant crops, Kām. **Sasyâd**, mfn. eating corn or fruit, AV. Paipp. **Sasyânanda**, m. N. of wk. **Sasyânte**, ind. when the grain is at an end, i. e. eaten up, Mn. iv, 27. **Sasyâvāpa**, m. sowing of crops, Yājñ., Sch. **Sasyêshṭi**, f. sacrifice offered on the ripening of new grain, W.

सस्य 2. *sasya*, m. (perhaps incorrect for *śasya*) a sort of precious stone, L.; n. a weapon, L.; virtue, merit, L.

Sasyaka, mfn. possessed of good qualities, perfect in its kind, Kāś. on Pāṇ. v, 2, 68; m. a sword, L.; m. n. a kind of precious stone, L.

सस्र *sasrá*, mf(*ā*)n. (fr. √*sṛi*) flowing, streaming, RV.

Sásri, mfn. running rapidly, speeding along, ib.

सस्रुत *sa-srut*, *sa-srotas*. See above.

सस्वर् *sasvár*, ind. (of unknown derivation), secretly, RV. (cf. Naigh. iii, 25).

Sasvártā, ind. id., ib.

सह् 1. *sah*, cl. 1. Ā. (Dhātup. xx, 22) *sáhate* (Ved. and ep. also °*ti* and exceptionally *sāhati*, once in MBh. 1. sg. *sahyāmi*; p. *sáhat*, *sáhamāna* [q. v.]; pf. *sehe*, *sasāha*; Ved. also *sasāhé* and *sāsāha*; *sāsáhat*; *sāsahishṭāḥ*, *sāsahyāma*; p. *sehāná*, *sāsahāná*, *sāsahvás* and *sāhvás* [q. v.]; aor. *asākshi*, *sākshi*, *sākshate*, RV.; *sákshīt*, GopBr.; *sakshati*, AV.; *sakshat*, *sā́kshāma*, RV.; Impv. *sakshi*, *sā́kshva*, ib.; p. *sákshat*, ib.; *ásahishṭa*, RV.; Prec. *sahyās*, *sāhyāma*, ib.; *sākshīya*, AV.; *sāhishīmáhi*, RV.; fut. *soḍhā*, MBh. &c.; *sahitā*, Gr.; *sakshyati*, MBh., °*te*, Br.; *sákshye* [?], AV.; *sahishyati*, °*te*, MBh.; Cond. *asahishyat*, ib.; inf. *sáhadhyai*, RV.; Kāṭh.; *sáḍhyai*, MaitrS.; *soḍhum*, *sahitum*, MBh.; ind. p. *soḍhvā*, ĀpŚr., Sch.; *sāḍhvā*, *sahitvā*, Gr.; *-sáhya*, RV. &c.; *sáham*, Br.), to prevail, be victorious; to overcome, vanquish, conquer, defeat (enemies), gain, win (battles), RV.; AV.; Br.; R.; Bhaṭṭ.; to offer violence to (acc.), AitBr.; ŚBr.; to master, suppress, restrain, MBh.; R. &c.; to be able to or capable of (inf. or loc.), ib.; to bear up against, resist, withstand, AV. &c. &c.; to bear, put up with, endure, suffer, tolerate (with *na*, 'to grudge'), MBh.; Kāv. &c.; to be lenient towards, have patience with any one (gen.), Bhag.; to spare any one, MārkP.; Pañcat.; to let pass, approve anything, Sarvad.; (with *kālam, kāla-kshepam* &c.) to bide or wait patiently for the right time, Kāv.; Kathās.: Caus. or cl. 10. *sāhayati* (aor. *asīshahat*), to forbear, Dhātup. xxxiv, 4: Desid. of Caus. *sisāhayishati*, Pāṇ. viii, 3, 62: Desid. *sīkshate* (p. *sīkshat*; accord. to Pāṇ. viii, 3, 61, also *sisahishate*), to wish to overcome, RV.; TS.: Intens. *sāsahyate, sāsoḍhi* (cf. *sāsahi*), Gr. [Cf. *sahas* and Gk. ἴσχω for σι-σχω; ἔχω, ἔ-σχον.]

2. Sah (strong form *sāh*), mfn. bearing, enduring, overcoming (ifc.; see *abhimāti-shāh* &c.)

1. Sahá, mf(*ā*)n. powerful, mighty, RV.; (ifc.) overcoming, vanquishing, MBh.; bearing, enduring, withstanding, defying, equal to, a match for (gen. or comp.), MBh.; Kāv. &c.; causing, effecting, stimulating, exerting, Śiś.; able to, capable of (inf. or comp.), Kālid.; Śiś.; Kathās.; m. the month Mārgaśīrsha (see *sahas*), VS.; ŚBr.; Car.; a partic. Agni, MBh.; a species of plant, AV.; N. of a son of Manu, Hariv.; of a son of Prāṇa and Ūrjasvatī, BhP.; of a son of Dhṛitarāshṭra, MBh.; of a son of Kṛishṇa and Mādrī, BhP.; (*ā*), f. the earth, L.; (with Buddhists) N. of a division of the world (with *loka-dhātu*, 'the world inhabited by men'), Kāraṇḍ.; N. of various plants (accord. to L. = Aloe Perfoliata, *daṇḍôtpalā, rāsnā* &c.), VarBṛS.; Suśr.; Unguis Odoratus, L.; n. = *bala*, L.; a kind of salt, L. — **1. -tā**, f., **-tva**, n. (for 2. see under 2. *saha*) sufferance, endurance, capacity of enduring, capacity, ability, Kām.; Rājat.; Kathās. — **pati**, m. 'lord of the world of men,' N. of Brahmā, Lalit. — **raksha** and °**kshas**, see under 2. *saha*, p. 1194, col. 2. **Sáhā-vat** or **sahā́-vat**, mfn. possessing strength, powerful, mighty, RV. **Sahā́-van**, mfn. (Padap. *sahá-van*), id., ib.

Sahaka, mfn. patient, suffering, enduring (gen.), Nalôd.

Sáhat, mfn. mighty, strong, RV. viii, 40, 1; lasting, solid, ib. v, 23, 1.

Sáhadhyai. See under √1. *sah*, p. 1192, col. 3.

Sahana, mf(*ā*)n. powerful, strong (in explanation of the etymology of *siṃha*), Nir. viii, 15; patient, enduring (see *a-s*°); m. (*saṃjñāyām*), g. *nandy-ādi*; n. patient endurance, forbearance, MārkP.; Sāh. — **śīla**, mfn. of a patient disposition, MW.

Sahanīya, mfn. to be borne or endured, pardonable, R.; Hariv.

Sáhantama, mfn. (superl. of *sahat*) strongest, most powerful, RV.

Sahantya, mfn. prevailing, conquering, ib.

Sáhamāna, mfn. (for *saha-m*° see under 2. *saha*) conquering, victorious, AV.; TBr.; (*ā*), f. a kind of plant, AV.; N. of that part of the frame enshrining the Universal Spirit which faces the south (the 3 others being *juhū, rājñī*, and *su-bhūta*), ChUp. xv, 2.

Sáhas, mfn. powerful, mighty, victorious (superl. -*tama*), RV.; m. the month Mārgaśīrsha or Agrahāyaṇa (November–December), the winter season, VS.; Suśr.; Pur.; n. strength, power, force, victory (*sahasas putra* or °*saḥ sūnu*, m. 'son of strength,' N. of Agni in RV.; *sahasā*, ind., see below; *sahobhiḥ*, ind. = 'mightily, intensely'), RV. &c. &c.; water, Naigh. i, 12; light, L.; N. of various Sāmans, ĀrshBr. [Cf. Goth. *sigis*; Angl. Sax. *sigor, sige*; Germ. *Sieg*.] — **kṛit**, mfn. bestowing strength or power, VS.; TS. (v.l.) — **kṛita** (*sáhas-*), mfn. produced by strength (said of Agni), RV.; invigorated, increased, excited, ib. — **vat** (*sáhas-*), mfn. powerful, mighty, victorious, RV.; AV.; BhP. (-*vat*, ind. mightily), RV.; containing the word *sahas*, AitBr.; m. N. of a king (v.l. *mahas-vat*), VP.; (*atī*), f., (prob.) N. of a plant, RV.; AV.

Sahasā (instr. of *sahas*), forcibly, vehemently, suddenly, quickly, precipitately, immediately, at once, unexpectedly, at random, fortuitously, in an unpremeditated manner, inconsiderately (with instr. = 'together with'). — **dṛishṭa**, m. 'seen fortuitously,' an adopted son, L. **Sahasôdgata**, m. N. of a man, Buddh.

Sahasāná, mfn. powerful, mighty, RV.; m. a peacock, Uṇ. ii, 87, Sch.; a sacrifice, oblation, ib.

Sahasānu, mfn. patient, enduring, L.; m. = prec., L.

Sahasā-vat, mfn. (= *sahas-vat*) strong, mighty (mostly said of Agni), RV.

Sahasin, mfn. powerful, mighty, RV.

Sahasyà, mfn. mighty, strong, RV.; AV.; m. the month Pausha (December–January), VS. &c. &c. — **candra**, m. the wintry moon, MW.

Sahā, sahā-vat. See under 1. *saha*, col. 1.

Sahānya, m. a mountain, L.

Sahām-pati, m. (rather fr. acc. of *sahā* than fr. gen. pl. of 2. *sah* + *p*°; cf. *saha-pati*) N. of Brahmā (with Buddhists), Lalit. (MWB. 210; 211); of a Bodhi-sattva, Kāraṇḍ.; of a serpent-demon, ib.; f. N. of a Kiṃ-narī, ib.

1. Sahita, mfn. (for 2. see p. 1195, col. 1) borne, endured, supported, W.

Sahitavya, mfn. to be borne or endured, MBh.

Sahitṛi, mfn. = *soḍhṛi*, Siddh.

Sahitra, n. patience, endurance, Pāṇ.; Vop.

Sahira, m. a mountain, L.

Sahishṭha, mfn. strongest, most mighty or powerful, RV.

Sahishṇu, mfn. patient, forbearing; bearing, enduring, putting up with (acc., gen., or comp.), MBh.; Kāv. &c.; m. N. of a Ṛishi, Hariv.; of one of the 7 Ṛishis under the 6th Manu, ib.; MārkP.; of a son of Pulaha, Pur.; of Vishṇu, RTL. 106, n. 1. — **tā**, f., **-tva**, n. patience, resignation, forbearance, MBh.; Kāv. &c.

Sáhīyas, mfn. more (or most) mighty or powerful, RV.; Kauś.; BhP.

Sáhuri, mfn. mighty, strong, victorious, RV.; m. the sun, Uṇ. ii, 73, Sch.; f. the earth, ib.; N. of Agni, L.

Saho, in comp. for *sahas*. — **já**, mfn. strength-born, produced by st°, RV. — **jit**, mfn. victorious by st°, AV. — **dá**, mfn. bestowing st°, RV. — **dairghatamasa**, n. du. N. of two Sāmans, ĀrshBr. — **bala**, n. great force or violence, cruelty, MW. — **bhári**, mfn. supporting st°, RV. — **rayishṭhiya**, n. N. of two Sāmans, ĀrshBr. — **van** (*sáho-*), mfn. mighty, superior, AV. — **vṛidh**, mfn. increasing strength, RV.

Sahya, mfn. to be borne or endured, endurable, tolerable, resistible, MBh.; R. &c.; able to bear, equal to, W.; powerful, strong, ib.; sweet, agreeable, W.; m. N. of one of the 7 principal ranges of mountains in India (see *kula-giri*); of a mountainous district (in which the Go-dāvarī rises in the N.W. of the Deccan), MBh.; VarBṛS. &c.; of a son of Vivasvat (v.l. *mahya*), MBh.; (*am*), n. help, assistance (oftener *sāhya*), MBh.; Hariv.; health, convalescence, L. — **karman**, n. help, assistance, MBh. — **tā**, f. endurableness, Mālav.; Kād. — **parvata** or **-mahībhṛit**, m. the Sahya range of mountains, MBh. — **varṇana**, n. N. of a ch. of the SkandaP. (containing a description of the Sahya mountains). — **vāsinī**, f. 'inhabiting the S° m°,' N. of Durgā, Mālatim. **Sahyâtmajā**, f. 'S°'s daughter,' N. of the river Kāverī, Cat. **Sahyâdri**, m. the S° mountain; -*khaṇḍa*, m. N. of a ch. of the SkandaP.

Sáhyas, mfn. = *sahīyas*, RV.

Sáhyu, mfn. conquering, victorious, RV.

Sahra, m. a mountain, L.

Sáhvan, mfn. powerful, mighty, ŚBr.

Sāḍhá, mfn. = *soḍhá*, overcome, conquered (cf. *a-shāḍha, ashāḷha*), RV.; AV. &c.

Sā́ḍhṛi or **sā́ḷhṛi**, mfn. = *soḍhṛi*, conquering, a conqueror, RV.

Sā́ḍhyai. See under √1. *sah*, p. 1192, col. 3.

Sāsahāná, mfn. (for *sa-s*°) overcoming, conquering, RV.

Sāsahi, mfn. (fr. Intens.) conquering, victorious, ib.; (ifc.) able to bear, Naish.

Sāsahvás and **sāhvás**, mfn. = *sāsahāna*, RV.

Síkshat. See Desid. of √1. *sah*.

Sehaná, mfn. = *sāsahāna*, RV.

Soḍha &c. See s.v.

सह् 3. *sah*, cl. 4. P. *sahyati*, to satisfy, delight, Dhātup. xxvi, 20; to be pleased, ib.; to bear, endure (cf. √1. *sah*), ib.

सह 2. *sahá*, ind. (prob. fr. 7. *sa* + *dhā*, which in Veda may become *dha*; cf. 1. *sadha*) together with, along with, with (with √*grah* and *ā*-√*dā*, 'to take with one;' with √*dā*, 'to give to take away with one;' with *kṛitvā* and acc., 'taking with one,' 'in the company of;' often as a prepos. governing instr. case, but generally placed after the governed word, e.g. *tena saha*, 'along with him;' exceptionally with abl., e.g. *aiśvaryāt saha*, 'with sovereignty,' Cāṇ. 104); in common, in company, jointly, conjointly, in concert (often used as a prefix in comp., expressing 'community of action,' e.g. *sahâdhyayana*, q.v.; or forming adjectives expressing 'the companion of an action,' e.g. *saha-cara*, q.v.); at the same time or simultaneously with (prefixed to adverbs of time, e.g. *saha-pūrvâhṇam*, q.v.; rarely ifc., e.g. *vainateya-s*°, 'with Vainateya,' Hariv.), RV. &c. &c.; m. a companion, L.; (*ā*), f. a female companion, BhP. — **ṛishabha**, mf(*ā*)n. (cf. *saharsh*°) together with a bull, ŚāṅkhŚr. — **kaṇṭhaka** (*saha-*), mf(*ikā*)n. with the throat, AV. — **karaṇa**, n. acting together, common action or performance, Saṃskārak. — **kartṛi**, m. a co-worker, assistant, Mn. viii, 206. — **kāra**, m. (for *sa-hakāra* see p. 1195, col. 1) acting with, co-operation, assistance, Kusum.; Bhāshāp., Sch.; a kind of fragrant mango tree, MBh.; Kāv. &c.; n. a m° blossom, Hariv.; m° juice, VarBṛS.; -*tā*, f. the state of a m° tree, Mālav.; -*taila*, m° oil, Suśr.; -*bhañjikā*, f. 'the breaking of m° blossoms,' a kind of game, Cat.; -*mañjarī*, f. N. of a woman, Vās.; °*rôpadeśa*, m. N. of wk. — **kārin**, mfn. acting together, co-operating, concurrent; m. a concurrent agent, expedient, assistant, Sāh.; Bhāshāp.; Sarvad.; (°*ri*)-*tā*, f. (Sāh.), -*tva*, n. (TS.), -*bhāva*, m. (Nilak.) concurrence, co-operation, assistance. — **kṛit**, mfn. co-operating, assisting, an assistant, W. — **kṛita**, mfn. co-operated with, accompanied by, assisted, aided, Kusum.; Bhāshāp.; Sarvad. — **kṛitvan**, mf(*arī*)n. co-operating, assisting, a coadjutor, Naish. — **kramya**, mfn. to be taken into or concluded in the Krama-text, RPrāt. — **khaṭvâsana**, n. sitting together on a bed, Mn. viii, 357. — **gata**, mfn. gone or going with, accompanied, associated, W. — **gamana**, n. going with or accompanying (esp. a widow's going with her deceased husband, i.e. burning herself with his dead body), ib. — **gāmin**, mfn. = -*gata*; (*inī*), f. a woman who burns herself with her deceased husband, ib. — **gu**, mfn. together with cows, AV. Paipp. — **guḍa**, mfn. provided with sugar, VarBṛS. — **gopa** (*sahá-*), mf(*ā*)n. with the cowherd, RV. — **candra-lalāma**, mfn. along with the moon-crested i.e. Śiva, BhP. — **cara**, mfn. going with, accompanying, associating with, Kālid.; Prab. &c.; belonging together, AitBr.; similar, like, Subh.; m. a companion, friend, follower, Kālid.; Śiś.; BhP.; a surety, W.; Barleria Prionitis and Cristata, Car.; = *pratibandhaka*, L.; (*ī*), f. a female companion or friend, mistress, wife, Kālid.; Kathās.; Barleria Prionitis or Cristata, L.; °*ra-bhinna*, m. (in rhet.) separation of what belongs together, joining discordant things or ideas (also °*nna-tā*, f., -*tva*, n.), Kpr.; Sāh.; (°*rī*)-*dharma*, m. 'the wife's duty,' sexual intercourse, Hariv. — **caraṇa**, mfn. going or belonging together, GopBr. — **carat**, mfn. going with, accompanying, attending, W. — **carita**, mfn. gone or going with &c.; congruent, homogeneous (-*tva*, n.), Pat.; Sāh.; TPrāt., Sch. — **cāra**, m. going together, AV.; agreement, harmony, congruence, concomitance (esp. in logic 'the invariable accompaniment of the *hetu* or middle term by the *sādhya* or major term,' as opp. to *vyabhicāra*; -*tva*, n.), Bhāshāp.; Kusum.; = *saha-gamana* (see -*vidhi*), N. of various phil. wks.; -*grantha-prakāśa*, m., -*rahasya*, n., -*vāda*, m. N. of wks.; -*vidhi*, m. N. of a wk. on the ceremonies enjoined upon a widow burning herself on the pyre of her husband. — **cārin**, mfn. going or living together, gregarious, Car.; connected or associated together, essentially belonging to (comp.), Sāh.; m. a follower, associate, companion, MBh.; R. &c.; (*iṇī*), f. a female companion, confidante, friend, R.; Kathās.; (°*ri*)-*grantha-rahasya*, n. N. of wk.; -*tva*, n. the being connected together, concomitance, inseparability, TPrāt., Sch. — **caitya-vat**, mfn. together with sanctuaries, R. — **cchandas** (*sahá-*), mfn. along with metre, RV. x, 130, 7. — **já**, mf(*ā*)n. born or produced together or at the same time as (gen.), TS.; Mn.; Kathās.; congenital, innate, hereditary, original, natural (ibc. = 'by birth,' 'by nature,' 'naturally;' with *deśa*, m. 'birthplace,' 'home'), MBh.; Kāv. &c.; always the same as from the beginning, Hariv. 4238; m. natural state or disposition (said to be also n.), L.; a brother of whole blood, L.; N. of various kings and other men, MBh.; Rājat. &c.; of a Tāntric teacher, Cat.; (*ā*), f. N. of various women, Rājat.; Buddh.; (*am*), n. N. of the third astrol. mansion (said to be also m.), VarBṛS.; emancipation during life, Cat.; -*kīrti*, m. N. of a Jaina author, Cat.; *-dhārmika*, mfn. innately honest, Hit.; *-pāla*, m. N. of various men, Rājat.; *-malina*, mfn. naturally dirty, spotty by nature, Kuval.; *-lalita*, m. N. of a man, Buddh.; *-mitra*, m. a natural friend (as a sister's son, cousin &c.), W.; *-vatsala*, mf(*ā*)n. fond or tender by nature, Hit.; *-vilāsa*, m. N. of a man, Buddh.; *-śatru*, m. (= °*jâri*), MW.; *-siddhi*, f. N. of wk.; *-suhṛid*, m. a natural friend, Prab.; °*jâdhinātha*, m. N. of a king, Cat.; °*jânanda*, m. N. of the founder of a Vaishṇava sect (also called Svāmi-nārāyaṇa, born about 1780 A.D.), RTL. 148; 149; of an author (also °*da-tīrtha* and *-nātha*), Cat.; °*jândha-dṛiś*, mfn. blind by nature or from birth, Śiś.; °*jâri*, m. a natural enemy, one hostile by birth (as the son of the same father by another mother, the son of a paternal uncle &c.), W.; °*jâshṭaka*, n. N. of a wk. by Saṃkarâcārya; °*jêtara*, mfn. other than natural, not innate or inherent or congenital, accidental, W.; °*jêndra*, m. N. of a man, Cat.; °*jôdāsīna*, m. one who is born neutral or who is naturally neither an enemy nor a friend, a common acquaintance, friend unconnected by birth, W. **-jagdhi**, f. eating together (used in explaining *sa-gdhi*), Nir. ix, 43. **-janman**, mfn. inherited from birth (as a servant), MārkP. **-janya**, m. N. of a Yaksha, BhP. (Sch.); (*ā*), f. N. of an Apsaras, MBh.; Hariv. &c. **-já**, mfn. born or produced together, RV. **-jāta**, mfn. born together or at the same time, equal in age, Kathās.; innate, natural, ib.; born from the same mother, twin-born, L. **-jāni** (*sahá-*), mfn. together with a wife, TS. **-jānusha** (*sahá-*), mfn. with offspring, RV. i, 108, 4. **-jit**, mfn. victorious at once (said of princes), MBh. **-jīvin**, mfn. living together, ib. **-joshaṇa**, mfn. (used in explaining *sa-joshas*), Nir. viii, 8. **-2. -tā**, f. (for 1. see 1. *saha*) association, connection, communion, MW. **-2. -tva**, n. (for 1. see ib.) id., ŚrS.; *-karman*, n. an action to be performed together, ĀpŚr. **-daṇḍa**, mfn. with an army, Bhaṭṭ. **-dāna**, n. common oblation (to various gods), Pāṇ. vi, 3, 26, Sch. **-dānu** (*sahá-*), mfn. with a Dānu or with Dānus, RV. **-dāra**, mfn. along with a wife, having a wife, married, MBh. **-dīkshitin**, mfn. undertaking the Dīkshā (q.v.) together, TāṇḍBr. **-deva** (*sahá-*), mfn. with the gods, MBh.; BhP.; m. N. of a Ṛishi (with the patr. *Vārshāgira*), RV. i, 107; of a man (with the patr. *Sārñjaya*), ŚBr.; of the youngest of the five Pāṇḍava princes (son of Mādrī and reputed son of Pāṇḍu, but really son of the Aśvins, and twin-brother of Nakula; see *mādrī*), MBh.; of a son of Haryaśvata, Hariv.; of a son of Harsha-vardhana, VP.; of a son of Haryavana, BhP.; of a son of Soma-datta, Hariv.; of a son of Jarā-saṃdha, ib.; of a son of Divā-kara, VP.; of a son of Devāpi, ib.; of a son of Divârka, BhP.; of a son of Su-dāsa, VP.; of a son of Su-prabuddha and uncle of Gautama Buddha, Buddh.; of a Rāja-putra (mentioned together with Yudhi-shṭhira), Rājat.; of an author (also with *bhaṭṭa*), Cat.; (*ā*), f. N. of various plants (accord. to L. Sida Cordifolia, Echites Frutescens, = *daṇḍôtpalā* &c.), Suśr.; VarBṛS. (v.l.); of a daughter of Devaka and wife of Vasu-deva, Hariv.; Pur.; (*ī*), f. N. of various plants (accord. to L. 'Sida Cordifolia and Rhombifolia, = *sarpâkshī* &c.'), VarBṛS.; Pañcat.; (°*va*)*-ja*, mfn. together with Deva-ja (or m. 'N. of Kṛiśâśva'), BhP.; *-śāstra*, n. N. of wk.; (°*vī*)*-gaṇa*, m. a collection of herbs used in certain ablutions at the consecration of an idol &c.), MW. **-devata** (*sahá-*), mfn. together with the deities, AV. **-devi**, w.r. for *sāhad*°, Rājat. **-droṇa**, mfn. along with Droṇa, MW. **-dharma**, m. community of duty or law, common usage or characteristic, MBh.; *-cara*, mfn. one following the same law or duties, MBh.; R.; (*ī*), f. a wife who helps in the fulfilment of duties, ib.; *-caraṇa*, n. the fulfilment of duties (in common with a husband), Śak.; *-cārin*, mfn. sharing the duties of (gen.), Śak.; (*iṇī*), f. a wife who helps a husband in fulfilling duties, a helpmate, lawful or legitimate wife, R.; Ragh.; Uttarar. **-dharman**, mfn. along with duties, sharing duties &c., BhP. **-dharmin**, mfn. following the same duties or customs, L.; (*iṇī*), f. a wife who shares duties, a lawful or legitimate wife, ib. **-dhānya**, mfn. provided with corn or grain or food, ŚāṅkhGṛ. **-nartana**, n. the act of dancing together, L. **-nirvāpa**, m. a common oblation, Pat. **-nivāsin**, mfn. dwelling together with (instr.; °*si-tā*, f.), Mālatim. **-nṛitya**, n. = *-nartana*, Gaut. **-nau**, mfn. with the ship, BhP. **-patni**, mfn. with a wife, R. **-patnī** (*sahá-*), f. along with a husband, AV. **-patnīka**, mfn. with a wife, ĀpŚr. **-pathin**, m. and f. (nom. *-panthās*, *-pathī*) going by the same road, a companion on a journey, fellow-traveller, MW. **-pāṇsu-kila**, m. 'one who has played with another in the dust or sand,' a friend from childhood, cotemporary, L. **-pāṇsu-krīḍana**, n. playing together with dust or sand (in childhood), Mālatim. **-pāṇsu-krīḍita**, mfn. one with whom another has played &c. (see above), a friend from childhood, Kād. **-pāṭha**, m. the being mentioned together, KātyŚr. **-pāna** (ib., Sch.) or **-pānaka** (L.), n. drinking t°. **-piṇḍa-kriyā**, f. offering of the Piṇḍa (q.v.) in common, Mn. iii, 248. **-pīti**, f. (used in explaining *sá-pīti*), Nir. ix, 43. **-putra**, mf(*ā*)n. with a son or children, MBh. **-purusha**, mfn. with men, ŚāṅkhŚr. **-pūrusha** (*sahá-*), mfn. id., AV. **-pūrvāhṇam**, ind. simultaneously with the beginning of forenoon, Pāṇ. vi, 3, 81, Sch. **-prakṛiti** or **-praklṛipti**, f. a precept about simultaneousness or concomitance, KātyŚr. (and v.l.) **-prama** (*sahá-*), mfn. with the measure, RV. x, 130, 7. **-prayāyin**, mfn. setting out t°, a fellow-traveller, Kathās. **-prayoga**, m. simultaneous practice or application, KātyŚr., Sch. **-pravāda**, mfn. with the case-forms (= *sa-pr*°), RPrāt. **-prasthāyin**, mfn. = *-prayāyin*, Kathās. **-bāndhava**, mfn. with relatives, R. **-bhaksha** (*sahá-*), mfn. eating or enjoying together, MaitrS.; AV.; Lāṭy. **-bhasman**, mfn. with the ashes, AitBr. **-bhārya**, mfn. with a wife, MW. **-bhāva**, m. the being together, companionship, community, Kuval.; connection together, concomitance, inseparability, Śaṃk.; Sarvad. **-bhāvanika**, mfn. along with Bhāvanikā, Kathās. **-bhāvin**, mfn. connected together, coherent, connected with (comp.), Śaṃk.; m. a friend, adherent, partisan, W. **-bhuj**, mfn. eating t° with (comp.), Kusum. **-bhū**, mfn. being together (used in explaining *sacā-bhū*), Nir. v, 5; appearing t° with (comp.), ĀpŚr., Sch.; innate, natural, Ratnâv.; Kād.; counterpart of (gen.), Kād. **-bhūta**, mfn. being together, joined, connected, Pat. **-bhūti**, f., AV. iv, 31, 6 (v.l. for *abhi-bh*° in RV.) **-bhojana**, n. eating t°, commensality with (comp.), Gaut.; common enjoyment or possession of (gen.), MBh. **-bhojin**, m. one who eats together, a messmate, ib. **-bhrātṛi**, mfn. t° with a brother or brothers, W. **-manas**, mfn. with intelligence, Rājat. **-maraṇa**, n. dying together, concremation, burning with the corpse of a husband, W. **-marmâsthi-saṃghāta**, mfn. with the joints and the whole frame of bones, R. **-mātṛika**, mfn. along with the mother, Vop. **-māda**, m. (used in explaining *sadha-m*°), Sāy. on RV. iii, 35, 4. **-māna**, mfn. (for *saham*° see p. 1193, col. 1) possessing pride, full of arrogance, MW. **-mārīca**, mfn. with Mārīca, R. **-mitra**, m. N. of a man, HPariś. **-mukha**, mfn. with the mouth, ĀpŚr. **-mūra** and **-mūla** (*sahá-*), mfn. along with the root (cf. *sa-mūla*), RV. **-mṛitā**, f. a woman who has burned herself with her dead husband (cf. *saha-maraṇa*), Pañcar. **-yajña**, mf(*ā*)n. with sacrifices, Bhag. **-yaśas** (*sahá-*), mfn. glorious, splendid, TS. **-yāta**, w.r. for *-jāta*, Kathās. **-yāyin**, mfn. going together, a fellow-traveller, Śak.; Kathās. **-yuj**, mfn. yoked or harnessed together, Nir. ix, 24. **-yudhvan**, mfn. fighting t°, a brother-in-arms, Śiś.; Bhaṭṭ. **-yoshit**, mfn. with a wife, R. **-yaugaṃdharāyaṇa**, mfn. with Yaugaṃdharāyaṇa, Kathās. **-raksha** (VP.) or **-rakshas** (*sahá-*, TS.), m. one of the three kinds of sacrificial fire (that which receives the offering to the Rakshasas; the latter also, 'a forest fire,' L). **-rasā**, f. Phaseolus Trilobus (a sort of bean), L. **-rājaka**, mfn. t° with the king, MBh. **-rshabha** (for *-ṛishabha*; *sahá-*), mf(*ā*)n. along with the bull, TS. **-lakshmaṇa**, mfn. with Laksh°, R. **-loka-dhātu**, m. the world inhabited by men, the earth, Buddh. **-vatsa**, mf(*ā*)n. with the calf, ĀpŚr. **-vartin**, mfn. being together, keeping company, MW. **-vasati**, f. dwelling t°, Śak. **-vasu** (*sahá-*), mfn. with wealth or with one's property (accord. to Sāy. 'N. of an Asura'), RV. ii, 13, 8. **-vah** (strong form *-vāh*), mfn. drawing together (said of horses), RV. vii, 97, 6. **-vācya**, mfn. to be spoken t°, Lāṭy. **-vāda**, m. 'speaking t°,' colloquy, disputation, MBh. **-vārshṇeya-jīvala**, mfn. with Vārsh° and Jīv°, MBh. **-vārshṇeya-bāhuka**, mfn. with V° and Bāhuka, ib. **-vārshṇeya-sārathi**, mfn. with the charioteer V°, ib. **-vāsa**, m. dwelling together, common abode, ib.; Hariv.; Kathās.; = next, MW. **-vāsika** or **-vāsin**, mfn. one who lives with another, a fellow-lodger or neighbour, MBh. **-vāhana**, mfn. along with vehicles, MBh. **-vivakshā**, f. the intention to utter anything together or at once, Pat. **-vīra** (*sahá-*), mfn. together with men or heroes, RV.; VS. **-vīrya**, n. fresh butter, L. **-vṛiddhi-kshaya-bhāva**, mfn. possessing or partaking of the increase and wane (of the moon), Subh. **-vaiśikya**, mfn. with the Vaiśikyas, MārkP. **-vrata**, mf(*ā*)n. having common observances or duties; (*ā*), f. = *-dharmacāriṇī*, col. 1, Hariv.; a religious community, sect, Lalit. **-śaya**, see *digdha-s*°. **-śayyā**, f. the lying together with, Āpast. **-śayyâsanâśana**, mfn. lying and sitting and eating together, BhP. **-śishṭa**, mfn. taught or enjoined together or at once (*-tva*, n.), ĀpŚr., Sch. **-śéyya**, n. = *-śayyā*, RV. **-saṃvāda**, m. speaking together, conversation, BhP. **-saṃvāsa**, m. dwelling t°, Rājat. **-saṃvega**, mfn. vehemently excited, MBh. **-saṃsarga**, m. carnal contact or intercourse with (instr.), MBh. **-saṃjāta-vṛiddha**, mfn. born and grown up together, ib. **-sambhalā** (*sahá-*), f. with (her) suitor, RV. **-sambhava**, mfn. born or produced together or at the same time (with *janmanā* = 'innate'), Kāv. **-sāman** (*sahá-*), mf(°*mnī*)n. accompanied with songs or hymns, rich in songs, RV. **-siddha**, mfn. innate (*-tva*, n.), Śaṃk. (quot.) **-sura-lalanā-lalāma-yūtha-pati**, mfn. with the leaders of the troops who form the ornament of the gods' wives, BhP. **-sûkta-vāka** (*sahá-*), mfn. accompanied with sacred hymns or formulas, AV. **-sevin**, mfn. having intercourse with, MBh. **-soma** (*sahá-*), mfn. with Soma draughts, VS. **-saumitri**, mfn. with Saumitri (i.e. Lakshmaṇa), R. **-stoma** (*sahá-*), mfn. with hymns, having h°, RV. **-stha**, mfn. being together with, being present; m. a companion, Kathās. **-sthāna**, n. (used in explaining *sadha-stha* and *sadana*), Nir. **-sthita**, mfn. = *-stha*, Kathās. **-sthiti**, f. abiding t° in (comp.), Naish. **-sphya**, mfn. with the sacrificial implement called Sphya (q.v.), ĀpŚr. **-huta**, mfn. with the oblation, Kauś. **Sahā-cara**, m. (for *saha-c*°) a Barleria with yellow flowers, Car. **Sahâjya**, mfn. along with clarified butter, KātyŚr. **Sahâdaram**, ind. with reverence, reverentially, Pañcar. **Sahâdhyayana**, n. studying together, companionship in study, MBh. **Sahâdhyāyin**, m. a fellow-student, condisciple, Kauś.; Hariv. &c.; one who studies the same science, VarBṛS. **Sahânugamana**, n. = *saha-maraṇa*, L. **Sahânuja**, mfn. with a younger brother, MW. **Sahânumaraṇa**, n. (= *saha-maraṇa*); *-viveka*, m. N. of a wk. on widow-burning. **Sahâpatya**, mfn. accompanied with offspring, Āpast. **Sahâpavâda**, mfn. containing contradictions, disagreeing, RPrāt. **Sahâmātya**, mfn. with a minister or councillor or c°s, attended by ministers, R. **Sahâya** &c., see p. 1195. **Sahâyatana**, mfn. with the fire-shrine, ĀśvGṛ. **Sahârambha**, mfn. beginning t°, GopBr. **Sahârogya** (?), mfn. possessing freedom from disease, healthy, L. **Sahârjuna**, mfn. with Arjuna, MBh. **Sahârtha**, m. accompanying or accessory matter, Kpr.; a common object, MW.; mfn. having the same object or meaning, synonymous, W.; *-tva*, n. (prob.) co-operation, Car.; *-nāśa*, mfn. one who is the same (i.e. unchanged) in profit and loss or fortune and misfortune, Kir.; °*rthī-√bhū*, P. *-bhavati*, to accompany, attend (°*rthī-bhāva*, m. 'companionship, community'), Pat. on Pāṇ. i, 4, 23, Vārtt. 3. **Sahârdha**, mfn. together with a half, Rājat. **Sahâlāpa**, m. colloquy, conversation with (comp.), Pañcar. **Sahâvasthita**, mfn. staying or being together (*-tā*, f.), Sarvad. **Sahâśrāya**, m. N. of a king, VP. **Sahâsana**, n. sitting or abiding t°, Mn.; MBh. &c. **Sahâsyā**, f. id. (with instr.), Suśr.; BhP. **Sahêti**, mfn. with the particle *iti*, followed by it; *-karaṇa* and *-kāra*, mfn. (or n., scil. *pada*, a word) followed by the particle *iti*, RPrāt. **Sahêndra**, mfn. with Indra, MBh. **Sahâika-sthāna**, n. the standing or being alone with (any one), Yājñ. ii, 284. **Sahôkti**, f. speaking together or at the same time, Vop.; (in rhet.) a comparison of many objects by using the word *saha* (opp. to *vinôkti*, q.v.), Kāvyâd.; Sāh. &c. (cf. IW. 458). **Sahôṭaja**, m. a kind of hut made of leaves (sometimes burnt with the body of an ascetic), L. **Sahôḍha**, m. (for *sa-hôḍha* see p. 1195) 'brought with (a woman pregnant at her marriage),' a son by another man than her husband, Vishṇ.; Mn.; MBh. &c.; *-ja*, id., Yājñ.; (*ā*), f. a woman married at the same time with another, R. **Sahôttha**, mfn. innate (= *saha-ja*), L.; m. N. of the third astrol. mansion, VarBṛS.

Sahôtthâyin, mfn. rising together, conspiring with, accomplice in a plot, Mudr. **Sahôtpatti**, f. simultaneous birth or origin, MBh. **Sahôdaka**, mfn. = *samânôdaka*, MārkP. **Sahôda-kumbha**, mfn. together with the water-jar, Gobh. **Sah'odana**, mfn. t° with rice, ĀśvGṛ. **Sahôdaya**, mf(*ā*)n. t° with the following (words, letters &c.), RPrāt. **Sahôdara**, mf(*ā* and *ī*)n. co-uterine, born of the same womb, Mn.; MBh. &c.; closely resembling or similar, Vcar.; Bālar.; m. a uterine brother, MBh.; Kāv. &c.; (*ā* or *ī*), f. a uterine sister, Mn.; MBh. &c. **Sahôdita**, mfn. said t°, declared comprehensively or collectively, W. **Sahôpadha**, mfn. t° with a penultimate sound or letter, RPrāt. **Sahôpapati-veśman**, mfn. living t° with a wife's paramour, Vishṇ.; Yājñ. **Sahôpamā**, f. 'comparison by the word *saha*,' = *sahôkti* above, MW. **Sahôpalambha**, m. simultaneous perception, Sarvad. **Sahôru**, mf(*ū*)n. = *saṃhitôru*, Pat. on Pāṇ. iv, 1, 70. **Sahôshita**, mfn. one who has dwelt with another, MBh.; Hariv. **Sahâñjas**, mfn. endowed with strength or power, VS.

Sahâya, m. (ifc. f. *ā*; prob. fr. *saha* + *aya*, cf. *sahâyana*; but, accord. to some, a Prākṛit form of *sakhâya*, see *sakhi*, p. 1130) 'one who goes along with (another),' a companion, follower, adherent, ally, assistant, helper in or to (loc. or comp.; ifc. = 'having as a companion or assistant, accompanied or supported by'), Mn.; MBh. &c.; (ibc.) companionship, assistance (see comp.); N. of Śiva, MBh.; the ruddy goose, L.; a kind of drug or perfume, L. — **karaṇa**, n. the act of rendering assistance, aiding, MW. — **kṛit**, m. 'rendering assistance,' a friend, companion, Kāśikh. — **kṛitya**, n. = *-karaṇa*, R. — **tā**, f. a number of companions &c., Pat. on Pāṇ. iv, 2, 43; = next, R.; Kālid. &c. — **tva**, n. companionship, association, friendship, assistance, help, R.; Pañcat.; Kathās. — **vat**, mfn. having a companion or assistant, accompanied or befriended or assisted by, provided with (comp.), MBh.; R. &c. **Sahâyârtham**, ind. for the sake of company, Mn. iv, 239. **Sahâyârthin**, mfn. seeking a companion, desirous of an ally, MW.

Sahâyaka (ifc.) = *sahâya*, MBh.

Sahâyana, n. going together, fellowship, company, R.

Sahâyin, mfn. going together, a companion, follower (mostly *inī*, f. 'a female companion'), R.; Pañcat.

Sahâyī, in comp. for *sahâya*. — **bhāva**, m. the being or becoming a companion, L. — √**bhū**, P. *-bhavati*, to be or become a companion, ib.

2. **Sahita**, mf(*ā*)n. (for 1. see p. 1193, col. 2) = *saṃhita* (cf. Pāṇ. vi, 1, 144, Vārtt. 1, Pat.), joined, conjoined, united (du. 'both together;' pl. [also with *sarve*] 'all t°'); accompanied or attended by, associated or connected with, possessed of (instr. or comp.), MBh.; Kāv. &c.; attached or cleaving to, KātyŚr.; being quite near, ib.; MBh.; (in astron.) being in conjunction with (instr. or comp.), VarBṛS.; (*ā*), f. N. of a river, VP.; n. a bow weighing 300 Palas, L.; (*am*), ind. together, along with, MBh.; near, close by, KātyŚr. — **kumbhaka**, m. a partic. mode of suppressing the breath (see *prâṇâyāma*). — **tva**, n. the being joined together, junction with (comp.), TPrāt. — **sthita**, mfn. standing together, Kathās. **Sahitâṅguli**, mfn. having fingers which have grown together, L. **Sahitôttara**, n. a bow weighing 500 Palas, L. **Sahitôru**, mf(°*rū*)n. = *saṃhitôru*, Pat. on Pāṇ. iv, 1, 70.

सहंसपात **sa-haṃsa-pāta**, mfn. (i.e. 7. *sa* + *h*°) accompanied with flights of swans or geese, Ragh.

Sa (to be similarly prefixed to the following): — **haṃsa-vāla-vyajana**, mf(*ā*)n. with swans as chowries or fly-whisks, ŚārṅgP. — **hakāra**, mfn. (for *saha-k*° see p. 1193, col. 3) having the sound *ha* (i.e. the sound used in calling), Nalôd. — **hanana**, mfn. with the drum-stick, ŚāṅkhŚr. — **haya**, mfn. with horses, MBh. — **hara**, m. N. of a Dānava (v.l. *saṃ-h*°), Hariv. — **hari**, m. a bull, L.; the sun, L.; ind. like Hari, i.e. Vishṇu, Pāṇ. ii, 1, 6, Sch. — **harsha**, mf(*ā*)n. joyful, glad (*am*, ind.), Kāv.; Kathās. (also w.r. for *sam-harsha*); *-mṛigayu-grāma-ninâda-maya*, mf(*ī*)n. resounding with the shouts of the joyful troop of hunters, Kathās.; *-vairâgyam*, ind. joyfully and (yet) with disgust, Dhūrtas.; *-sâdhvasam*, ind. with joy and (yet) trepidation, Mālatim.; °*shâkûtam*, ind. with joy and eagerness, ib. — **harshita**, mf(*ā*)n. joyful, glad, MBh. — **halanīya**, m. (prob.) a plough-mate (used in explaining *sāmanta*), IndSt. — **hasa**, mf(*ā*)n. having laughter, laughing, smiling, Śiś. vi, 57. — **hasta**, mfn. having hands, BhP.; dexterous or skilled in handling weapons, L.; *-tālam*, ind. with clapping of hands, Mṛicch. — **hasra**, see below. — **hālin**, m. 'plough-mate (?),' N. of a man, Buddh. — **hārda**, mf(*ā*)n. feeling or betraying affection, affectionate, Śiś.; MārkP. — **hāva**, mfn. employing amorous gestures, wanton (*am*, ind.), Bhaṭṭ. — **hāsa**, mf(*ā*)n. accompanied with a laugh, laughing (*am*, ind.), Śiś.; MārkP.; *-rabhasa*, (ibc.) laughingly and violently, Amar.; *-hā-kāram*, ind. laughing and uttering the exclamation *hā*, Śiś. — **hima**, mfn. having ice or snow, Rājat.; Kathās.; cold (as wind), R. — **hiraṇya** (*sá-*), mfn. provided with gold, ŚBr.; Kauś.; *-pātra* (*sá-h*°), mfn. with a golden vessel, ŚBr. — **hila**, m. 'having semen (?),' N. of a man, Rājat. — **huḍa**, mfn. having a ram, with rams, MBh. — **hūti** (*sá-*), f. (instr. °*tī*) conjoint or united invocation, RV. — **hṛid**, mfn. accompanied with the formula *hṛidā hṛit*, Kāśikh.; (*-hṛil*)*-lekha*, mfn. 'having distress of heart,' doubtful, restless, MBh.; questionable, causing doubt or suspicion, suspected, Prâyaśc.; n. questionable food, MW. — **hṛidaya** (*sá-*), mf(*ā*)n. with the heart, TBr.; Vikr.; hearty, sincere, AV.; possessing a heart, good-hearted, full of feeling, sensible, intelligent, Kāv.; Daśar.; Sāh.; m. a learned man, W.; m. or n. (?) N. of a wk. on Ācāra; *-līlā*, f. N. of a rhet. wk. by Rucaka; *-hṛidayâloka*, m. N. of a wk. also called Dhvany-āloka. — **hṛishṭakam**, ind. with bristling hair, with a thrill, Kāv. — **hetu**, mfn. having a cause or reason, well-founded, reasonable, Kāvyâd. — **hetuka**, mfn. id., Bhāshāp.; together with a reason, Rājat. — **hemaka**, mfn. t° with the gold pieces, Kathās. — **hema-kakshya**, mfn. having golden girths, MW. — **hela**, mfn. full of play or sport, wanton, careless, unconcerned (*am*, ind.), Kāv.; Kathās. &c.; m. N. of a man (also °*laka*), Rājat. — **hôḍha**, mf(*ā*)n. (for *sahôḍha* see p. 1194, col. 3) one who has the stolen property with him, Vaś.; Mn. &c. — **hautra**, mfn. together with the functions of the Hotṛi, ŚāṅkhŚr.; *-nakshatra-sattva-prayoga*, m. N. of wk. — **hlādam**, ind. joyfully, gladly, Prab.

सहण्डुक **sahaṇḍuka**, n. a partic. condiment prepared with meat &c., L.

सहम **sahama**, n. (fr. Arabic سهم) good or evil luck arising from the influence of the stars. — **kalpalatā**, f., **-candrikā**, f. N. of wks.

सहर **sa-hara**, °*ri* &c. See col. 1.

सहस् **sahas**, °*sā* &c. See p. 1193, col. 1.

सहस्र **sahásra**, n. (rarely) m. (perhaps fr. 7. *sa* + *hasra* = Gk. χίλιοι for χεσλοι; cf. Pers. *hazār*) a thousand (with the counted object in the same case sg. or pl., e.g. *sahasreṇa bāhunā*, 'with a thousand arms,' Hariv.; *sahasraṃ bhishajaḥ*, 'a thousand drugs,' RV.; or in the gen., e.g. *dve sahasre suvarṇasya*, 'two th° pieces of gold,' Rājat.; *catvāri sahasrāṇi varshāṇām*, 'four th° years,' Mn.; sometimes in comp., either ibc., e.g. *yuga-sahasram*, 'a th° ages,' Mn.; or ifc., e.g. *sahasrâśvena*, 'with a th° horses;' *sahasram* may also be used as an ind., e.g. *sahasram ṛishibhiḥ*, 'with a th° Ṛishis,' RV.; with other numerals it is used thus, *ekâdhikaṃ sahasram* or *eka-sahasram*, 'a th° + one,' 1001; *dvy-adhikaṃ s*°, 'a th° + two,' 1002; *ekādaśâdhikaṃ s*° or *ekādaśaṃ s*° or *ekādaśa-s*°, 'a th° + eleven' or 'a th° having eleven,' 1011; *viṃśaty-adhikaṃ s*° or *viṃśaṃ s*°, 'a th° + twenty,' 1020; *dve sahasre* or *dvi-sahasram*, 'two th°; *trīṇi sahasrāṇi* or *tri-sahasram*, 'three th°' &c.), RV. &c. &c.; a thousand cows or gifts (= *sahasraṃ gavyam* &c., used to express wealth; *sahasraṃ śatâśvam*, 'a th° cows and a hundred horses,' ŚāṅkhŚr.), RV.; VS.; ŚBr. (in later language often = '1000 Paṇas,' e.g. Mn. viii, 120; 336 &c.); any very large number (in Naigh. iii, 1 among the *bahu-nāmāni*; cf. *sahasra-kiraṇa* &c. below); mf(*ī*)n. a thousandth or the thousandth (= *sahasra-tama* which is the better form; cf. Pāṇ. v, 2, 57). — **ka**, mfn. (for *sahasraka* see p. 1196) thousand-headed, Yājñ. — **kaṃdhara-rāmāyaṇa**, n. N. of wk. — **kara**, m. 'thousand-rayed,' the sun, VarYogay.; Kathās. — **kara-pan-netra**, mfn. having a th° hands and feet and eyes, Yājñ. — **kalaśa-snapanâdi**, **-kalaśâbhisheka-prayoga**, m. N. of wks. — **kalā**, f. N. of a woman, Uttamac. — **kavaca**, m. N. of a mythical personage, Virac. — **kāṇḍa** (*sahásra-*), mfn. consisting of a th° parts, AV.; (*ā*), f. white-flowering Dūrvā grass, L. — **kiraṇa**, m. = *-kara*, Śak.; VarBṛS.; Pañcat.; N. of a man, Cat.; (*ī*), f. N. of wk.; °*ṇâvali*, f. N. of wk. — **kuṇapa** (*sahásra-*), mf(*ā*)n. having a th° dead bodies, AV. — **kṛitvas**, ind. a th° times, Mn.; Gaut. — **ketu** (*sahásra-*), mfn. having a th° forms, RV.; thousand-bannered, MW. — **gaṇa-nāman**, n., **-gīti**, f. N. of wks. — **gu**, mfn. possessing a th° cows, Mn.; Gaut.; th°-rayed, L.; th°-eyed, L.; m. the sun, Var.; N. of Indra, Vām. — **guṇa**, mfn. a th°fold (*-tā*, f.), Ragh.; Rājat. — **guṇita**, mfn. multiplied a th° times, MBh.; Pañcat.; Vet. — **godāna-paddhati**, f. N. of wk. — **ghātin**, mfn. killing a th°; n. a partic. engine of war, VarBṛ., Sch. — **ghnī**, mfn. killing a th°, AV. (v.l. *-ghnyá*). — **cakshas** (*sahásra-*), mfn. th°-eyed, RV. — **cakshu**, mfn. id., AV. — **cakshus**, mfn. id.; m. N. of Indra, R.; VarBṛS. — **caṇḍī-vidhāna**, n., **-caṇḍī-vidhi**, m., **-caṇḍī śata-caṇḍī-vidhāna**, n., **-caṇḍy-ādi-prayoga-paddhati**, f. or **-caṇḍy-ādi-vidhi**, m. N. of wks. — **caraṇa**, mfn. th°-footed (said of Vishṇu), MBh.; R. — **citya**, m. N. of a king, MBh. — **cetas** (*sahásra-*), mfn. having a th° aspects or appearances, RV. — **jaladhāra**, m. 'having a th° clouds,' N. of a mountain, Hariv. — **jit**, mfn. conquering or winning a th°, RV.; m. N. of Vishṇu, L.; of a king, MBh.; of a son of Indu, VP.; of a son of Kṛishṇa, BhP.; = *sahasrā-jit*, MW. — **jihva**, mfn. th°-tongued, Hāsy. — **jyotis**, m. N. of a son of Su-bhrāj, MBh. — **ṇī**, m. (fr. *s*° + *nī*) a leader of a th° or th°s, BhP. — **ṇīti** (*sahásra-*), mfn. (fr. *s*° + *nīti*) having a th° ways and means, RV. — **ṇītha** (*sahásra-*), mfn. (fr. *s*° + *nītha*) having a th° expedients or artifices, RV.; praised in a th° hymns, MW.; skilled in a th° sciences, ib. — **tamá**, mf(*ī*)n. the thousandth, TS.; ŚBr.; Pāṇ., Sch. — **da**, mfn. giving a thousand (cows), Mn.; R.; m. N. of Śiva, MBh.; of a son of Indu, Hariv. — **daṃshṭra**, mfn. th°-toothed, L.; m. = next, Suśr. — **daṃshṭrin**, m. a sort of sheat fish, L. — **dakshiṇa** (*sahásra-*), mfn. accompanied with a fee or recompense of a th° (kine), containing or giving a th° (kine), RV.; AV.; GṛŚrS. &c.; m. or n. (?) a partic. ceremony, Vait. — **dala**, mfn. having a th° petals, Pañcar. — **dá**, mfn. giving a th°, VS.; SV.; *-tama*, mfn., RV. — **dātu** (*sahásra-*), mfn. th°fold, RV. — **dāna** (*sahásra-*), mf(*ā*)n. bestowing a th° gifts, RV. — **dávan**, mfn. giving a th°, RV.; m. a giver of th°s, MW. — **dīdhiti**, m. 'th°-rayed,' the sun, Kād.; Nāg.; Priy. — **dṛiś**, mfn. th°-eyed, R.; N. of Indra, MBh.; RāmatUp.; of Vishṇu, A. — **dos**, mfn. having a th° arms; m. N. of Arjuna Kārtavīrya, L. — **dvār** (*sahásra-*), mfn. th°-gated, RV. — **dvāra** mf(*ā*)n. id., MBh. — **dhā**, ind. th°fold, in a th° ways or parts, RV. &c. &c. — **dhāman** (*sahásra-*), mfn. having th°fold splendour, AV.; TBr.; m. the sun, Mudr. — **dhāyas**, mfn. nourishing or sustaining a th°, TĀr. — 1. **-dhāra** (*sahásra-*), mf(*ā*)n. 'th°-streamed,' discharging a th° streams, RV.; flowing in a th° st°, MW.; (*ā*), f. a st° of water conveyed through a vessel pierced with a th° little holes, L. — 2. **-dhāra**, mfn. having a th° edges; m. the discus of Vishṇu, L. — **dhī**, mfn. th°-witted; m. N. of a fish, Pañcat. — **dhauta**, mfn. cleansed a th° times, Car. — **nayana**, mfn. th°-eyed; m. N. of Indra, MBh.; R. &c.; of Vishṇu, A. — **nāman** (*sahásra-*), mf(*mnī*)n. th°-named, containing a th° names, AV.; Pañcar.; n. pl. (or *-nāma*, ibc.) the th° names (of any deity, esp. of Vishṇu), Cat.; °*ma-kārikā*, f., °*ma-bhāshya*, n., °*ma-vivaraṇa*, n., °*ma-sarayu*, f., °*ma-stuti*, f., °*ma-stotra*, n., °*mârtha-śloka-sahasrâvalī*, f. N. of wks. — **nirṇij** (*sahásra-*), mfn. having a th° ornaments, RV. — **nītha**, see *-ṇītha*. — **netra**, mfn. th°-eyed, MBh.; BhP.; m. (ifc. f. *ā*) N. of Indra, MBh.; Ragh.; Vās.; of Vishṇu, A.; °*trânana-pāda-bāhu*, mfn. having a th° eyes and faces and feet and arms, Cat. — **pati**, m. chief of a th° (villages), Mn.; MBh. — **pattra**, m. N. of a mountain, Satr.; m. 'having a th° petals,' a lotus, MBh.; Hariv.; Ragh.; °*trâbharaṇa*, mfn. adorned with lotuses, MW. — **pad** (*sahásra-*; strong base *-pād*), mfn. th°-footed, RV.; AV.; Br. &c.; having a th° columns, MBh.; m. N. of Purusha, MW.; of Vishṇu, ib.; of Śiva, ib.; of Brahmā, W.; of a Ṛishi, MBh. — **parama**, mf(*ā*)n. the most excellent among th°, TĀr. — **parṇa** (*sahásra-*), mf(*ī*)n. th°-feathered (said of an arrow), RV.; th°-leafed, AV.; (*ī*), f. (prob.) a kind of plant, ib. — **parvā**, f. white Dūrvā grass, L. — **pākya**, m. 'boiled a th° times,' (with *sneha*) a partic. kind of oil, Car. — **pājas** (*sahásra-*), mfn. glittering in a th° ways, RV. — **pāthas** (*sahásra-*), mfn. appearing in a th° places, ib. — **pād**, see *-pad*. — **pāda**, m. 'th°-footed' or 'th°-rayed,' the sun, L.; a sort of duck, L.; N. of Vishṇu, L.; °*dâkshi-śirôru-bāhu*, mfn. having a th° feet and eyes and heads and thighs and arms, Siṇhâs. — **pāśa**, mf(*ā*)n. forming a thousand fetters, MantraBr. — **pūraṇa**, mfn. the thousandth, (and) obtaining a thousand, Śiś. (Sch.) — **pṛishṭha** (*sahásra-*), mfn. having a th° level places, AV. — 1. **poshá**, m. (RV.; AV.; VS.; TS.) or **-poshā**, f. (Kauś.) welfare or wealth (increased) a th°fold; (°*sha*)-*kāma*, mfn. 'desirous of a th°fold w°,' Lāṭy.; (°*sha*)-*púshi* (?), mfn., MaitrS. — 2. **posha**, mfn. prosperity (increasing) a th°fold, GṛŚrS. — **poshín**, mfn. thriving a th°fold, RV. — **poshyà**, n. = *-poshá*, m., RV. — **prakāra**, mf(*ā*)n. a th°fold, Kauś. — **pradhana** (*sahásra-*), mfn. having a th° prizes gained in battle, RV.; one who has experienced a th° battles, MW. — **prāṇa** (*sahásra-*), mfn. having a thousand lives, AV. (not in MS.) — **bala**, m. N. of a king, VP. — **bāhavīya**, n. (with *Indrasya*) N. of a Sāman, ĀrshBr. — **bāhu** (*sahásra-*), mfn. having a th° arms, th°-armed, MantraBr.; (also applied to AV. xix, 6, beginning with the above word); m. N. of Śiva, MBh.; of Arjuna, R.; of one of Skanda's attendants, MBh.; of the Asura Bāṇa, MW.; m. or f. a N. (others, 'battle, war'), RV. viii, 45, 26. — **buddhi**, mfn. th°-witted; m. N. of a fish, Pañcat. (cf. *-dhī*). — **bhakta**, n. a partic. festival at which th°s are treated, Rājat. — **bhara** (*sahásra-*), mfn. carrying off a th° as spoil, RV. — **bharṇas** (*sahásra-*), mfn. (prob.) a th°fold, RV. — **bhāgavatī**, f. N. of a divinity, SV. — **bhānu**, mfn. th°-rayed, Śiś. — **bhāva**, m. the becoming a th°, ĀśvŚr. — **bhid**, m. musk, Bhpr. — **bhuja**, mf(*ā*)n. th°-armed, Devīm.; m. N. of Vishṇu, MW.; of a Gandharva, Kāraṇḍ.; (*ā*), f. N. of Durgā, MW.; *-jihvâksha*, mfn. having a th° arms and tongues and eyes, MBh.; *-rāma-dhyāna*, n. N. of wk. (w.r. *-dhyāna-rāma*). — **bhṛishṭi** (*sahásra-*), mfn. th°-pointed, RV. — **bheda-śas**, ind. in a th° different ways, th°fold, Hcat. — **maṅgala**, N. of a place, Rājat. — **manyu** (*sahásra-*), mfn. having a th°fold courage, SV. — **marīci**, m. 'th°-rayed,' N. of the sun, MW. — **mīḍha** or **-mīḷha** (*sahásra-*), mfn. characterized by a thousand combats (said of a battle), RV. — **mukha**, mfn. having a th° exits, Pañcat.; *-rāvaṇa-caritra*, n. N. of wk. — **mushka** (*sahásra-*), mfn. having a th° testicles, RV. (accord. to Sāy. also 'having many flames'). — **m-ūti** (*sahásra-*), mfn. helping a th°fold, RV. (cf. *sahasrôti*). — **mūrti**, mfn. appearing in a th° forms, BhP.; Siṇhâs. — **mūrdha**, m. 'th°-headed,' N. of Vishṇu, MBh.; *-śravaṇâkshi-nāsika*, mfn. having a th° heads and ears and eyes and noses, BhP. — **mūrdhan**, mfn. th°-headed, ib.; Pañcar.; m. N. of Śiva, MBh.; of Vishṇu, A. — **mūla** (*sahásra-*), mfn. having a th° roots, AV.; (*ī*), f. Anthericum Tuberosum, L. — **mauli**, m. 'th°-crested,' N. of Vishṇu, MBh. — **m-bhará**, mfn. bringing a th°, RV. — **m-bhari**, mfn. nourishing a th°, Siṇhâs. — **yajñá**, m. a sacrifice of a th°, MaitrS.; N. of a man, Lalit.; *-tīrtha*, n. N. of a Tīrtha, Cat. — **yāj**, mfn. = next, PañcavBr.; m. one who sacrifices a th° victims, MW. — **yājin**, mfn. one who conducts a sacrifice for a recompense of a th° (cows), TS.; Br. — **yāman** (*sahásra-*), mfn. having a th° paths, RV. — **yuga**, n. a period of a th° ages, MBh. — **yoga**, m., **-yoga-cikitsā**, f. N. of wks. — **yojaná**, n. a distance of a th° Yojanas, VS.; MaitrS. — **raśmi**, mfn. th°-rayed; m. the sun, MaitrUp.; MBh.; Kāv.; MārkP.; *-tanaya*, m. 'son of the sun,' the planet Saturn, VarBṛS. — **ruc**, m. the sun, Harav. — **retas** (*sahásra-*), mfn. having th°fold seed, RV. — **roman**, n. 'having a th° hairs,' a blanket, W. — **liṅgī**, f. a th° Liṅgas, Rājat. — **locana**, mfn. th°-eyed; m. N. of Indra, Kāv.; of Vishṇu, A. — **vaktra**, mfn. th°-mouthed, Pañcar. — **vat** (*sahásra-*), mfn. a th°-fold, RV.; containing the word *sahasra*, ŚBr.; KātyŚr. — **vadana**, mfn. id.; m. N. of Vishṇu, L. — **varcas** (*sahásra-*), mfn. having th°fold power or efficacy, RV. — **vartani**, mfn. having a th° paths, MW. — **vartanin**, mfn. having a th° wheels; n. N. of a Sāman, ShaḍvBr. — **vartman**, mfn. having a th° paths, Śiś. — **valiśa** or **-valśa** (*sahásra-*), mfn. th°-branched, RV.; MaitrS. — **vāka**, mfn. containing a th° words or verses, Gaut. — **vāc**, m. N. of a son of Dhṛita-rāshṭra, MBh. — **vāja** (*sahásra-*), mfn. having th°fold vigour or energy, RV. — **vīra** (*sahásra-*), mfn. sufficient for a th° men, RV. — **vīrya** (*sahásra-*), mf(*ā*)n. having a th° energies, VS.; AV.; (*ā*), f. a kind of plant, Suśr.; Car.; Dūrvā grass (with white or blue flowers), L.; Bhpr.; = *mahā-śatāvarī*, Bhpr.; Asa Fœtida, A. — **vṛit**, mfn. including th°s, TĀr. (accord. to Sch. *vṛit* = *vriyamāṇa*, *prârthyamāna*). — **vedha**, n. a kind of sorrel, MW.; a kind of sour gruel, L. — **vedhin**, m. a kind of sorrel, Bhpr.; musk, ib.; Calamus Fasciculatus, W.; n. Asa Fœtida, Bhpr. — **śakti**, mfn. able to give a th°, MBh. — **śatá-dakshiṇa**, mfn. accompanied with a fee of a hundred th° (cows), ŚBr.; Mn. — **śala** (*sahásra-*), a distance of a th° Śalas, MaitrS.; Kāṭh. — **śas**, ind. by thousands, AV. &c. &c. — **śākha**, mfn. having a th° branches (also fig.), TUp.; Kusum. — **śikhara**, mfn. th°-peaked; m. N. of the Vindhya mountains, MārkP. — **śiras**, mfn. th°-headed, R.; BhP.; Pañcar. — **śirasa**, mfn. id., MBh.; °*sôdara*, mfn. having a th° heads and abdomens, ib. — **śīrsha**, mfn. th°-headed, TĀr.; Up.; (*ā*), f. a partic. Mantra or the N. of the Ṛig-veda hymn x, 90 (usually called the Purusha hymn), Yājñ., Sch.; cf. RTL. 17. — **śīrshan** (*sahásra-*), mfn. th°-headed, RV.; ShaḍvBr. &c. — **śṛiṅga** (*sahásra-*), mfn. th°-horned, RV.; AV. — **śokas** (*sahásra-*), mfn. emitting a th° flames, RV. — **śravaṇa**, m. 'th°-eared,' N. of Vishṇu, MW. — **śruti**, m. N. of a mountain, BhP. — **saṃvatsara** (*sahásra-*), n. a sacred rite of a th° years, Br.; KātyŚr. &c. — **saṃkhya**, mfn. numbering a th°, MBh.; (*ā*), f. the sum of a th°, MW. — **saṃkhyāka**, mfn. amounting to a th°, ib. — **saní**, mfn. gaining or bestowing a th°, Br.; GṛS.; f. a gift of a th°, ŚBr. — **sama**, mfn. lasting a th° years (as a sacred rite), BhP. — **sammita** (*sahásra-*), mfn. measuring a th°, TS.; Br. — **sava**, mfn. having a th° libations, MW. — **sā**, mfn. gaining or granting a th°, RV.; *-tama*, mfn. giving th°s, ib.; AV. — **sāvá**, m. th°fold Soma-pressing, RV. — **sāvya**, n. a partic. Ayana, ĀśvŚr.; Nir.; Maś. — **sīta**, mfn. having a th° furrows, ĀśvGr. — **starī** (*sahásra-*), mfn. having a th° barren cows, RV. — **stuka** (*sahásra-*), mf(*ā*)n. having a th° tufts or curls of hair, AV. — **stuti**, f. N. of a river, BhP. — **stotriya**, mfn. consisting of a th° Stotriyas, ŚāṅkhŚr. — **sthūṇa** (*sahásra-*), mfn. supported by a th° columns, RV. — **srota** or °**tas**, m. N. of a mountain, BhP. — **há**, mfn. slaying a th°, AV. — **hary-aśva**, m. (MW.) or **-hary-āśva** (?), m. (L.) 'having a th° bay horses,' the car of Indra. — **hasta**, mfn. th°-handed, AV.; m. N. of Śiva, MW.

Sahasrâṅśu, mfn. th°-rayed; m. the sun, Mn.; MBh.; R. &c.; *-ja*, m. 'sun-born,' N. of Saturn, VarBṛS.; *-sama*, mfn. sun-like, Ml. **Sahasrâkshá**, mfn. th°-eyed, RV.; VS.; TS. &c.; all-perceiving, all-inspecting, W.; m. N. of Indra (so called from the curse of Gautama who detecting Indra in a desire to seduce his wife Ahalyā covered him with a thousand marks of the female organ, afterwards changed to eyes; a different legend is in Rām. i, 48), MBh.; Kāv.; Pur.; of Indra in the 9th Manv-antara, MārkP.; of Purusha, MW.; of Vishṇu, ib.; of Fire and Rudra, ib.; of Śiva, ib.; a clear sky, VarBṛS.; N. of a partic. Mantra, Baudh.; m. or n. (?) of a place, Cat.; of wk.; (*ī*), f. N. of a goddess, ib.; *-jit*, m. N. of a son of Rāvaṇa, RāmatUp.; *-dhanush-mat*, mfn. provided with a rainbow, R.; °*kshêśvara*, m. N. of a Liṅga, Kāśīkh. **Sahásrâkshara**, mf(*ā*)n. having a th° syllables, RV.; AV.; PañcavBr. **Sahasrâkhya**, m. 'having a th° names,' N. of a mountain, Śatr.; n. N. of wk. **Sahasrâṅka** (?), m. the sun, L. **Sahasrâcāra**, m. Barleria Prionitis, MW. **Sahasrājit**, m. N. of a son of Bhajamāna, Hariv.; Pur. **Sahasrâṇīka**, m. = °*rânīka*, MW. **Sahasrâtṛiṇṇa**, mfn. pierced with a th° holes, Kauś. **Sahasrâtman**, mfn. having a th° natures, Yājñ. **Sahasrâdhipati**, m. the leader of a th° men, MBh.; the chief of a th° villages, Mn. vii, 119. **Sahasrânana**, m. 'th°-faced,' N. of Vishṇu, MBh.; *-śīrsha-vat*, mfn. having a th° faces and heads, BhP. **Sahasrānīka**, m. N. of a king, Kathās.; BhP. **Sahasrāposhá**, m. = *sahasra-p*°, AV. **Sahásrâpsas**, mfn. th°-shaped, RV. (Sāy.) **Sahásrā-magha**, mfn. having a th° treasures or gifts, RV. **Sahasrâyu**, mfn. living a th° years, AitBr. **Sahasrāyutīya**, n. du. (with Indrasya) N. of two Sāmans, ĀrshBr.; SV. **Sahasrâyudha**, mfn. having a th° weapons, Sāh.; m. N. of a man, Kathās.; °*yudhīya*, Nom. P. °*yudhīyati*, to resemble one who has a th° weapons, Sāh.; Kpr. **Sahásrâyus**, mfn. = °*râyu*, AV.; ŚBr.; Pañcar.; m. N. of a man, Kathās.; °*râyush-ṭva*, n. the living a thousand years, KātyŚr., Sch. **Sahasrâra**, mfn. th°-spoked, BhP.; m. n. a kind of cavity said to be found in the top of the head and to resemble a lotus reversed (fabled as the seat of the soul), L.; *-ja*, m. pl. N. of a class of gods (with Jainas), L. **Sahasrârghá** or **sahásrârgha**, mfn. equivalent to a th°, RV.; AV. **Sahasrârcis**, mfn. th°-rayed, Śivag.; m. the sun, Ragh. **Sahasrârha**, mfn. worth a th° (cows), ŚBr. **Sahasrâvara**, m. a fine below a th° or from five hundred to a th° Paṇas, W. **Sahasrâvartaka-tīrtha**, n. N. of a Tīrtha, Cat. **Sahasrâvartā**, f. (with Buddhists) N. of a goddess. **Sahasrâśva**, m. 'having a th° horses,' N. of a king, VP. **Sahasrâśvīna**, n. a distance equivalent to a th° days' journey for a horse, AitBr. **Sahasrâsya**, m. 'th°-faced,' 'th°-headed,' N. of the Serpent Ananta, Kāśīkh. **Sahasrâha**, n. a th° days, MaitrUp. **Sahasrâhnyá**, n. a thousand days' journey, AV. **Sahasrêkshaṇa**, mfn. th°-eyed; m. N. of Indra, Siṇhâs. **Sahásrêdhma**, a th° pieces of wood, MaitrS. **Sahásrôti**, mfn. = *sahásram-ūti*, RV. **Sahasrôpanishad**, f. N. of an Upanishad. **Sahasrôrv-aṅghri-bāhv-aksha**, mfn. having a th° thighs and feet and arms and eyes, BhP.

Sahasraka, n. (for *sahasra-ka* see p. 1195, col. 2) a th°, Hariv.; Pañcar.; (ifc.; f. *ikā*) amounting to a thousand, having a thousand, MBh.; R.; Pañcar.

Sahasrataya, mfn. a thousandfold, MW.; n. a thousand, Śiś.

Sahasrika, n. a thousand, Hariv. (prob. w.r. for *sahasraka*); mf(*ī*)n. (ifc., after *varsha* or *abda*) lasting a thousand years, MBh.; Hariv.

Sahasrin, mfn. numbering a thousand, th°fold, RV.; BhP.; gaining a th°, RV.; ŚBr.; containing a th° different things, RV.; having a th° (also ifc.), MBh.; Hariv. &c.; paying a th° (Paṇas as a fine), Mn. viii, 376; consisting of a thousand soldiers, L.; amounting to a th° (as a fine), MW.; m. a body of a th° men &c., W.; the commander of a th°, ib.

Sahasriya, mfn. a thousandfold, RV.; giving thousandfold, VS.; TS.

Sahasrīya, mfn. giving thousandfold (v.l. °*riya*; cf. *varsha-s*°), MaitrS.

सहाय *sahāya* &c. See p. 1195, col. 1.

सहार *sahāra*, m. (prob. a Prākṛit form for *saha-kāra*) a species of mango tree, Uṇ. iii, 139, Sch.; universal dissolution (= *mahā-pralaya*; prob. w.r. for *saṃ-h*°), L.

सहित *sahita*. See p. 1193, col. 2.

सहोढ *sahôḍha*. See p. 1194, col. 3.

सहोर *sahora*, mfn. (accord. to Uṇ. i, 66, Sch. fr. √1. *sah*) good, excellent, L.; m. a saint, pure or pious man, W.

सहोहा *sahohā*, N. of a Sāman, Lāṭy.

सह्ल *sahla*, *sahlaṇa*. See *salh*°, p. 1190.

सा 1. *sā*, f. of 4. *sa*, q.v.

सा 2. *sā́*, f. of 6. *sa*, q.v.

सा 3. *sā* (weak form of √*san*), giving, bestowing, granting (cf. *ap-*, *aśva-sā* &c.)

1. **Sātá**, mfn. gained, obtained, RV.; Br.; granted, given, bestowed, RV.; n. a gift, wealth, riches, ib.

1. **Sāti**, f. gaining, obtaining, acquisition, winning of spoil or property, RV.; a gift, oblation, L.; N. of a teacher (having the patr. *Aushṭrâkshi*), Cat.

Sātu, m. (prob.) the womb (as conceiving), RV.

Sānasi, mfn. bringing wealth or blessings, laden with spoils, victorious, RV.

Sānin, mfn. gaining, procuring (ifc.), Nir.

Sānuká, mfn. eager for prey, RV.

सा 4. *sā* = √*so*, q.v.

2. **Sāta**, mfn. (for 3. see p. 1200, col. 1) ended, destroyed, W.

2. **Sāti**, f. end, destruction, L.; violent pain, ib.

सांयमन *sāṃyamana*, mfn. (fr. *saṃyamana*) relating to restraint or self-control, KaushUp. (v.l.)

Sāṃyamani, m. (fr. id.) patr. of Śala, MBh.

Sāṃyamanika, mfn. = *saṃyamana*, Mahāvy.

सांयाति *sāṃyāti*, g. *kāśy-ādi*.

Sāṃyātika, mf(*ā* and *ī*)n. (fr. prec.), ib.

सांयात्रिक *sāṃyātrika*, m. (fr. *saṃ-yātrā*) a voyaging merchant, one who trades by sea &c.,

Hariv.; Kāv.; Kathās.; n. any vehicle, L.; the morning dawn, L.

सांयुग sāṃyuga, mf(ī)n. (fr. sam-yuga) relating to battle (with ku, f. 'a battle-field'), Śiś.

Sāṃyugīna, mfn. relating to war or battle, war-like, martial, Kālid.; m. a hero, great warrior, ib.

Sāṃyogika, mfn. = samyogāya prabhavati, g. saṃtāpâdi.

Sāṃyaugika, mfn. related, being in relation, connected, Nir. i, 2.

सांरक्ष्य sāṃrakshya, n. (fr. sam-raksha), g. purohitâdi.

सांराविण sāṃrāviṇa, n. (fr. sam-rāvin) general acclamation or calling out of a number of people together, a general shout, uproar, Mālatīm.; Naish.

सांवत्सर sāṃvatsara, mf(ī)n. (fr. sam-vatsara) yearly, annual, perennial, lasting or occupying a year (with bhṛiti, f. 'annual wages'), ŚrS.; MBh.; BhP.; m. an astrologer, almanac-maker, MBh.; Kāv. &c.; a lunar month, L.; black rice, L.; (with dīkshita) N. of an author, Cat.; (ī), f. a funeral ceremony performed a year after a person's death, L. **-ratha**, m. the sun, L. **-sūtra**, n. N. of a ch. of Bhaṭṭôtpalas Comm. on VarBṛS.

Śāṃvatsaraka, mfn. yearly, payable in a year (as a debt), Pāṇ. iv, 3, 50; m. an astrologer (in a-s°), VarBṛS. ii, 12, v. l.

Sāṃvatsarika, mfn. yearly, annual, relating to a year, produced in a year &c. (with bali, m. 'annual revenue;' with riṇa, n. 'a debt payable in a year'), AitBr. &c. &c.; relating to an annual sacrifice, Lāṭy.; m. an astrologer, Pañcat. **-śrāddha**, n. an annual funeral ceremony in honour of deceased ancestors (also N. of wk.), Cat. **Sāṃvatsarikâikôddishṭa-śrāddha-prayoga**, m. N. of wk.

Sāṃvatsarīya, mfn. = sāṃvatsara above; (ā), f. (with siṇhī) a partic. personification, IndSt.

सांवरण sāṃvaraṇa, m. (fr. sam-varaṇa) patr. of the Vedic Ṛishi Manu, RAnukr.

Sāṃvaraṇi, m. id., RV. viii, 51, 3.

सांवर्ग sāṃvarga, m. (fr. sam-varga) N. of a Sāman (with Indrasya), ĀrshBr.

Sāṃvargajita, m. pl. (fr. samvarga-jit) patr. of the Gotamas, Lāṭy.

सांवर्त sāṃvarta, mfn. written or composed by Sam-varta, Cat.; n. N. of various Sāmans (also with Indrasya), ĀrshBr. **-smṛiti**, f. N. of a law-book.

Sāṃvartaka, mfn. (fr. sam-vartaka = sam-varta) relating to or appearing at the dissolution of the universe (as fire, the sun &c.), R.; BhP.

सांवहित्र sāṃvahitra, mfn. (fr. sam-vahitṛi = sam-voḍhṛi), Pāṇ. iv, 3, 120, Vārtt. 8, Pat.

सांवादिक sāṃvādika, mfn. (fr. sam-vāda) colloquial, controversial, causing discussion, L.; m. a disputant, controversialist, logician, L.

Sāṃvādya, n. (fr. sam-vādin), g. brāhmaṇâdi.

सांवाशिन sāṃvāśina, n. (fr. sam-vāśin) bellowing together (of cows and calves), KātyŚr.

सांवासिक sāṃvāsika, mfn. = sam-vāsāya prabhavati, g. saṃtāpâdi.

Sāṃvāsyaka, n. = sam-vāsa, dwelling together, community of abode, MBh.

सांवाहिक sāṃvāhika, mf(ā and ī)n. (fr. sam-vāha), g. kāśy-ādi and guḍâdi.

सांवित्तिक sāṃvittika, mfn. (fr. sam-vitti) based on a (mere) feeling or perception, subjective, Kap., Sch.

1. **Sāṃvidya**, n. (fr. 1. sam-vid) mutual understanding, agreement, TS.; PañcavBr.

सांविद्य 2. sáṃvidya, n. (fr. 2. sam-vid) = (or prob. w. r. for) sáṃ-vidya, AV.

Sāṃvaidya, n. (cf. 2. sam-vedya) finding each other, meeting, Vait.

सांवृत्ति sāṃvṛitti, °ttika, w. r. for sam-vṛitti and sāṃvittika.

सांवेशनिक sāṃveśanika, mfn. = sam-veśanāya prabhavati, g. saṃtāpâdi.

Sāṃveśya, n. (fr. sam-veśin), g. brāhmaṇâdi.

सांवेषिक sāṃveshika, mfn. = sam-veshāya prabhavati, g. saṃtāpâdi.

सांव्यवहारिक sāṃvyavahārika, mf(ī)n. (fr. sam-vyavahāra) current in every-day life, generally intelligible, Lāṭy., Sch.

सांश sâṅśa, mfn. having or consisting of parts or shares, Sāṃkhyapr.

सांशंसिक sāṃśaṅsika, mfn. (fr. sam-śaṅsā) that which is recited together, GopBr.

सांशयिक sāṃśayika, mf(ī)n. (fr. sam-śaya) doubtful, dubious, Nir.; Āpast.; MārkP.; hazardous, Kām. (v. l.); in doubt, uncertain, irresolute, sceptical, L. **-tva**, n. doubtfulness, uncertainty, Bādar.

सांशित्य sāṃśitya, m. patr. fr. sam-śitu (see sam-√śo), g. gargâdi.

सांसर्गविद्य sāṃsargavidya, mfn. = saṃsarga-vidyām adhīte veda vā, Kāś. on Pāṇ. iv, 2, 60.

Sāṃsargika, mf(ī)n. produced by or resulting from contact (saṃsarga) or intercourse, Kām.; BhP.

सांसारिक sāṃsārika, mfn. (fr. sam-sāra) connected with or dependent on mundane existence, worldly, Kāv.; Śaṃk.; BhP.; being still subject to mundane existence, Karaṇḍ.

सांसिद्धिक sāṃsiddhika, mf(ī)n. (fr. saṃ-siddhi) effected naturally, belonging to nature, natural, native, innate, MBh.; Kāv. &c.; self-existent, existing by its own nature or essence, existing absolutely, absolute, Śaṃk.; effected by supernatural means (as spells &c.), MW. **-drava**, m. natural (as opp. to 'generated') fluidity (e. g. that of water), ib.

Sāṃsiddhya, n. the state of having attained the highest object, perfection, BhP.

सांसृष्टिक sāṃsṛishṭika, mfn. (fr. sam-sṛishṭi) directly or immediately connected, direct, L.

सांस्कारिक sāṃskārika, mfn. (fr. sam-skāra) belonging to or requisite for a funeral ceremony or other rite &c., R.

सांस्थानिक sāṃsthānika, mfn. (fr. saṃ-sthāna) relating or belonging to a common place of abode, a fellow-countryman (or countrywoman), Pāṇ. iv, 4, 72.

सांस्पर्शक sāṃsparśaka, n. (fr. sam-sparśa) touch, contact, MānGṛ.

सांस्फीयक sāṃsphīyaka, mfn. (fr. sam-sphīya), g. dhūmâdi.

सांस्राविण sāṃsrāviṇa, n. (fr. sam-srava) a general stream (of water &c., = vṛikshasya vṛiksham vyāpya samyak-srāvaḥ), L.

सांहत्य sāṃhatya, n. (fr. sam-hata; see sam-√han) connection, union, Kap.

Sāṃhananika, mfn. (fr. sam-hanana) relating to the body, bodily, corporeal, MW.

Sāṃhātika, n. (for sam-hāta) N. of the sixteenth Nakshatra after that in which the moon was situated at a child's birth, L.

सांहार sāṃhāra, w. r. for sam-hāra.

सांहित sāṃhita, mf(ī)n. relating to the Saṃhitā, found in the S° text or based upon it &c., Prāt.; Pāṇ., Sch. **Sāṃhitôpanishad-bhāshya**, n. N. of wk.

Sāṃhitika, mfn. = sāṃhita, g. ukthâdi; m. the author of an astrological Saṃhitā, Gaṇit.

साक sāka, n. = 2. śāka, a vegetable, herb, culinary herb, Uṇ. iii, 43, Sch.

साकच् sâkac (in gram.), having the Taddhita affix akac (cf. Pāṇ. v, 3, 71 &c.)

साकम् sākám, ind. (prob. fr. 7. sa + 2. añc; cf. sācī) together, jointly, at the same time, simultaneously, RV. &c. &c.; along with, together with, with (with instr.), ib. **-aśva**, m. N. of a man, ĀrshBr.; n. N. of a Sāman (-tva, n.), ib. **-úksh**, mfn. sprinkling together, RV. **-edhá**, m. pl. N. of the third Parvan of the Cāturmāsyas, TS.; ŚBr.; ŚrS.; a partic. Soma sacrifice lasting three days, ŚāṅkhŚr. **-prasthāyīya** (TS.) or **-prasthāyya** (ŚrS.), m. a partic. ceremony (also °yya-yajña, Vait.)

Sākam, in comp. for sākam. **-yúj**, mfn. joined together, RV. **-vṛit**, mfn. rolling t° (said of wheels), PañcavBr. **-vṛidh**, mfn. growing t°, RV. **-garbha**, mfn. pregnant t°, Kauś. **-já**, mfn. being born together or at the same time, RV.; ŚBr.

साकरुण्ड sākaruṇḍa, w. r. for sākuruṇḍa.

साकर्णकायन sākarṇakāyana, mfn. (fr. sa-karṇaka), g. pakshâdi.

Sākarṇakya, mfn. (fr. id.), g. saṃkāśâdi.

साकल sākala, n. N. of a town in Madras (also written śākala), MW.

साकलायन sākalāyana, mfn. (fr. sa-kala), g. pakshâdi.

Sākalya, n. totality, completeness, entireness (ena, ind. 'entirely,' 'completely'), the whole, Mn.; MBh. &c. **-vacana**, n. complete perusal, L.

साकलि sākali and °likā, f. N. of a woman, Divyâv.

साकल्यक sâkalyaka, mfn. sick, unwell (w. r. sākalpaka), Kathās.

साकाङ्क्ष sâkâṅksha, mfn. having a wish or desire, wishing, desirous, longing (am, ind. 'longingly'), Kāv.; Hit.; requiring a complement, correlative, Pāṇ.; Sāh.; having significance, MW. **-tā**, f. (Sāh.), **-tva**, n. (KātyŚr.) correlation.

साकाम्प्रात्तायन sākāmprāttāyana (?), m. (only pl.) a patr., Saṃskārak.

साकार sâkāra, mf(ā)n. having form, having any shape or definite figure, Kathās.; Sarvad.; having a fair form, beautiful (am, ind.), Hariv.; Pañcat.; MārkP. **-jñāna-vāda**, m. the doctrine (held by the Yogâcāras) that ideas consist of forms or images which exist independently of the external world, Sarvad. **-siddhi**, f. N. of wk., ib.

साकाश sâkāśa, mfn. with or having the light shining towards (an object), ĀśvGṛ.

साकुरुण्ड sākuruṇḍa, m. a kind of plant (cf. sa-k°), L.

साकुल sâkula, mfn. perplexed, bewildered, Kathās.

साकूत sâkūta, mf(ā)n. having significance, significant, having meaning, intentional, Kāv.; Kathās.; (am), ind. intentionally, emphatically, Kathās.; accurately, attentively, ib.; n. (prob.) a desired object, Prasannar. **-smita**, n. a significant or meaning smile, wanton glance, W. **-hasita**, n. id., Gīt.

साकेत sāketa, n. N. of the city Ayodhyā or Oude (prob. also of other cities), Pat.; Kāv.; VarBṛS. &c.; m. pl. the inhabitants of Sāketa, Cat. **-purāṇa** or **-māhātmya**, n. N. of a wk. (also called Ayodhyā-māhātmya).

Sāketaka, mfn. (fr. prec.), g. dhūmâdi.

Sāketana, n. the city of Sāketa, Buddh.

Sāketu, m. or f. (?), id., VP.

साकोक sākoka, m. N. of a poet, Cat.

साकोटक sākoṭaka, w. r. for śākhoṭaka.

साक्तव sāktava (fr. saktu), a beverage prepared from barley, L.

Sāktuka, mfn. = saktuni sādhuḥ, g. guḍâdi; = saktave prabhavati, g. saṃtāpâdi; m. barley, W.; = saktuka, a partic. vegetable poison, L.; n. a quantity of fried barley or barley-meal, ib.

Sāktusaindhava, mfn. = saktu-sindhushu bhavaḥ, Pāṇ. vii, 3, 19, Sch.

साक्ष् sāksh, cl. 1. P. sākshati = āpnoti (used in explaining pra-sākshate fr. pra-√sah), Nir. xi, 21.

साक्ष 1. sâksha, mfn. (fr. 7. sa + 1. aksha) furnished with a yoke (of oxen), Kauś.

साक्ष 2. sâksha, mfn. (fr. 7. sa + 2. aksha) having the seeds (of which rosaries are made), having a rosary, MW.

साक्ष 3. sâksha (fr. 7. sa + 4. aksha), having eyes (only in abl.; see next).

Sâkshát, ind. (abl. of sâksha above) with the eyes, with one's own eyes, Kāv.; Kathās.; Sarvad.; before one's eyes, evidently, clearly, openly, manifestly, AV. &c. &c.; in person, in bodily form, personally, visibly, really, actually, MBh.; Kāv. &c.; immediately, directly, Sarvad.; Kull. **-purushôttama-vākya**, n. N. of a wk. by Vallabhâcārya.

Sâkshāt, in comp. with forms of √*kṛi*. **-kara**, mfn. putting before the eyes, making evident to the senses, Cat. **-karaṇa**, n. the act of putting b° the e°, ib.; intuitive perception, actual feeling, MW.; immediate cause of anything, Kap. **-kartavya**, mfn. to be made fully perceptible or evident, Mahāv. **-kartṛi**, mfn. one who sees everything, Cat. **-kāra**, m. evident or intuitive perception, realization (*-tā*, f.), Vedântas.; Sarvad.; the experiencing a result of or reward for (gen.), BhP.; *-vat*, mfn. having a clear perception of (comp.), Sarvad. **-kārin**, mfn. = *-kara*, Sarvad.; Kap., Sch. **-√kṛi**, P. *-karoti* (ind. p.; *-kṛitvā* or *-kṛitya*, Pāṇ. i, 4, 74), to look at with the eyes, make visibly present before the eyes, realize, Kathās.; Sāh. **-kṛita**, mfn. clearly placed before the eyes or the mind's eye; *-dharman*, mfn. one who has an intuitive perception of duty, MW. **-kṛiti** (Sarvad.), **-kriyā** (SaddhP.), f. intuitive perception, realization.

Sâkshād, in comp. for *sâkshāt*. **-dṛishṭa**, mfn. seen with (one's own) eyes, Kum. **-dṛishṭi**, f. the act of seeing with (one's own) eyes, Sarvad. **-dharma**, m. the personified incarnation of law, Justice himself, MW. **-bhū**, P. *-bhavati*, to appear before the eyes, appear personally, Kathās.

1. **Sâkshi**, m. (m.c. for *sâkshin*, in *loka-* and *samasta-s°*, q. v.)

2. **Sâkshi**, in comp. for *sâkshin*. **-tā**, f. (Mn.; Kathās.), **-tva**, n. (Kap.; Suśr.) the office of any legal witness, evidence, testimony, attestation. **-dvaidha**, n. discrepancy between witnesses, contradictory evidence, MW. **-parīkshā**, f., **°kshaṇa**, n. examination of a w°, ib. **-pratyaya**, m. the evidence or testimony of an eye-w°, ib. **-praśna**, m. interrogation of w°s; *-vidhāna*, n. the rule or law about examining w°s, Mn. i, 115. **-bhāvita**, mfn. proved by an eye-w°, established by testimony, W. **-bhūta**, mfn. (cf. *sâkshī-√bhū*) being a w°, BhP.; Pañcar. **-mat**, mfn. having a w°, witnessed, Yājñ. ii, 94. **-mātra**, mfn. the simple Ego or subject (as opp. to the object or what is external to the Ego), Nir. xiv, 10; *°trā-√kṛi*, P. *-karoti*, to make a simple eye-w°, HPariś. **-lakshaṇa**, mfn. defined or proved by testimony, W. **-vat**, ind. like a witness, MW.

Sâkshika (ifc.; *ā*, f., *am*, ind.) = *sâkshin* (see *a-*, *agni-s°* &c.)

Sâkshin, mfn. seeing with the eyes, observing, witnessing; an eye-witness, witness (in law) of or to (gen., loc., or comp.), Gaut.; Mn.; MBh. &c.; m. (in phil.) the Ego or subject (as opp. to the object or to that which is external to the mind, AshṭāvS.; cf. *sâkshi-mātra*); N. of a man (also pl.), Saṃskārak.

Sâkshī, in comp. for *sâksha*. **-√kṛi**, P. *-karoti*, to call to witness, cause to attest, Kathās. **-√bhū**, P. *-bhavati*, to be an eye-witness, R.

Sâkshīka, m. N. of a man (cf. *sâkshin*), Saṃskārak.

Sâkshya, mfn. visible to (comp.), BhP.; n. testimony, evidence, attestation (*°aṃ-√kṛi*, 'to give evidence for'), Mn.; MBh. &c.

साक्षत **sâkshata**, mfn. containing uncrushed or whole grain (not deprived of husk), having grains of barley, Ragh.; (*am*), ind. without hurting (applied to a gentle kiss), Dhūrtas. **-pātra-hasta**, mfn. holding a vessel full of grain, MW.

साक्षर **sâkshara**, mf(*ā*)n. containing syllables or letters, L.; eloquent (*-tā*, f.), Kāv.

साक्षिप्तम् **sâkshiptam**, ind. with absence of mind, thoughtlessly, MBh.

Sâkshepa, mfn. containing an objection or limitation, Kāvyâd.; conveying reproach or irony, taunting (*am*, ind. tauntingly), Kathās.; Rājat.

साखि **sākhi**, m. N. of a people (cf. *śākhi*), L.

साखिदत्तेय **sākhidatteya**, mfn. (fr. *sakhi-datta*) belonging to a friend's gift, g. *sakhy-ādi*.

साखिल्य **sākhilya**, n. (fr. *sakhila*) friendship, Mahāv.

साखेय **sākheya**, mfn. (fr. *sakhi*) relating to a friend, friendly, amicable, Pāṇ. iv, 2, 80.

Sākhya, n. association, party, RV.; KātyŚr.; friendship (prob. w.r. for *sakhya*), L.; mfn. = *sākheya*, KātyŚr.

सागम **sâgama**, mfn. acquired in an honest manner, legitimate, Vishṇ.

Sâgamaka, mfn. having the grammatical augment, Pat.

सागर **sāgara**, m. (ifc. f. *ā*; fr. 2. *sa-gara*) the ocean (said to have been named so by Bhagīratha after his son Sagara [see 2. *sa-gara*, p. 1125]; another legend asserts that the bed of the ocean was dug by the sons of Sagara; 3 or 4 or 7 oceans are reckoned, cf. 1. *sam-udra*; *sāgarasya phenaḥ* = *samudra-ph°*), Mn.; MBh. &c.; an ocean (as expressing any vast body or inexhaustible mass; often ifc., cf. *guṇa-*, *śoka-*, *saṃsāra-s°*); a symbolical expression for the number 'four' (like other words signifying 'ocean'), Gaṇit.; a partic. high number (= 10 Padmas), Pur.; a sort of deer, L.; N. of a serpent-demon, Kāraṇḍ.; (with Jainas) of the third Arhat of the past Utsarpiṇī, L.; of one of the 10 orders of mendicants traced back to disciples of Śaṃkarâcārya, Cat.; of various persons, HPariś.; of two authors and of a wk. on Dharma, Cat.; of a place, ib.; (pl.) the sons of Sagara, MBh.; R.; n. N. of a town, Buddh.; mf(*ī*)n. relating to the sea, marine, Hariv. **-kukshi**, f. N. of a serpent-maiden, Kāraṇḍ. **-ga**, mf(*ā*)n. going to the ocean; (*ā*), f. a river, stream, (esp.) the Ganges, MBh.; (*-gā*)*-suta*, m. 'son of Gaṅgā,' metron. of Bhīshma, ib. **-gama**, mf(*ā*)n. = *-ga*, ib. **-gāmbhīra**, m. a partic. Samādhi, Kāraṇḍ.; (*ā*), f. N. of a serpent-maiden, ib. **-gāmin**, mfn. = *-ga*, R.; Ragh.; Rājat.; (*inī*), f. a river, R.; small cardamoms, L. **-m-gama**, mfn. = *-ga*, MBh.; Hariv. **-candra**, m. N. of a Jain poet, Gaṇar. **-tva**, n. the state of (being) the ocean, Hariv. **-datta**, m. 'Ocean-given,' N. of a king of the Gandharvas, Kathās.; of a Śākya, Buddh.; of a merchant, Pañcat.; of various other men, HPariś. **-deva**, m. N. of a mythical person, Vīrac. **-dhara**, m. N. of a poet, Cat. **-dhīra-cetas**, mfn. one whose mind is as firm or as deep as the ocean, MW. **-nandin**, m. N. of a poet, Uṇ. iv, 121, Sch. **-nāga-rāja-paripṛicchā**, f. N. of wk. **-nemi** or **-nemī**, f. 'sea-encircled,' the earth, L. **-paripṛicchā**, f. N. of wk. (cf. *sāgara-nāga-rāja-p°*), Buddh. **-paryanta**, mf(*ā*)n. bounded by the sea (as the earth), MBh.; R. **-pāla**, m. 'guardian of the ocean,' N. of a serpent-king, Buddh. **-pura**, n. N. of a town, Kathās. **-plavana**, n. navigating the ocean, leaping across or traversing the sea (also applied to a partic. pace of horses), R. **-buddhi-dhāry-abhijña-gupta**, m. N. of a Buddha, SaddhP. **-mati**, m. N. of a Bodhi-sattva, Kāraṇḍ.; of a serpent-king, ib.; of a man, Buddh. **-mudrā**, f. a partic. Samādhi, Buddh. **-mekhala**, mf(*ā*)n. sea-girt (cf. *sapta-sāgara-m°*); (*ā*), f. the earth, L. **-megha**, m. N. of a man, Buddh. **-lipi**, f. a partic. mode of writing, Lalit. **-vat**, ind. like the ocean, MW. **-vara-dhara**, m. the ocean, Lalit.; *-buddhi-vikrīḍitâbhijña*, m. N. of Ānanda (as Buddha), SaddhP. **-varman**, m. N. of a king, Inscr. **-vāsin**, mfn. dwelling on the sea-shore, MBh. **-vīra**, m. 'sea-hero,' N. of a man, Kathās. **-vyūha-garbha**, m. N. of a Bodhi-sattva, Buddh. **-śaya**, mfn. lying or resting on the ocean (said of Vishṇu), Śiś. **-śukti**, f. a sea-shell, Bhartṛ. **-saṃhitā**, f. N. of wk. **-sūnu**, m. 'son of the Ocean,' patr. of the Moon, Kāv. **Sāgarânukūla**, mfn. situated on the sea-coast, MW. **Sāgarânūpaka**, mfn. = *sāgara-vāsin*, MBh. **Sāgarânta**, m. the sea-shore, R.; mf(*ā*)n. bounded by the ocean, sea-girt (as the earth), MBh.; R.; VarBṛS. **Sāgarântargata**, mfn. living in the ocean, R. **Sāgarâpâṅga**, mf(*ī*)n. bounded by the sea (as the earth), MBh. **Sāgarâmbara**, mf(*ā*)n. sea-clad (as the earth), R.; Ragh.; Rājat.; (*ā*), f. the earth, Siṃhās. **Sāgarâmbu-raśana**, mf(*ā*)n. sea-girt, VarYogay. **Sāgarâlaya**, mfn. living in the ocean, R.; m. N. of Varuṇa, L. **Sāgarâvarta**, m. a bay of the sea, MBh. **Sāgarêśvara-tīrtha**, n. N. of a Tīrtha, Cat. **Sāgarôttha**, n. 'produced in the sea,' sea-salt, L. **Sāgarôdaka**, n. sea-water (prob. N. of a Tīrtha), MBh. xiii, 1696. **Sāgarôdgāra**, m. the swelling or heaving of the sea, flowing tide, flood (as opp. to 'ebb'), R. **Sāgarôddhūta-niḥsvana**, mfn. raising a sound like the ocean, MW. **Sāgarôpama**, m. or n. (?) a partic. high number, Jain.

Sāgaraka, m. pl. 'inhabitants of the sea-coast,' N. of a people, MBh.; (*ikā*), f., see above.

Sāgarāya, Nom. Ā. *°yate*, to resemble the ocean, Kāv.

Sāgarika, mf(*ī*)n., see *cātuḥ-s°*.

Sāgarikā, f. N. of a woman, Ratnāv. **-maya**, mf(*ī*)n. consisting of nothing but Sāgarikās, ib. (in Prākṛit).

सागस् **sâgas**, mfn. guilty of a sin or offence, Kāv.; Rājat.

सागुण्य **sāguṇya**, n. (fr. *sa-guṇa*) excellence, superiority, AVPariś.

साग्नि **sâgni**, mfn. together with the fire, KātyŚr.; Kauś.; maintaining a sacred fire, Pur.; connected with fire, Pāṇ. vi, 3, 80, Sch.; (*i*), ind. as far as the section on f°, Pāṇ. ii, 1, 6, Sch. **-citya**, mfn. connected with the piling of the sacred fire, IndSt. **-dhūma**, mfn. accompanied with fire and smoke, Hariv. **-purogama**, mfn. preceded by Agni, MBh. **-ratnâkara**, m. N. of wk.

Sâgnika, mfn. possessing or maintaining a sacred fire, associated with Agni, MBh.; witnessed by Agni, R. **-vidhi**, m. N. of a wk. (containing rules for the Śrâddha ceremonies of householders who maintain a sacred fire).

साग्र **sâgra**, mf(*ā*)n. with the tip or point, ŚBr.; KātyŚr.; = *sam-agra*, whole, entire, MBh.; having a surplus, more than, Āryabh.; (*am*), ind. for a longer period, for a whole life, MW.

साग्रयणाग्न्याधानप्रयोग **sâgrayaṇâgny-ādhāna-prayoga**, m. N. of wk.

साग्रह **sâgraha**, mfn. with pertinacity, insisting on anything, persistent (*am*, ind.), Daś.; HPariś.

सांकथिक **sāṃkathika**, mfn. (fr. *saṃ-kathā*) excellent in conversation, g. *kathâdi*.

Sāṃkathya, n. (fr. id.) talk, conversation (cf. *dharma-s°*), Car.; Kāraṇḍ.

सांकरिक **sāṃkarika**, mfn. (fr. *saṃ-kara*) sprung from a mixture of castes, the offspring of an illegitimate marriage, MBh.

Sāṃkarya, n. mixing or blending together confusedly, confusion, mixture, Sāh.; BhP., Sch. **-khaṇḍana**, n., **-vāda**, m. N. of wks.

सांकल **sāṃkala**, mfn. (fr. *saṃ-kala*) effected or produced by addition, accumulated &c., W.

सांकल्पिक **sāṃkalpika**, mf(*ī*)n. (fr. *saṃ-kalpa*) based on or produced by the will or imagination, Kap.; Śaṃk.

सांकारिका **sāṃkārikā**, f. a girl said to be unfit for marriage (as having applied fire to her father or other person's house), L. (v.l. *sāṃkāśikā*).

सांकाशिन **sāṃkāśina**, n. (fr. *saṃ-kāśin*) full visibility or appearance (instr. = 'straightway,' 'immediately,' 'directly'), KātyŚr.

Sāṃkāśya, m. (fr. *saṃ-kāśa*) N. of a man, MBh.; n. and (*ā*), f. N. of the town of Kuśa-dhvaja (brother of Janaka), R. **-nātha**, m. 'lord of Sāṃkāśya,' N. of Kuśa-dhvaja, ib.

सांकुचि **sāṃkuci**, m. and **°cī**, f. (perhaps fr. *saṃ-kuca*, but cf. *śaṅkuci*) a partic. aquatic animal, Bhpr.

Sāṃkucita, mfn. derived from Saṃ-kucita, g. *takshaśilâdi*.

साङ्कुर **sâṅkura**, mfn. possessing shoots or buds, budding, in bud, W.

सांकूटिन **sāṃkūṭina**, n. (of unknown meaning), Pat.; Pāṇ., Sch.

सांकृत **sāṃkṛita**, mfn. relating or belonging to Saṃ-kṛiti, derived from him &c., Cat.; (*ī*), f. of *sāṃkṛitya*.

Sāṃkṛiti, m. (fr. *saṃ-kṛiti*) patr. of a sage (son of Viśvāmitra and founder of the Vaiyāghrapadya family), ĀpŚr.; MBh.

Sāṃkṛiti-pútra, m. N. of a preceptor, ŚBr.

Sāṃkṛitya, m. patr. fr. *saṃ-kṛiti*, ĀśvŚr.; N. of a grammarian, TPrāt.

Sāṃkṛityāyana, m. patr. fr. *sāṃkṛitya*, Car.; (*ī*), f. N. of a Parivrājikā, Kathās.

सांकेतिक **sāṃketika**, mfn. (fr. *saṃ-keta*) consisting of signs, based on agreement, indicatory, conventional, Sāh.

Sāṃketya, n. agreement, appointment, assignation (esp. with a loved person), BhP.

सांक्रन्दनि *sāṃkrandani*, m. (fr. *sam-krandana*) patr. of Vālin, Mcar.

सांक्रामिक *sāṃkrāmika*, m. (fr. *sam-krāma*; cf. g. *guḍâdi*) passing over or being transferred (to others), Kām.

सांक्षेपिक *sāṃkshepika*, mfn. (fr. *sam-kshepa*) abridged, contracted, concise, summary, short, Kull.

सांख्य *sāṃkhya*, mfn. (fr. *sam-khyā*) numeral, relating to number, W.; relating to number (in gram. as expressed by the case-terminations &c.), Pat.; rational, discriminative, W.; m. one who calculates or discriminates well, (esp.) an adherent of the Sāṃkhya doctrine, CūlUp.; MBh. &c.; N. of a man, Car.; patr. of the Vedic Ṛishi Atri, Anukr.; N. of Śiva, MBh.; n. (accord. to some also m.) N. of one of the three great divisions of Hindū philosophy (ascribed to the sage Kapila [q.v.], and so called either from 'discriminating,' in general, or, more probably, from 'reckoning up' or 'enumerating' twenty-five Tattvas [see *tattva*] or true entities [twenty-three of which are evolved out of Prakṛiti 'the primordial Essence' or 'first-Producer,' viz. Buddhi, Ahaṃkāra, the five Tan-mātras, the five Mahā-bhūtas and Manas; the twenty-fifth being Purusha or Spirit [sometimes called Soul] which is neither a Producer nor Production [see *vikāra*], but wholly distinct from the twenty-four other Tattvas, and is multitudinous, each separate Purusha by its union with Prakṛiti causing a separate creation out of Prakṛiti, the object of the philosophy being to effect the final liberation of the Purusha or Spirit from the fetters caused by that creation; the Yoga [q.v.] branch of the Sāṃkhya recognizes a Supreme Spirit dominating each separate Purusha; the Tantras identify Prakṛiti with the wives of the gods, esp. with the wife of Śiva; the oldest systematic exposition of the S° seems to have been by an author called Pañca-śikha [the germ, however, being found in the Shashṭi-tantra, of which only scanty fragments are extant]; the original Sūtras were superseded by the S°-kārikā of Īśvara-kṛishṇa, the oldest manual on the S° system that has come down to us and probably written in the 5th century A.D., while the S°-sūtras or S°-pravacana and Tattva-samāsa, ascribed to the sage Kapila, are now thought to belong to as late a date as the 14th or 15th century or perhaps a little later), ŚvetUp.; MBh. &c.; IW. 73 &c.; RTL. **-kārikā**, f. N. of a collection of 72 memorial verses or stanzas by Īśvara-kṛishṇa (also called *sāṃkhya-saptati*; the oldest extant systematic exposition of the S° system; cf. above); *-bhāshya*, n. N. of a Commentary on prec. by Gauḍa-pāda (8th cent.) **-kaumudī**, f. N. of a Comm. on the S°-kārikā by Rāma-kṛishṇa Bhaṭṭâcārya. **-krama-dīpikā**, f. N. of a Comm. on the Tattva-samāsa. **-candrikā**, f. N. of a Comm. on the S°-kārikā by Nārayaṇa-tīrtha. **-jñāna**, n. knowledge of the S° system, MBh. **-tattva-kaumudī**, f. N. of a Comm. on the S°-kārikā by Vācaspati-miśra. **-tattva-candrikā**, f. = *sāṃkhya-c°* above. **-tattva-pradīpa**, m., **°pikā**, f. N. of a brief exposition of the S° system by Kavirāja-yati. **-tattva-vilāsa**, m. N. of a Comm. by Raghunātha-tarkavāgīśa Bhaṭṭâcārya on the S°-tattva-kaumudī. **-taraṃga**, m. N. of a modern Comm. on the S°-sūtra. **-darśana**, n. N. of a ch. of the Sarva-darśana-saṃgraha. **-padârtha-gāthā**, f. N. of a wk. by Rāmânanda-tīrtha. **-purusha**, m. the spirit or soul in the S° system, Śiś. **-pravacana**, n. = *yoga-sūtra* or = *sāṃkhya-sūtra* [qq. vv.]; *-bhāshya* (or *sāṃkhya-bh°*), n. N. of a Comm. on the S°-sūtra by Vijñāna-bhikshu. **-bhikshu**, m. a kind of mendicant, MW. **-mata**, n. N. of wk. **-maya**, mf(ī)n. consisting of the S°-doctrine, BhP. **-mīmāṅsā**, f. N. of wk. **-mukhya**, m. N. of Śiva, MBh. **-yoga**, m. 'adherent of the S° and Yoga,' N. of a Ṛishi, MBh. xiii, 7123 (v.l. *-yogau*); 'application of the S° doctrine to the knowledge of spirit,' N. of the 2nd ch. of the Bhagavad-gītā; the so-called theistical S°-yoga, Śaṃk.; (*am*), n. the S° and the Y°, MBh.; *-dīpikā*, f. N. of wk.; *-pravartin*, m. N. of Śiva, MBh.; *-vat*, mfn. acquainted with S° and Y°, ib.; *-vādin*, m. an adherent of the theistical S°-Y°, Śaṃk. **-vṛitti**, f. (= *-tattva-vilāsa*); *-prakāśa*, m., *-sāra*, m. N. of wks. **-śāstra**, n. the S° doctrine or any treatise upon it. **-saptati**, f. = *-kārikā*. **-sāra** or **-sāra-viveka**, m. N. of a wk. by Vijñāna-bhikshu. **-sūtra**, n. N. of six books of aphorisms of the S° philosophy (ascribed to Kapila, but prob. written in the 14th or 15th century A.D.); *-prakshepikā*, f., *-vivaraṇa*, n., *-vṛitti*, f., *-vṛitti-sāra*, m. N. of wks. **Sāṃkhyâcārya**, m. a teacher of the S° (also N. of an author), BhP.; Sarvad.; N. of Vishṇu, Vishṇ. **Sāṃkhyârtha**, m. meaning or doctrine of the S° (in comp.); *-tattva-pradīpikā*, f. N. of a brief exposition of the S° system by Bhaṭṭa-keśava; *-sāṃkhyāyika* = *sāṃkhya-tattva-vilāsa*. **Sāṃkhyâlaṃkāra**, m. = *sāṃkhya-krama-dīpikā*.

Sāṃkhyāyana, m. (patr. fr. *sāṃkhya*; cf. *śāṅkhāyana*) N. of a teacher, (pl.) his school, TĀr.; ĀśvGṛ. **-gṛihya**, n., **-tantra**, n., **-brāhmaṇa**, n., **-sūtra**, n. N. of wks.

साङ्ग *sâṅgá* or *sâṅga*, mfn. having limbs or a body, Kathās.; together with the limbs, AV.; ŚBr.; with all its Aṅgas or supplements, KātyŚr.; complete, entire, MBh.; concluded, finished, Uttarar. **-glāni**, mfn. with an exhausted body, Śāntiś. **-ja**, mfn. having hair, together with hair, covered with hair, MW. **-rāga**, mfn. having the body anointed with unguents, R. **-sena**, m. N. of a man, Cat. **Sâṅgôpâṅga**, mfn. (the Vedas) with the Aṅgas and Upâṅgas, MBh. **Sâṅgôpâṅgôpanishad**, mfn. along with the Aṅgas and Upâṅgas and Upanishads, R.

सांगतिक *sāṃgatika*, mfn. (fr. *sam-gati*) relating to society, social, associating, W.; m. a new comer, visitor, guest, acquaintance, Vishṇ.; Mn.; one who comes to transact business, MW.

Sāṃgatya, n. (fr. *sam-gata*) meeting, intercourse with (*saha*), Hit.; Subh.

Sāṃgama, m. = *sam-gama*, L.

Sāṃgamaná, m. (fr. *saṃ-g°*) patr. of Agni Anaśnat, ŚBr.

Sāṃgamishṇú, mfn. (fr. *sam-g°*) a kind of sand (or expressive of some quality belonging to it), TBr.

साङ्गद *sâṅgada*, mfn. along with (the monkey) Aṅgada, R.

साङ्गारक *sâṅgāraka*, mfn. attended by the planet Mars, MW.

साङ्गुष्ठ *sâṅgushṭha*, mfn. together with the thumb (*am*, ind.), ĀśvGṛ.; (*ā*), f. Abrus Precatorius, L.

सांग्रहणा *sāṃgrahaṇá*, mf(ī)n. (fr. *saṃgrahaṇa*) relating to the act of taking possession or occupying, TS.; TBr. **Sāṃgrahaṇêshṭi**, f. N. of a Śrauta wk.

Sāṃgrahasūtrika, mfn. (fr. *saṃgraha-sūtra*) = *saṃgraha-sūtram adhīte veda vā*, Pāṇ. iv, 2, 60, Sch.

Sāṃgrahika, mfn. (fr. *saṃ-graha*) = *saṃgrahe sādhuḥ*, g. *kathâdi*; = *saṃ-graham adhīte veda vā*, g. *ukthâdi*.

Sāṃgrāhika, mfn. obstructing, constipating, Car.

सांग्राम *sāṃgrāma*, mfn. (fr. *sam-grāma*), g. *vyushṭâdi*.

Sāṃgrāmajitya, n. (fr. *saṃ-grāma-jit*) victory in battle, AV.

Sāṃgrāmika, mf(ī)n. relating to war, warlike, martial (with *ratha*, m. 'a war-chariot;' with *mṛityu*, m. 'death in battle;' with *vitta*, n. 'spoils of war'), Gaut.; Kauś.; MBh. &c.; m. a commander, general, W. **-guṇa**, m. the martial qualities of a king (consisting of the 3 Śaktis, the Shāḍguṇya, and the Astrâdy-abhyāsa), L. **-tva**, n. state of war, militarism, Daś. **-paricchada**, m. implements of war, Hariv. **-vidhi-jña**, mfn. familiar with war affairs or military concerns, ib.

सांघटिक *sāṃghaṭika*, mfn. (fr. *sam-ghaṭa*) = *sam-ghaṭam adhīte veda vā*, g. *ukthâdi* (v.l.)

Sāṃghaṭikā, f. (cf. *sam-ghāṭikā*) a pair, couple, L.; a bawd, procuress, L.: Trapa Bispinosa, L.

सांघट्टिक *sām-ghaṭṭika*, mfn. = *sam-ghaṭṭam adhīte veda vā*, g. *ukthâdi*.

सांघात *sāṃghāta*, mfn. (fr. *sam-ghāta*) = *sam-ghāte dīyate* or *kāryam*, g. *vyushṭâdi*.

Sāṃghātika, mfn. = *saṃ-ghāte sādhuḥ*, g. *guḍâdi*; = *sam-ghātāya prabhavati*, g. *saṃtāpâdi*; belonging to a group, ŚāṅkhŚr.; n. (scil. *bha*) the 16th Nakshatra after the Janmarksha, L.

Sāṃghātya, n. = *saṃ-hātya* and *sam-ghātya*, Daśar.

सांघिक *sāṃghika*, mf(ī)n. (fr. *sam-gha*) relating to the brotherhood of monks, Kāraṇḍ.

साङ्मुखी *sâṅmukhī*, f. N. of a partic. Tithi, L.

साच् *sāc*, strong form of 2. *sac* (q.v.)

Sācayá, mfn. joined, united (cf. *prishṭi-* and *rātri-s°*), ŚBr.

1. **Sāci**, mfn. following, accompanying, ŚBr.; m. N. of Agni, L.

Sācin. See *savya-s°*.

Sāceya, mfn. belonging to, suitable or fit for (comp.), ŚāṅkhBr.

Sācya, mfn. to be assisted or served or honoured, RV. i, 140, 3.

साचार *sâcāra*, mfn. well-conducted, well-behaved, well-mannered, Kāvyak.

साचि 2. *sācí*, ind. (perhaps fr. 7. *sa* + 2. *añc*) crookedly, awry, obliquely, sideways, askance, RV. x, 142, 2 (?); PañcavBr.; Kir. **-vāṭikā**, f. the white-flowered hogweed, L. **-vilokita**, n. a side-long glance, W. **-sthita**, mfn. standing unevenly or across, ib. **-smita**, n. a smile aside, Bhām.

Sācī, in comp. for 2. *sāci*. **-√kṛi**, P. *-karoti*, to make crooked, distort, bend or turn aside, Kāv., Kathās. **-kṛita**, mfn. made crooked, bent sideways, distorted, averted (*am*, ind. 'crookedly'), MBh.; Kāv. &c. (*-dṛiś*, mfn. having averted eyes, Kathās.; *°tānana*, mfn. having an averted face, looking sideways, MBh.); n. distortion, perversion, prejudice, W. **-guṇa**, N. of a place, AitBr. **-sūtra**, n. frenum præputii, Gal.

Sācīna, mfn. approaching sideways or from the side, Pāṇ. i, 1, 58, Vārtt. 1, Pat.

साचिकाण्ड *sāci-kāṇḍa*, n. (corrupted fr. *saṃciti-k°*) N. of the ninth chapter of the Śatapatha-Brāhmaṇa.

साचिव्य *sācivya*, n. (fr. *saciva*) companionship, assistance, (esp.) ministry, ministership, the office of the counsellor or friend of a king, MBh.; Kāv. &c. **Sācivyâkshepa**, m. (in rhet.) an objection under the form of assent or approval, Kāvyâd. ii, 145, 146.

साचीवित् *sācīvít*, ind. swiftly, rapidly (= *kshipram*), Naigh. ii, 15.

साज *sâja*, mfn. together with the lunar mansion Pūrva-bhadra-padā, VarBṛS.

साजात्य *sâjātya*, n. (fr. *sa-jāti*) community of race with (gen.), MaitrS.; equality of kind, homogeneousness, Sāh.; Bhāshāp. **-lakshaṇa-prakāśa**, m. N. of wk.

साजोक *sājoka*, m. N. of a poet, Cat.

साज्य *sâjya*, mfn. having clarified butter, KātyŚr.

साञ्चाधर *sāñcādhara*. See *sañcādhara*.

सांचारिक *sāṃcārika*, mfn. (fr. *sam-cāra*) movable, moving, MBh.

साञ्ज *sāñja*, m. N. of a lexicographer, L.

साञ्जन *sâñjana*, mfn. having pigment, having impurities, not pure, Sarvad.; m. a lizard, L.

साञ्जलि *sâñjali*, mfn. with hands hollowed and joined (in supplication, see *añjali*), R.

सांजीवीपुत्र *sāṃjīvī-pútra*, m. N. of a teacher, ŚBr.

सांज्ञायनि *sāṃjñāyani*, m. metron. fr. *saṃjñā*, g. *tikâdi*.

साञ्झनन्दिन् *sāñjha-nandin*, m. N. of a poet, Cat.

साट् *sāṭ*, cl. 10. P. *sāṭayati*, to make visible or manifest, Dhātup. xxxv, 84.

साटोप *sâṭopa*, mfn. puffed up, self-conceited, proud, arrogant, Vās.; rumbling (as clouds), Pañcat.; (*am*), ind. haughtily, Mṛicch.; Ratnâv.; with a rumbling sound, Śiś.; angrily, furiously, MW.

साट्टहास *sâṭṭahāsa*, mfn. with loud laughter (*am*, ind.), MārkP.

साट्टाल *sâṭṭāla*, m. or n. (?) a palace (v.l. for *saddāla*), Bhadrab.

साठल *sāṭhala*, m. N. of a person, Cat.

साठोक *sāṭhoka*, m. N. of a poet, Cat.

साड *sāḍa*, mfn. having a point or sting (as a stick, a scorpion &c.), Pat.

साडखान *sāḍa-khāna*, m. N. of a king, Cat.

साडि *sāḍi*, m. patr. fr. *saḍa*, Pāṇ. viii, 3, 56, Sch.

साड्भूत *sāḍ-bhūta*, mfn. (in gram.) taking the form *sāṭ* or *sāḍ* (said of 2. *sah*).

साढ *sāḍha*, *sāḍhṛi* &c. See p. 1193, col. 2.

साण्ड *sāṇḍa*, mfn. having testicles, uncastrated, MaitrS.; TāṇḍBr.; GṛŚrS.

सात् 1. *sāt*, a Taddhita affix which when put after a word denotes a total change of anything into the thing expressed by that word (see *agni-*, *bhasma-sāt* &c.)

सात् 2. *sāt*, a Sautra root meaning 'to give pleasure,' Pāṇ.; Vop.

3. **Sāt**, n. N. of Brahman, L.

3. **Sāta**, n. (for 1. and 2. see p. 1196, col. 3) pleasure, delight, L.

Sātaya, mfn., Pāṇ. iii, 1, 138.

सातत्य *sātatya*, n. (fr. *sa-tata*) continuity, constancy, uninterruptedness (*ena*, 'continually, permanently'), MBh.; Suśr. &c. **-catushka-ṭīkā**, f. N. of wk.

सातल *sātala*, m. N. of a poet, Cat.

सातला *sātalā*, f. = *saptalā*, Car.

सातवाह *sātavāha* or °*hana*, m. N. of a king (fabled to have been discovered, when a child, riding on a Gandharva called Sāta, who, accord. to one legend, was changed into a lion; also = *śāli-vāhana*, q.v.), Hcar.; Kathās.; Rājat.

सातसङ्का *sātasaṅkā*, f. N. of a district, Kshitîś.

सातागिरि *sātā-giri*, m. N. of a Yaksha, Jātakam.

साति 3. *sāti* (for 1. and 2. see p. 1196, col. 3), N. of a metre, Piṅg.

सातिरात्र *sâtirātra*, mfn. together with the Atirātra, Vait.

सातिरिक्त *sâtirikta*, mfn. having excess, excessive, increased, more abundant, Divyâv.

Sâtireka, mfn. id., ib.

सातिलक *sātilaka*, w.r. for *sātīlaka* below.

सातिशय *sâtiśaya*, mfn. superior, better, best, eminent, Mn.; Hariv.; Kathās.

सातिसार *sâtisāra*, mfn. suffering from diarrhœa, L.; sinful, guilty, Divyâv.

सातीकाश *sâtīkāśa*, mfn. with or having excessive light, ĀśvGṛ.

सातीन *sātīna* and *sātīlaka*, m. a kind of pea, L.

सातु *sātu*. See p. 1196, col. 3.

सातोबार्हत *sātobārhata*, mfn. relating or belonging to the Sato-bṛihatī metre, Lāṭy.

सात्कार्य *sāt-karya*, n. (fr. *sat-kara*) the effecting anything well, effectiveness, Kap., Sch.

सात्त्र *sāttra* and *sāttrika*, mfn. (fr. *sattra*) belonging to a sacrifice, sacrificial, ŚrS.

सात्त्व *sāttva*, mfn. (fr. *sat-tva*) relating to the quality Sattva &c., MārkP.

Sāttvaki, m. patr. fr. *sattvaka*, g. *bāhv-ādi*.

Sāttvika, mf(*ī*)n. (fr. *sat-tva*) spirited, vigorous, energetic, Mn.; MBh. &c.; relating to or endowed with the quality Sattva (i.e. 'purity' or 'goodness'), pure, true, genuine, honest, good, virtuous (also applied to partic. Purāṇas which exalt Vishṇu, IW. 513), MaitrUp.; Mn.; MBh. &c.; internal, caused by internal feeling or sentiment, Mālatim.; natural, not artificial, unaffected (as style), Sāh.; m. a state of body caused by some natural emotion (constituting a class of 8 Bhāvas holding a middle place between the Sthāyi- and Vyabhicāri-bhāvas, viz. *stambha*, *sveda*, *româñca*, *svara-vikāra*, *vepathu*, *varṇa-vikāra*, *aśru*, *pralaya*, qq. vv.), ib.; N. of Brahmā, L.; of the eighth creation by Prajā-pati, MW.; (*ī*), f. N. of Durgā, L.; a partic. kind of Pūjā practised by the worshippers of Durgā, MW.; (scil. *tushṭi*) N. of one of the five kinds of external acquiescence (in Sāṃkhya), ib.; an autumn night, L.; n. an offering or oblation (without pouring water), L. **-purāṇa-vibhāga**, m., **-brahma-vidyā-vilāsa**, m. N. of wks.

सात्पुडा *sātpuḍā*, f. N. of a mountain, VP.

सात्म 1. *sâtma*, mfn. (fr. 7. *sa*+*ātman*) together with one's own person, BhP.

2. **Sātma**, in comp. for *sâtman*. **-tā** (*sâtmá-*), f. community of essence or nature with (gen., instr., or comp.), ŚBr.; MBh.; absorption into the essence (of Brahmă), MW. **-tvá**, n. the having a soul or essence, AV.; TS. &c. **Sâtmârpaṇa**, mfn. connected with self-sacrifice, Kād.

Sâtman, mfn. having a soul or spirit, together with the soul, ŚBr.; TS.; united to the Supreme Spirit, MW.

Sâtmī, in comp. for *sâtma*. **-kṛita**, mfn. one who has made anything part of his nature, i.e. become accustomed to (acc.), Suśr. **-bhāva**, m. the becoming a custom or habit, conduciveness, suitableness, Car. **-bhū**, P. *-bhavati*, to become a custom or habit, become suitable or salutary, Jātakam.

Sâtmya, mfn. agreeable to nature or natural constitution, wholesome, Suśr.; Car.; m. suitableness, wholesomeness, ib.; habit, habituation, diet (°*tas*, ind. 'from habit;' ifc. = 'used to'), ib.; community of essence or nature with (instr. or gen.), BhP.

सात्य *sātyá*, mfn. (fr. *satya*, of which it is also the Vṛiddhi form in comp.) one whose nature is truth, ŚBr.; n. N. of a Sāman, ĀrshBr. **-kāmi**, m. (patr. fr. *satya-kāma*), TS. (w.r. *sātyaṃkāmi* in g. *pailâdi*). **-m-kārya**, m. patr. fr. *satyaṃkāra*, g. *kurv-ādi*. **-dūta**, mfn. (fr. *satya-dūta*) 'belonging to the trusty messengers' (said of partic. oblations presented to Sarasvatī and other deities), TS., Sch. **-m-ugra**, m. pl. the school of Sātyamugri, AV.Pariś. **-m-ugri**, m. (°*grī* or °*gryā*, f.) patr. fr. *satyam-ugra*, Pāṇ. iv, 1, 81. **-m-ugrya**, m. pl. N. of a school of the Sāma-veda (q. v.) **-muni**, m. a patr. (perhaps w.r. for *sātyamugri*), Saṃskārak. **-yajñá**, m. (fr. *satya-y*°) N. of a teacher, ŚBr. **-yajñi**, m. (*sâtya-*; fr. id.) patr. of Soma-śushma, ib. **-rathi**, m. patr. fr. *satya-ratha*, VP. **-vata** or **-vateya**, m. (fr. *satyavatī*) metron. of Vyāsa, L. **-havyá**, m. (fr. *satya-h*°) N. of a Vāsishṭha, TS.; AitBr.

Sātyaka, m. patr. = *sātyaki*, MBh.; Hariv.

Sātyakāyana, m. (only pl.) a patr., Saṃskārak.

Sātyaki, m. (fr. *satyaka*) patr. of Yuyudhāna (a warrior in the Pāṇḍu army who acted as the charioteer of Kṛishṇa and belonged to the Vṛishṇi family), MBh.; Hariv.; BhP.

Sātyakin, m. (m.c.) = prec., MBh.

सात्राजित *sātrājitá*, m. (fr. *satrā-jit*) patr. of Śatânīka, ŚBr.; (*ī*), f. patr. of Satya-bhāmā, MBh.; Hariv.

सात्रासाह *sātrāsāhá*, m. (fr. *satrā-sāha*) 'all-subduing,' N. of a serpent, AV.; patr. of Śona, ŚBr.; N. of a place, g. *dhūmâdi*.

Sātrāsāhaka, mfn. (fr. prec.), g. *dhūmâdi*.

सात्वत् *sātvat*, m. pl. (cf. *satvat*) N. of a people, Hariv.; Śiś. (= *yadu*, Sch.)

Sātvata, mf(*ī*)n. relating to the Satvats or the Sātvatas, belonging or sacred to Sātvata or Kṛishṇa &c., MBh.; Pur.; containing the word *satvat*, g. *vimuktâdi*; m. a king of the Satvats (N. of Kṛishṇa, Bala-deva &c.), MBh.; BhP.; (pl.) N. of a people, Śiś. (= *yādava*, Sch.); an adherent or worshipper of Kṛishṇa, L.; a partic. mixed caste (the offspring of an outcaste Vaiśya; accord. to L., 'the son of an outcaste V° and a V° woman who was formerly the wife of a Kshatriya'), Mn. x, 43; N. of a son of Āyu or Aṃśu, Pur.; (*ī*), f., see below. **-saṃhitā**, f. N. of a wk. (treating esp. of Vaishṇava worship); *-prayoga*, m. N. of wk. **-siddhânta-śataka**, n. N. of a Vedânta wk. **Sātvatâcāra-vādârtha**, m. N. of a wk. (also called *bhakti-vilāsa-tattva-dīpikā*, deprecating the slaughter of animals even in sacrifices, by Mahêśa-nārāyaṇa).

Sātvatī, f. a princess of the Satvats (N. of the mother of Śiśu-pāla), MBh.; Śiś.; (scil. *vṛitti*, q. v.) one of 4 divisions of dramatic style (expressive of 'bravery, generosity, cheerfulness, and the marvellous;' it is of four kinds, viz. *utthāpaka*, *saṃghātya*, *parivartaka*, and *saṃlāpa*), Bhar.; Daśar.; Sāh. **-sūnu**, m. 'son of Sātvatī,' N. of Śiśu-pāla, Śiś.

Sātvatīya, m. an adherent of Sātvata, i. e. Kṛishṇa, BhP.

सात्विक *sātvika* &c. See *sāttvika*, col. 1.

साद *sāda*, *sādana* &c. See p. 1139, col. 1.

सादर *sâdara*, mf(*ā*)n. having or showing respect, respectful, reverential; considerate, attentive or devoted to (ifc.), intent upon (*am*, ind. 'respectfully' &c.), Kāv.; Kathās. &c. **-pūrvakam**, ind. with respect, respectfully, reverentially, Pañcar.

सादसत *sādasata*, mfn. containing the words *sat* and *asat*, g. *vimuktâdi*.

सादाशिव *sādāśiva*, mf(*ī*)n. relating or belonging to Sadā-śiva, i. e. Śiva, Kāśīkh.

सादि *sâdi*, mfn. having a beginning (*-tva*, n.), Kap.

Sâdy-anta, mfn. having beginning and end, complete, entire (*am*, ind. 'from beginning to end'), MW.

सादि *sādi*, *sādita*, *sādin* &c. See p. 1139, col. 1.

सादीनव *sâdīnava*, mfn. having torments, subject to pains, Lalit.

सादृश *sādṛiśa*, mfn. = *sa-dṛiśa*, like, similar, ŚāṅkhŚr.; proper, Divyâv.; (*ī*), f. = *sādṛiśya*, Śiś.

Sādṛiśīya, mfn. (fr. *sa-dṛiśa*), g. *kṛiśâśvâdi*.

Sādṛiśya, n. likeness, resemblance, similarity to (comp.), Āpast.; R.; Hariv. &c. **-vāda**, m. N. of various phil. wks.

सादेय्य *sādeyya*, w.r. for *sôdarya*, MBh.

साद्गुण्य *sādguṇya*, n. (fr. *sad-guṇa*) the having good qualities, excellence, superiority, Car.

साद्दाल *saddāla* (?), m. a palace (v.l. *sāṭṭāla*), Bhadrab.

साद्भुत *sâdbhuta*, mfn. astonished, surprised, Kathās.

साद्य *sādya*. See p. 1139, col. 1.

साद्यस्क *sādyaska*, mfn. (fr. *sa-dyas*) taking place immediately, MBh.

Sādyaskra (g. *kaskâdi*) or **sādyaḥkra**, mfn. (fr. *sadyaḥ-krī*) performed with Soma bought on the same day; m. N. of a partic. Ekâha, ShaḍvBr.; ŚrS.; MBh. **-prayoga**, m. N. of wk.

Sādyoja, mfn. (fr. *sadyo-ja*), g. *saṃkalâdi*.

साध् 1. *sādh* (connected with √2. *sidh*), cl. 1. P. Ā. *sâdhati*, °*te*; accord. to Dhātup. xxvi, 71 and xxvii, 16, cl. 4. *sādhyati*, cl. 5. *sādhnoti* (in JaimBr. also *sadhnoti*); pf. *sasādha*; aor. *asātsīt*; fut. *sāddhā*, *sātsyati*; inf. *sāddhum*, in later language *sādhitum*; Ved. inf. *sâdhase*, q.v.), to go straight to any goal or aim, attain an object, to be successful, succeed, prosper, RV.; to bring straight to an object or end, further, promote, advance, accomplish, complete, finish, ib.; to submit or agree to, obey, ib.; (*sādhyati*) to be completed or accomplished, Dhātup.: Caus. *sādhayati* (m.c. also °*te*; aor. *asīshadhat*; Ved. also *sīshadhati*, °*dhaḥ*, °*dhema*, °*dhātu*; Pass. *sādhyate*, MBh. &c.), to straighten, make straight (a path), RV.; to guide straight or well, direct or bring to a goal, ib.; to master, subdue, overpower, conquer, win, win over, RV. &c. &c.; to summon, conjure up (a god or spirit), Kathās.; (in law) to enforce payment, recover (a debt), collect (taxes), Mn.; Yājñ. &c.; to subdue a disease, set right, heal, cure, Suśr.; to bring to an end or conclusion, complete, make perfect, bring about, accomplish, effect, fulfil, execute, practice (with *vākyam*, 'to execute any one's [gen.] order;' with *naishkarmyam*, 'to practise inactivity;' with *marum*, 'to pr° abstinence;' with *mantram*, 'to pr° the recitation of spells'), GṛŚrS.; Mn.; MBh. &c.; to attain one's object, be successful, MBh. iii, 1441; to produce, make, render (two acc.), Śak.; BhP.; to establish a truth, substantiate, prove, demonstrate, Tattvas.; Sarvad.; to make ready, prepare, MBh.; to gain, obtain, acquire, procure, ŚBr. &c.; to find out (by calculation), Gaṇit.; to grant, bestow, yield, MBh.; Kāv. &c.; to put or place in (loc.), BhP.; to set out, proceed, go (in dram. accord. to Sāh. = √*gam*), MBh.; Kāv. &c.: Desid. of Caus. *sishādhayishati* or *sisādhayishati*, to desire to establish or prove, Sāh.; Sarvad.: Desid. *sishātsati*, Gr.: Intens. *sāsādhyate, sāsāddhi*, ib.

2. **Sādh,** (ifc.) accomplishing, performing (see *yajña-sādh*).

Sādha, m. accomplishment, fulfilment, RV.

Sādhaka, mf(*ikā*)n. effective, efficient, productive of (gen. or comp.), accomplishing, fulfilling, completing, perfecting, finishing, MBh.; Kāv. &c.; energizing (said of the fire supposed to burn within the heart and direct the faculty of volition), Suśr.; adapted to any purpose, useful, advantageous, MBh.; Pur.; effecting by magic, magical, Pañcat.; Rājat.; demonstrating, conclusive, proving, Sarvad.; m. an assistant, Kāv.; an efficient or skilful person, (esp.) an adept, magician, Kathās.; a worshipper, Mālatīm.; (*akā*), f. N. of Durgā, L.; (*ikā*), f. very deep or profound sleep (= *su-shupti*), L.; a skilful or efficient woman, MW.; n. (prob.) = *sādhana*, proof, argument, Kap. **-tama,** mfn. most effective (*-tva*, n.), Kap.; Śaṃk. **-tā,** f. usefulness, suitableness, Kull. **-tva,** n. magic, jugglery, Daś.; conclusiveness, Sarvad. **-varti,** f. a magical wick, Pañcat. **-sarvasva,** n. N. of wk.

Sādhad-ishṭi, mfn. (fr. pr. p. of √*sādh* + 3. *ishṭi*) having effective sacrifices or prayers, RV.

Sādhana, mf(*ī* or *ā*)n. leading straight to a goal, guiding well, furthering, RV.; effective, efficient, productive of (comp.), MBh.; Kāv. &c.; procuring, Kāv.; conjuring up (a spirit), Kathās.; denoting, designating, expressive of (comp.), Pāṇ., Sch.; m. N. of the author of RV. x, 157 (having the patr. *Bhauvana*), Anukr.; (*ā*), f. accomplishment, performance (see *mantra-s°*); propitiation, worship, adoration, L.; (*am*), n. (ifc. f. *ā*), the act of mastering, overpowering, subduing, Kir.; Pañcat.; subduing by charms, conjuring up, summoning (spirits &c.), MBh.; Kathās.; subduing a disease, healing, cure, Suśr.; MBh. &c.; enforcing payment or recovery (of a debt), Daś.; bringing about, carrying out, accomplishment, fulfilment, completion, perfection, Nir.; MBh. &c.; establishment of a truth, proof, argument, demonstration, Yājñ.; Sāh.; Sarvad.; reason or premiss (in a syllogism, leading to a conclusion), Mudr. v, 10; any means of effecting or accomplishing, any agent or instrument or implement or utensil or apparatus, an expedient, requisite for (gen. or comp.), Mn.; R. &c.; a means of summoning or conjuring up a spirit (or deity), Kālac.; means or materials of warfare, military forces, army or portion of an army (sg. and pl.), Hariv.; Uttar.; Rājat.; conflict, battle, Śiś.; means of correcting or punishing (as 'a stick,' 'rod' &c.), TBr.; Sch.; means of enjoyment, goods, commodities &c., R.; efficient cause or source (in general), L.; organ of generation (male or female), Sāh.; (in gram.) the sense of the instrumental or agent (as expressed by the case of a noun, opp. to the action itself), Pat.; preparing, making ready, preparation (of food, poison &c.), Kathās.; MārkP.; obtaining, procuring, gain, acquisition, Kāv.; BhP.; finding out by calculation, computation, Gaṇit.; fruit, result, Pañcat.; the conjugational affix or suffix which is placed between the root and terminations (= *vikaraṇa*, q.v.), Pāṇ. viii, 4, 30, Vārtt. 1; (only L. 'matter, material, substance, ingredient, drug, medicine; good works, penance, self-mortification, attainment of beatitude; conciliation, propitiation, worship; killing, destroying; killing metals, depriving them by oxydation &c. of their metallic properties [esp. said of mercury]; burning on a funeral pile, obsequies; setting out, proceeding, going; going quickly; going after, following'). **-kriyā,** f. the act of performing &c.; an action connected with a Kāraka, Pāṇ.; a finite verb, ib.; a Kṛid-anta affix, ib. **-kshama,** mfn. admitting of proof or evidence, Yājñ., Sch. **-catushṭaya,** n. (in phil.) four kinds of proof, MW. **-tā,** f. the being a means of (comp., cf. *bahu-s°*), Sarvad.; Bhāshāp. **-tva,** n. efficacy, Sāh.; = prec., Sarvad.; the being a proof or argument, Kull. on Mn. viii, 56; state of perfection, MW. **-dīpikā,** f. N. of a wk. on Bhakti by Nārāyaṇa-bhaṭṭa. **-nirdeśa,** m. production of proof (in law); the statement of premisses leading to a conclusion, W. **-pañcaka,** n. N. of five stanzas giving rules for the attainment of Praśānti or quietude. **-pattra,** n. any written document used as evidence or proof, MW. **-paddhati,** f. N. of a wk. on the worship of Rādhā and Kṛishṇa. **-bhāga,** see *mahā-s°*. **-mālā-tantra,** n., **-muktâvalī,** f. N. of wks. **-rūpin,** mfn. having the form or character of an instrument or expedient, MW. **-vat,** mfn. furnished with proof or evidence, Sarvad. **-sāgara,** m., **-subodhinī,** f. N. of wks. **Sādhanâdhyaksha,** m. superintendent of the military forces, Pañcat. (B.) **Sādhanārha,** mfn. worthy of being accomplished, MW. **Sādhanâvyāpaka,** mfn. (in logic) not invariably inherent in the proof, MW.; *-tā*, f., *-tva*, n. non-invariable inherence in the proof, ib.

Sādhanaka, (ifc.) = *sādhana*, a means, expedient (e.g. *paśu-s°*, '[a sacrifice] offered by means of cattle'), Śaṃk. on BṛĀrUp.

Sādhanī, in comp. for *sādhana*. **-√kṛi,** P. *-karoti*, to employ as a means for (loc.), Jātakam. **-bhūta,** mfn. becoming or being a means or expedient, Jaim., Sch.

Sādhanī-dvādaśī, f. N. of wk.

Sādhanīya, mfn. to be accomplished or performed, MBh.; Ragh.; to be formed (as words), Uṇ. iii, 131, Sch.; to be acquired (as knowledge), Kathās.; to be proved (*-tva*, n.), Sarvad.

Sādhanta, m. a beggar, mendicant, Uṇ. iii, 128, Sch.

Sādhaya, Nom. P. °*yati* (fr. *sādhu* = *bāḍha*; cf. *sādhishṭha, sādhīyas*), to make hard or firm, Vop. (see also Caus. of √*sādh*).

Sādhayitavya, mfn. (fr. Caus. of √*sādh*) to be accomplished or performed, Hit.

Sādhayitṛi, mfn. (fr. id.) one who brings about, an accomplisher, performer, Nir.

Sādhava, n. (fr. *sādhu*), g. *pṛithv-ādi*.

Sādhase (Ved. inf.) for levelling or preparing land (with *kshaitrāya*), RV. viii, 71, 12.

Sādhita, mfn. brought about, accomplished, perfected &c.; mastered, subdued, MārkP.; proved, demonstrated, Pañcat.; made, appointed, BhP.; punished by a fine, made to pay (= *dāpita*), L.; awarded (as a punishment or fine), W.; recovered (as a debt), ib.

Sādhin, mfn. accomplishing, performing (see *bhāra-s°*).

Sādhiman, m. (fr. *sādhu*) goodness, perfection, excellence, g. *pṛithv-ādi*.

Sādhishṭha, mfn. (superl. of *sādhu*) straightest (as a path), RV.; most effective (as a sacrifice), ib.; very fit, most proper or right, ChUp.; hardest, very hard or firm (= *dṛiḍha-tama*; in these senses regarded as irreg. superl. of *bāḍha*, Pāṇ. v, 3, 63), L.

Sādhīyas, mfn. (compar. of *sādhu*) more right or proper, Kusum.; more pleasant or agreeable, Sāh.; harder, firmer, very hard or firm, Daś. (in these senses regarded as an irreg. compar. of *bāḍha*, Pāṇ. v, 3, 63); ind. more eagerly, AitBr.; in a higher degree, excessively, Āpast.; Śiś.

Sādhú, mf(*vī*)n. straight, right, RV; AV.; BhP.; leading straight to a goal, hitting the mark, unerring (as an arrow or thunderbolt), RV.; ŚBr.; straightened, not entangled (as threads), Kauś.; well-disposed, kind, willing, obedient, RV.; R.; successful, effective, efficient (as a hymn or prayer), RV.; Kām.; ready, prepared (as Soma), RV.; AitBr.; peaceful, secure, RV.; powerful, excellent, good for (loc.) or towards (loc., gen., dat., acc. with *prati, anu, abhi, pari*, or comp.), ŚBr. &c. &c.; fit, proper, right, VarBṛS.; good, virtuous, honourable, righteous, ŚBr.; Mn.; MBh. &c.; well-born, noble, of honourable or respectable descent, W.; correct, pure, classical (as language), ib.; m. a good or virtuous or honest man, ŚBr.; Mn.; MBh. &c.; a holy man, saint, sage, seer, Kālid.; (with Jainas) a Jina or deified saint, W.; a jeweller, Hit.; a merchant, money-lender, usurer, L.; (in gram., accord. to some) a derivative or inflected noun; (*vī*), f. a chaste or virtuous woman, faithful wife, Mn.; MBh. &c.; a saintly woman, W.; a kind of root (= *medā*), L.; n. the good or right or honest, a good &c. thing or act (*sādhu asti* with dat., 'it is well with —;' *sādhu-√man* with acc., 'to consider a thing good, approve'), RV. &c. &c.; gentleness, kindness, benevolence, ŚBr.; MBh. &c.; (*ú*), ind. straight, aright, regularly, RV.; AV.; well, rightly, skilfully, properly, agreeably (with √*vṛit* and loc., 'to behave well towards' [once *sādhu*, in RV. viii, 32, 10]; with √*kṛi*, 'to set right;' with √*ās*, 'to be well or at ease'), RV. &c. &c.; good! well done! bravo! ŚBr.; MBh. &c.; well, greatly, in a high degree, R.; Kām.; BhP.; well, enough of, away with (instr.)! MBh.; Pañcat.; well! come on! (with Impv. or 1. pr.), MBh.; Kāv. &c.; assuredly, indeed, R.; Kām. **-karman** (*sādhú-*), mfn. acting well or rightly, RV.; doing kind actions, beneficent, MW. **-kāra,** n. the exclamation *sādhu* (i.e. well! well done!), applause (°*raṃ* √*dā*, 'to applaud'), R.; Kāraṇḍ. **-kārin,** mfn. acting well or rightly, skilled, clever, ŚBr.; MBh. &c. **-kīrti,** m. N. of an author, Cat. **-kṛit,** mfn. = *-kārin*, ŚBr. **-kṛita,** mfn. (ifc.) well or rightly done, BhP. **-kṛitya,** n. compensation, requital, ib.; advantage, Kām.; (*ā*), f. good or right manner of acting, VS.; TS.; ŚBr.; KātyŚr. **-gata,** mfn. resorted to by the good, respectable, virtuous, MW. **-caraṇa,** mfn. well-conducted, righteous, Lāṭy. **-caritra,** n. N. of wk. **-ja,** mfn. well-born, 'good conduct,' W. **-jana,** m. a g° person, honest man, Kāv.; Dhūrtas. (*a-s°*). **-jāta,** mfn. of a g° kind, beautiful, MBh.; R. **-tama,** mfn. best, most excellent, MBh. **-tara,** mfn. better than (abl.), Kām. **-tas,** ind. from a good man, Mn. iv, 252. **-tā,** f. rightness, correctness, Āpast.; honesty, uprightness, Kām.; Daś. &c. **-tva,** n. rightness, correctness, Lāṭy.; TPrāt., Sch.; goodness, excellence, Uttarar.; kindness, Kāv.; honesty, uprightness, Pañcat.; Uttarar. &c. **-datta,** m. a proper N., Campak. **-darśin,** mfn. seeing well, TĀr., Sch.; well-discerning (*a-s°*), Śak. **-dāyin,** mfn., Pāṇ. iii, 2, 78, Vārtt. 1, Pat. **-devin,** mfn. playing skilfully or fortunately, AV.; MBh. **-devī,** f. a mother-in-law, L. **-dvitīya,** mfn. having a merchant as second, accompanied by a m°, MW. **-dhī,** f. a good understanding, MW.; good disposition, ib.; mfn. having a good und°, wise, well-disposed, ib.; (*īs*), f. a mother-in-law, L. **-dhvani,** m. sound of applause or acclamation, Kād. **-nigūhin,** mfn., Kāś. on Pāṇ. vi, 4, 89. **-nigraha,** mf(*ā*)n. having a convenient handle, Suśr. **-padavī,** f. the path or way of the good, Bhartṛ. **-putra,** m. N. of a man, Buddh. **-pushpa,** n. a beautiful flower, MW.; the flower of the Hibiscus Mutabilis, L. **-pratikramaṇa-sūtra,** n. N. of wk. **-phala,** mfn. bearing good fruit, having good results or consequences, Śak. vii, 25, 26 (v.l.) **-bhāva,** m. good nature, goodness, kindness, MBh. **-mat,** mfn. good, MW.; (*atī*), f. one of the ten grades of a Bodhisattva, Cat.; N. of a Tantra deity, Buddh. **-mata,** mfn. well thought of, highly prized, MW. **-mantra,** m. an effective prayer or spell, Kām. **-mātrā,** f. the right measure (°*rayā*, 'in due measure'), Kām. **-m-manya,** mfn. thinking one's self good or virtuous, W. **-ratna-sūri,** m. N. of an author, Cat. **-randhin,** mfn., Kāś. on Pāṇ. vii, 1, 61. **-1. -vat,** mfn. right, correct, RPrāt. **-2. -vat,** ind. as if good, as if correct, MW. **-vandana,** n. N. of wk. **-vācaka,** mfn. telling or expressing what is good, VP. **-vāda,** m. exclaiming 'well done!' (°*daṃ* √*dā*, 'to applaud'), MBh.; Śiś.; Kathās. &c.; the name of an honest man, good renown, fame, reputation, BhP.; a right sentence, ib. **-vādin,** mfn. speaking rightly or justly, Gaut.; applauding, Hariv.; w.r. for *-vāhin*, MBh. vii, 7786. **-vāha,** m. a good or well-trained horse, MW. **-vāhin,** mfn. drawing (a carriage) well, MBh.; Hcat.; m. a good or well-trained horse, W.; mfn. having good h°s, W. **-vigarhita,** mfn. blamed or censured by the good, R. **-vṛiksha,** m. a good tree, ib.; Nauclea Cadamba, L.; Cratæva Roxburghii, ib. **-vṛitta,** mfn. well rounded, R.; Bhartṛ.; well-conducted, having good manners, MBh.; Kāv.; Gaut.; m. a well-conducted person, virtuous or honest man, MW.; n. good conduct, honesty, R.; *-tā*, f. the being well-conducted, honourableness, Kathās. **-vṛitti,** f. good means of living, MW.; g° exposition, excellent commentary, ib.; good or moral practice or observance, W.; mfn. well rounded, Bhartṛ. (v.l.); well-conducted, ib. (v.l.); *-tā*, f. the being well-cond°, MBh. **-vesha,** mfn. well dressed, Car. **-śabda,** m. = *-kāra*, MBh. **-śīla,** mfn. well-disposed, virtuously inclined (*-tva*, n.), Hit.; virtuous, righteous, W. **-śukla,** mfn. quite white, MBh. **-shṭhāna** (*s°* + *sthāna*), n. the right point of view, right way, Āpast. **-saṃsarga,** m. association with the good, MW. **-saṃskṛitá,** mfn. well prepared or arranged, ŚBr. **-samaksharūpa,** mfn. well before the eyes, Śak. vii, 31 (v.l.) **-samācāra,** m. 'conduct of the righteous,' N. of wk.; mfn. well-behaved, Pañcat. **-sammata,** mfn. approved by the good, R. **-siddha,** mfn. quite finished or perfect, Suśr. **Sādhûkta,** mfn. said or declared by the good, W.

Sādhuka, m. N. of a low or degraded tribe, ib.

Sādhuyā́, ind. in a straight course, directly towards any mark or aim, RV.; plainly, simply, AV.;

rightly, duly, RV.; VS.; TS.; kindly, properly, amicably, MW.

Sādhyá, mfn. to be subdued or mastered or won or managed, conquerable, amenable, MBh.; R. &c.; to be summoned or conjured up, L.; to be set to rights, to be treated or healed or cured, Suśr.; MBh.; Kathās.; to be formed (grammatically), Vop.; to be cultivated or perfected, Kāv.; to be accomplished or fulfilled or brought about or effected or attained, practicable, feasible, attainable, Mn.; MBh. &c.; being effected or brought about, taking place, Kāś.; to be prepared or cooked, Car.; to be inferred or concluded, Sarvad.; Bhāshāp.; Kpr.; to be proved or demonstrated, Ragh.; Sāh.; to be found out by calculation, VarBṛS.; Gaṇit.; to be killed or destroyed, MW.; relating to the Sādhyas (see below), MBh.; BhP.; m. (pl.) 'they that are to be propitiated,' N. of a class of celestial beings (belonging to the *Gaṇa-devatā*, q. v., sometimes mentioned in the Veda [see RV. x, 90, 16]; in the ŚBr. their world is said to be above the sphere of the gods; according to Yāska [Nir. xii, 41] their locality is the Bhuvarloka or middle region between the earth and sun; in Mn. i, 22, the Sādhyas are described as created after the gods with natures exquisitely refined, and in iii, 195, as children of the Soma-sads, sons of Virāj; in the Purāṇas they are sons of Sādhyā, and their number is variously twelve or seventeen; in the later mythology they seem to be superseded by the Siddhas, see *siddha;* and their names are Manas, Mantṛi, Prāṇa, Nara, Pāna, Vinirbhaya, Naya, Daṉsa, Nārāyaṇa, Vṛisha, Prabhu), RV. &c. &c.; the god of love, L.; N. of a Vedic Ṛishi, IndSt.; of the 21st astronomical Yoga, L.; (*ā*), f. N. of a daughter of Daksha and wife of Dharma or Manu (regarded as the mother of the Sādhyas), Hariv.; Pur.; (*am*), n. accomplishment, perfection, W.; an object to be accomplished, thing to be proved or established, matter in debate, ib.; (in logic) the major term in a syllogism, ib.; silver, L.; N. of a Sāman, ĀrshBr. **–kośa**, m. N. of a dictionary. **–tā**, f. practicableness, feasibility, MW.; conquerableness (see *a-s°*); curableness (see *a-s°*); *°tâvacchedaka*, n. the distinguishing property of the thing to be proved, MW. **–tva**, n. curableness, Suśr.; perfectibility, Sarvad.; practicability, Kāv.; KapS.; Bhāshāp. **–paksha**, m. the side of the thing to be proved (in a lawsuit), MW. **–pramāṇa-saṃkhyā-vat**, mfn. containing the number of the things to be proved and of the proofs, Yājñ., Sch. **–rshi** (*°ya + ṛishi*), m. N. of Śiva, MW. **–vat**, mfn. comprehending the point to be proved, Yājñ., Sch.; containing the major term (in logic), W.; m. the party on whom the burden of proof in a lawsuit rests, W. **–vyāpaka**, mfn. (in log.) invariably inherent in that which is to be proved, ib.; *-tā*, f. invariable inherence in what is to be pr°, ib. **–sama**, m. an assertion identical with the point to be proved, petitio principii, Sarvad.; Nyāyad.; *-tva*, n. sameness with the point to be pr° (*°tvāt*, 'because it is the same with what is to be pr°'), Nilak.; Nyāyad. **–sādhana**, n. the means of establishing what is to be proved (e. g. a Hetu or reason), effecting what has to be done &c., W.; *-kaumudī*, f., *-khaṇḍa*, N. of wks. **–siddha**, mfn. to be still accomplished and already accomplished, R. **–siddhi**, f. accomplishment of what has to be done, MW.; the establishing of what has to be proved, IW.; the success of an undertaking, accomplishment, fulfilment, ib.; proof, conclusion, ib.; *-pāda*, m. the fourth stage or division of a suit at law, judgment, decision, ib. **Sādhyâbhāva**, m. absence of the thing to be proved, ib.; impossibility of cure, ib.

2. **Sādhyā́**, ind. (for 1. see under *sādhyá*) = *sādhuyā́*, TS.; TBr.

Sādhv, in comp. for *sādhu*. **–anindita**, mfn. unblamed by the good, of irreproachable character, W. **–apāsana-vidhi**, m. N. of wk. **–aryá**, mf(*ā́*)n. (prob.) truly faithful, RV. **–alaṃkṛita**, mfn. beautifully adorned, MW. **–asādhú**, mfn. good and bad (*-tva*, n.), VarBṛS.; m. pl. the good and the wicked, MBh.; n. du. good and bad things, ŚBr.; R. **–ācāra**, m. the conduct of the good, virtuous c°, VarBṛS.; mfn. well-conducted c°, Mn.; MBh.

Sādhvī, f. See under *sādhú*, p. 1201, col. 2.

Sādhvika. See *sa-sādh°*, p. 1192, col. 2.

साधमित्रिक *sādhamitrika*, mf(*ā* or *ī*)n. (fr. *sadha-mitra*), g. *kāśy-ādi*.

साधय *sādhaya*. See p. 1201, col. 2, and √*sādh*, p. 1200, col. 3.

साधर्मिक *sādharmika*, m. (fr. *sa-dharma*) one of the same faith or religion, HPariś.

Sādharmya, n. community or equality of duty or office or properties, sameness or identity of nature, likeness or homogeneousness with (gen. or comp.), MBh.; Kāv. &c.; the being of the same religion, MW.; *-sama*, m. (in Nyāya) a pretended or sham objection, Nyāyas.

साधान *sâdhāna*, mfn. together with the receptacle, ŚBr.

साधार *sâdhāra*, mfn. having a support or basis or foundation, NṛisUp.; Pañcar. (cf. *niḥ-* and *bahu-s°*).

Sâdhāraṇa, mf(*ī* or *ā*)n. 'having or resting on the same support or basis,' belonging or applicable to many or all, general, common to all, universal, common to (gen., dat., instr. with and without *saha*, or comp.), RV. &c. &c.; like, equal or similar to (instr. or comp.), Hariv.; Kālid.; behaving alike, Dhūrtas.; having something of two opposite properties, occupying a middle position, mean (between two extremes, e. g. 'neither too dry nor too wet,' 'neither too cool nor too hot'), Suśr.; Kām.; VarBṛS.; (in logic) belonging to more than the one instance alleged (one of the three divisions of the fallacy called *anaikāntika*, q. v.); generic, W.; m. N. of the 44th (or 18th) year of Jupiter's cycle of 60 years, VarBṛS.; (*ī*), f. a key, L.; a twig of bamboo (perhaps used as a bolt), MW.; m. or n. (?) N. of a Nyāya wk. by Gadā-dhara; (*am*), n. something in common, a league or alliance with (comp.), Subh.; a common rule or one generally applicable, W.; a generic property, a character common to all the individuals of a species or to all the species of a genus &c., ib.; (*am*), ind. commonly, generally, L. **–kroḍa**, m., **-grantha**, m. N. of wks. **–tā**, f. commonness, community (*°tāṃ* √*nī*, 'to make common property'), Rājat. **–tva**, n. universality, Nyāyam., Sch.; temperateness, Suśr. **–deva**, m. N. of an author, Cat. **–deśa**, m. common land, MW.; a wild marshy country, ib. **–dhana**, n. joint or common property, ib. **–dharma**, m. com° or universal duty, conduct or duty binding on all castes and orders alike (as humanity &c.), IW. **–nyāsa**, m. N. of wk. **–paksha**, n. common side or party, middle side, the mean (between two extremes), MW. **–pūrva-paksha-rahasya**, n., **-prāyaścitta-saṃgraha**, m., **-rahasya**, n., **-vāda**, m., **-vrata-pratishṭhā-prayoga**, m. N. of wks. **–strī**, f. a common woman, harlot, Sāh. **Sādhāraṇâsādhāraṇânupasaṃhāri-virodha-grantha**, m. or *°rodhin*, n. N. of wk.

1. **Sâdhāraṇī**, f. See under *sâdhāraṇa*.

2. **Sâdhāraṇī**, in comp. for *°ṇa*. **–√kṛi**, P. *-karoti*, to make common property, share with (*saha*), R.; Kād.; to make equal with (comp.), MBh. **–√bhū**, to become equal, Ragh.

Sâdhāraṇya, n. commonness, universality, Sāh.; Sarvad. &c.; equalness, analogy, Sāh.; = *kuñcikā*, MW.; (*ā́*), ind. commonly, all together, RV.

Sâdhārita, mfn. supported, Campak.

Sâdhṛita, n. 'what is held together,' a stall, shop, W.; an umbrella, parasol, ib.; a flock of peacocks, ib.

साधिक *sâdhika*, mf(*ā*)n. (for *sādhikā* see *sādhaka*, p. 1201, col. 1) having excess or a surplus, excessive, increased, more than full or complete, Gobh.; Pur.; Divyâv.

साधिक्षेप *sâdhikshepa*, mfn. having or showing contempt, taunting, ironical (as language), MBh.

साधिदैव *sâdhidaiva*, mfn. (united or identified) with supreme deity, W.

Sâdhidaivata, mfn. having a tutelary deity, Śak. (v. l.)

साधिभूत *sâdhibhūta*, mfn. (identified) with the Being who is 'the substratum of all material objects,' W. **Sâdhibhūtâdhidaiva**, mfn. identical with the Adhibhūtas and Adhidaivas (qq. vv.), Bhag.

साधिमान *sâdhimāna*, mfn. with the surplus or excess, ŚBr.

साधियज्ञ *sâdhiyajña*, mfn. one with the Being who presides over sacrifice, Bhag.

साधिवास *sâdhivāsa*, mfn. having perfume, fragrant, MBh.

साधिष्ठ *sādhishṭha*, *sādhīyas*. See p. 1201.

साधिष्ठान *sâdhishṭhāna*, mfn. having a solid basis, possessing a firm foundation, R.

साधु *sādhu* &c. See p. 1201, col. 2.

साध्य *sādhya* &c. See col. 1.

साध्यवसाना *sâdhyavasānā* or *°nikā*, f. (in rhet.) an elliptical figure of speech (in which the meaning is left to be implied), Sāh.; Sarvad.

Sâdhyavasāya, mfn. elliptical, Pratāp.

साध्यास *sâdhyāsa*, mfn. having an addition, Lāṭy.

साध्याहार *sâdhyāhāra*, mfn. having or with something to be supplied, ĀpGṛ., Sch.

साध्र *sādhra*, n. N. of various Sāmans, ĀrshBr.

साध्वस *sādhvasa*, n. (ifc. f. *ā*; fr. *sa* + *dhvasa* = *dhvaṉsa*) consternation, perturbation, alarm, terror, fear of (gen. or comp.; *°sam* √*gam*, 'to become terrified'), MBh.; Kāv. &c.; (in dram.) false alarm, sudden fright, panic (one of the 7 divisions of the Bhaṇikā, q. v.), Sāh. **–vipluta**, mfn. overwhelmed with consternation, MW.

सानग *sā́naga*, m. (fr. *sanaga*) N. of a teacher, MaitrS.

सानत्कुमार *sānatkumāra*, mfn. relating to Sanat-kumāra; m. pl. a partic. class of gods, Dharmaś.; n. N. of an Upa-purāṇa.

सानत्सुजात *sānatsujāta*, mfn. relating to Sanat-sujāta, MBh.

सानन्द *sânanda*, mf(*ā*)n. having joy or happiness, joyful, glad, delighted with (comp.), Kāv.; Kathās.; m. a kind of tree, L.; N. of a youth attendant on Rādhā, Pañcar.; (with *miśra*) N. of an author, Cat.; (*ā*), f. a form of Lakshmī, ib.; (*am*), ind. joyfully, with delight, Kāv.; Sāh. **–gadgada-padam**, ind. speaking indistinctly through joy, Gīt. **–govinda**, N. of various wks. **–nī**, f. N. of a river, MārkP. **Sânandâśru**, n. tears of joy, Pañcar.

सानन्दूर *sānandūra*, N. of a Tīrtha, Cat. **–māhātmya**, n. N. of a ch. of the VarP.

सानल *sânala*, mfn. containing fire, MW.; together with the Nakshatra Kṛittikā, VarBṛS.; m. the resinous exudation of the Śāl tree, W.

सानसि *sānasí*, *sānin*. See p. 1196, col. 3.

सानाथ्य *sānāthya*, n. (fr. *sa-nātha*) assistance, aid, help, Kathās.

सानिका *sānikā*, f. (of unknown derivation) a flute, pipe, L.

Sāneyikā and **sāneyī**, id., L.

सानिबाप *sānibāpa* (of unknown meaning), Pañcad.

सानु *sā́nu*, m. n. (accord. to Uṇ. i, 3 fr. √*san;* collateral form 3. *snu*) a summit, ridge, surface, top of a mountain, (in later language generally) mountain-ridge, table-land, RV. &c. &c. (L. also, 'a sprout; a forest; road; gale of wind; sage, learned man; the sun'). **–ja**, m. (for *sânuja* see p. 1203, col. 1) 'produced on table-land,' Xanthoxylon Alatum, Bhpr.; n. the flower of Hibiscus Mutabilis, L. **–prastha**, m. N. of a monkey, R. **–mat**, mfn. having a summit or ridge, R.; m. a mountain, hill, Kāv.; Rājat.; (*atī*), f. N. of an Apsaras, Śak. **–ruha**, mfn. growing on a mountain-ridge (as a wood), R.

Sānuká, mfn. elevated, arrogant (Sāy.; but see p. 1196, col. 3).

सानुकम्प *sânukampa*, mf(*ā*)n. full of pity, compassionate, tender, kind (*am*, ind.), Daś.; Kathās.

सानुकूल *sânukūla*, mfn. (= *anukūla*) favourable, agreeable, Cāṇ.

Sânukūlya, n. favour, service, assistance, Sāh.

सानुक्रोश *sânukrośa*, mf(*ā*)n. full of compassion, compassionate, merciful, kind (*am*, ind.; *-tā*, f.), MBh.; R. &c.

सानुग *sânuga*, mfn. having attendants, with followers, Mn. iii, 87.

सानुचर *sânucara*, mf(*ī*)n. id., Kauś.; Car.

सानुज *sânuja*, mfn. (for *sānu-ja* see p. 1202, col. 3) accompanied by or along with a younger brother, R.

सानुतर्षम् *sânutarsham*, ind. by or through thirst, Śiś.

सानुताप *sânutāpa*, mf(*ā*)n. feeling repentance, Kathās.; Rājat.

सानुनय *sânunaya*, mf(*ā*)n. having courtesy, courteous, polite, civil, kind (*am*, ind.), R.; Daś.

सानुनासिक *sânunāsika*, mfn. nasalized (as a vowel), Vop.; singing through the nose, Saṃgīt. **–vākya**, mfn. speaking with a nasal sound (*-tva*, n.), Suśr.

Sânunāsikya, mfn. nasalized, nasal, TPrāt., Sch.; n. nasality, ib.

Sânunāsyam, ind. with a nasal sound, in a nasal tone, IndSt.

सानुप्रास *sânuprâsa*, mf(*ā*)n. containing alliteration, Kāvyâd.

सानुप्लव *sânuplava*, mfn. accompanied by followers or attendants, MW.

सानुबन्ध *sânubandha*, mf(*ā*)n. possessing connection or continuity, uninterrupted, continuous, Ragh.; Suśr.; having results or consequences, R.; together with one's (or its) belongings, R.; Suśr.

Sânubandhaka, mfn. having an indicatory letter or syllable (see *anubandha*), Pat.

सानुमान *sânumāna*, mfn. (in phil.) dependent on or associated with an inference (opp. to *nir-anumāna*), Tattvas.

सानुयात्र *sânuyātra*, mfn. attended by followers, with a retinue, R.

सानुराग *sânurāga*, mf(*ā*)n. feeling or betraying passion, affectionate, enamoured of (loc.), Kāv.; Kathās.; MārkP.

सानुवक्रग *sânuvakra-ga*, mfn.= *anuvakra-ga*, Sūryas.

सानुवषट्कार *sânuvashaṭ-kāra*, mfn. accompanied with the exclamation Vashaṭ, ĀpŚr.

सानुशय *sânuśaya*, mfn. filled with remorse, Rājat.; irritable, angry (*am*, ind. 'remorsefully'), Bālar.; affected by the remainder of the consequences of action which brings the soul back to the earth, Śaṃk.

सानुषक् *sânushák*, ind. (prob.) = *ānushak*, continually, perpetually (accord. to Sāy. = next; accord. to others *sa ānushag* are two separate words), RV. i, 176, 5.

Sânushaṅga, m. an uninterrupted series, Sāy. on RV. i, 176, 5.

सानुष्टि *sānushṭi*, m. pl., a patr., Saṃskārak.

सानुसार *sânusāra*, mf(*ā*)n. together with all followers or belongings, Hariv. (Nīlak.)

सानुस्वरित *sânusvarita*, mfn. (prob.) resounding, re-echoing, Hariv.

Sânusvāra, mfn. having the nasal mark Anusvāra, RPrāt.

सानूकाश *sânūkāśa*, mfn. together with the after-light or after-glow, ĀśvGṛ.

सानूप *sânūpa*, mfn. having well-watered soil, Hariv.; Kām.

सानेयिका *sāneyikā*, °*yī*. See p. 1202, col. 3.

सान्त *sânta*, n. (perhaps w.r. for *śānta*) joy, L.

सान्तःस्थ *sântaḥstha*, mfn. having (or along with) semivowels, RPrāt.

सान्तक *sântaka*, mf(*ā*)n. together with Antaka, i.e. Yama, Rājat.

सांततिक *sāṃtatika*, mfn. (fr. *sam-tati*) bestowing offspring, Hariv.

सांतपन *sāṃtapaná*, mfn. (fr. *sam-tapana*) heating, warming, warm (said of the Maruts), RV.; AV.; Br.; ŚrS.; relating to the sun, VS. (Mahīdh.); sacred to the Sāṃtapana Maruts, ŚāṅkhŚr.; m. or n. (with and without *kṛicchra*) a kind of penance, Baudh.; Mn. xi, 124 &c.

Sāṃtapanāyana, m. pl., a patr., Saṃskārak.

Sāṃtapanīya, mfn. relating or belonging to the Sāṃtapana Maruts, ŚBr.; KātyŚr.; (*ā*), f. (scil. *ishṭi*) a sacrifice offered to the above, Jaim.

Sāṃtāpika, mfn. able to warm or heat, Pāṇ. v, 1, 101.

सान्तर *sântara*, mf(*ā*)n. having an interval or interstices, MBh.; different (opp. to *eka-rūpa*), VarBṛS.; having an intervening clause or appendix, MBh.; not close or compact, open in texture, L.; mixed or mingled with others, L. **–pluta**, n. a manner of jumping, MBh. (= *plavanântaritā gatiḥ*, Nīlak.) **Sāntarôttara**, n. receiving (as a gift) more than one under and upper garment (in contravention of monastic rules), Buddh.

सान्तराय *sântarāya*, mfn. separated by an interval of time from (abl.), Sāh. (*-tā*, f., ib.)

सान्तराल *sântarāla*, mfn. having an interval &c.; together with the intermediate or mixed (castes), Mn. ii, 18.

सान्तर्दीप *sântardīpa*, mf(*ā*)n. having a lamp placed within or inside, Suśr.

सान्तर्देश *sântardeśa*, mfn. together with the intermediate regions, AV.

सान्तर्निदाघज्वरम् *sântarnidāgha-jvaram*, ind. with an internal burning fever, Śāntiś.

सान्तर्हास *sântarhāsa*, mfn. with an inward laugh (*am*, ind.), Megh.; Kathās.

सांतान *sāṃtāna*, mfn. (fr. *sam-tāna*) derived or taken from the Kalpa tree (called Saṃtāna), Hariv.

Sāṃtānika, mf(*ī*)n. stretching, extending, W.; desirous of offspring, Hcat.; = prec., Kir.; m. a Brāhman intending to marry for the sake of issue, W.; (pl.) N. of partic. worlds, MBh.

सान्त्व *sāntv* (also written *śāntv*, q.v.), cl. 10. P. Ā. (Dhātup. xxxii, 33; rather Nom. fr. *sāntva* below) *sāntvayati*, °*te* (pr. p. once in MBh. [viii, 243] *sāntvamāna* and once [vi, 4910] *sāntvayāna*; aor. *asasāntvat*, Gr.; ind. p. *sāntvayitvā*, MBh.; *sāntvayya*, BhP.: Pass. *sāntvyate*, MBh.; Hariv.), to console, comfort, soothe, conciliate, address kindly or gently, Mn.; MBh. &c.

Sāntva, n. (sg. and pl.) consolation, conciliation, mild or gentle language or words, MBh.; Kāv. &c.; mfn. mild, gentle, R.; sweet (as sound), L.; (*ayā*), ind. with mild or kind words, in a gentle manner, BhP. **–tas**, ind. with kind words, Kathās. **–da**, mfn. giving comfort or peace to (gen.), MBh. **–pūrva**, mfn. coaxing, conciliatory (as speech; *am*, ind.), ib. **–vāda**, m. sg. and pl. speaking in a kindly and affectionate manner, Amar.

Sāntvana, n. (sg. and pl.) or °**nā**, f. the act of appeasing or reconciling, soothing with kind words, consolation or conciliation of (gen. or comp.), MBh.; R. &c.

Sāntvanīya, mfn. to be soothed or comforted, serving for soothing or comforting, Car.

Sāntvayitṛi, mfn. one who comforts or speaks or acts kindly, R.

Sāntvita, mfn. soothed, comforted, conciliated, MBh.

सान्दिल्य *sāndilya*, w.r. for *śāṇḍilya*.

सांदीपनि *sāṃdīpani*, m. (fr. *sam-dīpana*) N. of a Muni (accord. to VP. he was the tutor of Kṛishṇa and Bala-rāma, and requested as his preceptor's fee that his son, supposed to be drowned in the sea but kept under the waters by the demon Pañca-jana, should be restored to him; Kṛishṇa plunged into the sea, killed the demon, and brought back the boy to his father), Hariv.; Kād.; Pur.

सांदृष्टिक *sāṃdṛishṭika*, mfn. (fr. *sam-dṛishṭi*) visible or perceptible at the same time, relating to present perception, appearing at once or immediately, L.; evident, undeniable, VarBṛS.; n. (scil. *phala*) present perception of a result, immediate consequence, L.

सान्द्र *sāndra*, mf(*ā*)n. (of unknown derivation) viscid, unctuous, oily, Suśr.; thick, solid, compact, dense, Kāv.; Kathās.; Pur.; strong, vehement, intense, Kālid.; Daś.; Prab.; studded or crowded with, full of (instr. or comp.), Naish.; Prab.; smooth, soft, bland, tender, Kālid.; Vās.; n. a wood, thicket, L.; a heap, cluster, W. **–kutūhala**, mfn. having intense curiosity, MW.; n. N. of a Prahasana. **–tama**, mfn. most compact or dense, Śiś. **–tara**, mfn. more (or most) vehement or intense (*am*, ind.), ib. **–tā**, f. thickness, denseness, vehemence, intensity, Gīt. **–tva**, n. id., MW. **–tvak-ka**, mfn. provided with a thick skin or covering, Śiś. **–pada**, n. a kind of metre, Ked. **–pushpa**, m. 'having thick clustering flowers,' the tree Terminalia Bellerica, L. **–prasāda-meha**, m. a kind of diabetes, Car. **–maṇi**, m. N. of a man, Saṃskārak. **–mūtra**, mfn. discharging a viscous urine, Car. **–meha**, m. a kind of diabetes, ib.; °*hin*, mfn. suffering from it, ib. **–snigdha**, mfn. thick and unctuous, L. **–sparśa**, mfn. unctuous or soft to the touch, Mālav.

Sāndrī, in comp. for *sāndra*. **–kṛita**, mfn. made thick or dense, Ragh.; increased, strengthened, Vās. **–√bhū**, P. *-bhavati*, to become thick, Car.

सांद्राविण *sāṃdrāviṇa*, n. (fr. *sam-drāvin*) running together from all sides, Pāṇ. iii, 3, 44, Sch.

सांध *sāṃdha*, mfn. (fr. *sam-dhi*) situated at the point of contact, Megh., Sch.

1. **Sāṃdhya**, mfn. produced by coalescence (as a syllable), Nir.

सांधिक *sāṃdhika*, m. (fr. *sam-dhā* or *sam-dhikā*) a distiller, L.

सांधिविग्रहिक *sāṃdhivigrahika*, m. (fr. *saṃdhi-vigraha*) a minister who decides upon peace and war, Kāv.; Rājat.

Sāṃdhivela, mfn. (fr. *saṃdhi-velā*), Pāṇ. iv, 3, 16; (*ī*), f. Hibiscus Rosa Sinensis, L.

सांध्य 2. *sāṃdhya*, mfn. (fr. *sam-dhyā*) relating to the evening twilight, vespertine, Kāv.; Kathās.; relating to the morning twilight or dawn, MW. **–kusumā**, f. Hibiscus Rosa Sinensis, L. **–bhojana**, n. an evening meal, Bhpr.

सान्न *sânna*, mf(*ā*)n. together with food, having food, Vishṇ.

सांनत *sāṃnata*, n. (fr. *sam-nati*) N. of two Sāmans, ĀrshBr.

Sāṃnatya, mfn. relating to natural bent or inclination, AAnukr.

सांनहनिक *sāṃnahanika*, mfn. (fr. *sam-nahana*) = next, Śiś.; m. an armour-bearer, shield-bearer, W.

Sāṃnāhika, mfn. (fr. *sam-nāha*) relating to the putting on of armour, preparation for battle, calling to arms (as a drum), MBh.; = next, ib.

Sāṃnāhuka, mfn. able to bear arms, AitBr.

सांनाय्य *sāṃnāyyá*, n. (fr. *sam-√nī*) any substance mixed with clarified butter &c. and offered as a burnt offering or oblation, (esp.) a partic. offering of the Agni-hotṛis (said to consist of milk taken from a cow on the evening of the new moon, mixed on the next day with other milk and offered with clarified butter), TS.; Br.; KātyŚr. **–kumbhī**, f. a jar or receptable for the Sāṃnāyya, ĀpŚr. **–tvá**, n. the being a S°, MaitrS. **–pātra**, n. the pan or receptacle for the S°, ĀpŚr. **–bhājana** (°*yyá-*), mf(*ā*)n. relating to the S°, ŚBr. **–vat**, ind. like (at) the S°, KātyŚr. **Sāṃnāyyôkhā**, f. the pan for the S°, TBr.

सांनिध्य *sāṃnidhya*, n. (fr. *sam-nidhi*) the being near, nearness, vicinity, presence, attendance (acc. with √*kṛi*, 'to make one's appearance, be or become present;' with Caus. of √*kṛi*, 'to cause to be near, call near;' with √*yā* or √*vraj*, 'to come near, approach;' *-pakshe* √*jan* with gen., 'to take the place of'), Mn.; MBh. &c. **–tas**, ind. from proximity, Mālatim. **–tā**, f. vicinity, neighbourhood, Hariv.

सांनिपातिक *sāṃnipātika*, mfn. (fr. *sam-nipāta*) coming into close contact or conjunction, coalescing, GṛŚrS.; complicated (esp. applied to a dangerous illness produced by a combined derangement of the three humours), Suśr. **–karman**, n. the treatment of the above illness, Kāv.; Suśr.; miscellaneous, promiscuous, collective, W.

Sāṃnipātin, mfn. (= *sam-n*°) falling together, meeting (°*ti-tva*, n.), KātyŚr.

Sāṃnipātya, mfn. (= *sam-n*°) to be joined or united, ib.

सांनिवेशिक *sāṃniveśika*, mfn. = *saṃ-niveśam samavaiti*, Pāṇ. iv, 4, 43, Sch.

सांनिहित्य *sāṃnihitya*, n. (fr. *saṃ-nihita*) close vicinity, anything near at hand, Saṃskārak.

सांन्यासिक *sāṃnyāsika*, mfn. (fr. *saṃ-nyāsa*) forming the original or correct text, Pat. on iii, 2, 107, Vārtt. 2; m. a Brāhman in the fourth stage of his life, religious mendicant, L.

सान्मातुर *sānmātura*, m. (cf. *san-m°* and *sāmm°*) the son of a virtuous mother, L.

सान्यपुत्र *sānya-putra*, m. N. of a teacher, Cat.

सान्वय *sânvaya*, mfn. along with family or descendants, Mn. ii, 168 &c.; being of the same family, of kin, related to or closely connected with, ib. viii, 198 ib.; full of meaning, significant, Daś.; having the same business (= *sa-kārya* or *karaṇa-sahita*), BhP. (Sch.); public, in presence of all, Kāty.

सान्वारम्भणीय *sânvārambhaṇīya*, mfn. having the Anvārambhaṇīyā (q.v.), ĀpŚr.

साप् *sāp*, strong form of 2. *sap*, q.v.

सापगम *sâpagama*, mfn. attended with or involving departures, Pañcat.

सापत्न *sāpatná*, mfn. (fr. *sa-patna* or *sa-patnī*) coming or derived from a rival, AV.; based on rivalry (as enmity), MBh.; born of a rival or co-wife; m. (with or without *bhrātṛi*, 'a half-brother on the mother's side'), R.; (pl.) the children of different wives of the same husband, MBh.

Sāpatnaka, n. rivalry among the wives of the same husband, MBh.; rivalry in general, enmity, ib.; Bālar.

Sāpatneya, mf(*ī*)n. born from a rival wife, Kull. on Mn. ix, 198.

Sāpatnya, mf(*ā*)n. based on rivalry (as enmity), Kām.; born from a rival or fellow-wife, R.; m. a half-brother, ib., a rival, enemy, L.; n. enmity or rivalry among wives of the same husband, Śiś.; relationship of children born from different wives of the same husband, R.

Sāpatnyaka, n. rivalry, enmity, Bālar.

सापत्य 1. *sâpatya*, mf(*ā*)n. possessing offspring, having progeny, MBh.; accompanied or attended by one's children, BhP.

सापत्य 2. *sāpatya*, m. = *sāpatnya*, the son of a rival wife, half-brother, Pat. on Pāṇ. vi, 3, 35, Vārtt. 11.

सापत्रप *sâpatrapa*, mf(*ā*)n. ashamed, embarrassed, Śiś.

सापद् *sâpad*, mfn. being in distress or misery, Pañcat.

सापदेशम् *sâpadeśam*, ind. under a pretext or pretence, Daś.

सापमान *sâpamāna*, mfn. treated or attended with contempt, Bhartṛ. (v.l.); (*am*), ind. contemptuously, MW.

सापर *sâpara*, mf(*ā*)n. together with the west, VarBṛS.

सापराध *sâparādha*, mf(*ā*)n. having faults, criminal, guilty, Kathās.; Rājat.; faulty, false, erroneous, VarBṛS., Sch.

सापरान्त *sâparânta*, mfn. together with the country of Aparânta, Kathās.

सापवादक *sâpavādaka*, mfn. having exceptions, liable to exception, Pat.

Sâpavādam, ind. with blame, reproachfully, Mālatīm.

सापह्नव *sâpahnava*, mf(*ā*)n. with dissimulation, dissembling, feigning, MBh.; Kathās.; dissembled, concealed, veiled, Sāh.

सापाय *sâpâya*, mf(*ā*)n. one who contends with adversity, Daśar.; attended with danger, dangerous, Kāv.; Pañcat.; Rājat.

सापाश्रय *sâpâśraya*, n. (scil. *vāstu*) a house with an open gallery at the back, VarBṛS.

सापिण्ड *sāpiṇḍa*, n. = *sāpiṇḍya*, Dattakac.

Sāpiṇḍi, m. (prob.) patr. fr. *sa-piṇḍa*, g. *aishukāry-ādi*. — **bhakta**, mfn. inhabited by Sāpiṇḍis, ib.

Sāpiṇḍī-mañjarī, f. N. of a wk. on law by Nāgêśa.

Sāpiṇḍya, n. (fr. *sa-piṇḍa*) connection or relationship by presenting offerings to the same deceased ancestors, consanguinity or relationship of a Sapiṇḍa, Saṃskārak.; Dattakac. — **kalpalatā**, f., -**kalpalatikā**, f., -**dīpikā**, f., -**nirṇaya**, m., -**mīmāṇsā**, f., -**vishaya**, m. N. of wks.

सापीड *sâpīḍa*, mfn. (perhaps w.r. for *sôtp°*) emitting or discharging a stream of water, R.

सापेक्ष *sâpêksha*, mfn. having regard or respect to (loc. or acc. with *prati*), MBh.; R.; requiring or presupposing anything, dependent on (comp.), Kathās.; Sāh.; Sarvad. — **tā**, f., -**tva**, n. dependence on, Sāh.; Sarvad.

साप्त 1. *sâpta* or *sāptá*, n. (fr. *saptan*, of which it is also the Vṛiddhi form in comp.) the number seven, a heptade, RV.; TS.; a team of seven horses (accord. to others m. and a proper N.), RV. viii, 55, 5. — **tantava**, m. pl. (fr. *sapta-tantu*) N. of a partic. sect, Vās., Introd. — **daśya**, n. (fr. *sapta-daśan*) the number seventeen, ŚāṅkhŚr. — **pada**, mfn. (fr. *sapta-pada*) belonging to seven steps, based or depending on seven steps (= 'sincere,' 'true'), MBh.; Pañcat.; BrahmaP. — **padīna**, mfn. = prec., Bālar.; n. friendship (formed with any one after taking seven paces together, or, accord. to others, after uttering only seven words), intimacy, Kum.; Pañcat.; circumambulation of the nuptial fire by the bride and bridegroom in seven steps, advance of the bride to meet the bridegroom in seven steps, MW. — **purusha**, mfn. (fr. *sapta-p°*) extending to or comprising seven generations, Saṃskārak. — **paurusha**, mf(*ī*)n. (fr. id.) = prec., Mn. iii, 146. — **rathavāhani**, m. a patr., ŚBr. — **rātrika**, mf(*ī*)n. (fr. *sapta-rātra*) lasting seven nights or days, SāmavBr.; Hariv.

Sāptatika, mfn. (fr. *saptati*) worth seventy &c., Pāṇ. v, 1, 19, Sch.

Sāptamika, mfn. (fr. *saptamī*) relating to the seventh day, Lāṭy.; relating to the seventh case, RPrāt.; taught in the seventh (Adhyāya of Pāṇini's grammar), Pat.

Sāptalāyana, m. patr. fr. *saptala*, g. *naḍâdi*.

Sāptaleya, mfn. (fr. id.), g. *sakhy-ādi*.

Sāpti, m. patr. fr. *saptan*, g. *bāhv-ādi*.

साप्त 2. *sāpta*, n. (fr. *sapti*) a horse-race, running-match for horses or the prize given for one, RV. ii, 19, 7.

साप्य *sāpyá*, m. patr. of Namī (v.l. *sāyyá*), RV.; PañcavBr.

साप्राय्य *sāprāyya*, n. (fr. *sa-prāya*) likeness, homogeneousness, Lāṭy.

साप्सरोगण *sâpsaro-gaṇa*, mfn. attended by a number of Apsarases, MW.

साफल्य *sāphalya*, n. (fr. *sa-phala*) fruitfulness, profitableness, advantage, result, success, Mn.; MBh. &c.

साबर्णिक *sābarṇika*(?), a proper N., Rājat.

साबाध *sâbādha*, mfn. suffering pain, unwell, Śak.

साब्दी *sābdī*, f. a kind of grape, L.

साब्रह्मचार *sābrahmacāra*, n. (fr. *sa-brahmacārin*), g. *yuvâdi*.

साभयदक्षिणम् *sâbhaya-dakshiṇam*, ind. with the gift of fearlessness or security, Jātakam.

साभापत *sābhāpata*, mfn. (fr. *sabhā-pati*), g. *aśvapaty-ādi*.

साभाव्य *sābhāvya*, n. (fr. *sa-bhāva*) homogeneousness, identity of nature, Bādar.

साभासंनयन *sābhāsaṃnayana*, mfn. (fr. *sabhā-s°*), Pat. on Pāṇ. i, 1, 73, Vārtt. 2.

साभिकाम *sâbhikāma*, mf(*ā*)n. having affection, loving, affectionate, Nal.

साभिचरणिक *sâbhicaraṇika*, mfn. possessing the same rules for exorcising or counteracting enchantments, ĀpŚr.

साभिज्ञान *sâbhijñāna* (ibc. or *am*, ind.), together with tokens of recognition, Megh.; Kathās. — **yuta**, mfn. furnished with tokens of r°, Pañcad.

साभिताप *sâbhitāpa*, mfn. suffering pain, distressed, afflicted, Kathās.

साभिनयम् *sâbhinayam*, ind. with dramatic gesture or gesticulations, pantomimically, Śak.

साभिनिवेश *sâbhiniveśa*, mfn. having or attended with a great inclination or predilection for anything, Sāh.

साभिप्राय *sâbhiprâya*, mfn. having a distinct aim or purpose, persevering, resolute, Kathās.; betraying a certain purpose, intentional, Pañcat.

साभिमान *sâbhimāna*, mf(*ā*)n. having pride, haughty, proud of (loc.; *am*, ind.), R.; Kathās.; Pañcat.; causing pride or self-satisfaction, MBh.; self-interested, egoistical (as an action), SārṅgP.

साभिलाष *sâbhilāsha*, mf(*ā*)n. having a desire or longing for (loc., acc. with *prati*, or comp.; *am*, ind.), Śak.; Kathās.; MārkP.

साभिशङ्क *sâbhiśaṅka*, mfn. distrustful, suspicious, Jātakam.

साभिसंस्कारपरिनिर्वायिन् *sâbhisaṃskāra-parinirvāyin*, mfn. (said of a kind of Anāgāmin, q.v.), Buddh.

साभिसर *sâbhisara*, mfn. along with followers or companions, Hcar.; Śiś.

साभ्यर्थन *sâbhyarthana*, mfn. with entreaties, Kād.

साभ्यसूय *sâbhyasūya*, mfn. envious, malicious, jealous of (loc.; *am*, ind.), Ragh.; Śiś.

साभ्यास *sâbhyāsa*, mfn. reduplicated, Nir.

साभ्र *sâbhra*, mfn. having clouds, cloudy, Megh. — **matī**, f. N. of a river flowing through Ahmedābād (commonly 'Sabermattee'), Śatr.; -*māhātmya*, N. of wk. — **vatī**, f. = -*matī*, Siṇhās.

साभ्रङ्गिका *sābhraṅgikā*, f. a kind of metre, Col.

साभ्रि *sâbhri*, mfn. together with a hoe or spade, KātyŚr.

साम् *sām*. See 1. *sāmaya*, p. 1205, col. 1.

साम 1. *sāma*, n. (fr. 1. *sama*, of which it is also the Vṛiddhi form in comp.) likeness, similarity, L. — **pushpi**, m. (prob. fr. *sama-pushpa*) a patr., Pravar. — **yugina**, mfn. (fr. *sama-yuga*), g. *pratijanâdi*. — **vaśa**, mfn. serving for or caused by the equality of the metre, RPrāt. — **stambi**, m. (prob. fr. *sama-stamba*) a patr., Pravar. — **sthya**, n. (fr. *sama-stha*) comfort, ease, welfare, g. *brāhmaṇâdi*.

Sāmācārika, mfn. (fr. *samācāra*), g. *vinayâdi*.

Sāmācārī, f. (fr. id.) customary practice or usage, right conduct or behaviour, HPariś.

1. **Sāmaka**, n. (for 2. see p. 1205, col. 2) the principal of a debt, Vishṇ.; m. (thought by some to be for *śāmaka* fr. √*śo*) a whetstone (esp. one for sharpening spindles), L.

Sāmātsāmya, n. (fr. *samāt-sama*) a series or succession of equal or similar beginnings and terminations, Lāṭy.

साम 2. *sâma*, mfn. undigested, crude, not sufficiently prepared or matured (a morbid state of the humours), Car.; Bhpr.

सामक्ष *sāmaksha*, n. (fr. *sam-aksha*) the being before the eyes, MaitrS.

Sāmakshya, n. id., TBr.; PañcavBr. (wrongly printed *sāmyaksha*).

सामग्री *sāmagrī*, f. (fr. *sam-agra*) totality, entirety, completeness, (esp.) a complete collection or assemblage of implements or materials, apparatus, baggage, goods and chattels, furniture, effects, Rājat.; Kathās.; Sarvad.; a means for (*kā te sāmagrī*, 'what means have you at your disposal?'), Hit. — **pratibadhyatā**, f., -**pratibandhakatā-vāda**, m., -**vāda**, m., -**vādârtha**, m., -**vicāra**, m., -**vyāpti**, f., -**vyāpti-vicāra**, m., -**sahacāra**, m. N. of wks.

Sāmagrya, n. = *sāmagrī*, MBh.; Hariv. &c.

सामञ्जस्य *sāmañjasya*, n. (fr. *sam-añjasa*) fitness, propriety, equity, justice, R. (B.), Sch. (*a-s°* Vedântas., Sch.)

सामन् 1. sā́man, n. (fr. √1. sā = 1. san) acquisition, possession, property, wealth, abundance, RV.; VS.

1. **Sāmana**, mf(*ā*)n. (for 2. see under 2. *sāman*) rich, affluent, abundant (others 'common, universal'), RV. iii, 30, 9.

सामन् 2. sā́man, n. (m. only in TBr.; prob. connected with √*sāntv;* accord. to some fr. √1. *sā;* cf. 3. *sāman*) calming, tranquillizing, (esp.) kind or gentle words for winning an adversary, conciliation, negotiation (one of the 4 Upâyas or means of success against an enemy, the other 3 being *dāna, bheda,* and *daṇḍa,* qq. vv.; ibc. or instr. sg. and pl., 'by friendly means or in a friendly way, willingly, voluntarily'), TBr. &c. &c.

3. **Sāma**, in comp. for 2. *sāman.* — **kalam**, ind. in a conciliatory or friendly tone, VP. — **gir**, mfn. speaking kind words, Śatr. — **dharmârtha-nīti-mat**, mfn. friendly and just and useful and wise (as speech), R. — **pūrva**, mfn. friendly, kind, gentle (*am,* ind.), R. — **pradhāna**, mfn. perfectly kind or friendly, Car. — **prayoga**, m. the use of kind or frº words, Dhātup. — **vāda**, m. a kind word, conciliatory speech, Śiś. — **sādhya**, mfn. to be accomplished in a conciliatory or peaceable way, Pañcat. — **siddha**, mfn. accomplished in a pº way, ib. — **siddhi**, f. the art of accomplishing something in a pº way, MW. **Sāmônmukha**, mfn. eager for conciliation, wishing to conciliate, ib. **Sāmôpacāra** or º**pâya**, m. a mild remedy, moderate measure, gentle means, ib.

2. **Sāmaná**, mfn. (for 1. see under 1. *sāman*) quiet, calm, RV. x, 85, 9.

1. **Sāmanya**, mfn. (for 2. see col. 2) friendly, favourable (in *a-s*º, q.v.)

1. **Sāmaya** (Nom. fr. *sāman* or fr. artificial √*sām;* for 2. *sâmaya* see col. 3), cl. 10. P. *sāmayati* (aor. *asasāmat* or *asīshamat*), to conciliate, appease, pacify, tranquillize, Dhātup. xxxv, 27.

सामन् 3. sā́man, n. (of doubtful derivation; accord. to Uṇ. iv, 152 fr. √*so* = 2. *sā,* as 'destroying sin;' in Nir. vii, 12 apparently connected with *sammita;* by others derived fr. √1. *san, sā, sāntv,* and perhaps not to be separated fr. 1. and 2. *sāman*) a metrical hymn or song of praise, (esp.) a partic. kind of sacred text or verse called a Sāman (intended to be chanted, and forming, with *ṛic, yajus, chandas,* one of the 4 kinds of Vedic composition mentioned first in RV. x, 90, 9), RV. &c. &c.; any song or tune (sacred or profane, also 'the hum of bees'), MBh.; Kāv. &c.; the faculty of uttering sounds (?), TBr. (Sch.) — **vat** (*sā́man-*), mfn. connected with a Sāman, TS. — **vin**, mfn. possessing the Sº, JaimBr.

4. **Sāma**, in comp. for 3. *sāman.* — **kārikā** (?), f. N. of wk. — **kārin**, mfn. making Sāmans, Shaḍv-Br. — **gá** or -**gā́**, m. a Brāhman who chants or recites the Sº-veda, RV. &c. &c.; (*ī*), f. the wife of a Sº-veda Brāhman, L.; *-gānām chandas,* n. a Pariśishṭa of the Sº-veda; (*-ga*)*-pūrvâpara,* m. or n., *-prayoga,* m., *-vṛishôtsarga,* m., º*gâhnika,* n. N. of wks. — **gaṇa**, m. the Sº collectively, IndSt. — **garbha**, m. N. of Vishṇu, L. — **gā**, see *-ga.* — **gāna**, m. a chanter of Sº, Cat.; n. Sº chant, KātyŚr.; *-priya,* m. N. of Śiva, Śivag. — **gāya**, m. Sº chant, Yājñ. iii, 112. — **gāyaka**, m. = *-ga,* MW. — **gāyin**, mfn. chanting the Sāma-veda, Saṃskārak. — **gīta**, n. = *-gāya,* MBh.; (also applied to the hum of bees), BhP. — **codanā**, f. an invitation to recite the Sāma-veda, ĀpŚr. — **ja**, mfn. occurring in the Sº-veda, Śiś.; m. an elephant, L. — **jāta**, m. an elephant, Śiś. — **jātaka**, n. N. of a Buddhist Sūtra. — **tantra**, n. N. of wk. (also *-bhāshya* and *-saṃgraha*). — **tás**, ind. from or concerning Sāma chants, ŚBr. — **tejas** (*sā́ma-*), mfn. having the glory of a Sāman, AV. — **tvá**, n. state or condition of (being) a Sº, ŚBr. — **darpaṇa**, m. N. of wk. — **dhvani**, m. the sound of the chanting of the Sº-veda, Mn. iv, 123 (see under *-veda,* col. 2). — **nidhaná**, n. the closing sentence of a Sº, ŚBr. — **patha**, m. the path of the Sº, JaimBr. — **pariśishṭa**, n. a Pariśishṭa belonging to the Sº-vº. — **pavitra**, n. N. of Sº-vº i, 2, 2, 3, 5, Āpast. — **prakāśana**, n. N. of wk. — **pragātha**, m. N. of partic. verses to be chanted by the three Hotrakas, Vait. — **prayoga**, m., **-prastotṛi-tva**, n., **-brāhmaṇa**, n. N. of wks. — **bhṛit**, mfn. bringing chants, RV. — **máya**, mf(*ī*)n. consisting of Sāmans, Br.; Up. — **yoni**, mfn. produced from the Sº-veda, Ragh.; m. an elephant, ib.; a Brāhman, L. — **rathaṃtara**, n. N. of a Sāman (said to have been created from Brahmā's mouth), MW. — **rāga**, m. a tune or air of the Sº-veda, Pāṇ. v, 2, 130, Sch. — **rāja**, m. N. of a king and various authors (also with *dīkshita*), Cat.; n. N. of a Sāman, Lāṭy. — **rājan**, n. N. of a Sº, PañcavBr. — **lakshaṇa**, n. N. of wk. — **vat**, mfn. connected with a Sº, TS., Sch.; m. N. of a son of Sārasvata (afterwards changed into a female), Cat. — **vid**, mfn. knowing the Sº-vº, Vait. — **vidhāna**, n. the employment of Sāmans (for religious or magical purposes), AgP.; *-brāhmaṇa,* n. N. of a Brāhmaṇa of the Sº-veda (and also called *sāma-vidhi*). — **vipra** (*sā́ma-*), mfn. skilled in Sāma chants, RV. — **vedá**, m. 'Veda of chants,' N. of one of the three principal Vedas (see *veda;* it contains a number of verses or stanzas nearly all of which [except about 78] occur in the Ṛig-veda and which, modified in various ways, are chanted, mostly, by the Udgātṛi priests at Soma sacrifices; the Saṃhitā of the Sāma-veda consists of two parts; the first, called Ārcika [or Pūrvârcika or Chando-grantha], contains 585 verses disjoined from their proper sequence in the Ṛig-veda and arranged in 59 Daśatis or decades, which again are subdivided into Prapāṭhakas and Ardha-prapāṭhakas; the second, called Uttarârcika or Uttarā-grantha, contains 1225 verses, also chiefly from the Ṛik-saṃhitā, but less disjointed than in the first part, and arranged in nine Prapāṭhakas with Ardha-prapāṭhakas, mostly, however, grouped in triplets; the directions for the formation of Sāmans or chants out of these verses are carefully laid down in the Gānas or manuals for chanting, two of which, viz. the Geya-gāna and Āraṇya-gº, are a directory for the Ārcika portion, and two, viz. Ūha-gº and Ūhya-gāna, for the Uttarârcikā; in Mn. i, 23 the Sāma-veda is described as drawn forth from the sun; in iv, 124 it is described as having a special reference to the Pitṛis or deceased ancestors, and its sound is therefore said to possess a kind of impurity, whereas the Ṛig-veda has the gods for his objects and the Yajur-veda men; the Sāma-veda is said to possess 8 Brāhmaṇas [see *brāhmaṇa*], Br.; ŚāṅkhŚr. &c. [IW. 25]; *-cchala,* n., *-pariśishṭa,* n., *-rahasya,* n., *-rahasyôpanishad,* f. N. of wks.; *-rāj,* m. N. of Vishṇu, Pañcar.; *-vid,* mfn. familiar with the Sº-vº; *-śikshā,* f. N. of a Śikshā; *-sāra,* m. N. of Vishṇu, Pañcar.; º*dântaga,* mfn. one who has gone through the Sº-vº, MBh.; º*dârtha,* m., º*dârtha-prakāśa,* m. N. of wks.; º*dīya-rudrī,* f., º*dīya-raudra-vidhi,* m., º*dôpanishad,* f. N. of wks. — **vaidika**, mfn. relating or belonging to the Sº-vº, KātyŚr., Sch. — **vairya**, n. the strength (?) of the Sº, JaimBr. — **śabda**, m. the sound of a chanted Sº, Gaut.; GṛS. — **śiras**, mfn. having the Sº as head, KaushUp. — **śravás**, m. N. of a man (pupil of Yājñavalkya), ŚBr. — **śravasa**, m. patr. fr. prec., PañcavBr. — **śrāddha**, n. N. of a ch. of the Smṛiti-tattva (also *-tattva*). — **śrauta-sūtra**, n. N. of wk. — **saṃhitā**, f. the continuous text of the Sº-veda, Hariv. — **saṃkshepa**, m. N. of a treatise on the Sº-veda. — **saṃkhyā**, f. N. of a Pariśishṭa of the Sº-veda. — **saṃgāyaka**, m. a chanter of the Sº-veda, W. — **saras** and **-sarasa**, n. N. of two Sāmans, ĀrshBr. — **sāvitrī**, f. N. of a partic. Sāvitrī, Gobh. — **surasa**, n. du., v.l. for *-saras.* — **sūkta**, n. N. of partic. hymns, Vait. — **sūtra**, n. a Sūtra wk. belonging to the Sº-vº (10 such works are enumerated), Cat.; *-vyākhyā,* f. N. of wk. **Sāmâṅga**, n. an Aṅga or part of the Sº-vº, NṛisUp. **Sāmâtāna**, m. = *sāma-pragātha,* ŚāṅkhŚr. **Sāmânta**, m. the end of a Sāman, Lāṭy. **Sāmântar-ukthya**, m. an Ukthya (q.v.) in a Sº, ŚāṅkhŚr. **Sāmêśvara-māhātmya**, n. N. of wk. **Sāmôdha**, mfn. having the Sº accent, Lāṭy. **Sāmôdbhava**, m. an elephant (cf. *sāma-jāta*), L.

5. **Sāma** (ifc.) = 3. *sāman* (see *anu-, ava-s*º).

2. **Sāmaka**, mf(*ikā*)n. (for 1. see p. 1204, col. 3) = *sāma adhīte veda vā,* g. *kramâdi.*

2. **Sāmanya**, mfn. (for 1. see col. 1) skilful in chanting or singing, RV.; Bhaṭṭ.

1. **Sāmika**, mfn. (for 2. see p. 1206, col. 2), (fr. 3. *sāman*), Lāṭy.; n. pronouncing verses over the sacrificial animal, L.

Sāmna, mf(*ī*)n. relating to Sāmans, IndSt.; (*ī*), f. a sort of metre (one of the classes occurring in the Sāma-veda); (*ī*), f. (cf. *sāmanī*) a rope for tying cattle, MW.

सामनसी sāmanasī, f. a verse containing the word *samanas,* ĀpŚr.

सामनी sāmanī, f. (cf. *sāmnī*) a rope or cord for tying cattle (v.l. *dāmanī*), L.

सामन्त sāmanta, mfn. (fr. *sam-anta*) being on all sides, KātyŚr.; bordering, limiting, W.; m. a neighbour, Kāṭh.; Mn.; Yājñ.; a vassal, feudatory prince, the chief of a district (paying tribute to a lord paramount), Mn.; MBh. &c.; a minister (?), Cāṇ. (v.l.); a leader, general, captain, champion, W.; N. of the author of the Tājika-sāra-ṭīkā (1620 A. D.), Cat.; n. a neighbourhood, Mn.; Śukas. — **cakra**, n. a circle of neighbouring princes, MW. — **ja**, n. (danger) arising from a vassal, Hariv. — **pāla**, m. N. of a king, Campak. — **pratyaya**, m. the evidence or testimony of near neighbours, MW. — **rāja**, m. (with *hari*) N. of the author of the Sūrya-prakāśa, Cat. — **vāsin**, mfn. dwelling on the borders, neighbouring, a neighbour, Mn. viii, 258.

Sāmantakena, ind. in the neighbourhood, Karaṇḍ.

Sāmanteya, m. N. of a man (v.l. *māmateya*), BhP.

सामय 2. sâmaya, mfn. (for 1. see col. 1) connected with or suffering from disease, Śaṃk.

सामयाचारिक sāmayācārika, mfn. (fr. *samayâcāra*) relating to conventional practice or usage, Gaut.; Āpast. — **sūtra**, n. N. of partic. Sūtras (treating of customs and rites sanctioned by virtuous men, and with the Gṛihya-sūtras, constituting the Smārta-sūtras which are based on Smṛiti or tradition, and opp. to the Śrauta-sūtras derived from Śruti, q.v.), IW. 145 &c.

Sāmayika, mfn. (fr. *sam-aya*) based on agreement, conventional, customary, Kaṇ.; Yājñ.; Nyāyam., Sch.; of the same opinion, like-minded, Rājat.; seasonable, timely, precise, exact, Mālav. (v.l.); Kir. (in *a-s*º); periodical, MW.; temporary, Sāṃkhyapr. — **tva**, n. conventionality, Nyāyam. **Sāmayikâbhāva**, m. temporary non-existence (as that of a water-jar which has been removed from its place to be again restored to it), MW.

सामर sâmara, mfn. with the immortals, accompanied by the gods, R.; BhP. **Sâmarâdhipa**, mfn. together with the lords of the gods, R.

सामरिक sāmarika, mfn. (fr. *sam-ara*) belonging to war or battle, martial, warlike, MW.

Sāmareya, mfn. (fr. id.), g. *sakhy-ādi.*

सामर्घ्य sāmarghya, n. (fr. *sam-argha*) cheapness, VarBṛS.

सामर्थ्य sāmarthya, n. (fr. *sam-artha*) sameness of aim or object or meaning or signification, belonging or agreeing together (in aim, object &c.), adequacy, accordance, fitness, suitableness, Pat.; Hariv.; Suśr. &c.; the being entitled to, justification for (loc. or comp.), MBh.; R. &c.; ability to or capacity for (inf., dat., loc., or comp.; acc. with √*kṛi,* 'to do one's utmost;' with √*bhaj,* 'to take pains,' 'exert one's self'), ib.; efficacy, power, strength, force (*āt* or *-tas* or *-yogāt,* 'through the force of circumstances,' 'by reason of,' 'in consequence of,' 'on account of,' 'as a matter of course'), ib.; the force or function or sense of a word, Kusum. — **bandhana**, mfn. having power as a bond of union, cemented by or contingent on power or fitness, MW. — **yoga**, see above. — **vat**, mfn. having power or strength, capable, MBh. — **hīna**, mfn. destitute of strength, weak, feeble, Hit.

सामर्ष sâmarsha, mfn. having impatience or anger, impatient, indignant, wrathful, enraged at (*prati*), Kāv.; Kathās. &c.; (*am*), ind. angrily, Mṛicch. — **tā**, f. angry impatience, wrath, Ragh. — **hāsam**, ind. with an ironical smile or laugh, MW.

Sâmarshaṇa, m. pl. N. of a family of Brāhmans (v.l. *agha-m*º), VP.

सामवायिक sāmavāyika, mfn. (fr. *samavâya*) belonging to or frequenting an assembly, Pāṇ. iv, 4, 43; closely connected with anything, concomitant, inherent, KātyŚr.; m. a minister or counsellor, Śiś.; member of an assembly, spectator, Mālav. (v.l. for *sāmājika*); chief of a company, W.

सामस्त sāmasta, n. (fr. *sam-asta*) the science or theory of word-composition, Pat. on Pāṇ. iv, 2, 104, Vārtt. 12.

Sāmastika, mfn. relating to the above, ib.

Sāmastya, n. totality, entirety, ŚāṅkhŚr., Sch.

सामाजिक *sāmājika*, mfn. (fr. *sam-āja*) relating to or frequenting an assembly, Pāṇ. iv, 4, 43; m. a member of or assistant at an assembly, spectator, Kāv.; Sāh. &c.

सामात्य *sā́mātya*, mfn. together with the inmates of the same house, ĀśvGṛ.; accompanied by ministers or counsellors, MBh. **-pramukha**, mfn. with the chief ministers, W.

Sâmātyaka, m. accompanied by ministers &c., R.

सामात्साम्य *sāmātsāmya*. See p. 1204, col. 3.

सामान *sāmāna*, Vṛiddhi form of 2. *samāna* in comp. **-grāmika**, mfn. (fr. *samāna-grāma*) belonging to or being in the same village &c., Pat. on Pāṇ. ii, 3, 60, Vārtt. 1. **-deśika**, mfn. coming or derived from the same village, ib. **Sāmānâdhikaraṇya**, n. (fr. *samānâdhikaraṇa*) common office or function, Hit.; the condition of relating to the same object or residing in the same subject, Sarvad.; grammatical agreement, identity of case-relation, correlation (opp. to *vaiyadh*°), Pāṇ., Sch.

Sāmānika, mfn. (fr. 2. *samāna*) of equal rank or dignity with (gen. or comp.), HPariś.; Pañcad.

Sāmānya, mf(*ā*)n. equal, alike, similar, MBh.; Śak.; shared by others, joint, common to (instr. with and without *saha*, or comp.), Yājñ.; MBh.; Suśr. &c.; whole, entire, universal, general, generic, not specific (opp. to *vaiśeshika*), Suśr.; VarBṛS.; common, common-place, vulgar, ordinary, insignificant, low, MBh.; Kāv. &c.; (*am*), n. equality, similarity, identity, MBh.; Suśr. &c.; equilibrium, normal state or condition, Nilak.; universality, totality, generality, general or fundamental notion, common or generic property (ibc., instr., or abl., 'in general,' as opp. to *viśesha-tas*, 'in particular'), Kaṇ.; Jaim.; Sarvad.; public affairs or business, W.; (in rhet.) the connection of different objects by common properties, Kpr.; Kuval.; (*ā*), f. a common female, prostitute, L.; (*am*), ind. after the same manner as, like (comp.), Kālid.; jointly, in general, in common, Mn. vii, 56. **-kavi-praśaṃsā**, f. praise of poets in general (not of single ones), Cat. **-krama-vṛitti**, f., **-ghaṭa**, m., **-candrikā**, f. N. of wks. **-cchala**, n. one of the three Vāk-chalas (i. e. too great generalization of the words of an opponent), Nyāyad.; Car. **-jñāna**, n. the perception of common or generic property, MW. **-tama**, mfn. most like or similar, GṛŚrS. **-tara**, mfn. more common, ib.; very common-place or insignificant, Pañcat. **-tas**, ind. equally, similarly, according to analogy, BhP.; KapS.; Sāṃkhyak.; in general, generally, Kaṇ.; Suśr.; BhP., Sch.; (*-to*)*-drishṭa*, n. (scil. *anumāna*; in log.) a partic. kind of induction or inference (e. g. generalizing from every day occurrences; accord. to the Sāṃkhya and Nyāya it furnishes evidence of what transcends the senses, such as the paths of the heavenly bodies, the existence of air, ether, soul, space, time &c.), generalization from particulars, Nyāyad. **-tva**, n. the state of generality, Kusum. **-deśa-vat**, ind. like any other country, Rājat. **-dhātrī**, f. a common nurse or foster-mother, Ragh. **-nāyikā**, f. = *-vanitā*, Sch. **-nirukti**, f. explanation of the meaning or idea of *sāmānya*, Cat.; N. of various wks.; *-kroḍa*, m., *-grantha-rahasya*, n., *-granthârtha*, m., *-ṭīkā*, f., *-dīdhiti-ṭīkā*, f., *-dvitīya-lakshaṇa*, n., *-pattra*, n., *-prathama-lakshaṇa*, n., *-lakshaṇa*, n., *-vivecana*, n., *-vyākhyā*, f.; °*ty-anugama*, m., °*ty-abhinava-vyākhyā*, f. N. of wks. **-paksha**, m. the general side, the middle or mean (between two extremes), MW. **-padârtha**, m. the category of Generality, ib. **-pūrvam**, ind. similarly, analogously, Kāty-Śr. **-praghaṭṭaka**, N. of part of a wk. **-prati-patti-pūrvam**, ind. after an equal elevation, after elevating to a common rank, MW. **-bhāva**, m., **-bhāva-grantha**, m., **-bhāva-ṭippaṇī**, f., **-bhāva-vyavasthâpana**, n. N. of wks. **-lakshaṇa**, n. a generic definition or sign, a definition comprising many individuals, a specific characteristic, W.; N. of various wks.; (*ā*), f. (in Nyāya) one of the three A-laukika or transcendental perceptions or Saṃnikarshas, MW.; N. of various wks.; (*ī*), f. N. of wk.; (°*ṇa*)*-kārya-kāraṇa-bhāva*, m., *-vyabhicāra*, m.; (°*ṇā*)*-grantha*, m., *-ṭippaṇī*, f., *-dīdhiti-ṭippaṇī*, f., *-dīdhiti-ṭīkā*, f., *-pūrva-paksha-prakāśa*, m., *-prakāśa*, m., *-rahasya*, n., *-vicāra*, m., *-vivecana*, n., *-vyabhicāra*, m. N. of wks. **-vacana**, mfn. expressing a common property, Pāṇ. ii, 1, 55; expressing a general or a wider notion, ib. iii, 4, 5; n. a substantive (as opp. to its attribute), Sāy. **-vat**, mfn. having generality, general (*-tva*, n.), Sarvad.; Kusum. **-vanitā**, f. a common woman, prostitute, MW. **-vāda**, m., **-vihita-dravya-vicāra**, m. N. of wks. **-śabda** (MBh.) or °**daka** (Cat.), m. a word of general meaning. **-śāsana**, n. a general edict or enactment, W. **-śāstra**, n. a general rule (in gram. = *utsarga*), MW. **-śrāddha-vidhi**, m., **-sūtra**, n., **-homa-paddhati**, f. N. of wks. **Sāmānyâdhikaraṇya**, w. r. for *sāmānâdh*° (q. v.)

Sāmānyâbhāva, m. N. of a Nyāya wk.; *-grantha*, m., *-ṭippaṇī*, f., *-prakāśa*, m., *-rahasya*, n., *-sādhana*, n.; °*vâloka*, m. N. of wks.

सामायिक *sāmāyika*, n. (fr. *samāya* = *samaya*) equanimity, HPariś.

सामासिक *sāmāsika*, mf(*ī*)n. (fr. *sam-āsa*) comprehensive, concise, succinct, brief, Mn.; BhP.; relating or belonging to a Samāsa or compound word, Pat.; m. or n. a compound word, Bhag.

सामि *sāmí*, ind. (g. *svar-ādi*) too soon, prematurely (with √*mush*, 'to steal in anticipation'), MaitrS.; TS.; Br.; incompletely, imperfectly, partially, half (often in comp. with a p. p., Pāṇ. ii, 1, 27), ib. &c. &c. [Cf. Gk. ἡμι-, ἥμισυς; Lat. *sēmi*, *sēmis*.] **-kṛita**, mfn. half-done, h°-finished, Śiś. **-gandharvá**, w. r. for *sāmi g*° (two words), MaitrS. **-cita** (*sā́mi-*), mfn. half piled up, ŚBr. **-pīta**, mfn. half-drunk, Kāś. on Pāṇ. ii, 1, 27. **-bhukta**, mfn. half-eaten, Ragh. **-saṃsthita** (*sāmí-*), mfn. half-finished, ŚBr.

सामिक 2. *sāmika* (?), m. (for 1. see p. 1205, col. 2) a tree, L.

सामित *sāmita*, mfn. (fr. *samitā*) made from or mixed with wheat-flour, Suśr.

सामित्य *sāmityá*, mfn. (fr. *sam-iti*) relating to an assembly or council, AV.

सामिधेन *sāmidhená*, mfn. (fr. *sam-idh*) relating to fuel and the kindling of the sacrificial fire, ŚBr.; (*ī*), f. (scil. *ṛic*) a verse recited while the sacrificial fire is kindled, VS.; Br.; MBh.; fuel, HPariś.

Sāmidheni, f. = *sāmidhenī*, Kauś.

Sāmidhenika (ifc.), id., ŚaṅkhBr.

Sāmidhenya, mfn. = *sāmidhena*, Vārtt. on Pāṇ. iv, 3, 120.

सामिन् *sāmin*, m. (? derivation) a person born under a partic. constellation (v. l. *sāvin*), VarBṛS.

सामिष *sâmisha*, mf(*ā*)n. possessed of flesh or prey, BhP.; provided with meat (as a Śrāddha), Mn. iv, 131.

सामीची *sāmīcī*, f. (fr. *samyañc*) praise, panegyric (= *vandanā*), L.; decency, politeness, civility, Mahāvy. **-karaṇīya**, mfn. to be civilly saluted, ib.

Sāmīcīnya, n. propriety, fitness, Kāv.

सामीप्य *sāmīpya*, mfn. (fr. *samīpa*) neighbouring, a neighbour, MBh.; n. neighbourhood, nearness, proximity (in space and time), Sāṃkhyak.; Sāh.; BhP.; nearness to the deity (as one of the four states of beatitude; cf. *sālokya*), MW.

सामीरण *sāmīraṇa*, mfn. (fr. *sam-īraṇa*) relating to the wind, Bālar.

Sāmīrya, mfn. (fr. *sam-īra*), g. *saṃkāśâdi*.

सामुत्कर्षिक *sāmutkarshika*, mf(*ī*)n. (fr. *sam-utkarsha*) most excellent, Buddh.

सामुदयिक *sāmudayika*, n. (m. c.) = next, VarYogay.

Sāmudāyika, n. (fr. *sam-udāya*) the eighteenth Nakshatra after that in which the moon was situated at the birth of a child, L.; mfn. belonging to a multitude or assemblage, collective, MW.

सामुदानिक *sāmudānika*, m. or n. (?) = *bhaiksha*, Śīl.

सामुद्ग *sāmudga*, m. (fr. *samudga*; cf. *mudga*) a joint with a socket like a cup (e. g. the shoulder-joint, hip-joint), Suśr.; n. medicine taken before and after a meal (and, as it were, enclosing the food), ib.

सामुद्र 1. *sāmudra*, mfn. (fr. *sam-udra*) relating to the sea, oceanic, marine, Kauś.; Suśr.; MBh. &c.; Vāgbh.; declared or related by Samudra, MW.; m. a mariner, voyager, sailor, Yājñ.; the son of a Karaṇa and a Vaiśyā (who lives from the produce of the sea), L.; a kind of gnat, Suśr.; patr. of Citra-sena, MBh.; (pl.) N. of a people, R.; (*ī*), f. N. of the daughter of Samudra and wife of Prācīna-barhis, Hariv.; Pur.; n. sea-salt, Car.; a cuttle-fish bone, L.; du. (with *Agneḥ*) N. of two Sāmans, ĀrshBr.; (m. or n.?) N. of a peculiar kind of rain-water (which falls in the month Āśvayuja or Āśvina), Suśr. **-nishkuṭa**, m. pl. inhabitants of the sea-coast (a people; cf. *samudra-n*°), MBh. **-bandhu**, m. 'sailor's friend,' the moon, Kathās. **-sthalaka**, mfn. (fr. *samudra-sthalī*), g. *dhūmâdi*.

1. **Sāmudraka**, mfn. oceanic, maritime, g. *dhūmâdi*; (*ikā*), f. a kind of leech, Suśr.; n. sea-salt, Suśr.; N. of a Tīrtha, MBh.

Sā́mudri, m. patr. fr. *sam-udra*, ŚBr.; HPariś.

1. **Sāmudrika**, mfn. belonging or relating to the sea, seafaring, MBh.; m. a mariner, ib.

सामुद्र 2. *sāmudra*, n. (fr. *sa-mudra*) an impression or mark on the body, L. **-tilaka**, m. N. of a wk. on palmistry (by Durlabha-rāja). **-vid**, mfn. familiar with palmistry, VarBṛS.

2. **Sāmudraka**, m. an interpreter of marks or spots on the body, fortune-teller, Siṃhâs. **-vidyā**, f. the art of interpreting marks on the body, palmistry, MW.

2. **Sāmudrika**, mfn. relating to marks on the body (°*kā guṇāḥ*, 'qualities denoted by marks on the b°'), MW.; relating to good or bad fortune (as indicated by marks on the b°), ib.; m. = 2. *sāmudraka*, Cat.; n. palmistry, Daś.; N. of a wk. on this subject. **-kaṇṭhâbharaṇa**, m., n., **-cintāmaṇi**, m. N. of wks. **-jña**, mfn. versed in palmistry, L. **-lakshaṇa**, n., **-śāstra**, n., **-sāra**, m. N. of wks. **Sāmudrikâcārya**, m. N. of Kāśi-nātha (the father of Rāghavêndra and grandfather of Ciraṃ-jīva), Cat.

सामूना *sāmūnā*, f. a black coloured deer ($1\frac{1}{2}$ cubits long, with shining long and soft hair), L.

सामूहिक *sāmūhika*, mfn. (fr. *sam-ūha*) collected in masses, arrayed in ranks, Kām.; m. a suffix forming collective nouns, Pat.; chapter treating of collective nouns, ib.

सामृत *sā́mṛita*, mfn. provided with nectar, Pat.

सामृद्ध्य *sāmṛiddhya*, n. (fr. *sam-ṛiddha*) prosperity, welfare, going on well, success (of a sacrifice), R.

सामोढ *sāmôḍha*, *sāmôḍbhava*. See p. 1205, col. 2.

सामोद *sâmoda*, mfn. joyful, pleased, Gīt.; possessing fragrance, fragrant, odoriferous, W.

साम्न *sāmna*, °*nī*. See p. 1205, col. 2.

साम्पद *sāmpada*, mfn. (fr. *sam-pad*) relating to the equipment or preparation of, requisite for (comp.), Kauś.

Sāmpannika, mfn. (fr. *sam-panna*) one who lives luxuriously, Car.

Sāmpādika, mfn. efficacious, Śaṃk.

साम्पराय *sāmparāya*, mfn. (fr. *sam-parâya*) required by necessity or calamity, VarYogay.; relating to war or battle, warlike, MW.; relating to the other world or to the future, ib.; m. the passage from this world into another, Up.; MBh. &c.; need, distress, calamity, MBh.; a helper or friend in need, ib. i, 723 (Nilak.); contention, conflict, Śiś.; the future, a future life, L.; inquiry into the future, MW.; investigation (in general), ib.; uncertainty, ib.

Sāmparāyaṇa, m. (fr. prec.) one who ushers a person into another world (said of Death), IndSt.

Sāmparāyaṇaka, m. (fr. prec.), g. *arīhaṇâdi*.

Sāmparāyika, mf(*ā* or *ī*)n. (g. *saṃtāpâdi*) relating to the future or to the passage into another world, future (with *phala*, n. 'reward in the next world;' °*kam* √*kṛi*, 'to prepare for death' or 'to perform funeral ceremonies for [gen.]'), Mn.; MBh. &c.; relating to or prepared for battle, martial, warlike, ib.; salutary or helpful in time of need, MBh.; Hariv.; R.; m. (with or scil. *ratha*) a war-chariot, L.; (*am*), n. war, battle, L. **-kalpa**, m. military form, strategic array, Mn. vii, 185.

साम्पातिक *sāmpātika*, mfn. (fr. *sam-pāta*) belonging or relating to contiguous hymns, ĀśvŚr.

साम्पीक *sāmpīka*, m. N. of a poet, Cat.

साम्प्रत *sāmprata*, mfn. (fr. *sam-prati*) seasonable, fit, proper, correct (cf. *a-s*°), Lāṭy.;

Sarvad.; belonging to the present time, present (not past or future), comp.; (*am*), ind. fitly, properly, MBh.; presently, now, ib. &c. &c. — **kāla**, m. the present time, Sāṃkhyak. **Sāmpratâdhipa**, m. a present or reigning sovereign, MārkP.

Sāmpratika, mf(*ī*)n. suitable, fit, proper, Uttarar.; present (not future), Kull.

साम्प्रदानिक *sāmpradānika*, mfn. (fr. *sam-pradāna*), g. *vinayâdi*.

Sāmpradāyika, mfn. (fr. *sam-pradāya*) based on tradition, traditional (cf. *a-s°*), Baudh.; Jaim.; standing upon or following tradition, RāmatUp.

साम्प्रयोगिक *sāmprayogika*, mfn. (fr. *sam-prayoga*) relating to use or application, Cat. **Sāmprayogikâdhikaraṇa**, n. N. of a Kāma-śāstra.

साम्प्रश्निक *sāmpraśnika*, mfn. (fr. *sam-praśna*), g. *chedâdi*.

साम्प्रियक *sāmpriyaka*, mfn. (fr. *sam-priya*) inhabited by people who are dear to one another, g. *rājanyâdi*.

साम्ब् *sāmb*, v.l. for √*samb*, q.v., p. 1177.

साम्ब 1. *sāmba*, m. (also written *śāmba*) N. of a son of Kṛishṇa and Jāmbavatī (in consequence of the curse of some holy sages who had been deceived by a female disguise which he had assumed, he was condemned to produce offspring in the shape of a terrific iron club for the destruction of the race of Vṛishṇi and Andhaka; he is said to have been instructed by Nārada in the worship of the sun, and by Vyāsa in the ritual of the Magi), MBh.; Hariv.; Pur.; (also with *śāstrin*) N. of various authors and teachers, Cat.; n. = *-purāṇa*, ib. — **carita**, n. N. of wk. — **pañcāśikā**, f. N. of a hymn by Sāmba (also called *sūrya-stotra*). — **pura**, n. or **-purī**, f. N. of a city founded by Sāmba (said to be situated on the banks of the Candra-bhāga), Cat. — **purāṇa**, n. = *sāmbôpapurāṇa*. — **pradyumna-prabandha**, m., **-muktâvalī-stotra**, n. N. of wks. — **mūrti**, mfn. having the form of Sāmba, Cat. — **vatī**, f. N. of a courtezan, Rājat. — **vijaya**, m. N. of wk. **Sāmbâditya**, m. a partic. form of the sun, Cat. **Sāmbêsvara**, m. N. of a temple founded by Sāmbavatī, Rājat. **Sāmbôpapurāṇa**, n. N. of an Upapurāṇa.

Sāmbi, m. patr. fr. *sāmba*, g. *bāhv-ādi*.

साम्ब 2. *sâmba*, mfn. attended by Ambā (q.v.), Kāsīkh. — **śiva**, m. N. of an author, Cat.

साम्बन्धिक *sāmbandhika*, n. (fr. *sam-bandha*) relationship by marriage, MBh.; conversation such as is fit for people related by marriage, ib.

साम्बर *sāmbara*, °*rī*. See *śāmb°*, p. 1065.

साम्बर्य *sāmbarya*, m. (prob. w.r. for *sām-varya*) a patr., Saṃskārak.

साम्बाधिक *sāmbādhika*, m. (fr. *sam-bādha*) the second Yāma (q.v.) of a night, L.

साम्बुवासर *sâmbu-vāsara*, mfn. (of doubtful meaning), Kathās. lxx, 59.

साम्भर *sāmbhara*, n. (fr. *sam-bhara*) a kind of salt, L.

साम्भल *sāmbhala*, mfn. bred in Sam-bhala (as a horse), L.

साम्भवी *sāmbhavī*, f. (fr. *sam-bhava*) possibility, probability, L.; the red Lodhra tree, W.

साम्भस् *sâmbhas*, mfn. having or containing water, watery, Bhaṭṭ.

साम्भाष्य *sāmbhāshya*, n. (fr. *sam-bhāshin*) conversation, g. *brāhmaṇâdi*.

साम्भूयि *sāmbhūyi*, m. patr. fr. *sam-bhūyas*, g. *bāhv-ādi*.

साम्मत्य *sāmmatya*, n. (fr. *sam-mati*) consent, agreement, g. *dṛiḍhâdi*.

साम्मद *sāmmadá*, m. (fr. *sam-mada*) patr. of Matsya (king of the aquatic animals), ŚBr.; ĀśvŚr.; of the author of RV. viii, 67, Anukr.

साम्मनस्य *sāmmanasyá*, n. (fr. *sam-manas*) concord, harmony, AV.; (*ānî*), n. pl. charms to secure harmony, AV., SBE. xlii, 134.

साम्मातुर *sāmmātura* and *sāmmātra*, m. patr. fr. 1. *sam-mātṛi*, Pat. on Pāṇ. iv, 1, 115.

साम्मार्जिन *sāmmārjina*, n. (fr. *sam-mārjin*), Pāṇ. v, 4, 15, Sch.

साम्मितिकायनि *sāmmitikāyani*, m. a patr., Pat.

साम्मुखी *sāmmukhī*, f. (fr. *sam-mukha*) a Tithi or lunar day extending till evening (see *tithi*), L.

Sāmmukhya, n. the state of being present face to face or in front (°*khyam ā-√dhā*, Ā., with gen. = 'to go to'), Sāh.; favour, fondness for (opp. to *vai-mukhya*), Rājat.; care for, attention to (comp.), ib.

साम्मेघ्य *sāmmeghya*, n. (fr. *sam-megha*) the cloudy season, TS.

साम्मोदनिक *sāmmodanika*, mfn. = *sammodanāya prabhavati*, g. *saṃtāpâdi*.

साम्य *sāmya*, n. (fr. 2. *sama*) equality, evenness, equilibrium, equipoise, equal or normal state (acc. with √*nī*, 'to bring to that st°,' 'calm'), MBh.; Kāv. &c.; likeness, sameness, identity with (instr. with and without *saha*, or gen., or loc., or comp.), MuṇḍUp.; MBh. &c.; equality of rank or position, Mn.; Yājñ.; VarBṛS.; homogeneousness (of sounds), Vop.; measure, time, MBh.; equability towards (loc. or *prati*), impartiality, indifference, Bhag.; Kum.; BhP.; justice (*sāmyam* √*kṛi*, 'to act justly towards [loc.]'), MBh.; v.l. for *śalyā*, Kāvyâd. i, 39. — **grāha**, m. one who beats time, R. — **tā**, f., **-tva**, n. equality, sameness, Mn.; MBh. &c. — **tāla-viśārada**, mfn. versed in time and measure, MBh. ii, 131 (B.) — **bodhaka**, mfn. expressive of similarity, MW. **Sāmyâvasthā**, f. a state of equipoise (of the 3 constituent ingredients of Prakṛiti; see *guṇa*), Sarvad.; Sāṃkhyak.; RTL. 32. **Sāmyâvasthāna**, n. id., Śaṃk.

साम्यक्ष *sāmyaksha*, *sāmyeksha* and °*kshya*, (prob.) w.r. for *sāmakshya*.

साम्राज्य *sā́mrājya*, n. (fr. *sam-rāj*) complete or universal sovereignty, empire, dominion over (gen., loc., or comp.), RV. &c. &c.; mfn. relating to sovereignty, TS.; (°*jyá*, m.) a universal sovereign, RV. viii, 25, 17 (accord. to g. *kurv-ādi*, 'the son of a un° s°.'). — **kṛit**, mfn. one who exercises imperial sway, MW. — **dīkshita**, mfn. consecrated to universal empire, ib. — **lakshmī-pīṭhikā**, f., **-lakshmī-pūjā**, f., **-siddhi**, f. N. of wks. — **siddhidā**, f. N. of the family deity of the Uddālakas, Cat.

साम्राणिकर्दम *sāmrāṇi-kardama*, n. a perfume or mixture of fragrant substances, civet, L.

Sāmrāṇi-ja, n. a kind of fruit-tree, L.

साय 1. *sāyá*, n. (prob. fr. √*so*, see *ava-sāya*, *avasāna*; but cf. 2. *sāya*, col. 3) the close of day, evening (*sāyaṃ* √*kṛi*, 'to spend the evening, make a stay'), RV. &c. &c.; Evening personified (as a son of Pushpârṇa and Doshā or as a son of Dhātṛi and Kuhū), BhP.; (*ám*), ind. in the evening, at eventide (*sāyaṃ sāyam*, 'every evening;' see also below), RV. &c. &c. [Cf., accord. to some, Lat. *sērus*.] — **tare**, ind. late in the evening, Pat. on Pāṇ. iv, 3, 23, Vārtt. 1. — **dhūrta**, m. a rogue, cheat or deceiver in the form of ev°, Naish. — **maṇḍana**, n. 'ev°-ornament,' sunset, W. **Sāyârambha**, mfn. beginning in the ev°, KātyŚr., Sch. **Sāyâśana**, n. an ev°-meal, ib. **Sāyâhan**, n. or °**hna**, m. eventide, TBr.; Mn.; MBh. &c.; (°*hna*)-*samaye*, ind. at eventide, R. **Sāyôdbhidura**, mfn. expanding or blossoming in the evening, L.

Sāyaṃ, in comp. for *sāyam*, col. 3. — **yâvan**, mfn. going or coming in the evening, TBr. — **saṃdhyā**, f. the evening twilight, RTL. 407; *-devatā*, f. 'deity of the ev° t°,' N. of Sarasvatī, L.; *-prayoga*, m. N. of wk. — **sūrya**, m. the ev° sun, MBh.; °*yôḍha*, mfn. brought by the ev° sun (said of a guest), Mn. iii, 105. — **homa**, m. the ev° oblation, ĀśvŚr., Sch. — **kāla**, m. eventide, evening, Naish., Sch. — **kālika** (Vās., Sch.) or **-kālīna** (Ragh., Sch.), mfn. belonging to evening, vespertine. — **gṛiha**, mfn. = *yatra-s°*, Prab. — **goshṭha**, mfn. brought into the fold at ev°, AitBr. — **tūrya**, n. drumming at ev°, L. — **dugdhá**, mfn. milked in the evening, ib.; ŚBr. — **doha**, m. milking the cows at evening, ev° milking or milk, ĀpŚr.; *-vat*, ind., ib. — **dhṛiti**, f. = *-homa*, MW. — **nivāsa**, m. ev° abode or resting-place, ib.

Sāyantana, mf(*ī*)n. relating to evening, vespertine, Kāv.; Pañcat.; SārṅgS. — **mallikā**, f. evening-jasmine, Ragh. — **samaya**, m. eventide, Pañcat.

Sāyam, ind. in comp. — **adhivāsa**, m. 'evening-decoration,' decorating an image of Durgā on the fifth day of the month Āśvina, MW. — **aśaná**, n. an ev° meal, MaitrS. — **āśa**, m. id., Kauś.; *-prātarāśa* (only loc. *e*), the ev° and morning m°, Gobh. — **āhuti**, f. an ev° oblation, ŚBr.; GṛŚrS. — **upâsana-vidhi**, m., **-aupāsana-prayoga**, m. N. of wks. — **posha**, m. food taken in the ev°, ŚāṅkhBr. — **prātar** (*sā-yám-*), ind. in the ev° and m° (also *sāyam prātaś ca*), AV. &c. &c.; *-agnihotra-prayoga*, m., *-agnihotra-homa*, m. N. of wks.; *-āśin*, mfn. eating (only) in the ev° and m°, ŚBr.; *-āhuti*, f. du. ev° and m° oblation, KātyŚr.; *-aupāsana-vidhi*, m. N. of wk.; *-doha*, m. ev° and m° milking, ib.; *-maya*, mf(*ī*)n. consisting of ev° and m°, Kāśikh.; *-homa*, m. du. ev° and m° oblation, Gobh. (also N. of wk.) — **bhava**, m. becoming evening, growing dark, AV. — **bhojana**, n. an evening meal, Kull. on Mn. iii, 105. — **mantra**, m. a Mantra to be used in the evening, Baudh.

Sāyamprātika, mfn. (fr. *sāyam-prātar*) belonging to evening and morning, Pāṇ. vi, 4, 144, Vārtt. 5, Pat.

साय 2. *sāya*, m. (fr. √2. *si*; for 1. see col. 2) a missile, arrow (= *sāyaka*), L.; (*sāyá*), n. unloosing, unyoking, turning in, RV. &c.

Sā́yaka, mfn. intended or fitted to be discharged or hurled, RV. (Naigh. ii, 20); m. (in RV. also n.) a missile, arrow, RV. &c. &c.; m. a symbolical expression for the number 'five' (from the 5 arrows of the god of love), Sāh.; a sword, MBh.; R.; the latitude of the sky, Gaṇit.; Saccharum Sara, L.; N. of a man, Pravar.; (*ikā*), f. a dagger, L.; the being or standing in regular order (= *krama-sthiti*; prob. w.r. for *śāyikā*), L. — **puṅkha**, m. the feathered part of an arrow, Ragh.; (*ā*), f. a partic. plant (= *śara-puṅkhā*), L. — **praṇutta** (*sā́y°*), mfn. driven away or put to flight by arrows, AV. — **maya**, mf(*ī*)n. consisting of arrows, MBh.; Hariv.

Sāyakāya, Nom. Ā. °*yate*, to resemble arrows, represent the arrows of (comp.), Daś.

Sāyakāyana, m. patr. fr. *sāyaka*, ŚBr. (g. *naḍâdi*).

Sāyakāyanin, m. pl. the school of Sāyakāyana, ib.

सायण *sāyaṇa*, m. (said to be a Drāviḍa word) N. of a learned Brāhman (also called Sāyaṇa-mādhava and Sāyaṇâcārya; he was son of Māyaṇa, pupil of Vishṇu Sarva-jña and of Saṃkarânanda; and flourished under Bukka I of Vijaya-nagara or Vidyā-nagara [A.D. 1350–1379] and his successor Harihara, and died in 1387; of more than a hundred works attributed to him, among which are commentaries on nearly all parts of the Veda, some were carried out by his pupils, and some were written in conjunction with his brother Mādhavâcārya or Vidyāraṇya-svāmin). — **mādhavīya**, mfn. written or composed by Sāyaṇa-mādhava, Sarvad.

Sāyaṇīya, mfn. relating to or composed by Sāyaṇa; n. a work of Sāyaṇa, Cat.

सायतन *sâyatana*, mfn. together with the place of abode &c., TS.

सायन *sâyana*, mfn. proceeding in the way of an Ayana (q.v.), ŚāṅkhŚr.; connected with the word *ayana*, ib.; n. (in astron.) with the precession or the longitude of a planet reckoned from the vernal equinoctial point, W.

सायवस *sāyavasa*, m. a patr., ŚBr.

सायास *sâyāsa*, mfn. beset with difficulties or trouble, Kathās.

सायिन् *sāyin*, m. (prob. w.r. for *sādin*) a horseman, W.

सायुज्य *sâyujya*, n. (fr. *sa-yuj*) intimate union, communion with (gen., loc., instr., or comp.); identification, absorption (into the divine Essence; this is one of the four grades or states of Mukti, cf. *sālokya*; RTL. 41), Kāṭh.; Br.; MBh. &c.; likeness, similarity, W. — **tā**, f. (Hcat.), **-tva**, n. (MaitrUp.) = prec. — **mukti**, f. emancipation consisting in the above absorption, Cat.

Sāyojya, n. = *sāyujya*, MaitrUp. (with *prāṇais* = 'abiding in life, living on,' MārkP.)

सायुध *sâyudha*, mf(*ā*)n. furnished with arms, armed, MBh. — **pragraha**, mfn. holding weapons in the hand, MW.

साय्य *sāyya*, m. a patr. (v.l. *sāpyá*), RV vi, 20, 6.

सार् sār. See √sār, p. 1066, col. 1.

सार 1. sāra (fr. √sṛi), m. course, motion (ifc. *pūrva-s°*); stretching out, extension, Kālac.; m. driving away, destroying, Bālar. ii, 86/87. **-sārin**, mfn. running courses or races, TB.

1. **Sāraka**, mfn. 'causing to go or flow,' cathartic, laxative, Bhpr.; m. Croton Jamalgota, L.

Sāraṇa, mf(*ī*)n. id., L.; cracked, split, L.; having five hair-tufts on the head, L.; m. dysentery, diarrhœa, L.; wind during the autumn, L.; Pæderia Fœtida, L.; Spondias Mangifera, L.; N. of a brother of Kṛishṇa, MBh.; Hariv.; MārkP.; of one of Rāvaṇa's ministers (sent as ambassador to Rāma), R.; (*ā*), f. stretching out, extension (only ifc.), Kathās.; (ifc. f. *ā*) producing a sound, striking a note on (loc.), ib.; a partic. process to which mineral substances (esp. quicksilver) are subjected (two others being given called *ṛitu-s°* and *prati-sāraṇā*; *°ṇā-traya*, n. 'the three Sāraṇā processes'), Sarvad.; (*ī*), f., see below; (*am*), n. leading home, Daś.; buttermilk (one fourth part of which is water), L.; a kind of perfume, L. **-sundara**, m. a partic. mixture, Cat. **Sāraṇêśa**, m. N. of a mountain, ib.

Sāraṇi, f. a stream, channel, water-pipe, HPariś.

Sāraṇika, m. a traveller, (esp.) a travelling merchant (v.l. *śār°*), MBh.; (*ā*), f. (in *cintāmaṇi-s°*) N. of wk. **-ghna**, m. 'killing travellers,' a robber, highwayman, L.

Sāraṇī, f. = *sāraṇi*, a stream, Bālar.; Pæderia Fœtida, L.; a poem consisting only of verses, L.; N. of wk. **-koshṭaka**, n., **-rāja**, m. N. of wks.

1. **Sārin**, mfn. going, running, hastening, MBh.; (ifc.) following, pursuing, AitBr. &c. &c.; (*iṇī*), f. a brook, channel, Vcar.; N. of various plants (Alhagi Maurorum, Pæderia Fœtida &c.), L.

Sārya, mfn. that which may be dropped or omitted (in pronunciation), MāṇḍS.

सार 2. sā́ra, m. n. (ifc. f. *ā*; perhaps to be connected with 1. *sāra* above; prob. fr. a lost root meaning 'to be strong') the core or pith or solid interior of anything, RV. &c. &c.; firmness, strength, power, energy, AV. &c. &c.; the substance or essence or marrow or cream or heart or essential part of anything, best part, quintessence (ifc. = 'chiefly consisting of or depending on &c.' [cf. *para*], e.g. *dharma-sāram jagat*, 'the world chiefly depends on justice;' *tūshṇīm-sāra*, mfn. 'chiefly silent;' *sārāt sāram*, 'the very best'), AitBr. &c. &c.; the real meaning, main point, MW.; a compendium, summary, epitome (often ifc. in titles of books); a chief ingredient or constituent part of the body (causing the peculiarities of temperament; reckoned to be 7, viz. *sattva, śukra, majjan, asthi, medas, māṅsa, rakta*), Suśr.; VarBṛS.; any ingredient, Suśr.; nectar, R.; BhP.; cream, curds, L.; worth, value (*eṇa*, 'in consideration of,' 'according to'), Mn.; Yājñ. &c.; wealth, property, goods, riches, Kāv.; Pur.; Rājat.; (in rhet.) a kind of climax (*uttarôttaram utkarshaḥ*), Sāh.; Kpr.; resin used as a perfume, Suśr.; ŚārṅgS.; water, Vās.; dung, Kṛishis.; the matter formed in a boil or ulcer, pus, MW.; impure carbonate of soda, ib.; a confederate prince, ally, VarBṛS.; (= 1. *śāra*) a piece at chess or backgammon &c.; (*ā*), f. a kind of plant (= *krishṇa-trivṛitā*), L.; Kuśa grass, L.; (*ī*), f., see under *sāri* and *sārī* (next p.); mf(*ā*)n. hard, firm, solid, strong, MBh.; Kāv. &c.; precious, valuable, Daś.; good, sound, best, excellent, BhP.; Pañcar.; sound (as an argument, thoroughly proved), W.; full of (instr.), VarBṛS.; motley, speckled (= *śāra*), Suśr.; Kād. **-kalikā**, f., **-kaumudī**, f., **-kshetra-māhātmya**, n., **-kshetra-māhātmya-sârôddhāra**, m. N. of wks. **-khadira**, m. 'hard Khadira,' a kind of Acacia Catechu, L. **-ga**, mfn. robust, strong, powerful, Śiś. (= *bhala-bhāj*, Sch.) **-gandha**, m. 'having perfection of scent,' sandal-wood, L. **-gātra**, mfn. strong-limbed, MBh. **-gītā**, f. N. of various wks. **-guṇa**, m. any chief or principal virtue, Siṅhâs. **-guru**, mfn. heavy with weight (as steps), Kum. **-graha-mañjarī**, f. N. of wk. **-grāha**, m. (with *karma-vipāka*) N. of a wk. on Dharma (composed by Kāṇhada-sūnu in 1384 A.D.) **-grāhin**, mfn. capable of extracting or apprehending the essence or best part of anything, R. **-grīva**, m. 'strong-necked,' N. of Śiva, MBh. **-caturviṅśatikā**, f., **-candrikā**, f., **-cintāmaṇi**, m. N. of wks. **-ja**, n. 'produced from cream,' fresh butter (cf. *sara-ja*), W. **-taṇḍula**, m. rice in whole grains slightly boiled, KātyŚr. **-tama**, mfn. the very best (*-tva*, n.), Saṃk. on ChUp. **-tara**, n. the better, something excellent (*sārāt sārataram*, 'the best or most excellent of all'), Cat.; mf(*ā*)n. better, more excellent, Śaṃk. on ChUp.; more precious, dearer, Śiś.; *-tā*, f. the being better or having more virtue, Divyâv. **-taru**, m. 'pith-tree,' the plantain (= *kadala*, 'Musa Sapientum;' so called as containing no hard wood), L. **-tas**, ind. according to the nature, Mn. viii, 405; vigorously, essentially, W. **-tā**, f. firmness, solidity, R.; strong confidence in (loc.), ib.; worth, value, Hit.; ŚārṅgP.; highest degree, R.; Rājat.; the being a chief ingredient (in the body; see *sāra*), Car. **-traya-culuka**, m. or n. N. of a Vedânta wk. **-tva**, n. hardness, firmness, solidity, ŚāṅkhGṛ.; MBh.; the being the main point or principal matter, Sāh. **-darśin**, mfn. having an eye for the good or important, R. **-dā**, f. = *śāradā* (q.v.) **-dāru**, n. hard wood, Hcat.; *-maya*, mf(*ī*)n. made of hard w°, ib. **-dīpikā**, f. N. of various wks. **-druma**, m. a tree having hard wood, VarBṛS.; the Khadira tree (Acacia Catechu), L. **-dhātṛi**, m. 'bestower of strength,' N. of Śiva, Hariv. **-dhānya**, n. the best grain or corn, VarBṛS. **-dhvaji**, m. a patr., Saṃskārak. **-pattra**, mfn. having hard or strong leaves (*-ka*, n.), g. *manojñâdi*. **-pada**, m. 'having strong feet,' a kind of bird reckoned among the Vishkiras (v.l. *śāra-p°*), Car. **-padyâvalī**, f. N. of wk. **-parṇī**, f. (cf. *śāla-p°*) Hedysarum Gangeticum, L. **-pāka**, n. a partic. poisonous fruit, Suśr. **-pādapa**, m. a partic. plant or tree (prob. = *dhāmanī*), L. **-prakāśikā**, f., **-pradīpikā**, f. N. of wks. **-phalgu**, mfn. strong and (or) weak, good and (or) bad, MBh.; *-tā*, f. (MBh.), *-tva*, n. (Mn. ix, 56) value and (or) worthlessness, goodness and (or) badness, comparative importance. **-bodhinī**, f. N. of a Comm. on the Kāvya-prakāśa. **-bhaṅga**, m. n. destruction or loss of vigour, W.; deprived of substance or strength, ib. **-bhaṭa**, N. of the fourth Muhūrta, Jyot. **-bhaṭṭāraka**, m. N. of an author, Cat. **-bhāṇḍa**, n. valuable merchandise, treasure, Yājñ.; Pañcat.; a natural receptacle (as a bag or skin for holding musk &c.), W.; *-gṛihaka*, m. or n. a treasure-house, treasury, Mālav. **-bhuj**, mfn. eating the essence or best part of anything, MW. **-bhūta**, mfn. being the chief thing, best, most excellent; n. the main or best thing, Kāv.; VarBṛS. &c. **-bhṛit**, mfn. taking or choosing what is best, BhP. **-bhoga**, m., **-mañjarī**, f. N. of wks. **-maya**, mf(*ī*)n. exceedingly firm or solid, BhP.; consisting of the chief or best part of anything (gen.), Cat. **-mahat**, mfn. very precious or valuable, Daś. **-mārgaṇa**, n. searching for pith or marrow, Yājñ. **-miti**, m. 'measure of all truth,' N. of the Veda, L. **-mūshikā**, f. a kind of plant (= *deva-dālī*), L. **-yoga**, m. possession of the essence or substance of anything, W. **-yodha**, mfn. consisting of excellent warriors, MBh. **-rūpa**, mfn. best, principal, most excellent, Chandom.; *-tā*, f. the being the best or first (*°tayā*, instr., 'especially, principally'), Sāh. **-laharī**, f. N. of a gram. wk. by Kavi-candra. **-loha**, n. 'essence of iron,' steel, L. **-vat**, mfn. hard, solid, firm, strong, steadfast, MBh.; R. &c.; substantial, nourishing (as food), Car.; valuable, precious, MBh.; Kām.; having pith or sap, containing resin, Suśr.; (*ī*), f. a kind of metre, Col.; a partic. Samādhi, Buddh.; *-tā*, f. hardness (of an arrow), Ragh.; force, strength, steadfastness, Kām.; Śiś., Sch. **-varjita**, mfn. 'devoid of substance,' pithless, sapless, W. **-vastu**, n. a valuable or important thing, Pañcat. **-vid**, mfn. knowing the substance or value of anything, Kāv. **-śūnya**, mfn. devoid of value, worthless, ib. **-saṃhitā**, f. N. of a wk. on music by Nārada. **-saṃgraha**, m. 'concentration of the essence of any work,' N. of various compendiums (also *-jñāna-bhūshaṇa-bhāshya*, n., *-nighaṇṭu*, m., *-saṃgraha*, m.) **-samuccaya**, m., **-sambandha-paddhati**, f., **-sāgara**, m., **-siddhânta-kaumudī**, f., **-sindhu**, m., **-sundarī**, f. N. of wks. **Sārâdāna**, n. picking out the best, Kap. **Sārâparādha**, m. du. the ability (of a criminal to suffer) and the nature of the crime (others, 'the greatness of the crime'), Mn. viii, 126; *-tas*, ind. according to the ability &c. (others, 'according to the greatness of the crime'), ib. ix, 262. **Sārâpahāra**, m. robbing of the substance or wealth of (gen.), Rājat. **Sārâmṛita**, n. N. of a grammar. **Sārâmbhas**, n. extracted juice, Suśr. **Sārârtha-saṃgraha**, m. N. of a Comm. on the Bhagavad-gītā. **Sārârthin**, mfn. desirous of deriving gain or profit from anything, MBh. **Sārâvalī**, f. N. of various wks.; *-jātaka*, n. N. of an astron. wk. **Sārâśīti**, f. N. of 80 choice stanzas, Subh. **Sārâsāra**, n. substance and (or) emptiness, strength and (or) weakness, relative strength, Hit.; worth and (or) worthlessness, relative quality (of goods), Mn. ix, 331; the good and (or) the best, Rājat.; mfn. strong and (or) weak, MBh.; *-tā*, f. the strong and (or) weak side of anything, Pañcat.; *-vicāra*, m. considering or weighing strong and weak points &c., MW.; *-viveka*, m. N. of two wks. **Sārâsvādinī**, f. N. of a Vedânta wk. **Sārêśvara**, m. (with *paṇḍita*) N. of a Jaina (author of the Liṅga-prakāśa, a gram. wk.) **Sārôddhāra**, m. N. of various wks. (also *-paddhati*, f., *-śakuna-parîkshā*, f., and *-saṃgraha*, m.)

2. **Sāraka**, mfn. (ifc.) full of, Kathās.; m. N. of a man, Divyâv.

Sārāt, (abl. of 2. *sāra*) in comp. **-sāra-tattva**, n., **-sāra-tattva-saṃgraha**, m., **-sāra-susaṃgraha**, m. N. of wks.

2. **Sārin** (for 1. see col. 1) in *trāṇa-s°* (q. v.)

Sārishṭha, mfn. the very best or most excellent (*-tva*, n.), Śaṃk.

सार 3. sā́ra, mfn. having spokes, Śulbas.

सारकायण sārakāyaṇa, mfn. (fr. *saraka*), g. *pakshâdi*.

Sārakeya, mfn., g. *sakhy-ādi*.

Sārakya, mfn., g. *saṃkāśâdi*.

सारघ sāraghá, mfn. (fr. *saragha*) coming or derived from the bee, RV.; AV.; ŚBr.; BhP.; m. a bee, RV. x, 106, 10; n. honey, Naish.; BhP.

सारङ्ग sāráṅga or sāraṅgá, mf(*ī*)n. (sometimes written *śār°*; either fr. *sa-raṅga*, 'having colour &c.,' or for *śārâṅga* or *sār°*, 'having a dappled body'), of a variegated colour, dappled, spotted (cf. *krishṇa-s°*, *lohita-s°*), AV.; Br.; MBh.; derived from the antelope called Sāraṅga, L.; m. (ifc. f. *ā*) a kind of spotted antelope, Kāv.; Kathās. &c.; N. of various birds (esp. a kind of Vishkira or Pratuda [qq. vv.]; a peacock; the Indian cuckoo; the Rāja-haṅsa; the Cātaka &c.), Kāv.; Suśr.; Car. &c.; a bee, BhP.; a kind of metre, Col.; (in music) a partic. Rāga, Saṃgīt.; (only L., 'an elephant; lion; cloud; tree; umbrella; parasol; garment; clothes; hair; lotus; flower; conch-shell; sort of musical instrument; ornament; jewel; gold; a bow; sandal; camphor; the earth; light; night'); N. of Śiva, MBh.; of Kāma-deva, L.; of the father of Bhaṭṭa Rāghava, Cat.; (with *kavi*) of a poet, ib.; (*ī*), f., see below. **-ja**, m. a deer; *-dṛiś*, f. a deer-eyed woman, Bhām. **-deva**, m. N. of a king, Cat. **-pāṇi**, m. N. of an author, ib. (cf. *-samuccaya*). **-raṅga-dā**, f. N. of a commentary on the Kṛishṇa-karṇâmṛita. **-locanā**, f. = *-dṛiś*, Naish. **-śabala**, mfn. dappled and spotted (said of horses), MBh. **-samuccaya**, m. N. of a wk. (also called *vivāha-paṭala*) by Sāraṅga-pāṇi. **-sāra**, N. of a poem. **-hāra**, m. a kind of Yogin, W. **Sāraṅgâkshā**, f. = *sāraṅga-dṛiś*, Mālav.

Sāraṅgika, m. a bird-catcher or deer-catcher, L.

Sāraṅgī, f. a kind of spotted doe or antelope (see *krishṇa-s°*); the female of a partic. bird, Mn. ix, 23 (cf. *śārṅgī*); a sort of violin, W.; a kind of metre, Col.; (in music) a partic. Rāgiṇī, Saṃgīt. **-sāra-samuccaya**, m. N. of wk.

सारण sāraṇa, sāraṇi &c. See col. 1.

सारण्ड sāraṇḍa, m. = *sarpâṇḍa*, a serpent's egg, L.

सारण्यक sā́raṇyaka, mfn. together with a forest, Pāṇ. i, 1, 7, Vārtt. 8, Pat.; (*sār°*) having the Āraṇyakas, MW.; (*am*), n. together with the Āraṇyakas, IndSt.

सारथि sā́rathi, m. (fr. *sa-ratha*) a charioteer, driver of a car, coachman (forming a mixed caste, commonly called Sārthī, and supposed to have sprung from a Kshatriya father and Brāhman mother), RV. &c. &c.; any leader or guide (see *nau-*, *vākya-s°*); a helper, assistant (see *karma-s°*); the son of a Saratha (q. v.), MW.; the ocean, ib.; N. of a town, Lalit. **-tva**, n. the office of a charioteer &c., Kathās. **-puri** (?), f. the town Sārathi, Lalit.

Sārathya, n. the office of a charioteer or coachman, charioteering &c., MBh.; Ragh.; BhP.

सारमेय sārameyá, m. (fr. *saramā*) a dog

(esp. one of the two four-eyed brindled watch-dogs of Yama, conjectured by some to have been originally Indra and Agni), R.; MBh.; R. &c.; N. of a son of Śva-phalka, BhP.; (*ī*), f. a female dog, bitch, L. **–gaṇâdhipa,** m. 'lord of the race of dogs,' N. of Kubera, Suśr. **–cikitsā,** f. the art of curing dogs, Cat. **–tā,** f. the being a dog, Kathās. **–vākya,** n. 'Sārameya's speech,' N. of the 56th ch. of the Uttara-kāṇḍa of the Rāmâyaṇa. **Sārameyâdana,** n. 'dog's-meal,' N. of a hell in which criminals are eaten by Yama's dogs, BhP.

सारम्भ *sârambha,* m. angry talk, Divyâv.

सारय *sāraya,* Nom. P. °*yati,* to be weak (*daurbalye*), Dhātup. xxxv, 16.

सारल्य *sāralya,* n. (fr. *sarala*) straightness, rectitude, sincerity, honesty, Rājat.

सारव *sārava,* mfn. (anomalously fr. *sarayū*) being in or belonging to the Sarayū river, Pāṇ. vi, 4, 174.

सारशन *sāraśana,* w. r. for *sārasana.*

सारस् *sāras* (m.c.) = 1. *sārasa,* the Indian crane, MBh. xiii, 736.

1. **Sārasa,** mf(*ī*)n. (fr. *saras*) relating or belonging to or coming from a pond or lake, Kāv.; VarBṛS.; Suśr.; m. (ifc. f. *ā*) the Indian or Siberian crane, Ardea Sibirica, Mn.; MBh. &c.; a swan = *haṃsa,* Śiś. xii, 44 (Sch.); a bird in general (cf. *rāja-s*°); the moon, L.; (in music) a kind of measure, Saṃgīt.; N. of a son of Garuḍa, MBh.; of a son of Yadu, Hariv.; of a hunchback (B. °*saka*), Mālav.; (*ī*), f. a female Indian crane, MBh.; Mṛicch.; (*am*), n. a lotus, Caurap.; a woman's zone or girdle (= *sārasana*), L. **–gṛidhra,** m. du. an Indian crane and a vulture, R. **–dvitīya,** mfn. accompanied by an Indian crane, MW. **–priyā,** f. the female of an Indian crane, L. **Sārasâksha,** n. a kind of ruby, L.; (*ī*), f. having the eyes of a *sārasa* or a lotus-eyed woman, Naish.

Sārasikā, f. a female Indian crane, Śiś.

सारस 2. *sârasa,* mfn. crying, calling, Nalôd.

1. **Sārasya,** n. (fr. prec.) a cry, shout, call &c., ib.

सारसन *sārasana,* n. (also written *sāraś*° and perhaps for *sa-raśana*) a woman's zone or girdle (said to be formed of 25 strings), Śiś.; a military belt or girdle, L.; a breast-plate, L.

सारसायन *sārasāyana,* mfn. (fr. *sa-rasa*), g. *pakshâdi;* m. (prob.) a patr., g. *aishukāry-ādi* (v.l. for *sārasyāyana*). **–bhakta,** mfn. inhabited by Sārasāyanas, ib.

Sāraseya, mfn., g. *sakhy-ādi.*

2. **Sārasya,** n. abundance of water, Nalôd.

Sārasyāyana. See *sārasāyana.*

सारस्वत *sārasvatá,* mf(*ī*)n. relating or belonging to Sarasvat (q. v.) or to Sarasvatī (the river or the goddess), derived or coming from them, RV. &c. &c.; relating to the Ṛishi Sārasvata, MBh.; belonging to the Sārasvata country, MBh.; eloquent, learned, W.; m. a Bilva stick, L.; N. of a Ṛishi (fabled to have sprung from the personified Sarasvatī river, MBh. (also °*tā gaṇāḥ*); Hariv.; of a Vyāsa, VP.; (pl.) N. of a people dwelling on the S° river (i. e. in the north-west part of the province of Delhi including part of the Panjāb), AV. Pariś.; MBh.; VarBṛS.; Pur.; (pl.) N. of a partic. tribe of Brāhmans (so called as coming from the above country or as supposed to be descended from the above Ṛishi), BhP.; (sg.) the twelfth Kalpa or day of Brahmā, Hcat.; a staff of the Bilva tree, L.; a partic. ceremonial in the worship of Sarasvatī, MW.; (*ī*), f. Cardiospermum Halicacabum, L.; (with or scil. *prakriyā*) N. of a grammar by Anubhūti-svarūpâcārya; (*am*), n. a partic. Sattra, Jaim.; eloquence, Prasannar.; N. of a grammar (= f.) **–kalpa,** m. the above Sarasvatī ceremonial, Cat. **–kośa,** m., **-tantra,** n. N. of wks. **–tīrtha,** n. N. of a Tīrtha, Cat. **–pura,** n. N. of a town, ib. **–prakriyā,** f. N. of a grammar (cf. above). **–prasāda-ṭīkā,** f., **-maṇḍana,** n., **-māhātmya,** n., **-vilāsa,** m. N. of wks. **–vyākaraṇa,** n. N. of a grammar. **–vrata,** n. a partic. observance in honour of Sarasvatī, Cat. **–sāra, -sāra-saṃgraha,** m., **-sūtra,** n. (cf. *sarasvatī-s*°) N. of wks. **Sārasvatâdarśa,** n. N. of a Nāṭaka by Appā-śāstrin. **Sārasvatâbhidhāna,** n. N. of a short vocabulary. **Sārasvatâlaṃkāra,** m. N. of a wk. on rhet. (prob. the Sarasvatī-kaṇṭhâbharaṇa). **Sārasvatôtsava,** m. the festival in honour of Sarasvatī, Tithyād. **Sārasvatâushadhī-√bhū,** P. *-bhavati,* to be a medicine for strengthening the voice in singing, HPariś.

Sārasvatīya, mf(*ā*)n. relating to or connected with the Sarasvatī-sūtra, Cat. **–śilpa-śāstra,** n. N. of wk.

Sārasvatya, mfn. = *sārasvata,* MBh.

सारागवस्त्र *sārāga-vastrá,* mfn. (fr. or for *sa-rāga-v*°) wearing red garments, TĀr.

साराघ्य *sārāghya* (perhaps w.r. for *sārârghya*) N. of an astron. wk.

सारामुख *sārāmukha* (?), m. a kind of rice, Cat.

सारायणीय *sārāyaṇīya,* m. pl. N. of a school, AV. Pariś.

साराल *sārāla,* m. the sesamum plant, L.

साराव *sârāva,* mfn. with a cry, crying, calling, Kathās.

सारि *sāri,* f. (= *śāri*) a kind of thrush-like bird, Kauś.; m. a chessman, piece at backgammon &c., Pañcad. **–phala** (Siṇhâs.) and **-phalaka** (L.), n. = *sāri-ph*°.

Sārika, m. (= *śārika*) the bird Turdus Salica, MBh.; N. of a Muni, ib.; (*ā*), f., see next.

Sārikā, f. (= *śārikā*) Turdus Salica, Mn.; MBh. &c.; a confidante, Vās.; the bridge of a stringed instrument, Saṃg.; the Viṇā of the Caṇḍālas, L.; N. of a Rākshasī, Cat. **–māhātmya,** n. N. of wk. **–mukha,** m. a partic. venomous insect, Suśr. **–vaṇa,** n., g. *koṭarâdi.*

Sārī, f. a kind of bird (= *sārikā; cf. viṭ-s*°), L.; a chessman, piece at backgammon &c. (= *śārī*); a kind of plant (= *saptalā*), L.; a frown, L. **–krīḍā,** f. a kind of game similar to chess &c., Siṇhâs.

सारिमेजय *sârim-ejaya,* mfn. together with Arim-ejaya (son of Śva-phalka), MBh.

सारिव *sāriva,* m. a kind of grain (reckoned among the *śāli* or *shashṭikā*), Car.; Vāgbh.; (*ā*), f. N. of two creeping plants (Hemidesmus Indicus and Ichnocarpus Frutescens), Suśr.

सारिष्ट *sârishṭa,* mfn. together with the Arishṭa trees, Vās.; having the symptoms of approaching death, Suśr.

सारिष्ठ *sārishṭha.* See p. 1208, col. 3.

सारिसृक्क *sārisṛikka* or °*kkva,* m. (prob. fr. Intens. of √*sṛij*) N. of a son of Manda-pāla or Śārṅgaka, MBh.

Sārisṛikta, m. N. of the author of RV. x, 142, 3; 6 (having the patr. Śārṅga), Anukr.

सारिस्थाखाँ *sāristhā-khāñ,* m. N. of a Khān, Kshitîś.

सारी *sārī.* See above.

सारु *sāru* (doubtful), a kind of metre, Col.

सारुन्धतीक *sârundhatika,* mfn. together with Arundhatī, Kum.

सारूढ *sārūḍha,* w.r. for *sv-arūḍha,* MBh.

सारूपवत्स *sārūpavatsa,* n. (fr. *sa-rūpa-vatsā*) milk from a cow that has a calf of the same colour, Vait.

Sārūpya, n. (fr. *sa-rūpa*) sameness or similarity of form, identity of appearance, resemblance, likeness, conformity with (gen.), Mn.; MBh. &c.; assimilation to or conformity with the deity (one of the grades of Mukti or beatitude, = *sarūpa-tā, sālokya*), BhP.; (in dram.) a mistake caused by the mutual resemblance of two persons (as in Veṇis. vi Yudhi-shṭhira takes Bhīma for Duryodhana and injures him), Bhar.; Sāh.; mf(*ā*)n. seasonable, fit, proper, suitable, Lalit. **–tas,** ind. in consequence of similarity of form, MW. **–tā,** f. likeness, resemblance, Hariv.

सारोप *sâropa,* mf(*ā*)n. containing an attribute to be supplied (in rhet.); (*ā*), f. (scil. *lakshaṇā*) an ellipsis containing an attribute to be supplied, Kpr.; Sāh.

सारोष्टिक *sāroshṭika* or *sāroshṭrika,* m. (corrupted fr. *saurāshṭrika*) a kind of poison, L.

सारोह *sâroha,* mf(*ā*)n. having elevation, elevated to (loc.), R.; together with a horseman, ib.

सार्क *sârka,* mfn. with the sun, sunny, VarYog.; Kathās.

सार्कण्डेय *sārkaṇḍeya,* m. patr. fr. *sṛikaṇḍu,* g. *śubhrâdi.*

सार्गड *sârgaḍa,* mfn. bolted, barred, ŚBr.

Sârgala, mfn. id., ib. (in the Kāṇva recension); Hariv.; obstructed, impeded, prevented, withheld, Ragh.

सार्गाल *sārgāla,* mf(*ī*)n. (fr. *sṛigāla*) relating or belonging to a jackal, MBh.

सार्गिक *sārgika,* mfn. = *sargāya prabhavati,* g. *saṃtāpâdi.*

साङ्गी *sārṅgī,* f. a kind of metre (= *sāraṅgī*), Col.

सार्चि *sârci,* mfn. flaming, burning, MBh.; R. **–mālin,** m. a partic. spell recited over weapons, R.

Sârcis, mfn. = *sârci,* MBh.

सार्ज *sārja,* m. = *sarjikā,* natron, L.

सार्जन *sārjana* (of unknown meaning), Pañcar.

सार्जनाक्षि *sārjanākshi,* m. a patr., Pravar.

सार्ञ्जय *sārñjayá,* m. (fr. *sṛiñjaya*) a patr., RV.; N. of a son of Saha-deva, Br.

सार्तरव *sârta-rava,* mfn. uttering wailing sounds, lamenting, R.

सार्ति *sârti,* mfn. suffering from some pain or injury, Bhpr.

सार्त्र *sārtra,* n. (said to be fr. √*sṛi*) a house, dwelling (= *ālaya*), L.

सार्थ *sârtha,* mf(*ā*)n. having an object or business, ŚāṅkhBr.; anything that has attained its object, successful (as a request), Śak., Sch.; having property, opulent, wealthy, Rājat.; having meaning or purport, significant, important, Kusum.; of like meaning or purport, W.; serving a purpose, useful, serviceable, MW.; m. a travelling company of traders or pilgrims, caravan, MBh.; R. &c.; a troop, collection of men, MBh.; a multitude of similar animals, herd, flock &c., Pañcat.; any company (*ena,* with gen. = 'in the company of,' Campak.), collection, multitude, MBh.; Kāv. &c.; a member of any company, W.; a wealthy man, W. **–ghnī,** see *-han.* **–ja,** mfn. born or reared in a caravan, tame (as an elephant), Nal. **–dhara,** m. N. of the leader of a c°, Kathās. **–pati,** m. the chief of a caravan, HPariś. **–pāla,** m. the guardian of a c°, MārkP. **–bhṛit,** m. = *-vāha,* Buddh. **–bhraṇśa-samudbhava,** mfn. arising from the loss of a c°, MBh. **–maṇḍala,** n. the circle or collected body of a c°, ib. **–vat,** mfn. having some meaning or purpose or intention, significant, W.; having a numerous company, ib. **–vāha,** m. the leader or conductor of a c°, a merchant, trader, MBh.; Kāv. &c.; the son of Māra (= *māra-putra*), Buddh.; a Bodhi-sattva, ib.; *-vacas,* n. the proclamation of the captain of a c°, MBh. **–vāhana,** m. the leader of a caravan, Kathās. **–saṃcaya,** mfn. possessing great wealth or riches, ib. **–han,** mf(*ghnī*)n. 'caravan-destroyer,' a robber who attacks a caravan, MW. **–hīna,** mfn. left behind by a caravan, R. **Sârthêśa,** m. = *sârtha-pati,* HPariś.

Sârthaka, mfn. having meaning, significant, important, RPrāt.; Sāh.; serviceable, useful, advantageous, BhP.; Pañcar. **–tā,** f. (Kāśikh.), **-tva,** n. (Sāh.) significance, importance; the being adapted to any purpose, serviceableness, MW.

Sârthaya, Nom. P. °*yati,* to make a profit or gain out of anything, Cat.

Sârthika, mfn. travelling with a caravan; m. a companion on a journey, merchant, trader, MBh.; BhP.

Sârthī-√kṛi, P. *-karoti* = *sârthaya* above.

सार्दागव *sārdāgava,* m. (fr. *sṛidāgu*) N. of a preceptor, Lāṭy.

सार्द्र *sârdra,* mfn. wet, moist, damp, MBh.; Naish.

सार्ध *sârdha,* mf(*ā*)n. joined with a half, plus one half, increased by one half, having a half over (e.g. *dve śate sârdhe*, 'two hundred together with a half,' i.e. 250), Mn.; MBh. &c.; (*ám*), ind. jointly, together, along with, with (instr. or comp.; with *ā-√dā*, 'to take with one'), ŚBr. &c. &c. — **m-vihārin**, mfn. dwelling together with a teacher, Divyâv. — **vārshika**, mfn. lasting a year and a half, Kull. on Mn. xi, 126. — **śata**, n. 'a hundred and a half,' 150, MW. — **saṃvatsara**, n. a year and a half, ib. — **saptan**, n. seven and a half, Sūryas., Sch.

Sârdha-candra, mfn. (fr. *sa + ardhac°*) together with the moon's crescent, Kum.

Sârdha-mātra, mfn. (fr. *sa + ardhamātrā*) having a half Mātrā, MW.

सार्प *sārpa*, mfn. (fr. *sarpa*, of which it is also the Vṛiddhi form in comp.) relating to snakes or serpents; n. (with or scil. *bha*) N. of the Nakshatra Āślesha, VarBṛS.; R. &c. — **rāja**, m. N. of various Sāmans, ĀrshBr. — **rājña**, mf(*ī*)n. belonging to or coming from Sarpa-rājñī (the serpent-queen), ŚrS.; (*ī*), f. N. of the authoress of RV. x, 189, ŚāṅkhBr.; pl. the verses attributed to Sarpa-rājñī, ŚrS. — **vidyika**, mfn. (fr. *sarpa-vidyā*) versed in ophiology or snake-science, Pat.

Sārpya, w.r. for *sārpa*, L.

सार्पाकव *sārpākava*, m. patr. fr. *sṛipāku*, g. *bidâdi*.

Sārpākavāyaṇa, m. patr. fr. *sārpākava*, g. *haritâdi*.

सार्पिणिका *sārpiṇikā*, f. (with *paṅkti*), Cat.

सार्पिष *sārpisha*, mfn. (fr. *sarpis*) containing clarified butter, cooked with ghee, L.

Sārpishka, mfn. id., L.

सार्य *sārya*. See p. 1208, col. 1.

सार्व *sārva*, mfn. (fr. *sarva*, of which it is also the Vṛiddhi form in comp.) relating to all, fit or good for all, Śiś. xiv, 4 (cf. Pāṇ. v, 1, 10); general, universal (see comp.); m. a Buddha or a Jina, L. — **m-saha**, m. (fr. *sarvaṃ-s°*) a kind of salt, L. — **karmika**, mfn. (fr. *sarva-karman*) fit for all actions (cf. *-kārmika* below), L. — **kāma**, mfn. (fr. *sarva-kāma*) designed for one who wishes for all things, ĀpŚr.; *-samṛiddha*, m. the sixth day in the Karma-māsa (prob. w.r. for *sarva-k°*), IndSt. — **kāmika**, mf(*ī*)n. (fr. id.) fulfilling all desires, gratifying every wish, GṛSrS.; MBh. &c. — **kāmya**, n. (fr. id.) fulfilment of every desire, Jaim. — **kārmika**, mfn. (cf. *-karmika* above) all-effective as a remedy against (gen.), Car. — **kāla**, mfn. (fr. *sarva-k°*) taking place at all times or seasons (as marriage), ĀśvGr. — **kālika**, mfn. (fr. id.) belonging to all times, suited to all seasons, everlasting, Āpast.; MBh. &c. — **kālya**, n. (fr. id.) occurrence at all times, Gaṇar. — **keśya**, mfn. coming or derived from Sarvakeśa, g. *śaṇḍikâdi*. — **kratuka**, mfn. (fr. *sarva-kratu*) relating to all sacrifices, Lāṭy., Sch. — **gaṇa**, n. (v.l. *sarva-g°*) salty soil, L. — **gāmin**, mfn. perhaps w.r. for *sarva-g°*) entering into the Universal Soul, Āpast. — **guṇika**, mfn. (fr. *sarva-guṇa*) endued with every good quality or excellence, MBh.; Hariv. — **carmīṇa**, mfn. (= *sarva-c°*) wholly made of leather, Pāṇ. v, 2, 5. — **janika**, mfn. (fr. *sarva-jana*) relating or belonging or suited to all men, universal, public, Pāṇ. v, 1, 9, Vārtt. 5, Pat. — **janīna**, mfn. (fr. id.) = prec., ib.; = *sarva-jane sādhuḥ*, g. *pratijanâdi*. — **janya**, mfn. (fr. id.) general, universal, VarBṛS. — **jña**, mf(*ī*)n. (fr. *sarva-jña*) coming from or relating to one who is omniscient, HPariś.; n., w.r. for next. — **jñya**, n. omniscience, Sarvad. — **dhātuka**, mfn. (fr. *sarva-dhātu*) applicable to the whole of a radical term or to the complete form of the verbal base (after the conjugational characteristics or Vikaraṇas are affixed in the four conj. or special tenses; in Veda often confounded with the Ārdhadhātukas, q.v.); n. N. of the verbal terminations of the four conj. tenses (Pr., Impf., Pot., and Impv.), and of all the root affixes (such as *śānac* and *śatṛi*) which have an indicatory *ś*, Pāṇ. i, 2, 4; iii, 4, 113 &c. — **nāmika**, mfn. (fr. *sarva-nāman*) relating to a pronoun or pronominal, Kāt. — **nāmnya**, n. (fr. id.) the being a name for everything, Nir. vii, 4. — **bhaṭṭa-bhaumâcārya**, m. N. of an author (prob. = *sārva-bhauma-bhaṭṭâcārya*), Cat. — **bhautika**, mfn. (fr. *sarva-bhūta*) relating to all elements or beings, comprising all animated beings, Mn. xii, 51. — **bhaumá**, mfn. (fr. *sarva-bhūmi*) relating to or consisting of or ruling over the whole earth, comprising the whole world, known throughout the world, ŚBr. &c. &c.; relating to all conditions of the mind, Yogas., Sch.; m. an emperor, universal monarch, AitBr. &c. &c.; N. of a son of Ahaṃ-yāti, MBh.; of a son of Su-dharman, Hariv.; of a son of Vidūratha, Pur.; of various authors (also with *bhaṭṭâcārya* and *miśra*), Cat.; of the elephant of Kubera (regent of the north), R.; Vās.; (*am*), n. sovereignty over the whole earth, universal empire, BhP.; *-gṛiha*, n. an imperial palace, L.; *-bhavana*, n. id., Śāntiś.; *-vrata*, n. a partic. religious observance, Cat.; *-sarvasve rāma-sūkta*, n., *-siddhânta*, m. N. of wks. — **bhaumika**, mfn. = *-bhauma*, spread over the whole earth, Kāśikh. — **medhika**, mfn. relating to the Sarva-medha (q.v.), R. — **yajñika**, mfn. (fr. *sarva-yajña*) relating to sacrifices of every kind, ŚāṅkhŚr. — **yaugika**, mfn. (fr. *sarva-yoga*) useful in diseases of every kind, Car. — **rātrika**, mfn. (fr. *sarva-rātra*) lasting the whole night (as a lamp), MatsyaP. — **rogika** or **-raugika**, mfn. (fr. *sarva-roga*) relating to or useful in diseases of every kind, Car.; Cat. — **laukika**, mf(*ī*)n. (fr. *sarva-loka*) prevailing throughout or common to the whole world, known by or permitted to every one, common, universal, MBh.; Kāv. &c. — **varṇika**, mfn. (fr. *sarva-varṇa*) of every kind or sort, Mn.; VarBṛS.; relating to every caste or tribe, Gaut.; MBh. — **varmika**, mfn. composed or written by Sarva-varman, Cat. — **vidya**, n. (fr. *sarva-vidyā*) omniscience, g. *catur-varṇâdi*. — **vibhaktika**, mfn. (fr. *sarva-vibhakti*) applicable or belonging to all the cases of a noun &c., R., Sch. — **vedasa**, mfn. (= and v.l. for *sarva-v°*) one who gives away all his wealth at a sacred rite, Mn. xi, 1; (*am*), n. a person's entire property; *-dakshiṇa*, mfn. (a sacrifice) at which one's whole property is given away as a fee to Brāhmans, Yājñ. — **vedya**, n. (fr. *sarva-veda*) all the Vedas collectively, g. *brāhmaṇâdi*; m. a Brāhman conversant with all the Vedas, W. — **vaidika**, mfn. (fr. id.) versed in all the Vedas, Kauś. — **saṃsarga-lavaṇa**, n. (v.l. *sarva-s°*), salty soil, L. — **saha**, v.l. for *sārvaṃ-s°*, q.v. — **surabhi**, mfn. (= or fr. *sarva-s°*) fragrant with all odours, ĀpGṛ. — **sūtra**, mfn. (fr. *sarva-s°*) consisting of threads of all colours, ĀpŚr. — **sena**, m. (fr. *sarva-s°*) a partic. Pañca-rātra, ĀśvŚr.; (*ī*), f. patr. of Su-nandā (the wife of Bharata), MBh.; *-yajña*, (prob.) w.r. for *sarva-seni-yajña*, Vait. — **seni**, m. (fr. id.) patr. of Śauceya, TS.; pl. N. of a warrior tribe, g. *dāmany-ādi*; *-yajña*, m. a partic. sacrifice, ĀpŚr., Sch. — **senīya**, m. a king of the Sārvasenis, g. *dāmany-ādi*. — **senya**, mfn. coming or derived from Sarva-sena, g. *śaṇḍikâdi*. **Sārvâtmya**, n. (fr. *sarvâtman*) the being the Universal Soul, Saṃk., Sch. **Sārvâyusha**, mfn. (fr. *sarvâyus*) possessing full vitality or vigour, AitBr.; ŚBr.

सार्षप *sārshapa*, mf(*ī*)n. (fr. *sarshapa*) made of or derived from mustard, Kauś.; n. (with or scil. *taila*) mustard oil, Suśr.

सार्ष्ट *sârshṭa*, mfn. (perhaps fr. 7. *sa + ā + ṛishṭa*, √2. *ṛish*) of equal rank or condition, ĀśvŚr.

Sârshṭi, mfn. (prob. connected with *ārsha* and *ṛishi* and *ṛishva*; cf. *ṛishi*) = prec., Pravar.; m. pl. N. of a Gotra, ĀśvŚr.; = next, BhP. — **tā**, f. equality in rank or condition or power (sometimes regarded as one of the grades of Mukti or beatitude; cf. *sālokya*, col. 3), TBr.; Up. &c.

Sārshṭya, n. a partic. state of Mukti (see above).

साल 1. *sāla*, m. (often incorrectly written for 1. *śāla*) the Sāl tree; a wall, fence &c.; for these and other meanings and compounds such as *sāla-grāma* &c., see 1. *śāla*; (*ā*), f., see next.

Sālā, f. (generally written *śālā*) a house (see *niḥ-sālā*). — **karī**, f. a female captive won in battle, W. — **vṛiká**, m. (in later language mostly *śālā-vṛika*) 'house-wolf (?),' a kind of wolf or hyena or jackal or similar animal, RV. &c. &c. — **vṛikīya**, w.r. for next. — **vṛikeyá**, m. the young of a wolf or hyena &c., MaitrS.; PañcavBr.; KaushUp.

साल 2. *sāla*, m. N. of a king, Rājat. — **candra**, m. N. of a prince, Buddh. **Sālêndra-rāja**, m. N. of a man, Lalit.

सालक *sâlaka*, mfn. adorned with locks (of hair), Kāvyâd.

सालकि *sālaki*, m. N. of a Muni, Cat.

सालक्तक *sâlaktaka*, mfn. dyed with lac, Kathās.

सालक्षण्य *sālakshaṇya*, n. (fr. *sa-lakshaṇa*) sameness of characteristics or attributes, Sarvad.

सालग *sālaga*, m. (in music) a partic. Rāga, Saṃgīt. — **sūḍaka**, m. pl. N. of partic. measures, ib. — **sūḍa-nṛitya**, n. a kind of dance, ib.

सालग्राम *sāla-grāma*, *sālaṅka* &c. See *śāl°*, p. 1067, cols. 1 and 3.

सालंकार *sâlaṃkāra*, mf(*ā*)n. having ornaments or decorations, decorated, adorned, Śrutab.

सालन *sālana*. See *śālana*, p. 1067, col. 2.

सालनिर्यास *sāla-niryāsa*, *sāla-pattrā* &c. See *śāl°*, p. 1067, col. 2.

सालबल *sālabala* (?), N. of a place, Buddh.

सालम्ब *sâlamba*, mfn. having anything as a support (comp.), Kathās.

Sâlambana, mfn. belonging to or connected with a partic. mental exercise (see *āl°*).

सालवन *sāla-vana*. See *bhadra-s°*.

सालवाहन *sālavāhana* or *sālivāhana*, v.l. for *sātav°* and *śālav°*, Siṃhâs.

सालस *sâlasa*, mfn. having languor, languid, tired, indolent, lazy, Ṛitus.

साला *sālā*, f. See 1. *sāla*, col. 2.

सालातुरीय *sālāturīya*. See *śāl°*, p. 1067.

सालिका *sālikā*, f. a flute, L.

Sāleyikā or **sāleyī**, f. id., L.

सालिङ्ग्य *sāliṅgya*, n. (fr. *sa-liṅga*) sameness of characteristics, ĀpŚr., Sch.

सालिमञ्जरि *sāli-mañjari*. See *śāl°*, p. 1068.

सालिवाहन *sālivāhana*. See *sālav°* above.

सालूर *sālūra*, *sāleya*. See *śāl°*, p. 1068.

सालोक्य *sālokya*, n. (fr. *sa-loka*) the being in the same sphere or world, residence in the same heaven with (instr. with *saha*, or gen., or comp.; this is one of the four stages of beatitude), MBh.; Hariv.; Pur. &c. — **tā**, f. id., MBh. **Sālokyâdi-catushṭaya**, n. the four (stages of beatitude), viz. Sālokya &c. (the others beings *sāmīpya*, *sārūpya*, and *sāyujya*; see also *sârshṭi*), RTL. 41.

सालोप *sālopa*, mfn. (? for *sa-l°* or = *sâl°*) having a bit or morsel (said of the mouth), Buddh.

सालोहित *sālohita*, m. (= *sa-l°*) a person related by blood, kinsman, Divyâv.

साल्व *sālva*, *sālvaṇa* &c. See *śālva*, p. 1068.

साल्ह *sālha*, m. N. of a man, Buddh.

साल्हण *sālhaṇa*, mfn. belonging or peculiar to Sālhaṇi (see next), Rājat.

Sālhaṇi, m. patr. fr. *salhaṇa*, ib.

साल्हृ *sālhṛi*. See p. 1193, col. 2.

साव *savá*, m. (fr. √3. *su*) a Soma libation (cf. *prātaḥ-* and *sahasra-s°*), RV.

Sāvana, mfn. (fr. 1. *savana*, p. 1190) relating to or determining the three daily Soma libations, i.e. corresponding to the solar time (day, month, year), VarBṛS., Sch.; m. an institutor of a sacrifice or employer of priests at a sacrifice (= *yajamāna*), L.; the conclusion of a sac° or the ceremonies by which it is terminated, L.; N. of Varuṇa, L.; n. scil. (*māna*) the correct solar time, Nidānas.

Sāvika, mfn. (fr. 1. *sava*) relating to the extraction of Soma, Vait.

Sāvin, mfn. preparing Soma (see *manyu-shāvin*); m. a kind of Mahā-purusha (v.l. *sāmin*), VarBṛS.; (*inī*), f. a river, Naish.

1. **Sāvya**, m. (for 2. see s.v.) in *sahasra-s°* (q.v.)

सावइसिरोले *sāvaïsirole*, N. of a district, Inscr.

सावक 1. *sāvaka*, mf(*ikā*)n. (fr. √2. *su* or 2. *sū*) one who has brought forth a child, Yājñ., Sch.; generative, productive, W.; parturient, ib.; (*ikā*), f. a midwife, ib.; m. the young of an animal (or for *śāvaka*), MW.

सावक 2. *sâvaka*, mf(*ā*)n. grown or covered over with the plant Blyxa Octandra, Lāṭy.

सावकाश *sâvakāśa*, mf(*ā*)n. having an opportunity, applicable (*-tva*, n.), Pat.; Saṃk.; Āp., Sch.; (*am*), ind. leisurely, MW.

सावग्रह *sâvagraha*, mfn. having an obstacle, having restraint, restrained, limited, Śaṃk.; (in gram.) having the mark of separation or elision called Avagraha (q.v.), being separated into its component parts or analyzed (as a word in the Pada-pāṭha q.v.), VPrāt.; withholding (its water, as a cloud), Subh.

सावचारण *sâvacāraṇa*, mfn. together with the application, Suśr.

सावज्ञ *sâvajña*, mfn. feeling contempt, despising, disdainful of (loc.), Kathās.; (*am*), ind. contemptuously, disdainfully, R.; Sāh.

सावदानम् *sâvadānam*, ind. (cf. 2. *avadāna*) with interruption (?), Buddh.

सावद्य *sâvadya*, mfn. liable to blame or censure, objectionable, MBh.; n. anything blamable or objectionable, HPariś.; (scil. *aiśvarya*) one of the three kinds of power attainable by an ascetic (the other two being *nir-avadya* and *sūkshma*), Cat.

सावधान *sâvadhāna*, mf(*ā*)n. having attention, attentive, heedful, careful, Bhartṛ.; HPariś.; intent upon doing anything (inf.), Uttamac.; (*am*), ind. attentively, cautiously, Śak. **-tā**, f. attention, carefulness, Pañcat. **-sāhitya**, n. N. of wk.

Sâvadhānaya, Nom. P. °*yati*, to make careful, put on one's guard, Kāśīkh., Sch.

Sâvadhānī, in comp. for *sâvadhāna*. **-√kṛi**, P. *-karoti*, to make attentive or careful, caution, MW. **-kṛita**, mfn. cautioned, apprized, made aware, ib. **-√bhū**, P. *-bhavati*, to be attentive or careful, Cat.

सावधारण *sâvadhāraṇa*, mfn. having a limitation or restriction, limited, restricted, Kād.

सावधि *sâvadhi*, mfn. having a boundary or limit, defined, circumscribed, Kathās.

सावन्तमिश्र *sâvanta-miśra*, m. N. of a man, Cat.

सावमर्द *sâvamarda*, mfn. painful or disagreeable or contradictory (as speech), R.

सावमान *sâvamāna*, mfn. accompanied with contempt or disdain, Bhartṛ.

सावयव *sâvayava*, mfn. having parts, composed of parts (in the Vaiśeshika phil. said of all things except the eternal substances). **-tva**, n. the being composed of parts, Saṃk.; Sarvad.

Sâvayavī-√kṛi, P. *-karoti*, to make into parts, divide into portions, Pañcar.

सावयस *sāvayasá*, m. (prob. fr. *sa-vayasa*) patr. of Ashāḍha, ŚBr.

सावर 1. *sâvara*, mfn. together with the afterbirth, ŚBr.

सावर 2. *sāvara*, °*raka*. See *sābara*, p. 1065.

सावरण *sâvaraṇa*, mfn. barred, bolted, locked up, Ragh.; concealed, secret, clandestine, ib.; **-sadāśiva-pūjā-vidhi**, m. N. of wk.

सावरोह *sâvaroha*, mfn. having shoots or roots sent down by the branches, Hariv.

सावर्ण *sāvarṇa*, mfn. (fr. *sa-varṇa*) relating or belonging to one of the same colour or tribe or caste, MW.; m. N. of a Ṛishi, VS.; MBh.; of the eighth Manu (cf. *sāvarṇi*), Hariv.; MārkP.; of the Saṃhitā traced back to Sāvarṇi (cf. under *sāvarṇaka*). **-lakshya**, n. 'mark of sameness of colour or caste,' the skin, L.

Sāvarṇaka, m. N. of a Manu, MārkP.; (*ikā*), f. N. of a partic. Saṃhitā, Cat.

Sávarṇi, m. N. of a Ṛishi, RV.; metron. of the eighth Manu (son of the Sun by Su-varṇā, q. v., and therefore younger brother of the seventh Manu or Vaivasvata; the succeeding Manus to the twelfth, or accord. to other authorities to the fourteenth inclusive, are all called Sāvarṇi; cf. *daksha-*, *brahma-*, *dharma-s*°), Hariv.; MārkP.

Sāvarṇika, mf(*ī*)n. belonging to the same tribe or caste, MārkP.; belonging to Manu Sāvarṇa or Sāvarṇi, Hariv.; (*ā*), f. N. of a village (printed *sābarṇ*°), Rājat.

Sāvarṇyá, mfn. relating to Manu Sāvarṇa or Sāvarṇi, Cat.; m. patr. fr. *sa-varṇa*, RV.; the eighth Manu (=*sāvarṇi*), MW.; n. identity of colour, Suśr.; identity of caste or class, W.; homogeneousness (of sounds), Pāṇ. i, 1, 69, Sch.; the Manv-antara presided over by the eighth Manu, MW.

सावलम्ब *sâvalamba*, mfn. having a support or prop, supported, leaning for support (on the arm of another), Ragh.

सावलेप *sâvalepa*, mfn. having pride, proud, haughty (*am*, ind.), Daś.; Kāvyâd.

सावशेष *sâvaśesha*, mf(*ā*)n. having a remainder, incomplete, unfinished, MBh.; Kāv. &c.; left, remaining (see comp.); n. a remainder, residue, MārkP. **-jīvita**, mfn. one whose life is not yet finished, having yet time to live, Pañcat. **-bandhana**, mfn. having bonds still remaining, still bound, ib.

सावष्टम्भ *sâvashṭambha*, mfn. possessing resolution, resolute, self-dependent, self-reliant, resolute (*am*, ind.), Kāv.; Kathās.; n. (scil. *vāstu*) a house with an open side-gallery, VarBṛS.

सावस *sāvasá*, mfn. supplied with provisions, ŚBr.

सावहित *sâvahita*, mfn. giving attention, attentive, Uttamac.

सावहेलम् *sâvahelam*, mfn. disdainful, contemptuous, careless (*am*, ind. 'carelessly, quite easily'), Kathās.; Rājat.

साविक *sāvika*. See p. 1210, col. 3.

सावित्र *sāvitrá*, mf(*ī*)n. (fr. *savitṛi*) relating or belonging to the sun, derived or descended from the sun, belonging to the solar dynasty, TS.; VS.; KātyŚr.; MBh.; Hariv.; relating to Sāvitra i. e. Karṇa, MBh.; accompanied or effected by the Sāvitrī verse (cf. below), BhP.; m. a partic. Agni, TBr.; a partic. kind of ladleful (cf. *graha*), TS.; ŚBr.; (scil. *homa*) a partic. oblation, Mn. iv, 150; (scil. *kalpa*) N. of the 10th Kalpa (q. v.), VP.; a Brāhman (accord. to some 'a Gṛiha-stha who possesses corn in a granary'), L.; an embryo or fetus, L.; the sun, L.; a son or descendant of Savitṛi (applied to Karṇa, Candra-ketu, Śiva, one of the Vasus, one of the Maruts, and one of the Rudras), MBh.; R.; Hariv.; N. of one of the peaks of Meru, VP.; (*ī*), f., see below; (*am*), n. (scil. *havis*) a partic. oblation, TS.; ŚBr. &c.; initiation into membership of the twice-born classes by reciting the Sāvitrī verse and investing with the sacred thread, BhP.; the sacred thread (=*yajñôpavīta*), L.; N. of various Sāmans, ĀrshBr.; of a Pariśishṭa of the Yajur-veda; of a partic. Muhūrta (q. v.), Cat.; of the Nakshatra Hasta (presided over by Savitṛi), MBh.; of a forest, MārkP. **-graha-homa**, m. N. of a partic. oblation, Vait. **-cayana**, n. 'arranging or preparing the Agni called Sāvitra,' N. of wk.; *-paddhati*, f., *-prayoga*, m. N. of wks. **-citi**, f. =*-cayana*, IndSt. **-vat** (°*trá*-), mfn. connected with verses addressed to Savitṛi, TS.

Sāvitrâgni-prayoga, m., **Sāvitrâdi-kāṭhaka-cayana**, n., **Sāvitrâdi-prayoga-vṛitti**, f. N. of wks.

Sāvitri, f. (m. c.) =*sāvitrī*, a partic. verse (cf. below), MBh.

Sāvitrikā, f. a partic. Śakti, Hcat.

Sāvitrī, f. a verse or prayer addressed to Savitṛi or the Sun (esp. the celebrated verse RV. iii, 62, 10; also called *gāyatrī*, q. v.), AitBr. &c. &c.; initiation as a member of the three twice-born classes by reciting the above verse and investing with the sacred thread (cf. under *sāvitrá*, and *upa-nayana*), Gaut.; Mn.; MBh. &c.; a partic. form of the Gāyatrī metre, Ked.; N. of Sūryā or a daughter of Savitṛi, AV.; Br.; MBh. &c.; N. of the wife of Brahmā (sometimes regarded as the above verse deified or as the mystical mother of the three twice-born classes, or as the daughter of Savitṛi by his wife Pṛiśni), MBh.; Kathās. &c.; of a wife of Śiva, L.; of a manifestation of Prakṛiti, Cat.; of the wife of Satya-vat (king of Śalva; she was daughter of Aśva-pati, king of Madra, and is regarded as a type of conjugal love; her story is the subject of a fine episode of the Mahā-bhārata; see *sāvitry-upâkhyāna*), MBh.; R.; BhP.; of the wife of Dharma (daughter of Daksha), VP.; of the wife of Kaśyapa, Cat.; of the wife of Bhoja (king of Dhārā), ib.; of a daughter of Ashṭāvakra, Kathās.; of the Yamunā river, Bālar.; of the Sarasvatī, R.; of another river, BhP.; a ray of light, solar ray, W.; the ring-finger, L. **-tīrtha**, n. N. of a Tīrtha, Cat. **-pañjara**, n. N. of wk. (cf. *gāyatrī-p*°). **-patita**, mfn. 'fallen from or deprived of the Sāvitrī,' not invested with the sacred thread at the proper time, Yājñ. i, 38. **-pariṇaya**, m. N. of a Kāvya by Varadâcārya. **-paribhrashṭa**, mfn. =*-patita*, Mn. x, 20. **-putra**, m. pl. N. of a warrior tribe, g. *dāmany-ādi*. **-putrīya**, m. a king of the Sāvitrī-putras, ib. **-bhāshya**, n. N. of wk. **-mahānāmya** (?), the ceremony of investiture with recital of the Sāvitrī, MW. **-vrata** or **-vrataka**, n. a partic. fast (kept by women on the fifth day of the second half of Vaiśākha, or of the dark half of Jyaishṭha, to preserve them from widowhood), Hariv.; °*ta-kathānaka*, n., °*ta-pūjā-kathā*, f., °*tôdyāpana*, n. N. of wks. **-sūtra**, n. the sacred thread (=*yajñôpavīta*), L.

Sāvitrīka. See *patita-s*°.

Sāvitreya, m. N. of Yama, L.

Sāvitry, in comp. for *sāvitrī*. **-avarajā**, f. the younger daughter of Sāvitrī, MW. **-upanishad**, f. N. of an Upanishad. **-upâkhyāna**, n. the story of Sāvitrī (MBh. iii, ch. 293-299; cf. above).

साविन् *sāvin*. See p. 1210, col. 3.

साविष्कार *sâvishkāra*, mfn. having manifestation, manifest, W.; making an exhibition of any power or talent, proud, haughty, arrogant, ib.

सावेगम् *sâvegam*, ind. with excitement or agitation, Mṛicch.; Śak.

सावेतस *sāvetasa*, m. a patr., ĀśvŚr.; Inscr.

सावेरी *sāverī*, f. (in music) a partic. Rāgiṇī, Saṃgīt.

साव्य 2. *sāvya*, mfn. (for 1. see p. 1210, col. 3) composed by Savya, ŚāṅkhŚr.

साशंस *sâśansa*, mfn. having desire, desirous, hopeful (*am*, ind. 'wishfully,' 'hopefully'), Mṛicch.; Kālid.; Kirāt.

साशङ्क *sâśaṅka*, mf(*ā*)n. having fear or anxiety, apprehensive, afraid of (loc.; *am*, ind. 'apprehensively'), MBh.; Kāv. &c. **-tā**, f. the state of being afraid or apprehensive, fear, terror, MW.

साशन *sâśana*, mfn. having food (see next).

Sâśanânaśaná, n. du. having and not having food, that which eats and does not eat, earthly and heavenly beings, RV.

साशनार *sāśanāra*, m. N. of a partic. Agrahāra or royal grant to Brāhmans, MW.

साशयन्दक *sāśayandaka* (?), m. a small house-lizard (=*jyeshṭhī*), L.

साशिक्य *sāśikya*, N. of a people or country (cf. *śāśika*), Daś.

साशिर *sâśira*, mfn. (fr. 7. *sa*+*āśira*=*āśir*) with admixture, mixed, TS.; ŚBr.

साशीति *sâśīti*, mfn. with eighty, increased by eighty, plus eighty, Yājñ.

साशीर्क *sâśīrka*, mfn. containing a prayer or blessing, TS. (a more correct form would be *sâśīshka*, but cf. *an-āśīrka*).

साशूक *sāśūka*, m. a blanket (=*kambala*), L.

साश्चर्य *sâścarya*, mfn. astonished, surprised by (comp.), Kathās.; wonderful, marvellous, astonishing, Bhartṛ.; (*am*), ind. with astonishment or surprise, Hit. **-kautuka**, mfn. astonished and curious, Kathās. **-carya**, mfn. of wonderful conduct, Bhartṛ.; Rājat. **-maya**, mf(*ī*)n. wonderful, full of marvels, MW.

साश्मवर्षिन् *sâśma-varshin*, mfn. accompanied by a shower of stones, BhP.

साश्र 1. *sâśra*, mfn. (fr. 7. *sa*+1. *aśra*) having angles or corners, angular, MW.

साश्र 2. *sâśra*, mfn. (fr. 7. *sa*+2. *aśra*; more correctly written *sâsra*) tearful, weeping, Kāśīkh.

Sâśru, mfn. accompanied by tears, tearful, shedding tears (*u*, ind.), MBh.; Kāv. &c. **-dhī**, f.

'having a sad heart,' a mother-in-law, L. **-nayana** or **-locana**, mfn. having tearful eyes, MBh.

साश्व *sâśva*, mfn. with horses, possessing horses, KātyŚr.; N. of a king, MBh.

Sâśva-medha, mfn. together with a horse-sacrifice, Vait.

साषीराजन् *sāshī-rājan*, m. pl. N. of partic. kings, Pañcad.

साष्ट *sâshṭa*, mfn. with eight, increased by eight, plus eight (with *śata*, n. = 108), L.

Sâshṭâṅga, mfn. performed with eight limbs or members (as a reverential prostration of the body so as to touch the ground with the hands, breast, forehead, knees, and feet), Prab.; (*am*), ind. with the above prostration (with *pra-√nam*, 'to make the above reverential prostration'), Hit. **-pātam**, ind. making the above prostration, ib.

साष्ट्रिक *sâshṭrika*, w.r. for *sôshṭ°*, MBh.

साष्ठी *sāshṭhī*, f. the small Banana, L.

सास *sâsa*, m. (√2. *as*) a bow, MW.

साසකර्णि *sāsakarṇi*, w.r. for *śāś°*, Saṃskārak.

सासद्यमान *sāsadyamāna*, pr. p. Ā. of √*sad*.

सासन्दीक *sâsandīka*, mfn. (see *āsandī*) together with a chair or stool, KātyŚr.

सासव *sâsava*, mfn. having spirituous liquor, filled with spirituous liquor, Śāntiś.

सासहि *sāsahi, sāsahvas*. See p. 1193.

सासार *sâsāra*, mf(*ā*)n. having showers, rainy, R.

सासि *sâsi*, mfn. having a sword, armed with a sword, MW. **-pāṇi** (Śiś.) and **-hasta** (R.), mfn. sword in hand.

सासु *sâsu*, mfn. having life, living, BhP.

Sâsusū, mfn. (see *asusū*), having arrows, Kir. xv, 5.

सासूय *sâsūya*, mfn. having envy, envious, disdainful, scornful, angry at or with (*prati*), Kāv.; Kathās.

सास्तरण *sâstaraṇa*, mf(*ā*)n. together with a carpet or rug, Lāṭy.

सास्थि *sâsthi*, mfn. having bones (said of any animal), see comp. **-tāmrârdha**, n. a kind of amalgam of zinc and copper, bell-metal (= *kāṅsya*), L. **-vadha**, m. the killing of any animal having bones, Yājñ. iii, 275. **-svānam**, ind. with the cracking sound of bones, Śiś.

सास्ना *sāsnā*, f. the dewlap of an ox, MaitrS.; Śiś. **-°di-mat** (*sāsnâd°*), mfn. having a dewlap &c., Sāh. **-lāṅgūla-kakuda-khura-vishāṇin**, mfn. having a dewlap (and) tail (and) hump (and) claws (and) horns, Pat. **-vat**, mfn. having a dewlap, Kaṇ.

सास्र 1. *sâsra*, mfn. (more correctly 1. *sâśra*, q.v.) having angles or corners, MW.

सास्र 2. *sâsra*, mfn. (cf. 2. *sâśra*) tearful, weeping, in tears (*am*, ind.), Kāv.; Kathās.

सास्रव *sâsrava*, mfn. (with Jainas) connected with the act called *āsrava* (q.v.), L.

सास्वादन *sâsvādana*, n. (scil. *sthāna*; with Jainas) N. of the second of the 14 stages towards supreme bliss, Cat.

साह् *sāh*. See 2. *sah*, p. 1193, col. 1.

1. **Sāha**, mfn. (fr. √*sah*) powerful, mighty, RV.; (also *shāha*, ifc.) resisting, conquering, subduing, MBh.

Sāhya, n. conquering, overthrowing, victory (see *abhimāti-*, *nṛi-*, and *pṛitanā-shāhya*); aid, assistance (often v.l. *sahya*; with √*kṛi* or √*dā*, 'to give assistance'), MBh.; R. &c.; conjunction, society, fellowship (in this meaning perhaps fr. *saha* or contracted from *sāhāyya*), L. **-kara**, mfn. rendering assistance, R. **-kṛit**, m. a companion, associate, W.

साह 2. *sāha*, m. = شاه (see *pradīpa-* and *madhukara-s°*).

Sāhi, m. = prec. (see *candra-*, *prema-s°* &c.) **-deva** and **-sujā**, m. N. of kings, Cat.

साहकायन *sāhakāyana*, mfn. (fr. *sahaka*, v.l. for *siṅhaka*), g. *pakshâdi*.

साहंकार *sâhaṃkāra*, mfn. having egotism or self-conceit, proud, arrogant, Rājat.; Kathās. **-tā**, f. self-conceit, arrogance, Pañcad.

Sâhaṃkṛita, mfn. self-conceited, proud, haughty, Siṅhâs.

साहचर *sāhacara*, mfn. (fr. *saha-c°*) belonging to the plant Saha-cara, Suśr.

Sāhacarya, n. companionship, fellowship, society, association with (instr. or comp.), Nir.; Kāv. &c.

साहजिक *sāhajika*, mfn. (fr. *saha-ja*) innate, natural, Vṛishabhān.; m. N. of a man, Rājat.

साहजित् *sāhajit*, m., v.l. for *sāhañji*, VP.

साहञ्ज *sāhañja*, m. N. of a king, Hariv.

Sāhañjanī, f. N. of a town built by Sāhañja, ib.

Sāhañji, m. = *sāhañja*, VP.

साहदेव *sāhadeva*, m. patr. fr. *saha-deva*, Pāṇ. iv, 1, 114, Sch.

Sāhadevaka, m. a worshipper of Saha-deva, Pāṇ. iv, 3, 99, Sch.

Sāhadevi, m. patr. fr. *saha-deva*, MBh.; Rājat.

Sāhadevyà, m. patr. of Somaka, RV.

साहन *sāhana*, n. (fr. Caus. of √*sah*) the act of causing to bear; sufferance, endurance, W.

Sāhantyá, mfn. = *sáhantya*, conquering, powerful, AV.; TS.

Sāhaya, mfn. causing or enabling to bear, Pāṇ. iii, 1, 138.

साहस *sāhasa*, mfn. (fr. *sahas*) over-hasty, precipitate, rash, inconsiderate, foolhardy, Hariv.; m. N. of Agni at the Pāka-yajña, Gṛihyas.; m. n. punishment, fine (regarded as of three kinds, the highest being called Uttama; half of that, Madhyama; and half of that, Adhama), Mn.; Yājñ. &c.; (*am*), n. (ifc. f. *ā*) boldness, daring, rashness, temerity, any precipitate or reckless act, MBh.; Kāv. &c.; overstraining, Car.; violence, force, rapine, rape, robbery, felony, aggression, cruelty, Gaut.; Āpast.; Nār.; adultery, Nār.; hatred, enmity, L. **-karaṇa**, n. violence, force, Daś. **-karma-tā**, f. rashness, temerity, Mṛicch. **-kārin**, mfn. acting inconsiderately or rashly, Ratnâv. **-lāñchana**, m. N. of a man (cf. *sāhasâṅka*), Vcar. **-vat**, mfn. inconsiderate, rash, foolhardy, VarBṛS. **Sāhasâṅka**, m. 'marked or characterized by daring,' N. of king Vikramâditya, Pañcad.; of a poet (mentioned by Rāja-śekhara); of a lexicographer, Cat.; *-carita*, n. N. of wk.; *°kīya*, mfn. relating to Sāhasâṅka, Cat. **Sāhasâdhyavasāyin**, mfn. acting with inconsiderate haste, MW. **Sāhasâṅka-rasika**, mfn. one whose only feeling or passion is cruelty, brutal, ferocious, W. **Sāhasâikânta-rasânuvartin**, mfn. one who follows or yields to the one passion of cruelty or rashness, MW. **Sāhasôpanyāsin**, mfn. suggesting violent deeds, Mālatim.

Sāhasika, mf(*ī*)n. bold, daring, impetuous, rash, reckless, inconsiderate, MBh.; Kāv. &c.; using great force or violence, perpetrated with violence, cruel, brutal, ferocious, rapacious, Mn.; MBh.; overstraining or overworking one's self, Car.; punitive, castigatory, W.; m. a robber, freebooter, ib.; N. of a cook, Kathās. **-tā**, f. cruelty, ferocity, impetuosity, ib.

Sāhasikya, n. rashness, foolhardiness, temerity, Naish.; Śiś.; violence, force, Pāṇ. i, 3, 32.

Sāhasin, mfn. rash, precipitate, inconsiderate, foolhardy, Kāv.; Kathās.; cruel, violent, ferocious, Nār.

साहस्र *sāhasrá*, mf(*ī* or *ā*)n. (fr. *sahasra*) relating or belonging to a thousand, consisting of or bought with or paid for a th°, thousandfold, exceedingly numerous, infinite, VS. &c. &c.; m. an army or detachment consisting of a th° men, W.; (pl.) N. of four Ekâhas at which a th° (cows) are given as a fee, ŚrS.; n. (ifc. f. *ā*) an aggregate of a th° or of many th°, TBr.; MBh. &c. **-cūḍika**, m. (with *loka-dhātu*) N. of a partic. world, Buddh. **-vat** (*°srá-*), mfn. containing a th°, TS. **-vedhin**, mfn. = *sahasra-v°*, Kālac. **-śas**, ind. by th°, ÂśvŚr. **Sāhasrâdya**, m. a partic. Ekâha, Vait. **Sāhasrānīka**, m. N. of a king (cf. *sahasrân°*), Buddh. **Sāhasrântya**, m. a partic. Ekâha, Vait.

Sāhasraka, mf(*ikā*)n. amounting to or containing a thousand, Cat.; n. the aggregate of a thousand, Pañcar.; N. of a Tīrtha, MBh.

Sāhasri, m. (prob.) a patr., Rājat.

Sāhasrika, mfn. consisting of a thousand, Hcat.

साहानुसाहि *sāhānusāhi*, m. N. of a king, Pañcad.

साहायक *sāhāyaka*, n. (fr. *sahāya*) assistance, aid, help, Kāv.; Kathās.; a number of associates or companions, MW.; auxiliary troops, ib.

Sāhāya, w.r. for *sahāya*.

Sāhāyya, n. help, succour (*°yyam* √*kṛi* and √*sthā*, 'to give assistance'), MBh.; Kāv. &c.; friendship, fellowship, alliance, W.; (in dram.) helping another in danger, Sāh. **-kara**, mfn. giving assistance, helping, Daś. **-dāna**, n. the giving of aid or assistance, ib.

Sāhāyyaka, n. aid, assistance, Daś.

साहि *sāhi*, m. = 2. *sāha* (see *candra-*, *prema-*, *rāma-s°* &c.)

साहिती *sāhiti*, f. See below.

साहित्य *sāhitya*, n. (fr. *sahita*) association, connection, society, combination, union with (instr. or comp.; *ena*, ind. 'in combination with, together with'), Kām.; Kap.; KātyŚr., Sch.; agreement, harmony, Prab.; literary or rhetorical composition, rhetoric, poetry, Sāh.; Cat. **-kaṇṭhôddhāra**, m., **-kalpadruma**, m., **-kalpapallavī**, f., **-kautūhala**, n., **-kaumudī**, f., **-candrikā**, f., **-cintāmaṇi**, m., **-cūḍāmaṇi**, m., **-taraṃgiṇī**, f. N. of wks. **-darpaṇa**, m. 'mirror of composition,' N. of a treatise on literary or rhetorical composition by Viśvanātha-kavi-rāja (15th century A.D.) **-dīpikā**, f., **-bodha**, m., **-mīmāṅsā**, f., **-muktāmaṇi**, m., **-ratnamālā**, f., **-ratnâkara**, m., **-vicāra**, m. N. of wks. **-vidhyādhara**, m. N. of Cāritra-vardhana Muni (author of a Comm. on the Naishadha-carita), Cat. **-śārṅgadhara**, m. (prob.) = *śārṅgadhara-paddhati*. **-śāstra**, n. a treatise on rhetoric or composition (or any work explaining the figures of rhetoric or giving rules for literary or poetical composition), MW. **-saṃgraha**, m., **-saraṇī-vyākhyā**, f., **-sarvasva**, n., **-sāmrājya**, n., **-sāra**, m., **-sudhā**, f., **-sudhā-samudra**, m., **-sūkshma-saraṇi**, f., **-sūcī**, f., **-hṛidaya-darpaṇa**, m. N. of wks.

Sāhitī, f. = *sāhitya* above, Cat.

Sāhya. See col. 1.

साहिल *sāhila*, m. N. of a poet, Cat.

साहिवीचि *sâhi-vīci*, mfn. having waves of serpents, MW.

साहुडियान *sāhuḍi-yāna* or *sāhuḍi-pāla*, m. N. of Śūla-pāṇi, Cat.

साहुल *sāhula* (?), m. N. of a man, Cat.

साहेब्राम् *sāheb-rām*, m. N. of the author of the Kāśmīra-rāja-vaṅśa (died before 1883), Cat.

साह्न *sâhná*, mfn. connected with a day, terminating with a day or lasting a day (opp. to 1. *ahīna*), Br.; m. = *ekâha*, TS.; TāṇḍBr.; ĀpŚr.

Sâhnâtirātrá, mfn. terminating with a day and exceeding a day, AV.

साह्नोक *sāhnoka*, m. N. of a poet, Cat.

साह्लाद *sâhlāda*, mfn. having joy or gladness, cheerful, glad (*am*, ind. 'joyfully'), Pañcat.

साह्व *sâhva*, mf(*ā*)n. having a name, named, called (see *ishu-*, *rathâṅga-s°* &c.)

Sâhvaya, mfn. = prec. (see *kāla-*, *gaja-s°* &c.); m. gambling with fighting animals, setting animals to fight for sport &c. (= *sam-āhvaya*), L.

साह्वन् *sāhvan*. See *viśva-s°*, p. 994, col. 1.

साह्वस् *sāhvas*. See p. 1193, col. 2.

साह्व्य *sāhvya*, m. N. of a village, Rājat.

सि 1. *si* (cf. √1. *sā*), cl. 5. 9. P. Ā. (Dhātup. xxvii, 2; xxxi, 5) *sinoti*, *sinute*; *sināti*, *sinīte* (really occurring only in pres. *sināti*, impf. *asinot*; pf. *sishāya*, RV.; aor. [?] *sishet*, ib.; *asaishīt*, *aseshṭa*, Gr.; fut. *setā*, ib.; *sishyati*, MBh.; *seshyati*, *°te*, Gr.; inf. *sétave*, AV.; *setum*, Gr.), to bind, tie, fetter, RV.; AV.; VS.; PārGṛ.; KaṭhUp.: Caus. *sāyayati* (aor. *asīshayat*), Gr.:

Desid. *sisīshati*, °*te*, ib.: Intens. *seshīyate*, *sesha-yīti*, *sesheti*, ib. [Cf. Gk. ἱ-μάς, ἱ-μονιά; Lett. *sinu*, 'to bind;' Angl.Sax. *sâl*; Germ. *Seil.*]

1. **Sitá**, mfn. (for 2. see below; for 3. p. 1214, col. 2) bound, tied, fettered, RV. &c. &c.; joined with, accompanied by (instr.), Prab.; Rājat.; BhP.

Sitaka, mfn., g. *ṛiśyādi*, Pāṇ. iv, 2, 80.

1. **Siti**, f. (for 2. see p. 1214, col. 3) binding, fastening (in 1. *prá-siti*, p. 697, col. 3).

1. **Sina**, mfn. (for 2. see s. v.) stuck fast (as food in the throat), Pat. on Pāṇ. viii, 2, 47, Vārtt. 4; m. a bond, fetter, L.

सि 2. *si* (see *sāyaka*, *senā*), to hurl, cast.

2. **Sita**. See 2. *prá-sita*, p. 697, col. 3.

सि 3. *si*, ind., g. *cādi*.

सिंसपा *siṇsapā*. See *śiṇśapā*, p. 1069, col. 3.

सिंह *siṇhá*, m. (ifc. f. *ā*; prob. fr. √*sah*) 'the powerful one,' a lion (also identified with *āt-man*), RV. &c. &c.; the zodiacal sign Leo or its Lagna, VarBṛS.; MārkP.; a hero or eminent person (ifc. = 'chief or lord of,' to express excellence of any kind; cf. *purusha-s*°, *rāja-s*°, and the similar use of *ṛishabha*, *vyāghra* &c.; sometimes also = 'prince, king,' e. g. *nāga-pura-s*°, the king of N°; cf. *siṇha-dvār* and *siṇhâsana*), MBh.; Kāv. &c.; a partic. form of temple, VarBṛS.; a partic. place prepared for the building of a house, Jyot.; a Moringa with red flowers (= *rakta-śigru*), L.; (in music) a kind of tune, Saṃgīt.; the symbol or emblem of the 24th Arhat of the present Avasarpiṇī, MW.; N. of a son of Kṛishṇa, BhP.; of a king of the Vidyā-dharas, Kathās.; of a king (the father of Sāhi-deva), Cat.; of the Veṅkata mountain, L.; (with *ācārya*) of an astronomer, VarBṛS., Sch.; of various other persons, Buddh.; Rājat.; a partic. mythical bird, R.; (*ā*), f. a partic. grass or plant (= *nāḍī*), L.; (*ī*), f., see below. — **karṇa**, (prob. m.) N. of a place, g. *takshaśi-lâdi*; (*ī*), f. a partic. position of the right hand in shooting an arrow, ŚārṅgP. — **karman**, mfn. acting like a lion, achieving lion-like deeds, Viddh. — **kal-pā**, f. N. of a (prob. imaginary) town, Divyâv. — **kāraka**, m. a creator of lions, Pañcat. — **ketu**, m. N. of a Bodhi-sattva, Lalit.; of another man, ib. — **keli**, m. N. of a celebrated Bodhi-sattva (= Mañ-ju-śrī), L. — **kesara** (less correctly -*kes*°), m. a lion's mane, W.; Mimusops Elengi, L.; a kind of sweet-meat, Śil. — **kesarin** (less correctly -*keśar*°), m. N. of a king, Buddh. — **kośa**, m. N. of a king, ib. — **ga**, m. 'going like a lion,' N. of Śiva, MBh. — **gāminī**, f. N. of a Gandharva maiden, Kāraṇḍ. — **giri**, m. (with Jainas) N. of a Sthavira, HPariś.; °*rîśvara*, m. N. of a teacher, W. — **gupta**, m. N. of a king, Kathās.; of the father of Vāg-bhaṭa, Cat. (v. l. *saṃgha-g*°). — **grīva**, mfn. lion-necked, MBh. — **ghosha**, m. N. of a Buddha, Buddh.; of various other men, Daś. — **candra**, m. N. of various men, MBh.; Buddh.; (*ā*), f. N. of a woman, Buddh. — **carman**, n. a lion's skin, ĀpŚr. — **jaṭi**, m. N. of a king, Buddh. — **tala**, m. the open hands joined, L. (cf. *saṃha-t*°). — **tā**, f. the being a lion, leonine state, MBh.; Kathās. — **tāla** or °**lākhya**, m. = -*tala*, L. — **tilaka-sūri**, m. N. of a Jaina author, Cat. — **tuṇḍa**, m. 'lion-faced,' a kind of fish, Mn. v, 16; Euphorbia Ligularia, Bhpr. — **tuṇḍaka**, m. a kind of fish (= -*tuṇḍa*), Yājñ. — **tva**, n. the state of a l°, MBh.; Ragh. &c. — **daṇshṭra**, mfn. l°-toothed, R.; m. a kind of arrow, ib.; m. N. of Śiva, MW.; of an Asura, Kathās.; of a king of the Śabaras, ib. — **datta**, m. 'lion-given,' N. of an Asura, ib.; of a poet, Cat. — **darpa**, mfn. having a lion's pride, MW. — **deva**, m. N. of a king, Rājat.; of an author, Cat. — **dvār**, f. a palace-gate, Kathās. — **dvāra**, n. id., ib.; Rājat.; a principal or chief gate, any gate or entrance, W. — **dvīpa**, m. N. of an island, Buddh. — **dhvaja**, m. N. of a Buddha, ib. — **dhvani**, m. the roar of a l°, W.; a sound like the roar of a l°, MW.; a cry challenging to battle, war-cry, Kum. — **nan-dana**, m. (in music) a kind of measure, Saṃgīt. — **nardin**, mfn. roaring like a lion, MW. — **nāda**, m. a lion's roar, R.; Hariv.; Kathās. &c.; a war-cry, MBh.; Kāv. &c.; a confident assertion, Pañcat.; recital of the Buddhist doctrine, Buddh.; a kind of bird, VarBṛS.; a kind of metre, Col.; (in music) a kind of time, Saṃgīt.; N. of Śiva, MBh.; of an Asura, Kathās.; of a son of Rāvaṇa, Bālar.; of a Śākya, Buddh.; of a king of Malaya, Mudr.; of the general of an army, Vās., Introd.; of a Buddhist saint, Buddh.; -*guggulu*, m. a partic. mixture, Bhpr.; -*nādin*, m. N. of a Bodhi-sattva, Buddh.; -*sādhana*, n. N. of wk. — **nādaka**, m. a lion's roar, L.; a war-cry, W.; (*ikā*), f. Alhagi Maurorum, L. — **nādin**, m. N. of a Māra-putra, Lalit. — **nṛipa**, m. N. of a king, Cat. — **parākrama**, m. N. of a man, Kathās. — **paripṛicchā**, f. N. of wk. — **parṇikā**, f. Phaseolus Trilobus, L. — **parṇī**, f. Justicia Ganderussa, L. — **pippalī**, f. a kind of plant (= *saiṇhalī*), MW. — **pucchikā**, f. Hemionitis Cordifolia, L. — **puc-chī**, f. id., ib.; Glycine Debilis, ib. — **pura**, n. N. of a town (Singapur), MBh.; Buddh. &c. — **puraka**, m. an inhabitant of that town, VarBṛS. — **pushpī**, f. Hemionitis Cordifolia, L. — **pūrvârdha-kāya-tā**, f. having the forepart of the body like a lion (one of the 32 signs of perfection), Dharmas. 83. — **pragar-jana**, mfn. roaring like a lion, MBh. — **pragar-jita**, n. the roaring of a lion, MW. — **praṇāda**, m. a war-whoop, R. — **pratīka** (*siṇhá*-), mfn. having a lion's appearance, AV. — **pradīpa**, m. N. of wk. — **bala**, m. N. of a king, Kathās.; -*datta*, m. N. of a man, Mudr. — **bāhu**, m. N. of the father of Vijaya (the founder of the first Buddhist dynasty in Ceylon), Buddh. — **bhaṭa**, m. N. of an Asura, Kathās. — **bhadra**, m. N. of a teacher, Buddh. — **bhū-pāla**, m. N. of an author, Cat. — **bhūbhṛit**, m. N. of a king, Rājat. — **mati**, m. N. of a Māra-putra, Lalit. — **mala**, n. a kind of brass (= *pañca-loha*), L. — **malla**, m. N. of an author, Cat. — **mahīpati**, m. N. of a king, Rājat.; of an author, Cat. — **māyā**, f. an illusory form shaped like a lion, Hariv. — **mu-kha**, mfn. l°-faced; m. N. of one of Śiva's attend-ants, Hariv.; of a scholar, Buddh.; (*ī*), f. Glycine Debilis, L.; Gendarussa Vulgaris, ib. — **yānā**, f. 'having a car drawn by lions,' N. of Durgā, L. — **ratha**, mf(*ā*)n. having a car dr° by l°, L.; m. N. of a man, Rājat.; (*ā*), f. N. of Durgā, Hariv. — **ra-va**, m. a lion's roar, Kāv.; a war-cry, MBh. — **raś-mi** (?), m. N. of a man, Buddh. — **rāj**, m. N. of a grammarian, MS. — **rāja**, m. N. of a king, Rājat.; of a grammarian, MS. — **rotsikā** (?), f. N. of a village, Rājat. — **rshabha** (°*ha* + *ṛish*°), m. a noble lion, R. — **lagna**, n. the Lagna (q. v.) of the sign Leo, MW. — **lamba**, m. N. of a place, Cat. — **līla**, m. (in music) a kind of time, Saṃgīt.; a partic. kind of sexual union, L. — **lomán**, n. a lion's hair, ŚBr. — **vaktra**, m. N. of a Rākshasa, R.; n. a lion's face, Cat.; N. of a town, Buddh. (w.r. -*vakta*). — **vatsa**, m. N. of a serpent-demon, ib. — **varman**, m. N. of a man, Inscr.; Kathās.; Daś. — **vāha**, mfn. riding on a l°, BhP. — **vāhana**, mfn. id.; m. N. of Śiva, MBh.; (*ā*), f. N. of Durgā, L. — **vāhin**, mfn. = -*vāha*; (*inī*), f. N. of Durgā, DevībhP. — **vi-krama**, m. a horse, L.; (in music) a kind of time, Saṃgīt.; N. of Candra-gupta, Inscr.; of a king of the Vidyā-dharas, Kathās.; of a thief, ib.; = *vikra-ma-siṇha*, MW. — **vikrānta**, mfn. valiant as a lion, MBh.; m. a horse, L.; n. a l°'s gait, Buddh.; a kind of metre, Col.; -*gati* or -*gāmin*, mfn. having a l°'s gait, MW.; -*gāmi-tā*, f. the having such a gait (one of the 80 minor marks of a Buddha), Dharmas. 84. — **vikrīḍita**, m. (in music) a kind of time, Saṃgīt.; a kind of Samādhi, Dharmas. 136; N. of a Bodhi-sattva, ib.; n. a kind of metre, Ked. — **vi-jṛimbhita**, m. (with Buddhists) a kind of Samādhi, Kāraṇḍ. (cf. -*vishkambhita*). — **vinnā**, f. Glycine Debilis, L. — **vishkambhita**, m. (with Buddhists) a kind of Samādhi, Kāraṇḍ. (perhaps only w.r. for -*vijṛimbhita*). — **vishṭara**, (prob.) a throne, Rājat. — **vyāghra**, 'lion and tiger,' a partic. philosophical term, Cat.; (*ī*), f. N. of various wks.; -*kroḍa*, m., -*ṭippaṇī*, f., -*ṭīkā*, f. N. of wks.; -*nishevita*, mfn. inhabited by lions and tigers, MW.; -*rahasya*, n., -*lakshaṇa*, n., -*lakshaṇa-prakāśa*, m., -*lakshaṇa-rahasya*, n., -*lakshaṇī*, f. N. of wks.; °*ghrāmi-shī*-√*kṛi*, to make a prey to lions and tigers, Kathās. — **vyāghrīya**, n. N. of wk. — **śāva** (Hariv.) or -**śiśu** (Śak.), m. a l°'s cub. — **śrī**, f. N. of a woman, Kathās. — **saṃhanana**, n. the killing of a lion, MW.; mfn. lion-shaped, having a strong and noble frame, MBh.; R. — **sāhi**, m. N. of a king, Inscr. — **siddhânta-sindhu**, m. N. of wk. — **sena**, m. N. of various men, MBh.; L. — **skandha**, mfn. having the shoulders of a lion, MBh.; R.; VarBṛS. — **stha**, m. 'being in the constellation Leo,' the planet Jupiter when so situated, (also) the festival celebrated at that time (called Siṇhasth), MW.; -*makarastha-guru-nirṇaya*, m., -*māhātmya*, n., -*snāna-paddhati*, f. N. of wks. — **svāmin**, m. N. of a temple erected in honour of Siṇha-rāja, Rājat. — **hanu**, mfn. having the jaws of a lion, Buddh. (-*tā*, f. one of the 32 signs of perfection, Dharmas. 83); m. N. of the grandfather of Gautama Buddha, ib. **Siṇhâksha**, m. N. of a king, Kathās. **Siṇhâ-cala**, m. N. of a mountain, Cat.; -*māhātmya*, n. N. of wk. **Siṇhâcārya**, m. N. of an astronomer, VarBṛS., Sch. **Siṇhâjina**, m. N. of a man, Pāṇ. v, 3, 82, Sch. **Siṇhâḍhya**, mfn. abounding in lions, W. **Siṇhânana**, m. Gendarussa Vulgaris, Bhpr. **Siṇhânuvāka**, m. N. of wk. **Siṇhâvaloka**, m. a kind of metre, Col. **Siṇhâvalokana**, n. a lion's backward look, BhP.; N. of wk.; (*ena* or °*kana-nyāyena*), ind. accord. to the rule of the lion's look (i.e. casting a retrospective glance while at the same time proceeding onwards), TPrāt., Sch.; ŚāṅkhBr., Sch.; MBh., Sch. **Siṇhâvalokita**, n. = prec., Gṛihyās.; Piṅg., Sch. **Siṇhâsana**, n. 'lion's-seat,' 'king's seat,' 'a throne,' MBh.; Kāv. &c.; a partic. sedent posture, Cat.; m. a kind of sexual union, L.; -*cakra*, n. N. of three astrological diagrams shaped like a man and marked with the 27 Nakshatras, MW.; -*traya*, n. N. of an astrological diagram, L.; -*dvātriṇśat* or °*śati* or °*śatikā* or °*śat-kathā* or °*śat-puttalika-vārttā* or °*śat-putrikā-vārttā* or °*śikā*, f. N. of a wk. consisting of 32 stories in praise of Vikramâditya (= *vikrama-carita*); -*bhrashṭa*, mfn. fallen from a throne, dethroned, MW.; -*raṇa*, m. n. a strife or struggle for the th°, R.; -*stha*, mfn. sitting on a throne, MBh. **Siṇhâstra**, n. N. of a mythical weapon, Dhanaṃj. **Siṇhâsya**, mfn. lion-faced, MW.; m. a kind of fish, Vajras.; Gendarussa Vulgaris, Bhpr.; Bauhinia Variegata, L.; a partic. position of the hands, Cat.; (*ā*), f. Gend° Vulg° or Adhatoda Vasika, L. **Siṇhêndra**, m. a mighty lion, Pañcar. **Siṇhôddhatā** (Piṅg.) or °**hônnatā** (ib.; Col.), f. a kind of metre.

Siṇhaka, m. endearing form of *siṇha*, Divyâv.; of *siṇhâjina*, Pāṇ. v, 3, 81 sq., Sch.; (*ikā*), f., see below.

Siṇhala, m. the island of Ceylon (perhaps so called as once abounding in lions), BhP.; Rājat. &c.; N. of a man, Buddh.; pl. the people of C°, AV.Pariś.; MBh.; VarBṛS. &c.; (*ā*), f. the island of C° (see -*sthāna*); n. id., W.; tin, L.; brass (more correctly *siṇhalaka*), L.; bark, rind, MW.; Cassia bark (more correctly *saiṇhala*), L. — **dvīpa**, m. the isl° of C°, Buddh.; Kathās. &c. — **stha**, mfn. being or dwelling in C°, MW.; (*ā*), f. a species of pepper, L.

Siṇhalā-sthāna, m. a kind of palm tree, L.

Siṇhalaka, mfn. relating to Ceylon (with *dvīpa*, m. 'Ceylon,' Cat.), VarBṛS.; n. C°, MW.; brass, L.

Siṇhāya, Nom. Ā. °*yate*, to behave like a lion, Hit.; Kathās.

Siṇhikā, f. N. of the mother of Rāhu (she was a daughter of Daksha [or Kaśyapa] and wife of Kaś-yapa [or Vipra-citti]), MBh.; Hariv.; Pur.; N. of a form of Dākshāyaṇī, Cat.; of a Rākshasī, R.; a knock-kneed girl unfit for marriage, L.; Gendarussa Vulgaris, L. — **tanaya**, m. 'son of Siṇhikā,' metron. of Rāhu, ŚārṅgP.; pl. N. of certain Asuras, MBh. — **putra** or -**suta**, m. metron. of Rāhu, A. — **sūnu**, m. ib., ŚārṅgP.

Siṇhikeya, m. metron. of Rāhu (w.r. for *saiṇh*°), Hariv.

Siṇhinī, f. (with Buddhists) N. of a goddess, W.

Siṇhiya or **siṇhila**, m. endearing forms of *siṇha*, Pāṇ. v, 3, 81, Sch.

1. **Siṇhī**, f. a lioness, RV.; VS.; TS. &c.; N. of the Uttara-vedi (nom. *siṇhīḥ*), TS.; of various plants (Solanum Jacquini; Sol° Melongena; Gendarussa Vulgaris; Hemionitis Cordifolia; Phaseolus Trilobus), PārGṛ.; Suśr.; a vein, L.; N. of the mother of Rāhu (= *siṇhikā*), L. — **latā**, f. the egg-plant, Bhpr.

2. **Siṇhī**, in comp. for *siṇha*. — √**kṛi**, P. -*karoti*, to turn into a lion, MBh.; NṛisUp. — √**bhū**, P. -*bhavati*, to become or be turned into a lion, Kathās.

सिंहाण *siṇhāṇa*, n. (corrupted fr. *śriṅkhā-ṇa*) the mucus of the nose, L.; rust of iron, L.; a glass vessel, L.

Siṇhāṇaka, m. the mucus of the nose, Divyâv. (printed *siṇhānaka*).

Siṅghāṇa, m. = *siṇhāṇa*, rust of iron, KātyŚr., Sch.

Siṅghāṇaka, m. the mucus of the nose, ib.; (*ikā*), f. id., Āpast.

Siṅghinī, f. = *śiṅghinī*, the nose, L.

सिक् *sik*, a Sautra root meaning 'to scatter about, sprinkle' (cf. √*sic*, *sik*).

Sikatā, f. (said to be fr. the above, but prob fr. √*sic*, p. 1214) sand, gravel (mostly pl., sg. also 'a grain of sand'), VS. &c. &c.; sandy soil, Pāṇ. v, 2, 105; gravel or stone (as a disease), Suśr.; pl. N. of a race of Ṛishis, MBh. (part of RV. ix, 86 is attributed to *Sikatā Nivāvarī*). **-tva**, n. the condition or nature of sand, Ragh. **-prâya**, n. a sandbank, L. **-maya**, mf(ī)n. consisting of sand, full of sand, sandy, L.; n. a sandbank or an island with sandy shores, W. **-meha**, m. a partic. urinary disease, gravelly sediment in the urine, Suśr.; °*hin*, mfn. suffering from the above disease, ib. **-vat** (*sik°*), mfn. abounding in sand, sandy, AV. **-vartman**, n. a partic. disease of the eyelid, ŚārṅgS. **-sindhu**, N. of a place, Rājat. **-setu**, m. a bank of sand, R. (v.l.)

Sikatôttara, mfn. abounding in sand, sandy, ĀśvGṛ.

Sikatila, mfn. consisting of sand, sandy, Bhart.; Prab.

Sikatyà, mfn. id., VS.

Sigatā, f. = *sikatā*, Kap.

सिक्त *sikta, sikti, siktha.* See below.

सिक्ष्य *sikshya*, m. crystal, glass, L.

सिगृडी *sigṛiḍī* or *sigruḍi*, f. (cf. *śimṛiḍī* and *śigru*) a kind of plant, L.

सिङ्गभूपाल *siṅga-bhūpāla*, m. N. of an author (cf. *siṅha-bh°*), Cat.

Siṅgā-bhaṭṭa, m. N. of an author (°*ṭīya*, n. his wk.), Cat.

सिङ्गापिदि *siṅgāpidi*, m. N. of a poet, ŚārṅgP.

सिङ्घणदेव *siṅghaṇa-deva*, m. N. of a king.

सिङ्घाण *siṅghāṇa* &c. See p. 1213, col. 3.

सिच 1. *sic*, cl. 6. P. Ā. (Dhātup. xxviii, 140) *siñcáti*, °*te* (once in RV. x, 96, 1, *sécate*; pf. *sisheca, sishice* [in RV. also *sisicuḥ, sisice*]; aor. *asicat*, °*cata* [Gr. also *asikta*]; Subj. *sicāmahe*, RV.; Prec. *sicyāt*, Br.; fut. *sekshyati*, °*te*, ib. &c.; inf. *sektum*, MBh.; *sektavai*, Br.; ind. p. *siktvā*, ib.; *-sícya*, AV.; *-secam* or *-sekam*, GṛŚrS.), to pour out, discharge, emit, shed, infuse or pour into or on (loc.), RV. &c. &c.; to emit semen, impregnate, RV.; AV.; Br.; Mn.; to scatter in small drops, sprinkle, besprinkle or moisten with (instr.), RV. &c. &c.; to dip, soak, steep, Bhpr.; to cast or form anything out of molten metal &c. (2 acc.), RV.; AV.; AitBr.: Pass. *sicyate* (ep. also °*ti*; aor. *aseci*), to be poured out or sprinkled, RV. &c. &c.: Caus. *secayati*, °*te* (ep. also *siñcayati*; aor. *asīshicat* or *asīsicat*), to cause to pour out &c.; to sprinkle, water (plants &c.), MBh.; Kāv. &c.: Desid. *sisikshati* or *sisikshati*; °*te*, Gr. (cf. *sisikshā*): Intens. *sesicyate, sesekti*. [Cf. Zd. *hincaiti*; Gk. ἰκμάς [?]; Angl.Sax. *seón*; Germ. *seihen, seichen*.]

Siktá, mfn. poured out, sprinkled, wetted, impregnated, RV. &c. &c.; (*ā*), f. = *sikatā*, L. **-tā**, f. the being sprinkled or watered, Rājat.

Sikti, f. sprinkling, discharge, effusion, RV.

Siktha, m. n. (ifc. f. *ā*) boiled rice from which the water has been poured off, Suśr.; a lump or mouthful of boiled rice kneaded into a ball, Kathās.; n. (also written *śiktha*) beeswax, Kālac.; a collection of pearls (weighing a Dharaṇa), VarBṛS.; indigo (= *nīlī*), L.

Sikthaka (ifc., f. *akā* or *ikā*), m. n. = prec., Hcat.; n. beeswax, L.

Sig, in comp. for 2. *sic*. **-vāta**, m. wind from the hem of a dress, ĀpGṛ.

2. **Sic**, f. the border or hem of a dress, RV.; AV.; ŚBr.; GṛŚrS.; (du.) the two borders or boundaries, i.e. the horizon, RV. i, 95, 7; (du. and pl.) the wings of an army, RV.; AV.

Sicaya, m. robe, raiment, cloth, clothes, Vikr.; Kād.; Rājat.; old or ragged raiment, W.

Siñcana, n. sprinkling, watering, Hcat.

Seka &c. See s. v.

सिच् 3. *sic*, f. = *śic*, a net, BhP.

सिजि *siji*, g. *yavâdi*. **-mat**, mfn., ib.

सिञ्चता *siñcatā*, f. long pepper (v.l. *siñcitā*), L.

सिञ्जा *siñjā, siñjâśvattha, siñjita*, incorrect for *śiñjā* &c.

सिट् *siṭ* (cf. √*śiṭ*), cl. 1. P. *seṭati*, to despise, Dhātup. ix, 18.

सिण्डाकी *siṇḍākī*, incorrect for *śiṇḍākī*.

सित 3. *sita*, mf(*ā*)n. (prob. formed fr. *a-sita* as *sura* fr. *asura*; for 1. and 2. *sita* see p. 1213, col. 1; for 4. see √1. *so*) white, pale, bright, light (said of a day in the light half of a month and of the waxing moon), MBh.; Kāv. &c.; candid, pure (see *-karman*); m. white (the colour), L.; the light half of the month from new to full moon, VarBṛS.; the planet Venus or its regent (= *śukra*), ib.; sugar, ib.; Bauhinia Candida, L.; N. of one of Skanda's attendants, MBh.; (*ā*), f. white sugar, refined sugar, Suśr.; Hcat.; moonlight, L.; a handsome woman, W.; spirituous liquor, L.; N. of various plants (a species of Aparājitā; white Kaṇṭakārī; white Dūrvā grass; Arabian jasmine &c.), Suśr.; bamboo juice, L.; N. of the Ganges (in *sitâsitā*, under *sitā*); one of the 8 Devīs (Buddh.), Kālac.; (*am*), n. silver, L.; sandal, L.; a radish, L. **-kaṭabhī**, f. a kind of tree, L. **-kaṇṭā** or **-kaṇṭārikā**, f. a white-blossomed Kaṇṭakārī, L. **-kaṇṭha**, mfn. white-necked, MW.; m. a gallinule, L. **-kamala**, n. a wh° lotus; *-maya*, mf(*ī*)n. consisting of wh° l°s, Kālac. **-kara**, m. 'wh°-rayed,' the moon, Rājat.; camphor, L.; °*rânana*, mf(*ā*)n. moon-faced, Rājat. **-karṇikā** (Suśr.) or **-karṇī** (L.), f. Gendarussa Vulgaris. **-karman**, mfn. pure in actions, MBh. **-kāca**, mfn. dark-yellowish white, L.; m. dark-y° whiteness, L.; rock-crystal, L. **-kācara**, mfn. dark-smoky white, L.; m. dark-s° whiteness, L. **-kuñjara**, m. a white elephant, L.; N. of Indra's el°, W.; mfn. riding on a white el°; m. N. of Indra, L. **-kumbhī**, f. a wh° Bignonia, L. **-krishṇa**, mfn. white and black, L.; m. wh° and b° colour, L. **-keśa**, m. 'wh°-haired,' N. of a Dānava, Hariv. **-kshāra**, n. a kind of Borax, L. **-kshudrā**, f. a white-blossomed Kaṇṭakārī, ib. **-khaṇḍa**, m. wh° lump-sugar, Hcat.; Dhūrtan. **-guñjā**, f. a white-blossomed Abrus Precatorius, L. **-cihna**, m. a sort of fish, L. **-cchattra**, n. a wh° umbrella, L.; (*ā* or *ī*), f. Anethum Sowa, ib. **-cchattrita**, mfn. turned into or representing a wh° umbrella, Naish.; m. having a wh° u°, possessed of the insignia of royalty, MW. **-cchada**, mfn. wh°-winged, having wh° leaves, L.; m. a goose, L.; (*ā*), f. wh° Dūrvā grass, ib. **-jā**, f. sugar in lumps, lump-sugar, ib. **-tara**, mfn. extremely wh°, Ml. **-turaga**, m. 'wh°-horsed,' N. of Arjuna, Kir. **-tejas**, mfn. having a wh° light, VP. **-darbha**, m. wh° Kuśa grass, L. **-dīdhiti**, m. 'wh°-rayed,' the moon, Śiś. **-dīpya**, m. wh° cumin, L. **-dūrvā**, f. wh° Dūrvā grass, ib. **-dru**, m. a kind of creeper, ib. **-druma**, m. (perhaps) a species of birch-tree, Hariv. **-dvija**, m. 'white bird,' a goose, Subh. **-dhātu**, m. a wh° mineral, MW.; chalk, L. **-paksha**, m. the light half of a month, VarBṛS.; a wh° wing, MW.; 'wh°-winged,' a goose, L. **-paṭa**, m. N. of an author, Praśnôt. **-padma**, n. a wh° lotus, BhP. **-parṇī**, f. a kind of plant (= *arka-pushpikā*), MW. **-pāṭalikā**, f. a wh° Bignonia, L. **-piṅgāṇa**, mfn. dark-yellowish-whitish white, L.; m. d°-y°-whitish whiteness, L. **-pīta**, mfn. white and yellow, Śaṃk.; *harin-nīla*, mfn. bluish-green, yellowish-white, L.; m. b°-g°-y° whiteness, L. **-puṅkhā**, f. a kind of plant, L. **-puṇḍarīka**, n. a wh° lotus, Kāv. **-pushpa**, m. Tabernæmontana Coronaria, L.; Saccharum Spontaneum, ib.; Acacia Sirissa, ib.; = *śveta-rohita*, ib.; (*ā*), f. a kind of jasmine (Jasminum Sambac or Sida Cordifolia), Suśr.; (*ī*), f. = *śvetâparājitā*, L.; n. Cyperus Rotundus, ib. **-pushpāya**, Nom. Ā. °*yate*, to resemble jasmine, Kāv. **-pushpika**, a kind of leprosy, L. **-prabha**, mf(*ā*)n. white, MBh.; n. silver, L. **-maṇi**, m. a crystal; *-maya*, mf(*ī*)n. made of cr°, Megh. **-manas**, mfn. pure-hearted, VP. **-marica**, n. white pepper, L. **-māraka**, (prob.) w.r. for *-sāraka*, Car. **-māsha**, m. Dolichos Catjang, L. **-megha**, m. a wh° cloud, R. **-yajñôpavītin**, mfn. invested with a wh° sacred thread, Hcat. **-yāminī**, f. a bright night, moonlight, Bhām. **-rakta**, mf(*ā*)n. wh° and red, NṛisUp. **-rañjana**, mfn. yellow, L.; m. yellow (the colour), W. **-raśmi**, m. 'wh°-rayed,' the moon, L. **-ruci**, mfn. bright-coloured, wh°, Śiś.; m. the moon, Subh. **-latā**, f. a kind of plant, L. **-lasuna**, garlic, L. **-lohita**, mfn. white and red, L.; m. wh° and r° colour, L. **-varman**, m. N. of a minister, Daś. **-varshābhū**, f. Bœrhavia Procumbens, L. **-vallija**, n. wh° pepper, ib. **-vājin**, m. 'having wh° horses,' N. of Arjuna, Kir. **-vāraṇa**, m. a wh° elephant, BhP. **-śarkarā**, f. white ground sugar, lump-s°, Sāh.; Pañcar. **-śāyakā**, w.r. for *-sāyakā*, L. **-śiṅśapā**, f. a kind of plant, L. **-śimbika**, m. a kind of wheat, ib. **-śiva**, n. rock-salt, ib. **-śūka**, m. barley, ib. **-śūraṇa**, m. or n. a species of Arum, ib. **-śmaśru**, mfn. having a white beard, MBh. **-śyāma**, mfn. blackish-white, L.; m. blackish-wh° colour, L. **-sapti**, mfn. having wh° steeds; m. N. of Arjuna, Kir. **-sarshapa**, m. white mustard, a grain of wh° m°-seed, VarBṛS. **-sāyakā**, f. a kind of plant, L. **-sāra** or °**raka**, m. Achyranthes Triandra, ib. (cf. *-māraka*). **-siṅhī**, f. a wh°-blossomed Kaṇṭakārī, ib. **-siddhârtha** or °**thaka**, m. wh° mustard (or a grain of wh° m°-seed), Pañcat. **-sindhu**, f. the Ganges, L. **-siva**, v.l. for *-śiva*, ib. **-sūraṇa**, v.l. for *-śūr°*, ib. **-hūṇa**, m. pl. the wh° Huns, VarBṛS. **Sitâṅśu**, m. 'wh°-rayed,' the moon, Bhartṛ.; Kuval.; camphor, L.; *-taila*, n. camphor-oil, ib. **Sitâṅśuka**, mfn. dressed in a wh° mantle or garment, Vikr. **Sitâkhya**, n. wh° pepper, L.; (*ā*), f. wh° Dūrvā grass, ib. **Sitâgra**, m. or n. a thorn (for *śit°*), ib. **Sitâṅka**, m. a kind of fish, ib. **Sitâṅga**, m. a kind of plant, ib.; camphor, ib.; N. of Śiva, ib. (printed *mit°*); *-rāga*, m. a white cosmetic or pigment for the limbs or body, Kum. **Sitâjājī**, f. wh° cumin, L. **Sitâtapatra**, n. a white umbrella (emblem of royalty), Siṅhâs. **Sitâtapavāraṇa**, n. id., Ragh. **Sitânana**, mfn. wh°-faced; m. N. of Garuḍa, L.; of one of Siva's attendants, Hariv. **Sitâpâṅga**, m. 'having wh° eye-corners,' a peacock, L. **Sitâbja**, n. a wh° lotus, ib. **Sitâbha**, m. 'wh°-looking,' camphor, ib.; (prob.) sugar, Pañcar.; (*ā*), f. a kind of shrub, L. **Sitâbhikaṭabhī**, f. (v.l. for *sitâlikaṭ°*). **Sitâbhra**, m. a white cloud, MBh.; m. n. camphor, Kāv. **Sitâbhraka**, m. or n. camphor, L. **Sitâmoghā**, f. a wh°-blossomed Bignonia, ib. **Sitâmbara**, mf(*ā*)n. clothed in wh° garments, ŚārṅgP.; m. 'a monk wearing wh° g°,' N. of one of the two great divisions of Jaina monks (= *śvet°*, q.v.), L. **Sitâmbuja** or °**tâmbhoja**, n. a wh° lotus, ib. **Sitâyudha**, m. a kind of fish, L. **Sitârkaka**, m. a wh°-blossomed Calotropis, L. **Sitârjaka**, m. wh° basil, L. **Sitâlaka**, m. a wh° Calotropis, L. (w.r. for °*tâlarka*). **Sitâlarka**, m. a wh° Calotropis, L. **Sitâli**, mfn. having wh° lines, MW.; *-kaṭabhī*, f. a species of Achyranthes, L.; °*likā*, f. 'wh°-lined,' a cockle, MW. **Sitâvara**, m. a species of culinary plant (also written *śit°*), Bhpr.; (*ī*), f. Vernonia Anthelminthica, L. **Sitâśva**, mfn. having wh° horses; m. N. of Arjuna, MBh.; the moon, L. **Sitâsita**, mfn. (for *sitâs°* see under *sitā* below) white and black, MaitrUp.; MBh.; Pur.; good and evil, MaitrUp.; m. N. of Bala-deva, L.; du. Venus and Saturn, ib.; *-kamala-dala-nayana-tā*, f. having eyes like the petals of a dark and wh° lotus (one of the 80 minor marks of a Buddha), Dharmas. 84; *-roga*, m. a partic. disease of the eyes, Cat. **Sitâhvaya**, m. 'white-named,' the planet Venus (cf. *śukra*), VarBṛS.; N. of various plants (= *śveta-rohita*; = *śveta-śigru*; a wh°-blossomed Tulasī), L. **Sitêkshu**, m. a species of sugar-cane, ib. **Sitêtara**, mfn. 'other than wh°,' black, dark, blue, Śiś.; Kum.; Laghuj.; white and black, BhP.; m. a kind of dark-coloured rice, L.; Dolichos Uniflorus, ib.; *-gati*, m. 'having a black course,' fire, ib.; *-saroja*, n. a blue lotus, Śiś. **Sitâiraṇḍa**, m. the white Ricinus, L. **Sitôtpala**, n. a white lotus, VarBṛS.; Hit.; Vet. **Sitôdaka**, w.r. for *śit°*, Kāraṇḍ. **Sitôdara**, m. 'wh°-bellied,' N. of Kubera, L. **Sitôdbhava**, mfn. produced from sugar, MW.; n. wh° sandal, L. **Sitôpala**, m. 'wh° stone,' chalk, L.; crystal, ib.; rock-crystal, ib.; (*ā*), f. sugar, Kāv.; Suśr.; Pañcar. (m. c. also °*pala*); white or refined sugar, MW.; n. chalk, ib. **Sitôshṇa-vāraṇa**, n. 'white heat-protector,' a white umbrella, ib.

Sitaka, mfn., g. *ṛiśyâdi*.

Sitā, f. of 3. *sita*, col. 2. **-khaṇḍa**, m. sugar in lumps, lump-sugar, L.; a kind of refined s° (said to be prepared from honey), MW. **-traya**, n. three kinds of white sugar (= *tri-sitā*), L. **-°di** (°*tâdi*), m. molasses, ib. **-pāka**, m. refined sugar, Bhpr. **-latā**, f. wh° Dūrvā grass, Car. **-°sita** (°*tâs°*), n. (for *sitâs°* see above) N. of Prayāga, Kāśīkh.; (*ā*), f. du. the Ganges and Jumnā rivers at Prayāga, ib.

2. **Siti**, mfn. (w.r. for *śiti*; for 1. see p. 1213, col. 1; for 3. see √1. *so*) white, L.; black, ib. **-kaṇṭha**, mfn. having a wh° throat, MW.; dark-necked, ib.; m. Śiva, ib. (cf. *śiti-k°*). **-māraka**, (prob.) w.r. for *sita-sāraka*, Car. **-vāra**, m. = *śiti-v°*, MW. **-vāsas**, mfn. clad in black, ib.; m. N. of Bala-rāma (for *siti-v°*), Śiś.

Sitiman, m. whiteness, Kāv.

Sitī-√kṛi, P. *-karoti*, to make white or bright, Sāh.; Naish.

Siti-vāra, a kind of plant (v.l. *sitāv°* [q.v.]; cf. *siti-v°* above), Kauś.

सिद्गुड *sidguṇḍa*, m. a person whose father is a Brāhman and whose mother is a Parājakī, L.

सिद्धार्थ *siddhârtha.* See col. 3.

सिध् 1. *sidh*, cl. 1. P. *sedhati*, to go, move, Dhātup. iii, 10; Naigh. ii, 14 (accord. to Pāṇ. vii, 3, 113 the *s* of this root is not changed to *sh* after prepositions; cf. *abhi-* and *pari-√sidh*).

सिध् 2. *sidh*, cl. 1. P. (Dhātup. iii, 11) *sédhati* (in later language also *°te*; pf. *sishedha*, ep. also *sishidhe*; aor. *asedhīt*, Gr. also *asaitsīt*; fut. *seddhā* or *sedhitā*, Gr.; *setsyati* or *sedhishyati*, MBh. &c.; inf. *seddhum*, Br. &c.; *sedhitum*, Gr.; ind. p. *-sídhya*, AV.), to drive off, scare away, repel, restrain, hinder, RV.; Kauś.; to punish, chastise, Bhaṭṭ.; to ordain, instruct, Dhātup.; to turn out well or auspiciously, ib.: Pass. *sidhyate* (aor. *asedhi*), to be driven or kept off or repelled, MBh. &c.: Caus. *sedhayati* (aor. *asīshidhat*), Gr.: Desid. of Caus. *sishedhayishati*, ib.: Desid. *sisedhishati*, *sisidhishati*, *sishitsati*, ib.: Intens. *seshidhyate*, *sesheddhi* (pr. p. *-séshidhat*, RV.), ib.

1. **Siddha**, mfn. driven off, scared away, PañcavBr.

1. **Siddhi**, f. driving off, putting aside, Yājñ.

सिध् 3. *sidh* (weak form of √*sādh*), cl. 4. P. (Dhātup. xxvi, 83) *sídhyati* (ep. and m.c. also *°te*; pf. *sishedha*, RV. i, 32, 13; aor. *asidhat*, Gr.; *saitsīt*, Sarvad.; Prec. *sidhyāsam*, Gr.; fut. *seddhā*, ib.; *setsyati*, *°te*, MBh. &c.; inf. *seddhum*, Gr.; ind. p. *sedhitvā*, *sidhitvā*, or *siddhvā*, ib.), to be accomplished or fulfilled or effected or settled, be successful, succeed, RV. &c. &c.; to hit a mark (loc.), Śak.; to attain one's aim or object, have success, MBh.; Kāv. &c.; to attain the highest object, become perfect, attain beatitude, R.; BhP.; to be valid or admissible, hold good, Mn.; Yājñ.; to be proved or demonstrated or established, result from, Pat.; Pañcat.; Sarvad.; to be set right, (esp.) be healed or cured, Suśr.; BhP.; to be well cooked, W.; to conform to a person's will, yield to (gen.), Kathās.; to fall to a person's (gen.) lot or share, Prab.; to come into existence, originate, arise, BhP.: Caus. *sedhayati* (aor. *asīshidhat*) or *sādhayati*, to show the knowledge or skill (of any one, the former, 'with reference to sacred things,' the latter, 'to secular things'), Pat. on Pāṇ. vi, 1, 49 (*sādh°*), to accomplish, effect, MW.: Desid. *sishitsati*, Gr.: Int. *seshidhyate*, *sesheddhi*, ib.

2. **Siddha**, mfn. accomplished, fulfilled, effected, gained, acquired, MBh.; Ragh.; one who has attained his object, successful, BhP.; one who has attained the highest object, thoroughly skilled or versed in (dat. or comp.), MBh.; R. &c.; perfected, become perfect, beatified, endowed with supernatural faculties (see 2. *siddhi*), ib.; sacred, holy, divine, illustrious, W.; hit (as a mark), Kathās.; prepared, cooked, dressed (as food), Mn.; MBh. &c.; healed, cured, Pañcat.; valid (as a rule in grammar, see *a-s°*); admitted to be true or right, established, settled, proved, Pat.; Mn.; Sāṃkhyak.; Sarvad.; resulting from, W.; adjudicated, decided, terminated (as a lawsuit), W.; paid, liquidated, settled (as a debt), ib.; ready for payment (as money), Hit.; well-known, notorious, celebrated (=*prasiddha*), ĀśvŚr.; R. &c.; effective, powerful, miraculous, supernatural, Cāṇ.; Rājat.; Vet.; subdued, brought into subjection (by magical powers), subject or obedient to (gen.), Pañcat.; Kathās.; peculiar, singular, Mālatīm.; invariable, unalterable, Pat.; m. a Siddha or semi-divine being of great purity and perfection and said to possess the eight supernatural faculties (see 2. *siddhi*; accord. to some, the Siddhas inhabit, together with the Munis &c., the Bhuvar-loka or atmosphere between the earth and heaven; accord. to VP. eighty-eight thousand of them occupy the regions of the sky north of the sun and south of the seven Ṛishis; they are regarded as immortal, but only as living to the end of a Kalpa [q.v.]; in the later mythology they are sometimes confused with the Sādhyas [q.v.] or take their place), ĀśvGṛ.; MBh. &c.; any inspired sage or prophet or seer (e.g. Vyāsa, Kapila &c.), ib.; any holy personage or great saint (esp. one who has attained to one of the states of beatitude, cf. *sālokya*), MBh.; Kāv. &c.; any great adept in magic or one who has acquired supernatural powers, ib.; (with Jainas) a Jina or Arhat; N. of the number 24 (cf. *jina*); the 21st of the astron. Yogas, L.; a lawsuit, judicial trial (=*vyavahāra*), L.; N. of a Deva-gandharva, MBh.; of a Rājarshi, ib.; of a king, Rājat.; of a brother of Jajja, ib.; of a Brāhman, Buddh.; of an author, Cat.; a kind of thorn-apple, L.; another plant or a sort of hard sugar (=*guḍa*), L.; (pl.) N. of a people, MBh.; VP.; (*ā*), f. a Siddhā or semi-divine female, R. (cf. comp.); N. of one of the Yoginīs (q.v.), L. (accord. to Sāh. *siddhā* is also used at the end of names of courtezans); a kind of medicinal plant or root (=*ṛiddhi*), L.; (*am*), n. magic, supernatural power, Pañcar.; sea-salt, L. **–kajjala**, n. magical lamp-black, Kāvyâd., Sch. **–kalpa** (?), m. N. of a partic. cosmic period, Buddh. **–kāma**, mfn. having the wishes fulfilled, R. **–kāmêśvarī**, f. one of the five forms of Kāmākhyā or Durgā, KālP. **–kārya**, mfn. one whose object is accomplished, Kathās. **–kerala**, n. 'perfect Kerala,' N. of a district, Cat. **–kshetra**, n. 'land of the Blest,' a region inhabited by the Siddhas (also as N. of various sacred regions), MBh.; Kathās.; Pur.; *-parvata*, m. N. of a mountain in Siddha-kshetra, Kathās. **–khaṇḍa**, m. a sort of sugar, L.; N. of various wks. **–kheṭi-sāriṇī**, f. N. of wk. **–gaṅgā**, f. the divine or heavenly Ganges (=*mandākinī*), L. **–gati**, f., g. *deva-pathâdi*. **–guru**, m. N. of an author, Cat. **–graha**, m. N. of a demon causing a partic. kind of seizure or madness, MBh. **–candra-gaṇi**, m. N. of the author of a Comm. on the Kādambarī. **–jana**, m. beatified people, the Blest, R. **–jala**, n. 'cooked water,' the fermented water of boiled rice, sour rice-gruel, L. **–tāpasa**, m. an ascetic endowed with supernatural power, Daś.; (*ī*), f. a female ascetic &c., Kathās. **–tva**, n. (or *-tā*, f.) perfection, perfect state, NṛisUp.; the condition of a Siddha, R.; Pañcar.; the establishment or validity of a rule or doctrine, APrāt.; Sarvad.; the being known or understood, BhP. **–darśana**, n. the seeing or sight of the Blest, Cat. **–deva**, m. 'perfected deity,' N. of Śiva, L. **–dravya**, n. any magical object, Cat. **–dhātu**, m. perfected mineral, quicksilver, L. **–dhāman**, n. the abode of the Blest, Kathās. **–nandin**, m. N. of a grammarian, Cat. **–nara**, m. a sorcerer, fortune-teller, Siṇhâs. **–nāgârjuna**, m. N. of an author, Gaṇar.; n. N. of a wk. on magic; *-tantra*, n.; *°nīya*, n. N. of wks. **–nātha**, m., **–nārāyaṇa**, m. N. of authors, Cat. **–paksha**, m. the logically proved side of an argument, MW. **–pati**, m. N. of a man (also called Mudgara-gomin), Buddh. **–patha**, m. 'path of the Blest,' the atmosphere, BhP. **–pada**, n. N. of a sacred place, ib. **–pātra**, m. N. of one of Skanda's attendants, MBh.; of a Deva-putra, Lalit. **–pāda**, m. N. of a teacher of the Yoga, Cat. **–pīṭha**, m. =*-kshetra*, L. **–putra**, m. the son of a Siddha, HPariś. **–pura**, n. or **-purī**, f. 'city of the Blest,' N. of a mythical city (located in the extreme north or, accord. to others, in the southern or lower regions of the earth), Sūryas.; Āryabh.; Gol. **–purusha**, m. =*-nara*, Siṇhâs.; a man who has attained perfection, MW. **–pushpa**, m. 'having perfect flowers,' the Kara-vīra plant, L. **–prayojana**, m. white mustard, L. **–prâṇêśvara**, m. a partic. mixture or preparation, Rasêndrac. **–prâya**, mfn. almost accomplished, nearly perfected, MW. **–buddha**, m. N. of a teacher of Yoga (v.l. *śuddha-buddhi*), Cat. **–bhūmi**, f. =*-kshetra*, Pañcat. **–mata**, n. the ideas or sentiments of the Blest, Cat. **–manorama**, m. N. of the second day of the civil month (Karmamāsa), IndSt. **–mantra**, m. a partic. efficacious Mantra, Vet.; Gīt.; N. of a medical wk. by Keśava-bhaṭṭa. **–mātṛikā**, f. N. of a partic. alphabet, L.; of a goddess, Cat. **–mānasa**, mfn. having a completely satisfied mind, R. **–mūlikā-nighaṇṭu**, m. N. of a dictionary. **–modaka**, m. sugar prepared from bamboo-manna, L. **–yātrika**, w.r. for *siddhi-y°*. **–yāmala**, n. N. of a Tantra. **–yoga**, m. magical agency, Kathās.; N. of a medical wk. by Vṛinda; *-mālā*, f., *-saṃgraha*, m. N. of wks.; *°gêśvara-tantra*, n. N. of a Tantra wk.; m. a partic. mixture or preparation, Rasêndrac. **–yogin**, m. N. of Śiva, MBh.; (*inī*), f. a sorceress, witch, fairy, Kathās.; N. of Manasā, Cat. **–yoshit**, f. a female Siddha, beatified woman, BhP. **–raṅga-kalpa**, m. N. of ch. of the Skanda-purāṇa. **–ratna**, mfn. possessing a magic jewel, Kathās. **–rasa**, m. 'perfected metallic fluid,' quicksilver, Naish.; one who by means of qu° becomes a Siddha even in the present life (and so acquires supernatural powers), Caṇḍ.; an alchemist, W.; mfn. possessing perfected metallic fluids, mineral, metallic, ib.; *-daṇḍa*, m. a kind of magic wand, Pañcad. **–rasâyana**, mfn. possessing an elixir (for prolonging life), Kathās. **–rāja**, m. N. of a king, Rājat.; *-varṇana*, n. N. of wk., Gaṇar. **–rātri** (?), f. N. of a medical wk. **–rudrêśvara-tīrtha**, n. N. of a Tīrtha, Cat. **–rūpa**, n. the right or correct thing, TPrāt., Sch. **–rshi**, m. (*°ddha + ṛishi*) N. of the author of the Siddha-yoga-mālā. **–laksha**, mfn. one who has hit the mark, Kathās. **–lakshmaṇa**, m. N. of an author, Cat. **–lakshmī**, f. (prob.) a form of Lakshmī; *-stotra*, n. N. of a ch. of various Purāṇas. **–loka**, m. the world of the Blest, BhP. **–vaṭa**, m. N. of a place, Cat.; (*ī*), f. N. of a goddess, ib.; (*°ṭa*)*-sthala-kalpa*, m. N. of a ch. of the Skanda-purāṇa (also called *śrī-śaila-dakshiṇa-dvāra-sthala-kalpa*). **–vat**, ind. as established or proved (with √*kṛi*, 'to regard as est° or pr°'), Sāy. **–vana**, n. 'grove of the Blest,' N. of a place, Cat. **–varti**, f. magical wick (v.l. *siddhi-v°*), Pañcat. **–vasti**, m. a strong injection (as of oil &c.), Suśr. **–vastu** (prob. n.) a spelling-book, Buddh. **–vāsa**, m. 'dwelling of the Blest,' N. of a place, Kathās. **–vidyā**, f. the doctrine relating to perfected beings, Pañcar.; a partic. form of the Mahā-vidyā, L.; *-dīpikā*, f. N. of a wk. on the worship of Dakshiṇa-kālī by Śaṃkara (pupil of Jagan-nātha). **–vīrya**, m. 'possessing perfect strength,' N. of a Muni, MārkP. **–śābara-tantra**, n. N. of a Tantra. **–saṃkalpa**, mfn. one whose wishes are accomplished, MW. **–saṃgha**, m. a company of Siddhas, assemblage of perfected beings, W. **–samâkhya**, mfn. called *siddha* (with *kshetra*, n. =*siddha-kshetra*), Cat. **–sambandha**, mfn. one whose kindred are well known, L. **–sarit**, f. 'river of the Blest,' N. of the Ganges, Bālar. **–salila**, n. =*-jala*, L. **–sādhana**, m. white mustard, L.; n. the performance of magical or mystical rites (for acquiring supernatural powers &c.), W.; the materials employed in those rites, ib.; the proving of anything already proved, Kap.; *-dosha*, m. the mistake of doing so, MW. **–sādhita**, mfn. one who has learned (the art of medicine) by practice (not by study), Car. **–sādhya**, mfn. who or what has effected what was to be done, W.; effected, accomplished, proved, ib.; m. a partic. Mantra, MW.; n. demonstrated proof or conclusion, ib.; *°dhyaka*, m. a partic. Mantra, Tantras. **–sāra-saṃhitā**, f. N. of a medical wk. **–sārasvata**, N. of a Tantra wk.; (with *śabdânuśāsana*) N. of a gram. wk.; *-dīpikā*, f. N. of a Comm. by Padma-nābha on the Bhuvanêśvarī-stotra; *-stotra*, n. another N. for *bhuvanêśvarī-stotra*. **–siddha**, mfn. thoroughly efficacious (said of a partic. Mantra), Tantras.; *°ddhâñjana*, n., *°ddhânta*, m., *°ddhânta-paddhati*, f. N. of wks. **–sindhu**, m. 'river of the Siddhas,' N. of the heavenly Ganges. **–susiddha**, mfn. 'exceedingly efficacious' (said of a partic. Mantra), Tantras. **–sena**, m. 'having a divine or perfect army,' N. of Kārttikeya (god of war), L.; of an astronomer, VarBṛS.; *-divākara* or *-divākṛit*, m. N. of a son of Sarva-jña and pupil of Vṛiddha-vāda-sūri (said to have induced Vikramâditya to tolerate the Jainas), Cat.; *-vākya-kāra* (Sarvad.), *-sūri* (Siṇhâs.), m. N. of authors. **–sevita**, m. 'honoured or worshipped by Siddhas,' N. of a form of Bhairava or Śiva (=*baṭuka-bhairava*), L. **–sopāna**, n. N. of wk. **–sthala** (Pañcar.), **-sthāna** (L.), n. the place or region of the Blest. **–sthālī**, f. the magical caldron of a great adept or sage (said to overflow with any kind of food at the wish of the possessor), MW. **–hema-kumāra**, m. N. of a king, Hemac., Sch. **–heman**, n. purified gold, Cat. **Siddhâgama**, m. N. of wk. **Siddhâṅganā**, f. a beatified woman, female Siddha, Megh.; Vās.; Kathās. **Siddhâcala**, m. 'mountain of the Blest,' N. of a mountain, Siṇhâs.; *-pūjā*, f. N. of wk. **Siddhâjña**, mfn. one whose orders are executed, VarBṛS. **Siddhâñjana**, n. magical ointment, Daś.; Kathās.; *°nāya*, Nom. Ā. *°yate*, to become a m° oi°, Dhanamj. **Siddhâdeśa**, m. the prediction of a seer, Mṛicch.; one whose predictions are fulfilled, prophet, soothsayer, fortune-teller, Mālav.; Ratnâv. **Siddhânanda**, m. N. of an author, Cat. **Siddhânta** &c., see s.v. **Siddhânna**, n. dressed food, cooked victuals, L. **Siddhâpagā**, m. =*siddha-sindhu*, L. **Siddhâmbā**, f. 'the blest mother,' N. of Durgā, Cat. **Siddhâri**, m. 'enemy of the Siddhas,' N. of a partic. Mantra, Tantras. **Siddhârtha**, mf(*ā*)n. one who

has accomplished an aim or object, successful, prosperous, MBh.; Kāv. &c.; leading to the goal, efficient, efficacious, Hariv.; R.; one whose aim or intention is known, L.; m. 'he who has fulfilled the object (of his coming),' N. of the great Buddha (Gautama or Śākya-muni, founder of Buddhism), MWB. 43; of a Māra-putra, Lalit.; of a Dānava, Kathās.; of one of Skanda's attendants, MBh.; of a king, ib.; of a councillor of Daśa-ratha, R.; of the father of Mahā-vīra (the 24th Arhat of the present Avasarpiṇī), Kathās.; of a poet, Subh.; (*ā*), f. N. of the mother of the 4th Arhat of the present Avasarpiṇī, L.; white mustard, Suśr.; VarBṛS. &c.; the Indian fig-tree, L.; the 53rd year in Jupiter's cycle of 60 years, VarBṛS.; n. (scil. *vāstu*) a building with two halls (one to the west and one to the south), VarBṛS.; *-kārin*, m. N. of Śiva, MBh.; *-carita*, n. N. of a poem; *-pricchā*, f. N. of a wk. on symbols belonging to deities, Hcat.; *-mati*, m. N. of a Bodhisattva, Lalit.; *-mānin*, mfn. one who thinks he has attained his object, Kathās.; *-saṃhitā*, f. N. of wk., Hcat. **Siddhârthaka**, m. white mustard (exceptionally also n.), Suśr.; VarBṛS. &c.; N. of two officials, Mudr.; n. a kind of ointment, Suśr. **Siddhârthin**, m. the 53rd year in Jupiter's cycle of 60 years, Cat. **Siddhâśrama**, m. 'hermitage of the Blest,' N. of a hº in the Himâlaya (where Vishṇu performed penance during his dwarf incarnation), R.; Ragh.; *-tīrtha*, n. N. of a Tīrtha, Śukas.; *-pada*, n. (the place of) the hermitage of the Blest, R. **Siddhâsana**, n. a partic. sedent posture in religious meditation (described as placing the left heel under the body and the right heel in front of it, fixing the sight between the eyebrows, and meditating upon the syllable *Om*), Cat.; m. N. of Skanda, L. **Siddhêcchā**, f. a partic. mode of livelihood, Baudh. **Siddhêśa**, m. lord of the Blest, BhP. **Siddhêśvara**, m. id., ib. (*ī*, f., VarP.); N. of various authors &c. (also with *bhaṭṭa*), Cat.; of a mountain, Inscr.; *-tantra*, n. N. of a Tantra; *-tīrtha*, n. N. of various Tīrthas, Cat.; *-stotra*, n. N. of a Stotra. **Siddhâika-vīra-tantra**, n. N. of a Tantra. **Siddhâiśvarya**, n. dominion over the Blest, Pañcar. **Siddhôdaka**, n. N. of a Tīrtha, Kathās. **Siddhâugha**, m. N. of certain Gurus (or teachers of mystical Mantras) revered by the Tāntrikas (named Nārada, Kāśyapa, Śambhu, Bhārgava, Kula-kauśika), Cat. **Siddhâushadha**, n. 'perfect drug,' a specific, panacea, Bhām.; *-saṃgraha*, m. N. of wk. **Siddhâushadhika**, n. a collection of five drugs or medicines (viz. *taila-kanda, sudhā-kº, kroḍa-kº, rudantikā*, and *sarpa-netrā*), L.

Siddhaka, m. a kind of tree (perhaps = Vitex Negundo or Vatica Robusta or the Sāl tree), Suśr.; (prob. n.) a kind of metre, Col.

Siddhânta, m. established end, final end or aim or purpose (cf. *sama-sº*), (cf. *rāddhânta*), demonstrated conclusion of an argument (or the 4th member of a syllogism following on the refutation of the *pūrva-paksha*, q. v.), settled opinion or doctrine, dogma, axiom, received or admitted truth (of four kinds, see *sarva-tantra-sº, prati-tantra-sº, adhikaraṇa-sº, abhyupagama-sº*), MBh.; Kap.; Sarvad. (cf. IW. 64); any fixed or established or canonical text-book or received scientific treatise on any subject (esp. on astronomy and mathematics; often ifc., as the following 9, Brahma-sº, Sūrya-sº, Soma-sº, Bṛihaspati-sº, Garga-sº, Nārada-sº, Parāśara-sº, Pulastya-sº, Vasishṭha-sº; or the following 5, Siddhântas, Pauliśa-sº, Romaka-sº, Vāsishṭha-sº, Saura-sº, and Paitāmaha-sº), VarBṛS.; Sarvad.; IW. 175; a partic. class of Buddhist and Jaina wks. **-kalpalatā**, f., **-kalpavallī**, f. N. of Vedânta wks. **-kalpavallī-vyākhyāna**, n. N. of an astron. wk. by Yallayâcārya. **-kārikā**, f. N. of a Nyāya wk. **-koṭi**, f. the conclusive point in an argument, MW. **-kaumudī**, f. N. of a celebrated grammar by Bhaṭṭoji-dīkshita (giving a particular arrangement of Pāṇini's Sūtras with Comm.); *-koṭi-pattra*, n., *-gūḍha-phakkikā-prakāśa*, m., *-vilāsa*, m., *-sāra*, m. N. of wks. **-garbha**, m. N. of a wk. by Mandanapāla. **-gītā**, f. N. of a Vedânta wk. **-gūḍhârtha-prakāśaka**, m., **-grantha**, m. N. of wks. **-candrikā**, f. N. of various wks. (also *-khaṇḍana*, n. and *-ṭīkā*, f.) **-candrôdaya**, m. a Comm. on the Tarka-saṃgraha (written in 1774 A.D. for Rājas-siṇha, son of king Gaja-siṇha of Vikrama-paṭṭana, by Kṛishṇa-dhūrjaṭi-dīkshita). **-cintāmaṇi**, m., **-cintāratna-saṃgraha**, m., **-cūḍāmaṇi**, m., **-jāhnavī**, f., **-jyotsnā**, f. N. of wks. **-tattva**, n. N. of various wks. (esp. of a Vaiśeshika wk., also called Padârtha-viveka); *-dīpa*, m., *-prakāśikā*, f., *-bindu* (or *siddhânta-bindu*), m., *-bindu-saṃdīpana*, n., *-viveka*, m., *-sarvasva*, n. N. of wks. **-tari**, f., **-darpaṇa**, m., **-dīpa**, m., **-dīpa-prabhā**, f., **-dīpikā**, f. N. of wks. **-dharmâgama**, m. an established traditional rule, Kāv. **-nirṇaya**, m., **-naiyāyika-mata**, n., **-nyāya-candrikā**, f. N. of wks. **-paksha**, m. the logically correct side of an argument, MW. **-pañcânana**, m. N. of the author of the Vākya-tattva. **-pañjara**, n. N. of a wk. by Saṃkarâcārya. **-paṭala**, m. n. N. of a wk. on the worship of Rāma. **-paddhati**, f. = *siddha-siddhânta-paddhati*. **-pīyūsha**, m. n., **-bindu**, m. (see *siddhânta-tattva-bº*), **-bindu-vyākhyā**, f., **-bhāshya**, n., **-makaranda**, m., **-mañjarī**, f., **-mañjūshā**, f., **-mañjūshā-khaṇḍana**, n., **-maṇi-mañjarī**, f., **-manoramā**, f. N. of wks. **-muktâvalī**, f. N. of various wks. (esp. of a Comm. by Viśva-nātha Pañcânana Bhaṭṭâcārya Tarkâlaṃkāra on the Bhāshā-pariccheda, IW. 61); *-prakāśa*, m. N. of a Comm. on that wk. **-mudrā**, f., **-ratna**, n., **-ratna-mālā**, f., **-ratnâkara**, m., **-ratnâvalī**, f., **-rahasya**, n. N. of wks. **-lakshaṇa**, n. N. of various wks. (also *ā*, f.); *-kroḍa*, m., *-ṭīkā*, f., *-dīdhiti-ṭīkā*, f., *-parishkāra*, m., *-prakāśa*, m., *-rahasya*, n., *-viveka-prakaraṇa*, n. N. of wks. **-laghu-khamāṇika**, m., **-lava**, m., **-leśa**, m. N. of wks. **-vāg-īśa**, m. (also with *bhaṭṭâcārya*) N. of various scholars, Cat. **-vāṅ-mālā**, f. N. of a Comm. (also called *vallabha-siddhânta-ṭīkā*) by Purushôttama. **-vācaspati**, m. N. of the author of the Śuddhi-makaranda, Cat. **-vilāsa**, m., **-viveka**, m., **-veda**, m., **-velā**, f., **-vaijayantī**, f., **-vyākhyā**, f., **-vyāpti**, f., **-vyutpatti-lakshaṇa**, n., **-śataka**, n., **-śikshā**, f., **-śikhāmaṇi**, m. N. of wks. **-śiromaṇi**, m. N. of an astron. wk. by Bhāskara (in 4 divisions called *Līlāvatī, Bīja-gaṇita, Gaṇitâdhyāya*, and *Golâdhyāya*), IW. 176; *-prakāśa*, m., *-vāsanā-vārttika*, n., and *ºny-udāharaṇa*, n. N. of Comms. on the above wk. **-śekhara**, m., **-saṃhitā-sāra-samuccaya**, m., **-saṃgraha**, m., **-saṃgraha-ṭīkā**, f., **-saṃdarbha**, m., **-samāsa**, m. N. of wks. **-sāra**, m. N. of various wks.; (with *kaustubha*) N. of a translation of the Almagest by Jagan-nātha; *-dīpikā*, f., *-saṃgraha*, m.; *ºrâvalī*, f. N. of wks. **-sārvabhauma**, m. or n., **-siddhâñjana**, n., **-sindhu**, m., **-sudhānidhi**, m., **-sundara**, m. or n. (also called *sundara-siddhânta*), **-sūkta-mañjarī**, f., **-sūtra-bhāshya-ṭīkā**, f., **-setukā**, f., **-svânubhūti-prakāśikā**, f., **-horā**, f. N. of wks. **Siddhântâcāra**, m. (with Tāntrikas) a perfect rule of action, MW.; one who practises this rule (said to consist in purity, quietism, and mental absorption in Durgā), ib. **Siddhântâdhikaraṇa-mālā**, f. N. of a wk. on the Vedânta (= *adhikaraṇa-mº*, q. v.) **Siddhântârṇava**, m. N. of another Vedânta wk. by Raghu-nātha Sārvabhauma.

Siddhântaya, Nom. P. *ºyati*, to establish or prove or demonstrate logically, Kap., Sch.

Siddhântita, mfn. established as true, logically demonstrated, Kull. on Mn. i, 8.

Siddhântin, m. one who establishes or proves his conclusions logically, one learned in scientific text-books, W.; = *mīmāṅsaka*, L.

Siddhântīya, n. N. of wk.

Siddhāyikā, f. (prob. for *siddha-dāyikā*) N. of one of the 24 goddesses (called Śāsana-devatās) who execute the commands of the 24 Arhats, L.

2. **Siddhi**, f. (for 1. see p. 1215, col. 1) accomplishment, performance, fulfilment, complete attainment (of any object), success, MBh.; Kāv. &c.; the hitting of a mark (loc.), Kām.; healing (of a disease), cure by (comp.), Yājñ.; coming into force, validity, ib.; settlement, payment, liquidation (of a debt), Mn. viii, 47; establishment, substantiation, settlement, demonstration, proof, indisputable conclusion, result, issue, RPrāt.; Up.; Sarvad.; decision, adjudication, determination (of a lawsuit), W.; solution of a problem, ib.; preparation, cooking, maturing, maturity, ib.; readiness, W.; prosperity, personal success, fortune, good luck, advantage, Mn.; MBh. &c.; supreme felicity, bliss, beatitude, complete sanctification (by penance &c.), final emancipation, perfection, L.; vanishing, making one's self invisible, W.; a magical shoe (supposed to convey the wearer wherever he likes), ib.; the acquisition of supernatural powers by magical means or the supº faculty so acquired (the eight usually enumerated are given in the following Śloka, *aṇimā laghimā prâptiḥ prākāmyam mahimā tathā | īśitvaṃ ca vaśitvaṃ ca tathā kāmâvasāyitā*; sometimes 26 are added, e.g. *dūra-śravaṇa, sarvajña-tva, agni-stambha* &c.), Sāṃkhyak.; Tattvas.; Sarvad.; any unusual skill or faculty or capability (often in comp.), Pañcat.; Kathās.; skill in general, dexterity, art, Car.; efficacy, efficiency, Kāv.; Pañcat.; understanding, intellect, W.; becoming clear or intelligible (as sounds or words), BhP.; (in rhet.) the pointing out in the same person of various good qualities (not usually united), Sāh.; (prob.) a work of art, Rājat. iii, 381; a kind of medicinal root (= *ṛiddhi* or *vṛiddhi*), L.; (in music) a partic. Śruti, Saṃgīt.; a partic. Yoga (either the 16th or 19th), Col.; Success or Perfection personified, MBh.; VarBṛS.; N. of Durgā, Kathās.; of a daughter of Daksha and wife of Dharma, Pur.; of the wife of Bhaga and mother of Mahiman, BhP.; of a friend of Danu, Kathās.; of one of the wives of Gaṇêśa, RTL. 215, 2; N. of Śiva (in this sense m.), MBh. **-kara**, mf(*ī*)n. producing success or good fortune, Kāv.; VarBṛS.; (*ī*), f. N. of a sorceress, Kathās. **-karaṇa**, n. the act of producing success or fortune; *-vidhāna*, n. N. of a Tantra wk. **-kāraka**, mfn. causing the attainment of the object of any one (gen.), leading to the desired goal, MBh.; producing an effect, effective, efficacious, MārkP. **-kāraṇa**, n. a cause of beatitude, means of obtaining felicity, MW. **-kārin**, mfn. causing the accomplishment of anything (gen.), Sāh. **-kshetra**, n. (cf. *siddha-kshº*) field of success, place of beatitude, seat of bliss, Śak.; Hcar.; N. of a sacred district, Hariv.; of a mountain, Śatr. **-cāmuṇḍā-tīrtha**, n. N. of a Tīrtha, Cat. **-jñāna**, n. knowledge of what is established, certain knº, Sarvad. **-traya**, n. N. of a Vedânta wk. by Yāmunâcārya. **-da**, mf(*ā*)n. conferring felicity or beatitude, VarYogay.; Mālatīm.; BhP.; N. of a form of Bhairava or Śiva, Śivag.; Putranjiva Roxburghii, L. **-darśin**, mfn. seeing (future) success, knowing future events, Mālav. **-dātrī**, f. 'giver of perfection,' N. of a form of Durgā, Cat. **-nṛisiṇha**, m. N. of a king (also *-malla*), Inscr. **-prada**, mfn. granting or promising success, Car. **-prâya**, mfn. (cf. *siddha-prº*) near to perfection, Ml. **-bīja**, n. the seed (i.e. source) of magical power, Pañcar. **-bhūmi**, f. the land of success or fortune, seat of bliss, BhP.; *-mārga*, v.l. for *siddhi-mº* (q.v.) **-bhairava-tantra**, n. N. of a Tantra. **-mat**, mfn. successful, Ragh.; accomplished, perfect, R.; Śak.; possessing magical power, Kathās. **-mantra**, m. a magical verse or formula, spell, charm, Cat. **-manv-antara**, n. N. of a place, Inscr. **-mārga**, m. the road leading to the land of the Blest, Pañcat. **-yātrika**, m. one who makes pilgrimages to learn magical arts or to gain good luck or beatitude, ib. **-yoga**, m. employment of magical arts, Kathās.; an auspicious conjunction of the planets, L. **-yoginī**, f. a kind of Yoginī, L. **-yogya**, mfn. necessary for success, Bhpr. **-rasa**, m. (prob.) w. r. for *siddha-rº*, quicksilver, Siṇhās. **-rasa-daṇḍa**, m. (prob.) w.r. for *siddha-rº* (q. v.) **-rāj**, m. N. of a mountain, Śatr. **-lābha**, m. acquirement of success or perfection, MW. **-varti**, f. magical wick (v. l. *siddha-vº*), Pañcat. **-vāda**, m. = *jñāna-goshṭhī*, MBh. xiii, 6525 (Nīlak.) **-vighna**, m. an obstacle to success or perfection, Rājat. **-vināyaka**, m. a form of Gaṇêśa; *-pūjana-vidhi*, m., *-vrata*, n. N. of wks. **-sādhaka**, m. or n. N. of a Vedânta wk. **-sādhana**, n. a means of obtaining beatitude or perfection or magical power, Pañcar. **-sopāna**, n. 'ladder of success,' N. of a Tantra wk. **-sthāna**, n. 'place of felicity,' any sacred spot where pilgrims may obtain beatitude (such as on the Ganges &c.), Pur.; Śukas.; the part of a medical work dealing with the efficacious treatment of disease, Car. **Siddhīśvara**, m. 'lord of magical power,' N. of Śiva, Kathās.; n. N. of a district sacred to Śiva, ib.

Siddhika (ifc.) = 2. *siddhi*, supernatural power, Kathās.

Siddhī-kṛita, mfn. accomplished, finished, Mṛicch.

Siddhy, in comp. for 2. *siddhi*. **-artham**, ind. for the sake of accomplishing or obtaining, Yājñ. **-asiddhi**, f. du. success and misfortune, Bhag.

1. **Sidhmá**, mfn. (for 2. see p. 1217, col. 1) going straight to a goal or object aimed at, RV. i, 33, 13.

Sidhya, m. 'auspicious,' N. of the asterism Pushya, L.

Sidhrá, mf(*ā́*)n. = 1. *sidhmá*, RV.; successful, efficacious, ib.; perfect, good, Uṇ. ii, 13, Sch.; m. a kind of tree, ib.

Sidhraka, m. a kind of tree, KātyŚr.

Sidhrakā, in comp. for *sidhraka*. — **vana**, n. (cf. g. *koṭarâdi*) N. of one of the celestial gardens, L. — **vat**, see *saidhrakāvata*.

सिध्म 2. *sidhmá*, mf(*ā*)n. (of doubtful derivation) white-spotted (accord. to others 'leprous'), TS.; (*ā*), f. a blotch, leprous spot, MW.; leprosy, ib.; m. n. one of the 18 forms of leprosy (= *mahā-kushṭha*), Car.; Bhpr.; n. a blotch, scab, W.

3. **Sidhma**, in comp. for *sidhman*. — **pushpikā**, f. a kind of mild leprosy, L. — **vat**, mfn. leprous, Pāṇ. v, 2, 97; blotchy, pock-marked, W.

Sidhman, m. n. one of the 18 varieties of leprosy (= *kshudra-kushṭha*), Suśr.; MBh. &c.

Sidhmalá, mfn. leprous, TBr.; Pāṇ. v, 2, 97; (*ā*), f. a kind of leprosy, Col.; dried or salt fish, L.

सिन 2. *sína*, n. (accord. to some fr. a √*sā* = *ā* in *ἅμεναι*; fr. which also *sinva*, *sinvat* in *a-s°*; for 1. *sina* see p. 1213, col. 1) provision, store (accord. to Naigh. = *anna*, 'food;' accord. to others = 'reward, pay'), RV.; m. (only L.) the body; a garment; Careya Arborea; (*ī*), f. = *sinīvālī*, Kāśikh.; mf(*ī*)n. white (= 3. *sita*), L.; blind, one-eyed (= *kāṇa*), L. — **vat** (*sína-*), mfn. abundant, copious, RV.

Sinī (f. of prec.), in comp. (?) — **pati**, m. N. of a warrior (v.l. *śin°*), Hariv. — **vāka**, m. N. of a man (v.l. *sil°*), MBh.

सिनीवाली *sinīvā́lī*, f. (of doubtful derivation) N. of a goddess (in RV. described as broad-hipped, fair-armed, fair-fingered, presiding over fecundity and easy birth, and invoked with Sarasvatī, Rākā &c.; in AV. she is called the wife of Vishṇu; in later Vedic texts she is the presiding deity of the first day of new moon, as Rākā of the actual day of full moon), the first day of new moon when it rises with a scarcely visible crescent, RV. &c. &c.; N. of a daughter of Aṅgiras, MBh.; of the wife of Dhātṛi and mother of Darśa, BhP.; of Durgā, L.; of a river, MārkP. — **kuhū-śānti**, f. N. of a religious ceremony (for averting the evil effects of being born on Sinīvālī and Kuhū days), Saṃskārak.

सिन्दुक *sinduka*, m. (of unknown derivation) = *sinduvāra*, L.; (*ā*), f. id., L.

Sinduvāra, m. (cf. *sindhu-v°*) Vitex Negundo, Kāv.; VarBṛS. (also *°raka*, L.); n. the berry of that plant, Kum.

सिन्दूर *sindūra*, m. (accord. to Uṇ. i, 69, fr. √*syand*) a sort of tree, L.; a proper N., Cat.; (*ī*), f. red cloth or clothes, L.; Grislea Tomentosa, L.; another plant (= *-pushpī*), L.; = *rocanī*, L.; n. red lead, minium, vermilion, Kāv.; Kathās. &c.; (= *rakta-śāsana*, *rāja-lekha*, and *rāja-lekhita-dakshiṇa*, L.) — **kāraṇa**, n. 'origin of minium,' lead, L. — **tilaka**, m. (ifc. f. *ā*) a mark on the forehead made with red lead, Kathās.; 'marked with red lead,' an elephant, L.; (*ā*), f. a woman whose forehead is marked with red lead (and therefore whose husband is living), L. — **nirgama**, m. N. of a ch. of GaṇP. ii. — **pushpī**, f. a kind of plant (= *vīra-pushpī*), L. — **prakāra**, m. N. of wk. (also *-ṭīkā*, f.), W. — **rasa**, m. a partic. preparation of quicksilver, L.

Sindūrikā, f. red lead, minium, W.

Sindūrita, mfn. reddened, made red, Śiś.

सिन्ध *sindha*. See *kús°*, p. 298, col. 1.

सिन्धि *sindhi*, n. (perhaps connected with next) rock-salt, L.

सिन्धु *sindhu*, m. and f. (prob. fr. √1. *sidh*, 'to go') a river, stream (esp. the Indus, and in this sense said to be the only river regarded as m., see *-nada*, col. 2), RV. &c. &c.; m. flood, waters (also in the sky), RV.; AV.; ocean, sea, RV. &c. &c.; a symbolical term for the number 4 (cf. 1. *samudra*), Gaṇit.; N. of Varuṇa (as god of the ocean), MW.; the moisture of the lips, Kum.; water ejected from an elephant's trunk (= *vamathu*), L.; the exudation from an elephant's temples, L.; the country around the Indus (commonly called Sindh; pl. 'the inhabitants of Sindh'), MBh.; Kāv. &c.; a king of Sindh (?), Cat.; N. of Vishṇu, RV.; MBh.; white or refined borax (= *śveta-ṭaṅkaṇa*), L.; = *sindhuka*, L.; (in music) a partic. Rāga, Saṃgītas.; N. of a king of the Gandharvas, R.; of a serpent-demon, Buddh.; of various men, Rājat. — **kanyā**, f. 'daughter of the ocean,' N. of Lakshmī, Pañcar. (also *kshīrôda-sindhu-k°*). — **kapha**, m. 'sea-foam,' cuttle-fish bone, L. — **kara**, n. a kind of borax, ib. (prob. incorrect). — **kārikā**, w.r. for *-vārikā*, Car. — **kshit**, m. N. of a Rājarshi (author of the hymn RV. x, 75 and having the patr. Praiyamedha), PañcavBr. — **khela**, m. 'played or flowed over by the Indus,' the country Sindh, L. — **gañja**, m. a treasury built by Sindhu, Rājat. — **ja**, mfn. ocean-born, river-born, aquatic, W.; born or produced in the country Sindh, MBh.; (*ā*), f. N. of Lakshmī (as produced at the churning of the ocean), Cat.; n. rock-salt, Suśr. — **janman**, mfn. ocean-born, MW.; produced in Sindh, ib.; m. the moon, L.; n. rock-salt, ib. — **ḍā** (?), f. N. of a Rāgiṇī, Saṃgīt. — **tás**, ind. from the Sindhu, AV. — **tīra-sambhava**, n. a kind of borax, L. — **datta**, m. N. of a man, Daś. — **deśa**, m. the country of Sindh, Cat. — **dvīpa**, m. N. of a king, MBh.; of the author of the hymn RV. x, 9 (having the patr. Āmbarīsha), Hariv.; VP.; of other men, MBh.; BhP. — **nada**, m. the river Indus, VarBṛS.; N. of a southern river, Cat.; of a country, ib. — **nandana**, m. 'son of the ocean,' the moon (one of the 14 precious things recovered by churning the ocean after the flood), L. — **nātha**, m. 'lord of rivers,' the ocean, Śiś. — **pati**, m. lord of the flood, RV.; 'lord of Sindh,' N. of Jayad-ratha, MBh. — **patnī** (*síndhu-*), f. having the Sindhu for mistress, AV. — **patha**, m., g. *deva-pathâdi*. — **parṇī**, f. Gmelina Arborea, L. — **pāra-ja**, mfn. born or produced on the Indus (said of a horse), L. — **piba**, m. N. of Agastya, Naish. — **putra**, m. 'son of the ocean,' the moon, L.; Diospyros Tomentosa, ib. — **pulinda**, m. pl. N. of a people, MW. — **pushpa**, m. 'sea-flower,' a conch-shell, L. — **prasūta**, n. rock-salt, Suśr. — **mathya**, mfn. produced at the churning of the ocean, BhP. — **madhya**, N. of a district, Cat. — **mantha**, m. the churning of the ocean, MW.; 'ocean churning-stick,' a mountain (accord. to some), ib.; *-ja*, n. rock-salt, L. — **mātṛi** (*síndhu-*), f. the mother of streams (said of the river Sarasvatī), RV.; mfn. having the sea as mother, ib. — **mitra**, m. N. of a man, g. *kāśyâdi*. — **mukha**, n. the mouth of a river, MW.; *°khâgata*, mfn. arrived at the mouth of a river, ib. — **rāja**, m. 'king of rivers,' the ocean, MaitrUp.; Kāv.; 'king of Sindh,' N. of Jayad-ratha, MBh.; Hariv. &c.; of a Muni, R. — **rājñī** (*síndhu-*), f. having the Sindhu as queen, AV. — **rāva**, m. Vitex Negundo, Pañcar. (w.r. for *-vāra*). — **lavaṇa**, n. rock-salt, L. — **vaktra**, N. of a place (see *saindhu-vaktraka*). — **vāra**, m. Vitex Negundo, MBh.; R.; Suśr.; Pañcar.; a horse (of a good breed) brought from Sindh, L. (cf. *-pāra-ja* above). — **vāraka**, m. (Suśr.) or **-vārikā**, f. (Car.) or **-vārita**, m. (L.) Vitex Negundo. — **vāsin**, mfn. living in Sindh, MW.; (*inī*), f. N. of the family-deity of the Māṇṭis, Cat. — **vāhas** (*síndhu-*), mfn. (perhaps) passing through the sea or navigating, RV. (accord. to Sāy. = *nadīnām pravāhayitā*). — **vīrya**, m. N. of a king of the Madras, MārkP. — **vṛisha**, m. N. of Vishṇu, L. — **veshaṇa**, m. Gmelina Arborea, L. — **śayana**, m. 'ocean-reclining,' N. of Vishṇu, ib. — **shāman** (for *-sāman*), n. N. of a Sāman, ĀrshBr.; Lāṭy. — **sheṇa** (for *-sena*), m. N. of a king of Sindh, Mudr. — **saṃgama**, m. 'sea-confluence,' the mouth of a river, Rājat. — **samudra-saṃgama**, m. N. of a place, MW. — **sarja**, m. the Sāl tree, L. — **sāgara**, the country between the mouths of the Indus and the sea, Inscr. — **sūnu**, m. patr. of Jālam-dhara, Cat. — **sṛitya**, n. the flowing in streams, AV. — **sauvīra**, m. pl. N. of a people inhabiting the country round the Indus (in comp. also N. of the country), AV.Pariś.; MBh.; R. &c.; a king of the above people, VarBṛS. — **sauvīraka**, m. pl. N. of a people (= prec.), ib. **Sindhûttama**, n. N. of a Tīrtha, MBh. **Sindhûttha**, m. the moon, L.; n. rock-salt, Suśr. **Sindhûdbhava** (ib.) or **°dhûpala** (L.), n. rock-salt.

Sindhuka, mfn. marine, W.; born or produced in Sindh, VP.; m. Vitex Negundo, VarBṛS.; N. of a king, VP.

Sindhura, m. an elephant, Rājat.; Śukas.; N. of the number eight, Gaṇit. — **dveshin**, m. 'elephant-hater,' a lion, L. **Sindhurā-giri-māhātmya**, n. N. of ch. of the Padma-purāṇa.

Sindhula, m. N. of the father of Bhoja, Cat.

सिन्व् *sinv*. See √*ninv*, p. 549, col. 2.

सिन्व *sinva*, *sinvat*. See *a-s°*, p. 121, col. 1.

सिपाहन *sipāhana*, N. of a place, Cat.

सिपिल *sipila*, m. N. of a man, Buddh.

सिपुना *sipunā*, f. a kind of plant, Kauś.

सिप्र *sipra*, m. (less correctly *śipra*; derivation unknown) sweat, perspiration, L.; the moon, L.; (*ā*), f. a woman's zone, L.; a female buffalo, L.; N. of a river near Ujjayinī, Kālid.; VarBṛS. &c.; n. N. of a lake, KālP.

Siprāya, Nom. Ā. *°yate*, to emit cold perspiration, Car.

सिफिन्ना *siphinnā*, f. N. of a village, Rājat.

सिभ् *sibh* or *simbh*. See √*sṛibh*.

सिम् 1. *sim*, ind., g. *câdi*.

सिम् 2. *sim*, (in Vedic gram.) a technical term for the eight simple vowels (viz. *a*, *ā*, *i*, *ī*, *u*, *ū*, *ṛi*, *ṛī*).

सिम 1. *simá*, mfn. (prob. connected with 1. *sama*; abl. *simásmāt*, dat. *simásmai*; voc. *simā* [Padap. *sima*, RV. viii, 41]; n. pl. *sime*) all, every, whole, entire (accord. to some = *śreshṭha*; accord. to others = *ātman*, 'one's self'), RV.

सिम 2. *síma*, m. = *śíma*, VS. (accord. to Mahīdh. = *sīmā*, *rekhā*).

सिमसिमाय *simasimāya* (onomat.), Ā. *°yate*, to bubble, simmer, crackle, Vās.; MārkP.

Simisimāya, Ā. *°yate*, to quiver (with irritability, itch &c.), Kathās.

सिमा *simā*, f. pl. a partic. Sāman (consisting of the Mahā-nāmnī verses; *-tva*, n.), Br.

सिमीक *simīka*, m. a kind of small worm or insect, L.

सिम्ब 1. *simba*, *simbala*, *simbi* &c. See *śimb°*, p. 1072, col. 2.

सिम्ब 2. *simba*, m. N. of a man, Rājat. — **rāja**, m. N. of an author, Cat.

सिम्बतिका *simbatikā*, f. (cf. *śimbikā*) a kind of pod or legume, Suśr.

सिम्भुक *simbhuka*, m. N. of a mythical bird, Pañcat.

सिर *sira*, m. = 1. *śira*, the root of Piper Longum, L.

सिरा *sirā*, f. (fr. √*sṛi*) a stream, water, RV. i, 121 (cf. Naigh. i, 12; often written *śirā*); any tubular vessel of the body, a nerve, vein, artery, tendon &c., Suśr.; Yājñ.; MBh. &c.; a vein-like channel or narrow stream of river water, VarBṛS.; lines which cross each other like veins, ib.; a bucket, baling-vessel, L. — **jāla**, n. a network of vessels or veins, MBh.; Suśr.; an enlargement of the vessels of the eye, W.; *-vat*, mfn. covered with a network of veins, Suśr. — **pattra**, m. the sacred fig-tree, L.; Phœnix Paludosa, L. — **praharsha**, m. = *sirā-harsha*, Suśr. — **bīja**, n., g. *rāja-dantâdi*. — **mūla**, n. 'root of the veins,' the navel, ib. — **moksha**, m. 'vein-loosing,' blood-letting, venesection, ib. — **°mbu** (*sirâmbu*), n. the fluid in the vessels of the body, blood &c., HPariś. — **vṛitta**, n. lead, L. — **vedha**, m. (Rāghav.), **-vedhana**, n. (Car.), **-vyadha**, m. and **-vyadhana**, n. (Suśr.) piercing the veins, venesection. — **harsha**, m. thrill of the nerves, MW.; an intensified form of *sirôtpāta* below, Suśr.; flow of discoloured tears, W. **Sirôtpāta**, m. a disease of the white of the eyes, redness of the veins, Suśr.; ŚārṅgS.

Sirāla, mf(*ā*)n. having numerous or large veins, VarBṛS.; m. pl. N. of a people, VP.; (*ā*), f. a kind of plant, L.; n. the fruit of Averrhoa Carambola, L.

Sirālaka, m. Vitis Quadrangularis, L.

Sirālu, mfn. = (or w.r. for) *sirāla*, VarBṛS.

सिरिध्र *siridhra* or *°rindhra*, g. *kulālâdi*.

सिरी *sirī́*, m. or f. (prob.) a shuttle (others, 'a weaver'), RV. x, 71, 9.

सिलक *silaka*, v.l. for *śilaka* (q.v.)

सिलाची *silācī́*, f. a partic. medicinal plant, AV.

सिलाञ्जाला *silāñjālā*, f. (prob.) a partic. plant, AV.

सिलिकमध्यम *sílika-madhyama*, mfn. (said of the horses of the Sun; accord. to Nir. = *saṃsṛita-madhyama* or *śīrsha-madhyama*), RV. i, 163, 10.

सिलिसिलिक *silisilika*, m. resin, Kauś. (Sch.)

सिलीवाक *silī-vāka*, v.l. for *sinī-v°* (q.v.)

सिल्लकी *sillakī*, f. = *śallakī*, Boswellia Thurifera, L.

सिल्लन *sillana*, m. N. of a man, Rājat.

Silla-rāja, m. N. of a man, ib.

सिल्ह *silha*, m. incense, olibanum, L. **-bhūmikā**, f. the olibanum tree, L. **-sāra**, n. olibanum, L.

Silhaka, m. (also written *sihlaka*) olibanum, L.; (*ī*), f. the olibanum tree, Liquidambar Orientale, Bhpr. **-maya**, mf(*ī*)n. made of olibanum, Hcat.

सिव् *siv*, cl. 4. P. (Dhātup. xxvi, 2) *sívyati* (Ved. also °*te*; pf. *sisheva*, Gr.; aor. *asevīt*, ib.; fut. *sevitā*, *sevishyati*, ib.; ind. p. *syūtva* or *sevitvā*, ib.; *-sīvya*, AV.), to sew, sew on, darn, stitch, stitch together, (fig.) join, unite, RV. &c. &c.: Caus. *sīvayati* (Lalit.) or *sevayati* (aor. *asīshivat*, Gr.), to sew, stitch: Desid. *sisevishati* or *susyūshati*, Gr.: Intens. *seshīvyate*, ib. [Cf. Gk. κασσύω = κατα-συω; Lat. *suere*, *sutor*; Slav. *šiti*; Goth. *siujan*; Angl.Sax. *seówian*; Eng. *sew*.]

Siva or **sivaka**, m. one who sews or stitches, a sewer, stitcher, L.

Sivasa, m. a verse, L.; cloth, L.

Sivāku, m. a Ṛishi, L.

Sīvaka, m. a sewer (*ikā*, f.), Kālac.

Sīvana, n. sewing, stitching, Suśr.; a seam, suture, MW.; (*ī*), f. a needle, ib.; the frenum of the prepuce, L.; the part of the body of a horse below the anus, L.

Sīvya, mfn. to be sewn, Car.

Sevaka, sevana. See 2. *sev°*, s. v.

सिवत *sivata* (?), m. pl. N. of a people, VP.

सिवर *sivara*, m. an elephant, L.

सिषंग्रामयिषु *sishaṃgrāmayishu*, mfn. = *sisaṃgr°* below, W.

सिषाधयिषा *sishādhayishā*, f. (fr. Desid. of Caus. of √1. *sādh*) the wish to establish or prove, Bhāshāp.

Sishādhayishu, mfn. (also written *sisādh°*) desirous of accomplishing or effecting, aiming at (acc.), Āpast.; Baudh.; BhP.; seeking to prove or demonstrate, Jaim., Sch.

सिषासतु *sishāsátu*, mfn. (fr. Desid. of √*sā* or *san*) wishing to gain or obtain (gen.), RV.

Sishāsáni, mfn. id., ib.

Sishāsú, mfn. id., ib.; ready to give, AV.; AitBr.

Sishṇu, mfn. ready to give, RV.

सिषेवयिषु *sishevayishu*, mfn. (fr. Desid. of Caus. of √*sev*) wishing to honour or worship, Cat.

सिष्णासु *sishṇāsu*, mfn. (fr. √*snā*) wishing to bathe, MBh. (C. *sisn°*).

Sisnāsu, mfn. id., Kād.

सिष्मियाण *sishmiyāṇa*, *sishvidāna*. See √*smi* and √*svid*.

सिसंग्रामयिषु *sisaṃgrāmayishu*, mfn. (fr. Desid. of √*saṃgrām*) wishing or intending to make war, eager or desirous to fight, Bhaṭṭ.

सिसनिस् *sisanis*, mfn. (fr. Desid. of √*san*), Pat.

सिसाधयिषु *sisādhayishu*. See *sishādh°*.

सिसिक्षा *sisikshā*, f. (fr. √*sic*) the desire of sprinkling or watering, Śiś.

सिसृक्षा *sisṛikshā*, f. (fr. Desid. of √*sṛij*) wish or purpose to create (with gen. or ifc.), Mn.; Hariv.; BhP.

Sisṛikshu, mfn. wishing to let flow or emit, MBh.; wishing or purposing to create, Mn.; MBh. &c.

सिस्नासु *sisnāsu*. See col. 1.

सिस्रत् *sisrat*. See √*sṛi*.

सिहुण्ड *sihuṇḍa*, m. (cf. *sih°*) a kind of spurge, Euphorbia Antiquorum (= *snuhi*), L.

सिह्ल *sihla*, *sihlaka* &c. See *silh°*, col. 1.

सी 1. *sī*, a word used in learning letters (?), Divyâv.

सी 2. *sī*, (either invented to account for *sītā* below or a lost root meaning) 'to draw a straight line'

Sītā, f. (less correctly written *śītā*; cf. *sīmán*, *sīra*) a furrow, the track or line of a ploughshare (also personified, and apparently once worshipped as a kind of goddess resembling Pomona; in RV. iv, 57, 6, Sītā is invoked as presiding over agriculture or the fruits of the earth; in VS. xii, 69–72, Sītā 'the Furrow' is again personified and addressed, four furrows being required to be drawn at the ceremony when the above stanzas are recited; in TBr. she is called *sāvitrī*, and in PārGṛ. *indra-patnī*, 'the wife of Indra;' in epic poetry S° is the wife of Rāmacandra and daughter of Janaka, king of Mithilā, capital of Videha, who was otherwise called Sīradhvaja; she was named Sītā because fabled to have sprung from a furrow made by Janaka while ploughing the ground to prepare it for a sacrifice instituted by him to obtain progeny, whence her epithet A-yoni-jā, 'not womb-born;' her other common names, Maithilī and Vaidehī, are from the place of her birth; according to one legend she was Vedavatī, q.v., in the Kṛita age; accord. to others she was an incarnation of Lakshmī and of Umā; the story of Rāma's bending the bow, which was to be the condition of the gift of Sītā, is told in R. i, 67; Sītā's younger sister Ūrmilā was at the same time given to Lakshmaṇa, and two nieces of Janaka, daughters of his brother king Kusa-dhvaja, to Bharata and Śatrughna), RV. &c. &c.; IW. 335, n. 1; 337 &c.; N. of a form of Dākshāyaṇī, Cat.; of a poetess, Cat.; of a river, MBh.; R. &c.; of the eastern branch of the four mythical branches of the heavenly Ganges (into which it is supposed to divide after falling on mount Meru; this branch is fabled to flow into the Varsha or Dvīpa called Bhadrâśva), L.; of an Upanishad, Cat.; spirituous liquor, W. **-kalyāṇa**, N. of a Kāvya. **-kuṇḍa**, N. of a small cavity or hollow in the ground consecrated to Sītā and filled with water, W. **-goptṛi**, m. a protector of the furrow, PārGṛ. **-gaurī-vrata**, n., **-caraṇa-cāmara**, N. of wks. **-jāni**, m. 'having Sītā as wife,' N. of Rāmacandra, Śukas. **-tīrtha-māhātmya**, n., **-divya-caritra**, n. N. of wks. **-dravya**, n. an implement of husbandry, Mn. ix, 293. **-nadī**, f. N. of a river, HPariś. **-nanda**, m., **-navamī-vrata-māhātmya**, n. N. of wks. **-pati** (or °*tāyāḥ-pati*), m. 'husband of Sītā,' N. of Rāma, RāmatUp. **-phala**, m. 'bearing Sītā's fruit,' Annona Squamosa, MW.; n. the fruit itself, ib. **-yajña**, m. a sacrifice offered to the Furrow, GṛS.; mfn. sacrificing to the Furrow, Hariv. **-rāghava-nāṭaka**, n. N. of a drama. **-rāma**, m. N. of various authors and other persons, Cat.; du. Sītā and Rāma, RTL. 184; *-candra*, m. f. N. of a king, ib.; *-tattva-prakāśa*, m., *-paddhati*, N. of wks.; *-paralīkara* (?), m. N. of an author, Cat.; *-yantrôddhāra*, m., *-vihāra* or °*ra-kāvya*, n. N. of wks.; *-śāstrin*, m. N. of various authors, Cat.; *-saṃkīrtana*, n. N. of wk.; *-sūri*, m. N. of an author, Cat.; *-stotra*, n.; °*mânujīya*, n., °*mâshṭaka*, n., °*mâshṭôttara-śata-nāman*, n. N. of wks. **-loshṭa** or **-loshṭha**, m. n. a clod taken from a furrow, Gobh. **-vana**, see *sītavana*. **-vallabha**, m. 'beloved by Sītā,' N. of Rāma, RāmatUp. **-vijaya-campū**, f., **-vivāha**, m. N. of wks. **-śruti**, f. news of Sītā, R. **-°shṭôttara-śata-nāmâvalī** (°*tâsh°*), f., **-sahasra-nāman**, n., **-sahasra-nāma-stotra**, n., **-stava**, m., **-stuti**, f., **-stotra**, n., **-svayaṃvara**, m. N. of wks. **-haraṇa**, n. 'the carrying off of Sītā,' N. of a ch. of R. **-°hāra** (°*tâh°*), m. 'Sītā's food,' Lycopodium Phlegmaria, ib. **Sītôpanishad**, f. N. of an Upanishad. **Sītôrmile**, f. du. Sītā and Ūrmilā, MW.

Sītya, mfn. ploughed, Pāṇ.; L.; n. corn, grain, L. [cf. prob. Gk. σῖτος].

सीक् *sīk* &c. See √*śīk*, p. 1077, col. 1.

सीक्ष् *siksh*, *sīkshati*. See √1. *sah*, p. 1192.

सीखा *sīkhā*, f. N. of a village, Inscr.

सीत् *sīt*. See *śīt*, p. 1077, col. 3.

सीतवन *sīta-vana* or *sītā-vana*, v.l. for *śīta-vana*.

सीतीनक *sītīnaka*, m. = *satīnaka*, pease, pulse, W.

Sītīlaka, m. id., L.

सीत्कार *sīt-kāra*, *sīt-kṛita*. See under *śīt*.

सीद् *sīd*, *sīdati*. See √2. *sad*, p. 1138, col. 2.

Sīda. See *kúsīda*, p. 298, col. 1.

Sīdantīya, n. (fr. *sīdantas*, the first word of RV. viii, 21, 5) N. of various Sāmans, ĀrshBr.

Sīdya, n. slothfulness, idleness, insolence, L.

सीधु *sīdhu*, m. (L. also f. and n.; less correctly *śīdhu*, of unknown derivation) spirituous liquor distilled from molasses, rum (or any similar spirit, also fig. = 'nectar'), MBh.; Kāv. &c. **-gandha**, m. 'having the smell of rum or spirituous liquor,' the plant or tree Mimusops Elengi (= *bakula*), L. **-pa**, mf(*ā* or *ī*)n. drinking spirits, Pāṇ. iii, 2, 8, Vārtt. 1. **-pāna**, n. the drinking of spirits, MBh. **-pushpa**, m. the Bakula tree, L.; the Kadamba tree, L.; (*ī*), f. Grislea Tomentosa (v.l. *svādu-p°*), L. **-rasa**, m. 'having juice like spirituous liquor,' the Mango tree, L. **-saṃjña**, m. the Bakula tree, L.

सीध्र *sīdhra*, n. the anus, L.

सीप *sīpa*, m. a vessel (for making libations), L.

सीपाल *sīpāla*, *sīpālila*. See *śīp°*, p. 1078.

सीबला *sībalā*, f. a partic. plant (growing on Hima-vat), TBr.

सीम् *sīm*, ind. (originally acc. of a pron. base and connected with *sa* as *kīm* with *ka*) him, her, it, them (employed for all genders, numbers and persons [cf. *id*, *īm*, and Gk. μιν, νιν]; and often weakened into a generalizing and emphasizing particle, which may become an enclitic particle after a pronoun or preposition, = περ or cunque, often translatable by 'ever'), RV.

सीमन् *sīmán*, m. (see 2. *sī* and *sītā*) a separation or parting of the hair so as to leave a line, AV.; Br.; AitUp.; a suture of the skull, L.; f. or n. a boundary, border, bounds, limit, margin, frontier (lit. and fig.), Yājñ.; Kāv.; Pur.; f. a ridge serving to mark the boundary of a field or village, Āpast.; VarBṛS.; a bank, shore, L.; the horizon, L.; the utmost limit of anything, furthest extent, summit, acme, ne plus ultra, Kāv.; Inscr.; the scrotum, Pat. on Pāṇ. ii, 3, 36; a partic. high number, Buddh.; the nape of the neck, L.

1. **Sīma** (only in loc. *sīme*) a boundary, limit, Inscr.

2. **Sīma**, in comp. for *sīman* (or sometimes a mere shortened form of 1. *sīmā*). **-tas**, ind. from the boundary or summit, VS. **-dhara-svāmin**, m. 'observing the bounds (of morality or decorum),' N. of a man, Śatr. **-liṅga**, n. (cf. *sīmā-l°*) a boundary-mark, land-mark, Mn. viii, 254.

Sīmaka (ifc.) = *sīman*, a boundary, limit, Pat.; Pañcar.

Sīmánta, m. (ifc. f. *ā*; cf. *sīmânta*) parting of the hair, AV.; GṛŚrS.; MBh. &c.; = *sīmantônnayana* below, Yājñ. i, 11; a line of separation on the human body (14 are enumerated, corresponding to the joints of the bones or Asthi-saṃghātas), Suśr.; a boundary, limit, MBh.; N. of a son of king Bhadra-sena, Cat.; of a poet, ib. **-karaṇa**, n. the act or ceremony of parting the hair, Gobh. **-karma-paddhati**, f. N. of wk. **-dṛiśvan**, mfn. (perhaps for *sīmânta-d°*) = *pāra-dṛiśvan*, Hcar. **-maṇi**, m. = *cūḍā-maṇi*, Prasannar. **-vat**, mfn. separated or parted by a straight line, Kir., Sch. **-vidhi**, m. N. of wk. **Sīmantônnayana**, n. 'the parting or dividing of the hair,' N. of one of the 12 Saṃskāras (observed by women in the fourth, sixth or eighth month of pregnancy), GṛS.; RTL.; *-prayoga*, m., *-mantra*, m. pl. N. of wks.

Sīmantaka, mf(*ikā*)n. having the hair parted (in pregnancy, see above), Gṛihyas.; m. hair-parting; (with Jainas) N. of a prince in one of the seven Jaina hells, L.; (*am*), n. red lead, vermilion (with which a mark is made along the division of the hair), L.; a kind of ruby, L.

Sīmantaya, Nom. P. °*yati,* to make a parting, traverse (the sea) in a straight line, Rājat.

Sīmantita, mfn. marked by a straight line, parted (as hair), Kir.; Kathās.

Sīmantin, mfn. parted (as hair), Suśr.; wearing the hair parted (as a pregnant woman), ŚāṅkhGṛ., Sch.; (*ī*), f. a woman, MBh.; Kāv. &c.; N. of a woman, Cat.

1. **Sīmā,** f. (ifc. f. *ā*) parting of the hair (see *su-sīma*); a boundary, landmark, Mn.; MBh. &c.; rule of morality (see comp.). **-krishāṇa,** mfn. ploughing on the border of a landmark, Yājñ. **-giri,** m. a boundary mountain, BhP. **-°jñāna** (°*māj*°), n. ignorance of boundaries, Mn. viii, 249. **-°tikramaṇôtsava** (°*mât*°), m. a festival at the passing of a boundary, Cat. **-°dhipa** (°*mâdh*°), m. a frontier-guardian, keeper of the borders, Pañcat.; a neighbouring king, MW. **-niścaya,** m. a legal decision in regard to landmarks and boundaries, ib. **-°nta** (°*mân*°), m. a border, boundary (*-bhūpāla,* m. 'a neighbouring king,' Campak. [*sīmāla* w.r.]), Bṛihasp.; Yājñ.; Kām. &c.; (fig.) bounds, MBh.; the boundary of a village, VarBṛS.; R.; mf(*ā*)n. bounded by a landmark, Hariv.; *-pūjana,* n. the act of honouring a village boundary &c., MW.; doing honour to a bridegroom when he arrives at the village boundary, A.; *-lekhā,* f. the utmost limit, Kād.; the extremity, ib. **-°ntara** (°*mân*°), n. the boundary of a village, MBh.; Ṛitus. **-°pahārin** (°*māp*°), mfn. one who takes away boundary-marks, Pañcar. **-pāla,** m. = *-°dhipa,* MārkP.; Pañcat. **-bandha,** m. a depository of rules of morality, Divyâv. **-liṅga,** n. a boundary-mark, landmark, Mn.; ib., Sch. **-vāda,** m. a dispute about boundaries, Mn.; Vcar. **-vinirṇaya,** m. (legal) decision of disputed questions about boundaries and landmarks, Mn. viii, 258; 266. **-vivāda,** m. litigation about bound°, Mn.; Yājñ., Sch.; *-dharma,* m. the law respecting disputes about bound°, MW. **-vṛiksha,** m. 'bound°-tree,' a tree serving as a bound°-mark, Mn. viii, 246; (fig.) one whose example is followed by others, MBh. **-saṃdhi,** m. the meeting of two boundaries, Mn. viii, 248; 261. **-setu,** m. a ridge or causeway serving as a boundary, ib. viii, 262; *-vinirṇaya,* m. (legal) decision about boundaries and barriers, MW. **Sīmôllaṅghana,** n. the transgressing of a boundary, trespass, passing a frontier, ib.

सीमा 2. *sīmā,* f. pl. = *simā,* ŚBr., Sch.

सीमिक *sīmika,* m. a kind of tree, L.; an ant or similar small insect, L.; an ant-hill, L.; (*ā*), f. an ant, L.

Sīmīka, m. (prob. w.r. for prec.) a kind of tree, L.

सीयक *sīyaka,* m. N. of a family of kings, Inscr.

सीर *sīra,* m. n. (for derivation see *sītā*) a plough, RV. &c. &c.; m. an ox for ploughing, draught-ox, Kauś.; the sun, Nir. ix, 40; Calotropis Gigantea, L. **-deva,** m. N. of a grammarian, Cat. **-dhvaja,** m. 'plough-bannered,' N. of Janaka, Bālar; of Bala-rāma, VP.; of a son of Hrasva-roman, ib. **-pati** (*sīra-*), m. lord of the plough, AV. **-pāṇi,** m. 'pl°-handed' or 'pl°-armed,' N. of Bala-rāma, L. **-bhṛit,** m. 'pl°-bearer,' id., MBh. **-yoga,** m. an ox yoked to a pl°, Kauś. **-vāhá,** mfn. drawing a plough, TS. **-vāhaka,** m. a plougher, ploughman, L. **Sīrâyudha,** m. 'plough-armed,' N. of Bala-rāma, Kād.; VP. **Sīrôtkashaṇa,** n. turning up the soil with a plough, ploughing, Megh.

Sīraka, m. a plough, MW.; a porpoise, L.; the sun, ib.

Sīrin, m. 'having or holding a plough,' N. of Bala-rāma, Hariv.

Sīrya. See *pari-s*°.

सीरज *sīraja,* N. of a place, Cat.

सील *sīla,* n. = *sīra,* a plough, Kapishṭh.

सीलन्ध *sīlandha* or *sīlandhra,* m. a kind of fish, Bhpr.

सीलमावती *sīlámāvatī,* f. (applied to the Indus; of doubtful meaning; accord. to Sāyaṇa 'rich in plants' [fr. *silanā,* 'a kind of plant of which ropes are made']; accord. to others 'rich in water'), RV. x, 75, 8.

सीलार *sīlāra,* m. N. of a family of kings (cf. *śilāra-vaṃśa*), Inscr.

सील्हन *sīlhana,* v.l. for *śilhana,* Cat.

सीवक *sīvaka, sīvana.* See p. 1218, col. 1.

सीस *sīsa,* n. (of doubtful derivation) lead (also used as money), VS. &c. &c.; the leaden weight used by weavers, VS.; mf(*ā*)n. leaden, of lead, VS.; LāṭyŚr. **-ja,** n. minium, red lead, L. **-pattra** or **-pattraka,** n. lead, L.

Sīsaka, m. n. lead, L.; m. = *śūla,* L.

सीसताण *sīsatāṇa,* N. of a place, Cat.

सीसर *sīsara,* m. N. of a mythical dog (the husband of Saramā), PārGṛ.

Sīsarama, m. N. of a dog-demon, Hir.

सीह *sīha.* See *sugandhi-s*°, p. 1222, col. 3.

सीहर *sīhara,* g. *sakhy-ādi.*

सीहुण्ड *sīhuṇḍa,* m. (cf. *seh*°) a kind of spurge, Euphorbia Antiquorum, L.

सु 1. *su,* cl. 1. P. Ā. *savati,* °*te,* to go, move, Dhātup. xxii, 42 (Vop. *sru*).

सु 2. *su* (= √1. *sū*), cl. 1. 2. P. (Dhātup. xxii, 43 and xxiv, 32; *savati, sauti,* only in 3. sg. pr. *sauti* and 2. sg. Impv. *suhi*) to urge, impel, incite, ŚBr.; KātyŚr.; to possess supremacy, Dhātup.

1. **Sutá,** mfn. impelled, urged, ŚBr.; allowed, authorized, ib.

1. **Suti,** (prob.) in *kuru-* and *pṛit-s*° (qq. vv.)

सु 3. *su,* cl. 5. P. Ā. (Dhātup. xxvii, 1) *sunóti, sunute* (in RV. 3. pl. *sunvánti, sunviré* [with pass. sense] and *sushvati*; p. *sunvát* or *sunvāná* [the latter with act. and pass. sense], ib.; pf. *sushāva, sushuma* &c., ib.; MBh.; p. in Veda *sushuvás* and *sushvāṇá* [the later generally with pass. sense; accord. to Kāś. on Pāṇ. iii, 2, 106, also *sushuvāṇa* with act. sense]; aor. accord. to Gr. *asāvīt* or *asaushīt, asoshṭa* or *asavishṭa;* in RV. also Impv. *sótu, sutám,* and p. [mostly pass.] *suvāná* [but the spoken form is *svāná* and so written in SV., *suv*° in RV.]; and 3. pl. *asushavuḥ,* AitBr.; fut. *sotā,* ib.; *soshyati,* KātyŚr.; *savishyati,* ŚBr.; inf. *sótave, sótos,* RV.; Br.; *sotum,* Gr.; ind. p. *-sútya,* Br.; *-sūya,* MBh.), to press out, extract (esp. the juice from the Soma plant for libations), RV.; AV.; ŚBr.; KātyŚr.; Up.; MBh.; to distil, prepare (wine, spirits &c.), Sch. on Pāṇ. ii, 2, 132: Pass. *sūyáte* (in RV. also Ā. 3. sg. *sunve* and 3. pl. *sunviré* with pass. sense; aor. *ásāvi,* ib.): Caus. *-sāvayati* or *-shāvayati* (see *abhi-shu* and *pra-*√3. *su;* aor. *asūshavat,* accord. to some *asīshavat*), Gr.: Desid. of Caus. *sushāvayishati,* ib.: Desid. *susūshati,* °*te,* ib.: Intens. *soshūyate, soshavīti, soshoti,* ib.

1. **Sut,** (ifc.; for 2. see col. 3) extracting juice, making libations (see *tīvra-sút, pra-sút, madhu-shút, soma-sút*); m. = *stotṛi,* a praiser, worshipper, Naigh. iii, 16.

2. **Sutá,** mfn. pressed out, extracted; m. (sg. and pl., once n. in ChUp. v, 12, 1) the expressed Soma-juice, a Soma libation, RV.; AV.; ŚBr.; ChUp.; BhP. **-kīrti,** f. mention of the (extracted) Soma, AitBr. **-pa,** m. (for *su-tapa* see p. 1223, col. 3) a drinker of the S°-juice; pl. N. of a class of deities, MW. **-pá** or **-pávan,** mfn. drinking the S°-juice, RV. **-péya,** n. the drinking of S°, ib. **-m-bhará,** mfn. carrying away Soma, RV.; m. N. of a Ṛishi (having the patr. Ātreya and author of RV. v, 11-14), Anukr. **-1. -vat,** mfn. (for 2. see under 3. *suta*) containing the word *suta* (*atī,* f. 'a verse c° the word *suta*'), AitBr.; m. a drinker of the S°-juice, W.; an offerer of a libation, MW. **-śravas,** m. N. of a teacher, Hir. **-soma** (*sutá-*), mfn. one who has extracted the S°, offerer of a S° libation, RV.; (a sacrifice) at which the S° is prepared, ib.; m. N. of a son of Bhīma-sena, MBh.; VP.; of a prince, Jātakam.; (*ā*), f. N. of a wife of Kṛishṇa (v.l. *śruta-s*°), Hariv.; *-jātaka,* n. N. of a Buddhist legend; *-vat* (*sutá-s*°), mfn. (pl.) joined with those who have prepared the Soma-juice, RV.; °*mâvadāna,* n. = °*ma-jātaka.* **Sutá-vat,** mfn. = *sutá-vat,* RV. **Sutâsutá,** n. du. what is extracted (as Soma) and what is not extracted (as milk), MaitrS.; °*tín,* mfn. having what is and what is not extracted, TBr.

2. **Suti,** f. extracting or pouring out (in *soma-s*°, q. v.)

Sute, (loc. of 2. *suta*) in comp. **-kara** (*suté-*), mfn. performing (recitation of certain texts) at the preparation of the Soma, RV. **-gṛibh,** mfn. taking hold of the Soma (for drawing it out of the vessel), ib. **-manas,** m. N. of a preceptor (having the patr. Śāṇḍilyāyana), IndSt. **-raṇa** (*suté-*), mfn. delighting in Soma, RV.

Sutya, n. (with or scil. *ahan*) the day of Soma extraction (also *sutyâha,* m.), ŚrS.; MBh.; (*ā*), f., see next.

1. **Sutyā,** f. (for 2. see below) the extraction or solemn preparation of Soma, VS.; Br.; ŚrS. **-kāla,** m. the time of, Nyāyam.; °*līna,* mfn. relating to that time (*-tva,* n.), ib., Sch. **-māsa,** m. a month in which the Soma is daily pressed, Lāṭy.

Sútvan, mf(*arī,* Pāṇ. iv, 1, 7)n. the extracting or preparing of Soma, RV.; AV.; m. a drinker of Soma, W.; a student who has performed his ablutions (before or after a Soma sacrifice), ib.; N. of a man (having the patr. Kairiśi), AitBr.

Sunvát, mfn. pressing out (the Soma) &c.; m. the offerer of a Soma sacrifice, Śiś.; N. of a son of Sumantu (also called Sunvāna), BhP.

Sushuvāṇa, sushvāṇá. See √3. *su,* col. 2.

Súshvi, mfn. pressing out or offering Soma (compar. *-tara*), RV.

Sūti, sūtya &c. See 3. *sūti,* p. 1241, col. 3.

Sotu, sotṛi &c. See p. 1248, col. 3.

सु 4. *su* (= √2. *sū*), (only in 3. sg. *sauti,* see *pra-*√2. *sū*) to beget, bring forth.

2. **Sut,** mfn. (for 1. see col. 2) begetting, generating, engendering, MW.

3. **Suta,** mfn. begotten, brought forth; m. (ifc. f. *ā*) a son, child, offspring (*sutau,* du. = 'son and daughter'), Mn.; MBh. &c.; a king, L.; N. of the 5th astrological house, VarBṛS.; N. of a son of the 10th Manu, Hariv.; (*ā*), f., see below. **-m-rayishṭhīya,** n. (with *Prajāpateḥ*) N. of two Sāmans, ĀrshBr. **-m-gama,** n. 'son-obtaining,' N. of a man (cf. *sautaṃgami*), Pāṇ. iii, 2, 47, Sch. **-jīvaka,** m. Putranjiva Roxburghii, L. **-m-jaya,** m. 'son-winning,' N. of a man (cf. *sutaṃ-gama*), MBh. **-tva,** n. condition of sonship (instr. with √*grah,* 'to adopt any one [acc.] as a son'), Kathās. **-dā,** f. 'son-giving,' N. of a divine being, Pañcar. **-nirviśesham,** ind. not differently from a son, exactly like a son, Ragh. **-pādikā** or **-pādukā,** f. a species of Mimosa, L. **-2. -vat,** mfn. (for 1. see under 2. *suta*) possessing sons or children, VarBṛS.; m. the father of a son, W. **-vatsala,** mfn. loving one's children; m. an affectionate father, Veṇīs. **-vallabha,** w.r. for prec. **-vaskarā,** f. the mother of seven children, L. **-śreṇī,** f. the plant Salvinia Cucullata, L. **-suta,** m. a son's son, a grandson, MārkP. **-hibuka-yoga,** m. junction of the 4th and 5th astrol. houses (said to be suitable for marriages), MW. **Sutâtmaja,** m. = *suta-suta,* L.; (*ā*), f. a granddaughter, L. **Sutârṇava,** m. N. of wk. **Sutârthin,** mfn. desirous of offspring, Mn. iii, 262. **Sutôtpatti,** f. birth of a son, Mn. iii, 16.

Sutā, f. (ifc. f. *ā*) a daughter, Mn.; MBh. &c.; the plant Alhagi Maurorum, L. **-dāna,** n. the gift (in marriage) of a daughter, Mn. iii, 26. **-pati,** m. 'daughter's husband,' a son-in-law, KātyŚr., Sch. **-putra,** m. du. a daughter and a son, L. **-bhāva,** m. the state of a daughter, Kathās.

3. **Suti.** See *sú-shuti.*

Sutin, mfn. having a son or sons (*inī,* f. 'a mother'), Hit.

1. **Sutī,** m. f. (abl. gen. *sutyus*) one who wishes for a son or treats any one like a son, Vop.

2. **Sutī,** in comp. for 3. *suta.* **-bhūta,** mfn. become a son, Kathās.

Sutīya, Nom. P. *-yati* (fr. 3. *suta* or *sutā*), to treat like a son, Sāh.; to wish for a son or for a daughter, MW.

2. **Sutyā,** f. (for 1. see above) bringing forth a child, parturition, MW.

सु 5. *sú,* ind. (opp. to *dus* and corresponding in sense to Gk. εὖ; perhaps connected with 1. *vásu,* and, accord. to some, with pron. base *sa,* as *ku* with *ka;* in Veda also *sū́* and liable to become *shu* or *shū* and to lengthen a preceding vowel, while a following *na* may become *ṇa;* it may be used as an adj. or adv.), good, excellent, right, virtuous, beautiful, easy, well, rightly, much, greatly, very, any, easily, willingly, quickly (in older language often with other particles; esp. with *u,* = 'forthwith, immediately;' with *mô,* i.e. *mā u,* = 'never, by no means;' *sú kam* often emphatically with an Impv., e.g. *tishṭhā sú kam maghavan mā́ párā gāḥ*, 'do tarry O Maghavan, go not past,' RV. iii, 53, 2; *su* always qualifies the meaning of a verb and is never used independently at the beginning of a verse; in later language it is rarely a separate word, but is mostly prefixed to substantives, adjectives, adverbs and participles, exceptionally also to an ind. p., e.g. *su-baddhvā*, 'having well bound,' Mṛicch. x, 50; or even to a finite verb, e.g. *su-nirvavau*, Śiś. vi, 58), RV. &c. &c. **-ūtí**, f. good protection or assistance, RV. **-kaksha**, m. N. of the author of RV. viii, 81; 82 (having the patr. Āṅgirasa), RAnukr. **-kaṅkavat**, m. N. of a mountain, MārkP. (v.l. *vaikaṅka*, VP.) **-kaṭam-kara**, mfn. very fit for making mats, Pat. **-kaṇṭakā**, f. Aloe Indica, L. **-kaṇṭha**, mf(*ī*)n. sweet-voiced, BhP.; m. N. of a singer, Cat.; (*ī*), f. the female or Indian cuckoo, L.; N. of an Apsaras, Bālar. **-kaṇḍu**, m. much-scratching, the itch, L. **-kathā**, f. a beautiful story, Kathās. **-kanda**, m. the root of Scirpus Kysoor, L.; an onion, W.; a yam, ib.; the root of Arum Campanulatum, MW.; other bulbous plants (= *vārāhi-kanda*; = *dharaṇī-k°*), ib.; *-ja*, v.l. for *su-kundana*, L. **-kandaka**, m. an onion, L.; a species of Arum, ib.; a yam, ib.; pl. N. of a people, MBh. **-kandin**, m. Amorphophallus Campanulatus, L.; Arum Campanulatum, MW. **-kanyaka**, mfn. having a beautiful daughter, Vop. **-kanyā́**, f. a beautiful girl, MW.; N. of a daughter of Śaryāta (or °ti) and wife of the Ṛishi Cyavana, ŚBr.; MBh.; Hariv. &c. (also °*yakā*). **-kanyāka**, mfn. = *-kanyaka*, Vop. **-kapardá**, mf(*ā́*)n. having beautiful braided hair, VS.; MaitrS. **-kapola**, mf(*ā*)n. having beaut° cheeks, BhP.; °*lâsya*, mfn. having a face with beaut° cheeks, ib. **-kamala**, n. a beaut° lotus flower, Kālac. **-kambala**, m. (ifc. f. *ā*) a beaut° dewlap, Hcat. **-kára**, mf(*ā*)n. easy to be done, easy for (gen.) or to (inf.), RV.; Mn. &c.; easy to be managed, tractable (as a horse or cow), L.; easily achieving, Vop.; m. a good-natured horse, L.; (*ā*), f. a tractable cow, W.; (*am*), n. doing good, charity, benevolence, ib.; *-taraka*, mfn. very easy to be done, Pat.; *-tva*, n. easiness, feasibleness, Sarvad.; Nilak.; *-saṃdhi*, mfn. easily joined or united, Pañcat. (v.l.) **-karīrá**, (prob.) w.r. for *-kurīrá*, MaitrS. **-karṇa**, m. a beautiful ear, BhP.; mfn. having beautiful ears; m. N. of a Rākshasa, R.; (*ā* or *ī*), f. a colocynth, L.; (*ī*), f. Salvinia Cucullata, ib. **-karṇaka**, mfn. = *-karṇa*, MW.; m. a kind of bulbous plant, L.; (*ikā*), f. Salvinia Cucullata, ib. **-karṇika**, mfn. having a beautiful film (as a lotus flower), Hcat. **-karma**, m. pl. N. of a class of deities, MW. **-karman**, n. a good work, Pañcar.; mfn. (*-kár°*) performing good works, virtuous, Rājat.; active, diligent, W.; m. a good or expert artificer or artist or architect, RV.; VS.; Nir.; N. of Viśva-karman (the architect of the gods), L.; the 7th of the 27 astronomical Yogas, ib.; N. of a king, MBh.; BhP.; of a teacher of the Sāma-veda, Pur.; pl. N. of a class of deities, ib. **-kala**, mfn. one who employs his property well both by giving and enjoying it, L.; m. N. of a man, Cat. **-kalatra**, n. a good wife, Kathās. **-kalita**, w.r. for next, MBh. **-kalila**, mfn. well filled with, ib. **-kálpa**, mfn. easy to be made, AV.; very qualified or skilled, BhP.; (w.r. for *-kalya*), ib. **-kalpita**, mfn. well equipped or armed, MBh. **-kalya**, mfn. perfectly sound, BhP. **-kavi**, m. a good poet, VarBṛS.; Kathās. &c.; *-tā*, f. the state of a good poet, poetical talent, Bhartṛ.; *-hṛidayânandini*, f. N. of wk. **-kashṭa**, mfn. very painful or dangerous (as a disease), Suśr. **-kāṇḍa**, mfn. having a good stem or stalk, MW.; well-jointed, ib.; Momordica Charantia, L. **-kāṇḍikā**, f. id., ib. **-kāṇḍin**, mfn. having good stems or stalks, MW.; beautifully jointed, ib.; m. a bee, L. **-kānta**, mfn. very handsome, Kathās. **-kānti**, m. N. of a man, Cat. **-kāma**, mfn. having good desires, MW.; (*ā*), f. Ficus Heterophylla, L.; (°*ma*)-*da*, mf(*ā*)n. abundantly granting desires, Hcat.; *-vrata*, n. a partic. religious observance, Cat. (v.l. *kāmya-v°*). **-kāla** (Hariv.) or **-kālin** (Mn.; Pur.), m. pl. N. of a class of Pitṛis. **-kālukā**, w.r. for *-vāl°*, L. **-kāśana**, mfn. shining beautifully, Nir. **-kāshṭha**, mfn. having good wood, MW.; (*ā*), f. the wild plantain, L.; = *kaṭvī*, ib.; n. fire-wood, A. **-kāshṭhaka**, mfn. having good wood, MW.; n. Pinus Deodora or another species, L. **-kiṃśuká**, mfn. (prob.) 'well made of Kiṃśuka wood' or 'bright with Kiṃśuka flowers' (said of the car of Sūryā), RV. x, 85, 20 (cf. Nir. xii, 8). **-kīrti**, f. good praise, hymn of praise, RV.; mfn. well or easily praised, ib.; glorious, Śivag.; m. N. of the author of RV. x, 131 (having the patr. Kākshīvata); of the above hymn, Br.; Vait. **-kukshi**, f. N. of a Gandharva maid, Kāraṇḍ. **-kucā**, f. having beautiful breasts, MBh. **-kuṭṭa**, m. pl. N. of a people, ib. **-kuṭya**, m. pl. N. of a people, ib. **-kuṇḍala**, m. N. of a son of Dhṛita-rāshṭra, ib. **-kuṇḍaka**, m. an onion, L. **-kundana**, m. a kind of plant (= *barbara*), L. **-kumala**, w.r. for *-komala*, Pañcat. **-kumāra**, mf(*ī*)n. very tender or delicate, MBh.; R. &c.; m. a delicate youth, ib.; tenderness, L.; sugar-cane and various other plants (Jonesia Asoka; the wild Campaka; Panicum Frumentaceum &c.), L.; N. of a serpent-demon, MBh.; of a Daitya, L.; of various kings, MBh.; Hariv.; Pur.; of a poet, Cat.; of a Varsha, MBh.; MārkP.; (*ā*), f. Jasminum Sambac or Grandiflorum, L.; Musa Sapientum, L.; Hibiscus Rosa Sinensis, L.; Trigonella Corniculata, L.; N. of a river, MW.; (*ī*), f. Jasminum Sambac or Grandiflorum, ib.; N. of a river, MBh.; VP.; *-tanu-tvac*, mfn. having very soft and delicate skin, MW.; *-tara*, mfn. more del°, Sāṃkhyak.; Vās.; *-tā*, f. (Kāvyâd. &c.) or *-tva*, n. (Kathās.) delicacy, tenderness; *-nakha-tvac*, mfn. having very del° nails and skin, MW.; *-vana*, n. N. of a forest, BhP.; °*râṅga*, mf(*ī*)n. having very del° limbs, MW. **-kumāraka**, mfn. very tender; m. a tender youth, Hariv.; Pañcar.; sugar-cane, L.; rice, MW.; N. of a son of Jāmbavat, VP.; (*am*), n. a partic. part of the ear, VarBṛS.; a cinnamon-leaf, L.; the Tamāla-pattra, MW. **-kumārīka**, mfn. having a handsome daughter, Pāṇ. vi, 2, 173, Sch. **-kumāla**, mfn. = *-kumāra*, Pañcad. **-kurīrá**, mf(*ā́*)n. having a beautiful head-dress, VS. **-kurkura**, m. N. of a dog-demon, Hir. **-kula**, n. a noble family, Kāv.; mf(*ā*)n. sprung from a n° f°, ib.; Pañcat.; *-ja*, mfn. id., Kāv.; *-janman*, n. n° birth, ib.; *-tā*, f. id., Prasaṅg.; *-strī*, f. a woman of good family, a respectable woman, MW. **-kulīna**, mfn. = *-kula-ja*, Pañcat. **-kusumā**, f. N. of one of the Mātṛis attending on Skanda, MBh. **-kūrkura**, m. N. of a demon hostile to children, PārGṛS. **-kṛit**, mfn. doing good, benevolent, virtuous, pious (compar. *-tara*; superl. *-tama*), RV.; AV.; VS. &c.; fortunate, well-fated, wise, W.; making good sacrifices or offerings, MW.; skilful, a skilful worker (said of Tvashṭṛi and Ṛibhu), RV.; m. pl. deceased fathers who enjoy the reward of virtue in the other world, RV.; AV. &c. **-kṛitá**, n. a good or righteous deed, meritorious act, virtue, moral merit (*-tas*, ind.), RV. &c. &c.; a benefit, bounty, friendly aid, favour, R.; Pañcat. &c.; the world of virtue, heaven, AV.; TS.; TBr.; fortune, auspiciousness, W.; reward, recompense, ib.; (*súkṛita*), mfn. well done or made or formed or executed, RV.; well arranged, adorned, made good (with *mati*, f. 'a well-taken resolution;' with *anartha*, m. 'an evil turned to good;' *kim atra sukṛitam bhavet*, 'what would be best done here?'), RV. &c. &c.; treated with kindness, befriended, MW.; well-conducted, virtuous, fortunate, ib.; (said to be) = *sva-k°*, TUp.; m. N. of a Prajā-pati, VP.; of a son of Pṛithu, Hariv.; (*ā*), f. N. of a river, VP.; *-karman*, n. a good or meritorious act (°*ma-kārin*, mfn. 'performing good acts'), Kām.; Kāv. &c.; mfn. doing g° deeds, virtuous, MBh.; R.; *-kṛit*, mfn. id., Mn. iii, 37; *-dvādaśī*, f. N. of a partic. 12th day (*-vrata*, n. N. of a relig. observance), Cat.; *-bhāj*, mfn. connected with merit, meritorious, Vās.; *-rasa*, m. the essence of merits or good deeds, JaimBr.; *-vrata*, n. N. of a religious observance, Cat.; °*tâtman*, mfn. one who has a well cultivated or refined mind, R.; °*târtha*, mfn. one who has fully attained his object, Kathās. (v.l. *sva-k°*); °*tâvāsa*, mfn. having a well-made or well-arranged residence, MW.; °*tâśā*, f. the hope of a reward for good acts, Āpast.; °*tôcchraya*, mfn. made very high, very lofty, MBh.; °*tôdīraṇa*, n. the proclaiming or blazoning abroad of good actions, MW. **-kṛiti**, f. well-doing, good or correct conduct, Pañcat.; acting in a friendly manner, kindness, MW.; virtue, ib.; the practice of religious austerities, ib.; mfn. righteous, virtuous, Cat.; m. N. of a son of Manu Svārocisha, Hariv.; of one of the 7 Ṛishis in the 10th Manv-antara, ib.; BhP.; of a son of Pṛithu, VP. **-kṛitin**, mfn. doing good actions, virtuous, generous (°*ti-tva*, n.), MBh.; Hariv.; R. &c.; prosperous, fortunate, Amar.; Kathās.; cultivated, wise, Kāv.; Hit.; m. N. of one of the 7 Ṛishis under the 10th Manu, MārkP. **-1. -kṛitya**, Nom. P. °*yati* (fr. *-kṛit*), Pat. **-2. -kṛitya**, n. a good work to be done, duty, BhP.; a good or correct action, Pañcat.; (°*tyá*), mfn. performing one's duties, TBr.; m. N. of a man (g. *naḍâdi*); *-prakāśa*, m. N. of wk. **-kṛityā́**, f. good or clever or righteous act, right or virtuous action, RV. **-kṛitvan**, mfn. acting skilfully or well, RV. **-kṛishṭa**, mfn. well-ploughed, AitBr.; R.; Pañcat. **-kṛishṇa**, mfn. very black, R. **-kéta**, mfn. having good intentions, benevolent, TS.; m. N. of an Āditya, ib. **-ketana**, m. N. of a son of Sunītha, BhP. **-ketú**, mf(*ú*)n. very bright, RV.; m. N. of a king of the Yakshas, Kāv.; of various kings, MBh.; Hariv.; R.; Pur.; *-sutā*, f. patr. of Tāḍakā, Bālar. **-ketṛi**, m. a partic. personification (identified with the sun), PārGṛ. (accord. to others *su-ketā*, f.) **-keśa**, mf(*ī* or *ā*)n. having beautiful hair, MBh.; R.; (prob.) thickly overgrown with a species of the Andropogon, Siddh.; m. N. of a Rākshasa, R.; (*ī*), f. N. of an Apsaras, MBh.; of a Surâṅganā, Siṇhâs.; of a daughter of Ketu-vīrya, MārkP.; °*śânta*, mf(*ā*)n. having beaut° locks of hair, MBh.; °*śī-bhārya*, mfn. one who has a beaut°-haired wife, Vop. **-keśan**, m. N. of a man, PraśnUp. **-keśi**, m. N. of a Rākshasa, Cat. **-keśin**, mfn. = *-keśa*, MW.; m. = *-keśi*, Cat.; (*inī*), f. a kind of plant, Npr. **-kesara**, m. Citrus Medica, L.; n. N. of two metres, Ked. **-komala**, mfn. very soft or tender, Kāv.; Pañcat.; Śukas. **-kolī**, f. a kind of bulbous plant, L. **-kośaka**, m. Mangifera Sylvatica, ib. **-kośā**, f. a species of Luffa, ib. **-kosalā**, f. N. of a town, Pat. **-krátu**, mfn. skilful, wise (said of various gods), RV.; m. N. of various kings, MBh. **-kratūya**, Nom. Ā. °*yate*, to show one's self skilful or wise, RV. **-kratūyā́**, f. intelligence, wisdom, skill, ib. **-kraya**, m. a fair bargain, Hcat. **-kriyā**, f. a good action, g° work, moral or religious observance, MW. **-krīḍā**, f. N. of an Apsaras, Kāraṇḍ. **-kruddha** (*sú-*), mfn. very angry, ŚBr.; R. **-krūra**, mfn. very dreadful, MBh. **-kleśa**, mfn. very distressing, Kathās. **-kvaṇa**, m. a beautiful sound, L. **-kshata** (*sú-*), mfn. greatly hurt or damaged, AV. **-kshatrá**, mfn. having a good dominion, ruling well, RV.; VS.; possessing or conferring power, strong, powerful, RV.; m. N. of a son of Niramitra, VP. **-kshatriya**, m. a good Kshatriya, Rājat. **-kshá́ya**, mfn. well-housed or well-sheltered, RV. **-kshití**, f. a good abode, secure dwelling, place of refuge, RV.; VS.; TS.; Br. **-kshubdha**, mfn. greatly agitated, Pañcar. **-kshétra**, n. an excellent field, RV.; Mn.; R. &c.; mf(*ā*)n. affording a good field or dwelling-place, RV.; Hariv.; having good fields, R.; sprung from a good womb, Suśr.; m. N. of a son of the 10th Manu, MārkP.; n. a house with three halls (towards the south, the west and the north), VarBṛS.; (°*trá*)-*tā*, f. the possession of a good field, AV. **-kshetriyā**, f. (the same form for instr.) desire of good fields, RV. **-kshema**, n. great prosperity or comfort or peacefulness (*-kṛit*, mfn.), VarBṛS. **-kshéman**, n. water, Naigh. i, 12. **-kshobhya**, mf(*ā*)n. easily agitated, Kathās. **-kshmá**, mf(*ā́*)n. consisting of good earth, VS. (Sch.) **-khá** &c., see *sukhá*, s.v. **-khallikā**, f. (perhaps) luxurious life, Lalit. **-khavi**, w.r. for *-shavi*, L. **-khādí**, mfn. (for *sukhâdi* see p. 1221, col. 3) wearing beautiful bracelets or rings (said of the Maruts), RV. **-khādita** (*sú-*), mfn. well masticated or eaten, VS. **-khura**, mf(*ā*)n. having beautiful hoofs, Hcat. **-khyāta**, mfn. very renowned, MW. **-khyāti**, f. good report, celebrity, ib.

सुक *súka* (for *śúka*), a parrot, AV. i, 22, 4.

सुक्कडि *sukkaḍi*, n. dry sandal-wood, L.

सुक्ति *sukti*, m. N. of a mountain (prob. w.r. for *śukti*), MārkP.

सुख् *sukh* (prob. Nom. fr. **sukha** below), cl. 10. 4. P. (Dhātup. xxxv, 75; xxxvi, 14) *sukhayati*, *sukhyati*, to make happy, please, delight, gladden, rejoice, comfort, MBh.; Kāv. &c.

Sukhá, mfn. (said to be fr. 5. *su* + 3. *kha* and to mean originally 'having a good axle-hole;' possibly a Prākṛit form of *su-stha*, q.v.; cf. *duḥkha*) running swiftly or easily (only applied to cars or chariots, superl. *sukhá-tama*), easy, RV.; pleasant (rarely with this meaning in Veda), agreeable, gentle, mild (comp. *-tará*), VS. &c. &c.; comfortable, happy, prosperous (= *sukhin*), R.; virtuous, pious, MW.; m. N. of a man, g. *śivâdi*; (scil. *daṇḍa*) a kind of military array, Kām.; (*ā*), f. (in phil.) the effort to win future beatitude, piety, virtue, Tattvas.; (in music) a partic. Mūrchanā, Saṃgīt.; N. of the city of Varuṇa, VP.; of one of the 9 Śaktis of Śiva, L.; (*am*), n. ease, easiness, comfort, prosperity, pleasure, happiness (in m. personified as a child of Dharma and Siddhi, MārkP.), joy, delight in (loc.; *sukhaṃ √kṛi*, 'to give pleasure;' *mahatā sukhena*, 'with great pleasure'), the sky, heaven, atmosphere (cf. 3. *kha*), L.; water, Naigh. i, 12; N. of the fourth astrol. house, VarBṛS.; the drug or medicinal root called Vṛiddhi, MW.; (*ám*), ind. (also *ena*, *āt*) easily, comfortably, pleasantly, joyfully, willingly (with inf. = 'easy to,' e. g. *sa bhavishyati sukhaṃ hantum*, 'he will be easy to kill;' *sukham – na punar*, 'rather – than,' e. g. *sukham asūn api saṃtyajanti na punaḥ pratijñām*, 'they rather renounce life than a promise;' *kadalī-sukham*, 'as easily as a Kadalī'), VS. &c. &c. **–kara**, mf(*ī*)n. causing pleasure or happiness, Nir.; easy to be done or performed by (gen.), R.; m. N. of Rāma, L.; (*ī*), f. N. of a Surâṅganā, Siṇhâs. **–kāra** (MW.), **-kārin** (Sāy.), **-kṛit** (MBh.), mfn. causing joy or happiness. **–kaumudī**, f. N. of a grammar. **–kriyā**, f. the act of causing delight or happiness, Dhātup. **–ga**, mfn. going easily, MW. **–gandha**, mf(*ā*)n. sweet-smelling, fragrant, R. **–gama** (MBh.), **-gamya** (Kām.), mfn. easy to be traversed or travelled over. **–grāhya**, mfn. easy to be grasped, Kathās.; easy to be comprehended or understood (see comp.); *-nibandhana*, n. a composition easy to be comprehended, easily intelligible language, Kum. **–ghātya**, mfn. easy to be killed, Pañcat. **–ṃ-kara**, mf(*ī*)n. causing joy or happiness, MW.; (*ī*), f. a kind of plant (= *jīvantī*), L. **–cara**, mf(*ī*)n. going or moving easily, MW.; m. N. of a village, L. **–cāra**, m. 'e°-going,' a good horse, L. **–citta**, n. mental ease; *-bhāj*, mfn. enjoying m° e°, Car. **–cchāya**, mfn. affording pleasant shadow, R. **–cchedya**, mfn. easy to be cut or destroyed, Kām.; Hit. **–jāta**, mfn. born or produced easily, W.; feeling easy or comfortable, Bhaṭṭ.; n. anything pleasant, Gīt. **–tama**, **-tara**, see above under *sukha*. **–tas**, ind. easily, comfortably, pleasantly, happily, R. **–tā**, f., **-tva**, n. ease, comfort, delight, happiness, prosperity, R.; Kathās.; Sarvad. **–da**, mf(*ā*)n. giving pleasure or delight, Kāv.; VarBṛS.; m. N. of Vishṇu, MBh.; a partic. class of deceased ancestors, MārkP.; (in music) a kind of measure, Saṃgīt.; (*ā*), f. Prosopis Spicigera or Mimosa Suma, L.; an Apsaras, L.; the river Ganges, MW.; (*am*), n. the abode of Vishṇu, L.; N. of a Varsha in Plaksha-dvīpa, VP. **–dāyaka**, mfn. giving or affording pleasure, Pañcar. **–duḥkha**, n. du. pleasure and pain, joy and sorrow, KaushUp.; *-maya*, mf(*ī*)n. consisting of pl° and p°, Kathās.; = next, ib.; *-samanvita*, mfn. feeling pl° and p°, Mn. i, 49; *-suhṛid*, m. a friend in joy and sorrow, Mṛicch.; °*khâtmaka*, mfn. consisting of pleasure and pain, MW.; °*khâdi*, mfn. (pl.) pl° and p° and the other (opposites; see *dvaṃdva*), Mn. i, 26; °*khin*, mfn. feeling pl° and p°, BhP. **–dṛiśya**, mfn. beautiful to look at, pleasant to see, Pañcar. **–deva**, m. N. of a man, Buddh.; (with *miśra*) N. of an author, Cat. **–dohā** (Hcat.) or **-dohyā** (L.), f. an easily milked cow. **–dhana**, n. pl. comfort and riches, VarBṛS.; m. sg. N. of a merchant, Kathās. **–nātha**, m. N. of a deity worshipped in Mathurā, Cat. **–nivishṭa**, mfn. comfortably seated, Pañcar. **–para**, mfn. fond of ease or comfort, intent on enjoyment, Śak. (v. l.); VarBṛS. **–parihīna**, mfn. destitute of comfort or happiness, VarBṛS. **–puṇyâha-ghosha**, m. the proclamation of a happy holiday, MW. **–peya**, mfn. easy or pleasant to drink, Subh. **–prakāśa**, m. (with *muni*) N. of an author, Cat. **–praṇāda**, mfn. sounding pleasantly, MBh. **–pratibandhin**, mfn. obstructing or interrupting happiness (°*dhi-tā*, f.), Vikr. v, $\frac{1}{1}\frac{8}{8}$. **–pratîksha**, mfn. looking for or expecting happiness, hoping for pleasure, W. **–pratyarthin**, mfn. opposed or hostile to happiness (*-tā*, f.), Vikr. v, $\frac{18}{18}$ (v. l. for *-pratibandhi-tā*). **–prada**, mfn. giving pleasure or happiness, MārkP. **–prabodhaka**, mf(*ikā*)n. easy to understand, Cat. **–pravicāra**, mfn. easily accessible, Car. **–pravepa**, mfn. easily trembling or shaken (as a tree), R. **–praśna**, m. inquiry as to welfare (°*śnam ud-ā-√hri* or *√dā*, 'to inquire after a person's welfare'), MBh. **–prasava**, mfn. bringing (or having brought) forth easily or happily, Śak. (v. l.); m. = next, Cat. **–prasavana**, n. easy birth or parturition, Kṛishṇaj. **–prasupta**, mfn. sleeping placidly, Ṛitus. **–prâpta**, mfn. one who has attained happiness, MW. **–prâpta-dhana**, mfn. one who has obtained wealth easily, Sāh. **–prâpya**, mfn. easy to be attained or won, Kathās. **–prêkshya**, mfn. easy to be caught sight of, MBh. **–plava**, mfn. offering a comfortable bath (v. l. *sukhâpl*°), R. **–baddha**, mfn. pleasantly formed, lovely, ib. **–bandhana**, mfn. attached to the pleasures or enjoyments of the world, Kām. **–buddhi**, f. easy understanding or knowledge, Cat. **–bodha**, m. id., ib.; perception or sensation of pleasure, MW.; *-kṛit*, mfn. causing to be easily understood, Śatr.; *-rūpa*, mfn. e° understood, Kāv. **–bodhana**, n. (= *-buddhi*); *-dīpikā*, f. N. of a Commentary. **–bodhikā**, f., **-bodhinī**, f. N. of wks. **–bhakshikā-kāra**, m. a maker of dainties or sweetmeats, confectioner, Campak. **–bhañja**, m. a kind of Moringa, L. **–bhāga**, m. a happy lot or portion, good fortune, MW. **–bhāgin** (R.), **-bhāj** (VarBṛS.), mfn. possessing or sharing in happiness, happy, fortunate. **–bhuj**, mfn. enjoying happiness, happy, lucky, VarBṛS. **–bhū**, mfn. (used in explaining *śam-bhu* and *mayo-bhū*), Nir. **–bhedya**, mfn. easy to be broken or destroyed, Kām. (v. l. for *-cchedya*); easily separated or disunited, Hit. **–bhoga**, m. the enjoyment of pleasure, MW. **–bhogin**, mfn. enjoying pleasure, ib. **–bhogya**, mfn. easy to be enjoyed or disposed of (as wealth), Kathās. **–bhojana**, n. dainty food, L. **–mada**, mfn. pleasantly intoxicating, Car. **–maya**, mf(*ī*, m. c. also *ā*)n. consisting of happiness, full of joy and pleasure, delightful, Kāv.; BhP. **–mānin**, mfn. thinking (anything) to be joy, seeing joy in (loc.), BhP. **–mārjana**, n. an auspicious ablution, Śak. (in Prākṛit). **–mālika**, m. (prob.) N. of the superintendent of a monastery, Pañcat. v, $\frac{1}{1}\frac{2}{2}$. **–mukha**, m. N. of a Yaksha, Buddh. **–m-edhas**, mfn. prospering well, Gaut.; MBh. **–modā**, f. the gum olibanum tree, L. **–yaśo-'rtha-vṛiddhi-kara**, mfn. causing increase of fortune (and) renown (and) wealth, VarBṛS. **–yoga-nidrā**, f. placid and quiet sleep, Kām. **–ratha** (*sukhá-*), mfn. having an easily running chariot, RV. **–rāja**, m. N. of various men, Rājat. **–rātri** or **-rātrikā**, f. a partic. night of new moon (when there is a festival in honour of Lakshmī, celebrated with lighted lamps), Cat.; a night when a wife may be legally approached (cf. Mn. iii, 47), MW.; a quiet or comfortable night (cf. *saurātrika*). **–rūpa**, mfn. having an agreeable appearance, Ml. **–lakshya**, mfn. easy to be seen or known, easily recognized, Hariv. **–lava**, m. a little pleasure, VarBṛS. **–lipsā**, f. desire of attaining pleasure or happiness, MW. **–lekhana**, n. N. of an orthographical wk. (by Bharata-sena, son of Gaurâṅga-mallika). **–leśa**, m. = *-lava*, MW. **–1. vat**, ind. like a joy or pleasure (with *√man*, 'to regard anything [acc.] as a pleasure'), BhP. **–2. -vat**, mfn. possessing ease or comfort (*-tā*, f. 'ease'), full of joy or pleasure, R. **–vatī**, f. N. of the heaven of Buddha Amitâbha (see under *sukhā-vat*, col. 3), Buddh.; *-vyūha*, m. N. of a Sūtra. **–varcaka** or **-varcas**, n. 'having a pleasant lustre,' natron, alkali, L. **–vartā**, w. r. for *-vat-tā* (q. v.) **–vartman**, mfn. having easy paths, MBh. **–varman**, m. N. of various men (esp. of a poet), Rājat.; Subh. **–vaha**, mfn. easily borne or carried, MBh. **–1. -vāsa**, m. a pleasant or comfortable abode (acc. with *√vas*, 'to live pleasantly at a place;' with *√dā*, 'to receive hospitably in one's house'), R.; Hcat.; mfn. one who has lived comfortably at a place, R. **–2. -vāsa**, mfn. 'sweet-smelling,' a water-melon, L. **–vāsana**, w. r. for *mukha-v*° (q. v.) **–vishṇu**, m. N. of a poet, Subh. **–vihāra**, m. an easy or comfortable life, SaddhP.; mfn. living easily, Car. **–vījya**, mfn. easy to be fanned or cooled (as a couch), Pañcar. **–vedana**, n. the consciousness of pleasure, W. **–śayana**, n. placid rest or sleep, L. **–śayā**, f. N. of a sorceress, Kathās. **–śayita**, mfn. lying or sleeping comfortably upon (comp.), Vās.; n. (= *-sayana*); *-pracchaka*, mf(*ikā*)n. inquiring whether any one has slept well, Śak. **–śayyā**, f. a comfortable couch, Vet.; pleasant rest or sleep, R. **–śarman**, m. N. of a poet, Cat. **–śāyin**, mfn. resting or sleeping pleasantly, Cat. **–śīta**, mfn. pleasantly cool; °*tôshna-māruta*, mfn. (a night) pleasant with cool and warm winds, R. **–śītala**, mfn. = *-śīta*, Cat. **–śobhârtham**, ind. for the sake of comfort and honour, MW. **–śrava**, mfn. sweetly sounding, pleasant to hear, Ragh. **–śravya**, mfn. id. (*-tā*, f.), Hariv. **–śruti**, f. agreeable to the ear, MW. **–saṃyāna**, n. comfortable journey or progress, R. **–saṃyoga**, m. gain of eternal bliss, Mn. vi, 64. **–saṃvāhya**, mfn. = *-vaha*, Pañcat. **–saṃvitti**, f. enjoyment or experience of happiness, Kir. **–saṃvṛiddha**, mfn. grown up in ease and comfort, MBh.; R. **–saṃveśa** (MBh.), **-saṃsupta** (R.), mfn. resting or sleeping well. **–saṃsevya**, mfn. easy to be approached or resorted to or attained, Kām. **–saṃstha** (Pañcat.), **-saṃsthita** (Mṛicch.), mfn. feeling comfortable or happy, Pañcat. **–saṃsparśa**, mf(*ā*)n. agreeable to the touch, pleasant to the feelings, gratifying, MBh.; R. &c. **–saṅga**, m. attachment to pleasure, Bhag. **–saṅgin**, mfn. attached to pleasure, MW. **–saṃcāra**, mf(*ā*)n. pleasant to be resorted to, inviting (*-tā*, f., *-tva*, n.), Hariv.; Sāh. **–saṃcārin**, w. r. for *-saṃcāra*. **–saṃjñā**, f. the term 'ease,' MW. **–saṃduhyā**, **-saṃdohyā**, f. = *-dohā*, *-dohyā*. **–samāja**, m. abundance of happiness or enjoyment, Gīt. **–sambandhi**, mfn. (m. c. for °*dhin*) joyful, happy, MBh. **–sambodhya**, mfn. easy to be taught or explained or to be reasoned with, Kathās. **–salila**, n. pleasant (i. e. tepid) water (*-nisheka*, m. 'a bath in t° w°'), Ṛitus. **–sāgara**, m. 'ocean of pleasure,' N. of a village, Kshitīś. **–sādhana**, n. means of obtaining pleasure, Bhām. **–sādhya**, mfn. easy to be accomplished or attained, Bhartṛ.; Saṃk.; easy to be cured, Suśr.; easy to be conquered or subdued, Hit. **–sukhena**, ind. most willingly, with all the heart, Pāṇ. viii, 1, 13. **–supta**, mfn. sweetly sleeping, comfortably asleep, MBh.; Rājat. **–supti**, f. placid sleep (cf. *saukhasuptikā*); *-prabodhita*, m. 'awakened from pl° sl°,' N. of Śiva, Śivag. **–suptikā**, f. (= *-supti*); *-praśna*, m. the question whether any one has slept well, Śak. (cf. *sukha-śayita-pracchaka*). **–secaka**, m. N. of a serpent-demon, MBh. (B. *mukha-s*°). **–sevya**, mfn. easy of access (*-tva*, n.), Rājat. **–stha**, mfn. = *-saṃstha*, Kāv.; Kathās. **–sparśa**, mf(*ā*)n. = *-saṃsparśa*, MBh.; R. &c.; *-vihāratā* (Divyâv.) or *-vihāritā* (Kāraṇḍ.), an easy life or state of existence. **–svāpa**, m. placid or quiet sleep, Kathās. **–hasta**, mfn. having a soft or gentle hand, R. **Sukhā-kara**, m. 'making happy, gladdening,' N. of a Buddhist world, SaddhP.; of the author of a Comm. on the Kādambarī. **Sukhā-√kṛi**, P. *-karoti*, to make happy, gladden, please, Pāṇ. v, 4, 63. **Sukhâgata**, n. welcome, Pañcat. **Sukhâjāta**, m. N. of Śiva, MBh. **Sukhâtmaka**, mf(*ikā*)n. consisting of pleasure, MW. **Sukhâdi**, mfn. (for *subhâdi* see p. 1220, col. 3) beginning with pleasure, pl° &c. (see *sukha-duḥkhâdi*). **Sukhâdhāra**, m. 'pleasure-seat,' Indra's heaven, paradise, L. **Sukhâdhishṭhāna**, n. a happy state, Divyâv. **Sukhânanda**, m. 'joy of happiness,' N. of an author. **Sukhânubhava**, m. perception or consciousness of pl°, W. **Sukhânta**, mfn. ending in happiness, MW.; subversive of h°, W. **Sukhânvita**, mfn. attended with h°, happy, VarBṛS. **Sukhâpa**, mfn. easily won or attained, BhP. **Sukhâpanna**, mfn. one who has attained or gained happiness, MW. **Sukhâpêta**, mfn. gradually deprived of pleasure (as opp. to *sukhād-ap*°), Pāṇ. ii, 1, 38, Sch. **Sukhâplava**, mfn. convenient for bathing (cf. *sukha-pl*°), R. **Sukhâbhiyojya**, mfn. easily assailable, Kām.; Hit. **Sukhâbhilāsha**, m. desire of pleasure, MW. **Sukhâbhyudayika**, mfn. causing joy or pl°, Mn. xii, 88. **Sukhâmbu**, n. = *sukha-salila*, Suśr. **Sukhâyata**, m. 'easily restrained or guided,' a well-trained horse, L. **Sukhâyana**, m. 'going easily or pleasantly,' a good horse, L. **Sukhârādhya**, mfn. easy to be conciliated or propitiated, BhP. **Sukhârohaṇa**, mfn. easy to be ascended, MBh. **Sukhârta**, mfn. (for °*kha-ṛita*) affected by joy, Pāṇ. vi, 1, 89, Vārtt. 6, Pat. **Sukhârtha**, m. anything that gives pleasure, Mn. vi, 26; *am* (Gaṇit.) and *āya* (Pañcat.), ind. for the sake of ease or pl°. **Sukhârthin**, mfn. seeking or wishing for pl° or happiness, Mn. vi, 49. **Sukhârha**, mfn. deserving of happiness, VarBṛS. **Sukhâloka**, mf(*ā*)n. pleasant-looking, beautiful (others 'easy to be seen'), Vikr. iv, 46. **Sukhâvagama**, m. easy perception or comprehension, Yogas., Sch. **Sukhâvagāha**, mfn. easy to be entered or dived into, Hir.; MBh. **Sukhā-vat**, mfn. = 2. *sukha-vat*; (with *varti*, f.) a kind of pill, Car.; (*vatī*), f. N. of the paradise or heaven of Amitâbha (situated in the western sky), Buddh.; SaddhP.; Kāraṇḍ.; MWB. 183, 204; of the wife of Sūrya-prabha, Kathās.; *-deva*, m. (with Śāktas) N. of a partic. class of authors of mystical prayers, Cat.; *-vyūha*, m. N. of a Buddhist wk.; °*tîśvara*, m. 'lord of Sukhā-vatī,' N. of Amitâbha, see above, L. **Sukhâvabodha**, m. easy comprehension, Śaṃk. **Sukhâvaha**, mfn. bringing or conferring pleasure, delightful, R. **Sukhâvṛita**, mfn. filled with joy or delight in (comp.), BhP. **Sukhâśa**, m. pleasant food, L.; cucumber, Cucumis Sativus (also °*śaka*), L.; mfn. eating dainty food (applied to Varuṇa), L. **Sukhâśaya**, w. r. for *sukhâśraya*. **Sukhâśā**, f. the hope of pl° or enjoyment, Pañcat.; (*su-kh*°) expectation which exists only in empty space (or is very remote). **Sukhâśraya**, mfn. connected with pl°, pleasant, gratifying, Pañcat.; Sāh. **Sukhâsakta**, m. 'devoted to happiness,' N. of Śiva, MBh. **Sukhâsana**, n. a comfortable seat, Siṇhâs. **Sukhâsikā**, f. well-being, comfort, ease, Rājat. **Sukhâsīna**, mfn. comfortably seated, R.; BhP.; Hit. **Sukhâsukha**, n. sg. pleasure and pain, Mn. xii, 19. **Sukhâsparśa**, mfn. = *sukha-sparśa*, MW. **Sukhâsvāda**, mfn. pleasantly flavoured, delightful, agreeable, Hit.; m. pleasant flavour, W.; enjoyment, ib. **Sukhâhara**, mfn. = *sukhâvaha*, MW. **Sukhâhāra**, n. ease and food, ib. **Sukhêcchā**, f. hope or desire of happiness, W. **Sukhêta**, mfn. affected by joy, Pāṇ. vi, 1, 89, Vārtt. 6, Pat. **Sukhêtara**, mfn. other than happy, unfortunate, MW.; n. pl. joys and sorrows, ŚvetUp. **Sukhêpsu**, mfn. desirous of ease, MW. **Sukhe-shṭha**, mfn. (loc. of *sukha* + *stha*) living in joy (applied to Śiva), Śivag. **Sukhâikāyatana**, n. sole abode of joy, MW. **Sukhâidhita**, mfn. one who has grown up or lived in easy circumstances, MBh. **Sukhâishin**, mfn. one who seeks (another's) happiness, wishing well to (comp.), MBh. **Sukhôcita**, mfn. accustomed to comfort or happiness, MBh.; Car. **Sukhôcchedya**, mfn. to be cut up or destroyed with ease, to be exterminated easily, Kām.; Rājat. **Sukhôtsava**, m. 'pleasure-feast,' a husband, L. **Sukhôdaka**, n. = *sukha-salila*, Suśr. **Sukhôdadhi**, m. N. of a Comm. on the Kāvyaprakāśa (usually called Sudhā-sāgara). **Sukhôdaya**, mfn. resulting in joy or happiness, Mn.; MBh. &c.; m. an intoxicating drink (made from honey or from the blossoms of the Bassia Latifolia), L.; realization or occurrence of pleasure, W.; N. of a son of Medâtithi, MārkP.; n. the Varsha ruled by Sukhôdaya, ib. **Sukhôdarka**, mfn. having happiness as a consequence, causing h°, Mn.; MBh. &c. **Sukhôdya**, mfn. to be uttered easily or agreeably, Mn. ii, 33. **Sukhôpagamya**, mfn. easy to be approached or reached, easy of access, Kām.; Mṛicch. **Sukhôpadhāna**, n. = *upakaraṇa*, L. **Sukhôpavishṭa**, mfn. comfortably seated, MBh.; R. &c. **Sukhôpasarpya**, mfn. easy to be approached, W. **Sukhôpâya**, m. an easy means, BhP.; (*ena*, instr. 'easily,' 'without pains or trouble,' Pañcat.); mf(*ā*)n. easy to be obtained, Pañcat. **Sukhôrjika**, m. natron (= *sarjikā-kshāra*). **Sukhôshita**, mfn. (also with *rajanīm*) one who has spent the night pleasantly, comfortably lodged, MBh.; R. &c; (*ā*), f. Sanseviera Roxburghiana, L. **Sukhôshṇa**, mfn. 'pleasantly warm,' tepid; n. tepid water, L. **Sukhôshya**, mfn. pleasant to be dwelt in, Hariv.

Sukhana, n. (used in explaining √*mṛid*), Dhātup.

Sukhanīya, mfn. causing ease or comfort, Kāty-Śr., Sch.

Sukhaya. See √*sukh*, p. 1220, col. 3.

Sukhayitṛi, m. one who gladdens or makes happy (gen.), Inscr.

Sukhayu, mfn. (used in explaining *śaṃyu*), Nir. iv, 21.

Sukhāya, Nom. Ā. °*yate*, to feel happy or pleased, be at ease or comfortable, Daś.; Kād.; to be pleasant or agreeable, Kād.

Sukhāvala, m. N. of Nṛi-cakshus (cf. *sukhīnala*), VP.

Sukhi, in comp. for *sukhin*. — **tā**, f. (Śak., v. l.), -**tva**, n. (Vedântas.) ease, comfort, happiness. — **svabhāva**, m. a happy or contented disposition, Hit.

Sukhita, mfn. pleased, delighted, comforted (*am*, ind.), Kāv.; Kathās. &c.; n. happiness, MW.

Sukhin, mfn. possessing or causing happiness or pleasure, happy, joyful, pleasant, comfortable, easy, MBh.; Kāv. &c.; m. a religious ascetic, W.

Sukhī, mfn. (prob.) one who loves pleasure, Vop. iii, 61.

Sukhīnala, m. N. of a son of Su-cakshus (cf. *sukhāvala*), BhP.

Sukhīlalita (?), f. N. of a virgin, Buddh.

Sukhīvala, m. = *sukhāvala*, VP.

1. **Sukhya**, mfn. belonging to pleasure, pleasurable, MW.

2. **Sukhya**, Nom. P. °*yati* (see √*sukh*).

सुखंसुण *sukhaṃsuṇa* or *sukhaṃghuṇa* (?), m. a kind of staff with a skull at the top considered as a weapon of Śiva (= *khaṭvâṅga*, q. v.), L.

सुग 1. *su-gá*, mf(*ā*)n. (i. e. 5. *su* + 2. *ga*; √*gam*) going well or gracefully, having a graceful gait, W.; easily passed, easy to traverse, RV.; AV.; TBr.; Lāṭy.; easy of access, Kathās.; Hcat.; easy to obtain, RV.; TS.; Pañcat.; easily understood, intelligible, MW.; n. a good path; easy or successful course, RV.; VS.; fæces, L. **Suge-vṛidh**, mfn. rejoicing in good progress, RV.

सुग 2. *su-ga*, mfn. (i. e. 5. *su* + 3. *ga*; √*gai*) singing well or beautifully, BhP.

Su (to be similarly prefixed to the following): — **gaṇ**, mfn. (a word formed artificially, see Pāṇ. iii, 2, 75, Sch.) counting well or easily or e° to be calculated. — **gaṇa**, mfn. = *ugaṇa*, Pat. on Pāṇ. vi, 1, 9, Vārtt. 4; m. N. of a Rāja-putra, Kathās.; (*ā*), f. N. of one of the Mātṛis attending on Skanda, MBh.; °*ṇôkti* (?), f. N. of wk. — **gaṇaka**, m. a good calculator or astronomer, Cat. — **gaṇita**, mfn. easily or accurately calculated, MW. — **gata**, mfn. going well, VarBṛS.; one who has fared well, Hit.; well-bestowed, MW.; m. a Buddha (-*tva*, n.), Kathās.; Jātakam., Introd.; a Buddhist, Bud° teacher, Hcat.; -*cetanā*, f. N. of a Buddhist nun, Buddh.; -*mitra*, m. N. of a man, ib.; -*śāsana*, n. the Bud° doctrine, Kathās.; °*tâyatana*, n. a Bud° temple or monastery, ib.; °*tâlaya*, m. id., L.; °*tâvadāna*, n. N. of a Bud° Sūtra wk. — **gati**, f. a good or happy condition, welfare, happiness, bliss, MBh.; Hariv.; MārkP. &c.; a secure refuge, Chandom.; mfn. having a good or auspicious position (as a planet), VarBṛS.; m. N. of a son of Gaya, BhP.; of an Arhat (prob. w. r. for *su-mati*), L.; -*sopāna*, n. N. of wk. — **gantva**, mfn. easily passed, Lāṭy. — **gandha**, m. a fragrant smell, fragrance, R.; a perfume, Yājñ.; VarBṛ. &c.; mf(*ā*)n. fragrant, MBh. &c. &c.; m. sulphur, L.; the chick-pea, ib.; Andropogon Schœnanthus, ib.; marjoram, ib.; a red-blossomed Moringa, ib.; = *tumburu*, ib.; a fragrant ointment (made of various substances), L.; N. of a mountain, Gol.; a trader, dealer, MW.; (*ā*), f. the ichneumon plant, L.; Curcuma Zedoaria, ib.; a fragrant grass, MW.; a sort of lime, ib.; sacred basil, Suśr.; Car.; N. of various other plants and trees (= *vandhyā*, *karkoṭakī*, *rudra-jaṭā* &c.), L.; a form of Dākshāyaṇī, Cat.; N. of an Apsaras, MBh.; Hariv.; of a Tīrtha, Vishṇ.; MBh.; of a woman, Rājat.; (*ī*), f. the small Banana, L.; N. of a female servant of Vasu-deva, VP.; n. small cumin seed, L.; the blue lotus, ib.; sandal, ib.; the Granthi-parṇa plant, ib.; = *kat-triṇa*, ib.; = *pattrâṅga*, ib.; = *gandha-triṇa*, ib.; civet, ib.; N. of a Tīrtha, MBh.; -*tā*, f. fragrance, perfume, MW.; -*taila-niryāsa*, n. (?) civet, L.; a partic. perfume made from roses &c., MW.; -*pattrā*, f. a kind of plant (= *jaṭā*), L.; = *rudra-jaṭā*, ib.; -*bhūtriṇa*, n. a kind of fragrant grass, ib.; -*mukha*, m. N. of a Bodhi-sattva, Kāraṇḍ.; -*mūlā*, f. Averrhoa Acida, L.; Hibiscus Mutabilis, ib.; = *rāsnā*, ib.; -*yukti*, f. preparation of perfumes (one of the 64 arts), BhP., Sch.; -*vat*, mfn. fragrant, MBh.; -*vanamāhātmya*, n. N. of wk.; °*dhâḍhya*, mfn. rich in fragrance, R.; (*ā*), f. Jasminum Sambac, L.; °*dhâditya*, m. N. of a man, Rājat.; °*dhâmalaka*, m. a kind of mixture of various herbs, L.; °*dhêśa*, m. N. of a temple erected by Su-gandhā, Rājat.; an image of the tutelary deity of Su-g°, MW. — **gandhaka**, m. 'having fragrance,' a kind of grain (perhaps of rice), Suśr.; a kind of culinary herb, ib.; the orange, L.; Momordica Mixta, ib.; red-blossomed basil, ib.; a kind of bulbous plant (= *dharaṇī-kanda*), ib.; sulphur, ib.; (*ikā*), f. a kind of plant, Suśr.; n. a kind of medicinal herb, L. — **gandhaya**, Nom. P. °*yati*, to make fragrant, scent, Śiś. — **gandhāra**, m. N. of Śiva (accord. to Nīlak. = *śobhano gandhāra-deśôdbhavaḥ*), MBh. — **gándhi** (or -*gandhi*), mfn. sweet-smelling, fragrant, RV.; MBh.; Hariv. &c.; virtuous, pious, MW.; m. a perfume, fragrance, MW.; the supreme Being (= *paramâtman*), ib.; a lion, L.; a sort of Mango, L.; a sort of Cyperus, L.; Ocimum Pilosum, L.; the root of Scirpus Kysoor, L.; n. sandal, L.; N. of various perfumes or fragrant plants (accord. to L. = *elavāluka*; = *kaśeru*; = *gandha-triṇa* &c.), Bhpr.; -*kusuma*, n. a fragrant flower, MW.; m. yellow oleander, L.; -*kusumā*, f. Trigonella Corniculata, ib.; -*tā*, f. fragrance, VarBṛS.; Śiś.; -*tejana*, m. or n. a kind of fragrant grass, TS.; Kāṭh.; Br. &c.; -*triphalā*, f. nutmeg, areca nut, and cloves, L.; -*mustaka*, n. a sort of Cyperus, Bhpr.; -*mūtra-patana*, m. a civet cat, L.; -*mūla*, n. a radish, L.; the root of Uśīra, MW.; -*mūlā*, f. Curcuma Zedoaria, L.; = *rāsnā*, ib.; -*mūshikā*, f. the musk rat, ib.; -*sīha*, m. N. of a man, Rājat. — **gandhika**, mfn. fragrant, Vishṇ.; m. a kind of grain (perhaps 'of rice'), Vāgbh.; Car.; olibanum, L.; sulphur, L.; a lion, L.; n. the white lotus, L.; the root of Andropogon Muricatus, L.; the root of Costus Speciosus or Arabicus, L.; a partic. medicinal herb, = *sura-parṇa*, L. — **gandhin**, mfn. fragrant, sweet-smelling, MBh.; R.; (*inī*), f. Pandanus Odoratissimus, L.; a kind of plant with fragrant leaves (= *ārāma-śītalā*), ib. — **ganman**, mfn., Vop. xxvi, 68. — **gabhasti** (*sú-* or *sugábh*°), mfn. having skilful hands (said of Tvashṭṛi), RV. — **gama**, mf(*ā*)n. easy to be traversed, BhP.; Kathās.; easy of access, Kathās.; Kuval.; easy to be ascertained or understood, obvious, MBh.; BhP. &c.; easy, practicable, MW.; m. N. of a Dānava, Kathās.; °*mânvayā*, f. N. of Comm. — **gamana**, mf(*ā*)n. easy of access, Nir. vi, 2; proceeding well, Sāy. on RV. i, 165, 8. — **gambhīra**, mf(*ā*)n. very deep, MBh. — **gamya**, mf(*ā*)n. easily traversed or passed, easy of access, Pañcar. — **gara**, n. cinnabar, L. — **garhita**, mfn. very blamable, R. — **galā**, f. N. of a woman, Rājat. — **gava**, m. a vigorous bull, MBh.; (-*gáva*), mfn. having fine cows, abounding in cattle, RV. — **gavi**, m. N. of a son of Prasuśruta, VP. — **gávya**, n. the possession of good or much cattle, RV.; mfn. = -*gáva*, MW. — **gahana**, mf(*ā*)n. very thick or close or impervious, L.; (*ā*), f. an enclosure round a place of sacrifice, W.; °*nâvṛiti*, f. id., MW. — **gāṅga**, m. or n. N. of a palace, Mudr. — **gắtu**, m. welfare, prosperity, AV. vi, 1, 3. — **gātuyắ**, f. (the same form for instr.) desire of welfare or prosperity, RV. — **gātra**, mf(*ī*)n. fair-limbed, graceful, Kathās.; (*ī*), f. a beautiful woman, Vcar.; (*am*), n. a fine or graceful figure, MW. — **gātriyā**, w. r. for -*gātuyắ*. — **gādhá**, mfn. easily fordable, RV. — **gārhapatyá**, m. a good householder, AV.; TBr. — **gīta**, n. good singing, BhP. — **gīti**, f. 'id.,' N. of a kind of Āryā metre, Col. — **gītha**, m. N. of a Ṛishi, Bālar. — **gú**, mfn. = -*gáva*, RV.; AV.; TBr. — **guṇa**, mf(*ā*)n. very virtuous or excellent, Caurap. — **guṇin**, mfn. id., Bhartṛ. — **gupta** (*sú-*), mfn. well guarded, ŚBr.; R.; well hidden or concealed, kept very secret, Kāv.; Pañcat.; (*ā*), f. Mucuna Pruritus, L.; (*am*), ind. very secretly or privately, Pañcat.; very carefully, MBh.; -*tara*, mfn. well hidden, Pañcat.; -*bhāṇḍa*, mf(*ā*)n. looking well after the household utensils (-*tā*, f.), Vishṇ.; -*lekha*, m. a very private letter or one written in cipher, MW. — **gupti**, f. good protection, great secrecy (acc. with *ā*-√*dhā*, 'to observe gr° s°'), Hit. — **guptī**-√**kṛi**, P. -*karoti*, to keep well, guard carefully, Pañcat. — **guru**, mfn. very heinous (as a crime), Mn. xi, 256; a good teacher, Jain. — **gulpha**, mf(*ā*)n. having beautiful ancles, Pāṇ. iv, 1, 54, Sch. — **gūḍha**, mfn. well guarded or concealed, very secret, MBh.; Pañcat.; (*am*), ind. very secretly, Daś. — **gṛiddha**, mf(*ā*)n. intensely longing for (loc.), MBh. — **gṛihá**, m. having a good or beautiful house or abode, AV.; m. 'having a good nest,' the taylor-bird, Sylvia Sutoria, L.; (*ī*), f. a partic. bird (reckoned among the Pratudas), Suśr. — **gṛihapati**, m. a good householder (said of Agni), VS. — **gṛihin**, mfn. well-housed, having a good nest (as a bird), Pañcat. — **gṛihīta**, mfn. held fast or firmly, seized, grasped, clung or adhered to, Śiś.; well apprehended or learnt, ib.; mentioned auspiciously (cf. next); -*nāman* (or °*ma-dheya*), mfn. one whose name is invoked auspiciously (also said of Yudhi-shṭhira and others who are invoked early in the morning to secure good luck), Kād.; Mudr. &c.; °*tâbhidha*, mfn. having an auspicious name, Rājat. — **ge-vṛidh**, see under 1. *su-ga*, col. 2. — **geshṇā**, f. 'singing well,' a Kiṃ-narī, L. — **gehinī**, f. a good housewife, Bālar. — **go**, f. an excellent cow, Pāṇ. v, 4, 69, Sch. — **gocara**, w. r. for *sva-g*°, Bcar. i, 13. — **gopá**, m. a good protector, RV.; mfn. well protected (superl. -*tama*), ib. — **gopya**, mfn. to be kept quite secret, Pañcar. — **gautama**, m. 'the good Gautama,' N. of G° Buddha, Lalit. — **gaurava**, mfn. very heavy or ponderous, L. — **gmya** (*sú-*), mfn. (√*gam*) advancing well, RV.; increasing, ib.; (*am*), n. happiness, prosperity, Naigh. iii, 6. — **grathita** (*sú-*), mfn. well fastened, ib. — **granthi**, mfn. well knotted, MW.; having beautiful joints, ib.;

m. a kind of perfume (=*coraka*), L.; n. the root of Piper Longum, L. **-graha**, mfn. having a good handle, MBh.; easy to be obtained, Kathās.; easy to be learnt or understood, Sāh. **-grahaṇa**, n. reverential clasping (of a person's feet), Inscr. **-grāma**, m. N. of a village in Magadha, HPariś. **-grāsa**, m. a dainty morsel, MW. **-grāhya**, mfn. easy to be taken, easily apprehensible &c., W. **-grīva**, mfn. handsome-necked, having a beautiful neck; m. (ifc. f. *ā*) N. of a monkey-king (who, with his army of monkeys headed by Hanumat, assisted Rāmacandra in conquering Rāvaṇa; he was believed to be the son of the Sun, and was re-established by Rāma in the throne of Kishkindha [q. v.], usurped by his brother Vālin), MBh.; R. &c.; of one of the four horses of Kṛishṇa or Vishṇu (the other three being Balāhaka, Megha-pushpa, and Śaivya), MBh.; Hariv.; BhP.; of a divine being, VarBṛS.; of the father of the ninth Arhat of the present Avasarpiṇī, L.; a kind of pavilion, Vāstuv.; (only L.) a conch; N. of Śiva or Indra; a goose; a hero; a piece of water; N. of a mountain; a sort of weapon; the countenance of a friend; a serpent of Pātāla, W.; (*ā* or *ī*), f. N. of an Apsaras, Hariv.; (*ī*), f. N. of a daughter of Daksha and wife of Kaśyapa (regarded as the mother of horses, camels, and asses), Hariv.; Pur.; °*vāgraja*, m. 'elder brother of Su-grīva,' N. of Vālin, L.; °*vêśa*, m. 'lord of S°,' N. of Rāma, L. **-grīshma**, m. a fine summer, GṛS. **-gla**, mfn. (√*glai*) very weary, Kāś. on Pāṇ. iii, 1, 136. **-ghaṭa**, mfn. easy contrived or accomplished (*-tva*, n.), Kusum. **-ghaṭita**, mfn. well joined or united or contrived or arranged, Hit.; *-ghaṭita*, mfn. id., Subh. **-ghaṭṭita**, mfn. well pressed down or levelled, MBh. **-ghana**, mfn. very dense (as a forest), Pañcat. **-gharikā-gṛihaka**, n. a kind of sieve, Śil. **-gharsha**, m. much rubbing, strong friction, L. **-ghora**, mf(*ā*)n. very fearful or terrible, MBh.; m. N. of a man, VP.; n. anything very dreadful or hideous, MBh. **-ghosha**, mfn. making a loud noise, very noisy, MBh.; having a pleasant sound, R.; m. a pleasant sound or cry, W.; N. of the conch of Nakula, Bhag.; of a Buddha, Lalit.; of an Agra-hāra (q. v.), Kathās.; a partic. form of a temple, Hcat.; *-grāma*, m. N. of a village, Cat.; *-ghosha*, mf(*ā*)n. sounding loud, MBh.; *-vat*, mfn. sounding pleasantly, ib. **-ghoshaka**, m. or n. (?), a partic. musical instrument, Divyâv. **-ghoshita**, mfn. proclaimed with loud voice, ib. **-ghná**, m. easy striking or killing, RV.

सुग्म्य *su-gmya* &c. See p. 1222, col. 3.

सुघट *su-ghaṭa* &c. See above.

सुचक्र *su-cakrá*, mfn. (i.e. 5. *su* + *c*°) having beautiful wheels, AV.; MBh.; m. a good chariot, RV.; N. of one of Skanda's attendants, MBh.; of a son of Vatsa-prī and Su-nandā, MārkP.; °*krôpaskara*, mfn. having good wheels and (other) equipment, MBh.

Su (to be similarly prefixed to the following): **-cákshas**, mfn. having good eyes, seeing well, RV.; ĀśvGṛ. **-cakshu** or **-cakshus**, N. of a river, R. **-cakshus**, mfn. having beautiful eyes (said of Śiva), Śivag.; seeing well, MW.; m. Ficus Glomerata, L.; a wise or learned man, W. **-cañcukā**, f. a kind of vegetable (=*mahā-cañcu*), MW. **-catura**, mfn. (accord. to native authorities fr. *catur*) very clever or skilful, Kām. **-candana**, m. a fine sandal tree, R. **-candra**, m. a partic. Samādhi, Buddh.; N. of a Deva-gandharva, MBh.; of a son of Siṃhikā, ib.; of a son of Hema-candra and father of Dhūmrâśva, R.; VP.; of various kings, R.; Kālac.; of a Bodhi-sattva, Buddh.; of a Ficus Indica, R. **-carā**, f. N. of an Apsaras, VP. **-1. -carita**, mfn. well performed (see comp.); n. (*sú-*; sg. and pl.) good conduct or behaviour, virtuous actions, VS. &c. &c.; *-carita*, mfn. one who leads a virtuous life, Mṛicch.; *-vrata*, mfn. well performing religious observances, Mn. xi, 116; °*târtha-pada*, mfn. (speech) containing well selected sense and words, Kum. **-2. -carita**, mf(*ā*)n. well-conducted, moral, virtuous, Mn. ix, 261; m. (with *miśra*) N. of an author, Cat.; (*ā*), f. a virtuous or faithful wife, L. **-caritra**, mf(*ā*)n. well-conducted, L.; (*ā*), f. a virtuous wife, L.; coriander, L.; n. good conduct, W. **-carman**, mfn. having beautiful skin or bark, L.; m. Betula Bhojpatra, L. **-cārā**, f. N. of a daughter of Śva-phalka, BhP. (B. *-cīrā*). **-cāru**, mfn. very lovely or beautiful, pleasing, delightful, MBh.; Kāv. &c.; m. N. of a son of Kṛishṇa and Rukmiṇī, MBh.; Hariv.; Pur.; of a son of Vishvaksena (adopted by Gaṇḍūsha), Hariv.; of a son of Pratiratha, ib.; of a son of Bāhu, VP.; *-tā*, f. loveliness, beauty, VarBṛS., Sch.; *-daśanā*, f. (a woman) having beautiful teeth, KāvP.; *-rūpa*, mfn. of beautiful form, MBh.; *-svana*, mfn. having a b° or melodious sound, W.; °*rv-aṅgī*, f. (a woman) having beautiful limbs, MārkP. **-citta**, mf(*ā*)n. well-minded, MBh.; m. (with *śailana*) N. of a teacher, JaimUp. **-citrá**, mf(*ā*)n. very distinguished, AV.; very manifold, Hariv.; very variegated, MW.; m. N. of a serpent-demon, MBh.; of a king, ib.; (*ā*), f. a kind of gourd, L.; (°*tra*)-*bījā*, f. Embelia Ribes, L. **-citraka**, mfn. very variegated; m. a kingfisher, L.; a kind of speckled snake, L.; N. of an Asura, Buddh. **-cintana**, n. the act of thinking well, deliberate consideration, W. **-cintā**, f. deep thought, due reflection or consideration, ib. **-cintita**, mfn. well thought about, well weighed or considered, ib.; *-cintin*, mfn. thinking quite well or right, Buddh.; °*târtha*, m. N. of a Māra-putra, Lalit. **-cintya**, mfn. well imaginable or conceivable, Hariv. **-cira**, mfn. very long (ibc., *am*, *āya*, and *ena*, 'for a very long time, a good while;' *āt*, 'after a very long time'), MBh.; R. &c.; *-śrama*, m. fatigue or exertion for a very long time, BhP.; °*râyus*, mfn. 'having a very long life,' a god, divinity, L.; °*rârpita*, mfn. fixed or directed for a long time, Amar.; °*rôtsuka*, mfn. anxious or desirous for a long t°, Kathās.; °*rôshita*, mfn. one who has dwelt or stayed for a long t°, R. **-cihnita**, mfn. distinctly marked, Vishṇ. **-cīrā**, see *-cārā*. **-cīrṇa-dhvaja**, m. N. of a king of the Kumbhâṇḍas, Buddh. **-cukrikā**, f. Tamarindus Indica, L. **-cuṭī**, f. 'cutting well,' a pair of scissors or nippers or tongs, L. **-cetaná**, mfn. very notable, distinguished, AV. **-cétas**, mfn. having great intelligence, sapient, wise, RV.; Śiś.; well-minded, benevolent, Rājat.; m. N. of a son of Gṛitsa-mada, MBh.; of a son of Pracetas, Hariv. **-cetī-kṛita**, mfn. made well-minded or well-disposed, Bhaṭṭ. **-cetúna**, mfn. = *-cetana*, ib. ix, 65, 30. **-cetúnā**, ind. (instr. of *-cetu*) with benevolence or favour, graciously, RV. **-cela**, mf(*ā*)n. well-clad, Hariv. **-celaka**, m. a fine garment, L. **-ceshṭa-rūpa**, m. N. of a Buddha, Lalit. **-cchattra**, m. N. of Śiva, MBh.; (*ā* or *ī*), f. the river Śata-dru or Sutlej, L. **-cchada**, mfn. having beautiful leaves, R. **-cchardís**, mfn. (superl. °*dísh-ṭama*) affording good shelter, RV. **-cchāya**, mfn. 'affording a good shadow' (and therefore beautiful), Kāvyâd.; shining very brightly (as a jewel), splendid, L.; (*ā*), f. N. of the wife of Ślishṭi, Hariv. **-jaghaná**, mfn. having beautiful hips, ib.; Hcat.; having a beautiful end or conclusion, TS.; a partic. ceremony, TBr., Sch. **-jaṅgha**, mf(*ā*)n. having beautiful legs, Śrutab. **-jatru**, mfn. having a beautiful collar-bone, MBh. **-jana**, m. a good or virtuous or kind or benevolent person (man or woman; often confounded with *sva-jana*), R.; Kathās. &c.; N. of the author of the ŚāṅkhŚr.; *-tā*, f. goodness, kindness, benevolence, Kāv.; Sāh.; a number of good men or respectable persons, W.; *-tva*, n. goodness, kindness, Śak. (v. l.); *-parivārā*, f. N. of a Gandharva maiden, Kāraṇḍ.; *-parisevitā*, f. N. of a Kiṃ-narī, ib.; °*nâkara*, m. N. of a man, Rājat.; °*nêtara-maitrī*, f. the friendship of a bad man, MW. **-janaya**, P. °*yati*, w. r. for *sva-j*°, Bālar. v, 40. **-jániman**, mfn. producing or creating fair things, RV. **-jantu**, m. N. of a son of Jahnu, VP. **-janman**, n. noble or auspicious birth (°*mâdi-vrata*, n. 'a partic. observance'), Kṛishṇaj.; (*-jánman*), mfn. = *-janiman*, RV.; of noble or ausp° birth, Kāv.; Kathās. **-jámbha**, mfn. having good jaws or strong teeth, RV. **-jambhan**, mfn. id., Pāṇ. v, 4, 125. **-jaya**, m. a great victory or triumph, BhP.; N. of a man, Buddh.; easy to be conquered by (instr.), MBh. **-jala**, mf(*ā*)n. having good or sweet water, R.; VarBṛS.; n. a lotus, L.; good water, W. **-jalpa**, m. good speech, a partic. kind of sp° (sincere, earnest, full of meaning and vivacity), L. **-javas**, mfn. very quick or swift, MW. **-jātá** (or *sú-*), mfn. well born or produced or made, of an excellent kind or nature, fine, beautiful, RV. &c. &c.; well grown, tall, MW.; nobly born, noble, RV.; ŚāṅkhGṛ.; genuine, sincere (as piety), BhP.; really born (i.e. not born in vain), Bhartṛ. (v. l. *sa jātaḥ*); m. N. of a son of Dhṛita-rāshṭra, MBh.; of a son of Bharata, VP.; of a bull, Lalit.; (pl.) of a people, Hariv.; (*ā*), f. aluminous slate, L.; a kind of plant (=*tuvarī*), MW.; N. of various women (esp. of a daughter of Uddālaka and wife of Kahoḍa), MBh.; Pur.; Lalit.; (*am*), n. good birth, b° under an auspicious constellation, MBh.; *-tā* (*sujātá-*), f. the being well born, nobility (also of mind), RV.; *-vaktra*, m. N. of a preceptor, ĀśvGṛ.; °*tâṅga*, mf(*ī*)n. having well-formed limbs, MW. **-jātaka**, m. or n. (?) beauty, splendour, Vās. **-jāti**, mfn. of good tribe or species, MW.; of a good race or caste, ib.; m. N. of a son of Vīti-hotra, ib. **-jātīya**, mfn. of good tribe or race, ib. **-jāmi**, mfn. rich in brothers and sisters or relatives, Kauś. **-jita** (*sú-*), n. an easy conquest, MaitrS.; *-śrama*, mfn. easily overcoming all fatigue, indefatigable, Kām. **-jihvá**, mfn. bright-tongued, sweet-voiced, RV.; m. fire or the god of fire, L. **-jīrṇa**, mfn. worn out, ragged, decayed; well digested, Hit.; *-śata-khaṇḍa-maya*, mf(*ī*)n. made of a hundred tattered rags, Bhartṛ. **-jīva**, n. it is an easy life for any one (gen.), R. **-jīvantī**, f. Hoya Viridiflora, L. **-jīvita**, n. a happy life, R.; it is easily lived by any one (instr.), Jātakam.; mfn. living happily, enjoying life, Kād. **-jushṭa** (*sú-*), mf(*ā*)n. well liked, welcome, RV. **-jūrṇi**, mfn. blazing or glowing brightly, ib. **-jña**, mf(*ā*)n. knowing well, conversant or familiar with anything, Kum. **-jñāna**, n. easy perception or intelligence, KaṭhUp.; good knowledge, Kām.; N. of various Sāmans, ĀrshBr.; mf(*ā*)n. possessing good knowledge, Kām. (cf. Siddh. on Pāṇ. iv, 1, 54); easy to be known or understood, Vām. ii, 1, 3; *-durgôdaya*, m. N. of a wk. on the 16 Saṃskāras by Viśvêśvara Bhaṭṭa; *-viṃśati*, f. N. of a Vedânta wk. by Mukunda Kavi. **-jyeshṭha**, m. N. of a king (son of Agni-mitra), Pur. **-jyaishṭhyá**, mfn. well entitled to primogeniture, AV. **-jyótis** (or *-jyotis*), mfn. shining very brightly, radiant, RV.; VS.

सुच्छत्त्र *su-cchattra*, *su-cchada* &c. See col. 2.

सुजघन *su-jaghana*, *su-jaṅgha* &c. See col. 2.

सुज्जक *sujjaka* and *sujji*, m. N. of two men, Rājat.

सुट् *suṭ*, (in gram.) a Pratyāhāra used as a technical expression for the first five inflections (i.e. nom. sg. du. pl., acc. sing. du. for masc. and fem. nouns; cf. *sarva-nāma-sthāna*).

सुटङ्क *su-ṭaṅka*, mfn. (cf. *ṭaṃ-kāra*) sharp, shrill (said of a disagreeable sound), Bālar. iv, ६१.

सुट्ट् *suṭṭ*, cl. 10. P. *suṭṭayati*, to slight, disregard, despise, Dhātup. xxxii, 26; to be small or low or shallow, Vop., ib.

सुडशब्दनृत्य *suḍa-śabda-nṛitya*, n. (in music) a kind of dance, Saṃgīt.

सुडीनक *su-ḍīnaka*, n. one of the modes of flight attributed to birds, MBh.

सुत् *sut*, *suta* &c. See √3. 4. *su*, p. 1219.

सुतनय *su-tanaya*, mfn. (i.e. 5. *su* + *tan*°) having beautiful children, VarBṛS.

Su (to be similarly prefixed to the following): **-tanu**, mfn. very thin or slender (*-tā*, f.), Dhūrtas. (v. l.); having a beautiful body, Kāv.; m. N. of a Gandharva, R.; of a son of Ugra-sena, Hariv.; of a monkey, R.; (*u* or *ū*), f. a fair woman (voc. *sutanu*, cf. Vām. v, 2, 49), Śak.; Śiś.; N. of a daughter of Āhuka (wife of Akrūra), MBh.; of a concubine of Vasu-deva, Hariv.; of a daughter of Ugra-sena, ib.; VP. **-tanuja**, mf(*ā*)n. having beautiful children, Kṛishṇaj. **-tantu**, m. 'having fair offspring,' N. of Vishṇu, MBh.; of Śiva, Śivag.; of a Dānava, Kathās. **-tantra**, mfn. 'well versed in doctrine' and 'commanding good troops,' VarYogay. **-tantri**, mfn. well accompanied on the lute (as a song), melodious, Ṛitus. **-tapa**, m. (for *suta-pa* see p. 1219, col. 2) 'practising great austerities,' N. of a class of gods under the eighth Manu, Pur. **-tápas**, mfn. very heating or warming, AV.; practising severe austerity, Kathās.; m. an ascetic, hermit, L.; the sun, L.; (pl.) N. of a class of gods under the eighth Manu (cf. *su-tapa*), BhP.; of various Ṛishis and their sons under various Manus, Pur.; of other persons, Vīrac. **-tapasvin**, mfn. practising great austerity or self-mortification, Kṛishṇaj. **-tapta** (*sú-*), mfn. very hot, much heated, ŚBr. &c. &c.; purified by heat (as gold), MBh.; greatly harassed or afflicted, Hit.; very severe (as a penance), Mn. xi, 239; (*ā*), f. Mucuna Pruritus, L. **—tamām**, ind. (superl.; cf. *-tarām*) most excellently, best, MW. **—tamisrā** (*sú-*), f. dense darkness, ŚBr. **—tara**, mfn. easy to be crossed, RV.; MBh.; easily passed (as a night), RV. **—taraṇá**, mfn. easy to be crossed (as a river), RV. **—tarām**, see s.v. **—tarkārī**, f. a kind of gourd (=*deva-dālī*), L. **—tardana**, m. the Koil or Indian cuckoo, L. **—tarpayat**, mfn. well satiating or satisfying, Hariv. **—tarpita**, mfn. well satiated or satisfied, MBh.; R. **—tárman**, mfn. easily conveying across (as a boat), RV. **—tala**, n. (L. also m.) 'great depth,' the second of the seven divisions of the regions under the earth (cf. *loka, pātāla*), Pur.; m. the base or foundation of a large building (=*aṭṭālikā-bandha*), L. **—talpa**, n. a beautiful couch, Pañcar. **—tashṭa** (*sú-*), mfn. well-fashioned, RV. **—tāna**, mfn. well-tuned, melodious, Pañcar. **—tāmra**, mfn. deep-red; °*r'oshṭha*, mfn. very ruddy-lipped, MBh. **—tāra**, mf(*ā*)n. very bright, R.; VarBṛS.; Kathās.; very loud, Bhartṛ.; having a beautiful pupil (as an eye), BhP.; m. a partic. perfume, Suśr.; N. of a preceptor, Cat.; (*ā*), f. (in Sāṃkhya) one of the nine kinds of acquiescence (*tushṭi*), one of the eight kinds of perfection (*siddhi;* also °*ram*, n.), Tattvas.; Sāṃkhyak., Sch.; N. of an Apsaras, Kālac.; of a daughter of Śva-phalka, VP.; n. a kind of cat's eye, L. **—tāraka**, mfn. having beautiful stars, MW.; (*ā*), f. N. of one of the 24 goddesses who execute the commands of the 24 Arhats, L. **—tāla**, m. (in music) a kind of time or measure, MBh. **—tikta**, mfn. very bitter or pungent, L.; m. Oldenlandia Herbacea, L.; (*ā*), f. a species of gourd (=*kośātakī*), L. **—tiktaka**, m. 'very bitter,' Gentiana Chirayita, L.; =*pāribhadra*, L. **—tintiḍā** or °*ḍī*, f. Tamarindus Indica, L. **—tīkshṇa**, mfn. very sharp or pungent, acutely painful (*am*, ind. 'excessively'), MBh.; R. &c.; m. Moringa Pterygosperma, L.; N. of a Muni (brother of Agastya), R.; Bhaṭṭ.; *-daśana*, m. 'very sharp-toothed,' N. of Śiva, MBh.; °*ṇâgra*, mfn. very sharp-pointed, MBh. **—tīkshṇaka**, m. a kind of tree (=*sushkaka*), L. **—tīrthá**, mfn. conveying well across or to a goal, VS.; easily crossed or traversed, MBh.; R. &c.; n. a good road, MaitrS.; a very sacred bathing-place, Pañcat.; an object of great adoration, BhP.; m. a good teacher (opp. to *ku-tīrtha*), VarYogay.; Mālav. i, 1½ (here, accord. to others, 'N. of a teacher'); N. of Śiva, MBh.; of a king (v. l. *su-nītha*), VP.; *-rāj*, m. N. of a mountain, Śatr. **—tīrthaka**, n. a very sacred bathing-place (as a proper N.), MBh. **—tīrthya**, mf(*ā*)n. affording s°b°-places, Hir. **—túka**, mf(*ā*)n. (fr. √*tuk*=*tak*) running swiftly, RV. **—tukana**, mfn. id. (used in explaining prec.), Nir. iv, 18. **—tuṅga**, mfn. very lofty or tall, W.; m. the culmination or culminating point of a planet, L.; the cocoa-nut tree, L.; N. of a place, MBh. (B. *sa-t°*). **—tumula**, mf(*ā*)n. very noisy or loud, MBh. **—tushṭa**, mfn. easily satisfied, Kāv. **—tus**, mfn. (nom. *-tūs*, instr. pl. *-tūrbhis*) well-sounding, Vop. **—tūlikā** or **-tūlī**, f. a beautiful mattress, L. **—tṛiṇa**, n. beautiful grass, Kāś. on Pāṇ. vi, 2, 195; N. of various kinds of grass, L. **—tṛishṇa** (?), N. of a country, Buddh. **—tejana**, mfn. well pointed or sharpened, MBh.; m. a well-pointed arrow, ib.; Alhagi Maurorum, L.; N. of a warrior, MBh. **—téjas**, mfn. very sharp or sharp-edged, AV.; very bright, splendid, ChUp.; m. N. of a son of the Gṛitsamada, MBh.; of the 10th Arhat of the past Utsarpiṇī (with Jainas), L. **—tejā** (?), f. Polanisia Icosandra (perhaps *-tejas* is meant), L. **—tejita**, mfn. =*-tejana*, MBh. **—tailā**, f. 'yielding good oil,' the plant Mahā-jyotishmatī, L. **—toya**, mf(*ā*)n. having beautiful water (as a river), VarBṛS.; m. N. of a king, VP. **—tosha** (R.), **-toshaṇa** (Hariv.), mfn. easy to be satisfied. **—tyáj**, mfn. easily letting loose or letting fly (others 'well hurling at,' said of Agni), RV. viii, 49, 6. **—tyaja**, mf(*ā*)n. easy to be abandoned or given up, Kir. **—trāta** (*sú-*), mfn. well guarded or protected, ŚBr. **—trātrá**, mfn. =prec. and next, RV. **—trāman**, mfn. guarding or protecting well, RV.; AV.; ŚBr.; ŚrS.; m. N. of Indra, L.; a protector, ruler (see *dharitrī-s°*); pl. a partic. class of gods under the 13th Manu, Pur.; (°*mā*), f. N. of Pṛithivī, MW. **—trāvan**, mfn. guarding well, AV. **—tvakka** (Suśr.), **-tvac** (Car.), mfn. having a beautiful skin. **—tsaru**, mfn. having a fine handle (as a sword), MBh. **—daṅśita**, mfn. well bitten, MW.; well armed (cf. *pari-d°*), ib.; very dense or close, crowded together, MBh. **—daṅshṭra**, mfn. having strong or beautiful teeth, MBh.; R.; m. N. of a Rākshasa, R.; of a son of Kṛishṇa, Hariv.; of a son of Śambara, Hariv.; of an adopted son of Asamañjas, ib.; (*ā*), f. N. of a Kiṃ-narī, Kāraṇḍ. **—dáṅsas**, mfn. accomplishing mighty or splendid actions, energetic, active, powerful, RV. **—dáksha**, mf(*ā*)n. very capable or clever or strong (mostly said of gods), RV.; TS.; m. N. of a man, g. *śubhrâdi*. **—dákshiṇa**, mfn. having an excellent right hand, RV.; very dexterous, MBh.; very courteous or polite, ib.; very sincere or upright, very liberal in sacrificial gifts, MW.; m. N. of a king of the Kambojas, MBh.; of a son of Pauṇḍraka, BhP.; (*ā*), f. N. of a wife of Dilīpa, Ragh. **—dagdhikā**, f. a kind of plant (=*dagdhā*), L. **—daṇḍa**, m. the ratan cane (=*vetra*), L. **—daṇḍikā**, f. the Go-rakshī plant, L. **—dat**, m. a handsome tooth, BhP.; mf(*atī*)n. having handsome teeth, MBh.; Kāv. &c.; (*ī*), f. N. of a Surāṅganā, Siṅhâs. **—datta**, mfn. well or properly given (cf. *sūtta*), Kār. on Pāṇ. vii, 4, 47; m. N. of a son of Śata-dhanvan (v. l. *su-dānta*), Hariv.; of the rich householder Anātha-piṇḍa-da, Lalit.; MWB. 407; of a village (also *-grāma*), Uttamac.; (*ā*), f. N. of a wife of Kṛishṇa, Hariv. **—dátra**, mfn. granting good gifts, RV. **—danta**, mfn. having good or handsome teeth, R.; m. a good tooth, MW.; a partic. Samādhi, Kāraṇḍ.; an actor, dancer, L.; N. of a man, g. *śubhrâdi;* (*ā*), f. N. of an Apsaras, VP.; (*ī*), f. the female elephant of the north-west quarter, L. **—dama**, mfn. =next, W. **—dambha**, mfn. easy to be subdued (used in explaining *dabhra*), Nir. iii, 20. **—dayita**, mfn. much beloved, very dear, MBh. **—daridra**, mfn. very poor, Hariv. **—darpaṇa**, mfn. having a beautiful mirror, reflecting well, Kathās. **—darbha**, mfn. having good Darbha or Kuśa grass, MW.; (*ā*), f. =*ikshu-darbhā*, L. **—dárśa**, mfn. easily seen, conspicuous (compar. *-tara*), RV.; MBh.; beautiful to see, lovely, MBh. (=*prasanna-vaktra*, Nīlak.); *-tā*, f. visibility, conspicuousness, Hcat. **—darśaka**, m. a partic. Samādhi, Kāraṇḍ. **—darśaná**, mf(*ā*)n. easily seen by (instr.), Vop.; good-looking, beautiful, handsome, lovely, MBh.; R. &c.; m. 'keen-sighted,' a vulture, L.; a fish, Bhpr.; (in music) a kind of composition, Saṃgīt.; N. of Śiva, MBh.; of a son of Agni and Sudarśanā, ib.; of a Vidyā-dhara, BhP.; of a Muni, ib.; of a Buddha, Lalit.; of a patriarch, Buddh.; of a serpent-demon, ib.; of a Cakravartin, ib.; of one of the 9 Jaina Śukla-balas or Bala-devas, L.; of the father of the 18th Arhat of the present Avasarpiṇī, L.; of a king of Mālava, MBh.; of a king of Ujjayinī, Cat.; of a king of Pāṭali-putra, Hit.; of a son of Śaṅkhana, R.; of a son of Artha-siddhi, Hariv.; of a son of Dhruva-saṃdhi, Ragh.; of a son of Dadhīci, Cat.; of a son of Aja-mīḍha, Hariv.; of a son of Bharata, BhP.; of a son-in-law of Pratika, ib.; of a gambler, Kathās.; of various authors &c. (also with *ācārya, kavi, bhaṭṭa, sūri* &c.), Cat.; of a Jambū tree, MBh.; of a mountain, TĀr.; MBh.; Kāraṇḍ.; of a Dvīpa, MBh.; m. n. N. of the *cakra* or circular weapon of Vishṇu-Kṛishṇa (or 'the disc of the sun'), MBh.; Kāv. &c.; of a mystical staff (carried by Saṃnyāsins as a defence against evil spirits, and consisting of a bamboo with six knots), RTL. xxi; (*ā́*), f. a handsome woman, a woman, W.; a night in the light half of a month, TBr.; an order, command, L.; Coculus Tomentosus, L.; a sort of spirituous liquor, L.; N. of a daughter of Duryodhana and Narmadā, MBh.; of a princess, Pañcat.; of a Gandharva maiden, Kāraṇḍ.; of a lotus pond, R.; of a Jambū tree, MBh.; of Indra's city Amarāvatī, Cat.; of a Comm. on the Tantra-rāja; (*ī*), f. N. of Indra's city (also °*nī-nagara*), Divyâv.; (*am*), n. (cf. m.) a partic. powder composed of various substances, Bhpr.; N. of Indra's city; of a Tīrtha, BhP.; *-kavaca*, n., *-kāla-prabhā*, f. N. of wks.; *-cakra*, n. Vishṇu's discus, Cat.; *-cūrṇa*, n. 'beautiful powder,' a medicinal compound used in fevers, ŚārṅgS.; *-jvālā-mantra*, m. N. of a Mantra; *-dvīpa*, n. Jambu-dvīpa, MW.; *-nṛisiṅhârādhana*, n., *-pañjarôpanishad*, f., *-pāñcajanya-pratishṭhā*, f. N. of wks.; *prīti-kara*, m. N. of a Kiṃ-nara prince, Buddh.; *-bhāshya*, n., *-mantra*, m., *-mahā-mantra*, m., *-māhātmya*, n., *-mīmāṅsā*, f., *-vijaya*, m., *-śataka*, n., *-shaḍ-akshara*, n., *-saṃhitā*, f., *-sampāta*, m., *-sahasra-nāman*, n., *-sukarṇaka-carita*, f., *-stava*, m., *-stotra*, n.; °*nâdi-yantra-vidhi*, m., °*nârādhana*, n., °*nârādhana-krama*, m., °*nâshṭaka*, n. N. of wks.; °*nôpanishad*, f. N. of an Upanishad. **—darśanīya**, mfn. easy to be seen, MBh. **—darśinī**, f. N. of a lotus pond, R. **—dala**, m. 'having good leaves,' Pterospermum Suberifolium, L.; a kind of creeper (=*kshīra-moraṭa*), L.; (*ā*), f. Rosa Glandulifera, L.; Glycine Debilis, L. **—daśana**, mf(*ā*)n. having handsome teeth, MārkP. **—daśârha-kula**, mfn. sprung from a race worthy of a happy fate (and 'from the noble race of the Daśârhas'), Kathās. **—dā́**, mfn. giving bountifully, munificent, RV. **—dā́tu**, mfn. (√*do*) easily divisible, RV. **—dātṛi**, mfn. =*-dā*, Sāy. **—dāna**, n. a rich or bounteous gift, Subh. **—dā́nu**, mfn. pouring out or bestowing abundantly, bounteous, munificent (said of various gods), RV.; AV. **—dānta**, mfn. well-tamed, well restrained (as horses), MBh.; m. 'very self-controlled,' a Pratyeka-buddha (q. v.), L.; a partic. Samādhi, Kāraṇḍ. (printed *su-danta*); N. of a son of Śata-dhanvan, Hariv.; *-sena*, m. N. of a medical writer, Cat. **—dāma**, m. 'giving well,' N. of a cowherd attendant on Kṛishṇa, Pañcar.; pl. N. of a people (v. l. for *su-dāsa*), R.; (*ā*), f. N. of one of the Mātṛis attendant on Skanda, MBh.; of a river (in the north of India), R. **—dāman**, mfn. giving well, bestowing abundantly, bountiful, RV.; m. a cloud, L.; the sea, L.; N. of a Gandharva, R.; of a king of the Daśārṇas, MBh.; of another king (prob. w. r. for *su-dās*), Kull. on Mn. viii, 110; of a cowherd attendant on Kṛishṇa, Cat.; of a poor Brāhman (who came to Dvārakā to ask Kṛishṇa's aid, and was made wealthy by him), BrahmavP.; of a garland-maker (cf. 3. *dāman*), BhP.; of Indra's elephant, Airāvata, L.; of a mountain (?), MBh.; of a river, PañcavBr.; pl. N. of a people, MBh. **—dāmana**, m. N. of a councillor of Janaka, R.; n. a partic. mythical weapon, R. (B. *su-dāruṇa*). **—dāminī**, f. N. of the wife of Śamīka, BhP. **—dāya**, m. a good or auspicious gift, a special gift on partic. occasions (e.g. a gift to a student at his investiture with the sacred thread or Yajñôpavīta, a nuptial present &c.), L.; mfn. one who makes the above gift (e.g. a father, mother, husband &c.), Dāyabh. **—dāru**, n. good wood, Pañcat. (B.); m. 'furnishing good wood,' N. of a part of the Vindhya mountains (called Pāriyātra, q. v.), L.; *-mūla*, m. Alhagi Maurorum, L. **—dāruṇa**, mf(*ā*)n. very cruel or dreadful or terrible (n. 'something terrible' or 'a partic. mythical weapon'), MBh.; R. &c. **—dā́van**, mfn. giving well, bounteous, munificent, RV. **—dā́s**, mfn. (prob. fr. a √*dās*=*dāś*) worshipping the gods well (bestowing rich gifts, Sāy.), RV. (compar. *-tara*, ib.); m. N. of a celebrated king of the Tṛitsus (son of Divo-dās, at whose court both Vasishṭha and Viśvāmitra appear to have acted as family priests; Sudās Paijavana is regarded as the author of RV. x, 133), RV.; AitBr.; GṛŚrS.; Mn. vii, 41. **—dāsa**, m. (perhaps identical with prec.) N. of a king, BhP.; of a grandson of Ṛitu-parṇa, Hariv.; of a son of Sarva-kāma, Pur.; of a son of Cyavana, ib.; of a son of Bṛihad-ratha, ib.; of the father of Mitra-saha, Cat.; pl. N. of a people (v. l. *-dāma* and *-dāman*), R. **—diti**, mfn. (in a formula as opp. to *a-diti*), Vait. (*su-dīti*, TS.) **—dina**, mf(*ā*)n. clear, bright (as a day or morning), RV.; n. a clear or fine or auspicious day, RV. &c. &c.; happy time, happiness (=*sukha*), Naigh. iii, 6; N. of a Tīrtha, MBh.; *-tā*, f. clear weather, Bhartṛ.; *-tvá*, n. state of fine weather, an auspicious time, RV.; °*nâha*, n. a bright or fine day, Pat. on Pāṇ. ii, 4, 30. **—dināya**, Nom. Ā. °*yate*, to become a fine day, clear up, Pāṇ. iii, 1, 17, Vārtt. 1. **—dív**, mfn. shining brightly, RV. **—divá**, n. (AV.), **-divasa**, m. (Bhartṛ.) a bright or fine day. **—divā**, ind. id., Kāśikh.; *-taṇḍi*, m. N. of a Ṛishi, MBh. **—dih**, mfn. well polished, bright, sharp (as teeth), Vait. **—dīkshā**, f. 'beautiful consecration,' N. of Lakshmī, Vishṇ. (=*yajñâdhikāra-siddhi*, Sch.) **—dīti**, f. bright flame, RV.; mfn. flaming, shining, brilliant, RV.; TS.; m. N. of a man (having the patr. Āṅgirasa and author of RV. viii, 71), Anukr. **—dī́diti**, mfn. flaming brightly, shining beautifully, RV. **—dīpta**, mfn. shining bright, MuṇḍUp. **—dīrgha**, mfn. very long (in time and space), very extended, Kāv.; Kathās.; (*ā*), f. a kind of cucumber, L.; (°*gha*)*-gharmā*, f. the plant Marsilia Quadrifolia, L.; *-phalakā*, f. a kind of egg-plant, L.; *-jīvaphalā*, f. a kind of cucumber, L. **—duḥkha**, n. great pain or sorrow, MBh.; mf(*ā*)n. very painful or troublesome, very difficult to (inf.), MBh.; R. &c.; (*am*), ind. very painfully, most uneasily, ib.; °*khârohaṇa*, mfn. very difficult of ascent, R. **—duḥkhita**, mfn. much grieved, greatly afflicted, MBh.;

Pur. — **duḥśrava,** mfn. very unpleasant to be heard, Uttarar. — **duḥsaha,** mfn. very difficult to be borne or endured, quite intolerable, Kālid. — **duḥsparśa,** mfn. very unpleasant to be touched or felt, BhP. — **dukūla,** mfn. made of very fine cloth, Ṛitus. — **dúgha,** mf(*ā*)n. milking well or easily, yielding much, abundant, bountiful, RV.; AV.; (*ā*), f. a good milch cow, RV. — **durācāra,** mfn. very ill-conducted, very badly behaved or wicked, a profligate, W. — **durādharsha,** mf(*ā*)n. quite intolerable, Hariv.; very hard to get at, unattainable, R. — **durāruha,** mfn. very hard to be ascended, inaccessible, W. — **durāvarta,** mfn. very hard to be dissuaded or convinced, MBh. — **durāsada,** mfn. very hard to be got at, unapproachable to (gen.), R. — **durukti,** f. very harsh language, BhP. — **durgama** or **-durgamya,** mfn. very difficult to be traversed or crossed or sailed over, MBh.; R. — **durjaya,** mfn. very difficult to be overcome or conquered, MBh.; Kāv. &c.; very d° to be won or obtained, BhP.; m. a kind of military array, Kām.; N. of a son of Suvīra, MBh.; of a Brāhman, Buddh.; (*ā*), f. (with Buddhists) N. of one of the 10 stages of perfection, Dharmas. 64. — **durjara,** mfn. very difficult to be digested, MBh. — **durjñeya,** mfn. very d° to become acquainted with, ib. — **durdarśa,** mfn. very d° to be discerned or seen or observed, unpleasant or intolerable to the eye, R., Sch. — **durdṛiśa,** mfn. id., R.; MārkP. — **durdharsha,** mfn. very d° to be approached or attacked, intangible, MBh. — **durnirīkshaṇa,** mfn. very d° to be looked at, BhP. — **durbala,** mfn. very weak or faint, MBh. — **durbuddhi,** mfn. very foolish or stupid, ib. — **durbhaga,** mf(*ā*)n. very unfortunate, BhP. — **durbhida,** mfn. very d° to be split or broken, MBh. — **durmati,** mfn. very foolish or evil-minded, ib. — **durmanas,** mfn. very dispirited or troubled in mind, R. — **durmarsha,** mf(*ā*)n. very or quite intolerable, BhP. — **durlabha,** mfn. very difficult to be attained, very scarce or rare, MBh.; R. &c.; very difficult to or to be (inf.), MBh. — **durvaca,** mfn. very d° to be answered, MBh.; Car. — **durvacas,** n. a very hard word, MārkP. — **durvaha,** mfn. very difficult to be borne, HPariś. — **durvida** (MBh.), **-durveda** (R.), mfn. very d° to be known or understood. — **duścara,** mfn. very d° of access, inaccessible, R.; very arduous or painful, Mn.; Sūryas. — **duścikitsa,** mfn. very d° to be healed or cured, BhP. — **dushkara,** mfn. very d° to be done, most arduous, MBh.; Bcar.; BhP. — **dushkula,** n. a very low or degraded race or family, R. — **dushkṛita,** mfn. a very great sin or crime, MBh. — **dushkha,** °**khita,** see *-duḥkha,* °*khita.* — **dushṭa,** mfn. very bad or wicked, R. — **dushpāra,** mfn. very difficult to be penetrated or investigated, Vishṇ. — **dushprabha,** m. a chameleon, L. — **dushprasādhya,** mfn. very d° to be mastered or conquered, Kām. — **dushprāpa,** mfn. very d° to be reached or attained, quite inaccessible, R. — **dushprêkshya,** mfn. very d° to be caught sight of, MBh. — **dustara** (Hit.; BhP.), **-dustāra** (MBh.), mfn. very d° to be passed or crossed. — **dustyaja,** mfn. very d° to be abandoned or quitted, MBh.; BhP. — **duha,** mfn. easy to be milked (cf. *su-dugha*), MBh. — **dūra,** mfn. very remote or distant (*-dūrāt,* 'from afar;' *-dūrāt sudūre,* 'very far away'), MuṇḍUp.; (*am*), ind. very far away, Ratnâv.; in a very high degree, Daś. — **dṛiḍha** (*sú-*), mfn. very firm or hard or strong, AV.; very tenacious (as memory), Kām.; well secured or locked, Kṛishṇaj.; (*am*), ind. very intensely, MBh.; *-tā,* f. firmness, Prab.; *-tvacā,* f. Gmelina Arborea, L.; *-vrata,* mfn. very rigid or strict in vows, MW.; *-harmya-vat,* mfn. having very strong fortresses, Hcat. — **dṛipta,** mfn. very proud or arrogant, R.; BhP. — **dṛiś,** mf(Ved. *-dṛiśī*)n. keen-sighted, RV.; Kām.; well-looking, handsome, RV.; having beautiful eyes (*-dṛik,* f. 'a pretty woman'), Kāv.; Pur.; m. pl. (with Buddhists) a partic. class of gods, Lalit. — **dṛiśīka,** mfn. looking beautiful, handsome, RV.; *-rūpa* (*-dṛiśīka-*), mfn. having b° colour, ib.; *-saṃdṛiś* (*-dṛiśīka-*), mfn. having a b° appearance, ib. — **dṛiśya,** mfn. easily seen, clearly visible, MBh.; looking beautiful, handsome, Pañcar. — **dṛishṭa,** mf(*ā*)n. well seen (acc. with √*kṛi,* 'to look at well or earnestly'), MBh.; R.; easy to be seen (compar. *-tara*), Jātakam.; m. pl. N. of a people (v. l. *sudeshṭa*), MBh. — **dṛishṭi,** mfn. keen-sighted, Bālar.; m. a vulture, L. — **devá,** m. a good or real god, RV.; ŚBr.; (accord. to some) 'sporting well,' a potent or highly erotic lover (in this meaning fr. √*div,* 'to play,' and opp. to *vi-deva,* 'impotent, unerotic'), RV. x, 95, 14; AV. xx, 136, 12; mfn. having the right gods, protected by them, RV.; TS.; destined for the r° gods, VS.; TBr.; m. N. of a Kāśyapa, TĀr.; of a Brāhman, MBh.; of a general of Ambarīsha, ib.; of a son of Hary-aśva and king of Kāśi, ib.; of a king of Vidarbha, R.; of a son of Akrūra, Hariv.; of a son of Pauṇḍra Vāsudeva, ib.; of a son of Cañcu, ib.; of a son of Campa, BhP.; of a son of Devaka, VP.; of a son of Vishṇu, BhP.; of a poet, Cat.; (*ā*), f. N. of the wife of Ari-ha (also called Āṅgeyī), MBh.; of the wife of Vikuṇṭhana (also called Dāśārhī), ib. — **devana,** n. ardent gambling, MBh. — **devi,** f. (m.c. for °*vī*) N. of the wife of Nābhi and mother of Ṛishabha, BhP. — **devikā,** f. (prob.) a proper N., Pat. — **devyà,** n. the whole body of good gods, RV. — **deśa,** m. a fit place, Kṛishṇaj. — **deśika,** m. a good guide, Bcar. — **deshṇa,** m. N. of a son of Kṛishṇa, Hariv.; of an adopted son of Asamañjas (v. l. *-daṇshṭra*), ib.; (pl.) N. of a people (v. l. *sudella*), MBh.; (*ā*), f. N. of the wife of Bali, MBh.; of the wife of Virāṭa, ib. — **deshṇu,** f. = *su-deshṇa,* Uṇ. iii, 16, Sch. — **deha,** m. a beautiful body, BhP. — **dogdhrī,** f. yielding much milk, MBh. — **dógha,** mf(*ā*)n. id., (fig.) bountiful, liberal, RV. — **dóha,** mfn. easy to be milked (compar. *-tara*), MaitrS. — **dohana,** mf(*ā*)n. id. (used in explaining *su-dugha*), Nir. xi, 43. — **dyu,** m. N. of a son of Cāru-pāda, BhP. — **dyút,** mfn. shining beautifully, RV. — **dyumná,** mf(*ā*)n. id., ib.; m. N. of a king, MaitrUp.; of a son of Manu Vaivasvata (supposed to have been born a female under the name of Iḍā [q. v.], and afterwards changed into a male through the favour of Mitra and Varuṇa), MBh.; Hariv.; of a son of Abhaya-da, BhP. — **dyótman,** mfn. shining bright, RV. — **dráviṇas,** mfn. having splendid riches or treasures, ib. — **drashṭṛi,** mfn. one who sees well, having good insight into (gen.), Pat. on Pāṇ. v, 4, 77. — **drú,** m. good wood or timber, RV. — **dvija,** mf(*ā*)n. having good teeth; °*jânana,* mfn. having a mouth containing good t°, MBh. — **dhána,** mfn. very rich, RV.; N. of various men, Buddh.; Śukas. — **dhanus,** m. N. of a son of Kuru, Hariv.; Pur.; of an ancestor of Gautama Buddha, Buddh. — **dhanva,** m. the 8th cubit (*aratni*) from the bottom or the 10th from the top of the sacrificial post, L. — **dhánvan,** mfn. having an excellent bow, RV. &c. &c.; m. the son of an outcaste Vaiśya by a woman of the same class, Mn. x, 23 (some read *sudhanvâcārya* in one word); N. of Vishṇu, L.; of Tvashṭṛi or Viśva-karman, L.; of an Āṅgirasa, ŚBr.; MBh.; of a son of Virāja and guardian of the east, Hariv.; of a king vanquished by Māndhātṛi, MBh.; of a son of Sambhūta, Hariv.; of a son of Ahīna-gu, ib.; of a son of Abhaya-da, ib.; of a son of Kuru, ib.; of a king of Sāṃkāśya, R.; of a son of Śāśvata, VP.; of a son of Satya-dhṛita, ib.; °*va-māhātmya,* n. N. of wk.; °*vâcārya,* m. a partic. mixed caste (= *sudhanvan*), L. (cf. Mn. x, 23); a worshipper of Īśāna i. e. Śiva, L. — **dhara,** m. N. of an Arhat, Buddh. — **dharma,** m. good law, justice, duty, R.; BhP.; 'maintaining law or justice,' N. of a man, Cat.; of a Mahā-brahman (q. v.), SaddhP.; one of the 10 disciples of the celebrated Jaina teacher and Arhat Mahā-vīra, W.; of a king of the Kiṃ-naras, SaddhP.; of a palace, Caurap.; pl. N. of a class of deities, MW.; (*ā*), f. the assembly hall of the gods (also *ī*), MBh.; Kāv.; Buddh.; N. of the wife of Mātali, MBh. — **dhárman,** mfn. well supporting or maintaining, VS.; practising justice, attending well to duty, Hariv.; m. the maintainer of a family (= *kuṭumbin*), L.; the assembly hall of the gods, Daś.; N. of a being reckoned among the Viśve Devāḥ, Hariv.; of a king of the Daśārṇas, MBh.; of a son of Dṛiḍha-nemi, Hariv.; of a son of Citraka, ib.; (with Jainas) of a Gaṇâdhipa (also °*ma-svāmin*), HPariś.; (pl.) N. of various classes of gods under various Manus, Pur. — **dharmin,** mfn. (in next; also w. r. for *-dharman*); °*mi-tā,* f. description of anything by mentioning its characteristics, Vās., Sch. — **dharmishṭha,** mf(*ā*)n. giving the strictest attention to one's duties, most virtuous, MBh. — **dharsha** or °**shaṇa,** mfn. (prob.) easy to be got at or laid hold of, Vop. — 1. **-dhā,** f. (√1. *dhā;* for 2. *su-dhā* &c., see s. v.) welfare, ease, comfort, AV.; AitBr. — **dhāta,** mfn. well-cleaned, ŚvetUp. (= *-dhauta,* Sch.) — **dhātu,** mfn. well-founded, secure, RV.; well off, wealthy, VS.; *-dakshiṇa* (*-dhā°*), mfn. (prob.) one on whom the sacrificial fee is well conferred, worthy of the sacrificial fee (accord. to Sch. 'one who receives precious metal as a s° fee'), VS.; Kāṭh.; Kauś. — **dhātṛi,** mfn. one who arranges or regulates well, PañcavBr.; KātyŚr. — **dhāma,** see next. — **dhāman,** m. N. of various Ṛishis, Pur.; of a son of Ghṛita-pṛishṭha, BhP.; of a mountain (v. l. *-dhāma*), VP.; pl. N. of a class of deities under the 10th Manu (v. l. *-dhāma*), ib. — **dhāya,** m. ease, comfort, TS. — **dhāyuka,** m. N. of a man; pl. his descendants, g. *upakâdi.* — 1. **-dhārá,** mfn. streaming beautifully, RV. — 2. **-dhāra,** mfn. well pointed (as an arrow), MBh. — **dhārin,** mfn. well maintaining (law or order), ib. — **dhi,** see *-dhī.* — **dhita** (*sú-*), mfn. (for *sudhita* see p. 1226, col. 1) well placed or fixed, RV.; well ordered or arranged or contrived, ib.; TBr.; well prepared or served, ready (as food), RV.; fixed upon, meant, intended, ib.; well-disposed, kind, benevolent, ib.; VS. — **dhī,** f. good sense or understanding, intelligence, Subh.; (*-dhī*), mfn. (nom. *īs, i*) having a good understanding, wise, clever, sensible, R.; Kathās. &c.; religious, pious, RV.; m. a wise or learned man, Pandit, teacher, L.; *-candrikā,* f. N. of wk.; *-°ndra-yati* (°*dhîndr°*), m. N. of an author; *-mayūkha,* m., *-vāda,* m., *-vilocana,* n., *-vilocana-sāra,* m., *-śṛiṅgāra,* m. N. of wks.; *-dhy-upâsya,* see *suddhyup°* (s. v.) — 1. **-dhīra,** mfn. very considerate or wise, MW. — 2. **-dhīra,** mfn. very firm or resolute, Pañcat. (v. l.) — **dhīvan,** mfn., Pāṇ. iii, 2, 74, Sch. — **dhúr** or **-dhúra,** mfn. going well under the yoke; m. a good draught-horse, RV. — **dhūpaka,** m. the resin of Pinus Longifolia, L. — **dhūpya** or **-dhūmya,** m. a partic. fragrant substance, L. — **dhūmra-varṇā,** f. N. of one of the seven tongues of Agni, Gṛihyās. — **dhṛit,** m. N. of a son of Mahā-vīrya (cf. *-dhṛiti*), BhP. — **dhṛita** (*sú-*), mfn. very constant or persevering, AV. — **dhṛiti,** m. N. of a king (son of Mahā-vīra or Mahā-vīrya; cf. *-dhṛit*), R.; of a son of Rājya-vardhana, Pur. — **dhṛishṭama,** mfn. very bold or resolute (?), RV. — **dhauta,** mfn. well cleaned or polished, MBh.

सुतराम् *su-tarām,* ind. (fr. 5. *su* + *tarām* = *taram*) still more, in a higher degree, excessively (*s° na,* 'still less;' *na s°,* 'very badly;' *mā s°,* 'in no way,' 'by no means'), MBh.; Kāv. &c.

सुतवत् *suta-vat, suta-soma* &c. See p. 1219, col. 2.

सुतार *su-tāra, su-tāraka* &c. See p. 1224, col. 1.

सुति *suti, sutī, sutīya, sutya* &c. See under 3. √*su,* 4. √*su,* p. 1219, cols. 2, 3.

सुदंष्ट्र *su-daṇshṭra, su-daṇsas* &c. See p. 1224, col. 2.

सुदि *sudi,* ind. (thought by some to be a contraction of *su-dina,* but really w. r. for *śudi,* q. v.)

सुदेल्ल *sudella, sudeshṭa.* See *su-deshṇa, su-dṛishṭa,* cols. 1, 2.

सुद्ध्युपास्य *suddhy-upâsya,* mfn. (euphonically for *sudhy-up°;* see *su-dhī*) 'to be worshipped by the intelligent' (said of the Supreme Being), Pāṇ. i, 1, 58, Sch.

सुधा 2. *su-dhā,* f. (fr. 5. *su* + √*dhe;* for 1. *su-dhā,* 'welfare,' see col. 2) 'good drink,' the beverage of the gods, nectar (cf. 2. *dhātu,* p. 514), MBh.; Kāv. &c.; the nectar or honey of flowers, L.; juice, water, L.; milk (also pl.), VarBṛS.; Pañcar.; whitewash, plaster, mortar, cement, MBh.; R. &c.; a brick, L.; lightning, L.; the earth, Gal.; Euphorbia Antiquorum or another species, Car.; Sanseviera Roxburghiana, L.; Glycine Debilis, L.; Emblica or yellow Myrobalan, L.; a kind of metre, Ked.; N. of the wife of a Rudra, BhP.; of the Ganges, L.; of various wks. — °**ṇśu** (°*dhâṇśu*), m. 'nectar-rayed,' the moon (as the supposed repository of nectar), Kāv.; Kathās. &c.; camphor, L.; *-taila,* n. camphorated oil, L.; *-bha,* n., *-ratna,* n. a pearl, L. — **kaṇṭha,** m. 'nectar-throated,' the Indian cuckoo, L. — °**kara** (°*dhâk°*), m. a mine or receptacle of n°, Naish.; the moon, ib. (*-tā,* f., Caurap.); N. of various wks. and authors. — **kalaśa,** m. N. of an author (pupil of Rāja-śekhara), Cat. — **kāra,** m. a plasterer, whitewasher, R. — **kir,** mfn. distilling nectar, Sāh. — **kshālita,** mfn. plaster-washed, whitewashed, Śiś. — **ṅga** (°*dhâṅga*), m. 'nectar-bodied,' the moon, L. — **jīvin,** m. 'living by plaster,' a plasterer, bricklayer, L. — **ṭippaṇī,** f. N. of a Commentary. — **dī-**

dhiti, m. = *sudhânśu*, Bālar. — 1. **-drava**, m. whitewash, plaster (°*vānulepa*), Mṛicch.; a nectar-like fluid, W. — 2. **-drava**, Nom. P. °*vati*, to appear white as plaster, Dhūrtas.; to flow like nectar, MW. — **dhavala**, mf(*ā*)n. white as plaster, Kād.; white-washed, plastered, stuccoed, Vās. — **dhavalita**, mfn. = prec., Hcat.; Kull. — **dhāman**, m. = *sudhânśu*, Vṛishabhān. — °**dhāra** (°*dhâdh*°), m. 'nectar-receptacle,' the moon, L. — **dhārā**, f. a stream of n°, Kāv.; *-kvatha-stotra*, n. N. of wk. — **dhauta**, mfn. white-washed, Kathās. — °**nanda-laharī** (°*dhân*°), f. N. of a poem. — °**nanda-sūri** (°*dhân*°), m. N. of a man, Cat. — **nidhi**, m. = *sudhâdhāra*, L.; N. of various wks. — °**ndhas** (°*dhân*°), m. = *suddhā-bhuj*, Pārśvan. — **pāṇi**, m. 'bearing n° in his hands,' N. of Dhanvantari (q.v.), L. — **pūra**, m. a stream of n°, Pañcat. — **bhavana**, n. a plastered or stuccoed house, W.; the fifth Muhūrta, ib. — **bhitti**, f. a whitewashed wall, Daś. — **bhuj**, m. 'feeding on nectar,' a god, deity, L. — **bhṛiti**, f. 'n°-bearing,' the moon, L.; sacrifice (v.l. *-sūti*), L. — **bhojin**, m. = *-bhuj*, Bālar. — **maya**, mf(*ī*)n. consisting of n°, Kāv.; Kathās.; made of cement or plaster &c., L.; m. (with or scil. *prāsāda*) a palace, mansion, brick or cemented or stone building, L. — **mayūkha**, m. = *sudhânśu*, Harav. — **mitra**, m. N. of a man, g. *kāśyâdi*. — **mukhī**, f. N. of an Apsaras, Pañcar. — °**mṛita** (°*dhâm*°), n. nectar, VP.; *-maya*, mf(*ī*)n. consisting of n°, ib. — **modaka**, m. bamboo manna, L.; *-ja*, m. a kind of sugar prepared from it, MW. — **yoni**, m. 'source of nectar,' the moon, MārkP. — **rañjinī**, f. N. of an astron. wk. by Keśavâcārya. — **raśmi**, m. = *sudhânśu*, Vṛishabhān. — **rasa**, m. nectar-juice, MBh.; Kathās.; milk, Pañcar.; N. of an astron. wk. by Ananta; mfn. tasting like n° (*-tva*, n.), Naish.; *-maya*, mf(*ī*)n. consisting of n°, containing nectar, Caurap. — **laharī**, f. N. of a poem (in praise of the sun) by Jagan-nātha Paṇḍita-rāja. — **vat**, m. N. of a man, g. *bāhv-ādi*; pl. a class of deceased ancestors (v.l. *svadhā-vat*), MBh. — °**vadāta** (°*dhâv*°), mfn. = *-dhavala*, MBh.; R.; N. of a mountain, Divyâv. — **varti**, m. collyrium made from nectar, HPariś. — **varsha**, m. a shower of n°, Kathās. — **varshin**, mfn. raining n°, HPariś. (v.l.); m. N. of Brahmā, W.; of a partic. Buddha, L. — °**vāsa** (°*dhâv*°), m. 'nectar-abode,' the moon, Kṛishṇaj.; (*ā*), f. a kind of cucumber (= *trapushī*), L. — **vṛishṭi**, f. a shower of nectar, W. — **śaśāṅka-dhavala**, mfn. white as cement and the moon, VarBṛS. — **śubhra**, mfn. whitewashed, Bhartṛ. — **śravā**, incorrect for *-sravā*. — **saṃgraha**, m. N. of a medical wk. — °**sava** (°*dhâs*°), m. a partic. cosmetic, BhP. — **sāgara**, m. 'ocean of nectar,' N. of various wks. — 1. **-sāra**, m. N. of a Commentary (also called *su-bodhinī*). — 2. °**sāra** (°*dhâs*°), m. a shower of nectar, Kathās. — **sita**, m. whitewashed, Śak. (v.l.); white as cement (*-tā*, f.), Kathās.; provided with n°, Kir. xv, 45. — **sindhu**, m. the ocean of n°, Ānand. — **sū**, m. 'producer of n°,' the moon, L. — **sūka** (?), m. N. of a king, VP. — **sūti**, f. 'producing n°,' the moon, Rājat.; sacrifice, oblation, L.; a lotus flower, L. — **seka**, m. sprinkling with n°, Kathās. — **spardhin**, mfn. vying with nectar, sweet as nectar (said of speech), Sāh. — **syanda**, mfn. distilling n°, W. — **syandin**, mfn. flowing with n°, Viddh. — **sravā**, f. 'water-distilling,' the uvula or soft palate, L.; the shrub Rudantī, L. — **hara**, m. 'nectar-stealer,' N. of Garuḍa (fabled to have stolen the moon's n° for the serpent children of Kadrū, wife of Kaśyapa, in return for which his mother Vinatā, also one of Kaśyapa's wives, was released from subjection to Kadru), L. — **hartṛi** (Kathās.), **-hṛit** (L.), m. = prec. — **hrada**, m. a nectar-lake, Kathās. **Sudhêndra**, m. (cf. *sudhîndra*) N. of an author. **Sudhôdaya**, m. 'n°-production,' N. of a Tantra wk. by Hari-vallabha. **Sudhôdgāra**, m. a flood of nectar; *-maya*, mf(*ī*)n. consisting of a flood of n°, Naish. **Sudhôdbhava**, m. 'nectar-source,' N. of Dhanvantari (q.v.), L.; (*ā*), f. Terminalia Chebula, L.

Sudhaya, Nom. P. °*yati*, to refresh, comfort (v.l. *svadh*°), BhP.

Sudhita, mfn. (for *su-dhita* see p. 1225, col. 3) nectar-like, BhP.

Sudhi-√kṛi, P. *-karoti*, to change into nectar, Naish.

सुधात *su-dhāta* &c. See p. 1225, col. 2.

सुधिति *sudhiti*, mfn. = *svadhiti*, an axe, hatchet, knife, L.

सुधी *su-dhī* &c. See p. 1225, col. 3.

सुधेष *sudhesha*, N. of a country, MW.

सुधौत *su-dhauta*. See p. 1225, col. 3.

सुनक्षत्र *su-nákshatra*, n. (i.e. 5. *su* + *n*°) a good or auspicious Nakshatra, AV.; m. 'born under an ausp° N°,' N. of a king (son of Maru-deva), BhP.; of a son of Niramitra, ib.; (*ā*), f. N. of the second night of the civil month (*karma-māsa*), MW.; of one of the Mātṛis attending on Skanda, MBh.

Su (to be similarly prefixed to the following): — **nat**, mfn., Pat. on Pāṇ. vi, 4, 40. — **nata**, mfn. hanging down very deep, Pat. on Pāṇ. ii, 1, 1, Vārtt. 27, and ii, 2, 24, Vārtt. 1. — **nati**, m. N. of a Daitya (v.l. *su-mati*), Hariv. — **nanda**, mfn. pleasing well, delighting, W.; m. a palace of a partic. form (v.l. *sundara*), L.; N. of a Deva-putra, Lalit.; of a Sātvata attending on Kṛishṇa, BhP.; of a Buddhist Śrāvaka, SaddhP.; (*ā*), f. a partic. Tithi, VarBṛS.; Sch.; Aristolochia Indica, L.; a white cow, L.; a partic. yellow pigment (= *go-rocanā*), L.; a woman, L.; N. of Umā or a friend of Umā (°*dā-sahita*, 'attended by S°'), L.; of a wife of Kṛishṇa (v.l. *su-vārttā*), Hariv.; of the mother of Bāhu and Vālin, L.; of Mudāvatī (q.v.), L.; of a sister of Su-bāhu (king of the Cedis), MBh.; of the wife of Sārvabhauma (also called Kaikeyī), ib.; of the wife of Bharata (also called Kāśeyī Sārvasenī), ib.; of the wife of Pratīpa (also called Śaibyā), ib.; of a female door-keeper, Ragh.; of a river, BhP.; n. N. of a club made by Tvashṭṛi, MārkP. — **nandaka**, n a partic. Gaṇa of Śiva, Harav. — **nandana**, m. N. of a son of Kṛishṇa, BhP.; of a son of Purīsha-bhīru, ib.; of a brother of Bhūnandana, Kathās.; (*ī*), f. N. of a river, L.; n. N. of the 12th Muhūrta, Cat. — **nandinī**, f. a kind of plant with fragrant leaves, L.; a species of the Ati-jagatī metre (= *mañju-bhāshiṇī*), Col. — **naya**, m. wise conduct or policy, MBh.; R. &c.; 'well-conducted,' N. of a son of Ṛita, Pur.; of a son of Pariplava, ib.; of a brother of Khanitra, ib.; pl. N. of a people, MBh.; *-śālin*, mfn. wise, clever, Mudr.; *-śrī* and *-śrī-mitra*, m. N. of two men, Buddh. — **nayaka**, m. (f. °*yikā*) a good leader, Pāṇ. vii, 3, 46, Vārtt. 1, Pat.; *-śrī*, m. N. of a man, Buddh. — **nayana**, mf(*ā*)n. having beautiful eyes, Kāv.; m. a deer, L.; f. a (fair-eyed) woman, Kālid. — **narda**, mfn. roaring vigorously, Parāś. — **nasa**, mfn. having a beautiful nose, MBh.; BhP.; (*ā*), f. N. of a river, MBh. — **nāga**, see *saunāga*. — **nāṭya**, n. a graceful dance, Hariv. — **nātha**, mfn. having or forming a good shelter, AV. — **nāda**, mfn. sounding well, harmonious, Saṃgīt. — **nādaka**, m. (orig. = prec.) a conch, L. — **nābha**, mfn. having a good nave or centre, MBh.; (also °*bhaka*) having a good handle, R.; m. a partic. spell recited over weapons, ib.; N. of a counsellor of Varuṇa, MBh.; of a son of Dhṛita-rāshṭra, ib.; of a son of Garuḍa, ib.; of a brother of Vajra-nābha, Hariv.; of a mountain, MBh.; R.; (prob.) n. a wheel, discus, BhP. — **nābhaka**, see prec. — **nā́bhi**, mfn. having a good nave, AV. — **nābhya**, mfn. id. (prob. w.r. for *-nābha*), Cat. — **nāmadheya**, mfn. having an auspicious name, Hcat. — **nā́man**, mfn. well-named, AV.; m. N. of one of Skanda's attendants, MBh.; of a Daitya (v.l. *su-manas*), Hariv.; of a son of Su-ketu, MBh.; of a son of Ugra-sena, ib.; of a son of Vainateya, ib.; (°*mnī*), f. N. of a daughter of Devaka and wife of Vasu-deva, Hariv.; (°*ma*)*-dvādaśī*, f. a partic. religious observance performed on the 12th day of the 12th month, VahniP. — **nāla**, n. 'having a beautiful stalk or stem,' a kind of Andropogon, Bhpr.; a red water-lily, L. — **nālaka**, m. 'id.,' Agati Grandiflora, L. — **nāsa**, mfn. = *-nasa*, BhP.; °*sâkshi-bhruva*, mfn. having a beautiful nose and eyes and brows (said of a face), MBh.; (*ā*), f. a handsome nose, MW. — **nāsika**, mfn. = *-nasa*, BhP.; having a good point or projection, MW.; (*ā*), f. Leea Hirta, L. — **nāsīra**, see s.v. — **nishṭhita**, mfn. well prepared or arranged, quite ready, R. (B. *-nishṭh*°). — **nikṛishṭa**, mf(*ā*)n. very low or mean, MBh. — **nikshipta**, mfn. well deposited with (loc.), Mṛicch. — **nikhāta**, mfn. dug very deep, L. — **nikhilam**, ind. very completely, Hariv. — **nigraha**, mfn. well controlled, easily restrained, Śiś. — **nitambinī**, f. having beautiful hips or buttocks, καλλίπυγος, Śukas. — **nidra**, mfn. sleeping well, Cāṇ.; (*ā*), f. sound sleep, Pañcar. — **nidhi**, m. a good place, RV. — **ninada**, mfn. sounding agreeably or pleasantly, Kir.; very noisy or loud (*am*, ind.), Pracaṇḍ. — **nibhṛitam**, ind. very secretly or privately, Hit. — **nimaya**, mfn. easily exchanged or bartered, Pāṇ. vi, 1, 50, Vārtt. 2, Pat. — **niyat**, f. = *śobhanā vidhā*, Hariv. (Nilak.) — **niyata**, mfn. well put together, R.; well disciplined or self-governed (with *vācā*, instr. 'suppressing speech'), MBh. — **niyukta**, mfn. well constructed or built (cf. *su-niry*°), R. — **nirája**, mfn. easy to be expelled or driven away, RV. — **nirūḍha**, mfn. well purged by an injection, Car. — **nirūpita**, mfn. well observed or inspected or examined, Hit. — **nirūhaṇa**, n. a good purgative, ŚārṅgS. — **nirgata**, mf(*ā*)n. well come forth or emerged from (abl.), Mcar. — **nirghṛiṇa**, mfn. very merciless or cruel, MBh. — **nirṇikta**, mfn. thoroughly cleansed, well washed off, MBh.; well polished, bright, Hcat. — **nirbhakta** (*sú-*), mfn. quite excluded from (abl.), ŚBr. — **nirmátha**, m. (instr. *ā*) complete production (of fire) by rubbing, RV. iii, 29, 12. — **nirmala**, mf(*ā*)n. perfectly clear or pure, Mṛicch. — **nirmita**, m. N. of a Deva-putra, Lalit. — **niryāsā**, f. 'having good exudation or resin,' Odina Wodier, Bhpr. — **niryukta**, mfn. = *-niyukta*, Hariv. — **nirlajja**, mf(*ā*)n. very shameless or impudent, R. — **nirviṇṇa**, mfn. quite depressed, altogether despondent, MārkP. — **nirvṛita**, mf(*ā*)n. quite at ease or happy in mind (w.r. *-nirvritta*), MBh. — **nivishṭa**, well stationed (as guardians), R.; well furnished with (instr.), ib.; well adorned or decorated, ib. — **niśita**, mfn. well whetted or sharpened, MBh. — **niścaya**, m. firm resolve, R.; mf(*ā*)n. perfectly sure or certain (*am*, ind.), Hariv.; Kathās. — **niścala**, mfn. 'quite immovable or unchangeable,' N. of Śiva, MW. — **niścita**, mfn. firmly resolved, R.; well ascertained or determined or fixed or settled (*am*, ind. 'most assuredly'), Kāv.; Hit.; m. a Buddha, L.; *-pura*, n. N. of a town, Rājat. — **nishaṇṇa** or °**ṇṇaka**, m. the herb Marsilea Quadrifolia, Car. — **nishká**, mfn. having beautiful ornaments, RV. — **nishkṛita**, n. a good atonement or expiation, BhP. — **nishṭapta**, mfn. well heated or liquefied, Hariv.; thoroughly cooked, R. — **nishṭhita**, mfn. (cf. *-niḥshṭh*°) well versed in or acquainted with (loc.), ib. — **nishṭhura**, mfn. very rough or harsh, MBh. — **nishphala**, mfn. quite useless or in vain, R. — **nistriṇśa**, m. a beautiful sword, MBh. — **nihita**, mfn. well fixed or established, ib. — **nīta**, mfn. well led or guided, MBh.; well managed or executed, ib.; well prepared (as a path), ib.; well-conducted, MBh.; m. N. of a king (son of Su-bala), VP.; n. good or wise conduct, wisdom, prudence, MBh.; R. &c. — **nīti** (or *sú-*), mfn. guiding well, RV.; Kauś.; well-conducted, MW.; m. N. of Śiva, Śivag.; of a son of Vidūratha, MārkP.; f. good conduct or behaviour, good policy, wisdom, discretion, RV. &c. &c.; N. of the mother of Dhruva (wife of Uttāna-pāda), BhP. — **nīthá**, mfn. giving or enjoying good guidance, RV.; well-conducted, righteous, moral, good, Uṇ. ii, 2, Sch.; m. a partic. verse, MBh.; a Brāhman, L.; N. of a man, RV. v, 79, 2; of a son of Kṛishṇa, Hariv.; of a son of Saṃnati or Saṃtati, ib.; of a son of Su-sheṇa, BhP.; of a son of Su-bala, ib.; of Śiśu-pāla, MBh.; of a Dānava, Kathās.; (*ā*), f. (also °*tha-kanyā*) N. of the first-born daughter of Mṛityu or death (wife of Aṅga), MBh.; Hariv.; BhP. — **nīla**, mfn. very black or blue, dark, W.; (only L.) m. the pomegranate tree; n. the root of Andropogon Muricatus; (*ā*), f. common flax; a partic. grass (= *caṇikā* or *jaraḍī*); Clitoria Ternatea. — **nīlaka**, m. 'very blue,' (only L.) Eclipta Prostrata; a partic. tree resembling the Terminalia Tomentosa; sapphire. — **nīhāra**, mfn. very misty or foggy, R. — **nu**, see *-nau*. — **nṛipa**, m. a good king, Vās. — **nṛiśaṅsa**, mfn. very mischievous; *-kṛit*, mfn. doing very m° things, very cruel, MBh. — **netṛi**, m. N. of one of the 16 Ṛitvij (cf. *un-netṛi*), Hariv. — **netra**, m. 'fair-eyed' or 'having a good leader,' N. of a Māra-putra, Lalit.; of a son of Dhṛita-rāshṭra, MBh.; of a son of Vainateya, ib.; of a son of the 13th Manu, Hariv.; of a son of Su-vrata, VP.; of a Cakra-vāka, Hariv.; (*ā*), f. (scil. *tushṭi*; in Sāṃkhya) one of the 9 kinds of acquiescence (cf. *su-pāra*), Tattvas.; °*trâdhipati*, m. N. of a serpent-demon, Buddh. — **nepathya**, mf(*ā*)n. having a beautiful costume, Sāh. — **naú**, f. a good ship, VS.; mfn. (nom. m. f. *aus*, n. *u*) having good ships, Vop.; (*u*), n. water, L. — **nyasta**, mf(*ā*)n. well laid down or stretched out, R.

सुनन्द *su-nanda, su-nandana.* See col. 2.

सुनफा *sunaphā*, f. (= Gk. συναφή; cf. *ana-*

phā) a partic. configuration of the planets (when any one of the planets, except the Sun, occupies a secondary position to the moon), VarBṛS. **-yoga,** m. the above configuration, MW.

सुनह *sunaha,* m. N. of a son of Jahnu (v.l. *sumaha*), Hariv.

सुनाकुत *sunākuta* or *sunākṛita,* m. zedoary, Curcuma Zerumbet, L.

सुनाभ *su-nābha* &c. See p. 1226, col. 2.

सुनार *sunāra,* m. the milk of a female dog, L.; the egg of a snake, L.; a sparrow, L.

सुनासीर *sunāsīra.* See *śunā-sīra,* p. 1082.

सुनिक *sunika,* m. N. of a minister of Ripum-jaya (v.l. *śunaka*), VP.

सुनिकृष्ट *su-nikṛishṭa, su-nikhāta* &c. See p. 1226, col. 2.

सुनु *su-nu.* See *su-nau,* p. 1226, col. 3.

सुनू *sunū.* See *su-lū,* p. 1232, col. 3.

सुन्द् *sund,* a Sautra root meaning 'to shine, be bright,' Vop.

Sunda, m. N. of Vishṇu, MBh.; of a Daitya (son of Ni-sunda and brother of Upa-sunda; the two brothers killed each other while quarrelling for a beautiful Apsaras named Tilôttamā), MBh.; R. &c.; N. of a monkey, R. **Sundâsura-vadhū,** f. the wife of the Asura Sunda (called Tāḍakā), Bālar. **Sundôpasunda,** m. du. the two Daityas Sunda and Upasunda, MBh.; Bcar.

Sundara, mf(*ī*)n. (perhaps for *su-nara* = *sū-nara; d* being inserted as in Gk. ἀνδρός fr. ἀνήρ) beautiful, handsome, lovely, charming, agreeable, MBh.; Kāv. &c.; noble, Subh.; (*am*), ind. well, right, Pañcat.; m. Clerodendron Phlomoides, L.; a palace of a partic. form, L.; N. of Kāma-deva, L.; of a serpent-demon, Buddh.; of a son of Pravilasena, VP.; of various authors (also with *ācārya, kavi, bhaṭṭa* &c.), Cat.; (*ī*), f., see below; (*am*), n. = *-kāṇḍa* below. **-kamalīya,** n. N. of wk. **-kāṇḍa,** n. a beautiful stalk, Vās.; 'b° section,' N. of the 5th book of the Rāmâyaṇa and of the Adhyātma-rāmâyaṇa. **-gaṇi,** m. (with *sādhu*) N. of an author, Gat. **-guru-kāvya,** n. N. of a poem. **-jāmātṛi-muni,** m. N. of an author, Cat. **-tara,** mfn. better, very good (*am,* ind.), BhP. **-tā,** f., **-tva,** n. beauty, excellence, Kāv. **-dāsa,** m., **-deva,** m. N. of authors, Cat. **-nanda,** m. (cf. *sundarân°*) N. of a man, Buddh. **-pāṇḍya-deva,** m. N. of a king (v.l. *sundara-vīra-pāṇḍya*), Kāv. **-pura,** n. 'beautiful town,' N. of a city; *-māhātmya,* n. N. of a ch. of the Brahmâṇḍa-purāṇa. **-bāhu-stava,** m. N. of a Stotra. **-maṇi-saṃdarbha,** m. N. of a wk. (on devotion to Rāma, by Madhurâcārya). **-miśra,** m. (with *Aujjāgari*) N. of the author of the Abhirāma-maṇi-nāṭaka. **-m-manya,** mfn. thinking one's self handsome or beautiful, Daśar. **-rāja,** m. N. of two authors, Cat.; °*jīya,* n. N. of an astron. wk. **-laharī,** f. N. of wk. **-vaṇśa,** m. N. of a race or people, MBh. **-vatī,** f. N. of a river, L. **-varṇa,** m. N. of a Deva-putra, Lalit. **-vīra-pāṇḍya,** see *sundara-pāṇḍya-deva.* **-śukla,** m. N. of the author of the Mauna-mantrâvabodha. **-śṛiṅgāra,** m., **-siddhânta,** m. N. of wks. **-sena,** m. N. of a king, Kathās.; of a grammarian, Cat.; *-bhāshya,* n. N. of wk. **-haci** (?), m. N. of a prince, Buddh. **Sundarânanda,** m. (cf. *sundara-n°*) N. of two persons, Buddh.; Col. **Sundarâraṇya,** n. N. of a forest; *-māhātmya,* n. N. of a ch. of the Brahmâṇḍa-purāṇa. **Sundarêśvara,** m. N. of a form of Śiva; *-stotra,* n. N. of a Stotra.

Sundaraka, m. N. of a man, Daś.; Kathās.; (*ikā*), f., see next.

Sundarika, f. N. of a woman, Buddh. **-tīrtha,** n., **-hrada,** m. N. of Tīrthas, MBh.

Sundarī, f. a beautiful woman, any woman (also applied to female animals), Kāv.; VarBṛS. &c.; a kind of tree, Vās.; turmeric, L.; a partic. metre, Col.; N. of a deity (= *tripura-sundarī*), L.; of a Yoginī, L.; of an Apsaras, Bālar.; of a daughter of Sva-phalka, Hariv.; of a daughter of Vaiśvānara, VP.; of the wife of Mālyavat, R.; of various other women, Kathās. **-kalpa,** m., **-kavaca,** m. n. N. of wks. **-tāpanī** or **-tāpinī,** f. N. of an Upanishad (belonging to the AV.) **-devī,** f. N. of a princess, Inscr. **-pūjā-paddhati,** f., **-pūjā-ratna,** n. N. of wks. **-bhavana,** n. N. of a temple, Rājat. **-mandira,** n. women's habitation or apartments, Daś. **-śakti-dāna-stotra,** n., **-svayaṃvara,** m. N. of wks.

सुन्न *sunna,* m. N. of a man, Rājat.

सुन्यस्त *su-nyasta.* See p. 1226, col. 3.

सुन्वत् *sunvat, sunvāna.* See √3. *su,* p. 1219, col. 2.

सुप् *sup,* (in gram.) technical expression for the termination of the loc. case plural, Pāṇ. iv, 1, 2 &c.; a Pratyāhāra used as a term for all or for any one of the 21 case-terminations, ib. i, 1, 71 &c. **-tiṅ-anta,** n. an inflected noun or verb as ending with a case-termination or verbal term° (see *tiṅ*); *-paribhāshā,* f., *-sāgara-samuccaya,* m. N. of wks.

Sub, in comp. for *sup.* **-anta,** n. technical expression for an inflected noun as ending with a case-termination, Pāṇ. iii, 1, 106, Sch.; *-prakāśa,* m., *-prakriyā-sarvasva,* n., *-rūpâvalī,* f., *-vāda,* m., *-vyākhyāna,* n., *-śiromaṇi,* m., *-saṃgraha,* m. N. of wks. **-artha,** m. (prob.) the meaning of a case-termination; *-tattvâvaloka,* m., *-nirṇaya,* m., *-saṃgraha,* m. N. of wks. **-vibhakty-artha-viveka,** m. N. of wk.

सुपक्क *sú-pakva,* mf(*ā*)n. (i. e. 5. *su* + *p*°; √2. *pac*) well-cooked or matured, thoroughly ripe (lit. and fig.), AV.; Suśr.; Pañcar.; a sort of fragrant Mango, L.

Su (to be similarly prefixed to the following): **-pakshá,** mfn. beautiful-winged, AV. **-pakshman,** mfn. having beautiful eyebrows, VarBṛS. **-paṅka,** m. or n. (?) good clay or mud, Śṛiṅgār. **-paṭṭaka,** mfn. having a beautiful girdle, Hcat. **-paṭha,** mf(*ā*)n. easy to read, legible, Naish. **-patana,** mfn. flying well (= *-parṇá*), Nir. **-pati,** m. a good husband, Hariv. **-pattra,** n. 'beautiful leaf,' the leaf of Laurus Cassia, L.; mfn. having beautiful wings, Śiś.; well-feathered (as an arrow), R.; having a beaut° vehicle, Śiś.; having beaut° leaves, L.; m. N. of a mythical bird, MārkP.; Helianthus Annuus, L.; a sort of grass, = *pallivāha,* ib.; a kind of plant (= *āditya-pattra*), MW.; (*ā*), f. Asparagus Racemosus, L.; Glycine Debilis, ib.; Prosopis Spicigera, ib.; Beta Bengalensis, ib.; a kind of creeper (= *rudra-jaṭā*), ib.; = *śāla-parṇī,* MW.; (*ī*), f. a kind of plant (= *gaṅgā-pattrī*), L. **-pattraka,** m. Moringa Pterygosperma, L.; (*ikā*), f. Glycine Debilis, L.; = *jatukā,* ib. **-pattrita,** mfn. well-feathered (as an arrow), MBh.; Hariv. **-pattrin,** mfn. id., MBh.; R. **-pátnī,** f. (a woman) having a good husband or lord, RV.; AV.; VS. &c. **-páth,** m. (nom. *-panthās*) a good path, VS.; ŚBr.; Kāv. **-pátha,** m. n. a good road, RV.; virtuous course, good conduct, Kathās.; mfn. having a good road, h° beaut° paths, MW.; m. N. of a man, Cat. **-pathin,** m. (nom. *-panthās*) a good road, MW.; mf(°*thī*)n. having good roads, ib.; (°*thin*)-*tara,* m. a better r°, Pāṇ. viii, 2, 17, Sch. **-pathyà,** mfn. very wholesome, MW.; (*ā*), f. a sort of spinage, L.; n. a good path, VS. **-pad** (strong base *-pâd*), mf(*-pádī*)n. having good or beautiful feet, swift-footed, RV. **-pada,** n. a good word, MBh.; the word *su,* VPrāt. **-padma,** mfn. having beautiful lotuses, MW.; m. N. of a grammar; (*ā*), f. (prob.) Acorus Calamus, L.; *-dhātupāṭha,* m., *-pariśishṭa,* n., *-makaranda,* m., *-shaṭkāraka-vyākhyāna,* n., *-samāsa-saṃgraha,* m. N. of wks. **-panthās,** see *su-pathin* above. **-paptani,** f. (*ī,* instr.) swift flight, RV. **-payas,** mfn. having beautiful water, Nāg.; *-vin,* mfn. abounding in milk, Hcat.; °*yo-dharā,* f. having a beaut° udder, ib. **-parama-turitā,** f. (with Buddhists) N. of a deity, Kālac. **-parâkrama,** mfn. very powerful, MBh. **-parâñc,** mf(*ācī*)n. following one another well, Lāṭy. **-pari,** g. *saṃkāśâdi.* **-parika,** m. endearing form of *-paridatta* &c., Pāṇ. v, 3, 84, Sch. **-pariklishṭa,** mfn. sorely distressed, grievously pained, MW. **-paricchanna,** mfn. well furnished with requisites, ib. **-parijñāta,** mfn. well ascertained, Ratnâv. **-pariṇata,** mfn. well developed or formed, L. **-pariṇīta,** mfn. well accomplished, MBh. **-paridatta,** m. N. of a man, Pāṇ. v, 3, 84, Sch. **-paripūjita,** mfn. highly honoured, L. **-paripūrṇa,** mfn. very full, ib.; very complete, Hcat.; °*nôttamâṅga-tā,* f. having the head well developed (one of the 80 minor marks of a Buddha), Dharmas. 84. **-paribhāsha,** mf(*ā*)n. (prob.) containing good general definitions or applications, Cat. **-paribhūta,** mfn. greatly humiliated, Vajracch. **-pariya,** m. = *-parika,* Pāṇ. v, 3, 84, Sch. **-parirakshita,** mfn. well guarded, R. **-parila,** m. = *-parika,* Pāṇ. v, 3, 84, Sch. **-parivishṭa** (*sú-*), mfn. well prepared, VS. **-parivrāj,** m. a good monk, VarBṛS. **-pariśuddha,** mfn. very pure, L. **-pariśrānta,** mfn. completely exhausted, MBh.; *-vāha,* mfn. having very wearied horses, MW. **-parishkṛita,** mf(*ā*)n. well prepared, MBh.; well adorned, ib. **-parisruta,** mfn. well filtered, Suśr. **-parihara,** mfn. easy to avoid, Bādar., Sch. **-parîkshaṇa,** n. thorough examination, Kām. **-parîkshita,** mfn. well examined, Mn.; Kām. **-parîkshya,** mfn. easy to examine, Bcar. **-parusha,** mfn. very rough or boisterous (as wind), VarBṛS. **-parus,** mfn. having good knots (as an arrow), Śiś. **-parṇa,** n. a beautiful leaf, R.; (°*ṇá*), mf(*ī*)n. having beaut° leaves, L.; having beaut° wings, RV.; m. any large bird of prey (as a vulture, eagle; also applicable to the sun or moon as 'having beaut° rays,' and to *soma* and clouds; du. 'sun and moon'), ib.; any mythical or supernatural bird (often identified with Garuḍa, and sometimes personified as a Ṛishi, a Deva-gandharva, and an Asura), RV.; TS.; Kāṭh.; MBh.; a ray, Naigh.; a horse, ib.; Nir.; a cock, MW.; a partic. array (as of an army), MBh.; Cassia Fistula, L.; N. of a son of Antariksha (v.l. *-varṇa*), VP.; of a mountain, BhP.; m. n. a partic. section of 103 Vedic verses, MBh.; (*ā*), f. a lotus plant, a pool abounding with lotuses, L.; N. of the mother of Garuḍa or of the Prājāpatya Āruṇi Suparṇeya, BhP.; NārUp.; of a river, VP.; (*ī*), f. a partic. personification (mentioned together with Kadrū, sometimes identified with Vāc and regarded as the mother of metres), TS.; Kāṭh.; ŚBr.; = *garuḍī,* MBh.; the mother of Su-parṇa, Suparṇ.; N. of one of the seven tongues of fire, Gṛihyās.; night, Nir.; a species of creeper (= *palāśī*), L.; a partic. drug (= *reṇukā*), ib.; *-ketu,* m. 'having Garuḍa for a symbol,' N. of Vishṇu-Kṛishṇa, MBh.; BhP.; Śiś.; *-cit,* mfn. heaped up or moulded into the form of the bird Su-parṇa, VS.; ŚBr.; *-citi,* f., *-citi-dīpikā,* f., *-citi-paddhati,* f. N. of wks.; *-citya,* mfn. = *-cit,* Cat.; *-yātu* (°*ṇá-*), m. a partic. demon, RV.; *-rāja,* m. N. of Garuḍa, R.; *-vāta,* m. the wind agitated by the wings of Garuḍa, MW.; *-sád,* mfn. sitting on the bird Su-p°, TS.; *-súvana,* mfn. serving as the breeding-place of eagles, AV.; °*ṇâkhya,* m. Mesua Roxburghii, L.; °*ṇâkhyāná,* n. the story of Su-p°, Suparṇ.; °*ṇâṇḍa,* m. the son of a Śūdra and a Sūta, L.; °*ṇâdhyāya,* m. N. of wk.; °*ṇī-tanaya,* m. 'son of Su-parṇī,' Garuḍa, L. **-parṇaka,** mfn. having beautiful leaves, W.; having good wings, ib.; m. Garuḍa or any supernatural bird, W.; Cassia Fistula, L.; Alstonia Scholaris, ib.; Echites Scholaris, W.; (*ikā*), f. Glycine Debilis, L.; Hoya Viridiflora, ib.; Vernonia Anthelminthica, Bhpr.; = *śāla-parṇī,* MW.; a partic. drug (= *reṇukā*), L.; *-kumāra,* m. pl. (with Jainas) a partic. class of deities, L. **-parṇin,** m. Garuḍa, Buddh. **-parṇeya,** m. (accord. to Sāy.) metron. fr. Su-parṇā, NārUp. **-paryavadāta,** mfn. very clean, ib. **-paryavasita,** mfn. well carried out, MBh.; °*târtha,* mfn. thoroughly acquainted with anything, ib. **-paryāpta,** mfn. very spacious (as a house), Mn. vii, 76; very plentiful, R.; well filled or fitted out (as a palace with various rooms and buildings), W.; perfectly equal to or a match for anything (dat.), R. **-paryāśīr-datta,** m. N. of a man, Pāṇ. v, 3, 84, Vārtt. 1, Pat. **-parvaṇa,** mfn. highly extolled, MBh. **-parvata,** m. N. of a Sādya, Hariv. **-parvan,** m. a good period of time, Kāśīkh.; mfn. having beautiful joints or knots, MBh.; R. &c.; having beautiful sections (said of books), Vās.; highly extolled, Kām.; Inscr.; m. cane, bamboo, L.; an arrow, ib.; smoke, ib.; a god, deity, Kāśīkh.; Kāv.; = *parvan,* L.; a special lunar day (in which religious ceremonies are performed, as the full and new moon, and the 8th and 14th days of each fortnight), MW.; N. of a being reckoned among the Viśve Devāḥ, Hariv.; of a son of the 10th Manu, MārkP.; of a son of Antariksha, VP.; of a teacher, Pat. **-parvā,** f. white Dūrvā grass, L. **-palāyita,** mfn. well fled, W.; n. skilful or well-managed retreat, total rout, MBh.; Hit. **-palāśá,** mfn. having many or beautiful leaves, RV.; Nir. **-pavi,** mfn. having good tires (said of wheels), AV. **-pavitra,** n. a kind of metre, Col. **-paścāt,** ind. very late in the evening, Baudh. **-pākaka,** mf(*ikā*)n., Pāṇ. vii, 3, 46, Vārtt. 2, Pat. **-pākinī,** f. a species of Curcuma, L. — **pākya**, n. a kind of salt, ib. — **pāñcālaka**, Pat. on Pāṇ. i, 1, 72, Vārtt. 17. — **pāṭala**, m. N. of a monkey, R. — **pāṭhaka**, mfn. reciting well, Hcat. — **pāṇi**, mfn. having good or beautiful hands, RV.; VS.; dexterous-handed, RV. — **pāṇḍara**, mfn. beautifully white, R. — **pātra**, m. (more correctly *-yātra*) N. of a man, Vās., Introd.; n. a beautiful cup or receptacle, Pañcar.; a very fit or worthy person (esp. to receive gifts), Kāv.; Pañcat. &c. — **pāda**, mfn. having handsome feet, MBh. — **pāna**, mfn. easy to be drunk, Pāṇ., Sch.; Vop.; °*nânna*, n. sg. good drinkables and eatables, VarBṛS. — **pāman**, m. N. of a man, g. *tikâdi*. — **pārá**, mf(*ā́*)n. easy to be crossed, RV.; easy to be borne, ib.; quickly passing off (as rain), ib.; leading to a prosperous issue, ib.; TS.; m. a partic. personification, SāmavBr.; Gaut.; (*ā*), f. (in Sāṃkhya) one of the 9 kinds of Tushṭi, Tattvas.; *-kshatra* (°*pā-rá-*), mfn. easily traversing his realm (said of Varuṇa), RV.; *-ga*, m. N. of the captain of a ship, Jātakam. (n. his abode). — **pāraṇa**, mfn. easy to be gone through or studied, Hariv. — **pārśva**, mf(*ā*)n. having beautiful sides, MBh.; m. a beaut° side, ib.; Ficus Infectoria, L.; Hibiscus Pupulneoides, L.; N. of a Rākshasa, R.; of a fabulous bird (son of Sampāti), ib.; of a son of Rukma-ratha, Hariv.; of a son of Śrutāyu, VP.; of a son of Dṛiḍha-nemi, BhP.; of the 7th Arhat of the present Avasarpiṇī, L.; of a mountain, MBh.; Pur. &c.; °*vôru*, mfn. having beautiful ribs and thighs, MW. — **pārśvaka**, m. Ficus Infectoria, Bhpr.; N. of a son of Citraka, Hariv.; of a son of Śrutāyu, BhP.; of the third Arhat of the future Utsarpiṇī, L. — **pāli**, mfn. (ifc.) well provided with, distinguished by, Hcat. — **pāvá**, mfn. well clarified (as Soma), TS. — **pāśa**, mfn. (prob.) having a good noose (said of Gaṇêśa), Cat.; (*ā́*), f. a strong noose, AV. — **piṅgalā**, f. Cardiospermum Halicacabum, L.; another plant (*=jīvantī*), ib. — **pitrya**, mfn. maintaining the paternal (character) well, RV. — **pidhāna**, mf(*ā*)n. well closed or locked up, MBh. — **pippalá**, mf(*ā́*)n. bearing good berries, RV.; VS.; AV. &c. — **píś**, mfn. (perhaps) having fine ornaments, well-formed, graceful, RV. — **pishṭa**, m. N. of a man, g. *śivâdi*; pl. his descendants, g. *upakâdi*. — **pis**, mfn. going well, Pāṇ., Sch.; Vop. — **pihita-vat**, mfn. having (the ears, acc.) carefully closed, Kāv. — **pīḍana**, n. the act of pressing strongly, L. — **pīḍita**, mfn. well pressed, MW. — **pīta**, mfn. quite yellow, MBh.; m. N. of the 5th Muhūrta, IndSt.; n. a carrot, L.; yellow sandal, ib. — **pīna**, mfn. very fat or big, R. — **pīvan**, mfn. id., Pāṇ. iii, 2, 74, Sch.; drinking well, L. — **pīvás**, mfn. *=-pīna*, RV. — **pú** or **-pū́**, mfn. clarifying well, VS.; AV. — **puṃsī**, f. a woman who has a good husband, Uṇ., Sch. — **puṅkha**, mfn. having a fine shaft, well-feathered (as an arrow), MBh.; R. — **puṭa**, mf(*ā*)n. having beautiful nostrils, VarBṛS.; m. N. of two bulbous plants, L. — **puṇya**, mfn. very excellent, MBh.; n. great religious or moral merit, Kāv.; *-gandha*, mfn. having an exc° smell, very fragrant, MBh.; *-da*, mfn. giving gr° merit, very meritorious, Pañcar. — **putra**, m. an excellent son, Kāv.; (°*trá*), mf(*ā́*)n. having exc° or many children, RV.; AV.; TBr. &c.; n. the fruit of the Flacourtia Cataphracta, L. — **putrikā**, f. a kind of Oldenlandia, L. — **pura**, n. a strong fortress, Hariv. — **purusha**, m. a partic. personification, SāmavBr.; Gaut. — **puru-hūti**, mfn. very much invoked, BhP. — **purodhas**, m. a good domestic priest, Inscr. — **pushkara**, m. a globe-amaranth, L.; (*ā*), f. Hibiscus Mutabilis, ib. — **pushkala**, mfn. very copious, MBh.; BhP. — **pushṭa**, mfn. well fed, Pañcat. — **pushṭi**, f. good prosperity, AV. — **pushpa**, n. 'good flower,' cloves, L.; the menstrual excretion, ib.; mfn. having beaut° flowers, Kāv.; m. Pterospermum Suberifolium, L.; globe-amaranth, ib.; *=rakta-pushpaka*, ib.; *=haridru*, ib.; the coral tree, W.; N. of a mythical king, Inscr.; (*ā*), f. (only L.) anise; (prob.) Phlomis Zeylanica; Clitoria Ternatea; *=kośātakī*; (*ī*), f. (only L.) Andropogon Aciculatus; Clitoria Ternatea; anise; Argyreia Speciosa; Phlomis Zeylanica; Musa Sapientum; a white-flowering Aparājitā; n. (only L.) Curcuma Longa; Hibiscus Mutabilis; Tabernæmontana Coronaria; *=tūla*. — **pushpaka**, m. Acacia Sirissa, L.; (*ikā*), f. (only L.) Argyreia Speciosa or Argentea; Bignonia Suaveolens; Anethum Sowa. — **pushpita**, mfn. having beautiful flowers, abounding with flowers (*e*, ind. 'on a place abounding with flowers'), MBh.; R.; having the hair bristling (with delight), MW. — **pushya**, m. N. of a Buddha, Lalit. — **pū́**, see *-pú*. — **pūjita**, mfn. highly honoured, MBh.; R.; (a cup) taken well care of, i. e. well cleansed, VarBṛS. — **pūta** (*sú-*), mfn. well clarified, ṚV. — **pūra**, mf(*ā*)n. easy to be filled, MBh.; Pañcat.; well filling, MW.; m. a citron, L. — **pūraka**, m. id., ib.; Agati Grandiflora, ib. — **pūrṇa** (*sú-*), mf(*ā*)n. well filled, quite full, RV.; VS.; ĀśvŚr. &c.; richly adorned with (instr.), MBh. — **pūrvam**, ind. very early in the morning, Baudh. (w.r. °*vām*); °*vâhṇe*, ind. early in the forenoon, AitBr.; ŚrS. — **pṛ́iksh**, mfn. abounding with food, RV. — **peśa**, m. fine woven cloth or texture of any kind, BhP.; mfn. *=-péśas*, ib. — **peśala**, mf(*ā*)n. very beautiful or handsome, ib. — **péśas**, mfn. well adorned, beautiful, handsome, RV.; VS.; TBr. &c. — **póśha**, mfn. prosperous, VS.; TBr.; easy to be maintained, not requiring much support (*-tā*, f.), L. — **pta** (fr. *su+ptā*; for *supta* see p. 1230), mfn. having beaut° braids of hair, Kād.; m. a wagtail with a black breast, L. — **prakāśa**, mf(*ā*)n. well-lighted, Kathās.; very or distinctly visible, Mn. viii, 245; very public, W. — **prakīrṇêndriya**, mfn. addicted to too frequent seminal effusion (i. e. to sexual excess), VarBṛS. — **praketá**, mfn. very bright, conspicuous, notable, RV.; very attentive, ib.; (*-prá-keta*), very considerate or wise, ib. — **prakshālita**, mfn. well washed, MBh.; Car.; Vishṇ. — **prakhya**, m. N. of a man (see *sauprakhya*). — **pragamana**, mfn. very accessible, Nir. — **pragupta**, mfn. well hidden, very secret, Kāv. — **pracāra**, mfn. going in a right course (also said of planets), Hariv.; appearing beautifully, MBh. — **prácetas**, mfn. very wise, RV. — **pracchanna**, mfn. well concealed, Daś. — **prajá**, mf(*ā*)n. having good or numerous children (*-tama*), RV.; MBh.; R. &c.; °*jā-pati*, m. a good Prajā-pati (Vishṇu), Vishṇ.; °*jâ-vat*, mfn. abounding in children, RV.; °*jā-vâni*, mfn. bestowing many children, VS.; TS. — **prajás**, mfn. *=-prajá*; having a good son ('in any one,' instr.; *-tva*, n.), RV.; AV.; VS. &c. — **prajāta**, mfn. having numerous offspring, Hariv. — **prajās-tvá**, n. the having many children, RV.; VS.; TS. — **prajña**, mf(*ā*)n. very wise, MBh.; Kathās. — **prajñāná**, mfn. easy to be perceived or found, MaitrS.; Kāṭh. — **práṇīti**, f. safe guidance, RV.; ŚāṅkhŚr.; mfn. guiding safely, RV.; AV.; Kauś.; following good guidance, RV. — **pratara**, mf(*ā*)n. easy to be crossed (as a river), Ragh.; easily crossing over, MW.; projecting far (?), ib. — **pratarka**, m. a sound judgment, good understanding or intellect, MW. — **pratardana**, m. N. of a king, ib. — **pratāra**, mf(*ā*)n. well conveying over (as a ship), R. — **pratikara**, mfn. easy to be requited, ib. — **pratigṛihīta** (*sú-*), mfn. well seized, ŚBr. — **praticáksha**, mfn. beautiful to look at, RV. — **praticchanna**, mfn. completely covered or enveloped (as with a garment), L.; (*am*), ind. in a very secret manner, MBh. — **praticchinna**, mfn. well distributed, L. — **pratijña**, m. N. of a Dānava, Kathās. — **pratipanna**, mfn. leading a virtuous course of life, well-conducted, L. — **pratipūjita**, mfn. well honoured or worshipped, MBh. — **pratibhā**, f. spirituous liquor, ib. — **pratima**, m. N. of a king, MBh. — **prativarman**, m. N. of a man, Pañcat. — **pratividdha**, mfn. well hit or pierced (with *dṛishṭyā*, 'well looked through'), L. — **pratiśraya**, mfn. possessing good shelter, R. — **pratishṭha**, mf(*ā*)n. standing firm, Sāy.; firmly supporting, Ml.; having beautiful legs, MBh.; very celebrated, famous, MW.; m. a kind of military array, Kām.; N. of the 2nd month, IndSt.; a partic. Samādhi, Buddh.; (*ā*), f. firm position, ŚvetUp.; good reputation, fame, W.; the establishment (of a temple, idol &c.), ib.; installation, consecration, ib.; a kind of metre, Nidānas.; RAnukr., Sch.; Chandom.; N. of one of the Mātṛis attending on Skanda, MBh. — **pratishṭhānā́**, mfn. standing firm, VS. — **pratishṭhāpita**, mfn. well established or set up (as an image), Kathās. — **pratishṭhita** (*sú-*), mf(*ā*)n. standing firm, AV.; MBh.; Pañcat.; properly set up or established, Hit.; thoroughly implanted in (loc.), ib.; well consecrated, W.; celebrated, ib.; faring well, R.; 'well supported,' having beaut° legs, MBh.; R.; m. Ficus Glomerata, L.; a partic. Samādhi, Kāraṇḍ.; N. of a Deva-putra, Lalit.; (*ā*), f. N. of an Apsaras, VP.; n. N. of a town in Pratishṭhāna, Kathās.; *-caraṇa*, m. a partic. Samādhi, Kāraṇḍ.; *-cāritra*, m. N. of a Bodhi-sattva, Buddh.; *-pāṇi-pāda-tala-tā*, f. the having the palms of the hands and soles of the feet well (and equally) placed (one of the 32 signs of perfection), Dharmas. 83; *-yaśas*, mfn. one whose renown is well established, Ratnâv.; °*tâsana*, m. a partic. Samādhi, Kāraṇḍ. — **pratishṇāta**, mfn. well bathed, MW.; thoroughly purified or cleared, ib.; well versed in, ib.; well investigated, clearly ascertained, ib.; *-sūtra*, m. a Brāhman well versed in the Sūtras, one who is well skilled in repeating or has clearly ascertained the (meaning of the) S°, ib. — **prátīka**, mf(*ā*)n. having a beautiful shape or form, handsome, lovely, RV.; AV.; VS. &c.; having a beautiful face, MW.; having a beaut° trunk, strong as an elephant's tr°, ib.; honest, BhP.; m. N. of Śiva, Śivag.; of Kāma-deva, L.; of a Yaksha, Kathās.; of various men, MBh.; Pur.; Kathās.; of a mythical elephant (°*kânvaya*, mfn., L.), MBh.; Ragh.; Vās.; n. N. of a pool, Kāśīkh.; °*kêśvara*, n. N. of a Liṅga, ib. — **pratīkinī**, f. the female of the elephant Su-pratīka, L. — **pratīta**, mfn. well known, Sāh.; m. N. of a preceptor, VBr. — **pratīpa**, m. N. of a king, VP. — **pratúr**, mfn. (nom. °*tū́s*) very victorious, RV. — **prátūrti**, mfn. id., ib.; TS.; TBr. — **prátyañc**, mf(*tīcī*)n. well turned back, VS. — **pratyavasita**, mfn. (perhaps) safely returned to one's own country, Kāś. — **pratyūḍha** (°*yūḷha*), mfn. properly pushed back, ŚāṅkhŚr. — **pradadi** (*sú-*), mfn. very liberal, AV. — **pradarśa**, mf(*ā*)n. of beaut° appearance, MBh. — **pradohā**, f. easily milked, ib. — **pradhṛishya**, mfn. easy to be injured or overpowered, ib. — **pranṛitta**, n. a beaut° dance, R. — **prapañca-hīna**, mfn. destitute of variety, NṛisUp. — **prapāṇá**, n. a good drinking-place, RV.; mfn. easy or fit for drinking, ib.; AV. — **prabala**, mfn. very powerful, MBh. — **prabuddha**, mfn. completely enlightened (as a Buddha), Buddh.; m. N. of a king of the Śākyas, ib. — **prabha**, mf(*ā*)n. having a good appearance, beautiful, MBh.; Hariv.; R.; very bright or splendid, glorious, W.; m. N. of a Dānava, Hariv.; of a Deva-putra, Kathās.; of one of the 9 Balas of the Jainas, L.; of various kings, VP.; Cat.; (*ā*), f. Vernonia Anthelminthica, L.; one of the 7 tongues of Fire, Tantras.; N. of one of the Mātṛis attending on Skanda, MBh.; of a Surâṅganā, Siṃhâs.; of various women, MBh.; Pur. &c.; of one of the 7 Sarasvatīs, MBh.; n. N. of a Varsha ruled by Su-prabha, VP.; *-deva*, m. N. of a man, Cat.; *-pura*, n. N. of a town, ib. — **prabhava-deva**, w.r. for *-prabha-d°*, Sis. — **prabhāta**, mf(*ā*)n. beautifully illuminated by dawn, R.; (*ā*), f. N. of a river, BhP.; n. a beautiful dawn or daybreak, Kāv.; the earliest dawn, MW.; a morning prayer, VāmP.; (*e*), ind. at earliest break of day, MW.; *-stotra*, n. N. of wk. — **prabhāva**, m. great might, omnipotence, R. — **prabheda-tantra**, n., **-prabheda-pratishṭhā-tantra**, n. N. of wks. — **pramadhu**, m. N. of a Brāhman, Buddh. — **pramaya**, mfn. easily measured, Pāṇ. vi, 1, 50, Vārtt. 2, Pat. — **pramāṇa**, mfn. large-sized, Hcat. — **prayás**, mfn. well regaled, RV.; VS.; food-bestowing, MW. — **prayā́**, mfn. pleasant to tread on, RV. — **prayâvan**, mfn. moving well along, swift (said of horses), ib. — **prayukta**, mfn. well discharged (as an arrow), L.; well recited, Sāh.; well planned (as a fraud), Pañcat.; Vet. &c.; well joined or applied or attached, W.; well managed, ib.; closely connected, ib.; *-śara*, m. one who fits an arrow skilfully on a bow, a good marksman, skilful archer, MW. — **prayoga**, m. good application, good management, ib.; dexterity, expertness, ib.; close contact, ib.; mfn. well discharged, L.; easy to be acted (as a drama), Sāh.; (*ā*), f. N. of a river, MBh.; Pur.; *-viśikha*, m. *= su-prayukta-śara*, MW. — **pralambha**, mfn. easily deceived, Pāṇ. vii, 1, 67, Sch.; easy of attainment, W. — **pralāpa**, m. good speech, eloquence, L. — **pravācaná**, mfn. worthy of much praise, RV. — **pravādita**, mfn. making good music, Hariv. — **pravṛikṇa**, mf(*ā*)n. well cut up (used in explaining *ūrj*), Nir. — **pravṛikti**, f. *=-vṛikti*, ib. — **pravṛitta**, mfn. being well in order, MBh.; acting well, Hariv. — **pravṛiddha**, mfn. full-grown, ib.; m. N. of a Sauvīraka, MBh. — **pravedita**, mfn. well made known, Buddh. — **pravepita**, mfn. trembling much, R. — **praveśa**, mf(*ā*)n. having a beautiful entrance, MBh. — **pravrajita**, mfn. wandering well about (as a mendicant), i. e. a good or proper monk, Buddh. — **praśaṃsita**, mfn. greatly praised, very famous, Pañcar. — **praśastá**, mfn. greatly praised, excellent, AV.; well known, very famous, Pañcar. — **praśna**, m. (prob.) *= su-kha-p°*, MBh. — **prasanna**, mf(*ā*)n. very clear (as water), ib.; R.; very bright or serene (as the face or mind), Pañcat.; Hit. &c.; very gracious or favourable, MārkP.; m. N. of Kubera, L. — **prasannaka,** m. Ocimum Pilosum, L.; = *kṛishṇârjaka*, MW. — **prasarā,** v.l. for *-prasārā*, L. — **prasava,** m. easy parturition, Sāy. — **prasāda,** m. extreme graciousness or propitiousness, MW.; mfn. easily placable, Mn.; MBh.; R.; very gracious or kind, auspicious, MW.; m. N. of Śiva, L.; of one of Skanda's attendants, MBh.; of an Asura, Hariv.; (*ā*), f. N. of one of the Mātṛis attending on Skanda, MBh. — **prasādaka,** mfn. = *-prasāda*, ib. — **prasādhita,** mfn. well adorned, Kathās. — **prasārā,** f. Pæderia Fœtida, L. — **prasārita,** mf(*ā*)n. widely extended, R. — **prasiddha,** mfn. well known, Sāh.; Kshitîś.; *-pada-mañjarī*, f. N. of wk. — **prasū,** f. well or easily bringing forth, ŚāṅkhGṛ. — **prahāra,** m. a well dealt blow, Hariv. (v.l. *samprah°*); N. of a fisherman, Kathās. — **prākāra,** m. a beautiful wall or rampart, Inscr. — **prākṛita,** mf(*ā*)n. very vulgar, R. — **prāñc** (*sú-*), mfn. (nom. *prāṅ*, *prācī*, *prāk*) going straight forward, RV.; VS. — **prāta,** mfn. (fr. next) dawning beautifully, Bhaṭṭ.; n. a fine morning, Śiś. — **prātár,** ind. fine dawn or morning, AV. — **prātiveśmika,** mfn. having a good neighbour, HYogay. — **prâpa,** mfn. easily obtainable, MBh.; R. — **prâpya,** mfn. id. (in *a-supr°*), Kathās. — **prâyaṇá,** mf(*ā́*)n. easily to be approached, pleasant to be trodden (superl. *-tama*), RV. — **prāvargá,** mfn. (for *su-prav°*) well distinguished, RV. — **prâví** or **-prâvyà,** mfn. very attentive or mindful, v° zealous, ib. — **priya** (*sú-*), mf(*ā*)n. very dear or pleasant, AV. &c. &c.; m. (in prosody) a foot of two short syllables, a pyrrhic, Col.; N. of a Gandharva, Buddh.; (*ā*), f. a lovely woman or favourite wife, MW.; N. of an Apsaras, MBh.; Hariv.; of a peasant girl, Lalit.; *°yâtman*, mfn. having a pleasant nature, very agreeable, R. — **prīta** (*sú-*), mf(*ā*)n. very delighted, well pleased with (loc.), RV. &c. &c.; much cherished, very dear or lovely, Pañcar.; very kind or friendly, MW. — **prīti,** f. great joy or delight; *-kara*, m. 'causing gr° d°,' N. of a king of the Kiṃnaras, Buddh.; *-yukta*, mf(*ā*)n. filled with great joy or delight, R. — **prâitu,** mfn. easy to be gone through or traversed, RV. — **prôkshita,** mfn. well sprinkled, Vishṇ. — **prauḍha,** mfn. full-grown; (*ā*), f. a marriageable girl, Subh. — **psáras,** mfn. enjoying a good meal, fond of dainty food (superl. *-tama*), RV. — **phála** or **-phalá,** mf(*ā*)n. yielding much or good fruit, fruitful, RV.; AV.; having a good blade (as a sword), MBh.; m. (only L.) the wood-apple tree, Feronia Elephantum; the citron tree; Pterospermum Acerifolium; the pomegranate tree; Zizyphus Jujuba; Phaseolus Mungo; (*ā*), f. (only L.) Momordica Mixta; Gmelina Arborea; a kind of brown grape; colocynth; Beninkasa Cerifera; Musa Sapientum. — **phalī-√kṛi** (*sú-*), P. *-karoti*, to cleanse well from husks, GṛŚrS. — **phālá** or **-phála,** m. a good ploughshare, AV.; MaitrS. — **phulla,** mfn. flowering beautifully, having beaut° blossoms, R. — **phena** (*sú-*), mf(*ā*)n. containing good foam, TS; m. a cuttle-fish bone, L. — **baddhá,** mf(*ā́*)n. bound fast, RV.; firmly closed, clenched, Hariv. — **bandha,** mfn. well bound or secured, having a good binding, W.; m. sesamum, L. — **bandhana-vimocana,** m. 'good deliverer from bonds,' N. of Śiva, MBh. — **bándhu** or **-bandhú,** mfn. closely connected or related, good friend, RV.; AV.; Bhartṛ.; m. N. of a Ṛishi (having the patr. Gaupāyana or Laupāyana and author of various hymns in RV.), Anukr.; N. of the author of the Vāsava-dattā (who prob. lived in 7th century A.D.); of a merchant, Kathās.; of various other persons, HPariś. — **babhru,** mfn. dark brown, MBh. — **barhís,** mfn. having good sacrificial grass, RV.; VS. — **bala,** m. 'very powerful,' N. of Śiva, MBh.; of a mythical bird (son of Vainateya), ib.; of a son of Manu Bhautya, MārkP.; of a son of Sumati, VP.; of a king of the Gāndhāras (father of Śakuni and the wife of Dhṛita-rāshṭra), MBh.; Hariv.; BhP.; *-candra*, m. (with *ācārya*) N. of an author, Cat.; *-putra*, m. 'son of Subala,' N. of Śakuni (cf. *saubala*), MBh.; *-vat*, mfn. very strong or powerful, Pracaṇḍ. — **bahu,** mf(*vī*)n. very much, very many, very numerous, Mn.; MBh. &c.; (*u*), ind. much, very much, greatly, BhP.; *-dhā*, ind. very much, often, frequently, Hcat.; *-śas*, ind. id., MBh.; MārkP.; *-śruta*, mfn. deeply versed in the Veda &c., R. — **bāndhava,** m. 'good friend,' N. of Śiva, MBh. — **bāla,** mfn. very childish, R.; m. a good boy, Bcar. xiii, 36; a god, L.; n. N. of an Upanishad; (*°lā*)-*grāma*, m. N. of a village, Cat. — **bālaka,** m. N. of the author of a Kāma-śāstra, ib. — **bāladhi,** see *-vāladhi*. — **bāliśa,** mf(*ā*)n. very childish or foolish, MBh. — **bāhú,** mfn. having strong or handsome arms, RV.; VS.; m. N. of a serpent-demon, MBh.; of one of Skanda's attendants, ib.; of a Dānava, Hariv.; of a Rākshasa, ib.; R. (cf. *-śatru*); of a Yaksha, VP.; of a son of Dhṛita-rāshṭra and king of Cedi, MBh.; of a king of Videhā, Buddh.; of a son of Mati-nāra, Hariv.; of a son of Citraka, ib.; of a son of Kṛishṇa, BhP.; of a son of Śatru-ghna, R.; of a son of Pratibāhu, BhP.; of a son of Kuvalayâśva, MārkP.; of a brother of Alarka, ib.; of a Bodhi-sattva and a Bhikshu, Buddh.; of a monkey, R.; (*ús*), f. N. of an Apsaras, MBh.; *-paripṛicchā*, f. N. of wk.; *-yukta*, m. N. of a king of the Gandharvas, Kāraṇḍ.; *-śatru*, m. N. of Rāma, Uttarar. — **bāhuka,** m. N. of a Yaksha, VP. — **bīja,** n. good seed, Mn. x, 69; m. 'having good seed,' N. of Śiva, MBh.; the poppy, L. — **bībhatsa,** mfn. very disgusting or hideous, MBh. — **buddhi,** f. good understanding, Pañcat.; mfn. of good und°, wise, clever, intelligent, Kāv.; Kathās. &c.; m. N. of a son of Māra-putra, Lalit.; of two kings, Kshitîś.; of a crow, Hit.; *-candra*, m. N. of a man, Buddh.; *-mat*, mfn. very intelligent or wise, Kathās.; *-miśra* and *-miśra-maheśvara*, m. N. of authors, Cat. — **búdha,** mf(*ā*)n. vigilant, AV. — **bodha,** m. right intelligence, good information or knowledge, BhP.; N. of an astron. wk.; (*ā*), f. N. of various Comms.; mf(*ā*)n. easy to be understood, easily taught, easy (*am*, ind.), Kāv.; Pañcat.; BhP.; *-kāra*, m. N. of an author, Cat.; *-jātaka*, n., *-pañcikā*, f., *-mañjarī*, f. N. of wks. — **bodhanā,** f. N. of a Tantra wk. — **bodhanī,** f. N. of various Comms. — **bodhikā,** f. N. of a Comm. on the Sārasvata-prakriyā. — **bodhinī,** f. N. of various Comms. (esp. on the Bhagavad-gītā, the Mitākshara, the Brahma-sūtras &c.); *-kāra*, m. the author of the Subodhinī (a gram. wk.), Cat. — **brahmaṇīya,** mfn. relating to the Subrahmaṇya (see next), Lāṭy., Sch. — **brahmaṇyá,** mfn. very kind or dear to Brāhmans (said of Vishṇu), Pañcar.; m. N. of one of the three assistants of the Udgātṛi priest, Br.; ŚrS.; MBh.; N. of Śiva, Śivag.; of Skanda or Kārttikeya, RTL. 211–218; of various authors &c. (also with *ācārya*, *paṇḍita*, *yajvan*, and *śāstrin*), Cat.; (*ā*), f. a partic. recitation of certain Mantras by the Udgātṛi priests (sometimes also the priest himself), Br.; ŚrS.; (*am*), n. (= f.) a partic. recitation, Hariv.; N. of a district in the south of India, Cat.; (*°ṇya*)-*kshetra-māhātmya*, n., *-pañca-ratna*, n., *-paddhati*, f., *-pūjā-vidhi*, m., *-prayoga*, m., *-māhātmya*, n., *-sahasra-nāman*, n., *-stotra*, n.; *°ṇyâshṭaka*, n. N. of wks. — **brahman,** m. a good Brāhman, ŚāṅkhŚr.; N. of a Deva-putra, Lalit.; n. the good Brahman, AitBr.; (*-bráhman*), mfn. attended with good prayers or having a good Brahman (priest), RV.; (*°ma*)-*bandhūka*, mfn., Kāś. on Pāṇ. vi, 2, 173; *-vāsudeva*, m. N. of the son of Vasu-deva in the form of Brahmā (i.e. of Kṛishṇa identified with the Creator), Tithyād. — **brāhmaṇa** (*sú-*), m. a good Brāhman, AV. — **bha,** n. (for *subha* see s. v.) an auspicious constellation, Bhadrab.; *-bodhârtha-mālā-paddhati*, f. N. of wk. — **bhaṃsas,** mfn. (prob.) having a beaut° mons Veneris, TBr. — **bhakti,** f. great devotion to or love for (*-tas*, 'out of great d°'), Hcat. — **bhakshya,** n. excellent food, Pañcat. — **bhága,** mf(*ā*)n. possessing good fortune, very fortunate or prosperous, lucky, happy, blessed, highly favoured, RV. &c. &c.; beautiful, lovely, charming, pleasing, pretty (voc. *subhaga* and *subhage*, often in friendly address), ib.; nice (ironical), Vās. (= *śobhana-paśu*, Sch.); liked, beloved, dear (as a wife), AV.; MBh.; R.; delicate, slender, thin, Car.; (ifc.) suitable for, Śak. (v.l.); (*am*), ind. beautifully, charmingly, Megh.; greatly, in a high degree (v.l. for *sutarām*), Śak.; m. N. of Śiva, Śivag.; borax, L.; Michelia Champaka, L.; Jonesia Asoka, L.; red Amaranth, L.; N. of a son of Subala, MBh.; (*ā*), f. good fortune (in this sense the loc. *āsu* seems to be used), PañcavBr.; a beloved or favourite wife, R. (cf. comp.); a five-year-old girl representing Durgā at festivals, L.; musk, L.; N. of various plants (a species of Musa; Glycine Debilis; Cyperus Rotundus &c.), L.; (in music) a partic. Rāgiṇī, Saṃgīt.; N. of a daughter of Pradhā, MBh.; of one of the Mātṛis attending on Skanda, ib.; of a kind of fairy, Buddh.; (*am*), n. good fortune; bitumen, L.; MW.; *-ṃ-karaṇa* (*°gáṃ-*), mf(*ī*)n. making happy, AV.; charming, enchanting, Rājat.; n. fascinating, winning (a woman), Cat.; *-tā*, f. love, conjugal felicity, VarBṛS.; *-tvá*, n. welfare, prosperity, RV.; PārGṛ.; favour, dearness (esp. of a wife), VarBṛS.; Vās.; *-mānin*, mfn. thinking one's self fortunate or pleasing, R.; Daś.; *-m-bhavishṇu*, mfn. becoming fortunate or pleasing, Pāṇ. iii, 2, 57; *-m-bhāvuka*, mfn. id., ib.; Dhūrtas.; *-m-manya*, mfn. (= *-mānin*), Daś. (*-bhāva*, m. 'self-conceit, vanity,' Megh.); *-saṃdeśa*, m. N. of a poem by Nārāyaṇa; *°gâkheṭa-bhūmi*, mfn. having fine hunting-grounds (*-tva*, n.), Kathās.; *°gā-tanaya*, m. the son of a beloved wife or of an honoured mother, R.; *°gânanda*, m. N. of a Prahasana (*-nātha*, m. N. of an author, Cat.); *°gârcana-candrikā*, f., *°gârcā-ratna*, n. N. of wks.; *°gā-suta*, m. (= *°gā-tanaya*), L.; *°gôdaya*, m. 'rise of prosperity,' N. of wk. (also *°ya-darpaṇa*, m.) — **bhagaya,** Nom. P. *°yati*, to make beautiful, adorn, BhP. — **bhaṅga,** mfn. easily broken, brittle, W.; m. the cocoa-nut tree, L. — **bhañjana,** m. a red species of Hyperanthera Morunga, L. — **bhaṭa,** m. a great warrior, champion, soldier, Kāv.; Kathās. &c.; N. of various men, Kathās.; of a poet (author of the drama Dūtâṅgada), Cat.; (*ā*), f. N. of a princess, Rājat.; (*°ṭa*)-*datta* and *-varman*, m. N. of two authors, Cat. — **bhaṭṭa,** m. a very learned man, MW.; a distinguished warrior (incorrect for *-bhaṭa*), ib. — **bhaṇita,** mfn. well spoken, Mālatīm. — **bhadra** (*sú-*), mf(*ā*)n. very glorious or splendid or auspicious or fortunate, RV.; MBh.; BhP.; m. Azadirachta Indica, L.; N. of Vishṇu, L.; (prob.) of Sanat-kumāra, Pañcar.; of a son of Vasu-deva, BhP.; of a son of Kṛishṇa, ib.; of a son of Idhma-jihva, ib.; of the last man converted by Gautama Buddha, SaddhP.; of a scholar, Jain.; of a mountain, Pañcar.; (*ā*), f. N. of various well-known plants (e.g. Ichnocarpus Frutescens; Curcuma Zedoaria; Prosopis Spicigera &c.), L.; (in music) a partic. Śruti, Saṃgīt.; a form of Durgā, Hcat.; N. of a younger sister of Kṛishṇa and wife of Arjuna (she was forcibly carried off by Arjuna from Dvārakā with Kṛishṇa's permission, as described in MBh. i, ch. 219; 220; her image is borne in procession with those of Jagannātha and Bala-rāma), MBh.; Hariv. &c.; of a wife of Durgama, MārkP.; of a daughter of Balin and wife of Avîkshita, ib.; of a granddaughter of Rukmin and wife of Aniruddha, VP.; of a daughter of the Asura Su-māya, Kathās.; of a mythical cow, MBh.; of a poetess, Cat.; n. fortune, welfare, BhP.; N. of a Catvara (q.v.), MBh.; of a Varsha in Plaksha-dvīpa ruled by Su-bhadra, BhP.; (*°drā*)-*dhanaṃjaya* and *-pariṇaya*, N. of two Nāṭakas; *-pūrvaja*, m. 'elder brother of Subhadrā,' N. of Kṛishṇa, Pañcar.; *-vijaya*, N. of a Nāṭaka; *-haraṇa*, n. 'the carrying off of Subhadrā,' N. of a section in the MBh. (cf. above) and of other poems; *°drêśa*, m. 'lord of S°,' N. of Arjuna, L. — **bhadraka,** m. the car or vehicle of a god for carrying his image in procession, L.; the plant Ægle Marmelos, L.; (*súbhadrikā*), f. a courtezan, VS.; a kind of metre, Ked.; of a younger sister of Kṛishṇa (see next), Pañcar.; (*am*), n. a kind of metre, Col. — **bhadrāṇī,** f. Ficus Heterophylla, L. — **bhayam-kara,** mfn. causing great fear or danger, MBh. — **bhayānaka,** mfn. causing great terror, very alarming, terrible, ib. — **bhára,** mf(*ā*)n. well compacted, solid, RV.; dense, abundant, ib.; easily carried or handled, ŚBr.; well practised, Mahāvy.; = *su-posha* (*-tā*, f.), ib. — **bhava,** mfn. = *uttama-janman*, VS. (Mahīdh.); m. N. of a king of the Ikshvākus, MBh. — **bhavas,** v.l. for prec., TS. — **bhavya,** mfn. very pretty or handsome, Hcat. — **bhasád,** mfn. having beaut° buttocks, καλλίπυγος (in compar. *°sáttarā*), RV. — **bhāgá,** mf(*ā́*)n. fortunate, wealthy, rich, RV.; (*ā*), f. N. of a daughter of Raudrâśva, VP. — **bhāgya,** mfn. very fortunate, enviable, R. — **bhājana,** n. a good receptacle or vessel of any kind, Suśr. — **bhānu,** mfn. shining beautifully or brightly, Kauś.; MBh.; m. N. of the 17th (or 51st) year of Jupiter's cycle of 60 years, VarBṛS.; of a son of Kṛishṇa, BhP. — **bhāvita,** mfn. well soaked, Suśr. — **bhāvi-tva,** n. the necessity of being good or excellent, Buddh. — **bhāshaṇa,** m. N. of a son of Yuyudhan, BhP. — **bhāshita,** mf(*ā*)n. spoken well or eloquently, MBh.; speaking or discoursing well, eloquent, ib.; m. a partic. Buddha, L.; (*am*), n. good or eloquent speech, witty saying, g° counsel, MBh.; Kāv. &c.; *-kāvya*, n., *-kaustubha*, m. N. of wks.; *-gaveshin*, m. N. of a king, Buddh.; *-candrikā*, f., *-nīvī*, f., *-prabandha*, m., *-mañjarī*, f. N. of wks.; *-maya*, mf(*ī*)n. consisting of good sayings, Pañcat.; *-muktâvali*, f., *-ratna-kośa*, m., *-ratna-saṃdoha*, m., *-ratnâkara*, m. N. of wks.; *-rasâsvāda-jāta-româñca-kañcuka*, mfn. having (as it were) armour consisting of bristling (or thrilling) hairs produced by tasting the flavour of delightful words, MW.; *-śloka*, m. pl., *-saṃgraha*, m., *-samuccaya*, m., *-sudhā*, f., *-sudhânanda-laharī*, f., *-sura-druma*, m., *-hārâvali*, f.; °*tārṇava*, m., °*tâvali*, f. N. of wks. **–bhāshin,** mfn. speaking friendly words, MBh.; spoken mildly or gently, Hariv. **–bhā́s,** mfn. shining beautifully, RV. **–bhāsa,** m. N. of a Dānava, Kathās.; of a son of Su-dhanvan, VP. **–bhāsvara,** mfn. shining brightly, radiant, splendid, R.; m. pl. N. of a class of deceased ancestors, VP. **–bhiksha,** mf(*ā*)n. having good food or an abundant supply of provisions, ChUp.; MBh. &c.; (*ā*), f. Lythrum Fructicosum or Grislea Tomentosa, L.; (*am*), n. abundance of food (esp. that given as alms), abundant supply of provisions, plenty (opp. to *dur-bh*°), MBh.; Kāv &c.; *-kara*, *-kārin*, *-kṛit;* °*kshâvaha*, mfn. causing abundance of food or good times, VarBṛS. **–bhishaj** (*sú-*), mfn. healing well (only superl. °*shak-tama*), AV. **–bhīta,** mfn. greatly afraid of (gen.), Pañcat. **–bhīma,** mfn. very dreadful or terrible, R.; m. N. of a malignant demon, MBh.; (*ā*), f. N. of a wife of Kṛishṇa, Hariv. **–bhīraka** or **-bhīrava,** m. the Palāśa tree, Butea Frondosa, L. **–bhīruka,** n. silver, L. **–bhukta,** mfn. well eaten, Pāṇ. vi, 2, 145, Sch. **–bhuja,** mfn. having handsome arms, Ragh.; (*ā*), f. N. of an Apsaras, VP. **–bhū́,** mfn. (n. pl. m. f. *-bhvàs*) of an excellent nature, good, strong, beautiful &c., RV. **–bhūtá,** mfn. well made or done (as food), Āpast.; (*ā*), f. that part of the frame enshrining the universal Spirit which faces the north, ChUp.; (*am*), n. welfare, well-being, AV.; Br.; *-kṛit*, mfn. causing w° or pr°, ĀpŚr. **–bhūti** (*sú-*), f. well-being, welfare; m. N. of a lexicographer (also called *-candra;* he wrote a Comm. on the Amara-kośa); of a Brāhman (son of Vasu-bhūti), Kathās.; of a teacher, Buddh.; *-pāla*, m. N. of a man, ib. **–bhūtika,** m. Ægle Marmelos, L. **–bhūma,** m. N. of Kārtavirya (as the 8th Jaina Cakra-vartin or universal emperor), L. **–bhūmi,** f. a good place, Gobh.; m. N. of a son of Ugra-sena (cf. next), VP.; *-pa*, m. N. of a son of Ugra-sena (v.l. *su-bhūshaṇa*), Hariv. **–bhūmika,** n. (or *ā*, f.) N. of a place near the Sarasvatī, MBh. **–bhūyas** (*sú-*), mfn. much more, far more, ŚBr. **–bhūshaṇa,** mf(*ā*)n. well adorned or decorated, Kām.; m., see *su-bhūmi-pa;* (*ā*), f. N. of a Kiṃnarī (cf. next), Kāraṇḍ.; *-bhūshitā*, f. N. of a Kiṃnarī, ib. **–bhṛita** (*sú-*), mfn. well borne or maintained, well cherished or protected, RV.; well paid, Kathās.; heavily laden, VarBṛS. **–bhṛiśa,** mfn. very vehement, very much, exceeding (*am*, ind. 'excessively'), MBh.; BhP. **–bheshaja** (*sú-*), mfn. a good remedy, AV.; TS.; n. 'collection of remedies,' N. of a Vedic book (perhaps the AV.), RPrāt. **–bhaiksha,** n. good alms, Hir. **–bhairava,** mf(*ī*)n. very fearful, W. **–bhogā,** f. N. of a Dikkumārī, Pārśvan. **–bhogīna,** mf(*ā*)n. very fit to be enjoyed, very desirable, Bhaṭṭ. **–bhogya,** mf(*ā*)n. easy to be enjoyed, Pañcat. **–bhoja,** mfn. eating well, MBh. **–bhojana,** n. good food, ib. **–bhójas,** mfn. bountiful, generous, plentiful, AV. **–bhrāj** (nom. *-bhrāṭ*) or **-bhrāja,** m. 'shining brightly,' N. of a son of Deva-bhrāj, MBh. **–bhrātṛi,** m. a good brother, Pāṇ. v, 4, 157, Sch. **–bhru** or **-bhrū,** f. a beautiful brow, Amar.; BhP.; mfn. (nom. sg. m. f. *-bhrū́s*, acc. m. f. *-bhruvam*, f. also *-bhrūm;* instr. f. *-bhruvā;* dat. *-bhruve* or °*vai;* abl. *-bhruvas* or °*vās;* gen. pl. *-bhrúvām* or *-bhrūṇām;* voc. sg. *-bhrūs* or generally *-bhru*, cf. Vām. v, 2, 50) lovely-browed, MBh.; Kāv. &c.; (*ūs*), f. a (l°-br°) maiden, ib.; N. of one of the Mātṛis attending on Skanda, MBh.; (*-bhrū́*)*-nāsâkshi-keśânta*, mfn. having handsome brows (and) nose (and) eyes (and) hair, MBh.

सुप्त *suptá*, mfn. (fr. √*svap;* for *su-pta* see p. 1228, col. 2) fallen asleep, slept, sleeping, asleep, VS. &c. &c.; lain down to sleep (but not fallen asleep), R. v, 34, 10; paralysed, numbed, insensible (see comp.); closed (as a flower), Kālid.; resting, inactive, dull, latent, BhP.; (*am*), n. sleep, deep or sound sleep, Kāv.; Kathās. **–ghātaka,** mfn. killing a sleeping person, murderous, L. **–ghna,** m. 'id.,' N. of a Rākshasa, R. **–cyuta,** mfn. fallen down in sleep, Kathās. **–jana,** m. a sleeping person, MW.; 'having every one asleep,' midnight (only in °*ne rātrau*, 'at midnight'), R.; *-prâya*, mfn. having almost every one asleep, MW. **–jñāna,** n. 'perceiving in sleep,' dreaming, a dream, L. **–tā,** f., **-tva,** n. sleepiness, numbness, insensibility (of a limb &c.), Suśr. **–tvac,** mfn. 'having the skin benumbed,' paralytic, ib. **–pūrva,** mfn. one who has slept before, MBh. **–prabuddha,** mfn. awakened from sleep, Kathās. **–pralapita,** n. pl. talking during sleep, Kām. (cf. Pāṇ. iii, 2, 149, Sch.) **–māṉsa,** mfn. 'having the flesh benumbed,' paralytic, Suśr. **–mālin,** m. N. of the 23rd Kalpa (q.v.) **–mīna,** mfn. (a pond) in which the fish are asleep, Ragh. **–vākya,** n. words spoken during sleep, Pañcat. **–vigraha,** mfn. 'having sleep for a body,' appearing as sleep (said of Kṛishṇa), Pañcar. **–vijñāna,** n. = *-jñāna*, L. **–vinidraka,** mfn. awaking from sleep, Kathās. **–stha** or **-sthita,** mfn. being in sleep, sleeping, ib. **Suptâṅga,** mfn. one who has a limb benumbed (*-tā*, f.), Suśr. **Suptâsupta,** mfn. asleep and awake, Mṛicch. **Suptôttitha,** mfn. arisen from sleep, Kāv.; Kathās.

Suptaka, n. sleep (*alīka-* or *vyāja-suptakam* √*kṛi*, 'to feign sleep'), Kathās.

Supti, f. sleep, (esp.) deep sleep, Śaṃk.; BhP.; sleepiness, drowsiness, Pratāp.; numbness, insensibility, paralysis, Suśr.; carelessness, confidence (= *viśrambha*), L.

सुप्लन् *súplan*, m. N. of a person (having the patr. Sārñjaya), ŚBr.

सुफल *su-phala* &c. See p. 1229, col. 1.

सुफालिह *suphāliha*, *suphālīha* or *suphāhila*, N. of a place, Cat.

सुबद्ध *su-baddha*, *su-bandha* &c. See p. 1229, col. 1.

सुब्रह्मण्य *su-brahmaṇya*, *su-brāhmaṇa*. See p. 1229, col. 2.

सुभ् *subh*, cl. 9. 6. P. *subhnāti*, *sumbhati*, (prob.) to smother (only impf. *asubhnan*, TS.; and pr. p. *sumbhan*, Kāṭh.); cl. 1. 6. P. *sobhati*, *sumbhati*, v.l. for √*śubh*, Dhātup. xi, 42.

Subdha, mfn. smothered, TS.

सुभ *subha*, mfn. (for *su-bha* see p. 1229, col. 2), often w.r. for *śubha*.

सुभक्ति *su-bhakti*, *-bhakshya*. See p. 1229, col. 2.

सुभग *su-bhaga*, *-bhaṅga* &c. See p. 1229, cols. 2, 3.

सुभाञ्जन *subhāñjana*, m. = *śobhâñjana*, Moringa Pterygosperma, L.

सुभ्वन् *súbhvan*, v.l. for *subhvan* (q.v.)

सुम *su-ma*, m. (i.e. 5. *su* + 4. *ma;* √3. *mā*) the moon, L.; the sky, atmosphere, L.; n. a flower (cf. *su-manas*), Cāṇ.; Śatr. **Sumâvali,** f. a garland of flowers (see *nīti-s*°).

Su (to be similarly prefixed to the following): **–makha** (*sú-*), mfn. very vigorous, very joyous or gay, RV.; having good sacrifices, Sāy.; n. a joyous festival or feast, ib. **–makhasya,** Nom. Ā. °*yate* (only pr. p. °*yámāna*), to be very joyous, make merry, TS. **–magadha,** m. pl. the happy Magadhas (*am*, ind.), Pat. on Pāṇ. ii, 1, 6; (*ā*), f. N. of a daughter of Anātha-piṇḍika, Buddh.; (*ī*), f. N. of a Buddhist Sūtra. **–maṅgala,** mf(*ī* or *ā*)n. bringing good fortune, very auspicious, RV. &c. &c.; well-conducted (= *sad-ācāra*), BhP.; m. N. of a preceptor, Cat.; (*ā*), f. a partic. medicinal root, L.; N. of one of the Mātṛis attending on Skanda, MBh.; of an Apsaras, Kāśīkh.; of a woman, Kathās.; of a river, KālP.; (*ī*), f. (*saṃjñāyām*), g. *gaurâdi;* n. an auspicious object, BhP.; *-nāman* (°*lá-*), mfn. bearing an auspicious name, ŚBr.; °*lâkhya-stotra*, n. N. of a Stotra. **–maṅgā,** f. N. of a river, VP. **–maṇi,** mfn. well adorned with jewels, AV.; m. N. of one of Skanda's attendants, MBh. **–maṇḍala,** m. N. of a king, MBh. **–mát** &c., see s.v. **–mata,** m. N. of a man, g. *naḍâdi*. **–matí,** f. good mind or disposition, benevolence, kindness, favour (acc. with √*kṛi*, 'to make any one the object of one's favour'), RV.; AV.; devotion, prayer, ib.; the right taste for, pleasure or delight in (loc.), R.; mfn. very wise or intelligent, Kāv.; Pañcat.; well versed in (gen.), Kathās.; m. N. of a Daitya, MBh.; Hariv.; of a Ṛishi under Manu Sāvarṇa, ib.; of a Bhārgava, MārkP.; of an Ātreya, Cat.; of a son or disciple of Sūta and teacher of the Purāṇas, VP.; of a son of Bharata, BhP.; of a son of Soma-datta, ib.; of a son of Su-pārśva, Hariv.; of a son of Janamejaya, VP.; of a son of Dṛiḍha-sena, BhP.; of a son of Nṛiga, ib.; of a son of Ṛiteyu, ib.; of a son of Vidūratha, MārkP.; of the 5th Arhat of the present Avasarpiṇī or the 13th Arhat of the past Utsarpiṇī, L.; of various other men, Kāv.; Kathās.; (also *ī*), f. N. of the wife of Sagara (mother of 60,000 sons), R.; Pur.; of a daughter of Kratu, VP.; of the wife of Vishṇu-yaśas and mother of Kalkin, KalkiP.; *-bodha*, m. N. of a wk. on music; *-bhadra*, m. N. of a man, Tantr.; *-meru-gaṇi*, m., *-ratnârya*, m. N. of two preceptors, Cat.; *-reṇu*, m. N. of a serpent-demon, Buddh.; *-vijaya*, m. N. of an author, Cat.; *-śīla*, m. N. of a preceptor, Buddh.; *-svāmin*, m. N. of a man, Inscr.; *-harsha*, m. N. of an author, Cat.; °*tīndra-jaya-ghoshaṇa*, n. N. of a poem; °*tīndra-yati*, m. N. of an author, Cat.; °*tī-vṛidh*, mfn. delighting in prayer or devotion, VS. **–matī-kṛita,** mfn. (see 1. *matya*) well harrowed or rolled, AitBr. **–mada,** mfn. very drunk or impassioned, W.; (*ā*), f. = next, L.; °*dâtmajā*, f. 'daughter of intoxication or passion,' an Apsaras, L. **–madana,** m. 'greatly delighting,' the Mango tree, L. **–madra,** m. pl. the happy Madras (*am*, ind.), Pat. on Pāṇ. ii, 1, 6. **–madhura,** mfn. very sweet or tender or gentle (*am*, ind.), MBh.; R. &c.; singing very beautifully (*am*, ind.), MBh.; BrahmaP.; m. a kind of potherb, L.; very soothing or gentle speech &c., MW. **–madhya,** mf(*ā*)n. good in the middle, containing good stuffing (as meat), R.; having a beaut° waist, slender-waisted, Hariv.; Pur. **–madhyama,** mf(*ā*)n. very middling or mediocre, Kām.; slender-waisted; (*ā*), f. a graceful woman, MBh.; R. &c. **–mana,** mfn. (prob. for *-manas*) very charming, beautiful, handsome, L.; m. wheat, L.; the thorn-apple, L.; N. of a mythical being, MBh.; of one of the 4 Bodhi-vṛiksha-devatās, Lalit.; of a serpent-demon, Buddh.; (*ā*), f. N. of various plants (accord. to L. 'great flowering jasmine, Rosa Glandulifera, or Chrysanthemum Indicum'), Suśr.; Mṛicch.; a spotted cow, L.; N. of a Kaikeyī, MBh.; of a wife of Dama, MārkP. **–manaḥ** (for *-manas*) in comp.; *-pattra*, n. (Suśr.), *-pattrikā*, f. (L.) the outer skin of a nutmeg; *-phala*, m. Feronia Elephantum, L.; n. nutmeg, L. **–manaka,** m. or n. (?) a flower, Pañcar. **–mánas,** mfn. good-minded, well-disposed, benevolent, gracious, favourable, pleasant, agreeable, RV.; AV.; Gobh.; KaṭhUp.; well pleased, satisfied, cheerful, easy, comfortable, RV. &c. &c.; wise, intelligent, Kāv.; Kathās.; m. a god, Śiś.; ŚārṅgP. (cf. *-manokasa* below); a good or wise man, L.; N. of various plants (accord. to L. 'wheat, a kind of Karañja, Azadirachta Indica, Guilandina Bonduc'), Suśr.; N. of a Dānava, Hariv.; of a son of Ūru and Āgneyī, ib.; of a son of Ulmuka, BhP.; of a son of Hary-aśva, VP.; of various other men, MBh.; Hariv.; Kathās.; (pl.) N. of a partic. class of gods under the 12th Manu, Pur.; f. (pl. or in comp.) flowers, Mn.; MBh. &c.; great-flowering jasmine, L.; N. of the wife of Madhu and mother of Vīra-vrata, BhP.; of various other women, Kathās.; n. a flower, Śatr. **–manaska,** mfn. in good spirits, cheerful, happy, Hcar.; (prob.) n. N. of a pleasure-grove, Divyâv. **–manasya,** Nom. Ā. °*yáte* (only pr. p. °*yámāna*), to be kind or gracious or favourable, RV.; AV.; VS.; to be in good spirits or cheerful or comfortable, ib.; TBr.; GṛŚrS. **–manā-mukha,** mf(*ī*)n. having a cheerful face, ŚāṅkhGṛ. **–manāya,** Nom. Ā. °*yate*, to become cheerful or happy, g. *bhṛiśâdi*. **–manāyana,** m. a patr. (perhaps w.r. for *saum*°), Saṃskārak. **–manâsya** (or °*nāsya;* cf. *-manā-mukha* and *-mano-m*°), N. of a serpent-demon, Hariv. **–manī-√kṛi,** P. *-karoti*, to make of good mind, make well-disposed, Bhaṭṭ. **–manī-√bhū,** P. *-bhavati*, to be of good mind, ib. **–mano** (for *-manas*) in comp.; *-*°*kasa*, n. (fr. *su-manas* + *okas*) the abode or world of gods (v.l. °*nâukasa*), Hariv.; *-jñaghosha*, m. N. of a Buddha, Lalit.; *-*°*ttarā*, f. (fr. *su-manas* + *utt*°) N. of a woman and the story about her, Pāṇ. iv, 3, 87, Vārtt. 1, Pat.; *-dāman*, n. a garland of flowers, Mṛicch.; *-bhara*, mfn. possessing or ornamented with flowers, W.; *-*'*bhirāma*, mf(*ā*)n. very captivating or agreeable, lovely, charming, R.; *-mattaka*, m. N. of a man, Rājat.; f. *-maya*, mf(*ī*)n. 'consisting of flowers' and 'being of pious disposition,' Śrīkaṇṭh.; *-mukha*, m. N. of a serpent-demon, MBh.; *-rajas*, n. the pollen of a flower, L.; *-rañjinī*, f. N. of wk.; *-latā*, f. a flowering creeper, Sāh. **–manorama,** mfn. very charming or lovely, R.; (*ā*), f. N. of two wks. **–manohara,** mf(*ā*)n.

very captivating or charming, beautiful, MBh.; Pur.; (*ā*), f. N. of a Comm. on the Kāvya-prakāśa. **-manoharaṇa**, mf(*ī*)n. id., MW. **-mántu**, mfn. easily known, well known, RV. x, 12, 6; 64, 1; m. friendly sentiment or invocation, ib. i, 129, 7; N. of a teacher (disciple of Vyāsa and author of a Dharma-śāstra), GṛS.; MBh. &c.; of a king, Kṛishṇaj.; of a son of Jahnu, VP.; *-nāman* (*-mántu-*), bearing a well-known name, RV.; *-sūtra*, n., *-smṛiti*, f. N. of wks. **-mantra**, mfn. following good advice, Kathās.; m. N. of a preceptor (having the patr. Bābhrava Gautama), IndSt.; of a minister and charioteer of Daśa-ratha, R.; of a counsellor of Hari-vara, Kathās.; of a son of Antarīksha, VP.; = *su-mantraka*, KalkiP.; *-jña*, mfn. well versed in sacred texts, MW. **-mantraka**, m. N. of an elder brother of Kalki, KalkiP. **-mantrita**, mfn. well advised, wisely planned (*am*, impers.), MBh.; R.; n. good counsel (°*tam* √*kṛi*, 'to take good c°'), MBh. **-mantrin**, mfn. having a good minister, ŚārṅgP. **-manda**, mfn. very slow or dull; (*ā*), f. N. of a partic. Śakti, Pañcar.; (°*da*)-*buddhi*, mfn. very dull-witted or much disheartened, MBh.; *-bhāj*, mfn. very unfortunate, ib. **-mánman**, n. pl. good wishes, RV.; mfn. uttering good w° or prayers, very devout, ib. **-manyu**, m. N. of a Deva-gandharva, MBh.; of a liberal man, ib. **-mara**, n. (impers.) it is easy to die (or as subst., 'an easy death'), R.; m. wind, L. **-marīcikā**, f. (scil. *tushṭi*; in Sāṃkhya) N. of one of the 5 kinds of external acquiescence, Tattvas. **-mardita**, mfn. much harassed or afflicted, MBh. **-marmaga**, mfn. deeply penetrating the vital organs (said of an arrow), BhP. **-marshaṇa**, mfn. easy to be borne, Kir. **-malakā**, f. N. of a town, Campak. **-malina**, mfn. very dirty or polluted, MBh. **-mallika**, m. pl. N. of a people, ib. **-mahat** (*sú-*), mfn. very great, huge, vast, abundant; (*at*, ind.) numerous, Nir.; MBh. &c.; = next, RV. vii, 8, 2. **-mahas**, mfn. (only in voc.) very glorious or sublime, RV. **-mahā** (for *mahat*) in comp.; *-kaksha*, mfn. very high-walled, MBh.; *-kapi*, m. N. of a demon, Hariv.; *-tapas*, mfn. performing very severe penance or austerities, extremely austere, MBh.; *-tejas*, mfn. very splendid or glorious, ib.; *-°tman* (°*hāt°*), mfn. very magnanimous, ib.; *-°tyaya* (°*hāt°*), mfn. causing very great evil or destruction, very pernicious, MBh.; *-prāṇa*, mfn. possessing excessive bodily strength or vigour, BhP.; *-bala*, mf(*ā*)n. v° strong or powerful, MBh.; Hariv.; *-bāhu*, mfn. having v° strong arms, very strong, MBh.; *-bhāga*, mfn. most excellent or glorious, MBh.; *-manas*, mfn. v° high-minded, ib.; *-ratha*, m. a very great or noble hero, ib.; *-°rha* (°*hār°*), mfn. v° splendid, Kathās.; *-vega*, mf(*ā*)n. very quick in motion, R.; *-vrata*, mfn. one who has undertaken v° solemn duties or vows, MBh.; *-sattva*, mfn. of v° noble nature or character, Hariv.; *-svana*, m. 'very loud-sounding,' N. of Śiva, MBh.; °*háujas*, mfn. very strong or powerful, R.; °*háushadha*, n. a herb of very strong efficacy, Pañcat. **-māgadha**, m. N. of a man, R.; (*ā*), f. N. of a daughter of Anātha piṇḍika, Divyâv.; (*ī*), f. N. of a river in Magadha, R. **-māgadhaka**, Pat. on Pāṇ. i, 1, 71, Vārtt. 17. **-1. -mātṛi**, f. a good or beautiful mother (see *saumātra*); (°*tṛi*), mfn. having a b° m°, RV. **-2. -mātṛi**, m. a good measurer (see *saumātra*). **-mānasa**, mfn. good-minded, L. **-mānikā**, f. N. of two metres, Col. **-mānin**, mfn. very proud or self-conceited (°*ni-tā*, f.), MBh. **-mānusha-vid**, mfn. one who knows men well, JaimBr. **-māyá**, mfn. (in Padap. for *sū-m°*) having excellent counsels or plans, very wise, RV.; m. N. of a king of the Asuras, Kathās.; of a Vidyā-dhara, ib.; (*ā*), f. N. of a daughter of Maya, ib. **-māyaka**, m. N. of a Vidyā-dhara (= prec.), ib. **-māruta**, n. the good troop or band of the Maruts, RV. **-mārtsna** (*sú-*), mfn. (see *mṛitsna*) very small or minute or fine, ŚBr. **-mārdava**, n. extreme softness, MW. **-māla**, m. N. of a people, MBh. (B. *cola*). **-mālatī**, f. N. of a metre, Col. **-māli** or **-mālin**, m. 'well-garlanded,' N. of a Rākshasa, R.; of a monkey, ib.; of a Brāhman (son of Veda-māli), Cat.; (*inī*), f. N. of a Gandharvī, Kāraṇḍ. **-mālya**, m. 'id.,' N. of a son of Mahā-padma or Nanda, Pur. **-mālyaka**, m. 'id.,' N. of a mountain, Gol. **-māsha** or **-māshaka**, mfn. possessing good beans, Pāṇ. vi, 2, 172 and 174, Sch. **-1. -mita** (*sú-*), mfn. (√*3. mā*) well measured out, RV. **-2. -mita** (*sú-*), mfn. (√*1. mi*) well fixed, ib. **-miti** (*sú-*), f. the being w° f°, ib. **-mitrá**, mf(*ā́*)n. having good friends, RV.; TS.; BhP.; m. a good friend, RV.; N. of a demon, MBh.; of the author of RV. x, 69, 70 (with patr. Vādhryaśva), Anukr.; of the author of RV. x, 105 (with patr. Kautsa), ib.; of a king of the Sauvīras, MBh.; of a king of Mithilā, Buddh.; of a king of Magadha (father of the Arhat Su-vrata), Śatr.; of the charioteer of Abhimanyu, MBh.; of a son of Gada, Hariv.; of a son of Śyāma, ib.; of a son of Śamīka (v. l. Samīka), BhP.; of a son of Kṛishṇa, ib.; of a son of Vṛishṇi, ib.; of a son of Agni-mitra, Vās., Introd.; of a son of Su-ratha (the last of the race of the Ikshvākus), BhP.; (*ā*), f. N. of a Yakshiṇī, Kathās.; of one of the wives of Daśa-ratha (mother of Lakshmaṇa and Śatru-ghna), R.; Ragh.; of the mother of Mārkaṇḍeya, Cat.; of the mother of Jaya-deva, ib.; (°*trā*)-*dhas*, mfn. one who makes good friends, MaitrS.; VS. (*śobhanāni mitrāṇi pushyati*, Mahīdh.); *-bhū*, m. N. of Sagara (as a Cakravartin), Jain.; of the 20th Arhat of the present era, ib.; (°*trā*)-*bhū* or *-tanaya*, m. 'son of Sumitrā,' N. of Lakshmaṇa, W. **-mitryà**, mfn. having good friends, RV.; VS. **-mīḍhá** (or *-mīḷhá*), m. N. of a man, RV.; of a son of Su-hotra, MBh. **-mīna**, m. pl. N. of a people, MārkP. **-mukta**, mfn. well thrown or hurled, MBh. **-mukha**, n. a good or beautiful mouth, Pañcat.; a bright face (instr. = 'cheerfully'), Kām.; mf(*ī* or *ā*)n. having a good or beautiful mouth, fair-faced, handsome, Kāv.; Kathās.; bright-faced, cheerful, glad, MBh.; R. &c.; inclined or disposed to (comp.; *-tā*, f.), Hariv.; Kāv.; Par.; gracious, favourable, kind to (gen.), R.; Car.; well pointed (as an arrow), MBh.; Hariv.; having a good entrance (in this and other fig. senses the fem. is only *ā*), Siddh.; Vop.; m. a learned man or teacher, W.; N. of various plants (accord. to L. 'a kind of herb, Ocimum Basilicum Pilosum and another species' &c.), Suśr.; Car.; a partic. gregarious bird (v. l. *su-mukhā*), Car.; N. of Śiva, MBh.; of Gaṇeśa, L.; of a son of Garuḍa (a mythical bird), MBh.; of a son of Droṇa, MārkP.; of a serpent-demon, MBh.; of an Asura, Hariv.; of a king of the Kiṃ-naras, Kāraṇḍ.; of a Ṛishi, MBh.; of a king (who perished through want of humility), Mn. vii, 41; of a monkey, R.; of a Haṃsa, Jātakam.; pl. N. of a class of gods, Buddh.; (*ā*), f., see m. above; (*ā* or *ī*), f. a handsome woman, W.; (*ī*), f. a mirror, L.; a kind of metre, Ked.; (in music) a partic. Mūrchanā, Saṃgīt.; Clitoria Ternatea, L.; Evolvulus Asinioides, L.; N. of an Apsaras, MBh.; Hariv.; (*am*), n. the mark or scratch of a finger-nail, L.; a kind of building, Gal.; *-sū*, m. 'father of Su-mukha,' N. of Garuḍa, L.; (°*khī*)-*pañcâṅga*, n. N. of a Tantra wk. **-mukhī-kṛita**, mfn. well tipped or pointed (as an arrow), MBh. **-muṇḍīka**, m. N. of an Asura, Kathās. **-mudita**, mfn. delighted with (instr.), enjoying, possessing, Hariv. **-mushita**, mfn. well cheated or deceived, Divyâv. **-mushṭi**, m., **-mushṭikā**, f. Hoya Viridiflora, L. **-muhūrta** (only loc. °*te*), a lucky hour, Siṇhâs.; mfn. occurring at a lucky h°, MBh. **-mūrti**, m. a partic. Gaṇa of Śiva, Harav. **-mūla**, m. Moringa Pterygosperma, L.; (*ā*), f. Glycine Debilis, L.; Hemionitis Cordifolia, L. **-mūlaka**, n. Daucus Carota, a carrot, L. **-mṛigá**, n. plenty of wild animals or game, good hunting, AV. **-mṛiḍīka** (or *-mṛiḷīka*), mf(*ā*)n. very compassionate or gracious, RV.; VS.; AV.; m. N. of a man, Cat.; n. pity, compassion, AV. **-mṛita**, mfn. stone-dead, Mṛicch. **-mṛityu**, m. an easy death, Pañcar. **-mṛishṭa**, mfn. well rubbed or polished, very bright or fine, MBh.; R.; BhP.; very dainty, Pañcat.; *-pushpâḍhya*, mfn. abounding in bright flowers, MW.; *-vesha*, mfn. dressed in well-brushed clothes, ib. **-méka**, mf(*ā*)n. (√*1. mi*) well fixed or established, firm, constant, unvarying, RV.; TS.; ŚBr. **-mekhala**, mfn. well girdled, MW.; Muñja grass (which forms the Brāhmanical girdle), Bhpr. **-megha**, m. 'well clouded,' N. of a mountain, R. **-medhá**, mf(*ā́*)n. very nourishing, loamy (as pasture land), RV.; (*-médha*), prob. = next, RV. x, 132, 7. **-medhás**, mfn. (acc. sg. *ásam* or *ām*) having a good understanding, sensible, intelligent, wise, RV. &c. &c.; m. N. of a Ṛishi under Manu Cākshusha, Cat.; of a son of Veda-mitra, ib.; pl. a partic. class of gods under the fifth Manu, Pur.; a partic. class of deceased ancestors, VP.; f. Cardiospermum Halicacabum, L. **-medhya**, mfn. very pure (in a ritual sense), R. **-meru**, m. N. of a mountain (= *meru*, q.v.), R.; Kālid.; Buddh. (cf. MWB. 120); N. of a Vidyā-dhara, Kathās.; of Śiva, W.; mfn. very exalted, excellent, ib.; *-jā*, f. 'sprung from Sumeru,' N. of a river, MārkP.; *-vatsa*, m. N. of a serpent-demon, Buddh. **-mla**, mfn. (prob.) very weak or feeble, Kāś. on Pāṇ. iii, 1, 136.

सुमङ्गा *sumaṅgā*, f. N. of a river, VP.

सुमत् *sumát*, ind. (prob. for *smat*) together, along with (instr.), RV. (accord. to native authorities fr. 6. *su* + *mat* = *kalyāṇa*, *śobhana*, or = *svataḥ*, *svayam*). **-kshara** (°*mát-*), mfn. oozing, juicy, VS.

Sumaj, in comp. for *sumat*. **-jani** (°*máj-*), mfn. together with his wife, RV.

Sumad, in comp. for *sumat*. **-aṅsu** (°*mád-*), mfn. together with the reins or harness, ib. **-gaṇa** (°*mád-*), mfn. together with the troop or band, associated with (instr.), ib. **-ga** (°*mád-*), mfn. together with the team (?), AV.

सुमतित्सरु *sumatí-tsaru*, mfn. (said of a plough), TS. (cf. *su-matī-√kṛi* and 1. *matya*; v. l. *somapitsaru*, VS.; Kāṭh., and *somasátsaru*, AV.)

सुमधुर *su-madhura*, *su-madhya* &c. See p. 1230, col. 3.

सुमागन्धा *sumāgandhā*, f. N. of a river (perhaps w. r. for *su-māgadhī*), Kāraṇḍ.

सुमित्र *su-mitra*, *su-mukha*, *su-medhas*. See cols. 1, 2.

सुम्न *sumná*, mfn. (prob. fr. 5. *su* and √*mnā* = *man*) benevolent, kind, gracious, favourable, RV. x, 5, 3; 7; (*am*), n. benevolence, favour, grace, RV.; TS.; devotion, prayer, hymn (cf. Gk. ὕμνος), RV.; satisfaction, peace, joy, happiness, ib.; N. of various Sāmans, ĀrshBr. **-āpi** (°*ná-*, for *summé-āpi*), mfn. near in favour, joined in affection (accord. to others a proper N.), RV. x, 95, 6. **-hū́**, mfn. invoking favour or protection, VS.; TS.

Sumnayā́, ind. devoutly, piously, RV.; kindly, graciously, AV.

Sumnāya, Nom. P. °*yati* (only p. °*nāyát*), to be gracious or favourable, RV.; to be glad or cheerful, triumph, ib.

Sumnāyú, mfn. gracious, favourable, RV.; AV.; devout, pious, ib.

Sumnāvárī, f. bringing favour or joy (applied to Ushas), RV.

Sumnín, mfn. gracious, favourable, TS.

Sumnyà, mfn. deserving grace or favour, MaitrS.

सुम्पलुण्ठ *sumpaluṇṭha*, m. zedoary, Curcuma Zerumbet, L.

सुम्भ् *sumbh*. See √*subh*, p. 1230, col. 2.

सुम्भ *sumbha*, m. pl. N. of a people, R.; sg. N. of a country (cf. *śumbha-deśa*), L.

सुम्मुनि *summuni*, m. N. of a king, Rājat.

सुयज् *su-yáj*, mfn. (i. e. 5. *su* + 2. *yaj*) worshipping or sacrificing well, RV.; VS.; f. a good or right sacrifice, VS.; TS.; Br.

Su (to be similarly prefixed to the following): **-yajus**, m. N. of a son of Bhumanyu, MBh. **-yajñá**, mfn. sacrificing well or successfully, RV.; m. a good or right sacrifice, R.; N. of a preceptor, GṛS.; of Utkala (son of Dhruva), Cat.; of a son of Ruci and Ākūti (an incarnation of Vishṇu), BhP.; of a son of Vasishṭha (and counsellor of Daśa-ratha), R.; of a son of Antara, Hariv.; of a king of the Uśīnaras, BhP.; of an author, Hcat.; (*ā*), f. N. of the wife of Mahā-bhauma (a descendant of Prasenajit), MBh. **-yata** (*sú-*), mfn. well restrained or governed or guided, RV.; well bound or fettered, AV.; °*tâtma-vat*, m. 'having the mind well controlled,' N. of a Ṛishi, MBh. **-yántu**, mfn. curbing or guiding well (as reins), RV. **-yantrita**, mfn. fast bound (*-tva*, n.), Pañcat.; well restrained or governed or self-controlled, Mn.; MBh. &c. **-yabhyā** (*sú-*), f. to be well embraced (sexually), AV. **-yáma**, mf(*ā*)n. easy to be guided, tractable (as a horse &c.), RV.; TBr.; easy to be restrained or controlled or kept in order, well regulated, RV.; AV.; VS.; m. pl. a partic. class of gods, BhP.; (*ā*), f. the Priyaṅgu plant, L. **-yávasa**, mf(*ā*)n. (in Padap. for *sū-y°*) having good pasturage, abounding in grass, RV.; m. N. of a man (cf. *sauyavasi*); n. beautiful grass, good pasturage (*e*, ind. 'when there is good p°'), RV.; TS.; ŚBr.; BhP.; °*sâd*, mfn. eating good grass, RV.; °*sín*, mfn. having good p°, ib.; °*sôdaka*, mfn.

abounding in good p° and water, MBh.; °*syú*, mfn. desirous of good p°, RV. **—yavasu**, m. N. of a Ṛishi, ĀrshBr., Sch. **—yaśa**, mfn. = *-yaśas* below, MW.; (*ā*), f. N. of a wife of Parīkshit, ib.; of an Apsaras, VP. **—yaśas**, n. glorious fame, Bcar.; (*sú-*), mfn. very famous (compar. *-tara*), SV.; BhP.; m. N. of a son of Aśoka-vardhana, Pur.; f. N. of a wife of Divo-dāsa, Hariv.; of the mother of an Arhat, L. **—yashṭavya**, m. N. of a son of Manu Raivata, MārkP. **—yāti**, m. N. of a son of Nahusha, Hariv. **—yāmá**, mfn. binding or restraining well (as reins), RV.; m. N. of a Deva-putra, Lalit.; pl. a partic. class of gods, MBh. **—yāman**, m. (with *cākshusha*) a partic. personification, AV. **—yāmuna**, m. a palace, L.; a kind of cloud, L.; N. of Vishṇu, L.; of a king (= *vatsa*), L.; of a mountain, Hariv. **—yā́su**, f. (a female) who receives excessive sexual embraces (comp. *-tarā*), RV. x, 86, 6. **—yukta**, mfn. well joined, harmoniously combined, MW.; well composed, attentive, MaitrUp.; very fit, R.; very auspicious, R. **—yukti**, f. a good appliance or contrivance, MW.; good argument, Cat. **—yúj**, mfn. well joined or yoked (*-yúk*, ind.), RV.; well placed or fixed, ib.; AV. **—yuta**, mfn. well accompanied by, well furnished or provided with, MW. **—yuddha**, n. a well-fought war or battle, Mn.; MBh. &c.; fair fighting, MBh.; Hariv. **—yoga**, m. a favourable juncture, good opportunity, MW. **—yojita**, mfn. well combined or prepared (as food), R. **—yodhana**, m. 'fighting well,' euphemistic N. of Dur-yodhana (q.v.), MBh. **—rakta**, mf(*ā*)n. well coloured, deeply dyed, W.; strongly affected or impassioned, ib.; deep red, crimson, Kāv.; very lovely or charming, R. **—raktaka**, m. a kind of Mango tree, Mangifera Sylvatica, L.; a sort of red or golden chalk, L. **—raksha**, m. 'good protector,' N. of a Muni, Cat.; of a mountain, MārkP. **—rakshaṇa**, n. careful protection, W. **—rakshita**, mfn. well protected, carefully guarded, PārGṛ.; MBh. &c.; m. N. of a man, Kathās. **—rakshin**, m. a good or faithful guardian, Kathās. **—rakshya**, mfn. easy to be preserved, MW. **—raṅga**, m. (for *sur*° see s. v.) a good colour or dye, W.; 'bright-coloured,' the orange tree, Subh.; a kind of fragrant grass, W.; crystal, ib.; (*ā*), f. a partic. plant (= *kaivartikā*), L.; (*ī*), f. Leea Hirta, L.; a Moringa with red flowers, L.; (*am*), n. red sanders, W.; vermilion, L.; *-da*, m. 'yielding a good colour,' red sanders, W.; Cæsalpinia Sappan, L.; *-dhātu*, m. red chalk, L.; *-dhūli*, f. the pollen of the orange tree, Subh. **—raṅgikā**, f. Sanseviera Roxburghiana, L. **—rajanī**, f. night, L. **—rajas**, mfn. having good or much pollen, g. *bhṛiśâdi*; °*jaḥ-phala*, m. the jack-fruit tree, L.; °*jāya*, Nom. Ā. °*yate*, to produce good or m° p°, g. *bhṛiśâdi*. **—rañjana**, m. the betel-nut tree, L. **—ráṇa**, mf(*ā*)n. joyous, gay, RV.; (*ā*), f. N. of a river, VP.; (*am*), n. joy, delight, RV. **—rata**, mfn. sporting, playful, Uṇ. v, 14, Sch.; compassionate, tender, L.; m. N. of a mendicant, Buddh.; (*ā*), f. a wife, Hariv. (Sch.); N. of an Apsaras, MBh.; (*am*), n. great joy or delight, ib.; (ifc. f. *ā*) amorous or sexual pleasure or intercourse, coition, Kāv.; Kathās. &c.; *-keli*, f. amorous sport or dalliance, Cat.; *-krīḍā*, f. id., Kathās.; *-gahvarā*, f. N. of a Surâṅganā, Siṇhâs.; *-glāni*, f. exhaustion from sexual intercourse, Megh.; *-janita*, mfn. produced by sexual int°, ib.; *-tālī*, f. a female messenger, go-between, L.; a chaplet, garland for the head, L.; *-nivṛitti*, f. cessation of sex° int°, Cat.; *-pradīpa*, m. a lamp burning during sex° int°, Kum.; *-prabhā*, f. N. of a woman, Kathās.; *-prasaṅga*, m. addiction to sex° int°, MW.; *-prasaṅgin*, mfn. addicted to sex° int°, Ṛitus.; *-priya*, mfn. id., VarBṛS.; N. of a woman, Dhūrtas.; *-bandha*, m. a kind of coition, L.; *-bheda*, m. a kind of c°, Cat.; *-mañjarī*, f. N. of a daughter of the Vidyā-dhara Mataṃga-deva and of the 16th Lambaka of the Kathā-sarit-sāgara (called after her); *-mṛidita*, mfn. worn out by sexual int°, Bhartṛ.; *-raṅgin*, mfn. (for *sura-t*° see p. 1234, col. 2), delighting in or addicted to sexual intercourse, Subh.; *-varṇana*, n. description of sex° intercourse, Cat.; *-vāra-rātri*, f. a night fit for sex° int°, Ragh.; *-vidhi*, m. performance or rule or mode of sex° int°, VarBṛS.; *-viśesha*, m. a partic. kind of sex° int°, Kir.; *-vyāpāra-jāta-śrama*, mfn. wearied by addiction to sex° int°, Subh.; *-sambhoga*, m. enjoyment of sex° int°, Vet.; *-saukhya*, n. the pleasure of sex° int°, ib.; *-stha*, mfn. engaged in sex° int°, Kathās.; °*tôtsava*, m. the joy of sexual int°, Subh.; °*tôtsuka*, mfn. desirous of sex° int°, VarBṛS.; °*tôpacāra-kuśala*, mfn. skilled in sex° int°, ib. **—rati**, f. great enjoyment or delight, MW.; *-miśra*, m. N. of the author of the Alaṃkāra-mālā. **—rátna**, mf(*ā*)n. possessing rich jewels or treasures, RV. **—rátha**, mfn. having a good chariot, a g° charioteer, RV.; yoked to a g° chariot (as horses), ib.; consisting in g° ch°s (as wealth), ib.; m. a good chariot, MBh.; 'having a good chariot,' N. of various kings, (e.g.) of the father of Koṭikâsya, MBh.; of a son of Dru-pada, ib.; of a son of Jayad-ratha, ib.; of a son of Su-deva, R.; of a son of Janam-ejaya, Hariv.; of a son of Adhiratha, Cat.; of a son of Jahnu, VP.; of a son of Kuṇḍaka, ib.; of a son of Raṇaka, BhP.; of a son of Caitra, BrahmavP.; (*ā*), f. N. of an Apsaras, Hariv.; of a river, MārkP.; (*am*), n. N. of a Varsha in Kuśa-dvīpa, MārkP.; *-deva*, m. N. of a messenger, Kathās.; *-vijaya*, m. N. of a ch. of the PadmaP.; °*thâkāra*, n. N. of a Varsha, MBh.; °*thôtsava*, m. N. of a poem. **—randhaka** and **-randhra**, N. of a place, Pañcar. **—rabhi, -rabhita**, see s. v. **—rasa**, mf(*ā*)n. rich in water, Bhām.; well-flavoured, juicy, sapid, savoury, R.; VarBṛS.; Vās.; sweet, lovely, charming, Kathās.; Bhām.; elegant (as composition), W.; m. Vitex Negundo, L.; Andropogon Schœnanthus, L.; the resin of Gossampinus Rumphii, L.; N. of a serpent-demon, MBh.; of a mountain, MārkP.; m. n. and (*ā*), f. holy basil, Hcar.; L.; (*ā*), f. N. of various plants (Anethum Panmori; Vitex Negundo; a kind of jasmine; = *rāsnā* &c.), L.; a kind of metre, Col.; (in music) a partic. Rāgiṇī, Saṃgīt.; N. of Durgā, L.; of a daughter of Daksha (wife of Kaśyapa and mother of the Nāgas), MBh.; R. &c.; of an Apsaras, MBh.; Hariv.; of a daughter of Raudrāśva, Hariv.; of a river, Pur.; (*ī*), f. a partic. plant, Vāgbh.; n. (only L.) resin; fragrant grass; gum-myrrh; Cassia bark; *-saṃgraha*, m. N. of wk.; °*sâgraja*, n. (prob.) = next, Suśr.; °*sâgraṇī*, m. white basil, L.; °*sâcchada*, m. (prob.) the leaf of the white b°, Suśr.; °*sâshṭa*, n. a collective N. of 8 plants (viz. Nirguṇṭī, Tulasī, Brāhmī &c.), L. **—rahas**, n. a very lonely place (also °*haḥ-sthāna*, n.), Pañcar. **—rājaka**, m. a kind of plant (= *bhṛiṅga-rāja*), m. **—rājan**, m. a good king, Pāṇ. v, 4, 69, Sch.; a divinity, MW.; mfn. having a good k°, L.; (°*jñī*), f. N. of a village, Pāṇ. iv, 1, 29, Sch. **—rājam-bhava**, n. the possibility of being a king, Śiś. **—rāji**, m. N. of a man, R. **—rājikā**, f. a small (white) house-lizard, L. **—rāṇāyanīya**, m. pl. N. of a school, IndSt. **—rātí**, mfn. rich in gifts, RV. **—rātri**, f. a fine night, W. **—rā́dhas**, mfn. granting good gifts, liberal, bountiful, RV.; receiving rich gifts, wealthy, ib.; m. N. of a Ṛishi (having the patr. Vārshāgira and author of RV. i, 100), Anukr.; of a man, ĀrshBr. **—rā́man**, mfn. very delightful, delicious, VS. **—rāva**, m. N. of a horse, MBh. **—rāshṭra** (*sú-*), mf(*ā*)n. having good dominion &c., TS.; m. N. of a country on the western side of India (commonly called Surat), MBh.; Hariv. &c.; of a minister of Daśa-ratha, RāmatUp.; (pl.) the country or the inhabitants of S°, MBh.; R. &c.; (*ā*), f. N. of a town (prob. 'the capital of S°'), AV.Pariś.; (°*shṭra*)*-ja*, mf(*ā*)n. born or produced in S°, MārkP.; m. a sort of black bean, L.; a kind of poison, L.; (*ā*), f. a sort of fragrant earth, L.; n. id., L.; *-brahma*, m. a Brāhman of S°, Pāṇ. v, 4, 104, Sch.; *-vishaya*, m. the country of S°, Hariv.; *-sauvīraka*, m. du. the countries of S° and Su-vīra, R.; °*trâdhipati*, m. a king of S°, MBh.; °*trâvanti*, m. pl. the inhabitants or the countries of S° and Avanti, ib.; °*trôdbhavā*, f. alum, Suśr. **—ri**, see *su-rai*. **—rukmá**, mfn. beautifully shining or adorned, RV.; VS. **—rúc**, f. bright light, RV.; mfn. shining brightly, ib.; BhP.; m. N. of a man, MBh. **—ruci**, f. great delight in (loc.), ŚārṅgP. (v.l.); m. N. of a Gandharva king, Hariv.; of a Yaksha, BhP. (Sch.); f. N. of a wife of Dhruva and mother of Uttama, Pur. **—rucira**, mf(*ā*)n. shining brightly, radiant, splendid, beautiful, MBh.; R. &c. **—ruja**, mfn. very sick, unwell, W. **—rūḍha**, mfn. standing well up or out, very prominent or projecting, ib. **—rūpá**, mf(*ā*)n. well-formed, handsome, beautiful, RV. &c. &c.; wise, learned, L.; m. N. of Śiva, MBh.; of an Asura, Hariv.; (pl.) a class of deities under Manu Tāmasa, Pur.; (*ā*), f. N. of various plants (Glycine Debilis; Jasminum Sambac &c.), L.; of an Apsaras, Hariv.; of the daughter of a serpent-demon, Kathās.; of a mythical cow, MBh.; (*am*), n. the mulberry tree, L.; N. of two Sāmans, ĀrshBr.; *-kṛitnú*, mfn. forming beautiful things, RV.; *-tā*, f. beauty, splendour, Hariv.; Kāv.; Pur.; *-varsha-varṇa*, mfn. beautifully coloured like a rainbow, TS. **—rūpaka**, mf(*ikā*)n. well-formed, beautiful, AgP. **—rūhaka**, m. 'easily mounted,' a horse resembling an ass, L. **—réknas**, mfn. having beautiful property, rich in possessions, RV. **—rekha**, mf(*ā*)n. forming beautiful lines, Kathās.; Prasannar.; (*ā*), f. a b° line, VarBṛS.; Kathās.; N. of a woman, Vās.; Pracaṇḍ. **—reṇu**, m. a sort of atom (= *trasa-reṇu*), Uṇ. iii, 38, Sch.; N. of an ancient king, Buddh.; f. N. of a daughter of Tvashṭṛi (wife of Vivasvat), Hariv.; of a river (sometimes regarded as one of the seven Sarasvatīs), MBh.; *-pushpa-dhvaja*, m. N. of a king of the Kiṃ-naras, Buddh. **—rétas**, mfn. having much semen, potent, RV.; VS.; ŚāṅkhŚr.; °*to-dhas* (or *-dhā*), mfn. bestowing potency or virility, PañcavBr.; KātyŚr. **—rebha**, mfn. (for *surêbha* see p. 1235, col. 2) fine-sounding, fine-voiced, Kir. xv, 16; n. tin, L. **—rai**, mfn. (nom. *-rās*, *-ri*) very rich, Vop. **—rocana**, mfn. (used in explaining *su-rukma*), Nir. viii, 11; m. N. of a son of Yajña-bāhu, BhP.; (*ā*), f. N. of one of the Mātṛis attending on Skanda, MBh.; n. N. of the Varsha ruled by Yajña-bāhu, BhP. **—rocis**, m. N. of a son of Vasishṭha, ib. **—rodha**, m. N. of a son of Taṃsu, Hariv. (v.l.) **—rodhas**, m. N. of a man, Pravar. **—roman**, m. 'fine-haired,' N. of a serpent-demon, MBh. **—rosha**, mfn. very angry, much enraged, R. **—roshaṇa**, m. 'id.,' N. of a warrior, Kathās. **—roha**, m. N. of a king of Cīna, ib. **—rohikā**, f. N. of a woman, g. *śivâdi*. **—rohiṇī**, f. beautifully red, ĀpŚr. **—rohitikā**, f. N. of a woman, g. *śivâdi*. **—lakkaṇa**, m. (prob. Prākrit for *-lakshaṇa*) N. of a man, Rājat. **—laksha**, mf(*ā*)n. having good or auspicious marks, fortunate, GopBr. **—lakshaṇa**, mfn. id., R.; Kathās.; (*ā*), f. N. of a wife of Kṛishṇa, Pañcar.; of a friend of Umā, L.; of the wife of Caṇḍa-ghosha, Daś.; of another woman, Viddh.; (*am*), n. the act of observing or examining carefully, ascertaining, determining, W.; a good or auspicious mark or characteristic, MBh.; *-tva*, n. the having ausp° marks or ch°, Kathās.; *-śūnyatā*, f. the absence of ausp° m°, Buddh.; *-sāra*, m. N. of a Tantra wk. **—lakshita**, mfn. well examined, well determined or ascertained, Mn. viii, 403. **—lagna**, mfn. firmly clinging to (loc.), Jātakam.; firmly adhering, Hcar.; m. or n. an auspicious moment (see *lagna*), Kathās. **—laṅghita**, mfn. one who has been made to fast properly (see √*laṅgh*), Suśr. **—labha**, mf(*ā*)n. easy to be obtained or effected, easily accessible or attainable, feasible, easy, common, trivial, MBh.; Kāv. &c.; fit or suitable for, answering to (mostly comp.), useful, advantageous, Kāv.; Kathās. &c.; w. r. for *su-bhaga*, Vikr. ii, 6; m. the fire at a domestic sacrifice, L.; N. of a man, Buddh.; (*ā*), f. sacred basil, L.; Glycine Debilis, L.; Jasminum Sambac, L.; = *dhūmra-pattrā*, L.; N. of a female teacher, GṛS.; of a female mendicant, MBh.; (°*bha*)*-kopa*, mfn. easily irascible, Śak.; *-tva*, n. the state of being easily attained &c., frequency, triviality, cheapness, VarBṛS.; Mālav. (in *a-sul*°); °*bhâvakāśa*, mfn. easily gaining room or admission, Śak.; °*bhī-bhāva*, m. = °*bhatva* (acc. with √*bhaj*, 'to be common or trivial'), Kāv.; °*bhêtara*, mfn. other than easy to be attained &c., difficult, rare, dear, Mālav. **—labhya**, mfn. easy to be obtained, R. **—lalāṭa**, mf(*ā*)n. having a beautiful forehead, ib. **—lalika**, m. a partic. mixed caste, L. **—lalita**, mf(*ā*)n. very playful or wanton or charming, MBh.; Kāv. &c.; greatly pleased or happy, W.; (*am*), ind. very sportively or wantonly, with delight, easily, ib.; *-latā-pallava-maya*, mf(*ī*)n. consisting of young sprouts of beautiful creepers, Bhartṛ.; *-vistara*, m. the beautiful Lalita-vistara (q. v.), Lalit. **—lavaṇa**, mf(*ā*)n. well salted, Suśr.; (*ā*), f. Coix Barbata, L. **—lasa**, m. N. of a man, HYog. **—lābha**, mfn. = *-labha*, Pāṇ. vii, 1, 68. **—lābhikā**, f. easy to be won, RV. **—lābhin**, m. N. of a man, g. *gargâdi*. **—likhita**, mfn. well written down, well registered, Suśr. **—lulita**, mfn. moving playfully or pleasantly to and fro, Suśr.; greatly hurt or injured, MBh. **—lū**, mfn. one who cuts well, Vop.; (as subst.) a partic. position in dancing (v. l. *sunū*), Saṃgīt. **—lekha**, mfn. having or forming auspicious lines, VarBṛS. **—locana**, mf(*ā*)n. fine-eyed, having beautiful eyes, MBh.; Rājat.; m. a deer, L.; N. of a Daitya, Hariv.; of a son of Dhṛita-rāshṭra (accord. to some of Dur-yodhana), MBh.; of a Buddha, Lalit.; of the father of Rukmiṇī, Cat.; (*ā*), f. N. of an Apsaras, Hariv.; of a Yakshiṇī, Kathās.; of the wife of king Mādhava, PadmaP.; of various other women, Daś.; Kathās. **—loma**, mfn. fine-haired, having beautiful hair or down, R.; (*ā*), f. N. of two plants (= *tāmra-vallī* or *māṃsa-ro-*

hinī), L. — **lomadhi,** m. N. of a king, BhP. (v. l.) — **loman,** mfn. = *-loma*, Pāṇ. vi, 2, 177. — **lomaśa,** mfn. having good hair or down, very hairy or downy, MW.; (*ā*), f. the plant Leea Hirta, L. — **lola,** mfn. ardently desirous of (comp.), Gīt. — **loha,** n. a kind of good iron, L. — **lohaka,** m. n. 'good metal,' brass, L. — **lohita,** m. a beautiful red colour, MW.; mfn. very red, L.; (*ā*), f. N. of one of the seven tongues of fire, MuṇḍUp.; MārkP. — **lohin,** m. N. of a man, g. *gargâdi.* — **vaṇśa,** m. 'having a good pedigree,' N. of a son of Vasu-deva, BhP.; *-ghosha,* mfn. sounding pleasantly like a flute, Hariv.; °*śékshu,* m. a kind of sugar-cane, L. — **vaktra,** n. a good mouth or face, MW.; good utterance or intonation, Śiksh.; mfn. having a handsome mouth or face (said of Śiva), MBh.; having good organs of pronunciation, Śiksh.; m. a kind of plant (= *su-mukha*), L.; N. of one of Skanda's attendants, MBh.; of a son of Danta-vaktra, Hariv. — **vakshas,** mfn. having a handsome breast, Uṇ. iv, 226, Sch.; m. N. of a man, g. *śubhrâdi.* — **vaca,** mfn. easy to be said, Nyāyas., Sch.; (*ā*), f. 'speaking well,' N. of a Gandharvī, Kāraṇḍ. — **vacana,** n. good speech, eloquence, Subh.; mfn. speaking well, eloquent, L.; (*ī*), f. N. of a goddess, L. — **vacas,** mfn. = prec., L. — **vacasyā,** f. a beautiful verse or hymn, RV. — **vájra,** mfn. having an excellent thunderbolt, RV. — **vajrin,** mfn. id., Lāṭy. — **vatsā,** f. N. of a Dik-kumārī, Pārśvan. — **vadana,** mf(*ā*)n. having a handsome or beautiful face, Kālid.; VarBṛS.; m. a kind of plant (= *sumukha*), L.; (*ā*), f. a beaut° woman, Ṛitus.; a kind of metre, Chandom.; N. of a woman, Veṇīs. — **vapus,** f. 'having a handsome body,' N. of an Apsaras, VP. — **vayas,** f. a hermaphrodite, L. — **varatrá,** mfn. having good thongs, RV. — **varūtha** or °**thin,** mfn. having a good protecting ledge (as a chariot), R. — **varga,** mfn. (for *suv*° see p. 1236, col. 2) having good society, MW. — **varcaka,** m. natron, alkali, L.; N. of an ancient sage (= *varca*), MBh. (Nilak.); (*ikā*), f. natron, Suśr.; a kind of plant (cf. *su-varjikā*), L. — **varcala,** m. N. of a country, W.; (*ā*), f. Ruta Graveolens, Vas.; MBh.; Suśr.; linseed, Linum Usitatissimum, L.; hemp, Polanisia Icosandra, L.; = *tri-saṃdhyā*, Kauś., Sch.; N. of the wife of the Sun, MBh.; R.; of Śiva (as a manifestation of the Sun), Pur.; of the wife of Parameshṭhin and mother of Pratīha, BhP.; of the wife of Pratīha, ib. — **várcas,** mfn. full of life or vigour, fiery, splendid, glorious, RV. &c. &c.; m. N. of a son of Garuḍa, MBh.; of one of Skanda's attendants, ib.; of a son of Dhṛita-rāshṭra, ib.; of a son of the tenth Manu, Hariv.; of a son of Khanī-netra, MBh.; of a Brāhman, ib.; of a brother of Bhūti, MārkP. — **varcasa,** mfn. fiery, splendid, radiant, TUp.; MBh.; m. N. of Śiva, MBh. — **varcasin,** m. N. of Śiva (cf. prec.), MBh.; natron, alkali, L. — **varcaska,** mfn. splendid, brilliant, Hariv. — **varcin,** m. natron, MW. — **varjikā,** f. a kind of plant (cf. *su-varcikā*), Car. — **varṇa** &c., see s. v. — **vartita,** mfn. well turned or rounded, R.; well arranged or contrived, MBh.; °*tôru,* mfn. having round thighs, Dharmas. 83. — **vartula,** m. a water-melon, L.; Gardenia Enneandra, L. — **vartman,** n. the right path or course, Pañcar.; mfn. following the r° p° or c°, Suśr. — **vardhayitṛi,** mfn. increasing well (used in explaining *su-vṛidh*), Sāy. — **várman,** n. good armour, AV.; m. 'having good armour,' N. of a son of Dhṛita-rāshṭra, MBh. — **varsha,** mf(*ā*)n. raining well, ŚāṅkhGṛ.; m. a good rain, R.; N. of a teacher, pl. his school (also °*shaka*), Buddh. — **valg,** mfn. jumping well, Vop. — **vallarī,** f. a partic. creeping plant, L. — **valli,** f. Vernonia Anthelminthica, L.; (*ī*), f. id., L.; another plant (= *kaṭvī*), ib.; (°*li*)-*ja,* n. a bulb, L. — **vallikā,** f. Vernonia Anthelminthica, L.; a red-colouring Oldenlandia, L. — **vaśa,** m. N. of a man, VP. — **vaśya,** mfn. easy to be subdued or controlled, R. — **vas,** mfn. (prob.) covering or clothing well, Vop. — 1. **-vasaná,** mf(*ā*)n. (√4. *vas*) = prec., RV.; well dressed or clothed, ChUp. — 2. **-vasaná,** n. (√5. *vas*) a good dwelling, RV. vi, 51, 4; N. of a place, Pañcar. — **vasanta,** m. a beautiful spring season, ŚāṅkhGṛ.; the day of full moon in the month Caitra, L.; a festival in honour of Kāma-deva in the m° C°, L. — **vasantaka,** m. a partic. festival (= prec.), L.; Gærtnera Racemosa, L. — **vasu** (?), f. N. of an Apsaras, L. — **vastu-sampad,** mfn. having abundant wealth, Daś. — **vastra,** mf(*ā*)n. well clothed, MBh.; (*ā*), f. N. of a river, VP. — **vah** (strong form *-vāh*), mfn. drawing or carrying well, Hcat. — **vaha,** mfn. id., L.; easy to be drawn or carried, L.; carrying well, bearing well, patient, W.; m. a partic. wind, Gol.; N. of various plants (Vitex Negundo; Cissus Pedata; Boswellia Thurifera &c.), L.; a Viṇā or lute, W. — **váhni,** mfn. having a good team (as a chariot), AV. — **váhman,** mfn. driving well, a good charioteer (said of Indra), RV. — **vākya,** mfn. speaking well, eloquent, MBh. — **vāgmin,** mfn. very eloquent, R. — **vāc,** mfn. id., RV.; AV.; worth mentioning, praiseworthy, RV. iii, 1, 19; sounding beautifully, MW.; making a loud noise, ib.; m. N. of a keeper of the Soma (v. l. *svāna*), MaitrS.; of a Brāhman, MBh.; of a son of Dhṛita-rāshṭra, ib. — **vā́cas,** mfn. very eloquent, RV. — **vācya,** mfn. easy to be read, MW. — **vājin,** mfn. beautifully feathered (as an arrow), Hariv.; (°*ji*)-*vāpu* (?), m. N. of an author, IndSt. — **vātā** (?), f. N. of an Apsaras, L. — **vātra,** n. N. of a Sāman, IndSt. — **vāditra,** n. beautiful music, Hariv. — **vānta,** mfn. (a leech) that has well vomited (i. e. disgorged sucked blood), Suśr. — **vāmā,** f. N. of a river, MBh. — **vār,** mfn. having beautiful water, MW. — **vārttā,** f. good news, MW.; N. of a wife of Kṛishṇa, Hariv. — **vāla,** mfn. having beaut° hair on the tail (said of an elephant), VarBṛS. — **vāladhi,** m. having a beautiful tail (as a cow), MBh.; *-khura,* mf(*ā*)n. having a beautiful tail and hoofs (as a cow), ib. — **vālukā,** f. Hoya Viridiflora, L. — 1. **-vāsa,** m. (√5. *vas*) a beautiful dwelling, MW. — 2. **-vāsa,** m. (√2. *vās*) an agreeable perfume, W. — 3. **-vāsa,** m. (√4. *vas*) 'well clad,' N. of Śiva, MBh.; a kind of metre, Col.; *-kumāra* or °*raka,* m. N. of a son of Kaśyapa, Kathās. — **vāsaka,** m. a water-melon, L. — **vāsana,** m. pl. N. of a class of gods under the tenth Manu, BhP. — **vāsarā,** f. cress, Bhpr. — **vā́sas,** mfn. having beaut° garments, well dressed, RV. &c. &c.; well feathered (as an arrow), MBh. — **vāsita,** mfn. well scented or perfumed, Hariv.; Pañcar. — **vāsin,** mfn. dwelling in a comfortable or respectable abode, W.; (*inī*), f. a woman married or single who resides in her father's house (cf. *sva-v*°), Gaut.; Mn.; Yājñ. (v. l.) &c.; a term of courtesy for a respectable woman whose husband is alive, MW. — **vā́stu,** f. N. of a river (Gk. Σόαστος; the modern Suwad), RV.; MBh.; Pur.; m. pl. the inhabitants of the country near the river Suvāstu, VarBṛS. — **vāstuka,** m. N. of a king, MBh. — **vāha,** mfn. easy to be borne (meaning also 'having beautiful horses' and 'having handsome arms;' cf. *bāha*), Vās.; m. a good stallion, ib.; N. of one of Skanda's attendants, MBh. — **vāhana,** m. N. of a Muni, Cat. — **vikrama,** mfn. having a beautiful gait, R.; very courageous or energetic or brave, MBh.; m. great prowess or valour, W.; N. of a son of Vatsa-prī, MārkP. — **vikrānta,** mfn. very valiant or heroic, bold, chivalrous, ŚārṅgP.; m. a hero, W.; n. valour, heroism, MBh.; *-vikramaṇa-paripṛicchā,* f. N. of a Buddhist wk.; *-vikramin* or *-vikrāmin,* m. N. of a man, Buddh. — **viklava,** mfn. very pusillanimous or irresolute, MBh. — **viguṇa,** mfn. destitute of all virtues or merits, very wicked, ib. — **vigraha,** mfn. having a beautiful body or figure, Kām.; Mṛicch.; m. N. of a messenger, Kathās. — **vicakshaṇa,** mfn. very clever, well discerning, skilful, wise, Kām.; Subh. — **vicāra,** m. good or deliberate consideration, W.; N. of a man, Cat. — **vicārita,** mfn. well weighed, deliberately considered, ŚārṅgP. — **vicārya,** ind. having well deliberated; *-kārin,* mfn. acting after due deliberation, Hit. — **vicita,** mfn. well searched through, R.; well examined, Āpast. — **vijñāná,** mfn. easy to be distinguished, RV.; well discerning, very clever or wise, Pañcat. — **vijñāpaka,** mfn. easy to be taught or instructed, Lalit. — **vijñeya,** mfn. well discernible, easy to be distinguished, KaṭhUp.; N. of Śiva, MBh. — **vita,** see s. v. — **vitata,** mfn. well spread (as a net), MBh. — **vitala,** m. a partic. form of Vishṇu, W. — **vittá,** n. great wealth or property, TBr.; mfn. very rich or wealthy, Pañcat. — **vitti,** m. N. of a divine being, Cat. — 1. **-vid,** m. (√1. *vid*) 'knowing well,' a Jina, Gal.; f. a shrewd or clever woman, L. — 2. **-vid,** m. (√3. *vid*) procuring or granting well (in *viśva-suvid,* q. v.) — **vida,** m. 'very knowing,' an attendant on the women's apartments (= *sauvida*), L.; a king, prince (cf. *su-vidat*), L.; a partic. tree (= *tilaka*), L. — **vidagdha,** mfn. very cunning, astute, Ratnāv. — **vidat,** m. a king, L. — **vidátra,** mfn. very mindful, benevolent, propitious, RV.; AV.; n. grace, favour, ib.; wealth, property, Nir. vii, 9; household, Uṇ. iii, 108, Sch. — **vidatriya,** mfn. propitious, gracious, favourable, RV. — **vidarbha,** m. pl. N. of a people, VP. — **vidalla,** n. the women's apartments, L.; (*ā*), f. a married woman, L. — **vidita** (*sú-*), mfn. well known or understood, ŚBr.; Mn.; MBh. — **vidīrṇa,** mfn. much torn or split, greatly expanded, MW.; n. (prob.) a great fight or slaughter, MBh. i, 5552. — **viddha,** mfn. well pierced or incised (as a vein), Suśr. — **vidyā,** f. good knowledge, Kāv. — **vidyut,** m. N. of an Asura, Cat. — **vidvas** (*sú-*), mfn. very intelligent or wise, RV. — **vidha,** mfn. of a good kind or nature, Subh.; (*am*), ind. in an easy way, easily, W. — **vidhāna,** n. good order or arrangement (*-tas,* ind. 'in right order, properly, duly'), Kām.; mfn. well arranged or contrived, L. — **vidhi,** m. a good rule or ordinance (instr. 'in the right manner, properly'), Kathās.; (with Jainas) N. of the 9th Arhat of the present Avasarpiṇī, L. — **vinaya,** mfn. well educated or disciplined, Lalit. — **vinashṭa,** mfn. quite disappeared or vanished, R.; quite worn out or emaciated, ib. — **vinirmala,** mfn. quite spotless or pure, Hariv. — **viniścaya,** m. a very firm resolution, R. — **viniścita,** mfn. thoroughly convinced, SaddhP. — **vinīta,** mf(*ā*)n. well trained (as horses), Kām.; properly behaved, very modest, Pañcar.; well executed, MBh.; (*ā*), f. a tractable cow, L. — **vineya,** mfn. easy to be trained or educated, Lalit. — **vinyasta,** mfn. well spread out or extended, R. — **vipina,** mfn. abounding in forests, richly wooded, MBh. — **vipula,** mf(*ā*)n. very great or spacious or numerous &c., MBh.; R.; very loud, MW. — **vipra** (*sú-*), mfn. very learned (esp. in sacred knowledge), RV. — **vibhakta,** mfn. well separated or distributed, Hariv.; Suśr.; BhP.; well proportioned, symmetrical, MBh.; Kāv. &c.; *-gātra,* mfn. having well separated or symmetrical limbs, MW.; *-tā,* f. good proportion, symmetry, Suśr.; °*ktâṅga-pratyaṅgatā,* f. having every limb and member well proportioned (one of the 80 minor marks of a Buddha), Dharmas. 84; °*ktânavadyâṅgī,* f. (a woman) having symmetrical and faultless limbs, MBh. — **vibhāta,** mfn. shining splendidly, very bright, MW.; thoroughly clear or distinct, NṛisUp. — **vibhīshaṇa,** mfn. very frightful, R. — **vibhu,** m. N. of a king (son of Vibhu), Hariv.; VP. — **vibhūshita,** mf(*ā*)n. beautifully adorned, Vishṇ.; Hariv.; R. — **vibhoka,** m. N. of a poet, Cat. — **vimala,** mf(*ā*)n. perfectly clear or pure, Suśr.; Śṛiṅgār. — **vimuc,** f. right unyoking or loosening, ŚrS. — **viraja,** mfn. thoroughly free from all passions, BhP. — **virūḍha,** mfn. fully grown up or developed, Bhag.; well ridden, MBh. — **vilaya,** mfn. (prob.) easily fusible or liquefying, Pat. on Pāṇ. vi, 1, 50, Vārtt. 2. — **vivaktṛi,** m. a good expositor or interpreter, ĀpŚr., Sch. — **vivartita,** mfn. well rounded, Lalit. — **vivikta,** mfn. very secluded or solitary (as a wood), MBh.; well decided or answered (as a question), BhP. — **vivṛit** or **-vivṛitá,** mfn. easily opened, RV. i, 10, 7. — **viśada,** mfn. very clear or distinct or intelligible, Mṛicch. — **viśārada,** mf(*ā*)n. very experienced or skilful, BhP. — **viśāla,** mfn. very large; m. N. of an Asura, Kathās.; (*ā*), f. N. of one of the Mātṛis attending on Skanda, MBh.; °*lâksha,* mfn. having very large eyes, ib. — **viśishṭa,** mfn. most distinguished or excellent, Hcat. — **viśuddha,** mfn. perfectly pure, MBh.; Subh.; (with Buddhists) N. of a partic. world, SaddhP. — **viśodhaka,** mfn. easily improved, Lalit. — **viśrabdha,** mfn. very beautiful or confident (*am,* ind.), R. — **viśvasta,** mfn. very confiding, quite unconcerned or careless, Pañcat.; very trusty, confidential, W. — **vishaṇṇa,** mfn. very dejected or sorrowful, R. — **vishāṇa,** mfn. having large tusks (as an elephant), MBh. — **vishṭambhin,** mfn. well-supporting (said of Śiva), Śivag. — **vishṭhita,** mfn. standing beautifully, R. — **vishṇu,** m. N. of a man, Buddh. — **vistara,** m. great extent, plenty, abundance (°*raṃ* √*yā,* 'to be richly supplied, become full'), Subh.; great diffuseness (°*rāt,* 'very fully, in great detail'), Pañcar.; mf(*ā*)n. very extensive or large, MBh.; Kathās.; very great or strong or intense, MBh.; Kāv. &c.; (*am*), ind. in great detail, at full length, Pañcar.; Hit.; very intensely or vehemently, R.; Hariv. — **vistīrṇa,** mfn. well spread or laid out, very extensive or large or broad, R.; Hit.; (*am*), ind. at full length, Cat. — **vispashṭa,** mfn. perfectly clear or manifest, NṛisUp. — **vismaya,** mf(*ā*)n. very astonished or surprised, Kathās. — **vismita,** mfn. id., BhP.; very surprising or wonderful (compar. *-tara*), R. — **vihita,** mfn. well done or performed or arranged or carried out,

MBh.; R. &c.; well supplied, richly provided with (instr.), ib.; well placed or deposited, MW.; *-prayogatā*, f. skilful arrangement or performance, Śak., Introd. — **vihvala**, mf(*ā*)n. very perturbed or distressed or wearied, MBh.; Kathās. — **vīthī-patha**, m. a partic. entrance to a palace, Hcar. — **vīra**, mf(*ā*)n. very manly, heroic, warlike, RV.; AV.; VS.; rich in men or heroes, having or containing or consisting in excellent offspring or heroes or retainers, ib.; TS.; ŚāṅkhGṛ.; m. a hero, warrior, RV.; m. the jujube tree, L.; another tree (= *eka-vīra*), L.; N. of Skanda, MBh.; of Śiva, Śivag.; of a son of Śiva, MW.; of various kings, (esp.) of a son of Dyutimat, MBh.; of a son of Kshemya, Hariv.; of a son of Śibi (ancestor of the Suviras), ib.; of a son of Deva-śravas, BhP.; n. = next, L.; *-ja*, n. sulphuret of antimony, L.; *-tā* (°*rá-*), f. abundance of heroes or warriors, AV.; TS.; °*rāmla*, n. sour rice gruel, L. — **vīraka**, m. Helminthostachys Laciniata, L.; n. a collyrium prepared from the Amomum Anthorhizon, W. — **vīrya**, n. manly vigour or deed, heroism, RV.; R.; abundance of heroes, host of warriors or brave men, RV.; TBr.; mfn. having great strength or power, very efficacious (herb or drug), Hit.; (*ā*), f. wild cotton, L.; the resin of the Gardenia Gummifera, L.; n. the fruit of the jujube, L. — **vṛikti**, f. (accord. to some for *su-ṛikti* = *su-ṛic*; cf. *su-vita* for *su-ita*) excellent praise or hymn of praise (also a form of instr.), RV.; mfn. singing or praising excellently, ib.; well praised, praiseworthy, glorious, ib.; TS. — **vṛiksha**, m. a fine tree, Cāṇ. — **vṛijána**, mf(*ā*)n. (prob.) dwelling in fair regions, RV. — **vṛit**, mfn. turning or running well (as a chariot), RV.; TBr. — **vṛitta**, mf(*ā*)n. well rounded, beautifully globular or round, MBh.; VarBṛS. &c.; well-conducted, virtuous, good (esp. applied to women), MBh.; R. &c.; composed in a beautiful metre, Kāv.; well done (n. impers.), Mālatīm.; m. a kind of round bulb, L.; (*ā*), f. a sort of grape, L.; N. of a plant (= *śata-pattrī*), L.; a kind of metre, Ked.; N. of an Apsaras, Hariv.; of a woman, Daś.; (*am*), n. welfare, BhP.; good conduct or behaviour, R.; Kathās.; *-tā*, f. 'round shape' and 'good conduct,' ŚārṅgP.; *-tilaka*, m. or n. N. of a wk. on metres. — **vṛitti**, f. a good way of living, good conduct or behaviour, MBh.; the life of a Brahma-cārin, life of chastity or continence, MW. — **vṛiddha**, mfn. very old or ancient (as a race), Kāv.; m. N. of the elephant of the southern quarter, L. — **vṛidh**, mfn. joyous, cheerful, RV. — **vṛidha**, mfn. growing well, thriving, prospering, AV. — **vṛiśc**, mfn. cutting well, Vop. — **vṛishabha**, m. an excellent bull, TBr. — **vṛishalīka**, mfn., Kāś. on Pāṇ. vi, 2, 173. — **vṛishṭa** (*sú-*), n. beautiful rain, TS.; Br. — **vṛishṭi**, f. id., ChUp.; VarBṛS. &c. — **vega**, mfn. moving very fast, fleet, rapid, Kām.; Hcat.; (*ā*), f. Cardiospermum Halicacabum, R.; N. of a female vulture, Bālar. — **vegin**, mfn. very swift or rapid (v. l. *-vegita*), MBh. — **veṇa**, m. (ifc. f. *ā*) N. of a man, Kathās.; (*ā*), f. N. of a river, Hariv. — **vetasa**, m. a good reed or cane, MBh. — 1. **-veda**, mfn. deeply versed in (sacred) science, MBh. — 2. **-véda**, mfn. easy to be found or obtained, GopBr. — **vedaná**, mfn. id., RV. — **vedas**, m. N. of a Ṛishi (having the patr. Śairīshi and author of RV. x, 147), Anukr. — **vena**, mf(*ī*)n. full of longing or desire, RV. — **vema**, mf(*ā*)n. (prob.) woven on a good loom (or 'having a good loom'?), MBh. — **vela**, mfn. greatly bowed or stooping, L.; humble, quiet, L.; m. N. of a mountain (= *tri-kūṭa* or *citra-kūṭa*), Mṛicch. — **veśa** &c., often w. r. for next. — **vesha**, m. a fine dress or garment; mf(*ā*)n. well dressed, well clad, beautifully adorned, MBh.; Kāv. &c.; *-tā*, f. the being well dressed &c., R.; *-dhara*, mfn. wearing fine clothes, VarBṛS.; *-vat*, mfn. beautifully dressed or adorned, Kām. — **veshin**, mfn. = prec., W. — **vyakta**, mfn. very clear or bright, R.; very plain or distinct or manifest (*am*, ind.), MBh.; R. &c. — **vyavasthita**, mfn. standing quite firmly, R. — **vyasta**, mfn. greatly dispersed or scattered (as an army), Hit. — **vyākhyāta**, mfn. well explained, Buddh. — **vyāhṛita**, n. a good saying or maxim, MBh. — **vyushṭa**, mfn. beautifully dawned, MBh. — **vyūha-mukhā** and **-vyūhā**, f. N. of two Apsarases, Kāraṇḍ. — **vratá**, mf(*ā*)n. ruling well, RV.; VS.; strict in observing religious vows, very religious or virtuous (often in voc.), MBh.; R. &c.; tractable (as a horse or cow), MBh.; m. a religious student, W.; N. of one of Skanda's attendants, MBh.; of a Prajā-pati, R.; of a son of Manu Raucya, MārkP.; of a son of Nābhāga, R.; of a son of Uśīnara, Hariv.; of a son of Kshemya, VP.; of a son of Priya-vrata, W.; of a scholar, Col.; of a historian, Rājat.; of a poet, Cat.; (with Jainas) of the 20th Arhat of the present Avasarpiṇī (also called Muni-suvrata) and of the 11th Arhat of the future Utsarpiṇī, L.; (*ā*), f. a partic. fragrant plant, Bhpr.; a cow that is easily milked, L.; a virtuous wife, W.; N. of an Apsaras, L.; of a daughter of Daksha, VP.; of the mother of the 15th Arhat of the present age, L.; of a princess, Dharmaś.; (°*ta*)*-datta*, m. N. of a poet, Cat.; *-svara*, m. N. of an Asura, Buddh.

सुय्य **suyya**, n. N. of a man (the foster son of Suyyā), Rājat.; (*ā*), f., see next.

Suyyā, f. N. of a woman, Rājat. — **kuṇḍala**, n. N. of a village, ib. — °**bhidhāna** (°*yâbh*°), mfn. called Suyyā, ib. — **setu**, m. N. of a dike, ib.

सुर् **sur** (rather Nom. fr. *sura* below), cl. 6. P. *surati*, to rule, possess supreme or superhuman power, Dhātup. xxviii, 50; to shine, ib.; cl. 10. P. *surayati*, to find fault (v. l. for *svar*), xxxv, 11.

Sura, m. (prob. fr. *asura* as if fr. *a-sura* and *sita* fr. *a-sita*; thought by some to be connected with 2. *svar*) a god, divinity, deity (*surāṇām hantṛi*, m. 'slayer of the gods,' N. of a partic. form of fire, son of Tapas), MaitrUp.; MBh. &c.; the image of a god, an idol, Vishṇ.; a symbolical N. for the number 'thirty-three' (from the 33 gods; see *deva*), Gaṇit.; a sage, learned man, L.; the sun, L.; (said to be) = *kshura*, MBh.; w. r. for *svara*, ib.; (*ā*), f., see s. v.; (*ī*), f. a goddess, Naish.; HPariś.; (*am*), n., see *surā*. — **ṛishi**, m. = *-rshi*, col. 3, BhP. — **karin**, m. an elephant of the gods, Kir.; °*rīndra-darpâpahā*, f. 'taking away the pride of the chief el° of the g°,' N. of the Ganges, KalkiP. — **kāminī**, f. an Apsaras (*-janāḥ*, 'the A° people'), Kum. — **kāru**, m. 'artificer of the gods,' N. of Viśva-karman, L. — **kārmuka**, n. 'bow of the gods,' the rainbow, Vikr. — **kārya**, n. work to be done for the gods, R. — **kāshṭha**, n. Pinus Deodora or another species, Suśr. — **kula**, n. a g°'s house, temple, Kathās. — **kṛit**, m. N. of a son of Viśvāmitra, MBh. (v. l. *sūra-k*°). — **kṛita**, mfn. made or caused by the g°, Kathās.; (*ā*), f. Cocculus Cordifolius, L. — **ketu**, m. the banner of the g° or of Indra, VarBṛS. — **khaṇḍanikā**, f. a kind of lute (v. l. *-maṇḍalikā*), L. — **gaja**, m. (= *-karin*) the gods' or Indra's elephant, Kāv. — **gaṇa**, m. sg. or pl. a host of g°, R.; VarBṛS.; Pañcar.; a class or company of divinities (see *gaṇa-devatā*), W.; N. of Śiva, MBh.; of a village, Vās., Introd. — **gaṇḍa**, m. a kind of boil, L. — **gati**, f. the being born as a god, W. — **garbha**, m. the child of a g°, MBh.; °*bhâbha*, mfn. like the sons of the g°, ib. — **gāyaka**, m. a singer of the g°, Gandharva, BhP. — **gāyana**, m. id., L. — **giri**, m. 'gods' mount,' mount Meru, ib.; Bālar. — **guru**, m. 'preceptor of the gods,' N. of Bṛihas-pati, VarBṛS.; Kathās. &c.; the planet Jupiter (°*ror divasaḥ*, 'Thursday'), VarBṛS.; Kālac.; *-divasa*, m. Thursday, VarBṛS. — **gṛiha**, n. = *-kula*, Rājat. — **grāmaṇī**, m. 'chief of the g°,' N. of Indra, L. — **cāpa**, m. n. = *-kārmuka*, VarBṛS.; Kir.; Kād. — **jana**, m. the race of gods, Siṅhās. — **jā**, f. N. of an Apsaras, MBh. — **jit**, m. N. of various authors, Cat. — **jyeshṭha**, m. 'oldest of the gods,' N. of Brahmā, ib. — **taraṃgiṇī**, f. (for *su-rata-r*° see p. 1232, col. 1) 'river of the gods,' the Ganges, Subh. — **taru**, m. tree of the gods, Pañcar.; Bhām.; = *kalpa-t*°, BhP. — **tā**, f. godhead, MBh.; the race of gods, Cat. — **tuṅga**, m. Elæocarpus Ganitrus, L. — **toshaka**, m. 'god-pleasing,' the jewel Kaustubha (worn by Kṛishṇa on his breast), L. — **dāru**, n. Pinus Deodora, Suśr.; VarBṛS.; BhP.; *-maya*, mf(*ī*)n. made of the Pinus D°, VarYogay. — **dīrghikā**, f. the celestial Ganges, L. — **dundubhi**, m. the god's drum, Kalyāṇam.; sacred basil, L.; (*ī*), f. id., MW. — **devatā**, f. a goddess, MBh. — **devin**, m. (prob.) N. of a partic. demon, Gobh. — **dru**, m. a tree of the gods, Chandom. — **druma**, m. id.; = *kalpa-vṛiksha*, Naish.; BhP. &c.; a kind of reed, Arundo Bengalensis, L.; the Deva-dāru pine, MW. — 1. **-dvipa**, m. an elephant of the g°, Ragh.; an el° of one of the quarters of the sky (see *dik-karin*), W.; Indra's el°, ib. — 2. **-dvipa**, Nom. P. °*pati*, to become an elephant of the gods, Subh. — **dvish**, m. 'enemy of the gods,' a demon, Asura, Daitya or Rākshasa, MBh.; Kāv. &c.; N. of Rāhu, Ragh.; VarBṛS. — **dhanus**, n. 'bow of the gods,' a rainbow, Kāv.; Var.; °*nur-lekhâya*, to resemble a rainbow (°*yita*, mfn.), Kāv. — **dhāman**, n. a place of the gods, Cat. — **dhunī**, f. 'river of the g°,' N. of the Ganges, Siṅhās. — **dhūpa**, m. 'incense of the g°,' the resin of the Shorea Robusta, L.; resin, turpentine, W. — **dhvaja**, m. = *-ketu*, VP., Sch. — **nadī**, f. 'river of the gods,' N. of the Ganges, MBh.; R. &c.; the celestial Ganges, W. — **nandā**, f. 'joy of the gods,' N. of a river, L. — **nāyaka**, m. 'leader of the gods,' N. of Indra, Rājat.; of an author of certain prayers (used by Tāntrikas), Cat. — **nāla**, m. a kind of reed, Arundo Bengalensis, L. — **nimnagā**, f. 'river of the gods,' N. of the Ganges, Kathās.; the celestial Ganges, MW. — **nirgandha**, n. the leaf of the Laurus Cassia (incorr. for *surabhi-gandha*), L. — **nirjhariṇī**, f. the celestial Ganges, Harav. — **nilaya**, m. 'abode of the gods,' N. of mount Meru, VarBṛS. — **pati**, m. 'lord of the gods,' N. of Indra, MBh.; Kāv. &c.; of Śiva, R.; *-guru*, m. 'Indra's teacher, Bṛihas-pati,' the planet Jupiter, Var.; *-cāpa*, n. 'bow of Indra,' the rainbow, VarBṛS.; *-tanaya*, m. 'Indra's son,' N. of Arjuna, MW.; *-tva*, n. lordship over the gods, Kāv.; *-dhanus*, n. (= *-cāpa*), Kāv.; Bhpr. — **patha**, m. 'path of the g°,' part of the atmosphere or sky, Kād.; the sky, heaven, L.; (prob.) the milky way, R. — **parṇa**, n. a kind of medicinal plant, L.; (*ī*), f. a kind of creeper, ib. — **parṇika**, m. a kind of Puṃ-nāga tree, MW. — **parṇikā**, f. Rottleria Tinctoria, L.; Elæocarpus Ganitrus, ib. — **parvata**, m. 'mountain of the g°,' Meru, ib. — **pāṅsulā**, f. an Apsaras (*-jana*, m. 'the A° people'), Vcar. — **pādapa**, m. a tree of the g°, BhP. — **pāla**, m. N. of an author, Cat. — **puṃnāga**, m. Elæocarpus Ganitrus, L. — **pura**, n. 'city of the gods,' Amarā-vatī, Kathās.; heaven (°*ram upa-√gam*, 'to go to heaven, die'), Jātakam.; (*ī*), f. Amarā-vatī, L. — **purodhas**, m. 'domestic priest of the g°,' N. of Bṛihas-pati, Kām. — **pushpa**, n. a flower of the g°, a celestial fl° (*-vṛishṭi*, f.), Kathās.; Kalyāṇam. — **pratishṭhā**, f. the setting up of an idol, Rājat. — **pravīra**, m. N. of a fire (son of Tapas), MBh. — **priya**, mfn. dear to the g°; m. a kind of bird (v. l. *saraḥ-p*°), Hariv.; Agati Grandiflora, L.; a species of Elæocarpus, ib.; N. of Indra, ib.; of Bṛihas-pati, ib.; of a mountain, Śatr.; (*ā*), f. an Apsaras, BhP.; Jasminum Grandiflorum, L.; = *svarṇa-rambhā*, ib. — **bhavana**, n. a god's abode, temple, VarBṛS.; Hcat. — **bhāva**, m. the dignity of a god, Kāv. — **bhī**, f. (for *surabhī* see p. 1235, col. 3) fear of the g°, Vās. — **bhuvana**, w. r. for *-bhavana*, Hcat. — **bhūya**, n. the becoming a deity, state of a deity, Śiś. — **bhūruha**, m. Pinus Deodora, Bhpr. — **bhūshaṇa**, n. 'ornament of the g°,' a necklace of pearls consisting of 1008 strings and 4 Hastas long, VarBṛS. — **maṇḍalikā**, see *-khaṇḍanikā*. — **mantrin**, m. 'counsellor of the g°,' N. of Bṛihas-pati, L. — **mandira**, n. a god's house, temple, Kāv.; Kathās.; Rājat. — **muni**, m. a divine Muni; pl. N. of the Pleiads, Śiś. — **mūla**, m. N. of a poet, Sadukt. — **mṛittikā**, f. alum-slate, L. — **medā**, f. a kind of medicinal plant, ib. — **mohinī**, f. N. of a Surâṅganā, Siṅhās. — **yāna**, n. a chariot of the g°, L. — **yuvati**, f. 'celestial maiden,' an Apsaras, Kāv.; VarBṛS. — **yoshit**, f. id., Kathās.; Vās.; BhP. — **rāj**, m. 'king of the g°,' N. of Indra, MBh.; BhP. — **rāja**, m. id., ib.; R.; Rājat.; *-guru*, m. (= *sura-pati-g*°), VarBṛS.; *-tā*, f. the state or rank of Indra, Kāv.; *-mantrin*, m. (= *sura-pati-guru*), VarBṛS., Sch.; *-vṛiksha*, m. 'Indra's tree,' N. of the Pārijāta, Ragh.; *-śarâsana*, n. 'Indra's bow,' a rainbow, Vās. — **rājan**, m. = *-rāj*, R. — **rājya**, n. dominion over the gods, ib. — **ripu**, m. an enemy of the g°, VarBṛS. — **rshabha** (°*ra + ṛish*°), m. 'best of the gods,' N. of Indra, L.; of Śiva, BhP. — **rshi** (°*ra + ṛishi*), m. a divine Ṛishi, a Ṛ° dwelling among the g°, MBh.; R.; BhP.; pl. the gods and Ṛishis, BhP. — **latā**, f. a kind of plant, L. — **lāsikā**, f. a flute (cf. *svara-l*°), L. — **loka**, m. the gods' world, heaven (*-nātha*, m. pl.), R.; BhP. &c.; *-rājya*, n. dominion over the w° of the g°, Bhartṛ.; *-sundarī*, f. 'celestial woman,' an Apsaras, Vikr.; N. of Durgā, MW. — **vadhū**, f. id., Ragh.; Kathās. — **vana**, n. a grove of the g°, BhP. — **vara**, m. 'best among the g°,' N. of Indra; *-nagara*, n. Indra's city, Cāṇ.; *-vanitā*, f. an Apsaras, BhP. — **varcas**, m. N. of an Agni (son of Tapas), MBh. — **vartman**, n. 'road of the gods,' the sky, atmosphere, Hāsy. — **varman**, m. N. of a king (v. l. *susthira-v*°), Hcar. — **vallabha**, m. Rottleria Tinctoria, L.; (*ā*), f. white Dūrvā grass, L. — **vallī**, f. sacred basil, ib. — **vāhinī**, f. 'river of the g°,' the heavenly Ganges, Kathās. — **vidvish**, m. an enemy of the g°, demon, Asura, W. — **vilāsinī**, f. a heavenly nymph, Apsaras, MW.; a proper N., ib. **-vīthī,** f. 'way of the gods,' N. of the way of the Nakshatras, MBh. **-velā,** f. N. of a river, L. **-veśman,** n. abode of the g°, heaven, ŚārṅgP.; a temple, Cāṇ.; Rājat. **-vairin,** m. an enemy of the g°, Asura, L. **-śatru,** m. id., Śiś.; *-guru,* m. the planet Venus, VarYogay.; *-han,* m. 'slayer of the enemy of the g°,' N. of Śiva, Śivag. **-śākhin,** m. 'tree of the gods,' the Kalpa tree, Naish.; Kāvyād.; ŚārṅgP. **-śilpin,** m. the artificer of the g°, L. **-śreshṭha,** m. 'best of the g°,' N. of Vishṇu, R.; of Śiva, ib.; of Indra, ib.; BrahmaP.; of Dharma, Hariv.; of Gaṇeśa, Pañcar.; (*ā*), f. a partic. plant, L. **-śvetā,** f. a small (white) house lizard, L. **-sakha,** m. 'friend of the gods,' N. of Indra, Śak.; pl. N. of the Gandharvas, Kir. **-saṃgha,** m. a company or assemblage of gods, Bhag. **-sattama,** m. the best of the g°, MW. **-sadana,** n. a god's house, temple, Kād. **-sadman,** n. abode of the g°, heaven, Śiś.; a god's house, temple, Kathās.; Rājat. **-sama,** mfn. equal to the g°, MW. **-samiti,** f. an assemblage of g°, W. **-sambhavā,** f. Polanisia Icosandra, L. **-sarit,** f. 'river of the gods,' the Ganges, Kāv.; Kād.; *-suta,* m. metron. of Bhīshma, Śiś. **-sarshapaka,** m. a kind of tree, L. **-sindhu,** f. = *-sarit,* Kathās.; = *mandākinī,* Śiś. (Sch.) **-suta,** m. a son of a g°, MBh.; R.; (*ā*), f. a daughter of a g°, R.; °*tôpama,* mfn. similar to the children of the g°, MW. **-sundara,** m. a beautiful deity, Bhag.; (*ī*), f. a lovely celestial female, Apsaras (*-jana,* m. pl.), ib.; Kāv.; Kathās.; N. of Durgā, L.; of a fairy, ib.; of a woman, Vet.; a partic. Yoginī, MW.; *-senā,* f. the army of the gods (*-gaṇa-pati,* m. 'the chief of the celestial host'), R.; N. of a woman, Daś. **-skandha,** m. N. of a demon, Buddh. (v.l. *khara-sk°*). **-strī,** f. a celestial woman, Apsaras, Vikr.; VarBṛS.; Kathās.; BhP.; °*strīśa,* m. 'lord of the A°,' N. of Indra, L. **-sthāna,** n. the place or abode of a god, MW.; a temple, Kām.; Hit. **-sravantī,** f. the heavenly Ganges, Harav. **-srotasvinī,** f. N. of the Ganges, Bhām. **Surâṅganā,** f. a celestial woman, Apsaras, Nal.; Kāv.; Kathās. &c. **Surâcārya,** m. 'preceptor of the gods,' N. of Bṛihas-pati, L. 1. **Surâjīva** (for 2. *surâj°* see below, col. 3), m. 'livelihood of the gods,' N. of Vishṇu, Pañcar. **Surâdri,** m. 'mountain of the gods,' the m° Meru, Śiś. **Surâdhama,** m. the lowest or worst of the gods, BhP. **Surâdhipa,** m. 'sovereign of the g°,' N. of Indra, MBh.; R.; Kathās. &c. **Surâdhīśa,** m. id., BhP.; Naish. **Surâdhyaksha,** m. 'sovereign of the g°,' N. of Brahmā, Hariv.; of Kṛishṇa, ib.; of Śiva, Śivag. **Surânaka,** m. a drum of the gods, BhP. **Surânanda,** m. N. of a teacher, Cat.; of a poet, ŚārṅgP.; (*ā*), f. N. of a Surâṅganā, Siṃhās. **Surâpagā,** f. 'river of the g°,' the Ganges, Kir.; Kathās.; Sāh. **Surâyudha,** n. a weapon of the g°, Kum. **Surâraṇi,** f. 'mother of the g°,' N. of Aditi (cf. *surâvani*), VP. **Surâri,** m. an enemy of the gods, an Asura (also a Rākshasa), Kāv.; Kathās. &c.; N. of a demon causing diseases, Hariv.; of a king, MBh.; the chirp of a cricket, W.; *-ghna,* m. N. of a demon causing diseases, Hariv.; *-sambhava,* mfn. caused by an enemy of the g°, MW.; *-han,* m. 'destroyer of the enemy of the g°,' N. of Śiva, MBh.; *-hantṛi,* m. 'demon-killer,' N. of Vishṇu, Tithyād. **Surârcana,** n. the act of worshipping the gods, worship, Yājñ. **Surârdana,** m. 'tormenter of the g°,' an Asura, MārkP. **Surârha,** n. 'worthy of the g°,' yellow sandal, L.; gold, ib.; saffron, MW. **Surârhaka,** m. a kind of fragrant plant, L. 1. **Surâlaya,** m. (for 2. *surâl°* see p. 1236, col. 1) abode of the gods, heaven, Hariv.; Kāv.; Kathās. &c.; Meru or Su-meru, L.; a god's abode, temple, Yājñ.; Car.; VarBṛS. &c.; wind (?), L. **Surâvani,** f. the Earth as mother of the gods or Aditi, MārkP. (cf. *surâraṇi*). **Surâvalī,** f. N. of wk. **Surâvāsa,** m. 'abode of the g°,' a temple, L.; N. of a temple, Rājat. **Surâśraya,** m. 'resort of the g°,' Meru, Sūryas.; Kathās. **Surâsura,** m. pl. or (prob. n.) sg. gods and Asuras, MBh.; Hariv.; R. &c.; *-guru,* m. N. of Śiva, MBh.; of Kaśyapa, Śak.; *-maya,* mf(*ī*)n. caused by the g° and As°, Cat.; *-vimarda,* m. a conflict or war between the g° and As°, R.; °*surâcārya,* m. N. of a teacher, W. **Surâspada,** n. 'god's abode,' a temple, Rājat. **Surâhva,** m. Pinus Deodora, Bhpr.; other plants (= *maruvaka*; = *hari-dru*), L.; (*ā*), f. a kind of creeping pl°, ib. **Surâhvaya,** m. marjoram, L.; n. Pinus Deodora, ib. **Surêjya,** m. 'preceptor of the gods,' N. of Bṛihas-pati, Jyot.; VarBṛS.; of the planet Jupiter, Var.; (*ā*), f. the sacred basil, L.; another plant, = *brāhmī,* ib. **Surêtara,** m. 'other than a Sura,' an Asura, BhP. **Surêndra,** m. chief of the gods (esp. N. of Indra), Mn.; Ragh.; BhP. &c.; N. of a king, Rājat.; of a teacher, Cat.; a kind of bulbous plant (Arum), L.; (*ā*), f. N. of a Kiṃnarī, Kāraṇḍ.; *-kanda,* m. a kind of bulbous plant (= °*rêndra*), Npr.; Suśr.; *-gopa,* m. cochineal, Suśr. (cf. *indra-g°*); *-cāpa,* n. 'Indra's bow,' the rainbow, ŚārṅgP.; *-jit,* m. 'conqueror of Indra,' N. of Garuḍa, L.; *-tā,* f. the rank of chief of the gods, Jātakam.; *-pūjya,* m. N. of Bṛihas-pati, the planet Jupiter, VarBṛS., Sch.; *-mālā,* f. N. of a Kiṃ-narī, Kāraṇḍ.; *-lupta,* morbid baldness of the head (= *indra-l°*), Car.; *-loka,* m. Indra's world, Bhag.; *-vatī,* f. N. of a princess, Rājat.; *-śishya,* m. N. of an author, Cat.; *-saṃhitā,* f. N. of wk. **Surêndraka,** m. a kind of bulbous plant (= °*rêndra*), Npr. **Surêbha,** m. (for *su-rebha* see p. 1232, col. 3) a celestial elephant, MW. **Surêśa,** m. a lord of the gods, BhP.; N. of a partic. god, MBh.; of a partic. Agni (son of Tapas), ib.; of Indra, VarBṛS.; Kathās.; BhP.; of Vishṇu-Kṛishṇa, Cat.; of Śiva, Śivag.; of a place, Pañcar.; (*ī*), f. N. of Durgā, Cāṇ.; *-loka,* m. Indra's world, BhP. **Surêśvara,** m. a lord of the gods, R.; BhP.; N. of Brahmā, R.; of Śiva, ib.; of Indra, Kāv.; BhP.; of a Rudra, MBh.; VP.; of a disciple of Śaṃkarâcārya and others, Buddh.; RāmatUp. &c.; (*ī*), f. N. of Durgā, Kathās.; Rājat.; of Lakshmī, Cat.; of Rādhā, Pañcar.; of the celestial Ganges, L.; *-dhanus,* n. 'Indra's bow,' the rainbow, Kāv.; *-paṇḍita,* m. N. of an author, Cat.; *-prabha,* m. N. of a king, Buddh.; *-vārttika,* n., *-vārttika-ṭīkā,* f. N. of wks.; *-svāmin*; °*varâcārya,* °*varâśrama,* m. N. of authors, Cat.; °*varī-kshetra,* n. N. of a region sacred to Durgā, Rājat.; °*varī-māhātmya,* n. N. of wk.; °*varôpâdhyāya,* m. N. of an author, Cat. **Surêshṭa,** mfn. beloved or desired by the gods, L.; m. Elæocarpus Ganitrus, L.; Vatica Robusta, ib.; Agati Grandiflora, ib.; = *vasuka,* ib.; Sesbana Grandiflora, W.; (*ā*), f. a kind of plant, = *brāhmī,* L.; Asclepias Acida, W. **Surêshṭaka,** n. the resin of the Vatica Robusta, L. 1. **Surôttama,** m. (for 2. *surôt°* see p. 1236, col. 1) chief of the gods, MBh.; N. of Vishṇu, Hariv.; of the Sun, L.; (*ā*), f. N. of an Apsaras, VP.; °*mâcārya,* m. N. of various authors, Cat. **Surôttara,** m. 'superior to g°,' sandal-wood, L. **Surôpama,** mfn. god-like, divine, MBh. **Surauḳas,** n. an abode of the gods, temple, Rājat.

Suraka. See p. 1236, col. 1.

Suralā, f. N. of a river, L.; of the Ganges, MW.

Surusura, mfn. 'ruling' or 'shining' (= *surat*), L.

सुरङ्गा *suraṅgā,* f. (for *su-raṅgā* see p. 1232, col. 1) a hole cut in the wall or made underground (= *suruṅgā,* q.v.), MBh.; Mudr.

सुरडा *suraḍā,* f. Ipomœa Turpethum, Car.

सुरत *su-rata* &c. See p. 1232, col. 1.

सुरभि *su-rabhí,* mf(*is* or *ī*)n. (prob. fr. 5. *su* + √*rabh,* = 'affecting pleasantly') sweet-smelling, fragrant, RV. &c. &c.; charming, pleasing, lovely, RV.; AV.; AitBr.; famous, celebrated, Kāvyād. ii, 176; best, excellent, L.; good, virtuous, L.; friendly, a friend, W.; m. fragrance, perfume, any sweet-smelling substance, L.; N. of various fragrant plants and substances (accord. to L. 'Michelia Champaka; Nauclea Cadamba; a kind of jasmine; nutmeg' &c. &c.), Suśr.; the season of spring, Kāv.; the month Caitra, L.; a fire lighted at the fixing of the sacrificial post, L.; (also *ī*), f. N. of various plants (Boswellia, Thurifera; Prosopis Spicigera or Mimosa Suma &c.), L.; spirituous liquor (cf. *surā*; v.l. *murā*), L.; N. of a fabulous cow (daughter of Daksha and wife of Kaśyapa, mother of cattle and of the Rudras, sometimes considered as one of the Mātṛis or as the cow of plenty; *surabheḥ sutāḥ,* 'the children of Surabhi,' i.e. 'cattle'), MBh.; Kāv. &c. (IW. 519); any cow (accord. to L. 'a brown cow'), Vās.; the earth, L.; (*i*), n. a fragrant smell or substance, perfume, ŚBr.; GṛŚrS.; ChUp.; R.; sulphur, L.; gold, L. **-kandara,** m. N. of a mountain, Vikr. **-kshetra-māhātmya,** n. N. of ch. of the Skandha-purāṇa. **-gandha,** m. a fragrant smell, BhP.; mfn. fragrant; (*ā*), f. Jasminum Grandiflorum, L.; n. the leaf of the Laurus Cassia, ib. **-gandhi** or °**dhin,** mfn. sweet-smelling, fragrant, MBh.; Kāv. &c. **-gandhita,** mfn. filled with sweet scents, R. **-gandhin,** see °*dhi.* **-ghṛita,** n. fragrant butter or ghee, W. **-cūrṇa,** n. perfumed powder, Kauś. **-cūla,** m. N. of a poet, Subh., Introd. **-cchada,** m. fragrant Jambu, L. **-tanaya,** m. 'son of Surabhi,' a bull, VarBṛS.; (*ā*), f. a cow, Megh. **-tā,** f. fragrancy, Cat. **-triphalā,** f. nutmeg (and) Areca nut (and) cloves, L. **-tvac,** f. cardamoms, L. **-dattā,** f. N. of an Apsaras, Kathās. **-dāru** (L.) or °**ruka** (Bhpr.), m. Pinus Longifolia. **-pattra,** m. marjoram, L.; (*ā*), f. Eugenia Jambolana, ib.; = *rāja-jambū,* ib. **-putra,** m. = *-tanaya,* VarBṛS. **-bāṇa,** m. 'having fragrant arrows' (as made of flowers), N. of the god of love, L. **-mát,** mfn. provided with perfumes, fragrant, TS.; ĀpŚr.; BhP.; containing the word *surabhi,* Br.; m. N. of Agni, AitBr.; (*atī*), f. a verse containing the word *surabhi,* Buddh. **-māruta,** n. 'having fr° winds,' N. of a forest, Kathās. **-māsa,** m. 'fragrant month,' spring, Vās.; Kād. **-mukha,** n. the opening of spring, MW. **-vatsa,** m. N. of a Vidyā-dhara, Kathās. **-valkala,** n. the bark of Laurus Cassia, L. **-shṭama** (°*bhi-*), mfn. (fr. the nom. °*bhis*) most fragrant or agreeable, RV. **-samaya,** m. the season of spring, Sāh. **-srag-dhara,** mfn. wearing fragrant garlands, MW. **-sravā,** f. the gum olibanum tree, L.

Surabhaya, Nom. P. °*yati,* to make fragrant, perfume, Subh.

Surabhikā, f. a sort of Musa, L.

Surabhita, mfn. rendered fragrant, perfumed, Kāv.; Vās. &c.; rendered famous, Daś.

Surabhin, mfn. perfumed, scented, fragrant (compar. °*bhin-tara*), RV.; Kauś.

Surabhī, f. (= °*bhi*), in comp. **-gandha,** n. the leaf of the Laurus Cassia, L. **-gotra,** n. 'race of Surabhī,' oxen, cattle, kine, MBh. **-paṭṭana,** n. N. of a town, ib. **-pattrā,** f. the rose-apple, W.; = *rāja-jambū,* MW. **-rasā,** f. the gum olibanum tree, L. **-suta,** m. pl. 'children of Surabhī,' oxen, cattle, R.

Surabhi-√kṛi, P. *-karoti,* to render fragrant, fill with fragrancy, Hariv.; Kāv. &c.; to divulge, Rājat.

Surabhy, in comp. for °*bhi.* **-āsya,** mfn. having the mouth fragrant (*-tva,* n.), ŚāṅkhŚr.

सुरस *su-rasa* &c. See p. 1232, col. 2.

सुरा *súrā,* f. (ifc. also *sura,* n.; prob. fr. √3. *su,* 'to distil,' and not connected with *sura,* 'a god') spirituous liquor, wine (in ancient times 'a kind of beer'); spirituous liquor (personified as a daughter of Varuṇa produced at the churning of the ocean), RV. &c. &c.; water, Naigh. i, 12; a drinking vessel, L.; a snake, L. **-°kara** (°*râk°*), m. 'mine of sp° liq°,' the cocoa-nut tree, L.; a distillery, Baudh. **-karman,** n. a ceremony performed with Surā, Lāṭy. **-kārá,** m. a distiller, VS. **-kumbha,** m. a vessel for spirituous liq°, Pañcar. **-°gāra** (°*râg°* or °*râg°*), m. (MārkP.) or **-gṛiha,** n. (L.) a tavern. **-grahá,** m. a cupful of Surā, ŚBr.; = *-kumbha,* MW. **-°grya** (°*râg°*), n. 'best liquor,' nectar, R. **-ghaṭa,** m. = *-kumbha,* R. **-** 2. **-°jīva** (°*râj°*), m. (for 1. *surâj°* see col. 1) = next. **-jīvin,** m. 'living by sp° liq°,' a distiller, tavern-keeper, Yājñ. **-dṛiti,** m. a leather bag for holding spirituous liq°, PañcavBr. **-dhara,** m. N. of an Asura, Kathās. **-dhāna,** mf(*ī*)n. containing S°, VS. **-dhvaja,** m. the flag or sign of a tavern, Mn.; MBh. **-** 1. **-pa,** mf(*ā* or *ī*)n. (fr. √1. *pā*) drinking sp° liq°, a spirit-drinker, ŚāṅkhŚr.; Kauś.; Mn. &c.; wise, sage, W.; pleasant, agreeable, ib. **-** 2. **-pa,** m. (fr. √3. *pā*) a preserver of sp° liq°, ib. **-pāna** or **-pāna,** n. the drinking of sp° liq°, TS.; ŚBr.; Nir. &c.; mfn. drinking sp° liq°, Cāṇ.; eating anything to excite thirst, W.; m. pl. N. of the people of eastern India (so called from their drinking sp° liq°), Pāṇ. viii, 4, 9, Sch.; (°*ṇa*)*-parikshīva,* intoxicated, MW.; *-prāyaścitta,* n. a penance for drinking spirits, ib. **-pātra,** n. a wine-glass or cup, A. **-pāna,** see *-pāna.* **-pin** (?), mfn. drinking Surā, Bhaṭṭ.; possessing wine-drinkers, MW. **-pīta,** mfn. one who has drunk S°, Pāṇ. iv, 1, 53, Sch. **-pītha,** m. the drinking of sp° liq°, AitBr.; mfn. dr° sp° liq°, BhP. **-priya,** mf(*ā*)n. fond of S°, Hariv. **-bali** (*surā-*), mfn. receiving an oblation of S°, TBr. **-bīja,** n. a substance serving for the preparation of beer; barm, Bhpr.; Suśr., Sch. **-°bdhi** (°*râb°*), m. the ocean of sp° liq°, MārkP. **-bhāga,** m. the scum or froth of beer, yeast, barm, L. **-bhājana,** n. a wine cup, Mn. xi, 148. **-bhāṇḍa,** n. = *-pātra,* A. **-°ma** (°*râma*), m. 'Surā-disease,' intoxication or its effects, RV. **-maṇḍa,** m. = *-bhāga,* L.; the scum or froth of beer, yeast, barm, W. **-matta,** mfn. intoxicated by Surā, Kāv. **-madá**, m. Surā-intoxication, ŚBr. **-maya**, mf(*ī*)n. consisting of S°, VS., Sch. **-mukha**, m. 'having S° in the mouth,' N. of a serpent-demon, MBh. **-mūlya**, n. drink-money, Śak. **-meha**, m. a kind of diabetes, ŚārṅgS. **-mehin**, mfn. suffering from diab°, Suśr. **-2.-°laya** (*°rā́l°*; for 1. *surā́l°* see p. 1235, col. 1), m. a tavern, Vās. **-vat** (*súrā-*), mfn. having spirituous liq°, RV.; ŚBr. **-vāri**, m. sp° liq°, L. **-vṛita**, m. 'surrounded with sp° liq°,' N. of the sun, ib. **-śū́**, mfn. swollen i.e. excited with sp° liq°, RV.; m. a drunkard, MW.; a heretic, ib. **-śodhana**, n. N. of wk. **-saṃspṛishṭa**, mfn. touched by sp° liq°, Mn. xi, 171. **-saṃdhāna**, n. the distilling of sp° liq°, MW. **-samudra**, m. the ocean of sp° liq°, KapS., Sch. **°sava** (*°rā́s°*), m. n. beer or sp° liq° produced by the fermentation of unripe corn, Mn.; MBh.; Hariv. &c.; n. Surā and Āsava, BhP., Sch.; sp° liq°, MW. **-somá**, m. Soma in the form of Surā, ŚāṅkhŚr.; du. Surā and Soma (*-vikrayin*, mfn.), VS.; KātyŚr. **-°hutí** (*°rā́h°*), f. libation of Surā, ŚBr. **2. Surôttama**, (prob.) n. (for 1. *surôtt°* see p. 1235, col. 2) the scum of Surā, Gobh. (Sch. 'excellent water'). **Surôda**, mfn. having Sūra for water, MBh.; VP.; m. the sea of S°, BhP.; Pañcar. **Súrôdaka**, mf(*ā*)n. = prec., AV.; m. = prec., VP. **Surôpayāmá**, m. a vessel for holding S°, MaitrS.

Suraka, mfn. = *surā-prakāra*, *surā-varṇa* (applied to a snake), g. *sthūlâdi*.

Surīya or **surya**, mfn., Pat. on Pāṇ. v, 1, 1, Vārtt. 4.

सुराति *su-rāti*, *su-rādhas* &c. See p. 1232, col. 2.

सुराल *surāla*, m. N. of a preceptor, Cat.

सुराष्ट्र *su-rāshṭra* &c. See p. 1232, col. 2.

सुरिस *surisa*. See *indra-s°*.

सुरीक *surīka*, m. N. of a poet, Cat.

सुरुङ्ग *suruṅga*, m. a kind of tree, Moringa Pterygosperma (cf. *su-raṅga*, p. 1232, col. 1), L.; (*ā*), f. (accord. to some = Gk. σύριγξ; cf. *suraṅgā*, p. 1235, col. 2) a hole made underground for military purposes or for house-breaking, mine, excavation, breach, subterranean passage, Mudr.; Kathās.; Divyâv. **-yuj**, m. = next, L. **Suruṅgâhi**, m. 'underground-serpent,' a house-breaker, L.

सुरुच् *su-ruc*, *su-ruci* &c. See p. 1232, col. 2.

सुरुन्दला *surundalā*, f. N. of a river, L.

सुरुण्ड *surūṇḍa*, m. pl. N. of a dynasty (v.l. *guruṇḍa*; cf. *muruṇḍa*), BhP.

सुरेज्य *surêjya*, *surêndra*. See p. 1235, cols. 1 and 2.

सुल् *sul* (only in *prá-sulāmi*, v.l. *prá-tilāmi*), VS. (= *pra-veśayāmi*, Sch.)

सुल *sula*, g. *balâdi*. **-vat**, mfn., ib.

Sulin, mfn. (fr. *sula*), g. *balâdi*.

सुलक्कण *su-lakkaṇa*, *su-laksha* &c. See p. 1232, col. 3.

सुलतान *sulatāna*, m. a sultan, L.

सुलेक *su-léka*, m. (cf. *leka*) N. of an Āditya, ĀpŚr.

सुलेख *su-lekha*, *su-locana* &c. See p. 1232, col. 3.

सुल्लण *sullaṇa*, w.r. for *sulhaṇa* below.

सुल्लाविहार *sullā-vihāra*, m. N. of a monastery, Rājat.

सुल्हण *sulhaṇa*, m. N. of the author of the Su-kavi-hṛidayânandinī (a Comm. on Kedāra's Vṛitta-ratnâkara), Cat.

सुल्हरी *sulharī*, f. N. of a place, Rājat.

सुवंश *su-vaṇśa*, *su-vaktra* &c. See p. 1233, col. 1.

सुवन *suvana*, m. (said to be fr. √2. *sū* = 5. *su*) the sun, Uṇ. ii, 80, Sch.; fire, L.; the moon, L.; n. in *pum-* and *suparṇa-s°*, q.v.

सुवर् *súvar*, ind. = 3. *svàr*, the sun, light, heaven, Āpast. **-gá** (for *su-varga* see p. 1233, col. 1) = *svargá*, TS.; TBr.; *-kāma* (*°gá-*), mfn. = *svarga-k°*, desiring heaven, TS. **-jāna**, mfn. born or produced in h°, TBr. **-jít**, mfn. winning h°, TS. **-dhāman** (*súvar-*), mfn. abiding in h° or light, ib. **-vat** (*súvar-*) and **-vid**, mfn. = *svàrvat* and *svar-víd*, ib.

Suvargéya or **suvargyà**, mfn. = *svargyà*, leading to heaven, celestial &c., TS.

सुवर्चक *su-varcaka*, *su-varcala* &c. See p. 1233, col. 1.

सुवर्ण *su-várṇa*, mf(*ā*)n. of a good or beautiful colour, brilliant in hue, bright, golden, yellow, RV. &c. &c.; gold, made of gold, TBr.; ChUp.; R.; of a good tribe or caste, MBh. xiii, 2607; m. a good colour, MW.; a good tribe or class, ib.; a kind of bdellium, L.; the thorn-apple, L.; a kind of metre, VarBṛS., Sch.; m. N. of a Deva-gandharva, MBh.; of an ascetic, ib.; of a minister of Daśa-ratha, R.; of a son of Antarīksha, VP.; of a king of Kāśmira, Rājat.; of a poet, Cat.; m. (rarely n.) a partic. weight of gold (= 1 Karsha, = 16 Māshas, = 80 Raktikās, = about 175 grains troy), Mn.; MBh. &c.; a gold coin, Mṛicch.; a kind of bulbous plant (= *suvarṇâlu*), L.; a kind of aloe, L.; a kind of sacrifice, L.; (*ā*), f. turmeric, L.; Sida Rhomboidea or Cordifolia, L.; another plant (= *svarṇa-kshīrī*), L.; a bitter gourd, colocynth, W.; N. of one of the seven tongues of fire, MW.; of a daughter of Ikshvāku (the wife of Su-hotra), MBh.; (*ī*), f. the plant Salvinia Cucullata (perhaps w.r. for *su-karṇī*), L.; (*am*), n. gold (of which 57 synonyms are given), AV. &c. &c.; money, wealth, property, riches, L.; a sort of yellow sandal-wood, L.; the flower of Mesua Roxburghii; a kind of vegetable (= *gaura-suvarṇa*), L.; red ochre (= *suvarṇa-gairika*), L.; the right pronunciation of sounds, ŚBr.; N. of a Tīrtha, MBh.; of a partic. world, ib. **-kakshya**, mfn. having a golden girdle, MBh. **-kaṅkaṇa** (Hit.), **-kaṭaka** (Mṛicch.), n. a gold bracelet. **-kaṇa**, m. a species of bdellium, L.; *-guggulu*, m. id., ib. **-kadalī**, f. a kind of plantain, ib. **-kartṛi**, m. a gold-worker, goldsmith, Mn.; MBh. **-karsha**, m. a Karsha weight of gold, MW. **-kāra**, m. id., Mn.; R.; Var.; Vās.; *°rânna*, n. food given by a goldsmith, Mn. iv, 218; *°rêśvara-varman*, m. N. of a poet, Subh. **-kṛit**, m. = *-kartṛi*, W. **-ketakī**, f. a kind of plant, (or) a Ketakī made of gold, Rājat. **-keśa**, m. N. of a serpent-demon, Buddh. **-kshīrī**, f. a kind of plant, Suśr. **-gaṇita**, n. computation of g° (of its weight and purity), Col.; a partic. method of calculation in arithmetic, W. **-garbha**, m. N. of a Bodhi-sattva, Buddh. **-giri**, m. N. of a mountain, ib. **-gairika**, n. red ochre, L. **-gotra**, n. N. of a kingdom, Buddh. **-granthi**, m. a pocket for keeping gold, Pañcat. **-cakravartin**, m. 'one who sets a golden wheel in motion,' a king, Buddh. **-campaka**, m. a yellow-flowering Campaka, Caurap., Sch. **-cashaka**, N. of Comm. **-cūḍa**, m. N. of a son of Garuḍa, MBh. **-cūla**, m. a kind of bird, Kathās. **-caura**, m. a stealer of g°, Mn. xi, 49. **-caurikā**, f. gold-stealing, Mṛicch. **-jīvika**, m. a g°-merchant (a partic. mixed caste, the son of a Māṇikī by a Kāṇsya-kāra), L. **-jyotis**, mfn. having a golden lustre, NṛisUp. **-tantra**, n. N. of wk. **-tāla**, m. a golden palm, MBh. **-dāna**, n. a gift of gold, Cat. **-dvīpa**, m. n. 'golden island,' (prob.) N. of Sumatra, Kathās.; Buddh. **-dhenu**, f. a golden offering in the shape of a cow, Cat.; *-dāna-vidhi*, m. N. of wk. **-nakulī**, f. a kind of plant, L. **-nashṭa-śānti**, f. N. of ch. of the Śānti-mayūkha. **-nābha**, mfn. having a golden centre (as a cup or vessel of any kind), Āpast.; Vishṇ.; m. N. of an author, Cat. **-nābhi**, m. or f. a golden navel, Vishṇ. **-paksha**, mfn. gold-winged, TĀr. **-pattra**, m. 'id.,' a kind of bird, MBh. **-padma**, n. a g°-coloured lotus flower, Suśr.; a golden lotus fl°, Cat.; *-dāna*, n. N. of wk. **-pārśva**, N. of a locality, Rājat. **-pālikā**, f. a kind of vessel made of gold, R. **-piñjara**, mfn. yellow like g°, Mṛicch. **-pura**, n. N. of a mythical city, Kād. **-pushpa**, mf(*ā*)n. having g° for flowers, MBh.; Pañcat.; Kuval.; m. the globe-amaranth, L.; n. its flower, VarBṛS.; (*ā* or *ī*), f. a kind of plant, ib. **-pushpita**, mfn. having g° for flowers, abounding in gold, Pañcat. **-pṛithvī-dāna-vidhi**, m. N. of wk. **-pṛishṭha**, mfn. having a golden surface, overlaid with gold, gilded, MBh. **-prabhāsa**, m. N. of a Yaksha, Buddh.; of a Buddhist Sūtra wk.; (*ā*), f. N. of the wife of the serpent-demon Kālika, Lalit. **-prasara**, n. the fragrant bark of the Feronia Elephantum, L. **-prasava**, n. id., MW. **-phalā**, f. a species of Musa, L. **-bala-ja**, see *sauvarṇabalaja*. **-bindu**, m. N. of Vishṇu, L.; of a temple, Hariv.; Mālatīm. **-bhāṇḍa** or **°ḍaka**, n. a jewel-box, Mṛicch.; *°ḍâgāra*, a treasury, ib. **-bhujêndra**, m. N. of a king, Buddh. **-bhū**, f. 'gold-country,' N. of a c° said to be in the north-east, VarBṛS. **-bhūmi**, f. = *-dvīpa*, Kathās.; Jātakam. **-maya**, mf(*ī*)n. made or consisting of gold, Pañcat. **-mākshika**, n. a bright yellow mineral substance (thought to be pyritic iron ore), Bhpr. **-mālikā**, f. 'g°-garlanded,' N. of a goddess, Cat. **-māsha**, m. (Prâyaśc.) or **°shaka** (Suśr.), a partic. weight (= 5 Kṛishṇalas or 12 Dhānya-māshas). **-muktā-vivāda**, m. N. of a Kāvya. **-mukharī**, f. N. of a river, Cat.; *-māhātmya*, n. N. of ch. of the Skanda-purāṇa. **-mukhī-māhātmya**, w.r. for prec. **-mushṭi**, f. a handful of g°, Lalit. **-mekhalī**, f. 'gold-girdled,' N. of an Apsaras, Kāraṇḍ. **-medinī**, f. the earth represented in gold (*-dāna*, n.), Cat. **-mocā**, f. a sort of Musa, L. **-yūthikā** or **°thī**, f. a species of jasmine, Mṛicch. **-rajatá**, mf(*ā́*)n. made or consisting of gold and silver, Br.; n. pl. g° and s°, R. **-ratnâkara-cchattra-kūṭa** or **°ttra-ketu**, m. N. of a future Buddha, Buddh. **-rambhā**, f. a species of Musa, L. **-rūpyaka**, mfn. abounding in gold and silver, MW.; m. N. of an island, R. **-rūpya-maya**, mf(*ī*)n. made or consisting of gold and silver, Kāraṇḍ. **-rekha**, m. N. of an author, Uṇ. iii, 136, Sch.; (*ā*), f. N. of a river, L. **-retas**, mfn. having golden semen (N. of Śiva), MBh. **-retasa**, m. N. of a man; pl. his descendants, Cat. **-roman**, mfn. having golden wool, L.; g°-haired, ib.; m. a ram, Pañcat.; N. of a son of Mahā-roman, VP. **-latā**, f. Cardiospermum Halicacabum, L. **-lekhā**, f. a streak of gold (on a touch-stone), Vās. **-vaṇij**, m. a gold-merchant, a partic. mixed caste (the son of a Vaiśya woman by an Ambashṭha), L. **-1. -vat**, mfn. 'containing or possessing gold' and 'having a correct pronunciation of sounds' (*-tā*, f.), BṛĀrUp., Sch.; beautiful, handsome, MW.; (*atī*), f. N. of various rivers containing g°, L.; of a town in Dakshiṇā-patha, Hit. **-2. -vat**, ind. like gold, L. **-varṇa**, mfn. golden coloured; m. N. of Vishṇu, L.; (*ā*), f. turmeric, ib.; (*°ṇa*)-*tā*, f. the having a golden colour (one of the 32 signs of perfection), Dharmas. 83. **-varsha**, m. N. of a king, Inscr. **-vastrâdi**, n. money and clothes &c., L. **-vijaya**, m. N. of a Kāvya. **-vṛishabha**, m. a bull made of g° (given as a present), Cat. **-śakaṭikā**, f. a golden toy-cart, Mṛicch. **-śiras**, mfn. having a golden head, MBh. **-śilêśvara-tīrtha**, n. N. of a Tīrtha, Cat. **-śekhara**, n. N. of a city, Vṛishabhān. **-shṭhivi** or **°vin**, m. 'spitting gold,' N. of a son of Sṛiñjaya, MBh. **-sānūra**, N. of a locality, Rājat. **-sāra**, N. of wk. **-siddha**, m. an adept in acquiring gold by magical means, Pañcat. **-sūtra**, n. a string of gold, Hariv.; Kum.; N. of Comm. **-steya**, n. the stealing of gold (one of the 5 Mahā-pātakas or great crimes), Mn. xi, 98 &c. **-steyin**, m. a stealer of gold, L. **-sthāna**, n. N. of a locality, Cat.; *-māhātmya*, n. N. of ch. of wk. **-hali**, m. a kind of tree, L. **Suvarṇâkarshaṇa-bhairava-stotra**, n. N. of a Stotra. **Suvarṇâksha**, m. 'golden-eyed,' N. of Śiva, MBh. **Suvarṇâkhya**, mfn. called Su-varṇa, MBh.; m. Mesua Roxburghii, L.; the thorn-apple, MW. **Suvarṇâbha**, m. Lapis Lazuli, Npr.; N. of a son of Śaṅkha-pada, MBh. **Suvarṇâbhisheka**, m. the sprinkling a bride and bridegroom with water containing a piece of gold, MW. **Suvarṇâlaṃkāra-vat**, mfn. having a golden ornament, Hcat. **Suvarṇâlu**, m. a kind of bulbous plant, L. **Suvarṇâvabhāsā**, f. N. of a Gandharva maiden, Kāraṇḍ. **Suvarṇâhvā**, f. yellow jasmine, L.

Suvarṇaka, mfn. golden, Harav.; of a beautiful colour, MW.; m. Cathartocarpus Fistula, Bhpr.; (ifc.) a Karsha of gold, MBh.; n. gold, ib.; R.; yellow brass, L.; lead, ib.; m. or n.(?) a kind of plant (v.l. *°ṇa-kshīrī*), Suśr.

Suvarṇasa, mfn., g. *tṛiṇâdi*.

Suvarṇâra, m. Bauhinia Variegata, Npr.

Suvarṇin. See *maṇi-ratna-suv°*.

Suvarṇī-√bhū, P. *-bhavati*, to become gold, Pañcat.; Kathās.

Suvarṇīya, mfn., g. *utkarâdi*.

Suvarṇya, mfn. = *suvarṇam arhati*, g. *daṇḍâdi.*

सुवर्धामन् *súvar-dhāman* &c. See p. 1236, col. 2.

सुवर्ष *su-varsha* &c. See p. 1233, col. 1.

सुवित *su-v-itá*, mfn. (fr. 5. *su* + *ita*; cf. *sv-itá*) easy of access or to traverse, prosperous (as a path), RV.; faring well, ib.; n. a good path, prosperous course (opp. to *dur-ita*), ib.; welfare, prosperity, fortune, good luck, ib.; AV.; TBr.

सुविद *su-vida*, *su-vidagdha* &c. See p. 1233, col. 2.

सुशंस *su-śáṇsa*, mfn. (i. e. 5. *su* + *ś°*) saying or wishing good things, blessing, RV.

Su (to be similarly prefixed to the following): **-śaṇsin**, mfn. announcing or wishing good things, W. **-śáka**, mf(*ā*)n. easy to be done or practicable, RV.; easy to or to be (inf.), Nyāyam. **-śakuna**, n. good birds, AV.; mf(*ā*)n. of good augury, auspicious, Bālar. **-śakta**, mfn. well able or capable, Pāṇ. v, 4, 121 (v. l.) **-śákti**, f. an easy possibility or feasibility, an easy affair, RV.; mfn. = prec., Pāṇ. v, 4, 121 (v. l.); m. N. of a man, Buddh. **-śaṭha**, mfn. very deceitful or false, Subh. **-śapha-gati-mukha**, mfn. having beautiful hoofs (and) gait (and) mouths, VarBṛS. **-śabda**, mfn. sounding well (as a flute), Mṛicch.; *-tā*, f. = *sauśabdya*, correct formation of grammatical forms, Pratāp. **-śama**, m. N. of a man (cf. *sauśami*), Siddh. **-śámi** or **-śámī**, ind. diligently, carefully, RV.; VS.; TS. **-śara**, mfn. easily broken, Nir. **-śaraṇá**, mfn. affording secure refuge or protection, RV.; MBh. xiii, 1173 (v. l. for *su-saraṇa*). **-śaraṇya**, mfn. id. (said of Śiva), Śivag. **-śarīra**, mfn. having a beautiful body, well shaped, VarBṛS. **-śárman**, n. good refuge or protection, AV.; mfn. granting secure r° or pr°, RV.; VS.; = *atisukha*, Vās. (Sch.); m. N. of an Asura, Kathās.; of a son of one of the Manus, Hariv.; MārkP.; of a king, MBh.; BhP.; of a Vaiśāli, MārkP.; of a Kāṇva, VP.; of Śāṇsapāyana, Cat.; pl. N. of a class of gods under the 13th Manu, MārkP.; (°*ma*)-*candra*, m. N. of a king, Inscr.; *-nagara* or *-pura*, n. N. of a town, ib. **-śalya**, m. Mimosa Catechu, L. **-śasta**, mfn. well recited (superl. *-tama*), AitBr. **-śastí**, f. good recitation, good hymn of praise (also as form of instr.), RV.; VS.; mfn. praiseworthy, RV. **-śāka**, m. 'good herb,' N. of various plants (Abelmoschus Esculentus; = *cañcu*; = *taṇḍulīya*), L.; n. = next, L. **-śākaka**, n. fresh ginger, L. **-śānta**, mfn. thoroughly allayed or extinguished, Kauś.; very calm or placid (as water), MBh.; (*ā*), f. N. of the wife of Śaśi-dhvaja, Pur. **-śānti**, f. perfect calm or tranquillity, MārkP.; m. N. of Indra under the third Manu, ib.; of a son of Aja-mīḍha, Hariv.; of a son of Śānti, VP. **-śārada**, m. N. of a teacher (with the patr. Śālaṅkāyana), IndSt. **-śāsana**, n. good government, MW. **-śāsita**, mf(*ā*)n. well governed or regulated, kept under good discipline, Hit. **-śāsya**, mfn. easy to be controlled or governed, MBh. **-śikshita**, mfn. well instructed, Mālav.; well trained or taught or disciplined, MBh. **-śikha**, mfn. having beautiful points or crests, L.; having a bright flame (as a lamp), Prab.; m. N. of Agni or fire, L.; (*ā*), f. a peacock's crest, MW.; cock's comb, L.; (°*khā*)-*samūha*, m. (a mass of) beautiful hair, BhP. **-śithila**, mfn. very loose, much slackened or lessened; °*lī-kṛita*, mfn. id., Mudr. **-śiprá** or **-śipra**, mfn. having beautiful cheeks or jaws, RV. **-śiprin**, mfn. id., MW. **-śimbikā**, f. a kind of plant, L. **-śiras**, mfn. having a fine head, R.; Hariv. **-śilpá**, mf(*ā*)n. beautifully decorated or variegated, RV.; VS. **-śiśvi** (*sú-*), mfn. swelling or growing well (in the womb), RV. **-śishṭa**, mfn. well governed or governing, MW.; m. a faithful minister or counsellor, ib. **-śishṭi** (*sú-*), f. good aid or assistance, RV. **-śishya**, m. a good pupil, Śak. **-śīghra**, mfn. very swift (*am*, ind.), MBh.; *-ga*, mfn. running very swiftly, R. **-śīta**, mfn. very cold or cooling, Suśr.; VarBṛS. &c.; m. Ficus Infectoria, L.; (*ā*), f. a partic. plant (= *śata-pattrī*), L.; n. great coldness, MW.; a kind of fragrant yellow sandalwood, L. **-śītala**, mfn. very cold or cooling, frigid, freezing, MBh.; Kāv. &c.; (*am*), n. coldness, Subh.; white sandal, L.; a kind of fragrant grass (= *gandha-tṛiṇa*), L. **-śīma**, mfn. good to lie or sit upon (opp. to *duḥ-ś°*), ŚBr.; ŚāṅkhBr.; (w. r. for *su-shīma* and *su-sīma*); *-kāma*, mf(*ā*)n. deeply in love (= *tīvra-manmatha*), Daś.; (of unknown meaning), Kauś. 77. **-śīla**, mfn. well-disposed, good-tempered, having an amiable disposition, MBh.; Kāv. &c.; tractable (as a cow), Yājñ.; well conducted, well made, well shaped, MW.; m. N. of a son of Kauṇḍinya, Hit.; of various kings, Kāv.; (*ā*), f. N. of a wife of Kṛishṇa, Hariv.; of a female attending on Rādhā, Pañcar.; of the wife of Yama, L.; of a daughter of Hari-svāmin, Cat.; n. good temper or disposition, MBh.; Pañcar.; *-guṇa-vat*, mfn. having an amiable temper and other good qualities, Subh.; *-tā*, f., *-tva*, n. excellence of temper or disposition, good morals, natural amiability, Kād.; Vet.; Hcat.; *-vat*, m. well-disposed, good-tempered, Mṛicch.; °*lântaka*, m. N. of a minister, Kautukar.; °*lin*, mfn. (= °*la-vat*), MārkP. **-śīvikā**, f. a kind of bulbous root or plant (= *vārāhī-kanda*), L. **-śukla**, mfn. very white, Mahāvy. **-śúkvan** (RV.) or **-śukváni** (VS.), mfn. shining brightly, brilliant. **-śuddha**, mfn. perfectly pure or bright, Vishṇ.; Hcat. **-śubha**, mfn. very beautiful or handsome (as an arm), R.; very lucky or auspicious (as a day), Kathās.; very noble (as a deed), R. **-śūlinī-daṇḍaka**, m. or n. (?) N. of wk. **-śṛiṅga**, mfn. having beautiful horns, TBr. **-śṛiṅgāra**, mfn. beautifully adorned, Pañcat. **-śṛita** (*sú-*), mfn. well cooked or prepared, AV. &c. &c. **-śéva**, mfn. very dear or kind or favourable, RV.; AV.; VS.; TS.; very auspicious or prosperous (as a path), AitBr. **-śévas**, mfn. very gracious or kind, AV. **-śévya**, mfn. dearly loved, RV. **-śóka**, mfn. shining beautifully, RV. **-śoṇa**, mfn. dark red, BhP. **-śodhita**, mfn. perfectly cleaned, Mahāvy. **-śopha**, mf(*ā*)n. much swollen, Siddh. on Pāṇ. iv, 1, 51. **-śobhana**, mf(*ā*)n. very handsome or beautiful, splendid, excellent, MBh.; Lalit.; Kathās. **-śobhamāna**, mfn. shining beautifully, handsome, splendid, MārkP. **-śobhita**, mfn. shining brightly, Nār.; beautified by (comp.), Pañcar. **-śoshita**, mfn. well dried, VarBṛS. **-ścandrá**, mfn. glittering beautifully, RV. **-śrápa**, mfn. easy to be cooked (compar. *-tara*), ŚBr. **-śrama**, m. N. of a son of Dharma (v. l. *suśruma*), VP. **-śrava**, mfn. worth hearing, Pañcar.; (*ā*), f. N. of a Vaidarbhi (the wife of Jayat-sena), MBh. **-śrávas**, mfn. abounding in glory, famous, RV.; AV.; BhP.; hearing well or gladly, gracious, kind (superl. *-tama*), RV.; Kāṭh.; ĀśvGṛ.; N. of a Prajā-pati, VP.; of a serpent-demon, Rājat.; of a man, RV. i, 53, 9 (Sāy.); of a Ṛishi (having the patr. Kaushya), ŚBr.; (°*vo*)-*mantra*, m. N. of a partic. Mantra, Saṃskārak. **-śravasyā́**, f. willingness to hear, RV. **-śrāta** (*sú-*), (= *su-śrita*) well cooked, RV. **-śrānta**, mfn. very tired, greatly exhausted, Cāṇ. (v. l.); Pañcat. **-śrī**, mfn. very splendid or rich, RV. **-śrīka**, mf(*ā*)n. id., Hariv.; Sāh.; (*ā*), f. the incense-tree, L. **-śrúk**, see *-śrút*. **-śrúṇa**, mfn. obtaining good hearing (Sāy. 'very famous'), RV. **-śrút**, mfn. (nom. *-śrúk*), hearing well, RV.; AV.; TBr.; m. N. of a man, Pat. on Pāṇ. i, 1, 3 &c. **-śruta** (*sú-*), mfn. very famous, RV.; well or correctly heard, Naish.; gladly heard, Mn. iii, 254; N. of the author of a system of medicine (reputed son of Viśvā-mitra and descendant of Dhanvantari; his work with that of Caraka, another older medical authority, is held in great esteem; it consists of six books); of a son of Su-bhāsa, VP.; of a son of Padmôdbhava, Daś.; (*am*), n. N. of the above medical work; also of the work of Caraka, Naish. iv, 116; 'well heard,' an exclamation at a Srāddha (cf. *śraushat*), Mn. iii, 254; *-pāṭha-śuddhi*, f. N. of wk.; *-saṃhitā*, f. Suśruta's medical work; *-sāra*, m. N. of wk. **-śruti** (*sú-*), f. a good or quick ear, AV. **-śroṇā**, f. N. of a river, Hariv. **-śroṇi**, mf(*ī*)n. having beautiful hips (= καλλίπυγος), MBh.; (*ī*), f. N. of a goddess, Cat. **-śrótu**, mfn. hearing willingly, RV. **-ślakshṇa**, mf(*ā*)n. very smooth or soft or tender (*am*, ind.), MBh.; very gracious (as speech), Bcar. **-ślishṭa**, mfn. closely adhering, well joined or contracted, close, tight, Kāv.; VarBṛS.; well ratified, Sāh.; very conclusive or intelligible, Mālatīm.; Jātakam.; *-guṇa*, mfn. having the strings tightly knotted (as a garland, *-tā*, f.), Mālatīm.; *-saṃdhi*, m. pl. very firm or strong joints, VarBṛS.; mfn. having very firm joints (*-tā*, f.), ib. **-ślesha**, m. close or intimate union, a close embrace, W.; mfn. having a close embrace (and 'having a beautiful play on words;' see *ślesha*), Vās. **-śloka** (*sú-*), mf(*ā*)n. well sounding or speaking, VS.; TBr. &c.; of good renown, famous, celebrated, BhP. **-ślokya**, mfn. very famous, BhP.; n. well sounding speech, praise, fame, GṛS. **-śva**, mfn. having a happy to-morrow, Pāṇ. v, 4, 120.

सुशवी *suśavī*. See *sushavī*, p. 1238, col. 1.

सुशिक्मन् *suśikman* (prob. w. r.), MaitrS.

सुशेरु *suśéru*, m. a kind of sand or gravel, TBr. (Sch.)

सुश्रवस् *su-śravas*, *su-śruta* &c. See col. 2.

सुषंसद् *su-shaṃsad*, mfn. (i. e. 5. *su* + *saṃ-sád*) having a good meeting, fond of good company, RV.

Su (to be similarly prefixed to the following, in which the initial *sh* stands for an orig. *s*): **-shakhí**, mfn. a good friend or having good friends, RV. **-sháṇa** or **-shaṇaṇá**, mfn. easy to be acquired, ib. **-shád**, mfn. addicted to sexual intercourse, AV. **-sháda**, mf(*ā*)n. easy to sit or dwell in, AV.; TS.; easy to be mounted or ridden (as a horse), VS. **-shadman**, m. N. of a man (cf. *saushadmana*). **-shaṃdhi**, m. (also written *su-s°*) N. of a son of Māndhātṛi, R.; of a son of Prasuśruta, VP. **-1. -shama**, mfn. very even &c. (= *sama*; cf. *su-sama*), L.; very beautiful, splendid, Pañcar.; easily intelligible, L.; (*ā*), f. exquisite beauty, splendour, Naish.; Bhām.; a partic. plant, Chandom.; a kind of metre, Col.; (with Jainas) the second Ara or spoke of a time-wheel in an Avasarpiṇī, and the fifth in an Utsarpiṇī (supposed to be a period in which continuous happiness is enjoyed by mankind; sometimes written *su-khamā*), L.; N. of a Surâṅganā, Siṇhās.; (*ī*), f., g. *gaurâdi*; (°*ma*)-*duḥshamā*, f. (with Jainas) N. of two spokes of a time-wheel (the third in an Avasarpiṇī and the fourth in an Utsarpiṇī), L. **-2. -sháma**, n. a happy year, ŚBr. **-shamiddha** (*sú-*), mfn. = *sú-samiddha* (q. v.) **-shamídh**, f. good fuel, RV.; TBr.; mfn. (also written *su-s°*) having good fuel, burning or lighting well, AitBr.; ŚāṅkhŚr. **-shavī**, see s. v. **-shavyá**, mfn. having a strong left hand (applied to Indra), RV. **-sháha** (or *-sháha*), mfn. easily subdued or conquered, RV. **-shā́**, mfn. (for *sushā* see s. v.) easily gaining or procuring, ib. **-shāḍha**, m. N. of Śiva, MBh. **-shāmán**, n. a beautiful song, RV.; (*-shā́man*), m. (also written *su-s°*), N. of a man, ib.; MBh. (cf. Pāṇ. vi, 4, 170, Sch.); mf(°*mnī*)n. peaceful, Bhaṭṭ. **-shārathi**, m. an excellent charioteer, RV. **-shā́ha**, see *-sháha*. **-shikta**, mfn. well sprinkled, R. **-shita**, mfn. = *-sita*, Pañcar. **-shirá**, see s. v. **-shīma**, mfn. cold, frigid, L.; pleasant, agreeable, L.; m. a sort of snake, L.; the Candra-kānta or moon gem, L.; (°*má*), prob. n. luck, welfare, Suparṇ. **-shút**, mfn. pressing out (Soma &c.) well (superl. *-shút-tama*), MaitrS. **-shuta** (*sú-*), mfn. well pressed out or prepared, RV. **-shuti** (*sú-*), f. a good or easy birth, RV. **-shupta** (*sú-*), mfn. fast asleep, ŚBr.; Kām. &c.; n. = next, Up.; Śaṃk.; BhP. **-shupti**, f. deep sleep (in phil. 'complete unconsciousness'), Vedântas.; *-vat*, ind. as in deep sleep, ib. **-shumát**, mfn. (prop.) very stimulating (accord. to Sāy. = *soma-vat* or *śobhana-prasava*), RV. x, 3, 1. **-shumṇá** or **-shumná**, mf(*ā*)n. very gracious or kind, RV.; VS.; m. N. of one of the 7 principal rays of the sun (supposed to supply heat to the moon), VP.; (*ā*), f. a partic. artery (prob. 'the carotid') or vein of the body (lying between those called *iḍā* and *piṅgalā*, and supposed to be one of the passages for the breath or spirit; cf. *brahma-randhra*), Up.; BhP.; Rājat. **-1. -shū́**, mfn. (prob.) very stimulating (accord. to others = *su-shuta*; superl. *-shū́tama*), VS. **-2. -shū́**, mfn. bringing forth easily, RV. **-shūta** (*sú-*), mfn. well begotten, ib. **-shūti**, f., Pāṇ. viii, 3, 88. **-shū́mā**, f. bringing forth easily, RV. **-shéka** and **-shecaná**, mfn. flowing or running well, ib. **-shéṇa**, mfn. having a good missile (said of Kṛishṇa and Indra), MBh.; VarBṛS.; m. 'having beautiful clusters,' Carissa Carandas, L.; Calamus Rotang, L.; m. N. of Vishṇu, MBh.; of a Gandharva, VS.; BhP.; of a Yaksha, VP.; of a serpent-demon, MBh.; of a Vidyā-dhara, Kathās.; of a monkey-chief (son of Varuṇa or Dhanvantari, father of Tārā, and physician of Su-grīva), MBh.; R. &c.; of a son of the second Manu, BhP.; of a son of Kṛishṇa, Hariv.; of a king of Śūra-sena, Ragh.; of a son of Parīkshit, MBh.; of a son of Dhṛitarāshṭra, ib.; of a son of Viśva-garbha, Hariv.; of a son of Vasu-deva, BhP.; of a son of Śambara, Hariv.;

of a son of Vṛishṭi-mat (or Vṛishṇi-mat), VP.; of a son of Karma-sena, Kathās.; of a physician of Prabhākara-vardhana, Vās., Introd.; (with *kavirāja-miśra*) of a grammarian, Cat.; (*ā*), f. N. of a princess, Kathās.; (*ī*), f. Ipomœa or Convolvulus Turpethum, L. — **sheṇikā**, f. N. of a plant (prob. = prec.), L. — **shedha**, mfn., g. *sushāmâdi*. — **shóma**, m. 'containing good sap,' N. of a partic. Soma vessel, RV.; (*ā*), f. id., ib.; N. of a river, ib.; BhP. — **shṭárīman**, mfn. forming an excellent bed or couch, VS.; TBr. — **shṭú**, mfn. highly praised or celebrated, RV. — **shṭuta** (*sú-*), mfn. id., ib.; correctly pronounced, ib.; Lāṭy. — **shṭutí**, f. excellent praise, a beautiful hymn, RV.; VS.; AV. — **shṭúbh**, mfn. uttering a shrill cry, RV.; ŚāṅkhŚr.; (prob. f.) a shrill cry, RV. — **shṭhāná**, mf(*ā*)n. standing firm, RV. — **shṭhā́man**, mfn. having a firm support or frame (as a chariot), ib. — **shṭhita**, incorrect for *su-sthita* (q.v.) — **shṭhú**, see below.

सुषवी *sushavī*, f. (also written *suśavī* and *susavī*) N. of various plants (Momordica Charantia; Nigella Indica &c.), Suśr.; Bhpr.

Sushā, f. (also written *śushā*; for *su-shā* see p. 1237, col. 3) black cumin or fennel, Car.

सुषि *sushi*, m. (also written *śushi*) the hole of a reed or cane, ĀpŚr., Sch.; m. a tube (cf. *deva-s*°). — **nandi**, m. N. of a king, VP.

Sushira, mf(*ā*)n. (prob. fr. *su + sirā*, q.v., also written *śush*°) 'having a good tube or channel,' perforated, pierced, hollow, RV. &c. &c.; having spaces, MW.; slow in articulation (= *vilambita*), id.; m. 'having a good flow of fluid or sap,' a reed, bamboo, cane, L.; fire (also n.), L.; a mouse, L.; (*ā*), f. a partic. fragrant bark, L.; a river, L.; (*am*), n. a hollow, hole, cavity, Kām.; MārkP.; a wind instrument, Saṃgīt.; the air, atmosphere, L.; cloves, L. — **ccheda**, m. a kind of flute, L. — **tā**, f. (Rājat.), **-tva**, n. (Śaṃk.) the being hollow, hollowness. — **vat**, mfn. hollow, ĀpŚr., Sch. — **vivara**, m. a hole (esp. of a snake), Kāv.; °*rin*, mfn. hollow, HPariś.

सुषिक *sushika* or *sushima*, m. coldness, L.; mfn. cold, ib.

सुषिलीका *sushilīkā*, f. a kind of bird, VS.; MaitrS.

सुषुत *su-shut* &c. See p. 1237, col. 3.

सुषुप्सा *sushupsā*, f. (fr. Desid. of √*svap*) desire of sleeping, sleepiness, MBh.; Naish.

Sushupsu, mfn. desirous of sleeping, sleepy, Suśr.; Śiś.; BhP.

सुषूय *sushūya*, Nom. Ā. °*yate* (also written *susūya*; cf. 1. *asūya*), to like, be fond of, enjoy (acc.), Car.

सुष्कन्त *sushkanta*, m. N. of a son of Dharmanetra (v.l. *sushmanta*), Hariv.

सुष्ठु *sushṭhú*, ind. (fr. √*sthā*; cf. *duḥ-shṭhu*) aptly, fitly, duly, well, excellently, exceedingly (*sushṭhu khalu*, 'most certainly'), RV. &c. &c. — **taram**, ind. still more, in a higher degree, Jātakam. — **tā**, f. welfare, prosperity, Mahāv. — **dvāra**, mfn. affording a good entrance (used in explaining *sukhá*), Sāy. on RV. iii, 35, 4. — **váh** (or *-vā́h*), mfn. carrying well, bearing along rapidly (as horses), RV.

सुष्म *sushma*, n. a rope, cord (v.l. for *śulba*), L.

सुष्मन्त *sushmanta*. See *sushkanta* above.

सुष्वय *sushváya*, Nom. P. Ā. °*yati*, °*te* (fr. next), to run, flow, RV.; AV.

Súshvi, mfn. (fr. 3. *su*) pressing or preparing Soma, RV.

सुसंयत *su-saṃyata*, mfn. (i.e. 5. *su* + *s*°) well governed or guided (as horses), MBh.; Prab.; BhP.; well restrained or controlled, well composed, Mn.; MBh. &c.

Su (to be similarly prefixed to the following): — **saṃyátta**, mf(*ā*)n. well prepared or ready or on one's guard (v.l. *-sampanna*), Hariv. — **saṃyukta**, mfn. closely joined or united, Hariv.; well or equally matched (in number), R.; well supplied or furnished with (instr.), ib. — **saṃyuta**, mfn. well composed or knit together (v.l. *-saṃhata*), R.; well joined with (comp.), BrahmaP. — **saṃrabdha** (*sú-*), mfn. firmly established, RV.; very angry, greatly enraged or agitated (compar. *-tara*), MBh.; R. &c.; n. = next, R. — **saṃrambha**, m. violent anger, R., Sch. — **saṃvigna**, mfn. greatly agitated or perplexed, MBh.; R. — **saṃvīta**, mfn. well covered or clothed or dressed, MBh.; well girt, well mailed, ib.; richly furnished with (comp.), R. — **saṃvṛita**, mfn. well covered or veiled or dressed, wrapped up or concealed in (instr. or comp.), Mn.; MBh. &c.; well girt with (instr.), R.; well surrounded or accompanied by (instr.), BhP.; well hidden, kept very secret, MBh.; R.; carefully guarding one's self, MārkP. — **saṃvṛiti**, mfn. well concealed, Śiś. xvi, 23. — **saṃvṛitta**, mfn. appearing in good or proper order, rightly sprung from (abl.), Hariv.; duly occurred, BhP.; well-rounded, Mahāv.; *-skandhatā*, f. having the shoulders well rounded (one of the 32 signs of perfection), Dharmas. 83. — **saṃvṛitti**, w.r. for *-saṃvṛiti*. — **saṃvṛiddha**, mfn. well thriven, prosperous, MBh. — **saṃśā́s** (*sú-*), mfn. well directing or instructing, AV. — **saṃśita**, mfn. well sharpened, very sharp, RV.; AV.; MBh.; of keen understanding, MBh. — **saṃśrita**, w.r. for prec. — **saṃślishṭa**, mfn. well composed (as a speech), R. — **saṃsád**, see *-shaṃsád*. — **saṃsṛishṭa**, w.r. for *-sammṛishṭa*. — **saṃskṛita** (*sú-*), mfn. beautifully adorned or decorated, RV.; well cooked or prepared, R.; Lalit.; kept in good order, R. (cf. comp.); correct Sanskṛit, Suśr.; (prob. m.) a sacred text or precept, MBh. (Nīlak.); °*tôpaskara*, mfn. keeping the household utensils in good order, Mn. v, 150; °*ra-tā*, f., Vishṇ. — **saṃsthā**, f. (only acc. with √*kṛi*, 'to duly discharge an obligation'), R. — **saṃsthāna**, mfn. well shaped or formed, VarBṛS. — **saṃsthita**, mfn. id., R.; well situated, W.; standing firmly, doing well, ib.; well brought together, circumscribed, ib.; m. N. of a man, Saddh. — **saṃhata**, mf(*ā*)n. firmly joined or combined, closely united, pressed against each other, MBh.; Kāv. &c.; well compacted, well knit together (acc. with √*kṛi*, 'to close very tightly'), R.; VarBṛS.; Mṛicch. — **saṃhati**, mfn. well combined, closely united, Śiś. — **saṃhita**, mfn. well united, MW.; *-pramāṇa*, mfn. having well united principals or chiefs, ib. — **saṃhṛishṭa**, mfn. greatly delighted, R. — **saktu**, m. pl. excellent groats, VarYogay. — **saktha** or **-sakthi**, mfn. having beautiful thighs, Pāṇ. v, 4, 121. — **sakhi**, m. (cf. *su-shakhi*) a good friend, Śiś. — **saṃkaṭa**, mfn. firmly closed, MBh.; hard to be explained, difficult, ib.; n. a great difficulty, very difficult matter or task, BhP. — **saṃkāśá**, mf(*ā́*)n. of beautiful appearance, handsome, RV. — **saṃkula**, m. N. of a king, MBh. — **saṃkruddha**, mfn. greatly enraged, MBh.; R. — **saṃkshepa**, m. N. of Śiva, MBh. — **saṅga**, mfn. very much adhered to or liked, MBh. — **saṃgatā**, f. N. of a woman, Ratnâv. — **saṃgama**, m. an excellent assembly or place of meeting, BhP. — **saṃgupta**, mfn. well kept or guarded or concealed, MBh. — **saṃgṛihīta**, mfn. well restrained or controlled or governed; *-rāshṭra*, mfn. one who governs his country well, Mn. vii, 113; well received, MBh.; well kept or preserved, W.; well abridged, ib. — **saṃgraha**, m. an excellent compendium, Hariv. — **saciva**, m. a good minister or counsellor, Mudr.; mfn. having a good m° or c°, Kām. — **sajjī-√kṛi**, P. *-karoti*, to make perfectly ready, Hit. — **saṃcita**, mfn. well gathered, carefully accumulated (*am*, ind.. with √*kṛi*, 'to gather or collect carefully'), ĀśvGṛ.; Pañcat.; amply provided with, Hcat. — **satkṛita**, mfn. well arranged, beautifully adorned or decorated, MBh.; received or treated with great hospitality, highly honoured, R.; one to whom the supreme honours have been duly rendered, R. — **sattra**, n. a well managed hospital or hospice, Kathās. — **sattva**, mfn. very resolute or courageous, ib. — **satyá**, mfn., AV. xx, 135, 4; (*ā*), f. N. of a wife of Janaka, KālP. — **sadṛiśa**, mf(*ī*)n. very like or similar, Veṇīs.; Nāg. — **sani**, mfn. very munificent or liberal (°*ni-tā*, f.), RV. — **sanitṛi**, m. a liberal giver, generous benefactor, ib. — **saṃtushṭa**, mfn. well satisfied, MBh. — **saṃtosha**, mfn. easy to be satisfied, ib. — **saṃtrasta**, mfn. greatly alarmed, R. — **saṃdīpta**, mfn. flaming beautifully, Pañcat. — **saṃdṛiś**, mfn. having a pleasing aspect, agreeable to look at, fair to see, RV. — **saṃdha**, mfn. true to a promise, keeping one's word, Kām. — **saṃdhi**, see *-shaṃdhi*. — **saṃdhita**, mfn. well reconciled, MW. — **sanna**, mf(*ā*)n. completely finished or done with, frustrated, foiled, Mṛicch. — **saṃnata** (*sú-*), mfn. well directed (said of an arrow), AV. — **saṃnipātita**, mfn. well hurled, R. — **sabhājita**, mfn. well honoured, treated with great attention or regard, R. — **sabheya** (*sú-*), mfn. skilful in council or company, TS. — **sama**, mf(*ā*)n. (cf. *su-shama*) perfectly level or smooth, VarBṛS.; well-proportioned, Vishṇ.; better than middling, VarBṛS.; °*mī-√kṛi*, to make perfectly smooth or even, MBh. — **samākṛita**, mf(*ā*)n. well furnished or supplied with (instr.), R. — **samāpta**, mfn. well finished or done, Mahāvy. — **samārabdha**, mfn. (prob.) very energetic in enterprise, ib. — **samāśrita**, mfn. well stationed, R. — **samāsīna**, mfn. comfortably seated, MBh. — **samāhita** (*sú-*), mfn. well laden (as a waggon), ŚBr.; well arrayed or repaired, beautifully adorned, R.; very intent or attentive, having the mind intently fixed or absorbed on a subject or object, MBh.; Kāv. &c.; perfectly fit or suitable, Mālatīm. — **samiddha** (*sú-*), mfn. well kindled or lighted, RV.; GṛŚrS. — **samidh**, see *-shamidh*. — **samīpa**, mfn. occurring in a short time, imminent, VarBṛS. — **samīhita**, mfn. much desired, very welcome, Mālatīm. — **samubdha** (*sú-*), mfn. well bound or fettered, RV. — **samṛiddha** (*sú-*), mfn. quite perfect, AV.; ŚBr.; very abundant, R.; very wealthy or prosperous, Mn. iii, 125; °*ddhârtha*, mf(*ā*)n. abundantly provided with everything, R. — **samṛiddhi**, f. great wealth or riches, MBh. — **sampad**, f. pl. plenty, abundance, great wealth or prosperity, Pañcad. — **sampanna**, mf(*ā*)n. well furnished or supplied, MBh.; Hariv.; full grown, Mṛicch. i, $\frac{55}{56}$. — **sampishṭa** (*sú-*), mfn. much crushed or shattered, RV. — **sampūrṇa**, mfn. completely filled, i.e. provided with (comp.), R. — **samprajña**, mfn. perfectly conscious, Lalit. — **sampratapta**, mfn. thoroughly harassed or afflicted, Kām. — **samprasthita**, m. N. of a man, Buddh. — **samprahṛishṭa**, mfn. greatly delighted, R. (B.) — **samprīta**, mfn. id., Bhaṭṭ. — **sambaddha**, mfn. well bound, closely united, MBh.; Pañcat. — **sambandha**, mfn. well joined, MW. — **sambhava**, m. N. of a king, Buddh. — **sambhāvya**, m. N. of a son of Manu Raivata (v.l. *sambhāvya*), VP. — **sambhṛit**, f. good or right collecting together, TS.; TBr. — **sambhṛita**, mfn. well collected or arranged or prepared, MBh. (printed *-saṃvṛita*). — **sambhṛiti**, f. right collection of requisites, Naish. — **sambhrama**, m. great agitation or hurry, Pañcat.; great reverence, MW. — **sambhramat** (Bcar.), or **-sambhrānta** (MBh.), mf(*ā*)n. greatly agitated or bewildered. — **sammata**, mfn. much honoured, highly approved, MBh. — **sammṛishṭa** (*sú-*), mfn. well rubbed or cleansed, RV.; MBh. — **saraṇa**, n. getting on well, easy progress, RV.; m. N. of Śiva (v.l. *-śaraṇa*), MBh. — **sarala**, mfn. perfectly straight, Gol. — **sártu**, f. N. of a river, RV. — **sarva** (*sú-*), mfn. quite complete, ŚBr. — **salila**, mf(*ā*)n. having good water, R. — **sava**, w.r. for *-hava*, AV. — **sasyá**, mf(*ā́*)n. well grown with corn, Hariv. — 1. **-saha** (*sú-*), ind. good company, RV. — 2. **-saha**, mfn. easy to be borne or suffered, W.; bearing or enduring well, ib.; m. N. of Śiva, MBh. (= *saumya*, Nīlak.) — **sahā́ya**, mfn. having a good companion or assistant, Mn. vii, 31; *-vat*, mfn. id., Suśr.; Kathās. — **sādhana**, mfn. easy to be proved (*-tva*, n.), Sarvad. — **sādhita**, mfn. well trained or educated, Hit. (v.l.); well cooked or prepared, Lalit. — **sādhu**, mfn. quite right or correct, Car. — **sādhya**, mf(*ā*)n. easy to be kept in order, obedient, amenable, Pañcar. — **sāntvita**, mf(*ā*)n. thoroughly conciliated, MBh. — **sāntvyamāna**, mf(*ā*)n. being thoroughly conciliated, ib. — **sāman**, n. conciliatory words, good negotiation, Pañcat. (v.l.); m., see *su-shāman*. — **sāyá**, n. a good evening (*am*, ind. 'early in the evening'), AV.; KātyŚr. — **sāra**, m. good essence or sap or substance, MW.; competence, ib.; mfn. having good ess° or sap, ib.; m. the red-flowering Khadira, Mimosa Catechu, L.; *-vat*, mfn. having good ess° or subst°, MW.; n. crystal, L. — **sārathi**, m. having a good charioteer, Śiś. — **sârtha-vāha**, m. N. of a man, Buddh. — **sāvitra**, n. good action or influence of Savitṛi, PañcavBr.; KātyŚr. — **sikatā**, f. (only L.) good sand; gravel; sugar. — **sikta**, mfn. (cf. *su-sh*°) well sprinkled, Mahāv. — **sic**, mfn. (of unknown meaning), MaitrS. — **sita**, mfn. pure white, Kathās. — **siddha**, mfn. well cooked, Suśr.; very efficacious, possessing great magical power, MBh.; °*ddhârtha*, mfn. one whose object is completely effected, ib. — **sīma**, mf(*ā*)n. having the hair well parted, GṛŚrS.; KaushUp.; having good boundaries, R.; m. N. of a son of Bindu-sāra, Divyâv.; (*ā*), f. a good boundary, MW.; N. of the mother of the sixth

Arhat, L.; of a town, Divyâv. **-sīman**, m. N. of a village, HPariś. **-sukha**, mf(*ā*)n. very pleasant or easy or comfortable (*am*, ind.), R.; Hariv.; feeling very comf° or happy, R.; *-dṛiśya*, mfn. very pleasant to see, Pañcar.; °*khôdaya*, mfn. causing great comfort or pleasure, R. **-sukhin**, mfn. very comfortable or happy, R. **-sugandha** or °**dhi**, very sweet-smelling or fragrant, MBh.; R. &c. **-sutama** (*sú-*), mfn. (used in explaining *su-shū́tama*), ŚBr. **-sundara**, mfn. very handsome, Buddh. **-subhiksha**, n. great abundance of food, R. **-sura-priyā**, f. jasmine, L. **-sūkshma**, mf(*ā*)n. very minute or small or delicate, MBh.; R. &c.; very subtle or keen (as understanding), MBh.; very difficult to be fathomed or understood, MuṇḍUp.; R.; m. or n.(?) an atom, Vishṇ., Sch.; *-pattrā*, f. a species of Valeriana, L.; °*mêśa*, m. 'lord of atoms,' N. of Vishṇu, Vishṇ. **-sūtra**, mfn. (prob. a word having a double sense), Cat. **-sena**, w. r. for *-sheṇa*. **-sevita**, mfn. well served (as a king), Hit. **-sevya**, mfn. (a road) to be well or easily followed, BhP. **-saindhavī**, f. a good mare from Sindh, Kathās. **-saubhaga**, n. conjugal felicity, BhP. **-skandana**, m. a partic. fragrant plant, L. **-skandha**, mfn. having a beautiful stalk or stem, VarBṛS.; *-māra*, v. l. for *skandha-māra* (q. v.) **-stanā** or °**nī**, f. (a woman) having beautiful breasts, Pāṇ. iv, 1, 54, Sch. **-stambha**, m. a good post or pillar, Pañcat. **-stuta**, m. (cf. *-shṭuta*) N. of a son of Supārśva, VP. **-strī**, f. a good chaste woman, Kāv.; Kathās. **-stha**, mf(*ā*)n. well situated, faring well, healthy, comfortable, prosperous, happy (compar. *-tara*), Mn.; MBh. &c.; *-kalpa*, mfn. almost well or at ease, Śak.; *-citta*, mfn. easy at heart, feeling happy or comfortable, MBh.; *-tā*, f. health, welfare, happiness, R.; *-tva*, n. id., MW.; *-mānasa*, mfn. (= *-citta*), R. **-sthaṇḍila**, n. a beautiful place, Kāś. on Pāṇ. vi, 2, 195. **-sthaya**, Nom. P. °*yati* (fr. *su-stha*), to establish or settle well, make comfortable, Bhaṭṭ. **-sthala**, m. pl. N. of a people (cf. *su-sthāla* in g. *bhargâdi*), MBh. **-sthāna**, n. a beautiful place, Kathās. (a partic. term in music), Inscr. **-sthāvatī**, f. (in music) a partic. Rāga, Saṃgīt. **-sthita**, mf(*ā*)n. well established, MBh.; R.; firm, unshaken (as a heart), R. (B.); being on the right path, innocent, Hariv.; being in good condition or well off, easy, comfortable, healthy, prosperous, fortunate, MBh.; Kāv. &c.; artless, simple (*e*, voc. f. in addressing a woman), R.; m. N. of various Jaina teachers, HPariś.; (*am*), n. a house with a gallery on all sides, VarBṛS.; *-tva*, n. ease, comfort, welfare, happiness, Śiś.; *-manas*, mfn. being in a happy frame of mind, contented, MW.; *-m-manya*, mfn. fancying one's self prosperous or well off, Hit. **-sthiti**, f. an excellent position, Ragh.; good condition, well-being, welfare, Bhadrab.; health convalescence, W. **-sthira**, mf(*ā*)n. very firm or steady, stable, MBh.; BhP.; resolute, cool, W.; (*ā*), f. a partic. vein or artery, Pañcar.; *-m-manya*, mfn. considering one's self firmly established, Śiś.; *-yauvana*, mf(*ā*)n. having perpetual youth, always young, Pañcar.; *-varman*, m. N. of a son of Sthira-varman (v. l. *sura-v*°), Hcar. **-stheya**, n. (impers.) easy to stand, MBh. **-snāta**, mfn. well purified by bathing, (esp.) one who has duly performed his ablutions, Vet.; BhP.; HPariś. **-snigdha**, mf(*ā*)n. very smooth or soft or gentle, VarBṛS.; Pañcar.; very loving or tender, Kāv.; (*ā*), f. a kind of creeper, L.; (°*dha*)-*gambhīra*, mfn. very soft and deep-toned, MW. **-snusha**, mf(*ā*)n. having a good daughter-in-law, RV. **-sparśa**, mfn. pleasant to the touch, very soft or tender, BhP. **-spashṭa**, mfn. very clear or distinct or manifest (*am*, ind.), Kathās.; Rājat. **-sphīta**, mfn. very thriving or flourishing or prospering, MBh.; Kāś. **-sphuṭa**, mfn. very clear, Virac. **-smita**, mf(*ā*)n. smiling sweetly, L. **-srag-dhara**, mfn. wearing a beautiful garland, BhP. **-sráj**, mfn. id., AV.; ŚBr. **-srás**, mfn. becoming loose or falling off easily, AV. **-sroṇi**, w. r. for *-śroṇi* (q. v.) **-srotas**, mfn. streaming beautifully, L.; m. N. of a man, Pat. on Pāṇ. vi, 1, 113; m. or f.(?) N. of a river (v. l. *su-śroṇā*), Hariv. **-svadha**, m. pl. N. of a partic. class of deceased ancestors, ib.; (*ā*), f. welfare, prosperity, MārkP. **-svana**, mfn. very loud (*am*, ind.), R. **-svapna**, m. a good or lucky dream, Rājat.; HPariś.; m. 'having good dreams,' N. of Śiva, MBh. **-svabhāva**, mf(*ā*)n. good-natured, MBh. **-svara**, m. the right tone or accent, Śiksh.; mf(*ā*)n. having a beautiful voice, MBh.; well-sounding, harmonious, melodious (*am*, ind.), Kāv.; Kathās.; loud (*am*, ind.), MBh.; R. &c.; m. a conch, L.; N. of a son of Garuḍa, MBh. **-sváru**, mfn. (of unknown meaning), RV. v, 44, 5 (= *śobhana-gamana* or *-stutika*, Sāy.) **-svāgata**, n. a hearty welcome (°*taṃ te 'stu*, a hearty w° to thee!), MBh.; R.; mf(*ā*)n. attended with a hearty w°, R. **-svāda**, mf(*ā*)n. having a good taste, well-flavoured, sweet, Pañcat.; Rājat. **-svādu**, mfn. id.; *-toya*, mfn. containing very sweet water, Hit. **-svānta**, mfn. having a good or happy mind, well-disposed, MW. **-svāpa**, m. deep sleep, L. **-svāmin**, m. a good lord or chief, Subh. **-svinna**, mfn. well boiled or cooked, Hariv. **-sveda**, mf(*ā*)n. sweating well, Siddh. on Pāṇ. iv, 1, 54.

सुस्थुषस् *susthushas* (to be pronounced in a partic. case for *tasthushas*), TāṇḍBr.

सुस्नयु *susnayu*, m. (said to be fr. √*snā*) the institutor of a sacrifice (= *yajamāna*), L.

सुस्ना *susnā*, f. a kind of pulse, Lathyrus Sativus, L.

सुस्मूर्षमाण *susmūrshamāṇa*, mfn. (fr. Desid. of √*smṛi*) wishing or trying to recollect, Bhaṭṭ.

Susmūrshā, f. the wish to recollect, Nyāyam., Sch.

सुस्रग्धर *su-srag-dhara* &c. See col. 1.

सुस्सल *sussala*, m. N. of a man (cf. *saussala*), Rājat.

सुह् *suh* (cf. √*sah*), cl. 4. P. *suhyati*, to satisfy, gladden, Dhātup. xxvi, 21; to be glad, rejoice, ib.; to bear, endure, support, ib.

सुहणमुख *suhaṇamukha* (?), N. of a place, Cat.

सुहत *su-hata*, mfn. (i. e. 5. *su* + *hata*; fr. √*han*) thoroughly beaten or slain, ShaḍvBr.; Pañcat.; justly slain or killed, Jātakam.

Su (to be similarly prefixed to the following): **-hána**, mfn. easy to be slain or killed, RV. **-hanu**, mfn. having handsome jaws, MBh.; R.; m. N. of an Asura, MBh. **-hántu**, mfn. = *-hána*, RV. **-haya**, see *mahā-suhayá*. **-hara**, m. 'seizing well,' N. of an Asura (v. l. *a-hara*), MBh. **-hala**, mfn. having an excellent plough (also °*li*), Pāṇ. v, 4, 121; m. N. of a physician and an ambassador (contemporaries of Maṅkha), Śrīkaṇṭh. **-halana**, m. (with *bhaṭṭa*) N. of the author of a Comm. on Halāyudha's Mṛita-saṃjīvanī, Cat. **-háva**, mf(*ā*)n. well or easily invoked, listening willingly, RV.; AV.; invoking well, ib.; AitBr.; n. an auspicious or successful invocation, RV.; AV. **-havis**, mfn. having or offering beautiful oblations, devout, pious, RV.; m. N. of an Āṅgirasa, PañcavBr.; of a son of Bhumanyu, MBh. **-hávītu-nāman**, mfn. one whose name is to be invoked auspiciously or successfully, RV. **-1. -havyá**, mf(*ā*)n. fit for invocation, RV. **-2. -havyá**, mfn. sacrificing well or successfully (applied to Agni), ib. **-hasânana**, mfn. having a cheerful smiling face, W. **-hásta**, mf(*ā*)n. having beautiful hands, RV.; TS.; skilful or clever with the h°, RV.; ŚāṅkhŚr.; trained in arms, disciplined, L.; m. N. of a Soma-keeper, VS.; of a son of Dhṛita-rāshṭra, MBh. **-hastin**, m. N. of a Jaina teacher, HPariś. **-hástya**, mfn. skilful-handed, clever, RV.; m. N. of a Ṛishi (having the metron. Gausheya and author of RV. x, 41), Anukr. **-hā́rd**, mfn. having a good interior, i. e. a good stomach &c. (said of Indra), RV.; having a good or loving heart, kind, benevolent, a friend (opp. to *dur-hā́rd*), AV. **-hāsa**, mf(*ā*)n. having a pleasant smile, Chandom. **-hāsin**, mfn. laughing, i. e. radiant or shining with (comp.), VarBṛS. **-hiṃs**, mfn. (nom. *-hin*) one who strikes well, Vop. **-hita** (*sú-*), mf(*ā*)n. very fit or suitable, Nir.; very salutary or beneficial, R.; thoroughly satiated or satisfied (esp. with food and drink), AV. &c. &c.; very friendly, affectionate, W.; (*ā*), f. one of the tongues of fire, L.; n. satiety, abundance, TS. **-hiraṇyá**, mfn. having beautiful gold, abounding in gold, RV.; VS. **-hiraṇya-vat** (*sú-*), mfn. id., AV. **-huta** (*sú-*), mf(*ā*)n. well offered or sacrificed, RV.; AV.; KātyŚr.; R.; well worshipped with sacrifices, BhP.; Pañcat.; (*am*), n. good or right sacrifice, ŚBr.; GṛŚrS.; *-kṛit* or *-hut*, mfn. offering a right s°, GṛŚrS.; °*tâd*, mfn. eating a right s°, RV. **-hū́**, mfn. calling or invoking well, VS. **-hūti**, see *svabhūti*. **-hṛid** &c., see s. v. **-hemanta**, m. a good winter, GṛS. **-hótṛi** (or *sú-h*°), m. a good sacrificer or priest, RV.; TS.; N. of a son of Bhumanyu, MBh.; of a son of Vitatha, Hariv. **-hotra**, m. N. of the author of RV. vi, 31, 32 (having the patr. Bhāradvāja), Anukr.; of a Bārhaspatya, IndSt.; of an Ātreya, MārkP.; of a preceptor, W.; of a Kaurava, MBh.; of a son of Saha-deva, ib.; of a son of Bhumanyu, ib.; of a son of Bṛihat-kshatra, Hariv.; of a son of Bṛihad-ishu, ib.; of a son of Kāñcana-prabha, ib.; of a son of Vitatha, ib.; of a son of Su-dhanvan, ib.; of a son of Su-dhanus, BhP.; of a son of Kshatra-vṛiddha, ib.; of a Daitya, MBh.; of a monkey, R.; pl. N. of a seat of fire-worshippers, Cat. **-hvāna**, mfn. (used in explaining *su-hava*), Nir.

सुहृद् *su-hṛid*, m. 'good-hearted,' 'kind-hearted,' 'well-disposed,' a friend, ally (also said of planets; *suhṛido janāḥ*, 'friends'), ŚrS.; Mn.; MBh. &c.; N. of the fourth astrol. mansion, VarBṛS.; f. a female friend, Gobh.; Kauś.; mfn. (only ifc.) fond of, liking or devoted to, Bālar.; very similar to, closely resembling, ib. **-āgama**, m. 'arrival of a friend,' N. of wk. **-bala**, m. the army of an ally, W. **-bheda**, m. separation of friends (N. of the 2nd book of the Hitôpadeśa). **-vadha**, m. the killing of a friend, Mn. xi, 56. **-vākya**, n. the speech or advice of a friend, MBh.

Suhṛic, in comp. for *suhṛid*. **-choka-vivardhana** (for *-śok*), augmenting the grief of a friend, MBh.

Suhṛij, in comp. for *suhṛid*. **-jana**, m. a friendly person, friend, MBh.; R.; (also pl.) friends, ib.

Suhṛit, in comp. for *suhṛid*. **-tama**, mfn. (superl.) very friendly or cordial, kind, affectionate, MBh. **-tā**, f., **-tva**, n. friendship, friendliness, affection, MBh.; Kāv. &c. **-tyāga**, m. the desertion of a friend, MW. **-prakāśâkhya-stava**, m. N. of wk. **-prâpti**, f. the acquisition of a friend, Sāṃkhyak.

Suhṛida, m. 'a friend,' N. of Śiva, MBh. **-druh**, mfn. (Nom. *-dhruk* or *-dhruṭ*) one who injures a friend, MW.

Su-hṛidaya, mfn. good-hearted, affectionate (superl. *-tama*), AitBr.

Suhṛin, in comp. for *suhṛid*. **-nārī**, f. a female friend, Cāṇ. (v. l.) **-mitra**, n. sg. friends and allies, MBh. **-mukha**, mfn. friendly-faced, Bcar.

Suhṛil, in comp. for *suhṛid*. **-liṅga-dhara**, mfn. having the mere appearance of a friend, BhP.

सुहोतृ *su-hotṛi* &c. See above.

सुह्म *suhma*, m. N. of a district or (pl.) a people in the west of Bengal (called after Suhma, the son of Dīrgha-tamas and Su-deshṇā, the wife of Bali, or the son of Kāñcanêshudhi, i. e. Bali in a former birth), MBh.; Hariv.; Pur. **-nagara**, n. the city of the Suhmas, Pāṇ. vi, 2, 89, Sch.

Suhmaka (ifc.) = *suhma*, Hariv.

सू 1. *sū* (not separable in all forms fr. √2. *sū*; cf. 1. *su-shū́*, *asu-sū*, and √4. *su*), cl. 6. P. (Dhātup. xxviii, 115) *suvā́ti* (in Br. also °*te*, and accord. to Dhātup. xxii, 43 and xxiv, 32 also *savati* and *-sauti*; pf. *sushuvé*, AV.; p. *sushuvāṇá*, q. v.; aor. *asāvīt*, *sāvishat*, RV.: Pass. *sūyáte*, Br. &c.), to set in motion, urge, impel, vivify, create, produce, RV. &c. &c.; to hurl upon, Bhaṭṭ.; to grant, bestow (esp. said of Savitṛi), RV.; to appoint or consecrate to (Ā. 'to let one's self be consecrated'), AV.; TS.; to allow, authorize, ŚBr.: Intens. *soshavīti*, to urge or impel violently (said of Savitṛi), RV.

Sūka, m. (cf. *sṛika*) an arrow, L.; air, wind, L.; a lotus, L.; m. N. of a son of Hrada (v. l. *mūka*), Hariv.

1. **Sūta**, mfn. urged, impelled &c. (cf. 3. *sūta*, p. 1241, col. 2, 1. *suta*, and *nṛi-shūta*).

1. **Sūti**. See 1. *pra-sūti*.

1. **Sūnu**, m. one who urges or incites, an inciter, Sāy. on RV. i, 103, 4; the sun (= *savitṛi*), L.

Sūshuvāṇá, mfn. (cf. Pāṇ. iii, 2, 106, Sch.) being consecrated, consecrated, TS.; Br.

सू 2. *sū* (cf. 1. *sū* and √5. *su*), cl. 2. Ā. (Dhātup. xxiv, 21) *sūte* (1. sg. pr. *suve*, 3. sg. impf. *asūta*; in later language also *sūyate* [xxvi, 31] and in comp. with *pra* also *-savati* and *-sauti* [cf. xxiv, 31]; pf. *sasūva*, RV.; *sushuvé*, AV. &c.; *susāva*, MBh. &c.; aor. *asushot*, MaitrS.; °*shavuḥ*, TBr.; *asoshṭa*, ChUp.; *asaushīt* and *asavishṭa*, Gr.; fut. *sotā*, *savitā*, ib.; *soshyáti*, °*te*, Br. &c.; *savishyati*, °*te*, MBh. &c.; p. f. *sū́shyantī*, RV.;

soshyántī [s. v.], ŚBr.; inf. *sū́tave*, RV.; *sūtavai*, AV.; *sávitave*, ib.; *sotum* or *savitum*, Gr.; ind. p. *sūtvā́*, Br.; *-sūya*, MBh. &c.; *-sū́ya*, ŚBr.), to beget, procreate, bring forth, bear, produce, yield, RV. &c. &c.: Pass. *sūyate* (aor. *asāvi*), to be begotten or brought forth, MBh.; Kāv. &c.: Caus. *sāvayati*, Gr.: Desid. *susūshati*, ib.

3. **Sū**, mfn. begetting, procreating, bringing forth, producing (mostly ifc.; see *a-*, *ambhaḥ-*, *karṇa-sū* &c.); m. one who begets, a father, RV.; VS.; a mother, RV. i, 32, 9; child-bearing, parturition, W. [Cf. Gk. ὗς, σῦς; Lat. *sus;* Angl.Sax. *sû;* Eng. *sow;* Germ. *Sau.*]

2. **Sūta**, mfn. (for 3. see p. 1241, col. 2) born, engendered (see *su-shūta*); one that has brought forth (young), Mn.; VarBṛS.; m. quicksilver, ŚārṅgS.; Sarvad.; the sun, W.; (*ā*), f. a woman who has given birth to a child, MW.; a young quadruped, L.; w. r. for *sutā*, Pañcat. iii, $\frac{1}{2}\frac{8}{4}\frac{6}{4}$. **-mahôdadhi**, m. N. of a wk. on medicine (cf. *sūtârṇava*). **-rāj**, m. quicksilver, L. **-vaśā** (*sūtá-*), f. a cow which remains barren after its first calf, AV.; MaitrS. **Sūtârṇava**, m. N. of a wk. on medicine (cf. *sūta-mahôdadhi*).

Sūtaka, n. birth (also 'the calving of a cow' &c.), GṛS.; Mn.; MBh. &c.; impurity (of parents) caused by child-birth or miscarriage, Yājñ.; Dhūrtas.; impurity (in general), Subh.; an obstacle, Tithyād.; (*akā* and *ikā*), f., see below; (*am*), m. n. quicksilver, mercury, Sarvad. **-bhojana**, n. a natal feast, ŚāṅkhGṛ. **-sāra** and **-siddhânta**, m. N. of wks. **Sūtakânna**, n. food rendered impure by child-birth or miscarriage, AitBr.; GṛŚrS. **Sūtakânnâdya**, n. id. &c., Mn. iv, 112.

Sūtakā, f. a woman recently delivered, Pāṇ. vii, 3, 45, Vārtt. 10, Pat. **-gṛiha**, n. a room set apart for a woman in child-birth, lying-in chamber, L. **-°gni** (*°kâgni*), m. a fire lighted at the ceremony performed after child-birth (cf. *sūtikâgni*), ĀpŚr.

Sūtakin, mfn. rendered impure by child-birth, Saṃskārak.

2. **Sūtí**, f. birth, production (generally ifc.), TBr.; MBh. &c.; parturition, delivery, lying in, Hariv.; Kathās.; yielding fruit, production of crops, BhP.; place or cause or manner of production, Kāv.; BhP.; offspring, progeny, MārkP.; m. a goose (?), L.; N. of a son of Viśvāmitra (v. l. *bhūti*), MBh. **-kāla**, m. the time of delivery, Hariv. **-gṛiha**, n. a lying-in chamber (also written *sūtī-gṛ°*), BhP. **-matī**, f. bringing forth children, MārkP. **-māruta**, m. the throes of child-birth (supposed to be caused by a partic. vital air), Yājñ.; BhP. **-mās** or **-māsa**, m. the month of delivery, the last month of gestation or pregnancy (= *vaijanana*), L. **-roga**, m. puerperal sickness, HPariś. **-vāta**, m. = *-māruta*, BhP.

Sūtika, g. *purohitâdi* (cf. *sautikya*).

Sū́tikā, f. a woman who has recently brought forth a child, lying-in woman, AV. &c. &c.; (with or scil. *go*) a cow that has recently calved, Yājñ.; MBh. **-gada**, m. puerperal sickness, fever or sickness of any kind supervening on child-birth, ŚārṅgS. **-°gāra** (*°kâg°*), n. a lying-in chamber, L. **-gṛiha** or **-geha**, n. id., L. **-°gni** (*°kâgni*), m. = *sūtakâgni*, ŚāṅkhGṛ. **-bhavana**, n. = *-gṛiha*, W. **-māruta**, m. vital air of child-birth, Ml. **-roga**, m. = *-gada*, MW. **-°vāsa** (*°kâv°*), m. = *-gṛiha*, L. **-shashṭhī**, f. a goddess worshipped on the sixth day after child-birth, MW.; *-pūjā*, f. the worship of the above goddess, ib. **Sūtikôtthāna**, n. a ceremony performed after the 10th day from delivery, Vishṇ.

Sūtī, in comp. for 2. *sūti*. **-gṛiha**, n. = *sūti-gṛ°*, BhP. **-māsa**, m. = *sūti-m°*, L. **-vṛitti**, f. N. of a Comm. on the Uṇādi-sūtra (v. l. for *satī-v°*), Cat.

Sūtu, f. child-bearing, pregnancy, AV.; TS.; Kāṭh.

Sūty, in comp. for 2. *sūti*. **-āśauca**, n. impurity caused by child-birth (continuing for ten days after regular parturition, and after miscarriage for a period of days equal to the number of months since conception), W.

Sūtrí, f. (prob.) the genitals (of a cow), AV.

Sūna, mfn. born, produced &c., Pāṇ. viii, 2, 45, Sch.; blown, budded (as a flower), W.; empty, vacant (prob. w. r. for *śūna*, *śūnya*), ib.; m. a son (prob. w. r. for 3. *suta*), Pañcat. iii, $\frac{2}{2}\frac{1}{1}\frac{7}{7}$; (*ā*), f. a daughter, L. (for other meanings see *sūnā*, p. 1242, col. 3); n. bringing forth, parturition, W.; a bud, flower (cf. *pra-sūna*), Śiś.; fruit, L. **-vat**, mfn. one who has borne or produced, W.; having budded or blossomed, ib. **-śara**, m. 'flower-arrowed,' the god of love, Ml.

2. **Sūnú**, m. a son, child, offspring, RV. &c. &c.; a younger brother, Kir. i, 24; a daughter's son, W.; N. of a Ṛishi (having the patr. Ārbhava or Kāśyapa, author of RV. x, 176), Anukr.; IndSt.; f. a daughter, Mn. i, 10. [Cf. Zd. *hunu;* Lith. *sūnùs;* Slav. *synŭ;* Goth. *sunus;* Angl. Sax. *sunu;* Eng. *son;* Germ. *Sohn.*] **-tā**, f. sonship, MBh. **-mát**, mfn. having sons, RV. **-rūpa** (?), mfn. having the form of a son, JaimBr.

Sūvan, mf(*arī*)n. bearing children, generating, producing (see *bahu-sūvarī*).

Sotṛi. See 2. *sotṛi*, p. 1248, col. 3.

सू 4. *sū*, ind., Ved. and in some comp. = 5. *su*, well, good &c. (cf. *sū-nara*, *sū-nṛita* &c.)

सूकर *sū-kará*, m. (prob. fr. *sū* + *kara*, making the sound *sū;* cf. *śū-kara* &c.; accord. to others fr. 3. *sū* and connected with Lat. *sū-culus*, *sū-cula*) a boar, hog, pig, swine (ifc. f. *ā; daṇshṭrā sūkarasya*, prob. 'a partic. plant,' Suśr.), RV. &c. &c.; a kind of deer (the hog-deer), L.; a partic. fish, L.; white rice, L.; a potter, L.; N. of a partic. hell, VP.; (*ī*), f. a sow, Yājñ.; R. &c.; a kind of bird, VarBṛS.; a small pillar above a wooden beam, L.; Batatas Edulis, L.; Mimosa Pudica, L.; Lycopodium Imbricatum, L.; N. of a goddess, Kālac. **-kanda**, m. 'hog's root,' a kind of bulbous plant, L. **-kshetra**, n. N. of a sacred district, Cat. **-gṛiha**, n. a pig-sty, Pañcat. **-tā**, f. the state or nature of a hog, Mn. iii, 190. **-daṇshṭra** or **°ṭraka**, m. 'hog's tusk,' N. of a kind of disease, Bhpr. **-nayana**, n. 'hog's eye,' N. of a hole of a partic. form in timber, VarBṛS. **-padī**, f., g. *kumbhapady-ādi*. **-pādikā**, f. a plant resembling Carpopogon Pruriens, L. **-pādī**, f. a kind of plant, VarBṛS. **-preyasī**, f. the beloved of the Boar (N. of the Earth as rescued from the flood by Vishṇu in the form of a boar), Kathās. **-mukha**, n. 'hog's mouth,' N. of a partic. hell, BhP. **-sadman**, m. N. of a man, Pāṇ. vi, 4, 144, Vārtt. 1. **Sūkarâkrāntā**, f. yam's root, L. **Sūkarâkshitā**, f. a disease of the eye (liable to be caused by surgical operations), Suśr. **Sūkarâsyā**, f. N. of a Buddhist goddess, Kālac. **Sūkarêshṭa**, m. 'liked by hogs,' the root of Scirpus Kysoor, L.

Sūkaraka, m. a species of rice, VarBṛS.; (*ikā*), f. a kind of bird, ib.; n. = *sūkara-nayana*, ib.

Sūkarika, m. or n. a kind of plant, VarBṛS.; (*ā*), f., see preceding.

सूक्त *sūktá*, mfn. (5. *su* + *ukta*) well or properly said or recited, RV. &c. &c.; speaking well, eloquent, MatsyaP.; (*ā*), f. a kind of bird, the Sārikā, L.; (*ám*), n. good recitation or speech, wise saying, song of praise, RV. &c. &c.; a Vedic hymn (as distinguished from a Ṛic or single verse of a hymn), Br.; ŚrS.; Mn.; BhP. **-cārin**, mfn. following a good word or advice, R. **-darśin**, m. 'hymn-seer,' the author of a Vedic hymn (*°śi-tva*, n.), MW. **-drashṭṛi**, m. id., ib. **-pañcaka**, n. N. of a Kāvya. **-bhāj**, mfn. one who has a hymn or hymns (addressed to him), Nir. **-mukhīya**, mf(*ā*)n. standing at the beginning of a hymn, ĀśvŚr. **-ratnâkara**, m. N. of a Mahā-kāvya (q. v.) **-vāká**, m. pronouncing a speech or hymn, recitation, RV.; VS.; Br.; ŚrS.; a partic. ceremony, MW. **-vākya**, n. a good speech or word, wise saying, BhP. **-vāc** (or *sūktá-vāc*), mfn. uttering a good speech &c., RV.; Br.; ĀśvŚr. **Sûktânukramaṇī**, f. an index of Vedic hymns (attributed to Śaunaka by Shaḍ-guru-śishya). **Sûktâmṛita-punaruktôpadaṅśana-daśana**, n. N. of a medic. wk. by Saj-jana. **Sûktâvali**, f. N. of an anthology by Lakshmaṇa. **Sûktâsi**, m. the sword of pleasant speech, MW. **Sûktôkti**, f. recitation of hymns, VS. **Sûktôcya**, mfn. to be pronounced in a hymn, TBr.

Sûkti, f. a good or friendly speech, wise saying, beautiful verse or stanza, Kāṭh.; R. &c. **-mañjarī-prakāśa**, m. N. of a Vedânta wk. **-mālikā**, f. N. of a poem. **-muktā**, f. pl. pearls of wise sayings, Kāv. **-muktâvali** or **°lī**, f. N. of various wks. **-ratnâkara**, m. a jewel-mine of beautiful sayings, Sāh.; N. of a Comm. on the Mahā-bhāshya. **-saṃgraha**, m. N. of a Kāvya by Kṛishṇa-dāsa Kāyastha. **-sahasra**, n. N. of a collection of a thousand beautiful verses. **-sādhutva-mālikā**, f. N. of a poem (perhaps identical with *sûkti-mālikā*).

Sûktika, m. (in music) a kind of cymbal, Saṃgīt.

Sûkty, in comp. for *sûkti*. **-ādarśa**, m. N. of a wk. on Bhakti by Kavi-tāṇḍava.

सूक्ष्म *sūkshma*, mf(*ā*)n. (prob. connected with *sūci*, p. 1241, col. 1) minute, small, fine, thin, narrow, short, feeble, trifling, insignificant, unimportant (with *artha*, m. 'a trifling matter'), Yājñ.; MBh. &c.; acute, subtle, keen (understanding or mental operation; *am*, ind.), KaṭhUp.; R. &c.; nice, exact, precise, Col.; subtle, atomic, intangible, Up.; Sāṃkhyak.; MBh. &c.; m. a partic. figure of rhetoric ('the subtle expression of an intended act'), Cat.; (with Śaivas) one who has attained a certain grade of emancipation, Hcat.; a mystical N. of the sound *ī*, Up.; N. of Śiva, MBh.; of a Dānava, ib.; Hariv.; m. or n. an atom, intangible matter, Sāṃkhyak.; Sarvad.; MBh. &c.; the subtle all-pervading spirit, Supreme Soul, L.; the Kataka or clearing-nut plant, L.; = *kṛitaka* or *kaitava*, L.; (*ā*), f. sand, L.; small cardamoms, L.; N. of two plants (= *yūthikā* or *karuṇī*), L.; of one of the 9 Śaktis of Vishṇu, L.; (*am*), n. the cavity or socket of a tooth, Vishṇ.; woven silk, L.; marrow, L.; the Vedânta philosophy, L. **-kṛiśa-phalā** or **-krishṇa-phalā**, f. a kind of tree (= *madhyama-jambu-vṛiksha*), L. **-ghaṇṭikā**, f. (prob.) = *kshudra-gh°*, L. **-cakra**, n. a partic. diagram, Cat. **-jātaka**, n. N. of a wk. of Varāha-mihira (= *laghu-j°*). **-ṭikka**, m. N. of a man (cf. *bṛihaṭ-ṭikka*), Rājat. **-taṇḍula**, m. 'having small seeds,' the poppy, L.; (*ā*), f. long pepper, L.; Andropogon Muricatus, W. **-tantra**, n. N. of a Tantra. **-tama**, mfn. very feeble, scarcely audible, TPrāt., Sch.; very subtle or minute, BhP. **-tara**, mfn. scarcely audible (v. l. for prec.); more (or most) subtle or minute, BhP. **-tā**, f. minuteness, subtlety, fineness, Mn. vi, 65. **-tuṇḍa**, m. a partic. biting insect, Suśr. **-tva**, n. = *-tā*, MBh.; Vedântas. **-darśin**, mfn. sharp-sighted, of acute discernment, quick, intelligent, KaṭhUp.; MBh.; (*°śi-*)*-tā*, f. quick-sightedness, acuteness, wisdom, Mālav. **-dala**, m. mustard, L.; (*ā*), f. Alhagi Maurorum, L. **-dāru**, n. a thin plank or board, L. **-dṛishṭi**, f. a keen glance, Pañcat.; mfn. keen-sighted, Kāśīkh. **-deha**, m. n. = *-śarīra* (q. v.), MW. **-dharma**, m. a subtle law or duty, MBh. i, 7246 (cf. IW. 387, n. 1). **-nābha**, m. N. of Vishṇu, L. **-pattra**, m. 'small-leaved,' N. of various plants (a kind of fennel or anise; a kind of sugar-cane; Ocimum Pilosum &c.), L.; (*ā*), f. Asparagus Racemosus and Argyreia Speciosa or Argentea, L.; (*ī*), f. a kind of Valerian, L.; n. coriander, L. **-pattraka**, m. 'id.,' Ocimum Pilosum, L.; (*ikā*), f. N. of various plants (Anethum Sowa; Asparagus Racemosus; Alhagi Maurorum &c.), L. **-parṇā**, f. 'id.,' N. of various plants (Hoya Viridiflora; Argyreia Speciosa; = *saṇa-pushpī*), L.; (*ī*), f. a kind of basil, L. **-pāda**, mfn. having small feet (*-tva*, n.), Kathās. **-pippalī**, f. wild pepper, L. **-pushpī**, f. 'having small flowers,' a kind of plant (= *yava-tiktā*), L. **-phala**, m. 'having small fruit,' Cordia Myxa, L.; (*ā*), f. Flaçourtia Cataphracta, L. **-badarī**, f. a kind of jujube, L. **-bīja**, m. 'having small seeds,' the poppy, L. **-bhūta**, n. a subtle element (= *tan-mātra*), Vedântas.; Sarvad. **-makshika**, m. (or *ā*, f.) a small fly, musquito, gnat, L. **-mati** or **-mati-mat**, mfn. acute-minded, Kāv. **-māna**, n. minute or exact measurement, precise computation, MW. **-mūlā**, f. 'having a slender root,' Sesbania Ægyptiaca, L. **-lobhaka**, n. (scil. *sthāna;* with Jainas) the tenth of the 14 stages leading to emancipation, Cat. **-vallī**, f. a kind of medicinal plant (= *tāmra-vallī*), L.; a red Oldenlandia, L.; Momordica Charantia, L. **-vāluka**, mfn. abounding in fine sand, R. **-śarīra**, n. (in phil.) the subtle body (= *liṅga-ś°*, q. v., opp. to *sthūla-ś°*, q. v.); n. pl. the six subtle principles from which the grosser elements are evolved (viz. Ahaṃ-kāra and the 5 Tan-mātras, see Mn. i, 17; accord. to other systems 'the 17 subtle principles of the 5 organs of sense, 5 organs of action, 5 elements, Buddhi and Manas'), IW. 53, n. 2; 198, n. 3. **-śarkarā**, f. fine gravel, sand, L. **-śāka**, m. Acacia Arabica, L. **-śākha**, m. 'having small branches,' a kind of plant (= *jāla-varvūra*), L. **-śāli**, m. a kind of fine rice, L. **-śiraska**, mfn. small-headed (applied as a nickname to a Buddhist), Cat. **-shaṭ-caraṇa**, m. a minute insect, a sort of tick or louse (said to infest the roots of the eyelashes), L. **-sphoṭa**, m. a kind of leprosy (= *vicarcikā*), Gal. **Sūkshmâksha**, mfn. keen-sighted, acute (applied to the mind; *-tā*, f.), Rājat. **Sūkshmâtman**, m. 'subtle-souled,' N. of Śiva, MBh. **Sūkshmêkshikā**, f. keen-sightedness, acuteness (prob. for *°kshi-tā*), Rājat. **Sūkshmâilā**, f. small cardamoms, L.

Sūkshmī, in comp. for *sūkshma*. — **√kṛi**, P. *-karoti*, to make thin or fine, subtilize, refine, MW. — **kṛita**, mfn. subtilized, made thin or minute, ib. — **bhūta**, mfn. become subtle or fine, minute, ib.

Sūkshmya (prob. w.r. for *sūkshma*), VarBṛS.

सूखर *sūkhara*, m. pl. N. of a Śaiva sect, W.

सूच् *sūc* (rather Nom. fr. *sūca* and *sūci* below), cl. 10. P. (Dhātup. xxxv, 21) *sūcayati*, to point out, indicate, show, manifest, reveal, betray (in dram. = 'to indicate by gesture, communicate by signs, represent'), MaitrUp.; MBh.; Kāv. &c.; to trace out, ascertain, espy, MW.: Pass. *sūcyate* (aor. *asūci*), to be pointed out or indicated, Kāv.; Kathās. &c.: Intens. *sosūcyate*, Pat. on Pāṇ. iii, 1, 22.

Sūca, mf(*ā*)n. pointing out, indicating &c. (ifc.), Jātakam.; m. a pointed shoot or blade of Kuśa grass (= *darbhâṅkura*), L.; (*ā*), f. pointing out, indication, Jātakam.; piercing, L.; gesticulation, L.; spying out, sight, seeing, L.

Sūcaka, mf(*ikā*)n. pointing out, indicating, showing, designating, MBh.; Kāv. &c.; pointing to (acc.), Hariv.; informing, betraying, treacherous, Car.; m. a denouncer, informer, Mn.; MBh. &c.; (the following only in L.) the manager or chief actor of a company; a narrator, teacher; the son of an Āyogava and a Kshatriyā; a Buddha; a Siddha; demon, imp; villain, dog; jackal; cat; crow; needle; balustrade, parapet; kind of rice.

Sūcana, mf(*ī*)n. pointing out, indicating (see *śubha-sūcanī*); (*ā*), f. (= *sūcā*) pointing out, indication, communication, Suśr.; Sāh.; piercing &c., L.; (*ī*), f. a short index or table of contents, L.; (*am*), n. indication, Jātakam.; bodily exertion, Car.

Sūcanīya, mfn. to be pointed out or indicated &c., Sāh.

Sūcayitavya, mfn. to be found out, Vikr.

Sūci or **sūcí**, f. (prob. to be connected with *sūtra*, *syūta* &c. fr. *√siv*, 'to sew,' cf. *sūkshma*; in R. once *sūcinā*, instr.), a needle or any sharp-pointed instrument (e.g. 'a needle used in surgery,' 'a magnet' &c.), RV. &c. &c.; the sharp point or tip of anything or any pointed object, Kāv.; Car.; BhP.; a rail or balustrade, Divyâv.; a small door-bolt, L.; 'sharp file or column,' a kind of military array (accord. to Kull. on Mn. vii, 187, 'placing the sharpest and most active soldiers in front'), Mn.; MBh.; Kām.; an index, table of contents (in books printed in India; cf. *-pattra* below); a triangle formed by the sides of a trapezium produced till they meet, Col.; a cone, pyramid, ib.; (in astron.) the earth's disc in computing eclipses (or 'the corrected diameter of the earth'), Sūryas.; gesticulation, dramatic action, L.; a kind of coitus, L.; sight, seeing (= *dṛishṭi*), L.; m. (only *sūcī*) the son of Nishāda and a Vaiśyā, L.; a maker of winnowing baskets &c. (cf. *sūnā*), L. — **kulāya**, Nom. Ā. *°yate*, to appear like a multitude of needles, Mahān. — **khāta**, m. a sharp pyramid or pyramidal excavation, a pyramid, cone, W. — **gṛihaka**, n. a n°-case, L. — **tā**, f. needle-work, ib. — **pattra**, n. an index (see above). — **pattraka** or **-pattrika**, m. Marsilea Quadrifolia, L. — **pushpa**, m. the Ketaka tree, Pandanus Odoratissimus, L. — **bhinna**, mfn. divided into needle-like points at the ends of the buds, Megh. — **bhedya**, mfn. capable of being pierced with a n°, very dense, palpable (as darkness), Megh.; Hit. — **mallikā**, f. Jasminum Sambac, L. — **radana**, m. 'n°-toothed,' the mungoose, L. — **roman**, m. 'having needle-like bristles,' a hog, L. — **vat**, m. N. of Garuḍa, L. — **vadana**, m. (perhaps w.r. for *-radana*) 'needle-faced,' the mungoose, L.; a musquito, L. — **śāli**, m. a sort of rice, L. — **śikhā**, f. the point of a needle, Naish. — **sūtra**, n. a thread for a needle or for sewing (v.l. *sūci-s°*), L.

Sūcika, m. one who lives by his needle, a tailor &c. (cf. *saucika*), VarBṛS.; (*ā*), f., see next.

Sūcikā, f. a needle, L.; an elephant's trunk or proboscis, L.; Pandanus Odoratissimus, L.; N. of an Apsaras (cf. *śucikā*), L. — **dhara**, m. 'having a trunk,' an elephant, L. — **°bharaṇa** (*°kâbh°*), n. a partic. drug (used as a remedy for the bite of a serpent), Rasendrac. — **mukha**, m. 'having a pointed end,' a shell, conch shell, L.

1. **Sūcita**, mfn. (for 2. *sûcita* see below) pointed out, indicated, hinted, communicated, shown, betrayed, made known by (instr. or comp.), MBh.; Kāv. &c.; pierced, perforated, MW.

Sūcitavya, mfn. = *sūcya*, MW.

Sūcin, mfn. spying, informing, W.; piercing, perforating, ib.; m. a spy, informer, MBh.; VP.; (*inī*), f. a needle, W.; night, ib.

Sūcī, f. (= *sūci*), in comp. — **kaṭāha-nyāya**, m. the rule of the needle and the caldron (a phrase implying that when two things have to be done, one easy and the other difficult, the easier should be done first), MW. — **kapiśa**, mfn. (applied to a kind of arrow the use of which is prohibited), MBh. — **karman**, n. needle-work (one of the 64 Kalās), BhP., Sch. — **khāta**, see *sūci-kh°*. — **tuṇḍa**, m. 'needle-mouthed,' a gnat, Bālar. — **dala**, m. Marsilea Quadrifolia, L. — **pattra**, m. a kind of sugar-cane (also *°ttraka*), L.; (*ā*), f. a kind of Dūrvā grass (= *gaṇḍa-dūrvā*), L.; (*am*), n., see *sūci-p°*. — **padī**, f., g. *kumbhapady-ādi*. — **padma**, n. a kind of military array (cf. under *sūci*), MBh. (v.l. *śūc°*). — **pāśa**, m. the eye of a needle, Suśr. — **pushpa**, see *sūci-p°*. — **prôta**, mfn. threaded, ĀpŚr., Sch. — **bhedya**, see *sūci-bh°*. — **mukha**, n. the point of a needle (also *°khâgra*), Kāv.; Suśr.; a partic. hell, BhP.; (*°cī-m°*), mf(*ī*)n. having a beak &c. as sharp as a n°, AV.; Pañcat.; pointed or sharp as a needle, MBh.; narrow (cf. *-vaktra*), Car.; ŚārṅgS.; (only L.) a bird (or a partic. bird or N. of a bird), Kathās.; Pañcat.; a kind of Kuśa grass; a gnat or some other stinging insect; a partic. position of the hands; (*ī*), f. a female bird, MW.; (*am*), n. a diamond, L.; *°khâgra-sambhedya*, mfn. very thick or dense (= *sūci-bhedya*, q.v.), Sarasv. — **roman**, see *sūci-r°*. — **vaktra**, mfn. having a mouth or aperture as pointed as a needle, too narrow, Suśr.; Bhpr.; m. N. of one of Skanda's attendants, MBh.; of an Asura, Hariv. — **vāna-karman**, n. pl. the arts of sewing and weaving, Cat. — **sūtra**, see *sūci-s°*.

Sūcīka, m. a stinging insect, R.

Sūcy, in comp. for *sūci* or *sūcī*. — **agra**, n. the point of a needle, MBh.; Pañcat.; as much land as is pierced by the point of a n°, i.e. very little (= *°gra-bhedyam bhūmi-talam*), MBh.; Inscr.; m. 'pointed or sharp as a n°,' a thorn, L.; *-viddha*, mfn. pierced by the p° of a n°, Pañcat.; *-sthūlaka*, m. Saccharum Cylindricum, L. — **āsya**, mfn. n°-mouthed, L.; m. a rat, L.; a gnat or musquito, L.; a partic. position of the hands, L. — **āhva**, m. a kind of culinary herb, L.

Sūcya, mfn. to be indicated or pointed out, to be made known or communicated, Sāh.

सूचित 2. *sûcita*, mfn. (5. *su*+*ucita*; for 1. *sūcita* see above) very fit or suitable, Nalôd.

सूच्चैस् *sûccais*, ind. (5. *su*+*uc°*) very loud, ĀpŚr.

सूच्छ्रित *sûcchrita*, mfn. well raised or lifted up or erected, R.

सूड *sūḍa* (of unknown meaning), Saṃgīt.

सूत् *sūt*, ind. (an imitative sound). — **kāra**, m. making the sound *sūt*, snorting, roaring &c., Kāv.; Kathās. — **kṛita**, n. id., Śiś.

सूत 3. *sūtá*, m. (of doubtful derivation, prob. to be connected with *√1. sū*; for 1. 2. *sūta* see pp. 1239 and 1240) a charioteer, driver, groom, equerry, master of the horse (esp. an attendant on a king who in earlier literature is often mentioned together with the *grāma-ṇī*; in the epics also a royal herald or bard, whose business was to proclaim the heroic actions of the king and his ancestors, while he drove his chariot to battle, or on state occasions, and who had therefore to know by heart portions of the epic poems and ancient ballads; he is the son of a Kshatriya by a Brāhmaṇī or of a Brāhman [accord. to Śāśvata also of a Śūdra] and a Kshatriyā; the most celebrated Sūta was Loma-harshaṇa who was a pupil of Vyāsa), AV. &c. &c. (IW. 510, n.); a carpenter or wheelwright, L.; N. of a son of Viśvāmitra, MBh.; (*yā*), f., g. *krauḍy-ādi*; (*ī*), f. the wife of a Sūta, MW.; a female bard, ib. — **karman**, n. the office or service of a charioteer, MBh. — **grāmaṇī**, m. pl. (cf. Kāś. on Pāṇ. vii, 1, 56) an equerry and the chief of a village, ŚBr. — **ja**, m. the son of a ch°, MBh.; = next, Hariv. — **tanaya**, m. 'son (i.e. adopted son) of the Sūta (Adhiratha),' N. of Karṇa, L. — **tā**, f., **-tva**, n. the business or condition of a ch°, MBh.; Hariv. — **duhitṛi**, f. = *-putrī*, Pāṇ. vi, 3, 70, Vārtt. 9, Pat. — **nandana**, m. 'son of Sūta,' N. of Ugra-śravas, MBh. — **putra**, m. the son of a ch° (also 'a charioteer'), MBh.; N. of Karṇa (cf. *sūta-ja*), ib.; N. of Kīcaka, ib.; (*ī*), f. the daughter of a ch°, Pāṇ. vi, 3, 70, Vārtt. 9, Pat. — **putraka**, m. N. of Karṇa (cf. *sūta-ja*), L. — **mukha** (*sūtá-*), mfn. having a Sūta for a head, MaitrS. — **vyasanin**, mfn. suffering some mishap from the unskilfulness of a ch°, MBh. v, 7223. — **saṃhitā**, f. N. of a ch. of the Skanda-purāṇa; *-tātparya-dīpikā*, f., *-vyākhyā*, f., *-saṃgraha*, m. N. of wks. — **sava**, m. N. of a partic. Ekâha, ŚāṅkhŚr.

सूतवे *sū́tave, sūtavaí*. See *√2. sū*.

सूति 3. *sūti*, f. (fr. *√3. su*; for 1. 2. *sūti* see pp. 1239 and 1240) pressing out the Soma-juice, or the place where it is pressed out, VP.

Sūtya, n. = *sutya*, MBh. v, 4802 (v.l. *sutya* and *sūya*); (*ā*), f. (cf. 3. *sūta*) = *sutyā*, L.

3. **Sūnú**, m. (for 1. 2. see under *√1. 2. sū*) one who presses out or extracts the Soma-juice, RV. iii, 1, 12 (= 1. *sotṛi*, Sāy.)

1. **Sūma**, m. (for 2. see s.v.) milk, water, L.

Sūya, n. extraction of the Soma-juice, libation, sacrifice (cf. *rāja-s°*), MBh.

सूति 4. *sūti*, f. (fr. *√siv*) = *syūti*, L.

सूत्त *sūtta*, mfn. (= *su-datta*) well given, entirely given (cf. *ātta, nītta*), Pāṇ. vii, 4, 47, Sch.

सूत्तर *sûttara*, mfn. (5. *su*+*uttara*) very superior, W.; well towards the north, northern, ib.

सूत्थान *sûtthāna*, mfn. (5. *su*+*utthāna*) good effort, MW.; mfn. making good efforts, clever, Kām.

Sûtthita, m. N. of a man (cf. *sautthiti*).

सूत्पर *sūtpara* (?), n. the distilling of spirituous liquor (= *surā-saṃdhāna*), L.

सूत्पलावती *sûtpalāvatī*, f. N. of a river, MārkP.

सूत्र् *sūtr* (rather Nom. fr. *sūtra* below), cl. 10. P. (Dhātup. xxxv, 54) *sūtrayati* (accord. to Gr. also *°te* and *sūtrāpayati*), to string or put together, Hcat.; to contrive, effect, produce, compose, Bālar.; Rājat.; Kathās.; to put in the form of a Sūtra (see below), teach as a Sūtra or aphorism, Śatr.; Kull.: Intens. *sosūtryate*, Pat. on Pāṇ. iii, 1, 22.

Sūtra, n. (accord. to g. *ardharcâdi* also m.; fr. *√siv*, 'to sew,' and connected with *sūci* and *sūnā*) a thread, yarn, string, line, cord, wire, AV. &c. &c.; a measuring line (cf. *-pāta*), Hariv.; VarBṛS. &c.; the sacred thread or cord worn by the first three classes (cf. *yajñôpavīta*), BhP.; a girdle, ib.; a fibre, Kālid.; a line, stroke, MBh.; VarBṛS.; Gol.; a sketch, plan, Rājat.; that which like a thread runs through or holds together everything, rule, direction, BhP.; a short sentence or aphoristic rule, and any work or manual consisting of strings of such rules hanging together like threads (these Sūtra works form manuals of teaching in ritual, philosophy, grammar &c.: e.g. in ritual there are first the Śrauta-sūtras, and among them the Kalpa-sûtras, founded directly on Śruti, q.v.; they form a kind of rubric to Vedic ceremonial, giving concise rules for the performance of every kind of sacrifice [IW. 146 &c.]; other kinds of S° works are the Gṛihya-sūtras and Sāmayācārika or Dharma-sūtras, i.e. 'rules for domestic ceremonies and conventional customs,' sometimes called collectively Smārta-sūtras [as founded on *smṛiti* or 'tradition,' see *smārta*]; these led to the later Dharma-śāstras or 'law-books' [IW. 145]; in philosophy each system has its regular text-book of aphorisms written in Sūtras by its supposed founder [IW. 60 &c.]; in Vyākaraṇa or grammar there are the celebrated Sūtras of Pāṇini in eight books, which are the groundwork of a vast grammatical literature; with Buddhists, Pāśupatas &c. the term Sūtra is applied to original text books as opp. to explanatory works; with Jainas they form part of the Dṛishṭi-vāda), IW. 162 &c.; a kind of tree, Divyâv. — **kaṇṭha**, m. 'having Sūtras in the throat ready to be repeated,' a Brāhman, L.; 'having lines on the throat,' a pigeon, dove, L.; a wagtail, L. — **karaṇa**, n. the composition of a Sūtra, ĀpŚr., Sch. — **kartṛi**, m. the author of a Sūtra manual, MBh. — **karman**, n. 'rule-work,' carpentry; (°*ma*)-*kṛit*, m. a carpenter, architect, R.; -*viśārada*, mfn. skilled in carpentry, ib. **-kāra**, m. a weaver or spinner (see *paṭṭa-s°*); a carpenter, R.; = next, MBh.; Ragh.; Sarvad. **-kṛit**, m. = -*kartṛi*, TPrāt., Sch. **-kṛitâṅga-vṛitti**, f. N. of wk. **-koṇa** or **-koṇaka**, m. a small drum shaped like an hour-glass and struck by a string and button (= *ḍamaru*), L. **-kośa**, m. a skein of yarn, L. **-krīḍā**, f. a partic. game with strings (mentioned among the 64 Kalās), Cat. **-gaṇita**, N. of an astron. wk. by Bhāskarâcārya. **-gaṇḍikā**, f. a kind of stick used by weavers in spinning threads, L. **-grantha**, m. a book of aphorisms, Sūtra work, Kāty., Sch. **-graha**, mfn. holding a thread, Pāṇ. iii, 2, 9, Vārtt. 2, Pat. **-grāha**, mfn. seizing a thread (but not holding it), ib. **-caraṇa**, n. N. of a class of Caraṇas or Vedic schools who introduced various Sūtra works, MW. **-jāla**, n. a net made of yarn or coarse string, MBh. **-tantu**, m. (once n.) a thread, string, line, Gobh.; ŚāṅkhGṛ.; Hariv.; perseverance, energy, L. **-tarkuṭī**, f. a distaff, spindle, L. **-daridra**, mfn. threadbare (-*tā*, f.), Mṛicch. **-dīpikā**, f. N. of wk. **-dhara**, mfn. wearing a string of (comp.), MBh.; m. one versed in the Sūtras, L. = next, L. **-dhāra**, m. 'rule or thread-holder,' an architect, carpenter, MBh.; VarBṛS.; a stage-manager (or principal actor who superintends the whole performance; accord. to some he was originally so called from holding the strings of puppets; his assistants are the *pāripārśvika* and *sthāpaka*, qq. vv.), Bhar.; Sāh. &c.; N. of Indra, L.; (*ī*), f. the wife of a stage-manager (also called *gṛihiṇī*), Mṛicch.; Mudr.; mf(*ī*)n. being the chief or leading person at any performance (comp.), Bālar.; -*maṇḍana*, m. (also simply called Maṇḍana) N. of an author (son of Śrī-kshetra and client of Kumbha-karṇa, king of Medapāṭa), Cat. **-dhṛik**, m. an architect (see *viśva-s°*); a stage-manager, Sāh. **-naḍa**, m. N. of a man (cf. *sautranāḍi*), g. *anuśatikâdi*. **-nyāsa**, m. N. of a gram. wk. **-pattra-kara** or **-pattrin**, mfn. liable to be made into threads or thin leaves, L. **-padī**, f. having feet as thin as thr°, g. *kumbhapady-ādi*. **-pāṭhânukrama**, m. N. of wk. **-pāta**, m. applying the measuring line (°*taṃ*-√*kṛi* or *car*, 'to measure, compare one thing with another'), Kathās. **-pāda**, m. N. of wk. **-piṭaka**, m. n. the basket or collection of Buddhist Sūtras (cf. *tri-piṭaka*). **-pushpa**, m. 'having thread-like flowers,' the cotton plant, L. **-prakāśa-bhāshya**, n., **-prakāśikā**, f., **-prasthāna**, n. N. of wks. **-prôta**, mfn. fastened with wires (as puppets), MBh. **-bhāshya**, n. N. of wk. (also °*shya-vyākhyā*, f.) **-bhid**, m. 'thread-cutter,' a tailor, L. **-bhṛit**, m. = -*dhāra*, a stage-manager, Daśar. **-madhya-bhū**, mfn. 'produced amid threads or fibres,' the resin of Shorea Robusta, L.; incense, W. **-mantra-prakāśaka**, N. of wk. **-maya**, mf(*ī*)n. consisting of threads, Hcat. **-muktā-kalāpa**, m. N. of a Vaishṇava wk. **-yantra**, n. a net (made) of yarn or coarse string, MaitrUp.; a weaver's loom, L.; a shuttle, W. **-rāja**, m. 'Sūtra-king,' a Sūtra of the first order, Kāraṇḍ. **-vāpa**, m. weaving (threads), L. **-vikrayin**, m. a dealer in yarn, R. **-vid**, m. 'Sūtra-knower,' one versed in Sūtras, L. **-vīṇā**, f. a kind of lute (= *lābukī*), L. **-veshṭana**, n. a weaver's shuttle, L.; the act of weaving, MW. **-śākha**, n. the body, Gal. **-saṃgraha**, m. one who grasps or holds the reins, L.; collection of Sūtras (in next); -*dīpikā*, f. N. of wks. **-samuccaya**, m. N. of wk. **-sthāna**, n. (in medic. wks.) the first general section (treating of the physician, disease, remedies, diet &c.) **Sūtrâtman**, m. 'thread-soul,' the soul which passes like a thread through the universe, Vedântas. (IW. 114). **Sūtrânta**, m. (formed like *vedânta*, *siddhânta* &c.) a Buddhist Sūtra or the doctrines contained in it, SaddhP.; Divyâv. **Sūtrântaka**, mfn. versed in the Buddhist Sūtras, Divyâv. **Sūtrârtha**, m. N. of a gram. and of a Vedânta wk.; -*candrikā*, f., -*darpaṇa*, m. N. of wks. **Sūtrâlaṃkāra**, m. N. of wk.; -*ṭīkā*, f., -*bhāshya*, n. N. of Commentaries. **Sūtrâlī**, f. a string of beads &c. worn round the neck, necklace, L. **Sūtrôta**, mfn. filed on a string, ĀpGṛ. **Sūtrôpanyāsa**, m. N. of a Vedânta wk.

Sūtraka, n. = *sūtra*, a thread, string &c., Pāṇ. i, 1, 1, Vārtt. 8, Pat.; (*ikā*), f. a kind of macaroni or vermicelli (shaped like thread), Pañcat. v, 3/34; a necklace (see *uraḥ-sūtrikā*).

Sūtraṇa, n. the act of stringing together &c.; arranging in aphorisms, Suśr.

Sūtraya, °*yati*. See √*sūtr*, p. 1241, col. 3.

Sūtrayitavya, mfn. to be composed or arranged in the form of Sūtras, Śaṃk.

Sūtralā, f. a spindle, distaff, L.

Sūtrika, in *sāṃgraha-s°*, q. v.; (*ikā*), f., see *sūtraka*, col. 1.

Sūtrita, mfn. strung, arranged &c.; directed or declared in a Sūtra, prescribed or delivered in aphorisms or axioms, MBh.; Śaṃk. **-tva**, n. the being said or enjoined in a Sūtra, Sāy.

Sūtrin, mfn. having threads or lines &c., Kālac.; m. a stage-manager, Daśar.; a crow, L.

Sūtrī-√kṛi, P. -*karoti*, to make or spin into thread, ĀpŚr., Sch.

Sūtrīya, mfn. relating to or concerning the Sūtras, Suśr.

सूत्रामन् *sū-trāman*, m. = *su-tr°*, N. of Indra, Rājat.

सूद् 1. *sūd* (prob. connected with √*svad*), cl. 1. Ā. (Dhātup. ii, 24) *sūdate* (occurring only in the reduplicated forms *sushūdima*, RV.; *sushūdati* or °*dat*, ib.; *sushūdáta*, AV.; Gr. also fut. *sūditā*, °*dishyati*), to put or keep in order, guide aright, RV.; AV.: Caus. or cl. 10. (cf. Dhātup. xxxiii, 43) *sūdáyati*, °*te* (p. *sūdayāna*, MBh.; aor. *asūshudat*, °*ta*), id.; RV.; AV.; VS.; to manage, arrange, prepare, effect, contrive, RV.; to settle, i. e. put an end to, kill, slay (also inanimate objects), MBh.; R. &c.; to squeeze, press, destroy, Śiś.: Desid. *susūdishate*, Gr.: Intens. *sosūdyate*, *sosūtti*, ib.

2. **Sūd.** See *havya-sūd*.

Sūda, m. a well, RV. (Naigh. iii, 25); the mud of a dried-up pool (others, 'sweetness, sweet drink,' esp. 'milk'), ib.; Br.; Kāṭh.; (prob.) a hot spring, Rājat.; a kind of sauce or broth (cf. *sūpa*), Kām.; Rājat.; a cook, MBh.; R. &c.; N. of a country in Kaśmīra (?), Rājat.; (*ī*), f., g. *gaurâdi*. **-karman**, n. a cook's work, cooking, MBh.; Kathās. **-tā**, f., **-tva**, n. the condition or business of a cook, ib. **-dohas** (*sū́da-*), mfn. yielding milk like a well, RV.; f. N. of a partic. verse, ŚBr.; ŚāṅkhŚr. **-vat** (*sū́da-*), mfn. containing the remains of liquids, MaitrS.; ĀpŚr. **-śālā**, f. 'cooking-room,' a kitchen, Kathās. **-śāstra**, n. the science or art of cooking (also N. of a wk. on cookery), Cat. **Sūdâdhyaksha**, m. a superintendent of cooking, director of the kitchen, MatsyaP.

Sūdaka, mfn. destroying, killing &c.

Sūdana, mf(*ā* or *ī*)n. putting in order, guiding aright, RV.; AV. Paipp.; (generally ifc.) killing, destroying, MBh.; R. &c.; n. the act of killing or slaying, destruction, Hariv.; the act of assenting or promising (= *aṅgī-karaṇa*), L.; the act of ejecting or throwing away (= *nikshepaṇa*), L.

Sūdayitnú, mfn. flowing, yielding sweetness (as waters), RV.

Sūdā-vatsa, m. N. of a man, Virac.

Sūdi or **sūdin**, mfn. streaming, overflowing (cf. *sūda-vat*), Kāṭh.

Sūdita, mfn. wounded, destroyed, killed, slain, MBh.; R. &c.

Sūditṛi, mfn. one who kills or destroys, Pāṇ. iii, 2, 153.

Sūdya, mf(*ā*)n. relating or belonging to a pool, VS.; TS.

सूदया *sūdayā*, f. (= *sūd°*?) a herb, Divyâv.

सूदर *sûdara*, mfn. having a well-formed belly, Pāṇ. vi, 2, 107, Vārtt. 1, Pat.

सूद्गातृ *sûdgātṛi*, m. an excellent Udgātṛi (q. v.), TS.

सून *sūna*. See p. 1240, col. 1.

सूनर *sū-nára*, mf(*ī*)n. (for *su-nara*, cf. *sundara*) glad, joyous, merry, RV.; delightful, MaitrS.

Sū-nṛita, mf(*ā*)n. joyful, glad, RV.; friendly, kind, Mn. (iii, 150); MBh. &c.; pleasant and true (in this sense supposed to be fr. 5. *su* + *ṛita*), Yājñ.; MBh. &c.; (*ā*), f., see below; (*am*), n. joy, gladness, delight, RV.; AV.; (with Jainas) pleasant and true speech (one of the five qualities belonging to right conduct), Sarvad. **-vāc**, mfn. truth-speaking, speaking politely and truthfully, MW. **Sūnṛitânṛita**, n. du. truth and falsehood, MBh.

Sū-nṛitā, f. gladness, joy, exultation, song of joy, glee (instr. pl. 'joyfully'), RV.; TS.; PārGṛ.; kindness, friendliness, kind and true speech, KaṭhUp.; MBh. &c.; truth (opp. to *an-ṛita*) personified as a goddess, RV.; AV. &c.; the wife of Dharma, BhP.; a daughter of Dharma and wife of Uttāna-pāda, Hariv.; VP.; of an Apsaras, L. **-vat** (*sūnṛitā-*), mfn. glad, joyous, RV. **-varī**, f. id. (said of Ushas), ib.

सूना *sūnā*, f. (prob. fr. √*siv*, 'to sew,' and connected with *sūci* and *sūtra*; cf. *sūna*, p. 1240, col. 1) a woven wicker-work basket or vessel of any kind, RV.; AV.; GṛŚrS.; a place for slaughtering animals, slaughter-house, butchery (wrongly *śūnā*; cf. *sūdanā*), MBh.; Kāv. &c.; the sale of flesh or meat, MW.; any place or utensil in a house where animals are liable to be accidentally destroyed (see *pañca-sūnā*); a stick fixed to an elephant's hook, L.; killing, hurting, injuring, BhP.; imminent death, danger of life (*sūnāyām api*, 'even in the last extremity'), ib.; the uvula or soft palate (in this and the next sense perhaps connected with *śūna*), L.; inflammation of the glands of the neck (commonly called 'mumps'), W. (accord. to some also, 'a zone, girdle;' 'a ray;' 'a river'). **-cakradhvaja-vat**, m. one who has a slaughter-house (and) an oil-press (and) a vintner's sign, Mn. iv, 84. **-taṭi** (?), f. a sl°-h°, L. **-dosha**, m. the guilt incurred by destroying animals in any of the 5 Sūnās (see *pañca-sūnā*), Mn. iii, 71. **-paricara**, mfn. flying around a slaughter-house (as a vulture), Mālav. **-stha**, mfn. being in a slaughter-house or in any place where animals are destroyed, Mn. xi, 155.

Sūnika, m. a butcher, flesh-seller, hunter, VarBṛS.

Sūnin, m. id., Yājñ.

सूनु 1. 2. 3. *sūnu*. See under √1. 2. *su*, and p. 1241, col. 3.

सूनृत *sū-nṛita*. See col. 2.

सून्नीय *sūnnīya*, mfn. (for *sūnneya*; see *un-√nī*) to be well or easily ladled out or drained out, TS.

सून्मद *sūnmada* or *sūnmāda*, (prob.) w.r. for *sônm°* (q. v.)

सूप *sūpa*, m. (of doubtful derivation, cf. *sūda*; in Uṇ. iii, 26 said to be fr √3. *su*, 'to distil') sauce, soup, broth (esp. prepared from split or ground pease &c. with roots and salt), MBh.; R.; Suśr. &c.; a cook, L. (*ī*, f., g. *gaurâdi*); a vessel, pot, pan, L.; an arrow, L. **-kartṛi** (MBh.), **-kṛit** (Kathās.), m. 'sauce-maker,' a cook. **-gandhi**, mfn. containing only a little sauce, Pāṇ. v, 4, 136, Sch. **-dhūpaka** or **-dhūpana**, n. 'flavouring sauce,' Asa Fetida, L. **-parṇī**, f. Phaseolus Trilobus, L. **-prati**, ind. nothing but s°, Pat. on Pāṇ. ii, 1, 9. **-rasa**, m. the taste or flavour of s°, Kāv. **-śāstra**, n. of a wk. on cookery (also called *pāka-s°*, by Bhīmasena). **-śreshṭha**, m. Phaseolus Mungo, L. **-saṃsṛishṭa**, mfn. mixed with s°, Āpast. **Sūpâṅga**, n. 'sauce-ingredient,' Asa Fetida, L. **Sūpâdanashashṭhī-pūjā**, f. N. of wk.

Sūpika, m. or n. (?) = *sūpa*, sauce, soup &c., L.

Sūpīya, mfn. = *sūpya*, g. *apūpâdi*.

Sūpe-śāṇa, m. (loc. of *sūpa* + *ś°*), Pāṇ. vi, 2, 64, Sch. (Kāś. *stūpe-ś°*).

Sūpya, mfn. fit for a sauce or soup &c., Car.; Vāgbh.; n. food consisting of soup, ib.

सूपचर *sûpacára*, mfn. easily accessible, complaisant, kind to (dat.), ŚBr.; easy to be had or got, ĀpŚr. (superl. -*tama*, KātyŚr., Sch., in a quotation); easily treated or cured, Suśr.

Sûpacaraṇá, mf(*ā*)n. easy of access or approach, TS.

Sûpacāra, mfn. easy to be dealt with, easily satisfied, MBh.

सूपत् *sūpat*, ind. (cf. *kūpat*), g. *câdi*.

सूपतीर्थ *sûpatīrtha*, mf(*ā*)n. having good steps for bathing, MBh.

Sûpatīrthya, mf(*a*)n. id., Lalit.

सूपदंश *sûpadvaṇśa*, m. good spice or condiment, R.

सूपद्वार *sûpadvāra*, mfn. having beautiful side-doors, R.

सूपयुक्त *sûpayukta*, mfn. well used or employed, Jātakam.

सूपवञ्चन *sûpavañcaná*, mf(*á*)n. easy of approach or access, not repellent, friendly, RV.

सूपविष्ट *sûpavishṭa*, mfn. comfortably seated, BhP.

सूपसंस्कृत *sûpasaṃskṛita*, mfn. well prepared, Car.

सूपसदन *sûpasadaná*, mfn. good or easy to be approached or stayed with, TS.

सूपसम्पन्न *sûpasampanna*, mfn. duly initiated, Buddh.

सूपसर्पण *sûpasarpaṇa*, mf(*á*)n. easy of access, AV.

सूपसिद्ध *sûpasiddha*, mfn. well-seasoned, made savoury or relishable, Car.

सूपस्कर *sûpaskara*, mfn. furnished with good implements or a good equipment, MBh.

सूपस्था *sûpasthá*, mfn. forming a good place of rest or shelter, RV.; VS.; ŚāṅkhŚr.

Sûpasthāná, mfn. willingly or gladly approached, TS.

सूपाय *sûpáya*, m. a good means or expedient, Kām.

Sûpâyaná, mf(*á*)n. easily accessible, RV.

सूपावसान *sûpávasāná*, mf(*á*)n. offering good rest or repose, TS.

सूपावृत् *sûpâvṛít*, mfn. willingly turning towards, MaitrS.; ĀpŚr.

सूभर्व *sū-bharva*, mfn. (for *su* + *bh°* fr. √*bharv*) eating or feeding well (as a bull; others 'well nourished,' fr. √*bhṛi*), RV.

सूम 2. *sūma*, m. (said to be fr. √2. *su*; for 1. *sūma* see p. 1241, col. 3) the sky, heaven, Uṇ. i, 144.

सूमय *sū-máya*, mfn. (for *su-m°*) well shaped or fashioned (as a bow), RV. (= *su-sukha*, Nir.)

सूय *sūya*. See p. 1241, col. 3.

सूयवस *sū-yávasa* &c. See *su-y°*, p. 1231, col. 3.

सूर् 1. *sūr* &c. See √*sūr*, p. 1086, col. 1.

सूर् 2. *sūr*, weak form of 2. *svàr*, q.v.

1. **Sūra**, m. the sun, RV.; AV.; Calotropis Gigantea (= *arka*), MW.; a wise or learned man, teacher (= *sūri*), L.; N. of the father of Kunthu (the 17th Arhat of the present Avasarpiṇī), L.; of various authors (also with *bhaṭṭa* and *miśra*), Cat.; (*ī*), f. N. of Kuntī (as married to the Sun before her marriage with Pāṇḍu), Pāṇ. iv, 1, 48, Vārtt. 9, Pat. **–kanda**, m. Amorphophallus Campanulatus, L. **–kṛit**, m. N. of a son of Viśvāmitra (v. l. *sura-kṛit*), MBh. **–cakshas** (*sū́ra-*), mfn. radiant as the sun, RV. **–candra**, m. N. of the Guru of Bhānu-candra, Cat. **–ji**, m. (with *gaṇaka*) N. of an author, ib. **–dāsa**, m. N. of a Commentator on Hari-vaṇśa. **–masa** (?), m. pl. N. of a people (cf. *sauramasā*), Pāṇ. iv, 1, 170. **–vat**, mfn. containing the word *sūra*, PañcavBr. **–varman**, m. N. of a poet, Cat. **–suta**, m. 'son of the Sun,' the planet Saturn, Mṛicch. **–sūta**, m. 'charioteer of the Sun,' N. of Aruṇa (or the Dawn personified), L. **–sena**, n. pl. N. of a people (prob. w. r. for *śūra-s°*), AV. Pariś. **Sūrâcārya**, m. N. of an author, Gaṇar. **Sūrâpagā**, w. r. for *sur°*. **Sūrâsana-deśa**, w. r. for *śūrasena-deśa*.

Sūraṇa, n. (also written *śūr°*) Amorphophallus Campanulatus (cf. *sūra-kanda*), L.

1. **Sūri**, m. a learned man, sage (often ifc. after names, esp. as a title given to Jaina teachers), Kālid.; VarBṛS. &c.; N. of Bṛihas-pati (the sage among the gods) or the planet Jupiter, VarBṛS.; of Kṛishṇa, W.; of a poet, Cat.; = *yādava* and *sūrya*, L.; (*ī*), f., Uṇ. iv 64, Sch. **–deva**, m. (with *budhêndra*) N. of a man (the father of Keśavārya), Cat. **–bhaṭṭa**, m. N. of an author, ib. **–saṃtosha**, m. N. of wk.

Sūrin, m. a wise or learned man, scholar, L.

Sū́rya, m. the sun or its deity (in the Veda the name Sūrya is generally distinguished from Savitṛi [q.v.], and denotes the most concrete of the solar gods, whose connection with the luminary is always present to the poet's mind; in Nir. vii, 5 he is regarded as one of the original Vedic triad, his place being in the sky, while that of Agni is on the earth, and that of Indra is in the atmosphere; ten hymns in the RV. are entirely in praise of Sūrya, e.g. i, 50, i, 115 &c., also AV. xiii, 2; he moves through the sky in a chariot drawn by seven ruddy horses or mares [see *saptâśva, harit, harid-aśva*]; in the later mythology Sūrya is identified with Savitṛi as one of the 12 Ādityas or emblems of the Sun in the 12 months of the year, and his seven-horsed chariot is said to be driven by Aruṇa or the Dawn as its charioteer, who is represented without legs; the Sun, whether named Sūrya or Vivasvat, has several wives, see *sūryā* below), RV. &c. &c. (cf. IW. 11; 16 &c.; RTL. 341); a symbolical expression for the number 'twelve' (in allusion to the sun in the 12 signs of the zodiac), Jyot.; Hcat.; the swallow-wort (either Calotropis or Asclepias Gigantea, = *arka*), L.; N. of the son of Bali, L.; of a Dānava, VahniP.; of an astronomer (= *sūrya dāsa*), Cat.; epithet of Śiva, MBh.; (*ā́*), f. the wife of Sūrya or the Sun (also called Saṃjñā, q. v.); the daughter of Sūrya or the Sun (see RV. i, 116, 17; also described as daughter of Prajāpati or of Savitṛi and wife of the Aśvins, and in other places as married to Soma; in RV. i, 119, 2 she is called Ūrjānī, and in vi, 55, 4, vi, 58, 4 the sister of Pūshan [q. v.], who is described as loving her, and receiving her as a gift from the gods; accord. to some she represents a weak manifestation of the Sun; Sūryā Sāvitrī is regarded as the authoress of the Sūryā-sûkta, RV. x, 85), RV.; AV.; AitBr.; Kauś.; = *vāc*, Naigh. i, 11; = *sūryā-sûktā* (q. v.), ŚāṅkhGṛ.; a new bride; a drug, L.; the colocynth or bitter gourd, L.; mfn. solar (perhaps w. r. for *saurya*), Jyot. [For cognate words see under 2. *svàr*.] **–kamala**, n. the sunflower, heliotrope, MW. **–kara**, m. a sunbeam, Pañcat.; *-miśra*, m. N. of an author, Cat. **–kalpa**, m., **-kavaca**, n. N. of wks. **–kavi**, m. N. of an author, Cat. **–kānta**, m. 'sun-loved,' the sun-stone, sun-crystal (a kind of crystal supposed to possess fabulous properties as giving out heat when exposed to the sun; there is a corresponding moon-stone, see *candra-k°*; also *°ta-maṇi*), MBh.; Kāv.; VarYogay.; crystal, W.; a kind of flower (= *āditya-parṇī*), Car.; Hibiscus Phœniceus, W.; N. of a mountain, MārkP. **–kānti**, f. sunlight, sunshine, W.; a partic. flower, L.; the flower of sesamum, W. **–kāla**, m. 'sun-time,' day-time, day, L.; *°lânala* or *°lânala-cakra*, n. a kind of astrological diagram for indicating good and bad fortune, L. **–ketu** (*sū́rya-*), mfn. having the sun for a flag (or 'bright as the sun'), AV.; m. N. of a king, Buddh. **–krānta**, m. (in music) a kind of measure, Saṃgīt. **–kshaya**, m. the sun's mansion, Bṛih. **–gaṅgā-tīrtha**, n. N. of a Tīrtha, Cat. **–garbha**, m. N. of a Bodhi-sattva, Kāraṇḍ.; of a man, Buddh.; of a Buddhist Sūtra. **–gupta** (?), m. N. of a man, Buddh. **–graha**, m. 'sun-planet,' the sun, W.; 'sun-seizure,' an eclipse of the sun, Tithyād.; 'sun-seizer,' N. of Rāhu and Ketu, W.; the bottom of a water-jar, ib. **–grahaṇa**, n. 'sun-seizure,' a solar eclipse, VarBṛS.; Inscr.; N. of wk. **–cakshus**, m. N. of a Rākshasa, R. **–candra**, m. N. of a man, Kathās.; du. the sun and moon, A.; *-grahaṇa*, n., *-vrata*, n., *-vrata-kalpa*, m., *-stotra*, n., *°candrôparāga-śānti*, f. N. of wks. **–candramas**, **°masa**, see *saurya-cāndramasa*. **–ja**, m. 'sun-born,' N. of the planet Saturn, VarBṛS.; of the monkey Su-grīva, L.; of the hero Karṇa, W.; (*ā*), f. the river Yamunā, L. **–jyotis**, mfn. having the sun's light, Vait. **–tanaya**, m. 'son of the Sun,' N. of Manu, MārkP.; of the planet Saturn, VarBṛS.; of Karṇa, W.; of Su-grīva, ib.; (*ā*), f. 'daughter of the Sun,' the river Yamunā, L. **–tapas**, m. N. of a Muni, Kathās. **–tāpinī**, f. N. of an Upanishad. **–tīrtha**, n. N. of a Tīrtha, MBh. **–tejas**, n. sunshine, Hit.; (*sū́rya-*), mfn. having the power or radiance of the sun, AV. **–tvac** (*sū́rya-*), mfn. having a skin or covering as bright as the sun, RV.; AV.; TBr. **–tvaca**, mfn. id., MW. **–tvacas** (*sū́rya-*), mfn. id., VS.; AV.; PañcavBr. **–datta**, m. N. of various men, MBh.; Cat. **–daśā-phala**, m. N. of wk. **–dāsa**, m. N. of various men, Col.; Cat. **–dṛiś**, mfn. looking at the sun, Yājñ. **–deva**, m. the god Sūrya, Kālac.; Buddh.; N. of an author, Cat. **–devatyà**, mfn. having the sun as a deity, MaitrS.; Kāṭh. **–dvādaśāryā**, f. pl. N. of wk. **–dhara**, m. N. of a poet, Sadukt. **–dhyāna**, n. N. of wk. **–dhvaja**, m. 'sun-bannered,' N. of a man, MBh.; *-patākin*, mfn. having the sun on his standard and flag (said of Śiva), MBh. **–nakshatra** (*sū́rya-*), n. 'sun-asterism,' a radiant ast°, ŚBr.; that Nakshatra in which the sun happens to be, Sūryapr.; *-yoga*, m. the conjunction of the sun with a N°, ib. **–nagara**, 'city of the Sun,' N. of the capital of Kaśmīr (commonly called Siri-nagar or Seri-nagar), MW. **–nandana**, m. 'son of the Sun,' N. of the planet Saturn, Hāyan. **–namaskāra**, m. adoration of the sun; *-mantra*, m., *-vidhi*, m. N. of wks. **–nāḍī**, f. N. of wk. **–nābha**, m. N. of a Dānava, Hariv. **–nārāyaṇa**, m. the Sun personified, MW.; N. of various authors and other men (also *°ṇa-kavi*), Cat.; *-kavaca*, n., *-pūjā*, f., *-vrata*, n., *-stotra*, n. N. of wks. **–netra**, m. N. of a son of Garuḍa, MBh. **–paksha-karaṇa**, n., **-paksha-śaraṇa**, n., **-pañcâṅga**, n., **-pañcâṅga-stotra**, n. N. of wks. **–paṇḍita**, m. N. of a scholar (= *-kavi*), Cat. **–pati**, m. the god Sūrya, W. **–pattra**, m. Calotropis Gigantea, L. **–patnī** (*sū́rya-*), f. having the Sun for husband, AV. **–parṇī**, f. a kind of plant, MBh.; Car. (w. r. *sūrpa-*); Vagbh.; Phaseolus Trilobus, Bhpr.; Glycine Debilis, ib. **–parvan**, n. the moment when the sun enters a new sign, Pañcar.; a solar festival (on the days of the solstices, equinoxes, eclipses &c.), MW. **–pāda**, m. a sunbeam, Hariv. **–putra**, m. patr. of the Aśvins, MBh.; of the planet Saturn, MBh.; VarBṛS.; of Yama, Tithyād.; of Varuṇa, L.; of Karṇa, W.; of Su-grīva, ib.; (*ī*), f. 'daughter of the Sun,' lightning, L.; the river Yamunā, Bālar. **–pura**, n. 'city of the Sun,' N. of a city (cf. *-nagara* above), Rājat. **–purāṇa**, n., **-pūjā**, f., **-pūjā-vidhi**, m., **-prakāśa**, m., **-prajñapti**, f. N. of wks. **–pratishṭhā**, f. the setting up of an image of the sun (*-māhātmya*, n.), Cat. **–pradīpa**, m. a kind of Samādhi, Buddh. **–prabha**, mfn. bright as the sun; m. a kind of Samādhi, Kāraṇḍ.; N. of the palace of Lakshmaṇā (wife of Kṛishṇa), Hariv.; of a serpent-demon, Buddh.; of a Bodhi-sattva, ib.; of various kings, Kathās.; Cat.; of the king after whom the 8th Lambaka of the Kathā-sarit-sāgara is called (*-tā*, f.), Kathās.; *°bhâ-tejas*, m. a partic. Samādhi, Buddh. **–prabhava**, mfn. sprung from the Sun, Ragh. **–prabhīya**, mfn. belonging to king Sūrya-prabha, Kathās. **–praśishya**, m. N. of Janaka, Bālar. **–phaṇi-cakra**, n. a kind of astrological diagram for indicating auspicious and inausp° moments for doing anything, MW. **–bali**, m. N. of wk.; *-rāma*, m. N. of an author, Cat. **–bimba**, m. or n. the disc of the sun, VarBṛS.; N. of a sacred place, Cat.; *-tīrtha*, n. N. of a Tīrtha, MW. **–bhakta**, mfn. worshipping the sun, one who worships the sun, Cat.; m. Pentapetes Phœnicea, L.; (*ā*), f. a kind of plant, ib. **–bhaktaka**, m. a sun-worshipper, W.; Pentapetes Phœnicea, L. **–bhaṭṭa**, m. N. of an author, Cat. **–bhaṭṭīya**, n. N. of wk. **–bhā**, mfn. bright as the sun, MW. **–bhāgā**, f. N. of a river, L. **–bhānu**, m. N. of a Yaksha, R.; of a king, Inscr. **–bhās**, m. N. of a man, MBh. **–bhrāj**, mfn. radiant as the sun, Kāṭh. **–bhrātṛi**, m. N. of Airāvata, L. **–maṇi**, m. the sun-stone, sun-gem (= *-kānta*), L.; a kind of flower (= *-kānta*), ib.; Hibiscus Phœniceus, ib.; *-vṛiksha*, m. the shrub Hib° Ph°, MW. **–maṇḍala**, m. N. of a Gandharva, R.; n. the orb or disc of the sun, TĀr.; MaitrUp. &c. **–mati**, f. N. of a princess, Rājat. **–mantra**, m. N. of wk. **–marut** or **°ta**, see *sauryamārutaka*. **–malla**, m. N. of a king, Śatr.; Inscr. **–māla**, mfn. sun-garlanded (said of Śiva), MBh. **–māsa**, m. a solar month, Sūryapr., Sch. **–mukhī**, f. Helianthus Annuus, MW. **–m-paśya**, in *a-s°*, mfn. never seeing the sun, Pat.; Viddh. (cf. *a-sūryam-paśyā*, f.) **–yantra**, n. 'sun-instrument,' a representation of the sun (used in worshipping the Sun or in taking solar observations), MW. **–yama**, see *sauryayāma*. **–ratha**, m. the chariot of the sun, R.; BhP. **–raśmi**, m. a sunbeam, Mn. v, 133; (*sū́rya-*), mfn. having the rays of the sun, RV.; VS.; m. N. of Savitṛi, MW. **–rahasya**, n. N. of wk. **–rājya**, n. the sun's dominion, MaitrS. **–rāma**, m. N. of an author, Cat. **–ruc**, f. sunlight, Śiś. **–rksha** (*°ya + ṛiksha*), n. the Nakshatra in which the sun happens to be, Jyot. **–rc** (*°ya + ṛic*), f. a hymn addressed to the sun, BhP. **–latā**, f. Polanisia Icosandra, L.; Calotropis Gigantea, Npr. **–loka**, m. the sun-world (a region or space supposed to exist round the sun, constituting a heaven of which the sun is regent), Inscr.; Kāśikh. **–locanā**, f. N. of a Gandharvī, Kāraṇḍ. **–vaṅśa**,

m. the solar race of kings (i.e. the royal dynasty of Rāma-candra, king of Ayodhyā, hero of the Rāmâyaṇa, who was descended from Ikshvāku, son of Vaivasvata Manu, son of the Sun; many Rājput tribes still claim to belong to this race; it is one of the two great lines of kings, the other being called 'lunar,' see *candra-v°*), Kshitīś.; Buddh. **-vanśya,** mfn. belonging to the above solar race, Ragh. **-vaktra,** m. a kind of medicament, Cat. **-vajra-pañjara,** n. N. of a ch. of a wk. **-vat** (*sūrya-*), mfn. sunny, AV.; TBr.; KātyŚr.; m. N. of a mountain, R.; (*atī*), f. N. of a princess, Vās., Introd. **-vana,** n. N. of a forest sacred to the Sun, Śatr. **-vara,** m. a partic. medicament, Cat.; *-locana,* m. a partic. Samādhi, Kāraṇḍ. **-varuṇa,** see *saurya-vāruṇa.* **-varga,** m. N. of wk. **-varcas** (*sūrya-*), mfn. resplendent as the sun, VS.; Yājñ.; R.; BhP.; m. N. of a Deva-gandharva, MBh.; Hariv.; BhP.; of a Ṛishi, ĀrshBr. **-varṇa,** mf(*ā*)n. sun-coloured, AV. **-varman,** m. N. of a king, MBh.; of a Ḍāmara, Rājat. **-vallī,** f. the plant Gynandropsis Pentaphylla, Suśr.; VarBṛS. **-vāra,** m. Sunday, Pañcat. **-vikāsin,** mfn. expanding at the appearing of the sun, L. **-vighna,** m. 'destroyer of the sun,' N. of Vishṇu, Pañcar. **-vilokana,** n. the ceremony of taking a child out to see the sun when four months old, MW. **-veśman,** n. the sun's mansion, IndSt. **-vaiśvānara,** see *sauryav°.* **-vrata,** n. a partic. ceremony, Cat.; a partic. diagram, ib.; N. of various wks.; *-kathā,* f., *-mahiman,* m. N. of wks. **-śataka,** n., **-śānti,** f. N. of wks. **-śishya,** m. N. of Yājñavalkya, Bālar.; *°yântevāsin,* m. N. of Janaka, ib. **-śobhā,** f. sunshine, MW.; a kind of flower, L. **-śrít,** v.l. for *-śvít,* AV. **-śrī,** m. N. of a being reckoned among the Viśve Devāḥ, MBh. **-śvít,** mfn. bright as the sun, RV. **-shaṭpadī,** f., **-shaḍ-aksharī,** f. N. of wks. **-saṃkrama** (Yājñ.) or **-saṃkrānti,** f. (Cat.) the sun's entrance into a new sign. **-saṃjña,** m. a kind of ruby, L.; n. saffron, ib. **-sadṛiśa,** m. N. of Līlāvajra, Buddh. **-saptati,** f., **-saptāryā,** f. pl. N. of wks. **-sama** (*sūrya-*), mfn. equal to the sun, VS.; Siṇhâs. **-sahasra-nāman,** n., **-sahasranāmâvalī,** f. N. of wks. **-sāman,** n. N. of various Sāmans, ĀrshBr. **-sārathi,** m. the Sun's charioteer, Dawn, L. **-sāvarṇi,** m. N. of a Manu; *°ṇika,* mfn. belonging to him, MārkP. **-sāvitra,** m. N. of a being reckoned among the Viśve Devāḥ, MBh. **-siṇha,** m. N. of a king, Cat. **-siddhânta,** m. a celebrated astronomical text-book (said to be a direct revelation from the Sun), IW. 175 &c.; of another wk.; *-ṭīkā,* f., *-dīpikā,* f., *-prakāśa,* m., *-pradīpikā,* f., *-bhāshya,* n., *-mañjarī,* f., *-rahasya,* n., *-vāsanā-bhāshya,* n., *-vyākhyā,* f., *-vyākhyāna,* n., *-vyākhyā-vivaraṇa,* n., *-sāraṇī,* f.; *°tôdāharaṇa,* n. N. of Comms. **-suta,** m. 'son of the Sun,' N. of the planet Saturn, Var.; of the monkey Su-grīva, Kām. **-sûkta,** n. N. of a partic. hymn to the Sun (RV. i, 50; RTL. 342; cf. *sūryā-s°*). **-sūta,** m. the charioteer of the Sun, BhP. **-sūri,** m. N. of an astronomer, Col.; Cat. **-sena,** m. N. of various men, Cat. **-stava-kapāla-mocana,** m., **-stavana,** n. N. of wks. **-stút,** m. a partic. Ekâha, ŚBr.; ŚrS.; Vait. **-stuti,** f. or **-stotra,** n. praise of the sun (N. of various wks.), Cat. **-hṛidaya,** n. N. of a hymn. **Sūryânśu,** m. a sunbeam, Vām.; Bhpr. **Sūryâkara,** m. N. of a man, Cat.; pl. N. of a people, R. **Sūryâksha,** mfn. sun-eyed, Hariv.; m. N. of a king, MBh.; Hariv.; of a monkey, R. **Sūryâgama,** m. N. of wk. **Sūryâgní,** m. du. Sūrya and Agni, TS. **Sūryā-candramásā** or **°sau,** m. du. the sun and moon (also characterized as Dānavas), RV.; AV.; ŚBr. &c. **Sūryâtapa,** m. the sun's heat (*°pe* √*dā,* 'to expose to the sun,' Ml.), Kāv.; *-cchinna-dṛishṭi,* mfn. having the sight dazzled by the sun's glare, MW.; *-parikshipta,* mfn. overspread by the sun's rays, ib. **Sūryâtmaja,** m. 'son of the Sun,' the planet Saturn, Var. **Sūryâtharva-śirshôpanishad,** f., **Sūryâtharvâṅgirasôpanishad,** f., **Sūryâdi-graha-prīty-artha-dāna,** n., **Sūryâdi-graha-phala-kuṇḍalī,** f., **Sūryâdi-graha-sādhana,** n., **Sūryâdi-pañcâyatana-pratishṭhā-paddhati,** f., **Sūryâdi-pratimā-pratishṭhā-vidhi,** m., **Sūryâdi-varsha-phalôkti,** f. N. of wks. **Sūryâdri,** m. N. of a mountain, MārkP. **Sūryânana,** m. 'sun-faced,' N. of a man, Lalit. **Sūryânuvādinī,** f. N. of Comm. **Sūryâpâya,** m. sun-departure, sunset, Megh. **Sūryâpīḍa,** m. N. of a son of Pārikshita or Parikshit, Hariv.; VP. **Sūryâbhinimrukta,** mfn. one upon whom (while sleeping) the sun has set, TBr. **Sūryâbhinimlukta,** mfn. id., Gobh. **Sūryâbhyudita,** mfn. one upon whom (while he is still sleeping) the sun has risen, TBr.; Gobh.; Gaut. **Sūryā-māsā,** m. du. the sun and moon, RV.; AV. **Sūryâruṇa-karma-vipāka,** m., **Sūryâruṇa-śataka,** n., **Sūryâruṇa-saṃvāda,** m., **Sūryâruṇa-smṛiti,** f. N. of wks. **Sūryârghya,** n. a respectful offering presented to the sun, Cat.; *-dāna-paddhati,* f., *-vidhi,* m. N. of wks. **Sūryârṇava,** m., **Sūryârṇava-karma-vipāka,** m., **Sūryâryā,** f. N. of wks. **Sūryâloka,** m. sunshine, L. **Sūryâvarta,** m. N. of two plants, Suśr.; ŚārṅgS.; Scindapsus Officinalis, L.; a kind of sunflower, Helianthus Indicus, ib.; Cleome Pentaphylla, ib.; Cleome Viscosa, W.; head-ache which increases or diminishes according to the course of the sun, Suśr.; a kind of Samādhi, Buddh.; N. of a water-basin, Śatr.; (*ā*), f. Polanisia Icosandra, L.; *-rasa,* m. a partic. preparation of copper, L. **Sūryâvalokana-prayoga,** m. N. of wk. **Sūryâvêkshaṇa,** n. the act of looking at the sun, W. **Sūryâśman,** m. the sun-stone (see *sūrya-kānta*), L. **Sūryâśva,** m. a horse of the sun, ib. **Sūryâshṭaka,** n., **Sūryâshṭa-śata-nāman,** n. pl., **Sūryâshṭôttara-śata-nāman,** n. pl. N. of wks. **Sūryâsta,** m. sunset, Pañcat.; *-m-gamana,* n. id., Cat.; *-m-aya,* m. id. (*-vat,* with *kāla,* m. 'the time of sunset'), Kuval., Sch.; Tithyād. **Sūryâhva,** mfn. named after the sun, MW.; m. Calotropis Gigantea, L.; n. copper, ib. **Sūryêndu-saṃgama,** m. conjunction of sun and moon, the night of new moon, L. **Sūryêshṭi-prayoga,** m. N. of wk. **Sūryôḍha,** mfn. brought by the (setting) sun; m. (with *atithi*) a guest who arrives at sunset, ĀpŚr.; Pur. &c.; m. the time of sunset, A. **Sūryôtthāna,** n. sunrise, MW. **Sūryôdaya,** m. id., MBh.; VarBṛS.; *-giri,* m. the mountain behind which the sun rises, MBh.; *-nibandha,* m., *-varṇana,* n., *-saṃkalpa-nāṭaka,* n. N. of wks.; *°dayâsta,* m. du. sunrise and sunset (*-kāla,* m. du. the times of them), Cat. **Sūryôdayana,** n. sunrise, Kauś. **Sūryôdyāna,** n. = *sūrya-vana,* Śatr. **Sūryôpanishad,** f. N. of an Upanishad. **Sūryôpasthāna-mantra,** m., **Sūryôpasthāna-vidhi,** m. N. of wks. **Sūryôpâsaka,** m. a sun-worshipper, MW. **Sūryôpāsanā,** f. the worship of the sun, Cat.; *-vidhi,* m. N. of wk.

Sūryaka, mfn. resembling the sun, Hariv. (v.l.); m. N. of various men, Rajat.; VP.

Sūryā, f., see *sūrya* above. **-vasu,** mfn. one whose wealth is Sūryā (said of the Aśvins), RV. **-vid,** mfn. knowing the Sūryā hymn (RV. x, 85), ĀśvGṛ. **-vivāha,** m. the marriage of S° (described in RV. x, 85), Kauś. **-sûkta,** n. the Sūryā hymn (RV. x, 85; describing the marriage of Sūryā; this hymn is also found with some variations in AV. xiv, 1), IndSt.

Sūryāṇī, f. the wife of the god Sūrya, Vop.

सूर 2. *sūra,* m. (fr. √1. *sū*) an inciter, propeller, RV. i, 121, 7 (Sāy.)

2. **Sūri,** m. 'inciter,' the institutor of a sacrifice (= *yajamāna* in later language), RV.; AV.; a lord, chief (also of gods), RV.; (*ī*), f., TS.

सूर 3. *sūra,* m. (fr. √3. *su*) the Soma-juice flowing from the Soma press, RV.; AV.

3. **Sūri,** m. a presser or extractor of Soma, Soma sacrificer, RV.

सूरत *sū-rata,* mfn. (for *su-r°*) well disposed towards, compassionate, tender, Uṇ., v, 14; tranquil, calm, ib.; (*ā*), f. a tractable cow, L. **-kalpa-taru,** m. N. of a Comm. on the Tarka-dīpikā by Śrīnivāsa Bhaṭṭa. **-siṇha,** m. N. of a king (patron of Śrī-nivāsa Bhaṭṭa), Cat.

सूरथ *sū-ratha,* m. (for *su-r°*) N. of an author, Cat.

सूरि 4. *sūrí,* m. (fr. √*sṛi;* cf. *sūrta*) a course, path (= *saraṇi*), RV. i, 141, 8 (Sāy.)

सूरी *sūrī.* See f. of 1. *sūra* and 1. 2. *sūri.*

सूर्क्ष् *sūrksh* or *sūrkshy,* cl. 1. P. (Dhātup. xxvii, 15; xv, 2) *sūrkshati* or *°shyati* (occurring only in pres. base; Gr. also pf. *susūrksha* or *°shya;* fut. *sūrkshitā,* *°shyitā* &c.), to heed, care or trouble about (acc. or gen.), MaitrS.; Kāṭh.; GopBr.; ĀpŚr.; to disrespect, slight, neglect (?), Dhātup. [Cf. accord. to some, Lith. *sergèti;* Goth. *saúrga;* Germ. *Sorge;* Angl. Sax. *sorh;* Eng. *sorrow.*]

Sūrkshaṇa, n. disrespect, contumely (more prob. 'respect,' 'regard'), L.

Sūrkshya, mfn. to be heeded or regarded, TBr.; m. a kind of bean, Phaseolus Radiatus, L.

सूर्जन *sūrjana,* m. N. of a king, Cat. **-carita,** n. a biography of king Sūrjana (by Candraśekhara), ib.

सूर्त *sūrta,* mfn. (fr. √*sṛi;* cf. Pāṇ. viii, 2, 61) walked, trodden (others, 'bright, illuminated;' cf. *a-sūrta*), RV.

सूर्प *sūrpa,* *°paka,* *°pāraka.* See *śūrp°.*

सूर्मि *sūrmi* or *sūrmī,* f. (rather fr. √*sṛi* than fr. *su* + *ūrmi;* also written *śūrmi* and *śūrmī*) a pipe for conveying water, RV.; ŚBr.; a kind of tube serving as a candlestick, RV.; TS.; Kāṭh.; a metal image, W.; a hollow metal column made red-hot for burning criminals (esp. adulterers) to death, Gaut.; Mn. &c.

Sūrmyà, mfn. being in tubes or pipes or channels, TS. (VS. *sūrvya*); (*ā*), f. N. of the wife of Anuhrāda, BhP.

सूर्य *sūrya* &c. See p. 1243, col. 1.

सूर्यन्ती *sūryantī,* w.r. for *tūryantī,* ĀpGṛ.

सूर्व्य *sūrvya,* mfn. being in beautiful vessels &c. (cf. under *sūrmya* above), VS.

सूलीक *sūlīka.* See *śūlika,* p. 1087, col. 1.

सूवन् *sūvan, sūvari.* See p. 1240, col. 2.

सूष् *sūsh* (also written *śūsh*), cl. 1. P. *sūshati,* to bring forth (a child), procreate, Dhātup. xvii, 28.

Sūshaṇā, f. 'the genitals' or 'a parturient woman,' AV.

Sūshā, f. (prob.) a parturient woman, ib.

Sūshyantī. See √2. *sū,* p. 1239, col. 3.

सूष *sūsha,* m. (prob. w.r. for *śūsha*) strength, vigour, energy, L.

सूषस् *sūshas,* mfn. one who enjoys a good dawn or happy morning, AV.

सृ *sṛi* (cf. √*sal*), cl. 1. 3. P. (Dhātup. xxii, 37; xxv, 17) *sárati* (ep. also *°te* and accord. to Pāṇ. vii, 3, 78 also *dhāvati*), and *sísarti* (the latter base only in Veda; 3. du. *sísrataḥ,* 3. pl. *sísrate,* RV.; p. *sísrat* [q.v.], ib.; pf. *sasā́ra, sasré,* ib. &c.; 1. du. *sasṛivá,* ŚBr.; p. *sasṛivás, sasrāṇá* and *sasṛimāṇá,* RV.; aor. *asārshīt,* Gr.; Subj. *sarshat,* AV.; Prec. *sṛiyāt,* Gr.; fut. *sartā,* ib.; *sarishyáti,* RV. &c.; inf. *sartum,* MBh. &c.; *sártave, °tavai,* RV.; ind. p. *sṛitvā́,* Br.; *-sṛítya, -sā́ram,* Br. &c.), to run, flow, speed, glide, move, go (with *uccakais,* 'to spring up;' with *vā́jam* or *ājim,* 'to run a race,' i.e. 'exert one's self'), RV. &c. &c.; to blow (as wind), Megh.; to run away, escape, R.; Mālav.; BhP.; to run after, pursue (acc.), RV.; to go towards, betake one's self to (acc. or *tatra* &c.), MBh.; BhP.; to go against, attack, assail, MBh.; to cross, traverse (acc.), R.; (Ā.) to begin to flow (said of the fluid which surrounds the fetus), AV.: Pass. *sriyate* (aor. *asāri,* Br.), to be gone &c., Gr.: Caus. *sārayati* or cl. 10. P. (Dhātup. xxxii, 107) to cause to run, Nir.; to set in motion, strike (a lute), Megh.; to remove, push aside (a braid of hair), ib.; put in array, to arrange (with *dyūtam,* 'the men on a chess-board'), Pañcad.; to make visible, show, manifest, Viddh.; to nourish, foster (gen.), HPariś.; Ā. *sārayate* (for *sarāyate* see *saraya,* p. 1182, col. 1), to cause one's self to be driven, drive (in a carriage), ĀśvGṛ.: Pass. *sāryate,* to be made to flow, discharge (excrement), Suśr.: Desid. *sisīrshati,* to wish to run (*vājam,* 'a race'), TS.: Intens. (cf. *sarisrará*) *sársṛite* (p. *sársrāṇa,* see *pra-*√*sṛi*) or *sarīsharti,* to stride backwards and forwards, Kāv.; to blow violently (as the wind), ib. [Cf. Gk. ὁρμή, ὁρμάω; ἅλμα, ἅλλομαι; Lat. *salire.*]

Sara, saraṇa &c. See p. 1182, col. 1.

Sísrat, mfn. running, swift, rapid, RV.

Sṛit, (ifc.) running &c. (see *adāra-, āji-sṛit* &c.)

Sṛitá, mfn. (cf. *sūrta*) going, running &c. (see *bhujaga-śiśu-sṛita*), Hariv.; gone, passed away (see comp.); (with *bahis*) one who has slipped or come out, Kathās.; n. (ifc. f. *ā*) going, moving; flight, escape, MBh. **-java** (*sṛitá-*), mfn. (an ass) whose swiftness or activity is gone, AitBr.; ŚBr. **-m-jaya,** m. N. of a son of Karma-jit, BhP.

Sṛiti, f. a road, path (*kha-sṛityā*, 'through the atmosphere'), RV. &c. &c.; wandering, transmigration, Mn.; BhP.; aiming at, producing, BhP.

Sṛitya, n. running, flowing (see *sindhu-s°*).

Sṛítvan, mf(*arī*)n. running, swift, nimble, RV.; Kāṭh.; m. the creator, Uṇ. iv, 113; = *visarpa* and *buddhi*, L.; (*arī*), f. a mother, L.

Sṛitvara, mf(*ī*)n. = *sṛitvan*, Pāṇ. iii, 2, 163.

Sṛimará, mfn. (Pāṇ. iii, 2, 160) going, going well or quickly, W.; m. a kind of animal frequenting damp places (accord. to some the 'Bos Grunniens' or 'a young deer'), MBh.; R. &c.; N. of an Asura (cf. *sṛimala*, *sṛima*, and *sṛipa*, col. 3), Hariv.

सृक् *sṛik*, an inarticulate sound. **-√kṛi,** P. *-karoti*, to make the sound *sṛik*, Vop.

सृक *sṛiká*, m. (usually derived fr. √*sṛi* or *sṛij*; but rather from an obsolete √*sṛik*, 'to be pointed') an arrow, spear, RV.; wind, L.; a lotus flower, L. **-vat,** mfn., v.l. for next, MaitrS. **Sṛi-ká-vat,** mfn. having an arrow or spear, TS.; Kāṭh. **Sṛiká-hasta,** mfn. holding an arrow &c. in the hand, VS.

Sṛikāyin or **sṛikāvin,** mfn. having an arrow or spear, VS.; Kāṭh.

Sṛikva, n. the corner of the mouth, L.; m. N. of a man, IndSt.

Sṛikvaṇī, f. the corner of the mouth, Suśr.; Kathās.

Sṛikvan, m. n. id., RV.; Yājñ.; MBh. &c.

Sṛikvi, n. id., Yājñ.; MBh.; Hariv. &c.

Sṛikviṇī, f. id., MBh.

Sṛiga, m. = *sṛika*, an arrow, spear, L. **-vat** (*sṛigá-*), mfn. having an arrow or spear (v.l. *sṛigá-vat*), MaitrS.

Sṛigāyin, mfn. = *sṛikāyin*, MaitrS.

सृकण्डु *sṛikaṇḍu*, m. N. of a man, g. *śubhrâdi*; f. = *kaṇḍū*, the itch, itching, L.

सृकाल *sṛikāla*, m. = *sṛigāla*, a jackal, L.

सृक्क *sṛikka*, *sṛikkaṇī* &c. = (or v.l. for) *sṛikva*, *sṛikvaṇī* &c. above.

सृकथा *sṛikthā*, f. (perhaps fr. √*sṛij*) a leech, L.

सृगाल *sṛigālá*, m. (also written *śṛigāla*; of doubtful derivation), a jackal, ŚBr. &c. &c.; a partic. tree, MBh. (Nīlak.); N. of a Vāsudeva (ruler of Karavīra-pura, Hariv.; of a Daitya, L.; a rogue, cheat, W.; a coward, poltroon, ib.; an ill-natured or harsh-speaking man, ib.; (*ī*), f. a female jackal, Pañcat.; Kathās.; a fox, W.; flight, retreat, L.; tumult, uproar (= *ḍamara*), L.; Asteracantha Longifolia, L.; (prob.) Batatas Paniculata (cf. *sṛigālikā*), L. **-kaṇṭaka,** m. 'jackal's thorn,' a kind of plant (Zizyphus Scandens or Argemone Mexicana), L. **-koli,** m. a sort of jujube (accord. to some = Zizyphus Œnoplia), L. **-garta,** m. N. of a place (°*tīya*, mfn.), Pāṇ. iv, 2, 137, Sch. **-ghaṇṭi,** f. Asteracantha Longifolia, L. **-jambu** or **-jambū,** f. a water-melon, L.; the fruit of the jujube, L. **-yoni,** m. the womb (or 'the being born in the w°') of a jackal, Mn. v, 154. **-rūpa,** mfn. 'jackal-formed,' N. of Śiva, MBh. **-vadana,** m. 'jackal-faced,' N. of an Asura, Hariv. **-vāṭī,** f. N. of a place, Hariv.; °*tīya*, mfn. inhabiting Sṛigāla-vāṭī, ib. **-vāstuka,** m. a kind of potherb, L. **-vinnā** or **-vṛintā,** f. Hemionitis Cordifolia, L. **Sṛigālâsthi-maya,** mf(*ī*)n. made of the bones of a jackal, Cat.

Sṛigālikā, f. a female jackal, Pañcat.; Kathās.; a fox, L.; running away, flight, L.; Batatas Paniculata, L.; riot, tumult, L.; N. of a woman, Das.

Sṛigālinī, f. a female jackal, MBh.

सृङ्का *sṛiṅkā*, f. (of unknown meaning), KaṭhUp.

सृज 1. *sṛij* (cf. √1. 2. *sarj*), cl. 6. P. (Dhātup. xxviii, 121) *sṛijáti* (Ved. and ep. also °*te*, and once in AV. *sárjati*; pf. *sasarja*, *sasṛijé* [2. sg. accord. to Pāṇ. vii, 2, 65, *sasarjitha* and *sasrashṭha*, in BhP. once *sasarktha*]; Vedic forms are *sasṛijmáhe*, °*jrire*, *sasṛijyāt*, *asasṛigram*; p. *sasṛijānā*, q.v.; *sasṛigmáhe*; aor. *asrākshīt*; *ásṛikshi*, *ásṛishṭa* [Ved. also *ásṛigram* or °*ran*; *ásarji*; *asrāk*, *asrāṭ*; *srās*; *srakshat*; p. *sṛijāná*, q.v.], ib.; fut. *srashṭā*, PañcavBr.; *srakshyati*, °*te*, Br. &c.; inf. *srashṭum*, MBh. &c.; ind. p. *sṛishṭvā*, Br.; *-sṛijya*, ib. &c.; *-sárgam* or *-sárjam*, Br.), to let go or fly, discharge, throw, cast, hurl at (acc. or dat.), RV. &c. &c.; to cast or let go (a measuring line), RV.; to emit, pour forth, shed, cause to flow (rain, streams &c.), ib. &c. &c.; to utter (a sound), Kathās.; to turn or direct (glances), Kum.; to let loose, cause (horses) to go quickly; Ā. 'to speed, run, hasten,' RV.; to release, set free, ib.; AV.; Kauś.; to open (a door), Kauś.; to publish, proclaim, AitBr.; to draw out and twist (a thread), twist, wind, spin (lit. and fig.; Ā. *sṛijyate*, 'for one's self;' cf. Pat. on Pāṇ. iii, 1, 87, Vārtt. 15, and Dhātup. xxvi, 69), TS.; AV.; ŚBr.; ŚrS.; (in older language only Ā.) to emit from one's self, i.e. create, procreate, produce, beget, RV. &c. &c.; to procure, grant, bestow, MBh.; R. &c.; to use, employ, Rājat.; to get, acquire, obtain, take (interest on money lent), Mn. viii, 140; to hang on, fasten to (loc.), MBh. iii, 2218 (perhaps *asṛijat*, w.r. for *asajat*; see √*sañj*): Pass. *sṛijyate* (aor. *ásarji*), to be let loose or emitted or created, RV. &c. &c.: Caus. *sarjayati*, °*te* (aor. *asasarjat* or *asīsṛijat*), to cause to let loose, let go, create &c., Br. &c.: Desid. *sisṛikshati*, °*te*, to wish to send forth or hurl or throw, Hariv.; (Ā.) to wish to produce or create, Kāṭh.; BhP.: Intens. *sarīsṛijyate*, *sarīsrishṭi* &c., Gr.

Sarga, sarja, °*jana* &c. See p. 1182, col. 3.

Sasṛijāná, mfn. being sent forth, let loose, let go, RV.

2. **Sṛij,** (ifc.) letting loose, emitting, discharging, MBh.; Kāv. &c.; producing, creating, begetting (also with gen.), Inscr.; MBh.; Rājat.

Sṛijati, m. (used as a substantive to denote the root *sṛij*, 'to create'), Śiś.

Sṛijatva-karman, n. begetting children, Saṃskārak.

Sṛijana, w.r. for *sarjana* (q.v.), Cat.

Sṛijayá, m. a kind of bird, VS. (Mahīdh.); (*ā́*), f. = *nīla-makshikā*, *śukla-sarpa*, or *nīla-mahisha*, TS. (Sch.)

Sṛijāná, mfn. let go, poured out, shed, emitted, sent forth, hurled, thrown, RV.

Sṛijikā-kshāra, w.r. for *sarj°* (q.v.), L.

Sṛijya, mfn. to be let go or emitted or created, BhP.; Sarvad.

Sṛishṭá, mfn. let go, discharged, thrown &c.; given up, abandoned (in *a-sṛ°*), Daś.; brought forth, produced, created, AV. &c. &c.; provided or filled or covered with (instr. or comp.), MBh.; R.; engrossed by, intent upon (instr.), MBh.; firmly resolved upon (loc. or dat.), Gaut.; ornamented, adorned, L.; abundant, much, many, L.; ascertained, W.; (*ā*), f. a kind of medicinal plant, L.; a musical instrument like a stick which produces a soft sound, L. **-māruta,** mfn. causing the discharge of wind, removing flatulence, Suśr. **-mūtra-purīsha,** mfn. promoting evacuations from the bladder and intestines, Suśr. **-vat,** mfn. one who has let go or created or made, W. **-viṇ-mūtra,** mfn. = *-mūtra-purīsha*, Suśr.

Sṛishṭi, f. (once in ŚBr. *sṛishṭí*) letting go, letting loose, emission, R.; production, procreation, creation, the creation of the world (*ā sṛishṭeḥ*, 'from the beginning of the world;' *sṛishṭiṃ kuru*, 'produce offspring;' cf. *manoratha-sṛ°*), TS. &c. &c.; nature, natural property or disposition, R.; the absence or existence of properties (?), W.; distribution of gifts, liberality, Mn. iii, 255; a kind of brick, TS.; ĀpŚr.; Gmelina Arborea, L.; m. N. of a son of Ugra-sena, BhP. **-karaṇa-ṭīkā,** f. N. of an astron. wk. **-kartṛi,** mfn. creating, a creator, MW. **-kṛit,** mfn. id.; m. (with *deva*) N. of Brahmā, MBh. **-khaṇḍa,** n. N. of the first ch. of the Padma-purāṇa. **-dā,** f. 'causing procreation,' a kind of bulb, L. **-dhara,** m. (with *śarman*), N. of the author of a Comm. on Purushôttama's Bhāshā-vṛitti. **-pattana,** n. a partic. magical power, Pañcar. **-pradā,** f. 'promoting procreation,' a partic. shrub (= *putra-dā*), L. **-prasaṅga,** m. N. of a Kāvya. **-mat,** mfn. engaged in the work of creation, MBh. **-saṃhitā,** f. N. of wk.

Sṛishṭy, in comp. for *sṛishṭi*. **-antara,** m. the offspring of intermarriage between the four original castes (created by Brahmā); *-ja*, m. the descendant of such offspring, Gaut.

सृजवान *sṛijavāna*, m. N. of a son of Dyuti-mat (v.l. *sṛijāvana*), VP.

सृञ्जय *sṛiñjaya*, m. N. of a son of Deva-vāta, RV.; of various other men, MBh.; Hariv. &c.; pl. N. of a family, AV.; Kāṭh. &c.; of a people (said to have been the allies of the Pañcālas), MBh.; (*ī*), f. N. of two wives of Bhajamāna (v.l. *sṛiñjarī*), Hariv.

सृञ्जरी *sṛiñjarī*. See preceding.

सृणि *sṛiṇi*, m. f. (said to be fr. √*sṛi*) an elephant-goad, Hcar.; Śiś.; m. the moon, Uṇ. iv, 104; an enemy, L.; (*sṛiṇī* and *sṛiṇí*), f. a sickle, RV.; ŚBr.

Sṛiṇika, m. an elephant-goad, L.; f. spittle, L.

Sṛiṇīka, m. (only L.) wind; fire; a thunderbolt; an intoxicated or frantic man; (*ā*), f. spittle, saliva, L.

Sṛiṇī-rāja, m. N. of a man, Virac.

Sṛiṇya, mfn. furnished with a sickle, RV. iv, 20, 5; (according to some) formed like a sickle, ib. i, 58, 4 (where *sṛiṇyā* for *sṛiṇyābhis*).

सृत् *sṛit*, *sṛita* &c. See p. 1244, col. 3.

सृदर *sṛidara*, m. a serpent, snake, Uṇ. v, 41, Sch.

सृदाकु *sṛídāku*, m. (said to be fr. √*sṛi*) the wind, Uṇ. iii, 78, Sch.; fire, L.; a forest-conflagration, L.; a kind of lizard, L.; a thunderbolt, L.; a river (accord. to some f.), L.; N. of a man (v.l. for next), MaitrS.

Sṛidāgu, m. N. of a man, MaitrS.

सृध् *sṛídh*, w.r. for *sṛídh*, AV.

सृप *sṛip*, cl. 1. P. (Dhātup. xxiii, 14) *sárpati* (ep. and m.c. also °*te*; p. *sárpat* [see s.v.] and *sarpamāṇa*; pf. *sasarpa* [1. du. *sasṛipiva*], Br.; aor. *asṛipat*, AV.; Br.; *asṛipta*, Br. &c.; *asārpsīt* or *asrāpsīt*, Gr.; fut. *sarptā* or *sraptā*, ib.; *sarpsyati*, Br.; *srapsyati*, ib. &c.; inf. *sarpitum*, MBh. &c.; *sarptum* or *sraptum*, Gr.; *-sṛ́pas*, Br.; ind. p. *sṛiptvā*, ib.; *-sṛ́pya*, AV. &c.; *-sarpam*, Br. &c.), to creep, crawl, glide, slink, move gently or cautiously (*sarpata*, 'depart!' Rājat.), RV. &c. &c.; to slip into (acc.), AitBr.; (in ritual) to glide noiselessly and with bended body and hand in hand (esp. from the Sadas to the Bahish-pavamāna), Br.; ŚrS.; ChUp.: Pass. *sṛipyate* (aor. *asarpi*), to be crept &c., MBh. &c.: Caus. *sarpayati* (aor. *asīsṛipat* or *asasarpat*), to cause to creep &c. (see *ava-*, *anu-pra-*, *vi-*√*sṛip*): Desid. *sisṛipsati* (see *ut-*√*sṛip*): Intens. *sarīsṛipyate* (AitĀr.), *sarīsarpti*, p. *sarīsṛipat* (BhP.), to creep along or hither and thither, glide about &c. [Cf. Gk. ἕρπω; Lat. *serpere*; see also *sarpa*.]

Sarpa &c. See p. 1184, col. 1.

Sṛipa, m. the moon (cf. *sṛipra*), L.; N. of an Asura (cf. *sṛima*), Hariv.

Sṛipta, mfn. crept, crawled &c.; slipped out of (abl.) or into (loc.), ŚBr.; ChUp.; n. a place crawled to, Kāś. on Pāṇ. ii, 3, 68.

Sṛipman, m. a serpent, L.; a child, L.; an ascetic, L.

Sṛiprá, mfn. slippery, oily (cf. *sarpís*), RV.; smooth, supple, lithesome, ib.; m. the moon, L.; (*ā*), f. N. of a river, L.; (*am*), n. honey, L. **-karasna** (°*prá-*), mfn. having smooth or supple arms, RV. **-dānu** (°*prá-*), mfn. sprinkling fat or oil, ib. **-bhojas** (°*prá-*), mfn. having fat or abundant food, ib. **-vandhura** (°*prá-*), mfn. having a smooth seat or box (as the chariot of the Aśvins), ib.

सृपाट *sṛipāṭa*, m. a small leaf of a flower &c., L.; (*ī*), f. a kind of measure, L.; a shoe, L.; base metal, L.; a small book, L.

Sṛipāṭikā, f. the beak of a bird, L.

सृबिन्द *sṛíbinda*, m. N. of a demon slain by Indra, RV.

सृभ् *sṛibh* or *sṛimbh* (cf. √*sibh*, *sribh*), cl. 1. P. *sarbhati*, *sṛimbhati*, to kill, slay, injure, Dhātup. xi, 40.

सृम *sṛima*, m. N. of an Asura (cf. *sṛipa* above and *sṛimara* col. 1), MaitrS.

Sṛimala, m. N. of an Asura (v.l. *samala*), Hariv.

सृष्ट *sṛishṭa* &c. See col. 2.

सॄ *sṝi* (cf. √*śṝi*, *svṝi*), cl. 9. P. *sṛiṇāti*, to hurt, injure, kill, Dhātup. xxxi, 22 (v.l.)

Sīrṇa, mfn. = *śīrṇa*, hurt, injured, L.

Sīrṇi, f. = *śīrṇi*, injury, hurt, L.

से 1. *se*, 2. sg. Ā. of √1. *as*.

से 2. *se*, m. and f., *si*, n. serving, L.; f. service, L.; N. of the wife of Kāma, L.

सेक् *sek* (cf. √*srek*), cl. 1. Ā. *sekate*, to go, move, Dhātup. iv, 7.

सेक *séka*, m. (fr. √*sic*) pouring out, emission, effusion (as of the seminal fluid; also 'the fluid itself'), RV.; Mn. xi, 120; sprinkling, besprinkling, moistening or watering with (comp.), Mn.; MBh. &c.; a shower-bath, Suśr.; ŚārṅgS.; a libation, offering, MW.; a drop of anything, ib.; pl. N. of a people, ib. – **m-dhara**, see *sekandhara*, s.v.; -*purī*, f., see ib. – **pātra** or -**bhājana**, n. a vessel for pouring out or holding water, watering-pot, bucket, L. – **miśrânna**, n. food mixed with curds, L. **Sekânta**, m. the end of the watering (of plants &c.), MW.

Sekima, mfn. sprinkled or watered with (comp.), Siṇhâs.; cast (as iron), Pāṇ. iv, 2, 20, Vārtt. 2, Pat.; n. a radish, L.

Sektavya, mfn. to be sprinkled or poured out &c., Hariv.; VarBṛS.

Séktṛi, mfn. sprinkling, a sprinkler, RV. iii, 32, 15; one who impregnates, impregnator (of cows or horses), Kull. on Mn. iii, 150; m. a husband, L.

Sektra, n. a vessel for holding or pouring out water, watering-pot, bucket, baling-vessel, L.

Seca, (ifc.) sprinkling, pouring out &c., Pat.

Secaka, m. 'sprinkler,' a cloud, L.

Secana, mfn. sprinkling, pouring out, emitting (see *visha-s°*); (*ī*), f., g. *gaurâdi*; (*am*), n. emission, effusion, Śaṃk.; sprinkling or watering with (comp.), MBh.; Mṛicch.; Suśr.; a shower-bath, Suśr.; casting (of metals), Cat.; a bucket, baling-vessel, L. – **ghaṭa**, m. a watering-pot, Śak.

Secanaka, n. a shower-bath, ŚārṅgS.

Secanīya, mfn. to be sprinkled or watered or poured out or effused, MW.

Secita, mfn. (fr. Caus. of √*sic*) sprinkled, watered, Hariv.; VarBṛS.

Secya, mfn. = *secanīya*, Car.

सेकन्धर *sekandhara*, m. = اسكندر, Iskandar (Alexander), Cat. – **purī**, f. Alexander's city, ib.

सेगव *segava*, m. (cf. *syagavi*) a young crab, L.

सेङ्गर *seṅgara*, m. (said to be = *śṛiṅgivara*) N. of a family, Cat.

सेचालिन् *secālin*, g. *suvāstv-ādi*, Kāś. (v.l. *sevālin*).

सेट *seṭa*, m. a partic. weight or measure, Col.

सेटु *seṭu*, m. a kind of water-melon or cucumber, L.

सेठ *seṭha*, m. (fr. *śreshṭha*, but = *śreshṭhin*), Siṇhâs.

सेतकी *setakī*, f., g. *nady-ādi*.

सेतव्य *setavya*. See col. 2.

सेतु *sétu*, mfn. (fr. √1. *si*) binding, who or what binds or fetters, RV.; m. a bond, fetter, ib.; a ridge of earth, mound, bank, causeway, dike, dam, bridge, any raised piece of ground separating fields (serving as a boundary or as a passage during inundations), RV. &c. &c.; Rāma's bridge (see *setu-bandha*), BhP.; a landmark, boundary, limit (also fig. = 'barrier, bounds'), Mn.; MBh. &c.; a help to the understanding of a text, an explanatory commentary (also N. of various commentaries), Cat.; an established institution, fixed rule, MW.; the Praṇava or sacred syllable Om (which is said to be *mantrāṇām setuḥ*), KālP.; Cratæva Roxburghii or Tapia Cratæva (= *varaṇa, varuṇa*), L.; N. of a son of Druhyu and brother of Babhru, Hariv.; of a son of Babhru, Pur.; of a place, MW. – **kara**, m. the builder of a bridge, VarBṛS. – **karman**, n. the work of building a bridge, R. – **kāvya**, n. N. of a poem. – **khaṇḍa**, m. n. N. of a ch. of the Skanda-purāṇa. – **ja**, m. pl. N. of a district of Dakshiṇā-patha, L. – **pati**, m. 'lord of the bridge or causeway,' an hereditary title belonging to the chiefs of Rāmnād as controlling the passage of the channel between Rāmêśvara and Ceylon, see col. 2. – **prada**, m. N. of Kṛishṇa, Pañcar. – **bandha**, m. the forming of a causeway or bridge, a dam or bridge (esp. the ridge of rocks extending from Rāmêśvara on the South-eastern coast of India to Ceylon, and supposed to have been formed by Hanumat as a bridge for the passage of Rāma's army), MBh.; R. &c.; N. of various wks. (esp. of the 13th ch. of the Bhaṭṭi-kāvya and of a Prākṛit poem on the history of Rāma, also called *rāma-setu* or *rāvaṇa-vaha*, attributed to Pravarasena and sometimes to Kālidāsa). – **bandhana**, n. the construction of a bridge or dam, MBh.; a bridge or dam, Kum.; a limit, barrier, Hariv.; N. of a Paurāṇic wk. – **bhettṛi**, m. the destroyer of a dam or bridge, MBh. – **bheda**, m. the breaking down of an embankment, Kāv. – **bhedin**, mfn. breaking down barriers, removing obstructions, MW.; m. Croton Polyandrum or Tiglium, L. – **maṅgala-mantra**, m., -**māhātmya**, n., -**yātrā-vidhi**, m. N. of wks. – **vṛiksha**, m. Cratæva Roxburghii, L. – **śaila**, m. a mountain or hill forming a boundary, BhP. – **shāman**, n. (with *svargya*) N. of a Sāman, ĀrshBr. – **saṃgraha**, m. N. of a Comm. on the Mugdha-bodha. – **saraṇi**, f. N. of a Sanskṛit translation of the Setu-bandha by Śiva-nārāyaṇa-dāsa. – **snāna-vidhi**, m. N. of wk.

Setavya, mfn. to be bound or fastened together, Nir. xi, 31, v.l.

Setuka, m. a causeway, bridge, W.; Cratæva Roxburghii, L.

Setṛi, mfn. binding, fettering, a bond or binder, RV.

Setra, n. a bond, ligament, fetter, Pāṇ. iii, 2, 182.

Seru, mfn. binding, fastening, Pāṇ. iii, 2, 159.

Saitava. See p. 1247, col. 3.

सेदि *sedí*, f. (fr. √*sad*) weariness, exhaustion, decay, VS.; AV.; Kauś.

Sedivas, pf. p. of √*sad*, q.v.

Seduka, m. N. of a king, MBh.

सेद्धव्य *seddhavya*, mfn. (fr. √2. *sidh*) to be kept off or prevented, MW.

Sedha, mf(*ā*)n. keeping or driving away (see *go-shedhā*); m. = *nishedha*, prohibition (see *vidhi-shedha*); (*ā*), f. 'prohibiting contact (?),' a hedgehog or porcupine, Yājñ.

Sedhaka, mfn. driving off, preventing, MW.

Sedhana, n., Kāś. on Pāṇ. iii, 1, 116.

Sedhanīya, mfn. = *seddhavya* above.

सेन 1. *séna*, mfn. (7. *sa* + *ina*) having a master or lord, dependent on another, Vās.

सेन 2. *sena* (?), n. the body, L.

सेना *sénā*, f. (fr. √2. *si*) a missile, dart, spear, RV.; AV.; N. of Indra's wife (or his thunderbolt so personified), TS.; AitBr.; Vait.; an army, armament, battle-array, armed force (also personified as wife of Kārttikeya; ifc. also *sena*, n.), RV. &c. &c.; a small army (consisting of 3 elephants, 3 chariots, 9 horse, and 15 foot), L.; any drilled troop or band or body of men, Bālar.; a kind of title or addition to the names of persons (also names of courtezans), Sāh. (cf. Pāṇ. iv, 1, 152 &c.); N. of a courtezan (abridged fr. *kubera-senā*), HPariś.; of the mother of Śambhava (the third Arhat of the present Avasarpiṇī, L. – **kaksha**, m. 'the flank of an army' and 'an army compared to dry wood,' MBh. – **karman**, n. the leading or managing of an army, ib. – **gopa**, m. the keeper of an army (a partic. office), ib. – °**gni** (°*nâgni*), m. the Agni of an army, Kauś. – **gra** (°*nâgra*), n. the front or van of an army, R.; -*ga* or -*gāmin*, m. 'going at the front of an army,' a general, ib. – °**ṅga** (°*nâṅga*), n. the component part of an army (supposed to consist of four divisions: elephants, chariots, cavalry, and infantry), Ragh.; VarBṛS.; a division of an army; -*pati*, m. the leader of a division, Kām. – **cara**, m. 'going with an army,' a soldier, warrior, MBh.; Rājat. – °**jīva** or °**vin** (°*nâj*°), m. 'living by or with an army,' id., MBh. – **jū**, mfn. swift as an arrow, RV. – °**dhinātha** (°*nâdh*°), m. the chief of an army (see *sarva-sen*°); N. of a man, Vās., Introd. – °**dhipa** (°*nâdh*°, VarBṛS.), -°**dhipati** (Jātakam.), -°**dhyaksha** (Hariv.), m. the commander of an army. – **nātha**, m. N. of an author, Cat. – **nī**, m. (nom. °*nīs*; dat. abl. pl. °*nībhyas*; Gr. also acc. sg. °*nyam*; loc. °*nyām* &c.) the leader of an army, commander, general, chief, RV. &c. &c.; N. of Kārttikeya (god of war), MBh.; Kāv. &c.; of one of the Rudras, Hariv.; of a son of Śambara, ib.; of a son of Dhṛita-rāshṭra, MBh.; of a die (the head of a host of dice), MW.; (-*nī*)-*bhogīna*, mfn., Pat. on Pāṇ. v, 1, 9, Vārtt. 3; (-*nī*)-*grāmaṇī*, du. the leader of an a° and the chief of a village, VS. – **pati**, m. the general of an a°, AitBr. &c. &c.; N. of Kārttikeya, L.; of Śiva, MBh.; of a son of Dhṛita-rāshṭra, ib.; -*tva*, n. generalship, ib.; -*pati*, m. the chief commander of an army, ib. – **patya**, n. (prob. w.r. for *sainâp*°) commandership, generalship, ib. – **paricchad**, mfn. surrounded by an a°, Ragh. – **pura**, n. N. of a city, Cat. – **pṛishṭha**, n. the rear of an army, MBh. – **praṇetṛi**, m. the leader of an a°, ib. – **bindu**, m. N. of a king, ib. – **bhaṅga**, m. the breaking of an a°, rout, disorderly flight, MW. – °**bhigoptṛi** (°*nâbh*°), m. the guardian of an army, Kām. – **mukhá**, n. the van of an a°, TBr.; ŚBr.; a division or company of an a° (consisting of 3 or 9 elephants, 3 or 9 chariots, 9 or 27 horses, 15 or 45 foot-soldiers), MBh.; a covered way leading to a city gate, L.; (*ī*), f. N. of a goddess, Rājat. – **yoga**, m. equipment of an a°, MBh. – **raksha**, m. 'army-protector,' a guard, sentinel, L. – **vāsa**, m. a camp, VarBṛS. – **vāha**, m. the leader of an army, MBh. – **vindu**, see -*bindu*. – **stha**, m. 'being in an army,' a soldier, L. – **vyūha**, m. battle-array, L. – **samudaya**, m. an assembled a°, MBh. – **sthāna**, n. a camp, L. – **han**, m. N. of a son of Śambara (v.l. *sena-h*°), Hariv.

3. **Sena** (for 1. 2. see col. 2), in comp. for *senā*. – **kula**, n. the family of the Senas (*i.e.* of persons and princes whose names end in *sena*; cf. under *senā*), Buddh. – **jit**, mfn. vanquishing armies, VS.; m. N. of a king, MBh.; of a son of Kṛishṇa, Hariv.; of a son of Viśva-jit, VP.; of a son of Bṛihat-karman, ib.; of a son of Kṛiśâśva, BhP.; of a son of Viśada, ib.; f. N. of an Apsaras, BhP. (Sch.) – **skandha**, m. N. of a son of Śambara, Hariv. – **han**, see *senā-han* above.

Senaka, m. N. of a grammarian, Pāṇ. v, 4, 112; of a son of Śambara, Hariv.

Senaya, Nom. P. °*yati* &c. See *abhi-shenaya*, p. 71, col. 2.

Seni. See *tīrtha-s*°, p. 449, col. 2.

Senīya. See *yukta-s*°, p. 853, col. 3.

Sénya, mfn. caused by the throw of a spear, AV.; m. a spearman, warrior, RV.

Sainaka &c. See p. 1247, col. 3.

सेन्दुक *sênduka*, °*duḍa* and °*dubha*, m. N. of poets, Cat.

सेन्द्र *sêndra*, mfn. accompanied by or together with Indra, TS. &c. &c. – **gaṇa**, mfn. together with Indra's troops, MBh. – **cāpa**, mfn. along with Indra's bow, MW. – **tā** (°*drá*-), f. (ŚBr.), -**tvá**, n. (TS.) union or connection with Indra. – **dhṛiti**, mfn. (?), Vās. **Sêndrâyudha-taḍit**, mfn. with a rainbow and lightning, MW. **Sendrâyudha-purogama**, mfn. preceded by the rainbow, ib.

Sêndraka, m. pl. N. of a family, Inscr.

सेन्द्रिय *sêndriya*, mfn. possessed of manly vigour or potency (-*tvá*, n.), MaitrS.; together with the organs of sense, Mn. i, 50.

सेपुर *sepura*, n. N. of a village of the Bāhīkas, Pat., Sch.

सेफ *sepha*, w.r. for *śepha*, q.v.

सेभ्य *sebhya* (?), m. coldness, L.; mf(*ā*)n. cold, L.

सेमन्ती *semantī*, f. the Indian white rose, L.

Semantikā, f. id., MW.

सेय 1. *seya*, n. (fr. √*san*) obtaining (see *śata-s*°).

सेय 2. *seya*, mfn. (fr. √*so*). See *ava-seya*.

सेयन *seyana*, m. N. of a son of Viśvāmitra (v.l. *sayana*), MBh.

सेर *sêra*, mfn. used in explaining *sīra*, ŚBr.

सेराल *serāla*, n. pale-yellowness, L.; mf(*ā*)n. pale-yellow, L.

सेराह *serāha*, m. a horse of milk-white colour, L.

Serurāha, m. a Serāha horse with a mark on the forehead, L.

सेरु *seru*. See col. 2.

सेर्ष्य *sêrshya*, mf(*ā*)n. full of envy, envious,

jealous of (comp.), Prab.; Kathās.; (*am*), ind. enviously, jealously, Pañcat.; BhP.

सेल् *sel*, v.l. for √*śel*, q.v.

सेल *sela*, m. or n. (prob. Prākṛit for *śaila*) a kind of weapon, Kād. (B.); a partic. high number (cf. *selu*), Buddh.

Sella, m. or n. (?) a kind of weapon, Pañcad.

सेलग *sélaga*, m. (perhaps fr. *sela*=*śaila* + *ga*) a waylayer, robber, AitBr.; ŚBr.; ĀśvŚr.

सेलिस *selisa*, m. a kind of white deer, L.

सेलु *selu*, m.=*śelu*, Cordia Myxa, Suśr.; a partic. high number (cf. *sela*), Buddh.

सेल्हार *selhāra*, m. N. of a family, Cat.

सेव् *sev*, cl. 1. Ā. (Dhātup. xiv, 30) *sevate* (rarely °*ti*; pf. *sisheve*, °*va*, MBh. &c.; fut. *sevitā*, Gr.; *sevishyate*, ib., °*ti*, MBh.; aor. *asishevat*, *asevishṭa*, Gr.; inf. *sevitum*, MBh. &c.; ind. p. *sevitvā*, *-sevya*, ib.), to dwell or stay near or in (loc.), ŚBr.; to remain or stay at, live in, frequent, haunt, inhabit, resort to (acc.), Mn.; MBh. &c.; to serve, wait or attend upon, honour, obey, worship, ib.; to cherish, foster (a child), Kathās.; to present with (instr.), Ragh.; to enjoy sexually, have sexual intercourse with (acc.), Mn.; MBh. &c.; to refresh by soft breezes, fan (said of the wind), R.; Kālid.; Pañcat.; to devote or apply one's self to, cultivate, study, practise, use, employ, perform, do, RV. &c. &c.; to exist or be found in anything (acc.), R.; Hariv.; Kathās.: Pass. *sevyate*, to be followed or served &c., MBh.: Caus. *sevayati* (aor. *asishevat*), to attend upon, serve, honour, Hit.; to tend, cherish (plants), Bhartṛ.: Desid. of Caus., see *sisevayishu*: Desid. *sisevishate*, °*ti*, Gr.: Intens. *seshevyate*, ib.

Seva (either fr. √*sev* or *siv*), g. *pacādi*; n. = 1. *sevi*, an apple, L.

1. **Sevaka**, mfn. (for 2. see col. 2) dwelling in, inhabiting (comp.), MBh.; practising, using, employing (comp.), Kāv.; Kathās.; revering, worshipping (mostly comp.), Yājñ.; BhP.; m. a servant, attendant, follower, R.; VarBṛS.; Rājat.; a votary, worshipper, Hariv.; Pañcar. **Sevakâlu**, m. a kind of plant (=*nīla-bhaṅga*; commonly called Dugdhapeyā), L. **Sevakôttama**, m. (and *ā*, f.) best of servants, MW.

1. **Sevana**, n. (for 2. see col. 2) the act of frequenting or visiting or dwelling in or resorting to (comp.), Kāv.; Pañcat.; BhP.; waiting upon, attendance, service, Mn.; MBh. &c.; honouring, reverence, worship, adoration (also *ā*, f.), Kāv.; VarBṛS. &c.; sexual enjoyment, intercourse with (comp.), Mn. xi, 178; devotion or addiction to, fondness for, indulgence in, practise or employment of (gen. or comp.), Mn.; R. &c. **-bhāvanā-kāvya**, n. N. of wk.

Sevanin, m. a ploughman (?), Hariv. (Nīlak.)

1. **Sevanīya**, mfn. (for 2. see col. 2) to be followed or practised, Bhartṛ.; to be served or waited upon or honoured, Hariv.; BhP.

Sevā, f. going or resorting to, visiting, frequenting, Cāṇ.; Subh.; service, attendance on (loc., gen., or comp.; *sevāṃ* √*kṛi*, with gen., 'to be in the service of'), Mn.; MBh. &c.; worship, homage, reverence, devotion to (gen. or comp.), ib.; sexual intercourse with (comp.), Hit.; Subh.; addiction to, indulgence in, practice or employment or frequent enjoyment of (comp.), Nir.; Mn.; MBh. &c. **-kāku**, f. change of voice in service (i.e. sometimes speaking loudly, sometimes softly, sometimes angrily, sometimes sorrowfully), Vikr. **-kaumudī**, f. N. of a wk. on Bhakti. **-jana**, m. a servant, attendant, VarBṛS. **-°ñjali** (°*vâñj*°), m. a servant's reverential salutation with hollowed hands (see *añjali*), Bhartṛ. **-tīrtha**, m. N. of an author, Cat. **-daksha**, mf(*ā*)n. skilled in service, Mālav. **-dharma**, m. the duties or functions of s°, Bhartṛ. **-phala-stotra**, n. N. of a hymn by Vallabhâcārya; *-vivṛiti*, f.; °*lôkti-vivṛiti*, f. N. of Comms. **-°bhirata** (°*vâbh*°), mfn. rejoicing in or fond of s°, VarBṛS. **-bhṛit**, mfn. maintaining s°, serving, honouring (comp.), R. **-°valamba** (°*vâv*°), mfn. depending on another's s°, Bhartṛ. **-°vasara** (°*vâv*°), m. opportunity for worship or adoration, Kum. **-vicāra**, m. N. of a wk. on Bhakti. **-vilāsinī**, f. a female servant, Nalac. **-vṛitti**, f. a livelihood gained by service, L. **-vyavahāra**, m. the practice of service, MW.

1. **Sevi**, n. the jujube (=*badara*), L.; an apple (in this sense prob. fr. Persian *seb*), L.

2. **Sevi**, in comp. for *sevin*. **-tā**, f. service, attendance, MārkP. **-tva**, n. seeking, resorting to (comp.), BhP.; honouring, deference towards (comp.), Kām.; the state of one who dwells in or inhabits, MW.

Sevikā, f. a partic. sweetmeat (a kind of vermicelli made of wheat-flour and boiled in milk and sugar), BhP.

Sevita, mfn. dwelt in, visited, frequented, followed, served &c. (see √*sev*); furnished or endowed with, abounding in (comp.), R.; n.=1. *sevi*, L. **-manmatha**, mfn. addicted to love or amorous enjoyments, MW.

1. **Sevitavya**, mfn. (for 2. see below) to be frequented or inhabited, Hariv.; to be followed or practised, TUp.; Mn. &c.; to be tended or taken care of, Cāṇ.; Mṛicch.

Sevitṛi, mfn. (only ifc.) one who honours or worships, MBh.; one who follows or pursues, ib.; m. a servant, attendant, Mālav. iv, 12.

Sevin, mfn. (only ifc.) going or resorting to, frequenting, inhabiting, MBh.; R. &c.; attending on, serving, a servant, Kālid.; Kir.; VarBṛS.; honouring, revering, deferential to, Mn.; MBh. &c.; having sexual intercourse with, Subh.; addicted to, fond of, enjoying, practising, employing, MBh.; Kāv. &c.

Sevya, mfn. to be resorted to or frequented or inhabited by (gen.), Hariv.; Pañcat.; Kathās.; to be followed (as a path), Rājat.; to be approached, Cāṇ.; to be waited upon or served or obeyed, a master (as opp. to 'a servant'), R.; Kālid. &c.; to be honoured, honourable, Yājñ.; MBh. &c.; to be enjoyed carnally, Subh.; to be practised or used or employed, MBh.; R. &c.; to be studied, Cat.; to be kept or hoarded, Hit.; to be taken care of or guarded, W.; m. the Aśvattha tree, Ficus Religiosa, L.; Barringtonia Acutangula, L.; a sparrow, L.; an intoxicating drink made from the blossoms of the Bassia Latifolia, L.; (*ā*), f. the parasitical plant Vandā, L.; Emblic Myrobolam, L.; a kind of wild grain or rice, L.; (*am*), n. the root of Andropogon Muricatus, Suśr.; red sandal-wood, L.; sea-salt, L.; the thick middle part of curds, L.; water, L. **-tā**, f., **-tva**, n. the state of being liable or worthy to be served or honoured or revered or followed or pursued, Kāv.; Rājat.; Sarvad. **-sevakau**, m. du. master and servant, Hit.

Sevyamāna, mfn. being dwelt in or served or used &c.

सेवक 2. *sevaka*, m. (fr. √*siv*; for 1. *sevaka* see col. 1) one that sews, a sewer, L.; a sack, L.

2. **Sevana**, n. (for 1. see col. 1) the act of sewing, darning, stitching, Suśr.; Vop.; ĀpŚr., Sch.; a sack, L.; (*ī*), f. a needle, L.; a seam, L.; a suture or peculiar seam-like union of parts of the body (seven in number, viz. five of the cranium, one of the tongue, and one of the glans penis), Br.; Suśr.; (*ī*), f. a kind of small jasmine, L.

2. **Sevanīya**, mfn. (for 1. see col. 1) to be sewn or stitched together, MW.

2. **Sevitavya**, mfn. (for 1. see above) to be sewn, Nir.

सेवती *sevati*, f. the Indian white rose, L.

सेवधि *seva-dhi*, w.r. for *śeva-dhi*.

सेवन्तिकापरिणय *sevantikā-pariṇaya*, m. N. of a Nāṭaka or a Kāvya, Cat.

सेवालिन् *sevālin*, mfn. (fr. *savāla*, see *śev*°), g. *suvāstv-ādi* (Kāś. *secālin*).

सेवासी *sevāsī*, ind. (with √1. *kṛi*), g. *ūry-ādi* (v.l.)

सेश्वर *sêśvara*, mfn. (7. *sa*+*īśvara*) having a god, theistical (see next). **-sāṃkhya**, n. the theistical branch of the Sāṃkhya school of philosophy, Sarvad.

सेषु *séshu*, mfn. (7. *sa*+*ishu*) having an arrow (see next). **-dhanvan**, mfn. having a bow and arrow, ŚāṅkhŚr.

Sêshuka, mf(*ā*)n. having an arrow, KātyŚr.

सेष्टि *sêshṭi*, mfn. (7. *sa*+3. *ishṭi*) provided with a sacrifice, ĀpŚr.

Sêshṭika, mfn. id., ĀpŚr., Sch.

सेष्मीयाण *seshmīyāṇa*. See √*smi*, Intens.

सेहान *sehāna*. See √1. *sah*, p. 1192, col. 3.

सेहु *sehu*, m. a partic. dry substance, AV.; a partic. organ in the body, Kāṭh.

सेहुण्ड *sehuṇḍa*, m. Euphorbia Ligularia (cf. *sīh*°), Kāśikh.; (*ā*), f. id., Bhpr.

सेह्नोक *sehnoka* or *sehloka*, m. N. of a poet (cf. *sohnoka*), Cat.

सै *sai* (cf. √3. *sā*, 1. *so*), cl. 1. P. *sāyati*, to waste away, decline, Dhātup. xxii, 18.

सैंह *saiṇha*, mf(*ī*)n. (fr. *siṇha*) belonging to lions, leonine, lion-like, MBh.; Hariv. &c.

Saiṇhakaroṇa, m. (cf. *ājaka-r*°), Pat. on Pāṇ. i, 1, 72, Vārtt. 14.

Saiṇhakarṇa, mfn. coming or derived from Siṇha-karṇa, g. *takshaśilādi*.

Saiṇhakāyana, mfn. (fr. *siṇhaka*), g. *pakshâdi*.

Saiṇhala, mf(*ī*)n. (fr. *siṇhala*) belonging to or produced in Ceylon, Singhalese, Śatr.; (*ī*), f. a kind of pepper, L.; n. Laurus Cassia, L.

Saiṇhādrika, m. pl. (fr. *siṇha-adri*) N. of a people, Inscr.

Saiṇhika, mfn. (fr. *siṇha*) lion-like, leonine, W.; m. (fr. *siṇhikā*), metr. of Rāhu or the personified ascending node (cf. next), L.

Saiṇhikeya, mfn. descended from Siṇhikā, Hariv.; m. a child of S° (also pl.; applied to a class of Dānavas), ib.; metr. of Rāhu (cf. prec.), Kāv.; VarBṛS.; BhP.

सैक *sâika*, mfn. added to one, plus one, Yājñ.; VarBṛS. **-dvi-saptaka**, mf(*ikā*)n. plus one (and) two (and) seven, Jyot. **Saikâvali**, mf(*ī*)n. having a necklace consisting of a single string of pearls, VarBṛS.

सैकत *saikatá*, mf(*ī*)n. (fr. *sikatā*) sandy, gravelly, consisting or made of sand, ŚBr. &c. &c.; m. pl. N. of a family of Ṛishis, MBh.; n. (ifc. f. *ā*) a sandbank, sandy shore or soil, any bank or shore, MBh.; Kāv. &c. **-vat**, mfn. possessing sandbanks, MW. **Saikatêshṭa**, n. 'liked by sandy soil,' ginger, L.

Saikatika, mfn. belonging or relating to sandbanks, MW.; living in doubt and error (=*bhrānti-jīvin* or *saṃdeha-j*°), L.; m. an ascetic or religious mendicant, L.; n. a thread worn round the wrist or neck to secure good fortune (=*maṅgala-sūtra*), L.; =*mātri-yātrā*, L.

Saikatin, mfn. having sandbanks or sandy shores, Kālid.

सैकयत *saikayata*, m., g. *krauḍy-ādi*. **-vidha**, mfn. inhabited by Saikayatas, g. *bhauriky-ādi*.

Saikayatyā, f. of *saikayata*, g. *krauḍy-ādi*.

सैक्य *saikya*, mfn. (fr. *seka*) connected with or dependent on sprinkling or watering, VarBṛS.

सैक्षव *sâikshava*, mfn. (7. *sa*+*aikshava*) sugared, sugary, Bhpr.

सैचालिन *saicālina*, mfn. (fr. *secālin*), g. *suvāstv-ādi* (Kāś. *saivālin*).

सैत *saita*, m. N. of a family of princes, Buddh.

सैतकेय *saitakeya*, mfn. (fr. *setakī*), g. *nady-ādi*.

सैतव *saitava*, mfn. (fr. *setu*) consisting of a dam or bridge, Kāv.; m. N. of a preceptor, ŚBr.

सैतवाहिनी *saitavāhinī*, f. (perhaps for *situ v*°) N. of the river Bāhu-dā, L.

सैद्धान्तिक *saiddhāntika*, mf(*ī*)n. (fr. *siddhānta*) connected with or relating to an established truth &c., W.; m. one who knows an established truth or is versed in a Siddhânta (q.v.), Siṇhâs.

सैध्रक *saidhraká*, mfn. (fr. *sidhraka*) made of the wood of the Sidhraka tree, TBr.

Saidhrakâvata, mfn. (fr. *sidhrakā-vat*), Pāṇ. iv, 2, 72, Kāś.

Saidhrika, n. a kind of tree, Sāy. **-maya**, mf(*ī*)n. made of Saidhrika wood, SāmavBr.

सैनक *sainaka*, n. (fr. *senā*; *saṃjñāyām*), g. *kulālâdi*.

Sainānīka, mfn. (fr. *senā + an°*) belonging to the van of an army, ŚāṅkhBr.

Sainānya, n. (fr. *senā-nī*) command of an army, generalship, AitBr.

Sainâpatya, n. (fr. *senā-pati*) id., Mn.; MBh. &c.

Sainika, mfn. relating or belonging to an army, military, martial, drawn up in martial array, MBh.; R. &c.; m. an army-man, soldier, guard, sentinel, a body of forces in array, ib.; N. of a son of Śambara, Hariv.

Sainya, mfn. belonging to or proceeding from an army, MBh.; Hariv.; m. (ifc. f. *ā*) a soldier (pl. 'troops'), R.; an army, MBh.; Rājat.; a sentinel, guard, L.; n. a body of troops, army, MBh.; R. &c.; a camp, VarBṛS. **-kaksha**, m. = *senā-k°* (q.v.), R. **-kshobha**, m. a mutiny in an army, VarBṛS. **-ghāta-kara**, mfn. causing the destruction of an army, ib. **-nāyaka**, m. the chief or leader of an army, general, Kathās. **-nigrāhikā**, f. (used in explaining *cakra-grahaṇī*), Nilak. **-niveśa-bhūmi**, f. place of the encampment of an army, VarBṛS. **-pati** (VarBṛS.), **-pāla** (R.), m. = *-nāyaka*. **-pṛishṭha**, n. the rear of an army, L.; *-bhāga*, m. id., L. **-maya**, mf(*ī*)n. consisting of troops, MBh. **-vāsa**, m. the camp of an a°, Daś. **-vyapadeśa**, m. the summons of an army, R. **-śiras**, n. the van of an a°, Prab. **-hantṛi**, m. 'army-destroyer,' N. of a son of Śambara, Hariv. **Sainyâdhipati** or **°nyâdhyaksha**, m. 'army-overseer,' a general, commander, W. **Sainyôpaveśana**, n. the halting or encampment of an army, Cat.

सैन्दूर *saindūra*, mfn. (fr. *sindūra*) coloured with red-lead or vermilion (*°rī-√kṛi*, 'to colour with vermilion'), Ratnāv.

सैन्धव *saindhavá*, mf(*ī*)n. (fr. *sindhu*) relating to the sea, oceanic, marine, aquatic, Buddh.; belonging to or produced in or coming from the Indus or Sindh, TS. &c. &c.; m. a king of Sindh, MBh.; Mudr.; BhP.; a horse (partic. one bred in S°), L.; N. of a teacher, Cat.; (pl.) the inhabitants of S°, AV.Pariś.; MBh. &c.; N. of a partic. school founded by Saindhavāyana, VP.; m. n. a kind of rock-salt (found in Sindh), any salt, ŚBr.; VarBṛS.; Suśr.; (*ī*), f. a partic. Rāgiṇī, Saṃgīt.; (*am*), n. (in dram.) a song in Prākṛit (accompanied with music expressive of a lover's disgust on being deserted by a loved woman), Sāh. **-khilyá** or **-ghaná**, m. a lump of salt, ŚBr. **-cūrṇa**, n. powdered rock-salt, Suśr. **-śilā-śakala**, n. a morsel of fossil salt, Ragh. **-sarpis**, n. clarified butter with salt, Suśr. **Saindhavâraṇya**, n. the jungly district of Sindh, MBh.

Saindhavaka, mfn. belonging or relating to the Saindhavas (with *nṛipa* or *rājan*, m. 'a king of the Saindhavas'), MBh.; m. a miserable inhabitant of Sindhu, MW.

Saindhavāyana, m. N. of a Ṛishi (pl. his family), MBh.; Hariv.

Saindhavāyani, m. patr. fr. *saindhava*, g. *tikâdi*.

Saindhukshita, n. (fr. *sindhu-kshit*) N. of various Sāmans, ĀrshBr.

Saindhumitrika, mf(*ā* or *ī*)n. (fr. *sindhu-mitra*), g. *kāśy-ādi*.

Saindhuvaktraka, mfn. (fr. *sindhu-vaktra*), Pāṇ. iv, 2, 126, Sch.

सैन्धी *saindhī*, f. spirituous liquor (esp. palm-juice), L.

सैमन्तिक *saimantika*, n. (fr. *sīmanta*) red-lead (so called because used to make a mark along hair-parting), L.

सैर *saira*, mf(*ī*)n. (fr. *sīra*) belonging to a plough, Āpast.; n. a kind of spirituous liquor, Prâyaśc.; = *sīrāṇām* (i. e. *pratisīrāṇām*) *samūhaḥ* (used in explaining *sairaṃdhrī*), Nīlak. on MBh. iii, 2586.

Sairakāyaṇa, mfn. (fr. *sīraka*), g. *pakshâdi*.

Sairamdhra, m. (prob. fr. an unused *sīram-dhra*, 'plough-holder;' cf. *mahī-dhra*, *aṇsa-dhrī*) a kind of menial or domestic servant (in the caste-system born from a Dasyu and an Āyogavī), Mn.; MBh. &c.; (*ī*), f. a maid-servant in the women's apartments, a woman of the above mixed caste, ib.; a female artisan who works in other person's houses, L.; N. of Draupadī (who became servant-maid in king Virāṭa's house, when her husbands, the five Pāṇḍava princes, entered his service in various disguises), MBh. iv, 77 &c.

Sairamdhrikā, f. a female servant, chamber-maid, Dhūrtan.

Sairi, m. the month Kārttika, L.; pl. N. of a people, VarBṛS. (v.l.)

Sairika, mfn. relating to a plough &c., Pāṇ. iv, 3, 124; m. a ploughman, W.; a plough-ox, ib.; the sky, atmosphere (cf. *sairibha*), L.; N. of a man (also written *śairika*), Cat.

Sairimdha, m. pl. N. of a people (v.l. *sairiḍya*, *°ritya*, *°ridya*, *°rimdhya*, *°rimdhra*), VarBṛS.

Sairimdhra, m. (and *ī*, f.), often v.l. for *sairaṃdhra*, *°dhrī*.

Sairimdhraka, mfn. (fr. *sirimdhra* and *sairimdhra*), g. *kulālâdi* (Kāś. *sairidhraka*).

Sairīya or **sairīyaka**, m. 'turned up by the plough,' Barleria Cristata, Suśr.

Saireya or **saireyaka**, m. id., ib.; (*°kam*), n. the flower of Barleria Cristata, Kir., Sch.

Sairyá, m. a kind of grass, RV.

सैरावत् *sairā-vat*, mfn. (accord. to Sāy. connected with *irā*, 'food,' accord. to others with *sīra*) having plenty of provisions (said of a ship), AitBr.

सैरिध्रक *sairidhraka*. See *sairimdhraka*.

सैरिभ *sairibha*, m. a buffalo, Hcar.; Bālar.; the sky, atmosphere (cf. *sairika*), L.; (*ī*), f. a female buffalo, L.

सैरिष्ठ *sairishṭha*, m. pl. N. of a people, MārkP.

सैलग *sailagá*, m. (fr. *selaga*, q.v.) a way-layer, robber, VS.

सैलि *saili*, m. pl. N. of a people, VarBṛS.

सैवाल *saivāla*. See *śaivāla*.

सैवालिन *saivālina* (or *śaiv°*), mfn. (fr. *sevālin* or *śev°*), g. *suvāstv-ādi* (v.l. *saicālina*).

सैस *saisa*, mfn. (fr. *sīsa*) leaden, made of lead, g. *rajatâdi*.

Saisaka, mfn. id., Mn. xi, 133.

सैसिकत *saisikata*, m. pl. N. of a people, MBh. (B. *saisiridhra*).

सैसिरिध्र *saisiridhra*. See preceding.

सैहरेय *saihareya*, mfn. (fr. *sihara*), g. *sakhy-ādi*.

सो 1. *so* (usually with prepositions; see *ava-*, *vy-ava-*, *adhy-ava-√so* &c.), cl. 4. P. (Dhātup. xxvi, 38) *syati* (pf. *sasau*, aor. *asāt* or *asāsīt* &c.), to destroy, kill, finish, Dhātup.: Pass. *sīyate* (aor. *asāyi*), Gr.: Caus. *sāyayati* or *sāpayati*, ib.: Desid. *sishāsati*, ib.: Intens. *seshīyate*, *sāsāti*, *sāseti*, ib.

Sāya, sita, siti, seya. See s.v.

सो 2. *so*, f. (nom. *sos*) N. of Pārvatī, L.

सो 3. *só*, = *sá* (f. of 6. *sa*) + *u*, ŚBr.

सोक्थ *sóktha*, mfn. with the Uktha (q.v.), TāṇḍBr.

Sôkthaka, mfn. id., ŚBr.

Sôkthya, mfn. with the Ukthya (q.v.), TāṇḍBr.

सोख *sókha*, mfn. with a caldron, ŚBr.

सोच्छ्रय *sôcchraya*, mfn. having height, high, lofty, L.

सोच्छ्वास *sôcchvāsa*, mfn. breathing hard, panting (*-tva*, n.), R.; Pratāp.; relaxed, loose (as a bandage), Suśr.; (*am*), ind. with a sigh of relief, Śak.; Prab.

सोटा *soṭā*, Pat. on Pāṇ. iii, 1, 27.

Soṭāya, Nom. Ā. *°yate*, ib.

सोढ *soḍha*, mfn. (fr. √1. *sah*; cf. *sāḍha*) borne, suffered, endured, tolerated, MBh.; Kāv. &c.; patient, enduring, W.; m. N. of a minister of Someśvara (king of Śākambarī), Cat.; n., see *avi-soḍha*. **-govinda**, m. N. of a poet, Cat. **-vat**, mfn. one who has borne or endured, MW. **Soḍhâmitra**, m. N. of a man (cf. *sauḍhāmitri*), Pat.

Soḍhavya, mfn. to be borne or endured, Pāṇ. vi, 3, 111, Sch.; to be put up with or excused (n. impers.), Hariv.; BhP.

Soḍhāya, Nom. Ā. *°yate*, to bear, endure, g. *sukhâdi*.

Soḍhin, mfn. one who has borne or endured, ib.

Soḍhṛi, mfn. bearing patiently, Bālar.; capable of resisting, a match for (gen.), MBh.; R.; Bhaṭṭ.; able, powerful (= *śakta*), L.

सोढल *soḍhala*, m. N. of various authors (v.l. *soṭhala*), Cat.

सोतु *sótu*, m. (fr. √3. *su*) extraction of Soma, libation (dat. *sótave* as inf.), RV.

1. **Sotṛi** or **sótṛi**, mfn. one who presses out or extracts Soma (loc. *sotári* as inf.), ib.

1. **Sótva**, mfn. to be pressed or extracted, RV.

2. **Sótva**, m. a Soma sacrificer, L.

सोतृ 2. *sotṛi*, mfn. (fr. √2. *sū*) engendering, generating, bringing forth children, MW.

सोत्क *sôtka*, mf(*ā*)n. full of desire or longing, Ṛitus.; Kathās.

सोत्कण्ठ *sôtkaṇṭha*, mf(*ā*)n. having an ardent desire, ardently longing for (*praiti*), Rājat.; bewailing, regretting, grieving at (comp.), Kathās.; (*am*), ind. longingly, regretfully, Kir.; Amar.

सोत्कम्प *sôtkampa*, mfn. trembling, tremulous, Megh.

सोत्कर्ष *sôtkarsha*, mfn. having eminence, excellent, Rājat.

Sôtkṛishṭa-hasita-svara, mfn. accompanied by loud laughter, R.

सोत्तर *sôttara*, mfn. with or connected with a wager or bet, Nār. **-paṇa**, mfn. id., ib.

सोत्पल *sôtpala*, mfn. possessing lotuses, MW.

सोत्पात *sôtpāta*, n. anointing with oil (?), L.

सोत्पीड *sôtpīḍa*, mfn. emitting a stream (as a mountain), R.; covered with foam or froth, MW.

सोत्प्रास *sôtprâsa*, mfn. exaggerated, ironical, derisive, scornful (*am*, ind. scornfully), Ratnâv.; Kād.; m. n. ironical exaggeration, sarcasm, ib. **-hasita**, n. derisive or sarcastic laughter, MW.

सोत्प्रेक्षम् *sôtprêksham*, ind. with indifference, carelessly, Veṇīs.

सोत्व 1. and 2. *sótva*. See above.

सोत्सङ्ग *sôtsanga*, mfn. deepened, depressed, Bhpr.

सोत्सव *sôtsava*, mfn. connected with a festival, festal (as a day), Kathās.; celebrating a festival, making merry, joyous, ib.

सोत्साह *sôtsāha*, mfn. making effort, vigorous, resolute, energetic, courageous (with *ghanāḥ*, 'threatening clouds'), Kāv.; Rājat.; Hit.; (*am*), ind. energetically, carefully, Pañcat.; much delighted, overjoyed (*am*, ind.), Kāv.; Vet. **-tā**, f. activity, energy, courage, Kathās.

सोत्सुक *sôtsuka*, mf(*ā*)n. regretful, sorrowful, anxious about, yearning or longing for (loc. or acc. with *prati*, or comp.), Kāv.; Kathās.

सोत्सेक *sôtseka*, mfn. haughty, arrogant, Kāvyâd.

सोत्सेध *sôtsedha*, mfn. high, lofty, R.; (*am*), ind. with a jerk or push upward, MBh.

सोदक *sôdaka*, mf(*ā*)n. having or containing water, TS.; GṛŚrS. &c.; = *samānôdaka*, MārkP.

Sôda-kumbha, m. a partic. ceremony in honour of deceased ancestors (also N. of wk.), Cat.

Sôda-pūrvam, ind. after sprinkling with water, Hcat.

सोदधिल *sôdadhi-la*, mfn. consisting of four (*udadhi* = 'the ocean' and 'the number 4') short syllables (*la*), VarBṛS., Sch.

सोदय *sôdaya*, mfn. having an increase of profit, accumulated, augmented by interest, Yājñ.; connected with the rise (of the heavenly bodies &c.), MW.; having a succession, having something coming after, followed by, ib.

Sôdayana, mfn. together with Udayana, Kathās.

सोदर *sôdara*, mf(*ī*)n. born from the same womb, co-uterine, of whole blood, Mn.; MBh. &c.

closely allied or connected with, next of kin to (e.g. *narmâka-sôdaram navam vayaḥ*, 'youth has only one brother, viz. amusement'), Kathās.; m. (with or scil. *bhrātṛi*) an own brother, Yājñ.; MBh. &c.; (*ī*), f. a co-uterine sister, Mālav. **-sneha,** v.l. for *sôdarya-sn°* (q.v.)

Sôdarīya, mfn. = *sôdara*, MBh.

Sôdarya, mfn. id., MBh.; Kāv. &c. **-vat,** mfn. having or together with a brother, MBh. **-sneha,** m. sisterly affection, Śak.

सोदर्क *sôdarka*, mfn. having elevations or turrets, MBh.; having the same burden or refrain, ŚāṅkhBr.; attended with results or consequences, MW.; n. a final refrain, ŚāṅkhGṛ.

सोद्धरण *sôddharaṇa*, mfn. together with sweetmeats which are taken home, MBh. (Nīlak.)

Sôddhāra, mfn. together with a selected portion, Kull. **-vibhāgin,** mfn. receiving an inheritance together with a selected portion, ib.

सोद्बाष्पम् *sôdbāshpam*, ind. with tears, tearfully, Kathās.

सोद्यम *sôdyama*, mfn. prepared or equipped for combat, ib.

सोद्योग *sôdyoga*, mfn. making active exertion, energetic, enterprising, Hit.; violent, dangerous (as a disease), Rājat.

सोद्वेग *sôdvega*, mf(*ā*)n. agitated, disturbed, anxious, fearful (*am*, ind.), Bcar.; Ratnâv.; Pañcat.

सोध *sodha*, m. pl. N. of a people (v.l. *go-dha*), MBh.

सोनह *sonaha*, m. garlic, L.

सोनि *soni*, m. or f. (fr. √3. *su*) = 1. *savana*, L.

सोनोदेवी *sono-devī*, f. N. of a woman, Cat.

सोन्माद *sônmāda*, mf(*ā*)n. mad, insane, R.

सोपकरण *sôpakaraṇa*, mfn. together with the implements, Mn. ix, 270; properly equipped, W.

Sôpakāra, mfn. furnished with necessary means or implements, well equipped or stocked, W.; (a deposit in pawn) from which profit accrues, beneficial, Mn. viii, 143; assisted, befriended, W.

Sôpakāraka, mfn. assisted, befriended, benefitted, Pañcat.

सोपक्रम *sôpakrama*, mfn. set about, undertaken, Cat.

सोपग्रहम् *sôpagraham*, ind. with conciliation, in a conciliatory or friendly manner, Kād.

सोपचय *sôpacaya*, mfn. connected with gain or advantage, profitable, Kathās.

सोपचार *sôpacāra*, mf(*ā*)n. with rules of conduct, MBh.; acting with politeness or civility, deferential (*am*, ind.), MBh.; Śiś.; embellished, ornamented, decorated, Hcat.

Sôpacārakam, ind. politely, courteously, MW.

सोपद्रव *sôpadrava*, mf(*ā*)n. visited with great calamities or afflictions, dangerous, ŚārṅgP.; wealthy, opulent, rich, Bṛihasp.

सोपध *sôpadha*, mfn. full of fraud or deceit, fraudulent, guileful (*aṁ*, ind.), MBh.; Hariv.; Hcat.; with the penultimate or preceding letter, VPrāt.

Sôpadhāna, mfn. possessing a pillow, cushioned, ŚrS.; id. (and 'possessing excellent qualities'), Śiś. ii, 77; furnished with a setting, set (as a jewel), ĀpGṛ.

Sôpadhi, mfn. fraudulent (*i*, ind.), Kir. **-śesha,** mfn. one in whom a residue of guile is left (opp. to *nir-upadh°*), Buddh.

सोपनिषत्क *sôpanishatka*, mfn. along with the Upanishads, Kull. on Mn. ii, 165.

सोपन्यास *sôpanyāsa*, mfn. well founded or substantiated (as speech), Hariv.

सोपपत्तिक *sôpapattika*, mfn. well founded or substantiated, correct, right, Nāg.; Sāh.; Nīlak.

सोपपद *sôpapada*, mfn. together with a secondary word, ŚāṅkhŚr.

सोपप्लव *sôpaplava*, mfn. eclipsed (as the sun or moon), L.; afflicted with any great calamity, overrun or attacked by enemies, MW.

सोपबर्हण *sôpabarhaṇa*, mf(*ā*)n. with a cushion or pillow, ŚBr.

सोपम *sôpama*, mf(*ā*)n. containing a simile or comparison, MBh.; dealing with (loc.) in the same way as with (instr.), ib.

सोपर *sôpara*, mfn. with the under part of the sacrificial post, KātyŚr.

सोपरोध *sôparodha*, mfn. obstructed, impeded, MW.; favoured, ib.; respectful, considerate, obliging (*am*, ind.), Kathās.

सोपवास *sôpavāsa*, mf(*ā*)n. one who fasts or has fasted, Yājñ.; Hcat.

Sôpavāsika, mfn. id., MW.

सोपसर्ग *sôpasarga*, mf(*ā*)n. having or meeting with difficulties or obstacles, R.; unbecoming, unpleasant (as speech), ib.; visited by portents or by great afflictions, portentous, MW.; possessed by an evil spirit, ib.; (in gram.) preceded by a preposition, RPrāt.; Kāś.

सोपस्वेद *sôpasveda*, mfn. having perspiration or moisture, moistened, wetted, MBh.

सोपहव *sôpahava*, mfn. with an invitation, KātyŚr., Sch.

सोपहास *sôpahāsa*, mfn. accompanied with derisive laughter, sneering, jocular, sarcastic (*am*, ind.), Sah. **Sôpahāsôtprâsa,** m. a jocular expression, MW.

सोपांशुयाज *sôpâṅśu-yāja*, mfn. with an oblation offered in secret or with a whisper, ŚāṅkhŚr.

सोपाक *sopāka*, m. (perhaps for *śva-pāka*) a man of a degraded caste (the son of a Caṇḍāla by a Pulkasī, and only to be employed as public executioner &c.), Mn. x, 38; a person who sells medicinal roots, L.

सोपाख्य *sôpâkhya*, mfn. 'one about whom anything can be affirmed,' having qualifications (cf. *nir-upâkhya*), Kaṇ., Sch.

सोपादान *sôpâdāna*, mfn. furnished with materials (as a carpenter who builds a house with wood), Nīlak.

सोपाधि *sôpâdhi*, mfn. restricted by some condition or limitation or stipulation, qualified by some condition (as liberality by the desire of receiving something in return), MW.; having some peculiar attribute or distinguishing title, ib.; (ind.) with limitations, conditionally.

Sopâdhika, mfn. = prec. (*-tva*, n.), Tarkas.; TPrāt., Sch.

सोपाध्यायगण *sôpâdhyāya-gaṇa*, mfn. with a multitude of teachers, R.

सोपान *sopāna*, n. (perhaps contracted fr. *sa* + *upâyana*) stairs, steps, a staircase, ladder to (gen. or comp.), MBh.; Kāv. &c. **-kūpa,** m. a well with steps, Rājat. **-tva,** n. the condition of a staircase (acc. with √*vraj*, 'to become a staircase'), Megh. **-paṅkti,** f. a line or flight of steps, staircase, ib. **-pañcaka,** n., **-pañca-ratna,** n. N. of wks. **-patha,** m. a way of steps, staircase, Ragh. **-paddhati,** f. id., Rājat. **-paramparā,** f. = *-paṅkti*, Ragh. **-bhūta,** mfn. become or being a staircase, Hariv. **-mārga,** m. = *-patha*, Ragh. **-mālā,** f. winding stairs, Jātakam. **-racanā,** f. N. of wk. **Sopānâlī,** f. = *-paṅkti*, Kuval.

Sopānaka, n. = *sopāna* (see next). **-paramparā,** f. a flight of steps, staircase, Uttamac.

सोपानह् *sôpānah*, mfn. (nom. *°nat*) furnished with shoes or sandals, having shoes, shod, Āpast.

Sopānatka, mfn. id., Gobh.; Mn.; Car.

सोपाय *sôpâya*, mfn. accompanied (as a song), Lāṭy.

सोपारकपत्तन *sopāraka-pattana*, n. N. of a town, Pañcad.

सोपालम्भ *sôpâlambha*, mfn. conveying a censure (*am*, ind.), Kathās.

सोपाश्रय *sôpâśraya*, mfn. having a support; n. a partic. posture in sitting (with Yogins), Yogas., Sch.; (*-nishadana*, n.), id., Sarvad.

सोपासन *sôpâsana*, mfn. having the sacred domestic fire (see 2. *upâsana*), MW.

सोभ *sobha*, n. N. of the city of the Gandharvas, IndSt.

Sóbhya or **sobhyà,** mfn. being in or belonging to Sobha; m. a partic. personification, MaitrS.; TS.; Gaut.

सोभय *sôbhaya*, mfn. comprehending both, RāmatUp.

सोभरि *sóbhari* (or *°rī*), m. N. of the author of the hymns RV. viii, 19–22 &c. (having the patr. *Kāṇva* or *Āṅgirasa*), RV.; AV.

Sobharīyû, mfn. seeking for Sobhari (or the Sobharis), RV.

सोभाञ्जन *sobhāñjana*, w.r. for *śobh°*.

सोम 1. *sóma*, m. (fr. √3. *su*) juice, extract, (esp.) the juice of the Soma plant, (also) the Soma plant itself (said to be the climbing plant Sarcostema Viminalis or Asclepias Acida, the stalks [*aṅśu*] of which were pressed between stones [*adri*] by the priests, then sprinkled with water, and purified in a strainer [*pavitra*]; whence the acid juice trinkled into jars [*kalaśa*] or larger vessels [*droṇa*]; after which it was mixed with clarified butter, flour &c., made to ferment, and then offered in libations to the gods [in this respect corresponding with the ritual of the Iranian Avesta] or was drunk by the Brāhmans, by both of whom its exhilarating effect was supposed to be prized; it was collected by moonlight on certain mountains [in RV. x, 34, 1, the mountain Mūja-vat is mentioned]; it is sometimes described as having been brought from the sky by a falcon [*śyena*] and guarded by the Gandharvas; it is personified as one of the most important of Vedic gods, to whose praise all the 114 hymns of the 9th book of the RV. besides 6 in other books and the whole SV. are dedicated; in post-Vedic mythology and even in a few of the latest hymns of the RV. [although not in the whole of the 9th book] as well as sometimes in the AV. and in the Br., Soma is identified with the moon [as the receptacle of the other beverage of the gods called Amṛita, or as the lord of plants, cf. *indu, oshadi-pati*] and with the god of the moon, as well as with Vishṇu, Śiva, Yama, and Kubera; he is called *rājan*, and appears among the 8 Vasus and the 8 Loka-pālas [Mn. v, 96], and is the reputed author of RV. x, 124, 1, 5–9, of a law-book &c.; cf. below), RV. &c. &c.; the moon or moon-god (see above); a Soma sacrifice, AitĀr.; a day destined for extracting the Soma-juice, ĀśvŚr.; Monday (= *soma-vāra*), Inscr.; nectar, L.; camphor, L.; air, wind, L.; water, L.; a drug of supposed magical properties, W.; a partic. mountain or mountainous range (accord. to some the mountains of the moon), ib.; a partic. class of Pitṛis (prob. for *soma-pā*), ib.; N. of various authors (also with *paṇḍita, bhaṭṭa, śarman* &c.; cf. above), Cat.; = *soma-candra* or *somêndu*, HPariś.; N. of a monkey-chief, L.; (*ā*), f. the Soma plant, L.; N. of an Apsaras, MBh.; of a river, MārkP.; of a queen, Inscr.; (*ī*), f., g. *gaurâdi*; (*am*), n. rice-water, rice-gruel, L.; heaven, sky, ether, L.; mfn. relating to Soma (prob. w. r. for *sauma*), Kāṭh. **-kanyā,** f. a daughter of Soma, MBh. **-karaṇī,** f. a partic. verse, ĀpŚr. **-karman,** n. the preparation of S°, Nir.; (*°ma*)*-paddhati* or *-pradîpikā*, f. N. of wk. **-kalaśa,** m. a jar for holding S°, Hariv. **-kalpa,** m. N. of the 21st Kalpa or world-period, L.; N. of wk. **-kavi,** m. N. of a poet, ŚārṅgP. **-kānta,** mfn. moon-beloved, MW.; lovely as the moon, ib.; m. the moon-gem, moon-stone (= *candra-k°*), ib.; N. of a king, Cat. **-kāma** (*sóma-*), mfn. desirous of S°, RV.; AV. **-kārikā,** f. sg. or pl. N. of various wks. **-kīrti,** m. N. of a son of Dhṛita-rāshṭra, MBh. **-kulyā,** f. N. of a river, MārkP. **-kratavīya,** n. N. of a Sāman, ĀrshBr. (v l. *saumak°*). **-kratu,** m. an offering of Soma (see *saumakratava*). **-krayaṇa,** mf(*ī*)n. serving as the price of the Soma plant, VS.; TS.; Br.; ĀpŚr.; (*ī*), f. a cow so serving, ib.; MaitrS.; n. the act of buying the Soma, TS. **-kshaya,** m. disappearance of the moon, new moon, MW. **-kshīrā,** f. = *-vallī*, L. **-kshīrī,** f. the Soma plant, Bhpr. **-khaddaka,** m. pl. N. of partic. Śaiva monks in Nepal, Inscr. **-gaṇaka,** m. N. of an author, Cat. **-garbha,** m. N. of Vishṇu, L. **-giri,** m. N. of a mountain,

MBh.; R.; of a teacher, Cat. **– gṛiha-pati** (*sóma-*), mfn. having the Soma for a Gṛiha-pati (q. v.), MaitrS. **– gopā** (*sóma-*), m. a keeper of S°, RV. **– graha**, m. a cup or bowl of Soma, TS.; ŚBr.; ĀpŚr.; an eclipse of the moon, VarBṛS. **– grahaṇa**, mf(*ī*)n. holding or containing S°, ĀpŚr., Sch.; n. an eclipse of the moon, Cat. **– ghṛita**, n. a partic. healing ointment, L. **– cakshas** (*sóma-*), mfn. looking like S°, TS. **– candra**, m. N. of a man (also °*rarshi*), HPariś.; *-gaṇi*, m. N. of an author, Cat. **– camasa**, m. a cup or ladle for taking up the S°, cup of Soma, PañcavBr.; ŚrS. **– cyuta** (*sóma-*), mfn. moved by S°, TS.; MaitrS. **– ja**, mfn. moon-produced, MW.; m. N. of the planet Mercury, Hāyan.; n. milk, L. **– jambhan** (Pāṇ. v, 4, 125) or °**bhā** (? GopBr.), m. N. of a man. **– já**, mfn. Soma-born, AV. **– jāmi** (*sóma-*), mfn. related to S°, RV. **– jushṭa** (*sóma-*), mfn. delighting in S°, AV. **– tilaka-sūri**, m. N. of a Jaina author, Cat. **– tīrtha**, n. N. of a place of pilgrimage, MBh.; Śak.; *-māhātmya*, n. N. of wk. **– tejas** (*sóma-*), mfn. having the splendour or power of S°, AV. **– tva**, n. the condition or state of the moon, TBr., Sch.; MārkP.; condition of S°, Ml. **– dakshá**, m. N. of a man, MaitrS. (also v.l. for *-raksha*). **– datta**, m. N. of various kings, MBh.; Hariv.; Pur.; of various Brāhmans, Kathās.; of a merchant, Śukas.; of a writer on Dharma, Cat.; (*ā*), f. N. of a woman, Cat. **– datti**, w.r. for *saumad*°, MBh. **– darśana**, m. N. of a serpent-demon, Buddh. **– dā**, f. N. of a Gandharvī, R.; of a Brāhman woman, Kathās. **– dīkshā-vidhi**, m. N. of wk. **– deva**, m. the god of the moon, R.; the god S°, Ml.; (also °*va-bhaṭṭa*) N. of the author of the Kathā-sarit-sāgara (who lived in Kaśmīr in the 11th century A.D.), IW. 531; of various authors and other men, Kathās.; Vcar. &c.; (*ī*), f. N. of a wife of Kāma-pāla, Daś.; *-śrī-kara-lāla-bhairava-pura-pati*, *-sūri*; °*vaika-nātha*, m. N. of authors, Cat. **– devata** (*sóma-*), mfn. having Soma as deity, ŚBr. **– devatya**, mfn. id., ĀśvGṛ. **– daiva-jña**, m. N. of an author, Cat. **– daivatya**, mfn. = *-devata* (with *nakshatra*, n. 'the lunar mansion Mṛiga-śiras'), MBh. **– dhāna**, mfn. holding or containing Soma, RV.; AV. **– dhārā**, f. the milky way, L.; the sky, heaven, W. **– dheya**, m. pl. N. of a people, MBh. **– nandin**, m. N. of one of Śiva's attendants, L.; of a grammarian, Cat. **– nandîśvara**, n. N. of a Liṅga, Cat. **– nātha**, m. N. of various scholars, Cat.; Col.; n. N. of a celebrated Liṅga of Śiva and of the place where it was set up by the god Soma (in the town described below; it was one of the 12 great Liṅga temples of India held in especial veneration [cf. IW. 322, n. 1], and was so famed for its splendour and wealth that it attracted the celebrated Mahmūd of Ghaznī, A.D. 1024, who, under pretext of destroying its idols, carried off its treasures along with its renowned gates), Vcar.; Vop.; Cat.; Col. &c.; *-tīrtha*, n. N. of a Tīrtha, Cat.; *-dīkshita*, m. N. of an author, ib.; *-dīkshitīya*, n. N. of wk.; *-paṭṭana*, n. (= *-pattana*), Cat.; *-paṇḍita*, m. N. of an author, ib.; *-pattana*, n. N. of a town on the western coast of India (commonly called Somnath Pattan in Kāthiāwār, celebrated for the Śiva temple above described), MW.; *-praśasti*, f. N. of wk.; *-bhaṭṭa*, m. N. of various authors, Cat.; *-bhāshya*, n. N. of wk.; *-mahā-pātra*, n. N. of an author, Cat.; *-rasa*, m. a partic. preparation of iron, L. **– nāthīya**, n., **-nīti**, f. N. of wks. **– netra** (*sóma-*), mfn. having S° as a guide, VS. **– pá**, mf(*ā*)n. drinking or entitled to drink Soma-juice, AV.; Kāṭh.; Br. &c.; m. a Soma sacrificer, any sacrificer, R.; N. of a being reckoned among the Viśve Devāḥ, MBh.; of one of Skanda's attendants, ib.; of an Asura, Hariv.; of an author, Cat.; pl. N. of a family of Ṛishis, MBh.; of a class of Pitṛis, ib.; Mn.; Hariv.; MārkP.; of a people, VarBṛS. **– pañcaka**, n., **-pañcaka-prayoga**, m., **-pañcikā**, f. N. of wks. **– paṇḍita**, m. N. of an author, Cat. **– pati** (*sóma-*), m. 'lord of S°,' N. of Indra, RV.; a lord of the moon, Kṛishṇaj. **– pattra**, n. Saccharum Cylindricum, L. **– patnī**, f. the wife of Soma, MBh. **– pada**, m. pl. N. of a Tīrtha, MBh.; °*dârtha-kathana*, n. N. of wk. **– paddhati**, f. N. of wk. **– paribādh**, mfn. removing the Soma, a despiser of the Soma, RV. i, 43, 8 (rather to be read *soma paribādho*). **– pariśrayaṇa**, n. a cloth with which the S° is pressed together, ĀpŚr. **– parṇá**, n. a S°-leaf, TBr. **– paryāṇáhana**, n. = *-pariśrayaṇa*, ŚBr.; KātyŚr. **– párvan**, n. (prob.) the time of a Soma-festival, RV. **– pá**, mfn. (cf. *-pá* above, acc. pl.

m. *-pas*; dat. sg. *-pe*) drinking or entitled to drink Soma-juice, RV.; MBh.; BhP.; a S° sacrificer or performer of any sacrifice, ib.; a Pitṛi of a partic. class (said to be esp. the progenitors of the Brāhmans), W.; a Brāhman, L.; *-tama*, mfn. drinking much S°, RV. **– pātra**, n. a vessel for holding Soma, ŚrS. **– pāthin** (?), m. a drinker of Soma, A. **– pāna**, n. the drinking of S°, Gaut.; Pañcat.; (*-pāna*), mfn. S° drinking, a S° drinker, TS.; ŚBr. **– pāyin**, mfn. id., AV.; MBh.; Śiś. **– pālá**, m. a guardian of S°, AitBr.; Suparṇ.; a preserver of S°, (prob.) a provider or seller of the S° plant, MW.; N. of various men, Rājat.; pl. N. of the Gandharvas (as keeping especial guard over the S°), MW.; *-vilāsa*, m. N. of wk. **– pávan**, m. a S° drinker, RV. **– pítsaru**, mfn. (said of a plough), VS.; MaitrS. **– pīḍā**, f. N. of a princess, Daś. **– píti** (*sóma-*), f. a draught of S°, RV.; AV.; a S° sacrifice, MW. **– pītin**, mfn. drinking S°, MBh. **– pīthá**, m. a draught of Soma, RV.; AV.; VS. &c.; mfn. drinking S°, BhP. **– pīthín**, mfn. drinking S°, TBr.; MBh. &c. **– pīvin**, m. (?) a S°-drinker, MW. **– putra**, m. 'son of S° or of the Moon,' the planet Mercury, Yājñ.; MārkP.; (*ī*), f. a daughter of S°, MBh.; mf(*ā*)n. having S° as son, AV. **– pura**, n. the city of Soma, MBh.; an ancient N. of Pāṭali-putra, Vīrac.; n. or (*ī*), f. N. of a temple, Buddh. **– purusha**, m. a servant of S°, ĀśvGr. **– purogava** (*sóma-*), mfn. having S° as a guide, VS.; ŚBr. **– pūjā**, f. N. of wk. **– pṛishṭha** (*sóma-*), mf(*ā*)n. bearing S° on the back (accord. to Sāy., 'one to whom the Pṛishṭhya-stotras, accompanied with S°, are dedicated'), RV.; AV. **– péya**, m. a sacrifice in which S° is drunk, Soma libation, MW.; n. a draught of S°, RV. **– pratiprasthātṛi-prayoga**, m. N. of wk. **– pratīka** (*sóma-*), mfn. having S° at the head, TBr. **– prathama**, mfn. having S° as the first, ĀpŚr. **– prabha**, mf(*ā*)n. having the splendour of the moon, Vās.; m. N. of various men, Kathās.; Cat.; (*ā*), f. a N., ib.; Vās. **– prayoga**, m., **-prayoga-kārikā**, f., **-prayoga-paddhati**, f., **-prayoga-prâyaścitta**, n., **-prayoga-mantra**, m. pl., **-prayoga-ratna-mālā**, f., **-prayoga-vṛitti**, f. N. of wks. **– pravāka**, m. the proclaimer of a S° sacrifice, PañcavBr.; GṛŚrS. **– praśna**, m., **-prâyaścitta**, n. N. of wks. **– bandhu**, m. 'friend of the moon,' the white esculent water-lily (as expanding at night), L. **– bṛihaspati**, m. du. S° and Bṛihaspati, JaimBr. **– bhaksha**, m. the drinking of S° (*-japa*, m. 'a prayer muttered while the Soma is drunk'), ĀśvŚr.; Nir.; N. of wk.; *-prayoga*, m., *-viveka*, m. N. of wks.; °*shayoḥ prayoga*, m. N. of wk. **– bhaṭṭa**, **-bhāgavatâcārya**, **-bhava**, m. N. of various persons, Cat. **– bhāva**, f. N. of the river Narma-dā, L. **– bhujagâvalī**, f. N. of wk. **– bhū**, mfn. 'Soma-born,' belonging to the family of the moon, W.; m. 'son of S°,' N. of Budha (regent of the planet Mercury), ib.; a son of Soma-candra, HPariś.; (with Jainas) N. of the 4th of the Black Vāsudevas, L.; *-pāla*, m. N. of a king, Col.; *-bhuj*, m. N. of a king, Cat. **– bhṛit**, mfn. bringing S°, VS. **– bhojana**, m. N. of a son of Garuḍa, MBh. **– makha**, m. a S° sacrifice, Hariv. **– mád** (strong form *-mād*), mfn. intoxicated with S°, RV. **– madá**, m. intoxication occasioned by S°, ŚBr. **– mantrânukramaṇikā**, f. N. of wk. **– maya**, mf(*ī*)n. made or consisting of Soma, Nir.; Pāṇ. **– māna**, n. measuring the S°, L. **– mitra**, m. N. of a man, g. *kāśyâdi*. **– miśra**, m. N. of an author, Cat. **– maitrāvaruṇa**, N. of wk. **– yajña**, m. a S° sacrifice, MBh.; ŚāṅkhGṛ., Sch. **– yaśas**, m. N. of a king, Śatr. **– yāga**, m. a S° sacrifice, BrahmavP.; ChUp., Sch.; a great triennial sac° at which Soma-juice is drunk, MW.; N. of wk.; *-kārikā*, f., *-prayoga*, m. N. of wks. **– yājamāna**, **-yājamāna-prayoga**, m. N. of wks. **– yājin**, mfn. offering S°, one who offers S°, TS.; Br. &c. **– yājyā**, f. the words spoken on taking out the S° for libation, ŚāṅkhŚr. **– yogá**, m. connection with S°, AV. **– yogin**, mfn. being in conjunction with the moon, MārkP. **– yoni**, m. (only L.) a god; a Brāhman; n. yellowish white sandal (very fragrant), L. **– rakshá**, mfn. preserving Soma, guardian of S°, ŚBr.; m. N. of a man, IndSt. **– rákshi**, mfn. = prec., Kāṭh.; MaitrS.; PañcavBr. **– rabhas** (*sóma-*), mfn. intoxicated with S° (only compar. *-tara*), RV. **– raśmi**, m. N. of a Gandharva, Daś. (Sch.) **– rasa**, m. the juice of the Soma plant, MW.; °*sôdbhava*, n. milk, L. **– rāga**, m. a partic. Rāga, Saṃgīt. **– rāja**, m. 'king Soma,' the moon, BhP.; N. of an author, Cat.; *-deva*, m. N. of an author, ib.; *-suta*, m. 'son

of the Moon,' the planet Mercury, BhP. **– rājaka**, m. pl. N. of a family, ĀśvŚr. (v.l. °*jaki*). **– rājan** (*sóma-*), mf(*jñī*)n. having S° as king, RV.; AV.; Br.; MBh.; m. N. of a Muni, Cat. **– rājikā**, f. Vernonia Anthelminthica, MW. **– rājin**, m. id., L. **– rājī**, f. a thin crescent of the moon, Chandom.; Vernonia Anthelminthica, VarBṛS.; Suśr.; a partic. metre, Chandom. **– rājya**, n. the dominion of S°, MaitrUp.; m. (w.r. for *saumar*°), Cat. **– rāta**, m. N. of a man, Śak. **– rāshṭra**, n. N. of a place, Cat. **– rūpa**, n. a form of Soma, Vait.; (°*pá*), mfn. Soma-shaped (*-tā*, f.), ŚBr. **– roga**, m. diabetes or a similar disease, Nid.; ŚārṅgS. **– raudra**, n. N. of a sacred text (cf. *somā-r*°), MW. **– rshi** (°*ma* + *ṛishi*), m. N. of a Ṛishi, = *-candra*, HPariś. **– latā**, f. the Soma plant (see 1. *sóma*); Ruta Graveolens, L.; = *-vallī*, Bhpr.; N. of the river Godāvarī, W. **– latikā**, f. Cocculus Cordifolius, L. **– lipta**, mfn. smeared with Soma; n. a Soma-utensil, ŚrS.; Vait. **– loka**, m. the world of the god of the moon, Up. **– vaṇśa**, m. the lunar race or dynasty (see *candra-v*°), Hariv.; Śatr. (cf. IW. 375; 411, n. 1); mfn. = *-vaṇśīya*; m. N. of Yudhi-shṭhira, L. **– vaṇśin**, m. a prince of the lunar race, MW. **– vaṇśīya** (MBh.) or **-vaṇśya** (Ragh.; Śatr.), mfn. belonging to the lunar race. **– 1. -vat** (*sóma-*), mfn. containing Soma, RV.; ŚBr.; KātyŚr.; attended &c. by Soma, RV.; TS.; ŚBr.; ĀśvŚr.; presided over by the moon (with *diś*, f. 'the north'), R.; having the moon, lunar, W.; °*vatī-kathā*, f. N. of a ch. of the Mahā-bhārata; °*vatī-tīrtha*, n. N. of a Tīrtha, Inscr.; °*vatī-vrata*, n., °*vatī-vrata-kathā*, f., °*vaty-amāvāsyā-kathā*, f. N. of chs. of wks. **– 2. -vat**, ind. like the moon, W. **– varcas** (*sóma-*), mfn. having the splendour of S°, AV.; m. N. of a being reckoned among the Viśve Devāḥ, MBh.; of a Gandharva, Hariv. **– valka**, m. N. of various plants (Acacia Arabica; a sort of the Karañja &c.), Car.; Suśr.; Bhpr.; (*ā*), f. a kind of plant, Suśr. **– vallari**, f. the Soma plant (see 1. *sóma*), W.; a kind of vegetable (= *brahmī*), ib. **– vallarī**, f. = prec., ib.; Ruta Graveolens, L. **– vallikā**, f. id., ib.; Vernonia Anthelminthica, ib. **– vallī**, f. the S° plant; Cocculus Cordifolius; Coc. Tomentosus &c., VarBṛS.; Bhpr. &c.; *-yogânanda*, m. N. of wk. **– vahana**, n. a vehicle or stand for supporting or carrying the S°, Lāṭy. **– vahni-prakāśa**, mfn. bright as the fire of the moon, MBh. **– vāmin**, mfn. vomiting S°, TS.; ŚBr.; ŚrS.; m. a priest who has drunk too much S°, MW. **– vāyavya**, m. pl. N. of a family of Ṛishis, MBh. **– vāra**, m. 'moon-day,' Monday, Inscr.; *-vrata*, n. a fast observed in the evening of a Monday in honour of Śiva and Durgā (°*ta-kalpa*, m., °*ta-vidhi*, m., °*tâcaraṇa-krama*, m., °*tôdyāpana*, n. N. of wks.), Cat.; °*râmāvāsya-pūjā-paddhati*, f., °*râmāvāsyā-vrata-kāla-nirṇaya*, m., °*râmāvāsyā-vrata-pūjā*, f. N. of wks. **– vāry-amāvāsyā-vrata**, n. N. of ch. of a wk. **– vāsara**, m. or n. Monday, Kṛishṇaj. **– vāha**, m. N. of a man, ĀśvŚr.; pl. his family, Cat. **– vikrayin**, mfn. selling Soma; m. a seller of Soma, TS.; Br.; ĀpŚr. &c. **– vidha**, mfn. being of the nature of Soma, ĀpŚr.; ib., Sch. **– vidhāna**, n., **-vihāra-kārikā**, f. sg. or pl. N. of wks. **– vīthī**, f. the orbit of the moon, MBh. **– vīrya**, mfn. having the power of S°, Suśr. **– vṛiksha**, m. N. of various plants (Acacia Arabica, = *kaṭphala* &c.), R. **– vṛiddha**, mfn. invigorated by S°, RV. **– vṛiddhi-vardhana**, n. a partic. fast regulated by the moon, = *cāndrāyaṇa* (q. v.), Vas. **– veśa** (prob. for *-vesha*), m. N. of a Muni, R. **– veshṭana**, mfn. enveloping Soma, ĀpŚr., Sch. **– vyāsa**, m. N. of an author, Cat. **– vrata**, n. a partic. religious observance; ib.; N. of various Sāmans, ĀrshBr. **– śakalā**, f. a kind of cucumber, L. (w.r. for *lomaśa-phalā*). **– śataka**, n., **-śata-dvayī**, f. N. of wks. **– śambha**, w.r. for next, Cat. **– śambhu**, m. N. of an author, Sarvad. **– śarman**, m. N. of various men, Pur.; Pañcat. &c. **– śita** (*sóma-*), mfn. sharpened by S°, RV. **– śushma** (*sóma-*) or °**man**, m. N. of a man, Br.; VS., Sch. **– śūra**, m. N. of a man, Kathās. **– śekharâkhya-nibandha**, m. N. of wk. **– śravas**, m. N. of various men, MBh.; Cat. **– śrī**, f. N. of a woman, Bhadrab. **– śreshṭha** (*sóma-*), mfn. having S° as the first, AV. **– śrauta**, n. N. of various wks. **– saṃsthā**, f. the basis or initial form of a Soma sacrifice, MBh.; Gaut.; MārkP. **– sakhi** (*sóma-*), mfn. having S° as a companion, VS. **– saṃjña**, n. camphor, L. **– sátsaru**, mfn. (said of a plough), AV. (v.l. *-pītsaru*, *sumatītsaru*). **– sad**, m. pl. N. of the Pitṛis of the Sādhyas, Mn. iii, 195. **–sapta-hautra-prayoga,** m. N. of wk. **–saraṇa,** mf(*ī*)n. leading to S°(as a way), TāṇḍyaBr.; ĀpŚr. **–salila,** n. Soma-water, Yājñ. **–sava,** m. 'pressure of S°,' a partic. sacrificial act, TBr., Sch. **–savana,** mfn. that from which Soma is pressed, ChUp. **–sāman,** n. N. of various Sāmans, ĀrshBr.; Lāṭy. **–sāra,** m. Acacia Arabica, L.; the white Khadira tree, MW. **–siddhânta,** m. a partic. heretical Tantra system (followed by a sect of Śaivas and personified in the 3rd Act of the Prabodha-candrôdaya), Prab.; N. of various astronomical wks., Cat.; of a partic. Buddha, ib. **–siddhântin,** m. a follower of the above system, W. **–sindhu,** m. 'ocean of S°,' N. of Vishṇu, L. **–sút,** mfn. pressing S°, RV.; TBr.; ĀśvŚr. &c.; m. a S°-distiller, a priest who offers the Soma-juice at a sacrifice, MW.; *-vat,* mfn. possessing offerers of Soma-juice (said of a hermitage, a sacrifice &c.), ib. **–suta,** m. 'a son of the Moon,' N. of Budha, Pur.; Śatr.; (*ā*), f. 'daughter of the M°,' the river Narmadā (Nerbudda), L. **–suti** (*sóma-*), f. the pressing of Soma, RV. **–sutyā́,** f. id., ŚBr. **–sútvan,** mfn. pressing Soma, RV.; m. one who offers S° libations, MW. **–sundara,** m. N. of an author, Cat. **–sûkta,** n. a hymn in honour of Soma, Cat.; N. of wk. **–sūkshman,** m. N. of a Ṛishi, VS. (v.l. *-śushma,* Sch.) **–sūtra,** n. a channel or receptacle for receiving the water with which a Liṅga has been bathed, L.; N. of various wks.; *-pañca-vidhāna,* n. N. of wk.; *-pradakshiṇā,* f. circumambulation around Śiva's idol in such a way as that the Soma-sūtra shall not be crossed, MW. **–sūrya-prakāśa,** mfn. bright as the sun and moon, MW. **–sena,** m. N. of a son of Śambara, Hariv.; of a king of Campaka-pura and Soma-pura, Cat. **–svāmin,** m. N. of a man, Kathās. **–hārá,** mfn. abstracting or robbing S°, Suparṇ. **–hārin,** mfn. id., MBh. **–hūti,** m. N. of a Ṛishi (w.r. for *somâhuti*). **–hotri-saptaka,** n., **-hotrâgni-shṭoma** (?), m., **-hautra,** n., **-hautra-prayoga,** m. N. of wks. **Somâṅśaka,** m. a part of the moon, R. **Somâṅśu,** m. a stalk or shoot of the Soma plant, VS.; ŚBr.; Kauś.; a moon-beam, KaushUp.; a part of the S° sacrifice, ŚāṅkhBr. **Somâkara,** m. N. of a Commentator, Jyot. **Somâkhya,** n. the red lotus, L. **Somâgni,** Soma and Agni (cf. *saumāgna*) in comp.; *-shṭoma,* m., *-yajamāna,* m.; °*gnîdhra-prayoga,* m. N. of wks. **Somâṅga,** n. a part of the Soma sacrifice, KātyŚr.; *-pāna-kārikā,* f. N. of wk. **Somâṇḍapille,** °**dabila,** f. N. of wks. **Somâtipavita,** mfn. excessively purged by the Soma-juice (which, if drunk in excess, is supposed to pass through the nose, ears, and other apertures of the body), PañcavBr.; ŚrS. **Sómâtipūta,** mfn. id., ŚBr.; ŚrS. **Somâtiriktá,** n. pl. the residue of S°, ŚBr. **Somâtmaka,** mf(*ikā*)n. having the nature of the moon, IndSt. **Somâd,** mfn. eating S°, RV. **Somâditya,** m. N. of a man, ŚārṅgP.; of a king, Inscr. **Somâdhāra,** m. pl. N. of partic. Pitṛis, MārkP. **Somâdhi,** v.l. for °*mâpi,* VP. **Somâdhvaryava,** n. N. of wk. **Somânanda** (Rājat.), °**da-nātha** (Sarvad.), m. N. of men. **Somânanda-bhāshya,** n. N. of wk. **Somânanda-sūnu,** °**dâcārya,** m. N. of men, Cat. **Somâ-pa,** mfn. or m., AitBr. (cf. *saumāpá*). **Somâpahṛitá,** mfn. one whose S° has been stolen, ŚBr. **Somâpi,** m. N. of a son of Sahadeva, Pur. **Somā-pūshán,** m. du. S° and Pūshan, RV.; TS. **Somā-paushṇá,** mfn. belonging to S° and Pūshan, TS. **Somâbha,** mfn. like the moon, MW.; (*ā*), f. = *candrâvalī,* L. **Somâbhishava,** m. the distilling or extracting of Soma-juice, MW. **Sómâbhishikta,** mfn. sprinkled or consecrated with S°, ŚBr. **Somâmbu-pa,** m. du. 'drinker of S°' and 'drinker of water,' N. of two divine beings, MārkP. **Somâyana,** n. a kind of penance, Yājñ., Sch. (cf. *cāndrâyaṇa*). **Somā-rudrá,** m. du. Soma and Rudra, RV.; TS.; ŚBr.; n. a hymn addressed to S° and R°, Cat.; *-sûkta,* n. N. of a Vedic hymn. **Somā-raudrá,** mfn. belonging to S° and Rudra, TS.; n. N. of the hymn RV. vi, 74, Mn. xi, 254. **Somârka-pratisaṃkāśa,** mfn. resembling the sun and moon, MBh. **Somârcis,** m. N. of a palace of the gods, R. **Somârthin,** mfn. desirous of S°, MBh. **Somârdha-hārin,** m. 'bearing a half-moon (on his forehead),' N. of Śiva, Cat. **Somârdhāya** (only p. p. °*yita*), to resemble the half-moon, Kāv. **Somârya,** m. N. of a Brāhman, Inscr. **Somârha,** mfn. entitled to Soma, MBh. **Somā-vatí,** f. containing Soma, VPrāt.; Pāṇ. **Somâvarta,** m. N. of a place, VP. **Somâśrama,** m. N. of a place of pilgrimage, MBh. **Somâśrayâyaṇa,** n. N. of a place of pilgrimage, ib. **Somâshṭamī,** f. N. of a partic. 8th day, Kṛishṇaj. **Somâsandī,** f. a stool or stand for the Soma, KātyŚr. **Somâha,** m. 'moon-day,' Monday, L. **Somâharaṇa,** n. the bringing or fetching of the Soma (°*haraṇá-ja*), Suparṇ. **Somâhāra,** m. a bringer of S°, ĀpŚr. **Sómâhuta,** mfn. one to whom S° is offered, RV. **Somâhuti,** f. a S° sacrifice, Br.; ĀpŚr.; BhP.; m. N. of the author of the hymns RV. ii, 4–7 (having the patr. Bhārgava), RAnukr. **Somâhvā,** f. the Soma plant, L. **Somêjyā,** f. a S° sacrifice, ŚrS. **Somêndu,** m. N. of a man (= *soma-candra*), HPariś. **Somêndrá** (?), mfn. belonging to S° and Indra, TS.; ĀpŚr. **Somêśvara,** m. N. of a divine being, Rājat.; of Kṛishṇa, L.; of a Cālukya and of various authors and other persons, Sarvad.; Vcar.; Cat. &c.; n. N. of a celebrated Liṅga of Śiva set up by Soma (= *soma-nātha,* q.v.) and of a Liṅga at Benares, Cat.; *-dīkshita, -deva, -bhaṭṭa,* m. N. of various persons, ib. **Somâindrá,** mfn. belonging to S° and Indra, TS. (incorrect for *saumendra*). **Somôtpatti,** f. the origin of S° (either the plant or the moon), Cat.; N. of various wks.; *-pariśishṭa,* n. N. of wk. **Somôdgīta,** n. N. of a Sāman, TāṇḍyaBr. **Somôdbhava,** mfn. moon-produced, sprung from the moon, L.; m. 'moon-producer,' N. of Kṛishṇa, Kṛishṇaj.; (*ā*), f. the river Narma-dā (or Nerbudda, supposed to be descended from the moon as the source of celestial nectar), Ragh. **Somôpanahana,** n. a cloth for tying up the Soma plant, ĀpŚr. **Somôshṇīsha,** n. a Soma-band, ib. **Somâudgātra,** n. N. of wk.

Sómaka, m. N. of a Ṛishi, VS.; of a king, RV.; AitBr.; MBh. &c.; of a son of Kṛishṇa, BhP.; of a partic. Bharaṭaka, Cat.; of a people or country, Kathās.; a king or native of Somaka, ib.; pl. the descendants of the king Somaka (*-tva,* n.), MBh.; Hariv.; VP.; the family of Drupada, MW.; (*ikā*), f. N. of a bird, Kathās. **Somakêśvara,** m. a king of the Somakas or Somaka, ib.

Somán, m. one who presses or prepares Soma, RV.; Naigh.; Nir.; a S° sacrificer, MW.; the moon, Uṇ. iv, 150, Sch.; a requisite for a sacrifice, ib.

Somala-devī, f. N. of a princess, Rājat.

Somāla, mfn. (accord. to some a Prākṛit corruption for *su-kumāra;* cf. *komala*) soft, bland, L.

Somālaka, m. a topaz, L.; (*ikā*), f. a partic. dish, ib.

Somin, mfn. having or possessing Soma, offering S°, performer of a S° sacrifice, RV.; inspired by S°, ib.; (*inī*), f. (*saṃjñāyām*), Pāṇ. v, 2, 137, Sch.

Somila, m. N. of a poet (also called *saumila*), ŚārṅgP.; of an Asura, Kathās.

Somilaka, m. N. of a weaver, Pañcat.

Somī-√kṛi, P. *-karoti,* to make into Soma, TS., Sch.

Somīya, in *agnī-shomīya* &c.

Somyá, mfn. offering S°, a S°-offerer, RV.; ĀśvŚr.; consisting of or containing or connected with or belonging to Soma, RV.; AV.; VS.; Gobh.; Soma-loving, inspired by S°, RV.; incorrect for *saumya,* q.v. (also *-tā,* f.), Up.; MBh.; MārkP.

Sauma &c. See s.v.

सोम 2. *sôma,* mfn. (prob.) together with Umā, IndSt.

सोर *sora,* m. a crooked movement, L.

सोरण *soraṇa,* mfn. astringent and sweet and sour and salt, L.; m. astringent &c. taste, ib.

सोरावास *sorāvāsa,* m. broth made of meat without salt, L.

सोराष्ट्रिक *sorāshṭrika,* w.r. for *saur°.*

सोर्णभ्रू *sôrṇa-bhrū,* mfn. having a circle of hair between the eye-brows, Bcar. i, 65 (conj.)

सोर्मि *sôrmi,* mfn. having waves, heaving, surging, Śiś.; Kathās.; speeding along, Vās.

Sôrmika, mfn. (printed *sau°*), id., L.

सोल *sola,* mfn. cold, L.; astringent and sour and bitter, ib.; m. coldness, ib.; astringent &c. taste, ib.

Solika, mfn. cold, L.; m. coldness, ib.

सोलङ्क *solaṅka,* m. N. of a family, Cat.

सोलूक *solūka,* m. N. of a poet, Cat.

सोल्कालातावपोथिक *sôlkâlātâvapothika,* mfn. with machines for hurling down fire-brands and lighted darts (on the enemy; these machines appear to have been a kind of catapult or ballista), MBh.

सोल्लास *sôllāsa,* mfn. rejoicing, delighted; (*am*), ind. glad, Bālar.; Kathās.

सोल्लुण्ठ *sôlluṇṭha,* mfn. ironical, sarcastic, Sāh.; m. irony, sarcasm, W. **–bhāshaṇa,** n. (L.), **-bhāshita,** n. (Sāh.), **-vacana,** n. (MW.); °**ṭhôkti,** f. (ib.) an ironical expression.

Sôlluṇṭhana, mfn. ironical, L.; n. irony, sarcasm, ib.

सोल्लेखम् *sôllekham,* ind. distinctly, Viddh.

Sôllekha-rekha, mf(*ā*)n. distinctly marked, not ambiguous, Bālar.

सोल्लोक *solloka,* m. N. of a poet (cf. *solūka* and *sohnoka*), Cat.

सोवाक *sovāka,* m. or n. (?) borax, Pañcad.

सोवाल *sovāla,* mfn. blackish or smoke-coloured, smoky, L.; m. smokiness, ib.

सोशीर *sôśīra,* mf(*ā*)n. abounding in roots of Andropogon Muricatus, Hcat.

सोष *sôsha,* mfn. mixed with salt earth (see *ûsha*), Yājñ.

सोष्ट्रिक *sôshṭrika,* mf(*ā*)n. together with earthen vessels of partic. shape (see *ushṭra*), MBh.

सोष्णीष *sôshṇīsha,* mfn. having a turban, MBh.; n. (scil. *vāstu*) a house with a verandah in front, VarBṛS.

सोष्मन् *sôshman,* mfn. having heat, hot, warm, Kāv.; Kathās.; (in gram.) having aspiration, aspirated (said of the sounds *kh, gh; ch, jh; ṭh, ḍh; th, dh; ph, bh;* of the sibilants, and *h*), Prāt.; Kāś. on Pāṇ. i, 1, 50; m. an aspirated sound, aspirate, ib.

Sôshma, in comp. for *sôshman.* **–tā,** f. heat, warmth, Śiś.; MārkP.; the state or condition of being aspirated, aspiration, RPrāt. **–vat,** mfn. aspirated, RPrāt. **–snāna-gṛiha,** n. a room containing hot baths, bath-room, Rājat.

सोष्यन्ती *soshyántī,* f. (fr. √2. *sū*) a parturient or lying-in woman, ŚBr. &c. &c. **–karman,** n. any religious act or observance relating to a parturient woman, Cat. **–savana,** n. a partic. Saṃskāra, KāṭhGṛ. **–homa,** n. an oblation on behalf of a parturient woman, Gobh.

सोहञ्जि *sohañji,* m. N. of a son of Kunti, BhP.

सोऽहम् *so 'ham,* nom. sg. m. I myself (see 6. *sa*).

सोहलग्राम *sohala-grāma,* m. N. of a village, Cat.

सोहाइच *sohāïca,* m. N. of a thief, Cat.

सोह्नोक *sohnoka,* m. (cf. *solloka*) N. of a poet, ib.

सौकन्य *saukanya,* mfn. relating to Sukanyā, MBh.; n. (scil. *ākhyāna*) the story of Sukanyā, BhP.

सौकर *saukara,* mf(*ī*)n. (fr. *sū-kara*) belonging or relating to a hog, hoggish, swinish, Kir.; Car.; BhP.; relating to Vishṇu (in his boar incarnation), RāmatUp.; n. = next, Cat. **–tīrtha,** n. N. of a Tīrtha (in which Vishṇu is worshipped as a boar), ib. **–sadma,** mfn. (fr. *sūkara-sadman*), Pāṇ. vi, 4, 144, Vārtt. 1.

Saukaraka, n. = *saukara* (also °*ka-tīrtha*), Cat.

Saukarika, m. a boar hunter, pig-dealer, R.; VarBṛS.; Buddh.; N. of a district, Cat.

Saukarīya, mfn. (fr. *sū-kara* and *su-kara*), g. *kṛiśâśvâdi.*

1. **Saukarya,** n. hoggishness, swinishness, Vās.

सौकरायण *saukarāyaṇa,* m. N. of a teacher, ŚBr.

सौकर्य 2. *saukarya,* n. (fr. *su-kara;* w.r. *saukārya*) easiness of performance, practicability, facility (dat. 'for greater facility;' instr. 'most easily'), Kāv.; Kathās. &c.; adroitness, MW.; easy preparation of food or medicine, W.

सौकुमारक *saukumāraka,* n. (fr. *su-kumāra*), g. *manojñâdi.*

Saukumārya, n. (ifc. f. *ā*) tenderness, delicacy, MBh.; Kāv. &c.; mfn. tender, delicate, MBh.

सौकृति *saukṛiti*, m. (fr. *su-kṛita*) a patr., Saṃskārak.

Saúkṛitya, n. acting well or religiously, piety, RV.

Saukṛityāyana, m. patr. fr. *su-kṛitya*, g. *naḍâdi.*

सौक्ति *saukti*, m. a patr., Saṃskārak.

Sauktika, mfn. (fr. *sûkta*), IndSt.

सौक्ष्म *saukshma* (fr. *sūkshma*), often w. r. for *saukshmya.*

Saukshmaka, m. a small insect, (perhaps) a grub or maggot, L.

Saukshmya, n. minuteness, fineness, subtlety, MaitrUp.; MBh. &c. **-tva**, n. id., MaitrUp.

सौख *saukha*, m. patr. fr. *sukha* (of which it is also the Vṛiddhi form in comp.), g. *śivâdi.* **-yānika**, m. (fr. *sukha-yāna*) a bard or other official who wishes a prince a prosperous march, L. **-rātrika**, mfn. (fr. *sukha-rātri*) one who asks another whether he has had a good night, g. *susnātâdi.* **-śayyika**, m. = *-śāyika*, L. **-śāyanika**, mfn. one who asks another whether he has slept well, g. *susnātâdi.* **-śāyika**, m. id. or an official who asks a prince whether he has slept well, R. **-suptika**, m. id., L.

Saukhavatī, w.r. for *sukhā-vatī.*

Saukhika, mfn. intent upon welfare &c., MBh.; = *sukhena jīvati*, g. *vetanâdi.*

Saukhīya, mfn. (fr. *sukha*), g. *kṛiśâśvâdi.*

Saukhya, n. (ifc. f. *ā*) welfare, comfort, health, happiness, felicity, enjoyment, Mn.; MBh. &c. **-da**, mfn. causing welfare &c., Kāvyâd. **-dāyaka**, m. Phaseolus Mungo, L. **-dāyin**, mfn. = *-da*, L. **-śāyika**, m. = (or w.r. for) *saukhaś°*, MBh.

Saukhyâspada, n. N. of a town, Cat.

सौगत *saugata*, mf(ī)n. (fr. *su-gata*) Buddhistic, Kathās.; Sarvad.; m. a Buddhist (said to be divided into 4 schools, MWB. 157); N. of a son of Dhṛita-rāshṭra, MBh.

Saugatika, m. (only W.) a Buddhist; a mendicant; an atheist; n. atheism, scepticism.

सौगन्ध *saugandha*, mf(ī)n. (fr. *su-gandha*) possessing a fragrant odour, sweet-scented, fragrant, MW.; m. a dealer in perfumes, MBh.; n. fragrance, W.; a partic. fragrant grass (= *kat-tṛiṇa*), L.

Saugandhaka, n. a blue water-lily, L.

Saugandhika, mfn. sweet-scented, fragrant, MBh.; R.; m. a dealer in perfumes, L.; a sexually weak man (who is stimulated by the smell of the female organs), Suśr.; a kind of worm infesting the bowels, Car.; (also n.) sulphur, L.; N. of a mountain, Cat.; (*ā*), f., see below; (*am*), n. a white or blue water-lily, Vās.; Jātakam.; a kind of fragrant grass (= *kat-tṛiṇa*), L.; a kind of Ocimum, Suśr.; a kind of unguent, TāṇḍBr.; a ruby, VarBṛS.; Hcat.; N. of a mountain, BhP. **-vana**, n. a thick cluster of water-lilies, MBh.; N. of a place of pilgrimage, ib. **-vat**, see *padma-* and *haima-sau°*.

Saugandhikā, f., in comp. **-pariṇaya**, m. N. of a Nāṭaka and a Kāvya. **-vivaraṇa-vyākhyā**, f. N. of a Commentary. **-haraṇa** (or *°kâh°*), n. fetching white water-lilies, MBh.; N. of a drama.

Saugandhya, n. sweetness of odour, fragrance, perfume, MBh.; Kāv. &c.

सौगम्य *saugamya*, n. (fr. *su-gama*) easiness of access or attainment, facility, MW.

सौचक्य *saucakya*, n. (fr. *sūcaka*), g. *purohitâdi.*

Sauci, m. = next, L.

Saucika, m. (fr. *sūci*) one who lives by his needle, a tailor (in the caste system he is the son of a Śauṇḍika and a Kaivartī), Kull. on Mn. iv, 214.

Saucikya, n. (fr. *sūcika*), g. *purohitâdi.*

सौचित्ति *saucitti*, m. (prob. fr. *su-citta*) patr. of Satya-dhṛiti, MBh.

सौचीक *saucīka*, m. N. of a partic. Agni, Sāy. in RV., Introd.

सौचुक *saucuka*, m. N. of the father of Bhūti-rāja (and grandfather of Indu-rāja), Cat.

सौजन्य *saujanya*, n. (fr. *su-jana*) goodness, kindness, benevolence, friendliness, Mṛicch.; Śiś.; Rājat. **-vat**, mfn. benevolent, kind, friendly, Prasaṅg.

सौजस् *saûjas*, mfn. strong, powerful, Bcar.

Saujaska, mfn. id., Jātakam.

सौजात *saujāta*, m. (fr. *su-jāta*) patr. of a Ṛishi, AitBr.

सौजामि *saujāmi*, m. (fr. *su-jāmi*) N. of a man, ĀśvGṛ.

सौडल *sauḍala*, m. (with *upâdhyāya*) N. of a preceptor, Cat.

सौढामित्र *sauḍhāmitri*, m. patr. fr. *soḍhāmitra*, Pat.

सौण्डी *sauṇḍī*, w.r. for *śauṇḍī*, q.v.

सौत *sauta*, mfn. fr. *sūta*, g. *saṃkalâdi.*

Sauti, m. patr. of Karṇa (so called from having been brought up by the Sūta Adhi-ratha; see *karṇa*), MBh.

1. **Sautya**, mfn. relating to a charioteer, BhP.; n. the office of a charioteer, ib.

सौतंगम *sautaṃgama*, mf(ī)n. (fr. *sutaṃgama*), Pāṇ. iv, 2, 80.

Sautaṃgamīya, mfn. (fr. *sautaṃgami*), Pāṇ. iv, 2, 112, Sch.

सौतिक्य *sautikya*, n. (fr. *sūtika*), g. *purohitâdi.*

सौत्थिति *sautthiti*, m. patr. fr. *sûtthita*, Pat.

सौत्य 2. *sautya*, mfn. (fr. *sutya* and *sutyā*) relating or devoted to Soma-pressing (with *ahan*, n. 'a day devoted to Soma-pressing'), ŚrS.; Hariv.; BhP.

सौत्र *sautra*, mf(ī)n. (fr. *sūtra*) consisting or made of threads, Gaut.; relating to a Sūtra, mentioned or declared (only) in a S°; (with *dhātu*, m.) a root given in a S° (for the sake of the derivation of a noun, but not used as a verb), Pat.; Siddh.; Pāṇ., Sch.; m. a Brāhman, L.

Sautranāḍi, m. patr. fr. *sūtra-nāḍa.*

Sautrāntika, m. a follower of the Sūtrânta (q.v.); pl. N. of one of the four great schools of Buddhism (said to admit the authority of the Buddhist Sūtras, but not of the Abhi-dharma), Sarvad.; MWB. 157.

Sautri, m. a weaver (perhaps w.r. for next), Campak.

Sautrika, m. a weaver, Prâyaśc.; a texture, anything woven (cf. *āvika-s°*), Yājñ.

सौत्रामण *sautrāmaṇa*, mf(ī)n. (fr. *su-trāman*) relating or belonging to Indra (with *diś*, f. 'Indra's quarter,' i.e. the east), Viddh.; m. a partic. Ekâha, ŚāṅkhŚr.; (*ī*), f., see below. **-dhanus**, n. 'Indra's bow,' the rainbow, Vās.

Sautrāmaṇi, m. = *sautrāmaṇī*, MBh.; Hcat.; N. of wk.

Sautrāmaṇika, mfn. being present or used at the Sautrāmaṇī, ŚBr.

Sautrāmaṇī́, f. a partic. sacrifice in honour of Indra (*su-trāman*; described as the 6th or 7th; of the 7 Havir-yajña-saṃsthās, q.v.; in the ŚBr. it is said that every one consecrated by the Sautrāmaṇī enters among the gods and is born *sarva-tanūḥ*, i.e. with his entire body; *-tvá*, n., ŚBr.), AV.; VS.; Br.; ŚrS.; BhP.; N. of a wk. by Deva-bhadra. **-paddhati**, f., **-prayoga**, m., **-viniyoga-sūtrârtha**, m., **-sūtra**, n., **-hautra**, n. N. of wks.

Sautrāmaṇīya, mfn. treating of the Sautrāmaṇī, IndSt.

सौत्वन *sautvana*, n. patr. fr. *sutvan*, Pāṇ. vi, 4, 167, Sch.

सौत्सुक्य *saûtsukya*, mf(ā)n. full of longing or expectation, Pañcat.

सौदक्ष *saudaksha*, mfn. (fr. *su-daksha*), g. *saṃkalâdi.*

Saudaksheya, m. (fr. id.) a patr., g. *śubhrâdi.*

सौदत्त *saudatta*, mfn. (fr. *su-datta*), g. *saṃkalâdi.*

सौदन्ति *saudanti*, m. (fr. *su-danta*) a patr., PañcavBr.

Saudanteya, m. (fr. id.) a patr., g. *śubhrâdi.*

सौदर्य *saudarya*, mfn. (fr. *sôdara*) brotherly or sisterly, Śak. (v.l.); n. brotherhood, BhP.

सौदर्शन *saudarśana*, m. (fr. *su-darśana*) N. of a village of the Bāhīkas, Pāṇ. iv, 2, 118, Sch.

Saudarśanika, mf(ī or ā)n. (fr. *saudarśana*), ib.

Saudarśanīya, mfn. (fr. id.), ib.

सौदामनी *saudāmanī*, f. (fr. *su-dāman*, 'Indra' or 'a cloud') lightning or a partic. kind of l°; perhaps forked l° (*vidyut saudāmanī yathā*, 'after the manner of f° l°'), MBh.; Kāv. &c.; N. of a daughter of Kaśyapa and Vinatā, VP.; of a Yakshiṇī, Kathās.; of a daughter of the Gandharva Hāhā, ib.; of an Apsaras, Bālar.; of a sorceress, Mālatīm.; of part of the Su-dāman mountain (accord. to some).

Saudāminī, incorrect for preceding.

Saudāminīya, mf(*ā*)n. (incorrect for *saudāmanīya*) like S° lightning, lightning-like, Bhām.

Saudāmeya, m. patr. fr. *su-dāman*, g. *śubhrâdi.*

Saudāmnī, f. = *saudāmanī*, L.

सौदायिक *saudāyika*, mfn. (fr. *su-dāya*) that which is given to a woman at her marriage by her father or mother or any relative and therefore becomes her property, Dāyabh.; Hcat.; relating to such a gift, MW.; n. a nuptial gift, ib.

सौदास *saudāsá*, m. (fr. *su-dās* and *su-dāsa*) N. of various kings (esp. of a son of king Su-dāsa, of the solar race, descendant of Ikshvāku and Sagara in the thirteenth generation, and also called Mitra-saha and Kalmāsha-pāda), TS.; MBh. &c.

Saudāsi, m. a patr., Pravar.

सौदेव *saudeva*, m. (fr. *su-deva*) patr. of Divo-dāsa, MBh.

Saudevika, mfn. (fr. *su-devikā*), Pat.

सौद्युम्नि *saúdyumni*, m. patr. fr. *su-dyumna* (applied to the Bharata Dauḥshanti), ŚBr.

सौध *saudha*, mfn. (fr. *sudhā*) having plaster or cement, plastered, stuccoed, R.; made of or coming from Euphorbia Antiquorum, Suśr.; Pañcar.; m. calcareous spar (= *dugdha-pashāṇā*), L.; n. (and m., g. *ardharcâdi*) a stuccoed mansion, any fine house, palace &c., MBh.; Kāv. &c.; n. silver, L.; opal (accord. to some). **-kāra**, m. a plasterer, the builder of a palace, MBh. **-tala**, n. the flat roof of a p°, Ragh. **-mūrdhan** (Prab.), **-mauli** (Cat.), m. the top or turret of a palace, Prab. **-vāsa**, m. a palatial dwelling, MW. **-śikhara**, m. n. = *-mūrdhan*, Prab. **Saudhâgra**, n. id., Rājat. **Saudhâṅgaṇa**, n. the court of a palace, Vās. **Saudhâlaya**, m. = *saudha-vāsa*, Inscr. **Saudhôtsaṅga**, m. the level roof of a palace, Megh.

Saudhākara, mfn. (fr. *sudhâkara*) relating or belonging to the moon, lunar, Naish.; N. of wk.

Saudhāmitrika, mf(*ā* or *ī*)n. (fr. *sudhā-mitra*), g. *kāśy-ādi.*

Saudhāya, Nom. Ā. *°yate*, to become nectar, Kāv.

Saudhāla, m. (prob. corrupted fr. *saudhâlaya*) a temple of Śiva (esp. in the form **Īśāna**), W.

Saudhāvatāna, g. *kāśy-ādi* (Kāś.)

Saudhāvatānika, mf(*ā* or *ī*)n., ib.

Saudhāvati, m. patr. fr. *sudhā-vat*, g. *bāhv-ādi.*

सौधन्य *saudhanya*, mfn. derived from Sudhana, Cat.

सौधन्वन *saudhanvaná*, m. 'son of Sudhanvan,' a Ṛibhu, RV.; TS.; a partic. mixed caste, KātyŚr.

सौधर्म *saudharma*, m. (fr. *su-dharma*) 'having rectitude,' a partic. abode of the gods (with Jainas), HPariś. **-ja**, m. pl. (with Jainas) a partic. class of gods, L. **Saudharmêndra**, m. N. of a Jaina saint, Śatr.

Saudharmya, n. rectitude, probity, honesty, Mahān.

सौधात *saudhāta*, m. the offspring of a Brāhman and a Bhṛijja-kaṇṭhī, L.

सौधातकि *saudhātaki*, m. patr. fr. *su-dhātṛi*, Pāṇ. iv, 1, 97.

Saudhātakyā, f. of prec., g. *krauḍy-ādi.*

सौधार *saudhāra* (?), m. N. of one of the 14 parts of a drama, W.

सौधृतेय *saudhṛiteya*, m. patr. fr. *su-dhṛiti*, BhP.

सौधोतकि *saudhotaki*, m. a patr. (prob. w. r. for *saudhātaki*), Pravar.

सौन *sauna*, mfn. (fr. *sūnā*; also written *śauna*) belonging or relating to a slaughter-house or to butchery &c., W.; m. a butcher, MBh.; BhP.; n. (with or scil. *māṅsa*) fresh butcher's meat, Mn.; Yājñ. **–dharmya**, n. 'law or rule of slaughter,' a state of deadly hostility, MBh. **–pāla**, m. having a butcher for a keeper, BhP.

Saunika, m. a butcher, Mn.; R. &c.; a hunter, Bhām.

सौनन्द *saunanda*, n. (fr. *su-nanda* and °*ndā*) N. of the club of Bala-rāma, L.; (*ā*), f. N. of the wife of Vatsa-prī, MārkP.

Saunandin, m. 'having Saunanda,' N. of Bala-rāma, L.

सौनव्य *saunavya*, m. patr. fr. *sūnu*, g. *gargâdi*.

Saunavyāyanī, f. of prec., g. *lohitâdi*.

सौनहोत्र *saunahotra*, incorrect for *śaun*°.

सौनाग *saunāga*, m. pl. the school of Su-nāga, Pat.; Kāś. &c.

सौनामि *saunāmi*, m. patr. fr. *su-nāman*, g. *bāhv-ādi*.

सौनीतेय *saunīteya*, m. (fr. *su-nīti*) metron. of Dhruva, Kāśikh.

सौनेत्र *saunetra*, mfn. (fr. *su-netra*), g. *saṃkalâdi*.

सौन्दर्य *saundarya*, n. (fr. *sundara*) beauty, loveliness, gracefulness, elegance, Kāv.; Kathās. &c.; noble conduct, generosity, R. **–purāṇa**, n., **-laharī**, f., **-vyākhyā**, f., **-stotra**, n. N. of wks.

सौप *saupa*, mfn. (fr. *sup*) relating to the case-terminations, Pāṇ. iv, 3, 66, Sch.

सौपथि *saupathi*, m. patr. fr. *su-patha*, Pravar.

Saupanthya, mfn. (fr. *su-path*), g. *saṃkāśâdi*.

सौपर्ण *saúparṇa* or *sauparṇá*, mf(ī)n. relating or belonging to or derived from or treating of or resembling the bird Su-parṇa (q. v.), AV. &c. &c.; (*ī*), f. a kind of creeping plant, L.; (*am*), n. an emerald, L.; dry ginger, L.; the Sauparṇa hymn (cf. RV. i, 164, 20 and IW. 39; a Vedic story relating the transformation of the metres into birds that they might fetch the Soma from heaven), Br.; GṛŚrS.; N. of various Sāmans, ĀrshBr. **–ketava**, mfn. relating or belonging to Vishṇu, Bālar. **–vrata**, n. N. of a partic. ascetic observance, ŚāṅkhGṛ.

Saúparṇīkādrava, mfn. relating to Su-parṇī and Kadrū, ŚBr.

Sauparṇeyá, m. (fr. *suparṇa* or °*ṇī*; cf. Pāṇ. iv, 1, 120, Sch.) a metron. (esp. N. of Garuḍa, q. v.), TS. &c.; pl. N. of the metres (regarded as children of Su-parṇī), MW.; (*ī*), f. a female descendant of Su-parṇa, Pāṇ. iv, 1, 15, Sch.

Sauparṇya, mfn. = *sauparṇa*, AitBr. (v. l.); n. the nature or state of an eagle or hawk (*-vat* with *cakshus*, 'an eye as sharp as an eagle's'), Suśr.

सौपर्य *sauparya*, mfn. (fr. *supari*), g. *saṃkāśâdi*.

सौपर्व *sauparva*, mfn. (fr. *su-parvan*), Pāṇ. vi, 4, 144, Vārtt. 1, Pat.

सौपस्तम्बि *saupastambi*, m. a patr., Pravar.

सौपाक *saupāka*, m. a partic. mixed tribe, MBh.

सौपातव *saupātava*, m. (only pl.) a patr., Saṃskārak.

सौपामायनि *saupāmāyani*, m. patr. fr. *su-pāman*, g. *tikâdi*.

सौपिक *saupika*, mfn. (fr. *sūpa*) sprinkled with sauce, Pāṇ. iv, 4, 26, Sch.

सौपिङ्गल *saupiṅgala*, mfn. (fr. *su-piṅgala*), g. *saṃkalâdi*.

सौपिष्ट *saupishṭa* (g. *śivâdi*) and *saupishṭi* (Pravar.), m. patr. fr. *su-pishṭa*.

सौपुष्पि *saupushpi*, m. patr. fr. *su-pushpa*, Pravar.

सौपूत *saupūta*, mfn. (fr. *su-pūta*), g. *saṃkalâdi*.

सौप्तिक *sauptika*, mfn. (fr. *supta*) connected with or relating to sleep, nocturnal, Mṛicch.; n. an attack on sleeping men, nocturnal combat, MBh.; R.; Kām. **–parvan**, n. N. of the 10th book of the Mahā-bhārata (describing how the three surviving Kuru warriors, Aśvatthāman, Kṛita-varman, and Kṛipa, after the destruction of their army, attacked the camp of the Pāṇḍavas by night and murdered them while asleep; the whole Pāṇḍava army was thus destroyed, except the five Pāṇḍu princes themselves, who, with Kṛishṇa and Sātyaki, were stationed at some distance from the camp).

सौप्रख्य *sauprakhya*, m. patr. fr. *su-prakhya*, Pāṇ. ii, 4, 54, Vārtt. 4, Pat.

Sauprakhyīya, mfn. (fr. prec.), ib.

सौप्रजास्त्व *sauprajāstvá*, n. = *su-pr*°, possession of good offspring, AV.

सौप्रतीक *saupratīka*, mfn. (fr. *su-pratīka*) relating or belonging to an elephant, L.

सौबल *saubala*, m. (fr. *su-bala*) patr. of Śakuni, MBh.; (*ī*), f. patr. of Gāndhārī (the wife of Dhṛita-rāshṭra), ib.; mfn. relating or belonging to Saubala, i. e. Śakuni, ib.

Saubalaka, m. = prec. m., MBh.; mfn. = prec. mfn., ib.

Saubaleya, m. N. of Śakuni, MBh.; (*ī*), f. N. of Gāndhārī, ib.

Saubalya, m. pl. N. of a people, MBh. (B. *śaub*°).

सौभ *saubha*, m. (also written *śaubha*) N. of the aerial city of Hari-ścandra (q. v.), MBh.; BhP.; of a town of the Śālvas, MBh.; a king of the Saubhas, ib.; pl. N. of a people, ib. **–dvār**, f., **-dvāra**, n. a gate of Saubha, ib. **–nivāsin**, m. pl. the inhabitants of S°, ib. **–pati**, **-rāj**, or **-rāja**, m. a lord or king of the Saubhas, ib.; BhP. **Saubhâdhipati**, m. a sovereign of the Saubhas, MBh.

Saubheya, m. an inhabitant of Saubha, BhP.

सौभकि *saubhaki*, m. N. of Drupada, MW.

सौभग *saúbhaga*, mfn. (fr. *subhaga*) 'auspicious,' coming from or made of the tree Su-bhaga, Car.; m. N. of a son of Bṛihac-chloka, BhP.; n. (ifc. f. *ā*) welfare, happiness, wealth, riches, enjoyment, RV.; loveliness, grace, beauty, BhP. **–tvá**, n. welfare, happiness, RV.

Saubhāgineya, m. (fr. *su-bhagā*) the son of a favourite wife or of an honoured mother, Bhaṭṭ.

Saúbhāgya, n. (fr. *su-bhaga*) welfare, good luck, good fortune, success, prosperity, happiness (esp. conjugal felicity), RV. &c. &c.; beauty, charm, grace, loveliness, MBh.; R. &c.; affection, favour, MW.; congratulation, good wishes, ib.; red lead, L.; borax, L.; a kind of plant, L.; the fourth of the astronomical Yogas, L. **–kalpa-druma**, m., **-kalpa-latā**, f., **-kavaca**, n., **-kāṇḍa**, n., **-krama-dīpikā**, f., **-gaurī-vrata-vidhi**, m. N. of wks. **–ghaṇṭā**, f. a kind of bell, Kād. **–cintāmaṇi**, m. a partic. drug, MW.; N. of various wks. **–cihna**, n. any mark of good fortune (esp. of wifehood, e. g. the marriage necklace, red pigment on the forehead), ib. **–tantu**, m. the marriage string (fastened round the bride's neck by the bridegroom at the wedding and worn till widowhood), ib. **–tantra**, n., **-tantra-pārāyaṇa-vidhi**, m. N. of wks. **–tṛitīyā**, f. the 3rd day of the light half of the month Bhādra, L. **–devatā**, f. a tutelary deity, MW. **–phala**, mfn. having happiness as a result, causing h° or delight, Kum. **–bhāskara**, N. of various wks. **–mañjarī**, f. N. of a Surāṅganā, Siṇhās.; N. of wk. **–mada**, m. intoxication (produced) by happiness or beauty, Kum. **–mālā-mantra**, m., **-ratnâkara**, m., **-lakshmī-kalpe śyāmalâmbā-stotra**, n., **-lakshmī-tantre śyāmalâmbā-varma-ratna**, n., **-lakshmy-upanishad**, f., **-latikā-paddhati**, f., **-laharī**, f. N. of wks. **–vat**, mfn. endowed with beauty, Sāy.; possessing good fortune, auspicious, fortunate, W.; (*atī*), f. a married and unwidowed woman, MW.; *-tā*, f. or *-tva*, n. auspiciousness, prosperity, W. **–vardhinī**, f. N. of Comm. **–vāyana**, n. auspicious offerings of sweetmeats &c., MW. **–vidyā**, f., **-vidyêśvara-stotra**, n. N. of wks. **–vilopin**, mfn. marring or impairing beauty, Kum. **–vrata**, n. a partic. religious observance, Cat. **–śayana-vrata**, n. id., ib.; *-kathā*, f. N. of ch. of wk. **–śuṇṭhī**, f., **-śubhôdaya**, m. N. of wks. **–sundarī-tīrtha**, n. N. of a Tīrtha, Cat.; of ch. of the Śiva-Purāṇa. **–sundarī-vrata-kathā**, f., **-hṛidaya**, n. N. of wks. **Saubhāgyârcana-kalpalatā**, f. N. of wk. **Saubhāgyâshṭaka**, n. N. of 8 substances which are said to cause prosperity &c., MatsyaP.; *-tṛitīyā-vrata*, n. a partic. religious observance (also prob. w. r. *-vrata-tṛitīyā-vrata*), Cat. **Saubhāgyôdaya**, m., °**gyôpanishad**, f. N. of wks.

सौभद्र *saubhadra*, mfn. relating to Su-bhadrā (q. v.), Pāṇ. iv, 2, 56, Sch.; m. metron. of Abhimanyu, MBh.; Hariv.; n. N. of a Tīrtha, MBh.; (scil. *yuddha*) the war occasioned by the carrying off of Su-bhadrā, ib.

Saubhadreya, m. metron. of Abhimanyu, L.; Terminalia Bellerica, L.

सौभर *saúbhara*, mf(ī)n. relating or belonging to Sobhari, RPrāt.; m. a patr. of Kuśika (author of RV. x, 127), Anukr.; n. N. of various Sāmans, ĀrshBr.; (*ī*), f. a verse composed by Sobhari, MW.

Saubharāyaṇa, m. patr. fr. *saubhara*, Pravar.

Saubhari, m. (fr. *sobhari*) N. of a Muni (married to the 50 daughters of Māndhātṛi and father of 150 sons), Pur.; of an author, Cat. **–saṃhitā**, f. N. of wk.

सौभव *saubhava*, m. N. of a grammarian, Cat.

सौभाग्य *saubhāgya* &c. See col. 2.

सौभाञ्जन *saubhāñjana*, m. = (or w. r. for) *śobhāñjana*, Moringa Pterygosperma, MBh.

सौभासिक *saubhāsika*, mfn. (fr. *su-bhāsa*) splendid, Divyâv.

Saubhāsinika, n. (with *ratna*) a kind of jewel, ib.

सौभिक *saubhika*, m. (cf. *śau*°) a juggler, L.

सौभिक्ष *saubhiksha*, mfn. (fr. *su-bhiksha*) bringing security and abundance of food, VarBṛS.

Saubhikshya, n. abundance of food or provisions, Bhadrab.

सौभूत *saubhūta*, mfn. (fr. *su-bhūta*), g. *saṃkalâdi*.

सौभेषज *saubheshaja*, mfn. consisting of the Su-bheshajas (q. v.), GopBr.

सौभ्रव *saubhrava*, n. N. of two Sāmans, ĀrshBr.

सौभ्रात्र *saubhrātra*, n. (fr. *su-bhrātṛi*) good brotherhood, fraternity, MBh.; Kāv. &c.

सौम *sauma*, mfn. (fr. *soma*, of which it is also the Vṛiddhi form in comp.) relating or belonging to Soma, VP. **–kratava**, n. (fr. *soma-kratu*) N. of a Sāman, ĀrshBr. **–kratavīya**, v. l. for *soma-kṛ*°, ib. **–datti**, m. patr. fr. *soma-datta*, MBh. **–pausha**, mfn. (cf. *saumāpaushṇa*) belonging or sacred to Soma and Pūshan, TāṇḍBr.; n. N. of a Sāman, IndSt.; °*shin*, m. N. of a Ṛishi, ib. **–mitrika**, mf(*ā* or *ī*)n. (fr. *soma-mitra*), g. *kāśy-ādi*. **–rājya**, m. patr. fr. *soma-rājaka*, ĀśvŚr. **–śushmāyana**, m. patr. fr. *soma-śushma*, VP. **Saumāgná**, mf(*ī*)n. (fr. *somâgni*) addressed to Soma and Agni, MaitrS. **Saumāpa**, m. patr. fr. *somā-pa*, ŚBr. **Saumāpaushṇá**, mfn. (fr. *somā-pūshan*, cf. *somā-paushṇa*) belonging to Soma and Pūshan, MaitrS.; n. N. of a Sāman, ĀrshBr. **Saumāraudrá**, mfn. (fr. *somā-rudra*) relating or belonging to Soma and Rudra, MaitrS.; ŚBr. **Saumendrá**, mfn. (fr. *somêndra*; cf. *somâindra*) belonging to Soma and Indra, MaitrS.

Saumaki, m. patr. fr. *somaka*, MBh.

Saumāyana, m. (fr. *soma*) patr. of Budha, PañcavBr.

Saumāyanaka, mfn. (fr. prec.), g. *arīhaṇâdi*.

Saumika, mf(*ī*)n. relating to Soma-juice or a Soma sacrifice, performed with Soma (with *makha*, m. 'a Soma sacrifice'), ŚrS; Mn.; Jaim.; relating to S° or the moon, lunar, W.; observing the Cāndrāyaṇa vow,

L.; (ī), f. the ceremony of pressing out the Soma-juice, L.; (am), n. a vessel for the Soma-juice, L.

Saumī, f. of next.

Saumyá (once in AV. saúmya), mf(ī, later ā; once in RV. saúmyā)n. relating or belonging to Soma (the juice or the sacrifice or the moon-god), connected or dealing with Soma, having his nature or qualities &c., RV. &c. &c.; cool and moist (opp. to āgneya, 'hot and dry'), Br.; Hariv.; Suśr.; northern (ena, 'to the north'), Hariv.; VarBṛS.; 'resembling the moon,' placid, gentle, mild (saumya, voc. = 'O gentle Sir!' 'O good Sir!' 'O excellent man!' as the proper mode of addressing a Brāhman, Mn. ii, 125), ŚBr. &c. &c.; auspicious (said of birds, planets &c.; esp. of the Nakshatras Mṛiga-śiras, Citrā, Anurādhā, and Revatī), R.; VarBṛS.; Hariv.; ŚārṅgS.; happy, pleasant, cheerful, MW.; m. a Soma sacrifice, L.; an adherent, worshipper, BhP.; a Brāhman, L.; patr. of Budha or the planet Mercury, VarBṛS.; of the Vedic Ṛishi Budha (author of RV. x, 1), RAnukr.; the left hand, Hcat.; Ficus Glomerata, L.; the fifteenth cubit (aratni) from the bottom or the third from the top of the sacrificial post, L.; (in anat.) the blood before it becomes red, serum, W.; the gastric juice, MW.; the month Mārgaśīrsha, Hcat.; N. of the 43rd (or 17th) year in the 60 years' cycle of Jupiter, VarBṛS.; (pl.) the people of Soma, ŚāṅkhGṛ.; a partic. class of deceased ancestors, Mn. iii, 199; m. n. a partic. penance (see -kṛicchra), Yājñ.; GāruḍaP.; N. of a Dvīpa of the earth or of Bharata-varsha, Pur.; of the 7th astrol. Yuga, Jyot.; (yā), f. N. of various plants (Abrus Precatorius; Glycine Debilis; Ruta Graveolens &c.), L.; a pearl, L.; the Nakshatra Mṛiga-śiras, Hariv.; N. of the five stars in Orion's head (also called ilvala, q.v.), W.; a species of the Āryā metre, Col.; N. of Durgā, Cat.; (ī), f. moonshine, MBh.; (am), n. the nature or condition of Soma, AV.; gentleness, MBh.; Pañcat.; the Nakshatra Mṛiga-śiras (presided over by the Moon), MaitrUp.; Hariv. (accord. to Nīlak. = 'Wednesday'); the left eye, L.; the middle of the hand, L.; N. of the fifth Muhūrta, Cat.; (scil. adbhuta) a partic. kind of omen or prodigy (occurring in the Diva or sky), MW. **–kṛicchra**, m. n. a kind of penance (described as subsisting for 5 days, severally, on sesamum, water of boiled rice, butter-milk, water, parched grain, and fasting on the 6th day), W. **–gandhā**, f. a kind of flower, L. **–gandhī**, f. id., ib.; the Indian white rose, MW. **–giri**, m. N. of a mountain, Hariv. **–gola**, m. the northern hemisphere, Gaṇit.; Gol. **–graha**, m. an auspicious or benign planet (such as Mercury, Jupiter, Venus, and the full moon), MW. **–jāmātṛi**, m. N. of a man, Cat.; -muni, m. N. of an author (°nīndra-stotra, n. N. of wk.), ib.; -yogīndra-stuti, f. N. of wk. **–tā**, f. the state of being cool and moist, MBh.; gentleness, placidity, ib.; R.; MārkP.; benevolence, MW.; beauty, ib. **–tva**, n. gentleness, mildness, Bhag.; R.; benevolence, MW.; beauty, ib. **–darśana**, mfn. pleasant to look at, Mn.; R.; (ā), f. N. of a princess, Kathās. **–dhātu**, m. 'Soma-like element,' the phlegmatic humour, Suśr. **–nāman**, mf(mnī)n. having a soft or agreeable name, Mn. iii, 10. **–prabhāva**, mfn. of gentle nature, Bcar. **–mukha**, mf(ā)n. pleasant-faced, Kāv. **–rūpa**, mfn. acting kindly towards (with gen.), VP. **–vapus**, mfn. having an agreeable form, MW. **–vāra**, m. 'Mercury's day,' Wednesday, ib. **–vāsara**, m. id., A. **–śānti**, f. N. of wk. **–śrī**, mfn. having agreeable beauty, Pracaṇḍ. **Saumyâkṛiti**, mfn. having an agr° appearance, Kathās. **Saumyârci**, mfn. having a gentle lustre, Bcar. **Saumyôpacāra**, m. a mild or gentle remedy or measure, MW. **Saumyôpayantṛi**, m. N. of an author, Cat.

सौमङ्गल saumaṅgala, mfn. (fr. su-maṅgala), g. saṃkalâdi.

Saumaṅgalya, n. welfare, prosperity, BhP.; an auspicious object (as an amulet &c.), ib.

सौमतायन saumatāyana, m. patr. fr. su-mata, g. naḍâdi.

Saumatāyanaka, mfn. (fr. prec.), g. arīhaṇâdi.

सौमदायन saumadāyana, m. (only pl.) patr. fr. su-mada (or w.r. for saumatāyana), Saṃskārak.

सौमन saumana, n. (fr. su-mana or °nas); m. or (ā), f. a flower, blossom, Suśr.; a partic. mythical weapon, R.

Saumanasá, mf(ī)n. (fr. su-manas) coming from or consisting of flowers, floral, flowery, Śiś.; Pārśvan.; agreeable to the feelings, pleasing, W.; m. cheerfulness, enjoyment, comfort, VS.; AV.; N. of the eighth day of the civil month (= karma-māsa), IndSt.; of the elephant of the western quarter, R.; of a mountain, ib.; Hariv.; (ā), f. the outer skin of the nutmeg, L.; N. of a river, R.; (ī), f. N. of the fifth night in the civil month, IndSt.; (am), n. benevolence, kindness, favour, RV.; pleasure, satisfaction, ib.; AV.; the nutmeg (cf. ī, f.), L.; N. of a peak of a mountain, R. (B.)

Saumanasāyana, m. patr. fr. su-manas, g. aśvâdi; (ī), f. the outer skin of the nutmeg, L. (°yinī, Car.)

Saumanasya, mfn. causing gladness or cheerfulness of mind, BhP.; m. N. of a son of Yajña-bāhu, ib.; n. satisfaction of mind, gladness, cheerfulness, Suśr.; Ragh.; Kathās.; right understanding, Śiś., Sch.; an offering of flowers placed in the hands of the priest at a Śrāddha, BhP.; N. of a Varsha in Plaksha-dvīpa (ruled by Saumanasya), BhP. **–vat**, mfn. cheerful, glad, Ragh.

Saumanasyāyanī, f. the blossom of the Mālatī or great-flowering jasmine, L.

Saumanāyana. See su-manāyana, p. 1230.

Saumanottarika, mfn. knowing the story of Sumanôttarā, Pāṇ. iv, 3, 87, Vārtt. 1, Pat.

सौमन्त saumanta, mfn. taught or enjoined by Su-mantu, Yājñ., Sch.

सौमन्त्रिण saumantriṇa, n. (fr. su-mantrin) having a good minister, Hit. (v.l.)

सौमात्र saumātra, m. patr. and metron. fr. su-mātṛi, Pāṇ. iv, 1, 115, Sch.

सौमित्र saumitra, m. (fr. su-mitrā) metron. of Lakshmaṇa, L.; n. (fr. su-mitra) friendship, Kāṭh.; N. of various Sāmans, ĀrshBr.

Saumitri, m. metron. of Lakshmaṇa (du. = 'L° and Śatru-ghna'), MBh.; R. &c.; N. of a teacher, Cat.

Saumitrīya, mfn. (fr. saumitri), g. gahâdi.

सौमिलिक saumilika, m. or n. (?) a partic. substance, Buddh.

सौमिल्ल saumilla, m. N. of a poet (also written saumila and saumalla; cf. somila), Mālav., Introd.

सौमिवि saumivi (?), m. pl. a patr., Saṃskārak.

सौमिश्रि saumiśri (?), m. a patr., Pravar.

सौमुक्तिवाद saumukti-vāda, m. N. of a Nyāya wk.

सौमुख्य saumukhya, n. (fr. su-mukha) cheerfulness, delight in (comp.), Bcar.; Jātakam.

सौमुचि saumuci, m. pl. a patr., Saṃskārak.

सौमेचक saumecaka, n. (prob. fr. su-mecaka) gold, W.

सौमेध saumedha, n. (fr. su-medha or °dhas) N. of various Sāmans, ĀrshBr.

Saumedhika, mfn. possessing supernatural knowledge or wisdom, W.; m. a sage, seer, ib.

सौमेरव saumerava, mf(ī)n. relating or belonging to Su-meru, Śiś.; n. N. of the country Ilâvṛita (q.v.), L.; gold, L.

Saumeruka, n. gold (prob. w.r. for prec.), L.

सौम्य saumya &c. See col. 1.

सौयज्ञक sauyajñaka, mfn. (fr. su-yajña), g. arīhaṇâdi.

सौयवस sauyavasa, n. (fr. su-yavasa) abundance of grass, ŚāṅkhBr.; (said to be fr. su-yavasu) N. of various Sāmans, ĀrshBr.

Sauyavasi, m. a patr., AitBr.

सौयामि sauyāmi, m. a patr., ŚāṅkhGṛ.

सौयामुन sauyāmuna, m. pl. (fr. su-yāmuna) a patr., Saṃskārak.

सौर 1. saura, mfn. (fr. surā) consisting of spirituous liquor, ŚrS.

सौर 2. saura, mf(ī)n. (fr. 1. sūra and sūrya; in some meanings perhaps fr. sura) relating or belonging or sacred to or coming from &c. the sun or the god Sūrya, solar, MaitrUp.; MBh. &c.; celestial, divine, W.; m. a worshipper of the sun, MBh.; Prab. (RTL. 342); 'son of the Sun,' N. of the planet Saturn, VarBṛS.; N. of the 20th Kalpa (q.v.); a solar day (while the sun is in one degree of the ecliptic), W.; a solar month (consisting of 30 risings and settings of the sun or the period during which the sun is in one sign of the zodiac), W.; a representation of a solar zodiacal sign used at marriage ceremonies, MW.; coriander, L.; Zanthoxylon Alatum, L.; N. of a Guru, MW.; (ī), f. the wife of the Sun, W.; patr. of Tapatī (the mother of Kuru; also called vaivasvatī), MBh.; a cow, Hcat.; Polanisia Icosandra, L.; (am), n. a collection of hymns addressed to Sūrya (extracted from the Ṛig-veda), Cat.; the right eye, Gal.; N. of a Sāman (= bṛihat-saura), ĀrshBr.; N. of wk. (prob. = saura-purāṇa), Kap., Sch. **–gaṇita-dvādaśa-horā-prakāśa**, m. N. of wk. **–ja**, m. coriander (v.l. saurabha), L. **–tantra**, n. N. of wk. **–tīrtha**, n. N. of a Tīrtha, Cat.; of a ch. of the Śiva-Purāṇa. **–divasa**, m. a solar day, MW. **–dharma**, m., **-dharmôttara**, N. of wks. **–dhrī**, f. a kind of stringed instrument, L. **–nakta**, n. a partic. religious observance, NarasP. **–paksha-gaṇita**, n. N. of wk. **–pata** (?), m. a worshipper of the sun, W. **–para**, N. of wk. **–pāta** (?), m. = -pata, W. **–purāṇa**, n., **-paurāṇika-mata-samarthana**, n. N. of wks. **–bhuvana**, n. = sūrya-loka (q.v.), MW. **–mantra**, m. N. of wk. **–māsa**, m. a solar month, MW. **–loka**, m. the sun's sphere, A. **–saṃvatsara**, m. a solar year, MW. **–saṃhitā**, f., **-siddhânta**, m. N. of wks. **–sûkta**, n. a hymn addressed to Sūrya (= sūrya-sûkta, q.v.) **Saurâṅga**, m. N. of a king, Inscr. **Saurâshṭâksharī-mantra**, m., **Saurôpapurāṇa**, n. N. of wks.

Sauraka, n. N. of a town founded by Surêndra, Rājat. **Saurakâyaṇôpanishad**, f. N. of an Up.

Sauramasa, m. a king of the Sūra-masas, Pāṇ. iv, 1, 170.

Saurasaindhava, mfn. (fr. sura-sindhu) belonging to the river Ganges, Gangetic, Śiś.; related to the Ganges (said of Bhīshma), MW.; m. a horse of the Sun (in this sense compounded of saura and saindhava, q.v.), ib.

Saúrāki, m. patr. of Vipūjana, MaitrS.

Saurāṭī, f. a partic. Rāgiṇī, Saṃgīt. (v.l. sauraṭī).

Sauri, m. N. of the planet Saturn (as son of the Sun), VarBṛS.; a patr., Saṃskārak.; Terminalia Tomentosa, L. (v.l. śauri); Polanisia Icosandra, ib. (more correctly saurī); N. of a locality, Buddh.; pl. N. of a people in the Deccan, VarBṛS. **–ratna**, n. sapphire, L.

1. **Saurika**, mfn. (for 2. see p. 1255, col. 1) heavenly, celestial, W.; m. the planet Saturn, MW.; heaven, paradise, L.

Saurī, f. See above under 2. saura.

Saurīya, mfn. solar, belonging or relating to the sun, Pat.; Vop.; m. a partic. tree with poisonous resin, Suśr.

Saureya or °yaka, m. a species of Barleria, L.

Saúrya, mf(saurī or sauryā)n. (fr. sūrya, of which it is also the Vṛiddhi form in comp.) relating or belonging to the sun, solar, Br.; GṛŚrS. &c.; (fr. sūra), g. saṃkāśâdi; m. a son of the sun, PraśnUp., Sch.; patr. of several Vedic Ṛishis, RAnukr.; a year, L.; n. N. of two summits of the Himâlaya, Pat.; of a town, Kaiy. **–cāndramasa**, mf(ī)n. (fr. sūrya-candramas or °masa) sacred to the sun and the moon, ĀśvŚr. **–pṛishṭha**, n. N. of a Sāman, Vait. **–prabha**, mfn. belonging to Sūrya-prabha, Kathās. **–bhagavat**, m. N. of a grammarian, Pat. **–mārutaka**, mfn. (fr. sūrya-marut or °ta) occurring in sunshine and wind (cf. vātâtapika), Car. **–yāma**, mfn. (fr. sūrya-yama) belonging to the sun and Yama, VS. **–varcasá**, m. patr. fr. sūrya-varcas, AV. **–vāruṇá**, mfn. (fr. sūrya-varuṇa) belonging to the sun and Varuṇa, MaitrS. **–vaiśvānara**, mf(ī)n. (fr. sūrya-vaiśvānara) addressed to the sun and Vaiśvānara, Nir.

Sauryāyaṇi, m. patr. fr. saurya, PraśnUp., Sch.

Sauryāyaṇin, m. N. of a man, PraśnUp.

Sauryin, m. N. of the Himâlaya, Pat.

Sauryodayika, mfn. (fr. sūryôdaya, 'sun-rise'), Buddh.

सौरटी sauraṭī, v.l. for saurāṭī above.

सौरण sauraṇa, mfn. (fr. sūraṇa, q.v.), ŚārṅgS.

सौरत *saurata*, mfn. (fr. *su-rata*) relating to sexual enjoyment, BhP.; n. sexual enjoyment, ib.; m. mild wind, L.

Sauratya, n. delight in (comp.), Jātakam.

सौरथ *sauratha* and °*theya*, m. (said to be metron. fr. *su-rathā*, but prob. w.r. for *saurabha*, °*bheya*), MBh. iii, 13297 and 13300.

Saurathī, f., patr. fr. *su-rathā*, Pat.

सौरपि *saurapi* (?), m. pl. a patr., Pravar.

सौरभ *saurabha*, mfn. (fr. *su-rabhi*) fragrant, BhP.; descended from (the cow) Su-rabhi, Hariv. (v.l. *saurasa*); m. coriander, Suśr.; a kind of Vesavāra (q.v.), L.; (*ī*), f. 'daughter of Su-rabhi,' a cow, MBh.; Hariv.; R.; (*am*), n. (ifc. f. *ā*) fragrance, perfume, Kāv.; Kathās. &c.; saffron, L.; myrrh (v.l. *staubhaka*), L.; N. of a Sāman, Lāṭy.; N. of various Comms.

Saurabhaka, n. a kind of metre, Col.

Saúrabheya, mfn. belonging or relating to Surabhi, MW.; m. 'son of Surabhi,' a bull, VS.; pl. a herd of cattle, MBh.; (*ī*), f. a cow, ib.; BhP.; N. of an Apsaras, MBh.; Hariv. **–tantra**, n. N. of a Tantra wk.

Saurabheyaka, m. a bull, L.

Saurabhya, n. fragrance, sweet-scentedness, odour (met. = 'universal diffusion'), Kāv.; Suśr.; BhP.; pleasingness, beauty, L.; good character, fame, L.; w.r. for *sauratya*; m. N. of Kubera, L. **–da**, n. a kind of perfume, Gal.

सौरस *saurasa*, mfn. (fr. *su-rasa*, °*sā*) coming from the plant Su-rasā, Car.; m. salted broth, L.; a partic. insect infesting the hair, Car.; metron. fr. *su-rasā*, Hariv.; (*ā*), f. the mountain jujube, L.; N. of a Vihāra founded by king Surêndra, Rājat.

Sauraseya, mfn., g. *sakhy-ādi*; m. N. of Skanda, L.

Saurasya, n. well-flavouredness, tastiness, savouriness, MW.; used in explaining *sauśāmya*, Nīlak.

सौरसेन *saurasena*, m. pl. N. of a people (= *śūra-sena*), Cat.

सौराज्य *saurājya*, n. (fr. *su-rājan*) good sovereignty, good government, Ragh.; Kathās. **–vat**, mfn. enjoying good government, Śatr.

सौराव *saurāva*, m. salted broth (cf. *saurasa*), Suśr.

सौराष्ट्र *saurāshṭra*, mf(*ā* or *ī*)n. (fr. *su-rāshṭra*) belonging to or coming from the country of Surāt, VarBṛS.; m. the resin of Boswellia Thurifera, L.; pl. the inhabitants of Surāt, AV.Pariś.; VarBṛS.; Rājat.; (*ā* or *ī*), f. a sort of fragrant earth found in S°, Suśr.; L.; (*am*), n. a kind of amalgam of zinc or copper, bell-metal, brass, L.; a kind of metre, Col. **–deśa**, m. the country of S°, Kathās. **–nagara**, n. the city of Surāt, Cat. **–maṇḍala**, n. the district of S°, ib. **–mṛittikā**, f. S° earth, MW.

Saurāshṭraka, mf(*ikā*)n. relating to or coming from Surāt, VarBṛS.; m. pl. the inhabitants of S°, ib.; n. a kind of metal, L.; a kind of poison (either of a snake or a vegetable or mineral poison), MW.

Saurāshṭrika, mfn. belonging to Surāt, VarBṛS.; m. pl. the inhabitants of Surāt, Car.; n. a kind of poison (cf. prec.), L.; bell-metal, brass, L.

Saurāshṭreya, mfn. belonging or relating to Surāt, R.

सौरिक 2. *saurika*, mfn. (fr. *surā*; for 1. *saurika* see p. 1254, col. 3) relating to or due for spirituous liquor (as money), Mn. viii, 159.

सौरिन्ध्र *saurindhra*, m. pl. N. of a people, VarBṛS.; (*ī*), f. a Saurindhra woman, MārkP.

सौरोहिक *saurohika*, m. metron. fr. *su-rohikā*, g. *śivâdi*.

Saurohitika, m. metron. fr. *su-rohitikā*, ib.

सौर्वल *saurvala*, w.r. for *sauvarcala*, Suśr.

सौलक्षण्य *saulakshaṇya*, n. (fr. *su-lakshaṇa*) the possession of auspicious marks, Kathās.

सौलभ *saulabha*, mfn. (fr. *su-labha*) written or composed by Su-labha, Pāṇ. iv, 3, 105, Vārtt. 1, Pat.

Saulabhāyana, mfn. id., Cat.

Saulabhya, n. easiness of attainment, Prab., Sch.

Saulābha, mfn. (fr. next), g. *kaṇvâdi*.

Saulābhya, m. patr. fr. *su-lābhin*, g. *gargâdi*.

सौलोह *sauloha*, mfn. (fr. next), g. *kaṇvâdi*.

Saulohya, m. patr. fr. *su-lohin*, g. *gargâdi*.

सौल्विक *saulvika*. See *śaulbika*, p. 1093.

सौव 1. *sauva*, mfn. (fr. *sva*) relating to self or to one's own property, Vop.; n. an order, edict, L.

Sauvagrāmika, mfn. (fr. *sva-grāma*) belonging or relating to one's own village, Vop.

Sauvādhyāyika, mfn. (fr. *svâdhyāya*), ib.

सौव 2. *sauvá*, mfn. (fr. *svar*) heavenly, celestial, VS.; TS.

सौवक्षसेय *sauvakshaseya*, m. patr. fr. *su-vakshas*, g. *śubhrâdi*.

सौवर *sauvará*, mfn. (fr. *svara*) relating to or treating of sound or accent, ŚBr.

सौवर्चनस *sauvarcanasá*, m. a patr., TS.

सौवर्चल *sauvarcala*, mfn. (fr. *su-varcala* or °*lā*) belonging to or coming from Su-varcala, MW.; n. (or m.) sochal salt (prepared by boiling down soda with emblic myrobolan), Kauś.; Suśr. &c.; natron, alkali, L.; (*ā*), f. N. of Rudra's wife, Hcat.

Sauvarcalīya, mfn. (fr. prec.), g. *aśvâdi*.

सौवर्चस *sauvarcasa*, m. (fr. *su-varcas*) shining, radiant, MānGṛ.

सौवर्ण *sauvarṇa*, mf(*ī* or *ā*)n. (fr. *su-varṇa*, of which it is also the Vṛiddhi form in comp.) made or consisting of gold, golden, ŚrS.; Yājñ.; MBh. &c.; weighing a Su-varṇa, W.; containing the word *suvarṇa*, g. *vimuktâdi*; m. a Karsha of gold, MBh.; a gold ear-ring, L.; n. gold, MBh. **–nābha**, m. pl. the disciples of Suvarṇa-nābha, Cat. **–parṇa**, mfn. having golden wings, Suparṇ. **–balaja** or **-bālaja**, mfn. (fr. *suvarṇa-balaja*), Pāṇ. vii, 3, 25, Sch. **–bhedinī**, f. the plant Priyaṅgu, L. **–retasa**, m. patr. fr. *suvarṇa-retasa*, Pravar. **–harmya**, n. a silver pavilion, Bcar.

Sauvarṇakāyana, mfn. (fr. *su-varṇaka*), g. *pakshâdi*.

Sauvarṇika, mfn. weighing or worth a Su-varṇa (ifc. after a numeral = 'w° a partic. number of S°s'), Hcat.; m. a worker in gold, goldsmith, Campak.; (*ā*), f. a partic. venomous insect, Suśr.

Sauvarṇya, n. a beautiful fresh colour, Jātakam.; 'the being gold' and 'the correct pronunciation of sounds,' Śaṃk.

सौवल्य *sauvalya*. See *saubalya*, p. 1253.

सौवश्व *sauvaśva*, m. a patr. fr. *sv-aśva*, Pāṇ. vii, 3, 3, Sch. **–bhārya**, mfn. one who has a Sauvaśvī as wife, Vop.

Sauvaśvi, m. a patr. fr. *sv-aśva*, Vop.

Saúvaśvya, n. a horse-race, RV.

सौवस्तिक *sauvastika*, mfn. (fr. *sv-asti*) benedictive, salutatory, W.; m. a family Brāhman or priest, L.; n. = *svasty-ayana*, L.

सौवात *sauvāta*, mfn. (fr. *svāti*), Pāṇ. iv, 2, 104, Vārtt. 8, Sch.

सौवादुमृदव *sauvādumṛidava*, n. (fr. *svādu-mṛidu*) sweetness and gentleness, Pāṇ. vii, 3, 4, Sch.

सौवास *sauvāsa*, m. (fr. **su** + 1. *vāsa*) a fragrant species of Tulasī, L.

सौवासिनी *sauvāsinī*, f. = *su-vāsinī*, ĀśvGṛ.

सौवास्तव *sauvāstava*, mf(*ī*)n. (fr. *su-vāstu*) having a good site, pleasantly situated, Pāṇ. iv, 2, 77.

सौविद *sauvida*, m. (fr. *suvida*) a guard or attendant on the women's apartments, L.

Sauvidalla, m. (fr. *suvidalla*) id., Śiś.; Bālar.; Kathās. **–tva**, n. the office of a chamberlain, Sāh.

Sauvidallaka, m. = *sauvidalla*, Hcar.

सौविष्टकृत् *sauvishṭakṛit*, mfn. dedicated to or treating of Agni Svishṭa-kṛit, ĀśvGṛ.

Sauvishṭakṛita, mf(*ī*)n. id., GṛŚrS.

Sauvishṭi, m. pl. a patr. (prob. fr. *sv-ishṭa*), Saṃskārak.

सौवीर *sauvīra*, m. pl. (fr. *su-vīra*) N. of a people inhabiting a district in the neighbourhood of the Indus, MBh.; Hariv. &c.; (sg.) a king of the Sauvīras, ib.; (*ā* or *ī*), f. (in music) a partic. Mūrchanā, Saṃgīt.; (*ī*), f. a princess of the Sauvīras, MBh.; MārkP.; (*am*), n. the fruit of the jujube, Suśr.; sour gruel, ib.; antimony, ib. **–pāṇa**, m. pl. (fr. *sauv°* + *pāna*) 'drinkers of *sauvīra*,' N. of the Bālhīkas, Pāṇ. viii, 4, 9, Sch. **–bhakta**, mfn. inhabited by S°s, g. *aishukāry-ādi*. **–rāja**, m. a king of S°, MW. **–sāra**, n. pure antimony, L. **Sauvīrâñjana**, n. a kind of antimony or collyrium, L. **Sauvīrâbhīra**, m. du. the S°s and the Ābhīras (collectively), BhP. **Sauvīrâmla**, n. sour gruel, L.

Sauvīraka, m. = *sauvīra*, MBh.; VarBṛS.; a contemptible Sauvīra, MW.; N. of Jayad-ratha, ib.; the jujube tree, L.; (*ikā*), f. id., L.; (*am*), n. sour gruel, MBh.; Suśr.

Sauvīrāyaṇa, m. (prob.) a descendant of the Sauvīras, g. *aishukāry-ādi*. **–bhakta**, mfn. inhabited by Sauvīrāyaṇas, ib.

Sauvīrya, m. a king of the Sauvīras, IndSt.; (*ā*), f. a princess of the Sauvīras, ib.; (*am*), n. great heroism or fortitude, MW.

सौव्रत्य *saúvratya*, n. (fr. *su-vrata*) faith, devotion, obedience, VS.

सौशब्द *sauśabda* or *sauśabdya*, m. (fr. *su-śabda*) the right formation of nominal and verbal forms (by case-terminations and tense-terminations; e.g. Śiś. i, 51), Pratāp.

सौशमि *sauśami*, m. (fr. *su-śama*) a patr., Pāṇ. ii, 4, 20, Sch. **–kantha**, n. ib.

Sauśāmya, n. (? for *sauśamya*) good pacification, reconciliation, MBh.

सौशर्मक *sauśarmaka*, mfn. (fr. *su-śarman*), g. *arīhaṇâdi*.

Sauśarmaṇa, mfn. proclaimed by Su-śarman, Kaiy.

Sauśarmi, m. patr. fr. *su-śarman*, g. *bāhv-ādi*.

सौशल्य *sauśalya*, m. pl. N. of a people (v.l. *saubalya*), MBh.

सौशिल्य *sauśilya*, w.r. for next, Pañcar.

सौशील्य *sauśīlya*, n. (fr. *su-śīla*) excellence of disposition, good morals, R.; BhP.

सौश्रव *sauśrava*, m. (fr. *su-śrava* or °*vas*) a patr., Hariv.

Sauśravasá, mfn. (fr. *su-śravas*) having a good reputation, ĀśvGṛ.; m. patr. of Upagu, PañcavBr.; n. high praise or renown, celebrity, RV.; a running-match, contest (?), ib.; N. of two Sāmans, ĀrshBr.

सौश्रिय *sauśriya*, n. (fr. *su-śrī*) great fortune or happiness, Saṃskārak.

सौश्रुत *sauśruta*, mfn. composed or written by Su-śruta, Cat.; m. (fr. *su-śrut* or °*ta*) a patr. (also pl.), Hariv. **–pārthava**, m. pl., g. *kārtakaujapâdi*.

सौश्रोमतेय *sauśromateyá*, m. a patr., ŚBr.

सौषद्मन *saushadmana*, m. a patr. fr. *su-shadman*, AitBr.

सौषध *saushadha*, mfn. (fr. 7. *sa* + *oshadhi* or *aushadha*) possessing or decorated with plants, MānGṛ.

सौषाम *saushāma*, n. (fr. *su-shāman*) N. of a Sāman, ĀrshBr.

सौषिर *saushira*, m. (fr. *su-shira*) a partic. disease of the teeth, Suśr.; n. wind-instruments (collectively), Saṃgīt.

Saushirya, n. hollowness, porosity, Vāgbh.

सौषुप्त *saushupta*, mf(*ā*)n. (fr. *su-shupta*; with *daśā*, f. 'deep sleep'), Kāśikh.; n. N. of the tenth book of the Mahā-bhārata (= *sauptikam parva*), Nīlak.

सौषुम्ण *saushumṇa*, m. (fr. *su-shumṇa*) a kind of sunbeam, VP.

सौष्टव *saushṭava*, w.r. for next.

सौष्ठव *saushṭhava*, n. (fr. *su-shṭhu*) excellence, superior goodness or beauty, extreme skilfulness, cleverness, MBh.; Kāv. &c.; a partic. position of the body (also in dancing; often with *lāghava*), ib.; Saṃgīt.; self-confidence, L.; a partic. division of dramatic composition, W.

सौष्मिकि *saushmiki*, m. pl. a patr., Saṃskārak.

सौसाम *sausāma*, m. patr. fr. *su-sāman*, Pāṇ. vi, 4, 170, Sch.

सौसायन *sausāyana*, g. *arihaṇâdi*.

Sausāyanaka, mfn. (fr. prec.), ib.

सौसुक *sausuka*, N. of a place, Pāṇ. iv, 2, 141, Vārtt. 1, Pat.

Sausukīya, mfn. relating to the preceding, ib.

सौसुम्न *sausumna*, incorrect for *saushumṇa*.

सौसुराद *sausurāda*, m. a kind of worm, Car.

सौस्त्र *saustra*, n. (fr. *su-strī*), g. *yuvâdi*.

सौस्थित्य *sausthitya*, n. (fr. *su-sthita*) an auspicious situation, VarBṛS.

Sausthya, n. (fr. *su-stha*) welfare, L.

सौस्नातिक *sausnātika*, mfn. (fr. *su-snāta*) one who asks whether an ablution has been successful or auspicious, Ragh. vi, 61 (cf. Pāṇ. iv, 4, 1, Vārtt. 3, Pat.)

सौस्वर्य *sausvarya*, n. (fr. *su-svara*) euphony, Śaṃk.

सौस्सल *saussala*, mfn. relating or belonging to Sussala, Rājat.

सौहविष *sauhavisha*, n. (fr. *su-havis*) N. of various Sāmans, ĀrshBr.

सौहार्द *sauhārda*, n. (fr. *su-hṛid*) good-heartedness, affection, friendship for or with (gen. or loc.), ŚāṅkhŚr.; MBh. &c.; m. the son of a friend, W. **-nidhi**, m. 'treasury of friendship,' N. of Rāma, MW. **-vyañjaka**, mfn. betraying friendship, Bcar.

Saúhārdya, n. friendship, affection, TS.; AitBr.

Sauhṛida, mfn. relating to or coming from a friend, R.; m. a friend, Pañcat.; pl. N. of a people, MBh.; n. (ifc. f. *ā*) affection, friendship for or with (loc. or *saha* or comp.), MBh.; R. &c.; liking for, fondness of (comp.), Jātakam.

Sauhṛidaya, n. cordial friendship, g. *yuvâdi*.

Sauhṛidayya, n. friendship, Pāṇ. vi, 3, 51, Sch.

Sauhṛidya, n. id., MBh.; Hit.

सौहित्य *sauhitya*, n. (fr. *su-hita*) satiety, satisfaction, ŚāṅkhŚr.; MBh. &c.; amiableness, loveliness, Sāh.; Tattvas.; fulness, completion, W.

सौहोत्र *sauhotra*, m. (fr. *su-hotra*) patr. of the Vedic Ṛishis Aja-mīḍha and Puru-mīḍha, RAnukr.

Sauhotri, m. a patr. of Jahnu, Hariv.

सौह्म *sauhma*, m. a king of the Suhmas, Pāṇ. iv, 1, 170, Sch.

Sauhmanāgara, mfn. (fr. *suhma-nagara*), ib.

स्कन्द् *skand* (cf. *skandh* and *skund*), cl. 1. P. (Dhātup. xxiii, 10) *skandati* (m. c. also °*te*; *caskánda*, RV. &c.; *caskande*, MBh. &c.; aor. *askan*, *skán*, RV.; *áskān*, *skān*, Br.; *askāntsīt*, ib.; *askadat*, Gr.; Prec. *skadyāt*, ib.; fut. *skanttā*, ib.; *skantsyati*, Br.; inf. *skanditum*, Gr.; *-skáde*, *-skádas*, RV.; ind. p. *skanttvā*, Gr.; *-skándya* or *-skádya*, Br.; *-skándam*, AV.; Br.), to leap, jump, hop, dart, spring, spurt out, be spilt or effused (esp. said of semen), RV. &c. &c.; (Ā.) to emit seminal fluid, VP.; to leap upon, cover (said of animals), TBr.; ŚBr.; to drop, fall down, perish, be lost, BhP.: Pass. *skadyate* (perf. *caskade* or *caskande*; aor. *askandi*), Gr.: Caus. *skandayati* (m. c. also °*te*; aor. *acaskándat*), to cause to jump or leap, R. (in explaining *skanda*); to pour out, effuse, shed, spill, emit (esp. seminal fluid), AitBr.; Mn.; to omit, neglect, Mn.; MBh. &c.; to cause to coagulate, thicken, Suśr.: Desid. *ciskantsati*, Gr.: Intens. *caniskadyate*, *canīskandīti* (Gr.), *kániskan*, *-canishkadat* (RV.), to leap, jump, hop &c. [Cf. Gk. σκάνδαλον; Lat. *scando*, *de-scendo*; *scāla* for *scant-(s)la*.]

Skanttṛi, mfn. one who leaps &c. (see *vi-shkanttṛi*).

Skandá, m. anything which jumps or hops (in *tṛiṇa-skandá*, 'grasshopper,' N. of a man), RV.; spurting, effusing, effusion, spilling, shedding (cf. *á-* and *ghrāṇa-sk*°); perishing, destruction, Gīt.; quicksilver, L.; 'Attacker,' N. of Kārttikeya (q. v., son of Śiva or of Agni; he is called god of war as leader of Śiva's hosts against the enemies of the gods; he is also leader of the demons of illness that attack children [cf. *-graha*], also god of burglars and thieves; cf. *-putra* and IW. 427, n. 1), MaitrS.; MBh. &c.; N. of Śiva, MBh.; a king prince, L.; a clever or learned man (cf. *skandha*), L.; the body, L.; the bank of a river, L.; MW.; N. of a man, g. *kuñjâdi* (pl., Saṃskārak.) **-kavaca**, n. N. of wk. **-gupta**, m. N. of a king, Inscr.; Vās., Introd.; of an elephant-keeper, Hcar. **-guru**, m. 'father of Skanda,' N. of Śiva, Śivag. **-graha**, m. the demon Skanda (causing disease), MBh.; Hariv.; Suśr. **-jananī**, f. 'Sk°'s mother,' Pārvatī, Kathās. **-jit**, m. 'conqueror of Sk°,' N. of Vishṇu, Pañcar. **-tā**, f. (MBh.) or **-tva**, n. (Bādar., Sch.) the condition of Sk°. **-dāsa**, m. N. of a merchant, Kathās. **-putra**, m. a son of Sk° (euphemistic term for a thief), Mṛicch. **-pura**, n. N. of a town, Rājat. **-purāṇa**, n. N. of a Purāṇa (consisting of several Saṃhitās, each of which contains a number of Khaṇḍas, the most celebrated being the Kāśī-khaṇḍa, chiefly intended to glorify Kāśī or Benares and exalt the sanctity of its shrines); *-samuccaya*, m. N. of wk.; °*nīya*, mfn. belonging to the Skanda-Purāṇa, Cat. **-bhaṭa**, m. N. of various persons, Inscr. **-bhaṭṭa**, m. N. of a man, Inscr. **-mātṛi**, f. 'mother of Sk°,' N. of Durgā, Cat. **-yāga**, m. N. of the 20th Pariśishṭa of the Atharva-veda. **-yāmala-tantra**, n. N. of wk. **-rāja**, m. the king Sk°, MBh. **-varman**, m. N. of various kings, Inscr. **-viśākha**, m. du. Sk° and Viśākha, g. *dadhi-paya-ādi*, Pat.; sg. N. of Śiva, MBh. (v. l. *skandha-v*°). **-shashṭhī**, f. the 6th day of the light half of the month Kārttika, Cat.; a festival in honour of Kārttikeya on the 6th day of the month Caitra, MW.; *-vrata*, n. a partic. religious observance, Cat.; N. of wk. **-sahasra-nāman**, n. 'the thousand names of Sk°,' N. of wk. **-skāra-śaṃkara** (?), m. N. of a poet, Subh. **-stotra**, n. N. of wk. **-svāmin**, m. N. of a Commentator, Cat. **Skandâṅśaka**, m. quicksilver, L. **Skandâgni**, w. r. for *skandhâgni*, L. **Skandâpasmāra**, m. a demon causing a partic. disease, MBh.; Suśr. **Skandâpasmārin**, mfn. attacked by the above disease, Suśr. **Skandârya**, m. N. of two Brāhmans, Inscr. **Skandêśvara-tīrtha**, n. N. of a Tīrtha, Cat. **Skandôpanishad**, f., **Skandôpapurāṇa**, n. N. of wks.

Skandaka, m. one who leaps or springs, MW.; a soldier, ib.; (prob.) n. a kind of metre, Sāh. (cf. *skandhaka*). **-grāma**, m. N. of a village, Rājat.

Skandana, n. spurting out, emission, effusion, dropping, Vait.; Yājñ., Sch.; failing to succeed, miscarrying, ŚrS.; TBr., Sch.; purging, evacuation of the bowels, L.; clotting or coagulation of blood, Suśr.; going, moving, W.

Skandanīya, mfn. to be emitted or poured out or effused, MW.

Skandita, mfn. emitted, effused, shed, Mn. ix, 50; going, W.

Skandin, mfn. (ifc.) effusing, shedding, Bālar.; Rājat.; coagulating (see *a-sk*°); leaping, jumping, MW.; bursting out, ib.

Skandola (?), mfn. cold, L.; m. coldness, ib.

Skandya, mfn. = *skanda iva*, g. *śākhâdi* (cf. *a-garta-sk*°).

Skanná, mfn. fallen, trickled down, emitted, sprinkled (as semen), RV.; Kāṭh.; ŚBr. &c.; gone, MW.; one who has failed, Hariv.; (accord. to Comm.) = *śushka*, *lambamāna*, or *unnata* (in *-skandhârdha-bhāga*), Hcar. (cf. *a-sk*°). **-tva**, n. the clotting or thickening of blood, Suśr.; Vāgbh. **-bhāga** (°*ná-*), mfn. one whose share is lost, Maitr.; Kāṭh.

Skānda, mfn. relating to Skanda &c., Sarvad.; composed by Skanda-svāmin (*-bhāshya*, n. N. of a Commentary); n. (with or scil. *purāṇa*) N. of the Skanda-purāṇa.

Skāndaviśākha, mfn. (fr. *skanda-v*°), Pāṇ. vii, 3, 21, Sch.

Skāndāyana, m. pl. (for next), g. *kuñjâdi*.

Skāndāyanya, m. patr. fr. *skanda*, ib.

स्कन्दिलाचार्य *skandilâcārya*, m. N. of a preceptor, Cat.

स्कन्ध् *skandh* (sometimes written *skand*), cl. 10. P. *skandhayati*, to collect, Dhātup. xxxv, 84.

स्कन्ध *skandhá*, m. (accord. to Uṇ. iv, 206, from √*skand* in the sense of 'rising'?) the shoulder, upper part of the back or region from the neck to the shoulder-joint (in men and animals), AV. &c. &c.; the stem or trunk of a tree (esp. that part of the stem where the branches begin), ŚāṅkhGṛ.; MBh. &c.; a large branch or bough, L.; a troop, multitude, quantity, aggregate (cf. *kari-*, *nara-sk*°), MBh.; BhP.; a part, division (esp. a division of an army or a form of military array), MBh.; Kāv. &c.; a chapter, section (of a book, system &c.), VarBṛS.; Car.; a tract, path, region (esp. of the winds, said to be seven), MBh.; Hariv.; (in phil.) the five objects of sense (see *vishaya*), W.; (with Buddhists) the five constituent elements of being (viz. *rūpa*, 'bodily form;' *vedanā*, 'sensation;' *saṃjñā*, 'perception;' *saṃskāra*, 'aggregate of formations;' *vijñāna*, 'consciousness or thought-faculty'), MWB. 109; (with Jainas) the body (in the widest sense, = *piṇḍa*), Sarvad.; a partic. form of the Āryā metre, Col.; a king, prince, L.; any article used at the coronation of a king (as a jar filled with consecrated water, an umbrella &c.), W.; a sage, teacher, ib.; war, battle, ib.; an engagement, agreement, ib.; a heron, ib.; equality of height in the humps of a pair of draught oxen, ib.; = *samparâya* and *bhadrâdi*, L.; N. of a serpent-demon, MBh.; of a poet, Cat.; often w. r. for *skanda*; (*ā*), f. a branch, L.; a creeper, L. **-cāpa**, m. 'shoulder-bow,' a sort of yoke or pole made of bamboo with a cord attached to either end for carrying burdens, L. **-ja**, mfn. growing from the stem, Āpast.; m. a tree growing from a principal stem (e. g. the gum olibanum tree &c.), MW. **-taru**, m. the cocoa-nut tree, L. **-deśa**, m. the region of the shoulder, MBh.; Śak.; the stem of a tree &c., Kathās.; the part about the shoulders or withers of an elephant (where the driver sits), MW. **-parinirvāṇa**, n. complete annihilation of the elements of being (with Buddhists), ib. **-pāda**, m. N. of a mountain, MārkP. **-pīṭha**, n. the sh°-blade, Kād. **-pradeśa**, m. the region of the shoulder, L. **-phala**, m. the cocoa-nut tree, L.; Ficus Glomerata, ib.; Aegle Marmelos, ib. **-bandhanā**, f. Anethum Panmorium, ib. **-maṇi**, m. a partic. amulet (= *asita-sk*°), Kauś., Sch. **-maya**, mf(*ī*)n., see *buddhi-skandha-m*°. **-mallaka**, m. a heron, L. **-māra**, m. (with Buddhists) one of the four Māras, Dharmas. 50. **-rāja**, w. r. for *skanda-r*°, MBh. **-ruha**, m. the Indian fig-tree, L. **-vat**, mfn. having a stem or a thick stem or many stems, MBh.; Hariv.; R.; MārkP. **-vaha**, **-vāha** or °**haka**, m. 'carrying burdens on the shoulders' (as an ox &c.), L. **-vāhya**, mf(*ā*)n. being carried on the shoulder of (ifc.), Hariv. **-viśākha**, w. r. for *skanda-v*°, MBh. **-śākhā**, f. a principal branch, L.; pl. the trunk and pr° branches, BhP. **-śiras**, n. the shoulder-blade, Kāv. **-śṛiṅga**, m. a buffalo, L. **-stambhi** (?), **-svāti** (?), m. N. of kings, VP. **-svāmin**, w. r. for *skanda-sv*° (q. v.) **Skandhâksha**, m. N. of one of Skanda's attendants, MBh. **Skandhâgni** or °**dhânala**, m. fire made with thick logs, L. **Skandhâvāra**, m. the king's camp or headquarters, royal residence, MBh.; R.; Kām. &c.; an army, L. **Skandhe-mukha**, mfn. having the face or mouth on the shoulders, MBh. **Skandhôpaneya**, mfn. to be carried on the sh°, W.; m. (scil. *saṃdhi*) a kind of treaty or alliance to maintain peace, a peace-offering, Kām.

Skandhaka, n. a kind of Āryā metre, VarBṛS.; Kāvyâd.

Skándhas, n. the shoulder, Uṇ.; the branching top or crown of a tree, RV.; TS.; AV.; the trunk of a tree, MW.

Skandhika, m. = *skandha-vāha*, L.

Skandhin, mfn. having a (big) stem, MBh.; m. a tree, L.

Skandhila, m. N. of a man, Buddh.

Skandhī-√kṛi, P. *-karoti*, to suspend over the shoulder, Nalac.

Skandho, in comp. for *skandhas*. **-grīvī**, f. N. of a partic. form of the Bṛihatī metre (v. l. °*vā*), RPrāt.; Nidānas. &c.

Skándhya, mf(*ā*)n. belonging &c. to the shoulder, AV.; AitBr.; = *skandha iva*, g. *śākhâdi*.

Skāndhin, m. pl. the disciples of Skandha, g. *śaunakâdi*.

स्कन्न *skanna*. See col. 2.

स्कम्भ् *skambh* or *skabh* (prob. a mere phonetic variety of √*stambh*, q. v.; in native lists written *skanbh*), cl. 5. 9. P. (Dhātup. xxxi, 8; Pāṇ. iii, 1, 82) *skabhnoti*, *skabhnāti* (accord. to Dhātup. x, 27 also cl. 1. Ā. *skambhate; pr.p. skabhnuvát*, Br.; *skabhát*, RV.; pf. *caskámbha*, 2. du. *-skambhdthuḥ*, ib.; p. *caskabhāná*, AV.; aor. *askambhīt*, Gr.; fut. *skambhitā, skambhishyati*, ib.; inf. *skambhitum*, ib.; *-skábhe*, RV.; ind. p. *skabhitví*, ib.), to prop, support, make firm, fix, establish, RV.; TS.; BhP.: Caus. *skambhayati* (aor. *acaskambhat*, Gr.; see *skambhita*) or *skabhāyáti* (Pāṇ. iii, 1, 84, Vārtt. 1, Pat.; see *skabhita*), to prop, support, fix, RV.; VS.; to impede, check, RV. x, 76, 4.

Skabdha. See *vi-shkabdha*, p. 998, col. 2.

Skabhana, n. = *śabda*, Vās. (Sch.)

Skabhitá, mfn. (fr. Caus.) supported, fixed, fastened, RV.

Skábhīyas, mfn. (compar.) supporting more or very firmly, ib.

Skambhá, m. a prop, support, pillar, buttress, fulcrum, the Fulcrum of the Universe (personified in AV. x, 7 and x, 8, and identified with Brahman, the Supreme Being, as well as with Purusha; see Muir's Sanskrit Texts, v, 378), RV.; AV.; N. of a man, g. *kuñjâdi*. **—deshṇa** (*skambhá-*), mfn. one whose gifts are firm, stable in giving (as the Maruts), RV. **—sárjana,** n. or °**nī,** f. a partic. part of a pillar, TS.; VS.

Skambhaná, n. a prop, pillar, RV.

Skambhaní or °**ní** (nom. °*nís*), id., TS.; VS.

Skāmbhāyana, m. pl. (of next), g. *kuñjâdi*.

Skāmbhāyanya, m. patr. fr. *skambha*, ib.

स्कवन *skavana*, see *danta-sk*°; cf. next.

स्कु *sku*, cl. 5. 9. P. Ā. (Dhātup. xxxi, 6; Pāṇ. iii, 1, 82) *skunoti, skunute; skunāti, skunīte* (only *-skunoti* and *-skauti* [ŚBr.] and *askunāt* [Bhaṭṭ.], *skutvā* [? ĀpŚr.] and *-skāvam* [TS.]; cf. *ā-√sku* and *niḥ-shku* [add.]), to tear, pluck, pick, poke; to cover, Bhaṭṭ.: Pass. *skūyáte*, to be stirred (as fire), MaitrS.: Caus. *skāvayati* (aor. *acuskavat*), Gr.: Desid. *cuskūshati*, °*te*, ib.: Intens. *coshkūyáte*, to gather up, collect, RV.; *coskūyate, coskoti*, Gr.

Coshkūyámāṇa, mfn., RV. i, 33, 3; Sāy. = *prayacchat* (Nir. vi, 22 = *dadat*), bestowing.

स्कुन्द् *skund* (= √*skand*), cl. 1. Ā. *skundate*, to jump (*āpravaṇe* or *āplavane*), Dhātup. ii, 8; to lift up (*uddharaṇe*; cf. *pra-skunda*), ib.

स्कुम्भ् *skumbh* (in native lists written *skunbh*; connected with √*skambh*), cl. 5. 9. P. (Dhātup. xxxi, 8; Pāṇ. iii, 1, 82) *skubhnoti, skubhnāti* (*skuptvā*, ind. p. [prob. w. r. for *skutvā* [ĀpŚr.]), to hold, stop, hinder (*rodhane*).

स्कृ *skṛi* = √1. *kṛi*, in *upa-, pari-*, and *saṃ-skṛi*.

Skṛit = *kṛit* in *kosa-skṛit*, q. v.

स्कृधोयु *skṛidhoyu*. See *á-skṛ*°.

स्कोटिका *skoṭikā*, prob. w. r. for *sphoṭikā*.

स्कोनगर *sko-nagara*, n. N. of a village of the Bāhikas, Kaiy.

Skaunagarika, mf(*ā* or *ī*)n. (fr. prec.), ib.

स्खद् *skhad*, cl. 1. Ā. *skhadate* (pf. *caskhade*; fut. *skhaditā* &c.), Dhātup. xix, 6: Caus. *skhādayati*, Dhātup. xix, 72; Vop. xviii, 24.

Skhadana, n. (only L.) cutting or tearing to pieces, hurting, killing, harassing, discomfiting; firmness.

Skhadā, f., g. *gavādi*.

Skhadyā, f. (fr. prec.), ib.

स्खल् *skhal*, cl. 1. P. (Dhātup. xv, 37) *skhalati* (rarely °*te*; pf. *caskhāla, caskhaluḥ*, MBh. &c.; fut. *skhalitā*, °*lishyati*, Gr.; aor. *askhālīt*, ib.; inf. *skhalitum*, ib.), to stumble, trip, totter, waver, fluctuate (with *na*, 'not to waver, remain steadfast, prevail'), MBh.; Kāv. &c.; to drop or slip down, trickle down, MW.; to stammer, falter (as speech), Yājñ.; Kālid.; BhP.; to make mistakes, blunder, err, fail, Kāv.; Car.; Rājat.; to gather, collect, Dhātup.; to move, MW.; to disappear, ib.: Caus. *skhalayati* (or *skhālayati*, Dhātup. xix, 59), to cause to falter, Kum.; to stop, arrest, BhP.

Skhala, m. stumbling, tottering, Prasaṅg. (cf. *apa-skhala*).

Skhalat, mfn. (pr. p.), see below.

Skhalad, in comp. for *skhalat* above. **—valaya,** mfn. one whose bracelet falls off or slips down, Bhartṛ. (v. l.) **—vākya,** mfn. making mistakes in speaking, stammering, faltering, blundering, Yājñ.

Skhalan, in comp. for *skhalat*. **—mati,** mfn. erring in judgment, weak-minded, MW.

Skhalana, n. stumbling, tottering, tripping, unsteady gait, Suśr.; Kām.; BhP.; faltering, stammering (in *vāk-skh*°), g. *khaṇḍv-ādi*; displacement (of a garment), Caurap.; rubbing, friction, touch, contact, collision, Śiś.; discharge, emission (of semen), Kull. on Mn. v, 63; falling into (comp.), BhP.; being deprived of (abl.), MBh.; mistake, blundering in (comp.), Amar.

Skhalita, mfn. stumbling, tripping, unsteady (as a gait), MBh.; Kāv. &c.; dropping, falling, dripping, trickling down, Mālatīm.; intoxicated, drunk, W.; stammering, faltering (speech), Kāv.; Kathās.; stopped, checked, obstructed, impeded, interrupted, frustrated, baffled, Kāv.; Pañcat.; BhP.; confounded, perplexed by (instr.), Śiś.; incomplete, deficient (opp. to *ulbaṇa*), ŚāṅkhBr.; erring, failing, blundering in (loc.), Śak.; awkward about (loc.), VarBṛS.; (*am*), n. the act of tripping, stumbling, staggering, MBh.; R. &c.; mistake, error, failure, blunder, blundering in (loc. or comp.), ib.; loss, deprivation, Ratnāv.; circumvention, stratagem (in war), L. **—gati,** mfn. having an unsteady gait, tottering, staggering, VarBṛS. **—vat,** mfn. gone astray, deviated from (*-tas*), Śāntiś. **—vīrya,** mfn. one whose heroism has been frustrated or disappointed, Ragh. **—subhagam,** ind. dashing or leaping along pleasantly (over a rocky bed, said of a stream), Megh.

स्खुड् *skhuḍ*, v. l. for √*sthuḍ*, q. v.

स्तक् *stak*, cl. 1. P. *stakati*, to strike against, Dhātup. xix, 20.

स्तन् *stan* (cf. √2. *tan*), cl. 1. P. (Dhātup. xiii, 18) *stanati* (once in BhP. *-stanase*; in RV. 3. sg. *stan* and 2. Impv. *stanihi*; pf. *tastāna, tastanuḥ*, Gr.; aor. *astānīt*, AV.; fut. *stanitā*, °*nishyati*, Gr.), to resound, reverberate, roar, thunder, RV. &c. &c.; to utter inarticulate sounds, Vās.: Caus. *stanáyati* (aor. *atishṭanat*), id. (*stanayati*, 'it thunders'), RV. &c. &c.; crackle (as fire), AitBr.: Desid. *tistanishati*, Gr.: Intens. *taṇstanyate, taṇstanti*, ib. (2. sg. Impv. *taṇstanīhi*, see *abhi-shṭan*). [Cf. Gk. στένω; Slav. *stenją*; Angl. Sax. *stunian*; Germ. *stöhnen*.]

Stána, m. (or n., g. *ardharcâdi*, ifc. *ā* or *ī*; derivation doubtful, but prob. connected with √*stan*, from the hollow resonance of the human breast), the female breast (either human or animal), teat, dug, udder, RV. &c. &c.; the nipple (of the female or the male breast), Suśr.; a kind of pin or peg on a vessel shaped like a teat, ŚBr. **—kalaśa,** m. a jar-like breast, Pañcat.; Vās.; N. of a bard (w. r. °*lasa*), Mudr. **—kuḍmala,** n. 'breast-bud,' a woman's br°, Hit. **—kuṇḍa,** n. (sg. or pl.) N. of a Tīrtha, MBh. **—kumbha,** m. = *-kalaśa* above, Vās. **—keśavatī,** f. having breasts and long hair, IndSt. **—koṭi,** f. the nipple of the br°, Ragh. **—koraka,** m. n. a bud-like br°, Gīt. **—graha,** m. the sucking or drawing of the br°, Kauś. **—cūcuka,** n. the nipple of the br°, Suśr. **—taṭa,** m. n. the projection of the female br°, Kāv. **—tyāga,** m. 'leaving the mother's breast,' weaning, Mālatīm. **—dātrī,** f. giving the breast, suckling, Pañcar. **—dveshin,** mfn. rejecting the br°, Suśr. **—ṃ-dha,** mfn. = *-ṃ-dhaya*, BrahmavP. **—ṃ-dhama,** mfn., Vop. **—ṃ-dhaya,** mf(*ī* or [L.] *ā*)n. sucking the breast; m. a suckling, infant, Kāv.; MantraBr. &c.; m. a calf, Śiś. **—pa,** mf(*ā*)n. drinking or sucking the breast; a suckling, Jātakam. **—patana,** n. flaccidity of the breast, Bhartṛ. **—pā,** mfn. = *-pa*, W. **—pātṛi,** mfn. sucking the breast of (comp.), Pañcar. **—pāna,** n. the drinking or sucking of the br°, MBh.; VarBṛS. &c. **—pāyaka,** mfn. = *-pa*, MW. **—pāyika,** m. pl., v. l. for *-poshika*, MBh.; (*ā*), f. a female child still unweaned, L. **—pāyin,** mfn. = *-pa*, Kṛishṇaj. **—poshika,** m. pl. N. of a people (v. l. *-yoshika* &c.), MBh. **—bāla,** m. pl. N. of a people, ib.; VP. **—bhara,** m. 'breast-weight,' a swelling bosom, Ratnāv.; a man with a br° like a woman's, W. **—bhava,** mfn. being on the breast, MW.; m. a partic. posture in sexual union, L. **—maṇḍala,** n. 'breast-orb,' = *-taṭa*, Dhūrtas. **—madhya,** m. a nipple, MW.; n. the space between the breast, Vikr. **—mukha,** m. (?) n. a nipple, L. **—mūla,** n. 'root of the breast,' the lower part of the female breast, Suśr. **—yodhika** (VP.) or **-yoshika** (MBh.), m. pl. N. of a people (v. l. *-poshika*). **—roga,** m. a disease of the female breast, Cat. **—rohita,** m. n. a partic. part of the female breast, Suśr. **—vatī,** f. possessing teats, TāṇḍyaBr.; a woman, Harav. **—vṛinta,** n. 'breast-stalk,' a nipple, L. **—vepathu,** m. the heaving of the breast, Śak. **—śikhā,** f. 'br°-point,' a nipple, L. **Stanâṇśuka,** n. a cloth covering the bosom, Vikr. **Stanâgra,** n. = °*naśikhā*, L. **Stanâṅga-rāga,** m. pigment on a woman's breast, MW. **Stanântara,** n. the space between the breasts, centre of the chest (of men and women), Kāv.; Suśr.; the heart (as between the br°s), W.; a mark on the breast (indicating future widowhood), ib. **Stanā-bhúj** (in Padap. *stana-bh*°), mfn. enjoying the udder (said of calves), RV. **Stanā-bhuja,** mfn. feeding or nourishing with the udder (said of cows), MW. **Stanâbhoga,** m. fulness of the br°, Prab.; the curve or orb of the breast, a man with projecting br° (like a woman's), W. **Stanâvaraṇa,** n. a breast-cloth (*-tā*, f.), Kāv. **Stanôttarīya,** n. id., ib. **Stanôpapīḍam,** ind. p. pressing the breast, Sāh.

Stanátha, m. roar (of a lion), RV.; thunder, MW.

Stanáthu, m. roar (of a lion), AV.

Stanana, n. the sound of a hollow cough, Car.; sounding, sound, noise, L.; the rumbling of clouds, ib.; = *kunthana, kunthita*, ib.; groaning, breathing hard, W.

Stanáyad-ama, mfn. (cf. 1. *ama*) having a roaring onset (said of the Maruts), RV.

Stanayitnú, m. (sg. or pl.) thunder (pl. personified as children of Vidyota, 'Lightning'), RV.; AV.; VS. &c.; a th°-cloud, Kāv.; BhP.; lightning, L.; sickness, ib.; death, ib.; a kind of grass (= *mustaka*), MW. **—ghosha,** mfn. loud as thunder, MW. **—mat** or (w. r.) **-vat,** mfn. connected with thunder, MBh. **—sáni,** mfn. bringing thunder, TS.; MaitrS.

Stanasyú, mfn. sucking the breast, a suckling, AV.

Stanita, mfn. thundering, sounding, MBh.; n. (ifc. f. *ā*) thunder, Kauś.; Mn.; MBh. &c.; loud groaning, Hariv.; the sound of a vibrating bow-string, BhP.; the noise of clapping the hands, L. **—kumāra,** m. pl. (with Jainas) a partic. class of gods, L. **—phala,** m. Asteracantha Longifolia, L. **—vimukha,** mfn. refraining from thunder, Megh. **—samaya,** m. the time of thundering, ib. **—subhagam,** ind. with pleasant rumbling sounds, Megh.

Stanín, mfn. having a breast or udder, MaitrS.; (said of a horse having a partic. deformity), L.

Stanya, mfn. contained in the female breast, RV., Sch.; n. (once m.) milk, MBh.; Suśr.; Kāv. &c. **—tyāga,** m. ceasing to drink a mother's milk, the being weaned, Kāv.; *-mātraka* (with *vayas*), n. the period immediately after weaning, Uttarar. **—da,** mfn. producing (good) milk, Bhpr. **—dāna,** n. the giving of milk from the breast, HPariś. **—pa,** mfn. drinking milk from the breast, a suckling, Suśr. **—pāna,** n. the drinking of milk from the breast, the period of early infancy, Kāv. **—pāyin** or **-bhuj,** mfn. sucking milk from the breast, unweaned, MW. **—roga,** m. sickness caused by unhealthy mother's milk, Bhpr. **Stanyâvataraṇa,** n. the inspissation of milk, Suśr.

स्तनुतृ *stanutṛi* (?), TPrāt.

स्तबक *stabaka*, m. (accord. to L. also n.; ifc. f. *ā*; also written *stavaka*; prob. connected with *stamba, stambaka*) a cluster of blossoms, bunch of flowers, nosegay, tuft, MBh.; R. &c.; a feather of a peacock's tail, BhP.; a tassel, Hariv.; a quantity, multitude, L.; a chapter or section (in such books as contain in their titles the words *latā, latikā, mañjarī* &c.) **—kanda,** m. a partic. bulbous plant, L. **—phala,** m. a partic. fruit-tree, L. **—saṃnibha,** mfn. resembling (clusters of) blossoms, R.

Stabakâcita, mfn. covered with blossoms, in blossom, MW.

Stabakaya, Nom. P. °*yati*, to provide with (clusters of) blossoms, Hcar.; Kād.

Stabakita, mfn. (g. *tārakâdi*) full of blossoms, Vās.

स्तब्ध *stabdha* &c. See p. 1258, col. 1.

स्तभ *stabha*, m. a goat or ram (cf. *stubha*), L.

स्तम् *stam*. See √1. *sam*, p. 1152, col. 1.

स्तम्ब *stambá*, m. (prob. phonetic variation of *stambha*) a clump or tuft of grass, any clump or bunch or cluster, AV. &c. &c.; a sheaf of corn, L.

a bush, thicket, L.; a shrub or plant having no decided stem (such as the Jhiṇṭī or Barleria), L.; the post to which an elephant is tied (wrongly inferred from *stambe-rama*, q.v.), L.; a mountain, L.; N. of various men, Hariv.; Pur.; n. (in these senses prob. w.r. for *stambha*, m.) a post, pillar i.g., W.; stupidity, insensibility, W. **–kari**, mfn. forming clumps or bunches, Hcar.; m. corn, rice, L.; *-tā*, f. formation of abundant sheaves or clusters of rice, Mudr. **–kāra**, mf(*ī*)n. making a clump, forming a cluster, W. **–ghana**, m. 'clump-destroyer,' a small hoe for weeding or eradicating clumps of grass, a sickle for cutting corn &c., L. **–ghāta**, m. cutting grass &c., L. **–ghna**, mf(*ī*)n. clump-destroying, weed-destroying, Bhaṭṭ.; m. = *-ghana*, L. **–já**, mfn. (prob.) bunchy, tufty, shaggy, AV. **–pur**, f. N. of the city Tāmalipta (q.v.), L. **–mitra**, m. (cf. *stambha-m°*) N. of a son of Jaritā, MBh.; (with *Śārṅga*) of the author of RV. x, 142, 7; 8, Anukr. **–yajus**, n. N. of a partic. formula and religious observance on removing clumps of grass, ŚrS. **–vatī**, f. N. of a woman, Hariv. **–vana**, m. N. of a man, ib. **–śás**, ind. by clumps or tufts, TBr. **–hanana**, n. and **-hananī**, f. = *-ghana*, L.

Stambaka, m. a clump, bunch, tuft, MBh.

Stambakāya, Nom. Ā. *°yate*, to become a bunch of flowers &c., Harav.

Stambakita, v.l. for *stabakita*, g. *tārakâdi*.

Stambin, mfn. clumpy, tufty, bunchy, bushy, shaggy, MaitrS.

Stambe-rama, m. (fr. loc. of *stamba* + *r°*) 'delighting in clumps of high grass,' an elephant, Kāv. **Stamberamâsura**, m. N. of an Asura (= *gajâsura*), Bālar.

स्तम्भ *stambh* or **stabh** (connected with √*skambh*, q.v.; in native lists written *stanbh*), cl. 5. 9. P. (Dhātup. xxxi, 7) *stabhnóti, stabhnā́ti* (cf. Pāṇ. iii, 1, 82), or cl. 1. Ā. (x, 26) *stámbhate* (pr.p. also *stambhat*, Hariv., *stabhamāna* [q.v.], AitĀr.; pf. *tastámbha*, *°mbhat*, *tastabhúḥ*; p. *tastabhvás*, *°vānā́*, RV.; *tastabhānā́*, *tastambhe*, MBh.; aor. *ástambhīt*; *astāmpsīt*, TBr.; *astabhat*, Gr.; fut. *stambhitā*, *°bhishyati*, ib.; inf. *stabdhum*, Kathās.; ind. p. *stabdhvā́*, AV. &c.; *stambhitvā*, MBh.; *-stábhya* and *-stambham*, Br.), to fix firmly, support, sustain, prop (esp. the heavens), RV.; AV.; Br.; to support or hold up by contact with, reach up to (acc.), MBh.; Hariv.; to stop, stop up, arrest, make stiff or immovable, paralyze, RV. &c. &c.; (Ā.) to rest or lean on (loc.), Hcar.; to become stiff or immovable, Bhaṭṭ.; to become solid, MBh. xii, 6807: Pass. *stabhyate* (aor. *astambhi*), to be firmly fixed or supported or propped &c., MBh.; Kāv. &c.: Caus. *stabhāyáti*, to make firm, support, RV.; to stop, arrest, ib.; *stambhayati*, *°te* (aor. *atastambhat*), to fix, establish, erect, MBh.; Kāv. &c.; to make stiff or rigid, paralyze, Suśr.; to make solid, ib.; to stop, arrest (also by magic), suppress, check, restrain, ib.: Desid. *tistambhishati*, Gr.: Intens. *tāstabhyate*, ib. [Cf. Gk. στέμφυλον, στέμβω, στείβω; Lith. *stambras*, *stimbras*; Germ. *stampfôn*, *stampfen*; Eng. *stamp*, *stump*.]

Stabdha, mfn. firmly fixed, supported, propped &c.; reaching up to (loc.), ŚvetUp.; MBh.; stiff, rigid, immovable, paralyzed, senseless, dull (*am*, ind.), MBh.; Kāv. &c.; solidified (as water), Hariv.; puffed up, proud, arrogant, ChUp.; Bhag. &c.; tardy, slack, slow (?), VarBṛS.; obstinate, stubborn, hard-hearted, MW.; coarse, ib. **–karṇa**, m. 'stiff-eared,' N. of an antelope, Hariv.; of a lion, Hit.; **-śirodhara**, mfn. holding the ears and the neck stiff, MBh. **–gātra**, mfn. holding the limbs stiff, Buddh. **–tā**, f. fixedness, rigidity, stiffness (of the membrum virile), Car.; pretentiousness, arrogance, MBh.; Kām. **–toya**, mfn. (a river) whose water has solidified, Hariv. **–tva**, n. stiffness (of the navel &c.), ŚārṅgS.; haughtiness, arrogance, Kathās. **–dṛishṭi**, mfn. having motionless (i.e. unwinking) eyes, Pañcat. **–nayana**, mfn. id., MBh. **–pāda**, mfn. one who has paralyzed legs, stiff-legged, lame (*-tā*, f.), Suśr. **–pūrṇa-koshṭha**, mfn. one who has a swollen or full abdomen (*-tā*, f.), ib. **–bāhu**, mfn. stiff-armed, Kathās. **–mati**, mfn. dull-minded, MārkP. **–meḍhra**, mfn. one whose sexual organ has become stiff (*-tā*, f.), Suśr. **–roma-kūpa**, mfn. one who has the pores of the skin stopped up (*-tā*, f.), ib. **–roman**, m. 'stiff-haired,' a boar, hog, L. **–locana**, mfn. having fixed or unwinking eyes (said of the gods), MBh. **–vapus**, mfn. one whose body is benumbed or paralyzed, HPariś. **–śrotra**, mfn. stiff-eared, Rājat. **–sakthi**, mfn. stiff-thighed, lame (*-tā*, f.), Suśr. **–sambhāra** (?), m. a Rākshasa, L. **–hanu**, mfn. having stiff or immovable jaws, Suśr. **Stabdhâksha**, mfn. = *stabdha-dṛishṭi*, Hariv. **Stabdhôda**, mfn. = *stabdha-toya*, ib. **Stabdhôrdhva-karṇa**, mfn. having the tips of the ears stiff or immovable, BhP.

Stabdhi, f. fixedness, hardness, rigidity, firmness, immobility, stupor, numbness, obstinacy, MW.

Stabdhī, in comp. for *stabdha*. **–karaṇa**, n. stiffening, making rigid, paralyzing, W. **–√kṛi**, P. *-karoti* (ind. p. *-kṛitya*), to make stiff or rigid, Hit. **–bhāva**, m. the becoming stiffened or rigid, torpidity, Vedântas.

Stabhamāna, mfn. making one's self stiff, behaving arrogantly, assuming an air of authority, AitĀr.

Stabhi, m. rigidity, L.

Stabhitá, mfn. fixed, established, supported, RV.; AV.

Stabhu (see next).

Stabhūya (fr. prec.), Nom. P. Ā. *°yáti*, *°yáte* (only in pr. p. *stabhūyát* and *°yámāna*), to stand firm, RV.

Stambha, m. (ifc. f. *ā*) a post, pillar, column, stem (as of a tree; also improperly applied to an arm), Kāṭh.; GṛŚrS.; MBh. &c.; support, propping, strengthening, Bhartṛ.; inflation, pretentiousness, arrogance, MBh.; R. &c.; fixedness, stiffness, rigidity, torpor, paralysis, stupefaction, MBh.; Kāv. &c.; becoming hard or solid, Rājat.; stoppage, obstruction, suppression (also the magical arresting of any feeling or force, as of hunger, thirst, or of the forces of water, fire &c. as taught in the Tantras), Kāv.; Suśr.; Pañcar.; filling up, stuffing, R.; N. of a partic. Adhyāya, Pat. on Pāṇ. v, 2, 60, Vārtt. 1; of a Ṛishi &c., VP. (cf. g. *kuñjâdi* and *śaunakâdi*). **–kara**, mfn. (prob.) causing obstruction, hindering, impeding (in *puṇya-st°*, q.v.), causing stiffness, paralyzing, MW.; m. a fence, railing, W. **–kāraṇa**, n. cause of obstruction or impediment, MW. **–tā**, f. stiffness, paralysis, Sāh. **–tīrtha**, n. N. of a place, Pañcat. **–pūjā**, f. worship of the posts (of the temporary pavilions erected for marriages or other festive occasions), MW. **–bhañjaka**, m. 'pillar-breaker,' N. of an elephant, Mṛicch. **–mitra**, m. N. of a Ṛishi (= *stamba-m°*), IndSt. **–vatī**, f. N. of a city, Siṇhâs. **Stambhôtkīrṇa**, mfn. carved out of a wooden post (as a statue), MW.

Stambhaka, mfn. stopping, arresting, R.; styptic, astringent, ŚārṅgS.; m. (prob.) a post, pillar, Mahāvy.; N. of one of Śiva's attendants, Kathās.; (*akī*), f. N. of a goddess, Kālac.; (*ikā*), f. the leg of a chair, Nalac.

Stambhakin, m. a kind of musical instrument covered with leather, L.

Stambhana, mf(*ī*)n. stiffening, making rigid or immovable, paralyzing, Kāv.; HPariś.; stopping, arresting, checking, restraining, MBh.; R.; styptic, astringent, Suśr.; m. 'paralyzer,' N. of one of the five arrows of Kāma-deva, Cat.; (*ī*), f. a kind of magic, Divyâv.; n. the act of turning into a pillar (see *rambhā-st°*); strengthening, supporting, Kāv.; Pañcar.; becoming stiff or rigid, Suśr.; making stiff or rigid, paralyzing, Vās.; Bālar.; a means of making stiff or rigid, Hcat.; stopping, arresting (also by magical means), MBh.; VP.; stopping flow of blood &c.; a styptic or astringent, Car.; a partic. magical art or faculty (see under *stambha* and cf. *jala-stambhana*). **–prakāra**, m. N. of a medic. work. **Stambhanâdi-vidhi**, m. N. of a Mantra.

Stambhanaka, mf(*ikā*)n. making solid, solidifying, HPariś.

Stambhanīya, mfn. to be fixed or stopped or checked (in *a-st°*), MBh.; to be treated with styptics, Car.

Stambhi, m. the sea, L.

Stambhita, mfn. (fr. Caus.) fixed, established, supported, Hariv.; stiffened, benumbed, paralyzed, Kathās.; stopped, brought to a standstill, suppressed, restrained, MBh.; Kāv. &c.; (ifc.) stuffed or filled with, Lalit. **–tva**, n. the being checked or impeded (in *sarva-loka-bhayâst°*). **–bāshpa-vṛitti**, mfn. suppressing the flow of tears, MW. **–rambha**, n. N. of a Troṭaka (cf. *rambhā-stambhana*), Sāh. **Stambhitâsru**, mfn. one who has suppressed his tears, ib.

Stambhin, mfn. provided with pillars or columns, Pracaṇḍ.; supporting, MW.; puffed up, arrogant, MBh.; stopping, restraining, MW.; m. the sea, L.; (*inī*), f. N. of one of the five Dhāraṇās or elements (= the earth; cf. *bhramaṇī*), Cat.

Stambhī-√bhū, P. *-bhavati*, to become a post, Hit.

Stambhīya, mfn. (said of a partic. Adhyāya), Pat. on Pāṇ. v, 2, 60, Vārtt. 1.

Stāmbhāyana, m. patr. fr. *stambha*, g. *naḍâdi*.

Stāmbhin, m. pl. the disciples of Stambha, g. *śaunakâdi*.

स्तर *stara*, *staraṇa*, *stariman* &c. See p. 1260, col. 1.

स्तरी *starī́*, f. (nom. *ī́s*, acc. *yàm*; pl. *yàs*) a barren cow, heifer, RV.; (with *rā́tri*) a night passed in vain, TS.; smoke, vapour, L. [Cf. Gk. στεῖρος, στέριφος; Lat. *sterilis*; Goth. *staira*; Germ. *stěr*, *stěro*; *Stärke*.]

Starī-√kṛi, P. *-karoti*, to render fruitless, Kāṭh.

स्तव 1. *stava*, m. or n. a partic. substance, Divyâv. **–karṇikā**, f. a lac-earring (?), ib. **–karṇin**, m. N. of Deva-trāta, ib.

स्तव 2. *stava*, *stavaka* &c. See p. 1259, col. 1.

स्तवत् *stavát*, mfn. (only in nom. sg. *stavā́n*; always applied to Indra and accord. to Sāy. RV. vi, 24, 8 = *stūyamāna*, 'being praised;' accord. to others = *stavas* = *tavas*, fr. √*stu* for √1. *tu*, and meaning 'strong, powerful;' others give it the sense 'thundering,' fr. √*stan*), RV.

स्तवरक *stavaraka*, m. a fence, railing (perh. w.r. for *āvaraka* or *stambha-kara*), L.

स्ताघ *stāgha*, mfn. shallow (see *a-stāgha*).

स्तामन् *stāmán*, m. (of unknown meaning; accord. to some w.r. for *srāman*, accord. to others for *sthāman*), AV. v, 13, 5.

स्तामु *stāmú*, mfn. (doubtful; accord. to Sāy. = *stotṛi*; accord. to others 'roaring, thundering,' fr. √*stan*, cf. *stavat*), RV. vii, 20, 3.

स्तायत् *stāyát*, *°yú*. See √*stai*, p. 1260.

स्ति *stí*, m. (only in acc. plur. *stī́n*; fr. √1. *as*, cf. *úpa-sti*, *abhí-* and *pári-shṭi*) a dependent, vassal, RV. **–pā́**, mfn. protecting dependents, ib.

स्तिघ *stigh*, cl. 5. P. *stighnoti* (accord. to Dhātup. xxvii, 18 Ā. *stighnute*; Pot. *stighnuyāt*, inf. *-stigham*; Gr. also pf. *tishṭige*; aor. *asteghishṭa*; fut. *steghitā*, *°ghishyate*; inf. *steghitum*), to step, stride, step up, mount (esp. in *ati-√stigh*, 'to step over, overstep,' and in *pra-√stigh*, 'to step up, rise up &c.'), MaitrS.: Desid. *tishṭighishati* (in *ati-tishṭighishan*, 'wishing to ascend'), ib. [Cf. Gk. στείχω; Slav. *stignąti*; Goth. *steigan*; Germ. *stîgan*, *steigen*; Eng. *sty*.]

स्तिप *stip* (cf. *step*), cl. 1. Ā. *stepate*, to ooze, drip, drop, Dhātup. x, 3.

स्तिपा *sti-pā́*. See above under *stí*.

स्तिभि *stibhi*, m. a clump, bunch, tuft (cf. *stabaka*, *stamba*), KātyŚr.; the sea, Uṇ. iv, 121, Sch.; an obstacle, obstruction (cf. *stambha*), L. **–vat**, mfn. = *phala-vat*, ĀpŚr. (Sch.)

Stibhini, f. a clump, tuft &c. = *stibhi*, Sch. on KātyŚr.

Stimbhi, m. = *stibhi*, L.

स्तिम् *stim* or *stīm* (cf. √*tim*), cl. 4. P. *stimyati* or *stīmyati*, to be or become wet or moist, Dhātup. xxvi, 17; to become fixed or immovable (see next).

Stimita, mfn. wet, moist, Naish.; Caurap.; fixed, motionless (cf. *stambhita*), MBh.; Kāv. &c.; still, calm, tranquil, soft, gentle (*am*, ind.), ib.; pleased, MW.; n. moisture, ib.; stillness, motionless, MBh. **–java**, mfn. advancing slowly or softly, Ragh. **–tā**, f. (Kād.), **-tva**, n. (Mālatīm.) steadiness, fixedness, stillness, absence of motion. **–nayana**, mfn. having the eyes intently fixed (cf. *stabdha-dṛishṭi*), Megh. **–pravāha**, m. flowing gently along, Ragh. **–vāyu**, m. still air, MW. **–samādhi-śuci**, mfn. pure through intense meditation, Kir. **–sthita**, mfn. standing still or motionless, Kathās. **Stimitâyatâksha**, mfn. keeping (his) large eyes intently fixed, MW.

Stimitaya, Nom. P. *°yati*, to make motionless or still, Kpr.

Stīmá, mf(*ā́*)n. (accord. to some fr. √*styai*) sluggish, slow, AV.

Stema, m. = *tema*, wetness, moisture, L.

Staimitya, n. (fr. *stimita*) fixedness, rigidity, immobility, numbness, Kāv.; Suśr.

स्तिया *stiyā*, f. stagnant water. See under √*styai*, p. 1260, col. 3.

स्तिरे *stire*. See √1. *stṛi*, p. 1260, col. 1.

स्तीम् *stīm*. See √*stim*, p. 1258, col. 3.

Stīmita, mfn. moist &c., L. (see *stimita*).

स्तीर्ण *stīrṇa* &c. See p. 1260, col. 2.

स्तीर्वि *stīrvi*, m. (said to be fr. √1. *stṛi*, only L.) an officiating priest (esp. an Adhvaryu, q. v.); a kind of grass; the sky, atmosphere; water; blood; the body; fear; N. of Indra.

स्तु 1. *stu*, cl. 2. P. Ā. (Dhātup. xxiv, 34; cf. Pāṇ. vii, 3, 95) *staúti* or *stavīti*, *stute* or *stuvīte* (in RV. also *stávate*, 3. sg. *stave* [with pass. sense], 1. 3. sg. *stushé*, Impv. *stoshi*, p. [mostly with pass. sense] *stuvāná*, *stávāna* or *stavāná*, *stávamāna*; in BhP. *stunvanti*, in Up. p. *stunvāna*; pf. *tushṭāva*, *tushṭuvús*, *tushṭuvé*, RV. &c. &c.; aor. *astāvīt* or *astaushīt*, Br. &c.; *stoshat*, *stoshāṇi*, RV.; *ástoshṭa*, ib. &c.; Prec. *stūyāt*, Gr.; fut. *stavitā* or *stotā*, Vop.; fut. *stavishyáti*, °*te*, RV.; *stoshyati*, °*te*, Br. &c.; Cond. *astoshyat*, Bhaṭṭ.; inf. *stotum*, ib. &c.; *stavitum*, Vop.; *stótave*, *stavádhyai*, RV.; ind. p. *stutvā́*, AV. &c.; *-stútya*, Br. &c.; *-stūya*, MBh. &c.), to praise, laud, eulogize, extol, celebrate in song or hymns (in ritual, 'to chant,' with loc. of the text from which the Sāman comes), RV. &c. &c.: Pass. *stūyáte* (aor. *astāvi*), to be praised or celebrated; *stūyamāna*, mfn. being praised, ib.: Caus. *stāvayati* (aor. *atushṭavat*, RV.; °*ṭuvat*, JaimBr.), to praise, celebrate; (*stāvayate*), to cause to praise or celebrate, BhP.: Desid. *tushṭūshati*, °*te* (p. p. *tushṭūshita*), to wish to celebrate, Śaṃk.: Intens. *toshṭūyate*, *toshṭoti*, Gr.

2. **Stáva**, m. (for 1. see p. 1258, col. 3) praise, eulogy, song of praise, hymn, panegyric, RV. &c. &c. **-cintāmaṇi**, m., **-daṇḍaka**, m. or n., **-mālā**, f. N. of wks. **-rāja**, m. 'chief of hymns,' a partic. mystical prayer or incantation (also as N. of wk.) **Stavâmṛita-laharī**, f. N. of wk. **Stavârha**, m. 'worthy of praise,' N. of a Pratyeka-buddhi, Divyâv. **Stavâvali**, f. N. of various collections of hymns or panegyrics.

Stavaka, m. praise, eulogium, L.; a panegyrist, praiser, W.

Stavát (nom. sg. *staván*). See p. 1258, col. 3.

Stavátha, m. praise, RV.

Stavádhyai. See above under root.

Stavana, n. praising, praise, Lāṭy.; BhP.; pl. songs of praise, BhP.

Stavanīya, mfn. to be praised, praiseworthy, Vop.

Stavanyà, mfn. id., Suparṇ.

Stavamāna, **stavāna**. See root.

Stavi, m. = *udgātṛi*, a chanter, L.

Stavitavya, mfn. to be praised &c., MW.

Stavitṛí, m. a praiser, singer, MaitrS.

Staveyya, m. N. of Indra, L.

Stavya, mfn. to be praised, praiseworthy, glorious, MBh.; Hariv. &c.

Stāva, m. praise, eulogy, Inscr.; a praiser, MW.; (*ā́*), f. N. of an Apsaras, VS.

Stāvaka, mfn. praising, extolling, Sāy. (*-tva*, n., Kull.); m. a praiser, panegyrist, BhP.; Sarvad.

Stāvya, mfn. to be praised or celebrated, Pāṇ. iii, 1, 123.

2. **Stu**. See *su-shṭú*, p. 1238, col. 1.

Stút, (ifc.) praising, celebrating (see *indra-*, *chandaḥ-*, *deva-stut* &c.); f. a hymn of praise, RV.

1. **Stutá**, mfn. (for 2. see col. 3) praised, eulogized, hymned, glorified, celebrated, RV. &c. &c.; recited with praise (as a hymn), ŚāṅkhŚr.; m. N. of Śiva, MBh.; n. praise, eulogy, RV.; Br.; ChUp.; (in ritual) = *stotra*, TS. **-vat**, mfn. having received praise, praised, celebrated, Hariv. **-śastrá**, n. du. Stotra and Śastra, TS.; Br. &c.; *-vat*, mfn. joined or connected with St° and Ś°, ĀpŚr. **-stoma** (*stutá-*), mfn. one whose praise has been sung, hymned, glorified, VS. **-svāmi-kshetra**, n. N. of a sacred place, Cat.

Stuti, f. (instr. once in Hariv. *stutinā*, with v.l. *stutibhiḥ*) praise, eulogy, panegyric, commendation, adulation, RV. &c. &c.; N. of Durgā, DevīP.; of Vishṇu, MBh.; of the wife of Pratihartṛi, BhP. **-kusumâñjali**, m. 'handful of flowers,' N. of a poem in praise of Śiva. **-gītaka**, n. a song of praise, panegyric, Kathās. **-candrikā**, f., **-ṭīkā**, f. N. of wks. **-pada**, n. an object of pr°, Subh. **-pāṭhaka**, m. 'praise-reciter,' a panegyrist, bard, herald (esp. of a prince, = 1. *bandin*), Pañcar. **-priya**, mfn. fond of praise, MW. **-brāhmaṇa**, N. of a wk. (or of a man), Buddh. **-bhāga**, m. N. of wk. **-maṅgala**, n. pl. praises and benedictions, Hariv. **-mat**, mfn. possessing or knowing hymns of pr°, ib. **-mantra**, m. a song or hymn of pr°, VarYogay. **-vacana**, n. (Pañcat.), **-vacas**, n. (Śiś.), **-vāda**, m. (MW.) laudatory speech, eulogy. **-vrata**, m. 'one whose duty is pr°,' a bard &c. (cf. *-pāṭhaka*), L. **-śabda**, m. a word of praise, R. **-śastra**, w. r. for *stuta-ś°* (q. v.) **-śīla**, mfn. skilful in praise (v. l. *śruti-ś°*), R. **-sāra**, m., **-sûkti-mālā**, f. N. of wks.

Stutya, mfn. to be praised, laudable, praiseworthy, MBh.; R. &c.; (*ā*), f. a partic. fragrant bark, L.; alum-slate, L. **-tva**, n. praiseworthiness, Sāy. **-vrata**, m. N. of a son of Hiraṇya-retas and the Varsha ruled by him, BhP.

Stuvat, mfn. (pr. p.) praising &c.; m. a praiser, worshipper, RV.

Stuvāna, mfn. praising (Sāy. 'being praised'). See root, col. 1.

Stuvi, m. a praiser, worshipper, L.; a sacrifice, L.

Stushéyya, mfn. (w. r. *stuveya* and *stushepya*) praiseworthy, excellent, RV.

Stotavya, mfn. to be praised or celebrated, MaitrUp.; MBh.

Stotṛí, mfn. praising, worshipping, RV.; AV.; m. N. of Vishṇu, MBh.

Stotrá, n. praise, eulogium, a hymn of praise, ode, RV. &c. &c.; (in ritual) N. of the texts or verses which are sung (in contradistinction to the Śastras [q. v.] which are recited), TS.; Br.; ŚrS. **-kārin**, mfn. reciting a Stotra, Jaim. **-jāla**, n., **-pāṭha**, m., **-prakaraṇa**, n., **-bhāshya**, n., **-ratna**, n. N. of wks. **-rāja**, m. N. of a Śaiva (author or wk.; cf. *stava-rāja*). **-vat**, mfn. accompanied by Stotras, Kāṭh.; ŚāṅkhŚr. **-varga**, m., **-vyākhyā**, f. N. of wks. **-samīshantī**, f. a partic. Vishṭuti, Lāṭy. **Stotrâdi-pāṭha**, m. N. of work. **Stotrârha**, mfn. worthy of praise, MW. **Stotrâvalī**, f. N. of wk.

Stotraya, Nom. P. °*yati*, to celebrate with a hymn of praise, Cat.

Stotríya and °**trīya**, mfn. relating or belonging or peculiar to a Stotra, SaṃhitUp.; m. (scil. *tṛica* or *pragātha*) the first part of the Bahish-pavamāna, Br.; ŚrS.; (*ā*), f. (scil. *ṛic*) a Stotra verse, ib.

Stóma, m. praise, eulogium, a hymn, RV.; AV.; GṛS.; Up.; BhP.; (in ritual) a typical form of chant (7 such forms are usually enumerated; but accord. to Lāṭy., Sch. the Stoma consists of 5 parts, viz. *prastāva*, *udgītha*, *pratihāra*, *upadrava*, and *nidhana*), TS.; Br.; ŚrS.; ChUp.; a Stoma day, TS.; PañcavBr.; a sacrificer, L.; N. of partic. bricks, ŚBr.; a heap, collection, number, multitude, quantity, mass, Kāv.; Rājat.; the letting of a dwelling, Āpast., Sch.; a measure of 10 Dhanv-antaras or of 96 inches, L.; n. (only L.) the head; riches, wealth; grain, corn; an iron-pointed stick or staff; mfn. crooked, bent, L. **-kshāra**, m. soap, L. **-citi**, f. piling up the bricks called Stoma, BhP. **-tashṭa** (*stóma-*), mfn. fashioned or formed into a hymn (or into the subject of a hymn), composed by poets, RV. **-purogava** (*stóma-*), mfn. having the Stoma as a leader or chief, MaitrS. **-pṛishṭha** (*stóma-*), mf(*ā*)n. having St° and Pṛishṭhas, VS.; TS. **-bhāga** (*stóma-*), mf(*ā*)n. one whose share is the Stoma, AitBr.; m. pl. N. of partic. verses (29 in number, which belong to the Soma sacrifice and are employed while laying the fifth layer of bricks), TS.; VS.; Br.; ŚrS.; (*ā*), f. pl. the bricks above mentioned, TS.; ŚBr.; °*gika*, mf(*ī*)n. belonging to the Stoma-bhāga verses, Vait. **-máya**, mf(*ī*)n. consisting of St°, ŚBr. **-yoga**, m. N. of wk. **-várdhana**, mfn. augmenting (or delighting in) hymns of praise, RV. **-vāhas** (*stóma-*), mfn. offering or receiving praise, RV. **-vṛiddhi**, f. enhancement of the St° (cf. *-vardhana*). **Stomâyaná**, n. N. of partic. sacrificial animals, ŚBr.

Stomaya, Nom. P. °*yati*, to praise, laud, hymn, Dhātup. xxxv, 69.

Stomīya, mfn. (ifc.) relating to a Stoma, ŚBr.

Stómya, mfn. id., PañcavBr.; worthy of a hymn of praise, laudable, RV.

Stauti, m. (used as a N. for √1. *stu*, 'to praise'), Śiś. xiv, 66.

स्तु 3. *stu* (prob. invented to serve as a root for the words below), to be clotted or conglomerated; to trickle.

4. **Stu** (= *stukā*) in *pṛithu-shṭu*, q. v.

1. **Stuka**, m. (= next) in *keśa-st°*, q. v.

Stúkā, f. a knot or tuft of hair or wool, thick curl of hair (esp. between the horns of a bull), RV.; AV.; ŚBr.; (?) a hip, thigh (= *jaghana*), Nir. xi, 32. **-vín**, mfn. having tufts of hair, shaggy, RV. **-sárgam**, ind. after the form of a curl or knot of hair, ŚBr.

Stukī, f. (v. l. for *śukī*) = *stoka-ghṛita-dhārā*, BhP. (Sch.)

2. **Stuta**, mfn. (for 1. see col. 1) dripping, oozing (v. l. *sruta*), L.

Stupá, m. (cf. *stūpa*) a knot or tuft of hair &c. (see *stúkā*), VS.; ŚBr.

Stūpa &c. See p. 1260, col. 1.

Stoká, m. (accord. to some for *skota* fr. √*ścut*; cf. Nir. ii, 1) a drop (of water &c.), RV.; AV.; Br.; ŚrS.; BhP.; a spark (see *agni-st°*); the Cātaka bird, L.; mf(*ā*)n. little, small, short (ibc. and *am*, ind. 'a little, slightly, gradually;' *bahutaram-stokam*, 'more-than;' *stokena na*, 'not in the least;' *stokena* and *stokāt* in comp. with a p. p. = 'hardly,' 'with some difficulty,' 'only just,' 'a little while ago' [cf. Pāṇ. ii, 1, 39; 3, 33]), MBh.; Kāv. &c. **-kāya**, mfn. 'little-bodied,' diminutive, W. **-tamas**, mfn. a little dark, Pracaṇḍ. **-tā**, f. (Uttamac.), **-tva**, n. (Campak.) littleness, insignificance. **-namra**, mf(*ā*)n. a little bent down, slightly depressed, Megh. **-pāṇḍura**, mfn. a little pale, BhP. **-śas**, ind. drop by drop, sparingly, AitĀr. **Stokâyus**, mfn. short-lived, BhP. **Stokâvaśesha-prāṇa**, mfn. id. (lit. 'having little breath left'), Rājat. **Stokônmishat**, mfn. feebly flickering, ib.

Stokaka, m. the Cātaka bird, MBh.; R. &c.; a kind of poison (= *vatsa-nābha*), L.

Stokīya or **stókya**, mf(*ā*)n. relating to or connected with drops (applied to the oblations of ghee and the verses employed while drops of it are falling), Br.; ŚrS.

स्तुक 2. *stuka* = *toka*, a child or young animal, TĀr.

स्तुच् *stuc*, cl. 1. Ā. *stocate*, to be bright or propitious (*prasāde*), Dhātup. vi, 15.

स्तुनक *stunaka*, m. (cf. *stubha*) a goat, L.

स्तुभ् 1. *stubh* (connected with √1. *stu* and *stumbh*), cl. 1. P. (Naigh. iii, 14) *stóbhati* (only in pres. base; 3. sg. *stobdhi*, JaimBr.; p. Ā. *stubhāna*, RV.; Gr. also pf. *tushṭubhe*; fut. *stobhitā* &c.), to utter a joyful sound, hum, make a succession of exclamations, shout (esp. applied to the chanted interjections in a Sāman), RV.; Br.; Lāṭy.; cl. 1. Ā. *stobhate*, to pause, stop, cause to stop, paralyze &c. (*stambhe*), Dhātup. x, 34: Caus. *stobhayati* (aor. *atushṭubhat*), to praise in successive exclamations, celebrate, RV. [Cf. Eng. *stop*.]

Stubdha, mfn. chanted, praised, hymned, Br.

2. **Stúbh**, (ifc.) uttering joyful sounds, praising (cf. *anu-*, *tri-shṭubh*, *vṛisha-stubh* &c.; accord. to some *stubh* in the first two comp. means 'stopping, pausing,' the metre requiring regular stoppages or pauses; but see *anu-shṭubh*); f. joyful exclamation or cry, praise, RV.; m. a praiser, Naigh. iii, 16.

Stúbhvan, mfn. trilling, shouting, praising, RV.

Stobdhavya, mfn. to be praised &c., JaimBr.

Stobha, m. a chanted interjection in a Sāman (such as *hum*, *ho*, *ohā* &c.), hum, hurrah, hymn, Br.; ŚrS.; MBh.; BhP.; a partic. division of the Sāma-veda (q. v.); torpor, paralysis = *ceshṭā-vighāta*, Nalac.; disrespect, contumely (= *helana*), L. **-cchalā**, f. N. of a ch. of the Sāma-veda-cchalā. **-pada**, n. N. of a treatise on the Stobha. **-prakṛiti**, f. N. of a part of the Sāma-veda. **-vat**, mfn. attended with Stobhas, L. **Stobhânusaṃhāra**, m. N. of a Pariśishṭa of the Sāma-veda.

Stobhana, mf(*ī*)n. (prob.) forming a Stobha, Nir. vii, 12 (in quot.). **-saṃhāra**, prob. w. r. for *stobhânusaṃhāra* (above).

Stobhita, mfn. (fr. Caus.) praised in successive exclamations or shouts, BhP.

Staubha, mf(*ī*)n. humming, making joyful exclamations, hurrahing, Lāṭy.

Staubhika, mfn. forming or containing a Stobha, ib.

स्तुभ *stubha*, m. N. of an Agni, MBh.; a goat (cf. *tubha*, *stábha* and *stunaka*), L.

स्तुम्प् *stump*. See *pra-s-√tump*, p. 699.

स्तुम्भ् *stumbh* (cf. *√stambh* and *stubh*; in native lists written *stunbh*), cl. 5. 9. P. *stubhnoti*, *stubhnāti*, to stop, stupefy; expel (Dhātup. xxxi, 7; Pāṇ. iii, 1, 82). Cf. Eng. *stop*, *stump*.]

स्तुव *stuva*, m. or n.(?) a partic. part of the head of a horse, L.

स्तुवेय *stuveya*, *stusheyya*. See p. 1259.

स्तू *stū*. See *āyata-* and *ghṛita-stū*.

स्तूणाकर्ण *stūṇākarṇa*, w.r. for *sthūṇ°*, q.v.

स्तूप् *stūp* (prob. invented as a root for *stūpa* below), cl. 4. 10. P. *stūpyati* or *stūpayati*, to heap up, pile, erect, Dhātup. xxvi, 127; xxxii, 133. [Cf. Gk. στύφω, στυφελός?.]

Stū́pa, m. (accord. to Sāy. fr. *√styai*, accord. to Uṇ. fr. *√3. stu*; prob. connected with *stupá*, under *√3. stu*) a knot or tuft of hair, the upper part of the head, crest, top, summit [cf. Gk. στύπος], RV.; TS.; PañcavBr.; a heap or pile of earth or bricks &c., (esp.) a Buddhist monument, dagoba (generally of a pyramidal or dome-like form and erected over sacred relics of the great Buddha or on spots consecrated as the scenes of his acts), MWB. 504; any relic-shrine or relic-casket (made of various materials, such as terra cotta, clay, elaborately formed brick or carved stone; often very small and portable, and enclosing a fragment of bone or a hair &c. of some saint or deceased relative, or inscribed with a sacred formula; these are carried long distances and deposited in hallowed spots such as Buddha-Gayā), MWB. 397, 504; any heap, pile, mound, tope, Hcat.; the main beam (of a house), ĀpGṛ.; (L. also, 'wind; fight; = *kūla*; = *bala*; = *nishprayojana*'). **-pṛishṭha**, m. 'hard-backed,' a turtle, tortoise, L. **-bimba**, n. = *-maṇḍala*, Kāraṇḍ. **-bhedaka**, m. the destroyer of a tope, ib. **-bhedana**, n. destruction of a tope, Buddh. **-maṇḍala**, n. the circumference or extent of a tope, Rājat. **Stūpêśāna**, m., Kāś. on Pāṇ. vi, 2, 64 (v.l. *sūp°*).

Staupika, n. = *buddha-dravya*, the relics deposited in a Stūpa or dagoba, L.; a kind of small broom carried by a Buddhist or Jaina ascetic, W.

स्तृ 1. *stṛi* (or *stṝi*), cl. 5. 9. P. Ā. (Dhātup. xxvii, 6; xxxi, 14) *stṛiṇóti*, *stṛiṇute* or *stṛiṇā́ti*, *stṛiṇīté* (Ved. and ep. also *stárati*, *°te*; pf. *tastā́ra*, *tastare* [3. pl. *tastaruḥ*, *tastarire*], Br. &c.; 3. sg. [with pass. sense] *tistiré*, RV.; 3. pl. *tastrire*, AV.; p. Ā. *tistirāṇá*, RV.; aor. *ástar*, *star*, ib.; *astṛishi*, *astṛita*, AitBr.; *astarīt*, AV.; *astārshīt*, *astarīshṭa*, *astīrshṭa*, Gr.; Prec. *stṛishīya*, AV.; *staryā́t* or *stīryā́t*; *stṛishīshṭa*, *starīshīshṭa*, *stīrshīshṭa*, Gr.; fut. *startā*, Gr.; *starishyati*, *te°* [Gr. also *starīsh°*], Br. &c.; inf. *startum* or *starītum*, Gr.; *stártave*, *°tavai*, *starītavai*, Br.; *stárītave*, AV.; *-stíre*, *-stṛiṇīshā́ṇi*, RV.; ind. p. *stīrtvā́* or *stṛitvā́*, Br.; *-stī́rya*, ib.; *-stṛitya*, MBh.), to spread, spread out or about, strew, scatter (esp. the sacrificial grass; in this sense in older language only cl. 9. P. Ā.), RV.; AV.; Br.; ŚrS.; R.; to spread over, bestrew, cover, KātyŚr.; MBh. &c.; (cl. 5. P. Ā.) to lay low, overthrow, slay (an enemy), RV.; AV.; Br.; Up.: Pass. *stīryate* (*°ti*) or *striyáte* (Gr. also *staryate*; aor. *ástāri*), to be spread or strewn &c., RV. &c. &c.: Caus. *stārayati* (aor. *atastarat*), to spread, cover, Bhaṭṭ.: Desid. *tistīrshate* or *tústūrshate* (Gr. also P. and *tistarīshati*, *°te*), to wish to spread or strew or lay low, Br.; Up.: Intens. *tāstaryate*, *testīryate*, *tāstarti*, Gr. [Cf. Gk. στορέννυμι, στρώννυμι; Lat. *sternere*; Goth. *straujan*; Germ. *streuen*; Angl. Sax. *streowian*; Eng. *strew*.]

Stara, m. (cf. *pra-*, *vi-*, *sva-stara*) a layer, stratum, Līl.

Staraṇa, n. the act of spreading or strewing or scattering (esp. the sacrificial grass), ŚrS.; the plastering (of a wall), ĀśvŚr. (Sch.)

Staraṇīya, mfn. to be spread or strewn or scattered, MW.

Stariman, m. 'that which is spread,' a bed, couch, Uṇ. iv, 147, Sch.

Stárīman, m. the act of spreading or scattering (only loc. *°maṇi* as inf.), RV.; = prec. (cf. *sushṭar°*), Uṇ. iv, 147, Sch.

Staru, m. 'overthrower,' an enemy, PārGṛ.

Startave, *°tavai*. See root.

Stárya, mfn. to be laid low or overthrown, ŚBr.

Stīrṇá, mfn. spread, strewn, scattered, RV.; AV. &c.; m. N. of a demon attendant on Śiva, ŚivaP. **-barhis** (*stīrṇá-*), mfn. one who has strewn the sacrificial grass, RV.

Stīrṇi, (prob.) f. = *sam-stara*, L.

2. **Strí**, m. (only in pl. nom. *stríṇas* [?], gen. *stṛiṇā́m* [v.l. *stṛīṇā́m*] and instr. pl. *stṛíbhis*; cf. *tṛí*, nom. pl. *tā́ras*) a star (as the 'light-strewer' or [pl.] the 'scattered ones'), RV.; Jyot.; a mark or star-like spot (on the forehead of a bull or cow), RV. [Cf. Lat. *stella*; Germ. *Stern*; Eng. *star*; accord. to some for *as-tṛi* (*√2. as*); cf. Gk. ἀστήρ, ἄστρον.]

Stṛiṇīshaṇi, inf. (with prep. *upa*). See root.

Stṛita, mfn. bestrewn, covered, MBh.; overthrown, Kāṭh.

Stṛiti, f. the act of bestrewing or covering, Vop.; striking down, overthrowing, TS.; Kāṭh.

Stṛitya, mfn. to be struck down or overthrown, AitBr.

Stairṇi, m. patr. fr. *stīrṇa*, Pat.

स्तृ 3. *stṛi*. See *√spṛi*, p. 1268, col. 3.

स्तृक्ष् *stṛiksh* (cf. *√tṛiksh*), cl. 1. P. *stṛikshati*, to go, Dhātup. xvii, 9.

स्तृण *stṛiṇa*. See *bhū-stṛiṇa*.

स्तृह् *stṛih* or *stṝih* (cf. *√tṛih*), cl. 6. P. (Dhātup. xxviii, 58) *stṛihati*, to injure, do harm, Āpast.

स्तेग *stegá*, m. (of unknown meaning; cf. *tega*), RV.; VS.

स्तेन् *sten* (prob. Nom. fr. *stena* below), cl. 10. P. (Dhātup. xxxv, 43) *stenayati*, to steal, rob, Mn. viii, 333; (with *vācam*) to misuse a word, be dishonest in speech, ib. iv, 256.

Stená, m. (prob. fr. *√stā*) a thief, robber, RV. &c. &c.; a kind of perfume, VarBṛS., Sch.; thieving, stealing, MW. **-nigraha**, m. the restraining or punishing of thieves, ib.; suppression of theft, ib. **-hṛidaya** (*stená-*), m. 'having the essence of a thief,' an incarnate thief, VS.

Staina, n. = next, L.

Stainya, n. (fr. *stena*) theft, robbery, MBh.; m. a thief, L.

स्तेप् *step* (cf. *√stip*), cl. 1. Ā. *stepate*, to flow, Dhātup. x, 4; cl. 10. P. *stepayati*, to send, throw, ib. xxxii, 132 (Vop.)

स्तेम *stema*. See p. 1259, col. 1.

स्तै *stai*, cl. 1. P. *stāyati*, to put on, adorn (v.l. for *√snai*, q.v.), Dhātup. xxii, 25; to steal, do anything stealthily (only in pr. p. *stā́yát* [AV.] and in the following derivatives).

Stāyú, m. = *tāyu*, a thief, robber, VS.

Stéya, n. theft, robbery, larceny, RV. &c. &c.; anything stolen or liable to be stolen, BhP.; anything clandestine or private, MW. **-kṛit**, mfn. committing theft, a thief, robber, stealer of (comp.), Mn. iv, 256; xi, 99. **-phala**, m. a partic. fruit-tree, L. **-saṃvāsika**, mfn. one who has stolen into any dwelling in the fictitious character of a monk, Buddh.

Steyi, in comp. for *steyin*. **-phala**, m. = *steyaph°*, L.

Steyin, m. a thief, robber, Mn.; MBh. &c.; a mouse, L.; a goldsmith, L.

स्तैमित्य *staimitya*. See p. 1259, col. 1.

स्तो *sto*. See *ghṛita-sto*.

स्तोक *stoka* &c. See p. 1259, col. 3.

स्तोतव्य *stotavya*, *stotra* &c. See p. 1259, col. 2.

स्तोभव्य *stobdhavya*, *stobha* &c. See p. 1259, col. 3.

स्तोम् *stom*. See *stomaya*, p. 1259, col. 2.

स्तौन *staunā́*, mfn. (of unknown meaning; accord. to Sāy. = *stena*, 'a thief, robber;' accord. to others, 'heavy, inert, slothful,' fr. *√stū* = *sthū* = *sthā*), RV. vi, 66, 5.

स्तौपिक *staupika*. See col. 1.

स्तौभिक *staubhika*. See col. 1.

स्तौला *staulā*, f. (of unknown meaning; accord. to Sāy. fem. of an adj. = *sthūla*), RV. vi, 44, 7.

स्त्येन *styena*, m. a thief, robber (cf. *stena*), L.; nectar (in this sense prob. fr. *√styai*), L.

Styaina, m. a thief, robber, L.

स्त्यै *styai*, cl. 1. P. *styāyati*, to be collected into a heap or mass, Dhātup. xxii, 14; to spread about, ib.; to sound, ib.; cl. 1. Ā. *styāyate* (pr. p. *styāna*, q.v.; ind. p. *-styāya*; see *ni-shtyai*), to stiffen, grow dense, increase, Uttarar.; Mcar.

Stiyā, f. (prob.) still or stagnant water, RV.

Styāna, mfn. grown dense, coagulated, Suśr.; Sāh.; stiffened, become rigid, Car.; soft, bland, unctuous, smooth (= *snigdha*), L.; thick, bulky, gross, W.; sounding, MW.; n. (only L.) density, thickness, grossness, massiveness; unctuousness; nectar; idleness, sloth, apathy; echo, sound.

Styāya. See *sam-styāya*.

Styāyana, n. collecting into a mass, aggregation, crowding together, Nir.

स्त्राट *strāṭa* (?), Pañcad.

स्त्रि *stri* (?) = 2. *stṛi*, a star (q.v.)

स्त्रितमा *stri-tamā*, *stri-tarā*. See *stri-t°* under *strī*.

स्त्री *strī́*, f. (perhaps for *sūtrī* or *sotrī*, 'bearer of children,' fr. *√2. sū*; accord. to some connected with Lat. *sator*; nom. *strī́*; acc. in later language also *strīm* and *strīs*, pl.) a woman, female, wife, RV. &c. &c.; the female of any animal (e.g. *śākhā-mṛiga-strī*, 'a female monkey'), ŚBr.; MBh.; a white ant, L.; the Priyaṅgu plant, L.; (in gram.) the feminine gender, Nir.; ŚBr. &c.; a kind of metre, Col. **-kaṭi** or **-kaṭī**, f. the female hip, L. **-karaṇa**, n. sexual connection, L. **-karman**, n. N. of the 2nd part of the 4th Adhyāya of the Kauśika. **-kāma** (*strī́-*), mfn. desirous or fond of women, TS.; AitBr. &c. (*-tama*, superl., Āpast.); desirous of female offspring, ĀśvGṛ.; m. desire for women or for a wife, MW. **-kārya**, n. attendance on women, Mn. x, 47. **-kitava**, m. a deceiver or seducer of women, L. **-kumāra**, n. sg. (g. *gavāśva*) or m. pl. (Virac.) w° and child. **-kṛita** (*strī́-*), mf(*ā*)n. made or done by women, AV.; n. sexual connection, Gaut. **-kośa**, m. 'w°'s treasure,' a dagger, L. **-kshīra**, n. mother's milk, Mn. v, 9. **-kshetra**, n. a female i.e. even (not odd) zodiacal sign (the 2nd, 4th &c.) or astrological mansion, Laghuj. **-ga**, see *anya-strī-ga*. **-gamana**, n. going to women, sexual union with w°, PārGṛ.; R.; *°nīya*, mfn. (see *guru-str°*). **-gavī**, f. a milch cow, Pāṇ. iii, 3, 71, Sch. **-guru**, m. a female Guru or priestess (who teaches initiatory Mantras), MW. **-graha**, m. a female planet (cf. *-kshetra*), IndSt. **-grāhin**, mfn. (in law) accepting (the guardianship over) a w°. **-ghātaka**, mfn. murdering a w° or wife, Vet. **-ghosha**, m. 'marked by the voices of women,' dawn, daybreak, L. **-ghna**, mfn. = *-ghātaka*, Mn. ix, 232. **-cañcala**, mfn. going after w°, VarBṛS. **-caritra**, n. the doings of w°, MW. **-citta-hārin**, mfn. captivating the heart of w°, L.; m. Moringa Pterygosperma, L. **-cihna**, n. 'w°'s mark,' the female organ, L. **-caura**, m. 'w°-thief,' a libertine, L. **-jana**, m. woman-kind, Kāv.; Rājat.; (in gram.) a feminine, R. vii, 87, 13. **-jananī**, f. bringing forth (only) daughters, Mn. ix, 81. **-janman**, n. the birth of a girl, VarBṛS.; (*°ma*)*-pattra-vicāra*, m. and *-pattrī-bhāvādhyāya*, m. N. of wks. **-jātaka**, n. the nativity of a girl, VarBṛS.; N. of various wks. (also *-ṭīkā*, f. and *-paddhati*, f.) **-jāti**, f. the female sex, MW. **-jita**, mfn. ruled by w° or by a wife, 'henpecked,' MBh.; R. &c. **-tamā** or **-tarā**, f. (superl. and comp.) a thorough or more thoroughly a woman (also *stri-t°*), Pāṇ. vi, 3, 44. **-tā**, f. = *-tva*, W. **-tānuka-roga**, m. a kind of disease, Cat. **-tva**, n. womanhood, wifehood, MBh.; R. &c.; (in gram.) feminineness, Cat. **-devata**, mf(*ā*)n. addressed to a female deity, ib. **-dehārdha**, m. 'he who has half of (his) body female,' N. of Śiva (cf. *ardha-nārīśa*), L. **-dvish** or **-dveshin**, m.

'w°-hating,' a mysogynist, VarBṛS. **-dhana**, n. 'w°'s wealth,' a wife's peculiar property (said to be of six kinds, *adhy-agnika, adhy-āvāhanika, ādhivedanika, prīti-datta, śulka, anv-ādheya*), Gaut.; Mn.; Yājñ. &c. (cf. IW. 267, n. 1); *-nirṇaya*, m., *-prakaraṇa*, n. N. of wk; *-lolupa*, mfn. coveting (another's) wife and property, Kām. **-dharma**, m. the duty of a woman, W.; the laws concerning w°, Mn. i, 114; copulation, Hariv.; VP.; menstruation, L.; *-paddhati*, f. N. of wk.; *-yoga*, m. the application of laws or customs relative to women, W. **-dharmiṇī**, f. a woman during menstruation, MBh.; Rājat. **-dhava**, m. a woman's husband, a man, L. **-dhūrta**, m. = *-kitava*, L. **-dhūrtaka**, n. sg. women and rogues, MBh. **-dhvaja**, m. 'having the mark of a female,' the female of any animal, L.; an elephant, L. **-nātha**, mfn. having a w° as lord or protector, MW. **-nāman**, mfn. bearing a female name, MBh. **-nibandhana**, n. a woman's peculiar province, domestic duty, housewifery, W. **-nirjita**, mfn. = *-jita*, VarBṛS.; BhP. **-°ndriya** (*strīnd°*), n. the female organ, Divyâv. **-paṇyôpajīvin**, m. one who lives by keeping prostitutes, MW. **-para**, m. 'devoted to women,' a libertine, L. **-parvata-deśa**, m. N. of a district, Cat. **-parvan**, n. N. of the 11th book of the Mahābhārata (describing the lamentations of queen Gāndhārī and the other women over the slain heroes), IW. 374. **-piśācī**, f. a fiend-like wife, Prab. **-puṃ-yoga**, m. the union of man and wife, Gaut. **-puṇs**, m. (nom. *-pumān*) man and wife, ŚBr.; Lāṭy. &c.; a woman who has become a man, MBh. **-puṇsa**, m. du. man and wife, Yājñ.; MBh. &c.; (in gram.) masculine and feminine, L.; (sg.) one who is both man and woman, MBh.; *-lakshaṇā*, f. a masculine w°, hermaphrodite, L.; *-liṅgin*, mfn. having the marks of man and w°, Car. **-puṃ-dharma**, m. the law (or duties) of husband and wife, Yājñ., Sch. (IW. 261). **-puṃnapuṇsaka**, (in gram.) feminine (and) masculine (and) neuter. **-pura**, n. the women's apartments, MBh. **-purusha**, n. sg. man and wife, Hcat. **-pushpa**, n. the menstrual excretion, Kālac. **-pūrusha**, n. = *-purusha*, Siṇhâs. **-pūrva**, mfn. = next, MBh.; = *strī-jita*, ib. **-pūrvaka** or **-pūrvin**, mfn. one who was a woman in a former birth (w. r. *°vika*), ib. **-prajñā**, f. having a w°'s understanding, ŚBr. **-pratyaya**, m. a feminine suffix, Pāṇ., Sch.; *-prakaraṇa*, n. N. of wk. **-pradhāna**, mfn. one to whom women are chief, devoted to w°, R. **-pramāṇa**, mfn. regarding w° as authorities, Laghuk. **-prasaṅga**, m. intercourse with w°, Suśr. **-prasū**, f. = *-jananī*, Yājñ. **-prâya**, mfn. mostly feminine, Āpast. **-priya**, mfn. dear to w°, L.; Mangifera Indica, L.; the Aśoka tree, L. **-bandha**, m. union with w°, sexual union, L. **-bādhya**, mfn. one who suffers himself to be distressed by a woman, MārkP. **-bāla-ghātin**, m. a murderer of w° and children, Mn. viii, 89. **-buddhi**, f. the female understanding, MW. **-bhaga**, n. the female organ, Nir. iii, 16. **-bhava**, m. state of a w°, womanhood, Subh. **-bhāga** (*strí-*), mfn. fond of w°, going after w°, AV. **-bhāva**, m. the becoming a wife (acc. with √*nī* or Caus. of √*labh*, 'to deprive of virginity'), Hariv. **-bhūshaṇa**, n. 'woman's ornament,' Pandanus Odoratissimus, L. **-bhṛitya**, m. pl. women and servants, MW. **-bhoga**, m. 'enjoyment of women,' sexual intercourse, MārkP. **-mat**, m. 'wife-possessor,' a married man, Bhaṭṭ. **-madhya**, n. society of w°, Car. **-mantra**, m. a female Mantra (i.e. one ending with *svāhā*), Sarvad.; a w°'s counsel, female stratagem, MW. **-maya**, mf(*ī*)n. feminine, Vās.; effeminate, womanish, Śaṃk. **-mānin**, m. N. of the son of Manu Bhautya, MārkP. **-māyā**, f. w°'s craft, Lalit. **-mukha**, n. a woman's mouth; *-pa*, m. or *-madhu*, n. or *-madhu-dohada*, m. or *-madhu-dohala*, m. drinking or desiring the nectar of a w°'s mouth, Mimusops Elengi (accord. to some also 'the Aśoka'), L. **-m-manya**, mfn. = *striyam-manya*, col. 2. **-yantra**, n. a woman regarded as the mere instrument or tool of man, Bhartṛ. **-yācita-putra**, m. a son obtained through a wife's solicitations, MW. **-rajas**, n. 'w°'s impurity,' menstruation, L. **-rañjana**, n. 'liked by w°,' betel (chewed with areca-nut and lime), L. **-ratna**, n. 'jewel of a woman,' an excellent woman, Kāv.; VarBṛS. &c. (with Buddhists, 'one of the seven treasures of monarchs,' Dharmas. 85); N. of Lakshmī, Śak.; *-kūṭā*, f. N. of a daughter of Raudrāśva, Hariv. **-rahas-kāma**, mfn. one who seeks to be alone with w°, Car. **-rājya**, n. 'women's realm,' a region (perhaps in Bhutān) peopled by Amazonian women, MBh.; VarBṛS. &c. **-rāśi**, m. = *-kshetra*, IndSt. **-rūpa** (*strí-*), mfn. having a w°'s form or shape, MaitrS. **-roga**, m. any disease incident to w°, Cat. **-lakshaṇa**, n. any characteristic of w°, MBh.; *-vid*, mfn. acquainted with those ch°, Jātakam. **-lampaṭa**, mfn. desirous of w°, Kathās. **-liṅga**, n. the female organ, MBh.; (in gram.) the feminine gender, Vop.; (*-vartin*, mfn. 'being in the f° g°, being a f°'), MW.; mfn. having the characteristics of a w°, ŚrS.; MBh. &c.; (in gram.) feminine (*-tva*, n.), IndSt. **-loka**, m. 'women's world,' N. of a country (cf. *-rājya*), R. **-lola**, mfn. = *-lampaṭa*, VarBṛS. **-laulya**, n. fondness for w°, Bhar. **-vadha**, m. the slaying of a woman, Kṛishṇaj. **-vaśa**, mfn. subject to w°, ruled by a woman, Subh.; n. submissiveness to w° &c., W. **-vaśya**, mfn. = prec. (*-tā*, f.), R.; Hariv. **-vākyâṅkuśa-prakshuṇṇa**, mfn. driven or urged on by the goad of a w°'s words, Pañcat. **-vāsa**, m. an ant-hill, L. **-vāsas**, n. a garment fit for sexual union, Āpast., Sch. **-vāhya**, m. pl. N. of a people, MārkP. **-vijita**, mfn. = *-jita*, VarBṛS. **-vitta**, n. property coming from a wife, L. **-vidheya**, mfn. submissive to a wife, uxorious, W. **-viyoga**, m. separation from a wife, MW. **-vivāha**, m. marriage with a woman, Mn. iii, 20. **-vishaya**, m. 'w°'s sphere,' sexual connexion, VP.; mfn. only feminine, Śāntiś. **-vṛita**, mfn. surrounded or attended by women, W. **-vesha-dhāraka** or **°rin**, mfn. wearing a w°'s garments, L. **-vyañjana**, n. pl. the bodily marks of womanhood (e.g. breasts &c.), ĀpŚr.; *-kṛitā*, mfn. a girl who has reached puberty, L. **-vraṇa**, m. the female organ, Kpr. **-śūdrâdi-dina-caryā-krama**, m., **-śūdrâdīnāṃ devârcana-vicāra**, m. N. of wks. **-śesha**, mfn. having only w° left (said of the world), MBh. **-śauṇḍa**, mfn. fond of w°, L. **-śroṇi**, f. a woman's hip, Suśr. **-shaṃsādá** (for *-saṃs°*), m. society of w°, TS. **-shakhá** (for *-sakha*), m. a friend of w°, VS. **-shū́** (for *-sū*), f. bringing forth females, MaitrS. **-shūya** (for *-sūya*), n. = *straishūya*, ŚāṅkhGṛ. **-saṃsarga**, m. female society, MW. **-saṃsthāna**, mfn. having a f° shape, ib. **-sakha**, mfn. accompanied by a w°, Siṇhâs. **-saṅga**, m. intercourse with w°, Subh. **-saṃgrahaṇa**, n. the act of embracing a w° (criminally), adultery, seduction, Yājñ., Sch. (IW. 261). **-saṃjña**, mfn. bearing a name with a feminine termination, VarBṛS. **-sabha**, n. an assembly of w°, L. **-sambandha**, m. connexion with a w°, Mn.; Rājat. **-sambhoga**, m. enjoyment of w°, sexual connexion, VP. **-sarūpin**, mfn. shaped like a w° (v. l. *-sva-r°*), MBh. **-sukha**, n. = *-sambhoga*, BhP. **-sevā**, f. devotion or addiction to women, Hit.; Subh. **-saubhāgya-kavala**, m. N. of wk. **-svabhāva**, m. the nature of w°, MBh.; Pañcar.; 'having a woman's nature,' a eunuch, L. **-svarūpa** or **°pa-vat**, mfn. having a w°'s shape or figure, MW. **-svarūpin**, mfn. id., MBh. **-hatyā**, f. the murder of a woman, Kathās. **-hantṛi**, m. the murderer of a woman, Mn. xi, 190. **-haraṇa**, n. the forcible abduction of a woman, rape, W. **-hārin**, m. the forcible abductor of a woman, ib. **-huta**, n. a sacrifice offered by a woman, Kauś.

Striyam-manya, mfn. (= *strīm-m°*) thinking oneself or passing for a woman, Pāṇ. vi, 3, 68, Sch.

Strīka (ifc.) = *strī* (see *sa-strīka*).

Strīya, Nom. P. *°yati*, to desire a woman or wife, Śāntiś.

Straiṇa, mf(*ī*)n. female, feminine, RV. &c. &c.; relating or belonging to women, subject to or ruled by women, being among w°, Kāv.; BhP.; worthy of a woman, L.; n. womankind, the female sex, AV. &c. &c.; the nature of w°, Uttarar.; BhP. **-tā**, f., **-tva**, n. effeminacy, MW.

Strairājaka, m. pl. the inhabitants of Strī-rājya, Cat.

Straishūya, n. (= *strī-sh°*) the birth of a girl, AV.

Stry, in comp. for *strī*. **-agāra**, n. the women's apartments, Gal. **-adhyaksha**, m. the superintendent of a king's wives, chamberlain, R. **-anuja**, mfn. born after a female child or sister, Pāṇ. iii, 2, 100, Sch. **-abhigamana**, n. the act of criminally approaching the wife of (comp.), Gaut. **-ākhyā**, f. 'called Strī,' the Priyaṅgu plant, L. **-ājīva**, m. one who lives by (prostitution of) his wife or other women, Mn. xi, 63. **-ādi-vyatyāsam**, ind. alternating with the wife so that the wife begins, MānGṛ.

स्थ *stha*. See p. 1262, col. 3.

स्थकर *sthakara* = *sthagara* below, Kauś.

स्थग् *sthag*, cl. 1. P. *sthagati*, to cover, hide, conceal, Dhātup. xix, 28: Caus. *sthagayati*, id., Kāv.; VarBṛS. &c.; to cover, veil, make invisible, cause to disappear, Mālatīm.; Bālar. [Cf. Gk. στέγω, στέγη, τέγος &c.; Lat. *tegere, toga, tugurium*; Lith. *stėgti, stógas*; Germ. *decken, Dach*; Eng. *thatch*.]

Sthaga, mfn. cunning, sly, fraudulent, dishonest, L.; (*ī*), f. a box (for holding betel and areca-nut), L.

Sthagana, n. the act of covering or hiding, concealment, Rājat.

Sthagayitavya, mfn. (fr. Caus.) to be hidden or concealed, Pañcat.

Sthagara, n. (also written *sthakara*, cf. *tagara, tagaraka*) a partic. fragrant substance or powder, TBr.; Gobh.

Sthagala, prob. = *sthagara*. See *sthāgala*.

Sthagikā, f. a kind of bandage, Suśr.; a box (for betel &c.), Hcat.; a courtezan (?), Śukas.

Sthagita, mfn. covered, concealed, hidden (*sthagitā Sarasvatī*, 'S° has hidden herself' = 'I cannot express myself'), Kāv.; VarBṛS.; Rājat.; closed, shut (as a door), MārkP.; stopped, interrupted, BhP.

Sthagu, m. a hump on the back (v. l. *sthaḍu*), L.

स्थगणा *sthagaṇā*, f. the earth, L.

स्थडु *sthaḍu*, m. See *sthagu* above.

स्थण्डिल *sthaṇḍila*, n. (of unknown derivation; accord. to some connected with √*sthal*) an open unoccupied piece of ground, bare ground (also with *kevala*), an open field, MBh. &c.; a piece of open ground (levelled, squared, and prepared for a sacrifice), ŚāṅkhBr.; ŚrS.; a boundary, limit, landmark, W.; a heap of clods, MW.; m. N. of a Ṛishi, Cat. **-śa**, mfn. (cf. *giri-śa* &c.) lying on the bare ground, L. **-śayyā**, f. the act of lying on the bare ground (as a penance), MBh. **-śāyikā**, f. id., Divyâv. **-śāyin**, mfn. = *-śa*; m. a devotee who sleeps on the bare ground or on the sacrificial ground (on account of a vow), R.; Bhaṭṭ. **-saṃveśana**, n. = *-śayyā*, BhP. **-sitaka**, n. an altar (= *vedi*), L.

Sthaṇḍilaka. See *sa-sth°*.

Sthaṇḍile (loc. of *sthaṇḍila*), in comp. **-śaya**, m. = *sthaṇḍila-śāyin*, Yājñ.; BhP.; N. of a Ṛishi, Cat. **-śayana**, n. = *sthaṇḍila-śayyā*, MBh.

Sthaṇḍileya, m. N. of a son of Raudrāśva, MBh.; Hariv.; Pur.

Sthaṇḍilya, w. r. for *sthaṇḍila*, ChUp.

Sthāṇḍila, mfn. sleeping on the bare ground (as a penance), Pāṇ. iv, 2, 15; raised (as a toll) from a Sthaṇḍila, g. *śuṇḍikâdi*; m. = *sthaṇḍila-śāyin*, L.

स्थपति *stha-pati*. See p. 1262, col. 3.

स्थपनी *sthapanī*, f. the space between the eye-brows (v. l. *sthapaṇī*), Suśr.

स्थपुट *sthapuṭa*, mf(*ā*)n. (of unknown derivation; cf. *sthagu, sthaḍu*) hunchbacked, unevenly raised, rugged, rough, Hcar.; Kāśikh.; being in difficult or distressed circumstances, W.; bent with pain, Mālatīm.; m. a hump, protuberance, an unevenly raised place, L. **-gata**, mfn. being or belonging to a hump (as flesh), Mālatīm.; being on raised places and in hollows, MW.

Sthapuṭaya, Nom. P. *°yati*, to make rough or uneven, dig or root up, Caṇḍ.; to raise or elevate by strewing or heaping, Āryav.

Sthapuṭita, mfn. made uneven &c., g. *tārakâdi*.

Sthapuṭī, in comp. for *sthapuṭa*. **-√kṛi**, P. *-karoti*, to make uneven, raise by strewing or heaping up, Hcar. **-kṛita**, mfn. made uneven &c., Kāśikh.

स्थल् *sthal* (connected with √1. *sthā*), cl. 1. P. *sthalati*, to stand firm, be firm, Dhātup. xx, 6. [Cf. Gk. στέλλω, στόλος; Germ. *stellen, still* &c.; Eng. *still*.]

Sthala, m. a chapter, section (of a book), Cat.; N. of a son of Bala, BhP.; (*sthálā*), f. a heap of artificially raised earth, mound, TS.; (*ī*), f. an eminence, tableland (also applied to prominent parts of the body), Lāṭy.; MBh.; Kāv. &c.; soil, ground, Kālid.; BhP.; place, spot, Ragh.; Prab.; (*am*), n. = *sthalī* above; dry land (opp. to damp low-land), firm earth (opp. to water), TS. &c. &c.; ground, soil, place, spot, Mn.; MBh.; R. &c.; a flat surface, roof (of a palace), Megh.; situation, circumstance, case (*tathāvidha-sthale*, 'in such a case'), Sāh.; Sarvad.; a topic, subject, W.; a text, ib. **–kanda,** m. a kind of plant, L. **–kamala,** n. the flower of Hibiscus Mutabilis, Gīt.; Dhanv.; Bhpr. **–kamalinī,** f. Hibiscus Mutabilis, Megh. **–kālī,** f. N. of a being attending on Durgā, W. **–kumuda,** m. Nerium Odorum, L. **–ga,** mfn. living on dry land, BhP. **–gata,** mfn. gone or left on dry l°, MW. **–cara,** mfn. = *-ga*, R.; Hit.; VarBṛS. **–gāmin,** mfn. id., VarBṛS. **–cārin,** mfn. id. (°*ri-tā*, f.), Kāśikh. **–cyuta,** mfn. fallen or removed from any place or position, MW. **–ja,** mfn. growing or living on dry land, Mn.; R.; Suśr. &c.; accruing from land-transport (said of certain taxes or duties), Yājñ.; (*ā*), f. licorice-root, L. **–tara,** n. a higher place, Lāṭy. **–tas,** ind. from dry land, MW. **–tā,** f. the state of being dry ground, ŚārṅgP.; Pañcat. **–devatā,** f. a local or rural deity, tutelary god presiding over some partic. spot, MW. **–nalinī,** f. Hibiscus Mutabilis (ifc. °*nika*, mfn.), BhP.; Kād. **–nīraja,** n. the flower of Hib° Mut°, Pañcar. **–pattana,** n. a town situated on dry land (opp. to *jala-p*°), Śil. **–patha,** m. a road by land (*ena*, 'by land'), Kalpas.; Kathās. &c.; commerce by l°, Kām., Sch. **–pathī-√kṛi,** P. *-karoti*, to make into dry l° or road by l°, Vcar. **–padma,** m. Arum Indicum, L.; the flower of Hibiscus Mutabilis, Pañcar.; Bhaṭṭ.; another plant (= *chattra-pattra, tamālaka*), MW. **–padminī,** f. Hibiscus Mut°, L. **–piṇḍā,** f. a kind of date, L. **–purāṇa,** n. N. of wk. **–mañjarī,** f. Achyranthes Aspera, L. **–mārga,** m. a way by land, MW. **–ruhā,** f. Hibiscus Mutabilis, L. **–vartman,** n. a road by land (°*nā*, 'by land'), Ragh. **–varman,** m. N. of a king, Hcar. **–vigraha,** m. a land-fight, Hit. **–vihaṃga** or °**gama,** m. a land bird, BhP. **–vetasa,** m. Calamus Rotang, Megh., Sch. **–śuddhi,** f. the cleansing of any place from impurity, MW. **–śṛiṅgāṭa** or °**ṭaka,** m. Tribulus Lanuginosus or a similar plant, L. **–sambhavâushadhi,** f. pl. plants growing on dry land, VarBṛS. **–sīman,** m. = *sthaṇḍila*, m.(?), L.; a land-mark, boundary, W. **–stha,** mfn. standing on dry ground, MBh.; R.; BhP. **Sthalântara,** n. another place, MW. **Sthalâravinda,** n. the flower of Hibiscus Mutabilis, Kum. **Sthalârūḍha,** mfn. standing on the ground (as opp. to one seated in a chariot), Mn. vii, 91. **Sthaleśvara,** n. N. of a locality, Kāśikh. **Sthalôtpalinī,** f. Hibiscus Mutabilis, Kād. **Sthalâukas,** m. an animal dwelling on dry land, BhP.

Sthalaya, Nom. P. °*yati*, to make into dry land, Subh.

Sthalāya, Nom. Ā. °*yate*, to become dry land, Naish.

1. **Sthalī,** f., see under *sthala* above. **–devatā,** f. a local deity, Megh. **–bhūta,** mfn. high-lying (as a country), Hariv. **–śāyin,** mfn. lying or sleeping on the bare ground, Bhartṛ.

2. **Sthalī,** in comp. for *sthala*. **–√bhū,** P. *-bhavati*, to become dry land, Naish., Sch.

1. **Sthalīya,** Nom. P. °*yati*, to regard as dry land, VarYogay.

2. **Sthalīya,** mfn. relating or belonging to dry land, terrestrial, MW.; belonging to a place, local, ib.; relating or bel° to a situation or case (in *uddeśya-vidheya-bodha-sthalīya-vicāra*, m. N. of wk.)

Sthale (loc. of *sthala*), in comp. **–jāta,** mf(*ā*)n. growing on dry land (with *padminī*, f. 'Hibiscus Mutabilis'), R.; n. licorice root, L. **–ruhā,** f. 'growing on dry land,' N. of two plants (= *gṛiha-kumārī* and = *dagdhā*), L. **–śaya,** m. 'sleeping on dry land,' a partic. (or any) amphibious animal, L.

Sthaleyu, m. N. of a son of Raudrāśva, Hariv.; VP.

Sthāla, n. (fr. *sthala*, of which it is also the Vṛiddhi form in comp.) any vessel or receptacle, plate, cup, bowl, dish, caldron, pot, ŚrS.; any culinary utensil, Rājat.; the hollow of a tooth, Yājñ.; (*ī*), f., see col. 2. **–patha,** mfn. (fr. *sthala-p*°) imported by land, Pāṇ. v, 1, 77, Vārtt. 3, Pat. **–pathika,** mfn. (fr. id.) imported or travelling by land, Pāṇ. ib., Vārtt. 1, Pat. **–rūpa,** n. the form or representation of a caldron or cooking-pot, MW.

Sthālaka, m. or n. (pl.) N. of partic. bones on the back, Vishṇ.; Car.

Sthālika, m. the smell of fæces, L.; mfn. smelling of fæces, L.

Sthālin, mfn. possessing any vessel or receptacle (cf. *kara-sth*°), Pāṇ. viii, 2, 83, Vārtt. 1, Pat.

Sthālī́, f. an earthen dish or pan, cooking-vessel, caldron, AV.; Br.; ŚrS.; a partic. vessel used in preparing Soma, MW.; the substitution of a cooked offering of rice &c. for a meat offering at the Māṅsâshṭakā (q. v.), ib.; Bignonia Suaveolens, L. **–graha,** m. a ladleful taken out of a cooking-vessel, KātyŚr. **–daraṇa,** n. the breaking of a dish or vessel, AdbhBr. **–druma,** m. Ficus Benjamina or Indica, L. **–pakva,** mfn. cooked or dressed in any vessel, boiled, W. **–parṇī,** w. r. for *śāli-p*°, q. v. **–pāká** (or *sthā́lī-p*°), m. a dish of barley or rice boiled in milk (used as an oblation), ŚBr.; GṛŚrS.; MBh. &c.; mfn. (= °*kīya*), Cat.; *-nirṇaya*, m., *-prayoga*, m., *-mantra*, m. pl. N. of wks.; °*kīya*, mfn. belonging to the above oblation, Gobh. **–purīsha,** n. the sediment or dirt sticking to a kettle or cooking-pot, BhP. **–pulāka,** m. boiled rice in a cooking-vessel; *-nyāya*, m. the rule of b° rice in a c°-v° (i. e. the inferring of the condition of a whole from that of a part, as of the good cooking of rice from tasting one grain), A. **–bila,** n. the interior or hollow of a cooking-vessel, Pāṇ. v, 1, 70; °*līya* or °*lya*, mfn. fit to be boiled in a cooking-vessel, ib., Sch. **–vṛiksha,** m. = *-druma*, L.

स्थविर *sthavira*, °*vishṭha*. See p. 1265.

स्था 1. *sthā*, cl. 1. P. Ā. (Dhātup. xxii, 30) *tishṭhati*, °*te* (pf. *tasthaú*, *tasthe*, RV. &c. &c.; aor. *ásthāt*, *ásthita*, ib.; 3. pl. *asthiran*, RV.; AV.; Br.; *ā́sthat* [?], AV.; *asthishi*, °*shata*, Br. &c.; Subj. *sthā́ti*, *sthā́thaḥ*, RV.; Prec. *stheyā́t*, ib.; *sthesham*, °*shuḥ* [?], AV.; *sthāsīshṭa*, Gr.; fut. *sthātā́*, MBh. &c.; *sthāsyati*, °*te*, Br. &c.; inf. *sthā́tum*, ib.; °*tos*, Br.; GṛŚrS.; *-sthitum*, R.; ind. p. *sthitvā́*, MBh. &c.; *-sthā́ya*, RV. &c. &c.; *-sthāyam*, Bhaṭṭ.), to stand, stand firmly, station one's self, stand upon, get upon, take up a position on (with *pādābhyām*, 'to stand on the feet;' with *jānubhyām*, 'to kneel;' with *agre* or *agratas* and gen., 'to stand or present one's self before;' with *puras* and with or without gen., 'to stand up against an enemy &c.'), RV. &c. &c.; to stay, remain, continue in any condition or action (e. g. with *kanyā*, 'to remain a girl or unmarried;' with *tūshṇīm* or with *maunena*, instr. 'to remain silent;' with *sukham*, 'to continue or feel well'), AV. &c. &c.; to remain occupied or engaged in, be intent upon, make a practice of, keep on, persevere in any act (with loc.; e. g. with *rājye*, 'to continue governing;' with *śāsane*, 'to practise obedience;' with *bale*, 'to exercise power;' with *sva-dharme*, 'to do one's duty;' with *sva-karmaṇi*, 'to keep to one's own business;' with *saṃśaye*, 'to persist in doubting;' also with ind. p., e. g. *dharmam āśritya*, 'to practise virtue'), AV.; Mn.; MBh. &c.; to continue to be or exist (as opp. to 'perish'), endure, last, TS.; Mn.; MBh. &c.; to be, exist, be present, be obtainable or at hand, AV. &c. &c.; to be with or at the disposal of, belong to (dat., gen., or loc.), Mn.; MBh. &c.; (Ā., m. c. also P., cf. Pāṇ. i, 3, 23; iv, 34) to stand by, abide by, be near to, be on the side of, adhere or submit to, acquiesce in, serve, obey (loc. or dat.), RV. &c. &c.; to stand still, stay quiet, remain stationary, stop, halt, wait, tarry, linger, hesitate (see under *sthitvā* below), RV. &c. &c.; to behave or conduct one's self (with *samam*, 'to behave equally towards any one,' loc.); to be directed to or fixed on (loc.), Hariv.; Kathās.; to be founded or rest or depend on, be contained in (loc.), RV.; AV.; MBh.; to rely on, confide in (loc., e. g. *mayi sthitvā*, 'confiding in me'), Bhaṭṭ.; to stay at, resort to (acc.), R.; to arise from (abl. or gen.), RV.; ChUp.; to desist or cease from (abl.), Kathās.; to remain unnoticed (as of no importance), be left alone (only Impv. and Pot.), Kāv.; Pañcat.: Pass. *sthīyate* (aor. *asthāyi*), to be stood &c. (frequently used impers., e. g. *mayā sthīyatām*, 'let it be abided by me,' i. e. 'I must abide'), Br. &c. &c.: Caus. *sthāpayati*, °*te* (aor. *átishṭhipat*; ind. p. *sthāpayitvā* [q. v.] and *-sthā́pam*: Pass. *sthāpyate*), to cause to stand, place, locate, set, lay, fix, station, establish, found, institute, AV. &c. &c.; to set up, erect, raise, build, MBh.; R.; to cause to continue, make durable, strengthen, confirm, MBh.; R.; Suśr. &c.; to prop up, support, maintain, MBh.; Hcat.; to affirm, assent, Sāh.; Nyāyas., Sch.; to appoint (to any office, loc.), Mn.; MBh. &c.; to cause to be, constitute, make, appoint or employ as (two acc.; with *dhātrīm*, 'to employ any one as a nurse;' with *rakshârtham*, 'to appoint any one as guardian;' with *sajjam*, 'to make anything ready;' with *su-rakshitam*, 'to keep anything well guarded;' with *svī-kṛitya*, 'to make anything one's own;' with *pariśesham*, 'to leave anyth° over or remaining'), ŚvetUp.; MBh.; Kāv. &c.; to fix, settle, determine, resolve, Mn.; MBh. &c.; to fix in or on, lead or bring into, direct or turn towards (loc., rarely acc.; with *hṛidi*, 'to impress on the heart;' with *manas*, 'to fix the mind on'), AV. &c. &c.; to introduce or initiate into, instruct in (loc., e. g. with *naye*, 'to instruct in a plan or system'), MBh.; Kathās.; to make over or deliver up to (loc. or *haste* with gen., 'into the hands of'), Yājñ.; Ratnâv.; Kathās.; to give in marriage, MBh.; to cause to stand still, stop, arrest, check, hold, keep in, restrain (with *baddhvā*, 'to keep bound or imprisoned'), ŚBr. &c. &c.; to place aside, keep, save, preserve, MBh.; Hariv.: Desid. of Caus. *-sthāpayishati* (see *sam-√sthā*): Desid. *tishṭhāsati*, to wish to stand &c., ŚBr.: Intens. *teshṭhīyate*; *tāstheti*, *tāsthāti*, Gr. [Cf. Gk. ἱ-στάναι; Lat. *stare*; Lith. *stóti*; Slav. *stati*; Germ. *stân*, *stehen*; Eng. *stand*.]

Tasthivás, mfn. (pf. p. of √1. *sthā*; nom. °*vā́n*, °*thúshī*, °*vát*) one who has stood, standing, remaining, continuing in, being on or in (loc.), RV.; Ragh.; one who has stood still or stopped or made a pause (used as pf. tense, 'he made a pause,' Hariv.), fixed, immovable, stationary (opp. to *jágat*), RV.; MBh. &c.; occupied with, engaged in (loc.), Ragh.; Rājat.; keeping on with (instr.), MBh.; persevering, constant, MBh.; ready to, prepared for (dat.), ib.

Stha (or *shṭha*), mf(*ā*)n. (only ifc.) standing, staying, abiding, being situated in, existing or being in or on or among (see *agni-*, *garbha-*, *jala-*, *naraka-*, *rājya-stha* &c.); occupied with, engaged in, devoted to, performing, practising (see *dhyāna-*, *yajña-*, *yoga-*, *savana-stha* &c.); a place, ground (ibc. = *sthala*), L. **–páti,** m. (accord. to some *sthapati*, fr. caus. of √1. *sthā*) 'place-lord,' a king, chief, governor, head official (accord. to KātyŚr., 'a Vaiśya or even a person of lower caste, who has celebrated the Go-sava sacrifice after being chosen king;' accord. to others, 'an Āyogava who is a town official;' cf. *nishāda-sth*°), AV.; VS.; Br.; ŚrS.; R.; Śiś.; an architect, master builder, carpenter, wheelwright, MBh.; R. &c. (IW. 185); one who sacrifices to Bṛihas-pati, L.; a guard or attendant on the women's apartments, chamberlain, L.; a charioteer, W.; N. of Bṛihas-pati, L.; of Kubera, L.; mfn. chief, best, principal, L. **–śás,** ind. according to (its) place, RV.

Sthapati. See *stha-pati* above.

Sthavi, sthavira. See p. 1265, col. 2.

2. **Sthā́** (or *shṭhā́*), mfn. (nom. m. n. *sthā́s*) standing, stationary (often ifc. = 'standing, being, existing in or on or among,' cf. *agni-shṭhā́*, *ṛita-sthā́* &c.), RV.; PañcavBr.; ŚāṅkhŚr. **–raśman** (*sthā́-*, Padap. *sthā́ḥ-*), having firm bridles (?), RV.

Sthāṇava, mfn. (fr. *sthāṇu* below) coming from the trunks or stems of trees, Hcar.

Sthāṇavīya, mfn. (fr. next) relating or belonging to Śiva, Bālar.

Sthāṇú, mfn. (accord. to some for *sthalnu*) standing firmly, stationary, firm, fixed, immovable, motionless, Mn.; MBh. &c.; m. (or n., g. *ardharcâdi*) a stump, stem, trunk, stake, post, pile, pillar (also as symbol of motionlessness), RV. &c. &c.; a kind of spear or dart, L.; m. a partic. part of a plough, Kṛishis.; the gnomon of a dial, MW.; a partic. perfume (= *jīvaka*), L.; a nest of white ants, W.; N. of Śiva (who is supposed to remain as motionless as the trunk of a tree during his austerities), MBh.; Kāv. &c. (RTL. 63); of one of the 11 Rudras, MBh.; Hariv.; of a Prajā-pati, R.; of a serpent-demon, RāmatUp.; of a Rākshasa, TāṇḍBr.; n. anything stationary or fixed, MBh. &c.; a partic. posture in sitting, Cat. **–karṇī,** f. a partic. species of large colocynth, L. **–ccheda,** m. one who cuts down the trunks of trees or clears away timber, Mn. ix, 44. **–tīrtha,** n. N. of a Tīrtha, MBh. **–diś,** f. 'Śiva's quarter,' the north-east, VarBṛS. **–bhūta,** mfn. become motionless as the trunk of a tree, MBh. **–bhrama,** m. mistaking anything for a post, Śāntiś. **–matī,** f. N. of a river, R. **–roga,** m. a partic. disease of horses, L. **–vaṭa,** N. of a Tīrtha, MBh. **–vat,** ind. like a post, MW. **–vanâukas,** mfn. inhabiting Śiva's forest, ib.

Sthāṇv, in comp. for *sthāṇu*. **–āśrama-māhātmya,** n. N. of wk. **–īśvara,** m. N. of a Liṅga of Śiva, VāmP.; n. N. of a town (cf. *sthāneśvara*), Hcat.

Sthātavya, mfn. (n. impers.) to be stood or stayed or remained or continued in or abided by (loc., rarely instr.), MBh.; Kāv. &c.

Sthā́tṛi, m. a guider, driver (of horses &c.), RV.; a guide, authority, MBh. iii, 12691; (°*trí*), mfn. (nom. n. °*tṛír*) what stands or stays stationary, immovable (as opp. to *jagat* or *caratha*), RV. i, 58, 8.

Sthātrá, n. station, place (cf. *bhūri-sth°*), RV. x, 125, 3.

Sthāna, n. (also said to be m., Siddh.) the act of standing, standing firmly, being fixed or stationary, AV. &c. &c.; position or posture of the body (in shooting &c.), R.; staying, abiding, being in or on (loc. or comp.), Daś.; Kām.; Hariv.; Sāh.; storing-place or storage (of goods), Mn. viii, 401; firm bearing (of troops), sustaining a charge (as opp. to *yuddha*, 'charging'), ib. vii, 190; state, condition (ifc. = 'being in the state of'), Up.; BhP.; continued existence, continuance in the same state (i. e. in a kind of neutral state unmarked by loss or gain), continuing as or as long as (with instr.), MBh.; R.; BhP.; a state of perfect tranquillity, Sarvad.; station, rank, office, appointment, dignity, degree, MaitrUp.; Mn.; MBh. &c.; place of standing or staying, any place, spot, locality, abode, dwelling, house, site (*sthāne sthāne* or *sthāne sthāneshu*, 'in different places,' 'here and there'), RV. &c. &c.; place or room, stead (*sthāne* with gen. or ifc. 'in place of,' 'instead of,' 'in lieu of;' *ripu-sthāne* √*vṛit*, 'to act in the place of an enemy;' *vilocana-sthāna-gata*, 'acting the part of eyes;' also *sthāna* ifc. = 'taking the place of,' 'acting as,' 'representing' or 'represented by,' e.g. *pitṛi-sth°*, 'acting as a father' or 'represented by a f°;' *iyaṅ-uvaṅ-sthāna*, 'repr° by *iy* or *uv*' [as *ī* and *ū*, Pāṇ. i, 4, 4]; in Pāṇini's grammar the gen. case is often used alone, when the word *sthāne* has to be supplied, e.g. *hanter jaḥ*, '*ja* is to be substituted in place of *han*,' i, 1, 49), AitBr.; GṛŚrS. &c.; place for, receptacle of (gen.), Mn.; MBh. &c.; proper or right place (*sthāne*, 'in the right place or at the right time, seasonably, justly'), PañcavBr. &c. &c. (cf. g. *svar-ādi*); province, region, domain, sphere (of gods or virtuous men; said to be in one of three places, viz. 'earth' or 'atmosphere' or 'heaven;' accord. to some that of virtuous Brāhmans is called Prājāpatya; of Kshatriyas, Aindra; of Vaiśyas, Māruta; of Śūdras, Gāndharva), Nir.; VarBṛS.; the main support or strength or chief constituent of a kingdom (said to be four, viz. 'army,' 'treasury,' 'city,' 'territory'), Mn. vii, 56; a stronghold, fortress, Pañcat.; the place or organ of utterance of any sound (said to be 8 in number, viz. *kaṇṭha*, 'throat;' *tālu*, 'palate;' *mūrdhan*, 'top of palate;' *danta*, 'teeth;' *oshṭha*, 'lips;' *kaṇṭha-tālu*, 'throat and palate;' *kaṇṭh'-oshṭha*, 'throat and lips;' *dant'-oshṭha*, 'teeth and lips;' to which are added *nāsikā*, 'nose,' said to be the place of utterance of true Anusvāra, and *uras*, 'chest,' of Visarga), Pāṇ. i, 9, Sch.; Prāt.; Sarvad.; any organ of sense (e.g. the eye), BhP.; the pitch or key of the voice, note, tone (of which, accord. to RPrāt., there are three [see *mandra*], or accord. to TPrāt., seven; *vīṇā cyutā sthānāt*, 'a lute out of tune'), ŚrS.; Prāt.; MBh. &c.; shape, form, appearance (as of the moon), VarBṛS.; the part or character of an actor, MW.; case, occurrence (*nê-daṃ sthānaṃ vidyate*, 'this case does not occur'), Yājñ.; Pañcat.; Vajracch.; occasion, opportunity for (gen. or comp.; *sthāne*, ind. 'occasionally'), ŚrS.; MBh. &c.; cause or object of (gen. or comp., e.g. *śulka-sthāna*, 'an object of toll;' *pūjā-* or *mānya-sth°*, 'an object of honour;' also applied to persons; *sthāne*, ind. 'because of,' 'on account of'), MBh.; Pañcat.; Kathās.; a section or division (e.g. of medicine), Car.; Suśr. &c.; an astrol. mansion or its subdivision, VarBṛS.; = *kāryôtsarga*, Śil.; an open place in a town, plain, square, W.; a holy place, MW.; an altar, ib.; N. of a Gandharva king, R. **–cañcalā**, f. Ocimum Pilosum, L. **–caturvidha-śloka**, m. N. of wk. **–cintaka**, m. one who provides quarters for an army, a kind of quarter-master, Pañcat. **–cyuta**, mfn. fallen or removed from any place or office &c., GāruḍaP. **–tas**, ind. according to place or station, MW.; in regard to the place or organ of utterance, ib. **–tā**, f. the state of being the receptacle of, possession of (gen.), Naish. **–tyāga**, m. abandonment of a dwelling-place, Cāṇ.; loss of rank or dignity, VarBṛS. **–tva** (in *eka-sthāna-tva*, 'the being pronounced with the same organ'), n., TPrāt., Sch. **–dātṛi**, mf(°*trī*)n. one who assigns a place to (gen.), Pañcar. **–dīpta**, mfn. (in augury) inauspicious on account of situation (see *dīpta*), VarBṛS. **–pata**, mfn. (fr. next), g. *aśvapaty-ādi*. **–pati**, m. lord of a pl°, (esp.) head of a monastery, Inscr. **–pāta**, m. occupying (another's) pl°, Nyāyam. **–pāla**, m. guardian of a pl° or region, Yājñ.; R.; Rājat.; chief guardian, superintendent, Hcar.; a keeper, watchman, policeman, W. **–pracyuta**, mfn. = *-cyuta*, R. **–prâpti**, f. obtainment of a place or situation, VarBṛS. **–bhaṅga**, m. ruin or fall of a place, Pañcat. **–bhūmi**, f. a dwelling-place, mansion, MW. **–bhraṇśa**, m. loss of place or station or rank, VarBṛS.; Hit. **–bhrashṭa**, mfn. = *-cyuta*, ib. **–māhātmya**, n. the greatness or glory of any place, the divine virtue supposed to be inherent in any sacred spot, MW. **–mṛiga**, m. N. of certain big animals (such as the turtle, crocodile, and Makara, supposed to frequent the same pl°), L. **–yoga**, m. assignment of suitable places or application of the best modes for preserving articles, Mn. ix, 332. **–yogin**, mfn. = *sthāne-yoga* (col. 3), VPrāt. **–rakshaka**, m. = *sthāna-pāla*, MW. **–vat**, mfn. being in the right place, well-founded (as doubt), Nyāyas. **–vid**, mfn. knowing places, having local knowledge, Kathās. **–vibhāga**, m. assignment of pl°, Bṛih.; (in alg.) subdivision of a number according to the position of its figures, Col. **–vīrâsana**, n. a partic. sedent posture, SaṃhUp. **–stha**, mfn. abiding in one pl°, immovable, VarBṛS.; staying at home, L. **–sthāna**, n. pl. every place (*eshu*, loc. pl. 'everywhere,' 'in every corner;' cf. *sthāna*, col. 1), Kathās. **–sthita**, mfn. standing in a (high) pl°, Kāv. **Sthānâṅga**, n. N. of the 3rd Aṅga (q. v.) of the Jainas. **Sthānâdhikāra**, m. the superintendence of a shrine, Inscr. **Sthānâdhipati**, m. = *sthāna-pati*, Inscr. **Sthānâdhyaksha**, m. the governor of a place, L. **Sthānânta**, mfn. ending in *sthāna*, Pāṇ. iv, 3, 35. **Sthānântara**, n. another pl°; *-gata*, mfn. gone to another place, gone away, MW.; °*râbhimukha*, mf(*ī*)n. facing another place turned away, Mālav. **Sthānânya-tva**, n. difference of pl°, MW. **Sthānâpatti**, f. taking the place of another person or thing, substitution, KātyŚr., Sch. **Sthānâpanna**, mfn. substituted in place of another (cf. prec.), ib. **Sthānâbhāva**, m. want of place or situation, MW. **Sthānâśraya**, m. the pl° on which anything stands, Suśr. (*eka-sth°*, mfn. 'being in the same pl°,' Kathās.) **Sthānâsana**, n. du. standing and sitting down, Mn. vi, 22; *-vihāra-vat*, mfn. (a pupil) occupying the habitation and seat and place of recreation (of his preceptor), ib. ii, 248; °*sanika*, mfn. standing or sitting, Āpast. **Sthānâsedha**, m. confinement to a place, local or personal arrest, Yājñ., Sch. **Sthānâsthāna-jñāna-bala**, n. the power of the knowledge of what is proper and what is improper, Buddh. **Sthāneśvara**, m. the governor of a pl°, Rājat.; n. (prob. incorrect for *sthāṇv-īśvara*) N. of a town and its territory (Thanesar), MBh.; Buddh.

Sthānaka, m. N. of a man, Rājat.; n. position, situation, rank, dignity, MBh.; a place, spot, Pañcat.; a city, town, L.; attitude of the body (in shooting &c.), Hcar.; Nalac.; a partic. point or situation in dramatic action, Vikr. iv, $\frac{1}{1}\frac{4}{8}$ (others 'a kind of posture;' but cf. *patākā-sth°*); a basin or trench dug for water at the root of a tree, L.; a division or section (esp.) of the Kāṭhaka (accord. to some 'a mode of recitation'); froth or bubbles on spirits or wine (prob. for *sthāsaka*), L.

Sthāni, in comp. for *sthānin*. **–bhūta**, mfn. (in gram.) being the original or primitive form, Pāṇ., Sch. **–vat**, ind. like the original or primitive element (the *ādeśa* or substituted form is said to be *sthāni-vat* when it is liable to all the rules which hold good for the primitive), Pāṇ. i, 1, 56; (*-vat*)-*tva*, n. the state of being like the original form or element, Pāṇ., Sch.; (*-vat*)-*sūtra-vicāra*, m. N. of wk.; (*-vad*)-*bhāva*, m. (= *-vat-tva*), Pat.

Sthānika, mfn. belonging to a place or site, local, W.; (in gram.) taking the place of anything else, substituted for (gen. or comp.), Pāṇ., Sch.; m. any one holding an official post, governor of a place, manager of a temple &c., L.

Sthānin, mfn. having a place, occupying a (high) position, Cat.; having fixedness, abiding, permanent, W.; being in the right place, appropriate, ĀśvŚr.; (in gram.) that which should be in the place or is to be supplied, Pāṇ. i, 4, 105; m. the original form or primitive element (for which anything is substituted, as opp. to *ādeśa*, 'the substitute'), Pāṇ., Sch.

Sthānīya, mfn. having its place in, being in (comp.; *kaṇṭha-sth°*, 'having its place in the throat'), Vedântas.; belonging to or prevailing in any place, local, W.; occupying the place of, representing (comp.), Āpast.; n. a town or a large village, L.

Sthāne (loc. of *sthāna*), in comp. **–patita**, mfn. occupying the place of another (person or thing; *-tva*, n.), Nyāyam., Sch. **–yoga**, mf(*ā*)n. (in gram.) implying the relation of 'instead' (said of the gen. case or *shashṭhī*, which designates that for which something is substituted), Pāṇ. i, 1, 49. **–yogin**, mfn. (cf. *sthāna-yoga*), id. (°*gi-tva*, n.), Pāṇ. i, 1, 47, Sch.

Sthāny, in comp. for *sthānin*. **–āśraya**, mfn. depending on the primitive form (said of an operation in gr.), MW.

Sthāpaka, mfn. (fr. Caus.) causing to stand, placing, fixing &c.; m. the erecter of an image, VarBṛS.; a depositor, Yājñ., Sch.; (ifc.) an establisher, founder, Cat.; (in dram.) a kind of stage-director (assistant of the Sūtra-dhāra [q. v.] but not clearly defined in his functions and not mentioned in any of the extant plays), Bhar.; Sāh.

Sthāpatya, m. (fr. *sthapati*) a guard of the women's apartments, L.; n. the office of the governor of a district, PañcavBr.; architecture, building, erecting, R.; BhP. **–veda**, m. 'science of architecture,' one of the four Upa-vedas (q. v.), IW. 184.

Sthāpana, mfn. (fr. Caus.) causing to stand &c.; maintaining, preserving (see *vayaḥ-sth°*); fixing, determining, Sāh.; (*ā*), f. the act of causing to stand firmly or fixing, supporting (as an attribute of the earth), MBh.; Hcat.; storing, keeping, preserving, Campak.; fixed order or regulation, ib.; establishing, establishment, dialectical proof (of a proposition), ib.; Car.; Sarvad.; arranging, regulating or directing (as a drama &c.), stage-management (cf. *sthāpaka*), W.; (*ī*), f. Clypea Hernandifolia, L.; (*am*), n. causing to stand, fixing, establishing, founding, instituting, raising, erecting (an image &c.), VarBṛS.; Inscr.; putting or placing or laying upon (comp.), Suśr.; Naish., Sch.; fastening, fixing, rendering immovable, BhP.; hanging, suspending, Cat.; strengthening (of the limbs), preservation or prolongation (of life) or a means of strengthening &c., Suśr.; Car.; a means of stopping (the flow of blood), styptic, ib.; storage (of grain), Kṛishis.; establishment or dialectical proof of a proposition, Madhus.; statement, definition, Sāh.; a partic. process to which quicksilver is subjected, Sarvad.; = *puṃ-savana*, L.; fixing the thoughts, abstraction, W.; a dwelling, habitation, ib. **–vṛitta**, mfn. one who is past all restoration to strength, Car.

Sthāpanika, mf(*ā*)n. deposited, laid up in store, Vet.

Sthāpanīya, mfn. to be fixed or established in a place, Kathās.; to be kept (as a cat &c.), ib.; to be treated with tonics or strengthening remedies, Suśr.

Sthāpayitavya, mfn. to be kept in a place, MBh.; to be kept in order or restrained, ib.

Sthāpayitṛi, mfn. one who causes to stand, establisher, founder, MBh.

Sthāpayitvā, ind. having placed or fixed &c.; having put aside = 'with the exception of' (acc.), Divyâv.

Sthāpita, mfn. caused or made to stand, fixed, established, founded &c.; handed over, deposited, Yājñ.; MBh. &c.; lodged, Kathās.; put aside, kept, stored, ib.; wedded, Mālatīm.; ordered, regulated, enjoyed, ordained, enacted, W.; settled, ascertained, certain, ib.; firm, steady, ib. **–vat**, mfn. one who has placed or fixed, ib.

Sthāpin, m. (prob.) the erecter (of an image), Pañcar.

Sthāpya, mfn. to be set up or erected (as an image), VarBṛS.; to be placed in or on (loc.), Yājñ.; MBh. &c.; to be installed in or appointed to (an office), R.; to be shut up or confined in (loc.), Kathās.; to be kept (*veśmani*, 'in the house,' i.e. 'as a domestic animal'), VarBṛS.; to be kept to (one's duty, loc.), MārkP.; to be plunged in (grief &c., acc.), Kathās.; to be kept in order or curbed or checked or restrained, MBh.; m. (prob.) the image of a god, Pañcar.; m. or n. a deposit, pledge (= *nikshepa*), L. **Sthāpyâharaṇa**, n. the stealing or embezzling of a deposit, MW.

Sthāma, in comp. for *sthāman*. **–vat**, mfn. powerful, strong, Lalit.; (ifc.) having the strength of, ib.

Sthā́man, n. station, seat, place, AV.; strength, power, Bālar.; Lalit.; SaddhP.; the neighing of a horse, MBh. i, 5116.

Sthāya, m. = *sthāman*, L.; a receptacle (in *jala-sth°*, q.v.); (*ā*), f. the earth, L.

Sthāyam. See √1. *sthā*, p. 1262, col. 2.

1. **Sthāyi**, f. the action of standing, Pāṇ. iii, 3, 95, Vārtt. 1, Pat.

2. **Sthāyi**, in comp. for *sthāyin.* — **tā**, f., **-tva**, n. constancy, stability, permanency, steadiness, durableness, invariableness, Suśr.; Sāh.; Sarvad. — **bhāva**, m. lasting or durable state of mind or feeling (said to be 8, viz. *rati, hāsa, śoka, krodha, utsāha, bhaya, jugupsā, vismaya* [qq. vv.], to which is sometimes added *śama*, 'quietism;' they are opp. to the *vyabhicāri-bhāvas* or 'transitory feelings'), Bhar.; Daśar.; Sāh. &c.

Sthāyika, mfn. lasting, enduring (in *ādy-anta-sth°*, 'lasting from the beginning to the end'), Siṉhâs.; faithful, trustworthy, Bhar.; (*ā*), f. the action of standing, Pāṇ. iii, 3, 95, Vārtt. 1, Pat.

Sthāyin, mfn. standing, staying, being or situated in or on (comp.), Nir.; MBh.; Kāv. &c.; being in a partic. place, resident, present, Kāv.; Kathās.; being in a partic. state or condition, Kāv.; MārkP.; permanent, constant, enduring, lasting (as a feeling or state; cf. *sthāyi-bhāva* above), ĀśvŚr.; MBh. &c.; persevering, steadfast, Śiś.; faithful, trustworthy, Bhar.; having the form of (comp.), VarBṛS.

Sthāyī-√bhū, P. *-bhavati*, to become lasting or permanent, Pañcat.

Sthāyuka, mf(*ā*)n. disposed to stay or last, staying, tarrying, stopping, abiding in (loc.), Bhaṭṭ.; lasting, enduring, constant, PañcavBr.; m. the overseer of a village, L.

Sthāla &c. See p. 1262, col. 1.

Sthāvan. See *sa-sthā́van.*

Sthāvará, mf(*ā́*)n. standing still, not moving, fixed, stationary, stable, immovable (opp. to *jaṅgama*, q.v.), TS. &c. &c.; firm, constant, permanent, invariable, Āpast.; R.; Hariv.; regular, established, W.; vegetable, belonging to the veg° world, Suśr.; relating to immovable property, Yājñ., Sch.; m. a mountain (cf. *-rāja*), Bhag.; Kum.; (*ā*), f. N. of a Buddhist goddess, Lalit.; (*am*), n. any stationary or inanimate object (as a plant, mineral &c.; these form the seventh creation of Brahmā, see under *sarga*), Up.; Mn.; MBh. &c.; stability, permanence (v. l. *sthira-tva*), Subh.; immovable property, real estate (such as land or houses), Yājñ.; a heir-loom, family-possession (such as jewels &c., which have been long preserved in a family and ought not to be sold), W.; a bow-string, L. — **kalpa**, m. a partic. cosmic period, Buddh. — **krayāṇaka**, (prob.) n. wooden goods, Campak. — **garala**, n. a partic. vegetable poison, L. — **jaṅgama**, n. (sg. or pl.) everything stationary and movable or inanimate and animate, ŚāṅkhGṛ.; Mn. &c. — **tā**, f fixedness, immobility; the state of a vegetable or mineral, Mn. xii, 9. — **tīrtha**, n. N. of a Tīrtha or a Tīrtha with stagnant water, Cat. — **tva**, n. fixedness, immobility, MBh. — **rāja**, m. 'mountain-king,' N. of Himâlaya; *-kanyā*, f. 'daughter of H°,' N. of Pārvatī, Kum. **Sthāvarâkṛiti**, mfn. having the form or appearance of a tree, Kathās. **Sthāvarâdi**, n. the poison called Vatsa-nābha (q.v.), MW. **Sthāvarâsthāvara**, n. everything stationary and movable, immovable and movable property, ib.

Sthāvira. See p. 1265, col. 3.

Sthāsu, n. bodily strength, W. (prob. w. r. for *sthāma*).

Sthāsnu, mfn. firm, stationary, immovable, Lāṭy.; Mn.; MBh. &c.; durable, permanent, eternal, Kāv.; BhP.; patient enduring (in *a-sth°*), Kathās.; a tree or plant (= *vṛiksha*; cf. *sthāvara*), MW. — **tā**, f. firmness, stability, durability, W.

Sthitá, mfn. standing (as opp. to 'going,' 'sitting,' or 'lying;' *parasparaṃ sthitam*, 'standing opposed to each other;' *sthitam tena*, 'it was stood by him' = 'he waited'), Mn.; MBh. &c.; standing firm (*yuddhe*, 'in battle'), Hariv.; standing, staying, situated, resting or abiding or remaining in (loc. or comp.; with *uccâvaceshu*, 'abiding in things high and low;' with *anityam*, 'not remaining permanently,' 'staying only a short time,' KātyŚr.; Mn.; MBh. &c.; being or remaining or keeping in any state or condition (loc., instr., abl., comp., or a noun in the same case, also ind. p. or adv.; *vyāpya sthitaḥ*, 'he keeps continually pervading,' Śak.; Vikr.; *upaviśya sthitaḥ*, 'he remains sitting,' Vikr.; *kathaṃ sthitâsi*, 'how did you fare?' Vikr.; *evam sthite*, 'it being so,' Pañc.; *puraḥ sthite*, 'it being imminent'), MBh.; Kāv. &c.; engaged in, occupied with, intent upon, engrossed by, devoted or addicted to (loc. or comp.), performing, protecting, Mn.; MBh. &c.; abiding by, conforming to, following (loc.), ib.; being in office or charge, Pañcat.; Rājat.; adhering to or keeping with (loc.), Hariv.; lasting, RPrāt.; firm, constant, invariable, Kathās.; settled, ascertained, decreed, established, generally accepted, ŚBr. &c. &c.; fixed upon, determined, Śak.; firmly convinced or persuaded, MBh.; Subh.; firmly resolved to (inf. or loc.), MBh.; R. &c.; faithful to a promise or agreement, L.: upright, virtuous, L.; prepared for or to (dat.), Yājñ.; Kum.; being there, existing, present, close at hand, ready (*sthito hy eshaḥ*, 'I myself am ready;' *agraje sthite*, 'when the elder brother is there'), Mn.; MBh. &c.; belonging to (gen.), R.; turned or directed to, fixed upon (loc. or comp.), VarBṛS.; Sarvad.; resting or depending on (loc.), MBh.; R. &c.; leading or conducive to (dat.), Pañcat.; one who has desisted or ceased, Pañcad.; left over, L.; (in Vedic gram.) not accompanied by *iti* (in the Pada-pāṭha), standing alone (*pade sthite*, 'in the Pada text'), Prāt.; (*am*), n. standing still, stopping, Bhartṛ.; staying, remaining, abiding, R.; manner of standing, ib.; perseverance on the right path, ib. — **tā**, f. the being in a place (v. l. *sthiti-tā*), BṛĀr. — **dhī**, mfn. steady-minded, firm, unmoved, calm, Bhag. — **pāṭhya**, n. (in dram.) recitation in Prākṛit by a woman standing, Sāh. — **prakaraṇa**, w. r. for *sthiti-pr°*. — **prajña**, mfn. firm in judgment and wisdom, calm, contented, Bhag. — **preman**, m. 'firm in affection,' a firm or faithful friend, L. — **buddhi-datta**, m. N. of a Buddha, Lalit. — **mati**, m. 'firm-minded,' N. of a teacher, Buddh. — **liṅga**, mfn. having the virile member erected (cf. *sthira-l°*), MBh. — **vat**, mfn. one who has stood or stayed &c.; being or situated in, Śiś.; (*sthitá-*), containing a form of √*sthā* (*-vatī*, f. 'a verse containing a form of √*sthā*'), ŚBr. — **saṃvid**, mfn. faithful to an agreement, keeping a promise, Kathās. — **saṃketa**, mfn. id., ib. **Sthitâsana**, n. the 5 standing postures (e.g. *daṇḍâsana* &c.) collectively, L. **Sthitôpasthita**, mfn. (a word) which stands with and without the particle *iti* (in the Pada text; see *sthita* above), Prāt.

Sthíti, f. standing upright or firmly, not falling, Kāvyâd.; standing, staying, remaining, abiding, stay, residence, sojourn in or on or at (loc. or comp.; *sthitiṃ* √*kṛi* or *vi-*√1. *dhā* or √*grah* or √*bhaj*, 'to make a stay,' 'take up one's abode'), Kāv.; Kathās. &c.; staying or remaining or being in any state or condition (see *rājya-sth°*); continuance in being, maintenance of life, continued existence (the 2nd of the three states of all created things, the 1st being *utpatti*, 'coming into existence,' and the 3rd *laya*, 'dissolution'), permanence, duration, ŚvetUp.; R.; Kālid.; BhP.; Sarvad.; duration of life, MārkP.; (in astron.) duration of an eclipse, Sūryas.; continued existence in any place, MBh.; Sāh.; that which continually exists, the world, earth, BhP.; any situation or state or position or abode, Kāv.; Pañcat.; Kathās.; station, high position, rank, Mn.; Yājñ.; Bhag. &c.; maintenance, sustenance, Mâlatîm.; settled rule, fixed decision, ordinance, decree, axiom, maxim, ŚBr. &c. &c.; maintenance of discipline, establishment of good order (in a state &c.), Ragh.; continuance or steadfastness in the path of duty, virtuous conduct, steadiness, rectitude, propriety, MBh.; R.; Ragh.; constancy, perseverance, Bhag.; Sarvad.; devotion or addiction to, intentness on (loc.), MBh.; R.; firm persuasion or opinion, conviction, Yājñ.; Kām.; settled practice, institution, custom, usage, Kathās.; Rājat.; settled boundary or bounds (esp. of morality, e.g. *sthitim* √*bhid*, 'to transgress the bounds of m°'), term, limit, R.; Kālid.; Bhaṭṭ.; standing still, stopping, halting (*sthitim ā-*√*car*, 'to remain standing'), Ragh.; Rājat.; Suśr.; standing-place, halting-place, stand or place or fixed abode, SBr.; Mn.; Rājat.; resistance to motion, inertia (in phil.); fixedness, immobility, stability, Ragh.; BhP.; depositing, laying down, Rājat.; Kathās.; form, shape, MārkP.; manner of acting, procedure, behaviour, conduct, Mn.; Śiś.; Hit.; occurrence, MBh.; regard or consideration for (loc.), Pañcat. v. l.; (in Vedic gram.) the standing of a word by itself (i.e. without the particle *iti*; see *sthita*). — **kartṛi**, mfn. causing stability or permanence, MārkP. — **jña**, mfn. knowing (and observing) the bounds of morality, Kum. — **tā** (*sthiti-*), f. fixity, stability, firm position, ŚBr. — **deśa**, m. place of abode, ŚārṅgP. — **pālana**, m. maintenance of stability or permanence (°*naṃ* √*kṛi*, 'to maintain stability'), MārkP. — **prakaraṇa**, n. N. of a ch. of the Vāsishṭha-rāmâyaṇa. — **prada**, mfn. bestowing firmness or stability, ib. — **bhid**, mfn. violating or transgressing the bounds of morality, Ragh. — **mat**, mfn. possessing firmness or stability, firm, stable, Kum.; lasting, enduring, Ragh.; keeping within limits (as the ocean), Vikr.; keeping within the limits of morality, virtuous, honest, Mn.; Kām.; Kum. — **varman**, m. N. of a king, Hcar. — **sthāpaka**, mfn. restoring anything to its original state or condition, W.; m. the capability of restoration to an original state or position, elasticity, Bhāshāp.

Sthity, in comp. for *sthiti.* — **atikrānti**, f. transgression of the bounds of morality or virtue, Kir.

Sthitvā, ind. having stood or stayed or stopped or waited &c. (sometimes used alone to express 'after some time;' *māsam sth°*, 'after a month;' *ciram api sth°*, 'after a long period' = 'sooner or later'), RV. &c. &c.

Sthin. See *tri-shṭhín* and *parame-shṭhín.*

Sthirá, mf(*ā*)n. firm, hard, solid, compact, strong, RV. &c. &c.; fixed, immovable, motionless, still, calm, ŚBr.; MBh. &c.; firm, not wavering or tottering, steady, R.; VarBṛS.; unfluctuating, durable, lasting, permanent, changeless, RV. &c. &c.; stern, relentless, hard-hearted, Kum.; constant, steadfast, resolute, persevering (*manas* or *hṛidayaṃ sthiraṃ* √*kṛi*, 'to steel one's heart, take courage,' R.; Kathās.); kept secret, Vet.; faithful, trustworthy, Yājñ.; MBh. &c.; firmly resolved to (inf.), MBh.; settled, ascertained, undoubted, sure, certain, Mn.; MBh. &c.; m. a partic. spell recited over weapons, R.; a kind of metre, VarBṛS.; N. of Śiva, MBh.; of one of Skanda's attendants, ib.; N. of a partic. astrol. Yoga, MW.; of certain zodiacal signs (viz. Taurus, Leo, Scorpio, Aquarius; so called because any work done under these signs is supposed to be lasting), ib. (L. also 'a tree; Grislea Tomentosa; a mountain; a bull; a god; the planet Saturn; final emancipation'); (*ā*), f. a strong-minded woman, MW.; the earth, L.; Desmodium Gangeticum, L.; Salmalia Malabarica, L.; = *kākolī*, L.; N. of the sound *j*, Up.; (*am*), n. steadfastness, stubbornness, resistance (acc. with *ava-*√*tan*, P. 'to loosen the resistance of [gen.];' Ā. 'to relax one's own resistance, yield;' with *ā-*√*tan*, Ā. 'to offer resistance'), RV. — **karman**, mfn. persevering in action, Ragh. — **kuṭṭaka**, m. (in alg.) a steady pulverizer, constant multiplier, common divisor (applied to a partic. kind of common div°), MW. — **gati**, m. 'moving firmly or slowly,' N. of the planet Saturn (cf. *śanaiś-cara*), L. — **gandha**, mfn. having durable perfume; m. Michelia Champaca, L.; (*ā*), f. Bignonia Suaveolens, ib.; Pandanus Odoratissimus, ib. — **cakra**, m. N. of Mañju-śrī, ib. — **citta** (R.) or **-cetas** (Śiś.), mfn. firm-minded, steady, resolute. — **cchada**, m. Betula Bhojpatra, L. — **cchāya**, m. a tree yielding permanent shadow, L.; any tree, ib. — **jaṅgama**, (prob.) n. (pl.) things stationary and movable, BhP. — **jihva**, m. 'firm-tongued,' a fish, ib. — **jīvita**, mfn. long-lived, tenacious of life; (*ā*), f. the silk-cotton tree, L. — **jīvin**, mfn. = prec.; m. N. of a crow, Pañcat. — **tara**, mfn. more (or most) firm or fixed or immovable; *-dṛiś*, mfn. with steady eyes, Bhartṛ. — **tā**, f. hardness, Suśr.; stability, steadfastness, permanence, Kāv.; Kathās. &c.; moral firmness, constancy, tranquillity (°*tām upa-*√*i*, 'to recover composure of mind'), MBh.; Śak. &c. — **tva**, n. hardness, Suśr.; immovableness, Mṛicch.; stability, constancy, MBh.; Suśr. &c. — **daṇshṭra**, m. 'strong-toothed,' a snake, L.; N. of Vishṇu in the boar-Avatāra, ib.; = *dhvani*, ib. (incorrect). — **deva**, m. N. of a Commentator, Cat. — **dhanvan** (*sthirá-*), mfn. having a strong bow (said of Rudra), RV. — **dhāman** (°*rá-*), mfn. belonging to a strong race, AV. — **dhī**, mfn. firm-minded, steadfast, Nāg. — **pattra**, m. Phœnix Paludosa, L. — **pada**, mf(*ā*)n. firmly rooted, Mudr. — **pāla-trilaksha**, m. N. of a man, Buddh. — **pīta** (°*rá-*), mfn. (prob.) having strong protection, RV. — **pushpa**, m. 'having firm flowers,' Michelia Champaca, L.; Clerodendrum Phlomoides, ib.; Mimusops Elengi, ib. — **pushpin**, m. 'id.,' Clerodendrum Phlomoides, ib. — **pratijña**, mfn. persisting in an assertion, faithful to a promise (*-tva*, n.), Kāv. — **pratibandha**, mfn. firm in resistance, offering an obstinate resistance, Śak. **— pratishṭhā**, f. a firm resting-place, fixed residence, MW. **— preman**, mfn. firm or steady in affection, L. **— psu**, mfn. (Ved.) having constant food, MW. **— phalā**, f. Benincasa Cerifera, L. **— buddhi**, mfn. steady-minded, resolute, steadfast, Cāṇ.; Rājat.; m. N. of an Asura, Kathās. **— buddhika**, m. N. of a Dānava, ib. **— mati**, f. a firm mind, steadfastness, L.; mfn. firm-minded, steady, Bhag.; m. N. of a Bhikshu, Buddh. **— mada**, mfn. intoxicating to such a degree as to cause lasting effects, Suśr.; intoxicated in that manner, L.; m. a peacock, L. **— manas**, mfn. firm-minded, steadfast, MBh.; Śiś. **— māyā**, f. a partic. spell, Cat. **— yoni**, m. a tree yielding permanent shade, L. **— yauvana**, n. perpetual youth, MārkP.; mf(*ā*)n. possessing perp° y°, ever youthful, ib.; Hariv.; Vikr.; m. a Vidyā-dhara, L. **— raṅgā**, f. 'having a durable colour,' indigo, L.; a sort of Curcuma, W. **— rāgā**, f. a kind of Curcuma, L. **— liṅga**, mfn. having a stiff virile organ, MBh.; *-pratishṭhā*, f. N. of wk. **— locana**, mfn. steady-eyed, MW.; (one) whose gaze is fixed, ib. **— varman**, m. N. of a man, Vās., Introd. **— vāc**, mfn. one whose word may be trusted, Nāṭyaś. **— vājin**, mfn. one whose horses stand still, MBh. **— vikrama**, mfn. taking firm strides, Bcar. **— śaṅku-karṇa**, mfn. having upright ears like spikes, ib. **— śrī**, mfn. having enduring prosperity, MW. **— saṃskāra**, mfn. thoroughly cultured; *-tā*, f. perfect culture, Mṛicch. **— saṃgara**, mfn. faithful to an agreement or promise, MBh. **— sattva**, mfn. having a steadfast character, R. **— sādhanaka**, m. Vitex Negundo, L. **— sāra**, m. Tectona Grandis, ib. **— sauhṛida**, mfn. firm in friendship, R.; VarBṛS.; n. firmness in fr°, MW. **— sthāyin**, mfn. standing firm, AmṛitabUp. **Sthirâṅhripa**, m. Phœnix Paludosa, L. **Sthirâghāta**, mfn. firm in bearing blows, (too) hard to be dug up, Gobh. **Sthirâṅghripa**, m. = *sthirâṅhripa*, L. **Sthirâtman**, mfn. firm-minded, stable, constant, VP.; steadfast, resolute, Kām.; Hit. **Sthirânurāga**, mfn. constant in affection or love; *-tva*, n. faithful attachment, Mudr. **Sthirânurāgin**, mfn. = °*rāga*; (°*gi*)*-tva*, n. = °*rāga-tva*, Mudr. **Sthirâpâya**, mfn. subject to constant decay, Kāv. **Sthirâyati**, mfn. of long extension or duration, lasting, Kir. **Sthirâyus**, mfn. long-lived; m. or f. the silk-cotton tree, L. **Sthirârambha**, mfn. firm or steadfast in undertakings, Mn.; ŚārṅgP.

Sthiraka, m. N. of a man, g. *naḍâdi*.

Sthiraya, Nom. P. °*yati*, to strengthen (with *hṛidi*; 'to impress deeply on the heart'), Caurap.

Sthirāya, Nom. Ā. °*yate*, to become fixed or immovable, Cat.; P. °*yati*, to remain firm, MW.

Sthirī, in comp. for *sthira*. **— kara**, mfn. making firm, Suśr. **— karaṇa**, mfn. id., Car.; n. hardening, Cat.; making firm or fixed, Sarvad.; making durable, corroboration, Sāh.; confirmation, Kull. on Mn. viii, 55. **— kartavya**, mfn. to be encouraged, Śak. **— kāra**, m. corroboration, Bādar., Sch. **— √kṛi**, P. *-karoti*, to make firm, strengthen, Pañcat.; to stop, ib.; to make permanent, establish, Kāv.; Kathās.; to corroborate, confirm, Mn., Sch.; MārkP.; to steel (the heart), Amar.; to encourage, comfort, MBh.; Pañcat. **— bhāva**, m. becoming stiff, immovableness, HYog. **— √bhū**, P. *-bhavati*, to become firm or stiff or hard, R.; Suśr.; to compose one's self, take courage, MBh.; R. &c.

Sthṛi. See *savya-shṭhṛi*, p. 1191, col. 3 (where read **-shṭhṛi**).

Sthema, in comp. for *stheman*. **— bhāj**, mfn. firm, strong, Śiś.

Sthemán, m. (fr. *sthira*) firmness, stability, TS.; Br.; Kāṭh.; continuance, duration (°*mnā*, ind. 'perseveringly'), HYog.; the state of standing or stopping still, rest, Naish.

Stheya, mf(*ā*)n. to be stationed or fixed or settled &c.; placed (as water in a jar), ŚāṅkhGṛ.; (*am*), n. (it is) to be stood still, R.; (it is) to be stood firm (in battle), BhP.; (it is) to be stayed or remained in (loc.), R.; Hariv. &c.; (attention) is to be fixed on (loc.), MBh.; R. &c.; (it is) to be behaved or acted or proceeded (with instr., ind. p., or adv.), Hariv.; Bhartṛ.; Rājat.; m. a person chosen to settle a dispute between two parties, an arbitrator, umpire, judge, Rājat.; Hit.; a domestic priest, L.

Sthéyas, mfn. (compar. of *sthira*) firmer, stronger, more important or worthy of consideration, very firm or strong, TS. &c.; very continuous or constant, Rājat.; very resolute, Sāh.

Stheyī-kṛita, mfn. (*stheyī* for *stheya*, m.) made an arbitrator or umpire or judge, Kathās.

Stheshṭha, mfn. (superl. of *sthira*) most fixed, very firm or strong or durable, Pāṇ. vi, 4, 157.

Sthairakāyaṇa, m. patr. fr. *sthiraka*, g. *naḍâdi*; (°*yana*), metron. of Mitra-varcas, IndSt.

Sthairabrahmaṇá, m. (prob.) N. of a man, MaitrS.

Sthairya, n. firmness, hardness, solidity, Yājñ.; MBh. &c.; fixedness, stability, immobility, Prab.; BhP.; Sarvad.; calmness, tranquillity, Pañcad.; continuance, permanence, Kāv.; Kathās.; steadfastness, constancy, perseverance, patience, MBh.; R. &c.; firm attachment to, constant delight in (loc.), Kāv.; Pañcat.; Kathās. &c. **— kara** or **-kṛit**, mfn. causing firmness or hardness, Suśr. **— vat**, mfn. having stability, standing still, fixed, immovable, Kāvyâd.; standing firm, not yielding, resolute, Sāy.; *-tva*, n. fixedness, firmness, concentration (of mind), MārkP. **— vicāraṇa**, n. N. of a wk. by Harsha.

स्थाग *sthāga*, m. (derivation doubtful) a dead body, L.; N. of one of Śiva's attendants, L.

स्थागर *sthāgara*, mfn. made of *sthagara*, q.v., TBr.

स्थागल *sthāgala*, m. or n.(?) = *sthagara* (cf. *sthagala*), g. *kisarâdi*.

Sthāgalika, mf(*ī*)n. dealing in the substance Sthāgala, ib.

स्थाघ *sthāgha*, m. (said to be fr. √1. *sthā*) a shallow, ford (= *gādha*), L.

स्थाजिरावती *sthājirāvatī*, f. (prob. w.r.), ŚāṅkhGṛ.

स्थाणव *sthāṇava*, *sthāṇu* &c. See p. 1262.

स्थाण्डिल *sthāṇḍila*. See p. 1261, col. 3.

स्थान *sthāna*, *sthānin*, *sthāpaka*, °*pana* &c. See p. 1263.

स्थाय *sthāya* &c. See p. 1264, col. 1.

स्थाल *sthāla* &c. See p. 1262, col. 1.

स्थावर *sthāvara* &c. See p. 1264, col. 1.

स्थाविर *sthāvira* &c. See col. 3.

स्थासक *sthāsaka*, m. smearing or perfuming the body with unguents (of sandal &c., cf. *sthakara*, *sthākara*), L.; a bubble of water or any fluid, L.; m. or n.(?) a bubble-shaped ornament on a horse's trappings, Śiś.; a figure made with unguents, Ratnâv.

स्थास्नु *sthāsnu*. See p. 1264, col. 1.

स्थिक *sthika*, m. (accord. to some fr. √1. *sthā*) the buttocks (= *kaṭi-protha*), L.

स्थित *sthita*, *sthiti* &c. See p. 1264.

स्थिर् *sthir*, cl. 1. P. *sthirati*, to stand firmly (in an etymol. explanation), Nir. ix, 11.

Sthiritvā, ind. having turned round (?), Hcar., Sch.

स्थिर *sthira* &c. See p. 1264, col. 3.

स्थिवि *sthivi*, m. (prob.) a bushel (others 'an ear') of grain, RV. x, 68, 3; = *sīmā*, L. **— mát**, mfn. provided with bushels (or 'ears') of grain, ib. 27, 15.

स्थु *sthu*. See *duḥ-shṭhu* and *su-shṭhú*.

स्थुड् *sthuḍ* (= √*thuḍ*), cl. 6. P. *sthuḍati*, to cover, Dhātup. xxviii, 94.

1. **Sthula**, n. (perhaps for *sthuḍa*, see prec.) a sort of long tent, Śiś.

स्थुरिका *sthurikā*, v.l. for *sthūrikā*, q.v.

स्थू *sthū* (collateral of √1. *sthā*, formed to account for the words below), prob. 'to be thick or solid or strong.'

Sthava, m. a he-goat (?), L.

Sthavi, m. (only L.) a sack, bag; heaven; a weaver; fire; a leper or the flesh of a leper; fruit.

Sthavimat, n. and **sthávimán**, m. the thick end, broad part, breadth (°*ma-tás*, ind. 'on the broad side'), MaitrS.; TS.; Br.; Kāṭh.

Sthávira, mf(*ā* or *ī*)n. (cf. *sthāvara*, p. 1264) broad, thick, compact, solid, strong, powerful, RV.; AV.; Br.; MBh.; Hariv.; old, ancient, venerable (°*re kāle* or *bhāve*, 'in old age'), Br. &c. &c.; m. an old man, W.; (with Buddhists) an 'Elder' (N. of the oldest and most venerable Bhikshus), MWB. 184; 255 &c.; N. of Brahmā, L.; (pl.) N. of a school (also *ārya-sth°*), Buddh.; (*ā*), f. an old woman, MW.; a kind of plant, L.; (*am*), n. benzoin, L. **— gāthā**, f. a partic. section of Buddhist writings, Divyâv. **— dāru**, n. a kind of wood, Bhpr. **— dyuti**, mfn. having the dignity of an 'Elder' (cf. above), MBh. **— sthavira**, m. pl. (prob.) the most venerable of the 'Elders,' Divyâv. **Sthavirâyus**, mfn. one who has attained to old age, Hariv. **Sthavirâvalī-carita**, n. N. of a Jaina wk.

Sthavirāya, Nom. Ā. °*yate*, to grow old, become old (said of time), Bhpr.

Sthávishṭha, mfn. (superl. of *sthūra*) very broad or thick or solid or strong, TS. &c. &c.

Sthávīyas, mfn. (compar. of id.) more (or most) broad or thick &c., Br. &c. &c.

Sthāvira, n. (fr. *sthavira*) old age (described as commencing at seventy in men and fifty in women, and ending at ninety, after which period a man is called *varshīyas*), Lāṭy.; MBh. &c.; mfn. (v.l. for *sthavira*) old, senile, MBh.; Hit.

Sthura. See *apa-shṭhura*, p. 53, col. 1.

Sthurin, m. = *sthaurin*, L.

2. **Sthula**. See *apa-shṭhula*, p. 53, col. 1.

Sthūṇa, m. (connected with *sthāṇu*; accord. to some for *sthulna*) N. of a son of Viśvāmitra, MBh.; of a Yaksha, ib.; (*ā*), f., see next; (*ī*), f. uncultivated land, Vop., Sch.; (*am*), n. a post, pillar, Siddh. **— karṇa**, m. N. of a Ṛishi, MBh.

Sthū́ṇā, f. the post or pillar or beam of a house, any post or stake or pillar or column, RV. &c. &c.; the trunk or stump of a tree, Kām.; an iron statue, L.; an anvil, = *śūrmi* or *sūrmi*, L.; (prob.) = *rajju*, a rope, cord, Hcat.; a kind of disease, L. [Cf. Gk. στήλη.] **— karṇá**, mf(*ī*)n. (said of cows whose ears are marked in a partic. manner), MaitrS.; m. a kind of military array, Kām.; N. of a Yaksha, MBh.; of a partic. demon of illness, Hariv.; m. (scil. *bāṇa*) or n. (scil. *astra*) a kind of missile, MBh. **— garta**, m. the pit or hole for a post, L. **— nikhanana-nyāya**, m. the rule of digging or fixing a post more deeply into the soil (applied to a disputant who adds corroborative arguments &c. to confirm an already strong position), A. **— paksha**, m. a kind of military array, Kām. **— padī**, f. one who has feet or legs like pillars, g. *kumbhapadyâdi*. **— bhāra**, m. the weight of a beam, g. *vaṃśâdi*. **— mayūkhá**, n. post and peg, ŚBr. **— rājá**, m. a principal post, ib **— virohaṇa**, n. the sprouting of a wooden stake (after it has been put in the ground to serve as a foot), ŚāṅkhŚr. **— śirsha**, n. the head or capital of a pillar, L. **Sthūṇâvaśesha**, mfn. having only the pillars left (said of a house), Sāh. **Sthūṇôpasthūṇaka**, m. du. N. of two villages, Divyâv.

Sthūṇīya (g. *apūpâdi*) or **sthūṇya** (Kāṭh.), mfn. relating to a post or pillar.

Sthūrá, mfn. (cf. *sthūla* below) thick, dense, heavy, big, bulky, stout, broad, strong, solid, RV.; m. du. the ankles or the buttocks; sg. the lower part of the thigh, L.; a child of Sthūrā, Pat. on Pāṇ. vi, 1, 103, Vārtt. 1; a man, L.; a bull, L.; (*ā*), f. N. of a woman, g. *gargâdi*. **— gudá**, f. (= *guda-kāṇḍe sthūlo bhāgaḥ*), TS. (Sch.) **— yūpa**, m. N. of a man (*-vát*, ind.), RV. **— vāku** = *ucca-dhvani*, L.

Sthūri, mfn. drawn by one animal, RV.; Br.; n. a waggon drawn by one animal, TBr.

Sthūrikā, f. (prob.) the nostril of a barren cow (v.l. *khurikā*, *churikā*, *sthurikā* &c.), Mn. vii, 325 (others 'an ox' or 'a load placed on an ox').

Sthūrin, m. (cf. *sthaurin*) a pack-horse, beast of burden, draught-ox, L. [Cf. Gk. ταῦρος; Lat. *taurus*; Goth. *stiur*, Eng *steer*.]

Sthūrī-pṛishṭha, m. a horse not yet ridden on or broken in by riding, Śiś.

Sthorā, f. the lading or cargo of a ship, Divyâv.

Sthorin, m. = *sthaurin*, L.

Sthauṇabhārika, mfn. (fr. *sthūṇā-bhāra*), g. *vaṃśâdi* (v.l. *sthauṇa-bh°*).

Sthauṇika, mfn. dragging beams of wood, L.

Sthauṇeya or °**yaka**, n. a kind of perfume, Car.; Suśr.; a carrot, L.

Sthaura, m. patr. of the Ṛishi Agni-yuta or Agni-yūpa (author of RV. x, 116), Anukr.; n. firmness, strength, power, W.; a sufficient load for a horse or ass, ib.

Sthaurin, m. a pack-horse, draught-ox, L.

Sthaurya, m. metr. fr. *sthūrā*, g. *gargâdi*.

स्थूण *sthūṇa*, *sthūṇā* &c. See p. 1265, col. 3.

स्थूम *sthūma*, m. (cf. *syūma*) light, L.; the moon, L.

स्थूल् *sthūl* (rather Nom. fr. *sthūla* below), cl. 10. Ā. *sthūlayate* (also P. *sthūlayati* accord. to some), to become big or stout or bulky, increase, grow fat, Dhātup. xxxv, 50.

Sthūlá, mf(*ā́*)n. (fr. √*sthū* = *sthā* and originally identical with *sthūra*) large, thick, stout, massive, bulky, big, huge, AV. &c. &c.; coarse, gross, rough (also fig. = 'not detailed or precisely defined;' cf. *yathā-sth*°), Mn.; MBh. &c.; dense, dull, stolid, doltish, stupid, ignorant (cf. comp.), MBh.; Pañcat.; (in phil.) gross, tangible, material (opp. to *sūkshma*, 'subtle'; cf. *sthūla-śarīra*); m. Artocarpus Integrifolia, L.; N. of one of Śiva's attendants, L.; m. n., g. *ardharcâdi*; (*ā*), f. Scindapsus Officinalis, L.; Cucumis Utilissimus, L.; large cardamoms, L.; n. 'the gross body' (= *sthūla-ś*°), Up.; MBh. &c.; sour milk, curds, L.; = *kūṭa*, L.; a heap, quantity, W.; a tent (prob. for 1. *sthula*), ib. **–kaṅgu**, m. a sort of grain or corn, L. **–kaṇā**, f. a kind of cumin, ib.; Nigella Indica, MW. **–kaṇṭaka**, m. a kind of acacia, L. **–kaṇṭakikā**, f. Salmalia Malabarica, ib. **–kaṇṭā**, f. the egg-plant, ib. **–kanda**, mfn. having a large bulb, Suśr.; m. Arum or a species of Arum, ib.; = *hasti-k*°, ib.; a kind of garlic (= *rakta-laśuna*) or onion, L. **–kandaka**, m. Arum, L. **–karṇa**, m. N. of a Ṛishi, MBh. (v.l. *sthūṇa-k*°). **–kāya**, mfn. large-bodied, corpulent, W. **–kāshṭha-dah** (nom. *-dhak*) or °**ṭhâgni**, m. fire made with thick pieces of timber, L. **–keśa**, m. N. of a Ṛishi, MBh.; Kathās. **–ksheḍa** (L.) or **-kshveḍa** (W.), m. an arrow. **–grīva**, mfn. thick-necked, MW. **–m-karaṇa**, mf(*ī*)n. making big &c., Pāṇ. iii, 2, 56. **–cañcu**, (prob.) f. a kind of culinary plant, L. **–cāpa**, w.r. for *tūla-c*°, L. **–cūḍa**, mfn. having big tufts of hair (said of the Kirātas), R. **–jaṅghā**, f. N. of one of the 9 Samidhs, Gṛihyās. **–jihva**, m. 'thick-tongued,' N. of a Bhūta, Hariv. **–jīraka**, m. a kind of cumin, L.; Nigella Indica, MW. **–taṇḍula**, m. large rice, L. **–tara**, mfn. more bulky, bigger, larger, very large, Pañcat. **–tā**, f. largeness, bigness, bulkiness, ib.; stupidity, clumsiness, ib. **–tāla**, m. Phœnix Paludosa, L. **–tomarin**, mfn. having a thick javelin, Hcat. **–tva**, n. bigness, bulkiness, MW.; stupidity, ib.; (in phil.) grossness, NṛisUp.; Sarvad. **–tvacā**, f. Gmelina Arborea, L. **–daṇḍa**, m. a sort of reed, ib. **–datta**, m. N. of a man, Kathās. **–darbha**, m. Saccharum Munja, Bhpr. **–dalā**, f. Aloe Perfoliata, L. **–deha**, m. n. = *-śarīra*, MW. **–dehin**, mfn. big-bodied, large (opp. to *alpa*), Bhpr. **–dhī**, mfn. dull-witted, stupid, W. **–nāla**, m. a kind of reed, L. **–nāsa**, m. 'large-nosed, thick-n°,' a boar, L. **–nāsika**, m. id., Śiś. **–nīla**, m. a hawk, falcon, L. **–paṭa**, m. n. coarse cloth, MW.; mfn. having coarse cloth or clothes, ib. **–paṭṭa**, m. cotton, L.; n. coarse cloth (accord. to some), MW. **–paṭṭāka**, m. id., L. **–pāda**, mfn. large-footed, club-f°, having swelled legs, MW.; m. an elephant, L.; a man who has elephantiasis, MW. **–piṇḍa**, m. N. of a man (see *sthaula-piṇḍi*). **–pushpa**, m. a kind of plant (= *baka*), L.; Aeschynomene Grandiflora, W.; (*ā*), f. a sort of Aparājitā growing on mountains, L.; Gomphrena Globosa, ib.; (*ī*), f. a kind of plant (= *yava-tiktā*), ib. (v.l. *sūkshma-pushpī*). **–pūlāsa**, n., g. *rāja-dantâdi*. **–pṛishata** (*sthūlá-*), mf(*ī*)n. composed of large drops, R.; coarsely spotted, VS.; MaitrS. **–prakaraṇa**, n. N. of wk. **–prapañca**, m. the gross or material world, Vedântas. **–phala**, n. the gross result of a calculation or measurement, MW.; m. 'having large fruit,' the silk-cotton tree, L.; (*ā*), f. a species of Crotolaria, L. **–bāhu**, m. 'strong-armed,' N. of a man, Kathās.; (*ū*), f. N. of a woman, Pāṇ. iv, 1, 67, Sch. **–buddhi**, mfn. dull-witted, stupid, Kād.; *-mat*, mfn. id., MBh. **–bhadra**, m. N. of one of the six Śruta-kevalins, Jain. **–bhāva**, m. bigness, coarseness, grossness, tangibility, ŚārṅgS. **–bhuja**, m. 'strong-armed,' N. of a Vidyā-dhara, Kathās. **–bhūta**, n. pl. (in phil.) the five grosser elements (see *sāṃkhya*). **–mati**, mfn. = *-buddhi* (accord. to some 'large-minded, intelligent'), VarBṛS. **–madhya**, mf(*ā*)n. thick in the middle, Suśr. **–maya**, mf(*ī*)n. consisting of the grosser elements, material, VP. **–marica**, n. a partic. fragrant berry (= *kakkola*), L. **–māna**, m. gross measure, rough computation, MW. **–mukha**, mfn. thick-mouthed, Pāṇ. vi, 2, 168. **–mūla**, n. 'large root,' a kind of radish, L. **–m-bhavishṇu** or **-m-bhāvuka**, mfn. liable to become large or stout, Pāṇ. iii, 2, 57. **–roma**, mfn. thick-haired, Cāṇ. **–laksha** or **-lakshya**, mfn. 'having large aims or attributes,' munificent, liberal, generous, Yājñ.; MBh. &c.; wise, learned, W.; mindful of both benefits and injuries, ib.; taking a wide aim, shooting at a large target (*-tva*, n.), Śiś. **–lakshi-tā**, f. munificence, liberality, Kām. **–vartma-kṛit**, m. Clerodendrum Siphonantus, L. **–valkala**, m. 'thick-barked,' the red Lodhra, L. **–vālukā**, f. 'having coarse sand,' N. of a river, MBh. **–vishaya**, m. a gross or material object, Vedântas. **–vṛiksha-phala**, m. a variety of Madana, L. **–vaidehī**, f. Scindapsus Officinalis, L. **–śaṅkhā**, f. a woman having a large vulva, MW. **–śara**, m. a kind of large reed, L. **–śarīra**, n. the gross or material and perishable body with which a soul clad in its subtle body is invested (opp. to *sūkshma-* and *liṅga-ś*°, qq.vv.), Vedântas.; RTL. 35; mfn. large-bodied, W. **–śalka**, mfn. large-scaled (as a fish), L. **–śākinī**, f. a kind of vegetable, L. **–śāṭa** and **-śāṭaka**, m., **-śāṭikā** and **-śāṭī**, f. thick or coarse cloth, L. **–śāli**, m. a kind of large rice, L. **–śimbī**, f. a kind of Dolichos, L. **–śiras**, m. 'large-headed,' N. of a Ṛishi, MBh.; Hariv.; of a Rākshasa, Kathās.; of a Yaksha, ib.; n. a large head or summit, W. **–śīrsha**, m. N. of an author, Cat. **–śīrshikā**, f. 'thick-headed,' a kind of small ant, L. **–śūraṇa**, m. or n. large Arum, Suśr. **–śopha**, mfn. greatly swollen (*-tva*, n.), Suśr. **–shaṭpada**, m. a kind of large wasp or bee, L. **–sāyaka**, m. a kind of large reed, L. **–sikta**, n. N. of a Tīrtha, Pat. **–sūkshma**, mfn. large and small, VP.; mighty and subtle (as God who sustains the universe and an atom), MW.; *-prakaraṇa*, n. N. of wk.; *-prapañca*, m. the gross and the subtle world, Vedântas.; *-śarīra*, n. the gross and s° body, ib. **–sūraṇa**, see *-śūraṇa*. **–skandha**, m. 'having a thick stem,' Artocarpus Locucha, L. **–sthūla**, mf(*ā*)n. excessively thick or fat, Kāv. **–hasta**, m. the thick trunk (of an elephant), Megh. 14; a large or coarse hand, ib. (accord. to some). **Sthūlâṅśā**, f. a kind of Curcuma, L. **Sthūlā-karṇa**, w.r. for *sthūṇā-k*°, q.v. **Sthūlâksha**, m. 'large-eyed,' N. of a Ṛishi, MBh.; of a Rākshasa, R.; (*ā*), f. = *veṇu-yashṭi*, Laghuk. **Sthūlâṅga**, mfn. large-bodied (as a fish), L.; m. l° rice, L. **Sthūlâcārya**, m. N. of a man, Bhadrab. **Sthūlântra**, n. the larger intestine near the anus, Yājñ.; Suśr. **Sthūlâmra**, m. the l° mango tree, L. **Sthūlârma**, m. N. of a place, TāṇḍBr. **Sthūlâshṭīva**, m. N. of a man (cf. *sthaulāshṭīvi*). **Sthūlâsthūla**, mfn. large and not large (compar. *-tara*), VP. **Sthūlâsya**, m. 'large-mouthed,' a snake, L. **Sthūlêccha**, mfn. having immoderate desires, Bhartṛ. **Sthūlâiraṇḍa**, m. the l° castor-oil plant, L. **Sthūlâilā**, f. large cardamoms, L. **Sthūlôccaya**, m. a rough heap or mass, large fragment of rock, L.; the middle pace of elephants (neither quick nor slow), Śiś.; (only L.) incompleteness, deficiency, defect; an eruption of pimples on the face; a hollow at the root of an elephant's tusks. **Sthūlôdara**, mfn. one who has a swollen belly, Bcar.

Sthūlaka, mfn., g. *ṛisyâdi*; m. Saccharum Cylindricum, L.

Sthūlin, m. (cf. *sthūrin*) a camel, L.

Sthūlī, in comp. for *sthūla*. **–karaṇa**, n. the act of making large or bulky, causing erections (of the male organ), Cat. **–kṛita**, mfn. made large, enlarged, fattened, MW. **–bhūta**, mfn. become large or thick, fattened, ib.

Sthaulá, mf(*ā́*)n. (= or for *sthūla*, of which it is also the Vṛiddhi form in comp.) stout, robust, RV. vi, 44, 7. **–piṇḍi**, m. (fr. *sthūla-piṇḍa*) a patr., Saṃskārak. **–lakshya**, n. (fr. *sthūla-l*°) munificence, liberality, Mn. vii, 211. **–śīrsha** (fr. *sthūla-śiras*), Pāṇ. vi, 1, 62, Sch. **Sthaulâshṭīvi**, m. (fr. *sthūlâshṭīva*) N. of a grammarian, Nir.

Sthaulaka, mfn. (fr. *sthūla*), g. *ṛisyâdi*.

Sthaulya, n. (fr. id.) stoutness, bigness, largeness, thickness, grossness, denseness (opp. to *saukshmya*), Suśr.; BhP.; Sarvad.; excessive size or length, BhP.; doltishness, density of intellect, MW.

स्थेमन् *stheman*, *sthairya* &c. See p. 1265.

स्थौणाभारिक *sthauṇābhārika*, *sthauṇika* &c. See p. 1265, col. 3.

स्थौर *sthaura*, °*rin*. See p. 1265, col. 3.

स्न *sna*, *snapana*. See below.

स्नव *snava*. See p. 1267, col. 3.

स्नस् *snas*, v.l. for √*snus*, q. v., p. 1268.

स्नसा *snasā*, f. a tendon, muscle, L.

स्ना 1. *snā* (cf. √*snu*), cl. 2. P. (Dhātup. xxiv, 44) *snā́ti*, cl. 4. P. (Nir. vii, 12) *snā́yati* (ep. also Ā. *snāyate*, Pot. *snāyāt*; ep. also *snāyita*; pf. *sasnau*, 3. pl. *sasnuḥ*, MBh.; BhP.; fut. *snātā*, Gr.; *snāsyati*, °*te*, MBh. &c.; aor. *asnāsīt*, Gr.; Prec. *snāyāt* [cf. above] or *sneyāt*, ib.; inf. *snātum*, Br. &c.; ind. p. *snātvā́*, *-snā́ya*, RV. &c.; Ved. also *snātvī*, Pāṇ. vii, 1, 49), to bathe, perform the ceremony of bathing or certain prescribed oblations (esp. on returning home from the house of a religious preceptor, or on concluding certain vows &c., also with *avabhṛitham*), RV. &c. &c.; to smear one's self with (instr.), Sarvad.: Pass. *snā́yate* (aor. *asnāyi*, impers.), Rājat.: Caus. *snāpáyati* or *snapáyati*, with prep. only *snāp*°), to cause to bathe, wash, cleanse, AV. &c. &c.; to wash away, AV. x, 1, 9; to steep or soak in (loc.), Bhpr.; to bathe with tears, weep for (?), MW.: Desid. *sisnāsati*, Pāṇ. viii, 3, 61 (but cf. *sishṇāsu*): Intens. *sāsnāyate*, *sāsnāti*, *sāsneti*, Gr. [Cf. Gk. νάω, νᾶμα; Lat. *nare*.]

Sna. See *nadī-shṇa*.

Snápana, mf(*ī*)n. (fr. Caus.) causing to bathe &c.; used for bathing (as water), AV.; n. the act of causing to bathe, bathing, ablution, ŚBr. &c. &c.

Snapita, mfn. (fr. id.) bathed, washed, sprinkled, wetted, cleansed, L.

Snaya, m. bathing, ablution, lustration, L.

2. **Snā** (or *shṇā*), mfn. bathing, bathed or immersed in (cf. *ghṛita-*, *su-snā* &c.)

Snātá, mfn. bathed, washed, cleansed or purified from (abl. or comp.), AV. &c. &c. (n. also impers.); immersed or versed in (loc. or comp.), Gaut.; R.; BhP.; m. one who has finished his religion, an initiated householder, GṛŚrS. **–vat**, mfn. having bathed or performed religious ablutions, Śiś. **–vasya**, mfn. to be put on after an ablution, KātyŚr. **–vrata**, mfn. = *snātaka-vr*°, R. **Snātânulipta**, mfn. one who is both bathed and anointed, Pāṇ. ii, 1, 49, Sch.

Snātaka, m. one who has bathed or performed ablutions (i.e. a Brāhman who, after performing the ceremonial lustrations required on his finishing his studentship as a Brahma-cārin under a religious teacher, returns home and begins the second period of his life as a Gṛiha-stha, see *samāvartana*; three kinds of Snātakas are named, 1. a *Vidyā-sn*°, q.v., 2. a *Vrata-sn*° [who has completed the vows, such as fasting, continence &c., without the Vedas], 3. a *Vidyā-vrata-sn*° or *Ubhaya-sn*° [who has completed both Vedas and vows], the last is the highest; in a wider sense there may be 9 Snātakas, see Mn. xi, 1), ŚBr.; GṛS.; Gaut.; Mn. iii, 4 &c. (IW. 296). **–vrata**, n. the vows and duties of a Snātaka (explained at full length in the Gṛihya-sūtras and giving a clear notion of what was considered good manners in well-educated persons), ĀśvGṛ.; Kauś.; Mn. &c.; mfn. = next, MBh. **–vratin**, mfn. fulfilling the vows and duties of a Snātaka, MBh.

Snātavya, n. (impers.) it is to be bathed &c., MBh.; Kathās.

Snātṛi. See *a-snātṛi*.

Snātra, n. a bath, ablution, bathing, Pārśvan.

Snātva, mfn. fit for ablutions, capable of being used for bathing, RV.; ŚBr.

Snātvā́, ind. having bathed &c. (see root). **–kālaka**, mfn., g. *mayūra-vyaṃsakâdi*.

Snāna, n. (ifc. f. *ā*) bathing, washing, ablution, religious or ceremonial lustration (as of an idol &c.), bathing in sacred waters (considered as one of the six daily duties [cf. *shaṭ-karman*] or as an essential part of some ceremonial, esp. the ablutions performed by a Brahma-cārin on becoming a householder, cf. *snātaka*), GṛŚrS.; Mn.; MBh. &c. (IW. 242; RTL. 394, n. 1 &c.); washing off, removal by washing, cleansing, BhP.; anything used in ablution (e.g. water, perfumed powder &c.), Kāv.; VarBṛS.; Vet.; BhP. **–kalaśa**, m., **-kumbha**, m. a jar or vessel containing lustral water, Rājat. **–gṛiha**, n. a bathing-house, bath-room, MBh.; Hariv. **–tīrtha**, n. a sacred bathing-place, Subh. **–tṛiṇa**, n. 'b°-grass,' Kuśa grass, L. **–dīpikā**, f. = *-sūtra-d*° (q.v.) **–droṇī**, f. a b°-tub, Rājat. **–paddhati**, f. N. of a Comm. on the

Snāna-sūtra-pariśishṭa by Hari-hara, Cat. — **bhū**, f. bathing-place, bath-room, Priy. — **bhūmi**, f. id., Car. — **yātrā**, f. 'bathing-procession,' a festival held on the day of full moon in the month Jyeshṭha (when images of Kṛishṇa as Jagan-nātha are carried out and bathed; in Orissa this festival is called Ratha-yātrā), MW.; °*trika*, mfn. a member of the above procession, ib. — **vastra**, n., -**vāsas**, n. a b°-dress, wet cloth, Kāv. — **vidhi**, m. 'rules of ablution,' N. of various wks.; -*kshama*, mfn. fit for ceremonial ablutions (said of water), fit for bathing, Kum.; -*paddhati*, f., -*sūtra-bhāshya*, n. N. of Comms. — **veśman**, n. = -*gṛiha*, Kathās. — **śāṭī**, f. (w.r. -*śāṭhī*) bathing-drawers, Mṛicch. — **śālā**, f. = -*gṛiha*, MBh. — **śīla**, mfn. fond of bathing, observing or performing ablutions (esp. in sacred waters), Gaut.; Hit. — **sūtra**, n. N. of a Sūtra wk. ascribed to Kātyāyana (also -*pariśishṭa*); -*dīpikā*, f., -*paddhati*, f., -*bhāshya-vyākhyā*, f. N. of Comms. **Snānâgāra**, n. = *snāna-gṛiha*, MW. **Snānâmbu**, n. bath-water, Kathās. **Snānôttīrṇa**, mfn. emerging from a bath, one who has just completed his ablutions, Śak. **Snānôdaka**, n. = *snānâmbu*, Kathās. **Snānôpakaraṇa**, n. any utensil used in bathing, any accessory of a bath, Pañcat.

Snānin, mfn. bathing, performing ablutions, Śatr.

Snānīya, mfn. fit or suitable for bathing, used in ablution; n. anything used in bathing (e.g. fragrant water &c.), Kauś.; MBh. &c. — **vastra**, n. a bathing-dress, Mālav.

Snāpaka, m. (fr. Caus.) 'bather,' a servant who bathes his master, R.; Car.

Snāpana, n. the act of causing to bathe, attending a person while bathing, Mn.; R.; Hariv. — **vidhi**, m. N. of wk. **Snāpanôcchishṭa-bhojana**, n. du. the act of bathing another person and eating his leavings, Mn. ii, 209.

Snāpita, mfn. caused to bathe, attended on while bathed, immersed, MW.

Snāyin, mfn. bathing, performing an ablution (°*yi-tā*, f.), Mn.; MBh. &c.

Snāsyat, mfn. (fut. p.) about to bathe or perform an ablution; m. a religious student about to become a Snātaka, Mn. ii, 245.

Snéya, n. to be bathed, Br.; Kathās.

स्नायु *snāyu*, f. n. (accord. to some fr. a √*snā* contracted from *sinā*, pres. base of √*si*, 'to bind;' cf. also √*snai*) any sinew or ligament in the human and animal body, tendon, muscle, nerve, vein, TBr.; Suśr.; Mn.; MBh. &c.; the string of a bow, Pañcat.; m. an eruption on the skin of the extremities, Bhpr. [? Cf. Germ. *sënawa, Sehne*; Eng. *sinew*.] — **jāla-vat**, mfn. covered with a network of sinews or nerves or veins, Suśr. — **nirmita**, mfn. made of sinews, Hit. — **pāśa**, m., -**bandha**, m. 's°-band,' a bow-string, Pañcat. — **bandhana**, n. a s°-ligament, MW. — **maya**, mf(*ī*)n. consisting or made of sinews, MBh.; Pañcat. — **marman**, n. the joint or place of junction of a sinew or tendon, Suśr. — **yuta**, mfn. possessed of s°s, Mn. vi, 76. — **rajju**, mfn. having s°s for cords (said of the body), MW. — **spanda**, m. the beat of the nerves, pulse, HPariś.

Snāyuka, m. a kind of parasitical worm, ŚārṅgS.; an eruption on the skin of the extremities, Bhpr.

Snāyv, in comp. for *snāyu*. — **arman**, n. a fleshy tumour of the white of the eye, Suśr.

1. **Snāva**, m. a tendon, sinew, muscle, nerve, L.

2. **Snāva**, in comp. for *snāvan*. — **saṃtata** (*snā́va*-), mf(*ā*)n. covered with sinews or tendons, TBr.

Snāvaka. See *a-snāvaka*.

Snā́van or **snāván**, n. a tendon, muscle, sinew, AV.; TS.; Br.; Kāṭh.; a bow-string, AV.

Snāvanyà, du. (gender unknown) partic. parts of the body of a horse, TS.

Snāvira. See *a-snāvirá*.

स्निग्ध *snigdha* &c. See col. 2.

स्निट् *sniṭ*, cl. 10. P. *sneṭayati*, to go, Dhātup. xxxii, 37; to love (cf. √1. *snih*), Vop.

स्निह् 1. *snih*, cl. 4. P. (Dhātup. xxvi, 91) *snihyati* (m. c. also °*te*; occurring only in pres. base; Gr. also pf. *sisneha*; fut. *snehitā*, *snegdhā*, *sneḍhā*; *snehishyati*, *snekshyati* &c.), to be adhesive or sticky or glutinous or viscid or moist, Car.; Bhpr.; to be fixed upon (loc.), Kathās.; to be attached to or fond of, feel affection for (loc. or gen.), MBh.; Kāv. &c.; cl. 1. P. *snehati*, see Caus.: Pass. *snihyate* (aor. *asnehi*), Gr.: Caus. (or cl. 10. P. Dhātup. xxxii, 36) *sneháyati* (aor. *asishṇihat*), to make unctuous or greasy or moist, Car.; KātyŚr., Sch.; to render pliant or subject, subdue, RV.; to kill, slay, Naigh. ii, 19 (v.l. *snehati*): Desid. *sisnehishati*, *sisnihishati*, *sisnikshati*, Gr.: Intens. *seshṇihyate*, *seshṇegdhi*, *seshṇeḍhi*.

Snigdha, mfn. sticky, viscous or viscid, glutinous, unctuous, slippery, smooth, MBh.; Kāv.; Suśr. &c.; glossy, resplendent, Kālid.; oily, greasy, fat, Suśr.; Subh.; treated or cured with oily substances, Car.; adhesive, attached, affectionate, tender, friendly, attached to or fond of (loc.), Mn.; MBh. &c.; soft, mild, bland, gentle (*am*, ind.), MBh.; Kāv. &c.; lovely, agreeable, charming, Kālid.; Uttarar.; thick, dense (as shade), Megh.; m. a friend, L.; Pinus Longifolia, L.; the red castor-oil plant, L.; (scil. *gaṇḍūsha*) a partic. mode of rinsing the mouth, MW.; (*ā*), f. marrow (= *medā*), L.; a partic. root similar to ginger, L.; (*am*), n. viscidity, thickness, coarseness, W.; bees'-wax, L.; civet, L.; light, lustre, W. — **kandā**, f. a species of plant (= *kandalī*), L. — **keśatā**, f. having soft hair (one of the 80 minor marks of a Buddha), Dharmas. 84 (v.l.) — **jana**, m. an affectionate person, friend, MW. — **taṇḍula**, m. a kind of rice of quick growth, L. — **tama**, mfn. very oily or unctuous, Kāv.; very affectionate, ib. — **tā**, f. unctuousness, oiliness, Kathās.; attachment to, fondness for, ib.; softness (of a vowel), TPrāt., Sch. — **tyāga**, m. abandonment of a beloved person, Bcar. — **tva**, n. unctuousness, oiliness, MW.; blandness, ib.; fondness for, attachment to (loc.), MBh. (v.l.) — **dala**, m. 'smooth-leaved,' a species of Karañja, L. — **dāru**, m. Pinus Deodora and Longifolia, L. — **nakhatā**, f. having soft nails (one of the 80 minor marks of a Buddha), Dharmas. 84. — **pattra**, m. = -*dala*, L.; (also *ā*, f.) Zizyphus Jujuba, L.; Beta Bengalensis, L. — **pattraka**, m. a kind of grass, L. — **parṇī**, f. Sanseviera Roxburghiana, L.; Gmelina Arborea, L. — **pāṇi-lekhatā**, f. having the lines of the hand soft (one of the 80 minor marks of a Buddha), Dharmas. 84. — **piṇḍītaka**, m. a kind of Madana tree, L. — **phalā**, f. the ichneumon plant (= *nākulī*), L. — **bhinnâñjana**, n. glossy pounded collyrium, Megh. — **mudga**, m. a kind of bean, Yājñ., Sch. — **rāji**, m. a kind of snake, ib. — **varṇa**, mfn. having a glossy or bright colour, MW.; having a soft or agreeable complexion, ib. — **śīta-rūksha**, mfn. glossy and cool and (yet) rough (-*tva*, n.), Suśr. **Snigdhâñjana**, n. glossy collyrium, Hariv. **Snigdhôshṇa**, mfn. oily and warm, Suśr.

2. **Snih**, f. (nom. *snik* or *sniṭ*) wetness, moisture, TĀr.; mfn. loving, affectionate, MW.

Snihiti, f. moisture, TĀr.

Sniḍha, mfn. bland, attached, tender, MW.

Snīhán, m. or **snīhā́**, f. the mucus of the nose, ŚBr.

Snīhiti, f. wetness, moisture, TĀr.; (prob.) slaughter, carnage, RV.

Sneha, m. (or n., g. *ardharcâdi*; ifc. f. *ā*) oiliness, unctuousness, fattiness, greasiness, lubricity, viscidity (also as one of the 24 Guṇas of the Vaiśeshika branch of the Nyāya phil.), Suśr.; Yājñ.; Tarkas.; Sarvad. (IW. 69); oil, grease, fat, any oleaginous substance, an unguent, ŚāṅkhBr. &c. &c.; smoothness, glossiness, VarBṛS.; blandness, tenderness, love, attachment to, fondness or affection for (loc., gen., or comp.), friendship with (*saha*), MaitrUp.; MBh.; Kāv. &c.; moisture, MW.; a fluid of the body, ib.; (pl.) N. of the Vaiśyas in Kuśa-dvīpa, VP. — **kartṛi**, mf(°*trī*)n. showing affection or love, Pañcar. — **kumbha**, m. an oil-vessel, a jug or receptacle for oil or grease, Suśr. — **kesarin**, m. castor-oil, Bhpr. — **guṇita**, mfn. endowed with love or affection, MW. — **guru**, mfn. heavy-(hearted) from love for (gen.), Mālatīm. — **ghaṭa**, m. = -*kumbha*, Suśr. — **ghnī**, f. a kind of plant, Car. — **ccheda**, m. interruption of friendship, cessation or loss of regard, Subh. — **dvish**, mfn. disliking oil, Suśr. — **pakva**, mfn. cooked or dressed with oil, W. — **pātra**, n. = -*bhāṇḍa*, L.; a worthy object of affection, Pañcar. — **pāna**, n. drinking oil (as a medicine), Suśr. — **pīta**, mfn. one who has drunk oil, ib. — **pūra**, m. a kind of vetch (?), L. — **pūrvam**, ind. preceded by affection, affectionately, tenderly, fondly, MW. — **pravṛitti**, f. 'course of friendship,' affection, love, Śak. — **prasara**, m. or -**prasrava**, m. flow or effusion or gush of love, Vikr. — **priya**, m. 'fond of oil,' a lamp, L. — **baddha**, mfn. bound by love or affection, MBh. — **bandha**, m. the bonds of love or affection, ib. — **bīja**, m. 'having oily seeds,' Buchanania Latifolia, L. — **bhaṅga**, m. = -*ccheda*, A. — **bhāṇḍa**, n. an oil-vessel, jar of oil, MW.; -*jīvin*, m. living by oil-vessels, an oilman, ib. — **bhū**, m. phlegm, rheum, the phlegmatic humour, L. — **bhūmi**, f. 'oil-source,' any substance yielding oil or grease, W.; any object of affection, one worthy of love, Mālatīm. — **bhūyishṭha**, mfn. consisting mostly of oil or oily substances, Suśr. — **maya**, mf(*ī*)n. full of love or affection, Kathās.; consisting of love or aff°, so called, Mṛicch.; Hcar. — **raṅga**, m. 'oil-coloured,' sesamum, L. — **rasana**, n. 'oil-taster,' the mouth, Gal. — **rekabhū**, m. 'receptacle for the discharge of moisture (or Amṛita),' the moon, L. — **lavaṇa**, n. a partic. mixture of oil and salt, Suśr. — **vacas**, n. words of love or affection, Bcar. — **vat**, mfn. unctuous, oily, fat, Śak.; Sch.; full of affection, loving, tender, MārkP.; Hit.; (*atī*), f. a partic. root similar to ginger, L. — **vara**, n. fat, L. — **varti**, f. a partic. disease of horses, L. — **vasti**, f. an oily injection, Suśr. — **viddha**, m. 'impregnated with oil,' Pinus Deodora, L. — **vimardita**, mfn. rubbed or anointed with oil, Suśr. — **vyakti**, f. manifestation of friendship, Megh. — **śarkarā**, f. a partic. plant or mixture, Car. — **saṃyukta**, mfn. mixed with oil, dressed with ghee, Mn. v, 24. — **saṃskṛita**, mfn. prepared with oil or grease, Suśr. — **saṃjvara-vat**, mfn. smitten with the fever of love, Mālatīm. — **sambhāsha**, m. a kind conversation, MW. — **sāra**, mfn. having oil for its chief ingredient, Suśr. **Snehâkula**, mfn. agitated by love, R. **Snehâkūta**, n. the feeling or passion of love, Mālatīm. **Snehâkta**, mfn. anointed with oil, oiled, greased, lubricated, Suśr. **Snehâṅkana**, n. a mark of affection, Mālatīm. **Snehânuvṛitti**, f. continuance of affection, affectionate or friendly intercourse, Hit. **Snehâbhyakta**, mfn. = *snehâkta*, Suśr. **Snehâśa**, m. 'oil-consumer,' a lamp, L. **Snehâśaya**, m. 'oil-receptacle,' id., L.

Snehaka, mfn. kind, affectionate, Divyâv.; causing affection, conciliating (gen.), MārkP.

Snehan, m. (only L.) a friend; the moon; a kind of disease.

Snehana, mf(*ī*)n. anointing, lubricating, Suśr.; Bhpr.; m. 'feeling affection,' N. of Śiva (cf. *a-sn°*), MBh.; n. unction, lubrication, rubbing or smearing with oil or unguents, Car.; unctuousness, being or becoming oily, Dhātup.; feeling affection, Sāy.

Snehanīya, mfn. to be anointed or lubricated, Car.; to be loved, MW.

Snehayitavya, mfn. to be anointed or lubricated, smeared with oil, Car.

Snehala, mfn. full of affection, fond of (loc.), tender, Śatr.; HPariś. — **tā**, f. affection, tenderness, Kād.

Snehita, mfn. (fr. Caus.) anointed, smeared with oil, MW.; loved, beloved, W.; kind, affectionate, ib.; m. a friend, ib.

Snehitavya, mfn. = *snehanīya*, MW.

Snéhiti, f. (prob.) slaughter, carnage (cf. *snīhiti*), RV.

Snehin, mfn. oily, unctuous, fat, W.; affectionate, friendly, attached to or fond of (comp.), Cat.; m. a friend, L.; a painter, L.

Snehu, m. a kind of disease, L.; the moon, W.

Snehya, mfn. to be anointed or lubricated, Car.

Snaigdhya, n. unctuousness, oiliness, smoothness, Suśr.; tenderness, fondness, affectionateness, W.

Snaihika, mf(*ī*)n. unctuous, oily, Car.

स्नु 1. *snu* (cf. √1. *snā*), cl. 2. P. (Dhātup. xxiv, 29) *snauti* (accord. to Vop. also *snute*; only in pres. base; Gr. also pf. *sushṇāva*, *sushṇuve*; fut. *snotā* or *snavitā* &c.), to drip, distil, trickle, emit fluid, yield milk, BhP. (cf. *pra*-√*snu*): Caus. *snāvayati* (aor. *asushṇavat*), Gr.: Desid. of Caus. *sisnāvayishati* or *susnāvayishati*, ib.: Desid. *susnūshati*, ib.: Intens. *soshṇūyate*, *sishṇavīti*, *soshṇoti*, ib. [Cf. Gk. νέω, νεύσομαι.]

Snava, m. oozing, dripping, trickling, L.

Snavana. See *pra-snavana*, p. 700, col. 1.

Snāvin. See *pra-snāvin*, p. 700, col. 1.

2. **Snu**, (ifc.) dripping, trickling, sprinkling (see *ghṛita-snu*).

Snuta, mfn. trickling, flowing (esp. said of milk flowing from a mother's breast), BhP.

Snuti, f. trickling, distilling, stream, flow, MW.

स्नु 3. *snú*, n. (accord. to L. also m., abridged fr. *sānu* and occurring only in instr. abl. sg., *snunā*, *snós;* and in instr. loc. pl. *snubhis, snushu*) the level summit or edge of a mountain, table-land, surface, height, RV.; VS.

स्नु 4. *snu*, f.=*snāyu*, a sinew, tendon, muscle (only occurring in *snu-tas*, 'from the sinews or muscles'), BhP.

स्नु 5. *snu*, a Kṛid-anta affix to roots forming adjectives expressive of an aptitude to do what is implied by the root, Vop.

स्नुघ्निका *snughnikā* (?), f. natron, mineral alkali, L.

स्नुच् *snuc* (prob. for √*stuc*), cl. 1. Ā. *snocate*, to be bright or clear, L.

स्नुषा *snushā́*, f. (accord. to some connected with *sūnu*) the son's wife, a daughter-in-law, AV. &c. &c.; the spurge plant (=*snuhī*), L. [Cf. Gk. νυός; Lat. *nurus*; Slav. *snŭcha*; Angl. Sax. *snoru*; Germ. *snura, snur, Schnur.*] **-ga**, mfn. having sexual intercourse with a daughter-in-law, Ml. **-tva**, n. the condition of a d°-in-law, Rājat. **-vat**, ind. like (with) a d°-in-law, Mn. viii, 62. **-śvaśurīyā**, f. (scil. *ishṭi*) a sacrifice intended to subdue an adversary as a daughter-in-law is subject to a father-in-law, ĀśvŚr.

स्नुस् *snus* (v.l. *snas*), cl. 4. P. *snusyati*, to eat, Dhātup. xxvi, 5; to disappear, ib.; to take, ib.

स्नुह् 1. *snuh*, cl. 4. P. *snuhyati*, to vomit, Dhātup. xxvi, 90; to be moist (=√*snih*, see *snūhan*).

Snuk, in comp. for 2. *snuh*. **-chada**, m. a kind of reed, Lipeocercis Serrata, L.

2. **Snuh**, mfn. (nom. *snuk* or *snuṭ*) vomiting, one who vomits, MW.; f. a kind of spurge, Euphorbia Antiquorum (its milky juice is used as an emetic &c.; it has 17 synonyms, cf. *sīhuṇḍa* &c.), Car.; Suśr.

Snuhā and **snuhi**, f. id., Hcar.

Snuhī, f. id., Suśr.

Snūhan, m. the mucus of the nose, ĀpŚr.

स्नेय *sneya*. See p. 1267, col. 1.

स्नेह *sneha* &c. See p. 1267, col. 2.

स्नै *snai* (v.l. *stai*), cl. 1. P. *snāyati*, to clothe, wrap round, envelop, adorn, Dhātup. xxii, 25.

स्नैग्ध्य *snaigdhya, snaihika*. See p. 1267, col. 3.

स्पन्द् *spand* (often confounded with √*syand*), cl. 1. Ā. (Dhātup. ii, 13) *spandate* (rarely °*ti*; only in pres. base and inf. *spanditum*; Gr. also pf. *paspande*; fut. *spanditā, spandishyate*; aor. *aspandishṭa*), to quiver, throb, twitch, tremble, vibrate, quake, palpitate, throb with life, quicken (as a child in the womb), PārGṛ.; Car.; MBh. &c.; to kick (as an animal), Br.; ĀśvŚr.; to make any quick movement, move, be active, Hariv.; to flash into life, come suddenly to life, BhP.: Caus. *spandayati* (aor. *apaspandat*), to cause to quiver or shake, MBh.; to move (trans.), ĀśvŚr.: Desid. *pispandishate*, Gr.: Intens., see *panishpadā*. [Cf. Gk. σφενδόνη, σφαδασμός, σφεδανός, σφοδρός; perhaps also Lat. *pendo, pondus*.]

Spanda, m. throbbing, throb, quiver, pulse, tremor, vibration, motion, activity, Kāv.; Rājat.; BhP.; N. of a Śaiva wk. by Abhinava-gupta. **-kārikā**, f. N. of a metrical version of the Spanda-sūtra (q.v.) **-caritra**, n. N. of a wk. on twitching of the limbs (regarded as a branch of the science of augury or prognostication; see *spandana*). **-nirṇaya**, m., **-nilaya**, m., **-pradīpa**, m., **-pradīpikā**, f., **-vivaraṇa**, n., **-vivṛiti**, f., **-śāstra**, n., **-saṃdoha**, m., **-sarvasva**, n. N. of wks. **-sūtra**, n. (also called *śiva-sūtra*) N. of aphorisms on the Śaiva philosophy by Vasu-gupta; *-vimarśinī*, f. N. of a Comm. on the above wk. **Spandârtha-sūtrâvalī**, f. N. of wk. (prob. the *spanda-kārikā*).

Spandaná, mf(*ā́*)n. making a sudden movement, kicking (as a cow), AV.; m. a kind of tree (the wood of which is made into bedsteads, chairs &c.), VarBṛS.; n. throbbing, pulsation, palpitation, quivering, twitching (twitchings and quiverings of the body are supposed to prognosticate good or bad luck, and are therefore minutely described in certain wks.; see above), trembling, agitation, ĀśvGṛ.; Mṛicch. &c.; throbbing with life, quickening (of a child in the womb), Yājñ.; Suśr.; quick movement, motion, Kathās.; w.r. for *syand*°, RV. iii, 53, 19.

Spandita, mfn. quivering, trembling, Sāh.; (fr. Caus.) set in motion, produced, Prab.; n. a pulsation, throb, trembling, Vikr.; movement or activity (of the mind), Prab.

Spandin, mfn. quivering, throbbing, pulsating, tremulous, Megh.; Rājat.

Spandolikā, f. (cf. *syand*°) swinging backwards and forwards, rocking one's self to and fro (as in a swing), BhP.

Spāndana, mfn. derived from the tree Spandana, made of it &c., g. *palāśâdi*.

स्पर *spara*, °*raṇa* &c. See col. 3.

स्परितृ *sparitṛi*. See p. 1269, col. 3.

स्परिश *spariśa*. See p. 1269, col. 1.

स्पर्ध् *spardh* (or *spṛidh*; cf. √*spṛih*), cl. 1. Ā. (Dhātup. ii, 2) *spárdhate* (m. c. also P. °*ti*; Subj. [*prá*]-*spūrdhán*, RV. vi, 67, 9; pf. *paspṛidhé*, °*dhānd*, *ápaspṛidhethām*, RV.; *paspardha*, MBh. &c.; aor. *aspṛidhran*, *spṛidhānd*, RV.; *aspardhishṭa*, Gr.; fut. *spardhitā*, *spardhishyate*, ib.; inf. *spárdhitum*, AV.; Br.; *spūrdháse*, RV.; ind. p. *-spṛidhya*, ib.), to emulate, compete, rival, vie or cope with (instr. with and without *saha*, or acc.), contend or struggle for (loc.), RV. &c. &c.: Caus. *spardhayati*, Gr.: Desid. *pispardhishate*, ib.: Intens. *pāspardhyate*, *pāspardhi*, ib. (*apāspāḥ*, Pāṇ. viii, 3, 14, Sch.)

Paspṛidhānā́. See above.

Spardha, mfn. emulous, envious (*-tā*, f.), W.; (*ā*), f., see below.

Spardhana, n. emulation, rivalry, envy, MW.

Spardhanīya, mfn. to be competed for, striven after, desirable, Nir.

Spardhas. See *vi-shpardhas*.

Spardhā, f. emulation, rivalry, envy, competition for or with (instr. with and without *saha*, gen., loc., or comp.; °*dhayā*, 'in rivalry or emulation'), MBh.; R. &c.; desire for (comp.), Bhartṛ. (v.l.) **-kara**, mf(*ī*)n. emulating, competing or vying with (comp.), Dhūrtan. **-vat**, mfn. id., Bālar.; Viddh.

Spardhita, mfn. contending or competing together, emulating, envious, jealous, MBh.; contended with, challenged, defied, R.

Spardhin, mfn. emulating, rivalling, vying with (comp.), MBh.; Kāv. &c.; proud, W.; superb, gorgeous, W.

Spardhya, mfn. to be competed for, desirable, valuable, MBh.; R. **Spardhyâstaraṇa-vat**, mfn. covered with a valuable carpet, MBh.

Spūrdháse. See root.

Spṛídh, f. contest, competition, battle, fight, RV.; a rival, adversary, ib.; m. a rival, enemy, BhP.; mfn. emulous, vying with (comp.), ib.; desirous of, ib.

Spṛidhānā́. See root.

Spṛidhya. See *mitha-spṛ*°.

स्पर्श् *sparś*. See √4. *spaś*, col. 3.

स्पर्श *sparśa*, °*śana* &c. See p. 1269.

स्पर्ष् *sparsh*, cl. 1. Ā. *sparshate* (*snehane*); see √*parsh*.

स्पश् 1. *spaś* (cf. √1. *paś*; only occurring in pf. *paspaśe*, p. *paspaśānā́*; aor. *áspashṭa*), to see, behold, perceive, espy, RV.: Caus. *spāśayati* (ĀpŚr.) and *spāśáyate* (RV.), to make clear, show; to perceive, observe. [Cf. Gk. σκέπ-τομαι, σκοπ-ή; Lat. *spicio*; Germ. *spëhôn*, *spähen*; Eng. *spy*.]

2. **Spáś**, m. one who looks or beholds, a watcher, spy, messenger (esp. applied to the messengers of Varuṇa), RV.; AV.; VS. [Cf. Lat. *spex* in *auspex*; Gk. σκώψ.]

Spaśa, m. = prec., ShaḍvBr.; Mn.; MBh.; Pañcat.; a fight, war, battle, L.; a kind of gladiator who fights with a savage animal for a reward, W. [Cf. Gk. σκοπός.]

1. **Spashṭá**, mfn. clearly perceived or discerned, distinctly visible, distinct, clear, evident, plain, intelligible, TS. &c. &c.; straight (opp. to 'crooked'), VarBṛS.; Kathās.; real, true, correct, Gaṇit.; Gol.; one who sees clearly, MW.; (*am*), ind. clearly, distinctly, Kāv.; Rājat.; straight out, openly, boldly, Amar.; Śukas. **-garbhā**, f. a woman who shows clear signs of pregnancy, MW. **-tara**, mfn. more or most evident or clear or intelligible, MBh. **-tā**, f. clearness, distinctness, evidence, Vishṇ. **-tāraka**, mfn. having stars distinctly visible (said of the sky), MW. **-pratipatti**, f. clear perception or ascertainment, ib. **-bhāshin** or **-vaktṛi**, mfn. speaking clearly or distinctly, plain-spoken, ib. **Spashṭâkshara**, mfn. 'containing distinct sounds or syllables,' distinctly pronounced or spoken, Ratnāv. **Spashṭârtha**, mfn. clear in meaning, distinct, obvious, perspicuous, intelligible, Cāṇ.; Yājñ., Sch. **Spashṭêtara**, mfn. 'other than clear,' indistinct, unintelligible, L.

Spashṭaya, Nom. P. °*yati*, to make clear, elucidate, ĀśvŚr., Sch.; Kull.; to make straight (cure a hump-back), Kathās.

Spashṭi, in comp. for 1. *spashṭa*. **-karaṇa**, n. making clear or intelligible, W.; **-kriti**, Gaṇit. **-√kṛi**, P. *-karoti*, to make distinct or clear, Sāy.; to rectify, correct (by calculation), Gaṇit. **-kṛita**, mfn. made clear, elucidated, exposed, W. **-kṛiti**, f. rectification, correction (by calculation), Gaṇit. **-bhūta**, mfn. become plain or evident, MW.

Spāśana, n. (fr. Caus.), see Nir. v, 3 and *pratispāśana*.

Spāśita, mfn. = 2. *spashṭa*, Pāṇ. vii, 2, 27.

स्पश् 3. *spaś* (cf. √3. *paś*), cl. 1. P. Ā. *spaśati*, °*te* (p. *paspāśa*, *paspaśe*; fut. *spaśitā* &c.), to bind, fetter, stop, hinder, Dhātup. xxi, 22: Caus. *spāśayati* (aor. *apaspaśat*), Gr.: Desid. *pispaśishati*, °*te*, ib.: Intens. *pāspaśyate*, *pāspashṭi*, ib.

Spaśā, f. girding a wife (at a sacrifice performed by her husband), L.

2. **Spashṭa**, mfn. (for 1. see col. 2) bound, fettered &c., Pāṇ. vii, 2, 27.

स्पश् 4. *spaś* (v.l. *sparś*; connected with √1. *spṛiś*), cl. 10. P. *spāśayati*, to take or take hold of, Dhātup. xxxiii, 7; to unite, join, embrace, ib.

स्पार्शन *spārśana*. See p. 1269, col. 2.

स्पार्ह *spārha* &c. See p. 1269, col. 2.

स्पूर्ध् *spūrdh*, collateral of √*spardh*, q. v.

स्पृ 1. *spṛi* (v.l. *stṛi* and *smṛi*), cl. 5. P. (Dhātup. xxvii, 13) *spṛiṇoti* (in Veda also *spṛiṇuté*; pf. *paspāra*, Br.; aor. *aspar*, Subj. *sparat*, Impv. *spṛidhi*, RV.; *áspārsham*, ib.; fut. *spartā*, *sparishyati*, Gr.; inf. *spárase*, RV.; ind. p. *spṛitvā*, Br.), to release, extricate or deliver from (abl.), save, gain, win, RV.; TS.; Br.; TUp.: Caus. *spārayati*, to attract to one's self, win, TBr.; to preserve, save, rescue, ib.; to gladden, delight, gratify, bestow, Dhātup.

Spára, n. N. of partic. Sāman days and the texts and sacrifices connected with them (*-tvá*, n.), TBr.

Spáraṇa, mf(*ī*)n. saving, delivering, AV.; TS.

Spárase. See under root.

Spartṛi. See *ava-sp*°.

Spṛit, mfn. (only ifc.) delivering one's self from, removing, avoiding (see *kilbisha-spṛit*); gaining, winning (see *dhana-* and *loka-spṛit*); f. a kind of brick, ŚBr.

Spṛita, mfn. saved, gained, won, PañcavBr.

Spṛiti, f. = *spara*, ŚBr.; KātyŚr.

स्पृ 2. *spṛi*, incorrect for √*spṝ*.

Sparitṛi, mfn. See p. 1269, col. 3.

स्पृक्का *spṛikkā*, f. Trigonella Corniculata, Suśr.; VarBṛS.

स्पृध् *spṛidh*. See √*spardh*, col. 2.

स्पृश् 1. *spṛiś*, cl. 6. P. (Dhātup. xxviii, 128) *spṛiśáti* (m.c. also °*te*; pr. p. *spṛiśāna*, MBh.; impf. *asparśat*, BhP.; pf. *pasparśa*, *paspṛiśuḥ*, *paspṛiśe*, ib. &c.; Subj. *paspārśat*, RV.; aor. *aspṛikshat*, AV.; Br.; *asprākshīt*, Br.; MBh.; *aspārkshīt*, Gr.; Prec. *spṛiśyāt*, MBh.; fut. *sprashṭā* or *sparshṭā*, Gr.; *sparkshyati*, ib.; *sprakshyati*, MBh.; inf. *sprashṭum*, ib. &c.; *-spṛíśe*, RV.; *-spṛíśas*, Br.; ind. p. *spṛishṭvā*, *-spṛiśya*, ib. &c.), to touch, feel with the hand, lay the hand on (acc. or loc.), graze, stroke, RV. &c. &c.; to handle, take hold of (*anyo'nyaṃ hastau spṛiśataḥ*, 'they mutually touch or shake hands'), MBh.; Kāv. &c.; (with *apáḥ, udakam, jalam*; or *adbhis* &c.) to touch or sip water, wash or sprinkle certain parts of the body with water, GṛŚrS.; Mn. ii, 60; MBh. &c.; to touch so as to hurt, injure, harm, Kathās.; to perceive or feel by touch, Up.; Mn.; VarBṛS.; to touch, come into contact (lit.; and fig. in astron. sense), VarBṛS.; to reach or penetrate to (loc. or acc.; with *karṇam*, 'to come to the ears;' with *kriyām*, 'to set about any action'), MBh.; R. &c.; to come up to, equal (acc.; with *girā*, 'to equal with words,' i.e. 'to be able to describe'), Kāv.; to act upon, affect, Sarvad.; BhP.; to touch i.e. endow or fill with (instr.), RV. iv, 3, 15; to touch i.e. befall, fall to the lot of, come upon, visit, afflict (acc.), ChUp.; MBh.; Kāv. &c.; to touch, take hold of, make one's own, appropriate, MBh. iv, 135; to attain to, obtain, experience, undergo, MBh.; Kām. &c.; to grant, bestow (cf. Caus.), BhP.: Pass. *spṛiśyate* (aor. *a-sparśi*), to be touched or seized or affected by, MBh. &c.: Caus. *sparśayati*, °*te* (aor. *apasparśat* or *api-spṛiśat*; Subj. *pispṛiśaḥ*, °*śati*, RV.), to cause to touch (two acc.), bring into immediate contact with (loc. or instr.), Mn.; MBh. &c.; to convey to (loc.), RV.; to fill or cover with (instr.) &c.; to perceive by touch, feel, MaitrUp.; to offer, present, give, Mn.; MBh. &c.: Desid. *pispṛikshati* (cf. *pispṛikshu*), Gr.: Intens. *parīspṛiśyate*, *parīsprashṭi*, *parīsparshṭi*, ib.

Spariśa, m. touch (= *sparśa*), L.

Sparśá, mfn. touching (in *a-bhūtala-sp*°, *manaḥ-sp*°, q.v.); m. (ifc. f. *ā*) touch, sense of touch (-*tas*, ind. e.g. *sparśa-taḥ sukham tat*, 'that is pleasant to the touch'), contact (fig. applied to the beginning of an eclipse or to any astron. contact), Mn.; MBh.; VarBṛS. &c.; (in gram.) collective N. of the twenty-five consonants constituting the five classes from *k* to *m* (so-called because formed by complete contact of the organs of utterance; cf. *sthāna* and *spṛishṭa*), Prāt.; ChUp.; BhP.; (in phil.) the quality of tangibility (which constitutes the skin's *vishaya*, q.v.), IW. 68; any quality which is perceptible by touching any object (e.g. heat, cold, smoothness, softness &c.), MBh. &c.; feeling, sensation (e.g. *sirah-śūla-sp*°, 'sensation of headache'), ŚBr. &c. &c.; pleasant feeling, MBh. v, 1366; unpleasant or morbid sensation, illness, Pāṇ. iii, 3, 16, Vārtt. 1, Pat.; air, wind, L.; (accord. to some) temperature, Nyāyad.; a kind of sexual union, L.; a gift, offering (see *kāka-sp*° and *sp*°-*yajña* below); w.r. for *spaśa*, a spy, MBh.; Śiś.; (*ā*), f. an unchaste woman, L.; (a word of unknown meaning), Hariv. 10243. **–klishṭa**, mfn. painful to the touch, Ml. **–kshama**, mfn. capable of touch, tangible, Śak. **–guṇa**, mfn. having the quality of tangibility (said of the air), Mn. i, 76. **–ja**, mfn. produced by touch, BhP. **–tanmātra**, n. the subtle element of tangibility (or of air), Sāṃkhyak. **–tā**, f. a state of contact or touch (in *a-bhū-tala-sparśatā*), Śak. **–tva**, n. a state of feeling, sensation, BhP.; -*jāti-pramāṇa*, n. N. of a Nyāya wk. **–dvesha**, m. sensitiveness to touch, Suśr. **–maṇi**, m. 'touchstone,' a kind of philosopher's stone (supposed to turn everything it touches to gold), L.; -*prabhava*, n. 't°-stone-production,' gold, L. **–yajña**, m. 't°-offering,' an of° consisting in the mere t° of the things offered, MBh. **–yoga-śāstra**, n. N. of a Yoga wk. **–rasika**, mfn. fond of sensation, sensual, lustful, Śāntiś. **–rūpa-vat**, mfn. pleasant to the t° and of beautiful appearance, MBh. **–repha-saṃdhi**, m. the junction of a Sparśa (q.v.) letter and *r*, RPrāt. **–lajjā**, f. 'shrinking from t°,' the sensitive plant, Mimosa Pudica, L. **–vat**, mfn. having tangibility, palpable (-*tva*, n.), Tarkas.; Bhāshāp. &c.; pleasant to the t°, smooth, soft, MBh.; Kum. **–varga**, m. the whole class of Sparśa consonants (see *sparśa*), RPrāt. **–vihāra**, m. a comfortable existence, Mahāvy. **–vedya**, mfn. to be known or apprehended by the sense of t°, MW. **–śabda-vat**, mfn. palpable and audible, BhP. **–śuddhā**, f. 'pure to the t°,' Asparagus Racemosus, L. **–saṃkocin**, m. 'closing at the t°,' Diascorea Globosa, L. **–saṃcārin**, mfn. passing (from one to another) by contact, contagious, infectious, Rājat. **–sukha**, mfn. pleasant to the touch, MW. **–snāna**, n. bathing or ablution at the entrance of the sun or moon into an eclipse, ib. **–spanda** (or, less correctly -*syanda*), m. 'starting at the t°,' a frog, L. **–hāni**, f. loss of feeling or of sensitiveness, Suśr.; red pustules (a kind of disease), ib. **Sparśājña**, mfn. devoid of all feeling or sensation, benumbed, paralyzed (-*tā*, f.), L. **Sparśānandā**, f. 'delighting the t°,' an Apsaras, L. **Sparśānukūla**, mfn. pleasant to the touch, cooling, Śak. **Sparśāśana**, m. pl. 'feeding on mere touch,' N. of a class of gods, MBh. **Sparśāsaha** or °**hishṇu**, mfn. intolerant of touch, sensitive to touch (-*tva*, n.), Suśr. **Sparśêndriya**, n. the sense of touch, Suśr. **Sparśôpala**, m. = *sparśa-maṇi*, Satr. **Sparśôshma-saṃdhi**, m. the junction of a Sparśa (q.v.) letter and sibilant &c. (cf. *ūshman*), RPrāt.

Sparśaka, mfn. touching, feeling, a toucher, L.

Sparśana, mf(*ī*)n. touching, handling, MW.; affecting, acting upon, afflicting, ib.; m. air, wind, L.; n. the act of touching, touch, contact, ŚvetUp.; Yājñ. &c.; sensation, sense of touch, organ of sensation or feeling, sensitive nerve, Mn.; MBh.; Sarvad.; gift, donation, L. **Sparśanêndriya**, n. the sense of touch, Suśr.

Sparśanaka, n. (in Sāṃkhya) that which touches (said of the skin), MW.

Sparśanīya, mfn. to be touched, Pañcat.; to be perceived or felt, MBh.

Sparśayitavya, mfn. (fr. Caus.) to be perceived or felt, PraśnUp.

Sparśāna, m. = *manas*, L.

Sparśika, mfn. tangible, palpable, perceptible, Pat. on Pāṇ. v, 2, 95.

Sparśitṛi, mfn. who or what touches or feels or perceives, MBh.

Sparśin, mfn. (only ifc.) touching, handling, GṛŚrS.; reaching or penetrating to, Rājat.; BhP.

Sparshṭavya, mfn. = *sprashṭavya*, MW.

Sparshṭṛi, mfn. = *sprashṭṛi*, L.

Spārśana, mfn. (fr. *sparśana*) what is touched or felt, palpable, tangible, Pāṇ. iv, 2, 92, Sch. **–pratyaksha**, n. tactile perception, perception by touching or feeling, MW.

2. **Spṛiś**, mfn. (generally ifc.; nom. *spṛik*) touching, coming into contact with (see *kshiti-*, *śava-spṛiś* &c.); reaching to (see *gagana-*, *bhū-spṛiś* &c.); experiencing, betraying, Kāv.; f. = *spṛikkā*, VarBṛS., Sch.

Spṛiśa, mfn. touching, reaching to (in *sarva-dvāra-sp*°), MBh.; m. touch, contact (in *duḥ-sp*°, q.v.); (*ā*), f. a kind of plant (= *bhujaṃga-ghātinī*), L.; (*ī*), f. the prickly nightshade, Solanum Jacquini, L.

Spṛiśi, mfn. = *vishaya-spṛiś*, Hariv. 7433 (Nīlak.)

Spṛiśya, mfn. to be touched or felt, tangible, sensible, MBh.; Hariv. &c.; to be taken in possession or appropriated, Rājat.; (*ā*), f. N. of one of the Samidhs (q.v.), KātyŚr., Sch.

Spṛishṭa, mfn. touched, felt with the hand, handled, AV. &c. &c., affected or afflicted or possessed by (instr. or comp.), MBh.; Kāv. &c.; defiled (cf. comp.); (in gram.) formed by complete contact of the organs of utterance (applied to all consonants except semivowels [called *īshat-spṛishṭa*, 'formed by slight contact'] and except sibilants and *h*, which are called *ardha-spṛishṭa*, 'formed by half-contact'), Prāt.; Śiksh. **–tā**, f. formation by contact (see prec.), VPrāt. **–pūrva**, mfn. felt or experienced before, MBh. **–mātra**, mfn. merely touched, MW. **–maithuna**, mfn. defiled by sexual intercourse, Mn. viii, 205.

Spṛishṭaka, n. a kind of embrace, L.; (*ikā*), f. touching parts of the body (as the feet &c., an asseveration or taking an oath), Mṛicch.; Mcar.

Spṛishṭavya, w.r. for *sprashṭavya*, Hit.

Spṛishṭā-spṛishṭi, ind. mutual touching, touching one another, L. (cf. Pāṇ. ii, 2, 27).

Spṛishṭi, f. touch, touching, contact, ŚBr.

Spṛishṭikā, f. See under *spṛishṭaka* above.

Spṛishṭin, mfn. (only ifc.) one who has touched, Gaut.

Sprashṭavya, mfn. to be touched or handled, Mn.; R.; Hit.; tangible, palpable, sensible, Vajracch.; n. touch, feeling, Mahāvy.

Sprashṭṛi, mfn. who or what touches or feels, ŚBr.; Up.; MBh.; m. any affection causing bodily pain, sickness, disease, morbid heat &c., L.

स्पृह् 1. **spṛih** (connected with √*spardh*, *spṛidh*), cl. 10. P. (Dhātup. xxxv, 19) *spṛiháyati* (m.c. also °*te*; pr. p. *spṛihayat* or *spṛihayamāṇa*, once in Āpast. *spṛihantī*; pf. *spṛihayām-āsa* or -*babhūva*, MBh. &c.; aor. *apaspṛihat*, inf. *spṛihayitum*, Gr.), to be eager, desire eagerly, long for (dat., gen., or acc.), RV. &c. &c.; to envy, be jealous of (dat., gen., or acc.), MBh.; Kāv. &c. [Cf. Gk. σπέρχω; Germ. *springen*; Eng. *spring*.]

Spārhá, mf(*ā*)n. desirable, enviable, excellent, RV.; BhP. **–rādhas** (*spārhá-*), mfn. possessing or bestowing enviable wealth (as Indra), RV. **–vīra** (*spārhá-*), mfn. consisting in excellent heroes or having excellent chiefs or guides, ib.

2. **Spṛih**. See *puru-spṛih* and *ni spṛih*.

Spṛihaṇa, n. (ifc.) longing for, coveting, striving after, MBh.

Spṛihaṇīya, mfn. to be wished or longed for, desirable, attractive to (gen. or instr.), MBh.; Kāv. &c.; enviable, to be envied by (gen.), R.; Kathās. **–tā**, f., **-tva**, n. desirableness, enviableness, Kāv.; Rājat. **–śobha**, mfn. having desirable or enviable beauty, MW.

Spṛihayád-varṇa, mfn. striving after or eager for any partic. appearance or form, vying in appearance or lustre, RV.

Spṛihayáyya, mfn. to be striven after or contended for, desirable, RV.; desiring, desirous (= *spṛihayālu*), Uṇ. iii, 96, Sch.; m. = *nakshatra*, ib.

Spṛihayālu, mfn. eagerly, desirous, eager, jealous, envious, longing for or to (dat., loc., or inf.), MBh.; Kāv. &c. **–tā**, f. (ifc.) desire of, longing for, Śāntiś.

Spṛihayītṛi, mfn. one who envies, an envier of (gen.), Nir., Sch.

Spṛihā, f. (ifc. f. *ā*) eager desire, desire, covetousness, envy, longing for, pleasure or delight in (dat., gen., loc., or comp.; acc. with √*kṛi* or *bandh*, 'to long for, be desirous of [loc. or comp.];' with √*kṛi*, 'to envy any one [loc.]'), MBh.; R. &c.; a kind of plant (v.l. *spṛiśā*), L. **–vat**, mfn. desirous of, longing for, delighting in (loc.), Ragh.; MārkP.

Spṛihālu, mfn. = *spṛihayālu*, L.

Spṛihita, mfn desired, wished for, longed for, MW.

Spṛihya, mfn. to be wished for or desired, W.; m. the citron tree, L.

स्पॄ **spṝi** (v.l. for √*śṝi*), cl. 9. P. *spṛiṇāti*, to hurt, kill, Dhātup. xxxi, 18.

Sparitṛi, mfn. one who injures or causes pain, L.

स्प्रष्टव्य *sprashṭavya*, *sprashṭṛi*. See col. 2.

स्फट् *sphaṭ* (= and v.l. for √*sphuṭ*), cl. 1. P. *sphaṭati*, to burst, expand &c., Dhātup. ix, 44: Caus. or cl. 10. P. to hurt, injure, Dhātup. xxxii, 90. [Cf. Goth. *spilda*; Germ. *spalten*.]

Sphaṭa, m. a snake's expanded hood, L.; (*ā*), f. id., L.; (*ī*), f. alum, L.

Sphaṭika, m. crystal, quartz, ŚvetUp.; Yājñ.; MBh. &c.; (*ā*), f. alum (accord. to some also °*kī*), L.; camphor, L. **–kuḍya**, n. a crystal wall, BhP. **–pātra**, n. a crystal vessel, Suśr. **–prabha**, mfn. glittering like crystal, crystalline, transparent, MW. **–bhitti**, f. = -*kuḍya*, Kir. **–maṇi**, m. crystal, Prab.; -*gṛiha*, n. a house of cr°, MW.; -*vat*, ind. like cr°, Prab.; -*śilā*, f. crystal, ib. **–maya**, mf(*ī*)n consisting or made of cr°, Kād.; Kathās. **–yaśas**, m. N. of a Vidyā-dhara, Kathās. **–śikharin**, m. 'crystal-mountain,' N. of Kailāsa, Bālar. **–śilā**, f. crystal; -*maṇḍapa*, m. or n. a cr°-bower, Ratnâv. **–skambha**, m. a cr° pillar, MW. **–harmya**, n. a cr° palace, Kathās. **Sphaṭikâksha-mālikā**, f. a cr° rosary, Kum. **Sphaṭikâcala**, m. = °*ka-śikharin*, L. **Sphaṭikâdri**, m. id.; -*bhidā*, m. camphor, L. **Sphaṭikâbhra**, m. 'cr°-cloud,' camphor, MW. **Sphaṭikâśman**, m. 'cr°-stone,' crystal, W.

Sphaṭikāri, °*rikā*, °*rī*, f. alum.

Sphaṭita, mfn. torn, Divyâv.

Sphāṭaka, m. a drop of water, L.; n. crystal, L.; (*ī*), f. alum, L.

Sphāṭi. See *viśva-sph*°.

Sphāṭika, mf(*ā* or *ī*)n. made of crystal, crystalline, MBh.; Kāv. &c.; n. crystal, MBh.; R.; a kind of sandal, ĀśvGṛPariś. **–saudha**, m. n. a crystal palace, Śiś. **Sphāṭikôpala**, m. crystal, L.

Sphāṭita, mfn. split open, expanded, made to gape, cleft, rent, torn, Suśr.; VarB S.; Hit.

Sphāṭika, m. = *sphaṭika*, crystal, quartz, L.

Sphāṇi. See *viśva-sph*°.

स्फण्ट् *sphaṇṭ*. See next and √*sphuṭ*.

स्फण्ड् *sphaṇḍ* (v.l. *sphaṇṭ*), cl. 10. P. *sphaṇḍayati*, to jest or joke with, laugh at, Dhātup. xxxii, 4.

स्फर् *sphar*, cl. 6. P. *spharati*, = (and v.l. for) √*sphur* (q.v.): Caus. *sphārayati*, to expand, open or diffuse widely (see below); to bend, discharge (a bow), R.

Sphara or **spharaka**, m. a shield, L. (accord. to some fr. Persian سپر).

Spharaṇa, n. = *sphuraṇa*, trembling, quivering, throbbing, vibration, L.; penetration, Mahāvy.

Spharitra, n. a partic. instrument, Mahāvy.

Sphāra, mf(*ā*)n. (accord. to Uṇ. ii, 13, fr. √*sphāy* below) extensive, wide, large, great, abundant, violent, strong, dense (as mist), loud (as a shout), Kāv.; HPariś.; Pañcad.; m. a shock, slap, bang, Kathās.; = *sphoraṇa*, Vop.; m. or n. a bubble or flaw (in gold &c.); m. n. much, abundance, L. [Cf. Gk. σφαῖρα.] **— phulla**, mfn. full blown, Mālatīm. **— sphāra**, mfn. very extensive &c., Sāh.

Sphāraṇa, n. = *spharaṇa*, L.

Sphārita, mfn. (fr. Caus.) opened wide, Mālatīm.; widely diffused, Bhartṛ.; throbbing, vibrating, MW.

Sphārī-√bhū, P. *-bhavati*, to open wide (intrans.), Kād.; to be spread or diffused widely, increase, grow, multiply, Mṛicch.; Pañcat.

स्फल् *sphal* (v. l. for √*sphul*, and occurring only with prepos., cf. √*skhal*), cl. 1. P. *sphalati*, to quiver, shake, vibrate, burst, break &c.: Caus. *sphālayati*, see *ā-√sphal*. [Cf. Gk. σφάλλω; Lat. *fallo*; Lith. *pùlti*; Germ. *fallen*; Eng. *fall*.]

Sphāla, m. quivering (= *spholana*), Vop.

Sphālana, n. (fr. Caus.) shaking, quivering, W.; flapping or flopping or striking against, slapping, Kull.; rubbing, friction, ib.

स्फवि *sphavi*. See below.

स्फाक *sphāka*. See *pīvaḥ-sphāka*.

स्फाटक *sphāṭuka*, *sphāṭika*. See p. 1269.

स्फाय् *sphāy*, cl. 1. Ā. (Dhātup. xiv, 16) *sphāyate* (Gr. also pf. *pasphāye*, aor. *asphāyishṭa* or *asphāshṭa*, fut. *sphāyitā* &c.), to grow fat, become bulky, swell, increase, expand, Hcar.; to resound, ib.: Pass. *sphīyate*, to become fat, SāmavBr.: Caus. *sphāvayati* (aor. *apisphavat*), to fatten, swell, strengthen, increase, augment, Bhaṭṭ. [? Cf. Gk. σφηλός; Lit. *spěti*; Slav. *spěti*.]

Sphavi, (prob.) m. a kind of tree, L.

Sphātí, f. fattening, breeding (of cattle), RV.; TS.; increase, growth, prosperity, Śatr. **— m-karaṇa**, n. du. N. of two Sāmans, ĀrshBr. **— mát**, mfn. thriving, fat (superl. *-máttama*), AV. **— hārin**, mfn. removing fat, AV.Paipp.

Sphāna, sphāyana. See *gaya-sph°*.

Sphāyat, mfn. (pr. p.) expanding &c. **— kairava**, Nom. P. *-vati*, to resemble an expanding lotus flower, Kāv.

Sphāvayitṛi, m. a fattener, breeder, AitBr.

Sphirá, mfn. fat, RV.; much, abundant, L. [? Cf. Lat. *pro-sper*.]

Sphivi, (prob.) m. a tree, L. = *uda-śvit*, L.

Sphīta, mfn. swollen, enlarged, Bhpr.; thriving, flourishing, successful, prosperous, rich, well off, abounding in, full of (instr. or comp.), MBh.; Kāv. &c.; heavy (with rain, as a cloud), Mṛicch.; dense (as smoke), Mālatīm.; much, abundant, many, numerous, MBh.; R. &c.; cold, L.; affected by hereditary disease, W. **— tā**, f. bulkiness, enlargement, MW.; prosperity, welfare, flourishing condition, Kām. **— nitambā**, f. having full buttocks, Hāsy.

Sphīti, f. welfare, prosperity, Rājat.

Sphītī, in comp. for *sphīta*. **— √kṛi**, P. *-karoti*, to enlarge, augment, Jātakam. **— kṛita**, mfn. enlarged, augmented, increased, R.

Spheman, m. (fr. *sphira*) fatness, abundance &c., Pāṇ. vi, 4, 157.

Spheyas, mfn. (compar. of *sphira*) more or most abundant, ib.

Sphesh̩ṭha, mfn. (superl. of *sphira*) very much, abundant, ib.

स्फार *sphāra*, *°raṇa*. See above.

स्फार्णि *sphārṇi*. See *viśva-sphārṇi*.

स्फाल *sphāla*, *°lana*. See above.

स्फिच् *sphic* or *sphij*, f. (nom. *sphik*; of doubtful derivation) a buttock, hip (*°cau* or *°jau*, du. 'the buttocks'), ŚāṅkhGṛ.; Mn.; MBh. &c. [Cf. Gk. πυγή, or accord. to some ὀσφύς.]

Sphik, in comp. for *sphic*. **— srāva**, m. a kind of disease, VarBṛS.

Sphig, in comp. for *sphic*. **— ghātaka**, m. a kind of tree (much used in medicine, = *kaṭ-phala*), L. **— daghna**, mfn. reaching to the hip, HirP.

Sphigī, f. = *sphic*, a buttock, RV.

स्फिञ्ज *sphiñja*. See *narma-sphiñja*.

स्फिट् *sphiṭ*, cl. 10. P. *spheṭayati*, to hurt, injure, kill, Dhātup. xxxii, 90 (v. l. for √*sphiṭṭ*; accord. to some also, 'to despise;' 'to love;' 'to cover').

Spheṭa. See *saṃ-spheṭa*.

स्फिट्ट् *sphiṭṭ* (cf. √*sphiṭ*, *sphaṭ*), cl. 10. P. *sphiṭṭayati*, to hurt, kill, Dhātup. xxxii, 90.

स्फिर *sphira*. See col. 1.

स्फीत *sphīta*, *sphīti*. See col. 1.

स्फुजिध्वज *sphuji-dhvaja*, m. N. of an astronomer, VarBṛ., Sch.

स्फुट् *sphuṭ* (cf. √*sphaṭ*), cl. 6. P., 1. P. Ā. (Dhātup. xxviii, 80; ix, 44; viii, 7) *sphuṭati*; *sphoṭati*, *°te* (Ā. only in Dhātup.; pf. *pusphoṭa*, Kathās.; aor. *asphoṭīt*, Gr.; fut. *sphoṭitā*, ib.; *sphuṭishyati*, MBh.; ind. p. *sphuṭitvā*, Vet.; *-sphoṭam*, Kathās.), to burst or become suddenly rent asunder, burst or split open (with a sound), part asunder, ŚBr. &c. &c.; to expand, blossom, bloom, Kāv.; BhP.; to disperse, run away, Bhaṭṭ.; to crack (as the joints of the fingers), Car.; to crackle (as fire), Ṛitus.; to burst into view, appear suddenly, Cat.; to abate (as a disease), Kathās.: Caus. *sphuṭayati* (Pass. *sphuṭyate*, Sarvad.), to burst open or into view, Dhātup. xxxv, 84; to make clear or evident, Saṃkar.; Sarvad.; Kull.; *sphoṭayati* (cf. Dhātup. xxxiii, 48; aor. *apusphuṭat*), to burst or rend suddenly, break, split, divide, MBh.; Kāv.; Kathās.; to put out (eyes), Pañcat.; to shake, wag, brandish, R.; Hariv.; Suśr. &c.; to push aside (a bolt), Kathās.; to crackle (as fire), MBh.; to hurt, destroy, kill, MW.; to winnow, ib.

Sphuṭa, mfn. open, opened, Suśr.; BhP.; expanded, blossomed, blown, MBh.; Uttarar.; plain, distinct, manifest, evident, clear, MBh.; VarBṛS. &c.; (in astron.) apparent, real, true, correct, Sūryas.; spread, diffused, extensive, wide, broad, Kum.; Bhartṛ.; Śiś.; extraordinary, strange, Kpr.; full of, filled with, possessed by (instr. or comp.), Divyâv.; Lalit.; white, L.; m. the expanded hood of a serpent, L. (also *ā*, f., Pañcat.); N. of a man, g. *aśvâdi*; (*am*), ind. distinctly, evidently, certainly, Kāv.; Kathās. **— karaṇa**, n. N. of wk. **— candra-tāraka**, mf(*ā*)n. radiant with the moon and stars (said of night), Kum. **— candrikā**, f., **-jyotisha**, n. N. of wks. **— tara**, mfn. more (or most) distinct or clear (*am*, ind.), Śiś.; *°râkshara*, mfn. having very clear words, perfectly clear or intelligible (cf. *sphuṭâksh°*), ib. **— tā**, f. manifestness, distinctness (acc. with √*gam*, 'to become manifest or evident'), Bhaṭṭ.; Kir.; reality, truth, correctness (in *a-sph°*), Gol. **— tāra**, mfn. having stars clearly seen, bright with stars, MW. **— tva**, n. the being open, openness, Suśr.; manifestness &c. (see *-tā*), Saṃk.; Sarvad.; Gaṇit. **— darpaṇa**, m. N. of an astron. wk. by Nārāyaṇâcārya. **— puṇḍarīka**, n. the expanded (lotus of the) heart, Bcar. i, 9. **— paurusha**, mfn. one who has displayed energy, MW. **— phala**, m. coriander or the fruit of Diospyros Embryopteris (= *tumburu*), L.; n. (in geom.) clear or precise result (of any calculation); distinct or precise area (of a triangle &c.) **— phena-rāji**, m. (the sea) bright with lines of foam, Kum. **— bandhanī**, v. l. for *-valkalī*. **— budbuda**, Nom. P. *°dati*, to apparently resemble a water-bubble, Kāv. **— bodha**, m. N. of a Vedânta wk. **— raṅgiṇī**, f. Cardiospermum Halicacabum, L. **— vaktṛi**, mfn. speaking distinctly or frankly, Cāṇ. **— valkalī**, f. Cardiospermum Halicacabum, Subh. **— vivaraṇa**, n. N. of an astron. wk. by Rudra-miśra. **— śabdam**, ind. with a clear sound, distinctly, audibly, Śiś. **— sāra**, m. (prob.) the true latitude of a star or planet, MW. **— siddhânta**, m. N. of an astron. wk. **— sūrya-gati**, f. apparent or true motion of the sun, MW.

Sphuṭâkshara, mfn. having clear words, perspicuous (as speech), Ratnâv. **Sphuṭâgas**, mfn. sinning openly (in the sight of every one), Śiś. **Sphuṭârtha**, m. clear sense or meaning, Śak., Sch.; mfn. having clear sense, perspicuous, intelligible (*tā*, f.), Śiś.

Sphuṭana, n. bursting, opening, expanding, Vāgbh.; Śatr.; cracking (of the joints &c.), Car.

Sphuṭanīya, mfn. to be broken open or split, MW.

Sphuṭi or **sphuṭī**, f. cracking or chapping of the skin of the feet, L.; the fruit of the Karkaṭī or Cucumis Momordica, L.

Sphuṭikā, f. a small bit or fragment, Daś.

Sphuṭita, mfn. burst, budded, blown &c.; laughed at (= *pari-hasita*; cf. √*sphuṇṭ*), MW. **— caraṇa**, mfn. having too flat or wide feet, splay-footed, ib.

Sphuṭī, in comp. for *sphuṭa*. **— karaṇa**, n. the act of making clear or evident, manifestation, Kād.; Saṃk.; making true or correct, correction, Sūryas. **— √kṛi**, P. *-karoti*, to make clear or evident or manifest, Kād.; Pratāp.; to sharpen (the senses), Car. **— bhāva**, m. becoming clear or evident, Nyāyam. **— √bhū**, P. *-bhavati*, to become evident or manifest, Naish.; Sarvad.

Sphoṭa, m. bursting, opening, expansion, disclosure (cf. *narma-sph°*), MBh.; Kāv. &c.; extension (see *kara-sph°*); a swelling, boil, tumour, Car.; Suśr.; a little bit or fragment, chip, L.; crackling, crash, roar, MBh.; VarBṛS.; (in phil.) sound (conceived as eternal, indivisible, and creative), Sarvad.; the eternal and imperceptible element of sounds and words and the real vehicle of the idea which bursts or flashes on the mind when a sound is uttered, Pat.; (*ā*), f. shaking or waving the arms, MārkP.; the expanded hood of a snake (= or w. r. for *sphaṭā*), L. **— kara**, m. Semecarpus Anacardium, L. **— cakra**, n. N. of a gram. wk. **— candrikā**, f. N. of a wk. (on the above philosophical Sphoṭa). **— jīvikā**, f. a kind of trade (perhaps one which involves the practice of splitting by explosive or other methods), HYog. **— tattva**, n., **-nirūpaṇa**, n. N. of wks. **— bījaka**, m. Semecarpus Anacardium, L. **— latā**, f. Gynandropsis Anacardium, L. **— vāda**, m. N. of various wks. (on the above Sphoṭa of phil.) **— hetuka**, m. Semecarpus Anacardium, L.

Sphoṭaka, m. a boil, tumour, Pat.; Car.; (*ikā*), f. id., Suśr.; a kind of bird, L.

Sphoṭana, mfn. breaking or splitting asunder, crushing, destroying, removing, Hariv.; MārkP.; m. 'Crusher,' N. of Śiva, MBh.; (in gram.) 'divider,' a kind of vocal sound audible between partic. conjunct consonants, APrāt.; (*ī*), f. an instrument for splitting or cleaving, a gimlet, auger, L.; (*am*), n. the act of breaking or tearing asunder &c., Āpast.; Suśr.; Pañcat.; winnowing grain &c., L.; shaking or waving (the arms), Sāh.; cracking (the fingers), Āpast.; (in gram.) the separation of certain conjunct consonants by the insertion of an audible vocal sound (cf. above), VPrāt.

Sphoṭāyana, m. N. of a grammarian, Pāṇ. vi, 1, 123.

Sphoṭikā. See *sphoṭaka* above.

Sphoṭita, mfn. (fr. Caus.) made to burst or open, rent or torn asunder, cleft, split, disclosed, MBh.; Kāv. &c.; n. crackling, VarBṛS. **— nayana**, mfn. having the eyes put out, Pañcat. **Sphoṭitârgala**, mfn. having the bolt pushed aside or the lock opened, Kathās.

Sphoṭinī, f. a cucumber, L.

Sphauṭāyana, m. patr. fr. *sphuṭa*, g. *aśvâdi*.

स्फुट्ट् *sphuṭṭ*, cl. 10. P. *sphuṭṭayati*, to despise, disrespect, Dhātup. xxxii, 37 (Vop.)

स्फुड् *sphuḍ*, cl. 6. P. *sphuḍati*, to cover, Dhātup. xxviii, 97.

स्फुण्ट् *sphuṇṭ*, cl. 1. P. *sphuṇṭati*, to open, expand, Dhātup. ix, 44; cl. 10. P. *sphuṇṭayati*, to jest, joke, laugh (v. l. for next), ib. xxxii, 4.

स्फुण्ड् *sphuṇḍ*, cl. 1. Ā. *sphuṇḍate*, to open, expand, Dhātup. viii, 25; cl. 10. P. *sphuṇḍayati*, to jest &c. (cf. prec.), ib. xxxii, 4.

स्फुत् *sphut*, an imitative sound (cf. *phut*), L. **— kara**, mfn. making a crackling sound (said of fire), MW. **— kāra**, m. a crackling sound, L.

स्फुर् 1. *sphur* (cf. √*sphar*), cl. 6. P. (Dhātup. xxviii, 95) *sphurátí* (m. c. also *°te*; p. *sphurat* and *sphuramāṇa* [qq. vv.]; only in pres. base, but see *apa-√sphur*; Gr. also pf. *pusphora*, *pusphure*; fut. *sphuritā*, *sphurishyati*; aor. *asphorīt*; Prec. *sphūryāt*; inf. *sphuritum*), to spurn, RV.; AV.; to dart, bound, rebound, spring, RV.; MBh.; Kāv.; to tremble, throb, quiver, palpitate, twitch (as the nerves of the arm, Śak.), struggle, Kauś.; MBh. &c.; to flash, glitter, gleam, glisten, twinkle, sparkle, MaitrUp.; R. &c.; to shine, be brilliant or distinguished, Rājat.; Kathās.; MārkP.; to break forth, burst out plainly or visibly, start into view, be evident or manifest, become displayed or expanded, NṛisUp.; MBh. &c.; to hurt, destroy, Naigh. ii, 19: Caus. *sphorayati* (aor. *apusphurat* or *apuspharat*), to stretch, draw or bend (a bow), Bhaṭṭ.; to adduce an argument, Śaṃk., Sch.; to cause to shine, eulogize, praise excessively, Pañcad.; *sphurayati*, to fill with (instr.), Lalit.: Desid. *pusphurishati*, Gr.: Intens. *posphuryate, posphorti*. [Cf. Gk. σπαίρω, σφυρόν; Lat. *sperno*; Lith. *spirti*; Germ. *sporo, spor, Sporn*; Eng. *spur, spurn*.]

2. **Sphur,** (ifc.) quivering, trembling, throbbing, Śiś. ii, 14.

Sphura, mfn. id., Pañcat.; m. quiver, throb &c. (in *sa-sphura*, 'throbbing,' i.e. 'living'), Bhaṭṭ.; = (and v.l. for) *sphara*, a shield, L.

Sphuraṇa, mfn. glittering, sparkling, VarBṛS.; n. the act of trembling, throbbing, vibration, pulsation (also *ā*, f.), Dhātup.; L.; quivering or throbbing of parts of the body (as indicating good or bad luck), MW.; springing or breaking forth, starting into view, expansion, manifestation, Sāh.; BhP.; Sarvad.; flashing, coruscation, twinkling, glittering, Megh.; Mālatīm.

Sphurat, mfn. (pr. p. P.) trembling, shaking &c. (see root and cf. comp.) **-taraṃga-jihva,** mfn. having tongue-like tremulous waves (said of a river), Rājat. **-prabhā-maṇḍala,** mfn. surrounded by a circle of tremulous light (said of a dart), Ragh.

Sphurad, in comp. for *sphurat*. **-adhar'oshṭha,** mfn. having quivering lips (*am*, ind.), MW. **-ulkā,** f. a shooting meteor, aerolite, ib.; °*kākṛiti*, mfn. having the form of a sh° meteor, ib. **-oshṭha,** mf(*ī*)n. with quivering lip, MBh. **-oshṭhaka,** mfn. id., L. **-gandha,** m. a diffused odour, Bhartṛ.

Sphuran, in comp. for *sphurat*. **-mīna,** mfn. having glittering fishes, gleaming with fishes, Rājat.

Sphuramāṇa, mfn. (pr. p. Ā.) trembling, quivering &c. **Sphuramāṇâdharoshṭha,** mfn. having quivering lips, R.

Sphurita, mfn. quivering, throbbing, trembling, palpitating, flashing &c., Kāv.; VarBṛS.; Pañcat.; struggling, Vās.; glittered, flashed (n. impers. 'it has been flashed by'), Hariv.; Kālid.; BhP.; broken forth, burst into view, suddenly arisen or appeared, Kathās.; Sarvad.; plainly displayed or exhibited, Śiś.; swelled, swollen, W.; (*am*), n. a tremulous or convulsive motion, quiver, throb, twitch, tremor, convulsion, Kālid.; Bhartṛ.; agitation or emotion of mind, MW.; flash, gleam, glittering, radiance, sheen, MBh.; Kathās.; sudden appearance, coming into being, Rājat. **-śatahrada,** mfn. having flashing lightning (said of a cloud), ib. **Sphuritâdhara,** mfn. having lips trembling with (comp.), Kum. **Sphuritôttarâdhara,** mfn. having trembling upper and under lip, ib.

Sphūrta, mfn. (accord. to some) throbbed, throbbing, MW.; suddenly risen into remembrance, ib.

Sphūrti, f. quivering, throbbing, throb, palpitation, tremor, vibration, Bhpr.; breaking forth visibly, sudden appearance or display, manifestation, Kāv.; Rājat.; bragging, boasting, Pañcad. **-mat,** mfn. throbbing, thrilling (with joy or excitement), tremulous, agitated, W.; tender-hearted, ib.; m. a follower or worshipper of Śiva (= *pāśupata*), L.

Sphoraṇa, n. throbbing, quivering (= *sphāra*), Vop.

स्फुर्छ् *sphurch, sphurj*. See √*sphūrch, sphūrj*.

स्फुल् *sphul* (later collateral of √*sphur*; only with prep., see *ni-, -niḥ-*, and *vi-*√*sphul*; cf. √*sphal*), cl. 6. P. (Dhātup. xxviii, 96) *sphulati* (pf. *pusphola*, fut. *sphulitā* &c., Gr.), to tremble, throb, vibrate, Dhātup.; to dart forth, appear, ib.; to collect, ib.; to slay, kill, Naigh. ii, 19. [For cognate words see under √*sphal*.]

Sphula, n. a tent (= *vastra-veśman*), L. **-mañjarī,** f. Achyranthes Aspera, L.

Sphulana, n. trembling, throbbing, vibration (= *sphuraṇa*), L.

Sphuliṅga, m. (accord. to L. also n. and *ā*, f.; perhaps for *sphulam-ga*) a spark of fire, MBh.; R. &c.; a fire-brand, ĀpŚr., Sch. **-vat,** mfn. scattering sparks, Śiś.

Sphuliṅgaka, m. a spark of fire, Yājñ.; BhP.

Sphuliṅgāya, Nom. Ā. °*yate*, to be or burn like sparks of fire, Kāv.

Sphuliṅgin, mfn. having sparks of fire, sparkling, MW.; (*inī*), f. N. of one of the seven tongues of Agni or fire, MuṇḍUp.; MārkP.

Spholana, n. = *sphāla*, Vop.

स्फूर्छ् *sphūrch* (also written *svūrch*), cl. 1. P. *sphūrchati*, to spread, extend, Dhātup. vii, 33; to forget, ib.

Sphūrchita, mfn. spread, Gr.; forgotten, ib.

1. **Sphūrṇa,** id., ib.

स्फूर्ज् *sphūrj*, cl. 1. P. (Dhātup. vii, 61) *sphūrjati* (only in pres.; Gr. also pf. *pusphūrja*, fut. *sphūrjitā* &c.), to rumble, roar, thunder, crash, Kāv.; Kathās.; to burst forth, be displayed, appear, ib.; Rājat.; Sāh.: Caus. *sphūrjayati* (aor. *apusphūrjat*), to crash, crackle, AV.; AitBr.: Desid. *pusphūrjishati*, Gr.: Intens. *posphūrjyate, posphūrkti*, ib. [Cf. Gk. σφαραγέομαι.]

Sphūrja, m. the crashing sound of thunder, thunder-clap, W.; Indra's thunderbolt, ib.; sudden outbreak (cf. *narma-sph*°); N. of a Rākshasa, BhāgP.; a kind of plant (= *sphūrjaka*), L. **Sphūrjā-vat,** mfn. thundering, Bhaṭṭ.

Sphūrjaka, m. a kind of plant (Diospyros Embryopteris, Strychnos &c., L.), ŚBr.; Car.; Suśr.

Sphūrjathu, m. thunder, a thunder-clap, Mcar.; Amaranthus Polygonoides, L.

Sphūrjana, m. = *sphurjaka*, L.; n. thundering, explosion, crash (Gk. σφάραγος), W.

Sphūrji. See *viśva-sph*°.

Sphūrjita, mfn. thundering; n. thunder, a thunder-clap, crash, roar &c., Kāv.

2. **Sphūrṇa,** mfn. (?) thundered, MW.

स्फेमन् *spheman* &c. See p. 1270, col. 1.

स्फैजायनि *sphaijāyani*, mfn. (fr. *sphij*), g. *karṇâdi*.

Sphaijika, mfn. (fr. id.) g. *vetanâdi*.

स्फोट *sphoṭa*, °*ṭaka* &c. See p. 1270, col. 3.

स्फ्य *sphyá*, n. an implement used in sacrifices (described as a flat piece of wood shaped like a sword for stirring the offerings of boiled rice, or, accord. to some, for trimming the mound used as an altar), AV.; TS.; Br.; GṛŚrS.; Mn.; MBh.; a spar or boom (of a ship's sails), ŚBr.; (also n.) a kind of oar, R. [Cf. accord. to some, Gk. σφήν; Germ. *spân, Span*.] **-kṛit,** mfn. making a Sphya, ĀpŚr.; m. N. of a man (cf. *sphaiyakṛita*). **-kṛita,** m. (prob. w.r. for prec.), g. *dvārâdi*. **-vartani,** f. the furrow or line made by the Sphya (in marking out the sacrificial ground), AitBr. **Sphyâgra,** mfn. having a point like the Sphya (said of a sacrificial post), ŚrS.

Sphaiyakṛita, m. patr. fr. *sphya-kṛit* or *sphya-kṛita* (cf. above), Kāś. on Pāṇ. vii, 3, 4.

स्व्रृ *sbṛi*. See √*svṛi*, p. 1285, col. 3.

स्म *sma, smā* (or *shma, shmā*), ind. a particle perhaps originally equivalent to 'ever,' 'always;' and later to 'indeed,' 'certainly,' 'verily,' 'surely' (it is often used pleonastically, and in earlier language generally follows a similar particle [esp. *ha, na*], or relative, or prep. or verb, while in later language it frequently follows *iti, na* and *mā́* [cf. 1. *mā́*]; it is also joined with a pres. tense or pres. participle to give them a past sense [e.g. *praviśanti sma*, 'they entered']; this use of *sma* is also found in the Brāhmaṇas and is extended to *veda* and *āha*, cf. Vām. v, 2, 46), RV. &c. &c.

स्मत् *smát*, ind. (prob. connected with prec.; accord. to Sāy. = *sumát*, q. v.) together, at the same time, at once (as a prep. with instr. = 'together or along with;' often in comp. = 'having,' 'possessing,' 'provided with'), RV. **-puraṃdhi** (*smát-*), mfn. having abundance, munificent (said of Indra), RV.

Smad, in comp. for *smat*. **-abhīśu** (*smád-*), mfn. having (beautiful) reins, RV. **-ibha** (*smád-*), n. 'having followers (?),' N. of a man (the enemy of Kutsa), ib. **-ishṭa** (*smád-*), mfn. having an errand, ib. **-ūdhnī** (*smád-*), f. (see *ū́dhas*) having a full udder, always giving milk (said of a cow), ib. **-dishṭi** (*smád-*), mfn. well trained or practised, ib. **-rātishac** (*smád-*; strong form °*shāc*), mfn. attended by givers or liberal men, ib.

स्मन् *smán*, m. (meaning unknown), MaitrS.

स्मय *smaya* &c. See col. 3.

स्मर *smara* &c. See p. 1272, col. 1.

स्मार्त *smārta* &c. See p. 1272, col. 2.

स्मि *smi*, cl. 1. Ā. (Dhātup. xxii, 51) *smayate* (m. c. also °*ti*; pf. *sismiye* or *sishmiyé* [p. *sishmiyāṇá*, cf. *upa-*√*smi*], ep. also *-smayām-āsa*; aor. *asmeshṭa*, Bhaṭṭ. 259; *asmayishṭhās*, MBh.; fut. *smetā, smeshyate*. Gr.; inf. *smetum*, ib.; ind. p. *smitvā*, Sāh.; *-smitya, -smayitya*, MBh.), to smile, blush, become red or radiant, shine, RV.; TS.; Kāṭh.; to smile, laugh, MBh.; Kāv. &c.; to expand, bloom (as a flower), Kāv.; to be proud or arrogant, BhP.: Pass. *smīyate* (aor. *asmāyi*), Gr.: Caus. *smāyayati*, °*te* (aor. *asismayat*; also *smāpayati* in *vi-*√*smi*, q. v.), to cause to smile or laugh &c.; (Ā.) to laugh at, mock, despise, Dhātup. xxxii, 37 (v.l. for *smiṭ*, q. v.): Desid. *sismayishate*, Gr.: Intens. *seshmīyate* (p. °*yamāna*, Nir. viii, 11), *seshmayīti, seshmeti*, ib. [Cf. Gk. φιλομμειδής for φιλο-σμειδης; μεῖδος, μειδάω; Lat. *mirus, mirari*; Slav. *smijati*; Eng. *smile*.]

Smaya, m. (ifc. f. *ā*) smiling at anything, wonder, surprise, astonishment, MBh.; Bhartṛ. (v.l.); arrogance, conceit, pride in or at (comp.), Ragh.; Daś.; BhP.; Pride (personified as the son of Dharma and Pushṭi), BhP. **-dāna,** n. an ostentatious donation, Hcat. **-nutti,** f. the driving away or pulling down of pride, MW. **Smayâdika,** mfn. beginning with (i.e. based chiefly on) arrogance, MBh.

Smayana, n. a smile, gentle laughter, ĀśvŚr.

Smayanīya, mfn. to be smiled (n. impers.), MW.

Smayāka, m. Panicum Miliaceum, L.

Smayin, mfn. smiling, laughing (in *antaḥ-sm*°, 'laughing inwardly'), Sukas.

Smita, mfn. smiled, smiling, MBh.; R. &c.; expanded, blown, blossomed, Śiś.; Pañcat.; n. a smile, gentle laugh (°*taṃ* √*kṛi*, 'to smile'), MBh.; Kāv. &c. **-dṛiś,** f. 'having a smiling look,' a handsome woman, W. **-pūrva,** mfn. 'preceded by a smile,' with a smile, smiling (*am*, ind.), MBh.; °*vâbhibhāshin*, mfn. addressing with a smile (°*shi-tā*, f.), Kād. **-mukha,** mfn. having a smiling face, R. **-vāc,** mfn. speaking with a smile, Kām. **-śālin,** mfn. having smiles, smiling, laughing, W. **-śobhin,** mfn. smiling beautifully, MW. **Smitôjjvala,** mfn. (an eye) bright with a smile, Mālatīm.

Smiti, f. smiling, a smile, laughter, MW.

Smetavya, mfn. to be smiled, TĀr.

Smera, mf(*ā*)n. smiling, friendly, Hariv.; Kālid.; Kathās. &c.; expanded, blown (as a flower), Vās.; Sāh.; proud (see comp.); evident, apparent, W.; (ifc.) gay, abounding in, full of, Hcar.; m. a smile, laugh (in *á-smera, sa-smeram*, qq. vv.); manifestation, appearance, W. **-tā,** f. smiling, a smile, Sāh. **-mukha,** mfn. having a smiling face, Kum.; Gīt. **-vishkira,** m. 'proud bird,' a peacock, L.

स्मिट् *smiṭ*, cl. 10. P. *smeṭayati*, to despise ('to go,' Śākaṭ.), Dhātup. xxxii, 37; to love, xxxii, 36 (Vop.)

स्मील् *smīl*, v.l. for √*śmīl*, q v.

स्मृ 1. *smṛi*, v.l. for √*spṛi*, q.v.

स्मृ 2. *smṛi*, cl. 1. P. (Dhātup. xxii, 35) *smárati* (m. c. also °*te*; pf. *sasmāra, sasmartha, sasmaruḥ*, MBh.; R. &c.; aor. *asmārshīt*, °*shuḥ*, ib.; fut. *smartā, smarishyati*, ib.; inf. *smartum*, ib.; ind. p. *smṛitvā*, GṛŚrS.; *smaritvā*, MBh.; *-smṛitya, smāram* [q. v.], ib. &c.), to remember, recollect, bear in mind, call to mind, think of, be mindful of (gen. or acc.; the action remembered is expressed by a p. p. or an impf. with *yad*, 'that,' or by a fut. without *yad*; the fut. may stand with *yad*, if there are two actions; cf. Pāṇ. ii, 3, 52; iii, 2, 112 &c.), RV. &c. &c.; to remember or think of with sorrow or regret, MBh.; to hand down memoriter, teach, declare, RPrāt.; Kāś.; Pañcat.; to recite, Hcat.: Pass. *smaryáte* (aor. *asmāri*; Prec. *smṛishīshṭa* or *smarishīshṭa*), to be remembered or recorded or declared (as a law) or mentioned in the Smṛiti (with *na*, 'to be passed over in silence'), Br.; Rājat.; Sarvad.; to be declared or regarded as, pass for (nom. or loc.), Āpast.; Kāś.: Caus. *smārayati* (rarely *smarayati*; m. c. also Ā.; aor. *asasmarat*; Pass. *smāryate*), to cause to remember or be mindful of or regret, MBh.; R. &c. (cf. Pāṇ. i, 3, 67, Sch.); to remind any one of (two acc. or acc. and gen. or rarely gen. of person), MBh.; Kāv. &c.: Desid. *susmūrshate* (Pāṇ. i, 3, 57), to wish to remember, Bhaṭṭ.: Intens. *sāsmaryate* or *sāsmarti*, Gr. [Cf. Gk. μέρμερος; Lat. *memor*, *mora*.]

Smara, mf(*ā*)n. remembering, recollecting (see *jāti-smara*); m. (ifc. f. *ā*) memory, remembrance, recollection, ChUp.; Uttarar.; loving recollection, love, (esp.) sexual love, AV. &c. &c.; Kāma-deva (god of love), Kālid.; Kathās. &c.; an interpreter or explainer of the Veda (and 'the god of love'), Naish.; the 7th astrol. mansion, VarBṛS. — **kathā**, f. love-talk, lover's prattle, VarBṛS. — **karman**, n. any amorous act, wanton behaviour, W. — **kāra**, mf(*ī*)n. exciting love, VarBṛS. — **kūpaka**, m. or -**kūpikā**, f. 'well of love,' the female organ, L. — **guru**, m. 'l°-preceptor,' N. of Vishṇu, L. — **gṛiha**, n. 'abode of love,' the female organ, L. — **cakra** or -**candra**, m. a kind of sexual union, L. — **cchattra**, n. the clitoris, L. — **jīvanī**, f. N. of a Surâṅganā, Siṃhâs. — **jvara**, m. 'love-fever,' ardent l°, Vet. — **tattva-prakāśikā**, f. N. of an erotic wk. — **tā**, f. state of recollection (see *jāti-sm°*). — **tāpa-maya**, mf(*ī*)n. consisting of the fire of l° (with *gada* = 'love-fever'), Naish. — **tva**, n. = -*tā* (see *jāti-sm°*). — **daśā**, f. state of the body produced by love (ten states are named: joy of the eyes, pensive reflection, desire, sleeplessness, emaciation, indifference to external objects, abandonment of shame, infatuation, fainting away, death), Megh. — **dahana**, m. 'burner of Kāma,' N. of Śiva (cf. under *an-aṅga*), Inscr. — **dāyin**, mfn. arousing love, Kir. — **dīpana**, mfn. id., Ragh.; m. N. of an author, Cat. — **dīpikā**, f. N. of an erotic wk. — **durmada**, mfn. intoxicated or infatuated by l°, BhP. — **dhvaja**, m. 'love-sign,' a partic. musical instrument, L.; the male organ, L.; a fabulous fish (regarded as Kāma's emblem), W.; (*ā*), f. a bright moonlight night, L.; (*am*), n. the female organ, L. — **nipuṇa**, mfn. skilled in (the art of) love, VarBṛS. — **pīḍita**, mfn. tormented by love, Pañcat. — **priyā**, f. 'dear to Kāma,' N. of Rati (q.v.), L. — **bāṇa-paṅkti**, f. the five arrows of Kāma (collectively), L. — **bhāsita**, mfn. inflamed by l°, MW. — **bhū**, mfn. arisen from l°, Śṛiṅgār. — **mandira**, n. = -*gṛiha*, L. — **maya**, mf(*ī*)n. produced by l°, Śiś. — **mush**, m. destroyer of Kāma, N. of Śiva, Kāv. — **moha**, m. infatuation of l°, W. — **mohita**, mfn. infatuated by l°, ib. — **ruj**, f. l°-sickness, BhP. — **lekha**, m. a love-letter, BhP. — **lekhanī**, f. the Śārikā bird, L. — **vatī**, f. a woman in love, L. — **vadhūya**, Nom. P. °*yati*, to resemble Kāma's wife, Kuval. — **vallabha**, m. 'love's favourite,' N. of A-niruddha, L. — **vīthikā**, f. 'l°-market,' a prostitute, harlot, L. — **vṛiddhi**, f. 'love-increase,' N. of a partic. plant (whose seed is an aphrodisiac), L.; -*saṃjña*, m. id., MW. — **śatru**, m. 'enemy of Kāma,' N. of Śiva (cf. *an-aṅga*), L. — **śabara**, m. 'love-barbarian,' cruel l°, MW. — **śara-maya**, mf(*ī*)n. abounding in Kāma's arrows (i.e. partic. flowers), Śukas. — **śāsana**, m. 'chastiser of Kāma,' N. of Śiva (cf. -*śatru*), Kum. — **śāstra**, n. a manual of erotics, Rājat. — **sakha**, m. 'love's friend,' the spring, Kum.; the moon, L. — **saha**, mfn. capable of exciting l°, Śiś. — **sāyaka-lakshya**, n. the aim of Kāma's arrows (-*tā*, f.), Kathās. — **stambha**, m. 'l°-column,' the male organ, L. — **smarya**, m. 'to be remembered by Kāma,' a donkey (noted for sexual power), L. — **hara**, m. 'love-destroyer,' N. of Śiva (cf. -*śatru*), Kautukas. **Smarâkula** or °**lita**, mfn. agitated by love, love-sick, Hit. **Smarâkṛishṭa**, mfn. attracted or overcome by love, Kathās. **Smarâgāra**, n. = *smara-gṛiha*, L. **Smarâṅkuśa**, m. 'love-hook,' a finger-nail, L.; a lascivious person, L. **Smarâtura**, mfn. love-sick, pining with love, VarBṛS. **Smarâdhivāsa**, m. 'love's abode,' the Aśoka tree, L. **Smarândha**, mfn. l°-blinded, infatuated by l°, W. **Smarâmra**, m. a species of Āmra, L. **Smarâri**, m. = *smara-śatru*, Kād. **Smarârta**, mfn. l°-sick, Naish., Sch. **Smarâsava**, m. 'love-liquid,' saliva, L. **Smarêshudhi-√kṛi**, P. -*karoti*, to turn into Kāma's quiver, Naish. **Smarôtsuka**, mfn. pining with l°, love-sick, W. **Smarôdgītha**, m. 'love-song,' N. of a son of Devakī, BhP. **Smarôddīpana**, m. 'love-kindler,' a sort of hair-oil, VarBṛS. **Smarônmāda**, m. amorous intoxication or folly, Daś. **Smarôpakaraṇa**, n. implement of love (as perfumes &c.), VarBṛS.

Smaraṇa, n. the act of remembering or calling to mind, remembrance, reminiscence, recollection of (gen. or comp.), MBh.; R. &c.; memory, BhP.; a kind of rhet. figure (cf. *smṛiti*), Kpr.; handing down by memory, tradition, traditional teaching or record or precept (*iti smaraṇāt*, 'from its being so mentioned in the Smṛiti,' q.v.), Kull.; Yājñ., Sch.; mental recitation (of the name of a deity), calling upon the name of a god, MW.; (*ī*), f. a rosary of beads (held in the hand, not worn as a necklace), ib. — **krama-mālā**, f. N. of a wk. (treating of meditation on Caitanya, Kṛishṇa, and Vṛindā-vana). — **padavī**, f. 'road of (mere) memory,' death (°*vīm gamitaḥ* = 'dead, killed'), Bhartṛ. — **bhū**, m. 'memory-born,' N. of Kāma-deva, Hariv. — **maṅgala** and °**lâṅkādaśaka**, (prob.) N. of wks. **Smaraṇânugraha**, m. the favour of remembrance, kind rem°, MW. **Smaraṇâpatya-tarpaka**, m. 'satisfying memory's offspring,' a turtle, tortoise, L. **Smaraṇâyaugapadya**, n. the non-simultaneousness of recollection, MW.

Smaraṇīya, mfn. to be remembered, memorable (°*yam smaram √kṛi*, 'to remind of Kāma;' °*yām gatim √nī*, 'to lead to the path of (mere) memory,' i. e. 'put to death'), Daś.; BhP.; Śatr.

Smartavya, mfn. to be remembered, memorable, MBh.; R. &c.; living only in the memory (of men), Jātakam.

Smartṛi, mfn. one who remembers or recollects (gen. or comp.), Hariv.; BhP.; a teacher, preceptor, Siṃhâs. — **tva**, n. remembrance, recollection, MW.

Smarya, mfn. to be remembered, memorable (cf. *smara-smarya*), Pañcar.

Smāra, m. remembrance, recollection of (comp.), TĀr.; (fr. *smara*) relating or belonging to the god of love, Naish.

Smāraka, mfn. (fr. Caus.) recalling, reminding of (comp.; -*tva*, n.), KātyŚr., Sch.

Smāraṇa, n. the act of causing to remember, reminding, calling to mind, Śaṃk.; Sāh.; (also *ā*, f.) counting or numbering again, calculating an account, checking, MBh.; (*ī*), f. a kind of plant, L.

Smāram, ind. (with *smāram* repeated) having remembered or recollected, Ghaṭ.; Uttamac. (cf. Vop. xxvi, 219).

Smārita, mfn. (fr. Caus.) reminded, called to mind, recalled to recollection, W.

Smārin, mfn. remembering (comp.), Rājat.; reminding, MW.

Smārta, mfn. (fr. *smṛiti*) relating to memory, memorial, MBh.; recorded in or based on the Smṛiti (q.v.), based on tradition, prescribed or sanctioned by traditional law or usage, legal, ĀśvGṛ.; Yājñ.; Sarvad.; versed in tradition, Pañcat.; m. an orthodox Brāhman versed in or guided by traditional law and usage (esp. a follower of Śaṃkarâcārya and of the Vedânta doctrine), RTL. 55; 95; = *smārta-bhaṭṭâcārya*, Cat.; (*am*), n. any act or rite enjoined by Smṛiti, legal act, MW. — **karman**, n. = *smārtam* above, ib. — **kāla**, m. the period to which memory may extend (i. e. a century, accord. to some lawyers), W. — **kutūhala**, n., -**dīpikā**, f. N. of wks. — **paṇḍita**, m. a Smārta scholar or Brāhman (cf. above), Hāsy. — **padârtha-saṃgraha**, m., -**pradīpikā**, f., -**prayoga**, m., °**ga-kārikā**, f., -**prâyaścitta**, n., °**tta-paddhati**, f., °**tta-vinirṇaya**, m., °**ttôddhāra**, m. N. of wks. — **bhaṭṭâcārya**, m. N. of Raghu-nandana (a celebrated Brāhman who lived at the beginning of the 16th century and wrote 28 Tattvas, the general name of which is Smṛiti-tattva), IW. 304, n. 2. — **rāma**, m. N. of the author of the Tripurā-paddhati. — **vyavasthârṇava**, m., -**samuccaya**, m. N. of wks. — **sūtra**, n. any Sūtra wk. based on Smṛiti (opp. to *śrauta-sūtra*, q.v.), IW. 145. — **homa-pariśishṭa**, n. N. of a Pariśishṭa of the Sāma-veda. **Smārtâṇḍa-billā**, f. (or °*ḍa-pille*, Cat.), N. of wk. **Smārtâdhāna**, n., °**tâdhāna-vidhi**, m., °**tânushṭhāna-paddhati**, f., °**tôpâsana-paddhati**, f. N. of wks.

Smārtika, mf(*ī*)n. based on tradition, traditional, Kull.

Smārya, mfn. to be remembered, memorable, Vop.

Smṛita, mfn. remembered, recollected, called to mind, thought of, NṛisUp.; R.; Kathās.; mentioned, KātyŚr., Sch.; handed down, taught, prescribed, (esp.) enjoined by Smṛiti or traditional law, declared or propounded in the law-books (*na smṛitam* = 'not allowed,' 'forbidden'), ĀśvŚr.; Mn.; Yājñ. &c.; declared as, passing for (nom., loc., or dat.), ChUp.; Mn.; MBh. &c.; termed, styled, named (nom. with or without *iti*), MaitrUp.; Mn. &c.; m. N. of a Prajā-pati, VP.; (*am*), n. remembrance, recollection, ĀśvGṛ. — **mātra**, mfn. only remembered or thought of, Pañcat.; °*trâgata*, mfn. come as soon as thought of or on merely being thought about, Kathās.

Smṛiti, f. remembrance, reminiscence, thinking of or upon (loc. or comp.), calling to mind (*smṛitim api te na yānti*, 'they are not even thought of'), memory, TĀr.; ChUp.; MBh. &c.; memory as one of the Vyabhicāri-bhāvas (q.v.), Daśar.; Memory (personified either as the daughter of Daksha and wife of Aṅgiras or as the daughter of Dharma and Medhā), Hariv.; Pur.; the whole body of sacred tradition or what is remembered by human teachers (in contradistinction to *śruti* or what is directly heard or revealed to the Ṛishis; in its widest acceptation this use of the term Smṛiti includes the 6 Vedâṅgas, the Sūtras both *śrauta* and *gṛihya*, the law-books of Manu &c. [see next]; the Itihāsas [e.g. the Mahābhārata and Rāmâyaṇa], the Purāṇas and the Nītiśāstras; *iti smṛiteḥ*, 'accord. to such and such a traditional precept or legal text'), IW. 144, 145; the whole body of codes of law as handed down memoriter or by tradition (esp. the codes of Manu, Yājñavalkya and the 16 succeeding inspired lawgivers, viz. Atri, Vishṇu, Hārīta, Uśanas or Śukra, Aṅgiras, Yama, Āpastamba, Saṃvarta, Kātyāyana, Bṛihas-pati, Parāśara, Vyāsa, Śaṅkha, Likhita, Daksha and Gautama; all these lawgivers being held to be inspired and to have based their precepts on the Veda; cf. IW. 203), GṛŚrS.; Mn.; Yājñ. &c.; symbolical N. for the number 18 (fr. the 18 lawgivers above); a kind of metre, L.; N. of the letter *g*, Up.; desire, wish, Pañcat. iii, 258 (v. l. for *spṛihā*). — **karaṇḍikā**, f., -**kalpadruma**, m. N. of wks. — **kārin**, mfn. arousing recollection, Śak. — **kāla-taraṃga**, m., -**kaumudī**, f., °**dī-ṭīkā**, f., -**gītā**, f., -**grantha-rāja**, m., -**candra**, m., -**candrikā**, f., -**candrôdaya**, m., -**caraṇa**, m. n., -**cintāmaṇi**, m. N. of wks. — **jāta**, m. 'memory-born,' the god of love, Dharmaś. — **tattva**, n. N. of a legal wk. by Raghu-nandana (cf. *smārta-bhaṭṭâcārya*); -*prakāśa*, m., -*viveka*, m. (also called °*ttvâmṛita*, n.), N. of wks. — **tantra**, n. a law-book, Kāv. — **da**, mfn. strengthening recollection, Bhpr. — **darpaṇa**, m., -**dīpa**, m., -**dīpikā**, f., -**nibandha**, m. N. of wks. — **patha**, m. the road to (mere) memory (*thaṃ √gā*, 'to go to the road of memory,' 'live only in the m° of men'), Bhartṛ. — **pariccheda**, m., -**paribhāshā**, f. N. of wks. — **pāṭhaka**, m. a lawyer, Pañcat. — **pāda**, m., -**prakāśa**, m. N. of wks. — **pratyavamarśa**, m. retentiveness of memory, accuracy of recollection, Hariv. — **pradīpa**, m. N. of wk. — **prabandha**, m. a Smṛiti composition, legal work, MW. — **prayojana**, mfn. having memory for object, helping or assisting m°, VPrāt. — **prâmāṇyârtha-vāda**, m., -**bhāskara**, m. N. of wks. — **bhū**, m. 'm°-born,' N. of Kāma-deva, Śiś. — **bhraṃśa**, m. loss of m°, Bhag.; loss of consciousness or discretion, Car. — **mañjarī**, f., -**mañjūshā**, f. N. of wks. — **mat**, mfn. having recollection or full consciousness, MBh.; Śak. &c.; having a good m°, Mn.; MBh. &c.; remembering a former life, Hariv.; prudent, discreet, Car.; Jātakam.; versed in tradition or law, Yājñ.; anything which causes recollection, BhagP. — **maya**, mf(*ī*)n. based upon Smṛiti or tradition, Pracaṇḍ. — **mahârṇava**, m., -**mīmāṃsā**, f., -**muktāphala**, n., -**muktâvalī**, f., -**rañjanī**, f., -**ratna**, n., -**ratna-kośa**, m., -**ratna-mahôdadhi**, m., -**ratna-viveka**, m., -**ratnâkara**, m., -**ratnâvalī**, f., -**rahasya**, n. N. of wks. — **rodha**, m. temporary obstruction or failure of memory, forgetfulness, Śak. — **lopa**, m. id., VarBṛS. — **vartman**, n. = -*patha*, Śiś. — **vardhanī**, f. 'strengthening m°,' a kind of plant (= *brāhmī*), L. — **vākyâpeta** (?), -**vāda**, m. N. of wks. — **vid**, mfn. versed in law or tradition, Kautukas. — **vinaya**, m. a reprimand given to a person by reminding him of his duty, Mahāvy. — **vibhrama**, m. confusion of m°, Bhag. — **viruddha**, mfn. contrary to law, illegal, unjust, W. — **virodha**, m. opposition to law, illegality, impropriety, W.; disagreement between two or more codes of law or legal texts (= *smṛityor vir°*, Yājñ. ii, 21), ib. — **vivaraṇa**, n., -**viveka**, m. N. of wks. — **vishaya**, m. the reach or range of m° (-*tām gamitaḥ* = 'died,' v. l. for *smaraṇa-padavīm g°*), Bhartṛ. — **vyavasthā**, f., -**śataka**, n. N. of wks. — **śāstra**, n. a law-book, code, digest (= *dharma-ś°*; cf. above under *smṛiti*), Hariv. — **śīla**, n. du. traditions and moral practices, MW. — **śekhara**, m. (or *kastūri-smṛiti*, f.) N. of a wk. on Ācāra (by Kastūri). — **śesha**, mf(*ā*)n. remaining only in memory, dead, gone (acc. with *√kṛi*, 'to destroy'), Rājat. — **śaithilya**, n. weakness or loss of memory, Śak. — **saṃskāra**, m. impression (caused) by memory (?); -*kaustubha*, m., -*rahasya*, n., -*vāda*, m., -*vicāra*, m. N. of wks.

-saṃhitā, f. N. of wk. **-saṃgraha**, m. N. of an ancient law-book (often quoted) and of other compilations; *-ratna-vyākhyāna*, n., *-sāra*, m. N. of wks. **-samuccaya**, m. 'law-collection,' N. of wk. **-sammata**, mfn. approved by law, MW. **-saroja-sundara**, m. or n.(?), **-sarvasva**, n., **-sāgara**, m., **°ra-saṃgraha** and **°ra-sāra**, m. N. of wks. **-sādhya**, mfn. capable of being proved by law, MW. **-sāra**, m., **°ra-vyavasthā**, f., **°ra-saṃgraha**, m., **°ra-samuccaya**, m., **°ra-sarvasva**, n., **°râvalī**, f. N. of wks. **-siddha**, mfn. established by law, MW. **-siddhânta-saṃgraha**, m., **-sindhu**, m., **-sudhâkara**, m. N. of wks. **-harā** or **-harikā**, f. 'memory-seizer,' N. of a daughter of Duḥ-saha (described as exercising an evil influence on the m°), MārkP. **-hīna**, mfn. 'destitute of m°,' oblivious, forgetful, R. **-hetu**, m. a cause of recollection, impression on the mind, association of ideas, recollection, W. **Smṛitô**, mfn. one who thinks on U (i. e. on Śambhu; = *uḥ Śambhuḥ smṛito yena saḥ*), Siddh. on Pāṇ. vii, 1, 90.

Smṛitika, n. water (= *udaka*), Naigh. i, 12 (v. l.)

Smṛity, in comp. for *smṛiti*. **-adhikaraṇa**, n. N. of wk. **-antara**, n. another law-book, MW. **-apêta**, mfn. departed from memory, forgotten, W.; illegal, unjust, ib. **-apramosha**, m. non-deprivation of recollection or of presence of mind, non-failure of discretion, Jātakam. **-artha-ratnâkara**, m. N. of a legal wk. (= *smṛiti-sāra*). **-artha-sāgara**, m. N. of a wk. by Nṛi-siṅha (composed in 1682 A.D.) **-artha-sāra**, m. 'essence of the meaning of Smṛiti,' N. of a wk. on Hindū ceremonies by Śrīdhara-svāmin (divided into Ācāra, Āśauca, and Prâyaścitta). **-ukta**, mfn. prescribed in codes of law, enjoined by the Smṛitis, canonical, W. **-upasthāna**, n. earnest thought, Divyâv.

स्मेर *smera* &c. See p. 1271, col. 3.

स्य 1. **syá**, pron. base of 3rd person (= *sá*; only in nom. m. *syás*, *syá*, f. *syā́*; cf. *tyá*, *tyád*), RV.

स्य 2. **sya**, n. a winnowing basket (= *śūrpa*), ŚāṅkhGṛ.

स्यगवि *syagavi* (?), m. a young crab (cf. *segava*), L.

स्यन्द *syand* (or *syad*; often confounded with *spand*), cl. 1. Ā. (Dhātup. xviii, 22) *syándate* (ep. and m. c. also °*ti*; pf. *sishyánda*, *sishyaduḥ*, AV.; Br.; *sasyande*, °*dire*, Gr.; aor. 2. 3. sg. *-asyán*, RV.; *asyandishṭa*, *asyantta*, *asyadat*, Gr.; fut. *syanttā*, *syanditā*, ib.; *syantsyáti*, Br.; *syandishyate*, *syantsyate*, Gr.; inf. *-syáde*, RV.; *syántum*, Br.; ind. p. *syanttvā́*, *syattvā́*, *-syadya*, ib.; *syanditvā*, Gr.), to move or flow on rapidly, flow, stream, run, drive (in a carriage), rush, hasten, speed, RV. &c. &c.; to discharge liquid, trickle, ooze, drip, sprinkle, pour forth (acc.), MBh.; Hariv. &c.; to issue from (abl.), Bhaṭṭ.: Caus. *syandayati* (aor. *ásishyadat*; Ved. inf. *syandayádhyai*), to stream, flow, run, RV.; Br. &c.; to cause to flow or run, Pāṇ. i, 3, 86, Sch.: Desid. *sisyandishate*, *sisyantsate*, *sisyantsati*, Gr.: Intens., see *acchā-√syand*, under 3. *accha*, and next.

Sanishyadá, mf(*ā*)n. (fr. Intens.) running, flowing, MS.; AV.

Syad. See *raghu-shyád* and *havana-syád*.

Syáda, m. driving, ŚBr.; rapid motion, speed, L.

Syanttavya, mfn. to be flowed &c., MW.

Syánttṛi, mfn. moving, driving, RV.

Syanda, m. flowing, running, streaming, trickling, oozing, Kāv.; Rājat.; fluxion, Suśr.; a partic. disease of the eyes, ib.; trickling perspiration, BhP.; the moon, L.

Syandaka, m. Diospyros Embryopteris (perhaps for *spana*°), L.; (*ikā*), f. N. of a river, R.

Syandaná, mf(*ā*)n. moving on swiftly, running (as a chariot), Kir.; dripping, sprinkling (ifc.), Kathās.; liquefying, dissolving, Suśr.; a war-chariot, chariot, car (said also to be n.), RV. &c. &c.; Dalbergia Ougeinensis, Kauś.; MBh. &c.; a partic. spell recited over weapons, R.; air, wind, L.; N. of the 23rd Arhat of the past Utsarpiṇī, L.; (*ī*), f. saliva, L.; the urinary passage, L.; (*am*), n. flowing, rushing, going or moving swiftly, Nir.; Bhāshāp.; circulation, Sāṃkhyak., Sch.; dropping, oozing, trickling, W.; water, L. **-druma**, m. Dalbergia Ougeinensis (so called from its wood being used to make wheels &c.), L. **-dhvani**, m. the rattling of carriage wheels, L. **Syandanâruḍha**, mfn. mounted on a chariot, W. **Syandanâroha**, m. a warrior who fights mounted on a chariot, L. **Syandanâlokabhīta**, mfn. terrified at the sight of a chariot, Śak.

Syandani, m. Dalbergia Ougeinensis, L.; N. of a man (pl.), Saṃskārak.

Syandanikā, f. a brook, rivulet, R.; a drop of saliva, MW.

Syandanīya, mfn. to be flowed or run or gone, MW.

Syandayádhyai. See root, col. 1.

Syanditâśva, Kāś. on Pāṇ. vi, 2, 108.

Syanditṛi, mfn. one who runs or rushes quickly, MW.

Syandin, mfn. flowing, running, VarBṛS.; Kuval.; emitting liquid, oozing, trickling, dropping (comp.), MBh.; Kāv. &c.; going, moving, W.; (*inī*), f. saliva, L.; a cow bearing two calves at once, W.

Syandolikā, f. swinging or a swing (prob. w.r. for *spand*°), L.

Syandyā, f. (prob. w.r. for *spandyā*), ĀpŚr.

Syandrá, mfn. running, rushing, swift, fleet, RV.; transient, transitory, ib.

Syanná, mfn. flowing, running, RV.; dropping, trickling, L.

Syédu, m. (prob.) phlegm, AV.

स्यपेटारिका *syapeṭārikā* (?), f. a kind of game, Divyâv.

स्यम् *syam*, cl. 1. P. (Dhātup. xix, 78) *syamati* (only in 3. pl. pf. *sasyamuḥ* and *syemuḥ*; Gr. also aor. *asyamīt*; fut. *syamitā*, *syamishyati*; ind. p. *syamitvā* or *syāntvā*; accord. to Vop. also cl. 10. P. *syamayati*), to sound, cry aloud, shout, cry, shriek, Bhaṭṭ.; (*syamati*), to go, Naigh. ii, 14; cl. 10. Ā. *syāmayate* (°*ti*), to consider, reflect, Dhātup. xxxiii, 20: Caus. *syamayati* (aor. *asisyamat*), Gr. (cf. above): Desid. *sisyamishati*, ib.: Intens. *sesimyate*, *saṅsyanti*, ib.

Syamana, n. (used in explaining *sīmikā*), Nir. iii, 20.

Syamika, m. an ant-hill, Uṇ. iii, 46, Sch.; a kind of tree, ib.

Syamīka, m. id., ib.; a cloud, L.; time, L.; N. of a race of kings L.; (*ā*), f. the indigo plant, L.; a kind of worm, L.; (*am*), n. water, L.

स्यमन्तक *syamantaka*, m. N. of a celebrated jewel (worn by Kṛishṇa on his wrist [cf. *kaustubha*], described as yielding daily eight loads of gold and preserving from all dangers; it is said to have been given to Satrā-jit [q.v.] by the Sun and transferred by him to his brother Prasena, from whom it was taken by Jāmbavat, and after much contention appropriated by Kṛishṇa, see VishṇuP. iv, 13), Hariv.; Pur.; Pañcar. **-prabandha**, m., **-maṇi-haraṇa**, n., **°tôpâkhyāna**, n. N. of wks.

स्यात् *syāt*, ind. (3. sg. Pot. of √1. *as*) it may be, perhaps, perchance (esp. used in Jaina wks. and occurring in 7 formulas, viz. 1. *syād asti*, 'perhaps it is [under certain circumstances];' 2. *syān nâsti*, 'perh° it is not, &c.;' 3. *syād asti ca nâsti ca*, 'perh° it is and is not [under c° c°];' 4. *syād avaktavyaḥ*, 'perh° it is not expressible in words;' 5. *syād asti câvaktavyaḥ*, 'perhaps it is and is not expressible in words;' 6. *syān nâsti câvaktavyaḥ*, 'perhaps it is not and is and is not expressible in words;' 7. *syād asti ca nâsti câvaktavyaḥ*), Sarvad.

Syād, in comp. for *syāt*. **-vāda**, m. 'assertion of possibility or non-possibility,' the sceptical or agnostic doctrine of the Jainas, Śatr.; *-mañjarī*, f., *-ratnâkara*, m. N. of wks.; *-vādin*, m. = next, L. **-vādika**, m. an adherent of the Jaina doctrine, L. **-vādin**, m. id., Sarvad.; N. of a Jaina, L.

स्यामन्तोपाख्यान *syāmantôpâkhyāna*, n. N. of wk. (prob. w.r. for *syamantakôp*°).

स्यामूल *syāmūla*, n. a sort of garment (prob. w.r. for *sāmūla*), ĀpŚr.

स्याल *syālá*, m. (also written *śyāla*, of doubtful derivation) the brother of a bride, a wife's brother (in later literature esp. the brother-in-law or favourite of a king, cf. 2. *śakāra*), RV. &c. &c.; (*ī*), f. a wife's sister, MW.

Syālaka, m. a wife's brother (= *svāla*), Cāṇ.; Prab.; (*ikā*), f. the younger sister of a wife, L.

स्युवक *syuvaka*, m. pl. N. of a people, VP.

स्यू *syū́*, f. (fr. √*siv*) a string, thread, VS. (a 'needle,' Mahīdh.)

Syutna, n. happiness, delight (cf. below), L.

Syumna, n. id. (cf. *syūmaká*, *syoná* below), L.

Syūtá, mfn. sewn, stitched, woven, RV. &c. &c.; sewn on, HPariś.; sewn or woven together, joined, fabricated, MW.; pierced, penetrated, ib.; m. a sack, coarse canvas bag, L.

Syūti, f. (only L.) sewing, stitching, weaving; a bag, sack; lineage, offspring.

Syūna, m. (only L.) a sack; a ray of light; the sun; (*ā*), f. a ray of light, L.; a girdle, L.

1. **Syūma**, m. n. (only L.) a ray of light; water.

2. **Syūma**, in comp. for *syū́man*. **-gabhasti** (*syū́ma-*), mfn. (prob.) having thongs for a pole, drawn by thongs (as a chariot), RV. **-gṛíbh**, mfn. (prob.) seizing the reins (with the teeth; said of a restive or runaway horse), ib. **-raśmi** (*syū́ma-*), m. 'having thongs for a bridle,' N. of a man, ib.

Syūmaká, n. delight, happiness, Naigh. iii, 6.

Syū́man, n. a band, thong, bridle, RV.; a suture (of the skull), AitBr.

Syūmanyú, mfn. (prob.) eager for the bridle, i.e. dragging at it, impatient, RV. i, 174, 5; desiring happiness, Sāy.

Syota, m. = *syūta*, a sack, L.

Syoná, mf(*ā́*)n. soft, gentle, pleasant, agreeable (esp. to walk upon or sit upon), mild, tender, RV.; TS.; Br.; GṛŚrS.; m. a sack, L.; a ray of light, L.; the sun, L.; (*am*), n. a soft couch, comfortable seat, pleasant site or situation, RV.; AV.; Lāṭy.; delight, happiness (= *sukha*), Naigh. iii, 6. **-kṛít**, mfn. one who causes comfort or happiness, RV. **-śī**, mfn. resting on a soft couch or comfortably, ib.

Syonāka, m. Bignonia Indica, L.

Syaukāmi, m. (an artificial patr.), Pat.

Syaumaraśma, n. du. (fr. *syūma-raśmi*; with *Indrasya*) N. of two Sāmans, ĀrshBr.

स्येदु *syedu*. See col. 2.

स्रंस 1. *sraṅs* (or *sras*; sometimes written *śraṅs* or *śraṅs*), cl. 1. Ā. (Dhātup. xviii, 15) *sraṅsate* (ep. and m. c. also °*ti*; pf. *sasraṅsa*, °*ṅsuḥ*, Br.; 3. pl. *-sraṅsire*, Hariv.; aor. *asrat*, Br.; *asrasat*, *srasema*, RV.; *asraṅsishṭa*, Br.; fut. *sraṅsitā*, *sraṅsishyate*, Gr.; Ved. inf. *-srásas*; *sraṅsitum*, Gr.; ind. p. *sraṅsitvā*, *srastvā*, ib.; *-sraṅsya*, *-srasya*, Br. &c.), to fall, drop, fall down, slip off, get loose from (abl.), VS. &c. &c.; to fall asunder or to pieces, TBr.; to hang down, dangle, droop, Ragh.; to be broken, perish, cease, Sāh.; to go, Naigh. ii, 14: Pass. *srasyate* (aor. *asraṅsi*), Gr.: Caus. *sraṅsayati* (aor. *asisrasat*; Pass. *sraṅsyate*), to cause to fall down, loosen, AV.; R. &c.; to let hang (the belly), AV.; to disturb, remove, destroy, Suśr.: Desid. *sisraṅsishate*, Gr.: Intens. *sanīsrasyate*, *sanīsraṅsti*, ib. (cf. next).

Sanisrasá, mfn. (fr. Intens.) falling down or asunder or to pieces, fragile, frail, AV. **Sanisrasâkshá**, mfn. one whose eyes fall out, ib.

Sanīsrasa, mfn. = *sanisrasa*, Pāṇ. iv, 2, 74, Vārtt. 1, Pat.

Sraṅsa. See *asthi-* and *paruḥ-sr*°.

Sraṅsana, mfn. laxative, purging, cathartic, Bhpr.; n. the act of falling or causing to fall, loosening, Naish., Sch.; premature abortion, Gaut.; a laxative, cathartic, Suśr.

Sraṅsita, mfn. (fr. Caus.) caused to fall or slip down, loosened, Uttarar.

Sraṅsin, mfn. becoming loose, falling down, slipping off, Kāv.; depending, pendulous, Suśr.; letting fall, miscarrying, Suśr.; m. Careya Arborea or Salvadora Persica, L.

Sraṅsinī-phala, m. the Sirisha tree, L.

Sras, mfn. falling, dropping (ifc.; see *vi-sras*, *su-sras*).

Srasta, mfn. fallen, dropped, slipped off, fallen from (abl. or comp.), R.; Kālid. &c.; loosened, relaxed, hanging down, pendent, pendulous, ib. &c.; sunk in (as eyes), Suśr.; separated, disjoined, W. **-kara**, mfn. having trunks hanging or dangling down, MW. **-gātra**, mfn. having relaxed or languid limbs, R. **-tā**, f. laxity, flaccidity, pendulousness, Kir., Sch. **-mushka**, mfn. having relaxed or pendulous testicles, Suśr. **-śarīra-saṃdhi**, mfn. having the joints of the body relaxed, Mṛicch. **-skandha**, mfn. having drooping shoulders (also = 'ashamed,' 'embarrassed'), Divyâv. **-hasta**, mfn. relaxing the grasp, letting go the hold, W. **Srastâṅsa**, mfn.

= *skandha*, Śak.; *-bāhu*, mfn. one who has drooping shoulders and arms, Bcar. **Srastâṅga**, mfn. = *srasta-gātra* (*-tā*, f.), Suśr. **Srastâpâna**, mfn. having prolapsus ani, Suśr. **Srastôttara-paṭa**, mfn. having the upper garment slipped down, MW.

Srastara, m. n. (ifc. f. *ā*) a couch or sofa for reclining (often v.l. *prastara*), PārGṛ.; Mn.; Kād.

Srasti, f. falling or hanging down, laxity, flaccidity &c., Pāṇ. iii, 3, 94, Vārtt. 2, Pat.

स्रंस् 2. *sraṅs*, v.l. for √*śrambh* (q.v.)

स्रंह् *sraṅh*, cl. 1. Ā. *sraṅhate*, to confide, trust, Dhātup. xviii, 8 (Vop.)

स्रक्ति *sraktí*, f. (accord. to some fr. √1. *sṛij*) a corner, edge (esp. of the Vedi), RV.; ŚBr.; ŚrS.

स्रक्त्य *sraktyá*, m. a partic. plant (= *tilaka*), AV.; Kauś.

स्रक्व *srákva*, m. or n. (cf. *sṛikva*) the corner of the mouth (also = 'mouth,' 'jaws'), RV.

स्रङ्क् *sraṅk*. See √*śraṅk*.

स्रज् *sráj*, mfn. (fr. √1. *sṛij*) turning, twisting, winding (ifc. nom. *-sraṭ*; cf. *rajju-sarja*), Pāṇ. viii, 2, 36, Sch.; f. (nom. *srak*) a wreath of flowers, garland, chaplet worn on the head, any wr° or g°, circle, series, chain (*audakī srak*, 'a watery g°,' i.e. 'one woven with water-flowers;' *loka-sraji*, 'in the circle of the worlds'), RV. &c. &c.; a kind of tree, Kauś.; a kind of metre, Piṅg.; N. of a partic. constellation (when the Kendras are occupied by three auspicious planets except the moon), VarBṛS.

Srag, in comp. for *sraj*. **-aṇu**, m. a Mantra or sacred text written in the form of a garland, Rāmat-Up. (Sch.) **-dāman**, n. the fillet or tie of a garland, MBh.; a g°, wreath, Ratnâv. **-dhara**, mf(*ā*)n. wearing a g°, crowned with (comp.; *surabhi-dh°*, 'wearing a fragrant g°'), MBh.; VarBṛS. &c.; (*ā*), f. a kind of metre (consisting of four times ‒‒‒‒◡‒‒, ◡◡◡◡◡◡‒, ‒◡‒‒◡‒‒), Piṅg.; N. of a goddess, Buddh. **-vat**, mfn. possessed of garlands, wearing a wreath, L. **-vin**, mfn. id., Mn.; MBh. &c.; (*iṇī*), f. N. of two metres, Piṅg.; of a goddess, Cat.

Sraja, (ifc.) a garland, MBh.; Hariv.; m. N. of one of the Viśve Devāḥ, MBh.

Srajaya, Nom. P. °*yati*, to garland, i.e. furnish with a garland, Bhaṭṭ.

Srajas, (ifc.) a garland, Hariv.

Srajin. See *pari-srajin*.

Sraji-vat, ind. as in (or with) a garland, BhP.

Srajishṭha, mfn. (superl. of *sragvin*) completely covered or profusely decorated with garlands, Pāṇ., Sch.

Srajīyas, mfn. (compar. of id.) well covered with garlands, ib.

Srajvan, m. a garland-maker, L.; a rope, L.

Srashṭavya, mfn. to be created, MārkP.

Srashṭāra, m. a creator (in °*rāya namaḥ*), MBh.

Srashṭṛi, m. one who emits or discharges (water &c.), MBh.; a maker, author, Nir.; Rājat.; a creator, the creator of the universe (applied to Brahmā, Śiva &c.), ŚvetUp.; R. &c. **-tā**, f., **-tva**, n. creatorship, MārkP.; Saṃk.

स्रद्धू *sraddhū*, f. (prob. for *śraddhū*, cf. *śardha*) breaking wind downwards, L.

स्रभिष्ठ *srábhishṭha*, mfn. = *surabhishṭha* (q.v.), ŚBr.

स्रम्भ् *srambh*. See √*śrambh*.

स्रव *srava* &c. See col. 2.

स्रस् *sras*, *srasta* &c. See p. 1273, col. 3.

स्राक् *srāk*, ind. = *drāk*, quickly, speedily, instantly, L.

स्राक्त्य *sráktya*, mfn. made from the plant Sraktya, AV.; Kauś.

स्राग्विण *srāgviṇa*, m. patr. fr. *sragvin*, Pāṇ. vi, 4, 166, Sch.; n., ib. 164, Sch.

स्राण *srāṇa*. See *aruḥ-srāṇa*.

स्राम *srāmá*, mfn. (of unknown derivation), lame, sick, RV.; AV.; ŚBr.; ChUp.; (*srā́ma*), m. lameness, sickness, disease (esp. of animals), RV.; TS.; Kāṭh.; ŚBr.

Srāmya, n. lameness, ChUp.

स्राव *srāva*, *srāvaka* &c. See col. 2.

स्रिध् 1. *sridh*, cl. 1. P. *srédhati* (aor. *sridhat*, p. *-sridhāna*; cf. *á-sredhat*, *á-sridhāna*), to fail, err, blunder, RV.

2. **Sridh**, f. erring, failing, a misbeliever, foe, enemy, RV.; AV.; VS.

स्रिभ् *sribh* or *srimbh*, cl. 1. P. *srebhati* or *srimbhati*, to hurt, injure, kill, Dhātup. xi, 40; 41.

स्रिम *sríma*, m. a kind of nocturnal spirit of evil, AV.

स्रिव् *sriv* or *srīv*, cl. 4. P. (Dhātup. xxvi, 3) *srīvyati* (Gr. also pf. *sisreva*; aor. *asrevīt*; fut. *srevitā*; ind. p. *srevitvā* or *srūtvā*), to fail, turn out badly, MaitrS.; AitBr.; (with *garbham*) to miscarry, ĀpŚr.; 'to go' or 'to become dry,' Dhātup.: Caus. *srevayati*, to cause to fail, lead astray, RV.; *srīvayati*, to frustrate, thwart, AV.: Desid. *sisrevishati*, *susrūshati*, Gr.: Intens. *sesrīvyate*, ib.

Srūta, mfn. gone; dried, withered, Pāṇ. vi, 4, 20.

स्रु *sru* (incorrectly written *śru*; cf. √2. *śru*), cl. 1. P. (Dhātup. xxii, 42) *srávati* (ep. and m. c. also °*te*; pf. *susrāva*, *susruvuḥ*, AV. &c.; *susruve*, MBh. &c.; aor. *ásusrot*, AV.; Br.; *asrāvīt*, JaimBr.; *asraushīt* [?], ŚBr.; fut. *srotā*, Gr.; *sroshyati*, ib.; *sravishyati*, MBh.; inf. *srotum*, Gr.; *srávitave*, *srávitavai*, RV.), to flow, stream, gush forth, issue from (abl., rarely instr.), RV. &c. &c.; to flow with, shed, emit, drop, distil (acc.), ChUp.; MBh. &c.; to leak, trickle, RV.; Br.; GṛŚrS.; Kathās.; to fail, not turn out well, TS.; Br.; to waste away, perish, disappear, MBh.; Kāv. &c.; to slip or issue out before the right time (said of a fetus), TBr.; MBh.; BhP.; (with *garbham*) to bring forth prematurely, miscarry, ĀpŚr.; to issue, arise or come from (abl.); to come in, accrue (as interest), Nār.: Caus. *srāvayati* (in later language also *sravayati*; aor. *asusravat* or *asisravat*), to cause to flow, shed, spill, AV.; Mn.; Suśr.; to set in motion, stir up, arouse, Kāṭh.: Desid. of Caus. *susrāvayishati* or *sisrāvayishati*, Gr.: Desid. *susrūshati*, ib.: Intens. *sosrūyate*, *sosroti*, ib. [Cf. Gk. ῥέω (for σρεϝω), ῥόσις &c.; Lith. *sravéti*; Germ. *stroum*, *Strom*; Angl.Sax. *stream*; Eng. *stream*.]

Srava, m. flowing, streaming, a flow of (comp.), MBh.; R. &c.; a waterfall, L.; urine, L.; (*ā*), f. N. of various plants (= *sruvā*, *madhu-sravā*, *madhu* &c.), L.; mf(*ā*)n. streaming or flowing with (comp.), MBh.; Kāv. &c. **-draṅga**, m. 'stirring town,' a fair, market, bazaar, L. **-mī**, mfn. (prob.) diminishing the morbid flow of urine, L.

Sravaka, mfn. flowing, dropping &c., L.

Sravaṇa, n. streaming, flowing, flowing off (also pl.; cf. *aśva-sr°*), R.; premature abortion, VarBṛS.; sweat, perspiration, L.; urine, L.

Sravat, mfn. (pr. p.) streaming, flowing &c.; (*át*), f. a river, RV.; AV.; (*antī*), f., see below. **-toyā**, f. a kind of shrub (= *rudantī*), L. **-pāṇi-pādā**, f. a girl with moist hands and feet (unfit for marriage), L. **-sveda-jala**, mfn. streaming with perspiration, W.

Sravátha, m. or n. flowing, streaming, running, RV.

Sravad, in comp. for *sravat*. **-garbhā**, f. a woman (or any female animal, as a cow) that miscarries, L.

Sravanta, mfn. flowing, dropping, MW.

Srávantī, f. (of *sravat*, q.v.) flowing water, a river, RV. &c. &c. (cf. Naigh. i, 13); a kind of herb, L.

Sravas, n. (ifc.) = *srava*, flow of (see *madhu-sravas*).

Sravitave. See root above.

Srāva, m. flow, (esp.) morbid flow or issue of (comp.), MBh.; Hariv.; Suśr.; (with or scil. *garbhasya*) miscarriage, Yājñ., Sch.; AgP.

Srāvaka, mfn. (fr. Caus.) causing to flow, shedding, exuding (*-tva*, n.), ĀpŚr., Sch.; n. black pepper, L.

Srāvaṇa, mfn. causing to flow, shedding (*rudhira-srāvaṇam* √*kṛi*, 'to shed any one's blood'), KātyŚr.; Suśr.; Kull.

Srāvayitavya, mfn. to be caused to flow or run, MaitrS.

Srāvita, mfn. caused to flow, liquefied, Suśr.

Srāvin, mfn. streaming, flowing (compar. °*vitara*), ŚBr.; VarBṛS.; flowing with, dripping, distilling (cf. *garbha-sr°*), MBh.; Hariv. &c.

Srāvya, mfn. to be caused to flow or run, Suśr.

Srut, mfn. flowing with, emitting, discharging, distilling (see *amṛita-*, *pari-srut* &c.)

Sruta, mfn. streaming, flowing, having flowed from (comp.), Mn.; MBh. &c.; flowed out, become empty (as a jar), VarBṛS.; flowed asunder, dissolved, ib.; Suśr.; (*ā*), f. a kind of medicinal plant (= *hingu-pattrī*), L.; (*ám*), n. flowing, a flow, AV. **-jala**, mfn. having the water flowed off, dried up, Mṛicch.

Sruti, f. a stream, flow or effusion of (comp.), Kāv.; VarBṛS.; BhP.; fall of (snow &c.), Ragh.; Kum.; a course, road, path, RV.; Br.; ŚāṅkhŚr.; a line drawn round the Vedi, ŚāṅkhŚr.

Srútya, mfn. relating to a road or path, VS.

Sruvá, m. (cf. *srúc*) a small wooden ladle (with a double extremity, or two oval collateral excavations, used for pouring clarified melted butter into the large ladle or Sruk [see *srúc*]; sometimes also employed instead of the latter in libations), RV. &c. &c.; a sacrifice, oblation, L.; (*ā*), f., see below. **-karṇa**, mfn. having the mark of a ladle on the ear, Pāṇ. vi, 3, 115. **-taru**, m. Flacourtia Sapida, L. **-daṇḍa**, m. the handle of the ladle Sruva, ĀśvŚr. **-druma**, m. = *-taru*, L. **-pūram**, ind. filling a l°, with a l°-full, ĀśvŚr. **-pragrahaṇa**, mfn. taking with a l°, i.e. taking all to one's self, appropriating all, MBh. **-lakshaṇa**, n. N. of the 27th Pariśishṭa of the AV. **-hasta**, m. N. of Śiva, ib. **-homa**, m. a libation offered with the Sruva, Lāṭy. **Sruvâhuti**, f. id., KātyŚr.

Sruvā, f. the ladle called Sruva, L.; Sanseviera Roxburghiana, L.; Boswellia Thurifera, L. **-vṛiksha**, m. the tree Sruvā, L.

Srū́, f. a stream (accord. to others, 'the leaden ball of a sling' = Zd. *srū*), RV. x, 96, 6; flow, effluence (= *srava*), L.; a spring, fountain, cascade, L.; a sacrificial ladle (= *sruva*), L.

1. **Srota**, m. n. (ifc. f. *ā*) = *srotas* (cf. *prati-* and *sahasra-sr°*). **-nadī-bhava**, n. antimony, L. **Srotâpatti**, f. = *srota-āpatti* below. **Srotôdbhava**, n. = *sroto-ja* (under *sroto*), L.

2. **Srota**, in comp. for *srotas*. **-āpatti**, f. entrance into the river (leading to Nirvāṇa), Buddh. **-āpanna**, mfn. one who has entered the above river, ib. (MWB. 132). **-īśa**, m. 'lord of streams,' the ocean, L.

Srótas, n. the current or bed of a river, a river, stream, torrent, RV. &c. &c.; water, Naigh. i, 12; rush, violent motion or onset of (comp.), Kāv.; Pur.; Sarvad.; the course or current of nutriment in the body, channel or course for conveying food (see *ūrdhva-* and *tiryak-sr°*); an aperture in the human or animal body (reckoned to be 9 in men and 11 in women), Suśr.; the spout of a jar, Suśr.; an organ of sense, ŚvetUp.; R. &c.; lineage, pedigree (?), MBh. **-tā**, f. flow, course (instr. = 'by degrees'), Śaṃk. **-vat**, mfn. possessing a stream or current; (*atī*), f. a river, L. **-vinī**, f. a river, Kād.; Śiś.

Srotasa (ifc.) = *srotas* (see *tri-*, *varuṇa-sr°*).

Srotasyà, mfn. flowing in streams, AV.; m. a thief, L.; N. of Śiva, L.

Sroto, in comp. for *srotas*. **-ja**, n. 'stream-produced,' antimony (cf. *sroto-'ñjana*), Suśr. **-java**, m. rapidity of a current, MW. **-'ñjana**, n. 'stream-collyrium,' antimony (esp. as a collyrium for the eyes, said to be produced in the river Yamunā), L. **-nadī-bhava**, n. id., L. **-'nugata**, m. a partic. Samādhi, Buddh. **-randhra**, n. the aperture of an elephant's trunk, Megh. **-vah** or **-vahā**, f. a river, Kālid.

Srotyá, f. flowing water, a wave, surge, stream, river, RV.; AV.; TS.; Br. (cf. Naigh. i, 13).

Srauta, n. N. of a Sāman (cf. *śrauta*), IndSt.

Srautika, m. a pearl-shell, L.

Srautovaha, mfn. (fr. *sroto-vahā*) relating to a river, Śak. (v.l.)

Srauva, mfn. relating to the sacrificial ladle (i.e. to the sacrifice), connected with or depending on the sacrifice, Vishṇ.

स्रुक्क *srukka*, *sruk-kāra* &c. See p. 1275.

स्रुघ्न *srughna*, m. N. of a town to the north of Hāstinapura, VarBṛS.; Buddh.; (*ī*), f. (also written *srug-ghnī*) natron, alkali, L.

Srughnikā, f. natron, alkali, L.

Sraughna, mf(*ī*)n. born or living in Srughna, coming from or leading to Srughna &c., Pāṇ. iv, 3, 25 and 86, Sch.

Sraughnī, f. of prec. **-pāśā**, f., **-bhāryā**, f., **-māninī**, f., Kāś. on Pāṇ. vi, 3, 39.

Sraughnīya, Nom. Ā. °*yate*, ib.

स्रुच् *srúc*, f. (nom. *srúk*; prob. connected with √*sru* and *sruvá*) a sort of large wooden ladle (used for pouring clarified butter on a sacrificial fire; and properly made of Palāśa or Khadira wood and about as long as an arm, with a receptacle at the end of the size of a hand; three are enumerated, viz. *juhū́*, *upabhṛ́t*, and *dhruvā́*, in which order they are used in sg., du., and pl.), RV. &c. &c.

Sruk, in comp. for *sruc*. — **kārá**, m. the exclamation 'Sruk,' AV. — **pātra**, n. the ladle Sruc and other sacrificial implements, R. — **praṇālikā**, f. the spout of a l°, KātyŚr., Sch. — **sammārjana**, n. cleaning the sacrificial l°, KātyŚr.; an implement for cleaning it, TBr. — **sruva**, n. sg. the two s° ladles Sruc and Sruva, Vait.; *-lakshaṇa*, n. N. of wk.

Srukka (ifc., f. *ā*) = *sruc*, R.

Srug, in comp. for *sruc*. — **ādāna**, n. the sacred text with which the Sruc is taken, ĀpŚr. — **āsādana**, n. the putting down of the Sruc, L. — **ghnī**, see *srughnī*. — **jihva**, m. 'ladle-tongued,' N. of Agni, L. — **daṇḍa**, m. the handle of the Sruc, Vait. — **dāru**, n. Flacourtia Sapida, L. — **bhāṇḍa**, m. or n. sg. the Sruc and other sacrificial implements, MBh.; Hariv. — **bheda**, m. the breaking of the Sruc, KātyŚr. — **mat**, see *sraugmata*. — **vat**, mfn. possessing a Sruc, Vop. — **vyūha**, m. the arranging of the different kinds of Sruc, KātyŚr.

Srucaya, Nom. P. °*yati* = *srugvantam ācashṭe* or *karoti*, Vop.

Srucāyani, m. a patr., Pat.

Srucishṭha and **srucīyas**, mfn. compar. and superl. of *srug-vat*, ib.

1. **Srucya**, Nom. P. °*yati*, Pāṇ. i, 4, 15, Sch.

2. **Srucya**, mfn. performed with the Sruc, ĀpŚr.; m. (with or scil. *āghāra*) the sprinkling of clarified butter so performed, ib.

Sraugmata, n. (fr. *srug-mat*) N. of a Sāman, Lāṭy.

स्रुह् *sruh*. See *vi-srúh*.

स्रेक् *srek* (also written *śrek*, *sek*, *svek*), cl. 1. Ā. *srekate*, to go, move, Dhātup. iv, 8.

स्रेकपर्ण *sreka-parṇa*, mfn. (said to =) resembling oleander, TBr.

स्रै *srai*. See √*śrai*, *śrā*.

स्व 1. *svá*, mf(*ā*)n. own, one's own, my own, thy own, his own, her own, our own, their own &c. (referring to all three persons accord. to context, often ibc., but generally declinable like the pronominal *sarva*, e.g. *svasmai*, dat. *svasmāt*, abl. [optionally in abl., loc., sing., nom. pl., e.g. *taṃ svād āsyād asṛijat*, 'he created him from his own mouth,' Mn. i, 94]; and always like *śiva* when used substantively [see below]; sometimes used loosely for 'my,' 'thy,' 'his,' 'our' [e.g. *rājā bhrātaraṃ sva-gṛihaṃ prêshayām-āsa*, 'the king sent his brother to his (i.e. the brother's) house']; in the oblique cases it is used as a reflexive pronoun = *ātman*, e.g. *svaṃ dūshayati*, 'he defiles himself;' *svaṃ nindanti*, 'they blame themselves'), RV. &c. &c.; m. one's self, the Ego, the human soul, W.; N. of Vishṇu, MBh.; a man of one's own people or tribe, a kinsman, relative, relation, friend (*svāḥ*, 'one's own relations,' 'one's own people'), AV. &c. &c.; (*ā*), f. a woman of one's own caste, MBh.; (*am*), n. (ifc. f. *ā*), one's self, the Ego (e.g. *svaṃ ca Brahma ca*, 'the Ego and Brahman'); one's own goods, property, wealth, riches (in this sense said to be also m.), RV. &c. &c.; the second astrological mansion, VarBṛS.; (in alg.) plus or the affirmative quantity, W. [Cf. Gk. ἕ, ὅς, σφός; Lat. *se, sovos, suus*; Goth. *sik*; Germ. *sich* &c.] (N.B. in the following comp. *o° own* stands for *one's own*). — **kampana**, m. 'self-moving,' air, wind, L. — **kambalā**, f. N. of a river, MārkP. — **karaṇa**, n. making (a woman) o° own, marrying, Pāṇ. i, 3, 56. — **karman**, n. o° own deed, Mn.; Hit.; o° own business or occupation, Kathās.; o° own occupation or duty, ŚāṅkhŚr.; Mn. &c.; °*ma-kṛit*, m. doing o° own business, an independent workman, W.; °*ma-ja*, mfn. arising from o° own act, R.; °*ma-vaśa*, mfn. subject to (the consequences of) o° own acts, W.; °*ma-stha*, mfn. minding o° own business or duty, Mn. x, 1. — **karmin**, mfn. selfish, A. — **kāmin**, mfn. following o° own wish, self-pleasing, ŚBr.; TĀr.; self-loving, selfish, MW. — **kārya**, n. o° own business or duty or function, W.; *-saha*, mfn. able to do o° own duty or effect o° own business, MW. — **kāla**, m. o° own time, proper time; (*e*), ind. at the right t°, ŚāṅkhŚr.; Mn. &c. — **kīrti-maya**, mf(*ī*)n. consisting of o° own fame, BhP. — **kuṭumba**, n. o° own household, Mn. — **kula**, n. o° own family or race, Kathās.; mfn. of o° own kin, Hit.; *-kshaya*, m. 'destroying (its) own family,' a fish, L.; *-ja*, mfn. born from o° own kin, Rājat. — **kulya**, mfn. id., ib. — **kuśala-maya**, mf(*ī*)n. relating to o° own welfare, Megh. — **kṛit**, mfn. doing o° own, performing o° own obligations, BhP. — **kṛita** (*svá-*), mf(*ā*)n. done or performed or built or composed or created or fixed by o° self, MBh.; Hariv.; R. &c.; spontaneous, TS.; ŚBr.; n. a deed done by o° self, MBh.; R.; °*tártha*, mfn. (prob.) w.r. for *su-kṛit*°, Kathās. — **ketu**, m. N. of a king, VP. — **kshatra** (*svá-*), mfn. master of o° self, independent, free, RV.; possessing innate strength, self-powerful, innately strong, MW. — **ga**, see *á-sva-ga*. — **gata**, mfn. belonging to o° self, own, Hariv.; Kāv.; Vedântas.; BhP.; passing in o° own mind, spoken to o° self, apart, W.; (*am*), ind. to o° self, aside (in dram.), Mṛicch.; Kālid. &c. — **gati**, f. a kind of metre, Ked. (v. l. *kha-g*°). — **garbha**, m. o° own womb, MW.; o° own embryo, ib. — **guṇa**, m. o° own merits, Kāv.; mfn. having o° own m°, appropriate, Śiś.; *-tas*, ind. from o° own personal m°, MW.; *-prakāśaka*, mfn. proclaiming o° own merits, boastful, ib. — **gupta**, mfn. self-defended, s°-preserved, W.; (*ā*), f. a kind of plant, VarBṛS.; Mimosa Pudica, L.; Mucuna Pruritus, ib.; cowach, W. — **gūrta** (*svá-*), mf(*ā*)n. exulting in themselves, RV.; boasting of (gen.), ib. — **gṛiha**, n. o° own house, Hariv.; Kāv.; Pañcat.; m. a kind of bird, L. — **gṛihīta**, w.r. for *su-g*°, L. — **gocara**, mfn. subject to o° self (°*raṃ* √*kṛi*, 'to subject to o° self'), Kām.; m. o° own sphere or range, Bcar. i, 13 (conj.) — **gopa** (*svá-*), mf(*ā*)n. guarding one's self, RV. — **graha**, m. N. of a demon attacking children, ŚārṅgS. — **grāma**, m. o° own village, Kāv. (cf. *sauvagrāmika*). — **cakshus**, n. o° own eye, Bhag. — **cara**, mfn. self-moving, having o° own motion, Horās. — **caraṇa-parshad**, f. a college or community of members of o° own Caraṇa or sect, MW. — **caryā**, f. o° own nature, Śrikaṇṭh. — **cetas**, n. o° own mind (°*sā*, 'out of o° own head'), Ratnâv. — **cchanda**, m. o° own or free will, o° own choice or fancy (ibc., °*dāt*, °*dena*, or °*da-tas*, 'at o° own will or pleasure,' 'spontaneously,' 'independently,' 'freely'), Up.; MBh.; Kāv. &c.; N. of wk.; mf(*ā*)n. following o° own will, acting at pleasure, independent, uncontrolled, spontaneous (*am*, ind.), Yājñ.; Kāv.; VarBṛS. &c.; uncultivated, wild, W.; m. N. of Skanda, AV.Pariś.; *-cara*, mf(*ā*)n. moving about at will, independent, R.; *-cārin*, mfn. id., Kuval.; ŚārṅgP. &c.; (*iṇī*), f. an independent woman, Kād.; a harlot, MW.; *-tantra*, n., *-tantra-rāja*, m. N. of wks.; *-tas*, ind. at will or pleasure, spontaneously, MBh.; *-tā*, f. independent action, uncontrolled behaviour, Kād.; *-naya*, m. N. of wk.; *-nāyaka*, m. a partic. Rasa, Rasêndrac.; *-paddhati*, f., *-bhaṭṭāraka-bṛihat-pūjā-pattrikā-vidhi*, m., *-bhairava*, m. N. of wks.; *-bhairava-rasa*, m. a partic. Rasa, Rasêndrac.; *-maraṇa*, n. dying at o° own will (a faculty bestowed on Bhishma), MBh.; R.; *-mṛityuka*, mfn. having death in o° own power, MBh.; *-vana-jāta*, mfn. growing spontaneously or wild in a forest, Hit.; *-śāktâgama*, m., *-saṃgraha*, m., *-sāra-saṃgraha*, m., °*cchandôddyota*, m. N. of wks. — **cchandaka**, mfn. = *-cchanda*, W. — **já**, mf(*ā́*)n. self-born, produced in or by o° self, own, akin, RV.; R.; m. a viper, AV.; AitBr.; ĀpŚr. (accord. to Sāy., 'a snake that has heads at both ends'); a son, L.; sweat, ib.; m. n. blood, ib.; (*ā*), f. a daughter, ib. — **jana**, m. (ifc. f. *ā*) a man of o° own people, kinsman; o° own people, own kindred, KātyŚr.; MBh.; Kāv. &c. (often confounded with *su-j*°); *-gandhin*, mfn. distantly related to (gen.), Mudr.; *-tā*, f. relationship to or with (gen.), Bhartṛ.; °*nâvṛita*, mfn. surrounded or accompanied by o° own people, MW. — **janaya**, Nom. P. °*yati*, to be related to (acc.), resemble, Bālar. (w. r. *su-j*°). — **janāya**, Nom. Ā. °*yate*, to become a relation, MBh.; Pañcat. — **janman** (*svá-*), mfn. self-begotten, own, RV. — **jā**, mfn. self-born, ĀpŚr. — **jāta**, mfn. self-begotten, L.; m. a child beg° by o° self, Prab. — **jāti**, f. o° own kind, Suśr.; o° own family or caste, Mn.; Pañcat.; mfn. of o° own kind, Pañcat.; *-dvish*, m. a dog, L. — **jātīya** (Mn.; Hariv. &c.) or **-jātya** (MBh.; Pañcat.), mfn. relating or belonging to o° own kind. — **jita**, mfn. self-conquered, BhP. — **jenya** (*svá-*), mfn. relating to o° own birth, RV. — **jñāti**, f. o° own kindred or kin, W.; m. a kinsman, ib. — **tantra**, n. self-dependence, independence, self-will, freedom, Pañcat.; Hit.; o° own system or school, Suśr.; o° own army, ib.; (with Buddh.) a partic. doctrine of free-will or independence, Buddh.; N. of wk. (also called °*tra-tantra*); mf(*ā*)n. self-dependent, self-willed, independent, free, uncontrolled (with *pada*, n. 'an ind° word'), Lāṭy.; Up.; Mn. &c.; of age, full grown, W.; m. N. of a Cakra-vāka, Hariv.; *-tantra*, n., see above; *-tā*, f. self-dependence, independence, freedom, Mn.; MBh.; Kathās.; MārkP.; originality, Cat.; wilfulness, W.; *-mukha mardana*, n., *-lekhana*, n. N. of wks.; *-vṛitti*, f. acting self-reliantly, independent action, L.; *-sāra*, N. of wk. — **tantraya**, Nom. (only °*yāṃ-cakre*), to make subject to o° own will, Ragh. — **tantrika**, m. the Sva-tantra school, Buddh. (prob. w. r. for *svāt*°). — **tantrin**, mfn. free, independent, uncontrolled, MBh. (accord. to Nilak. = *sva-śāstrânusārin*). — **tavas** (*svá-*), mfn. (nom. *-tavān*) self-strong, inherently powerful, valiant, RV.; Kāṭh.; VS. &c.; firmly rooted (said of a mountain), RV. — **tas**, ind. = *svasmāt* (e.g. *svato 'ṇśāt*, 'from o° own share;' *raksher apacāraṃ tvaṃ svato vā parato 'pi vā*, 'ward off injury from thyself and from others'), Mn.; Kathās.; of o° own self, of o° own accord (applicable to all three persons), MBh.; Ragh.; Kathās. &c.; by nature, Kathās.; out of (their) own estate, Mn. viii, 166; (*ca svataḥ*, w. r. for *śāśvataḥ*, Pañcat. iii, 96); °*taḥ-pramāṇa*, mfn. self-proved, self-evident, Sarvad.; °*taḥ-siddha*, mfn. s°-accomplished, MW.; s°-proved, s°-demonstrated, ib.; °*tas-tva*, n. the being s°-proved, Sarvad. — **tā**, f. the state of belonging to one's self, ownership (*-tām paśyati*, 'he thinks it belongs to him;' *rāja-svatām upapadyate*, 'it accrues to the king's ownership'), Śak.; = *-tva*, MW. — **tulya**, mfn. equal to one's self, Inscr. — **tṛitīya**, mf(*ā*)n. having o° own as the third, KātyŚr. — **tejas**, n. o° own splendour, Bhag.; °*jo-raśmi-mālin*, mfn. surrounded with a garland of rays of o° own splendour, R. — **tra**, mfn. self-preserving, W.; m. a blind man, L. — **tvá**, n. proprietary right to, property in (loc.), Kathās.; BhP.; self-existence, independence, Kāṭh.; MaitrS.; relationship to o° self, MW.; *-nivṛitti*, f. cessation or loss of proprietary right, W.; *-bodhana*, n. declaration or proof of ownership, ib.; *-rahasya*, n. N. of wk.; *-vat*, mfn. having propr° right, MW.; m. an owner, ib.; *-vāda*, m., *-vicāra*, m. (= *-rahasya*) N. of wks.; *-vyabhicārin*, mfn. departing or deviating from ownership (°*ri-tva*, n. 'uncertainty of own°'), W.; *-vyavasthârṇava-setu-bandha*, m. N. of wk.; *-hāni*, f. loss of proprietary right, forfeiture of title, W.; *-hetu*, m. ground or cause of propr° r°, ib.; °*tvâbhāva*, m. non-existence of propr° right, ib.; °*tvâvagama*, m. determination or ascertainment of ownership, ib.; °*tvâspada*, n. site of own°, that in which any one has proprietorship, ib.; °*tvâspadī-bhūta*, mfn. become the subject of proprietary right, MW.; °*tvôtpatti*, f. the arising of propr° right, origin of ownership, W. — **dāna**, n. the giving of o° own property, Jaim. — **dāra**, m. o° own wife; *-gāmin*, mfn. cohabiting with o° own wife, ŚāṅkhGṛ.; *-nirata*, mfn. attached to o° own wife, uxorious, Mn. iii, 45. — **diṅ-mukham**, ind. towards (its) own place or quarter, Sūryas. — **duhitṛi**, f. one's own daughter, MW. — **dṛiś**, mfn. seeing o° self or the soul, BhP. — **dṛishṭa**, mfn. self-seen (?), Hariv. (v.l. *saṃhṛishṭa*). — **deśa**, m. o° own place or country or home, Mn.; Kathās.; Rājat. &c.; pl. the inhabitants of o° own country, o° own subjects, BhP.; *-ja*, m. 'born in o° own country,' a countryman, L.; *-paridhi*, m. circumference of a circle of longitude in any place that has latitude, W.; *-bandhu*, m. (= *-ja*), A.; *-madhya-paridhi*, m. circumf° of the terrestrial equator, W.; *-smārin*, mfn. yearning for o° own country, home-sick, Rājat. — **deha-dāna**, n. the gift of o° own body, L. — **dosha-ja**, mf(*ā*)n. due to o° own fault, MBh. — **dharma**, m. o° own rights (°*maṃ* √*labh*, 'to get justice'), MBh.; o° own duty, MaitrUp.; Mn.; Yājñ. &c.; peculiar property, peculiarity, W.; *-cyuta*, mfn. deprived of o° own rights, fallen from or neglecting o° own duty, W.; *-tyāga*, m. dereliction or neglect of o° own duty, ib.; abandoning o° own religion, apostasy, ib.; *-vartin*, mfn. applying o° self to o° duties (°*ti-tva*, n.), MBh.; *-skhalana*, n. falling from or neglect of o° own duty, W.; *-stha*, mfn. abiding in o° own duty, ib.; °*mâcaraṇa*, n. the practising o° own duties, ib.; °*mâdhva-bodha*, m. N. of wk.; °*mânapaga*, mfn. not swerving from o° d°, MW.; °*mârtha-viniścaya*, m.

the knowing or ascertaining one's own duty and interest, ib. —**dharman**, mfn. abiding in one's own customs, RV. —**dhā**, see p. 1278, col. 1, and s.v. —**dhāman**, m. N. of a son of Satya-sahas and Sūnṛitā, BhP.; pl. N. of a class of gods under the 3rd Manu, Pur. —**dhur**, mfn. self-dependent, indep°, PañcavBr. (Sch.); n. (acc. *-dhūr* ?) N. of a Sāman, ib. —**dhṛiti** (*svá-*), f. standing still of o° self, VS.; Br.; ĀśvŚr. —**dhenava** (*svá-*), mfn. coming from o° own cows, RV. —**nagara**, n. o° own town or native city, Śak. —**nābhaka**, m. N. of a spell pronounced over weapons, R. —**nābhya**, mfn. issuing from o° own navel, BhP. —**nāman**, n. o° own name, Gaut.; mfn. having a name or reputation through o° self, Cāṇ.; °*mâṅka*, mfn. marked with or called after o° own name, MW. —**nāśa**, m. self-destruction, L. —**nishṭha**, mfn. being in o° own person (*-tva*, n.), KapS., Sch. —**paksha**, m. o° own wings, Kathās.; o° own party, MBh.; Mālav.; Pañcat. &c.; a man of o° own party, friend (also pl.), MBh.; Suśr.; BhP.; o° own opinion or assertion, Kathās.; Madhus. —**pakshīya**, mfn. belonging to o° own party, Saṃskārak. —**pañcaka**, mfn. (perhaps) multiplied 5 times with itself, Jyot. —**paṇa**, m. o° own stake, Yājñ. —**pati** (*svá-*), m. o° own lord, RV.; (*-pati*), mfn. having an own consort, AV.; *-bhrāntimatī*, f. (a woman) mistaking anything for her husband, Prâyaśc. —**patita**, mfn. dropped off of its own accord, Var. —**patī-√kṛi**, P. *-karoti*, to make any one her husband, Naish. —**pada**, n. one's own place or abode, Kathās.; o° own position or rank, ib. —**para-pratāraka**, mfn. deceiving one's self and others, Bhartṛ. —**para-maṇḍala**, n. one's own and an enemy's country, MW. —**piṇḍā**, f. a kind of date tree, L. (w. r. for *sthala-p°*). —**pitṛi**, m. (for *svapitṛi* see p. 1280, col. 1) o° own father, Prab.; Sarvad. &c.; pl. o° own deceased ancestors, MBh. —**piś**, m. N. of a man (cf. *svāpiśi*). —**putra-vat**, ind. like o° own children, MW. —**pura**, n. o° own city, L.; N. of a suburb of Vajra-nagara, Hariv. —**puras**, ind. before o° self, ib. —**pū́**, see s. v. —**pūrṇa**, mfn. perfectly satisfied with or through o° own acts, BhP. —**posham**, ind. (with √*push*) to prosper in o° person, Pāṇ. iii, 4, 40. —**prakāśa**, mfn. clear or evident by itself (*-tva*, n.), Up.; Sāh. &c.; self-luminous, A.; N. of Comm.; *-jñāna-vādârtha*, m., *-tā-vicāra*, m., *-pradīpikā*, f., *-rahasya*, n., *-vādârtha*, m. N. of wks. —**pratikara**, w. r. for *su-p°*, R. —**pratinidhi**, m. a substitute for one's self (*-tvena*, ind. instead of him, her, them &c.), Sāy. —**pratishṭha**, mfn. astringent, L.; m. astringent taste, L. —**pradhāna**, mfn. self-dependent, independent, L.; *-tā*, f. self-dependence, Kām.; o° own natural state, MW. —**prabhā**, f. N. of Comm. —**prabhutā**, f. own or arbitrary power (*ayā*, ind. 'arbitrarily'), Pañcat. —**pramāṇânurūpa**, mfn. suited to o° strength, Śak. —**prayogāt**, ind. by means of o° self, without assistance, Kathās. —**prayojana-vaśa**, m. the force of o° own object or purpose, MW. —**prasāra**, m. opening o° own mouth, Vop. —**bandhu**, m. one's own relation or friend, Mn. ii, 207; *-paddhati*, f. N. of wk. —**balâśraya**, mfn. depending on o° own strength, MW. —**bāndhava**, m. o° own relation, Mn. viii, 29. —**bāhu**, m. o° own arm; *-bala*, n. strength of o° own arm, MBh. —**bīja**, n. o° own seed or cause, MW.; m. the soul, L. —**brāhmaṇyā**, w. r. for *su-brāhmaṇyā*, Mn. ix, 126. —**bhaksha**, mfn. (perhaps) drawing nourishment from one's self, ĀpŚr. —**bhaṭa**, m. o° own warrior or body-guard, MW. —**bhadrā**, f. Gmelina Arborea, L. (v. l. *subh°*). —**bhavas** (*svá-*), mfn. (prob.) being in the Self (said of the breath), TS. —**bhājana**, w. r. for *sabhājana*, L. —**bhānu** (*svá-*), mfn. self-luminous, RV. —**bhāva**, m. (ifc. f. *ā*) native place, Vishṇ.; own condition or state of being, natural state or constitution, innate or inherent disposition, nature, impulse, spontaneity; (°*vāt* or °*vena* or °*va-tas* or ibc.), from natural disposition, by nature, naturally, by o° self, spontaneously), ŚvetUp.; Mn.; MBh. &c.; *-kṛita*, mfn. done by nature, natural, VarBṛS.; *-kṛipaṇa*, m. 'naturally mean,' N. of a Brāhman, Pañcat.; *-ja*, mfn. produced by natural disposition, innate, natural, R.; Sāh. &c.; *-janita*, mfn. id., Kāv.; *-tas*, ind., see above; *-tā*, f. (Jātakam.) or *-tva*, n. (TPrāt., Sch.) the state of innate disposition or nature; *-daurjanya*, n. natural or innate wickedness, W.; *-dvesha*, m. natural hatred, L.; *-prabhava*, mfn. (= *-ja* above), VarBṛS.; *-bhāva*, m. natural disposition, Pañcat.; *-vāda*, m. the doctrine that the universe was produced and is sustained by the natural and necessary action of substances according to their inherent properties, MW.; *-vādin*, m. one who maintains the above doctrine, ib.; *-śūra*, mfn. possessing natural heroes (others, 'valiant by nature'), Hit.; *-siddha*, mfn. established by nature, natural, innate, ĀśvŚr.; Bhartṛ.; self-evident, obvious, Kāś.; °*vârtha-dīpikā*, f. N. of Comm.; °*vôkta*, mfn. said or declared spontaneously, Yājñ., Sch.; °*vôkti*, f. statement of the exact nature (of anything), accurate description of the properties (of things), Kāvyâd.; Pratāp. &c.; spontaneous declaration, A.; °*vônnata-bhāva*, mfn. high-minded by nature (*-tva*, n.), Hariv. —**bhāvikī**, (prob.) w.r. for *svābhāvikam*, Cat. —**bhāshita**, (prob.) w.r. for *su-bh°*, Kathās. —**bhū**, mfn. self-existent, RāmatUp.; ĀpŚr.; m. N. of Brahmā, BhP.; of Vishṇu, L.; of Śiva, MW.; f. one's own country, home, Rājat.; *-tyāga*, m. abandonment of o° own c°, L. —**bhūta**, mfn. being o° own, belonging to (gen.), Sāy. —**bhūti**, f. o° own welfare (°*tyartham*, 'for the sake of one's own interest'), Pat.; mfn. arising spontaneously, VS.; °*ty-ojas* (*svá-bhūty°*), mfn. possessing energy derived from inherent power, RV. —**bhūmi**, f. = *-bhū*, f., Hit.; o° own land, own estate, W.; o° own or proper place, VarBṛS.; m. N. of a son of Ugra-sena, VP. —**bhyasa**, mfn. spontaneously frightened, AV. —**mat**, mfn., in *alpa-sva-m°*, having little property, Śatr. —**manīshā**, f. own judgment or opinion, Nyāyad., Sch. —**manīshikā**, f. id., Bādar., Sch.; indifference, L. —**mano-bodha-vākya**, n. pl. N. of wk. —**māṇsa**, n. own flesh or body, Mn.; R. —**mātreṇa**, ind. by or through one's self, Inscr. —**māyā**, f own cunning or magical art or skill, MW. —**mārga-marma-vivaraṇa**, n. N. of wk. —**yata** (*svá-*), mfn. self-guided, RV. —**yatna**, m. o° own exertion, L. —**yaśas** (*svá-*), mfn. glorious or illustrious through o° own (acts), self-sufficient (compar. *-tara*), RV.; AV. —**yāvan**, mfn. self-moving, going one's own way, RV. —**yú**, see p. 1278, col. 3. —**yukta** (*svá-*), mfn. self-yoked (said of the horses of the Maruts), ib. —**yukti** (*svá-*), f. own yoke or team of horses, ib.; mfn. self-yoked, MW.; (°*tyā* or °*ti-tas*), ind. in natural course, of course, naturally, Kathās. —**yúgvan**, m. 'any one joined to one's self,' an ally, RV. —**yúj**, m. id., RV.; AV. —**yuti**, f. the line which joins the extremities of the perpendicular and diagonal, Col. —**yūthya**, m. a relation, one's belongings (pl.), MBh. —**yoni**, f. own womb, o° own birthplace or source, Mn.; MBh.; Hariv. &c.; womb of o° own caste, Mn. x, 27 sq.; w.r. for *śvay°*, MBh.; mf(*ī*)n. related by blood, consanguineous, Mn.; Yājñ.; issuing or arising out of self, Hariv.; (*is*), f. a sister or near female relative, W.; n. (with *kaśyapasya*) N. of a Sāman, ĀrshBr.; du., Lāṭy.; *-guṇa-kṛit*, mfn. operating like that from which it is derived, Bhpr. —**rasa**, m. own (unadulterated) juice or essence, MBh.; Car. &c.; natural or peculiar flavour, W.; proper taste or sentiment in composition, ib.; a partic. astringent juice or decoction, MW.; the sediment of oily substances ground on a stone, W.; own inclination (*-tas*, 'through own incl°,' 'for pleasure'), ĀpŚr., Sch.; feeling for one's own people, Kāv.; instinct of self-preservation (?), Yogas.; analogy, L.; mf(*ā*)n. agreeable or pleasant to one's taste, congenial, Kathās.; TPrāt., Sch.; m. N. of a mountain, Pur. —**rasī-√kṛi**, P. *-karoti*, to make into sap or juice, Car. —**rā́j**, mfn. (nom. *-rāṭ*) self-ruling, m. a self-ruler, RV.; TS.; AV. &c.; mfn. self-resplendent, self-luminous, MW.; m. N. of Brahmā, Pur.; of Vishṇu-Kṛishṇa, MBh.; BhP.; Pañcar.; of a Manu, BhP.; of an Ekâha, ŚāṅkhŚr.; Vait.; of one of the 7 principal rays of the sun, VP.; f. various kinds of metre, AV.; Br. &c. —**rā́jan**, mf(*jñī*)n. self-ruling, s°-guiding, a s°-ruler, TS.; TBr.; Lāṭy. —**rājya**, n. independent dominion or sovereignty, RV.; AV.; own dominion or kingdom, R.; Kathās.; (with *Indrasya*) N. of a Sāman, ĀrshBr. —**rāshṭra**, n. own kingdom, Mn.; Hit.; m. N. of a king, MārkP.; pl. N. of a people, MBh.; VP.; *-cintā*, f. care for one's own country or p°, L. —**rāshṭrīya**, mfn. belonging to o° own kingdom (*-jana*, m. pl. 'own subjects'), Mn., Sch. —**ruci**, f. own will or pleasure, Śiś.; mfn. following o° own pl°, MārkP.; (*yā*), ind. according to o° own will, Yājñ.; Mn., Sch. —**ruh**, mfn. self-growing, s°-increasing, MW. —**rūpa**, n. (ifc. f. *ā*) o° own form or shape, the f° or sh° of (gen. or comp.; with or without *śabdasya* or *śabda-sva-r°*, 'a word itself or in its own form' [opp. to its synonyms or varieties]; with *nāmnām* = 'names themselves'), MBh.; Pañcat.; BhP. &c.; own condition, peculiarity, character, nature (*eṇa* or ibc., 'by nature,' 'in reality,' 'by itself'), RPrāt.; NṛisUp.; Mn. &c.; peculiar aim, W.; kind, sort, ib.; a partic. relation (in phil., see under *sambandha*), MW.; occurrence, event, Campak.; Uttamac.; Siṃhâs.; mfn. having o° own peculiar form or character, MW.; having a like nature or char°, similar, like, Sāṃkhyak. (w.r. for *sa-r°*); pleasing, handsome (for *su-r°*), L.; wise, learned, L.; m. N. of a Daitya, MBh.; of a son of Su-nandā, MārkP.; of a pupil of Caitanya, W.; m. or n. N. of a place, Cat.; (*ā*), f. N. of a place, MW.; *-gata*, mfn. endowed with o° own form or nature, having a like character, W.; *-tas*, ind. in o° own form, BhP.; according to o° own f°, analogously, similarly, identically, MW.; by nature, in reality, by itself, MārkP.; (°*to go-dāna-prayogaḥ*, N. of wk.); *-tā*, f. (or *-tva*, n.) the state of o° own form or nature (°*tayā*, 'literally,' 'in reality'), MBh.; BhP.; Śak., Sch.; Sāh.; the having a natural form, identity of form or nature, W.; w.r. for *su-rūpa-tā*, Rājat.; *-dhārin*, mfn. having one's own form, MBh.; *-nirūpaṇa*, n., *-nirṇaya*, m., *-prakāśa*, m. N. of wks.; *-bhāva*, m. (a short word) whose essence is of the same efficacy (as that of the full form), Mn. ii, 124; *-vat*, mfn. having the form of (comp.), MBh.; *-sambandha-rūpa*, n., *-sambodhana*, n., *-sambodhana-pañca-viṇśati-vṛitti*, f., °*-rūpâkhya-stotra*, n. N. of wks.; °*-rūpâcārya*, m. N. of a teacher, Cat.; °*-rūpânusaṃdhāna*, n., °*-rūpânusaṃdhāna-stotra*, n. N. of wks.; °*-rūpâsiddhi*, f. a form of non-proof (where the quality alleged to belong to a subject is not really proved), Tarkas.; °*-rūpôtprêkshā*, f. a kind of simile, Sāh.; Kuval.; °*-rūpôpanishad*, f. N. of an Upanishad. —**rūpaka**, n. or (*ikā*), f. an image of (gen.), Hcat.; (ifc.) own condition, peculiarity, character, nature, Pañcar. —**rūpin**, mfn. having one's own or natural form, MBh.; appearing in the form of (ifc.), R.; Pur.; Pañcar.; embodied, MBh.; Inscr.; having essential properties, MW.; identical, ib. —**rocas** (*svá-*), mfn. self-shining, TBr. (v.l. *-rocis*). —**roci**, f. own ray, MārkP. (pl.) —**rocisha**, w.r. for *svār°*, ib. —**rocis**, mfn.; n. own light, BhP.; (*svá-*), mfn. self-shining, RV.; BhP.; m. N. of a son of the Gandharva Kali by the Apsaras Varūthinī, MārkP. —**lakshaṇa**, n. peculiar characteristic or property, MBh.; mfn. having its own specific characteristics, Sarvad.; *-prakāśa*, m. N. of wk. —**likhita**, n. any document or receipt written with one's own hand, Vishṇ. —**liṅga**, mfn. preserving (its) own grammatical gender, L. —**līna**, m. N. of a Dānava, L. —**vaṇśa-ja**, mfn. sprung from the immediate family of any one (gen.), Hariv. —**vaṇśin**, mfn. belonging to the imm° family of any one (gen.), ib. —**vaṇśya**, mfn. belonging to one's own family, MBh.; Rājat. —**1. -vat** (*svá-*), mfn. possessing property, wealthy (*-tā*, f.), TS.; Jaim. (for *svavān* nom. of *sv-avas* see p. 1282). —**2. -vat**, ind. as if it were o° own property, Gaut. —**vargīya**, mfn. belonging to o° own kindred, Pañcat.; bel° to (its) own group (of consonants), VPrāt. —**vargya**, mfn. id., ĀśvŚr.; bel° to one's own tribe, MW. —**vaśa**, mf(*ā*)n. (for *sv-avaśa* see p. 1282) having control of one's self, self-controlled, subject to one's self or to one's own will, independent, free (*-tā*, f.), MBh.; R. &c.; °*śaṃ-kṛita*, mfn. brought into subjection by (instr.), R. —**vaśinī**, f. a kind of metre, RPrāt.; Nidānas. —**vaśya**, mfn. subject or submissive to o° own self, R. —**vasu** (*svá-*), v.l. of the Pada-pāṭha for *svá-v°*, RV.; AV. —**vahita**, mfn. self-impelled, self-moved, W.; alert, active, ib. —**vāñchā**, f. one's own desire (°*chayā*, 'according to o° own wish'), Hit. —**vāra**, m. o° own place (see 2. *vāra*), R. —**vārtta**, n. o° own condition or welfare, MW. —**vāsin**, n. du. (with *Jamad-agneḥ*) N. of two Sāmans, ĀrshBr.; (*inī*), f. a woman whether married or unmarried who continues to dwell after maturity in her father's house, Yājñ.; Vcar. (cf. *su-v°*). —**vikatthana**, mfn. self-praising, boasting of o° own acts, R. —**vigraha**, m. o° own body (°*ham*, 'one's self'), Rājat. —**vicchandas**, mfn. = *sva-cch°* + *vi-cch°*, Lāṭy. —**vidyut** (*svá-*), mfn. 'self-lightning,' flashing forth l° by o° own power, RV. —**vidhi**, m. 'own rule or method;' (*inā*), ind. in o° own way, BhP.; in the right w°, duly, VarBṛS. —**vidheya**, mfn. to be done by one's self, Naish. —**vināśa**, m. self-destruction, suicide, MW. —**vishaya**, m. o° own country, home (*kasmiṅś-cit sva-vishaye*, 'in some part of his kingdom'), MBh.; R.; Pañcat. &c.; one's own sphere or province, BṛĀrUp., Sch. **-vîkshita**, w.r. for *sv-avêkshita*, R. **-vîrya-tas**, ind. according to one's power, MW. **-vṛikti** (*svá-*), f. self-appropriation (°*tibhis*, 'exclusively for ourselves'), RV.; mfn. self-cleansing, having cl° properties, MW.; f. a hymn, ib. **-vṛij**, mfn. appropriating to one's self (others, 'suffering one's self to be appropriated or won over,' said of Indra), RV. **-vṛiti**, w.r. for *-vṛitti*, MBh.; R. **-vṛitta**, n. one's own business or occupation, MW. **-vṛitti**, f. one's own way of life, R.; o° own subsistence or existence (also pl.; °*ttyā*, 'at the sacrifice of o° own life'), MBh.; Kām.; self-dependence, Cāṇ.; mfn. subsisting by c° own exertions, MW.; *-vāda*, m. N. of wk. **-vṛishṭi** (*svá-*), mfn. retaining rain for one's self, rain-appropriating, RV. **-vairitā**, f. hostility towards o° self (*nijâyushaḥ sva-vairitām* √*kṛi*, 'to cause the destruction of o° own life'), Naish. **-śakti**, f. own power or strength, Mn. ix, 298; own energy (of a god), BhP.; (*yā*), ind. to the best of one's ability, Pañcat.; Siṇhās. **-śarîra**, n. o° own body or person, R. **-śiras**, w.r. for *svaḥ-ś°*, Hariv. **-śocis** (*svá-*), mfn. self-radiant, RV. **-ścandra** (*svá-*), mfn. s°-glittering, s°-brilliant, ib. **-ślāghā**, f. s°-praise, L. **-saṃyukta**, mfn. connected with o° self, Sāh. **-saṃvid**, f. the knowledge of one's own or the true Essence, BhP.; mfn. knowing only o° self, ib. **-saṃvṛita**, mfn. self-guarded, Mn. vii, 104. **-saṃvedana**, n. knowledge derived from one's self, HYog.; Buddh. **-saṃvedya**, mfn. intelligible only to one's self, Rājat.; Daś.; Pañcar. **-saṃsthā**, f. the abiding in self, s°-possession, absorption in self, MW. **-saṃhitā**, f. connection (only) with self, being by o° self or alone, IndSt. **-sattā**, f. the being in one's own possession or at o° own disposition, KātyŚr., Paddh. **-sadṛiśa**, mf(*ā*)n. like or suitable to o° self, R.; Rājat. **-samāna**, mfn. id., Rājat. **-samuttha**, mfn. arising within self, MBh.; produced or existing by s°, natural, MārkP. **-sambhava**, mfn. being o° own origin or source, BhP.; =next, ib. **-sambhûta**, mfn. produced from o° self, Kathās. **-sammukha**, mfn. facing o° self, turning to o° self, Cat. **-sara**, see s.v. **-sarva**, n. the whole of o° own property, Cat. **-sāra** (*svá-*), n. = *-sara*, RV. **-sic**, mfn. pouring out spontaneously, VS.; TS.; (cf. *su-sic*). **-siddha**, mfn. spontaneously effected, BhP.; naturally one's own, belonging to o° self by nature, ib. **-sû**, f. 'self-created,' the earth, L. **-sṛit**, mfn. going o° own way, RV. **-setu** (*svá-*), mf(*u*)n. forming o° own embankment or bridge, ib. **-sainya**, n. one's own army, L. **-skanda**, m. a person who has gained his liberty by redeeming a pledge, L. **-stara**, m. self-strewn grass (as a couch), ĀśvGṛ.; Gobh.; Āpast. **-stha**, mf(*ā*)n. self-abiding, being in o° self (or 'in the self,' Sarvad.), being in one's natural state, being o° self, uninjured, unmolested, contented, doing well, sound, well, healthy (in body and mind; often v.l. for *su-stha*), comfortable, at ease (compar. *-tara*), MaitrUp. &c. &c.; relying upon one's self, confident, resolute, composed, W.; self-sufficient, independent, ib.; (*am*), ind. composedly, MW.; *-citta*, mfn. sound in mind, Jātakam.; *-tā*, f. well-being, health, ease, Pañcat.; HYog.; *-vṛitta*, n. medical treatment of a healthy person, Car.; °*thârishṭa*, n. a death-token in a healthy person, Aśvav. **-sthāna**, n. one's own place, own home, KātyŚr.; Gobh.; MBh. &c.; mfn. being in o° own place, Lāṭy.; *-stha*, mfn. standing in or occupying one's own condition, MW. **-sthita**, mfn. independent, Nir. **-sthî-√kṛi**, P. *-karoti*, to make o° self, make well, reduce to one's natural condition, Pañcad. **-sthî-√bhû**, P. *-bhavati*, to become o° self, return to one's natural condition, become well or sober, Prab. **-sva-kāla**, m. the proper time for each, Kāv. **-svadha**, m. pl. N. of a partic. class of Pitṛis, Cat. **-sva-prāṇa**, m. pl. the respective breath or life of each, Sāy. **-svabhāva**, m. one's natural disposition, Mṛicch. **-sva-ruci**, mfn. pl. every one brilliant in his own way, Siṇhâs. **-svarûpa**, n. one's true character, Vedântas.; HYog.; N. of wk. **-svāmi-bhāva**, m. the relation of possession and possessor, KapS. **-svāmi-sambandha**, m. id., Sāṃkhyak., Sch. **-hantṛi**, m. a suicide, Siṇhâs. **-haraṇa**, n. confiscation of property, Gaut. **-hasta**, m. one's own hand (°*taṃ* √*dā*, 'to offer one's hand for aid [loc.]'), Ratnâv.; Hit. &c.; own handwriting, autograph, Vishṇ.; *-gata*, mfn. fallen into or being in o° own hands, L.; *-svastika-stanî*, f. covering (her) breasts with crossed hands, Kathās.; °*hastôllikhita*, mfn. drawn or painted by o° own h°, MW. **-hastikā**, f. a hoe, mattock, pickaxe, Pañcat. **-hastita**, mfn. held or supported by o° own hand, Naish. **-hita**, mfn. beneficial to o° self, Kāv.; well disposed to o° self, Pañcat.; n. o° own welfare, Śiś.; °*tâishin*, mfn. seeking o° own good or advantage, W. **-hetu**, m. o° own cause, own sake (°*tunā*, 'for o° own s°'), ib. **-hotṛi** (*svá-*), m. o° own Hotṛi, AV. **Svâkāra**, m. (for *sv-āk°* see p. 1283) o° own nature, natural disposition, Pañcat.; mfn. having o° own form, W.; *-kara*, m. a partic. Samādhi, Kāraṇḍ. **Svâkṛiti**, mfn. (for *sv-āk°* see p. 1283) = °*kāra*, MW. **Svâksha-pāda**, m. a follower of the Nyāya philosophy, L. **Svâkshara**, m. one's own handwriting, autograph, L. **Svâkhyāta**, mfn. self-announced (*-tā*, f.), HYog. **Svâkhyā-śataka**, n. N. of wk. **Svâgata**, mfn. (for *sv-āg°* see p. 1283) come of o° self, MW. **Svâṃ-kṛita**, mfn. made o° own, seized, TS. **Svâṅga**, n. a limb of o° own body, o° own b°, limb or body in the strict (not metaphorical) sense, Kāv.; Yogas. &c.; m. a proper N., MW.; *-bhaṅga*, m. injury to o° own body, Ml.; *-śîta*, mfn. cooled in all parts, Bhpr. **Svâjñā**, f. o° own command (°*jñām* √*grah*, 'to submit to one's com°'), Uttamac. **Svâñjalyaka**, n. the joining of one's hands in supplication, supplication, MBh. **Svâtman**, m. o° own self, o° self (= reflexive pron.), o° own nature (°*ma-tā*, f.), NṛisUp.; R.; Kathās. &c.; (°*ma*)*-nirûpaṇa*, n., *-nirûpaṇa-prakaraṇa*, n., *-pûjā*, f., *-prakāśikā*, f., *-prabodha*, m., *-prayoga-pradîpikā*, f., *-yoga-pradîpa*, m. N. of wks.; *-vadha*, m. suicide, Kathās.; *-saṃvitty-upadeśa*, m., *-saṃvid-upadeśa*, m., °*mânanda-prakaraṇa*, n., °*mânanda-prakāśa*, m., °*mânanda-vivardhinî*, f., °*mânanda-stotra*, n., °*mânandôpadeśa*, m., °*mânubodha*, m., °*mânubhava*, m., °*mânurûpaṇa*, n. N. of wks.; °*mârāma*, mfn. taking pleasure in or contented with o° self, Pañcar.; m. (also *-yogin* or *-yogîndra*) N. of an author, Cat.; °*mâvabodha*, °*môpadeśa*, m. N. of wks. **Svâtmi-bhāva**, m. v.l. for *ātmî-bh°*, q.v., Bhartṛ. **Svâdāna**, n. (for *sv-ād°* see p. 1283) taking what belongs to o° self or o° own due, Mn. viii, 172. **Svâdhikāra**, m. o° own office, special charge, peculiar station, Megh.; Pañcat. **Svâdhipatya**, n. own supremacy, supreme sway, sovereignty, W. **Svâdhishṭhāna**, n. o° own place, VP., Sch.; one of the 6 mystical circles of the body (see *cakra*), Pañcar.; Ānand. **Svâdhîna**, mf(*ā*)n. dependent on one's self, independent, free, Hariv.; R.; being in o° own power or control, being at o° own disposal, MBh.; Kāv. &c.; *-kuśala*, mfn. having prosperity in o° own power, Śak.; *-tā*, f. subjection to (only) one's self, independence, freedom, Kāv.; *-tva*, n. (= *-tā*), ib.; *-patikā* (Pratāp.) or *-bhartṛikā* (Sāh.), f. a woman whose husband is under her own control. 1. **Svâdhyāyá**, m. reciting or repeating or rehearsing to o° self, repetition or recitation of the Veda in a low voice to o° self, ŚBr. &c. &c.; repeating the V° aloud (acc. with caus. of √1. *śru*, 'to cause the V° to be repeated aloud'), Mn. iii, 232; recitation or perusal of any sacred texts, W.; the Veda, L.; a day on which sacred recitation is resumed after its suspension, MW.; N. of wk.; mfn. studying the V° (*-tama*, perhaps w.r. for *svâdhyâyi-t°*), Divyâv.; *-dhṛik*, mfn. one who repeats or recites the V°, Āpast.; *-brāhmaṇa*, n. N. of ch. in the Taittirîyāraṇyaka; *-vat*, mfn. (= *-dhṛik*), Yājñ.; MBh.; Hariv.; m. a repeater or student of the V°, W.; °*yâyârthin*, m. one who seeks a maintenance for himself during his studentship, Mn. xi, 1. 2. **Svâdhyāya**, Nom. P. °*yāyati*, to study, recite, read to (acc.), Divyâv.; SaddhP. **Svâdhyāyana**, m. N. of a man; pl. his family, Cat. **Svâdhyāyanikā**, f. a certain portion of a sacred work or sacred texts which have to be repeated or studied, Divyâv. **Svâdhyâyin**, mfn. repeating or reciting the Veda, MBh.; (cf. *nitya-sv°*); m. one who recites or repeats any sacred texts to himself, (esp.) a repeater of the Veda, W.; a tradesman, shopkeeper, dealer, L. **Svâdhyâyinikā**, f. = *svâdhyāyanikā*, Divyâv. **Svânanda**, m. delight in one's self, Cat.; *-candrikā*, f. N. of wk.; *-pûrṇa*, m. N. of an author, Cat. **Svânubhava**, m. o° own personal experience or observation, Cat.; °*vâdarśa*, m. N. of wk. **Svânubhāva**, m. enjoyment of or love for property, Kathās. **Svânubhûti**, f. o° own experience, Cat.; self-enjoyment (see comp.); *-prakāśa*, m., *-prakāśa-vivṛiti*, f., *-vākya*, n., *-bhûty-abhidha-nāṭaka*, n. N. of wks.; °*bhûty-eka-sāra*, mfn. whose only essence consists in self-enjoyment, Bhartṛ. **Svânurûpa**, mfn. resembling one's self, suited to o° character, Kathās.; natural, innate, W. **Svânusāra**, m. (only *eṇa*, 'according to o° property'), Hcat. **Svânta**, m. (accord. to Pāṇ. vii, 2, 13 fr. √*svan*) own end, BhP.; own death, Śiś.; own territory or domain or province, Kām.; n. 'seat of the Ego,' the heart (as s° of the emotions; ifc. f. *ā*), Kāv.; Kathās.; MārkP. &c.; a cavern, L.; *-ja*, m. 'heart-born,' love, Gît.; *-vat*, mfn. having a heart, Kathās.; *-stha*, mfn. being in the heart (perhaps w.r. for *svântaḥ-stha*, 'being in one's interior'), BhP. **Svânyadîya-tva**, n. the state of being o° own or some one else's, MW.; *-saṃdeha*, m. doubt about 'meum' and 'tuum,' ib. **Svâparādha**, m. offence against o° self, Hariv. **Svâpyayá**, m. turning into o° self (as an explanation of *svápna*), ŚBr.; Bādar. **Svâbhāva**, m. own non-existence, Nilak. **Svâbhicārin**, (prob.) w.r. for *vyabhic°*, Kathās. **Svâbhîshṭa**, mfn. loved by o° self, Pañcar. **Svâyatta**, mfn. dependent on o° self, being under o° own control (*-tva*, n.), Kathās.; Daś.; Rājat. &c.; uncontrolled by others, o° own master, MW. **Svâyatti-√kṛi**, P. *-karoti* &c., to make subject to o° self, Uttamac. **Svâyoga**, m. the not being contained in o° self, TPrāt., Sch. **Svârabdha** or °**rambhaka**, mfn. self-undertaken, BhP. 1. **Svâ-rāj**, mfn. (for 2. see p. 1282) = *sva-r°*, Prab. **Svârāma**, mfn. delighting in o° self, BhP. **Svâ-rúh** (or *svâr°*?), mfn. growing from (its) own root, firm-rooted, TS.; (nom. °*rut* fr. °*rudh*, Kāṭh.) **Svârjita**, mfn. self-acquired, Kāv. **Svârtha**, m. o° own affair or cause, personal matter or advantage, self-interest, o° own aim or object (also pl.), MaitrUp.; MBh.; R. &c.; o° own property or substance, MW.; own or original meaning, Sāh.; Vedântas.; TPrāt., Sch.; similar meaning (prob. for *sârtha*), a pleonasm, MW.; = *liṅgârtha-viśesha*, L.; mf(*ā*)n. directed to o° self, egoistical (*-tā*, f.), Kum.; Tarkas. &c.; adapted to (its) purpose, Car.; having one's object, expressing (its) own inherent or true meaning, hav° a natural or literal meaning, hav° a similar m° (= *sârtha*), pleonastic, MW.; (*am* or *e*), ind. on o° own account, for o° self, Kāv.; Kathās.; KapS. &c.; *-paṇḍita*, mfn. clever in o° own affairs, MBh.; *-para*, mfn. intent on o° own advantage, self-interested, Śiś. (*-tā*, f. 'selfishness,' MW.); *-parâyaṇa*, mfn. id., MW.; *-prayatna*, m. a self-interested project, Ratnâv.; *-bhāj*, mfn. managing one's own affairs, HPariś.; *-bhraṇśin*, mfn. ruinous to o° own interests, Pañcat.; *-lipsu*, mfn. wishing to gain o° own object, self-seeking, MW.; *-vighāta*, m. frustration of one's object, ib.; *-sādhaka*, mfn. effective of or promoting one's own object, Cāṇ.; BhP.; Nir.; *-sādhana*, n. accomplishment of one's own object or desire, Mn.; Rājat.; (°*na*)*-tatpara*, mfn. intent upon it, Mn. iv, 196; *-siddhi*, f. (= *sādhana*), Rājat.; °*thânumāna*, n. 'inference for o° self,' (in log.) a partic. process of induction, MW.; °*thêt*, mfn. attending to one's own affairs, TS.; °*thôpapatti*, f. the gaining o° own object, Ragh. **Svârthika**, mfn. having o° own object, MW.; preserving an original meaning unchanged, pleonastic, Pāṇ., Sch.; Sāy.; done with one's own wealth, MW. **Svârthin**, mfn. pursuing o° own objects, self-seeking, Siṇhâs. **Svâvamānana**, n. (L.) or °**mānanā**, f. (Sāh.) self-contempt, despair of o° self. **Svá-vasu**, mfn. guarding one's possessions, RV. (cf. *svá-v°*). **Svâśishâtman**, mfn. (*āśishā*, instr. of *āśis*) thinking only of o° own wishes, BhP. **Svâśraya**, mfn. relating or referring to the thing itself or to the point in question, Pāṇ., Sch. **Svâśrita**, mfn. self-dependent, MW. **Svâhata**, mfn. struck or coined by o° self, Rājat. **Svêccha**, ibc. (Daś.) or °**cham**, ind. (Kathās.; Chandom.) accord. to o° own wish, at will or pleasure, of o° own accord, voluntarily. **Svêcchā**, f. o° own wish or will, free will, Kāv.; Rājat.; Pañcar.; ibc. or (*ayā*), ind. accord. to o° own wish, at pleasure, of o° own free will, VarBṛS.; Kathās.; MārkP. &c.; °*-cāra* (°*châc°*), m. acting as one likes, doing what is right in o° own eyes, MW.; *-tas*, ind. (= *svêcchayā* above), Kathās.; Hit.; *-°dhîna* (°*châdh°*), mfn. dependent on o° own will or inclination, MW.; *-maya*, mf(*î*)n. endowed with free will, BhP.; Pañcar.; *-mṛityu*, mfn. having death in o° own power, dying at o° own will; m. N. of Bhîshma (who had received from his father the power of fixing the time of his own death), Pañcar.; *-°hāra* (°*châh°*), mfn. eating anything at one's pleasure (°*ra-vihāra*, m. 'feeding and roaming accord. to one's inclination'), Hit. **Svêshṭa**, mfn. dear to one's self; *-devatā*, f. (Kathās.; Vet.) or *-daivata*, n. (Kathās.) a favourite deity. **Svâitu** (*svá-etu*), mfn. (perhaps) going o° own gait or way, RV. **Svâishá**,

m. o° own or free choice, ŚBr. **Svôkta**, mfn. spoken by o° self (°*tam âkshipati*, 'he corrects his own previous remark'), Śak., Sch. **Svôcita**, mfn. suitable to o° self, Kathās.; Rājat.; Daś., Sch. **Svôttha**, mfn. arising or originating in o° self, innate, ChUp., Sch. **Svôtthita**, mfn. originating in or caused by o° self, Kathās. **Svôdaya**, m. the rising of a sign or of any heavenly body at any partic. place (determined by adding to or deducting from the *laṅkôdaya* or time of rising at Ceylon), MW. **Svôdara-pūraka**, mfn. filling only one's belly, thinking only of eating, L. **Svôdara-pūraṇa**, n. the filling of o° own belly, eating one's fill, Pañcad. **Svôpajña**, mfn. self-invented, s°-composed, Hemac.; *-dhātu-pāṭha-vivaraṇa*, m. N. of wk. **Svôpadhi**, m. self-support, MW.; (prob.) a fixed star, ib. **Svôpârjita**, mfn. self-acquired, Dāyat. **Svôras**, n. o° own breast, Nal. **Svâujas**, mfn. having natural or peculiar energy, MW.; m. N. of a minister, Nyāyam.

2. **Sva**, Nom. P. *svati* (pf. *svām-āsa*) = *sva ivâcarati*, he acts like himself or his kindred, Vop. xxi, 7.

Svaka, mf(*akā* or *ikā*)n. = 1. *sva*, one's own, my own &c., Mn.; MBh. &c.; m. one of one's own people, a relation, kinsman, friend; pl. one's own people, friends, Mṛicch.; BhP.; n. one's own goods, property, wealth, riches, MBh.; Kāv. &c.

Svaka-svaka, mfn. = *svaka*, Kāraṇḍ.

Svakīya, mfn. = 1. *sva*, one's own, own, proper, belonging to one's self or family or people, MBh.; Kāv. &c.; m. (pl.) one's own people, followers, friends, MBh.; (*ā*), f. one's own wife, MW.

Svadhaya, Nom. P. °*yati*, to propitiate, conciliate, BhP. (Sch.)

Sva-dhā́, f. (for *svadhā́* see p. 1280) self-position, self-power, inherent power (accord. to some, N. of Nature or the material Universe; *sva-dháyā*, 'by self-power'), RV.; own state or condition or nature, habitual state, custom, rule, law, RV.; ease, comfort, pleasure (*ánu svadhā́m*, *svadhā́m ánu* or *svadhā́ ánu*, *svadháyā*, or *svadhā́bhiḥ*, 'according to one's habit or pleasure, spontaneously, willingly, easily, freely, undisturbedly, wantonly, sportively'), RV.; AV.; VS.; TBr.; own place, home (*svadhé*, du. 'the two places or homes,' heaven and earth, Naigh. iii, 30), ib.; 'own portion or share,' the sacrificial offering due to each god, (esp.) the food or libation, or refreshing drink (cf. 2. *su-dhā*) offered to the Pitṛis or spirits of deceased ancestors (consisting of clarified butter &c. and often only a remainder of the Havis; also applied to other oblations or libations, and personified as a daughter of Daksha and wife of the Pitṛis or of Aṅgiras or of a Rudra or of Agni), RV. &c. &c.; (*-dhā*), ind. (with dat. or gen.) the exclamation or benediction used on presenting (or as a substitute for) the above oblation or libation to the gods or departed ancestors (accord. to Mn. iii, 252 the highest form of benediction at a Śrāddha; with √*kṛi*, 'to pronounce the exclamation or benediction *sva-dhā*;' *svadhâstu*, 'let there be a blessing on it' [cf. RTL. 104, n. 1]), RV. &c. &c. **-kara**, mfn. offering libations and oblations to deceased ancestors or deified progenitors, Mn. ix, 127; = next, MW. **-kārá**, m. pronouncing the benediction *svadhā* or the exclamation itself, AV.; TS.; ĀpŚr.; Mn.; MārkP. **-°dhipa** (°*dhâdh*°), m. 'lord of the Sv°, N. of Agni, Hariv. **-ninayana**, n. performance of a Śrāddha rite with Sv°, Mn. ii, 172; °*yanīya*, mfn. relating to it, Gobh. **-pati**, m. lord of the Sv° (Indra), RV. **-prâṇa** (°*dhā́*-), mfn. breathing Sv°, AV. **-priya**, m. 'fond of Sv°,' Agni or fire, W.; black sesamum (= *tila* or ses° offered to the Pitṛis), L. **-bhājin**, m. pl. 'Sv°-eating,' the Pitṛis, R. **-bhuj**, m. 'id.,' a god, L.; pl. = prec., Ragh.; MārkP. **-maya**, mf(*ī*)n. 'full of Sv°,' the female breast, MārkP. **-°mṛita-maya** (°*dhâmṛ*°), mfn. consisting of Sv° and nectar (said of a Śrāddha), MBh. **-vat** (°*dhā́*-), mfn. adhering to custom or law, regular, constant, faithful, RV.; containing oblations or refreshment, AV.; containing the word *svadhā*, ŚāṅkhŚr.; m. pl. a class of Pitṛis, MBh. (B. *sudhāvat*). **-°śana**, m. pl. 'Svadhā eaters,' the Pitṛis, L.

Svadhāmahe (formed like *yajāmahe*) a sacrificial exclamation or benediction, ĀpŚr.

Svadhāyin, mfn. owning the Svadhā (said of the Pitṛis; v.l. *svadhāvin*), VS.; TBr.

Svadhā́van, mf(*arī*)n. lawful, constant, faithful, RV.; containing homes (as heaven and earth), ib.

Svadhāvín, mfn. containing refreshment, TS.; owning the Svadhā (see *svadhāyin*).

Svayam, in comp. for *svayam*. **-yāna**, n. 'advance of one's own accord,' offensive warfare, Mahāvy. **-vara**, mf(*ā*)n. self-choosing (with *kanyā*, 'a girl who chooses her husband herself'), Mn.; MBh. &c.; m. self-choice, the election of a husband by a princess or daughter of a Kshatriya at a public assembly of suitors, MBh.; R. &c.; *-kathā*, f. the declaration of a Svayaṃ-vara, MW.; *-kṛita-kshaṇā*, f. a maiden who has fixed the moment for a Sv°, ib.; *-pati*, m. a husband chosen at a Sv°, Kathās.; *-prabhā*, f. N. of the wife of the Daitya Trailokya-mālin, ib.; *-vadhū*, f. a self-chosen wife, Śak.; *-vāpī*, f. (?), Pañcat.; *-vṛita*, mfn. self-chosen, elected by one's self, ib.; *-sakhī*, f. a self-chosen female friend, ib.; *-suhṛid*, m. a self-chosen friend (°*hṛit-tva*, n.), ib.; *-stha*, mfn. engaged in a Sv°, Ragh.; °*râgata*, mfn. come of one's own free will, Kathās. **-varaṇa**, n. the free choice of a husband (= *-vara*), Bālar. **-varayitrī**, f. a maiden who herself chooses her own husband, Pracaṇḍ. **-vaśa**, mfn. subject to one's self, self-dependent, free, MBh. **-vaha**, mfn. self-moving, Sūryas., Sch.; n. (scil. *yantra*) a self-moving machine or instrument, Gol. **-vāda**, m. one's own statement, Rājat. **-vānta**, mfn. vomited by one's self, HPariś. **-vikrīta**, mfn. sold by one's self, Vet. **-vilīná**, mfn. self-dissolved, MaitrS. **-viśīrṇa**, mfn. self-fallen, dropped spontaneously, Kum. **-vṛita**, mfn. self-chosen, Vikr. **-vedana**, n. spontaneous consciousness, Sarvad. **-vyakta-sthala-stotra**, n. N. of a Stotra. **-śīrṇa**, mfn. = *-viśīrṇa*, Gaut. **-śṛita**, mfn. ripened spontaneously, Kāṭh. **-śreshṭha**, mfn. best or most excellent by nature (said of Śiva), MBh. **-saṃyoga**, m. voluntary (matrimonial) union with (instr.), Gaut. **-saṃviddha**, mfn. complete in itself, AitBr. **-sambhṛita**, mf(*ā*)n. self-composed, ŚBr. **-siddha**, mfn. perfect in itself (the world), HYog. **-sras**, mfn. dropping spontaneously, AV. **-srasta**, mfn. dropped or fallen sp°, Kauś. **-hāra-karī**, **-hārikā**, and **-hārī**, f. 'self-seizing,' N. of a daughter of Nirmārshṭi (and Duḥsaha; she is described as exercising an evil influence on certain substances, e.g. by abstracting the colour from saffron and the thread from cotton), MārkP. **-hotṛi**, m. one who himself sacrifices, ShaḍvBr. **-homa**, m. a sacrifice offered by one's self, a simple (non-formal) sacr°, ŚāṅkhBr.; °*min*, mfn. offering a sacr° of the above kind, ib. **-kartṛika**, mfn. self-performed, ĀpŚr., Sch. **-kṛitá** (or *svayáṃ-k*°), mf(*ā́*)n. made or performed or effected or committed or composed by one's self, natural, spontaneous (with *vigraha*, 'a war undertaken on one's own account'), TBr. &c. &c.; adopted, Yājñ. **-kṛitin**, mfn. acting spontaneously, Suśr. **-kṛishṭa**, mfn. ploughed by one's self, Parāś. **-krānta**, mfn. mounted by one's self (as a throne), Rājat. **-khāta**, mfn. dug by one's self, Gobh. **-guṇa-parityāga**, m. spontaneous abandonment of 'the thread' and of 'virtue,' Bhartṛ. **-guptā**, f. 'self-preserved,' Mucuna Pruritus or Carpopogon Pruriens, Car. **-gurutva**, n. (its) own weight, Subh. **-graha**, m. the taking for one's self (without leave), forcible seizure, Śiś. **-grahaṇa**, n. id., Veṇīs. **-grāha**, m. id., Mālatīm.; mf(*ā*)n. one who takes or seizes forcibly, MBh.; spontaneous, voluntary (see comp.); (*am*), ind. forcibly, violently, Hariv.; *-nishakta-bāhu*, mfn. putting the arms spontaneously round (loc.), embracing ardently, Kum.; *-praṇaya*, mfn. spontaneously or ardently affectionate, Mṛicch. **-grāhya**, mfn. suffering force or constraint, MBh. **-citi**, f. piling up on one's own account, TS. **-já**, mf(*ā́*)n. spontaneously produced (waters), RV. **-jāta**, mfn. self-born, s°-produced, brought into any state spontaneously, KātyŚr. **-jyotis** (*svayáṃ-*), mfn. self-shining, ŚBr.; BhP. **-tyakta**, mfn. voluntarily abandoned, Bhartṛ. **-datta**, mfn. self-given (said of a child who has given himself for adoption; one of the 12 kinds of children recognized in law-books), Gaut.; Mn.; Yājñ. **-dāna**, n. spontaneous gift (of a daughter in marriage), Kathās. **-diná**, mfn. (see 1. *dina*) self-cut, self-torn, TS. **-dṛiś**, mfn. visible or clear by itself, self-evident, BhP. **-nirdishṭá**, mfn. self-marked or indicated, ŚBr.

Svayám, ind. (prob. orig. a nom. of 1. *sva*, formed like *aham*) self, one's self (applicable to all persons, e.g. myself, thyself, himself &c.), of or by one's self, spontaneously, voluntarily, of one's own accord (also used emphatically with other pronouns [e.g. *ahaṃ svayaṃ tat kṛitavān*, 'I myself did that']; sometimes alone [e.g. *svayaṃ tat kṛitavān*, 'he himself did that;' *svayaṃ tat kurvanti*, 'they themselves do that']; connected in sense with a nom. [either the subject or predicate] or with instr. [when the subject] or with a gen., and sometimes with acc. or loc.; often in comp.), RV. &c. &c. **-agurutva**, n. state of lightness existing in one's self, Subh. **-adhigata**, mfn. self-acquired, VarBṛS. **-anushṭhāna**, n. o° own performance or achievement, Hit. **-apôdita**, n. that from which one is by o° self exempted, AitBr. **-abhigūrta** (*svayám-*), mfn. self-welcomed, TS. **-arjita**, mfn. acquired or gained by o° self, Gaut.; Mn.; Yājñ. &c. **-avadīrṇa**, n. a natural fissure on the surface of the earth, Kauś. **-avapanná**, mf(*ā́*)n. self-fallen, dropped down spontaneously, TS. **-āgata**, mfn. come of o° own accord, intruding, Pañcat. **-ātṛiṇṇa**, mf(*ā́*)n. full of natural holes, ĀpŚr.; (*ā*), f. a kind of brick, TS.; °*ṇṇa-vat*, mfn. full of n° holes, ŚBr. **-ānīta**, mfn. self-brought, brought by o° self, HPariś. **-āsana-ḍhaukana**, n. fetching o° self a seat or chair, HYog. **-āhṛita**, mfn. brought by o° self, HPariś. **-āhṛitya-bhojin**, mfn. enjoying things brought by one's self, MBh. **-indriya-mocana**, n. spontaneous emission of semen, Gobh. **-īśvara**, m. one's own lord, an absolute sovereign, NṛisUp. **-īhita-labdha**, mfn. gained by one's own effort, Mn. ix, 208. **-ukti**, m. a deponent or witness who volunteers to give evidence in a lawsuit, Nār.; f. voluntary declaration or information, W.; (in law) voluntary testimony or evidence, ib. **-ujjvala**, mfn. self-radiant, VarBṛS. **-uditá**, mfn. risen spontaneously, ŚBr. **-udgīrṇa**, mfn. unsheathed by itself (said of a sword), VarBṛS. **-udghāṭita**, mfn. opened spontaneously (as a door), ib. **-udyata**, mf(*ā*)n. offered spontaneously, MBh. **-upasthita**, mf(*ā*)n. come voluntarily or of one's own accord, BhP. **-upâgata**, mfn. id.; m. a child who offers himself voluntarily for adoption, MW. **-upêtá**, mfn. approached of one's own accord, ŚBr. **-patita**, mfn. = *-avapanna*, Kull. on Mn. vi, 21. **-pāṭha**, m. an original text, TPrāt., Sch. **-pāpa** (*svayám-*), mfn. (prob.) injuring one's self, TS. **-prakāśa**, mfn. self-manifesting, BhP.; m. N. of various authors (also with *yati*, *yogêndra*, *muni*, *sarasvatī* &c.), Cat.; °*tīrtha*; °*śâtman* (*sarasvatī*), °*śânanda* (*muni*), °*śêndra* (*sarasvatī*), m. N. of authors, ib. **-prakāśamāna**, mfn. self-luminous (*-tva*, n.), Vedântas. **-prajvalita**, mfn. self-kindled, Kauś. **-pradīrṇa**, n. = *-avadīrṇa*, KātyŚr. **-prabha**, mfn. self-shining, MBh.; Hariv.; BhP.; m. (with Jainas) N. of the fourth Arhat of the future Utsarpiṇī, L.; (*ā*), f. N. of an Apsaras, MBh.; of a daughter of Hemasāvarṇi, R.; of a daughter of Maya, Kathās. **-prabhu**, m. self-powerful, R. **-prasīrṇá**, mfn. = *-avapanna* ŚBr. **-prastutá**, mfn. self-praised, ib. **-prôkta**, mfn. s°-announced, HirP. **-bodha**, m. N. of a Vedânta wk. **-bhagna**, mf(*ā*)n. broken spontaneously, KātyŚr.; R. **-bhu**, m. 'self-existent,' N. of Brahman, MBh.; R.; of Śiva, Pañcar.; (*-bhú*), n. of *-bhū* (q.v.); *-caitanya*, n. N. of a temple of Ādi-buddha, IndAnt. **-bhuva**, mfn. = *-bhū*, MBh.; R.; m. N. of the first Manu (w.r. for *svāyam-bh*°), W.; (*ā*), f. a kind of shrub, L. **-bhū́**, mfn. self-existing, independent; RV.; TS.; KaṭhUp.; Suśr.; m. N. of Brahman, Mn.; MBh. &c.; of Śiva, Kathās.; of Vishṇu, ib.; of Buddha, Buddh.; of Ādi-buddha, ib.; of a Pratyeka-buddha, L.; of Kāla or time, L.; of Kāmadeva, L.; of Vyāsa, Cat.; (with Jainas) of the third black Vāsudeva, L.; of various plants, L.; the air (= *antariksha*), L.; mfn. relating or belonging to Buddha, Kathās.; *-kshetra-māhātmya*, n., *-purāṇa*, n., *-mātṛikā-tantra*, n. N. of wks.; *-liṅga*, n. N. of a Liṅga (= *jyotir-l*?), Cat.; *-liṅga-sambhūtā*, f. a partic. plant (= *liṅginī*), L. **-bhūta**, m. 'self-created,' N. of Śiva, MW. **-bhṛita**, mfn. self-maintained or nourished, BhP. **-bhoja**, m. N. of a son of Pratikshatra, Hariv.; of a son of Śini, BhP. **-bhrami** or °**min**, mfn. self-revolving, ib. **-mathitá**, mfn. self-churned, TS. **-mūrtá**, mfn. self-curdled, self-coagulated, ib. **-mṛita**, mfn. one who has died a natural death (lit. of his own accord), Pañcat.; Hit. **-mlāna**, mfn. faded or withered of itself (i.e. naturally), Kauś.

Svayú, mfn. left to itself (as cattle), RV.; ruling of one's own free will or own right (as Indra), ib.

Svāpaya, Nom. P. °*yati* (cf. Caus. of √*svap*), Vop.

Svāmin. See p. 1284, col. 1.

Svāya (cf. 2. *sva*), Nom. Ā. °*yate* = *sva ivâcarati*, he acts like himself or his own kindred, Vop.

Svikā. See *svaka*, col. 1.

Svin. See *śata-svin* and *śrotra-svin*.

Svī, in comp. for 1. *sva*. **—karaṇa**, n. making one's own, appropriating, accepting, acquiring, Nir.; Yājñ.; Rājat.; taking to wife, marrying, Kālid.; assenting, agreeing, promising, Sarvad.; *-karman*, mfn. whose function is to appropriate, Kull. **—karaṇīya**, mfn. to be appropriated or accepted or assumed or assented to or promised, W. **—kartavya**, mfn. to be accepted, VarBṛS.; to be assented or agreed to, Sarvad. **—kartṛi**, mfn. one who wishes to make one's own or win any one, Rājat. **—kāra**, m. making one's own, appropriation, claiming, claim, BhP.; Siddh.; reception, Kathās.; assent, agreement, consent, promise, Sarvad.; *-graha*, m. robbery, forcible seizure, Mcar.; *-pattra*, n. a written document or will disposing of one's property, RTL. 531; *-rahita*, mfn. devoid of assent, not agreed to, W.; °*rânta*, mfn. ended or concluded by assent, agreed to, ib. **—kārya**, mfn. to be appropriated or taken possession of, Rājat.; to be received, Kathās.; to be got in one's power or won over, ib.; to be agreed or assented to, Pat. **—√kṛi** (*svī-*), P. Ā. *-karoti*, *-kurute* (the latter older and more correct), to make one's own, win, appropriate, claim, ŚBr. &c. &c.; to take to one's self, choose (with or without *bhāryârthe*, 'to take for a wife; marry;' *snushā-tvena*, 'for a daughter-in-law'), R.; Kathās.; Rājat.; to win power over (hearts &c.), Daś.; BhP.; (Ā.) to admit, assent or agree to, ratify, Hit.; Sarvad.: Caus. *-kārayati*, to cause any one to appropriate, present any one with (two acc.), Rājat. **—kṛita**, mfn. appropriated, accepted, admitted, claimed, agreed, assented to, promised, Kāv.; Pur. &c. **—kṛiti**, f. taking possession of, appropriation, HPariś.

Svīya, mf(*ā*)n. relating or belonging to one's self, own, proper, peculiar, characteristic, Kāv.; Pur. &c.; m. (pl.) one's own people or kindred, ib.; (*ā*), f. 'one's own wife,' a wife solely attached to her husband, Sāh. **Svīyâkshara**, m. one's own handwriting or signature, autograph, L.

Svaira, mf(*ā*)n. (prob. fr. *sva* + *īra*, 'going, moving') going where one likes, doing what one likes, self-willed, wilful, independent, unrestrained, L.; walking slowly or cautiously, Kāv.; voluntary, optional, MW.; (*am*), n. wilfulness, ib.; (*am*), ind. according to one's own inclination or will or pleasure, of one's own accord, freely, unconstrainedly, easily, spontaneously, at random, Vas.; MBh.; Kāv. &c., slowly, softly, gently, cautiously, Kāv.; Kathās. &c.; unreservedly, confidingly, ib.; (*eṇa*), ind. at will, at random, R.; BhP.; (*eshu*), ind. in optional or indifferent matters, MBh.; R. **—kathā**, f. unreserved or unconstrained conversation, Bhartṛ. **—gati**, mfn. going about freely, Śak. **—cārin**, mfn. acting at will, free, independent, MBh.; Hariv.; R. **—tā**, f. wilfulness, independence, Vet. **—vartin**, mfn. acting as one likes, following one's own inclinations, BhP. **—vihārin**, mfn. roaming about at pleasure, Yājñ.; unimpeded, meeting with no resistance, Rājat. **—vṛitta**, mf(*ā*)n. = *-vartin*, MBh.; R. **—vṛitti**, mfn. acting wilfully or without restraint, MBh.; BhP.; f. wilfulness, unbridledness, L. **—stha**, mfn. remaining indifferent or unconcerned, Kathās. **Svairâcāra**, mfn. of unrestrained conduct or behaviour, MBh. **Svairâlāpa**, m. = *svaira-kathā*, Bhartṛ. **Svairâhāra**, m. as much food as one likes, abundant food, Rājat.

Svairakam, ind. freely, unreservedly, unrestrainedly, straight out, plainly, Mṛicch.

Svairatha, m. (perhaps for *svaira-ratha*, 'whose chariot moves freely') N. of a son of Jyotishmat, VP.; n. N. of the Varsha ruled by Svairatha, ib.

Svairi, in comp. for *svairin*. **—karman**, n. (prob. w. r. for *svaira-k°*) an action accomplished for one's own profit, Āpast. **—tā**, f. wilfulness, independence, L.

Svairin, mfn. going where one likes, free, independent, unrestrained (esp. said of unchaste women), ChUp.; MBh. &c.; (*iṇī*), f. a bat, L.

स्वःकाम्य *svaḥ-kāmya*, *svaḥ-pati* &c. See p. 1281, col. 2.

स्वकम्पन *sva-kampana*, *sva-kambalā* &c. See p. 1275, col. 1.

स्वक्क् *svakk*. See √*shvakk*.

स्वक्त *sv-akta*, mfn. well smeared or anointed, Car.

स्वक्ष 1. *sv-aksha*, mfn. having a beautiful axle, R.; m. a chariot having a beautiful axle, MBh.

स्वक्ष 2. *sv-aksha*, mfn. having perfect organs of sense, Śiś.

स्वक्ष 3. *sv-aksha*, mf(*ī*)n. handsome-eyed, MBh.; R.; m. pl. N. of a people, MBh.

स्वगत *sva-gata*, *sva-guṇa* &c. See p. 1275, col. 2.

स्वगा *svagā*, ind. a sacrificial exclamation (expressing desire for prosperity), VS.; ŚBr.; TBr. **—kartṛi**, mfn. uttering the excl° Svagā, TS. **—kārá**, m. the excl° Svagā, VS.; TBr. **—√kṛi**, P. *-karoti*, to utter the excl° Svagā, TS.; ŚBr. **—kṛita** (*svagā́-*), mfn. one over whom the excl° Svagā has been pronounced, ŚBr.; finished, done, TS. **—kṛiti** (*svagā́-*), m. the use of the excl° Svagā, MaitrS.; TBr.

स्वग्नि *sv-agní*, mfn. one who has a good Agni or fire, RV.

स्वङ्ग् *svaṅg* (cf. √*śvaṅg*), cl. 1. P. *svaṅgati*, to go, move, Dhātup. v, 44, Vop.

स्वङ्ग *sv-áṅga*, mfn. having a beautiful body, well-shaped, fair-limbed, RV.; n. a good or handsome limb, MW.

स्वङ्गारिन् *sv-aṅgārin*, mfn. having beautiful coals (said of fire), Hcat.

स्वङ्गुरि *sv-aṅgurí*, mfn. handsome-fingered (said of Savitṛi and Sinīvālī), RV.

स्वचर *sva-cara*, *sva-cetas* &c. See p. 1275, col. 2.

स्वच्छ *sv-accha*, mf(*ā*)n. very transparent or clear, pellucid, crystalline, R.; Pañcat. &c.; bright-coloured, Kathās.; clear, distinct (as speech), ib.; pure (as the mind or heart), ib.; healthy, sound, convalescent (in this sense perhaps Prākrit for *svastha*), L.; m. rock-crystal, L.; the jujube tree, L.; (*ā*), f. white Dūrvā grass, L.; (*am*), n. a pearl, L.; an alloy or amalgam of silver and gold, L.; pure chalk &c. (= *vimalôparasa*), L. **—tā**, f., **-tva**, n. perfect clearness or transparency or purity, Kāv.; Śaṃk.; BhP. **—dravya**, n. the crystalline humour, MW. **—dhātuka**, n. an alloy of silver and gold, L. **—pattra**, n. 'transparent leaf,' talc, L. **—bhāva**, m. transparence, Viddh. **—maṇi**, m. 'clear-gem,' crystal, L. **—vāluka**, n. a kind of semi-metal, L.

Svacchaka, mfn. very clear or bright (said of cheeks), Pañcat.

स्वच्छन्द *sva-cchanda* &c. See p. 1275, col. 2.

स्वच्छिका *svacchikā*, f. = *aṅguli-saṃdaṅśa* (see add.), L.

स्वज् *svaj* or *svañj* (cf. *pari-shvaj*), cl. 1. Ā. (Dhātup. xxiii, 7) *svájate* (rarely °*ti*; p. *svajāmana* and *svajāna*, MBh.; pf. *sasvaje*, RV. &c. &c. [3. pl. °*juḥ*, BhP.]; *sasvañje*, Gr.; aor. *ásasvajat*, RV.; *asvaṅkshi*, Gr.; fut. *svaṅktā*, *svaṅkshyate*, ib.; *svajishyate*, MBh.; inf. *-svájé*, RV.; *svaktum*, MBh.; ind. p. *svajitvā*, *-svajya*, ib.), to embrace, clasp, encircle, twist or wind round, MBh.; Kāv. &c.: Pass. *svajyate* (aor. *asvañji*), Gr.: Caus. *svañjayati* (aor. *asishvañjat*), ib.: Desid. *sisvaṅkshate*, ib.: Intens. *sāsvajyate*, *sāsvaṅkti*, ib.

Svakta, **svaṅga**, **svañjana**. See *pari-shv°*.

स्वज *sva-ja*, *sva-jana* &c. See p. 1275, col. 2.

स्वञ्च् *sv-añc*, mfn. going well, moving swiftly or gracefully, nimble, swift, rapid, RV.

Svañcana, mfn. (used in explaining *sv-añcas* and *sv-arka*), Nir.

Sv-añcas, mfn. = *sv-añc*, RV.

स्वञ्ज *svañja*, (prob.) w. r. for *sañja*, L.

स्वठ् *svaṭh* = √2. *śvaṭh*, Dhātup. xxxii, 28 (Vop.)

स्वतन्त्र *sva-tantra*, *sva-tavas* &c. See p. 1275, col. 3.

स्वद् *svad* or *svād* (prob. fr. 5. *su* + √*ad*), cl. 1. Ā. (Dhātup. ii, 17) *svádate* (Ved. also P. *svádati*; pf. *sasvade*, Śiś.; *sasvāde*, Gr.; fut. *svāditā*, *svādishyate*, ib.; Ved. inf. *-sŭde*; ind. p. *-svădya*, R.), to taste well, be sweet or pleasant to (dat. or gen.), RV. &c. &c.; to taste with pleasure, relish, enjoy, like (acc.), delight in (loc.), RV.; MBh.; (P.) to make palatable, season, RV.; VS.; to make sweet or pleasant or agreeable, VS.; TBr.; to be pleasant or wholesome, VS.; P. Ā. *svādati*, °*te* (cf. Dhātup. ii, 27), to taste, relish, enjoy (generally v. l. *khād*, q. v.), R.; Hariv.; Subh.: Caus. *svadáyati*, °*te* (aor. *asishvadat*), to make savoury or palatable, sweeten, season, prepare, cook, RV.; TS.; Br.; Mn.; to propitiate, conciliate, MaitrS.; *svādayati* (cf. Dhātup. xxxiii, 130), to eat, relish, taste, enjoy, Suśr.; Śiś.: Desid. of Caus. *sisvādayishati*, Gr.: Desid. *sisvādishate*, ib.: Intens. *sāsvādyate*, *sāsvātti*, ib. [Cf. Gk. ἥδομαι; Lat. *suadeo*, and under *svādu*.]

Svadana, n. the act of tasting, licking, eating, enjoying, L.

Svadayitṛi, mfn. one who seasons or makes palatable, TS.

Svadāvan, mfn. (formed analogously to *svadhāvan*; prob.) 'having a good taste' or 'enjoying dainty food,' RV.

Svaditá, mfn. well seasoned or prepared, savoury, VS.; TBr.; n. 'may it be well tasted or eaten!' (an exclamation used at a Śrāddha after presenting the oblation of food to the Pitṛis; cf. *su-śruta*, *sva-dhā*), Mn. iii, 251; 254.

Svāda, m. taste, flavour, savour, Hariv.; Kāv.; Kathās.; the beauty or charm (of a poem), Sāh.

Svā́dana, mfn. seasoning, making (food) savoury, RV.; n. the act of tasting, Śiś.; tasting i. e. enjoying (a poem &c.), Sāh.

Svādanīya, mfn. palatable, savoury, MBh.

Svādava, n. agreeable taste or relish, L.

Svādas. See *prá-svādas*.

Svādita, mfn. tasted, relished, W.; sweetened, MW.; pleased, ib.

Svādin, mfn. tasting, enjoying (ifc.), Nalôd.

Svādiman, m. (g. *pṛithv-ādi*) savouriness, sweetness, KātyŚr., Sch.

Svā́dishṭha, mf(*ā*)n. sweetest, very sweet or pleasant, RV. &c. &c.; sweeter than (abl.), Bhartṛ.

Svā́dīyas, mfn. sweeter, more savoury or pleasant than (abl.), RV. &c. &c.

Svādú, mf(*vī́*)n. sweet, savoury, palatable, dainty, delicate, pleasant to the taste, agreeable, charming (also as compar. 'sweeter than &c.,' with abl.), RV. &c. &c.; m. sweet flavour, sweetness, L.; sugar, molasses, L.; N. of various plants (= *jīvaka*, *gandha-dhūma-ja* &c.), L.; (*us* or *vī*), f. = *drākshā*, a grape, L.; (*u*), n. sweet taste, sweetness, Megh.; pleasantness, charm, beauty, Subh. [Cf. Gk. ἡδύς; Lat. *suavis*; Old Sax. *swôti*; Angl. Sax. *swête*; Eng. *sweet*; Germ. *süss*.] **—kaṇṭa**, m. 'sweet-thorn,' Asteracantha Longifolia, L. **—kaṇṭaka**, m. id., L.; Flacourtia Sapida, ib. **—kanda**, m. 'having a sweet root,' a kind of arum, L.; (*ā*), f. Batatas Paniculata, L. **—kandaka**, m. a kind of vegetable, L. **—kara**, m. 'seasoner, cook,' a kind of mixed caste, MBh. **—kāma**, mfn. liking sweets (*-tā*, f.), R. **—kāra**, mfn. causing relish, dainty, W. **—kshádman**, mfn. having or providing sweet or dainty food, RV. **—khaṇḍa**, m. lump sugar, sugar in small pieces, L. **—gandha**, m. a Moringa with red flowers, L.; (*ā*), f. id. or Convolvulus Paniculatus, L. **—m-kāram**, ind. (Pāṇ. iii, 4, 26) making savoury, sweetening, Śiś.; Naish. **—tama**, mfn. very sweet or pleasant, Sāy. **—tara**, mfn. sweeter or very sweet, Vās. **—tā**, f. savouriness, sweetness, MBh.; Kathās. **—tiktakashāya**, mfn. sweet and astringent and bitter, L.; m. sweet and ast° and b° taste, L. **—tuṇḍikā**, f. Momordica Monadelpha, L. **—dhanvan**, m. 'having a sweet bow,' N. of Kāma-deva (whose bow is said to be made of sugar-cane), L. **—parṇī**, f. 'sweet-leafed,' a kind of plant (= *dugdhikā*). **—pāka**, mfn. sweet or good to be cooked or digested (*-tva*, n.), Suśr.; (*ā*), f. Solanum Indicum, L. **—pākin**, mfn. = *-pāka*, Suśr. **—piṇḍā**, f. a kind of date tree, L. **—pushpa**, m. 'having pleasant flowers,' a kind of plant (= *kaṭabhī*), L.; (*ī*), f. Grislea Tomentosa, L. **—phala**, n. 'sweet fruit,' the fruit of the jujube, L.; (*ā*), f. the jujube tree, L. **—majjan**, m. a sort of mountain Pilu tree, L. **—māṅsī**, f. the root Kākolī (q.v.), L. **—mustā**, f. a species of water-creeper, L. **—mūla**, n. 'sweet root,' Daucus Carota, L. **—mṛidu**, mfn. sweet and delicate (cf. *sauvādumṛidava*). **—yukta**, mfn. possessing sweetness, sweet, Megh. **—yogin**, mfn. id., MBh. **—rasa**, mf(*ā*)n. having a sweet or agreeable taste, Suśr.; (*ā*), f. (only L.) spirituous liquor; Asparagus Racemosus; a grape; the root of

Spondias Mangifera; = *kākolī*. **-rātí**, mfn. bestowing agreeable gifts, RV. **-latā**, f. Batatas Paniculata, L. **-luṅgī**, f. the sweet citron, L. **-vāri**, m. the sea of sweet water, L. **-vivekin**, mfn. distinguishing dainties (from other food), Rājat. **-śuddha**, n. 'sweet and pure,' rock or river salt, W. **-shaṃsád**, mfn. 'sitting round dainties' or 'forming an agreeable company,' RV. **-sammud** (*svādú-*), mfn. delighting in dainty food, AV. **-svādu**, mfn. exceedingly sweet or savoury, HPariś. **Svādûda**, m. = *svādu-vāri*, R. **Svādûdaka**, mfn. having sweet water, BhP.; *-samudra*, m. = *svādu-vāri*, Sāṃkhyas., Sch.

Svādukā, f. Tiaridium Indicum, L.

Svādumán, m. sweetness, MaitrS.

Svādushkiliyā, f. pl. N. of the verses beginning with *svādush kila* (RV. vi, 47, 1 &c.), ŚāṅkhBr.

Svādū-√kṛi, P. *-karoti*, to make sweet, sweeten, MW.

Svādmán, m. sweetness, RV.; (*svā́°*), n. id., dainty food or drink, ib.

Svādya, mfn. to be tasted, MBh.; savoury, palatable, Bālar.; astringent and salt, L.; m. astringent and salt taste, L.

Svādv, in comp. for *svādu*. **-anna**, n. sweet or choice food, dainties, delicacies, W.; mfn. having or providing delicacies, MW. **-amla**, m. 'sweet and sour,' the pomegranate tree, L.; *-tikta-tubara*, mfn. sweet and sour, bitter and astringent, L.; m. sweet and sour and bitter and astringent taste, L.

स्वदान *sva-dāna, sva-dāra* &c. See p. 1275, col. 3.

स्वधय *svadhaya*, °*yati*. See p. 1278, col. 1.

स्वधर्म *sva-dharma* &c. See p. 1275, col. 3.

स्वधा *svadhā́*, f. (for *sva-dhā* see p. 1278, col. 1) an axe, knife, TS.

Svádhiti, m. f. (also written *sv°*) an axe &c. (in Naigh. ii, 20 among the *vajra-nāmāni*; *devī́ svádhitiḥ*, 'heavenly axe,' thunderbolt), RV.; AV.; TS.; GṛŚrS.; a saw, L.; (according to some) a large tree with hard wood, RV. v, 32, 10; ix, 96, 6. **-hetika**, m. 'axe-armed,' a soldier armed with an axe, L.

Svádhitī-vat, mfn. furnished with axes or knives (said of the chariot of the Maruts; accord. to some, 'made of Svadhiti wood,' see above), RV. i, 88, 2.

स्वधिचरण *sv-adhicaraṇá*, mf(*ā́*)n. good to be walked upon, TS.

स्वधित *svádhita*, mfn. = 1. *su-dhita*, firm, solid, TBr.

स्वधिष्ठान *sv-adhishṭhāna*, mfn. having a good standing-place (said of a war-chariot), MBh.

Sv-adhishṭhita, mfn. good to be stood on or lived in (acc.), BhP.; well-guided (as an elephant), Kām.

स्वधीत *sv-adhīta*, mfn. well-recited or repeated or studied (as the Veda), well read, well instructed, MāṇḍS.; n. anything well repeated or learned, R.; BhP.

Sv-adhīti, mfn. good repetition or recitation (as of the Veda or other sacred work), MBh.

स्वध्यक्ष *sv-adhyakshá*, mf(*ā́*)n. good to be inspected, TS.; ŚBr.

स्वध्यवसान *sv-adhyavasāná*, mf(*ā́*)n. good to be striven after, TS.

स्वध्वर *sv-adhvará*, m. n. a good sacrifice, RV.; BhP.; mfn. performing a sacrifice well, well adapted to a sacrifice, RV.

Sv-ādhvaryu, mfn. having a good Adhvaryu priest, TS.

स्वन् 1. *svan*, cl. 1. P. (Dhātup. xix, 79) *svanati* (m.c. also °*te*; pf. *sasvāna*, 3. pl. *sasvanuḥ* [Gr. also *svenuḥ*], MBh. &c.; aor. *asvanīt, svānīt*, RV. [for aor. P. *sváni* see *adhi-* and *anu-shvan*]; fut. *svanitā, svanishyati*, Gr.; inf. *svanitum*, ib.), to sound, make any noise, roar, yell, hum, sing, RV. &c. &c.: Caus. *svanayati* (aor. *asisvanat*), to sound, resound, RV.; BhP.; to adorn (in this sense also *svānayati*), Dhātup. xix, 62; Desid. *sisvanishati*, Gr.: Intens. *saṃsvanyate; saṃsvanti* (cf. *pari-shvan*), ib. [Cf. Lat. *sonit, sonus, sonare*; Angl. Sax. *swin*; Eng. *swan*; Germ. *Schwan*.]

2. **Svan**. See *tuvi-shván*.

Svaná, m. (ifc. f. *ū*) sound, noise (in the older language applied to the roar of wind, thunder, water &c.; in later l° to the song of birds, speech, and sound of any kind, cf. Naigh. i, 11), RV. &c. &c.; a partic. Agni, MBh.; (*sváná*), roaring water, VS.; TBr.; mfn. ill-sounding, L. **-cakra**, m. a form of sexual union, L. **-vat**, mfn. sounding, resounding, loud (*vat*, ind. 'aloud'), MaitrUp.; MBh. &c. **Svanôtsāha**, m. a rhinoceros (= *gaṇḍaka*), L.

Svanád-ratha, mfn. (pr. p. of √*svan* + *r°*) having a rattling chariot, RV.

Svanas. See *tuvi-shvanás*.

Svanābhaka (perhaps connected with *svaná* above, but see under 1. *sva*, p. 1276, col. 1).

Svani, mfn. (in *tuvi-* and *mahi-shváṇi*); m. fire, L.

Svanika. See *pāṇi-svanika*.

Svanita, mfn. sounded, sounding &c.; n. sound, noise, Śiś.; a thunderclap, W. **Svanitâhvaya**, m. a kind of herb (= *taṇḍulīya*), L.

Svāná, m. (cf. √3. *su*, p. 1219) sounding, making a noise, rattling (as a chariot), panting (as a horse), RV.; m. sound, noise, rattle, ib.; twang (of a bowstring), Śiś.; N. of one of the seven guardians of Soma, VS.

Svāni, mfn. (fr. *svana*), g. *sutaṃgamâdi*.

Svānín, mfn. noisy, turbulent, RV.

Svānta. See *svā́nta*, p. 1277, col. 3.

स्वनगर *sva-nagara, sva-nābhya* &c. See p. 1276, col. 1.

स्वनडुह् *sv-anaḍuh*, mfn. having excellent bulls, Vop.

स्वनय *svanáya*, m. N. of a man (son of Bhāvayavya), RV.

स्वनवेक्षणीय *sv-anavêkshaṇīya*, mfn. not at all to be hoped for, past all hope, R.

स्वनीक *sv-anīka*, mfn. having a fair or radiant countenance (as Agni), RV.

स्वनुगुप्त *sv-anugupta*, mfn. well hidden, MBh.

स्वनुजा *sv-anujā*, f. having a beautiful younger sister, ĀpGṛ.; Baudh.

स्वनुरक्त *sv-anurakta*, mfn. truly devoted to (loc.), R.

स्वनुरूप *sv-anurūpa*, mfn. well suited, MW.

स्वनुष्ठित *sv-anushṭhita*, mfn. well observed, duly practised or performed, R.; BhP.

स्वन्त *sv-anta*, mfn. having a good end, terminating well, MBh.; Ragh.; Kathās.; auspicious, fortunate, MBh.

स्वन्न *sv-anna*, n. good food, BhP.

स्वप् *svap*, cl. 2. P. (Dhātup. xxiv, 60) *svapiti* (Ved. and ep. also *svápati*, °*te*; Impv. *svápitu*, AV.; Pot. *svapīta*, MBh.; pf. *sushvā́pa* [3. pl. *sushupuḥ*; p. *sushupvás* and *sushupāṇá*, qq. vv.], RV. &c. &c.; aor. *asvāpsīt*; Prec. *supyāt*, GṛS.; fut. *svaptā*, MBh.; *svapishyati*, AV.; °*te*, R.; *svapsyati*, Br. &c.; °*te*, MBh. &c.; inf. *svaptum*, Br. &c.; ind. p. *suptvā́*, AV. &c., *-svā́pam*, RV.), to sleep, fall asleep (with *varsha-śatam*, 'to sleep for a hundred years, sleep the eternal sleep'), RV. &c. &c.; to lie down, recline upon (loc.), Mn.; MBh. &c.; to be dead, MBh.; R.; Pass. *supyate* (aor. *asvāpi*), MBh.; Kāv. &c.; Caus. *svāpáyati* or (m. c.) *svapayati* (aor. *asūshupat*; in RV. also *sishvapaḥ, sishvap*; Pass. *svāpyate*), to cause to sleep, lull to rest, RV.; AV.; PañcavBr.; to kill, RV.; Bhaṭṭ.: Desid. of Caus. *sushvāpayishati*, Gr.: Desid. *sushupsati*, to wish to sleep, Nir. xiv, 4: Intens. *soshupyate, sāsvapīti, sāsvaptī, soshupīti, soshopti*, Gr. [Cf. Gk. ὕπ-νος; Lat. *somnus* for *sop-nus, sopor, sopire*; Slav. *sŭpati*; Lith. *sápnas*; Angl. Sax. *swefan*, 'to sleep.']

Supta, supti. See p. 1230, cols. 1, 2.

Sushupāṇá and **sushupvás**, mfn. sleeping, asleep, RV.

Sushupsā, sushupsu. See p. 1238, col. 1.

Svapaná, mfn. sleepy, drowsy, VS.; n. the act of sleeping, dreaming, sleep, Kāv.; Suśr.; numbness (of the skin), Suśr.

Svapanīya, mfn. to be slept, MW.

Svapitṛi, mfn. (for *sva-pitṛi* see p. 1276, col. 1) asleep, a sleeper, Kām.

Svaptavya, mfn. = *svapanīya*, PañcavBr.; MBh.

Svaptṛi, mfn. = *svapitṛi*, MW.

Svápna, m. (once in R., n., ifc. f. *ā*; for *sv-apna* see p. 1281, col. 1) sleep, sleeping, RV. &c. &c.; sleepiness, drowsiness, Caurap.; sleeping too much, sloth, indolence, Mn. ix, 13; xii, 33; dreaming, a dream (acc. with √*dṛiś*, 'to see a vision, dream,' RV. &c. &c. **-kalpa**, mfn. dream-like, R. **-kāma**, mfn. wishing for sleep, MW. **-kṛit**, mfn. causing sleep, somniferous, soporific, L.; m. Marsilea Quadrifolia, L. **-gata**, mfn. fallen asleep, sleeping, dreaming, R. **-giri**, m. N. of a place, Vcar. **-gṛiha**, n. a sleeping apartment, bed-chamber, L. **-cintāmaṇi**, m. N. of a wk. on oneiromancy. **-ja**, mfn. produced in sleep, dreamt, Megh. **-jñāna**, n. perception in a dream, Kap., Sch. **-tandritā**, f. languor produced by drowsiness, MBh. **-darśana**, n. dream-vision, vision in a dream, Hariv. **-dṛiś**, mfn. (nom. *k*) having a vision, dreaming, BhP. **-dosha**, m. 'sleep fault,' pollutio nocturna, L. **-dhī-gamya**, mfn. perceptible by the mind (only when) in a state of sleep, Megh. **-naṅśana**, mfn. destroying sleep (others 'acquiring riches,' cf. *sv-apna*), RV. x, 86, 21. **-niketana**, n. = *-gṛiha*, L. **-nidarśana**, n. = *-darśana*, ChUp.; °*nīya*, mfn. treating of visions and dreams, Suśr. **-parîkshā**, f. N. of wk. **-paryantam**, ind. till the end of sleeping-time, Āpast. **-prakaraṇa**, n. N. of wk. **-prapañca**, m. the illusions of sleep, the world spread out like a dream, MW. **-phalâdhyāya**, m., **-phalâphala**, n. N. of wks. **-bhāj**, mfn. enjoying sleep, Subh. **-mantra-paṭala**, m. n. N. of wk. **-māṇava** or °*vaka*, m. 'dream-charm,' a kind of charm effecting the realisation of dreams Kathās. **-mukhā** (*svápna-*), f. (prob.) phantom or illusion of a dr°, AV.; KātyŚr. **-labdha**, mfn. obtained or appeared in a dr°, Megh. **-vat**, ind. (risen) as (from) a dr°, BhP. **-vārāhī-kalpa**, m., **-vāsavadattā-nāṭaka**, n. N. of wks. **-vikāra**, m. change (produced) by sleep, Buddh. **-vicārin**, mfn. interpreting dr°s, L. **-vidhi**, m. N. of wk. **-vinaśvara**, mf(*ī*)n. evanescent as a dream, Siṃhâs. **-viparyaya**, m. transposed order of sleeping-time, Bhpr. **-vṛitta**, mfn. occurring in a dr°, Ragh. **-śīla**, mfn. disposed to sleep, sleepy, drowsy, W. **-saṃdarśana**, n. = *-darśana*, Megh. **-sṛishṭi**, f. the creation of dr°s, MW. **-sthāna**, n. the site or locality of a dream, ŚBr.; a bed-chamber, Kathās.; mfn. sleeping, dreaming, NṛisUp. **Svapnâdeśa**, m. an order given by a dream, Kathās. **Svapnâdhyāya**, m. 'dr°-chapter,' N. of the 68th Pariśishṭa of the Atharva-veda and other wks.; *-vid*, m. an interpreter of dreams, Śaṃk. **Svapnânayana-mantra**, m. N. of wks. **Svapnântá**, m. a state of sleep or dreaming, ŚBr.; R. **Svapnântara**, n. id.; *-gata*, mfn. occurred during sleep, dreamt, L. **Svapnântika**, n. consciousness in dr°, Kaṇ. **Svapnâbhikāraṇa**, n. a soporific remedy, AV. **Svapnâvasthā**, f. a state of dreaming (applied to life as an illusion), W. **Svapnêśvara**, m. N. of two authors, Cat. **Svapnôpabhoga**, m. enjoyment in a dream, Bcar. **Svapnôpama**, mfn. resembling sleep or a dream, MW.

Svapnaj, mfn. (nom. *k*) sleepy, asleep (cf. *á-sv°*), MBh.; Bhaṭṭ.

Svapnayā́, ind. in dream, AV.

Svapnāya, Nom. Ā. °*yate*, to wish to sleep, be sleepy, MBh.; to resemble a dream, BhP.

Svapnālu, mfn. sleepy, drowsy, Suśr.

Svapne-duḥshvapnyá, n. (loc. of *svapna* + *d°*) a bad dream during sleep, AV.

Svápnya, n. a vision in a dream, AV.

Svapnyáyā, ind. = *svapnayā́*, ŚBr.

Svāpa, m. sleeping, sleep, Suśr.; Kathās.; BhP.; dreaming, a dream, Prab.; BhP.; sleepiness, sloth, W.; the sleep of a limb, numbness, Suśr.; loss of sensation, ignorance, L. **-vyasana**, n. somnolency, lethargy, Mcar.

Svāpaka, mfn. (fr. Caus.) causing to sleep, soporiferous, soporific, Pāṇ. vii, 4, 67, Vārtt. 2, Pat.

Svāpakīya, Nom. P. °*yati* = *svāpakam icchati*, ib.

Svāpana, mfn. (fr. Caus.) causing to sleep, making sleepy (said of a mystic weapon), Śiś.; n. a soporific (remedy), Kauś.

Svāpin, mfn. causing sleep, lulling to sleep, MW.

Svāpna, mfn. (fr. *svapna*) relating to sleep, Sāṃkhyapr., Sch.

स्वप् *sv-ap*, mfn. having good water, Vop.

स्वपक्ष *sva-paksha, sva-pañcaka* &c. See p. 1276, col. 1.

स्वपत्य *sv-apatyá*, n. good offspring (also applied to good work or deeds; dat. °*tyaí*), RV.; mfn. having good offspring, ib.

स्वपराद्ध *sv-aparāddha*, mfn. very faulty, MW.

स्वपस् *sv-ápas*, mfn. doing good work, skilful, artistic (said of Tvashṭṛi, the Ṛibhus &c.), RV.; VS.; artificially fashioned (superl. *-tama*, said of Indra's thunderbolt), RV. i, 61, 6; m. a good artificer, RV.; N. of a man, IndSt.

1. **Svapasyà**, mfn. active, industrious (said of Indra), RV.; ŚBr.

2. **Svapasya**, Nom. Ā. °*yáte*, to work well, be active or industrious, RV.; TS.

Svapasyā́, f. (only in instr. which is of the same form) activity, diligence, skill, RV.

Svapā́ka, mfn. (*su-ap*° in Padap.) skilful, industrious, RV. iv, 3, 2 (Sāy.; others, 'coming willingly from afar,' fr. 5. *su* + *apā́ka*).

स्वपिवात *sv-apivāta*, mfn. (see *api-√vat*) understanding or meaning well (said of Rudra), RV. vii, 46, 3 (accord. to Nir. 'whose speech is trustworthy or authoritative;' accord. to others, 'much desired,' fr. *api-√van*).

स्वपू *sva-pū́*, f. (prob.) a broom, RV.

स्वप्न *sv-ápna*, mfn. (for *svapna* see p. 1280) = next (accord. to some), RV. i, 120, 12; viii, 2, 18.

Sv-ápnas, mfn. wealthy, rich, RV.

स्वब्दिन् *svabdin*, mfn. (prob.) roaring, panting, RV. viii, 33, 2 (= *svabhūta-śabda, śabdam kurvat*, Sāy.)

स्वभक्ष *sva-bhaksha, sva-bhadrā* &c. See p. 1276, col. 1.

स्वभिगूर्त *sv-àbhigūrta*, mfn. well applauded, greeted with acclamations or cheers, TBr.

स्वभिराम *sv-abhirāma*, mfn. very pleasant or delightful, R.

स्वभिष्टि *sv-abhishṭí*, mfn. helpful, favourable, RV.; favoured, well-aided, ib. **-sumna** (°*shṭí-*), mfn. affording favourable assistance, ib.

स्वभीशु *sv-abhīśú*, mfn. well bridled or caparisoned, RV.

स्वभ्यक्त *sv-àbhyakta*, mfn. well anointed, AV.

स्वभ्यग्र *sv-abhyagra*, mfn. very imminent or impending or near at hand, MBh.; very swift, ĀśvŚr. (Sch.)

स्वभ्यस्त *sv-abhyasta*, mfn. much practised, Jātakam.

स्वमनीषा *sva-manīshā* &c. See p. 1276.

स्वमेक *svameka* (?), m. n. (cf. *su-mekha*) a year, L.

स्वयंवर *svayam-vara* &c. See p. 1278.

स्वयशस् *sva-yaśas, sva-yāvan* &c. See p. 1276, col. 2.

स्वर् 1. *svar* (= √*sur*), cl. 10. P. *svarayati*, to find fault, blame, censure, Dhātup. xxxv, 11.

स्वर् 2. *svar* (prob. = a lost √*sur*; cf. √*svṛi*), cl. 1. P. *svarati*, Caus. *svarayati*, to shine.

Svaḥ, in comp. for 3. *svàr* below. **-kāmya**, Nom. P. °*yati*, to wish for heaven, Siddh. **-pati**, m. the lord of h°, MW. **-patha**, m. 'way to h°,' death, BhP. **-pāla**, m. a guardian of h°, ib. **-pṛishṭha**, n. N. of various Sāmans, ĀrshBr. **-śiras**, mfn. having h° for a head, Hariv. **-sad**, m. 'dwelling in heaven,' a god, Naish. **-sarit**, f. river of h°, the Ganges, Bh. **-sāman**, n. N. of a Sāman, IndSt. **-sindhu**, f. = *-sarit*, Bhartṛ. **-sundarī** (Bālar.), **-strī** (R.), f. 'celestial woman,' an Apsaras. **-syandana**, m. celestial chariot, Indra's chariot, BhP. **-sravantī**, f. = *-sarit*, Cat.

3. **Svàr** (in Yajur-veda also *súvar*), ind. (used in Veda as nom., acc., loc., or gen., in Naish. vi, 99 also as abl.; from the weak base *sū́r* the RV. forms the gen. *sū́ras* and the dat. *sūré* [iv, 3, 8]), the sun, sunshine, light, lustre, RV.; AV.; VS.; bright space or sky, heaven (as distinguished from *div*, which is regarded as the vault above it; often 'heaven' as a paradise and as the abode of the gods and the Blest, in AV. also of the Asuras; *svaḥ prayātaḥ*, 'gone to heaven,' i. e. 'departed this life'), RV. &c. &c.; the space above the sun or between the sun and the polar star, the region of the planets and constellations (regarded as the 3rd of the 7 worlds [see *loka*] and the 3rd of the three Vyāhṛitis [i. e. *bhū́r bhúvaḥ sváḥ*]; *svar* is pronounced after *Om* and before the Gāyatrī by every Brāhman on beginning his daily prayers), Mn.; MBh. &c.; water, Naigh. i, 12; N. of Śiva, MBh. [Cf. Gk. ἠέλιος, ἥλιος; Lat. *sol;* Lith. *sáulė;* Goth. *sauil;* Angl. Sax. *sôl*.] **-atikrama**, m. stepping beyond heaven, i. e. reaching Vaikuṇṭha, BhP. **-adhîta**, mfn. 'reaching h°,' the mountain Meru, Vāgbh.; *-sāra*, m. N. of Indra, ib. **-āpagā**, f. 'river of h°,' = *-gaṅgā*, L. **-ārūḍha**, mfn. ascended to h°, Bhaṭṭ. **-ālu**, m. a kind of root (= *vacā*), L. **-iṅgaṇa**, m. shaking h°, a strong wind, L. **-ga**, see below. **-gaṅgā**, f. the heavenly Ganges, the Milky Way, L. **-gata**, mfn. being in h°, BhP.; gone to h°, dead, MBh.; R. &c. **-gati**, f., **-gamana**, n. 'going to h°,' death, future felicity, ib. **-giri**, m. 'mountain of h°,' Su-meru, L. **-cakshas** (*svàr-*), mfn. brilliant as light, RV. **-canas** (*svàr-*), mfn. 'lovely as light' or 'pleasing to h°,' ib. **-jit**, mfn. winning or procuring light or heaven, RV.; m. a kind of sacrifice, Mn. xi, 74; N. of a man (with patr. Nāgnajita), ŚBr. **-jeshá**, m. the winning of light &c., RV. **-jyotis** (*svàr-*), mfn. shining with h°'s light, VS.; n. N. of two Sāmans, ĀrshBr.; (°*tir*)*-nidhana* (*svàr-*), mfn. having *svar-jyotis* as final part, ŚBr.; n. N. of a Sāman, ĀrshBr. **-ṇadī**, f. = *-āpagā*, Śāntiś.; Pañcar.; a kind of shrub (prob. w. r. for *svarṇa-dā*), L. **-ṇara** (*svàr-*), m. lord of h° (applied to Agni, the sun, Soma &c.), RV.; a partic. sun, TĀr.; n. bright space, ether, RV. **-ṇidhana**, n. *svar* as a conclusion, TāṇḍBr.; Lāṭy. **-ṇīta**, mfn. led to h°, Pañcar. **-ṇṛi** (*svàr-*), m. lord of h° (applied to Agni and the Maruts), RV. **-ṇetṛi**, mfn. guide to heaven (as a N. of a king), MBh. **-da**, mfn. bestowing heaven, Hariv. **-dantin**, m. a celestial elephant, Dharmaś. **-dā**, mfn. bestowing h°, ĀpŚr. **-dṛiś**, mfn. (nom. *k*) seeing light or the sun (applied to gods and men), RV. **-deva**, m. N. of a man, Cat. **-dhāman** (*svár-*), mfn. abiding in light, TS. **-dhunī**, f. = *-āpagā*, BhP. **-dhenu**, f. = *kāma-dhenu*, Kāv. **-nagarī**, f. 'town of h°,' N. of Amarāvatī, Kathās.; *-kṛita*, mfn. turned into Am°, ib. **-nadī**, f. = *-ṇadī*, L. **-nayana**, mfn. leading to h°, R. **-pati** (*svàr-*), mfn. lord of light, RV.; N. of Indra, BhP. **-bhāṇu**, m. = *-bhānu*, i. e. Rāhu, HPariś. **-bhānava**, m. a kind of gem, L.; (*ī*), f. a daughter of Svar-bhānu, MBh. **-bhānavīya**, mfn. relating or belonging to Svar-bhānu, Subh. **-bhānu** (*svàr-*), m. N. of a demon supposed to eclipse the sun and the moon (in later language applied to Rāhu or the personified ascending node), RV. &c. &c.; of a Kaśyapa, VP.; of a son of Kṛishṇa, BhP.; *-sūdana*, m. 'destroyer of Rāhu,' N. of the Sun, MBh. **-maṇi**, m. 'sky-jewel,' the sun, Bālar. **-madhya**, n. the central point of the sky, zenith, MW. **-mīḷha**, mfn. having light or the sun as its reward or prize, RV.; n. a contest for light, ib. **-yaśas**, n. the glory of heaven, BhP. **-yāta**, mfn. gone to h°, dead, Yājñ.; MBh. &c. **-yātṛi**, mfn. going to h°, dying, MBh. **-yāna**, n. the act of going to h°, dying, death, Cat. **-yoshit**, f. a celestial woman, an Apsaras, Bālar. **-līna**, N. of a place, Cat. **-loka**, m. the world of h°, i. e. a partic. h°, the region called Svar (cf. *bhuvar-, bhūr-l*°), R.; Pur.; N. of mount Meru (also *-śikhara*), Daś.; m. an occupant of h°, a god, one of the Blest (*-tā*, f.), BhP. **-vat** (*svàr-* or *súvar-*), mfn. bright, shining, celestial, RV.; TS.; containing the word *svar* (°*van-nidhana*, mfn. applied to a Sāman; cf. *svar-ṇidhana*), PañcavBr.; Lāṭy. **-vadhū**, f. = *-yoshit*, HPariś. **-vāpī**, f. 'stream of h°,' the Ganges, L. **-vāhinī**, f. = *-āpagā*, Bālar. **-vid**, mfn. winning or possessing or bestowing light or h°, celestial, RV.; VS. **-vīthi**, f. N. of the wife of Vatsara, BhP. **-veśyā**, f. 'courtezan of h°,' an Apsaras, Rājat. **-vaidya**, m. 'physician of h°,' N. of either of the two Aśvins (*-pratima*, 'A°-like'), Git. **-shā́**, mfn. = *-vid*, RV. **-shāti** (*svàr-*), f. the acquiring light or heaven, ib.

Svargá (or *suvargá*), mfn. going or leading to or being in light or heaven, heavenly, celestial (with *loká*, m. or pl. = 'the world of light, heavens'), AV. &c. &c.; m. heaven, the abode of light and of the gods, heavenly bliss, (esp.) Indra's heaven or paradise (to which the souls of virtuous mortals are transferred until the time comes for their re-entering earthly bodies; this temporary heaven is the only h° of orthodox Brāhmanism; it is supposed to be situated on mount Meru, q.v.; acc. with √*gā, ā-√sthā*, or *ā-√pad*, 'to go to heaven,' 'die'), RV. (only x, 95, 18), AV. &c. &c.; a partic. Ekāha, ŚāṅkhŚr.; N. of a son of the Rudra Bhīma, VP. **-kāma**, mfn. desirous of heaven, Br.; Up. **-khaṇḍa**, n. N. of the 3rd book of the Padma-purāṇa. **-gata**, mfn. gone to h°, W. **-gati**, f., **-gamana**, n. going to h°, death, MBh.; R. &c. **-gāmin**, mfn. going to h°, Hit. **-giri**, m. 'mountain of h°,' Meru, MW. **-cyuta**, mfn. fallen or descended from h°, Cāṇ. **-jit**, mfn. winning h° (superl. *-tama*), MBh. **-jīvin**, mfn. dwelling in h°, Āpast. **-taraṃgiṇī**, f. 'river of h°,' the Ganges, Kathās. **-taru**, m. a tree of h°, Sarasv. **-tarsha**, m. eager desire for heaven, Bcar. **-da**, mfn. h°-giving, procuring paradise, Pañcat. **-dvāra**, n. heaven's gate, Āpast.; N. of a Tīrtha, MBh.; of Śiva, ib.; °*rêshṭi*, f. N. of wk. **-naraka**, n. pl. the h°s and hells, JaimUp. **-pati**, m. 'lord of h°,' Indra, Hit. **-patha**, m. 'road of h°,' (prob.) the Milky Way, R. **-pada**, n. N. of a Tīrtha, Vishṇ. **-para**, mfn. desirous of heaven, W. **-parvan**, n. N. of the 18th book of MBh. (in which is described the journey of the five Pāṇḍava princes towards Indra's h° in mount Meru). **-purī**, f. 'city of h°,' Amarāvatī, R. **-prada**, mfn. = *-da*, Kāv. **-pradhāna**, mfn. having heaven as the best, Bcar. **-bhartṛi**, m. = *-pati*, Śiś. **-mandākinī**, f. the celestial Ganges, Pañcar. **-mārga**, m. the road to h°, MBh.; road of h°, Milky Way, R.; Śak.; N. of a Tīrtha, MBh.; *-didṛikshu*, mfn. wishing to see the road to h°, MW. **-yāṇa**, mf(*ī*)n. going or leading to heaven, AitĀr.; n. the road to heaven, AitBr. **-yoni**, f. cause or source of h°, MBh. **-rājya**, n. kingdom of h°, Pañcat. **-rodaḥ-kuhara**, m. the void or hollow space between h° and earth, Bālar. i, 49. **-loka**, m. (also in pl.) the celestial world, Indra's h°, ĀśvGṛ.; MBh. &c.; (*svargá-*), mfn. belonging to or dwelling in h°, ŚBr.; KaṭhUp.; °*kêśa*, m. 'lord of h°,' Indra, MW.; the body (as enjoying felicity in Indra's h°), L. **-vat**, mfn. possessing or enjoying heaven, R. **-vadhū**, f. 'celestial nymph,' an Apsaras, L. **-vāsa**, m. residence in heaven, Suśr. **-śrī**, f. the glory of h°, MW. **-saṃkrama**, m. a bridge or ladder to h°, Pañcat. **-sattra-prayoga**, m. N. of wk. **-sad**, m. 'heaven-dweller,' a god or one of the Blest, MBh. **-sampādana**, mfn. procuring or gaining heaven, MBh. **-sarid-varā**, f. 'best of heavenly rivers,' the Ganges, L. **-sādhana**, mfn. means of attaining h°, MW. **-sukha**, n. the bliss of heaven, MBh. **-strī**, f. = *-vadhū*, Rājat. **-stha**, mfn. 'dwelling in h°,' dead, R. **-sthita**, mfn. id., Sarvad.; = *-sad*, Subh. **-hetau**, ind. for the sake of heaven, Bcar. **-hvāya**, mfn., Pāṇ. iii, 2, 2, Sch. **Svargâpagā**, f. 'heavenly river,' the Ganges, L. **Svargâpavarga**, m. du. h° and emancipation, Bcar. **Svargâbhikāma**, mfn. desirous of h°, ib. **Svargârūḍha**, mfn. ascended to h°, W. **Svargârohaṇa**, n. ascension to h°, N. of partic. funeral ceremonies, Cat.; *-parvan*, n. = *svarga-parvan* (q.v.), MBh.; °*haṇika*, mfn. relating to the 18th book of MBh. (with *parvan* = prec.), ib. (IW. 374). **Svargârgala**, m. or n. bar to (the gate of) h°, Hit. **Svargârtham**, ind. for the sake of h°, Bc. **Svargâvāsa**, m. abode in h°, Hariv. **Svargêpsu**, mfn. desirous of obtaining h°, MW. **Svargôpaga**, mfn. going or coming to h°, Kāraṇḍ. **Svargaukas**, m. 'h°-dweller,' a god, one of the Blest, Hariv.; Kum.

Svargaya, Nom. Ā. °*yate*, to be like heaven, Mṛicch.

Svargi, in comp. for *svargin*. **-giri**, m. the heavenly mountain, Meru, L. **-vadhū** and **-strī**, f. a celestial woman, Apsaras, L.

Svargin, mfn. belonging to or being in heaven, SaṃhUp.; gone to heaven, deceased, dead, Ragh.; m. an occupant of heaven, a god, one of the Blest, MBh.; Hariv. &c.

Svargīya, mfn. relating or belonging to heaven, leading to heaven, heavenly (with *kārya*, n. = 'cremation of the dead'), MBh.; Hariv.; R.

Svargyà, mfn. = prec., VS. &c. &c.; occupying or dwelling in heaven, MārkP.; n. (with *setu-shāman*) N. of a Sāman, IndSt.

Svaryú, mfn. desirous of light or splendour, RV.

Svaś, in comp. for *svar*. **-cūḍāmaṇi**, m. the crest-jewel of heaven, BhP.

Svā, in comp. for *svar*. **-2. -rāj**, m. (for 1. see p. 1277, col. 3) 'king of heaven,' N. of Indra, L.

स्वर *svara, svaraṇa* &c. See p. 1285.

स्वरक्षु *svarakshu*, f. N. of a river, MārkP.

स्वरंकृत *sv-araṃkṛita*, mfn. well arranged or prepared (as a sacrifice), RV.

स्वरतिक्रम *svar-atikrama, svar-adhīta* &c. See p. 1281, col. 2.

स्वरस *sva-rasa, sva-rāj* &c. See p. 1276, col. 2.

स्वरित्र *sv-aritrá*, mf(*ā*)n. having good oars, well rowed, RV.

स्वरु *sváru*, m. (of doubtful derivation) a large piece of wood cut from the trunk of a tree, stake, (esp.) sacrificial post or a strip of wood from it, RV.; AV.; Br.; KātyŚr.; a sacrifice, L.; sunshine, L.; a thunderbolt, L.; an arrow, L.; a kind of scorpion, L. **-mocana**, m. the third cubit from the bottom or the fifteenth from the top of the sacrificial post, L.

Svarus, m. = *svaru*, a thunderbolt, L.

स्वरूप *sva-rūpa* &c. See p. 1276, col. 2.

स्वरेणु *svareṇu*, f. N. of a wife of the sun (v.l. *sureṇu* and *saraṇyū*), L.

स्वर्क *sv-arká*, mfn. (fr. 5. *su+arka*, √*arc*) singing or praising beautifully, RV.

Sv-arcana, mfn. (used in explaining prec.), Nir. xi, 14.

Sv-arcí (RV.) or **sv-arcis** (Hcat.), mfn. flashing beautifully.

स्वर्ग *svarga* &c. See p. 1281, col. 2.

स्वर्जि *svarji*, f. (= *sarji*) natron, nitrate of potash, Suśr. **-kshāra**, m. id., ib.

Svarjika, m. (Suśr.) or °**kā**, f. (Car.) or °**kā-kshāra**, m. (Suśr.) id.

Svarjin, m. id., L.

स्वर्जित् *svar-jit* &c. See p. 1281, col. 2.

स्वर्ण *svarṇa*, m. (contracted from *su-varṇa*) a partic. Agni, Hariv.; n. gold (as a weight = one Karsha of gold), Yājñ.; Kāv.; Kathās. &c.; a kind of red chalk, R.; a kind of plant (accord. to L., 'a kind of herb = *gaura-suvarṇa*,' 'the thorn-apple,' 'a kind of cocoa palm,' and 'the flower of Mesua Roxburghii'), BhP. **-kaṇa**, m. a kind of bdellium (= *kaṇa-guggulu*), L. **-kaṇikā**, f. a particle or grain of gold, KālP. **-kāya**, m. 'g°-bodied,' N. of Garuḍa, L. **-kāra**, m. a g°-worker, g°smith (forming a partic. caste; *-tā*, f.), Yājñ.; R.; Kathās. **-kāraka**, m. id., HPariś. **-kūṭa**, N. of a place, Cat. **-kṛit**, m. = *-kāra*, HPariś. **-ketakī**, f. Pandanus Odoratissimus, L. **-kshīriṇikā** or **-kshīrī**, f. Cleome Felina, L. **-khaṇḍāya**, Nom. Ā. °*yate*, to become a lump of g°, Rājat. **-gaṇapati**, m. N. of a partic. form of Gaṇeśa, Cat. **-giri**, m. N. of a mountain, Śatr. **-gairika**, n. a kind of yellow ochre or red chalk, Suśr. **-gaurī-vrata**, n. N. of a partic. religious observance, Cat.; *-pūjā*, f. N. of a ch. of the BhavP. **-grāma**, m. N. of a country situated to the east of Dacca, Col. **-grīva**, m. 'g°-necked,' N. of one of Skanda's attendants, MBh.; (*ā*), f. N. of a river issuing from the eastern side of the Nāṭaka mountain, KālP. **-gharma**, m. N. of a partic. Anuvāka, BhP. **-cūḍa**, m. 'g°-crested,' the blue jay, L.; a cock, W.; N. of a king, Hcat. **-cūḍaka**, m. the blue jay, L. **-cūla**, m. (prob.) id., Kathās. **-ja**, n. 'gold-produced,' the metal tin, L. **-jātikā** or **-jātī**, f. a kind of jasmine, Bhpr. **-jīrī** (?), f. a partic. mixture, Cat. **-jīvantikā** or **-jīvā**, f. Hoya Viridiflora, L. **-tantra**, n. N. of a Tantra. **-da**, mfn. giving gold, Rājat.; (*ā*), f. Tragia Involucrata, L. **-dāmā**, f. 'g°-girdled,' N. of a goddess, Cat. **-dīdhiti**, m. 'g°-rayed,' fire, L. **-dugdhā** or **-dugdhī**, f. Cleome Felina, L. **-dru**, m. Cassia Fistula, L. **-dvīpa**, m. n. 'g°-island,' (prob.) N. of Sumatra, Kathās.; Śatr. **-dhātu**, m. red ochre, L. **-nābha**, m. ammonite, MBh.; a partic. spell recited over weapons, R. **-nibha**, n. a kind of red chalk, L. **-paksha**, m. 'gold-winged,' N. of Garuḍa, L. **-padmā**, f. 'bearing gold lotuses,' the heavenly Ganges, L. **-parṇī**, f. 'gold-leaved,' Hoya Viridiflora, L. **-pāṭhaka**, m. borax, L. **-pārevata**, n. a kind of fruit tree, L. **-puṅkha**, mfn. gold-feathered (as an arrow), MBh.; m. a g°-f°arrow, Śiś. **-pushpa**, m. 'g°-flowered,' Cassia Fistula, L.; Michelia Campaka, L.; (*ā* and *ī*), f. N. of various plants (Methonica Superba, Cassia Fistula &c.), L. **-pushpikā**, f. jasmine, L. **-prastha**, m. N. of an Upadvīpa in Jambu-dvīpa, BhP. **-phalā**, f. 'having g° fruit,' a kind of Musa, L. **-bandha** or °**dhaka**, m. a deposit of g°, MW. **-bindu**, m. a spot of yellow or g°, L.; N. of Vishṇu, L.; of a Tīrtha, MBh. **-bhāj**, m. a partic. sun, VP., Sch. **-bhūmikā**, f. ginger or cassia bark, L. **-bhūshaṇa**, m. Cassia Fistula, Bhpr.; n. a kind of red chalk, L. **-bhṛiṅgāra**, m. a golden vase, Rājat.; a kind of plant, L. **-maya**, mf(*ī*)n. consisting or made of g°, Siṃhâs. **-mahā**, f. N. of a river, KālP. **-mākshika**, n. a kind of mineral substance, Bhpr. **-mātṛi**, f. a kind of plant, L. **-mukharī-māhātmya**, n. N. of wk. **-mūla**, m. 'g°-rooted,' N. of a mountain, Kathās. **-mūshikā**, f. a kind of plant (prob. w. r. for *-yūthikā*), L. **-yūthī**, f. yellow jasmine, L. **-rambhā**, f. a kind of plant, L. **-rāga** or **-rāja**, m. white lotus, L. **-rīti**, f. gold-like brass, bell metal, L. **-rūpin**, mfn. g°-coloured, Hcat. **-rekhā**, f. a gold streak (on a touchstone), Kuval.; N. of a Vidyā-dharī, Hit.; of a river, VP. **-retas**, mfn. having golden seed (said of the sun), RāmatUp. **-roman**, m. 'g°-haired,' N. of a king, R.; BhP. **-latā**, f. 'g° creeper,' Cardiospermum Halicacabum, L.; Hoya Viridiflora, L. **-lābha**, m. a partic. spell recited over weapons (cf. *-nābha*), R. **-vaṅga**, m. a partic. preparation made of tin, L. **-vajra**, n. a sort of steel, L. **-vaṇij**, m. a gold merchant, money-changer (forming a partic. caste), BrahmavP. **-varṇa**, n. turmeric (also *ā*, f.), L.; *-bhāj*, f. Terminalia Chebula, L.; °*ṇābhā*, f. a species of plant, L. **-valkala**, m. 'having g° bark,' Bignonia Indica, L. **-vallī**, f. a kind of plant (= *rakta-phalā*), L. **-vidyā**, f. (prob.) the art of making gold, Cat. **-śikha**, m. a partic. bird (= *-cūḍa*), Kathās. **-śuktikā**, f. g° from Suvarṇa-dvīpa, L. **-śṛiṅga**, mfn. g°-horned, MW.; °*gin*, m. N. of a mountain, MārkP. **-śephālikā**, f. Cassia Fistula, Bhpr. **-śaila**, m. N. of a mountain, Pañcad. **-shṭhīvin**, m. = *suvarṇa-shṭh°*, MBh. **-saṃcayā**, f. N. of a town, Pañcad. **-sindūra**, m. a partic. medicinal preparation, L. **-sū**, mfn. producing g° (as a mountain), Rājat. **-stha**, mfn. set in g°, Pañcar. **Svarṇâkara**, m. a gold-mine, Rājat. **Svarṇâkarshaṇa** and °**shaṇa-bhairava-vidhāna**, n. N. of wks. **Svarṇâṅga**, m. 'g°-bodied,' Cassia Fistula, L. **Svarṇâdri**, m. 'g°-mountain,' Meru, L. **Svarṇâri**, n. 'enemy of gold,' lead, L.; sulphur, L. **Svarṇâhvā**, f. a kind of plant, L.

Svarṇaka, m. a kind of tree, Hariv.; gold, Yājñ.; golden, of gold, W.

स्वर्णली *svarṇalī* or *svarṇulī*, f. a kind of plant, L.

स्वर्त् *svart*, v.l. for √*śvart*, q.v.

स्वर्थ *sv-ártha*, mf(*ā*)n. pursuing or serving worthy ends, RV.

स्वर्द् *svard* (cf. √*svad*), cl. 1. Ā. *svardate*, to taste; to please, Dhātup. ii, 18; to be pleasing, ib.; (also *sañcarane*.)

स्वर्द *svar-da, svar-dṛiś* &c. See p. 1281.

स्वर्धिन् *sv-ardhín*, m. a good partisan (or 'one who has chosen the good side'), AV.

स्वर्य *svarya*. See p. 1285, col. 3.

स्वर्वत् *sv-arvat*, m. a good or swift courser, MānGṛ.

स्वर्हण *sv-arhaṇa*, n. great reverence, BhP.

Sv-arhat, mfn. very honourable (*-tama*, superl.), ib.

स्वलक्षण *sva-lakshaṇa, sva-likhita* &c. See p. 1276, col. 3.

स्वलक्षित *sv-alakshita*, mfn. altogether unseen, not thoroughly observed, BhP.

स्वलंकृत *sv-alaṃkṛit* and °*kṛita*, mfn. beautifully adorned, MBh.

स्वलदा *svaladā*, f. N. of a daughter of Raudrāśva.

स्वलीन *svalīna*, m. N. of a Dānava, VahniP.

स्वल्प *sv-alpa*, mf(*ā*)n. very small or little, minute, very few, short (*ena*, 'in a short time'), Mn.; MBh. &c. **-kaṅka**, m. a species of heron (= *bhū-kāka*), MW. **-keśin**, m. 'having small fibres,' the root of sweet flag, L. **-kesarin**, m. 'having small filaments,' Bauhinia Variegata, L. **-jātaka**, n. N. of a wk. by Varāha-mihira (also called *sūkshma-j°*). **-tantra**, mfn. consisting of short sections, concisely written (*-tva*, n.), Kathās. **-tara**, mfn. very insignificant or unimportant, Mn.; Pañcat. **-tas**, ind. quite gradually, MBh. xii, 5221 (v.l.) **-duḥkha**, n. very little pain, Ml. **-dṛiś**, mfn. very short-sighted (metaphorically), Rājat. **-dehā**, f. a dwarfish girl unfit for marriage, L. **-drāvaka**, n. a partic. mineral preparation, L. **-pattraka**, m. 'small-leaved,' a kind of Madhūka or Bassia Latifolia, L. **-phalā**, f. 'having small-sized fruit,' Andersonia Rohitaka, L. **-bala**, mfn. extremely weak or feeble, Hit. **-yātrā**, f. the shorter Yātrā (by Varāha-mihira), VarBṛS., Sch. **-vayas**, mfn. very young, Kathās. **-vitta-vat**, mfn. possessing very little property, Hcat. **-vishaya**, m. a very small matter or object, W.; a small part, ib. **-vyaya**, m. very little expenditure, MW.; mfn. spending very little, very niggardly, ib. **-vrīḍa**, mfn. having little shame, shameless, impudent, W. **-śarīra**, mfn. having a very diminutive body, small in stature, L. **-śilā**, f. a very small stone; °*lāya*, Nom. Ā. °*yate*, to become a very small stone, Bhartṛ. **-smṛiti**, mfn. having a short memory, Mṛicch. **Svalpâṅguli**, f. the little finger, L. **Svalpâtivistara**, mf(*ā*)n. very concise and very diffuse, Cat. **Svalpântara**, mfn. little different, Bc. **Svalpâpahāra**, mfn. eating very little, most abstemious, MW. **Svalpâyu** or °**yus**, mfn. short-lived, Hāsy. **Svalpêccha**, mfn. having few wishes, unpretentious, unassuming (*-tā*, f.), Car.

Svalpaka, mf(*ikā*)n. very small or minute or short, AV. &c. &c.

Svalpī-√bhū, P. *-bhavati* (p.p. *-bhūta*), to become small, melt away (as merit), Megh.

Svalpīyas, mfn. very little (property), Mn. xi, 8.

स्ववंशज *sva-vaṇśa-ja* &c. See p. 1276.

स्ववक्लिन्न *sv-avaklinna*, mfn. well soaked or macerated, Car.

स्ववग्रह *sv-avagraha*, mfn. easily checked or restrained, Kām.

स्ववच्छन्न *sv-avacchanna*, mfn. well covered, Car.

स्ववश *sv-avaśa*, mfn. (for *sva-v°* see p. 1276, col. 3) not at all master of one's self, Vās.

स्ववस् *sv-àvas*, mfn. (nom. °*vān*) having or affording good protection, RV.

स्ववेक्ष *sv-avêksha*, mf(*ā*)n. well provided for, R.

Sv-avêkshita, mfn. well considered, ib.

स्वव्याज *sv-avyāja*, mfn. thoroughly sincere or honest, MBh.

स्वश *svaśa*, m. pl. N. of a people (prob. w. r. for *khaśa*), Buddh.

स्वशक्ति *sva-śakti* &c. See p. 1277, col. 1.

स्वश्व *sv-áśva*, mf(*ā*)n. having excellent horses, well mounted, well yoked, RV.

Sv-aśvayú, mfn. fond of good steeds (others, 'wishing to be a good courser'), RV.

Sv-áśvya, n. possession of good horses, RV.; skill in horses, ib.

स्वष्ट्र *sv-áshṭra*, mfn. armed with an excellent goad, RV.

स्वसंयुक्त *sva-saṃyukta, sva-saṃvid* &c. See p. 1277, col. 1.

स्वसर *svásara*, n. (perhaps fr. *sva + sara*, 'one's own resort') a stall, fold, RV.; one's own place, home, ib.; ŚBr.; nest of birds, RV.; day, Naigh.

Svasāra, n. = *svasara*, RV. i, 178, 2.

स्वसित *sv-asita*, mfn. very black (in °*tâyata-locana*, 'having very black and long eyes'), Mal.

स्वसृ *svásṛi*, f. (of doubtful derivation) a sister (also applied to closely connected things of the fem. gender, as to the fingers, the waters &c.), RV. &c. &c. [Cf. Gk. ἔορ; Lat. *soror*; Lith. *sesū*; Goth. *swistar*; Germ. *Schwester*; Eng. *sister*.] **-tvá**, n. sisterhood, RV. x, 108, 10.

Svasā, f. (m. c.) = *svasṛi*, MBh.

Svasrīya, m. a sister's son, nephew, TS. &c. &c.; (*ā*), f. a sister's daughter, niece, Mn. xi, 171.

Svasreya, m. (and *ī*, f.) = prec., MW.

Svāsṛika, mfn. (fr. *svasṛi*), Pat.

Svāsrīya, m.pl. = *svāsrīyeryūnaś chāttrāḥ*, ib.

Svāsrīyi, m. a son of a sister's son, ib.

स्वस्क् *svask.* See √*shvashk.*

स्वस्तक *sv-astaká*, mfn. having a good or comfortable home, AV.

स्वस्तमित *sv-astamitá*, n. a beautiful sunset, AV.

स्वस्ति *sv-astí*, n. f. (nom. *svastí*, °*tís;* acc. *svastí*, °*tím;* instr. *svastí*, °*tyā́;* dat. *svastáye;* loc. *svastaú;* instr. *svastíbhis;* also personified as a goddess, and sometimes as Kalā, cf. *svasti-devī*), well-being, fortune, luck, success, prosperity, RV.; VS.; ŚBr.; MBh.; R.; BhP.; (*í*), ind. well, happily, successfully (also = 'may it be well with thee! hail! health! adieu! so be it!' a term of salutation [esp. in the beginning of letters] or of sanction or approbation), RV. &c. &c. – **kara**, m. N. of a man, Pravar. – **karman**, n. causing welfare or success, R. – **kāra**, m. the bard who cries *svasti*, R.; = prec., MBh.; the exclamation *svasti*, Kathās. – **kṛit**, mfn. causing welfare or prosperity (said of Śiva), Śivag. – **gav-yūti** (*svastí-*), mfn. having happy pastures or fields, MaitrS. – **gā́**, mfn. leading to fortune or prosperity, RV. – **tā**, f. a state of welfare, AitBr. – **da** (Śivag.), -**dā́** (RV.), mfn. conferring happiness. – **devī**, f. N. of a goddess (represented as wife of Vāyu and said to have sprung from the essence of Prakṛiti), MW. – **pura**, n. N. of a Tīrtha, MBh. – **bhāva**, m. N. of Śiva, ib. – **mát**, mfn. being or faring well, happy, fortunate, RV. &c. &c.; conferring happiness, RV.; containing the word *svasti*, AitBr.; (*atī*), f. N. of one of the Mātṛis attending on Skanda, MBh. – **mukha**, mfn. having the word *svasti* in the mouth, wishing joy or fortune, L.; m. a Brāhman or a bard, L.; a letter (beginning with *svasti*), L. – **vacana**, n. pronouncing the word *svasti*, benediction, MBh. – **vah** (or -*vāh*), mfn. carrying auspiciously (as a carriage; others, 'conferring happiness'), RV. – **vāc**, f. (Vcar.) or -**vācaka**, m. (BhP.) benediction, congratulation. – **vācana** or °**naka**, n. a religious rite preparatory to a sacrifice or any solemn observance (performed by scattering boiled rice on the ground and invoking blessings by the repetition of certain Mantras; also applied to the fee or complimentary present of flowers, sweetmeats &c. offered to Brāhmans on such occasions), MBh.; Kāv. &c.; -*paddhati*, f., -*mantra*, m. pl. N. of wks. – **vācanika**, mfn. pronouncing a blessing on anything, Mcar. – 1. -**vācya**, mfn. to be called upon to pronounce a blessing on anything, MBh.; n. = -*vācana*, Yājñ. – 2. -**vācya**, ind. calling upon any one to pronounce a blessing on anything, Gobh. – **vāda**, m. = -*vāc*, Dhanaṃj. – **vā́hana**, mfn. leading auspiciously (as a road), AV.

Svastika, m. a kind of bard (who utters words of welcome or eulogy), R.; any lucky or auspicious object, (esp.) a kind of mystical cross or mark made on persons and things to denote good luck (it is shaped like a Greek cross with the extremities of the four arms bent round in the same direction; the majority of scholars regard it as a solar symbol; that is, as representing a curtailed form of the wheel of the Solar Vishṇu, consisting of four spokes crossing each other at right angles with short fragments of the periphery of the circle at the end of each spoke turning round in one direction to denote the course of the Sun; accord. to the late Sir A. Cunningham it has no connexion with sun-worship, but its shape represents a monogram or interlacing of the letters of the auspicious words *su asti* [*svasti*] in the Aśoka characters; amongst Jainas it is one of the 24 auspicious marks and is the emblem of the seventh Arhat of the present Avasarpiṇī), Hariv.; Kāv.; Pur.; the crossing of the arms or hands on the breast, MBh.; Mālatīm.; Kathās.; a bandage in the form of a cross, Suśr.; a dish of a partic. form, MBh.; R.; Pañcar.; a kind of cake, ib.; a triangular crest-jewel, L.; the meeting of four roads, W.; a partic. symbol made of ground rice and formed like a triangle (it is used in fumigating the image of Durgā, and is said to symbolize the Liṅga), MW.; a species of garlic, L.; a cock, L.; a libertine, L.; N. of a serpent-demon, MBh.; of one of Skanda's attendants, ib.; of a Dānava, Hariv.; of a poet, Cat.; of another man, Buddh.; m. n. a mansion or temple of a partic. form, VarBṛS.; Marsilea Quadrifolia, L.; a partic. mode of sitting practised by Yogins (in which the toes are placed in the inner hollow of the knees), MārkP.; Pañcar. – **karṇa**, mfn. marked on the ear with the figure called Svastika, L. – **dāna**, n. crossing the hands, Bālar. – **yantra**, n. a surgical instrument of a partic. form, Suśr. **Svastikâṅka**, mfn. marked with the Svastika cross, Bc. **Svastikâdi-cakra**, n. pl. N. of wk. **Svastikâsana**, n. a mode of sitting (see above), Sarvad.

Svastikī-kṛita, mfn. crossed (as hands), Cat.

Svastī, ind. (with √*as* = *svasti*), Siddh.

Svasty, in comp. for *svasti.* – **akshara**, n. expressing thanks for anything, Hcat. – **ayana**, n.sg. and pl. (ifc. f. *ā*) auspicious progress, success, Jātakam.; blessing, benediction, congratulation (with Caus. of √*vac*, 'to ask for a blessing'), AV. &c. &c.; a Mantra recited for good luck or the recitation of such a Mantra, W.; a means of attaining prosperity, Jātakam.; a vessel full of water borne in front of a procession, L.; mf(*ī*)n. bringing or causing good fortune, auspicious (°*tama*, superl.), TBr. &c. &c.; -*gaṇa*, m. a collection of Mantras recited for good luck, AV. Pariś. – **artha-carita**, mfn. one who has happily attained his aim, SāmavBr. – **ātreya**, m. N. of an ancient sage (supposed author of RV. v, 50, 51; pl. = 'the family of Sv°-ātr°'), MBh.; Hariv.; the hymn composed by Sv°-ātr°, ĀśvŚr.; a mirror, Lāṭy.

Svastya, mfn. happy, fortunate, Kauś.

स्वस्थ *sva-stha* &c. See p. 1277, col. 1.

स्वहतवासस् *sv-ahata-vāsas*, mfn. clothed in beautiful and unwashed (i. e. new) garments, Hcat.

स्वहन्तृ *sva-hantṛi*, *sva-haraṇa* &c. See p. 1277, col. 1.

स्वाकार *sv-ākāra*, mfn. (for *svâkāra* see p. 1277, col. 2) of decent or respectable appearance, Hcar.

Sv-ākṛiti, mfn. good-looking, handsome, Kathās.

स्वाकूति *sv-ākūti*, m. N. of a divine being enumerated among the Jayas, Cat.

स्वाक्त *sv-ākta*, n. good ointment (for the eyes), AV.

स्वाक्षर *svâkshara*, *svâṅga* &c. See p. 1277, col. 2.

स्वाख्यात *sv-ākhyāta*, mfn. well proclaimed (often applied to *dharma*), Divyâv.

स्वागत *sv-āgata*, mfn. (for *svâgata* see p. 1277, col. 2) well come, welcome, R.; lawfully-earned (as money), Mn. iv, 226; m. N. of a Buddha, Lalit.; of a king, VP.; of another man, Buddh.; (*ā*), f. a kind of metre, Srutab.; (*am*), n. welcome, greeting, salutation (*svāgatam te* with or without *astu*, 'I wish you welcome'), MBh.; Kāv. &c.; welfare, health (see next). – **praśna**, m. enquiry as to health, Śukas. – **vacana**, n. the uttering of welcome, the word welcome, MW.

Svāgatika, mfn. bidding welcome to any one, Pāṇ. vii, 3, 7, Sch.

Svāgatī-√kṛi, P. -*karoti* (ind. p. -*kṛitya*), to make into a cry of welcome, Megh.

Svāgama, m. welcome, salutation, MBh.

स्वाग्रयण *sv-āgrayaṇa*, mfn. forming a good Āgrayaṇa (Graha), VS.

स्वाङ्किक *svāṅkika*, m. (perhaps fr. *sva* + *aṅkī*) a drummer, L.

स्वाचरण *sv-ācaraṇa*, n. good conduct or behaviour, MBh.; mfn. well-conducted, ib.

Sv-ācāra, m. (Subh.) and mf(*ā*)n. (Yājñ.) = prec. – **vat**, mfn. well-behaved, VarYogay.

स्वाचान्त *sv-ācānta*, mfn. one who has sipped water well or according to rule, Vishṇ.

स्वाच्छन्द्य *svācchandya*, n. (fr. *sva-cchanda*) independence, freedom (instr. = 'by one's own will, voluntarily'), Mn. iii, 31.

स्वाजन्य *svājanya*, n. (fr. *sva-jana*) kinship, relationship, HPariś.

स्वाजीव *sv-ājīva* (R.), °*vya* (Mn.), mfn. yielding an easy subsistence.

स्वाढ्यंकर *sv-āḍhyaṃ-kara*, mfn. easy to make rich, Pāṇ. iii, 3, 127, Sch.

Svāḍhyaṃ-karaṇa, mfn. easily enriching, Pāṇ. i, 1, 72, Vārtt. 9, Pat.

Svāḍhyam-bhava, mfn. easy to become rich, Pāṇ. iii, 3, 127, Sch.

स्वातत *sv-ātata*, mfn. well stretched or fixed, RV.; well aimed, ib.

स्वातन्त्र्य *svātantrya*, n. (fr. *sva-tantra*) the following one's own will, freedom of the will, independence (*āt* and *ena*, 'by one's own will, of one's own free choice, voluntarily, freely'), Lāṭy.; MaitrUp.; MBh. &c.

स्वाति *svāti*, f. (of unknown derivation) N. of the star Arcturus (as forming the 13th and 15th lunar asterism; also *svātí*, pl. *svātyaḥ*), AV. &c. &c.; N. of one of the wives of the Sun, L.; a sword, L.; m. N. of a son of Uru and Āgneyī (v. l. *khyāti*), Hariv.; VP.; of Megha-svāti, VP.; mfn. born under the star Arcturus, Pāṇ. iv, 3, 34. – **karṇa**, m. N. of a king, VP. – **kārī**, f. (?) N. of a goddess presiding over agriculture, PārGṛ. – **giri**, f. N. of a serpent-maiden, Kāraṇḍ. – **mukha**, m. a partic. Samādhi, ib.; N. of a Kiṃ-nara king, ib.; (*ā*), f. N. of a serpent-maiden, ib. – **yoga**, m. conjunction with Svāti, MW. – **sheṇa**, m. (for -*sena*), N. of a king, VP.

स्वात्त *svāttá*, mfn. (fr. √*svad*) seasoned, spiced, VS. (cf. *agni-shvāttá*).

स्वात्मन् *svâtman* &c. See p. 1277, col. 2.

स्वाद *svāda*, *svādu* &c. See p. 1279, col. 3.

स्वादर *sv-ādara*, mfn. very regardful, very considerate, MBh.

स्वादान *sv-ādāná*, mfn. (for *svâdāna* see p. 1277, col. 2) easy to be taken, MaitrS.

स्वादित्य *sv-ādityá*, mfn. any one befriended by the Ādityas, RV.; n. the favour or protection of the Ādityas, ib.

स्वाधी *sv-ādhí*, mfn. well-minded, thoughtful, heedful, devout, pious, RV.

स्वाधीन *svâdhīna*, *svâdhyāya* &c. See p. 1277, col. 2.

स्वाध्वरिक *svādhvarika*, mfn. (fr. *sv-adhvara*), g. *svāgatâdi.*

स्वान *svāna.* See √3. *su*, and p. 1280, col. 2.

स्वानम *sv-ānama*, mf(*ā*)n. easy to be attracted or captivated, Śiś.

स्वान्त *svânta.* See √*svan* and p. 1277, col. 3.

स्वाप *svāpa* &c. See p. 1280, col. 3.

स्वापतेय *svāpateya*, n. (fr. *sva-pati*) one's own property, wealth, riches, MBh.; Kāv. &c.

स्वापद *svāpada.* See *śvā-pada.*

स्वापि *sv-āpí*, m. a good friend or comrade, RV.; VS.; AitBr. – **mat**, mfn. containing the word *svāpi*, AitBr.

Svāpika, n. N. of a fortress, Rājat.

स्वापिशि *svāpiśi*, m. patr. fr. *sva-piś*, g. *raivatikâdi.*

Svāpiśīya, mfn. (fr. prec.), ib.

स्वाप्त *sv-āpta*, mfn. very abundant, MBh.; very skilful or trustworthy, Kām. – **vacana**, mfn. (used in explaining *sv-apivāta*), Nir. x, 7.

स्वाभाविक *svābhāvika*, mf(*ī*)n. (fr. *svabhāva*) belonging to or arising from one's own nature, natural, native, spontaneous, original, peculiar, inherent (-*tva*, n.), Up.; MBh. &c.; m. pl. N. of a Buddhistic school (cf. Buddhac. ix, 48; 51). **Svābhāvikêtara**, mf(*ā*)n. not natural or inherent, Sāh.

Svābhāvya, mfn. self-existent, existing spontaneously (said of Vishṇu), MBh.; n. own peculiarity, own nature, Śaṃk.

स्वाभास *sv-ābhāsa*, mfn. very illustrious or splendid, Kir.

स्वाभील *sv-ābhīla*, mfn. very formidable, MBh.

स्वाभू sv-ābhū́, mfn. very abundant or ready to hand, RV.; ready to help, ib.

स्वामिन् svāmin, m. (fr. 1. sva + min) an owner, proprietor, master, lord or owner of (gen., loc., or comp.), Mn.; MBh. &c.; a chief, commander (of an army), Vikr.; Subh.; a husband, lover (du. 'husband and wife'), Āpast.; Mn.; MBh. &c.; a king, prince (in dram. used as a form of address = *deva*); a spiritual preceptor, learned Brāhman or Pandit (used as a title at the end of names, esp. of natives of the Carnatic); the image or temple of a god (often ifc.; see *śrīdhara-, vishṇu-sv°* &c.); N. of Skanda, Yājñ. i, 293; of Vishṇu, L.; of Śiva, L.; of Garuḍa, L.; of the Muni Vātsyāyana, L.; of the 11th Arhat of the past Utsarpiṇī, L.; of various authors (also with *miśra* and *śāstrin;* sometimes abridged from names ending in *svāmin*, e. g. for *kshīra-* and *śabara-svāmin*), Cat.; (*inī*), f., see next.

Svāmi, in comp. for *svāmin*. **-kārttika**, m. N. of an author; °*kânuprêkshā*, f. N. of wk. **-kārya**, n. the business of a king or master, MW.; °*ryârthin*, mfn. desirous of or seeking a master's interest, ib. **-kumāra**, m. N. of Skanda, Kathās.; of an author (?), Cat. **-giri-māhātmya**, n. N. of wk. **-guṇa**, m. the virtue of a ruler, Ml. **-jaṅghin**, m. N. of Paraśu-rāma, L. **-janaka**, m. the father of a husband, f°-in-law, L. **-tā**, f. (VarBṛS.), **-tva**, n. (MBh.) ownership, mastership, lordship of (gen. or comp.) **-datta**, m. N. of a poet, Cat. **-pāla**, m. du. the owner and the tender (of cattle), Mn. viii, 5; *-vivāda*, m. a dispute between the owner and tender (of c°); °*da-taraṃga*, m. N. of wk. **-prasāda**, m. (*āt*, ind. 'by your majesty's leave'), Ml. **-bhaṭṭāraka**, m. a noble lord, Mṛicch. **-bhāva**, m. ownership, mastership, lordship, R. **-mūla**, mfn. originating or derived from a master or lord, depending on a m° or husband, W. **-vaśī-kara-stotra**, n. N. of wk. **-vātsalya**, n. affection for a lord or husband, MW. **-śāstrin**, m. N. of an author, Cat. **-śaila-māhātmya**, n. N. of wk. **-sad-bhāva**, m. existence of a master or owner, W.; amiability of a master or lord, ib. **-sevā**, f. the service of a master, respect or reverence for a master or husband, ib.

Svāmika, (in comp.) = *svāmin* (cf. *niḥ-, pranashṭa-sv°* &c.) **-rāja**, m. N. of a king, Inscr.

Svāminī, f. a proprietress, mistress, lady (used in addressing a queen or a king's favourite wife), MBh.; Kāv. &c. **-stotra**, n. N. of a Stotra.

Svāminy, in comp. for *svāminī*. **-ashṭaka**, n. N. of wk.

Svāmy, in comp. for *svāmin*. **-artham**, ind. for a master's sake, MW. **-asammata**, mfn. unpermitted by a master, one who has not obtained an owner's permission, ib. **-upakāraka**, m. 'serviceable to a master,' a horse, W.

Svāmya, n. mastership, lordship, ownership, dominion or power over any one, Mn.; MBh. &c. **-kāraṇa**, n. the cause of lordship or supremacy, MW.

स्वाम्नाय sv-āmnāya, mfn. well handed down by tradition, Śiksh.

स्वायत्त svâyatta &c. See p. 1277, col. 3.

स्वायम्भुव svāyambhuva, mfn. (fr. *svayambhū*) relating to Svayam-bhū or the Self-existent, derived from the Self-existent (i. e. Brahman), MBh.; Kāv. &c.; relating to or derived from Manu Svāyambhuva, MBh.; Hariv.; Pur.; m. 'son of Svayam-bhū,' N. of various sages (esp. of the first Manu, of Marīci, Atri, Nārada &c.), ib.; (*ī*), f. Ruta Graveolens, L.; (*am*), n. N. of a Śaiva Tantra. **-manupitṛi**, m. 'father of Manu Svāyambhuva,' N. of Brahmā, MW.

Svāyambhū = *svāyambhuva* above, MW. **-kshetra-māhatmya**, w. r. for *svayambh°* (q. v.)

स्वायस sv-āyasá, mfn. made of good metal (as a knife), RV.; AV.

स्वायु sv-ā́yu, mfn. having good people (subjects), VS.; m. N. of a man (see next).

Svāyava, m. patr. fr. *sv-āyu*, PañcavBr.

Sv-āyús, n. full vigour or life, VS.

स्वायुज् sv-āyúj, mfn. easy to be yoked, RV.

स्वायुध sv-āyudhá, mfn. well-armed, having good weapons, RV.

स्वार svāra &c. See p. 1285, col. 3.

स्वारक्ष्य sv-ārakshya, mfn. easy to be protected or defended, MBh.

स्वारब्ध svârabdha, svârāma &c. See p. 1277, col. 3.

स्वारसिक svārasika, mfn. (fr. *sva-rasa*) possessing inherent flavour or sweetness (as a poem &c.), MW.; natural, self-evident, Naish.

Svārasya, n. naturalness, self-evidence, ĀpŚr., Sch.

स्वाराज् 1. 2. svā-rāj. See p. 1277, col. 3, and p. 1282, col. 1.

स्वाराज्य svā́rājya, n. (fr. *sva-rāj*) independent rule, uncontrolled dominion, sovereignty (accord. to some 'Indra's heaven,' fr. 2. *svā-rāj;* also *Indrasya svārājyam*, N. of a Sāman), TS. &c. &c.; union with Brahma, identification with the self-refulgent, state of self-effulgence, MW.; mfn. procuring sovereignty or heaven, PañcavBr. **-kāma**, mfn. desirous of sovereignty or heaven, ŚāṅkhBr. **-siddhi**, f. N. of a Vedānta wk.

स्वाराधित sv-ārādhita, mfn. well propitiated, faithfully served, Hit.

स्वारूढ sv-ārūḍha, mfn. riding well, Hariv.; well ridden (as horses), MBh.

स्वारूपा svārūpā, f. (fr. *sva-rūpa*, q. v.) N. of a place, Cat.

स्वारोचिष svārocisha, m. (fr. *sva-rocis*) patr. of the second Manu, Mn.; MBh. &c.; mfn. relating or belonging to Manu Svārocisha, Hariv.; Pur.

Svārocis, m. = prec., Cat.

स्वार्जित svârjita, svârtha &c. See p. 1277.

स्वार्द्र sv-ārdra, mfn. very wet or moist, Bhartṛ. (v. l.)

स्वालक्षण sv-ālakshaṇa, mfn. easily perceived or discerned, MBh.

Svālakshya, mfn. id., Hariv.

स्वालक्षण्य svālakshaṇya, n. (fr. *sva-lakshaṇa*) specific characteristics, natural disposition, Mn. ix, 19.

स्वाल्प sv-ālpa, mfn. (fr. *sv-alpa*) very little or small, few, W.; n. littleness, paucity, ib.

स्वावश्य svāvaśya, n. (fr. *sva-vaśa*) self-will, self-determination, AitBr.

स्वावृज् sv-ā́vṛij, mfn. easily acquired, RV.

स्वावृत् sv-āvṛít, mfn. willingly turning towards, MaitrS.

स्वावेश sv-āveśá, mf(*ā́*)n. easy of access or approach, RV.; VS.

स्वाशित sv-āśita, mfn. well fed or satiated, RV.; R.

स्वाशिर् sv-āśir, mfn. well mixed (°*śir āmarkaḥ*, 'N. of a Sāman'), ĀrshBr.

स्वाशिस् sv-āśís, mfn. well praising, RV.

स्वाशु sv-āśú, mfn. very swift, RV.

स्वाश्लिष sv-ā-√ślish, P. -*ślishyati*, to embrace firmly or closely (v. l. *vâślishyet* for *sv-āśl°*), Mn. xi, 103.

स्वास् sv-ā́s, mfn. fair-mouthed (as Agni), RV.; keen-edged, sharp (as an axe), ib.

स्वासद् sv-āsád, mfn. sitting happily by, AV.

Sv-āsáda, mf(*ā́*)n. (used in explaining *sv-āsasthá*), ŚBr.

स्वासन sv-āsana, n. a good seat, KātyŚr.

Sv-āsa-sthá, mf(*ā́*)n. sitting on a good seat, RV.; TS.; offering or supplying a good seat, VS.; ŚBr.

Sv-āsīna, mfn. comfortably seated, Hariv.

स्वासृक svāsṛika, svāsriya, svāsriyi. See p. 1283, col. 1.

स्वास्तर sv-āstara, m. good straw for a couch, R.

Sv-āstaraṇa, mfn. having a fair couch or cushion, Subh.

Sv-āstīrṇa, mfn. well-spread, ĀśvGṛ.; MBh. &c.

स्वास्थ्य svāsthya, n. (fr. *sva-stha*) self-dependence, sound state (of body or soul), health, ease, comfort, contentment, satisfaction, MBh.; Kāv. &c.

स्वाहा sv-ā́hā, ind. (prob. fr. 5. *su* and √*ah;* cf. *dur-āhā*) hail! hail to! may a blessing rest on! (with dat.; an exclamation used in making oblations to the gods; with √*kṛi* [ind. p. -*kā́ram* or -*kṛitya*] and acc. 'to pronounce the exclamation Svāhā over'), RV. &c. &c.; f. an oblation (offered to Agni, Indra &c.) or Oblation personified (as a daughter of Daksha and wife of Agni; she is thought to preside over burnt-offerings; her body is said to consist of the four Vedas, and her limbs are the six Aṅgas or members of the Veda; she is represented also as a wife of the Rudra Paśu-pati), RV. &c. &c. **-karaṇa**, n. consecration by uttering Svāhā, APrāt. **-kārá**, m. (ifc. f. *ā*) utterance of or consecration by uttering Sv° (also as a deity presiding over the Prayāja), ŚBr. &c. &c.; *-vashaṭ-kāra*, m. du. the exclamations Svāhā and Vashaṭ, JaimUp. **-kṛit**, mfn. consecrating with Sv°, a sacrificer, Hariv. **-kṛita** (*svā́hā-*), mfn. consecrated or offered with Sv°, RV.; AV.; Br. **-kṛiti** or **-kṛitī** (*svā́hā-*), f. consecration with Sv° (also as a deity presiding over the Prayāja), Br.; ŚrS. **-pati** (Hariv.), or **-priya** (L.), m. 'lord or lover of Sv°,' N. of Agni. **-bhuj**, m. 'Sv°-eater,' a god, L. **-°rha** (*svāhârha*), mfn. worthy of the consecration with Sv°, R. **-vana**, n. N. of a forest, Pañcar. **-vallabha**, m. = *-pati*, Bālar. **-°śana** (*svāhâś°*), m. = *svāhā-bhuj*, L. **-sudhâkara**, m. N. of a poem.

Svāhi, m. N. of a son of Vṛijinī-vat, Hariv.

Svāheya, m. metron. of Skanda, MBh.

Svāhyà, mfn. worthy of an oblation with Svāhā, AV.

स्वाहार sv-āhāra, mfn. easy to be obtained or procured, R.; m. good food, MW.

स्वाहुत sv-à̄huta, mfn. well sacrificed or honoured with sacrifice, RV.

स्वाह्वान sv-āhvāna, mfn. easy to be invoked (used in explaining *su-hava*), Sāy.

स्विका svikā. See under svaka, p. 1278.

स्वित sv-itá, n. = *suvita*, welfare, luck, VS.

स्विद् 1. svid, ind. (prob. fr. 5. *su* + *id;* cf. *kuvid*) a particle of interrogation or inquiry or doubt, often translatable by 'do you think?' 'perhaps,' 'pray,' 'indeed,' 'any' (esp. used after the interrogative *ka* and its derivatives, e. g. *kaḥ svid eshām brāhmaṇānām anūcāna-tamaḥ*, 'pray who [or "who do you think"] is the most learned of these Brāhmans?' ŚBr.; but also without another interrogative, e. g. *tvaṃ svin no yājñavalkya brahmishṭho 'si*, 'do you think, Yājñavalkya, you are the greatest Brāhman among us?' ib.; also used after *uta, api, āho*, and *utâho*, and disjunctively in the first or second or both parts of a double interrogation, thus: *kiṃnu – svid; kiṃsvid – svid; svid – svid; svid – utâho; nu – svid; svid – nu; svid – uta; svid – vā; svid – kimu; svid – kim – nukim;* sometimes making a preceding interrogative indefinite, e. g. *kvá svid*, 'anywhere;' *káḥ svid*, 'whoever,' 'any one;' similarly with *yad*, e. g. *yad svid dīyate*, 'whatever is given,' MaitrS.; sometimes apparently a mere expletive), RV. &c. &c.

स्विद् 2. svid, cl. 1. Ā. 4. P. (Dhātup. xviii, 4; xxvi, 79) *svedate* or *svidyati* (Ā. *svidyate*, Yājñ.; p. *svidyamāna*, Suśr.; pf. *sishveda*, Gr.; *sishvide*, MBh.; p. *sishvidānā́*, RV.; aor. *asvidat*, Śiś.; fut. *svettā, svetsyati*, Gr.; ind. p. *-svedam*, Br.), to sweat, perspire, AitĀr.; ChUp.; KātyŚr.; MBh. &c.; (*svedate*), to be anointed, Dhātup.; to be disturbed (?), ib.: Caus. *svedayati* (aor. *asishvidat*), to cause to sweat, treat with sudorifics, Suśr.; to foment, soften, SāmavBr.: Desid. of Caus. *sisvedayishati*, Gr.: Desid. *sisvitsati*, ib.: Intens. *seshvidyate, seshvetti*, ib. [Cf. Gk. ἱδρώς; Lat. *sūdor, sūdare;* Angl. Sax. *swât;* Eng. *sweat;* Germ. *Schweiss, schwitzen.*]

3. **Svid**, (ifc.) sweating, perspiring, Śiś.

Svidita, mfn. sweated, melted, W.; sweating, perspiring, ib.

Svinná, mfn. sweating, perspiring, VS. &c. &c.; sweated, treated with sudorifics, Suśr.; seethed, boiled, Hariv.; MārkP. **Svinnâṅguli**, mfn. having perspiring or moist fingers, Suśr.

Svéda, m. (ifc. f. *ā*) sweating, perspiring, sweat, perspiration (pl. 'drops of p°'), RV. &c. &c.; a sudorific, Car.; Suśr.; warmth, heat, L.; warm vapour, steam (see comp.); mfn. sweating, perspiring, toiling, W. — **cūshaka**, m. 'perspiration sucker,' a cooling breeze, L. — **cchid**, mfn. cutting i.e. allaying p°, cooling, W. — **ja**, mfn. sweat-produced, engendered by heat and moisture, generated by warm vapour or steam (said of insects and vermin), AitUp.; Mn.; MBh. &c.; *-dūshita*, mfn. defiled by vermin, BhP. — **jala**, n. (ifc. f. *ā*) 'sweat-water,' perspiration, Pur.; *-kaṇa*, m. (Śiś.), *-kaṇikā*, f. (Vās.) = next. — **bindu**, m. drop of p°, Vās. — **malôjjhita-deha**, m. 'one whose body is freed from p° and impurity,' a Jina, L. — **mātṛi**, f. chyle, L. — **leśa**, m. a drop of p°, Śak. — **vāri**, n. = *-jala*, Śiś. — **viprush**, f. = *-bindu*, ib. **Svédâñji**, mfn. moist with p°, RV. **Svedâmbu** (Kathās.), °**mbhas** (Hāsy.), n. = *sveda-jala*. **Svédâyana**, n. 'sweat-passage,' a pore, ŚBr.; Yājñ. **Svedôda** or °**daka**, n. = *sveda-jala*, W. **Svedôdgama**, m. the breaking out of perspiration, Ratnāv.

Svedana, mfn. perspiring, inclined to perspire, Suśr.; causing to perspire, ib.; (*ī*), f. an iron plate or pan, L.; (*am*), n. the act of sweating or perspiring, L.; any instrument or remedy for causing perspiration, a diaphoretic, sudorific, Suśr.; softening, fomenting, Hit.; a partic. process to which quicksilver is subjected, Sarvad.; mucus, Gal. — **tva**, n. inclination to perspire, Suśr. — **yantra**, n. a steam-bath (for metals), L.

Svedanikā, f. an iron plate or pan used as a cooking utensil, L.; a room for cooking, kitchen, MW.

Svedayú, mfn. sweating, perspiring, MaitrS.

Svedita, mfn. (fr. Caus.) caused to sweat &c.; fomented, softened (said of a dog's tail), Hit.

Svedin, mfn. sweating, perspiring (in *a-sv°*), MBh.

Svédu-havya, mfn. (prob.) offering the sweat (caused by labour) as a sacrifice, toiling, exerting one's self, RV.

Svedya, mfn. to be sweated or treated by sudorific means, Śiś.; Pañcat.

स्विध्म *sv-idhmá*, mf(*ā*)n. consisting of good or dry wood, RV.

स्विषु *sv-ishú*, mfn. having good or swift arrows, RV.

स्विष्ट 1. *sv-ishṭa*, mfn. (√3. *ish*) much desired or loved, R.

स्विष्ट 2. *sv-ìshṭa*, mfn. (√*yaj*) well or properly sacrificed, correctly offered, RV. &c. &c.; well worshipped or honoured, VS.; BhP.; n. a right sacrifice, VS.; ŚBr.; MBh. &c. — **kṛit**, mfn. offering a right sacrifice (esp. applied to Agni; superl. *-tama*), VS. &c. &c.; = *-kṛita*, GṛŚrS.; (*-kṛic*)*-caturtha*, mf(*ā*)n. having Agni Svishṭa-kṛit as fourth, ĀpGṛ.; (*-kṛid*)*-bhāga*, m. the share of Agni Sv°, AitBr.; *-bhājanā*, n. the substitute for Agni Sv°. — **kṛita**, mfn. belonging or offered to Agni Sv°, Gṛihyas.

Sv-ishṭi, f. a successful sacrifice, AV.; TS.; Kauś.; mfn. sacrificing well or with success, MBh.

स्वी *svī*, *svī-karaṇa* &c. See p. 1279, col. 1.

स्वूर्छ् *svūrch*. See √*sphūrch*.

स्वृ *svṛi* (also written *svar*), cl. 1. P. (Dhātup. xxii, 34) *svárati* (pf. *sasvāra*; 3. sg. Subj. [?] *sasvár*, RV.; aor. *asvār*, *asvārshṭām*, ib.; *asvārīḥ*, JaimBr.; *asvārīt* and *asvārshīt*, Gr.; fut. *svaritā*, *svartā*, *svarishyati*, ib.; inf. *svaritos*, JaimBr.; *svaritum*, *svartum*, Gr.; ind. p. *-svāram*, ŚāṅkhŚr.), to utter a sound, sound, resound, RV.; JaimBr.; ChUp.; to make (acc.) resound, RV.; to sing, praise, RV.; to shine, Kauś.; ChUp.: Caus. *svarayati* (aor. *asisvarat*; Pass. *svaryate*), to pronounce or mark with the Svarita accent, Prāt.; Lāṭy.: Desid. *sisvarishati*, *susvūrshati*, Gr.: Intens. *sāsvaryate*, *sāsvarti*, ib. [Cf. Gk. σῦριγξ; Lat. *susurrus*; Germ. *schwirren*, *Schwarm*; Eng. *swarm*.]

Svára or **svará**, m. (ifc. f. *ā*) sound, noise, RV. &c. &c.; voice, Mn.; MBh. &c.; tone in recitation &c. (either high or low), accent (of which there are three kinds, *udātta*, *anudātta* qq. vv., and *svarita*, col. 3), a note of the musical scale (of which seven [rarely six or eight] are enumerated, 1. *nishāda*; 2. *ṛishabha*; 3. *gāndhāra*; 4. *shaḍja*; 5. *madhyama*; 6. *dhaivata*; 7. *pañcama* [described as resembling respectively the notes of an elephant, bull, goat, peacock, curlew or heron, horse, and Koïl; and designated by their initial letters or syllables thus, *ni*; *ṛi*; *ga*; *sha*; *ma*; *dha*; *pa*], but the order is sometimes changed, *shaḍja* being placed first, and *nishāda* last), Prāt.; ŚrS.; Saṃgīt; MBh. &c.; a symbolical expression for the number 'seven,' VarBṛS.; a vowel (either *dīrgha*, 'long;' or *hrasva*, 'short;' or *pluta*, 'prolated'), Prāt.; ŚrS.; MBh. &c.; air breathed through the nostrils, ChUp.; N. of Vishṇu, Vishṇ.; (*ā*), f. N. of the chief wife of Brahmā, L.; (*am*), n. a musical note, Sāy. on RV. x, 146, 2; N. of various Sāmans, ĀrshBr. — **kampa**, m. trembling of tone, L. — **kara**, mfn. producing voice, Suśr. — **kshaya**, m. loss of v°, Car. — **gatâdhyāya**, m. N. of the first ch. of the Saṃgīta-darpaṇa and of the Saṃgīta-ratnâkara. — **grāma**, m. the musical scale, gamut, MW. — **gupti**, f. depth of v°, Divyâv. — **ghna**, m. 'voice-destroyer,' N. of a partic. disease of the throat, Suśr. — **cintā**, f. N. of a wk. on vowels, Sarvad. — **cchidra**, n. the sound-hole of a flute, Saṃgīt. — **tattva-camatkāra**, m., **-tattvôdaya**, m., **-tantra**, n. N. of wks. — **tā**, f. the state of (being) voice or a musical sound, Cat. — **dīpta**, mfn. (in augury) inauspicious with regard to voice or sound, VarBṛS. — **nābhi**, m. a kind of flute, Saṃgīt. — **nirṇaya**, m. N. of a wk. (on the accents of the Ṛig-veda, in 21 Ślokas, by Jayanta-svāmin). — **paksha**, mfn. 'sound-winged,' possessing sound as wings, JaimUp. — **pañcāśat**, f. N. of a wk. on Vedic accents. — **pattana**, n. 'abode of accents,' N. of the Sāma-veda. — **paribhāshā**, f. N. of a wk. (on the more ancient notation of the accents or tones in the Sāma-veda, used in South India). — **parivarta**, m. change or modulation of the voice, Mṛicch. — **puraṃjaya**, m. N. of a son of Śesha, VP. — **pṛishṭha**, mfn. having the Svara-sāman for a Pṛishṭha (q. v.), ŚrS. — **prakaraṇa**, n., **-prakriyā**, f., **-prastāra**, m. N. of wks. — **baddha**, mfn. composed in musical measure (said of a song &c.), MW. — **brahman**, n. 'Brahman as manifested in sound,' the sacred texts, BhP. — **bhakti**, f. 'vowel-separation,' a vowel-sound phonetically inserted between *r* or *l* and a following consonant (e. g. *varsha* pronounced *varisha*), Prāt. — **bhaṅga**, m. 'broken articulation,' stammering, L.; hoarseness, HYog. — **bhaṅgin**, m. 'note-separating,' a kind of bird, L. — **bhūta**, mfn. become a vowel (i. e. changed from a semivowel followed by a vowel into *i* or *u*), VPrāt. — **bheda**, m. indistinctness of utterance, hoarseness, Suśr.; simulation of voice (instr. 'in a feigned v°'), Pañcat.; betrayal by one's voice (*-bhaya*, n. 'fear of betraying one's v°'), ib.; difference of accent, Kāś.; difference of musical tones, Inscr. — **bhairava**, m. N. of Tantra wk. — **mañca-nṛitya**, n. (in music) a kind of dance, Saṃgīt. — **mañjarī**, f. N. of a wk. on Vedic accents. — **maṇḍala**, m. or °**ḍalikā**, f. a kind of Viṇā or stringed musical instrument, L. — **mantra-kāṇḍa**, n., **-mela-kalā-nidhi**, f. N. of wks. — **mātrā**, f. strength of sound, Vait. — **yoga**, m. 'sound-combination,' voice, Kād. — **yoni**, m. or f. the Ṛic on which the Svara-sāman is based, ŚāṅkhŚr. — **ratna-kosa**, m., **-ratna-bhāṇḍa**, n. N. of wks. — **lakshaṇa**, n. N. of a treatise (on the accents of the Taittirīya, by Keśa-vārya). — **lāsikā**, f. a flute, pipe, L. — **vat** (*svára-*), mfn. having sound, sonorous, loud, AitBr.; Vait.; having a melodious voice, ŚBr.; having an accent, accentuated, ib.; containing a vowel, SaṃhUp. — **vidhi**, m. N. of a med. wk. — **vibhakti**, f. separation of a vowel (in Sāman-chanting), PañcavBr. — **vaidika**, n., **-vyākhyā**, f. N. of wks. — **śas**, ind. according to the accent, Pat. — **śāstra**, n. N. of a class of wks. on the modulation of sounds or on the passage of the air through the nostrils (esp. as bearing on the prognostication of future events); N. of a wk. on Vedic accents. — **śikshā**, f. N. of wk. — **śuddha**, mfn. correct in musical measure, MW. — **śūnya**, mfn. unmelodious, unmusical, W. — **saṃyoga**, m. = *-yoga*, Mṛicch.; a song, Śak.; the junction of vowels, MW. — **saṃsvāra-vat**, mfn. correct in accent, Ragh. — **saṃkrama**, m. succession of tones (applied to the musical scale, MW.), rise and fall of the voice, modulation of tone, Mṛicch. — **saṃgraha**, m. N. of a wk. on suppression of the voice and breath (for attaining beatitude). — **saṃdarbha**, m. = *-saṃkrama*, Cat. — **saṃdeha-vivāda**, m. a kind of round game, Kād. — **saṃdhi**, m. the junction or coalition of vowels, MW. — **samuccaya**, m. N. of wk. — **sampad**, f. euphony or melody of voice, R. — **sampanna** (*svára-*), mf(*ā*)n. melodious, harmonious, ŚBr.; having a melodious voice, R. — **sāman** (*svára-*), m. N. of the three days before and after the Vishuvat of the Gavām-ayana (i. e. the last three days of the first, and the first three days of the second half-year), Br.; ŚrS.; n. N. of a Sāman, IndSt. — **sāra**, m., **-siṃha**, m., **-siddhânta-kaumudī**, f., **-siddhânta-candrikā**, f., **-siddhânta-mañjarī**, f., **-subodhinī**, f., **-svarūpa**, n. N. of wks. — **han**, m. = *-ghna*, ŚārṅgS. **Svarâṇśa**, m. a half or quarter tone in music, L.; a seventh (see under *svara*), VarBṛS. **Svarâṅka**, m. a kind of musical composition, Saṃgīt. **Svarâṅkuśa**, m. N. of a wk. (= *svara-nirṇaya*). **Svarânta**, mfn. ending in a vowel, VPrāt.; having the Svarita accent on the last syllable, ShaḍvBr. **Svarântara**, n. 'vowel-interval,' the interval between two vowels, hiatus (= *vivṛitti*), MW.; (*e*), ind. between two vowels, ib. **Svarârṇava**, m., °**râvadhāna**, n., °**râshṭaka**, n. N. of wks. **Svarôdaya**, mfn. followed by a vowel, RPrāt.; m. n. N. of a class of wks. (= *svara-śāstra*, q. v.); *-yuddha-nirṇaya*, m., *-vicāra*, m. N. of wks. **Svarôpaghāta**, m. 'voice-destruction,' hoarseness, Hcat.; °*tin*, mfn. suffering from it, ib. **Svarôpadha**, mfn. having a vowel as penultimate letter, RPrāt.

Sváraṇa, mfn. loud-sounding, clear-voiced, RV. i, 18, 1.

Svaras. See *gharmá-svaras*.

Svarí, mfn. noisy, boisterous, RV.

Svarita, mfn. caused to sound, BhP.; sounded, having an accent, accentuated, Lāṭy.; having the Svarita accent, Vait.; Prāt.; Pāṇ.; added, admixed (*-tva*, n.), Naish.; m. n. the Svarita accent (a kind of mixed tone, produced by a combination of high and low tone, and therefore named in Pāṇ. i, 2, 31 *sam-āhāra*, the high and low tones being called *ud-ātta*, 'raised' or 'acute,' and *an-udātta*, 'low' or 'grave;' the Sv° corresponds to the Greek circumflex and is of four kinds, viz. *kshaipra* [as in *vy-āpta* for *vi-āpta*], *jātya* [as in *kvà* for *kúa*], *praślishṭa* [as in *divìva* for *diví iva*], or *abhinihita* [as in *tè'bruvan* for *té abruvan*]; it is marked in RV. by a small upright stroke above a syllable; and when produced by an *udātta* immediately preceding is sometimes called 'a dependent Svarita,' and, when it properly belongs to a word, an 'independent Svarita'), ĀśvŚr.; Prāt.; Pāṇ. — **tva**, n. the state of having the Svarita, TPrāt. — **vat**, mfn. containing the Svarita, VP. — **vākya-paddhati**, f. N. of wk.

Sváritṛi, mfn. sounding, noisy, loud, boisterous, RV.

Svarīyas, v. l. for *svaryas*, ĀrshBr.

Svaryà, mf(*ā*, Ved. *ī*)n. resounding, roaring, crashing, loud, RV.; beneficial to the voice, Suśr.

Svaryas, n. (with Vishṇoḥ) N. of Sāmans, ĀrshBr.

Svārá, m. sound, noise (of a snorting horse), RV.; tone, accent, RPrāt.; the Svarita accent, TPrāt.; mfn. relating to sound or accent, MW.; having the Svarita accent; n. a Sāman ending with the Svarita accent, VS.; PañcavBr.; Lāṭy.

Svāra-sāmika, mfn. (fr. *svara-sāman*), Lāṭy.

Svārāyaṇa, m. patr. fr. *svara*, g. *aśvādi*.

स्वृक्ष *sv-ṛiksha*, n. an auspicious asterism, Hcat.

स्वृत *sv-ṛita* (√*ṛi* used in explaining *svàr*), Nir. ii, 14.

स्वृतीक *svṛitīka*, n. = *udaka*, water (cf. *smṛitīka*), Naigh. i, 12.

स्वृद्ध *sv-ṛiddha*, mfn. very prosperous or fortunate, BhP.

स्वॄ *svṝ*, v. l. for √*sṝ*.

स्वेक् *svek*, v. l. for √*srek*.

स्वेक *sveka*, m. (used in explaining *su-meka*), ŚBr.

स्वेच्छ *svéccha* &c. See p. 1277, col. 3.

स्वेतव्य *sv-ètavya*, n. (impers.) it is easy to be gone, TS.

स्वेद *sveda* &c. See col. 1.

स्वेष्ट *svéshṭa*, *svâitu*, *svâisha*. See p. 1277, col. 3.

स्वैर *svâira* &c. See p. 1279, col. 1.

स्वैरिन्ध्री *svairindhrī*, f. = *sairindhrī*, L.

स्वोचित *svôcita, svôttha* &c. See p. 1278, col. 1.

स्वोजस् *sv-ójas*, mfn. very strong or powerful, RV.

स्वोपश *sv-opaśa*, mf(*ā*)n. having beautiful locks of hair(?), MaitrS. (v. l. *sv-aupaśa*). **Sv-aupaśá**, mf(*ā*)n. id., VS.

स्वोरस् *svôras*, n. See p. 1278, col. 1.

स्वोरस *svorasa*, m. a husk, shell; n. the sediment of oily substances ground with a stone, L.

स्वोवश्वीय *svovaśvīya*, w.r. for *śvo-vasīyasa* (q. v.)

ह HA.

ह 1. **ha**, the thirty-third and last consonant of the Nāgarī alphabet (in Pāṇini's system belonging to the guttural class, and usually pronounced like the English *h* in *hard;* it is not an original letter, but is mostly derived from an older *gh*, rarely from *dh* or *bh*). — **kāra**, m. the letter or sound *ha*, MW. — **tva**, n. the state of the letter *ha*, ib.

ह 2. *ha* (only L.), m. a form of Śiva or Bhairava (cf. *nakulīśa*); water; a cipher (i. e. the arithmetical figure which symbolizes 0); meditation, auspiciousness; sky, heaven, paradise; blood; dying; fear; knowledge; the moon; Vishṇu; war, battle; horripilation; a horse; pride; a physician; cause, motive; = *pāpa-haraṇa*; = *sakopa-vāraṇa*; = *śushka*; (also *ā*, f.) laughter; (*ā*), f. coition; a lute; (*am*), n. the Supreme Spirit; pleasure, delight; a weapon; the sparkling of a gem; calling, calling to; the sound of a lute; (ind.) = *aham* (?), IndSt.; mfn. mad, drunk.

ह 3. *ha*, ind. (prob. orig. identical with 2. *gha*, and used as a particle for emphasizing a preceding word, esp. if it begins a sentence closely connected with another; very frequent in the Brāhmaṇas and Sūtras, and often translatable by) indeed, assuredly, verily, of course, then &c. (often with other particles, e. g. with *tv eva, u, sma, vai* &c.; *na ha*, 'not indeed;' also with interrogatives and relatives, e. g. *yad dha*, 'when indeed;' *kad dha*, 'what then?' sometimes with impf. or pf. [cf. Pāṇ. iii, 2, 116]; in later language very commonly used as a mere expletive, esp. at the end of a verse), RV. &c. &c.

ह 4. *ha*, mf(*ā*)n. (fr. √*han*) killing, destroying, removing (only ifc.; see *arāti-, vṛitra-, śatru-ha* &c.)

ह 5. *ha*, mf(*ā*)n. (fr. √3. *hā*) abandoning, deserting, avoiding (ifc.; see *an-oka-* and *vāpī-ha*); (*ā*), f. abandonment, desertion, L.

हंस 1. *haṇsá*, m. (ifc. f. *ā*; accord. to Uṇ. iii, 62 fr. √1. *han*, 'to go?') a goose, gander, swan, flamingo (or other aquatic bird, considered as a bird of passage; sometimes a mere poetical or mythical bird, said in RV. to be able to separate Soma from water, when these two fluids are mixed, and in later literature, milk from water when these two are mixed; also forming in RV. the vehicle of the Aśvins, and in later lit° that of Brahmā; ifc. also = 'best or chief among'), RV. &c. &c.; the soul or spirit (typified by the pure white colour of a goose or swan, and migratory like a goose; sometimes 'the Universal Soul or Supreme Spirit,' identified with Virāj, Nārāyaṇa, Vishṇu, Śiva, Kāma, and the Sun; du. 'the universal and the individual Spirit;' accord. to Sāy. resolvable into *ahaṃ sa*, 'I am that'), Up.; MBh.; Hariv. &c.; one of the vital airs, L.; a kind of ascetic, MBh.; Hariv.; BhP.; a man of supernatural qualities born under a partic. constellation, VarBṛS.; an unambitious monarch, L.; a horse, Naigh. i, 14; an excellent draught-ox (accord. to some, 'a buffalo'), VarBṛS.; a mountain, L.; a temple of a partic. form, VarBṛS.; a kind of Mantra or mystical text, Cat.; silver, L.; envy, malice, L.; N. of two metres, Col.; (in music) a kind of measure, Saṃgīt.; a mystical N. of the letter *h*, Cat.; a spiritual preceptor, W.; N. of a Deva-gandharva, Hariv.; of a Dānava, ib.; of a son of Brahmā, BhP.; of a son of Vasu-deva, ib.; of a son of A-rishṭā, MBh.; of a son of Brahma-datta and general of Jarā-saṃdha, ib.; of various authors &c., Cat.; of one of the Moon's horses, VP.; of a mountain, Pur.; pl. N. of the Brāhmans in Plaksha-dvīpa, BhP.; (*ī*), f. a female goose, Mṛicch.; Kathās.; N. of various metres, Śrutab.; Chandom.; Col.; of a daughter of Bhagīratha and wife of Kautsa, MBh.; of a courtezan, Rājat. [Cf. Gk. χήν; Lat. *anser* for *hanser;* Lit. *żąsìs;* Germ. *Gans;* Angl. Sax. *gôs;* Eng. *goose*.] — **kākīya**, mfn. (fr. *haṇsa-kāka*) relating to a goose and a crow (as a partic. fable), MBh. — **kāntā**, f. 'gander-loved,' a female goose, L. — **kālī-tanaya**, m. a buffalo (see *kālī-t°*), L. — **kīlaka**, m. a partic. form of sexual union (v. l. *-nīlaka*), L. — **kūṭa**, m. 'swan's peak,' N. of one of the peaks of the Himâlaya, MBh.; Hariv.; the hump on the shoulder of the Indian ox, L. — **ga**, m. 'going or riding on a swan,' N. of Brahmā, L. — **gati**, mfn. having a swan's gait, Vikr. — **gadgadā**, f. 'prattling like a swan,' a sweetly speaking woman, L. — **gamana**, n. the gait of a swan or goose, MW.; (*ā*), f. N. of a Surâṅganā, Siṇhâs. — **gāminī**, f. 'walking like a swan,' a graceful woman, Mn. iii, 10. — **guhya**, n. 'the mystery of the Universal Soul,' N. of a partic. hymn, BhP. — **cakra-praśna**, m. N. of wk. — **candrâṇśu**, m. pl. the rays of the sun and the moon, MBh. — **cara-svârôdaya**, m. N. of wks. — **cihna-dukūla-vat**, mfn. clad in a garment woven with representations of geese, Ragh. — **cūḍa**, m. N. of a Yaksha, MBh. — **cchattra**, n. dry ginger, L. — **ja**, m. 'swan-born,' N. of one of Skanda's attendants, MBh. — **jātīya**, mfn. belonging to the tribe of birds called Haṇsa, anserine, Pañcat. — **jihva**, m. 'goose-tongued,' N. of a man, pl. his family, Saṃskārak. — **tā**, f. the being a goose, Kathās. — **tīrtha**, n. N. of a Tīrtha, Cat. — **tūla**, n. (L.), — **tūlikā**, f. (Nalac.) 'g°-cotton,' the soft feathers or down of a goose. — **tva**, n. = *-tā*, Kathās. — **dāhana**, n. aloe wood, L. — **dūta**, m. n. N. of two poems (by Kavīndrâcārya Sarasvatī and by Rūpa Gosvāmin). — **dvāra**, n. N. of a pass near Lake Mānasa. — **dvīpa**, m. n. N. of an island, Kathās. — **dhvaja**, m. N. of a king, Cat. — **nāda**, m. the cackling or cry of a goose or swan (thought to have something of a sacred character); (in music) a kind of measure, Saṃgīt.; N. of a Vidyā-dhara, Bālar.; °*dôpanishad*, f. N. of an Upanishad (= *haṇsôp°*). — **nādin**, mfn. making a noise like a g° or swan, cackling; (*inī*), f. a graceful woman (one of the various classes into which women are divided), L. — **nābha**, m. N. of a mountain, MārkP. — **nidāna**, n. N. of a med. wk. — **nīlaka**, see *-kīlaka*. — **paksha**, m. a partic. position of the hand, Cat. — **patha**, m. pl. N. of a people (v. l. *-pada*), MBh. — **pada**, n. goose-foot (as a mark), Nar.; a partic. weight (= *karsha*), ŚārṅgS.; m. pl., see prec.; (*ā*), f. a kind of Svara-bhakti, MāṇḍŚ.; (*ī*), f. N. of various plants (accord. to L. 'a species of Mimosa and Cissus Pedata'), Car.; a kind of metre, Col.; N. of an Apsaras, VP. — **padikā**, f. N. of the first wife of Dushyanta (v. l. *haṇsa-vatī*), Śak. — **paramêśvara**, m. N. of a Tantra wk. — **pāda**, m. the foot of a goose, MW.; (*ā*), f. N. of an Apsaras, VP.; w. r. for *haṇsa-padā*; (*ī*), f. N. of a plant = (or w. r. for) *haṇsa-padī*; (*am*), n. vermilion, L.; quicksilver, L. — **pādikā**, f. a kind of plant (= *-padī*), L. — **pāla**, m. N. of a king, Inscr. — **pura**, n. N. of a town, L. — **prapatana**, n. N. of a Tīrtha, MBh. — **poṭṭalī**, f. a partic. mixture, Rasêndr. — **prabodhā**, f. N. of a Surâṅganā, Siṇhâs. — **bīja**, n. a goose's egg, L. — **bhūpāla**, m. N. of an author, Cat. — **maṇḍūraka**, n. a partic. mixture, Cat. — **mārga**, m. pl. N. of a people (B. *hanyamāna*), MBh. — **mālā**, f. a line or flight of Haṇsas, flock of wild geese &c., Kum.; a kind of goose or duck (with dark grey wings), L.; a kind of metre, Col. — **māshā**, f. Glycine Debilis, L. — **māhêśvara**, m. N. of a Tantra wk. (cf. *-paramêśv°*). — **mukha**, mf(*ī*)n. formed like a goose's beak, ŚrS. — **mauna**, n. N. of wk. — **yāna**, n. a goose or swan as a vehicle, a car drawn by swans, Kathās.; BhP.; mf(*ī*)n. riding on a swan, Cat. — **yukta**, mfn. drawn by swans (said of the chariot of Brahmā), MW. — **yuvan**, m. a young goose or swan, ib. — **ratha**, m. 'whose vehicle is a Haṇsa,' N. of Brahmā, L.; of a man, Rājat. — **rāja**, m. 'king of geese,' a large gander, Hit.; N. of a man, Rājat.; of various authors, Cat. — **rāma-praśna**, m. N. of a treatise on augury (cf. *cakra-pr°*). — **ruta**, n. the cackling of geese, Suśr.; a kind of metre, Col. — **roman**, n. = *-tūla*, HPariś. — **lipi**, f. a partic. mode of writing, Jain. — **līla**, m. (in music) a kind of measure, Saṃgīt. — **lomaśa**, n. green sulphate of iron, L. — **lohaka**, n. brass, L. — **vaktra**, m. 'swan-beaked,' N. of one of Skanda's attendants, MBh. — **vat**, mfn. possessing geese &c.; containing the word *haṇsa*, AitBr.; (*atī*), f. a verse containing the word *haṇsa* (applied to RV. iv, 40, 5, in which the sun in the form of Dadhi-krā, here called Haṇsa, is identified with Para-brahman or the Supreme Being; this verse is also found in VS. x, 24; xii, 14 &c.), ĀpŚr.; Cissus Pedata, L.; N. of the first wife of Dushyanta (v. l. for *-padikā*), Śak.; of the murderess of Vīra-sena, Hcar.; of a town and district (= Pegu), Buddh. — **vāraṇa-gāminī**, f. a woman who walks like a swan and young elephant, MW. — **vāha**, mfn. riding on a Haṇsa, BhP. — **vāhana**, m. 'id.,' N. of Brahmā, ib. — **vikrānta-gāmitā**, f. having a walk like the gait of a swan (one of the 80 minor marks of a Buddha), Dharmas. 84. — **viveka**, m. N. of wk. — **vega**, m. N. of a man, Hcar. — **śyeta**, mf(*enī*)n. white like a swan, Kir. — **śreṇi**, f. a line or row of geese, Ragh. — **saṃghârāma**, m. N. of a temple, Buddh. — **saṃdeśa**, m. N. of a poem by Vedântâcārya. — **sāci**, m. a kind of bird, TS. **Haṇsâṇśu**, mfn. 'swan-rayed,' swan-coloured, white, MW. **Haṇsâkāra**, mfn. having the form of a Haṇsa, VarBṛS. **Haṇsâṅghri**, m. 'goose-footed,' vermilion, L.; (*ī*), f. a kind of Mimosa, L. **Haṇsâdhirūḍhā**, f. 'mounted on a swan,' N. of Sarasvatī (as wife of Brahmā), L. **Haṇsâbhikhya**, n. 'bright as a swan,' silver, L. **Haṇsârūḍha**, mf(*ā*)n. mounted on a swan (applied to Varuṇa, Brahmā, and Sarasvatī), L. **Haṇsâvatī**, f. N. of a woman, Daś.; of Pegu, Inscr. **Haṇsâvalī**, f. = *haṇsa-śreṇī*, Kathās.; N. of a woman, Vīrac. **Haṇsâshṭaka**, n. N. of a poem. **Haṇsâsya**, m. a partic. position of the hand, Cat. **Haṇsâhvayā**, f. a kind of Mimosa, Suśr. **Haṇsêśvara-tīrtha**, n. N. of a Tīrtha, Cat. **Haṇsôdaka**, n. a kind of cordial liquor (described as a sort of infusion of cardamoms), Car. **Haṇsôpanishad**, f. N. of an Upanishad belonging to the Atharva-veda (cf. *haṇsanādôp°*).

2. **Haṇsa**, Nom. P. °*sati*, to act or behave like a swan, Subh.

Haṇsaka, m. a goose, gander, swan, flamingo (also 'a little or poor goose &c.'), Kāv.; BhP.; (in music) a kind of measure, Saṃgīt.; N. of a son of Brahma-datta, Hariv.; m. n. an ornament for the feet or ankles (said to be formed like a goose's foot), Śiś. vii, 23; (*ikā*), f. a female goose, Kathās.; N. of a mythical cow, MBh. — **vatī**, f. a proper N., g. *ajirâdi* (v. l.)

Haṇsakāyana, m. pl. N. of a people (cf. *hāṇs°*), MBh.

Haṇsāya, Nom. Ā. °*yate*, to be like a goose or swan, Prasannar.

Haṇsin, mfn. (prob.) containing the Universal Soul (said of Kṛishṇa), Pañcar.; (*inī*), f. a partic. manner of walking, Saṃgīt.

Haṇsira, m. a kind of mouse (cf. *hasira*), Suśr.

Haṇsī, f. a female goose &c. (see 1. *haṇsa*). — **yugala**, m. a pair of geese or ducks, MW.

Haṇsīya, mfn., g. *gahâdi*.

हंहो *haṃho*, ind. (cf. *ham*) a vocative particle (corresponding to 'ho!' 'hollo!' accord. to some also expressing haughtiness or contempt; in dram. a form of address used by equals to each other), MBh.; Kāv. &c.

हक् *hak*, ind. (onomat.) the sound *hak*. — **kāra**, m. making the sound *hak*, calling, calling to, L.

Hakka, m. calling to an elephant, L.; (*ā*), f. an owl, VarBṛS.

Hakkaya, Nom. P. °*yati*, to call, call to, Pañcad.

Hakkā-pradhānā, f. (used in explaining *nishṭhura-bhāshā*), Śil.

Hakkā-hakka, m. calling on, challenging, Pañcat.

हचि *haci*. See *sundara-haci*, p. 1227, col. 1.

हचिपुर *haci-pura*, n. N. of a town, Buddh.

हजदेश *haja-deśa*, m. N. of a district, Cat.

Hajāja and **hajāji**, N. of a place, ib.

हञ्चा *hañcā*. See *karahañcā*, p. 255, col. 1.

हञ्ज *hañja*, f. (accord. to some = *kanyā*) a female servant (voc. °*je*, often used in dram. as a particle of address), L.

Hañjikā, f. a female attendant, chamber-maid (-*tva*, n.), Kāśīkh.; Clerodendrum Siphonantus, L.

हञ्जि *hañji*, m. a sneeze, sneezing (= *kshut*), L.

हट् *haṭ*, cl. 1. P. *haṭati*, to shine, be bright, Dhātup. ix, 25.

हट *haṭa*, w.r. for *haṭha*.

हटक *haṭaka*, w.r. for *hāṭaka*.

हटपर्णी *haṭaparṇī*, w.r. for *haṭha-parṇī*.

हट्ट *haṭṭa*, m. (cf. *aṭṭa*) a market, fair, Pañcat.; Vet.; (*ī*), f. a petty market or fair, L. **-candra**, m. N. of a grammarian (often quoted). **-cauraka**, m. a thief who steals from fairs and markets, L. **-vāhinī**, f. a gutter in a market-place, Subh. **-vilāsinī**, f. 'dallying in market-places,' a wanton woman, prostitute, W.; a sort of perfume (= *dhamanī*), L.; turmeric (= *haridrā*), L. **-veśmālī**, f. a row of market houses, L. **Haṭṭâdhyaksha**, m. the surveyor of a market, L.

हठ् *haṭh* (only in Dhātup. ix, 50; prob. artificial), cl. 1. P. *haṭhati*, to leap, jump; to be wicked; to treat with violence, oppress (cf. next); to bind to a post.

Haṭha, m. violence, force (ibc., *ena*, and *āt*, 'by force, forcibly'), R.; Rājat.; Kathās. &c.; obstinacy, pertinacity (ibc. and *āt*, 'obstinately, persistently'), Pañcat.; Kathās.; absolute or inevitable necessity (as the cause of all existence and activity; ibc., *āt*, and *ena*, 'necessarily, inevitably, by all means'), MBh.; Kāv. &c.; = *haṭha-yoga*, Cat.; oppression, W.; rapine, ib.; going in the rear of an enemy, L.; Pistia Stratiotes, L. **-karman**, n. an act of violence, Siṇhâs. **-kāmuka**, m. a violent suitor of (comp.), Kathās. **-tattva-kaumudī**, f., **-dīpa**, m., **-dīpikā**, f. (= *-pra-dīpikā*) N. of wks. **-parṇī**, f. Blyxa Octandra, L. **-pra-dīpikā**, f. (cf. *-yoga*) N. of wk. **-yoga**, m. a kind of forced Yoga or abstract meditation (forcing the mind to withdraw from external objects; treated of in the Haṭha-pradīpikā by Svātmārāma and performed with much self-torture, such as standing on one leg, holding up the arms, inhaling smoke with the head inverted &c.); *-viveka*, m., *-saṃgraha*, m. N. of wks. **-yogin**, m. an adherent of the Haṭha-yoga, Cat. **-ratnâvalī**, f. N. of wk. **-vidyā**, f. the science or method of forced meditation, Cat. **-śarman**, m. N. of a Brāhman, Kathās. **-saṃketa-candrikā**, f. N. of two wks. **Haṭhâdeśin**, mfn. prescribing forcible measures against (gen.), Mcar. **Haṭhâyāta**, mfn. become absolutely necessary, indispensable, Kathās. **Haṭhâlu**, m. Pistia Stratiotes, L. **Haṭhâśleshа**, m. a forcible embrace, Ml.

Haṭhāt-kāra, m. = *balāt-kāra*, ŚivaP.

Haṭhikā, f. (prob.) great noise or din, Daś.

Haṭhin, mfn. obstinately insisting on, Nīlak.

हड *haḍa*, (prob.) w.r. for next, Kāraṇḍ.

हडि *haḍi*, m. wooden fetters, Divyâv.; = next, Cat.

Haḍika, m. a servant of the lowest caste, L.

Haḍḍaka, haḍḍi, haḍḍika, haḍḍipa, m. id., L.

हड्ड *haḍḍa*, n. a bone, L. **-ja**, n. 'produced from bones,' marrow, L.

हड्डचन्द्र *haḍḍa-candra*, m. = *haṭṭa-c°*, Col.

हढक्क *haḍhakka*, m. n. a small hand drum, rattle, L.

हण्ड *haṇḍa*. See *kūla-haṇḍa*.

Haṇḍaka. See *kūla-haṇḍaka*.

Haṇḍikā, f. an earthen pot or boiler, Subh. **-suta**, m. a small earthen pot, L.

Haṇḍī, f. = *haṇḍikā*, MW.

हण्डा *haṇḍā*, f. (in dram.) a low-caste female (voc. °*de* often in address; cf. *hañjā*), L.

हत *hata* &c. See col. 2.

हथिण्डवग्राम *hathiṇḍavagrāma*, m. N. of a village, Inscr.

हद् *had*, cl. 1. P. Ā. (Dhātup. xxiii, 8) *hadati*, °*te* (pf. *jahade*; aor. *ahatta* &c., Gr.), to evacuate, discharge excrement, BhP.; Sarasv.; Kathârṇ.: Caus. *hādayati*, Gr.: Desid. *jihatsate*, ib.: Intens. *jāhadyate*, *jāhatti*, ib. [Cf. Gk. χέζω.]

Hadana, n. evacuation of excrement or ordure, L.

Hanna, mfn. evacuated (as excrement), L.

Hādi, m. or f. a spider (= *lūtā*), L.

हद्द *hadda*, m. or *haddā*, f. (Arab.) N. of a division of a zodiacal sign (thirty such divisions or degrees are specified; cf. *triṇśâṇśa*), IndSt.; Cat. **Haddêśa**, m. 'lord of a thirtieth division of a zodiacal sign,' (prob.) a planet, ib.

हन् 1. *han*, cl. 2. P. (Dhātup. xxiv, 2) *hanti* (3. du. *hatáḥ*, 3. pl. *ghnanti*; rarely Ā. *hate*, 3. pl. *ghnate*; and cl. 1. *hanati*, Ved. also *jighnate*, °*ti*; Pot. *hanyāt*, Br. also *hánīta*, *ghnīta*; Impv. *jahí*, TĀr. *handhí*; impf. *áhan*, Ved. and ep. also *ahanat*, *ahanan*, *aghnanta*; p. *jaghnat*, *ghnamāna*, MBh.; pf. *jaghā́na*, *jaghnúḥ*, Br. and ep. also *jaghne*, °*nire*, Subj. *jaghánat*, RV.; p. *jaghnivás*, Ved. also *jaghanvás*; aor. *ahānīt*, JaimBr. [cf. √*vadh*]; fut. *hantā*, MBh.; *haṇsyati*, ib.; *hanishyáti*, °*te*, AV. &c.; inf. *hántum*, Ved. also *hántave*, °*tavaí*, °*toḥ*; ind. p. *hatvā́*, Ved. also °*tvī́*, °*tvāya*, *-hatya*; *-hanya*, MBh.; *-ghā́tam*, Br. &c.), to strike, beat (also a drum), pound, hammer (acc.), strike &c. upon (loc.), RV. &c. &c.; to smite, slay, hit, kill, mar, destroy, ib.; to put to death, cause to be executed, Mn.; Hit.; to strike off, Kathās.; to ward off, avert, MBh.; to hurt, wound (the heart), R.; to hurl (a dart) upon (gen.), RV.; (in astron.) to touch, come into contact, VarBṛS.; to obstruct, hinder, Rājat.; to repress, give up, abandon (anger, sorrow &c.), Kāv.; BhP.; (?) to go, move, Naigh. ii, 14: Pass. *hanyáte* (ep. also °*ti*; aor. *avadhi* or *aghāni*), to be struck or killed, RV. &c. &c.: Caus. *ghātayati*, °*te* (properly a Nom. fr. *ghāta*, q. v.; aor. *ajīghatat* or *ajīghanat*), to cause to be slain or killed, kill, slay, put to death, punish, Mn.; MBh. &c.; to notify a person's death (*kaṇsaṃ ghātayati* = *kaṇsa-vadham ācashṭe*), Pāṇ. iii, 1, 26, Vārtt. 6, Pat.; to mar, destroy, MBh.; Pañcat. (v. l.): Desid. *jighāṇsati*, °*te* (Pot. *jighāṇsīyat*, MBh.; impf. *ajighāṇsīḥ*, ŚBr.), to wish to kill or destroy, RV. &c. &c.: Intens. *jáṅghanti* (RV.; p. *jaṅghanat*, *jáṅghnat* or *ghánighnat*), *jaṅghanyate* (with pass. sense, MuṇḍUp.), *jeghnīyate* (Pāṇ. vii, 4, 31), to strike = tread upon (loc. or acc.), RV.; to slay, kill, ib.; to dispel (darkness), destroy (evil, harm), ib.; to hurt, injure, wound, MuṇḍUp. [Cf. Gk. θείνω, θάνατος; φόνος, ἔπεφνον, πέφαται; Lat. *de-fendere*, *of-fendere*; Lit. *genu*, *gìti*; Slav. *gŭnati*.]

Ha. See 4. *ha*, p. 1286, col. 1.

Hatá, mfn. struck, beaten (also said of a drum), smitten, killed, slain, destroyed, ended, gone, lost (often ibc. = 'destitute of,' 'bereft of,' '-less'), RV. &c. &c.; injured, marred, hurt, wounded (lit. and fig.), MBh.; Kathās.; struck off (as a head), R.; knocked out (as an eye), ib.; hit by (instr. or comp.), Kāv.; Kathās.; whirled up, raised (as dust), Śak.; visited or afflicted or tormented by, struggling with, suffering from (instr. or comp.), ŚBr.; ChUp.; MBh. &c.; (in astron.) touched, come into contact, VarBṛS.; violated (sexually, as a woman), MBh. viii, 2037; ruined, undone, hopeless, miserable, wretched (of persons and things; cf. comp.), Mn.; MBh. &c.; worthless, useless, ib.; defective, Sāh.; cheated, deceived, Kuval.; deprived of, lapsed from (*-tas* or comp.), MBh.; R.; (in arithm.) multiplied, Āryabh.; (*ā*), f. a violated woman (see above); a despised girl unfit for marriage, L.; (*am*), n. striking, killing, hurting, W.; multiplication, ib. [Cf. Gk. φατός, 'slain.'] **-kaṇṭaka**, mfn. freed from thorns (or enemies), MBh. **-kilbisha**, mfn. freed from sins, Mn. iv, 243. **-citta** (W.), **-cetas** (R.), mfn. bereft of sense, mad, dispirited, perplexed, confounded. **-cchāya**, mfn. dimmed in lustre, bereft of beauty, Kathās. **-jalpita**, n. pl. useless talk, Sāh. **-jīvana**, n. a blighted or wrecked life, Daś. **-jīvita**, n. id., Amar.; despair of life, W.; mfn. deprived of life or hope, overcome with despair, ib. **-jñāna**, mfn. deprived of consciousness, MW. **-jyotir-niśītha**, m. a night in which the stars are extinguished, starless night, ib. **-tāpa**, mfn. freed from heat, cooled, W. **-trapa**, mfn. devoid of shame, shameless, BhP. **-tvishа** or **-tvish**, mfn. = *-cchāya*, MBh.; R.; Bcar. **-daiva**, mfn. ill-fated, ill-starred, luckless, MW. **-dvish**, mfn. one who has slain his enemies, ib. **-dhī**, mfn. = *-citta*, BhP. **-dhvānta**, mfn. freed from darkness, ib. **-paramârtha**, mfn. neglectful of the highest truth (said of the senses), Bhartṛ. **-pitṛi**, mfn. one whose father has been slain, Pāṇ. v, 4, 158, Sch. **-putra** (*hatá-*), mfn. one whose son or sons have been killed, TS.; ŚBr. **-prabha**, mfn. = *-cchāya*, MBh. **-prabhāva**, mfn. bereft of power, MW. **-pramāda**, mfn. freed from carelessness, Kir. **-pravīra**, mfn. whose chief warriors are slain, MW. **-prâya**, mfn. almost killed, ib. **-bāndhava**, mfn. deprived or destitute of relations, ib. **-buddhi**, mfn. = *-citta*, Śiś. **-bhaga**, mfn. ill-starred, ill-fated, luckless, BhP. **-bhāgya**, mfn. id., MW. **-bhrātṛi** (*hatá-*), mfn. one whose brother has been slain, AV. **-mati**, mfn. = *-citta*, Dhūrtan. **-mātṛi** (*hata-*), mfn. one whose mother has been slain, AV. **-māna**, mfn. free from pride or arrogance, BhP. **-mānasa**, mfn. = *-citta*, Vcar. **-mūrkha**, m. an excessive fool, blockhead, L. **-medhas**, mfn. = *-citta*, MW. **-yuddha**, mfn. destitute of martial spirit, BhP. **-ratha**, m. a chariot whose horses and charioteer are slain, MW. **-lakshaṇa**, mfn. deprived of auspicious marks, unlucky, MārkP. **-varcas** (*hatá-*), mfn. bereft of vigour or power, decayed, AV. **-vikramôdyama**, mfn. bereft of strength and energy, Ṛitus. **-vidhi**, m. evil fate, Bhartṛ.; Śiś. &c.; mfn. ill-fated, ill-starred, Dharmav. (conj.) **-vinaya**, mfn. lost to a sense of propriety, MW. **-vīrya**, mfn. one who has lost his virility or vigour, Kum. **-vṛitta**, mfn. defective in metre (*-tā*, f.), Kpr.; Sāh. **-vṛishṇi** (*hatá-*), f. whose bull or lord (i.e. Vṛitra) has been slain (said of the waters), RV. iv, 17, 3. **-vega**, mfn. whose impetus or force has been impeded, R. **-vrīḍa**, mfn. = *-trapa*, Amar. **-śishṭa**, mfn. left or remaining out of the slain, left surviving, MBh.; *-jana*, m. a survivor, ib. **-śesha**, mfn. = *-śishṭa*, ib. **-śrī**, mfn. whose prosperity is blighted, reduced to penury, MW. **-sampada**, mfn. id., ib. **-sammada**, mfn. whose pleasures are destroyed or marred, ib. **-sarva-yodha**, mfn. having all the warriors slain, ib. **-sâdhvasa**, mfn. freed from fear, ib. **-sūta**, mfn. one whose charioteer is slain, ib. **-strīka**, mfn. one who has killed a woman, Mṛicch. **-svara**, mfn. one who has lost his voice, hoarse, Bhpr. **-svasṛi** (*hatá-*), mfn. one whose sister has been slain, AV. **-hima**, mfn. one who has destroyed frost (accord. to others, m. 'hard frost'), Mālav. v, 7. **-hṛidaya**, n. a cursed or broken heart, Śāntiś. **Hatâghaśaṇsa**, mfn. one whose enemies are destroyed, VS. **Hatâdhimantha**, mfn. free from disease of the eye or from loss of sight, Suśr. **Hatâroha**, mfn. (an elephant) whose riders are slain, MW. **Hatâvaśesha**, m. pl. those left of the slain, ib. **Hatâśa**, mf(*ā*)n. whose hopes are destroyed, desperate, Amar.; hopeless, i. e. wretched, foolish, stupid, wicked, miserable, Ratnâv.; Prab.; unfruitful, infertile, barren, W. **Hatâśraya**, mfn. one whose refuge is destroyed (others, 'whose camp is destroyed'), Bcar. xiii, 70. **Hatâśva**, mfn. one whose horse or horses have been killed, W. **Hatêkshaṇa**, mfn. one whose sight is destroyed, blind, Bcar. viii, 7. **Hatâinas**, mfn. = *hata-kilbisha*, BhP. **Hatôttara**, mfn. giving no answer, Kāv. **Hatôdyama**, mfn. one whose efforts are crushed, broken in purpose, Bcar. xiii, 71 (conj.) **Hatâujas**, mfn. whose vigour is destroyed, weakened, debilitated, MBh.; R.; m. a kind of fever, Suśr.

Hataka, mf(*ikā*)n. struck, hit, afflicted by (ifc.; see *daiva-*); cursed, wretched, miserable (ifc., e. g. *Cāṇakya-h°*, 'the wretched Cāṇakya'), Mṛicch.; Mudr. &c.; m. a low person, coward, L.

Hati, f. striking, a stroke or blow with (comp.), Git.; Sarasv.; killing, destroying, destruction, removal, MBh.; Kāv. &c.; disappearance, loss, absence, Kap.; (in arithm.) multiplication, Āryabh., Sch.

Hatu, (prob.) m. winter, L.

Hatnú, mfn. destructive, fatal, mortal, RV.; m. a weapon, L.; disease, L.

Hatya, n. (ifc.) and **hatyā**, f. killing, slaying, slaughter, Mn.; MBh. &c.

Hatru, mfn. hurtful, mischievous (= *hiṇsra*), L.

Hatvāya, hatvī. See root, col. 2.

Hátha, m. a blow, stroke, RV.; killing, slaughter, ib.; a man stricken with despair, Uṇ. ii, 2, Sch.

2. **Han**, mf(*ghnī*)n. killing, a killer, slayer (only ifc.; see *ari-*, *tamo-han* &c.)

Hana, mf(*ī*)n. id. (see *vīra-hana*); m. killing, slaughter (see *su-hana*); (*ā*), f. (see *dur-hánā*).

Hanana, mf(*ī*)n. killing, a killer, slayer, Hariv.; (prob.) m. a drum-stick, ŚāṅkhŚr.; a kind of worm, L.; n. the act of striking or hitting, Nir. i, 1; 7; striking off, Mālatīm.; killing, destroying, removing, dispelling, Hariv.; Kāv.; BhP.; multiplication, Āryabh., Sch. **-śīla**, mfn. of a murderous disposition, cruel, MW.

1. **Hananīya**, mfn. to be struck or beaten or killed, worthy of death, W.

2. **Hananīya**, Nom. P. °yati = hananam icchati (Desid. *jihananīyishati*), Pāṇ. vii, 3, 55, Vārtt. 1, Pat.

Hananīyaka, mfn. (fr. prec.), Pat.

Hani, m. or f. a weapon, L.

Hániyas, mfn. more or most destructive, MaitrS.

1. **Hanu**, f. (only L.) 'anything which destroys or injures life,' a weapon; death; disease; various kinds of drugs; a wanton woman, prostitute; m. N. of a partic. mixed tribe, L.

Hanusha, m. anger, wrath, L.; a Rākshasa, L.

Hanūsha, m. a Rākshasa, L.

Hantave, °tavai. See root, p. 1287, col. 2.

Hantavya, mfn. to be slain or killed, to be punished with death, Mn.; MBh. &c.; to be violated (as justice), Mn. viii, 15; to be refuted, Hcat.

Hanti, f. the root or verb *han*, Nyāyam.

Hantu, m. killing, slaying (cf. *su-h°* and root), BhP.; m. a bull, L. — **kāma**, mf(*ā*)n. (*hantu* for °*tum*) desirous of killing, Kathās. — **manas**, mfn. intending to kill, MW.

Hantṛi or **hántṛi**, mf(*trī*)n. (the former with gen., the latter with acc.) slaying, killing, a slayer, killer, murderer, robber, disturber, destroyer (*-tva*, n.), RV. &c. &c.; m. a partic. measure of food, W.; (°*trī*), f., see next.

Hantrī-mukha, m. N. of a partic. demon hostile to children, PārGṛ.

Hántva, mfn. to be killed or slain, RV.

Hánman, m. or n. a stroke, blow, thrust, RV.

Hanyamāna, mfn. (pr. p. Pass.) being killed or slain &c.; m. pl. N. of a people (v. l. *haṃsa-mārga*), MBh.

Hānuka, mfn. killing, hurting, mischievous (= *ghātuka*), L.

Hāntra, n. dying, death (= *maraṇa*), Uṇ. iv, 159, Sch.; a Rākshasa, L.; dying, death, L.; war, fight, L.

Hāndra (?), n. dying, death, W.

हनील *hanīla*, m. Pandanus Odoratissimus, L.

हनु 2. *hánu*, f. (accord. to L. also m.; not fr. √*han*, see cognate words below) a jaw (also *hánū*), RV. &c. &c.; n. 'cheek,' a partic. part of a spear-head, ŚBr. [Cf. Gk. γένυς, γένειον, γενείας, γνάθος; Lat. *gena*, *genuīnus*; Goth. *kinnus*; Germ. *Kinn*; Eng. *chin*.] — **graha**, m. 'jaw-seizure,' lock-jaw, Suśr. — **bheda**, m. the gaping or parting asunder of the jaws, BhP.; N. of a partic. form of the end of an eclipse, VarBṛS. — **mat** &c., see below. — **moksha**, m. relaxation of the jaws, Suśr. — **shkambha**, m. = *-graha*, Car. — **saṃhati**, f. (Bhpr.), **-saṃhanana**, n. (Suśr.) a partic. form of lock-jaw. — **stambha**, m. = *-graha*, L. — **svana**, m. sound made with the jaws, Bcar.

Hanavyà, mf(*ā̀*)n. relating to the jaws, AV.

Hanukā, f. a jaw, VarBṛS.

Hanumac, in comp. for °*mat*. — **chata** (for *-śata*), n. N. of a wk. on Bhakti by Śrī-nivāsâcārya.

Hanumaj, in comp. for °*mat*. — **jayantī**, f. the day of full moon of the month Caitra (being the supposed birthday of Hanumat), MW.

Hanu-mat, m. 'having (large) jaws,' N. of a monkey-chief (one of the most celebrated of a host of semi-divine monkey-like beings, who, according to R. i, 16, were created to become the allies of Rāma-candra in his war with Rāvaṇa; Hanumat was held to be a son of Pavana or Māruta, 'the Wind;' and is fabled to have assumed any form at will, wielded rocks, removed mountains, mounted the air, seized the clouds, and rivalled Garuḍa in swiftness of flight; according to other legends, Hanumat was son of Śiva; his mother's name was Añjanā, q.v.; in modern times Han° is a very common village god in the Dekhan, Central and Upper India, cf. RTL. 220), MBh.; R. &c.; a particular sort of monkey, Simia Sinica, W. — **kalpa**, m. N. of a ch. of the Sudarśana-saṃhitā. — **kavaca**, n. 'Hanumat's breast-p[la]te,' N. of various hymns (addressed to the five-headed Han° in various Purāṇas). — **kāvya**, n., **-kīrtana**, n., **-taila-vidhi**, m., **-pañcâṅga**, n., **-paṭala**, m. n. N. of wks. — **paddhati**, f. N. of a wk. in 5 chapters (four of which are taken from the Sudarśana-saṃhitā and the last from the Rāmâyaṇa) describing the rites to be observed in the worship of Hanumat. — **pratishṭhā**, f., **-pratishṭhā-kalpa**, m., **-prabandha**, m., **-prātaḥ-stotra**, n. N. of wks. — **saṃhitā**, f. N. of a poem describing the festivities on the occasion of the presence of Rāma and Sītā at a pastoral dance (*rāsôtsava*) on the banks of the Sarayū. — **sahasra-nāman**, n., **-stotra**, n. N. of wks.

Hanumad, in comp. for °*mat*. — **aṅgada-saṃvāda**, m., **-ashṭaka**, n., **-ashṭôttara-śata-nāman**, n., **-upanishad**, f., **-eka-mukha-kavaca**, n., **-gahvara**, n. (= °*man-mantra-g°*), **-daṇḍaka**, m. or n., **-dīpa**, m., **-durga**, n., **-dvādaśa-nāman**, n., **-bali**, m., **-bāhuka**, m., **-bhāshya**, n., **-rāmâyaṇa**, n., **-vishaya-mantra**, m., **-vrata-kalpa**, m. N. of wks.

Hanumadīya, mfn. written or composed by Hanumat, Cat.; n. N. of wk.

1. **Hanuman**, m. c. for °*mat* (in *hanumâdi*), R.

2. **Hanuman**, in comp. for °*mat*. — **nāṭaka**, n. N. of a drama (containing the story of the Rāmâyaṇa dramatized, = *mahā-n°*, q. v.) — **nighaṇṭu**, m., **-mantra-gahvara**, n. (= °*mad-gahvara*), **-mantrôddhāra**, m., **-mālā-mantra**, m. N. of wks.

Hanumanta, in comp. for °*mat*. — **bhaṭṭīya**, n. N. of a poem. **Hanumantêśvara** and °**ratīrtha**, n. N. of a Tīrtha, Cat.

Hanula, mfn. having strong jaws, g. *sidhmâdi*.

Hanū-mat &c. = *hanu-mat*.

Hānavya, mfn. being in the jaws (as a tooth), Suśr.

Hānu, m. a tooth (v. l. *hālu*), L.

हन्त *hánta*, ind. an exclamation or inceptive particle (expressive of an exhortation to do anything or asking attention, and often translatable by 'come on!' 'here!' 'look!' 'see!' in later language also expressive of grief, joy, pity, haste, benediction &c. and translatable by 'alas!' 'ah!' 'oh!' &c.; often repeated or joined with other particles, e.g. *hā hanta*, *hanta hanta*, *hanta tarhi*), RV. &c. &c. — **kārá**, m. the exclamation *hanta* (a partic. formula of benediction or salutation; also explained as 16 mouthfuls of alms, in ŚBr. among the four teats of the cow, Vāc.), ŚBr.; PārGṛ.; Pur. **Hantôkti**, f. 'saying alas!' tenderness, compassion, MW.

हपुषा *hapushā* or *habushā*, f. N. of a partic. substance forming an article of trade (commonly called Habush, and said to be of a long form and black colour, and smelling like raw meat or fish; it is of two kinds), Car.; Suśr. &c.

हबसोर *habasora*, N. of a place, Cat.

हम् *ham*, ind. an exclamation expressive of anger or courtesy or respect (also *ham bho* or *ham bhoḥ*; cf. *haṃho*), Divyâv.; Jātakam.

हम *hama*, m. a partic. personification, Gaut.

हमीआण *hamīāṇa*, N. of a place, Cat.

हमीपुर्य *hamī-purya*, mfn. coming or derived from Hamī-pura (cf. *hammīra*), Cat.

हम्ब *hamba*, m. N. of a man, Rājat.; (*ā*), f., v. l. for *hambhā*.

Hambīrā. See *naṭṭa-h°*.

Hambhā, f. lowing or bellowing of cattle, MBh.; R. &c. — **rava**, m. id. (*-virāvin*, 'making a lowing or bellowing sound'), MBh. — **śabda**, m. id., Siṇhās.

Hambhāya, Nom. Ā. °*yate*, to low, bellow, MBh.

हम्म् *hamm*, cl. 1. P. *hammati*, to go (accord. to Pat. used in Surāshṭra), Naigh. ii, 14; Dhātup. xiii, 24.

हम्मीर *hammīra*, m. N. of a king of Śākambharī (who ruled from 1301–1365 A.D. and patronized Rāghava-deva, the grandfather of Śārṅgadhara, the author of the anthology, one stanza of which is attributed to him). — **carita**, n. 'Hammīra's deeds,' N. of a Mahā-kāvya by Naya-candra.

हय् *hay*, cl. 1. P. *hayati*, to go, move, Dhātup. xv, 5 (accord. to Vop. also, 'to be weary,' and accord. to others, 'to worship' or 'to sound'). In Naigh. ii, 14 *hayantāt* is enumerated among the *gati-karmāṇah* (cf. *hayat* under √2. *hi*).

हय *háya*, m. (ifc. f. *ā*; fr. √1. *hi*) a horse, RV. &c. &c.; a symbolical expression for the number 'seven' (on account of the 7 horses of the Sun), Śrutab.; the zodiacal sign Sagittarius, VarBṛS.; (in prosody) a foot of four short syllables, proceleusmaticus, Col.; a man of a partic. class, L.; the Yak or Bos Grunniens, L.; N. of Indra, L.; of one of the horses of the Moon, L.; of a son of Sahasra-da, Hariv.; of a son of Śatā-jit, VP.; pl. the family of Haya, MBh.; (*ā* or *ī*), f. a female horse, mare, Hariv.; Kathās.; Physalis Flexuosa, L.; mfn. urging on, driving (see *aśva-hayá*). — **kantharā** and °**rikā**, v. l. for *-kātarā*, °*rikā*, q. v. — **karman**, n. practice or knowledge of horses, MBh. — **kātarā** and °**rikā**, f. a kind of plant, L. — **gandha**, n. black salt (v. l. *hṛidya-g°*), L.; (*ā*), f. (v. l. *hṛidya-g°*) Physalis Flexuosa, L.; another plant (= *aja-modā*), L. — **gardabhi**, m. N. of Śiva, L. — **grīva**, m. 'horse-necked,' N. of a form of Vishṇu (manifested, accord. to one legend, in order to recover the Veda carried off by two Daityas called Madhu and Kaiṭabha), Pañcar.; of a Daitya (also called *Brahma-veda-prahartṛi*, as having carried off the Vedas at the dissolution of the universe caused by Brahmā's sleep at the end of the past Kalpa; in order to recover them, Vishṇu became incarnate as a Matsya or fish, and slew Haya-grīva), Hariv.; Kathās. &c.; of a Rākshasa, R.; of a Tantra deity, Buddh.; of a Rājarshi, MBh.; of a wicked king of the Videhas, MBh.; of a Muni, Cat.; of the supposed author of the Chāndogya Upanishad and various other writers &c., ib.; (*ā*), f. N. of Durgā, L.; (°*va*)*-gadya* and *-daṇḍaka*, n. N. of Stotras; *-pañca-rātra*, n., *-pañjara*, n. N. of wks.; *-prôkta*, mfn. proclaimed or taught by H°, Cat.; *-ripu*, m. 'enemy of H°,' N. of Vishṇu, L.; *-vadha*, m. N. of a poem by Bhartṛi-meṇṭha, Rājat.; *-saṃhitā*, f., *-sahasra-nāma-stotra*, n., *-stotra*, n. N. of wks.; *-han*, m. 'slayer of H°,' N. of Vishṇu, L.; °*vopanishad*, f. N. of an Up°. — **ghna**, m. = *-māra*, L. — **ṃ-kasha**, m. 'impelling horses,' N. of Mātali, L. — **caryā**, f. the roaming of the sacrificial h°, R. — **ochaṭā**, f. a troop of horses, L. — **jña**, m. one who understands the points of a h°, a h°-dealer, groom, jockey (*-tā*, f.), MBh. — **jñāna**, n. knowledge of horses, ib. — **tattva**, n. id.; *-jña*, mfn. acquainted with the nature of horses, ib. — **dānava**, m. 'Dānava in the form of a h°,' N. of Keśin, Hariv. — **dvishat**, m. 'h°-hater,' a buffalo, L. — **nirghosha**, m. the clatter of a horse's hoofs, MW. — **pa**, m. 'horse-keeper,' a groom, VarBṛS.; = next, Kathās. — **pati**, m. 'id.,' N. of a prince, ib. — **puccha**, m. or n. a horse's tail, W.; (*ī*), f. = next, Bhpr. — **pucchikā**, f. Glycine Debilis, L. — **priya**, m. 'dear to h°s,' barley, L.; (*ā*), f. Physalis Flexuosa or Phoenix Sylvestris, L. — **māra** or **-māraka**, m. 'h°-killer,' Nerium Odorum, L. — **māraṇa**, m. 'id.,' Ficus Religiosa, L. — **mukha**, n. a horse's face, R.; N. of a country, Buddh.; (*ī*), f. N. of a Rākshasī, R. — **medha**, m. a h° sacrifice (see *aśva-m°*), VP.; *-yāj*, m. (nom. *-yāṭ*) one who performs a h° s°, MW. — **rūpin**, mfn. horse-shape, ib. — **lālā**, f. h°'s saliva, L. — **līlāvatī**, f. N. of a wk. on h°s (quoted by Malli-nātha). — **vāhana**, m. N. of Revanta (son of the Sun), L.; of Kubera, L.; *-śaṃkara* or *-sa°*, m. Bauhinia Variegata. — **vidyā**, f. = *-jñāna*, Rājat. — **śālā**, f. a horse-stable, L. — **śāstra**, n. (MBh.), **-śikshā**, f. (MatsyaP.) the art of training or managing h°s, hippology. — **śiras**, n. a h°'s head, MBh.; R. &c.; mfn. having a h°'s head (as the sun), MBh.; m. N. of Vishṇu (in the form of Haya-grīva), Hariv.; BhP.; f. N. of a daughter of Puloman, Hariv.; of a daughter of Vaiśvānara (also *-śirā*), Pur.; n. a partic. mythical weapon, R.; Hariv. — **śiśu**, m. a young h°, foal, VarBṛS. — **śīrsha** or °**shan**, mfn. having a horse's head, BhP.; m. Vishṇu in a partic. form (prob. as Haya-grīva; cf. *-śiras*), ib.; *-pañcarātra*, n. N. of a Vaishṇava wk. (chiefly treating of the erection of images and their consecration). — **saṃgrahaṇa**, n. the restraining or curbing or checking of h°s, MBh. — **skandha**, m. a troop of horses, L. — **hartṛi**, m. the stealer of a horse, VP. **Hayâṅga**, m. Sagittarius (the zodiacal sign), VarBṛS. **Hayâdhyaksha**, m. 'superintendent of h°s,' a head groom, L. **Hayânanā**, f. 'horse-faced,' N. of a Yoginī, Hcat. **Hayâyur-veda**, m. veterinary science, MW. **Hayâri**, m. 'h°-foe,' Nerium Odorum, L. **Hayârūḍha**, m. 'mounted on a horse,' a rider, W. **Hayâroha**, m. id., MBh.; Kathās.; n. horsemanship, riding, W. **Hayâlaya**, m. a horse-stable, L. **Hayâśanā**, f. Boswellia Thurifera, L. **Hayâsya** or °**syaka**, m. 'horse-mouthed,' Vishṇu in a partic. manifestation (cf. *haya-grīva* and *-śiras*), BhP. **Hayêshṭa**, m. 'loved by horses,' barley, L. **Hayôttama**, m. an excellent horse; *-yuj*, drawn by excellent horses, MBh.

Hayana, m. a year (cf. *hāyana*), L.; n. a covered

carriage or palanquin (also read *ḍayana;* see under √*ḍī*), L.

Hayi, m. or f. wish, desire, L.

Hayin, m. a horseman, rider, MBh.; MārkP.

Hayushā, f. a herb, plant (= *oshadhi*), L.

हये *hayé*, ind. an exclamation ('O, ho!'), RV.; ŚBr.; Gobh.

हर *hara*, mf(*ā*, rarely *ī*)n. (only ifc.; fr. √1. *hṛi*) bearing, wearing, taking, conveying, bringing (see *kavaca-, vārttā-h°*), taking away, carrying off, removing, destroying (see *bala-, śakti-h°*); receiving, obtaining (see *aṇśa-h°*); ravishing, captivating (see *mano-h°*); m. 'Seizer,' 'Destroyer,' N. of Śiva, ĀśvGṛ.; Mn.; MBh. &c.; of a Dānava, MBh.; Hariv.; of a monkey, R.; of various authors &c., Cat.; (in arithm.) a divisor, Col.; the denominator of a fraction, division, ib.; a stallion (?), L.; an ass, L.; fire, L. **–kumāra-ṭhakkura**, m. N. of a modern author, Cat. **–keli**, N. of a drama (composed by Vigraha-rāja-deva A.D. 1153). **–keśa**, incorrect for *hari-keśa*. **–kośa**, m. N. of a dictionary. **–kshetra**, n. N. of a district sacred to Śiva, Inscr. **–gaṇa** and **-gupta**, m. N. of poets, Cat. **–govinda**, m. (also with *vācaspati* and *śarman*) N. of various authors, ib. **–gaurī**, f. one of the forms of Śiva or of Śiva and Pārvatī conjoined (= *ardhanārīśa*); *-saṃvāda*, m. N. of wk. **–carita-cintāmaṇi**, m. N. of a poem. **–cāpâropaṇa**, n. N. of a drama. **–cūḍāmaṇi**, m. 'Śiva's crest-gem,' the moon, L. **–jit**, m. N. of a man, Cat. **–jī**, m. (with *bhaṭṭa*) N. of the father of Hara-datta, ib. **–tejas**, n. 'Śiva's energy,' quicksilver, L. **–dagdha-mūrti**, m. 'whose body has been burnt by Ś°,' Kāma-deva (also 'sexual love'), VarBṛS. **–datta**, m. N. of various writers &c. (esp. of the author of the Pada-mañjarī, a Comm. on the Kāśikā-vṛitti, and the Mitâksharā, a Comm. on Gautama's Dharma-sūtra), Cat.; *-caritra*, n. N. of wk.; *-siṇha*, m. N. of a modern author, Cat.; *°ttâcārya*, m. N. of a preceptor, Sarvad.; *°ttīya*, n. N. of wk. **–dāsa**, m. N. of an author (perhaps w.r. for *hari-d°*), Cat. **–nartaka**, n. a kind of metre (= *hariṇa-pluta*), Ked. **–nātha** and **-nārāyaṇa** (also spelt *hari-n°*), m. N. of authors, Cat. **–netra**, n. Śiva's eye, Kathās.; a symbolical expression for the number 'three,' L. **–pati**, m. N. of an author, Cat. **–pradīpikā**, f. N. of a medic. wk. **–priya**, m. Nerium Odorum, L. **–bala**, m. N. of a man, Kathās. **–bīja**, n. 'Śiva's seed,' quicksilver, L. **–mukuṭa-māhātmya**, n., **-mekhalā**, f. N. of wks. **–mekhalin**, m. a partic. class of artisans, Gol. **–mohana** and **-rāta**, m. N. of authors, Cat. **–rūpa**, m. 'having the form of Hara,' N. of Śiva, L. **–vijaya**, m. N. of a poem by Ratnâkara. **–vilāsa**, m. a kind of musical composition, Saṃgīt.; N. of a poem. **–śūra**, N. of a place, Vīrac. **–śṛiṅgārā**, f. (in music) a partic. Rāgiṇī, Saṃgīt. **–śekharā**, f. 'Ś°'s crest,' the Ganges, L. **–sakha**, m. 'S°'s friend,' N. of Kubera, Daś. **–siṇha**, m. N. of a king, Cat. **–siddhi-pradā**, f. N. of a partic. family-deity, Cat. **–sūnu**, m. 'Śiva's son,' N. of Kārttikeya, Ragh. **–svāmin**, m. N. of a man, Kathās. **–hāra**, m. 'Śiva's necklace,' N. of the serpent-demon Śesha, Alaṃkārat. **–hūrā** (?), f. = *hāra-h°*, grape, L. **Harâksha**, n. = *rudrâksha*, the berry of Elæocarpus Ganitrus, L. **Harâdri**, m. 'Ś°'s mountain,' Kailāsa (the favourite resort of Śiva), Kathās. **Harânata**, m. N. of Rāvaṇa, L. **Harânanda**, N. of an author or of a wk., Cat. **Harâyatana**, n. a temple of Śiva, Rājat. **Harârdha**, Śiva's half (*-tā*, f.), Śiś. **Harâvatī**, f. N. of a country, Inscr. **Harâvāsa**, m. Ś°'s abode, Kailāsa, Rājat. **Harâspada**, n. id., Kathās. **Harâhara**, m. N. of a Dānava (du. *°rau*, also = 'Hara and Ahara'), MBh. **Harêśvara**, m. Śiva and Vishṇu forming one person, Inscr. **Harôdbheda**, m. N. of a Tīrtha, MatsyaP.

Haraka, m. a taker, seizer, conveyer, W.; a rogue, cheat, ib.; a reflecting person, ib.; N. of Śiva, ib.; a divisor or division, ib.; a long flexible sword, ib.

Haraṇa, mf(*ā* or *ī*)n. (only ifc.) carrying, holding, containing (e.g. *bali-haraṇī darvī*, 'a ladle containing an oblation'), ĀśvGṛ.; taking away, removing (e.g. *rajo-h°*, 'removing dust'), Kauś.; m. 'taker,' a hand, L.; an arm, L.; Michelia Champaca, L.; n. the act of carrying or bringing or fetching, KātyŚr.; MBh. &c.; offering, KātyŚr.; Gaut.; carrying off, robbing, abduction, Gaut.; Mn.; MBh. &c.; removing, destroying, Suśr.; VarBṛS.; dividing, division, Col.; a nuptial present (= *yautaka*), MBh.; a gift to a student at his initiation, W.; fodder given to a stallion (= *vāḍaba-h°*), Kāś. on Pāṇ. vi, 2, 65; (L. also 'a partic. gesture' [esp. of an archer in shooting]; 'boiling water;' 'semen virile;' 'gold'). **–bhāga** (*háraṇa-*), mfn. entitled to partake (said of deceased ancestors), TBr. **–hārika**, n. (or *ā*, f.) fetching the nuptial present, MBh. **Haraṇâharaṇa**, n. id., ib.

Haraṇi, f. a water-channel, gutter, L.; death, L.

Haraṇīya, mfn. to be taken or seized &c., Pāṇ. vi, 1, 217, Sch.

Hárayāṇa, m. N. of a man, RV.

Háras, n. a grasp, grip, AV.; a draught, drink, beverage, RV.; AV.; flame, fire (accord. to some also 'anger,' 'fury'), ib. [Cf. Gk. θέρος.] **–vat** (*háras-*), mfn. seizing (or 'fiery'), RV. ii, 23, 6; f. (pl.) rivers (?), Naigh. i, 13. **–vin**, mfn. fiery, energetic, TS.; Br.; ĀśvGṛ.

Harā-śayá, mf(*ā*)n. (for *haraḥ-ś°* as *rajā-ś°* for *rajaḥ-ś°*) fiery, energetic, MaitrS.; (*ā*), f. (applied to a partic. formula), ib.; ĀpŚr.

1. **Hari**, mfn. (for 2. see col. 3) bearing, carrying (see *dṛiti* and *nātha-h°*).

1. **Harika**, m. (for 2. see p. 1291, col. 2) a thief, gambler, W.

1. **Hariman**, m. (for 2. see p. 1292, col. 1) death, illness, L.; time, W.

Harīman, m. = *mātariśvan*, L.

Harta, (m. c.) = *hartṛi*, destroying, MBh.

Hártave, *°tavai*. See √*hṛi*.

Hartavya, mfn. to be taken or seized or appropriated or acquired, Mn.; Pañcat.

Hartu, m. 'seizer,' death, L.; great love, L.

Hartṛi, m. one who brings or conveys, a bearer, bringer, Āpast.; Kauś.; MBh. &c.; one who seizes or takes away, a robber, thief, Yājñ.; MBh. &c.; one who severs or cuts off (only *°tā* as fut., 'he will cut off'), BhP.; one who imposes taxes (a king), ib.; a remover, dispeller, destroyer, MBh.; Hariv.; Kathās.; the sun, MW.

Harman, n. gaping, yawning, L.

Harmita, mfn. thrown, L.; burnt, L.

1. **Hāra**, mf(*ī*)n. bearing, carrying, carrying away, stealing (e.g. *kshīra-h°*, 'stealing milk'), MārkP.; levying, raising (e.g. *kara-h°*, 'raising taxes'), BhP.; ravishing, charming, delightful (or 'relating to Hari i.e. Vishṇu'), ib.; relating to Hara or Śiva, Nalac.; m. taking away, removal, ib.; confiscation, forfeiture (of land, money &c.), Mn.; MBh.; Kathās.; waste, loss (see *kāla-h°*); war, battle, W.; a carrier, porter, ib.; (in arithm.) a divisor or division, Col.; (in prosody) a long syllable, ib.; a garland of pearls, necklace (accord. to some, one of 108 or 64 strings), MBh.; Kāv. &c.; (*ā*), f., Pāṇ. iii, 3, 104; (*ī*), f. a pearl, L.; a girl of bad reputation (unfit for marriage), L.; a kind of metre, Col. **–guṭikā**, f. the bead or pearl of a necklace, MW. **–phala** or **-phalaka**, n. a necklace of five strings, L. **–bhūrā** (?), f. a grape (cf. *-hūrā*), L. **–bhūshika**, m. pl. N. of a people, MārkP. **–muktā**, f. pl. the pearls of a necklace, Vās. **–yashṭi**, f. (ifc. f. *i* or *ī*) a string of pearls, necklace, Hariv.; Kāv.; Kathās. **–latā**, f. id., Vās.; Kathās.; N. of a woman, Kathās.; of a wk. on law by Aniruddha. **–varsha**, m. N. of a king, Cat. **–hārā**, f. a kind of brown grape, L. **–hūṇa**, m. pl. N. of a people, MBh. **–hūra** (?), n. a partic. intoxicating beverage, L.; (*ā*), f. a grape (cf. *hara-h°* and *hāra-bhūrā*), L. **–hūrikā**, f. a grape, L. **–haura** (?), m. N. of the prince of a partic. people, VarBṛS. **Hārâvalī**, f. a string of pearls, Kāv.; N. of a vocabulary of uncommon words by Purushôttama-deva.

2. **Hāra** (for 3. see p. 1292, col. 1), Nom. P. *°rati*, to be like a string of pearls, Dhūrtas.

Hāraka, mf(*ikā*)n. taking, seizing, robbing, stealing (see *artha-, aśva-h°*); removing, taking upon one's self (see *samagra-mala-h°*); ravishing, captivating (in *gopī-nayana-h°*, 'captivating the eyes of the Gopīs,' Pañcar.); m. a thief, robber, L.; a gambler, cheat, rogue, Rājat.; a divisor, Āryabh., Sch.; a string of pearls, Pañcat.; Trophis Aspera, L.; a kind of prose composition, L.; a kind of science, L.; (*ikā*), f. a kind of metre, Col.

Hāraṇā, f. (fr. Caus.) causing to take or seize &c., Pāṇ. iii, 3, 107, Sch.

Hāram, ind. seizing, destroying (cf. *sarvasva-h°*), Kusum.

Hārāpaya, *°yati*. See √*hṛi*.

Hārāya, Nom. Ā. *°yate*, to become a string of pearls, Pārśvan.

Hāri, m. = 1. *hāra* (see *aṅga-h°*); a caravan, L.; losing a game (in gambling), L.; mfn. captivating, charming, beautiful, W.

Hāri-kaṇṭha, mfn. (fr. *hārin* + *k°*) 'having a charming throat (i.e. voice),' and 'having a string of pearls round the neck,' Vās.; m. 'having a ring on the throat,' the Koïl or Indian cuckoo, L.

1. **Hārita**, mfn. (fr. Caus.; for 2. see p. 1292, col. 1) caused to be taken or seized &c.; brought, conveyed, Kum.; robbed, carried off, Kathās.; made away with, lost, relinquished, Mṛicch.; Rājat. &c.; deprived of (acc.), Kām.; surpassed, exceeded, Gīt.; captivated, fascinated, MW.

Hārin, mfn. taking, carrying, carrying away, stealing, robbing (gen. or comp.), Yājñ.; MBh. &c.; removing, dispelling, destroying, Kāv.; Kathās.; taking to one's self, appropriating, levying or raising (taxes), Bhartṛ.; Rājat.; surpassing, exceeding, VarBṛS.; ravishing, captivating, attracting, charming (*°ri-tva*, n.), Mn.; MBh. &c.; (fr. 1. *hāra*) having or wearing a garland of pearls, Bhartṛ.; BhP.

1. **Hārīta**, m. (for 2. see p. 1292, col. 1) a thief, cheat, rogue, MW.; roguery, cheating, fraud, ib.

Hāruka, mf(*ā*)n. seizing, consuming, TS.

Hārtra, n. (fr. *hartṛi*), g. *udgātr-ādi*.

Hārtrya, m. patr. fr. *hartṛi*, g. *kurv-ādi*.

Hārya, mfn. to be borne or carried, Hariv.; Kālid.; Kathās.; to be taken away or carried off or robbed or appropriated, ŚBr. &c. &c.; to be shaken or altered (see *a-h°*); to be won over or bribed, Mṛicch.; Vās.; to be acted (as a play), Bhar.; (in arithm.) to be divided, the dividend, Āryabh., Sch.; captivating, charming, MBh. xiii, 1429; m. a serpent, MW.; Terminalia Bellerica, L.; (*ā*), f. a kind of sandal wood, L. **–putra**, m. N. of Rāma (?), MW.

हरमुज *haramuja*, N. of a place, Cat.

हरवे *harave*, N. of a place (= Herāt), Cat.

हरस् *haras* &c. See col. 2.

हराक *harāka*, N. of a place, Cat.

हराक्ष *harâksha* &c. See col. 1.

हरि 2. *hári*, mfn. (prob. fr. a lost √*hṛi*, 'to be yellow or green;' for 1. *hari* see above, col. 2) fawn-coloured, reddish brown, brown, tawny, pale yellow, yellow, fallow, bay (esp. applied to horses), green, greenish, RV. &c. &c.; m. yellow or reddish brown or green (the colour), L.; a horse, steed (esp. of Indra), RV. &c. &c.; a lion, MBh.; Kāv. &c.; the sign of the zodiac Leo, VarBṛS.; the sun, ib.; = *hari-nakshatra*, ib.; a monkey, MBh.; R. &c.; (L. also, a ray of light; the moon; Phaseolus Mungo; a jackal; a parrot; a peacock; the Koïl or Indian cuckoo; a goose; a frog; a snake; fire); the wind or N. of Vāyu (god of the wind), R.; of Indra, ib. &c.; (esp.) N. of Vishṇu-Kṛishṇa (in this sense thought by some to be derived from √*hṛi*, 'to take away or remove evil or sin'), MBh.; Kāv. &c.; of Brahmā, TĀr.; of Yama, L.; of Śiva, L.; of Śukra, L.; of Su-parṇa, L.; of a son of Garuḍa, MBh.; of a Rākshasa, ib.; of a Dānava, Hariv.; of a son of Akampana (or Anukampana), MBh.; of a son of Tārakâksha, ib.; of a son of Parājit, Hariv.; of a son of Parāvṛit, VP.; of a worshipper of Vishṇu, BhP.; of various authors and scholars (esp. of the poet Bhartṛi-hari as the author of the Vākya-padīya; also with *miśra, bhaṭṭa, dīkshita* &c.), Cat.; of a mountain, VP.; of a world (cf. *hari-varsha*), L.; of a metre, Col.; of a partic. high number, Buddh.; pl. men, people (= *manushyāḥ*), Naigh. ii, 3; a partic. class of gods under Manu Tāmasa, Pur.; (*ī*), f. N. of the mythical mother of the monkeys, MBh.; R. [Cf. Lat. *holus, helvus, fulvus*; Lith. *žalias, želti*; Slav. *zelenŭ*; Germ. *gëlo, gelb*; Eng. *yellow*.] **–kaṇṭha**, m. N. of an author, Cat. **–kathâmṛita**, n. N. of wk. **–karṇa**, m. N. of a man (see *hārikarṇa*). **–kavi, -kavîndra**, m. N. of authors, Cat. **–kānta**, mfn. beloved by Indra, MW.; beautiful as a lion, ib. **–kārikā**, f. Bhartṛi-hari's Kārikā (= *vākya-padīya*) and another wk. **–kāla-deva**, m. N. of a king, Col. **–kālā-vrata** (?), n. a partic. religious observance, Cat. **–kāli-tṛitīyā**, f. a partic. day (*-vrata*, n.), ib. **–kīrtana**, n. N. of a Stotra. **–kutsa**, m. N. of a man; pl. his family, Pravar. **–kṛishṇa**, m. N. of various authors &c., Cat.; *-samuddhāra*, m. N. of a man, Kshitīś.; *-siddhânta*, m. N. of an author, Cat. **–kelīya**, m. 'sported in by Kṛishṇa,' the country of Bengal, W.; pl. the people of B°, L.; mfn. belonging to or dwelling in Bengal, MW. **-keśa** (*hári-*), mfn. fair-headed, RV.; VS.; MBh.; m. N. of one of the 7 principal rays of the sun, VP.; of Savitṛi, RV.; of Śiva, MBh.; of a Yaksha (who propitiated Śiva and was made by him a leader of his Gaṇas and a guardian of fields and fruits; see *daṇḍa-pāṇi*), Cat.; of a son of Śyāmaka, BhP. **-krāntā**, f. Clitoria Ternatea, L.; (°*taḥ* w.r. for *hariḥ krāntaḥ*, L.) **-kshetra**, n. N. of a territory, Cat. **-gaṇa**, m. a troop of horses, Rājat.; N. of various persons, ib.; ŚārṅgP.; Subh. **-gati**, f. N. of wk. **-gandha**, m. yellow sandal, L. **-giri**, m. N. of a mountain, MBh. **-gītā**, f. a kind of metre, Col.; pl. the doctrine communicated by Nārāyaṇa to Nārada, MBh. **-guṇa-maṇi-darpaṇa**, m., **-guru-stava-mālā**, f. N. of wks. **-gṛiha**, n. 'abode of Hari,' N. of a city (= *eka-cakra*), L. **-gopaka**, m. cochineal (cf. *indra-g*°), Subh. **-ghosha**, m. N. of a man, Kathās. **-candana**, m. n. a sort of sandal tree, Śiś.; BhP.; Śatr.; yellow sandal, MBh.; Kāv. &c. (in this sense prob. only n.); one of the five trees of paradise (the other four being Pārijāta, Mandāra, Saṃtāna, and Kalpa), Pañcar.; Pañcat.; n. the pollen or filament of a lotus, L.; saffron, ib.; moonlight, ib.; the person of a lover or mistress, ib.; °*danâspada*, n. a place where yellow sandal grows, Kum. **-candra**, m. N. of various authors and other persons, Hcar.; Subh. &c. **-caraṇa-dāsa**, m. N. of an author, Cat. **-caraṇa-purī**, m. N. of a teacher, ib. **-cāpa**, m. n. 'Indra's bow,' a rainbow, VarBṛS. **-ja**, see p. 1292, col. 2. **-jāta**, mfn. (prob.) = *hári*, yellow, RV. **-jit**, **-jīva**, **-jīvana-miśra**, m. N. of various men, Cat. **-naigumeshin** (?), m. N. of one of Indra's attendants, Col. (cf. *naigamesha*). **-tattva-muktâvali** or °**lī**, f. N. of a Comm. **-turaga**, m. a horse of I°, Bcar.; N. of I°, id., ib. **-turaṃgama**, m. id., MW.; °*mâyudha*, n. I°'s thunderbolt, ib. **-toshaṇa**, n. N. of wk. **-trāta**, mfn. protected by Hari, MW. **-tvac**, mfn. yellow-skinned, ĀpŚr. **-datta**, m. N. of a Dānava, Kathās.; of various authors &c., ib.; Pañcat.; Śukas. &c.; (*ā*), f. N. of a woman, Śukas.; *-daivajña*, *-bhaṭṭa*, *-miśra*, m. N. of authors, Cat. **-darbha**, m. a sort of Kuśa grass, L. (cf. *harid-garbha*). **-dāsa**, m. a slave or worshipper of Vishṇu, BhP.; N. of various authors &c., Vet.; Cat.; *-tarkâcārya* (Cat.), *-nyāya-vācaspati-tarkâlaṃkāra-bhaṭṭâcārya* (ib.), *-bhaṭṭa* (ib.), *-bhaṭṭâcārya* (Kusum.), *-miśra* (Cat.), *-vijaya* (ib.), m. N. of authors. **-dina**, n. 'day sacred to Vishṇu,' the 11th day in a fortnight, L.; Vop.; *-tilaka*, N. of wk. **-diś**, f. 'Indra's quarter,' the east, Gol. **-dīkshita**, m. N. of various authors, Cat. **-dūta**, m. N. of a drama. **-dṛiśvan**, mf(*arī*)n. (prob.) one who has seen Vishṇu, Vop. **-deva**, m. the asterism Śravaṇā (presided over by Vishṇu), L.; N. of various men, Cat.; *-miśra*, *-sūri*, m. N. of authors, ib. **-drava**, m. green fluid, MW.; (perhaps) Soma, ib.; a powder made from Mesua Roxburghii, L. **-1. -dru** (*hari-*), mfn. moving in the yellow (Soma; said of the Soma-stones), RV. (more correctly accentuated *hari-drú*). **-2. -dru** (*hari-*), m. a kind of tree (accord. to L. 'Chloroxylon Swietenia; a sort of Pinus; Curcuma Aromatica'), ŚBr.; KātyŚr.; Hariv.; a tree (in general), L.; (*hari-dru*), N. of a pupil of Kalāpin, Pāṇ. iv, 3, 104, Sch.; *-mat*, m. N. of a man, ChUp., Sch. **-druka**, mfn. dealing in Curcuma Aromatica, g. *kisarâdi*. **-dvāra**, n. 'Vishṇu's gate,' N. of a celebrated town and sacred bathing-place (commonly called Hardvār, where the Ganges finally leaves the mountains for the plains of Hindūstān, whence it is sometimes called Gaṅgā-dvāra; it is called 'Hari's gate,' as leading to Vaikuṇṭha or Vishṇu's heaven), Rudray.; Buddh.; *-māhātmya*, n. N. of wk. **-dvish**, m. 'hater of Hari,' an Asura, L. **-dhāyas** (*hári-*), mfn. having or giving yellowish streams (as the sky), RV. **-dhārita-grantha** (?), m. N. of wk. **-dhūmra**, mfn. yellowish brown, Hariv. **-nakshatra**, n. the Nakshatra Śravaṇā, VarBṛS. **-nadī**, f. N. of a river; *-ramya*, m. N. of a village, Cat. **-nanda**, m. N. of a pupil of Devânanda, W. **-nandana**, m. N. of various authors, Cat. **-nandin**, m. a proper N., g. *kshubhnâdi*. **-nātha**, m. N. of various men, Cat.; *-gosvāmin*, *-mahôpâdhyāya*; °*thâcārya*, °*thôpâdhyāya*, m. N. of authors, ib. **-nânâkṛiti**, f. N. of wk. **-nābha**, m. N. of an author, Cat. **-nāman**, n. the name of Hari or Vishṇu, Col.; Cat.; m. the kidney-bean, Phaseolus Mungo, L.; °*ma-kavaca*, n., °*ma-mālā*, f., °*ma-vyākhyā*, f., °*mâmṛita*, n., °*mâmṛita-vaishṇava-vyākaraṇa*, n., °*môpanishad*, f. N. of wks. **-nāyaka**, m. N. of an author, Cat. **-nārāyaṇa**, m. N. of various persons, Inscr.; Kshitîś.; *-śarman*, m. N. of an author, Cat. **-nārāyaṇīya**, n. N. of wk. **-nīla**, mfn. yellowish-blue, JaimUp. **-netra**, n. the eye of Vishṇu, MārkP.; a white lotus, L.; an eye of a greenish colour, MW.; mfn. having yellow eyes, MBh.; m. an owl, L. **-pañcaka-vrata**, n. a partic. religious observance, Cat. **-pañcâyudha-stotra**, n. N. of wk. **-paṇḍita**, m. N. of an author, Cat. **-paṇḍitīya**, n. Hari-paṇḍita's work, ib. **-pada**, n. (accord. to some) the vernal equinox, MW. **-parṇa**, mfn. green-leaved, ib.; n. a radish, L. **-parvata**, m. N. of a mountain, MārkP. **-pā́**, mfn. drinking the yellow (Soma), RV. **-pāla** (Gaṇar.), **-pāla-deva** (Cat.), **-pāla-bhaṭṭa** (ib.), m. N. of men. **-piṅga**, mfn. yellowish-brown, MBh. **-piṅgala**, mfn. id., ib.; R. **-piṇḍā**, f. N. of one of the Mātṛis attending on Skanda, MBh. **-pura**, n. N. of a town, VP. **-pūjana-vidhi**, m., **-pūjā-paddhati**, f., **-prabodha**, m. N. of wks. **-prabha**, mfn. fallow-coloured (*-tva*, n.), Car. **-prasāda**, m. N. of various men, Col.; Cat.; *-māhātmya*, n. N. of wk. **-priya**, mfn. liking bay horses (or 'dear to them,' said of Indra), RV.; liked or loved by Vishṇu or Kṛishṇa, L.; m. Nauclea Cadamba, L.; Nerium Odorum, ib.; a yellow-flowered Eclipta, ib.; = *bandhūka*, ib.; = *vishṇu-kanda*, ib.; a conch-shell, ib.; a fool, blockhead, W.; a mad person, MW.; armour, mail, W.; N. of Śiva, ib.; (*ā*), f. (only L.) Lakshmī; the earth; sacred basil; spirituous liquor; the 12th day of a lunar fortnight; n. the root of Andropogon Muricatus, L.; red or black sandal, L. **-babhru**, m. N. of a man, MBh. **-bala**, m. N. of a king, Campak. **-bābā**, m. N. of an author, Cat. **-bīja**, n. 'Vishṇu's seed,' yellow orpiment, L. (see *haritāla*). **-buṅga-pura**, n. N. of a town, Cat. **-bodha**, m. the awaking of Vishṇu; *-dina*, n. N. of a festival day, Kathârṇ. **-brahman**, m. N. of an author, Cat. **-bhakta**, m. a worshipper of Vishṇu, BrahmavP. **-bhakti**, f. the worship of Vishṇu, Cat.; N. of wk.; *-kalpa-latā*, f., *-kalpa-latikā*, f., *-taraṃgiṇī*, f., *-dīpikā*, f., *-bhāskara-sadvaishṇava-sāra-sarvasva*, n., *-bhāskarôdaya*, m., *-rasâmṛita-sindhu*, m., *-rasāyana*, n., *-rahasya*, n., *-latā*, f., *-latikā-stava*, m., *-vilāsa*, m., *-samāgama*, m., *-sāra*, *-sudhā-rasa*, m., *-sudhôdaya*, m. N. of wks. **-bhaṭa**, m. N. of an Asura, Kathās. **-bhaṭṭa**, m. N. of various scholars, Subh.; Cat. &c.; *-dīkshita*, m. N. of an author, Cat. **-bhadra**, m. N. of various men, Buddh.; Cat.; n. the fragrant bark of Feronia Elephantum, L.; *-sūri*, m. N. of an author (*-kathā*, f. N. of wk.), Cat. **-bhānu**, **-bhānu-śukla**, **-bhāratī**, m. N. of authors, Cat. **-bhāvinī** or °**vinī**, f. a woman who meditates on Vishṇu, MW. **-bhāskara** or °**ra-śarman**, m. N. of an author, Cat. **-bhuj**, m. 'frog-eater,' a snake, L. **-bhūta**, m. N. of a poet, Subh. **-maṇi**, m. a smaragd, Bhaṭṭ. **-maṇḍalâksha**, mfn. having eyes like the disk of the sun, Bcar. **-mat**, m. 'having bay horses,' N. of Indra, MBh. **-madhyā**, f. having a yellowish waist (and so reminding of Vishṇu), Rājat.; N. of a Surâṅganā, Siṇhâs. **-mantha**, m. Premna Spinosa (the wood of which by attrition produces flame), L.; the chick-pea, ib.; N. of a partic. country, ib.; *-ja*, m. 'produced in the district Hari-mantha,' the chick-pea, ib.; (m.) n. a sort of kidney-bean, Suśr. **-manthaka**, m. the chick-pea, L. **-mandira**, n. a temple of Vishṇu, W.; the world of V°, Kṛishṇaj. **-manyu-sāyaka** (*hári-*), mfn. stimulating the mettle of the bay horses (said of Indra), RV. **-mahiman**, m., **-mālā**, f., **-māhātmya-darpaṇa**, m. N. of wks. **-mitra**, **-miśra**, m. N. of various men, Cat. **-m-īḍe**, 'I praise Hari' (or °*ḍe-stotra*), n. N. of a hymn. **-muktâvalī**, f. N. of wk. **-medha**, m. N. of Nārāyaṇa or Vishṇu-Kṛishṇa, MBh.; N. of wk. **-medhas**, m. N. of Vishṇu-Kṛishṇa, MBh.; BhP.; of the father of Hari (Vishṇu), BhP.; of a man, MBh. **-m-bhará**, mfn. bearing the yellow-coloured (thunderbolt), RV. **-yaśas**, **-yaśo-miśra**, m. N. of authors, Cat. **-yūpīyā**, f. N. of a locality, RV. **-yoga** (*hári-*), mfn. having a yoke of bay horses, yoked with horses, ib. **-yójana**, n. the harnessing of the bay horses, ib.; m. Indra, MW. (cf. *hāriy*°). **-yoni**, mfn. produced from Hari or Vishṇu, MBh. **-ratna**, **-rasa-kavi**, m. N. of authors, Cat. **-rāja**, m. N. of a king, Rājat. **-rāma**, m. N. of various men, Cat.; *-cakra-vartin* (Col.), *-tarka-vāg-īśa*, *-tarka-vāg-īśa-bhaṭṭâcārya*, *-tarkâlaṃkāra*, *-tarkâlaṃkāra-bhaṭṭâcārya*, *-bhaṭṭâcārya*, *-vācas-pati* (Cat.), m. N. of various men. **-rāya**, °**ya-śarman**, m. N. of various men, Cat. **-ripu**, m. a kind of plant, Kālac. **-rudra**, m. Hari and Rudra (i.e. Vishṇu and Śiva) in one person, MBh. **-roman**, mfn. having fair hair on the body, ib. **-lāla**, **-lāla-miśra**, m. N. of authors, Cat. **-līlā**, f. 'Hari's play,' N. of Vopa-deva's index to the Bhāgavata-Purāṇa; *-kṛishṇa-kautaka*, n., -°*mṛita* (°*lâm*°), n., *-vivaraṇa-saṃgraha*, m., *-viveka*, m. N. of wks. **-locana**, mfn. brown-eyed, L.; m. a crab, L.; an owl, ib.; N. of a demon causing disease, Hariv.; *-candrikā*, f. N. of a Comm. **-loman**, mfn. yellow-haired, Car. **-vaṇśa**, m. the family of Kṛishṇa, Śatr.; the race of monkeys, R.; N. of various men, Sadukt.; Cat.; m. n. (scil. *purāṇa*) N. of a celebrated poem supplementary to the Mahā-bhārata on the history and adventures of Kṛishṇa and his family (it is usually regarded as part of the greater epic, though really a comparatively modern addition to it; cf. IW. 418); *-kavi*, m. N. of an author, Cat.; *-kṛishṇa-līlā*, f. N. of wk.; *-gosvāmin*, m. N. of an author, Cat.; *-catushka*, n. N. of wk.; *-candra-gosvāmin*, m. N. of an author, Cat.; *-deva*, m. N. of a teacher, ib.; *-nyāsa*, m. N. of wk.; *-paṇḍita*, m. N. of an author, Cat.; *-purāṇa*, n. N. of wk.; *-bhaṭṭa* (?), m. N. of an author, Cat.; *-vilāsa*, m., *-śravaṇa-vidhāna*, n., *-śravaṇa-vidhi*, m., *-sāra-carita*, n. N. of wks. **-vaṇśya**, mfn. belonging to Hari's family, Śatr. **-vat** (*hári-*), mfn. possessing Hari, MW.; poss° bay horses (m. N. of Indra), RV.; VS.; AitBr.; connected with the yellow (Soma), RV.; containing the word *hari* ([*atī*], f. 'such a verse'), Br.; Lāṭy. **-vana**, n. a proper N., g. *kshubhnâdi*. **-vandana**, n. N. of wk. **-vara**, mfn. the best of the monkeys, R.; m. N. of a king, Kathās.; n. N. of a town, ib. **-varṇa**, m. N. of a man, PañcavBr.; n. N. of a Sāman (w.r. for *hāriv*°). **-varpas** (*hári-*), mfn. having a yellowish or greenish appearance, RV. **-varman**, m. N. of various men, Inscr.; Buddh.; Cat.; °*ma-deva*, m. N. of a king, Inscr. **-varsha**, n. one of the 9 divisions of Jambu-dvīpa (the country between the Nishadha and Hema-kūṭa mountains; see *varsha*), MBh.; Pur.; Śatr.; m. N. of a king of Hari-varsha, Pur. **-vallabha**, m. 'beloved by Vishṇu,' N. of various men (also *-rāya*), Kshitîś.; Col.; Cat.; (*ā*), f. N. of Lakshmī, MW.; sacred basil, L.; another plant (= *jayā*), ib. **-vāghala**, m. N. of a man, Cat. **-vāyu-stuti**, f. N. of wk. **-vāluka**, n. the fragrant bark of Feronia Elephantum, Bhpr. **-vāsa**, mfn. (prob.) wearing a yellow garment (Vishṇu), MBh.; m. Ficus Religiosa, L. **-vāsara**, n. Vishṇu's day (the 11th or 12th lunar day, or accord. to some, the first quarter of the 12th l° d°), Kṛishṇaj. **-vāsuka**, n. = *-vāluka*, L. **-vāhana**, m. 'Vishṇu-bearer,' N. of the bird Garuḍa, L.; 'having bay horses,' N. of Indra, MBh.; R.; of the sun, L.; *-diś*, f. Indra's quarter, i.e. the east, Vikr. **-vijaya**, m. N. of a wk. by Sarva-sena; *-kāvya*, n. N. of wk. **-vinoda**, m., **-vilāsa**, m., **-vilāsa-kāvya**, n. N. of wks. **-vṛiksha**, m. a kind of tree, Suśr. (cf. 2. *-dru*). **-vṛisha** (?), n. = *-varsha*, n., L. **-vyāsa** (W.), **-vyāsa-deva**, **-vyāsa-miśra**, **-vyāsa-muni** (Cat.), m. N. of various men. **-vrata** (*hári-*), mfn. (perhaps) one whose sphere or whose surroundings are yellow, RV. **-śaṃkara**, m. N. of various men, Cat.; of a place, ib. **-śayā́**, mf(*ā́*)n. resting or being in gold, VS. v, 8; (*ā*), f. N. of the verse *yā́ te agne hari-śayā́ tanū́ḥ*, ib. **-śayana**, n. Vishṇu's sleep, L. **-śara**, m. having Vishṇu for an arrow, N. of Śiva (Śiva having Vishṇu as the shaft which set the cities of Tripura on fire), L. **-śarman** (Kathās.), **-śarmârya** (Inscr.), **-śikha** (Kathās.), m. N. of various persons. **-śipra** (*hári-*), mfn. having yellow (golden) cheek-guards on (his) helmet, RV.; m. 'ruddy-jawed,' N. of Indra, MW. **-ścandra** (*hári-*), mfn. (see *candra*) having golden splendour, RV.; m. N. of the 28th king of the solar dynasty in the Tretā age (he was son of Tri-śaṅku, and was celebrated for his piety; accord. to the Mārkaṇḍeya-Purāṇa he gave up his country, his wife and his son, and finally himself, to satisfy the demands of Viśvā-mitra; after enduring incredible sufferings, he won the pity of the gods and was raised with his subjects to heaven: accord. to MBh. ii, 489 &c., his performance of the Rāja-sūya sacrifice was the cause of his elevation, and in the Aitareya-Brāhmaṇa quite another legend is told about him, see under *śunaḥ-śepa*, p. 1082, col. 3: in later legends Hari-ścandra is represented as insidiously induced by Nārada to relate his actions with unbecoming pride, whereupon he was degraded from Svarga, one stage at each sentence, till stopping in time and doing homage to the gods he was fixed with his capital in mid-air; his aerial city is popularly believed to be still visible in the skies at particular times; cf. *saubha*), Br.; MaitrUp.; MBh. &c.; N. of various authors &c., Inscr.; Cat.; m. or n. (?) N. of a place, Cat.; n. N. of a Liṅga, MW.; *-caritra*, n. N. of wk.; *-tīrtha*, n. N. of a Tīrtha, MW.; *-pura*, n. the city of Hariścandra (= *saubha*), L.; a mirage, VarBṛS.; *-purāṇa*, n., *-yaśaś-candra-candrikā*, f., °*ścandrâkhyāyikā*, f., °*ścandrôpâkhyāna*, n. N. of wks. **–śmaśāru** (*hári-*), mfn. having a ruddy or yellow beard, RV. **–śmaśru**, mfn. id., MBh.; Hariv.; R.; m. N. of a Dānava, BhP. **–śrama**, m. N. of a man, Cat. **–śravā**, w.r. for next, VP. **–śrāvā**, f. N. of a river, MBh. **–śrī́**, mfn. beautifully yellow, gold-coloured, RV.; PañcavBr.; blessed with Soma, RV.; bl° with or abounding in horses, MW.; *-nidhana*, n. N. of a Sāman, PañcavBr. **–shác** (*-shā́c*), mfn. occupied with the yellow (Soma), RV. **–sheṇa**, m. (*sheṇa* for *sena* fr. *senā*) N. of a son of the 10th Manu, VP.; of the 10th of the Jaina Cakra-vartins in Bhārata, L. **–shṭhā́**, mfn. (*shṭhā* for *sthā*) borne along by bay horses, RV.; one who stands over horses, a guider of horses, MW. **–saktha**, n., *saṃjñāyām*, Pāṇ. viii, 3, 99, Sch. **–sakha**, m. 'friend of Indra,' a Gandharva, Kir. **–saṃkīrtana**, n. the act of pronouncing or repeating the name of Vishṇu (supposed to possess great efficacy), Cat.; N. of wk. **–sādhana-candrikā**, f. N. of wk. **–siṇha**, m. N. of a king, Kathās.; *-deva* (*śrī-hari-*), m. N. of a king, Inscr. **–siddhi**, f. N. of a goddess, Pañcad. **–suta**, m. 'son of Hari,' N. of Arjuna, MW.; of the 10th Cakra-vartin (= *-sheṇa*), L. **–sûkta**, n. N. of a partic. hymn addressed to Hari, Cat. **–sūnu**, m. 'son of Hari,' N. of Arjuna, MW. **–sena**, m. N. of a minister of Samudra-gupta, Inscr.; of an author, Cat. **–sevaka-miśra**, m. N. of an author, ib. **–soma**, m. N. of a man, Kathās. **–stava**, mfn. one whose bay horses are praised, ŚāṅkhBr. **–stuti**, f., **-stotra**, n. N. of hymns (in praise of Vishṇu). **–svāmin**, m. N. of various men, Kathās.; Cat.; (°*mi*)*-putra*, m. N. of an author, Cat. **–haya**, m. a horse of Indra, R.; 'having bay or gold-coloured horses,' N. of Indra, MBh.; R.; of the Sun, W.; of Skanda, ib.; of Gaṇêśa, ib.; °*yânuja*, m. 'Indra's younger brother,' N. of Vishṇu-Kṛishṇa, R. **–hara**, m. 'Vishṇu-Śiva,' a partic. form of deity consisting of V° and Ś° conjoined, Kāv.; RTL. 65; (du. or in comp.) Vishṇu and Śiva, Hariv.; Hit.; N. of various persons, Tattvas.; Kshitîś. &c.; of a river, Prâyaśc.; *-kathā*, f. the repeating of the names of Vishṇu and Śiva, Hit.; *-kshetra*, n. 'sacred place of V° and Ś° conjoined,' N. of a place of pilgrimage, MW.; *-khāna*, *-tarkâlaṃkāra-bhaṭṭâcārya*, m. N. of certain men, Cat.; *-tāratamya*, n. N. of various wks.; *-dīkshita*, m. N. of a man, Cat.; *-dīkshitīya*, n. N. of wk.; *-deva* (ŚārṅgP.; Inscr.), *-deva-hindū-pati*, *-paṇḍita* (Cat.), m. N. of certain men; *-paddhati*, f. N. of wk.; *-purī*, m. N. of an author, Cat.; *-praśaṇsā*, f. N. of wk.; *-prasāda*, *-brahman*, m. N. of authors, Cat.; *-brahma-mānasika-snāna-vidhi*, m. N. of wk.; *-bhaṭṭa*, *-bhaṭṭâcārya*, m. N. of authors, Cat.; *-bhāshya*, n., *-bheda-dhik-kāra*, m., *-maṇḍala-shoḍaśa-liṅgôdbhava*, m. N. of wks.; *-mahā-rāja*, m. N. of a man, Cat.; *-māhātmya*, n. N. of ch. of the Skanda-Purāṇa; *-miśra*, m. N. of a man, Cat.; *-yoga*, m., *-vilāsa*, m. N. of wks.; *-sarasvatī*, m. N. of a teacher, Cat.; *-stotra*, n. N. of various Stotras; *-svāmin*; °*râgni-hotrin*, m. N. of authors, Cat.; °*râtmaka*, mfn. consisting of or comprising V° and Ś° in their united state, relating to V° and Ś°, Hariv.; VarP.; m. the bull of Śiva, L.; N. of Garuḍa, ib.; of Daksha, ib.; n. = *hari-hara-kshetra*, MW.; °*râtmaka-stotra*, n. N. of various Stotras; °*rânanda*, m. N. of various men, Cat.; °*rânusaraṇa-yātrā*, f. N. of wk.; °*rârya*, m. N. of a teacher, Cat.; °*râshṭôttara-śata-nāman*, n., °*râshṭôttara-śata-nāmāvali*, f., °*rôpâdhi-vivecana*, n. N. of wks.; °*rôpâdhyāya*, m. N. of an author, Cat. **–hari-hari-vāha**, m. (with Buddhists) N. of a Lokêśvara, W. **–hari-hari-vāhana-sādhana**, N. of wk. **–heti**, f. Indra's weapon, i.e. the rainbow, (or) Vishṇu's w°, i.e. the Cakra; *-mat*, mfn. adorned with a rainbow, Mālatīm.; *-hūti*, m. 'named after the Cakra,' Anas Casarca, Śiś. (cf. *cakra-vāka*). **Harindra-vaiśeshika**, N. of wk. **Harîśa**, m. a king of the monkeys, R. **Harī-śayá**, mf(*ā*)n. = *hari-śayá*, VPrāt. **Hare-kṛishṇa-mahāmantrârtha-nirūpaṇa**, n. N. of wk.

2. **Harika**, m. (for 1. see p. 1289, col. 2) a horse of a yellowish or reddish brown colour, W.

Hariṇá, mf(*ī́*)n. (the fem. *háriṇī* belongs to *harita*) fawn-coloured, yellowish, tawny (also said of unhealthy complexion), greenish, green, MaitrUp.; MBh.; m. yellowish (&c.) the colour, L.; a deer, antelope, fawn, stag (one of 5 kinds, others being called *ṛishya*, *ruru*, *pṛishata*, *mṛiga*), RV. &c. &c.; an ichneumon, MaitrS.; a goose, L.; the sun, L.; a minor division of the world, W.; N. of Vishṇu or Śiva, L.; of a Gaṇa of Śiva, L.; of a serpent-demon, MBh.; of an ichneumon (v.l. *harita*), ib.; (*ī*), f., see below. **–kalaṅka**, m. 'deer-spotted,' the moon, L. **–carman**, n. a d°-skin, Kauś. **–dhāman**, m. 'd°-abode,' the moon, Rājat. **–nayanā**, f. a d°-eyed woman, Daś. **–nartaka**, m. a Kiṃnara, L. **–pṛiṇākā**, f. a young female deer, ĀpŚr. **–pluta**, n., **-plutā**, f. N. of two metres, Piṅg. **–lakshaṇa** (Gol.), **-lakshman** (Bālar.), **-lāñchana** (Kād.), m. 'd°-marked,' the moon. **–locanā**, f. = *-nayanā*, R. **–lolâkshī**, f. a woman with eyes rolling like a deer's, ib. **–hṛidaya**, mfn. 'deer-hearted,' timid, L. **Hariṇâkrīḍana** or °**ḍita**, n. a partic. children's game, Hariv. **Hariṇâksha**, m. 'deer-eyed,' the moon, L.; (*ī*), f. a deer-eyed woman, Hcat.; a kind of perfume, L. **Hariṇâṅka**, m. 'd°-marked,' the moon, W. **Hariṇâdhipa**, m. 'deer-king,' a lion, Jain. **Hariṇântara**, m. a species of deer, MW. **Hariṇâyatêkshaṇā**, f. a woman with eyes long as a deer's, Vcar. **Hariṇâri**, m. d°-enemy, a lion, Anarghar. **Hariṇâśva**, m. 'deer-horse,' the wind, Vās.; N. of a man, MBh. **Hariṇêkshaṇā**, f. a deer-eyed woman, Naish.; Prasannar. **Hariṇêśa**, m. 'deer-lord,' a lion, Hcar.

Hariṇaka, m. a small deer, deer, Kād.

Hariṇāya, Nom. Ā. °*yate*, to become a deer, Śṛiṅgār.

Hariṇī́, f. a female deer, doe, TS. &c. &c.; Rubia Munjista, L.; yellow jasmine, L.; one of the four kinds of beautiful women (corresponding to the kind of man termed *mṛiga*), L.; a golden image, Rājat.; a kind of metre (four times ⏑⏑⏑⏑⏑–, – – – –, ⏑–⏑⏑–⏑–), Piṅg.; a kind of Svara-bhakti (q.v.), TPrāt., Sch.; N. of an Apsaras, Ragh.; of a Yakshiṇī, Buddh.; of the mother of Hari (Vishṇu), BhP.; pl. N. of the verses AV. xviii, 2, 11–18, Kauś. **–dṛiś** or **-nayanā**, f. a doe-eyed woman, Kāv. **–rūpāya**, Ā. °*yate*, to resemble a doe, Gīt. **–vṛitta**, n. the Hariṇī-metre, MW.

Harít, mfn. fawn-coloured, pale yellow, yellowish, pale red, fallow, bay, tawny, greenish, RV. &c. &c.; m. pale yellow, reddish, bay (the colour), L.; a horse of the Sun (*harito hariṇś ca*, acc. pl. 'the horses of the Sun and of Indra'), Śak.; emerald, BhP.; a lion, L.; the sun, L.; N. of Vishṇu, L.; Phaseolus Mungo (prob. w.r. for *hari*), L.; f. a female horse of a reddish colour, a bay mare (applied to the horses of Soma, Indra, and Tvashṭṛi, and esp. to *sapta-haritaḥ*, 'the 7 horses of the Sun,' thought to symbolize the days of the week), RV.; TS.; MBh.; R.; BhP.; a quarter of the sky, RV.; ŚBr.; Kāv. &c.; pl. rivers (= *nadyas*), Naigh. i, 13; grass or a species of grass, L.; turmeric, W. **–pati**, m. the regent of a quarter of the sky, Naish. **–parṇa**, n. 'green-leaved,' a radish, L. **–mat**, mfn., g. *yavâdi*. **–vat** (*hárit-*), mfn. gold-coloured, RV.

Hárita, mf(*ā* or *háriṇī*)n. yellowish, pale yellow, fallow, pale red, pale (also, 'pale with fright'), greenish, green (also; 'verdant' as opp. to *śushka*, 'dry'), RV. &c. &c.; m. yellowish (the colour), L.; Phaseolus Mungo or Lobatus, L.; a lion, L.; N. of a son of Kaśyapa, ŚBr.; of a son of Yadu, Hariv.; of a son of Rohita, BhP.; of a son of Rohitâśva, ib.; of a son of Yuvanâśva, ib.; of a son of Parāvṛit, ib.; of a son of Vapushmat, MārkP.; of an ichneumon (v.l. *hariṇa*), MBh.; pl. the descendants of Harita (also called *harītāḥ*), ĀśvŚr. (cf. Pāṇ. ii, 4, 67, Vārtt. 1, Pat.); N. of partic. verses of the AV. (also *haritā mantrāḥ*), Cat.; of a class of gods in the 12th Manvantara, Pur.; (*ā*), f. Dūrvā grass, Śiś. (= *nīla-dūrvā*, L.); turmeric, L.; a brown-coloured grape, L.; Sesbaṇa Aegyptiaca, L.; a kind of Svara-bhakti, TPrāt., Sch.; (*am*), n. a yellowish or greenish substance, ŚBr.; gold, AV.; Kāṭh.; greens, vegetables, Vishṇ. ('unripe grain,' Sch.); a kind of fragrant plant (= *sthauṇeyaka*), L. **–kapiśa**, mfn. yellowish-brown, Megh. **–kātya**, m. N. of a man, Pāṇ. i, 1, 73, Vārtt. 8. **–garbha**, mf(*ā*)n. containing a golden germ, Āp Śr. **–gomaya**, m. pl. fresh cow-dung, Kauś.; Gobh. **–cārika**, mfn. (perhaps) using supernatural means of locomotion, Divyâv. **–cohada**, mf(*ā*)n. having green leaves, MBh.; m. a tree, plant, L. **–jambhan**, mfn., Pāṇ. v, 4, 125. **–tṛiṇa**, n. green grass, MW. **–tva**, n. yellowish green (the colour), Car. **–dhānya**, n. green i.e. unripe corn, Gaut. **–nemin**, mfn. having (a chariot with) golden fellies (Śiva), R. **–pattra-maya**, mf(*ī*)n. formed of green leaves, Śiś. **–pattrikā**, f. a species of plant, L. **–pāṇḍu**, mfn. yellowish-pale, Suśr. **–prabha**, mfn. appearing yellowish or pale, Hariv. **–bheshajá**, n. a remedy against jaundice, AV. **–yajña**, m. N. of a man (see *hāritay*°). **–yava**, m. green barley, ĀpŚr. **–latā**, f. = *pattrikā*, L. **–śāka**, m. Moringa Pterygospermum, L. **–sena**, m. N. of a king, Buddh. **–spṛiśa**, mfn. (?), JaimUp. **–sraj** (*hárita-*), mfn. wearing or forming yellow (green) garlands, AV.; adorned with a golden chain or garland, AitBr. **–hari**, m. 'having reddish or bay horses,' the Sun, Kāv. **Haritâruṇa**, mfn. yellowish-red, Kum. **Haritârdhakāya**, mfn. having half the body green, Bcar. **Haritâśma**, n. 'green-coloured stone,' a turquoise or emerald, L.; sulphate of copper or blue vitriol, L. **Haritâśmaka**, n. a turquoise, Hcat. **Haritâśva**, mfn. having reddish or bay horses (the Sun), MBh.; m. N. of a son of Su-dyumna, VP. **Haritôpala**, m. 'green stone,' an emerald, BhP.

Haritaka, mfn. greenish (applied to the 6th unknown quantity), Col.; m. or n. a green herb, Car.; (*ī*), f. Terminalia Chebula, Divyâv.; (*am*), n. grass, Śiś. **–śāka**, n. Moringa Pterygospermum, Suśr.

Haritāya, Nom. P. Ā. °*yati* or °*yate*, to become or appear green, Bhaṭṭ.; Kād.

Haritāla, m. a kind of pigeon of a yellowish green colour, Columba Hurriyala, L.; (*ī*), f. Panicum Dactylon, L.; the blade of a sword, L.; the fourth (or third) day in the light half of the month Bhādra, L.; a streak or line in the sky, L.; the atmosphere, L.; (*am*), n. yellow orpiment or sulphuret of arsenic (described as the seed or seminal energy of Vishṇu, = *harer vīryam*), MBh.; Hariv. &c. **–janaka**, m. orpiment-producer (a word employed in modern Sanskṛit to express the metal arsenic). **–maya**, mf(*ī*)n. consisting or made of orpiment, Kum.

Haritālaka, m. a kind of pigeon (= *haritāla*), L.; n. yellow orpiment, L.; painting the person, theatrical decoration, W.; (*ikā*), f., see next.

Haritālikā, f. Panicum Dactylon, L.; the fourth (or third) day of the light half of the month Bhādra, L. **–kathā**, f., **-pūjana**, n. N. of wks. **–vrata**, n. a partic. religious observance on the above day, Cat.; *-kathā*, f., *-nirṇaya*, m. N. of wks.

Haritī-kṛita, mfn. painted green, Hit.

Harid, in comp. for *harit*. **–ambara**, mfn. wearing a yellow or green garment, Cat. **–aśva**, m. 'having fallow horses,' the Sun, Ragh.; Śiś. **–garbha**, m. a kind of Kuśa grass (prob. w.r. for *harid-darbha*), L. **–dantāvala**, m., **-rañjanī**, f. turmeric, L. **–varṇa**, mfn. green-coloured, of a yellowish golden colour, MW.

Haridra, m. the yellow sandal tree, VarBṛS.; N of a deity, Col.; (*ā*), f., see below.

Haridraka, m. the yellow sandal tree, VarBṛS.; N. of a serpent-demon, MBh.

Haridrā, f. Curcuma Longa, turmeric or its root ground to powder (46 synonyms of this plant are given), Kauś.; MBh.; Suśr. &c.; N. of a river, Col. **–°kta** (°*drâkta*), mfn. smeared or stained with t°, MW. **–gaṇa-pati**, m. a partic. form of the god Gaṇêśa (in whose honour a Mantra is repeated with offerings of t°); *-prakaraṇa*, n. N. of wk. **–gaṇêśa**, m. = *gaṇa-pati*, Cat. **–°ṅga** (°*drâṅga*), m. a kind of pigeon (= *haritāla*), L. **–dāna**, n. N. of wk. **–dvaya**, n. Curcuma Longa and C° Aromatica, L. **–°bha** (°*drâbha*), mfn. resembling t°; of a yellow colour, L.; m. Curcuma Zerumbet or Terminalia Tomentosa, L. **–meha**, m. yellow diabetes, Suśr.; °*hin*, mfn. suffering from it, ib. **–rāga** or **-rāgaka**, mfn. 't°-coloured,' unsteady in affection or attachment, fickle, capricious (like the colour of turmeric, which does not last), L.

Haridrika, mfn. dealing in turmeric, g. *kisarâdi*.

1. **Harin**, m. (m. c. for *hari*, only in gen. pl. *hariṇām*) a monkey, R. (B.) iv. 44, 16.

2. **Harin**, in comp. for *harit*. **–maṇi**, m. 'green gem,' an emerald, Śiś.; BhP.; *-maya*, mf(*ī*)n. made or consisting of emerald, Dharmaś. **–mudga**, m. Phaseolus Mungo, L.

2. Harimán, m. (for 1. see p. 1289, col. 2) yellow colour, yellowness (as a disease), jaundice, RV.; AV.

Hariya, m. a horse of a reddish or bay colour, L.

Hariśa, mfn., g. *lomâdi*.

Harītakī, f. (rarely °*ka*, m. n.) the yellow Myrobalan tree, Terminalia Chebula (28 synonyms and seven varieties are enumerated; the fruit is used for dyeing yellow and as a laxative), Suśr.; Hariv.; VarBṛS. **–cūrṇa**, n. the powdered seed of the Myrobalan tree, VarBṛS. **Harītaky-ādi**, N. of a medic. wk.

Hary, in comp. for *hári*. **–akshá**, mfn. yellow-eyed, VS.; MBh.; m. a lion, MBh.; R.; the zodiacal sign Leo, Cat.; a monkey, R.; N. of Kubera, L.; of a demon causing diseases, PārGṛ.; of an Asura, BhP.; of a son of Pṛithu, ib.; of Śiva, MW. **–akshan**, mfn. = *-aksha*, MBh. **–aṅka-kula**, mfn. born in the family whose symbol is the lion (i. e. the solar race), Bcar. **–aṅga**, m. N. of a son of Campa, Hariv.; VP. **–amara**, m. N. of a man, Virac. **–avana**, m. N. of a son of Kṛita, BhP. **–aśva**, m. a bay horse (of Indra), MBh.; R.; (*háry-*), mfn. possessing bay horses, RV.; m. N. of Indra, BhP.; of Śiva, MBh.; of various men, ib.; Hariv.; R.; Pur.; pl. N. of the sons of Daksha, Hariv.; Pur.; *-cāpa*, 'Indra's bow,' the rainbow, Hariv.; *-prasūta* (*háry-aśva-*), mf(*ā*)n. impelled or instigated by him who possesses bay horses, RV. **–ashṭaka**, n. N. of wk. **–ātman**, m. N. of a Vyāsa, VP. **–ānanda**, m. N. of a pupil of Rāmânanda, W.

Haryajvāyana, m. (prob. for *hari-y*°) N. of a teacher, JaimUp.

3. **Hāra**, mfn. (for 1. and 2. see p. 1289, col. 2) relating to Hari or Vishṇu, BhP.

Hārika, mfn. being like Hari (= *harir iva*), g. *aṅguly-ādi*; m. pl. N. of a people, MārkP.

Hārikarṇa, m. patr. fr. *hari-karṇa*, Pravar.

Hā́rikarṇī-pútra, m. N. of a preceptor, ŚBr.

Hārikeyī, f. a patr., Pāṇ. iv, 1, 15, Vārtt. 1, Pat.

Hāriṇa, mfn. belonging or relating to or derived from deer, Kauś.; MBh. &c.; n. venison, MW.

Hāriṇaka, mfn. hunting deer, Pāṇ. iv, 4, 35, Sch.

Hāriṇāśvā, f. (fr. *hariṇâśva*) a partic. Mūrchanā, Saṃgīt.

2. **Hārita**, m. (fr. *harit* and *harita*) green (the colour), W.; a moderate wind neither too gentle nor too strong, L.; the Haritāla pigeon, L.; 'descendant of Harita,' N. of a son of Viśvāmitra (pl. his family, also called *haritāḥ*), MBh.; Hariv.; VP.; (*ā*), f. a kind of Svara-bhakti (v. l. *haritā*), TPrāt., Sch.; (*ī*), f. a patr. (*-putra*, m. a son of Hārītī), Lalit.

Hāritaka, n. = *haritaka*, a green vegetable, L.

Hāritakāta, m. pl. the descendants of Harita-kātya, Pāṇ. i, 1, 73, Vārtt. 8.

Hāritayajña, mfn. relating or belonging to Harita-yajña, L.

Hāritāyana, m. patr. fr. *hārita*, Pāṇ. iv, 1, 100.

Hāritāsra, m. N. of a man, Cat.

Hāridrá, mfn. (fr. *haridrā*) coloured with turmeric, yellow, ŚBr. &c. &c.; m. a yellow colour, L.; the Kadamba tree, L.; a kind of vegetable poison, Bhpr.; a kind of fever (also of animals), ib. **–tva**, n. yellowness, Car. **–meha**, °*hin* = *haridrā-m*°, ib.

Hāridraka, mfn. yellow, VarBṛS.; m. a kind of tree, L.; N. of a serpent-demon, Hariv.

Hāridravá (or *hā́r*°), m. (fr. *hari-dru*) a kind of yellow bird, RV.; AV.; pl. the disciples of Hari-dru, Nir.; (also °*vika*) m. or n. a work of the Hāri-dravas, ib.

Hāridravin, m. the disciples of Hari-dru, Pāṇ. iv, 3, 104, Sch.

Hāridravīya or °*veya*, m. pl. id., IndSt.

Hāridrumata, m. patr. fr. *haridru-mat*, ChUp.

Hāriyojaná, mf(*ī*)n. (fr. *hari-y*°) one who harnesses bay horses (Indra), RV.; m. a partic. Soma-graha, VS.; ŚBr.; ŚrS.

Hārivarṇa, n. (fr. *hari-v*°) N. of various Sāmans, ĀrshBr.

Hārivāsa, m. (fr. *hari-v*°) N. of a deity, W.

Hārisheṇi and °*ṇya*, m. patr. fr. *hari-sheṇa*, Pāṇ. iv, 1, 152 and 153, Sch.

2. **Hārīta**, m. (for 1. see p. 1289, col. 3) = *harita*, the Haritāla pigeon, MBh.; Suśr. &c.; N. of various authors &c. (esp. of a lawyer often quoted), Āpast.; TPrāt.; MBh. &c.; pl. the descendants of Hārīta, VP.; N. of a people, R.; (*ī*), f. N. of a deity (*-putra*, m. N. of a family, IndSt.) **–dharma-śāstra**, n. Hārīta's law-book, Cat. **–bandha**, m. a kind of metre, Col. **–śikshā**, **-saṃhitā**, **-smṛiti**, f. N. of wks.

Hārītaka, m. the Haritāla pigeon, Pañcat.; N. of an author, VP.

Hārīti, m. pl. patr. fr. *hārīta*, Pravar.

Hāryaśva, m. patr. fr. *hary-aśva*, g. *bidâdi*.

Hāryojaná, v. l. for *hāriyojana*, MaitrS.

हरि 3. *hari*, ind. (for 1. see p. 1289, col. 2; for 2. ib., col. 3) an exclamation ('alas!'), MW.

हरिज *harija*, n. (= Gk. ὁρίζων) the horizon, VarBṛS.; the longitudinal parallax, Sūryas.

हरिभ *haribha*. See *hariva*.

हरिमन्त *harimanta*, m. N. of an Āṅgirasa (author of RV. ix, 72), Anukr.

हरिले *harile*, ind. (in dram.) a vocative particle used in addressing a female slave, W.

हरिव *hariva*, m. or n. a partic. high number, Buddh.

हरिष *harisha*, m. = *harsha*, joy, L.

हरीशय *harīśaya*. See *hari-śaya*, p. 1290.

हरीषा *harīshā*, f. a partic. kind of seasoning or condiment (v. l. *harīsā*), Bhpr.

हरुण *haruṇa*, m. or n. a partic. high number, Buddh.

हरेणु *hareṇu*, m. a kind of pea or pulse (with slightly globular seeds), Suśr.; a creeper marking the boundary of a village, L.; N. of Laṅkā, L.; f. a sort of drug or perfume (= *reṇukā*), L.; a respectable woman, L.; a copper-coloured deer, L.

Hareṇuka, m. (or *ā*, f.) a kind of pea or pulse, Lalit.; Suśr.

हर्त *harta*, °*tavya*, °*tṛi* &c. See p. 1289, col. 2.

हर्तालिकाव्रतनिर्णय *hartālikā-vrata-nirṇaya*, m. N. of wk.

हर्मन् *harman*. See p. 1289, col. 2.

हर्मित *harmita*, mfn. thrown, cast, sent, L.; burnt (cf. *gharma*), L.

हर्मुट *harmuṭa*, m. a tortoise, L.; the sun, L.

हर्म्य *harmyá*, n. (ifc. f. *ā*; said to be fr. √*hṛi*, 'to captivate or charm the mind;' but rather connected with √2. *ghṛi* and *gharma*, and perhaps originally signifying 'the domestic fire-hearth'), a large house, palace, mansion, any house or large building or residence of a wealthy person, RV. &c. &c.; a stronghold, prison, RV. v, 32, 5; viii, 5, 23; a fiery pit, place of torment, region of darkness, the nether world, MW.; mfn. living in houses, ib. **–cara**, mfn. moving or living in a mansion or palace, Kṛishṇaj. **–tala** (Suśr.), **-pṛishṭha** (Hariv.), n. the flat roof or upper room of any mansion or palace. **–bhāj**, mfn. living in a p°, MW. **–valabhī**, f. = *-tala*, VarBṛS. **–stha**, mfn. being in a house or palace, MW. **–sthala**, n. = *-tala*, Megh. **Harmyâgra**, n. = *harmya-tala*, Ragh. **Harmyâṅgana**, n. the court of a palace, MW.

Harmikā, f. a summerhouse on a Stūpa, Divyâv.

Harmye-shṭhā́, mfn. (fr. loc. of *harmya* + *sthā*) being in a house or stall (cf. *gharmye-shṭhā*), RV.

हर्य् *hary*, cl. 1. P. (Dhātup. xv, 7) *haryati* (rarely Ā. °*te*; pr. p. P. *háryat* or *haryát* [see below], Ā. *háryamāṇa*), to like, delight in, be fond of or pleased with, yearn after, long for (acc. or loc.), RV.; to go, Naigh. ii, 14; to threaten, Dhātup.: Intens. *jāharyīti*, *jāharti*, *jāharyati*, Siddh. [Cf. Gk. χαίρω.]

Háryat or **haryát**, mfn. eager, willing, glad, RV.

Haryatá, mfn. desired, wished for, pleasant, dear, precious, RV.; m. a horse (accord. to some, 'a steed fit for the Aśva-medha sacrifice'), L.; N. of the author of RV. viii, 72 (having the patr. Prāgātha), Anukr.

हर्यक्ष *hary-aksha*, *hary-aṅga* &c. See above, col. 1.

हर्यत्वत *haryatvata*, m. N. of a son of Kṛita (v. l. *haryaśvata*), VP.

हर्याीत *haryāta*, m. pl. N. of a people, VP.

हर्ष *harsha*, m. (ifc. f. *ā*; fr. √*hṛish*) bristling, erection (esp. of the hair in a thrill of rapture or delight), MBh.; Kāv. &c.; joy, pleasure, happiness (also personified as a son of Dharma), KaṭhUp.; MBh. &c.; erection of the sexual organ, sexual excitement, lustfulness, Suśr.; ardent desire, MBh.; N. of an Asura, Kathās.; of a son of Kṛishṇa, BhP.; of various authors &c. (also with *dīkshita*, *miśra*, *sūri* &c.; cf. *śrī-harsha*); mfn. happy, delighted, W. **–kara**, mf(*ī*)n. causing joy or happiness, BhP. **–kīrti**, m. N. of an author, Cat. **–kīlaka**, m. a kind of sexual enjoyment, L. **–kula**, **-kulâgraṇī**, **-kuśala**, m. N. of authors. **–kṛit**, m. N. of a man, VP. **–kaumudī**, f. N. of a Commentary. **–krodha**, m. du. joy and anger, Hit. **–gaṇi**, m. N. of an author, Cat. **–gadgada**, mfn. (a voice) faltering with joy, MBh. **–garbha**, mfn. full of joy, blissful, Daś. **–gupta**, m. N. of a man, Kathās. **–carita**, n. N. of a poem by Bāṇa (containing the life of king Harsha-vardhana of Sthāṇvīśvara); *-vārttika*, n., *-saṃketa*, m. N. of Comms. on the above wk. **–cala**, mfn. trembling with joy, Ragh. **–ja**, mfn. arising from joy, MBh.; n. semen, L. **–jaḍa**, mfn. paralyzed with joy, MW. **–datta**, **-datta-sūnu**, m. N. of authors, Cat. **–dāna**, n. a gift joyfully offered, Hcar. **–deva**, m. N. of a poet and king (also called *śrī-h*°, q. v.) **–dohala**, m. or n. lustful desire, Mālav. **–dhara** and **-nātha-śarman**, m. N. of authors, Cat. **–nāda**, m. a shout of joy, R. **–niḥsvana** (Ragh.), **-nisvana** (R.), m. id. **–pura**, n. N. of a town, Kathās.; (*ī*), f. (in music) a partic. Rāga, Saṃgīt. **–pūrṇa-vaktra**, mfn. having a face full of joy, Bcar. **–bhāj**, mfn. partaking of joy, joyful, glad, Pañcat. **–máya**, mf(*ī*)n. whose essence or nature is joy, ŚBr. **–malla**, m. = *-deva*, Vās., Introd. **–mitra**, m. N. of a king, Rājat. **–yukta**, mfn. filled with joy, joyful, VarBṛS. **–ratna** and **-rāma**, m. N. of two authors, Cat. **–vat**, mfn. full of joy (ind. = 'joyfully'), Śatr.; Kathās.; HParis.; (*atī*), f. N. of a princess, Kathās.; of a town, ib. **–vardhana**, m. a kind of musical composition, Saṃgīt.; m. N. of a powerful king of Northern India (said to have founded an era, A. D. 605 or 606); pl. N. of a people, MārkP. **–varman**, m. N. of a king, Kathās. **–vivardhana**, mfn. increasing or promoting joy, MBh. **–vivṛiddha-sattva**, mfn. one whose vigour is increased by happiness, MW. **–vishāda**, m. joy and depression, Mālav. **–vihvala**, mfn. agitated with joy, overjoyed, W. **–veṇuka**, m. a festival, L. **–śoka**, m. du. joy and sorrow, KaṭhUp. **–samanvita**, filled with joy, joyful, W. **–sampuṭa**, m. a kind of sexual enjoyment, L. **–svana**, m. a cry of joy, sound of pleasure, L. **Harshâkula**, mfn. agitated with joy, R. **Harshâtiśaya**, m. excess of joy, Bcar. **Harshânvita**, mfn. full of joy, happy, MBh. **Harshâvishṭa**, mfn. penetrated or filled with joy, Pañcat. **Harshâśru**, n. tears of joy, Daś. **Harshêśvara-māhātmya**, n. N. of wk. **Harshôtkarsha**, m. excess of happiness, W. **Harshôtphulla-locana**, mfn. one whose eyes are opened wide in rapture, Ratnâv. **Harshôdaya**, m. rise of joy, occurrence of pleasure, W.

Harshaka, mfn. thrilling, setting on edge (see *danta-h*°); gladdening, delighting, R.; m. N. of a mountain, L.; of a son of Citra-gupta, Cat.; of a king belonging to the Śaiśunāga dynasty, ib.

Harshaṇa, mfn. causing the hair of the body to stand erect, thrilling with joy or desire, gladdening, delightful, pleasant, MBh.; Hariv. &c.; m. 'gladdener,' N. of one of the five arrows of Kāma-deva, Bcar.; of a man, VP. (L. also, 'a partic. disease of the eyes;' 'a partic. Śrāddha;' 'a deity presiding over Śrāddhas;' 'the 14th of the astron. Yogas'); n. bristling, erection, Suśr.; erection of the sexual organ, sexual excitement, ib.; the act of delighting, delight, joy, happiness, MBh.; R. **–tā**, f. joyful excitement, Bālar.

Harshaṇīya, mfn. delightful, pleasant, Lalit.

Harshayitnu, mfn. gladdening, causing delight, W.; m. a son, L.; n. gold, L.

Harshāya, Nom. Ā. °*yate*, to be glad, MW.

Harshita, mfn. (fr. Caus.) made to stand erect, bristling (as hair &c.), Cat.; gladdened, delighted, charmed, pleased, happy, R.; Hariv.; n. joy, delight (see *sa-h*°).

Harshin, mfn. (prob.) becoming rigid or firm (see *viḍu-h*°); joyful, joyfully, anticipating (comp.), Hariv.; Pañcar.; rejoicing, delighting, MBh.; (*iṇī*), f. a partic. plant, L.

Harshuka, mfn. gladdening, delighting, L.

Harshu-mát, mfn. (prob.) exciting, stimulating, RV.

Harshula, mfn. disposed to be cheerful or happy, delighted, MBh.; Rājat.; m. a lover, L.; a deer, L.; N. of Buddha, L.; (*ā*), f. a girl with a beard (unfit for marriage), L.

Hárshyā, ind. (instr.) in impatient excitement, RV.

Hārshṭeya, m. (prob.) metron. fr. *hrishṭi*, g. *grishty-ādi.*

Hārshṇi, f. = *haraṇa*, L.

हर्षीका *harshīkā*, f. a kind of metre, RPrāt.

हल् 1. *hal* (prob. invented as a source for *hala*), cl. 1. P. *halati*, to plough, make furrows, Dhātup. xx, 7.

Hala, m. n. (ifc. f. *ā*) a plough (also as a weapon, and as a land measure), MBh.; Kāv. &c.; m. N. of an author, Cat.; pl. N. of a country and people in the north, VarBṛS.; (*ā*), f. the earth, L.; water, L.; spirituous liquor, wine, L.; (*ī*), f. Methonica Superba, L.; (*am*), n. a plough, L.; a partic. constellation (reckoned among the Ākriti-yogas), VarBṛS.; ugliness, deformity (= *vairāgya*), R.; hindrance, obstruction (= *prati-shedha*), L.; quarrel (= *vivāda*), L. **-kakud,** f. the projecting beam of a plough, BhP. **-golaka,** m. a kind of insect, MBh. (Nīl.) **-daṇḍa,** m. the shaft or pole of a pl°, L. **-dhara,** m. 'plough-holder,' N. of Bala-rāma (as carrying a peculiar weapon shaped like a ploughshare), MBh.; Śiś.; of various authors &c., Vcar.; Rājat. **-bandha,** g. *khaṇḍikādi.* **-bhūti,** m. N. of Śaṃkarācārya, Gal. **-bhṛit,** m. = *-dhara* (N. of Bala-rāma), MBh.; Megh. **-bhṛiti,** f. ploughing, agriculture, husbandry, L.; m. = *-bhūti*, L. **-mārga,** m. a furrow, Hariv. **-mukha,** n. a ploughshare, R.; (*ī*), f. a kind of metre, Piṅg. **-muhūrta,** n. N. of a partic. hour, Cat. **-rada,** mfn. having teeth shaped like a plough, Bhām. **-rāksha,** n. Tabernæmontana Coronaria, L. **-vaṅśa,** m. = *-daṇḍa*, L. **-vāhā,** f. 'plough,' a partic. land-measure, Inscr. **-sīra,** m. (prob.) a ploughshare (others, 'a furrow'), Divyāv. **-hati,** f. striking (the soil) with a plough, ploughing, furrowing, W. **Halābha,** m. 'plough-like,' a piebald horse with a black stripe along its back, L. **Halābhiyoga,** m. application of a plough, the beginning of ploughing, Gobh. **Halāyudha,** m. 'pl°-weaponed,' N. of Bala-rāma (see above; also transferred to Vishṇu-Kṛishṇa), MBh.; Hariv.; (also with *bhaṭṭa, miśra* &c.) N. of various writers (esp. of a poet, of the author of the Abhidhāna-ratnamālā, of the author of the Purāṇa-sarvasva &c.), Cat.; *-cchāndogya* (?) and *-stava*, m. N. of wks. **Hal'īshā,** f. = *halēshā*, the pole of a plough, Pat.

Halaka, m. N. of a man, Divyāv.

Halakā, f., g. *prēkshādi.*

Halakin, mfn. (fr. prec.), ib.

Halaya, Nom. P. °*yati*, to plough (= *halaṃ gṛihṇāti*), Vop.

Halahala, mfn. ploughing, making furrows, L.

Halāha, m. (prob. for *halābha*) a piebald horse, L.

1. **Hali,** m. a large plough (see *śata-h*°); a furrow, W.; agriculture, ib.; N. of a man, g. *gṛishṭy-ādi.*

2. **Hali,** in comp. for *halin.* **-priya,** m. Nauclea Kadamba, L.; (*ā*), f. spirituous liquor, L. **-rāma,** m. (with *śarman*) N. of an author.

Halika, m. a ploughman, husbandman, L.; N. of a serpent-demon, MBh.

Halin, m. a ploughman, agriculturist, Vās.; N. of Bala-rāma, MBh.; Hariv.; of a Ṛishi, R.; (*inī*), f. a number of ploughs, L.; Methonica Superba, L.

Halī. See *hala.*

Hale-dvipadikā, f. (fr. loc. of *hala* + *dv*°) N. of a partic. tax, Pāṇ. vi, 2, 63, Sch.

Halya, mfn. ploughed, tilled (see *tri-* and *dvi-h*°); m. ploughing, agriculture, Pāṇ. vi, 4, 97; (*ā*), f. a multitude of ploughs, g. *pāśādi*; (*am*), n. a ploughed field, arable land, MW.; deformity, R.

Hāla, m. = *hala*, a plough, L.; a 'scraper' (kind of bird), Suśr., Sch.; N. of Bala-rāma (cf. *haladhara*), L.; of Sātavāhana, Cat.; of a king (son of Arishṭa-karman), VP.; (*ā*), f. spirituous liquor (a provincial term accord. to Vām. v, 1, 13; (*ī*), f. a wife's younger sister, L. **-bhṛit,** m. N. of Bala-rāma (= *hala-bhṛit*), MW. **-bandha,** n. (fr. *hala-b*°), g. *khaṇḍikādi.* **-sapta-sataka,** n. N. of an anthology (containing 700 Prākṛit stanzas). **Hālāsya,** N. of a place sacred to Śiva; *-khaṇḍa*, m. n., *-māhātmya*, n., °*syāshṭaka*, n. N. of wks.

Hālaka, m. a horse of a yellowish brown or tawny colour, L.

Hālāha, m. = *halāha*, L.

Hālika, mfn. relating or belonging to a plough, Pāṇ. iv, 3, 124; m. a ploughman, agriculturist, Rājat.; Pañcat.; a slaughterer (used in explaining *go-vikarta*), KātyŚr., Sch.

Hālinī, f. a kind of lizard, L.

Hālu, m. a tooth, Uṇ. i, 1, Sch.

Hāleya, m. (fr. *hali*) N. of a king, BhP.

हल् 2. *hal*, m. n. (in Pāṇini's system) a technical expression for all the consonants or for any consonant. **-anta,** mfn. ending in a consonant; m. or n. N. of wk.

हलदी *haladī* or *haladdī*, f. turmeric (= *haridrā*), L.

हलहला *halahalā*, ind. an exclamation of applause or approbation, MBh.; R. **-śabda,** m. the exclamation *halahalā*, halloo, hallooing, shout, ib.

हला *halā*, ind. (in dram.) a vocative particle (used in addressing a female friend who is an equal), Daśar.; Sāh.

हलाहल *halāhala*, m. n. a kind of deadly poison (produced at the churning of the ocean by gods and demons), Kāv.; Pañcat.; m. (only L.) a kind of lizard; a kind of snake; a Jaina or Bauddha sage.

Hālahala (Jātakam.) and **hālahāla** (L.), n. the above poison.

Hālāhala, m. a partic. poisonous plant (the seed of which is said to resemble a cow's teat), Bhpr.; a kind of lizard, L.; a kind of spider, L.; n. (rarely m.), a deadly poison prepared from the roots of the above plant, accord. to R. and BhP. produced at the churning of the ocean (cf. *halāhala*), Kāv.; Suśr.; BhP.; (*ā*), f. a kind of small mouse, L.; (*ī*), f. spirituous liquor, L. **-dhara,** m. 'having venom,' a small black snake, L.

Hāhala or **hāhāla,** n. the above poison, L.

हलिक्ष्ण *halíkshṇa*, m. a kind of lion, VS. (Mahīdh.)

Hálikshṇa, m. a kind of animal, TS. (Sch.); m. or n. a partic. intestine, AV.

हलिङ्गु *haliṅgu*, m. N. of a man (see next).

Háliṅgava, m. patr. fr. *haliṅgu*, ŚBr.

हलिभ *halibha*, m. or n. a partic. high number, Buddh.

हलिमा *halimā*, f. N. of one of the seven mothers of Skanda, MBh.

हलीन *halīna*, m. Tectona Grandis, L.; = next, L.

Halīma, m. Pandanus Odoratissimus, L.

Halīmaka, m. id., L.; a partic. form of jaundice (in this sense prob. connected with *hariman*), Suśr.; N. of a serpent-demon, MBh.

हलुआण *haluāṇa* or *halūāṇa*, N. of a place, Cat.

हलुहार *haluhāra*, m. a horse with black testicles and a mark on its forehead, L.

हल्ल *halla*, m. N. of a man, Buddh.

हल्लक *hallaka*, n. the red lotus, Hāsy.

हल्लन *hallana*, n. rolling or tossing about, rolling about in sleep, L.

हल्लीश *hallīśa*, m. one of the eighteen Uparūpakas or minor dramatic entertainments (described as a piece in one act, consisting chiefly of singing and dancing by one male and 7, 8, or 10 female performers; perhaps a kind of ballet), Sāh.; n. a circular dance (performed by women under the direction of a man), Kāvyād.

Hallīśaka, m. n. a kind of dance (= prec.), Kāvyād.

Hallīsha, °**shaka,** m. n. id., L.

Hallīsa, m. n. id., HPariś.

Hallīsaka, m. n. id., Pañcad.; a kind of musical instrument (v. l. *jhallīshaka*), Hariv.

Hallīsakāya (only °*yita*, n., also impers.) to perform the above dance, Kāśīkh.

हल्ह *halha.* See *vihálha.*

हव 1. *hava*, m. (fr. √*hu*) an oblation, burnt offering, sacrifice, Śiś.; fire or the god of fire, L.

1. **Havana,** m. (for 2. see p. 1294, col. 1) fire or Agni the god of fire, L.; a fire-receptacle (= f.), L.; (*ī*), f. the sacrificial ladle, ŚBr.; KātyŚr.; a hole made in the ground for the sacrificial fire which is to receive a burnt-oblation, L.; (*am*), n. the act of offering an oblation with fire, sacrifice, MBh.; Hariv.; a sacrificial ladle, Vait. **-paddhati,** f. N. of a Tantra wk. **Havanāyus,** m. 'having the burnt-offering for its life,' fire, L.

Havanīya, mfn. to be offered with fire, sacrificial, W.; m. (?) an oblation, Śiś. (Sch.); n. anything fit for an oblation, clarified butter, ghee, W.

Haviḥ, in comp. for *havis.* **-śālā,** f. a room where oblations are prepared, L. **-śesha,** m. the remnant of a sacrifice; *-bhaksha*, mfn. eating the r° of a sacrifice, KātyŚr. **-śravas,** m. N. of a son of Dhṛita-rāshṭra, MBh. **-saṃsthā,** f., see *havir-yajña-s*°.

Havitrī, f. a hole made in the ground for receiving the sacred fire for an oblation, L.

Havin. See under 2. *hava.*

Havir, in comp. for *havis.* **-ád** (RV.), **-adá** (AV.), mfn. eating the oblation. **-ádya,** n. the act of eating or tasting the obl°, RV.; TBr. **-antarāṇa,** n. passing over an obl°, KātyŚr. **-aśana,** m. 'consuming oblations,' fire, L. **-ātañcana,** n. a kind of rennet for coagulating an obl° of milk &c., ŚBr.; KātyŚr. **-āhuti,** f. offering an obl°, GṛŚrS. **-ucchishṭá,** n. the residue of an oblation, ŚBr.; *-bhuj*, mfn. eating the res° of an obl°, ŚrS.; *-śesha*, m. what is left from the res° of an obl°, Gobh.; °*ṭāśa* (ŚBr.), °*ṭāśana* (ŚāṅkhŚr.), mfn. = °*ṭa-bhuj.* **-gandhā,** f. 'smelling like clarified butter,' Prosopis Spicigera, L. **-gṛiha** or **-geha,** n. any house or chamber in which an oblation is offered, sacrificial hall, L. **-grahaṇī,** f. a sacrificial ladle, KātyŚr. **-dá,** mfn. giving or bringing oblations, RV. **-dāna,** n. the gift of an oblation, Mn.; R. **-dhā́na,** m. N. of the author of RV. x, 11–15, Anukr.; of a son of Antar-dhāna (cf. *havir-dhāman*), BhP.; (*ī*), f. N. of the mythical cow Surabhi or Kāma-dhenu, ib.; of the wife of Havir-dhāna, ib.; (*am*), n. 'oblation-receptacle,' the vehicle in which the Soma plants are conveyed to be pressed (generally in du.), AV.; VS.; ŚBr.; a shed for the Soma vehicles, ib.; KātyŚr.; a place of sacrifice, MBh.; Hariv.; the earth (as the depository of obl°s), AV.; (*e*), du. (with *Prajāpateḥ*) N. of two Sāmans, ĀrshBr. **-dhānin,** mfn. possessing a Soma car or shed, TS. **-dhāman,** m. N. of a son of Antardhāman (cf. *havir-dhāna*), MBh. **-dhūma,** m. the smoke from an oblation, Bcar. **-nirvapaṇa,** n. (with *pātra*) the vessel in which an obl° is offered, ĀpŚr. **-bhāga** (*havír-*), m. the share in an obl°, ŚBr. **-bhāj,** mfn. partaking of an oblation, Nir. **-bhuj,** m. 'eating the obl°,' fire or Agni the god of fire (also applied to Śiva and other gods), Hariv.; Kāv.; BhP.; pl. N. of the Pitṛis of the Kshatriyas, Mn. iii, 197. **-bhū,** f. the place of sacrifice (personified as daughter of Kardama and wife of Pulastya), BhP. **-bhūta** (*havír-*), mfn. become an obl°, ŚBr. **-máthi,** mfn. destroying or disturbing sacrifices, RV. **-mantha,** m. Premna Spinosa or Longifolia, L. **-yajñá,** m. the offering of an obl°, a simple oblation of clarified butter &c. (as opp. to a *soma-y*°), Br.; GṛŚrS.; *-kāṇḍa*, n. N. of the first (or second) book of the ŚBr.; *-ṛtvij* (for *-ṛitvij*), a priest officiating at a Havir-y°, KātyŚr.; *-vidha* (°*jñá-*), mfn. of the nature of the Havir-y°, ŚBr.; *-saṃsthā*, f. primary or essential form of the Havir-y° (7 are enumerated, viz. Agny-ādheya, Agni-hotra, Darśa-pūrṇamāsau, Cāturmāsyāni, Paśu-bandha, Sautrāmaṇī, and Pāka-yajña), Lāṭy. **-yājin,** m. 'oblation-offerer,' a priest, W. **-varsha,** m. N. of a son of Agnīdhra and the Varsha ruled by him, MārkP. **-vah,** mfn. (nom. *-vāṭ*) conveying the sacrifice, RV. **-huti,** f. offering an oblation, L.

Havish, in comp. for *havis.* **-káraṇa,** n. the act of preparing an oblation, TS.; Br. **-kṛit,** mfn. preparing the oblation, RV.; ŚBr.; ŚrS.; m. the exclamation *hávish-kṛid éhi* (VS. i, 15), ŚBr.; ŚrS.; N. of an Āṅgirasa (cf. *hāvishkṛita*), TS. **-kṛita** (*havísh-*), mfn. made into an obl°, TS.; ŚBr.; Mn. **-kṛiti** (*havísh-*), f. preparation of the obl°, RV. **-ṭas,** ind. (= abl.) from the obl°, ŚāṅkhŚr. **-ṭva,** n. the being an oblation, Nyāyam., Sch. **-paṅkti** (*havísh-*), f. five obl°s collectively, Br.; mfn. consisting of 5 obl°s, Kāṭh.; AitBr. **-pati** (*havísh-*), m. lord of the obl°, RV.; VS.; ShaḍvBr. **-pā́,** mfn. drinking the obl°, RV. **-pātrá,** n. a vessel for the obl°, ŚBr.; KātyŚr. **-pānta-sūkta,** n. the hymn RV. x, 88 (cf. next), Cat. **-pāntīya,** mfn. beginning with *havish-pāntam* (RV. x, 88), Nir. vii,

23; Mn. xi, 252 (v. l. *havishyantīya*). **-mat** (*havísh-*), mfn. possessing or offering an obl°, RV.; AV.; KaṭhUp.; attended with or containing obl°s, RV.; VS.; m. N. of an Āṅgirasa, TS.; of a Devarshi, MBh.; of one of the 7 Ṛishis in the 6th Manv-antara or of one (or two) in the 11th, Hariv.; Pur.; pl. N. of a class of Pitṛis (regarded as progenitors of Kshatriyas and as descended from Aṅgiras), Mn. iii, 197; 198; (*atī*), f. N. of the mythical cow Kāma-dhenu, BhP.; of a daughter of Aṅgiras, MBh.

Havishyà, mfn. fit or prepared for an oblation, RV.; TS.; worthy of an oblation or sacrifice (as Śiva), MBh.; m. n. anything fit for an oblation (esp. rice or other kinds of grain), sacrificial food (cf. comp. n. = *ghṛita, havis* &c.), GṛŚrS.; Mn.; MBh. &c.; (*ā*), f., Pāṇ. iv, 4, 122. **-bhaksha**, mfn. eating sacrificial food (rice or other grain, clarified butter &c.; *-tā*, f.), ŚāṅkhGṛ. **-bhuj**, mfn. id., Mn. xi, 78. **-śanna**, n. the refuse of a sacrifice, KātyŚr.

Havishyânna, n. food fit to be eaten during certain festival days, any particularly sacred food, Yājñ.

Havishyâśin, mfn. = *havishya-bhuj*, Mn. xi, 219.

Havishyantīya. See *havish-pāntīya.*

Havishyanda, m. (for *haviḥ-sy°*) N. of a son of Viśvāmitra (v. l. *havishpanda* and *havisyanda*), R.

Havís, n. an oblation or burnt offering, anything offered as an oblation with fire (as clarified butter, milk, Soma, grain; *havish* √*kṛi*, 'to prepare an oblation,' 'make into an oblation'), RV. &c. &c.; water, Naigh. i, 12; fire, Kālac.; N. of a Marut-vat (?), Kālac.

1. **Havyá**, n. (for 2. see col. 2) anything to be offered as an oblation, sacrificial gift or food (in later language often opp. to *kavya*, q. v.), RV. &c. &c. **-kavya**, n. oblations both to the gods and to the spirits of deceased ancestors, Mn. iii, 190; *-vaha*, mfn. receiving both oblations (cf. above), MBh.; conveying both oblations, ib.; *°vyâśa*, mfn. eating both obl°s, Pañcar. **-jushṭi** (*havyá-*), f. delight in or enjoyment of an oblation, RV.; AitBr. **-dāti** (*havyá-*), mfn. conveying or presenting oblations (to the gods; said of Agni), RV.; f. sacrificial gift, oblation, ib. **-pa**, m. 'protector of oblations,' N. of one of the 7 Ṛishis in the 13th Manv-antara, Hariv. **-pāka**, m. = *caru*, L. **-bhuj**, m. 'obl°-eater,' fire or the god of fire, VarBṛS. **-mantrâdhikṛita**, m. du. 'superintendent of the sacrifice and of the council,' a priest and a minister, Bcar. x, 1. **-yoni**, m. 'source of the sacrifice,' a deity, L. **-lehin**, m. 'obl°-licker,' fire, the god of fire, Bālar. **-váh**, m. (nom. *-vāṭ*) bearing the oblation (to the gods), RV.; MBh.; R.; fire or the god of fire, ib. **-vaha**, m. fire, L. **-vāhá** (or *-vāha*), mfn. = *-vah* (also applied to the Aśvattha tree of whose wood the Araṇi is made), AV.; TBr.; m. Agni or fire, MBh.; MārkP. **-váhana**, mfn. = *-vah*, RV.; ŚrS.; m. N. of Agni, TS.; ŚBr.; fire, MBh.; R. &c.; N. of the 9th Kalpa (q. v.); of one of the 7 Ṛishis under Manu Rohita or Sāvarṇa, Hariv.; MārkP. **-vāhinī**, f. 'obl°-bearer,' N. of the tutelary deity of the family of Kapila, Cat. **-śódhana**, mfn. purifying the obl°, TBr. **-sūkti** (*havyá-*), f. a sacrificial verse or formula, VS.; TBr. **-sūd** (RV.), **-sūda** (TS.), or **-sūdana** (VS.), mfn. preparing or providing the oblation. **Havyâd**, mfn. eating the oblation, RV. **Havyâda**, mfn. id., Hariv.; m. N. of a Ṛishi, Cat. **Havyâśa** (Rājat.), **havyâśana** (L.), m. 'oblation-eater,' fire.

1. **Hāvaka**, m. (fr. Caus.) the institutor of a sacrifice, Siṇhâs.

Hāvanīya, mfn. (fr. id.) to be caused to sacrifice or to be sacrificed, Baudh.

Hāvin, mfn. offering an oblation, sacrificing (in *eka-h°*), ŚāṅkhŚr.

Hāvirdhāna, mfn. containing the word *havir-dhāna*, g. *vimuktâdi*.

Hāvirdhāni, m. patr. fr. *havir-dhāna*, BhP.

Hāvir-yajñika (Lāṭy.), **°yajñiya** (KātyŚr.), mfn. relating or belonging to or destined for the Havir-yajña.

Hāvishkṛita (fr. *havishkṛit*), n. N. of a Sāman, ĀrshBr.

Hāvishmata, n. (fr. *havish-mat*) N. of a Sāman, ĀrshBr.

हव 2. *háva*, mfn. (fr. √*hve* or *hū*; for 1. see p. 1293, col. 2) calling, RV.; m. call, invocation, ib.; AV.; direction, order, command, L. **-vat**, mfn. containing the word *hava*, AitBr.

2. **Hávana**, m. N. of a Rudra, MBh.; Hariv.; n. calling, invocation, summons, RV.; Pañcar.; challenging or challenge to battle, MW. **-śrút**, mfn. listening to or hearing invocations, RV.; ŚāṅkhŚr. **-syád**, mfn. hastening to an invocation or challenge, RV.

Havás, n. an invocation, call, RV.

Havín, mfn. calling, invoking, AV.; looking for help, AitBr. ('skilled in sacrifice,' Sāy.)

Havītu. See *su-havītu-nāman* and √*hve* (for dat. *hávītave*).

Hávīman, m. or n. call, invocation, RV.

2. **Hávya** (or *havyá*), mf(*ā*)n. to be called or invoked, RV.; AV.; VS.; m. N. of a son of Manu Svāyambhuva, Hariv.; of a son of Atri, VP.

Hāva, m. calling, alluring, dalliance, blandishment (collective N. of ten coquettish gestures of women, beginning with *līlā*, q. v.), MBh.; Kāv. &c.

2. **Hāvaka**, m. a caller, summoner, (in nuptial ceremonies) one who summons the bride, an attendant on the bridegroom.

हवङ्ग *havaṅga*, m. (fr. *havam*+*ga*?) eating rice and curds from a metal cup, L.

हवल *havala* and *havava*, N. of partic. high numbers, Buddh.

हविध्र *havidhra*, m. N. of a king, MBh.; of a son of Manu Svārocisha, Hariv.

हविष्ठ *havishṭha*, m. N. of a Dānava, Hariv.

हस् 1. *has*, cl. 1. P. (Dhātup. xvii, 72) *hasati* (m. c. also *°te*; pf. *jahāsa*, *jahase*, MBh. &c.; aor. *ahasīt*, Gr.; fut. *hasitā*, ib.; *hasishyati*, MBh. &c.; inf. *hasitum*, ib.; ind. p. *hasitvā*, *-hasya*, ib.), to laugh, smile, laugh at (instr.), ShaḍvBr.; Gobh.; MBh. &c.; to deride, mock, ridicule (acc.), MBh.; R. &c.; to surpass, excel, Kāvyâd.; to expand, open (as a blossom), Kuval.: Pass. *hasyate* (aor. *ahāsi*), to be laughed or smiled at, MBh.; Kāv. &c.: Caus. *hāsayati* (aor. *ajīhasat*), to cause to laugh, Hariv.; Kum.: Desid. *jihasishati* (cf. √1. *jaksh*), Gr.: Intens. *jāhasyate* (p. *°yamāna*, MBh.), *jāhasti*, to laugh continuously or immoderately, ib.

2. **Has**, ind. an exclamation of laughter or loud merriment (also employed as a Nidhana in the Sāman). **-kartṛí**, m. a stimulator, inciter (others, 'illuminator'), RV. **-kārá**, m. 'smile (of the sky),' sheet-lightning, ib. **-kṛiti** (*hás-*), f. loud merriment, laughter, ib.

Hása (or *hasá*), m. (ifc. f. *ā*) mirth, laughter, RV. &c. &c. **-kṛit**, mfn. causing mirth or laughter, Śṛiṅgār. **-vajra**, m. N. of a man, Buddh. **Hasāmud**, mfn. laughing merrily, Hir. **Hasā-mudá**, mfn. id., AV.

Hasat, mfn. (pr. p. of √*has*) laughing, smiling &c.; mocking, scorning, excelling, Śiś. v, 63; (*antī*), f. a portable fire-vessel, small furnace, chafing-dish, L.; Arabian jasmine, L.; a partic. female demon, L.; N. of a river (= *hasanī*), Divyâv.

Hasana, mf(*ā*)n. laughing, Nir. iii, 5; jesting or sporting with, Pañcar.; m. N. of one of Skanda's attendants, MBh.; (*ā*), f. a jest, encouraging shout (others, 'lightning'), RV. ix, 112, 4; (*ī*), f., see next; (*am*), n. laughter, a laugh (accord. to some, 'with tremulous lips'), VarBṛS.; Suśr.

Hasanī, f. a portable fire-place or chafing-dish, L.; N. of a mythical river (= *hasantī*), Divyâv. **-maṇi**, m. 'hearth-jewel,' fire, L.

Hasanīya, mfn. to be laughed at or derided by (gen.)

Hasantikā, f. a portable fire-vessel, small fire-place, Vcar., Rājat.

Hasikā, f. laughter, derision, jesting, L.

Hasita, mfn. laughing, jesting, smiling, Kathās.; one who has laughed (m. 'he laughed' = *jahāsa*), Vet.; mocked, ridiculed, surpassed, excelled, Kāv.; blown, expanded, L.; (*am*), n. laughing, laughter (also impers. = 'it has been laughed'), TĀr.; Kāv.; Kathās. &c.; the bow of Kāma (god of love), W.

Hasitṛi, mfn. one who laughs, a laugher, smiler, MW.

Hasrá, mf(*ā́*)n. laughing, smiling, RV.; foolish, stupid, L.

Hāsa, m. (ifc. f. *ā*) laughing, laughter, mirth (often in pl.), MBh.; Kāv. &c.; mocking, derision of (gen.), R.; a jest, joke, fun (*ākhyāna-h°*, 'a funny story'), Kathās.; dazzling whiteness (regarded as laughter in which the teeth are shown), R.; Kathās.; Sāh.; pride, arrogance, BhP.; (*ā*), f. N. of Durgā, L. **-kara**, mfn. provoking laughter, causing to laugh, Śiś.; laughing, merry, W. **-bhūta**, mfn. representing the laughter of (gen.), Jātak. **-vatī**, f. N. of a Tantra deity, Buddh. **-śīla**, mfn. prone to mirth or laughter, Kathās. **Hāsâspada**, n. an object of jest or laughter, Kathās.

Hāsaka, m. one who causes laughter, a buffoon, jester, MBh.; R.; Subh.; a laugher, MW.; (*ikā*), f. laughter, mirth, merry-making, L.

Hāsana, mfn. (fr. Caus.) causing laughter, funny, comical, Kathās.

Hāsanika, m. a play-fellow, L.

Hāsin, mfn. laughing, smiling at (comp.), MBh.; Hariv. &c.; dazzlingly white (cf. under *hāsa*), brilliant or adorned with, ib.; (*inī*), f. N. of an Apsaras, MBh.

Hāsya, mfn. to be laughed at, laughable, ridiculous, funny, comical, MBh.; Kāv. &c.; laughing, laughter, mirth (in rhet. one of the 10 Rasas or of the 8 Sthāyi-bhāvas, qq. vv.), Yājñ.; MBh. &c.; jest, fun, amusement, Mn.; MBh. &c. **-kathā**, f. a funny tale, BhP. **-kara** (Sāh.), **-kāra** (R.), mfn. provoking laughter, causing to laugh. **-kārya**, n. a ridiculous affair, Pañcat. **-kṛit**, mfn. = *-kara*, Daś. **-tara**, mfn. more ridiculous, MBh. **-tā**, f., **-tva**, n. laughableness, ridiculousness, MBh.; Kāv. &c. **-didṛikshu**, mfn. curious to see something ridiculous, Kathās. **-padavī**, f. the road of laughter (*°vīṃ* √*yā*, 'to incur ridicule'), Pañcat. (*-bhāva*, m. = *-tā*, Kathās.); a jest, joke (pl.), Hariv. **-ratnâkara**, m. 'jewel-mine of mirth,' N. of a drama. **-rasa**, m. the sense of humour (see *rasa*); *-vat*, mfn. funny, comical, Bālar. **-sthāyi-bhāva**, m. the permanent sense of humour (see *sthāyi-bh°*). **-hīna**, mfn. destitute of a smile (or 'of blossom'), Hāsy. **Hāsyârṇava**, m. 'ocean of mirth,' N. of a Prahasana by Jagad-īśvara. **Hāsyâspada**, n. a laughing-stock, butt (*-tva*, n.), Kāv.

हसिर *hasira*, m. a kind of mouse (cf. *haṇsira*), Cat.

हसुराज *hasurāja*, m. N. of a man, Buddh.

हस्कर्तृ *has-kartṛi* &c. See col. 2.

हस्त *hásta*, m. (ifc. f. *ā*, of unknown derivation) the hand (ifc. = 'holding in or by the hand;' *haste* √*kṛi* [as two words], 'to take into the hand,' 'get possession of;' *haste-*√*kṛi* [as a comp.], 'to take by the hand, marry;' *śatru-hastaṃ* √*gam*, 'to fall into the hand of the enemy'), RV. &c. &c.; an elephant's trunk (ifc. = 'holding with the trunk'), AitBr.; MBh. &c.; the fore-arm (a measure of length from the elbow to the tip of the middle finger, = 24 Aṅgulas or about 18 inches), VarBṛS.; Rājat. &c.; the position of the hand (= *hasta-vinyāsa*), VPrāt.; hand-writing, Yājñ.; Vikr.; the 11th (13th) lunar asterism (represented by a hand and containing five stars, identified by some with part of the constellation Corvus), AV. &c. &c.; a species of tree, L.; (in prosody) an anapest, Col.; quantity, abundance, mass (ifc. after words signifying 'hair;' cf. *keśa-h°*); N. of a guardian of the Soma, Sāy.; of a son of Vasudeva, BhP.; of another man, Rājat.; (*hástā*), f. the hand, AV. xi, 124; the Nakshatra Hasta, Pur.; (*am*), n. a pair of leather bellows, L.; mfn. born under the Nakshatra Hasta, Pāṇ. iv, 3, 34. [Cf., accord. to some, Gk. ἀγοστός.] **-kamala**, n. a lotus carried in the h° (as symbolizing good fortune or prosperity; thus when Lakshmī was churned out of the ocean, she appeared holding a lotus), Mālav.; a lotus-like hand, A. **-kārya**, mfn. to be done or made with the hand, PañcavBr. **-kṛita** (*hásta-*), mf(*ā*)n. made with the h°, AV. **-kohali** (?), f. the binding of the string round the fore-arm of the bride and bridegroom, L. **-kauśala**, n. skilfulness of hand, manual dexterity, MW. **-kriyā**, f. any manual performance, ib. **-ga**, mf(*ā*)n. being in one's (comp.) hand or possession, Kathās.; Pañcat. **-gata**, mfn. come to hand, fallen into one's possession, procured, obtained, secured (*para-hasta-g°*, 'being in the hand or possession of another'), Hariv.; Ragh. &c. **-gāmin**, mfn. = *-ga*, Ragh. **-giri**, m. N. of a mountain (*-māhātmya*, n.), Cat. **-gṛíhya**, ind. having taken the h°, RV.; AV. **-graha**, m. the taking of the hand, BhP.; Kathās.; the marriage ceremony, Kathās.; the putting h° to or engaging in, Pracaṇḍ. **-grābhá**, mfn. one who takes or has taken a girl's h° (= 'one who marries or has married a wife'), RV. **-grāha**, mfn. taking (or able to take) any one by the h° (= 'being in the immediate neighbourhood,' R.; *hasta-grāhaṃ* √*grah*, 'to take any one by the hand,' Pāṇ. iii,

4, 39); m. a husband (cf. -*grābhá*), Nir.; BhP. **-grāhaka,** mfn. taking any one by the hand (= very importunate), Rājat. **-ghná,** m. a kind of hand-guard (protecting the h° in archery), RV. **-caraṇa,** m. du. hands and feet, Mn. ix, 277. **-cāpa,** w.r. for -*vāpa*, MBh. **-cāpalya,** n. = -*kauśala*, MW. **-cchedana,** m. the amputation of a h°, Mn. viii, 322. **-cyuta** (*hásta-*), mfn. shaken or moved with the h°, RV. **-cyuti** (*hásta-*), f. quick motion of the h°, RV.; MaitrS. **-jyoḍi,** m. a kind of plant, L. **-tala,** n. the (palm of the) h° (see comp.); the tip of an elephant's trunk, MW.; -*gata*, mfn. being (already) in one's hand, Mudr. **-tāla,** m. clapping the h°s together (see *sa-hasta-tālam*). **-tulā,** f. the h° as a balance or instrument for weighing anything, Pañcat. **-tra,** m. or n. a hand-guard (cf. -*ghná*), Lāṭy. **-traya-sammite,** ind. at a distance of 3 Hastas, VarBṛS. **-dakshiṇa,** mfn. situated on the right h° (as a road), Pat.; right, correct, MBh. **-datta,** mfn. reached with the h°, Cat. **-dīpa,** m. a h°-lantern, Kathās. **-dosha,** m. a slip of the h°, mistake committed by the h°, MW. **-dvaya,** n. a distance of 2 Hastas or 48 inches, L. **-dhātrī,** f. N. of wk. **-dhāraṇa,** n. holding by the hand, supporting, helping, L.; warding off a blow, MW.; stopping a bl° with the hand, ib.; (*ā*), f. supporting, helping, MBh.; taking to wife, marrying, Hariv.; Naish. **-parṇa,** m. Palma Christi or Ricinus Communis, L. **-pāda,** m. du. or n. sg. hands and feet, Mn.; Yājñ.; °*ādi*, the h° and feet, the extremities, limbs of the body, MW. **-puccha,** n. the h° below the wrist, L. **-pṛishṭha,** n. the back of the hand (also called *apa-pṛ°*), L. **-prada,** mfn. giving the h°, supporting, helping, MBh. **-prâpta,** mfn. = -*gata*, MBh.; R. &c. **-prâpya,** mfn. to be reached with the h°, R.; Megh. **-bandha,** m. = *haste-b°*, Pāṇ. vi, 3, 13, Sch. **-bimba,** n. anointing the body with perfumes, L. **-bhraṇśin** (Śak.), **-bhrashṭa** (Kathās.), mfn. slipped from the h°, escaped **-maṇi,** m. a jewel worn on the wrist, MW. **-mātra,** a cubit in length, ib. **-muktâvalī,** f. N. of wk. **-yata** (*hásta-*), mfn. held or guided by the hand, RV. **-yugala,** n. the two hands, MW. **-yoga,** m. employment or practice of the h°, MBh. **-ratnâvalī,** f. N. of a wk. on mimetic gestures with one or both h°. **-rekhā,** f. a line on the h°, MW. **-lakshaṇa,** n. N. of the 28th Pariśishṭa of the AV. **-lāghava,** n. lightness of hand, manual readiness, cleverness (reckoned among the 64 Kalās), Cat.; a real injury, MBh. **-lekha,** m. hand-drawing (°*khī-√kṛi*, 'to draw, sketch'), Naish. **-lepana,** n. an ointment for the hands, L. **-vat** (*hásta-*), mfn. having h°s, RV.; dexterous with the h°s (as an archer or thief), MBh.; Ragh.; Daś. **-vartam,** ind. (with Caus. of *√vṛit*) to turn or crush with the h°s, Bhaṭṭ. **-vartin,** mfn. being or remaining in the h°, seized, held, caught hold of, W.; m. N. of a prince, Daś. **-vāpa,** m. scattering or shooting a shower of arrows with the h°, MBh. **-vāma,** mfn. situated on the left hand (also = 'wrong'), MBh. **-vāraṇa,** n. taking or holding by the hand, L.; warding off a blow, L. **-vinyāsa,** m. position of the h°s, VPrāt. **-veshya,** n. handiwork, manual labour, TāṇḍBr. **-śrāddha,** n. N. of wk. **-saṃlagnikā,** f. (instr.) with the h°s put together, Mahāvy. **-saṃvāhana,** n. rubbing or shampooing with the h°s, MW. **-saṃjīvanī,** f. N. of a wk. on palmistry. **-saṃjñā,** f. a sign with the h°, Jātakam. **-saṃdhunakam,** ind. tossing or shaking the h°s, Mahāvy. **-siddhi,** f. earnings gained by manual labour, salary, VP. **-sūtra** (Kum.) or **-sūtraka** (L.), n. a bangle or ornament put on the wrist of a girl before her wedding. **-stha,** mfn. being in or held with the h°, Kathās.; -*yuga*, mfn. holding a yoke in the h°, Bcar. **-sthita,** mfn. being in h°, held, MW. **-svara-lakshaṇa,** n. N. of wk. **-svastika,** m. (ifc. f. *ā*) crossing the h°s, Mālatīm.; Bālar. **-hārya,** mfn. to be grasped with the hands, manifest, Bālar. **-homa,** m. an oblation offered with the h°, Kauś. **Hastâkshara,** mfn. written with the h° (opp. to *mudrâṅkita*, 'printed'), L. **Hastâgni,** m. N. of a man; pl. his family, Saṃskārak. **Hastâgra,** n. 'tip of the h°,' the fingers (-*lagnā*, f. [with gen.] = 'clasping the fingers of,' i.e. 'married to'), Pañcat.; the tip of the trunk of an elephant, Śiś. **Hastâṅguli** or °**lī,** f. a finger of the hand, Hariv.; GāruḍaP. **Hastâñjali,** m. the hands joined together and hollowed (see *añjali*), Mṛicch. **Hástâdāna,** mfn. taking or seizing with the hand (or trunk, as men, monkeys, or elephants), TS.; n. the act of seizing with the h°, Pāṇ. iii, 3, 40. **Hastâbharaṇa,** n. an ornament for the hand, MBh.; a kind of snake, Suśr. **Hastâmalaka,** n. 'the fruit or seed of the Myrobalan in the hand' (as a symbol of something palpable or clear), R.; N. of a work on the Vedānta by the next; m. N. of a son of Prabhākara (pupil of Śaṃkarâcārya); -*ṭīkā*, f., -*bhāshya*, n., -*vedânta-prakaraṇa*, n., -*saṃvāda-stotra* or °*ka-stotra*, n. N. of wks. **Hastârūḍha,** mfn. lying on the h°, clear, manifest, Hariv. **Hastâlamba,** m. 'h°-support,' material support or refuge, Kathās. **Hastâlambana,** n. id., Pañcat. **Hastâliṅgana** or °**naka,** n. an embrace, Hariv. **Hastâvanéjana,** n. water for washing the h°s, AV. **Hastâvalamba,** m. (ifc. f. *ā*) = *hastâlamba*, Vikr.; Ratnâv.; mfn. supported by the h° of another, MW. **Hastâvalambana,** n. = prec., HPariś. **Hastâvalehakam,** ind. licking the hands, Mahāvy. **Hastâvāpa,** m. 'hand-covering,' a hand-guard or finger-guard (used by archers), MBh.; R. &c.; seizing an arrow with the h°, L. **Hastâvāpin,** mfn. provided with a hand-guard, MBh.; Jātakam. **Hastā-hasti,** ind. (cf. *keśā-keśi* &c.) hand to hand, in close fight, MBh. **Hastā-hastikā,** f. close fight, Anarghar. **Hastôcchraya,** m. 'lifting up the hand,' an oblation (?), Divyâv. **Hastôdaka,** n. water held in the hand, Kathās.

Hastaka, m. the hand (ifc. with f. *ikā* = 'holding in the hand'), MBh.; Kāv. &c.; the h° as a support, Gīt.; the h° as a measure of length, ŚārṅgS.; position of the h°s, Cat.; a turn-spit (v.l. *hastika*), Hcar.; (*ikā*), f. a kind of stringed instrument, Saṃgīt. **-vapra,** N. of a place, Inscr.

Hastakita, mfn. (fr. *hastaka*), g. *tārakâdi*.

Hasti, in comp. for *hastin*. **-kaksha,** m. a kind of venomous insect, Suśr.; n. N. of wk. **-kakshya,** m. a lion, L.; a tiger, ib.; n. N. of wk. **-kaccha,** m. N. of a serpent-demon, Buddh. **-kanda,** m. a kind of bulbous plant, L. **-karañja** or °**jaka,** m. Galedupa Piscidia, L. **-karkoṭaka,** m. a kind of big Momordica Mixa, L. **-karṇa,** m. 'elephant-eared,' N. of various plants (accord. to L. 'the castor-oil tree [also the red kind]; Butea Frondosa; Arum Macrorrhizum'), Suśr.; VarBṛS.; of one of Śiva's attendants, L.; a partic. class of semi-divine beings (forming one of the Gaṇa-devatās, q.v.), MW.; N. of a Rākshasa, R.; of a serpent-demon, Buddh.; of a locality, Rājat.; -*dala*, m. a sort of Butea, L.; -*palāśa*, m. Butea Frondosa, Suśr. **-karṇaka,** m. a sort of Butea, L. **-karṇika,** n. a partic. sedent posture (with Yogins), Cat. **-karshū,** g. *kāśy-ādi*. **-kāśyapa,** m. N. of a man, MBh. **-kumbha,** m. N. of a grotto, Inscr. **-koli,** m. or f. a sort of jujube, L. **-kośātakī,** f. a kind of Cucurbitaceous plant, L. **-gartā,** f. N. of a cavity in the earth, Buddh. **-gavâśva,** n. sg. elephants (and) cows (and) horses, MBh.; °*śvôshṭra-damaka*, m. a trainer of el° and cows and h° and camels, Mn. iii, 162. **-giri,** m. the city and district of Kāñcī (q.v.), L.; N. of a mountain (see comp.); -*campū*, f., -*māhātmya*, n., °*rîśa-maṅgalâśāsana*, n. N. of wks. **-gaurī-vratôdyāpana-vidhi,** m. N. of wk. **-ghaṭa,** m. N. of the 7th book of the Śata-patha-Brāhmaṇa. **-ghāta,** mfn. killing elephants, Pāṇ. iii, 2, 54, Sch. **-ghoshā** or **-ghoshātakī,** f. a kind of Cucurbitaceous plant, L. **-ghna,** mfn. able to kill elephants, Pāṇ. iii, 2, 54. **-carma,** (Ved.) the skin of an el°, Pāṇ. v, 4, 103. **-cāra,** m. a kind of weapon (resembling a Śarabha and used for frightening elephants), L. **-cārin,** m. an el°-driver, Śiś.; (*iṇī*), f. Galedupa Piscidia, L. **-jana-prakāśa,** m. N. of wk. **-jāgarika,** m. a keeper of el°, Hcar., Sch. **-jihvā,** f. 'el°-tongue,' a partic. vein, Cat. **-jīvin,** m. an el°-driver, Hariv. **-danta,** m. the tusk of an el° (see *hāstidanta*); a pin or peg projecting from a wall, MW.; m. or n. a radish, L.; (*ī*), f. a radish, Suśr.; Tiaridium Indicum, Car.; n. ivory, MW.; -*phalā*, f. Cucumis Utilissimus, L.; -*vastra-maya*, mf(*ī*)n. made of ivory or cloth, Hcat. **-dantaka,** m. n. a radish, L. **-dāya,** m. N. of a man (see *hāstidāyi*). **-dvayasa,** mf(*ī*)n. as high or as big as an el°, Pāṇ. v, 2, 37, Sch. **-nakha,** m. 'elephant's nail,' a sort of turret or raised mound of earth or masonry protecting the access to the gate of a city or fort (described as furnished with an inner staircase and with loopholes for discharging arrows &c.), Śiś. **-nāga,** m. a princely el°, Divyâv. **-nāyaka,** m. N. of a man, Buddh. **-nāsā,** f. an el°'s trunk, L. **-nishadana,** n. a partic. posture in sitting, Yogas., Sch. **-pa,** m. an elephant-driver, el°-keeper, VS.; MBh.; Hariv.; Pur. **-paka,** m. id., Śiś.; Hit. &c.; N. of a poet, Subh. **-pattra,** m. = -*kanda*, L. **-pada,** n. the track of an el°, MBh.; m. 'el°-footed,' N. of a serpent-demon, ib. **-parṇikā** or **-parṇinī,** f. Luffa Fœtida or another species, L. **-parṇī,** f. N. of two plants (= *karkaṭī* or = *moraṭā*), ib. **-pāda,** mfn. el°-footed, Pāṇ.; Vop. **-pādikā,** f. a kind of medicinal plant, L. **-pāla,** m. = next, Kathās.; N. of a king, Col.; Buddh. **-pālaka,** m. an elephant-keeper, el°-driver, Kathās. **-piṇḍa,** m. N. of a serpent-demon, MBh. **-pippalī,** f. Scindapsus Officinalis, Suśr.; Car. **-pūraṇī,** f. a kind of very small hogweed, L. **-pṛishṭhaka,** n. the back of an el°, MW.; N. of a village, R. **-bandha,** m. a place for entrapping el°s, Vāś. **-bhadra,** m. N. of a serpent-demon, MBh.; Hariv. **-makara,** m. a sea-monster shaped like an el°, L. **-mat,** mfn. provided with el°, Pat. **-mada,** m. the exudation from an el°'s temples, L. **-malla,** m. N. of Airāvata (Indra's el°), Śiś.; of Gaṇeśa, L.; of Śaṅkha (the 8th of the chief Nāgas or serpents of Pātāla), W.; a heap of ashes, ib.; a shower of dust, ib.; frost, cold, ib.; -*sena*, m. N. of an author, Cat. **-mātra,** mfn. as great as an el°, MW. **-māyā,** f. N. of a charm, Hariv. **-mukha,** m. 'elephant-faced,' N. of Gaṇeśa, L.; of a Rakshasa, R. **-mṛiḍitā,** f., *saṃjñāyām*, Pāṇ. vi, 2, 146, Sch. **-meha,** m. a kind of diabetes (°*hin*, mfn. = 'suffering from it'), Car. **-yaśas,** n. the magnificence of an el°, PārGṛ.; °*śasi-hasti-varcasin* (?), mfn. having an elephant's m° and splendour, Hir. **-yūtha,** n. a herd of el°s, MBh. **-ratha,** n. sg. el°s and chariots, ib.; -*dāna*, n. N. of the 13th Pariśishṭa of the AV. **-rāja,** m. a powerful el°, Śiś.; the chief of a herd of elephants, Hit. **-ruci,** m. N. of an author, Cat. **-rodhraka,** m. Symplocos Racemosa, L. **-rohaṇaka,** m. Galedupa Piscidia, ib. **-lodhraka,** m. Symplocos Racemosa, ib. **-vaktra,** m. 'el°-faced,' N. of Gaṇeśa, Daś. **-vadha,** m. the killing of an el° (esp. by a lion, which incurs the guilt of murder, whilst others carry off the spoils, such as the tusks and the pearls said to be found in the head), MW. **-varcasá,** n. the vigour of an el°, AV.; the magnificence of an el°, MW. **-varman,** m. N. of a king, Inscr. **-vātiṅgaṇa,** m. Solanum Melongena, L. **-vānara,** mfn. (a battle) in which el°s and monkeys take or took part, R. **-vāha,** m. an elephant-driver, MW.; a hook for driving el°s, L. **-vishāṇī,** f. Musa Sapientum, ib. **-vaidyaka,** n. the art of healing el°s (as N. of wk.); -*kāra*, m. the composer of such a wk. **-śālā,** f. an el°-stable, MBh.; Kathās.; N. of a place, Rājat. (could be also -*śāla*). **-śikshaka,** m. a breaker in or trainer of el°s, MBh. **-śikshā,** f. the art of training el°s, R.; Mṛicch.; Kād. **-śiras,** m. N. of a man (see *hāsti-śīrshi*). **-śuṇḍa,** m. an el°'s trunk, MW.; (*ā*), f. id., ib.; Heliotropium Indicum, L.; (*ī*), f. id., ib.; colocynth, Npr. **-śyāmāka,** m. a kind of millet, Car. **-shaḍgava,** n. a yoke or collection of 6 el°s, MBh. **-sūtra,** n. a Sūtra treating of elephants, ib. **-sena,** m. N. of a king, Śatr. **-somā,** f. N. of a river, MBh. **-snāna,** n. the washing of an el°, Hit. **-hasta,** m. an el°'s trunk, MBh.; -*parāmṛishṭa*, mf(*ā*)n. seized or struck by the trunk of an el°, ib.

Hastika, n. a multitude of elephants (or m. 'an elephant'), MBh. ix, 2839 (B.); m. a toy-elephant, Jātakam.; a turn-spit (v.l. for *hastaka*), Hcar.

Hastin, mfn. having hands, clever or dexterous with the h°s, RV.; AV.; (with *mṛiga*, 'the animal with a h° i.e. with a trunk,' an elephant; cf. *danta-h°*), ib.; having (or sitting on) an el°, MārkP.; m. an elephant (four kinds of el°s are enumerated; see *bhadra, mandra, mṛiga, miśra*; some give *kiliñja-h°*, 'a straw el°,' 'effigy of an el° made of grass'), AV. &c. &c.; (ifc.) the chief or best of its kind, g. *vyāghrâdi*; a kind of plant (= *aja-modā*), L.; N. of a son of Dhṛita-rāshṭra, MBh.; of a son of Suhotra (a prince of the Lunar race, described as founder of Hastinā-pura), ib.; VP.; of a son of Bṛihat-kshatra, BhP.; of a son of Kuru, Śatr.; (*inī*), f. a female elephant, AV. &c. &c.; a kind of drug and perfume (= *haṭṭa-vilāsinī*), L.; a woman of a partic. class (one of the 4 classes into which women are divided, described as having thick lips, thick hips, thick fingers, large breasts, dark complexion, and strong sexual passion), Siṅhās.; N. of Hastinā-pura, L.

Hastinā-pura, n. (less correctly *hastina-p°* or *hastinī-*) N. of a city founded by king Hastin, q.v. (it was situated about fifty-seven miles north-east of the modern Delhi on the banks of an old channel of the Ganges, and was the capital of the kings of the Lunar line, as Ayodhyā was of the Solar dynasty;

hence it forms a central scene of action in the Mahābhārata; here Yudhi-shṭhira was crowned after a triumphal progress through the streets of the city; see MBh. xii, 1386–1410: other names for this celebrated town are *gajâhvaya, nāga-sâhvaya, nāgâhva, hāstina*), MBh.; Hariv.; Pur. &c.

Hastī-√kṛi, P. *-karoti*, to hand over, deliver, Mālatīm.

Hastīna. See *antar-h°*, p. 43, col. 3.

Haste (loc. of *hasta*), in comp. **—karaṇa**, n. taking (the bride's) hand, marrying, L. **—√kṛi**, P. *-karoti*, to take in hand, take possession of, make one's own, MW. **—gṛihya**, ind. (= *hasta-gṛ°*), g. *mayūra-vyaṇsakâdi*. **—bandha**, m. = *hasta-b°*, Pāṇ. vi, 3, 13, Sch.

Hasty (before vowels), in comp. for *hasti*. **—adhyaksha**, m. a superintendent of elephants, MW. **—asanā**, f. Boswellia Serrata or Thurifera, L. **—aśva**, n. sg. el° and horses, R.; VarBṛS.; *-dīkshā*, f. N. of the 16th and 17th Pariśishṭas of the AV.; *-ratha-ghosha*, m. the sound of chariots (and) horses (and) elephants, Ml.; *-ratha-sambādha*, mfn. crowded with carriages (and) horses (and) el°, R.; *°vāroha-bandhaka*, m. pl. el°-riders (and) horsemen (and) their servants, ib. **—ājīva**, m. an el°-driver, MBh. **—āyurveda**, m. a work on the treatment of el° diseases, Cat. **—āroha**, m. an el°-rider, el°-driver, MBh.; VarBṛS. &c. **—āluka**, n. a kind of large bulbous plant, Suśr. **—ṛishabha**, mfn. accompanied by an elephant-like bull (as cows), ŚBr.

Hástya, mf(*ā*)n. being on the hand (as the fingers), TS.; Br.; prepared with the hand, RV.; held in the hand, TBr.

Hāsta, mfn. formed with the hands (with *mukula*, n. = *añjali*), Naiâd.

Hāstāyana, mfn. (fr. *hasta*), g. *pakshâdi*.

Hāstika, mfn. consisting of elephants, Ratnâv.; m. an el°-rider, el°-driver &c., W.; n. a multitude of el°s, MBh. ix, 2839 (B. *hastika*); Pāṇ. iv, 2, 47; a multitude of female el°s, Pāṇ. vi, 3, 35, Vārtt. 11, Pat.

Hāstikarshūka, mf(*ā* or *ī*)n. (fr. *hasti-karshū*), g. *kāśy-ādi*.

Hāstidanta, mfn. (fr. *hasti-d°*) consisting or made of ivory, Kauś.

Hāstidāyi, m. patr. fr. *hasti-d°*, Pravar.

Hāstina, mfn. belonging to an elephant, AV.; having the depth of an elephant (as water), Daś.; n. = next, L. **—pura**, n. = *hastinā-pura* (*-tva*, n.), MBh.; R. &c.

Hāstināyana, mfn. (fr. *hastin*), g. *pakshâdi*; m. a patr., g. *naḍâdi*.

Hāstipada, m. (fr. *hasti-p°*) N. of a man, Pāṇ. iv, 3, 132; mfn. relating or belonging to Hasti-pada, ib.

Hāstiśīrshi, m. patr. fr. *hasti-śiras*, Pāṇ. vi, 1, 62, Vārtt. 3, Pat.

हस्र **hasra.** See p. 1294, col. 2.

हहल **hahala**, n. a sort of deadly poison (cf. *halāhala*), L.

हहव **hahava**, n. a partic. hell (cf. *hāhava*), Buddh.

हहा 1. **hahā**, ind. an exclamation (= 'alas!' in *hahā dhik*), Ratnâv.

हहा 2. **hahā**, m. N. of a Gandharva (m. c. for *hāhā*), MBh.; R.

हहाल **hahāla**, m. pl. N. of the Caidya country, L.

हहाहा **hahāhā**, ind. = 1. *hahā*, Sāh.

हहे **hahe**, ind., g. *câdi*.

हा 1. **hā**, ind. an exclamation expressive of pain, anger, astonishment, satisfaction &c. (= ah! alas! oh! ha! often before or after a voc. case, also repeated *hā-hā*, cf. 1. *hahā* above, or followed by other particles, esp. *dhik, hanta, kashṭam* &c.), MBh.; Kāv. &c. **—kashṭa-śabda**, m. the exclamation *hā kashṭam*, Kād. **—kāra**, m. the excl° *hā*, Śiś. **—hā-kṛita**, mfn. filled with cries, Bcar. **—hā-rava** or **-hā-śabda**, m. the exclamation *hā hā*, Kathās.

हा 2. **hā** (not always separable fr. √3. *hā*), cl. 3. Ā. (Dhātup. xxv, 7) *jihīte* (p. *jíhāna* [q.v.]; pf. *jahiré*, AV.; aor. *ahāsta*, RV. &c.; fut. *hātā*, Gr.; *hāsyate*, Br.; MBh.; inf. *-hātum*, ib.; ind. p. *hātvā*, Gr.; *-hāya*, RV.), to start or spring forward, bound away, give way to (dat.), RV.; to spring or leap upon(?), RV. x, 49, 5; to go or depart or betake one's self to have recourse to (acc.), Nalôd.; to fall or come into any state, Kir.: Pass. *hāyate* (aor. *ahāyi*), Gr.: Caus. *hāpayati* (aor. *ajīhapat*), ib.: Desid. *jihāsate*, ib.: Intens. *jāhāyate*, *jāhāti*, *jāheti*, ib.

Jíhāna, mfn. bounding forward (as a horse), RV.; flying (as an arrow), Kir.

1. **Hāna**, mfn. gone or departed &c. (in *sáṃhāna*, 'risen'), VS.

Hāyas. See *ví-* and *sárva-hāyas*.

1. **Heya**, mfn. (for 2. see p. 1297, col. 1) to be gone &c., MW.

हा 3. **hā**, cl. 3. P. (Dhātup. xxv, 8) *jáhāti* (rarely cl. 1. *jahati*; 3. du. *jahītaḥ*, Impv. *jahīhi* [or *jahāhi*, Pāṇ. vi, 4, 117]; *jahītāt*, AV.; Pot. *jahyāt*, AV. &c.; pf. *jahau*, *jahúḥ*, RV. &c.; *jahe*, Br.; aor. *ahāt*, ib. &c.; *ahāsīt*, Gr.; 3. sg. *ahās*, RV.; *áhāsi*, AV.; *hāsishṭa*, ib.; fut. *hātā*, Gr.; *hāsyati*, *°te*, AV. &c.; *jahishyati*, MBh. &c.; inf. *hātum*, ib.; ind. p. *hitvā* [q.v.], RV. &c.; *hitví*, *°tvāya*, RV.; *-hītvā*, Gr.; *-hāya*, Br., *-hīyam*, TS.), to leave, abandon, desert, quit, forsake, relinquish (with *śarīram, deham, prāṇān, asūn, jīvitam* &c. = 'to die'), RV. &c. &c.; to discharge, emit, ib.; to put away, take off, remove, lay aside, give up, renounce, resign, avoid, shun, abstain or refrain from, Mn.; MBh. &c.; to disregard, neglect, ib.; to lose, be deprived of, R.; Kām.; to get rid of, escape from, Up.; MBh. &c.; to cause to emit (with *śardham*, 'to cause to break wind'), Vop.: Pass. *hīyáte* or *hī́yate* (ep. also *hīyati*; aor. *ahāyi*), to be left or abandoned or deserted &c.; to be left behind, fall short of (abl.), RV. &c. &c.; to be excluded from or bereft of (abl. or instr.; with *prāṇaiḥ*, 'to die'), KaṭhUp.; Mn.; MBh. &c.; to be overtaken by (instr.), MBh.; to be deficient or wanting, suffer loss or injury, fail (also in a lawsuit), decrease, wane, decline, come to an end, ChUp.; Mn.; MBh. &c.; to weigh less (at the ordeal of the balance), Yājñ., Sch.; to be given up or avoided, Bhartṛ. (v.l.); to be subtracted, VarBṛS.; to become detached from (with abl. or instr.), fall out (as hair), BhP.: Caus. *hāpayati* (m. c. also *°te*, aor. *ajīhapat*; *-jīhipaḥ*, RV.), to cause to leave or abandon &c.; to omit, neglect, Mn.; MBh. &c.; to fall short of, be wanting in (acc.), MBh.; Cāṇ.; to give up (*asūn*, 'life'), Hariv.; to lose (*kālam*, 'time'), Kām.; to abandon (*pratijñām*, 'a thesis'), Jātakam.: Desid. *jihāsati*, to wish to leave or abandon, Daś.; BhP.; HPariś.; to wish to reject or disdain, Prab.; to wish to escape, Sarvad.: Intens. *jehīyate*, *jāhāti*, *jāheti*, Gr.

Jahitá, mfn. rejected, forsaken, forlorn, RV.; ĀpŚr.

Ha. See 5. *ha*, p. 1286, col. 1.

Hāta, mfn. given up, abandoned, BhP. **—vat**, mfn. abandoned by, deprived of (acc.), Kām. (v.l.)

Hātavya, mfn. to be abandoned or left, relinquishable, Mn.; MBh. &c.; to be left behind i. e. overtaken, MBh.

Hātu, m. or f. death, L.; a road, L.

2. **Hāna**, n. the act of abandoning, relinquishing, giving up, escaping, getting rid of, Gaut.; Saṃk.; Sarvad.; want, lack, Kap.; cessation, ib.; Bhartṛ. (v.l.)

Hāni, f. (accord. to some fr. √*han*) abandonment, relinquishment, Kuval.; taking off, laying aside (ornaments), Subh.; decrease, diminution, MBh.; Kāv. &c.; deprivation of (abl.), Gaut.; damage, loss, failure (also in a lawsuit), ruin, Yājñ.; MBh. &c.; insufficiency, deficit, a minus, ĀśvGṛ.; MBh.; cessation, disappearance, non-existence, Kāv.; Kathās. &c. **—kara**, mfn. injurious, detrimental, Pañcat.; causing to disappear, Śiś. **—kṛit**, mfn. causing loss, prejudicial, destructive, Kathās.

Hānīya, mfn. = *hātavya*, MW.

Hāpana, n. (fr. Caus.) the act of causing to quit or abandon &c.; diminution, Suśr.

Hāpita, mfn. (fr. id.) caused to be left or abandoned &c.; injured (as a deposit), Yājñ.; deprived of (instr.), BhP.

Hāyaka, mfn. giving up, abandoning, MBh.

1. **Hāyana**, mf(*ā* or *ī*)n. (for 2. see p. 1297, col. 1) quitting, leaving, MW.; passing away, ib.

Hāyin, mfn. leaving, abandoning, neglecting, ib.

Hāsas, m. the moon, Uṇ. iv, 220, Sch.

Hitvā, ind. having left or abandoned &c.; letting alone, slighting, disregarding, R.; Kathās.; excepting, with the exception of (acc.), VarBṛS.

Hīná, mfn. left, abandoned, forsaken, RV.; left behind, excluded or shut out from, lower or weaker than, inferior to (abl.), Mn.; MBh. &c.; left out, wanting, omitted, MBh.; defeated or worsted (in a lawsuit), Yājñ.; deficient, defective, faulty, insufficient, short, incomplete, poor, little, low, vile, bad, base, mean, ŚBr. &c. &c.; bereft or deprived of, free from, devoid or destitute of, without (instr., abl., loc., acc., or comp.; *prāṇair hīnaḥ*, 'bereft of breath or life;' *mantrād* or *mantrato h°*, 'devoid of sacred knowledge'), MuṇḍUp.; KātyŚr.; Mn.; MBh. &c.; lost or strayed from (a caravan), Pāṇ. i, 4, 23, Kāś.; brought low, broken down in circumstances, ŚrS.; m. a faulty or defective witness (of five kinds, viz. *anya-vādin, kriyā-dveshin, nôpasthāyin, nir-uttara, āhūta-prapalâyin*), Yājñ., Sch.; subtraction (= *vyavakalana*), MW.; Mesua Ferrea, L.; (*ā*), f. a female mouse (w. r. for *dīna*), L.; (*am*), n. deficiency, want, absence (*velā-hine* = 'before the right time,' 'unseasonably'), VarBṛS.; Yājñ. **—karman**, mfn. engaged in low practices, neglecting or omitting customary rites or religious acts, Gaut.; Mn.; MBh. **—kula**, mfn. of low family, base-born, plebeian (*-tva*, n.), MW. **—kushṭa**, n. (prob.) = *kshudra-k°*, Cat. **—kośa**, mfn. having an empty treasury, MBh. **—kratu**, mfn. one who neglects to sacrifice, Mn. xi, 12. **—krama**, m. diminishing series or order of succession, Suśr. **—kriya**, mfn. = *-karman*, Mn. iii, 7. **—guṇa**, mfn. of inferior virtue or merit, R. **—cakshus**, mfn. one who has lost an eye or whose sight is dimmed, R. **—carita**, n. (pl.) base or mean conduct, Śāntiś. **—ja**, mfn. low-born, MBh. **—jāti**, mfn. of low caste, outcaste, degraded, vile, Mn. iii, 15. **—tara**, mfn. worse, inferior, MuṇḍUp. **—tarpita**, mfn. insufficiently satiated, ŚārṅgP. **—tas**, ind. = *hīnena* or *hīnāt*, MBh.; of less value, Vas. **—tā**, f., **-tva**, n. defectiveness, deprivation, destitution, the state of being without, want or absence of (instr. or comp.), Mn.; MBh. &c. **—dagdha**, mfn. insufficiently burned or cauterized, Suśr. **—darśana-sāmarthya**, mfn. destitute of the power of seeing, blind, Rājat. **—dīnânukampaka**, mfn. feeling compassion for the wretched and miserable, Kāraṇḍ. **—nāyaka**, mfn. having a low or base hero (said of a drama), MW. **—paksha**, mf(*ā*)n. unprotected, Yājñ., Sch. **—pratijña**, mfn. faithless, Hariv. **—bala**, mfn. deficient in strength, weak, feeble, Pañcat. **—bāhu**, m. N. of one of Śiva's attendants, L. **—buddhi**, mfn. of weak understanding, R. **—mūlya**, n. a low price, Yājñ. **—yāna**, n. 'simpler or lesser vehicle,' N. of the earliest system of Buddhist doctrine (opp. to *mahā-yāna*; see *yāna*). **—yoni**, m. or f. an inferior womb, low birth or origin, MW. **—rātra**, mf(*ā*)n. having shorter nights, Gaut. **—rūpa**, mf(*ā*)n. deficient in form or beauty, R. **—roman**, mfn. deprived of hair, bald, MBh. **—varga** (Jātak.), **-varṇa** (Hit.), mfn. of low caste, outcaste. **—vāda**, m. defective statement, insufficient or contradictory evidence, prevarication, W. **—vādin**, mfn. defeated or worsted (in a lawsuit), Pañcat.; making a defective statement, insufficient or inadmissible (as a witness; see *hīna* above), W.; contradictory, prevaricating, ib.; destitute of speech, speechless, dumb, ib. **—vīrya**, mfn. = *-bala* (*-tva*, n.), R.; Bhpr. **—vṛitti**, mfn. of base conduct, MBh. **—vyañjana**, mfn. (speech) deficient or indistinct in its consonants, R. **—sakhya**, n. making friends with low people, L. **—saṃdhi**, mfn. destitute of peace or reconciliation, W. **—sevā**, f. attendance on base or low people, Cāṇ.; Hit. **—svara**, mfn. defective in sound, soundless (*-tā*, f.), Suśr. **Hīnâṇśu**, mfn. destitute of rays, dark, Kāv. **Hīnâṅga**, mf(*ā* or *ī*)n. defective in limb, crippled, lame, mutilated, ShaḍvBr.; Mn.; VarBṛS.; incomplete in parts, imperfect, KātyŚr., Sch. **Hīnâtirikta**, mfn. defective or excessive, too few or too many; *-kāle*, ind. too late or too soon, VarBṛS.; *-gātra* (Mn.) or *°tâṅga* (f. *ī*, Yājñ.), mfn. having a limb too few or too many. **Hīnâdhika**, mfn. smaller or greater than (abl.), VarBṛS.; too little or too much; (*e*), ind. too late or too soon, ib.; *-tā*, f. (Kāvyâd.), *-tva*, n. (ib., Sch.) deficiency or excess; *°kâṅga*, mf(*ī*)n. having too few or too many limbs, VarBṛS. **Hīnânna-vastra-vesha**, mfn. (a Brahma-cārin) eating less food (than his preceptor) and wearing an inferior dress, Mn. ii, 194. **Hīnârtha**, mfn. one who has fallen short of his object or lost his advantage, MBh. **Hīnôdgata**, mfn. insufficiently emerged or come forth, Suśr. **Hīnôpamā**, f. comparison with something inferior, Śaṃkar.; Pratāp.

Hīnaka, mfn. deprived of (see *kara-saṃdaṇśa-h°*, add.)

Hīnita, mfn. deprived of one's own, MBh. i, 3558; iv, 226 (conj.); separated from (comp.), Hariv.; subtracted (= *vy-avakalita*), L.

Hīyamāna, mfn. being left or deserted &c.; weaker, inferior, MBh.; being lost, MW.; sinking, giving in, ib.

2. **Heya,** mfn. (for 1. and 3. see p. 1296 and 1304) to be left or quitted or abandoned or rejected or avoided (*-tva*, n.), Kāv.; Kathās. &c.; to be subtracted, L.

हाइकार *hāi-kāra*, m. the exclamation *hāi*, Lāṭy.

हाउकार *hāü-kāra*, m. the exclamation *hāü*, Lāṭy.

हाउयवादारसृत् *hāüyavādāra-sṛit* and *hāü-huvaivā-sāman*, n. N. of Sāmans, IndSt.

हांस *hānsa*, mfn. (fr. *hansa*) relating to a goose or swan, Car.

Hānsakāyana, mfn. (fr. *hansaka*), g. *pakshâdi*; m. a patr., g. *naḍâdi*.

हाकिनी *hākinī*, f. a partic. female demon (cf. *ḍākinī* and *śākinī*), Tantras.

हाङ्गर *hāṅgara*, m. a large fish, shark, L.

हाज्यखान *hājya-khāna*, m. N. of a Khan, Cat.

हाट *hāṭa.* See *karahāṭa*, p. 255, col. 1.

हाटक *hāṭaka*, m. (said to be fr. √*haṭ*; perhaps connected with *hiraṇya*) N. of a country and people, MBh.; a partic. magical drink, BhP.; (*ī*), f. N. of a river in the lower world, BhP.; n. 'found in Hāṭaka,' gold, MBh.; Kāv. &c.; mf(*ī*)n. = next, Śiś. **-maya,** mf(*ī*)n. golden, made of gold, Hcar.

Hāṭakêśa or °**kêśāna,** m. N. of a form of Śiva (worshipped on the banks of the Go-dāvarī), Kathās.

Hāṭakêśvara, m. id., ib.; Pur.; n. a partic. incantation, Rājat.; *-māhātmya*, n. N. of wk.

Hāṭakīya, mfn. made or consisting of gold, Alaṃkāraś.

हाडि *hāḍi*, m. N. of a man, Rājat.; (*ī*), f. a kind of written character, Jaim. **-grāma,** m. N. of a village, Rājat.

Hāḍikā, f. an earthen pot (cf. *handikā*), Kathārṇ.

हात *hāta, hātavya, hātu.* See p. 1296, col. 2.

हात्कृत *hāt-kṛita*, n. uttering the sound *hāt*, L.

हात्र *hātra* (?), n. wages, hire, L.; = (or w. r. for) *hāntra*, L.

हान *hāna, hāni* &c. See p. 1296, col. 2.

हानव्य *hānavya, hānu.* See p. 1288, col. 2.

हानुक *hānuka, hāntra.* See p. 1288, col. 1.

हान्दण *hāndaṇa*, N. of a place, Cat.

हापन *hāpana, hāpita.* See p. 1296, col. 2.

हापुत्री *hāputrī*, f. a kind of wagtail, L.

Hāputrikā, f. id., W.

हाफिका *hāphikā*, f. gaping, yawning, L.

हामिग्राम *hāmi-grāma*, m. N. of a village, Rājat.

हाम्फ *hāmpha* (?), Pañcad.

हाम्बीरी *hāmbīrī*, f. (in music) a kind of Rāgiṇī (cf. *naṭṭa-hambīrā*), Saṃgīt.

हायक *hāyaka, hāyin.* See p. 1296, col. 2.

हायति *hāyati*, m. N. of a man, Saṃskārak.

हायन 2. *hāyaná*, m. n. (accord. to native authorities fr. √1. or 2. *hā*; but cf. *hayana*) a year (ifc. f. *ī*, and accord. to Pat. on Pāṇ. iv, 1, 27 also *ā*), AV. &c. &c.; m. a sort of red rice (pl. its grains), MaitrS.; ŚBr.; KātyŚr.; a flame, ray, L.; (*ī*), f. a year, AV. xii, 1, 36; mfn. lasting a year or returning every year (applied to Takman, q.v.), AV. **-grantha,** m., **-phala,** n., **-ratna,** n., **-sindhu,** m., **-sundara** and °**nôttama,** m. or n. N. of wks.

Hāyanaka, m. a kind of red rice, Car.

हायि *hāyi*, ind. an exclamation used in chanting a Sāman (cf. *hāï*), MBh. **-kāra,** m. the exclamation *hāyas*, Lāṭy. **Hāyī-śabda,** m. id., Nyāyam., Sch.

हार *hāra, hāraka, hārin* &c. See p. 1289, cols. 2 and 3.

हारयु *hārayu*, N. of a place, Cat.

हारव *hārava*, m. N. of an inhabitant of hell, L.

हारायण *hārāyaṇa*, n. N. of various Sāmans, ĀrshBr.

हारिक *hārika, hāriṇa, hārīta, hāridra* &c. See p. 1292, col. 1.

हारिस *hārisa*, m. or n. a partic. high number, Buddh.

हार्ग *hārga* (?), m. (said to be fr. √1. *hṛi*) satisfaction, L.

हार्द् *hārd* (fr. and = *hṛid*). See *dur-* and *su-hārd*.

Hārda, mfn. relating to or being in the heart, Suparṇ.; Śaṃk.; BhP.; (*am*), n. love, kindness, affection for (loc. or comp.), MBh.; R. &c.; meaning, intention, purpose, BhP. **-vat,** mfn. feeling affection for (loc.), MārkP. **-vidyā,** f. N. of wk.

Hārdi, m. the heart, AV.; contentment, ease, comfort, VarBṛS.; n. the heart or interior of the body (also applied to the intestines), RV.

Hārdikā. See *yama-h°*.

Hārdikya, m. patr. of Kṛita-varman, MBh.; Hariv.; friendship, R.

Hārdin, mfn. feeling affection for (loc.), MārkP.

Hārdivan (TĀr.) or **hārdvan** (VS.), mfn. hearty, cordial, having an affection for (loc.)

हार्म्य *hārmyá*, n., v. l. for *harmyá*, TĀr.

हार्य *hārya.* See p. 1289, col. 3.

हार्ष्टेय *hārshṭeya, hārshṇi.* See p. 1293, col. 1.

हाल *hāla, hālaka, hālika* &c. See p. 1293, cols. 1 and 2.

हालहल *hālahala, hālāhala, hāhala* &c. See p. 1293, col. 2.

हावक *hāvaka, hāvanīya, hāvin* &c. See p. 1294, cols. 1 and 2.

हावु *hāvu*, ind. an exclamation of joy (used in chanting a Sāman), TUp.

हास *hāsa, hāsya.* See p. 1294, cols. 2 and 3.

हास्त *hāsta, hāstika, hāstina.* See p. 1296, col. 1.

हाहव *hāhava*, m. a kind of hell (cf. *ha-hava*), Kāraṇḍ.

हाहस् *hāhas*, m. a Gandharva, L.

Hāhā, m. (for *hā hā* see under 1. *hā*, p. 1296, col. 1) a Gandharva or N. of a Gandharva, ŚrS.; MBh.; Hariv. &c.; a partic. high number, ten thousand billions (*mahā-hāhā*, 'a hundred thousand billions'), MW.

हि 1. *hi* (cf. √*hay*), cl. 5. P. (Dhātup. xxvii, 11) *hinóti* (Ved. also *hinuté, hinvati* and *hinváti*, °*te*; p. *hinvāná* [with act. and pass. sense], RV.; *háyat*, RV.; TS.; 1. sg. *hishe*, RV.; pf. *jighāya, jighyuḥ*, Br. &c.; *jighye* [with pass. sense], Bhaṭṭ.; aor. *áhema, ahyan, heta*; p. *hiyāná* [with pass. sense], RV.; *ahyam* [?], *áhait*, AV.; *ahaishīt*, Br.; *aheshata*, RV.; fut. *hetā*, Gr.; *heshyati*, MBh. &c.; inf. *-hyê*, RV.), to send forth, set in motion, impel, urge on, hasten on (Ā. also intrans.), RV.; AV.; ŚBr.; KātyŚr.; to stimulate or incite to (dat.), RV.; to assist or help to (dat.), ib.; to discharge, hurl, cast, shoot, RV.; to convey, bring, procure, ib.; ŚBr.; to forsake, abandon, get rid of, Bhaṭṭ.; (*hinvati*), to gladden, delight, Dhātup. xv, 82: Pass. *hīyate* (aor. *ahāyi*), Gr.: Caus. *hāyayati* (aor. *ajīhayat*), ib.: Desid. of Caus. *jighāpayishati*, ib.: Desid. *jighīshati*, ib.: Intens. *jeghīyate, jeghayīti, jegheti*, ib.

Haya, hayana &c. See p. 1288, cols. 2, 3.

1. **Hitá,** mfn. (for 2. see p. 1298, col. 2) sent, impelled, urged on, set in motion &c.; going, running, speeding, RV.; AV.

Hiti, f. sending, errand, direction (see *asmé-* and *devá-h°*).

Hitvan, mfn. speedy, swift, RV.

Hinvá, m. 'Inciter,' N. of Indra's father (*prīṇayitri*, Sāy.), RV.

Hinvāná, hiyāná. See root, col. 2.

Hetí, hetú &c. See p. 1303, col. 3.

हि 2. *hí*, ind. (used as a particle [cf. *ha* and *gha*] and usually denoting) for, because, on account of (never standing first in a sentence, but generally after the first word and used enclitically, sometimes after pronouns; e.g. *sárvo hí pṛitanā jigīshati*, 'for everybody wishes to win battles;' *bhavān hi pramāṇam*, 'for your honour is the authority;' *tathā hi*, 'for example,' 'accordingly;' *ná hí* or *nahí*, 'for not,' 'not at all'), RV. &c. &c.; just, pray, do (with an Impv. or Pot. emphatically; sometimes with Indic., e.g. *paśyāmo hi*, 'we will just see'), ib.; indeed, assuredly, surely, of course, certainly (*hí vai*, 'most assuredly;' *hi-tu* or *hi-punar*, 'indeed—but;' often a mere expletive, esp. to avoid a hiatus, sometimes repeated in the same sentence; *hī* is also said to be an interjection of 'envy,' 'contempt,' 'hurry' &c.), ib.

Hiná, ind. for, because (= 2. *hí*), RV. vi, 48, 2.

हिंस 1. *hins* (orig. Desid. of √*han*), cl. 1. 7. P. (Dhātup. xxix, 19; xxxiv, 23) *hinsati, hinásti* (Ved. and ep. also Ā. *hinsate, hinste*; 2. sg. *hinsi* for *hinassi*, MBh. iii, 13269; pf. *jihinsa*, °*simá, jihinsiḥ*, AV.; aor. *ahinsīt, hinsīt*, RV. &c.; fut. *hinsitā*, Gr.; *hinsishyati*, °*te*, Br. &c.; inf. *hinsitum* [Ved. also *hinsitoḥ*], ib.; ind. p. *hinsitvā*, AV.; Br.; *-hinsya*, MBh.), to injure, harm, wound, kill, destroy, RV. &c. &c.: Pass. *hinsyate* (aor. *ahinsi*), to be injured or killed, RV. (in *á-hinsyamāna*) &c.: Caus. or cl. 10. P. (Dhātup. xxxiv, 23) *hinsayati* (aor. *ajihinsat*), to injure, harm, kill, slay, MBh.: Desid. *jihinsishati*, to wish to injure &c., ŚBr.: Intens. *jehinsyate, jehinsti*, Gr.

2. **Hins,** mfn. injuring, striking (see *su-hins*).

Hinsa, mfn. injuring, injurious, mischievous, hostile, RV.; (*ā*), f., see below.

Hinsaka, mfn. = prec., Yājñ.; MBh. &c.; m. (only L.) a noxious animal, beast of prey; an enemy; a Brāhman skilled in the magical texts of the Atharva-veda (cf. *hinsā-karman*).

Hinsana, m. an enemy, L.; n. the act of hurting, injuring, killing, slaying, Mn.; MBh. &c.

Hinsanīya, mfn. to be hurt or injured, MBh.; to be killed (as cattle), Kull. on Mn. v, 41.

Hinsā, f. injury, harm (to life or property), hurt, mischief, wrong (said to be of three kinds, 1. mental, as 'bearing malice;' 2. verbal, as 'abusive language;' 3. personal, as 'acts of violence'), Mn.; Yājñ.; MBh. &c.; Injury or Mischief personified (as the wife of Adharma and daughter of Lobha and Nishkṛiti), Pur.; Asteracantha Longifolia, L. **-karman,** n. any injurious or hostile act (esp. employment of magical spells and mystical texts such as those of the Atharva-veda for the injury of an enemy, q.v.), L. **-**°**tmaka** (*hinsât°*), mfn. intent on doing harm, R. **-**°**tman** (*hinsât°*), mfn. id., Bcar. **-prāṇin,** m. a savage or noxious animal, MW.; (°*ṇi*)-*pracura*, mfn. abounding in n° an°s, ib. **-prâya,** mfn. generally or for the most part injurious, Mn. x, 83. **-rata,** mfn. delighting in doing harm or mischief, Mn. iv, 170. **-ruci,** mfn. id. (*-tva*, n.), R. **-**°**rtha-vāda** (*hinsârth°*), m., **-lakshaṇa,** n., **-vāda,** m. N. of wks. **-vihāra,** mfn. taking pleasure in mischief, roaming about to do harm, MW. **-samud-bhava,** mfn. arising from injury (i.e. from the sin of hurting living creatures), ib.

Hinsāru, m. a destructive animal, a tiger, L.

Hinsālu, mfn. mischievous, hurting, murderous, W.

Hinsāluka, m. a mischievous animal, savage dog, L.

Hinsitá, mfn. hurt, injured, wounded, killed, destroyed, AV. &c. &c.; n. injury, harm, Pañcat.

Hinsitavyà, mfn. to be harmed or injured, AV.

Hínsitos. See under the root above.

Hinsīna, m. a savage animal, beast of prey, L.

Hinsīra, mfn. mischievous, destructive, L.; m. a tiger, L.

Hinsya, mfn. to be hurt or injured or killed, ŚāṅkhGṛ.; Mn.; MBh. &c.

Hinsrá, mf(*ā́*)n. injurious, mischievous, hurtful,

destructive, murderous, cruel, fierce, savage (ifc. 'acting injuriously towards'), RV. &c. &c.; m. a man who delights in injuring living creatures, Mn. iii, 164; a savage animal, beast of prey, Ragh.; N. of Śiva, MBh.; of Bhīma-sena, L.; of a certain cruel Brāhman, Hariv.; (*ā*), f. a mischievous woman, Mn. ix, 80; N. of various plants (accord. to L., Nardostachys Jatamansi, Coix Barbata, = *kākādanī* and *elāvalī*), Suśr.; fat, L.; a vein, L.; (*am*) n. cruelty, Mn. i, 29. **-jantu** or **-paśu**, m. a savage animal, beast of prey, Kāv. **-yantra**, n. an implement for injuring or wounding, trap, Yājñ.; a mystical text used for injurious purposes, MW. **Hinsrātmatā**, f. malevolence, Bcar. **Hinsrâhinsra**, n. noxiousness and harmlessness, Mn. i, 29.

Hinsraka, m. a savage animal, beast of prey, L.

हिक *hika*, n. (with *Prajāpateḥ*) N. of a Sāman, ĀrshBr.

हिक्क् *hikk*, cl. 1. P. Ā. (Dhātup. xxi, 1) *hikkati*, °*te* (Gr. also pf. *jihikka*, °*kke* &c.), to hiccup (hiccough), sob, make a spasmodic sound in the throat, Pat.; VarBṛS.; Suśr.: Caus. P. *hikkayati* (aor. *ajihikkat*), to cause to hiccup, Suśr.; (Ā.) *hikkayate*, to injure, kill, Dhātup. xxxiii, 12 (v.l. *hikk* for *kishk*).

Hikkā, f. hiccup (cf. *hekkā*), sob, a spasmodic sound in the throat, Suśr.; R.; Hariv.; an owl, L. **-śvāsin**, mfn. = *śvāsa-hikkin* (q.v.), Car.

Hikkikā, f. hiccup, MBh.; stertorous breathing, KātyŚr., Sch.

Hikkita, n. hiccup, spasmodic catch and sound in the breath, Pat.

Hikkin, mfn. suffering from hiccup, hiccupping, Suśr.

हिक्कल *hikkala* (?), the staff of a Buddhist monk, Buddh.

हिक्मत्प्रकाश *hikmat-prakāśa*, m. (fr. حكمت) N. of a med. wk. translated from the Arabic by Mahā-deva Paṇḍita.

Hikmat-pradīpa, m. N. of a med. wk. by the same author.

हिक्वा *hikvā*, f., w.r. for *hikkā* above.

हिङ् *hiṅ*, ind. the lowing sound or cry made by a cow seeking her calf, RV. i, 164, 28. **-kartṛi**, m. one who makes the sound *hiṅ*, TS. **-kārá**, m. the sound or cry *hiṅ* (used also in ritual), VS.; Br.; ŚrS.; a tiger (as making a lowing or roaring sound), L. **-√kṛi**, P. *-karoti* (ind. p. *-kṛitya*; p. p. *-kṛita*), to make the sound *hiṅ*, RV.; AV.; Br.; ŚrS. **-kriyā**, f. making the sound *hiṅ*, a lowing cry, Harav.

हिङ्ग *hiṅga*, m. pl. N. of a people, MārkP.

हिङ्गलाची *hiṅgalācī*, f. N. of a Yakshiṇī, Buddh.

हिङ्गु *hiṅgu*, m. Ferula Asa Fœtida, Buddh.; BhP.; n. a fluid or resinous substance prepared from the roots of the Asa Fœtida (used as a medicine or for seasoning), MBh.; Hariv.; Suśr. &c. **-nāḍika**, f. the resin of Gardenia Gummifera (cf. *nāḍī-hiṅgu*), L. **-niryāsa**, m. the fluid extracted from Asa Fœtida (see above), L.; the Nimba tree, L. **-pattra**, m. the Iṅgudī tree, L.; (*ī*), f. = *-parṇī*, L.; (*am*), n. the leaf of the Asa Fœtida, L. **-parṇī**, f. Gardenia Gummifera, L. **-rāta**, m. N. of a man, Mudr. **-śirāṭikā** (prob. w.r.) or **-śivāṭikā**, f. a partic. plant (= *vanśa-pattrī*), Bhpr.; Car. **Hiṅgûjjvalā**, f. a kind of perfume, Mṛicch.

Hiṅguka, m. the Asa Fœtida plant, MBh.

Hiṅgudī, f. Solanum Melongena, L.

Hiṅgula, m. n. a preparation of mercury with sulphur, vermilion, VarBṛS.; (*ā*), f., see below; (*ī*), f. Solanum Melongena or some other species, L.

Hiṅgula a, (prob.) n. vermilion, cinnabar, MBh.; VarBṛS.; (*ikā*), f. Solanum Jacquini, L.

Hiṅgulā, f. N. of a country, VāmP.; of the tutelary deity of the Dadhi-parṇas, Cat. **-jā**, f. N. of a goddess, ib.

Hiṅguli, m. vermilion, L.

Hiṅgulu (L.) or °**luka** (VarBṛS.), m. n. id.; (°*lu*), f. Solanum Melongena, L.

Hiṅgūla, m. a kind of plant (v.l. *hijjala*), Pañcar.; n. the edible root of Amorphophallus Campanulatus, L.

हिङ्गोलाष्टक *hiṅgoláshṭaka*, n. N. of wk.

हिज्ज *hijja*, m. the tree Barringtonia Acutangula (commonly called Hijjal), L.

Hijjala, m. the Hijjal tree, Pañcar. (v.l.); L.

हिञ्जीर *hiñjīra*, m. a rope or chain for fastening an elephant's foot, L.

हिट् *hiṭ*, v.l. for √*biṭ* (q.v.)

हिडिम्ब *hiḍimba*, m. N. of a gigantic Rākshasa slain by Bhīma, MBh.; (*ā*), f., see below. **-jit**, m. 'conqueror of Hiḍimba,' Bhīma, L. **-dvish**, m. 'enemy of H°,' Bhīma, Dhanaṃj. **-nisūdana** and **-bhid**, m. 'destroyer of H°,' Bhīma, ib. **-vadha**, m. 'the killing of Hiḍimba,' an episode of the Mahā-bhārata (i, 152–156).

Hiḍimbā, f. Hiḍimba's sister (who changed herself into a beautiful woman and married Bhīma; he had a son by her named Ghaṭôtkaca), MBh.; Kām.; BhP.; the wife of Hanumat (see comp.) **-pati** or **-ramaṇa**, m. 'husband or lover of Hiḍimbā,' N. of Bhīma or of Hanumat, L.

हिण्ड् *hiṇḍ*, cl. 1. Ā. (Dhātup. viii, 15) *hiṇḍate* (only impf. *ahiṇḍanta* and pf. *jihiṇḍe*), to go, move, wander or roam about (cf. *ā-* and *pari-√hiṇḍ*); to disregard, slight, Dhātup.

Hiṇḍaka, m. = *nāḍī-taraṃga* (cf. *rata-h°*), L.

Hiṇḍana, n. (only L.) wandering, roaming; sexual intercourse; writing.

Hiṇḍi, (prob.) f. = *rātrau rakshā-cāra*, L.

Hiṇḍika, m. an astrologer, L.

Hiṇḍira, m. = *hiṇḍīra*, L.

Hiṇḍī, f. N. of Durgā, L. **-kānta** or **-priyatama**, m. 'beloved by Durgā,' N. of Śiva, L.

Hiṇḍīra, m. cuttle-fish bone (supposed to be the congealed foam of the sea, = *samudra-phena*), Sāh.; a man, male, L.; a tonic or stomachic (= *rucaka*), L.; Solanum Melongena, L.; n. the pomegranate, L.

Hiṇḍuka, m. N. of Śiva, MBh.

हित 2. *hitá*, mf(*ā́*)n. (p. p. of √1. *dhā*, cf. *dhita*; for 1. *hita* see p. 1297, col. 2) put, placed, set, laid, laid upon, imposed, lying or situated or contained in (loc.), RV.; AV.; Up.; set up, established, fixed (as a prize), RV.; planned, arranged (as a race or contest), ib.; prepared, made ready, ib.; held, taken, MW.; assigned to, destined for (dat. or gen.), ib.; reckoned among (loc.), TS.; constituted or appointed as (nom.), RV.; given (as a name), AV.; beneficial, advantageous, salutary, wholesome, suitable, agreeing with (often said of diet, regimen, medicines &c.), convenient, suitable, fit, agreeable to or for (dat., gen., loc., or comp.), RV. &c. &c.; well-disposed, favourable, friendly, affectionate, kind, Mn.; MBh. &c.; m. a friend, benefactor, ib.; (*ā́*), f. a causeway, dike (see *hitā-bhaṅga*); pl. N. of partic. veins or arteries, ŚBr.; KaushUp.; Yājñ.; (*am*), n. (sg. or pl.) anything useful or salutary or suitable or proper, benefit, advantage, profit, service, good, welfare, good advice &c., Mn.; MBh. &c. **-kara**, mfn. doing a service, furthering the interests of (gen.), favourable, useful, a benefactor, R.; VarBṛS. **-kāma**, mfn. wishing well to, desirous of benefiting, Pañcat.; Hit. **-kāmyā**, f. (only in instr.) desire for another's (gen.) welfare, Mn.; MBh.; Hariv. &c. **-kāraka**, mfn. = *-kara*, Pañcat. **-kārin**, mfn. id. (°*ri-tā*, f.; °*ri-tva*, n.), Āpast.; R.; Rājat. &c. **-kṛit**, mfn. id., VarBṛS.; BhP.; Kathās. &c. **-nāman**, m. N. of a man, Pāṇ. vi, 4, 170, Vārtt. **-pathya**, mf(*ā*)n. useful and salutary, Vās.; = *hitā* (i.e. *prâptā*) *pathyā* (i.e. *harītakī*) *yena*, ib. **-praṇī**, m. 'executing what is advantageous,' a spy, L. **-prayas** (*hitá-*), mfn. one who has offered an oblation of food or for whom an oblation has been offered, RV. **-pravṛitta**, mfn. intent on the welfare of (loc.), Bcar. **-prêpsu**, mfn. = *-kāma*, Mn. v, 46. **-buddhi**, f. friendly intention (°*dhyā*, 'with fr° int°'), R.; mfn. friendly-minded, well-disposed, Hit. **-mitra**, m. a benevolent friend, MW.; (*hitá-*), mfn. having ben° friends, RV. **-lāla-śarman** (*miśra-hita-l°*), m. N. of an author, Cat. **-vacana**, n. friendly advice, good counsel, Hit. **-vat**, mfn. favourable, useful, Hit. **-vākya**, n. = *-vacana*, Cat.; *-sūtra*, n. N. of wk. **-vādin**, mfn. speaking good counsel or friendly advice, a friendly counsellor or adviser, Jātakam. **-sūtra**, n. N. of wk. **-harivanśa** or **-harivanśa-gosvāmin**, m. = *hari-vanśa-gosv°*, Cat. **-hita**, m. N. of a man, Rājat. **Hitâtman**, mfn. quite intent upon the welfare of (comp.), Bcar. **Hitâdhāyin**, mfn. = *hita-kara* (°*yi-tā*, f.), Rājat. **Hitânukārin**, mfn. acting conformably to what is right or kind, W. **Hitânubandhin**, mfn. having welfare as a consequence, having salutary con°s, Kām. **Hitânveshin**, mfn. seeking the welfare of another (gen.), MBh. **Hitā-bhaṅga**, m. the breaking of a dike (v.l. *iḍā-bh°*), Mn. ix, 274. **Hitârtham** (R.) or °**thāya** (MBh.; R.), ind. for the sake of another's welfare. **Hitârthin**, mfn. seeking or desiring one's (own) or another's welfare or advantage, MBh.; R. &c. **Hitâvalī**, f. a partic. drug, L. **Hitâśansā**, f. wishing well, congratulation, ib. **Hitâśva**, m. N. of a man, VP. **Hitâhita**, mfn. good and (or) evil, beneficial and (or) disadvantageous, Mn.; Suśr.; (*ā*), f. pl. N. of partic. veins, Yājñ.; n. sg. advantage and (or) disadvantage, Pur. **Hitâhitīya**, mfn. treating of what is beneficial and disadvantageous, Suśr. **Hitêcchā**, f. wishing well, good-will, good wishes, MW. **Hitâishin**, mfn. well-wishing, desiring another's welfare (°*shi-tā*, f.), MBh.; Pañcat.; Kathās.; Jātakam. **Hitôkti**, f. kind or good advice, Dhanaṃj. **Hitôpadeśa**, m. friendly advice, salutary instruction, MBh.; Pañcat. &c.; N. of a popular collection of fables intermixed with didactic sentences and moral precepts (compiled by Nārāyaṇa, and supposed to be narrated by a Brāhman named Vishṇu-śarman to some young princes; it is chiefly founded on the Pañca-tantra, q.v.); N. of two wks. on medicine. **Hitôpadeshṭṛi**, mfn. instructing on what is salutary, a friendly instructor, kind adviser, Kāv.

Hitaka, m. a child, the young of any animal, L.

Hitāya, Nom. Ā. °*yate*, to avail, be of use or advantage, Vās.

Hitâvat, mfn. one who has put away or hidden his property, RV.

हिति *hiti*, *hítvan*. See p. 1297, col. 3.

हित्वाय *hitvā́ya*, *hitvī́*. See √3. *hā*.

हिन *hiná*. See under 2. *hí*, p. 1297, col. 3.

हिन्ताल *hintāla*, m. the marshy date tree, Phœnix or Elate Paludosa (cf. *tāla* and *bṛihat-tāla*), Hariv.; Vās.; Jātakam.

हिन्दु *hindu*, m. (fr. the Persian هندو) a Hindu (more properly Hindū). **-dharma**, m. the Hindū religion, MW. **-sthāna**, n. the country of the Hindūs, Hindūstān (properly restricted to the upper provinces between Benares and the Sutlej), Cat.

हिन्दोल *hindola*, m. (or *ā*, f.) a swing, swinging cradle or hammock, Śṛiṅgār.; an ornamental swing or litter in which figures of Kṛishṇa are carried during the Swing-festival in the light half of the month Śrāvaṇa, MW. (cf. RTL. 430); m. (in music) a partic. Rāga, Saṃgīt.; (*ī*), f. a partic. Rāgiṇī, ib.

Hindolaka, m. a swing, Pañcad.

Hindolaya, Nom. P. °*yati*, to swing, rock about (cf. *andolaya*), Pañcad.

हिन्व् *hinv*, *hinvá*, *hinvāná*. See √1. *hi*.

हिन्विधेनामन् *hinvidhe-nāman*, mfn. (of unknown meaning), MaitrS.

हिबुक *hibuka*, n. (= ὑπόγειον) N. of the fourth Lagna or astrological sign, fourth astrological house (= *pātāla*), VarBṛS.

हिम् 1. *hím*, ind. an exclamation (interchangeable with *hín*, q.v.)

हिम् 2. *hím* (only in instr. *himā́*), cold, frost, hoar-frost, snow, RV. x, 37, 10; 68, 10.

Himá, m. cold, frost, RV. &c. &c.; the cold season, winter, Kālid.; MārkP.; the sandal tree, L.; the moon (cf. *hima-kara* &c.), L.; camphor, L.; (*himā́*), f. (only with *śatá*) the cold season, winter (also = 'a year;' cf. *varshá*), RV.; VS.; AV.; (*himā́*), night, Naigh. i, 7; (*himā*, only L.), cardamoms; Cyperus Rotundus and another species; Trigonella Corniculata; a partic. drug (= *reṇukā*); N. of Durgā; (*am*), n. frost, hoar-frost, snow (rarely 'ice'), ShaḍvBr. &c. &c.; sandal-wood (of cooling properties), Suśr.; the wood of Cerasus Puddum, L.; tin, L.; a pearl, L.; fresh butter, L.; a lotus, W.; N. of a Varsha, VP.; mf(*ā*)n. cold, cool, Jātakam. [Cf. Zd. *zima*; Gk. (δύς-)χιμος; χιών, χειμών; Lat. *bīmus* for *bi-himus*; *hiems*; Slav. *zima*; Lit. *žëmà*.] **-ṛitu**, m. the winter season, Śiś. **-kaṇin**, mfn. mixed with snow-flakes (as wind), Kāv. **-kara**, mfn. causing or producing cold, cold, W.; m. the moon, Hariv.; Kāv.; Var. &c.; camphor, L.; *-tanaya*, m. 'son of the Moon,' N. of the planet Mercury, VarBṛS. **– kashāya**, m. a partic. cool drink, Suśr.; ŚārṅgS. **– kiraṇa**, m. 'cold-rayed,' the moon, Dhūrtan. **– kūṭa**, n. a snowy summit, BhP.; m. the winter season, L. **– kshmādhara**, m. snowy mountain, Himâlaya, VarBṛS. **-khaṇḍa**, n. a hail-stone, MārkP. **– garbha**, mfn. laden with snow, Śak. **– giri**, m. the Himâlaya mountain, ib.; ŚārṅgS.; Kathās. &c.; *-sutā*, f. patr. of Pārvatī, Kāv.; Kathās.; °*tā-kānta*, m. 'loved by P°,' N. of Śiva, Kathās. **– gu**, m. 'cold-rayed,' the moon, Var. **– gṛiha** or °**haka**, n. a room furnished with cooling appliances, Kād. **– gaura**, mfn. white as snow, Kir. **– ghna**, mfn. keeping off snow, R. **– ja**, mfn. produced by cold, W.; born or prod° in the Himâlaya mountain, ib.; m. the mountain Maināka, L.; (*ā*), f. a kind of plant, = *kshīriṇī*, L.; the plant called Zedoary, L.; sugar prepared from Yava-nāla, L.; N. of Pārvatī, ib.; of Śacī, ib. **– jyotis**, mfn. cold-rayed (as the moon), Hariv. **– jvara**, m. fever with cold paroxysms, ague, MW. **– jhati** or **-jhanti**, f. cold dew, hoar-frost, mist, fog, L. (cf. *ku-jjhaṭi*). **– tala**, N. of a kingdom, Buddh. (more correctly *hema-tāla*). **– taila**, m. camphor oil, L. **– tvish** (Kathās.) or **-dīdhiti** (ib.; Var.; Śiś.), m. 'having cool rays,' the moon. **– dugdhā**, f. a kind of plant (= *kshīriṇī*), L. **– durdina**, n. a snowy day, cold and bad weather, L. **– dyuti**, m. 'having cool radiance,' the moon, Śiś. **– druma**, m. Melia Bukayun, L. **– druh**, m. 'dew-dispeller,' the sun, MW. **– dhara**, mfn. bearing snow (on its head, said of the Himâlaya), R.; m. the Him° m°, Cat. **– dhātu**, m. 'having cold minerals,' L. **– dhāman**, m. 'cold-rayed,' the moon, Śiś.; Bālar. **– dhvasta**, mfn. withered by cold, frost-bitten, frost-nipped (as a lotus &c.), MW. **– nirjhara-viprushmat**, mfn. mixed with or having drops of icy cold water-falls, BhP. **– nirmukta**, mfn. freed from frost, Ragh. **– pāta**, m. fall of snow, Ṛitus.; VarBṛS.; Pañcat. **– prastha**, m. 'having snowy table-land,' the Himâlaya mountain, L. **– bāluka**, °**kā**, see *-vāluka*, °*kā*. **– bhānu**, m. 'having cool lustre,' the moon, Kautukar. **– bhās**, m. id., MW. **– bhūbhṛit**, m. 'snow-m°,' the Himâlaya, MārkP. **– mayūkha**, m. 'cool-rayed,' the moon, VarBṛS. **– mitra**, m. N. of a man, Cat. **– yukta**, m. a kind of camphor, L. **– raśmi**, m. 'cool-rayed,' the moon, Śiś.; *-ja*, m. patr. of the planet Mercury, Var. **– rāja**, m. N. of a king, Rājat. **– ruci**, m. = *-raśmi*, Śiś.; Kām. &c. **– ṛtu**, m. = *-ṛitu*, Rājat. **– vat** (*himá-*), mfn. having frost or snow, snowy, frosty, icy, snow-clad, AV.; R.; exposing one's self to coldness or enduring it, Baudh.; m. a snowy mountain, RV.; AV.; the Himâlaya, AV. &c. &c.; Kailāsa, L.; (*atī*), f. Hoya Viridiflora, ib.; (*-vac*)*-chiras*, n. (for *-śiras*) the summit of the Himâlaya, Bcar. v, 45 (conj.); (*-vat*)*-kukshi*, m. a valley of the Him°, MW.; *-khaṇḍa*, n. N. of a book of the Skanda-Purāṇa; *-pura*, n. the town on the Him°, Kum.; *-prabhava*, mfn. springing from or belonging to the Him°, R.; *-suta*, m. 'son of the Him°,' the mountain Maināka, L.; (*-sutā*), f. the Ganges, Dhanamj.; Pārvatī, A.; (°*vad*)*-giri*, m. a snowy mountain (*-saṃśraya*, m. 'taking refuge in the Him°,' N. of Śiva), MW.; (°*van*)*-māhātmya*, n. N. of wk.; (°*van*)*-mekhalā*, f. the Him° chain of mountains, Uttamac. **– vata** (m.), (ifc.) = *-vat*, g. *śarat-prabhṛiti*. **– vāri**, n. cold water, MārkP. **– vāluka**, m. or °**kā**, f. camphor, L. **– viddha**, mfn. penetrated with frost (as the west wind in the cold season), MW. **– vṛishṭi**, f. fall of snow, Hariv. **– śarkarā**, f. a kind of sugar produced from Yava-nāla, L. **– śikharin**, m. 'snow-mountain,' the Himâlaya, Vcar. **– śītala**, mfn. very cold or frosty, freezing, W. **– śuci-bhasma-bhūshita**, mfn. adorned with ashes white as snow, ib. **– śubhra**, mfn. white as snow, Śiś. **– śaila**, m. 'snow-mountain,' the Himâlaya, Cat.; *-ja*, mfn. produced on the Him°, Yājñ.; (*ā*), f. 'daughter of Him°,' N. of Pārvatī, L.; *-sutā*, f. id., Prab. **– śratha**, m. the loosening or melting of snow, Pāṇ.; Vop.; 'shedding cold,' the moon, W. **– śrathana** or **-śranthana**, n. melting of snow, Pāṇ.; Vop. **– saṃhati**, f. a mass of ice or snow, deep snow, L. **– saṃkhāta** (w. r. for) **-saṃghāta**, m. id., Rājat. **– saras**, n. cold water, Mālatim. **– srut**, m. 'distilling cold,' the moon, Kād. **– sruti**, f. a snow-shower, Ragh. **– hāna-kṛit**, m. 'causing cessation of cold,' fire, W. **– hāsaka**, m. Phoenix Paludosa, L. **Himâṅśu**, m. 'cool-rayed,' the moon, Kāv.; VarBṛS. &c.; camphor, W.; *-mālin*, m. 'encircled by cold rays,' the moon, Kām.; °*māṅśv-abhikhya*, n. 'called after the moon,' silver, L. **Himâga**, m. 'snow-mountain,' the Himâlaya, ib. **Himâgama**, m. approach of cold, beginning of winter, MBh.; R. &c. **Himâṅka**, m. camphor, L. **Himâcala**, m. 'snow-mountain,' the Himâlaya, Śiś.; Kathās.; MārkP. &c.; °*lêndra*, m. id., Kathās. **Himâtyaya**, m. passing off or end of the cold season, R. **Himâdri**, m. the Himâlaya mountain, Kāv.; Kathās. &c.; *-jā*, f. 'daughter of Him°,' Pārvatī, MW.; the Ganges, A.; a kind of plant (= *kshīriṇī*), L.; *-tanayā*, f. 'daughter of Him°,' Pārvatī (*-pati*, m. 'husband of P°,' Śiva), Kavik.; the Ganges, A. **Himâdrīya**, Nom. to represent the Himâlaya (°*yita*, n. impers.), Cat. **Himânaddha**, mfn. frost-bound, frozen, Suśr. **Himânila**, m. a cold or frosty wind, L. **Himânta**, m. end of the cold season, MBh. **Himâpaha**, m. 'removing cold,' fire, Agni, ib. **Himâbja**, n. a blue lotus, L. **Himâbha**, mfn. resembling cold, like snow or frost, W. **Himâbhra**, m. camphor, L. **Himâmbu**, n. cold water, MW.; dew, A. **Himâmbhas**, n. cold water, Ragh.; BhP.; dew, A. **Himârāti**, m. 'enemy of cold,' fire, L.; the sun, ib.; a kind of plant (= *citraka*), MW.; another plant (= *arka*), ib. **Himâri**, m. 'enemy of cold,' fire, Bhaṭṭ.; *-śatru*, m. 'enemy of fire,' water, Bcar. xi, 71. **Himâruṇa**, mfn. grey with frost, R. **Himârta**, mfn. pinched with cold, suffering from cold, chilled, frozen, Śak.; Hit. **Himârdita**, mfn. pinched or pained by cold, MW. 1. **Himâlaya**, m. 'abode of snow,' the Himâlaya range of mountains (bounding India on the north, and containing the highest elevations in the world; in mythology personified as husband of Menā or Menakā [by whom he had a son Maināka] and father of Pārvatī, 'daughter of the Mountain,' and of Gaṅgā, who, as the personified Ganges, is generally regarded as his eldest daughter), Bhag.; Kāv. &c.; the white Khadira tree, L.; (*ā*), f. Flacourtia Cataphracta, L.; *-sutā*, f. 'daughter of Him°,' Pārvatī, Kavik. 2. **Himâlaya**, Nom. P. °*yati*, to resemble the Himâlaya, Dhūrtas. **Himā-vatī**, f. a kind of plant, L. **Himâvila**, mf(*ā*)n. covered with snow, HPariś. **Himâśrayā**, f. Hoya Viridiflora, L. **Himâhati**, f. fall of snow, Kathās. **Himâhva**, m. 'called after ice,' camphor, L.; n. N. of a Varsha in Jambu-dvīpa, Pur. **Himâhvaya**, m. camphor, L.; n. = prec., n., MārkP.; a lotus, W. **Himôttarā**, f. a kind of grape, L. **Himôttarīya**, mfn. having snow for an over-garment, Jātakam. **Himôtpanna**, mfn. produced by cold, MW.; (*ā*), f. = *hima-śarkarā*, L. **Himôdaka** or °**daki**(?), m. N. of a man, Cat. **Himôdbhavā**, f. 'cold-produced,' Curcuma Zedoaria, L.; another plant (= *kshīriṇī*), ib. **Himôpacāra**, m. application of cooling remedies or refrigerants, Vcar. **Himôsra**, m. 'cool-rayed,' the moon, Bhaṭṭ.

Himaka, m. Flacourtia Sapida, L.; N. of a man, Rājat.; (*ikā*), f. hoar-frost, L.

Himavala, n. a pearl, L. (v. l. *hem°*).

Himā, f. See under *hima*, p. 1298, col. 3.

Himānī, f. a mass or collection of snow, Rājat.; Pārśvan. &c.; = *hima-śarkarā*, L. **– viśada**, mfn. white as a snow-drift, MW.

Himāya, Nom. Ā. °*yate*, to resemble snow, Kāv.

Himāla, m. the Himâlaya mountain, L.

Himikā, f. See *himaka* above.

Himita, mfn. changed into snow or ice, Naish.

Himi-√kṛi, P. *-karoti*, to change into snow or ice, Śiś.

Himerú, mfn. (prob.) = next, MaitrS.

Himelu, mfn. chilly, suffering from cold, Pāṇ. v, 2, 122, Vārtt. 8.

Himna, m. the planet Mercury (= *hemna*), Cat.

Himya, mfn. snowy, covered with snow, Pāṇ. v, 2, 120, Vārtt., Sch.; (*ā́*), ind. by cold, RV.

Héman &c. See 2. *héman*, p. 1304, col. 1.

हिम्न *himna*, m. = *hemna*, the planet Mercury, Cat.

हिम्पतिवर्मन् *himpati-varman* or *himmati-varman*, m. N. of a man, Cat.

Himmaka, m. N. of a man, Cat.

हिर *híra*, m. a band, strip, fillet, ŚBr. (= *mekhalā*, Sch.); (*a*), f., see next.

Hirā́, f. a vein, artery (cf. *hitā* and *sirā*), AV.; VS.; Gmelina Arborea, L. [Cf., accord. to some, Lat. *haru(-spex)*.] **– dhara**, m. N. of a man, Cat.

Hirôdaka, n. blood, Divyāv.

हिरकुत् *hirakut.* See *híruk*, p. 1300.

हिरङ्गु *hiraṅgu*, m. N. of Rāhu (the personified ascending node), L.

हिरण *hiraṇa*, n. (= *híranya*) gold, L.; semen, L.; a cowry, L.

Hiraṇin, mfn. (prob. for *hiraṇyin*) golden, adorned with gold, RV.

Hiraṇ-máya, mf(*ī*)n. (for *hiraṇya-maya*) golden, gold-coloured, TS. &c. &c.; m. N. of Brahmā (see *hiraṇya-garbha*), L.; of a Ṛishi, MBh.; of a son of Agnīdhra and ruler of a Varsha, BhP.; m. n. one of the 9 Varshas or divisions of the continent (said to be between the mountainous ranges Śveta and Śṛiṅga-vat; see *varsha* and *śveta*), Pur.

Híraṇya, n. (ifc. f. *ā*; prob. connected with *hari*, *harit*, *hiri*) gold (orig. 'uncoined gold or other precious metal;' in later language 'coined gold' or 'money'), RV. &c. &c.; any vessel or ornament made of gold (as 'a golden spoon,' Mn. ii, 29), RV.; AV.; VS.; Kauś.; a gold piece or coin (generally with *suvárṇa* as opp. to base metal), Br.; a cowry, L.; semen virile, L.; substance, imperishable matter, L.; a partic. measure, W.; the Datura or thorn apple, MW.; N. of a Varsha (= *hiraṇ-maya*), MārkP.; m. a kind of bdellium, L.; N. of a Daitya, MBh.; Pañcar.; of a son of Agnīdhra (= *hiraṇ-maya*, q. v.), MārkP.; of a king of Kaśmīra, Rājat.; (*ā*), f. one of the seven tongues of fire, L.; mfn. golden, made of gold, Mn.; MBh. **– kaksha** (MBh.; R.) or **-kakshyá** (TĀr.; ĀśvŚr.), mfn. wearing a g° girdle. **– kaṇṭha**, mfn. g°-necked, MBh. **– karṇa** (*híraṇya-*), mfn. wearing gold in the ear, RV. **– kartṛi**, m. a goldsmith, MBh. **– kavaca**, mfn. having golden armour (said of Śiva), ib.; °*côdbhava*, m. N. of Śiva, MW. **– kaśipú**, m. a golden cushion or seat or clothing, Br.; Lāṭy.; (*híraṇya-*), mfn. having a g° cushion or clothing, AV.; m. N. of a Daitya king noted for impiety (he was son of Kaśyapa and Diti, and had obtained a boon from Brahmā that he should not be slain by either god or man or animal; hence he became all-powerful; when, however, his pious son Prahlāda praised Vishṇu, that god appeared out of a pillar in the form Nara-siṇha, 'half man, half lion,' and tore Hiraṇya-kaśipu to pieces; this was Vishṇu's fourth Avatāra; see *pra-hlāda*, *nara-siṇha*), MBh.; Hariv.; Pur. (cf. IW. 328; 392, n. 2); *-cchedin* (Pañcar.), *-dāraṇa* (L.), or *-han* (MW.), m. N. of Vishṇu. **– kāma-dhenu**, f. a golden figure representing the Kāma-dhenu (one of the 16 Mahā-dānas; see *mahā-dāna*, *tulā-purusha*), Cat.; *-dāna*, n., *-dāna-prayoga*, m. N. of wks. **– kārá**, m. a goldsmith, VS.; R. **– kukshi**, mfn. g°-bellied, Kauś. **– kubja**, m. N. of a man, Vcar. **– kula**, m. N. of a king, Rājat. **– kṛit**, mfn. making or bringing forth gold (said of Agni), MBh. **– kṛita-cūḍa**, mfn. one whose tuft of hair is golden (said of Śiva), ib. **– kṛishṇala**, n. a small piece of gold, Kāṭh.; Anup. **– ketu**, m. N. of an author, Madanap. **– keśa** (*híraṇya-*), mf(*ī*)n. gold-haired, g°-maned, RV.; AV.; BhP.; m. N. of Vishṇu, L.; pl. a partic. school, IndSt.; (*ī*), f. (scil. *śākhā*) id., ib. **– keśin**, m. N. of the author of certain Sūtras, Cat.; (°*si*)*-kārikā*, f., *-śākhīya-brāhmaṇa*, n., *-śrauta-sūtra*, n., *-sūtra*, n., *-sūtra-vyākhyāna*, n., (°*śy*)*-āhnika*, n. N. of wks. **– keśīyâgny-ādhāna-paddhati**, f. N. of wk. **– keśya** (*híraṇya-*), mfn. golden-haired, golden-maned, RV. **– kośa**, m. wrought and unwrought gold and silver (?), L. **– khādi**, mfn. wearing golden brooches, ŚāṅkhŚr. **– gadā**, f. a golden club, Cat.; *-dāna*, n. N. of wk. **– garbhá**, m. a golden fetus, Cat.; N. of Brahmā (so called as born from a golden egg formed out of the seed deposited in the waters when they were produced as the first creation of the Self-existent; according to Mn. i, 9, this seed became a golden egg, resplendent as the sun, in which the Self-existent Brahmā was born as Brahmā the Creator, who is therefore regarded as a manifestation of the Self-existent, RV. x, 121), RV.; AV.; ŚBr. &c. (cf. RTL. 14 &c.); N. of the author of the hymn Ṛig-veda x, 121 (having the patr. Prājāpatya), Anukr.; of a Vedânta teacher, Tattvas.; of various other persons, Cat.; of Vishṇu, MBh.; of a flamingo, Hit.; (in phil.) the soul invested with the Sūkshma-śarīra or subtle body (= *sūtrâtman*, *prāṇâtman*), Vedântas.; (*ā*), f. N. of a river, Cat.; (prob.) n. N. of a Liṅga, ib.; mfn. relating to Hiraṇya-garbha or Brahmā, IndSt.; *-tantra*, n., *-dāna*, n., *-dāna-prayoga*, m., *-dāna-vidhi*, m. N. of wks.; *-vatī* (*-garbhá-*), f.

a verse containing the word *hiraṇya-garbha*, ŚBr.; *-vidhi*, m. N. of the 12th Pariśishṭa of the Atharva-veda; *-saṃhitā* (or °*bha-parāśara-saṃhitā*), f., *-hṛidaya*, n. N. of wks. **-gupta**, m. N. of various men, Kathās. **-cakra** (*hiraṇya-*), mfn. g°-wheeled, RV. **-jā́**, mfn. sprung from g°, golden, AV. **-jit**, mfn. gaining gold, RV.; AV. **-jihva** (*hiraṇya-*), mfn. g°-tongued, RV. **-jyotis**, n. splendour of g°, ŚBr.; (*hiraṇya-jyotis*), mfn. having golden spl°, AV.; TS.; Kāṭh. **-tusha**, m. = *-śakala*, Lāṭy., (Sch.) **-téjas**, n. = *-jyotis*, AV. **-tvac** (*hiraṇya-*), mfn. having a g° covering, coated with gold, RV. **-tvaca**, mfn. having skin bright as gold, MW. **-tvacas** (*hiraṇya-*), mfn. having a golden skin, (or) having a g° caparison, AV. **-da**, mfn. yielding gold, Mn. iv, 230; m. the ocean, L.; (*ā*), f. the earth, ib.; N. of a river, Hariv. **-daṇshṭra**, mfn. having g° teeth, ChUp. **-dakshiṇa**, mfn. having a fee or wage of gold, KātyŚr. **-dat** (*hiraṇya-*), mfn. having g° teeth, RV.; m. N. of a Baida, AitBr. **-datta**, m. N. of various men, Kathās. **-danta**, mfn. = *-dat*, Hir. **-dā́**, mfn. = *-da*, RV. **-dāna**, n. the granting of g°, Cat.; N. of wk. **-devī-sûkta**, n. N. of wk. **-dyū**, mfn. playing for gold or money, Pat. **-drāpi** (*hiraṇya-*), mfn. wearing a golden mantle, AV. **-dhanus**, m. 'g°-bowed,' N. of a king, MBh. **-nābha**, m. 'having a g° navel,' N. of Vishṇu, L.; of various men, PraśnUp.; MBh.; Hariv. &c.; of the mountain Maināka, R.; n. a building having three halls (viz. towards the east, west, and south), VarBṛS. **-nikāsham**, ind. rubbing in or mixing gold, ĀśvGṛ. **-nidhi**, m. a g° treasure, ChUp. **-nirṇij** (*hiraṇya-*), mfn. adorned with g°, bright as g°, RV. **-nemi**, mfn. having golden fellies or wheels, RV. **-paksha** (*hiraṇya-*), mfn. g°-winged, RV.; VS. &c. **-pati**, m. a lord of g°, TĀr.; MBh. **-parṇa** (*hiraṇya-*), g°-winged, RV.; PārGṛ.; g°-leafed, VS.; TBr.; Nir. **-parvata**, m. N. of a mountain, Buddh. **-pāṇi** (*hiraṇya-*), mfn. golden-handed, RV.; g°-hoofed, RV.; m. N. of various men, ShaḍvBr.; Buddh. **-pātrá**, n. a g° vessel, TS.; Br.; VP. **-pāvá**, mfn. purifying with g°, RV., (Sāy.) **-piṇḍá**, m. a lump of g°, RV. **-pura**, n. N. of an Asura town floating in the air or situated beyond the ocean, MBh.; Hariv. &c.; of a town in Kāśmīra, Kathās.; Rājat. **-purusha**, m. the figure of a man made of g°, KātyŚr.; Vait. **-pushpi**, m. N. of a man, Cat. **-pushpī**, f. a kind of plant, Suśr. **-peśas** (*hiraṇya-*), mfn. adorned with g°, having golden lustre, RV. **-praüga** (*hiraṇya-*), mfn. having a golden fore-part (said of a chariot-pole), RV. i, 35, 5. **-pratipūrṇa**, mfn. full of g°, Hariv. **-prākārā**, f. having a golden rampart, MānGṛ. **-bandhana** (*hiraṇya-*), mf(*ā*)n. having golden bands (said of the cordage of a ship), AV. **-bāhu** (*hiraṇya-*), mfn. golden-armed, VS.; TĀr.; m. N. of Śiva, MBh.; the river Śoṇa (v.l. *-vāha*), Hcar.; N. of a serpent-demon, MBh.; of a man, Cat. **-bindu**, m. fire, MW.; N. of a mountain, MBh.; of a Tīrtha (also *-bindos tīrtham*), ib. **-máya**, mf(*ī*)n. made of g°, ŚBr. **-mālin**, mfn. having a golden garland, KātyŚr., Sch. **-mūrdhan** (*hiraṇya-*), mf(*dhnī*)n. g°-headed, TS. **-yashṭi**, f. a golden tree, ĀpŚr. **-yoni**, mfn. having a g° womb, ib. **-rathá**, m. a chariot full of g°, RV.; AitBr.; a ch° made of g°, Cat.; (*hiraṇya-*), mfn. riding in a g° ch°, RV.; m. N. of a king, VP. **-raśana**, mfn. having a g° girdle, BhP. **-rūpa** (*hiraṇya-*), mfn. g°-shaped, gold-like, RV. **-retas**, mfn. having golden seed; m. N. of Agni or fire, MBh.; Kāv. &c.; of the sun, L.; of Śiva, ib.; of one of the 12 Ādityas, RāmatUp.; of various men, BhP.; Cat.; a kind of plant (= *citraka*), MW. **-retasa**, m. N. of a man; pl. his family, Cat. **-roman**, m. 'golden-haired,' N. of a Loka-pāla (son of Marīci), MW.; of Bhishmaka, MBh.; of a son of Parjanya, Hariv.; VP.; of various Ṛishis, Hariv.; BhP. **-lakshmī-sûkta**, n. N. of wk. **-loman**, m. N. of a Ṛishi in the 5th Manv-antara, MārkP. **-vakshas** (*hiraṇya-*), mfn. g°-breasted, holding g° (as the earth), AV. **-vat** (*hiraṇya-*), mfn. possessing g°, RV.; consisting of g°, ib.; connected with g°, GṛŚrS.; m. N. of Agni, MW.; (*atī*), f. N. of Ujjayinī in the third age, Kathās.; of a river, Buddh.; of various women, Kathās.; Cat.: n. the possession of g°, RV. **-vandhura** (*hiraṇya-*), mfn. having a g° seat or framework (as a chariot), RV. **-varcasa**, mfn. shining with golden lustre, Hir. **-varṇa** (*hiraṇya-*), mf(*ā*)n. g°-coloured, g°-like, RV.; AV.; TBr. &c.; containing the word *hiraṇya-varṇa* (as a verse), TS.; Kauś.; Baudh.; (*ā*), f. a river, L. **-varṇīya**, mfn. beginning with *hiraṇya-varṇa*, TPrāt. **-vartani** (*hiraṇya-*), mfn. having a golden path, RV.; VS. **-varman**, m. 'having g° armour,' N. of a king, MBh. **-varsha**, m. N. of a man, Bcar.; Kathās. **-vāśī** (*hiraṇya-*), mfn. wielding a gold axe or knife, RV.; *-mat*, mfn. id. (only superl. *-tama*, 'most skilful wielder of the g° knife'), ib. **-vāha**, m. 'bearing g°,' N. of the river Śoṇa (cf. *-bāhu*), Hcar.; of Śiva, MBh. **-víd**, mfn. possessing or granting g°, RV. **-vimitá**, n. a golden palace, ŚBr. **-ví́**, mfn. covered with g°, RV. **-vīrya**, mfn. having golden seed (fire), BhP. **-vṛishabha**, m. a small g° bull, Cat.; *-dāna*, n., *-dāna-prayoga*, m. N. of wks. **-śakalá**, m. a small piece of g°, ŚBr. **-śaklá**, v.l. for *-śalká*, TS. **-śamya** (*hiraṇya-*), mfn. having g° pegs, RV. **-śarīra**, mfn. having a g° body, AitBr. **-śalká**, m. a fragment of gold, TS. **-śipra** (*hiraṇya-*), mfn. having a g° helmet (or visor), RV. **-śīrshan**, mf(*shṇī*)n. g°-headed, Kāṭh. **-śṛiṅga** (*hiraṇya-*), mfn. g°-horned, RV.; AV.; m. N. of a mountain, MBh. **-śmaśru**, mfn. g°-bearded, Cat. **-śrāddha**, n. N. of wk. **-shṭhīva**, m. N. of a mountain, BhP. **-shṭhīvin**, mfn. vomiting gold (said of a bird), MBh. **-saṃkāśa** (*hiraṇya-*), mfn. resembling gold, shining like g°, ŚBr. **-saṃdṛiś** (*hiraṇya-*), mfn. id., RV. **-saras**, n. N. of a Tīrtha, MBh. **-stuti**, f. a partic. hymn, IndSt. **-stūpa** (*hiraṇya-*), m. N. of an Āṅgirasa (author of RV. i, 31-35; ix, 4; 69), RV.; ŚBr.; pl. N. of a family, MW. **-sthāla**, n. a g° bowl, Lāṭy. **-sraj**, f. a g° garland or ring or chain, GṛŚrS.; (*hiraṇya-*), mfn. having a g° garland or chain, AV.; PañcavBr. &c. **-hasta** (*hiraṇya-*), mfn. g°-handed, RV.; AV.; m. N. of Savitṛi, ib.; of a man, RV.; MBh. **-heman**, n. gold, HYog. **Hiraṇyâkshá**, mfn. golden-eyed, RV.; TĀr.; m. N. of a noted Daitya (twin brother of Hiraṇya-kaśipu, and killed by Vishṇu, in his third or Varāha Avatāra), MBh.; Hariv.; Pur. (IW. 327); N. of Savitṛi, RV.; of a Ṛishi and various other men, MBh.; Hariv. &c.; of a place, Cat.; pl. N. of a family, Hariv.; *-ripu* (Ragh.) or *-hara* (Pañcar.), m. N. of Vishṇu. **Hiraṇyâṅga**, m. N. of a Ṛishi, Cat.; pl. his family, ib. **Hiraṇyâbja**, n. a g° lotus, Kathās. **Hiraṇyâbhīśu**, mfn. having g° reins, RV. **Hiraṇyâśva**, m. the image of a horse made of g° (one of the 16 Mahā-dānas, q.v.), Cat.; *-dāna*, n. N. of wk.; *-ratha*, m. a horse and chariot made of g° (one of the 16 Mahā-dānas, q.v.), Cat. **Hiraṇyêshṭaká**, f. a golden brick, TS.; ŚBr.; ĀpŚr.

Hiraṇyaka, m. eagerness for gold, Pāṇ. v, 2, 65; N. of a king of the mice, Hit.

Hiraṇyáya, mf(*ī*)n. golden, abounding in gold (*hiraṇyáyā*, instr. f., RV. viii, 1, 32), RV.; VS.; AV.; ŚBr.

Hiraṇyayá, f. desire for gold (only *hiraṇyayā́*, instr.), RV.

Hiraṇyayú, mfn. desiring gold, ib.

Hiraṇyava, m. the property of a god or of a temple (= *deva-sva*), L.; golden ornament (cf. *sú-* and *a-h°*, add.)

Hiraṇyin, mfn. abounding in gold, g. *prêkshâdi*; (*inī*), f. a gold-mine, region abounding in gold, g. *pushkarâdi*.

Hiraṇye-śaya, mfn. (i.e. loc. of *hiraṇya* + *ś°*) lying or reposing in gold, MBh.

Hiraṇ-vat, m. (for *hiraṇya-vat*) N. of a son of Āgnīdhra, VP.; (*atī*), f. N. of various rivers, MBh.; R.; MārkP.

हिरम्य *híramya*, n. (a word formed for explaining *hiraṇya*), ŚBr.

हिरि *hiri*, mfn. (= *hari*, 'yellow, golden') in the following words: **-śiprá**, mfn. 'golden-cheeked' or 'having a golden visor' (applied to Agni and Indra), RV. (= *haraṇa-śīla-hanu*, 'one whose jaws carry away or seize,' or = *dīptôshṇīsha*, 'having a bright head-dress,' Sāy.) **-śmaśru** (*híri-*), mfn. golden-bearded (said of Agni), ib.

Hiri-mat, mfn. 'tawny-horsed' (= *hari-vat*), ib.

Hirīmaśá, mfn. golden-bearded, RV. x, 105, 7 (Sāy.)

हिरिवेर *hirivera*, n. = *hrivera* (q.v.), L.

हिरु *hiru* or *hiruka*, m. N. of a man, Divyâv.

हिरुक् *híruk*, ind. (cf. *huruk*) off, away, out of sight of (abl.), RV.; AV.; aside, apart, without, Śaṃk.; in the midst of, amongst, L.; near, L.; below, L.

Hirakut, ind. (dimin. fr. *hiruk*), Pāṇ. v, 3, 72, Kâś.

हिल् *hil* (prob. artificial), cl. 6. P. *hilati*, to sport amorously, dally, wanton, express amorous inclination, Dhātup. xxviii, 69.

Hilihila, mfn. sporting, dallying, L.

हिल *hila*, m. N. of a mountain and a town (cf. *hetu-h°*), Buddh.

हिलमोचि *hilamoci*, °*cikā*, and °*cī*, f. Enhydra Hingcha, L.

हिलिमा *hilimā*, f. (of unknown meaning), Divyâv.

हिलीसमुद्र *hilī-samudra*, N. of a place, Cat.

हिल्ल *hilla*, m. a kind of aquatic bird, L.; N. of a man, Rājat.

हिल्लाज *hillāja*, m. N. of an astronomer, Cat. **-graha-phala**, n., **-jātaka**, n., **-tājika**, n., **-dīpikā**, f. N. of wks.

हिल्लोल *hillola*, m. (cf. *hindola*) a wave, surge, MW.; a whim, ib.; a partic. form of sexual union, ib.; (in music) one of the Rāgas, ib.

Hillolaya, Nom. P. °*yati*, to swing or rock or roll about (v.l. for *hindolaya*), Dhātup. xxxv, 84, 6.

हिवुक *hivuka*. See *hibuka*, p. 1298, col. 3.

हिष्क् *hishk*, v.l. for √*hikk* and *kishk*.

हिष्का *hishkā*, w.r. for *hikkā*.

हिहि *hihi*, ind. = *hīhī* (cf. next).

ही *hī*, ind. (an exclamation of surprise or astonishment or horror or sorrow or hilarity or satisfaction, usually translatable by) ah! oh! alas! &c.; (also said to be so used in giving a reason or cause, and translatable by) therefore, so, because, for (cf. 2. *hi*) &c.; (it is sometimes repeated, cf. *hīhī*), Hariv.; Bhaṭṭ.

हीक *hīka*, m. N. of a Piśāca, MBh.

हीड् *hīḍ*, *hīl* (cf. √*heḍ*), P. Ā. *hīḍati* or *hīlati*, °*te*, P. (only in *jihīḍa*, AV.; *jihīla*, RV.; and *ahiḍat*, GopBr.), to pull, tear, make angry, vex, offend; Ā. (only in [*á-*]*hīḍamāna*, ŚBr.; *jihiḍe*, °*dire*; *jihīḷe*, RV.; AV.; *jihīḍāná*, RV.; *hīḍishātām*, TĀr.), to be angry or wroth: Caus. (only *ajīhiḍat*) to pull out (hair), AV.

Hīḍá or **hīḷá**, m. an instigator, stimulator, RV. viii, 8, 19.

Hīḍitá or **hīḷitá**, mfn. angry, wroth, RV.; Br.

हीन *hīna* &c. See p. 1296, col. 2.

हीन्ताल *hīntāla*, m. = *hintāla*, L.

हीर *hīra*, m. a diamond, L.; a thunderbolt, L.; a serpent, L.; a lion, L.; a string of pearls (connected with 1. *hāra*), L.; N. of Śiva, L.; of the father of Harsha, Vās., Introd.; (*ā*), f. a kind of ant or moth, L.; Gmelina Arborea, L.; N. of Lakshmī, L.; of a woman, Cat.; m. n. a diamond, L.; a kind of metre, Col. **-kārya**, m. N. of a man, Bhadrab. **-jit**, m. N. of a poet, Cat. **-bhaṭṭa**, m. N. of a man, ib.

Hīrâṅga, m. 'diamond-bodied,' Indra's thunderbolt, L. **Hīrânanda**, m. N. of two authors, Cat.

Hīrârāma, m. (with *kavi*) N. of a poet, ib.

Hīraka, m. or n. a diamond (the gem is supposed to be presided over by Śukra or Venus), Pañcar.; a kind of metre (= *hīra*), Col.

Hīrā-devī, f. N. of a queen, Inscr.

Hīroka, m. N. of a poet, Cat.

हील *hīla* or *hīlaka*, n. (perhaps fr. √*hil*) semen virile, L.

Hīluka, n. a kind of rum or spirit distilled from molasses, L.

हीलना *hīlanā*, f. (cf. *helana*) injury, Śīl.

हीष् *hīsh*, ind. an exclamation introduced in chanting, PañcavBr.

Hīshī-svara, n. N. of a Sāman, Lāṭy.

हीही *hīhī*, ind. (an exclamation of joy &c., translatable by) ha! ha! hee! hee! ah! or any similar sound (as in laughing &c.), Ratnâv. **-kāra**, m. the above exclamation, Lalit.

हु 1. *hu*, cl. 3. P. (Dhātup. xxv, 1) *juhóti* (Ved. and ep. also Ā. *juhuté*; 3. pl. pr. *júh-*

vati, °te, RV. &c.; 2. sg. Impv. juhudhí, Br. &c.; hoshi, RV.; p. P. júhvat; Ā. júhvāna [also with pass. sense]; 3. pl. impf. ájuhavuḥ, ib.; pf. P. juhāva, juhuvuḥ, MBh.; Ā. juhuve, R.; juhvé, juhuré, RV.; juhvire, Br.; juhavām-cakāra, ib.; Up.; juhavām-āsa, Vop.; aor. ahaushīt, Br. &c.; Prec. hūyāt, Gr.; fut. hotā, ib.; hoshyáti, °te, AV. &c.; Cond. ahoshyat, Br.; inf. hótum, °tos, °tavai, and ind. p. hutvā, ib. &c.), to sacrifice (esp. pour butter into the fire), offer or present an oblation (acc. or gen.) to (dat.) or in (loc.), sacrifice to, worship or honour (acc.) with (instr.), RV. &c. &c.; to sprinkle on (loc.), Yājñ.; to eat, Vop.: Pass. hūyáte (aor. áhāvi), to be offered or sacrificed, RV. &c. &c.: Caus. hāvayati (aor. ajūhavat), to cause to sacrifice or to be sacrificed or to be honoured with sacrifice, GṛŚrS. &c.: Desid. juhūshati, to wish to sacrifice, MBh.; R.: Intens. johavīti (impf. ajohavīt or ajuhavīt, BhP.), johūyate, johoti (Gr.), to offer oblations repeatedly or abundantly. [Cf. Gk. χυ- in χέω (for χέϝω), χυλός, χυμός; Lat. fūtis, 'water-pot.']

1. **Hava, havana** &c. See p. 1293, col. 2.

Hut, mfn. sacrificing (ifc.; see agni-h° &c.)

Hutá, mfn. offered in fire, poured out (as clarified butter), burnt (as an oblation), sacrificed, AV. &c. &c.; sacrificed to, one to whom an oblation is offered, RV. vi, 50, 15 (if not for hūta [cf. v, 5], as sometimes in abhi-, ā-, sam-ā-huta, qq. vv.), MBh.; R. &c.; m. N. of Śiva, MBh.; n. an oblation, offering, sacrifice, AV. &c. &c. – **jātavedas**, mfn. one who has made an oblation to fire, MW. – **bhaksha**, m. 'eating the obl°,' N. of Agni or fire, Car. – **bhāga** (hutá-), mfn. partaking of or entitled to an oblation, AV. – **bhuj**, m. 'oblation-eater,' fire, Kāv.; Suśr. &c. (-bhuk-priyā, f. 'Agni's wife,' L.; -bhug-diś, f. 'Agni's quarter,' i. e. the south-east, VarYogay.); Plumbago Ceylanica, Suśr.; N. of a partic. star (β Tauri), Sūryas. – **bhoktṛi** (R.), **-bhojana** (BhP.), m. = -bhaksha. – **vaha**, m. (ifc. f. ā) 'obl°-bearer,' Agni or fire, MBh.; Kāv. &c.; -jvālā-sama, mfn. like flames of fire, Ml. – **vahāya**, Nom. Ā. °yate, to be or act like fire, Mālatīm. – **śishṭa**, n. remnant of an obl°; °tâśana, mfn. feeding on the r° of an obl°, MBh. – **śesha**, m. = -śishṭa, GṛŚrS. – **saṃvikta**, m. (accord. to some) one who has sacrificed his individuality or blended it with the Universal Soul (see saṃvitka), MW. – **havya-vaha**, m. N. of a son of Dhara, MBh. – **homa**, m. one who has offered obl°s, Mn. vi, 45. **Hutâṇsa**, m. a part of an obl°, VarBṛS. **Hutâgni**, mfn. one who has offered oblations in fire, Mn. vii, 145; m. fire with which an obl° is made, W. **Hutâd**, mfn. eating the obl°, TS.; AitBr. **Hutâśa**, m. obl°-eater, fire, MBh.; Kāv. &c.; N. of the number 'three,' Gaṇit.; Plumbago Ceylanica, Suśr.; fear, alarm (?), L.; -vṛitti, f. subsistence gained by working with fire (as at a forge), VarBṛS.; mfn. subsisting by fire, ib.; -veśa, m. N. of a medic. authority (= agni-veśa), Cat.; -śālā, f. = agni-śālā, Pañcar.; -śauca, n. purification by fire, Rājat.; -suta, m. pl. 'Agni's sons,' N. of partic. Ketus, VarBṛS. **Hutâśana**, m. 'obl°-eater,' fire, Gṛihyas.; Yājñ.; MBh. &c.; (ā), f. N. of a Yoginī, Hcat.; (°na)-maya, mf(ī)n. consisting of fire, having the nature or property of fire, Cat.; -vat, mfn. provided with fire, Kāv.; Kathās.; -sahāya, m. 'friend of fire,' N. of Śiva, MBh.; °nāya, Nom. Ā. °yate, to become fire, appear as fire, Kād. **Hutâśin**, mfn. feeding on oblations, MBh. **Hutâhutá** (?), mfn. sacrificed and (or) not sacrificed, TBr.; ĀpŚr. **Hutâhuti**, mfn. having an obl° just offered, MW. **Hutôcchishṭa**, mfn. left from an obl°, ŚBr.; -bhaksha, mfn. = hutaśishṭâśana, KātyŚr. **Hutôccheshaṇa**, n. = huta-śishṭa, Hir.

Huti, f. a sacrifice (see sarva- and havir-h°).

Hutmat. See vi-hútmat, p. 953, col. 2.

Hotavyà, mf(ā)n. to be offered or sacrificed, AitBr. &c. &c.; to be sacrificed to or worshipped with sacrifices, TS. &c. &c.; (am), n. (impers.) it is to be sacrificed, MaitrS.

Hótṛi &c. See p. 1306, col. 1.

हु 2. hu, ind. an exclamation in huṃ hu, hūṃ hu &c., Sarasv.

हुंहुंकार huṃhuṃ-kāra. See under hum.

हुक्कार huk-kāra, m. the sound huk (supposed to be made by a drum), Inscr.

हुगलि hugali, °lī, or huguli, °lī, f. N. of a town in Bengal (= Hūgli), Kshitîś.

हुग्ग hugga, m. N. of a lexicographer, Cat.

हुंकार huṃ-kāra, huṃ-kṛita &c. See hum.

हुञ्जिका huñjikā, f. a partic. Rāga, Saṃgīt.

हुड् huḍ, cl. 6. P. huḍati, to collect, accumulate (= √huṇḍ), Dhātup. xxviii, 102; to dive, sink, be submerged, ib.; cl. 1. P. hoḍati, to go (= √hoḍ, hūḍ), ib. ix, 70.

Huḍa, m. a ram, L.; VarBṛS. (v. l.); a partic. implement of war, MBh.; a bar or iron rod for keeping out thieves, MW.; (accord. to some) a place for voiding excrement, ib. – **româśraya-phalā**, f. a kind of shrub, L.

Huḍu, m. a ram, L.

हुडुक् huḍuk, ind. an onomat. sound, Sarvad. – **kāra**, m. (with Pāśupatas) a kind of chuckling, ib.

Huḍukka, m. a kind of rattle or small drum, L.; a kind of bird in rut (Gallinula Madraspatana, = dātyūha), L.; a drunken man, L.; a stick or staff bound with iron, L.; the bar or bolt of a door, L.; (ā), f. a kind of drum, Saṃgīt. – **hikkā**, f. the sound of a little hand-drum, L.

Huḍut, ind. = huḍuk, Kāśīkh.; the noise of a bull, L. – **kāra**, m. = huḍuk-k°, Kāśīkh.

Huḍum = huḍut (in huḍuṃ-kṛitya), ib.

Huḍumba, m. = bhrashṭa-cipiṭa, L.

Huḍḍuka, v. l. for huḍukka.

हुण huṇa, m. N. of Vishṇu, L.

हुण्ड् huṇḍ, cl. 1. Ā. huṇḍate (accord. to Pāṇ. vii, 1, 58, Sch., also huṇḍati), to collect, accumulate, Dhātup. viii, 16; to select, choose, take (cf. √bhuṇḍ), ib. 24 (v. l.)

Huṇḍa, m. a ram (cf. huḍa), Kāśīkh.; a tiger, L.; a village hog, L.; a blockhead, L.; a Rākshasa, L.; (prob.) an ear (of corn), Siṇhâs.; (pl.) N. of a people (v. l. pauṇḍra), MBh.; (ā), f. crackling (of fire), Kāśīkh., Sch.

Huṇḍana, m. N. of one of Śiva's attendants (cf. vi-huṇḍana), Kāśīkh.; n. becoming benumbed or paralyzed, Car. **Huṇḍanêśa**, m. N. of Śiva, Kāśīkh.

Huṇḍi, m. or f. a heap or lump of rice (= piṇḍita odanaḥ), L.

हुण्डिका huṇḍikā, f. (Pers. هندي) a bill of exchange, bond, Rājat.; assignment or order (for the maintenance of soldiers), ib.

Huṇḍī, f. = prec., MW.

हुन् hun (only in 3. sg. Pot. hunet) = √1. hu, to sacrifice, Pañcar.; Hcat.

हुम् hum or hūm, ind. an exclamation (of remembrance, doubt, interrogation, assent, anger, reproach, fear &c., not translatable); a mystical syllable used in spells and magical texts or sentences; in Vedic ritual used immediately before the singing of the Prastāva or prelude as well as during the chanting of the Pratihāra or response, ŚrS.; MBh.; Kāv. &c. – **phaḍ-anta**, m. pl. (scil. mantrāḥ) mystical texts ending in the exclamations hum and phaṭ, MW.

Huṃ, in comp. for hum. – **huṃ-kāra**, m. the exclamation huṃ-hum, Lalit. – **kāra**, m. the sound hum (esp. expressive of menace or contempt &c.; also applied to the trumpeting of an elephant, to the roaring or grunting &c. of other animals, to the twang of a bow &c.), MBh.; R. &c.; (ā), f. N. of a Yoginī, Hcat.; (ī), f. id. or N. of a similar being, Pañcad.; -garbha, mfn. filled with groaning or menacing sounds, MW.; -tīrtha, n. N. of a Tīrtha, Cat. – √**kṛi**, P. -karoti (ind. p. -kṛitya), to utter the sound hum, to hum, ŚārṅgP.; to address roughly, Yājñ.; to utter a sound of disgust at (acc.), Car.: Caus. -kārayati, to give vent to one's anger, MBh. – **kṛita**, mfn. roaring, bellowing, bleating, VarBṛS.; addressed roughly (v. l. hūṃ-kṛita), MBh.; uttered with a mystical sound, pronounced as an incantation, MW.; n. an exclamation of anger, R.; BhP.; roar (of thunder), lowing (of a cow) &c., Kāv.; an incantation, MW.

हुमाउं humāüṃ, m. Humāyūn (emperor), Inscr.

हुम्भा humbhā, f. = hambhā, R. (B.)

हुम्मा hummā, ind. an interjection in a Sāman, PañcavBr.

हुरिञ्जक huriñjaka, m. N. of a mixed tribe (the son of a Nishāda and a Kavaṭī), L.

हुरुक् hurúk, ind. = hiruk, RV. ix, 77, 5.

हुरुट्टक huruṭṭaka, m. a kind of curved bolt or iron hook (for elephants), L.

हुरुष्कर hurushkara, m. pl. = yavana, L.

हुर्छ् hurch (or hūrch, prob. connected with √hvṛi), cl. 1. P. (Dhātup. vii, 31) húrchati (pf. juhūrcha, fut. hūrchitā &c., Gr.), to go crookedly, creep stealthily, totter, fall; to fall off from (abl.), MaitrS.; Kāṭh.: Caus. hūrchayati, to cause to fall from (abl.), Kāṭh.

Huraś, in comp. for huras. – **cit**, mfn. lurking surreptitiously, going crookedly, a deceiver, thief, RV.

Hurás, ind. surreptitiously, stealthily, secretly, ib.

Hūrchana, n. going crookedly, crookedness, cunning, Dhātup.

Hūrchita or **hūrṇa**, mfn. (p. p.) gone crookedly, Gr.

Hūrchitṛi, mfn. one who goes crookedly &c., ib.

हुल् hul, cl. 1. P. holati, to go, Dhātup. xx, 14; to cover, conceal, ib.; to kill, ib.

Hula, m. a partic. kind of warlike implement (cf. huḍa), MBh.; n. a double-edged knife with two sharp edges, L. – **mātrikā**, f. a long dagger, L. **Hulâgrakā**, f. a kind of weapon, L.

Huluhula, mfn. (fr. √hul), L.

हुलहुली hulahulī, f. inarticulate sounds made by women on joyful occasions (= mukha-ghaṇṭā), L.

Hulihulī, f. nuptial music, L.; roaring, howling, Mṛicch. viii, 22/23.

Huluhulu, ind. an exclamation of joy, L.

हुलिङ्ग huliṅga, m. N. of a country belonging to Śālva in Madhya-deśa, L.

हुलु hulu, m. a ram (cf. huḍu), L.

हुल्ल hulla, n. (in music) a kind of dance, Saṃgīt.

हुल्लुर hullura, m. N. of a king of the Nāgas, Kāraṇḍ.

हुवध्यै huvádhyai, huvānā. See √hve.

हुवन्य huvanya, Nom. P. °yati (prob. fr. huvana = havana), to call, cry, RV.

हुवा huvā, ind. an exclamation, MBh.

हुविष्क huvishka, m. N. of a king, Inscr.

हुष्क hushka, m. N. of a king, Rājat. – **pura**, n. the town founded by king Hushka, ib.

हुष्टुत hushṭuta, m. a sword with irregular longitudinal white marks, L.

हुस्स् huss, ind. an exclamation, JaimUp.

हुहव huhava or huhuva, m. a partic. hell (cf. hahava), Divyâv.

हुहु huhu or huhū or hūhu or hūhū, m. (nom. huhūs, gen. huhos), N. of a Gandharva, ŚāṅkhŚr.; MBh. &c.

हू 1. hū, weak form of √hve, p. 1308.

2. **Hū**, mfn. calling, invoking (see indra-, deva-, pitṛi-hū &c.)

हू 3. hū, ind. an exclamation of contempt, grief &c. (hū hū, the yelling of a jackal, VarBṛS.) – **rava**, m. 'making the sound hū,' a jackal, L.

हूंकार hūṃ-kāra, hūṃ-kṛiti. See under hum, col. 2.

Hūṃhūṃkāra-pāra or **hūṃhūṃkāra-priya**, m. N. of Śiva, MBh.

हूड् hūḍ (cf. √hruḍ, huḍ, hoḍ &c.), cl. 1. P. hūḍati, to go, Dhātup. ix, 68.

हूण hūṇa, m. pl. N. of a barbarous people, the Huns (sg. = a king of the Huns), Inscr.; Buddh.; MBh. &c.; N. of a family, Cat.; of a people living in Bhārata-varsha, MW.

हूत hūta, hūti. See √hve, p. 1308.

हून *hūna*, m. (often incorrectly for *hūṇa*) a kind of gold coin current in the kingdom of Mādra (commonly called a Pagoda and worth about 8 shillings), MW.

हूम् *hūm*, ind. an exclamation or interjection &c.; see *hum*.

हूम्फ *humpha* (of unknown meaning), Pañcad.

हूय *hūya*. See *deva-* and *pitṛi-hūya*.

हूरलोप *hūra-lopa*(?), m. a humming sound made for lulling children to sleep, Vās., Sch.

हूरव *hū-rava*. See under 3. *hū*, p. 1301.

हूरहूण *hūra-hūṇa*, m. N. of a people, Vās., Introd.

हूरा *hūrā*. See *hara* and *hāra-hūrā*.

हूर्छ् *hūrch*. See √*hurch*, p. 1301.

हूर्णि *hūrṇi*, m. or f. (fr. √*hṛi*?) a small stream, channel, L.

हूलुण्ट *hūluṇṭa*, m. N. of a serpent-demon, Buddh.

हूष्कपुर *hūshka-pura*, incorrect for *hushka-p°* (q. v.)

हूहू *hūhū*. See *huhu* and 3. *hū*, p. 1301.

हृ 1. *hṛi*, cl. 1. P. Ā. (Dhātup. xxii, 2) *hárati*, °*te* (once in RV. *harmi*, and once in Sch. on ĀpŚr. *-jiharti*; pf. P. *jahāra*, *jahártha*, *jahruḥ* [*-jaharuḥ*?], AV. &c.; Ā. *jahre*, Br. &c.; aor. *ahār*, *ahṛithās*, AV.; Br.; *ahārshīt*, RV. &c. &c.; 3. pl. Ā. *ahṛishata*, RV.; Prec. *hriyāt*, *hṛishīshṭa*, Gr.; fut. *hartā*, Br. &c.; *harishyati*, °*te*, ib.; Cond. *aharishyat*, ib.; inf. *hártum*, °*tos*, °*tave*, °*tavai*, ib.; *haritum*, R.; ind. p. *hṛitvā*, *-hāram*, Br. &c.; *-hṛitya*, AV. &c.), to take, bear, carry in or on (with instr.), carry, convey, fetch, bring, RV. &c. &c.; to offer, present (esp. with *balim*), AV. &c. &c.; to take away, carry off, seize, deprive of, steal, rob, ib.; to shoot or cut or hew off, sever (the head or a limb), Mn.; MBh. &c.; to remove, destroy, dispel, frustrate, annihilate, ib.; to turn away, avert (the face), Ratnâv.; Śiś.; Ā. (older and more correct than P.), to take to one's self, appropriate (in a legitimate way), come into possession of (acc.), receive (as an heir), raise (tribute), marry (a girl), ŚBr.; GṛŚrS. &c.; to master, overpower, subdue, conquer, win, win over (also by bribing), Mn.; MBh. &c.; to outdo, eclipse, surpass, Bālar.; to enrapture, charm, fascinate, MBh.; R. &c.; to withhold, withdraw, keep back, retain, Yājñ.; MBh. &c.; to protract, delay (with *kālam*, 'to gain time'), AitBr.; ĀśvŚr.; Kathās.; (in arithm.) to divide, VarBṛS.; Gol.: Pass. *hriyáte* (ep. also °*ti*; aor. *ahāri*), to be taken or seized &c., AV. &c. &c.: Caus. *hārayati*, °*te* (aor. *ajīharat*; Pass. *hāryate*), to cause to be taken or carried or conveyed or brought by (instr. or acc.; cf. Pāṇ. i, 4, 53, Sch.) or to (dat.), Mn.; MBh. &c.; to cause to be taken away, appropriate, seize, rob, Kathās.; to have taken from one's self, be deprived of, lose (esp. at play), Kāv.; Kathās.; (*harayate*), see *pra-√hṛi*; (*hārāpayati*), to lose (at play), Pañcad.: Desid. *jihīrshati*, °*te* (cf. *jihīrshā*, °*shu*), to wish to take to one's self or appropriate, covet, desire, long for, AV. &c. &c.; (with *kālam*), to wish to gain time, MBh.: Intens. *jehrīyate*; *jarharīti*, *jarīharīti*, *jarharti*, *jarīharti* (cf. *sam-√hṛi*), Gr. [Cf. Gk. χείρ.]

Hara, haraka, haraṇa &c. See p. 1289.

Hṛit, mfn. (only ifc.) bringing, carrying, carrying away, seizing &c. (see *bali-*, *taila-*, *pāpa-*, *bhaya-hṛit* &c.)

Hṛitá, mfn. taken, taken away, seized (often ibc. = 'deprived or bereft of,' 'having lost,' '–less'); ravished, charmed, fascinated, Ratnâv.; n. a portion, share, MW. — **candra**, mf(*ā*)n. bereft of the moon (lotus), Ragh. — **jñāna**, mfn. bereft or void of knowledge, MW. — **dāra**, mfn. bereft of one's wife, R. — **dravya**, mfn. stripped of everything, deprived of one's property, Nal. — **dhana**, mfn. spoiled of wealth, MW. — **prasāda**, mfn. deprived of calmness, ib. — **mānasa**, mfn. deprived of mind, robbed of one's senses, ib. — **rājya**, mfn. stripped of a kingdom, MBh. — **vāsas**, mfn. one whose dress is taken away, deprived of clothes, ib. — **vitta**, mfn. = *-dravya*, BhP. — **śishṭa**, mfn. spared from pillage, Daś. — **sarvasva**, mfn. robbed or stripped of all personal property, entirely ruined, MBh. — **sāra**, mfn. robbed of the best part, R. **Hṛitâdhikāra**, mfn. deprived of an office or right, turned out, Rājat. **Hṛitôttara**, mfn. deprived of an answer, left without a reply, W. **Hṛitôttarīya**, mfn. stripped of upper garments, MW. **Hṛitôraga**, mfn. freed from or devoid of snakes, ib.

Hṛiti, f. taking away, seizure, robbery, VarBṛS.; undoing destruction (as opp. to *kṛiti*), Vop.; (in astron.) a portion or division (of a partic. side of a triangle on the celestial globe), Gaṇit.

हृ 2. *hṛi* or *hrī*, cl. 9. Ā. *hṛiṇīte* (only p. *hṛiṇāná*, RV. i, 25, 2 &c.; Pot. [*abhi*]-*hṛiṇīthāḥ*, ib. viii, 2, 19, and [?] *ahṛiṇāt*, ŚāṅkhBr. xxiii, 4), to be angry or wroth.

Hṛiṇāya, °**yati** (only p. °*yát*), id., RV. i, 132, 4.

Hṛiṇāyu. See *dur-hṛiṇāyú*.

Hṛiṇi, m. anger (= *krodha*), Naigh. ii, 13; flaming (among the *jvalato nāmadheyāni*), ib. i, 17.

Hṛiṇiyā or **hṛiṇīyā**, f. (only L.) censure, aversion; shame, bashfulness.

Hṛiṇīya, Nom. Ā. °*yate* (only in *hṛiṇīyathās* [SV. for *hṛiṇīthāḥ*, RV.; see above under √2. *hṛi*] and *hṛiṇīyamāna* [cf. *á-hṛ°*], RV.), to be angry.

हृद् *hṛíd*, n. (optionally substituted for *hṛidaya* in the weak cases, i. e. in all except the first five inflexions; thought to be connected with *śrad* q. v.) the heart (as the seat of feelings and emotions), soul, mind (as seat of thought and intellectual operations; *hṛidy avedin*, 'having no capacity of knowledge in the heart or mind,' said of animals), breast, chest, stomach, interior (also in older language, 'interior of the body'), RV. &c. &c. [Cf. Gk. καρδία, κραδίη; Lat. *cor* (*cordis*); Germ. *Herz*; Eng. *heart*.] — **ambhoja**, n. a lotus-like heart, Kathās. — **āmaya**, m. sickness of h°, Car. — **āvarta**, m. a curl or lock of hair on a horse's chest, L. — **utkleda** or **-utkleśa**, m. sickness of h° or stomach, nausea, Suśr. — **ga**, mf(*ā*)n. reaching up to the breast (as water), Mn. ii, 62. — **gata**, mfn. gone to or being in the h°, MBh.; R. &c.; cherished, dear, pleasant, agreeable, ib.; come to mind, conceived, designed, W.; n. design, meaning, intent, ib. — **gada**, m. = *-āmaya*, L. — **gama**, mfn. going to the h°, Saṃskārak. — **gola**, m. N. of a mountain, Pāṇ. iv, 3, 91, Sch.; °*līya*, n. pl. the inhabitants of the above m°, ib. — **grantha**, m. = *-vraṇa*, L. — **graha**, m. 'heart-seizure,' spasm of the heart, Car. — **ghaṭana**, n. a partic. disease of the heart (perhaps w. r. for *-ghaṭṭana*), ib. — **dāha**, m. h°-burning, ib. — **deśa**, m. the region of the h°, W. — **dyotá**, m. an internal disease, AV.; *-bheshajá*, n. a remedy against int° d°s, ib. — **dyótana**, mfn. (cf. √3. *dyut*) breaking or crushing the heart, ib. — **drava**, m. too rapid throbbing of the h°, too quick pulsation, Car. — **dvāra**, n. the entrance into the h°, AmṛitUp. — **dhātrī**, f. a partic. medicament (prob. w. r. for *bṛihad-dh°*), L. — **dhita**, mfn. (for *-hita*), beneficial to the heart or stomach, L. — **balá**, mfn. subduing (i. e. hitting) the h° (said of a bow), AV. — **bheda-tantra**, n. N. of a Tantra. — **ruj**, f. a kind of disease, L.; h°-ache (lit. and fig.), sorrow, grief, BhP. — **rogá**, m. (for *hṛidroga* see s. v.) id., RV.; Suśr.; VarBṛS. &c.; *-pratikāra*, m. N. of wk.; *-vairin*, m. 'hostile to heart-ache,' Pentaptera Arjuna, L.; °*gin*, mfn. suffering from h°-ache, Suśr. — **vaktrâvartin**, mfn. having a curl or lock of hair on the chest and head (as a horse), L. — **vaṇṭaka**, m. 'dividing the h° or chest,' the stomach, L. — **vartin**, mfn. dwelling in the h°, Jain. — **vidāha**, m. = *-dāha*, Car. — **vyathā**, f. beating of the heart, Vāgbh. — **vraṇa**, m. a heart-wound, heart-sore, L.

Hṛic, in comp. for *hṛid*. — **chaya**, mfn. (for *-śaya*) lying or abiding in the heart (with *muniḥ purāṇaḥ*, 'the eternal Monitor in the heart,' i. e. 'the conscience'), MBh.; BhP.; m. 'h°-dweller,' Kāma-deva or love, ib.; *-pīḍita*, mfn. tormented by l°, love-sick, MBh.; *-vardhana*, mfn. augmenting love, ib.; °*yâvishṭa-cetana*, mfn. having a h° penetrated by love, ib. — **chūla**, m. n. (for *-śūla*) h°-pain, (prob.) spasm of the h°, Car.; Suśr. — **choka**, m. (for *-śoka*) heart-ache, sorrow, grief, a pang, AV. Paipp. — **chosha**, m. (for *-śosha*) internal dryness, Suśr.

Hṛij, in comp. for *hṛid*. — **ja**, mfn. arisen or being in the heart, L.

Hṛit, in comp. for *hṛid*. — **kamala**, see *śiro-hṛ°*. — **kampa**, m. heart-throb, palpitation, L. — **tás**, ind. from the h°, RV. — **tāpa**, m. heart-pain, a pang, MBh.; BhP. — **toshaṇī**, f. N. of a poem. — **paṅkaja**, n. the heart compared to a lotus-flower, Bhag. — **pati**, m. the lord of hearts, BhP. — **padma**, n. = *-paṅkaja*, Kathās. — **piṇḍa**, n. 'h°-mass,' the h°, W. — **pīḍana**, n. or **-pīḍā**, f. oppression of the h°, Suśr. — **puṇḍarīka** or **-pushkara**, n. = *-paṅkaja*, Up. — **prátishṭha**, mfn. standing or dwelling in the h°, VS. — **priya**, mfn. dear to the heart, L. — **stambha**, m. paralysis of the h°, Car. — **stha**, mfn. standing or abiding in the h°, Bhag. — **sphoṭa**, m. breaking of the h°, broken h°, Kathās.; (*am*), ind. (to die) of a broken heart, Prab.

Hṛitsv (for *hṛitsu*, loc. pl. of *hṛid*) in comp. — **ás**, mfn. (fr. √2. *as*) throwing into the heart, RV. — **āśaya**, m. 'dwelling in the hearts,' N. of a preceptor (having the patr. *Āllakeya*), JaimUp.

Hṛida = *hṛid* (in *su-hṛida*, q. v.)

Hṛidam-sáni, mfn. (fr. acc. of prec. or of a masc. or fem. *hṛid*) winning the heart of (gen.), RV. (others 'giving heart to,' 'encouraging,' 'inspiring').

Hṛídaya, n. (ifc. f. *ā*) the heart (or region of the heart as the seat of feelings and sensations; *hṛidaye* √*kṛi*, 'to take to heart'), soul, mind (as the seat of mental operations; *capala-hṛidaya*, 'fickle-minded'), RV. &c. &c.; the heart or interior of the body, RV.; AV.; TBr.; MBh.; the heart or centre or core or essence or best or dearest or most secret part of anything, AV. &c. &c.; true or divine knowledge, MW.; the Veda, ib.; science, ib.; (with *Prajāpateḥ*) N. of a Sāman, IndSt.; m. a partic. Sunday, BhavP.; (*ā*), f. N. of a mare, Hariv.; mfn. going to the heart, BhagP. (fr. *hṛid* + *aya*, Sch.) — **kampa**, m. tremor or throb of the heart, palpitation, MW. — **kampana**, mfn. stirring or agitating the heart, MBh.; n. throbbing or palpitation of the h°, MW. — **klama**, m. weakness of the h°, Suśr. — **kshobha**, m. agitation of the h°, Veṇīs. — **gata**, mfn. dwelling in the h°, VP. — **granthi**, m. 'heart-knot,' anything which binds the soul or grieves the h°, Vedântas.; BhP. — **graha**, m. seizure or spasm of the h°, Car. — **grāha**, m. learning the secret of (gen.), MārkP. — **grāhaka**, mfn. seizing i. e. convincing the mind, Jātakam. — **grāhin**, mfn. captivating the h°, R.; Kir. — **m-gama**, mf(*ā*)n. touching the h°, MBh.; R. &c.; coming from the h° (*-tā*, f.), Bhaṭṭ. — **candra**, m. N. of a king, Inscr. — **cora** or **-caura**, m. a stealer of hearts, Hcar. — **cchid**, mfn. h°-piercing, MBh.; R. — **já**, mfn. belonging or corresponding to the interior, TBr.; m. 'h°-born,' a son, BhP. — **jña**, mfn. knowing i. e. agreeing with the heart, ChUp.; (ifc.) knowing the secret of (*-tva*, n.), MBh.; Hariv.; Pur. — **jvara**, m. anguish of h°, Veṇīs. — **datta**, m. N. of a lawyer, Cat. — **darpaṇa**, m. N. of a rhet. wk. — **dāhin**, mfn. h°-burning, Bhartṛ. — **dīpa** or **-dīpaka**, m. N. of a glossary of materia medica by Vopadeva. — **dūta**, m. N. of a poem by Hari-hara Bhaṭṭa. — **deśa**, m. the region of the heart, GṛŚrS. — **daurbalya**, n. weakness of h°, faintheartedness, Bhag. — **drava**, m. too rapid throbbing of the h°, Car. — **dhara**, m. N. of a man, Cat. — **narapati**, m. N. of a king, Inscr. — **nātha**, m. (with *śarman*) N. of an author. — **nārāyaṇa-deva**, m. N. of an author, Cat. — **pīḍā**, f. = *hṛit-p°*, Suśr. — **puṇḍarīka**, n. = *hṛit-p°*, Sarvad. — **purusha**, m. pulsation or beating of the h°, Gobh., Sch. — **prakāśa**, m., **-prabodha**, m. N. of wks. — **pramāthin**, mfn. agitating or disturbing the h°, Mālav. — **prastara**, mfn. stone-hearted, cruel, Śak. — **priya**, mf(*ā*)n. dear to the heart, beloved, Hit.; pleasant, dainty (as food), Suśr. — **bandhana**, mfn. captivating or winning the h°, Bcar. — **bodhikā**, f. N. of a wk. — **rajju**, f. (in geom.) the semidiameter of a circle in contact with the angles of a trapezium, Col. — **rāma**, m. (also with *dīkshita*, *deva*, and *miśra*) N. of various authors &c., Cat. — **roga**, m. heart-disease, Pāṇ. vi, 3, 51. — **lekha**, m. 'h°-impression,' knowledge, MW.; 'h°-furrow,' anxiety (cf. *hṛil-l°*), ib. — **lehya**, mfn. to be 'licked' i. e. enjoyed by the h°, delightful, Pracaṇḍ. — **vat**, mfn. having a heart, tender-hearted, kind, W. — **vallabha**, m. the beloved of the h°, Ratnâv. — **virodha**, m. oppression of the h°, Car. — **vṛitti**, f. disposition or inclination of heart, Bhartṛ. — **vedhin**, mfn. h°-piercing, MW. — **vyathā**, f. heart-pang, mental anguish, MBh. — **vyādhi**, m. h°-ache (lit. and fig.), Kshem. — **śalya**, n. a thorn or wound in the h°, MW. — **śūlá**, m. a spit for roasting the heart of a victim (also applied to the act of roasting; °lānta, m. 'the end of the act of roasting;' mfn. 'ending with it'), TS.; ŚBr.; GṛŚrS. **—śaithilya**, n. faintheartedness, depression, BhP. **—śoka**, m. h°-sorrow, a pang of grief, Pāṇ. vi, 3, 51. **—śoshaṇa**, mfn. h°-withering, MW. **—śrish**, mfn. clinging to or laying hold of the h°, AV. **—saṃsarga**, m. union of h°s, ĀpGṛ. **—saṃghaṭṭa**, m. paralysis of the h°, Campak. **—saṃdhi**, m. a place of juncture of the heart, Suśr. **—saṃnihita**, mfn. placed or deposited near the heart (voc. f. *e*, 'oh, beloved of my heart!'), Śak. **—sammita**, mfn. breast-high, as high as the h°, ŚāṅkhŚr. **—sāhi**, m. N. of a king, Cat. **—stha**, mfn. being in the heart (as wishes), Pañcat.; being in the body (as worms), Suśr. **—sthalī**, f. 'heart-region,' the breast, Dharmaś. **—sthāna**, n. id., L. **—sthāyin**, mfn. being in the interior of the body, Car. **—spṛiś**, mfn. touching (the region of) the h°, Gobh. **—hārin**, mfn ravishing or fascinating the h°, Rājat.; Śārṅg. **Hṛidayâkāśa**, m. the hollow or cavity of the h°, IndSt. **Hṛidayâgra**, mfn. having the heart as its point, JaimUp. **Hṛidayâtman**, m. a heron, L. **Hṛidayânanda**, m. (with *vidyâlaṃ-kāra*) 'h°'s joy,' N. of an author, Cat. **Hṛidayânuga**, mf(*ā*)n. gratifying the h°, Kām. **Hṛidayâbharaṇa**, m. N. of an author, Cat. **Hṛidayâmayā**, m. = *hṛid-ām°*, AV. **Hṛidayâmbuja**, n. = *hṛit-paṅkaja*, Jain. **Hṛidayârāma**, m. N. of an author, Cat. **Hṛidayârṇava**, m. a partic. mixture, L. **Hṛidayâvagāḍha**, mfn. plunged into the h°, Bcar. **Hṛidayâvarjaka**, mfn. winning the h° of any one, Rājat. **Hṛidayā-vídh**, mfn. h°-piercing, RV.; Bhaṭṭ.; sore in h°, AV. **Hṛidayêśa**, m. 'h°'s-lord,' a husband, Kāv.; N. of a king, Inscr.; (*ā*), f. a mistress, wife, L. **Hṛidayêśvara**, m. = °*yêśa*, Kāv.; Inscr. **Hṛidayôdaṅka**, m. upheaving the h°, MW.; mfn. heart-disturbing, ib. **Hṛidayôdvartana**, m. 'h°-splitting,' N. of a demon, Hariv. **Hṛidayôdveshṭana**, n. contraction of the heart, Suśr. **Hṛidayônmāda-kara**, mfn. bewitching hearts, Bcar. **Hṛidayônmādinī**, f. (in music) a partic. Śruti, Saṃgīt. **Hṛidayôpakartin**, mfn. suffering from a partic. heart-disease, Car. **Hṛidayôpalepa**, m., °*yôpasaraṇa*, n. N. of partic. diseases of the h°, Car. **Hṛidayaṃpaśá**, m. a partic. fleshy part of the h°, VS.; (du.) heart and pericardium, TS. (Sch.)

Hṛidayālu, mfn. tender-hearted, warm-hearted, affectionate, Pāṇ. v, 2, 122, Vārtt. 5, Pat. °**yāvin**, mfn. id. (in Veda), ib., Vārtt. 1, Pat.

Hṛidayika, mfn. good-hearted, warm-hearted, hearty, Pāṇ. v, 2, 122, Vārtt. 5, Pat.

Hṛidayitnu, mfn., Vop. xxvi, 166.

Hṛidayin, mfn. having a heart, tender-hearted, hearty, Pāṇ. v, 2, 122, Vārtt. 5, Pat.

Hṛidaye-śaya, mfn. (loc. of *hṛidaya* + *ś°*) lying or being in the heart, inward (as anger), R.

Hṛidayyà, mf(*ā*)n. being in the heart, heart-felt, RV.; AV.; dear to the heart, BhP.

Hṛidi (loc. of *hṛid*), in comp. **—śaya**, mfn. lying or remaining in the heart, MBh. **—stha**, mfn. being in the heart, ŚvetUp.; Suśr. &c.; beloved, dear, R.; BhP. **—spṛiś**, mfn. touching the heart, charming, lovely, RV.; ĀśvŚr.; BhP. **—spṛiśa**, mfn. id., BhP.

Hṛidika, m. N. of the father of Kṛita-varman (cf. *hārdikya*), MBh.

Hṛidīka, m. = prec., BhP.

Hṛidya, mf(*ā*)n. being in the heart, internal, inward, inmost, innermost, RV.; pleasing or dear to the heart, beloved, cherished, RV.; TBr.; BhP.; grateful, pleasant, charming, lovely, Mn.; MBh. &c.; pleasant to the stomach, savoury, dainty (as food), ib.; proceeding from or produced in the heart. L.; m. the wood-apple tree, L.; a Vedic Mantra employed to effect the subjection of an enemy or rival, L.; (*ā*), f. a partic. medicinal root (= *vṛiddhi*), L.; red arsenic, L.; a she-goat, L.; (*am*), n. white cumin, L.; the aromatic bark of Laurus Cassia, L.; thick sour milk, L.; intoxicating drink made from honey or the blossoms of Bassia Latifolia, L. **—gandha**, mfn. smelling sweet, fragrant, Suśr.; m. the Bilva tree, L.; (*ā*), f. Jasminum Grandiflorum, L.; (*am*), n. small cumin, L.; sochal salt, L. **—gandhaka**, n. a kind of salt (= *sauvarcala*), L. **—gandhi**, m. small cumin, L. **—tama**, mfn. most pleasant or dear to the heart, MBh. **—tara**, mfn. more pleasant or lovely, MBh. **—tā**, f., **-tva**, n. heartiness, cordiality, agreeableness, delightfulness, Suśr.; Kām.; Jātakam. **Hṛidyâṃśu**, m. 'pleasant-rayed,' the moon, L.

Hṛidyota, °**tana**. See *hṛid-dy°*.

Hṛin, in comp. for *hṛid*. **—mantra**, m. a partic. Mantra, Cat. **—moha**, m. (prob.) contraction or oppression of the heart, Car.

Hṛil, in comp. for *hṛid*. **—lāsa** or °**saka**, m., °**sikā**, f. palpitation of heart (accord. to some also 'hiccup'), Mālatīm.; Suśr.; Car. **—lekha**, m. 'heart-furrow,' anxiety of the mind, disquietude (accord. to some also *ā*, f.), MBh.; 'heart-impression,' knowledge, reasoning, W.

हृद्रोग *hṛidroga*, m. (fr. Gk. ὑδροχόος; for *hṛid-roga* see p. 1302, col. 2) the zodiacal sign Aquarius, VarBṛS.

हृद्वर्तिन् *hṛid-vartin* &c. See p. 1302, col. 2.

हृल्लकालोल *hṛillakālola*, m. N. of a Rākshasa, Vcar.

हृष् *hṛish*, cl. 1. P. Ā. *hárshati*, °*te* (fr. P. only p. *hárshat*), to be excited or impatient, rejoice in the prospect of, be anxious or impatient for (dat.), RV.; to speak or affirm falsely, lie, Dhātup. xvii, 59; cl. 4. P. (Dhātup. xxvi, 119) *hṛishyati* (ep. and m. c. also °*te*; pf. *jaharsha*, *jahṛishuḥ*; *jahṛishe*, °*shire*, MBh. &c.; aor. *a-hṛishat*, ib.; fut. *harshitā*, *harshishyati*, Gr.; inf. *harshitum*, ib.; ind. p. *-hṛishya*, MBh. &c.), to thrill with rapture, rejoice, exult, be glad or pleased, PārGṛ.; Mn.; MBh. &c.; to become sexually excited, Suśr.; to become erect or stiff or rigid, bristle (said of the hairs of the body &c.), become on edge (like the teeth), MBh.; BhP.: Pass. *hṛishyate* (aor. *aharshi*), Gr.: Caus. *harsháyati*, °*te* (aor. *ajīhṛishat* or *ajaharshat*), to excite, make impatient or eager for (victory &c.), RV. &c. &c.; to rejoice, be glad, Mn.; MBh.; to cause to bristle, Cat.: Desid. *jiharshishati*, Gr.: Intens. *jarīhṛishyate*, *jarharshṭi* &c. (Ved. forms *jarhṛishanta*, *járhṛishāṇa* and *jā́hṛishāṇá*), to be impatient or excited, RV.; VS.; ĀśvŚr.; to excite violently, RV. [Cf. Lat. *horreo* for *horseo*.]

Harsha, harshaka &c. See p. 1292.

Hṛishi, m. f. joy, satisfaction, L.; splendour, L.; a liar, L.; m. du. Agni and Soma, L. **Hṛishī-keśa**, see below under *hṛishīka*. **Hṛishī-vat**, mfn. full of joy, glad, happy, RV.

Hṛishitá, mfn. cheerful, glad, happy, RV.; MBh.; bristling, erect (as the hair of the body), MBh.; not drooping, fresh (as flowers), MBh.; dulled, blunted, set on edge (= *pratihata*), Pat. on Pāṇ. vii, 2, 29; surprised, astonished (= *vismita*), ib.; bent, bowed (= *praṇata*), L.; armed, accoutred (= *varmita*), L. **—srag-rajo-hīna**, mfn. having fresh garlands and free from dust, Nal.

Hṛishīka, n. (Uṇ. iv, 27) an organ of sense, Hariv.; BhP. **—nātha**, m. 'lord of the senses,' N. of Vishṇu-Kṛishṇa, Pañcar. **Hṛishīkêśa**, m. (perhaps = *hṛishī-keśa*, cf. *hṛishī-vat* above), id. (*-tva*, n.), MBh.; Hariv. &c.; N. of the tenth month, VarBṛS.; of a Tīrtha, Cat.; of a poet, ib.; lord of the senses (said of Manas), BhP.; °*śâśrama*, m. N. of a man, Cat. **Hṛishīkêśvara**, m. = *hṛishīka-nātha*, BhP.

Hṛishu, mfn. glad, happy, L.; telling lies, L.; m. Agni or fire, L.; the sun, L.; the moon, L.

Hṛishṭa, mfn. thrilling with rapture, rejoiced, pleased, glad, merry, Mn.; MBh. &c.; bristling, erect, standing on end (said of the hairs of the body), MBh.; R. &c.; rigid, stiff, Hariv.; blunted (cf. *hṛishita*), Pat.; surprised, astonished, ib. **—citta** (Megh.), **-cetana** or **-cetas** (R.), mfn. rejoiced in heart. **—tanu**, mfn. = next, BhP. **—tanūruha**, mfn. = *-roman*, MBh. **—tushṭa**, mfn. pleased and satisfied, Kāraṇḍ. **—pushṭa**, mfn. happy and well-fed; °*ṭâṅga*, mfn. happy and fat (in body), Hit. **—manas** (Pañcat.), **-mānasa** (MBh.), mfn. = *-citta*. **—rūpa**, mfn. thrilling with happiness, in a happy or cheerful mood, MBh. **—roman**, mfn. having the hair of the body bristling or thrilling (with delight or rapture), Bhag.; m. N. of an Asura, Kathās. **—vat**, ind. cheerfully, MBh. **—vadana**, mfn. merry-faced, having a cheerful countenance, MW. **—saṃkalpa**, mfn. pleased in mind, contented, glad, MBh. **—hṛidaya**, mfn. joyous-hearted, light-hearted, happy, W.

Hṛishṭi, f. delight, joy, rapture, Mālatīm.; pride, arrogance, L. **—yoni**, m. a kind of semi-impotent man (= *īrshyaka*, q. v.), Bhpr.

Hṛishyaka, f. (in music) a partic. Mūrchanā, Saṃgīt.

Hṛishya-jihva, n. a kind of leprosy (w. r. for *ṛiśya-j°*, q. v.), ŚārṅgS.

हे *he*, ind. a vocative particle ('oh!' 'ho!' &c.; also said to express envy or ill-will or disapprobation), ŚBr. &c. &c.

हेक्का *hekkā*, f. = *hikkā*, hiccup, L.

हेठ् *heṭh* (also written *heṭ*, *heḍh*), cl. 1. P. Ā. *heṭhati*, °*te*, to be wicked; vex, harass, hurt, injure, Dhātup. viii, 13; ix, 35; cl. 9. P. *heṭhnāti*, see √*heḍh*: Caus. *heṭhayati*, see *vi*-√*heṭh*.

Heṭha, m. vexation, obstruction, hurt, injury, L.

हेड् *heḍ* or *hel* (cf. √*hel* and √*hīḍ*), cl. 1. Ā. *heḍate*, *helate*, *helate*, to be or make angry or hostile (*krudhyati-karman*, Naigh. ii, 14; only occurring in *á-heḷat*, °*ḷamāna*, and °*ḷayat*, qq. vv.); to act or treat carelessly or frivolously (*anādare*, Dhātup. viii, 32; only in *heḍamāna*, R.; *helamāna*, MBh.; and Caus. *helayati*, °*te* [cf. *vi*-√*hel*], pf. *helayām-āsa*, ib.); cl. 1. P. *heḍati* (pf. *jiheḍa* &c., Gr.), to surround, clothe, attire, Dhātup. xix, 16: Caus. *heḍayati* (aor. *ajiheḍat* or *ajīhiḍat*; cf. under √*hīḍ*), Gr.

Héḍa, héla, m. anger, passion, hatred, RV.; AV. **—ja**, m. id., L.

Heḍana, helana. See *deva-h°*.

Heḍas, helas, n. = *heḍa*, RV.; AV.; VS.

Helana &c. See p. 1305, col. 2.

हेडावुक *heḍāvuka* (Yājñ., Sch.) or °*vukka* (L.), m. a horse-dealer, horse-seller.

हेडिइव *heḍiëva*, m. N. of a man, Inscr.

हेड्डेशहरिहर *heḍḍeśa-hari-hara*, m. N. of an author, Cat.

हेढ् *heḍh* (Vop. *heṭh*), cl. 9. P. *heḍhnāti* or *heṭhnāti*, to be born again, Dhātup. xxi, 60; to produce happiness or prosperity, ib.; to purify, ib.

हेति *hetí*, f. (fr. √1. *hi*; in later language also m.) a missile weapon, any weapon (also personified), RV. &c. &c.; stroke, wound, Sāy.; Agni's weapon, flame, light, MBh.; Kāv. &c.; a ray of the sun, L.; rapid motion, shot, impact (of a bow-string), RV.; an implement, instrument, BhP.; a young shoot or sprout, L.; m. N. of the first Rākshasa king (represented as occupying the Sun's chariot in the month Caitra or Madhu), R.; of an Asura, BhP. **—mát**, mfn. armed with missiles, possessed of weapons, AV.; illuminated by the sun, BhP. **—mantra**, m. N. of a Mantra, Cat.

Hetika, (ifc.) = *heti* (cf. *śakti-*, *svadhiti-h°*).

Hetú, m. 'impulse,' motive, cause, cause of, reason for (loc., rarely dat. or gen.; *hetunā*, *hetoḥ*, *hetave*, *hetau*, 'for a cause or reason,' 'by reason of,' 'on account of' [with gen. or comp., e.g. *mama hetoḥ* or *mad-dhetoḥ*, 'on account of me']; *kaṃ hetum* or *ko hetuḥ*, 'wherefore?' 'why?' Pāṇ. ii, 2, 23, Pat.; *yato hetoḥ*, 'because;' *anena hetunā* or *iti hetoḥ*, 'for this reason;' *mṛityu-hetave*, 'in order to kill;' *hetur alaukikaḥ*, 'a supernatural cause;' ifc. *hetu* also = 'having as a cause or motive,' 'caused or effected or actuated or attracted or impelled by,' e.g. *karma-hetu*, 'caused by the acts [of a former existence],' Mn. i, 49; *māṇsa-hetu*, 'attracted by [the smell of] flesh,' MBh. x, 496; *karma-phala-hetu*, 'impelled by [the expectation of] the consequences of any act,' BhP. ii, 47; 49), RV. &c. &c.; a logical reason or deduction or argument, the reason for an inference (esp. applied to the second member or Avayava of the five-membered syllogism, see *nyāya*), Nyāyad.; IW. 61; logic (in general, see *hetu-vidyā*); (in gram.) the agent of the causal verb, Pāṇ. i, 4, 55 &c.; (with Buddhists) primary cause (as opp. to *pratyaya*, q. v.), Sarvad.; (with Pāśupatas) that which causes the bondage of the soul, i.e. the external world and the senses, ib.; a means (*hetubhiḥ*, ifc. 'by means of'), MBh.; mode, manner (*hetubhiḥ*, ifc. 'according to'), ib.; Suśr.; Yājñ.; price, cost, Rājat. v, 71; condition, MBh.; (in rhet.) = *kāvya-liṅga* (q. v.), Bhar.; Kpr.; Sāh. **—tā**, f., **-tva**, n. the state of being a *hetu*, causation, causativeness, existence of cause or motive, Kāv.; Kathās.; Sarvad.; (*-tva*)-*khaṇḍana*, n. N. of wk. **—dushṭa**, mfn. inconvincible by reasons, unreasonable (said of persons), MBh. **—dṛishṭi**, f. examination of reasons, scepticism, Lalit. **—balika**, mfn. strong in argument, Sukh. i. **—mat**, mfn. having a reason or cause, proceeding from a cause, Pāṇ.; Sāṃkhyak.; Sarvad.; accompanied with arguments, provided with reasons or proofs, well-founded, Bhag.; R.; Bhāshāp.; having the Hetu (or second Avayava of a syllogism), MW.; controverted by arguments, ib.; open to arg°, reasonable, MBh. **-mātra-tā**, f. the being a mere pretext, Kathās. **-mātra-maya**, mf(ī)n. serving only as a pretext, ib. **-yukta**, mfn. provided with reasons, well-founded, MBh. **-rūpaka**, n. a metaphor accompanied with reasons (e. g. *gāmbhīryeṇa samudro 'si*, 'because of thy profundity thou art a sea'), Kāvyâd. ii, 83; 86. **-lakshaṇa**, n. the characteristics of a Hetu; *-ṭīkā*, f., *-prakāśa*, m., *-vivecana*, n.; *°nâloka*, m. N. of wks. **-vacana**, n. a speech accompanied with arguments, R. **-vāda**, m. a statement of reasons or arg°, assigning a cause, disputation, MBh.; R. **-vādika** or **-vādin**, m. a disputant, sceptic, MBh. **-vidyā**, f. 'science of causes,' dialectics, logic (also *-śāstra*), Daś.; Buddh. **-viśeshôkti**, f. (in rhet.) a 'mention of difference (see *viś°*)' accompanied with reasons, Kāvyâd. ii, 328; 329. **-śāstra**, n. (= *-vidyā*); *°trâśraya*, m. reliance on the science of dialectics, Mn. ii, 12. **-śūnya**, mfn. devoid of reason, unfounded, Pratāp. **-ślishṭa**, n.? (in rhet.) the combining of causes (a method of describing similarity by using epithets common to two objects), MW. **-hāni**, f. omission of argument, Kāvyâd. iii, 127. **-hila**, n. a partic. high number, Buddh. **-hetumad-bhāva**, m. the relation subsisting between cause and effect, MW. **Hetûtprêkshā** (Sāh.) or **hetûpamā** (Kāvyâd.), f. a simile accompanied with reasons. **Hetûpanyāsa**, m. the assignment of reasons or motives, statement of an argument, MW.

Hetuka, mf(ī)n. (only ifc.) causing, effecting, R.; Suśr.; Hit.; caused or effected or conditioned by, MBh.; VarBṛS. &c.; destined for, MBh.; Sāṃkhyak.; m. a cause, instrument, agent, W.; a logician, MW.; N. of an attendant of Śiva, L.; of a Buddha, L.; of a poet, Cat.

Hetū-√kṛi, P. *-karoti*, to make or consider anything a cause or motive &c., Sarvad.

Hétṛi or **hetṛi**, mfn. urging on, inciting, an inciter, RV.

Hetv, in comp. for *hetu*. **-antara**, n. another argument, Car. **-apadeśa**, m. the adducing or mentioning of a reason, Nir.; the second Avayava in a syllogism (cf. under *hetu*), MW. **-avadhāraṇa**, n. (in dram.) reasoning, Bhar. **-ākshepa**, m. (in rhet.) an objection accompanied with reasons, Kāvyâd. ii, 167; 168. **-ābhāsa**, m. (in logic) a mere appearance of a reason, fallacious semblance of an argument, fallacious middle term, fallacy (said to be of 5 kinds, viz. *vyabhicāra* or *sa-vyabhicāra*, *viruddha*, *asiddha*, *sat-pratipaksha*, *bādha* or *bādhita*), Nyāyas.; Tarkas.; Sarvad.; N. of various wks.; *-dīdhiti-ṭippaṇī*, f., *-nirūpaṇa*, n., *-parishkāra*, m., *-rahasya*, n., *-vyākhyā*, f., *-sāmānya-lakshaṇa*, n. N. of wks.

Hétva, mfn. to be urged on or incited, RV.

1. **Hemán**, n. impulse, RV. ix, 97, 1 (Sāy. 'gold'); water, Naigh. i, 12.

3. **Heya**, mfn. (for 1. and 2. see p. 1296 and 1297), id., MW.

Haituka, mf(ī)n. having a cause or reason, founded on some motive (in *a-h°*), Bhag.; BhP.; (ifc.) caused by, dependent on, MBh.; BhP.; m. a reasoner, rationalist, sceptic, heretic (*ī*, f.), Mn.; Yājñ.; MBh. &c.; a follower of the Mīmāṃsā doctrines, W.

Haitukya, n. causality, causativeness (*a-h°*, n. absence of interested motives'), MW.

हेमन् 2. *héman* (see *himá* and next), winter (only used in loc., 'in the winter'), TS.; Kāṭh.; ŚBr.

Hemantá, m. winter, the cold season (comprising the two months Agra-hāyaṇa and Pausha, i. e. from middle of November to middle of January), RV. &c. &c.; (*ī*), f. id., L. **-ṛitu-varṇana**, n. 'description of the winter season,' N. of wk. **-jabdha** (*°tá-*), mfn. swallowed by winter (i. e. 'hidden away or disappeared in w°'), AV. **-nātha**, m. 'lord of winter,' the wood-apple tree (= *kapittha*), L. **-pratyavarohaṇa**, n. redescending into winter (a kind of ceremony), ĀpGṛ., Sch. **-megha**, m. a winter-cloud, Pañcat. **-śiśirá**, m. du. (cf. Pāṇ. ii, 4, 48) winter and spring, TS.; ŚBr. **-samaya**, m. w° time, Pañcat. **-siṇha**, m. N. of a king of Karṇapura, Cat. **Hemantânila**, m. a winter wind, Rājat.

Hemantânta, m. (only in loc. *°nte*) the end of winter, MBh.

Hemavala, n. a pearl (= *hima-v°*; cf. next), L.

1. **Haima**, mfn. wintry, brumal, caused or produced by snow or ice, Ragh.; covered with s°, MBh.; relating to or coming from the Himâlaya (as pearls), MBh.; VarBṛS.; m. N. of a mountain, MBh.; n. hoar-frost, dew, W.

1. **Haimaná**, mf(ī)n. relating or belonging or suitable to winter, winterly, wintry, cold, AV. &c. &c.; m. the month Mārgaśīrsha (November-December), L.; a kind of rice which grows in winter (= *shashṭika*), L.; m. n. winter, cold, L.

Haimantá, mf(ī)n. (fr. *hemanta*) wintry, relating or suitable to or growing in winter, VS.; Suśr. &c.

Haimantika, mfn. = prec., VS.; Br.; ŚrS.; Car.; = *hemantam adhīte veda vā*, g. *vasantâdi*.

Haimala, m. n. winter (prob. w. r. for *haimana*), L.

Haimavat, m. N. of the 8th month (prob. w. r. for *hima-vat* or *haimavata*), Sūryapr.

Haimavatá, mf(ī)n. (fr. *hima-vat*) belonging to or situated or growing on or bred in or coming or flowing from the Himâlaya mountains, AV. &c. &c.; snowy, covered with snow, MW.; m. a kind of vegetable poison, L.; a kind of demon, MānGṛ.; pl. the inhabitants of the Himâlaya mountains, MBh.; Hariv.; N. of a school, Buddh.; (*atī*), f. N. of various plants (Vacā with white flowers, Terminalia Chebula, Linum Usitatissimum &c.), Car.; Suśr.; a kind of drug or perfume (= *reṇukā*), L.; patr. of Gaṅgā, MBh.; Bālar.; of Pārvatī or Umā, JaimUp.; of the wife of Kauśika, MBh.; of the wife of Saṃhatâśva, Hariv.; (*am*), n. a pearl, L.; N. of a Varsha, MBh.; Śatr.

Haimavatika, m. pl. the inhabitants of the Himâlaya mountains, MBh.

Haimâcala, m. = (or perhaps w. r. for) *himâcala* (q. v.), Subh.

हेमन् 3. *heman*, n. (of doubtful derivation) gold, Naigh. i, 2; Mn.; MBh. &c.; a gold piece, Kathās.; (pl.) golden ornaments, Kuval.; Mesua Roxburghii, Car.; the thorn-apple, MW.

1. **Hema**, in comp. for 3. *heman*. **-kaksha**, m. a golden girdle, Vās.; mf(ā)n. having g° walls, R.; = next, MBh. **-kakshya**, mfn. having a g° girdle, R. **-kaṇṭha**, m. a proper N., Cat. **-kandala**, m. having g° shoots, coral, L. **-kamala**, n. a g° lotus, Kathās. **-kampana**, m. N. of a man, MBh. **-kara**, m. 'g°-worker,' N. of Śiva, ib.; (with *maithila*) N. of an author, Cat. **-karaka**, m. a g° vase, L. **-kartṛi**, m. a goldsmith, Mn. xii, 61; a kind of bird, MW. **-kalaśa**, m. a g° pinnacle or cupola, Inscr. **-kānti**, mfn. having a g° lustre, VarBṛS.; f. Curcuma Aromatica or another species, L. **-kāra**, m. a goldsmith, Mn.; MBh. &c. **-kāraka**, m. id., Yājñ.; (*ikā*), f. a kind of plant, L. **-kiñjalka**, m. n. g° filaments, R.; n. 'having g° f°,' the Nāgakesara flower, L. **-kirīṭa-mālin**, mfn. garlanded with a g° diadem, MBh. **-kuḍya**, **-kuṇḍya**, N. of a place, VarBṛS. **-kumbha**, m. a g° jar, MW. **-kūṭa**, m. 'g°-peaked,' N. of one of the ranges of mountains dividing the known continent into 9 Varshas (situated north of Himâlaya and forming with it the boundaries of the Kiṃnara or Kimpurusha Varsha; see *varsha*), MBh.; Hariv. &c.; of a monkey, R.; *-māhātmya*, n. N. of wk. **-kūṭhya** = *-kuḍya* above. **-ketakī**, f. Pandanus Odoratissimus, L. **-keli**, m. 'golden sport,' N. of Agni or fire, L. **-keśa**, m. 'g°-haired,' Śiva, W. **-kshīrī**, f. a kind of plant, Suśr. **-gandhinī**, f. the perfume Reṇukā, L. **-garbha**, mfn. containing g° in the interior, Hcat. **-giri**, m. 'g° mountain,' N. of mount Meru, Bhartṛ.; of another mountain, VarBṛS. **-guha**, m. N. of a serpent-demon, MBh. **-gaura**, mfn. of a g° yellow colour (*°râṅga*, mfn. having g° y° limbs), SkandaP.; m. a kind of tree (= *kiṃkirāta*), L. **-ghna**, n. lead, L.; (*ī*), f. turmeric, L. **-cakra**, mfn. having g° wheels, MW. **-candra**, mfn. decorated with a g° crescent (as a chariot), R.; m. N. of a king (son of Viśāla), ib.; Pur.; of a celebrated Jaina author (pupil of Deva-candra Sūri and teacher of king Kumāra-pāla; he lived between 1089 and 1173 A.D. and is the author of a great many works, esp. of the Anekârtha-keśa, the Abhidhāna-cintāmaṇi, the Uṇādi-sūtra-vṛitti, the Deśī-nāma-mālā, a Sanskrit and Prākṛit grammar &c.) **-citra**, n. N. of a mythical town, VP. **-cūrṇa**, n. g°-dust, Suśr. **-cūlin**, mfn. having a g° crest or top, Hariv. **-cchanna**, mfn. covered with g°; n. a g° covering, g° trappings (of an elephant &c.), ib. **-ja**, n. tin, L. **-jaṭa**, m. pl. N. of a class of Kirātas, Kād. **-jālâlaṃkṛita**, mfn. 'adorned with a g° net,' N. of a Bodhi-sattva, Lalit. **-jīvantī**, f. a kind of plant, L. **-jvāla**, m. 'g°-flamed,' Agni or fire, L. **-taru**, m. 'g° tree,' the Datura or thorn-apple, W. **-tāra**, n. blue vitriol, L. **-tāraka**, m. pl. N. of a people, MārkP. **-tāla**, N. of a mountainous district in the north, VarBṛS. **-tilaka-sūri**, m. N. of a man, Cat. **-dantā**, f. 'g°-toothed,' an Apsaras, Hariv. **-dīnāra**, m. a g° Dīnāra, Kathās. **-dugdha**, m. 'g°-juiced,' Ficus Glomerata, Car.; (*ā* or *ī*), f. = *svarṇa-kshīrī*, L. **-dugdhaka** or **-dugdhin**, m. Ficus Glomerata, L. **-dhanvan**, m. 'having a golden bow,' N. of a son of the 11th Manu, MārkP. **-dharma** or **°man**, m. N. of a man, ib. **-dhānya**, n. sesamum grain (cf. *homa-dh°*), L. **-dhānyaka**, m. a partic. weight (= 1½ Māshakas), ŚārṅgS. **-dhāraṇa**, n. a partic. weight of g° (= 8 Palas), L. **-nābhi**, m. a g° nave, Kauś.; mfn. having a g° nave or centre, MW. **-netra**, m. 'g°-eyed,' N. of a Yaksha, MBh. **-parvata**, m. an (artificial) mountain made of g° (as a gift; cf. *mahādāna*), Cat.; N. of mount Meru, L. **-piṅgala**, mfn. g° yellow, R. **-pīṭhâdhi-devatā**, f. the tutelary deity of a g° footstool (applied to a monarch's foot), MW. **-puñjaka**, m. N. of a man, MBh. (B. *-kampana*). **-pushkara**, n. a lotus-flower of g°, Hariv. **-pushpa** (only L.), m. 'bearing g° flowers,' Michelia Champaka; Jonesia Asoka; Mesua Roxburghii; Cassia Fistula; (*ī*), f. Rubia Munjista; Hoya Viridiflora; Curculigo Orchioides; a colocynth; = *kaṇṭakārī* and *svarṇalī*; (*am*), n. the flower of Michelia Champaka &c. (see above). **-pushpaka** (only L.), m. Michelia Champaka; Symplocos Racemosa; (*ikā*), f. yellow jasmine; Linum Usitatissimum. **-pṛishṭha**, mfn. overlaid with g°, gilded, Hariv. **-pratimā**, f. a golden statue or image, L. **-prabha**, m. 'having a g° lustre,' N. of a Vidyādhara (*ā*, f.), Kathās.; of a king of the parrots, ib. **-phalā**, f. 'having g° fruit,' a kind of plantain, L. **-bhadrika**, mf(ā)n. wearing a g° amulet, MBh. **-bhastrā**, f. a gold purse or purse containing gold, Kathās. **-maya**, mf(ī)n. made of gold, golden, MBh.; R. &c. **-marīci-mat**, mfn. having g° rays, MBh. **-mākshika**, n. pyrites, L. **-mālā**, f. 'g°-garlanded,' N. of the wife of Yama, L. **-mālikā**, f. a g° necklace, Jātak. **-mālin**, mfn. garlanded or adorned with g° (as elephants, a Rākshasa &c.), R.; m. the sun, MW. **-māshā**, f. a partic. weight of g°, L. **-mṛiga**, m. a golden deer (according to a story told in R. iii, the Rākshasa Mārīca transformed himself into a golden deer and so captivated Rāma and his wife Sītā, that the former left his forest-home to pursue it; during his absence Rāvaṇa, q. v., disguised as a mendicant, presented himself before Sītā and carried her off). **-yajñôpavīta-vat**, mfn. furnished with a g° sacrificial thread, Hariv. **-yūthikā**, f. yellow jasmine, L. **-ratna-maya**, mf(ī)n. consisting of g° and jewels, Kathās. **-ratna-vat**, mfn. id., ib. **-rāgiṇī**, f. 'gold-coloured,' turmeric, L. **-rāja**, m. (with *miśra*) N. of an author, Cat. **-reṇu**, m. 'gold dust,' a kind of atom (= *trasareṇu*), L. **-latā**, f. 'g° creeper,' a kind of plant (accord. to some, Hoya Viridiflora), BhP.; N. of a princess, Kathās. **-lamba** or **°baka**, m. N. of the 31st (or 5th) year of Jupiter's cycle of 60 years, VarBṛS. **-1. -vat**, ind. like g°, Siṇhâs. **-2. -vat**, mfn. adorned with gold, R. **-varṇa**, mfn. g°-coloured, R.; m. N. of a son of Garuḍa, MBh.; of a Buddha, Lalit. **-vala**, n. a pearl, L. **-vallī**, f. 'golden creeper,' Hoya Viridiflora, L. **-vijaya**, m. N. of a poet, Inscr. **-vibhrama-sūtra**, n. N. of wk. (cf. *haim°*), Cat. **-vishāṇin**, mfn. golden-horned, MBh. **-vyākaraṇa**, n. Hema-candra's grammar, Cat. **-śaṅkha**, m. 'having a g° conch,' N. of Vishṇu, L. **-śikhā** or **-śikā** (?), f. 'g°-crested,' the plant Svarṇa-kshīrī, L. **-śīta**, n. id., L. **-śṛiṅga**, n. a g° horn, Ratnâv.; m. 'g°-peaked,' N. of a mountain, Hariv. **-śṛiṅgin**, mfn. having g° 'tusks' and 'peaks,' MBh. **-śaila**, m. 'g°-peaked,' N. of a mountain, VP. **-sabhā-nātha-māhātmya**, n. N. of wk. **-sāra**, n. blue vitriol (cf. *-tāra*), L. **-sāvarṇi**, m. N. of a man, R. **-siṇha**, m. a throne of g°, BhP. **-sūtra** or **°traka**, n. 'g°-thread,' a necklace, R.; Vikr. **-sūri**, m. N. of a scholar (= *hema-candra*), Col. **-haṇsa-gaṇi**, m. N. of an author (pupil of Ratna-śekhara), Cat. **-hasti-ratha**,

m. 'g°-elephant-chariot,' N. of one of the 16 Mahā-dānas (q.v.) **Hemâṅka,** mfn. adorned with g° (v.l. *hemâṅga*), Mudr. **Hemâṅga,** mf(*ī*)n. having g° limbs or parts, golden, R.; Mudr. (v.l. *hemâṅka*); Bhām.; m. Michelia Champaka, Suśr.; a lion, L.; the mountain Meru, Rājat.; N. of Brahmā, L.; of Vishṇu, L.; of Garuḍa, L.; (*ā*), f. a partic. plant (= *svarṇa-kshīrī*), L. **Hemâṅgada,** m. 'having a g° bracelet,' N. of a Gandharva, Cat.; of a king of the Kaliṅgas, Ragh.; of a son of Vasudeva, BhP. **Hemâcala,** m. = *hema-parvata* (in both meanings), Subh.; Inscr.; Cat. **Hemâḍhya,** mfn. abounding in gold, MW. **Hemâṇḍa** (Rājat.) or °**ḍaka** (Dharmaś.), n. the golden world-egg (cf. *brahmâṇḍa*). **Hemâdri,** m. 'g° mountain,' Meru or Sumeru, L.; N. of an author (son of Kāma-deva; he lived in the 13th century A.D. and wrote the encyclopædical wk. Catur-varga-cintāmaṇi, divided into 5 Khaṇḍas, Vrata, Dāna, Tīrtha, Moksha, and Pariśesha), Cat.; (with *bhaṭṭa*) N. of the author of a Comm. on Raghu-vaṇśa; *-jaraṇa*, m. (= *hemâdrikā*), *-dāna-khaṇḍa-sāra*, m. or n., *-prayoga*, m., *-prâyaścitta*, n. N. of wks. **Hemâdrikā,** f. the plant *svarṇa-kshīrī*, L. **Hemâbha,** mfn. looking like g°, MBh.; (*ā*), f. N. of the palace of Rukmiṇī, Hariv. **Hemâmbu,** n. liquid g°, Vṛishabhān. **Hemâmbuja** (Kathās.) or °**mbhoja** (Megh.), n. a g° lotus-flower. **Hemâlamkāra,** m. a g° ornament, Ratnâv.; °*rin*, mfn. adorned with g°, Hcat. **Hemāvatī-māhātmya,** n. N. of wk. **Hemâhva,** m. 'called after gold,' Michelia Champaka, L.; (*ā*), f. Hoya Viridiflora, L.; = *svarṇa-kshīrī*, L. **Hemêśvara-māhātmya,** n. N. of wk.

2. **Hema,** m. a partic. weight of gold (= *māshaka*), L.; a horse of a dark or brownish colour, L.; N. of Buddha, L.; of a son of Ruśad-ratha, Pur.; of the father of Su-tapas, ib.; = *hema-candra*, Cat.; (*ā*), f. Hoya Viridiflora, L.; the earth, L.; a handsome woman, L.; N. of an Apsaras, Hariv.; R.; of a river, MBh.; (*am*), n. gold, L.

Hemaka, n. gold, R.; a piece of gold (in *sa-h°*), Kathās.; N. of a forest, Cat.; of a Daitya (?), VP.

Hemala, m. a goldsmith, L.; a touchstone, L.; a chameleon, lizard, L.

Hemāya, Nom. Ā. °*yate*, to be or become gold, Harav.

Hemyá-vat, mfn. having golden trappings or a golden girth (?), RV. iv, 2, 8 (Sāy.)

2. **Haima,** mf(*ī*)n. (fr. 3. *heman*, of which it is also the Vṛiddhi form in comp.) golden, consisting or made of gold, Mn.; MBh. &c.; of a golden yellow colour, MW.; m. N. of Śiva, MBh.; Gentiana Cherayta, L.; (scil. *kośa*) the lexicon of Hema-candra, Cat.; (*ā*), f. yellow jasmine, L.; (*ī*), f. id., L.; Pandanus Odoratissimus, L. **-kūṭa,** m. pl. the inhabitants of Hema-kūṭa, MārkP. **-kośa,** m. Hema-candra's lexicon. **-girika,** m. pl. the inhabitants of Hema-giri, MārkP. **-candri,** m. patr. fr. *hema-candra*, R. **-carci,** m. (prob. w.r. for *-varci*) a patr., Pravar. **-citra-samutsedha,** mfn. enchased with golden pictures, MBh. **-prākṛita-ḍhuṇḍikā,** f. N. of wk. **-mudrā** or **-mudrikā,** f. a g° coin, MW.; (°*drika*), mfn. having or possessing a g° coin, ib. **-valkala,** mfn. clothed in gold, MW. **-vibhrama-sūtra,** n. = *hema-v°*, Cat. **-śaila,** m. N. of a mountain (v.l. *hema-ś°*), VP. **-saugandhika-vat,** mfn. furnished with g° lotus-flowers (v.l. *padma-s°*), MBh. **Haimâṅgikī-gaurâṅga-deva-stuti,** f. N. of wk. **Haimâcala,** see p. 1304, col. 2. **Haimânekârtha,** N. of Hema-candra's lexicon.

2. **Haimana,** mfn. golden (v.l. *haimaja*), Bhpr.

Haimī-bhūtâ, mfn. become gold, turned into gold, Kum.

हेमन् 4. *heman*, m. the planet Mercury, L.

हेमन्त *hemanta, hemavala.* See p. 1304, cols. 1 and 2.

हेमात्र *hemâtra*, m. or n. a partic. high number, Buddh.

हेम्न *hemna*, m. (Gk. Ἑρμῆς) the planet Mercury, VarBṛS.; (*ā*), f. id. (?), L.

हेय *heya.* See pp. 1296, 1297, and 1304.

हेर *hera*, n. (of unknown derivation) a sort of crown or tiara, L.; turmeric, L.; demoniacal illusion, L.

Heraka, m. a spy, L.; N. of a demon attending on Śiva, L.

Herika, m. a spy, secret emissary, L.

Hairika, m. id., Hcar. ('a superintendent of the goldsmiths,' Sch.); a thief, L.

हेरम्ब *heramba*, n. N. of Gaṇeśa, MBh.; Kathās. &c. (RTL. 218); a buffalo, Mālatim; a boastful hero, L.; a partic. Buddha (= *heruka*), L. **-kānana-māhātmya,** n. N. of wk. **-jananī,** f. 'mother of Gaṇeśa,' Durgā, L. **-pāla,** m. N. of a Kanouj king, Inscr. **-mantra,** m. a partic. Mantra (sacred to Gaṇeśa). **-sena,** m. N. of a medic. author. **-haṭṭa,** m. N. of a country (said to be one of the provinces of the Deccan), L. **Herambôpanishad,** f. N. of an Upanishad.

Herambaka, m. pl. N. of a people, MBh. **-sena,** m. N. of an author, Cat.

Herambha, w.r. for *heramba*, Kathās.

Hairamba, mfn. relating to or connected with Gaṇeśa, Cat.; m. pl. N. of a sect, W.

हेरुक *heruka*, m. N. of Gaṇeśa, KālP.; of an attendant on Mahā-kāla or Śiva, L.; of an inferior Buddha, Buddh.; pl. N. of a class of heretics, L.; (*ā*), f. a species of plant, AV. Paddh.

हेल् *hel* (in the meaning 'to sport, play,' prob. not identical with √*hel, heḍ*, although sometimes confounded with it; only in the following derivatives; cf. √*hil, avahelā, prahelā*).

Helana, n. the act of slighting, disregard, contempt, MBh.; BhP.; sporting amorously, wanton dalliance (cf. √*hil*), W.

Helanīya, mfn. to be slighted or derided, Nilak.

Helā, f. (ifc. f. *ā*) disrespect, contempt (cf. *avahelā*); wanton sport, frivolity, amorous dalliance (of women; in dram. one of the 20 natural graces [*sattva-ja alaṃkāra*] of the Nāyikā), Daśar.; Sāh. &c.; sport, pastime, carelessness, ease, facility (ibc. and instr. sg. or pl. 'in sport,' 'sportively,' 'easily,' 'at once;' *tṛiṇa-helayā*, 'as if it were a straw'), Kāv.; Kathās. &c.; moonlight, L.; = *prastāva*, L. **-cakra,** m. N. of a man, Rājat. **-rāja,** m. N. of a historian (used by Kalhaṇa for his Rāja-taraṃgiṇī) and of a grammarian, Cat. **-vat,** mfn. careless, taking things easily, Pañcar.

1. **Heli,** f. = *helā*, L.; an embrace, L.; a marriage-procession in the street, L.

Helitavya, n. (impers.) it is to be acted carelessly or frivolously, MBh.

Helihila or **hailihila,** mfn. of a sportive or wanton nature, L.

हेलक *helaka*, n. a partic. measure of weight (= 10 Hoḍhas), L.

हेलञ्चि *helañci*, f. a kind of herb, L.

हेलावुक *helāvuka*, °*vukka*, m. = *heḍāv°*, L.

हेलि 2. *heli*, m. (Gk. ἥλιος; for 1. *heli* see above) the sun, VarBṛS.; Pur.

Helika, m. id., Kāśīkh.

हेलु *helu*, N. of a village in Kaśmīra, Rājat. **-grāma,** m. the village Helu, ib.

हेलुग *heluga* and *heluya*, a partic. high number, Buddh.

हेळ् *heḷ, heḷa, heḷas.* See √*heḍ*, p. 1303.

हेवज्र *hevajra*, m. N. of a Buddhist god, W.

हेवर *hevara*, a partic. high number, Buddh.

हेवाक *hevāka*, m. (said to be fr. Marāṭhī *hevā*, 'ardent desire') a whim, caprice, Vcar.; Āryav.

Hevākasa, mfn. whimsical, capricious (as love), Daśar.

Hevākin, mfn. devoted to, absorbed in, engrossed by (comp.; °*ki-tā*, f.), Uttamac.

हेष् 1. *hesh* (cf. √*hresh*), cl. 1. Ā. (Dhātup. xvi, 20) *héshate* (Ved. ep. also °*ti*; p. *héshat*, RV.; MBh.; *heshamāṇa*, Hariv.; pf. *jiheshire*, Śiś.; fut. *heshitā* &c., Gr.), to neigh, whinny, RV. &c. &c.

Heshā, f. neighing, whinnying, Kir.; MārkP.

Heshāya, Nom. Ā. °*yate*, to neigh, whinny, Pañcat.

Heshita, n. = *heshā*, MBh.; Hariv. &c.

Heshin, m. 'neighing,' a horse, L.

हेष् 2. *hesh* (prob. connected with √1. *hi*), to be quick or strong or fiery (in the following derivatives):

Heshá, mfn. quick, strong (in *heshá-kratu*, 'of strong power,' others 'roaring mightily,' applied to the Maruts), RV. iii, 26, 5.

Héshas, n. quickness, vigour, fire (others 'wound'), RV. x, 89, 12. **-vat** (*héshas-*), mfn. quick, strong, fiery, RV. vi, 3, 3.

है *haí*, ind. (g. *svar-ādi*) a vocative particle (used in calling or vociferating), AV.; TBr. &c.

हैंसकायन *haiṇsakāyana*, mfn. (fr. *hiṇsaka*), g. *pakshâdi*.

हैङ्गुल *haiṅgula*, mfn. (fr. *hiṅgula*) having the colour of vermilion, Naish.; coming or derived from Hiṅgulā, VāmP.

हैडिम्ब *haiḍimba*, mfn. relating to or treating of Hiḍimba, MBh.; = next, ib.

Haiḍimbi, m. 'son of Hiḍimbā,' metron. of Ghaṭôtkaca, MBh.

हैतनामन् *haitanāman*, m. patr. fr. *hitanāman*, Pāṇ.

Haitanāmaná, m. id., MaitrS.

हैतुक *haituka*, °*kya.* See p. 1304, col. 1.

हैदरशाह *haidaraśāha*, m. = حيدر شاه, Cat.

हैम *haima, haimana* &c. See col. 1.

हैमहा *haimahā*, ind. an exclamation, ŚrS.

हैमिनी *haiminī*, f. N. of a woman, MārkP.

हैयंगव *haiyaṃgava*, n. (fr. *hyas* + *go*) = next, BhP.

Haiyaṃgavīna, n. clarified butter prepared from yesterday's milking, fresh butter, Hariv.; Ragh.; Bhaṭṭ.

हैरण्य *hairaṇyá*, mf(*ā*)n. (fr. *hiraṇya*, of which it is also the Vṛiddhi form in comp.) golden, consisting or made of gold, AV.; R.; bearing gold (said of a river), MBh.; offering gold (said of hands or arms), ib. **-garbha,** mfn. relating or belonging to Hiraṇya-garbha, Śaṃk.; m. patr. of Manu (son of Brahmā), Mn. iii, 194; of Vasishṭha, MBh.; a worshipper of Hiraṇya-garbha, Cat. **-nābhá,** m. patr. fr. *hiraṇya-n°*, ŚBr. **-bāheya,** m. patr. fr. *hiraṇya-bāhu*, Pat. **-vāsas,** mfn. (fr. *hiraṇya-v°*) clothed with golden feathers (as an arrow), MBh. **-stūpa,** mf(*ī*)n. written or composed by Hiraṇya-stūpa (also °*pīya*), Nir.; ŚāṅkhGṛ.; m. patr. of Arcat (author of RV. x, 149), Anukr.

Hairaṇyaka, m. a goldsmith, VarBṛS.; an overseer of gold, guardian of golden treasure, L.; n. N. of a Varsha, MBh.

Hairaṇyika, mf(*ā* or *ī*)n. (fr. *hiraṇya*), g. *kāśy-ādi*; m. a goldsmith, Divyâv.

Hairaṇvatī, f. (cf. *hiraṇvatī*) N. of a river, MBh.

हैरम्ब *hairamba, hairika.* See above, col. 2.

हैवम् *haivam*, ind. = Pāli *hevam*, Divyâv.

हैहय *haihaya*, m. N. of a race (said to have been descendants of Yadu; they are described in the Purāṇas as separated into 5 divisions, viz. the Tālajaṅghas, Viti-hotras, Āvantyas, Tuṇḍikeras, and Jātas; they are said to have overrun parts of India along with the Śakas or Scythian tribes), MBh.; R.; Pur. &c.; a king of the Haihayas (esp. applied to Arjuna Kārtavīrya, who is said to have had a thousand arms; see *kārtavīrya*), ib.; N. of a son of Sahasrada, Hariv.; of a son of Śata-jit, Pur.; (?) of a medical author, Cat. **Haihayêndra-kāvya,** n. N. of a poem.

Haiheya, m. N. of Arjuna Kārtavīrya (cf. above), L.

हो *hó*, ind. (a vocative particle [g. *câdi*] used in calling to a person or in challenging) ho! hallo! &c. (also expressive of surprise &c.), TS. &c. &c.

होइड *hoïḍa*, n. N. of a Sāman, Kāṭh.

होटा *hoṭā*, f., v.l. for *hoḍhā*.

होड् *hoḍ* (cf. √*huḍ, hūḍ*), cl. 1. Ā. *hoḍate*, to disregard, disrespect (= √*heḍ*), Dhātup. viii, 33; (also *hauḍ*) to go, move, Vop.

Hoḍa, m. a raft, float, boat, L.; a title of a partic. class of Kāyasthas and of Śrotriya Brāhmans in Bengal, L.; (*ā*), f., g. *ajâdi* (Kāś. *hoḍhā*).

Hoḍiman, m. (fr. prec.), g. *pṛithv-ādi*.
Hauḍa, n. (fr. id.), ib.

होड्ड *hoḍṛi* (?), m. a robber, highway-robber, L.

होढ 1. *hoḍha*, mfn. (thought by some to be fr. *ha* + *ūḍha*) stolen; m. n. and (*ā*), f. stolen goods, Mn. ix, 270, Sch. on Yājñ. ii, 5.

2. **Hoḍha**, Nom. Ā. *hoḍhate*, *hoḍhāyate*, Vop. xxi, 7.

होतृ *hótṛi*, m. (fr. √1. *hu*) an offerer of an oblation or burnt-offering (with fire), sacrificer, priest, (esp.) a priest who at a sacrifice invokes the gods or recites the Ṛig-veda, a Ṛig-veda pr° (one of the 4 kinds of officiating priest, see *ṛitvij*, p. 224; properly the Hotṛi priest has 3 assistants, sometimes called Purushas, viz. the Maitrā-varuṇa, Acchā-vāka, and Grāva-stut; to these are sometimes added three others, the Brāhmaṇācchansin, Agnīdhra or Agnīdh, and Potṛi, though these last are properly assigned to the Brahman priest; sometimes the Neshṭṛi is substituted for the Grāva-stut), RV. &c. &c.; N. of Śiva, MBh.; mf(*trī*)n. one who sacrifices (gen. or comp.), sacrificer, Mn.; MBh. &c. **-karman**, n. the work or function of the Hotṛi, ĀśvŚr. **-camasá**, m. the ladle or other vessel used by the Hotṛi, TS.; Br.; ŚrS.; °*síya*, mfn. (fr. prec.), ĀpŚr. **-japa**, m. murmured recitation of the H°, AitBr. **-tvá**, n. condition or office of the H°, Br. **-pravara**, m. election of a H° (also N. of wk.), ĀpŚr. **-mat** (*hótṛi-*), mfn. provided with a H°, RV. **-várya** (ŚBr.), **-vū́rya** (RV.), n. election of the H° **-veda**, m. the Veda, i.e. ritual of the H°, Sāy. **-shádana** (for *-sad*°), n. the Hotṛi's seat or place where the Hotṛi sits at a sacrifice (said to be near the *uttara-vedi*), RV.; AV.; Br.; ŚrS. **-shāman**, n. N. of Sāmans, Lāṭy. **-samsthā-japa**, m. N. of a liturgical treatise.

Hotar-yaja, m. the Praisha (q.v.) consisting of the words *hotar yaja*, ŚāṅkhŚr.

Hotâdhvaryū, m. du. the Hotṛi and Adhvaryu priests, KātyŚr.

Hotā-potārau, m. du. the Hotṛi and Potṛi priests, Pāṇ. vi, 3, 25, Sch.

Hotā-yaksha, m. the Praisha (q.v.) consisting of the words *hotā yakshat*, ŚāṅkhŚr.

Hotur-antevasin, m. the pupil of a Hotṛi priest, Pāṇ. vi, 3, 23, Sch.

Hótṛika, m. = *hotraka*, ŚBr.; Lāṭy. &c.

Hótos. See √1. *hu*.

Hotrá, n. sacrificing, the function or office of the Hotṛi, RV.; AV.; ŚBr.; Kāṭh.; a burnt-offering, oblation with fire, sacrifice, RV.; PañcavBr.; ŚāṅkhŚr.; MBh.; (*ā*), f., see below. **-prayoga**, m. N. of wk. **-vā́h** (or *-vā́h*), mfn. bearing the sacrifice, RV. **-vāhana**, m. (id.) N. of a Brāhman and of a Rājarshi, MBh.

Hotraka, m. an inferior Hotṛi priest or an assistant of the H° (in a wider sense applied to all the chief priests; cf. under *hotṛi*), AitBr.; GṛŚrS.; N. of a son of Kāñcana, BhP.

1. **Hótrā**, f. (for 2. see p. 1308, col. 3) the function or office of a priest (esp. of the Hotrakas, also applied to the persons of the Hotrakas), Br.: ŚrS. **-camasa**, m. the ladle or other vessel used by the Hotrakas, ŚBr. **-śaṅsin**, m. 'reciting the part of the Hotṛi,' an assistant of the Hotṛi, Hotraka, Br.; ŚrS.

Hotrin. See *agni-hotrin*.

Hotriya, n. the office or function of a priest, RV.

Hotrī. See under *hotṛi* above.

Hotrī́ya, mfn. relating or belonging to the Hotṛi or the Hotrakas, TS.; ŚBr.; KātyŚr.; n. = *havir-geha*, L.

Hótva, mfn. to be sacrificed or offered in sacrifice, MaitrS.

Hotvan, m. a sacrificer, L.

Hóma, m. the act of making an oblation to the Devas or gods by casting clarified butter into the fire (see *deva-yajña* and IW. 245), oblation with fire, burnt-offering, any oblation or sacrifice (*ayuta-h*°, 'a sacrifice of 10,000 burnt-offerings to the planets'), AV. &c. &c. **-karman**, n. sacrificial act or rite, Kathās. **-kalpa**, m. mode or manner of sacrificing, Hir. **-kāla**, m. the time of sacrifice, GṛŚrS.; MBh.; R.; °*lātikrama-prâyaścitta-prayoga*, m. N. of wk. **-kāshṭhī**, f. an implement for blowing on fire, L. **-kuṇḍa**, n. a hole in the ground for the sacred fire for oblations (= *agni-k*°), L. **-tattva-vidhi**, m., **-tarpaṇa-vidhi**, m. N. of wks. **-turaṃga**, m. the sacrificial horse, Ragh. **-darpaṇa-vidhi**, w.r. for *-tarp*° (q.v.) **-darvī**, f. the sacrificial ladle, ĀpGṛ., Sch. **-duh**, mfn. (a cow) giving milk for an oblation, Hariv.; Bcar. **-dravya**, n. anything employed for a Homa-sacr° or oblation, KātyŚr.; *-pariṇāma*, N. of a Pariśishṭa of the Sāma-veda. **-dvaya-prayoga** and **-dvaya-samāsa-prayoga**, m. N. of wks. **-dhānya**, n. 'sacrificial grain,' sesamum, L. **-dhūma**, m. the smoke of a burnt-offering, L. **-dhenu**, f. a cow yielding milk for an oblation, MBh.; Kālid.; MārkP. **-nirṇaya**, m., **-paddhati**, f., **-prâyaścitta**, n. N. of wks. **-bhasman**, n. the ashes of a burnt-offering, L. **-bhāṇḍa**, n. a sacrificial implement, Kathās. **-mantra-bhāshya**, n. N. of wk. **-yūpa**, m. the sacrificial post at the Homa, L. **-lopa-prâyaścitta-prayoga**, m. N. of wk. **-vat**, mfn. one who has offered an oblation or performed a sacrifice, Bhaṭṭ. **-vidhāna**, n., **-vidhi**, m. N. of wks. **-velā**, f. = *-kāla*, BhP. **-śālā**, f. a chamber or place for keeping the sacred fire for oblations, RTL. 365. **-svarôttara**, n. N. of a Tantra wk. **Homâgni**, m. sacrificial fire, Pañcat. **Homânala**, m. id., Daś. **Homârjunī**, f. = *homa-dhenu*, Bālar. **Homêndhana**, n. sacrificial firewood, L.

Homaka, m. = *hotraka* (8 in number), MatsyaP.

Homi, m. fire, L.; clarified butter, L.; water, L.

Homin, mfn. offering, presenting an oblation of (only ifc.; see *kshīra-*, *tila-h*° &c.); (*inī*), f., *saṃjñāyām*, Pāṇ. v, 2, 137, Kāś.

Homīya, mfn. relating or belonging to or fit or destined for an oblation or sacrifice, ChUp.; Gobh. &c. **-dravya**, n. anything used for an oblation (as clarified butter), MW.

Homya, mfn. = *homīya*, Kauś.; MBh.; n. clarified butter, L.

Hoshin. See *pajra-hoshin*.

Hauta, Vṛiddhi form of *huta* in comp. **-bhuja**, mfn. (fr. *huta-bhuj*) relating or belonging to or presided over by Agni, VarBṛS.; n. the Nakshatra Kṛittikā, ib. **Hautâśana**, mfn. (fr. *hutâś*°) = prec.; m. (with *loka*) Agni's world, Hcat.; (with *koṇa*) 'Agni's corner or quarter,' the south-east, VarBṛS. **Hautâśani**, m. (fr. id.) patr. of Skanda, R.; of the monkey Nīla, ib.

Hautṛika, mfn. relating or belonging to or coming from the Hotṛi priest, sacerdotal, Pāṇ. iv, 3, 78, Sch.; n. the office of the Hotṛi, Cat.

Hautna, mfn. = *yajamāna*, Uṇ. iv, 105, Sch.

Hautra, mfn. = *hautṛika*, KātyŚr.; n. the function or office of the Hotṛi (also as N. of wk.), ŚrS. **-kalpa-druma**, m., **-prayoga**, m., **-mañjarī**, f., **-sūtra**, n., °**trâvaloka**, m. N. of wks.

Hautraka, n. N. of the 16th Pariśishṭa of Kātyāyana.

Hautrika, mfn. relating to the office or function of the Hotṛi, sacerdotal, Kāty.

Haumīya, mfn. = *homīya*, Saṃskārak.

Haumya, mfn. id., ShaḍvBr.; GṛŚrS.; MBh.; n. clarified butter, L. **-dhānya**, n. = *homa-dh*°, L. **-pariśishṭa-vivecana**, n. N. of wk.

Haushya, m. pl. a partic. school of the Yajur-veda, AV. Pariś.

होरा *horā*, f. (fr. Gk. ὥρα) an hour (the 24th part of an Aho-rātra), VarBṛS.; MārkP.; the half of a zodiacal sign, Var.; horoscope or horoscopy, ib. &c. **-kandarpa-jātaka**, n., **-cūḍāmaṇi**, m., **-°dhyāya** (*horâdh*°), m., **-prakaraṇa** (?), n., **-prakāśa**, m., **-pradīpa**, m., **-makaranda**, m., °**ndôharaṇa**, n., **-ratna**, n. N. of wks. **-vid**, mfn. versed in horoscopy, VarBṛS., Sch. **-śāstra**, n. horoscopy, astrological science (also as N. of wk.); *-sāra*, m. n., *-sudhā-nidhi*, m.; °*trârṇava-sāra*, m. n. N. of wks. **-shaṭ-pañcāśikā**, f., **-sāra**, m. n., **-sāra-sudhā-nidhi**, m., **-setu**, m. N. of wks.

होरिलमिश्र *horila-miśra*, m. N. of the author of a Smṛiti-saṃgraha, Cat.

होरिलसिंह *horila-siṅha*, m. N. of a man (perhaps = prec.), Cat.

होल *hola*, m. N. of a man, Rājat.; pl. a country belonging to Udīcya, L.; (*ā*), f. N. of a town, Rājat. **-siṅha**, m. N. of a man, Cat.

Holaḍa and **Holarā**, N. of places, Rājat.

होलक *holaka*, m. half-ripe pulse cooked over a light fire, Bhpr.

होलाक *holāka*, m. a kind of vapour-bath (induced over hot ashes for the cure of partic. diseases, by sweating; also with *sveda*), Car.; (*ā*), f., see next.

होलाका *holākā*, f. (perhaps from a cry or shout or sound in singing), the spring festival at the approach of the vernal equinox (commonly called Hūlī or Holī, and said to be dedicated to Kṛishṇa and the Gopīs; it is celebrated during the ten days preceding the full moon of the month Phālguna, when people sprinkle red powder in sport and light fires; in some parts of India the Holī festival corresponds to or immediately precedes the Dolā-yatrā, q.v.), RTL. 430.

Holā, f. the Holī festival, MW. **-khelana**, n. the frolics practised at the Holī festival, ib.

Holikā, f. the Holī festival (also applied to a Rākshasī worshipped at it), W. **-pūjana**, f., **-pūjā**, m., **-prayoga**, m., **-māhātmya**, n., **-vidhāna**, n.; °**kôtpatti**, f. N. of wks.

Holi-nirṇaya, m. (prob. for *holī-n*°) N. of wk.

Holī. See above under *holākā*.

होलीर *holīra*, *hosiṅga-kṛishṇa*, and *hositaka-bhaṭṭa*, m. N. of authors, Cat.

होहौ *hohau* and *hau*, ind. vocative particles (used in calling and challenging), L.

हौड् *hauḍ*, *hauḍa*. See √*hoḍ*.

हौणिक्या *hauṇikyā*, f. a patr., Pāṇ. iv, 1, 79, Sch.

हौण्डिन *hauṇḍina*, m. N. of partic. transpositions of verses (*vihāra*), ĀśvŚr.

हौतभुज *hautabhuja*, *hautra*, *haumīya* &c. See col. 2.

ह्नु *hnu*, cl. 2. Ā. (Dhātup. xxiv, 73) *hnuté* (Ved. and ep. also *hnauti* and *hnavati*, °*te*; pf. *juhnuve*, Gr.; aor. *ahnoshṭa*, ib.; fut. *hnotā*, *hnoshyate*, ib.; inf. *hnotum*, Mālatīm.; ind. p. *hnutya*, Daś.; generally with prepositions; cf. *apa-*, *api-*, *ni-* √*hnu* &c.), to hide from (dat.), Pāṇ. i, 4, 34; to drive or take away, Bhaṭṭ.: Pass. *hnūyate* (aor. *ahnāvi*), Gr.: Caus. *hnāvayati* (aor. *ajuhnavat*), ib.: Desid. *juhnūshate*, ib.: Intens. *johnūyate*, *johnoti*, ib.

Hnava, m., **hnavana**, n. secreting, hiding, concealing (see *apa-* *ni-hn*° &c.)

Hnavāyya. See *a-hnavāyyá*.

Hnuta, mfn. taken away, withheld, secreted &c. (see *apa-*, *ni-hnuta* &c.)

Hnuti, f. abstraction, concealment, denial, MW.

Hnotavya, mfn. to be secreted or concealed &c., ib.

ह्मल् *hmal* (cf. √*hval*), cl. 1. P. *hmalati*, to shake, move, Dhātup. xix, 45; to go, xx, 14 (v.l.): Caus. *hmalayati* or *hmālayati* (the former when prepositions are prefixed), Dhātup. xix, 45; 67.

Hmala and **hmāla**, g. *jvalâdi*.

ह्यस् *hyás*, ind. (g. *svar-ādi*) yesterday, RV. &c. &c. [Cf. Gk. χθές; Lat. *hesternus*, *heri*; Goth. *gistra* (*-dagis*); Germ. *gëstaron*, *gestern*; Angl.Sax. *geostra*; Eng. *yester*(*-day*).]

Hyaḥ, in comp. for *hyas*. **-kṛita**, mfn. done or happened yesterday (*-vat*, ind.), HPariś.

Hyastana, mf(*ī*)n. hesternal, belonging to or produced or occurred yesterday, MBh.; (*ī*), f. (scil. *vibhakti*) the personal terminations of the imperfect, Kāty. **-dina**, n. the day just past, yesterday, L.

Hyastya, mfn. hesternal, of yesterday, Pāṇ. iv, 2, 105.

Hyo, in comp. for *hyas*. **-go-doha**, m. yesterday's cow's milk, L.

ह्रग् *hrag* (cf. √*hlag*), cl. 1. P. *hragati*, to cover, conceal, Dhātup. xix, 25.

ह्रणिया *hraṇiyā* or *hraṇīyā*, f. = *hṛiṇ*°, L.

ह्रद 1. *hradá*, m. (once n.; ifc. f. *ā* rather to be connected with √*hlād*, but cf. √*hrād*; for 2. *hrada* see p. 1307) a large or deep piece of water, lake, pool (rarely applied to the sea; with *gāṅga*, 'the water of the Ganges'), RV. &c. &c.; (*ā*), f. the incense tree, L.; (*ī*), f., g. *gaurâdi*. **-graha**, m. 'lake-monster,' a crocodile, alligator, L. **Hradântara**, n. another lake, MW. **Hradâlayêśa-māhātmya**, n. N. of wk. **Hradôdara**, m. 'lake-bellied,' N. of a Daitya, MBh.

Hradayyá, mfn. being in a pond or lake, TS.

Hradavya, mfn. id., Pāṇ. vi, 1, 83, Vārtt. 2, Pat.

Hradin, mfn. abounding in pools or in water (as

a river), MBh.; Hariv.; R.; (*inī*), f. a river, VarBṛS.; BhP.

Hrade-cákshus, mfn. (prob.) mirrored in a lake, RV.

Hrádya, mf(*ā*)n. being in a pond or lake, TS.

1. **Hrādin,** mfn. (for 2. see col. 2) = *hradin*, R.; (*inī*), f. a river, L.; N. of a river (v.l. *hradinī*), R. (Sch.)

ह्रप् *hrap*, v.l. for √*hlap*, q.v.

ह्रस् *hras*, cl. 1. P. Ā. *hrasati*, °*te* (only in present base; Gr. also pf. *jahrāsa* &c.), to become short or small, be diminished or lessened, Mn.; MBh. &c.; to descend from (abl.), MBh.; (P.) to sound, Dhātup. xvii, 61: Caus. *hrāsayati* (aor. *ajihrasat*), to make small or less, shorten, curtail, diminish, Gobh.; Mn. &c.: Desid. *jihrasishati*, Gr.: Intens. *jāhrasyate*, *jāhrasti*, ib.

Hrasita, mfn. shortened, curtailed, diminished, Bhaṭṭ.; BhP.; sounded, W.

Hrasiman, m. shortness, smallness, g. *pṛithv-ādi*.

Hrásishṭha, mfn. (superl. fr. *hrasva*) shortest or smallest, very short or small, ŚBr.

Hrásīyas, mfn. (compar. fr. id.) shorter (also prosodially) or smaller, very short or small, ŚBr.; ĀśvŚr.; RPrāt. &c.; (*ī*), f. a variety of the Gāyatrī metre (containing two lines of six syllables and one line of seven), VS. Anukr. [Cf. Gk. χερείων.]

Hrasta. See *nir-hrasta*.

Hrasvá, mf(*ā*)n. short, small, dwarfish, little, low (as an entrance), weak (as a voice), VS. &c. &c.; unimportant, insignificant, BhP.; less by (abl.), Car.; prosodically or metrically short (as opp. to *dīrgha*; cf. *laghu*), ŚrS.; RPrāt.; Pāṇ. &c.; m. a dwarf, W.; a short vowel, Prāt.; N. of Yama, L.; (*ā*), f. a female dwarf, MW.; N. of various plants (Phaseolus Trilobus; = *nāga-balā* and *bhūmi-jambū*), L.; of a Sāman, ĀrshBr.; (*am*), n. a kind of vegetable, L.; green or black sulphate of iron, L.; a partic. short measure, MW. **-karṇa,** m. 'short-eared,' N. of a Rākshasa, R. **-karshaṇa,** n. a partic. Svara, Saṃh-Up. **-kuśa,** m. Kuśa grass or a kind of short Kuśa g° (cf. *-darbha*), L. **-gavedhukā,** f. Uraria Lagopodioides, L. **-jambū,** f. a species of Jambū with small black fruit, L. **-jātya,** mfn. of a small sort or kind, Suśr. **-taṇḍula,** m. a kind of rice, L. **-tā,** f. shortness (of stature), R. **-tva,** n. id., Suśr.; Sarvad.; prosodial shortness, Kāś. on Pāṇ. ii, 3, 56. **-darbha,** m. = *-kuśa*, L. **-dā,** f. the incense-producing-tree (v.l. *hradā*), L. **-nirvaṇśaka,** m. a small sword, L. **-pattraka,** m. 'having short leaves,' a kind of Bassia, L.; (*ikā*), f. the small Pippala tree, L. **-parṇa,** m. 'id.,' Ficus Infectoria, L. **-pūrva,** mfn. preceded by a short vowel, VPrāt. **-plaksha,** m. a species of small Plaksha tree, L. **-phala,** m. 'having small fruit or kernels,' the date tree, L.; (*ā*), f. the tree Bhūmi-jambū. **-bāhu,** mfn. short-armed, MārkP.; m. N. of Nala (while in the service of king Ṛitu-parṇa), Kathās. **-bāhuka,** mfn. short-armed, MBh. **-mūrti,** mfn. short in stature, dwarfish, MW. **-mūla,** m. 'having a small root,' the red sugar-cane, L. **-mūlaka,** m. (prob.) id., Suśr. **-roman,** m. 'short-haired,' N. of a king of Videha (son of Svarṇa-roman), BhP. **-śākhā-śipha,** m. 'having short branch roots,' a small tree, shrub, L. **-śigruka,** m. a species of Moringa, Suśr. **-sabhā,** f. a small or narrow hall, MW. **Hrasvâgni,** m. Calotropis Gigantea, L. **Hrasvâṅga,** mfn. short-bodied, dwarfish, BhP.; m. a dwarf, W.; the medicinal plant and root Jīvaka, L. **Hrasvâiraṇḍa,** m. red Ricinus, L. **Hrasvôdaya,** mfn. followed by a short vowel, RPrāt. **Hrasvôpadha,** mfn. having a short penultimate, AV.

Hrasvaka, mfn. very short or small, MBh.; Hariv. &c.

Hrāsa, m. shortening, diminution, decrease, deterioration, detriment, Mn.; Yājñ. &c.; paucity, scarcity, MBh.; Hariv. &c.; sound, noise, L. **Hrāsânveshaṇa-vat,** mfn. connected with diminution and searching, Sāh.

Hrāsaka, mf(*ikā*)n. shortening, diminishing, decreasing, MW.

Hrāsana, n. shortening, diminution, Gṛihyās.; Suśr.

Hrāsanīya, mfn. to be made shorter or diminished, ŚārṅgS.

Hrāsva, n. (fr. *hrasva*), g. *pṛithv-ādi*.

ह्राद् *hrād* (cf. √*hlād*), cl. 1. Ā. (Dhātup. ii, 25) *hrādate* (pf. *jahrāde* as Pass. impers., Bhaṭṭ.; Gr. also aor. *ahrādishṭa* &c.), to sound, roar, make a noise (mostly with a preposition, cf. *nir-*, and *sam-√hrād*): Caus. *hrādayati*, to cause to sound, ĀpGṛ.; to refresh, delight (= or w.r. for *hlādayati*), MārkP. [Cf. Gk. χάλαζα.]

2. **Hrada,** m. (ifc. f. *ā*; for 1. see p. 1306, col. 3) sound, noise, L.; a ray of light (see *śata-hr°*); a ram, L.; N. of a son of Hrāda, Hariv.

Hradaka, mfn. = *hrade kuśalaḥ*, g. *ākarshâdi*.

Hrāda, m. sound, noise, roar (of thunder), ChUp.; MBh.; Kir.; sound (in a phonetical sense), Pat.; N. of a serpent-demon, MBh.; of a son of Hiraṇya-kaśipu, Hariv.; Pur.

Hrādaka, mfn. = *hrāde kuśalaḥ*, g. *ākarshâdi*.

2. **Hrādin,** mfn. (for 1. see col. 1) sounding, noisy, very loud, MBh.; VarBṛS.; Śiś.; (*inī*), f. lightning, MBh.; Hcar.; Indra's thunderbolt, L.

Hrādúni or °**nī,** f. 'rattling,' hail, RV.; VS.; Br.; ChUp. **-hata** (°*dúni-*), mfn. struck by hail, MaitrS. **-vṛit** (°*dunī-*), mfn. covered or hidden by hail, RV.

ह्राम् *hrām*, ind. an exclamation, BhP.

ह्रास *hrāsa*, *hrāsana*. See col. 1.

ह्रिणिया *hriṇiyā*, *hriṇīyā*, f. = *hrin°*. I

ह्रिणीय *hriṇīya*, Nom. Ā. °*yate* (cf. *hṛiniya*) to be ashamed of (instr.), Naish.; (with *na*) to be unashamed before (abl. = to bear comparison with), Bhaṭṭ.

ह्रित *hrita*, w.r. for *hṛita* or *hrīta*.

Hriti, f. = *hṛiti*, taking, conveying, L.

ह्रिवेर *hrivera*, n. = *hrīvera*, L.

ह्री 1. *hrī*, cl. 3. P. (Dhātup. xxv, 3) *jihreti* (*jihriyat*, MaitrS.; pf. *jihrāya*, Ragh.; *jihrayām-cakāra*, °*yām-āsa*, Gr.; aor. *ahraishīt*, ib.; Prec. *hrīyāt*, ib.; p. *hrayāṇa*, see *a-hr°*; fut. *hretā*, *hreshyati*, Gr.), to feel shame, blush, be bashful or modest, be ashamed of any one (gen.) or anything (abl.), Kāv.; Kathās.: Caus. *hrepayati* (aor. *ajihripat*), to make ashamed, cause to blush, confound, put to shame (also fig. = 'surpass, excel'), ib.: Desid. *jihrīshati*, Gr.: Intens. *jehrīyate* (p. °*yamāṇa*, SaddhP.), *jehrayīti*, *jehreti*, to be greatly ashamed, ib.

2. **Hrī́,** f. shame, modesty, shyness, timidity (also personified as daughter of Daksha and wife of Dharma), VS. &c. &c. **-jita,** mfn. overcome by shame, modest, ashamed, L. **-deva,** m. N. of a Buddhist deity, Lalit. **-dhārin,** mfn. feeling shame, bashful, Pañcad. **-nirāsa,** m. abandonment of sh°, shamelessness, W. **-nisheva,** mfn. practising modesty, modest (also °*vaka* and °*vin*), MBh.; m. N. of a prince, ib. **-pada,** n. cause of sh°, Kum. **-bala,** mfn. strong in modesty, extremely modest, Jātakam. **-bhaya,** n. fear of sh°, Rājat. **-mat,** mfn. bashful, modest, ashamed, embarrassed (*-tva*, n.), MBh.; R. &c.; m. N. of a being reckoned among the Viśve Devāḥ, MBh. **-mūḍha,** mfn. perplexed or confused by sh°, Megh. **-yantraṇā,** f. torment of sh°, constraint of bashfulness, Ragh. **-sanna-kaṇṭha,** mfn. having the throat or the utterance broken by shame, MW.

Hrīka, (ifc.) = 2. *hrī* (cf. *nir-hrīka*); m. a mongoose, L.; (*ā*), f. shame, bashfulness, L.

Hrīku, mfn. ashamed, bashful, modest, L.; m. a cat, L.; lac, L.; tin, L.

Hrīṇa, mfn. ashamed, bashful, shy, R. **-mukha,** mfn. shame-faced, blushing, ib.

Hrīta, mfn. ashamed, modest, shy, timid, MBh.; Kathās. **-mukha,** mfn. = *hrīṇa-m°*, PañcavBr. **-mukhin,** mfn. id., TS.

Hrīti, f. shame, bashfulness, modesty, MBh.

Hrepaṇa, n. (fr. Caus.) shame, embarrassment, Kathās.

Hrepita, mfn. ashamed, put to shame, surpassed, Ragh.

ह्रीछ् *hrīch*, cl. 1. P. *hrīcchati*, to be ashamed or modest, blush, Dhātup. vii, 30.

ह्रीम् *hrīm*, ind. an exclamation, BhP.

ह्रीवेर *hrīvera*, n. a kind of Andropogon (accord. to some, Pavonia Odorata), Suśr.

Hrīvela and °**laka,** n. id., L.

ह्रु *hru* (collateral form of √*hvṛi*), cl. 9. P. *hruṇāti* (see *vi-√hru*).

Hrút, f. any cause of going wrong or falling, stumbling-block, trap &c., RV.; AV.

Hruta, mfn. crooked, KātyŚr. ('ill,' Sch.)

ह्रुड् *hruḍ* or *hrūḍ*, cl. 1. P. *hroḍati* or *hrūḍati* (accord. to some also Ā. °*te*), to go, Dhātup. ix, 71 (v.l.)

Hrū́ḍu or **hrū́ḍru** (applied to Takman), AV. i, 25, 2; 3.

Hroḍa. See *jyā-hroḍa*.

ह्रुम् *hrum*, ind. an exclamation, BhP.

ह्रेप् *hrep*, cl. 1. Ā. *hrepate*, to go, Dhātup. x, 11 (v.l.); *hrepayati*, see √*hrī*.

ह्रेष् *hresh* (cf. √1. *hesh*), cl. 1. Ā. (Dhātup. xvi, 21) *hreshate* (m.c. also P. °*ti*; pf. *jihreshe* &c., Gr.), to neigh (as a horse), whinny, MBh.; Kāv. &c.; to go, move, Dhātup. xvi, 18 (v.l. for *presh*): Caus. *hreshayati*, to cause to neigh, MBh.

Hreshā, f. neighing (of a horse), whinnying, MBh.

Hreshita, mfn. neighed, ib.; n. = prec., ib.

Hreshin, mfn. neighing, whinnying, ib.

ह्रेषुक *hreshuka*, m. an instrument for digging, a kind of spade, MBh.

ह्रौड् *hrauḍ* (cf. √*hruḍ*, *hrūḍ*), cl. 1. P. *hrauḍati*, to go, Dhātup. ix, 71 (v.l.)

ह्रौम् *hraum*, ind. an exclamation, Cat.

ह्लग् *hlag* (cf. √*hrag*), cl. 1. Ā. *hlagate*, to cover, hide, Dhātup. xix, 26.

ह्लन्न *hlanna*. See under √*hlād*.

ह्लप् *hlap* (v.l. *hrap*), cl. 10. P. *hlāpayati*, to speak, Dhātup. xxxii, 115; to sound, creak, ib.

ह्लस् *hlas* (cf. √*hras*), cl. 1. P. *hlasati*, to sound, Dhātup. xvii, 62.

ह्लाद् *hlād* (cf. √*hrād*), cl. 1. Ā. (Dhātup. ii, 26) *hlādate* (perhaps orig. 'to make a cry of joy'), to be glad or refreshed, rejoice, Nir.; MBh.; to sound, shout (for joy), ib.: Caus. *hlādayati*, °*te* (aor. *ajihladat*; Pass. *ahlādayishata*, Daś.; Bhaṭṭ.), to refresh, gladden, exhilarate, delight, TĀr.; MBh.; R. &c. [Cf. Gk. κέχλαδα, καχλάζω; Old Germ. *glat*; Eng. *glad*.]

Hlatti, hlanna, hlanni. See *pra-hl°*

Hlāda, m. refreshment, pleasure, gladness, joy, delight, R.; VarBṛS. &c.; N. of a son of Hiraṇya-kaśipu (= and v.l. for *hrāda*), VP.

Hlādaka, mf(*ikā*)n. refreshing, gladdening, cooling, RV.; AV. **Hlādikā-vatī,** f. rich in refreshments or enjoyments, RV.

Hlādana, mfn. id., MBh.; R.; Suśr.; n. refreshing, refreshment, Vāgbh.; Kāvyâd.

Hlādanīya, mfn. fit for refreshment, MBh.

Hlādita, mfn. refreshed, gladdened, delighted, MBh.; R. &c.

Hlādin, mfn. refreshing, comforting, gladdening, exhilarating (°*di-tva*, n.), MBh.; Suśr. &c.; very noisy or loud (v.l. *hrādin*), VarBṛS.; (*inī*), f. (cf. *hrādi-nī*) lightning, L.; Indra's thunderbolt, L.; the incense-tree, L.; a partic. Śakti, BhP., Sch.; a mystical N. of the sound *d*, Up.; N. of a river, R.

Hlāduka, mf(*ā*)n. exhilarating, cooling, fresh, TĀr.

Hlādukā-vatī, f. = *hlādikā-vatī*, ib.

Hlāduni, f. (used in explaining *hrāduni*), Śaṃk.

ह्ली *hlī* = √*hrī*, in the following derivatives:

Hlī́ka, mfn. bashful, modest, TBr.; Kāṭh.; (*ā*), f. shame, modesty, L.

Hlīku, mfn. ashamed, modest, shy, L.; m. lac, L.; tin, L.

ह्लेष् *hlesh* = √*hresh*, in the following derivatives:

Hleshā, f. = *hreshā*, neighing, whinnying, L.

ह्वल् *hval* (cf. √*hvṛi*), cl. 1. P. (Dhātup. xix, 44) *hvalati* (m.c. also °*te*; pf. *jahvāla*, aor. *ahvālīt* &c., Gr.; inf. *hvālitos*, ŚBr.; ind. p. *-hvālam*, ib. &c.), to go crookedly or astray or wrong or deviously, stumble, fall, fail, ŚBr.; Bhaṭṭ.: Caus. *hvalayati* or *hvālayati* (the former when prepositions are prefixed; aor. *ajihvalat*), to cause to tremble, shake, Bhaṭṭ.

Hvala, mfn. stumbling, staggering, PārGṛ.; (*á*), f. going astray or wrong, failure, ŚBr.

Hvalana, mfn. stumbling, staggering, PārGṛ.

Hvāla, m. failure, cessation, KātyŚr. ('dying,' Sch.)

ह्वृ *hvṛi* or *hvṝ* (cf. √*hval*, √*dhvṛi*), cl. 1. P. (Dhātup. xxii, 23) *hvárati* (in RV. also *hvárate*; and accord. to Dhātup. xxxi, 21 also *hvṛiṇāti*; pf. *jahvāra*, °*vartha*, °*varuḥ*, Gr.; aor. *ahvārshīt*, *hvārshīt*, *hvār*, *hvārishuḥ*, VS.; Br.; Kāṭh.; Prec. *hvaryāt*, Gr.; fut. *hvartā*, *hvarishyati*, ib.; inf. *hvartum*, ib.), to deviate or diverge from the right line, be crooked or curved, bend, go crookedly or wrongly or deviously, stumble, fall down, VS. &c. (see above): Caus. *hvārayati* (aor. *jihvaraḥ*, °*ratam*; *juhuraḥ*, *juhūrthāḥ*, *juhurāṇá*), to cause to go crookedly, lead wrong or astray, RV.; (Ā.) to go wrong or astray, ib.: Desid. *juhvūrshati*, Gr.: Intens. *jāhvaryate*, *jāhvarti*, ib.

Hvara. See *dhariṇa-hvara.*

Hvaraka, m. pl. N. of a school, IndSt.

Hvāras, n. (pl.) crookedness, deceit, intrigue, ib.; VS.; a partic. contrivance attached to the Soma-sieve (perhaps the curved rods fixed round the rim), RV.; a trap, snare (?), RV. ii, 23, 6.

Hvarita, mfn., Pāṇ. vii, 2, 31 &c.

Hvārá, m. 'going crookedly or deviously,' a serpent, RV.; AV.

Hvāryá, mfn. serpentine, winding, RV.; m. a serpent, Sāy. on RV. v, 9, 4; a horse, Naigh. i, 14.

Hvṛita, mfn., Pāṇ. vii, 2, 31 &c.

ह्वे *hve*, cl. 1. P. Ā. (Dhātup. xxiii, 39) *hváyati*, °*te* (Ved. also *hávate* and *huváti*, °*te*; other present forms are *hve*, AV.; *hvāmahe*, VS.; *hóma*, *hūmáhe*, *juhūmási*, RV.; p. *huvāná* [with pass. sense], ib., *hvayāna*, MBh.; pf. *juhāva*, *juhuvuḥ*, ŚBr. &c.; *juhvé*, *juhūré*, RV.; *juhuve*, *juhurire*, Br.; *hvayām-āsa* and *hvayām-cakre*, MBh.; aor. *áhvat*, *ahvata* [or *ahvāsta*, Pāṇ. iii, 1, 54], RV. &c. &c.; *ahvi*, AV.; *áhūmahi*, *ahūshata*, RV.; *ahvāsīt* [?], GopBr.; fut. *hvātā*, Gr.; *hvayishyati*, °*te*, Br.; *hvāsyate*, ŚāṅkhŚr.; inf. Class. *hvātum*; Ved. *hávitave*, *hváyitum*, °*tavai*; *huvádhyai*; ind. p. Class. *hūtvā*; Ved. *-hūya* and *-hāvam*), to call, call upon, summon, challenge, invoke (with *nāmnā*, 'to call by name;' with *yuddhe*, 'to challenge to fight'), RV. &c. &c.; to emulate, vie with, W.: Pass. *hūyáte* (aor. *áhāvi* or *ahvāyi*), to be called &c., RV.: Caus. *hvāyayati* (aor. *ajūhavat* or *ajuhāvat*), to cause any one (acc.) to be challenged by (instr.), Vop.: Desid. *juhūshati*, °*te*, Gr.: Intens. *johūyate* or *jóhavīti* (*johuvanta*, *ajohavuḥ*, *jóhuvat*, *jóhuvāna*, RV.; AV.; BhP.) or *johoti* (Gr.), to call on, invoke &c. [Cf. Gk. γοάω.]

2. **Hava, hāva** &c. See p. 1294, cols. 1 and 2.

Huta (for *hūta*?). See p. 1301, col. 1.

Hūtá, mfn. called, summoned, invited, RV.; Prab.; n. the act of calling, Pāṇ. viii, 2, 84. **-vat**, mfn. containing the word *hūta*, ŚrS.

Hūti, f. calling; invocation &c.

Hūya. See *devi-* and *pitri-hūya.*

2. **Hótrā**, f. (for 1. see p. 1306, col. 1) calling, call, invocation (also personified), RV.; TBr.; (*hotrābhiḥ*), ind. by good words, MBh. iii, 1332. **-vid**, mfn. knowing invocation, RV.

Hvayana, hvayitavya. See *ā-hv°.*

Hvā, f. a name, appellation (see *giri-hvā*).

Hvātavya, mfn. to be called, Nir.

Hvātṛi, m. (used in explaining *hotṛi*), ib.

Hvāna, n. calling, calling near, MBh.; a cry, noise (see *ku-hvāna*).

Hvānīya, mfn. to be called or invoked, MW.

Hvāya. See *svarga-hvāya.*

Hvāyaka, mfn. calling &c., Pat.

Hvāyakīya, Nom. P. °*yati* = *hvāyakam icchati*, ib.: Desid. *jihvāyakīyishati*, ib.

Hvāyayitavya. See *ā-hv°.*

Hvāyin, mfn. calling, invoking, challenging, MW.

Hveya, mfn. to be called or invoked, ib.

ADDITIONS AND CORRECTIONS.

Obs. *When no meaning is given some addition or rectification of accent is intended. The word* **Pra-kriyā** *has been accidentally omitted at p. 654, but will be found at p. 1330.*

Aṅśa-rūpiṇī, f. (with *śakti*) a female personification of the divine energy, RTL. 187. **Aṅśu** (col. 2, l. 1, for 'array' read 'a ray'). **Aṅsa** (in comp.); *-dhrī* (read, 'applied to the Vedi'), AV. xi, 1, 23; *-pīṭha*, m. the shoulder-blades, Suśr.; °*sôccaya*, m. du. the shoulder-blades, ĀpŚr. **Aṅhana**, n. (fr. √1. *aṅh*) the act of moving or creeping (like a snake), L. **Aṅho** (in comp. for *aṅhas*); *-liṅga*, mfn. characterized by the word *aṅhas* (said of a series of texts), Kauś. **A-kaṇaka**, mfn. (rice) without red particles adhering to the husks, Divyâv. **Akabara** or **Akabbara** or **Akavara**, m. (emperor) Akbar, Inscr. **A-karishyat**, mfn. not intending to do, Drāhy. **A-karṇīya**, mfn. not to be heard, MBh. **A-karmikā**, f. idle, Divyâv. **A-kali**, mfn. not quarrelling Śiś. **A-kalita**, mfn. incalculable, immeasurable, Mālatīm. **A-kalmasha**, (also) m. N. of the fourth Manu, MatsyaP. **A-kalmāsha**, mf(*ī*)n. spotless, ŚBr. **A-kalya**, (also) not to be guessed, Daś. **A-kasya-vid**, mfn. not attending to anything, MaitrS. **A-kāma-saṁjñapana**, n. unintentional killing of a victim before a sacrifice, ĀpŚr. **A-kāyikā**, f. a kind of game, Divyâv. **A-kāla**, (also) night, ib.; *-kaumudī*, f. an irregular festival, ib. **A-kālaka**, n. food eaten at irregular times, ib. **Akāvaṅká**, n. water (= *aṅkâṅká*), MaitrS. **A-kiṁcid**, n. nothing, MBh. **A-kilina**, mfn. (for *a-klinna*) not moist or wet, Gobh. **A-kuṇḍala**, mfn. without ear-rings, Bcar. **A-kutaś** (in comp. for *a-kutas*); *-cana*, m. N. of Śiva, L.; *-cid*, ind. not for any reason, unintentionally, MBh.; (°*to*)-*mṛityu*, mfn. not threatened by death from any quarter, BhP. **A-kutūhala**, mfn. not taking interest in (loc.), Bcar. **A-kutsayat**, mfn. not abusing or reproaching, Mn. ii, 54. 2. **A-kupya**, n. (impers.) anger must not be shown, MBh. **A-kupyat**, mfn. not boiling, AV. **A-kumbha**, m. 'no water-jar,' anything singular of its kind, Jātakam. **A-kula**, (also, in astron.) N. of Sunday, Monday, Thursday, and Saturday; (also *ā*, f.) the 1st, 3rd, 5th, 7th, 9th, 11th, and 13th days of a half-month; n. N. of partic. lunar mansions. **A-kulaka**, mfn. (fruit) without stone, Car. **Á-kuśala** (ŚBr.); n. (with Buddhists) demerit, sin, MWB. 124. **A-kushṭhi-pṛishat**, mfn. neither leprous nor spotted, ĀśvGṛ. **A-kūja**, mfn. noiseless, MBh. **A-kūjana**, n. noiselessness, silence, ib.; mfn. not creaking (as the axle of a car), ib. **A-kūrma-pṛishat**, mfn. not spotted like a turtle, ĀśvGṛ. **A-kṛita** (in comp.); *-kārya* (Divyâv.) or *-kṛitya* (Siṅhâs.), mfn. one who has not done his duty; *-cūḍa*, mfn. untonsured, Mn. v, 67; *-śmaśāna* (*ákṛita-*), mfn. one who has not established a burning-ground, ŚBr. **A-kṛimi-parisṛipta**, mfn. not crawled over by worms, Gobh. **A-kṛiśa-kīrti**, mfn. of undiminished glory, Bcar. **A-kṛishṭa**, (also) not prolonged or drawled (in pronunciation), SaṃhUp. **A-kopya**, mfn. (fr. Pāli *akuppa*) not to be disregarded, Divyâv. **Akkā**, f. a procuress, Pañcat. **Akkā-devī**, f. N. of a queen, Inscr. **Akti**, f. ointment, L. 2. **Akrá**, (accord. to some also) a horse, RV. **A-krandita**, mfn. not pressed (as *tila*), Divyâv. **A-krama**, (also) *am*, ind. not by degrees, simultaneously, Naish.; °*ma-śas*, ind., id., Kap.; °*môḍhā*, f. a woman married out of the regular order (as the younger sister before the elder &c.), KātyŚr. **Á-krīta**, mfn. not bought, ŚBr. **Á-krudhyat**, mfn. not being angry, ŚBr. **Á-krūra**, **Á-krodha** (ŚBr.). **A-klība**, mfn. not impotent, manly, Bcar. √**Aksh**, *akshṇute*, *akshṇuyāt*, (also) to mark (esp. cattle on the ear; *akshitá*, mfn. 'marked;' *akshitavyà*, mfn. 'to be marked;' cf. *ashṭa-karṇa* and Gk. ὀξύς), MaitrS. 1. **Aksha**, (also) a chariot, Dharmaś.; *-dhurā*, f. an axle-pin, Āpast.; *-śabda*, m. the creaking of an axle, ĀpŚr.; 2. **Aksha** (in comp.); *-dharma*, m. the laws or rules of gambling, Pracaṇḍ.; *-mālikā*, f. a rosary, Kathās.; *-śikshā*, f. the art of gambling, Pracaṇḍ.; *-śīla*, mfn. addicted to gambling, Āpast.; *-sūtra-valayin*, mfn. having a rosary for a bracelet, Caṇḍ. 4. **Aksha** (in comp.); *-prapātana*, n. casting glances, Hariv. **Akshatā**, mfn. (also) unthrashed, Gobh.; m. n. (also) a boil or sore not produced by cutting, Kauś.; °*tâmaya*, m. disease without any external injury, ŚBr. **Akshan-vat**, see *akshaṇ-vat*. **A-kshama**, (also) unfit, improper, Jātakam.; (*ā*), f. (in dram.) sensitiveness, irritability, Sāh.; °*min*, mfn. intolerant, cruel, Bhartṛ. **A-kshaya-vaṭa**, m. 'undecaying Banyan,' N. of a very ancient sacred tree, RTL. 337. **Akshayiṇī** (read, 'N. of a river'), Rājat. **Akshara**, n. (also) an indelible mark incised on metal or stone; (also) m. N. of a Sāman, ĀrshBr.; (erase 'Achyranthes Aspera'); *-vat*, mfn. possessing syllables, JaimUp.; *-śikshā*, f. alphabetic science, Daś.; *-saṁhāta* or *-saṁghāta*, (in dram.) accidental putting together or arranging of letters or syllables, Bhar.; *-saṁhitā*, f. the Saṁhitā of syllables, TPrāt.; *-sadhātu*, n. a partic. manner of singing, Lāṭy.; *-sampád*, f. fitness or completeness of the number of syllables, ŚBr.; °*rântara*, n. another letter, transliteration, L. **A-kshānta**, mfn. impatient, Bcar. **Akshi** (in comp.); *-bandha*, m. binding the eyes, Naish.; *-lakshī-√kṛi* (P. *-karoti*), to make anything an object for the eyes, look at, Naish.; *-saṁskāra*, m. painting the eyes, L.; collyrium, L. **A-kshiṇvat**, mfn. not injuring, Mn. ii, 100. **Á-kshīyamāṇa**, mfn. imperishable, inexhaustible, RV. **A-kshuṇṇa-vedha**, the act of throwing a spear so as to touch the mark lightly, Divyâv. **Á-kshetra-jña** (ŚBr.). **Á-kshodhuka**, mfn. not hungry, MaitrS. **A-kshobha** (insert n. before 'freedom'). **A-kshobhya** (in comp.); *-tīrtha*, m. N. of a disciple of Ānanda-tīrtha (q.v.), Cat. **A-kshobhyā**, f. N. of a Yoginī, Hcat. **Akshṇayâpacchedana**, n. transverse division, Śulbas. **A-khaṇḍa** (in comp.); *-kala*, mfn. full (as the moon), Mālatīm.; *-maṇḍala*, mfn. possessing the whole country, Rājat.; °*ḍôpadhi*, m. a quality not to be defined by words, Sāṃkhyak. **A-kharvan** (?), mfn. unmutilated, unimpaired, Hcat. **A-khinna**, mfn. unwearied, Bcar. **Á-gatâsu**, mfn. not dead, alive, MaitrS. **A-gatyā**, ind. unavoidably, indispensably, Bcar.; Jātakam. **Agada**, (also) a magic jewel, Divyâv. **A-gadita**, mfn. untold, unasked, Śiś. **A-gandha-sevin**, mfn. not addicted to perfumes, Āpast. **A-gandhi** (or °*dhin*), mfn. without smell, scentless, Vishṇ. **A-gama**, mfn. impassable, MBh. **A-gamya-rūpa**, mf(*ā*)n. difficult to be traversed, Kir. **A-garbha**, mfn. not rooted in another tree, KātyŚr.; (*ā*), f. not pregnant, ŚBr. **Agastya** (in comp.); *-gṛihaspatika*, mfn. having Agastya for a householder, ĀpŚr.; *-śāsta*, mfn. ruled by Agastya (with *diś*, f. 'the south'), MBh. **Agāra**, (also) a partic. high number, Buddh.; *-vinoda*, m. N. of a wk. on architecture; *-stūpa*, m. the chief beam of a house, ĀpGṛ.; *-sthūṇā-virohaṇa*, n. the sprouting of the post of a house, Buddh.; °*râvakāśa*, m. ground fit for (building) a h°, ĀpGṛ. **A-gālita**, mfn. unfiltered, Suśr. **A-gīta**, mfn. unsung (in *gītâgīta*), JaimUp. **A-guṇin**, mfn. devoid of merit, ŚBr.; not requiring the Guṇa change, KātyŚr., Sch.

A-gṛihīta, mfn. untwisted (?), MānGṛ.; *-diś,* mfn. missing, L. **A-gṛihṇat,** mfn. not biting (as a leech), Suśr. **Á-gṛihya,** mfn. imperceptible, ŚBr.; independent (=*sva-tantra*), Bhaṭṭ. **A-goḥ-prâpaṇam,** ind. not within the reach of a cow, KātyŚr. **A-gocara,** insert m. after 'Brahma;' °*carī-√kṛi* (P. *-karoti*), to make unfit to collect alms in, Divyâv. **A-gó-tā,** f. want of cows, RV.; AV. **Agnā́-vishṇu** (ŚBr.). **Agni,** (also) = next, ĀpŚr.; *-kshetra,* n. the place for the fire-altar, IndSt.; *-godāna,* m. one at whose hair-cutting ceremony Agni is the chief deity, ĀpGṛ.; *-cakra,* n. the sphere or range of fire, IndSt.; *-jā,* f. a brown cow, L.; *-jyeshṭha* (°*ni-jy*°), mfn. having Agni for a chief, TBr.; *-jyotis,* mfn. flaming, KātyŚr.; *-tanu,* f. pl. N. of partic. texts, ĀpŚr.; *-tuṇḍa,* m. a partic. fire-spitting animal (existing in a hell), Vishṇ.; *-nāmán,* n. a name of Agni, ŚBr.; *-nārāyaṇa,* m. N. of Agni (as worshipped by the Agni-hotṛi-brāhmans), RTL. 50; *-nidhāna,* n. the placing of the fire, KātyŚr.; *-nyakta* (°*ni-ny*°), mfn. mingled with Agni (i.e. having Agni incidentally mentioned), TBr.; *-patana,* n. throwing one's self into fire, Pañcat.; *-pāta,* m. id., Kālac.; *-pānīya,* n. the observance of throwing one's self first into water and then into fire, Hāla, Sch.; *-putra,* m. 'Agni's son,' N. of Skanda, AV.Pariś.; *-praṇayana,* n. vessels for conveying the sacrificial fire, MānŚr.; *-pradāna,* n. throwing into the fire, Pañcat.; *-bhāṇḍa,* n. the vessel for the Aupāsana fire, HirP.; *-bhūti* (see also Pāṇ. viii, 2, 107, Vārtt. 2, Pat.); *-madana,* n. the fire of sexual love, MBh.; *-man,* m. fieriness, Vām. v, 2, 56; *-m-īyāma,* m. N. of a Sāman, Lāṭy.; Drāhy.; *-yauna,* mfn. produced from fire, MBh.; *-rahasya-kāṇḍa,* n. N. of the 10th (or 12th) book of the ŚBr.; *-locana,* m. fiery-eyed, N. of Śiva, Gal.; *-vaha,* mfn. exposing one's self to heat, MBh.; *-viś,* f. coal, L.; *-śakaṭī,* f. 'fire-vehicle,' a portable furnace, Alaṃkārat.; *-śakti,* f. the force of digestion, VarBṛS.; *-śauca-vastra,* n. a fine muslin garment, Kāraṇḍ.; *-saṃdīpana,* mfn. stimulating digestion, Bhpr.; *-samādhāna,* n. kindling fire, Gobh.; *-sthala,* n. the fire-place, IndSt.; *-sparśa,* mfn. scalding hot, Āpast.; *-hotṛi-brāhmaṇa,* m. N. of a class of Brāhmans (who regard Agni as chief deity), RTL. 50; *-hotrá-prâyaṇa,* mfn. beginning with the Agni-hotra, TS.; *-hotra-velā,* f. the time of the Agni-hotra, JaimUp.; °*ny-arci,* m. the flame of fire, JaimUp.; °*ny-āyatana,* n. a fire-shrine, MānGṛ.; °*ny-upasthā́na* (MaitrS.); °*nau-karaṇa,* n. burnt offering, KātyŚr., Sch. **Agnīya,** mfn. relating to Agni or fire, g. *utkarâdi.* **Agneyānī,** f. a kind of brick, TS. **Agra,** n. (also) rest, remainder, Līl.; *-gaṇanā,* f. the reckoning or placing uppermost, Naish., Sch.; *-cchada,* n. the point of a leaf, Viddh.; *-tala-saṃcāra,* m. a partic. posture in dancing, Saṃgīt.; *-devī,* f. a chief queen, Bcar.; *-drava-saṃhati,* f. the thin upper part of milk or curds, L.; *-dharma,* m. high spiritual state, Divyâv.; *-pāka,* m. the firstlings of fruit, KātyŚr.; *-bodhi,* m. N. of a king of Ceylon, Buddh.; *-bhojya,* mfn. enjoying the best of anything, MBh.; *-yāna,* n. the first vehicle, Buddh.; *-śikha,* mfn. having a pointed flame, MBh.; *-śrāvaka,* m. (and *ikā,* f.) 'chief disciple,' N. of some followers of Buddha, MWB. 47; *-saṃkhyā,* f. (acc. with Caus. of *sam-ā-√ruh,* 'to put at the head'), Ragh. **Agra-ṇī-√kṛi,** P. *-karoti,* to send before, VP. **A-grasta,** mfn. not swallowed (said of sounds), ChUp. **A-graha,** mfn. (also) where no ladleful is drawn, ĀpŚr. **A-grahaṇa,** n. not meaning, Paribh.; (*á-gṛ*°), mfn. not afflicted by disease, MaitrS. **Agrâgra,** mf(*ā*)n. pointed in front, ĀpŚr. **Agrânta,** m. or n. the product added to the ultimate term, Col. **Agrima-vatī,** f. the verse RV. ix, 62, 25 (beginning with '*pávasva vācó agriyáḥ*'), Lāṭy. **A-ghaṭita-ghaṭita,** mfn. badly put together, Subh. **A-ghaṇṭa,** m. (cf. *ghaṇṭa*) N. of Siva, MBh. **Aghaya,** Nom. P. °*yati,* to do evil, sin, Dhātup. **Agharikā,** f. a kind of game, Divyâv. **A-ghūrṇa,** mfn. not tottering, ĀpŚr. **A-ghôdaka,** n. (prob.) the daily bath during the period of uncleanness, BaudhP. **A-ghora-ghaṇṭa,** m. N. of an adherent of a partic. sect worshipping Devī, Mālatīm. (cf. IW. 500). **Aghnya-tvá,** n. the state of being a cow, MaitrS. **Aṅka,** (also) a kind of regnal year (used in Orissa and usually spoken of as Onko year; the peculiarity of it is that in counting the years of the reign of a king certain numbers are omitted, thus, accord. to one system, the numbers ending with 6 or 0, excepting 10, are dropped, so that the sequence of the years would be—1, 2, 3, 4, 5, 7, 8, 9, 10, 11, 12, 13, 14, 15, 17, 18, 19, 21 &c.); *-gata,* mfn. lying in the lap, Bcar.; *-ccheda,* m. (in dram.) interruption (of the action) by the close of an Act, Bhar.; *-pāla,* m. an account-book, Kāv.; *-lakshaṇa,* n. a mark, brand, ŚāṅkhGṛ.; *-saṃjñā,* f. N. of a wk. on the numerical value of words expressing numerals (by Rāmânanda-tīrtha); °*kâsya,* n. (=*aṅka-mukha*), Daś.; Sāh. **Aṅkāya,** Nom. Ā. °*yate,* to resemble the marks on the moon, Bhām. **Aṅkâvaṅká,** n. water (=*aṅkâṅká,* cf. *akāvaṅká*), MaitrS. **Aṅku,** du. a partic. part of a chariot, Gobh. 1. **Aṅkura** (in comp.); *-vat,* mfn. abounding in sprouts or buds, MBh.; °*râropaṇa* or °*rârpaṇa,* n. 'planting a shoot,' a kind of nuptial ceremony, GṛS. 2. **Aṅkura,** Nom. P. °*rati,* to shoot, sprout, bud, Pārv. **Aṅkuraṇa,** n. shooting, sprouting (lit. and fig.), Sāh. **Aṅkuraya,** Nom. P. °*yati,* to cause to sprout or bud, effect, produce, Subh. **Aṅkurāya,** Nom. Ā. °*yate,* to shoot, sprout, Kāv. **Aṅkulī,** f. a cat (v.l. *akulī*), TāṇḍBr. **Aṅkūraya** = *aṅkuraya,* Kāśīkh.; Pārv. **Aṅkri,** m. or f. a mark, sign, L. **Aṅga** (in comp.); *-kriyā,* f. anointing the body, Daś.; *-bhañjana,* n. side-ache, Suśr.; *-bheda,* (also) m. self-betrayal, Kāś.; *mantra,* m. an unessential or secondary text, IndSt.; *-vāhaka,* mfn. rubbing or shampooing the body, MatsyaP.; *-samākhyāyam,* ind. calling the limbs by name, AitBr.; *-sphuraṇa-vicāra,* m. N. of a wk. on prognosticating events from quiverings of the limbs; °*gâṅgi-bhāva-saṃkara,* m. confusion of essential and secondary ideas, Kuval. **Aṅgadin,** mfn. wearing a bracelet, MBh.; °*dīya,* mfn. belonging to Aṅgada, R. **Aṅgareja,** mfn. English, Inscr. **Aṅgāra,** (in comp.); *-karmânta,* m. charcoal-burning, MBh.; *-jīvikā,* f. subsistence by ch°-b°, HYog.; *-varsha,* n. a shower of sparks from burning charcoal, Bcar.; *-vāra,* m. the day of the planet Mars, Thursday, Cat.; *-śakaṭī,* f. a portable fire-receptacle, L.; *-sāt-√kṛi,* P. *-karoti,* to reduce to charcoal, lay anything upon coals, ĀpŚr.; °*râvakshepaṇa,* n. an instrument for putting on coals, tongs, Nīlak. **Aṅgāraka-yantra** (or *bhauma-y*°), n. a kind of auspicious diagram, Inscr. **Aṅgiraḥ-smṛiti,** f. N. of a law-book. **Áṅgiro-dhāman,** mfn. abiding with the Aṅgiras, MaitrS. **Aṅgu,** m. or f. (?) a limb of the body, L.; a bird, L. **Aṅgula-rāji,** m. a kind of snake, Suśr. **Aṅguli** (in comp.); *-ja,* m. a finger-nail, Gal.; *-praṅéjana,* n. water for washing the fingers, ŚBr.; *-prâśana,* n. eating with the fingers, ĀpGṛ., Sch.; *-mātrá,* mfn. of the size of a finger, MaitrS.; *-saṃdeśa* (read *-saṃdaṃśa*); °*lī-granthi,* m. a finger-joint, KātyŚr.; °*lī-bhaṅga,* m. curving the fingers (in scorn), MatsyaP.; °*lī-veshṭa,* m. (prob.) a glove, R. **Aṅgulikā,** f. a kind of ant, Suśr. **Aṅgushṭha-vibhedaka,** m. 'thumb-separator,' a mitten, Kāraṇḍ. **Aṅgūsha,** m. (also) a kind of bird, L.; an elephant, L.; speed, L. **Áṅghâri** (VS.). **Aṅghri,** (also) division, branch, sphere, AgP.; *-pāta,* m. setting down the feet, a footstep, BhP.; *-saṃdhi,* m. 'foot-joint,' the ancle, L.; °*ghry-avanejana,* mf(*ī*)n. washing the feet (*-tva,* n.), BhP.; fit for washing the feet, ib. √1. **Ac,** (also) to adorn, Dharmaś. **Á-cakrivas,** mfn. not guilty of a Kṛityā (q.v.), AV. **A-cakravarta,** see *cakra-vṛitta.* **A-caṇḍa-marīci,** m. 'cool-rayed,' the moon, Naish. **A-cara,** (also) impassable, Hariv. **Á-caraṇa,** n. improper conduct, ŚBr.; mf(*ā*)n. **A-caraṇīya,** mfn. (prob.) not to be associated with, Gobh. **A-carama-vayas,** n. 'not the last age,' youth, Uttarar. **A-carita,** n. not eating, abstinence from food (accord. to Sch. on Yājñ. ii, 40, but in Mn. viii, 49 rather read *ā-carita,* q.v.). **A-carishyat,** mfn. one who will not keep his vow, Gobh. **A-cākrika,** mfn. having no accomplice (*-tā,* f.), Rājat. **A-cirôḍhā,** f. a newly-married woman, Śiś. **Acchaṭā-śabda** or °*ṭā-saṃghāta,* m. the sound of a snap, a snap with the fingers, Divyâv. **A-cchandáska,** mfn. having no metre, MaitrS. **A-cchidrôktha,** mfn. having (its) verses complete, AitBr. **Acchéra** (or *añśéra*), mfn. (said of the waters), MaitrS. **A-cyāvin,** mfn. firm, unchanging, Bcar. ix, 14 (conj.). **A-cyuta-cakravartin,** m. N. of the author of a Comm. on the Dāya-bhāga, IW. 304. **Aja** (in comp.); *-gati,* mfn. 'accessible (only) to goats,' steep (as a road), MBh.; *-pāla,* (also) N. of a partic. tree (under which Buddha meditated), MWB. 39; *-loman,* (also) mf(*mnī*)n. hairy as a goat, MaitrS. **A-janman,** mfn. not subject to birth, Ragh. **Ajaya** (in comp.); *-pāla, -varman, -siṇha,* m. N. of kings, Inscr. **A-jāti,** f. sham or bad merchandise, Yājñ. **A-jina-ratna,** n. a lucky-bag, Daś. **Ajira,** n. (with *ājeḥ*) a field of battle (cf. *samarâjira*), Śiś. **A-jīryat,** mfn. not subject to old age or decay (*-tā,* f.), KaṭhUp. **A-jū,** mfn. not rushing forward, Sāy. (in a quotation). **Ajjū,** f. a mother, L. **A-jñāna** (in comp.); *-bodhinī,* f. N. of a Comm. on the Ātma-bodha by Śaṃkarâcārya; *-vidhvaṇsana,* m. N. of a Tathāgata, Sukh. i. **Á-jyāyas,** mfn. not greater than (abl.), TBr. **Añjishṭhu,** m. fire, L.; the sun, L. **Aṭaṭa** or *aṭaṭá* (for *a-taṭa*?) a partic. hell, Divyâv.; Dharmaś. **Aṭaṭyā,** f. constant roaming (= *aṭāṭyā*), Subh. **Aṭṭa-pālaka,** m. overseer of a market, L. **Aḍara,** m. a tree, L. **Aḍuva,** m. a boat (= *plava*), L. **Aṇasa,** m. a bird, L. **Aṇi,** (also) half of a lunar month, L. **A-ṇikāsham,** (prob.) w.r. for *a-nik*° (below). **Aṇima-tás,** ind. from the thin side, MaitrS. **Aṇīci,** m. or f. bamboo, cane, L.; a carter, L. **Aṇīcin,** m. N. of a man (having the patr. Mauna), ŚāṅkhBr. **Aṇu,** m. (also) the soul, life (=*ātman*), Harav.; sea-salt, L.; a sacred text, single verse or Mantra (cf. *srag-aṇu*); *-priyaṅgu* (*áṇu-*), m. or f. pl. Panicum Miliaceum and Panicum Italicum, ŚBr.; *-vrata,* read 'five' for 'twelve.' **Aṇḍa,** (also) a pinnacle or cupola, VarBṛS.; a partic. part of a Stūpa, Divyâv.; a sword with irregular longitudinal white marks, L. **Aṇḍika,** m. fever in an elephant or lion, L.; unwholesome condition of water, L. **Aṇḍuka,** m. (only L.) a kind of bird; a frog; the scrotum. **A-tandrī,** mfn. (nom. *īs*) = *a-tandrin,* MBh. (B.). **A-tamâvishṭa** (ŚBr.). **A-tara-paṇyena,** ind. without paying toll, Divyâv. **A-tarka,** (also) mfn. incomprehensible, ib. **Atarkitôpapanna,** mfn. occurred unexpectedly, Kum. **A-taskará,** mfn. free from robbers, AV. **Ati-kṛicchra,** (also) mfn. (said of Vishṇu), MBh.; (*am*), ind. with great difficulty, BhP. **Ati-kṛitârtha,** mfn. very clever or skilful, MBh. **Ati-kṛiti,** f. excess, Veṇīs. **Ati-kramaṇa,** (also) mf(*ī*)n. committing excess or sin (sexually), Vishṇ. **Ati-krāntâtikrānta,** mfn. one who has crossed the stream of sorrow, Divyâv. **Ati-gārgya,** m. an excellent Gārgya, Pat. on Pāṇ. vi, 2, 191. **Ati-citrīya,** Nom. Ā. °*yate,* to cause great astonishment, Daś. **Ati-ciraya,** Nom. P. °*yati,* to linger, Divyâv. **Ati-cchanda,** m. (prob.) too much wilfulness or criticism, MBh. (B. *-ccheda*). **Ati-tamām,** ind. (superl. of *ati*) in a very high degree, Naish., Sch. **Á-titikshamāṇa,** mfn. unable to endure, ŚBr. **Áti-tṛiṇṇa,** mfn. (√*trid*) cleft, split, penetrated, VS. **Atithī** (in comp. for *atithi*); *-√kṛi* (P. *-karoti*), to grant anything (acc.) to a guest, Naish.; to cause anything (acc.) to be a guest, i.e. to make it arrive at (loc.), ib.; *-√bhū* (P. *-bhavati*), to become the guest of (gen.), ib.; °*thy-artha,* mfn. hospitable, L. **Ati-√daṅh** (only in *-daṅhiḥ,* used in explaining *adhi-dhak*), Nir. i, 7. **Ati-digdha,** a poisoned arrow, Bcar. v, 1. **Ati-dosham,** ind. after dusk (v.l. *abhi-d*°), ĀpŚr. **Ati-dvaya,** mfn. unparalleled, unique, Kād. **Ati-√nam** (Caus. *-nāmayati*), to pass time, Divyâv. **Ati-pādá,** m. going too far, overstepping, TBr. **Ati-pāraya,** mfn. carrying across, RV. vi, 47, 7. **Ati-pra-√śridh** (Caus. *-śardhayati*), to obtrude or force anything upon any one (dat.), RV. viii, 13, 6. **Ati-prasaṅga,** m. (also) too much diffuseness, Veṇīs.; Rājat. **Ati-prasanna,** n. (impers.) too much grace has been shown, Mālatīm. **Ati-bodhi-sattva,** mfn. exceeding a Bodhi-sattva, Mālatīm. **Ati-bhāra,** (also) excess; *-bhūta,* mfn. exceeding, surpassing (gen.), Bcar. ii, 2. **Ati-manoratha-krama,** m. excess of desire, ib. v, 35. **Ati-māya,** mfn. past illusion, Kir. **Ati-māla,** mfn. excelling a necklace (in beauty), Laghuk. 1017. **Ati-mukti,** f. (also) a partic. class of oblations, ĀpŚr. **Ati-yātrā,** f. passing over, Saṃk.; fare for crossing (?), Divyâv. **Ati-rātra-yājin,** m. N. of a dramatic author (of the 16th century A.D.). **Ati-roká,** m. a passage for light, vista, MaitrS. **Ati-vara,** m. an extra donation, ĀpŚr. **Ati-vīrya-prabha,** m. N. of a Tathā-gata, Sukh. i. **Ati-vyasta,** mfn. too widely separated, TPrāt. **Ati-śaṅsana,** n. (Vait.), °*nā,* f. (AitĀr.) continued recitation. **Atiśaya** (in comp.); *-vat,* mfn. excessive, Daś.; °*śayôpamā,* f. (in rhet.) an exaggerated simile, Kāvyâd. **Ati-śāta,** mfn. causing great joy, delightful, Gīt. **Ati-śrama,** see *śramâpanayana* (p. 1096). **Ati-sarasvatī,** f. a partic. personification, MānGṛ. **Ati-sarga,** (also) remnant, Divyâv. **Ati-sāra,** (also) transgression (in *sâti-s*°), ib. **Ati-sitâṅga-vihaṃga,** m. a swan, Śiś. **Ati-suhita,** mfn. perfectly satiated, ĀpŚr.

Ati-svinna, mfn. caused to perspire abundantly, Suśr. **Ati-hasita,** n. (in rhet.) excessive or foolish laughter, Sāh. **Ati-hāra,** m. addition, SaṃhUp. **Atīkāśá,** m. brightness, lustre, TS.; an aperture, ib. **Atī-cāra,** m. = *ati-c°* (p. 13). **Á-tīrṇa,** mfn. not crossed, endless, RV. **Á-tīrtha,** n. a wrong way or manner (*ena,* 'not in the right or usual manner'), ŚBr.; Lāṭy.; unseasonable time, BhP. **Atī-vāda,** m. = *ati-vāda,* Vait. **Atīśa,** m. N. of a learned Buddhist (the re-founder of Lāmism), MWB. 273. **A-tulya-prabha,** m. = *amitâbha,* Sukh. i. **A-taijasa,** mfn. not made of metal, Mn. vi, 53. **Á́t-ka,** (accord. to some also = *tejas*). **Attrīṇi,** m. or f. (said to be fr. √*ad*) a kind of worm, L. **Á́tya,** (also) mfn. rapid, swift, RV. ii, 34, 13. **Aty-akshara,** mfn. inarticulate, MānGṛ. **Aty-antaśas,** ind. in an exaggerated manner, excessively, Baudh. **Aty-aya,** m. (also) confession of sins, Lalit. **Atyayika-piṇḍa-pāta,** m. special or occasional alms (of 5 kinds), Divyâv. **Aty-ākhaṇḍala-vikrama,** mfn. surpassing Indra in heroism, Ragh. **Aty-āyus,** mfn. very old, Veṇīs. **Aty-urvīśa,** m. a supreme sovereign, VarBṛS. **Aty-ūrjitam,** ind. very much, in a high degree, Mālatīm. **Aty-ūrdhvâksha,** mfn. with uplifted eyes, TĀr. **Aty-ūha,** m. (also) the penis of an elephant, L. **Aty-ṛishabha,** m. an excellent bull (applied to Prajā-pati), Hir. **Atyetavai,** see *atī* (p. 16). **Atra-sad,** mfn. sitting here, JaimUp. **A-trasyat,** mfn. not trembling, W.; not having a flaw (as a gem), Śiś. iv, 53. **A-trāsita,** mfn. not frightened, Veṇīs. **A-trirātra-yājin,** mfn. not taking part in the Trirātra sacrifice, Drāhy. **A-tvara,** mfn. not hasty, deliberate, Yājñ.; MBh. **A-tsaruka,** mfn. (a vessel) having no handle, TāṇḍyaBr. **Atharí,** (accord. to some) an elephant, RV. iv, 6, 8. **Atharví,** (accord. to some) fiery (cf. *Viśpalā* below), RV. i, 112, 10. **A-daṇḍa,** mfn. having no handle, Āpast. **A-daṇḍana,** n. not punishing, Yājñ. **A-dattâdāna,** n. stealing (with Buddhists one of the ten sins), Dharmas. 56. **A-dattâdāyika** (Divyâv.) and *°dāyin* (Mn.), m. a thief. **A-danta-jāta,** mfn. one who has not teethed, ĀśvGṛ. **A-dantâghātin,** mfn. not striking against the teeth (as a sound), Lāṭy. **Á-dabdha-cakshus,** mfn. one whose eyes do not fail, AV. **A-dayīya** (p. 18, col. 2, l. 1 read *a-dasīya*). **A-daridra,** mf(*ā*)n. having no beggars, Kathās. **A-darśana-patha,** (also) non-admission to (the king's) presence (?), disgrace, Divyâv. **A-darśanī-√bhū,** to become invisible, Pañcat. **Adás,** (also) then, AV. xii, 1, 55. **Á-dasta,** mfn. unexhausted, imperishable, TBr.; Kāṭh. **A-dākshiṇātya,** m. pl. 'not Southerners,' the Gauḍas, Kāvyâd. **A-dānava,** m. 'not a Dānava,' a god, MBh. **A-dāniya,** mfn. unworthy of a gift, ĀpŚr. **A-dāny̆á** (read, 'not deserving a gift'). 2. **A-dāmán,** mfn. unbound, RV. vi, 24, 4. **Á-dāsyat,** mfn. not wishing to give, AV. **Aditi-kuṇḍalâharaṇa,** n. N. of a Nāṭaka by Kādamba. **Á-dipsat,** mfn. not wishing to injure, AV. **A-divā** (in comp.); *°vâsin,* not eating by day, Āpast.; *°vā-svāpin,* not sleeping by day, ib. **A-dīna-gātratā,** f. having no defective members (one of the 80 minor marks of a Buddha), Dharmas. 84. **A-dīrgha-darśin,** mfn. not far-sighted, Bcar. **A-duḥkha-sukha-vedanā,** f. the non-perception of either pain or pleasure, Sukh. i. **A-duhāna,** mfn. yielding no milk, KātyŚr. **A-deśika,** mfn. guideless, homeless, MBh. **A-deha,** m. 'bodiless,' the god of love, Gal. **A-daiteya,** m. 'not a Daiteya,' a god, Hariv. **A-dosha,** mfn. faultless, guiltless, Ragh.; Kathās.; *-darśin,* mfn. seeing or thinking no harm, Bcar. **Adbhuta** (in comp.); *-kṛishṇa-rāja* (or *Kṛ°*?), N. of a chief, Inscr.; *-darpaṇa,* N. of a Nāṭaka; *-raṅga,* N. of a Prahasana; *°târtha,* mfn. containing wonderful things, Kāvyâd.; *°tôtpāta,* m. pl. miracles and prodigies, ApGṛ.; *°bhutôpamā,* f. (in rhet.) a simile implying a miracle, ib. **Adma-sád,** (also) a fly (= *makshikā*), Nir., Sch. **Adya** (in comp.); *-tas,* ind. from to-day, Dhūrtan.; *-tva,* n. the present time, Pat.; *-yajña,* m. to-day's sacrifice, ĀpŚr., Sch. **Adyâgreṇa,** ind. henceforth, Divyâv. **A-dyotaka,** mfn. not expressing or denoting, Pāṇ. i, 4, 93, Sch. **Adri-dhṛit,** m. 'mountain-holder,' N. of Kṛishṇa (cf. *govardhana,* p. 366), L. **Adri-bhedana,** n. the splitting of the Soma stone, KātyŚr. **A-druta,** mfn. not accelerated, TPrāt. **A-dvaya-vāda,** m. assertion of non-duality, Naish. **A-dvādaśâha,** mfn. not twelve days old, ŚāṅkhŚr. **A-dvi-yoni,** mfn. not produced by two (vowels), not diphthongal, RPrāt. **A-dvi-varsha,** mfn. not two years old, PārGṛ. **A-dvīpa,** mf(*ā*)n. having no refuge or protector, Kāraṇḍ. **A-dvaita** (in comp.); *-dīpikā,* f., *-brahma-siddhi,* f., *-makaranda,* m. N. of wks.; *-vādin,* m. (also) N. of Śaṃkara, Gal.; of Buddha, Divyâv. **A-dvaitin,** m. 'non-dualist,' an adherent of Śaṃkara, Sāṃkhyas., Sch. **Adha-īsha,** n. draught-cattle, TS. **Adhaḥ** (in comp. for *adhas*); *-kumba,* mf(*ā*)n. having the thick end downwards, ĀpŚr., Sch.; *-khāta,* mfn. dug deep (as a furrow), Vishṇ.; *-śāyin,* mfn. lying on the ground (*°yi-tā,* f.), Gaut.; *-saṃveśin,* mfn. id., Lāṭy.; *-sthānâsana,* mfn. standing or sitting lower, Gaut. **Adhamâdhama,** mfn. lowest of all, Pañcat. **Adhara** (in comp.); *-dala,* n. a lip, Kpr.; *-mūla* (*ádh°*), mfn. having the roots downwards, ŚBr.; *-rucaka,* n. lovely lips, Kād.; *°râmbara,* n. (ifc. f. *ā*) an under-garment, Śiś.; *°rôshṭha-rucaka,* n. lovely lips, R. **Adharima,** mfn. lowest, Divyâv. **Adharma** (in comp.); *-caraṇa,* n. (Gaut.), *-caryā,* f. (Āpast.) practice of wickedness, injustice; *°mâstikāya* (accord. to some Jaina authorities, 'the category which is the determinant cause of rest'); *°môttaratā,* f. prevalence of injustice, MBh. **Adhastān** (in comp. for *°stāt*); *-nābhi,* ind. below the navel, MaitrS.; *-nirbādham* (*adhástān-*), ind. (with the knobs) turned downwards, ŚBr. **Á-dhārayamāṇa,** mfn. not resisting, ŚBr. **A-dhārāgraha,** m. a ladleful or cupful not drawn from flowing water, ĀpŚr. **Adhâsana-śāyin,** mfn. (for *adha-ās°*) sitting or lying on the ground, Āpast. **Adhi-kaṇṭham,** ind. on or round the neck, Mālatīm.; Naish. **Adhikaraṇa-lekhaka,** m. a clerk at a hall of justice, Kād. **Adhi-karṇam,** ind. on the ear, Śiś. **Adhi-kalpin,** (accord. to others, 'supreme umpire'). **Adhika-vayas,** mfn. advanced in age, Veṇīs. **Adhi-kashṭa,** n. great misery, BhP. **Adhikâkshara,** mfn. having a redundant syllable, Nir. **Adhikâdhi,** mfn. full of sorrow, Daś. **Adhikāra** (in comp.); *-purusha,* m. an official, Ragh.; *-vat,* m. id., Mudr.; *-saṃgraha,* m. N. of a wk. on Bhakti (Rāmānuja school). **Adhikāraka,** mfn. introductory, TPrāt. **Adhi-√kṛi,** Ā. *-kurute,* (also) to define, Bcar. xii, 36. **Adhi-ketanam,** ind. on a flag, Śiś. **Adhikôpama,** mfn. containing a redundant simile, Sarasv. **Adhi-kshiti,** ind. on the earth, Naish. **Adhi-gopam,** ind. on a cowherd, Laghuk. 970. **Adhi-goptṛi,** see *dhanâdh°*. **Adhi-cara,** mfn. redundant, superfluous, ŚāṅkhBr. **Adhicitta-śikshā,** f. (with Buddhists) training in higher thought (one of the 3 kinds of training), Dharmas. 140. **Adhi-jaṅgham,** ind. on the legs, Naish. **Adhi-jarāyu,** f. (a cow) having the after-birth in itself or part of it, AV. Paipp. **Adhi-√jāgṛi** (only *-jāgarat*), to watch over (loc.), Hir. **Adhi-√ji** (Prec. 1. pl. *-jīyāsma*), to overcome, Bhaṭṭ. **Adhi-jigāṃsu,** mfn. (fr. Desid. of *adhi-√gam*) wishing to learn, HPariś. **Adhi-daivatya,** n. the highest divine rank among (abl.), MaitrUp. **Adhi-dyo,** f. (nom. *aus*) a kind of brick, MaitrS. **Adhi-nāgam,** ind. 'on elephants' and 'on snakes,' Śiś. **Adhi-niśam,** ind. by night, ib. **Adhi-paśya,** m. an overseer, AV. Paipp. **Adhi-pāṇi,** ind. in the hand, Kir. **Adhi-pāśa,** m. a short stick, Kauś. **Adhi-prajñam,** ind. with regard to knowledge, KaṭhUp. **Adhi-prajñā-śikshā,** f. (with Buddhists) training in higher knowledge, Dharmas. 140. **Adhi-bala,** n. (in dram.) a violent altercation, Bhar.; Daśar.; Sāh.; pursuing an aim by an indirect course, ib. **Adhi-makham,** ind. in regard to a sacrifice, BhP. **Adhi-mitra,** n. an occasional friend (*-tā,* f.), VarBṛS. **Adhi-mukta,** mfn. also 'intent on,' Divyâv.; m. a partic. Samādhi, Kāraṇḍ. **Adhi-moksha,** m. = *adhi-mukti,* Buddh. **Adhi-yoga,** m. a partic. constellation, VarBṛS. **Adhi-rajani,** ind. by night, Śiś. **Adhi-ruh,** (ifc.) mounting or riding on, ib. **Adhi-rūḍhaka,** m. a parasitical plant, Hcat. **Adhi-rūḍhā,** f. (also) a woman from her 33rd to her 50th year, Bhpr. **Adhi-rūḍhi,** f. becoming thicker upwards, Naith. **Adhi-rodhavya,** n. (impers.) it is to be mounted on (loc.), Kathās. **Adhi-ropaṇa,** (also) transferring to (loc.), Sarasv. **Adhi-laṅkam,** ind. over Laṅkā, Mcar. **Adhi-√2. luṭh** (P. *-luṭhati*), to leap up and down, spring about, Bālar. x, 54. **Adhi-vakshas,** ind. on the breast, Śiś. **Adhi-varcas,** n. a latrine (v. l. *°rca*), Gobh. **Adhi-varjana,** n. placing near the fire, Sāy. **Adhi-vartana.** n. rolling on, Āpast. **Adhi-√5. vas** (Caus. *-vāsayati*), to accept (esp. an invitation), Divyâv. **Adhi-vasati,** f. a dwelling, habitation, Sāh. **Adhi-vāsanā,** f. obedience, compliance, Lalit. **Adhi-vāsanīya,** mfn. to be consecrated (cf. 1. *adhi-vāsana,* p. 22), Hcat. **Adhi-vāha,** m. the leader of a team, Kuval. **Adhi-vivāham,** ind. with regard to marriage, GṛS. **Adhi-vīra,** m. the chief hero among (comp.), Uttamac. **Adhi-vṛiksha-sūrye,** ind. when the sun is (still) shining on the tops of trees (*°rya-,* in comp.), Gaut. **Adhi-veśma,** in the house, Śiś. **Adhi-vyatikrama,** m. passing over or through (comp.), ĀpGṛ. **Adhi-vrata,** n. anything accessory to a vow or observance, MaitrS. **Adhi-śiras,** ind. on the head, Kauś. **Adhi-śirodharam,** ind. on the neck, Kir. **Adhi-śīla-śikshā,** f. (with Buddhists) training in higher morality (cf. *adhicitta-ś°* above), Dharmas. 140. **Adhi-śrī,** mfn. being at the height of fortune or glory, Kālid. **Adhi-śrotram,** ind. over the ears, Rājat. **Adhi-shavaṇa-phalaka,** n. du. N. of two boards used in pressing the Soma, ŚrS. **Adhi-shādam,** ind. sitting down upon, Kāṭh. **Adhi-shṭhā** (√*sthā*; P. *-tishṭhati*), to bless (?), Divyâv. **Adhishṭhāna,** (also, with Buddhists) steadfast resolution (one of the 6 or 10 Pāramitās, q. v.) MWB. 128; a king's court, Divyâv. **Adhi-shṭhita** (in Bhag. xiii, 17, the text has *dhi-shṭhita,* with elision of *a*). **Adhi-senāpati,** f. the chief commander of an army, MBh. **Adhi-syada,** mfn. very swift, Kir. **Adhi-hastya,** n. a present &c. held in the hand, Āpast. **Adhī-kshepa,** m. = *adhi-ksh°,* Hāla, Sch. **A-dhīta-rasa,** mfn. having the juice not sucked out, AitBr. **Adhī-vāsa,** m. = *adhi-v°,* MBh. **Adhîśitṛi,** m. a chief lord, Śiś. **Adhîsh** (*adhi-√3. ish,* Ā. *adhy-eshate*), to seek, Divyâv. **A-dhūnvat,** mfn. not moving, not agitating, ib. **Adho** (in comp. for *adhas*); *-'ṃśuka,* n. a lower garment, L.; *-nāpita,* m. the son of a Karaṇa and an Ambashṭhā (who catches fish), L.; *-nivīta,* mfn. having the sacred thread hanging down, ĀśvGṛ. (cf. IW. 196); *-nīvī,* f. having the girdle slipped down, MBh.; *-bāṇa,* m. N. of a mountain, Divyâv.; *-mayūkha,* mfn. shining downwards, Kum.; *-vāsas,* n. an under garment, Mahān. **Adhy-adhvam,** ind. on the road, Śiś. **Adhyayana,** also going over, recitation, repetition (of the Veda &c.); *-saṃvṛitti,* f. community of occupation in reciting (the Veda &c.), Āpast. **Adhy-ardhôpā,** f. an Ūpā and a half, Drāhy., Sch. **Adhy-avasāya,** (also) clinging to (earthly things), Divyâv. **Adhy-avaseya,** mfn. only to be conceived in the mind, Buddh. **Adhy-ākāśam,** ind. in the air, Śiś. **Adhy-ākramaṇa,** n. stepping over, Jātakam. **Adhy-ācāra,** m. reach, range, PārGṛ. **Adhy-ājya,** mfn. sprinkled with ghee, MānGṛ. **Adhyātma-cintāmaṇi,** m. N. of a Vedānta wk. **Adhyāyôpâkarman,** n. the opening ceremony of the annual course of Vedic recitation, Hir. **Adhy-ārohaṇa,** n. ascending, Svapnac. **Adhy-āśaya,** m. inclination, disposition, Lalit.; an imagination, Bcar. i, 9; purpose, Divyâv. **Adhy-āsyā,** f. (scil. *ṛic*) an additional verse, Lāṭy. **Adhy-āhāriṇī,** f. (with *lipi*) a kind of written character (v. l. *madhyāh°,* q. v.), Lalit. **Adhy-ud-√yam,** to put down, BaudhP. **Adhy-upêksh** (*-upa-√īksh;* P. *-upêkshati*), to disregard, Divyâv. **Adhy-upêkshā,** f. disregard, neglect, indifference, Jātakam. **Adhy-uras,** ind. on the breast, Śiś. **Adhy-usha,** m. a kind of measure (= two Prasritas, q. v.), L. 1. **Adhyeya,** mfn. (it is) to be studied or learned (n. impers.), Mn.; Naish. 2. **A-dhyeya,** mfn. not to be thought of, Hcat. **Adhy-ôḍha,** m. = *adhy-ūḍha,* MBh. **Adhri** (AV. v, 20, 10 read *adri* with the MSS.; *grâvā ádriḥ* = 'press-stone'). **Adhva** (in comp. for *adhvan*); *-gacchat,* m. a traveller, Jātakam.; *-gaṇa,* m. (perhaps for *adhvaga-gaṇa*) a crowd of travellers, Divyâv.; *-gati,* m. travelling, a journey, Sāh.; *-darśin,* m. 'way-indicator,' a leader, guide, Daś.; *-loshṭa,* n. a clod from the road, MānGṛ.; *-śīla,* mfn. fond of travelling, Āpast.; *-śrama,* m. fatigue of travel, Megh.; *-saha,* m. an indefatigable traveller, VarBṛS.; *°dhvâpanna,* mfn. one who has started on a journey, Āpast. **Adhvará-kalpa,** mfn. equivalent to a sacrifice called Adhvara, MaitrS. **Adhvara-guru,** m. N. of Vishṇu, Vishṇ. **Adhvara-śrī,** (accord. to some) turning towards the sacrifice, RV. i, 47, 8 &c. **A-dhvarás,** mfn. = *adhvara,* ŚBr. **A-dhvartavyà,** mfn. not to be bent or broken, TS. **Adhvaryu** (in comp.); *-patha,* m. the path on which the Adhvaryu priest walks up to the fire, ŚrS.; *-pātrá,* n. the vessel of the Adhvaryu priest, MaitrS. 1. **Adhvāna,** m. = *adhvan,* MBh. 2. **A-dhvāna,** m. uttering no sound, silence (°*nam gataḥ*, 'become silent'), Mṛicch. 1. **Anaka,** mfn. (for *aṇaka*) inferior (cf. *rājâṇaka*). **A'n-akshita,** mfn. unmarked (see √*aksh*), MaitrS. **Anaṅga** (in comp.); *-bhīma*, m. N. of two kings, Inscr.; *-maṅgala*, N. of a Bāṇa by Sundara Kavi; *-latikā*, f. N. of Nāṭaka; *-vidyā*, f. (= *kāma-śāstra*), Daś.; *-harsha*, m. N. of a dramatic poet, Cat. **An-aṅgushṭha,** mfn. without the thumb, Gaut. **Ana-ḍud** (in comp. for °*ḍuh*); *-arha*, mfn. worth an ox, ĀpŚr.; *-yajña*, m. a sacrifice for oxen, MānGṛ. **A'n-atidagdha,** mfn. not burned all over, ŚBr. **A'n-atidāha,** m. not too much burning, ib. **A'n-atidṛiśna,** mfn. = (or w. r. for) *an-atidṛiśyá*, TS. **An-atipraśnyá,** mfn. not to be too much questioned about, BṛĀrUp. **A'n-atimānin,** mfn. not too self-conceited, ŚBr. **A'n-atisṛishṭa,** mfn. not allowed, AV. **An-adhîtya,** mfn. without going over or repeating, Mn. ii, 168. **An-adhîyat** (AitĀr.), °**yāna** (Āpast.), mfn. not repeating or learning. **An-adhîshṭa,** mfn. not asked for instruction, Divyâv. **An-adhyavasita,** mfn. irresolute, Jātakam. **An-adhyâtmavid,** mfn. not knowing the Supreme Spirit, Mn. vi, 82. **An-adhyāya,** (also) non-recitation, silence, Naish. **An-adhyāsa,** mf(*ā*)n. without an addition or appendix, Lāṭy. **An-anuyoga,** mfn. not inquired after, Āpast. **An-anuvākya,** mfn. not teaching recitation of the Veda, Vishṇ. **An-anûtthāna,** n. the not following, Kum. **An-antaḥpādam,** ind. not within the Pāda of a verse, Pāṇ. iii, 2, 66. **An-antara,** m. (also) the next (younger) brother after (abl.), MBh. **A'n-antarhiti,** f. the not being covered or concealed, MaitrS. **Ananta-śāyin,** m. 'reclining on (the serpent) Ananta,' N. of Vishṇu, L. **Ananya** (in comp.); *-kārya*, mfn. having no other business, Ragh.; *-parâyaṇa*, mfn. devoted to no other, Śak.; *-rādhas*, mfn. striving after nothing else, BhP.; *-vandin*, mfn. not praising anybody else, Kum. **A'n-anvagbhāva,** m. the not following after, MaitrS. **A'n-anvavajaya,** m. the not winning subsequently, ib. **A'n-anvāgata,** mfn. not visited or attacked by (instr.), ŚBr. **An-anvāgama,** m. the not going after, JaimUp. **An-apakshepyá,** mfn. not to be rejected, MaitrS. **An-apacâyitṛi,** mfn. not revering, ŚāṅkhBr. **A'n-apacāyyamāna,** mfn. not being revered, TBr. **An-apatrapā,** f. shamelessness, Dharmas. 69. **An-apadoshyá,** mfn. not to be wasted, MaitrS. **An-aparuddha,** mfn. unexcluded, JaimUp. **An-apâya-dṛishṭa,** mfn. free from all visible danger, secure, Bcar. ii, 42. **A'n-apinaddha,** mfn. unbound, ŚBr. **A-napuṇsaka,** n. not neuter, Pāṇ. **A'n-apêkshamāṇa,** mfn. not looking about, ŚBr. **An-abhigata,** mfn. not understood, ŚBr. **A'n-abhijita,** mfn. not (yet) won, TS. **An-abhilulita,** mfn. not pressed upon (v. l. for *an-atil*°), Śak. **An-abhiśasti,** mfn. = °*sti*, Hir. **An-abhishekya** (Drāhy.), °**shecanîya** (ŚBr.), mfn. not worthy of inauguration. **An-abhihitavācya,** omission of a particle required by the sense, Kpr. **A'n-abhyavacāruka,** mfn. not rushing against, MaitrS. **A-nama,** mf(*ā*)n. not to be overthrown, Śiś. **An-amin,** mfn. not ill, Nalac. **An-ambu,** m. 'waterless,' the bird Cātaka, L. **An-artha** (in comp.); *-kāma*, mfn. wishing evil to (gen.), Bcar.; *-bhīru*, mfn. afraid of evil, ib.; °*thâvêksha*, mfn. regardless of (worldly) objects, ĀpGṛ. **An-ardhuka,** mfn. not fulfilling wishes, Gobh. **Anarmán,** w. r. for *an-arvan*, AV. vii, 7, 1. **A-narman,** mfn. 'not (merely) jocular,' sarcastic, ironical, MBh. 1. **Anala** (in comp.); *-sakha*, m. 'fire's friend,' the wind, ib.; °*lânanda*, read *amal*°; °*lôpala*, m. 'fire-stone,' crystal, L. 2. **Anala,** Nom. P. °*lati*, to become fire, Subh. **An-alam,** (also) unable to (inf.), Śiś. **Analāya,** Nom. Ā. °*yate*, to be or act like fire, Kathās. **A'n-avagata,** mfn. not acquired, TS. **An-avagîta,** (also) not become tedious, Jātakam. **A'n-avacchitti,** f. uninterruptedness, TBr. **An-avadânîya** (or °*nîyá*), f. not fit for distribution, MaitrS.; TBr. **An-avama-darśin,** m. N. of one of the 24 mythical Buddhas, MWB. 136, n. 1. **An-avarâgra,** mfn. without beginning or end (?), Divyâv. **A'n-avaruddha,** mfn. not fallen to the share of, not given or accorded to (gen.), ŚBr. **An-avarodhya,** mfn. not to be constrained or forced, Gaut. **An-avarṇa,** mfn. not ugly, fair, beautiful, TĀr. **An-avarti,** mfn. not being in need, TāṇḍBr. **An-avalopa,** mfn. not fallen short of, ib. **An-avasnātā,** f. a woman that has not (yet) bathed (i. e. has not yet had her monthly courses), ĀpGṛ. **A-navîkṛita,** 'non-innovation,' (in rhet.) motonony in the construction of a phrase, Kpr. **A'n-avṛitta** (p. 28, col. 3), read *A'n-āvṛitta*. **An-avêkshitam,** ind. without looking at, Gobh. **A'n-avêta,** mfn. not gone away or run off, TS. **A'n-avêshṭa,** mfn. not averted by sacrifice, MaitrS. **A-nashṭa,** n. 'I hope you have not lost anything' (used in greeting a Vaiśya), Āpast. **Anasvin,** mfn. going in a cart, TS. **Anaha,** mfn. (said to be fr. √*an*) breathing freely, healthy, well (= *nīroga*), L. **A'n-āktâksha,** mfn. not having the eyes anointed, AV. **An-ākshepam,** ind. without reproaching (loc.), Bcar. vi, 51. **An-ākhyāya,** ind. without telling, Mn. viii, 224. **An-āgarta,** mfn. without holes (?), BaudhP. **An-āgāmin** (see MWB. 133). **An-ācîrṇa,** mfn. not undertaken before, R. **A'n-āchṛiṇṇa,** read *án-ācch*° (p. 27). **Anāṭa,** m. (said to be fr. √*an*, but prob. for *an-āṭa*, 'not walking') a child or any young woman (= *śiśu*), L. **An-ātmatā,** f. want of common sense, Pārv. **An-ātman,** (also) unreal, Divyâv. **An-ādarâkshepa,** m. (in rhet.) objection to anything by feigned indifference, Kāvyâd. ii, 140. **An-ādi,** (also) ind. perpetually, incessantly, Naish. **An-āntarīyaka,** mfn. immediate, ĀpGṛ., Sch. **An-āpatti,** mfn. guiltless, Divyâv. **A'n-āprīta,** mfn. not consecrated with the Āprī verses, ŚBr.; untouched by water, i. e. not used before (as a water-vessel), GṛS. **An-ābhogá,** mfn. having or offering no enjoyments, TĀr. **An-āyatana,** (also) groundless, Divyâv. **A'n-āyuvāna,** mfn. not drawing in (the wings), ŚBr. **An-ārūḍhá,** mfn. not contained in, Kap., Sch.; not fallen into (acc.), Veṇīs. **An-āroka,** mfn. without interstices, dense, MānŚr. **A-nāla,** mfn. having no stalk, Śiś. **An-ālabdha,** mfn. not taken hold of, MBh.; not killed, ŚBr. **An-ālayana,** mfn. abodeless, JaimUp. **An-āviddha,** (also) not containing long compounds, Vām. i, 3, 25. **An-āvṛita,** (also) unlimited, free, MBh. **An-āvṛitti-bhaya,** mfn. having no fear of return to worldly existence, Kum. **An-āśakin,** m. 'not eating,' an ascetic, L. **An-āśita,** mfn. one who has not eaten, hungry, R. **An-āśvāsika,** mfn. untrustworthy, Divyâv. **An-āsaṅga,** m. uncertainty, Mālatīm. **An-āstika,** mfn. atheistic, MBh.; °*kya*, n. atheism, ib. **An-āstha,** mfn. indifferent, Bcar.; Kathās. **An-āsrava,** mfn. free from mundane inclinations, Lalit.; *-prakāra*, mfn. free from the various kinds of m° incl°, Bcar. v, 10. **A'n-āhita,** mfn. not kindled (as fire), MaitrS. **Ani,** m. the pin of an axle tree (cf. *aṇi*), L. **A-nihshṭubdha,** mfn. unhallowed, ĀpŚr. **A-nikāsham,** ind. without rubbing out, ĀpŚr. **A-nikṛiti,** f. honesty, MBh. **A-nikshipya,** mfn. without having deposited, Mn. viii, 191. **A-nigupta,** mfn. not hidden or concealed, generally open or accessible, Hir. **An-iṅgana,** mfn. immovable, MāṇḍUp., Sch. **A'n-iṅgyamāna,** mfn. not being shaken or moved, ŚBr. **A-nicaya,** m. not storing up, Gaut.; mfn. having no stores, ib. **An-iṭ-kārikā,** f. pl. N. of 11 gram. Kārikās (as given in Kāś.). **A'n-itthaṃ-vid,** mfn. not knowing thus, ŚBr. **A-nidāgha-dīdhiti,** m. the moon, Śiś. **A-nipāna,** n. not drinking, thirst, BhP. **A-nibandhana,** mfn. causeless, accidental, Uttarar. **A-nibhṛita,** mfn. violently moved or shaken, Jātakam.; violent, intense, strong, ib. **A-nimitta,** (also) m. (scil. *vimoksha*) unconditioned salvation (with Buddhists one of the three kinds of s°), Dharmas. 73; n. a bad omen, Mṛicch.; *-lipi*, f. a partic. mode of writing, Jaim. **A-nimisha,** (also) m. N. of Vishṇu, RTL. 106, n. 1. **A-nimishita,** mfn. = *a-nimisha*, Daś. **A-niyantraṇam,** ind. unconstrainedly, freely; °*ṇânuyoga*, mfn. to be questioned unreservedly, Śak. **A-niyamôpamā,** f. (in rhet.) a kind of simile (in which the Upamāna is not restricted to a certain person or thing), Kāvyâd. ii, 20. **A'-niyasita,** mfn. relaxed, ŚBr. **A'-niraśita,** mfn. not eaten up, ŚBr. **A-nirākaraṇa,** n. the not forgetting, PārGṛ.; °*karishṇu*, mfn. not forgetting, ib.; °*âkṛitin*, mfn. one who does not forget what he has learned, ĀśvŚr. **A-niruddha,** m. (also) N. of various writers (esp. of the author of a Comm. on the Sāṃkhya-sūtras, about 1500 A.D.). **A-nirghātya,** mfn. not to be brought out by force, Suśr. **A-nirdaya,** (in comp.) tenderly, softly, Śak. **A'-nirdāhuka,** mfn. not burning or scorching, MaitrS. **A'-nirmārga,** m. not wiping off, ib. **A-nirvartin,** (also) unalterable, MBh. **A-nirvāpa,** m. N. of Bṛihaspati, L. **A-nirvāhaṇa-śīla,** mfn. not disposed to accomplish anything, irresolute, Mṛicch. **A-nirvedita,** mfn. not depressed, self-reliant, bold, Mṛicch. **A'-nirhata,** mfn. not expelled from (abl.), ŚBr. **A-nila,** (also) a kind of sword, L.; °*lâśana*, m. 'air-eater,' a serpent, MBh.; °*lâhata*, mfn. moved by the wind, Bcar. **A-nilambha,** m. a kind of meditation, Buddh. **A-niveshṭyamāna,** mfn. not being fettered or hindered, ŚāṅkhBr. **A-niśānta,** mfn. unextinguished, Śiś. **A-niścara,** mfn. not wavering, firm, resolute, Divyâv. **A-niśceya,** mfn. not to be decided or ascertained, Sāy. **An-ishucārin,** mfn. one who does not go hunting with arrows (but with snares), Gaut. **An-ishṭaká,** mfn. without bricks, ŚBr. **An-ishṭa-yajña,** mfn. one who has not sacrificed (with success), GopBr. **A-nishpanna,** mfn. not become ripe (*-tva*, n.), Pāṇ. iii, 3, 133, Vārtt. 2. **A-nisṛishṭa,** mfn. not allowed, unauthorized, Mn. ii, 205. **A-nistishṭhat,** mfn. not bringing to an end, ChUp. **An-iha,** mfn. one who has or knows no 'here,' Āpast. **A-nihita,** mfn. not set down, KātyŚr.; not ending with a consonant, VPrāt. **A-nihūta,** mfn. (prob. w. r. for *anu-hūta*, 'called after'), Hir. **Anī,** f. the double panel of a door (cf. *aṇi*, *aṇī*, p. 11), L. **An-īkshaka,** mfn. not seeing, blind, Jātakam. **A-nīcaistana,** mfn. not low, Dharmaś. **An-īrita,** mfn. unstirred, Bcar. **A-nīla,** mfn. white, Jātakam.; m. N. of a serpent demon, MBh. **An-īhamāna,** mfn. not exerting one's self, indifferent, Mn. iv, 22. **Anu-kaccham,** ind. along or on the shore, Megh. **Anu-kaṇṭhī,** f. a necklace consisting of one string, L. **Anu-kanakhalam,** ind. over Kanakhala, Megh. **Anu-kampya,** m. (also) a relative, friend, ĀpGṛ. **Anu-karshaṇa,** (also) a drinking vessel, L. **Anu-kalám,** ind. by the sixteenth (part), ŚBr. **Anu-**√**3. kā,** P. *-kāyati* = *abhidhatte*, Pat. **Anu-kāra,** (also) dancing, a dance, Harav. **An-ukta-siddhi,** f. (in dram.) a veiled or indirect compliment, Bhar.; Sāh. **Anu-krośâkshepa,** m. (in rhet.) an objection based on compassion or sympathy, Kāvyâd. ii. 158. **Anu-krośin,** mfn. compassionate, sympathetic, ĀśvŚr. **Anu-gaṇḍikā,** f. a chain of hills, MBh. **Anu-gantī,** f. (for *anu-gantrī*?) a message, Divyâv. **Anu-gara,** m. invitation addressed to a reciter, Kāś. on Pāṇ. i, 4, 41. **Anu-**√**1. gā,** (also) to undergo, MBh. iii, 373. **Anu-gāna,** n. 'after-song,' (*-śas*, ind.), SāmavBr. **Anu-gāpana,** n. causing to sing after, Gobh. **Anu-gīta,** mfn. (also) sung after, JaimUp.; n. an imitative song, Ratnâv. **Anu-geya,** mfn. to be sung after, Gobh. **Anu-goptṛi,** m. a protector, defender, R. **Anu-grahaṇa,** (also) practising, practice, MBh.; °*grahîtṛi*, m. a favourer, furtherer, Śaṃk. **Anu-ghaṭana,** n. continuation (of a tale), Kād. **Anu-caraṇa,** n. going after, wandering, Kauś.; *-carita*, n. acts, deeds, adventures, BhP. **An-uccalat,** mfn. not moving or going from (abl.), Śak. **Anujā-sutā,** f. the son of a younger sister, Bcar. **Anu-jñâkshepa,** m. (in rhet.) an objection expressed by a feigned consent, Kāvyâd. ii, 136. **Anu-jñāpana,** (also) taking leave, Siṇhâs.; asking l°, ĀpŚr., Sch.; °*jñāpya*, mfn. to be allowed or permitted, Pañcad. **Anu-tarsha,** m. 'thirst' and 'an intoxicating drink,' Śiś. x, 2. **Anu-tāpaka,** mf(*ikā*)n. causing repentance, Naish. **Anu-tāpâṅka,** N. of a drama. **Anu-tishṭhāsu,** mfn. intending to perform anything, Kull. on Mn. ii, 104. **Anu-toda,** m. repetition (of a song), TāṇḍBr.; n. (with *Gautamasya*) N. of a Sāman, ĀrshBr. **A'-nutta,** (accord. to some) = *ánu-tta* (for *anu-datta*), admitted. **An-uttaraṃga,** mfn. not surging or billowy, Kum. **An-uttara-pūjā,** f. (with Buddhists) highest worship (of seven kinds; cf. *vandana*), Dharmas. 14. **An-uttuṇḍita,** mfn. not having the front protruding, Suśr. **An-utpattika-dharma-kshānti,** f. (with Buddhists) resignation to consequences which have not yet arisen, Sukh. i (cf. Dharmas. 107). **An-utpāda,** (also) mfn. having no origin, Sukh. i. **An-utpūta,** mfn. not completely purified, MānGṛ. **A'n-utsikta,** mfn. not overflown or filled up, ŚBr. **An-utsṛishṭa,** mfn. not letting loose a sacrificial victim, ĀśvGṛ.; not discontinued, incessantly celebrated, TāṇḍBr. **An-uda-pāna,** n. 'non-water-drinking,' thirst, BhP. **Anu-darśa,** m. representation, admonition, MBh. **An-udgṛihṇat,** mfn. not ceasing, AitĀr. **An-udghāta,** m. no blow or jolt or jerk, Kālid. **An-uddhāna,** n. non-abandonment, TāṇḍBr. **Anu-dravaṇa,** n. quick recitation, ĀśvŚr., Sch. **Anu-drashṭavyà** (ŚBr.). **A'n-udvāta,** mfn. unextinguished, TBr. **Anu-dvāra,** mfn. having a door or entrance behind, Gobh. **Anu-dvîpa,** m. N. of six islands (as Aṅga-dvipa &c.), L. **An-udvejayat,** mfn. not stimulating,

Mṛicch. **Anu-nadi**, ind. along the river, Dharmaś. **Anu-nidhānam**, ind. according to position, in right order, Gobh. **Anu-ninīshā**, f. the wish to propitiate, HPariś. **An-upakiñca**, mfn. 'having nothing defective,' not hoarse, not faltering (voice), Hir. **An-upagata-jara**, mfn. not impaired by old age or infirmity, Bcar. **An-upagṛihīta**, mfn. unchanged, SaṃhUp. **An-upacarita**, mfn. not transferred, Sāṃkhyas., Sch. **An-upadeshṭavya**, mfn. not to be commended, Mālatīm. **Á́n-upadhmāta**, mfn. not blown upon, ŚBr. **An-upanata**, mfn. not occurred, ĀśvŚr., Sch. **An-upanāha**, m. not a perpetual enmity, Lalit. **An-upayat**, mfn. not going to (a wife; v. l. °*yāt*), Mn. ix, 4. **An-uparāga**, mfn. free from passion, MBh. **Anu-pari-√grah**, to grasp all round, surround, Divyâv.; to favour, befriend, Vajracch. **Anu-pari-√plu** (Caus. -*plāvayati*), to wash, Hir. **Anu-pari-√mṛij** (Caus. ind. p. -*mārjya*), to wipe all round, Divyâv. **Anupari-vārita**, mfn. surrounded, ib. **Anu-pari-√sic**, to pour round, MaitrS. **An-uparodha**, m. not prejudicing or injuring (-*tas*, with gen. = 'without prejudice to'), PārGṛ.; Mn. **Anu-parvata**, m. a promontory, headland, Hcat. **Anupalipta**, m. N. of a Tathāgata, Sukh. i. **Anupalīḍha**, mfn. unlicked, Kauś. **An-upastīrṇa-śāyin**, mfn. lying upon the bare ground, Kathās. **An-upahata-karṇêndriyatā**, f. having the organ of hearing uninjured (one of the 80 minor marks of a Buddha), Dharmas. 84. **An-upahita**, mfn. unconditioned, Veṇīs. **An-upâkrushṭa**, mfn. irreproachable, Jātakam. **Anu-pāta**, m. splitting or cutting down (a kind of torture), Divyâv. **Anupâtta**, mfn. not caught (as fire), Nir. vii, 23; not mentioned explicitly, Sāh. **An-upâdāna**, n. not mentioning, omission, ib. **Anu-pāde**, ind. behind (a person's feet), MBh. **An-upâdhi-rāmaṇīya**, see 1. *upâdhi* (p. 213). **An-upâya**, m. bad means (*ena*, 'to no purpose'), MBh.; mfn. (a Stobha) in which the chorus of chanting priests does not join, Drāhy. (Sch.) **Anu-pālya**, mfn. to be guarded or kept or maintained (as truth), Kathās. **Anu-piṇḍam**, ind. at every Piṇḍa (q. v.), ĀpŚr. **Anu-pūraṇa**, n. subsequent filling, Sāṃkhyas., Sch. **Anu-pūrva** (in comp.); -*gātratā*, f. having regular members (one of the 80 minor marks of a Buddha), Dharmas. 84; -*daṇshṭratā*, f. having r° eye teeth (id.), ib.; °*vâṅgulitā*, f. having regular fingers (id.), ib.; °*vena*, (also) gradually, by degrees, Jātakam. **An-upêta**, (also) not affected by, devoid of (comp.), Bcar.; °*upêya*, mfn. not to be married, Mn. xi, 173; °*upêyamāna*, mfn. not being approached (sexually), MBh. **Á́n-upôpta**, mfn. not filled up or covered by heaping up, TS. **Anu-pradātṛi**, m. an increaser, TS. **Anu-prapattavya**, n. (impers.) it is to be followed or conformed to, AitBr. **Anu-pra-√1. vap** (Ā. -*vapate*), to shave or be shaved in turn, TāṇḍBr. **Anu-pravartana**, n. urging to (loc.), Bcar.; °*vartita*, mfn. set going again, Divyâv.; °*vṛitti*, f. (acc. with √*kṛi*, 'to pay attention to'), ib. **Anu-pra-√viś** (Caus. -*veśayati*), to send home, ib. **Anu-pra-√vraj**, to become an ascetic after, ib. **Anu-pravrajana**, n. the becoming an ascetic after (another), ib. **Anu-prashṭṛi**, mfn. (fr. *anu-√prach*) inquiring after all things, desirous of knowledge, MBh. **Anu-prasarpaka** (Lāṭy., Sch.), °**pin** (Jaim.), mfn. creeping after; °*sṛiptin*, mfn. one who has crept after, Lāṭy. **Anu-prahita**, (also) shot off, Kir. **Anu-prahṛita** (in comp.); -*bhājaná*, n. the substitute for what is thrown into the fire, ŚBr.; °*prahṛitya*, mfn. to be th° into the fire, ib. **Anu-priya**, mfn. liked, dear, MBh. **Anu-prêshaṇa**, n. sending after, Prab., Sch. **Anu-bimba**, m. n. reflected image, Naish.; °*mbana*, n. the being a refl° im°, ib.; °*mbita*, mfn. reflected, ib. **Anu-bodha**, (also) perception, ĀpŚr. **An-ubha**, mfn. (du.) neither, no one (of two), MBh.; °*ubhaya*, mfn. id., Sarvad.; °*yâtman*, mfn. of neither kind (°*tma-tā*, f.), Sāh. **Anu-bhava**, (also) cognition, consciousness, L.; custom, usage, Lalit.; (*am*), ind. at every birth, BhP.; °*bhāvya*, mfn. to be (or being) perceived, Sarvad. **Anu-bhāshita**, n. spoken words, talk, speech, BhP. **Á́numata-vajra**, mfn. one who has received the thunderbolt by consent (?), MaitrS. **Anu-mantavya**, mfn. to be consented to or acknowledged, Inscr. **Anu-mātṛi**, mfn. drawing inferences, Śaṃk., Sch. **Anu-√mārg**, to search through, R. **Anu-mārga**, m. following, seeking (*eṇa*, with gen. = 'after'), Kād.; Kathās.; °*gâgata*, mfn. met half-way, Jātakam. **Anu-mālinī-tīram**, ind. on the bank of the Mālinī, Śak. **Anu-mṛit**, mfn. dying after, following in death, Ragh. **Anu-modin**, mfn. causing pleasure to (gen.), Jātakam. **Anu-mroka**, see *mrokânumroka* (p. 837). **Anu-√yam**, (also) to give over, Divyâv. **Anu-yiyāsu**, mfn. wishing to follow, HPariś. **Anu-yoktavya**, mfn. to be questioned, MBh. **Anuyogadvāra**, N. of a sacred book, Jain. **Anu-lamba**, mfn. dependent, subordinate, TāṇḍBr. **Anu-lepin**, mfn. (ifc.) smeared or anointed with, MBh. **Anuloma-pratiloma** (said of a mythical sea and mountain), Divyâv. **Anu-lomaya**, (also) to make favourable, MBh. **Anu-lomikī**, f. (with *kshānti*) resignation to natural consequences, Sukh. i (cf. *an-utpattika-dharma-kshānti*, and *ghoshânugā*, Dharmaś. 107). **Anu-vaṇśa-śloka**, mpl. Ślokas containing genealogies (e. g. MBh. i, 3759 &c.), IW. 511, n. 1. **Anu-vanântam**, ind. along or in the forest, Kir. **Anu-vapram**, ind. along the shore, ib. **Anu-vartitā**, f. compliance, Bcar.; °*vartya*, mfn. to be followed, Kathās.; to be supplied from the preceding, Pat.; °*vṛitti*, f. (in dram.) politeness, courtesy, Sāh. **Anu-√7. vas** (only -*vāvase*), to rush at, RV. viii, 4, 8. **Anu-vāda** (used in explaining *dhvani*), Kpr. **Anu-vādinī**, f. a lute, L. **Anu-vāsaram**, ind. day by day, Ragh. **Anu-vidha**, mfn. conforming or adhering to, BhP.; °*vidheya*, mfn. to be followed, Bhartṛ.; to be prescribed according to (instr.), Pat. **Anu-vi-√lok** (P. -*lokayati*), to survey, Divyâv. **Anu-vishṇu**, ind. after Vishṇu, Laghuk. 972. **Anu-vyāpin**, mfn. (ifc.) spreading over, covering, filling, Jātakam. **Anu-vyāhṛita**, n. curse, imprecation, MBh. **Anu-śaṇsa**, m. speaking ill, TĀr.; comfort, privilege, Divyâv.; -*śaṇsana*, n. subsequent recitation, TāṇḍBr., Sch. **Anuśayâkshepa**, m. (in rhet.) objection expressing (or resulting from) repenting, Kāvyâd. ii, 162. **Anu-śayin**, (also) indifferent to everything, Kap. **Anu-śāsin**, (also) ruling, VarP.; °*śāsti*, f. instruction, L.; °*śishṭa*, mfn. giving false evidence (?), L. **Anu-śiksha**, f. learning or striving after, Jātakam. **Anu-śuśrūshā**, f. obedience, MBh. **Anu-√śru** (Caus. -*śrāvayati*), to announce, Divyâv.; °*śrotavya*, mfn. to be heard, Suśr. **Á́nu-śloka**, m. N. of a Sāman, TS. **Anusha**, m. a demon, L. **Anu-shakti**, f. clinging to, adherence, Cat. **Anu-shṭubh**, see 2. *stúbh* (p. 1259); °*shṭup-sampád*, f. completion of an Anu-shṭubh, ŚBr. **An-ushṭra**, (also) mfn. that from which camels are excluded, Mn. v, 18. **Anu-shṭhānika**, m. N. of a class of Theistic Reformers, RTL. 524. **Anu-sam-√varṇ**, to approve of, Divyâv. **Anu-saṃvṛijin** or °**jina**, mfn. blameless (?), Hir. **Anu-sam-√sṛi**, (Caus., also) to make progress through, ib. **Anu-saktham**, ind. along the thigh, Lāṭy. **Anu-samjñapti**, f. explanation, Divyâv. **Anu-saṃtāna**, m. offspring, a son, Gaut. **Anu-saṃdhānīya**, mfn. to be attended to, Kāvyâd. **Anu-saṃdhi**, m. (in dram.) juncture of a Patākā or episode, Bhar. **Anu-saraṇa**, (also) visiting, Vishṇ.; °*sartavya*, mfn. to be followed, MBh.; n. (impers.) it is to be conformed to, Kpr.; °*sartṛi*, mfn. (ifc.) visiting in turn, MBh.; following, seeking, Daśar.; °*sṛita-vatsā*, f. (scil. *vivṛitti*) hiatus between a long or short syllable, PratijñāS. **Anu-sarga**, m. secondary creation, BhP. **Anu-sarpaṇa**, n. following, Daśar. **Anu-stanita**, n. continual thundering, Āpast. **Anu-spandyam**, ind. along the cord, BaudhP. **Anu-smṛiti**, (also) N. of a poem (consisting of 72 verses from MBh. on the necessity of remembering Vishṇu at death). **Anu-srotasa**, mfn. in the direction of the current of a river, ĀpGṛ. **Anu-√svan** (3. sg. aor. Pass. -*shvāṇi*), to roar after, RV. vi, 46, 14. **Anu-haraṇa**, (also) inheriting, Vishṇ. **Anu-√hṛi**, (also) to carry behind, ĀpGṛ. **Anu-homa**, m. after-oblation, ŚrS. **Anū-kāśin**, mfn. viewing, beholding, TBr. **Anûtthātṛi**, m. an attendant, Jaim.; °*tthāna*, see *an-anûtth*° (add.). **An-ūtsarga**, m. non-abandonment, Āpast. **An-ūdara**, mfn. having no belly, MBh.; m. N. of one of the sons of Dhṛita-rāshṭra, ib. **Anûddeśa**, (also) subsequent indication, Kāvyâd. **An-ūdbhāsin**, mfn. not shining forth, Āpast. **An-ūdhás**, (also, accord. to some) having no breasts, a young girl, RV. **Anūna-vastuka**, mfn. complete in substance or essence, Mālav. **Anūpâlu**, n. a kind of poisonous root, Gal. **Anū-bandhyā** (MaitrS.). **An-ūrdhva-jñu**, mfn. not raising the knees, ŚāṅkhGṛ. **An-ūsha-rih**, mfn. not licking salt, MaitrS. **An-ūshman**, mfn. not aspirated, APrāt. **An-ūha**, (also) m. absence of modification, ŚāṅkhŚr. **An-ṛigveda-vinīta**, mfn. not versed in the Ṛig-veda, R. **Anṛiṅga** (?), n. a small town, L. **An-ṛiṇī-karaṇa**, n. releasing from debt, HPariś. **An-ṛita** (in comp.); -*katha*, mfn. telling untruths, VP.; -*paśu*, m. not a real animal, MaitrS.; -*saṃhita*, mfn. not true to a contract or stipulation, AitBr.; -*saṃgara*, mfn. id., Āpast.; -*sarvasva*, m. N. of a man, Kautukas.; °*tâtmaka*, mf(*ikā*)n. of faithless disposition, Mālatīm. **An-ṛitika**, mfn. untruthful, Bcar. ii, 11. **An-ṛishabha**, mfn. without the male, TāṇḍBr. **Aneka** (in comp.); -*dhṛit*, m. N. of Rudra-Śiva, Hcat.; -*varṇa*, mfn. many-coloured, Bhag.; -*varshika*, mfn. many years old, R.; -*saṃsthāna*, mfn. wearing various disguises (as spies), Mn. ix, 261; -*saṃkhya*, mfn. very numerous, Kir.; °*kâtma-vādin*, mfn. asserting a plurality of souls, Sāṃkhyas., Sch. **An-edhas**, m. fire, L.; the wind, L. **Anela-mūka**, (prob.) = *an-eḍa-m*°, Hcar. **An-evam**, ind. not so, Bādar.; (*án-evaṃ*)-*vid* or -*vidvas*, mfn. not having such knowledge, ŚBr. **An-aikântika-tā**, f. variableness, Bcar. **Á́n-aiḍaka**, mf(*ī*)n. not coming from the animal called Eḍaka, ŚBr. **An-aitihya**, mfn. not based on tradition, MBh. **An-aindava**, mfn. not coming from the moon, not lunar, Bālar. **A-naibhṛitya**, n. inconstancy, MBh.; want of modesty, Jātakam. **A-naiścārika**, mfn. not averting or distracting, Āpast. **An-ojas** or °**ska**, mfn. powerless, weak, Jātakam. **Ano-yukta**, n. a cart with a pair of oxen, Drāhy., Sch. **An-aucitī**, f. indecorous conduct, Naish. **An-aupama**, mfn. = °*mya*, Hcar. **An-aupâdhika**, mfn. (with *sambandha*), IW. 63. **An-aushadha**, irremediable, incurable, Kāv. **Anta** (add, *antena*, 'finally,' MānGṛ.; *antāya-√kṛi*, 'to fight obstinately,' MBh.; *antād antam parikramya*, 'walking to and fro,' ib.); -*karaṇa*, n. causing an end of, abolishing (comp.), Bcar.; -*karman*, mfn. (= *anta-kara*), ib. iii, 59; -*tvāshṭrī*, see *tvāshṭrī-sāman* (p. 464); -*dīpaka*, n. a partic. rhetorical figure (e. g. Bhaṭṭ. x, 23); -*dvīpa*, N. of a country to the north of Madhya-deśa (°*pin*, m. an inhabitant of it), Cat.; -*nāman* (*ánta*-), mfn. denoting 'the end,' TS.; TāṇḍBr.; -*netra*, n. the hem of a garment, Nalac.; -*pluta*, mfn. pronounced with prolation of the last syllable, Vait.; -*śas*, ind. even down to, Divyâv. **Antaḥ** (in comp. for *antar* below); -*kratu*, ind. during a sacrifice, Jaim.; -*kraurya*, n. inward cruelty, Ragh., Sch.; -√*khyā* (read 'to inquire into, investigate'); -*parimārjana*, n. an internal remedy, Car.; -*pātin*, mfn. (ifc.) occurring in the interior of anything, ĀpŚr., Sch.; -*pārśva* (*ántaḥ*-) = *antaḥ-pārśvyá*, TS.; -*puracārikā*, f. a female attendant in the women's apartments, Kathās.; -*pura-vṛiddhā*, f. an old female att° in the w°'s ap°, Kād.; -*purâdhipatya*, n. supremacy over the w°'s ap°, Vishṇ.; -*purâvacara*, m. an attendant in the w°'s ap°, Jātakam.; -*purīya*, Nom. P. °*yati*, to behave as in the w°'s ap°, Sāh.; -*purevāsa*, mfn. living in the w°'s ap°, HPariś.; -*pūjā*, f. inward or silent worship, Cat.; -*pūya*, mfn. containing pus, Suśr.; -*pracalita*, mfn. inwardly moved, Mṛicch.; -*pratihāram*, ind. within the syllables forming a Pratyāhāra, Lāṭy.; -*pramoda*, m. inner joy, Mālatīm.; -*praveśa*, m. entering within, Suśr.; -*prâṇin*, m. a worm (v. l. *aṇu-pr*°), VP.; -*śava*, mfn. containing a corpse, Gaut.; -*śānti*, f. inner calm, Bhām.; -*śīrṇa*, mfn. withered or rotten within, Mālatīm.; -*śailaja*, m. a native of Antar-giri, VarBṛS.; -*śri* (*ántaḥ*-), ind. (said of a partic. pronunciation), ŚBr.; -*sattva*, n. inner nature, ŚārṅgP.; -*sadas*, n. the interior of an assembly hall, BhP.; ind. (= -*sadasam*), ŚāṅkhŚr.; -*salila*, mf(*ā*)n. having its waters hidden (said of the Sarasvatī), Ragh.; (*am*), ind. in the w°, Veṇīs.; (°*la-stha*, mfn. standing in w°, Pañcat.); -*sānu*, ind. in the mountain ridge, Kir.; -*sāma*, ind. within a Sāman, Lāṭy.; -*sāmika*, mfn. appearing within a S°, SaṃhUp.; -*sushirin*, mfn. hollow in the interior, HPariś.; -*stobha*, mfn. containing a Stobha, ĀrshBr.; -*stoma-bhāgám*, mfn. within the bricks called Stoma-bhāgā, ŚBr.; -*sthībhāva*, m. transition into a semivowel, VPrāt.; -*spandya*, mfn. situated within the measuring cord, Śulbas.; -*smayin* (see *smayin*, p. 1271); -*smita*, n. inward smile, Caurap.; -*smera*, mfn. smiling inwardly, Bhām. **Antaka** (in comp.); -*pura*, n. the city or dwelling of Death (acc. with Caus. of √*gam*, 'to kill'), Daś.; °*kânana*, n. the jaws of Death, ib. **Antama-sthā**, f. a metre of 46 syllables, Nidānas. **Antar** (in comp.); -*antaḥstha*, mfn. containing a semivowel, Hir.; -*āgamana*, n. passing between,

Mn. iv, 126; *-iti* (*antár-*), excluding, MaitrS.; *-gaṇa*, m. a Gaṇa contained in another G°, Pāṇ. i, 1, 74, Sch.; *-gala-gata*, mfn. sticking in the throat, Pañcat.; *-jana*, m. pl. the inhabitants of a house, Lalit.; *-jalâugha*, m. an inner mass of water, Megh.; *-divākīrtya*, m. concealing a Caṇḍāla, PārGṛ.; *-dhana*, n. a hidden or inner treasure, Kāv.; *-dhināman*, mfn. named concealment, JaimUp.; *-dhairya*, n. inner firmness or constancy, Mcar.; *-dhvānta*, n. inner darkness, Bhām.; *-nikhāta*, mfn. engraven, Mālatīm.; *-niveśana*, n. an inner apartment, Mn. vii, 62; *-nihita*, mfn. placed within, put in (*-vacana*, mfn. 'having words inserted,' 'containing or expressing, as it were, words'), Mālav.; *-bhāva*, m. disappearance, Daś.; *-bhinna*, mfn. inwardly divided or torn, Mālatīm.; *-bhūta*, mfn. (ifc.) being or contained in anything, ib.; *-bheda*, m. inner division, Mcar.; *-madâvastha*, mfn. having latent or unmanifested ruttish desires, Ragh.; *-mandira*, n. inner apartments (reserved for women), Daś.; *-marman*, n. the innermost heart, Uttarar. v, 16; *-mukha*, (also) mfn. turned inwards, Mcar.; n. the interior of the mouth, Vām.; (*am*), ind. inwardly, Sūryas.; *-moda*, m. inner joy, Mālatīm.; *-yukshu* (used in explaining *antariksha*), JaimUp.; *-yajana*, n., *-yāga*, m. inner sacrifice, Cat.; *-yāma*, (also) speaking to one's self, unheard by another, L.; *-vartinī*, f. pregnant, Divyâv.; *-vâvat* (others 'far apart, far and wide'), RV.; *-vṛitti*, f. internal condition, Mālatīm.; *-hiti* (*antár-*), f. concealment, TBr.; (°*taś*)-*cakshus*, n. the inner eye, Ragh.; (°*taś*)-*caṇḍāla* (= *antar-divākīrtya*), Āpast.; (°*taś*)-*cara*, mfn. penetrating within, Kum. **Antará** (in comp.); *-kośá*, m. an interior case or sheath; *-tás*, ind. internally, inside, within, ŚBr.; Śulbas.; R.; within (as prepos. with gen.), ŚBr.; *-dvīpa*, m. N. of the seven Dvīpas south of Bhārata-varsha, L.; *-patita*, mfn. 'fallen between,' unimportant, indifferent, Kād.; *-prêkshin*, mfn. perceiving a weak point, MBh.; R.; *-bhāvanā*, f. composition by the difference, Col.; *-vāsaka*, n. the inner garment (of a Buddhist monk), MWB. 83; °*rântarāt*, ind. here and there, Divyâv.; °*rânveshin*, mfn. waiting for an opportunity, Śak. **Antarā** (add, *antarā ca – antarā ca*, with two accusatives of places = 'between – and –,' Divyâv.); *-bhakta*, n. medicine taken between two meals, Suśr.; *-śṛiṅgám* (MaitrS.); *-śṛiṅgīya*, mfn. being between the horns, ib.; °*rêsha*, m. the space between the two shafts of a carriage, ĀpŚr. **Antariksha** (in comp.); *-nāman*, mfn. called atmosphere, JaimUp.; °*kshâsana*, n. a partic. posture in sitting, L. **Antarī-√kṛi** (P. *-karoti*), to take in the middle, Hariv. **Antarīya** (also Gobh. i, 2, 21). **Anti** (in comp.); *-tara*, mfn. standing in the very front, MBh.; *-deva*, m. N. of an ancient king and sage, ib.; Bcar. **Antikāt**, ind. in comparison with, than (gen.), Divyâv. **Antu**, m. (said to be fr. √*am*) a guardian, protector, L.; a mark, characteristic, L. **Antya** (in comp.); *-maṇḍana*, n. a funeral ornament, Kum.; °*tyârdha*, the hinder part, Mālatīm. **Andha** (in comp.); *-hārin*, mfn. dark, Git.; *-kāla*, m. a partic. hell, Kāraṇḍ.; *-caṭaka-nyāya*, m. the rule of the blind man catching a sparrow (cf. *ghuṇâkshara-ny*°), A.; *-tāmisra*, n. darkness, Mcar.; *-paramparā-nyāya*, m. the rule of the blind following the blind (applied to people following each other thoughtlessly), ib.; *-mehala*, n. the smell of being stained by urine, L.; mfn. having the above smell, ib.; *-vyūha*, m. a partic. Samādhi, Kāraṇḍ.; °*dhī-karaṇa*, n. making blind, Jātakam. **Andhakântaka**, m. N. of Śiva, Kir. **Andhakī**, f. the south-west quarter, L. **Anna** (in comp.); *-kāraṇa*, mfn. preparing food, MaitrS.; *-kāśin*, mfn. (?) yearning for food, JaimUp.; *-jā*, f. a kind of hiccup, ŚārṅgS.; *-drava-śūla*, n. a kind of colic, Bhpr.; *-paryāyam*, ind. so that all dishes go round in turn, PārGṛ.; *-pāśa*, m. the binding power of food (as binding soul and body together), Gobh.; *-bhuj*, m. (also) fire (of digestion), MārkP.; *-yoni*, 'produced out of rice,' arrack, Kāv.; *-vikṛiti*, f. (= *-vikāra*), MBh.; *-vidvesha*, m. 'disgust of food,' want of appetite, Suśr.; *-śubha*, mfn. pleasant through food, JaimUp.; *-saṃskartṛi*, m. 'preparer of food,' a cook, Āpast.; *-saṃdeha* (*anná-*), m. cementing of food, ŚBr.; *-hāra*, mfn. containing food, AgP.; °*nâda*, (also) m. fire (at the end of a religious rite), L.; °*nâbhiruci*, f. desire of food, appetite, Suśr.; °*nâśana*, n. (= *anna-prâśana*), AgP. **Annikā**, f. N. of a woman, HPariś. **Annīya**, Nom. P. °*yati*, to desire food, Āpast. **Anya** (in comp.); *-kāra* or *-kriya*, mfn. intent on other business, Bcar.; *-cchāyā-yoni*, mfn. 'having its source in another's light,' borrowed, Vām. iii, 2, 7; *-janátā*, f. fellowship with others, MaitrS.; *-tīrthika*, mfn. belonging to another sect, heterodox, Jātakam.; *-padârtha-pradhāna*, mfn. having as chief sense that of another word (as a Bahu-vrīhi), Pāṇ. ii, 2, 24, Sch.; *-parigraha*, m. the wife of another, Mn. v, 162; *-bandhu*, mfn. related to another, ĀpŚr.; *-bhāva*, m. change of state, Suśr. (°*vin*, mfn. changed, altered, ib.); *-mātṛika*, mf(*ā*)n. having another mother, Kathās.; *-mānasa* (see *an-any*°); *-yajña*, m. another's sacrifice, ĀpŚr.; *-rāshṭriya*, mfn. (= °*trīya*), Kāṭh.; *-lokya*, mfn. destined for another world, VP.; *-loha* or °*haka*, m. brass-metal, L.; *-śaṅkita*, mfn. (= *anyathā-sambhāvin*), Ratnâv.; *-śākhā-stha*, mfn. one who studies in another Śākhā, L.; *-śṛiṅgá*, n. the horn (by which an animal is tied), MaitrS.; °*yâpadeśa*, m. (= *anyôkti*), Subh.; °*yârtha*, m. another's affair, Jaim.; mf(*ā*)n. one who has another aim or object (*-tva*, n.), ib.; having another sense or meaning (also *-vat*), Daśar., Sch.; n. the use of a word in an uncommon sense, Vām. ii, 1, 12; °*yôkti*, f. allegorical expression, Cat. (*-kaṇṭhâbharaṇa*, n., *-pariccheda*, m. pl., *-śataka*, n. N. of wks.); °*yôpatâpin*, mfn. paining others, Kāvyâd. **Anyat** (in comp.); *-kāma*, mfn. desirous of something else, Up.; *-pārśva*, mf(*ā*)n. showing another side, Kauś.; *-sthāna-gata*, mfn. being at another place, Lāṭy. **Anyataḥ** (in comp. for *anyatas*); *-siti-bāhu* (*anyátaḥ-*), mfn. having the fore-feet white only on one side, VS.; *-siti-randhra* (*anyátaḥ-*), mfn. having the ear-cavities white only on one side, ib.; (°*to*)-*ghātin*, mfn. striking against another, ŚBr.; *-jyotis* (*anyáto-*), mfn. having light or a Jyotis day only on one side, ib.; *-dvāra* (°*to-*), mfn. having doors only on one side, JaimUp.; *-mukha* (*anyáto-*), mfn. having a face only on one side, ŚBr. **Anyatara**, (also) a certain one, Divyâv.; °*ráto-yukta*, mfn. yoked only on one side, ŚBr.; °*rânyatara*, mfn. of whatever kind, Vajracch. **Anyatra-karaṇa**, m. the son of a paramour, Gaut. **Anyathā** (in comp.); *-karaṇa*, n. (Campak.), *-kṛiti*, f. (L.) changing, change; *-jātīyaka*, mfn. of another kind, Pat.; *-darśana*, n. false trial (of a lawsuit), Yājñ., Sch.; *-°bhidhāna* (°*thâbh*°), n. false statement or deposition, ib.; *-śīlika*, mfn. accustomed to act differently from (*atas*), GopBr.; *-sambhāvin*, mfn. suspecting something else, distrustful, Ratnâv. **Anyâdṛiśa**, (also) uncommon, strange, Kād. **Anyā-ya**, mfn. having intercourse with another's wife, Nalac. **A-nyāya** (in comp.); *-tas*, ind. irregularly, improperly, BhP.; *-mati*, mfn. having improper thoughts, Bcar.; *-vṛitti*, mfn. (= *-vartin*), Daś.; *-samāsa*, m. an irregular compound, VPrāt.; °*yin*, mfn. badly behaved, Uttamac. **A-nyūna** (in comp.); °*nâṅga*, mfn. not defective in limbs or organs, Lāṭy.; °*nâtiriktâṅga*, mfn. having neither too few nor too many limbs or organs, ĀśvGṛ.; °*nârtha-vādin*, mfn. adequately expressive, Kāvyâd. **Anyedyushka** (Suśr.) or °**dyuska** (Car.), mfn. relating or belonging to the other day. **Anyonya** (in comp.); *-kṛitya*, n. mutual services, Śak.; *-gata*, mfn. mutual, reciprocal, Vikr.; *-darśana*, n. an interview, ib.; *-dharmin*, mfn. possessing mutually each other's qualities, MBh.; *-bhāva*, m. mutual exchange of condition, Śāntiś.; *-mithuna*, mfn. living by couples, Hariv.; *-spardhā*, f. mutual emulation (°*dhin*, mfn. = rivalling), Mn.; °*nyânurāga*, m. mutual affection, Śak.; °*nyâpatita-tyāgin*, mfn. deserting each other without either losing caste, Vishṇ.; °*nyôpamā*, f. a reciprocal simile, Kāvyâd. **Anv-aksharam**, ind. according to the sound or letter, SaṃhUp. **Anv-ak-sthānin** or °**nīya**, mfn. inferior in dignity, Āpast. **Anvag-jyeshṭha**, mfn. the next eldest, ib. **Anv-agram**, ind. from below to above, ib. **Anv-aṅgám**, ind. for every part of an action, ŚBr. **Anv-√at** (P. *-atati*), to go after, follow, ĀpŚr. **Anvabhy-ava-√car**, to come near, MaitrS. **Anv-abhyavacâram**, ind. creeping after, MaitrS. **Anvayâgata**, mfn. inherited, Pañcat. **Anv-avalamba**, mfn. hanging down along (acc.), Gobh. **Anv-avêkshaṇa**, n. looking after, inspection, MBh. **Anv-avêkshin**, mfn. circumspect, considerate, ib. **Anv-ākarshaka**, mfn. attracting from the preceding, TPrāt. **Anv-ākhyāyaka**, mfn. stating exactly or explicitly, Pat. **Anv-ādhi**, m. a deposit delivered to another person to be handed over to a third, Gaut. **Anv-āpadina**, m. N. of a king (v.l. *allāp*°), Sāh. **Anv-ā-√vṛit** (Caus. *-vartayati*), to change, Divyâv. **Anv-āvṛitám**, ind. with regard to order or succession, ŚBr. **Anv-āsecana**, n. sprinkling, Kauś. **Anv-āsthāna**, n. (TBr., Sch.), °**sthāya**, m. (TBr.) attainment. **Anv-ā-√hiṇḍ** (P. *-hiṇḍati*), to wander, Divyâv. **Anv-icchā**, f. seeking after, ib. **Anv-īkshaka**, mf(*ikā*)n. careful, anxious, R. **Anv-īta**, mfn. = *anv-ita*, Bālar. **Anv-eshṭṛi**, mfn. searching, pursuing, L. **Apa-kaṇṭaka**, mf(*ā*)n. free from thorns or dangers, Dharmaś. **Apa-kartana**, n. cutting in pieces, dismembering, Mcar. **Apa-karshin**, mfn. drawing along (as a plough), Pañcat. **Apa-kashāya**, mfn. sinless (*-tva*, n.), MārkP. **Apa-kṛit**, mfn. doing harm or injury, Mcar. **Apa-kṛitya**, (also) mfn. deserving to be harmed or injured, ib. **Apa-kośa**, mfn. unsheathed, Bhojac. **Apa-krama-maṇḍala**, n. ecliptic, Āryabh., Sch. **Apa-krānta**, (also) abused (?), Divyâv.; *-medha* (*ápa*°*-*), mfn. sapless, pithless, ŚBr. **Apa-krámam**, ind. going away, MaitrS. **A-pakshapātin**, mfn. not flying with wings (and 'a partisan of A i. e. Vishṇu'), Vās. **Apa-khyāti**, f. disgrace, Bhojac. **Apa-gata-kālaka**, mfn. (a robe) free from black spots, Divyâv. **Apa-gṛihya**, mfn. being outside a house, ŚāṅkhGṛ. **Apa-grāma**, mfn. ejected from a village or community, ŚāṅkhŚr. **Apa-ghāṭilā**, f. a kind of musical instrument (cf. *ava-ghaṭarikā*), Lāṭy. **Apa-ghṛiṇa**, mfn. pitiless, cruel, Kāv. **A-paṅka**, mfn. mudless, dry (*-tā*, f.), Kir. **A-pacana**, n. the not being cooked, MBh. ix, 2780; °*camāna* (Mn.), °*camānaka* (Gaut.), mfn. one who does not cook for himself. **Apa-cāyaka**, mfn. honouring, Divyâv. **Apa-cikīrshu**, mfn. wishing to do harm or injury, Kāśīkh. 2. **Apa-cit** (read, 'a sore, boil,' = *apacī*, fr. 2. *apa-√ci*, AV.). **Ápa-cetas**, mfn. averse from (abl.), TBr. **Apa-√ji**, (also) to win from (with *punaḥ*, 'to reconquer'), TS. **Apa-jihīrshā**, f. the wish to take away, Kathās. **Apa-jvara**, mfn. free from fever, MBh. **A-pañcama**, m. not a nasal, VPrāt. **A-pañca-yajña**, mfn. one who does not perform the 5 Mahā-yajñas (q. v.), L. **Apaṭīkā**, f. dissimulation, L. **Apa-taṇsana**, n. falling out, Cat. **A-patana-dharmin**, mfn. not liable to fall out (*-tva*, n.), Suśr. **A-patanīya**, mfn. not causing loss of caste, Āpast. **Apatanta** = *āpatantá* (p. 1319), MānŚr. **Apa-tarám**, ind. farther away, MaitrS. **Apa-tāna**, m. cramp, Divyâv. **A-patita** (in comp.); °*tânyonya-tyāgin*, mfn. deserting one another (as the father deserting a son, the teacher a pupil &c.) without (the latter) being ejected from caste, Yājñ. ii, 237. **Apa-turīyá**, mfn. not containing the last quarter, MaitrS. **Apa-tushāra**, mfn. free from mist or fog (*-tā*, f.), Ragh. **Apatya** (in comp.); *-nātha*, mfn. accompanied or protected by one's own child, Bcar. i, 92; *-sneha*, m. love for one's own children, Mālatīm. **A-patha** (in comp.); *-dāyin*, mfn. not going out of a person's (gen.) way (cf. *a-pantha-d*°), Vishṇ.; *-hara*, mfn. choosing the wrong road, Kir. **Apa-darpa**, mf(*ā*)n. free from pride or self-conceit, Naish. **A-padânta**, m. not the end of a word, Pāṇ. viii, 3, 24; *-stha*, mfn. not standing at the end of a word, not final, ib., Sch. **Apa-dālaka**, m. the sheat fish, L. **A-padi-baddha**, mfn. not bound on the foot, ĀpŚr. **Apa-dūshaṇa**, mfn. faultless, blameless, Dharmaś. **Apa-dṛishṭi**, f. a look of displeasure, Naish. **A-padma**, mf(*ā*)n. having no lotus-flower, Mṛicch. **Apa-nayin**, mfn. behaving improperly or indiscreetly, Kathās. **Apa-nāma**, m. a curve, Śulbas. 1. **Apa-nidra**, (also) bristling, erect (as the hair on the body), Naish. **Apa-nidhi**, mfn. treasureless, poor, MBh. **Apa-ninīshā**, f. the wish to expel, Dharmaś.; °*shu*, mfn. wishing to expel (acc.), Kād. **Apa-nishâduka**, mfn. lying down apart, MaitrS. **Apa-neya**, mfn. to be taken back, Nār. **Apa-nodaka**, mfn. removing, dispelling, Vishṇ. **A-pantha-dāyin**, mfn. = *a-pathad*°, Gobh. **Apa-nyāyya**, mfn. improper (*-tva*, n.), KātyŚr., Sch. **Apapa**, m. (with Buddhists) a partic. cold hell, Dharmas. 122. **Apa-payas**, mfn. waterless, Kir. **Apa-pīḍā**, f. a sudden and dangerous attack of illness, Rājat. **Apa-prasara**, mfn. checked, restrained, Dharmaś. **Apa-bhāshaṇa**, (also) false expression or diction, Kāvyâd. **Apa-bhāshitavai**, inf. (with *na*, 'it should not be spoken ungrammatically'), Pat. **Apa-maṅgala**, mfn. inauspicious, Subh. (conj.). **Apa-mada**, mfn. free from pride or arrogance, Kāv. **Apa-mala**, mfn. spotless, clean, Śāntiś. (v.l.). **Apama-śiñjinī**, f. = *apama-jyā*, Gaṇit. **Apa-mārin**, mfn. dying or pining away,

TS. **Apa-mud**, mfn. joyless, pitiable, Śiś. **Apa-mṛiga**, mfn. deerless (as a wood), VP. **Apa-mṛishṭi**, f. wiping off, AV. Anukr. **A-payasya**, mfn. without coagulated milk, KātyŚr. **Apa-yāṇya**, n. (prob. w. r. for *apa-yāpya*), Vas. **Apa-yātavya**, n. possibility of escaping; *-naya*, m. a device for escaping, Jātakam. **Apara**, also (*e*), m. pl. others (= *anye*, used to indicate a various reading), Hāla, Sch.; (*ā*), f. (with *vidyā*) the exoteric Vedânta doctrine (as opp. to *parā v°*, 'the esoteric'), IndSt.; *-gandhikā*, f. N. of a country (= *ketu-māla*), L.; *-godāni* (?), m. N. of one of the four Dvipas, Dharmas. 120; *-tas*, ind. elsewhere, Uttarar.; on the west side, Śulbas.; *-dīkshin*, mfn. undergoing the later consecration, AitBr.; *-rātri*, f. the second half of the night, TS., Sch.; *-vallabha*, m. N. of a people, MBh., *-vedanīya*, n. (Karman) manifesting itself at a subsequent period, Dharmas. 132; *-śvas*, ind. the day after to-morrow, Gobh.; *°rāśā*, f. the western quarter, Vcar. **A-para-yoga**, mfn. without another addition, unmixed, Āpast. **Á-paraśu-vṛikṇa**, mfn. not hewn off with an axe, TS.; ŚBr. **A-paraspara-sambhūta**, mfn. not produced one from another or in regular order, Bhag. **A-parāktva**, n. the not being averted, ŚāṅkhBr. **A-parāṅmukha**, also (*am*), ind. unreservedly, freely, Vikr. **Á-parājayin**, mfn. never losing (at play), TBr. **A-parājita-gaṇa**, m. N. of a Gaṇa of martial hymns, Kauś. **Aparādha-vat**, mfn. missing an aim, Car. **Á-parāpāta**, m. not passing away, MaitrS. **A-parābhava**, m. not succumbing, victory, MBh. **A-parāmṛishṭa**, mfn. not touched by or come into contact with (instr.), Suśr. **A-parâyaṇa**, mf(*ā*)n. having no refuge, Kāraṇḍ. **A-parârdhya**, mfn. having no highest possible number, unlimited, ĀpŚr. **Á-parāvapishṭha**, mfn. not to be removed at all, TS. **A-parāvāpa**, m. not scattering, MaitrS. **A-parāvṛitta** (in comp.); *-bhāgadheya*, mfn. one to whom fortune does not return, miserable, Vikr. **A-parāvṛitti** (in comp.); *-vartin*, mfn. turned away not to return, deceased, Hariv. **A-paricalita**, mfn. unmoved, immovable, Śiś. **A-parijāta**, mfn. not fully born, born prematurely, ĀśvGṛ. **A-parijīrṇa**, mfn. undigested, Suśr. **A-paritta** (?), for *á-paritta* (below), MaitrS. **A-parityajya**, mfn. = (or v. l. for) *a-parityājya*. **A-paribādha**, mfn., v. l. for *a-parivāha*. **A-paribhaksha**, m. not passing over another at a meal, Lāṭy. **A-paribhāshita**, mfn. not explicitly mentioned, Bālar. **A-paribhogam**, ind. without being eaten, Divyâv. **A-parimita-kṛitvas**, ind. innumerable times, TĀr. **A-parimlāna-lalāṭatā**, f. the having an unwrinkled forehead (one of the 80 minor marks of a Buddha), Dharmas. 84. **A-parilupta**, mfn. not invalidated, RPrāt., Sch. **A-pariśrita**, n. not an enclosure, TāṇḍBr. **A-parisaṃkhyāna**, n. innumerableness, infinite difference, Nyāyas. **A-parisaṃkhyeya**, mfn. innumerable, infinitely different, ib., Sch. **A-paristhāna**, mfn. improper; n. impropriety, Mālatim. **A-parihita**, n. an unworn or clean garment, Āpast. **A-parihīṇa-kālam**, ind. without loss of time, at once, Bālar. **A-parihīyamāṇa**, mfn. not being omitted (*°naṃ √kṛi*, 'to supply deficiencies'), MBh. **A-parîkshya-kārin**, mfn. acting inconsiderately, Mṛicch. **Á-parītta**, mfn. not delivered, MaitrS. **A-parîtya**, mfn. not to be walked round, KāṭyŚr. **Apa-rujā**, f. 'free from sickness or harm,' N. of Pārvatī, L. **Apa-rush**, mfn. free from anger, Ragh. **A-parusha-keśatā**, f. having soft hair (one of the 80 minor marks of a Buddha), Dharmas. 84. **Apa-ródhya**, mfn. to be expelled or excluded from, TĀr. **A-parkya-pṛishṭha**, m. a partic. Ekāha, ŚāṅkhŚr. **A-paryāgata**, mfn. not a year old (grain), Suśr. **A-paryāṇa**, mfn. unsaddled, Kād. **A-paryupya**, ind. without clipping or shaving round, ĀśvGṛ. **A-paryushita**, mfn. quite fresh or new, Veṇis.; not inveterate, expiated at once (as sin), MBh. **A-paryeshita** or **°eshṭa**, mfn. unsought, SaddhP. **A-parvaṇi**, ind. (loc. of *a-parvan*) at the wrong time, out of season, Kir. **A-parvata** or **°tīya**, mfn. without hills, level, R. **Apa-lakshmaṇa**, mfn. without Lakshmaṇa (Rāma's brother), Bālar. **Apa-vaṅśa**, m. the hairless upper part of an elephant's tail, L. **Apa-vaktra** or **°traka**, n. a kind of metre (cf. *apara-v°*), Sāh. **Apa-vatsa**, mf(*ā*)n. having no calf, MBh. **Apa-varga**, (also) shooting off (an arrow), Kir.; opp. to *svarga* (in phil.); *-mārga*, m. the path of emancipation, Bcar. **Apa-varjana**, (also) gift, donation, L.; *-varjita-taila-pūra*, see *taila-p°* (p. 455). **Apa-varṇa**, mfn. faulty or incorrect as to sound, Śiksh. **Apa-vartikā**, f. = *nīvi*, KātyŚr., Sch. **Apa-vartya**, mfn. to be reduced (by division) to the smallest quantity, Bīj. **Apa-vātā**, f. a cow which has lost the love for its calf, Kauś. **Apa-vāda**, m. (also) the withdrawal of the *adhyāropa* or superimposed attribute (in the Vedânta). **Apa-√vij**, to start away from (acc.), AV. xii, 1, 37. **A-pavitra-ḍākinī**, f. a disgusting female imp, Mṛicch. **Apa-vidyā**, f. bad knowledge, ignorance, MārkP. **Apa-vipad**, mfn. free from misfortune or calamity, Nalac. **Apa-vṛiktatva**, n. the having finished, KātyŚr., Sch. **Apa-vṛitta**, (also) badly conducted, ill-behaved, BhP.; *-bhāva*, m. aversion, Jātakam. **Apa-vyavastha**, mfn. unsettled, changing, Naish. **Apa-vyākhyā**, f. false explanation, KātyŚr., Sch. **Apa-vyāpāra**, mfn. having no occupation or business, L. **Apa-vyāhāra**, m. profane or bad language, KātyŚr., Sch. **Apa-śabda**, m. ungrammatical language (compared to a deer as grammar to a lion), Subh.; *°dita*, mfn. spoken ungrammatically, R. **Apa-śastra**, mfn. weaponless, Kathās. **Apa-śālīna**, mfn. unembarrassed (*-tā*, f.), Naish. **Apa-śīla**, mfn. ill-natured, mean, low, Kāśīkh. **A-paśútā**, f. want of cattle, MaitrS. **A-paśu-bandha-yājin**, mfn. one who does not perform the Paśu-bandha sacrifice, HirP. **Apa-śushka**, mf(*ā*)n. averse, unfavourable, TS. (Sch.). **Apa-śūla**, mfn. having no spear, Ragh. **Apa-śrama**, mfn. indefatigable, Naish. **Apa-śruti**, mfn. unpleasant to the ear, MBh. **Apa-sarpya**, mfn. (prob.) to be driven away, Pañcat. iii, 241. **Apa-savya**, m. (scil. *agni*) the sacrificial fire at the birth of a son, L. **Apa-sāritā**, f. (fr. *°rin*) issue, end, Mālav. **Apa-skambhá** (accord. to some, 'the tearing [arrow],' AV. iv, 6, 4). **Apa-stana**, mfn. far from the mother's breast, MBh. **Apa-spaśa**, mf(*ā*)n. without spies (and *a-paspaśa*, 'without the introduction to the Mahābhāshya'), Śiś. ii, 112. **Apa-smaya**, mfn. free from arrogance or pride, BhP. **Apa-smāra**, (also) want of memory, confusion of mind (in rhet. one of the Vyabhicāribhāvas, q. v.), Sāh. **Apa-svara**, (also) mfn. singing out of tune, Saṃgīt. **Apa-haraṇa**, (also) keeping off all contrarieties, Jātakam. **Apa-harsha**, mfn. showing or feeling no joy, Kād. **Apa-hasita**, n. (also) smiling in tears, Daśar. **Apa-hastaka**, mfn. handless, ŚāṅkhGṛ. **Apa-hāra**, (also) a thief, L.; a shark or a crocodile, L.; *-varman*, m. N. of a man, Daś.; *°hārya*, mfn. one from whom anything (acc.) is to be taken, Āpast. **Apa-hita**, mfn. entrusted, L.; charged (with a crime), L. **Apa-√hṛi**, (also) to captivate, Divyâv.; *°hṛit*, mfn. taking away (comp.), Kāv. **Apa-helana**, n. = *ava-h°*, L. **Apa-hnavana**, n. denial, Śīl. **Apa-hrepaṇa**, n. putting to shame, Car. **Apa-hvara**, m. a partic. demon causing illness, PārGṛ. **Apâṅga-viśāla-netra**, mfn. casting side glances with wide-opened eyes, Mṛicch. **A-pāñcālya**, n. destruction of the Pañcālas, MBh. **A-pāṭha**, m. 'cessation of recital or of study,' a holiday, Divyâv. **A-pāṇi**, mfn. handless (*-tva*, n.), MBh.; *-grahaṇa*, (also) mfn. unmarried, Kathās. **Ápātta**, mfn. (fr. *apâ-√1. dā*) taken off or away, ŚBr. **A-pātra** (in comp.); *-varshaṇa*, n. liberality towards the undeserving, Kām.; *°shin*, mfn. liberal towards the und°, Hit.; *°trī-√bhū*, to become unfit for (gen.), Jātakam. **Apâdya**, m. N. of AV. iv, 33, 1 &c., Kauś. **Apânika**, m. speaking to one's self without another being able to hear, L. **A-pānīya**, mfn. without water to drink, MBh. **Apā-nunutsu**, mfn. wishing to remove or dispel, Kāśīkh. **Apâpad** or **°pada**, mfn. = *apa-vipad*, Jain. **Apâpāya**, mfn. free from calamity or danger, Jain. **Apâya-saṃvartanīya**, mfn. leading to destruction or hell, Vajracch. **A-pāra**, (also) difficult to be got at, R.; *-pāra*, (also) whose farther shore is difficult to be reached, Bcar. xii, 93. **Apâri-jāta**, mfn. free from hosts of enemies, Jain. **Apârthaya**, Nom. P. *°yati*, to render useless, Naish. **Apālu**, (prob.) m. (said to be fr. *√āp*) the wind, L. **Apâśrayaṇa**, n. leaning against anything, Gaut.; *°ya-vat* or *°yin*, mfn. having a support in (instr. or comp.), MBh. **Api**, (also) suppose that, perhaps, Jātakam.; (*api-api*), as well-as, ib.; *-drashṭṛi*, m. a superintendent, ŚāṅkhŚr., Sch.; *-naddhâkshá*, mfn. one who has the eyes covered, hoodwinked, MaitrS.; *-somapītha*, mfn. partaking of Soma drink, ŚāṅkhBr. **A-piśāca-dhīta**, mfn. (prob. right reading) not drunk or sucked by Piśācas, Hir. i, 25, 1. **A-puñja**, m. a spark, L. **A-putrya**, sonless, childless, MantraBr. **A-punar** (in comp.); *-ābhāva* (*á-p°*), m. not appearing again, MaitrS.; *-bhāvin*, mfn. the last, Veṇis. **A-purusha**, (also) a cruel man or servant (of Yama), Jātakam.; *°shâparādha*, m. not an offence of the person, Gaut.; *°shâbhivīta* (*á-p°*), mfn. not impelled by men, ŚBr. **Apuvāya**, **°yate**, see *apvā* (p. 59, col. 3). **Apusha**, m. (said to be fr. *√āp*) fire, L.; mfn. ill, sick (in this meaning prob. fr. *a* + *√2. push*), L. **A-pushkala**, (also) empty of meaning, shallow, flat, Hcar. **A-pushṭârtha**, mfn. (in rhet.) of irrelevant purport or meaning (*-tva*, n.), Sāh. **Apūpa** (in comp.); *-śālā*, f. a bakehouse, Mn. ix, 264. **Apūpaka**, m. (MBh.), *°pikā*, f. (Kathās.) = *apūpá*, a cake &c. **A-pūra**, mfn. not to be filled or satisfied, not to be quenched (as thirst), BhP. **A-pūraṇa**, mf(*ī*)n. insatiable, MBh.; (ifc.) not completing, defective, BhP. **A-pūrva**, (also) mfn. not married before, Āpast.; m. a novice, Kir. vi, 39; *-karaṇa*, n. (with Jainas) N. of the 8th stage leading to perfection; *-darśana*, mfn. never seen before, Kād.; *-pada*, mfn. not preceded by another word (i. e. not standing at the end of a compound), Pāṇ. iv, 1, 140; *-vāda*, m. N. of a Nyāya wk.; *°rvin*, mfn. one who has not done (anything) before, MBh.; unmarried, R. **A-pṛithak** (in comp.); *-tvin*, mfn. not asserting a separate existence, MBh.; (*°thag*)*-jita*, mfn. not conquered singly, Mn. vii, 97; (*°thag*)*-dharmin*, mfn. having no separate qualities, MaitrUp.; (*°thag*)*-vivekya*, mfn. not to be distinguished, ib. **Apêkshaṇa**, (also) mfn. not looking at (comp.), Subh. (conj.). **Apêta** (in comp.); *-prajanana*, mfn. one who has lost his generative energy, KātyŚr.; *-prāṇa*, mfn. lifeless, Kathās. **Apô-√sṛij**, to relinquish, Divyâv. **Aptúr**, (accord. to others = *ap-túr*, 'vanquishing the waters in speed,' i. e. 'swift, rapid'). **Aptúrya**, (accord. to others = *ap-t°*, 'victorious fight, victory'). **Ap-pūrvam**, ind. after a libation of water, ĀśvGṛ. **A-prakāśat** or **°śin**, mfn. invisible, MBh. **A-prakṛita**, mfn. not being in question, not belonging to the matter, KātyŚr. **A-pragādha**, mfn. not shallow, deep, Divyâv. **A-praguṇa**, (also) obstinate, refractory, Vām. iv, 2, 7. **Á-praghnatī**, f. (prob.) not driving onward, ŚBr. **A-pracchanna**, n. courtesy, courteous treatment of a friend or guest, L. **Apracchāya**, mfn. shadeless, Jātakam. **A-prajana**, mfn. not begetting (*-tva*, n.), Gaut. **A-praṇihita**, mfn. free from desire, Sukh. i; (prob.) n. purposelessness, ib. **A-pratikṛishṭa**, mfn. unruffled (as a garment), Āpast. **A-pratibhaṭa**, mfn. irresistible, Daś. **A-pratimalla**, mfn. unrivalled, Mcar. **A-pratilomayat**, mfn. not adverse or contrary, Āpast. **A-prativāṇi**, mfn. unhindered, Divyâv. **A-pratisaṃkhyā**, (also) inconsiderateness, Jātakam. **A-pratisādhya**, mfn. incurable, Vishṇ., Sch. **A-pratihata-raśmi-rāga-prabha**, m. = *amitâbha*, Sukh. i. **A-pratībhā**, f. not thinking of anything, Āpast. **A-pratta-devata** (or *-daivata*), mfn. not yet offered to a deity, ĀpŚr. **A-pratyutthāyuka**, mfn. not rising before (w. r. *°yika*), GopBr.; Vait. **A-prapaśya**, mfn. not looking, JaimUp. **A-prayujyamāna**, mfn. not being added, Kāś.; not being borrowed (on interest), Pañcat. **Á-pravartin**, mfn. immovable, ŚBr.; ChUp. **A-pravṛitta**, mfn. not due, unjust (as taxes), Bcar. ii, 44. **A-pravṛitti**, (also) want of news about (gen.), R.; mfn. inactive, KaushUp. **A-praśama**, m. tumult, uproar, Bcar.; Jātakam. **A-prasanna**, mfn. not reconciled, angry with (loc.), Śiś. **A-prahṛishṭaka**, m. a crow, L. **A-prātirūpya**, n. incomparableness, MBh. (*a-prat°*, C.). **A-prāstāvika**, v. l. for *a-prast°*. **A-priyâkhyāyin**, m. teller of bad news (a post at court), Divyâv. **Ap-liṅga**, n. N. of a Liṅga, RTL. 446. **Apva**, mf(*ā*)n. abounding in water, MānGṛ. **Apvā́** (read, 'Impurity,' N. of a deity presiding over evacuation from fright). **Apsu-mat**, (also) having always water, ChUp. **A-phenila**, mfn. frothless, Vishṇ. **A-baddha**, (also) not yet appeared or visible, Ragh. xviii, 47. **Abadhā**, f. a segment of the basis of a triangle, Līl. **A-bandhura**, mfn. high, elevated, Uttarar.; (*am*), ind. dejectedly, sadly, Śiś. **A-bala**, (also) a wife's elder brother, L.; *°lâgni*, mfn. badly digested, Car.; *°liman*, m. enfeeblement, weakness, ChUp.; *°līyas-tva*, n. non-predominance, Vām. i, 3, 11. **Abāla**, m. cocoa-nut, L. **Abja** (in comp.); *-pāṇi*, m. N. of a Buddha, W.; *-samudgata* (?), Bcar. i, 33; *-sambhava*, m. N. of Brahmā, MBh.; *-saras*,

n. a lotus pond, Hit.; °*jâsana*, n. a partic. posture in sitting (=*padmâsana*), HYog. **Abjala**, m. a horse of very low breed, L. **Abda** (in comp.); -*bhū*, mfn. coming from a cloud, Śiś.; -*paryaya*, m. the change of the year, Mn. xi, 27. **Abdhi** (in comp.); -*kanyā*, f. patr. of Lakshmī, Kuval.; -*tanaya*, m. du. the two Aśvins, Kathās.; -*mathana*, n. N. of a wk. in Apabhraṅśa; -*vastrā*, f. the earth, L. **Abbā**, f. a mother, L. **Ab-bindu**, m. a drop of water, BhP. **A'-brahmavarcasin**, m. not an excellent theologian, MaitrS. **A-bhaṅga-ślesha**, m. an ambiguity without any different analysis of the words, Kpr. **A-bhaṅgura**, mf(*ā*)n. level, flat, Suśr.; imperishable, durable, Kathās. **A-bhaya** (in comp.); -*gaṇa*, m. a list of hymns that secure from danger, AV.Pariś.; -*giri-vihāra*, m. N. of a monastery, Inscr.; -*datta*, m. N. of a physician, Mudr. **A-bhavani**, f. non-existence, death, Subh. **A-bhavya**, (also) ugly, R.; wicked, MBh.; unhappy, miserable, Kathās. **A-bhāgadheyá**, mfn. receiving no share, MaitrS. **A-bhājana**, n. not a worthy object for (gen.), Kād. **A-bhāna**, n. non-appearance, Vedântas. **A-bhāvayat**, mfn. unconscious, unwise, Bhag. 2. **A-bhi**, mfn. fearless, MBh. **Abhi-kara**, m. a performer, executor, GopBr. **Abhi-karṇa-kūpam**, ind. into the auditory passage, Naish. **Abhi-karman**, mfn. performing, bringing about, Dharmaś. **Abhi-krishṇam**, ind. towards Kṛishṇa, Śiś. **Abhi-krāmam** (MaitrS.). **Abhi-kshepa**, m. a partic. manner of handling a club, Nīlak. **Abhi-khya**, mfn. like, similar to (comp.), L. **Abhi-khyāna**, (also) groundless demand, L. **Abhi-gīta**, n. a song, Divyâv. **Abhi-gopāya**, Nom. P. °*yáti*, to guard, protect, ŚBr. **Abhi-grāhin**, mfn. seizing, Hir. **Abhi-ghosham**, ind. towards a station of herdsmen, Kir. **Abhi-caraṇa**, n. spell, incantation (see *sâbhicaraṇika*); °*carita*, n. exorcising, incantation, Kāṭh. **Abhi-√cumb**, to kiss, Daś. **Abhi-ceshṭā**, f. activity, Kap. **Abhi-cchāyā**, f. a dark line formed by a cloud's shadow, ĀpŚr. **Abhi-jāta**, (also) distinguished by (comp.), Jātakam.; -*vāc*, mfn. pleasant-voiced, Kum. **Abhi-jñā**, f. (read, 'of which *five* or *six* are enumerated,' and cf. *shaḍ-abh*°, p. 1109); °*jña*, Nom. P. °*jñati*, to become wise, Kulârṇ.; °*jñāta*, mfn. known, famous, Lalit.; acquainted with, Sukh.; °*jñetara*, mfn. not familiar with (comp.), Śaṃk. **Abhi-tashṭīya**, n. N. of the hymn RV. iii, 38 (beginning *abhí táshṭeva*), ŚāṅkhŚr. **Abhi-tāḍana**, n. striking, a stroke, Śiś. **Abhi-tāpin**, mfn. intensely hot, Dharmaś. **Abhi-tsārá** (MaitrS.). **Abhi-dūtam**, ind. towards the messenger, Śiś. **Abhi-dosham**, ind. about dusk, ĀpŚr. **Abhi-dhyālu**, mfn. covetous, Divyâv. **Abhi-nāmadheya**, n. a surname, R. **Abhi-nigadana**, n. the act of talking or reciting to, Kauś. **Abhi-nimroka**, m. (ĀpŚr., Sch.), °**mlocana**, n. (KātyŚr., Sch.) the setting of the sun upon anything. **Abhi-niyama**, m. definiteness as to (comp.), Āpast. **Abhi-nir-√mi**, P. -*minoti*, to cause by a miracle, Divyâv.; to assume a shape, ib. **Abhi-niryāṇa**, n. = *abhi-nishkramaṇa*, Bcar. **Abhi-nir-√hṛi**, to obtain (?), ib. **Abhi-nivishṭaka**, mfn. (prob.) stale, flat, MānGṛ. **Abhi-ni-√vṛit**, to become, ib. **Abhi-niveśana**, n. application to, intentness on (comp.), Car. **Abhi-niścikramishā**, f. desire of going forth from home, Bcar. **Abhi-ni-shic** (√*sic*), to pour out, effuse, ib. **Abhi-nīti**, (also) persuasion, Kir. **Abhi-nīla-netratā**, f. having dark-blue eyes (one of the 32 signs of perfection), Dharmas. 83. **A-bhinna** (in comp.); -*kāla*, mfn. occurring at the same time, BhP.; -*vela*, mfn. not breaking bounds, Kāvyâd.; °*nnâṇḍa*, mfn. having a whole egg, MānGṛ. **Abhi-patti**, (also) possession; -*mat*, mfn. possessed of, Jātakam. **Abhi-paryāvartá**, m. turning towards, coming near, MaitrS. **Abhi-pāṇḍu**, mfn. quite pale (-*tā*, f.), Kir. **Abhi-pālin**, see *gṛihâbh*° (p. 362). **Abhi-pitva** (read, 'see *abhi*-√*2. pat*'). **Abhi-pra-√driś**, Caus. -*darśayati*, to point to (acc.), Jātakam. **Abhi-pra-√budh**, Ā. -*budhyate*, to feel, experience, Hir. **Abhi-pravrajana**, n. advancing, ĀpŚr. **Abhi-prasanna**, mfn. believing in (loc. or gen.), Divyâv. **Abhi-priyatamam**, ind. in the presence of a beloved person, Śiś. **Abhi-prêshaṇa**, n. sending out (messengers), Daś. **Abhi-plava**, (also) a kind of aquatic bird, Vishṇ. **Abhi-bhāshita**, (also) n. pl. words, BhP. **Abhi-bhūti**, (also) a partic. Ekâha, Vait. **Abhi-√bhūsh**, to adorn, Vṛishabhān. **Abhi-maṅgala**, mfn. auspicious, PārGṛ. **Abhi-manāya**, Nom. (also) to recover consciousness or calmness, Daś. **Abhi-marśa**, m. consideration, Jātakam.; °*śin*, mfn. = °*śaka*, Daś. **Abhi-mārgaṇā**, f. tracking, searching out, Jātakam. **Abhi-mukhaya**, Nom. (also) to conciliate (?), Kir. **Abhi-muni**, ind. before the eyes of the Muni, ib. **Abhi-yukta**, (also) m. pl. N. of the Vaiśyas of Kuśa-dvīpa, BhP. **Abhi-raśmimāli**, ind. towards the sun, ib. **Abhirūpa** (in comp.); -*prajāyinī*, f. the mother of beautiful children, MBh.; -*bhūyishṭha*, mfn. for the most part composed of learned men, Śak. **Abhi-lambha**, m. acquisition, Nalac. **Abhi-lashitârtha-cintāmaṇi**, m. N. of an encyclopædia by Bhū-loka-malla Sômêśvara-deva (who reigned from 1127–1138 A.D.). **Abhi-vandya**, mfn. praiseworthy, Naish. **Abhi-vardhana**, n. strengthening, increasing, Kād. **Abhi-vātā**, f. (√*van*) a cow that nourishes her calf, Lāṭy. **Abhi-vijñeya**, mfn. perceivable, visible, R. **Abhi-√vī**, to urge, impel (cf. *a-purushâbhivīta*, p. 1314). **Abhi-vyāhāra**, (also) speaking to, addressing, Jātakam. **Abhi-vratin**, mfn. bent on (comp.), Bcar. **Abhi-śatru**, ind. against the enemy, Śiś. **Abhi-śiro 'gra**, mfn. turned with the points towards the head, Gobh. **Abhi-śrad-√dhā**, to believe in, Vajracch. **Abhi-shava**, (also) consecration, Dharmaś.; °*shavaṇa*, (also) bathing, Kir. **Abhi-sheka-bhūmi-pratilambha**, m. attainment of the royal station, Sukh. i. **Abhi-sam-√yam**, to hold against, Gobh. **Abhi-saṃhṛitya**, ind. conjointly, Mālatīm. **Abhi-sam-√cūrṇ**, to grind, pulverize, Car. **Abhi-sam-pra-√2. hā** (only ind. p. -*hāya*), to forsake, Divyâv. **Abhi-samplava**, m. fluctuation, Bcar. **Abhi-sam-√budh** (with *samyak-sambodhin*), to obtain the highest perfect knowledge, Sukh. i. **Abhi-sambhava**, m., °*vana*, n. attainment, Śaṃk. **Abhi-√2. sū**, to bring forth, Bālar. **Abhi-skanda** (accord. to some, 'm. the mounting [buck],' AV. v, 14, 11). **Abhi-staraṇa**, n. scattering, strewing, TBr., Sch. **Abhi-hāra**, (also) offering, sacrifice, Jātakam. **Abhi-hiṅsana**, n. harming, injuring, R. **Abhi-√2. hṛi** (only in 2. sg. -*hṛiṇīthās*), to be angry with (acc.), RV. viii, 2, 19. **A-bhī-ga**, mfn. unterrified, Śiś. **Abhishṭa-tṛitīyā**, f. the third day in the light half of Mārga-śīrsha, Cat. **A-bhugna-kukshitā**, f. the having the loins not bent (one of the 80 minor marks of a Buddha), Dharmas. 84. **A-bhujaṃga-vat**, mfn. without snakes (and 'without libertines'), Kāvyâd. ii, 322. **A-bhūta** (in comp.); °*tôpamā*, f. a simile implying an impossibility, ib. ii, 38. **A-bhūtala-sparśatā**, f. not touching the ground, Śak. **A-bhedya**, (also) not to be seduced, Kām. **A-bhaishajya**, n. unwholesome food, Divyâv. **Abhy-adhikâdhika**, mfn. always or progressively increasing, Naish. **Abhy-adhyayana**, n. studying (the Veda &c.) at any place (comp.), Gaut. **Abhy-anujñeya**, mfn. to be admitted or assented to, Nyāyam. **Abhy-anumodana**, n. agreement with, approval, Jātakam. **Abhy-antara**, m. 'on intimate terms,' a lover, Divyâv.; -*cārin*, mfn. moving inside, Bhag. **Abhy-ardhám**, ind. beside, apart from (abl.), MaitrS. **Abhy-ava-√gāh**, (also) to enter, Divyâv. **Abhy-avapāta**, m. gravitation, Bcar. xii, 24. **Abhy-avaskanda**, (also) judgment, L. **Abhy-avahāra**, (also) food, R.; °*avahṛita*, mfn. eaten, L. **Abhy-avâyin**, mfn. going down, Āpast. 2. **Abhy-ākāram**, ind. (√*1. kṛī*) sweeping together, ĀpŚr. **Abhy-āgāmin**, mfn. approaching, Ked. **Abhy-ā-nandya**, ind. having thanked and praised, Divyâv. **Abhy-āmnāya**, m. mentioning, mention, Nir. **Abhy-ārūḍha**, (also) very fortunate, L. **Abhy-āvartín** (VS.). **Abhy-āśrāvaṇa**, n. (in ritual) calling out or to, Vait. **Abhy-āsāriṇī**, f. = *abhi-s*°, Kāṭh. **Abhy-āhitâgni**, mfn. (a house) containing a sacred fire, MānGṛ. **Abhy-ujjayini**, ind. towards Ujjayinī, Kathās. **Abhy-uj-√jval**, Caus. -*jvalayati*, to inflame, BaudhP. **Abhy-utthiti**, f. rising from a seat, Naish. **Abhy-utsāha**, m. energy, exertion, Buddh. **Abhy-udayâvaha**, m. bringing prosperity, Bcar. **Abhy-udācārin**, mfn. rising against (acc.), AitBr. **Abhy-udgati**, f. going to meet, Daś. **Abhy-uddravaṇa**, n. running forth, TBr., Sch. **Abhy-uddharaṇa**, n. (MBh.), °**dhāra**, m. (Divyâv.) rescuing, deliverance. **Abhy-unmodanīya**, mfn. to be assented to or acquiesced in, Col. **Abhy-upapatti**, f. (also) confession of faith, Divyâv.; °*upapattṛi*, m. one who approaches to help, Car.; °*upapādana*, n. coming to aid, Daś. **Abhra** (in comp.); -*kūṭa*, m. n. the top of a cloud, Bcar.; Śak.; -*khaṇḍa*, m. n. a portion of a cl°, Mṛicch.; -*ga*, m. 'cloud-goer,' a bird, AgP.; -*giri*, m. N. of a mountain, Hcat.; -*m-ga*, mfn. cloud-going, JaimUp.; -*phullaka*, m. an actor, L.; -*maṅsī* (read -*māṅsī*); -*maya*, mf(*ī*)n. hidden in clouds, HPariś.; °*bhrâgama*, m. 'cl°-approach,' beginning of the rainy season, Mālatīm. **Abhramu-jīvitêśa** (Dharmaś.), °**mū-pati** (Vcar.), m. N. of Indra's elephant. **A-bhrāja**, n. N. of a Sāman, ĀrshBr. **Amaṭha**, m. (fr. √*3. am*) a stately gait (=*prakarsha-gati*), L. **Amamri** or °**rī**, f. a kind of plant, Kauś. **A-mara** (in comp.); -*gaṇanā-lekhya*, n. the list (or number) of the gods, Ragh. viii, 94; -*garbha*, m. a divine child, MBh.; -*giri* (Kālac.), -*parvata* (Hcat.), m. Mount Meru; -*druma*, m. the Pārijāta tree, Śiś.; -*maya*, mf(*ī*)n. consisting of gods, VarBṛS.; -*mṛigīdṛiś* (Kathās.), -*rāja*, m. N. of a Prākṛit poet; -*vadhū* (Hcat.), an Apsaras; -*varṇin*, mfn. of divine colour or beauty, MBh.; °*râgāra*, n. a god's house, temple, Kād. **A-marī**, f. a goddess, HPariś. **A-mala** (in comp.); -*paksha-vihaṃgama*, m. a swan, Śiś.; °*lânvaya*, mfn. of pure or noble race, Mālatīm. **A'ma-vishṇu** (RV.). **Amā-putra**, mf(*ā*)n. together with the son or daughter; (*ā*), f. (with *dṛishad*) the larger with the smaller mill-stone, Kauś. **A-māpya**, mfn. immeasurable, Vajracch. **A-mita** (in comp.); -*dhvaja*, (also) N. of a Tathāgata, Sukh. ii; -*prabha* or -*prabhāsa*, m. (=*amitâbha*), Sukh. i; -*mati*, mfn. of unbounded wisdom, Bcar.; -*skandha*, m. N. of a Tathāgata, Sukh. ii; °*tâbha* (see MWB. 183 &c.); °*tâśanā*, f. 'immoderate in eating,' N. of one of the Mātṛis attending on Skanda, MBh.; °*tâyur-dhyāna-sūtra*, n. N. of a Buddhist Sūtra. **A-mitodana**, m. (for *a-mṛit*°) N. of a king, Buddh. **A-mitra** (in comp.); -*karman*, n. an unfriendly act, Bcar.; -*karshaṇa* (MBh.), °*shin* (R.), mfn. harassing enemies. **A-mithuna**, mfn. (pl.) not both sexes promiscuously, ĀśvGṛ. **A-mithyā-√kṛi**, to make true, confirm, MBh. **A-mīmāṅsaka**, mfn. uncritical, Jātakam. **Amukīya**, mfn. belonging to such and such a person, IndSt. **A-mukta-viśrambha**, mfn. with unshaken confidence (*am*, ind.), Bcar. **Amútaḥ-pradāna**, n. an offering from there, TBr. **Amudā**, ind. then, at that time, Śaṃkar. **A-mudra**, mfn. having no seal (by which to prove one's self legitimate), MBh.; Hariv.; having no impression or image of one's self, having no equal, Kathās. **Amudryañc** or **amumuyañc**, mfn. turned in that direction, Vop. **A-mūlā**, f. (accord. to some, 'movable property,' AV. v, 31, 4). **A-mṛita** (in comp.); -*cit*, mfn. heaped or piled up like nectar, MaitrS.; -*dhāyin*, mfn. sipping n°, VP.; -*pāyin*, mfn. = prec.; listening to delightful speech, SivaP.; -*plavana*, n. a stream or flow of n°, Mālatīm.; -*bhāshaṇa*, n. words like n°, Kāv.; -*megha*, m. a cloud of n°, Mālatīm.; -*saras*, n. 'lake of nectar,' N. of a city in the Panjāb (commonly called Amritsar); °*tâtman*, mfn. consisting of nectar, Kāvyâd.; °*tī-√bhū*, to become n°, Yājñ. **A-meghôpaplava**, mfn. not covered with clouds, Śiś. **A-medhya-pratimantraṇa**, n. conjuring of unlucky omens, ĀpY. **A-meni** (accord. to others, 'inflicting no punishment'). **A-mogha**, (also) m. a shark, L.; -*tā*, f. unerringness (of a weapon), Kir.; -*deva*, m. N. of a poet, Cat.; -*rāghava*, m. N. of a drama, ib.; -*vatī*, f. N. of a river, RV.; °*ghârtha*, mfn. of unerring purpose, ib. **A-moha**, m. (with Buddhists) freedom from ignorance (one of the three roots of virtue), Dharmas. 138. **A-mauktika**, mfn. having no pearls, Mṛicch. **Amnás**, ind. = *amnás*, MaitrS. **Ambaka**, m. N. of a poet, Subh. **Amba-pālī**, f. N. of a courtezan (converted by Gautama Buddha), MWB. 409. **Ambara** (in comp.); -*khaṇḍa*, m. n. a rag (and 'a cloud'), Bhartṛ.; -*mālā*, f. N. of a woman, Viddh.; -*lekhin*, mfn. touching the sky, Ragh. **Ambika**, m. N. of a man, Kāṭh.; Anukr. **Ambikā** (in comp.); -*khaṇḍa*, m. n. N. of a ch. of the SkandaP.; -*pariṇaya*, m. N. of a Campū; -*māhātmya*, n. N. of a ch. of the SkandaP.; -*vana*, n. N. of a forest, BhP. **Ambu** (in comp.); -*kapi*, m. Delphinus Gangeticus, L.; -*kapha*, m. cuttlefish-bone, L.; -*kāntāra*, m. N. of Varuṇa, L.; -*kukkuṭa*, m. a water-fowl, L.; -*ja-bāndhava*, m. 'lotus-friend,' the sun, Kuval.; -*jâsanā*, f. 'l°-seated,' Lakshmī, Daś.; -*jīvin*, mfn. living by water (as a fisherman &c.), Vishṇ.; -*dhakāminī*, f. 'ocean-lover,' a river, Bhām.; -*dhāra*, m. a cloud, Bcar.; -*priya*, m. a kind of ratan (also called *vidula*), L.; -*bhakshya*, mfn. subsisting on water, Up.; *-maya*, mf(*ī*)n. consisting of w°, Kāśīkh.; *-līlā-geha*, n. a pleasure-house standing in water, Kathās.; *-vardhana*, n. high sea-tide, L.; *-vallī*, f. Momordica Charantia, L.; *-vāsa*, m. N. of Varuṇa, L.; *-vega*, m. a current of w°, BhP.; *-samplava*, m. a flow of w°, ib.; *-sūkara*, m. a kind of porcine crocodile, L.; *-hasta*, m. a water-elephant (cf. *jala-dvīpa*), L.; °*ûrmi-gata*, mfn. gone to (i. e. reflected by) waves of water (as the moon), Bcar. iii, 45. **Ambujinī**, f. a lotus plant, Naish. **Ambeka**, m. N. of a Commentator, Cat. **Ambhastas**, ind. out of the water, Śiś. **Ambho** (in comp. for *ambhas*); *-garbha*, mfn. containing water (as a cloud), Mālatīm.; *-ja-bandhu*, m. 'lotus-friend,' the sun, Hcat.; *-ja-vadanā*, f. a lotus-faced woman, Kautukas. **Ammarā**, f. the second beam of timber over a door, L. **Amla** (in comp.); *-juṇḍī*, f. the fourth change in warm milk when mixed with Takra (v. l. *amla-duṇḍī*), L.; *-tikta-kashāya*, mfn. astringent (and) bitter (and) sour; m. astr° (and) sour (and) bitter taste, L. **Ámloṭa**, m. ebony, Diospyros Ebenaster, L. **Ayaḥ-śalākā**, f. an iron dart, L. **A-yathāvṛitta**, mfn. behaving improperly, Daś. **Ayam-āsya**, m. (said to be the fuller form of *a-yāsya*, q. v.), JaimUp. **Ayas-kīla**, m. N. of a mountain, Divyâv.; (*ā*), f. N. of a river, ib. **Ayātrika** or °**trīya**, mfn. inauspicious (?), Hāla, Sch. **A-yuk-pāda-yamaka**, n. = *a-yugma-p*°, Bhaṭṭ., Sch. **A-yuga** (in comp.); *-cchada*, m. Echites Scholaris, L.; *-sapti*, m. the sun (= *sapta-s*°), Śiś. **A-yuja** (in comp.); *-kāram*, ind. in an odd number of times, HirP.; °*jâkshara*, mfn. having an odd number of syllables, ĀpGṛ. **A-yuta** (in comp.); *-dhā*, ind. ten thousandfold, JaimUp.; *-dhāra*, mfn. possessing ten thousand streams, ib. **A-yūthika**, mfn. separated from the herd or flight, KāṭhGṛ. **Ayo** (in comp. for *ayas*); *-ga*, mfn. relating to iron, Nalac.; *-'ni*, m. a pestle, L.; *-maṇi*, m. f. a magnet, L.; *-miśra*, mfn. set with iron, Āpast. **A-yoga-peśala**, mfn. unskilled in emergencies, Bcar. viii, 35. **A-yogin**, mfn. separated (from a beloved object), Naish. **A-yaugika**, (also) not being applied, Kām. **Ay-man**, n. (√*ay*) = *saṃgrāma*, L. **A-rakta**, mfn. undyed, Mn. x, 87; *-tāmra*, mfn. unstained by red, Bcar. viii, 22. **Araṃ-gamá** (accord. to some, 'going fast,' 'quick'). **A-rajanī-kṛita**, mfn. not coloured or dyed, Baudh. **A-rajaska**, (also) dustless, HPariś.; free from impurity (others, 'meek, gentle'), Bcar. ii, 5. **A-rajo-viṭṭā**, f. not yet having the monthly courses, Kauś. **A-raḍa**, m. (said to be fr. √*ṛi*) a tree, L. **Araṇā-vihārin**, mfn. dwelling in virtue (others, 'dwelling in a forest'), Buddh. 2. **Áraṇi** (accord. to some, 'uncouthness' [Sāy. reads *araṇim*], AV. i, 18, 2). **Araṇya** (in comp.); *-nitya*, mfn. used to dwell in a forest, MBh.; °*nyôpanishad*, f. N. of an Upanishad. **Á-radhra** (accord. to others, 'rich, liberal;' cf. *radhra*). **A-rasaná**, mfn. having no girdle, MaitrS. **A-rākshasa**, mfn. freed from Rākshasas, MBh. **A-rāga-dvesha** (in comp.); *-tas*, ind. not from passion or anger, Bhag.; °*shin*, mfn. neither loving nor hating, Vishṇ. **Arāṭakī**, f. a kind of plant, AV. **Arāḍa**, m. N. of a Muni, Bcar. **A-rântara-gatā**, f. (with *nābhi*) N. of a mythical place, Divyâv. **Arāla** (in comp.); *-keśī*, f. a woman with curled hair, Ragh.; *-hasta*, m. a partic. position of the hands, Cat. **Ari-śāsin**, mfn. chastising enemies, Hariv. **Arishṭa** (in comp.); *-nemi*, (also) N. of Vishṇu, L.; *-roga*, m. a partic. disease, KātyŚr., Sch. (also °*ty-āmaya*, KātyŚr.). **Arishṭaka**, mfn. suffering from the disease Arishṭa, Kauś. **A-rīṇa**, mfn. not wanting, full of, Naish. **Aruḥ-sráṇa** (accord. to some read *aruḥ-srāṇa* [fr. √*śrā*, to cook] = 'a remedy which causes a wound to ripen or heal,' AV. ii, 3, 3). **Aruṇa**, (also) coarse (as food), Jātakam.; full of, mixed with (instr. or comp.), ib.; *-datī*, f. a girl with reddish teeth, ĀpGṛ. **Arundhatī-darśana-nyāya**, m. the rule of the view of the star Arundhatī, A. **Arula**, n. water, L.; a small boat, L. **A-rūḍha-mūlatva**, n. state of not having taken root, insufficient foundation, Mālav. **A-rūpa**, (also) emancipation (= *nirvāṇa*), MWB. 137; *-rāga*, m. longing for immaterial life in the higher heavens, ib. 127; *-loka*, m. a formless heaven (4 classes enumerated), ib. 213; °*pâvacara*, m. pl. (with *devāḥ*) the gods of the formless heaven, Dharmas. 129. **A-repa**, mfn. = *a-repas*, Baudh. **A-romaśa**, n. absence of a partic. faulty pronunciation of the sibilants, MāṇḍŚ. 1. **Arka** (in comp.); *-dugdha*, n. the milk of Calotropis Gigantea, L.; *-netra*, mfn. twelve-eyed, Kālac.; *-bandhu*, m. 'belonging to the kindred of the Sun,' N. of Buddha, Bcar.; °*kâtmajā*, f. 'daughter of the Sun,' N. of Yamunā, L.; °*kêshṭa*, n. yellow sandal-wood, L. 2. **Arka**, Nom. P. °*kati*, to become a sun, Subh. **Arghya** (in comp.); *-dāna*, n. a partic. act of homage to the sun, RTL. 407; *-śīla*, mfn. of deferential character or disposition, R. **Arcas**, n. worship, praise, L. **Arcā** (in comp.); °*cârha* (MBh.), °*cârhaka* (Bcar.), mfn. worthy of honour or praise; °*cā-viḍambanā*, f. false or feigned worship, BhP. **Arcicayishu**, mfn. (fr. Desid. of √*arc*) wishing to praise or worship, Kir. **Arj** (erase 1. before root). **Arjin**, mfn. acquiring, Śiś. **Arṇava-śakkarī**, f. (incorrect for *-śakvarī*) sea-girt (the earth), Kāvyâd. iii, 149. **Arṇikā**, f. a partic. weight (= 2 Māshas), L. **Artha** (in comp.); *-kathā*, f. (fr. Pāli *aṭṭha-kathā*) 'explaining meanings,' a class of Buddhist wks., MWB. 65; *-kartṛi* (Kālac.), *-kārin* (R.), mfn. useful, profitable; *-kāmya*, Nom. P. °*yati*, to wish for money, Śiś.; *-gati*, f. meaning, sense, SaddhP.; *-caryā*, f. doing business, ĀśvGṛ.; promoting another's affairs (one of the 7 elements of popularity), Jātakam. (Dharmas. 19); *-darpaṇa*, m. N. of a wk. on ŚāṅkhGṛ.; *-darśin*, m. N. of one of the 24 mythical Buddhas, MWB. 136, n. 1; *-dāyâda*, m. an heir to wealth, Bcar.; *-dyotanikā*, f. N. of a wk. on dramatic art; *-nāśaka*, mfn. wasting money, prodigal, Daś.; *-pañcaka*, n. N. of a wk. on Bhakti; *-padavī*, f. the path of advantage (°*vīṃ* √*gam*, 'to be intent on one's adv°'), BhP.; *-para*, mfn. greedy, covetous, R.; *-pāṭha*, m. the reading required by the sense, ĀpGṛ., Sch.; *-punarukta*, n. (in Nyāya) repetition of the same meaning in other words; *-pūrvaka*, mfn. having a particular aim or object (*-tva*, n.), VPrāt., Sch.; *-yogya*, mfn. useful, profitable, Daś.; *-racana*, n. pursuing an aim, exertion, endeavour, BhP.; *-rūpa*, n. a thing, matter, Pat.; *-lāghava*, n. taking a thing easily, Naish.; *-lopa*, (also) loss of property, MBh.; *-lola*, mfn. coveting money, Kālac.; *-vaśa*, cause and effect, Sukh. i; *-vāda*, (also) speaking for gain, L.; *-viśeshaṇa*, n. (prob.) specification of any matter, Sāh.; *-vyavahāra*, m. a pecuniary suit, Yājñ., Sch.; *-ślesha*, m. a pun or quibble based upon the sense (not upon the form of words, as opp. to *śabda-śl*°), Śiś. ix, 31, Sch.; *-saṃdeha*, m. a dubious or critical matter, Hit. (v. l.); *-sama*, mfn. having the same sense, synonymous, L.; *-samāhartṛi*, m. a collector of money, Mn. vii, 60; *-sambhava*, mfn. (a meaning) derived from the (mere) object of thought (without regard to the sense or context of the phrase), Kpr.; Sāh.; *-sādhana*, n. accomplishment of a purpose, means of attaining an object, Ragh.; Kathās.; °*thâkshipta*, mfn. effected by any cause, Śaṃk.; °*thâdhinātha*, m. 'lord of wealth,' N. of Kubera, Kāv.; °*thânartha*, m. du. what is expedient or not expedient, Mn. viii, 24; °*thântarya*, n. repetition required by the sense of one or more words successively, IndSt.; °*thâpêksha*, mfn. pursuing (worldly) objects, Hir.; °*thâbhipatti*, f. resulting from the facts, MBh.; °*the-ga*, mfn. following one's business or vocation, Āpast.; °*thôddyotanikā*, f. N. of a Comm. on Śak. by Rāghava-bhaṭṭa. **Arthāpaya**, (accord. to others) to esteem highly, make much of anything, Naish. **Arthushya**, mfn. having a purpose, desirous of &c. (= *arthin*), L. **Ardha** (in comp.); *-kapiśa*, mfn. half-brown, brownish, Daśar., Sch.; *-daṇḍa*, m. h° the fine, Mn. viii, 243; *-devatā*, f. a half-deity, demigod, JaimUp.; *-dvi-caturaska*, n. a partic. posture, Vikr.; *-nākula*, n. a kind of Yoga posture, L.; *-nishpanna*, mfn. h°-finished, Rājat.; *-phālaka*, m. or n. N. of a partic. garment, Bhadrab.; m. pl. a partic. Jaina sect (*-mata*, n. its doctrine), ib.; *-makuṭa*, m. N. of Śiva, L.; *-mānava*, m. an actor dressed like Kṛishṇa, L.; *-mānusha*, m. an actor dressed as a god, L.; *-māyūrī*, f. (in music) one of the three Mārjanās (q. v.), L.; *-muṇḍa*, mfn. h°-bald, Bcar.; *-rūpa*, mfn. forming a h° (*-tā*, f.), Sarvad.; *-rcasya* (for *-ṛic*°), n. recitation by half-verses, Vait.; *-vaiśasa*, n. h° a murder, Kum.; *-suptaka*, mf(*ikā*)n. h°-asleep, Kṛishṇaj.; *-spṛishṭa*, mfn. (in gram.) half-touched (see *spṛishṭa*), VPrāt., Sch.; *-hara*, mfn. inheriting half a property, Vishṇ.; *-hastaka*, m. a distance of 120 inches, L.; °*dhânta-râika-vācaka*, m. (scil. *dosha*) = *ardhântarâikapadatā*, Kpr.; °*dhâvishṭa*, mfn. h°-faltering (speech), Kathās.; °*dhâsi*, m. 'half-sword,' a dagger, MBh. ('a one-edged sword,' Nīlak.); °*dhêshṭakā*, f. half a brick, Śulbas.; °*dhôcchishṭa*, mfn. having the half left, Kathās.; °*dhôpā*, f. half an Ūpā, Drāhy., Sch. **Ardhaya**, Nom. P. °*yati*, to halve, Līl. **Arpaṇa-mīmāṃsā**, f. N. of wk. **Arpima**, n. milk from a cow which has a diminutive calf, L. **Arpiśa**, n. = prec. and next, L. **Arpisha**, n. fresh meat, L. **Arbuda**, (also) the cartilage of a rib, Vishṇ.; (with Buddhists) N. of one of the 8 cold hells, Dharmas. 122; *-dhā*, ind. millionfold, JaimUp.; *-māhātmya*, n. N. of a ch. of the SkandaP.; °*dô-dāsarpiṇī*, f. 'creeping near of Arbuda,' N. of a partic. sacrificial path, AitBr. **Arbhaka**, (also) N. of a poet, Subh. **Arma-kapālá**, m. n. a potsherd from a heap of rubbish, TS. **Aryaka**, m. N. of a demon causing disease, Hariv. **Aryama-nandana**, m. patr. of Yama, Naish. **Arvāk-srotas**, mfn. turned downwards in moving (as an animal), MBh. **Arhaka**, mfn. entitled to (comp.), Hcat.; little, small (for *arbhaka*), L. **Arhaṇīya**, mfn. worthy to be honoured (superl. *-tama*), MBh. **Arhasāna**, m. the moon, L.; a horse, L. **A-lakshaṇaka**, mfn. undefinable, incomparable (said of Buddha), Divyâv. **A-lakshman**, mfn. inauspicious, MBh. **Alaṃ-kāra**, (also) N. of a minister of Jaya-siṃha of Kaśmīr (1129–1150 A.D.; he is also called Laṅkaka); *-bhāṇḍa*, n. a jewel-box, Mṛicch.; *-ratnâkara*, m., *-sarvasva*, n., °*rânusāriṇī*, f. N. of wks. **A-laṅghita**, mfn. not reached or touched, Mṛicch.; *-pūrva*, mfn. not infringed or violated before, Vikr.; °*tâtman*, mfn. not forgetting one's self, Kathās. **A-latikā**, f. a soil destitute of creeping plants, Kām. **A-labdha** (in comp.); *-gādha*, mfn. one who has not reached the ground, Jātakam.; *-pada*, mfn. one who has found no place in or has made no impression upon (loc.), Ragh. **A-labhya**, (also) unintelligible, Sah. **Alam** (in comp.); *-artha-vacas*, n. a word of refusal or prohibition, Śiś. x, 75; *-ārya*, mfn. very generous, Lalit.; *-bhavishṇu*, mfn. being able to (inf.), BrahmaP. **A-lavaṇa** (read, 'not salt'); °*ṇâśin*, mfn. not eating salt food, ŚrS. **Alasaya**, Nom. °*yati*, to slacken, relax (trans.), Subh. **A-lāghava**, n. (with *manasaḥ*) no ease or relief of conscience, Mn. xi, 234. **Alātacakra**, n. a fire-brand carried around (*-vat*, ind.), MBh.; R. &c. **A-lābha-lābha**, loss and gain, Bcar. xi, 43. **A-lipi**, mfn. unstained (and 'unwritten'), Jain. **Ali-mat**, mfn. swarming with bees, Kāvyâd. **Alīka**, (also) *ā*, f. a courtezan, L.; (°*ka*)-*vāda-śīla*, mfn. inclined or disposed to tell untruths, Daś. **A-luñca**, mfn. not plucking or tearing, Bhar. **Aluma**, m. (said to be fr. √*al*) decoration, L.; a barber, L.; fire, L. **Á-lūna**, m. no remnant or remaining particles, MaitrS. **A-lepa**, m. = prec., IndSt.; mfn. unstained, clean, pure, MBh. **A-lopī**, f. 'Non-destroyer,' N. of a goddess, RTL. 226. **Algáṇḍu**, v. l. for *alāṇḍu* (q. v.). **Alpa** (in comp.); *-kaṇṭha*, mfn. having a feeble voice, Śiksh.; *-kāya*, mfn. thin, emaciated (*-tva*, n.), Suśr.; *-cchada*, mfn. scantily clad, Mṛicch.; *-deśa-vṛitti-tva* (see *vyā-vṛitta*, p. 1039); *-nidāna*, mfn. originating from a trifling cause, Suśr.; *-paricchada*, mfn. possessing little property, poor, Divyâv. (conj.); *-pushpaka*, m. 'small-flowered,' the Tilaka tree, L.; (*ā*), f. the small Banana, L.; *-phala*, mf(*ā*)n. yielding little fruit, of small results or consequences, MānGṛ.; *-bhujântara*, mfn. narrow-chested, Vikr.; *-vat* or *-vitta-vat*, mfn. possessing little, poor, Hcat.; *-sparśa*, mf(*ā*)n. insensible, Suśr. (v. l.); *-sva-mat*, mfn. possessing little, poor, Śatr.; *-svara*, mfn. having a feeble voice, Kathās.; containing few vowels, Bhāshik.; *-hariṇa*, m. a kind of small red deer, L.; °*pâṅga*, mfn. small-bodied (*-tva*, n.), Ratnâv.; °*pâtaṅka* or °*pâbādha*, mfn. having little pain, well, healthy, Kāraṇḍ.; °*pâlpa*, mfn. very little, Śak. (*-bhās*, mfn. 'of very l° splendour,' Megh.); °*pâvaśishṭa*, mfn. having little left (*-tva*, n.), MBh.; °*pâvaśesha*, mfn. id., R.; °*pī-bhāva*, m. decrease, diminution, Dhātup. **Alpakát**, ind. (also) nearly, almost, ŚBr. **Allaṭa**, m. N. of the author of the last part of the Kpr. **Allāḍa-laharī**, f. N. of a Comm. on the Kir. **Allāpadīna**, m. = العابدين, N. of a king, Sāh. (v. l.). **Ava-kara**, (also) a kind of plant (growing on garbage heaps), Kauś. **Ava-kalana**, n. burning with Kuśa grass, Baudh. **Ava-kāśe**, ind. (prob.) about dawn, MānGṛ. **Ava-kīrṇa**, mfn. = *ā-k*°, Divyâv. **Ava-keśin**, m. a barren tree, Naish. **A-vakra-gamitā**, f. having a straight gait (one of the 80 minor marks of a Buddha), Dharmas. 84. **Ava-khāda** (accord. to others fr. √*khad* = *khid*, 'hindrance, annoyance'). **Ava-gamana**, (also) attachment, devotion, Kauś. **Ava-gītha**,

n. early recitation at a sacrifice, L. **Ava-graha,** (also) mark of the elision of an initial *a; -śaka,* N. of a Pariśishṭa of the SV. **Ava-ghoshaṇā,** f. announcement, publication, Jātakam. **Ava-caraka,** m. a footman, runner, Divyâv. **Ava-cāraṇa,** mfn. running, ib. **Ava-cīra-vicīraka,** mfn. dilapidation, ib. **Ava-cchādana,** n. covering, Drāhy. (Sch.). **Ava-jayana,** n. means of subduing or healing a disease, Car. **Ava-jāta,** mfn. misborn (?), Divyâv. **Ava-jihva,** mfn. tongueless, Hir. **Ava-jvalana,** n. illumining, ĀpŚr., Sch. **Ava-jvāla,** m. hot infusion, Kauś. (Sch.). **A-vañcanatā,** f. honesty, Cāṇ. **Avaḍa,** m. a kind of field, L. **Ava-tarpaṇa,** n. a soothing remedy, palliative, Suśr. **Ava-tāḍana,** n. striking, a stroke, blow, Mālatīm. **Ava-tāra** (acc. with √*labh*, 'to get an opportunity'), Divyâv.; *-prêkshin,* mfn. watching opportunities, espying faults, ib. **Avatká** (accord. to some = 'spring water,' AV. ii, 3, 1). **A-vatsala,** mf(*ā*)n. not tender, harsh, cruel to (loc.), Ratnâv. **A-vatsā,** f. a cow whose calf is dead, Yājñ. i, 170. **Ava-dāta-vasana,** mfn. 'clothed in white,' laical, Divyâv. **Ava-dāna-kalpalatā,** f. 'storehouse of legends of Buddha's life and acts,' N. of a celebrated wk., MWB. 326, n. 1. **Ava-dola,** m. swinging, Ragh. ix, 46 (accord. to Sch. *nava-d°*). **Ava-draṅga,** an earnest (?), Divyâv. **Ava-dhāna,** (also) fixing, fastening, MBh.; *-vat,* mfn. attentive (*-tā,* f.), Naish., Sch. **Avadhika** (?), mfn. occurring after (comp.), Daś. **Ava-√dhīr** (read *ava-dhīraya*). **Avana,** (also) mfn. preserving, a preserver, Dharmaś. **Ava-niḥsaraṇa,** n. keeping away from (abl.), Lalit. **Avanī-mukha,** mfn. turned towards the earth, R. **Avanti-mihira,** m. N. of Varāha-mihira, Hcar. **A-vapana,** n. not shaving, ParGṛ. **A-vapus,** mfn. bodiless, formless, MBh. **Ava-pūraṇa,** n. filling or covering with (comp.), Car. **Ava-pṛishṭhī-kṛita** or **°ṭhībhūta,** mfn. set on the path of Buddhahood (?), Divyâv. **Ava-bharjita,** mfn. (√*bhṛij,* Caus.) roasted, parched, i.e. burned, destroyed, BhP. **Avabhartsana,** n. scolding, threatening, Jātakam. **Ava-bhāsya,** mfn. to be (or being) illumined, Śaṃk. **Ava-mūrdhaka,** mfn. with hanging head, Divyâv. **Ava-mocana,** n. (also) putting on (?), Nalac. **Avamohana,** n. a narcotic, Car. **Avara** (in comp.); *-kaṅka,* f. N. of a city, Jain.; *°rârdha,* mfn. belonging to the lower half, KaushUp. **A-vartin,** mfn. behaving improperly, MBh. **A-varshatarkye,** ind. when no rain is to be expected, when the sky is clear, ĀpGṛ. **A-valita,** mfn. not bent or curved, VarBṛS. **Ava-lipsa,** m. a kind of amulet, AV. Paipp. **Ava-lokanaka,** mfn. having a fine view, ib.; *°lokita,* m. (also) N. of a poet, Subh. **Avalopa,** (also) hurting, wounding, Śiś. **Ava-lopana,** n. cutting off, destruction, Vās. **A-valka,** m. Gymnema Sylvestre, L. **A-valgu-kārin,** mfn. not dealing fairly with (loc.), MBh. **Ava-vādaka,** m. a spiritual instructor, Divyâv. **Ava-visraṃsita,** mfn. (√*sraṃs,* Caus.) fallen down, Bcar. **Avaśānta,** mfn. (√*śam*) extinguished, AitBr. **Ava-√śṛidh,** P. *-śardhayati,* to break wind against, mock, defy, Mn. viii, 282; *°śardhayitṛi,* m. one who breaks wind upon or against, Vishṇ. **A-vaśya,** (also) disobedient, KaṭhUp.; Pañcat.; *-bhāgīyaka,* mfn. inevitable, Divyâv.; *-yātavyatā,* f. necessity of marching against an enemy, Kām.; *°śyêndriya,* mfn. one who does not control his senses, MBh. **Avaśyāya-kiraṇa,** m. 'cold-rayed,' the moon, Dhūrtan. **Ava-shṭabdhatā,** f. stiffness, rigidity, Śaṃk. **Avasara** (in comp.); *-pāṭhaka,* m. a bard, panegyrist, Nalac. **Ava-sárpaṇa** (ŚBr.). **Ava-sādanā,** f. humiliation, discouragement; *-vineya,* mfn. to be taught by disc°, Divyâv. **Ava-sāraṇā,** f. rehabilitation of a monk, Buddh. **Avasita** (in comp.); *-kārya,* mfn. one who has finished what had to be done, satisfied, Vikr.; *-maṇḍana,* mfn. entirely adorned or dressed, Śak.; *°târtha,* mfn. (= *°takārya*), Daś.; *°siti,* f. conclusion, end, Ked. **Avasushirā,** f. the neck, L. **Ava-skandana,** n. (also) attack, onset, rushing on (*prati*), Kpr. **Ava-sthātavya,** n. (impers.) it is to be stayed or remained, Kād. **Ava-sphūrjathu,** m. rolling of thunder, Kaṇ. (v.l.). **Ava-sphoṭana,** n. cracking the fingers, Gaut. **Ava-sraṃsana,** n. falling down, Dhātup. **Ava-svāpanikā** or **°panī,** f. (the magical art of) lulling to sleep, HPariś. **A-vahat,** mfn. not flowing, stagnant (as water), ĀśvGṛ. **Ava-hārika,** n. booty, plunder, MBh. **Avahita-pāṇi,** mfn. holding in the hand, Āpast. **Avahni,** mfn. (prob.) not sacrificing, Nir. **Avâṇśa,** m. the penis, SāmavBr. **Avāk** (in comp. for *avāñc*); *-chruti,* mfn. deaf and dumb, L.; *-phala,* mfn. having evil consequences, MBh.; *-srotas,* mfn. tending downwards, MBh. **A-vāg** (in comp. for *avāk* above); *-ja,* mfn. not produced from the voice (sound), DhyānabUp.; *-dushṭa,* mfn. not using coarse words, Hariv. **A-vācaṃ-yama,** mfn. not suppressing the voice, not silent, TBr. **A-vācāla,** mfn. not talkative or boastful, Rājat. 1. **A-vācya,** (also) not deserving censure, unblamable, irreproachable, Mṛicch. **Avāñc,** (more correctly *avāñc,* also) southern, Daś. **Avâptu-kāma,** mfn. desirous of attaining, Bcar. **Á-vāruṇa,** mfn. not relating or belonging to Varuṇa, TBr. **A-vārtta,** mfn. not worthless, important, Sarvad. **Avâlamba,** m. = *apâl°,* ĀpŚr. **A-vikalpaka,** mfn. not hesitating, MBh. **A-vikāra,** (also) m. a partic. Samādhi, Buddh. **A-vikuṇṭha,** mfn. not blunt or obtuse, sharp, penetrating, BhP. **A-vikūṇita,** mfn. not kept contracted (nose), HPariś. **A-vikṛishita** or **°shṭa,** mfn. not kept asunder, contracted (as vowels), Prāt. **A-vikopita,** mfn. uninjured (relics), Divyâv. **A-vikramaṇa,** n. suppression of the Krama-pāṭha (q.v.), Prāt. **A-vikrayya,** mfn. not to be sold, Kull. **A-viklishṭa,** mfn. distinct, intelligible, R. (B.) iv, 19, 10 (v.l.). **A-vikhaṇḍana,** n. non-violation, Jātakam. **A-vikhyāta-dosha,** mfn. one who has not manifestly committed a crime, Gaut. **A-vigaṇayya,** ind. taking no notice of, RPrāt. **A-vighna-maṅgala,** n. prayer for undisturbedness or security, Mālatīm. **Á-vicita,** mfn. not piled up, MaitrS. **A-vijānaka,** mfn. not knowing, not familiar with, MBh. **A-vitaraṇa,** n. not transferring, Suśr. **A-vitāna,** mfn. not empty (and 'without an awning'), Śiś. iii, 50. **Avida,** ind. an exclamation of surprise and grief (also repeated and with *bho*), Mṛicch. **A-vidvishāvat,** mfn. unhostile (?), Hir. (conj.). **A-vidhāyin,** mfn. not docile or compliant, Bhpr. **A-vidhura,** mfn. not bereft or lonely, Śaṃk.; 'not deprived of a carriage-pole' and 'cheerful,' Śiś. xii, 8. **A-vidhya,** mfn. not to be pierced or wounded, invulnerable, MBh. **Avina,** (also) a bird, L.; the elbow, L. **A-vinyasta,** mfn. untrodden, Jātakam. **A-viprapañca,** mfn. (prob.) inexplicable, Buddh. **A-viplava,** mf(*ā*)n. uninterrupted, Yogas.; uncorrupted, chaste, MBh. (v.l.). **A-vibarha,** m. not scattering, ŚāṅkhBr. **A-vibudha,** (also) not surrounded by learned men, Kāvyâd. ii, 322. **Á-vibhakta** (MS.). **A-vibhajya** (read, 'Kum. iv, 37'). **A-vibhavat,** mfn. not existing or present, KātyŚr. **A-vibhraṃśa,** mfn. not fallen or stumbled upon, R. **A-vimanas,** (also) not dejected, in good spirits, Jātakam. **A-vimarśa,** mfn. inconsiderate, thoughtless, Kathās.; *°śitavya,* mfn. not to be considered, unimportant, Mālatīm. **A-vimuktôpanishad,** f. N. of an Upanishad. **A-vimukham,** ind. without averting the face, straightforward (v.l. *abhi-m°*), MBh. **A-vimocana,** n. (also) insolubleness, Hir. **A-virala-dantatā,** f. the having teeth without gaps (one of the 32 signs of perfection), Dharmas. 83. **A-viralita,** mfn. not separated, closely united or joined, Uttarar. **A-virūḍha,** mfn. not deeply rooted, wavering, Jātakam. **A-viroddhṛi,** mfn. not opposing or contending, MBh. **A-vilamba-sarasvatī,** f. N. of a poetess, Cat. **A-vilambya,** ind. without delay, Kathās. **Avi-loman,** n. sheep's wool, Pat. **A-vivarta,** m. a partic. Samādhi, Buddh. **A-vivāha,** mfn. not living in wedlock (as cattle), AitBr. **A-viśaṅkita,** (also) not doubted or distrusted, R. **A-viśāla-bhāva,** m. narrowness, Bcar. **A-viśrabdha,** mfn. not inspiring confidence, BhP. **A-viśrama,** mfn. unceasing, unremitting, Śak. (v.l.). **A-viśrānta-vidhyādhara-vyākaraṇa,** n. N. of a grammar by Vāmana (prob. w.r. for *viśr°*), Cat. **A-vishama-padatā,** f. having equal feet (one of the 80 minor marks of a Buddha), Dharmas. 84. **A-vishṭāva,** mfn. without a Vishṭāva (see below), Drāhy. **Avishṭhu,** m. (said to be fr. √*av*) a horse, L.; a priest, L. **A-visaṃvādita,** mfn. undisputed, generally approved, MārkP. **A-visṛishṭa,** mfn. not removed or put aside, Lāṭy.; not dismissed, HPariś. **A-viskanttṛi,** mfn. not leaping to and fro, Bhaṭṭ. **A-viheṭhita,** mfn. unhurt, undamaged, Buddh. **A-vītaka,** not an inclosed place, Yājñ. ii, 271. **A-vīra-ghna,** mfn. not killing men, Hir.; *-stha,* mfn. not standing out heroes, cowardly, Kāth. 2. **A-vṛitta,** mfn. of bad conduct or behaviour, R. **A-vṛintaka,** mfn. without a handle, KātyŚr., Sch. **A-vṛishaṇa,** mfn. having no testicles (*°ṇī-kṛita,* mfn. 'castrated'), R. **A-vṛishṭa,** mfn. not rained, Pañcat. **Avêkshatā,** f. foresight, Divyâv. **A-veśa-sadṛiśa,** mfn. not like prostitution, Mṛicch. **A-vaivartika,** mfn. never returning (for a new birth; *-tva,* n.), Sukh. i. **A-vaiśāradya,** n. want of confidence, Car. **A-vaishamya,** n. symmetry, Vām. iii, 2, 5. **Avôksh** (*ava-√uksh*), to besprinkle, Hir. **Avôkshaṇīya,** mfn. fit for sprinkling (as water), JaimUp. **A-voḍhṛi,** m. not a husband, Kull. **A-vyakta,** m. (also) a young monk who has not finished his studies, Śil.; *-nirmāṇa,* mfn. not yet full-grown, R.; *-bhāshin,* mfn. speaking indistinctly, Mṛicch.; *-mūrti,* mfn. of imperceptible form, Bhag. **A-vyañjana,** mfn. (a girl) who has not yet attained to puberty, Pañcat.; having no consonants, AmṛitUp. **Á-vyatī,** f. not desirous (of sexual intercourse), RV. x, 95, 5. **A-vyathin,** mfn. not discomposed, Śiś. **A-vyavastha,** (also) not lasting or enduring, Kālid.; (*ā*), f. unsettled state, Rājat.; *°sthita,* (also) unsettled, uncertain, Bcar. **A-vyavahāra,** m. improper conduct or practice, Hāsy.; *°hṛita,* mfn. (= *°hārya*), BhP. **A-vyavêta,** mfn. not separated by (instr.), RPrāt.; separated by *a,* VPrāt. **A-vyāghāta,** m. no contradiction, Drāhy. **A-vyābādha,** mfn. unobstructed, unimpeded, Mahāvy. **A-vyāla-ceshṭita,** mfn. not acting like a snake, not deceitful, R. **Á-vyupta** (in comp.); *-keśa,* mfn. having unshorn hair, MaitrS.; *-vaha,* mfn. (a horse) whose shoulder is unshaven, ib. **A-śakta-bhartṛika,** mfn. having an impotent husband, Vishṇ. **Aśana** (in comp.); *-kriyā,* f. the taking of food (*°yāṃ √kṛi,* 'to eat'), Pañcat. **A-śani,** (also) a hail-stone, Kauś.; *-grāvan,* m. a diamond, Prab.; *°nīśa,* m. N. of Rudra-Śiva, Hcat. **A-śayya,** m. 'having no bed,' a partic. class of ascetics, R. **A-śābda,** mfn. not based on a Vedic text, Jaim. **A-śikha,** mfn. having no topknot of hair, L. **A-śila,** mfn. stoneless, R. **A-śiślikshu,** see *śiśl°* (p. 1076). 1. **A-śishṭha** (erase 1.). **A-śishya-vṛitti,** mfn. not behaving like a pupil, MBh. **Aśīty-akshara,** mfn. containing eighty syllables (*-tva,* n.), MaitrS. **A-śīrta-tanu,** mfn. having an indestructible body, Kāṭh. **A-śuci-vrata,** mfn. making unholy vows, Bhag. **A-śuddha-prakṛiti,** mfn. having dishonest ministers, Pañcat. **A-śubha** (in comp.); *-cintaka,* m. N. of a fortune-teller, Kautukar.; *°bhâtmaka,* mfn. evil-minded, Kām. **A-śūdrôcchishṭin,** mfn. not giving the remnants of food to a Śūdra, Hir. **A-śoka** (in comp.); *-bhāṇḍa* or *-bhāṇḍaka,* n. jewels given to one's bride, Lalit.; *-malla,* m. N. of various authors, Cat.; *-vanikā-nyāya,* m. the rule of the grove of Aśoka trees (applied to cases in which a preference of any particular thing among many cannot be accounted for, just as Rāvaṇa kept Sītā in an Aśoka grove, but might equally well have kept her in a grove of other trees), A.; *-śrī,* m. N. of a son of Bindu-sāra, HPariś.; *°kântara* (*âś°*), mfn. not mingled with sorrow, ŚBr.; *°kī-√kṛi,* to turn into an Aśoka (and 'to free from sorrow'), ŚārṅgP.; *°kêśvara,* m. N. of two temples built by Aśoka, Rājat. **A-śobhana,** mfn. not beautiful, VarBṛS., Sch.; disagreeable, vicious, bad, VarBṛS.; BhP.; inauspicious, Suśr. **Aśma** (in comp. for *aśman*); *-garbha-maya,* mf(*ī*)n. consisting of emerald, Dharmaś.; *-cūrṇa,* n. ground or powdered stone, KātyŚr.; *-plava,* m. a boat of stone, Mn. iv, 190; *-yokta,* N. of a tree (perhaps w.r. for *-yoktra*), Kauś.; *-loshṭra-nyāya,* m. the rule of the stone and clod of earth (used to denote the relative importance of two things, both of which may be unimportant), A.; *-varshavat,* mfn. raining stones, R. **Aśmayu,** (prob.) m. a ray of light (= *mayūkha*), L. **A-śmaśāna-cit,** mfn. not piled up in the form of a pyre, MaitrS.; (*á-śm°*), mfn. not piling up &c., TS. **A-śmaśru,** mfn. unbearded, GopBr. **A-śraddhya,** n. unbelief, Divyâv. **A-śrānta,** (also) eternal, continual, L. **Aśru** (in comp.); *-dhārā,* f. a flow of tears, Pañcat.; *-netra,* mfn. with tears in the eyes, MBh.; *-pariplutâksha,* mfn. having the eyes filled with t°, Bcar.; *-pramārjana,* n. wiping away tears, MBh. xii, 5263; consoling, comforting, MBh.; R.; Hariv.; *-maya,* mf(*ī*)n. consisting of tears, Naish.; *-leśa,* m. a tear-drop, Megh.; *-vadana,* mf(*ā*)n. tear-faced, BhP.; *-vaha,* mfn. full of tears, Bcar. **A-ślishṭa,** mfn. incoherent, MBh.; *°ṭârtha,* mfn. inconsistent, contradictory, L. **A-śleshā-vidhi,** m. N. of a Pariś. of MānGṛ. **Aśva** (in comp.); *-kanda,* m. Physalis Flexuosa, L.; *-kuñjara,* m. an excellent horse, Pāṇ. ii, 1, 62, Kāś.; *-krānta,* mfn. trodden by h°s, TĀr.;

-gopa, m. the attendant of a h°, Bcar.; *-ghosha*, m. N. of the author of the Buddha-carita (2nd or 3rd cent. A.D.); *-caryā*, f. following the (sacrificial) h°, R.; *-dāya*, mfn. intending to present with a horse, Pāṇ. iii, 12, Kāś.; *-deva*, m. N. of a poet, Cat.; *-dvādaśa*, mf(*ā*)n. pl. (eleven cows and) a h° as the twelfth, ŚrS.; *-dhāṭī*, f. N. of a poem by Jagannātha Paṇḍita-rāja; *-nāga*, m. (= *kuñjara*), Pāṇ. ii, 1, 62, Kāś.; *-nāman*, n. a horse's name, Hir.; *-panya*, m. a h°-dealer (in the caste system the son of a Kshatriya and an unmarried Vaiśyā), L.; *-pad* (or *-pād*), m. a h°'s foot, Vait.; *-pada*, n. the print of a h°'s foot, KātyŚr.; *-parśu*(?), m. the rib of a h°, MaitrS.; *-pūrṇa*, mfn. abounding in h°, MānGṛ.; *-pota*, m. a foal, L.; *-poshaka*, m. a groom, KātyŚr., Sch.; *-prakāṇḍa*, n. (= *kuñjara*), Pāṇ. ii, 1, 66, Kāś.; *-prapatana*, °*nīya* (read *prapad*°); *-priya*, m. 'dear to h°,' barley, L.; *-pluta*, n. a h°'s leap, Vet.; *-ballava* and *-manimda*, m. a groom, Pāṇ. vi, 2, 66, Kāś.; *-matallikā* and *-macarcikā*, f. (= *-kuñjara*), ib. ii, 1, 66, Kāś.; *-mahisha*, n. sg. a h° and a buffalo, ib. ii, 4, 9, Kāś.; *-yukta*, mfn. relating to a h°, KātyŚr.; *-ratna*, n. a jewel of a h° (one of the 7 treasures of a Cakra-vartin), Dharmas. 85; *-ratha-dāna*, n. N. of the 14th Pariś. of the AV.; *-ripu*, (also) a buffalo, L.; *-lavaṇa*, n. salt given to a h°, Pāṇ. vi, 2, 4, Kāś.; *-vāṇija*, m. a h°-dealer, ib. 13, Kāś.; *-vāhyâlī*, f. a riding-school, Uttamac.; *-vṛindāraka*, m. (= *-kuñjara*), Pāṇ. ii, 1, 62, Kāś.; *-vṛindin*, mfn. consisting of a large number of horses, MBh.; *-śiśna*, m. a horse's penis, KātyŚr.; *-saṃkhya*, m. 'counting h°s' (= *ballava*), Pāṇ. vi, 2, 66, Kāś.; *-sādhana*, mfn. effective by horses, Ragh. iv, 62; *-sūta*, m. a charioteer, MBh.; *-sravaṇa*, n. the flowing off (of water) from a wet horse, KātyŚr.; °*vājaneya*, m. a h° belonging to a Cakra-vartin, Divyâv.; °*vânana*, m. pl. 'h°-faced,' N. of a mythological people, Pracaṇḍ.; °*vânusaraṇa*, n. (= *aśva-caryā*), MBh.; °*vânṛita*, n. false testimony concerning h°s, Mn. viii, 98; °*vâpad*, f. an accident occurring to a sacrificial horse, KātyŚr.; °*vā-mukha*, m. submarine fire, Naish.; °*vâvatāra*, m. N. of the 10th Avatāra of Vishṇu (as Kalki or Kalkia), RTL. 114; °*vâikaviṇśa*, mf(*ā*)n. pl. (twenty cows and) a h° as twenty-first, KātyŚr. **Aśvaka**, (also) a toy-horse, Jātakam. **Aśvattha** (in comp.); *-kalpa*, m., *-pūjā*, f., *-vivāha*, m. N. of wks.; *-śākhā*, f. a branch of the holy fig-tree, MaitrS.; °*tthôdyāpana*, n. the ceremony of raising a bank of earth round a holy fig-tree, Cat. **Aśvi** (in comp. for *aśvin*); *-sālokya*, n. attainment of heaven by those who have offered Aśva-medha sacrifices, Mn. iv, 231; *-suta*, m. du. the two sons of the Aśvins (Nakula and Saha-deva), MBh. **Ashṭa** (in comp. for *ashṭan*); *-karma-paribhrashṭa*, m. a Jaina, L.; *-pada*, (also) consisting of 8 words, Mālatīm., Sch.; *-bhoga* (a fiscal term), Inscr.; *-ratni*, m. 8 Aratnis long, MBh.; *-vārshika*, mf(*ī*)n. lasting 8 years, Hcat.; °*tôṅga* and °*ṭā-daśa*, see below; °*ṭâprush* (TS.); °*ṭâratni*, mfn. 8 Aratnis long, ŚBr.; °*ṭârdha*, mfn. half of half of 8 = 2, Pratāp.; °*ṭâśvasamādhi*, m. a team of 8 horses, R.; °*ṭôttara*, mfn. more than 8, Yājñ., Sch. **Ashṭakā-śrāddha**, n. a Śrāddha performed at the Ashṭakā festival, ĀpGṛ. **Ashṭakyā**, f. a cow employed at the A° f°, Kauś. **Ashṭama-deśa**, m. intermediate region (= *antarā-diś*), Gobh. **Ashṭâṅga**, (also) all the perfections, Divyâv.; *-praṇipāta*, m. prostration of the 8 parts of the body (= *-praṇāma*), PārGṛ.; *-mārga-deśika*, m. 'guide of the eightfold path,' N. of a Buddha, Divyâv.; *-yoga*, m. the eightfold Yoga (consisting of *yama*, *niyama*, *āsana*, *prâṇâyāma*, *pratyāhāra*, *dhyāna*, *dhāraṇa*, and *samādhi*, qq. vv.), Up.; *-samanvāgata*, mfn. (said of a feast), Divyâv.; °*gôpêta*, mfn. (said of excellent water), ib. **Ashṭā-daśa** (in comp. for °*śan*); *-prakṛiti*, 18 officials, Inscr.; *-rcá* (for *-ṛicá*), a stanza or hymn of 18 verses, AV.; *-vakra*, m. N. of a mountain, Divyâv.; *-vakrikā*, f. N. of a mythical river, ib. **Ashṭā-pada**, (also) a chess-board on which each line has 8 squares or 64 in all, MW. **Ashṭika**, mfn. having the length of eight, Śulbas. **Ashṭhī**, f. the bone of the knee or elbow, L. **A-saṃyatta**, (also) unprepared, BhP. **A-saṃyogôpadha**, mfn. (a word) the penultimate letter of which is not a conjunct consonant, Pāṇ. iv, 1, 54. **A-saṃlulita-keśatā**, f. having the hair not tangled (one of the 80 minor marks of a Buddha), Dharmas. 84. **A-saṃvṛitta-vidheya**, (in rhet.) the insertion into a compound of a word which ought to be independent, Kpr. **A-saṃvlaya** (TBr.). **A-saṃsûkta-gila** (accord. to some = 'swallowing without pronouncing a blessing,' AV.). **A-saṃskārya**, mfn. not worthy to receive a Saṃskāra (q.v.), Mn. x, 68. **A-saṃhata-vihārin**, m. N. of a Buddha, Divyâv. **A-sakta**, (also) eternal, continual, L. **A-saṃkīrṇa**, (also) not densely populated, R. **A-saṃklṛipta**, mfn. not desired, MBh. **A-saṃkhya-śas**, ind. in countless numbers, BhP. **A-saṃgata-prabha**, m. = *amitâbha*, Sukh. i. **A-saṃgītakam**, ind. without music (with √*nṛit*, to dance without m°, i. e. 'to do anything without cause or reason'), MBh. **A-saṃgraha**, m. refraining from begging, L. **A-saṃgrāha**, mfn. not prancing (said of a horse), MBh. v, 5262 (Nīlak.). **A-sajāti**, mfn. not of the same caste (v. l. *a-svajāti*), Mn. ix, 86. **A-saṃjñika**, n. unconsciousness, ecstatic state, Divyâv.; *-sattva*, m. pl. N. of certain ecstatic beings, ib. **A-sat** (in comp.); *-kriyā*, f. bad conduct, Jātakam.; *-pratigraha*, m. (= *-parigraha*), Mn.; Yājñ. **A-sanāma**, mf(*ā*)n. not having the same name, MBh. **A-sanidarśana**, mfn. (prob.) indefinable, Buddh. **A-saṃdadhāna**, mfn. not making peace, Pañcat. **A-saṃdarśana**, n. not seeing (i. e. absence of intercourse with) people, MBh. **A-saṃnipātin**, mfn. not producing an immediate effect, ĀpY. **A-saṃnyupta**, mfn. (√2. *vap*) not thrown together, ĀpŚr. **A-samanvāhāra**, m. thoughtlessness(?), Divyâv. **A-samaya-vyukta**, mfn. (said of a Śrāvaka at a partic. stage of development), Buddh. **A-samāpta-prabha**, m. = *amitâbha*, Sukh. i. **A-samparigraha**, mfn. not accepted, refused, Jātakam. **A-sampusha**, m. N. of Indra, L. **A-sampṛikta**, mfn. secret, L. **A-samprajñāta**, mfn. unconscious, Yogas., Sch. **A-samprajñāna**, n. want of knowledge, Buddh. **A-sampramāṇa**, mfn. not too spacious, ŚāṅkhGṛ. **A-sambhava**, m. non-coition, impotence, ĀpGṛ. **A-sambhūta**, mfn. not existing, fictitious, R. **A-sammosha-dharman**, m. N. of Buddha, Divyâv. **A-sarva-homa**, m. not offering the whole of an oblation (keeping back a portion), L. **A-sasya**, mf(*ā*)n. not grown with corn, Hariv. **A-sahat**, mf(*antī*)n. unable to (inf.), ib. **A-sahṛidaya**, mfn. not sensible of what is beautiful, Sāh. **A-sahya**, (also) lost beyond aid (as a sinking ship), Divyâv. **A-sādhāraṇôpamā**, f. a kind of comparison (in which a person or thing is said to be only comparable to himself or itself?), Kāvyâd. ii, 37. **A-sādhu**, mfn. (in rhet.) not grammatically correct (as *anya-kāraka* for *anyat-k*°), Vām. ii, 1, 5. **A-sāra**, mfn. (also) faithless, L. **Asālati-prakāśa**, m. N. of a dictionary (written under Asālati, king of Kaśmīr). **A-sāhacarya**, n. unsimultaneousness, Nyāyas., Sch. **Asi**, m. (also) a shark, alligator, L.; *-jala*, n. blood dripping from a sword, Dharmaś.; *-jihva*, m. 'sword-tongued,' N. of an Asura, Hariv.; *-tāla*, m. N. of a plant (from which the shafts of arrows are made), Kauś.; *-plava*, m. a kind of porpoise, L.; *-baddha*, mfn. girt with a dagger or sword, ŚāṅkhŚr.; *-mārga*, m. pl. the various ways of handling a sword, MBh.; *-sūnā*, f. (= *sūnā*), Divyâv.; (*asy*)*-agra*, n. the point of a knife, Śāṅkh.; (*asy*)*-ākṛiti*, mfn. formed like a sw°, KātyŚr. 2. **Asita**, m. (also) the dark half of a lunar month, L.; a partic. intoxicating drink, L.; *-gati*, m. 'having a black course,' fire (*-dyuti*, 'shining like fire'), Bcar. v, 79; *-ratna*, n. a sapphire, Kir.; *-skandha*, m. a kind of amulet, Kauś.; °*tânana*, m. a black-faced monkey, L.; °*têkshaṇa*, mfn. black-eyed, MBh. **A-sīma** = *a-sīman*, Naish. **A-sukhāya**, Nom. Ā. °*yate*, to be uneasy, Jātakam. **A-supratāra**, mfn. difficult to be crossed, ib. **Asura** (in comp.); *-lokā* (MaitrS.); *-viśa*, n. the race of Asuras, AitBr.; °*rârdana*, m. 'harasser of A°,' a god, MBh. **Asuri**, (prob.) m. (said to be fr. √2. *as*) war, battle (= *saṃgrāma*), L. **Asu-vyaya**, m. sacrifice of one's own life, Prab. **A-sūci-saṃcāra**, mfn. impenetrable even to a needle, very dense, Bhartṛ.; Rājat. **A-sūta**, mfn. having no charioteer, R. **Asṛig-bhājana**, mfn. receiving blood as a share, ŚāṅkhBr. **Asṛij** (for 'a kind of religious abstraction,' read, 'N. of the 16th of the astrological Yogas, also called Siddhi'). **A-sṛiṇya** (v.l. *asṛ*°) = *a-sriṇi*, BhP. **A-secanaka-darśana**, mfn. lovely to see, Divyâv. **A-sodha**, (also) m. an elephant with thick and short tusks, L. **A-saunāman** (erase and read in ŚBr. *asau n*°). 1. **Asta** (in comp.); *-karuṇa*, mfn. pitiless, cruel, Mālatīm. 2. **Asta** (in comp.); *-gāmin*, mfn. going down, Hāsy.; *-m-gacchat*, m. (= *lagna*), Sūryas.; *-m-ayâcala*, m. (= *asta-giri*), L.; *-m-itôditā*, f. (scil. *paurṇa-māsī*) the day on which the moon rises full after sunset, Gobh.; *-lagna*, n. the western horizon, Sūryas., Sch.; °*tâbhi-lāshin*, mfn. verging towards sunset, Mudr. **A-stanā**, f. having no breast or udder, MaitrS. **Astaryà**, mfn. not to be laid low, unconquerable, ŚBr. **Asti-nâsti-tva**, n. being and not being, Kaṭy. **Astika**, m. (commonly written *āstīka*, q. v.), L. **Astu**, (also) existence, reality (= *asti-bhāva*), L. **Astra**, (also) the art of throwing missiles, MBh.; *-kshati-mat*, mfn. wounded by arrows, Śiś.; *-jīvana*, m. (= *-jīva*), L.; *-veda*, m. the science of archery, Dhanaṃj. **A-strīka**, mfn. without women, HPariś.; having no wife, Bhaṭṭ. **A-sthāna**, (also) impossibility, Divyâv.; an army which has lost its chief, L.; mfn. deep, L. **Asthi** (in comp.); *-kara*, m. fat, serum of flesh, L.; *-kumbha*, m. an urn for preserving the bones of burned bodies, ĀpŚr.; *-khāda*, m. 'bone-eater,' a dog, L.; *-cit*, mfn. not piled up like bones, MaitrS.; *-bhaṅga*, m. N. of a poet, Cat.; *-yantra-vat*, like skeletons, Divyâv.; *-vilaya-tīrtha*, n. N. of a sacred place at Nāsik, RTL. 301; *-śuddhi*, f. N. of wk.; *-śesha*, mfn. having only bones left (*-tā*, f.), Kathās.; *-saṃyoga*, m. a joint, Car.; *-saṃghāta* and *-saṃnahana*, m. N. of plants, L.; *-saṃcaya* (see RTL. 284 &c.); °*thy-uddharaṇa*, n. N. of wk. **A-spandana-sthiti**, f. fainting, L. **A-spṛishṭa-purushântara**, mfn. not belonging to another, Kum. **A-sphuṭa-bhāshaṇa**, mf(*ā*)n. lisping, L. **Asmád-rāta**, mfn. given by us, TS. **Asmādṛiśa**, mfn. like us, ŚāṅkhBr. **Asy-agra** &c., see under *asi* (col. 2). **A-syūta-nāsika**, mfn. (a draught ox) whose nose is not pierced, Baudh. **A-sruta**, mfn. imperishable, Pār. **A-svagátā** (accord. to some = *a-svasthatā*, 'ill health,' others, 'dependence,' AV. ix, 2, 3). **A-svatā**, (also) unselfishness, Bcar. vi, 10. **A-svarya**, mfn. not good for the voice, Suśr. **A-svar-yogya**, mfn. unworthy of heaven, VP. **A-svasthāna**, mfn. occurring out of its proper place, Drāhy. **A-svāmi-vikraya**, m. sale of property by one who is not the rightful owner, Mn. viii, 4 (cf. IW. 261). **A-svârtha**, mfn. useless, BhP. 1. **Aha**, (also) a particle answering to *ha* in a preceding sentence (*ha-aha* = μὲν—δέ), Gaṇar. 4. **Ahaḥ** (in comp. for *ahar*); *-kshānta*, mfn. patient during the day, Hir.; *-stoma*, m. a Stoma belonging to a partic. day, Drāhy. **A-hata-mārga**, mfn. one whose course is free, Mṛicch. **Aham** (in comp.); *-indra*, m. N. of a divine being, Dharmaś.; *-padârtha*, m. the Ego, Sāṃkhyas., Sch.; *-mati*, (also) mfn. egoistic, arrogant, BrahmavP.; (*m*)*-ghāta*, m. a self-murderer, Kāraṇḍ. **Ahamada**, m. = Ahmad, Cat. **Ahar** (in comp.); *-ādi*, m. daybreak, Śiś.; *-pati* (MaitrS.). **Ahalyā** (in comp.); *-kāmadhenu*, f. N. of a modern law-book; *-saṃkrandana*, n. N. of a drama. **A-hāpayat**, mfn. not omitting or losing, Kām.; MārkP. **Ahi** (in comp.); *-kañcuka*, m. a snake's skin, Svapnac.; *-jambhana*, n. a means of destroying snakes, MantraBr.; *-nilvayanī*, f. (cf. *-nirvlayanī*) a snake's skin, L.; *-prishṭha*, n. an iron machine like a snake's backbone, L.; *-vidvish*, m. N. of Indra, Kir.; *-vratin*, mfn. one who lives like a snake (only on air), L. **A-hiṃkāra** or °**kṛiti**, mfn. not accompanied by the exclamation *hiṅ*. **Ahīna** = 1. *áhīna*, MaitrS. **A-hima-rocis**, m. 'hot-rayed,' the sun, Śiś. **A-hiraṇyava**, mfn. possessing no golden ornaments, ŚāṅkhŚr. **A-hīnâha**, mfn. one whose days are not lessened, BaudhP. **Ahī-ramaṇī**, f. a two-headed snake (= *ahīraṇī*), Hcar. **A-hutâbhyudite**, ind. when the sun has risen before the sacrifice, KātyŚr. **A-hedamāna**, mfn. not sporting or joking, being in earnest, R. **A-hetu-vāda**, m. the doctrine of the Cārvākas, Jātakam.; °*din*, m. an adherent of it, ib. **Ahedhma**, m. (with *Paiḍvasya*) N. of a Sāman, ĀrshBr. **A-helin**, mfn. not dallying, ib. **Aho-bala**, m. N. of various authors (also with *śāstrin* or *sūri*), Cat. **A-hrasta**, mfn. (for *-hrasita*) not shortened, Vait.

Ā-kapiśa, mfn. brownish, Kir. **Ā-kampra**, mfn. somewhat trembling, Śiś. **Ā-karṇaka**, m. n. (and *ikā*, f.) the sheath of a knife, L. **Ā-karsha**, (also) an instrument for collecting ashes, shovel, Kauś. (Sch.); a partic. part of an elephant's trunk, L. **Ā-kalusha**, mfn. a little turbid, Jātakam. **Ā-kāśa** (in comp.); *-garbha*, m. N. of a Bodhisattva, Buddh.; *-cakra*, n. the region of ether, Vīrac.; *-plavā*, f. N. of a Kiṃ-narī, Kāraṇḍ.; *-maṇi*, m. the sun, Dharmaś.; *-vacana*, n. (in dram.) a voice from the sky, Bhar.; °*śânantyâyatana*, (also) m. pl. N. of a class of gods, MWB. 213 (also °*tanôpaga*, Dharmas. 129); °*śôpanyāsa*, m. N. of a Vedânta wk. **Ākiṃcanya,** (also) m. a nihilist, Bcar. xii, 63; °*nyâyatana*, (also) m. pl. N. of a class of gods, MWB. 213 (also °*tanôpaga*, Dharmas. 129). **Ā-kīṭa-pataṃga-pipīlakam,** ind. down to worms (and) flying insects (and) ants, ChUp. **Ā-√kuṭ** (Caus. -*koṭayati*), to break, Divyâv.; °*koṭana*, n. smoothing, Mahâvy.; (*ā*), f. punishment, Nār., Sch. **Ā-kuṭila,** mfn. a little bent, Śak.; a little curled, Kād. **Ā-kuḍmali-kṛita,** mfn. half expanded, Prasannar. **Ā-√1. kṛi** (Caus. -*kārayati*, also) to imply by signs, Divyâv. **Ā-kṛiti-loshṭa,** a clod from the field in its natural shape, Kauś. **Ā-kṛishṭa,** m. a magical diagram scratched on the ground (?), ib. **Āké** (accord. to some, 'visibly' [cf. *akshi*, √*īksh*], RV. ii, 1, 10; -*nipá*, read *ā kenipâso*, ib. iv, 45, 6). **Ā-koshṭham,** ind. down to the abdomen, BhP. **Ā-kshepa** (in comp.); -*valana*, n. tossing about (the arms &c.), Ratnâv.; -*sūtra*, n. a string for filing pearls, Ragh. vi, 28 (v.l.); °*piṇī*, f. (with *siddhi*) the magical power of attraction, Mālatīm. (= *ākarshiṇī siddhiḥ*, Sch.). **Ā-kshveḍita,** n. humming, buzzing, R. **Ā-khaṇḍala,** (also) the ruler of (gen.), Vīrac.; -*kakubh*, f. 'Indra's quarter,' the east, Vās.; °*lâśā*, f. id., Prasannar. **Ākhu** (in comp.); -*yāna*, m. Gaṇêśa (cf. -*ga*), L.; -*han*, m. 'mouse-killer,' a cat, Pat. on Pāṇ. iii, 2, 84, Vārtt. 4. **Ā-khedana,** n. drawing to one's self, ĀpŚr., Sch. **Ā-khyātôttara,** mfn. (a name) the second part of which is a verb, ĀpGṛ. **Ā-khyāna-vid,** m. a knower of stories, Mālatīm. **Ā-khyāyanī,** f. a message, L. **Ā-gata** (in comp.); -*vismaya*, mfn. filled with wonder, Bcar.; °*tâstha*, mfn. full of interest, ib. **Á-gadhita,** mfn. (√*gadh*) clung to, pressed close to, RV. i, 126, 6. **Ā-gama** (in comp.); -*kalpadruma*, m., -*kaumudī*, f., -*candrikā*, f., -*tattva-saṃgraha*, m., -*prakāśa*, m., -*rahasya*, n. N. of wks. (cf. IW. 524; RTL. 185–208); -*virodha*, m. conflict with tradition, Kāvyâd.; -*saṃhita*, mfn. agreeing with tr°, Bcar.; °*mika*, mfn. acquired by tr°, Nyâyas., Sch.; °*mya*, (also) with reference to, owing to (gen.), Divyâv. **Ā-gará** (accord. to others = *āgāra*). **Ā-garbham,** ind. down to the child in the womb, Vīrac. **Āgasvin,** m. an evil-doer, Alaṃkārav. **Āgāra,** (also) a partic. high number, Buddh.; °*rika*, m. a householder, layman, Buddh. **Āgīgrāma,** m. N. of a family, Inscr. **Ā-gīta,** mfn. sung unto, JaimUp. **Āgnīdhra,** (also) m. pl. N. of a people, VarBṛS.; (*ī*), f. kindling or feeding the fire, L. **Āgneya,** mfn. (also) inflammable, combustible, MBh. **Ā-grathana,** n. tying round, girding, Ragh. **Ā-granthana,** n. a knot (= *granthi*), Bcar. i, 78. **Āgrayaṇiya,** m. pl. the firstfruits destined for oblation, ŚāṅkhBr. **Āghaṭṭalikā,** f. a horn for blowing, L. **Ā-ghargharam,** ind. snarlingly, growlingly, Mālatīm. **Ā-gharsha,** m. rubbing, friction, Śiś. **Ā-ghāta-kāla,** m. a critical or dangerous time, Car. **Ā-ghāraṇa,** m. a partic. sacrificial ladle, L. **Ā-ghoshiṇī,** f. pl. N. of a class of demons, ŚāṅkhGṛ., Sch. **Āṅgalaukika,** m. a dream caused through bile or phlegm, L. **Āṅgirasa,** (also) m. a partic. magical implement, Kauś. **Āṅgula,** mf(*ī*)n. sticking to the fingers, Baudh. **Ā-cakshas,** mfn. eloquent (= *vāgmin*), L. **Ā-cañcala,** mfn. moving slowly to and fro, Prasannar. **Á-carita,** distress for debt (in the legal sense), Mn. viii, 49. **Ācāra-maya,** mf(*ī*)n. wholly addicted to ceremonial usages, Kād. **Ācārya,** m. (also) the son of an outcast Vaiśya and a Vaiśyā who was before a Brāhman's wife, Mn. x, 23 (accord. to some, read *cārya*); -*tarpaṇa*, n. a rite supplementary to the *ṛishi-t*°, RTL. 410; -*mushṭi*, f. 'a teacher's closed hand,' constraint, force, Mahâvy.; °*ryâsandī*, f. a t°'s seat, Hir. **Ācikhyâsôpamā,** f. a kind of simile (in which it is left uncertain whether praise or censure is meant), Kāvyâd. ii, 32. **Ā-citra,** mfn. decorated with many-coloured ornaments, R. **Ā-√2. cumb,** to kiss, Daś. **Ā-cchoṭita,** mfn. (fr. Caus. of √*chuṭ*) torn off, Hcat. **Ājakeśin,** m. pl. N. of a family, JaimUp. **1. Āji** (in comp.); -*bhūmi*, f. a field of battle, Śiś.; -*śobhin*, mfn. distinguished in battle, MBh. **Ā-jihmita,** mfn. turned or bent a little aside, Kād. **Ā-jīrṇantam,** ind. to the end of digestion, Baudh. **Āñchita,** mfn. provided or furnished with, Harav. **Āñjaneya,** (also) N. of an author; -*purāṇa*, n., -*stava*, m., -*stotra*, n. N. of wks. **Āṭaka,** (also) m. a sparrow, L. **Āṭika,** m. pl. N. of a School of the Yajus, AV. Pariś. **Ā-ṭopa,** m. (also) haste, L. **Āḍambarita,** mfn. accompanied with sounds of a drum, Nalac.; highly increased, Siṇhâs. **Āḍindikā,** f. clean shaving of the whole body, L. **Ā-√ḍval,** cl. 10. P. -*ḍvālayati*, to mix, mingle; °*ḍvālana*, n. mixing, mingling, KātyŚr., Sch. **Āḍhā,** f. a centipede, L. **Āḍhārikā,** f. = (or v.l. for) *ḍhārikā*, ĀpGṛ. **Āḍhika,** n. bone, L. **Āṇuka** or **āṇūka,** n. dirt in the eye, L. **Āṇḍa** (in comp.); -*kośa*, (also) mfn. enclosed in an egg, BhP.; -*pīta* (*āṇḍá-*), mfn. one who has sipped eggs, TĀr. **Ā-√taksh,** (also) to cut, carve, form by carving, Jātakam. **Ā-tati,** f. darkness, L. **Ā-tapa,** (also) moonshine, Daś.; Harav.; -*nivāraṇa*, n. a parasol, VarYog. **Ātijagata,** mfn. composed in the metre Ati-jagatī, TāṇḍBr., Sch. **Ā-titāṅsu,** mfn. (Desid. of √*tan*) wishing to overspread or cover, Śiś. **Ātivāhika,** (also) m. an inhabitant of the other world, L. **Ātiśayika,** (also) extraordinary, Jātakam. **Ātisārika,** mf(*ī*)n. like diarrhœa, Car. **Ā-tṛipti,** ind. to satiety or satisfaction, Bālar. **Ātta** (in comp.); -*kānti*, mfn. deprived of splendour, Prab.; -*vidya*, mfn. one who has acquired knowledge from (abl.), Vop.; -*vibhava*, mfn. one who has acquired wealth, Gaut.; -*somapīthīya* (*ātta-*), mfn. deprived of the Soma drink, ŚBr.; -*sva*, mfn. d° of one's property (-*tva*, n.), Ragh. **Ātma** (in comp. for *ātman*); -*kāma*, mfn. desirous of emancipation, Jātak.; -*cintā*, f. meditation on the soul, Mn. xii, 31; -*jit*, mfn. master of one's self, Bcar.; -*jñānôpanishad*, f., -*jyotir-upanishad*, f., -*tattva-viveka*, m. N of wks.; -*dhāraṇī*, f. (with Buddhists) one of the four Dhāraṇīs, Dharmas. 52; -*nirāloka*, n. (with *muni*) N. of Śiva, MBh. xiii, 1183; -*nirūpaṇa* and -*pañcaka*, n. N. of wks. by Śaṃkarâcārya; -*saṃyukta*, mfn. being in the body, Āpast.; -*saṃyoga*, mfn. connexion with one's self, ib.; -*sambhāvita*, mfn. self-conceited, proud, ib.; °*mâbhimarśana*, n. rubbing one's self, ĀpY.; °*mâyāsa*, m. self-torture, Nāg.; °*mâvāsya*, mfn. filled by the Universal soul, BhP.; °*mêcchā*, f. desire of (union with) the Un° soul, Śaṃk.; °*môllāsa*, m. N. of a Vedânta wk. **Ātmanikā,** f. N. of a woman, Kathās. **Ā-dadhici,** ind. including Dadhīci, Naish. **Ā-darin,** mfn. full of respect or regards, Naish. **Ā-daśâham,** ind. for ten days, Baudh. **1. Ā-dāna,** (also) resumption of the object of action (one of the 13 members of the Vimarśa, q.v.), Sāh. **1. Ādi,** (also) the third part in the 7-partite Sāman, ChUp.; -*keśavâshṭaka*, n. N. of a Stotra; -*guru*, m. 'first father,' N. of Brahmā, Bhag.; -*grantha*, m. N. of the first division or principal section of the sacred book of the Sikhs, RTL. 161; 169; IW. 325, n. 1; -*tā*, f. the being the beginning of anything, Śiś.; -*dīpa*, m. N. of a Rudra, Hcat.; -*pitāmaha*, m. N. of Brahmā, Prasaṅg.; -*bhavānī*, f. the Śakti of Parama-purusha, W.; -*yāmala*, n. N. of a Tantra; -*vaktṛi*, m. the first propounder of a doctrine, Āryabh., Introd.; -*varāha*, m. N. of Bhoja (Kanouj king), Inscr.; -*śūra*, m. N. of a king of Bengal (also called Ādîśvara), IW. 210, n.; -*siṇha*, m. N. of a king, Inscr.; -*sthāyika*, see *sthāyika* (p. 1264); -*svarita*, mfn. having the Svarita accent on the first syllable, VPrat., Sch. **Āditya** (in comp.); -*kīlaka*, m. a partic. phenomenon in the sky, ĀpGṛ., Sch.; -*gata*, mfn. being in the sun, Bhag.; -*dhāman* (°*tyá*), mfn. having a place among the Ādityas, MaitrS.; -*rāma*, m. N. of a king, Inscr.; -*vardhana*, m. N. of a Kanouj king, Inscr.; -*vāra*, m. Sunday, IW. 178, n. 1; -*vidhi*, m. N. of wk.; -*śakti*, m. N. of a chief, Inscr. **Ādinava-darśá** (VS.). **Ā-dinântam,** ind. till the close of day, Kathās. **Ā-deya,** (also) acceptable, agreeable (-*tara-tā*, f.), Jātakam. **Ā-deśá,** (also) a guest (= *prāghūrṇika*), Śīl. **Ā-deha-dāham,** ind. from the cremation of the body, Naish. **1. Ādya** (in comp.); -*kālaka*, mf(*ikā*)n. relating only to this day, MBh.; °*yâdya*, mfn. each or every preceding (element), Mn. i, 20. **Ādhārin,** mfn. forming the place for (gen.), ĀpŚr., Sch. **Ādhārshṭya,** n. cowardice, Dhātup. **Ādhirathīya,** n. N. of various Sāmans, ĀrshBr. **Ādhirājya** (AV.). **Ādhi-stena,** m. the stealer of a deposit, Mn. viii, 144. **Ādhomukhya,** n. going downwards, Śiś. **Ānaka-dundubhi,** m. N. of Vishṇu, L. **Ānana-cara,** mf(*ī*)n. falling into the mouth of (gen.), Mālatīm. **Ānantarya,** (also) an unpardonable sin (said by Buddhists to be five, viz. 'matricide,' 'parricide,' 'killing an Arhat,' 'shedding the blood of a Buddha,' 'causing divisions among the brotherhood'), Dharmas. 60; -*samādhi*, m. a partic. Samādhi, ib. 101. **Ānanda,** (also) N. of one of the chief disciples of Gautama Buddha, MWB. 47 &c.; of various authors &c., Cat.; -*cid-ghana*, mfn. consisting only of joy and thought, NṛisUp.; °*dâtman* (ŚBr.). **Ā-nābhi,** ind. up to the nave, MBh.; up to the navel, Vishṇ. **Ā-nāya,** (also) investiture (= *upanaya*), L. **Ā-nīla-nishadhâyata** or °**dhâyāma,** mfn. stretching from the Nīla to the Nishadha mountains, Hcat. **1. Ā-√1. nu** (read 1. *ā*-√4. *nu*). **Ānubandhika,** mfn. of continued influence or efficacy, Car. **Ānuyājika,** mf(*ī*)n. relating to the after-sacrifice, MānŚr. **Ānushák** (accord. to some also, 'regularly,' 'thoroughly'), RV. **Ānṛitika,** mfn. addicted to lying, MBh. **Ā-netrī** (RV.). **Ā-neya,** mfn. to be brought, R. **Ānobhadra-sûkta,** n. N. of RV. i, 89, Cat. **Āntarālika,** m. the son of an Anuloma by a woman of superior caste, L. **Á'ntya** (VS.). **Āntrī-mukha,** m. N. of a demon, Hir. **Āndīḍa** or °**dīra,** m. N. of a king, VP. **Āndolikā,** f. a swing-cot, palanquin, Daś. **Āndhā-svara,** n. a partic. mode of singing, Drāhy. **Ānvīkshikī,** (also, with *buddhi*) an argumentative mind, R. **Āpaṇa** (add 'fr. 4. *ā* + √*paṇ*'). **Āpaṇīya,** mfn. coming from the market, Āpast. **Āpatantá,** a species of grain, MaitrS. **Á'pati,** m. a present lord (?), ib. **Á-pattos** (Ved. inf. of *ā*-√*pad*), to fall or get into, ŚBr. **Āpatsahāya,** m. a friend in need, Rājat. **Āpadika,** m. 'a bolt' or 'a sapphire' (*indra-kīla* or *indra-nīla*), L. **Ā-parusha,** mfn. a little rough, Jātakam. **1. Ā-pāda** (p. 143, col. 1, erase 1. and parenthesis on next line); °*din*, mfn. falling into, incurring (comp.), Lāṭy. **Ā-pāda-tala-mastakam,** ind. from the sole of the foot to the head, Sāṃkhyapr. **Ā-pārshṇi,** ind. down to the heels, Mālav. **Á'pāshṭhi,** m. a patr., ŚBr. **2. Ā-pí,** mfn. (fr. *ā*-√*pyai*, accord. to some, 'swelling,' 'refreshing,' RV. v, 53, 2). **Ā-piṅgala** (= *ā-piṅga*); °*lâksha*, mfn. having reddish eyes, Bcar. **Ā-piṅgalaka,** m. a bull which has been set at liberty, L. **Āpīḍaka-jāta,** mfn. (said of a tree in full flower), Divyâv.; °*din*, mfn. decorated on the head with (comp.), MBh. **Āpeyá** and °**yatvá** (MaitrS.). **Āpoda,** m. patr. of the Ṛishi Dhaumya (v.l. *āyoda*), MBh. **Āpo-máya** (ŚBr.). **Āpta** (in comp.); -*kṛit*, mfn. trustworthy, MBh.; -*kriya*, m. a trusty agent, Inscr.; -*cchandas*, mfn. complete as to metre, TāṇḍBr.; -*vacana* (cf. IW. 82); -*vāda*, m. (= -*vacana*), Siṇhâs.; -*vibhaktika*, mfn. complete as to case-terminations, TāṇḍBr.; -*stoma*, mfn. complete in the Stomas, ib., Sch. **Āptavyà** (ŚBr.). **Āpti,** (also) trustworthiness, Sāṃkhyapr. **Āptor-yāma,** °**man** = *apt*°, MBh.; Pur. **Á'pnāna** (RV.). 1. **Āpya,** (also) mfn. friendly, kind, RV. iii, 2, 6. **Āpyâna-vat** and **āpyâyana** (ŚBr.). **Ā-pravartana,** n. general outbreak (of perspiration), BhP. **Ā-prâsa,** m. covering the Vedi with Darbha grass, L. **Ābravantī,** f. N. of a town, R. (B.). **Ābharaṇa-sthāna,** n. a place (on the body) for ornament, Mṛicch. **Ābhijñānika,** mfn. relating to recognition, Daś. **Ābhimukhya-karaṇa,** n. addressing a person, Kāś. on Pāṇ. ii, 3, 47. **Ābhirāmika,** mfn. amiable, Mudr. **Ā-bhīshaṇa,** n. a weapon, Kāty. **Ā-bhugna-saktha,** mf(*ī*)n. crooked-thighed, Suśr. **2. Ā-bhū́** (RV.). **Ā-bhūka,** mfn. (prob.) forceless, feeble, AV. **Ā-bhūti** (RV.). **1. Ābhogin,** (also) of great extent, Subh. **Ābhyantara-nṛitta,** n. perfect dancing (according to the Nāṭya-śāstras), L. **Á'm** (MaitrS.). **1. Āma** (in comp.); -*maya*, mf(*ī*)n. unbaked, BaudhP.; -*vidhi*, m. a partic. observance, Cat.; -*śrāddha*, n. a Śrāddha at which raw food is presented, L.; °*mâjīrṇa*, n. a partic. form of indigestion, Bhpr.; °*mâśraya* (read °*mâśaya*); °*mêshṭaka*, mfn. made of raw bricks, Mṛicch. **3. Āma,** ind. yes, HParis. **Ā-majjam,** ind. to the marrow, Naish. **Ā-mantraṇika,** n. N. of the fifth Saṃskāra (= *nāma-karman*), L. **Āmardaka-tīrtha-nātha,** m. N. of a Śaiva ascetic, Inscr. **Āmalakī** (cf. RTL. 339; 568). **Ā-mikshā-payasya,** n. a kind of Prātar-doha (q.v.), ĀpŚr. **Āmitra,** (also) belonging to an enemy, MBh.; -*śocani* (*ām*°), m. a patr., MaitrS. **Āmisha** (in comp.); -*dāna*, n. (with Buddhists) gift of material things (one of the three kinds of charity, the others being *dharma-d*° and *maitrī-d*°), Dharmas. 105. **Ā-mīvā,** f. disease, L. **Ā-muktā** or °**tikā,** f. a jewel, Divyâv. **Ā-mukha,** (also) mfn. being in front or before the eyes, Jātakam. **Ā-mur** &c. (read *mṛī* for *mṛi*). **Ā-moṭana,** n. cracking, breaking, Mālatīm. **Āmnāya** (in comp.); -*para*, mfn. honouring sacred tradition, Mn. vii, 80; -*yoni*, m. N. of Brahmā, Kāv. **Āmrá,** n. (ŚBr.); -*kavi*,

m. N. of a poet, Inscr.; *-prasāda*, m. N. of a Guhila king, ib. **Āmreḍita-yamaka**, n. a Yamaka (in which every Pāda ends with a word repeated twice), Bhar. **Ā-mlócantī**, f. N. of an Apsaras, MaitrS. **Ā-yata** (in comp.); *-pakshmala*, mfn. (an arrow) with long feathers, Kathās.; *-pāṇi-lekhatā*, f. having long lines on the hand (one of the 80 minor marks of a Buddha), Dharmas. 84; *-pārshṇitā*, f. having a long heel (one of the 32 signs of perfection), ib. 83; *-bhrūkatā*, f. having long eye-brows (one of the 80 minor marks of a Buddha), ib. 84; *-vikrama*, mfn. far-striding, Bcar.; *-sama-lamba*, mfn. right-angled, Col. **Ā́yavas** (MaitrS.). **Āyasī**, f. (also) an iron vessel, Vishṇ. **Ā-yasta**, (also) n. resoluteness, R. (B.). **Ā-yācana**, n. a prayer (to the gods), Divyâv. **Ā-yāna**, (also) a partic. ornament for horses, Hcar. **Ā-yāpita**, mfn. (Caus. of √*yā*) brought up, ib. **Ā-yāmatas**, ind. in length, ĀpGṛ. **Ā-yāsá** (VS.); *-dāyin*, mfn. causing affliction, Bcar.; °*sana*, n. (prob.) excitation, irritation, Car. (v.l.); °*sita*, n. exertion, endeavour (v.l. *pra-y*°), Mālatīm.; °*sya*, n. N. of various Sāmans, PañcavBr. **Ā-yukta**, m. (in dram.) an official appointed by a king, Bhar.; (*ā*), f. a woman appointed as treasurer &c., ib. **Ā-yudha-piśācikā** (MBh.) or °**cī** (Bālar.), f. the fondness of a demon for fighting; °*dhika* or °*dhīyaka*, n. making or dealing in weapons, Baudh. **Āyushya-gaṇa**, m. N. of a class of hymns for prolonging life, AV.Pariś. **Ā́yogava** (ŚBr.). 1. **Āra** (in comp.); °*rāgrā*, f. an arrangement of 11 sacrificial posts (making the middlemost and the others lower by degrees on both sides), ĀpŚr. 3. **Āra**, n. a multitude of enemies, Śiś. xix, 27. **Āraṭṭa**, (also) mfn. cracked, split, L.; m. an Araṭṭa horse of very low breed, L. **Āraba** or °**va**, m. an Arabian (*ī*, f.), Jain.; °*bya-yāminī*, f. Arabian Nights (translated into Sanskṛit by Jagad-bandhu). **Ā-rambaṇa**, (also) a railing, balustrade, Mahāvy.; *-cchedana*, m. a partic. Samādhi, ib. **Ā-rambha** (in comp.); *-yajña*, m. a kind of sacrifice, Vishṇ. **Āralu**, m. Bignonia Indica, L. **Ārāgaya**, Nom. P. °*yati*, to gladden highly, Vajracch.; to obtain, Lalit.; to relish, Divyâv.; °*gita*, mfn. pleased, ib. **Ārād-upakāraka** or °**rin**, mfn. indirectly effective, Nyāyam., Sch. **Ārādhya-karpūra**, m. N. of a poet, Subh. **Ārāma** (in comp.); *-parigraha*, m. landed property (of monasteries), Sukh. i; °*mâdhipati*, m. a head gardener, Bhām. 2. **Ārāva**, n. a partic. high number, Buddh. **Ā-rāsa**, m. a scream, shout, Śiś. **Āruṇiyôpanishad**, f. N. of an Upanishad (also called *āruṇikôp*° or *āruṇeyôp*° or *āruny-upanishad*). **Ā-rūḍha**, (also) one who has taken a vow, Divyâv.; m. barley, L.; a partic. Samādhi, Kāraṇḍ.; n. leaping upon, covering, Hariv. **Ārūpya**, n. deformity, ugliness, Mahāvy. **Ā-ropa**, m. the rhet. figure 'super-imposition,' IW. 458. **Ā-rohá** (MaitrS.; also) a chief elephant-driver, L. **Arka**, (also) m. an amulet made of the Arka plant, Kauś. **Ārkshākāyaṇa**, see *galūnasa* (p. 1326). **Ārkshyá** (SV.). **Ārcika**, m. patr. of Jamad-agni, Bālar. **Ārjika**, m. (and *ā*, f.) mutual term of address for husband and wife, L. **Ārṇava**, mfn. come from the sea, Naish. **Ārta** (in comp.); °*tâyana*, m. help in need, MBh.; °*tāyani*, m. N. of Śalya, ib. 1. **Ārti** (erase 1. and 2.). **Ārtos** (Ved. inf. of 2. *ar*), to fall into, TS. **Ārdra** (in comp.); *-pāda*, mfn. having wet feet, Mn. iv, 76; *-vāsas*, mfn. dressed in wet clothes, ib. vi, 23; °*drânulepana*, mfn. wet with unguents, Bcar. **Ārpayitṛí**, **ā́rbhava** (ŚBr.). **Ārya** (in comp.); *-karman*, mfn. doing noble actions, acting like an Āryan, Bcar. viii, 54; *-dhana*, n. (with Buddhists) a noble treasure (7 in number), Divyâv.; *-dharma*, m. religion of the Āryans, RTL. 20 &c.; *-pāla*, m. 'protector of the Ā°,' N. of Avalokitêśvara or Padma-pāṇi, MWB. 199; *-mārga-pudgala-nāyaka*, m. N. of Buddha, Divyâv.; *-rūpa*, m. having the appearance of an Āryan, Mn. x, 57; *-vajra*, m. N. of a grammarian, Cat.; *-śūra*, m. N. of the author of the Jātaka-mālā; *-sthavira*, m. pl. a partic. Buddhist sect, Mahāvy. **Āryā**, f. (also) N. of a Stotra &c.; *-triśatī*, f. N. of a Kāvya by Sāma-rāja Dīkshita; *-pañcāśat*, f. N. of a Vedânta wk.; *-rāmâyaṇa* (or *ārsheya-r*°), n. N. of the Yoga-vāsishṭha; *-saptaśatī*, f. N. of a Kāvya by Govardhana Ācārya. **Ārsheya** (in comp.); *-brāhmaṇa*, n. N. of a Brāhmaṇa (belonging to the Sāma-veda and originally a mere list of names of Sāmans); *-vát* (ŚBr.). **Āla**, (also) a disease affecting wheat, Kauś. (Sch.); *-jāla*, n. (prob.) a great fraud, Kād. **Ā-lakshita**, (also) n. N. of a wood, R. (B.). **Ālaṃkārika**, m. a writer on rhetoric, Śiś., Sch. **Ā-lapita**, n. talk, conversation, Ratnâv. **Ā-laptaka**, mfn. talkative, affable, Mahāvy. **Ā-labhyà** (TBr.). **Ā-lambhá** (ŚBr.). **Ālasya-vat**, mfn. idle, lazy, slothful, L. **Ā́-lāpá** (AV.). **Ālāla**, a partic. slimy substance in the human body, Car.; *-mehin*, mfn. discharging the above with the urine, ib. **Ā-√liś** (only pf. *-liliśire*) = *ā-√riś* (p. 150), ŚBr. **Āluka**, m. (also) mixture of 5 of the 6 flavours (see *rasa*) excepting sour, L.; mfn. sweet (and) salt (and) pungent (and) bitter (and) astringent, L. **Ā-loka** (in comp.); *-kara*, (also) m. a partic. Samādhi, Mahāvy.; *-suvega-dhvaja*, m. N. of a serpent-demon, ib.; *-sthāna*, n. reach or range of sight, Mālatīm. **Ā-lolikā**, f. a humming sound made for soothing a child to sleep, Vās. **Āllakeya**, see *hṛitsv-āśaya*. **Ā-√van**, (add) Desid. *-vivāsate*, to seek to win, attract, propitiate, RV. i, 41, 8. **Ā-varaṇa**, n. (also) envelopment (in phil.), Divyâv. 378, 4; Dharmas. 115; IW. 109; °*rītri*, mfn. one who veils or covers, Kir. **Ā-varjana**, (also) pouring out a fluid, L. **Ā-vartá** (ŚBr.); °*taka*, (also) mfn. bringing back (?), Bcar. ix, 6; °*tam*, ind. repeating, KātyŚr. **Āvaśyaka-bṛihad-vṛitta** (read *-vṛitti*, f.). **Ā-vāpa**, (also) a receptacle (cf. *vyasanâv*°). **Ā-vāridhi**, ind. as far as the sea, Kir. **Ā-vāsika**, mfn. staying or abiding in (loc.), Jātakam. **Āviḥ** (in comp. for *āvis*); *-sūryé*, ind. when the sun shines, MaitrS. **Āvika**, n. (ŚBr.). 3. **Ā-√2. vid** (read √3. *vid*); *-vévidāna*, attaining, RV. **Ā-vutta**, see *ābutta*. **Āvṛitī-śayāna**, mfn. lying covered, JaimUp. **Ā́-voḍhavai** (Ved. inf. of *ā-√vah*), to bring near, ŚBr. **Ā-vyathā́**, f. slight emotion, ib. **Ā-vyushám** (AV.). **Ā-vraska**, (also) a fissure, place of cutting &c., Kauś. **Ā-śaṇsa**, mfn. expecting (comp.), Divyâv. **Ā-śaṅkita**, (also) n. fear, doubt, Jātakam. **Ā-śayá** (ŚBr.); *-tas*, ind. with intent, Divyâv. 1. **Āśā** (in comp.); *-pūrā*, f. N. of one of the 139 mothers of Gujarāt (who satisfies the hopes of wives by giving children), RTL. 227. 2. **Āśā** (in comp.); *-pālīya*, n. N. of the hymn AV. i, 31, Kauś.; *-mukha*, n. (= *diṅ-m*°), Mṛicch.; °*śâsa*, mfn. filling the regions of the sky, Śiś. **Ā-śātanā**, f. injury, violation, Śīl.; temptation, ib. **Āśāvarī**, and °**varītarī**, f. a partic. Rāgiṇī or musical mode, L. **Ā-śāsti**, f. a prayer, Mcar. **Ā-śikham**, (also) from head (to foot), Naish. **Āśīna**, mfn. = *āśiná* (p. 157), MaitrS. **Āśīvishá** (AV.); (*ā*), f. N. of a mythical river, Div.; (°*sha*)-*nadī*, f. id., ib.; *-parvata*, m. one of the 7 myth° mountains, ib. **Āśu** (in comp.); *-kavi*, m. an extempore versifier, Nalac.; *-gandha*, m. N. of a Bodhi-sattva, Mahāvy. **Ā-śocani**, m. fire, L.; the moon, L. **Āścarya** (in comp.); *-mañjarī*, f., *-rāmāyaṇa*, n. N. of two Kāvyas. **Āśyà**, mfn. to be eaten, TS. **Ā-śyāma**, mfn. dusky, dark-coloured, Hcat. **Āśrama** (in comp.); *-viḍambaka*, mfn. profaning a hermitage, BhP. 2. **Ā-śrava**, w.r. for *ā-srava*, see col. 3. **Ā-śravaṇam**, ind. up to the ear, Naish. **Ā-śrāva**, w.r. for *ā-srāva*. **Āśrāvita-pratyāśrāvita**, n. du. address and response, JaimUp. **Ā-śretṛi**, mfn. leaning on, resorting to (gen.), MBh. **Āśvapadika**, mfn. come into contact with a horse's foot, ĀpŚr., Sch. **Ā́śvamedhika**, ŚBr.; (*ī*), f., MānGṛ. **Ā-śvāsana-śīla**, mfn. disposed to encouraging another (*-tā*, f.), Mālatīm. **Ā-śvāsanī**, f. N. of a Kiṃnarī, Kāraṇḍ. **Āśvika**, m. a horse-dealer, L. **Āśvina**, n. (also) a cup of Soma consecrated to the Aśvins, Lāṭy.; °*nâgra*, mfn. beginning with a cup &c., Kāṭh. **Āśvīya**, n. a multitude of horses, L. **Ashāḍha**, (also) N. of Śiva (cf. *su-sh*°), MBh. **Āshṭrā-daṇshṭrá**, n. N. of a Sāman, MaitrS. **Ā-sakta**, (also) n. darkness, L. **Ā-saṅga**, (also) a cloak (see *citrâs*°, p. 397); a sword, L.; one of the 7 islands of Antara-dvīpa, L.; *-kāshṭha*, n. a peg, Bcar. xi, 45. **Ā-sáñjana** (ŚBr.). **Āsaṃjñika**, n. unconsciousness, Mahāvy. **Āsaṭa**, m. N. of a king (also *-deva*), Inscr. **Āsaḍa**, m. N. of the author of a Comm. on Megh. (12th cent. A.D.). **Āsanapaṭṭi**, m. a flat seat, KātyŚr., Sch. **Āsandí-vat** (ŚBr.). **Āsanna** (in comp.); *-kālika*, mfn. near in time, Pāṇ. v, 4, 20, Sch.; *-yodhin*, mfn. (an arrow) employed in close fight, MBh. **Āsa-puṭá**, m. (fr. 2. *āsa* + *p*°) ashes wrapped in a leaf, TBr. **Āsapha-khāna**, m. = Āsaf Khān, Inscr. **Ā-samāpti**, ind. (from the beginning) to the end, Rājat. **Āsarvā**, f. N. of a queen of Kṛishṇapa, Inscr. **Ā-sāda**, m. an eating-room, kitchen, Kauś.; °*danā*, f. attacking, assailing, Jātakam. **Ā-sāvin**, mfn. one who is about to generate, L. **Āsura-sva**, n. the property of the A°, Mn. xi, 20; (°*rī*)-*kalpa*, (also) N. of the 35th Pariśishṭa of the AV. **Ā-sṛishṭi**, ind. since the creation of the world, Kathās. **Ā́-sthita**, (also) n. a bodily defect (?), AV. **Ā-sphānaka**, n. a partic. meditation (?), Lalit. **Ā-sphura**, m. a place for gambling with dice (cf. *ā-sphāra*), MBh. **Āsya** (in comp.); *-garta*, m. the hollow of the mouth, Mālatīm.; *-jāha*, n. (= *-mukha*), Gaṇar. 354, Sch.; *-prayatna* (see *pra-yatna*, p. 687); *-maithunika*, mfn. using the mouth as a vulva, MBh.; *-vairasya*, n. bad taste in the mouth, Suśr.; *-sammita*, mfn. on a level with the mouth, ĀśvŚr. **Āsra**, m. distress, L.; n. 'a tear' or 'blood' (cf. 1. 2. *asra*), L. **Ā-srava**, m. (with Buddh.) impurity, defilement, sin; (with Jainas) the influence or action of body and mind and speech in impelling the soul to generate Karma. **Ā-srāvá** (accord. to some in AV. = 'diarrhœa'). **Ā-svādanīya**, mfn. pleasant, Mahāvy.; *-dya*, (also) n. food, Daś. **Ā-svāpana**, n. sleep, Divyâv. **Āhava-śobhin**, mfn. distinguished in battle, MBh. **Ā-hasa**, m. a quiet laugh, Vās. **Ā-√hiṇḍ**, to roam, Divyâv. **Ā-hita**, (also) n. a partic. mode of fighting (v.l. *a-h*°), Hariv. **Ā-hiti**, f. placing or what is placed, ŚBr. **Āhinta**, m. N. of a man, Mṛicch. 1. **Ā-huti** (in comp.); *-parimāṇa*, mfn. (fuel) containing as many pieces of wood as there are oblations to be made, Hir.; (°*tī*)-*shahi*, mfn. strong in sacrifice, Kauś. **Ā-hūrya** (RV.). 2. **Ā-hṛitya**, mfn. to be fetched, TāṇḍBr.; to be offered, ib. **Āhrīkya**, n. shamelessness, Mahāvy. **Ā-hlādá** (TS.); *-laharī*, f. N. of a poem. **Ā-hvātṛi**, m. a caller, summoner, Sāy. **Ā-hvānana**, n. calling near, Nalac. **Ā-hvāyitavya** (read *ā-hvāyayitavya*).

Ikshu (in comp.); *-bhañjam*, ind. as if breaking sugar-cane, Prasannar.; *-bhañjikā*, f. a kind of game, Cat.; *-yashṭi*, f. the stalk of the s°-c°, ib.; *-śalākā*, f. a thin stick of s°-c°, MaitrS. **Ikshvāku-candramas**, m. N. of Buddha, Bcar. **√iṅk** = *iṅg* (see *viṅg*, *viṅgita*). **Iṅgita** (in comp.); *-maraṇa*, n. a partic. manner of dying (among Jainas), Śīl.; *-lakshya*, n. a partic. rhet. figure, Hāla, Sch. **Iṅguda-taila**, n. the oil of the Iṅguda nut, Pāṇ. v, 2, 29, Vārtt. 3, Pat. **Icchā** (in comp.); *-maraṇa*, m. 'dying at will,' N. of Bhīshma, Gal. (cf. IW. 403); *-sadṛiśa*, mfn. corresponding to the wish of (gen.), Śiś. **Icchāpita**, mfn. (fr. √3. *ish*) caused to love, Divyâv. **Ijjā-devī**, f. N. of a queen of Vishṇugupta of Magadha, Inscr. **Itat**, N. of a Kāvya, Kauś. **Iḍa-prajas**, f. pl. = *iḍā-pr*°, MaitrS. **Iḍā** (in comp.); *-daḍha* (read *-dadha*); *-°nta* (*iḍânta*), mfn. ending with the Iḍā libation, ŚBr.; *-prāśitrá*, n. sg. Iḍā and Prāśitra, ŚBr.; *-bhaṅga* (v.l. for *hitābh*°), Mn. ix, 274; °*ḍôpahavana*, n. one of the sacrificial utensils, BaudhP. **Itaḥ** (in comp. for *itas*); *-pradāna* (*itáḥ-*; also) n. oblation from hence, TS.; *-prabhṛiti*, ind. from hence, MBh.; (°*to*)-*gata*, mfn. relating to this, Śak.; (°*to*)-*mukham*, ind. hitherwards, ib. **Itarátas**, °**rāthā** (ŚBr.). **Itânta**, mfn. gone to the end, Śiś. **Iti**, (also) 'and so forth' (*iti cêti ca*, 'thus and thus,' 'in this and that manner'), MBh.; *-krameṇa*, ind. in this manner, Ragh.; *-niścaya*, mfn. one who has thus resolved, Bcar. xii, 104; *-prabhṛiti*, mfn. thus beginning and so forth, Kauś.; *-hâsa*, see below; *-héti*, mfn. telling news, ŚāṅkhGṛ.; °*tîti*, the hymn RV. x, 119 (quoted), Mn. xi, 252; °*tyahé*, ind. on this or that day, ŚBr. **Itihā́sá** (ŚBr.); *-purāṇa*, n. the Itihâsas and the Purāṇas, Hir.; *-samuccaya*, m. N. of a wk. containing 32 legends from the MBh.; °*sôpanishad*, f. N. of an Upanishad. **Itthā́** (accord. to some also 'here, hither,' 'there, thither,' = Prākṛit *ettha*). **Idam** (in comp. for 2. *idám*); *-yú* (Naigh. iv, 3); *-yugīna*, mfn. belonging to this cosmic period, Siṇhâs.; *-śabda*, m. the word *idam* (to be used in assigning the oblation to each deity), ĀpY. **Idamīya**, mfn. belonging to him or her, Naish. **Idahā**, f. N. of a cow (v.l. *iḍā*), Drāhy. **Iddha**, (also) vehement, fierce, Kir. **Idhma** (in comp.); *-prôkshaṇa*, n. sprinkling the firewood, L. **Idhman**, n. fuel, L. **Indirā-dayita**, m. N. of Vishṇu, Dhanaṃj. **Indīvara-dṛiś**, f. a lotus-eyed woman, Bhām. **Indu**, (also) the weight of a silver Pala, L.; *-kalâvataṇsa*, m. N. of Śiva, Daś.; *-gaura*, m. N. of Śiva, Siṇhâs.; *-pāda*, m. a moon-ray, Bcar. **Indukā**, f. N. of a river, Hcat. **Indra** (in comp.); *-karman*, n. a sacrifice to Indra, Sāy.; *-kalpa*, mfn. resembling I°, Bcar.; *-gāthā*, f. pl. songs in praise of Indra, AitBr.; *-gṛiha*, n. Indra's house, i.e. hiding-place, TāṇḍBr.; *-nata*, mfn. bent by Indra (said of a tree which has grown crooked), Drāhy.; *-prayāṇa*, n. the sinking down of I°'s banner, Vishṇ.; *-bala* and *-bhaṭṭāraka*, m. N. of kings, Inscr.; *-magha-śrī*, f. N. of a Gandharvī, Kāraṇḍ.; *-rāja*, m. N. of various kings, Inscr.; *-śatru* (p. 167, col. 1), for (*as*) read (*us*) and after Indra's enemy add: in this sense the accent is *Indra-śatrú* (cf. Introd. p. xviii); *-sakha* (*índra-*), m. a friend of I°, Suparn.; *-sabhā*, f. 'I°'s court,' N. of a drama; *-sarasvatī*, m. N. of an author, Cat.; *-suparṇá*, m. du. Indra and Suparṇa, Suparṇ.; °*drâvasikta*, m. pl. 'watered by Indra,' N. of a class of ascetics who subsist only on vegetables, Baudh. **Indrāṇī** (in comp.); *-gaurī-pūjā*, f. 'worship of Indrāṇī and Gaurī,' a partic. nuptial ceremony, ĀpGṛ., Sch.; °*ṇya*, mfn. consecrated to I°, MānGṛ.; °*ṇy-upanishad*, f. N. of the hymn RV. x, 145 (= AV. iii, 18), Sāy. **Indriya** (in comp.); *-parimocana*, m. a partic. Samādhi, Kāraṇḍ.; *-bhāvanā*, f. mental exercise, Jātakam.; *-vāda*, m. N. of a Nyāya wk.; *-vikalatā*, f. defect of the senses (one of the 8 imperfect births), Dharmas. 134; *-saṃyamá* (ŚBr.); *-sevana*, n. sensual enjoyment, Pañcar.; *-sparśa*, m. touching parts of the body (in the Nyāsa ceremonial), RTL. 406; °*yâśva*, m. pl. the senses compared to (restive) horses, Bcar.; °*yâshyā*, f. a cow one year old with reddish eyes, TāṇḍBr. **Indhita**, mfn. (fr. Caus. of √*indh*) inflamed, kindled, Car. **Ibha**, m. (accord. to some also in RV. = 'elephant'); *-nimīlikā* (for the meaning given read '= *gaja-n*°'). **Iyádhyai** (Ved. inf. of √5. *i*), to come, RV. vi, 20, 8. **Iriṇa** (in comp.); *-loshṭa*, m. a clod from salt soil, MānGṛ. **Ilā** (in comp.); *-sutā*, f. metron. of Sītā, Bhām. **Ishīkâñji**, mfn. having stripes like reeds, Kauś. **Ishu**, m. du. (also) N. of two Vishṭutis, ŚrS.; *-nibandhana*, a quiver, R.; *-pad* (strong form *-pād*), m. N. of an Asura (v.l. *-pa*), MBh.; *-parshin*, mfn. showering arrows, ŚBr.; *-pāta*, m. an arrow's flight (as a measure of distance), MBh.; *-mukha*, n. the point of an arrow, TĀr.; *-varsha*, m. a shower of arrows, Daś.; *-vikshepa*, m. (= *-pāta* above), VP.; (*ishū*)*-guha*, mfn. hiding arrows, Kauś.; (*ishv*)*-árga* (for *ishu-várga*), m. an averter of arrows, TS. 1. **Ishṭa** (in comp.); *-devatā* (cf. RTL. xiv; 370 &c.); *-vrata* (*ishṭá-*), TS.; *-sāhasa*, mfn. violent, Śiś.; °*ṭâthititva*, n. delight in (showing) hospitality, Bcar. vii, 45. **Ishṭakā-purāṇa**, n. N. of the 10th Pariś. of Kāty. **Ishṭáni** (RV.; accord. to others = *isham tanvan*). 3. **Ishṭi** (in (comp.); *-kāla-nirṇaya*, m. N. of wk.; *-maya*, mf(*ī*)n. consisting of sacrifices, VP.; *-rūpá*, n. the property of the Ishṭi, ŚBr. **Ishṭvā** (AV.). **Ishṭvīnam**, ind. = *ishṭvā*, Pāṇ. vii, 1, 48, Sch. **Ishva**, m. (fr. √3. *ish*) desire, L.; a Vedic teacher, L.; (*ā*), f. offspring, L. **Iha** (in comp.); *-manas*, mfn. having the mind turned hither, ĀpŚr.; °*hârtha*, mfn. useful here (i.e. for this world), MBh.; (*am*), ind. for the sake of this world, Bcar.; °*hârthin*, mfn. busy in worldly objects, Mn. ii, 37; °*hêha-mātṛi* (others, 'born at the same time'). **Iheda**, n. N. of a Sāman, TBr.

√**Īksh**, (also) to be seen, Jātakam. **Īkshita**, mfn. (also) approved, ib. **Īm** (in comp. for *īm*); *-kārá*, m. uttering the exclamation *īm*, TS.; *-kṛita* (*īm-*), mfn. one who has uttered *īm*, ib. 2. **Īḍ** (RV.). **Īdṛig-avastha**, mfn. being in such a situation, Vṛishabhān. **Īdṛiśa-bhūta**, mfn. being such a one (*-tā*, f.), Naish. **Īra**, (also) mfn. driving, chasing, Nalac. **Īrayádhyai** (Ved. inf. of Caus. of √*īr*), to set in motion, RV. iv, 2, 1. **Īrmánta** (RV.). **Īlikā**, f. a nerve, tendon, gut, L. **Īśa** (in comp.); *-gocara*, m. 'Śiva's region,' the north-east, AgP.; *-śakti*, f. the personified female energy of Ś°, L. (cf. RTL. 187); °*śâcala*, m. the Himavat, Git.; °*śâdhara*, m. (with Buddhists) N. of one of the 8 mountains, Dharmas. 125; °*śêśvara*, N. of a temple, Rājat. **Īśake**, ind. in the north-east, AgP. **Īśāna** (in comp.); *-diś*, f. 'Śiva's region,' the north-east, Hcat.; *-hata*, mfn. killed by fever (= *jvara-hata*), Kauś. (Sch.). **Īśvara** (in comp.); *-kāraṇika* (Jātakam.), *-kāraṇin* (Sāṃk.), or *-kārin* (Hcar.), m. a theist; *-pratyabhijñā-sūtra*, n. N. of a Śaiva wk. by Utpala; *-priya*, m. a partridge, L. **Īshat** (in comp.); *-saṃjña*, mfn. slightly conscious, R.; *-sadṛiśa*, mfn. a little like, ĀpY. **Īshânta-bandhana**, n. a yoke, L. **Īhā** (in comp.); *-lih*, mfn. reading (any one's) wish (*nayanayoḥ*, 'in his eyes'; cf. 2. *lih*, p. 903), Sāh.

Uktá (RV.); *-bhāva*, mfn. having the sense already expressed, Hāla, Sch.; *-mātra*, mfn. merely uttered, MBh.; *-rshi* (for *-ṛishi*), m. the Ṛishi mentioned, Anukr.; °*târtha*, mfn. (= *-bhāva* above), Vām. **Ukti** (in comp.); *-posha*, m. a pleonastic expression, Mālatīm., Sch.; *-pratyuktikā*, f. speech and answer, Mcar. **Uksha-vaśā́** (TS.). **Ukshāṇa**, m. (= *ukshan*) a bull, R. (B.). **Ukshṇo-randhra**, m. N. of a Ṛishi, TāṇḍBr. **Ukha-cchid** (RV.; accord. to some, 'one who has broken his hip'). **Ukhaḍa**, N. of a place, Kshitīś. **Ugra** (in comp.); *-dhṛitâyudha*, mfn. armed with terrible weapons, Bcar.; *-pūti*, mfn. excessively fetid, Mālatīm.; *-rush*, mfn. dreadfully enraged, Kum.; °*râtapa*, mfn. dreadfully hot, Śak.; °*rânna*, n. the food of an Ugra, Mn. iv, 212. **Ucita-darśitva**, n. (prob.) the knowing what is fit or proper, Bcar. iv, 37. **Ucca** (in comp.); *-kalpa*, m. N. of a town, Inscr.; *-taratā*, f. surplus, excess, Naish.; *-saṃrāga*, mfn. 'highly reddened' and 'much inflamed,' R.; *-saṃśraya*, mfn. situated at a high elevation (as a star), ib. **Uccakais**, (also) greatly, in a high degree, Kir. **Uc-cala**, mfn. springing forth, Hcat. **Uc-cicīshā**, f. (fr. Desid. of √1. *ci*) desire of plucking or gathering, Śiś. **Uc-citraṇa**, n. decorating, embellishing, Vcar.; °*trita*, mfn. richly decorated or furnished with (instr.), ib. **Uccilliṅga**, m. (= *dāḍimī*), L. **Uc-√culump**, to sip, drink in, Mcar. **Uccaiḥ** (in comp. for *uccais*); *-śravya-karṇaka*, m. N. of a demon, Hir.; *-svara*, mfn. crying aloud, VarBṛS. **Uccair** (in comp. for *uccais*); *-abhijana*, mfn. of noble descent, Mudr.; *-gati*, f. going up, ascending, Mcar.; *-māna*, m. haughtiness, Naish. **Uccaistana**, mfn. high, lofty, Dharmaś. **Uc-chalana**, n. breaking forth, L. **Uc-chiṅhana** (read = *uc-chiṅghana*). **Uc-chiṅkhana** (read *uc-chiṅghana*). **Uc-chishṭita**, mfn. made impure, defiled, Parāś. **Uc-chuna**, m. N. of Vaiśākha, L. **Uc-chushma**, TS.; (*ā*), f. N. of a plant, Kauś. **Uc-cheda-vāda**, m. the doctrine that death causes extinction, Jātakam.; °*din*, m. an adherent of the above doctrine, ib. **Uc-chopha** (?), m. = *uc-chotha*, Mālatīm. **Uc-chvayana**, n. swelling, Sāṃk. **Uc-chvasana**, n. becoming loose (as a girdle), Mālatīm. **Uj-jigamishā**, f. (fr. Desid. of √*gam*) desire of coming forth, Kāvyâl. **Uj-jighra**, mfn., Vop. 26, 34 (cf. *jighra*, p. 421). **Uj-jihāna-jīvita**, mfn. one whose life is departing, about to die, Mālatīm. **Uj-jihīrshu** (fr. Desid. of *ud* + √*hṛi*), wishing to extricate or rescue, MBh. **Uj-jīvita-madâlasa**, N. of a drama. **Uj-jhaṭita**, mfn. disturbed, confounded, Rājat. **Ujjhita-karṇaka**, mfn. destitute of ear-rings, Bcar. **Uñcha** (in comp.); *-dharman* (MBh.) and *-bhuj* (Kāśīkh.), mfn. (= *-vartin*); *-śila* (add, Mn. iv, 5). **Uṭ-ṭaṅkita**, mfn. marked by, showing traces of (comp.), Vcar. **Uṭ-ṭikita**, n. jumping, Rājat. **Uḍupa** (in comp.); *-bhṛit*, m. N. of Śiva, Kāv.; *-sahā*, f. pl. the female companions of the moon, BhP. **Ut-kaṇṭhā-nirbharam**, ind. longingly, yearningly, Ratnâv. **Ut-kalikā-vallarī**, f. N. of a poem. **Ut-kīrtana**, n. (in dram.) awakening of the remembrance of former events, Sāh. **Ut-kīlaya**, Nom. P. °*yati*, to uproot, Divyâv. **Ut-√kū**, P. *kauti*, to cry out, Sarasv. **Ut-kūlaya**, Nom. P. °*yati*, to cause to overflow a bank, Pārv. **Ut-ketana**, n. a raised flag, Dharmaś. **Ut-kopa**, mfn. enraged, angry, Alaṃkāras. **Ut-koraka**, mfn. having sprouting buds, HPariś. **Ut-krama**, (also) dying, L. **Ut-krāthinī**, f. N. of one of the Mātṛis attending on Skanda, MBh. **Ut-krośa**, m. a watchman, Divyâv. **Ut-kvātha**, m. a decoction, Car. **Ut-kshepa**, (also) a partic. mode of lengthening vowels, TBr., Sch.; *-lipi*, m. a kind of written character, Buddh. **Ut-khaṇḍita**, mfn. broken, destroyed, Mālatīm. **Ut-khanana**, n. digging or tearing out, Kathās. **Utkhalī** or °*khilī*, f. N. of a goddess, Buddh. **Ut-khātam**, ind. digging up, Lāṭy. **Ut-kheda**, m. grief, sorrow, L. **Ut-tanū-ruha**, mfn. with bristling hair, Jātakam. **Ut-tapanīya**, mfn. (said of a kind of fire), BaudhP. **Uttapta-vaidūrya-nirbhāsa**, m. N. of a Tathāgata, Sukh. i. **Uttama** (in comp.); *-gāya*, mfn. (either fr. 2. *gāya*) highly celebrated (or fr. 1. *gāya*) wide-striding (said of Vishṇu), BhP.; *-caritra*, m. N. of a prince, Uttamac.; *-vid*, mfn. having supreme knowledge, Bhag.; °*môttamaka* (or °*mika*), n. a kind of song or conversation in a play, Bhar. **Uttara** (in comp.); *-krama*, m. objection, refutation, Jātakam.; *-gārgya*, the younger Gārgya (N. of wk.); *-ghṛita*, mfn. sprinkled over with ghee, Gobh.; *-tas*, ind. from the north, Baudh.; *-pūjā*, f. highest worship (sevenfold with Buddhists), Dharmas. 14; *-rāma-campū*, f. N. of a poem; *-vayasá* (ŚBr.); *-śalaṅkaṭa* (see *śal*°, p. 1059); °*rârdha-paścârdha*, m. north-west, MānŚr.; °*rârdhá-pūrvârdha* (ŚBr.); °*rī́ya* (erase accent). **Ut-taraṃgi**, mfn. surging, heaving, Mālatīm. **Ut-taraṇa-setu**, m. a bridge for crossing over (gen.), Mṛicch. **Ut-tarjanika**, mfn. threatening, menacing, Vcar. **Ut-tāpana**, n. paining, distressing, Hcat. **Uttiṅga**, m. a partic. insect, Śīl. **Ut-tīram**, ind. on the shore, Kir. **Ut-tuṅgita**, mfn. lifted up, raised, Śiś. **Ut-√tṛī**, (Caus. also) to remove (the nails), HPariś. **Ut-tejana**, n. (in dram.) challenging, provocation, Sāh. **Ut-thāpana**, n. (in dram.) defiance, ib. **Ut-pakva**, mfn. over-ripe, swollen, Mālatīm. **Ut-paksha**, mfn. with outspread wings, HPariś. **Ut-patín**, mfn. flying up, MaitrS. **Ut-pattra**, mfn. leafed, Jātakam. **Ut-pathaya**, Nom. P. °*yati*, to lead astray, Nalac. **Ut-paryāṇita**, mfn. unsaddled, HPariś. **Utpala** (in comp.); *-dṛiś*, mfn. lotus-eyed, Mālatīm.; *-pattra-nīla*, mfn. blue as a lotus-petal, Bcar. **Ut-pāta-lakshaṇa**, n. N. of the 64th Pariś. of the AV. **Ut-pātin**, mfn. flying up, Naish. **Ut-pālikā**, f. a dam, dyke, Dharmaś. **Ut-pipāna** (fr. 2. *ut-√pā*; accord. to others, 'with swelling sound'). **Ut-piba**, (also) m. a kind of partridge, L. **Ut-puṉsana**, n. wiping off, effacing, removing, Alaṃkārar. **Ut-puplushā**, f. (fr. *ut* + Desid. of √*plu*) the wish to fly up, HPariś. **Ut-prâsaya**, Nom. P. °*yati*, to mock, Divyâv. **Ut-prishṭi**, mfn. with prominent ribs, MaitrS. **Ut-prabhâtīya**, see *śrī-vallabha* (p. 1100). **Ut-prêkshā** (in comp.); -°*kshepa* (°*kshâk*°), m. a partic. figure of speech, Vās., Sch.; *-dhvani*, m. a partic. figure of sp°, Hāla, Sch. **Ut-prêkshita**, (also) invented (as opp. to 'borrowed'), Daśar.; °*tôpamā*, f. a kind of comparison, Kāvyâd. ii, 23. **Ut-plava**, m. flying up, Naish. **Ut-saṅga-pādatā**, f. (?) having an arched foot or high instep (one of the 32 signs of perfection), Dharmas. 83. **Ut-saṅgita**, mfn. held in the lap, Dharmaś. **Ut-sada**, mfn. excellent, Divyâv.; m. excellence, ib. **Ut-sargam**, ind. 'leaving off (everything else),' at once, immediately, ŚāṅkhBr. **Ut-sava** (in comp.); *-priya*, mfn. fond of festivals, Śak. **Ut-sādhana**, n. cleaning with perfumes, L. **Ut-sārin**, mfn. extending towards, Git. **Ut-sāha** (in comp.); *-gātratā*, f. having vigorous members (one of the 80 minor marks of a Buddha), Dharmas. 84. **Ut-sikta-manas**, mfn. of disordered mind, Mn. viii, 71. **Ut-sisṛikshu**, (also) desirous to diffuse, Bcar. ii, 50. **Ut-sū** (read, *ud-√1. sū*). 2. **Ut-sṛijya**, mfn. to be leapt over or left out, not to be observed, TS.; TāṇḍBr. **Ut-sṛishṭikâṅka**, a species of drama, Bhar. (cf. IW. 471). **Ut-sekin**, mfn. arrogant, proud, Mudr. **Ut-svedana**, n. watering, Śīl. **Uda** (in comp.); *-kaṅsya*, n. a copper vessel with water, MānGṛ.; *-gāha*, mfn. diving into water, Pāṇ. vi, 3, 60; *-dhānâyatana*, n. the place for a w°-reservoir, ĀpGṛ.; *-purā*, f. a kind of brick, MaitrS. **Udak** (in comp. for 2. *udañc*); *-śiras*, mfn. one who has his head directed towards the north, Gobh.; (*g*)*-āvṛitta*, mfn. turned to the n°, ĀpY. **Udaka** (in comp.); *-kṛicchra*, m. a kind of penance, Suśr.; *-candra*, m. N. of a Tathāgata, Sukh. i; *-rakshikā*, f. a leech, Kauś.; *-secana*, n. sprinkling w° (accord. to others, 'a shower of rain'), Mṛicch.; °*kâbhyavâyin*, mfn. going down into w°, bathing, Baudh.; °*kôtsecana*, n. a water-libation, Gobh.; °*kya*, m. or n. a water-plant, Kauś. **Udadhi** (add, N. of the number 4); *-nemi*, mfn. ocean-encircled, Ragh.). **Ud-aya**, (also) N. of a mountain near Rāja-gṛiha, MWB. 403, n. 1; *-varman*, m. N. of a Para-māra king, Inscr.; *-vyayin* (see *vyayin*, p. 1032); °*yâstamaya*, m. rising and setting, KaṭhUp.; °*yin*, mfn. victorious, triumphant, Śiś. **Udara** (in comp.); *-tāḍam*, ind. so as to beat the belly, Prab.; *-vistāra*, m. corpulence, Mṛicch.; *-stha* (MBh.), *-sthita* (HPariś.), mfn. being in the womb. **Ud-āraṇa**, n. (√*ṛi*) rising, ascending, MaitrS. **Udâj** (*udā* + √*aj*), to drive towards (dat.), Hir. **Ud-ājá** (read, 'a selected portion,' = *uddhāra*). **Udāttôkti**, f. accentuated speech, IW. 473. **Udāná** (AV.), also (with Buddhists) one of the 9 divisions of sacred scriptures, Dharmas. 62 (MWB. 63); *-bhṛit*, f. N. of partic. bricks, ŚBr. **Udīcīna-kumba**, mf(*ā*)n. with the broad end to the north, Hir. **Udīcī-patha**, m. N. of Northern India, Inscr. **Ud-ubja**, mfn. having the face turned upwards, L. **Udumbara**, (also) a toothpick made of Udumbara wood, ĀpGṛ. **Ud-ūrmi**, mfn. having surging waves, HPariś. **Ud-garjita**, n. roaring, grunting,

Mālatīm. **Ud-gāla**, m. vomiting (cf. *ud-gāra*), L. **Ud-gūrṇa**, mfn. raised, exerted, L. **Ud-√grah**, (also) to comprehend, Divyâv. **Ud-grivikā**, f. lifting up the neck, Vās. **Ud-ghṛishṭa**, (also) n. a partic. fault in pronunciation, Śiksh. **Uddaṇḍa-kavi** or °**ḍa-raṅga-nātha**, m. N. of the author of the drama Mallikā-māruta. 2. **Ud-dā** (read 2. *ud-√3. dā*). **Ud-dāla**, (also) a wicker basket for catching fish, L. **Ud-dāha**, m. heat, fire, Mālatīm. **Ud-dīkshā**, f. conclusion of the Dīkshā, MānGṛ. **Ud-deha**, m. an ant-hill, AV.Paipp. **Uddhati-śrit**, mfn. 'towering' and 'arrogant,' Śiś. xii, 56. **Ud-dhana**, m. (*√han*) a wooden sword-like instrument for stirring boiled rice, L. **Ud-dhūti**, f. shaking, brandishing, Mālatīm. **Ud-dhūmāyita**, mfn. filled with vapour, Mālatīm. **Ud-bandha**, m. (also) the son of a Khanaka and a Śūdrā, L. **Ud-bhava-kośaka**, m. the womb, MārkP. **Ud-bhuja**, mfn. with uplifted arms, Dharmaś. **Ud-yata-daṇḍa**, mfn. 'ready to strike' or 'having his army ready,' Mn. vii, 102, 103. **Udrāyaṇa**, m. N. of a disciple of Buddha, Divyâv. **Ud-roka**, m. shining forth, Vās. **Ud-vastra**, mfn. throwing off clothes, Suśr. **Ud-vāsaniya**, mfn. to be taken away or removed, Vas. **Ud-vāsya** (MaitrS.). **Ud-vāha-maṅgala**, n. a marriage-feast, Mālatīm. **U'd-vita**, mfn. (*√1. vī*) driven out, expelled, AV. **Ud-vega**, (also) absence of passion or emotion, L.; *-kartarī*, f. an Areca nutcracker, L. **Ud-vecam**, ind. picking out, Gobh. **Ud-vepin**, mfn. trembling, R. (B.). **Ud-vellana**, n. rolling, Dharmaś. **Ud-veshṭana**, n. (also) relieving a besieged town, HPariś. **Ud-vyūḍha**, mfn. dropped from (comp.), Śak. (v. l.). **Undanī**, f. (prob.) a reservoir of water for irrigation, Inscr. **Unda-pura**, n. N. of a town, ib. **Un-natêccha**, mfn. magnanimous, Ragh. **U'nnīta-śikha** (Suparṇ.). **Un-nīpam**, ind. up-hill, VS., Sch. **Un-majjaka**, m. a partic. class of ascetics, Baudh. **Un-matta-citta**, mfn. disordered in mind, a maniac, Bcar. **Un-mathana**, (also) harassing, afflicting, Kir. **Un-mādin**, (also) intoxicating, Dharmaś. **Un-miñja**, m. a question (?), Sukh. i. **Un-mīlita**, (also) made public by an inscription, Inscr. **Un-meshin**, mfn. starting up, Mālatīm. **Un-moksha**, f. deliverance, MaitrS. **Upa-kakshadaghná**, mfn. reaching up to the shoulder, ŚBr. **Upa-karaṇa**, (according to some also) heaping earth (fr. *√kṛī*), Vishṇ. **Upa-kartavya**, n. (impers.) a service is to be rendered to (gen.), R. (B.). **Upa-kalpin**, mfn. prepared or ready for (dat.), Baudh. **Upa-kāśinī**, f. N. of a demon, Hir. **Upa-krama**, (also) effort, endeavour, Campak. **Upa-gandhin**, mfn. fragrant, R. (B.). **Upa-geya** (put 2. before *upa-geya* on p. 197, col. 1; for 1. *upa-geya* see p. 196, col. 3). **Upa-grāmam**, ind. towards the village, Kir. **Upa-caturam**, ind. nearly four, Gaṇar. 135, Sch. **Upa-caraka**, m. a spy, Śil. **Upa-caradhyai** (Ved. inf. of *upa-√car*), Pāṇ. iii, 4, 9, Sch. **Upa-caryā**, f. medical treatment, L. **Upacīkā**, f. = *upajīkā* below, AV. Paipp. **Upajanam**, ind. before men, in presence of others, Kir. **Upa-jijñāsya**, (also) to be informed of all, MBh. **Upa-jika** &c. (read, *upajīkā*, f. a kind of ant, AV.). **Upa-jīvitṛi**, mfn. living on (gen.), Mn., Sch. **Upa-jvalana**, mfn. fit for kindling fire, ĀpŚr. **Upa-tapana**, mfn. harassing, oppressing, Kir. **Upa-talpam**, ind. upon the turret, Śiś. **Upa-triṅśa**, mfn. (pl.) nearly thirty, L. **Upa-dadhí**, mfn. placing upon, TS. **Upa-√dambh**, (also) to fail, ĀpŚr. **Upa-dāsa**, m. destruction, ĀpŚr., Sch. **Upa-didikshu**, mfn. (*√diś*) intending to teach, Gṛihyās., Introd. **Upa-dehikā**, f. the white ant, L. **Upa-dhāna**, n. (also) fetching, procuring, Jātakam.; a jewel-case, ib.; *-liṅga*, mfn. (a verse) containing the word *upa-dhāna*, ĀpGṛ. **Upadhi**, (also) one of the requisites for the equipment of a Jaina ascetic (said to be 6, viz. 3 garments, 1 jar, 1 broom, and 1 screen for the mouth), Śīl. **Upa-dhenu**, ind. near the cows, Kir. **Upa-nadi**, ind. on the river, ib. **Upa-nāyin**, mfn. bringing near, fetching, MBh.; taking as apprentice, Nār. **Upa-nigrāham**, ind. placing near to (loc.), ĀpŚr. **Upa-nidhyātavya**, mfn. (cf. *ni-√dhyai*) to be considered, Mahāvy. **Upa-ninīshu**, mfn. (Desid. of *√nī*) wishing to present, ĀpŚr., Sch. **Upa-nimantraṇa**, (also) singing the two Sāmans Śyaitana and Audhasa, L. **Upa-nirgama**, (also) departure from (comp.), Mālatīm. **Upa-nir-√hṛi**, to take away, Hir. **Upa-nivartam**, ind. repeatedly, ŚāṅkhBr. **Upa-niveśinī**, f. the fifteenth day of the light half of Jyeshṭha, L. **Upa-neya**, mfn. to be adduced as an example, Jātakam. **Upa-patti**, (also) origin, birth, Śiś.; use, employment, KātyŚr., Sch. **Upa-pannârtha**, mfn. having good reasons, MBh. **Upa-parîksha**, mfn. examining, Divyâv. **Upa-pātra**, n. a subsidiary vessel, MWB. xiii, n. 1. **Upa-pādin**, mfn. = °*daka*, Kathās. **Upa-pāyana**, n. giving to drink, watering, MānGṛ. **Upa-bilam**, ind. to the brim, ĀpŚr. **Upa-bhaimi**, ind. besides Bhaimī (i. e. Damayantī), Naish. **Upa-manthana**, n. stirring up, Kauś. **Upa-√mṛī** (Pass. *-mūryate*), to be destroyed, ŚBr. **Upa-yoga**, (also) calculation (°*gam √kṛi*, 'to calculate'), HPariś. **Upa-rakta**, (also) m. N. of Rāhu, L. **Upa-rathyā**, f. a side-street, L. **Upa-ravá** (TS.). **Upa-rāga-vat**, mfn. eclipsed, obscured, Śiś. **Upa-ri-martya** (accord. to some, 'raising mortals'). **Upárishṭāt** (in comp.); *-kāla*, m. a later period, ĀpŚr. **Upa-rudita**, n. wail, lament, Mudr. **Upa-rodham**, ind. having locked in or shut up, Pāṇ. iii, 4, 49. **Upa-lakshmī**, f. a goddess mentioned with Lakshmī, MānGṛ. **Upa-laya**, m. a hiding-place, Jātakam. **Upalâśa**, m. (prob.) = *upalā* (*aśa* = *aśan*, 'a stone'), MānGṛ. **Upa-√van** (Desid. *-vivāsati*), to propitiate, seek to win or render gracious, RV. vi, 15, 6. **Upa-vapana**, n. scattering, ĀpŚr. **Upa-varṇa**, m. an inferior caste, L. **Upa-vastra**, n. upper clothing, RTL. 415. **U'pa-vahas** (for *upa-vaha*, ŚBr., Kāṇva recension). **Upa-vāsana**, n. (*√4. vas*) attire, covering, AV. **Upa-viṅśa**, mfn. (pl.) nearly twenty, L. **Upa-vindhyâdri**, ind. near the Vindhya mountains, HPariś. **Upa-veṇu**, m. (prob.) common reed, Hcat. **Upa-vedi**, ind. near the altar, Kir. **U'pa-veśi** (ŚBr.). **Upa-vyākhyāna** (read, 'a supplementary explanation'). **Upa-vrata**, n. a minor vow or observance, Baudh. **Upa-śānta**, n. tranquillity, peace, Sukh. i. **Upa-śikshaṇa**, n. taking into discipleship or apprenticeship, ĀpŚr., Sch. **Upa-śushka**, mfn. dry, ib. **Upa-śaila**, m. a hill, Hcat. **Upa-śosha**, mfn. drying up, withering, R. (B.). **Upa-saṃhata**, mfn. collected, Divyâv. **Upa-saṃhāra**, (also) that part of a drama which usually precedes the Bharata-vākya, Bhar. **Upasad-dhoma**, m. (for *-homa*) the oblation of the Upasad ceremony, ŚrS. **Upa-sarga**, (also) an eclipse of sun or moon, Gobh. **Upa-sāgaram**, ind. towards the (Ṛishi) Sāgara, HPariś. **Upa-siddha**, mfn. (*√3. sidh*) ready, prepared (food; cf. *sūpasiddha*), Gobh. **Upa-hāsanīyatā**, f. ridiculousness, Mṛicch. **Upāṅśu-ghātaka**, m. an assassin, Bṛihasp. **Upâtta-sāra**, mfn. having the best part taken or enjoyed, Mālav. **Upâdhāyyà-pūrvaya** (see *pūrvaya*, p. 645). **Upâya-kauśalya**, n. skill in the choice of means, SaddhP. **Upâyôpeya**, means and object, Mālav. **Upâlipsu**, mfn. wishing to reproach or blame, Kāś. on Pāṇ. viii, 2, 94. **Upâsaka-daśa** (read, '*-daśā*, f. pl.'). **Upâ-√hiṇḍ**, to wander, ib. **Upâhita**, (also) m. a meteor, L. **Upêta-pūrva**, mfn. one who has gone to a teacher before, ĀśvGṛ. **Upôttara**, mfn. later, ĀpŚr., Sch. **Upôndana**, n. wetting, watering, ib. **Upolava**, N. of a plant, Kauś. **Upôshaṇīya-prabha**, m. = *amitâbha*, Sukh. i. **Upta-keśa**, mfn. one who has his hair shorn, MānGṛ. **Ubh**, (also) cl. 7. *unábdhi*, to bind, compress, confine, contain, include. **Ubhaya** (in comp.); *-pārśvatas*, ind. on both sides, Bcar.; *-vartanin*, mfn. having both wheels (or two wheels), TāṇḍBr.; (°*yataḥ*)*-kshṇú*, mfn. two-edged, TS.; (°*yataḥ*)*-praṇava*, mfn. having the syllable Om at the beginning and end, Baudh.; (°*yato*)*-dhāra*, mfn. two-edged, BhP. 2. **Ubhayā** (in comp.); *-cakra*, mfn. two-wheeled, JaimUp.; *-pad*, mfn. two-legged, JaimUp. **Umā** (in comp.); *-vṛishâṅka*, m. du. Umā and Śiva, Ragh. **Umbhita**, mfn. included or contained in (see *√ubh* above), Bhām. **Urandhrā**, f. N. of a goddess, ĀpŚr. **Urarī-√kṛi**, to begin with (acc.), Mālatīm. **Uralli**, roaring, a roar (?), ib. **Uras** (in comp.); *-peśa*, mfn. wearing ornaments on the breast, Hir.; (*uraḥ*)*-śiras*, n. sg. head and br°, Kauś.; (*uraḥ*)*-stha*, mfn. being in the chest (as the voice), R. (B.); (*uro*)*-grīva*, n. sg. breast and neck, Suśr. **Urī-√kṛi** = *urarī-√kṛi* (above), Mālatīm. **Uru** (in comp.); *-dhāra*, mfn. broad-edged, BhP.; *-puṇya-kośa*, m. a great treasure of merit, Gobh., Sch. **Urváśī** (RV.). **Ula**, a kind of vegetable, Kauś. **Ulūkâri**, m. 'owl's enemy,' a crow, L. **Uloká** (prob. a collateral form of *loka*, p. 906). **Ulkā** (in comp.); *-pāta*, m. the falling of meteors, Gobh.; *-lakshaṇa*, n. N. of the 58 Pariś. of the AV. **Ul-baṇa-tāpa**, mfn. much burnt, Kum. **Ulmuka-mathyā** (read *-mathyà*). **Ullaka**, the juice of a partic. fruit, Hcar. **Ul-lalana**, mfn. swarming (as bees), Śiś. **Ul-lāsaka**, n. a kind of inferior drama, Bhar. **Ul-likhita**, (also) painted, Bcar. **Ul-liṅganâshṭaka**, n. N. of a poem by Kāmêśa. **Ul-lekhanīya**, m. a kind of clearing nut, L. **Ul-lola**, mfn. (also) lovely, Dharmaś. 2. **U'sh** (RV.). **Ushā** (in comp.); *-carita*, n., *-nidāna*, n., *-pariṇaya*, m., *-haraṇa*, n. N. of wks. **Ushṇa** (in comp.); *-naraka*, m. a hot hell (said to be 8 in number), Dharmas. 11. **Ushṇīsha** (in comp.); *-vijaya*, m. a partic. prayer, Buddh.; (*ā*), f. a Tantra deity, ib.; *-śiraskatā*, f. having a turbaned head (one of the 32 signs of perfection), Dharmas. 83 (cf. MWB. 475). **Usmita**, m. (?) N. of a Vināyaka, MānGṛ. **Uhlaṇa**, m. N. of the author of a Comm. on Suśr.

Ūkha, m. a buttock (cf. *ukha*), L. 1. **Ūḍha** (read 1. and 2. *ūh*); *-pūrvā*, f. a woman married before, Śak.; *-ratha*, mfn. drawing a chariot, Laghuk.; *-vayas*, mfn. full grown, BhP. **Ūti-máti**, f. the verse RV. i, 30, 7, MaitrS. **Ūdalêśvara**, m. N. of a god, Inscr. **Ūna** (in comp.); *-dvivārshika*, mfn. not yet two years old, Mn. v, 68; *-varṇatā*, f. defectiveness by one syllable, Kāvyâd. iii, 157; *-vāda*, m. improper speech, Baudh.; *-shoḍaśa-varsha*, mfn. not yet sixteen years old, R.; °*nêndu-pūrṇimā*, f. the moon on the day before the full moon, L. **Ūnī-√bhū**, to become less, diminish (intrans.), Kālac. **Ūpā**, f. a kind of Nidhana, ŚrS.; *-svara*, n. the way in which the Ūpā is sung, ib., Sch. **Ūbadhya**, (also) breaking wind, L. **Ūma**, m. (also) the sky, L. **Ūrī-√kṛi**, to incur, undergo, HPariś. **Ūru** (in comp.); *-grāhá*, m. (= *-graha*), AV.; *-cchinna*, mfn. one who has broken a leg, KaushUp.; *-bhaṅga*, m. fracture of the thigh, Vās.; *-bhitti*, f. the region of the hips, Śiś. ix, 75; *-mūla*, n. the groins, L. **Ūrjáyat** (RV.). **Ūrjayanta-tīrtha**, n. N. of a place, Inscr. **Ūrjas-pati**, m. N. of Vishṇu, Vishṇ. **Ūrjâhuti**, f. a nourishing or strengthening oblation, MaitrS. **Ūrjita**, (*am*), ind. haughtily, arrogantly, Nāg. **Ūrṇa** (in comp.); *-vāhi*, m. (= *-vābhi*), L. **Ūrṇā** (in comp.); *-mṛidu* (*ūrṇā-*), mfn. soft as wool, TBr.; °*-lam-kṛita-mukhatā* (*ūrṇâl*°), f. having soft hair between the brows (one of the 32 signs of perfection), Dharmas. 83; *-mradas*, mfn. (= *-mṛidu*), ĀpŚr.; *-vāhi*, m. (= *ūrṇa-v*°), L. **Ūrṇāyú**, mfn. woollen, VS.; m. a ram, L.; a blockhead, Kshem.; a spider, L.; a woollen blanket, L.; N. of a Gandharva, MBh.; Hariv.; f. a ewe, L. **Ūrdhva**, also (*ā*), f. the upper region (zenith), L.; *-cūḍa*, mfn. (hair) tied up in a tuft, Mṛicch.; *-jānu* or *-jñu*, mfn. long-shanked, L.; *-jvalana*, n. flaming upwards, Śiś.; *-jhampa*, m. a jump upwards, Kathās.; *-nāpita*, m. a barber who shaves the upper part of the body; *-pravarshin*, mfn. raining i. e. sacrificing upwards (to the sky), MBh. xii, 2147; *-bhāga-hara*, mfn. emetic (cf. *ūrdhva-bhāga*), Suśr.; *-mūla*, mfn. having the roots upwards, TĀr.; *-vāsin*, m. pl. N. of a class of ascetics, R. (B.); *-śushi*, f. (scil. *samidh*) grown dry on the tree, Kauś.; *-sūcikā*, f. an upper iron bolt of a door, L.; °*dhvâgra*, mf(*ā*)n. with the point upwards, Hir. (*-romatā*, f. having the hairs of the body erect [one of the 32 signs of perfection], Dharmas. 83). **Ūrdhvakam**, ind. at the top of the voice, aloud, Mṛicch. 1. **Ūrva** (RV.; prob. identical with 2. *ūrva*, and accord. to some also, 'a fold,' 'herd,' 'cattle;' 'a mountain'). **Ū'rvya**, mfn. being in ponds or lakes &c., VS. **Ūlī**, f. an onion, L.; *-bhaksham*, ind. (with *√bhaksh*) so as to eat hot, Kauś.; *-bheda* and *-viveka*, m. N. of two wks. on the proper spelling of words containing a sibilant.

Ṛik &c. (in comp. for 2. *ṛic*); *-pada*, n. a part of a Ṛic, JainUp.; (*ṛig*)*-aśīti*, 80 Ṛicas, ŚBr.; (*ṛig*)*-yajus*, n. du. the Ṛig and Yajur-vedas, Mn. iv, 123. 2. **Ṛiksha** (in comp.); *-karṇī*, f. N. of a Yogini, Hcat.; *-bila*, n. N. of a cavern, R. (B.); *-varṇa*, mfn. bear-coloured, MBh. **Ṛiju** (in comp.); *-gātratā*, f. having all the limbs straight (one of the 32 signs of perfection), Dharmas. 83; *-yodhin*, m. a fair-fighter (opp. to *jihma-y*°), MBh. (cf. IW. 408); *-vyākaraṇa*, n. N. of a grammar; (°*jv*)*-āgata*, mfn. in front (= en face), Nalac.; (°*jv*)*-āyata*, mfn. straight and extended, Kum. **Ṛijūyat** (fr. *ṛijūya*; read *ṛijūyát*). **Ṛiṇa** (in comp.); *-kāti* (*ṛiṇá-*) *-cit*, n. (read, 'revenging guilt'); *-cyút* (read, 'removing guilt'). **Ṛita** (in comp.); *-śrī*, f. true beauty, ĀpŚr.; *-sadhastha*, mfn. standing in the right manner, ib.; °*tâmṛita*, n. du. lawful gleaning and unsolicited alms, Mn. iv, 4; °*tôkti*, f. telling the truth, ib. viii, 104. **Ṛitavyà-vat** (ŚBr.). **Ṛitu** (in comp.); *-karmán*, n. a right action, TBr.; *-ketu-lakshaṇa*, n. N. of the 55th Pariśishṭa of the AV.; *-gamana*, n. approaching (a woman) at the right time, ĀpŚr.; *-devata*, mfn. having the seasons for a deity, ĀśvGṛ.; *-paryaya*, m. (= *-paryāya*), Mn. i, 30; *-maṅgala*, n. an auspicious omen for the s°, Śak.; *-vyāvṛitti*, f. the end of a s°, ĀpŚr.; *-samā-veśana*, n. cohabitation during the fortnight after menstruation, ĀpGṛ. **Ṛite** (in comp.); *-bhaṅga*, mf(*ā*)n. (prob.) without separation (i.e. analysis), Gobh.; *-sphya*, mfn. without the Sphya, ĀpŚr. **Ṛitvan**, m. N. of a Gandharva, MBh. **Ṛitvig-āśis**, f. a wish or prayer uttered by the officiating priest, ŚrS. **Ṛiddhi** (VS.; also) N. of Gaṇeśa's wife, RTL. 215; *-lakshmī*, f. N. of a Nepāl queen, Inscr. (°*dhy*)-*abhisaṃskāra*, m. a phantom produced by magical art, Jātakam. **Ṛiśyapad**, mf(*ī*)n. deer-footed, AV. **Ṛishabha**, (also) m. N. of one of the 24 Jaina saints or Jinas; (*ā*), f. a masculine (bullish) girl unfit for marriage, ĀpGṛ.; *-carmá*, n. a bull's skin, TBr.; *-datta*, m. N. of various persons, HPariś.; *-vikrama*, m. a bull in prowess, Bcar.; °*bhâikādaśa*, n. ten cows and a bull, Baudh.; °*bhâikâdhika*, mfn. having one bull added, ib. **Ṛishi** (in comp.); *-vāṭa*, m. a hermitage of Ṛishis. **Ṛishvá-vīra** (RV.).

Eka (in comp.); *-karman* (Daś.) or *-kriya* (Mcar.), mfn. having one and the same business; *-kriyā-vidhi*, m. employment of the same verb, Kāvyâd.; *-ga*, mfn. attentive to only one object, L.; *-garbha*, mfn. bringing forth only one child, BhP.; *-grantha*, m. an aggregate of 32 letters, L.; *-cchāyā-pravishṭa*, mfn. jointly liable, Kāty.; *-tīr-thin* (L.), *-tīrthya* (Baudh.), m. one who has the same teacher, fellow-student; *-triṇśa*, °*śaka*, °*śat* (read *éka-triṇśa*, °*śaka*, °*śat*); *-dvāra*, mf(*ā*)n. having (only) one access or approach, MBh.; *-nibha*, mfn. uniform, VarBṛS.; *-pati*, f. having only one husband (*-tva*, n.), HPariś.; *-padam*, ind. (= *-pade*), Mālatīm.; *-palâdhika*, n. one Pala more, Mn. viii, 397; *-pātin*, (also) flying (only) in one manner, MBh., being alone or solitary, ib.; *-bhūyas*, mfn. having one over, odd, Gobh.; *-bhoga*, m. and °*gya*, n. sole and entire right of enjoyment, Inscr.; *-mūrti*, f. one person, Subh.; *-loka* (*éka-*), mfn. possessing one world, MaitrS.; *-vartanin*, mfn. one-wheeled, ShaḍvBr.; *-viṇśati-cchadi* (*éka-*), mfn. having 21 roofs, TS.; *-vṛikshīya*, mfn. derived from the same tree or wood, KātyŚr.; *-veda*, mfn. knowing (or studying) only one V°, ib.; *-vyūha*, mfn. appearing (only) in one form, Vishṇ.; *-śarīrin*, mfn. standing alone, i.e. having no relatives, Daś.; *-śūla*, mfn. one-pointed, Hir.; *-śesha*, mfn. of which only one is left, MBh.; *-śnushṭi* (v.l. for *-śrushṭi*, AV. iii, 30, 7); *-saptati-guṇa*, mfn. multiplied by 71, Mn. i, 79; *-sampratyaya*, m. having the same signification, VarBṛS.; *-sthânâśraya* (see *sthān*°, p. 1263). **Ekató-mukha**, mf(*ā*)n. turned to one side, TBr.; (a vessel) having a spout only on one side, ĀpŚr., Sch. **Ekâkshi-piṅgalin**, m. N. of Kubera, R. **Ekâṅga-graha**, m. paralysis, L. **Ekâtma-pak-sha**, m. the Vedânta doctrine, Sāṃkhyas., Sch.; *-vāda*, m. a teacher of the Vedânta, ib. 2. **Ekā-daśa** (in comp.); *-rcá* (fr. *ṛic*), a hymn of 11 verses, AV.; *-varsha*, mfn. 11 years old, Hir.; *-vyūha*, mfn. appearing in 11 forms (Rudra), BhP. **Ekânta** (in comp.); *-duḥkha*, mfn. absolutely unhappy, Bcar. xi, 43. **Ekântaritin** (?) or °*rin*, mfn. one who fasts every second day, L. **Ekâmra** (in comp.); *-candrikā*, f. N. of wk.; *-nātha* (cf. RTL. 446), *-pu-rāṇa*, n., *-vana-māhātmya*, n. N. of wks. **Ekâ-yanī-bhāva**, m. unanimity, Mcar. **Ekârtha-dīpaka**, n. a Dīpaka (q.v.) of simple meaning, Kāvyâd. ii, 112. **Ekârsheya**, mfn. having only one sacred ancestor, MānŚr. **Ekâha-dhanin**, mfn. having food for one day, Baudh. **Ekâhan**, n. a single day (= *ekâha*), MBh. xvii, 67. **Ekī-bhāva-stotra**, n. N. of a Stotra. **Ekīya**, (also) single in its kind, Jātakam. **Ekâika** (in comp.); *-tra*, ind. singly, ĀpŚr., Sch.; *-vat*, mfn. possessing (only) one (of several things), ib. **Ekôti-bhāva** (read, 'the thread-like continuity of personality or individual life running through the whole cycle of re-births,' Buddh.). **Ejana**, n. tremor, L. **Eṇika**, °**kīya**, Pat. on Pāṇ. ii, 4, 14. **Etat-prabhṛiti**, mfn. beginning with this, Gobh. **Etad** (in comp.); *-upanishad*, mfn. following this Upanishad, ChUp. **Etāvatitha**, mf(*ī*)n. the so-manieth (v.l. °*tima*), Drāhy., Sch. **Etāvad-āvāsa**, mfn. having so many abodes, JaimUp. **Éti-vat**, mfn. containing a form of √5. *i* (*eti*), TBr. **Éd**, ind. (accord. to some = 2. *ā* + *íd*) behold! (followed by a partic. with an acc. and preceded by a verb of motion, e.g. *éyāya Vāyúr éd dhatám Vṛitrám*, 'Vāyur went [to see, and] behold Vṛitra was slain;' sometimes the verb of motion must be supplied, sometimes the substantive, and sometimes the participle), Br. **Edhinī**, f. the earth (= *medinī*), L. **Eraṇḍa-palla**, N. of a town, Inscr. **Eraṇḍā**, (also) N. of a charm, Divyâv. **Erā**, f. a ewe (= *eḍakā*), L. **Éru** (accord. to some, 'the penis'). **Elā-rasālaka**, mf(*ikā*)n. astringent (and) pungent (and) bitter, L. **Elā-vāluka**, n. a kind of perfume (cf. *elav*°), L. **Evam** (in comp. for *evam*); *-vi-dus*, mfn. (= *vidvas*), Kāṭh.; *-śīla*, mfn. of such a character or disposition, MBh.; *-karman*, mfn. one who has done so, Mn. viii, 314; *-klṛipta*, mfn. so prescribed or enjoined, RPrāt.; *-gotra* and *-jāti*, mfn. of such a family, Lalit. **Evam** (in comp.); *-pariṇāma*, mfn. having such a conclusion, Mcar.; *-pratyaya*, mfn. having such a belief, Śaṃk.; *-pra-vāda*, mfn. having such a grammatical form, RPrāt. **Evāvadá** (RV.). **Évāsha**, m. a kind of small animal (cf. *yév*° and *yav*°), MaitrS. **Eshâìshyà** (accord. to some the word is *eshâìshá*, 'impetuous,' and °*shyà* the instr. of the fem. °*shí*). **Éshṭavai** (Ved. inf. of *ā*-√3. *ish*), ŚBr. **Êshṭrí**, mfn. hastening on, advancing, ib. **Êshyà** (AV.). **Êhi'bhikshukā**, f. the call *êhi bhiksho*, 'come, monk!,' Divyâv.

Aikamantrya, n. the having the same Mantras, ĀpŚr., Sch. **Aikamukhya**, n. unanimity, Mcar. **Aiṇeya-jaṅghatā**, f. having legs like those of a deer (one of the 32 signs of perfection), Dharmas. 83. **Aindra-nighaṇṭu**, N. of a glossary by Vararuci. **Airyāpathikī**, f. (fr. *īryā-patha*), HPariś. **Aila-vaṇśa**, m. the race of Aila, i.e. the lunar race, MBh. (IW. 511, n. 1). **Aivamarthya**, n. the having such a sense, MānGṛ., Sch. **Aiśi**, m. patr. of Skanda, Kum. xi, 44. **Aiśvarakāraṇika**, m. a theist of the Nyāya school, Hcar. **Aiśvarika**, N. of one of the 4 philosophical systems in Nepal (the other 3 being *kārmika*, *yātnika*, and *svābhāvika*), Buddh. (cf. MWB. 204). **Aiśvarya-kādambinī**, f. N. of a poem in praise of Kṛishṇa by Vidyā-bhūshaṇa.

Okivás (RV.). **Ogaṇá** (accord. to some for *ava-gaṇa* = 'lonely, forsaken, wretched, miserable'). **Ogha**, m. pl. the (four) floods (of worldly passion), Divyâv.; *-deva*, m. N. of a chief, Inscr. **Ótsūryám** (add 'i.e. *ā* + *utsūryam*'). **Ódatī** (others, 'lustful, wanton'). **Odana** (in comp.); *-pac*, mfn. (nom. *-pak*), Pāṇ. vi, 4, 15, Sch.; *-piṇḍa*, m. a ball of boiled rice, ĀpGṛ.; *-prati*, ind., Pat. on Pāṇ. ii, 1, 9. **Ódman**, (also) wetness, rain, ŚāṅkhBr. **Opaśá** (accord. to some also, 'a horn'). **Ōpya** (ŚBr.). **Osha-dávan**, mfn. (prob.) giving quickly, AV. xix, 42, 3 (cf. *oshishṭha-d*°). **Oshadhi** (in comp.); *-nāmâvalī*, f. N. of wk.; *-vallabha*, m. the moon, Alaṃkārar.; *-homa*, m. a kind of oblation, ĀpŚr.; °*dhîśvara*, m. the moon, Dharmaś. **Oshṭha** (in comp.); *-mudrā*, f. sealed i.e. closed lips, Uttarar.; *-rucaka* (Hariv.), *-rucira* (Vishṇ.), n. lovely lips; *-śataka*, n. N. of a poem.

Aujasa, (also) N. of a Tīrtha (v.l. *ausaja*), Vishṇ. **Aujjāgari** (see *sundara-miśra*, p. 1227). **Autkaṭya**, n. excess, superabundance, Śiś., Sch. **Audarcisha**, mfn. directed to Agni, Śiś. **Audā-rika** (in comp.); *-śarīra*, n. the coarse body (perishing at death), Śil. **Audārya-cintāmaṇi**, m. N. of a Prākṛit grammar. **Audumbarāyaṇa**, (also) a married Brāhman, L. **Audumbarī**, f. (with *saṃhitā*) N. of a wk. on Bhakti (accord. to Nimbârka). **Auddhatya**, (with Buddhists) self-exaltation (one of the 10 fetters which bind a man to existence), MWB. 127. **Audrāyaṇa**, m. (for Prākṛit *Uddāyaṇa*) N. of a prince, HPariś. **Aunnidrya**, n. sleeplessness, L. **Aupakārika**, mfn. beneficial, useful, Daś. **Aupakārya**, n. a preparatory or secondary action, ĀpGṛ. **Aupacāyika**, n. a kind of Śrāddha, L. **Aupajaṅghani**, m. N. of a teacher (cf. °*jandhani*), Baudh. **Aupāsaná** (ŚBr.). **Aumā-pendra**, mfn. relating to Vishṇu, Śiś. **Aumā-pata**, (also) n. N. of a wk. (on music, apparently by Umā-pati). **Aurabhrika**, m. (also) a sheep-butcher, L. 1. **Aúrva** (RV.). **Aushadha** (in comp.); *-kalpa-grantha*, *-prakāra*, *-prayoga*, m. N. of wks. on medicine. **Aushṭhīna**, mfn. being on the lips, Caurap. **Aushṇa**, n. heat, Śaṃk.

Kaṇsa (in comp.); *-dhvaṇsana*, m. (— *-jit*), Gīt.; *-nidhana*, n. N. of a poem (without labial letters, in 17 cantos); *-parimṛij*, Kāś. on Pāṇ. viii, 2, 36. **Kakárdu** (accord. to some *kakárdave* is w.r. for *kapardavé* = *kapardiné*). **Kakāṭika** (AV.). **Kakuca**, a kind of plant or fruit, Kauś. **Kákutsala** (AV.). **Kakudin**, m. a bull, Baudh. **Kakúd-mat** (RV.). **Kakún-mat** (TS.). **Ka-kúbhvat** (MaitrS.). **Kakum-mukha**, n. a region of the sky, Śiś. **Kakuhá** (accord. to some also m. 'a horse of the Aśvins,' RV. i, 184, 3). **Kak-kinda**, m. a lizard, L. **Kakha-tīra**, Pāṇ. iv, 2, 104, Vārtt. 2, Pat. **Kaṅka** (in comp.); *-deva*, m. N. of a Para-māra king, Inscr.; *-parvan* (*kaṅ-ká-*), AV.; *-raṅka*, m. a hungry or half-starved crane, Prab.; *-vājita*, mfn. having heron's feathers (as an arrow), MBh.; *-hrada*, m. N. of a tank, SahyKh. **Kaṅkaṭīka**, m. N. of Śiva, L. **Kaṅ-kaṇa**, (also) a drop of water, Dharmaś.; N. of a poet, Cat.; °*ṇâbharaṇa*, mfn. wearing a golden bracelet, Mṛicch. **Kaca** (cf. RTL. 194, n. 1); *-rūpin*, mfn. having the form of Kaca, MBh. **Ka-cāra**, m. or n. a pond, Bhadrab. **Kacchapa-ghā-ta** or °**pâri**, m. N. of a family, Inscr. 3. **Káṭ**, ind. a particle of exclamation, TĀr. **Kaṭa** (in comp.); *-kaṭa*, (also) n. sea-salt, L.; *-kara* or *-karman*, m. a straw-mat maker (the son of a Vaiśya and a Śūdrā), L.; °*ṭâkshaya*, Nom. P. °*yati*, to regard with a side glance, Pārv. **Kaṭakaṭaya**, P. Ā. °*yati* or °*yate* (onomat.) to gnash, grate, Mālatīm. **Kaṭani**, m. or f. a mountain-slope, L. **Kaṭi-stha**, mfn. borne on the hip or in arms, HPariś. **Kaṭha-sūtra**, n. N. of Sūtras, KātyŚr., Sch. **Kaṭhina**, n. (also) a garment made in a day and offered to a monk as a present, Buddh.; *-tāraka-nātha*, m. the full moon, Śṛiṅgār. **Kaḍaṅgara**, a partic. weapon, MBh. **Kaṇa-kukkuṭa**, m. the son of a Vaidehaka and a Pulkasī, L. **Kaṇṭaka-praticchedana**, m. a two-edged battle-axe, L. **Kaṇṭha** (in comp.); *-taṭinī*, f. the throat, Siṇhâs.; *-trāṇa*, n. a neck-protector, MBh.; *-nālikā*, f. the windpipe, Mahāvy.; *-pra-ṇālikā*, f. id., Bālar.; *-sūtra*, n. a necklace, MBh.; *-sthānīya*, mfn. (see *sthānīya*, p. 1263); °*ṭhe-guḍa*, m. the apple or protuberance in the throat, L. **Kaṇṭhya**, mfn. clear, evident, Jain. **Kaṇḍa**, n. an ornament, L.; a joint (= *parvan*), L.; *-gopāla*, m. N. of a king, Inscr. **Kaṇḍu**, f. an itching or ardent desire, Śiś.; °*dūla*, mfn. itching, ardently desiring, Car.; Śiś., Sch. **Katarátas** (ŚBr.). **Katarathā**, ind. in which of two manners or ways?, ShaḍvBr. **Katham-kathā**, f. doubt and questioning, Divyâv. 1. **Kathā** (in comp.); *-trayī*, f. N. of a wk. (containing the substance of the R., MBh. and BhP.); *-prastāvatas*, ind. in the course of conversation, Kathās.; *-saṃdhi*, f. a joint in a tale (i.e. the place where it is joined to another tale), Kathās. 2. **Kad** (in comp.); *-adhvaga*, m. a heretic, Bhadrab.; *-artha* (*kád-*), RV.; *-āśaya*, mfn. deceitful, intriguing, Campak.; *-īśitṛi*, m. a bad ruler, Kautukar. **Kadamba** (in comp.); *-koraka-nyāya*, m. the rule of the Kadamba buds (i.e. simultaneous appearance or action), A.; *-gola*, m. a K° blossom, Mālatīm. **Kadru**, f. daughter of Daksha (read *Kadru*). **Kadrú** (RV.). **Kadvindu** (?), N. of a reed plant (in °*du-koshṭha*), Kauś. **Kanaka** (in comp.); *-śṛiṅga-maya* (see *śṛiṅg*°, p. 1087); °*kâ-kshī*, f. an owl, L.; °*kâbja*, n. a gold lotus, Mālatīm.; °*kôjjvala*, mfn. radiant with gold, MBh. **Kánīyaḥ-stana**, mfn. having fewer teats, ŚBr. **Kanīyo 'kshara**, mfn. having fewer syllables, TāṇḍBr. **Kanthaka**, m. (= *kaṇṭhaka*) Buddha's horse, Bcar. **Kandala**, mfn. filled with (comp.), Nalac.; °*li*, a sprout, ib. **Kanduka** (in comp.); *-līlā*, f. a game at ball, Kum.; °*kôtsava*, m. a pastime consisting in playing at ball, Daś. **Kanyā** (in comp.); *-°gāra* (°*nyâg*°) or *-gṛiha*, n. the women's apartments, Daś.; *-darśam*, ind. at the sight of a girl, Pāṇ. iii, 4, 29, Sch.; *-pipīlikā*, f. a very small ant, L.; *-pra-vahaṇa*, n. (= *pradāna*), SāmavBr. **Kanyākā**, f. a girl, L.; the pupil of the eye, AitĀr. **Kapaṭa** (in comp.); *-kāpaṭikā*, f. fraud, deceit, Mṛicch.; *-nāṭaka*, n. a comedy (as it were) of a deceit, Mālatīm. **Kapaná** (RV.). **Kapāṭa-mudrā**, f. shutting a door, Vcar. **Kapāla** (in comp.); *-hasta*, mfn. bearing a skull in the hand, Bcar.; °*lêśvara*, m. 'lord of skulls,' N. of Śiva (esp.) as worshipped at a temple in Nāsik; (*ī*), f. N. of Śiva's wife, Inscr. **Kapi** (in comp.); *-ketu*, m. N. of Arjuna, Śiś.; *-lalāṭa*, m. an arm, Kauś.; *-vaná* (MaitrS.). **Ka-piñjala-nyāya**, m. the rule of the Kapiñjalas (with whom even 'three' is a large number), Say. on RV.

iii, 56, 5. **Kapilâhvaya,** n. (with or without *pura*) the city of Kapila-vastu, Bcar. **Kapota** (in comp.); *-karbura,* mfn. spotted like a dove, Kum.; *-pada-darśana,* n. the sight of the foot-print of a dove, ĀpGṛ.; *-peṭaka,* n. a flight of doves, Hcar. **Kamaṭa,** m. a dwarf, L. **Kamaṇḍalu** (in comp.); *-caryā,* f. the practice of carrying a water-jar, Baudh. **Kamala** (in comp.); *-mukha,* mf(*ī*)n. lotus-faced, Mālatīm.; °*lā* or °*lâtmikā,* f. N. of one of the 10 Mahā-vidyās (q. v.). **Kampanā,** f. (prob.) an army in motion; °*nâdhipati,* m. the leader of an army in motion, Rājat. v, 446. **Kampita,** n. trembling, tremor, L. **Kambā,** f. (prob.) a kind of mash, Uttarar. **Kayā-śubhīya,** n. the hymn RV. i, 165 (MaitrS.). 1. **Kara** (in comp.); *-tantu,* m. (see *kāratantavika*); *-rudh,* mfn. warding off a hand (and 'a ray'), Megh.; *-saṃdaṇśa,* m. the thumb and forefinger of the hand (°*śa-hīnaka,* mfn. deprived of the thumb and f°), Yājñ. ii, 274; °*rânta,* m. the tip of a finger, R.; °*rârpaṇa,* n. marriage, Mālatīm. 2. **Kara** (in comp.); *-gṛihīti,* f. levying taxes (and 'shaking hands'), Hcar.; *-dāyaka,* mfn. paying tribute, Hariv. **Karaṇa,** n. (also) a sinew, tendon, muscle, Kir.; *-mantra,* m. a Mantra pertaining to any sacred rite, ĀpŚr., Sch.; *-vigama,* m. death (= *deha-tyāga*), Megh. **Karaṇīya,** n. an affair, business, matter, Ragh. **Karad,** onomat. (with *iti*), MānGṛ. **Karabhīya,** mfn. tending camels, Hcar. **Karalāya,** Nom. Ā. °*yate,* to become terrible, Vās. **Karitva,** mfn. fit for work or business, L. **Karīshaṇī,** f. (applied to the goddess of fortune), MānGṛ. **Karuṇa** (in comp.); *-varuṇâlaya,* m. a sea of compassion, Kāv.; *-veditṛi,* mfn. (= *-vedin*), MBh. **Karoṭa-pāṇi,** m. pl. a class of gods, Divyâv. **Karkándhu-rohita** (VS.). **Karkāra,** m. a tree, L. **Karkī,** f. a white calf, Kauś. **Karṇa** (accord. to some also, *karṇá,* mfn. 'cropped or defective on the ears') in comp.; *-dārin,* mfn. ear-rending, MBh.; *-deva,* m. N. of a king, Inscr.; *-nirvāka,* m. N. of a man, MBh.; *-pāśa,* m. a beautiful ear, Daś. (cf. Gaṇar. on Pāṇ. ii, 1, 66); *-bhaṅga,* m. bending the ears, Śak. (v. l.); a partic. ear-disease, Suśr.; *-rasâyana,* n. a feast for the ears, Rājat. **Karṇāṭa-kalaha,** m. a quarrel about nothing, Mālatīm. **Karta,** (also) a spindle (?), MānGṛ. (v. l.). **Kartana-bhāṇḍa,** n. id., L. **Kartu,** mfn. (= *karma-kāra*), L. **Karttikā,** f. a dagger, HPariś. **Kardamila,** (also) mfn. slippery, Nalac. **Karpaṭaka,** a village, Divyâv. **Karpaṭi,** mfn. indigent, poor, L. **Karma** (in comp. for *karman*); *-kośa,* m. a store of good actions, MBh.; *-janya,* mfn. produced by acts (*-tā,* f.), Vedântas.; *-jita,* mfn. won or acquired by acts, ChUp.; *-daṇḍa,* m. control of actions, MārkP.; *-dāyâda,* m. heir of works (i. e. one who has to bear their consequences), Buddh.; *-deha,* m. the active body, Kap.; *-nivṛitti,* f. the end of a rite, ĀpGṛ.; *-pātaka,* n. a sinful deed, R.; *-ploti,* f. the thread of action, Divyâv.; *-phala-hetu,* mfn. one who is actuated by the (thought of the) result of his acts, Bhag.; *-rāshṭra,* N. of a country, Inscr.; *-vāda,* m. a text relating to sacrificial rites, Baudh.; *-saṅga,* m. attachment to action, Bhag.; °*gin,* mfn. attached to action, ib.; *-sūtra,* n. N. of wk.; *-svaka,* mfn. one who has to bear the consequence of his acts, Buddh.; °*mâṅga,* (also) a partic. Śrāddha, RTL. 305; °*mâbhyāsa,* m. the performance of a sacred rite, Āpast.; °*mâvadāna,* n. a great deed, exploit, Jātakam. **Karmaṇya-kṛit,** mfn. working for hire, a hireling, L. **Karśanīya,** (also) to be ill-treated, Jātakam. **Kala,** m. N. of a poet, Subh. **Kalaṅkêśa,** m. the moon, Caurap. **Kalaca** (? for *kalaka*), m. an arithmetician, calculator (= *gaṇaka*), L. **Kalacuri-saṃvatsara** (= *Cedi-saṃvat*), a year of the Kalacuri (or Cedi) era (beginning on September 5, A.D. 248). **Kala-pralāpa,** mfn. speaking pleasantly, Bcar. **Kalama** (in comp.); *-kedāra,* m. a rice-field, Mṛicch.; °*mâudana,* n. boiled rice, ib. **Kalambhi,** m. a Ṛishi, L. **Kalala,** (also) a leather-bag, L.; a bone, ib. **Kalaviṅka-svara,** (also) mfn. having a voice (soft) as a sparrow's, Bcar. **Kalahaṇsa-gāminī,** f. a woman with a gait like a swan's, Mṛicch. **Kalā** (in comp.); *-°ṇśa-rūpiṇī* (°*lâṇś°*) and *-rūpiṇī,* f. N. of partic. female personifications, RTL. 187; *-keli,* (also) mfn. one who exercises an art for pleasure, Gīt.; *-virodha,* m. incompatibility with (the rules of) art, Kāvyâd. **Kalāpi,** m. or f. a bunch, tuft, ŚāṅkhŚr. **Kali** (in comp.); *-varjya,* mfn. (in law) to be avoided in the present Kali age, obsolete; *-vishṇu-vardhana,* m. N. of a king, Inscr.; *-śatru,* m. an evil enemy (?), Bcar. v, 75.

Kalita-kusuma, mfn. budded, blossomed, Mālatīm. **Kalinda-jā,** f. N. of the river Yamunā, Bhām. **Kalevara-push,** m. a man, human being, ib. **Kalpa** (in comp.); *-nātha,* m. N. of Indra, Dharmaś.; *-vrata,* n. a partic. observance, AV. Paddh.; °*pâtyaya,* m. the end of a Kalpa, Bcar. **Kalpitôpamā,** f. an imaginary comparison (as of an elephant with a walking mountain), Bhar.; Hāla, Sch. **Kalpusha,** mfn. fit for work, capable, L. **Kalyacitta,** mfn. sound in mind, Bcar. **Kalyāṇa-lakshaṇa,** mfn. having auspicious marks, Daś. **Kava,** m. sound, L. **Kavaca-śiva,** m. N. of a Śaiva ascetic, Inscr. **Kavaṭa,** m. remainder of food (= *uccishṭa*), L. **Kavalya,** mfn. to be bitten or swallowed, Nalac. **Kavi** (in comp.); *-kaṇṭhâbharaṇa,* n. N. of a wk. on rhet. by Kshemêndra; *-krama,* m. N. of a wk. on metres; *-jana-śevadhi,* N. of a lexicon; *-tā-ratnâkara,* m. N. of a poem; *-tâvali,* f. N. of an anthology; *-pūrṇa* (read *-pūra*); °*vîndra-karṇâbharaṇa,* n. N. of wk. 1. **Kavya** (erase 1); *-havya-bhuj,* m. N. of Agni, Kathās. **Kavyát,** mfn. wise, TS. **Kaśā-pāta,** m. the stroke of a whip, Bcar. **Kaśikā,** f. a whip, Mṛicch. **Kashaka** (?), m. N. of a god or demon, Hir. **Kashākasha,** m. a kind of worm, L. **Kastūri,** m. N. of the author of a law-book. **Kāṇsa,** (also) a kind of measure, Gobh., Sch. **Kāṇsikā,** f. a metal vessel (others, 'a partic. musical instrument'), Divyâv. **Kākaṇī,** f. = *kākiṇī,* ib. **Kākatīya,** m. N. of a dynasty, Inscr. **Kāka-śaṅkin,** mfn. timid as a crow, MBh. **Kāku-vakrôkti,** f. a partic. figure of speech, Hāla, Sch. **Kākesa-parvata,** m. the mountain Caucasus, Āryav. **Kākhatīra,** mfn. (fr. *kakh°*), Pāṇ. iv, 2, 104, Vārtt. 2, Pat. **Kājala,** n. unguent (for *kajjala,* q. v.?), Daś. **Kāṇa,** Nom. P. °*ṇayati,* to make blind, destroy the sight, HPariś. **Kāṇāda,** m. a follower of Kaṇāda, Śaṃk. **Kāṇelī-suta,** m. a bastard (= °*lī-mātṛi*), Mṛicch. **Kāṇḍa,** m. (also) abundance, Vcar.; (*ī*), f. a piece, Kauś.; *-kāra,* (also) a kind of artisan, R.; *-nāman,* n. pl. the names of the Kāṇḍas, Hir.; *-visarga,* m. the completion of (the study of) a K°, ib.; °*ḍôpakaraṇa,* n. the beginning of (the study of) a K°, ib. **Kātarâkshī,** f. a woman with timid eyes, Kāvyâd. ii, 156. **Kāna,** n. sound (cf. *kvāṇa*), L. **Kāpālika-tva,** n. barbarousness, cruelty, Mālatīm. **Kāpila,** mfn. derived from a brownish cow, Parāś. **Kāpileya-bābhrava,** m. pl. the Kāpileyas and the Bābhravas, AitBr. **Kāpeya,** mf(*ī*)n. customary among the Kāpis, ĀpŚr., Sch. **Kāpota,** m. (also) a Vānaprastha who has collected food (like a pigeon) for a year, L.; *-vṛitti,* mfn. one who subsists like a pigeon, Baudh. **Kāma** (in comp.); *-kānana,* n. Kāma's grove, Mālatīm.; *-krodha,* m. du. desire and anger, Mn. xii, 11; *-da,* m. 'gracious lord,' Jātakam.; *-dughâkshiti,* mfn. 'possessing wish-granting imperishableness,' JaimUp.; *-push,* mfn. granting wishes, Dharmaś.; *-lubdha,* mfn. libidinous, MBh.; *-vaktavya-hṛidaya,* mfn. enamoured (?), R.; *-varsha,* mfn. (= *-varshin*), BhP.; *-vādin,* mfn. speaking according to pleasure, Baudh.; *-vihārin,* mfn. roaming at will, MBh.; *-veśin,* mfn. entering at will, Hariv.; *-samuttha,* mfn. sprung from desire, Mn. vii, 45; °*mâgāyin,* mfn. singing a wish, JaimUp.; °*mândha-saṃjña,* mfn. one whose intellect is blinded with pleasure, Bcar.; °*mâbhishvaṅga,* mfn. amorous inclination, Mālatīm.; °*mârṇava,* m. N. of various kings, Inscr.; °*mârtha,* m. an object or matter of pleasure, MBh.; °*môpabhoga,* m. enjoyment of pleasures, Bcar. **Kāmukī,** f. (ifc.) a mistress, Mṛicch. **Kāmya** (in comp.); *-śrāddha,* n. a kind of Śrāddha, RTL. 305; °*myêshṭi,* f. a sacrifice performed for the obtainment of a partic. object, TS., Sch. **Kāmrā,** f. a whip, L. **Kāya** (in comp.); *-klama,* m. bodily fatigue, Bcar.; *-gata,* mfn. dwelling in the body, Mn. xi, 98; *-vyūha,* m. the supernatural power of assuming several bodies simultaneously, Sāṃkhyapr.; *-sthiti,* f. support of the body, keeping alive, taking food, Bhadrab.; °*yâvatāra,* m. N. of a town, Inscr. **Kāyādhavá,** m. (fr. *kayādhu*) metron. of Prahrāda, TBr. **Kāyôḍha-ja,** mfn. (for °*ḍhā-ja*) born from a woman married according to the Prajā-pati rite, Mn. iii, 38. 1. **Kāra** (accord. to some in RV. also, 'gain, prize, booty;' 'contest, war'); *-yantrika,* m. a kind of artisan, R. 1. **Kāraka** (erase accent). **Kāraveya,** m. pl. a class of Ṛishis, Bādar., Sch. **Kārā-dvīpa,** m. N. of an island, Jātakam. **Kárādhunī** (accord. to some °*ni,* m. [fr. *kārā* = 3. *kāra* + *dhuni*], 'a bard'). **Kārāpaka,** m. (prob.) an agent (cf. next), Inscr.

Kārāvī, f. a small-sized house that may be taken to pieces, Gal. 1. **Kārin** (accord. to some in RV. also, *kārín,* 'conquering, victorious'). 3. **Kārin,** mfn. (fr. √*kṛī*) scattering, destroying, Śiś. **Kārīrādi,** m. pl. N. of a family, JaimUp. **Kāruṇika,** (also) N. of a Tathāgata, Sukh. i. **Kāruṇya** (in comp.); *-dhenu* (applied to Buddha), Divyâv.; *-maya,* mf(*ī*)n. full of compassion, Jātakam.; *-laharī-stava,* m. N. of wk. **Kāru-vindu,** m. the son of a Brāhman and a Vaidehakī, L. **Kārtavīrya-campū,** f. N. of a poem. **Kārttika-pūrṇimā,** f. N. of a festival, RTL. 432. **Kārpāsika,** (also) a kind of artisan, R. 1. **Kārya,** (also) to be caused to do, Naish.; *-karaṇa,* n. the doing one's duty, MBh.; *-padavī,* f. the way to action, Mālatīm. 2. **Kāryà,** mfn. (fr. √*kṛī*) to be bought (?), MaitrS. 1. **Kāla** (in comp.); *-tama,* mfn. quite black, Daś.; *-hasta,* m. N. of a pious forester, RTL. 441. 2. **Kāla** (add, *kālena kālam,* 'from time to time,' Divyâv.; *kāla-kāleshu,* 'at every time, always,' R.) in comp.; *-kshama,* mfn. 'bearing time,' lasting, durable, Śak.; *-caryā,* f. seasonable occupation, Āpast.; *-nātha,* m. N. of an author, Cat.; *-nirṇaya-dīpikā,* f. N. of wk.; *-pakva,* mfn. ripe for death, MBh.; *-paraśu-dhāra,* m. 'bearing the axe of Death,' an executioner, Mṛicch.; *-prakāśikā,* f. N. of wk.; *-praṇālikā,* f. a water-clock, Nalac.; *-bheda,* m. N. of wk.; *-yukta* (Bcar.), *-yuta* (R.), mfn. fit for the (present) time, seasonable; *-rūpin,* mfn. 'having the appearance of Death,' N. of Śiva, MBh.; *-varshin,* mfn. raining seasonably, Mṛicch.; *-viprakarsha,* m. distance in time, interval, APrāt.; *-virodha,* m. contradiction as to time, Kāvyâd.; *-velā-yoga,* m., *-horā,* f. N. of wks.; *-saṃvara,* m. N. of Vishṇu, Pañcar.; °*lôdayin,* m. N. of a disciple of Buddha, Sukh. ii. **Kālindī-mukunda,** m. N. of wk. **Kāliyāri,** m. N. of Kṛishṇa, Pracaṇḍ. **Kālī** (in comp.); *-ghaṭṭa,* m. the Ghāt near the temple of Kālī at Calcutta (whence probably the N. Calcutta); *-caturdaśī,* f. N. of a festival (kept on the 14th day of the second half of Āśvina), RTL. 204; *-pūjā,* f. N. of another festival (kept in the month Kārttika), ib. 431; *-sûkta,* n., *-stava,* m., *-stotra,* n. N. of wks. **Kālpya,** mfn. pertaining to ritual, Kauś. **Kāvya** (in comp.); *-bandha,* m. a poetical work, poem, Sāh.; *-ratna,* n., *-saṃgraha,* m. N. of wks.; °*vyâloka-locana,* n. N. of a rhet. wk. by Abhinavagupta. **Kāśi-vardhana,** n. (with *nagara*) the city of Benares, Buddh. **Kāśmīra-vāṇija,** m. a merchant who goes to Kaśmīra, Pāṇ. vi, 2, 13, Kāś. **Kāśyapa,** (also) N. of a Buddha, Inscr. **Kāśyapībālākya-māṭharī-pútra** (ŚBr.). **Kāshi,** m. a ploughman (= *karshaka*), L. **Kāshṭha** (in comp.); *-kalāpa,* m. a bundle of fire-wood, Hir.; *-śālika,* m. (prob.) a dealer in wood, Campak. **Kāshṭhāgata,** mfn. excessive, vehement, Kum. iii, 35. 1. **Kāsa,** m. (also) going, motion, Śiś. xix, 27. **Kiṃstya** (accord. to Sch., 'a conch-shell' = *śaṅkha*). **Kikivi,** m. or f. a kind of bird, L. **Kiṭa,** (also) the son of a Vaiśya and a Kilushī (cf. *kīlusha* below), L. **Kim** (in comp.); *-adyaka,* mfn. not valuing the present day, MBh.; *-pavitra* (*kim-*), mfn. purified by what?, TS.; (*kiṃ*)*-stha,* mfn. occupied with what?, Rājat. **Kimba,** m. a kind of tree, Nalac. **Kilina,** mfn. = *klinna,* Gobh., Sch. **Kilbishī,** f. a courtezan, L.; night, ib.; a Piśācī, ib. **Kishkuru,** a staff, club (v. l. *kiṃk°* and *kiṃk°*), Kauś. **Kīcaka,** (also) a kind of bird, R. **Kīri,** °**rin** (accord. to some the base is always *kīrí,* and the meaning is 'humble, poor, miserable, wretched, a miser' [cf. *karuṇa*], except RV. v, 52, 12, where *kīrín* = 'shouting, singing'). **Kīrtana,** (also) a monument, Jātakam.; a temple, Inscr. **Kīrti,** (also) an edifice, palace, temple, Inscr.; *-taraṃgiṇī,* f. N. of wk.; *-nāśin,* mfn. destroying reputation, Mn. viii, 127. **Kīlinī,** f. the earth (cf. *adri-kīlā*), L. **Kīlusha,** m. a monkey, L. 1. **Ku** (in comp.); *-cāru,* m. a kind of bull-like deer, L.; *-tapa-vinyāsa,* m. arranging musical instruments and musicians, Bhar.; *-tapa-hāra,* m. a partic. implement, (prob.) a sickle, Baudh.; *-dhṛiti,* mfn. one who has little or no control over himself, Bcar.; *-lagna,* mfn. ominous, inauspicious, Kathās.; *-sthala-pura,* n. N. of a town, Inscr. **Kukkuṭa-dhvaja,** m. N. of Skanda, L. **Kukkuha,** m. a partic. aquatic bird, Dharmaś. **Kukshi** (in comp.); *-kūjita,* n. belching, L.; *-bheda* (read 'an eclipse' for 'darkness'); *-matī,* f. far advanced in pregnancy, Divyâv.; (°*shy*)*-agni,* m. the (digestive) fire of the stomach, L. **Kuca-śataka,** n. N. of a Kāvya. **Kuñjikā,** (also) a kind of drum, L.

Kuṭvuḍī, m. N. of a Sultān (Qutb-ud-dīn), Inscr. **Kuṇapa**, m. (also) a partic. hell, Buddh.; *-bhuj*, m. 'carcase-eater,' a Rākshasa, Mālatīm. **Kuṇḍa**, (also) crippled, lame, Mahāvy.; °*ḍâśin*, mfn. (also) one who eats out of a jar (Gaut., Sch.) or as much as a jar holds, Vishṇ., Sch. **Kuṇḍala** or °**laka**, (also) a rope, Jātakam. **Kuṇḍi**, m. or f. a water-jar, L. **Kutas-tana**, mfn. coming from whence, i.e. not possible, Bhadrab. **Kutūhala-śālā**, f. a room for recreation, Divyâv. **Kutsa**, m. (also) a distance of about 30 inches, L. **Kudrīcī**, f. (prob.) N. of a shrub (=*guḍūcī*), Kauś. **Kuntā-kunti**, ind. spear against spear, in close fight, Campak. **Kuptu**, f. a fire-place, hearth, ĀpGṛ. **Kupya-vetanin** (see *vetanin*, p. 1014). **Kubera-senā**, f. N. of a courtezan, HPariś. **Kubjī**, f. (prob.) a tiger's den, MaitrS. **Kubhanyú** (accord. to some = *ku-bhanyú*, 'chattering, noisy'). **Kumāra** (in comp.); *-deshṇa* (rather 'whose gifts are like those of children,' i.e. 'who gives and takes back'); *-pitṛi-mesha*, m. a partic. demon hostile to children, Suśr.; *-brahmacārin*, mfn. chaste from infancy, Mn. v, 159; *-rāja*, m. N. of Harsha-vardhana, Buddh.; *-vat* (°*rá-*), m. N. of a man, MaitrS.; (°*rī*)-*bhāva*, m. maidenhood, virginity, Mālatīm. **Kumuda** (in comp.); *-śyenī*, f. a woman with a white complexion like a lotus (cf. *śyenī* under *śyeta*, p. 1095), Pāṇ. vi, 2, 2, Sch.; *-sakhī*, f. 'lotus-friend,' moonshine, Jātakam. **Kumba** (accord. to some also, 'the horn or point of anything'). **Kumbha** (in comp.); *-dhārikā*, f. a female slave, L.; °*bhânta*, mfn. concluding with the (ceremony of interring the) urn, HirP. **Kumbhī** (in comp.); *-kapāla*, *-nadāla*, and *-bhagāla*, n. (prob.) a potsherd or fragment of a broken jar, Pāṇ. vi, 2, 137, Kāś.; *-pākya*, mfn. boiled in a jar, ĀpŚr. **Kumbhya**, mfn. being in jars, ĀpŚr. **Kuraṅga-mada**, m. musk, Gīt. **Kuru** (in comp.); *-kshetra*, m. pl. (w.r. for *kauruksh*°); *-piśaṅgilá* (VS.). **Kurvát**, °**vāṇá** (AV.). **Kula** (in comp.); *-kumārī*, f. a girl of good family, Mālatīm.; *-gotra*, n. du. f° and tribe, Mn. iii, 109; *-pāṃsana*, mf(*ī*)n., °*sin*, and °*sula*, mfn. disgracing a f°, MBh.; R. &c.; *-pālin*, mfn. maintaining (the honour of) a f°, R.; *-pravāla*, m. the scion or offspring of a f°, Bcar.; *-bhaṭa*, m. N. of a Śūrasena chief, Inscr.; *-rājadhānī*, f. chief residence, Ragh.; *-śekhara-deva*, m. N. of a king, Inscr.; *-saṃgata*, m. (= *-mitra*), Gaut.; *-stambha*(?) and °*lâditya*, m. N. of chiefs, Inscr.; °*lôcita*, mfn. customary in a f°, Bcar. **Kulaṅgâpa-mārin**, m. a kind of demon, MānGṛ. **Kulika**, (also) a judge, Nār. **Kulmi**, (also) cow's hair, ĀpŚr., Sch. **Kuśa** (in comp.); *-cīrin*, mfn. wearing a garment of Kuśa grass, MBh.; *-pavitra*, n. Kuśa grass as a means of purification, KātyŚr.; *-prasū*, f. flowering K° gr°, ib.; *-bhāra*, m. a load of K° gr°, ŚāṅkhŚr.; *-mālin*, m. N. of an ocean, Jātakam.; °*śêṇḍva*, n. a covering for the hands made of K° gr°. **Kuśala**, n. (also) religious merit, Inscr.; MWB. 124; *-campū*, f., *-mata-prasaṅga*, m. N. of poems; *-mūla*, n. a stock of merit, Sukh. i; °*lâvasānatā*, f. a happy result, Mālatīm.; °*lêtara*, n. misfortune, calamity, BhP. **Kushapa**, m. the Vindhya mountains, L. **Kusuma** (in comp.); *-dāyin*, mfn. putting forth buds, Śak.; *-prabha*, m. N. of a Tathāgata, Sukh. i; *-mālā*, f. a wreath of flowers, Mālatīm.; *-lāvī*, f. a female gatherer of fl°, Sāh.; *-vṛishṭy-abhiprakīrṇa*, *-sambhava*, -°*mâbhijña*, m. N. of Tathāgatas, Sukh. i; °*mâpīḍa*, m. = °*ma-mālā*, Mālatīm. **Kuhara-bhāj**, mfn. dwelling in dens, Mālatīm. **Kuharin**, mfn. having holes, Caṇḍ. **Kūṭa** (in comp.); *-ghaṭita-lakshaṇa*, n. N. of a Nyāya wk.; *-danta*, mfn. having prominent teeth, Hir. **Kūḍí** (accord. to Kauś., Sch. = *badarī*, 'Christ's thorn'). **Kūpa** (in comp.); *-daṇḍa*, m. a mast, Daś.; *-yantra-ghaṭikā-nyāya*, m. the rule of the buckets attached to a water-wheel (i.e. the vicissitudes of worldly existence), A.; *-rājya*, n. N. of a country, Inscr.; (°*pe*)-*piśācaka*, m. a frog in a well, L. **Kūpaka**, m. N. of a people, Inscr. **Kūrpāsa**, (also) a kind of plant, Kād. **Kūrma-pitta** (erase the meaning 'a vessel with water'). **Kūlyā**, f. a stream, Hir. **Kṛicchra** (in comp.); *-dvitīya*, m. a friend in need, Car.; *-vartin*, mfn. performing a penance, Kām.; °*rôdya*, mfn. difficult to be pronounced, Kāvyâd. 1. **Kṛita** (in comp.); *-kshaṇa*, (also) ready to, prepared for, intent upon, engrossed by (comp.), Jātakam.; *-ṃ-jaya*, m. N. of a teacher, Hir.; *-pada*, mfn. being about to (inf.), Subh.; *-yāma*, mfn. whose function is performed, useless, Kauś.; *-lakshaṇa*, (also) caused by, R.; *-vadhya-cihna*, mfn. bearing the marks of death, Mālatīm.; *-vaira*, mfn. one who has become an enemy, Mṛicch.; *-spṛiha*, (also) desirous of (dat.), Bcar.; *-smaya*, mfn. awakening admiration, Jātakam.; °*tâdhikāra*, mfn. superintending, watching over (loc.), Bcar.; °*tâdhipatya*, mfn. possessed of sovereignty or power, Kir.; °*tânuyātra*, mfn. accompanied by, Bcar.; °*tâbhiyoga*, mfn. taking pains, Mālatīm.; °*tâbhyanujña*, mfn. one who has obtained leave, Bcar.; °*tâvṛitti*, mfn. moving to and fro, oscillating, ib.; °*tâśraya*, mfn. resorted to, Jātakam.; °*tôpavāsa*, mfn. one who has fasted, MBh. **Kṛitā**, f. (also) a skin, hide (= *kṛiti*), MānGṛ. **Kṛittikâñji** (ŚBr.). **Kṛitnú** (accord. to some also, 'winning the prize, victorious'). **Kṛityā** (in comp.); *-pratiharaṇa*, n. pl. N. of a series of hymns for counteracting spells, AV. Pariś.; *-hata*, mfn. stricken by a spell, Mn. iii, 58. **Kṛitvya** (accord. to some also, 'bringing or containing a prize'). **Kṛipāṇa** (in comp.); *-pāṇi*, mfn. holding a sword in the hand, Mālatīm.; *-pāta*, m. the fall or stroke of a sword, ib.; *-putrī*, f. a dagger, Dharmaś.; *-yashṭi*, f. a sword-blade, ib. **Kṛipâtman**, mfn. tender-hearted, Bcar. **Kṛiptu**, f. a hearth (prob. w.r. for *kuptu*), ĀpGṛ. **Kṛivī**, f. scissors, L. **Kṛiśānu-śakala**, m. a spark of fire, Śiś. **Kṛishāku**, m. a ploughman, L. **Kṛishīṭa**, n. water, L. **Kṛishṇa** (in comp.); *-khura*, m. having black hoofs, HirP.; *-gava*, mfn. drawn by black oxen, ib.; *-dhṛiti*, m. (with *sātyaki*) N. of a teacher, JaimUp.; *-nandin*, m. N. of a poet, Inscr.; *-padâmṛita*, *-bhūshaṇa*, *-māhātmya*, n. N. of wks.; *-rāja* and *-rāya*, m. N. of various kings, Inscr.; *-śakuná*, m. a crow, TS.; *-śīrshan* (°*shṇá-*), mfn. black-headed, MaitrS.; *-sūtra*, (also) n. a black thread, HirP.; *-stuti*, f., *-stotra*, n. N. of hymns; °*ṇâkshi*, mfn. black-eyed, HirP. **Kṛishya-kāra**, m. a ploughman, husbandman, Vet. **Kekôtkaṇṭha**, m. fond of uttering cries (as a peacock), Mālatīm. **Ketri**, m. a partic. personification (perhaps Agni), PārGr. **Kedārikā**, f. (also) a small field, Inscr. **Kenipá** (accord. to some fr. *keni* [√3. *ci*] + *pa*, 'attending to the worship or sacrifice'). **Kerā**, f. a kind of plant, Kauś. **Keśa** (in comp.); *-kalpanā*, f. arranging a horse's mane, Mṛicch.; *-kūṭa*, m. braided hair, L.; *-nidhāna*, n. the burying of hair, ĀpGṛ.; *-pratigraha*, m. a barber, Gobh.; *-vāpa*, m. hair-cutting, MānGṛ.; *-śesha-karaṇa*, n. leaving a remnant of hair, PārGṛ.; *-śmaśru-loma-nakha*, n. pl. hair and beard and down of the body and nails, Hir.; *-saṃvardhana* (see *saṃv*°, p. 1116). **Keśa-vâyudha**, (also) n. a wheel, L. **Keśānī**, f. a kind of creeper, Kauś. **Késara-pāśa**, mf(*ā*)n. having fetters of hair, MaitrS. **Kesarāya**, Nom. Ā. °*yate*, to become hair, Nalac. **Kesarin**, (also) N. of a Tathāgata, Sukh. i. **Kaiñjalka**, mfn. consisting of lotus fibres, Jātakam. **Kaideva**, m. N. of a writer on botany, Nirṇayas. **Kokalla** or **Kokkala**, m. N. of a king, Inscr. **Kokkili**, m. N. of a king, Inscr. **Kocava** or °**vaka**, a covering of soft goat's hair, Buddh. **Koṭara-vat**, mfn. having cavities, Mālatīm. **Koṭṭabhañja**, m. N. of a chief, Inscr. **Koṭṭūra**, m. N. of a village, ib. **Koṭhī**, f. N. of a tank, SkandaP. **Koṇa** (in comp.); °*ṇâgamana*, m. (= *kanaka-muni*), Inscr.; MWB. 136 n.; °*ṇe-piśācaka*, m. a house-frog, L. **Koneri-tīrtha**, n. N. of a Tīrtha, Inscr. **Kopa-saṃdhukshaṇa**, mfn. inflaming anger, Uttarar. **Komala**, (also) of like colour, Kir. **Kolamba-varsha**, m. a year of the Kollam era (used in Southern India; it is converted into the corresponding A.D. by adding 824–25; thus Kollam 336 = A.D. 1160–61). **Kośa** (in comp.); *-gata-vasti-guhyatā*, f. having the pudenda hidden in the abdomen (one of the 32 signs of perfection), Dharmaś. 83; *-daṇḍa*, m. du. treasury and army, Mn. ix, 294. **Kosalā-nandinī**, f. N. of Ayodhyā, L. **Kauṇḍinya**, (also) one of the 24 mythical Buddhas, MWB. 136. **Kautuka**, (also) the place for a partic. nuptial ceremony, MānGṛ. **Kautūla**, m. the husband of a h°'s sister, L. **Kaunṛitika**, mf(*ī*)n. wicked, perverse, L. **Kaunteya-vṛitta**, n. N. of wk. **Kaupīnâcchādana**, n. a cloth for covering the pudenda, Baudh. **Kauberaka**, m. a servant of Kubera, Hir. **Kaumāra-bandhakī**, f. a courtezan, Mālatīm. **Kaumudī-maha** or °**hôtsava**, m. the festival of full moon, ib. **Kaurukshetra**, m. pl. the inhabitants of Kuru-kshetra (w.r. *kur*°), Mn. vii, 193. **Kaula**, m. (also) a boat, raft (cf. *kola*), Mahāvy.; °*lêśī*, f. N. of a female personification, RTL. 188. **Kauśika-gṛihya-sūtra**, n. N. of wk. **Kauśikī-vara-prasāda**, m. the favour of a boon from Kauśikī i.e. Durgā, Inscr. **Kausuma**, n. a heap of flowers, Dharmaś. **Kaustubha-dūshaṇa**, n. N. of a Vedānta wk. **Krama** (in comp.); *-gata*, mfn. come into the way of (gen.), Mālatīm.; *-vyatyaya*, m. inverted order, Subh. **Kramaṇêshṭakā**, f. N. of a brick (close to the Adhvaryu-patha), Drāhy., Sch. **Krivirdatī**, f. (prob.) sharp-toothed (cf. *krivī*), RV. **Krīḍā** (in comp.); *-biḍālikā*, f. a cat to play with, Rājat.; *-yoga*, m. arrangement of games or sports, Mālatīm. **Kruśika**, m. a jackal, L.; an owl, L. **√kroñc**, P. *kroñcati*, to trumpet (as an elephant), Divyâv. **Krodha** (in comp.); *-vinayana*, n. appeasing anger, Hir.; *-vivaśā*, f. a bad-tempered girl (unfit for marriage), L. **Krauśna**, m. a beast of prey, L. **Kvadhastha** (accord. to some read *sadhastham*). **Kshaṇa** (in comp.); *-kshapā*, f. a night of full moon, Dharmaś.; *-dâdhinātha*, m. the moon, ib.; *-rajanī*, f. (= *-kshapā*), ib.; °*ṇâṃśu*, f. lightning, L. **Kshaṇitu**, m. = *kshaṇanu*. **Kshatra** (in comp.); *-jāta* or *-yoni*, mfn. born from the military caste, MBh. **Kshatriya-yoni**, f. a Kshatriya's form of existence, ChUp. **Kshapā-kshaya**, m. 'night's end,' morning, Mṛicch. **Kshamā-śipha**, mfn. having patience as fibres (said of the tree of knowledge), Bcar. xiii, 65. 1. **Ksháya** (RV.). 3. **Kshayá** (the accent is on the last syllable in the sense 'destruction,' accord. to Pāṇ. iii, 3, 56 and vi, 1, 63). **Kshā** (in comp.); *-trāṇa*, m. N. of a demon, Kauś.; *-pavitra*, m. or n. N. of a partic. text, Baudh. **Kshānti-varṇa-vādin** or **kshānti-vādin**, mfn. praising patience, Jātakam. **Kshāma-kukshitā**, f. having thin loins (one of the 80 minor marks of a Buddha), Dharmas. 84. **Kshāra**, (also) flowing water, flow, MānGṛ.; *-lavaṇâvarânna-saṃsṛishṭa*, n. salt or pungent food or such as has an admixture of inferior food, ĀpGṛ. 2. **Kshiti** (in comp.); *-kshamā-vat*, mfn. patient as the earth, R.; *-vṛishan*, m. a king, Rājat. **Kshitikā**, f. a partic. part of a lute, Kauś. **Kshitvarī**, f. night, L. **Kshipaṇa**, mfn. one who throws, L. **Kshipram-suvana**, n. a partic. ceremony for causing easy birth, ĀpGṛ. **Kshipra-prasavana**, n. id., Hir. **Kshīṇa** (in comp.); *-kalmasha*, mfn. freed from sin, Bhag.; °*ṇâsrava*, mfn. id., Divyâv. **Kshīrâbdhi-mandira**, mfn. dwelling in the ocean of milk, Pañcar. **Kshudra** (in comp.); *-miśra*, mfn. mixed up with small (stones), BaudhP.; *-sūtra*, n. N. of wk.; °*drânukshudra*, n. pl. (with *śikshāpadāni*) minor observances of discipline, Divyâv.; °*drôpāya*, m. the three minor stratagems (viz. *māyā*, *upêkshā*, *indra-jāla*), L. **Kshudri**, m. the ocean, L. **Kshudhāru**, mfn. = *kshudhālu*. **Kshullaká-vaiśvadeva**, m. a small cup for the Vaiśvadevas, MaitrS. **Kshūṇa**, n. transgression, offence, L. **Kshetra** (in comp.); *-gṛiha*, n. sg. field and house, Mn. xi, 164; *-ja*, mfn. (a quarrel) arisen about land, Nār.; *-bhāga*, m. a piece of land, ChUp.; *-vitṛiṇṇī*, f. a clod of earth taken from the field, BaudhP.; *-sádhas* (accord. to some, 'bestowing a field'); *-siṃha* (or *kheta-s*°), m. N. of various kings, Inscr. **Kshemaṇīya-tara**, n. better health, Divyâv. **Kshema-siṃha** (or *khema-s*°), m. N. of a king, Inscr. **Kshaitrá** (accord. to some the accent should be on the last syllable). **Kshaitrapatya**, n. (also) a sacrifice offered to the lord of the soil, ĀpGṛ. **Kshoṇí** (accord. to some also, 'a partic. class of goddesses or semi-divine females;' accord. to others, 'flood, stream of water or Soma &c.'). **Kshotṛi**, m. a pestle, L. **Kshobha**, (also) a strong current of water, MBh. **Kshauṇī** (in comp.); *-dhara*, m. a mountain, Daś.; *-nātha*, m. a king, Kautukas. **Kshaudra-paṭala**, m. or n. a honey-comb, Ragh. **Kshauma-daśā**, f. a fringed linen cloth, Gobh. **Kshṇū**, f. the pointed end of a scraper or shovel, L. **Kshmā-vṛisha** (read *-vṛishan*). **Kshveḍita**, (also) chewed, SaddhP.

Kha (in comp.); *-ḍīna* or *-pariḍīnaka*, n. a partic. mode of flying, MBh.; *-puṭa*, mfn. one who eats out of his own hands, L.; *-latā*, f. 'creeper in the air,' anything impossible, Śiś.; *-stha*, mfn. standing in the air, MBh.; *khâṅka* and *khâdhvanīna*, m. the sun, L. **Khaṭvâṅga** (in comp.); *-ghaṇṭā*, f. a bell fastened to the Khaṭvâṅga staff, Mālatīm.; *-hasta*, mfn. = *-bhṛit*, Bcar. **Khaḍga** (in comp.); *-ratna*, n. an excellent sword (one of the 7 precious things of a king), Dharmas. 85; *latā-*, f. a sw°-blade, Mālatīm.; *-vāri*, n. blood dripping from a sword, Vcar.; *-vi-*

shāṇa, m. a rhinoceros, Divyâv.; *-śataka*, n. N. of wk.; °*gâṅga*, m. a fire-spark, L.; °*gā-khaḍgi*, ind. sword against sword, in close fight, Campak. **Khaḍgaka**, mfn. (fr. *khaḍga*), Parāś. **Khaṇḍa-saṃsthāpaka** (see *saṃsth*°, p. 1121). **Khaṇḍika**, (also) a partic. measure of grain, Inscr. **Khaṇḍila**, a short chapter of a book, MānGṛ. **Khadana**, (also) firmness, solidity, Dhātup. **Khanya-vādin**, m. a mineralogist, Mahāvy. **Khamāṇika** (see *siddhânta-laghu-kh*°, p. 1216). **Khara** (in comp.); *-graha*, (also) N. of various kings and chiefs, Inscr.; *-turagīya* (with *samparka*, m.), sexual union of a donkey and a horse, Kull.; *-mukha*, n. a horn for blowing, L.; °*râri*, m. 'Khara's enemy,' N. of Rāma, L. **Kharaka**, m. roaring of water, L. **Kharaṭa**, mfn. hard, L.; m. hardness, ib. **Kharvaya**, Nom. P. °*yati*, to cut or break in pieces, destroy, Nalac. **Khalī-kṛitya**, in spite of (acc.), Jātakam. **Khale-kapota-nyāya**, m. or **-kapotikā**, f. the rule of the doves alighting upon a threshing-floor, Śiś., Sch. **Khalvaṅga**, a kind of pea (=*krishṇa-caṇaka*), Kauś. (Sch.). **Khāḍgika**, m. a swordsman, L. **Khātra**, (also) a breach, hole in the wall, Campak. **Khidrá**, n. (rather, 'weight, burden'). **Khinna-mānasa**, mfn. distressed in mind, Bcar. **Khilá** and **khilyá** (accord. to some also 'pasture-land'). **Khura** (in comp.); *-nyāsa*, m. the print of a hoof, Ragh.; *-mālin*, m. N. of an ocean, Jātakam.; °*râgra*, n. the tip of a hoof, Bcar. **Kheṭana**, n. chase, hunting (cf. *ākheṭa*), L. **Kheta-siṇha**, **Khema-siṇha**, see *Kshetra-s*°, *Kshema-s*° (above).

Gagana (in comp.); *-paridhāna*, mfn. 'sky-clothed,' stark-naked, BhP.; *-siṇha*, m. N. of a Kacchapa-ghāta king, Inscr.; °*nâṅgaṇa*, n. the celestial vault or sky, Vās. **Gaṅga**, (also) m. a kind of deer, L.; N. of a dynasty, Inscr. **Gaṅgama**, mfn. going, moving, L.; restless, inconstant, L. **Gaṅgā** (in comp.); *-vilāsa*, m. N. of wk.; -°*shṭaka* (°*gâshṭ*°), n. a hymn consisting of 8 verses and addressed to Gaṅgā whilst bathing, RTL. 399; °*geshṭi*, f. a pearl, L. **Gaja** (in comp.); *-pūrva* (see *gaja*, p. 643); *-prayantṛi*, m. an el°-driver, MBh.; *-māna*, m. N. of a man, Mṛicch.; *-ratha-pura*, n. N. of a town, Inscr.; *-vadhū*, f. a female elephant, Mālatīm.; °*jâlāna*, n. a rope for fettering an elephant, Ragh. **Gaṇa** (in comp.); *-pati-nāga*, m. N. of a king in Āryâvarta, Inscr.; *-pūraṇa*, mf(ī)n. forming a number or assembly, L.; *-bhogya*, mfn. to be possessed in joint tenure by a number of persons (as opp. to *eka-bhogya*), Inscr.; °*ṇêśa*, m. (with Jainas) a disciple who is put in charge of a few others. **Gaṇaka-mahāmātra**, m. a finance minister, Mahāvy. **Gaṇanâvarta-lipi**, f. a kind of writing, Lalit. **Gaṇitra**, n. a partic. astrological instrument, Divyâv. **Gaṇḍa**, (also) a pledge, Mṛicch.; *-kāsha*, m. (=*kapola-k*°), Śiś.; *-pālī*, f. the region of the cheeks, Mālatīm. **Gaṇḍuka**, m. a ball for playing with, L. **Gata** (in comp.); *-praja*, mfn. one whose children are dead, Baudh.; °*tôdaka*, mfn. waterless, dry, MBh. **Gadā-pāṇi**, m. N. of Vishṇu, L. **Gadga**, mfn. stammering, L. **Gadgada-ruddha**, mfn. (speech) stopped by sobs, Bcar. **Gandha** (in comp.); *-kuṭī*, (also) a chamber devoted to Buddha's use, Inscr. (cf. MWB. 404, n. 2); *-pushpa-dhūpa-dīpa*, m. pl. perfumes (and) flowers (and) incense (and) lamps, Hir.; *-prabhāsa*, m. N. of a Tathāgata, Sukh. ii; *-lipta*, mfn. anointed with perfumes, ĀpGṛ.; *-hastin* and °*dhôttama*, m. N. of Tathāgatas, Sukh. ii; °*dhôddāma*, mfn. thoroughly perfumed or fragrant, Mṛicch. **Gandharva** (in comp.); *-pratyupasthita*, mfn. pregnant, Divyâv.; °*vôpâdhyāya*, m. a music master, Hcar. **Gandhi-vṛitta**, (in rhet.) =*vṛitta-gandhi*, AgP. **Gabhasti**, m. (also prob. 'a pole,' in *syūma-g*°, p. 1273); *-vāra*, m. Sunday, Cat. **Gamanâgamana**, n. sg. going and coming, death and re-birth, Baudh. **Gamika**, mfn. being on a journey, travelling, Divyâv. **Gambhīra** (in comp.); *-kukshitā*, f. having a deep abdomen (one of the 80 minor marks of a Buddha), Dharmas. 84; *-dhīra*, mfn. deep and solemn, Bcar.; *-nābhitā*, f. the having a deep navel (cf. above), Dharmas. 84; *-pāṇi-lekhatā*, f. the having deep lines in the hand, ib.; (°*rá*)*-vepas* (accord. to some, 'singing in a deep tone' or 'constantly speeding'). **Gayā-kāśyapa**, m. N. of a disciple of Buddha, Sukh. i. **Gayāsadīna**, m. N. of a Sultān, Inscr. **Gardabha-kshīra**, n. the milk of a she-ass (cf. *mṛiga-ksh*°), MBh. (v. l.). **Garbha** (in comp.); *-gata*, an embryo, Bcar.; *-prāvaraṇa*, n. the membrane encircling the fetus, ĀpGṛ., Sch.; *-mṛit*, mfn. dying in the womb, MaitrS.; *-saṃskāra*, m. a partic. ceremony, ĀpGṛ., Sch.; *-saṃdhi*, m. (in dram.) a partic. juncture, Bhar. **Garvi**, f. arrogance, L. **Garhitânnâśana**, mfn. eating forbidden food, Mn. x, 35. **Gala** (in comp.); *-granthi*, m. a noose or sling for the neck, Dharmaś.; *-moṭana*, n. wringing the neck, Śukas.; *-randhra*, n. the throat, Campak. **Galūnasa**, m. (with *ārkshākāyaṇa*) N. of a teacher, JaimUp. **Gálda** (accord. to some in RV. viii, 1, 20, mfn. = 'ardent, eager'). **Galla-pūraṇa**, mfn. filling or swelling the cheeks, Mālatīm. 1. **Gava** (erase 1.); °*vâlambha*, m. 'killing a cow,' hospitality, ĀpSr., Sch. **Gavâsthi** (said of partic. arrows not to be employed in fair fighting), MBh. **Gavīnī**, (also) f. sg. the womb, MānGṛ. **Gáv-yūti** (accord. to some, 'road for the cows;' 'any road or way;' 'a herd of cattle'). **Gahane-shṭhá**, mf(*ā*)n. being in the depth, MaitrS. **Gáhya**, m. N. of an Agni, TS. **Gāṅgeya-deva**, m. N. of a Kalacuri king, Inscr. **Gājara**, a carrot, BrahmaP. **Gāḍhôdvega**, mfn. extremely anxious, Mālatīm. **Gātra** (in comp.); *-ceshṭa*, n. posture of the limbs, Bcar.; *-vigharshaṇa*, n. itching of the limbs, Dhātup.; *-śayya*, mfn. (said of a class of ascetics), R. (B.); *-saṃkocin*, m. a cat, L. **Gāndhāri-vāṇija**, m. a merchant who goes to the Gāndhāris, Pāṇ. vi, 2, 13, Kāś. **Gāyatrī-mukha**, n. the mouth of the Gāyatrī, JaimUp. **Gāyikī**, f. a songstress, Bhar. **Gārbhiṇa**, (also) = *sīmantônnayana* (p. 1218). **Gārhya**, n. (with *nāman*) the domestic name, ĀpY., Sch. **Giri** (in comp.); *-jādevī*, f. N. of a queen of Pūna-paksha, Inscr.; *-rāja-ghoshka* and °*shêśvara*, m. N. of a Tathāgata, Sukh. i; *-lakshmaṇa*, m. a fig-tree, L.; *-stanī*, f. 'mountain-breasted,' the earth, L. **Gītāgīta**, mfn. sung and unsung, JaimUp. **Gīti-śataka**, n. N. of wk. **Guṅguma**, humming (cf. *ghuṅgh*°), L. **Guccha-gulma**, n. bushes and shrubs, Mn. i, 48. **Guñjā**, f. a drum, Bhaṭṭ. **Guḍā-keśatā**, f. having the hair crisp or curly (one of the 80 minor marks of a Buddha), Dharmas. 84. **Guṇa** (also 'power, might;' *āt*, 'by virtue of,' 'in consequence of,' 'by means of'); *-kathā*, f. (in rhet.) eulogy, Rasat.; *-gandhavat*, mfn. having the fragrance of (i.e. resembling) virtue, Bcar.; *-guru*, mfn. respectable through v°, Mālatīm.; *-dhṛita*, mfn. upheld by virtue (and 'by ropes'), Mṛicch.; *-vat-payaska*, mfn. producing excellent milk, Bcar.; *-vad-vapus*, mfn. of excellent form, ib.; *-vipramukta*, mfn. freed from qualities, BhP.; *-hārya*, mfn. to be won by virtues, Mṛicch.; °*ṇâtipāta*, m. acting against nature, Bhar.; °*ṇôjjvala*, mfn. shining with virtues, Mālatīm.; °*ṇôdaya*, m. rising or development of v°, Mn. vii, 211. **Gudânila**, m. breaking wind, L. **Gupta**, m. (also) the era named after the Gupta dynasty (beginning A.D. 319; hence the Gupta year 165 corresponds to A.D. 484–85; in later times the years are called *Valabhī-saṃvat* from the rulers of Valabhī, and the era is spoken of as the Gupta-Valabhī era). **Gupti** (a 'rampart,' read, 'Kum. vi, 38') in comp.; *-gupta*, m. N. of a Jaina teacher; *-pālaka*, m. a jailer, Mṛicch. **Gumphanikā**, f. 'word-garland,' a literary composition, Subh. **Guru** (in comp.); *-caryā*, f. attendance on a teacher, Mālatīm.; *-dina*, n. Thursday, Cat.; *-mukhī*, f. N. of a partic. alphabet used by the Sikhs (a modification of Devanāgarī), RTL. 164; *-yoshit*, f. a teacher's wife, Mn. ii, 210; *-śuśrūshin*, mfn. (=*-śuśrūshu*), Baudh.; (°*rv*)*-aṅganâgama*, m. adultery with a t°'s wife, Mn. xi, 55. **Guruṇḍa** (see *suruṇḍa*, p. 1236). **√guh** (read, 'ind. p. *gūḍhvī*'). **Guhya-dhārā**, f. the urethra, L. **Gūḍha** (in comp.); *-gulphatā*, f. the having the ankle hidden (one of the 80 minor marks of a Buddha), Dharmas. 84; *-mantra*, mfn. having secret intentions, Śṛiṅgār.; *-sira*, mfn. having the arteries hidden, Bcar.; (°*ra-tā*, f. one of a Buddha's marks, Dharmas. 84). **Gṛiddhi**, f. greediness, Mahāvy. **Gṛiha**, (also) domestic or family life, Jātakam.; *-kakshyā*, f. a court-yard, Bcar.; *-dvār* (=*-dvāra*), Baudh.; *-nirvāha*, m. housekeeping, Kathās.; *-paṭala*, the thatch of a house, VarBṛS.; *-pati-vadana*, n. a partic. religious recitation, ĀpGṛ., Sch.; *-pūjā*, f. a partic. nuptial ceremony, ib.; *-pṛishṭha*, n. the flat roof of a house, VarBṛS.; *-prapadana*, n. (solemn) entrance into a h°, ĀśvGṛ.; *-mayūra*, m. a domestic or tame peacock, Mṛicch.; *-śreṇī*, f. a street, L.; °*he-śūra*, m. 'bold at home,' a cowardly bully, L.; °*hôdaka*, n. rice-gruel, L. **Gṛihaka**, a small house, hut, R. **Gṛihīta** (in comp.); *-cāpa*, *-dhanus* or *-dhanvan*, mfn. armed with a bow, Śak.; *-nāmadheya*, mfn. named, mentioned, Mālatīm.; *-paścāttāpa*, mfn. penitent, Ratnâv.; *-pātheya*, mfn. supplied with victuals for a journey, Śak.; *-śūla*, mfn. armed with a spear, Bcar.; °*tâvaguṇṭhana*, mfn. veiled, covered, Mṛicch. **Geha**, (also) family life, Jātakam.; *-pārāvata*, m. a domestic pigeon, Mṛicch. **Go** (in comp.); *-opaśa* (*gó-*), accord. to some, '(a goad) having a cow-horn as its point,' RV. vi, 53, 9; *-kṛicchra*, n. a kind of penance in which barley cooked in cow's urine is eaten, L.; *-cara*, (also) a place where birds are fed, Jātakam.; *-carma-mātra*, mfn. (land &c.) measuring a bull's hide, Baudh.; *-dāna-vrata*, n. a vow taken at the Go-dāna ceremony, ĀpGṛ.; *-paksha-netratā*, f. having eyes with lids like those of a cow (one of the 32 signs of perfection), Dharmas. 83; *-pa-nanda*, m. 'son of a cowherd,' N. of Krishṇa, Subh.; *-pâcala* or *-pâdri*, m. N. of Gwalior, Inscr.; *-pāla-dāraka*, m. a cowherd boy, Mṛicch.; *-pitṛi*, m. a guardian, protector, Jātakam.; *-pītilaka* (?), m. a kind of bird, Kauś., Paddh.; *-pucchâgra*, 'end of a cow's tail,' a kind of dramatic composition, IW. 471; (*gô*)*-purogava* (rather = *gó-agra*, 'a cow which is chief of all'); *-bīja-kāñcana*, n. pl. cows (and) grain (and) gold, Mn. viii, 88; *-bhaga*, mfn. cow-protecting, JaimUp.; *-vāṇija*, m. a cattle-dealer, Pāṇ. vi, 2, 13, Kāś.; *-vāhin*, m. Bos Gavæus, L.; *-vidhā*, f. food for cows, Pat.; *-śālā*, f. N. of a Krishṇa temple, Inscr.; *-śru* (?), m. N. of a Brahma-cārin (having the patr. Jābāla), JaimUp.; *-shṭha-gata*, mfn. gone into the cow-stall or stable, Hir.; *-shṭhôdumbara*, m. a kind of tree, ĀpGṛ., Sch. **Goṇikā**, (also) N. of the mother of Patañjali, IW. 167. **Golikā**, (also) a partic. insect, ĀpGṛ., Sch. **Gautamīya**, n. N. of a Tantra wk., RTL. 207. **Granthi**, (also) the point of a moustache, Nalac. **Grahaṇaka**, (also) containing, including, Siddh. **Grahaṇântam**, ind. until (the Veda) has been thoroughly apprehended or learned, Baudh. **Grahântar-ukthya**, n. a partic. Ekâha, ŚrS. **Grāma** (in comp.); *-deva*, m. (=*-devatā*), Inscr.; *-maryādā*, f. the boundary of a village, HirP.; *-yājana*, n. sacrificing for many, Baudh.; *-luṇṭhaka*, m. a village robber, PadmaP.; *-śakaṭika*, n. a village cart, Mṛicch.; *-sīmanta* (=*-sīmā*), Baudh.; °*mya*, (accord. to some also) venereal disease, Kauś. **Grāsa** (in comp.); *-pātrī-√kṛi*, P. *-karoti*, to swallow anything as a good morsel, Subh.; °*sâcchādana*, n. food and raiment, Mn. ix, 202; °*sâvarârdhya*, n. at least one morsel, ĀpGṛ. **Grāhaka-tva**, n. the power of perception or comprehension, Mālatīm. **Grāha-melaka**, m. conjunction of planets, Sūryas. **Grīva-baddhá**, mfn. fastened round the neck, TS. **Glātu**, mfn. ill, sick, L.

Ghaṭa-jānu, mfn. having knees swollen like jars, Bcar. **Ghaṭana**, m. an actor, L.; a wicked or shameless person, L. **Ghana** (in comp.); *-dundubhi-svana*, mfn. deep as the sound of a drum or of a cloud, Bcar.; *-pada*, (also) water, L.; °*nâbhoga*, m. the orb or circumference of a cloud, Bcar. **Ghargaraka**, m. (also) a hooting owl, L. **Ghāṭā**, f. a pot (cf. *ghaṭa*), Car. **Ghārikā**, f. a kind of food or dish, Nalac. **Ghuṅghuma**, humming, Subh. **Ghṛita** (in comp.); *-prikta*, mfn. full of ghee, MBh.; *-samudra*, m. the ocean of ghee, Sāṃkhyas., Sch. **Ghora**, m. (also) a jackal, L.; °*rita*, n. snorting, L. **Ghoshavad-ādi**, mfn. beginning with a sonant, Hir. **Ghoshita**, m. N. of a man, Divyâv. **Ghnu** (see *śata-ghnu*, p. 1049).

Cakadra (see *viś-c*°, p. 991). **Cakita-gati**, mfn. walking timidly or hurriedly, Bcar. **Cakra** (in comp.); *-cara*, m. 'circle-goer,' one who goes by turns (to the houses of Brāhmans, Kshatriyas and Vaiśyas, scil. for alms), Baudh. (Sch.); *-dhāraṇa*, n. an axle, L.; *-paksha*, m. a goose, L.; *-patha*, m. a road for wheels, carriage-road, MBh.; *-bandha*, m. all that holds a wheel together, ib.; *-ratna*, n. an excellent wheel or disk (one of the 7 treasures of a king), Dharmas. 85; °*krâṅkita-pāṇi-pāda-talatā*, f. having the palms of hands and feet marked with a wheel (one of the 32 signs of perfection), Dharmas. 83; °*krâṅkita-pāda*, mfn. having the feet marked with a wheel, Bcar. i, 65. **Cakraka**, m. (also) the ring on an umbrella, Subh. **Cakshuḥ-śrotra**, mfn. possessing sight and hearing, JaimUp. **Cañcala**, m. (also) a wagtail, L. **Cañcu**, mfn. (add 'skilled' or 'clever in,' and *-tā*, f., *-tva*, n. 'skill,' 'cleverness).' **Caṇava**, m. an inferior kind of grain, L. **Catuḥ** (in comp. for *catur*); *-shashṭy-upacāra-mānasa-pūjā-stotra*, n. N. of wk.; *-suvarṇaka* (or *-sauv°*), mfn. having the weight of four Suvarṇas, Mn. viii, 137. **Catur** (in comp.); *-asra-yāna*, mfn. moving regularly (others 'four-wheeled'), Ragh. vi, 10; *-asra-śobhin*, mfn. beautifully symmetrical, Kum. i, 32; *-daṅshṭra*, m. (also) N. of Airāvata, L.; *-viṅśaty-akshara*, mfn. having 24 syllables, JaimUp.; *-vyavasita-yamaka*, n. a kind of Yamaka (in which the four quarters of a stanza are homophonous), Bhar. **Caturthi-prabhṛiti**, mfn. (for *°thī-pr°*) beginning with the fourth night, ĀpGṛ. **Catuś-catvāriṇśad-akshara**, mfn. having 44 syllables, JaimUp. **Catush-putra**, mfn. having four sons, ib. **Catvarī**, f. a street, L. **Catvāraka**, n. a collection of four, Inscr. **Candana** (in comp.); *-gandha*, m. N. of a Tathāgata, Sukh. i; *-gaura*, mfn. white as the moon, Bcar.; *-bhānu*, (also) N. of a Tathāgata, Sukh. i; *-vanī*, f. a sandal wood, Sāh. **Candra** (in comp.); *-bhīru*, n. silver, L.; *-varcasa*, n. moonshine, Suśr.; *-vyākaraṇa*, n. Candra's grammar (published under Abhimanyu), Rājat. i, 176; *-śakala*, m. n. the half-moon, Kād.; *°drâgra* (accord. to some, 'having gold as the chief part, containing or yielding g°'); *°drârka-mardana*, m. 'tormenter of sun and moon,' N. of Rāhu, MW. **Campaka-śreshṭhi-kathānaka**, n. N. of a tale. **Cayana** (in comp.); *-kārikā*, f., *-paddhati*, f., *-prayoga*, m., *-sūtra*, n. N. of wks.; *°nânta*, mfn. concluding with (the erection of) a Śmaśāna, HirP. **Cara** (in astron., read, 'the difference of time between the rising of a heavenly body at Laṅkā or Ceylon, over which the first meridian passes, and that of its rising at any partic. place'). **Caraṇaka**, n. a small foot, Śiś. **Caritrâvaśesha**, mfn. having only virtue left, Mṛicch. **Carmâmbara**, mfn. clothed in leather, Bcar. **Caryâcaraṇa**, n. the practice of discipline, Sukh. i. **Calat-saṭa**, mfn. with flying mane, Bcar. **Calâtman**, mfn. fickle-minded, ib. **Cashakāya**, Nom. Ā. *°yate*, to become a cup, Nalac. **Cākrika**, m. a secretly born son of a Śūdra and a Vaiśyā, L. **Cāṇḍikā**, f. N. of one of the 6 Yoginīs, Dharmas. 13. **Cāndramasāyani**, (also) N. of Buddha, L. **Cāpa**, (also) a partic. measure of length, Daś.; *-nigama*, m. archery, Bālar.; *-rava*, m. the whizzing of a bow, R. **Cāmuṇḍarāja**, m. N. of several kings, Inscr. **Cāritrapushpa**, mfn. whose flowers are moral actions, Bcar. **Cāru** (in comp.); *-gāmitā*, f. having a graceful gait (one of the 80 minor marks of a Buddha), Dharmas. 84; *-gīta*, n. N. of wk.; *-payodhara*, mf(*ā*)n. fair-bosomed, Bcar.; *-śriṅgin* (see *śriṅgin*, p. 1088). **Cārya**, (also) m. the son of an outcaste Vaiśya (v.l. for *ac°* or *ācārya*), Mn. x, 23. **Cālukya-vikrama-kāla**, m. N. of an era established by the Western Cālukya king Vikramâditya VI; (its first year corresponds to the expired Śaka year 998 = A.D. 1076–77). **Cāhuyāna**, m. N. of a dynasty, Inscr. **Ci** (large Sanskṛit type should have been used for the roots 1. *ci* and 2. *ci*, and the aor. *cikayām akaḥ* put under the latter). **Cikitsanīya**, mfn. curable, Jātakam. **Cikitsā-prābhṛita** (see *prābhṛita*, p. 702). **Citântarâṅsatā**, f. the having the place between the shoulders well filled out (one of the 32 signs of perfection), Dharmas. 83. **Citi**, (also) N. of a plant (v.l. *citti*), Kauś. **Citta** (in comp.); *-dhāraṇa*, n. concentrated attention, Sāṃkhyas., Sch.; *-dhārā-buddhi-saṃkusumitâbhyudgata*, m. N. of a Tathāgata, Sukh. i; *-pāvan* (or *cit-p°*), m. N. of a class of Brāhmans in Koṅkan, RTL. 271, n. 1; *-virāga*, m. irritation of the mind, Pāṇ. vi, 4, 91; *°ttâdhipatya*, n. control over the mind, Bcar. **Citra**, (also) leaping to and fro, Jātakam.; *-katha*, mfn. full of varied converse, Bcar.; *-keśatā*, f. the having beautiful hair (one of the 80 minor marks of a Buddha), Dharmas. 84; *-javanikā*, f. a painted curtain, Mālatim.; *-pakshmatā*, f. the having beautiful eyelashes (cf. *-keśatā*), Dharmas. 84; *-sudhā-nidhi*, m. N. of wk.; *-hetu*, m. a partic. rhet. figure, Kāvyâd. ii, 253; *°trâkṛiti*, f. a picture, Mṛicch.; *°trâṅgulitā*, f. the having beautiful fingers (cf. *-keśatā*), Dharmas. 84; *°trâyudha*, (also) N. of Kāma-deva, Bcar.; *°trâhuti*, f. an offering to Citra, RTL. 425. **Cintā** (in comp.); *-parīta* or *-vaśa*, mfn. lost in thought, thoughtful, Bcar.; *-vidheya*, mfn. influenced by a thought, Bcar.; *-vivikta*, mfn. alone with, i.e. immersed in thought, MBh. **Cira** (in comp.); *-vāsa*, m. a long sojourn, MBh.; *-saṃsthita* (Yājñ.) or *-sthita* (Mn.), mfn. having stood for a long time. **Cīra** (in comp.); *-cīvara*, n. a bark garment, Mālatim.; *°râmbara*, mfn. = *°ra-bhṛit*, Bcar. **Cīvara-vat**, mfn. = prec., Pracaṇḍ. **Cuṭī**, f. cutting, in *su-c°*, q.v. **Cuṇḍikā**, f. cutaneous eruption (see *saṃcāri-c°*). **Culla-patka**, m. N. of a disciple of Buddha, Sukh. i. **Cūrṇavṛiddhi**, m. N. of a man, Mṛicch. **Cedi-saṃvat** (see *kalacuri-saṃvatsara*, p. 1324). **Cesṭāpṛithaktva-nivartin**, mfn. to be (or being) carried out by separate (repeated) acts, ĀpY. **Caitra** (in comp.); *-kuṭī*, f. N. of a wk. on Kṛit suffixes (attributed to Vara-ruci); *-saṃkrānti*, f. N. of a festival usually celebrated early in April (in Bengal). **Corikā-vivāha**, m. a secret marriage, Mṛicch. **Cola-bhāṇa**, n. N. of a drama. **Caudrāyaṇa** &c. (erase and cf. *audr°*, p. 1323). **Caura-kilbisha**, n. the crime or guilt of a thief, Mn. viii, 300.

Chadis-tṛiṇa, n. straw for a roof, L. **Chándaḥ-pratishṭhāna**, mfn. based on metre, MaitrS. **Chala** (in comp.); *pāta*, m. gliding out, Dharmaś.; *-vāc*, f. deceitful speech, L. **Chāga-māṅsa**, n. goat's flesh, Mn. iii, 269. **Chāṇaka**, m. a partic. mixed caste, L. **Chittapa** (or *cit°*), m. N. of a grammarian and a poet, Gaṇar.; Subh. **Chinna** (in comp.); *-karṇá*, mf(*ī*)n. (ŚBr.); *-dvaidha*, mfn. one whose doubts have been destroyed, Bhag.; *-sthūṇa*, mfn. having broken legs, MBh.; *°nnâbhra*, n. a cloud torn asunder, Bhag. **Churikābandha-prayoga**, m. the ceremony of providing a Śūdra with a bill-hook, Cat. **Chūrikā** (cf. *sthūrikā*, p. 1265).

Jakshā, f. chewing, L. **Jakshita**, mfn. chewed, eaten, L. **Jagat** (accord. to some also 'a river,' RV. x, 75, 2); *-prakāśa*, (also) N. of a poem in praise of king Jagat-siṇha. **Jagad** (in comp. for *jagat*); *-ābharaṇa*, n. N. of a poem by Jagannātha Paṇḍita-rāja; *-īśa*, (also) N. of the author of the Hāsyârṇava; *-dhitâtman* (for *-hit°*), mfn. having the heart set on the salvation of the world, Bcar.; *-bhaya*, n. terror of the universe, BhP.; *-yātrā*, f. worldly affairs, ib.; *-rāma*, m. N. of an author, Cat. **Jagamyā** (read *°myāt*, Hir. i, 8, 4). **Jagdha** (in comp.); *-tṛiṇa*, mfn. one who has eaten grass, KaṭhUp.; *°dhârdha*, mfn. half-eaten, Mālatim. **Jaṅghā**, (also) the leg; *-nalaka*, a bone of the leg, Mālatim. **Jaṭā** (in comp.); *-jhāṭa*, m. N. of Śiva, L.; *-varman*, m. N. of a king, Inscr. **Jaṭharôtsava**, m. a festive dinner, L. **Jatukā**, f. a cockroach, L. **Jana** (in comp.); *-kāya*, m. a crowd of people, Jātakam.; *-śrī*, f. beautiful women (coll.), Bcar. iv, 102; *-sammarda*, m. a throng of people, Mṛicch.; *°nârṇava*, m. 'id.,' a caravan, MBh. **Janayitnu**, m. a father, L. **Janikā**, f. a mother, Divyâv. **Janitra** (with *paramá*, accord. to some, 'origin on high,' AV. i, 25, 1). **Jani-vid**, m. knowing or winning women, ĀpGṛ. **Janīna**, mfn. kind to people, Inscr. **Janma** (in comp. for *janman*); *-jarântaka*, m. destroyer of birth and old age, Bcar.; *-parigraha*, m. birth (acc. with √*kṛi*, 'to be born'), Jātakam.; *-mṛityu*, m. du. birth and death, KaṭhUp.; *-vātsalya*, n. love for one's native country, Hit.; *°mântakara*, m. destroyer of birth, Bcar. **Janya-vṛitti**, f. contest, fight, Daś. **Japāpīḍa**, m. a garland of China roses, Mālatim. **Jabdha**, mfn. swallowed (see *hemanta-j°*). **Jambū-dvīpêśvara**, m. a sovereign of India, Sukh. i. **Jambha** (in comp.); *-nisumbhana*, m. N. of Indra, Nalac.; *°bhârāti*, m. id., Dharmaś. **Jaya** (in comp); *-kṛishṇa*, m. N. of various authors (also with *bhaṭṭa*, *upâdhyāya* &c.), Cat.; *-nāman*, m. N. of a Jaina teacher, Inscr.; *-lakshmaṇa*, n., *-vilāsa*, m. N. of wks.; *°yôttara*, mfn. certain of victory, MBh.; *°yôdāharaṇa*, n. report or praise of v°, R. **Jaraṭha**, (also) full-grown, Mālatim. **Jarāyujá**, mfn. (accord. to some in AV. i, 12, 1 = 'sprung from the womb of a cloud,' said of lightning). **Jarâyudha**, mfn. having old age as his weapon (said of Death), Bcar. **Jarishṇu** (?), Hir. i, 4, 6. **Jarjara-pūjā**, f. (in dram.) homage to the banner of Indra (a kind of ceremony). **Jala** (in comp.); *-garbha*, mfn. wet with dew, Bcar. xiii, 72; *-gāhana*, n. entering the water, Kāvyâd.; *-taraṃgiṇī*, f. a series of cups filled with water in varying quantities and played on as a musical instrument by striking them successively with a wand or light hammer, MW.; *-taskara*, m. 'water-thief,' the sun, L.; *-pavitra*, n. a water-strainer, filter, Baudh.; *-pālikā*, f. lightning, L.; *-pūrṇa*, (also) filled with tears, Bcar. viii, 74; *-pṛikta*, mfn. touching water, swimming, R.; *-bṛiṅhaṇa*, n. a flood of water, L.; *-bhauta*, mfn. one who is infatuated or silly in regard to w°, Kathās.; *-mitra*, m. the moon, Dhūrtan.; *-hīna*, mfn. waterless, dry, Mṛicch. **Jalpa** (in comp.); *-kalpataru*, m., *-kalpalatā*, f., *°pêśvara-māhātmya*, n. N. of wks. **Jalhaṇa**, m. N. of a poet (contemporary of Maṅkha), Subh. **Javás** (accord. to some, 'swift, rapid,' RV. iii, 50, 2; iv, 27, 1). **Jáhā**, (prob.) an exclamation (others, read *jáhāko* = *jahako*), RV. viii, 45, 37. **Jahāṅgīra** or **Jihāṅgīra**, m. Jahāngir (emperor), Inscr. **Jāgaritadeśa**, m. place of waking, ŚBr. **Jāgrat-prapañca**, m. the world as it appears to one who is awake, Sāṃkhyapr. **Jāṅmāyana**, a kind of water vessel (v.l. *jāgm°*), Kauś. **Jāta** (in comp.); *-tarsha*, mfn. thirsty, desirous, Bcar.; *-pūrva*, mfn. born before, Mṛicch.; *-rāga*, mfn. enamoured, Bcar.; *-rūpa*, (also) m. N. of a Commentator on the Amarakośa; *-vidyā*, f. (accord. to some, 'innate or peculiar knowledge'); (*°tá*)*-vedas* (accord. to some, 'sage, wise'); *°tânukampa*, mfn. compassionate, Bcar. **Jātaka** (in comp.); *-darpaṇa*, m., *-bhūshaṇa*, n., *-mañjarī*, f., *-ratna*, n., *-lakshaṇa*, n., *-saṃgraha*, m. N. of wks. **Jāti** (in comp.); *-tas*, ind. according to caste, Mn. x, 11; *-nirṇaya*, m., *-vicāra*, m., *-sāṃkarya*, n. N. of wks.; (*°ty*)*-antarīyaka*, mfn. belonging to another (future) birth, Jātakam.; (*°ty*)*-utpatti-krama*, m. N. of a ch. of the Skanda-purāṇa. **Jānakī-gītā**, f. N. of a wk. on Bhakti by Śrī-Harsha. **Jānu** (in comp.); *-nikuñcana*, n. a partic. posture in Yoga, L.; (*°nv*)*-antarā*, ind. between the knees, Baudh. **Jāyānya** (accord. to some = 'syphilis'). **Jārin**, m. one whose wife has a paramour, Hir.; (*iṇī*), f. having a paramour, enamoured, RV. **Jāla** (in comp.); *-bhūshaṇa*, m. the son of a Maitreya and a Kshatriyā, L.; *-mārga*, m. the way through the window, Mālatim.; *°lâbaddhâṅguli-pāṇi-pāda-talatā*, f. the having the soles of the feet and palms and fingers covered with nets (or cross-lines; one of the 32 signs of perfection), Dharmas. 83; *°lôpajīvin*, m. a fisherman, Śak. **Jita-manyu**, m. N. of a poet, Cat. **Jihma-kārin**, mfn. acting crookedly or deceitfully, R. (B.). **Jihvā-pāvan**, m. 'drinking with the tongue,' a dog, L. **Jīva**, m. (also) N. of a famous physician, Buddh.; *-koshaṇī*, f. the skin from a living animal, Kauś. (Sch.); *-ghātya* (read, 'a living animal fit to be killed'); *-cūrṇa*, n. pl. living animals (such as 'centipedes,' Sch.) ground to powder, GṛS.; (*°vá*)*-dhanya* (accord. to some, 'blessing or befriending living creatures'); *-nāśa*, m. state between life and death, R.; *-śriṅga*, n. the horn of a living animal, Hir.; *-sūvarī*, f. bringing forth a living child, MānGṛ.; *°vânanda*, N. of a Nāṭaka. **Jīvad-vibhāga**, m. partition while (the father is still) living, Bṛihas. **Jīvita** (in comp.); *-gupta*, m. N. of two kings of Magadha, Inscr.; *-tṛishṇā*, f. thirst for life, Mālatim.; *-pradāyin*, mfn. life-preserving, ib.; *-maraṇa*, n. death in life, ib.; *-sarvasva*, n. the whole essence of l°, Śak.; *°tâvasāna*, n. end of life, death, Mālatim.; *°tôdvahana*, n. carrying on l°, continuing to live, ib. **Jīvin** (also, 'vivifying'), MBh. **Jīvī**, f. N. of a plant, Kauś. **Jushṭā** or **Jushṭi**, f. also N. of a cow, Lāṭy.; Drāhy. **Juhoti** (in comp.); *-codana*, mfn. impelled by the word *juhoti*, ĀpY.; *-yajati-kriyā*, f. pl. the offering of burnt oblations and (other) sacrifices, Mn. ii, 84. **Jñāna** (in comp.); *-kautūhala*, n. desire of knowledge, Jātakam.; *-nidhi*, m. N. of the teacher of Bhavabhūti, Mālatim., Introd.; *-panya*, m. a dealer in kn°, Mālav.; *-pradīpa*, m. a lamp of kn°, Kum.; N. of a metrical dialogue on the Vedânta between Hara and Hari, Cat.; *-mārga*, m. the way of kn° (one of the 3 roads to salvation; cf. *karma-* and *bhakti-m°*), RTL. 63; *-sūryôdaya*, m. N. of a Jaina drama. **Jñāpakâvalī**, f. N. of a gram. wk. **Jñeyârṇava**, m. the ocean of knowledge, Bcar. vii, 56. **Jyā** (in comp.); *-nivāraṇa*, n. a leathern fence for the arm, L.; *-°rohaṇa* (*jyâr°*), n. the fixing a bow-string, Cat. **Jyâyas-vat** (others, 'following a leader, obedient;' others, 'excellent, superior'). **Jyāyu**, a bow-string, Kauś. **Jyeshṭha** (in comp.); *-brāhmaṇa*, (also) n. the chief Brāhmaṇa, JaimUp.; *-lakshmá*, n. the principal mark or sign, MaitrS.; *-sāmaka*, m. one who knows the Jyeshṭha-sāman, Baudh. **Jyotaya-māmaká** (some read *-mānaká*, 'little shiner'). **Jyotsnâḍhya**, mfn. full of light, Mṛicch. **Jráyas** (accord. to some, 'onset, haste, hurry, course'). **Jvalac-charīra**, mfn. having a radiant body, Bcar. **Jvalanâdhipati**, m. N. of a Tathāgata, Sukh. i. **Jvālá**, m. (also) a hot infusion, MaitrS. **Jvālāyana**, m. N. of a teacher, JaimUp. **Jvālā-lakshaṇa**, n. N. of the 29th Pariśishṭa of the AV.

Jhaṅki or **jhaṅkī**, f. N. of a kind of dram.

entertainment (tableaux vivants). **Jhaṭiti** (repeated = 'no sooner-than,' Mālatīm.). **Jhaṇaj-jhaṇatkārin**, mfn. making a rattling or tinkling, Pracaṇḍ. **Jhiṇikā**, f. hiccough, L.

Ṭiṭṭibhâsana, n. a partic. posture in Yoga, L. **Ṭippaṇy-āśaya**, m. N. of a Vedânta wk. **Ṭīkā** (in comp.); *-samuccaya*, m., *-sarvasva*, n. N. of wks. **Ṭeka**, m. N. of a demon causing disease (v.l. *ṭaka*), Hir. **Ṭoḍara-prakāśa**, m. and **Ṭolaka-māhātmya**, n. N. of wks.

Ṭhuṇṭhu-paddhati, f. N. of wk. **Ṭhepaka** or **Ṭhevaka**, m. N. of a chief, Inscr.

Ḍaṅka-māhātmya, n. (? for *Ḍhaṅka-m°*) N. of wk. **Ḍamara**, m. (also) a portent, evil omen, L. **Ḍamaru**, m. (add 'a sacred drum, shaped like an hour-glass, used by the god Śiva and by Buddhist mendicant monks for a musical accompaniment in chanting,' cf. MWB. 384, 385). **Ḍambara-siṅha**, m. (with *Para-māra*) N. of a king, Inscr. **Ḍāla-candra**, m. N. of a king, Cat. **Ḍiṇḍika**, m. a partic. mixed caste, L. **Ḍuṇḍura**, m. an upper bedroom, L. **Ḍuṇḍhi**, (also) N. of various authors, Cat. **Ḍval** (see *ā-ḍval*, p. 1319, col. 2).

Ḍhilī or **Ḍhillī** or **Ḍhillikā**, f. the city Delhi, Inscr. **Ḍhaukana**, n. (also) bringing near (in *svayam-āsana-ḍh°*, see p. 1278).

Takarī (also *tagara*, °*raka* or *tagarī*) = *sthakara* or *sthagara*, a partic. fragrant powder (Bloomfield's AV., p. 311). **Takma-nāśana-gaṇa**, m. a series of Mantras or texts used as a protection against fevers &c., AV. Pariś. **Taj-jalān** (ChUp. iii, 14, 1, read, accord. to some, *taj-jānāntī*, 'thinking, may I know that;' cf. IW. 102, 1). **Taḍit-pati**, m. a cloud, L. **Taṇḍaka**, n. (also) a ship, Nalac. **Tat** (in comp.); *-kṛite*, ind. therefore, MBh.; *-kriya*, mfn. working without wages, L.; *-kshaṇikā*, f. a courtezan, Mahāvy.; *-parâyaṇa*, mfn. having that as chief object, Bhag.; *-prakṛita*, mfn. made or consisting of that, Pāṇ. v, 4, 21; *-pratyayam*, ind. to make anything sure (°*ya-tva*, n.), Āpast.; Baudh.; *-pradhāna*, mfn. depending chiefly on that, Mn. iii, 18; *-sad*, mfn. sitting there, Hir. **Tatra-loka**, m. the other world, HirP. **Tathârtha-vāc**, f. truth, L. **Tadātva-mātra-śraddheya** (see *śr°*, p. 1096). **Tad-dharma**, mfn. having the same qualities, ĀpY. **Tanu** (in comp.); *-jihvatā*, f. the having a thin tongue (one of the 80 minor marks of a Buddha), Dharmas. 84; *-dīrgha-ghoṇa*, mfn. one who has a thin long nose, Bcar.; *-varman*, n. armour for the body, MBh. **Tanman**, n. (prob.) = *tardman*, a fissure, hole, MānGṛ. **Tapaḥ** (in comp. for *tapas*); *-pradhāna*, mfn. pre-eminent in penance, Bcar.; *-sahāya*, m. companion in penance, ib.; (°*pas*)*-tanu*, mfn. having p° as a body, JaimUp. **Tapo** (in comp. for *tapas*); *-da*, (also) any sacred place, Bcar.; *-nidhāna*, n. a treasury of penance, ib.; *'nta*, mfn. ending with p°, Mn. xi, 235; *-yoga*, m. the practice of p°, ib. i, 41; *-varishṭha*, mfn. excellent in p°, Bcar. **Tamaḥ** (in comp.); *-pracchādaka*, mfn. covering with darkness (said of an evil demon), MārkP.; *-saṃghāta*, m. dense d°, Ratnâv. **Tamo** (in comp.); *-nishṭha*, mfn. founded on d°, Mn. xii, 95; *-viśāla*, mfn. full of darkness, Sāṃkhyak. **Taraṃga-dattā**, f. N. of a comedy, Daśar. **Taraṇḍaka**, m. (also) a raft, float, L. **Tarī**, f. = *starī*, a barren cow, MaitrS. **Taruṇâditya**, m. the newly-risen sun, MBh. **Tarumastaka**, the top of a tree, Bcar. **Tarka** (in comp.); *-kutūhala*, n., *-cūḍāmaṇi*, m., *-vāda*, m. N. of wks. **Tarṇa**, (also) any young animal, Dhūrtan. **Tarda** (accord. to some, 'a field insect'). **Tasthu** (rather 'n. that which is stationary, i.e. plants and animals'). **Tājika**, (also) Arab, Inscr. **Tāpasa-vatsarāja**, N. of a Nāṭaka (by Anaṅga-harsha, written before 850 A.D.). **Tāmra** (in comp.); *-jīva*, m. the son of a Māgadha and a Brāhmaṇī (who works in copper), L.; *-nakha*, mf(*ī*)n. having red nails, MBh. (*-tā*, f., Dharmas. 84); °*râdhar'oshṭha*, mfn. having a red lower lip, Bcar. **Tārā** (in comp.); *-candrôdaya*, m. N. of a poem; *-maitraka*, n. 'star-friendship,' spontaneous love, Mālatīm.; Uttarar.; *-vartman*, n. the sky, L. **Tārkshyâsana**, n. N. of a partic. posture in Yoga, L. **Tāla-pramāṇa**, mfn. as tall as a palm tree, Bcar. **Tāvad-vidha**, mfn. of such kind, Jātakam. **Titiru**, m. or f. = *pataṃga*, L. **Tibeṭa** (said to be fr. *trivishṭapa*), Tibet, Āryav. **Timirâugha**, m. deep darkness, L. **Timi-śatru**, m. a partic. marine monster, L. **Tiraścīna-vaṅśa**, m. a cross-beam (?), ChUp. iii, 11. **Tirumalêśa**, m. N. of Vishṇu, Inscr. **Tiruvânanda-pura**, n. N. of a town, Inscr. **Tiryag** (in comp.); *-ākṛiti*, m. any creature like an animal, Jātakam.; *-valana*, n. oblique movement, deflection, Mālatīm. **Tilâśana**, mfn. eating sesamum grains, Baudh. **Tilitsaka**, m. a hyæna, L. **Tishyâmra-tīrtha**, n. N. of a place, Inscr. **Tīkshṇa** (in comp.); *-daṃshṭratā*, f. the having sharp eye-teeth (one of the 80 minor marks of a Buddha), Dharmas. 84; °*ṇâmla*, mfn. bitter and sour, Mṛicch. **Tíkshṇīyas**, mfn. sharper, AV. **Tīra** (in comp.); *-vilagna*, mfn. come ashore, landed, Kathās. **Tīrtha** (in comp.); *-pratipādana*, n. = *sat-pattra-dāna*, Daś. (Sch.). **Tuk** (= √*tak*, see *su-tuka*, p. 1224). **Tuṅga-nakhatā**, f. the having prominent nails (one of the 80 minor marks of a Buddha), Dharmas. 84. **Tuṇḍin**, m. a bird, L. **Tunnā**, f. (also 'a violated woman'). **Tumbakī**, f. a kind of drama of an inferior order (containing exhibitions of jugglery), Sāh. **Turaga** (in comp.); *-pālaka*, m. a groom, Bcar. **Turaṃgin**, (also) consisting of horses or horsemen, MBh. **Tulaji**, m. N. of a king of Tanjore (1765–1788 A.D.) and reputed author of various wks. **Tulā** (in comp.); *-puṃs*, m. (= *-purusha*), Baudh.; *-māna*, n. weights and measures, Mn. viii, 403. **Tulya** (in comp.); *-krama*, mfn. keeping the same pace, Jātakam.; *-gariman*, mfn. of the same dignity with (instr.), Pracaṇḍ.; *-codana*, n. an equally important rule, Drāhy.; *-vat*, ind. like, ĀpY.; °*lyâbhidhāna*, mfn. of equal name (i.e. having a name corresponding to one's qualities), Bcar. **Tuvara** (see *tubara*). **Tuvi-grá**, mfn. (accord. to some = 'roaring loud,' fr. √2. *gṛī*). **Tushṭūshita** (see √*stu*, p. 1259). **Tūrya** (in comp.); *-ghosha*, m. the sound of musical instruments, Mn. vii, 225; N. of a Tathāgata, Sukh. i. **Tūla-sadṛiśa-sukumāra-pāṇitā**, f. the having hands soft as cotton (one of the 80 minor marks of a Buddha), Dharmas. 84. **Tṛiṇa** (in comp.); *-kāshṭha*, n. grass and wood, Mn. v, 122; *-cchedin*, mfn. one who plucks grass, ib. iv, 71; *-pañcikā*, f. straw, L.; *-prâsana*, n. throwing grass into the fire, Drāhy.; *-saṃvara*, m. red deer, ib.; *-saṃcaya*, m. a bundle of grass or straw, ib.; *-skandá*, m. a grasshopper (see *skandá*). **Tṛishṇā** (in comp.); *-°rta* (°*ṇârta*), mfn. tormented by thirst, Mṛicch.; *-saṅga*, m. attachment to desire, Bhag. **Tejo** (in comp. for *tejas*); *-mātrā*, f. a particle of light, ŚBr.; *-vaidagdhya-śīlavat*, mfn. having energy (and) cleverness (and) a good character, Sāh.; *-hara*, mfn. taking away or wasting strength, Bcar. **Taila**, (also) m. N. of a king, Inscr.; *-ghṛita*, n. ghee mixed with sesamum oil, Mṛicch. **Toyâhāra**, m. a partic. class of ascetics, Baudh. **Tauvilikā**, f. a female demon causing disease, AV. vi, 16, 3 (Sāy.). **Tyakta** (in comp.); *-punaḥ-svī-kṛita*, (in rhet.) resuming what has been suspended, Kpr.; °*tâgni*, mfn. one who has abandoned the sacred fire, Mn. iii, 153. **Trayī-nishkarsha**, m. the extract or essence of the three Vedas, Mn. iv, 125. **Trayodaśa-māsa**, mfn. extending over thirteen months, JaimUp. **Trāsa** (add 'fr. √2. *tras*'). **Tri** (in comp.); *-divin*, m. a god, Kāv.; *-pāda*, (also) a vessel with three feet, Kauś.; *-putra*, mfn. having three sons, JaimUp.; *-pura-vighna*, m. the destroyer of Tripura, MBh.; *-prakāra*, mfn. of three kinds, threefold, Mn. xii, 51; *-vastu*, n. the triple object (viz. Buddha, Dharma, and Saṃgha), Divyâv.; *-vishūka*, mfn. diverging into three directions, HirP.; *-veda*, m. (with *krishṇa-rāta-lauhitya*) N. of a teacher, JaimUp.; *-śūla-paṭṭiśa-dhara*, m. N. of Śiva, Hariv.; *-shaṃdhi* (in AV., prob. the personification of a three-pointed weapon as a 'battle-god'). **Trish-prakāra** (or *triḥ-pr°*), mfn. = *tri-prakāra*, MārkP.; APrāt., Sch. **Traidhātuka-samatā**, f. equilibrium of the three elements, Sukh. i. **Try-ambaka**, (also) N. of a sacred bathing-place at the source of the Godāvarī (commonly called Trimbak, and renowned for a temple of the three-eyed god Śiva). **Tvag-asthi-śesha**, mfn. having only skin and bone remaining, a mere skeleton, Bcar. **Tvāyā** (accord. to some = *te, tvé*).

Daṃshṭrâyudha, mfn. having tusks for weapons, Bhag. **Dakshiṇā** (in comp.); *-pada*, mf(*ī*)n. having the feet towards the south, Hir.; *-pratigraha*, m. N. of partic. Mantras, HirP.; *-pravaṇa*, mfn. sloping down southwards, Hir.; *-prâñc*, mfn. directed towards the south-east, ib.; *-varjam*, ind. with the exception of the sacrificial gift, ĀpGṛ. **Dagdha** (in comp.); *-kilbisha*, mfn. one whose sins are burnt away or destroyed, MBh.; °*dhânna*, n. scorched rice, L. **Daṇḍa** (in comp.); *-padmâsana*, n. a partic. posture in Yoga, L.; *-pāśika*, m. a police-officer, constable, Nalac.; *-vidhi*, m. a mode of punishment, Mn. viii, 221; *-śūra*, m. N. of a man, Mṛicch.; °*ḍôpānaha*, n. sg. a staff and sandal, JaimUp. **Daṇḍāya**, (also) to resemble the stem of (comp.), Mālatīm. **Daṇḍika**, m. (also) a kind of arrow, L. **Dattôttara**, (also) pronouncing a judgment, Mālatīm. **Dadā**, ind. an exclamation, JaimUp. **Daditthá**, (also) N. of a monkey, Bālar. **Dadda**, m. N. of various kings (of Gurjara &c.), Inscr. **Dan** (accord. to some fr. √*daṃs*, 'to make straight,' either 'to raise, erect,' or 'to put right, rule, guide, manage;' in some places probably = 'a guide, manager, institutor'). **Danta** (in comp.); *-kośa*, m. the tusk of an elephant compared to a flower-cup, Ragh.; *-pāñcālikā*, f. an ivory doll, Mālatīm.; *-līna*, mfn. that to which the teeth adhere (?), VS., Sch. **Daphara-khāna**, m. Zaphar Khān (Sultān), Inscr. **Dama** (in comp.); *-dāna*, n. du. self-control and liberality, Mn. iv, 246; °*môpêta*, mfn. endowed with self-control, MBh. **Damanâropaṇa**, n. a partic. ceremony, Inscr. **Damayantī-pariṇaya**, m. N. of a poem. **Dám-pati** (accord. to some = 'lord, master,' fr. √*daṃs* + *p°* [cf. *dan* above]; *ī*, du. 'master and mistress'). **Dayā** (in comp.); *-pūrvam*, ind. compassionately, Baudh.; *-°lasa* (*dayâl°*), mfn. disinclined to pity, Bcar. viii, 30. **Daraka**, mfn. timid, afraid, L. **Darbha** (in comp.); *-grumushṭi*, m. a firmly closed hand full of Darbha grass, ĀpGṛ. (Sch.); °*bhêṇḍva*, covering for the hands made of Darbha grass (?), ib. **Darśana** (in comp.); *-kāṅkshin*, mfn. longing for the sight of (comp.), Bhag.; °*nôtsuka*, mfn. id., Mālatīm. **Dala-nagara**, n. N. of a town, Inscr. **Daśa** (in comp.); *-nakha*, mfn. having ten finger-nails, Mṛicch.; *-putra*, mfn. having ten sons, JaimUp.; *-rātra-paryushita*, mfn. having stood for ten nights or days, Suśr.; *-sāhasram*, (also) ten thousand times, Parāś.; °*śâvayava*, m. N. of Śiva, L.; °*śâvasthā*, f. (in rhet.) the ten conditions (of a lover, viz. *abhilāsha*, *cintana*, *smṛiti*, *guṇa-kathā*, *udvega*, *pralāpa*, *unmāda*, *saṃcara*, *jaḍatā*, and *maraṇa*, qq. vv.), Daśar. iv, 48; °*śôttara*, m. the eleventh, MBh. **Daśana-śikhara**, the point of a tooth, Gīt. **Daśamī-stha**, mfn. between 90 and 100 years old, Mn. ii, 138. **Daśā-vipāka**, m. fulfilment of destiny, Mālatīm. **Daśra**, m. a tooth, L.; a serpent, L. **Dashṭa-mātra**, mfn. just bitten or stung, Mālatīm. **Dashṭavya**, n. the act of biting, Jātakam. **Dahana** (in comp.); *-kalpa*, m. a crematory rite, HirP.; *-vat*, ind. as (at) cremation, ib.; *-sārathi*, m. the wind, Daś. **Dahyu**, m. fire, L. **Dākshâyya**, m. a vulture, L. **Dākshiṇeya**, mfn. having a claim on the sacrificial gift, ĀpŚr. **Dākshiṇya**, (also) dexterous, energetic, strong, capable, Jātakam. **Dāḍima-phala**, n. the kernel or seed of a pomegranate, Amar. **Dātṛi-pratîcchaka**, m. du. giver and receiver, Mn. iv, 194. **Dātrā-karṇa**, mf(*ī*)n. having ears formed like a sickle, MaitrS. **Dātreyá**, m. a patron., ib. **Dāda-da** (erase x after 'Śiś.'). 1. **Dāna** (in comp.); *-paṭṭaka*, n. a deed of donation, Rājat.; *-pratibhū*, a surety for payment, Mn. viii, 160; *-viśodhana*, n. du. addition and subtraction, VarBṛS.; *-vīra*, m. (in rhet.) liberal heroism, Bhar.; *-saṃvanana*, n. encouraging liberality, R. **Dānâpnas** (RV.). **Dāya-vīra**, m. (in rhet.) compassionate or liberal heroism (cf. *dāna-v°* above), Sāh. **Dāra-gupti**, f. guarding a wife, Hir. 3. **Dāru** (in comp.); *-citi*, f. a pile or pyre of wood, HirP.; *-puttrikā*, *-puttrī* (read *-putrikā*, *-putrī*). **Dārḍhajayanti** (see *vaipaścita*, p. 1332). **Dārbhyūsha** (applied to a bow; v.l. °*usha*), Kauś. **Dālbhyāyana**, m. N. of a teacher, Prasannar. **Dāśeraka**, (also) a camel, L. 2. **Dās** (= 2. *dāś*, see *su-dās*, p. 1224). **Dāha-vadānya**, mfn. burning intensely (*-tā*, f.), Hcar. **Dik-pāla-stuti**, f. (in dram.) praise of the guardians of the world (a kind of introductory ceremony). **Digdha-phala**, n. the point of a poisoned arrow, Kum. iv, 25. **Dig-valaya**, m. n. the universe, Śiś. **Ditya-váh** (VS.). **Dinam-manyā**, f. a full-moon night, L. **Divasa** (TBr.). **Diva-stambhana**, mf(*ī*)n. sky-supporting, JaimUp. **Divā-sthāna**, mfn. standing during the day, Baudh. **Divi-dhuvaka**, N. of a tree, Kauś. **Divya** (in comp.); *-kālinī*, f. a kind of non-poisonous snake, L.; °*vyônmāda*, m. N. of a modern drama. **Diśāna**, m. an instructor in sacred knowledge, L. **Dishṭa-gamana**, n. dying, death (cf. *dishṭā gatiḥ*), HirP. **Dīna-cintāmaṇi**, f. N. of a princess, Inscr. **Dīpta** (in comp.); *-phala*, mf(*ā*)n. bearing glorious fruit, Bcar.; °*tâgra*, mfn. flame-pointed, JaimUp. **Dīrgha** (in comp.); *-nir-vaṇśa*, m. a long sword, L.; °*ghâṅgulitā*, f. the having long fingers (one of the 32 signs of perfection), Dharmas. 83; °*ghâbhinishṭhânânta*, mfn. ending in a long vowel or in Visarga, ĀpGṛ. **Dīr-ṇâṅga**, m. N. of the planet Saturn, L. **Duḥkha** (in comp.); *-pratīkāra*, m. a remedy for pain, Bcar.; *-bhūyishṭha*, consisting mostly of p°, abounding with sorrow, ib.; °*khêta*, mfn. affected with sorrow, Pāṇ. vi, 1, 89, Vārtt. 6, Pat. **Dundubhi-svara-nirghosha**, m. N. of a Tathâgata, Sukh. i. **Dur** (in comp. for *dus*); *-anuga*, mfn. difficult to be followed, Baudh.; *-anusamprâpya*, mfn. d° to be completely attained, JaimUp.; *-anūcāna*, mfn. ignorant, ib.; *-gandha-rasa*, mfn. having a bad smell or taste, Baudh.; *-yodhanâsana*, n. a kind of posture (=*vīrâsana*, p. 1006). **Dush** (in comp. for *dus*); *-kuha*, mfn. disbelieving, incredulous, Bcar. i, 18; *-pratīti-kara*, mfn. suggesting an offensive meaning, Kāvyâd. i, 66; *-pradharsha*, m. (also) N. of a Tathâgata, Sukh. i. **Dū** (in comp. for *dus*); *-rūpa*, mfn. of evil form, JaimUp. **Dūra-kārya**, mfn. having a remote effect, Kāvyâd. **Dūre-devata**, mfn. having far distant divinities, JaimUp. **Dṛik** (in comp. for 2. *dṛiś*); *-cchada*, m. an eyelash, L.; *-śravas*, m. (=*-karṇa*), L.; (*dṛig*)-*āyudha*, m. N. of Śiva, L. **Dṛiśāna**, m. (also) the sun, L. **Dṛiśīku**, mfn. one who has gone to see a sacrifice, L. **Dṛishṭâdṛishṭa**, (also) dimly seen, Inscr. **Dṛishṭi** (in comp.); *-prapāta*, m. a glance, Kum.; *-bandha*, m. the tip of the nose, L. **Deva** (in comp.); *-gama*, mfn. going to the gods, Baudh.; *-jana*, (also) N. of a Guhyaka, L.; *-tara*, m. (with *cyāvasāyana kāśyapa*) N. of a teacher, JaimUp.; *-pāṇi*, (also) N. of the author of a Comm. on Daśar., Vikr., Sch.; *-yaśasá*, n. divine glory, TS.; *-yashṭi* (see *veda-y*°, p. 1017); *-rāya*, m. N. of a king, Inscr.; *-saṃyukta*, mfn. connected with the gods, ĀpGṛ.; °*vêndra-varman*, m. N. of various kings, Inscr.; °*vâinasá* (accord. to some, 'sin committed by the gods'). **Devatā-nigama**, m. address of a deity, ĀpY. **Devī**, f. (also) = *gāyatrī*, Parāś.; = *nāgī*, Buddh. **Deśa** (in comp.); *-bhraṇśa*, m. ruin of a country, VarBṛS.; *-viruddha* (Vām.) or *-virodhin* (Kāvyâd.), mfn. contradictory as to time. **Deha** (in comp.); *-baddha*, mfn. embodied, Kum.; *-vimukti*, f. abandonment of the body or of life, ib. **Dehalī-dīpa-nyāya**, m. the rule of the lamp placed over the threshold (i.e. giving light to both sides, and so serving a twofold purpose), A. **Dai** (i.e. under √*dai*, p. 497, col. 1; for √5. *dā* read √7. *dā*). **Dor-vishâda**, m. languor or lassitude of the arms, Mālatīm. **Dohada** or **dohala** (accord. to Lüders fr. *duhalī* = *dvihṛid*, 'pregnant'). **Daundubhi**, f. deceit, L.; (*ī*), the journey of the bridegroom to the bride, ib. **Daurmatya**, n. bad disposition, L. **Dauhṛidinī**, f. a woman with two hearts (i.e. a pregnant woman, = *dvihṛidayā*; cf. *dohada*), Suśr. **Dyut** (under √1. *dyu* at p. 499 read 1. **Dyut**, and at p. 500 read 2. **Dyut** and 3. **Dyút**). **Dyuvan**, m. heaven, L.; the sun, ib. **Dyu-stha**, mfn. dwelling in heaven, Baudh. **Drá** (accord. to some in AV. xi, 7, 3, 'that which is free,' opp. to *vrá*). **Drava-rāga**, mfn. dropping or wet with unguent, Kum. vii, 58. **Draviṇa** (in comp.); *-pati*, m. N. of Kubera, Bcar.; °*ṇêndrâtmaja*, m. K°'s son, ib. **Dravya** (in comp.); *-guṇa*, m. pl. the accessories of (i.e. unimportant) things, Bcar. xi, 36; *-śaktimat*, mfn. possessed of the power to produce matter, BhP.; *-samuccaya*, m. accumulation (of things), ĀpY. **Druma** (in comp.); *-ccheda-prâyaścitta*, n. N. of wk.; °*mâksha*, m. N. of a king, Bcar. ix, 60; °*mâbja-ketu*, m. 'having the sign of a tree and a lotus,' the moon, ib. v, 3. **Drumala**, n. a wood, L. **Draupadī-pariṇaya-campū**, f. N. of a poem. **Dvārakā-nātha**, m. 'lord of Dv°,' N. of Kṛishṇa, RTL. **Dvārā-vatī**, (also) N. of Bangkok, Inscr. **Dvi** (in comp.); *-khurin*, mfn. having cloven hoofs, Baudh.; *-garta*, N. of a country in the extreme north of India (between two lakes), MW.; *-gotra*, mfn. belonging to two families, Baudh.; *-jāti-pravara*, m. a man bel° to the first twice-born caste, ib.; *-pa-rāja-vikrama*, mfn. having the gait of the king of elephants, Bcar.; *-modakikā* (see *mod*°, p. 835); *-yajñôpavītin*, mfn. wearing two sacrificial threads, Baudh.; *-rada-gāmin*, mfn. walking like an elephant, Ragh.; *-rada-maya*, mf(*ī*)n. consisting or made of ivory, Bcar. **Dvesha-kalpa**, m. a ceremony intended to cause injury to an enemy, Lāṭy.; Drāhy. **Dvy-avara**, mfn. at least two, ĀpGṛ.

Dhánu (accord. to some also, 'water, juice &c.;' cf. √*dhanv*, *dhanutri*). **Dhanôtpatti**, f. income, L. **Dhandhuka**, m. N. of various kings, Inscr. **Dharīyas**, mfn. stronger or very strong, Hir. **Dharuṇí** (accord. to some, 'a supporter'). **Dharma**, (also) a thing, Sukh. i; *-kīrti*, m. N. of a teacher, Buddh.; *-cakra-pravartana*, n. setting in motion the wheel of the law, ib.; MWB. 42; *-dhṛít*, mfn. (rather, 'upholding order,' applied to the gods); *-mati-vinandita-rāga*, m. N. of a Tathâgata, Sukh. i; *-matsara*, mfn. jealous of merit, Bcar.; *-vallabha*, m. a lover of religion, ib.; *-vahikā*, f. an account-book of charitable expenditure, Jain.; *-vīra*, n. virtuous heroism, Sāh.; *-saṃśraya*, m. the practice of religion, Bcar.; *-sāgara*, m. N. of a preceptor, Sukh. i; °*môlkā*, f. the torch of the law, ib. **Dhātu**, (also) a cause, Sukh. i. **Dhāman** (accord. to some in RV. also = *muhūrta*, 'an hour'). **Dhāyine**, n. du. two doors, folding doors (?), Kauś. **Dhārshṭya-bhūmi**, f. a prodigy of impudence, L. **Dhāvanī**, f. (also) a personification of the goddess of fortune, L. 1. **Dhi** (for 'abstracted' read 'formed'). **Dhi-shṭhita** (substituted for *adhi-shṭhita*, Bhag. xiii, 17). **Dhishṇya-viharaṇa**, n. the distribution of the Dhishṇya fires, Lāṭy.; Drāhy. **Dhīr** (see *ava-√dhīr*). **Dhī-saṃtati**, f. continued meditation, Prab. **Dhūmra-karṇa**, m. a donkey, L. **Dhūrṇi**, f. = *dhṛiti*, L. **Dhūrta-prahasana**, n. N. of a comedy by Jyotir-īśvara. **Dhṛitâtapatra**, mfn. holding the (royal) umbrella, Bcar. **Dhṛitisheṇa**, m. N. of a Jaina teacher, Inscr. **Dhṛishāṇa**, m. a god, L. **Dhṛishṭá** (read *dhṛ́ishṭa* and cf. Introd. p. xviii). **Dhotra**, n. a rope, cord, L. **Dhyānâspada**, n. place of meditation, Kum. **Dhrūṇā**, f. sound, L. **Dhvaja-praharaṇa**, m. N. of Vāyu, L. **Dhvasrá** (also, 'waterless, shallow,' applied to rivers). 1. **Dhvānta**, (also) mfn. sounding, roaring, MānGṛ. 2. **Dhvānta** (in comp.); *-maṇi*, m. a firefly, L.; *-saṃtati*, f. a dense or deep darkness, Rājat.

Nakshatra (in comp.); *-nāma*, mf(*ā*)n. having the name of a Nakshatra, ĀpGṛ.; *-nirdeśa*, m. astrology, Baudh. **Nagara-mosha**, m. the sacking of a town, Daś. **Nagôtsaṅga**, m. a mountain-top, Ragh. **Naṭiti**, f. dancing, L. **Naṭêśa-vijaya**, m. N. of a poem. **Naṭa-jānu**, f. a knock-kneed girl unfit for marriage, L. **Nadá** (accord. to some also, 'the penis'). **Nadanu**, m. a cloud, L. **Nadī** (in comp.); *-nāma*, mf(*ā*)n. having the name of a river, ĀpGṛ.; *-vapra*, m. n. a high river-bank, R.; *-sīsa*, a mass of foam, Kauś. **Nandayitnu**, m. joy, L.; a son, L.; mfn. joyful, ib. **Na-bhrāj** (read *nabh-rāj*). **Namatra**, n. an implement used by blacksmiths, L. **Namāka**, m. pl. a tribe of barbarians, L. **Nara** (in comp.); *-durācara*, mfn. difficult (for men) to perform, Bcar.; *-pati-jaya-sūra*, m. N. of a king, Inscr.; °*rêndra* (and *-rāja*), m. N. of Tathâgatas, Sukh. i. **Narāci** (accord. to some, 'personal possession'). **Nalinī-saṃvartikā**, f. the young leaf of a water-lily, Kād. 1. **Nava** (in comp.); *-nīta-piṇḍa*, a lump of fresh butter, JaimUp.; *-vrata*, mfn. one who has recently taken his vow, Bcar.; °*vôtthāna*, mfn. recently risen, Ragh. **Nava-ratna**, nine gems (for 'lapis lazuli' read 'cat's eye' [= *vaiḍūrya*], and for *go-medha* read *go-meda*, 'zircon' or 'jacinth;' the 9 gems are sacred to the five planets with the Sun and Moon, Rāhu and Ketu). **Nasaratha**, m. Nasrat Shāh (Sultān), Inscr. **Nasra**, m. a nostril, L. **Nāga** (in comp.); *-tithi*, N. of the fifth Tithi of the light half of the month Caitra, Inscr.; *-dantaka*, (also) n. a partic. posture in Yoga, L.; *-paṭṭana*, n. N. of a town, Inscr.; *-bhaṭa* or *-bhaṭṭa*, m. N. of various kings and chiefs, ib.; *-vikrānta-gamitā*, f. having a walk like the gait of an elephant (one of the 80 minor marks of a Buddha), Dharmas. 84; *-hrada*, (also) N. of a town, Inscr. **Nāti** (in comp.); *-rūḍha*, mfn. not quite conventional or commonly understood, Kāvyâd.; (°*ty*)-*āyata-vacanatā*, f. the not having too loud a voice (or 'not having a large mouth,' one of the 80 minor marks of a Buddha), Dharmas. 84. **Nāth**, (also) to harass, destroy, Dhātup. **Nānā** (in comp.); -°*vastha* (*nānâv*°), mfn. differently conditioned, Kāvyâd.; -°*śraya* (*nānâśr*°), mfn. wearing different forms (or, 'resorting to various means'), Bcar. xiii, 18. **Nāpita-karman**, n. a barber's work, HirP. **Nābhi-deśa**, m. the region of the navel, Hir. **Nāmadheya-grahaṇa**, n. the mentioning of the name (of partic. sacrificers), ĀpY. **Nāmana**, mfn. (fr. Caus. of √*nam*) bending down, humiliating, Kāvyâd.; depression under the horizon, Gol. **Nārāśaṇsa**, m. (also) a Soma vessel. **Nār-medha** (read *śaka-pūta*). **Nāsika**, N. of a sacred town in Western India on the Godāvarī (called Nāsik, because Lakshmaṇa here cut off the nose of Rāvaṇa's sister, the female Rākshasa Śūrpa-ṇakhā, q.v.), IW. 353. **Nāsikâropaṇa**, n. placing on the nose, Kathās. **Niḥ-shku** (√*sku*), to tear, rend (only ind. p. *-shkāvam*), TS. **Niḥ-shṭhu** (only aor. *-nir-ashṭhavisham*), to spit, GopBr.; Vait. **Niḥ-spṛihā**, f. a passionless girl unfit for marriage, L. **Ni-kāyin**, m. (read) a series of sacrifices having all the same name but different rewards, ĀpY. **Ni-gha**, m. (also) a pointed instrument for boring holes in jewels &c., L. **Ni-jihvika**, mfn. = (or w.r. for) *nir-j*°, tongueless, Hir. i, 15, 5. **Ni-tara**, mfn. deeply fixed (in the earth), standing firm, MānGṛ. **Nitya** (in comp.); *-bhaktika*, mfn. regularly fed by another, Āpast.; *-śaṅkin*, m. 'always afraid,' a deer, antelope, L.; *-śatru-ghna*, mfn. killing one's constant enemies (i.e. passions), R. **Nidrā-mudrā**, f. the seal of sleep, Mālatīm.; °*drita*, mfn. fallen asleep, Daś. **Nidhana** (in comp.); *-kṛita*, mfn. put to an end, destroyed, JaimUp.; *-vāda*, m. a word used as Nidhana, Lāṭy.; Drāhy. **Nindya-veśa**, mfn. (a convent) the entrance into which is faulty, Daś. **Nipuṇī**, m. or f. N. of an evil demon, Hir. **Nimi**, m. N. of a Tathâgata, Sukh. i. **Nimitta-grahaṇa**, n. taking aim, L. **Ni-√mih** (add, 'in RV. also pr. p. *-méghamāna*'). **Ni-√mṛi** (read, '√*mṛī*'). **Ni-mrúc** (in AV. iv, 3, 6, accord. to some, 'crusher, destroyer;' accord. to others, 'out of sight'). **Niyamôjjhita**, f. spontaneousness, L. **Nir** (in comp. for *nis*, see p. 539, col. 2); *-√aksh* (only Impv. *-akshṇuhi*), to castrate, emasculate, AV. iv, 22, 1; *-aṅgushṭha*, mfn. not touched with the thumb, Baudh.; *-upajīvitā*, f. want of subsistence, Dhūrtas.; *-granthi-siratā*, f. the having veins without knots (one of the 80 minor marks of a Buddha), Dharmas. 84; *-√dham*, (also) to drive away from (abl.), Baudh. iv, 1, 20; *-dhamana*, n. expulsion, ib. i, 18, 18; *-māta*, mfn. well instructed, Śil.; *-māra* (said to = *animan*), BaudhP.; *-mita-rāga*, mfn. painted, Kum. iv, 19; *-muda*, mfn. (prob.) joyless, Bcar. viii, 3; *-mumukshu*, mfn. longing for liberation, v, 39; *-√4. yu* (read 3. *yu*); *-vaṇśaka* (see *hrasva-nirv*°); *-vidhitsu*, mfn. wishing to perform, MBh.; *-vikshu*, mfn. (=°*kshat*), Kāvyâd. ii, 270; *-vṛita* with √*bhū*, P. *-bhavati*, to attain Nirvāṇa, Sukh. i; *-huta*, mfn. completely sacrificed, MBh. **Ni-√lī** (erase here perf. *ni-layāṃ cakre* and put it under *nilay* = *nir-√i*). **Ni-vāsita**, mfn. (√3. *vas*) put to death (v. l. for *ni-pātita*), Pañcat. **Niśā** (in comp.); *-maṇi*, m. a fire-fly, L.; °*śêta-vaktrā*, f. a moon-faced woman, Dhūrtan. **Niśītha-caṇḍa**, mfn. (prob.) sounding harsh by night, Bcar. v, 80. **Niś-cikramishā**, f. (fr. Des. of *nish-√kram*) desire to escape, Bcar.; °*shu*, mfn. wishing to escape or leave (esp. worldly life), ib. **Nish** (in comp. for *nis*); *-ṭâkvarī* (rather 'roaming, vagrant'); *-paridāha*, (also) free from pain, Sukh. i. **Ni-shaṅgathi**, (also) a quiver, Kāṭh. **Ni-shur** (√*sur*; aor. *ny-ashorīt*), Pāṇ. vii, 2, 2, Sch. **Nish-pesha** (in comp.); *-vat*, mfn. put down with a stamp, Bcar. i, 33. **Nish-shapin** (RV.). **Ni-hrāda-vat**, mfn. sounding, loud, Bcar. **Nī-kāśa**, mfn. like, similar (= *ni-kāśa*), Kāvyâd. ii, 57. **Nī-caistana**, mfn. low, MW. **Nīḍin**, m. 'having a nest,' a bird, L. **Nīti-sumâvali**, f. N. of wk. **Nīlâlaka-varūthin**, mfn. encircled by a mass of dark locks, BhP. **Nī-varaṇa**, n. an obstacle (= *ni-v*°, p. 559), Sukh. i. **Nṛi** (in comp.); *-pa-nāpita-putra-nyāya*, m. the rule of the king and the barber's son (i.e. the rule of innate fondness for one's own, like the barber, who when asked by the king to bring him a fine boy, brought his own ugly son), A.; *-pa-rshi*, m. a royal sage, Bcar.; *-viḍamba*, mfn. imitating or representing a man, BhP.; *-sūrya*, m. the sun of mankind, Bcar. **Netra-saṃkocana**, n. closing of the eyes, Sāh. **Nepāla-varsha** (or °*lâbda* or *Naipālikâbda* &c.), a year of the Newar era (which begins on the 20th October, A.D. 879). **Naîka** (in comp.); *-dharma*, m. pl. several properties, Kāvyâd.; *-mukha*, mfn. many-faced, Bcar. **Naidāghī**, f. N. of a summer month, HirP. **Naibhṛitya**, n. modesty, MW. **Nairañjanā**, f. N. of a river, Bcar. **Nôtseka,** mfn. not proud, humble, modest, Ragh. **Nau** (in comp.); *-vimāna,* m. n. an aerial car resembling a ship, Ragh.; *-sārathi,* m. a helmsman, pilot, Jātakam. **Nyagrodha-parimaṇḍalatā,** f. the having a waist like a fig-tree (one of the 32 signs of perfection), Dharmas. 83. **Ny-astaka** (accord. to others, 'clinging to the ground'). **Ny-ā-√dru,** P. *-dravati,* to run downwards, MaitrS. **Nyāya** (in comp.); *-viruddha* or *-virodhin,* mfn. inconsistent with logical argument, Kāvyâd.; *-virodha,* m. inconsistency with logical argument, ib. **Nyā-vicchāy** (see *√vich,* p. 959). **Nva** (see *sadā-nva,* p. 1139).

Paṅka-prakshâlana-nyāya, m. the rule of washing off the mud (instead of avoiding it, i. e. of curing a disease instead of preventing it), A. **Pacatra,** n. a cooking-vessel, boiler, L. **Pajrá** (accord. to some also = 'shining, bright' [cf. *pājas,* p. 614]; also 'clear, loud,' said of a voice; *-hoshin,* mfn. = 'called loudly'). **Pañca** (in comp. for *pañcan*); *-gūḍha,* m. a turtle, tortoise, L.; *-parva,* mfn. (also) fivefold, Bcar.; *-putra,* mfn. having five sons, JaimUp.; *-maṇḍala-namaskāra,* m. prostrate reverence, Sukh. i; *-varga,* m. also the square of five, VarBṛS.; *-śala* (accord. to some = *pañca-śara,* 'five-arrowed'); *-havis,* mfn. consisting of five oblations, HirP.; °*câcalâṅka,* mfn. distinguished by five hills, Bcar. **Paṭula,** mfn. eloquent, L. **Paṇya-siddhi,** f. prosperity in trade, Hir. **Patanu,** m. a falcon, L. 2. **Pati,** f. = *gati,* going, motion. **Páttra** (add, 'sometimes spelt *patra*'). **Patnyodana,** m. n. a wife's rice, Hir. **Pada** (in comp.); *-ccheda,* (also) separation of words at a particular place, cæsura, Kāvyâd.; *-valmīka,* m. elephantiasis, L.; *-saṃtāna,* m. combination of words, Kāvyâd.; *-saṃdhāna,* n. putting together words (writing them into one word), ib.; *-hita,* m. the substitute for a husband, BaudhP. **Padira,** m. a road, L. **Padma-sadman,** (also, prob.) the sun, Inscr. **Padyamātṛikā,** f. a poem consisting only of verses, L. **Payaḥ** (in comp. for *payas*); *-prasravin,* mfn. yielding milk, giving suck to, Rājat.; (°*yo*)*-garbha,* m. a cloud, L.; *-vikāra,* m. a preparation of milk, Baudh. **Para** (in comp.); *-kula,* m. an otter, L.; *-citta-jñāna,* n. knowledge of the thoughts of others, Sukh. i; *-vākya,* n. words referring to something else, ĀpY. **Parama** (in comp.); *-brahmaṇya,* mfn. most kind to Brāhmans, Inscr.; *-bhaṭṭāraka,* m. a paramount sovereign, ib.; °*mâhlādana,* mfn. most delightful or agreeable, Daś. **Parākrama-bāhu,** m. N. of various kings in Ceylon, Buddh. **Parākrānti,** f. marching forward (?), JaimUp. **Parāsedha** (read, 'fr. √2. *sidh*'). **Pari-kshata-vrata,** mfn. one who has broken his vow, Bcar. **Párigadhitā,** f. firmly embraced, RV. i, 126, 6. **Parighaṭṭanā,** f. (in dram.) striking (or tuning ?) the musical instruments, Bhar. **Pari-járbhurāṇa,** mfn. (fr. Intens. of *√bhur*) quivering, flickering, RV. i, 140, 10. **Pári-takmyā** (accord. to some also, 'going round or overtaking an adversary's chariot'). **Pari-tapta-mukha,** mfn. having the face overwhelmed with grief, Bcar. **Pari-nir-mita** (p. 596, col. 2, read '*-vaśa-vartin*' and 'cf. *para-nirmita-v°-v°*'). **Pari-pūrṇa-sattva,** mfn. having absolute perfection, Bcar. **Pari-√8. vas** (read 3. *vas*). **Parivesha-bandhin,** mfn. forming a circle, Ragh. **Pari-√vraj,** Desid. *-vivrajishati,* to wish to wander about as a mendicant, Bcar. **Pari-hāra,** (also) a ring, Inscr. **Pari-hārikā,** f. a kind of riddle, Kāvyâd. **Pari-hūta,** mfn. called all round (?), Hir. **Parī-tāna,** m. the act of stretching the cord round, HirP. **Parito-yoni,** mfn. a Sāman (having the verse RV. (beginning with *parito*) ix, 196, 1 for its Yoni, Drāhy. (Sch.). **Parī-dā** = *pari-√1. dā,* ĀpGṛ. **Paru,** (also) Bos Grunniens, L. **Paruḥ-śraṅsā,** m. the fracture of a joint, AV. **Pary-ādhānêjya,** n. du. kindling the sacred fire and offering oblations previously (to an elder brother), Baudh. **Párynkta** (accord. to Sāy. = *pari-yukta* = *viniyukta*). **Parvata** (in comp.); *-pūrusha,* m. the demon of the mountain (?), Hir.; *-saṃnirodha,* m. a m°-rift, MBh. **Palôdbhava,** n. fat, L. **Palpūlī** (see *vāsaḥ-p°,* p. 947). **Palli-gupta,** m. (with *lauhitya*), N. of a teacher, JaimUp. **Pavitra** (in comp.); *-kāma,* mfn. desirous of purification, Baudh.; °*trâtipavitra,* mfn. most pure or holy, ib. **Paśu** (in comp.); *-meḍhra,* m. N. of a disciple of Viśvāmitra, Anarghar.; *-vāṭi,* f. an enclosed place for cattle to graze, Kāty.; *-vṛiddhi-kara,* mf(*ī*)n. causing increase of cattle, Mn. vii, 212; *-saṃsthā* (see *saṃsthā,* p. 1121); *-saṃkhya,* mfn. counting over cattle, Pāṇ. iii, 2, 7, Sch.; *-sādhanaka,* mfn. (a sacrifice) performed by means of cattle, Śaṃk. **Pastyā** (accord. to some also, 'river or N. of a river'). **Pā,** add √5. *pā,* cl. 3. Ā. *pipīte,* to rise against, be hostile (see 2. *anû-√5. pā,* p. 41; 2. *ut-pā,* p. 181; *praty-ut-√5. pā,* p. 677). **Pāṅsu-sikatā,** f. pl. (prob.) dust and sand, Kauś. **Pāgala,** (also) m. a partic. mixed caste, L. **Pāja,** (also) boiled rice, L. **Pāṭala-romaka,** mfn. red-maned (as a horse), R. **Pāṭūra,** (also) the 14th day of a half-month, L. **Pāṇḍavâbhyudaya,** m. N. of a Chāyā-nāṭaka by Rāma-deva. **Pātāna-prastha,** N. of a village, Pat. on Pāṇ. iv, 2, 104, Vārtt. 26. **Pātu,** m. a protector, L.; N. of Brahmā, ib. **Pātra** (p. 612, col. 3, read 1. *pātra*) in comp.; *-caya,* m. (HirP.), *-cayana,* n. (BaudhP.) the act of putting the sacrificial utensils on the pyre by the side of the deceased; *-prôkshа,* m. the sprinkling of the vessels, ĀpGṛ. **Pāthi,** m. the sun, L. **Pāthikṛitī,** f. (scil. *ishṭi*) a sacrifice to Agni Pathi-kṛit, HirP. **Pāda** (in comp.); *-kula,* n. (prob.) a family of attendants, Inscr.; *-padmôpajīvin,* m. a dependent, feudatory, ib.; *-puṭī* or *-phalā,* f. a stirrup, L. **Pādavī** (see under *padá,* p. 583, cols. 2, 3). **Pāna-mantra,** m. N. of Mantras attached to the Sāvitrī verse when drinking the Madhuparka, Drāhy., Sch. **Pānīya** (p. 613, col. 1, read 1. *pānīya*). **Pārāvata,** m. (also) N. of a flute-player (teacher of Bāṇa), Hcar. **Pārthuśravasa,** m. N. of a demon, JaimUp. **Pārshṇa,** m. (with *śailāna*) N. of a teacher, ib. **Pāla,** (also) N. of a dynasty (that reigned over Gauḍa and the adjacent countries from about 800–1050 A. D.). **Pāśa,** (also) a partic. land-measure, Inscr. **Piṭa** and °**ṭaka,** a basket (add, 'from *√piṭ* in the sense of gathering together'). **Pindūsha,** m. ear-wax, L. **Piyaroja** or **Peroja** or **Piroja** (with *sāha, sāhi*), m. N. of a Sultān (Fīrōz Shāh), Inscr. **Piśaṅka,** (prob.) = *piśaṅga,* Hir. **Pishṭa-saṃyavana,** n. one of the sacrificial utensils, HirP. **Pishpala** (or *piḥpala,* Sch.) = *pippala,* Drāhy. **Pīnāha,** m. the cover of a well, L. **Pum-vishaya,** m. du. subject and object, Sarvad. **Puṇya** (in comp.); *-nāman,* (also) mfn. having a holy name, Baudh.; *-vaha,* mfn. causing felicity, MBh.; °*nyôkta,* mfn. called pure, ĀpGṛ. **Putra-lālasa,** mfn. devotedly fond of a son, Bcar. **Punar** (in comp.); *-ātta* (see *samāpta-pun°,* p. 1161); *-dahana,* n., *-dāha,* m. burning again, Baudh.; *-yuvan,* (also) the moon, L.; (°*naḥ*)*-sará* (accord. to some also, 'attacking' or 'defending'). **Purushânna,** n. food for men, Baudh.; °*shâhuti,* (also) the oblation of a man, HirP. **Pulinda-sena,** m. N. of a Kaliṅga king, Inscr. **Pushkara-vishṭara,** m. 'having a lotus-seat,' N. of Brahmā, BhP. **Pūrṇa-mukha,** (also) n. a full face, Hir. **Pūrṇi,** f. a flood, stream (= *pūra*), L. **Pūrva** (in comp.); *-kāma-kṛitvan,* (rather 'having fulfilled wishes in the past'); *-dhyāna,* n. the first (stage of) contemplation, Bcar.; *-vat,* n. add, 'reasoning from cause to effect' (one of the 3 kinds of *anumāna,* cf. *śesha-vat,* p. 1332). **Pṛithak-salila,** mfn. possessing separate oceans (?), JaimUp. **Pṛithivī** (in comp.); *-pratishṭha,* mfn. having the earth as a support, JaimUp.; (°*vy*) *-upara,* mfn. higher than the earth, ib. **Pṛiśnibāhu** (erase, 'm. &c.'). **Pṛishṭha** (in comp.); *-vaṅśa,* (also) the beam of the roof of a house, Hir.; *-śikhara,* m. n. the hump on the back, a protuberant back, high back (as of an elephant), ŚārṅgP.; *-homa,* m. a libation connected with the singing of the Pṛishṭha Sāman, Lāṭy.; Drāhy. **Peṭa,** °**ṭaka** (add, 'fr. *piṭa,* °*ṭaka,* q. v.'). **Péshṭra** (AV.). **Potha,** (also) a big ship, L. **Pautrya,** mfn. = 1. *pautra,* Baudh. **Paupika,** m. a baker, L. **Paulushita** (see *satya-yajña*). **Pnā** (read *ptā*). **Pyāna,** m. the sea, L.; the moon, L. **Pra-karaṇa,** (also) typical performance, ĀpY. **Pra-kīrṇa-vāc,** mfn. talking of different objects, Bcar. x, 6. **Pra-kriyā,** f. production, creation, origin, Sarvad.; form, procedure, method, mode, manner, MBh.; a ceremony, Hariv.; Kathās.; formality, Rājat.; prerogative, privilege, high rank or position, excellence, superiority, MBh.; Kathās. &c.; the insignia of high rank or dignity, Rājat.; Gīt.; characterization, Nyāyas.; a chapter, section (often at the end of titles of books); medical prescription, Bhpr.; *-kaumudī,* f., *-pradīpa,* m., *-bhūshaṇa,* n., *-mañjarī,* f., *-ratna,* n., *-saṃgraha,* m., *-sarvasva,* n. N. of gram. wks. **Pra-√kshṇu,** P. *-kshṇauti,* (also) to cut or dash to pieces, Baudh.

Pra-khyāta, mfn. 'told (by others),' i. e. borrowed, not original, Daśar. **Pra-gaṇikā,** f. a female favourite of a king, L. **Pra-gayaṇa,** n. (in dram.) a kind of dialogue, Bhar. **Pra-cátā** (accord. to others, 'away, off'). **Pra-cerita** (?), Bcar. viii, 52; 75. **Pra-cyāvanī,** f. (with *kumbhī*) a large jar used for sprinkling a pyre, BaudhP. **Pra-jānuka,** m. the body, L. **Prajā́-pati** (in comp.); *-cita* (*prajā́p°*), mfn. heaped up by Prajāpati, MaitrS.; *-mātra,* mfn. having the measure of Pr°, JaimUp. **Prajôtpatty-ānupūrvyeṇa,** ind. according to seniority, Hir. **Prajñātâgra,** mfn. 'having the top-end conspicuous,' thinner at the top, Lāṭy.; Drāhy. (Sch.). **Pra-ṇetri,** (also) a charioteer, Bcar. **Pra-taṅkam** (accord. to others, acc. of *pra-taṅka,* 'a hiding-place'). **Pra-tárdana** (MS.). **Pratāpa** (in comp.); *-vat,* (also) N. of a Tathāgata, Sukh. i; *-vilāsa,* m. N. of a Nāṭaka by Gaṅgā-dhara. **Prati-mantraṇa,** (also) magic, conjuring, ĀpY. **Prati-runshita,** mfn. covered with dust, Anarghar. **Prati-loḍita,** mfn. (fr. Caus. of *√luḍ*) disarranged, spoiled, MBh. **Prati-loma,** see under *prati,* p. 663, col. 1. **Prati-√1. vidh,** to honour, worship, RV. vii, 63, 5. **Prati-śaucam,** ind. at each purification, Baudh. **Prati-shiddha-vāma** (rather, 'intent upon forbidden things'). **Prati-saṃvādin** (?), m. an adversary (prob. for *prati-vādin*), Hir. i, 15, 6. **Prati-saṃkucita,** mfn. closed, Bcar. **Prati-satkṛita,** mfn. honoured in return, MBh. **Pratīcya-vāṭa,** the western district, Daś. **Pratīvartá** (accord. to others, 'attacking, assailing'). **Praty-aṅsa,** see under *praty,* p. 663. **Pratyak** (in comp.); *saṃstham,* ind. so as to end in the west, Drāhy.; (*g*)*-apavarga,* mfn. ending in the west, Hir. **Praty-ā-cchid** (*√chid*; only in Caus. ind. p. *-cchedya*), to break to pieces, Baudh. **Praty-ā-√sic,** to pour in again, Kauś. **Praty-eka,** see p. 664, col. 2. **Prathama** (in comp.); °*mâtka-rekhā,* f. the first and best of its kind, Caurap.; °*môttama,* mfn. (du.) the first and last, Hir.; °*môdbhava,* mfn. first produced, Baudh. **Prathita-prabodha,** mfn. of celebrated understanding, Ragh. **Pra-dhānâhuti,** f. a chief oblation, ĀpGṛ. **Pra-dhārya,** mfn. to be regarded as (nom.), Bcar. **Pra-patishṇu,** mfn. flying forth, JaimUp. **Pra-parīksh** (*√īksh*), to reflect further, Bcar. **Pra-baddha-vilūna,** mf(*ā* or *ī*)n. Pāṇ. iv, 1, 52, Vārtt. 4, Pat. **Prabhācandra,** m. N. of a teacher, Jain. **Pra-yata** (in comp.); *-vastra,* mfn. clothed in clean garments, Hir.; °*tâñjali,* mfn. closely joining the hands, Baudh. **Pra-lambâri,** m. N. of Bala-rāma, L. **Pra-√likh** (erase the meaning 'to scrape together'). **Pra-vacana-kartṛi,** m. a proclaimer, Hir. **Pravát** (accord. to some also, 'a river, stream;' °*vátvat,* 'swift, rapid'). **Pra-viśālaya,** Nom. P. °*yati,* to make longer, lengthen, Subh. **Pra-vishṭa-dīksha,** mfn. one who has undertaken religious observances, Bcar. **Praśna-moksha,** m. the settlement of a question, Kālid. **Pra-sam-√paś,** to consider thoroughly, MānŚr. **Pra-sava-dharman,** mfn. subject to the condition of birth, Bcar. **Prasiddhi-vidyā-viruddha,** mfn. contrary to common sense and science, Kpr. **Prasū-tāta,** m. du. father and mother, L. **Prasūna-vitati,** f. a nosegay, Cāṇ. **Prasṛita-yāvaka,** m. n. gruel prepared from a handful of barley, Baudh. **Pra-sekam,** (ind. p. of *pra-√sic*) pouring out, BaudhP. **Pra-√stigh,** to rise, MaitrS. **Pra-hasana-nāṭaka,** n. N. of a comedy ascribed to Kālidāsa. **Pra-hoshá** (accord. to some = *pra-ghoshá,* 'a hymn of praise;' °*shín,* 'accompanied by h°s of pr°'). **Prācīna-śāli,** m. N. of a teacher, JaimUp. **Prācya-vāṭa,** m. n. the eastern district, Daś. **Prāṇa** (in comp.); *-pratishṭhā,* f. the ceremony of putting life into an idol by the recitation of certain Mantras, consecration of an image or idol, RTL. 70; *-prada,* (in rhet.) 'vivifying,' Kpr.; *-saṃhita,* mfn. connected with breath, JaimUp.; °*nâgnihotra,* n. a sacrifice to the vital airs, Baudh. **Prātipāna,** mfn. (a jar) containing water to drink, MānGṛ. **Prāpaṇikā,** f. a bold girl unfit for marriage, L. **Prāptavyamartha** (read, 'a man obtains what he is destined to obtain'). **Priya** (in comp.); *-kalpa,* m. a ceremony intended to cause blessing to a friend, Lāṭy.; Drāhy.; *-viprayoga,* m. separation from friends, Bcar.; *-śaṅsā,* f. glad tidings, R.; °*yâbhidheya,* mfn. worthy to be called a lover, Bcar. **Prukshi,** (prob.) m. fire, L.; a well, L. **Prêkshârtham,** ind. for looking at, for show, Kāvyâd. **Prêta** (in comp.);

-patnī, f. a widow, Baudh.; *-saṃsthā* (see *saṃsthā*, p. 1121). **Prêshyântevâsin**, m. pl. servants and pupils, Hir. **Praishya-saṃyuta**, mfn. implying servitude, Mn. ii, 32. **Prôta-ghana** (read *-ghana*). **Protsāraṇa** (read *prôts°*). **Plugi** and **Plok**, ind. onomat. sounds used for a Nidhana, Drāhy.

Phala (in comp.); *-kriyā*, f. acting with an object in view, L.; *-pravritti*, f. id., Bcar.; *-stha*, mfn. useful (cf. *-saṃstha*), ib.; *°lêpsā*, f. desire of future reward, ib. **Phalī-karaṇa** (in comp.); *-miśra*, mfn. mixed with rice-chaff, ĀpGṛ.; *-mushṭi*, f. a handful of rice-chaff, ib. **Phāli**, m. or f. a leaf, L.

Baṭṭa (see *vaṭṭa*). **Bandhu** (in comp.); *-varman*, m. N. of a prince, Inscr.; *-śoka*, m. mourning for a relative, Bcar. **Bandhûraḥ** (pl. of *bandhur?*), AV. iii, 9, 3. **Babiru**, Babylon (cf. *Bāveru*). **Babhrū-mūtra**, n. urine of a red cow, ĀpGṛ. **Bamba-viśvayás** (MaitrS.). **Balâbhijña**, m. N. of a Tathāgata, Sukh. i. **Bali** (in comp.); *-vāhana*, mfn. carrying tribute, JaimUp.; *-śesha*, m. the remains of an oblation, Mn. iii, 91; *-hṛit*, (also) offering oblations, MānGṛ. **Bava**, N. of a Karaṇa (half a Tithi), Inscr. **Bahiḥ** &c. (in comp. for *bahis*); *-prayāṇa*, n. going outside, Bcar.; *-śauca*, n. external purification, Baudh.; (*°hir*)*-mālā*, f. an outer, i. e. visible garland, Baudh.; *-vaiśravaṇa*, m. N. of a partic. divinity, MānGṛ. **Bahu** (in comp.); *-kshīra-duh*, mfn. yielding much milk, Bcar.; *-devatā*, f. an offering for many deities, ĀpY.; *-pratigrāhya*, mfn. one who is able to give presents to many, Baudh.; *-vidhâkāra*, mfn. multiform, manifold, R.; *-vista* or *-vaistika*, mfn. weighing many Vistas, L.; *-velam*, mfn. oftentimes, Pañcad.; *-saṃsthita*, mfn. much frequented, Mn. viii, 371; *-sūvarī* (read *-sûvarī*); *°hûpamā*, f. a kind of comparison (in which many Upamānas are contained), Kāvyâd. **Bālin**, see *vālin*. **Bāveru** = *Babiru*, Babylon, MW. **Bāshpa** (in comp.); *-grathita*, mfn. choked by tears, Bcar.; *-hatêkshaṇa*, mfn. blinded by tears, ib. **Bāsteya**, see *vāsteya*. **Bāhuleya**, (also) a bull, Inscr. **Bila-vat**, n. a hollow vessel, Hir. (Sch.). **Bisa** (in comp.); *-guṇa*, mfn. (a bow) strung with a lotus fibre, Kum.; *-lāvam*, ind. (with √*lū*) so as to cut off like a lotus fibre, Bālar. **Bīja** (in comp.); *-dharman*, mfn. having the condition of a seed, Bcar.; *°jâṅkura-nyāya*, m. the rule of seed and sprout (i. e. of the relation of both cause and effect), A. **Bīṭaka** (see *vīṭaka*). **Buddha-bhadra**, m. N. of a Buddhist mendicant, Inscr. **Bṛihac-chiras** (for *-śiras*), m. a kind of fish, Baudh. **Bodhi-parinishpatti**, f. perfect knowledge, Sukh. i. **Brahma** (in comp. for *brahman*); *-ghosha*, m. N. of a Tathāgata, Sukh. i; *-hṛidaya*, (also) N. of a partic. Anuvāka (TĀr. x, 28), Baudh.; *°mâsandī*, f. the throne of Brahman, JaimUp. **Brahmôttara**, n. (also, prob.) the sanctuary of a temple, Inscr. **Brāhmaṇa** (in comp.); *-bhakta*, mfn. apportioned to Brāhmans, JaimUp.; *-yoni*, f. a Brāhman's form of existence, ChUp.; *-varṇin*, mfn. belonging to the caste of Br°s, Pāṇ. v, 2, 132, Sch.; *-sambhāshu*, mfn. speaking with a Br°, Hir.; *°ṇâvêksha*, mfn. based on the Brāhmaṇas, ĀpGṛ. **Bruḍ**, **brūs** (see *vruḍ*, *vrūs*).

Bhaksha (in comp.); *-cchandas*, n. a metre used while eating the sacrificial food, Lāṭy.; Drāhy.; *-vikāra*, m. pl. various dishes of food, MBh. **Bhagadatta**, m. N. of a mythical king, Inscr. **Bhañj** (√2. *bhañj*, cl. 10. P. *bhañjayati*), 'to speak' or 'to shine,' Dhātup. xxxiii, 86. **Bhaṭila**, m. a servant, L.; a dog, L. **Bhandra**, n. = *bhadra*, L. **Bharaṇḍakeshṇa** (of unknown meaning), JaimUp. i, 54, 2. **Bharata** (in comp.); *-ṭīkā*, f. N. of Abhinava-gupta's Comm. on Bharata's Nāṭya-śāstra; *-samuccaya*, m. (a partic. rhet. figure consisting of an) accumulation of dramatic terms, Kshem.; *°târjuna-nāṭaka*, n. N. of a drama by Hasti-malla-sena. **Bharjū**, a preparation of barley, L. **Bhartṛi-sûkta**, n. N. of partic. Mantras (in the TĀr.). **Bhaveṇu**, mfn. = *bhavya*, L. **Bhānu-bhṛit**, m. the sun, Bcar. **Bhāra-voḍhṛi**, m. a bearer of burdens, carrier, MBh. **Bhā-vat**, mfn. possessing light, JaimUp. **Bhāvayú** (others, 'ruttish, wanton'). **Bhāskara** (in comp.); *-dina*, n. Sunday, Inscr.; *-putra-vāsara*, m. Saturday, ib. **Bhikshôpabhogin**, mfn. living on alms, Bcar. **Bhidatha**, m. an arrow, L. **Bhidā-kara**, mfn. causing a distinction, Kāvyâd. **Bhuktôcchishṭa**, mfn. left after being used, Bcar. **Bhujaṃgadīrgha**, mfn. as long as a snake, ib. **Bhujâṅsa-deśa**, m. the upper end of the arm, Bcar. 2. **Bhujyú** (p. 759, col. 2, read 1. *bhujyú*). **Bhū**, f. (also) a partic. land-measure, Inscr.; *-s-tṛiṇa*, m. Andropogon Schoenanthus, Mn.; Suśr.; *-sthita*, mfn. (= *-stha*), Baudh. **Bhūta-han**, mfn. creature-slaying, Baudh. **Bhūmi**, f. (also) = *bhū* (above); *-ga*, mfn. (= *-gata*), Baudh.; *-cchidra*, land unfit for cultivation, Inscr.; *-tanaya*, Tuesday, Cat. **Bhṛishṭī**, f. (prob.) raised ground near a tank for planting Piper Betel upon, Inscr. **Bherī-śaṅkha-vāda**, mfn. sounding the drum and the conch-shell, MBh. **Bhaikshāka**, n. mendicancy, Bcar. **Bhaikshârthin**, mfn. seeking for alms, Baudh.; *°kshâhāra*, mfn. living on alms, ib. **Bhrātṛi-saṃghāta-vat**, mfn. keeping together with brothers, Kām. **Bhrū** (in comp.); *-vañcita*, n. pl. stolen glances (others *-kuñcita*), Bcar.; *-vijṛimbha*, m., *°bhaṇa*, n. the bending or knitting of the brows, BhP.

4. **Ma** (add, 'connected with √3. *mā*'). **Magadhâjira**, n. the court of Magadha, Bcar. **Mañju-nandin**, m. N. of a poet, Inscr. **Mañjulā**, f. = *mañju-bhāshiṇī*, L. **Maṇi-tsaru**, mfn. jewel-handled, Bcar. **Maṇḍana-deva**, m. N. of a prince, Inscr. **Maṇḍayitnu**, m. one who adorns, L.; a lover, L. **Maṇḍalâgāra**, n. a round apartment, Hir. **Mati-saciva**, m. a wise counsellor, Bcar. **Madana-viklava**, mfn. bewildered by passion, Bcar. **Madguśa**, m. an ichneumon, L. **Madhu** (in comp.); *-dhāna*, n. a vessel for holding honey, JaimUp.; *-saṃślishṭa*, mfn. connected with h°, MaitrS.; *°dhv-ālopa*, m. a bite of honey, JaimUp. **Madhurântaka**, m. N. of various kings, Inscr. **Madhyama** (in comp.); *-pada-lopin* &c. (read 'member' for 'number'); *-sva-bhāva*, mfn. indifferent, neutral, Bcar. **Manaḥ** &c. (in comp. for *manas*); *-kshobha-kara*, mfn. mind-disturbing, ib.; *-śama*, m. tranquillity of mind, ib.; *-śalya*, mfn. heart-piercing, Kum. ii, 22; *-svāsthya*, n. health of mind, Bcar. **Manushya** (in comp.); *-kāya*, mfn. having a human body, Bcar.; *-rāj*, m. a king of men, MaitrS.; *°shyâmanushya*, m. pl. men and not men, Sukh. i. **Mano** (in comp. for *manas* above); *-jvara*, m. heart-ache, Bcar.; *-netra*, mfn. having the mind as a guide, JaimUp.; *-ratha* (accord. to some orig. Prākṛit for *mano 'rtha*, 'heart-matter'); *-rūpa*, n. character of mind, JaimUp. **Mantra** (in comp.); *-baddha*, mfn. bound by spells, Bcar.; *-samnāma*, m. altering the Mantras, ĀpGṛ. **Manthana-yantraka**, n. an implement for kindling fire, Kāty. **Manda-rogin**, mfn. rarely ill, MBh. **Manv-ādi**, N. of partic. Tithis (which are anniversaries of the 14 Manus), Inscr. **Mámat** (repeated, rather = 'no sooner–than'). **Mayūra-kiśora**, m. a young peacock, Vās. **Maraṇâdhvan**, m. the path of death, Bcar. **Marīci**, f. a ray, JaimUp. **Maruta**, (prob.) the god of war, MānGṛ. ii, 15, 6. **Malinī-kara**, mfn. defiling, Bcar. **Mahat-tarā**, f. (in dram.) a woman superintending the gynaeceum, Bhar. **Mahā** (in comp.); *-dharma-dundubhi*, m., *-dharma-dhvaja*, m. N. of Tathāgatas, Sukh. i; *-praṇidhāna*, n. the great prayer, ib.; *-prabha*, m., *-meru*, m., *-ratna-ketu*, m. N. of Tathāgatas, Sukh. ii; *-buddha-rūpa*, n. a great image of Gautama Buddha, Inscr.; *-°bhra-ghosha* (*mahâbhr°*), mfn. sounding deep like thunder, Bcar.; *-sādhanika*, m. (an official title), Inscr.; *-sudarśa*, m. N. of a king, Bcar.; *°hôpêkshā*, f. great forgiveness, Sukh. i; *°hôrmimat*, mfn. forming great waves, Bcar. 4. **Mā** (for 751 read 771). **Mâghona**, (also) mfn. belonging to or ruled by Indra, RV. vi, 43, 4. **Mātrâpacāra**, m. wanting of the measure, ĀpY. **Mādhyā-varsha**, mfn. celebrated in the middle of the rainy reason, Hir. 2. **Māna** (accord. to some in RV. i, 39, 1 = 'light, sheen'). **Mānastokīya**, a partic. text (beginning with *mā nas toke*). **Mānâbharaṇa**, m. N. of a king, Inscr. **Mānusha-nikāśana**, mfn. human-like, JaimUp. **Māra-varman**, m. N. of a king, Inscr. **Mārga-pranashṭa**, mfn. one who has lost his way, Bcar. **Mārjāra-vaktra**, mfn. cat-faced, ib. **Mālava**, (also) N. of an era identical with the Vikrama era (see *Vikramâditya*), Inscr. **Mālā-yamaka**, n. a Yamaka in which the whole stanza consists of one consonant combined with all vowels, Bhar. **Māsha-vāpa** and **°pin**, mfn., Pāṇ. viii, 4, 11, Sch. **Māsârdha-māsa**, m. pl. months and fortnights, Hir. **Miñjā** (= *majjan*); *°jâstha* or *°jâsthi*, n. the marrow of a bone, Gaṇar. **Mitra-bhūti**, m. N. of a teacher, JaimUp. **Mithū-kṛit** (accord. to others, 'imitated, feigned, sham'). **Mithyā** (in comp.); *-tva-niyata*, mfn. bent on falsehood, Sukh. i; *-dūta*, m. a false or lying messenger, Pañcat. **Miśra** (in comp.); *-bhāṇa*, m. a kind of Bhāṇa (q. v.), Cat.; *-vishkambhaka* (= *saṃkīrṇa-v°*, p. 1126), Bālar. **Mihira-lakshmī**, f. N. of a queen of Ravi-sheṇa, Inscr. **Mīnâkshī**, f. 'fish-eyed,' N. of a goddess worshipped at Madurā (commonly called Mīnācī), Inscr.; RTL. 228; 442. **Mukha** (in comp.); *-padma*, n. a lotus-face, Bcar.; *-vāta*, m. 'mouth-wind,' breath, Hir.; *°khenâdâyin*, m. pl. N. of a partic. class of self-mortifying devotees, Baudh. **Muni-śāvaka**, m. a young Brāhman, Cat. **Mushma**, m. a mouse, L. **Muhur-dīkshin**, mfn. consecrating repeatedly, JaimUp. **Mūrti-saṃcara**, mfn. going about with a body, embodied, incarnate, Uttarar. **Mṛigâjira**, n. an arena of deer, Bcar. **Mṛita**, 'begging for food' (for L. read Mn. iv, 5); *-saṃjīvaka*, mfn. reviving the dead, BhP. **Mṛityu** (in comp.); *-śrama*, m. the pain of death, Bcar.; *-sūkta*, n. N. of partic. Mantras in the TĀr. **Megha-kālī**, f. N. of a female demon, Bcar. **Meru** (in comp.); *-guru*, mfn. firm as Mount Meru, ib.; *-dhvaja*, m., *-pradīpa*, m., *-prabhāsa*, m. N. of Tathāgatas, Sukh. ii. **Moksha** (in comp.); *-kāma*, mfn. (= *-kāṅkshin*), Bcar.; *-dvish*, m. 'enemy of final beatitude,' N. of Kāma-deva, ib. **Mogha-bāshpa**, mfn. shedding vain tears, ib. **Moha** (in comp.); *-kara*, mfn. causing bewilderment, infatuating, ib.; *-kārin*, (also) bewildering, confounding, puzzling, Kāvyâd. iii, 99; *-citta*, n. perplexity of mind (?), Bcar. xiii, 49 (some read *moha-citram*, others *citta-moham*). **Maujadīna**, m. N. of a Sultān, Inscr.

Yajunā, f. anything fit for a sacrifice, L. **Yajña** (in comp.); *-lopa*, m. disturbance of a sacrifice, HirP.; *-saṃstara* (see *saṃst°*, p. 1121); *-samṛiddhi*, f. success of a s°, R. **Yathā** (in comp.); *-gavam*, ind. as has been done with the cows, BaudhP.; *-gīta*, mfn. as sung, JaimUp.; *-°dhyāyam* (*yathâdh°*), ind. according to the chapter, i. e. in the same ch°, Hir.; *-puroḍāśam*, ind. like a Puroḍāśa, ib.; *-bālam*, ind. accord. to youth, so that the youngest begins, Baudh.; *-bhūta-pratijñā*, f. the true promise, Sukh. i; *-°śraya* (*yathâśr°*), mfn. as fit or appropriate, Bcar. viii, 15; *-saṃvādam*, ind. as appointed or stipulated, KātyŚr.; *-sushṭhu*, ind. so as to make thoroughly smooth, BaudhP.; *°thôpapadam*, ind. as it happens, Hir. **Yad-vidvas**, mfn. knowing which, JaimUp. **Yavâcāma**, m. barley-gruel, Baudh. **Yaśaḥ** &c. (in comp. for *yaśas*); *-prabha* and *-prabhāva*, m. N. of Tathāgatas, Sukh. ii; (*°śo*)*-dharman* and *-dhavala*, m. N. of kings, Inscr.; (*°śo*)*-viśāla*, mfn. far-famed, Bcar. **Yahvā**, f. understanding, intelligence (= *buddhi*), L. **Yātrā-saṃdhāna**, n. marching away after making peace (cf. *saṃdhāya-gamana*, p. 1144), MBh. xii, 2662. **Yāvatima**, mfn. (v. l. for *yāvatitha*), Drāhy., Sch. **Yāvad** (for *yāvat*); *-āvāsa*, mfn. having as many abodes (correl. to *tāvad-āv°*), JaimUp.; *-grahaṇam*, ind. (also) until understanding, Hir.; as long as possible, BaudhP. **Yuga** (in comp.); *-cchidra*, n. a hole in a yoke, ĀpGṛ.; *-pradhāna*, m. N. of a patriarch, Jain.; *-mātra-darśin* (= *-m°-dṛiś*), Bcar. **Yuddha-śauṭīratā**, f. heroism in battle, R. **Yūropa-khaṇḍa**, the continent of Europe, Aryav. **Yoni** (in comp.); *-shad*, mfn. dwelling in the womb, Hir.; *-saṃkalusha* (see *saṃk°*, p. 1125); (*°ny*)*-ajāta*, mfn. not born from a womb, Bcar. i, 30.

Ráṇhi (accord. to some also, 'glory, might, power &c.'). **Raksho-rāja**, m. the king of demons, Hir. **Rajaḥ** &c. (for *rajas*); *-snāta*, mfn. immersed in clouds or gloom, Bcar.; (*°jo*)*-viśāla*, mfn. full of passion, Sāṃkhyak. **Rají** (accord. to some also, 'straight, erect, upright'). **Rajjv-ambara**, mfn. wearing rope-garments, Bcar. **Raṇam-gaha**, m. N. of a Tathāgata, Sukh. i. **Ratna** (in comp.); *-caura*, m. a stealer of jewels, Bcar.; *-deva*, m. N. of a prince, Inscr.; *-parvata*, m. a jewel-mountain, Sukh. i; *-mañjarī*, f. N. of a Sanskṛit translation of the Karpūra-mañjarī; *-śrī* and *°tnâbhibhāsa*, m. N. of Tathāgatas, Sukh. i. **Ratha** (in comp.); *-praṇetṛi*, m. a charioteer, Bcar.; *-sâhvayā*, f. a (female) ruddy goose, ib.; *°thâshṭamī*, f. the 8th lunar day in the bright half of the month Māgha, Inscr. **Rathar-ví**, mfn. (prob.) taking the form of a wheel (said of a serpent), AV. x, 4, 5. **Ramatha**, m. joy, delight, L. **Rampā**, f. the implement of a worker in leather, L. **Ravi** (in comp.); *-ja-putra-dina*, n. Saturday, Inscr.; *-vardhana-*

gaṇi, m. N. of an author, Jain.; *-sheṇa*, m. N. of a chief (cf. *mihira-lakshmī*), Inscr. **Raśmi-dhāra**, m. a charioteer, Bcar. **Rasâvaha**, mfn. causing enjoyment, delighting, Kāvyâd. **Rahasya-vid**, mfn. one who knows (the texts called) Rahasya, Baudh. **Rāka**, m. a quiver, L.; wealth, money, ib.; the sun, ib. **Rāga-dosha**, (prob.) = *rāga-dvesha*, Bcar. **Rāja** (in comp. for *rājan*); *-praśasti-mahākāvya*, n. N. of a poem, Inscr.; *-ṛddhi*, f. (for *-ṛiddhi*) royal pomp, Bcar.; *-vatsa*, m. (= *-putra*), ib.; *-varman* (Kāvyâd.), *-siṃha-pāṇḍya* (Inscr.), m. N. of kings. **Rājanīya-prabha**, m. = *amitâbha*, Sukh. i. **Rāti-kula**, n. a house (whose inhabitants are) disposed to give (alms), Hir. **Rāmâdhipati**, m. N. of a king, Inscr. **Rāśi**, (also) a division of beings, Sukh. i. **Rāshṭrôḍa**, m. N. of a family (= *rāshṭra-kūṭa*), Inscr. **Rāhu** (in comp.); *-sapatna-vaktra*, mfn. moon-faced, Bcar.; °*hûpasarga*, m. 'contact of Rāhu,' an eclipse, ib. **Ripu-haṇa**, mfn. killing enemies, MBh. **Rukma-pattra**, mfn. decorated with gold-leaf, Bcar. **Rukmala**, n. gold, L. **Rudrâmbā**, f. N. of a princess, Pratāp., Sch. **Rudrâikādaśikā**, f. = °*daśinī*, Baudh. **Rūḍha-mūla**, mfn. one who has taken root, Bcar. **Repha-lakārôpânta**, mfn. having a name whose last letter but one is *r* or *l*, ĀpGṛ.

Lakshmaṇa-sena, m. a king of the Sena dynasty of Eastern India (founder of an era, beginning on October 7, A.D. 1119). **Lamba** (in comp.); *-saṭa*, mfn. (a horse) with flying mane, Bcar.; *-sraj*, mfn. wreaths dangling down, ib. **Lalaha**, mfn. sportive, dallying, L. **Lalita-vigraha-rāja**, N. of a Nāṭaka. **Lavaṇôdaka-miśra**, mfn. mixed with salt water, Hir. **Lashmi-deva**, m. N. of a chief (= *lakshmī-d*°), Inscr. **Lāṅgalêsha**, f. the pole of a plough, Lāṭy.; Drāhy. **Lājâhuti**, f. a burnt-oblation of parched grain, Baudh. **Lāsaka-yuvan**, m. a young dancer, L. **Linduma**, m. a partic. fragrant substance, L. **Loka** (in comp.); *-virodhin*, mfn. (= *-viruddha*), Kāvyâd.; *-sâkshi* (= *-sâkshin*), R.; *-sīmânurodhin*, mfn. conforming to ordinary limits, moderate, Kāvyâd.; °*kânanda*, (also) N. of a Buddhist drama; °*kêndra*, m. N. of a Tathāgata, Sukh. i. **Loshṭa-citi**, f. = *śmaśāna-karaṇa*, BaudhP. **Loha** (in comp.); *-cumbaka-nyāya*, m. the rule of iron and magnet (i.e. of a very close affinity between two things), A.; °*hârya*, m. N. of a Jaina teacher, Inscr. **Lohita** (in comp.); *-bindu-citra*, mfn. covered with red spots, Bcar.; *-stoka*, m. a drop of blood, JaimUp.

Vaktra-pāṇi, (in dram.) preparation of mouth and hands (a kind of introductory ceremony), Bhar. **Vaṅka**, mfn. (for *vakra*) crooked, deceitful, Bcar. xi, 46. **Vaṅkú** (accord. to some also, 'false,' 'deceitful'). **Vacatra**, n. speech, L. **Vajra** (in comp.); *-dhvani*, m. the crash of a thunderbolt, Bcar.; *-saṃsparśa*, mfn. as hard as adamant, MBh. **Vati**, = *vadi*, Inscr. **Vatsa-bhaṭṭi**, m. N. of a poet, Inscr. **Vadhū-yāna**, n. a woman's vehicle, Mṛicch. **Vadhūyú** (accord. to some also, 'a paramour'). **1. Vana** (in comp.); *-cchandatā*, f. longing for the forest, Bcar.; *-pratishṭha*, mfn. abiding in a f°, ib.; *-śakuni*, m. a f°-bird, ib.; *-saṃśraya*, m. resort to the forest, ib. **Vanitā-sakha**, mfn. united with a wife, Kum. i, 10. **Vandin** (p. 919, col. 2, read, 'praising, honouring,' = 1. *bandin*, 'a praiser,' 'bard'). **Vapatra**, m. a field, L. **Vapur-guṇa**, m. personal beauty, ib. **Vamuka**, m. a cloud, L. **Vayaḥ** (in comp. for *vayas*); *-prakarsha*, m. prolongation of life, ib.; *-sukha*, n. the pleasures of youth, ib.; (°*yo*) *-'nurūpa*, mfn. suitable to one's age, ib. **Vara-sampad**, f. the accomplishments of a bridegroom, ĀpGṛ. **Varīya** (read, *vārīya*, p. 943, col. 3). **Varuṇa-pariyatana**, mfn. enclosed by Varuṇa, JaimUp. **Varṇa** (in comp.); *-saṃvarga*, m. (prob. = *-saṃsarga*), Vas.; °*nânupūrveṇa*, ind. according to the order of caste, ĀpGṛ. **Varsha-pavitra**, mfn. having the rain as means of purification, JaimUp. **Varshimán** (VS.). **Vallūra**, (also) m. N. of a clan of Brāhmans, Inscr. **Vastī**, f. an act in the practice of Yoga (see *shaṭ-karman*, p. 1108). **Vahni** (in comp.); *-dhūma-nyāya*, m. the rule of fire and smoke (i.e. of invariable concomitance), A.; *-stambha*, m. the (magical) quenching of fire. **Vāk** (in comp. for *vāc*); *-pati-vāra*, m. Thursday, Cat. **Vākya-saṃcāra**, m. way or manner of speaking, MBh. **Vācam-niyama**, mfn. silent, Hir. **1. Vāji** (in comp.); *-bhṛit*, m. a groom, Bcar.; *-ratna*, m. N. of a teacher, Hir. **Vāta** (in comp.); *-cala*, mfn. fluttering in the wind, Bcar.; *-yāna*, n. (= *vātâyana*), ib. iii, 20; °*tâjira*, mfn. swift as wind, Hir.; °*têshu*, mfn. wind-arrowed, ib. **Vānara** (accord. to some for *vana-nara*). **Vārī**, f. water, Kāṭh. **Vāsa-vṛiksha**, m. a roosting tree, Bcar. **Vijaya-bāhu**, m. N. of a king, Buddh. **Vi-jāman** (read, 'corresponding to each other,' i.e. 'being in pairs,' 'symmetrical'). **Vidátha** (accord. to some for *vidhátha* fr. √*vidh*, and orig. = 'homage, worship, sacrifice;' accord. to others also = 'house, household, &c.'). **Vi-devam**, ind. unerotically (cf. *su-deva*), ŚBr. **Vidhya**, mfn. (fr. √*vyadh*) to be pierced or perforated, MW. **Vi-nivṛitti**, (also) cessation of work, inactivity, Bcar. **Vindhya-vāsaka** or °**sin**, m. N. of a Sāṃkhya teacher. **Vipas**, n. inspiration (see *vipaś-ci* &c., p. 972, col. 3). **Vi-prasanna**, mfn. tranquil, calm, Bcar. **Vibhā-vāyu**, m. morning-wind, Ragh. **Vi-mṛigvan**, mf(*arī*)n. pure, AV. **Viyūshka**, mfn. being without gravy, HirP. **Vi-rajaḥ-prabha**, m. N. of a Tathāgata, Sukh. i. **Vi-luptí**, f. miscarrying (conj. for *vi-liptī*), AV. xii, 4, 41. **Vivatsā**, f. (fr. Desid. of √5. *vas*) desire of dwelling, Bcar. **Vi-vi-√han** (only in pr. p. *-ghnat*), to scatter, disperse, Hir. **Viśpálā** (accord. to some, 'N. of a mare'). **Viśva** (in comp.); *-varman*, m. N. of a prince, Inscr.; °*śvâbhirakshaṇa*, mfn. all-defending, JaimUp. **Vi-shṭāva**, m. a subdivision of the periods of a stoma, Lāṭy. **Vi-shṭimin**, mfn. (√*stīm*) making or becoming wet, VS. **Vi-sraṇsikā**, f. N. of a plant, BaudhP. **Vīṇā-vat**, mfn. = *pra-vīṇa*, Drāhy., Sch. **Vīra** (in comp.); *-peśas*, (°*rá-*; accord. to some, 'consisting in male children'); *-ravi-varman* and *-rāja-varman*, m. N. of various kings, Inscr.; *-līla*, mfn. playing at being a hero, Bcar.; *-sena*, (also) N. of a poet (400 A.D.), Inscr. **Vīryâ-sammita**, mfn. corresponding to strength, MS. **Vṛiksha** (in comp.); *-nāma*, mfn. having the name of a tree, ĀpGṛ.; *-mūlika* (also Baudh. ii, 18, 24). **Vṛiṅga**, m. a paramour, L. **Vṛitti-vallabha**, N. of a Nāṭaka. **Vṛitra-hátha** (RV.). **Vṛish**, to rain, add, [cf. Gaelic *pas*, a shower]. **Vṛishṭi-tāḍita**, mfn. beaten by rain, Bcar. **Vetasvin**, mfn. = °*vat*, Hir. **Veda** (in comp.); *-vikraya*, mfn. = °*yin*, Baudh.; *-saṃnyāsin*, mfn. abandoning the Veda, ib. **Vedispṛiś**, mfn. touching the Vedi, KātyŚr. **Vedyā́** (accord. to some also, 'art, dexterity &c.'). **Vaikhānasa-śāstra**, n. the institutes of Vaikhānasa, Baudh. **Vaiṇavata** (for 'a bow' read 'skill,' and cf. *vīṇā-vat* above), Lāṭy.; Drāhy. (Sch.). **Vaipaścita** (with *dārḍha-jayanti*), m. N. of a teacher, JaimUp. **Vaiśvantara**, N. of a hermitage, Bcar. **Vy-atishikta**, mfn. separated, ĀpY. **Vy-avadāra-prâpaṇa**, n. the attainment of full age, Baudh. **Vy-ava-√stṛi**, to spread out below, ĀpGṛ. **Vy-avahārya** (p. 1034, col. 3, read 'see *a-vyav*°'). **Vy-ākula-veshṭana**, mfn. having the hair-covering in confusion, Bcar. **Vy-ādhi-dharmin**, mfn. subject or liable to pain, ib. **Vy-ā-√bhram**, to be dispersed in different directions, BaudhP. **Vyeman**, n. a garment, L. **Vyomânta**, 1000 billions, JaimUp. **Vrá** (accord. to some, 'that which is confined'). **Vrata** (in comp.); *-cārya*, n. performance of vows, JaimUp.; °*tâvritti*, f. repetition of a vow, Baudh.; °*tôpêta*, mfn. one who has undertaken a religious vow, ib. **Vrā́** (accord. to some also, 'a woman, esp. a wanton or lustful w°'). **Vrīhi-śarāva**, n. a shallow cup of rice, Hir.

Śakuni-mitra, m. N. of a teacher, JaimUp. **Śakṛid** (in comp. for *śakṛit*); *-dhata*, a dung-heap, Hir.; *-rasa*, m. liquid cow-dung, Baudh.; *-rīti*, f. a heap of excrement, ĀpGṛ. **Śakti-vishaya**, m. the range of possibility (*e*, 'if possible'), ib. **Śaṅku-karṇa**, add, (becomes *śaṅkū-karṇa* when it means 'having the ear marked with a *śaṅku* or like a *ś*°, Pāṇ. vi, 2, 112; vi, 3–115). **Śacī-puram-dara**, m. du. Śacī and Indra, Ragh. **Śabdôpātta**, mfn. stated explicitly, Kāvyâd. **Śama** (in comp.); *-vihāra*, mfn. living a tranquil life, Bcar.; °*mâśraya*, m. the having recourse to a tr° life, ib.; °*mêpsu*, mfn. desirous of a tr° life, ib. **Śarat-payoda**, m. an autumnal cloud, ib. **Śarmaṇya-deśa**, m. the country of Germany (°*śīya*, mfn. born in G°), Āryav. **Śarma-varūtha**, n. du. guard and protection, Hir. **Śarmishṭhā-vijaya**, m. N. of a Nāṭaka. **Śalālu-grapsa** (Hir.) or **-glapsa** (ĀpGṛ.), m. = *udumbara-phala-stabaka* (Sch.). **Śaśa** (in comp.); *-dhara*, m. (with *vāra*) Monday, Inscr.; °*śâṅkâtmaja-vāsara*, m. Wednesday, ib. **Śaśi** (in comp.); *-vāsara*, m. Monday, ib. **Śāka-jañjabha**, m. du. Śāka and Jañjabha (two divine beings), Hir. **Śāṇḍikera**, m. N. of a demon, ib. **Śānti** (in comp.); *-mat*, mfn. tranquil, calm, JaimUp.; *-sheṇa* (for *-sena*), m. N. of a Jaina scholar, Inscr. **Śārada-tilaka**, N. of a Bhāṇa by Śaṃkara. **Śāhā-jyāhām**, m. Shāh Jahān (emperor), Inscr. **Śikhara-svāminī**, f. N. of a queen, ib. **Śikhin** (AV.). **Śibinta**, m. N. of a teacher, Hir. **Śilaka**, m. N. of a man, ChUp. **Śiśu** (accord. to some also = *śiśna*, 'membrum virile'); *-pramāṇa*, mfn. of a child's size, Bcar. **Śishṭânuśishṭa**, mfn. taught by learned men, Kāvyâd. **Śukra** (in comp.); *-dina*, n., *-vāsara*, m. Friday, Inscr. **Śukla** (also for *śukra*, Venus); *-dharma*, m. the pure law, Sukh. i. **Śuṇḍhi**, (prob.) mfn. pure, bright, splendid, MānGṛ. **Śuti** = *śudi*, Inscr. **Śuddha** (in comp.); *-raśmi-prabha*, m. N. of a Tathāgata, Sukh. ii; °*ddhâdhivāsa*, mfn. inhabiting pure abodes, Bcar.; °*ddhâujas*, mfn. pure in valour, ib. **Śubha** (in comp.); *-jāla-hasta*, mfn. having a hand with beautifully reticulated lines, ib.; *-bhrū*, mfn. fair-browed, ib.; °*bhôrṇa-bhrū*, mfn. having a beautiful curl of hair between the brows, ib. **Śesha**, add 'effect;' *-vat*, n. an argument from effect to cause (one of three kinds of *anumāna* or inference, the other two being *pūrva-vat* and *sāmānyato-dṛishṭa*). **Śmaśāna** (in comp.); *-loshṭa*, n. a clod of earth from a cemetery, ĀpGṛ.; °*nâdhivyatikrama*, m. passing over a cemetery, ib. **Śyāma-jayanta** and **-sujayanta**, m. N. of teachers, JaimUp. **Śyāvâśva-stuta** (RV.). **Śyenī** (accord. to Sāy. and others in RV. i, 140, 9 = 'black, dark'). **Śravaṇā-paksha**, m. the fortnight that precedes the Śravaṇā full moon, Hir. **Śrāddhâbhimarśana**, n. touching in the way prescribed at the Śrāddha ceremony, ib. **Śruta-graha**, m. the perception of sacred knowledge, Bcar. **Śreṇya**, (also) = *bimbi-sāra*, ib. **Ślokârdha**, m. n. half a Śloka, Kāvyâd. **Śva** (in comp. for *śvan*); *-graha-gṛihīta*, mfn. attacked by the dog-demon (epilepsy), ĀpGṛ.; *-graha-prâyaścitta*, n. expiation for epilepsy, Hir.; *-lominī*, f. N. of a female demon, ib. **Śvadhiti** (see *svadh*°, p. 1280). **Śvetârdha-vaktra**, mfn. having half the face white, Bcar.

Shaḍ-vishāṇa, mfn. armed with six tusks, Bcar. **Shuduvadīna**, m. N. of a Sultān, Inscr.

Saṃyuktâkshara, n. a conjunct letter, Prāt. **Sam-vatsarântarhita**, mfn. separated for a year, MaitrS. **Sam-vanin**, mfn. concordant, Hir. **Sam-varaṇa-nāṭaka**, n. N. of a drama. **Sam-varta-vāta**, m. a whirlwind, Hir. **Sam-vardhayitṛi**, mfn. rearing, bringing up, Bcar. **Sam-vādâbhijayana**, n. obtaining the victory in disputes, Hir. **Sam-vāditṛi**, mfn. holding a colloquy, HirP. **Saṃśayâtiśaya**, m. exaggeration in the way of suggesting doubts, Kāvyâd. **Saṃsāra-devī**, f. N. of a queen or princess, Inscr. **Sam-hotrá** (rather, 'concourse of priests for disputations &c.'). **3. Sád** (erase 'm.;' *sádā* = 'ever' in AV. iv, 4, 7). **Sa-nishyadá** (erase and see *sanishyadá* under √*syand*, p. 1273). **Sa-nisrasa**, see under √*sraṇs*, p. 1273. **Sa-nūpura**, mfn. adorned with anklets, Drāhy. **Sánemi** (accord. to some an instr. of *sana* = 'from of old, always'). **Saṃ-dashṭa-yamaka**, n. a Yamaka in which each quarter of the stanza begins with a word twice repeated, Bhar. **Sam-nyupta**, mfn. (fr. *sam-ni-*√2. *vap*) thrown together. **Sa-patnī-bādhana**, n. overcoming rivals or co-wives, ĀpGṛ. **Sapta-muñja**, mfn. formed out of seven blades of Muñja grass, MānGṛ. **Saptarshi-saṃvat**, a year of the Saptarshi era (the 1st year of which corresponds to the expired year 26, i.e. the 27th current year of the Kali-yuga; the hundreds of this era are often omitted, e.g. the Saptarshi year 4869 will be called simply 69; the corresponding year of one of the centuries A.D. is found by adding 24–25; thus 69 [for 4869] corresponds to A.D. 1793–94). **Sama** (in comp.); *-dṛishṭi-pāta*, m. 'an equal glance' and 'a glance with even (not three) eyes,' Bcar. i, 10; *-m-bhūmi*, mfn. being on a level with the ground, BaudhP. **Samid-dhārin**, mfn. carrying a load of fuel, Baudh. **Sa-muñja**, mfn. furnished with reeds, MānGṛ. **Sam-úd** (accord. to some = 'conversation,' AV. viii, 1, 15). **Samudra** (in comp.); *-vastra*, mfn. (= *vasana*), Bcar.; *-saṃyāna*, n. going to sea, Baudh. **Sam-ūḍha-rūpin**, m. N. of a partic. form of the Dvādaśāha sacrifice, Drāhy. (Sch.). **Sampari-√stṛi**, to scatter all round, Hir. **Sarpir-miśra**, mfn. mixed with clarified butter, ib. **Sárva** (in comp.); *-kuśala-mūla-pāramitā*, f. perfection of all the sources of merit, Sukh. i; *-pūrusha*, mfn. (a house) containing all men, Hir.; *°vârtha-darśa*, m. N. of a Tathāgata, Sukh. ii. **Sarshapa-miśra**, mfn. mixed with mustard seeds, Hir. **Sahasra-putra**, mfn. having a thousand sons, JaimUp. **Sāṃgrāmika**, n. pl. (scil. *sûktāni*) hymns containing charms for use in battle, AV.Pariś. **Sātyā-dhivāka**, m. (with *caitrarathi*) N. of a teacher, JaimUp. **Sāṃnāyyâpidhānī**, f. one of the utensils used at the Sāṃnāyya offering, BaudhP. **Sā-hapadīna** or **Sāhav°** m. N. of a Sultān, Inscr. **Siṇha-saṃvat**, a year of the Siṇha era (used in Gujarāt and converted into the corresponding A.D. year by the addition of 1113–14; e.g. the Siṇha year 96 corresponds to A.D. 1209–10). **Sikatôpôpta**, mfn. strewn with sand, Hir. **Su-caritin**, mfn. well-conducted, moral, MānGṛ. **Su-pratīka**, (also) m. an elephant, Parāś. **Su-varṇa-stainya**, n. the stealing of gold, Baudh. **Su-hemanta**, (also) mfn. having a good winter, MānGṛ. **Sṛish-ṭārtha**, mfn. having power or authority, Sāh. **Staru** (prob. incorrect; the voc. *staro* seems to be w.r. for *suge*). **Sthira-śaṅku-karṇa**, mfn. having upright ears like spikes, Bcar. **Snānīyôcchādita-snāta**, mfn. one who has bathed and rubbed himself with unguents &c., ĀpGṛ. **Svayaṃ-vakra**, mfn. 'crooked by itself,' grown crooked (not artificially bent), Drāhy. **Sv-avôkshita**, mfn. well-sprinkled, BaudhP.

Havyā, f. N. of a cow, Drāhy.

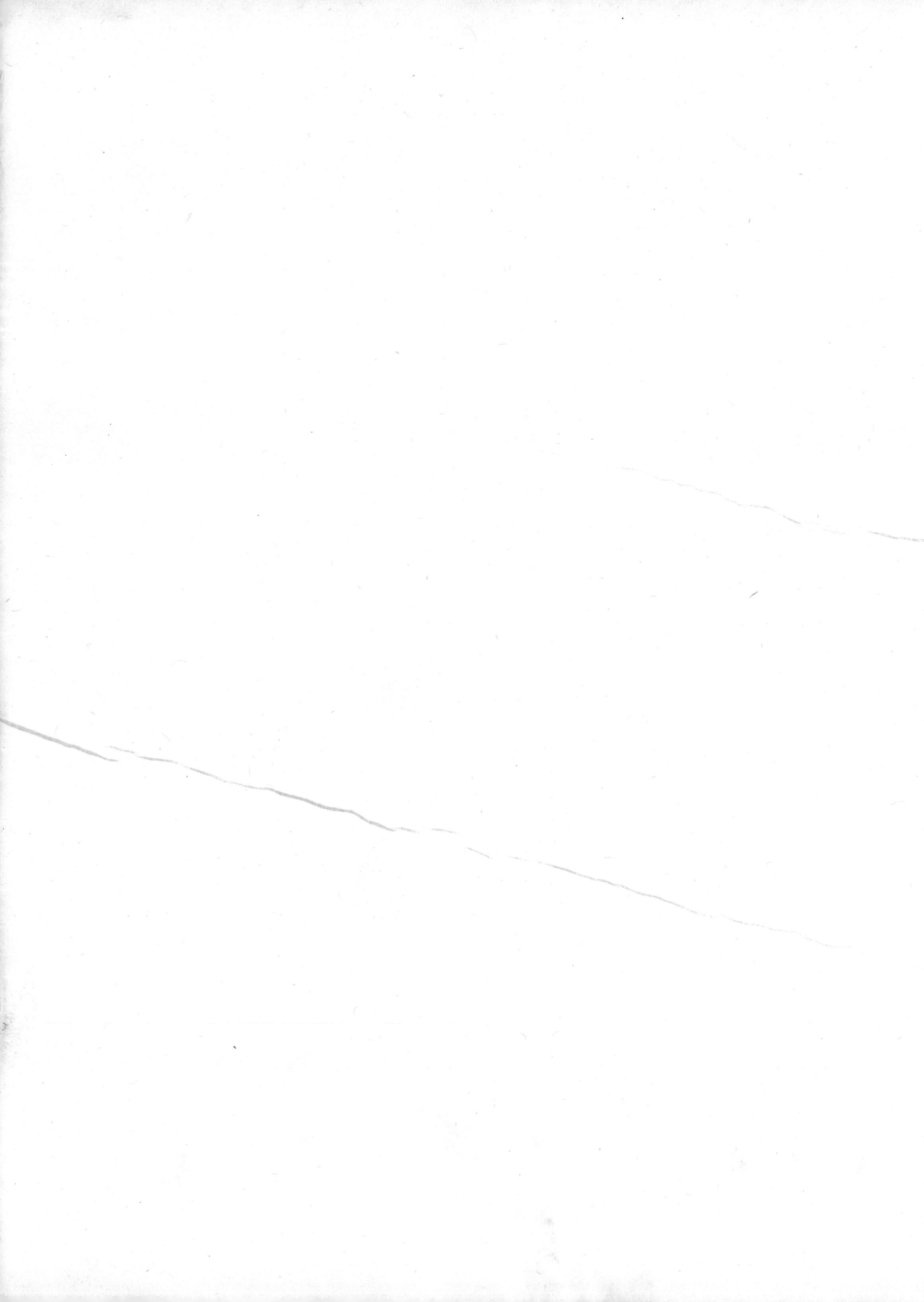